W9-BKS-139

WEBSTER'S
NEW UNIVERSAL
UNABRIDGED DICTIONARY

DELUXE
SECOND EDITION

BASED UPON THE BROAD FOUNDATIONS LAID DOWN BY

Noah Webster

EXTENSIVELY REVISED BY THE PUBLISHER'S EDITORIAL STAFF UNDER THE GENERAL SUPERVISION OF

JEAN L. McKECHNIE

INCLUDING ETYMOLOGIES, FULL PRONUNCIATIONS, SYNONYMS, AND AN ENCYCLOPEDIC SUPPLEMENT OF GEOGRAPHICAL AND BIOGRAPHICAL DATA, SCRIPTURE PROPER NAMES, FOREIGN WORDS AND PHRASES, PRACTICAL BUSINESS MATHEMATICS, ABBREVIATIONS, TABLES OF WEIGHTS AND MEASURES, SIGNS AND SYMBOLS, AND FORMS OF ADDRESS

ILLUSTRATED THROUGHOUT

Dorset & Baber

WEBSTER'S NEW TWENTIETH CENTURY DICTIONARY

Second Edition

Published by New World Dictionaries/Simon and Schuster
A Simon & Schuster Division of Gulf & Western Corporation
Simon & Schuster Building
Rockefeller Center
1230 Avenue of the Americas
New York, New York 10020

Dictionary Editorial Offices
New World Dictionaries
850 Euclid Avenue
Cleveland, Ohio 44114

Manufactured in the United States of America

10 9

Library of Congress Catalog Card Number: 83-42537

ISBN 0-671-41819-X

Previous editions of this book were published by The World Publishing Company, William Collins +World Publishing Co., Inc. and William Collins Publishers, Inc.

PRINTED IN THE UNITED STATES OF AMERICA

CONTENTS

INTRODUCTORY

SUPPLEMENTS

INTRODUCTION

WITH THE publication of this new, extensive revision of WEBSTER'S NEW UNIVERSAL UNABRIDGED DICTIONARY, the publisher is continuing his tradition of making available to the general public scholarly but practical reference works at a reasonable cost. This dictionary has had a long and honorable history. From its earliest progenitor, Noah Webster's COMPENDIOUS DICTIONARY OF THE ENGLISH LANGUAGE, through the various excellent editions of George W. Ogilvie, and continuing into the numerous revisions prepared by the present publisher, the editorial staffs involved have striven constantly to retain that which has remained lexicographically sound, at the same time building in the light of constantly increasing linguistic knowledge. The result has been at all times a work that has served the needs of its own period as the first Webster dictionary served early nineteenth-century America.

With the accelerated growth and change in our language in recent times, and especially in the years following World War II, it became clear that the time had arrived for something more ambitious than the regular annual revision. Rapid advances in the sciences, and especially in the fields of nuclear physics and medicine, had introduced hundreds of new concepts and the words that gave them currency. War and the political and economic changes that followed had brought into the language additional hundreds of new words and phrases and had given new meanings to other, well-established terms. But especially the accumulation of gradual, but by now surely perceptible, changes in the syntax and idiom of American speech had lent an air of encroaching obsolescence to the otherwise sound, Websterian definitions of much of the general vocabulary.

The time had come for a complete re-evaluation of the dictionary; and so members of the publisher's permanent lexicographical staff under the general supervision of Jean L. McKechnie, set to work examining every definition and revising where the passage of time had left its mark in a now obscure definition or in a prolixity not in keeping with the staccato tempo of mid-twentieth-century America. The staff was fortunate in having available for its use the resources and files of *Webster's New World Dictionary of the American Language,* an advantage which made possible the elimination of much of the backbreaking work involved in the recasting of new, up-to-date definitions.

The entire list of entries in the dictionary was re-examined on the basis of modern word-count lists. Words whose increased use in recent years had established them as a part of the active vocabulary of American English were inserted, and such rare or esoteric words as had virtually disappeared from active use were dropped from the word stock to make room for the newer, more pertinent entries. The constant criterion for entry selection was the probability of usefulness to the reader. Consequently, in these days of increased emphasis upon adult education, it was found advisable to include a considerable number of obsolete, archaic, and rare words that are likely to be encountered in the earlier standard literature. At no time, however, was the dictionary allowed to become a mere repository of the rare obsolete words and variant forms that are frequently to be met up with only in some of the unabridged dictionaries. As a result, the several hundred thousand vocabulary entries in WEBSTER'S NEW UNIVERSAL UNABRIDGED DICTIONARY include virtually all those words that a prolific reader in English will ever be likely to investigate.

Because of the general familiarity of the reading public with the diacritical markings for indicating pronunciation already in use in this dictionary, it was decided to retain this system with some minor modifications to allow for a more nearly precise transcription. The pronunciations themselves have been carefully restudied, and where some radical change, as in the stress pattern, has taken place in the prevailing pronunciation, this has been recorded. Variant pronunciations have been given only where these are heard with some degree of frequency. Because the system of diacritical markings, based on that used by Webster, was designed to avoid, wherever possible, the necessity of respelling for pronunciation, some of the diacritics have deliberately been given an elasticity that will accommodate the phonetic patterns of speakers from different parts of the country. A full pronunciation key and a guide to the pronunciation system will be found on p. xii. For the additional convenience of users of this dictionary, an abbreviated key has been included at the bottom of every two-page spread of the text.

In the etymologies, the aim has been to show the origin and line of development of the word in the simplest manner possible, with a minimum of distracting details. Doubtful forms and hypothetical roots have been omitted as of little interest to the lay user of the dictionary. Where a number of related words deriving from a single source appear in close proximity to one another, the etymological treatment is often given only with the basic or most important word of the group. Etymologies have been given for obsolete words only when such words occur commonly in the standard literature, especially when the derivation helps make clear the meaning of the word. To conserve space, the etymologies of some compounded words, especially of scientific terms, indicate only the various combining forms of which they are composed. All such combining forms have been entered in their proper alphabetical order, traced to their sources, defined, and exemplified in usage.

The aim of the editors has been to construct definitions that would be accurate, clear, and simple, and would yet contain sufficient information or explanatory notation so that their meanings would be thoroughly understood by the general reader. Illustrative phrases showing a word in use have been added where it was felt that these would help give the connotative force of the word. In addition, many citations from literature have been included to illustrate the usage of our finest writers. Following many of the entries will be found lists of synonymous or closely related words and, where it was thought helpful, some of these terms have been discriminated in a brief paragraph following the list of synonyms.

No fixed, arbitrary arrangement of the senses within a given entry has been attempted. Any effort to arrange each entry so that the prevailing current meaning is given first is doomed to failure, since for most words there are a number of senses, on different levels and in different fields, that have equal currency. The editors have therefore allowed practicality to determine their practice. Where the historical order of senses seemed advisable, this order has been followed; where one meaning flows logically into another or others, this too has been indicated. Introductory phrases indicating specialized fields of knowledge introduce those meanings that are restricted to these special fields. Labels indicating variation in usage help the reader judge the usability of a term (e.g., *slang, colloquial, obsolete, archaic, rare, British, dialectal*).

Careful attention has been paid to the idiomatic phrasal units that are such a basic feature of English, and hundreds of additional phrases (such as *to burn the candle at both ends, up in arms, bed of roses*) have been added to this revision of the dictionary. Such phrases have been inserted following the entry for that word which is regarded as basic in the phrase, and under the pertinent part of speech. In addition to such idioms, compound noun phrases which have specialized meanings have been entered either under the key word or, where necessary, as individual entries properly alphabetized.

Several thousand illustrations, including hundreds of new ones, appear throughout the dictionary to help clarify the definitions. These illustrations have been carefully selected to show the function, relative size, or appearance of the object being defined. Full captions and explanatory legends are included as an additional aid to the user of the dictionary.

The entire work has been reset in a new modern format and in a clear, legible type of a size that is uniquely large for unabridged dictionaries. Following the dictionary text proper will be found an encyclopedic supplement of useful information, including an exhaustive listing of biographical entries, lists of foreign countries, provinces, and cities, with their population figures, charts of other geographical data, the air distances between principal cities, a list of foreign words and phrases, a complete listing of abbreviations in common use, tables of weights and measures, signs and symbols, and forms of address.

It is the express wish and expectation of the publisher and editors that this new revision of WEBSTER'S NEW UNIVERSAL UNABRIDGED DICTIONARY will serve its users as well as Webster's original work served the people of his time.

THE EDITORS

OUTLINE HISTORY OF THE ENGLISH LANGUAGE

HAROLD WHITEHALL, B. A., Ph. D.

PROFESSOR OF ENGLISH, CHAIRMAN LINGUISTICS, INDIANA UNIVERSITY

I

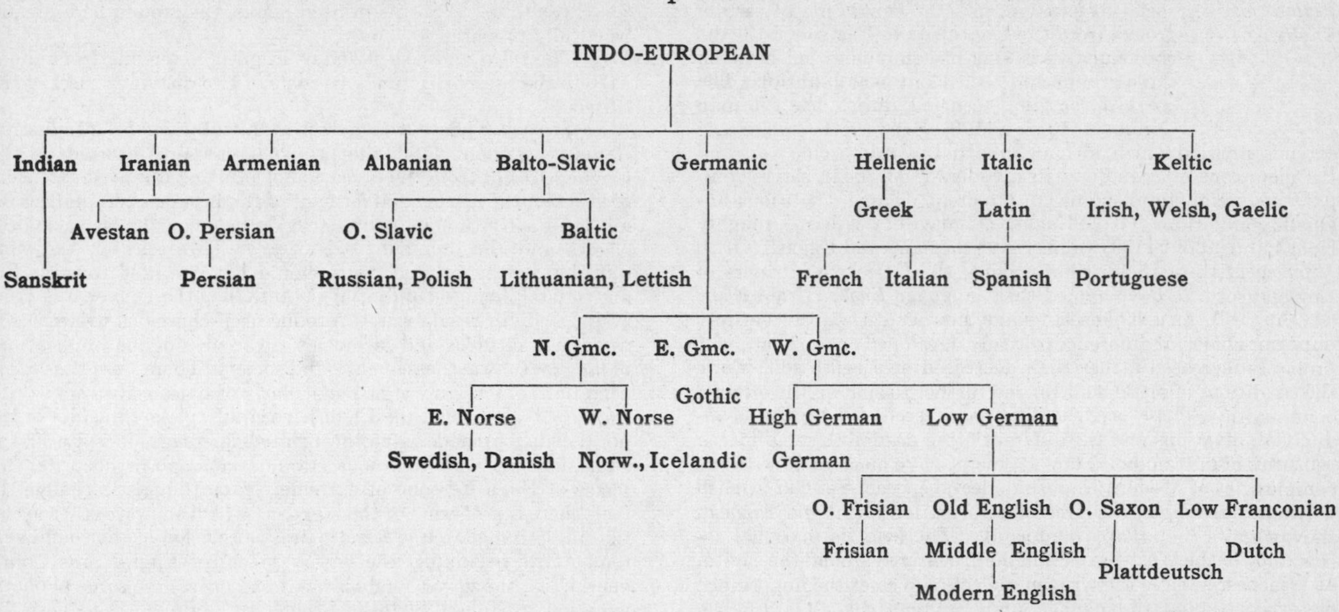

THE ULTIMATE origins of the English language, as modern scholarship sees them, can best be grasped from some such schema as that above. Whatever the demerits of this schema, it at least suggests the connection of English with the West Germanic sub-branch of the Germanic branch of the linguist's conception of a parent language called Indo-European. It also suggests that English is closely connected with Dutch and Frisian, more remotely with German, more remotely still with Latin, Greek, Welsh, and Russian, and very remotely with Sanskrit and Iranian. Consideration of series of cognate forms like English *brother*, Dutch *broeder*, German *Brūder*, Old Saxon *brōthar*, Lithuanian *broter-*, Greek *phrātēr*, Latin *frāter*, Irish *brathair*, Sanskrit *bhrātar-* underlines these relationships and gives a hint of the comparative method by which their existence was established. To the philologist, versed in the principles of phonetic differentiation, the interconnections between so unlikely a series as Latin *canō* 'I sing,' English *hen*, Old English *hana*, Old Icelandic *hane* 'cock,' German *Hahn*, Greek *kanássein* 'to sound,' and Sanskrit *kankani* 'bell' are equally apparent and significant.

The significant history of the English language, however, goes back no further than the 5th century A.D. when tribes from the northwestern Continental fringe, speaking a form of West Germanic, invaded and conquered Romano-Keltic England. To trace the development of the English language is to trace the process by which the dialects this handful of invaders spoke became the mighty instrument of communication, emotion, and literature now used by upwards of 190 million of the world's inhabitants. And the more we trace this phenomenon, the more we shall realize that the history of our language is merely one aspect of the social and cultural history of the invaders' descendants.

Change in Language Language is, in fact, the predominant factor in the social organization of humanity. Its real existence lies not so much in the printed book, not even in a dictionary such as this, as in the sense of community or community of feeling of those who habitually use it. Inevitably, therefore, any dislocation of the community—whether geographical by extension or vertical by class-differentiation—will cause marked changes in the pattern of the language itself. But even within a stable community, linguistic change is constantly at work. Analyzed into its simplest elements, spoken language is no more than an organized and closely knit system of sound-signals produced by certain correlated movements of specific bodily organs. The child acquires this system from those around him by a process of trial and error, but not as a number of isolated sounds. He hears words; he tries, with imperfect results at first, to adjust his vocal apparatus to the series of complicated and minute adjustments that every word occasions; eventually, these adjustments, through self-training, become more or less automatic. But always the child will articulate a little differently from his parents, and although he is not conscious of it, his sound-system will differ in some particulars from that used by his parents. Curiously enough, the differences will tend to be most marked in the sounds which are most difficult to articulate and which are least closely correlated with the remainder of the sound-system. And, what is still more striking, in any speech community, at the same moment, and under the same conditions, the youngest generation will tend to modify the same sounds *in the same direction*. It is this fact that makes a science of language, and hence a history of the English language, possible.

Carried to its logical conclusion, this principle would imply that any speech community speaks differently from all other speech communities, and that within each community there is a difference in the speech of successive generations. And to some degree, that is true. The constant tendency towards change, however, is partially offset by tendencies that oppose it. Since the necessity for communication is the well-spring of language, too varied a differentiation would obviously defeat the primary purpose for which language was developed. The impulse towards differentiation is mainly supported by the complexity of social relationships; the impulse towards uniformity is supported by those elements of social and mental organization that make for unity—writing, education, the Church, the political organization of the community, and on the psychological plane, the principle of analogy. At any given moment, therefore, there tends to develop a kind of equilibrium between differentiation on the one hand and uniformity on the other. When great social upheavals or racial intermixtures occur, that equilibrium may be destroyed, and linguistic change will appear to be comparatively rapid; in periods of social stability, linguistic change will operate more gradually. It is this fact that justifies the customary and arbitrary time-divisions in the history of any single language.

The Principal Periods of English (*a*) The origins of the English language lie in a social dislocation, i.e., the emigration of certain groups from the Continent to England, with the consequent breaking of communication between these groups and their Continental kinsfolk. The great dislocation occurred during the Norman Conquest (1066–c.1120). Between the two events extends a period which, although marred by internecine wars and the incursions of Scandinavian invaders (850–1042), shows comparative social stability and an apparent if largely fictitious linguistic equilibrium. To the English language of this period, roughly from 450 to about 1150, we may give the name Old English (OE.).

Irrespective of their tribal origins, the Germanic invaders of England seem to have named their language *Englisc* (from *Engle* 'the Angles'). As a spoken language, however, it was not entirely uniform. Dialectal differences already developed on the Continent probably increased rather than decreased on English soil, where the conditions of settlement tended further to split up the original communities. These original differences, seconded by the Scandinavian invasions and the differentiation natural to some fifteen centuries of untrammeled development, have much to do with the complexities of Modern English dialectal speech. Yet Old English writings, our only real source of information about Old English, show a quite remarkable uniformity. The eventual national ascendancy of the West-Saxon kingdom, centered around the capital at Winchester, gave the written dialect of Wessex the importance of a written standard language; and the great bulk of Old English literature was either written originally in West-Saxon or was transcribed into it from its original Northumbrian and Mercian sources. Written West-Saxon is, therefore, an arresting example of the crystallizing power exerted by a powerful written standard upon the free stream of linguistic development.

(*b*) The next great period of the language, that of Middle English (ME.), cannot be fitted as neatly between dates as the preceding period. Time was needed to absorb the great historical shock of the Norman Conquest, and the terminal date for Middle English can be fixed only in the most arbitrary manner. The adoption of the limits 1150–1475 is dependent upon the emerging of a distinctive Post-Conquest literature and upon the social effects of the invention of printing.

It would be an error to regard the Conquest as producing a clean break in the history of English; it merely released and accelerated tendencies towards differentiation that must already have been in operation. Its most immediate result was to replace English, as an authoritative language, by the Norman-French of the conquerors for well over two hundred years. In the meantime, the effects upon the English language itself were three-fold: (1) The social prestige of Norman-French and the extension in the ecclesiastical, administrative, and scholarly use of Latin brought into English an enormous number of words borrowed from these languages; (2) the loss of the West-Saxon written standard allowed free-play to the dialectal peculiarities and disturbed the linguistic equilibrium of English; (3) the influence of French and Latin spelling did much to revise the traditional orthography of English.

The first part of the Middle English period is something like linguistic chaos. Important literary works were written in half a dozen dialects sufficiently diverse in themselves, and doubly diverse as a result of the frantic spelling expedients of their authors. Early Middle English is not one but a group of languages, each of which must be mastered separately by the student. The resolution of this confusion, which was the adoption of London English as a basis for a new *written* standard language, came about under the pressure of many disparate factors: (1) the break-down of direct English authority over Normandy (1204–65); (2) the gradual establishment of nationalism (1272–1400); (3) the rise to importance of the middle- and laboring-classes (1348–1430); (4) the intrusion of English into the conduct of government (from about 1337), law (1344–62), and education (1349–85); (5) the growing centralization of administration at the capital; (6) the timely appearance of important works by Chaucer, Lydgate, and Occleve, all of whom wrote London English. By 1420, at the latest, a written form of the South East Midland dialect used in and around London was on its way to becoming a written standard for the entire country. Although much fine literature continued to be produced in the rival literary dialects of the Northwest and the North, the predominance of written London English was never afterwards seriously challenged. When, in the years 1476–90, Caxton chose to use it for his printed books, the ground had already been fully prepared for him.

(*c*) The third and last period of English, extending from about 1476 to the present, actually consists of two distinct phases of the language.

In the earlier phase, which ends in the full tide of the Industrial Revolution about 1780, the principal pressures exerted on the language result from the invention of printing, the vast extension of literacy, the intellectual ferment of the Renaissance, and, above all, from a continuous social struggle between the rising middle classes and the dominant aristocracy. Theoretically, the wide diffusion of the printed word should have worked towards linguistic stability and uniformity. Actually, the converse is true. Its immediate result was to produce self-conscious awareness—awareness of ideas and ideologies, awareness of the implications of language, awareness of class and society. There were thus rapid accretions of foreign words, particularly of Latinic abstract words, that greatly modified the English vocabulary. And in spite of the normalizing tendencies of the printed language, in spite of the efforts of many self-conscious grammarians and orthoëpists, this phase of English is one of extremely rapid linguistic change. In fact, there is no period of the language which shows greater variation in pronunciation or a more drastic revision of the sound-system. At its beginning, the vowel system of English was Continental, i.e., the vowel symbols had more or less the same phonetic values as in Italian, Spanish, French, or German. At its end, the vowel distribution of English had undergone so thorough a regrouping that the sounds were completely divorced from the Continental values of the symbols and consequently from the system of orthography—still the basis of modern English spelling—fixed by Caxton and his followers.

Changes as violent as this are likely to have violent social causes. Insofar as any single social cause can be considered responsible, it would appear to lie in the dislocation of the community along vertical lines, the clash of phonetic system against phonetic system resulting from the clash of the aristocratic and middle classes. As early as 1400, the powerful bourgeoisie of England's first industrial stronghold, East Anglia, had developed a kind of generalized *lingua franca*, based on the local spoken dialect of that region, through which they were enabled to carry out their business affairs. Wherever industry later extended, this *lingua franca*, no longer purely regional, seems to have followed. In the 17th century, the settlement of the New England Colonies by immigrants drawn principally from South Eastern England brought this type of English to the New World, where it formed the basis for the Eastern American speech of today.

Yet for all its wide distribution, the middle-class *lingua franca* had the phonetic system of the East Anglian dialects; and that system varied greatly from the phonetic system used by the London aristocracy. Thus during the entire period 1476–1780—the so-called period of Early Modern English (EMnE.)—we have the spectacle of two important class dialects existing, often in the same localities, side by side, and influencing the formative years of each successive youngest generation from two directions at once. And it is from the unconscious attempts of each youngest generation to reconcile the conflicting signalling-systems of the two class dialects, to achieve a workable synthesis between them, that the Great Vowel Shift of the Early Modern English period seems to arise and continue.

Within the limits of the Early Modern period itself, no such synthesis was achieved. The social struggle went on. Linguistic change lost nothing of its rapidity. The two great class dialects of English not only held their ground, but even gained it; for if the middle-class type became standard for the New England Colonies, the aristocratic type became standard in the Southern Colonies, where it formed the basis of the Southern American of today. The final phase of the English language, the phase of Late Modern English (LMnE.), was not ushered in until the Industrial Revolution, by securing enormous material gains for the middle-classes, had secured their social, political, and economic victory and an authoritative predominance for their type of English.

Upon that type, pruned and 'regularized' by grammarians and lexicographers, both the cultivated British and the cultivated American of today are firmly rooted. As spoken English, the older aristocratic type lingers in Tidewater, Virginia, and a few other Southern localities—lingers also, in piecemeal fashion, in such conservative linguistic 'islands' as the Ozark Mountains and the Great Smokies where it is rediscovered by scholars under the strange guise of 'folk-dialect.' From England, it has disappeared almost without a trace. Thus the history of English between 1750 and 1850 is not the history of an evolution but the history of a replacement.

Within the actual limits of the Late Modern phase of English, from 1780 to the present, something like linguistic equilibrium has been re-established. Apart from certain necessary phonological generalizations, change has been slight and gradual. Individual, regional, and to some extent, class-divergencies still exist; but the written word, fostered by democratic social institutions, by popular education, and by the accessibility of grammars and dictionaries, has come to be of paramount importance. Even though modern methods of communication and organization have immensely extended the limits of the speech community, the tendencies towards uniformity are sufficient—or were recently sufficient—to balance the tendencies towards differentiation. How long this balance will continue remains to be seen.

II

Characteristics of English in the Old English Period (450–1150)

Old English differs very considerably from Modern English in orthography, pronunciation, vocabulary, and grammar. Yet many of the characteristics and a good many of the words of MnE. are clearly recognizable in their OE. form, and the difficulties of OE. may easily be overstressed. The following short passage, containing an unusual proportion of words still present in MnE., suggests some of the outstanding points of similarity.

Ic eom munuc, and ic singe ælce dæg sofon tīda mid
I am monk, and I sing each day seven tides (with)
gebrōþrum; and ic eom gebysgod on rædinga and on sange;
brothers; and I am busied (in) reading and (in) song;
ac ic wolde betwēonum leornian sprecan on Englisc ongemong
(but) I would between learn (to) speak (in) English among
mīnum oþrum manigfaldum bysgum. . . .
mine other manifold businesses. . . .

(a) Orthography and Pronunciation

Although OE. had the so-called 'Continental' values for its vowel-symbols, and although many of its sounds have since been modified by sound-change, one of the chief difficulties is the actual form of OE. spelling. As a result of palatalizations that occurred after the OE. spelling system was already fixed, a single consonantal symbol may represent several sounds. Moreover, the priests who originally reduced OE. to writing tended to be almost too careful in expressing the vowels, even to the little glides which enable the vocal organs to pass smoothly between two points of articulation. The following summary should aid recognition:

(1) *C* = MnE. *k* in *cynn* 'kin,' *munuc* 'monk,' and MnE. *ch* in *cild* 'child,' *ceorl* 'churl.' (2) *G* = MnE. *y* in *gēar* 'year,' *gīet, gēt* 'yet,' *fæger* 'fair,' MnE. *g* in *grund* 'ground,' *gold* 'gold,' and German spirant *g* (not unlike MnE. *w*) in *boga* 'bow,' *folgian* 'follow.' (3) *H* = MnE. written *-gh* (no longer pronounced) in *niht* 'night,' and *sōhte* 'sought,' but had the phonetic values of *ch* in G. *ich* and *nacht.* (4) *Cg* = MnE. *-dge* in *brycg* 'bridge'; *sc* = MnE. *sh* in *scip* 'ship,' *Englisc* 'English.' (5) *F* = MnE. *f* in *fetor* 'fetter,' but had the value of MnE. *v* in *heofon* 'heaven,' *æfre* 'ever.' (6) MnE. *th,* as in *with, then* was expressed indifferently by the Runic symbols *ð, þ* as in *wiþ* 'with,' *ðū* 'thou.' (7) OE. *y,* always a vowel with the sound of *u* in Fr. *une,* corresponds chiefly to MnE. *i* as in *fyr* 'fire,' occasionally to MnE. *u* as in *bysig* 'busy,' *cycgel* 'cudgel,' and very occasionally to MnE. *e* as in *cnyll* 'knell.' (8) OE. *æ* = MnE. *a* in *bæc* 'back,' but OE. *æ* may correspond to MnE. *ea* as in *dælan* 'to deal,' or to MnE. *ee* as in *dæd* 'deed.' (9) Certain OE. diphthongs, like the *ea, eo* of *earm* 'arm,' *weorc* 'work, ME. *werk,*' are no more than ultra-accurate recordings of the simple vowels *æ* and *e* (*i*); others, like the *īe* of *stīele* 'steel,' and the *ea* of *ceald* 'cold,' are found only in West Saxon and have no influence on the later history of our forms for these words, which are derived from Anglian *stele, cāld;* all OE. diphthongs, irrespective of origin, were simplified in ME. and are therefore of no importance in the general development of English.

(b) Vocabulary

About 85 per cent of the Old English vocabulary has been lost to MnE. partly because of later replacements from French and Latin, partly because of the development of idiomatic phrases. In estimating this loss, however, it should never be forgotten that the OE. words which managed to survive—the bulk of our prepositions, pronouns, auxiliaries, conjunctions, as well as our words of fundamental concept—occur more frequently in spoken and written MnE. than most other elements in our vocabulary. Moreover, much of this lost vocabulary consists of synthetic compounds of which the simplex elements still survive. *Dōm-bōc* 'law-book,' *eorþ-cræft* 'geometry,' and *gaderscipe* 'marriage' may be gone, yet *doom, book, gather, earth, craft* are still with us, and *-ship* is still an active formative suffix. The flexible formation of compounds from words and particles in current use, a feature still operative in German, is rightly considered to be one of the distinguishing marks of OE. vocabulary. Nowadays, English makes comparatively little use of it. Yet even today, formations like *steamboat, motor car, fire insurance* keep alive the method by which OE. *mōdcaru* 'sorrow,' and *glædmodnes* 'kindness' were formed.

(c) Grammar and Morphology

OE. was what is usually termed an 'inflected' or 'synthetic' language like modern German, i.e., the functional relationship between meaningful words was largely expressed by suffixal phonetic elements which served to denote such categories as number, gender, case, tense, and voice. Like most Indo-European languages, OE. possessed 'grammatical gender,' a device only remotely connected with sex, which served to classify nouns along analogical lines in such a manner that the determination of agreement was not impossible to the speaker and writer. Thus *mægden,* 'maiden' is neuter, *swāt* 'sweat' masculine, and *tīd* 'time, tide' feminine. Theoretically, the noun and adjective have inflections for four cases in the singular and the plural, and the latter has, in addition, forms for each of the three genders and variant forms according to whether it is accompanied by the article or not. The pronoun, the keystone to any system based upon inflectional agreement, is even more complex: it possesses not only distinctive forms for all genders, persons, and cases, but also preserves, in addition to the normal singular and plural, a dual number. The practical purpose of this serried array of inflections amounts simply to this: that the relationship between meaningful words expressed in MnE. partly through word-order and partly through the use of words empty of meaning—prepositions like *on, of, to* or words like *concerning, according* used as prepositions—is expressed in OE. by the addition of predetermined phonetic elements to the meaningful word. In OE. I should write *Hē wæs ān þara twelfa;* in MnE. *He was one of the twelve.* In OE. I might write *Lēof, þæs mē þyncþ þū eart wītega;* in MnE., to express the same relationship, I should have to write *Dear one,* according to *that* (or from *that*) *it seems to me you are a prophet.* Since inflections are phonetic elements, any phonetic changes which level and confuse them may finally result in a complete breakdown of the entire system and its replacement by the analytical expression of relationship that we find in MnE. That is precisely what happened to OE. From the first written records onwards, the inflections of noun and adjective lacked clarity and distinction; when final vowels became weakened, these inflections were rendered practically useless. Those of the pronoun (with the exception of the dual number) and, to some extent, those of the verb, still retained sufficient distinctiveness to continue their usefulness in ME. and MnE.

Characteristics of English in the Middle English Period (1150–1475)

Consideration of the bewildering scope of the Middle English dialects lies outside the scope of this discussion. Even the great Northern literary dialect, lineal ancestor of the language of Burns, and that of the Northwest used by the *Gawain* poet must be passed over in silence. For the historian of the whole English language, the one important variety of ME. is that of the South Eastern Midland area particularly as written by Chaucer.

(a) Orthography and Pronunciation

If the ME. of Chaucer resembles MnE. more closely than OE., the fact is due partly to a series of orthographic adaptations brought about by the influence of Fr. The most important of these are: (1) The use of *ch* for OE. *c* in *child;* (2) the use of *qu-* for OE. *cw-* in *quene, queen,* OE. *cwēn;* (3) the partial displacement of *þ, ð* by *th* in *with,* OE. *wiþ;* (4) the introduction of *v* for medial voiced *f* in *love,* OE. *lufu;* (5) the use of *sh, ssh* for OE. *sc* in *shal,* OE. *sceal,* and *wasshe,* OE. *wascan;* (6) the use of *k* before front vowels for OE. *c* in *kepen* 'keep,' OE. *cēpan,* beside the retained *c* before back vowels as in *cot;* (7) the eventual introduction of consonantal *y* for OE. *g* in *yere,* OE. *gēar* 'year,' etc.; (8) the use of *ou* for OE. *ū* to discriminate it from Fr. *u* and OE. *y,* spelled *u,* as in *mouth,* OE. *mūþ* beside *muchel,* OE. *mycel* 'much'; the use of *o* for the sake of clarity in the neighborhood of *v, u, m, n, w,* as in *monk,* OE. *munuc,* and *sone,* OE. *sunu;* (9) in the latest ME. the symbols *ea* and *oa,* imported from the Low Countries, began to be employed in words like *deal, boat* to distinguish the vowels from those of *deed, boot* which had a different pronunciation; (10) it is uncertain whether the replacement of OE. *æ* by ME. *a,* as in *that,* OE. *þæt,* is merely orthographic or a symbol of an actual sound-change; (11) equally uncertain is the replacement of OE. *æ* in *hælan* 'to heal' by ME. *e,* as in *hēlen.*

Actual phonetic changes as distinct from mere changes of orthography are also apparent: (1) OE. *ā* in *hām* 'home,' *stān* 'stone,' etc., shifted to the sound of the vowel in MnE. *law* and was spelled *o, oo* as in ME. *home, hoom* and *stone, stoon;* (2) the OE. diphthongs, where they survived in OE. itself, became simple vowels as in OE. *dēop,* ME. *depe, deep,* and OE. *strēam,* ME. *streem;* (3) OE. *y* as in *hyll, fyr* became *i* in South East Midland, as in *hill, fire;* (4) OE. spirant *g,* as in *boga,* already closely analogous to *w,* became and was written *w,* as in ME. *bowe;* (5) vowels of unstressed syllables lost their distinct character and became levelled, for the most part, under a sound written *e,* very like the sound we give the final *-a* of *sofa;* (6) long vowels were shortened before two or more consonants (whence MnE. *kept* beside *keep, depth* beside *deep*), and when they occurred in the first syllable of trisyllabic words (whence *holiday, halidom* beside *holy*); (7) the short vowels *a, e, o* were lengthened in open syllables, as in OE. *nama,* ME., MnE. *name,* and OE. *mete,* ME. *mēte,* MnE. *meat.*

(b) Vocabulary

The ME. vocabulary differs from that of OE. by the accretion of a vast number of words borrowed from other languages and by the consequent loss of many OE. words. The process had already commenced during the 10th and 11th centuries, i.e., during the latter part of the OE. period, with borrowings from the Scandinavian settlers resident in Eastern and Northern England. Because of the rigid traditions of the West-Saxon written language, comparatively few of such borrowings appear in OE.; we first realize their number and importance only after the Conquest. Permanent additions to the English language from this source include common nouns like *axle-tree, bull, dirt, law, leg, root, skin, want, window,* adjectives like *ill, rotten, tight, weak,* and verbs like *call, crawl, die, raise, scowl, take.*

Much more impressive, however, are the borrowings of words of Romance origin from the Norman conquerors, more especially during the years after about 1240 when the Norman-French were forced by political circumstances to reconcile themselves to their English neighbors. There is no other period of the language that shows the accession of so many alien, and on the whole, useful words as the period 1250–1450. Among them were the mundane *air, bacon, bucket, fry, gum, pork, push, sound, stew, stubble,* and *trip,* as well as the more abstract *beauty, color, heritage, honor, judgment, noble,* and *tragedy.* Some, like *abbey, cardinal, clerk, image, parson, penance,* and *piety,* are drawn from the special vocabulary of the Church; some, like *assize, attorney, fine, forfeit, pillory, plea, suit,* from that of the law; some from medicine, like *anatomy, balm, ointment, poison, stomach;* some from the army, like *ambush, archer, chieftain, dart, lance;* some from the table, like *appetite, taste, veal, venison;* some from the home, like *basin, lamp, lantern, towel.*

Side by side with these French words, many of which were ultimately of Latin origin, occur direct borrowings from Latin itself. But whereas the French words bear in many cases the stamp of actual usage, actual speech, most of the Latin words were plainly literary and scholarly borrowings: *custody, genius, immune, lucrative, necessary, private, rational, subjugate, temperate,* etc.

(c) Grammar and Morphology

The eventual result of the weakening of unstressed final vowels (see *b.* immediately above) was the disintegration of the complicated OE. inflectional system. In the English of Chaucer, 'grammatical' is completely replaced by 'natural' gender; the complex OE. article has become the invariable *þe, the;* the adjective is indeclinable; inflectional expression of case is limited to the genitive singular of nouns; a single ending *-es* has completely superseded the great variety of endings once used to indicate the genitive singular and the plural. To trace these changes in detail would require a volume of paradigms. Here, the practical results can be summarized in a single sentence: OE. was a 'synthetic,' while late ME. is an 'analytical' language. Of the once highly organized inflectional system of article, noun, and adjective, all that is left in MnE. is a group of fossil forms: *for the nonce, Atterbury, Nash, Noakes, Nalder,* and *Nelm* (earlier *for þen ones, æt þære byrig, at þen asche, at þen okes, at þen aldre, at þen elme*).

The pronoun and verb also underwent considerable phonetic modification during the ME. period, but partly because of adaptation and partly because of their importance in determining the categorical relationships within the analytical sentence, their main features are remarkably well-preserved. In the pronoun, the outstanding developments were: (1) Loss of the dual; (2) replacement of the masculine third person accusative *hine* by the dative *him;* (3) appearance of a mysterious feminine *she* to replace the original *hēo;* (4) intrusion of the Scandinavian plurals *they, their, them* to replace the English *hi, he, hir, hem.* Most of these changes were very gradual; Chaucer, for instance, still retains *hir, hem,* and the latter has still a kind of fictitious survival in MnE. *'em.* The net result of all the changes was to level off distinctions no longer needed and at the same time to reinforce distinctions that the operation of phonetic change threatened with obliteration.

Similarly with the verb. OE. had possessed two great classes of verbs, usually distinguished as *weak* and *strong.* In the first class the preterit and past participle were formed by adding to the present stem the dental suffixes *-ede, -ode, -de* and *-ed, -od, -d;* in the second, tense change was indicated by a modification (ablaut, gradation, or 'internal inflection') of the stem vowel itself. Cf. MnE. *talk—talked* or *drop—dropped* with *sing—sang—sung.* In the strong verbs, never important in numbers but extremely frequent in occurrence, the phonetic changes of the early ME. period brought about the loss of distinction between preterit singular and preterit plural, and seriously weakened the distinction between preterit and past participle. In the weak verbs, the operation of the sound change that weakened the vowels of final unstressed syllables obliterated the distinction between the class which added the suffixes *-ede, -ed* and that which added *-ode, -od* to indicate tense changes. By the end of the ME. period, therefore, the verb was fairly close to its modern development. One other important change concerns the personal ending of the third person singular indicative. The *-eth* that would be the regular development of OE. *-þ* still lingers on in verse, but during the late ME. period it had already been replaced in common usage by the ending *-es, -s,* borrowed from the Northern dialect.

III

The English language after the end of the ME. period does not lend itself to any such schematic treatment as we have attempted for Old and Middle English. The varied and flexible instrument used by Shakespeare, Milton, and, eventually, by ourselves, is altogether too gigantic to be compressed neatly into mnemonic schedules. Moreover, most of us have read the great authors of the EMnE. period and we are at least aware of the external appearance of EMnE. To proceed further, to delve beneath the spelling in order to explore the progress of the Great Vowel Shift during the 16th, 17th, 18th, and 19th centuries, would require the use of some such probe as the alphabet of the International Phonetic Association. And even if we familiarized ourselves with some such alphabet, we might well end by knowing at once too much and too little. While it is easy to visualize the phonetic direction of the changes—to state, in phonetic terms, that long low- and mid-tongue vowels were raised, long high-tongue vowels diphthongized, short vowels centralized—the complicated correlations of vowel with vowel during the period of the changes would still elude us.

With the fixation of English spelling, which commenced with Caxton and was achieved about 1650, the English language acquired its modern external form. With the introduction of thousands of new words from various sources during the same period, it completed most of the circle of its vocabulary. Thanks to these facts, the modern reader may approach most English authors from Dryden onwards without being conscious of any particular sense of archaism. And this annihilation of time is perhaps the greatest benefit conferred on humanity by standard written language. Yet, consideration of this and other benefits should not blind us to events below the surface. For the user of the English language there is both illumination and an implicit warning in the famous simile of J. Vendryes:

"The ice borrows its substance from the river, it is indeed the actual water of the river itself—and yet it is not the river. A child, seeing the ice, thinks that the river exists no more, that its course has been arrested. But this is only an illusion. Under the layer of ice, the river continues to flow down to the plain. Should the ice break, one sees the water suddenly bubble up as it goes gushing and murmuring on its way. This is an image of the stream of language. The written tongue is the film of ice upon its waters; the stream which still flows under the ice that imprisons it is the popular and natural language; the cold which produces the ice and would fain restrain the flood is the stabilizing action exerted by grammarians and pedagogues; and the sunbeam which gives language its liberty is the indomitable force of life, triumphing over rules, and breaking the fetters of tradition."*

* J. Vendryes, *Language: A Linguistic Introduction to History*, translated by Paul Radin (New York, 1925), pp. 275–6.

GUIDE TO PRONUNCIATION

PRONUNCIATION in this dictionary is indicated directly on the entry word by a system of symbols, or diacritical marks. Thus, the symbol c̱ is used to indicate the sound of the hard **c** in **cat**, and the word is entered in the vocabulary as **c̱at**. The Key to Pronunciation printed below gives a complete description of the symbols used and the sounds they represent. The modified sounds are unmarked, as the **e** in **cent**, the **a** in **apply**, the **i** in **pin**, the **u** in **tub**, the **o** in **on**, and the **y** in **myth**.

When two vowels stand together, only the one which indicates the sound of the word is marked, as in **strēak, brāin, mōat**. The clusters **ae** and **oe** ending a syllable are pronounced as ē; when followed by a consonant in the same syllable they are pronounced as e in **met**.

In a few instances it is impossible to indicate the pronunciation on the word itself; in such cases the word, or part of it, is respelled in parentheses immediately following the entry. The word is respelled phonetically, that is, according to its sound, regardless of the letters that compose it. Examples of respelling are **e̱ight** (āt); **guīde** (gīd); **heir** (ãr); and **här′le-quin** (-kin *or* -kwin).

The accents are indicated thus: primary ′, secondary ″. The secondary accent or subordinate stress is normally indicated only when it falls at an irregular interval from the primary or main stress, that is, at an interval other than two syllables.

Although full vowel quality is indicated in all syllables, it should be understood that in totally unstressed syllables the vowel quality is variously reduced, or weakened, in colloquial speech to a more or less neutral sound. To avoid the confusion of excessive diacritical marks, sounds in non-English words are indicated by the English sounds most nearly approximating these.

KEY TO PRONUNCIATION

ā as in fāte, āle, ā′corn, be-rāte′, nat″u-ral-i-zā′tion.
ä " " fär, fä′ther, ärch, mär′shal, cär-toon′; also as in whät, wänt.
ȧ " " fȧst, glȧss, a-lȧs′; also as in so′dȧ, ȧ-dapt′ȧ-ble.
a̤ " " fa̤ll, pa̤w, a̤w′ful, ap-pla̤ud′.
ă " " fi′năl, sea′măn, tol′er-ănt, men′ăce.
ã " " cãre, ãir, mil′i-tãr-y, de-clãre′.
a " " at, ac-cord′, com-par′i-son, car′ry.

ē " " ēve, mēte, hē, Ē′den, in-ter-vēne′; also as in hēre, drēar′y.
e̱ " " pre̱y, e̱ight, o-be̱y′.
ẽ " " hẽr, vẽrse, sẽr′vice, in-tẽr′.
e " " met, ebb, en-dorse′, mon′e-tar-y, dis-tend′.
ee " " feed, pro-ceed′, lee′way.

ī " " pīne, ī-de′a, īce′berg, de-cīde′, al-lī′ance.
ï " " clïque, ma-rïne′; also as in Mar-tï′ni.
ĩ " " bĩrd, stĩr, ex′tĩr-pate, fĩrm′a-ment.
i " " it, hit, re-mit′, cit′y; also as in pos′si-ble, grav′i-ty, pu′pil.

ō " " nōte, ōat, sō, ō′pen, hel-lō′; also as in ren′ō-vate, prō-pel′.
ö " " möve, pröve, tömb.
ọ " " lọng, crọss, ọff, ọrb, fọr-bid′, dọr′mer.
ŏ " " at′ŏm, plŏv′er; also as in ac′tŏr, wŏrd, wŏrk.
o " " not, for′est, non′sense; also as in dog, broth, cost; also as in con-fess′, con-cur′.
ọọ " " mọọn, cọọ, fọọd, brọọd′er.
oo " " book, hood, foot, look, cook′y.

ū " " ūse, fūse, ū-til′i-ty, fū′tile, im-mūne′.
ụ " " bụll, pụt, fụl-fil′, boun′ti-fụl.
u̇ " " bru̇te, ju̇′ry; also used for the German ü.
ũ " " tũrn, fũr, bũr-lesque′, de-mũr′.
u " " up, rub, sun′set, in-sult′.

ȳ " " crȳ, eȳe.
y " " myth, cit′y.

c̱ " " c̱at, to-bac̱′c̱o.
ç " " ma-çhine′.
c " " ace, ce′dar.
ch " " church.
c̱h " " c̱hord.

ġ as in ġem.
ñ " " añ′ger, sphiñx.
ṅ " " French boṅ.
ng " " ring.
ş " " mi′şer, aş.

th " " this.
th " " thin.
z̧ " " az̧ure.

au " " umlaut.
aw " " straw.

ou " " out.
oi " " oil.
oy " " boy.

ew " " new, few.

ow " " now.

-tūre as -chẽr (in picture).
-tion, **-sion** as -shun (in nation, tension).

-ciăn, **-tiăn**, **-siăn** as -shun (in Martian, Melanesian, mortician).

-şiăn, **-şion** as -zhun (in Persian, fusion).

-liŏn as -lyun *or* -yun (in million).

-ceous, **-(s)cious** as -shus (in cretaceous, delicious, conscious).

qu as kw (in queen).
-ous as -us (in porous).

ph- as f- (in phone, etc.).

-le as -l (at end of syllable, as in able, cycle, etc.).

-iȧ as -yȧ (in pharmacopoeia).

wh- as hw- in whale, etc.

kh as in German doch (dokh).

LIST OF ABBREVIATIONS USED IN THIS DICTIONARY

a. or adj. … adjective
abbrev. … abbreviation, abbreviated
abl. … ablative
Abyss. … Abyssinian
acc. … accusative
act. … active
A.D. … Anno Domini (in the year of the Lord)
adv. … adverb
Afr. … African
alt. … alternate(ly)
Am. … America, American
Am. Ind. … American Indian
Am. Sp. … American Spanish
anat. … anatomy
anc. … ancient
Anglo-Fr. … Anglo-French
Anglo-Ind. … Anglo-Indian
Anglo-Ir. … Anglo-Irish
Anglo-N. … Anglo-Norse
Anglo-Norm. … Anglo-Norman
aor. … aorist, aoristic
Ar. … Arabic
Aram. … Aramaic
arch. … architecture
archaeol. … archaeology
arith. … arithmetic
Arm. … Armoric
art. … article
AS. … Anglo-Saxon
Assyr. … Assyrian
astron. … astronomy
at. wt. … atomic weight
aug. … augmentative
aux. … auxiliary

b. … born
Bab. … Babylonian
B.C. … before Christ
biol. … biology
Bohem. … Bohemian
bot. … botany
Braz. … Brazilian
Bret. … Breton
Brit. … British
B.T.U. … British thermal unit(s)
Bulg. … Bulgarian

c. … circa (about), century
Canad. … Canadian
Catal. … Catalonian
caus. … causative
Celt. … Celtic
cf. … *confer* (compare)
Ch. … Chaldean, Chaldee
Chin. … Chinese
Chron. … Chronicles
chron. … chronology
Col. … Colossians
colloq. … colloquial
comp. … comparative, compound, composition
conch. … conchology
conj. … conjunction
contr. … contraction, contracted
Cor. … Corinthians
Corn. … Cornish
cub. … cubic
Cym. … Cymric

D. … Dutch
Dan. … Danish, Daniel
dat. … dative
def. … definite
deriv. … derivation
Deut. … Deuteronomy
dial. … dialect, dialectal
dict. or dic. … dictionary
dim. … diminutive
distrib. … distributive
Dr. … Doctor
dyn. … dynamics

E. … English
Eccles. … Ecclesiastes
eccles. … ecclesiastical
e.g. … *exempli gratia* (for example)
Egypt. … Egyptian
E. Ind. … East Indian
encyc. … encyclopedia
Eng. … English
Eph. … Ephesians
Esk. … Eskimo

esp. … especially
Est. … Esther
et al. … *et alii* (and others)
etc. … et cetera (and so forth)
Eth. … Ethiopic
ethn. … ethnography, ethnology
etym. … etymology
Eur. … European
Ex. … Exodus
exclam. … exclamation
Ezek. … Ezekiel

F. or Fahr. … Fahrenheit
f. … feminine
fig. … figuratively
Finn. … Finnish
Fl. … Flemish
fl. … flourished
Fr. … French
Frank. … Frankish, Franconian
freq. … frequentative
Fris. … Frisian
ft. … foot, feet
fut. … future

G. … German
Gael. … Gaelic
Gal. … Galatians
Gen. … Genesis, General
genit. … genitive
geog. … geography
geom. … geometry
Gmc. … Germanic
Goth. … Gothic
Gr. … Greek
gram. … grammar

Hab. … Habbakuk
Hag. … Haggai
Haw. … Hawaiian
Heb. … Hebrews, Hebrew
her. … heraldry
Hind. … Hindustani, Hindu, Hindi
hist. … historical, history
hort. … horticulture
Hos. … Hosea
Hung. … Hungarian
hyp. … hypothetical

Ice. … Icelandic
i.e. … *id est* (that is)
illus. … illustration
imper. … imperative
imperf. … imperfect
impers. … impersonal
in. … inch
incept. … inceptive
Ind. … Indian
ind. … indicative
indef. … indefinite
Indo-Eur. … Indo-European
inf. … infinitive
intens. … intensive
interj. … interjection
Ir. … Irish
Iran. … Iranian
Is. or Isa. … Isaiah
It. … Italian

Japan. … Japanese
Jer. … Jeremiah, Jeremy
Josh. … Joshua
Jud. … Judges

Kin. … Kings

L. … Latin
Lev. … Leviticus
L.G. … Low German
L.Gr. … Low Greek
lit. … literal, literally
Lith. … Lithuanian
LL. … Low Latin, Late Latin

mag. … magazine
masc. … masculine
math. … mathematics
Matt. … Matthew
M.D. … Middle Dutch
ME. … Middle English
mech. … mechanics
Med. … medieval
med. … medicine, medical
metal. … metallurgy

Mex. … Mexican
MFr. … Middle French
MGr. … Medieval Greek, Middle Greek
M.H.G. … Middle High German
Mic. … Micah
milit. … military
mineral. … mineralogy
ML. … Medieval Latin
M.L.G. … Middle Low German
MnE. … Modern English
Mod. … Modern
Mongol. … Mongolian
myth. … mythology

N. … Norse
n. or n. … noun
N.Am. … North American
nat. ord. … natural order
neg. … negative
Neh. … Nehemiah
neut. … neuter
nom. … nominative
Norm. … Norman
Norw. … Norwegian
Num. … Numbers

obj. … objective
obs. … obsolete
occas. … occasionally
O.Celt. … Old Celtic
O.D. … Old Dutch
OE. … Old English
OFr. … Old French
O.H.G. … Old High German
ON., O.N. … Old Norse
O.Norm. Fr. … Old Norman French
O.Pers. … Old Persian
orig. … origin, originally
ornith. … ornithology
OS. … Old Saxon
O.Slav. … Old Slavic
O.Sp. … Old Spanish
oz. … ounce

p. or part. … participle
pass. … passive
Per. … Persic, Persian
perf. … perfect
perh. … perhaps
pers. … person
pert. … pertaining
Peruv. … Peruvian
Pet. … Peter
phar. … pharmacy
Phil. … Philemon
Philip. … Philippians
philol. … philology
philos. … philosophy
Phoen. … Phoenician
phr. … phrase
phys. geog. … physical geography
Pid. Eng. … Pidgin English
pl. … plural
poet. … poetic
Pol. … Polish
pol. econ. … political economy
Port. … Portuguese
poss. … possessive
pp. … past participle
ppr. … present participle
Pr. … Provençal
pred. … predicate
prep. … preposition
pres. … present
priv. … privative
prob. … probably
Prof. … Professor
pron. … pronoun, pronunciation, pronounced
pronun. … pronunciation
pros. … prosody
Prov. … Proverbs
prov. … provincial
Prov. Eng. … Provincial English
Prov. Scot. … Provincial Scottish
Ps. … Psalms
psychol. … psychology
pt. … past tense

q.v. … *quod vide* (which see)

R.C. … Roman Catholic
redupl. … reduplication, reduplicative
Rev. … Revelation
rhet. … rhetoric

ABBREVIATIONS

Rom.	Roman, Romans
Russ.	Russian
S.Afr.	South African
S.Am.	South American
Sam.	Samaritan, Samuel
Sans.	Sanskrit
sb.	substantive
Scand.	Scandinavian
Scot.	Scottish, Scotch
Scrip.	Scripture
Sem.	Semitic
Serb.	Serbian
Shak.	Shakespeare
sing.	singular
Slav.	Slavonic, Slavic
sp.	spelling
Sp.	Spanish
Sp. Am.	Spanish American
sp. gr.	specific gravity
sq.	square
SS.	Saints
subj.	subjunctive
superl.	superlative
surg.	surgery
Sw.	Swedish
sym.	symbol
syn.	synonym
Syr.	Syrian, Syriac
Tag.	Tagalog
Tamil.	Tamilian
Tart.	Tartar
Tat.	Tatar
term.	termination
Teut.	Teutonic
T. H.	Territory of Hawaii
theol.	theology
Thess.	Thessalonians
Tim.	Timothy
trans. or transl.	translation
Turk.	Turkish
typog.	typography
U.S.	United States
U.S.S.R.	Union of Soviet Socialist Republics
var.	variant, variety
v. or v.	verb
v.i.	verb intransitive
v.t.	verb transitive
W.	Welsh
W. Ind.	West Indian
yd.	yard
Yid.	Yiddish
Zech.	Zechariah
Zeph.	Zephaniah
zool.	zoology

A, a (ā), *n.*; *pl.* **A's, a's, As, as** (āz), 1. the first letter of the Roman and English alphabet: from the Greek *alpha*, a borrowing from the Phoenician.

2. a sound of A or a.

3. a type or impression for A or a.

4. *a symbol for* the first in a sequence or group.

A, a (ā), *a.* 1. of A or a.

2. first in a sequence or group.

3. first-class; A 1: see *A one.*

Among logicians, A, as an abbreviation, stands for a universal affirmative proposition. A asserts; E denies.

The Romans used A to signify a negative or dissent in giving their votes, A. standing for *antiquo*, I oppose or object to the proposed law. Opposed to this letter were U. R., *uti rogas*, be it as you desire—the words used to express assent to a proposition. These letters were marked on wooden ballots, and each voter had an affirmative and a negative put into his hands, one of which, at pleasure, he gave as his vote. In criminal trials, A. stood for *absolvo*, I acquit; C. for *condemno*, I condemn; and N. L. for *non liquet*, it is not evident; and the judges voted by ballots thus marked. In inscriptions, A. stands for *Augustus*; or for *ager, aiunt, aurum, argentum*, etc.

A. is used for *anno*, as in A. D., for *anno Domini*, in the year of our Lord, and A. M., for *anno mundi*, in the year of the world; and also for *ante*, as in A. M., for *ante meridiem*, before noon; and for *artium*, as in A. M., for *artium magister*, master of arts.

In algebra, *a* and other first letters of the alphabet usually represent known quantities —the last letters being used to represent unknown quantities.

In pharmacy, *ā* or *āā*, abbreviations of the Greek *ana*, signifies *of each separately*, or, that the things mentioned should be taken in quantities of the same weight or measure.

In commerce, A stands for *accepted*, as in case of a bill of exchange. Merchants also number their books by the letters A, B, C, instead of figures. Public officers number their exhibits in the same manner; as, the document *A* or B.

A (ā), *n.* 1. an object shaped like A.

2. in chemistry, *the symbol for* argon.

3. in education, a grade first in quality; as, an *A* in history.

4. in music, (a) the sixth tone or note in the scale of C major, or the first in the scale of A minor; (b) a key, string, etc. producing this tone; (c) the scale having A as the keynote.

A (ā), *a.* shaped like A.

a (ȧ *or* ā), *a., indef. art.* an abbreviation of Anglo-Saxon *an* or *ane*, one, used before words beginning with a consonant sound or a sounded *h*; as, *a* table, *a* home, *a* unicorn. [see *an.*]

a-, a combining form in many English words, as in *a*sleep, *a*wake, *a*foot, *a*ground, *a*going. In some cases, this is a contraction of the Teutonic *ge-*, as in *a*ware, from the Anglo-Saxon *gewaer*. Sometimes it is a corruption of the Anglo-Saxon *on*, as in *a*gain, from *ongean*; *a*wake, from *onwacian*, to watch or wake. In some words, *a-* may be a contraction of *at, of, in, to*, or *an*.

In some words of Greek origin *a-* is privative, giving to them a negative sense, as in *agastric*, from *a* and *gaster*, stomach. In some words derived from the Greek and Latin, *a* is used as a prefix and as a suffix; as, *a*spire, *a*mend, *a*byss, com*a*, Afric*a*, etc.

A 1 (ā wun), see *A one.*

ä·ä′, *n.* [Hawaiian.] a bed of lava that has become solidified with a rough surface.

äal, *n.* [Hind. *āl*, a plant.] a plant of the genus *Morinda*: it is commonly called *Indian mulberry.*

äam, *n.* [D.] a measure of liquids among the Dutch, varying in different cities from thirty-seven to forty-one English wine gallons.

äard′värk, *n.* [D., earth pig.] an African anteater, *Orycteropus capensis.*

AARDVARK

äard′wolf (-wulf), *n.* [D., earth wolf.] a digitigrade, carnivorous quadruped, *Proteles lalandi*, of South Africa, somewhat like the hyena and the civet.

Ăa·ron′iç, Ăa·ron′iç·ăl, *a.* pertaining to Aaron, the first high priest of the Hebrews, or to the priesthood of which he was the head.

Ăar′ŏn's bēard, the flowered St. John's-wort, *Hypericum calycinum.*

Ăar′ŏn's rod, 1. a rod with a serpent twined round it, used in architecture as an ornament.

2. any of several plants with flowers on a long stem, as the goldenrod.

ab-, a combining form used with words of Latin origin, as in *ab*duct: it is the Latin preposition *ab*, the Greek *apo*, and the English *of*, and denotes *from, from off, away, down, down from.*

Ab, *n.* the eleventh month of the Jewish civil year, and the fifth of the ecclesiastical year. In the Syriac calendar, it is the name of the last summer month.

Ab, in chemistry, alabamine.

ä′bȧ, *n.* [Ar.] 1. a woven fabric of camel's or goat's hair.

2. a loose, sleeveless robe worn by Arabs.

ab ab·sūr′dō, [L., lit., from absurdity.] obviously absurd: said of an argument that a statement is false because it is absurd.

ab′ȧ·çȧ, *n.* the native Filipino name for the manila hemp plant; also, its fiber.

ȧ·bac′i·nāte, *v.t.* [from LL. *ab*, and *bacinus*, a basin.] to destroy the sight of by placing a red-hot copper basin close to the eyes. [Rare.]

ȧ·bac·i·nā′tion, *n.* the act of destroying eyesight by placing a red-hot copper basin close to the eyes: a form of medieval torture.

ab·ȧ·cis′çus, *n.* in ancient architecture, a tile or square in a mosaic pavement.

ab′ȧ·cist, *n.* [L. *abacus*, a counting board.] one who casts accounts with an abacus; a calculator.

ȧ·back′, *adv.* [AS. *on bæc*, at, on, or toward the back.] toward the back; on the back part; backward. Now archaic except in nautical usage, where it signifies the situation of the sails when pressed back against the mast by the wind.

laid aback; having the sails purposely placed aback to give the ship sternway.

taken aback; having the sails carried back suddenly by the wind; hence, surprised.

ab·aç′ti·năl, *a.* [L. *ab*, from; and *actinal.*] pertaining to or situated at the opposite extremity from the mouth, especially in a radiate animal.

ab·aç′tion, *n.* a stealing of herds of cattle.

ab·aç′tŏr, *n.* [L. *abigere*, to drive from.] in law, one who steals herds of cattle, in distinction from one who steals a head or two.

ab·aç′ū·lus, *n.* same as *abaciscus.*

ab′ȧ·çus, *n.* [L. *abacus*, anything flat, as a sideboard, a bench, a slate, a table or board for games; Gr. *abax*, a counting board.]

ABACUS

1. among the Romans, a cupboard or buffet.

2. an instrument for doing or teaching arithmetic. On this are drawn lines; a counter on the lowest line is one; on the next, ten; on the third, a hundred, etc. On the spaces, counters denote half the number of the line above. Other schemes are called by the same name, as the calculating frame employed by the Chinese, which consists of wires stretched in a framework, with counters sliding on the wires.

ABACUS

3. in architecture, a slab atop the capital of a column. It is square in the Tuscan, Doric, and Ionic orders, but its sides are arched inward in the Corinthian and Composite. The name is also given to a concave molding on

the capital of the Tuscan pedestal, and to the plinth above the boltel in the Tuscan and Doric orders.

IONIC CAPITAL
A. the abacus

DORIC CAPITAL
A. the abacus

abacus major; a trough used for washing ore in mines.

A·bad′dŏn, *n.* [Heb., from *abad*, to perish.]
 1. the destroyer, or angel of the bottomless pit. Rev. ix. 11.
 2. the bottomless pit.

ȧ·băft′, *adv.* [AS. *be*, by, and *æftan*, behind.] on or toward the stern or rear of a ship; astern; aft.

ȧ·băft′, *prep.* in nautical usage, behind; back of.
 abaft the beam; in that arc of the horizon which is between a line drawn at right angles with the keel, and the point to which the stern is directed.

ȧ·bāi′sănce, *n.* obeisance. [Obs.]

ȧ·bāi′sẽr, *n.* ivory black or animal charcoal.

ab·āl′ien·āte (-yen-), *v.t.*; abalienated, *pt.*, *pp.*; abalienating, *ppr.* 1. to transfer the title of: a civil law term.
 2. to alienate or estrange, in general sense.
 3. in medicine, to cause aberration of (the mind). [Obs.]

ab·āl′ien·ā·ted, *a.* transferred, as a title to property; estranged.

ab·āl·ien·ā′tion, *n.* 1. mental derangement. [Obs.]
 2. the act of abalienating; transfer of title.
 3. estrangement.

ab·ȧ·lō′nē, *n.* [Sp. origin.] name used on Pacific coast of United States to designate the univalve shellfish commonly called ear shells.

ab·am′pēre, *n.* [*ab*solute, and *ampere*.] a C.G.S. electromagnetic unit, 10 amperes.

ȧ·ban′dŏn, *v.t.*; abandoned (-dund), *pt.*, *pp.*; abandoning, *ppr.* [Fr. *abandonner*; *a-*, to, and *bandon*, decree, authority, ban; that is, to place under a ban or authority of another.]
 1. to forsake entirely; as, to *abandon* a hopeless enterprise.
 2. to renounce and forsake; to leave with a view never to return; to desert as lost or desperate; as, to *abandon* a cause or party.
 3. to give up or resign (oneself) completely, without restraint; as, to *abandon* oneself to intemperance.
 4. to resign; to yield, relinquish, or give over entirely; as, to *abandon* a throne.
 5. in commerce, to relinquish to insurers (all claim to a ship or goods insured), as a preliminary toward recovering for a total loss.
 Syn.—desert, forsake, leave, quit, forego, give up, take leave of, evacuate.

ȧ·ban′dŏn, *n.* a relinquishment. [Obs.]

ȧ·bȧn·dọn′, *n.* [Fr.] 1. unrestrained freedom of activity.
 2. surrender to one's feelings or impulses.

ȧ·ban′dŏned (-dund), *a.* 1. wholly forsaken or deserted.
 2. given up, as to a vice; hence, extremely wicked, or sinning without restraint; irreclaimably wicked.
 3. unrestrained.
 Syn.—corrupt, depraved, forsaken, profligate, reprobate.

ȧ·ban·dŏn·ee′, *n.* in law, one to whom anything is abandoned.

ȧ·ban′dŏn·ẽr, *n.* one who abandons.

ȧ·ban′dŏn·ing, *n.* a forsaking; total desertion.

ȧ·ban′dŏn·ment, *n.* 1. an abandoning.
 2. the fact or state of being forsaken.
 3. in commerce, the relinquishment to underwriters of all property saved from loss by shipwreck, capture, or other peril stated in a policy. This *abandonment* must be made before the insured can demand indemnification for a total loss.

ȧ·ban′dum, *n.* in old law, anything forfeited or confiscated.

ab·an·ni′tion (-nish′un), *n.* [LL.] banishment. [Rare.]

ȧ·bap·tis′tŏn, *n.* the perforating part of the old trephine, an instrument used in trepanning. [Obs.]

ab″ăr·tiç″ū·lā′tion, *n.* in anatomy, that kind of articulation or structure of joints which allows free motion in the joint: called also *diarthrosis* and *dearticulation*.

ȧ·bāse′, *v.t.*; abased (-bāst′), *pt.*, *pp.*; abasing, *ppr.* [Fr. *abaisser*, from LL. *abassare*, to lower.]
 1. literally, to lower or depress; to throw or cast down; as, to *abase* the eye. [Archaic.]
 2. to cast down; to reduce low; to depress; to humble; to degrade: applied to the passions, rank, office, and condition in life.
 Syn.—debase, degrade, depress, disgrace, humble, humiliate, lower.

ȧ·bāsed′ (-bāst′), *a.* 1. reduced to a low state; humbled; depressed.
 2. in heraldry, a term used of the wings of eagles when the tops are turned downward toward the point of the shield.

ȧ·bāse′ment, *n.* the act of humbling or bringing low; also, a state of depression, degradation, or humiliation.

ȧ·bash′, *v.t.*; abashed (-basht′), *pt.*, *pp.*; abashing, *ppr.* [OFr. *esbahir*, to astonish.] to disconcert; to discomfit; to make ashamed; to confuse or confound, as by exciting suddenly a consciousness of guilt, error, or unworthiness.
 Syn.—disconcert, confuse, shame.

ȧ·bash′ed·ly, *adv.* in a confused manner.

ȧ·bash′ment, *n.* 1. the fact or state of being abashed.
 2. a feeling of shame or uneasiness.

ȧ·bā′si·ȧ, *n.* inability to walk properly, due to lack of co-ordination of the leg muscles.

ȧ·bas′si, ȧ·bas′sis, ab·bas′si, *n.* [Per., from Shah *Abas* II.] a silver coin formerly current in Persia, worth about twenty-nine cents.

ȧ·bāt′ȧ·ble, *a.* that may or can be abated; as, an *abatable* writ or nuisance.

ȧ·bāte′, *v.t.*; abated, *pt.*, *pp.*; abating, *ppr.* [Fr. *abattre*, to beat down.]
 1. to beat down; to pull down; to put an end to in any manner; as, to *abate* a nuisance.
 2. to lessen; to diminish; to moderate; as, to *abate* zeal; to *abate* pride; to *abate* a demand.
 3. to lessen; to mitigate; as, to *abate* pain, sorrow, or misery.
 4. to overthrow; to cause to fail; to frustrate by judicial sentence; as, to *abate* a writ.
 5. to deject; to depress; as, to *abate* the soul. [Obs.]
 6. to deduct from; to lower; as, to *abate* a price.
 7. to cause to fail; to annul. By the English law, a legacy to a charity is *abated* by a deficiency of assets.
 8. to remit; as, to *abate* a tax.

ȧ·bāte′, *v.i.* 1. to decrease, or become less in strength or violence; as, pain *abates*; a storm *abates*.
 2. to fail; to be defeated, or come to naught; as, a writ *abates*.
 3. in law, to enter into a freehold after the death of the last possessor and before the heir or devisee takes possession: with *in* or *into*.
 4. in horsemanship, to perform well a downward motion. A horse is said to *abate*, or take down his curvets, when, working upon curvets, he puts both his hind legs to the ground at once, and observes the same exactness in all his motions.
 Syn.—decrease, diminish, lessen, lower, reduce, subside, decline, intermit.

ȧ·bä′te, *n.*; *pl.* **ȧ·bä′ti,** [It.] a title given in Italy to ecclesiastics not otherwise designated. Compare *abbé*. Also written *abbate*.

ȧ·bāt′ed, *a.* lessened; decreased; destroyed; mitigated; defeated; remitted; overthrown; depressed.

ȧ·bāte′ment, *n.* 1. the act of abating; the state of being abated.
 2. in law, a reduction, removing, or pulling down, as of a nuisance.
 3. diminution, decrease, or mitigation, as of grief or pain.
 4. deduction; the sum withdrawn, as from an account.
 5. overthrow, failure, or defeat, as of a writ.
 6. in law, the entry of a stranger into a freehold after the death of the last possessor, before the heir or devisee.
 7. in heraldry, a mark of dishonor in a coat of arms by which its dignity is debased for some stain on the character of the wearer.

ȧ·bāt′ẽr, *n.* a person or thing that abates.

ab′ȧ·tis, ab′ȧt·tis, *n.sing.* and *pl.* [Fr. *abatis*.]
 1. in fortification, piles of trees or branches of trees sharpened and laid with their points outward, in front of ramparts, to prevent assailants from mounting the walls: an old form of barricade.
 2. a barbed-wire entanglement for defense; device that admits or deflects light from above.

ȧ·bat·jour′ (ä-bä-zhör′), *n.* [Fr. *abattre*, to throw down, and *jour*, daylight.] skylight;

ȧ·bāt′ŏr, *n.* in law, a person who enters into a freehold on the death of the last possessor before the heir or devisee; also, one who abates anything, as a nuisance.

A bat′tẽr·y, an electric battery of low voltage used to light the filament of certain radio tubes, etc.

ȧ·bat·toir′ (ȧ-bȧt-twär′), *n.* [Fr.] a building for the slaughtering of cattle; a slaughterhouse.

ab′ȧ·tūre, *n.* [Fr.] the track left in grass or herbage by any animal of the chase.

ȧ·bat·voix′ (ȧ-bä-vwä′), *n.* [Fr. *abattre*, to throw down, and *voix*, the voice.] a canopy or sounding board over a pulpit or rostrum.

ab·ax′i·al, *a.* [*ab-*, from, and *axial*.] away from the axis; as, an *abaxial* ray of light.

ab′bȧ, *n.* [Syr., a father.]
 1. in the Syriac, Coptic, and Ethiopic churches, a title given to the bishops.
 2. [A–] in the New Testament, God. Mark xiv. 36.

ab′bȧ·cy, *n.* [from *abba*.] the position, rights, privileges, or term of office of an abbot.

Ab·bas′sid, *n.* and *a.* Abbasside.

Ab·bas′sīde, *n.* any caliph of the dynasty that ruled at Bagdad (750–1258 A.D.) and claimed descent from Mohammed's uncle, Abbas.

Ab·bas′sīde, *a.* of the dynasty that ruled at Bagdad (750–1258 A.D.).

ab·bä′te, *n.* same as *abate, n.*

ab·bā′tiăl (-shăl), *a.* belonging to an abbey.

ab·bat′iç·ăl, *a.* abbatial.

ȧb·bé′ (ȧ-bā′), *n.* [Fr., from *abba*.] in a monastic sense, an abbot; the superior of an abbey: but more generally, a title given to Roman Catholic clergy without any determinate rank or office.

ab′bess, *n.* a female superior or governess of a nunnery, or convent of nuns, having the authority over the nuns which the abbots have over the monks.

ab′bey, *n.*; *pl.* **ab′beys,** [Fr. *abbaye*, abbey.]
 1. a monastery headed by an abbot or a nunnery headed by an abbess.
 2. the monks or nuns in such a place, collectively.
 3. a church connected with a monastery.
 Syn.—cloister, convent monastery, nunnery, priory.

ab′bey lub′bẽr, a name formerly given to an idle monk or abbey pensioner.

ab′bŏt, *n.* [AS. *abbod*; L. *abbas*, from Syr. *abba*, father.]
 1. the superior or governor of an abbey or monastery.
 2. a title sometimes borne by bishops whose sees were formerly abbeys.

ab′bŏt·ship, *n.* same as *abbacy*.

ab·boz′zō (-bot′sō), *n.* [It., a sketch.] a rough sketch or outline of anything, as of a picture or a poem; a preliminary draft.

ab·brē′vi·āte, *v.t.*; abbreviated, *pt.*, *pp.*; abbreviating, *ppr.* [L. *abbreviare*; *ad*, to, and *breviare*, from *brevis*, short.]
 1. to shorten; to make shorter.
 2. to shorten (a word or phrase) by the omission or substitution of letters.
 3. in mathematics, to reduce to lower terms.
 Syn.—abridge, condense, shorten, contract.

ab·brē′vi·ā·ted, *a.* shortened; reduced to lower terms; abridged. In botany, an *abbreviated* perianth is shorter than the tube of the corolla.

ab·brē·vi·ā′tion, *n.* 1. the act of shortening or contracting.
 2. the state or fact of being made short.
 3. a letter or letters used for a word or phrase; as, *Gen.* for Genesis; *U. S. A.* for United States of America.
 4. the reduction of fractions to lower terms.
 5. in music, one dash, or more, through the stem of a note, dividing it respectively into quavers, semiquavers, or demisemiquavers.

written played
ABBREVIATION

 6. a summary; an abridgment; a contracted or abbreviated form.
 Syn.—contraction, abridgment, curtailment.

ab·brē′vi·ā·tŏr, *n.* 1. one who abridges or reduces to a smaller compass.
 2. one of a number of secretaries in the chancery of Rome whose duty is to draw up the pope's briefs and reduce petitions, when granted, to a due form for papal bulls.

ab·brē′vi·ȧ·tō·ry, *a.* shortening; contracting.

ab·brē′vi·ȧ·tūre, *n.* a letter or character for shortening; an abridgment; a compend.

ab·brŏch′ment, *n.* the act of monopolizing goods or forestalling a market. It was formerly a criminal offense in England. [Obs.]

A B C, *pl.* **A B C's,** the first three letters of the alphabet; hence, usually in the plural, the whole alphabet; also used to denote the rudiments or first principles of anything; as, the *A B C* of farming.
A B C book; a little book or primer for teaching the elements of reading.
A B C Powers; Argentina, Brazil, and Chile.
A B C soil; a vertical section of soil made up of three layers; the top layer (*A-horizon*) is mostly humus, the middle layer (*B-horizon*) is of clay and other oxidized material, and the bottom layer (*C-horizon*) consists of loose rock and other mineral materials.

ab·çä′ree, *n.* see *abkari*.

ab·çou·lomb′ (-lom′), *n.* [*ab*solute, and *coulomb*.] a C.G.S. electromagnetic unit, 10 coulombs.

ab′dȧl, *n.* in Persia and other Asiatic countries, a Mohammedan devotee or fanatic.

ab·dȧ·lä′vï, ab·dē·lä′vi, *n.* the Egyptian muskmelon.

Ab·dē′ri·ăn, *a.* [Gr. *Abdera*, a Thracian town, birthplace of Democritus, the Laughing Philosopher.] given to foolish and immoderate laughter.

Ab′dē·rīte, *n.* an inhabitant of Abdera, a town in Thrace, home of Democritus, the Laughing Philosopher, called *the Abderite*.

ab′dest, *n.* [Per. *abdast*; *ab*, water, and *dast*, hand.] purification by washing: a Mohammedan rite.

ab·dev′en·ham, *n.* astrological term applied to the ruler of the twelfth house of the heavens.

ab′di·çȧ·ble, *a.* able to be abdicated.

ab′di·çănt, *a.* abdicating; renouncing.

ab′di·çănt, *n.* an abdicator.

ab′di·çāte, *v.t.*; abdicated, *pt.*, *pp.*; abdicating, *ppr.* [L. *abdicare*; *ab-*, and *dicare*, to proclaim.]
1. to relinquish, renounce, or abandon.
2. to give up formally or by default (a high office, throne, authority, etc.).
3. to reject, renounce, or abandon, as a right or power.
4. in the civil law, to disclaim and expel from the family, as a father his child; to disinherit during the life of the father.
Syn.—resign, renounce, abandon, give up, vacate, quit, relinquish.

ab′di·çāte, *v.i.* to renounce, abandon, cast off, or relinquish a right, power, or trust.

> Though a king may *abdicate* for his own person, he cannot *abdicate* for the monarchy. —Burke.

ab′di·çā·ted, *a.* renounced; relinquished; abandoned.

ab·di·çā′tion, *n.* 1. the act of abdicating; the act of giving up a high office, authority, or function, especially that of a king.
2. a casting off; rejection; disinheritance.

ab′di·çā·tive, *a.* causing or implying abdication.

ab′di·çā·tŏr, *n.* a person who abdicates.

ab′di·tive, *a.* [L. *abdere*, to hide.] having the ability to hide; hiding. [Rare.]

ab′di·tō·ry, *n.* a place for secreting or preserving goods. [Rare.]

ab′dō·men (*or* ab-dō′men), *n.* [L.]
1. in higher vertebrates, the belly, or that part of the body which lies between the diaphragm and the pelvis. It is lined with a membrane called the peritoneum, and contains the stomach, liver, spleen, pancreas, kidneys, bladder, and intestines. It is separated from the breast internally by the diaphragm and externally by the extremities of the ribs.
2. in insects, the posterior or hind part of the body, below the thorax. In some species, it is covered with wings and a case. It is divided into segments, or rings, on the sides of which are small spiracles by which the insect respires.

RH E LH RL U LL RI H LI

ABDOMINAL REGIONS
E, epigastric; RH, LH, right and left hypochondriac; RL, LL, right and left lumbar; U, umbilical; RI, right iliac; H, hypogastric; LI, left iliac

ab·dom′i·năl, *a.* 1. of, in, or for the abdomen; as, the *abdominal* regions.
2. having ventral fins under the abdomen: said of fishes.
abdominal ring; an oblong tendinous ring in each groin, through which pass the spermatic cord in men and the round ligaments of the uterus in women: called also *inguinal ring*.

ab·dom′i·năl, *n.* [L. *abdominalis*; pl., *abdominales*.] a member of a former large group of fishes whose ventral fins are placed behind the pectoral, and which belong to the division of bony fishes. The group contained, among other fishes, the salmon, pike, mullet, flying fish, herring, and carp.

ab·dom·i·nos′çō·py, *n.* [L. *abdomen*, and Gr. *skopein*, to look at.] inspection of the abdomen in order to detect disease.

ab·dom′i·nō·thō·rac′iç, *a.* pertaining to the abdomen and the thorax.

ab·dom′i·nous, *a.* 1. relating to the abdomen.
2. having a large belly.

ab·dūce′, *v.t.*; abduced (-dūst′), *pt.*, *pp.*; abducing, *ppr.* [L. *abducere*, to lead away.] to draw from; to withdraw, or draw to a different part: formerly used in anatomy. [Archaic.]

ab·dū′cens, *n.*; *pl.* **ab·dū·cen′tēs,** one of the abducent nerves.

ab·dū′cent, *a.* in physiology, abducting. The *abducent* muscles, called *abductors*, are opposed to the *adducent* muscles, or *adductors*.
abducent nerves; the sixth pair of cranial nerves.

ab·duçt′, *v.t.*; abducted, *pt.*, *pp.*; abducting, *ppr.* 1. to take (a person) away unlawfully and by force; kidnap.
2. in physiology, to move or pull (a part of the body) away from the median axis or from another part.

ab·duç′tion, *n.* 1. an abducting or being abducted.
2. in logic, a kind of argumentation, called by the Greeks *apagoge*, in which the major is evident, but the minor is so obscure as to require further proof.
3. in law, the unlawful taking and carrying away of a child, a wife, etc., either by fraud, persuasion, or open violence.
4. in physiology, (a) the moving of a part of the body away from the median axis or from another part; (b) the changed position resulting from this.

ab·duç′tŏr, *n.* 1. in physiology, a muscle or nerve which abducts.
2. a person who abducts; a kidnaper.

ȧ·bēam′, *adv.* 1. on the beam: a nautical term signifying at right angles to the keel of the ship.
2. opposite a ship's side (with *of*).

ȧ·beãr′, *v.t.* [AS. *aberan*.] to bear; to endure. [Dial.]

ȧ·beãr′ănce, *n.* behavior: only in *good abearance*.

ȧ·beãr′ing, *n.* demeanor. [Obs.]

ā″bē·cē·dâr′i·ăn, *n.* [formed from the first four letters of the alphabet.] one who teaches the letters of the alphabet; also, a learner of the letters; hence, a novice.

ā″bē·cē·dâr′i·ăn, ā·bē·cē′dȧ·ry, *a.* pertaining to or formed by the letters of the alphabet; hence, elementary.

ā·bē·cē′dȧ·ry, *n.*; *pl.* **ā·bē·cē′dȧ·rieș,** same as *abecedarian*, *n.*

ȧ·bed′, *adv.* on or in a bed.

ȧ·begge′, *v.t.* an obsolete form of *aby*.

ȧ·bēle′, ā′bel tree, [D. *abeel*; OFr. *abel*; LL. *albellus*, dim. of L. *albus*, white.] the white poplar.

Ā·bel′i·ăn, *a.* relating to or named after the Norwegian mathematician Abel (1802–1829); as, *Abelian* equations; *Abelian* integrals.

Ā·bel′ian (-yan), **Ā·bel·ō′ni·ăn, Ā′bel·īte,** *n.* in church history, one of a temporary sect in Africa, mentioned only by Augustine, who states that the members married, but lived in continence, after the alleged manner of Abel, and attempted to maintain the sect by adopting the children of others.

Ā·bel·mos′çhus, *n.* former name of a genus of plants to which the okra and abelmosk belong.

ā′bel·mosk, *n.* [Ar. *abu al misk*, lit., father of musk.] a species of *Hibiscus*, or Syrian mallow. The plant rises on a herbaceous stalk to a height of three or four feet, sending out two or three side branches. The seeds are used to make perfume.

Ab′ẽr·deen An̄′gus, [after *Aberdeen*, Scotland, and *Angus*, a proper name.] any of a breed of black, hornless cattle, originally from Scotland.

Ab′ẽr·deen ter′ri·ẽr, a Scottish terrier.

ab″ẽr·dē·vīne′, *n.* the European siskin, *Carduelis spinus*, a small green and yellow finch.

ab·er′rănce, *n.* [L. *aberrans*, from *ab*, and *errare*, to wander.] the quality or state of being aberrant; deviation.

ab·er′răn·cy, *n.*; *pl.* **ab·er′răn·cieș,** same as *aberrance*.

ab·er′rănt, *a.* wandering; straying from what is true, correct, normal, or typical.

ab′ẽr·rāte, *v.i.* to wander.

ab·ẽr·rā′tion, *n.* 1. a departure from what is right, true, correct, etc.; deviation from truth or moral rectitude; deviation from a straight line.
2. in astronomy, a slight apparent motion or displacement of the fixed stars, occasioned by the progressive motion of light and the earth's motion in its orbit.
3. in optics, (a) the failure of light rays from one point to converge to a single focus; (b) an error in a lens or mirror causing such failure.
4. mental derangement or lapse.
See *chromatic aberration*, *spherical aberration*.
Syn.—insanity, delusion, divergence, mania, alienation, illusion, deviation.

ab·ẽr·rā′tion·ăl, *a.* marked by aberration.

ab·ē·run̄′çāte, *v.t.* [L. *aberuncare*, to weed out.] to pull up by the roots; to extirpate completely. [Obs.]

ab·ē·run̄′çā·tŏr, *n.* 1. a weeding machine.
2. same as *averruncator*.

ȧ·bet′, *v.t.*; abetted, *pt.*, *pp.*; abetting, *ppr.* [OFr. *abeter*, to incite, to deceive.] to encourage, sanction, help, etc.: now used chiefly in a bad sense; as, to *abet* an evildoer.
Syn.—aid, encourage, countenance, incite, instigate, assist, connive at.

ȧ·bet′, *n.* the act of aiding or encouraging in a crime. [Obs.]

ȧ·bet′ment, *n.* the act of abetting.

ȧ·bet′tăl, *n.* same as *abetment*.

ȧ·bet′tŏr, ȧ·bet′tẽr, *n.* one who abets, or incites, aids, or encourages another to commit a crime. The legal form of the word is *abettor*.
Syn.—accessory, accomplice, ally, assistant.

ab·ē·vaç·ū·ā′tion, *n.* in medicine, a partial evacuation.

ȧ·bey′ănce, *n.* [OFr. *abeance*, expectation; Fr. *bayer*, to gape, stare at.]
1. in law, a state of not having been determined or settled. The fee simple or inheritance of lands and tenements is in *abeyance* when there is no person in being in whom it can vest; so that it is in a state of expectancy or waiting until a proper person shall appear. Thus, if land is leased to A for life, remainder to the heirs of B, the remainder is in *abeyance* till the death of B. —Blackstone.
2. a state of temporary suspension, as of an activity or function.

ȧ·bey′ăn·cy, *n.* abeyance.

ȧ·bey′ănt, *a.* in a state of suspense.

ab·far′ad, *n.* [*ab*solute, and *farad*.] a C.G.S. electromagnetic unit, 10^9 farads.

ab′grē·gāte, *v.t.* to separate from a herd. [Obs.]

ab′hăl, *n.* an East Indian berry, the juniper.

ab·hen′ry, *n.* [*ab*solute, and *henry*.] a C.G.S. electromagnetic unit, 10^{-9} henry.

ab·hom′i·năl, *a.* not human. [Obs.]

ab·hor′, *v.t.*; abhorred, *pt.*, *pp.*; abhorring, *ppr.* [L. *ab*, from, and *horrere*, to shrink.]
1. to hate extremely or with contempt; to loathe, detest, or abominate.
2. to be opposed or averse to.

ab·horred′, *a.* hated extremely; detested.

ab·hor′rence, *n.* 1. extreme hatred, detestation, or great aversion.
2. something abhorred or repugnant.
Syn.—antipathy, aversion, hatred, dislike.

ab·hor′ren·cy, *n.* abhorrence. [Obs.]

ab·hor′rent, *a.* 1. hating; detesting; struck with abhorrence.
2. contrary; odious; inconsistent with, or expressive of extreme opposition; as, slander is *abhorrent* to all ideas of justice. In this sense, followed by *to*.
3. exciting horror; as, *abhorrent* scenes.
Syn.—loathsome, odious, hateful, detestable, abominable, revolting, repugnant.

ab·hor′rent·ly, *adv.* with abhorrence.

ab·hor′rẽr, *n.* one who abhors.

ab·hor′ring, *n.* 1. loathing; the feeling of abhorrence.
2. an object of abhorrence; as, an *abhorring* to all flesh. [Obs.]

A′bib, *n.* [Heb. *abib*, an ear of corn.] the first month of the Jewish ecclesiastical year, seventh of the civil year, afterwards called *Nisan*.

ȧ·bīd′ănce, *n.* continuance; stay. [Rare.]

ȧ·bīde′, *v.i.*; abode, *pt.*, *pp.*; abiding, *ppr.* [AS. *abidan*, to abide.]
1. to rest, or dwell. [Archaic or Poetic.]
2. to tarry or stay for a short time. [Obs.]

3. to continue permanently, or in the same state; to be firm and immovable.

4. to remain; to continue.

Syn.—inhabit, dwell, live, lodge, rest.

ȧ·bīde′, *v.t.* 1. to wait for; to be prepared for; to await.

2. to endure or sustain.

To *abide* the indignation of the Lord.
—Joel ii. 11.

3. to bear or endure; to bear patiently; as, I cannot *abide* his impertinence.

In general, *abide by* signifies to adhere to, maintain, or defend; as, to *abide by* a bargain, a promise, or a friend; or to suffer the consequences of; as, to *abide by* the event.

ȧ·bīd′ẽr, *n.* one who dwells or abides.

ȧ·bīd′ing, *a.* without change.

Syn.—continuing, lasting, enduring, durable, steadfast, changeless, remaining, awaiting.

ȧ·bīd′ing·ly, *adv.* in a manner to continue; permanently.

Ā′bi·ēṣ, *n.* [L.] a genus of trees, the conifers, including some of the best known fir trees.

ab′i·ē·tēne, *n.* [from L. *abies,* a fir tree.] a hydrocarbon obtained by distilling the resin of the nut pine of California.

ab·i·et′iç, *a.* relating to the products of the fir tree; pertaining to the genus *Abies.*

ab′i·ē·tin, ab′i·ē·tine, *n.* a neutral resin, extracted from the turpentine of some species of *Abies.*

ab″i·ē·tin′iç, *a.* relating to abietin.

ab′i·ē·tīte, *n.* a kind of sugar obtained from the silver fir, the *Abies pectinata* of Europe.

ab′i·gāil, *n.* [originally a Hebrew proper name.] a lady's maid: from the name of a lady's maid in a popular play by Beaumont and Fletcher.

ȧ·big′ē·at, *n.* [L. *abigeatus,* cattle stealing.] the crime of cattle stealing.

a·bil′i·ment, *n.* an obsolete form of *habiliment.*

ȧ·bil′i·ty, *n.*; *pl.* **ȧ·bil′i·tieṣ,** [Fr. *habileté;* L. *habilitas,* ableness, fitness.]

1. power to do (something physical or mental).

2. riches, wealth, or substance, which are the means, or which furnish the power, of doing certain acts. [Rare.]

3. the state or quality of being able.

4. [*usually in pl.*] power of the mind; also, special skill.

5. talent.

6. civil or legal power; the power or right to do certain things; as, *ability* to inherit.

Syn.—capacity, skill, talent, aptitude.

ȧ·bīme′, ȧ·byme′ (-bēm′), *n.* abyss. [Obs.]

ab i·ni′ti·ō (i-nish′i-ō), [L.] from the beginning.

ab·in·tes′tāte, *a.* [L. *ab,* and *intestatus,* dying without a will, from *in,* and *testari,* to bear witness.] in the civil law, inheriting from one dying without a will.

ab in′trȧ, [L.] from within.

ab″i·ō·gen′e·sis, *n.* [Gr. *a* priv., *bios,* life; *genesis,* generation.] generation of living from nonliving matter; spontaneous generation: a former theory, now rejected.

ab″i·ō·ġē·net′iç, *a.* of or pertaining to abiogenesis.

ab″i·ō·ġē·net′iç·ăl·ly, *adv.* by spontaneous generation.

ab·i·oġ′e·nist, *n.* one who holds the doctrine of abiogenesis.

ab·i·oġ′e·nous, *a.* produced by abiogenesis.

ab·i·oġ′e·ny, *n.* same as *abiogenesis.*

a″bī·ō·log′iç·ăl, *a.* relating to the study of lifeless matter; not biological.

ā·bī·ol′ō·ġy, *n.* the science of inanimate things: in contradistinction to biology.

ab′i·on, *n.* inanimate things in the aggregate, as contrasted with animate beings.

ab·i·ō′sis, *n.* existence of a state of lifelessness; absence of life.

ab·ir′ri·tănt, *a.* relieving or lessening irritation.

ab·ir′ri·tănt, *n.* something, especially a medicine or a drug, that allays irritation.

ab·ir′ri·tāte, *v.t.*; abirritated, *pt., pp.*; abirritating, *ppr.* to deaden sensibility in; to debilitate.

ab·ir·ri·tā′tion, *n.* debility; low vitality.

ab·ir′ri·tā·tive, *a.* characterized by debility.

ab·jeçt′, *v.t.* to throw away; to cast down. [Obs.]

ab′jeçt, *a.* [L. *abjectus; abjicere,* to throw away, from *ab,* and *jacere,* to throw.]

1. sunk to a low condition: applied to persons or things.

2. worthless; mean; despicable; low in estimation; without hope or regard.

Syn.—low, degraded, contemptible, pitiful.

ab′jeçt, *n.* a person in the lowest condition [Obs.]

ab·jeçt′ed·ness, *n.* a very low or despicable condition. [Obs.]

ab·jeç′tion, *n.* a state of being cast away; hence, a low state; meanness of spirit; baseness.

ab·jeçt′ly, *adv.* in a contemptible manner; meanly; servilely.

ab·jeçt′ness, *n.* meanness; servility.

ab·judġe′, *v.t.* to reject or remove by law. [Rare.]

ab·jū′di·çāte, *v.t.* to abjudge. [Rare.]

ab·jū·di·çā′tion, *n.* rejection or deprivation by judgment.

ab′jū·gāte, *v.t.* [L. *abjugatus.*] to unyoke. [Obs.]

ab·junç′tive, *a.* isolated. [Rare.]

ab·jū·rā′tion, *n.* 1. the act of abjuring; a renunciation upon oath; as, an *abjuration* of the realm, by which a person swore to leave the country and never to return. Formerly, in England, felons, taking refuge in a church and confessing their guilt, might save their lives by abjuring the realm.

2. a formal rejection or denial; a solemn renunciation; as, an *abjuration* of heresy.

oath of abjuration; an oath whereby an alien seeking naturalization renounces allegiance to all foreign sovereignties; also formerly, in England, an oath asserting the right of the present royal family to the crown and disclaiming such right in the descendants of the house of Stuart.

ab·jū′rȧ·tō·ry, *a.* abjuring.

ab·jūre′, *v.t.*; abjured, *pt., pp.*; abjuring, *ppr.* [L. *abjurare,* to deny upon oath.]

1. to renounce upon oath; to abandon; as, to *abjure* allegiance to a prince.

2. to renounce or reject with solemnity; to reject; as, to *abjure* errors; to *abjure* reason.

3. to recant or retract.

Syn.—abnegate, recant, renounce, retract, deny, recall, revoke, forswear.

ab·jūre′, *v.i.* to take an oath of abjuration. [Rare.]

ab·jūr′ẽr, *n.* one who abjures.

ab·kä′rī, *n.* [Hind. *abkar,* a distiller.] in India, the manufacture and traffic in intoxicating liquors; also, the government tax paid by distillers and dealers. Also written *abcaree, abkary,* etc.

ab·laç′tāte, *v.t.* [L. *ablactare; ab,* and *lac,* milk.] to wean from the breast. [Rare.]

ab·laç·tā′tion, *n.* 1. the weaning of a child from the breast.

2. the old name of a method of grafting, in which the scion is not separated from the parent stock until it is firmly united to that in which it is inserted: now called grafting by approach or inarching.

ab·lā′quē·āte, *v.t.* to lay bare, as the roots of a tree or vine. [Obs.]

ab·lā·quē·ā′tion, *n.* [L. *ablaqueare.*] a laying bare the roots of trees or vines to expose them to the air and water.

ab·las·tem′iç, *a.* [Gr. *a* priv., and *blastēma,* sprout.] nongerminal.

ȧ·blas′tous, *a.* [Gr. *ablastos,* barren.] having no bud or germ.

ab·lā′tion, *n.* [L. *ablatus,* pp. of *auferre,* to carry away.]

1. a carrying away.

2. in medicine, the surgical removal of a part of the body.

3. in chemistry, the removal of whatever is finished or no longer necessary.

4. in geology, the melting of a glacier, the wasting away of rocks, etc.

ab·lȧ·ti′tious (-tish′us), *a.* lessening.

ab′lȧ·tive, *n.* [L. *ablativus,* from *ablatus,* pp. of *auferre,* to carry away.] in linguistics, (a) the case which chiefly signifies a taking away, removal, and direction from; (b) a word or phrase in this case; (c) in Latin, the case expressing source, cause, agency, and instrument, as well as deprivation; (d) a Latin word or phrase in this case.

ablative absolute; in Latin grammar, a construction somewhat resembling the *nominative absolute* in English, in which a noun or pronoun, combined with a participle expressed or understood, or with some other qualifying word, forms an adverbial clause which, if omitted, leaves a perfect or complete sentence.

ab′lȧ·tive, *a.* 1. taking away or tending to remove. [Obs.]

2. in grammar, of or in the ablative.

ab′laut, *n.* [G. *ab,* off, and *laut,* sound.] vowel gradation expressing changes of tense, aspect, etc., such as takes place in the verb, *sing, sang, sung.*

ab′laut, *a.* of or characterized by ablaut.

ȧ·blāze′, *adv.* on fire; in a blaze.

ā′ble, *a.*; *comp.* abler; *superl.* ablest, [OE. *abil, habil;* OFr. *able,* Fr. *habile,* from L. *habilis,* suitable, fit, from *habere,* to have, hold.]

1. having sufficient power or strength, bodily or mental (to do something); as, a man *able* to perform military service; a child is not *able* to reason on abstract subjects.

2. having strong or unusual powers of mind, or intellectual qualifications; as, an *able* minister.

3. having large or competent property, or simply having property or means; as, he is *able* to support a wife.

4. having competent strength or fortitude; as, he is *able* to sustain great pain.

5. having competent legal power or qualifications; as, *able* to take by inheritance.

6. in nautical usage, seaworthy.

Syn.—capable, efficient, skillful, clever, strong, powerful, effective.

ā′ble, *v.t.* to enable. [Obs.]

-a′ble, [L. *-abilis.*] a combining form very common as a termination of adjectives, especially those based on verbs, and signifying *able to, having qualities of, tending to, capable of, worthy of,* etc.; as, toler*able,* obtain*able,* laud*able.*

ā′ble-bod″ied (-id), *a.* having a sound, strong body, or a body of competent strength for service. In marine language, it denotes skill in seamanship.

ā″ble-bod′ied·ness, *n.* physical soundness; robustness.

ā′ble-bod″ied sēa′măn, a trained, skillful sailor.

ab′lē·gāte, *n.* in the Roman Catholic Church, a papal envoy of high rank, entrusted with important diplomatic missions; also, the envoy who bears to a newly created cardinal his insignia of office.

ab·lē·gā′tion, *n.* the act of sending abroad. [Obs.]

ā′ble-mīnd″ed, *a.* having mental power.

ā″ble-mīnd′ed·ness, *n.* intellectual ability.

ab′len, ab′let, *n.* [Fr. *ablette,* from L. *albus,* white, hence the name *bleak.*] a small freshwater fish, the bleak.

ā′ble·ness, *n.* ability of body or mind; force; vigor.

ab·lep′si·ȧ, ab′lep·sy, *n.* [Gr. *ablepsia,* blindness.] blindness.

ā′ble sēa′măn, an able-bodied seaman.

ab′li·gāte, *v.t.* [L. *abligare.*] to keep from by tying up. [Obs.]

ab·lig·ū·ri′tion (-rish′un), *n.* [L. *abliguritio,* feasting.] extravagance in the preparation and serving of food. [Obs.]

ā′bliṇṣ, *adv.* see *aiblins.*

ȧ·bloom′, *adv.* in bloom.

ab·lūde′, *v.i.* [L. *ab,* and *ludere,* to play.] to be unlike; to differ. [Obs.]

ab′lū·ent, *a.* [L. *abluere,* to wash away.] washing clean; cleansing by water or liquids.

ab′lū·ent, *n.* in medicine, that which purifies the blood; also, that which removes filth or viscid matter from the skin, ulcers, etc.

ȧ·blush′, *adv.* and *a.* rosy; blushing.

ab·lū′tion, *n.* 1. in a general sense, the act of washing; a cleansing or purification by water.

2. the washing of the body as a preparation for religious duties.

3. in chemistry, the purification of bodies by the affusion of a proper liquid, as water to dissolve salts. [Obs.]

4. in medicine, the washing of the body externally, as by baths, or internally, by diluting fluids. [Obs.]

5. the water used in cleansing. [Rare.]

6. in the Roman Catholic Church, a small quantity of wine and water which is used to wash the chalice and the priest's fingers after the Communion, and which then, as containing portions of the consecrated elements, is drunk by the priest.

ab·lū′tion·ā·ry, *a.* pertaining to ablution.

ab·lū′vi·ŏn, *n.* that which is washed off. [Rare.]

ā′bly, *adv.* in an able manner; with great ability.

-a′bly, a combining form for adverbs; as, accept*ably.*

ab′nē·gāte, *v.t.*; abnegated, *pt., pp.*; abnegating, *ppr.* to deny; to renounce.

Syn.—abjure, disown, disclaim, surrender.

ab·nē·gā′tion, *n.* [L. *ab,* from, and *negare,* to deny.] a denial; a renunciation; self-denial.

Syn.—denial, renunciation, abjuration.

ab′nē·gā·tŏr, *n.* one who denies, renounces, or opposes anything.

ab·nẽrv′ăl, *a.* [L. *ab*, from, and *nervus*, nerve.] from a nerve.

ab′net, *n.* in ancient times, the girdle of a Jewish priest.

ab·neū′răl, *a.* situated in or pertaining to the region opposite to the neural axis.

ab′nō·dāte, *v.t.* [L. *abnodare*; *ab*, from, and *nodare*, to cut.] to cut knots from (trees). [Obs.]

ab·nō·dā′tion, *n.* the act of cutting away the knots of trees. [Obs.]

ab·nọr′măl, *a.* [L. *abnormis*; *ab*, from, and *norma*, rule.] not normal; not average; not typical; irregular; varying from an established standard; anomalous; as, an *abnormal* appetite or thirst.

Syn.—eccentric, strange, unusual, unnatural, irregular, anomalous.

ab·nor·mal′i·ty, *n.* 1. the state of being abnormal.

2. *pl.* **ab·nor·mal′i·tieṣ,** that which is abnormal.

ab·nọr′măl·ly, *adv.* in an abnormal manner.

ab·nọr′măl psy̆·chol′ō·gy̆, the study of the behavior of abnormal people, especially that of the neurotic, psychotic, or feeble-minded.

ab·nọr′mi·ty, *n.*; *pl.* **ab·nọr′mi·tieṣ,** [L. *abnormis*, irregular.]

1. abnormality.

2. monstrosity.

ab·nọr′mous, *a.* abnormal.

ȧ·bōard′, *adv.* 1. within a ship, vessel, or boat; on board; as, he came *aboard* at midnight; also, within or on a train or streetcar.

2. by the side of; as, to lie close *aboard*.

aboard main tack; an order to draw a corner of the mainsail down to the chesstree.

all aboard; an imperative phrase notifying passengers to get upon a train or other vehicle; an announcement of the intention of starting.

to fall aboard; to strike a ship's side.

to get aboard; to get foul of, as a ship.

to go aboard; to enter a ship; to embark.

ȧ·bōard′, *prep.* 1. on board of; as, *aboard* a ship.

2. alongside.

ȧ·bō′brȧ, *n.* a South American gourd.

ȧ·bōd′ănce, *n.* an omen. [Obs.]

ȧ·bōde′, past tense and past participle of *abide*.

ȧ·bōde′, *n.* [see *abide*.]

1. stay; a staying in a place; residence for a longer or shorter time.

2. a place of residence; a dwelling; a habitation.

to make abode; to dwell or reside.

Syn.—dwelling, domicile, residence, house, home, sojourn, stay.

ȧ·bōde′, *v.t.* bode. [Obs.]

ȧ·bōd′ing, *n.* presentiment. [Obs.]

ä·bō·gä′dō, *n.* [Sp.] a lawyer or advocate.

ab·ōhm′ (-ōm′), *n.* [*ab*solute, and *ohm*.] a C.G.S. electromagnetic unit, 10^{-9} ohm.

ȧ·bol′ish, *v.t.*; abolished (-isht), *pt.*, *pp.*; abolishing, *ppr.* [Fr. *abolir*; L. *abolere*, from *ab*, and *olere*, to grow.]

1. to make void; to annul; to abrogate: applied chiefly to established laws, contracts, customs, and institutions.

2. to destroy, or put an end to.

Syn.—abrogate, nullify, annul, repeal, revoke, cancel, destroy, do away with, annihilate.

ȧ·bol′ish·ȧ·ble, *a.* that may be annulled, abrogated, or destroyed, as a law, rite, custom, etc.

ȧ·bol′ish·ẽr, *n.* one who abolishes.

ȧ·bol′ish·ment, *n.* the act of annulling; abrogation; destruction.

ab·ō·li′tion, *n.* 1. the act of abolishing, or the state of being abolished; an annulling; abrogation; utter destruction; as, the *abolition* of laws, decrees, ordinances, rites, customs, debts, etc.

2. [sometimes A-] the putting an end to slavery in the United States.

ab·ō·li′tion·iṣm, *n.* the principles of an abolitionist; belief in the abolition of slavery.

ab·ō·li′tion·ist, *n.* a person who favors abolition; specifically, one who favored the abolition of slavery in the United States.

ab·ō·li′tion·īze, *v.t*; abolitionized, *pt.*, *pp.*; abolitionizing, *ppr.* to teach abolitionism; to imbue with belief in abolitionism.

ȧ·bol′lȧ, *n.* [L.] a garment worn by the ancient Greeks and Romans.

ab·ō·mā′sum, ab·ō·mā′sus, *n.* [L. *ab*, from, and *omasum*, a third stomach.] the fourth stomach of a ruminant animal, lying next to the omasum, or third stomach.

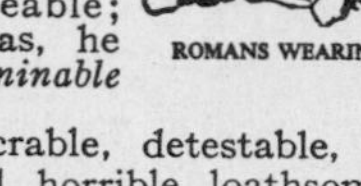

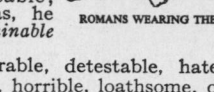

ROMANS WEARING THE ABOLLA

Ā′-bomb, *n.* an atomic bomb,

ȧ·bom′i·nȧ·ble, *a.* [see *abominate*.]

1. very hateful; detestable; loathsome; odious to the mind; offensive to the senses.

2. disagreeable; very bad; as, he shows *abominable* taste.

Syn.—execrable, detestable, hateful, abhorrent, foul, horrible, loathsome, odious.

ȧ·bom′i·nȧ·ble·ness, *n.* the quality or state of being odious; hatefulness.

ȧ·bom′i·nȧ·bly, *adv.* in an abominable manner.

ȧ·bom′i·nāte, *v.t.*; abominated, *pt.*, *pp.*; abominating, *ppr.* [L. *ab*, from, and *ominari*, to regard as an omen.]

1. to hate extremely; to abhor; to detest.

2. to dislike very much.

Syn.—abhor, detest, execrate, hate, loathe.

ȧ·bom·i·nā′tion, *n.* 1. extreme hatred; detestation.

2. the object of detestation.

The way of the wicked is an *abomination* unto the Lord. —Prov. xv. 9.

3. hence, any object of extreme hatred.

ȧ·bom′i·nā·tŏr, *n.* one who abominates.

ȧ·bọọn′, *prep.* and *adv.* [Scot.] above.

ab·ō′răl, *a.* [L. *ab*, from, and *os* (*oris*), mouth.] away from the mouth.

ȧ·bōrd′, *n.* [Fr.] literally, arrival, but formerly used for first appearance, manner of accosting, or address. [Obs.]

ȧ·bōrd′, *v.t.* 1. to approach. [Obs.]

2. to accost. [Archaic.]

ab·ō·rig′i·năl, *a.* [L. *ab*, from, and *origo*, origin.]

1. first; original: *aboriginal* people are the first inhabitants of a country.

2. of or characteristic of aborigines.

Syn.—native, indigenous, original.

ab·ō·rig′i·năl, *n.* 1. an original inhabitant. The first inhabitants of a country are called *aboriginals*, as the Indians in America.

2. an aboriginal plant or animal.

ab·ō·rig·i·nal′i·ty, *n.* the state of being aboriginal.

ab·ō·rig′i·năl·ly, *adv.* in an aboriginal manner; originally.

ab·ō·rig′i·nēs, *n.pl.*; *sing.* **ab·ō·rig′i·nē,** 1. the first inhabitants of a country.

2. the flora and fauna native to a region.

ȧ·bọrn′ing, *adv.* while being born or created; as, the plan died *aborning*.

ȧ·bọrse′ment, *n.* abortion. [Obs.]

ȧ·bọrt′, *v.i.*; aborted, *pt.*, *pp.*; aborting, *ppr.* [L. *ab*, from, and *oriri*, to rise.]

1. to miscarry; to give birth prematurely; hence, to come to nothing.

2. in biology, to remain undeveloped, as the organs of an animal or plant.

ȧ·bọrt′, *v.t.* 1. to cause to have an abortion.

2. to check (a disease) before fully developed.

3. to cut short (an action or operation of an aircraft, guided missile, etc.), as because of some failure in the equipment.

ȧ·bọrt′, *n.* an abortion. [Obs.]

ȧ·bọr′ti·cīde, *n.* [L. *abortus*, and *cidium*, from *caedere*, to kill.]

1. the act of destroying a fetus; feticide.

2. an abortifacient.

ȧ·bọr·ti·fā′cient (-shent), *a.* [L. *abortio*, miscarriage, and *facere*, to make.] causing abortion.

ȧ·bọr·ti·fā′cient, *n.* that which causes abortion.

ȧ·bọr′tion, *n.* [L. *abortio*, a miscarriage.]

1. the act of miscarrying, or producing young before the natural time, or before the fetus is perfectly formed: called *criminal abortion* when unlawful.

2. the fetus brought forth before it is perfectly formed; hence, anything misshapen or imperfectly developed; a monstrosity.

3. in a figurative sense, any fruit or produce that does not come to maturity, or anything which fails in its progress before it is matured or perfect, as a design or project.

4. in biology, (a) the incomplete or arrested development of an organ; (b) an organ whose development has been arrested.

ȧ·bọr′tion·ăl, *a.* abortive.

ȧ·bọr′tion·ist, *n.* one who causes or seeks to cause abortion, especially a criminal abortion.

ȧ·bọr′tive, *a.* 1. brought forth in an immature state; failing, or coming to naught, before it is complete.

2. failing in its effect; miscarrying; producing nothing; as, an *abortive* scheme.

3. productive of nothing; chaotic; as, the *abortive* gulf. [Rare.]

4. pertaining to abortion; as, *abortive* vellum is made of the skin of an *abortive* calf.

5. in medicine, (a) producing abortion; as, *abortive* drugs; (b) cutting short a disease process.

6. in biology, incompletely developed; imperfect or stunted, as an organ.

ȧ·bọr′tive, *n.* 1. that which is brought forth or born prematurely. [Obs.]

2. a drug used to cause abortion; an abortifacient. [Obs.]

ȧ·bọr′tive·ly, *adv.* immaturely; in an untimely manner.

ȧ·bọr′tive·ness, *n.* the state of being abortive; want of success.

ȧ·bọrt′ment, *n.* an untimely birth. [Obs.]

ȧ·bōu′li·ȧ, *n.* same as *abulia*.

ȧ·bound′, *v.i.*; abounded, *pt.*, *pp.*; abounding, *ppr.* [L. *abundare*, to overflow.]

1. to have or possess in great quantity; to be wealthy (*in*); as, to *abound in* good things.

2. to be in great plenty; to be very prevalent; as, vice *abounds*, game *abounds*.

3. to be filled; teem (*with*); as, woods that *abound with* game.

Syn.—flourish, luxuriate, teem, overflow, swarm.

ȧ·bound′ing, *n.* increase; abundance.

ȧ·bout′, *prep.* [AS. *abutan*, *onbutan*, *embutan*, about, around.]

1. around, on the exterior part or surface of; as, a girdle *about* the waist.

2. near to in place, with the sense of circularity; close to; as, enemies *about* him on every hand.

3. near to in time, number, quantity, degree, etc.; as, *about* 12 o'clock; *about* three weeks; *about* 500 men; *about* a bushel; *about* the best; *about* my height.

4. near to in action, or near to the performance of some act; as, Paul was *about* to open his mouth.

5. near to the person of; appended to the clothes; as, everything *about* him is in order.

6. concerned in; engaged in; as, what is he *about?*

7. around, referring to compass or circumference; as, two yards *about* the stem.

8. here and there, in different parts and directions of; as, the gossip *about* the village; a man *about* town.

9. in relation to; having regard to; as, they will talk *about* you; much ado *about* nothing.

ȧ·bout′, *adv.* 1. near to in quality, degree, etc.; as, *about* as high, or as cold.

2. on every side; all around.

3. here and there; around; in one place and another; as, wandering *about*.

4. in circumference; as, ten miles *about*.

5. around, or by the longest way: opposed to *across*, or by the shortest way; as, a mile *about*, and half a mile *across*.

6. near; as, standing somewhere *about*.

7. in an opposite direction; as, to face or turn *about*.

8. in readiness; as, *about* to sail; *about* to begin.

9. in succession or rotation; as, turn and turn *about* is fair play.

10. almost; all but; as, just *about* done.

about face; a military command ordering soldiers to turn about or face oppositely.

about ship, *ready about*; orders to sailors to prepare for tacking.

to bring about; to bring to the end; to effect or accomplish (a purpose).

to come about; to happen; to change or turn; to come to the desired point. In a like sense, seamen say *go about* when a ship changes her course to go on the other tack.

to go about; to enter upon; also, to prepare; to seek the means.

ȧ·bout′-fāce, *n.* the act of turning about, or facing oppositely. Figuratively, a reversal of opinion; a decided change of attitude.

ȧ·bout″-fāce′, *v.i.*; about-faced, *pt.*, *pp.*; about-facing, *ppr.* to effect an about-face.

ȧ·bout″-ship′, *v.i.* to put a ship on the other tack.

ȧ·bŏve′, *prep.* [AS. *abufan*; *a*, on, and *bufan*, *beufan*; *be*, by, and *ufan*, above.]
1. literally, higher than; over; as, *above* the earth.
2. figuratively, superior in any respect; as, *above* reproach; the colonel is *above* the captain in rank.
3. more in number or quantity; as, the weight is *above* a ton; *above* five hundred members.
4. more in degree; in a greater degree; as, happiness is to be preferred *above* riches.
5. beyond in place or position; as, the road *above* the town.
6. beyond; in a state to be unattainable; as, things *above* comprehension.
7. too elevated in mind or rank; having too much dignity for; as, this man is *above* mean actions.

ȧ·bŏve′, *adv.* 1. overhead; in a higher place; as, the stars *above*; the powers *above*.
2. before; in a former place; as, what was said *above*.
3. higher in authority; as, an appeal to the court *above*.
4. more than; as, *above* a score.
above all; most of all; mainly.

ȧ·bŏve′, *a.* preceding; foregoing; as, the *above* citation.

ȧ·bŏve′, *n.* something that is above.

ȧ·bŏve′bōard, *a.* and *adv.* above the board or table; in open sight; without trick, concealment, or deception.

ȧ·bŏve′deck, *a.* and *adv.* on deck; aboveboard.

ȧ·bŏve′ground, *adv.* and *a.* not buried; not dead.

ȧ·bŏve′-men″tioned, *a.* mentioned before.

ȧ·bŏve′-said (-sed), *a.* mentioned or recited before.

ȧ·bŏve′stāirs, *adv.* upstairs; on the floor above.

ȧ·bŏve′-wat′ẽr, *a.* above the surface of a body of water.

ab ō′vō, [L., from the egg.] from the beginning.

ȧ·box′, *adv.* and *a.* in the position of a vessel's headyards when the headsails are laid aback.

ab″rȧ·cȧ·dab′rȧ, *n.* any cabalistic word or formula supposed to have magic powers; hence, unmeaning language; jargon.

ab·rā′dănt, *a.* abrading.

ab·rā′dănt, *n.* a substance used for polishing or grinding, as emery.

ab·rāde′, *v.t.*; abraded, *pt.*, *pp.*; abrading, *ppr.* [L. *abradere*; *ab*, away, and *radere*, to scrape.] to rub or wear off; to waste by friction.
Syn.—scrape off, wear away, wear off, waste away, erase.

Ā′brȧ·ham, *n.* [Heb., lit., father of many: see Gen. xvii. 5.] in the Bible, the first patriarch and ancestor of the Hebrews: Gen. xii–xxv.

Ā·brȧ·ham′iç, Ā″brȧ·ham·it′iç, *a.* pertaining to Abraham, the patriarch; as, the *Abrahamic* covenant.

Ā′brȧ·ham-man, Ā′brȧm-man, *n.* one of a class of impostors, in England, who wandered about the country, pretending lunacy.
to sham Abraham; to feign sickness.

Ā′brȧ·ham's bos′ŏm (booz′um), the repose of bliss after death.

A·brañ′çhi·ȧ, *n.pl.* [Gr. *a* priv., and *branchia*, gills.] a term applied to an order of *Annelida*, because the species composing it have no special organs of respiration.

ȧ·brañ′çhi·ăn, *a.* abranchiate.

ȧ·brañ′çhi·ăn, ȧ·brañ′çhi·āte, *n.* one of the *Abranchia*.

ȧ·brañ′çhi·āte, *a.* pertaining to the *Abranchia*; having no gills.

ȧ·brañ′çhi·ous, *a.* abranchiate. [Rare.]

Ab′rȧ·sax, *n.* see *Abraxas*.

ab·rāse′, *v.t.*; abrased, *pt.*, *pp.*; abrasing, *ppr.* to wear away; to smooth; to abrade.

ab·rā′sion, *n.* 1. the act of scraping or rubbing off, as of skin.
2. a wearing away by rubbing or scraping, as of rock by wind, water, etc.
3. substance worn off by attrition or rubbed off.
4. an abraded spot or area.

ab·rā′sive, *a.* 1. tending to cause abrasion.
2. tending to provoke anger, ill will, etc.; aggressively annoying; irritating.

ab·rā′sive, *n.* a substance used for grinding, polishing, etc., as sandpaper or emery.

ab′raum, *n.* [G. *ab*, off, and *raumen*, to take.] a red ocher used to color mahogany.
abraum salts; a combination of salts found at Stassfurt, Prussia, used largely in the manufacture of potassic salts.

Ab·rax′ăs, Ab′rȧ·sax, *n.* [the Greek letters *a, b, r, a, x, a, s*, as numerals express 365.]
1. a word denoting a power which presides over 365 others, the number of days in a year, and used as a mystical term to express the supreme God, under whom the Basilidians supposed 365 dependent deities. It was the principle of the Gnostic hierarchy, whence sprang their multitude of eons.
2. in antiquities, a gem or stone with the word *abraxas* engraved on it.

ab″rē·aç′tion, *n.* [*ab-*, and *reaction*, after G. *abreagierung*.] in psychoanalysis, the relieving of a repressed emotion, as by talking about it.

ȧ·breast′ (-brest′), *adv.* and *a.* side by side (in going or facing forward).
abreast of (or *with*); in line with; not behind.

ȧ·bridġe′, *v.t.*; abridged, *pt.*, *pp.*; abridging, *ppr.* [Fr. *abréger*, from L. *abbreviare*; *ad*, to, and *brevis*, short.]
1. to make shorter; to epitomize; to shorten by using fewer words, yet retaining the sense in substance: used of writings; as, Justin *abridged* the history of Trogus Pompeius.
2. to shorten in duration, extent, scope, etc.; to diminish; lessen; curtail; as, to *abridge* power or rights.
3. to deprive; to cut off: followed by *of*; as, to *abridge* one *of* his rights or enjoyment.
Syn.—abbreviate, contract, shorten, cut down, prune.

ȧ·bridġed′, *a.* condensed; shortened; epitomized; curtailed.

ȧ·bridġ′ẽr, *n.* one who or that which abridges.

ȧ·bridġ′ment, ȧ·bridġe′ment, *n.* 1. an abridged or condensed form of a book, etc.
2. diminution; contraction; reduction; as, an *abridgment* of expenses.
3. curtailment, as of rights.
Syn.—abstract, abbreviation, compend, compendium, contraction, digest, epitome, summary, synopsis.

ā′brin, *n.* [Gr. *habros*, graceful.] a vegetable toxin obtained from the seed of the wild licorice and used in treating trachoma.

ȧ·brōach′, *adv.* 1. broached; opened so that the liquid contents can come out.
2. astir; as, set mischief *abroach*.

ȧ·broad′, *adv.* 1. in a general sense, at large; widely; not confined to narrow limits.
2. beyond the walls of a house; outdoors; as, to walk *abroad*.
3. beyond the limits of a camp or fortified place.
4. beyond the bounds of a country; in foreign countries; as, to go *abroad* for an education.
5. extensively; before the public at large; as, to tell the news *abroad*.
6. widely; with expansion; as, a tree spreads its branches *abroad*.

ab′rō·gȧ·ble, *a.* that may be abrogated.

ab′rō·gāte, *v.t.*; abrogated, *pt.*, *pp.*; abrogating, *ppr.* [L. *abrogare*, to repeal; *ab*, from, and *rogare*, to ask or propose.] to repeal; to annul by an authoritative act; to abolish by the authority of the maker or his successor: applied to the repeal of laws, decrees, or ordinances, the abolition of established customs, etc.
Syn.—abolish, nullify, rescind, annul, repeal.

ab·rō·gā′tion, *n.* the act of abrogating; repeal (of a law, etc.).

ab′rō·gā·tive, *a.* causing repeal; tending to abrogate.

ab′rō·gā·tŏr, *n.* one who abrogates.

A·brō′ni·ȧ, *n.* [Gr. *habros*, delicate.] a genus of North American trailing plants, bearing heads of fragrant verbenalike flowers.

ȧ·brood′, *adv.* brooding. [Dial.]

ȧ·brook′, *v.t.* to brook; to endure. [Obs.]

ab·rot′ȧ·num, *n.* [Gr. *abrotonon*.] a species of evergreen plants classified under the genus *Artemisia*: called also *southernwood*.

ab·rupt′, *a.* [L. *abruptus*, from *abrumpere*, to break off.]
1. literally, broken off, or broken short.
2. steep; craggy: applied to rocks, precipices, and the like.
3. figuratively, sudden; without notice to prepare the mind for the event; as, an *abrupt* entrance or address.

1. ABRUPT ROOT
2. ABRUPT LEAF
3. ABRUPT-PINNATE LEAF

4. sudden and short in behavior or speech; gruff; brusque.
5. unconnected; having sudden transitions from one subject to another; as, an *abrupt* style.
6. in botany, terminating suddenly; ending as if broken or cut off; as, an *abrupt*-pinnate leaf is one which has neither leaflet nor tendril at the end.
Syn.—sudden, unexpected, blunt, bluff, unceremonious.

ab·rupt′, *n.* a chasm; an abrupt place. [Poetic.]
Over the vast *abrupt*. —Milton.

ab·rupt′ed, *a.* torn off; torn asunder. [Obs.]

ab·rup′tion, *n.* a sudden breaking off; a violent separation of parts of a mass.

ab·rupt′ly, *adv.* suddenly; in an abrupt manner.

ab·rupt′ness, *n.* the state or quality of being abrupt.

Ā′brus, *n.* [Gr. *habros*, graceful.] a genus of papilionaceous plants, including the Jamaica wild licorice.

abs-, ab-: used before *t* or *c*, as in *abstract*, *abscond*.

ab′scess, *n.* [L. *abscessus*, from *ab*, and *cedere*, to go from.] a swollen, inflamed area in body tissues, in which pus gathers.

ab′scess, *v.i.* to form an abscess.

ab′scessed, *a.* [pp. of *abscess*.] having an abscess or abscesses.

ab·sces′sion, *n.* departure. [Obs.]

ab·scind′, *v.t.*; abscinded, *pt.*, *pp.*; abscinding, *ppr.* [L. *ab*, off, and *scindere*, to cut.] to cut off. [Archaic.]

ab·scis′sȧ, *n.*; *pl.* **ab·scis′sae** (-sē), [L. *abscissa (linea)*, (a line) cut off; fem. of *abscissus*, pp. of *abscindere*; *ab-*, off, and *scindere*, to cut.] in geometry, the line or part of a line drawn horizontally on a graph, by which a point is located with reference to a system of co-ordinates: distinguished from *ordinate*.

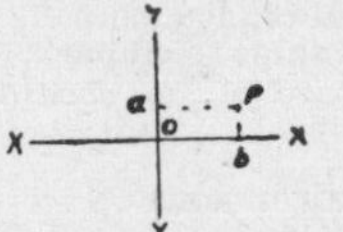

O is the origin. *XX* is axis of abscissae. *YY* is axis of ordinates. *aP* is abscissa. *bP* is ordinate.

ab·sciṣ′ṣion (-sizh′un), *n.* [L. *abscissio*, from *ab*, and *scindere*, to cut off.]
1. a cutting off, as by surgery.
2. in rhetoric, a device in which the speaker, having begun to say a thing, stops abruptly, as if supposing the matter sufficiently understood; thus, "He is a man of so much honor and candor, and such generosity—but I need say no more."

ab·sçond′, *v.i.*; absconded, *pt.*, *pp.*; absconding, *ppr.* [L. *abscondere*; *abs*, from or away, and *condere*, to hide.]
1. to go away hastily and secretly; run away and hide, especially in order to escape the law.
2. to hide, withdraw, or be concealed.
The marmot *absconds* in winter. —Ray.

ab·sçon′ded (-did), *a.* concealed; withdrawn; hidden.

ab·sçond′ence, *n.* concealment. [Obs.]

ab·sçond′ẽr, *n.* one who absconds.

ab′sence, *n.* [L. *absentia*, being away.]
1. a state of being away or not present; as, speak well of one in his *absence*.
2. the time of being away.
3. want; destitution; lack.
In the *absence* of conventional law. —Kent.
4. heedlessness; inattention to things present; as, *absence* of mind.

ab′sent, *a.* 1. not present; not in company; away.
2. heedless; inattentive to persons present, or to subjects of conversation in company.
3. lacking; nonexistent.
absent (or *absentee*) *voter*; one duly qualified to vote, and permitted, because of illness, disability, travel, etc., to vote by mail at general elections.
Syn.—abstracted, dreamy, inattentive, listless.

ab·sent′, *v.t.*; absented, *pt.*, *pp.*; absenting, *ppr.* [L. *absentare*, from *absens* (*-entis*), *ppr.* of *absum*, *abesse*; *ab*, away, and *esse*, to be.] to take or hold (oneself) away; to retire or withdraw; to forbear to bring into presence; as, let a man *absent himself* from the company.

ab·sen·tā′nē·ous, *a.* pertaining to absence. [Obs.]

ab·sen·tā′tion, *n.* the act of remaining away or absenting oneself.

ab·sen·tee′, *n.* 1. one who withdraws or absents himself from his country, office, work, duty, etc.

2. a landowner or capitalist who derives his revenue from one country and resides in and expends it in another.

ab·sen·tee′, *a.* of the nature of an absentee; by an absentee; as, *absentee* ownership.

ab·sen·tee′ism, *n.* absence from duty, work, or station; especially, such absence when deliberate or habitual.

ab·sen·tee′ land′lọrd, a person who owns land, buildings, etc. in some city or region other than that in which he lives: often implying neglect of tenants or workmen.

ab·sent′ẽr, *n.* one who absents himself.

ab′sent·ly, *adv.* in an absent manner.

ab·sent′ment, *n.* the state of being absent. [Obs.]

ab″sent-mīnd′ed, *a.* characterized by inattention to present needs or surroundings; preoccupied; abstracted.

ab″sent-mīnd′ed·ly, *adv.* in an absent-minded or preoccupied manner.

ab″sent-mīnd′ed·ness, *n.* the state of being preoccupied or abstracted.

ab″sent·ness, *n.* absent-mindedness.

ab′sent with·out′ lēave, in military usage, absent from duty without official permission but with no intention of deserting.

ab·sid′i·ōle, *n.* same as *apsidiole.*

ab′sinthe, ab′sinth, *n.* [L. *absinthium.*]

1. wormwood or its essence.

2. an aromatic liqueur of an opaline-green color, flavored with wormwood and other plants containing absinthin.

ab·sin′thi·ăl, *a.* bitter; pertaining to wormwood.

ab·sin′thi·ăn, *a.* of the nature of wormwood.

ab·sin′thi·āte, *v.t.*; absinthiated, *pt., pp.*; absinthiating, *ppr.* to compound or impregnate with absinthe.

ab·sin′thi·ā·ted, *a.* impregnated with or containing absinthe.

ab·sin′thiç, *a.* pertaining to absinthe; as, *absinthic* acid.

ab·sin′thin, *n.* the crystalline bitter principle of wormwood.

ab′sin·thişm, *n.* absinthe poisoning, a diseased condition caused by habitually drinking too much absinthe.

ab·sin′thi·um, *n.* [L.] the common wormwood, *Artemisia absinthium,* a bitter plant, used as a bitter tonic, etc.

ab′sis, *n.* same as *apsis.*

ab·sist′, *v.i.* [L. *ab,* from, and *sistere,* to stand.] to stand apart; to desist. [Obs.]

ab·sist′ence, *n.* a standing apart. [Obs.]

ab′sō·lūte, *a.* [L. *absolutus,* from *ab,* and *solvere,* to loose.]

1. literally, in a general sense, free or independent of anything extraneous.

2. complete in itself; whole.

3. unconditional; as, an *absolute* promise.

4. existing independent of any other cause; as, God is *absolute.*

5. unlimited by extraneous power or control; as, an *absolute* government or monarch.

6. not relative; as, *absolute* space.

7. in chemistry, pure; unmixed; as, *absolute* alcohol.

8. free from imperfection; perfect.

9. actual; real; as, an *absolute* truth.

10. in grammar, (a) independent; as, the *absolute* case: applied to a word or member of a sentence not immediately dependent on the other parts of the sentence in government; (b) used without an explicit object: said of a verb; (c) with the noun understood: said of a pronoun or an adjective, as in "Ours are the brave."

absolute equation; in astronomy, the sum of the optical and eccentric equations.

absolute numbers; in algebra, numbers that have no letters annexed; as, $2a + 36 = 48$. The two latter numbers are *absolute* or pure.

absolute space; in physics, space considered without relation to any object.

absolute temperature; temperature measured from absolute zero.

absolute velocity; the velocity of a body with reference to a body not in motion.

absolute zero; in thermodynamics, a point of temperature, theoretically equal to −273.18° C. or −459.72°F.: the hypothetical point at which a substance would have no molecular motion and no heat.

Syn.—arbitrary, positive, imperious, despotic, peremptory, tyrannous, tyrannical, autocratic, supreme.

Ab′sō·lūte, *n.* 1. the independent, unrestricted, and perfect Being; God: generally with *the*; as, the power of *the Absolute.*

2. [a−] that which is perfect or unrestricted; a condition of perfection.

ab′sō·lūte al′ço·họl, ethyl alcohol containing not over one per cent by weight of water.

ab′sō·lūte cēil′ing, the greatest altitude above sea level at which aircraft can keep normal horizontal flight.

ab′sō·lūte·ly, *adv.* 1. completely; wholly; as, this thing is *absolutely* unintelligible.

2. without dependence or relation; in a state unconnected.

3. without restriction or limitation.

4. without condition.

5. positively; peremptorily.

Syn.—completely, unrestrictedly, unconditionally.

ab′sō·lūte mū′şiç, music that does not try to tell a story, describe a scene, etc.: distinguished from *program music.*

ab′sō·lūte·ness, *n.* 1. independence; completeness in itself.

2. despotic authority, or that which is subject to no extraneous restriction or control.

3. positiveness.

ab′sō·lūte pitch, 1. the pitch of a tone as determined by its rate of vibration.

2. the ability to recognize the pitch of any tone heard, or to reproduce a given tone without having it sounded beforehand.

ab·sō·lū′tion, *n.* 1. the act of absolving or freeing from the consequences of sin or crime.

2. in civil law, an acquittal, or decision of a judge declaring an accused person innocent.

3. in the Roman Catholic and Orthodox Eastern Churches, a remission of sins, formally given by a priest after penance by the sinner.

4. in the Roman Catholic Church, the act of absolving from excommunication or freeing a person from its penalties on his reconciliation to the church.

5. in some Protestant churches, a declaration of remission of sins on the ground of repentance.

ab′sō·lū·tişm, *n.* 1. the quality of being absolute, or certain.

2. the doctrine or system of absolute government.

3. the doctrine of predestination.

ab′sō·lū·tist, *n.* one who favors absolutism.

ab′sō·lū·tist, ab″sō·lū·tis′tiç, *a.* of the nature of absolutism.

ab·sol′ū·tō·ry, *a.* giving absolution; absolving; as, an *absolutory* sentence.

ab·solv′ȧ·ble, *a.* capable of being absolved.

ab·solv′ȧ·tō·ry, *a.* conferring absolution, pardon, or release; having power to absolve. [Rare.]

ab·solve′, *v.t.*; absolved, *pt., pp.*; absolving, *ppr.* [L. *ab,* from, and *solvere,* to loose.]

1. to set free or release from some obligation, debt, or responsibility, or from that which subjects a person to a burden or penalty; as, to *absolve* a person from a promise.

2. to pronounce free from guilt or blame; acquit.

3. to give religious absolution to.

Syn.—acquit, clear, exculpate, exonerate, forgive, pardon, remit.

ab·solv′ent, *a.* having the power to absolve; absolving.

ab·solv′ent, *n.* a person who absolves.

ab·solv′ẽr, *n.* one who absolves; one who pronounces sin to be remitted.

ab′sō·nănt, *a.* [L. *ab,* from, and *sonans,* ppr. of *sonare,* to sound.] discordant; harsh; contrary.

ab·sọrb′, *v.t.*; absorbed, *pt., pp.*; absorbing, *ppr.* [L. *absorbere*; *ab,* from, and *sorbere,* to drink in.]

1. to drink in; to suck up like a sponge or the lacteals of the body.

2. to drink in, swallow up, or engulf completely.

3. to engross or engage wholly; to interest greatly.

4. to receive or take up by chemical or molecular action; as, to *absorb* gases.

5. to take in and incorporate; assimilate.

Syn.—consume, engulf, imbibe, drink in, suck up, engross.

ab·sọrb·ȧ·bil′i·ty, *n.* the state or quality of being absorbable.

ab·sọrb′ȧ·ble, *a.* that can be absorbed.

ab·sọrbed′, *a.* [pp. of *absorb.*]

1. taken in; sucked up.

2. engulfed.

3. assimilated.

4. greatly interested; wholly occupied; as, *absorbed* in reading.

ab·sọrb′ed·ly, *adv.* in an absorbed manner.

ab·sọr″be·fā′cient, *a.* [from L. *absorbere,* and ppr. of *facere,* to make, cause.] in medicine, inducing absorption of fluids.

ab·sọr″be·fā′cient, *n.* a drug that induces absorption.

ab·sọrb′en·cy, *n.* the quality of being absorbent.

ab·sọrb′ent, *a.* capable of absorbing moisture, light rays, etc.

absorbent cotton; cotton made absorbent for surgical use, with the fatty substance removed.

absorbent ground; in painting, a prepared ground that absorbs the oil of the colors used and thus hastens drying.

ab·sọrb′ent, *n.* 1. in anatomy, a vessel which absorbs, as the lacteals and lymphatics.

2. in medicine, a substance used to absorb acidity in the stomach, as magnesia, chalk, etc.

3. any substance that absorbs.

ab·sọrb′ẽr, *n.* a person who or a thing which absorbs.

shock absorber; any device which lessens, by absorbing, the force of shocks and jarring, as on the springs of an automobile.

ab·sọrb′ing, *a.* 1. imbibing; taking in.

2. engrossing.

ab·sọrb′ing·ly, *adv.* in an absorbing manner.

ab·sọr·bi′tion (-bish′un), *n.* absorption. [Obs.]

ab·sọrp·ti·om′e·tẽr (-ti- *as* -shi-), *n.* [L. *absorptio,* absorption, and Gr. *metron,* a measure.] an instrument invented by Bunsen for measuring the extent to which particular gases may be absorbed by certain liquids.

ab·sọrp′tion, *n.* 1. an absorbing or being absorbed.

2. entire occupation or engrossment of mind; as, *absorption* in business.

3. in physiology, one of the vital organic functions, the conveying to the blood stream or lymph of the materials of nutrition, by means of the lacteals or the lymphatics.

4. a taking in or incorporating; assimilation, as of a gas by a liquid, a minority group by dominant group, etc.

5. in physics, (a) a taking in and not reflecting; (b) partial loss in power of light or radio waves passing through a medium.

ab·sọrp′tive, *a.* 1. having power to absorb.

2. relating to absorption.

ab·sọrp′tive·ness, *n.* the power of absorption.

ab·sọrp·tiv′i·ty, *n.* 1. the quality of being absorptive.

2. in physics, the fraction of a radiant energy absorbed by the surface that it strikes.

ab·squät′ū·lāte, *v.i.* to leave suddenly; to decamp; also, to squat; sit. [Slang.]

abs′quē hoc, [L., without this or that.] in law, words used in traversing what has been alleged and is repeated.

ab·stāin′, *v.i.*; abstained, *pt., pp.*; abstaining, *ppr.* [L. *abstinere,* to keep from; *abs,* and *tenere,* to hold.] in a general sense, to forbear, or refrain *from,* voluntarily; to refrain from indulgence; as, to *abstain* from the use of intoxicating liquors; to *abstain* from luxuries.

Syn.—forbear, cease, refrain, give up, withhold, relinquish.

ab·stāin′, *v.t.* to prevent. [Obs.]

Abstain men from marrying. —Milton.

ab·stāin′ẽr, *n.* one who abstains, particularly from intoxicants.

ab·stē′mi·ous, *a.* [L. *abstemius,* abstaining from intoxicating liquor; *abs,* from, and *temetum,* strong drink.]

1. sparing in diet; refraining from a free use of food and strong drink.

2. sparing in the enjoyment of appetites or pleasures of any kind.

3. sparingly used, or used with temperance; marked by abstinence; as, an *abstemious* diet.

Syn.—sober, temperate, abstinent.

ab·stē′mi·ous·ly, *adv.* temperately; with a sparing use of food or strong drink.

ab·stē′mi·ous·ness, *n.* the quality of being temperate or sparing in the use of food and strong drink.

ab·sten′tion, *n.* the act of abstaining.

ab·sten′tious, *a.* characterized by abstinence.

ab·stẽrġe′, *v.t.*; absterged, *pt., pp.*; absterging, *ppr.* [L. *abstergere*; *abs,* away, and *tergere,* to wipe.] to wipe or make clean by wiping; to cleanse by lotions or similar applications; to purge.

ab·stẽr′ġent, *a.* wiping; cleansing.

ab·stẽr′ġent, *n.* anything which cleans, as lotions or soap.

ab·stẽrse′, *v.t.* to clean. [Obs.]

ab·stẽr′sion, *n.* [from L. *abstergere, abstersus.*] the act of wiping clean; a cleansing by lotions or similar applications.

ab·stẽr′sive, *a.* [see *detersive.*] cleansing; having the quality of removing foulness.

ab·stẽr′sive, *n.* that which cleanses.

ab·stẽr′sive·ness, *n.* the quality of being abstersive.

ab′sti·nence, *n.* [L. *abstinentia,* abstinence from anything.]

1. in general, the act or practice of voluntarily refraining from, or forbearing, any action.

2. the refraining from an indulgence of appetite, or from customary gratifications of one's appetites: it denotes a total forbearance, as in fasting or in giving up the drinking of alcoholic liquors.

total abstinence; the act or practice of refraining from the use of any intoxicating liquors.

ab′sti·nen·cy, *n.* abstinence. [Rare.]

ab′sti·nent, *a.* refraining from indulgence of one's appetites.

ab′sti·nent·ly, *adv.* with abstinence.

Ab′sti·nents, *n.pl.* a sect which appeared in France and Spain in the third century A.D., opposing marriage and the eating of flesh, and placing the Holy Spirit in the class of created beings.

ab·stort′ed, *a.* [L. *abs,* from, and *tortus,* twisted.] forced away. [Obs.]

ab·stract′, *v.t.*; abstracted, *pt., pp.*; abstracting, *ppr.* [L. *abstractus,* dragged away, pp. of *abstrahere,* to draw from or separate.]

1. to draw from, or to separate; as, to *abstract* a criticism from one's own bias.

2. to separate (ideas) by the operation of the mind; to think of (a quality) apart from any particular instance or material object that has it.

3. to select or separate (the essential material of a book or writing); to epitomize or reduce to a summary.

4. to take secretly for one's own use from the property of another; to purloin; as, to *abstract* goods from a parcel.

5. to draw away the attention or interest of; as, he was *abstracted* by thoughts of the morrow.

ab′stract, *a.* [L. *abstractus,* pp. of *abstrahere*; *abs,* from, and *trahere,* to draw.]

1. thought of apart from any particular instances or material objects; not concrete.

2. expressing a quality thought of apart from any particular or material object; as, beauty is an *abstract* word.

3. not easy to understand; abstruse.

4. loosely, theoretical; not practical.

5. in art, characterized by design or form that is geometric or otherwise not representational.

6. mentally abstracted.

abstract idea; in metaphysics, an idea separated from a complex object, or from other ideas which naturally accompany it.

abstract or *pure mathematics*; mathematics that treats of magnitude or quantity without restriction to any species of particular magnitude.

abstract numbers; numbers used without application to things, as six, eight, ten: when applied to anything, as six feet, ten men, they become concrete.

ab′stract, *n.* 1. a summary, or epitome, containing the substance, a general view, or the principal heads of a treatise or writing.

2. in grammar, a noun used as a general term; an abstract noun, as virtue, goodness, paternity.

3. in pharmacy, a solid preparation in which two parts of the drug are represented by one part of the *abstract,* which is compounded with milk sugar. *Abstracts* are double the strength of the fluid extracts.

4. that which is abstract; an abstract idea, etc.

abstract of title; a summary of the successive title deeds to a piece of real estate.

in the abstract; in a state of separation; as, a subject considered *in the abstract,* i.e., without reference to particular persons or things.

Syn.—abridgment, summary, digest, synopsis, compendium, epitome.

ab·stract′ed, *a.* separated; removed; abstruse; absent in mind.

Syn.—absent, preoccupied, absorbed.

ab·stract′ed·ly, *adv.* in an abstracted state.

ab·stract′ed·ness, *n.* the state of being abstracted.

ab·stract′ẽr, *n.* 1. one who makes an abstract or summary.

2. specifically, one who engages in the business of making abstracts of title.

ab′stract ex·pres′sion·ism, a post-World War II movement in painting characterized by emphasis on the artist's spontaneous and self-expressive application of paint in creating a nonrepresentational composition.

ab·strac′tion, *n.* [L. *abstractio,* from *abs,* away, and *trahere,* to draw.]

1. the act of abstracting or state of being abstracted.

2. the operation of the mind when occupied by abstract ideas, as when we contemplate some particular part or property of a complex object as separate from the rest. Thus, when the mind considers the branch of a tree by itself, or the color of the leaves as separate from their size or figure, the act is called *abstraction*; so, also, when it considers whiteness, softness, virtue, existence, etc. as separate from any particular objects. *Abstraction* is the groundwork of classification, by which things are arranged in orders, genera, and species. We separate in idea the qualities of certain objects which are of the same kind, from others which are different in each, and arrange the objects having the same properties in a class, or collected body.

3. a separation from worldly objects; a recluse life; as, a hermit's *abstraction.*

4. absence of mind; inattention to present objects; as, a fit of *abstraction.*

5. a taking for one's own use the property of another.

6. something abstract; an abstract idea; an impracticable notion.

ab·strac′tion·ăl, *a.* pertaining to abstraction.

ab·strac′tion·ism, *n.* the theory and practice of the abstract, especially in art; cult of abstract pictures, statues, etc.

ab·strac′tion·ist, *n.* 1. a person who deals with abstractions.

2. a person who makes, or is in favor of, abstract paintings, statues, etc.

ab·strac·ti′tious (-tish′us), *a.* obtained by distillation. [Obs.]

ab·strac′tive, *a.* having the power or quality of abstracting.

ab·strac′tive·ly, *adv.* in the abstract; separately.

ab·strac′tive·ness, *n.* the quality of being abstractive.

ab′stract·ly, *adv.* separately; absolutely; in an abstract state or manner; as, matter *abstractly* considered.

ab′stract·ness, *n.* the state or quality of being abstract.

ab·strict′ed, *a.* cut off by abstriction.

ab·stric′tion, *n.* [L. *abstringere*; *abs,* from, and *strictio,* from *stringere,* to bind.] in botany, a cutting off of spores from a spore-bearing branch by the formation of dividing tissues (septa), as in some algae and fungi.

ab·stringe′, *v.t.* [L. *abs,* from, and *stringere,* to bind.] to unbind. [Obs.]

ab·strūse′, *a.* [L. *abstrusus,* pp. of *abstrudere,* to thrust away, to conceal; *abs,* away, and *trudere,* to thrust.]

1. hidden; concealed. [Obs.]

2. remote from apprehension; difficult to be comprehended or understood: opposed to what is obvious and not used of material objects; as, metaphysics is an *abstruse* science.

Syn.—complex, mysterious, obscure, recondite.

ab·strūse′ly, *adv.* in an abstruse manner; in a manner not to be easily understood.

ab·strūse′ness, *n.* the state or quality of being difficult of understanding.

ab·strū′sion, *n.* the act of thrusting away.

ab·strū′si·ty, *n.* 1. abstruseness.

2. that which is abstruse.

ab·sũrd′, *a.* [L. *absurdus,* from *ab,* and *surdus,* deaf, insensible.] clearly untrue or unreasonable; ridiculously inconsistent with reason, or the plain dictates of common sense; logically contradictory. An *absurd* man acts contrary to the clear dictates of reason or sound judgment. An *absurd* proposition contradicts obvious truth.

Syn.—foolish, irrational, ridiculous, preposterous, silly, unreasonable, nonsensical.

ab·sũrd′i·ty, *n.* 1. the quality of being inconsistent with obvious truth, reason, or sound judgment and therefore laughable or ridiculous.

2. that which is absurd: in this sense the word has a plural; as, the *absurdities* of men.

ab·sũrd′ly, *adv.* in a manner ridiculously inconsistent with reason or obvious propriety.

ab·sũrd′ness, *n.* same as *absurdity.*

ab·tẽr′mi·năl, *a.* [L. *ab,* from, and *terminalis,* end.] proceeding inward from the end toward the center: applied to electrical currents traversing a muscle, etc.

ab′thāin, ab′thāne, *n.* [Gael.] a Scottish abbacy.

ȧ·bū′li·ȧ, ȧ·böu′li·ȧ, *n.* [Gr. *aboulia*; *a,* priv., and *boule,* advice.] loss of will power.

ȧ·bū′nȧ, *n.* [Eth. and Ar., our father.] the established head of the Christian church in Abyssinia.

ȧ·bun′dănce, *n.* [Fr. *abondance*; L. *abundare*; *ab,* and *unda,* wave.]

1. great plenty; an overflowing quantity; ample sufficiency: strictly applicable to quantity only, but sometimes used of number; as, an *abundance* of laborers.

2. abundant wealth or means; as, to give of one's *abundance.*

3. fullness; overflowing; as, the *abundance* of the heart.

Syn.—plenteousness, exuberance, plenty, plentifulness, plentitude, riches, affluence, copiousness, wealth.

ȧ·bun′dănt, *a.* [L. *abundans* (*-antis*), from *abundare,* to overflow.]

1. plentiful; in great quantity; fully sufficient; as, an *abundant* supply.

2. abounding (*in* something).

abundant number; in arithmetic, a number the sum of whose aliquot parts exceeds the number itself. Thus, 1, 2, 3, 4, 6, the aliquot parts of 12, make the sum of 16. This is opposed to a *deficient* number, as 14, whose aliquot parts are 1, 2, 7, the sum of which is 10; and to a *perfect* number, which is equal to the sum of its aliquot parts, as 6, whose aliquot parts are 1, 2, 3.

Syn.—ample, copious, exuberant, luxuriant, plentiful, plenteous.

ȧ·bun′dănt·ly, *adv.* fully; amply; plentifully.

ȧ·bũrst′, *a.* bursting.

ȧ·bũr′tŏn, *adv.* and *a.* a nautical term applied to casks, boxes, etc. placed athwartships.

ȧ·būs′ȧ·ble, *a.* capable of being abused.

ȧ·būs′āge, *n.* abuse. [Obs.]

ȧ·būse′, *v.t.*; abused, *pt., pp.*; abusing, *ppr.* [Fr. *abuser*; It. *abusare*; L. *abutor, abusus*; *ab,* and *uti,* to use.]

1. to use ill; to maltreat; to misuse; to use with bad motives or to wrong purposes; as, to *abuse* rights or privileges.

2. to violate; to defile.

3. to deceive; to impose on. [Archaic.]

Nor be with all these tempting words *abused.* —Pope.

4. to treat harshly; to use insulting, coarse, or bad language about or to; to revile.

Syn.—misuse, insult, revile, traduce.

ȧ·būse′, *n.* 1. ill use; improper treatment or employment; application to a wrong purpose; as, an *abuse* of our natural powers; an *abuse* of civil rights, or of religious privileges; *abuse* of advantages, etc.

2. a corrupt practice or custom; as, the *abuses* of government.

3. rude speech; rudely contemptuous language addressed to a person; insulting or coarse language.

4. violation; defilement. [Obs.]

ȧ·būse′ful, *a.* using or practicing abuse; abusive.

ȧ·būs′ẽr, *n.* one who abuses.

ȧ·bū′sion, *n.* abuse; evil or corrupt usage; deception. [Obs.]

ȧ·bū′sive, *a.* 1. abusing; mistreating.

2. coarse and insulting in language; scurrilous; harshly scolding; as, *abusive* words.

Syn.—insolent, insulting, offensive, opprobrious, reproachful, rude, scurrilous.

ȧ·bū′sive·ly, *adv.* in an abusive manner; rudely; reproachfully.

ȧ·bū′sive·ness, *n.* ill usage; the quality of being abusive; rudeness of language or violence to a person.

ȧ·but′, *v.t.*; abutted, *pt., pp.*; abutting, *ppr.* [Fr. *aboutir*; *a,* to, and *bout, but,* end.] to border upon; to be contiguous to; to meet; strictly, to end at.

ȧ·but′, *v.i.* to touch at one end; border; terminate: used with *on, upon,* or *against*; as, the building *abuts on* the highway.

Ȧ·bū′tȧ, *n.* a genus of tropical American climbing plants of the moonseed family.

Ȧ·bū′ti·lon, *n.* [Ar. *aubutilun.*] a genus of plants, chiefly tropical, belonging to the mallow family, or *Malvaceæ.*

a̤·but′ment, *n.* 1. a part that supports an arch or strut, as of a bridge.

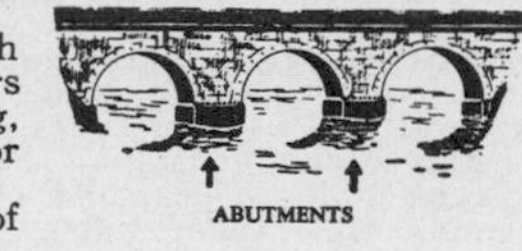
ABUTMENTS

2. that which abuts or borders on another thing, as a building or piece of land.
3. the state of abutting.
4. the point of contact between the support and the thing supported.

a̤·but′tăl, *n.* 1. the butting or boundary of land at the end: used in the plural.
2. an abutment.

a̤·but′tẽr, *n.* a person who or a thing which abuts: said of a building or land, or its owner.

a̤·but′ting, *a.* 1. touching at the end; contiguous; as, *abutting* property.
2. resting on or against; as, *abutting* rocks.
Syn.—adjacent, neighboring, next.

a̤·buzz′, *a.* [*a-*, in, and *buzz*.]
1. filled with buzzing.
2. full of activity.

ab·vōlt′, *n.* [*ab*solute, and *volt*.] a C. G. S. electromagnetic unit, 10^{-8} volt.

ab·wätt′, *n.* [*ab*solute, and *watt*.] a unit of power, 10^{-7} watt.

a̤·bȳ′, a̤·bȳe′, *v.t.* [AS. *a*, out, and *bycgan*, to buy.] to pay for; atone for. [Obs.]

a̤·bȳ′, a̤·bȳe′, *v.i.* to last; endure. [Obs.]

a̤·bysm′, *n.* [Fr. *abisme*; L. *abyssus*, from Gr. *abyssos*; *a* priv., and *byssos*, depth.] a gulf; a chasm; an abyss. [Poetic.]

a̤·bys′măl, *a.* of or like an abyss; bottomless; unfathomable; immeasurable.

a̤·bys′măl·ly, *adv.* deeply; to the lowest depths; as, sunk *abysmally* in crime.

a̤·byss′, *n.* [Gr. *abyssos*, bottomless; *a* priv., and *byssos*, bottom.]
1. a bottomless gulf; also, a deep mass of waters, according to the Bible supposed to have encompassed the earth in the beginning; as, the face of the *abyss*, in the Septuagint.
2. that which is immeasurable; that in which anything is lost.

Thy throne is darkness, in the *abyss* of night. —Milton.

3. the bottomless pit; hell; Erebus.
4. an immensity of time, space, depth, or scope; as, an *abyss* of ignorance; an *abyss* of crime.
5. in heraldry, the center of an escutcheon; as, he bears azure, a fleur-de-lis, in *abyss*.
6. the ocean depths.
Syn.—chasm, cleft, crevasse, gorge, gulf, pit.

a̤·byss′ăl, *a.* 1. pertaining to an abyss; immeasurably deep; unfathomable.
2. pertaining to the ocean's greatest depths; as, the *abyssal* fauna and flora.

Ab·ys·sin′i·ăn, *a.* pertaining to Abyssinia (Ethiopia), a country of Africa, east of the upper reach of the Blue Nile; Ethiopian.

Ab·ys·sin′i·ăn, *n.* 1. a native of Abyssinia (Ethiopia)
2. the language of the Abyssinians.

Ab·ys·sin′i·ăn Chūrch, a sect of Christians in Abyssinia, which admits but one nature in Jesus Christ and rejects the council of Chalcedon. It is governed by a bishop, or metropolitan, called the **abuna**.

aç-, [AS. *ac*, *ake*, *oke*, oak.] a prefix used in place names; as, *Ac*ton (*oak*town), etc.

aç-, a variant of *ad-*, used before *c* and *q*, as in *ac*cuse, *ac*quire.

-aç, [L. *acus*, Gr. *akos*.] a suffix meaning *characteristic of*, *pertaining to*, *having*; as, mani*ac*, demoni*ac*. It is preceded by *i* and may be followed by *al*.

Ac, in chemistry, actinium.

A·çā′cia̤ (-sha̤ *or* -shi-a̤), *n.*; *pl.* **A·çā′cia̤ṣ** (-sha̤z); L. *pl.* **A·çā′ciae** (-shi-ē), [L. *acacia*, a thorn, from Gr. *akakia*, a point.]
1. a genus of plants of the mimosa family, natural order *Leguminosæ*, suborder *Mimoseæ*, for the most part natives of warm regions. As objects of ornament the *acacias* are usually of striking beauty. Some of the species produce catechu, as *Acacia Catechu*, and some exude gum arabic, as *Acacia Verek*, *Acacia Arabica*, *Acacia vera* (Egyptian thorn), *Acacia Adansoni*; the bark of others yields a large quantity of tannin, as *Acacia decurrens* and *Acacia mollissima*. Several species furnish timber of good quality.

ACACIA ARABICA

2. [a–] gum arabic.
3. [a–] the locust tree.
4. [a–] among antiquaries, a name given to an object resembling a roll or bag, seen on medals, in the hands of several emperors and consuls.

A·çā′ciănṣ, *n.pl.* in church history, certain sects, so called from their leaders, Acacius, bishop of Caesarea, and Acacius, patriarch of Constantinople.

aç′a̤·cin, aç′a̤·cine, *n.* gum arabic.

aç·a̤·dēme′, *n.* [L. *academia*.]
1. an academy; a school. [Poetic.]
2. [A–] the Academy, or school of Plato.

aç·a̤·dē′mi·ăl, *a.* academic. [Rare.]

aç·a̤·dē′mi·ăn, *n.* a member of an academy; a student in an academy. [Obs.]

aç·a̤·dem′iç, *a.* 1. of schools or colleges and their learning; scholastic; scholarly.
2. having to do with general or liberal rather than technical or vocational education.
3. of or belonging to a learned society.
4. too far from immediate reality; not practical enough; too speculative.
5. formal; pedantic.
6. [A–] pertaining to the school or philosophy of Plato; as, the *Academic* sect.
academic costume; a costume worn by students of a college or university, by those holding an academic degree, or by the faculty. The costume usually consists of a cap and gown.
academic rank; the rank or official standing of instructors in a college or university; as, professor, associate professor, assistant professor, instructor, tutor, and lecturer.
academic year; the period, usually from late September to late June, in which academic institutions are in session.

aç·a̤·dem′iç, *n.* 1. a person belonging to a college or university.
2. [A–] one who belonged to the school or adhered to the philosophy of Plato.

aç·a̤·dem′iç·ăl, *a.* academic.

aç·a̤·dem′iç·ăl·ly, *adv.* in an academic manner.

aç·a̤·dem′iç·ălṣ, *n.pl.* the cap and gown or other traditional costume worn at some colleges.

aç″a̤·de·mi′cian (-mish′un), *n.* [Fr. *académicien*.] a member of an academy, or society for promoting arts and sciences; particularly, [A–], a member of the French Academy, the English Royal Academy, or the American Academy of Arts and Letters.

aç·a̤·dem′i·cişm, *n.* 1. [A–] a principle of Academic philosophy.
2. a custom or mode peculiar to an academy.
3. the quality of being academic; formal or pedantic quality, spirit, etc.

a̤·çad′e·mişm, *n.* academicism (sense 3).

a̤·çad′e·mist, *n.* 1. a member of an academy for promoting arts and sciences; academician.
2. [A–] an Academic philosopher.

a̤·çad′e·my, *n.* [L. *academia*; Gr. *akademeia*: originally a garden, grove, or villa, near Athens, where Plato taught.]
1. [A–] the school of Plato; hence, Plato's followers or philosophy.
2. an institution of higher learning.
3. a private secondary or high school.
4. a school for teaching a particular art or particular sciences; as, a military *academy*.
5. a building in which the students or members of an academy meet; a place of education.
6. a society of men united for the promotion of arts and sciences in general, or of some particular art or science.
7. specifically, an institution for the cultivation and promotion of the fine arts, partaking of the character both of an association of artists for mutual improvement and of a school of instruction.
academy figure; in art, a drawing or photograph after a living model.
Syn.—college, institute, school, seminary.

a̤·çā′di·ăl·īte, *n.* [*Acadia*, Nova Scotia, and *-lite*, from Gr. *lithos*, stone.] a kind of mineral; chabazite.

A·çā′di·ăn, *n.* an inhabitant of Acadia or Nova Scotia.

A·çā′di·ăn, *a.* pertaining to Acadia or its people.

aç′a̤·jöu, *n.* [Fr.] 1. the cashew tree.
2. the fruit of this tree.

aç′a̤·jöu, *n.* [Fr.] mahogany.

aç′a̤·leph, *n.* any of the *Acalephæ*.

Aç·a̤·lē′phae, *n.pl.* [Gr. *akalēphē*, a nettle.] in former zoological classifications, a large class of marine, radiate animals or zoophytes, including the medusa, sea nettle, jelly fish, etc.: so called from the property, possessed by most of the species, of irritating and inflaming the skin when touched. The most typical of the *Acalephæ*, the *Medusidæ*, are gelatinous, free-swimming animals, consisting of an umbrella-shaped disk, containing canals which radiate from the center.

ACALEPHÆ
1. *Medusa pellucens*
2. *Rhizostoma cuvieri*

aç·a̤·lē′phăn, *a.* pertaining to the *Acalephæ*.

aç·a̤·lē′phăn, *n.* one of the *Acalephæ*.

aç·a̤·lēphe′, *n.* an acaleph.

aç·a̤·lē′phoid, *a.* resembling an acalephan.

a̤·çal′y·cine, aç·a̤·lyc′i·nous, *a.* [Gr. *a* priv., and *kalyx*, calyx.] without a calyx or flower cup.

aç·a̤·lyc′ū·lāte, *a.* without a calycle.

A·çal′y·pha̤, *n.* [Gr. *akalēphē*, nettle.] a genus of herbaceous plants, family *Euphorbia*, some of which are cultivated while others grow as weeds, as *Acalypha virginica*, the three-seeded mercury.

aç·a̤·nā′ceous, *a.* [Gr. *akanos*, from *akē*, point, a prickly shrub.] prickly.

a̤·çan′tha̤, *n.* [Gr. *akantha*, from *akē*, a spine or thorn.]
1. in botany, a prickle.
2. in zoology, a spine or prickly fin; the spinous process of the vertebrae.

Aç·an·thā′cē·ae, *n.pl.* a family of plants of which the acanthus is a type.

aç·an·thā′ceous, *a.* 1. spiny; prickly.
2. pertaining to the *Acanthaceæ*.

a̤·çan′thine, *a.* pertaining to or resembling the acanthus.

a̤·çan′thīte, *n.* silver sulfide, Ag_2S.

a̤·çan·thō·çär′pous, *a.* [Gr. *akantha*, thorn, and *karpos*, fruit.] having spiny fruit.

A·çan·thō·ceph′a̤·la̤, *n.pl.* [Gr. *akantha*, thorn, and *kephalē*, head.] an order of intestinal worms having the proboscis covered with spinelike hooks.

a̤·çan·thō·ceph′a̤·lăn, *n.* any of the *Acanthocephala*.

a̤·çan·thō·ceph′a̤·lous, *a.* [Gr. *akantha*, thorn, and *kephalē*, head.] pertaining to the *Acanthocephala*.

aç·an·thoç′la̤·dous, *a.* [Gr. *akantha*, thorn, and *klados*, branch.] having thorny branches.

a̤·çan′thoid, *a.* formed like or resembling a spine.

aç·an·thoph′ō·rous, *a.* [Gr. *akantha*, thorn, and *pherein*, to bear.] bearing spines.

a̤·çan′thō·pod, *n.* [Gr. *akantha*, a spine, and *pous*, foot.] a term applied to clavicorn coleopterous insects, including those species with spiny feet.

aç·an·thop′ō·dous, *a.* [Gr. *akantha*, thorn, and *pous*, foot.] in zoology, having spine-bearing feet.

Aç·an·thop′tẽr·ī, *n.pl.* [Gr. *akantha*, thorn, and *pteron*, wing.] same as *Acanthopterygii*.

aç·an·thop′tẽr·ous, *a.* pertaining to the *Acanthopterygii*.

aç″an·thop·tẽr·yġ′i·ăn, *a.* and *n.* (of) any of the *Acanthopterygii*.

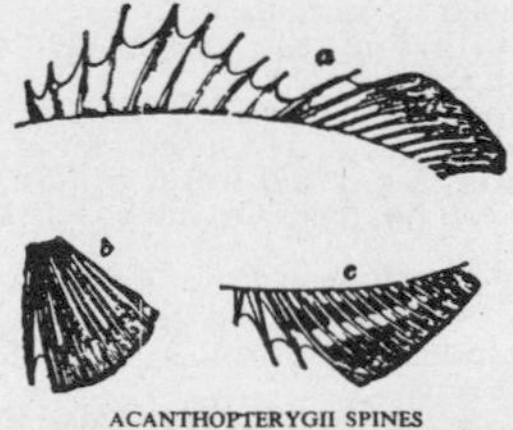

ACANTHOPTERYGII SPINES
a, dorsal spine *b*, anal spine
c, ventral spine

Aç″an·thop·tẽr·yġ′i·ī, *n.pl.* [Gr. *akantha*, a thorn, and *pterygion*, the fin of a fish, from *pteryx*, a wing.] one of the two primary divisions of the osseous fishes as classified by Cuvier, and including by far the greatest number of common fishes. They are characterized by having one or more of the first rays of the fins in the form of unjointed spines. In some species the first dorsal fin is represented by a few unconnected spines. The first rays of the anal fins consist of simple spines, and each ventral fin usually has one. The swim bladder in all is a shut sac. The division includes the perch, mackerel, gudgeon, bass, flying fish, mullet, braize, tunny, etc. Many fishes belonging to this division are used as food.

aç″an·thop·tẽr·yġ′i·ous, *a.* in zoology, having the characteristics of the *Acanthopterygii* or spiny-finned fishes; belonging to the *Acanthopterygii.*

ȧ·çan′thous, *a.* acanthoid.

Ȧ·çan′thus, *n.* [L. *acanthus*; Gr. *akanthos*, from *akantha*, a prickle or thorn.]

1. a genus of prickly plants with large leaves, natural order *Acanthaceæ* found in the Mediterranean region.

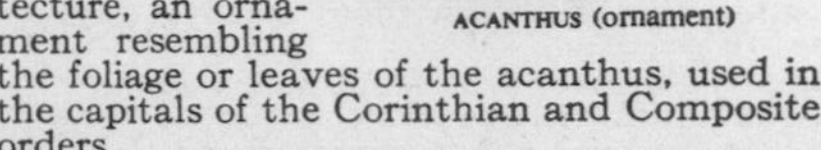

ACANTHUS (ornament)

2. [a–] in architecture, an ornament resembling the foliage or leaves of the acanthus, used in the capitals of the Corinthian and Composite orders.

3. [a–] any plant of the genus *Acanthus.*

ä çäp·pel′lä, [It., from L. *ad*, to, according to, and *capella*, chapel.] in the style of church or chapel music, especially in the old style, without accompaniment: said of choral singing.

ä çä·pric′ciō (kä-prē′chō), [It.; *a*, at, and *capriccio*, whim, fancy.] in music, at pleasure; at whatever tempo and with whatever expression the performer likes.

ȧ·çär′di·aç, *a.* [Gr. *a* priv., and *kardia*, heart.] without a heart.

aç·ȧ·rī′ȧ·sis, *n.* infestation by acarids.

aç′ȧ·rid, *n.* any of the *Acarida.*

Ȧ·çar′i·dȧ, *n.pl.* [Gr. *akarēs*, too short to be cut, small, tiny; *a* priv., and *keirein*, to cut.] a division of *Arachnida*, including the mites, ticks, and water mites. Of the true mites, the domestic or cheese mite and the itch mite are examples. The garden mites and spider mites live upon plants; the wood mites and harvest ticks are found amongst moss and herbage or creeping on trees and stones, while the true ticks (*Ixodidæ*) attach themselves parasitically to the bodies of various mammals, as sheep, oxen, dogs, etc. The water mites (*Hydrachnidæ*) are parasitic for at least a portion of their existence upon water beetles and other aquatic insects. The mouth in all is formed for suction. Also called *Acarina.*

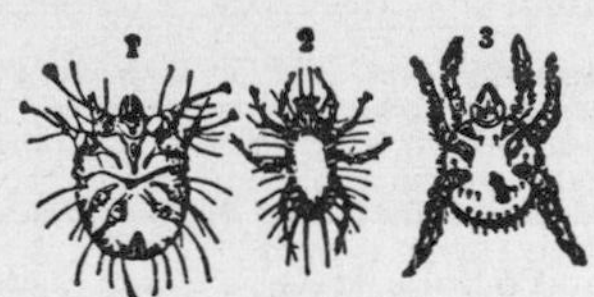

ACARIDA
1. itch mite (*Sarcoptes scabiei*)
2. cheese mite (*Acarus domesticus*)
3. harvest tick (*Leptus autumnalis*)

ȧ·çar′i·dăn, *a.* of or pertaining to the *Acarida.*

ȧ·çar′i·dăn, *n.* one of the *Acarida.*

Aç·ȧ·rī′nȧ, *n.pl.* same as *Acarida.*

aç′ȧ·rine, *a.* [Gr. *akari*, a mite.] of, belonging to, or caused by mites.

aç′ȧ·roid, *a.* having the appearance of or resembling a mite.

aç′ȧ·roid res′in (or **gum**), a resin taken from some kinds of grass tree, used in varnish, etc.

ȧ·çär′pel·ous, ȧ·çär′pel·lous, *a.* [Gr. *a* priv., and L. *carpellum*, from Gr. *karpos*, fruit.] without carpels.

ȧ·çär′pous, *a.* in botany, not fruitful.

Aç′ȧ·rus, *n.* 1. the typical genus of the *Acarida*: it includes the mites.

2. [a–] a mite.

ȧ·çat·ȧ·leç′tiç, *a.* [Gr. *akatalēktos*, incessant, from *a* priv., and *katalēgein*, to stop.] having the complete number of syllables or metrical feet, without defect or superfluity.

ȧ·çat·ȧ·leç′tiç, *n.* an acatalectic line or verse.

ȧ·çat′ȧ·lep·sy, ȧ·çat·ȧ·lep′si·ȧ, *n.* [Gr. *a* priv., and *katalambanein*, to comprehend.]

1. impossibility of complete discovery or comprehension; incomprehensibility.

2. in medicine, uncertainty in the diagnosis or prognosis of disease. [Obs.]

ȧ·çat·ȧ·lep′tiç, *a.* [Gr. *akatalēptos*; *a* priv., and *kata*, down, and *lambanein*, to seize.] incomprehensible.

aç·ȧ·thär′si·ȧ, (*or* -shȧ), *n.* [Gr. *akatharsia*, impurity, from *a* priv., and *kathartos*, pure.] impurity; filth.

ȧ·çau′dăl, *a.* [L. *a*, without, and *cauda*, tail.] without a tail.

ȧ·çau′dāte, *a.* same as *acaudal.*

aç·au·les′cent, ȧ·çau′line, *a.* 1. having no stem.

2. having only a very short stem.

ȧ·çau′lous, *a.* [Gr. *a* priv., and *kaulos*, a stalk.] same as *acaulescent.*

Aç·çā′di·ăn, *n.* an inhabitant of Accad, or Akkad, an ancient country north of Babylonia.

aç·çēde′, *v.i.*; acceded, *pt.*, *pp.*; acceding, *ppr.* [L. *accedere*; *ad*, to, and *cedere*, to yield.]

1. to agree or assent, as to a proposition, or to terms proposed by another (used with *to*).

2. to become a party, by agreeing to the terms of a treaty, convention, etc.

3. to attain, as to an office or rank; to enter upon the duties (of an office): used with *to.*

Syn.—acquiesce, agree, consent, assent, comply, succeed, attain, enter upon.

aç·çēd′ence, *n.* the act of acceding.

aç·çēd′ẽr, *n.* one who accedes.

aç·cel′ẽr·ȧ·ble, *a.* capable of acceleration.

aç·cel·ẽr·an′dō (*or* ät-chā-le-rän′do), *adv.* [It.] in music, with gradually quickening tempo.

aç·cel′ẽr·ănt, *a.* [L. *accelerans*, ppr. of *accelerare.*] accelerating.

aç·cel′ẽr·ănt, *n.* 1. something that increases the speed of a process.

2. in chemistry, a catalyst.

aç·cel′ẽr·āte, *v.t.*; accelerated, *pt.*, *pp.*; accelerating, *ppr.* [L. *accelerare*; *ad*, to, and *celerare*, to hasten.]

1. to cause to move faster; to hasten; to quicken (motion); to add to the velocity of (a moving body).

2. to hasten the working of (a process, etc.); as, to *accelerate* the growth of a plant.

3. to bring nearer in time; to shorten (the time) between the present time and a future event; as, to *accelerate* a crisis.

accelerated motion; in mechanics and physics, motion with a continually increasing velocity.

accelerating force; the force that causes accelerated motion, as gravity.

Syn.—hasten, expedite, further, quicken, forward, advance.

aç·cel′ẽr·āte, *v.i.* to increase in speed; to go faster.

aç·cel·ẽr·ā′tion, *n.* 1. an accelerating or being accelerated.

2. change in velocity, either increase (*positive acceleration*) or decrease (*negative acceleration*).

3. the rate of such change.

acceleration of the moon; the increase in the speed of the moon's mean motion around the earth (less than 1/3 minute per century).

acceleration of the planets; the increasing velocity of the planets in proceeding from the aphelion to the perihelion of their orbits.

acceleration of the tides; priming of the tides, which occurs in the first and third quarters of the moon.

diurnal acceleration of the fixed stars; the time which the fixed stars gain on the apparent mean diurnal revolution of the sun, nearly three minutes, fifty-six seconds of mean time.

aç·cel·ẽr·ā′tion of grav′i·ty, the acceleration of a freely falling object, caused by the force of gravity: it is expressed in terms of the rate of increase each second of velocity per second (32 + ft. per second per second).

aç·cel′ẽr·ȧ·tive, *a.* of, causing, or increasing acceleration.

aç·cel′ẽr·ā·tŏr, *n.* [L. *ad*, to, and *celerare*, to hasten.]

1. one who or that which accelerates; anything that increases speed.

2. a device, such as the foot throttle of an automobile, for increasing the speed of a machine.

3. in anatomy, a muscle or nerve that speeds up a motion.

4. in chemistry, a substance that speeds up a reaction.

5. in photography, a chemical that speeds up developing.

aç·cel′ẽr·ȧ·tō·ry, *a.* accelerative.

aç·cel·ẽr·om′e·tẽr, *n.* [L. *accelerare*, to hasten, and Gr. *metron*, measure.] an instrument for measuring and recording the acceleration of an aircraft.

aç·cend′, *v.t.* [L. *accendere*; *ad*, to, and *candare*, to kindle.] to kindle; to set on fire. [Obs.]

aç·cend·i·bil′i·ty, *n.* the state or quality of being accendible.

aç·cend′i·ble, *a.* capable of being kindled; combustible; inflammable.

aç·cen′sion, *n.* the act of kindling or setting on fire, or the state of being kindled. [Rare.]

aç′cent, *n.* [L. *accentus*, from *ad*, to, and *canere*, to sing.]

1. originally, the modulation of the voice in reading or speaking, as practiced by the ancient Greeks, involving variation of musical pitch.

2. a particular stress or force of voice upon a certain syllable or word, which distinguishes it from the others. There are two kinds of *accent* in many English words, the primary and the secondary; thus, in uttering the word *aspiration*, the first and third syllables are distinguished—the third by a full sound, which constitutes the primary *accent*; the first, by a degree of force in the voice which is less than that of the primary *accent*, but evidently greater than that which falls on the second and fourth syllables.

3. a mark used in writing or printing to direct the stress of the voice in pronunciation, as in the primary (′) and secondary(″) accenting of English (*as″pi-ra′tion*).

4. a mark used to distinguish between various sounds of the same letter; as, in French there are acute (´), grave (`), and circumflex (^) *accents.*

5. a modulation of the voice expressive of feeling or sentiments; as, the tender *accents* of love.

6. manner of speaking; as, a man of plain *accent.*

7. [*pl.*] poetically, words, language, or expressions in general.

Winds! on your wings to heaven her *accents* bear. —Dryden.

8. the pitch contour of a phrase.

9. a distinguishing style of expression; as, the *accent* of Beethoven.

10. a striking or prominent feature of any artistic composition; as, the classical *accent* of a pillar.

11. in music and prosody, rhythmic stress or beat.

12. in music, (a) emphasis or stress on a note or chord; (b) a mark showing this.

13. a distinguishing regional or national style of pronunciation; as, a French *accent.*

14. in mathematics, a mark used to distinguish magnitudes of the same or similar kind, expressed by the same letter, but differing in value; as, *a′*, *a″*.

15. a mark at the right hand of a number used to express a minute of a degree: two such *accents* express a second, etc.; thus, 26° 43′ 58″ (twenty-six degrees, forty-three minutes, fifty-eight seconds) west longitude; similar, *accents* are used to denote feet and inches, respectively.

Syn.—cadence, intonation, emphasis, stress, tone.

aç·cent′, *v.t.*; accented, *pt.*, *pp.*; accenting, *ppr.*

1. to give accent to; to utter (a syllable, word, or phrase) with a particular stress or modulation of the voice; to emphasize.

2. to stress or emphasize.

3. to mark with an accent in writing or printing.

aç′cent·less, *a.* devoid of accent.

aç·cen′tŏr, *n.* [L. *ad*, to, and *canere*, to sing.]

1. in music, one who sings or performs the leading part. [Obs.]

2. [A–] a genus of insessorial birds, so named from their sweetness of song. It includes the English hedge sparrow.

aç·cen′tū·ȧ·ble, *a.* capable of being accented.

aç·cen′tū·ăl, *a.* 1. pertaining to accent.

2. having rhythm based on stress; as, German poetry is basically *accentual.*

aç·cen·tū·al′i·ty, *n.* the quality or state of being accentual.

aç·cen′tū·ăl·ly, *adv.* with due observance of accent; rhythmically.

aç·cen′tū·āte, *v.t.*; accentuated, *pt.*, *pp.*; accentuating, *ppr.* [L. *accentuatus*, pp. of *accentuare*; *ad*, to, and *canere*, to sing.]

1. to mark or pronounce with an accent or with accents.

2. to emphasize; heighten the effect of.

aç·cen·tū·ā′tion, *n.* an accentuating or accenting.

aç·cept′, *v.t.*; accepted, *pt.*, *pp.*; accepting,

ppr. [L. *acceptare,* from *accipere*; *ad,* to, and *capere,* to take.]
1. to take or receive (what is offered) with a consenting mind.
2. to receive with approval or favor.
3. to consent or agree to; as, to *accept* the terms of a contract.
4. to understand; to have a particular idea of; to receive in a particular sense; as, how is this phrase to be *accepted?*
5. in commerce, to agree, as by a signed promise, to pay; as, to *accept* a bill of exchange.
6. to receive as true, valid, proper, etc.; as, to *accept* an apology.
7. to respond to in the affirmative; as, he will *accept* an invitation.
8. in law, to receive in person, as service of a writ.
9. in parliamentary procedure, to receive (a committee report) as satisfactory.
Syn.—receive, take, admit.

aç·cept·ȧ·bil′i·ty, *n.* the quality of being acceptable.

aç·cept′ȧ·ble, *a.* [L. *acceptabilitas,* from *ad,* to, and *capere,* to take.]
1. that may be received with pleasure; pleasing to a receiver; gratifying; as, an *acceptable* present.
2. agreeable or pleasing in person; as, a man makes himself *acceptable* by his services or civilities.
Syn.—agreeable, grateful, pleasing, welcome.

aç·cept′ȧ·ble·ness, *n.* the quality of being acceptable.

aç·cept′ȧ·bly, *adv.* in an acceptable manner.

aç·cept′ănce, *n.* 1. an accepting or being accepted.
2. a receiving with approval or satisfaction; favorable reception; as, the *acceptance* of gifts.
3. the receiving of a bill of exchange or order, in such a manner as to bind the acceptor to make payment. This must be by express words; to charge the drawer with costs, in case of nonpayment, the *acceptance* must be in writing, under, across, or on the back of the bill.
4. a signed bill of exchange accepted; as, a merchant receives another's *acceptance* in payment.
5. an agreeing to terms or proposals in commerce, by which a bargain is concluded and the parties bound.
6. an agreeing to the act or contract of another by some act which binds the person in law; as, a landlord's taking rent agreed upon in a lease made by his predecessor is an *acceptance* of the terms of the lease.

aç·cept′ăn·cy, *n.* acceptance.

aç·cept′ănt, *a.* accepting.

aç·cept′ănt, *n.* one who accepts. [Archaic.]

aç·cep·tā′tion, *n.* 1. kind reception; a receiving with favor or approbation. [Archaic.]
2. a state of being acceptable; favorable regard. [Archaic.]

Some things are of great dignity and *acceptation* with God. —Hooker.

3. the meaning or sense in which a word or expression is understood, or generally received; as, a term is to be used according to its usual *acceptation.*

aç·cept′ed, *a.* generally regarded as true, valid, proper, etc.; conventional; approved.

aç·cept′ẽr, *n.* [L. *acceptor,* one who receives; from *accipere*; *ad,* to, and *capere,* to take.] a person who accepts: see *acceptor.*

aç·cep′ti·lāte, *v.t.* to remit (a debt) by acquittance without receiving the money.

aç·cep·ti·lā′tion, *n.* [L. *acceptilatio,* from *accipere,* to receive or take, and *latio,* from *latus,* pp. of *ferre,* to bear.] remission of a debt by an acquittance from the creditor without receiving the money.

aç·cep′tion, *n.* acceptation, specifically in sense 3.

aç·cept′ive, *a.* acceptable.

aç·cept′ŏr, *n.* same as *accepter,* but more used in commerce and law.

aç′cess, *n.* [L. *accessus,* approach.]
1. a coming toward or near; approach.
2. admittance; admission; as, to gain *access* to an important official.
3. the way or means by which a thing may be approached; as, the *access* is by a neck of land.
4. liberty to approach, come into, or use (with *to*): often implying previous obstacles.
5. in law, admission to sexual intercourse.
6. addition; increase by something added; as, an *access* of territory: in this sense *accession* is more generally used.
7. the onset of a disease; attack.
8. an outburst; paroxysm; as, an *access* of anger.
9. in the Anglican and Protestant Episcopal Churches, the prayer before consecration of the Eucharistic elements; the prayer of humble *access.*
Syn.—admission, approach, entrance, admittance, increase.

aç′cess, *v.t.*; accessed, *pt., pp.*; accessing, *ppr.* to gain or have access to; as, branch officials can *access* the central data bank.

aç·ces′sȧ·ry, *a.* and *n.* see *accessory.*

aç·ces·si·bil′i·ty, *n.* the quality or condition of being accessible.

aç·ces′si·ble, *a.* 1. that may be approached or entered.
2. easy to approach or enter.
3. that can be got; obtainable.
4. open to the influence of (with *to*); as, he is not *accessible to* pity.
Syn.—attainable, complaisant, courteous, sociable, friendly.

aç·ces′si·bly, *adv.* so as to be accessible.

aç·ces′sion, *n.* [L. *accessio,* an approach, from *accedere*; *ad,* to, and *cedere,* to move.]
1. a coming to and joining; as, a king's *accession* to a confederacy.
2. (a) increase by something added; (b) that which is added; augmentation; as, an *accession* of wealth or territory.
3. in law, (a) addition to property by improvements or natural growth; (b) the owner's right to the increase in value due to such additions.
4. the act of attaining a throne, an office, or dignity; as, the *accession* of a new president; the *accession* of the house of Hanover.
5. the onset of a disease; attack; as, an *accession* of fever.
Syn.—addition, augmentation, growth, increase.

aç·ces′sion·ăl, *a.* additional.

aç·ces′sit, *n.* [L., 3d pers. sing., perf. ind. of *accedere,* to come near, and meaning "he came near."] in England, a certificate or prize awarded to a student second in merit.

aç·ces·sō′ri·ăl, *a.* [L. *accessorius,* from *accessus,* pp. of *accedere*; *ad,* to, and *cedere,* to yield.] pertaining to or resembling an accessory; as, *accessorial* agency, *accessorial* guilt.

aç·ces′sō·ri·ly, aç·ces′sȧ·ri·ly, *adv.* in the manner of an accessory; by subordinate means, or in a secondary character; not as principal, but as a subordinate agent.

aç·ces′sō·ri·ness, aç·ces′sȧ·ri·ness, *n.* the state of being accessory, or of being or acting in a secondary character.

aç·ces′sō·ry, aç·ces′sȧ·ry, *a.* [L. *accessorius,* from *accessus,* pp. of *accedere*; *ad,* to, and *cedere,* to yield.]
1. aiding in certain acts or effects in a secondary or subordinate manner; additional; extra; as, *accessory* sounds in music.
2. in law, acting as an accessory; helping in an unlawful act.
accessory fruit; fruit formed with a part of the floral envelope attached to the pericarp as additional substance; pseudocarp: the mulberry and checkerberry are examples.
accessory nerves; in anatomy, the eleventh pair of cranial nerves.

aç·ces′sō·ry, *n.*; *pl.* **aç·ces′sō·rieṣ,** 1. something extra; thing added to help in a secondary way.
2. any article of clothing worn to complete one's outfit, as purse, gloves, stockings, etc.
3. equipment, usually demountable and replaceable, for convenience, comfort, safety, or completeness; as, the *accessories* of an automobile.
4. in law, a person who, though absent, helps another to break or escape the law.
5. in music, any mechanical device which helps to control the tonal effects of an organ.
accessory before (or *after*) *the fact*; a person who, though absent at the commission of a felony, aids or abets the accused before (or after) its commission.
Syn.—abettor, accomplice, ally, confederate, assistant, associate, coadjutor, companion, helper, henchman, partner, auxiliary, participator, appurtenance, attachment, appendage, ornament, decoration.

ac·ciac·ca·tū′ra (ät-chäk-kä-tö′rä), *n.* [It.] 1. in music, a short grace note sounded very quickly just before a principal note: it has a small line through the stem, and is shown as smaller.

2. in phonetics, the unemphasized first sound in a rising diphthong.

aç′ci·dence, *n.* [misspelled plural of *accident*; L. *accidentia,* from *accidere,* to happen.]
1. a book containing the fundamentals of grammar.
2. the part of grammar treating of the accidents, or inflection of words.
3. the fundamentals of any language, art, science, etc.

aç′ci·dence, *n.* [L. *accidens,* ppr. of *accidere*; *ad,* to, and *cadere,* to fall.] a happening by accident; a chance. [Obs.]

aç′ci·dent, *n.* [L. *accidens,* falling, from *ad,* to, and *cadere,* to fall.]
1. a happening; an event that takes place without one's foresight or expectation; an event which proceeds from an unknown cause, or is an unusual effect of a known cause, and therefore not expected; chance; casualty; contingency.
2. an unfortunate occurrence or mishap, especially one resulting in an injury.
3. in logic, a property, or quality of a thing, which is not essential to it, as whiteness in paper: also applied to all qualities in opposition to substance, as sweetness and softness, and to things not essential to a body, as clothes.
4. in grammar, something belonging to a word, but not essential to it, as gender, number, and case.
5. in heraldry, a point or mark not essential to a coat of arms.
6. in geography and geology, an irregular formation.
Syn.—casualty, contingency, misadventure, mischance, misfortune, mishap, disaster.

aç·ci·den′tăl, *a.* 1. happening by chance; not expected; casual; fortuitous; taking place not according to the usual course of things: opposed to that which is constant, regular, or intended; as, an *accidental* visit.
2. nonessential; not necessarily belonging; as, the songs are *accidental* to the play.
accidental colors; in optics, the imaginary complementary colors seen after fixing the eye for a short time on a bright-colored object, and then turning it suddenly to a white or light-colored surface. If the object is blue, the accidental color is yellow; if red, the accidental color is green.

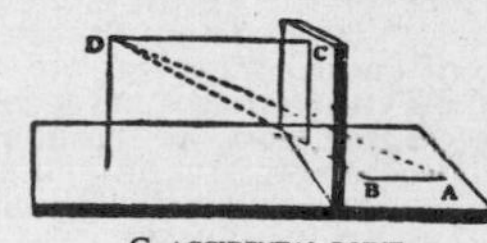

C. ACCIDENTAL POINT

accidental point; in perspective, that point (C) where a line (DC) drawn from the eye (D) parallel to a given right line (BA) meets the perspective plane.
Syn.—casual, chance, contingent, fortuitous, incidental.

aç·ci·den′tăl, *n.* 1. anything happening, occurring, or appearing accidentally, or as if accidentally; a property not essential. [Rare.]
2. in music, a sharp, flat, or natural which does not occur in the clef, and which implies some change of pitch in the note before which it is placed.
3. in painting, one of those chance effects, occurring from luminous rays falling on certain objects, by which they are brought into stronger light than they otherwise would be, so that their shadows are consequently deeper.

aç·ci·den′tăl·ism, *n.* accidental character.

aç″ci·den·tal′i·ty, *n.* the quality of being accidental.

aç·ci·den′tăl·ly, *adv.* by chance; casually; fortuitously; not essentially.

aç·ci·den′tăl·ness, *n.* the quality of being accidental; casualness.

aç′ci·den·ted, *a.* varied and uneven in surface: applied to land.

aç′ci·dent in·sūr′ănce, insurance against injury due to accident.

aç·cip′i·ent, *n.* [L. *accipiens,* ppr. of *accipere*; *ad,* to, and *capere,* to take.] one who receives. [Obs.]

aç·cip′i·tẽr, *n.* [L., a bird of prey, from *accipere*; *ad,* to, and *capere,* to take or seize.]
1. in ornithology, any of an order of birds of prey, the *Raptores.*
2. a bandage for the nose: so called from its resemblance to a hawk's claw.

aç·cip′i·trăl, *a.* of or like an accipiter.

Aç·cip′i·trēṣ, *n.pl.* the *Raptores.*

Aç·cip·i·trī′nae, *n.pl.* a subfamily of *Raptores,* including the hawks, family *Falconidæ,* having the wings shorter than the tail and the bill short and hooked from the base.

aç·cip′i·trine, *a.* of or like an accipiter.

aç·cis′mus, *n.* [Gr. *akkismos,* coyness.] in rhetoric, a feigned refusal.

aç·cīte′, *v.t.* [L. *accitus,* pp. of *accire; ad,* to, and *cire,* to go, with causative force of *cieri,* cause to go.] to call; to cite; to summon. [Obs.]

aç·clāim′, *v.t.;* acclaimed, *pt., pp.;* acclaiming, *ppr.* [L. *acclamare; ad,* to, and *clamare,* to cry out.]

1. to applaud.

2. to salute or declare by acclamation; as, to *acclaim* the President on his inauguration.

3. to cry aloud or shout; as, he *acclaimed* his grief.

aç·clāim′, *v.i.* to shout approval; as, the people *acclaimed* with one voice.

aç·clāim′, *n.* loud approval; acclamation.

aç·clāim′ẽr, *n.* one who acclaims.

aç·clȧ·mā′tion, *n.* [L. *acclamatio,* a shouting, from *ad,* and *clamare,* to cry out.]

1. loud applause; an eager expression of approval; a token of public approbation. Anciently, *acclamation* was a form of words, uttered with vehemence, somewhat resembling a song, sometimes accompanied with applause. In modern times, *acclamation* is expressed by hurrahs, by clapping of hands, and often by repeating words expressive of joy and good wishes.

2. in archaeology, a representation, in sculpture or on medals, of people expressing joy. *Acclamation medals* are those on which laudatory acclamations are recorded.

3. spontaneous and unanimous action by a multitude or meeting in favor of a person or proposition; as, he was nominated, and the platform was adopted, by *acclamation.*

Syn.—applause, plaudit, acclaim, approval, cheer, exultation, shouting.

aç·clam′ȧ·tō·ry, *a.* expressing joy or applause by acclamation.

aç·clī′mȧ·tȧ·ble, *a.* capable of being acclimated.

aç·clī·mȧ·tā′tion, *n.* same as *acclimatization.*

aç·clī′māte, *v.t.;* acclimated, *pt., pp.;* acclimating, *ppr.* [Fr. *acclimater,* from L. *ad,* to, and *climat,* climate; Gr. *klima(t),* a belt or zone of the earth, from *klinein,* to slope or lean.] to accustom to a new climate or different environment.

aç·clī′māte·ment, *n.* acclimation. [Rare.]

aç·cli·mā′tion, *n.* 1. the process of becoming accustomed to a new climate.

2. the state of being habituated or accustomed to a climate.

aç·clī′mȧ·tī·zȧ·ble, *a.* acclimatable.

aç·clī″mȧ·tī·zā′tion, *n.* acclimation.

aç·clī′mȧ·tīze, *v.t.;* acclimatized, *pt., pp.;* acclimatizing, *ppr.* to accustom to a new climate or different environment; acclimate.

aç·clī′mȧ·tīzed, *a.* accustomed to a new climate.

aç·clī′mȧ·tūre, *n.* the act of acclimating, or state of being acclimated. [Rare.]

aç′cli·nāte, *a.* [L. *acclinatus,* pp. of *acclinare; ad,* to, and *clinare,* to lean.] bending upward.

aç·cliv′i·ty, *n.* [L. *acclivitas,* a slope, from *ad,* to, and the root *kli,* to lean.] a slope or inclination of the earth, as the side of a hill, considered as *ascending,* in opposition to *declivity,* or a side *descending;* rising ground; ascent.

aç·clī′vous, aç·cliv′i·tous, *a.* rising with a slope, as a hill.

aç·cloy′, *v.t.;* accloyed, *pt., pp.;* accloying, *ppr.* [Fr. *encloyer,* to drive in a nail, from L. *in,* and *clavus,* nail.] to fill; to stuff; to fill to satiety. [Obs.]

aç·cōast′, *v.t.* and *v.i.* to lie or sail along the coast (of). [Obs.]

aç·coil′, *v.i.;* accoiled, *pt., pp.;* accoiling, *ppr.* [OFr. *acoillir,* from L. *ad,* to, and *colligere,* to collect.]

1. to collect; to gather together. [Obs.]

2. in nautical language, to coil up.

aç·cō·lāde′, *n.* [Fr. *accolade,* from L. *ad,* to, and *collum,* neck.]

1. a ceremony used in conferring knighthood, originally consisting of an embrace or kiss, now done by touching the shoulder with the flat of a sword.

2. in music, a vertical line connecting several staves.

3. an approving or praising mention.

aç′cō·lā·ted, *a.* bearing two or more profile heads, one overlapping another; as, an *accolated* coin.

aç′cō·lent, *a.* [L. *accolere,* to dwell by, from L. *ad,* and *colere,* dwell.] dwelling in the same vicinity.

aç′cō·lent, *n.* one who dwells near by; a neighbor.

aç·com·bi·nā′tion, *n.* combination. [Rare.]

aç·com′mō·dȧ·ble, *a.* [Fr. *accomodable.*] that may be accommodated or fitted. [Rare.]

aç·com′mō·dȧ·ble·ness, *n.* the ability to be accommodated. [Rare.]

aç·com′mō·dāte, *v.t.;* accommodated, *pt., pp.;* accommodating, *ppr.* [L. *accommodatus, pp.;* from *ad,* to, and *commodare,* to fit; *con,* and *modus,* a measure.]

1. to fit, adapt, or make suitable; as, to *accommodate* ourselves to circumstances; to *accommodate* the choice of subjects to the occasion.

2. to supply with or furnish: followed by *with;* as, to *accommodate* a man *with* apartments.

3. to supply with conveniences; as, to *accommodate* a friend.

4. to reconcile (things which are at variance); to adjust; as, to *accommodate* differences.

5. to show the fitness or agreement of; to apply; as, to *accommodate* prophecy to events.

6. to lend money to, or give commercial credit to.

Syn.—adapt, adjust, fit, suit, serve, oblige.

aç·com′mō·dāte, *v.i.* 1. to be in or come to adjustment, as the eye in order to see distinctly at a certain distance.

2. to conform. [Rare.]

aç·com′mō·dāte, *a.* suitable; fit: adapted; as, means *accommodate* to the end. [Obs.]

aç·com′mō·dāte·ly, *adv.* suitably; fitly. [Obs.]

aç·com′mō·dāte·ness, *n.* fitness. [Obs.]

aç·com′mō·dāt·ing, *a.* obliging; yielding to the desires of others; disposed to comply, and to oblige another; as, an *accommodating* man.

aç·com·mō·dā′tion, *n.* 1. fitness; adaptation: followed by *to.*

2. adjustment of differences; reconciliation, as of parties in dispute.

3. the provision of conveniences.

4. [*pl.*] conveniences; things furnished for use: chiefly applied to board, lodging, etc.; as, the *accommodations* at a hotel.

5. in mercantile language, a loan of money, or an extension of credit.

6. in theology, the application of a passage to something not originally intended by it, on the ground of resemblance or analogy.

> Many of those quotations were probably intended as nothing more than *accommodations.* —Paley.

7. automatic adjustment or the power of conforming, as that of the eye to see at different distances.

accommodation bill or *note;* a bill of exchange or a note made or endorsed without consideration by one or more persons to enable the drawer to get credit or raise money on it.

accommodation ladder; in nautical language, a ladder hung over the side of a ship at the gangway.

accommodation train; a railroad train that stops at all or most stations.

aç·com′mō·dā·tive, *a.* furnishing accommodation; accommodating.

aç·com′mō·dā·tive·ness, *n.* the state or quality of being accommodative.

aç·com′mō·dā·tŏr, *n.* one who or that which accommodates.

aç·cŏm′pȧ·nȧ·ble, *a.* sociable. [Obs.]

aç·cŏm′pȧ·ni·ẽr, *n.* one who or that which accompanies.

aç·cŏm′pȧ·ni·ment, *n.* [Fr. *accompagnement;* L. *ad,* to, with, and *compania,* associate; from *con,* together, and *panis,* bread.]

1. that which attends as a circumstance, or which is added to the principal thing by way of ornament or for the sake of symmetry.

2. in music, the subordinate part or parts accompanying the voice or a principal instrument; also, the harmony of a figured bass.

aç·cŏm′pȧ·nist, *n.* the performer in music who takes the accompanying part.

aç·cŏm′pȧ·ny, *v.t.;* accompanied, *pt., pp.;* accompanying, *ppr.* 1. to go with or attend as a companion or associate on a journey, walk, etc.; as, a man *accompanies* his friend to church, or on a tour.

2. to be with, as connected; to attend; as, pain *accompanies* disease.

3. in music, to act as an accompanist for.

Syn.—attend, escort.

aç·cŏm′pȧ·ny, *v.i.* 1. to attend; to be an associate; as, to *accompany* with others. [Obs.]

2. to cohabit. [Obs.]

3. in music, to perform the accompanying part in a composition.

aç·com′plē·tive, *a.* tending to accomplish. [Rare.]

aç·com′plice, *n.* [L. *ad,* to, and *complex,* from *con,* together, and *plectere,* to twist, also *plicare,* to fold.] an associate in a crime; a partner or partaker in guilt. It was formerly used in a good sense for *co-operator,* but this sense is wholly obsolete. It is followed by *of* or *with* before a person; as, A was an *accomplice of* B in the murder of C. Sometimes used with *to* before a thing, but *in* is generally used.

Syn.—accessory, abettor, ally.

aç·com′plice·ship, *n.* the state of being an accomplice. [Rare.]

aç·com·plic′i·ty, *n.* complicity. [Rare.]

aç·com′plish, *v.t.;* accomplished, *pt., pp.;* accomplishing, *ppr.* [Fr. *accomplir,* to finish, from L. *ad,* and *complere,* to complete, to fill up.]

1. to do; to succeed in doing; to complete; to finish entirely.

2. to execute; as, to *accomplish* a vow.

3. to gain; to obtain or effect by successful exertions; as, to *accomplish* a purpose.

4. to fulfill or bring to pass; as, to *accomplish* a prophecy.

5. to furnish thoroughly; to render accomplished.

Syn.—achieve, complete, effect, do, execute, finish, fulfill, perform, realize, bring about, carry out, consummate.

aç·com′plish·ȧ·ble, *a.* capable of being accomplished.

aç·com′plished, *a.* 1. finished; completed; fulfilled; executed; effected.

2. well endowed with good qualities and manners; complete in acquirements; educated and polished.

Syn.—skilled, proficient, polished, refined, cultured, educated.

aç·com′plish·ẽr, *n.* one who accomplishes.

aç·com′plish·ment, *n.* 1. completion; fulfillment; entire performance; as, the *accomplishment* of a prophecy.

2. the act of carrying into effect, or obtaining an object designed; attainment; as, the *accomplishment* of our desires or ends.

3. acquirement; that which constitutes excellence of mind, or elegance of manners, acquired by education or training; as, full of *accomplishments.*

accomplishment quotient (or *ratio*); achievement quotient.

aç·compt′ (-count′), *n.* account. [Archaic.]

aç·compt′ănt, *n.* accountant. [Archaic.]

aç·cord′, *n.* 1. agreement; harmony of minds; consent or concurrence of opinions or wills.

> They all continued with one *accord* in prayer. —Acts i. 14.

2. harmony of sounds; agreement in pitch and tone; as, the *accord* of notes.

3. agreement; just correspondence of things; as, the *accord* of light and shade in painting.

4. will; voluntary or spontaneous motion: preceded by *own.*

> Being more forward of his own *accord.* —2 Cor. viii. 17.

5. in law, an agreement between parties in controversy, by which satisfaction for an injury is stipulated, and which, when executed, bars a suit.

6. an informal agreement between countries.

aç·cord′, *v.t.;* accorded, *pt., pp.;* according, *ppr.* [OE. *acord;* Fr. *accorder;* from L. *ad,* to, and *cor, cordis,* heart.]

1. to make to agree or correspond; to adjust.

> Her hands *accorded* the lute's music to the voice. —Sidney.

2. to bring to an agreement; to settle, adjust, or compose; as, to *accord* suits or controversies.

3. to grant; to give; to concede; as, to *accord* due praise.

aç·cord′, *v.i.* 1. to agree; to be in correspondence; as, his dress *accords* with his duties.

2. to be in harmony.

aç·cord′ȧ·ble, *a.* agreeing; suitable.

aç·cord′ănce, *n.* 1. agreement with a person; conformity with a thing.

2. an agreeing.

3. a granting.

Syn.—agreement, concord, harmony.

aç·cord′ăn·cy, *n.* accordance.

aç·cord′ănt, *a.* corresponding; consonant; agreeable.

aç·cord′ănt·ly, *adv.* in an agreeable manner; suitably.

aç·cord′ẽr, *n.* one who accords.

aç·cord′ing, *a.* 1. agreeing; harmonizing.

2. suitable; congruous; in accordance: used with *to;* as, *according to* the rules. [Obs.]

ac·cord'ing, *adv.* accordingly; agreeably.
according as; agreeably, conformably, or proportionately as.
according to; (a) in a way consistent with; (b) in proportion to; (c) on the authority of; as stated by.

ac·cord'ing·ly, *adv.* agreeably; suitable; in a manner conformable to; consequently; as, to be rewarded *accordingly*.
Syn.—therefore, wherefore, conformably, consequently, then.

ac·cor'di·on, *n.* a musical instrument with keys, metal reeds, and a bellows which is alternately pulled out and pressed together between the hands of the player to force air through the reeds and thus produce tones.

ACCORDION

ac·cor'di·on, *a.* pleated or folded like an accordion; as, *accordion* pleats, an *accordion* booklet.

ac·cor'di·on·ist, *n.* a person who plays the accordion.

ac·cor'di·on plēats or **plāits,** narrow pleats like the folds in the bellows of an accordion.

ac·cor'pō·rāte, *v.t.* to incorporate. [Obs.]

ac·cost', *v.t.*; accosted, *pt., pp.*; accosting, *ppr.* [Fr. *accoster*; L. *accostare*, to bring side by side; *ad*, to, and *costa*, rib, side.]
1. to approach and speak to; to speak to first; to address; as, he *accosted* the lady.
2. to solicit for sexual purposes: said of prostitutes, etc.

ac·cost', *v.i.* to adjoin. [Obs.]

ac·cost'á·ble, *a.* easy of access; approachable.

ac·cost'ed, *a.* in heraldry, side by side: a term used when charges are placed on each side of another charge.

ac·cöuche'ment, *n.* [Fr.] delivery in childbirth.

ac·cöu·chēur', *n.* [Fr.] a medical practitioner who attends women in childbirth.

ac·cöu·chēuse', *n.* [Fr.] a midwife.

ac·count', *n.* [OE. *acounten*; Fr. *aconter*; **L.** *ad*, to, and *computare*, to reckon.]
1. a sum stated on paper; a business transaction, especially one in which credit is used; an entry in a book or on paper of things bought or sold, of payments, services, etc., including the names of the parties to the transaction, date, and price or value of the thing. An *account* may be either a single entry, or charge, or a statement of a number of particular debts and credits.
2. a computation of debts and credits, or a general statement of particular sums; as, the *account* stands thus; let them exhibit his *account*.
3. a computation or mode of reckoning applied to things other than money or trade; as, the Julian *account* of time.
4. [*pl.*] the books containing entries of financial transactions: generally used in connection with a particular set of books; as, his *accounts* are neatly kept.
5. narrative; relation; statement of facts; recital of particular transactions and events, verbal or written; as, an *account* of the revolution in France.
6. an assignment of reasons; explanation by a recital of particular transactions, given by a person in an employment, or to a superior, sometimes implying responsibility; an answering for conduct; a report; as, the congressman came home to give an *account* of his activities.
7. reason or consideration as a motive; as, on all *accounts*; on every *account*.
8. value; importance; estimation; worthy of more or less esteem; as, men of *account*.
9. a general statement in explanation of some event or phenomenon; as, no satisfactory *account* of the matter has yet been given.
10. profit; advantage; a result or production worthy of regard; as, to turn to *account*.
11. behalf; sake; as, I have incurred this trouble on your *account*.
account current, running account, open account; an account continuing between two parties without formal balancing or settlement; the statement of items of such an account.
account rendered; a bill or account presented by a creditor to his debtor for settlement.
account sales; a statement of daily transactions between two firms or individuals on a board of trade, or similar institution indicating the sales made by one on the other's behalf; also, a separate account given to a merchant by his broker, showing goods sold, prices obtained, and the net result after deduction of all necessary expenses; also, a similar account given by a merchant to the consigner of goods, showing the net proceeds of each consignment, after deduction of freight, commission, etc.
account stated, or *stated account*; an account presented by the creditor and accepted as correct by the debtor.
bank account; the balance on deposit in a bank and subject to withdrawal by the depositor.
payment on account; partial payment of a debt.
private accounts; individual accounts.
public accounts; accounts of public institutions or offices of government.
settled account; an account which has been ischarged.
statement of account; the periodical statement which a business firm sends to every debtor showing the amount due: usually contracted to *statement*.
to close an account; to settle an account with the object of discontinuing further credit or business with a firm.
to open an account; to begin financial transactions with a banker or merchant; to enter an account for the first time in a ledger or other book.
writ of account; in law, a writ which the plaintiff brings, demanding that the defendant should render his just account or show good cause to the contrary: called also an *action of account*.
Syn.—record, report, sum, balance, statement, recital, narrative, relation, explanation, rehearsal.

ac·count', *v.t.*; accounted, *pt., pp.*; accounting, *ppr.* 1. to deem, judge, consider, think, or hold in opinion; as, he is *accounted* a learned judge.
2. to reckon, or compute. [Obs.]
3. to give an account of; to account for; to explain; as, a way of *accounting* the solidity of ice. [Obs.]

ac·count', *v.i.* 1. to render an account of money received and paid out; as, an officer must *account* to the treasurer for money received.
2. to give reasons; to assign the causes; to explain (with *for*); as, idleness *accounts for* poverty.
3. to make satisfactory amends for; as, we must *account* for our crime.
4. to dispose of, as by killing; put out of action (with *for*); as, he *accounted for* five of the enemy.

ac·count·á·bil'ity, *n.* the state of being accountable, responsible, or liable; accountableness.

ac·count'á·ble, *a.* 1. liable to be called to account; answerable to a superior; as, every man is *accountable* to God for his conduct.
2. capable of being accounted for; explicable.
3. that may be counted or counted for. [Obs.]
Syn.—amenable, responsible, answerable, liable.

ac·count'á·ble·ness, *n.* liability to answer or to give account; the state of being answerable, or liable for the payment of money or damages; responsibility.

ac·count'á·bly, *adv.* in an accountable manner.

ac·count'ăn·cy, *n.* the position or business of an accountant.

ac·count'ănt, *n.* [OFr. *acomptant*, ppr. of *acompter*; L. *ad*, to, and *computare*, to reckon.] a trained person whose work is to inspect, keep, or adjust accounts.

ac·count'ănt ġen'ēr·ăl, the principal or responsible accountant in a public office or in a mercantile or banking house or company, as in the Bank of England, etc.

ac·count'ănt·ship, *n.* the office or employment of an accountant.

ac·count' book, a book in which business accounts are kept.

ac·count'ing, *n.* 1. the system, science, or art of keeping, analyzing, and explaining commercial accounts.
2. a statement of debits and credits.
3. a settling or balancing of accounts.

ac·cou'ple (-kup'pl), *v.t.* [Fr. *accoupler*, to join; L. *accopulare*; *ad*, to, and *copulare*, to join.] to couple; to join or link together. [Obs.]

ac·cou'ple·ment (-kup'pl-), *n.* 1. a coupling or joining. [Obs.]
2. something that couples, as a brace.

ac·cöu'tēr, ac·cöu'tre (ak-kǫǫ'tēr), *v.t.*; accoutered, *pt., pp.*; accoutering, *ppr.* [Fr. *accoutrer*, to dress; L. *ad*, to, and *custos*, keeper.] in a general sense, to dress; to equip; specifically, to array in a military dress; to put on, or to furnish with, a military dress and arms; to equip for military service.
Syn.—arm, equip, outfit, furnish, prepare, provide, supply.

ac·cöu'tēr·ments, ac·cöu'tre·ments (-kǫǫ'-tēr-), *n.pl.* 1. dress; furnishings; specifically, military dress and arms; accessories for military service.
2. the regulation equipment which a soldier carries in addition to his clothes and weapons.

ac·coy', *v.t.* [OFr. *acoyer*, to appease; L. *ad*, to, and *quietus*, pp. of *quiescere*, to rest.] to render quiet or shy; to soothe; to subdue. [Obs.]

ac·cred'it, *v.t.*; accredited, *pt., pp.*; accrediting, *ppr.* [Fr. *accréditer*, to give authority or reputation; L. *ad*, to, and *creditum*, a belief, from *credere*, to lend, to believe.]
1. to bring into credit or favor; to trust; to esteem or have a high opinion of; as, his most considerable and *accredited* assistant.
2. to confer credit or authority on; to stamp with authority.
3. to authorize; to give credentials to, as an envoy; as, the minister *accredited* by France.
4. to believe; to put credit in; as, they *accredited* stories of witchcraft.
5. to attribute.
to accredit with; to give credit for; as, statesmen are often *accredited with* sentiments they do not hold.

ac·cred·i·tā'tion, *n.* the act of accrediting, or state of being accredited.

ac·cred'it·ed, *a.* accepted as valid or credible; publicly or officially authorized; as, our *accredited* representatives abroad.

ac"crē·men·ti'tial (-tish'ăl), *a.* relating to accrementition.

ac"crē·men·ti'tion, *n.* [L. *accrementum*, from *ad*, to, and *crescere*, to grow.] growth by the addition of new cells exactly like those from which they developed.

ac·cresce', *v.i.* to accrue. [Obs.]

ac·cres'cence, *n.* continuous growth; accretion.

ac·cres'cent, *a.* 1. increasing; growing.
2. in botany, continuing to grow larger after flowering.

ac·cres·ci·men'tō, *n.* [It., from L. *accrescere*, to increase.] in music, the addition to a note of half its length in time: indicated by placing a small dot after it.

ac·crēte', *v.i.* 1. to grow together.
2. to grow by being added to.

ac·crēte', *v.t.* to cause to adhere; to add.

ac·crēte', *a.* 1. formed by accretion.
2. in botany, grown together.

ac·crē'tion, *n.* [L. *accretio*, increase, from *ad*, to, and *crescere*, to grow.]
1. growth in size, especially by addition or accumulation.
2. an increase by accumulated matter; as, a mineral vein is augmented by *accretion*.
3. in civil law, an increase to property without cost to the owner, as an increase of land by flood or alluvial deposit, or change in the course of a stream; increase of inheritance by death, surrender, or failure on the part of a coheir.
4. in medicine, the union by gradual growth of organs or parts naturally separate, as the fingers.

ac·crē'tive, *a.* increasing by growth; growing; adding to by growth; as, the *accretive* motion of plants.

aç·crim′i·nāte, *v.t.* [L. *ad*, to, and *criminari*, to accuse.] to accuse of a crime. [Obs.]

aç·crim·i·nā′tion, *n.* accusation of a crime. [Obs.]

aç·crōach′, *v.i.* [Fr. *accrocher*, to fix on a hook; from *croc, crochet*, a hook, from the same elements as *crook*.]
1. to draw to oneself; acquire. [Obs.]
2. to encroach.

aç·crōach′ment, *n.* encroachment, especially in the sense of usurpation. [Obs.]

aç·crụ′ăl, *n.* act or process of accruing; accretion.

aç·crụe′, *v.i.*; accrued, *pt.*, *pp.*; accruing, ppr. [Fr. *accroitre, accru*, to increase; L. *accrescere*; *ad*, to, and *crescere*, to grow.] literally, to come as a natural growth or advantage (with *to*); to be added, as increase, profit, or damage; as a profit *accrues* to government from the coinage of copper; a loss *accrues* from the coinage of gold and silver.

accrued interest; in accounting, such interest as has become due since the time of the last payment.

accrued liability; that portion of an accruing liability which has already become chargeable, its actual payment as yet not having become due.

aç·crụe′, *n.* something that accrues; accession. [Obs.]

aç·crụ′ẽr, *n.* in law, accretion; as, title by *accruer*.

aç·crụ′ment, *n.* accrual.

aç·cū·bā′tion, *n.* [L. *accubatio*, a reclining, from *ad*, to, and *cubare*, to lie down.] a lying or reclining on a couch, as the ancients at their meals, with the head resting on a pillow or on the elbow.

aç·cul·tū·rā′tion, *n.* [prefix *ac-*, and *culture*.] the transfer of culture from one ethnic group to another.

aç·cumb′, *v.i.* to recline, as at table. [Obs.]

aç·cum′ben·cy, *n.* state of being accumbent or reclining. [Obs.]

aç·cum′bent, *a.* [L. *accumbens*, ppr. of *accumbere*, from *ad*, to, and *cubare*, to recline.]
1. lying down.
2. leaning or reclining, as the ancients at their meals.
3. in botany, lying against anything: said of leaves, organs, etc.; as, an *accumbent* ovule.

ACCUMBENT OVULE (*Thlaspi arvense*)

aç·cum′bent, *n.* one who reclines at table.

aç·cū′mū·lāte, *v.t.*; accumulated, *pt.*, *pp.*; accumulating, *ppr.* [L. *accumulatus*, pp. of *accumulare*; *ad*, to, and *cumulare*, to heap.]
1. to heap up; to pile; to amass; as, to *accumulate* earth and stones.
2. to collect or bring together; as, to *accumulate* causes of misery; to accumulate wealth.

Syn.—amass, collect, gather, heap up, hoard.

aç·cū′mū·lāte, *v.i.* to grow to a great size, number, or quantity; to increase greatly; as, public evils *accumulate*.

aç·cū′mū·lāte, *a.* collected into a mass or quantity.

aç·cū·mū·lā′tion, *n.* 1. the act of accumulating; the state of being accumulated; an amassing; as, an *accumulation* of earth, or of evils.
2. in law, the concurrence of several titles to the same thing, or of several circumstances to the same proof.
3. that which is accumulated; a collection; as, a great *accumulation* of sand at the mouth of a river.
4. the addition to capital of interest or profits.

accumulation of power; in physics, the storing of energy or power as by the lifting of weights, by causing chemical changes, etc.

aç·cū′mū·lā·tive, *a.* 1. resulting from accumulation.
2. given to accumulating; heaping up; accumulating.

aç·cū′mū·lā·tive·ly, *adv.* in an accumulative manner; collectively.

aç·cū′mū·lā·tive·ness, *n.* the quality of being accumulative.

aç·cū′mū·lā·tõr, *n.* one who or that which accumulates, gathers, or amasses; specifically, an apparatus for storing power or energy, as a storage battery.

aç′cū·rȧ·cy, *n.* [L. *accuratio*, from *accurare*, to take care of; *ad*, to, and *curare*, to take care; *cura*, care.]
1. exactness; exact conformity to truth, or to a rule or model.
2. freedom from mistake; correctness; precision; as, the *accuracy* of ideas or opinions is conformity to truth; the value of testimony depends on its *accuracy*.

aç′cū·rāte, *a.* [L. *accuratus*, pp. of *accurare*, to take care.]
1. in exact conformity to truth, or to a standard or rule, or to a model; free from error or defect; as, an *accurate* account; *accurate* measure.
2. exact, correct, or precise; as, an *accurate* accountant.

Syn.—exact, correct, precise.

aç′cū·rāte·ly, *adv.* exactly; in an accurate manner; with precision; without error or defect; as, a writing *accurately* copied.

aç′cū·rāte·ness, *n.* accuracy; exactness; nicety; precision.

aç·cũrse′, *v.t.*; accursed *or* accurst, *pt.*, *pp.*; accursing, *ppr.* [AS. *a* and *cursian*; *acursien*.] to doom to destruction; to imprecate misery or evil upon: now only in the past participle.

aç·cũrsed′ (*or* ak-kũrs′ed), **aç·cũrst′,** *a.* 1. worthy of curses; detestable; execrable; cursed; as, deeds *accursed*.
2. doomed to evil of any kind; under a curse; ruined; blasted.

Thro′ you my life will be *accurst*.
—Tennyson.

aç·cũrs′ed·ly, *adv.* execrably; detestably; in an accursed manner.

aç·cũrs′ed·ness, *n.* the state or quality of being accursed.

aç·cūṣ′ȧ·ble, *a.* [L. *accusabilis*, from *accusare*, to call to account.] that may be accused; blamable; liable to censure (followed by *of*); as, *accusable of* being a heretic.

aç·cūṣ′ăl, *n.* accusation.

aç·cūṣ′ănt, *n.* one who accuses.

aç·cū·ṣā′tion, *n.* 1. the act of charging with a crime or offense; the act of accusing of any wrong or injustice.
2. the charge of an offense or crime; the declaration containing the charge; that which is charged.

They set up over his head his *accusation*.
—Matt. xxvii. 37.

Syn.—charge, impeachment, arraignment, indictment, crimination.

aç·cū·ṣȧ·tī′văl, *a.* relating to the accusative case.

aç·cū′ṣȧ·tive, *n.* the accusative case: in English grammar, the objective case; in Latin and Greek, the fourth case.

aç·cū′ṣȧ·tive, *a.* 1. of or in the accusative case.
2. charging with offense or crime. [Obs.]

aç·cū′ṣȧ·tive çase, in linguistics, the case expressing the goal of an action or motion: in Latin grammar, the case occurring in the direct object of a verb and after certain prepositions; in English grammar, the objective case.

aç·cū′ṣȧ·tive·ly, *adv.* 1. in an accusative manner.
2. in relation to the accusative case in grammar.

aç·cū·ṣȧ·tō′ri·ăl, *a.* of an accuser.

aç·cū·ṣȧ·tō′ri·ăl·ly, *adv.* in an accusatorial manner.

aç·cū′ṣȧ·tō·ry, *a.* accusing; containing an accusation; as, an *accusatory* libel.

aç·cūṣe′, *v.t.* [Fr. *accuser*; L. *accusare*, to call to account, from *ad*, to, and *causa*, a reason, case, or suit at law.]
1. to charge with, or declare to have committed a crime; to charge with an offense against the laws, judicially or by a public process; as, to *accuse* one of a high crime or misdemeanor.
2. to find at fault; to blame: followed by *of* before the subject of accusation; as, to *accuse* one *of* greed.

Syn.—charge, indict, arraign, impeach, blame.

aç·cūṣed′, *n.* one charged with a crime (with *the*); as, *the accused* was seen to enter the house. It has the same form in the plural; as, *the accused* are charged with conspiring.

aç·cūṣe′ment, *n.* an accusation. [Obs.]

aç·cūṣ′ẽr, *n.* one who accuses or blames; one who brings an accusation against another in court.

aç·cūṣ′ing·ly, *adv.* in an accusing manner.

aç·cus′tõm, *v.t.*; accustomed *pt.*, *pp.*; accustoming, *ppr.* [Fr. *accoutumer*, from *ad* and *coutume, coustume*, custom; L. *consuetumen*, habit, from root in *consuescere*; *con* and *suere*, to make one's own, from *suus*, one's own.] to make familiar by use; to habituate or inure; as, to *accustom* oneself to a diet.

aç·cus′tõm, *v.i.* 1. to be wont, or habituated to do anything. [Obs.]
2. to cohabit. [Obs.]

aç·cus′tõm, *n.* custom. [Obs.]

aç·cus′tõm·ȧ·ble, *a.* of long custom; habitual; customary. [Obs.]

aç·cus′tõm·ȧ·bly, *adv.* according to custom or habit. [Obs.]

aç·cus′tõm·ănce, *n.* custom; habitual use or practice. [Obs.]

aç·cus′tõm·ā·ri·ly, *adv.* customarily. [Obs.]

aç·cus′tõm·ā·ry, *a.* customary. [Obs.]

aç·cus′tõmed, *a.* 1. customary; habitual; usual; often practiced; as, in their *accustomed* manner.
2. wont or used (*to*); as, he is *accustomed to* obeying orders.

aç·cus′tõmed·ness, *n.* the quality or state of being accustomed.

āce, *n.* [L. *as*, a unit or pound.]
1. a unit; a single point on a card or die, or the card or die so marked.
2. a very small quantity; a particle; an atom.
3. a single point in scoring various games, as tennis.
4. an expert in anything, especially in combat flying.

āce, *a.* first-rate; expert; as, an *ace* salesman. [Colloq.]

-ā′ce·a (-ā′she-ȧ), [LL. neut. pl. of *aceus*.] a plural suffix for names of classes or orders of animals; as, Crust*acea*, Cet*acea*: properly agreeing with *animalia* (animals) understood.

-ā′cē·ae (-ā′cē-ē), [L. f. pl. of *aceus*.] a plural suffix for names of orders or families of plants; as, Lili*aceæ*, Ros*aceæ*: properly agreeing with L. *plantæ* (plants) understood.

-a′ce·an, same as *-aceous*.

ȧ·cē′di·ȧ, *n.* [Gr. *akēdia*, from *akēdos*; *a* priv., and *kēdos*, care.] melancholia; sloth; boredom; listlessness; a mental condition marked by apathy.

āce′high′, *a.* of a hand in poker or brag, having an ace, but having neither a pair nor anything better; hence, unexcelled, ranking highest. [Colloq.]

āce′high′, *adv.* unexcelled in favor, in the highest esteem. [Colloq.]

āce in the hōle, 1. in stud poker, an ace dealt and kept face down until the deal is over.
2. any thing or person serving as an advantage held in reserve until needed. [Slang.]

A·cel′dȧ·mȧ, *n.* [L. *Aceldama*, from Gr. *Akeldama*, for Aram. *ōkēl damō*, field of blood.]
1. a field said to have lain south of Jerusalem, the same as the potter's field purchased with the bribe which Judas took for betraying Jesus, and therefore called the field of blood. See Acts i. 19, Matt. xxvii. 8.
2. a place of bloodshed.

ac·ē·naph′thēne, *n.* crystalline hydrocarbon, $C_{12}H_{10}$, obtained from coal tar by distillation.

ȧ·cen′triç, *a.* [Gr. *a* priv., and *kentron*, a center.] off center; without a center.

-ā′ceous (-ā′shus), [L. *-aceus*, of the nature of.] of the nature of; belonging to; characterized by; like, as in crust*aceous*, farin*aceous*.

Ȧ·ceph′ȧ·lȧ, *n.pl.* [Gr. *a* priv., and *kephalē*, head.] a class of mollusks, having no apparent head, as the oyster; the *Lamellibranchiata*.

ȧ·ceph′ȧ·lăn, *n.* one of the *Acephala*.

Ȧ·ceph′ȧ·lī, *n.pl.* [LL. nom. pl. of *acephalus*, from Gr. *a* priv., and *kephalē*, head.]
1. any of various Christian groups without a leader; especially, a fifth-century Egyptian sect, which separated with the patriarch of Alexandria.
2. a class of levelers in the reign of Henry I of England, who would acknowledge no head or superior.
3. an imaginary African people, reported by ancient writers to have no heads.

ȧ·ceph′ȧ·list, *n.* one who acknowledges no head or superior; one of the Acephali.

ȧ·ceph′ȧ·lō·cyst, *n.* [Gr. *akephalos*, headless, and *kystis*, bladder.] a headless larval tapeworm embedded in the liver, etc. of its host.

ȧ·ceph″ȧ·lō·cys′tiç, *a.* pertaining to or of the nature of an acephalocyst.

ȧ·ceph′ȧ·lous, *a.* [Gr. *a* priv., and *kephalē*, head.]
1. without a head; headless.
2. in botany, a term applied to ovaries, the style of which springs from their base instead of their apex.

3. in zoology, having no part of the body differentiated as the head.

4. in prosody, defective or lacking something at the beginning: applied to a verse or line of poetry.

5. of or pertaining to the *Acephala*.

6. having no chief or leader.

ȧ·ceph′ȧ·lus, *n.* [Gr. *a* priv., and *kephalē*, head.] a headless monster.

ä·ce′qui·ä (ä-sā′kē-ä), *n.* [Sp.] an irrigating ditch.

Ā′cẽr, *n.* [L., a maple tree, so called from its sharp leaves; from root *ak*, sharp, appearing in *acid*, *acetic*, etc.] a large genus of trees and shrubs including the maples and box elder. *Acer saccharinum* is the sugar maple.

Ac·e·rā′cē·ae, *n.pl.* [L. *acer*, maple, and suffix *-aceae*.] a family of trees and shrubs, the maple family, having opposite leaves and small clustered flowers: they are found in the temperate parts of Europe and Asia, the north of India, and North America. They yield a sweet, sticky sap, from which sugar is often made. The bark is astringent and yields yellow and reddish dyes.

ac·e·rā′ceous, *a.* of or pertaining to the *Aceraceæ*.

ac′ẽr·āte, *n.* [L. *acer*, maple.] a salt of aceric acid.

ac′ẽr·āte, *a.* needle-shaped.

Ac·e·rā′tēs, *n.* a genus of North American herbs of the milkweed family.

ȧ·cẽrb′, *a.* [Fr. *acerbe*, L. *acerbus*, bitter, sour, from *acer*, sharp.] sour, bitter, and harsh to the taste; sour, with astringency or roughness: a quality of unripe fruits.

ac′ẽr·bāte, *v.t.*; acerbated, *pt.*, *pp.*; acerbating, *ppr.* 1. to make sour, bitter, or harsh to the taste.

2. to embitter; to exasperate.

ȧ·cẽrb′iç, *a.* sour; harsh; severe.

ȧ·cẽrb′i·ty, *n.* 1. a sourness with bitterness and astringency.

2. harshness, bitterness, or severity of temper, words, etc.

ȧ·cer′iç, *a.* [L. *acer*, a maple tree.] pertaining to the maple; obtained from the maple; as, *aceric* acid.

ȧ·cer′iç ac′id, an acid which exists in the sap of the maple.

ac′ẽr·ōse, ac′ẽr·ous, *a.* [L. *acerosus*, chaffy, from *acus*, genit. *aceris*, needle.]

1. in botany, chaffy; resembling chaff.

2. having a sharp, stiff point like a needle, as the leaves of the pine, juniper, etc.

ACEROSE LEAVES

ȧ·cẽr′rȧ, *n.* [L.] in Roman antiquity, a container in which incense was burned; a censer.

ȧ·cẽr′văl, *a.* [L. *acervalis*, from *acervus*, heap.] pertaining to a heap. [Obs.]

ȧ·cẽr′vāte, *v.t.* [L. *acervatus*, pp. of *acervare*, to heap up, from *acervus*, heap.] to heap up. [Obs.]

ȧ·cẽr′vāte, *a.* in botany, heaped, or growing in heaps, or in closely compacted clusters.

ac·ẽr·vā′tion, *n.* the act or process of heaping up.

ȧ·cẽr′vȧ·tive, *a.* tending to heap up.

ȧ·cẽr′vū·line (*or* -lin), *a.* shaped like little heaps.

ȧ·ces′cence, *n.* [Fr. from L. *acescens*, ppr. of *acescere*, to become sour.] the process of becoming sour.

ȧ·ces′cen·cy, *n.* the quality or state of being acescent.

ȧ·ces′cent, *a.* turning sour; readily becoming tart or acid; hence, slightly sour; acidulous; subacid.

ȧ·ces′cent, *n.* any substance which is slightly acid, or likely to become sour.

acet-, [see *aceto-*.] combining form of *acetic*, *acetyl*, before vowels.

ac·e·tab′ū·lăr, *a.* cup-shaped.

Ac·e·tab·ū·lif′ẽr·ȧ, *n.pl.* [L. *acetabulum*, a cup, and *ferre*, to bear.] see *Dibranchiata*.

ac·e·tab·ū·lif′ẽr·ous, *a.* having cup-shaped suckers like the cuttlefish.

ac·e·tab′ū·li·form, *a.* acetabular.

ac·e·tab′ū·lum, *n.* [L. *acetabulum*, a vinegar cup, from *acetum*, vinegar.]

1. among the Romans, a vinegar cruet or similar container; also, a measure of about one-eighth of a pint.

2. in anatomy, the cup-shaped socket of the hip bone, into which the thigh bone fits.

3. a cotyledon in the placenta of ruminating animals.

4. socket on the trunk of an insect, in which the leg is inserted.

5. a sucker of the cuttlefish and others of the *Dibranchiata*.

ȧ·cē′tăl, *n.* [*acet-*, *-ic*, and *al*(cohol).] a colorless liquid, $C_6H_{14}O_2$, obtained by the imperfect oxidation of alcohol, used in medicine as a hypnotic.

ac·et·al′dē·hȳde, *n.* [*acet-*, and *aldehyde*.] a colorless, soluble, volatile liquid, C_2H_4O, used as a solvent and in manufacturing various organic compounds.

ac·et·am′id, ac·et·am′īde, *n.* [*acet-*, *-ate*, and *amid*.] a white crystalline organic substance, CH_3CONH_2, the amide of acetic acid.

ac·et·an′i·lid, ac·et·an′i·līde, *n.* [Eng. *acetyl*, and *anilid*.] a white crystalline organic substance, $CH_3CONHC_6H_5$, produced by the action of acetic acid on aniline: used as a drug to lessen pain and fever.

ac·e·tā′ri·ous, *a.* used in salads, as lettuce, etc.

ac′e·tȧ·ry, *n.* an acid pulpy substance in certain fruits, as the pear, enclosed in a small gritty mass toward the base of the fruit.

ac′e·tāte, *n.* [L. *acetum*, vinegar, from *acere*, to be sour.] a salt or ester of acetic acid.

ac′e·tā·ted, *a.* combined with acetic acid.

ȧ·cē′tiç (*or* ȧ-set′-), *a.* [L. *acetum*, vinegar.] relating to vinegar; having the properties of acetic acid or vinegar; sour.

acetic acid; a sour, colorless, liquid compound, CH_3COOH, having a sharp odor: it is found in vinegar.

acetic ether; any ester of acetic acid.

ȧ·cet″i·fi·cā′tion, *n.* an acetifying.

ȧ·cet′i·fi·ẽr, *n.* a device used in acetifying.

ȧ·cet′i·fȳ, *v.t.*; acetified, *pt.*, *pp.*; acetifying, *ppr.* to convert into acid or vinegar.

ȧ·cet′i·fȳ, *v.i.* [L. *acetum*, vinegar, and E. *-fy*.] to turn acid.

ac·e·tim′e·tẽr, *n.* an acetometer.

ac·e·tim′e·try, *n.* the act or method of ascertaining the strength of vinegar or the proportion of acetic acid contained in it.

ac′e·tin, *n.* a mixture of acetic acid and glycerin.

ac′e·tīze, *v.i.* to acetify. [Rare.]

ac′e·tō-, acet-, [L. *acetum*, vinegar.] a combining form used in chemistry to indicate compounds derived from acetic acid, acetyl, etc.; as, *aceto*-gelatin; *aceto*-bromide.

ac″e·tom′e·tẽr, *n.* [*aceto-*, and *-meter*.] an instrument used to find the amount of acetic acid in a definite quantity of vinegar or other liquid.

ac″e·tō·nae′mi·ȧ, *n.* [E. *acetone*, and Gr. *aima*, blood.] in pathology, a diseased condition due to the presence of acetone in the blood.

ac′e·tōne, *n.* [*acet-*, and *-one*.] a colorless, inflammable, volatile liquid, CH_3COCH_3, used as a paint remover and as a solvent for certain oils and other organic compounds: also called *dimethyl acetone*.

ac′e·tōne bod′y, a ketone body.

ac·e·ton′iç, *a.* derived from acetone.

ac″e·tō·phē′nōne, *n.* a chemical compound derived from acetic and benzoic acids.

ac′e·tōse, *a.* acetous.

ac·e·tos′i·ty, *n.* sourness.

ȧ·cē′tous (*or* ac′e-tous), *a.* of, producing, or like vinegar; sour; acid.

acetous acid; term formerly applied to impure and dilute acetic acid, under the notion that it was composed of carbon and hydrogen in the same proportions as in acetic acid, but with less oxygen. [Obs.]

acetous fermentation; the process by which alcohol or sugar is changed into acetic acid.

ȧ·cē′tum, *n.* [L. *acere*, to be sour.] vinegar.

ac′e·tyl, *n.* [L. *acetum*, vinegar, and *hylē*, substance.] the radical CH_3CO derived from acetic acid.

ȧ·cet′y·lāte, *v.t.*; acetylated, *pt.*, *pp.*; acetylating, *ppr.* [*acetyl*, and *-ate*.] to combine an acetyl radical with (an organic compound).

ac″e·tyl·chō′line, *n.* [*acetyl*, and *choline*.] an alkaloid, $C_7H_{17}O_3N$, extracted from ergot and used in medicine to lower blood pressure and increase peristalsis.

ȧ·cet′y·lēne, *n.* a colorless gaseous hydrocarbon, C_2H_2, prepared by the reaction of water with calcium carbide: it is used as the starting material in the synthesis of many organic compounds, for lighting, and, with oxygen in a blowtorch, for welding, etc.

ac′e·tyl·sal″i·cil′iç ac′id, aspirin.

āce′y-deūc′y, *n.* [from *ace*, and *deuce*.] a variation of the game of backgammon.

A·çhae′ăn, *a.* of Achaia, its people, or its culture; Greek.

A·çhae′an, *n.* 1. a native or inhabitant of Achaia.

2. A Greek: so used in Homer.

The Achaeans are thought to have been a people from the northern Danube region who migrated into Greece about 1300 B.C.

Aç̈h·ae·men′i·ăn, *n.* a Persian of the period of Achaemenes; also, the language of his dynasty.

ȧ·çhae′tous, *a.* [Gr. *a* priv., and *chaitē*, hair.] without hairs, as some caterpillars, plants, etc.

A·çhā′iȧ, *n.* a province of ancient Greece, in the Peloponnesus.

A·çha′ian, *adj.* and *n.* Achaean.

ȧ·chär′, *n.* [Per.] an Anglo-Indian name for a pickle or relish.

açh′āte, *n.* agate (the stone). [Rare.]

ȧ·çhāte′, *n.* [Fr. *achat*, purchase, from *acheter*; LL. *accaptare*; *ad*, to, and *captare*, to take.]

1. purchase; bargaining. [Obs.]

2. [*pl.*] same as *cates*.

A·çhā′tēş, *n.* [L.] in Virgil's *Aeneid*, a loyal friend and companion of Aeneas; hence, any loyal friend.

Açh·ȧ·tī′nȧ, *n.* a genus of land snails, popularly called agate snails. Some of them have shells nine or ten inches long.

ä·çhä·töur′, *n.* [Fr.] a purchaser or buyer of provisions; a caterer. [Obs.]

āçhe (āk), *v.i.*; ached, *pt.*, *pp.*; aching, *ppr.* [AS. *ace*, *ece*, ache, from *acan*, to ache.]

1. to suffer pain; to have or be in pain, or in continued pain; as, the head *aches*.

2. to yearn or long (with *for* or an infinitive); as, his heart *aches for* her.

āçhe (āk), *n.* a dull, continuous pain, as distinguished from a sudden twinge, or spasmodic pain.

A·çhē′ăn, *a.* see *Achaean*.

ȧ·çheī′lȧ·ry, *a.* same as *achilary*.

ȧ·çheī′lous, *a.* same as *achilous*.

ā·çhēne′, *n.* [Gr. *a-*, not, and *chainein*, to gape.] any small, dry fruit with one seed, whose thin outer covering (pericarp) does not burst when ripe.

ā·çhē′ni·ăl, *a.* pertaining to an achene.

ā·çhē′ni·um, *n.* an achene.

Açh′e·ron, *n.* fabled river of hell; hence, the lower regions.

Açh·e·ron′tiç, *a.* dark and forbidding, like the lower regions.

ACHENE—lettuce and buttercup

Ȧ·cheu′le·ăn, Ȧ·cheu′li·ăn (-shōō′), *a.* [Fr. *Acheulien*, from *St. Acheul*, France, where remains were found.] of or designating a type of paleolithic culture characteristic of the Heidelberg and Piltdown man.

ȧ·chiēv′ȧ·ble, *a.* that may be achieved.

ȧ·chiēve′, *v.t.*; achieved, *pt.*, *pp.*; achieving, *ppr.* [Fr. *achever*, *achiever*, to finish, from L. *ad*, to, and Fr. *chief*, from L. *caput*, head.]

1. to perform or execute; to accomplish; to finish, or carry on to a final close; as, he *achieved* his laborious task.

2. to gain or obtain as the result of exertion; to bring about by effort.

ȧ·chiēve′, *v.i.* to effect a desired result.

Syn.—accomplish, consummate, realize, attain, effect, execute, finish, fulfill, gain, perform, win.

ȧ·chiēve′ment, *n.* [Fr. *achevement*, from *achever*, to end.]

1. the performance of an action; the act of achieving; an obtaining by exertion.

FUNERAL ACHIEVEMENT

2. a great or heroic deed; a feat; something accomplished by valor, or boldness.

3. a tablet or panel bearing a coat of arms, granted for the performance of a great or honorable action. Especially applied to the escutcheon of a deceased person, it is displayed at the funeral and over the tomb: also called a *hatchment*.

achievement quotient; in educational psychology, the ratio of a person's achievement age (as shown by testing what has been learned) to his mental age: also called *accomplishment quotient*.

à·chiēv′ēr, *n.* one who achieves or accomplishes.

à·chi′là·ry, *a.* [Gr. *a*. priv., and *cheilos*, lip.] in botany, without a lip, or labellum.

Ach·il·lē′à, *n.* a genus of herbs of the thistle family, including the yarrow.

Ach·il·lē′ăn, *a.* unconquerable, like Achilles.

A·chil′lēs, *n.* [L., from Gr. *Achilleus*.] in Homer's *Iliad*, the Greek hero of the Trojan War, who killed Hector and was killed by Paris.

A·chil′lēs′ heel, a vulnerable point. Achilles' mother held him by the heel when she dipped him in the Styx to make him invulnerable. He was, however, fatally wounded by Paris, who shot an arrow into his heel, the one vulnerable point on his body.

A·chil′lēs′ ten′dŏn, the tendon connecting the back of the heel to the muscles of the calf of the leg.

a·chī′lous, *a.* in anatomy and botany, possessing no lips or only rudimentary ones.

āch′ing, *n.* continued pain or distress.

āch′ing, *a.* continuously painful.

ä·chï·ō′te, *n.* [Sp. *achiote*, from Indian *achiotl*.] same as *arnotto*.

ach′i·rīte, *n.* an old name for dioptase.

A·chit′ŏ·phel, *n.* same as *Ahithophel*.

à·chlam′y·dāte, *a.* [Gr. *a* priv., and *chlamys*, cloak.] having no mantle: a term applied to certain gastropods.

Ach·là·myd′ē·ae, *n.pl.* a group of plants having no perianth, as the willow, oak, and birch.

ach·là·myd′ē·ous, *a.* [Gr. *a* priv., and *chlamys*, a garment.] in botany, having no floral envelope.

à·chō′li·à, *n.* [Gr. *a* priv., and *cholia*, bile.] lack of bile.

à·chol′iç, *a.* acholous.

ach′ō·lous, *a.* lacking bile.

ach′ŏr, (*or* ā′chŏr), *n.* [Gr. *achōr*, dandruff.]
1. a disease of infants, the face, and often the neck and breast, becoming covered with scabs.
2. a scaly eruption of the scalp.
3. a pustule.

à·chor′dăl, *a.* [Gr. *a*. priv., and *chordē*, a chord.] having no notochord.

Ach·or·dā′tà, *n. pl.* a general rame for the animals which have no notochord.

à·chō′ri·ŏn, *n.* [LL. *achor*, from Gr. *achōr*, scurf.] the parasitic fungus which causes favus in man.

Ach·rō·an′thēs, *n.* same as *Malaxis*.

ach′rō·īte, *n.* [Gr. *achroos*, from *a* priv., and *chroa*, color.] a colorless variety of tourmaline.

ach·rō·mā′si·à (-zhi-à), *n.* lack of pigment in the skin.

ach·rō·mat′iç, *a.* [Gr. *a* priv., and *chrōma*, *chrōmatos*, color.] 1. colorless.
2. forming visual images whose outline is free from prismatic colors: said of a lens.
3. in biology, (a) staining poorly with the usual stains; (b) made of achromatin.
4. in music, without accidentals; as, an *achromatic* scale.

achromatic lens; a compound lens so made and adjusted as to transmit light without breaking it up into its primary colors.

ach·rō·mà·tic′i·ty, *n.* the state or quality of being achromatic.

à·chrō′mà·tin, *n.* organic tissue not easily colored or stained.

à·chrō′mà·tism, *n.* the state or quality of being achromatic; lack of color.

à·chrō″mà·ti·zā′tion, *n.* the process of achromatizing.

à·chrō′mà·tīze, *v.t.*; achromatized, *pt.*, *pp.*; achromatizing, *ppr.* [Gr. *a* priv., and *chrōma*, color.] to make achromatic; to rid of color.

à·chrō·mà·top′sy, à·chrō·mà·top′si·à, *n.* [Gr. *a* priv., and *chrōma*, color, and *opsis*, sight.] color blindness.

à·chrō·mà·tō′sis, *n.* a disease characterized by absence of coloring matter, as albinism.

à·chrō′mà·tous, à·chrō′mous, *a.* lacking color; colorless.

ā·chrō′miç, *a.* [from Gr. *achrōmos*; *a*-, not, and *chrōma*, color, and *-ic*.] without color.

ā·chrō′mous, *a.* [Gr. *achrōmos*, colorless; *a*-, not, and *chrōma*, color.] without color.

ach·rō·ō·dex′trine, *n.* [Gr. *achroos*, colorless, and Eng. *dextrine*.] dextrine not colorable by iodine.

ach·rō′ous, *a.* achromatic.

à·chȳ′lous, *a.* [Gr. *a* priv., and *chylos*, juice.] without chyle.

à·chȳ′mous, *a.* without chyme.

à·ciç′ū·là, *n.*; *pl.* **à·ciç′ū·lae,** [L. *acicula*, a small needle.] in biology and geology, a needlelike spine, prickle, or crystal.

à·ciç′ū·lăr, *a.* [L. *acicula*, a small needle.] slender and pointed; resembling a needle, as certain leaves and crystals.

à·ciç′ū·lăr·ly, *adv.* in an acicular manner.

à·ciç′ū·lāte, à·ciç′ū·lā·ted, *a.* [L. *acicula*, a needle.] 1. having aciculae.
2. having marks like scratches made by a needle.

à·ciç′ū·li·fọrm, *a.* having the form of a needle.

à·ciç′ū·lite, *n.* same as *aikinite*.

à·ciç′ū·lum, *n.*; *pl.* **à·ciç′ū·là.** an acicula; a needlelike part.

ac′id, *a.* [L. *acidus*, sour, from root *ak*, sharp.]
1. sour, sharp, or biting to the taste.
2. of or like an acid.

ac′id, *n.* 1. a sour substance.
2. LSD. [Slang.]
3. in chemistry, a compound that can react with a base to form a salt, the hydrogen of the acid being replaced by a positive ion. The majority of *acids* contain oxygen, and are known as *oxyacids*; those not containing oxygen are termed *hydrogen acids. Acids* usually have the following properties: (a) a sour taste; (b) solubility in water; (c) the ability to turn blue litmus red; (d) the power of uniting in definite proportions with the metals, called bases, forming salts, the metal replacing the hydrogen of the *acid*; (e) the power of decomposing most carbonates, causing effervescence: according to modern theory an *acid* is a compound which yields hydrogen ions (protons) to a base in a chemical reaction. *Acids* vary in their terminations according to the quantity of oxygen or other electronegative constituent. Those having the maximum of oxygen end in *-ic*; those of a lower degree in *-ous. Acids* that end in *-ic*, as sulfur*ic acid*, form salts terminating in *-ate*; those ending in *-ous* form salts terminating in *-ite*.

ac′id-fȧst″, *a.* not readily decolorized by acids when stained, as the tubercle bacillus.

ac′id-fọrm·ing, *a.* 1. forming an acid in chemical reaction; acidic.
2. yielding a large acid residue in metabolism: said of foods.

à·cid′iç, *a.* 1. acid-forming.
2. in geology, containing a high percentage of silica: opposed to *basic*.

ac·id·if′ēr·ous, *a.* [L. *acidus*, sour, and *ferre*, to bear.] containing or yielding an acid.

à·cid′i·fī·à·ble, *a.* capable of conversion into an acid.

ac·id·if′iç, *a.* producing an acid or acidity.

à·cid″i·fi·çā′tion, *n.* the act or process of changing into an acid.

à·cid′i·fī·ēr, *n.* 1. one who or that which acidifies.
2. in chemistry, that which has the property of changing a substance into an acid, as oxygen, chlorine, etc.

à·cid′i·fȳ, *v.i.* and *v.t.*; acidified, *pt.*, *pp.*; acidifying, *ppr.* [*acid*, and L. *facere*, to make.]
1. to make or become acid; specifically, to convert into an acid.
2. to make or become sour.

ac·id·im′e·tēr, *n.* [L. *acidus*, sour, acid, and Gr. *metron*, measure.] an instrument for ascertaining the strength of acids.

ac·id·im′e·try, *n.* the measurement of the strength of acids; especially, the process of estimating the amount of acid in any liquid by finding how much of a standard alkaline solution is required to neutralize a measured quantity of the given solution.

ac′id in·tox·i·çā′tion, same as *acidosis*.

à·cid′i·ty, *n.* [Fr. *acidité*, from L. *aciditas*, sourness.]
1. the quality of being sour; sourness.
2. the degree of this.
3. hyperacidity.

ac′id·ly, *adv.* in an acid manner.

ac′id·ness, *n.* acidity.

ac″i·doph′i·liç, *a.* [from *acid*, and *-phile*, and *-ic*.] staining readily with acid dyes, as some bacteria.

ac″i·doph′i·lus milk, milk with acidophilic bacteria added: used for medicinal purposes.

ac″i·dō′sis, *n.* in medicine, a condition in which the alkali reserve (blood bicarbonates) of the blood is lower than normal: loosely called *acid intoxication*, *autointoxication*.

ac″i·dot′iç, *a.* of or having acidosis.

ac′id rāin, rain with a high concentration of acids produced by sulfur dioxide, nitrogen oxide, etc. emitted during the combustion of fossil fuels: it has a destructive effect on plant and aquatic life, buildings, etc.

ac′id test, a crucial, final test of the value or quality of a thing or person: originally, a test of gold by acid.

à·cid′ū·lae, *n.pl.* [L.] an old name for medicinal springs impregnated with carbonic acid.

à·cid′ū·lāte, *v.t.*; acidulated, *pt.*, *pp.*; acidulating, *ppr.* [L. *acidulus*, slightly sour, and *-ate*.] to make somewhat acid or sour.

à·cid′ū·lent, *a.* having an acid quality; tart.

à·cid′ū·lous, *a.* [L. *acidulus*, slightly sour.] slightly sour; subacid, as oranges, etc.

ac′i·ēr·āġe, *n.* [Fr., from *acier*, steel.] the process of coating another metal with a layer of iron or steel, by electricity: stereotypes are sometimes steel-faced in this way.

ac′i·fọrm, *a.* [L. *acus*, a needle, and *forma*, form.] shaped like a needle.

à·cil′i·āte, *a.* without cilia.

ac·i·nā′ceous, *a.* [L. *acinus*, grapestone, and *-aceous*.] containing kernels.

à·cin′à·cēs, *n.* [L., from Gr. *akinakēs*, a short sword.] a short straight dagger worn by the Scythians, Medes, and Persians.

ac·i·nac′i·fọrm, *a.* [L. *acinaces*, a scimitar; Gr. *akinakēs*, and *-form*.] in botany, formed like or resembling a scimitar.

Ac·i·nē′tae, *n.pl.* [L., from Gr. *a* priv., and *kinētos*, movable.] in zoology, an order of the *Infusoria* having shells and suctorial tentacles.

ac·i·net′i·fọrm, *a.* having the form of *Acinetæ*.

à·cin′i·fọrm, *a.* [L. *acinus*, a grapestone, and *-form*.] having the form of grapes, or being in clusters like grapes.

ac′i·nous, ac′i·nōse, *a.* consisting of, containing, or resembling an acinus or acini.

ac′i·nus, *n.*, *pl.* **ac′i·nī,** [L. *acinus*, grapestone.]
1. in botany, any of the small parts (drupelets) which compose the fruit of the blackberry, and other similar plants.
2. in anatomy, any of the small sacs of a compound or racemose gland.

-ā′clous, [L. *-ax*, *-acis*; It. *-ace*, and OFr. *-ous*.] a suffix meaning full of, characterized by; added to verb stems to form adjectives; as, cap*acious*, aud*acious*, ten*acious*.

Ac·i·pen′sēr, *n.* [L., from Gr. *akkipēsios*, a sturgeon.] a genus of cartilaginous ganoid fishes, distinguished by the bony scales or plates arranged at intervals along the body in five longitudinal rows. The gills are free, the snout long and conical, and the mouth retractile, toothless, and projecting from the under surface of the head. The genus in-

ACIPENSER
head of sturgeon

cludes the sturgeon, sterlet, huso, etc.

-ac′i·ty, [Fr. *-acité*, from L. *-acitas*.] a suffix used to form nouns corresponding to adjectives in *-acious*; as, ten*acity*.

Açk-Açk, açk-açk, *n.* 1. an antiaircraft gun.
2. its fire.

aç·knōw′, *v.t.* to avow; to acknowledge. [Obs.]

aç·knowl′edge (ak-nol′ej), *v.t.*; acknowledged, *pt.*, *pp.*; acknowledging, *ppr.* [OE. *ac-* (*a*-), *knowlechen*, *knoulechen*, acknowledge, from *knouleche*, *cnawleche*, know, *knowlage*, *knowen*, to know.]
1. to own, avow, or admit to be true, by a declaration of assent; as, to *acknowledge* the being of a God.
2. to own or notice with particular regard.
3. to own or confess, as implying a consciousness of guilt.
4. to admit or receive with approbation.
5. to own with gratitude, or as a benefit; as, to *acknowledge* a favor, or receipt of a gift.
6. to own or admit to belong to oneself; as, to *acknowledge* a son.
7. to receive with respect.
8. to confirm receipt of; as, please *acknowledge* this letter.
9. to show recognition of by an act, as by a bow, nod, smile, lifting of the hat, etc. as a mark of friendship or respect; to salute; as, she met him in the street, but barely *acknowledged* him.

10. to own, avow, or assent to (an act) in a legal form, to give it validity; as, to *acknowledge* a deed.

Syn.—allow, avow, confess, concede, admit, grant, own, recognize, accept, indorse, certify, profess.

aç·knowl'edġed, *a.* avowed, recognized, accepted, admitted, indorsed, confessed.

aç·knowl'edġed·ly, *adv.* avowedly.

aç·knowl'edġ·ẽr, *n.* one who acknowledges.

aç·knowl'edġ·ment, *n.* 1. the act of admitting; confession; as, the *acknowledgment* of a fault.

2. the act of recognizing with approbation, or in the true character; as, the *acknowledgment* of God or of a public minister.

3. concession; admission of the truth, as of a fact, position, or principle.

4. the owning of a benefit received, accompanied with gratitude; an expression of thanks; hence, something given or done in return for a favor.

5. a declaration or avowal of one's own act to give it legal validity; as, the *acknowledgment* of a deed before a proper officer.

acknowledgment money; in some parts of England, a sum paid by a tenant on the death of his landlord, as an acknowledgment of his new lord.

Syn.—admission, avowal, concession, recognition, confession.

à·clas'tiç, *a.* [Gr. *aklastos*, unbroken, from *a* priv., and *klastos*, from *klaein*, to break.] unable to refract light.

aç'lē, *n.* a tree of the bean family, native to India, Burma, and the Philippine Islands. The timber is one of the hardest known woods, close-grained, heavier than water, and is used largely for furniture and cabinet work.

à·clin'iç, *a.* [Gr. *a* priv., and *klinein*, to bend.] not dipping or bending; as, the *aclinic* line, an imaginary line around the earth near the equator, where the magnetic needle ceases to dip.

aç'lys, *n.*; *pl.* **aç'ly·dēş,** [L. a javelin.] an ancient weapon consisting of a short club studded with sharp points and attached to a cord, which enabled the thrower to draw it back after having launched it against an enemy.

aç'mē, *n.* [Gr. *akmē*, a point.]

1. the top or highest point; the height or crisis of anything.

2. the period of fullest development in the history of a species of an animal.

3. in medicine, the crisis of a disease.

4. mature age; people of mature age collectively. [Obs.]

Syn.—apex, height, culmination, climax, zenith.

aç'mīte, *n.* [Gr. *akmē*, a point.] a mineral of the augite family, occurring in long, pointed crystals, of a dark brownish color and a bright and somewhat resinous luster.

aç'nē, *n.* [perhaps altered from Gr. *akmē*, point.] a skin disease characterized by chronic inflammation of the sebaceous glands, usually causing pimples on the face, back, and chest.

aç·nō'dăl, *a.* pertaining to an acnode or acnodes.

aç'nōde, *n.* [L. *acus*, needle; *nodus*, a node.] in mathematics, the point of a curve where the curve turns sharply back on itself.

à·çock', *adv.* in a cocked or tilted manner.

à·çock'bill, *adv.* [*acock* and *bill*, point, edge.] with the ends cocked or tilted up; a nautical term, used of the anchor when hanging at the cathead, and of the yards when tipped at an angle with the deck.

A·coe'là (à-sē'là), *n. pl.* [L. *acœlus*, from Gr. *akoilos*; *a* priv., and *koilos*, hollow.] a group of worms belonging to the *Turbellaria*, having no digestive tract.

à·coe'lō·māte, *a.* without a body cavity.

ac·oe·lom'à·tous, *a.* same as *acœlomate*.

à·coe'lō·mous, *a.* acoelomate.

à·coe'lous, *a.* without an alimentary canal.

A·coem'ē·tī, A·coem'ē·tae (-sem-), *n.pl.* [Gr. *akoimetoi*, the sleepless ones, from *a* priv., and *koimasthai*, to fall asleep.] an order of Eastern monks and nuns of the fifth century who kept up a continuous service of prayer and praise by sleeping in relays. In the sixth century the monks embraced Nestorianism and their order became extinct, but the nuns maintained their organization until the sixteenth century.

à·cōld, *a.* cold; very cold; as, Tom's *acold*. [Obs.]

aç·ō·log'iç, *a.* relating to acology.

à·col'ō·ġy, *n.* [Gr. *akos*, remedy, and *logos*, discourse.] the science of medical remedies. [Rare.]

aç·ō·lyç'tine, *n.* an alkaloid obtained from aconite.

aç'ō·lȳte, *n.* [Gr. *akolouthos*, a follower.]

1. one who waits on a person; an attendant.

2. in the Roman Catholic Church, the highest of the inferior orders of clergy, whose office it is to follow and serve the superior orders in the ministry of the altar, light the candles, prepare the elements of the sacrament, etc.

ACOLYTES

3. in astronomy, an attendant or accompanying star or other heavenly body; a satellite.

à·col'y·thist, *n.* an acolyte. [Obs.]

à·cō'mi·a, *n.* [Gr. *a* priv.; *komē*, hair.] absence of hair; baldness, usually due to skin disease.

à·çon'dy·lōse, à·çon'dy·lous, *a.* [Gr. *a* priv., and *kondylos*, joint.] having no condyles or joints.

aç·ō·nī'tăl, *a.* having the quality of aconite.

aç'ō·nīte, *n.* [L. *aconitum*; Gr. *akoniton*, a poisonous plant, probably from *akōn*, a dart, it having been used to poison darts.]

1. the herb called wolfsbane, or monkshood, a poisonous plant.

2. any plant of the genus *Aconitum*.

3. a drug made from dried roots of monkshood.

aç·ō·ni'ti·à (-nish'i-à), *n.* aconitin.

aç·ō·nit'iç, *a.* pertaining to aconite.

à·çon'i·tin, à·çon'i·tine, *n.* a poisonous, narcotic alkaloid, extracted from several species of aconite.

Aç·ō·nī'tum, *n.* [L.] a genus of poisonous plants, natural order *Ranunculaceæ*, comprising the aconites.

à·çon'ti·à (-shi-à), *n.pl.* [L., from Gr. *akōntion*.] the defensive organs of the sea anemone.

A·çon'ti·as, *n.* [Gr. *akontias*, a dart, from *akōn*, a dart, *akontion*, dim.] a genus of reptiles, having rudimentary hind limbs, and allied to the slowworm of Great Britain. *Acontias meleagris*, sometimes called *dart snake* from its manner of darting on its prey, is about three feet in length, of a light gray color, with black spots resembling eyes. It is a native of Africa and the Mediterranean isles.

à·çop'iç, *a.* [Gr. *a* priv., and *kopos*, a striking, weariness, from *koptein*, to strike.] in medicine, relieving weariness; restorative.

ā'çorn (*or* ā'kẽrn), *n.* [ME. *akorn*, *eykorn*, *akecorn*, *okecorn*, *akern*; AS. *æcern*, acorn, an adj. form of *æcer*, field; Ice. *akarn*, from *akr*, a field; properly, any fruit of the field.]

1. the seed or fruit of the oak; an oval nut which grows in a hard, woody cup.

2. in nautical language, a small ornamental piece of wood, of a conical shape, fixed on the point of a spindle above the vane, on the masthead, to keep the vane from being blown off.

ACORNS AND LEAVES

3. see *acorn shell*.

ā'çorn çup, the capsule which holds the acorn.

ā'çorned, *a.* bearing acorns, as the oak.

ā'çorn shell, 1. the shell of the acorn.

2. one of the cirripeds of the genus *Balanus*, allied to the barnacles, called by this name from a supposed resemblance of some of the species to acorns.

ā'çorn squăsh, a kind of squash shaped like an acorn.

Aç'ō·rus, *n.* [L., from Gr. *akoros*, sweet flag.] a genus of plants of the natural order *Araceæ*. The aromatic calamus of the druggists, *Acorus calamus*, or sweet flag, is widely prevalent in northern temperate regions.

à·çoş'miṣm, *n.* [Gr. *a* priv., and *kosmos*, world, and *-ism*.] a belief which denies the existence of a universe as distinct from God.

à·çoş'mist, *n.* one who professes acosmism.

à·çot·y·lē'dŏn, *n.* [Gr. *a* priv., and *kotylēdōn*, cavity, cup.] in botany, a plant in which the seed lobes, or cotyledons, are not present, or are very indistinct. The *acotyledons* form a grand division of the vegetable kingdom, including the ferns, lichens, etc., and correspond to the *Cryptogamia* of Linnaeus.

à·çot·y·lē'dŏn·ous, *a.* having either no seed lobes, or such as are indistinct.

à·çöu'çhy, *n.* [Fr. *acouchi*, *agouchi*, from the native name in Guiana.] a rodent of the genus *Dasyprocta*, found in the West Indies and South America; the olive agouti, or Surinam rat; it is related to the guinea pig.

à·çöu'me·tẽr (*or* -kow'), n. [Gr. *akouein*, to hear, and *metron*, measure.] an instrument for determining the acuteness of the hearing.

à·çöu'me·try, *n.* the measurement of the acuteness of hearing.

aç·öu·sim'e·tẽr (*or* -kow-), *n.* same as *acoumeter*.

à·çöus'tiç (*or* -kows'), *a.* [Gr. *akoustos*, heard, from *akouein*, to hear.] pertaining to the ears, to the sense of hearing, or to the doctrine of sounds.

acoustic duct; in anatomy, the *meatus auditorius*, or external passage of the ear.

acoustic vessels; in ancient theaters, brazen tubes or vessels shaped like a bell, used to project the voices of the actors, so as to make them audible to a great distance.

à·çöus'tiç, *n.* any remedy or remedial agent designed to assist in hearing.

à·çöus'tiç·ăl, *a.* of or pertaining to acoustics.

à·çöus'tiç·ăl·ly, *adv.* in relation to sound or hearing.

à·çöus·ti'cian (-tish'un), *n.* one skilled in acoustics.

à·çöus'ti·cŏn, *n.* [L. *acousticus*, Gr. *akoustikos*, relating to hearing, from *akouein*, to hear.] an adjustable apparatus for transmitting sounds to deaf persons, consisting of an ear piece, a transmitter, and a small electric battery. It is capable of nearly 3,000 different adjustments in applying it to various individual needs. A trade-mark (**Acousticon**).

à·çöus'tiçs (*or* -kows'), *n. pl.* 1. the qualities of a room, theater, etc. that have to do with how clearly sounds can be heard or transmitted in it.

2. [construed as sing.] the science of heard sound.

à·çöus·tom'e·tẽr (*or* -kows-), *n.* an apparatus for testing the acoustic properties of a room.

à" cou"vert' (à"çöu"vãr'), [Fr.] under cover; secure; sheltered.

aç·quāint', *v.t.*; acquainted, *pt.*, *pp.*; acquainting, *ppr.* [ME. *acquentin*, Fr. *acointer*, from L. *adcognitare*, to make known, from *ad*, and *cognitus*, pp. of *cognoscere*, to know thoroughly; *con*, and *gnoscere*, to know.]

1. to make familiar: usually followed by *with*.

2. to inform; to communicate notice to; as, a friend in the country *acquaints* me *with* his success.

Syn.—apprise, enlighten, inform, make aware, tell.

aç·quāint'à·ble, *a.* affable; easily approached. [Obs.]

aç·quāint'ănce, *n.* 1. a state of being acquainted, or of having more or less intimate knowledge: used with reference both to persons and things.

2. a person known to one, especially a person with whom one is not on terms of great intimacy; as, he is not a friend, only an *acquaintance*.

3. the whole body of those with whom one is acquainted; as, my *acquaintance* is large.

Syn.—familiarity, fellowship, intimacy. —*Intimacy* is the result of close connection, and hence is the stronger word; *familiarity* springs from close acquaintance.

aç·quāint'ănce·ship, *n.* the state of being acquainted.

aç·quāint'ănt, *n.* an acquaintance. [Obs.]

aç·quāint′ed, *a.* having acquaintance; having personal knowledge of; fairly familiar with.

aç·quāint′ed·ness, *n.* extent of acquaintance. [Rare.]

aç·quest′, *n.* [OFr. *acquest*, L. *acquæsitum*, anything acquired, from *acquisitum*, pp. of *acquirere*, to acquire.]
 1. acquisition; the thing gained. [Obs.]
 2. conquest; a place acquired by force. [Obs.]
 3. in English law, property not descended by inheritance, but acquired by purchase or donation.

aç·qui·esce′ (-wi-es′), *v.i.*; acquiesced, *pt.*, *pp.*; acquiescing, *ppr.* [Fr. *acquiescer*, to yield to, from L. *acquiescere*; *ad*, to, and *quiescere*, to rest.]
 1. to rest satisfied, or apparently satisfied, or to rest without opposition and discontent: usually implying previous opposition, uneasiness, or dislike, but ultimate compliance, or submission; as, to *acquiesce* in the dispensations of Providence.
 2. to assent to, upon conviction; as, to *acquiesce* in an opinion; that is, to rest satisfied of its correctness or propriety.
 Syn.—accede, agree, consent, submit, yield, comply, concur, conform.

aç·qui·es′cence, *n.* a quiet assent; a silent submission, or submission with apparent consent: distinguished on the one hand from avowed consent, and on the other, from opposition or open discontent; as, an *acquiescence* in the decisions of a board of arbitration.

aç·qui·es′cen·cy, *n.* acquiescence. [Obs.]

aç·qui·es′cent, *a.* resting satisfied; submitting; disposed to submit.

aç·qui·es′cent·ly, *adv.* in an acquiescent manner.

aç·quī′et, *v.t.* to ease. [Obs.]

aç·quīr·ȧ·bil′i·ty, *n.* capability of being acquired or possessed.

aç·quīr′ȧ·ble, *a.* that may be acquired.

aç·quīre′, *v.t.*; acquired, *pt.*, *pp.*; acquiring, *ppr.* [L. *acquirere*; *ad*, to, and *quærere*, to seek.]
 1. to get or gain by one's own efforts or actions.
 2. to gain, by any means, as a thing which is in a degree permanent, or which becomes vested or inherent in the possessor; as, to *acquire* a title, estate, learning, habits, skill, dominion, etc.; plants *acquire* a green color from the rays of the sun.
 Syn.—attain, compass, earn, gain, get, obtain, procure, realize, win.

aç·quīred′ çhar″aç·tēr·is′tiç, in biology, a modification of structure or function caused by environmental factors: now generally regarded as not inheritable: also *acquired character*.

aç·quīre′ment, *n.* 1. the act of acquiring.
 2. that which is acquired; attainment. It is used in opposition to natural gifts; as, eloquence and skill in music are *acquirements*.

aç·qui·ṣi′tion (-zish′un), *n.* [L. *acquisitio*, the act of acquiring, from *acquirere*, to seek for.]
 1. the act of acquiring; as, a man takes pleasure in the *acquisition* of property.
 2. a thing or person acquired, or gained; as, learning is an *acquisition*.

aç·quiṣ′i·tive, *a.* 1. acquired, as distinguished from native. [Obs.]
 2. naturally inclined to obtain or possess property, knowledge, etc.; as, a man of *acquisitive* disposition.

aç·quiṣ′i·tive·ly, *adv.* in an acquisitive manner.

aç·quiṣ′i·tive·ness, *n.* desire of possession; propensity to acquire.

aç·quiṣ′i·tŏr, *n.* a person who acquires. [Rare.]

aç·quit′ *v.t.*; acquitted, *pt.*, *pp.*; acquitting, *ppr.* [Fr. *acquitter*, to free, from L. *acquitare*, to settle a claim, from *ad*, to, and *quietare*, to quiet.]
 1. to pay (a debt or claim).
 2. to release from a duty, obligation, etc.
 3. to declare (a person) not guilty (*of* something); exonerate.
 4. to bear or conduct (oneself); behave.
 Syn.—absolve, discharge, justify, clear, release, exonerate, forgive, set free.

aç·quit′ment, *n.* the act of acquitting or the state of being acquitted. [Rare.]

aç·quit′tăl, *n.* 1. an acquitting; discharge (of duty, obligation, etc.).
 2. in law, a setting free or being set free.

aç·quit′tănce, *n.* 1. a discharge or release from a debt; the state of being so discharged or released.
 2. the writing which is evidence of a discharge; a receipt in full, which bars a further demand.

aç·quit′tēr, *n.* a person who acquits.

ȧ·crā′ni·ȧ, *n.* [Gr. *a* priv., and *kranion*, skull.]
 1. a malformation characterized by total or partial absence of the bones and integuments of the cranium.
 2. [A–] [*pl.*] the lowest group of vertebrates: also called *Acephala*.

ȧ·crā′ni·ăl, *a.* without a skull.

A·cras′pē·dȧ, *n.pl.* [Gr. *a* priv., and *kraspedon*, border.] a group of jellyfishes; the *Discophora*.

aç′rȧ·sy, ȧ·crā′si·ȧ, *n.* [L. *acrasia*, from Gr. *a* priv., and *krasia*, power, temperance.] excess; irregularity; intemperance. [Obs.]

ȧ·crāze′, ȧ·crāṣe′, *v.t.* [see *craze*.] to make crazy; to infatuate. [Obs.]

ā′çre (-kẽr), *n.* [ME. *aker*, AS. *æcer*, L. *ager*, Gr. *agros*, all meaning field, and from Sans. root *ajra*.]
 1. originally, an open, plowed, or sowed field.
 2. a measure of land, containing 160 square rods or perches, or 4,840 square yards. This is the statute *acre* in the United States and Great Britain. The Irish *acre* is 7,840 square yards. The *acre* of Scotland contains 6,150²/₆ square yards.
 3. [*pl.*] lands; estate.
 God's acre; a burial ground; a churchyard.

ā′çre·ȧ·ble, *a.* according to the acre; measured or estimated in acres or by the acre.

ā′çre·āġe, *n.* 1. extent of a piece of land in acres; acres taken collectively; as, the *acreage* of New York State.
 2. land sold or distributed by the acre.

ā′çred (-kẽrd), *a.* possessing acres or landed property: often in hyphenated compounds; as, wide-*acred* landlords.

ā′çre-foot′, *n.* the quantity of water (43,560 cu. ft.) that would cover one acre to a depth of one foot.

ā′çre-inch′, *n.* one twelfth of an acre-foot, or 3,630 cubic feet.

aç′rid, *a.* [L. *acer*, *acris*, sharp.]
 1. sharp; pungent; bitter; sharp or biting to the taste; as, *acrid* salts.
 2. stinging, sharp, bitter, or caustic of temper, speech, etc.; as, an *acrid* temper.

ȧ·çrid′i·ăn, *n.* one of the *Acrididæ*.

A·çrid′i·dae, *n.pl.* [Gr. *akridion*, dim. of *akris*, locust.] a family of orthopterous insects, including the grasshoppers: all the species of this family can leap.

aç′rid·ine, *n.* a colorless, crystalline compound, $C_{13}H_9N$, found in coal tar: certain dyes and drugs are made from it.

ȧ·çrid′i·ty, *n.* 1. the state or quality of being bitter, sharp, or acrimonious; acridness.
 2. *pl.* **ȧ·çrid′i·tieṣ,** an acrid remark.

aç′rid·ly, *adv.* bitterly; sharply.

aç′rid·ness, *n.* the state or quality of being acrid.

aç·ri·mō′ni·ous, *a.* [L. *acrimoniosus*, from *acrimonia*, sharpness.]
 1. sharp; bitter; corrosive; abounding with acrimony. [Archaic.]
 2. severe, sarcastic of speech, temper, etc.

aç·ri·mō′ni·ous·ly, *adv.* with sharpness or bitterness.

aç·ri′mō′ni·ous·ness, *n.* the state or quality of being acrimonious.

aç′ri·mō·ny, *n.* [L. *acrimonia*, sharpness.]
 1. sharpness; a quality of bodies which corrodes, dissolves, or destroys others; harshness or bitterness of taste; pungency. [Archaic.]
 2. *pl.* **aç′ri·mō·nieṣ,** sharpness or severity of temper; bitterness of expression proceeding from anger, ill nature, or petulance.
 Syn.—harshness, asperity, smartness, bitterness, tartness.

aç′ri·sy, ȧ·çris′i·ȧ, *n.* [Gr. *akrisia*, from *a* priv., and *kritos*, discernible, from *krinein*, to judge, to separate.]
 1. a state or condition of which no right judgment can be formed; matter in dispute; also, inability to judge. [Obs.]
 2. in medicine, the undecided character of a disease, making prognosis doubtful. [Obs.]

Aç′ri·tȧ, *n. pl.* [neut. pl. of Gr. *akritos*, undecided, from *a* priv., and *krinein*, to judge.] a term applied to that division of radiate animals in which there is no distinctly discernible nervous system, and no separate alimentary canal, as the sponges, polyps, etc.

aç′ri·tăn, *a.* pertaining to the *Acrita*.

aç′ri·tăn, *n.* one of the *Acrita*.

aç′rīte, *a.* acritan.

ȧ·çrit′iç·ăl, *a.* 1. in medicine, without crisis or indications of crisis.
 2. not critical; having no tendency to criticism or critical judgment.

aç″ri·tō·chrō′mȧ·cy, *n.* [Gr. *akritos*; *a* priv., and *kritos*, distinguishable, and *chrōma*, color.] achromatopsy or color blindness.

aç′ri·tūde, *n.* an acrid quality; bitterness to the taste; biting heat. [Obs.]

aç′ri·ty, *n.* sharpness; eagerness. [Obs.]

aç′rō-, a combining form from Gr. *akros*, summit, extreme, topmost, meaning:
 1. pointed, as in *acro*cephaly.
 2. highest, topmost, as in *acro*spire.

aç″rō·ȧ·mat′iç, aç″rō·ȧ·mat′iç·ăl, *a.* see *acroatic*.

aç″rō·an·es·thē′si·ȧ, *n.* loss of feeling or sensation in the extremities.

aç·rō·at′iç, *a.* [L. *acroaticus*, Gr. *akroatikos*, connected with hearing, from *akroasthai*, to hear.] abstruse; pertaining to deep learning, and opposed to *exoteric*. Aristotle's lectures were of two kinds, *acroatic* (also *acroamatic*, or *esoteric*), which were delivered privately to a class of select disciples, who had been previously instructed in the elements of learning; and *exoteric*, which were delivered in public. The former were concerned with being, God, and nature; the principal subjects of the latter were logic, rhetoric, and policy. The abstruse lectures were called *acroatics*.

aç′rō·bat, *n.* [Fr. *acrobate*, Gr. *akrobatos*, to walk on tiptoe, to go aloft; from Gr. *akros*, high, tip, and *bainein*, to go.] a gymnast; a tumbler; one who practices daring and difficult feats of agility and strength on the tightrope, trapeze, horizontal bar, and other apparatus, or on the ground.

Aç·rob′ȧ·tēṣ, *n.* [L.] a genus of marsupial animals found in Australia, including the opossum mouse; the flying phalanger.

OPOSSUM MOUSE
(*Acrobates pygmæus*)

aç·rō·bat′iç, *a.* pertaining to an acrobat.

aç·rō·bat′iç·ăl·ly, *adv.* in an acrobatic manner.

aç·rō·bat′içs, *n. pl.* 1. [construed as sing.] the art of an acrobat.
 2. the performances of an acrobat.
 3. stunts; as, the *acrobatics* of aviation.

aç′rō·bat·işm, *n.* the art of acrobats.

aç′rō·blast, *n.* see *mesenchyma*.

Aç·rō·çär′pi, *n.pl.* [*acro-*, and Gr. *karpos*, fruit.] a division of the mosses containing the species in which the capsule terminates the growth of a primary axis.

aç·rō·çär′pous, *a.* bearing fruit at the end of the stalk; specifically, of mosses, having a capsule terminate the growth of a primary axis.

aç″rō·cē·phal′iç, *a.* of or having acrocephaly.

aç″rō·cē·phal′iç, *n.* a person who has acrocephaly.

aç″rō·ceph′ȧ·lous, *a.* acrocephalic.

aç·rō·ceph′ȧ·ly, *n.* [*acro-*, and Gr. *kephalē*, head.] an abnormal condition in which the skull is pointed.

Aç″rō·cē·rau′ni·ăn, *a.* [*acro-*, and Gr. *keraunos*, thunderbolt.] an epithet applied to certain mountains which project into the Adriatic and are often struck by lightning.

aç·rō·daç′tyl·um, *n.* [*acro-*, and Gr. *daktylos*, finger.] the upper surface of each digit of a bird's foot.

aç′rō·dont, *n.* [*acro-*, and Gr. *odous* (*odontos*), tooth.] a lizard characterized by having the bases of the teeth attached to the edge of the jaw without sockets.

aç′rō·dont, *a.* resembling an acrodont or its teeth.

aç′rō·drōme, *a.* [*acro-*, and Gr. *dromos*, course.] in botany, having the nerves, or veins, ending at the tip of the leaf.

ȧ·çrod′rō·mous, *a.* acrodrome.

aç·rō·dyn′i·ȧ, *n.* an epidemic disease marked by disturbances of the alimentary canal and the nervous system.

aç′rō·ġen, *n.* [*acro-*, and Gr. *genēs*, from *gignesthai*, to bear.] a plant, such as a fern or moss, having a perennial stem with the growing point at the tip.

aç·rō·ġen′iç, *a.* acrogenous.

ȧ·çroġ′e·nous, *a.* in botany, 1. increasing by growth at the tip.
 2. of the acrogens.

aç·roġ′rȧ·phy, *n.* [*acro-*, and Gr. *graphia*, from *graphein*, to write.] the art of producing designs in relief on metal or stone by etching, as in making an electrotype.

ȧ·çrō′lē·in, *n.* [L. *acer*, *acris*, sharp, and *olere*, to smell, and *-in*.] a yellowish or colorless, pungent liquid, C_3H_4O, a decomposition product of glycerol and glycerides, used as a tear gas in chemical warfare, etc.

aç'rō·lith, *n.* [Gr. *akros*, summit, and *lithos*, stone.] in Grecian sculpture, a statue whose head and extremities only were of stone, the body and limbs being of wood covered with fabric or thin metal.

ȧ·çrol'i·thăn, *a.* of or formed like an acrolith.

aç·rō·lith'iç, *a.* acrolithan.

aç'rō·logue (-log), *n.* a symbolic letter or picture employed in acrology.

ȧ·çrol'ō·ġy, *n.* [*acro-*, and Gr. *logia*, from *legein*, to say.] the science of denoting names by means of initials, pictorial representations, etc.

aç"rō·mā'ni·ȧ, *n.* a violent form of mania, or insanity.

aç"rō·me·gal'iç, *a.* of or having acromegaly.

aç"rō·me·gal'iç, *n.* a person who has acromegaly.

aç·rō·meg'ȧ·ly, *n.* [Gr. *akros*, extremity, and *megas* (*megalē*), large.] a disease which permanently enlarges the bones of the extremities, caused by abnormal activity of the pituitary gland.

ȧ·çrom'e·tẽr, *n.* [L. *acer*, sharp, and Gr. *metron*, measure.] an instrument for ascertaining the density of oil.

ȧ·çrō'mi·ăl, *a.* in anatomy, of the acromion.

ȧ·çrō'mi·on, *n.* [Gr. *akromion*, from *akromia*, the point of the shoulder.] in anatomy, the outer extremity of the scapula.

aç"rō·mon"ō·gram·mat'iç, *a.* in poetry, having each line or verse begin with the letter with which the preceding line or verse ends.

aç"rō·när·çot'iç, *n.* a drug that is both narcotic and acrid.

ȧ·çron'i·çăl, ȧ·çron'y·çăl, *a.* [Gr. *akronychos*, at sunset, from *akros*, highest, and *nyx*, night.] in astronomy, happening at sunset or in the evening: also spelled *acronichal*, *acronychal*.

ȧ·çron'i·căl·ly, *adv.* in an acronical manner.

aç·rō·nyç'tous, *a.* acronical.

aç'rō·nym, *n.* [*acro-*, and homo*nym*.] a word formed from the first (or first few) letters of several words, as *radar*, from *ra*dio *d*etecting *a*nd *r*anging.

ȧ·çrook', *adv.* in a crooked manner. [Rare.]

ȧ·çrop'e·tăl, *a.* in botany, developing upward from the base toward the apex.

aç·rō·phō'bi·ȧ, *n.* [Gr. *akros*, high, and *phobos*, fear.] an abnormal fear of high places.

aç·roph'ō·ny, *n.* [*acro-*, and Gr. *phōnē*, sound.] the science of using picture symbols to represent the initial sound of the name of an object.

aç·rō·pō'di·um, *n.* [*acro-*, and Gr. *pous* (*podos*), foot.] in zoology, the whole of the upper surface of the foot.

ȧ·çrop'ō·lis, *n.* [Gr. *akropolis*, *akros*, high, and *polis*, city.] a citadel; specifically [A—] the citadel in Athens.

aç·rō·pol'i·tăn, *a.* pertaining to an acropolis.

aç·rō·sär'çum, *n.* [L., from Gr. *akros*, extreme, and *sarx* (*sarkos*), flesh.] in botany, a berry resulting from an ovary with an adnate calyx, as the cranberry.

aç'rō·sōme, *n.* [*acro-*, and Gr. *sōma*, body.] a very small body at the anterior end of a spermatozoon.

aç'rō·spīre, *n.* [Gr. *akros*, extreme, and *speira*, spire, coil.] the sprout at the ends of seeds when they begin to germinate; the plumule, so called from its spiral form.

aç'rō·spīre, *v.i.* to grow the first leaf; to sprout.

aç'rō·spōre, *n.* [*acro-*, and Gr. *spora*, seed.] in some fungi, a naked spore borne at the end of the mother cell.

ȧ·çros'pō·rous, *a.* bearing acrospores.

ȧ·çross', *prep.* 1. from one side to the other side of; athwart; as, a bridge is laid *across* a river.

2. intersecting; passing over at any angle; as, a line passing *across* another.

3. on or to the other side of; as, *across* the ocean.

4. opposite; as, the window *across* from mine.

5. in contact with; as, he came *across* an old friend.

ȧ·çross', *adv.* 1. crosswise; transversely from one side to the other; as, his arms were folded *across*.

2. from one side to the other.

3. on or to the other side.

ȧ·çros'tiç, *n.* [Gr. *akrostichos*, from *akros*, extreme, and *stichos*, order, line, verse.]

1. a composition, usually in verse, in which certain letters of the lines, taken in order, form a name, title, motto, etc. which is the subject of the composition.

2. a Hebrew poem of which the initial letters of the lines or stanzas formed the alphabet in order. Twelve of the psalms are of this character, of which Psalm cxix. is the best example.

ȧ·çros'tiç, ȧ·çros'tiç·ăl, *a.* relating to or containing an acrostic; as, *acrostic* verses.

ȧ·çros'tiç·ăl·ly, *adv.* in the manner of an acrostic.

aç·rō·tär'si·um, *n.* [L., from Gr. *akros*, highest, and *tarsos*, tarsus.] the instep, or upper surface of the tarsus.

aç"rō·te·leū'tiç, *n.* [Gr. *akros*, extreme, and *teleutē*, end, and *-ic*.] in ecclesiastical usage, anything added to the end of a psalm or hymn, as a doxology.

aç·rō·tē'ri·ăl, *a.* pertaining to an acroterium; as, *acroterial* ornaments.

aç·rō·tē'ri·um, *n.*; *pl.* **aç·rō·tē'ri·ȧ,** [L., from Gr. *akrōtērion*, pl. *akrōtēria*.] in classical architecture, any of the pedestals, usually without a base, placed at the two extremes or in the middle of pediments or frontispieces, serving to support statues, etc. The term is also applied to a figure placed as an ornament on the top of a church or other building.

AAA, ACROTERIA

aç·rō·thym'i·ŏn, *n.* [Gr. *akros*, extreme, and *thymos*, thyme.] a species of wart with a narrow base and broad top, having the color of thyme: also called *thymus*.

ȧ·çrot'iç, *a.* [Gr. *akrotēs*, an extremity.] relating to or affecting external surfaces.

aç'rō·tism, *n.* in medicine, absence or imperceptibility of the pulse beat.

ȧ·çrot'ō·mous, *a.* [*acro-*, and Gr. *temnein*, to cut.] in mineralogy, having a cleavage parallel with the top.

aç'ryl, *n.* in chemistry, a hypothetical radical of acrolein.

ȧ·çryl'iç, *a.* [*acr*olein, and *-yl*, and *-ic*.] 1. designating or of a colorless, pungent acid, $C_3H_4O_2$, obtained by the oxidation of acrolein.

2. designating or of a series of olefin acids with the general formula $C_nH_{2n-2}O_2$.

açt, *v.i.*; acted, *pt.*, *pp.*; acting, *ppr.* [Fr. *acte*; L. *actum*, a thing done, neut. of pp. of *agere*, to do; Gr. *agein*, to do, drive, lead.]

1. to perform on the stage; to play a role; to follow the profession of an actor.

2. to be suited to performance: said of a play or a role.

3. to behave; to comport oneself.

4. to do a thing; to function.

5. to have an effect (often with *on*); as, acids *act* on metal.

6. to seem or pretend to be; as, he *acted* angry.

act as; to perform the functions of.

act for; (a) to do the work of; (b) to act in behalf of.

act on; (a) to obey; (b) to act in regard to; (c) to have an effect on.

act up; to behave playfully or mischievously. [Colloq.]

açt, *v.t.* 1. to perform; to represent (a character) on the stage; to simulate or play (a role); hence, to feign or counterfeit; as, to *act* the villain.

2. to transact; to do or perform. [Obs.]

3. to put in motion; to actuate; to regulate movements. [Obs.]

to act one's age; to behave in a manner proper to one's age.

Syn.—personate, simulate, perform, feign, work, make, move, execute, effect, do.

açt, *n.* 1. the exertion of power; as, the *act* of giving or receiving. In this sense it denotes an operation of the mind as well as of the body. Thus, to discern is an *act* of the understanding; to judge is an *act* of the will.

2. a thing done; a deed, exploit, or achievement, whether good or bad, as, all the *acts* of a man's career.

3. an action; performance; production of effects; as, an *act* of charity.

4. a state of reality or real existence, as opposed to a possibility. [Obs.]

5. in general, action completed: preceded by *in* it denotes incomplete action; as, he was taken *in the act*.

6. a main division of a drama or opera.

7. a short performance on a program, as in vaudeville.

8. a piece of affected or feigned behavior. [Colloq.]

9. a decision (of a legislative body, council, court of justice, or magistrate); a law, judgment, resolve, award, determination; as, an *act* of congress or of parliament.

10. the book, record, or writing containing the laws and determinations.

11. any instrument in writing to verify facts; as, this is my *act* and deed.

act of faith; see *auto-da-fé*.

act of God; in insurance and law, an inevitable, accidental or extraordinary episode in the course of events, which cannot be foreseen and guarded against, as the consequences arising from storms, lightning, etc.

act of grace; a general public pardon or amnesty to a number of offenders, as at the accession of a sovereign, etc.

Syn.—action, accomplishment, performance, achievement, transaction, proceeding, exertion, exercise, doing, effect, feat, work, deed.

aç'tȧ, *n.pl.* [L., pl. of *actum*, neut. of *actus*, pp. of *agere*, to do.] acts; the proceedings of ecclesiastical or judicial bodies.

Acta Sanctorum; collections of accounts of the lives of saints and martyrs of the Roman Catholic and Orthodox Eastern churches.

açt"a·bil'i·ty, *n.* the quality of being actable.

açt'ȧ·ble, *a.* capable of being acted.

Aç·taē'ŏn, *n.* [L., from Gr. *Aktaion*.] in Greek mythology, the hunter who made Artemis angry by watching her bathe; she changed him into a stag, and he was torn to pieces by his own dogs.

ACTH, [from *a*drenocorti*c*o*t*ropic *h*ormone.] a pituitary hormone used experimentally in the treatment of rheumatoid arthritis and certain other diseases.

Aç'ti·ăn, *a.* relating to Actium, a town and promontory of Epirus; as, *Actian* games, which were instituted by Augustus to celebrate his naval victory over Antony near that town, Sept. 2, B. C. 31: they were celebrated every five years.

aç·tin-, see *actino-*.

aç'ti·năl, *a.* [*actin-*, and *-al*] in zoology, of the oral region of a radiate animal, the region from which the rays or tentacles grow.

aç'tine, *n.* a ray, as those in the spicule of a sponge.

aç·ti·neñ'çhy·mȧ, *n.* [L., from *actin-* and Gr. *enchyma*, a pouring together; *en*, in, and *chein*, to pour.] in botany, the radiated cellular tissue of some medullas; stellate cellular tissue.

açt'ing, *a.* 1. performing or adopted for performance; as, the *acting* version of a play.

2. functioning.

3. temporarily taking over the duties or position of someone else; as, the *acting* chairman.

açt'ing, *n.* 1. the act of performing on the stage; the art of an actor.

2. affected or simulated behavior.

Aç·tin'i·ȧ, *n.* [L., from Gr. *aktis* (*aktinos*), a ray.]

1. a genus of radiate zoophytes, the sea anemones, having a circle of tentacles or rays around the mouth.

2. [a—] any sea anemone or any animal related to it.

aç·tin'i·ăn, *a.* pertaining to or resembling the *Actinia*.

aç·tin'i·ăn, *n.* any sea anemone.

aç·tin'iç, *a.* pertaining to actinism.

actinic focus; the focus at which the actinic rays are brought together by a lens.

aç·tin'iç rāys, light waves of short wave length, occurring in the violet and ultraviolet parts of the spectrum, that produce chemical changes, as in photography.

aç·tin'i·fōrm, *a.* [Gr. *aktis*, a ray, and *-form*.] having radial form, like one of the *Actinia*.

aç·tin'i·ō·chrōme, *n.* [*actino-*, and Gr. *chrōma*, color.] a red pigment obtained from certain radiate zoophytes.

aç'tin·ism, *n.* [Gr. *aktis*, *aktinos*, a ray.]

1. that branch of science which treats of the radiation of heat or light. [Obs.]

2. in chemistry, that property of ultraviolet light, Xrays, etc. by which chemical reactions are produced.

aç·tin'i·um, *n.* [Mod. L., from Gr. *aktis*, *aktinos*, a ray], a radioactive chemical element found with uranium and radium in pitchblende and other minerals: symbol, Ac; at. wt., 227 (?); at. no., 89.

aç'ti·nō-, aç'ti·ni-, aç'tin-, [Gr. *aktis*, *aktinos*, a ray.] a combining form denoting: (a) in zoology, the possession of tentacles, or a radiated structure; (b) in physics and chemistry, the presence of actinic rays.

aç″ti·nō·çhem′is·try, *n.* the chemistry of the action of actinic rays.

aç″ti·nō·çrī′nīte, *n.* a fossil species of radiate crinoid.

aç·tin′ō·gram, *n.* an actinograph.

aç·tin′ō·gràph, *n.* [*actino-*, and Gr. *graphein*, to write.] in photography, an actinometer.

aç′tin·oid, *a.* radiated, as one of the *Actinia*.

aç·tin′ō·līte, *n.* [*actino-*, and Gr. *lithos*, a stone.] a bright green type of amphibole of which asbestos is the fibrous variety.

aç″tin·ō·lit′iç, *a.* like or containing actinolite.

aç·tin′ō·logue (-log), *n.* any part in a radiate animal that has a homologous relation to another in a different segment of the animal.

aç·ti·nol′ō·ġy, *n.* [*actino-*, and Gr. *logos*, from *legein*, to say.]
1. the science which treats of the action of actinic rays.
2. the homologous relation of similar segments in a radiate animal.

aç·ti·nom′e·tẽr, *n.* [*actino-*, and Gr. *metron*, measure.]
1. an instrument for measuring the intensity of the sun's rays, or the actinic effect of light rays.
2. in photography, an exposure meter.

aç″ti·nō·met′riç, *a.* of or having to do with an actinometer or actinometry.

aç·ti·nom′e·try, *n.* the measurement of the intensity of actinic rays with an actinometer.

aç″ti·no·mor′phiç, *a.* [*actino-*, and *-morphic*.] in biology, having radial symmetry, as a flower or a starfish.

aç″ti·no·mor′phous, *a.* actinomorphic.

aç″ti·nō·mȳ′cēṣ, *n.* [*actino-*, and Gr. *mykēs*, a mushroom.] a bacterium which causes actinomycosis in cattle.

aç″ti·nō·mȳ·çō′sis, *n.* [*actino-*, and Gr. *mykēs*, a mushroom, excrescence, and *-osis*.] an infectious disease of cattle, hogs, and people, that affects the mouth, jaw, skin, bones, and viscera.

aç″ti·nō·mȳ·çot′iç, *a.* of actinomycosis.

aç·tin′ō·phōre, *n.* [Gr. *aktinophoros*, ray-bearing.] one of the bones that support the fin rays of a fish.

aç·ti·noph′ō·rous, *a.* having radiating spines.

aç″tin·ō·sō′mȧ, *n.* [*actino-*, and Gr. *soma*, body.] the body of an actinozoan, whether simple or compound.

aç′tin·ost, *n.* [*actin-*, and Gr. *osteon*, bone.] one of the bones at the base of the paired fins of certain fishes.

aç·tin′ō·stōme, *n.* [*actino-*, and Gr. *stoma*, mouth.] the mouth of a coelenterate.

aç·ti·nō·ther′ȧ·py, *n.* same as *radiotherapy*.

aç·ti·not′rō·chȧ, *n.* [*actino-*, and Gr. *trochos*, wheel.] the larva of certain marine worms of the genus *Phoronis*.

Aç″ti·nō·zō′ȧ, *n.pl.* [*actino-*, and Gr. *zoon*, animal.] a class of *Cœlentera*, including the sea anemones, corals, etc.; *Anthozoa*.

aç″ti·nō·zō′ăl, *a.* pertaining to the *Actinozoa*.

aç″ti·nō·zō′ăn, aç″ti·nō·zō′on, *n.* one of the *Actinozoa*.

aç·tin′ū·lȧ, *n.* [L., dim. of Gr. *aktis*, *aktinos*, ray.] a larval stage of certain hydroids.

aç′tion, *n.* [ME. *accion*; OFr. *action*; L. *actio* (*n*), from *agere*, to do, drive.]
1. the doing of something; hence, the state of acting or moving; exertion of power or force, as when one body acts on another.
2. the effect or influence of something (on something else); as, the *action* of a drug; motion produced.
3. an act or thing done; a deed.
4. in mechanics, operation; the way of working, moving, etc., as of a machine.
5. the moving parts or mechanism, as of a gun, piano, etc.
6. [*pl.*] habitual conduct; behavior; demeanor.
7. the series of events in a story or play.
8. the posture, gesture, gesticulation, etc. of an actor or speaker.
9. in physiology, the motions or functions of a part or organ of the body; as, the *action* of the heart and lungs.
10. in law, a lawsuit or legal process; a claim made before a court. *Actions* are civil, criminal, or penal; *civil*, when instituted solely in behalf of private persons to recover debts or damages; *criminal*, when instituted by a government for the punishment of a crime; *penal*, when instituted to recover a penalty imposed by way of punishment. The word is also used for a *right of action*; as, the law gives an *action* for every claim.
11. in painting and sculpture, an attitude or position which suggests animation, as the arm extended to represent the act of giving
12. a battle; a fight; an engagement between enemies in war.

Syn.—act, deed, accomplishment, behavior, feat, performance, exploit, achievement, exercise, proceeding, transaction.—In many cases, *action* and *act* are synonymous; but some distinction between them is observable. *Action* seems to have more relation to the power that acts, and its operation and process of acting; and *act*, more relation to the effect or completed operation.

bring action; to start a lawsuit.

in action; (a) active; in motion or operation; (b) participating; (c) in combat.

see action; to participate in military combat.

take action; (a) to become active; start to move, work, etc.; (b) to start a lawsuit.

aç′tion·ȧ·ble, *a.* furnishing ground, or cause, for an action, or lawsuit.

aç′tion·ȧ·bly, *adv.* in an actionable manner.

aç′tion·less, *a.* without action.

aç′tion pāint′ing, a form of abstract expressionism in which such methods as the spattering or dripping of paint are used to create bold, fluid, apparently random compositions.

aç′ti·vāte, *v.t.* activated, *pt.*, *pp.*; activating, *ppr.* 1. to make active; cause to engage in activity; hence, to create or organize (a military unit, governmental bureau, etc.).
2. to make radioactive.
3. to make capable of reacting or of accelerating a chemical reaction.
4. to treat (sewage) with air so that aerobes will become active in it, thus purifying it.

aç′ti·vā′tion, *n.* an activating or being activated.

aç′ti·vā″tŏr, *n.* 1. a thing or person that activates.
2. in chemistry, a catalyst.

aç′tive, *a.* [ME. *actif*; OFr. *actif*; L. *activus*, from *agere*, to act.]
1. acting; functioning; moving; working.
2. capable of acting, functioning, etc.
3. causing action, motion, or change.
4. characterized by quick motion or the disposition to move with speed; nimble; lively; brisk; agile; as, an *active* animal.
5. busy; constantly engaged in action; pursuing business with vigor; diligent; energetic; as, an *active* life.
6. requiring action or exertion; practical; producing real effects: opposed to *theoretical*, *ideal*, or *speculative*; as, *active* duties.
7. in grammar, (a) indicating the voice or form of a verb whose subject is shown as performing the action of the verb: opposed to *passive*; (b) in or of the active voice; (c) showing action rather than state of being: said of verbs like *throw* and *walk*.
8. in business, producing profit or interest; as, *active* funds.
9. in medicine, effective and quick; as, an *active* remedy; also, progressive; as, an *active* disease.

active bonds; bonds having fixed interest payable from date of issue: distinguished from *passive bonds*, which bear no interest but entitle the holder to a future benefit.

active capital; money, or property that may readily be converted into money.

active immunity; immunity (to a disease) due to the production of antibodies.

active list; a list of officers serving in or available for service in the armed forces.

active service; service on the active list or in the armed forces in wartime.

Syn.—agile, alert, assiduous, brisk, busy, lively, nimble, quick, spirited, vigorous, sprightly, prompt, energetic, operative, industrious.

aç′tive·ly, *adv.* in an active manner; by action; nimbly; briskly.

aç′tive·ness, *n.* the quality or state of being active.

aç′tiv·iṣm, *n.* the doctrine or policy of being active or doing things with decision.

aç′tiv·ist, *n.* an individual who favors, incites, or demands intensified activities, especially in time of war.

aç·tiv′i·ty, *n.*; *pl.* **aç·tiv′i·tieṣ.** 1. the quality or state of being active; action; motion; use of energy.
2. normal power of mind or body; energetic action; nimbleness; agility; animation.
3. an active force.
4. any specific action or pursuit; as, outside *activities*.

Syn.—briskness, liveliness, animation.

aç′tiv·īze, *v.t.* activized, *pt.*, *pp.*; activizing, *ppr.* to activate.

açt′less, *a.* without action or spirit. [Rare.]

açt of wạr, an act of aggression by one nation, group of nations, etc. against another without a declaration of war.

aç′tŏn, *n.* [OFr. *aketon*, *hoqueton*, a quilted jacket; Sp. *alcoton*, cotton.] a stuffed vest or tunic formerly worn under a coat of mail.

aç′tŏr, *n.* [L. *actor*, a doer, an advocate.]
1. one who acts or performs; an active agent.
2. one who acts a part in a play, moving picture, etc.
3. in law, an advocate or proctor in civil courts or causes; also, a plaintiff.

bad actor; (a) a person who misbehaves; (b) an unscrupulous or dangerous person; criminal. [Slang.]

aç′tŏr-aç′tion çŏn·struç′tion, a sentence or clause containing both subject (actor) and predicate (action).

aç′tŏr-man′ȧ·ġẽr, *n.* the manager of a theater who acts in plays his company produces.

aç′tress, *n.* a woman or girl who acts; specifically, a woman or girl who acts a part in a play, moving picture, etc.

Acts, *n.pl.* [construed as sing.] a book of the New Testament, ascribed to Luke, and describing the beginnings of the Christian church: full title, *Acts of the Apostles*.

aç′tū·ăl (ak′chụ̈-ăl), *a.* [ME. *actuel*, active; L. *actualis*, from *actus*, pp. of *agere*, to do.]
1. existing in act; real: in opposition to *speculative*, or existing in theory only; as, an *actual* crime; *actual* receipts.
2. existing at the present time; as, the *actual* condition of the country.

actual cautery; burning by a red-hot iron, etc.: opposed to *potential cautery*: see *cautery*.

actual sin; that which is committed by a person himself: opposed to *original sin*.

Syn.—certain, genuine, positive, real, true, authentic, veritable, unquestioned.

aç′tū·ăl, *n.* in finance, something actually in hand or received, as distinguished from estimated assets or receipts.

aç′tū·ăl·ist, *n.* a realist; one who believes in actualities.

aç·tū·al′i·ty, *n.*; *pl.* **aç·tū·al′i·tieṣ.** 1. the state of being actual; reality.
2. an actual thing or condition; fact.

aç″tū·ăl·i·zā′tion, *n.* an actualizing or being actualized.

aç′tū·ăl·īze, *v.t.*; actualized, *pt.*, *pp.*; actualizing, *ppr.* 1. to make actual or real; realize in action.
2. to make realistic.

aç′tū·ăl·ly, *adv.* 1. in fact; really.
2. as a matter of fact; indeed.

aç′tū·ăl·ness, *n.* the state of being actual.

aç·tū·ā′ri·ăl, *a.* 1. relating to an actuary or the business of an actuary.
2. calculated by actuaries.

aç′tū·ȧ·ry, *n.*; *pl.* **aç′tū·ȧ·rieṣ.** [L. *actuarius*, clerk, from *actus*, pp. of *agere*, to do.]
1. a registrar or clerk: a term of the civil law, and used originally in courts of civil law jurisdiction.
2. an official statistician and computer of an insurance company; one who calculates insurance risks and premiums.

aç′tū·āte, *a.* put in action. [Obs.]

aç′tū·āte, *v.t.*; actuated, *pt.*, *pp.*; actuating, *ppr.* [L. *actuatus*, pp. of *actuare*, to act.]
1. to put into action or motion; hence, to move or incite to action; as, men are *actuated* by motives.
2. to carry out; to execute. [Obs.]

Syn.—act upon, impel, induce, instigate, move, prompt.

aç·tū·ā′tion, *n.* an actuating or being actuated.

aç′tū·ā·tŏr, *n.* a person or thing that actuates.

aç′ū·āte, *v.t.* acuated, *pt.*, *pp.*; acuating, *ppr.* [L. *acuatus*, pp. of *acuare*, from *acuere*, to sharpen.] to sharpen; to make pungent, or corrosive. [Obs.]

aç′ū·āte, *a.* sharp at the end; having a point.

aç·ū·ā′tion, *n.* the act of sharpening. [Obs.]

ȧ·çū′i·ty, *n.*; *pl.* **ȧ·çū′i·tieṣ.** sharpness; acuteness; keenness, as of thought or vision.

ȧ·çū′lē·āte, *a.* [L. *aculeatus*, from *aculeus*, a sting.]
1. in botany, having prickles, or sharp points.
2. in zoology, having a sting, or prickles.

ȧ·çū′lē·ā·ted, *a.* aculeate.

ȧ·çū′lē·i·fọrm, *a.* [L. *aculeus*, prickle, and *-form.*] in botany, resembling a prickle.

ȧ·çū′lē·ō·lāte, *a.* in botany, having small prickles.

ȧ·çū′lē·ous, *a.* aculeate. [Obs.]

ȧ·çū′lē·us, *n.*; *pl.* **ȧ·çū′lē·ī.** [L., dim. of *acus*, needle.]

1. in botany, a prickle, or rigid point, growing from the epidermis of a plant: distinguished from a thorn, which grows from the wood.

2. in zoology, a sting, as of a bee or wasp.

ȧ·çū′men, *n.* [L. *acumen*, a point, a sting.]

1. quickness of perception; keenness of mind or discrimination; sagacity.

2. in botany, a tapering point.

ȧ·çū′mi·nāte, *a.* having a long, projecting, and highly tapering point, as certain leaves.

ȧ·çū′mi·nāte, *v.t.*; acuminated, *pt.*, *pp.*; acuminating, *ppr.* [L. *acuminatus*, pp. of *acuminare*, to sharpen.] to make sharp.

ȧ·çū′mi·nāte, *v.i.* to come to, or end in, a sharp point.

ȧ·çū·mi·nā′tion, *n.* 1. an acuminating or acuminate condition.

2. a tapering point.

ȧ·çū′mi·nōse, *a.* nearly acuminate.

ȧ·çū′mi·nous, *a.* 1. keen; possessing acumen.

2. acuminate.

ACUMINATE LEAF

aç·ū·min′ū·lāte, *a.* somewhat acuminate.

aç′ū·pres·sūre, *n.* [*acu*puncture and *pressure.*] a practice analogous to acupuncture but involving the application of manual pressure to parts of the body rather than the insertion of needles.

aç″ū·punç″tū·rā′tion, *n.* same as *acupuncture.*

aç′ū·punç·tūre, *n.* [L. *acus*, needle, and *punctura*, a pricking.] the ancient practice, especially as carried on by the Chinese, of piercing parts of the body with needles in seeking to treat disease or relieve pain.

ȧ·çūt′aṅ″gū·lăr, *a.* acute-angled.

ȧ·çūte′, *a.* [L. *acutus*, pp. of *acuere*, to sharpen.]

1. sharp at the end; ending in a sharp point: opposed to *blunt* or *obtuse.*

2. keen or quick of mind; having nice discernment; perceiving or using minute distinctions: opposed to *dull* or *stupid*; as, an *acute* reasoner.

3. sensitive to impressions; as, a man of *acute* eyesight, hearing, or feeling.

4. severe and sharp, as pain.

5. in medicine, sharp; severe; coming speedily to a crisis: said of some diseases: the opposite of *chronic.*

6. critical; crucial.

7. in music, shrill; high in tone or pitch: said of sound: opposed to *grave.*

8. under 90 degrees: said of angles.

acute accent; a mark (′) used to show: (a) the quality or length of a vowel, as in *idée*; (b) primary stress, as in *type′writer*; (c) any stress on a spoken sound or syllable, as in scanning poetry; (d) high rising tone or pitch, as in the Chinese language.

acute angle; in geometry, an angle which is less than a right angle, or less than ninety degrees.

Syn.—keen, penetrating, shrewd, sagacious, piercing, pointed, sharp.

ACUTE ANGLE

ȧ·çūte′, *v.t.* to give an acute sound or accent to. [Obs.]

ȧ·çūte′-aṅ″gled, *a.* having an acute angle or angles.

ȧ·çūte′ly, *adv.* sharply; keenly; with nice discrimination.

aç″ū·tē·naç′ū·lum, *n.*; *pl.* **aç″ū·tē·naç′ū·lȧ,** [L. *acus*, needle, and *tenaculum*, holder.] in medicine, an instrument for facilitating the use of a needle in surgical operations.

ȧ·çūte′ness, *n.* sharpness; the state or quality of being acute.

Syn.—sharpness, sagacity, penetration, keenness, shrewdness.

ȧ·çū′ti-, a combining form, from L. *acutus*, sharp, meaning *sharp, sharp-pointed.*

ȧ·çū·ti·fō′li·āte, *a.* [*acuti-*, and L. *folium*, leaf.] in botany, having sharp-pointed leaves.

ȧ·çū·ti·lō′bāte, *a.* [*acuti-*, and L. *lobus*, lobe.] in botany, having acute lobes: said of certain leaves.

-ăcy, [L. *-acia.*] a combining form used in forming abstract nouns, meaning *quality, position, condition,* etc.; as, democr*acy*, cur*acy*.

ȧ·cyç′liç (*or* -sīk′), *a.* 1. not cyclic; not in cycles.

2. in chemistry, having the structure of an open chain rather than a closed ring.

ac·y·rol′ō·ġy, *n.* [L. *acyrologia*, from Gr. *akyrologia*; *a* priv., and *kyros*, authority, and *logos*, word.] faulty diction.

ad, *n.* an advertisement. [Colloq.]

ad, *n.* [short for *advantage.*] in tennis, advantage: said of the first point scored after deuce.

ad in; server's advantage.

ad out; receiver's advantage.

ad-, [L. *ad*, to, unto, toward.] a combining form meaning, in general, *motion toward, addition to, nearness to,* as in *ad*mit, *ad*join, *ad*renal: it has been assimilated in Latin to the first letter of the word to which it is prefixed; thus, in *ac*claim, *af*firm, *al*ligation, *ap*prove, *ar*rive, *at*trition, etc. the *ac-, af-, al-, ap-, ar-, at-*, etc. are all modified forms of *ad-*. In *a*scend, *a*scribe, the *d* has been lost altogether.

-ad, [Gr. *-as, -ad.*] a combining form meaning *of* or *relating to*, used in forming: (a) the names of collective numerals, as in mon*ad*; (b) the names of some poems, as in Ili*ad*; (c) the names of some plants, as in cyc*ad*.

-ad, [L. *ad*, to.] a combining form meaning *toward*: used especially in anatomical terms; as, dors*ad*, toward the back.

ad ăb·sũr′dum, [L.] to the point of absurdity.

ȧ·daç′tyl, *a.* [Gr. *a* priv., and *daktylos*, a digit.] adactylous.

ā″daç·tyl′i·ȧ, *n.* same as *adactylism.*

ȧ·daç′tyl·iṣm, *n.* congenital lack of fingers or toes.

ȧ·daç′tyl·ous, *a.* without fingers or toes; having no claws.

ad′āġe, *n.* [Fr. *adage*; L. *adagium, adagio*, from *ad*, and *aio*, I say.] a proverb; an old saying.

Syn.—maxim, proverb, saw, saying, dictum, motto, aphorism, byword, axiom.

ȧ·dā′ġi·ăl, *a.* proverbial.

ä·dä·ġiet′tō (-jet′), *a.* and *adv.* [It.] not quite so slow as adagio.

ȧ·dä′ġiō (-jō), *n.*; *pl.* **ä·dä′ġiōṣ,** [It. *ad*, to, at, and *agio*, leisure.]

1. in music, a slow movement; a piece of music to be performed in adagio tempo.

2. a slow ballet dance requiring skill in balancing.

ä·dä′ġiō, *adv.* in music and dancing, slowly; leisurely, and with grace. When repeated, *adagio, adagio*, it directs the movement to be very slow.

ä·dä′ġiō, *a.* slow.

Ad′ăm, *n.* in Hebrew, Chaldee, Syriac, Ethiopic, Arabic, *man*; primarily, the name of the human species, mankind; specifically, in the Bible, the first man, the progenitor of the human race.

Adam's ale; water.

Adam's apple; (a) the thyroid cartilage, the prominent part in the front of the throat, particularly in males: so called from the superstition that it was caused by the forbidden apple sticking in Adam's throat; (b) a variety of the lime, *Citrus limetta.*

Adam's needle; the *Yucca filamentosa*, or bear grass.

Ad′ăm, *a.* [after Robert and James *Adam*, 18th-c. British architects.] relating to a style of English furniture and architecture with straight lines and ornamentation of garlands, etc.

Ad′ăm-and-Ēve′, *n.* a kind of orchid bearing clusters of yellowish-brown flowers and one leaf at the base; puttyroot.

ad′ȧ·mant, *n.* [OF.; L. *adamas, adamantis*, the hardest metal, from Gr. *adamas, adamantos*; *a* priv., and *damān*, to subdue.]

1. a stone imagined by some to be of impenetrable hardness: a name formerly given to the diamond and other substances of extreme hardness.

2. unbreakable hardness. [Poetic.]

ad′ȧ·mant, *a.* 1. too hard to be broken.

2. unyielding; firm.

ad″ȧ·man·tē′ăn, *a.* hard as adamant.

ad·ȧ·man′tine, *a.* 1. made of adamant.

2. resembling adamant; very hard; unbreakable; unyielding; firm.

3. resembling the diamond in hardness or sparkling luster.

adamantine spar; a variety of corundum, with gray, brown, or greenish shades.

ad·ȧ·man′toid, *n.* a hexoctahedron; a crystal bounded by forty-eight equal triangles.

ad·am·bū·lā′çrăl, *a.* [L. *ad*, to, and *ambulacrum*, a walk.] in zoology, next to the ambulacra.

A·dam′iç, A·dam′iç·ăl, *a.* of, pertaining to, or resembling Adam.

Ad′ăm·īte, *n.* 1. a human being, thought of as a descendant of Adam; one of mankind.

2. [a–] a hydrous arsenate of zinc, named after Adam, a French mineralogist: called also *adamine.*

3. in church history, a member of a sect of visionaries who pretended to establish a state of innocence and, like Adam, went naked.

Ad′ămṣ·īte, *n.* [from Major Roger *Adams* (1889–), Am. army officer who invented it.] a yellow, odorless crystalline compound, $NH{\cdot}(C_6H_4)_2{\cdot}AsCl$, used in a vaporous form as a lung-irritant in chemical warfare: symbol, DM (no period).

Ad·an·sō′ni·ȧ, *n.* [from M. *Adanson*, a French botanist who traveled in Senegal.] a genus of large low trees, of which *Adansonia digitata* is the African calabash tree, or baobab tree of Senegal. *Adansonia Gregorii*, the only other species, is the cream-of-tartar tree of North Australia.

ȧ·dapt′, *v.t.*; adapted, *pt., pp.*; adapting, *ppr.* [L. *ad*, to, and *aptare*, to fit.]

1. to make suitable; to fit, or suit; as, to *adapt* an instrument to its uses; we have provisions *adapted* to our wants.

2. to change (oneself) so that one's behavior, attitudes, etc. will conform to new or changed circumstances.

3. specifically, to remodel, work up, and render fit for representation on the stage, as a novel, or a play from a foreign language.

Syn.—accommodate, adjust, suit, arrange, fit, conform.

ȧ·dapt·ȧ·bil′i·ty, *n.* the quality of being adaptable.

ȧ·dapt′ȧ·ble, *a.* 1. capable of being adapted or made suitable.

2. able to change without difficulty so as to conform to new or changed circumstances.

ȧ·dapt′ȧ·ble·ness, *n.* suitableness; adaptability.

ad·ap·tā′tion, *n.* 1. an adapting or being adapted.

2. a thing resulting from adapting: as, this play is an *adaptation* of a novel.

3. in biology, a change in structure, function, or form that produces better adjustment of an animal or plant to its environment.

4. in physiology, the power that the eye has of adjusting to variations in light.

5. in sociology, a change in behavior to conform to cultural patterns.

ȧ·dapt′ȧ·tive, *a.* adaptive.

ȧ·dapt′ed·ness, *n.* state or quality of being adapted; suitableness.

ȧ·dapt′ēr, ȧ·dapt′ŏr, *n.* 1. one who or that which adapts; specifically, one who translates, remodels, or works up, rendering fit to be represented on the stage, as a play from a foreign tongue or from a novel.

2. a contrivance for adapting apparatus to new uses.

3. a connecting device; specifically, in chemistry, a tube used in connecting two pieces of apparatus, as a retort with a receiver.

ȧ·dap′tion, *n.* adaptation; the act of fitting.

ȧ·dapt′ive, *a.* 1. able to adapt.

2. showing adaptation.

ȧ·dapt′ive·ly, *adv.* in an adaptive manner.

ȧ·dapt′ive·ness, *n.* the state or quality of being adaptive; suitableness.

ȧ·dapt′ly, *adv.* in a suitable or convenient manner. [Obs.]

ȧ·dapt′ness, *n.* the state of being fitted. [Obs.]

ȧ·dap′tŏr, *n.* an adapter.

Ā·där′, *n.* [Heb. *adār.*] the sixth month of the Jewish year.

Ā·där′ She̩′ni, [Heb., lit., second Adar.] same as *Veadar.*

ad as′trȧ pēr as′pe·rȧ, [L.] to the stars through difficulties.

ȧ·dāy′, ȧ-dāy′, *adv.* [*a-*, on, and *day.*] daily.

ad çap·tan′dum, [L. *ad*, to, and gerund of *captare*, to take.] for the purpose of catching: often applied as an adjective to specious attempts to catch popular favor or applause; as, *ad captandum* oratory.

ad captandum vulgus; to please and catch the crowd.

add, *v.t.*; added, *pt., pp.*; adding, *ppr.*, [L. *addere*, from *ad*, to, and *dare*, to give.]

1. to join or unite (to) so as to increase the number, size, quantity, etc.; as, *add* this to your store.

2. to state further; to subjoin; as, let me *add* this.
3. to combine (numbers) into a sum; calculate the total of.
to add up to; (a) to reach a total of; (b) to mean; signify.
Syn.—annex, adjoin, adduce.

add, *v.i.* 1. to be or serve as an addition; to be added; to augment (with *to*); as, the consciousness of folly often *adds to* one's regret.
2. to perform the arithmetical operation of addition; as, he *adds* very rapidly.
Syn.—augment, increase, cast up, total, sum up.

add'ȧ·ble, *a.* same as *addible.*

ad'dax, *n.* a species of north African and Arabian antelope, *Hippotragus nasomaculatus*, and one of the largest of the genus: the horns of the male are about four feet long and twisted.

HEAD OF ADDAX (*Hippotragus nasomaculatus*)

add'ed līne', in music, an extra line above or below the staff, for showing high or low notes that cannot be shown on the staff: also called *ledger line.*

ad·deem', *v.t.* to award; to sentence. [Obs.]

ad'dend, *n.* [from *addendum*], in mathematics, a number or quantity to be added to another.

ad·den'dum, *n.*; *pl.* **ad·den'dȧ.** [L. gerund of *addere*, to add, place.]
1. a thing added or to be added.
2. an appendix or supplement to writing.
3. the part of a gear tooth that projects beyond the pitch circle.
4. the addendum circle.
addendum circle; in mechanics, the circle which might be described around the outer ends of gear teeth on a wheel.

ad'dẽr, *n.* [ME. *adder, addre*, from *nadder, neddre*, by faulty separation of *a nadder*, an adder; AS. *nædre*; G. *natter*; Ice. *nathra*, a snake.]
1. a poisonous serpent of several species, belonging to the viper family. The common European *adder*, *Pelias berus* or *Vipera communis*, attains a length of from two to three feet and is the only poisonous snake found in Great Britain. Its bite is rarely fatal to man.
2. any one of several harmless American snakes, as the milk *adder*, the spreading *adder*, etc.
3. a large, poisonous snake of Africa; puff *adder.*
4. a European fish; the sea *adder*, or fifteen-spined stickleback.

add'ẽr, *n.* one who or that which adds; specifically, an adding machine.

ad'dẽr bōlt, a dragon fly. [British.]

ad'dẽr flȳ, the dragon fly or *Libellula*: sometimes called *adder bolt.*

ad'dẽr pīke, the lesser weever, *Trachinus vipera*: also called *sting fish, etter pike*, etc.

ad'dẽr's-mēat, the wake robin or cuckoo pint; also, the chickweed. [British dial.]

ad'dẽr's-mouth, a delicate North American orchid, *Microstylis ophioglossoides.*

ad'dẽr's-spēar, same as *adder's-tongue.*

ad'dẽr's-tongue (-tung), 1. a variety of fern, genus *Ophioglossum*, whose seeds are produced on a spike, supposed to resemble a serpent's tongue.
2. the dogtooth violet.

ad'dẽr-wŏrt, ad'dẽr's wŏrt, snakeweed, *Polygonum bistorta*, so named from its supposed virtue in curing the bite of serpents: called also *bistort.*

add·i·bil'i·ty, add·ȧ·bil'i·ty, *n.* the condition of being addible; the capability of being added.

add'i·ble, add'ȧ·ble, *a.* that may be added.

ad'dice, *n.* an adz. [Obs.]

ad·dict', *v.t.*; addicted, *pt., pp.*; addicting, *ppr.* [L. *addictus*, pp. of *addere*, to devote, to deliver over.] to apply habitually; to devote or give (oneself) up habitually (with *to*); to habituate; to attach closely: generally with a reflexive pronoun and sometimes in a good sense, but, as now used, generally in a bad sense; as, to *addict* oneself to intemperance, to gambling, or the like: most frequently used in the past participle; as, she was *addicted* to gossip.
to addict oneself to a person, to attach or devote oneself to a person, as to a master or leader. [Obs.]

ad·dict', *a.* addicted. [Obs.]

ad'dict, *n.* one who is addicted to some habit, as to the use of a drug.

ad·dict'ed, *a.* devoted or given up (*to* a practice or habit, especially a bad habit).
Syn.—devoted, accustomed, prone, attached, habituated, disposed, inclined, abandoned.

ad·dict'ed·ness, *n.* the quality or state of being addicted.

ad·dic'tion, *n.* 1. the condition of being addicted (*to* a habit); habitual inclination.
2. among the Romans, a making over of goods to another by sale or legal sentence; also, an assignment of debtors in service to their creditors.

add'ing mȧ·chīne', a machine that prints numbers and automatically adds them as the operator presses its keys: some adding machines can also subtract, multiply, and divide.

ADDING MACHINE

Ad·di·sō'ni·ăn, *a.* of or like Joseph Addison (1672–1719), English essayist and poet; specifically, of or like his literary style, characterized by clarity, restraint, urbanity, etc.

Ad'di·son's dis·ēase'. [after Dr. Thomas *Addison* (1793–1860) of England, its discoverer.] a disease of the adrenal glands, characterized by anemia, peculiar skin discoloration, etc.

ad·dit'ȧ·ment, *n.* [L. *additamentum*, an increase.] an addition; a thing added.

ad·di'tion (-dish'un), *n.* [L. *additio*, from *addere*; *ad*, to, and *dare*, to give.]
1. the act of adding; opposed to *subtraction*, or *diminution*; as, a sum is increased by *addition.*
2. a thing or part added; an increase.
3. in arithmetic, an adding of two or more numbers to obtain a number called a sum; also the branch of arithmetic which treats of adding numbers.
4. in law, a title annexed to a man's name to show his rank, occupation, or place of residence; as, Adam Brown, *Esq.*; John Jones, *electrician*; George Johnson *of Chicago.*
5. in music, a dot at the right side of a note, to lengthen its sound one half.
6. in heraldry, something added to a coat of arms as a mark of honor; opposed to *abatement*; as bordure, quarter, canton, gyron, pile, etc.
7. anything added by way of improvement.
Syn.—increase, accession, augmentation, annexation, additament, increment, appendage, adjunct.

ad·di'tion·ăl, *a.* supplemental; added; increased or increasing in any manner.

ad·di'tion·ăl·ly, *adv.* in addition.

ad·di'tion·ā·ry, *a.* additional. [Obs.]

ad·di·ti'tious (-tish'us), *a.* additive. [Rare.]

ad'di·tive, *a.* 1. to be added.
2. showing or relating to addition. Opposed to *subtractive.*

ad'di·tō·ry, *a.* adding, or capable of adding; making an addition. [Obs.]

ad'dle (ad'l), *a.* [ME. *adel*; AS. *adela*, mud, filth.]
1. having lost the power of development; rotten; putrid: applied to eggs.
2. barren; confused; muddled.
His brains grow *addle.* —Dryden.

ad'dle, *v.t.*; addled, *pt., pp.*; addling, *ppr.* 1. to make rotten.
2. to muddle; confuse.

ad'dle, *v.i.* 1. to become rotten.
2. to become muddled or confused.

ad'dle, *n.* 1. mire; liquid manure. [Obs.]
2. dregs; the dry lees of wine.

ad'dle·brāined, *a.* stupid; muddled.

ad'dled (ad'ld), *a.* 1. rotten, corrupt, putrid, or barren; as, an *addled* egg.
2. muddled; confused.

ad'dle·pāte, *n.* a stupid, muddled fellow.

ad'dle·pā"ted, *a.* addlebrained.

ad'dle·pā"ted·ness, stupidity; denseness; obtuseness; silliness.

ad·dọọm', *v.t.* to adjudge. [Obs.]

ad·dorsed', *a.* [from L. *ad*, and *dorsum*, back.] in heraldry, placed back to back, as two animals or figures.

ad·dress', *v.t.*; addressed, *pt., pp.*; addressing, *ppr.* [ME. *addressen*; OFr. *addresser, adrecer*; from L. *ad*, to, and *directio*, from *dirigere*, to lay straight, to direct.]
1. to apply (oneself); direct (one's energies *to*); as, he now *addressed* himself to the business.
2. to aim or direct (spoken or written words *to*).
3. to aim or direct; to throw or hurl. [Obs.]
4. to direct words to; to talk to; as, he *addressed* the judges; he *addressed* himself to the speaker.
5. to direct in writing, as a letter; to write the destination on (a letter or parcel); as, he *addressed* a letter to the governor.
6. to present a letter of thanks or congratulation, a petition, etc. to; as, the legislature *addressed* the president.
7. to court or approach as a lover.
8. in commerce, to consign or intrust to the care of another as agent; as, the ship was *addressed* to a merchant in Baltimore.
9. in golf, to take a stance and aim the club at (the ball).
10. to use a proper form in speaking to; as, *address* the judge as *Your Honor.*
11. in law, to remove (a judge) from office by executive action following a formal request by a legislative body.
Syn.—approach, salute, hail, accost, apostrophize, greet, court, woo.

ad·dress', *n.* 1. a written or spoken speech; a discourse; as, the president made a short *address.*
2. a written or formal message of respect, congratulation, thanks, petition, etc.; as, an *address* of thanks; an *address* to constituents.
3. manner of speaking to another; as, a man of pleasing *address.*
4. courtship: more generally in the plural, *addresses*; as, he makes or pays his *addresses* to a lady.
5. skill; dexterity; skillful management; as, the envoy conducted the negotiation with *address.*
6. (*also* ad'dress), the place to which mail, etc. can be sent to one.
7. (*also* ad'dress), delivery directions on a letter, parcel, etc., including the name, title, and place of residence of the person for whom it is intended.
Syn.—direction, superscription, discourse, speech, harangue, oration, lecture, sermon, tact, skill, ability, ingenuity, adroitness.

ad·dress·ee', *n.* one to whom anything is addressed, as a letter.

ad·dress'ẽr, ad·dress'ŏr, *n.* one who addresses.

ad·dress'ing mȧ·chīne", a mechanical device for addressing envelopes and newspaper wrappers automatically.

ad·dres'sion, *n.* the act of laying out one's route or course. [Obs.]

ad·dres'sō·graph (-graf), *n.* an addressing machine; a trade-mark (**Addressograph**).

ad·dūce', *v.t.*; adduced, *pt., pp.*; adducing, *ppr.* [L. *adducere*, to lead or bring to; *ad*, to, and *ducere*, to lead.] to give, present, or offer as a reason or proof; to cite, name, or introduce as an example.
Syn.—advance, allege, assign, cite, quote, bring forward, urge, name, mention.

ad·dū'cent, *a.* [L. *adducens*, *ppr.* of *adducere*; see *adduce.*] in physiology, adducting: opposed to *abducent.*

ad·dū'cẽr, *n.* one who adduces.

ad·dū'ci·ble, ad·dūce'ȧ·ble, *a.* capable of being adduced.

ad·duct', *v.t.* [L. *adductus*, pp. of *adducere*, to lead to.] in physiology, to move or pull (a part of the body) toward the median axis or toward another part: opposed to *abduct.*

ad·duç′tion, *n.* 1. an adducing.
2. in physiology, (a) an adducting; (b) the position (of a part) resulting from adducting.

ad·duç′tive, *a.* 1. adducting.
2. of adduction.

ad·duç′tŏr, *n.* [L. *adducere,* to lead to.]
1. a muscle which adducts; as, the *adductor* of the eye, which turns the eye toward the nose; the *adductor* of the thumb, which draws the thumb toward the fingers.
2. in zoology, one of the muscles which bring together the valves of the shell of the bivalve mollusks.

ad·dulce′, *v.t.* [Fr. *adoulcir*; L. *adulcir,* from *ad,* to, and *dulcis,* sweet.] to sweeten. [Obs.]

-āde, [Fr. *-ade*; Pr., Port., or Sp. *-ada*; It. *-ata*; L. *-ata,* fem. ending of pp. of verbs of the first conjugation.] a suffix meaning: (a) *the act of,* as in block*ade*; (b) *the result or product of,* as in pom*ade*; (c) *participant in an action,* as in brig*ade*; (d) [after *lemonade,* etc.] *drink made from,* as in lime*ade.*

ȧ·deem′, *v.t.* in Roman law, to revoke, as a legacy.

ä″de̤·län·tä′dō, *n.* [Sp.] formerly, a Spanish title for a governor of a province; a lieutenant governor; a commander.

ad·ē·las′tẽr, *n.* [Gr. *adēlos,* not manifest, and *aster,* star.] in botany, a name proposed for any plant that has come into cultivation without its flower being known and has not therefore been referred to its genus.

ad′el·ing, *n.* see *atheling.*

ad″ē·lō·ço·don′iç, *a.* [Gr. *a* priv., *dēlos,* manifest, and *kōdon,* bell.] describing a gonophore having no umbrella developed.

ad″ē·lō·mor′phous, *a.* [Gr. *adēlos,* not manifest, and *morphē,* form.] of indistinct form: said of certain glandular cells.

ȧ·del′ō·pod, *n.* [Gr. *a* priv., *dēlos,* apparent, and *pous,* foot.] an animal whose feet are not apparent.

ȧ·del′phi·ȧ, *n.* [Gr. *adelphos,* brother.] in botany, a bunch or bundle of stamens: used of those plants in which the stamens, instead of growing singly, combine by the filaments into one or more parcels.

ȧ·del′phous, *a.* in botany, forming an adelphia or adelphias; uniting by the filaments into one or more parcels: said of stamens.

ȧ·dempt′, *a.* [L. *ademptus,* pp. of *adimere,* to take away.] taken away. [Obs.]

ȧ·demp′tion, *n.* [L. *ademptio,* from *adimere,* to take away.] in law, the revocation of a grant, donation, or the like.

aden-, aden·i-, aden·o-, [Gr. *adēn,* gland.] a combining form signifying *of a gland* or *glands.*

ad·ē·nal′ġi·ȧ, ad·ē·nal′ġy, *n.* [*aden-,* and Gr. *algos,* pain.] pain in a gland.

ad·e·neç′tō·my, *n.* the surgical removal of a gland.

ȧ·dē′ni·a, *n.* enlargement of the glands.

ȧ·den′i·form, *a.* [*adeni-,* and *-form.*] shaped like a gland.

ad′e·nïne, *n.* [*aden-,* and *-ine.*] a white, crystalline purine base, $C_5H_5N_5$, derived from nucleic acid formed in the pancreas, spleen, etc.

ad·e·nī′tis, *n.* glandular inflammation.

ad″e·nō·graph′iç, *a.* pertaining to adenography.

ad·e·nog′rȧ·phy, *n.* [*adeno-,* and Gr. *graphein,* to describe.] that part of descriptive anatomy which treats of the glands.

ad′e·noid, *a.* [*aden-,* and Gr. *eidos,* form.]
1. glandlike; glandular.
2. of or like lymphoid tissue.

ad″e·noi′dal, *a.* 1. adenoid.
2. having adenoids.
3. having the characteristic mouth-breathing, nasal tone, etc. due to adenoids.

ad′e·noids, *n. pl.* growths of adenoid tissue in the upper part of the throat, behind the nose; hypertrophy of a pharyngeal gland.

ADENOIDS

ad″e·nō·log′iç·ăl, *a.* pertaining to adenology.

ad·e·nol′ō·ġy, *n.* [*adeno-,* and Gr. *logos,* discourse.] the study of glands.

ad·e·nō′mȧ, *n.* [*aden-,* and *-oma.*] a benign tumor of glandular origin, or with a glandlike cell arrangement.

ȧ·den′ō·phōre, *n.* the stalk of a nectar gland.

ad·e·noph′ō·rous, *a.* [*adeno-,* and Gr. *phoros,* from *pherein,* to bear.] in botany, gland-producing.

ad·e·noph′yl·lous, *a.* [*adeno-,* and Gr. *phyllon,* leaf.] bearing glands upon the leaves.

ad′e·nōse, ad′e·nous, *a.* pertaining to or resembling a gland; full of glands.

ad″e·nō·tom′iç, *a.* relating to adenotomy.

ad·e·not′ō·my, *n.* [*adeno-,* and Gr. *tomē,* from *temnein,* to cut.] in surgery, a cutting or incision of a gland.

ȧ·deph′ȧ·gous, *a.* [Gr. *adēphagos,* gluttonous.] gluttonous: applied to certain voracious beetles.

ad′eps, *n.* [L.] fat; animal oil; the contents of the cells of the adipose tissue.

ȧ·dept′, *n.* [L. *adeptus,* pp. of *adipisci,* to arrive at, from *ad,* to, and *apisci,* to pursue.] one fully skilled or well versed in any art; a proficient; a master. The term was originally used of alchemists who claimed to have found the philosopher's stone or the panacea.

ȧ·dept′, *a.* highly skilled; completely versed in or acquainted with.
Syn.—expert, dexterous, skillful, versed in.

ȧ·dep′tion, *n.* [L. *adeptio.*] an obtaining; acquirement. [Obs.]

ȧ·dept′ist, *n.* an adept. [Obs.]

ȧ·dept′ness, *n.* the quality of being adept.

ad′ē·quȧ·cy, *n.* the state or quality of being adequate; a sufficiency for a particular purpose; as, the *adequacy* of supply to demand.

ad′ē·quāte, *a.* [formerly, *adæquate,* from L. *adæquatus,* pp.; from *ad,* to, and *æquare,* to make equal.]
1. equal to a requirement or occasion; sufficient; suitable; as, we have no *adequate* tools.
2. barely satisfactory; acceptable but not remarkable.

ad′ē·quāte·ly, *adv.* in an adequate manner.

ad′ē·quāte·ness, *n.* the state of being adequate; sufficiency.

ad·ē·quā′tion, *n.* the act of making equal; the resulting equivalence; an equivalent.

ȧ·des′my, *n.* [Gr. *a* priv., and *desmos,* fetter.] in botany, the separation of an organ that is usually entire, or of parts that are usually united.

Ad·es″sē·nā′ri·ăns, *n.pl.* [L. *adesse,* to be present.] in church history, a sect which held the real presence of Christ's body in the Eucharist, but not by transubstantiation.

Ad·es′te Fi·de′lis (-dā′lis), [L.] a Latin hymn beginning *Adeste fidelis* (O Come All Ye Faithful).

à deux (à doo), [Fr.] for two; of two; hence, intimate or intimately.

ad ex·trē′mum, [L., at the extreme.] at last; finally.

ad·feçt′ed, *a.* see *affected* (sense 4).

ad·fil′i·āte, *v.t.* and *v.i.* to affiliate. [Obs.]

ad·fil·i·ā′tion, *n.* affiliation. [Obs.]

ad fī′nem, [L.] to the end; at the end.

ad·flux′ion (-fluk′shun), *n.* see *affluxion.*

ad·hā′mănt, *a.* [L. *adhamare,* to catch; from *ad,* to, and *hamus,* hook.] holding tightly, as by hooks.

ad·hēre′, *v.i.*; adhered, *pt., pp.*; adhering, *ppr.* [L. *adhærere*; *ad,* to, and *hærere,* to stick.]
1. to stick fast, as glutinous substances; to become joined by natural growth; to cleave; as, the lungs sometimes *adhere* to the pleura; a stamp *adheres* to an envelope.
2. to hold to, be attached, or remain fixed, either by personal union or conformity of faith, principle, or opinion; as, men *adhere* to a party, a leader, a cause, etc.
3. to be consistent; to hold together as the parts of a system. [Obs.]
Syn.—attach, cling, stick, cleave, fasten, unite, join.

ad·hēr′ence, *n.* 1. the quality or state of sticking or adhering; the state of being adherent.
2. a being fixed in attachment; devotion and support; steady attachment; as, an *adherence* to a party or opinions.

ad·hēr′en·cy, *n.* adherence. [Rare.]

ad·hēr′ent, *a.* 1. sticking; uniting, as glue or wax.
2. in botany, attached: used of parts that are normally separate; as, an *adherent* ovary, an ovary attached or united by its whole surface to the tube of the calyx.
3. attached as a circumstance; accidentally connected with; not belonging to the nature of a thing; not inherent in.

ad·hēr′ent, *n.* a person who adheres; one who follows a leader, party, etc.; a follower, or partisan; a believer in a particular faith or cause.
Syn.—follower, partisan, supporter, friend, aid, ally, companion, backer.

ad·hēr′ent·ly, *adv.* in an adherent manner.

ad·hēr′ẽr, *n.* one who adheres; an adherent.

ad·hē′şion, *n.* [Fr. *adhesion*; L. *adhæsio,* from *ad,* to, and *hærere,* to stick.]
1. the act or state of sticking, or being united and attached to; as, the *adhesion* of glue, or of parts united by growth, cement, and the like.
2. adherence; union; steady attachment; firmness in opinion; as, *adhesion* to vice; *adhesion* to party or principles.
3. in physics, the force that holds together the unlike molecules of substances whose surfaces are in contact: distinguished from *cohesion.*
4. in medicine, (a) the growing together of normally separate tissues; (b) [*pl.*] the bands of fibrous tissue by which such tissues are connected.
5. in botany, the union of parts or organs normally separate.
6. agreement to adhere in loyal union; assent; concurrence.

ad·hē′sive, *a.* sticky; tenacious, as glutinous substances; apt or tending to adhere.
adhesive inflammation; in medicine, that kind of inflammation which causes union by adhesion without suppuration.
adhesive slate; a variety of slaty clay, adhering strongly to the tongue, and rapidly absorbing water.
adhesive tape (or *plaster*); tape with a sticky substance on one side, variously used, as for holding bandages in place.

ad·hē′sive, *n.* an adhesive substance.

ad·hē′sive·ly, *adv.* in an adhesive manner.

ad·hē′sive·ness, *n.* 1. the quality of sticking or adhering; stickiness; tenacity.
2. in phrenology, the tendency to make and maintain attachment to persons, to promote lasting friendships or social intercourse, etc.

ad·hib′it, *v.t.* [L. *adhibere*; *ad,* to, and *habere,* to have.] to use or apply; to affix or fasten, as a label. [Rare.]

ad·hi·bi′tion (-bish′un), *n.* application; use.

ad hoç, [L., to this.] for this specific purpose; for this case only.

ad hom′i·nem, [L., to the man.]
1. appealing to one's prejudices, selfish interests, etc. rather than to reason.
2. attacking one's opponent rather than dealing with the subject under discussion.

ad·hort′, *v.t.* to exhort. [Obs.]

ad·hor·tā′tion, *n.* [L. *adhortatio,* advice.] advice. [Obs.]

ad·hor′tȧ·tō·ry, *a.* [L. *adhortari,* to advise.] advisory; containing counsel or warning. [Obs.]

ad″i·ȧ·bat′iç, *a.* [Gr. *adiabatos,* not able to go through, from *a* priv., *dia,* through, and *bainein,* to go.] of or denoting change in volume or pressure without loss or gain of heat.

ad″i·ȧ·bat′iç·ăl·ly, *adv.* in an adiabatic manner.

ad″i·aç·tin′iç, *a.* [Gr. *a* priv., *dia,* through, and *aktis,* a ray.] impervious to the actinic rays of light.

Ad·i·an′tum, *n.* a large genus of ferns, including the common maidenhair fern.

ad″i·aph″ō·rē′sis, *n.* lack of perspiration.

ad·i·aph′ō·rişm, *n.* theological indifference.

Ad·i·aph′ō·rist, *n.* [Gr. *adiaphoros,* from *a* priv., *dia,* through, and *pherein,* to bear.] a moderate or indifferent person; specifically, a name given in the sixteenth century to certain followers of Melanchthon, who held some opinions and ceremonies to be indifferent which Luther condemned as sinful or heretical.

ad″i·aph″ō·ris′tiç, *a.* pertaining to adiaphorism.

Ad·i·aph′ō·rīte, *n.* same as *Adiaphorist.*

ad·i·aph′ō·ron, *n.pl.* **ad·i·aph′ō·rȧ.** an indifferent moral or religious principle.

ad·i·aph′ō·rous, *a.* 1. indifferent; neutral.
2. in medicine, neither harmful nor helpful.

ad″i·ȧ·thẽr′măn·cy, *n.* [Gr. *a* priv., *dia,* through, and *thermē,* heat.] imperviousness to heat waves.

ad″i·ȧ·thẽr′miç, *a.* impervious to heat waves.

ad″i·ȧ·thet′iç, *a.* [Gr. *a* priv., *diathesis,* from *diatithenai,* to place separately.] not chargeable or due to diathesis, or constitutional predisposition to certain diseases.

A·dic′ē·ȧ, *n.* a genus of plants, of the nettle family, but without nettles: also called *Pilea.*

ȧ·dieū′, *interj.* [OE. *adew*; OFr. *à Dieu*; L. *ad,*

to, and *Deum*, acc. of *Deus*, God.] farewell: an expression of kind wishes at the parting of friends.

à·dieū′, *n.*; *pl.* **à·dieūs′** *or* **à·dieūx′** (-dūz′). a farewell; good-by.

Syn.—good-by, farewell, valediction, valedictory.

à·dīght′ (-dīt′), *v.t.* to put in order; to dress; to equip. [Obs.]

ad in·fi·nī′tum, [L., to infinity.] without end or limit.

ad i·nĭ′ti·um (i-nish′i-um), [L.] at the beginning.

ad in′te·rim, [L.] 1. in the meantime.

2. temporary.

ä·dī·ōs′, *interj.* [Sp.] adieu; farewell; good-by.

ad·i·pes′cent, *a.* [L. *adeps* (*adip*), fat, and *-escent*.] growing fatty.

à·dip′iç, *a.* [L. *adeps*, fat.] pertaining to or derived from fat; as, *adipic* acid.

ad·i·poc′ẽr·āte, *v.t.*; adipocerated, *pt.*, *pp.*; adipocerating, *ppr.* to convert into adipocere.

ad″i·poc″ẽr·ā′tion (-ā′shun), *n.* the act or process of being changed into adipocere.

ad′i·pō·cēre″, *n.* [Fr. *adipocire*; L. *adeps* (*adip*), fat, and *cera*, wax.] a fatty or waxy substance of a light brown color into which the muscular fibers of dead animal bodies are converted by long exposure to moisture.

ad″i·pō·cēr′i·form, *a.* resembling adipocere.

ad·i·poc′ẽr·ous, *a.* pertaining to or of the nature of adipocere.

ad·i·poġ′e·nous, *a.* [L. *adeps*, *adipis*, fat, and *genous*, producing.] capable of producing fat.

ad″i·pō·lyt′iç, *a.* [L. *adeps*, fat, and Gr. *lytikos*, able to loose, from *lyein*, to loose.] effecting the digestion of fats.

ad·i·pō′mȧ, *n.* a fatty tumor; lipoma. [Obs.]

ad·i·pom′a·tous, *a.* composed mostly of fatty tissue, as a tumor. [Obs.]

ad′i·pōse, *a.* [L. *adiposus*, fatty, from *adeps*, fat.] fatty; consisting of, or resembling, fat.

adipose fin; in zoology, a soft, fatty dorsal fin.

adipose tissue; an aggregation of minute cells (*adipose cells* or *vesicles*), which draw fat or oily matter from the blood, dispersed in the interstices of common areolar tissue, or forming distinct masses. *Adipose tissue* underlies the skin, surrounds the large vessels and nerves, invests the kidneys, etc.

ad′i·pōse, *n.* fat in general; specifically, the fat on the kidneys.

ad′i·pōse·ness, *n.* adiposity.

ad·i·pos′i·ty, *n.* 1. the state of being adipose; obesity.

2. a tendency to become obese.

ad′i·pous, *a.* fat; of the nature of fat; adipose.

à·dip′si·ȧ, ad′ip·sy, *n.* [Gr. *a* priv., and *dipsa*, thirst.] a total absence of thirst.

à·dip′sous, *a.* thirst-quenching, as certain fruits.

Ad·i·ron′daçks, *n.pl.* one of the groups of the Appalachian mountain system in New York State: the name is from a Mohawk word and means "they eat bark."

ad′it, *n.* [L. *aditus*, pp. of *adire*, to approach; *ad*, and *ire*, to go.] an entrance or passage; specifically, in mining, the more or less horizontal opening giving access to the shaft of a mine, or by which water and ores can be carried away: also called *tunnel*.

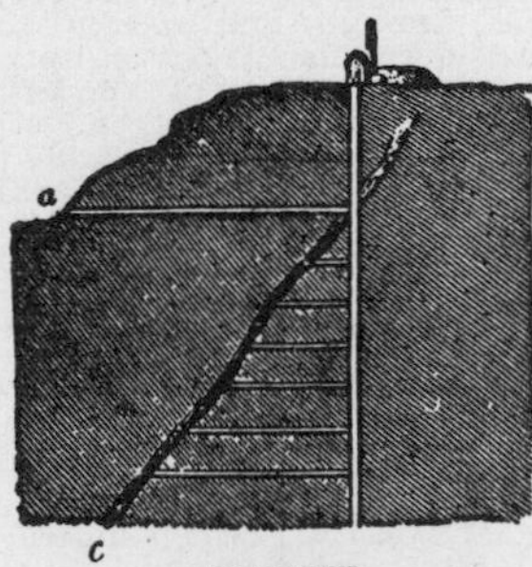

ADIT OF MINE
a. adit *c.* vein

ad·jā′cence, *n.* the quality or state of being adjacent; adjacency.

ad·jā′cen·cy, *n.* 1. the quality or state of being adjacent; nearness.

2. *pl.* **ad·jā′cen·cies**, an adjacent thing.

ad·jā′cent, *a.* [L. *adjacens*, ppr. of *adjacere*, to lie near.] lying near or close (*to* something); bordering upon.

Syn.—adjoining, approximating, contiguous, bordering, close to, near to, abutting.

ad·jā′cent, *n.* That which is next to or contiguous. [Obs.]

ad·jā′cent an′gles, two angles having the same vertex and a line in common.

ad·jā′cent·ly, *adv.* so as to be adjacent.

ad·jeçt′, *v.t.* [L. *adjectus*, pp. of *adjicere*, to throw to; *ad*, to, and *jacere*, to throw.] to add or join, as one thing to another. [Rare.]

ad·jeç′tion, *n.* the act of adding, or thing added. [Rare.]

ad·jeç·ti′tious (-tish′us), *a.* added. [Rare.]

ad·jeç·tī′văl (*or* ad′jec-tiv-al), *a* 1. pertaining to an adjective.

2. having the nature or function of an adjective.

3. added to an adjective base; as, an *adjectival* suffix.

ad·jeç·tī′văl·ly, *adv.* as an adjective.

ad′jeç·tive, *n.* [L. *adjectivus*, a grammatical term, from *adjectus*, pp. of *adjicere*, to add to.]

1. in grammar, a word used with a noun to express a quality of the thing named, or something attributed to it, or to limit or define it, or to specify or describe a thing as distinct from something else. It is called also an *attributive* or *attribute*. Thus, in the phrase a *wise* ruler, *wise* is the *adjective*, or attribute, expressing a particular quality of ruler.

2. any phrase or clause similarly used.

ad′jeç·tive, *a.* pertaining to an adjective; as, the *adjective* use of a noun.

2. having the nature or function of an adjective.

3. dependent or subordinate.

adjective color; a color which requires fixation by some mordant or base to make it permanent.

ad′jeç·tive, *v.t.*; adjectived, *pt.*, *pp.*; adjectiving, *ppr.* to make an adjective of (a word). [Rare.]

ad′jeç·tive·ly, *adv.* adjectivally. [Rare.]

ad′jeç·tiv·īz′ẽr, *n.* [*adjective*, and *-ize*, and *-er*.] in linguistics, a suffix that forms adjectives from other parts of speech.

ad·join′, *v.t.*; adjoined, *pt.*, *pp.*; adjoining, *ppr.* [ME. *adjoinen*; Fr. *ajoindre*; L. *adjungere*; *ad*, to, and *jungere*, to join.]

1. to join or add; to put in addition; to unite, annex, or append.

2. to lie or be next to, or in contact with; to be contiguous to; as, my house *adjoins* the church.

ad·join′, *v.i.* to lie close together; to be in contact or proximity: formerly used with prepositions, as *to*, *on*, *with*; as, one man's land *adjoins to* another's.

ad·join′ing, *a.* joining to; adjacent.

ad·joint′, *n.* one joined with another in company or an enterprise. [Obs.]

ad·joūrn′ (-jūrn′), *v.t.*; adjourned, *pt.*, *pp.*; adjourning, *ppr.* [ME. *ajournen*; Fr. *ajourner*; L. *adjurnare*, to fix a day, from *ad*, to, and *diurnus*, belonging to a day.] to put off, or defer, to another day; suspend; as, the court *adjourned* the consideration of the question.

Syn.—suspend, defer, postpone, put off.

ad·joūrn′, *v.i.* 1. to suspend business for a time, as from one day to another or for a longer period.

2. to go away from a place (*to* another place); as, let's *adjourn* to the veranda [Colloq.]

ad·joūrn′ăl, *n.* adjournment. [Rare.]

ad·joūrn′ment, *n.* 1. the act of adjourning, as in legislatures.

2. the putting off till another specified day or time; as, the *adjournment* of a debate.

3. the time or interval during which a public body defers business.

ad·judġe′, *v.t.*; adjudged, *pt.*, *pp.*; adjudging, *ppr.* [ME. *adjugen*; Fr. *adjuger*; L. *adjudicare*; *ad*, to, and *judicare*, to judge, decide.]

1. to decide or determine by law.

2. to decree or declare by law.

3. to pass sentence on; to sentence or condemn (with *to*); as, the criminal was *adjudged* to jail.

4. to give or award by law, as costs, etc.

5. to deem; to regard; as, he *adjudged* him unworthy of his friendship. [Rare.]

Syn.—decree, award, assign, decide, determine, settle, adjudicate.

ad·judġ′ẽr, *n.* one who adjudges.

ad·judġ′ment, *n.* the act of judging; sentence.

ad·jū′di·çāte, *v.t.*; adjudicated, *pt.*, *pp.*; adjudicating, *ppr.* [L. *adjudicatus*, pp. of *adjudicare*; *ad*, to, and *judicare*, to judge.] in law, to adjudge; to hear and decide (a case).

ad·jū′di·çāte, *v.i.* to hear and decide judicially; give judgment (*in* or *on* a matter, dispute, etc.).

ad·jū·di·çā′tion, *n.* 1. the act of adjudicating; the act or process of hearing and deciding judicially; as, a ship was taken and sent into port for *adjudication*.

2. a judicial sentence; judgment or decision of a court.

3. specifically, in law, the act of a court declaring a person bankrupt.

4. in Scots law, an action by which a creditor attaches the estate of his debtor, in payment or security of his debt.

ad·jū′di·çā·tive, *a.* adjudicating.

ad·jū′di·çā·tŏr, *n.* a person who adjudicates; judge.

ad·jū′di·çā·tūre″, *n.* an adjudication.

ad′jū·gāte, *v.t.*; adjugated, *pt.*, *pp.*; adjugating, *ppr.* to yoke to. [Obs.]

ad′junçt, *n.* [L. *adjunctus*, pp. of *adjungere*; *ad*, to, and *jungere*, to join.]

1. something added to another thing, but not essentially a part of it; as, water absorbed by a sponge is its *adjunct*.

2. in logic, a nonessential attribute, as the color of the body.

3. in grammar, a modifying word or phrase; as, the history *of the American Revolution*: the words in italics are the *adjuncts* of *history*.

4. an associate or assistant in work or duty to be done.

5. in music, a relative scale or key; an attendant key.

Syn.—appurtenance, attribute, addition, complement, help.

ad′junçt, *a.* added to or united with; attending.

ad·junç′tion, *n.* 1. the act of joining.

2. the thing joined.

ad·junç′tive, *a.* joining; having the character of an adjunct.

ad·junç′tive, *n.* that which is joined.

ad·junç′tive·ly, *adv.* in an adjunctive manner.

ad·junçt′ly, *adv.* in connection with; consequently.

ad·jū·rā′tion, *n.* the act of adjuring; specifically, (a) a solemn charging on oath, or under penalty of a curse; (b) an earnest entreaty.

ad·jū′rȧ·tō·ry, *a.* containing an adjuration.

ad·jūre′, *v.t.*; adjured, *pt.*, *pp.*; adjuring, *ppr.* [ME. *adjuren*; L. *adjurare*; *ad*, to, and *jurare*, to swear.]

1. to charge, bind, or command on oath, or under the penalty of a curse; as, Joshua *adjured* the children of Israel.

2. to entreat earnestly and solemnly; to charge, urge, or summon impressively; as, the mayor *adjured* the people to keep the peace.

I *adjure* thee by the living God.
—Matt. xxvi.

ad·jūr′ẽr, ad·jūr′ŏr, *n.* one who adjures.

ad·just′, *v.t.*; adjusted, *pt.*, *pp.*; adjusting, *ppr.* [Fr. *adjuster*, to join fitly or dispose in an orderly manner; L. *adjuxtare*, to put side by side; *ad*, and *juxta*, near. Influenced by L. *adjustus*.]

1. to make exact; to fit; to make correspondent or conformable: generally with *to*; as, to *adjust* a garment *to* the body, or things *to* a standard.

2. to put in order; to regulate or reduce to system.

3. to make accurate, as a watch.

4. to settle or bring to a satisfactory state.

5. to decide how much is to be paid in settling (an insurance claim).

6. in military usage, to correct (the gun sight, one's aim, etc.) in firing.

Syn.—accommodate, adapt, settle, conform, regulate, classify, arrange, fit, suit.

ad·just′, *v.i.* to come into conformity; become suited or fit.

ad·just′ȧ·ble, *a.* that can be adjusted.

ad·just′ȧ·bly, *adv.* so as to be adjustable.

ad·just′ẽr, ad·just′ŏr, *n.* one who or that which adjusts; specifically, (a) one whose business it is to adjust differences, grievances, or claims; as, an insurance *adjuster*; (b) a thing or device that adjusts something, as in a machine.

ad·just′ive, *a.* tending to adjust.

ad·just′ment, *n.* 1. the act of adjusting; regulation; a reducing to just form or order; a making fit or conformable; settlement.

2. the arrangement of the different parts of an instrument into their proper places; as, the microscope is out of *adjustment*.

3. a means or device by which parts are adjusted to one another; as, the *adjustment* on a micrometer.

4. a lowering of price, as of damaged or soiled goods.
5. in insurance, the settling of the amount of indemnity which the party insured is entitled to receive under the policy, and, in marine insurance, the fixing of the proportion of that indemnity which each underwriter is liable to bear.
Syn.—arrangement, regulation, settlement, adaptation, disposal, disposition.

ad′jū·tāge, *n.* the tube out of which water flows in a fountain.

ad′jū·tăn·cy, *n.* 1. the office or rank of an adjutart.
2. skillful arrangement. [Rare.]

ad′jū·tănt, *n.* [L. *adjutans*, ppr. of *adjutare*, freq. of *adjuvare*, to help, assist.]
1. in military affairs, an officer whose duty is to assist the commanding officer of a regiment or garrison by receiving and communicating orders, handling correspondence and records, etc.
2. a helper; an assistant; an aid.
A fine violin must be the best *adjutant* to a fine voice. —W. Mason.
3. the adjutant bird.

ADJUTANT BIRD

ad′jū·tănt bīrd, [so called because of its stiff figure in walking.] a very large grallatorial bird, *Ciconia argala*, allied to the storks and a native of the warmer parts of India. Called also the *adjutant crane* or *adjutant stork*.

ad′jū·tănt ġen′ēr·ăl; *pl.* **ad′jū·tănts ġen′ēr·ăl, ad′jū·tănt ġen′ēr·ăls.** 1. in military affairs, a staff officer, the chief aid to a commanding general of a corps or higher echelon.
2. an officer in charge of the militia of a State or Territory of the United States.
3. [A- G-] in the United States Army, the general in charge of the department that handles all records, circulars, correspondence, etc.

ad·jū′tŏr, *n.* [L., from *adjuvare*, to assist.] a helper. [Obs.]

ad′jū·vănt, *a.* [L., ppr. of *adjuvare*, to assist.] helping; assisting.

ad′jū·vănt, *n.* 1. an assistant.
2. in medicine, a substance added to a drug to aid the operation of the principal ingredient.

ad Kă·len′dăs Grae′çăs, [L.] at the Greek Calends; hence, never: the Greeks did not reckon dates in the Roman way, by calends.

ad·lē·gā′tion, *n.* [L. *adlegatio*, from *adlegare*; *ad*, to, in addition to, and *legare*, to send on an embassy.] in the law of the old German empire, a right claimed by the states of joining their own ministers with those of the emperor in public treaties and negotiations relating to the common interests of the empire.

ad′-lib′, *v.t.* and *v.i.;* ad-libbed, *pt., pp.*; ad-libbing, *ppr.* [from *ad libitum*.] to improvise (words, gestures, etc. not in the script); extemporize. [Colloq.]

ad lib′i·tum, [L., at one's pleasure.]
1. as one desires; at pleasure; as much as one pleases.
2. in music, a direction indicating that the passage may be interpreted as one pleases, or may be omitted. Usually shortened to *ad lib.*

ad lit′tēr·ăm, [L., lit., to the letter.] literally; exactly.

ad lō′çum, [L.] at or to the place.

ad·lō·çū′tion, *n.* same as *allocution*.

ad·mär′ġin·āte, *v.t.* [L. *ad*, to, and *margo*, margin, and *-ate*.] to make marginal notes on. [Rare.]

ad·max′il·lā·ry, *a.* connected with the maxilla.

ad·mea′şūre (ad-mezh′ūr), *v.t.* [ME. *amesuren*; OFr. *admesurer*; L. *admensurare*, from *ad*, to, and *metiri*, to measure.]
1. to measure or ascertain dimensions, size, or capacity; to measure.
2. to apportion; to assign to each claimant his right; as, to *admeasure* dower or common of pasture.

ad·meaş′ūre·ment, *n.* 1. the measuring of dimensions, as of a ship, cask, or the like; measurement; mensuration.
2. the measure, or dimensions, of a thing ascertained.
3. the adjustment of proportion, or ascertainment of shares, as of dower or pasture held in common.

ad·meaş′ūr·ēr, *n.* one who admeasures.

ad·men·sū·rā′tion, *n.* [see *mensuration*] admeasurement.

Ad·mē′tus, *n.* [L.; Gr. *Admētos*, lit., wild, unbroken.] in Greek legend, a king of Thessaly whose wife, Alcestis, sacrificed her life for him but was brought back from Hades by Hercules.

ad·min′i·çle, *n.* [L. *adminiculum*, support; originally, a support for the hand; *ad*, to, and *manus*, hand, with dim. ending *-culum*.]
1. help; support; an auxiliary.
2. in law, corroborative or explanatory proof. In Scots law, any writing helpful in establishing the existence or terms of a lost deed.

ad·mi·niç′ū·lăr, *a.* 1. supplying help; helpful.
2. corroborative.

ad·mi·niç′ū·lā·ry, *a.* adminicular.

ad·mi·niç′ū·lāte, *v.t.* in Scots law, to support by corroborative evidence.

ad·min′is·tēr, *v.t.*; administered, *pt., pp.*; administering, *ppr.* [OE. *aministren*; Fr. *administrer*; L. *administrare*; *ad*, to, and *ministrare*, to serve.]
1. to have charge of as chief agent in managing, as public affairs; conduct; direct. A president *administers* the laws when he executes them, or carries them into effect. A judge *administers* the laws when he applies them to particular cases or persons.
2. to dispense; as, to *administer* justice.
3. to give or furnish; as, to *administer* relief, medicine, etc.
4. to give, as an oath.
5. in law, (a) to manage (an estate of one who has died intestate, or without a competent executor); (b) to manage (an estate of a deceased person as an executor).
Syn.—manage, conduct, minister, furnish, supply, dispense, distribute, direct, control, execute, superintend.

ad·min′is·tēr, *v.i.* 1. to act as manager or administrator.
2. to furnish help or be of service (with *to*); as, to *administer* to an invalid's needs.

ad·min·is·tē′ri·ăl, *a.* pertaining to administration, or to executive duties.

ad·min′is·tră·ble, *a.* capable of being administered.

ad·min′is·trănt, *n.* a person who administers.

ad·min′is·trănt, *a.* managing; governing; executive.

ad·min′is·trāte, *v.t.*; administrated, *pt., pp.*; administrating, *ppr.* [L. *administratus*, pp. of *administrare*; *ad*, to, and *ministrare*, to serve.] to administer.

ad·min·is·trā′tion, *n.* 1. the act of administering; direction; management.
2. the management of governmental or institutional affairs.
3. [often A–] the executive officials of a government or institution and their policy.
4. dispensation; distribution; as, the *administration* of justice, of the sacrament, or of grace.
5. the management and settling of the estate of an intestate person, under a commission from the proper authority. Also, the management and settling of a deceased person's estate by an executor under a will or the administering of the estate of a minor, mental incompetent, etc.
6. the power, office, or commission of an administrator.
7. the term or period during which an administrative official or officials hold office; as, the war with Spain occurred during President McKinley's *administration*.
8. the act of prescribing medically.
9. the act of tendering, as an oath.
administration with the will annexed; administration granted in cases where a testator makes a will without naming executors, or where the executors named in the will are incapable of acting or refuse to act.
letters of administration; the commission from a probate court or other proper authority, under which an administrator proceeds.

ad·min′is·trā·tive, *a.* pertaining to administration; executive; as, *administrative* ability.

ad·min′is·trā·tive·ly, *adv.* in an administrative manner.

ad·min′is·trā″tŏr, *n.* 1. one who, by virtue of a commission from a surrogate, probate court, or other proper authority, has charge of the settling of a deceased person's estate where there is no executor.
2. one who administers, or who executes, directs, manages, distributes, or dispenses, as in civil, political, judicial, or ecclesiastical affairs.

ad·min′is·trā·tŏr·ship, *n.* the office of an administrator.

ad·min″is·trā′tress, *n.* a woman administrator.

ad·min″is·trā′trix, *n.* a woman administrator.

ad″mi·ră·bil′i·ty, *n.* admirableness. [Rare.]

ad′mi·ră·ble, *a.* [L. *admirabilis*, from *admirari*; *ad*, to, at, and *mirari*, to wonder.]
1. worthy of admiration; having qualities to excite wonder, with approbation, esteem, reverence, or affection; excellent: used of persons or things; as, an *admirable* work of art, an *admirable* teacher.
What a piece of work is a man! How noble in reason! How infinite in faculty! In form and moving, how express and *admirable*! —Shak.
2. causing wonder; strange; amazing. [Obs.]
Syn.—wonderful, excellent, pleasing, worthy, choice.

ad′mi·ră·bly, *adv.* in an admirable manner.

ad′mi·răl, *n.* [ME. *admiral*, *admiralle*; OFr. *admiral*; from Ar. *amir al*, ruler of; sp. influenced by *admirable*.]
1. a naval commander in chief; the commander of a navy or of a fleet.
2. a naval officer of the highest rank or of a specified high rank. In the United States Navy, there are four grades of admiral, in order of rank, Admiral of the Fleet, full admiral, vice-admiral, and rear-admiral.
3. the ship which carries the admiral; the flagship; also, the principal ship of a fleet of merchantmen, of yachts, or of fishing vessels.
4. a name given to two species of butterflies: *Vanessa atalanta*, or red admiral, and *Limenitis camilla*, or white admiral.
Admiral of the Fleet, the highest rank in the United States Navy, having the insigne of five stars.
Lord High Admiral; in Great Britain, formerly, an officer at the head of the naval administration.

ad′mi·răl·ship, *n.* 1. the office of an admiral.
2. the seamanship or naval skill of an admiral.

ad′mi·răl·ty, *n.* 1. the office, functions, or jurisdiction of an admiral.
2. the branch of jurisprudence which deals with maritime cases; as, a suit in *admiralty*.
3. [often A–] the governmental department or officials in charge of naval affairs, as in England.
4. [A–] the building in London in which British naval affairs are administered.
admiralty court, or *court of admiralty*; a court for the trial of cases arising on the high seas, as suits for damage by collision, and the like. In the United States, there is no admiralty court distinct from others, but the Federal district courts are invested with admiralty powers.

ad·mi·rā′tion, *n.* [L. *admiratio*, from *admirari*, to admire.]
1. an admiring; wonder mingled with approbation, esteem, love, or delight, excited by something fine, skillful, beautiful, etc.
2. wonder or a wondering. [Archaic.]
Your boldness I with *admiration* see. —Dryden.
3. high esteem.
4. that which is admired; as, the picture is the *admiration* of all beholders.
note of admiration; the exclamation point(!).
Syn.—wonder, approval, adoration, reverence, appreciation.

ad·mī′rā·tive, *a.* pertaining to or expressing admiration. [Rare.]

ad·mīre′, *v.t.*; admired, *pt., pp.*; admiring, *ppr.* [L. *admirari*; *ad*, at, and *mirari*, to wonder; Fr. *admirer*; It. *ammirare*.]
1. to regard with wonder, delight, and pleased approval; to feel admiration for; to look on or contemplate with pleasure; as, to *admire* virtue; to *admire* a landscape or a statue; to *admire* a woman.

2. to have a high regard for.
3. to wonder at; to regard with wonder. [Archaic.]
Syn.—approve, commend, applaud, esteem, adore, respect, revere, love, praise.

ad·mīre′, *v.i.* 1. to be surprised; to marvel; to wonder; often followed with *at*; as, he *admired at* his own contrivance. [Archaic.]
2. to feel pleasure; as, I should *admire* to go with you. [Dial.]
3. to feel admiration.

ad·mīred′, *a.* regarded with admiration; as, a greatly *admired* novel.

ad·mīr′ẽr, *n.* 1. one who admires.
2. a man who admires, or is in love with, a woman; a suitor.

ad·mīr′ing·ly, *adv.* with admiration; in the manner of an admirer.

ad·mis·si·bil′i·ty, *n.* the quality or state of being admissible.

ad·mis′si·ble, *a.* that may be admitted, allowed, accepted, or conceded; as, the testimony is *admissible.*

ad·mis′si·ble·ness, *n.* admissibility.

ad·mis′si·bly, *adv.* so as to be admitted; in an admissible manner.

ad·mis′sion, *n.* [ME. *admyssion*; L. *admissio(n)*, from *admissus*, pp. of admittere, to admit.]
1. the act or practice of admitting, or allowing to enter; as, the *admission* of aliens into our country; also, the state or fact of being admitted.
2. power or permission to enter; right of entry; entrance; access; as, the free *admission* of air.
3. the granting of an argument or position not fully proved; a conceding.
4. confession; acknowledgment; as, an *admission* of guilt.
5. a fact, assertion, etc. that is conceded, acknowledged, or confessed.
6. a fee or price charged for entrance; as, the *admission* is fifty cents.
7. in law, an essential fact or matter, the necessity of proving which is removed by the opposite party admitting it. *Admissions* are either upon the record or by agreement between the parties to a suit.
Admission Day, any of several legal holidays celebrated individually by certain States commemorating their admission into the Union.
Syn.—access, admittance, entrance, confession, acknowledgment.

ad·mis′sive, *a.* admitting or tending to admit.

ad·mis′sō·ry, *a.* pertaining to admission.

ad·mit′, *v.t.*; admitted, *pt.*, *pp.*; admitting, *ppr.* [ME. *admitten*; L. *admittere*; *ad*, to, and *mittere*, to send.]
1. to permit to enter or use; let in; as, to *admit* a student into college.
2. to give right of entrance; as, a ticket *admits* one to a theater.
3. to permit, allow, or be capable of; as, the words do not *admit* of such a construction. In this sense, *of* may be used after the verb, or omitted.
4. to have room for; hold; as, the hall *admits* 2,500 people.
5. to concede; grant; as, she *admitted* he might be right.
6. to acknowledge; confess; as, to *admit* one's culpability.
7. to permit to practice certain functions; as, he was *admitted* to the bar.
Syn.—acknowledge, allow, assent, grant, concede, own.

ad·mit′, *v.i.* 1. to give entrance to a place.
2. to allow or warrant (with *of*).

ad·mit′tȧ·ble, *a.* that may be admitted or allowed.

ad·mit′tănce, *n.* 1. the act of admitting.
2. permission to enter; the power or right of entrance; hence, actual entrance; as, he gained *admittance* into the church.
3. concession; admission; allowance; as, the *admittance* of an argument. [Obs.]
4. the state of being personally acceptable. [Obs.]
Sir John, you are a gentleman of excellent breeding, of great *admittance.* —Shak.
5. in electricity, the current divided by the voltage; the reciprocal of impedance.

ad·mit·tā′tũr, *n.* [L., let him be admitted.] a certificate of admission in some colleges.

ad·mit′ted, *a.* allowed; granted; conceded.

ad·mit′ted·ly, *adv.* by admission or general agreement; confessedly.

ad·mit′tẽr, *n.* one who or that which admits.

ad·mix′, *v.t.* to mingle with something else; mix (a thing) in.

ad·mix′tion (-chun), *n.* [L. *admixtio*, from *admiscere*; *ad*, to, and *miscere*, to mix.] a mingling of bodies; a union by mixing different substances together.

ad·mix′tūre, *n.* [see *mixture.*] 1. the act of mixing.
2. that which is formed by mixing; a compound of substances mixed together.
3. a thing or ingredient added in mixing.

ad·mon′ish, *v.t.*; admonished, *pt.*, *pp.*; admonishing, *ppr.* [ME. *admonyshen*; OFr. *admonester*, advise; ML. *admonitare*, freq. of L. *admonere*; *ad*, to, and *monere*, to warn, advise.]
1. to warn; caution against specific faults.
2. to reprove with mildness.
3. to advise; exhort.
4. to inform or remind by way of a warning.
Syn.—caution, rebuke, counsel, censure, advise, reprove, forewarn, warn.

ad·mon′ish·ẽr, *n.* one who reproves or counsels.

ad·mon′ish·ment, *n.* admonition.

ad·mō·ni′tion (-nish′un), *n.* [OE. *amonicioun*; Fr. *admonition*; L. *admonitio*, from *admonere*, to warn, advise.]
1. an admonishing.
2. a mild rebuke; reprimand.
Syn.—warning, caution, rebuke, reproof, advice, counsel, censure.

ad·mon′i·tive, *a.* containing admonition. [Rare.]

ad·mon′i·tive·ly, *adv.* by admonition.

ad·mon′i·tŏr, *n.* [L.] an admonisher.

ad·mon·i·tō′ri·ăl, *a.* admonitory. [Rare.]

ad·mon′i·tō·ri·ly, *adv.* in an admonitory manner.

ad·mon′i·tō·ry, *a.* containing admonition; admonishing.

ad·mon′i·trix, *n.*; *pl.* **ad·mon·i·trī′cēṣ**, [L.] a woman admonitor. [Rare.]

ad·mọr·ti·zā′tion, *n.* same as *amortization.*

ad·nas′cent, *a.* [L. *adnascen(t)s*, *ppr.* of *adnasci*; *ad*, to, and *nasci*, to be born, to grow.] growing on something else.

ad′nāte, *a.* [L. *adnatus*, pp. of *adnasci*, to be born, to grow to.] in botany and zoology, congenitally joined together: said of unlike parts. Thus *adnate* anthers are such as are united to their filaments throughout their whole length, as in the ranunculus. *Adnate* stipules are such as grow to the petiole or leaf stalk, as in the rose.

1. ADNATE ANTHER
2. ADNATE STIPULE

ad·nā′tion, *n.* the condition of being adnate.

ad nạu′se·am (-shi-am), [L., to nausea.] to the point of disgust; to a sickening extreme.

ad·nẽr′văl, *a.* [L. *ad*, to, and *nervus*, nerve.] moving toward the nerve: applied to an electrical current passing along a muscle fiber.

ad·nex′ȧ, *n.pl.* in anatomy, parts that are conjoined; appendages.

ad·nom′i·năl, *a.* of, or having the nature of, an adnoun.

ad·nom′i·năl·ly, *adv.* as an adnoun.

ad′noun, *n.* [*ad-* and *noun.*] in grammar, an adjective; especially, an adjective used as a noun; as, "the lame, the halt, and the blind" are *adnouns.*

ad·nū′bi·lā·ted, *a.* [L. *adnubilatus*, pp. of *adnubilare*; *ad*, to, and *nubilare*, to cloud.] clouded; obscure. [Obs.]

ȧ·dō′, *n.* [OE. *ado*, *at do*, to do.] bustle; trouble; fuss; as, to make a great *ado* about nothing; to persuade one with much *ado.*

ȧ·dō′bē, *n.* [Sp. *adobe*, dried brick.]
1. the sun-dried brick used in Mexico, Arizona, California, and elsewhere, for building houses.
2. the clay used in making the bricks.
3. a building made of adobe.

ADOBE HOUSES

ȧ·dō′bē, *a.* built of sun-dried bricks; as, an *adobe* house.

ad·ō·les′cence, *n.* [Fr. *adolescence*; L. *adolescentia*, from *adolescen(t)s*, ppr. of *adolescere*, to grow; *ad*, to, and incept. form of *olere*, to grow, from *alere*, to nourish.]
1. the quality of being youthful; adolescency.
2. the period of life between puberty and maturity.

ad·ō·les′cen·cy, *n.* youthfulness.

ad·ō·les′cent, *a.* [L. *adolescen(t)s*, ppr. of *adolescere*; *ad*, to, and *olescere*, to grow.]
1. growing up; developing from childhood to maturity.
2. of or characteristic of adolescence; youthful.

ad·ō·les′cent, *n.* a boy or girl from puberty to adulthood; person in his teens.

Ad·ō·nā′ī, *n.* [Heb., my lord.] God; Lord: used in Hebrew reading as a substitute for the "ineffable name" JHVH (see *Jehovah*).

Ad·ō·nē′ăn, *a.* pertaining to Adonis.

Ȧ·dō′ni·ȧ, *n.pl.*; [L., from Gr. neut. pl. of adj. *Adōnios*, pertaining to *Adōnis.*] a festival celebrated anciently in honor of Adonis, by women who spent two days in alternate lamentation and feasting.

Ȧ·don′iç, *n.* a verse, consisting of a dactyl and a spondee or trochee, as those used in bewailing the death of Adonis.

Ȧ·don′iç, *a.* pertaining to Adonis.

Ȧ·dō′nis (*or* Ȧ·don′is), *n.* 1. in Greek mythology, a young man loved by Aphrodite because he was so handsome: he was killed by a wild boar.
2. any very handsome young man.
3. a genus of plants belonging to the natural order *Ranunculaceæ.* In the pheasant's-eye, *Adonis autumnalis*, the petals are bright scarlet, and are considered as emblematical of the blood of Adonis, from which the plant is fabled to have sprung.

Ȧ·dō′nist, *n.* [Hebrew, Chaldee, and Syriac, *adōn*, Lord, a scriptural title of the Supreme Being.] one who maintains that the word *Adonai* should always be read for the ineffable name Jehovah. [Obs.]

ad′ō·nīze, *v.t.*; adonized, *pt.*, *pp.*; adonizing, *ppr.* to beautify: used of males. [Rare.]

ȧ·dōor′, **ȧ·dōorṣ′**, *adv.* at the door. [Obs.]

ȧ·dopt′, *v.t.*; adopted, *pt.*, *pp.*; adopting, *ppr.* [L. *adoptare*; *ad*, to, and *optare*, to desire, choose.]
1. to take (a child of other parents) as one's own in affection and law.
2. to choose and receive (an adult person) into a relationship, as a friend, heir, or citizen.
3. to take or receive as one's own (that which is not so naturally); as, to *adopt* the opinions of another.
4. to select and take; as, to *adopt* a style.
5. to choose and follow (a course).
6. to vote to accept (a committee report, motion, etc.).
Syn.—affiliate, embrace, choose, select, elect, assume, appropriate, arrogate.

ȧ·dopt′ȧ·ble, *a.* capable of being adopted; suitable for adoption, or selection.

ȧ·dopt′ed, *a.* taken by adoption; as, an *adopted* child, an *adopted* style.

ȧ·dopt′ed·ly, *adv.* in the manner of something adopted.

ȧ·dopt′ẽr, *n.* 1. one who adopts.
2. in chemistry, an adapter.

ȧ·dop′tion, *n.* [L. *adoptio*, from *adoptare*, to adopt.] the act of adopting or the state of being adopted; specifically, (a) the taking and treating of the child of another as one's own; (b) the taking into fellowship or a close relationship; as, the *adoption* of a person into a society; (c) the receiving as one's own of what is new or not natural to one; acceptance.

Ȧ·dop′tion·ist, *n.* in ecclesiastical history, one who maintained that Jesus was the son of God by adoption only.

ȧ·dop′tious, *a.* adoptive. [Obs.]

ȧ·dopt′ive, *a.* [L. *adoptivus*, from *adoptare*, to adopt.]
1. that adopts; as, an *adoptive* father.
2. that is adopted; as, an *adoptive* son.

ȧ·dopt′ive·ly, *adv.* by adoption.

ȧ·dōr·ȧ·bil′i·ty, *n.* adorableness.

ȧ·dōr′ȧ·ble, *a.* [Fr. *adorable*; L. *adorabilis*, from *adorare*, to adore.]
1. worthy of being adored, or worshiped; worthy of divine honors.
2. worthy of the utmost love or respect.
3. delightful; charming. [Colloq.]

ȧ·dōr′ȧ·ble·ness, *n.* the quality or state of being adorable.

à·dōr′à·bly, *adv.* in a manner worthy of adoration.

ad·ō′răl, *a.* [L. *ad,* to, and *oral,* from *os, oris,* mouth.] in anatomy and zoology, near the mouth.

ad·ō·rā′tion, *n.* [Fr. *adoration,* L. *adoratio,* from *adorare,* to worship.]
1. the act of paying honors, as to a divine being; the worship paid to God. *Adoration* consists in external homage, accompanied by the highest reverence.
2. homage paid to one in high esteem; profound reverence; great love and respect.
3. a mode by which the cardinals in conclave sometimes elect the pope.
4. in art, a pictorial representation of the *adoration* of the infant Jesus by the magi and the shepherds.

à·dōre′, *v.t.;* adored, *pt., pp.;* adoring, *ppr.* [ME. *adouren;* OFr. *adoren,* from L. *adorare,* to worship; *ad,* to, and *orare,* to speak, from *os, oris,* mouth.]
1. to worship with profound reverence; to pay divine honors to; to honor as a god, or as divine.
2. to love greatly; to regard with the utmost esteem, affection, and respect; idolize.
3. to like very much. [Colloq.]

à·dōre′ment, *n.* adoration. [Obs.]

à·dōr′ẽr, *n.* 1. one who worships, or honors as divine.
2. an admiring lover.

à·dōr′ing·ly, *adv.* with adoration.

à·dorn′, *v.t.;* adorned, *pt., pp.;* adorning, *ppr.* [OE. *adornen;* Fr. *adorner,* from L. *adornare; ad,* to, and *ornare,* to deck out.]
1. to deck or decorate; to add to the beauty of, by dress; to deck with external ornaments; as, a bride *adorns* herself for the altar.
2. to set off to advantage; to add beauty, splendor, honor, or distinction to; to embellish by anything external or adventitious; as, to *adorn* sentiments with elegance of language.

Syn.—deck, decorate, embellish, ornament, bedeck, garnish, beautify, grace, exalt, honor.

ad·or·nā′tion, *n.* adornment. [Obs.]

à·dorn′ẽr, *n.* one who adorns.

à·dorn′ing, *n.* ornament; decoration.

à·dorn′ing·ly, *adv.* by way of adorning.

à·dorn′ment, *n.* 1. an adorning or being adorned.
2. an ornament or decoration.

ad·os·çū·lā′tion, *n.* [L. *adosculatio,* from *adosculari,* to kiss.]
1. in botany, the impregnation of plants by the falling of the pollen on the pistil.
2. in zoology, impregnation by external contact merely, as in most fishes.

à·down′, *adv.* from a higher to a lower situation; downward. [Poetic.]

à·down′, *prep.* down. [Poetic.]

A·dox′à, *n.* [Gr. *adoxos; a* priv., and *doxa,* glory.] a genus of plants, the *Adoxaeæ:* the moschatel is the only species.

ad pā′trēs, [L.] to (one's) fathers; dead.

ad·press′, *v.t.* to press close to.

ad′quem′, [L.] to or at which or whom: opposed to *a quo.*

ad·rā′di·ăl, *a.* [L. *ad,* to, *radius,* ray, and *-al.*] located near a ray: a term applied to certain processes in some hydrozoans.

ad·rā′di·ăl·ly, *adv.* so as to be adradial.

ad·reç′tăl, *a.* [L. *ad,* to, *rectum,* and *-al.*] in zoology, situated near the rectum.

ad′rem′, [L., to (the) thing.] to the point at issue; to the matter in hand.

ad·rē′năl, *n.* [L. *ad,* to, *ren,* kidney, and *-al.*] an adrenal gland.

ad·rē′năl, *a.* 1. near the kidney.
2. of or from the adrenal glands.

ad·rē′năl glands, the two small ductless glands on the upper part of the kidneys in mammals: also called *suprarenal glands.*

ad·ren′ăl·in, *n.* [*adrenal,* and *-in.*]
1. a hormone produced by the adrenal glands.
2. a drug, $C_9H_{13}NO_3$, with this hormone in it, made from the adrenal glands of animals or synthetically, and used to raise blood pressure, stop bleeding, etc.: a trade-mark (**Adrenalin**). Also called *epinephrine.*

ad·ren′ăl·ine (-in *or* -ēn), *n.* adrenalin.

Ā′dri·ăn, *a.* relating to the Adriatic.

Ā·dri·at′iç, *a.* [L. *Adriatus, Hadriaticus,* from *Adria, Hadria,* a town of the Venetians.] of or in the Adriatic Sea.

à·drift′, *a.* or *adv.* 1. literally, floating without mooring or direction, at the mercy of winds and currents; drifting: as an adjective it always follows its noun.
2. figuratively, swayed by any chance impulse; without direction or purpose.

à·drip′, *a.* and *adv.* dripping. [Rare.]

ad′rō·gāte, *v.t.* to adopt by adrogation.

ad·rō·gā′tion, *n.* [L. *adrogatio,* from *ad,* to, and *rogare,* to ask.] a kind of adoption in ancient Rome, by which a person capable of choosing for himself was admitted into the relation of a son.

à·droit′, *a.* [Fr. *adroit,* from L. *directus,* pp. of *dirigere,* to set in a straight line.] dexterous; skillful and clever in the use of the hands, and figuratively, in the exercise of the mental faculties; ingenious; ready in invention or execution; as, an *adroit* mechanic, an *adroit* plan.

Syn.—expert, artful, clever, skillful, dexterous, proficient.

à droite (à′drwȧt′), [Fr.] to the right; on the right.

à·droit′ly, *adv.* in an adroit manner.

à·droit′ness, *n.* the state or quality of being adroit.

ad·sci·ti′tious (-tish′us) *a.* [L. *adscitus,* pp. of *adsciscere,* to take knowingly; *ad,* to, and *sciscere,* to approve, from *scire,* to know.] added; supplemental; additional.

ad·sci·ti′tious·ly, *adv.* in an adscititious manner.

ad′script, *n.* [L. *adscriptus,* pp. of *adscribere,* to enroll.] one who is held as a feudal serf by adscription.

ad′script, *a.* written after.

ad·sçrip′tion, *n.* 1. attachment to an estate or to a feudal lord.
2. an ascription.

ad·sçrip·ti′tious (-tish′us), *a.* adscriptive.

ad·sçrip′tive, *a.* attached to and transferable with land, as a feudal serf.

ad·sig″ni·fi·çā′tion, *n.* added signification. [Rare.]

ad·sig′ni·fȳ, *v.t.* [L. *adsignificare,* from *ad,* to, and *significare,* to point out.] to add meaning to (a word). [Rare.]

ad·sorb′, *v.t.* [L. *ad-,* to, and *sorbere,* to drink in, suck.] to collect (a gas, liquid, or dissolved substance) in condensed form on a surface.

ad·sorb′ent, *a.* [L. *ad,* to, and *sorbens,* ppr. of *sorbere,* to drink in, suck.] adsorbing.

ad·sorb′ent, *n.* a thing or substance that adsorbs.

ad·sorp′tion, *n.* [from *adsorb,* after *absorption.*] an adsorbing or being adsorbed; adhesion of the molecules of a gas, liquid, or dissolved substance to a surface.

ad·sorp′tive, *a.* 1. able to adsorb.
2. Relating to adsorption.

ad·sorp′tive, *n.* an adsorbent.

ad·stip′ū·lāte, *v.i.* [L. *adstipulari; ad,* to, and *stipulari,* to stipulate.] in Roman law, to stipulate, as a second or accessory party to an agreement.

ad·stip′ū·lā·tŏr, *n.* in Roman law, one who stipulates, as a second or accessory party to a contract.

ad·sū′ki bēan, adzuki bean.

ad′sum, [L.] I am present.

ad·tẽr′mi·năl, *a.* [L. *ad,* to, and *terminalis,* from *terminus,* end.] passing toward the extremities of a muscle: said of electrical currents.

ad·ū·lā′ri·à, *n.* [from *Adula,* a mountain in the Swiss Alps.] a translucent variety of feldspar, commonly called *moonstone,* from the play of light exhibited in its crystalline structure.

ad′ū·lāte, *v.t.;* adulated, *pt., pp.;* adulating, *ppr.* [L. *adulatus,* pp. of *adulari,* to flatter.] to flatter servilely; praise too highly.

ad·ū·lā′tion, *n.* servile flattery; praise in excess, or beyond what is merited.

Syn.—flattery, sycophancy, blandishment, obsequiousness.

ad′ū·lā·tŏr, *n.* one who offers praise servilely.

ad′ū·lā·tō·ry, *a.* flattering fulsomely; containing excessive praise; servilely praising.

ad′ū·lā·tress, *n.* a female adulator.

A·dul′lăm·īte, *n.* 1. a dweller in the ancient village of Adullam in Canaan.
2. in English politics, one of a party of Liberals who seceded from their own leaders in 1866, and were likened to the political outlaws who took refuge with David in the cave of Adullam: cf. 1 Sam. xxii. 1, 2.

à·dult′ (*or* ad′ult), *a.* [L. *adultus,* pp. of *adolescere; ad,* to, and *olescere,* from *alere,* to nourish.]
1. having arrived at mature years or having grown to full size and strength; as, an *adult* person or plant.
2. pertaining to adults; suitable for adults; as, *adult* behavior, an *adult* school.

adult education; formal education for adults, including vocational and cultural courses, whether by correspondence or attendance.

à·dult′ (*or* ad′ult), *n.* 1. a person grown to full size and strength, or to the years of manhood or womanhood; a mature person.
2. an animal or plant that is full grown.
3. in law, a person who has come of age.

à·dul′tẽr, *v.i.* 1. to commit adultery. [Obs.]
2. to adulterate. [Obs.]

à·dul′tẽr·ănt, *n.* that which adulterates.

à·dul′tẽr·ănt, *a.* adulterating; making inferior or impure.

à·dul′tẽr·āte, *v.t.;* adulterated, *pt., pp.;* adulterating, *ppr.* [L. *adulteratus,* pp. of *adulterare,* from *adulter,* an adulterer; *ad,* to, and *alter,* another.] to corrupt, debase, or make impure by adding a poor or improper substance; as, to *adulterate* liquors; to *adulterate* drugs.

Syn.—alloy, debase, defile, corrupt, vitiate, contaminate.

à·dul′tẽr·āte, *a.* 1. guilty of adultery; adulterous.
2. debased by foreign admixture; adulterated.

à·dul′tẽr·āte·ly, *adv.* in an adulterate manner.

à·dul′tẽr·āte·ness, *n.* the quality or state of being adulterated.

à·dul·tẽr·ā′tion, *n.* 1. the act of adulterating, or the state of being adulterated; the use of ingredients in the production of any professedly genuine article, which are cheaper and of a worse quality, or which are not considered so desirable as the ingredients for which they are substituted. The *adulteration* of many articles, especially of food, is punishable by law.
2. an adulterated product.

à·dul′tẽr·ẽr, *n.* a person, especially a man, guilty of adultery.

à·dul′tẽr·ess, *n.* a woman guilty of adultery.

à·dul′tẽr·ine, *a.* of or resulting from adultery or adulteration.

à·dul′tẽr·ine, *n.* in law, a child issuing from an adulterous relationship. [Rare.]

à·dul′tẽr·īze, *v.i.* to commit adultery. [Archaic.]

à·dul′tẽr·ous, *a.* 1. guilty of adultery.
2. pertaining to adultery.
3. spurious; corrupt; adulterated. [Obs.]
4. born of adultery. [Obs.]

à·dul′tẽr·ous·ly, *adv.* in an adulterous manner.

à·dul′tẽr·y, *n.* [L. *adulterium,* from *adulter,* an adulterer.]
1. violation of the marriage bed; sexual intercourse between a married man and a woman not his wife, or between a married woman and a man not her husband. *Adultery* is a common legal ground for divorce.
2. in Scripture, all manner of lewdness or unchastity; also, idolatry or apostasy.
3. in ecclesiastical affairs, the intrusion of a person into a bishopric during the life of the bishop.

à·dult′hood, *n.* the state of being adult.

ad·um′brăl, *a.* shady.

ad·um′brănt, *a.* giving a faint shadow.

ad·um′brāte, *v.t.;* adumbrated, *pt., pp.;* adumbrating, *ppr.* [L. *adumbratus,* pp. of *adumbrari,* to shade; *ad,* and *umbra,* shade.]
1. to outline in a shadowy way; sketch.
2. to foreshadow.
3. to overshadow.

ad·um·brā′tion, *n.* 1. an adumbrating or being adumbrated.
2. a faint sketch or outline; an imperfect representation of a thing.
3. in heraldry, the shadow of a figure, outlined and painted in a color darker than the field.
4. a foreshadowing; indication in advance.
5. an overshadowing.

ad·um′brà·tive, *a.* faintly indicative; lightly sketched; adumbrating.

ad·ū·nā′tion, *n.* [L. *adunatio,* from ppr. of *adunare,* to make one; *ad,* to, and *unare,* from *unus,* one.] the state of being united; union. [Obs.]

à·duñç′, *a.* aduncous.

à·duñ′çāte, à·duñ′çā·ted, *a.* [L. *aduncatus,* pp. of *aduncare,* to hook; *ad,* to, and *uncare,* to hook, from *uncus,* a hook.] aduncous.

à·duñ′ci·ty, *n.* [L. *aduncitas,* hookedness; *ad,* to, and *uncus,* a hook.] hookedness; a curving inward.

à·duñ′çous, *a.* [L. *aduncus,* hooked.] hooked; curving inward, as a parrot's beak.

à·dūre′, *v.t.* [L. *adurere; ad,* to, and *urere,* to burn.] to burn up. [Obs.]

à·dust′, *a.* [L. *adustus,* burnt up, pp. of *adurere,* to burn.]

1. burnt; scorched; dried or parched by heat; hot and fiery.
2. sunburnt.
3. in medicine, formerly, characterized by great body heat and dryness; hence, sallow and melancholy.

ȧ·dust'ed, *a.* adust. [Obs.]

ȧ·dus'tion, *n.* the act of burning, scorching, or heating to dryness, or a state of being thus heated or dried. [Obs.]

ad va·lō'rem, [L.] according to the value: a term applied to (a) a duty laid upon goods at a certain rate per cent according to their invoiced value, rather than upon the quantity of pieces; (b) an assessment of taxes laid on the value of a property.

ad·vȧnce', *v.t.*; advanced, *pt., pp.*; advancing, *ppr.* [ME. *advaunce, avauncen, avancen*; OFr. *avancer*, to forward, promote, from L. *abantiare, ab* and *ante*, before; Fr. *avant*. The *a* was made *ad* on the supposition that it came from L. *ad*.]
1. to bring forward; to move further in front.
2. to promote; to raise to a higher rank; as, to *advance* one from the bar to the bench.
3. to improve or make better; to benefit; to promote the good of; further; as, to *advance* one's true interests.
4. to cause to happen earlier; to accelerate; as, to *advance* the growth of plants.
5. to offer or propose; to bring to view or notice; as, to *advance* an argument.
6. in commerce, to supply beforehand; to furnish on credit, or before goods are delivered or work is done; as, to *advance* money on loan or contract, or toward a purchase or enterprise.
7. to furnish for others; to supply or pay for others, in expectation of repayment; lend.
8. to raise the rate of; as, to *advance* the price of goods.
Syn.—forward, promote, further, raise, elevate, exalt, improve, heighten, accelerate.

ad·vȧnce', *v.i.* 1. to move or go forward; to proceed; as, the troops *advanced*.
2. to improve, or make progress; develop; as, to *advance* in knowledge, in stature, in wisdom, or in years.
3. to rise in rank, office, quality, importance, etc.; as, to *advance* from captain to colonel.
Syn.—proceed, progress, rise, increase.

ad·vȧnce', *a.* being before, in time or place; as, an *advance* agent.
advance sheets; in printing, unbound sheets of a book submitted in advance of publication, as for review.

ad·vȧnce', *n.* 1. movement forward, or toward the front; the act of advancing.
2. the front; the position before anything.
3. the first approach, or overture, toward opening negotiations, getting acquainted, etc.: used in the plural; as, *advances* with a view to matrimony.
4. improvement; progress; as, an *advance* in religion or knowledge.
5. advancement; promotion; preferment; as, an *advance* in rank or office.
6. in trade, a rise in value or cost.
7. a giving beforehand; a furnishing of something, on contract, before an equivalent is received, as money or goods toward a capital or stock, or on loan; also, the money or goods thus furnished.
8. a furnishing of money or goods for others, in expectation of reimbursement; also, the property so furnished; a loan.
I shall, with great pleasure, make the necessary *advances*. —Jay.
in advance; (a) in front; before; (b) beforehand; before an equivalent is received; before due; as, to be paid *in advance*.

ad·vȧnced', *a.* 1. moved forward; furnished beforehand; in front; in advance.
2. far on in life; old.
3. ahead of the times; very progressive or uncoventional; as, *advanced* ideas.

ad·vȧnced' stand'ing, credits toward a degree allowed to a student by a college for courses taken at another college.

ad·vȧnce' guärd, a detachment of troops sent ahead to reconnoiter and protect the line of march.

ad·vȧnce' man, a person hired to travel in advance of a theatrical company, political candidate, etc. to arrange for publicity, schedule appearances, etc.

ad·vȧnce'ment, *n.* 1. the act of moving forward or advancing.
2. the state of being advanced; promotion in rank or excellence.
3. provision made, as by a parent for a child, by gift of property during the parent's life, to which the child would be entitled as heir after his parent's death.
4. the payment of money in advance; also, money paid in advance.
Syn.—improvement, progress, progression, promotion, exaltation, elevation, preferment, enhancement.

ad·vȧn'cēr, *n.* 1. one who or that which advances.
2. the second start or branch of the horns on the head of a stag or similar animal.

ad·vȧn'cive, *a.* tending to advance. [Rare.]

ad·vȧn'tāġe, *n.* [ME. *avantage, avauntage*; Fr. *avantage*, an advantage, benefit.]
1. any state, condition, or circumstance specially favorable to success, prosperity, interest, etc.; as, the enemy had the *advantage* of elevated ground.
2. benefit; gain; profit.
3. opportunity; convenience for obtaining benefit; as, students enjoy great *advantages* for improvement.
4. favorable state or circumstances; as, jewels set to *advantage*.
5. superiority over: with *of* or *over*; as, to get the *advantage of* an enemy.
6. in tennis, the first point scored after deuce: often shortened to *ad* or *vantage*.
to take advantage of; (a) to use for one's own benefit or for a special purpose; (b) to abuse the confidence of, to impose upon.
Syn.—benefit, good, profit, gain, avail, emolument, interest, help, vantage.

ad·vȧn'tāġe, *v.t.*; advantaged, *pt., pp.*; advantaging, *ppr.* to benefit; to yield profit or gain to; to promote; to advance the interest of.

ad·vȧn'tāġe·ȧ·ble, *a.* profitable; convenient; gainful. [Obs.]

ad·vȧn'tāġe ground, vantage ground. [Rare.]

ad·vǎn·tā'ġeous, *a.* being of advantage; furnishing convenience, or opportunity to gain benefit; favorable; useful; beneficial; as, an *advantageous* position of the troops; trade is *advantageous* to a nation.

ad·vǎn·tā'ġeous·ly, *adv.* in an advantageous manner.

ad·vǎn·tā'ġeous·ness, *n.* the quality or state of being advantageous.

ad·veç'tion, *n.* [L. *advectio*, a conveying, from *advectus*, pp. of *advehere*, to convey; *ad-*, to, and *vehere*, to carry.] the transference of heat by horizontal currents of air.

ad·veç'tion, *a.* of or due to advection.

ad·vēne', *v.i.* [L. *advenire*, to come to.] to accede, or come (*to*); to be added or become a part, though not essential.

ad·vēn'ient, *a.* advening; coming from outward causes. [Obs.]

Ad'vent, *n.* [L. *adventus*, pp. of *advenire*; *ad*, to, and *venire*, to come.]
1. [a—] a coming; approach; visitation.
2. specifically, the coming of Christ.
3. in the church calendar, the period including the four Sundays before Christmas.
4. Christ's second coming to earth, on Judgment Day: also called *Second Advent*.

Ad'vent·iṣm, *n.* [*Advent* + *-ism*.] the belief that Christ's second coming to earth and the Last Judgment will soon occur.

Ad'vent·ist, *a.* of Adventism or Adventists.

Ad'vent·ist, *n.* a member of a Christian sect based on Adventism.

ad·ven·ti'ti·ȧ (-tish'i-a), *n.* [L., f. sing. of *adventitius*, coming from abroad, extraneous; with *membrana* understood; from *ad*, to, and *venire*, to come.] in anatomy, any membranous structure covering an organ.

ad·ven·ti'tious, *a.* [L. *adventitius*, extraneous.]
1. added extrinsically; accidental; not inherent; casual.
2. in botany, occurring in an abnormal position, as leaf buds on the surface of a stem, or roots from aerial stems or branches.
3. in zoology, occurring away from its natural position or habitat.

ad·ven·ti'tious·ly, *adv.* accidentally; in an adventitious manner.

ad·ven·ti'tious·ness, *n.* the quality or state of being adventitious.

ad·ven'tive, *a.* 1. accidental; adventitious. [Rare.]
2. in botany, not native to the environment.

ad·ven'tive, *n.* a plant that is not native to the environment.

Ad'vent Sun'dāy, the first of the four Sundays in Advent.

Ad·ven'tū·ǎl, *a.* relating to the season of Advent. [Obs.]

ad·ven'tūre, *n.* [OE. *aventure*; Fr. *aventure*; L. *adventura*, from *advenire*; *ad*, to, and *venire*, to come.]
1. hazard; risk; chance. [Obs.]
2. a bold undertaking, in which hazards are to be encountered and the issue is staked upon unforeseen events.
3. a remarkable occurrence in one's personal history; a stirring experience, often of a romantic nature.
4. a speculative business enterprise.
5. the encountering of danger.
6. a liking for danger, excitement, etc.

ad·ven'tūre, *v.t.*; adventured, *pt., pp.*; adventuring, *ppr.* 1. to risk or hazard; to venture.
2. to venture on; to attempt.

ad·ven'tūre, *v.i.* 1. to engage in daring undertakings.
2. to take risks.

ad·ven'tūre·fųl, *a.* given to adventure; full of enterprise. [Rare.]

ad·ven'tūr·ēr, *n.* 1. one who has or likes to have adventures.
2. a soldier willing to fight for the side that pays most; soldier of fortune.
3. a speculator.
4. one who gains or strives to gain social standing, wealth, etc. by questionable means.

ad·ven'tūre·sǒme, *a.* bold; daring; adventurous.

ad·ven'tūre·sǒme·ness, *n.* the quality of being bold and adventurous.

ad·ven'tūr·ess, *n.* a female adventurer; specifically, a woman who seeks to gain wealth or social position by fraudulent means, by exploiting her charms, etc.

ad·ven'tūr·ous, *a.* [ME. *aventurous*; Fr. *aventureux*, from *aventurer*, to venture.]
1. inclined or willing to incur hazard; fond of adventure; daring; courageous; enterprising: applied to persons.
2. full of hazard; attended with risk; exposing to danger; requiring courage: applied to things; as, an *adventurous* undertaking.
Syn.—rash, audacious, brave, enterprising, venturesome, hazardous, reckless.

ad·ven'tūr·ous·ly, *adv.* boldly; daringly; in an adventurous manner.

ad·ven'tūr·ous·ness, *n.* the fact or quality of being adventurous.

ad'vērb, *n.* [L. *adverbium*; *ad*, to, and *verbum*, word.] in grammar, (a) a word used to modify a verb, adjective, or other adverb, by expressing time, place, manner, degree, cause, etc.; (b) any phrase or clause similarly used.

ad·vēr'bi·ǎl, *a.* 1. pertaining to an adverb.
2. having the nature or function of an adverb.
3. added to an adverb base; as, an *adverbial* suffix.

ad·vēr·bi·al'i·ty, *n.* the quality of being adverbial.

ad·vēr'bi·ǎl·īze, *v.t.* to use as an adverb; to give the quality or form of an adverb to.

ad·vēr'bi·ǎl·īz"ēr, *n.* a suffix that forms adverbs from other words.

ad·vēr'bi·ǎl·ly, *adv.* in the manner of an adverb.

ad vēr'bum, [L.] to a word; word for word; verbatim.

ad·vēr·sā'ri·ȧ, *n. pl.* [L. *adversaria*, neut. pl. of *adversarius*, opposing, turned toward.]
1. a commonplace book.
2. a miscellaneous collection of notes, remarks, or selections: sometimes used as a title of books or papers of such character.

ad·vēr·sā'ri·ous, *a.* antagonistic; inimical. [Obs.]

ad'vēr·sā·ry, *n.* [OE. *adversie*; OFr. *adversier*, from L. *adversarius*, turned toward, opponent.]
1. an enemy or foe; one who opposes another. In Scripture, Satan is called *the Adversary*.
2. an opponent or antagonist, as in a contest of any kind.
Syn.—opponent, antagonist, enemy, foe.—Unfriendly feelings mark the *enemy*; habitual hostility, the *adversary*; active hostility, the *foe*. *Opponents* are those who are pitted against each other; *antagonists*, those who struggle in the contest with all their might.

ad'vēr·sā·ry, *a.* 1. opposed; opposite to; adverse. [Archaic.]
2. in law, having an opposing party; in distinction from case, in law or equity, to which no opposition is made; as, an *adversary* suit.

ad·vērs'ȧ·tive, *a.* [L. *adversativus*, from *adversatus*, pp. of *adversari*, to be opposed to.] expressing some difference, contrariety, or opposition; as, in the sentence "John works hard but he makes very little money," *but* is called an *adversative* conjunction.

ad·vērs′ȧ·tive, *n.* an adversative word, such as *but, yet, however.*

ad·vērs′ȧ·tive·ly, *adv.* in an adversative manner or sense.

ad′vērse (*or* ad·vērse′), *a.* [ME. *adverse*; Fr. *adverse*; L. *adversus*, pp. of *advertere*; *ad*, to, and *vertere*, to turn.]

1. opposite; opposing; acting in a contrary direction; conflicting; counteracting; opposed to; hostile; as, *adverse* winds, an *adverse* party, *adverse* criticism.

2. contrary to one's interests or supposed good; hence, unfortunate; calamitous; pernicious; unprosperous; as, *adverse* fate or circumstances.

3. in botany, turned toward the stem: applied to leaves.

adverse possession; in law, possession of land by a person not the owner but exercising the rights of ownership: when such possession is uncontested over a certain period of years, unimpeachable title to the land is gained.

Syn.—opposite, opposing, contrary, inimical, hostile, unfortunate, calamitous, unprosperous.

ad·vērse′, *v.t.* to oppose. [Obs.]

ad′vērse·ly, *adv.* in an adverse manner; oppositely; unfortunately; unprosperously.

ad′vērse·ness, *n.* the quality or state of being adverse; opposition; adversity; unprosperousness.

ad·vērs·i·fō′li·āte, ad·vērs·i·fō′li·ous, *a.* [L. *adversus*, opposite, and *folium*, a leaf.] in botany, having the leaves opposite to each other on the stem.

ad·vēr′si·ty, *n.*; *pl.* **ad·vēr′si·tieṣ.** [ME. *adversite*; L. *adversitas*, from *adversus*, pp. of *advertere*, to oppose.]

1. misfortune; calamity; affliction; distress; state of unhappiness.

Sweet are the uses of *adversity*. —Shak.

2. an instance of misfortune; a calamity.

Syn.—disaster, misfortune, calamity, bad luck, misery, distress.

ad·vērt′, *v.i.*; adverted, *pt., pp.*; adverting, *ppr.* [L. *advertere*; *ad*, to, and *vertere*, to turn.] to turn the mind or attention; to refer or allude (*to* something); as, he *adverted to* what was said, or *to* a circumstance that occurred.

ad·vērt′ence, ad·vērt′en·cy, *n.* [OFr. *advertence*; L. *advertentia*, from *advertens*, ppr. of *advertere*, to turn to.] a direction of the mind to; attention; notice; regard; consideration; heedfulness.

ad·vērt′ent, *a.* attentive; heedful.

ad·vērt′ent·ly, *adv.* in an advertent manner.

ad′vēr·tīṣe, ad′vēr·tīze (*or* ad·vēr·tīz′), *v.t.*; advertised, *pt., pp.*; advertising, *ppr.* [ME. *advertisen*; OFr. base *advertiss-*, from *advertir*, to inform, certify.]

1. to take note of; to observe. [Obs.]

2. to inform; to give notice, advice, or intelligence to, whether of a past or present event, or of something yet to come.

I will *advertise* thee what this people will do to thy people. —Num. xxiv. 14.

3. to publish a notice of; to give conspicuous notice or information of to the public, through newspapers, signs, circulars, posters, periodical publications, radio, television, etc.; especially, to praise publicly in this way to encourage buying; as, to *advertise* goods for sale, entertainments to occur, etc.

Syn.—announce, proclaim, publish, make known, apprise, inform.

ad′vēr·tīṣe, ad′vēr·tīze, *v.i.* 1. to call the public's attention to things for sale, help wanted, etc., as by printed notices or announcements.

2. to ask for publicly by printed notice, etc. (with *for*); as, to *advertise* for a servant.

ad·vēr′tīṣe·ment, ad·vēr′tīze·ment (*or* -tīz′-ment), *n.* 1. information; admonition; notice given. [Obs.]

2. a public notice or announcement, usually paid for, as of things for sale, needs, etc.

ad′vēr·tīṣ·ēr, ad′vēr·tīz·ēr (*or* -tīz′-), *n.* one who or that which advertises.

ad′vēr·tīṣ·ing, ad′vēr·tīz·ing (*or* -tīz′-), *a.* 1. that advertises.

2. having to do with advertising.

ad′vēr·tīṣ·ing, ad′vēr·tīz·ing (*or* -tīz′-), *n.* 1. printed or spoken matter that advertises.

2. the business or profession of preparing and issuing advertising matter, or of securing contracts for the publication of advertisements.

ad′vēr·tīṣ·ing man, a man whose work or business is advertising: often colloquially abbreviated to *ad man.*

ad·vīce′, *n.* [ME. *advyse*, *avys*; OFr. *avis*; L. *advisum*, a view, opinion, from *advisus*, pp. of *advidere*; *ad*, to, and *videre*, to see.]

1. counsel; an opinion offered as worthy to be followed in a particular situation.

We may give *advice*, but we cannot give conduct. —Franklin.

2. prudence; deliberate consideration. [Obs.]

3. information as to the state of an affair or affairs; notice; intelligence: usually in the plural; as, we have late *advices* from China.

4. in commerce, a notification by one person to another, usually by mail, as of a draft drawn or other business transacted in which both are interested; as, letters of *advice*.

to take advice; to follow the counsel of others.

Syn.—counsel, instruction, information, notice, admonition, recommendation, exhortation, intelligence.

ad·vīce′ bōat, a dispatch boat. [Archaic.]

ad·vīṣ·ȧ·bil′i·ty, *n.* the quality of being advisable; expediency.

ad·vīṣ′ȧ·ble, *a.* 1. proper to be advised; prudent and wise; proper to be done or practiced; as, it is not *advisable* to proceed at this time.

2. open to advice. [Rare.]

Syn.—prudent, expedient, proper.

ad·vīṣ′ȧ·ble·ness, *n.* the quality of being advisable or expedient.

ad·vīṣ′ȧ·bly, *adv.* in an advisable manner; prudently; wisely.

ad·vīṣe′, *v.t.*; advised, *pt., pp.*; advising, *ppr.* [OE. *avisen*; L. *advisare*; *ad*, to, and *visare*, from *videre*, to see.]

1. to give advice or counsel to; to offer an opinion as worthy or expedient to be followed; as, I *advise* you to be cautious of speculation.

2. to give information to; to communicate notice to; to make acquainted with; followed by *of* before the thing communicated; as, the merchants were *advised of* the risk.

Syn.—counsel, admonish, inform, apprise, acquaint.

ad·vīṣe, *v.i.* 1. to deliberate, weigh well, or consider. [Obs.]

2. to consult with others; to join others in deliberating: followed by *with*; as, I shall *advise with* my friends.

ad·vīṣ′ed·ly, *adv.* with deliberation or advice; with due consideration; as, an enterprise *advisedly* undertaken.

ad·vīṣ′ed·ness, *n.* deliberate consideration; prudent procedure.

ad·vīṣe′ment, *n.* 1. counsel. [Archaic.]

2. consultation; deliberation; as, to take a case under *advisement*.

ad·vīṣ′ēr, ad·vīṣ′ọr, *n.* one who gives advice; as, a legal *adviser*.

ad·vīṣ′ing, *n.* advice; counsel.

ad·vī′ṣō, *n.* [*ad*, for *a*, Sp. *aviso*, advice.]

1. advice; suggestion. [Obs.]

2. an aviso, or advice boat. [Obs.]

ad·vī′ṣō·ri·ly, *adv.* in an advisory manner or capacity.

ad·vī′ṣō·ry, *a.* 1. advising or having power to advise; as, an *advisory* board.

2. relating to advice.

ad′vō·cȧ·cy, *n.* 1. the act of pleading for or supporting; an advocating (*of* something).

2. advowson.

ad′vō·çāte, *n.* [OE. *avocat*; L. *advocatus*, a counselor, from *advocare*; *ad-*, to, and *vocare*, to call.]

1. one who pleads the cause of another in a court of law; a counsel or counselor; as, he is a learned lawyer and an able *advocate*.

2. one who defends, vindicates, or espouses a cause by argument; one who is friendly to; an upholder; a defender; as, an *advocate* of peace, or of the oppressed.

ad′vō·çāte, *v.t.*; advocated, *pt., pp.*; advocating, *ppr.* 1. to plead in favor of; to defend by argument before a tribunal or the public; to support or vindicate; be in favor of; as, to *advocate* total abstinence.

2. in Scottish law, to appeal from a lower to a higher court.

Syn.—plead for, favor, support, maintain.

ad′vō·çāte, *v.i.* to act as an advocate (*for*). [Obs.]

ad′vō·çāte·ship, *n.* the office or duty of an advocate.

ad′vō·çȧ·tess, *n.* a female advocate. [Rare.]

ad·vō·çā′tion, *n.* 1. a pleading for; plea; apology; advocacy. [Obs.]

2. in Scottish and papal law, the transfer by a superior court to itself of an action pending in an inferior court.

ad′vō·çā·tọr, *n.* a person who advocates.

ad·voç′ȧ·tō·ry, *a.* 1. of an advocate.

2. of advocacy; advocating.

ad·vō·çā′tus dī·ab′ō·lī, [L.] the devil's advocate.

ad·vō·lū′tion, *n.* [L. *advolvere*; *ad*, to, and *volvere*, to roll.] a rolling toward something. [Obs.]

ad·vou′trēr, *n.* [ME. *advouter*, OFr. *avouter*, *avoltre*, L. *adulter*, adulterer.] an adulterer. [Obs.]

ad·vou′tress, *n.* an adulteress. [Obs.]

ad·vou′try, ad·vow′try, *n.* adultery. [Obs.]

ad·vow·ee′, *n.* one who has the right of advowson.

ad·vow′ṣon, *n.* [ME. *advowson*, *avowiesoun*; OFr. *avoeson*; L. *advocatio*, a summoning, a calling to, from *ad*, to, and *vocare*, to call.] in English law, a right of presentation to a vacant benefice; a right of nominating a person as rector or vicar of a vacant parish.

ad·y·nā′mi·ȧ, *n.* [L., from Gr. *adynamia*, want of strength, from *a* priv., and *dynamis*, power.] in medicine, weakness; lack of strength occasioned by disease; a deficiency of vital power.

ad·y·nam′iç, *a.* [Gr. *adynamia*, without power, and *-ic*.]

1. of or characterized by adynamia; weak; destitute of strength.

2. in physics, characterized by the absence of force.

ȧ·dyn′ȧ·my, *n.* same as *adynamia*.

ad′y·tum, *n.* [L., from Gr. *adyton*, neut. of *adytos*, not to be entered, from *a* priv., and *dyein*, to enter.] in ancient temples, an innermost room or shrine where oracles were given.

adz, adze, *n.* [ME. *adis*, *adse*, AS. *adesa*, an adze, ax.] an axlike tool with an arching blade at right angles to the handle, ground from a base on its inside to the outer edge: used for dressing wood, etc.

ad·zụ′ki bēan, [Japan.] 1. a bushy bean plant of China and Japan, with black or white pods.

2. its small, smooth, brownish bean.

Also written *adsuki*.

ae (ā), *a.* [from AS. *an*, whence Eng. *one*.] [Scot.] one.

æ, (ē, i, *or* e) 1. a diphthong in some Latin words, equivalent to *ai* in Greek, usually written *ae* or replaced by *e* in modern spelling of derived English words, as in *demon* (*daemon*), *ether* (*aether*), etc.

2. an Anglo-Saxon character symbolizing a low front unrounded vowel like that in Modern English *hat*, *add*, *rack*, etc.

3. a character in the International Phoenetic Alphabet symbolizing the vowel sound described in sense 2.

Ae′ȧ·çus, *n.* [L.; Gr. *Aiakos*.] in Greek mythology, a king of Aegina who after he died became one of the three judges of the dead in the lower world, with Minos and Rhadamanthus.

Ae·cid″i·ō·mȳ·çē′tēṣ, *n.pl.* [L. *æcidium*, dim. of Gr. *aikia*, injury, and *mykētes*, pl. of *mykēs*, a fungus.] a group of minute parasitic rust fungi infesting cultivated plants.

ae·cid′i·ō·spōre, *n.* [L. *æcidium*, dim. of Gr. *aikia*, injury, and *spora*, seed.] a spore formed by a process of abstriction in certain parasitic fungi.

ae·cid′i·ō·stāġe, *n.* same as *acciostage*.

Ae·cid′i·um, *n.* [Mod. L., from dim. of Gr. *aikia*, injury.]

1. aecium.

2. [A–] a genus of parasitic fungi, commonly called rusts, which infest plants.

ae′ci·ō·stāġe, *n.* [from *æcium*, and *stage*.] in botany, the period in their life cycle during which certain rusts produce aecia.

ae′ci·um, *n.*; *pl.* **ae′ci·a,** [Mod. L. from Gr. *aikia*, injury.] in botany, a cuplike spore fruit produced by certain rusts, in which chains of spores are developed.

A·ē′deṣ (ā-ē′dēz), *n. sing.* and *pl.* [Mod. L.; Gr. *aēdēs*, unpleasant, from *a-*, not, and *hēdys*, sweet.] a genus of mosquitoes, one species of which can carry the virus of yellow fever.

ae′dīle, ē′dīle, *n.* [L. *ædilis*, from *ædes*, building, temple.] in ancient Rome, an officer or magistrate who had the care of the public buildings, streets, highways, public spectacles, etc.

ae·gȧ·grop′i·lȧ, ae·gag′rō·pīle, *n.* [Mod. L., from Gr. *aigagros*, a wild goat, and L. *pila*, ball, from *pilus*, hair.] a concrete mass of hair, etc., found in the stomach of some ruminants.

Ae·ġē′ăn, *a.* [L. *Ægeum*; Gr. *Aigaion*.] of or pertaining to the arm of the Mediterranean Sea east of Greece, or the Archipelago.

Ae·ġē′ăn civ″il·i·zā′tion (or **çul′tūre**), the civilization of the people who lived in the Aegean Islands and near-by regions before the ancient Greeks: it flourished in the Bronze Age.

Ae·gē′ri·ăn, Ē·gē′ri·ăn, *a.* of or pertaining to the *Ægeriidæ*, commonly called clearwings.

Ae·gē·rī′i·dae, Ē·gē·rī′i·dae, *n.pl.* [Mod. L., after *Ægeria*, a prophetic nymph of Roman legend.] in entomology, a typical genus of *Lepidoptera*, consisting of bright-colored moths with transparent wings.

Ae′ġeus, *n.* [L., from Gr. *Aigeus*.] in Greek legend, a king of Athens who killed himself when he thought his son Theseus was dead.

ae·ġi·crā′ni·ȧ, *n.pl.* [Mod. L., from Gr. *aix*, *aigos*, goat, and *kranion*, skull.] in classical architecture, the heads of rams or goats sculptured in ornamentation.

ae′ġi·lops, ē′ġi·lops, *n.* [L., from Gr. *aigilōps*; *aix*, *aigos*, goat, and *ōps*, eye.]
1. in medicine, goat eye; an abscess in the inner canthus of the eye.
2. [A–] in botany, a genus of grasses growing wild in southern Europe.

Ae′ġir, *n.* [ON.] in Norse mythology, the god of the sea.

ae′ġir·ite, ae′ġir·ïne, *n.* [Ice. *Ægir*, the god of the sea, and *-ite*, *-ine*.] same as *acmite*.

ae′ġis, ē′ġis, *n.* [L. from Gr. *aigis*, a goatskin, from *aix*, *aigos*, a goat.]

PALLAS WEARING THE AEGIS

1. in Greek mythology, a shield or breastplate: originally applied to the shield worn by Jupiter. In later times, part of the armor of Pallas Athena, appearing as a kind of breastplate covered with metal scales and the head of the Gorgon Medusa, and fringed with serpents.
2. figuratively, any power or influence which protects or shields; as, under the *aegis* of American citizenship.
3. sponsorship; auspices.

Ae·ġis′thus, *n.* in Greek legend, the son of Thyestes and lover of Clytemnestra: he helped her to kill her husband, Agamemnon.

Ae·ġi·thog′nȧ·thae, *n.pl.* [Mod. L., from Gr. *aigithos*, a bird, and *gnathos*, a jaw.] a large group or suborder of birds of the order *Carinatæ*.

ae·ġi·thog′nȧ·thiṣm, *n.* the state or quality of being aegithognathous; a condition of some birds, in which the bony palate is formed by the union of the vomer with the alinasal walls and turbinals: it is characteristic of the large group *Ægithognathæ* including the passerine and gallinaceous birds.

ae·ġi·thog′nȧ·thous (-thus), *a.* in ornithology, having the structure of the palate disposed as in the sparrow and other passerine birds.

Ae′glē, *n.* [L., from Gr. *aiglē*, splendor.] in botany, a small genus of trees of the family *Rutaceæ*, found in tropical Asia and Africa, and resembling the citrus or orange tree. *Ægle Marmelos* produces the golden orange of India.

ae·gō·phon′iç, ē·gō·phon′iç, *a.* of or like aegophony.

ae·goph′ō·ny, ē·goph′ō·ny, *n.* [Gr. *aix* (*aigos*), a goat, and *phōnē*, voice.] the sound of the voice of a person affected with pleurisy, when heard through the stethoscope: so called because it is tremulous and broken, so as to suggest the bleatings of a goat.

Ae·ġyp′tus, *n.* in Greek legend, a king of Egypt whose fifty sons married the fifty daughters of his brother Danaus: cf. *Danaides*.

-ae′mï·ȧ, -emia.

Ae·nē′ăs, *n.* [L.; Gr. *Aineias*.] in Greek and Roman legend, a Trojan, son of Anchises and Venus, and hero of Virgil's *Aeneid*: escaping from ruined Troy, Aeneas wandered for years before coming to Latium.

Ae·nē′id, *n.* [L. *Æneis*, *Æneidos*.] the epic poem by Virgil, of which Aeneas is the hero.

a·ē′ne·ous (a-ē′nē-us), *a.* [L. *aeneus*, of bronze.] colored like, or having the appearance of, bronze: a term used in zoology.

ae·nig′mȧ·tite, *n.* [L. *ænigma*, enigma.] an amphibolic mineral which crystallizes in the triclinic system.

Ae·ō′li·ăn, Ē·ō′li·ăn, *a.* [L. *Æolius*; Gr. *Aiolios*.]
1. pertaining to Aeolus, the god of the winds.
2. of Aeolia, or Aeolis, in Asia Minor.
3. [a–] of the wind; produced by or blown by the wind; Aeolic.

aeolian harp; a simple stringed instrument that is made to sound by the currents of air. It is usually placed at or near an open window, and consists of a box of thin wood in which are stretched numerous strings of equal length, tuned in unison. Also called *aeolian lyre*.

Ae·ol′iç, Ē·ol′iç, *a.* same as *Aeolian*.

Ae·ol′iç, Ē·ol′iç, *n.* the Aeolian Greek dialect.

ae·ō·lī′nȧ, *n.* [L. *Æolus*; Gr. *Aiolos*, god of the winds.] a small free reed musical instrument, the forerunner of the accordion.

ae′ō·līne, *n.* same as *aeolina*.

ae·ol′ï·pīle, ae·ol′ī·pȳle, ē·ol′i·pīle, *n.* [L. *æolipilæ*; *Æolus*, god of the winds, and *pila*, a ball.] a simple apparatus, invented by Hero of Alexandria, for demonstrating the force of steam under pressure: it consists of a hollow metal ball connected to a boiler and having short bent pipes as outlets for the steam, which, as it is expelled, causes the ball to revolve.

Ae′ō·lis, Ē′ō·lis, *n.* [L., from Gr. *Aiolis*, from *aiolos*, quick-moving.] a genus of sluglike mollusks with gull-like papillae in clusters along the back.

ae″ō·lō·trop′iç, *a.* [Gr. *aiolos*, changeful, and *tropē*, from *trepein*, to turn.] in physics, having different properties in different directions; not isotropic.

ae·ō·lot′rō·py, *n.* the state or quality of being aeolotropic.

Ae′ō·lus, *n.* [L., from Gr. *Aiolos*.]
1. in Greek and Roman mythology, the god of the winds.
2. a king of Thessaly, the Aeolians' forefather.

ae′ŏn, *n.* an extremely long, indefinite period of time; thousands and thousands of years. Also spelled *eon*.

ae·ō′ni·ăn, *a.* lasting forever; eternal. Also spelled *eonian*.

ae·py·ọr′nis, ē·py·ọr′nis, *n.* [Gr. *aipus*, high, and *ornis*, bird.] a gigantic ostrichlike bird found in a fossil state in Madagascar.

ae′quō an′i·mō, [L.], with calm mind; with equanimity.

ā·ẽr- (*or* är), aero-: words beginning with *aer-* may also be spelled *aër-*.

ae·rā′ri·ăn, *a.* [L. *ærarius*, from *æs*, *æris*, pertaining to ore, money.] of the Roman public treasury; fiscal.

ae·rā′ri·ăn, *n.* a Roman citizen of the lowest class of freemen, who paid only a poll tax and was not qualified to vote.

ā′ẽr·āte, *v.t.*; aerated, *pt.*, *pp.*; aerating, *ppr.* [Gr. *aēr*, air, and *-ate*.]
1. to expose to air; cause air to circulate through.
2. to combine oxygen with (the blood) by breathing.
3. to charge (liquid) with gas, as in making soda water.
4. in agriculture, to expose (soils) to the action of the air by plowing, harrowing, etc.

ā·ẽr·ā′tion, *n.* an aerating or being aerated.

ā′ẽr·ā·tŏr, *n.* 1. a person or thing that aerates.
2. an apparatus for forcing gas into combination with liquids, as in making soda water.
3. an apparatus for blowing a stream of air or gas upon wheat, etc., to destroy fungi or injurious insects; a fumigator.

ā·ẽr·eñ′çhy·mȧ, *n.* [Gr. *aēr*, air, and *enchyma*, an infusion.] in botany, a form of cellular tissue found in the stems of some marsh and aquatic plants: it resembles the tissue of cork.

ā·ē′ri- (*or* ā′ẽr-i, *or, now commonly*, är′i), aero-: words beginning with *aeri-* may also be spelled *aëri-*.

ā·ē′ri·ăl (*or, now usually*, är′iă-l), *a.* [*aeri-*, and *-al*.]
1. belonging to the air; of the air.
2. consisting of or having the nature of air; light as air.
3. growing, existing, or happening in air.
4. inhabiting or frequenting the air.
5. placed in the air; high; lofty; elevated.
6. possessed of a light and graceful beauty.
7. ethereal; visionary; as, *aerial* fancies.
8. of or for aircraft or flying; as, an *aerial* map.

aerial ladder; a ladder that can be mechanically extended for reaching high places, mounted on a fire engine, etc.

aerial railway; an arrangement of overhead cables or rails with cars suspended from them, used to carry people or things across a canyon, river, etc.

aerial sickness; the nausea caused by the movement of an aircraft.

aer′i·ăl (är′i-ăl), *n.* in radio and television, a wire or set of wires, often high in the air, for sending or receiving the electromagnetic waves; antenna.

ā·ē′ri·ăl·ist, *n.* an acrobat who performs on a trapeze, high wire, etc.

ā·ē′ri·ăl·ly, *adv.* 1. in an aerial manner.
2. in the air.

ā·ē′ri·ăl tọr·pē′dō, a bomb shaped like a torpedo, dropped from an airplane.

A·ē′ri·ănṣ, *n.pl.* in church history, a branch of Arians, so called from Aerius, who maintained that there is no difference between bishops and priests.

ae′rie (ē′rē *or* ā′ẽr-y), *n.* [ME. *aire*; ML. *aeria*, *eyria*; OFr. *aire*; Pr. *agre*; prob. from L. *ager*, field, but influenced by L. *aer*, air & ME. *ei*, egg.]
1. the nest of an eagle or other bird of prey that builds in a high place.
2. a house or stronghold on a high place.
3. the young (of an eagle, hawk, etc.) in the nest.
Also spelled *aery*, *eyrie*, *eyry*.

ā·ẽr·if′ẽr·ous, *a.* [*aeri-*, and *ferous*, from L. *ferre*, to bear.] conveying or containing air; air-bearing, as the larynx and bronchial tubes, and the trachea of insects.

ā″ẽr·i·fi·cā′tion, *n.* an aerifying or being aerified.

ā′ẽr·i·fọrm, *a.* 1. having the form or nature of air or gas.
2. like air; insubstantial.

ā′ẽr·i·fȳ, *v.t.*; aerified, *pt.*, *pp.*; aerifying, *ppr.*
1. to fill with air, or to combine air with.
2. to change into an aeriform state.

ā′ẽr·ō (*or* är′ō), *n.*; *pl.* **ā′ẽr·ōṣ,** any form of airship. [Colloq.]

ā′ẽr·ō (*or* är′ō), *v.i.* to travel by airship. [Colloq.]

ā′ẽr·ō- (*or, now usually*, är′ō), [Gr. *aēr*, air.] a combining form meaning:
1. *air, of the air*, as in *aero*lite.
2. *of aircraft, connected with flying*, as in *aero*batics.
3. *gas, of gases*, as in *aero*dynamics.
Words beginning with *aero-* may also be spelled *aëro-*.

ā″ẽr·ō·bat′içs, *n. pl.* [*aero-*, and acro*batics*.]
1. spectacular feats done in flying, as loops, rolls, etc.
2. [construed as sing.] the art of doing such feats in flying.

ā′ẽr·ōbe, *n.* [*aero-*, and Gr. *bios*, life.] a microorganism that lives in contact with the air and absorbs oxygen from it.

ā·ẽr·ō′biç, *a.* 1. of the nature of an aerobe.
2. of or produced by aerobes.
3. designating or involving exercise, such as running or swimming, that conditions the heart and lungs by increasing the efficiency of oxygen intake by the body.

ā·ẽr·ō′biç·ăl·ly, *adv.* in the manner of the aerobes.

ā·ẽr·ō′biçs, *n.* aerobic exercises.

ā″ẽr·ō·bī·ō′sis, *n.* life in and by means of air or oxygen.

ā·ẽr·ō′bi·um, *n.*; *pl.* **ā·ẽr·ō′bi·a,** [Mod. L.; see *aerobe*.] an aerobe.

Ā″ẽr·ō·brañ′çhi·ȧ, *n. pl.* [*aero-*, and Gr. *branchia*, gills.] a former subclass of *Arachnida*, including the scorpions and spiders.

ā″ẽr·ō·brañ′çhi·āte, *a.* of the *Aerobranchia*.

ā″ẽr·ō·bus′, *n.* [*aero-*, and *bus*.] an aeroplane of sufficient size to carry many passengers. [Colloq.]

ā′ẽr·ō·çurve, *n.* an aeroplane having a curved sustaining surface.

ā′ẽr·ō·cyst, *n.* [*aero-*, and Gr. *kystis*, bladder.] an air cell or air bladder of an alga.

ā″ẽr·ō·dō·net′içs, *n.* [from *aero-*, and Gr. *donetos*, agitated, from *donein*, to shake, and *-ics*.] the branch of aviation that has to do with gliding.

ā′ẽr·ō·drōme, *n.* [*aero-*, and Gr. *dromos*, course.] same as *airdrome*.

ā″ẽr·ō·dȳ·nam′iç, *a.* relating to the force of air in motion.

ā″ẽr·ō·dȳ·nam′içs, *n.* [*aero-*, and Gr. *dynamis*, power.] the science relating to the effects produced by air or other gases in motion.

ā′ẽr·ō·dȳne, *n.* [*aero-*, and *-dyne*.] any aircraft that is heavier than air.

ā″ẽr·ō·em′bō·liṣm, *n.* [*aero-*, and *embolism*.] a condition caused by a sudden, considerable lowering of air pressure, as in flying at high altitudes, characterized by the formation of nitrogen bubbles in the blood, acute pain in the joints and lungs, etc.

ā'ĕr·ō·foil, *n.* same as *airfoil.*

ā'ĕr·ō·gram, *n.* [*aero-*, and Gr. *gramma*, a writing.]
1. a message sent by radio; radiogram.
2. a letter sent by airmail.

ā'ĕr·ō·graph, *n.* [*aero-*, and Gr. *graphos*, a description or writing.] an apparatus, or a process, for conducting wireless telegraphy. [Rare.]

ā·ĕr·og'rȧ·phĕr, *n.* one versed in the science of aerography; an aerologist.

ā''ĕr·ō·graph'iç·ăl·ly, *adv.* by means of aerography.

ā''ĕr·ō·graph'içs, *n. pl.* [construed as sing.] the study of atmospheric phenomena.

ā·ĕr·og'rȧ·phy, *n.* [*aero-*, and Gr. *graphein*, to describe.] a description of the air or atmosphere.

ā'ĕr·ō·gun'', *n.* an antiaircraft gun.

ā''ĕr·ō·hȳ''drō·dȳ·nam'iç, *a.* [*aero-*, Gr. *hydor*, water, and *dynamis*, power.] acting by the force of air in water; as, an *aerohydrodynamic* wheel.

ā'ĕr·ō·līte, *n.* [*aero-*, and Gr. *lithos*, a stone.] a meteorite of stone.

ā''ĕr·ō·li·thol'ō·ġy, *n.* [*aero-*, Gr. *lithos*, stone, and *logos*, word, description.] the science dealing with aerolites.

ā''ĕr·ō·lit'iç, *a.* of or pertaining to aerolites.

ā''ĕr·ō·loġ'iç, ā''ĕr·ō·loġ'iç·ăl, *a.* of aerology.

ā·ĕr·ol'ō·ġist, *n.* one versed in aerology.

ā·ĕr·ol'ō·ġy, *n.* [*aero-*, and Gr. *logos*, description.] that branch of physics which treats of the air, its constituent parts, properties, and phenomena.

ā'ĕr·ō·man''cy, *n.* [*aero-*, and Gr. *manteia*, divination.] divination by means of the air and winds; hence, humorously, the science of forecasting weather.

ā''ĕr·ō·mȧ·rine', *a.* [*aero-*, and *marine.*] of the navigation of aircraft above the ocean.

ā''ĕr·ō·mē·çhan'iç, *n.* [*aero-*, and *mechanic.*] a mechanic whose work is repairing and adjusting aircraft.

ā''ĕr·ō·mē·çhan'iç, *a.* relating to aeromechanics.

ā''ĕr·ō·mē·çhan'içs, *n.* the science of air or other gases in motion or equilibrium: it has two branches, aerodynamics and aerostatics.

ā''ĕr·ō·med'i·cine, *n.* a branch of medicine concerned with the diseases and disorders that are incident to flight in the earth's atmosphere.

ā''ĕr·om'e·tĕr, *n.* [*aero-*, and Gr. *metron*, measure.] an instrument for weighing air or other gases, or for ascertaining the density of air and gases.

ā''ĕr·ō·met'riç, *a.* pertaining to aerometry.

ā''ĕr·om'e·try, *n.* the science of measuring the weight, density, etc. of air and gases; pneumatics.

ā'ĕr·ō·naut, *n.* [*aero-*, and Gr. *nautes*, a sailor.] the pilot or navigator of a balloon or dirigible.

ā''ĕr·ō·naut'iç, ā''ĕr·ō·naut'iç·ăl, *a.* 1. of aeronautics.
2. of aeronauts.

ā''ĕr·ō·naut'içs, *n.* the science or art of making and flying aircraft; aviation.

ā''ĕr·ō·neū·rō'sis, *n.* a nervous condition of aviators under severe stress, with severe stomach pains, digestive disturbances, etc.

ā''ĕr·ō·phā'ġi·ȧ, ā''ĕr·oph'ȧ·ġy, *n.* an abnormal, spasmodic swallowing or gulping of air.

ā''ĕr·ō·phō'bi·ȧ, ā·ĕr·oph'ō·by, *n.* [*aero-*, and Gr. *phobos*, fear.] an abnormal fear of air, especially of drafts.

ā'ĕr·ō·phōne, *n.* [*aero-*, and Gr. *phōnē*, voice.]
1. an apparatus for intensifying sound waves in the air, used to detect approaching aircraft.
2. A trumpetlike appliance for the relief of the deaf.

ā'ĕr·ō·phōre'', *n.* [*aero-*, and *-phore.*] an apparatus for supplying air or oxygen through a face mask, as to workers in mines, under water, etc.

ā''ĕr·ō·phō·tog'rȧ·phy, *n.* the science, art, or practice of taking photographs of the ground, etc. from an aircraft.

ā'ĕr·ō·phȳte (-fīt), *n.* [*aero-*, and Gr. *phyton*, a plant.] same as *epiphyte.*

ā'ĕr·ō·plāne, *n.* [*aero-*, and L. *planus*, flat, level.] same as *airplane.*

ā'ĕr·ō·pulse'', *n.* [*aero-*, and *pulse* (throb).] a jet engine in which the high pressure developed in the burning of the fuel closes the air-intake valves of the combustion chamber: when the air is expelled from the jet, the pressure is lowered enough to open the valves for a fresh air supply.

ā'ĕr·ō·sçep''sy, ā''ĕr·ō·sçep'sis, *n.* [*aero-*, and Gr. *skepsasthai*, to explore.] the faculty of perception by the medium of the air, supposed to be a function of the antennae of insects.

ā'ĕr·ō·sçōpe, *n.* [*aero-*, and Gr. *skopein*, to look out.] in biology, a device for gathering dust, bacteria, etc. from the atmosphere, for microscopic examination.

āe·rōse', *a.* resembling copper or brass.

ā''ĕr·ō·sid'ĕr·īte, *n.* [*aero-*, and Gr. *sidērites*, of iron.] a meteorite consisting chiefly of iron.

a''ĕr·ō·sid'ĕr·ō·līte, *n.* [*aero-*, and Gr. *sidēros*, iron, and *lithos*, stone.] a meteorite containing both iron and stone.

ā'ĕr·ō·sol'', *n.* [*aero-*, and *sol* (solution).] a suspension of colloidal particles in a gas.

ā'ĕr·ō·sol'' *a.* 1. designating or of a small container in which gas under pressure is used to aerate and dispense liquid through a valve in the form of a spray or foam.
2. dispensed by such a container; as, an *aerosol* insecticide, *aerosol* shaving cream.

ā'ĕr·ō·spāce'', *n.* [altered from *air-space*, from *air* and *space.*] the earth's atmosphere and the space outside it considered as one continuous field.

ā'ĕr·ō·spāce'', *a.* of aerospace, or of spacecraft or missiles designed for flight in aerospace.

ā'ĕr·ō·sphēre, *n.* [*aero-*, and *sphere*, from Gr. *sphaira*, a ball.] the air surrounding the earth; the atmosphere.

ā'ĕr·ō·stat, *n.* [*aero-*, and Gr. *statos*, sustaining.] a dirigible, balloon, or other lighter-than-air craft.

ā''ĕr·ō·stat'iç, ā''ĕr·ō·stat'iç·ăl, *a.* 1. of aerostatics.
2. aeronautic.
3. used in aerostats.

ā''ĕr·ō·stat'içs, *n.* the science that treats of the equilibrium of air or other gases, or of bodies sustained in them.

ā''ĕr·ō·stā'tion, *n.* 1. aerial navigation of lighter-than-air craft.
2. the science of aerostatics.

ā''ĕr·ō·ther''ȧ·peū'tiçs, *n.pl.* [construed as sing.], [*aero-*, and *therapeutics.*] the treatment of disease by the use of air, especially by exposing the patient to changes of atmospheric pressure.

ā''ĕr·ō·trop'iç, *a.* [*aero-*, and Gr. *tropē*, from *trepein*, to turn.] of, characterized by, influenced by, or having the nature of, geotropism.

ā·ĕr·ot'rō·pişm, *n.* in botany, the deviation of roots from the natural direction of growth, by the action of gases.

ae·rū'ġi·nous (ē-), *a.* [L. *æruginosus*, adj. from *ærugo*, rust of copper, from *æs*, copper.] pertaining to or resembling copper rust; bluish-green.

ae·rū'gō (ē-), *n.* [L., from *æs*, brass, copper.] the rust of brass or copper; verdigris.

ā'ĕr·y, *a.* airy; ethereal; spiritual. [Poetic.]

āer'y, (*also pronounced* ē'rē, ā'ĕr-y), *n.* same as *aerie.*

aes'çhy·nīte (es'), *n.* [Gr. *æschynē*, shame.] a rare mineral found in the Ural Mountains, an ore containing titanium, thorium, cerium, etc.

Aes·çhy·nom'e·nē, *n.* [L., a sensitive plant, from Gr. *aischynomenē*, f. ppr. of *aischynein*, to disfigure.] in botany, a genus of plants of the pea family, *Fabaceæ*, mostly found in South America.

aes·çhy·nom'e·nous, *a.* sensitive, as the leaves of some varieties of *Æschynomene.*

Aes·çū·lā'pi·ăn, Es·çū·lā'pi·ăn, *a.* relating to Aesculapius or the art of healing.

Aes·çū·lā'pi·us, Es·çū·lā'pi·us, *n.* [L., from Gr. *Asklēpios.*] in Roman mythology, the god of medicine, the son of Apollo by the nymph Coronis: identified with the Greek Asclepius.

aes'çū·lin, *n.* see *esculin.*

Ae'sir (ā'sir *or* ē'sir), *n.pl.* [Ice. pl. of *ass*, a god.] the principal gods of Norse mythology, including Odin, Thor, Balder, Loki, Freya, and Tyr.

Ae·sō'pi·ăn, E·sō'pi·ăn, *a* pertaining to Æsop, the famous Greek fabulist, or to his fables.

Ae·sop'iç, E·sop'iç, *a.* same as *Aesopian.*

aes'thȧ·cȳte, *n.* [Gr. *aisthanesthai*, to feel, and *kytos*, cell.] one of the sensory cells of a sponge.

aes''thē·mȧ·tol'ō·ġy, es''thē·mȧ·tol'ō·ġy, *n.* [Gr. *aisthēma*, *aisthēmatos*, sensation, and *logos*, description.] formerly, the branch of physiology treating of the senses and their organs.

aes·thē'si·ȧ, es·thē'si·ȧ, *n.* [Gr. *aisthēsis*, sensation, from *aisthanesthai*, to perceive.] in physiology, perception, feeling, or sensibility.

aes·thē'si·ō·ġen, es·thē'si·ō·ġen, *n.* [Gr. *aisthēsis*, feeling, and *genēs*, producing.] a substance supposed to produce great sensitivity in the nervous system.

aes·thē·si·ol'ō·ġy, es·thē·si·ol'ō·ġy, *n.* the branch of physiology which treats of the sensations.

aes·thē''si·ō·mā'ni·ȧ, *n.* [Gr. *aisthēsis*, feeling, and *mania*, madness.] insanity accompanied by hallucinations. [Obs.]

aes·thē·si·om'e·tĕr, es·thē·si·om'e·tĕr, *n.* [Gr. *aisthēsis*, feeling, and *metron*, measure.] in medicine, an instrument for testing the tactile sensibility of the human body by ascertaining, through the application of the points of the instrument to the skin, the shortest distance at which two points can be perceived as distinctly separate.

aes·thē'sis, es·thē'sis, *n.* aesthesia.

aes·thē·sod'ic, *a.* [Gr. *aisthēsis*, feeling, and *hodos*, a way.] conveying sensory impulses: said of the nerves.

aes'thēte, es'thēte, *n.* [Gr. *aisthētēs*, one who perceives.]
1. a person highly sensitive to art and beauty.
2. a person who exaggerates the value of artistic sensitivity or makes a cult of art and beauty; believer in art for art's sake.

aes·thet'iç, aes·thet'iç·ăl, es·thet'iç, es·thet'iç·ăl, *a.* 1. of aesthetics.
2. of beauty.
3. sensitive to art and beauty; showing good taste; artistic.

aes·thet'iç·ăl·ly, es·thet'iç·ăl·ly, *adv.* 1. According to the principles of aesthetics, with reference to the sense of the beautiful.
2. in an aesthetic manner.

aes·thē·ti'ciăn, es·thē·ti'ciăn (-tish'un), *n.* one versed in aesthetics; an authority in matters of taste.

aes·thet'i·cişm, es·thet'i·cişm, *n.* 1. the doctrine or principles of aesthetics.
2. attachment to aesthetics; a proneness to indulge and cultivate the sense of the beautiful.
3. sensitivity to art and beauty.

aes·thet'içs, es·thet'içs, *n.* [Gr. *aisthētikos*, perceptive by feeling.] the theory of the fine arts and of people's responses to them; the science or that branch of philosophy which deals with the beautiful; the doctrines of taste.

aes''thō·phys·i·ol'ō·ġy, *n.* [Gr. *aisthanesthai*, to perceive, and *physiologia*, *physis*, nature, and *logos*, discourse.] the physiology of sensation and of the organs of sense.

aes·tif'ĕr·ous, *a.* same as *estiferous.*

aes'ti·văl, *a.* [L. *æstivalis*, from *æstas*, summer.] same as *estival.*

aes'ti·vāte, *v.i.* [L. *æstivare*, *æstivatum*, to spend the summer.] same as *estivate.*

aes·ti·vā'tion, *n.* same as *estivation.*

aes'tū·ȧ·ry, *n.* same as *estuary.*

aes'tū·āte, es'tū·āte, *v.i.* [L. *æstuatus*, pp. of *æstuare*, to burn, boil up.] to be agitated; to rage; to boil. [Obs.]

aes·tū·ā'tion, es·tū·ā'tion, *n.* agitation, as of a fluid in boiling; hence, mental agitation or excitement. [Obs.]

aes'tūre, es'tūre, *n.* violent commotion. [Obs.]

Ae·thā'li·um, *n.*, *pl.* **Ae·thā'li·ȧ,** [L., from Gr. *aithalos*, smoke, soot.]
1. a genus of slime molds, *Myxomycetes*, often found in greenhouses: sometimes called *flowers of tan.*
2. [a–] a sporiferous body in slime molds, produced by the fusing of plasmodia.

ā·ē·thē·og'ȧ·mous, *a.* [Gr. *aēthēs*, *a* priv., *ēthos*, custom, and *gamos*, marriage.] in botany, cryptogamous.

ae'thĕr, *n.* same as *ether.*

ae·thē'rē·ăl, *a.* same as *ethereal.*

ae'thi·ops, *n.* formerly, in chemistry, any of certain mineral preparations, black or very dark in color.
aethiops martial; black oxide of iron.
aethiops mineral; a combination of mercury and sulfur, of a black color; black sulfide of mercury.

aeth'ō·ġen, *n.* [Gr. *aithos*, fire, and *genēs*, producing.] in chemistry, boric nitride: it burns with a greenish phosphorescence.

ae'thri·o·sçōpe, *n.* [Gr. *aithrios*, clear, and *skopein*, to observe.] an instrument, including a differential thermometer, for measuring minute changes in the heat radiated from the sky.

Ae·thū′sȧ, *n.* [Gr. *aithousa*, f. ppr. of *aithein*, to burn.] a genus of poisonous plants of the parsley family, *umbelliferæ*.

ae″ti·ō·log′iç·ăl, *a.* same as *etiological*.

ae″ti·ō·log′iç·ăl·ly, *adv.* same as *etiologically*.

ae·ti·ol′ō·ġy, *n.* [Gr. *aitia*, cause, and *logos*, description.] same as *etiology*.

ā·ē·tī′tēs, *n.* [L., from Gr. *aetitēs*, from *aetos*, eagle.] eaglestone; a variety of bog iron.

Ae·tō′li·ăn, *a.* of Aetolia, a region in the western part of ancient Greece, or of its people, customs, etc.

Ae·tō′li·ăn, *n.* a native or inhabitant of Aetolia.

af-, *ad-* in an assimilated form before *f*, as in *affix*.

ȧ·fär′, *adv.* at a distance in place; to or from a distance, used absolutely or with *from* preceding, or *off* following. [Poetic or Archaic.]

ȧ·fēard′, ȧ·fēared′, *a.* [AS. *afæred*, pp. of *afæran*, to frighten, from *a*, and *fær*, terror.] afraid. [Archaic or Dial.]

ā·fē′brile, *a.* [*a-*, not, and *febrile*.] having no fever.

A′fēr, *n.* [L., African] the southwest wind.

af·fȧ·bil′i·ty, *n.* the quality or state of being affable; readiness to converse; civility and courteousness in receiving others and in conversation; winning sociability.

Syn.—civility, courtesy, politeness, sauvity, urbanity, benignity.

af′fȧ·ble, *a.* [Fr. *affable*; L. *affabilis*, easy to be spoken to, from *ad*, to, and *fari*, to speak.]

1. easy to approach and talk to; courteous; complaisant; of easy manners.

2. kindly of aspect; benign; gracious; as, an *affable* mien: opposed to *forbidding*.

Syn.—courteous, civil, complaisant, accessible, mild, benign, gracious, urbane, polite.

af′fȧ·ble·ness, *n.* affability.

af′fȧ·bly, *adv.* in an affable manner.

af·fāir′, *n.* [ME. *afere*; OFr. *afaire*; Fr. *affaire*, from *à faire*, to do; L. *ad*, to, and *facere*, to do.]

1. business of any kind; that which is done, or is to be done.

2. [*pl.*] transactions in general; as, human *affairs*, political or ecclesiastical *affairs*, public *affairs*, a man of *affairs*.

3. [*pl.*] matters of business.

4. any matter, occurrence, or thing.

5. [from *love affair*] an amorous relationship or episode between two people not married to each other; an amour.

Syn.—business, concern, matter, subject, transaction, occurrence.

ȧf·fāire′ d'ȧ·moūr′, [Fr.] a love affair.

ȧf·fāire′ dē coeur (koor), [Fr., an affair of the heart.] a love affair.

ȧf·fāire′ d'hon·neur′ (dọ-noor′), [Fr., an affair of honor.] a duel.

af·fam′ish, *v.t.* [see *famish*.] to starve. [Obs.]

af·fam′ish·ment, *n.* a starving. [Obs.]

af·fat′ū·āte, *v.t.* to infatuate. [Obs.]

af·fēar′, *v.t.* to frighten. [Obs.]

af·feçt′, *v.t.*, affected, *pt.*, *pp.*; affecting, *ppr.* [Fr. *affecter*; L. *affectare*, to strive after.]

1. to act upon; to produce an effect or change upon; as, cold *affects* the body; loss *affects* our interests.

2. to move or stir the emotions of; as, *affected* by grief.

3. to aim at; aspire to; to put on a pretense of; as, to *affect* imperial sway.

4. to frequent or haunt; as, the deer *affects* the forest.

5. to love, or regard with fondness. [Obs.]

Think not that wars we love and strife *affect*. —Fairfax.

6. to be pleased with or take a fancy to [Obs.]

Study what you must *affect*. —Shak.

7. to imitate or assume the character of; as, he *affects* the airs of his superiors.

8. to make a pretentious display of; as, he *affects* a style of dress that is ridiculous.

9. to attempt to imitate, in a manner not natural; to assume a fake appearance of; to feign; as, to *affect* to be grave; *affected* friendship.

Spencer, in *affecting* the ancients, writ no language. —B. Jonson.

Syn.—assume, arrogate, pretend, feign, put on, influence, move, interest, act on, concern.

af·feçt′, *n.* 1. a disposition or tendency. [Obs.]

2. in psychology, (a) an emotion, feeling, or mood as a factor in behavior; (b) a stimulus arousing an emotion, feeling, or mood.

af·feç·tā′tion, *n.* [L., *affectatio(n)*, from *adfectare*, to strive after, imitate.] an attempt to assume or exhibit what is not natural or real; false pretense; artificial appearance, or show; as, an *affectation* of wit or virtue.

af·feçt′ed, *a.* 1. attacked by disease; afflicted.

2. influenced; acted upon.

3. emotionally moved or touched.

4. disposed.

5. given to false show; assuming, or pretending to possess what is not natural or real; as, an *affected* young woman.

6. assumed for effect; artificial; not natural; as, *affected* airs.

7. in algebra, designating or of an equation in which there are two or more powers of the unknown quantity.

af·feçt′ed·ly, *adv.* in an affected manner; hypocritically; with more show than reality; as, to walk *affectedly*; *affectedly* civil.

af·feçt′ed·ness, *n.* the quality of being affected; affectation.

af·feçt′ēr, af·feçt′ŏr, *n.* a person who affects something.

af·feçt·i·bil′i·ty, *n.* the state of being affectible. [Rare.]

af·feçt′i·ble, *a.* that may be affected. [Rare.]

af·feçt′ing, *a.* 1. exciting or touching the emotions; moving; pathetic; as, an *affecting* address.

The most *affecting* music is generally the most simple. —Mitford.

2. full of affectation. [Obs.]

Syn.—moving, pathetic, touching, tender, impressive, exciting.

af·feçt′ing·ly, *adv.* in an affecting manner; in a manner to excite the emotions.

af·feç′tion, *n.* [Fr. *affection*; L. *affectio*, from *afficere*, to affect.]

1. the state of being affected.

2. a mental state or tendency; disposition.

3. fond or tender feeling; warm liking; as, the *affection* of a parent for his child. The word is also often used in this sense in the plural; as, he won her *affections*.

4. in a general sense, an attribute, quality, or property; as, love, fear, and hope are *affections* of the mind; form, weight, and dimensions are *affections* of bodies.

5. the state of the mind toward a thing; disposition toward; inclination.

6. a disease, or any diseased state, as, a gouty *affection*.

Syn.—fondness, attachment, kindness, love, liking, tenderness.

af·feç′tion·ăl, *a.* of the affections.

af·feç′tion·āte, *a.* 1. having great love, or affection; fond; as, an *affectionate* brother.

2. warm in feeling; zealous. [Obs.]

Man, in his love to God, and desire to please him, can never be too *affectionate*. —Sprat.

3. proceeding from affection; indicating love; benevolent; tender; as, the *affectionate* care of a parent; an *affectionate* disposition.

4. strongly inclined: used with *to*. [Obs.]

Syn.—tender, attached, loving, devoted, warm, fond, earnest, kind, ardent.

af·feç′tion·āte·ly, *adv.* with affection; fondly; tenderly; kindly.

af·feç′tion·āte·ness, *n.* the quality of being affectionate.

af·feç′tioned, *a.* disposed; inclined. [Rare.]

Kindly *affectioned* one to another. —Rom. xii.

af·feç′tive, *a.* that affects or excites emotion; emotional.

af·feç′tive·ly, *adv.* in an affective manner.

af·feç·tiv′i·ty, *n.* in psychology, sensitivity to emotional stimuli; tendency to affects, or emotional responses.

af·feç′tū·ous, *a.* full of affection. [Obs.]

af·feer′, *v.t.* [ME. *affeer*; OFr. *affeurer*; L. *afforare*, to fix a price; from *ad*, to, and *forum*, market.]

1. in old English law, to fix the amount of (an amercement); to assess.

2. to confirm. [Obs.]

af·feer′ment, *n.* the act of affeering.

af·feer′ŏr, af·feer′ēr, *n.* a person who affeers.

af′fēr·ent, *a.* [L. *afferens*, ppr. of *afferre*, *ad*, to, and *ferre*, to bear.] in physiology, bringing inward to a central part; as, *afferent* nerves.

af·fet·tū·ō′sō, *a.* [It.] tender; affecting: in music, a direction to the performer.

af·fī′ănce, *n.* [ME. *affiance*, *afiance*; OFr. *afiance*, from *afier*, to trust in.]

1. the marriage contract or promise; betrothal.

2. trust, reliance, or faith.

The Christian looks to God with implicit *affiance*. —Atterbury.

af·fī′ănce, *v.t.*; affianced, *pt.*, *pp.*; affiancing, *ppr.* 1. to betroth; to pledge in marriage, or to promise marriage to.

2. to promise solemnly; to pledge.

af·fī′ănced (-ănst), *n.* one betrothed; a future husband or wife.

I with my *affianced*. —Tennyson.

af·fī′ăn·cēr, *n.* one who makes a contract of marriage between two persons.

af·fī′ănt, *n.* [OFr. *affiant*, ppr. of *affier*, to pledge one's faith.] in law, one who makes an affidavit.

af·fiçhe′, *n.* [Fr. *afficher*, to fasten to.] a paper or bill posted in a public place; a poster.

af·fi·dā′vit, *n.* [L. he has made oath. Perf. tense of *affidare*.] a declaration upon oath; a declaration in writing signed by the party and sworn to, usually before a notary public.

af·file′, *v.t.* [Fr. *affiler*; L. *ad*, to, and *fil*, thread.] to sharpen. [Obs.]

af·fil′i·ȧ·ble, *a.* capable of being affiliated.

af·fil′i·āte, *v.t.*; affiliated, *pt.*, *pp.*; affiliating, *ppr.* [Fr. *affilier*, from L. *adfiliare*, to adopt as a son, *ad*, to, and *filius*, son.]

1. to adopt as a member or branch.

2. to connect or associate (oneself).

3. to trace the origin and connections of.

4. to determine legally the paternity of (an illegitimate child).

Syn.—adopt, admit, initiate, receive.

af·fil′i·āte, *v.i.* to unite or associate oneself; as, to *affiliate* with a political party.

af·fil·i·ā′tion, *n.* 1. adoption; association, as with organizations, clubs, etc.

2. in law, the fixing of the paternity of a child.

3. the assignment of anything to its origin; connection by way of descent.

af·fī′năl, *a.* [OFr. *affin*, *afin*, a kinsman or ally; L. *affinis*, from *ad*, to, and *finis*, border, end.] related by marriage.

af·fine′, *v.t.* to refine. [Obs.]

af·fīned′, *a.* joined in affinity.

af·fin′i·tȧ·tive, *a.* of the nature of affinity.

af·fin′i·tȧ·tive·ly, *adv.* by means of affinity.

af·fin′i·tive, *a.* closely connected.

af·fin′i·ty, *n.* [L. *affinitas*, from *affinis*, adjacent, related by marriage; *ad*, to, and *finis*, end.]

1. the relation contracted by marriage: distinguished from *consanguinity*, or relation by blood.

Solomon made *affinity* with Pharaoh. —1 Kings iii. 1.

2. a condition of close relationships; conformity; resemblance; connection; as, the *affinity* of sounds, of colors, or of languages.

3. in chemistry, that force by which atoms of certain elements combine and stay combined.

4. a resemblance in general plan or structure, or in the essential structural parts, existing between species, languages, etc., implying common origin.

5. a mutual attraction between individuals of opposite sex; also, either of the individuals so attracted; as, there is an *affinity* between us; she is my *affinity*.

6. companionship; acquaintance. [Obs.]

Syn.—alliance, kindred, relationship.

af·firm′, *v.t.*; affirmed, *pt.*, *pp.*; affirming, *ppr.* [ME. *affermen*; OFr. *affirmer*; L. *affirmare*, to present as fixed; *ad*, to, and *firmare*, to make firm.]

1. to assert positively; to tell with confidence; to aver; to declare the existence of; to maintain as true: opposed to *deny*.

Affirming each his own philosophy. —Tennyson.

2. to establish, confirm, or ratify; as, the supreme court *affirmed* the judgment.

Syn.—aver, protest, assert, asseverate, assure, protest, avouch, confirm, establish, ratify, declare, pronounce.

af·firm′, *v.i.* 1. to make a positive statement, as of fact.

2. to declare formally and solemnly before a court without taking an oath; to make a legal affirmation.

af·firm′ȧ·ble, *a.* capable of being asserted or declared: followed by *of*; as, charity in judgment is *affirmable of* every just man.

af·firm′ȧ·bly, *adv.* in a way capable of affirmation.

af′firm′ănce, *n.* 1. confirmation; ratification; as, the *affirmance* of a judgment; a statute in *affirmance* of common law.

2. declaration; affirmation. [Rare.]

They swear it till *affirmance* breeds a doubt. —Cowper.

3. in law, an upholding by an upper court of a lower court's judgment.

af·firm′ănt, *n.* one who affirms; one who makes a legal affirmation.

af·fīr·mā′tion, *n.* [L. *affirmatio*, from *affirmare*, to affirm.]

1. the act of affirming or asserting as true: opposed to *negation* or *denial*.
2. that which is asserted; positive declaration.
3. confirmation; ratification.
4. a solemn declaration made, under the penalties of perjury, by persons who conscientiously decline taking an oath: such *affirmation* is in law equivalent to an oath.

af·firm′ȧ·tive, *a.* [Fr. *affirmatif*; L. *affirmativus*, from *affirmare*, to affirm.]
1. affirming or asserting: opposed to *negative*; as, an *affirmative* proposition.
2. confirmative; ratifying; as, an act *affirmative* of common law.
3. in mathematics, positive: a term applied to quantities to be added: opposed to *negative*.
4. positive; dogmatic. [Obs.]

af·firm′ȧ·tive, *n.* 1. that side in a debate which upholds the proposition being debated: opposed to the *negative*.
2. a short expression of assent, as the word *yes*.
3. a statement in which anything is affirmed; an affirmative proposition; an affirmation.

af·firm′ȧ·tive aç′tion, a policy or program for correcting the effects of discrimination in the employment or education of members of certain groups, as women, blacks, etc.

af·firm′ȧ·tive·ly, *adv.* in an affirmative manner; positively; on the affirmative side of a question: opposed to *negatively*.

af·firm′ȧ·tō·ry, *a.* affirmative; assertive.

af·firm′ẽr, *n.* one who affirms.

af·fix′, *v.t.*; affixed, *pt.*, *pp.*; affixing, *ppr.* [L. *affixare*, freq. of *affigere*, to fasten.]
1. to add at the end; to subjoin; to annex; as, to *affix* a syllable to a word; to *affix* a signature to a letter.
2. to attach, unite, or connect with; as, names *affixed* to ideas, or ideas *affixed* to things.
3. to fix or fasten in any physical manner.
Syn.—attach, add, annex, subjoin, connect, adjoin, append, fasten, fix.

af′fix, *n.* 1. a thing affixed; an addition; an attachment; that which is joined.
2. a syllable or a group of syllables added to a word or root; a prefix, suffix, or infix.
3. in decorative art, any small ornament added or attached, as the dragons on Japanese bronzes.

af·fix·ā′tion, *n.* 1. an affixing or being affixed.
2. in linguistics, the adding of affixes to roots or bases in order to vary function, modify meanings, etc.

af·fix′ion (-fik′shun), *n.* the act of affixing, or the state of being affixed. [Obs.]

af·fix′tūre, *n.* that which is affixed; affixion.

af·flā′tion, *n.* [L. *afflatus*, pp. of *afflare*, to blow, or breathe upon; *ad*, to, and *flare*, to blow.] a blowing or breathing on.

af·flā′tus, *n.* 1. breathing.
2. inspiration or powerful impulse as of a poet, artist, etc.

af·fliçt′, *v.t.*; afflicted, *pt.*, *pp.*; afflicting, *ppr.* [L. *afflictare*, to trouble, agitate, freq. of *affligere*, to strike down.]
1. to cause pain or suffering to; to trouble, grieve, or distress; as, one is *afflicted* with the gout, or with melancholy, or with losses and misfortunes.
2. to humiliate; to humble. [Obs.]
Syn.—torment, distress, trouble, grieve, harass, pain, disquiet.

af·fliçt′ed·ness, *n.* the state of being afflicted; affliction. [Obs.]

af·fliç′tion, *n.* [Fr. *affliction*; L. *afflictio(n)*, from *affligere*, to strike down.]
1. the state of being afflicted; a state of pain, distress, or grief; as, some virtues are seen only in *affliction*.
2. the cause of continued pain or distress, as sickness, losses, calamity, adversity, persecution.

Many are the *afflictions* of the righteous.
—Ps. xxxiv. 19.

Syn.—trouble, distress, sorrow, adversity, misfortune, grief, regret, sadness, tribulation, trial.

af·fliç′tion·less, *a.* having no affliction.

af·fliç′tive, *a.* giving pain; causing continued or repeated pain or grief; painful; distressing.

af·fliç′tive·ly, *adv.* in an afflictive manner, so as to give pain or grief.

af′flū·ence, *n.* [Fr. *affluence*; L. *affluentia*, abundance, from *affluere*, to flow to; *ad*, to, and *fluere*, to flow.]
1. a flowing to or toward; influx; as, an *affluence* of new settlers.
2. abundance; specifically, abundance of riches; wealth; as, a man of *affluence*.

Many new men rose rapidly to *affluence*.
—Macaulay.

Syn.—abundance, wealth, opulence, plenty, exuberance, prosperity, riches.

af′flū·en·cy, *n.* affluence. [Obs.]

af′flū·ent, *a.* 1. flowing freely.
2. wealthy; plentiful; abundant.
Syn.—rich, opulent, fluent.

af′flū·ent, *n.* [L. *affluens*, ppr. of *affluere*, to flow to.] a tributary stream.

af′flū·ent·ly, *adv.* in abundance; abundantly.

af′flū·ent·ness, *n.* the state of being affluent.

af′flux, *n.* [L. *affluxum*, pp. of *affluere*, to flow to; *ad*, to, and *fluere*, to flow.] the act of flowing to; a flowing to, or that which flows to; as, an *afflux* of blood to the head.

af·flux′ion (-fluk′shun), *n.* afflux.

af·fōrce′, *v.t.* [OFr. *afforcier*; L. *affortiare*, from *ad*, to, and *fortis*, strong.] to reinforce; to strengthen.

af·fōrd′, *v.t.*; afforded, *pt.*, *pp.*; affording, *ppr.* [ME. *aforthen*; AS. *gefarthien*, further, advance; *ge-*, and *farthian*, further.]
1. to give forth, yield, or produce; as, the earth *affords* grain; trade *affords* profit.
2. to yield, grant, or confer; as, a good life *affords* consolation in old age.
3. to be able to sell at a profit. [Obs.]
4. to have the means for; to be able to bear expenses, or the price of, without serious inconvenience; as, one man can *afford* to buy a farm, which another cannot: in this sense, generally preceded by *can* or *be able*.
Syn.—spare, supply, give, impart, furnish, bestow.

af·fōrd′ȧ·ble, *a.* that can be afforded.

af·for′est, *v.t.* [L. *afforestare*, to convert into a forest; *ad*, to, and *foresta*, forest.] to convert (ground) into forest; to plant many trees on.

af·for·es·tā′tion, *n.* the act or result of turning ground into forest or woodland.

af·fọrm′ȧ·tive, *n.* a formative added to the stem; an affix, as *-ly* in king*ly*, *-ous* in virtu*ous*.

af·fran′chīṣe, *v.t.*; affranchised, *pt.*, *pp.*; affranchising, *ppr.* [Fr. *affranchir*, to make free; *a* for L. *ad*, to, and *franc*, free.] to free from any controlling power; to liberate; to make free; to enfranchise.

af·fran′chīṣe·ment, *n.* the act of making free, or liberating from dependence or servitude.

af·frāy′, *n.* [ME. *affray*, terror, brawl; OFr. *esfrai*; Fr. *affray*, from *affrayer*, to disquiet.]
1. in law, a public fight or riot. A private fight is not an *affray* in the legal sense.
2. popularly, any fight, quarrel, or brawl; tumult; disturbance.
Syn.—quarrel, brawl, scuffle, encounter, fight, contest, tumult, disturbance.

af·frāy′ẽr, *n.* one who engages in affrays.

af·frei̤ght′ (-frāt′), *v.t.*; affreighted, *pt.*, *pp.*; affreighting, *ppr.* [Fr. *affreter*; *a*, and *freter*, freight, charter.] to hire for the transportation of goods or freight, as a vessel.

af·frei̤ght′ẽr, *n.* a person who hires or charters a ship to convey goods.

af·frei̤ght′ment, *n.* the act of hiring a ship for the transportation of goods.

af′friç·āte, *n.* [L. *affricatus*, pp. of *affricare*, to rub against, from *ad-*, to, and *fricare*, to rub.] in phonetics, any of the complex sounds produced when slowly released stop consonants are followed immediately by fricatives (spirants) at the same point of articulation: the English affricates are those in *latch* and *judge*.

af″friç·ā′tion, *n.* in phonetics, the slow release of stop consonants causing the formation of affricates.

af·friç′a·tive, *n.* an affricate.

af·friç′a·tive, *a.* of or forming an affricate.

af·frīght′ (-frīt′), *n.* 1. sudden or great fear; terror. [Archaic.]
2. the cause of terror; a frightful object. [Archaic.]

The gods upbraid our suff'rings,
By sending these *affrights*. —B. Jonson.

af·frīght′, *v.t.*; affrighted, *pt.*, *pp.*; affrighting, *ppr.* [ME. *afrighten*; AS. *afyrhtan*, to terrify.] to impress with sudden fear; to frighten; to terrify or alarm. [Archaic.]
Syn.—alarm, appall, dismay, shock, terrify.

af·frīght′ed·ly, *adv.* with fright. [Archaic.]

af·frīght′en, *v.t.* to frighten. [Archaic.]

af·frīght′ẽr, *n.* one who frightens. [Archaic.]

af·frīght′ful, *a.* terrifying; terrible; that may excite great fear; dreadful. [Archaic.]

af·frīght′ment, *n.* fright; terror; the state of being frightened. [Archaic.]

af·frŏnt′, *v.t.*; affronted, *pt.*, *pp.*; affronting, *ppr.* [Fr. *affronter*, to encounter face to face; L. *affrontare*; *ad*, to, and *frons*, front, forehead.]
1. literally, to meet or encounter face to face, in a good or bad sense. [Obs.]

The seditious *affronted* the king's forces.
—Milton.

2. to insult openly; to offer abuse or insult in any manner, by words or actions; to slight.
3. to confront defiantly.

af·frŏnt′, *n.* 1. an open or intentional insult; anything reproachful or contemptuous that excites or justifies resentment, as foul language, or personal abuse; incivility.
2. shame; disgrace; anything producing a feeling of shame or disgrace; an indignity.
Syn.—insult, abuse, offense, annoyance, indignity, wrong, outrage.

af·frọn·té′ (-tā′), *a.* [Fr.] in heraldry, face to face: an epithet applied to animals that face each other on an escutcheon; also, facing the spectator, as the lion in the crest of Scotland.

af·frŏnt′ed·ly, *adv.* affrontingly. [Obs.]

af·frŏnt′ẽr, *n.* one who affronts.

af·frŏnt′ing·ly, *adv.* in an affronting manner.

af·frŏnt′ive, *a.* giving offense; tending to offend; abusive. [Rare.]

af·frŏnt′ive·ness, *n.* the quality of being affrontive. [Rare.]

af·fūṣe′, *v.t.* [L. *affusus*, pp. of *affundere*, to pour to; *ad*, to, and *fundere*, to pour.] to pour upon; to sprinkle, as with a liquid. [Rare.]

af·fū′ṣion, *n.* 1. a pouring on, or sprinkling with, a liquid, as water upon a child in baptism.
2. in medicine, the act of pouring water, etc. on the whole or part of the body as a treatment for fevers.

af·fȳ′, *v.t.* to betroth; to bind or join. [Obs.]

af·fȳ′, *v.i.* to trust or confide. [Obs.]

Af′ghȧn (-gȧn), *n.* 1. a native of Afghanistan.
2. the language of Afghanistan.
3. [a–] a kind of woolen blanket or shawl.

Af′ghȧn, *a.* pertaining to Afghanistan.

ä·fi·ciọ·nä′dọ (ä-fi-thyọ-nä′thọ), *n.* [Sp.] a devotee.

ȧ·fiēld′, *adv.* to the field; in the field; abroad; astray.

ȧ·fīre′, *adv.* and *a.* on fire.

ȧ·flāme′, *adv.* and *a.* flaming; ablaze.

ȧ·flat′, *adv.* and *a.* flat.

af″lȧ·tox′in, *n.* [from *Aspergillus flavus*, (the fungus), and *toxin*.] any of several carcinogenic substances produced by a fungus found especially on peanuts.

ȧ·flaunt′, *adv.* in a flaunting manner.

ȧ·flick′ẽr, *adv.* in a flickering state or condition.

ȧ·flōat′, *a.* 1. floating on the surface; as, the ship is *afloat*.
2. on board ship; at sea; as, much wheat is *afloat*.
3. moving; in circulation; passing from place to place; as, a rumor is *afloat*.
4. unfixed; moving without guide or control; as, our affairs are all *afloat*.
5. flooded; awash; as, the deck is *afloat*.

ȧ·flōw′, *adv.* and *a.* flowing.

ȧ·flush′, *adv.* and *a.* 1. flushed or blushing.
2. on the same level.

ȧ·flut′tẽr, *adv.* and *a.* in a flutter.

ȧ·fōam′, *adv.* in a foaming state.

ȧ fōnd (ȧ fōn′), [Fr.] 1. to the bottom or foundation.
2. thoroughly; completely.

ȧ·foot′, *adv.* and *a.* 1. on foot; traveling or moving on the feet.
2. in action; astir; about.
3. in a state of preparation; as, a design is *afoot*.

ȧ·fōre′, *adv.* [ME. *aforn*; AS. *onforan*; *on*, on, and *foran*, at the front.]
1. before. [Archaic or Dial.]
2. in the fore part of a vessel.

ȧ·fōre′, *prep.* before; as, *afore* God; *afore* the mast. [Archaic or Dial.]

ȧ·fōre′, *conj.* rather than; before; as, *afore* I'll endure tyranny I'll die. [Archaic or Dial.]

ȧ·fōre′cīt·ed, *a.* previously quoted.

ȧ·fōre′gō·ing, *a.* going before; referring to something previous.

ȧ·fōre′hand, *adv.* in time previous; by previous provision: beforehand. [Archaic or Dial.]

ȧ·fōre′men·tioned, *a.* mentioned before or previously.

ȧ·fōre′nāmed, *a.* named before or previously.

ȧ·fōre′said (-sed), *a.* said before or previously.

ȧ·fōre′thought (-thạt), *a.* premeditated; thought out beforehand; as, malice *aforethought*.

ȧ·fōre′thought, *n.* previous deliberation; forethought.

à·fōre′tīme, *adv.* in time past; in a former time.

ā fọr·ti·ō′rī (-shi-),all the more: said of a conclusion that follows with even greater logical necessity than another already accepted in the argument.

à·foul′, *adv.* or *a.* entangled; in a collision.
to run afoul of; (a) to collide with so as to cause entanglement or injury; (b) to get into trouble with.

Afr-, Afro-.

à·frāid′, *a.* [ME. *afraied*, pp. of *afraien*, to frighten.] fearful; frightened; timid; stricken with fear; apprehensive of disaster; dreading: followed by *of, that*, or an infinitive. It is often used colloquially to indicate regretful realization; as, I'm *afraid* he lies.
Syn.—alarmed, apprehensive, cautious, timid, fearful, timorous, cowardly, frightened.

Af″rà·mer′i·căn, *a.* and *n.* same as *Afro-American.*

Af·rā′siăn, *a.* [*Afr-*, and *Asian.*] of Afrasia.

Af·rā′siăn, *n.* the offspring of an African and an Asiatic.

af′reet, af′rĭt, *n.* [Ar. *'ifrit*, a demon.] in Arabic mythology, a powerful, evil demon.

à·fresh′, *adv.* anew; again; once more.

Af′riç, *a.* and *n.* same as *African.*

Af′ri·căn, *a.* [L. *Afer*, an African.]
1. pertaining to Africa, its peoples, culture, etc.
2. Negro or Negroid.

Af′ri·căn, *n.* 1. a native or inhabitant of Africa.
2. a member of an African race; Negro or Negroid.

Af″ri·can′dēr, *n.* same as *Afrikander.*

Af′ri·căn·ism, *n.* a word, idiom, custom, or other characteristic of natives of Africa.

Af′ri·căn·īze, *v.t.* 1. to staff with native Negro Africans.
2. to give an African character, etc. to.

Af′ri·căn lil′y, an African plant of the lily family, having straplike leaves and clusters of blue or white, funnel-shaped flowers.

Af′ri·căn sleep′ing sick′ness, same as *sleeping sickness.*

Af′ri·căn vī′ō·let, any of a group of tropical African plants with violet or pinkish flowers.

Af″ri·käans′, *n.* [S.Afr.D., from *Afrika*, Africa.] the Dutch dialect spoken in South Africa: also called *Cape Dutch, Taal.*

Af″ri·kan′dēr, *n.* [S.Afr.D., from D. *Afrikaner*, with *d* after *Hollander.*]
1. Afrikaner: an earlier name.
2. a breed of cattle, originally from Africa.

Af″ri·kä′nēr, *n.* [D.] a South African of European, especially Dutch, ancestry; Boer.

Af′rō, *a.* [from L. *Afer*, an African.]
1. designating or of a full bouffant hair style, as worn by some Negroes.
2. Afro-American. [Colloq.]

Af′rō, *n.* an Afro hair style.

Af′rō-, a combining form meaning; (a) Africa; (b) African.

Af″rō-À·mer′i·căn, *a.* of Negro Americans, their culture, etc.

Af″rō-À·mer′i·căn, *n.* a Negro American.

à·frŏnt′, *adv.* in front.

à·frŏnt′, *prep.* in front of.

àft, *a.* or *adv.* [AS. *æftan*, behind, in the rear.] in nautical use, at, toward, or in the stern of a ship; abaft; astern.

àft′ēr, *a.* [ME. *after*; AS. *æfter*, after; Ice. *aptr*; Gr. *apōterō*, further off.]
1. more aft, or toward the stern of the ship; as, *after*sails; *after* hatchway.
2. next later in time; as, in *after*life.
After hands shall sow the seed.
—Whittier.

àft′ēr, *prep.* 1. behind; as, men placed in line one *after* another.
2. later in time; as, *after* supper.
3. in pursuit of; moving behind; following; in search of; as, the police are *after* him.
4. in imitation of; as, to make a thing *after* a model; a portrait *after* Vandyke.
5. according to; as, consider a thing *after* its intrinsic value.
6. according to the direction and influence of.
To live *after* the flesh. —Rom. viii. 12.
7. in honor of; for the sake of; as, to name a boy *after* his father.
8. below in order of rank or excellence; as, Milton comes *after* Shakespeare.
9. in consequence of; as, *after* this experience, I will take greater precautions.
10. in opposition to; as, *after* all warnings, he persisted.
11. concerning; about; as, to inquire *after* one who is absent.

àft′ēr, *adv.* subsequently; later in time; also, behind; in the rear; as, he comes *after*. This is really an elliptical use of the preposition, the object being understood.

àft′ēr, *conj.* following the time when; later than.

àft″ēr·aç·çount′, *n.* a subsequent reckoning.

àft′ēr·act, *n.* a subsequent act.

àft′ēr·āġ″eṣ, *n.pl.* later ages; succeeding times.

àft′ēr·bīrth, *n.* 1. the placenta and fetal membranes expelled from the womb after childbirth.
2. in law, a child born after the father's death or final will.

àft′ēr·brāin, *n.* the posterior part of the hindbrain; myelencephalon.

àft′ēr·bŭrn″ēr, *n.* 1. a device attached to the tail pipe of some jet engines, using hot exhaust gases to burn extra fuel for added thrust.
2. an auxiliary device, as on internal-combustion engines and incinerators, for burning undesirable exhaust gases produced during the original combustion.

àft′ēr·çlap, *n.* an unexpected subsequent event; something disagreeable happening after an affair is supposed to be at an end.

àft′ēr·çost, *n.* later cost; expense after the execution of the main design.

àft′ēr·çōurse, *n.* a following course at a meal; a dessert.

àft′ēr·çrop, *n.* the second crop in the same year.

àft′ēr·damp, *n.* an asphyxiating gas left in a mine after an explosion of firedamp.

àft′ēr·dāyṣ, *n.pl.* future days.

àft′ēr·deçk, *n.* the part of a ship's deck toward the stern.

àft′ēr·din′nēr, *a.* following a dinner.

àft′ēr·ef·feçt″, *n.* an effect that is realized later, or as a secondary result.

àft·ēr·eȳe′, *v.t.* to keep (one) in view; to look after. [Rare.]

àft′ēr·gāme, *n.* a second game played in order to reverse or improve on the results of the first; hence, a subsequent scheme, or expedient.

àft′ēr·glōw, *n.* 1. the glow remaining after a light has gone, as in the western sky after sunset.
2. the pleasant feeling one has after an enjoyable experience.

àft′ēr·gràss, *n.* a second crop of grass.

àft′ēr·grōwth, *n.* second growth; figuratively, development.

àft′ēr·guärd, *n.* seamen stationed on the poop or afterpart of ship, to attend aftersails.

àft′ēr·hōpe, *n.* future hope.

àft′ēr·im″āġe, *n.* in psychology, an image or sensation retained after the external stimulus is withdrawn.

àft′ēr·ings, *n.pl.* the last milk drawn in milking a cow.

àft′ēr·līfe, *n.* 1. future life, or life after death.
2. a later period of life; subsequent life.

àft′ēr·math, *n.* a second crop of grass in the same season; hence, a result, usually an unpleasant one.

àft′ēr·mōst, *a. superl.* hindmost; nearest the stern: opposed to *foremost.*

àft·ēr·noon′, *n.* the part of the day between noon and evening.

àft·ēr·noon′, *a.* of, in, or for the afternoon.

àft′ēr·pāins, *n.pl.* the pains which follow childbirth.

àft′ēr·pärt, *n.* the latter part; in nautical usage, the part of a ship toward the stern.

àft′ēr·piēçe, *n.* a piece performed after a play; a short dramatic production.

àft′ēr·sāilṣ, *n.pl.* sails on the mizzenmast.

af′tēr·sen·sā″tion, *n.* in psychology, an afterimage of peripheral origin.

àft′ēr·shàft, *n.* a feather springing from the posterior side of the stem of another feather; the shaft of such a feather; the hypoptilum.

àft′ēr·swärm, *n.* a swarm of bees which leaves the hive after the first swarm.

àft′ēr·tāste, *n.* 1. the taste left in the mouth after eating or drinking.
2. the feeling remaining after an experience.

àft′ēr·thought (-thọt), *n.* reflection after an act or experience; a later thought; a thought or expedient occurring too late to be useful.

àft′ēr·tīme, *n.* succeeding time; the future.

àft′ēr·wărd, àft′ēr·wărdṣ, *adv.* in later or subsequent time.

àft′ēr·wit, *n.* subsequent wit; wisdom that comes too late.

af′tēr·wŏrld″, *n.* a world after this one; world supposedly existing after death, for spirits, etc.

àft′mōst, *a.* in nautical usage, nearest to the stern.

ag-, ad-: used before *g*, as in *ag*grade.

Ag, *argentum*, [L.], in chemistry, silver.

ä′gȧ, ä′ghȧ, *n.* [Turk. *agha*, commander.] in Moslem countries, a title of respect given to various chief officers, whether civil or military.

à·gain′ (à-gen′), *adv.* [ME. *agen*; AS. *ongegn*, *ongean*; *on*, for *an*, on, and *gean*, like G. *gegen*, against.]
1. back toward a former position, place, or person; as, bring us word *again.*
2. back; in return, as a reply, etc.; as, to answer *again*. [Rare.]
3. moreover; further; in addition; as, *again*, let me add; *again*, it is further to be considered.
4. once more; anew; another time; as, if a man die, shall he live *again?*—Job xiv. 14.
5. on the other hand; from a contrary standpoint.
6. in the opposite direction; back. [Obs.]
again and again; often; repeatedly.
as much again; as much more; twice the amount or number.
now and again; now and then; occasionally.

à·gain′, *prep.* against; toward; in order to meet. [Obs.]

à·gainst′ (-genst′), *prep.* [ME. *againest, again*, from AS. *ongegn*, and *es*, a genit. ending, and *t*, intensive.]
1. so as to contradict or refute; as, a decree *against* law, reason, or public opinion.
2. in competition with, as between different sides or parties; as, there are twenty votes in the affirmative *against* ten in the negative.
3. in an opposite direction to; as, to ride *against* the wind.
4. opposite in place; abreast; as, a ship is *against* the mouth of a river. In this sense it is often preceded by *over.*
5. in opposition to; adverse to; as, this change of measures is *against* us.
6. toward so as to come in contact with or strike; as, throw the ball *against* the wall.
7. in contrast with; as, green *against* the gold.
8. in preparation for; as, have things ready *against* our return.
9. as a debit or charge on; as, many bills were entered *against* his account.

ag·à·laç′ti·à, *n.* [Gr. *agalaktia*, from *a* priv., and *gala, galaktos*, milk.] a deficiency in the secretion of milk by the mother after childbirth.

ag·à·laç′tous, *a.* characterized by agalactia.

à·gal′lō·chum, à·gal′lŏch, *n.* [L., from Gr. *agallochon*, the fragrant aloe.] a very soft, resinous, East Indian wood with a highly aromatic smell. It is burnt as a perfume and is the aloes of the Bible. Also called *agalwood.*

ag·al·mat′ō·līte, *n.* [Gr. *agalma, agalmatos*, image, and *lithos*, stone.] a soft variety of pinite carved into images by the Chinese, and hence called figure stone: also called *steatite* and *pagodite.*

Ag′à·mà, *n.* a genus of lizard that changes color like the chameleon.

ag′à·mà, *n.* [Guiana name.] a species of the genus *Agama.*

Ag·à·mem′non, *n.* [Gr.] in Greek legend, king of Mycenae and commander in chief of the Greek army in the Trojan War, killed by his wife Clytemnestra.

ag′à·mï, *n.* [Fr., from the Guiana name.] a long-legged, long-necked wading bird of Central America; trumpeter.

AGAMI
(*Psophia crepitans*)

à·gam′iç, *a.* [Gr. *agamos*; *a* priv., and *gamos*, married.] produced without sexual union; asexual.

à·gam′iç·ăl·ly, *adv.* in an agamic manner.

ag′à·mist, *n.* [Gr. *agamos*; *a* priv., and *gamos*, married.] an unmarried person, or one who is opposed to marriage and advocates celibacy. [Obs.]

ag″à·mō·ġen′e·sis, *n.* [Gr. *agamos*; *a* priv., and *gamos*, married, and *genesis*, reproduction.] in biology, asexual reproduction.

ag″à·mō·ġē·net′iç, *a.* produced asexually.
ag″à·mō·ġē·net′iç·ăl·ly, *adv.* by or with asexual reproduction.
ag′à·moid, *n.* an agama.
ag′à·moid, *a.* pertaining to or having the characteristics of lizards of the genus *Agama.*
à·gam′ō·spōre, *n.* [Gr. *agamos*; *a* priv., and *gamos,* married, and *spora,* seed.] a spore produced asexually.
ag′à·mous, *a.* [Gr. *a* priv., and *gamos,* marriage.]
1. in botany, having no flowers or seeds; cryptogamous.
2. in biology, asexual.
à·gan̄·gli·on′iç, *a.* having no ganglia.
ag·à·pan′thus, *n.* [Gr. *agapē,* love, and *anthos,* flower.] any of a number of related African plants of the lily family, with clusters of white, purple, or blue flowers.
à·gāpe′, *adv.* or *a.* gaping, as with wonder, expectation, or eager attention; having the mouth wide open.
ag′à·pē, *n.*; *pl.* **ag′à·pae,** [Gr. *agapē,* love.]
1. a meal that early Christians ate together: see *love feast.*
2. in Christian theology, (a) God's love for man; (b) spontaneous, altruistic love.
Ag·à·pem′ō·nē, *n.* [Gr. *agapē,* love, and *monē,* abode.] an association of men and women living promiscuously on a common fund; specifically, the association formed in England in 1846.
ā′gär, *n.* [Malay.]
1. agar-agar.
2. a substance containing agar-agar.
ā′gär-ā′gär, *n.* 1. the native Malay name for a seaweed—the *Gracilaria lichenoides*—much used in the East for soups and jellies.
2. a gelatinous product made from this, and used as a base for bacterial cultures, as a laxative, etc.
ag′à·riç (*or* à·gar′ic), *n.* a fungus of the genus *Agaricus.*

AGARIC
(*Agaricus disseminatus*)

à·gar·i·çā′ceous, *a.* belonging to the gill fungi family, including most toadstools and mushrooms.
à·gar′i·cin, *n.* an extract of the white agaric, *Polyporus officinalis.*
à·gar′i·çoid, *a.* of the nature of an agaric; mushroomlike.
À·gar′i·çus, *n.* [L. *agaricum,* from Gr. *agarikon.*] in botany, a genus of fungi containing numerous species, including many of the most common mushrooms, some of which are edible while others are poisonous.
In pharmacy, either of two species of fungus belonging to the genus *Polyporus*; that of the larch, *Polyporus laricis,* called also *male agaric*; and that of the oak, *Polyporus igniarius,* called also *female agaric.* The former was used as a cathartic; the latter as a styptic, and also for tinder and in dyeing.
agaric mineral; a light, chalky deposit of carbonate of lime formed in caverns or fissures of limestone.
à·gäsp′, *adv.* and *a.* in a gasping manner; out of breath.
à·gäst′, *a.* obsolete spelling of *aghast.*
À·gas′tri·à, *n.pl.* [Gr. *a* priv., and *gastēr,* stomach.] a division of *Metazoa* without intestines.
à·gas′triç, *a.* without a stomach or digestive canal, as the tapeworm.
à·gāte′, *adv.* on the way; going. [British Dial.]
ag′ăte, *n.* [Fr. *agate*; L. *achates*; Gr. *achatēs,* an agate.]
1. a hard semiprecious variety of chalcedony having various tints in the same specimen. Its colors are arranged in stripes or bands, or are blended in clouds. Some varieties are *fortification agate, moss agate, ribbon agate, zone agate, star agate,* etc.
2. an instrument used by gold wire drawers, as a polishing tool with a tip of agate.
3. in printing, type of a size, 5½ point, between pearl and nonpareil. In England it is called *ruby.*
This line is printed in agate.
4. in bookbinding, a burnisher.
5. a playing marble made of agate, or of some material in imitation of agate.
6. a very small person: from the little figures carved on *agate* seals.
ag′ăte, *a.* resembling agate; agate-colored.
ag′ăte glass, a variegated glass made by blending glass of various colors in melting.
ag′ăte grāy, a color yellow in hue and of very low saturation.
ag′ăte jas′pẽr, a variety of quartz made up of jasper and agate.
ag′ăte ō′păl, opalized agate.
ag′ăte shell, a shell of the agate snail: some of these shells are among the largest of land shells.
ag′ăte snāil, a land snail of the genus *Achatina.*
ag′ăte·wāre, *n.* 1. pottery made to resemble agate, by veining and marbling the colors.
2. pots and pans of iron or steel enameled to look like agate.
Ag′à·this, *n.* [Gr. *agathis,* a ball of thread.] same as *Dammara.*
ag′à·thiṣm, *n.* [Gr. *agathos,* good, and *-ism.*] the doctrine that all things tend toward ultimate good.
ag·à·tif′ẽr·ous, *a.* composed of or producing agates.
ag′à·tine, *a.* pertaining to agate.
ag′à·tīze, *v.t.* to change to or make to resemble agate.
ag′à·tīzed, *a.* made into or resembling agate.
ag′à·ty, *a.* of the nature of agate.
à gauche (à gōsh′), [Fr.] to the left; on the left.
À·gā′vē, *n.* [Gr. *agauos,* noble.]
1. a genus of related plants of the amaryllis family, including especially the century plant of American deserts, also called *maguey* in Mexico: it attains maturity in from ten to fifty or sixty years at which time a flowered stem shoots up from the center to a height of about forty feet. The plant has many uses. From its sap *pulque* is made. An extract from its leaves serves as soap, and the withered flower stem is cut up for razor strops. Thread, rope, and paper are made from the fiber of its leaves.

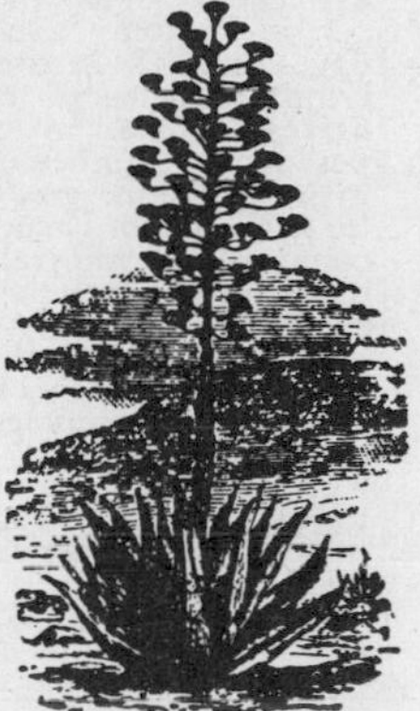

AGAVE
American aloe

2. [a–] any plant of the genus *Agave.*
à·gāze′, *adv.* and *a.* [*a-,* on, and *gaze.*] gazing.
à·gāzed′, *a.* struck with amazement; aghast. [Obs.]
āġe, *n.* [OFr. *aage*; Fr. *âge*; L. *æta(t)s*; Gr. *aiōn,* a period of existence.]
1. the whole duration of a person or thing since birth or beginning.
2. that part of the duration of a being which is between its beginning and any given time; as, what is the present *age* of a man, or of the earth?
3. the latter part of a normal lifetime; senility; old age; as, the eyes of Israel were dim for *age.*
4. a certain period of human life, as infancy, youth, manhood, and old age; the *age* of youth; the *age* of manhood.
5. the period when a person of either sex attains full legal rights, adult responsibilities, etc.; as, in the United States, both males and females are of *age* at twenty-one years.
6. a particular period of time, as distinguished from others; as, the golden *age*; the *age* of iron; the *age* of heroes or of chivalry.
7. the people who live at a particular period; hence, a generation; as, *ages* yet unborn.
8. a geological period marked by certain classes of rocks and animal or vegetable forms; as, the Carboniferous *age*; the Silurian *age.*
9. in the game of poker, the position of the player first to the left of the dealer, his being the oldest hand: he has the right to bet or drop out.
age distribution; in statistics, the distribution of conditions and other qualifying factors, in accordance with age classes.
age limit; a limit according to chronological age.
age norm; the norm, as for physical and mental qualities, of a given chronological age.
Syn.—epoch, era, generation, period.
āġe, *v.i.*; aged (ājd), *pt., pp.*; aging, *ppr.* 1. to grow old; to show signs of age.
2. to ripen or become mature.
āġe, *v.t.* 1. to make, or make seem, old or mature.
2. to cause to ripen or become mature over a period of time under fixed conditions.
-aġe, [OFr.; LL. *-aticum,* belonging to, related to.] a noun-forming suffix added to verbs and nouns meaning, in general:
1. *that which belongs or relates to the act of,* as in pass*age,* marri*age*; hence, (a) *amount of,* as in drink*age,* wast*age*; (b) *cost of,* as in post*age,* porter*age*; (c) *place of,* as in steer*age.*
2. *that which belongs or relates to the state or condition of,* as in pupil*age,* sav*age* [L. *silvaticus.*], voy*age* [L. *viaticum.*]; hence, (a) *collection of,* as in peer*age,* baron*age,* acre*age,* foli*age,* root*age*; (b) *place for,* as in orphan*age.*
Senses 1 and 2 are often inextricably blended in the same word.
ā′ġed, *a.* 1. old; grown old; made old; as, an *aged* man, or an *aged* oak.
2. (ājd), having a certain age; having lived; as, a man *aged* forty years.
3. pertaining to old age; as, *aged* wrinkles.
Syn.—elderly, old, senile.
ā′ġed, *n.* old persons, collectively: preceded by *the.*
ā′ġed·ly, *adv.* like an aged person.
ā′ġed·ness, *n.* the state of being aged; oldness.
à·gee′, *adv.* and *a.* [*a-,* intens., and *gee* (command to a horse to turn).] on or to one side; away; askew. [British Dial.]
āġe′iṣm, āġ′iṣm, *n.* discrimination against people on the basis of age; specifically, discrimination against, and prejudicial stereotyping of, older people.
āġe′less, *a.* without limit of existence; not growing old.
āġe′lonġ, *a.* 1. lasting long.
2. lasting forever.
à·gen′, *adv.* and *prep.* see *again.*
ā′ġen·cy, *n.*; *pl.* **ā′ġen·cieṣ,** [L. *agentia,* from *agen(t)s,* ppr. of *agere,* to act.]
1. active force; action; power.
2. that by which something is done; means; instrumentality.
3. the business of any person, firm, etc. empowered to act for another.
4. the business office or district of such a person, firm, etc.
5. an administrative division of government with specific functions.
à·ġen′dà, *n.pl.*; *sing.* **à·ġen′dum,** [L., neut. of the gerundive of *agere,* to act.]
1. things to be done.
2. the service or office of a church; matters of ecclesiastical ritual or liturgy.
3. [also construed as sing.] a list of items of business to be brought before a meeting, etc.
ag″en·ē′si·à, *n.* same as *agenesis.*
aġ·e·nes′iç, *a.* imperfectly developed.
à·ġen′e·sis, *n.* [Gr. *a* priv., and *genesis,* birth.] any imperfect development of an organ or other part.
ā′ġent, *a.* acting: opposed to *patient.* [Archaic.]
ā′ġent, *n.* [L. *agens, agentis,* ppr. of *agere,* to act; Gr. *agein,* to drive.]
1. one who performs actions, exerts power, or has the power to act; as, a moral *agent.*
2. an active power or force; that which has the power to produce an effect; as, heat is a powerful *agent.*
3. one entrusted with the business of another; one empowered to act for another.
4. a representative of a government agency; as, a revenue *agent.*
Syn.—deputy, substitute, actor, factor.
ā·ġen′tiăl (-shăl), *a.* pertaining to an agent or agency.
ā′ġen·tive, *a.* [*agent,* and *-ive,* after *genitive, accusative,* etc.] of or producing a grammatical form denoting the doer of some action.
ā′ġen·tive, *n.* an agentive affix or form, as the suffix *-ant,* in *servant.*
á′ġent prō·vŏc·à·teūr′ (*or* à′zhäṅ). [Fr.] one who associates with persons of a group in order to incite them to acts which will make them or their group liable to penalty.
ā′ġent·ship, *n.* the office of an agent; agency.
āġe of çŏn·sent′, in law, the age of a girl before which sexual intercourse with her, regardless of whether she has consented, is considered rape.
āġe′-ōld, *a.* ages old; centuries old, ancient.
A·ġẽr′à·tum, *n.* [L., from Gr. *ageraton,* a plant; *a* priv., and *geras,* age.] a genus of plants of the thistle or aster family, having small thick heads of blue or white flowers.

ȧ·geū′si·ȧ, *n.* same as *ageustia.*

ȧ·geūs′ti·ȧ, *n.* [L., from Gr. *ageustia,* a fasting, from *ageustos;* *a* priv., and *geustos,* tasting.] in medicine, loss or impairment of the sense of taste.

ag·gen·ẽr·ā′tion, *n.* [L., from *aggenerare,* to beget in addition.] the state of growing to another. [Obs.]

ag′gẽr, *n.* [L.] a fortress, or mound. [Obs.]

ag′gẽr·āte, *v.t.* [L. *aggeratus,* pp. of *aggerare,* to heap up.] to heap up. [Rare.]

ag·gẽr·ā′tion, *n.* a heaping; accumulation; as, *aggerations* of sand. [Rare.]

ag·gẽr·ōse′, *a.* in heaps, or formed in heaps.

ag·gest′, *v.t.* to heap up. [Obs.]

ag·glom′ẽr·āte, *v.t.* and *v.i.;* agglomerated, *pt., pp.;* agglomerating, *ppr.* [L. *agglomeratus,* pp. of *agglomerare;* *ad,* to, and *glomerare,* to form into a ball.] to gather, grow, or collect into a ball or mass.

ag·glom′ẽr·āte, ag·glom′ẽr·ā·ted, *a.* wound or collected into a ball.

ag·glom′ẽr·āte, *n.* 1. a jumbled mass or ball.

2. a mass of volcanic fragments compacted by heat.

ag·glom·ẽr·ā′tion, *n.* the state of being gathered into a mass; an agglomerated mass or cluster.

ag·glom′ẽr·ā·tive, *a.* having a tendency to agglomerate.

ag·glū′ti·nănt, *n.* [L. *agglutinans,* ppr. of *agglutinare,* to glue to.] any viscous substance which unites other substances by adhesion: an adhesive.

ag·glū′ti·nănt, *a.* sticking together; adhesive; tending to cause adhesion.

ag·glū′ti·nāte, *v.t.;* agglutinated, *pt., pp.;* agglutinating, *ppr.* [L. *agglutinatus,* pp. of *agglutinare,* to cement to; *ad,* to, and *glutinare,* from *gluten,* glue.]

1. to unite, or cause to adhere, as with glue or other viscous substance; to unite by causing an adhesion of substances.

2. in linguistics, to form (words) by agglutination.

3. in medicine and bacteriology, to clump, as microorganisms, blood cells, etc.

ag·glū′ti·nāte, *a.* 1. cemented together, as with glue.

2. forming words by agglutination; as, *agglutinate* languages.

ag·glū·ti·nā′tion, *n.* 1. the act of uniting by glue or other adhesive substance; the state of being thus united.

2. in linguistics, a forming of compounds in which the form and meaning of the root words remain practically unchanged.

ag·glū′ti·nā·tive, *a.* 1. that tends to unite, or has power to cause adhesion.

2. formed or distinguished by agglutination, as a language.

ag·glū′ti·nin, *n.* a substance causing agglutination (of bacteria, blood cells, etc.).

ag″glū·tin′ō·gen, *n.* [from *agglutinin,* and *-gen.*] any antigen which stimulates the production of agglutinins.

ag·grȧ·dā′tion, *n.* the act of aggrading, specifically, in physiography, the deposition of sediment by running water, as in the channel of a river: opposed to *degradation.*

ag·grāde′, *v.t.* [L. *aggradi;* *ad,* to, and *gradi,* to step, from *gradus,* step.] in geology, to build up the grade or slope of (the earth) by deposition of sediment, as in the bank of a stream.

ag′gran·dī·zȧ·ble, *a.* that may be aggrandized.

ag·gran·di·zā′tion, *n.* aggrandizement. [Obs.]

ag′gran·dīze, *v.t.;* aggrandized, *pt., pp.;* aggrandizing, *ppr.* [Fr. *agrandir,* to augment, from L. *ad,* to, and *grandire,* to increase, from *grandis,* great.]

1. to make great or greater in power, rank, or honor; to exalt; as, to *aggrandize* a family.

2. to enlarge; make seem greater; as, to *aggrandize* our conceptions.

Syn.—exalt, promote, advance.

ag′gran·dīze, *v.i.* to enlarge or become great. [Obs.]

ag·gran′dize·ment (-diz-), *n.* the act of aggrandizing; also, the state of being exalted in power, rank, or honor.

ag′gran·diz·ẽr, *n.* one who aggrandizes.

ag·grāte′, *v.t.* [It. *aggratare;* from L. *ad,* to, and *gratus,* pleasing.] to please. [Obs.]

ag′grȧ·vāte, *v.t.;* aggravated, *pt., pp.;* aggravating, *ppr.* [L. *aggravatus,* pp. of *aggravare;* *ad,* to, and *gravis,* heavy.]

1. to make heavy. [Obs.]

2. to make worse, more severe, or less tolerable; as, to *aggravate* the evils of life.

3. to make more enormous, or less excusable; as, to *aggravate* a crime.

4. to exaggerate; to give coloring in description; as, to *aggravate* a charge against an offender.

5. to irritate; provoke; tease. [Colloq.]

Syn.—intensify, irritate, enhance, increase, magnify.

ag′grȧ·vā·ting, *a.* 1. increasing in severity, enormity, or degree, as evils, misfortunes, pain, punishment, crimes, guilt.

2. provoking; exasperating; vexing. [Colloq.]

ag′grȧ·vā·ting·ly, *adv.* in an aggravating manner.

ag·grȧ·vā′tion, *n.* [Fr. *aggravation;* L. *aggravatio,* a making heavy.]

1. the act of making worse; the act of increasing severity or enormity; as, an *aggravation* of pain or a crime.

2. a thing or circumstance that aggravates.

3. irritation; provocation; the act of irritating or provoking. [Colloq.]

ag′grȧ·vā·tive, *a.* tending to aggravate. [Rare.]

ag′grȧ·vā·tive, *n.* anything causing aggravation. [Rare.]

ag′grē·gāte, *v.t.;* aggregated, *pt., pp.;* aggregating, *ppr.* [L. *aggregatus,* pp. of *aggregare,* to lead to a flock, add to; *ad,* to, and *gregare,* to herd; *grex, gregis,* a herd.]

1. to bring together; to collect into a sum, mass, or body.

2. to unite to, as a person to a society.

3. to make the sum total of; to amount to.

Syn.—accumulate, collect, pile, heap up.

ag′grē·gāte, *a.* 1. formed into a whole, mass, or sum; united; combined; total; as, the *aggregate* amount of charges.

2. in anatomy, zoology, botany and geology, clustered or associated together, as the lymph follicles of the conjunctiva, called *aggregate glands;* an *aggregate* animal is composed of a number of individuals combined in one organism; an *aggregate* flower is formed by a cluster of carpels; an *aggregate* rock is composed of mineral fragments or crystals mixed in one rock.

ag′grē·gāte, *n.* 1. a mass, assemblage, or collection of distinct things; as, a house is an *aggregate* of stones, brick, timber, etc.

2. sand and pebbles added to a cement to make concrete.

3. a mass formed by the union of homogeneous particles; an agglomerate of different minerals which are separable by mechanical means.

4. the total sum, quantity, or number of anything; as, in the *aggregate.*

ag′grē·gāte·ly, *adv.* collectively; taken in a sum or mass.

ag·grē·gā′tion, *n.* [Fr. *aggregation.*]

1. the act of aggregating; also, the state of being collected into a sum or mass.

2. a collection of particulars; an aggregate.

3. in logic, the combination of terms into a term true of anything of which any of its parts are true.

ag′grē·gā·tive, *a.* taken together; collective.

ag′grē·gā·tŏr, *n.* 1. one who joins with others.

2. one who brings together, collects, etc.

ag′grē·gȧ·tọ·ry, *a.* 1. relating to an aggregate.

2. aggregated.

ag·grēge′, *v.t.* to aggravate. [Obs.]

ag·gress′, *v.i.;* aggressed, *pt., pp.;* aggressing, *ppr.* [L. *aggressus,* pp. of *aggredi,* to attack, to go to; *ad,* to, and *gradi,* to step, from *gradus,* step.] to make a first attack; to commit the first act of hostility or offense; to begin a quarrel or controversy; to assault first, or invade.

ag·gress′, *v.t.* to attack; to set upon. [Rare.]

ag·gress′, *n.* aggression. [Obs.]

ag·gres′sion, *n.* [L. *aggressio,* from *aggredi,* to attack.]

1. an unprovoked attack, or act of hostility.

2. the practice or habit of being aggressive.

ag·gres′sive, *a.* 1. tending to aggress; starting fights or quarrels.

2. full of enterprise and initiative; bold and active; pushing.

ag·gres′sive·ly, *adv.* in an aggressive manner.

ag·gres′sive·ness, *n.* the quality of being aggressive or quarrelsome.

ag·gres′sŏr, *n.* the person, nation, etc. who starts a fight or makes an unprovoked attack; an assaulter; an invader.

ag·griēv′ănce, *n.* oppression; hardship; injury. [Obs.]

ag·griēve′, *v.t.;* aggrieved (-grēvd′), *pt., pp.;* aggrieving, *ppr.* [ME. *agreven;* OFr. *agrever, aggraver,* to aggravate; L. *aggravare,* to make heavy; *ad,* to, and *gravis,* heavy.]

1. to give pain or sorrow to; to afflict.

2. to oppress or injure in one's legal rights; to vex or harass by civil or political injustice.

ag·griēve′, *v.i.* to grieve. [Obs.]

ag·griēved′, *a.* [pp. of *aggrieve.*]

1. having a grievance; offended; slighted.

2. injured in one's legal rights.

ag·grōup′, *v.t.;* aggrouped (-gröpt′), *pt., pp.;* aggrouping, *ppr.* [Fr. *agrouper;* It. *aggruppare;* *a,* to, and *gruppo,* a knot, heap, group.] to bring together; to group.

ag·grōup′ment, *n.* arrangement in one or more groups; subdivision; grouping.

ag′gry, ag′gri, *n.* a kind of colored glass bead, supposed to be of ancient Egyptian origin, found among the natives of Africa.

ä′ghȧ (ä′gȧ), *n.* aga.

ȧ·ghȧst′ (ȧ-gȧst′), *a.* [ME. *agast,* full form, *agasted,* pp. of *agasten,* to terrify; *a,* AS. *ā,* and *gasten,* AS. *gæstan,* to terrify.] struck with amazement; stupified with sudden fright or horror.

ȧ·ghȧst′, *v.t.* to terrify.

ag′i·ble, *a.* [L. *agibilis,* from *agere,* to do.] possible; practicable. [Obs.]

ag′ile, *a.* [Fr. *agile;* L. *agilis,* from *agere,* to move, to act.] nimble; apt or ready to move; brisk; active.

And bending forward struck his *agile* heels.
—Shakespeare

Syn.—active, nimble, quick, spry, alert.

ag′ile·ly, *adv.* in an agile manner.

ag′ile·ness, *n.* agility.

ȧ·gil′i·ty, *n.* [Fr. *agilité;* L. *agilitas, agilis,* from *agere,* to move, to do.] the quality or condition of being agile; nimbleness; briskness; quickness of motion.

ag′i·ō, *n.* [It. *aggio,* exchange, premium.]

1. in commerce, a fee paid to exchange one kind of money for another, or to exchange depreciated money for money of full value.

2. premium; sum given above the nominal value, as the *agio* of exchange.

3. the rate of exchange between the currencies of different nations.

4. agiotage.

ag′i·ō·tăge, *n.* [Fr. *agiotage,* from *agioter,* to job in stocks; from *agio,* premium.]

1. the exchange business.

2. the business of a stockbroker; speculation in stocks.

ȧ·gist′, *v.t.* [OFr. *agister;* *a* (L. *ad*), to, and *gister,* to assign a lodging; L. *gistum,* from *jacitum,* pp. of *jacere,* to lie.]

1. to feed or pasture (cattle) for a fee.

2. to assess for any public service.

ag′is·tā·tŏr, *n.* same as *agistor.*

ȧ·gist′ment, *n.* 1. the taking and feeding of other men's cattle for a fee; also, the fee paid.

2. any burden, charge, or tax laid against land.

ȧ·gist′ŏr, ȧ·gist′ẽr, *n.* 1. one who is hired to take cattle to feed or pasture.

2. formerly, an officer of the king's forest who had the care of agisted cattle and collected the money for the same.

ag′i·tȧ·ble, *a.* that may be agitated.

ag′i·tāte, *v.t.;* agitated, *pt., pp.;* agitating, *ppr.* [L. *agitatus,* pp. of *agitare,* to put in motion; from *agere,* to move.]

1. to stir violently; to move back and forth with a quick motion; to shake or move briskly; as, to *agitate* water in a vessel.

2. to disturb, or excite; to fluster; as, to *agitate* the mind or passions.

3. to discuss; to debate; to controvert; as, to *agitate* a question.

4. to consider on all sides; to revolve in the mind, or view in all its aspects; to contrive; as, politicians *agitate* desperate designs.

5. to move or actuate. [Obs.]

Syn.—disturb, rouse, ruffle, discompose, deliberate upon, debate, canvass, excite.

ag′i·tāte, *v.i.* to seek to stir up the public on any subject; as, to *agitate* in every state of the Union.

ag′i·tāt·ed, *a.* [pp. of *agitate.*] shaken; perturbed; excited.

ag′i·tā·ted·ly, *adv.* in an agitated manner.

ag·i·tā′tion, *n.* 1. an agitating or being agitated; the state of being moved with violence, or with irregular action; commotion; as, the sea after a storm is in *agitation.*

2. emotional disturbance; perturbation; excitement of passion with physical disturbance.

3. discussion; examination of a subject in controversy.

4. public excitement over any matter; as, the free-silver *agitation;* the *agitation* for municipal ownership.

Syn.—disturbance, emotion, tremor, debate, discussion.

ag·i·tā′tion·ăl, *a.* relating to agitation.

ag′i·tā·tive, *a.* having a tendency to agitate.

ä·gi·tä′tō, *a.* and *adv.* [It., from L. *agitatus;* see *agitate.*] in music, fast and with excitement: a direction to the performer.

aġ'i·tā·tŏr, *n.* 1. one who agitates; especially, one who tries to arouse or increase dissatisfaction so as to produce changes.
 2. in English history, one of certain officers appointed by the army to manage its concerns.
 3. an apparatus for shaking or mixing.

aġ'it·prop, *a.* [*agitation* and *propaganda.*] serving the purposes of both agitation and propaganda: said of anything used to excite public opinion.

Ȧ·glā'iȧ, *n.* [L.; Gr. *Aglaia,* lit., brightness.] in Greek mythology, one of the three Graces.

ȧ·glēam', *adv.* and *a.* [*a-,* on, and *gleam.*] gleaming.

ag'let, āig'let, *n.* [OFr. *aguillette;* Fr. *aiguillette,* a point, dim. of *aiguille;* L. *acucula,* dim. of *acus,* needle.]
 1. formerly, an ornament at the ends of laces, tabs, points, braid, or cord, used in dress.
 2. a metal tip on a ribbon or lace.
 3. a staylace, round and white, used in haberdashery.
 4. in botany, any pendant part of a flower; specifically, a pendant anther; a loose catkin.

ag'let hōle, an eyehole.

ȧ·gleȳ' (-glī'), *adv.* [*a-,* on, and *gley,* squint.], [Scot.] awry; off to one side.

ȧ·glim'mẽr, *a.* and *adv.* glimmering.

Ä''gli·paȳ'ăn (-pī'ăn), *a.* of or pertaining to a movement started in the Philippines in 1902 by the Rev. Gregorio Aglipay, a Filipino priest, to establish a "Philippine Independent Catholic Apostolic Church."

ȧ·glit'tẽr, *adv.* and *a.* in a glitter; sparkling.

ȧ·glob'ū·liṣm, *n.* [Gr. *a* priv., and L. *globulus,* dim. of *globus,* a ball.] in pathology, a condition in which there is a diminution of the proportion of red corpuscles in the blood.

Ȧ·glos'sȧ, *n.pl.* [Gr. *a* priv., and *glōssa,* tongue.] a suborder of amphibians that are without a tongue.

ȧ·glos'săl, ȧ·glos'sāte, *a.* [Gr. *aglōssos,* without tongue.] tongueless; as, *aglossal* toads.

ȧ·glos'sāte, *n.* a member of the *Aglossa.*

ȧ·glōw', *adv.* and *a.* in a glow (of color or emotion); glowing; as, the horizon all *aglow.*

ag·lū·ti'tion (-tish'un), *n.* [Gr. *a* priv., and L. *glutitio,* from *glutire,* to swallow.] inability to swallow.

ȧ·glȳ', *adv.* [Scot.] agley.

ȧ·glyph'ō·dont, *a.* [Gr. *aglyphos,* uncarved; *a* priv., and *glyphein,* to carve, and *odous, odont,* tooth.] having no grooved teeth for venom: applied to snakes.

ag'mi·nāte, ag'mi·nā·ted, *a.* [L. *agmen, agminis,* a train, crowd.] arranged in a cluster or clusters; grouped together; as, *agminate* glands.

ag'nāil, *n.* [ME. *agnayle, angnail;* AS. *angnægle,* a corn, wart.]
 1. a whitlow; an inflammation around a fingernail or toenail.
 2. a hangnail; a piece of half-severed skin beside or at the base of a nail.

ag'nāmed, *a.* [L. *ag, ad,* to, and *name.*] designated by an epithet added to the surname.

ag'nāte, *a.* 1. related through male descent or on the father's side.
 2. allied; from a common source; akin.

ag'nāte, *n.* [L. *agnatus,* pp. of *agnasci,* to be born in addition to; *ad,* to, and *nasci,* to be born.] a relative through male descent or on the father's side.

ag'nȧ·thous, ag·nath'iç, *a.* [Gr. *a* priv., and *gnathos,* jaw.] without jaws.

ag·nat'iç, *a.* 1. of agnation.
 2. related through male descent or on the father's side.

ag·nā'tion, *n.* relationship through male descent or on the father's side: distinct from *cognation,* which includes descent in the male and female lines.

ag'nel, *n.* [OFr. *agnel,* a lamb; L. *agnellus,* dim. of *agnus,* a lamb.] an ancient French gold coin: it was called also *mouton d'or* and *agnel d'or.*

ag'nī, *n.,* pl. of *agnus.*

Äg'ni, *n.* [Sans. *agni,* fire.] in Hindu mythology, the Vedic god of fire and guardian of man: he is shown as having two faces.

ag·ni'tion (-nish'un), *n.* [L. *agnitio,* from *agnoscere,* to acknowledge.] acknowledgment. [Obs.]

ag·nīze', *v.t.* to acknowledge. [Archaic.]

Ag·no·ē'tae, *n.pl.* [L., from Gr. *agnoētai,* ignorant, from *agnoein,* to be ignorant.]
 1. a sect of the fourth century who denied the omniscience of God: also called *Theophronians,* after their leader.
 2. a sect of the sixth century who denied the omniscience of Christ: also called *Themistians,* after their leader.

ag·noi·ol'ō·ġy, *n.* [Gr. *agnoia,* ignorance, and *logia,* from *legein,* to say.] the metaphysical study of ignorance.

ag·nō'men, *n.; pl.* **ag·nom'i·nȧ, ag·nō'menṣ,** [L. *ad,* to, and *nomen,* name.]
 1. in ancient Rome, a name added to a cognomen, especially as an epithet honoring some exploit or event: as *Africanus* added to *Publius Cornelius Scipio.*
 2. a nickname.

ag·nom'i·nāte, *v.t.* to name. [Obs.]

ag·nom·i·nā'tion, *n.* [L. *agnominatio,* from *ad,* to, and *nomen,* name.]
 1. a name or title added to another, as expressive of some act, achievement, etc.; a surname.
 2. similarity of sound in two or more words, usually made apparent by alliteration.

ag·nos'tiç, *n.* [Gr. *a* priv., and *gnōstikos,* knowing, from *gignōskein,* to know.] one who believes in agnosticism; one who thinks it is impossible to know whether there is a God or a future life, or anything beyond material phenomena. The name was suggested by Huxley in 1869.

ag·nos'tiç, *a.* of or characteristic of an agnostic or agnosticism.

ag·nos'tiç·ăl·ly, *adv.* 1. in an agnostic manner.
 2. from an agnostic point of view.

ag·nos'ti·ciṣm, *n.* 1. the doctrine of an agnostic: distinguished from *atheism.*
 2. in theology, the doctrine that God is unknown and unknowable.
 3. in philosophy, the doctrine that a first cause and the essential nature of things are unknowable to man.

> By *agnosticism,* I understand a theory of things which abstains from either affirming or denying the existence of God; all it undertakes to affirm is that, upon existing evidence, the being of God is unknown. —G. J. Romanes.

ag'nus, *n.; pl.* **ag'nus·eṣ** or **ag'nī,** [L., a lamb.] an image of a lamb as emblematic of Christ; Agnus Dei.

Ag'nus Dē'ī, [L., Lamb of God.]
 1. a representation of Christ as a lamb, often holding a cross or a flag with a cross on it.
 2. in the Roman Catholic Church, a medallion of wax, or other object, stamped with the figure of a lamb, supporting the banner of the cross. Blessed by the Pope, it is worn as a talisman to preserve the wearer from diseases and other calamities. Also, a prayer in the Mass or the music for it.
 3. the Anglican anthem beginning with these words.

AGNUS DEI

Ag'nus Scyth'i·çus (sith'), [L., Scythian lamb.] a name applied to the roots of a species of fern, *Dicksonia Barometz,* covered with brown, woolly scales, and in shape resembling a lamb: found in Russia and Tartary.

ȧ·gō', *a.* [OE. *ago, agon,* pp. of *agon,* to go; AS. *āgān,* to pass away; *ā* and *gān,* to go.] past; gone by: used following the noun; as, a year *ago.*

ȧ·gō', *adv.* in the past; as, long *ago.*

ȧ·gog', *adv.* and *a.* [earlier form, *on gog;* Fr. *en gogue,* mirth, glee.] in a state of eager excitement, anticipation, or interest.

> The gaudy gossip, when she's set *agog.* —Dryden.

-a·gogue (a-gog), [from Gr. *agōgos,* leading.] a combining form meaning *leading, directing, inciting,* as in dem*agogue,* myst*agogue*: also spelled *-agog.*

ȧ·gō'ing, *adv.* in motion; as, to set a mill *agoing.*

ȧ·gom'phi·ous, *a.* [Gr. *a* priv., and *gomphios,* molar.] having no teeth.

ag'ōn, *n.; pl.* **ȧ·gō'nēs,** [Gr.] 1. the contest for a prize at public games.
 2. the conflict of characters in a drama.

ag'ō·năl, *a.* in medicine, of or pertaining to the death agony.

ȧ·gone', *a.* and *adv.* ago; past; since. [Archaic.]

ā'gōne, *n.* an agonic line.

ȧ·gon'iç, *a.* [Gr. *agōnos,* without angles; *a* priv., and *gōnia,* angle.] not forming an angle.
 agonic line; an imaginary line on the earth's surface on which true north and magnetic north are identical, and a compass needle makes no angle with the meridian. There are two principal *agonic lines;* one, called the *American agone,* is in the western hemisphere, and the other, or *Asiatic,* is in the eastern hemisphere. Although they extend from south to north, they do not coincide with meridians.

ag'ō·niṣm, *n.* [Gr. *agōnismos,* from *agonizesthai,* to contend for a prize.] contention for a prize. [Obs.]

ag'ō·nist, *n.* [Gr. *agōnistēs,* contestant.]
 1. in ancient Greece, one who contended for a prize in the public games.
 2. in church history, any of the disciples of Donatus.

ag·ō·nist'iç, ag·ō·nist'iç·ăl, *a.* 1. pertaining to ancient Greek contests of strength or athletic combats.
 2. contesting; combative.
 3. strained for effect.

ag·ō·nist'iç·ăl·ly, *adv.* in an agonistic manner.

ag·ō·nist'içs, *n.* the science of athletic contests, or contending in public games.

ag'ō·nīze, *v.i.;* agonized, *pt., pp.;* agonizing, *ppr.* [Fr. *agonizer;* L. *agonizare,* labor, strive; Gr. *agonizesthai,* to contend for a prize.]
 1. to writhe with extreme pain; to suffer violent anguish.

> To smart and *agonize* at every pore. —Pope.

 2. to struggle; to contend; to strive.

ag'ō·nīze, *v.t.* to cause extreme pain to; to torture.

ag'ō·nīz·ing, *a.* 1. that agonizes.
 2. giving extreme pain.

ag'ō·nīz·ing·ly, *adv.* with extreme anguish.

ȧ·gō'nō·thēte, *n.* [Gr. *agōnothetēs; agon,* contest, and *tithenai,* to appoint.] an officer who presided over the public games in Greece.

ag''ō·nō·thet'iç, *a.* pertaining to an agonothete.

ag'ŏ·ny, *n.; pl.* **ag'ŏ·nieṣ,** [ME. *agonie;* L. *agonia;* Gr. *agōnia,* a contest or struggle, from *agon,* a struggle for a prize.]
 1. pain so extreme as to cause writhing or contortions of the body, similar to those made in the athletic contests in Greece.
 2. extreme pain of body or mind; anguish; especially, the suffering of Jesus in the garden of Gethsemane.
 3. the pangs of death.
 4. violent striving or contest.
 5. any violent emotion; a paroxysm.
 agony column; a newspaper column devoted to personal advertisements, as to missing relatives, etc.

 Syn.—anguish, pang, distress, suffering, pain, torture.—*Agony* and pang denote a severe paroxysm of pain (*agony* being the greater); *anguish* is prolonged suffering; as, the *anguish* of remorse.

ag'ŏ·rȧ, *n.; pl.* **ag'ŏ·raē** (-rē), **ag'ŏ·raṣ,** [Gr.]
 1. the public square and market place in an ancient Greek city.
 2. a place of assembly, especially a market place.

ag''ō·rȧ·phō'bi·ȧ, *n.* [*agora,* and *-phobia.*] an abnormal fear of being in open or public places.

ä·gō·stä·de̱'rō, *n.* [Sp. Am.] a cattle pasture.

ä·gou·ä'rȧ, *n.* [S. Am. name.] a species of racoon, *Procyon cancrivorus,* commonly called crab-eating raccoon.

ȧ·gou'tȧ, *n.* [native name.] an insectivorous mammal, about the size of a rat, peculiar to Haiti, of the *Centetes* family, and belonging to the genus *Solenodon.* Its tail is devoid of hair and scaly, its eyes are small, and its nose elongated.

ȧ·gou'ti, ȧ·gou'ty, *n.; pl.* **ȧ·gou'tiṣ, ȧ·gou'tieṣ,** [Fr. *agouti, acouti;* Sp. *aguti,* native Am. *aguti, acuti.*] a quadruped of the order *Rodentia,* genus *Dasyprocta,* related to the guinea pig and found in the West Indies and Central and South America. It is of the size of a rabbit.

AGOUTI
(*Dasyprocta agouti*)

ȧ·graffe′ (-graf′), *n.* [Fr. *agrafe, agraffe,* a clasp, hook; also, *agrappe; a* (L. *ad*), to, and *grappe,* L. *grappa;* O.H.G. *chrapfo;* G. *krapfe,* a hook.]
1. an ornamental hook or clasp for armor or costumes.
2. a device for clasping a piano string so as to prevent vibration.
3. a builder's cramp iron.

ȧ·gram′mȧ·tism, *n.* in pathology, a form of aphasia characterized by inability to form normal connected sentences.

ȧ·gram′mȧ·tist, *n.* [Gr. *agrammatos,* illiterate; *a* priv., and *grammata,* letters, from *graphein,* to write.] an illiterate person. [Obs.]

ȧ·graph′i·ȧ, *n.* [Gr. *a* priv., and *graphein,* to write.] a form of aphasia in which there is a partial or total loss of the ability to write.

ȧ·graph′iç, *a.* of or having agraphia.

ȧ·grappes′ (-graps′), *n.pl.* [see *agraffe.*] hooks and eyes for fastening armor. [Obs.]

ȧ·grā′ri·ăn, *a.* [L. *agrarius,* from *ager,* a field, country.]
1. relating to land, particularly public land; especially, denoting or pertaining to an equal division of lands; as, the *agrarian* laws of Rome, which distributed the conquered and other public lands equally among all the citizens.
2. pertaining to agrarianism.
3. of agriculture.
4. in botany, wild; growing without cultivation: said of plants growing in the fields.

ȧ·grā′ri·ăn, *n.* one in favor of a more equitable division of land.

ȧ·grā′ri·ăn·işm, *n.* 1. the doctrine or methods of agrarians.
2. agitation or political movement for more equitable division of land.

ȧ·grā′ri·ăn·īze, *v.t.*; agrarianized, *pt., pp.*; agrarianizing, *ppr.* 1. to imbue with the principles of ideas of agrarianism.
2. to distribute lands equally among all.

ȧ·grē′, ȧ·gree′, *adv.* [Fr. *agre.*] in good part; kindly. [Obs.]

ȧ·gree′, *v.i.*; agreed, *pt., pp.*; agreeing, *ppr.* [ME. *agreen;* Fr. *agréer,* to receive kindly, from OFr. phrase, *à gré,* favorably; *à,* L. *ad,* to, and *gre,* good will, from L. *gratus,* pleasing.]
1. to be of one mind; to harmonize in opinion; as, all the parties *agree* in the decision.
2. to be or live in concord, or without contention.
3. to consent or accede (*to* something); as, to *agree to* an offer, or *to* an opinion.
4. to arrive at a satisfactory understanding (*about* prices, terms, etc.).
5. to come to a compromise of differences; to be reconciled; as, they have *agreed* at last.
6. to be consistent; to harmonize; not to contradict; as, this story *agrees* with what has been related by others.
7. to resemble; to be similar; as, the picture does not *agree* with the original.
8. to be suitable, healthful, etc. (followed by *with*); as, the same food does not *agree* with every constitution.
9. in grammar, to correspond in number, case, gender, or person; as, a verb *agrees* with its subject.

Syn.—accede, acquiesce, accept, coincide, concur, consent, harmonize, correspond, promise, engage, contract.

ȧ·gree′, *v.t.* 1. to admit, or come to one mind concerning; as, to *agree* the fact.
2. to grant or acknowledge (followed by a noun clause); as, we *agreed* that the food was good.

ȧ·gree·ȧ·bil′i·ty, *n.* the quality or state of being agreeable.

ȧ·gree′ȧ·ble, *a.* [ME. *agreable;* OFr. *agreable,* from *agreer,* to accept, to please.]
1. suitable; conformable. [Obs.]
2. in pursuance of; in conformity with; as, *agreeable* to the order of the day, the house took up the report of the committee: also used adverbially in this sense for *agreeably.*
3. pleasing; pleasant, either to the mind or senses; as, *agreeable* manners; fruit *agreeable* to the taste.
4. willing or ready to agree; as, we found the opposition *agreeable* to our suggestion.

Syn.—acceptable, grateful, pleasant.

ȧ·gree′ȧ·ble·ness, *n.* 1. suitableness; conformity. [Obs.]
2. the quality of pleasing; that quality which gives satisfaction or moderate pleasure to the mind or senses; as, an *agreeableness* of manners; there is an *agreeableness* in the taste of certain fruits.

ȧ·gree′ȧ·bly, *adv.* 1. pleasingly; in an agreeable manner; in a manner to give pleasure; as, to be *agreeably* entertained with a discourse.
2. suitably; consistently. [Obs.]

Marriages grow less frequent, *agreeably* to the maxim above laid down. —Paley.

3. alike; in the same manner. [Obs.]

ȧ·greed′, *a.* mutually determined or decided upon; as, an *agreed* amount.

ȧ·gree′ing·ly, *adv.* in conformity to. [Obs.]

ȧ·gree′ment, *n.* 1. concord; harmony; conformity; as, to live in *agreement* with one's neighbors.
2. unity of opinion or sentiment; as, a good *agreement* is found among the members of the council.
3. resemblance; conformity; similitude.

Expansion and duration have this further *agreement.* —Locke.

4. an understanding or arrangement between two or more people, countries, etc.; bargain; compact; contract; as, he made an *agreement* for the purchase of a house.
5. the terms in which a contract or bargain is set down in writing; a written contract.
6. in grammar, correspondence in number, gender, case, or person.

Syn.—accordance, bargain, concurrence, compact, contract, covenant, harmony.

ȧ·grē′ẽr, *n.* one who agrees.

ȧ·gres′tiăl (-chăl), *a.* 1. agrestic.
2. growing wild.

ȧ·gres′tiç, *a.* [L. *agrestis,* rural, from *ager,* field.]
1. rural; rustic.
2. crude; unpolished.

ag′ri·busi″ness (-biz″nes), *n.* [*agri*culture, and *business.*] farming and the businesses associated with farming, as the processing of farm products, the manufacturing of farm equipment and fertilizers, etc.

ȧ·griç·ō·lā′tion, *n.* cultivation of the soil. [Obs.]

ȧ·griç′ō·list, *n.* a husbandman; an agriculturist. [Obs.]

ag′ri·cul·tŏr, *n.* [L. *ager,* a field, and *cultor,* a cultivator.] one whose occupation is to till the ground; a farmer; a husbandman; one skilled in husbandry. [Obs.]

ag·ri·cul′tūr·ăl, *a.* of agriculture; pertaining to farming, husbandry, tillage, or the culture of the earth; as, *agricultural* implements, *agricultural* pursuits.

agricultural ant; a species of ant, the best known of which is the *Pogonomyrmex barbatus* of Texas, which clears large spaces around its nest.

agricultural college; a college specializing in the teaching of agriculture and its allied sciences. In the United States, these institutions are under State control.

agricultural economics; the study of economic principles applied to agriculture.

agricultural geology; the study of geology as it affects agriculture.

ag″ri·cul′tūr·ăl·ist, *n.* an agriculturist.

ag·ri·cul′tur·ăl·ly, *adv.* as regards agriculture; for agricultural purposes.

ag′ri·cul·tūre, *n.* [L. *ager,* a field, and *cultura,* cultivation.] the science and art of farming; tillage; the cultivation of the ground, for the purpose of producing vegetables and fruits; the art of preparing the soil, sowing and planting seeds, caring for the plants, and harvesting the crops. In a broad sense, the word includes gardening, or horticulture, and also the raising of livestock.

ag·ri·cul′tūr·ist, *n.* 1. an agricultural expert.
2. a farmer.

ȧ·grief′, *adv.* in grief; amiss. [Obs.]

Ag·ri·mō′ni·ȧ, *n.* [ME. *agrimony;* OFr. *aigremoine;* L. *agrimonia,* for *argemonia;* Gr. *argemōnē.*] a genus of plants of the rose family, having several species, of which the *eupatoria* and the *odorata* were formerly used in medicine.

ag′ri·mō·ny, *n.* any plant of the genus *Agrimonia.*

ag″ri·mō′tŏr, *n.* a mechanical field tractor chiefly used by farmers for hauling harvesters or reaping machines.

ȧ·grin′, *adv.* and *a.* [AS. *a,* on, and *grin.*] grinning.

ag″ri·ō·loġ′i·căl, *a.* pertaining to agriology.

ag·ri·ol′ō·ġist, *n.* one versed in agriology.

ag·ri·ol′ō·ġy, *n.* [Gr. *agrios,* wild, savage, and *logia,* from *logos,* word, description.] the comparative study of the customs of primitive peoples.

ag′rō-, [Gr. from *agras,* a field.] a combining form meaning *field, earth, soil,* as in *agro*biology.

ag″rō·bī·ol′ō·ġy, *n.* the science of biology, plant nutrition, and growth as applied to agriculture in the improvement of crops and control of the soil.

ȧ·grol′ō·ġy, *n.* the science of soils in relation to crop production.

ag′rŏm, *n.* [native name.] a disease indigenous to the East Indies, in which the tongue chaps and cracks.

ag·rō·nom′iç, ag·rō·nom′i·căl, *a.* of agronomy.

ag·rō·nom′içs, *n.pl.* [construed as sing.] agronomy.

ȧ·gron′ō·mist, *n.* a student of or specialist in agronomy.

ȧ·gron′ō·my, *n.* [Gr. *agronomos,* an overseer of the public lands; *agros,* field, and *nomos,* from *nemein,* to deal out, manage.] the art and science of crop production; the management of farm land.

ȧ·grōpe′, *adv.* in the act of groping.

Ag·rō·stem′mă, *n.* [Gr. *agros,* field, and *stemma,* wreath.] a genus of plants of several species, including the common corn cockle, wild lychnis or campion, etc.

A·gros′tis, *n.* [Gr. *agrōstis,* grass.] a genus of bent grasses.

ag·ros·tog′rȧ·phẽr, *n.* one who writes about grasses; an agrostologist.

ȧ·gros·tō·graph′iç, ȧ·gros·tō·graph′iç·ăl, *a.* pertaining to agrostography.

ag·ros·tog′rȧ·phy, *n.* [Gr. *agrōstis,* grass, and *graphia,* from *graphein,* to write.] a description of grasses.

ag·ros·tō·loġ′iç, ag·ros·tō·loġ′iç·ăl, *a.* pertaining to agrostology.

ag·ros·tol′ō·ġist, *n.* a specialist in agrostology; an authority upon grasses.

ag·ros·tol′ō·ġy, *n.* [Gr. *agrōstis,* grass, and *logos,* discourse.] that branch of botany which deals with grasses.

ȧ·ground′, *adv.* 1. on or onto the ground, as a boat in shallow water; on or onto a beach, reef, etc.
2. figuratively, stopped; impeded by insuperable obstacles.

ȧ·group′ment, *n.* see *aggroupment.*

ȧ·gryp′ni·ȧ, *n.* [Gr. *agrypnia,* from *agrypnios,* sleepless; *agreuein,* to hunt, and *hypnos,* sleep.] sleeplessness; insomnia.

ȧ·gryp·nō·çō′mȧ, *n.* [Gr. *agrypnos,* sleepless, and *kōma,* coma.] lethargy, without actual sleep.

ag·ryp·not′iç, *a.* preventing sleep.

ag·ryp·not′iç, *n.* in medicine, any agency or drug which tends to prevent sleep.

ä′guȧ (-gwȧ), *n.* [native name.] a large, voracious, bellowing toad, the *Bufo marinus,* found in the West Indies and South America.

ä·guȧ·çä′tẹ, *n.* [Sp.] a tropical tree bearing a pear-shaped fruit; the avocado.

ä·guȧ·ji′ (-gwȧ-hē′), *n.* [Sp. Am.] the gag, a large food fish of the Florida reefs.

ä·guär·dï·en′tẹ (ä-gwär-), *n.* [Sp., contraction of *agua ardiente,* burning water; L. *aqua,* water, and *ardens,* burning.]
1. a popular brandy of Spain and Portugal, distilled from native red wines.
2. any common alcoholic liquor, especially Mexican pulque. In the southwestern United States, the term is often applied to inferior whisky.

ā′gūe, *n.* [ME. *agu, ague;* OFr. *agu,* f. *ague;* L. *acutus,* f. *acuta,* sharp, violent; L. *febris acuta,* a violent fever.]
1. an acute fever. [Obs.]
2. a chill, or fit of shivering.
3. a fever, usually malarial, marked by regularly recurring chills.

ā′gūe, *v.t.*; agued, *pt., pp.*; aguing, *ppr.* to cause a shivering in; to affect with an ague. [Rare.]

ā′gūe çāke, an enlargement and hardening of the spleen from the effect of intermittent fevers.

ā′gūed (-gūd), *a.* having a fit of ague; shivering with cold or fear.

ā′gūe drop, Fowler's solution.
ā′gūe fit, a paroxysm of cold, or shivering; chilliness.
ā′gūe grass, in botany, the colicroot, *Aletris farinosa*; star grass: it is of the bloodwort family.
ā′gūe root, same as *ague grass.*
ā′gūe spell, a charm or spell supposed to cure or prevent ague.
ā′gūe tree, the sassafras. [Obs.]
ā′gūe·weed, 1. thoroughwort, or boneset, *Eupatorium perfoliatum.*
2. the stiff gentian, *Gentiana quinqueflora.*
ȧ·guilt′ (-gilt′), *v.t.* to be guilty of; to sin against; to offend; to wrong. [Obs.]
ȧ·guilt′ (-gilt′), *v.i.* to be guilty; to sin; to offend: followed by *with, against, to.* [Obs.]
ȧ·guīse′ (-gīz′), *v.t.* to dress; to adorn. [Obs.]
ȧ·guīse′, *n.* dress. [Obs.]
ā′gū·ish, *a.* 1. chilly; somewhat cold or shivering; also, having the qualities of an ague.
2. of or productive of ague; as, an *aguish* district.
3. subject to ague.
ā′gū·ish·ly, *adv.* in the manner of ague, or of a person affected by ague.
ā′gū·ish·ness, *n.* chilliness; the quality of being aguish.
ȧ·gū′jȧ (-hȧ), *n.* [Sp., literally, needle.]
1. the spearfish of the West Indies.
2. a large, voracious garfish, *Tylosurus fodiator.*
ȧ·gush′, *adv.* and *a.* in a gushing state.
aġ′y·nā·ry, *a.* [Gr. *a* priv., and *gynē*, woman.] in botany, without female organs: said of flowers.
aġ′y·nous, *a.* same as *agynary.*
ȧ·ġȳ′rāte, *a.* [L. *agyratus*, pp. of *agyrare*; Gr. *a* priv., and *gyros*, circle.] in botany, without whorls.
äh, *interj.* [ME. *a*; OFr. *ah*; G. *ach*; L. *ah*; Gr. *a.*] an exclamation expressive of surprise, pity, complaint, contempt, dislike, joy, exultation, etc., according to the manner of utterance.
ȧ·hä′, *interj.* an exclamation expressing triumph, contempt, simple surprise, etc., often mixed with irony or mockery.
ȧ·hä′, *n.* a sunk fence: more commonly called *ha-ha.*
Ā′hab, *n.* [Heb., lit., father's brother.] in the Bible, a wicked king of Israel, led astray by his wife Jezebel. I Kings xvi. 22.
Ȧ·has″ū·ē′rus, *n.* [of Per. origin.] in the Bible, either of two kings of the Medes and Persians, especially the one who took Esther as his wife. Est. i; Ez. iv. 6.
à haute voix (ȧ ōt′ vwȧ′), [Fr., in high voice.] aloud.
ȧ·head′ (ȧ-hed′), *adv.* and *a.* [*a-*, on, and *head.*]
1. further forward than another thing; in front; originally, in nautical usage, further forward than another ship, or on the point to which the stem is directed, in opposition to *astern.*
2. onward; forward; as, move *ahead.*
3. in advance.
4. headlong; without restraint; precipitantly.
ahead of; in advance of; before.
be ahead; (a) to be winning or profiting; (b) to have as a profit, benefit, or advantage. [Colloq.]
ȧ·heap′, *adv.* in a heap.
ȧ·height′ (-hīt′), *adv.* aloft; on high. [Archaic.]
ȧ·hem′, *interj.* a cough or similar noise in the throat used to attract the attention of someone, give a warning, fill a pause, etc.
ȧ·hīgh′ (-hī′), *adv.* on high. [Obs.]
A·him′sä, *n.* [Hind.] Gandhi's doctrine of passive resistance.
Ȧ·hith′ō·phel, Ȧ·hit′ō·phel, *n.* [Heb. *'achīthōphel*, lit., brother is foolishness.] in the Bible, a counselor of David, who joined with Absalom in rebellion against him. II Sam. xv-xvii: also *Achitophel.*
ȧ·hōld′, *adv.* near the wind; as, to lay a ship *ahold.* [Obs.]
ȧ·horse′, *adv.* and *a.* [*a-*, on, and *horse.*] on horseback.
ȧ·hoy′, *interj.* [interj. *a*, and *hoy*, var. of *hey.*] in nautical usage, a call used in hailing a person or a vessel; as, ship *ahoy!*
Äh′ri·mȧn, *n.* [Per. *Ahrīman*; prob. from Avestan *aṅra mainyu*, the evil (lit., hostile) spirit.] in the Zoroastrian religion, the spirit of evil. See *Ormazd.*
ä′hu, *n.* [Per. *āhū*, deer.] the Persian gazelle.
ä′hu·atle (ä′ō-atl), *n.* [Mex.] the eggs of a fly, used as a food by Mexican Indians.
ȧ·hull′, *adv.* in nautical usage, with the sails furled and the helm lashed: applied to ships in a storm.
ȧ·hun′gẽred, *a.* hungry. [Archaic.]
Ā′hụ·rȧ-Maz′dȧ, *n.* same as *Ormazd.*
ȧ·hyp′ni·ȧ, *n.* insomnia; sleeplessness.
ai (ī), *interj.* an exclamation of pain, sorrow, pity, etc.
ä′i, *n.*; *pl.* **ä′iṣ,** [Braz. *ai, hai*, from the animal's cry.] the three-toed South American sloth.
aī·aī′ä, aī·aī′aī, *n.* [Sp. Am.] 1. a species of *Platalea*, or spoonbill: called also the *roseate spoonbill.*
2. the American jabiru, genus *Mycteoria*, of Paraguay.
āi′bliṇṣ, ā′bliṇṣ, *adv.* [Scot.] perhaps.
Aich·met′al, a kind of gun metal.
āid, *v.t.*; aided, *pt., pp.*; aiding, *ppr.* [ME. *aiden*; OFr. *aider*; L. *adjutare*, freq. of *adjuvare*, to help, assist; *ad*, to, and *juvare*, to help.]
1. to help; to assist; to support, as by furnishing strength or means to effect a purpose.
2. to forward; to facilitate.
3. in law, to correct (a fault) subsequently in proceedings, so that it may be eliminated from consideration.
Syn.—abet, assist, help, relieve, support, succor, cooperate.
āid, *v.i.* to help; to assist.
āid, *n.* 1. help; succor; support; assistance.
2. a person who aids, or gives support; a helper; an auxiliary; also, a thing that aids.
3. in English law, (a) a subsidy or emergency tax granted by parliament and making a part of the king's revenue; (b) an exchequer loan.
4. in English feudal law, a tax paid by a tenant to his lord; originally, a mere gift, which afterward became a right demandable by the lord.
5. in law, a remedy of defect in pleadings or procedure.
6. the help of whip, rein, spur, heel, etc., by which a horseman aids the action of his horse.
7. an officer in the army, navy, etc. who is assistant to a superior; an aide.
aid grant; a grant in aid, as aid given to a student at a college or university.
aid station; a dressing station.
āid′ănce, *n.* aid; help; assistance. [Rare.]
āid′ănt, *a.* helping; helpful; supplying aid.
āide, *n.* [Fr.] an officer in the army, navy, etc. who is assistant to a superior.
āide′-de-camp, āid′-de-camp (Fr. *pron.* ed′d'-käṅ), *n.*; *pl.* **āideṣ′-de-camp, āidṣ′-de-camp,** [Fr. *aide*, aid, *de*, L. *de*, of, and *camp*, L. *campus*, field.] in military affairs, an officer serving as assistant and confidential secretary to a general, marshal, etc.
aide-mé·moire′ (ed″me″mwȧr′), *n.* [Fr.] a memorandum of a discussion, proposed agreement, etc.
āid′ing, *a.* helping; assisting.
āid′less, *a.* helpless; without aid; unsupported; undefended.
āid-mā′jŏr, a regimental adjutant. [Obs.]
āig′let, *n.* same as *aglet.*
āi′gre (-gẽr), *a.* [Fr.] sour; sharp. [Obs.]
āi′gre·mōre (-gẽr-), *n.* [Fr.; origin unknown.] prepared charcoal used in making gunpowder.
āi·grette′, āi′gret, *n.* [Fr., a heron with a tuft of feathers on its head; tufted.]
1. a tuft formed of feathers, diamonds, etc., surmounting a headdress.
2. any ornament resembling this.
3. the small white heron, with a tufted head: usually *egret.*
4. a crown of feathery seed, as the dandelion or thistle top.
āi·guière′ (ā-gyãr′), *n.* [Fr.] a tall pitcher, with handle and tall spout.
āi·guille′ (-gwēl′), *n.* [Fr., a needle.]
1. a sharp, rocky mountain peak; especially, any of the Alpine peaks in the neighborhood of Mont Blanc.
2. a needlelike instrument for boring.
āi·guil·lette′ (-gwil-let′), *n.* [Fr., dim. of *aiguille*, needle.]
1. a gilt cord hung in loops from the shoulder of certain military uniforms; aglet.
2. in cookery, a side dish served on a small ornamental skewer.
āi′gū·let, *n.* [Fr.] an aglet. [Obs.]
āi′kin·īte, *n.* [named after Dr. A. *Aikin.*] a mineral containing lead, copper, and bismuth: also called *needle ore, aciculite.*
āil, *v.t.*; ailed (āld), *pt., pp.*; ailing, *ppr.* [ME. *ailen, aylen*; AS. *eglian, eglan*, trouble, pain.] to be the cause of pain to; to be the trouble with; as, what *ails* the man?
āil, *v.i.* to be ill or indisposed; to be affected with pain or uneasiness; to be in trouble; as, one day the child began to *ail.*
āil, *n.* indisposition or disease.
āi·lan′thiç, āi·lan′tiç, *a.* of or resembling an ailanthus.
Āi·lan′thus, Āi·lan′tus, *n.* [L., from *ailanto*, tree of heaven; Malacca name.] a genus of trees native to the East Indies and cultivated in America and Europe for their leaves, which are fed upon by silkworms; tree of heaven; also [a-], a tree of this genus.
āi·lan′thus moth, a large silk-producing moth native to China and cultivated in the eastern United States: its larvae feed on ailanthus leaves.
āi·lan′tine, *n.* silk obtained from the silkworm that feeds on the ailantus.
āi·lan′tine, *adj.* of or pertaining to the Ailanthus or to the silkworm that feeds on it.
āi′lẽr·on, *n.* [Fr.] a movable hinged section of the wing of an airplane, for banking in turns.
āi·lette′ (ā-let′), *n.* [Fr. *ailette*, dim. of *aile*, wing; L. *ala*, wing.] a metal shield formerly worn upon the shoulder by knights: the original form of the modern epaulet.
āil′ing, *a.* sickly; ill.
āil′ment, *n.* any bodily or mental disorder; illness, especially one that is not severe.
Āi·lū·roid′ē·ȧ, *n.pl.* [L., from Gr. *ailouros*, cat, and Gr. *eidos*, form.] in zoology, a group of carnivorous mammals that includes the cats, civets, and hyenas.
āil′weed, *n.* a parasitic plant that attaches itself to clover.
āim, *v.i.*; aimed, *pt., pp.*; aiming, *ppr.* [ME. *aymen, amen*; OFr. *amer, esmer*; L. *æstimare*, to estimate.]
1. to point a weapon, as a lance or a gun, or direct a remark, blow, etc. so as to hit.
2. to direct one's efforts; to attempt to reach or accomplish an object or purpose; to try or purpose to be or do something.
3. to guess or conjecture. [Obs.]
āim, *v.t.* 1. to direct (a blow, remark, etc.) with the intention of hitting; as, to *aim* a blow with a club.
2. to point, direct, or level, as a gun or other weapon, at any object.
3. to estimate; to conjecture; to consider. [Obs.]
Syn.—aspire, endeavor, direct, purpose.
āim, *n.* 1. the pointing or directing of a weapon; the direction of anything at a particular point or object, so as to strike or affect it.
2. the point intended to be hit, or object intended to be affected; as, he missed his *aim.*
3. a purpose; intention; design; scheme; as, men often fail to achieve their *aims.*
4. sighting in pointing a weapon.
5. conjecture; guess. [Obs.]
take aim; to point a weapon; to sight along a gun at the target; to direct a missile, blow, etc.
āim′ẽr, *n.* one who aims.
āim′less, *a.* without aim or purpose; having no end or object in view.
āim′less·ly, *adv.* in an aimless or purposeless manner.
āim′less·ness, *n.* the state of being without aim or purpose, or of having no object in view.
āin, *a.* [Scot.] own.
Aī′nō, *n.* Ainu.
ain't (ānt), [early assimilation of *amn't*, contr. of *am not*; later confused with *a'nt* (*are not*), *i'nt* (*is not*), *ha'nt* (*has not, have not*).] am not. [Colloq.] Also a dialectal or substandard contraction for *is not, has not,* and *have not*: *ain't* was formerly standard for *am not* and is still defended by some authorities as a proper contraction for *am not* in interrogative constructions; as, I'm going too, *ain't* I?
Aī′nu, *n.* [*Ainu*, lit., man.]
1. a member of a primitive, light-skinned race of Japan, now living mostly in Karafuto and part of Hokkaido.
2. the language of this race.
Aī′nu, *a.* of the Ainus, their language, etc.
āir, *adv.* and *a.* [Scot. dial. form of *ere*, from AS. *aer.*] early; before.
āir, *n.* [ME.; OFr. *air*, air, breath; L. *aer*; Gr. *aēr*, air, mist, from *aein*, to breathe, blow.]
1. the elastic, invisible mixture of gases (nitrogen, oxygen, hydrogen, carbon dioxide, argon, neon, helium, etc.) that surrounds the earth; atmosphere.
2. space above the earth; sky.
3. air of a certain kind or condition; as, night *air*; bad *air.*

4. any aeriform or gaseous body. [Obs.]
5. a breeze, zephyr, or gentle wind.
Let vernal *airs* through trembling osiers play. —Pope.
6. publicity; public utterance.
You gave it *air* before me. —Dryden.
7. a report; advice; news. [Obs.]
8. the characteristic look, appearance, manner, or mien of a person; as, the *air* of a youth; a lofty *air*.
9. the general character or outward appearance of anything; as, the room had an *air* of refinement.
10. [*pl.*] an affected manner; show of pride; haughtiness; as, he puts on *airs*.
11. anything light or uncertain.
12. in music, a melody or tune; especially, the main melody in a harmonized composition, usually the soprano or treble part.
13. in the Greek church, a delicate veil spread over the paten and the chalice together, in addition to the individual veils of those vessels.
14. in radio, the medium through which signals and broadcasts reach the audience: a figurative use.
air castle; a castle in the air; a castle existing only in fancy; hence, any fanciful, ambitious plan.
get the air; to be dismissed; to be rejected. [Slang.]
give the air to; to dismiss unceremoniously; to discharge. [Slang.]
in the air; (a) current or prevalent; (b) not decided; not settled; still imaginary.
on the air; in radio, broadcasting or being broadcast.
up in the air; (a) not settled; not decided; still imaginary; (b) angry; highly excited, upset, agitated, etc.
walk on air; to feel very happy, very lively, or exalted.
Syn.—appearance, bearing, mien, carriage, demeanor, behavior, expression, look, manner, style.

ãir, *a.* in aeronautics, of or pertaining to anything occurring in the air; as, *air* fight, *air* line, *air* routes.

ãir, *v.t.*; aired, *pt.*, *pp.*; airing, *ppr.* 1. to expose to the air; to put where air can dry, cool, freshen, etc.; to ventilate; as, to *air* clothes; to *air* a room.
2. to expose to heat or fire to expel dampness; as, to *air* linen by the fire.
3. to make known or publicize, generally with the suggestion of ostentation; as, to *air* a grievance.
4. to make a vain display of in public or before others; as, she *aired* her charms.

Aī′rȧ, *n.* [L., from Gr. *aira*, a kind of darnel.] a genus of perennial grasses, including the hair grass.

ãir at·tack′, an attack by aircraft; an air raid.

ãir bag, a bag of nylon, plastic, etc. that inflates automatically within an automobile at the impact of a collision, to protect riders from being thrown forward.

ãir bāse, a base for aircraft, especially military aircraft, consisting of a landing field, repair facilities, etc.

ãir bȧth, 1. an apparatus for applying air to the body.
2. an arrangement for drying substances in air of regulated temperature.

ãir blad′dẽr, 1. a sac filled with air or gas, as the cells of the lungs: also called *air cell.*
2. the bladder of a fish, containing air, by which it is enabled to maintain its equilibrium in the water: also called *swimming bladder.*

ãir′-bọrne, *a.* 1. borne in or by the air.
2. transported by aircraft, as *air-borne* military forces.

ãir brāke, a brake operated by the action of compressed air on a piston, as in a bus or railroad car.

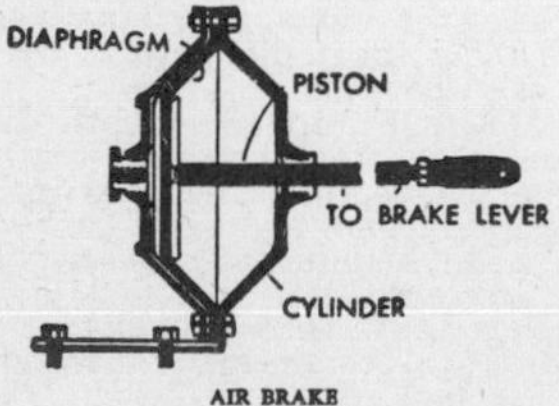

AIR BRAKE

ãir′brā′sive, *n.* a method of preparing teeth for filling by wearing down the surface with an abrasive substance blown into the cavity by a jet of air.

ãir′brush, *n.* a kind of atomizer, operated by compressed air: used to apply paint or liquid color. Also *air brush.*

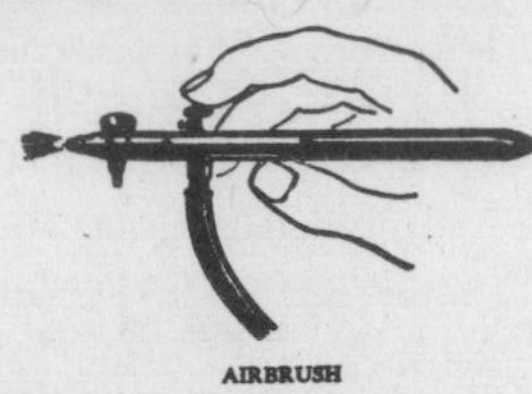
AIRBRUSH

ãir′-built (-bilt), *a.* fanciful; having no solid foundation; chimerical; as, *air-built* hopes.

ãir′bus, *n.* [*air*plane, and *bus*.] an airplane designed for mass transportation of passengers; especially, an extremely large, short-range airplane of this kind.

ãir cell, in botany and zoology, a cavity or cell containing air.

ãir chām′bẽr, a cavity or compartment full of air, especially one used in hydraulics to equalize the flow of a fluid.

ãir çock, a faucet to regulate air supply to a pipe, chamber, etc.

ãir çŏm·press′ŏr, an apparatus for compressing air for mechanical purposes.

ãir çŏn·dens′ẽr, an air compressor.

ãir′-çŏn·di″tiŏn, *v.t.* to provide with air conditioning.

ãir′-çŏn·di″tiŏned, *a.* having air conditioning.

ãir çŏn·di′tiŏn·ing (-dish′un-ing), the process of cleaning the air and controlling its humidity and temperature in buildings, cars, etc.

ãir′-çọọl″, *v.t.* to cool by passing air over, into, or through.

ãir′-çọọled″, *a.* cooled by having air passed over, into, or through it; as, an *air-cooled* engine.

ãir çor′ri·dọr, a passage in the air for aircraft, especially one established by international agreement.

ãir′çraft, *n. sing.* and *pl.* any machine or machines for flying or sailing through the air, whether heavier or lighter than air.

ãir′çraft çar′ri·ẽr, a flat-topped naval vessel which carries, and serves as a base for, aircraft, usually small airplanes.

ãir çrew, the crew of an aircraft in flight.

ãir çross′ing, a passage for air in a mine, running over or under another one.

ãir çush′iŏn (-un), 1. a bag inflated with air and used as a cushion or pillow.
2. in mechanics, a device for lessening shock by means of compressed air.

ãir cyl′in·dẽr, an air-filled cylinder fitted with a piston, for absorbing the recoil of a gun.

ãir′drawn, *a.* drawn in air; imaginary.

ãir′drōme, *n.* [from *air*, and Gr. *dromos*, course.] the physical facilities of an air base, excluding personnel.

ãir′drop, *n.* the act of delivering supplies or troops by parachuting them from an aircraft in flight.

ãir′-drȳ″, *v.t.*; air-dried, *pt.*, *pp.*; air-drying, *ppr.* to dry by exposing to the air.

Āire′dāle, *n.* a dog of the terrier family, characterized by brown, black, or gray wiry hair.

AIREDALE
(24 in. high at shoulder)

ãir en′ġine, an engine operated by heated air.

ãir′ẽr, *n.* 1. one who exposes to the air.
2. a frame on which clothes are aired.

ãir′fiēld″, *n.* a field where aircraft can take off and land.

ãir fleet, a fleet of aircraft, especially one for military purposes.

ãir flōw, a flow of air.

ãir′foil″, *n.* a part with a flat or curved surface made to be moved through the air so as to keep an aircraft up or control its movements; the wing, rudder, etc. of an aircraft.

ãir fōrce, 1. the aviation branch of the armed forces of a country.
2. the largest unit of this branch.

ãir foun′tain (-tin), a device for producing a jet of water by the power of compressed air.

ãir freight (frāt), the carrying of heavy goods by aircraft; also, goods so carried.

ãir fũr′năce, a furnace that works with a natural draft of air and has no forced draft.

ãir gas, dry air charged with vapor from petroleum or from some other hydrocarbons, used for lighting or heating.

ãir gun, a pneumatic gun that shoots a projectile by means of compressed air.

ãir hōld′ẽr, an instrument for holding air, as for the purpose of counteracting the pressure of a decreasing column of mercury.

ãir hōle, 1. an opening to admit or discharge air.
2. an unfrozen or open place in the ice on a body of water.
3. an air pocket.

ãir′i·ly, *adv.* in an airy manner; breezily.

ãir′i·ness, *n.* 1. the quality or state of being airy, or full of fresh air.
2. gaiety; levity; as, the *airiness* of girls.

ãir′ing, *n.* 1. an exposure to the air, or to a fire, for warming or drying.
2. a walk or ride in the open air; a short excursion; the exercise of horses in the open air.
3. exposure to public knowledge.

ãir jaçk′et, 1. a jacket having airtight cells or cavities which can be filled with air, to make persons buoyant in swimming.
2. a compartment containing air surrounding some part of a machine, especially for checking the transmission of heat.

ãir lāne, a route for travel by air; an airway.

ãir′less, *a.* 1. not open to a free current of air; without fresh air.
2. without wind or breeze; still and humid.

ãir lev′el, a spirit level.

ãir′līke, *a.* resembling air.

ãir līne, 1. straight line; a bee line; shortest distance between two points.
2. a system of air transport.
3. an organization in the business of providing transportation by air.
4. a route for travel by air.

ãir′-līne, *a.* 1. of an air line.
2. direct; straight.

ãir lī′nẽr, a large aircraft for carrying passengers.

ãir loçk, 1. an airtight compartment, with adjustable air pressure, between places that do not have the same air pressure, as between the working part of a caisson and the outside.
2. a blockage, as in a water pipe, caused by an air bubble.

ãir māil, 1. the system of carrying mail by aircraft.
2. the mail so carried.

ãir′măn, *n.*; *pl.* **ãir′men,** an aviator.

ãir mass, in meteorology, a large body of air having virtually uniform conditions of temperature and moisture in a horizontal cross section.

Āir Med′ăl, a United States military decoration awarded for heroism or meritorious service while participating in an aerial flight.

ãir mē′tẽr, an airometer.

ãir·mīn′ded, *a.* interested in aircraft or in air activities in general.

ãir·om′e·tẽr, *n.* 1. an instrument for measuring the speed of the flow of air.
2. a gasometer.

ãir pas′sāġe, 1. a passage or space with air in it or through which air can pass.
2. a journey by air.
3. accommodations for such a journey.

ãir pīpe, any pipe used to conduct air into or out of close places, for ventilation, etc.

ãir′plāne, *n.* [altered, after *air*, from earlier *aeroplane*.] an aircraft that is kept aloft by the aerodynamic forces upon its wings and is driven forward by a screw propeller or by other means, as jet propulsion: also ***aeroplane.***

AIRPLANE

ãir′plāne çar′ri·ẽr, see *aircraft carrier.*

ãir′plāne clọth, 1. a strong, plain-weave cloth, originally of linen but later of cotton, used for airplane wings.
2. a similar cotton cloth used for pajamas, sport shirts, etc.

ãir′plāne spin, in wrestling, a hold in which an opponent is lifted up and spun around before being thrown.

ãir plant, a plant that grows on the trunk or

branches of another plant, but not as a parasite, and gets nourishment from the air and the rain; an epiphyte.
āir pock'et, an atmospheric condition that causes an aircraft to make sudden, short drops while in flight.
āir pore, in botany, a stoma.
āir pōrt, on board ship, a porthole or scuttle to admit air.
āir'pōrt, *n.* a place where aircraft can land and take off, usually equipped with hangars, facilities for refueling and repair, various accommodations for passengers, etc.
āir pres'sūre, the pressure of atmospheric or compressed air.
āir'proof, *a.* not penetrable by air.
āir'proof, *v.t.* to make airproof.
āir pump, a machine, of varying construction, for exhausting the air from a vessel or enclosed space, for forcing air through something, or for compressing air in any enclosed place.
āir rāid, an attack from the air by aircraft, usually bombers.
āir-rāid shel'tēr, a cellar, subterranean tunnel, or bombproof metal cubicle for protection during an air raid.
āir-rāid wạr'den, a person responsible for various tasks in an air raid, as warning people, directing traffic, protecting property, giving first aid, etc.
āir rī'fle, a rifle operated by compressed air; it usually shoots small pellets.
āir rōute, a line of travel by airplane.
āir saç, in birds, a receptacle for air, or one of the vesicles lodged in the fleshy parts, in the hollow bones, and in the abdomen, all communicating with the lungs.
āir'sçāpe", *n.* [*air,* and land*scape.*] a view of the earth from a high position, as from an aircraft.
āir sçout, an aviator who flies to reconnoiter.
āir sēr'vice, 1. transportation by aircraft.
2. the aviation branch of the armed forces.
āir shaft, a passage for air into a tunnel, mine, etc., usually opened in a perpendicular direction, and meeting horizontal passages, to cause a free circulation of fresh air through the mine.
āir'shed", *n.* [*air,* and water*shed.*] an area of varying size that is dependent on a single air mass and that is uniformly affected by the same sources of air pollution.
āir'ship, *n.* 1. a self-propelled aircraft that is lighter than air; a dirigible.
2. occasionally, an airplane.
āir'sick", *a.* sick or nauseated because of traveling by air.
āir'-slacked (-slakt), *a.* slacked or pulverized by exposure to the air; as, *air-slacked* lime.
āir spāce, 1. a space with air in it.
2. the amount of breathable air in a room or building.
3. space for maneuvering an aircraft flying in formation.
āir speed, the speed of an aircraft determined by its relationship to the air rather than the ground.
āir'-sprāyed", *a.* sprayed by means of compressed air.
āir spring, a spring or shock absorber that operates by the elasticity of air.
āir'strip", *n.* an airfield, usually for temporary use, consisting of one or more runways made of prepared metal mats, gravel, etc.
āirt, *n.* [from Gael. *aird,* height, direction.], [Scot.] any of the cardinal points of the compass; direction.
āirt, *v.t.* [Scot.] to guide or direct.
āir tax'i, a small or medium-sized commercial airplane that carries passengers, and often mail, to places not regularly served by scheduled airlines.
āir thēr·mom'e·tēr, a kind of thermometer in which the changes of temperature are measured by the expansion and contraction of atmospheric air.
āir'tīght (-tīt), *a.* 1. too tight for air or gas to enter or escape.
2. giving no opening for attack; as, an *airtight* alibi.
āir tīght, a stove with a draft which can be shut off almost entirely.
āir trap, a contrivance for the escape of foul air from drains, sewers, etc.
āir valve, a valve to regulate the admission or escape of air; especially, a valve to admit air to a steam boiler.
āir ves'i·çle, in botany, a space filled with air, found in many water plants.
āir ves'sel, a tube, duct, cell, or chamber for conveying or holding air.
āir'wărd, āir'wărds, *adv.* up into the air.
āir'wāy, *n.* 1. the specially marked way or route along which aircraft fly from airport to airport; airlane.
2. an air shaft.
the airways; in radio, the air; broadcasting.
āir well, an air shaft.
āir'wom"ăn (-woom"), *n.*; *pl.* **āir'wom"en** (-wim"), a woman flyer.
āir'wŏr"thy, *a.* fit to be flown: said of aircraft.
āir'y, *a.* 1. consisting of air.
2. of or belonging to air; high in the air; as, an *airy* flight.
3. open to a free current of air.
4. light as air; like air; thin; unsubstantial; without solidity; delicate or graceful in appearance or quality; ethereal; immaterial.
5. without reality; having no solid foundation; vain; trifling; as, an *airy* scheme.
6. gay; sprightly; full of vivacity and levity; light of heart; lively; as, an *airy* girl.
7. having affected manners; putting on airs. [Colloq.]
aīsle (īl), *n.* [Fr. *aile,* a wing; L. *ala,* wing.]
1. a part of a church alongside the nave, choir, or transept, set off by a row of columns, pillars, or piers.
2. a passageway between rows of seats.
3. a narrow passageway or corridor, as in a theater, between rows of trees, etc.
aīsled (īld), *a.* having an aisle or aisles.
aīsle'less, *a.* without an aisle.
āit, *n.* [Scot.] oat.
āitch (āch), *n.*; *pl.* **āitch'eṣ,** [ME. and OFr. *ache.*] H or h.
āitch, *adj.* shaped like an H.
āitch'bōne, *n.* [by faulty separation of ME. *a nache bone*; OFr. *nache,* the buttock; L. *natica,* from *natis,* buttock.]
1. the rump bone.
2. the cut of meat around the rump bone. Also called *edgebone.*
āi·ti·ol'ō·ġy, *n.* etiology. [Obs.]
Ā"ï·zō·ā'cē·ae, *n.pl.* [L., prob. from Gr. *aei,* always, and *zoos,* alive.] a family of apetalous plants, with opposite leaves; the carpet weed family, with 22 genera and 500 species.
ā"ï·zō·ā'ceous, *a.* of the *Aizoaceæ.*
ȧ·jär', *adv.* and *a.* [ME. *on char,* on the turn; AS. *cerr, cyrr,* turn.] partly open, as a door.
ȧ·jär', *adv.* and *a.* out of harmony.
Ā'jax, *n.* [L.; Gr. *Aias.*] in Homer's *Iliad,* (a) a strong, brave Greek warrior who killed himself when Achilles' armor was given to Odysseus: called *Ajax Telamon*; (b) one of the swiftest runners among the Greek warriors: called *Ajax the Less.*
ȧ·jog', *adv.* moving leisurely along; on the jog.
aj'ū·tāġe, *n.* same as *adjutage.*
ȧ·kä'lȧ, *n.* [Hawaiian.] a shrub of the family *Rosaceæ* growing in the Hawaiian Islands, producing large, edible red berries.
A·kē'bi·ȧ, *n.* [L., from Japan., *akebi.*] a genus of hardy Japanese climbing plants, of which *Akebia quinata* is much cultivated and admired.
ȧ·kēne', *n.* same as *achene.*
ȧ·kim'bō, *a.* and *adv.* [ME: *in kenebowe,* lit., in keen bow, i.e., in a sharp curve; a folk etym. from ON. *kengboginn,* bow-bent, from *keng,* bent, and *bogi,* a bow.] with hands on hips and elbows bent outward; as, with arms *akimbo.*
ȧ·kin', *a.* [*a-,* of, and *kin.*]
1. related; of one kin.
2. allied by nature; having similar qualities; similar; as, envy and jealousy are near *akin.*
ak·i·nē'si·ȧ, *n.* [Gr. *akinēsia, akinēsis,* from *a* priv., and *kinein,* to move.] paralysis of the motor nerves; loss of the control of movement.
ak·i·nē'siç, ak·i·net'iç, *a.* pertaining to akinesia.
Ak'kad, *n.* 1. a native or inhabitant of ancient Akkad.
2. any of several Semitic dialects spoken by the Akkads: also spelled *Accad.*
Ak'kad, *a.* Akkadian: also spelled *Accad.*
Ak·kā'di·ăn, *a.* 1. of ancient Akkad, its people, or its culture.
2. of the Semitic dialects spoken by the Akkads.
Ak·kā'di·ăn, *n.* Akkad.
ȧ·knee' (-nē'), *adv.* on the knees. [Rare.]
ak·nōw', *v.t.* acknow. [Obs.]
al-, in Arabic, a prefix, corresponding to the Italian *il,* and the Spanish *el* and *la,* equivalent to the English definite article, *the*; as, *Al*koran, the Koran, or the book; *al*cove, *al*chemy, *al*embic, *al*manac.
al-, ad-: used before *l,* as in *al*lude.
-al, [L. *-alis.*] an adjectival suffix meaning *belonging to, of,* or *pertaining to,* etc. It also appears as part of nouns which were originally adjectives, used as substantives, as riv*al,* anim*al,* etc., and is used to form nouns of action from verbs, as arriv*al,* acquitt*al,* etc.
-al, [from *al*dehyde.] in chemistry, a suffix signifying *the presence of the aldehydes,* as in chlor*al.*
Al, in chemistry, aluminum.
äl, *n.* [Hind.] an Indian plant, *Morinda citrifolia,* yielding a madder, used in Madras for dyeing: written also *aal, awl.*
ā'lȧ, *n.*; *pl.* **ā'lae** (-lē), [L., a wing.]
1. in anatomy and zoology, (a) a wing; (b) a winglike structure, as a lobe of the ear.
2. in botany, (a) one of the side petals of a butterfly-shaped corolla; (b) a thin wing on some seeds.
à lä (ä' lä), [Fr.] to the, at the, or in the; hence, according to, or in the fashion of; as, *à la carte,* according to the menu card, or bill of fare; *à la française,* in the French fashion.
Al"ȧ·bam'ȧ çlāims, claims made upon England by the United States for damages to American shipping during the Civil War by Confederate privateers sailing from England, especially the *Alabama*; a tribunal of arbitration, sitting at Geneva, 1872, awarded **$15,000,000** to the United States: also known as the *Geneva award.*
Al"ȧ·bam'i·ăn, *a.* of Alabama.
Al"ȧ·bam'i·ăn, *n.* a native or inhabitant of Alabama.
al"ȧ·bam'ïne, *n.* [*Alabama,* and *-ine.*] a name given to chemical element 85, supposedly found in monazite sands in 1931: symbol, Ab: see *astatine.*
al·ȧ·ban'dīte, al·ȧ·ban'dine, *n.* manganese sulfide: named after *Alabanda,* an old city of Asia Minor, which produced it.
al'ȧ·bas·tēr, *n.* [L. *alabaster*; Gr. *alabastros.*]
1. a hydrated sulfate of calcium, or variety of gypsum, of fine texture, and usually white and translucent, but sometimes yellow, red, or gray. It is soft and costly and carved into statuettes, vases, mantel ornaments, etc. The finest variety is found near Florence, Italy.
2. a somewhat translucent, hard stone, or variety of calcite, found in large masses formed by the deposition of calcareous particles in caverns of limestone rocks. These concretions have a foliated, fibrous, or granular structure, and are of a pure white color, or are striped or spotted with shades of yellow, red, or brown. Also called *stalagmite, stalactite,* and *travertine.*
3. among the ancients, a vessel in which odoriferous liquors or ointments were kept: so called from the stone of which it was made.
al'ȧ·bas·tēr, *a.* made of alabaster, or resembling it.
al·ȧ·bas'tri·ăn, al·ȧ·bas'trine, *a.* pertaining to or like alabaster.
al·ȧ·bas'trum, *n.*; *pl.* **al·ȧ·bas'trȧ,** [L.] 1. a flower bud.
2. a small, pear-shaped, wide-lipped vessel used by the ancient Greeks as a receptacle for perfumes and unguents.
à lȧ cärte (çärt'), [Fr.] by the bill of fare; with a separate price for each item on the menu: opposed to *table d'hôte.*
ȧ·lack', *interj.* an exclamation of regret, surprise, dismay, etc. [Archaic.]
ȧ·lack' ȧ·dāy, *interj.* alack. [Archaic.]
à lȧ çrē·ōle', [Fr., after the fashion of the Creoles.] prepared with tomatoes and highly seasoned.
ȧ·laç'ri·fȳ, *v.t.* to arouse. [Rare.]
ȧ·laç'ri·ous, *a.* brisk. [Obs.]
ȧ·laç'ri·ous·ly, *adv.* briskly. [Obs.]
ȧ·laç'ri·ous·ness, *n.* briskness. [Obs.]
ȧ·laç'ri·tous, *a.* showing alacrity.
ȧ·laç'ri·ty, *n.* [Fr. *alacrité*; L. *alacritas,* briskness, from *alacer, alacris,* brisk, lively.]
1. cheerfulness; gaiety; sprightliness.
2. a readiness or promptness to act or serve; cheerful willingness; as, he responded with *alacrity* to the demand.
3. quickness or facility of thought or action.
A·lad'din, *n.* the young man in the *Arabian Nights* who obtains a magic lamp and ring, the rubbing of which causes a jinni to appear, who does the bidding, or fulfills the wish, of the one who has the lamp and ring in his possession at the time.
A·lad'in·ist, *n.* a freethinker among the Mohammedans: so named from *Aladdin* (meaning *height of religion*), a learned priest of the time of Mohammed II. Also spelled *Aladdinist.*

à lȧ frăṅ·çaiṣe′ (-sez′), [Fr.] in the French manner.

à lȧ jụ·lienne′ (zhụ·lyen′), [Fr.; see *julienne.*] cut into thin strips, as fried potatoes, cheese, etc.

à lȧ king′, [Fr., lit., in kingly style.] served in a sauce containing diced mushrooms, pimentos, and green peppers.

à lȧ let′tre, [Fr.] to the letter; literally.

ȧ·lā′li·ȧ, *n.* [L., from Gr. *alalia*, from *a* priv., and *lalein*, to talk.] a paralysis of the larynx or muscles of speech: loss of the ability to speak is the result.

al′ȧ·līte, *n.* [*Ala*, a valley in Piedmont, and *-lite*, Gr. *lithos*, stone.] a bright green variety of pyroxene, in prisms: first obtained in the valley of Ala.

al·ȧ·loṅ′gȧ, al·i·loṅ′ghi (-gi), *n.* [L. *ala*, wing, fin, and *longa*, long.] the tunny.

à lȧ ly·on·naiṣe′ (lyọ-neṣ′), [Fr., in the manner of *Lyons*, France.] fried with sliced onions.

Al·ă·man′nī, *n.pl.* Germanic tribes which invaded and settled in Alsace and part of Switzerland in the early 5th century A.D.: also spelled *Alemanni.*

Al·ă·man′niç, *a.* Alemannic.

ä·lȧ·mẹ′dȧ, *n.* [Sp.] a walk or public promenade shaded by trees, especially by poplar and cottonwood trees.

ä·lȧ·mī′rẹ, *n.* [formed from *a, la, mi, re,* names of notes in the musical scale.] the lowest note but one in Guido Aretino's scale of music.

al′ȧ·mō″, *n.*; *pl.* **al′ȧ·mōṣ″,** [Sp. *ālamo*, poplar tree.]

1. a poplar tree.
2. a cottonwood tree.

al″ȧ·mō·dal′i·ty, *n.* [Fr. *à la mode*, and *-ality.*] conformity to the fashion.

al′ȧ·mōde, *a.* [Fr. *à la mode*, after the fashion.]

1. according to the fashion or prevailing mode.
2. made or served in a certain style, as pie with ice cream, or beef braised and prepared with vegetables in sauce. Also *à la mode, a la mode.*

al′ȧ·mōde, *n.* a thin, glossy black silk for hoods, scarfs, etc.

à lȧ mọrt′, [Fr.] very ill; depressed; melancholy; in a moribund state.

ȧ·lăn′, *n.* [OFr. *alant*; L. *alanus*, a hunting dog.] a wolf dog. [Obs.]

ȧ·land′, *adv.* at or on land.

ȧ·lāne′, *a.* and *adv.* [Scot.] alone.

à lȧ New′bŭrg, [Fr. *à la*; and Newburg, after *Newburgh*, Scotland.] served in a sauce of creamed egg yolks, wine, and butter.

al′ȧ·nïne, *n.* a compound derived from aldehyde ammonia.

al′ant çam″phŏr camphor obtained from elecampane.

ȧ·lan′tin, *n.* an amylaceous or starchy substance extracted from the root of the *Angelica Archangelica*; inulin.

ā′lăr, *a.* [L. *alaris*, from *ala*, wing.]

1. possessing wings or alae.
2. of or relating to a wing or ala.
3. shaped like or resembling wings.
4. in botany, located in the forks of a plant or a stem; axillary.
5. in anatomy, of or pertaining to the armpit; axillary.

Al Ä′răf, in Mohammedan belief, the wall that separates heaven from hell, as described in the Koran.

A·lā′ri·ȧ, *n.* [L. *alarius*, from *ala*, wing.] a genus of seaweeds.

ȧ·lärm′, *n.* [ME. *alarme*; OFr. *alarme*; It. *allarme*, fright, alarm; from *all' arme*, to arms! *a*, L. *ad*, to; *le*, L. f. pl. of *ille*, the; *arme*, L. *arma*, neut. pl., arms.]

1. any sound, outcry, or information, intended to give notice of approaching danger; as, to sound an *alarm.*
2. a summons to arms.
3. a warning of danger.
4. sudden surprise with fear or terror; as, the fire of the enemy excited *alarm.*
5. terror; a sensation excited by an apprehension of danger, from whatever cause; as, we felt *alarm* at the cry of fire.
6. a mechanical contrivance for rousing attention or warning of danger.
7. the bell or buzzer of an alarm clock.
8. in fencing, an appeal or challenge.

Syn.—fright, terror, consternation, apprehension, affright, dread, fear, panic.—*Alarm* is the dread of impending danger; *apprehension*, fear that it may be approaching; *terror* is agitating and excessive fear; *consternation* is terror which overpowers the faculties.

ȧ·lärm′, *v.t.*; alarmed, *pt., pp.*; alarming, *ppr.*

1. to give notice of danger to; to rouse to vigilance and exertions for safety.
2. to call to arms for defense.
3. to surprise with apprehension of danger; to disturb with terror; to frighten.

ȧ·lärm′ȧ·ble, *a.* liable to be alarmed; easily alarmed.

ȧ·lärm bell, a bell that gives notice of danger.

ȧ·lärm bīrd, see *turacou.*

ȧ·lärm çlock, a clock with a bell or buzzer, which can be so set to sound at a particular hour, as to wake one from sleep.

ȧ·lärmed′, *a.* notified of sudden danger; surprised with fear; roused to vigilance or activity by apprehension of approaching danger; frightened.

ȧ·lärm′ed·ly, *adv.* in an alarmed manner.

ȧ·lärm′ing, *a.* exciting apprehension; terrifying; awakening a sense of danger; as, an *alarming* message.

ȧ·lärm′ing·ly, *adv.* with alarm; in a manner to excite apprehension.

ȧ·lärm′ist, *n.* 1. a person who habitually spreads alarming rumors, exaggerated reports of danger, etc.

2. a person easily frightened and likely to anticipate the worst.

ȧ·lärm′ist, *a.* of or like an alarmist.

ȧ·lärm pōst, a place to which troops are to repair in case of an alarm.

ȧ·lärm wätch (wäch), a watch that can be so set to sound at a designated time, like an alarm clock.

ȧ·lär′um, *n.* alarm. [Archaic or Poetic.]

ā′lȧ·ry, *a.* [L. *alarius*, from *ala*, wing.] pertaining to wings; winglike.

ȧ·lȧs′, *interj.* [ME. *alas, allas*; OFr. *a las, ha las*; Fr. *hélas*; *a*, ah, and *las*, wretched; L. *lassus*, weary.] an exclamation expressive of sorrow, grief, pity, concern, or apprehension of evil: formerly, sometimes followed by *day* or *while*; *alas the day*, like alackaday; or *alas the while.*

Ȧ·las′kăn, *a.* of Alaska.

Ȧ·las′kăn, *n.* a native or inhabitant of Alaska.

ȧ·lāte′, *adv.* lately. [Archaic.]

ā′lāte, ā′lā·ted, *a.* [L. *alatus*, winged, from *ala*, wing.] having wings or winglike attachments.

al·ȧ·tēr′nus, al′ȧ·tērn, *n.* the popular name of a species of *Rhamnus* or buckthorn.

ȧ·lā′tion, *n.* the state or manner of being winged.

ȧ·lạunt′, *n.* alan. [Obs.]

alb, *n.* [OE. *albe*; L. *alba*, f. of *albus*, white.] a tunic or vestment of white linen reaching to the feet, worn by the Roman Catholic clergy. Also, a white garment worn in the early church by new converts from the Saturday before Easter until the first Sunday after Easter, which is called *Alb* Sunday.

ALB

al′bȧ, *n.* [L. *alba*, f. of *albus*, white.] the white nerve tissue of the brain and spinal cord.

äl′bȧ, *n.* [Pr., dawn, from L. *albus*, white.] the conventionalized morning song of Provençal troubadour literature, a lyric in which a lover voices regret at parting from his beloved; aubade.

al′bȧ·çore, *n.*; *pl.* **al′bȧ·çoreṣ, al′bȧ·çore,** [Port., from Ar. *al*, the, and *bukr*, young camel.] any of a number of related salt-water fishes of the mackerel family, including the tunny or tuna, the bonito, etc.

al′băn, *n.* [L. *albus*, white.] a crystalline substance obtained from gutta percha.

Al·bā′ni·ăn, *a.* of Albania, its people, language, etc.

Al·bā′ni·ăn, *n.* 1. a native or inhabitant of Albania.

2. the language of the Albanians.

al·bā′tȧ, *n.* [L. *albatus*, pp. of *albare*, to make white, from *albus*, white.] a silvery alloy of zinc, copper, and nickel.

al′bȧ·tross, *n.* [altered, prob. after L. *albus*, white, from Port. *alcatraz*, a cormorant; Sp. *alcatruz*, a pelican, from Ar. *al*, the, and *qādūs*, bucket; Gr. *kados*, bucket.] an aquatic bird of the petrel family. The bill is straight; the upper mandible crooked at the point, and the lower one truncated; the nostrils are oval, open, and placed on the sides; the wings are pennated, and there are three webbed toes on each foot. The upper part of the body is sometimes white, but usually of a spotted brown, and the belly white. It is the largest sea bird known and preys on fish and small water fowl. The *albatross* is found chiefly in the South Seas. It is sometimes called the *great gull.*

WANDERING ALBATROSS
(*Diomedea exulans*)

al′bȧ·tross çloth, a kind of thin woolen cloth.

ạl·bē′, ạl·bee′, *conj.* albeit. [Archaic.]

al·bē′dō, *n.* [L. *albus*, white.] in astronomy, the ratio between the light reflected from a surface and the total light falling upon the surface; as, the *albedo* of the moon.

ạl·bē′it, *conj.* [ME. *al be it*; *al*, all, and *be it.*] be it so; even though; although; notwithstanding.

Albeit so mask'd, madam, I love the truth.
—Tennyson.

al′bērt·īte, *n.* [after *Albert*, New Brunswick, and *-ite.*] a bituminous mineral closely resembling asphaltum.

al′bēr·type, *n.* 1. a process of printing a picture in ink from a photographic plate: the invention of Joseph Albert.

2. a picture produced by this process.

al·bes′cence, *n.* the condition or quality of being albescent.

al·bes′cent, *a.* [L. *albescens*, ppr. of *albescere*, to become white, from *albus*, white.] becoming white, or whitish; moderately white.

al′bi·çănt, *a.* [L. *albicans*, ppr. of *albicare*, to be white.] turning white.

al·bi·çā′tion, *n.* the process of turning white.

al′bi·çōre, *n.* same as *albacore.*

al·bi·flō′rous, *a.* [L. *albiflorus*; *albus*, white, and *flos, floris*, flower.] bearing white flowers.

Al·bi·gen′sēṣ, Al·bi·geois′ (-zhwä′), *n.pl.* [L. from Fr. *Albigeois*, inhabitants of *Albi.*] a religious sect that opposed the Church of Rome in the twelfth century: so called from Albi, a town in the south of France, where they resided. Although confused with the Waldenses, they were a branch of the Cathari. The *Albigenses* defied the authority of the church, discarded sacraments, and looked upon marriage as sinful. They were exterminated during the Crusades and the Inquisition.

Al·bi·gen′sian (-shun), *a.* pertaining to the Albigenses.

Al·bi·gen′sian (-shun), *n.* any member of the Albigenses.

al′bin, *n.* [L. *albus*, white.] a variety of opaque white apophyllite found in Bohemia.

al·bī′ness, *n.* a female albino.

al·bin′iç, *a.* of or having albinism.

al′bi·niṣm, *n.* the state of being an albino; leukopathy; albinoism.

al·bi·nis′tiç, *a.* of or pertaining to albinism.

al·bī′nō, *n.*; *pl.* **al·bī′nōṣ,** [Port. *albino*, from L. *albus*, white.]

1. a person having, through deficiency of coloring matter, abnormally white skin and hair and pink eyes.
2. any plant or animal having the same abnormal lack of color.

al·bī′nō·iṣm, *n.* the state of being an albino.

al·bi·not′iç, *a.* albinistic.

Al′bi·ŏn, *n.* [L., from Gaul; understood as if from L. *albus*, white: the cliffs of southern England are white.] England: used in poetry.

al′bīte, *n.* [L. *albus*, white, and *-ite.*] a sodium-bearing, whitish mineral of the feldspar group. It is a constituent of many varieties of granitic rocks.

Al·biz′zi·ȧ (-bit′si-ȧ), *n.* [L. from It. *Albizzi*, a noble family in Tuscany.] a genus of plants of the *Mimoseæ* family, allied to the *Acacia.*

al′bō·lith, al′bō·līte, *n.* [L. *albus*, white, and Gr. *lithos*, stone.] artificial stone or cement composed of magnesia and silica. It is used as a fireproofing and for plastic decorations in buildings.

Al′bō·rak, *n.* [Ar. *al-buraq*, from *baraqa*, to shine.] the fabled white mule on which Mohammed is said to have journeyed to heaven.

al′bronze, *n.* an alloy of copper and aluminum.

al·bū·gin′ē·ȧ, *n.* [L., f., as if from *albugineus*,

white, with *tunica* understood.] a white fibrous tissue covering certain organs or parts, as the eye, ovary, and testis.

al·bū·ġin′ē·ous, *a.* pertaining to or resembling the albuginea, especially the white of the eye.

al·bū′gō, *n.*; *pl.* **al·bū′ġi·nēs,** [L., whiteness, from *albus*, white.] a disease of the eye in which a white opaque spot grows on the cornea and obstructs vision: also called *leucoma.*

al′bum, *n.* [L., neut. of *albus*, white.]
1. among the Romans, a white tablet on which the names of public officers and records of public transactions were entered.
2. a book for collecting autographs, pictures, stamps, etc.
3. a booklike holder for phonograph records.
4. a set of phonograph records in such a holder.

al·bū′men, *n.* [L. *albumen*, from *albus*, white.]
1. the white of an egg.
2. in botany, the nutritive matter in seeds of plants between the skin and embryo; the endosperm, or perisperm.
3. albumin. [Rare.]

al·bū′men·īze, *v.t.*; albumenized, *pt., pp.*; albumenizing, *ppr.* to cover or treat with albumen or an albuminous solution.

al·bū′min, *n.* a protein substance found in animal tissue, blood, milk, egg, muscle, and in plant tissue. Heat coagulates it; water dissolves it. Nitrogen, hydrogen, carbon, oxygen, and sulfur are its component elements. It was formerly called *albumen.*

al·bū′mi·nāte, *n.* a compound of an albumin with an acid or base.

al·bū″mi·nif′ẽr·ous, *a.* [*albumin*, and *-ferous*, from L. *ferre*, to bear.] producing albumin.

al·bū″mi·nim′e·tẽr, *n.* [*albumin*, and Gr. *metron*, measure.] an instrument for discovering the amount of albumin in a liquid.

al·bū′mi·nin, *n.* the substance of the cells in the tissue that surrounds the white of a bird's egg.

al·bū″mi·nip′ȧ·rous, *a.* [*albumin*, and L. *parere*, to bring forth.] yielding albumin.

al·bū′min·īze, *v.t.* same as *albumenize.*

al·bū′mi·noid, *a.* resembling albumin.

al·bū′mi·noid, *n.* 1. a protein.
2. any of the scleroproteins, a group of simple proteins including keratin and collagen, characterized by insolubility.

al·bū·mi·noid′ăl, *a.* relating to or having the nature of an albuminoid.

al·bū′mi·nōne, *n.* peptone.

al·bū′mi·nōse, *n.* same as *albumose.*

al·bū′mi·nous, al·bū′mi·nōse, *a.* relating to or containing albumin.

al·bū′mi·nous·ness, *n.* the condition of being albuminous.

al·bū″mi·nū′ri·ȧ, *n.* [L. *albumen*, whiteness, and Gr. *ouron*, urine.] the presence of albumin in the urine.

al′bū·mōse, *n.* a compound derived from albumin by the action of certain enzymes.

al′būrn, *n.* [L. *alburnus*, whitish, from *albus*, white.] the bleak, a small fish.

al·būr′nous, *a.* relating to alburnum.

al·būr′num, *n.* [L., neut. of *alburnus*, whiteish, from *albus*, white.] the white and softer part of wood, between the inner bark and the heartwood; sapwood. This annually acquires firmness, and thus becomes heartwood.

ALBURNUM
aa. Alburnum or sapwood. *bb.* Heartwood. *c.* Pith. *dd.* Bark.

Al′byn, *n.* [see *Albion.*] Scotland. [Poetic.]

alc-, some words beginning *alc-* are also spelled *alk-*.

al·çāde′, *n.* alcalde.

al′çȧ·hest, *n.* alkahest.

Al·çā′iç, *a.* pertaining to Alcaeus, a lyric poet of Mitylene, in Lesbos, who flourished about 600 B. C., or to his poetry.

Al·çā′iç̣s, *n.pl.* verse by Alcaeus or in his metrical patterns: he wrote four-stanza odes, with four lines to a stanza and four feet to a line.

al·çāide′, *n.* [Sp. *alcaide, alcayde*, a governor, from Ar. *al-qāīd*; *al*, the, and *qāīd*, leader, from *qāda*, to lead.] among the Moors, Spaniards, and Portuguese, a governor of a castle or fort; also, a jailer.

äl·cäl′de, *n.* [Sp. *alcalde*, from Ar. *al-qāḍī*, judge, from *qada*, to judge.] in Spain and Spanish countries, a magistrate or judge; a chief magistrate or mayor.

äl·cäl·dī′ȧ, *n.* [Sp.] the territory in which an alcalde has jurisdiction; also, the office in which he conducts business.

al·çȧ·lim′e·tẽr, *n.* alkalimeter.

al·çan′nȧ, *n.* [Sp. *alcana, alhena*; Ar. *alhinnā*; *al*, the, and *hinnā*.] a plant, a species of *Lawsonia*; also, a powder, prepared from its leaves, used in eastern countries to give a reddish-orange color to the nails and hair. Also called *henna.*

al·çap′ton, *n.* alkapton.

al·çär·rä′zȧ (*Sp.* äl-kä-rä′thä), *n.* [Sp., from Ar. *al-kurrāz*; *al*, the, and *kurrāz*, earthen vessel.] an earthenware vessel for cooling liquids.

äl·çāyde′, *n.* an alcaide.

al·çä′zär (*Sp.* äl-kä′thär), *n.* [Sp., from Ar. *al qacr*; *al*, the, and *qacr*, a fortified place.] a fort or royal residence.

Al·cē′dō, *n.* [L.; Gr. *Alkyōn*; see *halcyon.*] a genus of brightly colored kingfishers.

Al·ces′tis, *n.* [L.; Gr. *Alkēstis.*] in Greek legend, the wife of Admetus, king of Thessaly, and heroine of a play by Euripides: she offered her life to save that of her husband, but was rescued from Hades by Hercules.

al·çhem′iç, al·çhem′iç·ăl, *a.* of or relating to alchemy.

al·çhem′iç·ăl·ly, *adv.* in the manner of alchemy.

Al·çhe·mil′lȧ, *n.* [Fr. *alchemille*; Port. *alchemila*, from Ar. *alkmelyeh*, alchemy. So called because it was thought to have alchemical virtues.] a genus of plants of the rose family.

al′çhe·mist, *n.* one who practiced alchemy.

al·çhe·mis′tiç, al·çhe·mis′tiç·ăl, *a.* practicing alchemy, or relating to it.

al′çhe·mis·try, *n.* alchemy. [Obs.]

al′çhe·mīze, *v.t.*; alchemized (-mīzd′), *pt., pp.*; alchemizing, *ppr.* to change by alchemy.

al′çhe·my, *n.* [L. *alchimia*; Gr. *archēmia*; Ar. *alkīmīa*; *al*, the, and *kīmīa*, Gr. *chēmia*, alchemy; *chēmia*, for *chymeia*, a pouring together; *chymos*, juice, from *cheein*, to pour.]
1. the doctrine, study, and practice of chemistry in the Middle Ages, which was chiefly concerned with transmutation of metals into gold and the finding of a universal remedy for diseases. The art was much practiced from the thirteenth to the seventeenth century.
2. any imaginary power or process of transmuting one thing into another.

Al·cī′dēṣ, *n.* [L.; Gr. *Alkeidēs.*] Hercules.

al′ci·dīne, *a.* [Mod. L. *alcidinus*, from *Alcidæ*, name of the family of birds; see *auk.*] belonging to a family of diving birds that have a stocky body, short tail and wings, and webbed feet, as the puffins, murres, etc.

Alç·mā′ni·ăn, *a.* pertaining to Alcman, a Spartan lyric poet of the seventh century B. C., or to his verse.

Alç·mē′nē, *n.* [L.; Gr. *Alkmēnē.*] in Greek mythology, the mother of Hercules: see *Amphitryon.*

al′çō, *n.* [native name.] a small dog native to Peru and Mexico, and domesticated by the aborigines.

al′çō·hol, *n.* [Fr. *alcohol*; Sp. *alcohol*, from Ar. *al*, the, and *kohl*, powder of antimony, used to color the eyebrows; *kahala*, to stain, paint.]
1. originally, powdered antimony; any impalpable powder. [Obs.]
2. a colorless, volatile, pungent liquid, C_2H_5OH; grain alcohol; ethyl alcohol; ethanol; it can be burnt as a fuel, is used in industry and medicine, and is the intoxicating ingredient in whiskey, gin, rum, and other distilled or fermented liquors.
3. any intoxicating liquor with this liquid in it.
4. the drinking of such liquors.
5. any of a series of organic compounds the simplest of which are like ethyl alcohol in construction, as methyl alcohol (or wood alcohol), CH_3OH, a very poisonous liquid, and amyl alcohol, $C_5H_{11}OH$, found in fusel oil: all alcohols contain a hydroxyl group and form esters in reactions with organic acids.

al′çō·hol·āte, al′çō·āte, al′çō·hāte, *n.* a compound derived from an alcohol by the substitution of a base for the hydroxyl hydrogen.

al·çō·hol′ȧ·tūre, *n.* [Fr. *alcoolature.*] an alcoholic tincture made from fresh plants.

al·çō·hol′iç, *a.* 1. pertaining to alcohol, or partaking of its qualities.
2. containing alcohol; as, an *alcoholic* thermometer.
3. suffering from alcoholism.

al·çō·hol′iç, *n.* 1. one addicted to the use of alcoholic liquors.
2. [*pl.*] alcoholic beverages.

al·çō·hol′i·căl·ly, *adv.* in an alcoholic manner.

al·çō·hol·ic′i·ty, *n.* the quality or state of being alcoholic.

al′çō·hol·iṣm, *n.* a diseased condition caused by the excessive or continuous use of alcoholic liquors.
2. alcohol poisoning.

al″çō·hol·i·zā′tion, *n.* 1. the act of saturating the system with alcoholic drinks.
2. the act of converting into alcohol.
3. the act of pulverizing. [Obs.]

al′çō·hol·īze, *v.t.*; alcoholized, *pt., pp.*; alcoholizing, *ppr.* 1. to convert into alcohol.
2. to pulverize. [Obs.]
3. to saturate with alcohol.

al″çō·hol·om′e·tẽr, al·çō·hol′me·tẽr, al·çō·hom′e·tẽr, al·çō·om′e·tẽr, *n.* [*alcohol*, and Gr. *metron*, measure.] an instrument for determining the percentage of alcohol in liquor.

al″çō·hol·ō·met′riç·ăl, al″çō·hol·met′riç·ăl, al″çō·hō·met′riç, al″çō·ō·met′riç·ăl, *a.* relating to the alcoholometer; as, *alcoholometrical* tables.

al″çō·hol·om′e·try, *n.* the act and method of determining the relative proportion of pure alcohol in liquor.

Al′çōr, *n.* [Ar.] a small star in Ursa Major.

Al·çō·ran′, *n.* the Koran.

Al·çō·ran′iç, *a.* pertaining to the Koran.

Al·çō·ran′ist, *n.* one who adheres strictly to the letter of the Koran.

äl·çor·nō′quẹ (-kā), *n.* [Sp., cork tree.] the bark of several Brazilian trees, used in medicine and tanning.

al′çōve, *n.* [Fr. *alcôve*; Sp. *alcoba*; Ar. *al-qobbah*; *al*, the, and *qobbah*, arch, vault, dome.]
1. originally, a recess in a room, as for a bed.

ALCOVE

2. a recess in a room, or a small room attached to a larger one, as a breakfast nook.
3. a small secluded building, or recess, in a garden.
4. a niche for a statue, a seat, etc.
5. any natural recess, as in a grove; a secluded spot.

al′cy·on, *n.*; *pl.* **al·cȳ′ō·nēṣ,** same as *halcyon.*

Al″cy·ō·nā′ce·ȧ, *n.pl.* group of *Alcyonaria.*

Al″cy·ō·nā′ri·ȧ, *n.pl.* an order of Anthozoa found only in deep water, usually attached to a foreign body.

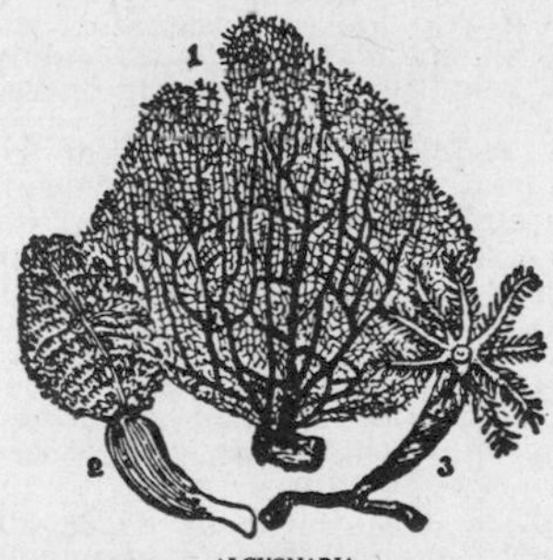

ALCYONARIA
1. Sea fan (*Gorgonia flabellum*). 2. Sea pen (*Pennatula phosphorea*). 3. *Cornularia rugosa.*

Al·cȳ′ō·nē, *n.* [L., from Gr. *Alkyonē*, a daughter of King Aeolus. She was changed into a kingfisher.] one of the stars in the Pleiades.

al·cy·on′iç, *a.* pertaining to the group or family of zoophytes, allied to the sponges.

al′cy·on·īte, *n.* a fossil zoophyte of or resembling the genus *Alcyonium.*

Al·cy·ō′ni·um, *n.* [L., from Gr. *alkyonion*, a zoophyte, so called from its resemblance to the nest of the *alkyon.*] a genus of zoophytes, branching somewhat like a plant and covered with small polyps.

al′cy·ō·noid, *a.* relating to the *Alcyonaria.*

ạl′dāy, *adv.* continually. [Obs.]

Al·deb′ȧ·ran, *n.* [Ar. *al-debarān*; *al*, the, and

debarān, following, from *dabar*, to follow.] a star of the first magnitude in the constellation Taurus, forming the Bull's Eye.

al′dē·hȳde, *n.* [abbrev. of *al*cohol, and L. *dehyd*rogenatus; L. *de*, from, without, and *hydrogen*.] a colorless, pungent, volatile liquid, CH_3CHO, produced by the oxidation of alcohol.

al·dē·hȳ′diç, *a.* pertaining to aldehyde.

äl den′te (-tā; *Eng.* al den′tē), [It., lit., to the tooth.] firm to the bite; chewy.

ąl′dẽr, *n.* [ME. *alder*, *aldir*, *aller*; AS. *alr*, *alor*; Ice. *ölr*, *elrir*; Norw. *older*; L. *alnus*, from Fr. *aune*, alder.]
1. a tree usually growing in moist land and belonging to the genus *Alnus*: the bark is used in dyeing and tanning, and the wood for bridges and piles because it resists underwater rot.
2. any of several species of other genera which resemble true alders.

ALDER
(*Alnus glutinosa*)

ąl′dẽr·măn, *n.*; *pl.* **ąl′dẽr·men**, [AS. *ealdorman*; *ealdor*, prince, chief, and *man*.]
1. among the Anglo-Saxons, a senior, or superior. The title was applied to princes, dukes, earls, senators, and presiding magistrates; also to archbishops and bishops; as, Ethelstan, duke of the East-Anglians, was called *alderman* of all England.
2. in many cities of the United States, a member of a municipal council elected by the people; a city councilor; a councilman.
3. in England, a municipal councilor or magistrate.

ąl′dẽr·măn·cy, *n.* the position of alderman.

ąl·dẽr·man′iç, *a.* characteristic of, or relating to, an alderman.

ąl′dẽr·măn·līke, *a.* like an alderman.

ąl′dẽr·măn·ly, *a.* pertaining to or like an alderman.

ąl′dẽr·măn·ry, *n.* a district having an alderman; a ward.

ąl′dẽr·măn·ship, *n.* an alderman's office.

ąl′dẽrn, *a.* made of alder. [Obs.]

Ąl′dẽr·ney, *n.* any of the breed of cattle originally raised on the island of Alderney in the English Channel. *Alderneys* are of a tawny color, much resembling Jerseys.

Ąl′dīne (*or* ąl′din), *a.* designating those editions, chiefly of the classics, published by Aldus Manutius of Venice in the sixteenth century.

ąl′dōse, *n.* [*ald*ehyde, and *-ose*.] in chemistry, any sugar containing the aldehyde group.

al·do′ste·rōne″, *n.* [*ald*ehyde, and *ster*ol, and *-one*.] a steroid hormone, $C_{21}H_{28}O_5$, produced synthetically and by the adrenal cortex glands: believed to be the chief regulator of sodium, potassium, and chloride metabolism.

al·do′ste·rōn″iṣm, *n.* the condition arising from too great a secretion of aldosterone, resulting in hypertension and excessive excretion of potassium.

al′drin, *n.* [G., after Kurt *Alder*, 20th-c. G. chemist.] an insecticide containing a naphthalene derivative, $C_{12}H_8Cl_6$, especially effective against insects resistant to DDT.

āle, *n.* [ME. *ale*; AS. *ealu*.]
1. a fermented drink made from malt and hops, like beer, but produced by rapid fermentation at a relatively high temperature.
2. a merry meeting in English country places, so called from the liquor drunk. [Rare.]
On ember eves and holy *ales*. —Shak.

ȧ·lēak′, *a.* and *adv.* leaking; in a leaking state.

ā″lē·ȧ·tō′riç, *a.* 1. same as *aleatory*.
2. designating music resulting from purely random successions of tones and noises.

ā′lē·ȧ·tō·ry, *a.* [L. *aleatorius*, pertaining to gaming; from *aleator*, a gamester; *alea*, a game with dice.]
1. of or depending on chance or luck.
2. in law, depending upon a contingency: applied to contracts, etc.

āle′bench, *n.* a bench in or before an alehouse.

āle′ber·ry, *n.* a beverage formerly made by boiling ale with spice, sugar, and sops of bread.

āle brew′ẽr, one whose occupation is to brew ale.

ȧ·lec′i·thăl, *a.* [Gr. *a* priv., and *lekithos*, yolk.] pertaining to certain eggs from which the food yolk is missing.

āle′çon·nẽr, *n.* [*ale* and *con*, to know or see.] an officer in London, in former times, whose business was to test the quality of ale and inspect the measures used in public houses.

āle′çost, *n.* [*ale* and L. *costum*; Gr. *kostos*, an oriental, aromatic plant.] costmary, a plant formerly used to flavor ale.

Ȧ·leç′tō, *n.* [L.; Gr. *Alēktō*.] in Greek mythology, one of the three Furies.

Al·eç·tor′i·dēṣ, *n.pl.* [L., from Gr. *alektoris*, pl. *alektorides*, f. of *alektōr*, a cock.] an order of birds including the cranes, rails, etc. and ordinarily understood to include the domestic fowls and pheasants.

ȧ·leç·try·om′ȧ·çhy, ȧ·leç·tō·rom′ȧ·çhy, *n.* [Gr. *alektōr*, a cock, and *machē*, a fight.] cockfighting.

ȧ·leç′try·ō·man″cy, ȧ·leç′tō·rō·man″cy, *n.* [Gr. *alektōr*, a cock, and *manteia*, divination.] an ancient practice of foretelling events by means of a cock. The letters of the alphabet were traced on the ground, and a grain of corn was laid on each; a cock was then permitted to pick up the grains, and the letters under the grains selected, being formed into words, were supposed to foretell the event desired.

ȧ·lee′, *adv.* and *a.* in nautical usage, on the side of a ship away from the wind.

al′e·gẽr, *n.* [*ale*, and *egar*; Fr. *aigre*, sour.] sour ale; the acid of ale; vinegar resulting from the fermentation of ale.

al′e·gẽr, *a.* [OFr. *alegre*; It. *allegro*; L. *alacer*, brisk, cheerful.] gay; cheerful; sprightly. [Obs.]

āle′hoof, *n.* [ME. *alehoofe*, a corruption of *haihove*; *hai*, a hedge, and *hoofe*, ivy; AS. *hofe*, ivy.] ground ivy.

āle′house, *n.* a house where ale is sold; tavern; saloon.

āle knīght, a drinking companion. [Obs.]

al′em, *n.* [Turk. *alem*, a flag, banner.] the standard of the Ottoman empire.

Al′e·man·nī, *n.pl.* the Alamanni.

Al·e·man′niç, *a.* [L. *Alemannicus*, pertaining to the Alamanni, from Goth. *alamans*, all men.] relating to the Alamanni.

Al·e·man′niç, *n.* the German dialect of the Alamanni.

ȧ·lem′biç, *n.* [L. *alambicus*; Ar. *alanbīq*; *al*, the, and *anbīq*, Per. *ambīq*, a still; Gr. *ambix*, a cup of a still.]
1. a chemical apparatus formerly used in distillation, and usually made of glass or metal. The bottom part, containing the substance to be distilled, was called the cucurbit; the upper part which received and condensed the steam was called the head, the beak of which was fitted to the neck of a receiver.
2. anything that refines, purifies, or works a change; as, the *alembic* of a vivid imagination.

ALEMBIC

ȧ·lem′broth, *n.* a double chloride of mercury and ammonium, formerly used by alchemists.

Ȧ·len′çon lāce, a delicate but durable lace of needle-point, originating in Alençon, France, in the seventeenth century. It has a solid floral pattern made in small sections and is pieced together so that the seams cannot be detected.

ȧ·length′, *adv.* at full length; along; stretched at full length; lengthwise.

ä′leph (-lif), *n.* [Heb., lit., ox, leader.] the first letter of the Hebrew alphabet, a neutral vowel: various diacritical marks determine its sound.

ȧ·lep′i·dōte, *n.* [Gr. *a* priv., and *lepis* (*lepidotis*), scale.] any fish whose skin is not scaly.

ȧ·lep′i·dōte, *a.* having no scales.

āle′pōle, *n.* a pole set up in front of an alehouse as a sign. [Obs.]

ȧ·lẽrce′, *n.* [Sp. *alerce*, the larch tree; L. *larix*; Gr. *larix*, the larch.]
1. a Chilean tree of the pine family.
2. the wood of the sandarac tree of Morocco.

ȧ·lẽrt, *a.* [Fr. *alerte*; It. *all' erta*, on the watch; *all'* for *alla*, for L. *ad* and *illam*, on the, and *erta*, watch, f. of *erto*, raised aloft, pp. of *ergere*, from L. *erigere*, to raise.]
1. watchful; vigilant; ready.
2. brisk; nimble; moving with promptness.
Syn.—active, brisk, lively, vigilant, watchful, wide-awake, prompt, ready.

ȧ·lẽrt, *n.* 1. a period of vigilance: used principally in the phrase *on the alert*; as, the watch stood *on the alert*.
2. an alarm; notice to stand in readiness, as for an air raid.

ȧ·lẽrt′, *v.t.* to issue an alarm to; to warn, as for an air raid; as, to *alert* a city.

ȧ·lẽrt′ly, *adv.* in an alert manner; promptly.

ȧ·lẽrt′ness, *n.* briskness; nimbleness; sprightliness.

-a′lēs, [L., pl. of *-alis*.] a suffix used in forming the scientific Latin names of orders of plants.

āle′tāst·ẽr, *n.* same as *aleconner*.

ȧ·lē·thi·ol′ō·ġy, *n.* [Gr. *alētheia*, truth, and *logos*, discourse.] the science or doctrine of truth; the branch of logic that deals with truth.

ȧ·leth′ō·sçōpe, *n.* [Gr. *alēthēs*, true, and *skopein*, to view.] an instrument for viewing pictures, producing a stereoscopic effect.

Al′e·tris, *n.* [L., from Gr. *aletris*, a grinder of corn, from *aletreuein*; *alein*, to grind.] a genus of plants of the lily family.

ȧ·lette′ (ȧ-let′), *n.* [dim. of L. *ala*, a wing.] the face of the pier of an arch, extending along the edge of the opening; especially, that portion between the edge of the opening and the pillar or pilaster used to decorate the arch.

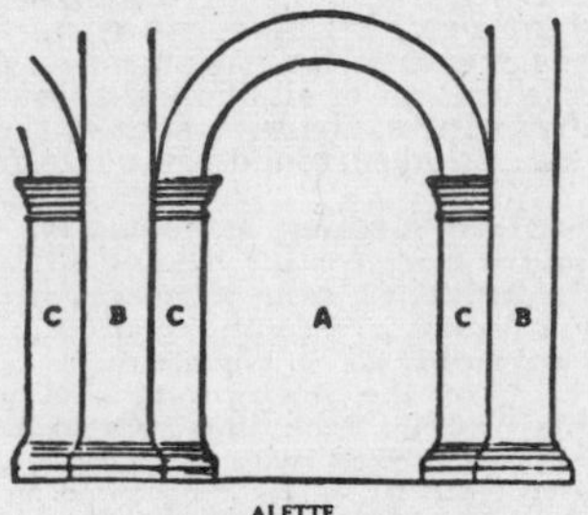

ALETTE
A. arch BB. pillars CC. alettes

Al·eū·rī′tēṣ, *n.* [L., from Gr. *aleuritēs*, pertaining to *aleuron*, meal, from *alein*, to grind.] a genus of cactuslike plants, including the candleberry tree.

ȧ·leū′rō·man·cy, *n.* [Gr. *aleuromanteion*, divination by meal; *aleuron*, meal, and *manteia*, divination.] a kind of divination by flour or meal.

al·eū·rom′e·tẽr, *n.* [Gr. *aleuron*, meal, and *metron*, measure.] an instrument for testing the quality of gluten in flour.

ȧ·leū′rō·nat, *n.* flour made of aleurone.

ȧ·leū′rōne, *n.* a protein substance found in small granules in ripening seeds, and forming an outer layer in cereals.

al·eū·ron′iç, *a.* pertaining to or resembling aleurone.

Al′ē·ŭt, *n.*; *pl.* **Al′ē·ŭts, Al′ē·ŭt**, 1. a native of the Aleutian Islands and part of Alaska.
2. the language of these natives.

Ȧ·leū′tian, *a.* 1. of the Aleutian Islands.
2. of the Aleuts, their culture, etc.

Ȧ·leū′tian, *n.* an Aleut.

al′e·vin, *n.* [Fr. *alevin*; OFr. *alever*; L. *adlevare*, to raise.] a young fish of any kind; especially a young salmon.

ȧ·lew′, *n.* halloo. [Obs.]

āle′wīfe, *n.*; *pl.* **āle′wīveṣ**, a fish, *Clupea vernalis*, of the herring family, found in the ocean and in some lakes and streams.

āle′wīfe, *n.* a woman who keeps an alehouse.

al·ex·an′dẽrṣ (-eg-zan′), *n.* [ME. *alisandre*; OFr. *alisaundre*; AS. *alexandrie*, from L. *Alexandria*.]
1. the *Smyrnium olusatrum*, a plant of the parsley family, formerly much cultivated in Europe for salads.
2. on the American continent, the *Thaspium aureum*, or meadow parsnip.

Al·ex·an′dri·ăn, *a.* 1. pertaining to Alexander the Great or his rule.
2. of Alexandria, Egypt, or the late Hellenic culture that flourished there.
3. in prosody, Alexandrine.

Al·ex·an′dri·ăn, *n.* a citizen of Alexandria.

Al·ex·an′drine, *n.* in prosody, an iambic line having normally six feet; iambic hexameter.

Al·ex·an′drine, *a.* of an Alexandrine or Alexandrines.

al·ex·an′drīte, *n.* [named after *Alexander II*, Czar of Russia.] a variety of chrysoberyl, emerald-green by daylight and deep red by artificial light.

ȧ·lex′i·ȧ, *n.* [L., from Gr. *a* priv., and *lexis*, speech, from *legein*, to speak.] inability to read, caused by lesions of the brain; word blindness.

ȧ·lex′in, *n.* [Gr. *alexein*, to ward off.] a substance found in the blood, capable of destroying bacteria.

ȧ·lex·i·phär′miç, ȧ·lex·i·phär′maç, *a.* [L., from Gr. *alexipharmăkon*; *alexein*, to ward off, and *pharmakon*, poison.] expelling or resisting poison; antidotal.

ȧ·lex·i·phär′miç, ȧ·lex·i·phär′maç, *n.* an antidote.

ȧ·lex·i·phär′miç·ăl, ȧ·lex·i·phär′maç·ăl, *a.* same as *alexipharmic*.

ȧ·lex″i·py̆·ret′iç, *a.* [Gr. *alexein*, to ward off and *pyretos*, fever; from *pyr*, fire.] aiding in reducing or removing fevers.

ȧ·lex″i·py̆·ret′iç, *n.* a medicine effective in reducing or removing fevers; a febrifuge.

ȧ·lex·i·ter′iç, ȧ·lex·i·ter′iç·ăl, *a.* [Gr. *alexitērios*, able to keep off, from *alexitēr*, one who defends, from *alexein*, to ward off.] resisting poison; counteracting the effects of poison.

ȧ·lex·i·ter′iç, *n.* a medicine to counteract the effects of poison; alexipharmic.

āle′yärd, *n.* an elongated form of drinking glass and measure for liquid, formerly used.

ALEYARDS

al′fȧ, *n.* the name of a North African grass of the genus *Stipa*; also, its fiber, used in the manufacture of paper, baskets, etc.

al′fȧ grȧss, alfa.

al·fal′fȧ, *n.* [Sp. *alfalfez*, from Ar. *al-façç*, *façah*, the best fodder.] a deep-rooted plant of the pea family, with small divided leaves, purple cloverlike flowers, and spiral pods, used extensively in the United States for fodder, pasture, and as a cover crop: also called *lucerne*.

al′fe·nid, al′fe·nīde, *n.* an alloy of silver and nickel with a thick silver electroplating.

al·fē′reẓ, *n.* [Sp. *alferez*, ensign, from Ar. *al-fāris*; *al*, the, and *fāris*, a knight, horseman.] a standard bearer. [Obs.]

al′fet, *n.* [L. *alfetum*; AS. *alfaet*, a pot to boil in.] an early English ordeal to determine the innocence or guilt of an accused person, who was required to plunge his arm into a pot of boiling water; also, the pot of boiling water used for this purpose.

al·fil″ȧ·ri′ȧ, al″fi·le·ril′lȧ, *n.* [Sp. Am.] the naturalized European plant, *Erodium cicutarium*, of the geranium family: a valuable forage grass in the United States; also called *pin grass* and *pin clover*.

ăl fī′ne, [It.] to the end.

al·fi·ō′nȧ, ȧl·fi·ō′ne̤, *n.* [Sp. Am.] the largest of the edible surf fish on the coast of California; the *Rhacochilus toxotes*.

al·for′jȧ (*also* Sp. äl-fo̤r′hä), *n.* [Sp., from Ar. *alkhorj*.]

1. a leather or canvas saddlebag used by cowboys.

2. a cheek pouch, as of a chipmunk.

al·fres′cō, *adv.* and *a.* [It.; *al*, for *a il*, in the, and *fresco*, fresh, cool.] out of doors.

al′gȧ, *n.*; *pl.* **al′gae,** [L., seaweed.] a seaweed; one of the algae.

al′gae (*or* -ġē), *n.pl.* [pl. of L. *alga*, seaweed.] a group of plants, one-celled, colonial, or many-celled, containing chlorophyl and having no true root, stem, or leaf: algae are found in water or damp places, and include seaweeds, pond scum, etc.

al′găl, *a.* pertaining to, or characteristic of, the algae.

algal fungus; a fungus of the group *Phycomycetes*.

al′gȧ·rot, al′gȧ·roth, *n.* [Fr. *algaroth*, from *Algarotti*, a Venetian scholar.] an emetic powder, antimony oxychloride, precipitated by compounding the trichloride and trioxide of antimony.

al·gär·rō′bȧ, al·gȧ·rō′bȧ, *n.* [Sp., from Ar. *al-kharrubah*; *al*, the, and *kharrubah*, the carob.]

1. an evergreen tree growing in the Mediterranean region, which bears an edible bean, known as St. John's bread.

2. the mesquite tree and its fruit.

3. the West Indian locust.

al″gär·rō·bil′lȧ, al″gȧ·rō·vil′lȧ, *n.* the seeds and husks of certain leguminous South American shrubs: used in tanning and dyeing.

a̤l′gāte, a̤l′gātes, *adv.* [ME. *al*, all, and *gate*, gate; AS. *algeats*, a gate, a way.] by all means; on any terms. [Obs.]

al′gȧ·zel, *n.* [Ar. *al*, the, and *ghazāl*, gazelle.] the gazelle. [Obs.]

al′ge·brȧ, *n.* [Fr. *algèbre*; Russ. *algebra*; Ar. *al-jabr*, *al-jebr*, the reunion of broken parts, from *jabara*, to reunite, bind together.]

1. a mathematical system used to generalize certain arithmetical operations by permitting letters or other symbols to stand for numbers: it is used especially in the solution of polynomial equations.

2. a special application of this system in which the fundamental arithmetical operations of addition and multiplication are replaced by general binary operations, with properties to be defined.

3. a textbook or treatise dealing with algebra.

al·ge·brā′iç, al·ge·brā′iç·ăl, *a.* pertaining to algebra; like or characteristic of algebra.

al·ge·brā′iç·ăl·ly, *adv.* by algebraic process.

al·ge·brā′iç num′bẽr, a root of a polynomial equation with coefficients that are whole numbers.

al′ge·brā·ist, *n.* an expert in algebra.

al′ge·brā·ize, *v.t.*; algebraized, *pt.*, *pp.*; algebraizing, *ppr.* to perform by algebra, or to reduce to algebraic form.

al·ġē·fā′cient (-shunt), *a.* [L. *algere*, be cold, and *faciens*, ppr. of *facere*, to make.] cooling.

Al·ġē′ri·ăn, *a.* relating to Algiers.

Al·ġē′ri·ăn, *n.* an inhabitant or native of Algiers.

Al·ġe·rīne′, *a.* Algerian.

Al·ġe·rīne′, *n.* 1. a native of Algeria, especially one of Berber, Arab, or Moorish descent.

2. a North African pirate.

3. a soft woolen cloth with bright stripes.

al·ġē′si·ȧ (*or* -zi-ȧ), *n.* [Gr. *algesis*, sense of pain, from *algein*, to suffer.] pain.

al·ġet′iç, *a.* causing pain.

-al′ġi·ȧ, -al′ġy, a suffix meaning *pain*, as in neur*algia*.

al′ġid, *a.* [L. *algidus*, cold, from *algere*, to be cold.] cold.

al·ġid′i·ty, al′ġid·ness, *n.* chilliness; coldness.

al·ġif′iç, *a.* producing cold.

al·ġin″ū·rē′sis, *n.* condition of painful urination.

al·ġiv′ŏ·rous (-rus), *a.* feeding on algae.

al′ġoid, *a.* resembling one of the algae.

Al′gol, *n.* [Ar. *al-ghūl*, destruction, from *ghala*, to destroy.] a fixed star in Medusa's head, in the constellation Perseus: it is binary and loses most of its brightness when eclipsed by its dark companion.

al·gŏ·lag′ni·ȧ, *n.* [Mod.L., from Gr. *algos*, pain, and *lagneia*, lust.] abnormal sexual pleasure derived from inflicting or suffering pain; masochism or sadism.

al·go·loġ′iç·ăl, *a.* pertaining to algology; of the nature of seaweeds or algae.

al·gol′ō·ġist, *n.* a specialist in algology.

al·gol′ō·ġy, *n.* [L. *alga*, seaweed, and Gr. *logos*, description.] the study of seaweeds or algae.

al·gom′e·tẽr, *n.* [Gr. *algos*, pain, and *metron*, measure.] an instrument for testing sensibility to pain.

al·gom′e·try, *n.* the science of pain sensibility.

Al·gon′ki·ăn, *a.* 1. Algonquian.

2. in geology, late Proterozoic.

Al·gon′qui·ăn (-ki- *or* -kwi-), *a.* designating or of a widespread and important family of approximately fifty languages used by a number of North American Indian Tribes, including the Arapaho, Cheyenne, Blackfoot, Chippewa, Shawnee, Ottawa, and others.

Al·gon′qui·ăn, *n.* 1. the Algonquian family of languages.

2. a member of any tribe using one of these languages.

Al·gon′quin, *n.* 1. a member of a tribe of Algonquian Indians who lived in the area of the Ottawa River, Canada: now called *Ottawa*.

2. the language of this tribe.

3. Algonquian.

al·gŏ·phō′bi·ȧ, *n.* [from Gr. *algos*, pain; and *-phobia*.] an extreme or abnormal fear of pain.

al′gor, *n.* [L., from *algere*, to be cold.] cold or a chill felt during a fever.

al′gŏ·riṣm, *n.* [ME. and OFr. *algorisme*; L. *algorismus*, from Ar. *al-Khowārazmī*, lit., a native of Khwarazm (Khiva), an Arabic mathematician of the ninth century.]

1. the Arabic system of numerals; decimal system of counting.

2. the act or skill of computing with any kind of numerals.

al′gŏ·rithm, *n.* [altered (after *arithmetic*) from *algorism*.] in mathematics, any special method of solving a certain kind of problem; specifically, the repetitive calculations used in finding the greatest common divisor of two numbers (called in full *Euclid's algorithm*).

al′gous, *a.* [L. *alga*, seaweed.] pertaining to seaweed; abounding with, or like, seaweed.

al·guȧ·zīl′ (-gwȧ-), *n.* [Sp., from Ar. *al-wazīr*; *al*, the, and *wazīr*, officer.] an officer of justice in Spain of inferior rank; a constable.

al′gum, *n.* a tree, probably sandalwood, which grew on Mount Lebanon in Biblical times, and was used in the construction of Solomon's temple.

Send me also cedar trees, fir trees, and *algum* trees, out of Lebanon. —2 Chron. ii. 8.

Al·ham′brȧ, *n.* a fortress and palace erected by the Moors near Granada, Spain, during the thirteenth and early fourteenth centuries.

ALHAMBRA

Al·ham·brā′iç, *a.* same as *Alhambresque*.

Al·ham·bresque′ (-bresk′), *a.* after the pattern of the decoration of the Alhambra.

al·hen′nȧ, *n.* same as *henna*.

ā′li·ăs, *adv.* [L.] otherwise named; called by the assumed name of; as, Smith *alias* Jones.

ā′li·ăs, *n.* [L., from *alius*, other.]

1. an assumed name.

2. a second writ issued when the first has failed.

A′li Bä′bȧ, in the *Arabian Nights*, a poor woodcutter who found the treasure of the forty thieves in a cave: he made the door of the cave open by saying "Open sesame!"

al′i·bī, *adv.* [L., locative case of *alius*, other.] elsewhere, or in another place.

al′i·bī, *n.* 1. in law, a plea that the person charged with an offense was in another place at the time it was committed.

2. the fact of being elsewhere at the time of an offense charged.

3. an excuse. [Colloq.]

al′i·bī, *v.i.* to offer an excuse. [Colloq.]

al·i·bil′i·ty, *n.* the state of being alible.

al′i·ble, *a.* [L. *alibilis*, from *alere*, to nourish.] nutritive; possessing nourishment.

Al·ice blūe, [after *Alice* Roosevelt Longworth, daughter of Theodore Roosevelt.] a light blue.

al′i·dāde, al′i·dad, *n.* [L. *alidada*, from Ar. *al-'idādah*, a rule.]

1. a part of an optical or surveying instrument, consisting of the vernier, indicator, etc.

2. a surveying instrument consisting of a telescope mounted on a rule marked off in degrees, used in topographic mapping.

āl′ien (-yen), *a.* [OFr. *alien*; L. *alienus*, from *alius*, another.]

1. foreign; not belonging to the same country, land, or government.

2. strange; not natural; as, cruel words *alien* to his lips.

3. opposed or repugnant; as, beliefs *alien* to one's religion.

4. of aliens.

Syn.—foreign, distant, unsympathetic, remote, irrelevant.

āl′ien (-yen), *n.* 1. foreigner; one born in, or belonging to, another country; an immigrant who has not become a naturalized citizen.

2. a stranger or outsider.

3. a hypothetical being from outer space, as in science fiction, that visits or invades the earth.

āl′ien, *v.t.*; aliened (-yend), *pt.*, *pp.*; aliening, *ppr.* 1. to sell or transfer (any property).

2. to alienate, as the affections.

āl″ien·ȧ·bil′i·ty, *n.* the fact of being alienable.

The *alienability* of the domain. —Burke.

āl′ien·ȧ·ble, *a.* capable of being sold, transferred, or conveyed, as real estate.

āl′ien·āġe, *n.* the state of being an alien.

āl′ien·āte (-yen-), *v.t.*; alienated, *pt.*, *pp.*; alienating, *ppr.* [L. *alienatus*, pp. of *alienare*, from *alius*, another.]

1. to transfer (title, property, or right) to another; as, to *alienate* lands, or sovereignty.

2. to estrange; to withdraw, as the affections; to make indifferent or averse, where love or friendship before subsisted; as, to

alienate the heart or affections; to *alienate* a man from the friends of his youth.

Syn.—estrange, transfer, wean, disaffect.

āl′ien·āte, *a.* estranged; withdrawn; strange.
O *alienate* from God, O spirit accurst!
—Milton.

āl′ien·āte, *n.* a stranger; an alien. [Obs.]

āl·ien·ā′tion, *n.* [Fr. *aliénation*; L. *alienatio*, from *alienare*; *alius*, another.]
1. in law, a transfer of title, or a legal conveyance of property to another.
2. the state of being alienated.
3. a withdrawing or estrangement, as of the heart or affections.
4. delirium; mental derangement; insanity.

āl′ien·ā·tŏr, *n.* one who alienates.

āl·iēne′ (-yēn′), *v.t.*; aliened, *pt., pp.*; aliening, *ppr.* same as *alien.*

āl·ien·ee′ *n.* one to whom the title of property is transferred.

āl′ien·ism, *n.* 1. the state of being an alien.
2. the quality or condition of being alien.
3. the science of mental alienation; psychiatry.

āl′ien·ist, *n.* a specialist in mental diseases; psychiatrist: term used in law.

āl·ien·or′, *n.* a person who transfers the ownership of property.

al·i·eth′moid, al″i·eth·moid′ăl, *a.* [L. *ala*, wing, and *ethmoid.*] relating to expansions of the ethmoid region.

ä′lif, *n.* [Ar.; akin to Heb. *āleph*; see *aleph.*] the first letter of the Arabic alphabet.

à·lif′ẽr·ous, *a.* [L. *ala*, wing, and *ferre*, to bear.] having wings. [Rare.]

al′i·form, *a.* [L. *ala*, wing, and *forma*, shape.] resembling a wing in shape.

à·lig′ẽr·ous, *a.* [L. *ala*, wing, and *gerere*, to carry.] having wings. [Rare.]

à·līght′ (-līt′), *v.i.*; alighted, *pt., pp.*; alighting, *ppr.* [ME. *alighten*; AS. *alīhtān*; *a*, out, off, and *līhtān*, to dismount, to render light.]
1. to get down or descend, as from horseback or from a carriage.
2. to descend and settle; as, a flying bird *alights* on a tree.
3. to hit (upon) accidentally or unexpectedly.

à·līght′, *a.* lighted; lighted up; as, the candles are *alight.*

à·līgn′, *v.t.*; aligned, *pt., pp.*; aligning, *ppr.* [Fr. *aligner*, from *à*, to, and *ligne*, line.]
1. to bring into a straight line; adjust by line.
2. to bring into agreement, close cooperation, etc.; as, he *aligned* himself with the liberals.

à·līgn′, *v.i.* to come or fall into line; to line up.

à·līgn′ẽr, *n.* a person who aligns.

à·līgn′ment, *n.* [Fr. *alignement*; see *align.*]
1. an aligning or being aligned.
2. arrangement in a straight line.
3. a line or lines formed by aligning.
4. in engineering, a ground plan, as of a fieldwork, railroad, etc.

à·līke′, *a.* [ME. *alike*; AS. *onlic* and *gelic*, similar, correspondent.] like one another; showing resemblance or similitude; similar.

à·līke′, *adv.* equally; in the same manner, form, or degree; in common; as, we are all *alike* concerned in the matter.

à·līke′-mīnd″ed, *a.* having the same mind; like-minded. [Obs.]

ä′līm, *n.* [Ar. *'ālim*, learned, from *'alama*, to know.] a Moslem religious teacher.

al′i·mà, *n.* [L., from Gr. *halimos*, of the sea.] the larval stage of a stomatopod.

al′i·ment, *n.* [L. *alimentum*, from *alere*, to nourish.]
1. that which nourishes; food; nutriment.
2. an allowance for support, as that of a pensioner.

al′i·ment, *v.t.*; alimented, *pt., pp.*; alimenting, *ppr.* 1. to nourish.
2. to provide means of support for.

al·i·men′tăl, *a.* supplying food; nourishing; furnishing the materials for natural growth; as, chyle is *alimental*; *alimental* sap.

al·i·men′tăl·ly, *adv.* so as to serve for nourishment or food.

al·i·men′tà·ri·ness, *n.* the quality of supplying nourishment. [Obs.]

al·i·men′tà·ry, *a.* 1. pertaining to aliment or food; nourishing; as, *alimentary* particles.
2. furnishing support or sustenance.
alimentary canal; the passage extending from the mouth to the anus, which receives the food and conveys and digests it, absorbing part and excreting the remainder.

al″i·men·tā′tion, *n.* [Fr. *alimentation*; L. *alimentatio*, from *alimentare*, to provide.]
1. the act or power of nourishing.
2. the state of being nourished.
3. support; sustenance.

al·i·men′tà·tive, *a.* of alimentation, or nourishment; nutritive.

al·i·men′tive·ness, *n.* in phrenology, the instinct for seeking food.

al·i·mō′ni·ous, *a.* nourishing; affording food. [Rare.]

al′i·mō·ny, *n.* [L. *alimonia*, food, support, from *alere*, to nourish.]
1. means of living; aliment.
2. an allowance made for the support of the wife in case of divorce or legal separation from the husband. It is granted at the discretion of the court, and when awarded must be paid out of the (former) husband's estate or income.
3. like payment to a man by his (former) wife.
alimony pendente lite; the maintenance awarded the wife out of the husband's income or estate while divorce proceedings are pending.
permanent alimony; alimony awarded the wife after divorce or legal separation obtained by her.

al·i·nā′săl, *a.* [L. *ala*, wing, and *nasus*, nose.] of or pertaining to the lateral nasal region.

à·līne′, *v.t.* and *v.i.*; alined, *pt., pp.*; alining, *ppr.* same as *align.*

à·lin·ē·ā′tion, *n.* 1. the act of bringing objects in line with each other; a method of locating remote or obscure objects by an imaginary line extending between two distinct objects; as a locating of the North Star by means of the pointers of the Great Dipper.
2. alignment.

à·līne′ment, *n.* same as *alignment.*

à·līn′ẽr, *n.* same as *aligner.*

Al′i·oth, *n.* [Ar. *alyāt*, the tail of a fat sheep.] a star in the tail of the Great Bear.

al′i·ped, *a.* [L. *ala*, wing, and *pes*, *pedis*, foot.] wing-footed; having wings formed by a membrane connected with the feet.

al′i·ped, *n.* an animal whose feet are connected by a membrane, which has the functions of a wing, as the bat.

al·i·phat′iç, *a.* [Gr. *aleiphar*, *aleiphatos*, fat.] in chemistry, fatty.

al′i·quănt, *a.* [L. *aliquantus*, some, moderate, from *alius*, other, and *quantus*, how great.] designating a part of a number that does not divide the number evenly but leaves a remainder; as, 5 is an *aliquant* part of 16.

al′i·quot, *a.* [L. *aliquot*, some, several, from *alius*, other, and *quot*, how many.] designating a part of a number that divides the number evenly and leaves no remainder; as, 5 is an *aliquot* part of 15.

al·i·sep′tăl, *a.* [L. *ala*, wing, and *sæptum*, *septum*, septum.] pertaining to the alisepta1.

al·i·sep′tăl, *n.* the cartilage which forms lateral expansions of the septum in the nasal cavity, as in the skull of an embryonic bird.

āl′ish, *a.* like ale; having the qualities of ale.

Al·is·mā′cē·ae, *n.pl.* [L., from Gr. *alisma*, plantain, and *-aceæ.*] a botanical family consisting of monocotyledonous aquatic or marsh plants, the leaves of which are elliptical, and the flowers white in color, regular in structure, and either monoecious or dioecious.

al·is·mā′ceous, *a.* pertaining or belonging to the family *Alismaceæ.*

al·i·sphē′noid, al″i·sphē·noid′ăl (-sfē-), *a.* [L. *ala*, wing, and *sphenoid.*] pertaining to the alisphenoid bones.

al·i·sphē′noid, *n.* in anatomy, either of the two bones which form the large winglike plates on the sides of the sphenoid bone.

à·lis′son, *n.* same as *alyssum.*

à·lit′, alternative past tense and past participle of *alight.*

al′i·truñk, *n.* [L. *ala*, wing, and *trunk.*] the segment of the body of an insect to which the wings are attached.

al·i·tũr′ġiç·ăl, *a.* without liturgy: an ecclesiastical term applied to those days on which the liturgy or eucharistic service is not performed.

ā·li·un′dē, *adv.* [L. *alius*, other, and *unde*, whence.] in law, from another source; as, evidence *aliunde* is evidence to support or contradict a document but not deriving from the document itself.

à·līve′, *a.* [ME. *alive*, *alyfe*, *on live*; AS. *on līfe*, *on*, in, and *līfe*, dat. case of *līf*, life.]
1. having life; living.
2. in a state of action; unextinguished; undestroyed; unexpired; in force or operation; as, to keep the interest *alive.*
3. cheerful; sprightly; lively; full of eagerness; as, the company were all *alive.*
4. aware of; perceiving (with *to*); as, he is *alive to* the newest developments.
5. of all living persons; as, the proudest man *alive.*

à·liz′à·rāte, *n.* a salt of alizarin obtained by the action of an alkali.

à·li·zä′ri, *n.* [prob. from Ar.] a Levantine name for madder.

à·li·zä′riç, *a.* pertaining to or containing alizari.

à·liz′à·rin, à·liz′à·rine, *n.* [from *alizari.*] a yellowish-red crystalline compound, $C_{14}H_8O_4$, formerly obtained from madder, but now made by the oxidation of anthracene. It is used in dyeing fabrics—silk, wool, or cotton.

al′kà·hest, *n.* a term supposed to have been invented by Paracelsus to designate an imaginary universal solvent capable of dissolving all substances.

al·kal·am′ide, al·kal·am′id, *n.* [from *alkali* and *amide.*] in chemistry, a compound in which the hydrogen in ammonia has been replaced by acidic or basic radicals.

al·kà·les′cence, al·kà·les′cen·cy, *n.* [*alkali* and *-escence.*] the process of becoming, or a tendency to become, alkaline.

al·kà·les′cent, *a.* 1. becoming alkaline.
2. slightly alkaline.

al′kà·lī, *n.*; *pl.* **al′kà·līs** *or* **al′kà·līes,** [ME. *alkaly*; OFr. *alcali*; Ar. *al-qalīy*; *al*, the, and *qalīy*, ashes of the plant saltwort; *qalay*, to roast in a pan.]
1. in chemistry, any base or hydroxide having the following properties: (a) solubility in water; (b) the power of neutralizing acids; (c) the property of altering the tint of many coloring matters. Alkalis turn red litmus blue and have an acrid taste. The more common alkalis include: hydrate of potassium (potash), hydrate of sodium (soda), hydrate of lithium (lithia), and hydrate of ammonium (an aqueous solution of ammonia). In a more general sense, *alkali* is applied to a large number of substances, both natural and artificial, formerly called vegetable alkalis, or now, alkaloids.
2. the saltwort, *Salsola kali.*
3. any soluble mineral salt or mixture of salts found in certain soils, as in some deserts, and capable of neutralizing acids.

al′kà·li·fī″à·ble, *a.* that may be alkalified, or converted into an alkali.

al′kà·li·fȳ, *v.t.*; alkalified, *pt., pp.*; alkalifying, *ppr.* to form or to convert into an alkali.

al′kà·li·fȳ, *v.i.* to become an alkali.

al·kà·liġ′e·nous, *a.* [*alkali*, and *-genous*; Gr. *genēs*, producing.] producing an alkali.

al′kà·lī land, an arid region, particularly in the western United States, where the soil is strongly impregnated with alkalis which are destructive to vegetation.

al′kà·lī″ met′ăl, any metal, such as sodium, potassium, or lithium, whose hydroxide is an alkali.

al·kà·lim′e·tẽr, *n.* [*alkali*, and Gr. *metron*, measure.] an instrument for measuring the quantity of alkali in any solution or mixture.

al″kà·li·met′riç, al″kà·li·met′riç·ăl, *a.* pertaining to alkalimetry.

al·kà·lim′e·try, *n.* the process of determining the strength of alkalis or the amount of alkali present in any mixture.

al′kà·līne (*or* -lin), *a.* pertaining to an alkali; having the properties of or containing an alkali.

al′kà·līne-ẽarth′ met′ăls, the group of chemical elements comprising calcium, strontium, barium, and sometimes, beryllium, magnesium, and radium.

al′kà·līne ẽarths, the oxides of the alkaline-earth metals.

al·kà·lin′i·ty, *n.* the quality or state of being alkaline.

al·kā′li·ous, *a.* alkaline. [Obs.]

al′kà·li·zāte, *a.* alkaline. [Obs.]

al″kà·li·zā′tion, *n.* the act of making alkaline; the process of converting into alkali.

al′kà·līze, *v.t.*; alkalized, *pt., pp.*; alkalizing, *ppr.* to make alkaline.

al′kà·loid, *n.* any of a class of organic compounds found in living plants, usually in combination with organic acids and having alkaline properties. Most alkaloids contain carbon, hydrogen, nitrogen, and usually oxygen. Their one common property is that of combining with acids to form salts. Many are used in drugs, as morphine, strychnine, quinine, etc.

al′kà·loid, *a.* of, pertaining to, or resembling an alkali; containing an alkali or alkaloid.

al·kà·loid′ăl, *a.* pertaining to or resembling an alkaloid.

al″kà·lō′sis, *n.* a diseased condition in which

the alkali reserve of the body is higher than normal.

al′kāneș, *n.pl.* [*alky*l, and meth*anes*.] a series of saturated hydrocarbons of the open-chain type having the general formula C_nH_{2n+2}; methane series.

al′kȧ·net, *n.* [Sp. *alcaneta, orcaneta*, dim. of *alcana*, henna.]

1. a deep-red dye, made from the roots of *Alkanna tinctoria* and other plants, as the *Anchusa officinalis* of England and *Lithospermum canescens*, commonly called puccoon, of America.

2. any of the various plants from which the dye is obtained.

Al·kan′nȧ, *n.* [L.; Sp. *alcana*.] a genus of perennial herbs of the family *Boraginaceæ*, found in Oriental and Mediterranean countries, including the dye-yielding *Alkanna tinctoria*.

al·kan′nin, *n.* [Mod. L. *Alkanna*, from Sp. *alcana* (see *alkanet*); and *-in*.] a powder made from the root of the alkanet: used in preparing a red dyestuff.

al·kap′ton, *n.* a substance, $C_6H_3(OH)_2$, found in the urine in certain diseases.

al·kär′ġen, *n.* [*alkar*sin and oxy*gen*.] cacodylic acid.

al·kär′sin, al·kär′sine, *n.* [*al*cohol, *ars*enic, and *-in*.] a liquid containing cacodyl together with its oxidation products: it is poisonous and spontaneously inflammable, and has an extremely offensive odor.

al·kä′zär, *n.* same as *alcazar*.

al·kē·ken′ġi, *n.* [Fr. *alkekenge*, from Ar. *al kākanj*, a kind of resin found in the mountains near Herat.] *Physalis alkekengi*, a plant of the nightshade family, found in southern parts of Europe; the ground cherry. The scarlet fruit enclosed in the enlarged red calyx makes the plant very ornamental in the beginning of winter.

al′kēne, *n.* [*alk*yl, and *-ene*.] any of a series of unsaturated open-chain hydrocarbons containing a double bond and having the general formula C_nH_{2n}: also called *olefin*.

al·ken′nȧ, *n.* same as *henna*.

al·kẽr′mes, *n.* [Fr. *alkermes*; Ar. *al-qirmiz*; *al*, the, and Sans. *krimija*, worm-begotten, from *krimi*, worm.] a former compound cordial to which a fine red color was given by the kermes insect.

Al·kō·răn′, *n.* same as *Koran*.

Al·kō·răn′iç, *a.* same as *Alcoranic*.

al′kyl, *n.* an alkyl radical; methyl, ethyl, etc.

al′kyl, *a.* [*alk*ali, and *-yl*.] in chemistry, formed by substituting an element or a group of elements for hydrogen in the molecule of a hydrocarbon: applied only to radicals.

al′kȳne, *n.* [from *alkyl*, and *-ine*.] any of a series of unsaturated open-chain hydrocarbons containing a triple bond and having the general formula C_nH_{2n-2}.

ąll, *a.* [AS. *all, al*; D. *al, alle*; W. *oll*; Arm. *oll*; Gr. *holos*; O.H.G. *alanc*, entire, complete.]

1. the whole number of, taken individually or together: used often with a collective noun; as, *all* sections should be indicated; *all* the Republicans favor the plan; *all* the company was uneasy.

2. the whole quantity of, with reference to extent, duration, amount, quality, or degree: used especially with singular nouns; as, *all* China; *all* the year.

3. every one of; as, *all* men must eat.

4. any; any whatsoever; as, beyond *all* doubt; free from *all* care.

5. every: used mostly with *kind, manner*, and *sort*; as, *all manner* of evil; *all kind* of experiences.

6. the greatest possible; as, said in *all* sincerity.

7. alone; nothing but; only; as, he was *all* soldier.

ąll, *adv.* 1. wholly; completely; entirely; in the highest degree; very; as, it is *all ready*; he is *all* for amusement; *all* too dear.

2. apiece; as, a score of thirty *all*.

all along; all the time; throughout.

all but; very nearly; almost.

all in all; considering everything; as a whole; everything.

all one; a matter of indifference; just the same.

all over; (a) everywhere; as, he searched *all over*; (b) [Colloq.] in every respect; exactly; as, that was his father *all over*; (c) entirely past; ended; as, the storm, or the bitter feeling, is *all over*.

all the better, worse, etc.; so much the better, worse, etc.

all the same; notwithstanding; nevertheless.

ąll, *conj.* albeit; although. [Obs.]

ąll, *n.* 1. a whole: a totality.

2. one's entire property or interest; as, he was fighting for his *all*.

ąll, *pron.* 1. [*construed as pl.*] everyone; as, *all* must die.

2. [*construed as pl.*] every one; as, when he wrote to his friends for help, *all* responded.

3. everything; the whole affair; as, *all* is over between them.

4. every part or bit; as, *all* of it is gone.

after all; even after everything is considered; nevertheless.

at all; in any degree, to any extent, for any reason; under any circumstances; as, he has no time *at all* for recreation.

for all; in spite of; despite.

ąll-, a combining form meaning: (a) *wholly, entirely, exclusively*, as in *all*-American; (b) *for every*, as in *all*-purpose; (c) *of everything, of every part*, as in *all*-inclusive.

ȧl′lä, *prep.* [It., dat. f. of the def. article, *la*; Fr. *à la*.] after the manner of; in the style of; as, *alla francese*, in the French style.

al′lȧ·ġīte, *n.* [Gr. *allagē*, change, from *allassein*, to change, and *-ite*.] an impure, brownish variety of rhodonite.

Al′läh, *n.* the Moslem name of the Supreme Being.

ąll-A·mer′i·căn, *a.* 1. entirely made up of Americans; representative of the United States as a whole; completely within the United States.

2. pertaining to the all-American, or a member thereof; as, he is an *all-American* quarterback.

ąll-A·mer′i·căn, *n.* 1. in sports, an imaginary team, particularly a football team, selected every year by various recognized authorities, and made up of men who in their opinion have done the best work in each position during the year.

2. a player chosen for such team.

all·ȧ·mort′, *a.* same as *alamort*.

Al·lăn·ȧ·dāle′, *n.* in English legend, a famous member of Robin Hood's band.

al′lăn·īte, *n.* [named after Thomas *Allan*, the discoverer.] an ore of the elements cerium and lanthanum, pitch-black or brownish in color.

al″lan·tī′ȧ·sis, *n.* same as *botulism*.

al·lan·tō′iç, *a.* pertaining to, or contained in, the allantois.

allantoic acid; an acid found in the liquid of the allantois of cows. This was formerly called amniotic acid.

al·lan′toid, al·lan·toid′ăl, *a.* [L. *allantoides*, from Gr. *allantoeidēs*, sausage-shaped.] in anatomy, of or like the allantois.

Al·lan·toid′ē·ȧ, *n.pl.* in zoology, a division of vertebrates including those reptiles, birds, and mammals which, when in embryo, have a complete allantois.

al·lan′tō·in, *n.* a crystalline compound, $C_4H_6N_4O_3$, found in the allantoic fluid of the cow, in the urine of most mammals, etc.

al·lan′tō·is, *n.* [Gr. *allas, allantos*, a sausage, and *eidos*, form.] a thin membrane situated between the chorion and amnion in mammals, birds, and reptiles, having to do with the formation of the umbilical cord and placenta.

al·lan·tū′riç, *a.* of, related to, or derived from allantoin or uric acid.

al·lär·gän′dō, *a.* and *adv.* [It.] in music, gradually slower and with more power: a direction to the performer.

ąll′-ȧ·round″, *a.* having many abilities, talents, or uses; not specialized; versatile.

al·las·sō·ton′iç, *a.* [Gr. *allassein*, to change, and *tonos*, tension.] designating the movements taking place under temporary stimulation of plant organs.

al′lȧ·trāte, *v.i.* [L. *allatratus*, pp. of *allatrare*, to bark.] to bark. [Obs.]

al·lāy′, *v.t.*; allayed, *pt., pp.*; allaying, *ppr.* [OE. *alaien*; AS. *ālecgan*; *ā*, out, and *lecgan*, to lay.]

1. to make quiet; to pacify or appease; as, to *allay* the tumult of the passions; to *allay* civil commotions.

2. to lessen, alleviate, relieve (pain, etc.).

3. to alloy. [Obs.]

Syn.—check, repress, assuage, appease, abate, subdue, compose, soothe, calm, quiet, alleviate.

al·lāy′, *v.i.* to weaken; to subside.

al·lāy′, *n.* 1. an alloy. [Obs.]

2. that which allays, or abates. [Obs.]

al·lāy′ẽr, *n.* one who or that which allays.

al·lāy′ment, *n.* the act of quieting, or a state of rest after disturbance; also, that which allays; abatement; as, the *allayment* of grief. [Rare.]

ąll′bōne, *n.* the stitchwort, *Alsine holostea*.

ąll-çlēar′, *n.* a siren or other signal that an air raid is over.

al′lē·cret, *n.* [OFr. *alecret, halecret*.] a kind of armor worn by the Swiss in the sixteenth century.

al·leçt′, *v.t.* to entice. [Obs.]

al·leç·tā′tion, *n.* enticement; allurement. [Obs.]

al·ledġe′, *v.t.* allege. [Obs.]

al·lē·gā′tion, *n.* 1. affirmation; positive assertion or declaration.

2. that which is alleged; assertion; that which is offered as a plea, excuse, or justification.

3. an assertion without proof.

4. in ecclesiastical courts, a formal complaint, or declaration of charges.

5. in law, the first plea of the plaintiff in a case testamentary; in criminal or civil proceedings, the statement which a party undertakes to prove.

ALLECRET ARMOR

al·leġe′ (-lej′), *v.t.*; alleged (-lejd′), *pt., pp.*; alleging, *ppr.* [OE. *alegen*, to bring forward as evidence; OFr. *esligier*, from L. *ex*, out, and *litigare*, to dispute at law.]

1. to declare; to affirm; to assert with positiveness; as, to *allege* a fact.

2. to assert or declare without proof.

3. to give as an argument, plea, or excuse; to cite or quote; as, to *allege* the authority of a judge.

Syn.—bring forward, adduce, advance, assign, produce, cite, quote, declare, affirm, assert.

al·leġe′, *v.t.* to mitigate; to lighten, as a burden. [Obs.]

al·leġe′ȧ·ble, *a.* that can be alleged or affirmed.

al·leġe′ănce, *n.* allegation. [Obs.]

al·leġ′ed·ly, *adv.* according to allegation.

al·leġe′ment, *n.* allegation. [Obs.]

al·leġ′ẽr, *n.* one who alleges.

al·lē′ġiănce (-juns), *n.* [ME. *alegeaunce*; *a*- and *legeaunce*, from OFr. *ligance*; L. *ligantia*, from *ligare*, to bind.]

1. the relationship of a vassal to his feudal lord.

2. the tie or obligation of a citizen or subject to his government or ruler; the duty of fidelity to one's ruler, government, or country. Natural or implied *allegiance* arises from the connection of a person with the society in which he is born, and from his duty to be a faithful citizen, independent of any express promise.

3. loyalty and devotion in general, as to a church, a political party, a principle, a leader.

express allegiance; that obligation which proceeds from an express promise, or oath of fidelity.

Syn.—devotion, fealty, loyalty, obedience.

al·lē′ġiănt, *a.* loyal.

al·le·gor′i·căl, al·le·gor′iç, *a.* 1. of, characteristic of, or in the manner of allegory; figurative; describing by resemblances.

2. that is or contains an allegory.

al·le·gor′iç·ăl·ly, *adv.* in a figurative manner; by way of allegory.

al·le·gor′iç·ăl·ness, *n.* the quality of being allegorical.

al′le·gō·rist, *n.* one who allegorizes, or uses allegory, as Bunyan or Spenser.

al″le·gor·i·zā′tion, *n.* the act of construing allegorically; the act of turning into allegory.

al′le·gō·rīze, *v.t.*; allegorized, *pt., pp.*; allegorizing, *ppr.* 1. to treat as allegory; to turn into allegory; as, to *allegorize* the history of a people.

2. to understand in an allegorical sense; as, when a passage in a writer may be understood literally or figuratively, he who gives it a figurative sense is said to *allegorize* it.

al′le·gō·rīze, *v.i.* to make or use allegory; as, a man may *allegorize* to please his fancy.

al′le·gō·rī″zẽr, *n.* one who allegorizes, or turns matter into allegory.

al′le·gō·ry, *n.*; *pl.* **al′le·gō·rieș,** [L. *allegoria*; Gr. *allēgoria*, description of one thing under the image of another; from *allos*, other, and *agoreuein*, to speak in the assembly; *agora*, a place of assembly.]

1. a story in which people, things, and happenings have another meaning, as in a fable or parable: allegories are used for teaching or explaining.

2. the presentation of ideas by means of such stories; symbolical narration or description.

3. in painting and sculpture, a symbolic representation.

4. any emblem or symbolic suggestion.

Syn.—fable, fiction, metaphor, illustration, parable, simile.

al·le·gresse′, *n.* [Fr. *allégresse*, from L. *alacer*, sprightly.] joy.

al·le·gret′tō, *a.* and *adv.* [It., dim. of *allegro.*] in music, faster than *andante* but not so quick as *allegro*: a direction to the performer.

al·le·gret′tō, *n.*; *pl.* **al·le·gret′tōs**, in music, a movement or passage in allegretto time.

al·le′grō, *a.* and *adv.* [It., from L. *alacer*, brisk, sprightly, cheerful.] in music, fast; faster than *allegretto* but not so fast as *presto*: a direction to the performer.

al·le′grō, *n.*; *pl.* **al·le′grōs**, in music, a movement or passage in allegro time.

al·lē′lo·morph″, *n.* [from Gr. *allēlōn*, of one another, and *morphē*, form.] in genetics, either of a pair of contrasting characters inherited alternatively according to Mendelian law.

al·lē·lū′ia, al·lē·lū′iah, *interj.* and *n.* [L.; Heb. *hallēlūyāh*, praise ye Jehovah.] same as *halleluiah.*

al·le·mande′, *n.* [Fr., lit., German.]

1. any of various stately German dances of the 16th, 17th, and 18th centuries, in 2/2 time.

2. the music for this.

3. a piece of music resembling this in rhythm, formerly used as the movement preceding the prelude in a suite.

al·lē·man′nic, *n.* and *a.* see *alemannic.*

al·len′ăr·ly, *adv.* only: a Scottish legal term.

al′lēr·gen, *n.* any substance which causes an allergic state or reaction.

al″lēr·gen′ic, *a.* of or acting as an allergen; inducing allergy.

al·lēr′gic, *a.* 1. having an allergy.

2. of or caused by an allergy.

al′lēr·gist, *n.* a physician specializing in the diagnosis and treatment of allergies.

al′lēr·gy, *n.* a condition of unusual sensitivity to a substance or substances which, in like amounts, do not affect others; it may be characterized by itching, sneezing, wheals, diarrhea, or other systemic disturbances. Allergens are usually protein substances, but nonorganic agents, such as light, cold, heat, and the like, are also causative factors.

al·le′ri·on, *n.* [etymology doubtful; Fr. *alérion*; L. *alarius*, from *ala*, wing.] in heraldry, an eagle or eaglet, displayed without beak and legs, with wings outspread and tips pointing downward.

al·lē′vi·āte, *v.t.*; alleviated, *pt.*, *pp.*; alleviating, *ppr.* [L. *alleviatus*, pp. of *alleviare*, from *allevare*; *ad*, to, and *levis*, light.]

1. to remove in part; to lessen, mitigate, or make easier to be endured; as, to *alleviate* sorrow, pain, care, etc.: opposed to *aggravate.*

2. to lessen the magnitude or criminality of. [Rare.]

Syn.—lessen, diminish, mitigate, assuage, allay, ameliorate, moderate, soften.

al·lē·vi·ā′tion, *n.* 1. the act of lightening, allaying, etc.; a lessening, or mitigation.

2. that which lessens, mitigates, or makes more tolerable.

al·lē′vi·ā·tive, *a.* alleviating or tending to alleviate.

al·lē′vi·ā″tive, *n.* anything that alleviates or makes more bearable.

al·lē′vi·ā·tŏr, *n.* a person or thing that alleviates.

al·lē′vi·ā·tō·ry, *a.* alleviative.

al′ley, *n.*; *pl.* **al′leys**, [OE. *aly*, *ally*; OFr. *alée*, *allée*, a going, passage, from *aler*, *aller*, to go.]

1. a narrow foot passage between buildings.

2. a narrow and rather obscure passageway, narrower than a street, for people or vehicles in cities and towns; a minor thoroughfare through the center of city blocks or squares.

3. a lane in a garden or park, between flower beds, shrubs, etc.

4. a passage between seats, counters, desks, shelving, or cases.

5. the space between rows of composing stands in a printing office.

6. in bowling, (a) a long, narrow lane, usually of polished wood, along which the balls are rolled; (b) [*usually pl.*] a building or hall for bowling.

7. in tennis, either of the two narrow lanes opposite each other on the long sides of the court, used in playing doubles.

blind alley; (a) an alley that has no rear outlet; hence, (b) any undertaking, idea, etc. that leads to nothing.

up one's alley; suited to one's tastes or abilities. [Slang.]

al′ley, *n.*; *pl.* **al′leys**, [said to be contracted from *alabaster*, from which it was formerly made.] a choice taw or large marble used as a shooter in playing marbles: also written *ally.*

al′ley cat, a homeless, mongrel cat that haunts alleys, etc. for food.

al′leyed (-lid), *a.* having an alley or alleys, or forming an alley.

al′ley-wāy, *n.* 1. any narrow passageway.

2. an alley between buildings.

al·lez-vouz en′ (à″le″ voo″zän′), [Fr.] go away! get out!

all-fīred′, *a.* [altered from *hell-fired.*] complete; total; as, an *all-fired* fool. [Slang.]

all-fīred′, *adv.* completely; extremely. [Slang.]

All Fools′ dāy, the first day of April; April Fools' Day: it is a day when practical jokes are played.

all fours, 1. a game of cards, played by two or four persons: so called from the four points for scoring: high, low, jack, and the game.

2. all four limbs of an animal or human being: as, the cat landed on *all fours.*

go on all fours; (a) to move on all four limbs; (b) to creep or crawl, as a baby; (c) to move along evenly.

all hāil, [*all* and AS. *hæl*, health.] all health: a greeting expressing a wish of health or safety to the person addressed.

all-hāil′, *v.t.* to salute; to greet. [Poet.]

Allhal′lond, *n.* Allhallows. [Obs.]

All·hal′lōw·mas, *n.* the feast of All Saints; Allhallows.

All·hal′lōwn, *a.* of or pertaining to the season of Allhallows. [Obs.]

All·hal′lōws, All·hal′lōw, *n.* All-Saints' Day, the first of November: a feast dedicated to all the saints in general.

Allhallow eve; Halloween.

All·hal′lōw·tīde, *n.* [AS. *tid*, time.] the time or season of Allhallows.

all′hēal, *n.* the valerian: a popular name.

al·lī′a·ble, *a.* capable of entering into an alliance.

al·li·ā′ceous (-shus), *a.* [L. *allium*, garlic, and *-aceous.*] 1. pertaining to the plants of the genus *Allium*, including garlic.

2. having the smell or taste of garlic, onions, etc.

al·lī′ănce, *n.* [OFr. *alliance*; L. *alligantia*, from *alligare*; *ad*, to, and *ligare*, to bind.]

1. the relation or union between families, contracted by marriage.

2. the union between nations, contracted by compact, treaty, or league.

3. the treaty, league, or compact, which is the instrument of confederacy between states or provinces; also, the act of confederating.

4. any union or connection of interests between persons, families, states, or corporations; as, an *alliance* between church and state.

5. the persons, countries, parties, etc. allied; as, men or states may secure any *alliances* in their power.

6. similarity or relationship in characteristics, structure, etc.; affinity.

7. formerly, a subdivision of the vegetable kingdom between a class and an order.

Syn.—connection, affinity, union, confederacy, league, coalition.

al·lī′ănce, *v.t.* to ally. [Rare.]

al·lī′ănt, *n.* an ally. [Obs.]

al′lice, al′lis, *n.* [L. *alosa*; Fr. *alose.*] the shad, *Clupea vulgaris.*

al·li′cien·cy (-lish′en-), *n.* hypnotic power; attraction: magnetism. [Obs.]

al·li′cient, *n.* [L. *alliciens*, ppr. of *allicere*, to draw gently to, to entice.] that which attracts. [Rare.]

al·li′cient, *a.* having power to attract.

al·līed′, *a.* 1. connected by marriage, treaty, agreement, etc.; united; joined.

2. closely related; as, anatomy and biology are *allied* sciences.

3. [A–], of the Allies of World War I or II.

4. [A–], of England and the United States jointly in World War II; as, the *Allied* High Command.

Al′līes, *n.pl.* [see *ally.*] 1. in World War I, the nations allied by treaty against Germany and the other Central Powers; originally, Great Britain, France, and Russia, later joined by the United States, Italy, Japan, etc.

2. in World War II, the nations associated against the Axis; especially, Great Britain, the Soviet Union, and the United States: sometimes only of the United States and Great Britain.

al′li·gāte, *v.t.*; alligated, *pt.*, *pp.*; alligating, *ppr.* [L. *alligatus*, pp. of *alligare*, to bind to; *ad*, to, and *ligare*, to bind.] to tie together; to unite by some tie. [Obs.]

al·li·gā′tion, *n.* 1. the act of tying together; also, the state of being tied. [Rare.]

2. a rule of arithmetic for finding the price or value of compounds of ingredients of different values and varying proportions.

alligation alternate; the process which ascertains what proportions of given price will produce a compound of given cost.

alligation medial; the process of finding the cost of a mixture, the prices and proportions of ingredients being given.

al′li·gā·tŏr, *n.* [Sp. *el lagarto*, lizard; L. *lacerta*, *lacertus*, lizard.]

1. any of a genus of saurian reptiles of the family *Crocodilidæ*; the American crocodile; the cayman. It has a long scaly body, four feet, armed with claws, and a serrated tail. The mouth is very large and furnished with sharp teeth. The largest grow to the length of about 12 feet. They live in and about the tropical rivers and marshes of the United States and China. The snout of the alligator is shorter and blunter than the crocodile's.

ALLIGATOR
(*Alligator lucius*)

2. a scaly leather made from an alligator's hide.

3. in mechanics, any machine, tool, or apparatus with a powerful, movable, often toothed, jaw.

al′li·gā·tŏr ap′ple, the edible fruit of a West Indian tree.

al′li·gā·tŏr fish, the *Podothecus acipenserinus*, a marine fish found along the northwestern coast of North America.

al′li·gā·tŏr gär, a very large gar pike found in the rivers of the South.

al′li·gā·tŏr peār (pār), see *avocado.*

al′li·gā·tŏr tūr′tle, 1. the common snapping turtle, *Chelydra serpentina.*

2. a fresh-water turtle of southern United States, the *Macrochelys lacertina*. It commonly attains a weight of fifty or sixty pounds, often more, and is esteemed for food.

al′li·gā·tŏr wood, a kind of West Indian timber.

al′li·gā·tŏr wrench, a kind of wrench with toothed, V-shaped jaws.

al·līgn′ment, *n.* same as *alignment.*

all′-im·pọr′tănt, *a.* highly important; necessary; essential.

all′-in·clū′sive, *a.* including everything; comprehensive.

al·lin′ē·āte, *v.t.* to align. [Rare.]

al·lin·ē·ā′tion, *n.* alignment. [Rare.]

al·li′sion, *n.* [L. *allisio*, from *allidere*, to strike against; *ad*, to, and *lædere*, to strike.] a striking against; as, the *allision* of the sea against the shore.

al·lit′ēr·ăl, *a.* alliterative; characterized by alliteration. [Rare.]

al·lit′ēr·āte, *v.t.*; alliterated, *pt.*, *pp.*; alliterating, *ppr.* to place (letters or words) so as to produce alliteration.

al·lit′ēr·āte, *v.i.* [L. *alliteratus*, pp. of *alliterare*; *ad*, to, and *litera*, *littera*, letter.]

1. to use alliteration.

2. to constitute or have alliteration.

al·lit·ēr·ā′tion, *n.* [Fr. *allitération*, from L. *alliterare*; *ad*, to, and *littera*, letter.] the repetition of the same sound, usually of a consonant, at the beginning of two or more words immediately succeeding each other, or at short intervals, as the repetition of *f* and *g* in the following line:

Fields ever fresh, and groves ever green.

al·lit′ēr·ā·tive, *a.* pertaining to, using, or showing alliteration.

al·lit′ẽr·ȧ·tive·ly, *adv.* in an alliterative manner.

al·lit′ẽr·ȧ·tive·ness, *n.* the state or quality of being alliterative.

al·lit′ẽr·ā·tŏr, *n.* one who uses alliteration.

Al′li·um, *n.* [L., the garlic.] a genus of bulbous plants of the lily family, having about three hundred species. It includes the garlic, onion, and leek.

all′mouth, *n.* a fish commonly known as the angler, *Lophius piscatorius.*

all′ness, *n.* entirety; totality.

all″nīght′, *n.* food, fuel, or light sufficient to last through the night. [Obs.]

al′lo-, [Gr. *allos,* other.] a combining form signifying *variation, departure from the normal, reversal,* as in *allo*nym, *allo*morph.

al′lō·că·ble, *a.* that can be allocated.

al′lō·çāte, *v.t.*; allocated, *pt., pp.*; allocating, *ppr.* [ML. *allocatus,* pp. of *allocare,* from L. *ad,* to, and *locare,* to place; *locus,* a place.]
1. to set apart for a specific purpose; as, they will *allocate* funds for housing.
2. to distribute by a plan; allot; assign.
3. to locate.

al·lō·çā′tion, *n.* 1. allotment, apportionment, assignment, or the act thereof; as, the *allocation* of shares in a stock company.
2. arrangement; disposition; the act of putting in place.
3. in England, an allowance made upon accounts in the exchequer.
4. a thing allocated.

al·lō·çā′tŭr, *n.* [ML., it is allowed, from *allocare,* to allow.] the endorsement of a judge on a writ or legal document to designate it as approved or allowed.

al·lō·chī′ri·ȧ, *n.* [*allo-,* and Gr. *cheir,* hand.] in pathology, a confusion of the two sides of the body in the localization of sensation.

al·loch′rō·ous, *a.* [Gr. *allochroos,* changed in color.] of a variety of colors: said of minerals.

al·lō·cryp′tiç, *a.* [*allo-,* and Gr. *kryptos,* hidden.] hiding from view by the use of extraneous objects of similar color to itself; imitating the color of plants or trees by changing colors, for the purpose of concealment, as the chameleon.

al·lō·çū′tion, *n.* [L. *allocutio,* from *alloqui,* to speak to; *ad,* to, and *loqui,* to speak.]
1. the act or manner of speaking to or of addressing in words, as in warning or advising.
2. an address; a formal address, as of a general to his troops, or of the pope to the clergy.

al′lod, al·lō′di·ȧl, al·lō′di·um, etc. same as *alod,* etc.

al·log′ȧ·mous, *a.* of, caused by, or relating to allogamy, or cross-fertilization.

al·log′ȧ·my, *n.* [*allo-,* and Gr. *gamos,* marriage.] fertilization of a flower by the pollen of another; cross-fertilization of flowers.

al·lō·ġē′nē·ous, *a.* [*allo-,* and Gr. *genos,* kind.] varying in nature or kind. [Rare.]

al′lō·ġraft, *n.* [*allo-* and *graft.*] a graft of tissue or an organ taken from an individual of the same species as the recipient but with different hereditary factors.

al′lō·graph, *n.* [*allo-,* and Gr. *graphein,* to write.] a signature made by proxy. In law, an instrument written by a person who is not a party to its execution.

al·lom′ẽr·işm, *n.* [*allo-,* and Gr. *meros,* part; and *-ism.*] in chemistry, a change in the chemical constituents or their proportions while the crystalline form remains unvaried.

al·lom′ẽr·ous, *a.* of or characterized by allomerism.

al′lō·mọrph, *n.* [*allo-,* and Gr. *morphē,* figure, form.]
1. in mineralogy, (a) any variety of a substance that has more than one crystalline form but always the same chemical constitution; (b) a kind of pseudomorph whose constituents have partly or completely changed.
2. in linguistics, any of the variant forms of a morpheme as conditioned by position or adjoining sounds.

al·lō·mọr′phiç, *a.* showing or pertaining to allomorphism.

al·lō·mọr′phişm, *n.* the state or quality of being or becoming an allomorph or allomorphs (sense 1).

al·lŏnġe′, *n.* [Fr. *allonger,* to lengthen, to thrust.]
1. a pass with a sword; a thrust made by stepping forward and sharply extending the arm: now contracted to *lunge.* [Obs.]
2. a long rein. [Obs.]
3. in commerce, the name applied to a slip or rider attached to a bill of exchange to receive endorsements when the reverse of the bill is filled.

al·lŏnġe′, *v.i.* [Fr. *allonger,* to lengthen; *a,* L. *ad,* to, and *longare,* from *longus,* long.] to make an allonge; to lunge. [Obs.]

ȧl·lōns′ (ȧ″lōṅ′), *interj.* [Fr.] 1. let us go; come on.
2. nonsense!

al′lō·nym, *n.* [*allo-,* and Gr. *onyma,* name.]
1. a pseudonym; especially, the name of another assumed by an author; a false name.
2. the work published under such a name.

al·lon′y·mous, *a.* published under a false name.

al′lō·path, *n.* 1. one who practices allopathy.
2. an advocate of allopathy.

al·lō·path′iç, *a.* of or using allopathy.

al·lō·path′iç·ăl·ly, *adv.* in a manner conformable to allopathy.

al·lop′ȧ·thist, *n.* an allopath.

al·lop′ȧ·thy, *n.* [*allo-,* and Gr. *pathos,* from *paschein,* to suffer.] that method of medical practice which seeks to cure disease by the production of a condition of the system either different from or opposite to the condition produced by the disease: distinguished from *homeopathy.*

al′lō·phāne, *n.* [Gr. *allophanēs,* appearing otherwise; *allos,* other, and *phanēs,* from *phaneisthai,* to appear.] a natural, translucent silicate of aluminum, $Al_2SiO_5 \cdot 5H_2O$, of various colors.

al·lō·phan′iç, *a.* pertaining to anything which changes its appearance or color.

al′lō·phōne″, *n.* [*allo-,* and *-phone.*] in linguistics, any of the variant forms of a phoneme as conditioned by position or adjoining sounds.

al·lō·phyl′i·ăn, al·lō·phyl′iç, *a.* [L. *allophylus,* from Gr. *allophylos*; *allos,* other, and *phylē,* tribe.]
1. neither Indo-European nor Semitic.
2. speaking allophylian languages.

al′lo·plașm, *n.* [*allo-,* and *plasm.*] in biology, a differentiated cell substance, as of flagella and cilia.

al·lot′, *v.t.*; allotted, *pt., pp.*; allotting, *ppr.* [OFr. *alloter*; *a,* to, and *loter, lotir,* to assign by lot; AS. *hlot*; O.H.G. *hlōz,* lot, share.]
1. to divide or distribute by lot.
2. to distribute or parcel out in parts or portions, or to distribute (a share) to each individual concerned.
3. to grant, as a portion; to give, assign, or appoint in general.

Syn.—distribute, assign, apportion, appoint, destine.

al′lō·thē·işm, *n.* [*allo-,* Gr. *theos,* god, and *-ism.*] the worship of other gods.

al·loth′i·ġēne, al·loth·i·ġen′iç, *a.* [Gr. *allothi,* elsewhere, and *-gene,* Gr. *genēs,* produced.] produced elsewhere; said of rock fragments found elsewhere than in their place of origin.

al·loth″i·ġē·net′iç, al″lō·thog′e·nous, *a.* same as *allothigene.*

al·lot′ment, *n.* 1. the act of allotting.
2. that which is allotted; a share, part, or portion granted or distributed; that which is assigned by lot.
3. a part, portion, or place assigned; as, an *allotment* of ground for a garden.
4. in the United States armed forces, a portion of one's pay regularly deducted, as for one's dependents, insurance premiums, etc.

al·lō·tri·oph′ȧ·ġy, *n.* [Gr. *allotrios,* another's, and *phagia,* from *phagein,* to eat.] in pathology, an appetite for unnatural foods.

al′lō·trōpe″, *n.* an allotropic form.

al·lō·troph′iç, *a.* [*allo-,* and Gr. *trophos,* nourishing.] modified in such a way as to be less nutritious.

al·lō·trop′iç, al·lō·trop′iç·ăl, *a.* relating to or characterized by allotropy.

al·lō·trop′iç·ăl·ly, *adv.* in an allotropical manner.

al″lō·trō·pic′i·ty, *n.* power of becoming allotropic.

al·lot′rō·pişm, *n.* allotropy.

al·lot′rō·pīze, *v.t.*; allotropized, *pt., pp.*; allotropizing, *ppr.* to make allotropic.

al·lot′rō·py, *n.* [Gr. *allotropos,* of or in another manner; *allos,* other, and *tropos,* way, manner.] the property exhibited by certain chemical elements of existing in more than one form and with different physical and chemical properties; for example, carbon crystallizes perfectly in the diamond, imperfectly in graphite, and is amorphous in anthracite and charcoal.

al·lot′tȧ·ble, *a.* capable of being allotted, or distributed.

ȧll′ ọt·tä′vä, [It., lit., according to the octave.] in music, to be played an octave higher or an octave lower, depending on whether the sign or abbreviation (*8, 8va~~~~~, 8va*) is above or below the staff.

al·lot′ted, *a.* distributed by lot; granted; assigned.

al·lot·tee′, *n.* the person to whom an allotment is made; one who receives a share.

al·lot′tẽr, *n.* one who allots.

al·lot′tẽr·y, *n.* allotment. [Obs.]

all′-out′, *a.* complete or wholehearted; as, an *all-out* effort. [Colloq.]

all′ō″vẽr, *a.* 1. over the whole surface.
2. with the pattern repeated over the whole surface; as, *allover* embroidery.

all′ō″vẽr, *n.* cloth, lace, etc. with such a pattern.

al·low′, *v.t.*; allowed, *pt., pp.*; allowing, *ppr.* [OE. *alouen*; OFr. *alouer*; Fr. *allouer*; L. *allocare,* to admit as approved, to place; *ad,* to, and *locare,* to place.]
1. to grant, give, or yield; as, to *allow* a servant his liberty.
2. to admit; as, to *allow* the truth of a proposition; to *allow* a claim.
3. to approve, justify, or sanction.
4. to afford, or grant, as a compensation; as, to *allow* a dollar a day for wages.
5. to permit; to grant license to; as, to *allow* a son to be absent.
6. to let enter; permit the presence of; as, dogs are not *allowed.*
7. to provide or keep (a certain amount or extra quantity) so as to have enough; as, *allow* an inch for shrinkage.
8. to think; give as one's opinion. [Dial.]

allow for; to make an allowance or allowances for; leave room, time, etc. for.

allow of; (a) to be subject to; (b) to tolerate.

Syn.—permit, suffer, tolerate.—*Allow* and *permit* are often used synonymously; but *permit* rather implies a formal sanction; *allow* implies that we merely do not hinder; *suffer* is still more passive than *permit,* and may imply that we do not prevent something, though we feel it to be disagreeable, or know it to be wrong; *tolerate* is always used in the sense of permitting or bearing something unpleasant.

al·low′, *v.i.* [OE. *alouen*; OFr. *alouer*; L. *allaudare,* to praise much; *ad,* to, and *laudare,* to praise.] to admit; to acknowledge; to concede.

al·low′ȧ·ble, *a.* permissible; lawful; admitted as true and proper; not forbidden; not unlawful or improper; as, a certain degree of freedom is *allowable* among friends.

al·low′ȧ·ble·ness, *n.* the quality of being allowable.

al·low′ȧ·bly, *adv.* in an allowable manner.

al·low′ănce, *n.* 1. the act of allowing or admitting.
2. permission; license; approbation; sanction.
3. admission; assent to a fact or state of things; a granting.
4. freedom from restraint; indulgence.
5. that which is allowed; a portion appointed; a stated quantity, as of food or drink; hence, a limited quantity of meat and drink when provisions fall short.
6. abatement; deduction; as, to make *allowance* for the inexperience of youth.
7. established character; reputation; as, a pilot of approved *allowance.* [Obs.]
8. in commerce, a customary deduction from the gross weight of goods, such as tare and tret.
9. a sum of money granted or allowed at stated intervals; as, his *allowance* is **$500** a year.

make allowance (or *allowances*); to take circumstances, limitations, etc. into consideration.

make allowance (or *allowances*) *for*; (a) to forgive or excuse because of mitigating factors; (b) to leave room, time, etc. for; allow for.

Syn.—concession, grant, permission, pay, stipend, consent, authority.

al·low′ănce, *v.t.*; allowanced (-ănst), *pt., pp.*; allowancing, *ppr.* [ME. *alouance*; OFr. *alouance,* from *allouer,* to grant, permit.] to put upon allowance; to restrain or limit to a certain amount of provisions; as, distress forced the captain to *allowance* his crew.

al·low′ed·ly, *adv.* admittedly; by acknowledgment.

al·low′ẽr, *n.* one who allows, permits, grants, or authorizes.

al·lox'ăn, *n.* [*all*antoin, *ox*alic, and *-an.*] a crystalline compound, $C_4H_2N_2O_4$, obtained by the action of strong nitric acid on uric acid.

al·lox'ȧ·nāte, *n.* a salt of alloxanic acid.

al·lox·an'iç, *a.* pertaining to alloxan.

al·lox·an'tin, *n.* a crystalline substance obtained by the action of reducing agents on alloxan.

al'loy, *n.* 1. in coinage, a baser metal mixed with a finer.

2. the relative purity of gold or silver.

3. in chemistry, a metal that is a mixture, generally by fusion, of different metals or of a metal and something else.

4. figuratively, that which detracts from the value of anything; as, no happiness is without *alloy*.

al·loy', *v.t.*; alloyed (-loid'), *pt., pp.*; alloying, *ppr.* [Fr. *aloyer*; OFr. *allier, allayer*; L. *alligare*; *ad*, to, and *ligare*, to bind.]

1. to reduce the purity of (a metal) by mixing with it a portion of one less valuable; as, to *alloy* gold with silver, or silver with copper.

2. to mix (metals) so as to form an alloy.

3. to debase by adding something inferior; as, to *alloy* pleasure with misfortunes.

al·loy', *v.i.* to unite to form an alloy.

al·loy'āġe, *n.* the act of alloying metals, or the mixture so made.

al·lō·zō'oid, *n.* a zooid differing from the parent organism.

ạll'-poṣ·ṣessed' (-zest'), *a.* wild; raging, as if possessed by evil spirits.

ạll'-pūr''pōse, *a.* for every purpose; useful in many ways.

ạll'-rīght'', *a.* 1. honest, honorable, dependable, etc. [Slang.]

2. good; excellent. [Slang.]

ạll rīght, 1. satisfactory; adequate; also, correct.

2. unhurt; uninjured.

3. yes; very well; certainly.

ạll'-round'', *a.* all-around.

Ạll Sāints' Dāy, Allhallows or Allhallowmas, a feast day celebrated on the first day of November.

ạll'seed, *n.* any of various plants having many seeds, as the goosefoot, *Chenopodium polyspermum*, found in waste places.

Ạll Sōuls' Dāy, the second day of November, a festival in the Roman Catholic Church, when prayers are publicly offered up for the release of souls from purgatory.

ạll'spīce, *n.* 1. the fruit of *Eugenia pimenta*, a tree of the West Indies.

2. the aromatic spice made from this berry: its odor and flavor are supposed to combine those of cinnamon, cloves, and nutmeg, hence the name.

ạll'-stär', *a.* made up entirely of outstanding or star performers.

al·lūde', *v.i.*; alluded, *pt., pp.*; alluding, *ppr.* [L. *alludere*, to joke, jest, refer to; *ad*, to, and *ludere*, to play.] to refer indirectly (*to*); to have reference; to hint by remote suggestions; as, that story *alludes* to a recent transaction.

Syn.—hint, refer, suggest, intimate.

al·lūde', *v.t.* to make an allusion to; to refer to indirectly. [Obs.]

al·lū·mette' (-met'), *n.* [Fr.] a slip of paper or splinter of wood for lighting lamps; especially, a match.

al·lū'mi·nŏr, *n.* an illuminator; an illustrator. [Obs.]

al·lūr'ănce, *n.* enticement. [Obs.]

al·lūre', *v.t.*; allured, *pt., pp.*; alluring, *ppr.* [OFr. *alurer, aleurer*, to attract, allure; *a*, to, and *lurer*, to lure; Fr. *leurre*, a decoy.] to tempt by the offer of some good; to invite by something flattering or acceptable; as, rewards *allure* men to brave danger.

Syn.—entice, decoy, seduce, attract, tempt, lead astray.—We are *allured* to evil by some promised good; we are *enticed* into it through our passions; we are *seduced* when drawn aside from the path of rectitude.

ȧl·lūre', *n.* [Fr.] bearing; mien; air.

al·lūre', *n.* the power to entice or attract; fascination.

al·lūre'ment, *n.* 1. an alluring.

2. that which allures; any real or apparent good held forth, or operating, as a motive to action; temptation; enticement; as, the *allurements* of pleasure, or of honor.

3. fascination; charm.

al·lūr'ẽr, *n.* one who or that which allures.

al·lūr'ing, *a.* inviting; attracting; tempting.

al·lūr'ing·ly, *adv.* in an alluring manner; enticingly.

al·lūr'ing·ness, *n.* the quality of alluring or tempting.

al·lū'ṣion, *n.* [Fr. *allusion*; L. *allusio(n)*, a playing or sporting with; from ppr. of *alludere*, to play or sport with.]

1. an indirect reference to something; casual mention.

2. in rhetoric, a reference to some striking incident in history, or passage in some writer, by way of illustration.

al·lū'sive, *a.* 1. containing an allusion.

2. using allusion; full of allusions.

al·lū'sive·ly, *adv.* by way of allusion; by implication, remote suggestion, or insinuation.

al·lū'sive·ness, *n.* the quality of being allusive.

al·lū'sō·ry, *a.* allusive. [Obs.]

al·lū'vi·ȧ, *n.* Latin plural of *alluvium*.

al·lū'vi·ăl, *a.* pertaining to or having the character of alluvium; deposited or thrown up by the action of waves or currents of water; as, *alluvial* deposits; *alluvial* soil.

al·lū'vi·ăl, *n.* alluvial soil.

al·lū'vi·ăl çōne (or **fan**), a cone-shaped deposit of alluvium made by a swift stream where it runs out into a level plain or meets a slower stream.

al·lū'vi·ŏn, *n.* [Fr. *alluvion*; L. *alluvio*, an overflowing, from *alluere*; *ad*, to, and *luere*, to wash.]

1. a gradual washing or carrying of earth or other substances to a shore or bank; also, the earth thus added.

2. in law, the gradual increase of earth on a shore or bank of a river, by the force of water, as by a current or by waves.

3. in physical geography, a tract of alluvial formation: particularly applied to the bottomlands and deltas of rivers.

4. a flood.

al·lū'vi·ous, *a.* alluvial. [Obs.]

al·lū'vi·um, *n.*; *pl.* **al·lū'vi·umṣ** or **al·lū'vi·ȧ,** [L. *alluvium*, from *alluere*, to wash upon.] earth, sand, gravel, and other transported matter which has been washed away and deposited by flowing water, especially along a river bed.

ạll'where, ạll'whereṣ (-hwãrz), *adv.* everywhere. [Rare.]

ạll'wŏrk, *n.* common manual work of all kinds, especially domestic work; as, a maid of *allwork*; a man of *allwork*.

al·lȳ', *v.t.*; allied, *pt., pp.*; allying, *ppr.* [OE. *alien*; OFr. *alier*; Fr. *allier*; from L. *alligare*; *ad*, to, and *ligare*, to bind.]

1. to unite, or form a relation, as between families by marriage, or between nations by treaty, league, or confederacy (with *to* or *with*): generally used reflexively or in the passive.

2. to form a relation between by similitude, resemblance, etc.: generally used in the passive form; as, hate is *allied* to fear.

al'lȳ, *n.*; *pl.* **al'lieṣ,** 1. a prince or state united to another by treaty or league; a confederate.

2. a helper; an auxiliary.

3. any organism akin to another by structure, etc.

See also *Allies*.

al'lyl, *n.* [L. *allium*, garlic, and *-yl.*] in chemistry, the univalent radical C_3H_5, found in oil of garlic and in other compounds.

al'ly·lēne, *n.* a colorless, gaseous hydrocarbon, C_3H_4.

al'mȧ, al'mȧh, *n.* [Ar. *'almah*, learned, knowing, from *'alama*, to know.] same as *alme*.

al·mȧ·çan'tăr, *n.* see *almucantar*.

al·mȧ·dī'ȧ, al'mȧ·die (-di), *n.* [Ar. *alma 'dīyah*; *al*, the, *ma 'dīyah*, ferryboat.] a bark canoe used by the Africans; also, a river boat used in India, shaped like a shuttle.

al'mȧ·ġest, Al'mȧ·ġest, *n.* [ME. *almagest*; L. *almageste*; Ar. *almajisti*; *al*, the, and Gr. *megistē*, greatest, superl. of *megas*, great.]

1. a vast work on astronomy and geography compiled by Claudius Ptolemy c. 150 A.D.

2. any of several medieval works like this, on astrology, alchemy, etc.

al·mā'grȧ, *n.* [Sp. *almagra*; Ar. *al-maghrah*, red ocher.] a fine deep-red ocher, with an admixture of purple, found in Spain: sometimes used as a paint, and for polishing silver and glass, under the name of *Indian red*.

Al'māin, *n.* 1. a German: also used adjectively. [Obs.]

2. [a–] the allemande.

Al'māin riv'et, *n.* a kind of light, flexible armor invented in Germany about 1450, and used in England in the sixteenth and seventeenth centuries. It consisted of overlapping plates sliding on rivets.

al'mȧ mā'tẽr, Al'mȧ Mā'tẽr (*or* mä'tẽr), [L., fostering mother.]

1. the college or university where one was educated.

2. its anthem, or hymn.

ạl'mȧ·naç, *n.* [Sp. *almanac*; L. *almanac*, probably from Ar. *almanakh*; *al*, the, and *manakh*, a calendar.] a book or table, containing a yearly calendar of days, weeks, and months, with the times of the rising and setting of the sun and moon, changes of the moon, eclipses, hours of full tide, stated festivals of churches, tables of useful information, weather forecasts, etc. for the year.

nautical almanac; an official annual publication for mariners, astronomers, and others, giving in advance the positions of the heavenly bodies, predictions of astronomical phenomena, and other calculations.

al'măn·dīne, *n.* [LL. *alamandina*, a corruption of *alabandina*.] the common garnet, a reddish iron-alumina stone found crystallized as a rhombic dodecahedron. Precious *garnet* is deep red and transparent. Written also *almandite*.

al'me, al'meh, *n.* an Egyptian dancing girl.

äl·men·drōn', *n.* [Sp., from *almendra*, almond.] the tree yielding the Brazil nut of commerce, *Bertholletia excelsa*.

al'mẽr·y, *n.* ambry. [Obs.]

älm'esse (äm'es), *n.* alms. [Obs.]

ạl·mīght'fụl, ạl·mīght'i·fụl, *a.* all-powerful. [Obs.]

ạl·mīght'i·ly, *adv.* with almighty power.

ạl·mīght'i·ness, *n.* omnipotence; infinite or boundless power.

ạl·mīght'y, *a.* [ME. *almighty*; AS. *ealmihtig*; *eal*, all, and *mihtig*, mighty.]

1. possessing all power; omnipotent.

2. great; terrible; enormous; astonishing; as, an *almighty* mistake. [Slang.]

almighty dollar; money regarded figuratively as a god, or source of great power: first used by Washington Irving in 1837. [Colloq.]

the Almighty; God.

älm'nẽr, (äm'), *n.* an almoner. [Obs.]

äl'mŏnd (ä'mund *or* am'und), *n.* [OE. *almande*; L. *amygdala*; Gr. *amygdalē*, an almond.]

1. the *Prunus* or *Amygdalus communis*, a tree of the rose family, or its popular edible nut, which is the kernel or stone of the fruit. The leaves and flowers of the *almond* tree resemble those of the peach.

2. anything having a close resemblance to an almond nut: applied specifically to a tonsil and various ornaments.

3. a light-tan color.

ALMOND
(*Amygdalus communis*)

äl'mŏnd-eyed, *a.* having eyes that look almond-shaped, or oval with pointed ends; slant-eyed.

äl'mŏnd fūr'nāce, [*almond* is probably a corruption of *Almain*, German.] a kind of furnace used in the refining process, to separate the metal from cinders and other foreign matter.

al'mŏn·dine, *n.* see *almandine*.

äl'mŏnd oil, a bland, fixed oil, obtained from almonds by pressure.

äl'mŏnd pēach, a hybrid between the almond and the peach, cultivated in France.

äl'mŏnd wil'lōw, the *Salix amygdalina*, the leaves of which are light green on both sides.

al'mŏn·ẽr, *n.* [OFr. *aumoniere, almosniere*; L. *eleemosyna*, alms.]

1. a functionary or agent who distributes alms or charity, as for a monastery, a noble's establishment, etc.

2. any one who dispenses charity, benefits, or blessings. [Archaic.]

al'mŏn·ẽr·ship, *n.* the office and duties of an almoner.

al'mŏn·ry, *n.*; *pl.* **al'mŏn·rieṣ,** the place where an almoner resides, or where alms are distributed.

äl'mōse, *n.* alms. [Obs.]

ạl'mōst, *adv.* [AS. *ēalmaēst*.] nearly; well-nigh; for the great part.

almost never; scarcely ever.

almost nothing; scarcely anything at all.

älm′ry, *n.* almonry. [Obs.]

älmṣ (ämz), *n., sing.* and *pl.* [ME. *alms, ælmesse*; AS. *ælmesse*; L. *eleemosyna*, alms; Gr. *eleēmosynē*, pity, compassion; *eleēmōn*, pitiful; *eleos*, pity.]
 1. anything given gratuitously to relieve the poor, as money, food, or clothing.
 2. a deed of mercy. [Obs.]
 tenure by free alms; frankalmoin.

älmṣ chest, a box with a slot, used in English churches to collect alms for the poor.

älmṣ′deed, *n.* an act of charity; a charitable gift.

älmṣ dish, 1. in the Anglican Church, a large plate on which offerings collected in the church are carried to the altar.
 2. a beggar's dish.

älmṣ fee, 1. Peter's pence.
 2. land held in frankalmoin; that is, land held by the church, usually in return for praying for the donor.

älmṣ′fōlk (ämz′fōk), *n.pl.* persons supported by alms. [Obs.]

älmṣ′giv″ẽr, *n.* one who gives to the poor.

älmṣ′giv″ing, *n.* the giving of charity.

älmṣ′house, *n.* a home for people too poor to support themselves; a poorhouse.

älmṣ′măn, *n.*; *pl.* **älmṣ′men,** 1. a man who lives by alms.
 2. one who gives alms. [Obs.]

älmṣ′wom″ăn, *n.*; *pl.* **älmṣ′wom″en,** a woman supported by alms.

al·mū·çan′tăr, *n.* [Sp. *almicantarat*; Ar. *almuqantarāt*; *al*, the, and *muqantarāt*, pl. of *muqantarah*, a sundial.] 1. any of the circles of the sphere parallel to the horizon, concieved of as passing through every degree of the meridian: stars on the same almucantar have the same altitude.
 2. a telescope floating in mercury, used to observe heavenly bodies as they cross a certain almucantar.

al·mū·çan′tăr stàff, an instrument having an arc of fifteen degrees, formerly used to take observations of the sun, about the time of its rising or setting, to find the variation of the compass.

al′mūce, au′mūce, *n.* [Sp. *almuce*; L. *almussa, almucia*.]
 1. a furred hood worn by the clergy in the thirteenth, fourteenth, and fifteenth centuries, when officiating in churches during inclement weather.
 2. a kind of tippet, a medieval garment, with a hood and a fur lining.
 Also written *amice*.

PRIEST WEARING ALMUCE

al·mụde′, *n.* [Port. *almude*; Ar. *al-mudd*, a dry measure.] a variable measure for liquids and grain in Spain, Portugal, Turkey, etc. ranging for liquids from three and one-half to five and one-half English gallons; for grain, from three and one-half to eleven pints.

al′mug, *n.* [Heb.] a tree or wood mentioned in the Bible, believed to have been the sandalwood of the East. I Kings x. 12.

al′nāġe, ạul′nāġe, *n.* [OFr. *aulnage*; Fr. *aunage, aulner*, to measure by the ell; *alne, aune*, ell.] a measuring of cloth by the ell.

al′nā·ġẽr, ạul′nā·ġẽr, *n.* formerly, in England, a sworn officer whose duty was to inspect and measure woolen cloth for duty.

al′ni·cō″, *n.* [*al*uminum, and *ni*ckel, and *co*balt.] an alloy containing aluminum, nickel, cobalt, and iron, used in making magnets.

Al′nus, *n.* [L. *alnus*, alder.] a genus of cupuliferous trees, commonly called alders.

al′od, *n.* alodium.

ȧ·lō′di·ăl, *a.* relating to an alodium; freehold.

ȧ·lō′di·ăl, *n.* any land or property held as a freehold.

ȧ·lō′di·ăl·iṣm, *n.* the alodial system.

ȧ·lō′di·ăl·ist, *n.* one who holds land alodially.

ȧ·lō′di·ăl·ly, *adv.* in alodial tenure.

ȧ·lō′di·ȧ·ry, *n.* an alodialist.

ȧ·lod″i·fi·çā′tion, *n.* the conversion of title from feudal tenure to freehold.

ȧ·lō′di·um, *n.* [ML. *allodium, alodium*, from O.H.G. *alod*, full and free possession, from *all*, all, and *-od*, orig., what fate assigned; hence possessions.] in law, land owned independently, without any rent, payment in service, etc.; a freehold estate: opposed to *feud*.

Al′ō·ē, *n.* [L. *aloe*; Gr. *aloē*, the aloe.] a genus of plants of the lily family, native to the southern part of Africa.

al′ōe, *n.*; *pl.* **al′ōeṣ,** any plant of the genus *Aloe*, as *Aloe socotrina*, one of the species used in medicine.

al′ōeṣ, *n.pl.* [construed as sing.] in medicine, a bitter, laxative drug obtained from the juice of aloe leaves.

al′ōeṣ·wood, *n.* see *agallochum*.

al·ō·et′iç, *a.* 1. pertaining to the aloe or aloes; having the qualities of aloes.

ALOE (*Aloe socotrina*)

 2. consisting chiefly of aloes; having aloes as a principal ingredient; as, an *aloetic* preparation.

al·ō·et′iç, *n.* a medicine containing aloes.

ȧ·lòft′, *adv.* 1. high up; in the air; high above the ground; as, the eagle soars *aloft*.
 2. in nautical language, at the masthead, or on the higher yards or rigging.
 3. on the upper part, as of a building.

ȧ·lòft′, *prep.* on top of; on the upper surface of. [Obs.]

A·lō′gi·ăn, *n.* [L. *Alogiani, alogii*; Gr. *alogos*; *a* priv., and *logos*, word.] in church history, a member of a sect of the second and third centuries, that rejected the Gospel and Revelation of St. John.

al″ō·gō·trō′phi·ȧ, al·ō·got′rō·phy, *n.* [Gr. *alogos*; *a* priv., and *logos*, reason, and *trophē*, nourishment, from *trephein*, to nourish.] a disproportionate nutrition and growth of the parts of the body, especially of the bones.

al′ō·ġy, *n.* [Gr. *a* priv., and *logos*, reason.] irrational behavior; unreasonableness. [Obs.]

ä·lō′hä, *n.* and *interj.* [Hawaiian] love: a word used as a greeting or farewell.

al′ō·in, *n.* a bitter, crystalline cathartic made from the aloe.

al′ō·man·cy, *n.* same as *halomancy*.

ȧ·lōne′, *a.* and *adv.* [*all* and *one*.]
 1. single; solitary; separate from others or from the mass; without the presence or aid of another; by oneself; as, he toiled *alone* and in the dark.
 2. only; exclusively; sole; with no person or thing else; as, he *alone* has the power of pardon.
 3. unequaled in attributes or position; peerless; as, among modern chemists, he stands *alone*.
 to leave alone; (a) to let be by oneself; (b) [Colloq.] not to bother or interfere with.
 to let alone; to leave unaltered or undisturbed; to refrain from interfering with.
 to let well enough alone; to be content with things as they are and not try to improve them.

ȧ·lōne′ly, *a.* and *adv.* only; merely; singly. [Obs.]

ȧ·lōne′ness, *n.* the condition of being alone.

ȧ·lọng′, *adv.* [ME. *along, anlong*; AS. *andlang*, along; *and*, over against, and *lang*, long.]
 1. by the length; lengthwise; in a line with the length; by the side.
 2. onward, in time or space; in a forward line, or with a progressive motion; as, let us walk *along*; the years creep *along* unnoticed.
 3. in connection or company: often used with *with*; as, he took his dog *along*; he carried the odor of sanctity *along with* him.
 all along; all the time; from the very beginning.
 to get along; (a) to go forward; (b) to contrive; (c) to thrive; succeed; (d) to be in harmony; agree; (e) [Colloq.] to go away.

ȧ·lọng′, *prep.* 1. by the length of; by the side of; as, the ship sailed *along* the coast.
 2. throughout the length of; in the line of; in the course of; as, the wagons moved slowly *along* the highway.

ȧ·lọng′, *adv.* on account; because: followed by *of* or *on*; as, all *along of* this change. [Obs. or Dial.]

ȧ·lọng′shōre, *adv.* along the shore; near or beside the shore.

ȧ·lọng′shōre·măn, *n.* see *longshoreman*.

ȧ·lọng′sīde, *adv.* by the side; along the side; side by side; as, their vessel lay *alongside* of the pier.

ȧ·lọng′sīde, *prep.* at the side of; side by side with.

ȧ·lọọf′, *n.* same as *alewife*, the fish. [Obs.]

ȧ·lọọf′, *adv.* [ME. *aloofe*; *a*, on, and *loof*, from D. *loef, luff*, to windward.] at a short distance; apart; aside; by oneself; as, to stand *aloof*.

ȧ·lọọf′, *a.* 1. at a distance; removed.
 2. distant in sympathy, interest, etc.; reserved and cool; as, her manner was *aloof*.

ȧ·lọọf′, *prep.* separate or clear from; as, *aloof* the crowd. [Obs.]

ȧ·lọọf′ness, *n.* the state or quality of keeping aloof.

al·ō·pē′ci·ȧ (-shi-ȧ), *n.* [L. *alopecia*; Gr. *alōpekia*, from *alōpēx*, a fox.] loss of the hair; baldness.

ȧ·lop′e·cist, *n.* one who gives treatment for the alleged prevention or cure of alopecia, or baldness.

al·ō·pē′çoid, *a.* [Gr. *alōpēx*, fox, and *eidos*, like.] foxlike; vulpine.

Al″ō·pē·çū′rus, *n.* [L., from Gr. *alōpēx*, fox, and *oura*, tail.] a genus of grasses, commonly called foxtail grass. The meadow foxtail, *Alopecurus pratensis*, furnishes valuable fodder, but some other species are troublesome as weeds.

ȧ·lọr′ciç, al·ọr·cin′iç, *a.* pertaining to or obtained from aloes.

ȧ·lōse′, *n.* [Fr., from L. *alosa*.] a shad, especially the European shad.

al·ŏu·atte′ (-at′), *n.* [Fr., from native name.] the South American howling monkey.

ȧ·loud′, *adv.* 1. loudly; with a loud voice, or great noise.
 2. audibly; out loud; as, to speak or read *aloud*.

ȧ·lōw′, *adv.* in nautical usage, below: opposed to *aloft*.

ȧ·low′, *adv.* and *a.* on fire. [Dial.]

alp, *n.*; *pl.* **alps,** [L. *alpes*, high mountains; Gael. *alp*; Ir. *ailp*, a high mountain; O.H.G. *Alpen*, the Alps.]
 1. a high mountain, especially in Switzerland.
 2. figuratively, something difficult of attainment or hard to surmount; an obstacle.
 3. in Switzerland, a mountain pasture.

alp, *n.* the common European bullfinch.

al·paç′ȧ, *n.* [Sp. *alpaca, alpaco*, from Ar. *al*, the, and *paco*, the Peruvian name of the animal.]
 1. a ruminant, native to the mountains of Bolivia and Peru, allied to the llama; the *Auchenia pacos*. It is somewhat like a sheep and can be domesticated. Its wool, called also *alpaca*, is very valuable, being long, fine, and dark in color.

ALPACA (*Auchenia pacos*)

 2. any fabric woven from alpaca wool, or made in part of it; also, a thin cloth made of cotton and wool, with a hard, shiny surface.
 3. any garment made of alpaca cloth.

al′pen, *a.* same as *alpine*. [Rare.]

al′pen·glōw, *n.* a reddish-purple glow often seen on mountain tops just before sunrise or after sunset.

al′pen·horn, *n.* [G. *Alpen*, genit. pl. of *Alp*, of the Alps, and *horn*.] a very long, powerful horn, nearly straight, but curving slightly and widening toward its extremity: used by Swiss mountaineers for signaling.

al′pen·stock, *n.* an iron-pointed staff used as an aid in mountain climbing.

al·pes′trine, *a.* [L. *alpestris*, pertaining to mountains, from *alp*, a mountain.]
 1. pertaining to high mountains, as the Alps.
 2. in botany, growing on mountain heights, but below the timber line.

al′phȧ, *n.* [L., from Gr. *alpha*, from Heb. *aleph*, an ox or leader.]
 1. the first letter in the Greek alphabet, corresponding to English A: used to denote first, beginning, or chief; as, Plato, the *alpha* of the wits.
 2. in cataloguing the stars, the symbol of the brightest in the constellation: as α Lyrae, α Tauri, etc.
 alpha particle; a positively charged particle given off by certain radioactive substances: it consists of two protons and two neutrons, and is converted into an atom of helium by the acquisition of two electrons.
 alpha rays; rays of alpha particles: they are less penetrating than beta rays.
 alpha test; an intelligence test originally used by the United States Army in World

War I: it is made up mainly of printed questions meant to examine one's understanding of number and word relations, as well as his general knowledge and judgment.

alpha wave; any of the brain waves given off as during relaxation with the eyes shut or in the absence of sensory stimulation.

al'phȧ and ō-mę'gȧ, 1. the first and last letters of the Greek alphabet.

2. the first and the last; the beginning and the end.

al'phȧ·bet, *n.* [L. *alphabetum*, from Gr. *alpha* and *beta*, the first two letters of the Greek alphabet.]

1. the letters of a language arranged in the customary order.

2. a system of characters which form the elements of a written language.

3. the simplest elements of anything; rudiments; first principles; fundamentals; as, the *alphabet* of science.

4. any series of signs representing letters or syllables; as, the Braille *alphabet*.

alphabet soup; a soup that has small noodles cut in the form of letters of the *alphabet*.

al'phȧ·bet, *v.t.* to arrange in the order of an alphabet; to designate by the letters of the alphabet. [Rare.]

al''phȧ·bet·ā'ri·ăn, *n.* a learner of the alphabet.

al·phȧ·bet'iç·ăl, al·phȧ·bet'iç, *a.* 1. of or pertaining to an alphabet; expressed by an alphabet; as, *alphabetic* languages.

2. in the usual order of the letters of a language; as, an *alphabetical* classification.

al·phȧ·bet'iç·ăl·ly, *adv.* in an alphabetical manner; in the customary order of the letters of a language.

al·phȧ·bet'içs, *n.* the science of the origin, growth, and use of alphabetic letters or symbols to represent spoken sounds.

al'phȧ·bet·işm, *n.* the representation of spoken sounds by alphabetic characters.

al'phȧ·bet·īze, *v.t.*; alphabetized, *pt.*, *pp.*; alphabetizing, *ppr.* 1. to arrange in the order of the letters of an alphabet.

2. to express by or furnish with an alphabet.

al''phȧ·nū·mer'iç, *a* [*alpha*bet and *numeric*al.] having or using both alphabetical and numerical symbols.

Al·phē'ụs, *n.* [L.; Gr. *Alpheios.*] in Greek mythology, a river god who pursued Arethusa until she was changed into a fountain by Artemis.

al·phit'ō·man·cy, *n.* [Gr. *alphiton*, barley, and *mantis*, a diviner, soothsayer; *manteia*, divination.] divination by barley meal.

alp'hǫrn'', *n.* an alpenhorn.

al'phōs, al'phus, *n.* [L. *alphus*, from Gr. *alphos*, white.] a form of psoriasis or leprosy.

al·phō'sis, *n.* [Gr. *alphos*, white, and *-osis.*] abnormal absence of pigment, as in some diseases, albinism, etc.

Al'pīne (*or* -pin), *a.* [L. *alpinus*, from *Alpes*, the Alps.]

1. of or pertaining to the Alps or their inhabitants.

2. [a–] resembling the Alps; very high; elevated; towering.

3. [a–] growing on mountain heights above the timber line; as, *alpine* plants.

4. in ethnology, designating or of one of the three main divisions of the Caucasian, or white, race.

Al'pīne, *n.* a member of the Alpine division of the Caucasian race.

al'pin·ist, Al'pin·ist, *n.* one who climbs the Alps or other high mountains.

al'pist, al'pi·ȧ, *n.* the seed of various kinds of canary grass or foxtail grass, used for feeding birds.

al''qui·fōu' (-ki-), *n.* [Fr. *alquifoux*; Sp. *alquifol*; Ar. *al-koh'l*, a fine powder.] a sort of lead ore (galena), found in Cornwall, England: used by potters to give a green glaze to their wares: called also *potter's ore*.

ạl·read'y (-red'), *adv.* by or before a certain time, past, present, or future; previously; beforehand; by the time specified; even now; as, it had been *already* discovered; the results are *already* apparent.

ạl''rīght', *adv.* all right: a spelling much used but still generally considered a substandard usage.

ạls, *adv.* also. [Obs.]

ạls, *conj.* as. [Obs.]

Al·sā'tiăn (-shăn), *n.* 1. a native or inhabitant of Alsace.

2. a frequenter of Alsatia, formerly a resort of criminals in London.

3. a variety of police dog.

Al·sā'tiăn, *a.* 1. of Alsace, its people, etc.

2. of Whitefriars, a district in London formerly frequented by criminals.

al'sīke *n.* [from *Alsike* in Sweden.] a European forage plant, *Trifolium hybridum*, commonly called Swedish clover: also *alsike clover*.

al''si·nā'ceous, *a.* [L. *alsine*, luxuriant plant, a chickweed, from Gr. *alsinē*; and *-aceous.*] of or like chickweed.

Al·sī'nē, *n.* [L., from Gr. *alsinē*, a kind of plant.] a large genus of herbs of the pink or chickweed family, *Caryophyllaceæ*.

Al Si·rät', [Ar., the road.] in the Moslem religion,

1. the true faith of the Koran.

2. the narrow bridge over hell-fire to Paradise.

ạl'sō, *adv.* [ME. *al so*, *al swo*, *al swa*, from AS. *eal swā*; *eal*, all, and *swa*, so.]

1. likewise; in like manner.

2. as something additional tending the same way or in the same direction; besides; as well; further; too; as, he is *also* an orator.

ạl'sō, *conj.* even as; so; as. [Obs.]

ạl'sō·ran'', *n.* a person defeated in a race, competition, election, etc.: a term borrowed from horse racing. [Colloq.]

Al·stō'ni·ȧ, *n.* [from Dr. *Alston*, a botanist of Edinburgh.] a genus of trees of the dogbane family.

ạl'stŏn·īte, *n.* same as *bromlite*.

alt, *a.* [It. *alto*; L. *altus*, high.] in music, having a high pitch; in the first octave above the treble staff.

alt, *n.* a high tone or note, especially one in the first octave above the treble staff; also, this octave.

äl'tȧ, *a.* [It.] in music, high: feminine of *alto*.

Al·tā'iç, Al·tā'iăn, *a.* 1. of the Altai Mountains or the peoples inhabiting them.

2. of their languages: see *Ural-Altaic*.

Al·tāir', *n.* [Ar. *al tā'ir*, the bird.] a star of the first magnitude in the constellation Aquila.

al·tā'īte, *n.* a mineral, telluride of lead, found first in the Altai Mountains, in central Asia.

ạl'tăr, *n.* [ME. *alter*; L. *altare*, an altar, a high place, from *altus*, high.]

1. a place, especially a raised platform, where sacrifices or offerings are made to an ancestor, a god, etc.

2. a table, stand, etc. used for sacred purposes in a place of worship, as the Communion table in Christian churches.

ANCIENT ALTARS

3. figuratively, a church; a place of worship.

4. in shipbuilding, one of the steps or ledges, the flights of which form the sides of a dry dock.

to lead to the altar; to marry.

ạl·tăr·āge, *n.* 1. the revenue accruing from offerings made at the altar.

2. offerings made upon an altar or to a church.

ạl'tăr boy, a boy or man who helps a priest, vicar, etc. at religious services, especially at Mass.

ạl'tăr çlọth, a cloth to lay upon an altar in churches.

ạl'tăr çush'iŏn (-un), a cushion laid upon the altar in some churches to support the service book.

ạl'tăr fīre, sacrificial fire on an altar; hence, figuratively, religious fervor, or religious service.

ạl'tăr·ist, *n.* a vicar; a chaplain.

ạl'tăr·piēce, *n.* a painting, mosaic, or piece of sculpture placed above and behind the altar in a church; a reredos.

ạl'tăr rāil, a low railing in front of the altar or communion table.

ạl'tăr sçreen, a wall or partition built behind an altar.

ạl'tăr stōne, the stone constituting the surface of an altar.

ạl'tăr thāne, a mass priest. [Obs.]

ạl'tăr tōmb, a raised monument surmounting a tomb, having a general resemblance to an altar: *altar tombs* are often surmounted by a recumbent effigy.

ALTAR TOMB

ạl'tăr·wīse, *adv.* in the usual position of an altar, at the east end of the church, with the front facing the west.

alt·az'i·muth, *n.* [*alt*itude and *azimuth.*] an instrument for simultaneously measuring the altitude and azimuth of a star so as to determine precisely its apparent position.

ạl·tēr, *v.t.*; altered, *pt.*, *pp.*; altering, *ppr.* [ML. *alterare*, to make other, from L. *alter*, other.]

1. to change; make different; modify; as, snow *altered* the landscape; age had *altered* the singer's voice.

2. to castrate. [Dial.]

3. to resew parts of (a garment) for a better fit.

Syn.—change, modify, metamorphose, transform, vary.

ạl·tēr, *v.i.* to become, in some respects, different; to vary; as, the weather *alters* almost daily.

ạl''tēr·ȧ·bil'i·ty, *n.* alterableness.

ạl'tēr·ȧ·ble, *a.* that can be altered.

ạl'tēr·ȧ·ble·ness, *n.* the quality of being alterable; variableness.

ạl'tēr·ȧ·bly, *adv.* in a manner that can be altered, or varied.

ạl'tēr·ănt, *a.* [L. *alteran(t)s*, ppr. of *alterare*, to make other.] altering; causing alteration.

ạl'tēr·ănt, *n.* 1. that which causes change or modification.

2. an alterative medicine. [Obs.]

3. in dyeing, a substance used to change a color.

ạl·tēr·ā'tion, *n.* [L. *alteratio.*]

1. the act of making different.

2. the state of being altered; as, a cold substance suffers an *alteration* when it becomes hot.

ạl'tēr·ā·tive, *a.* causing alteration; specifically, in medicine, having the power to gradually restore the normal functions of the body.

ạl'tēr·ā·tive, *n.* a medicine or treatment which gradually restores to health.

ạl'tēr·çāte, *v.i.*; altercated, *pt.*, *pp.*; altercating, *ppr.* [L. *altercatus*, pp. of *altercari*, to dispute, from *alter*, other.] to contend in words; to dispute with zeal, heat, or anger; to wrangle.

ạl·tēr·çā'tion, *n.* warm contention in words; dispute carried on with heat or anger; controversy; wrangle.

ạl'ter·çā·tive, *a.* wrangling; disputing; scolding. [Obs.]

ạl'tēred çhord, in music, a chord in which one or more tones have been chromatically altered by sharps, flats, or naturals foreign to the key.

al'tēr ē'gō, [L., literally, other I.]

1. another self; another aspect of oneself.

2. a bosom friend; a close companion.

al'tēr ī'dem, [L.] another of the same kind; second self.

al·ter'i·ty, *n.* the state or quality of being different; oppositeness. [Rare.]

al'tērn, *a.* [L. *alternus*, from *alter*, other.]

1. acting by turns; succeeding one another; alternate.

2. in crystallography, exhibiting, on two parts, an upper and a lower part, faces which alternate among themselves in the position of their sides and angles but which, when the two parts are compared, correspond with each other in form.

al·tẽr′nȧ·cy, *n.* performance or action by turns. [Obs.]

al·tẽr′nănt, *a.* [L. *alternans,* ppr. of *alternare,* to alternate.] alternating; having alternate layers.

Al·tẽr·nan′the·rȧ, *n.* [Mod.L., from *alternus,* alternate, and *anthera,* anther.] a genus of dwarf tufted plants having opposite leaves and small tribracteate flowers arranged in heads. Some of the species have richly colored foliage.

al·tẽr·nȧt′ (-nȧ′), *n.* [Fr.] rotation in precedence, as among diplomats of equal rank, in signing treaties and in international conventions.

al′tẽr·nāte, *a.* [L. *alternatus,* pp. of *alternare,* to do by turns.]

1. occurring by turns; following each the other in succession of time or place; hence, reciprocal.

And bid *alternate* passions fall and rise. —Pope.

2. every other, as the odd and even numbers in a numerical list.

3. in botany, (a) growing along the stem singly at various intervals: opposed to *opposite;* (b) placed at intervals between other parts.

ALTERNATE LEAVES

alternate alligation; see *alligation.*

alternate angles; in geometry, two angles at opposite ends and on opposite sides of a line crossing two others. If the two lines are parallel, the alternate angles are equal. Thus, if the parallels *AB, CD,* be cut by the line *EH,* the angles *BFG* and *CGF* are equal alternate angles, as are also the angles *AFG* and *FGD.*

ALTERNATE ANGLES

al′tẽr·nāte, *n.* 1. that which happens by turns with something else; vicissitude. [Rare.]

2. a regularly appointed substitute for a delegate or appointee; as, he attended the national convention as an *alternate.*

3. an alternative. [Obs.]

4. in linguistics, an allomorph.

al′tẽr·nāte, *v.t.;* alternated, *pt., pp.;* alternating, *ppr.* to perform by turns, or in succession; to cause to succeed by turns; to change (one thing for another) reciprocally; as, congress *alternated* a high tariff with a low one.

al′tẽr·nāte, *v.i.* 1. to follow one another in time, place, or condition, reciprocally: often followed by *with;* as, the flood and ebb tides *alternate with* each other.

2. to take turns.

3. to exchange places, etc. regularly.

4. in electricity, (a) to reverse direction regularly and continually, as a current; (b) to make, or be operated by, such a current.

al′tẽr·nāte·ly, *adv.* in an alternate manner: (a) in reciprocal succession; by turns; in the same way as night follows day and day follows night; (b) with the omission or intervention of one between each pair; as, read the lines *alternately.*

al′tẽr·nāte·ness, *n.* the quality of being alternate, or of following in succession.

al·tẽr·nā′tion, *n.* [L. *alternatio,* ppr. of *alternare,* to do by turns.]

1. the reciprocal succession of things, in time or place; the act of following and being followed in succession.

2. in mathematics, same as *permutation.* [Rare.]

3. in church ritual, the response of the congregation speaking alternately with the minister.

al″tẽr·nā′tion of gen·ẽr·ā′tions, the occurrence of generations in alternate order, first one that reproduces sexually, then one that reproduces asexually, and so on.

al·tẽr′nā·tive, *a.* [Fr. *alternatif;* ML. *alternativus.*]

1. providing or necessitating a choice between two (or, loosely, more than two) things.

2. something remaining to be chosen; as, is there an *alternative* to going?

al·tẽr′nā·tive, *n.* 1. that which may be chosen or omitted as one of two things, so that if one is taken, the other must be left. Thus, when two things offer a choice of one only, the two things are called *alternatives.* When one thing only is offered it is said there is no *alternative.*

2. the choice between two things.

3. by extension, a choice between a number; as, one of numerous *alternatives;* hence, any one of the things to be chosen.

al·tẽr′nā·tive ço̤n·junç′tion, a conjunction joining elements, which, it implies, are not to be taken together, as *or, neither . . . nor,* etc.

al·tẽr′nā·tive·ly, *adv.* 1. in an alternative manner; with a choice.

2. as an alternative; on the other hand.

al·tẽr′nā·tive·ness, *n.* the quality or state of being alternative.

al′tẽr·nā″tŏr, *n.* an electric generator or dynamo producing alternating current.

Al·thae′ȧ, *n.* [L., from Gr. *althaia,* wild mallow.]

1. a genus of the mallow family, including the common garden hollyhock, *Althæa rosea,* and the common marsh mallow, *Althæa officinalis.*

2. [a–] the flowering shrub *Hibiscus syriacus:* called also *rose of Sharon* and *shrubby althaea.*

Al′thing (-ting), *n.* [Ice. *allr,* all, and *thing,* office, court.] the parliament of Iceland.

Al′thing·măn, *n.* a member of the Icelandic parliament.

alt′ho̤rn, *n.* a brass-wind instrument used extensively in military bands, often in place of the French horn. It is of the saxhorn class.

ALTHORN

al·thōugh′ (thō′), *conj.* [*all,* and *though.*] in spite of the fact that; granting that; though: now sometimes spelled *altho.*

al′ti·grȧph″, *n.* [*alti-,* from L. *altus,* high, and *-graph.*] an altimeter for recording automatically on a chart the altitude or height above the ground.

al·til′ō·quence (-kwens), *n.* [L. *altus,* high, and *loqui, loquens,* speaking.] lofty speech; pompous language.

al·til′ō·quent, *a.* high-sounding. [Obs.]

al·tim′e·tẽr, *n.* [L. *altus,* high, and *metrum;* Gr. *metron,* measure.] an instrument for taking altitudes, as a quadrant, sextant, theodolite, or, in aeronautics, an aneroid barometer with a dial marked in feet or meters.

al·tim′e·try, *n.* the art of measuring altitudes by means of an altimeter.

al·tin′çär, *n.* see *tincal.*

al′ti·sçōpe, *n.* [L. *altus,* high, and Gr. *skopein,* to look at.] an instrument consisting of mirrors and lenses arranged in a telescopic tube, so designed as to permit a view around an obstacle; a kind of periscope.

al·tis′ō·nănt, al·tis′ō·nous, *a.* [L. *altus,* high, and *sonans,* ppr. of *sonare,* to sound.] high-sounding; lofty or pompous, as language.

al·tis′si·mō, *a.* [It., superl. of *alto,* high.] in music, in the second octave above the treble staff.

al′ti·tūde, *n.* [L. *altitudo,* from *altus,* high.]

1. the elevation of an object above a certain level, especially above the earth's surface or sea level.

2. a high place or region.

3. in astronomy, the angular height of a planet, star, etc. above the horizon, measured by the arc of a vertical circle intercepted between such object and the horizon. It is either *apparent* or *true. Apparent altitude* is that which appears by observations made at any place on the surface of the earth; *true altitude,* that which results by correcting the apparent for refraction, parallax, and dip of the horizon.

4. in geometry, the perpendicular distance from the base of a figure to its highest point or to the side parallel to the base.

5. a high degree of authority, rank, etc.

6. elevation of spirits; haughty air: in this sense generally used in the plural. [Colloq.]

The man of law began to get into his *altitudes.* —Scott.

meridian altitude; an arc of the meridian between the horizon and any star or point on the meridian.

al·ti·tū′di·năl, *a.* of, relating, or pertaining to altitude.

al″ti·tū·di·nā′ri·ăn, *a.* aspiring to great heights.

al·tiv′ō·lănt, *a.* [L. *altus,* high, and *volans,* flying.] flying high. [Obs.]

al′tō (*or* äl′tō), *n.;* *pl.* **al′tōṣ,** [It., from L. *altus,* high.]

1. the range of the lowest female voice (contralto) or the highest male voice.

2. a voice or singer with such a range.

3. an instrument having a similar range, as an althorn.

4. a part for such a voice or instrument.

al′tō, *a.* 1. singing or playing within the range of an alto.

2. for this range.

al′tō çlef, *n.* the C clef, placed on the third line of the staff.

al′tō-çū′mū·lus, *n.* [*alto-,* from L. *altus,* high; and *cumulus.*] a formation of high, fleecy clouds in round, white or grayish, partly shaded masses.

al·tō·geth′ẽr, *adv.* [ME. *altogedere.*]

1. wholly; entirely; completely; without exception; as, *altogether* foolish ideas.

2. everything being considered; on the whole.

Distinguished from *all together.*

al·tō·geth′ẽr, *n.* the entire effect; the whole taken together.

in the altogether; nude. [Colloq.]

al′tō ho̤rn, an althorn.

al·tom′e·tẽr, *n.* [L. *altus,* high, and *metrum;* Gr. *metron,* measure.] an altimeter.

al″tō-ri·liē′vō, *n.* [It. *alto,* high, and *rilievo,* relief.] sculpture in which the figures project from a background by half their thickness or more; high relief.

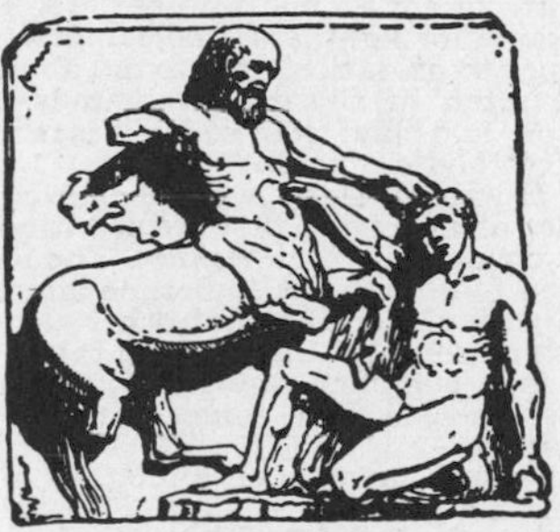

ALTO-RELIEVO

äl′to̤-ri·liḙ′vo̤, [It.] alto-relievo.

al′tō-strā′tus, *n.* [*alto-,* from L. *altus,* high; and *stratus.*] a formation of gray or bluish sheetlike clouds, like the cirro-stratus but lower and heavier.

al·tri′ciăl (-trish′ăl), *a.* of, pertaining to, or having the characteristics of the Altrices.

Al·trī′cēṣ, *n.pl.* [L., pl. of *altrix,* nurse.] a division of birds characterized by young which remain in the nest for a comparatively long time.

al′trụ·iṣm, *n.* [Fr. *altruisme,* from It. *altrui,* of or to others, from L. *alter,* another. A term first employed by the Positivists, or followers of the French philosopher Comte.] unselfish concern for the welfare of others: opposed to *egoism.*

al′trụ·ist, *n.* an exponent of altruism.

al·trụ·is′tiç, *a.* of or exhibiting altruism; unselfish.

al·trụ·is′tiç·ăl·ly, *adv.* in an altruistic manner; unselfishly.

al′ū·del, *n.* [Sp. *aludel,* from Ar. *al-uthāl,* for *ithāl,* pl. of *athla,* utensil.] one of a series of pear-shaped vessels, generally of earthenware, with open ends which fit into each other, making a continuous tube used as a condenser in sublimation.

al′ū·lȧ, *n.;* *pl.* **al′ū·lae,** [dim. of L. *ala,* a wing.]

1. the bastard wing of a bird.

2. a membranelike flap having a basilar attachment, on the wings of certain flies; also, a like structure similarly placed on certain beetles.

al′ū·lär, *a.* pertaining to the alula.

al′ū·let, *n.* same as *alula,* 2.

al′um, *n.* [L. *alumen,* alum.]

1. a double sulfate of ammonium or a univalent metal (as sodium or potassium) and of a trivalent metal (as aluminum, iron, or chromium): it is used as an astringent, as an emetic, and in the manufacture of baking powders, dyes, and paper. The commonest form is potash alum (potassium aluminum sulfate), $KAl(SO_4)_2 \cdot 12H_2O$.

2. aluminum sulfate: in this sense an erroneous usage.

al′um, *v.t.* to subject to the action of alum.

ȧ·lū′mi·nȧ, *n.* [L., from *alumen*, alum.] an oxide of aluminum, Al_2O_3, present in bauxite and clay and found as different forms of corundum, including emery, sapphires, rubies, etc.

ȧ·lū′mi·nāte, *v.t.*; aluminated, *pt.*, *pp.*; aluminating, *ppr.* [L. *alumen*, alum; *-ate*.] to treat with alum or alumina; to wash with alum water.

ȧ·lū′mi·nāte, *n.* a compound formed by replacing the hydrogen in the trihydrate of aluminum by a metal.

al·ū·min′iç, *a.* of, pertaining to, or containing, aluminum.

ȧ·lū″mi·nif′ẽr·ous, *a.* [L. *alumen*, alum, and *-ferous*, from *ferre*, to bear.] yielding or containing alum or aluminum.

ȧ·lū·min′i·fọrm, *a.* having the form of an alum.

ȧ·lū′mi·nīte, *n.* a hydrous aluminum sulfate occurring in small, white, roundish or reniform masses.

al·ū·min′i·um, *n.* see *aluminum*.

ȧ·lū′mi·nīze, *v.t.*; aluminized, *pt.*, *pp.*; aluminizing, *ppr.* to treat or impregnate with aluminum.

ȧ·lū′mi·nō·thẽr″my, *n.* [from *aluminum*, and Gr. *thermē*, heat.] a metallurgical process in which aluminum reduces another metal from its compounds, simultaneously releasing great heat.

ȧ·lū′mi·nous, *a.* pertaining to or containing alum, alumina, or aluminum.

ȧ·lū′mi·num, *n.* [L. *alumen*, alum.] a silvery metallic chemical element: symbol, Al; atomic weight, 26.97; atomic number, 13. It is remarkable for lightness, malleability, and resistance to oxidation. It is found abundantly, most often in silicate compounds such as feldspar and clay, from which it is reduced by an electrolytic process.

Sir Humphry Davy, who recognized the existence of the metal, first termed it *alumium*, later changed it to *aluminum*. The form was altered to *aluminium* sometime later to conform with the spellings of other elements in the same series of the periodic table. *Aluminum* is in popular usage today, although the British people and some scientists prefer *aluminium*.

ȧ·lū′mi·num, *a.* of, containing, or made of aluminum.

ȧ·lū′mi·num hȳ·drox′īde, a soluble compound, $Al(OH)_3$, obtained by treating the solution of an aluminum salt with an alkali, and used as a mordant in dyeing.

ȧ·lū′mi·num ox′īde, alumina.

al′um·ish, *a.* having the nature of alum; somewhat resembling alum.

ȧ·lum′nȧ, *n.*; *pl.* **ȧ·lum′nae,** [L., fem. of *alumnus*.] a girl or woman who has attended or been graduated from a specified or implied school, college, or university.

ȧ·lum′nus, *n.*; *pl.* **ȧ·lum′nī,** [L., from *alere*, to nourish.] a boy or man who has attended or been graduated from a specified or implied school, college, or university.

al′um·rọọt, *n.* any of several plants of the saxifrage family, genus *Heuchera*, having tiny, bell-shaped flowers and an astringent root.

al′um sçhist, al′um shāle, a fissile rock of varying colors, often glossy, composed chiefly of iron pyrites and aluminum silicate, and the source of the greater part of the alum of commerce.

al′um stōne, alunite.

al′ū·nīte, *n.* [Fr., from *alun*; L. *alumen*, alum.] a mineral containing hydrated potassium aluminum sulfate.

ȧ·lū′nō·ġen, *n.* [Fr. *alun*, alum, and *-gen*, Gr. *-genēs*, producing.] the native hydrous aluminum sulfate common in clays.

ȧ·lū′tȧ, *n.* [L.] a pliable, alum-dressed leather.

al·ū·tā′ceous, *a.* leatherlike in quality or color.

al′vē·ā·ry, *n.*; *pl.* **al′vē·ā·rieṣ,** [L. *alvearium*, a beehive, bulging vessel; *alveus*, a hollow vessel.]

1. a beehive; hence, anything like a beehive.
2. the hollow of the external ear, where the wax is contained.

al′vē·ā·ted, *a.* formed like a conical beehive.

al·vē″ō·lā′bi·ăl, *a.* [*alveolo-* and L. *labia*, lip.] relating to the lips and alveoli.

al·vē′ō·lăr, al·vē′ō·lā·ry, *a.* [L. *alveolus*, a small hollow or cavity, dim. of *alveus*, a hollow vessel.]

1. of or like an alveolus or alveoli; socketlike.
2. in anatomy, (a) relating to the part of the jaws containing the sockets of the teeth; (b) relating to the air pockets in the lungs.
3. in phonetics, formed, as English *t*, *d*, *s*, by touching or approaching the upper alveoli with the tongue.

alveolar processes; the processes of the maxillary bones containing the sockets of the teeth.

al·vē′ō·lăr, *n.* in phonetics, a sound articulated by the tongue on or near the upper alveoli; teethridge sound.

al·vē′ō·lāte, *a.* deeply pitted, so as to resemble a honeycomb; full of many small cavities.

al·vē′ō·lāt·ed, *a.* alveolate.

al′vē·ōle, *n.* same as *alveolus*.

al·vē′ō·li·fọrm, *a.* having the form of an alveolus.

al·vē′ō·lō-, [L. *alveolus*, a socket.] a combining form denoting connection with, or relation to, an alveolus or alveolar process.

al·vē″ō·lō·den′tăl, *a.* [*alveolo-* and L. *dens*, *dentis*, tooth.] relating to the tooth sockets.

al·vē″ō·lō·lin′guăl (-gwăl), *a.* [*alveolo-*, and L. *lingua*, tongue.] relating to the alveolar processes and the tongue.

al·vē′ō·lus, *n.*; *pl.* **al·vē′ō·lī,** [L., dim. of *alveus*.]

1. a small cell, cavity, or hollow in a surface.
2. in anatomy and zoology, a small cavity or hollow, as a cell of a honeycomb, air cell of a lung, tooth socket, etc.
3. [*usually pl.*] in phonetics, the ridge of the gums above and behind the upper front teeth; teethridge.

al′vē·us, *n.*; *pl.* **al′vē·ī,** [L.]

1. the channel or bed of a river.
2. in anatomy, a tube or canal through which some fluid flows, as the thoracic duct.

al′vine, *a.* [Fr. *alvin*, from L. *alvus*, the belly.] pertaining to the abdomen or intestines; as, *alvine* discharges.

ạl′wāy, *adv.* [ME. *alway*, *alle wey*; AS. *ealne weg*; *ealne*, acc. of *eal*, all, and *weg*, acc. of *weg*, way; all the way.] always. [Archaic or Poetic.]

ạl′wāyṣ, *adv.* [ME. *alwayes*, the genit. sing. with an adverbial *s* added.]

1. perpetually; throughout all time; as, the sun has *always* held the earth in its orbit.
2. continually; all the time; as, to do *always* the things that please.
3. at all times; on all occasions; invariably: opposed to *sometimes*; as, he is *always* kind to strangers.

Syn.—ever, constantly, continually, permanently, perpetually.

ȧ·lys′sŏn, *n.* any plant of the genus *Alyssum*. [Obs.]

Ȧ·lys′sum, *n.* [L., from Gr. *alysson*, neut. of *alyssos*, a cure for canine madness; *a* priv., and *lyssa*, madness.]

1. an extensive genus of cruciferous plants, bearing grayish leaves and white or yellow flowers.
2. [a–] any plant of this genus.
3. [a–] a dwarf plant with small spikes of flowers, usually white; sweet alyssum.

am, [AS. *am*, *eom*.] the first pers. sing. of the verb *to be*, in the indicative mood, present tense.

I *am* that I *am*. —Ex. iii. 14.

Am, in chemistry, americium.

ā′mȧ, *n.* [L. *ama*, *hama*; Gr. *hamē*, a water-bucket.] in the early Christian church, a vessel for mixing and storing wine for the Eucharistic service. The wine was poured from the *ama* into smaller vessels when it was required for the service. Now called *cruet*.

AMAS

am·ȧ·bil′i·ty, *n.* [Fr. *amabilité*; L. *amabilitas*, lovableness.] lovableness.

am′ȧ·dȧ·vat′, *n.* [E. Ind.] a singing cage bird of India, often also kept for fighting: also called *strawberry finch* and *red waxbill*.

Am′ȧ·dis, *n.* [Sp., lit., love of God.] a faithful lover: from Amadis of Gaul, hero of several medieval romances in Spanish, French, and English literature.

am′ȧ·dōu″, *n.* [Fr.; Pr., perhaps from Port. *amador*; L. *amator*, lover.] a spongy material made from certain fungi and used as punk for lighting fires or as a styptic.

ä′măh, *n.* [Anglo-Ind., from Port. *ama*.] in the Orient, a woman servant or nurse, especially one who nurses or takes care of babies; a wet nurse.

ȧ·māin′, *adv.* 1. with force, strength, or vigor; violently; furiously.

2. suddenly; at once.
3. at or with great speed.

[Archaic or Poetic in all senses.]

Am′ȧ·lek·īte, *n.* [from Heb. *'amālēqī*, an ancient Bedouin tribe said to be descended from Amalek, grandson of Esau; and *-ite*.]

1. a member of a Syrian Bedouin tribe.
2. in the Bible, a member of a tribe descended from Esau: Gen. xxvi. 12–16.

ȧ·mal′găm, *n.* [Fr. *amalgame*; ML. *almagama*; prob. from Ar. *al malgham*; Gr. *malagma*, a poultice, an emollient, from *malassein*, to soften.]

1. any metallic alloy of which mercury forms an essential constituent part: silver amalgam is used as a dental filling.
2. a native compound of mercury and silver found in fine crystals in mines.
3. a mixture of different things; combination; blend.

ȧ·mal′găm, *v.t.* and *v.i.* 1. to amalgamate. [Archaic.]

2. to coat with amalgam.

ȧ·mal′gȧ·mȧ, *n.* amalgam. [Obs.]

ȧ·mal′găm·ȧ·ble, *a.* that can be amalgamated.

ȧ·mal′gȧ·māte, *v.t.* and *v.i.*; amalgamated, *pt.*, *pp.*; amalgamating, *ppr.* 1. to combine in an amalgam; to alloy with mercury.

2. to mix; to blend; to unite; to combine; to consolidate.

ȧ·mal′gȧ·māte, ȧ·mal′gȧ·mā·ted, *a.* 1. alloyed with mercury.

2. blended; coalesced; combined; united.

ȧ·mal·gȧ·mā′tion, *n.* 1. an amalgamating or being amalgamated.

2. the result of amalgamating; mixture; blend; combination.
3. the union or combination of two or more companies or organizations into one.

ȧ·mal′gȧ·mā·tive, *a.* tending to amalgamate.

ȧ·mal′gȧ·mā·tŏr, *n.* one who or that which amalgamates; specifically, an apparatus used in mining for extracting silver from pulverized ore by amalgamating it with mercury.

ȧ·mal′gȧ·mīze, *v.t.* amalgamate. [Rare.]

Am·ăl·thaē′ȧ, Am·ăl·thē′ȧ, *n.* [L.; Gr. *Amaltheia*.] in Greek and Roman mythology, the goat that nursed Zeus (Jupiter): one of its horns was called the *cornucopia*, or *horn of plenty*, because it would become full of whatever its owner wanted.

ȧ·mȧnd′, *n.* [L. *amandare*.] to send away. [Obs.]

am′ăn·din, *n.* [Fr. *amande*, almond.]

1. the albumin of sweet almonds.
2. a kind of paste or cold cream for chapped hands, containing almond extract.

Am·ȧ·nī′tȧ, *n.* [L.] 1. a genus of *Agaricus*, containing the poisonous mushrooms, as the fly agaric.

2. [a–] any fungus belonging to this genus.

ȧ·man′i·tin, ȧ·man′i·tine, *n.* [Gr. *amanitai*, pl., a sort of fungi.] an organic base, the poisonous principle of certain mushrooms, as *Agaricus muscarius*, *Agaricus bulbosa*, etc.

ȧ·man·ū·en′sis, *n.*; *pl.* **ȧ·man·ū·en′sēṣ,** [L. *amanuensis*; *a*, *ab*, from, and *manu*, abl. of *manus*, hand, and *–ensis*, relating to.] one whose employment is to write what another dictates, or to copy what another has written; secretary.

ȧ·mar′ȧ·çus, *n.* [L.] an aromatic plant of the Mediterranean region; dittany.

am′ȧ·rȧnt, *n.* amaranth.

am′ȧ·ranth, *n.* [L. *amarantus*; Gr. *amarantos*, unfading; *a* priv., and *marainein*, to fade.]

1. a plant of the genus *Amaranthus*, usually with colorful leaves and, in some instances, showy, tassellike heads of flowers, as the love-lies-bleeding, pigweed, tumbleweed, etc.
2. an imaginary flower that never fades. [Poetic.]
3. a dark purple; purplish red.

Am″ȧ·ran·thā′cē·ae, Am″ȧ·ran·tā′cē·ae, *n.* *pl.* a family of plants, including the amaranths.

am″ȧ·ran·thā′ceous, am″ȧ·ran·tā′ceous, *a.* of or pertaining to the *Amaranthaceæ*.

am·ȧ·ran′thad, am·ȧ·ran′tad, *n.* any plant related to the amaranth family.

am·ȧ·ran′thine, *a.* 1. of or like the amaranth.

2. never-fading, like the amaranth of the poets; imperishable.
3. deep-purple; purplish-red.

Am·ȧ·ran′thus, Am·ȧ·ran′tus, *n.* [L.] a

genus of plants of which the amaranths are typical.

ȧ·mär·gō′sō, *n.* [Sp., bitter.] the bark of the goatbush, *Castela erecta*, a shrub of southern Texas and northern Mexico. It is very bitter.

am′ȧ·rine, am′ȧ·rin, *n.* [L. *amarus*, bitter.] a poisonous, acrid, crystalline substance obtained by treating the oil of bitter almonds with ammonia.

ȧ·mar′i·tūde, *n.* [L. *amaritudo*, from *amarus*, bitter.] bitterness. [Obs.]

Am″ȧ·ryl″li·dā′cē·ae, *n.pl.* [L. *Amaryllis* (*id*), and *-aceæ*.] in botany, an order of plants, the amaryllis family, closely allied to the *Liliaceæ*, and comprising several hundred species, including the snowdrop, narcissus, daffodil, etc.

am″ȧ·ryl″li·dā′ceous, am″ȧ·ryl·lid′ē·ous, *a.* of or pertaining to the *Amaryllidaceæ*.

Am·ȧ·ryl′lis, *n.* [Gr., a shepherdess' name in Virgil and Theocritus.]
1. a large genus of plants, the type genus of *Amaryllidaceæ*.
2. [a–] any plant of this genus.
3. in pastoral poetry, a shepherdess: a conventional name.

ȧ·mȧss′, *v.t.*; amassed, *pt.*, *pp.*; amassing, *ppr.* [Fr. *amasser*; L. *amassare*; *ad*, to, and *massa*, heap, mass.]
1. to collect into a heap; to gather a great quantity of; to pile up.
2. to collect together; accumulate, especially for oneself; as, he *amassed* a fortune.
Syn.—accumulate, aggregate, heap together, hoard, lay up.

ȧ·mȧss′ȧ·ble, *a.* capable of being amassed.

ȧ·mȧss′ẽr, *n.* one who amasses.

ȧ·mas·sette′ (-set′), *n.* [Fr.] a kind of spatula used by painters in scraping pigments together before grinding them.

ȧ·mȧss′ment, *n.* the act or result of amassing.

am·as·then′iç, *a.* [Gr. *hama*, together, and *sthenos*, strength.] in optics, uniting the actinic rays of light into one focus.

ȧ·mas′ti·ȧ, *n.* [L., from Gr. *amastos*; *a* priv., and *mastos*, breast.] in anatomy, congenital absence of the mammae, or breasts.

ȧ·māte′, *v.t.* [OFr. *amatir*, to subdue.] to terrify; to dishearten. [Obs.]

ȧ·māte′, *v.t.* to be a mate to. [Obs.]

am′ȧ·teūr (-chụr *or* -tụr *or* -tyụr), *n.* [Fr., from L. *amator*, a lover, from *amare*, to love.]
1. one who cultivates any study or art, from taste or attachment, without pursuing it professionally.
2. in modern athletic sports, an athlete who has never used any athletic art professionally or as a means of livelihood; one who has not taken part in contests open to professionals. The term is variously and more specifically defined by different athletic associations.
3. a person who does something more or less unskillfully.

am·ȧ·teūr′ish, *a.* characteristic of an amateur; inexpert; unskillful.

am·ȧ·teūr′ish·ly, *adv.* in an amateurish manner; crudely; unskillfully.

am·ȧ·teūr′ish·ness, *n.* the quality of being amateurish.

am′ȧ·teūr·işm, *n.* 1. state of being an amateur.
2. an amateurish method or quality.

Ä·mä′ti, *n.* a violin made by Nicolo Amati (1596–1684) or his family, in Cremona, Italy.

am·ȧ·tī′tō, *n.* [It. *amatita*, lead or chalk for pencils; L. *hæmatites*, hematite.] a red pigment derived from hematite.

am′ȧ·tive, *a.* [L. *amatus*, pp. of *amare*, to love.] amorous.

am′ȧ·tive·ness, *n.* in phrenology, a faculty which is supposed to influence sexual desire.

am′ȧ·tol″, *n.* [from *ammonium*, and *toluene*.] a powerful explosive containing ammonium nitrate and trinitrotoluene (TNT).

am·ȧ·tō′ri·ăl, *a.* [L. *amatorius*, from *amare*, to love.]
1. relating to love; as, *amatorial* verses.
2. designating the oblique muscles of the eye: so called humorously from their use in ogling.

am·ȧ·tō′ri·ăl·ly, *adv.* in an amatorial manner; by way of love.

ä·mä·tō′ri·ō, *n.* [It.] a love gift; specifically, a gift bearing the portrait of a lady and a complimentary inscription.

am·ȧ·tō′ri·ous, *a.* amatory. [Obs.]

am′ȧ·tō·ry, *a.* pertaining to, expressing, or causing love, especially sexual love.

am·ạu·rō′sis, *n.* [Gr. *amaurosis*, from *amauros*, dark, dim.] partial or total blindness without visible organic change, caused by disease of the optic nerve.

am·ạu·rot′iç, *a.* pertaining to or having the characteristics of amaurosis.

ȧ·mau′site, *n.* felsite or petrosilex.

ȧ·māze′, *v.t.*; amazed, *pt.*, *pp.*; amazing, *ppr.* [ME. *amasen*; *a* and *masen*, to confuse, perplex.]
1. to confound with great surprise or sudden wonder; to astound, perplex, or astonish; to awe; as, he *amazes* people by his boldness.
2. to puzzle; to daze; to bewilder. [Obs.]
Syn.—astonish, astound, bewilder, dumbfound, surprise, perplex, confound.

ȧ·māze′, *v.i.* to be astounded or bewildered. [Archaic.]

ȧ·māze′, *n.* amazement. [Poetic.]

ȧ·māz′ed·ly, *adv.* with amazement; in an amazed manner.

ȧ·māz′ed·ness, *n.* the state of being amazed.

ȧ·māze′fụl, *a.* full of or tending to cause amazement. [Obs.]

ȧ·māze′ment, *n.* 1. an amazed condition; great surprise or wonder; astonishment.
2. frenzy; madness. [Obs.]
3. bewilderment. [Obs.]
Syn.—wonder, admiration, astonishment, surprise, confusion, perturbation, awe.

Am·ȧ·zil′i·ȧ, *n.* [Mod. L., from *amazili*, a word of probable South American origin.] a genus of hummingbirds, native to Mexico and Central and South America. Their coloring is mostly green and chestnut.

ȧ·māz′ing, *a.* causing amazement; wonderful; astonishing; almost unbelievable.
Syn.—wonderful, marvelous, astonishing, surprising, incredible.

ȧ·māz′ing·ly, *adv.* in an amazing manner or to an amazing degree.

Am′ȧ·zŏn, *n.* [L., from Gr. *Amazōn*; *a* priv., and *mazos*, breast. Derived by Greek folk etym. from the legend that the Amazons cut off the right breast to facilitate the use of the bow and javelin.]
1. in Greek mythology, a female warrior of a race supposed to have lived in Scythia, near the Black Sea.
2. [a–] a woman or girl soldier.
3. [a–] a large, strong, masculine woman; a virago.

AMAZONS

4. a South American parrot of the genus *Chrysotis*.
5. any of various South American hummingbirds.
6. an Amazon ant.

Am′ȧ·zŏn ȧnt, a species of red ant, found in Europe and North America. It robs the nests of other ants, capturing the young in the larval or nymph state, and making slaves of them.

Am·ȧ·zō′ni·ăn, *a.* 1. pertaining to or resembling an Amazon; hence, of masculine manners; warlike: applied to females.
2. belonging to the River Amazon in South America, or to the country around it.

am′ȧ·zŏn·īte, *n.* Amazon stone.

Am′ȧ·zŏn stōne, a bright green variety of microlite, used as a gem, found on the banks of the Amazon River and elsewhere.

am′bāġe, *n.* [Fr. *ambages*, from L. *amb*, around, and *agere*, to drive.]
1. a winding pathway.
2. [*usually pl.*] a roundabout, indirect way of talking or doing things.

am·baġ′i·nous, *a.* ambagious. [Rare.]

am·bā′ġious (-jus), *a.* [L. *ambagiosus*.] characterized by circuitous methods; using ambages; roundabout; devious.

am·baġ′i·tō·ry, *a.* ambagious. [Rare.]

am′bȧ·ri, *n.* [Hind.] a covered seat on the back of an elephant or camel; a howdah.

Am·bär·vā′li·ȧ, *n.pl.* [L.] an ancient Roman festival in which sacrifices were offered to Ceres as an invocation for fertile fields. The sacrificial animals were first led about the fields.

am·bä′ry, am·bä′rï, *n.* [native name.]
1. an East Indian fiber plant, *Hibiscus cannabinus*; brown Indian hemp.
2. its tough fiber, used in making rope.

am′bash, *n.* [prob. native name.] in botany, a leguminous African shrub, *Herminiera elaphroxylon*, valued for its light white wood: called also the *pith tree of the Nile*.

am′băs·sāde, em′băs·sāde, *n.* the mission or functions of an ambassador; an embassy. [Obs.]

am·bas′sȧ·dŏr, em·bas′sȧ·dŏr, *n.* [Fr. *ambassadeur*; transmitted from Celt. via L. (Gaul.) *ambactus*, helper, henchman, and Goth. *andbahts*, servant.]
1. the highest diplomatic representative that one sovereign power or state sends officially to another.
2. a special representative: an *ambassador-at-large* is one accredited to no particular country; an *ambassador extraordinary* is one on a special diplomatic mission; an *ambassador plenipotentiary* is one having the power to make treaties.
3. an official herald, messenger, or agent with a special mission.

am·bas·sȧ·dō′ri·ăl, *a.* pertaining or belonging to an ambassador or embassy.

am·bas′sȧ·dŏr·ship, *n.* the office, term of office, dignity, or functions of an ambassador.

am·bas′sȧ·dress, *n.* 1. a female ambassador.
2. the wife of an ambassador.

am′bē, *n.* [Gr. *ambē*, ridge.] an obsolete surgical instrument for reducing dislocated shoulders.

am′bẽr, *n.* [Fr. *ambre*; from Ar. *'anbar*, ambergris.]
1. a yellow or brownish-yellow translucent fossil resin found in alluvial soils and on some seashores, and used in jewelry, pipestems, etc. It is hard, easily polished, and quickly electrified by friction.
2. the color of amber.
3. liquidambar, a balsam.
4. ambergris: the original meaning. [Obs.]
black amber; jet.
white amber; spermaceti. [Obs.]

am′bẽr, *a.* 1. consisting of, made of, or resembling amber; as, *amber* bracelets.
2. having the color of amber.

am′bẽr, *v.t.*; ambered, *pt.*, *pp.*; ambering, *ppr.*
1. to scent or flavor with ambergris.
2. to encase or preserve in amber; as, an *ambered* fly.
3. to give an amber or yellowish color to.

am′bẽr·fish, *n.* one of several brilliantly colored fishes, genus *Seriola*, found in tropical waters. Some are valued as food.

am′bẽr·grēase, *n.* ambergris. [Rare.]

am′bẽr·gris, *n.* [Fr. *ambre gris*; *ambre*, amber, and *gris*, from OS. *gris*, gray.] a grayish waxy substance that is a morbid secretion in the intestines of the sperm whale and is usually found floating on the surface of the ocean in regions frequented by whales, sometimes in masses of from 60 to 225 lbs. in weight. It is highly valued in making perfumes.

am′bẽr jack, an amberfish, *Seriola lalandi*.

am′bẽr·oid, *n.* a material made to resemble amber, formed of small pieces of amber or some other resin pressed together: also *ambroid*.

am′bẽr seed, musk seed, a seed somewhat resembling millet. It has a bitterish taste, and is found in Egypt and the West Indies.

am′bẽr tree, a shrub of the genus *Anthospermum*, with evergreen leaves, which, when bruised, emit a fragrant odor.

am′bi-, [from L. *ambo*, both.] a combining form meaning *both*, as in *ambi*dextrous.

am·bi·dex′tẽr, *n.* [*ambi-*, and L. *dexter*, the right hand.]
1. a person who uses both hands with equal facility.
2. a double-dealer; one equally ready to act on either side in disputes.
3. in law, a person who takes money or bribes from both sides.

am·bi·dex′tẽr, *a.* 1. able to use both hands with equal ease.
2. on both sides of a dispute at the same time; deceitful.

am″bi·dex·ter′i·ty, *n.* the state or quality of being ambidextrous.

am·bi·dex′trăl, *a.* belonging to both sides, as a noun modified by adjectives directly before and after it.

am·bi·dex′trous, *a.* 1. having the faculty of

using both hands with equal ease; hence, very skillful or versatile.

2. siding with both parties; double-dealing; treacherous.

am·bi·dex′trous·ly, *adv.* in an ambidextrous manner.

am·bi·dex′trous·ness, *n.* ambidexterity.

am′bi·ent, *a.* [L. *ambiens*, ppr. of *ambire*, to go round.] surrounding; encompassing on all sides; investing; as, the *ambient* air.

am′bi·ent, *n.* that which encompasses on all sides.

am·biġ′e·năl, *a.* [*ambi-*, and L. *genus*, born.] of two kinds: used only in the Newtonian phrase *ambigenal hyperbola*, one of the triple hyperbolas of the third order, having one of its infinite legs falling within an angle formed by the asymptotes, and the other without.

am·biġ′e·nous, *a.* of two kinds: specifically applied in botany to certain perianths having the inner members petaloid and the outer calycine.

am′bi·gū, *n.* [Fr. *ambigu*, doubtful.] a banquet or feast, consisting of a medley of dishes served at once.

am·bi·gū′i·ty, *n.* [L. *ambiguitas*, from *ambiguus*, doubtful.]

1. the quality or state of being ambiguous.

2. [*pl.*] **am·bi·gū′i·tieṣ,** an ambiguous remark; an expression with more than one possible meaning.

am·big′ū·ous, *a.* [L. *ambiguus*, from *ambigere*, to wander; *ambi*, about, around, and *agere*, to drive.] having two or more possible meanings; being of uncertain signification; susceptible of different interpretations; hence, obscure; not clear; not definite; uncertain or vague.

Syn.—doubtful, indefinite, dubious, equivocal, uncertain, involved.

am·big′ū·ous·ly, *adv.* in an ambiguous manner; with doubtful meaning.

am·big′ū·ous·ness, *n.* the quality or condition of being ambiguous; uncertainty of meaning; ambiguity.

am·bi·lē′vous, *a.* [*ambi-*, and L. *lævus*, left.] awkward, as though both hands were the left: opposed to *ambidextrous*. [Rare.]

am·bip′à·rous, *a.* [*ambi-*, and L. *parere*, to bear.] in botany, containing the beginnings of both flowers and leaves: said of a bud.

am′bit, *n.* [L. *ambitus*, a circuit, from *ambire*, to go about.]

1. a circuit or circumference.

2. the limits or scope.

am″bi·tend′en·cy, *n.* [*ambi-*, and *tendency*.] in psychology, the existence of conflicting tendencies in the same individual.

am·bi′tion (-bish′un), *n.* [L. *ambitio*, from *ambire*, to go about: from the practice of Roman candidates for office, who went about the city to solicit votes.]

1. an eager and sometimes inordinate desire for something, as preferment, honor, superiority, power, fame, wealth, etc.; or desire to distinguish oneself in some way.

2. object of ambitious desire or effort.

am·bi′tion·less, *a.* devoid of ambition.

am·bi′tious, *a.* 1. full of or showing ambition.

2. greatly desirous (*of* something); eager for.

3. showing great effort; aspiring.

am·bi′tious·ly, *adv.* in an ambitious manner.

am·bi′tious·ness, *n.* the quality of being ambitious.

am′bi·tus, *n. sing.* and *pl.* [L.] 1. the circumference or exterior edge or border, as of a leaf.

2. in Roman history, a canvassing for votes.

am·biv′à·lence, *n.* [*ambi-*, and *valence*.] in psychology, the simultaneous existence of conflicting emotions, as love and hate, in one person toward another person or thing.

am·biv′à·lent, *a.* of or having ambivalence.

am″bi·vẽr′sion, *n.* [*ambi-*, and intro*version*.] in psychology, a condition or character trait midway between introversion and extroversion.

am′bi·vẽrt, *n.* [*ambi-*, and intro*vert*.] a person who has ambiversion.

am′ble, *v.i.*; ambled (-bld), *pt.*, *pp.*; ambling, *ppr.* [Fr. *ambler*, from L. *ambulare*, to walk.]

1. to move smoothly and easily by raising first both legs on one side, then both on the other: said of horses, etc.

2. to go easily and unhurriedly; walk in a leisurely manner.

am′ble, *n.* 1. a horse's ambling gait.

2. a leisurely walking pace.

am′blẽr, *n.* a person or animal that ambles.

am′bling·ly, *adv.* with an ambling movement.

am·blō′sis, *n.* [L., from Gr. *amblōsis*, abortion.] abortion; miscarriage.

am·blot′iç, *a.* causing, or tending to cause, abortion.

am·blot′iç, *n.* a drug that induces abortion.

am·bly·ā′phi·à, *n.* [L., from Gr. *amblys*, dull, and *haphē*, touch, from *haptein*, *haptesthai*, to touch.] in pathology, dullness or insensibility of touch.

am′bly·gon, *n.* [Gr. *amblys*, dull, obtuse, and *gōnia*, an angle.] an obtuse-angled triangle; a triangle with one angle of more than ninety degrees. [Obs.]

am·blyg′ō·năl, *a.* containing an obtuse angle. [Obs.]

am·blyg′ō·nīte, *n.* [Gr. *amblygōnios*, having an obtuse angle, and *-ite*.] a pale-green crystalline mineral, $Li(AlF)PO_4$.

am″bly·ō·cär′pous, *a.* [Gr. *amblys*, dull, and *karpos*, fruit.] in botany, having abortive seeds: applied to fruit.

am·bly·ō′pi·à, am′bly·ō·py, *n.* [L., from Gr. *amblys*, dull, and *ōps*, eye.] dullness or obscurity of sight, without any apparent organic change in the eyes: the first stage of amaurosis.

am·bly·op′iç, *a.* relating to or having amblyopia.

am·bly·op′sid, *n.* a fish of the family *Amblyopsidæ*.

Am·bly·op′si·dae, *n.pl.* a family of fishes, including the blindfish of Mammoth Cave and other caves of North America.

am·bly·op′sis, *n.* [L., from Gr. *amblys*, dull, dim, and *opsis*, sight.] the typical genus of *Amblyopsidæ*.

am·bly·op′soid, *a.* characteristic of the *Amblyopsidæ*.

am·bly·op′soid, *n.* an amblyopsid.

am′bly·ō·py, *n.* same as *amblyopia*.

Am·blyp′ō·dà, *n.pl.* [L., from Gr. *amblys*, blunt, and *pous*, *podos*, foot.] a group of extinct ungulate mammals whose fossil remains are found in the Eocene beds of North America.

Am·bly·rhyn′çhus, *n.* [L., from Gr. *amblys*, dull, and *rhynchos*, snout.] a genus of blunt-snouted lizards of the family *Iguanidæ*, found only in the Galapagos Islands.

Am·blys′tō·mà, *n.* [L., from Gr. *amblys*, dull, and *stoma*, mouth.] a genus of salamanders, the type of the family *Amblystomidæ*. Also called *Ambystoma*.

am·blys′tō·mid, am′bly·stōme, *n.* one of the amphibian *Amblystomidæ*.

Am·bly·stom′i·dae, *n.pl.* a family of amphibians of which *Amblystoma* is the typical genus. They are salamanders found only in America.

am′bō, *n.*; *pl.* **am′bōṣ,** [L., from Gr. *ambōn*, a stage, platform.] an oblong, elevated pulpit, in the early Christian churches.

am′bō·cep·tŏr, *n.* [from L. *ambo*, both, and *receptor*, a taker or receiver.] in bacteriology, a substance present in the blood during infection, believed to help in the destruction of the disease-causing microorganism by connecting it with another substance in the blood (the *complement*).

am·bō·dex′tẽr, *a.* and *n.* ambidexter. [Obs.]

Am·boi′nà wood, [from *Amboina*, an island of the Moluccas.] the mottled, curled wood of an Asiatic tree, used in making furniture.

Am·boi·nēse′, Am·boy·nēse′ (*or* -nēz′), *n.* a native or natives of Amboina, the most important of the Moluccas or Spice Islands.

am·bol′iç, *a.* [Gr. *ambolikos*. from *anabolikos*, *anabolē*, that which is thrown up.] causing abortion.

am′bon, am′bō, *n.* [Gr.] in anatomy, a circumferential fibrocartilage, as the glenoid fossa of the scapula.

am′brē·āte, *n.* a salt of ambreic acid.

am·brē′iç, *a.* pertaining to or obtained from ambrein; as, *ambreic* acid.

am′brē·in, *n.* a fatty, crystalline substance, the chief constituent of ambergris.

am·brette′, *n.* [Fr., dim. of *ambre*, amber.]

1. same as *amber seed*.

2. a kind of pear with the odor of musk.

am′brīte, *n.* [Eng. *amber*, and *-ite*.] a fossil resin occurring in parts of New Zealand in large masses.

am′broid, *n.* same as *amberoid*.

am·brol′ō·ġy, *n.* [L. *ambra*, and Gr. *logia*, from *legein*, to speak.] the natural history of amber.

am′brōṣe, *n.* 1. ambrosia. [Obs.]

2. the Jerusalem oak; also, the wood sage.

am·brō′ṣià (*or* -zhi-à), *n.* [Gr. *ambrosia*, f. of *ambrosios*, immortal, from *abrotos*; *a* priv., and *brotos*, mortal; Sans. *amrita*, immortal.]

1. in Greek and Roman mythology, the food of the gods, supposed to confer immortality on mortals who ate it.

2. figuratively, anything very pleasing to taste or smell.

3. [A–] in botany, a genus of the aster family, with lobed leaves, as the ragweed.

4. beebread.

am·brō′ṣi·aç (*or* -zhi-ak), *a.* ambrosial. [Obs.]

am·brō″ṣi·ā′ceous, *a.* in botany, of or pertaining to the *Ambrosia*, the ragweed family.

am·brō′ṣiăl (-zhăl *or* -zhi-ăl), *a.* 1. pertaining to or having the nature of ambrosia; fragrant; delicious.

We have only to live right on and breathe the *ambrosial* air. —Thoreau.

2. of or befitting the gods; heavenly; divine.

am·brō′ṣiăl·ly, *adv.* deliciously; delightfully.

Am·brō′ṣiăn (*or* -zhăn), *a.* 1. pertaining to St. Ambrose (340?–397 A.D.), Bishop of Milan.

2. [a–] ambrosial.

Ambrosian chant; a mode of singing or chanting introduced by St. Ambrose. It was superseded by the Gregorian chant.

Ambrosian ritual; a formula of worship instituted in the church of Milan by St. Ambrose.

am′brō·ṣin, *n.* [L. *Ambrosinus nummus*.] in the middle ages, a coin struck by the dukes of Milan, on which St. Ambrose was represented on horseback.

am′brō·tȳpe, *n.* [Gr. *ambrotos*, immortal, and *typos*, type.] an old style of photograph, consisting of a glass negative backed by a dark surface so as to appear positive.

am′bry, *n.* [OE. *ambry*, *amrie*; OFr. *almarie*; L. *armarium*, a chest for tools or arms.]

1. a storage place, as a chest, cupboard, pantry, or the like.

2. an almonry: an improper use of the word.

3. a niche or closet in the wall of a church, for sacramental vessels, etc.

AMBRY

āmbṣ′āce (āmz′ās), *n.* [ME. *ambesas*; OFr. *ambes as*; L. *ambas as*; *ambas*, both, and *as*, unit.]

1. double aces, the lowest number in throwing dice.

2. the most worthless or least thing possible; bad luck. Also spelled *amesace*.

am·bū·lā′çrà, *n.*, pl. of *ambulacrum*.

am·bū·lā′çrăl, *a.* of or pertaining to an ambulacrum or to ambulacra.

am·bū·lā′çri·fọrm, *a.* shaped like an ambulacrum.

am·bū·lā′çrum, *n.*; *pl.* **am·bū·lā′çrà,** [L., a walk, avenue, from *ambulare*, to walk.] in zoology, an external section or division extending from the apex to the base of a ray of an echinoderm, as the sea urchin, and containing a series of perforations through which the tube feet or tentacles are protruded and withdrawn.

am′bū·lănce, *n.* [Fr., from *ambulant* in *hôpital ambulant*, from L. *ambulare*, to walk, move.]

1. a movable hospital; a hospital establishment designed to accompany an army in the field.

2. a vehicle especially adapted to carry the sick or wounded: used on the battlefield, by hospitals, etc.

ambulance chaser; a lawyer who encourages accident victims to sue for damages as his clients. [Slang.]

am′bū·lănt, *a.* [L. *ambulans*, ppr. of *ambulare*, to walk.] walking; moving about.

am′bū·lāte, *v.i.*; ambulated, *pt.*, *pp.*; ambulating, *ppr.* [L. *ambulatus*, pp. of *ambulare*, to walk.] to walk; to move about.

am·bū·lā′tion, *n.* a walking or moving about.

am′bū·lā·tive, *a.* walking. [Rare.]

am′bū·lā·tŏr, *n.* 1. one who walks or moves about.

2. a device for measuring distance walked; pedometer.

am′bū·lā·tō·ry, am″bū·lā·tō′ri·ăl, *a.* 1. pertaining to walking or a person who walks.

2. able to walk or move about.

3. adapted to walking.

4. moving from one place to another; not stationary; as, *ambulatory* jurisdiction.

5. in medicine, designating or of patients who are not bedridden.

6. in law, not fixed; able to be altered, as a will during the life of the testator.

am′bū·lā·tō·ry, *n.*; *pl.* **am′bū·lā·tō·rieṣ,** any covered or sheltered place for walking.

am′bŭr·y, *n.* same as *anbury.*

am·bus·çāde′, *n.* [Fr. *ambuscade;* Port. and It. *ambuscado, emboscata;* L. *imboscata,* an ambush, f. of pp. of *imboscare,* to set in ambush.]
1. a hiding or lying in wait in order to make an unexpected attack: used generally with reference to a body of soldiers or other fighting men.
2. a place where men lie concealed, with a view to attacking an enemy; an ambush.
3. a body of men lying in ambush.

am·bus·çāde′, *v.t.* and *v.i.;* ambuscaded, *pt., pp.;* ambuscading, *ppr.* 1. to hide for a surprise attack; ambush.
2. to attack from hiding; waylay.

am·bus·çā′dō, *n.* an ambuscade. [Obs.]

am′bụsh, *n.* [OFr. *embusche,* from *embuschier;* L. *imboscare,* to set in ambush; *in,* in, and *boscus,* wood, bush.]
1. a hiding or lying concealed, for the purpose of attacking; a lying in wait; a snare; a trap.
2. the person or body of persons posted in a concealed place.
3. a place of concealment from which an unexpected attack may be made; an ambuscade.

am′bụsh, *v.t.* and *v.i.;* ambushed, *pt., pp.;* ambushing, *ppr.* 1. to hide for a surprise attack.
2. to attack from hiding; waylay.

am′bụsh·ẽr, *n.* one who ambushes.

am′bụsh·ment, *n.* an ambush.

am·bus′tion (-chun), *n.* [L. *ambustio,* from *amburere,* to burn or scorch; *amb-,* about, and *urere,* to burn.] a burn or scald. [Obs.]

Am·bys′tō·mȧ, *n.* same as *Amblystoma.*

ȧ·mē′bȧ, am·ē·bē′ăn, ȧ·mē′biç, ȧ·mē′bi·fọrm, ȧ·mē′bō·cȳte, ȧ·mē′boid, etc. same as *amœba,* etc.

ȧ·meer′, *n.* same as *amir.*

ȧ·meer′ship, *n.* same as *amirship.*

am′el, *n.* and *v.* enamel. [Obs.]

am′el·çorn, *n.* [Gr. *amelkorn;* O.H.G. *amar,* amelcorn; L. *amylum,* starch; Gr. *amylon.*] a kind of wheat grown as stock feed.

ȧ·mēl′iō·rȧ·ble (-yō-), *a.* capable of betterment.

ȧ·mēl′iō·rănt, *n.* a thing that ameliorates.

ȧ·mēl′iō·rāte, *v.t.;* ameliorated, *pt., pp.;* ameliorating, *ppr.* [L. *amelioratus,* pp. of *ameliorare,* to make better; *ad,* to, and *meliorare,* from *melior,* better.] to make better; to improve; to meliorate.

ȧ·mēl′iō·rāte, *v.i.* to grow better or less severe.

ȧ·mēl·iō·rā′tion, *n.* a making or becoming better; improvement.

ȧ·mēl′iō·rā·tive, *a.* tending to produce improvement.

ȧ·mēl′iō·rā·tŏr, *n.* one who or that which ameliorates.

ā′men′ (*also* ä′men′), *n.* [L. *amen;* Gr. *amēn;* Heb. *āmēn,* truly, certainly.]
1. [A–] a term used in Scripture to denote Christ.

These things saith the *Amen,* the faithful
and true witness. —Rev. iii. 14.

2. a speaking or writing of *amen;* an expression of formal assent, concurrence, or conviction.
3. the conclusion, in word or act; the end.

ā′men′, *interj.* so be it: used as an expression of hearty assent or formal confession of faith; also, as the formal conclusion of prayers, etc.

ā′men′, *adv.* truly; verily.

ā′men′, *v.t.* to assent to or concur in; to sanction; to say *amen* to; to conclude.

Ä′men, *n.* [Egypt., lit., hidden one.] the ancient Egyptian god of life and reproduction: also spelled *Amon, Ammon.* See also *Amen-Ra.*

ȧ·mē·nȧ·bil′i·ty, *n.* the state or quality of being amenable.

ȧ·mē′nȧ·ble (*also* ȧ-men′ȧ-ble), *a.* [Fr. *a,* L. *ad,* to, and *mener,* L. *minare,* to drive.]
1. responsible or answerable.
2. willing to follow advice; open to suggestion; responsive; submissive.
3. that can be tested by (with *to*): as, *amenable* to the laws of physics.

ȧ·mē′nȧ·ble·ness, *n.* amenability.

ȧ·mē′nȧ·bly, *adv.* in an amenable manner.

am·ē·nāġe′ (-näzh′), *v.t.* to manage. [Obs.]

am′ē·nănce, *n.* conduct; behavior. [Obs.]

ā′men′ çor′nẽr, those seats to the side of and facing the pulpit of certain churches, especially in some small towns of the United States, where those leading the responsive amens usually sit.

ȧ·mend′, *v.t.;* amended, *pt., pp.;* amending, *ppr.* [Fr. *amender;* L. *emendare,* to free from fault; *e, ex,* from, without, and *mendum,* fault, blemish.]
1. to make better by some change; improve.
2. to correct errors in; to supply deficiencies in, or to free from whatever is faulty or wrong.
3. to alter (a motion, law, etc.) by formal action of an authorized body.

Syn.—correct, reform, rectify, better, improve, mend.—To *amend* is literally to take away blemishes, and hence to remove faults; to *reform* is to form over again for the better; to *correct* is to make accurate or right; to *rectify* is to set right. We *rectify* abuses, mistakes, etc.; *correct* errors; and *reform* or *amend* our lives.

ȧ·mend′, *v.i.* to improve one's conduct.

ȧ·mend′ȧ·ble, *a.* capable of correction; as, an *amendable* fault.

ȧ·mend′ȧ·ble·ness, *n.* the state or quality of being amendable.

ȧ·mend′ȧ·tō·ry, *a.* of or pertaining to amendment.

ȧ·mende′ (*Fr. pron.* ȧ-moṅd′), *n.* [Fr., a fine, penalty.] a fine or other penalty; also, any recantation or making of amends.

amende honorable; an open recantation or apology, with reparation to the injured person.

ȧ·mend′ẽr, *n.* a person who amends.

ȧ·mend′fụl, *a.* amending. [Obs.]

ȧ·mend′ment, *n.* 1. an alteration or change for the better; improvement.
2. correction of a fault or faults.
3. in legislative or deliberative proceedings, a revision or change proposed or made in a bill, motion, or law; also, a statement of this.
4. in law, the correction of an error in a writ or process.

Syn.—correction, improvement, reformation, amelioration, betterment.

ȧ·mendṣ′, *n.pl.* [Fr. *amendes,* pl. of *amende.*] [construed also as sing.], payment made or compensation given for injury, insult, loss, etc.; as, he made *amends* for his rudeness.

Syn.—reparation, restitution, restoration, compensation.

ȧ·men′i·ty, *n.; pl.* **ȧ·men′i·tieṣ,** [Fr. *aménité;* L. *amœnitas,* from *amœnus,* pleasant, delightful.]
1. pleasantness; attractiveness.
2. [*pl.*] attractive or desirable features, as of a place, climate, etc.
3. [*pl.*] courteous acts; civilities.

ȧ·men·or·rhē′ȧ, ȧ·men·or·rhoe′ȧ, *n.* [Gr. *a* priv., *mēn,* month, and *rheein,* to flow.] abnormal absence or suppression of the menses.

ȧ·men·or·rhē′ăl, ȧ·men·or·rhoe′ăl, *a.* pertaining to amenorrhea.

Ä′men-Rä, *n.* [Egypt. *Amen-Rā; Amen,* lit., hidden one, and *Rā,* sun.] the ancient Egyptian sun god: also spelled *Amon-Ra.*

ā men′sȧ et thō′rō, [L.] from bed and board: legal phrase used in divorce proceedings.

am′ent, *n.* [L. *amentum,* a thong, or strap.] a tassellike spike of small, closely clustered, unisexual flowers lacking petals and sepals, as on a willow, birch, or poplar; catkin.

AMENTS
(of the willow, male and female, with separate flowers)

ā′ment, *n.* [L. *amens,* senseless, mad; *a-,* away, and *mens,* mind.] in psychology, a person who has a mental deficiency; feeble-minded person.

ȧ·men′tȧ, *n.;* pl. of *amentum.*

Am·en·tā′cē·ae, *n.pl.* [LL., from *amentum,* strap.] in botany, a former classification of plants which bear flowers in aments.

am·en·tā′ceoụs, *a.* 1. in botany, growing in an ament or aments; resembling an ament; as, an *amentaceous* inflorescence.
2. bearing aments; having flowers arranged in aments; as, *amentaceous* plants.

ȧ·men′tăl, *a.* in botany, relating to or bearing aments.

ȧ·men′tăl, *n.* a plant bearing aments.

ȧ·men′ti·ȧ (-shi-), *n.* [L., want of reason; *a,* away, from, and *mens, mentis,* mind.]
1. congenital subnormality of intelligence; feeble-mindedness: distinguished from *dementia.*
2. a type of temporary confusional insanity.

am·en·tif′ẽr·ous, *a.* [L. *amentum,* a strap, and *ferre,* to bear.] bearing aments, or catkins.

ȧ·men′ti·fọrm, *a.* resembling an ament in shape.

ȧ·men′tum, *n.; pl.* **ȧ·men′tȧ,** in botany, an ament.

ȧ·men′ty, *n.* amentia. [Obs.]

am′ē·nūṣe, *v.t.* to diminish. [Obs.]

ȧ·mẽrce′, *v.t.;* amerced, *pt., pp.;* amercing, *ppr.* [ME. *amercen, amercien;* OFr. *amercier,* from *a merci,* at the mercy of, liable to punishment.] to fine or inflict other penalty upon as legal punishment.

ȧ·mẽrce′ȧ·ble, *a.* subject to amercement; justifying amercement.

ȧ·mẽrce′ment, *n.* 1. a penalty imposed on an offender at the discretion of the inflicter, specifically, the court. It differs from a fine, in that the latter is, or was originally, a fixed and certain sum prescribed by statute for an offense, while an *amercement* is at the discretion of the court.
2. the imposing of such a penalty.

ȧ·mẽr′cẽr, *n.* one who amerces.

ȧ·mẽr′ci·ȧ·ment (*or* -shȧ-), *n.* same as *amercement.*

A·mer′i·căn, *a.* [from *America,* and *-an:* derived from *Americus* Vespucius, the Latin name of Amerigo Vespucci (1451–1512), Italian navigator.]
1. of or in North or South America, or North America, South America, and Central America considered together.
2. of, in, or characteristic of the United States, its people, etc.; as, the *American* language.

American aloe; a century plant.

American Beauty; a variety of hybrid, perennial red rose.

American cheese; a kind of fairly hard, mild Cheddar cheese, popular in the United States.

American eagle; the bald eagle of North America, shown on the coat of arms of the United States.

AMERICAN EAGLE
(30 in. long)

American English; the English language as spoken and written in the United States: usually distinguished from *British English.*

American Indian; a member of any of the aboriginal races of North America, South America, or the West Indies: they were named Indians from the belief, held by early explorers, that these regions were part of Asia.

American ivy; the Virginia creeper.

American Labor Party; a political party of New York State, founded in 1936.

American leopard; a jaguar.

American Party; a secret political party in existence from 1853 to 1856, whose object was to exclude foreign-born citizens from participating in government: called also the *Know-Nothing* party because members professed ignorance of the party's activities.

American plan; a system of hotel operation in which the price charged to guests covers room, service, and meals: distinguished from *European plan.*

American Protective Association; a secret society formed in Iowa, in 1887, for the purpose of keeping Roman Catholics out of public office, professedly to protect American institutions.

American Revolution; (a) a sequence of actions by American colonists from 1763 to 1783 protesting British domination and culminating in the Revolutionary War; (b) the Revolutionary War (1775–1783), fought by the American colonies for independence from England.

American screw gauge; a standard gauge for checking the diameter of wood screws and machine screws.

American system; the original name for the protective tariff system of the United States.

Native American Party; a short-lived political party, organized about 1843, whose object was somewhat similar to that of the American (Know-Nothing) Party.

A·mer′i·căn, *n.* 1. a native or inhabitant of America; originally, any of the aboriginal natives.
2. a citizen of the United States.
3. the English language as spoken in the United States.

A·mer″i·căn′ȧ (*or* -kan-ȧ, -kän-ȧ), *n.pl.* matter relating to America, as in history, ethnography, geography, literature, culture, etc.

A·mer′i·căn Fed·ẽr·ā′tion of Lā′bŏr, a federation of labor unions of the United States and Canada, founded in 1881.

A·mer′i·căn·ism, *n.* 1. devotion or loyalty to the United States, its interests, institutions, etc.

2. any custom, trait, or idea peculiar to or originating in the United States.

3. a word, phrase, or idiom original with or peculiar to American English.

A·mer′i·căn·ist, *n.* 1. a person who makes a study of America, its history, geology, etc.

2. an anthropologist specializing in the study of American Indians and their culture.

3. a linguist specializing in the language of the American Indians.

4. a person sympathetic toward the United States, its policies, etc.

A·mer″i·căn·i·zā′tion, *n.* an Americanizing or being Americanized.

A·mer′i·căn·īze, *v.t.* and *v.i.*; Americanized, *pt.*, *pp.*; Americanizing, *ppr.* to make or become American in character, manners, methods, ideals, etc.; to assimilate to United States customs, speech, etc.

am″ėr·ic′i·um, *n.* [Mod. L., from *America.*] a chemical element, one of the transuranium elements produced by atomic fission; symbol, Am; atomic weight, 243.13; atomic number, 95.

Am′ėr·ind, *n.* an American Indian or Eskimo.

Am·ėr·in′di·ăn, *n.* an Amerind.

Am·ėr·in′di·ăn, *a.* of the Amerinds or their culture.

Am·ėr·in′diç, *a.* Amerindian.

am·e·ris′tiç, *a.* [Gr. *a* priv., and *meristos*, divided, from *merīzein*, to divide; *meros*, part.] unsegmented, undifferentiated, or undeveloped: specifically applied to ferns lacking certain parts.

āmeş′āce (āmz′ās), *n.* same as *ambsace.*

Am·ē·tab′ō·là, Am″ē·tab·ō′li·à, *n.pl.* [L., from Gr. *ametabolos*, unchangeable.] a group of insects, consisting of those which do not pass through regular metamorphosis.

à·met·à·bō′li·ăn, *a.* pertaining to the *Ametabola.*

à·met·à·bō′li·ăn, *n.* one of the *Ametabola.*

à·met·à·bol′iç, *a.* not subject to metamorphosis.

am·ē·tab′ō·lous, *a.* ametabolic.

à·meth′ō·dist, *n.* one lacking method; a quack. [Obs.]

am′ē·thyst, *n.* [L. *amethystus*; Gr. *amethystos*, not drunken: the Greeks believed the stone and plant of that name to be preventives of intoxication; *a* priv., and *methystos*, drunken, from *methyein*, to be drunk; *methy*, strong drink.]

1. a purple or violet variety of quartz, used in jewelry.

2. purple; violet.

Oriental amethyst; the purple variety of transparent crystallized corundum.

am′ē·thyst, *a.* 1. of or containing amethyst.

2. purple; violet.

am·ē·thys′tine, *a.* [Gr. *amethystinos*, pertaining to amethyst.]

1. pertaining to or resembling amethyst, especially in color.

2. composed of amethyst; as, an *amethystine* cup.

am·ē·trom′e·tėr, *n.* [Gr. *ametros*, irregular, and *metron*, measure.] an instrument used for determining and examining conditions of ametropia.

am·ē·trō′pi·à, *n.* [L., from Gr. *ametros*, irregular, and *ops*, eye.] any condition of imperfect refraction of the eye, as nearsightedness, farsightedness, or astigmatism.

am·ē·trop′iç, *a.* pertaining to or produced by ametropia.

Am′ex, *n.* the American Stock Exchange.

Äm·for′täs, *n.* [M.H.G. *Anfortas*] the leader of the knights of the Holy Grail: cf. *Parsifal.*

am′gärn, *n.* [W., ferrule.] a stone implement probably used as the ferrule of a spear shaft by the ancient inhabitants of Europe.

Am·har′iç, *a.* pertaining to Amhara, in Ethiopia, its people, or their language.

Am·har′iç, *n.* the Southern Semitic language used officially in Ethiopia.

Am·hėrs′ti·à, *n.* [LL., named after the Countess of *Amherst.*] a genus of Burmese plants, with but a single species (*Amherstia nobilis*), bearing large vermilion flowers spotted with yellow. It is regarded as sacred to Buddha.

à″mī′, *n.*; *pl.* **à″mīs′** (à″mē′), [Fr.] a (man or boy) friend.

Am′i·à, *n.* [L., from Gr. *amia*, a kind of tunny.] a genus of fishes found in North American waters, and including only the bowfin, *Amia calva.*

ā″mi·à·bil′i·ty, *n.* amiableness; excellence of disposition.

ā′mi·à·ble, *a.* [Fr. *aimable*, from L. *amicabilis*, friendly; *amicare*, to make friendly, from *amicus*, a friend.]

1. friendly; amicable; kindly. [Obs.]

2. possessing sweetness of temper; having a pleasant disposition; good-natured.

Syn.—charming, lovable, pleasing, obliging.

ā′mi·à·ble·ness, *n.* the quality of being amiable.

ā′mi·à·bly, *adv.* in an amiable manner.

am′i·anth, *n.* amianthus. [Poetic.]

am·i·an′thi·form, *a.* having the form or structure of amianthus.

am·i·an′thoid, *a.* resembling amianthus.

am·i·an′thus, *n.* [L. *amiantus*, from Gr. *amiantos*; *a* priv., and *miainein*, to stain.] a kind of asbestos with long, silky fibers: also *amiantus.*

am′iç, *a.* of an amide.

amic acid; a nitrogenized acid of the nature of an amide.

am″i·cà·bil′i·ty, *n.* the quality or state of being amicable; friendliness; conciliation.

am′i·cà·ble, *a.* [L. *amicabilis*, from *amicus*, a friend, from *amare*, to love.] friendly; peaceable; characterized by good will; harmonious; as, nations can come to an *amicable* adjustment of their differences.

amicable action; in law, an action entered in court by the amicable arrangement of both parties, for the purpose of obtaining a decision on a point of law connected with it.

amicable numbers; in mathematics, any two numbers each of which is equal to the sum of all the aliquot parts of the other.

Syn.—friendly, peaceable.—*Amicable* always supposes two or more parties, as an *amicable* arrangement. A single individual would not be described as *amicable*, though he may be called *friendly*. *Amicable* rather implies a negative sentiment, and *friendly* a positive feeling of regard, the absence of indifference.

am′i·cà·ble·ness, *n.* the quality of being peaceable, friendly, or disposed to peace; friendliness; amicability.

am′i·cà·bly, *adv.* in a friendly manner; with harmony or good will; as, the dispute was *amicably* adjusted.

am′ice, *n.* see *almuce.*

am′ice, *n.* [Fr. *amict*, from L. *amictus*, a cloak.] an oblong white linen cloth worn as a collar by Roman Catholic priests at Mass, with the upper edge fastened round the neck under the alb.

1. AMICE (round the neck) 2. AMICE (worn as a hood)

am′içt, *n.* an amice (piece of cloth). [Obs.]

à·mī′çus çū′ri·ae, [L., friend of the court.] in law, a person, either an attorney or a layman, called in to advise the court on some legal matter.

à·mid′, *prep.* [ME. *amid*, *on midde*, *on midden*; AS. *on middan*; *on*, in, and *middan*, dat. of *midde*, middle.] in the midst or middle of; amidst; among.

am′id, *n.* same as *amide.*

am′ide (*or* -id), *n.* [*am*monia and *-ide.*] in chemistry, (a) any of a group of organic compounds containing the $CO·NH_2$ radical (e.g., acetamide) or an acid radical in place of one hydrogen atom of an ammonia molecule (e.g., sulfanilamide); (b) any of the ammono bases in which one hydrogen atom of the ammonia molecule is replaced by a metal (e.g., sodamide).

à·mid′iç, *a.* of or made from an amide.

am′i·din, *n.* [Fr. *amidon*, from L. *amylum*, starch; and *-in.*] in chemistry, a transparent, water-soluble substance made by heating a mixture of starch and water.

à·mī′dō (*or* am′i-dō), *a.* [from *amide.*] of an amide or amides.

à·mī′dō- (*or* am′i-dō), [from *amide.*] a combining form indicating that a chemical compound has had one hydrogen atom in the ammonia molecule replaced by an acid radical.

à·mī′dŏ·ġen, *n.* [*amido-* and *-gen.*] the hypothetical monovalent radical NH_2.

am′i·dōl (*or* -dol), *n.* [*amido-* and *phenol.*] a colorless crystalline compound, $C_6H_3ON_2·HCl$, used as a developer in photography.

à·mid′ship, *adv.* same as *amidships.*

à·mid′ships, *adv.* in or toward the middle part of a ship; midway between bow and stern.

à·midst′, *prep.* [AS. *on-middan*, in the middle; OE. *amidde*, *amiddes* (*es* being an adverbial genitive termination), and unhistoric *t.*] in the middle or midst of; among; amid; as, *amidst* the trees, *amidst* the enemy.

à·mie′ (à-mē′), *n.*; *pl.* **à·mies′** (-mē′), [Fr.] a (woman or girl) friend.

à·mī′gō, *n.*; *pl.* **à·mī′gōs** (*or Eng.* -gōz), [Sp.] a friend.

am′in, *n.* same as *amine.*

à·mīne′ (*or* am′in), *n.* [*am*monia, and *-ine.*] in chemistry, a derivative of ammonia in which hydrogen atoms have been replaced by radicals containing hydrogen and carbon atoms.

à·mī′nō (*or* am′i-nō), *a.* [from *amine.*] of an amine or amines.

à·mī′nō- (*or* am′i-nō), [from *amine.*] a combining form indicating that a chemical compound has had one hydrogen atom in the ammonia molecule replaced by an alkyl or other nonacid radical.

à·mī′nō ac′ids, 1. a group of nitrogenous organic compounds that serve as units of structure of the proteins and are essential to human metabolism.

2. chemical compounds in which a hydrogen atom in the alkyl group attached to the COOH (carboxyl) group of an organic acid is replaced by an NH_2 group.

à·mī′nō reş′in, a thermosetting resinous product made by condensation of a compound containing an amine (e.g., melamine or urea) with an aldehyde (e.g., formaldehyde).

à·mīr′, *n.* [Ar. *amīr.*] in Moslem countries, a ruler or prince: also written *ameer.*

à·mīr′ship, *n.* the rank or authority of an amir: also written *ameership.*

Am′ish (*or* äm′ish), *n.pl.* Mennonites of a sect founded by Jacob Ammann (or Amen) in the 17th century.

Am′ish, *a.* of or designating the Amish.

à·miss′, *adv.* [*a-*, at, and *miss.*]

1. away from the mark; astray.

2. incorrectly; wrongly.

3. faultily; defectively.

à·miss′, *a.* wrong; faulty; out of order; improper: used in the predicate.

à·mis·si·bil′i·ty, *n.* the quality of being amissible; liability to be lost. [Rare.]

am·i·tō′sis, *n.* [Mod. L.; *a-*, not, and *mitosis.*] in biology, direct or simple cell division; cell division in which the nucleus divides without structural change: opposed to *mitosis.*

am·i·tot′iç, *a.* pertaining to or by amitosis.

am′i·ty, *n.* [Fr. *amitié*; a supposed LL. *amicitas* from L. *amicus*, friendly; from *amare*, to love.] friendship between individuals, societies, or nations; harmony; good understanding.

Syn.—friendship, attachment, esteem, good will, comity, harmony, peace.

am′mà, *n.* [L. *amma*; Gr. *amma*, mother in a convent; Syr. *ama*, mother, nurse; Anglo-Ind. *amah.*] an abess or spiritual mother.

am′măn, *n.* [G. *amtmann*; AS. *ambaht*, or *embeht*, office, duty, charge, and *man.*] in certain cantons of Switzerland, an executive or judicial official.

Am′măn·īte, *n.* a member of the Amish sect of Mennonites.

am′me·līne, am′me·lin, *n.* a white crystalline chemical compound, $C_3H_5N_5O$.

am′mē·tėr, *n.* [*am*pere, and *-meter.*] an instrument for measuring the strength of an electric current in terms of amperes.

Am′mī, *n.* [L.] a genus of umbelliferous plants found around the Mediterranean.

am·mi·ā′ceous, *a.* [L. and Gr. *ammi*, umbelliferous plant; and *-aceous.*] belonging to the *Umbelliferae* family, a group of plants with hollow stems and generally edible roots.

am′mīne, *n.* [*ammo*nia, and *-ine.*] in chemistry, (a) a molecule of ammonia (NH_3) as found in certain complex compounds; (b) any of certain complex compounds containing this molecule.

am·mī′nō-, [from *ammine.*] a combining form used in the names of certain chemical compounds, meaning *containing one or more ammines.*

am′mō, *n.* ammunition. [Slang.]

am′mō·çhryse (-kris), *n.* [Gr. *ammos*, sand, and *chrysos*, gold.] a substance, probably sand, anciently used as a blotter.

am′mō·dȳte, *n.* a sand eel; also, a European viper commonly called the *sand natter.*

Am·mō·dȳ′tēş, *n.* [Gr. *ammos*, sand, and *dytēs*, a diver, from *dyein*, to dive.] a genus of fishes (sand eels) of the family *Ammodytidæ*, about a foot in length, with a long, slender body and a compressed head.

Am'mŏn, *n.* [L. *Ammon*; Gr. *Ammōn*; Heb. *'Amōn*; Egypt. *Amūn, Amen*, he who is hidden.]

1. same as *Amen*.

2. in ancient Egypt, a name for Zeus or Jupiter.

3. [a–] the argali, a species of wild sheep.

Am'mŏn, *n.* [Heb. *'ammōn*, lit., prob. populous.] in the Bible, a Semitic tribe descended from Lot's son (Gen. xix. 38; Deut. ii. 19–20).

am·mō'ni·å, *n.* [Gr. *Ammoniakos*, pertaining to Ammon; L. *sal ammoniacum*, the salt from which it is manufactured.]

1. a colorless, pungent gas, NH_3, composed of hydrogen and nitrogen.

2. a water solution of this gas: called also *ammonia water, aqua ammonia*, or *spirits of hartshorn*.

am·mō'ni·aç, am·mō·nī'å·çăl, *a.* pertaining to ammonia, or possessing its properties.

ammoniacal engine; an engine whose motive power is derived from the expansion of ammonia vapor.

am·mō'ni·aç, *n.* [Fr.; L. *ammoniacum*; Gr. *ammōniakon*, gum resin from a plant said to grow near the temple of Jupiter *Ammon* in Libya.] a pungent gum resin obtained from an herb found in Mediterranean countries: it is used as a cement for porcelain, a stimulant, etc. It has a fetid smell, and a nauseous, sweet taste, followed by a bitter one. It is inflammable and soluble in water and spirit of wine; called also *gum ammoniac*.

Am·mō'ni·ăn, *a.* 1. relating to Ammonius Saccas, who flourished at the end of the second century A.D. and was one of the founders of Neoplatonism.

2. relating to Ammonius of Alexandria, a Christian philosopher of the third or fourth century A.D., who divided the gospels into the *Ammonian* sections.

Am·mō'ni·ăn, *a.* of the Egyptian deity Ammon, or his temple and worship.

am·mō'ni·āte, *n.* any of several compounds containing ammonia.

am·mō'ni·āte, *v.t.*; ammoniated, *pt., pp.*; ammoniating, *ppr.* to mix or combine with ammonia.

am·mō'ni·ā·ted, *a.* combined, saturated, or impregnated with ammonia.

am·mō'niç (*or* -mon'iç), *a.* of or pertaining to ammonium or ammonia.

am·mŏn''i·fi·çā'tion, *n.* 1. infusion with ammonia or ammonium compounds.

2. the production of ammonia by bacterial action in the decay of nitrogenous organic matter.

am·mon'i·fȳ, *v.t.*; ammonified, *pt., pp.*; ammonifying, *ppr.* to cause to undergo ammonification.

am·mon'i·fȳ, *v.i.* to undergo ammonification.

am·mō'ni·ō-, a combining form denoting the presence of ammonia or ammonium in a chemical compound.

Am'mŏn·īte, *n.* a member of the Semitic tribe Ammon.

Am'mŏn·īte, *a.* of the tribe Ammon.

am'mŏn·īte, *n.* [L. *cornu Ammonis*, horn of Ammon, from *Jupiter Ammon*, whose statues were represented with ram's horns.] the serpent stone, or *cornu Ammonis*, a fossil shell, curved into a spiral like a ram's horn, ranging in size from five inches to six feet in diameter. Fossils are found in strata of limestone and clay, and in argillaceous iron ore.

AMMONITE (5 in.-6 ft.)

am''mŏn·i·tif'ēr·ous, *a.* [from *ammonite*, and *ferous*, from L. *ferre*, to bear.] containing the remains of ammonites.

am·mō'ni·um, *n.* in chemistry, the radical NH_4, present in salts produced by the reaction of ammonia with an acid: its compounds are like those of the alkali metals.

am·mō'ni·um çhlō'rīde, a white crystalline compound, NH_4Cl, produced by the reaction of ammonia with hydrochloric acid; sal ammoniac: it is used in dry cells, fertilizers, dyes, etc., and as a flux in soldering.

am·mō'ni·um hȳ·drox'īde, an alkali, NH_4OH, formed by dissolving ammonia in water.

am·mō'ni·um nī'trāte, a colorless, crystalline salt, NH_4NO_3, used in some explosives.

am·mō'ni·um sul'fāte, an ammonium salt, $(NH_4)_2SO_4$, made chiefly from synthetic ammonia and used in making fertilizers, in treating water, in tanning hides, etc.

am'mō·nō'', *a.* 1. of or containing ammonia.

2. derived from ammonia: used to describe compounds bearing the same relation to ammonia as certain other compounds bear to water; as, sodium amide, $NaNH_2$, is an *ammono* base corresponding to sodium hydroxide, NaOH.

am'mō·nō''-, [from *ammonia*.] a combining form meaning *of ammonia, containing ammonia*.

am''mō·nō·tel'iç, *adj.* [*ammono-*, and *telic*] excreting ammonia as the main nitrogenous waste: characteristic chiefly of freshwater fishes, frogs, etc.

Am·moph'i·lå, *n.* [L., f. of *ammophilus*; Gr. *ammos*, sand, and *philos*, loving.]

1. a genus of hymenopterous insects, popularly called sand wasps.

2. a genus of grasses growing on the sandy coasts of North America and northern Europe.

am·moph'i·lous, *a.* sand-loving; growing in sandy places.

am·mū·ni'tion (-nish'un), *n.* [Fr. *amunition*, from L. *munitio*, from *munire*, to fortify; the *a* is due to mistaking *la munition* for *l'amunition*.]

1. bullets, gunpowder, shot, shells, bombs, grenades, rockets, and other projectiles and missiles.

2. any resources that may be used for attack and repulse, considered either literally or figuratively; as, boys use snow for *ammunition*; facts are his *ammunition*.

3. any military supplies; munitions. [Archaic.]

am·mū·ni'tion, *v.t.*; ammunitioned, *pt., pp.*; ammunitioning, *ppr.* to provide or equip with ammunition.

am·nē'si·å (*or* -zhå), *n.* [L., from Gr. *a* priv., and *mnasthai*, to remember.

1. partial or total loss of memory caused by brain injury, or by shock, repression, etc.

2. loss of memory for certain kinds of words: a variety of aphasia: in full, *verbal amnesia*.

am·nē'siç, *a.* characterized by amnesia.

am·nē'siç, *n.* a person suffering from amnesia.

am·nes'tiç, *a.* producing amnesia.

am'nes·ty, *n.* [L. *amnestia*, from Gr. *amnēstia*, forgetfulness, *amnestos*, forgotten; *a* priv., and *mnasthai*, to remember.]

1. an act of oblivion; a general pardon of offenses against a government, or the proclamation of such pardon.

2. a deliberate overlooking, as of an offense.

Syn.—absolution, exoneration, pardon, acquittal, oblivion.

am'nes·ty, *v.t.*; amnestied, *pt., pp.*; amnestying, *ppr.* to grant pardon or amnesty to.

am'niç, *a.* same as *amniotic*.

am''ni·ō·cen·tē'sis, *n.* [Mod. L., from *amnion*, and Gr. *kentēsis*, a pricking.] the surgical procedure of inserting a hollow needle through the abdominal wall into the uterus of a pregnant woman and extracting amniotic fluid for analysis to determine the presence of disease, genetic defects, etc.

am'ni·ŏn, *n.*; *pl.* **am'ni·ŏnş** *or* **am'ni·å,** [Gr. *amnion*, the membrane around the fetus, dim. of *amnus*, lamb.]

1. the innermost membrane surrounding the fetus in mammals, birds, and reptiles.

2. a similar membrane of certain invertebrates, especially insects.

false amnion; in anatomy, the outer layer of the amnion, which, in a state of maturity, unites with the chorion.

Am·ni·ō'tå, *n.pl.* the group of vertebrates having an amnion during the embryo stage.

am·ni·ot'iç, *a.* pertaining to the amnion; contained in the amnion; as, the *amniotic* fluid.

amniotic acid; allantoin. [Obs.]

amn't, am not: see also *ain't*. [Colloq.]

å·moe'bå, *n.*; *pl.* **å·moe'båş** *or* **å·moe'bae,** [Mod. L., from Gr. *amoibē*, change, from *ameibein*, to change.]

1. a microscopic, one-celled animal, that absorbs its food at every point of its body by means of processes which are also locomotive, being protruded and withdrawn at will, so that it constantly changes its shape: written also *ameba*.

AMOEBAS

2. [A –] a genus of microscopic protozoans, of which *Amœba proteus* is common.

am·oe·bae'um, *n.*; *pl.* **am·oe·bae'å,** [L., neut. of *amœbæus*, from Gr. *amoibaios*, alternate; *amoibē*, change.] a poem in which persons are represented as speaking alternately.

Am·oe·bē'å, *n.pl.* in zoology, the division, in some classifications, of the protozoans which includes the amoebas and similar organisms.

am·oe·bē'ăn, *a.* same as *amoebic*: written also *amebean*.

am·oe·bē'ăn, am·oe·bae'ăn, *a.* [see *amœbæum*.] alternately answering or responding.

å·moe'bi·ăn, *n.* a protozoan of the genus *Amœba*.

å·moe'biç, *a.* 1. of or like an amoeba or amoebas.

2. caused by amoebas.

Written also *amebic*.

å·moe'biç dy'sen·ter''y, a form of dysentery caused by a certain kind of amoeba.

å·moe'bi·form, *a.* of or characteristic of an amoeba: written also *amebiform*.

å·moe'bō·cȳte, *n.* see *leucocyte*: written also *amebocyte*.

å·moe'boid, *a.* like or characteristic of an amoeba, as in constantly changing shape: written also *ameboid*.

amoeboid movements; the alternate prolongation and retraction of an amoeba or other simple mass of protoplasm, as a colorless blood corpuscle.

å·moe'bous, *a.* resembling an amoeba: written also *amebous*.

å·moe'bū·lå, *n.* a diminutive amoeba: written also *amebula*.

å·mŏk', *a.* and *adv.* same as *amuck*.

å·mŏk', *n.* among Malayans, the condition of being amuck.

å·mō'lę, *n.* [Mex.] 1. the roots of any of several plants of the southwestern U. S. and Mexico, used as a substitute for soap.

2. any of these plants.

A·mō'mum, *n.* [L., from Gr. *amōmon*, an Eastern plant.] a genus of aromatic plants of the ginger family, growing in warm climates and characterized by pungency. It includes species yielding cardamoms and grains of paradise.

Ä'mŏn, *n.* same as *Amen*.

å·mŏng', å·mŏngst', *prep.* [ME. *among, amang*; AS. *amang, onmang, gemang*, contr. for *ongemang*; *on*, in, and *gemang*, crowd, company.]

1. mixed or mingled with; surrounded by; as, tares *among* wheat.

2. associated with; making part of the number of.

Blessed art thou *among* women.
—Luke i. 28.

3. from place to place in; as, he passed *among* the crowd.

4. by many; with many; as, popular *among* businessmen.

5. as compared with; as, one *among* thousands.

6. with a portion for each of; as, the estate was divided *among* the relatives.

7. with one another; as, don't quarrel *among* yourselves.

8. by the concerted or joint action of; as, we have, *among* us, made him a success.

Syn.—amid, amidst, between, betwixt.

Ä'mon-Rä', *n.* same as *Amen-Ra*.

å·mon·til·lä'dō, *n.* [Sp.] a dry sherry, light in color and of aromatic bouquet.

am·ō·rä'dō, *n.* [Sp. *enamorado*; L. *inamorare*; *in*, in, and *amāre*, to love.] a lover. [Obs.]

ā·mor'ăl, *a.* [*a-*, not, and *moral*.] not concerned with moral standards; not to be judged by criteria of morality; neither moral nor immoral.

am'ŏ·ret, am·ŏ·rette', *n.* [OFr. *amorette, amourette*; It. *amoretta*, a little love, dim. of *amor*.]

1. an amorous girl; paramour. [Obs.]

2. a love knot, love song, or love sonnet. [Obs.]

am·ŏ·ret'tō, *n.*; *pl.* **am·ŏ·ret'ti,** [It., dim. from *amore*, love.] an infant cupid: especially common in Italian art of the 16th century.

äm·ō·rī'nō, *n.*; *pl.* **äm·ō·rī'nī,** [It., dim. from *amore*, love, cupid.] same as *amoretto*.

am'ŏ·rist, *n.* a lover; a gallant; an inamorato.

å·mọrn'ingş, *adv.* in the morning; every morning. [Obs.]

am·ō·rō'så, *n.* [It.] an amorous woman; a sweetheart or mistress.

am·ŏ·ros'i·ty, *n.* the quality of being amorous; amorousness. [Rare.]

am·ō·rō'sō, *n.* [It.] a lover; a man enamoured.

am·ō·rō'sō, *adv.* [It.] in music, in a soft and tender manner.

am'ŏ·rous, *a.* [ME. *amorous*; OFr. *amorous*; L. *amorosus*, full of love; *amor*, love.]

1. inclined to love or to making love; loving; fond.
2. in love; enamoured (*of* a person or thing.)
3. pertaining to love; produced by love; indicating love; as, *amorous* delight, *amorous* airs.
4. of sexual love or love-making.
Syn.—loving, fond, affectionate.

am′ō·rous·ly, *adv.* in an amorous manner; fondly; lovingly.

am′ō·rous·ness, *n.* the quality of being amorous; fondness; lovingness.

ā′mōr pā′tri·ae″, [L.] love of one's country; patriotism.

Ȧ·mor′phȧ, *n.* [L., f. of *amorphus*, without form, irregular, from Gr. *amorphos*.] a genus of leguminous plants; bastard indigo.

ȧ·mor′phiç, *a.* same as *amorphous*.

ȧ·mor′phiṣm, *n.* that state or property of matter in which it is without regular or definite shape; the state of being noncrystalline.

ȧ·mor′phous, ȧ·mor′phiç, *a.* [Gr. *amorphos*, from *amorphē*; *a* priv., and *morphē*, form.]
1. having no determinate form; of irregular shape.
2. having no regular structure; noncrystalline.
3. formless; characterless; unorganized; vague.

ȧ·mor′phous·ly, *adv.* in an amorphous manner.

ȧ·mor′phous·ness, *n.* the quality of being amorphous, or without regular shape.

Ȧ·mor·phō·zō′ȧ, *n.pl.* [Mod. L., from Gr. *amorphos*, without form, and *zōon*, animal.] a name for the *Protozoa*.

ȧ·mor·phō·zō′iç, *a.* relating to the *Amorphozoa*.

ȧ·mor′phy, *n.* irregularity of form; shapelessness. [Rare.]

ȧ·mort′, *a.* [from Fr. *à la mort*, to the death, after the manner of death.] not alive; spiritless. [Archaic.]

ȧ·mor′tiṣe, ȧ·mor·ti·ṣā′tion, ȧ·mor′tiṣ·ȧ·ble, ȧ·mor′tiṣe·ment, same as *amortize*, etc.

ȧ·mor′tīz·ȧ·ble, *a.* [Fr. *amortissable*.] capable of being settled or cleared, as a debt.

ȧ·mor·ti·zā′tion, ȧ·mor′tize·ment, *n.* 1. the act or right of transferring or selling property in mortmain.
2. the settling of a debt, especially by a sinking fund.

ȧ·mor′tīze, *v.t.*; amortized, *pt., pp.*; amortizing, *ppr.* [Sp. *amortizare*; OFr. *amortir*, to extinguish, to deaden; LL. *admortizare*, from L. *ad*, to, and *mors*, death.]
1. in law, to transfer or sell (property) in mortmain.
2. to deaden; to destroy. [Obs.]
3. to apply to a debt for the purpose of settling it, as by a sinking fund.
4. in accounting, to write off (expenditures) by prorating over a fixed period.

ȧ·mor′tize·ment, *n.* 1. same as *amortization*.
2. in architecture, the crown or finial at the top of any member or part, whether in itself an ornament or not.

ȧ·mor′we, *adv.* [ME.] in the morning. [Obs.]

Ā′mōs, *n.* 1. a Hebrew prophet of the eighth century B.C.
2. a book of the Old Testament containing prophesies attributed to him.

ȧ·mō′tion, *n.* [L. *amotio*, from *amovere*; *a*, *ab*, from, and *movere*, to move.]
1. removal; especially, the ousting of a person from office.
2. in law, deprivation of possession.

ȧ·mō′tus, *a.* [L., withdrawn, pp. of *amovere*.] drawn up so that it does not touch the ground; elevated: said of the hind toe of some birds. [Rare.]

ȧ·mount′, *v.i.*; amounted, *pt., pp.*; amounting, *ppr.* [ME. *amounten*, to mount up to; OFr. *amounter*, from *amont*, *a mont*; L. *ad montem*, to a mountain, *ad*, to, and *montem*, acc. sing. of *mons*, mountain.]
1. to add up (*to* a sum, quantity, etc.); as, the interest on the several sums *amounts* to fifty dollars.
2. to rise, reach, or extend (*to*); to be equal (*to* something) in value, meaning, or effect; as, the testimony of these witnesses *amounts* to very little.
3. to ascend; to go up. [Obs.]

ȧ·mount′, *v.t.* to imply; to amount to. [Obs.]

ȧ·mount′, *n.* 1. the total of two or more particular sums or quantities; as, the *amount* of 7 and 9 is 16.
2. the effect, substance, or result; the meaning; the import; as, the *amount* of the testimony is this.
3. a principal plus its interest.
4. a quantity; as, he met a fair *amount* of resistance.

ȧ·mōur′, *n.* [Fr., from L. *amor*, love.] a love affair, especially one of an illicit or secret nature.

ȧ·mōu·rette′, *n.* same as *amoret*.

ȧ·mōur-prō′pre, *n.* [Fr.] self-love; self-esteem.

ȧ·mōv·ȧ·bil′i·ty, *n.* liability to removal from office. [Rare.]

ȧ·mōv′ȧ·ble, *a.* removable.

ȧ·mōv′ăl, *n.* removal. [Obs.]

ȧ·mōve′, *v.t.*; amoved, *pt., pp.*; amoving, *ppr.* [L. *amovere*; *a*, *ab*, from, and *movere*, to move.]
1. to remove. [Obs.]
2. in law, to remove from a post or station.

ȧ·mōve′, *v.t.* to set in motion; to excite; to arouse. [Obs.]

äm·pä′rō, *n.* [Sp. and Port., defense, protection.] a preliminary certificate of title to land.

Am″pe·li·dā′cē·ae, *n.pl.* [LL., from Gr. *ampelis*, dim. of *ampelos*, vine.] in botany, *Vitaceæ*, an order of woody vines.

am″pe·li·dā′ceous, *a.* of or relating to the *Ampelidaceæ*.

am′pe·līte, *n.* [L. *ampelitis*; Gr. *ampelites*, from *ampelos*, vine.]
1. an earth containing pyrites, used by the ancients to kill insects, etc., on vines.
2. cannel coal.

Am·pe·lop′siṣ, *n.* [Gr. *ampelos*, vine, and *opsis*, appearance.]
1. a genus of plants, natural order *Vitaceæ*, nearly identical with *Vitis*, except that the flowers have a ring around the base of the ovary.
2. [a–] a plant of this genus, widely grown as an ornamental.

am′pēr·äġe, *n.* the strength of an electric current, measured in amperes.

am′pēre, *n.* [named after André Marie *Ampère*, French electrician.] the standard unit for measuring the strength of an electric current. It is the amount of current that would be produced by an electromotive force of one volt acting through a resistance of one ohm.

am′pēre bal′ănce, a form of ammeter.

am′pēre-foot′, *n.* a unit of electrical measurement, equal to a current of one ampere flowing through one foot of a conductor.

am′pēre-hour′, *n.* the quantity of electricity produced by a current of one ampere in one hour.

am′pēre mē′tēr, same as *ammeter*.

am′pēre tūrn, a unit of magnetomotive force, equal to the force resulting from the effect of one ampere passing around a single turn of a wire coil.

am·pē·rom′ē·tēr, *n.* same as *ammeter*.

am′pēr·sand, *n.* [a corruption of *and per se and*; *per se*, L., by itself. The first *and* is equivalent to the character & or &, made by combining the letters of L. *et*, and.] the symbol &, meaning *and*.

am·phet′ȧ·mīne, *n.* [*a*lpha-*m*ethyl-beta-*phen*yl-*et*hyl-*amine*.] a colorless, volatile liquid, $C_9H_{13}N$, used in its sulfate or phosphate forms as a drug to overcome mental depression, fatigue, etc., and to lessen the appetite in dieting.

am′phi-, [Gr. *amphi*, on both sides.] a combining form meaning *on both sides*; *round about*; *on all sides*.

am″phi·är·thrō′di·ăl, *a.* of or pertaining to amphiarthrosis.

am″phi·är·thrō′sis, *n.* [*amphi-*, and Gr. *arthrosis*, a jointing, from *arthron*, a joint.] in anatomy, a form of articulation in which the bones are connected by cartilaginous substance permitting slight motion, as the articulation of the vertebrae.

am′phi·as·tēr, *n.* [*amphi-*, and Gr. *astēr*, a star.] in mitosis, the long spindle with asters at either end that forms during the prophase, or first stage.

Am·phib′i·ȧ, *n.pl.* [*amphi-*, and Gr. *bios*, life.]
1. in zoology, a class of vertebrate animals whose young usually have gills and live in the water and later develop lungs. They include (a) the frogs, or *Anura*; (b) the tailed *Amphibia* (*Urodela*), as the salamanders and the sirens (*Sirenoidea*); and (c) the toads, or *Bufos*.
2. [a–] amphibious animals in general; amphibians.

am·phib′i·ăl, *a.* amphibian. [Rare.]

am·phib′i·ăn, *a.* 1. of or pertaining to the *Amphibia*; as, *amphibian* reptiles.
2. amphibious.

am·phib′i·ăn, *n.* 1. one of the *Amphibia*.
2. any plant that lives and grows either on land or in water.
3. a person or thing of double or doubtful nature.
4. in aeronautics, an airplane equipped with adjustable pontoons, capable of landing or taking off on land or on water.
5. a tank or other vehicle that can travel on either land or water.

am·phib′i·ō·līte, *n.* [*amphi-*, and Gr. *bios*, life, and *lithos*, stone.] a fossil of the *Amphibia*.

am·phib″i·ō·loġ′iç·ăl, *a.* pertaining to amphibiology.

am·phib·i·ol′ō·ġy, *n.* [*amphi-*, and Gr. *bios*, life, and *logos*, discourse.]
1. the branch of zoology which deals with the study of amphibious animals.
2. a treatise on amphibious animals, or the history and description of such animals.

am″phi·bī·ot′iç, *a.* that lives in water in one stage of development, and on land in another.

Am″phi·bi·ot′i·çȧ, *n.pl.* [*amphi-*, and Gr. *bios*, life, and *-ōtikos*.] a division of insects comprising those with aquatic larvae.

am·phib′i·ous, *a.* 1. that can live both on land and in water, as frogs, crocodiles, beavers, and the like.
2. of a mixed nature; partaking of two natures; as, an *amphibious* breed.
3. that can operate on both land and water.

am·phib′i·ous·ly, *adv.* in an amphibious manner.

am·phib′i·ous·ness, *n.* the quality of being amphibious.

am·phib′i·um, *n.*; *pl.* **am·phib′i·ȧ** *or* **am·phib′i·umṣ,** an amphibian. [Rare.]

am·phi·blas′tiç, *a.* [*amphi-*, and Gr. *blastikos*, tending to sprout.] in embryology, segmenting unequally.

am·phi·blas′tū·lȧ, *n.* a blastula in which the cells of one hemisphere differ greatly from those of the other, as in some sponges.

am′phi·bōle, *n.* [Gr. *amphibolos*, doubtful, from *amphiballein*, *amphi-*, and *ballein*, to throw.] a mineral, including tremolite, asbestos, actinolite, and hornblende, of many colors and of varied composition, occurring in both massive and crystalline form, composed mainly of silica, magnesium, and calcium, often with some aluminum and iron.

am·phi·bol′iç, *a.* pertaining to or resembling amphibole.

am·phi·bol′iç, *a.* 1. relating to amphibology; ambiguous; doubtful.
2. fluctuating.

am·phib′ō·līte, *n.* [from *amphibole*, and *-ite*.] a rock consisting largely of hornblende.

am″phib·ō·loġ′iç·ăl, *a.* doubtful; of doubtful meaning.

am″phib·ō·loġ′iç·ăl·ly, *adv.* with a doubtful meaning.

am·phi·bol′ō·ġy, *n.*; *pl.* **am·phi·bol′ō·ġieṣ,** [Gr. *amphibolos*, doubtful, and *logia*, from *legein*, to speak.]
1. double or doubtful meaning; ambiguity.
2. a sentence, etc. capable of double meaning, because of doubtful syntax; as, "the Duke yet lives that Henry shall depose."

am·phib′ō·lous, *a.* [Gr. *amphibolos*, doubtful.] doubtful in meaning; ambiguous; equivocal.

am·phib′ō·ly, *n.*; *pl.* **am·phib′ō·lieṣ,** 1. uncertain meaning of a proposition, phrase, etc. owing to faulty syntax or ambiguity.
2. employment of ambiguous language; quibbling.

am′phi·braçh, am·phib′rȧ·çhys, *n.* [Gr. *amphibrachys*; *amphi*, on both sides; and *brachys*, short.] in poetry, a foot of three syllables, a short, a long, and a short (⏑—⏑).

Am-phib-ra- | *chys* **hastes with** | **a state-ly** |
stride. —Coleridge.

am·phi·cär′piç, am·phi·cär′pous, *a.* [*amphi-*, and Gr. *karpos*, fruit.] bearing two kinds of fruit, differing either in shape or in the time of maturing.

am·phi·chrō′iç, *a.* [*amphi-*, and Gr. *chroa*, color.] having the power to bring out two different colors in the same substance, as red and blue in litmus paper.

am·phi·coe′lous, am·phi·coe′li·ăn, *a.* [Gr. *amphikoilos*, hollowed all around; *amphi-*, and *koilos*, hollow.] concave on both sides; biconcave: said of the vertebrae of fishes.

am′phi·cōme, *n.* [Gr. *amphikomos*, with hair all around; *amphi-*, and *komē*, hair.] a kind of figured stone, of a round, rugged shape: used by the ancients in divination. [Obs.]

am″phi·crē·at′i·nin, *n.* a leucomaine derived from muscle tissue.

am·phiç′ty·on, *n.* [Gr. *Amphictyones,* prob. from *amphiktiones; amphi,* around, and *ktiones,* dwellers.] in ancient Greece, a member of an amphictyonic council.

am·phiç·ty·on′iç, *a.* pertaining to the amphictyons or an amphictyony.

amphictyonic council; in ancient Greece, an assembly composed of delegates from the states associated in an amphictyony.

am·phiç′ty·ō·ny, *n.* in ancient Greece, a confederation of states established around a religious shrine or center, as at Delphi.

am′phid, *n.* in early chemistry, a salt formed by combining an acid with a base, as distinguished from a *haloid* compound. [Obs.]

am′phi·disk, *n.* [*amphi-,* and Gr. *discos,* a round plate.] a spicule with a finely notched disklike wheel at each end, characteristic of fresh-water sponges.

am·phi·drō′mi·à, *n.pl.* [Gr. *amphidromia,* running around, from *amphidromos,* a running around.] a ceremony in ancient Greece, in which a child was first carried around the hearth and then given a name. [Obs.]

am·phi·drom′iç·ăl, *a.* pertaining to the amphidromia. [Obs.]

am·phi·ġē′ăn, *a.* [*amphi-,* and Gr. *gē, gaia,* earth.] in biology, covering the earth; found throughout the world. [Rare.]

am′phi·ġen, *n.* [*amphi-,* and Gr. *genēs,* producing.]

1. in chemistry, any element that may combine with a metal or metals to form acids and bases, as sulfur or oxygen. [Obs.]

2. in botany, any cryptogamous plant that grows by cellular accretion alone, as the lichens.

am′phi·ġēne, *n.* same as *leucite* (a mineral).

am·phi·ġen′e·sis, *n.* [*amphi-,* and Gr. *genesis,* generation.] same as *amphigony.*

am·phiġ′e·nous, *a.* in botany, growing and spreading in every lateral direction, as lichens.

am·phi·gon′iç, *a.* relating to amphigony. [Rare.]

am·phig′ō·nous, *a.* relating to both parents.

am·phig′ō·ny, *n.* sexual reproduction; propagation by the sexes.

am·phi·gor′iç, *a.* relating to an amphigory; meaningless.

am′phi·gō·ry, *n.* [Fr. *amphigouri,* perhaps from Gr. *amphi,* about, and *gyros,* circle.] a nonsensical poem, as in parody or burlesque.

am·phil′ō·ġişm, am·phil′ō·ġy, *n.* [Gr. *amphilogia,* doubt; *amphi,* on both sides, and *logia,* from *legein,* to speak.] an ambiguous mode of speech; equivocation; amphibology.

am·phim′à·cēr, *n.* [Gr. *amphimakros,* long on both sides; *amphi-,* and *makros,* long.] in Greek and Latin poetry, a foot of three syllables, the middle one short and the others long, as in *cāstĭtās.*

am·phi·mix′is, *n.* [Mod. L., from Gr. *amphimixis; amphi-,* and *mixis,* mingling.] in biology, (a) the uniting of male and female germ cells from two individuals in reproduction; (b) crossbreeding.

Am·phi·neū′rà, *n.pl.* [L., from Gr. *amphineuron; amphi,* around, and *neuron,* nerve.] a class of sea mollusks, characterized by the symmetrical arrangement of the nerves along the sides of the body.

Am·phī′ŏn, *n.* [L.; Gr. *Amphiōn.*] in Greek mythology, the son of Zeus and Antiope: with a lyre that Hermes gave him he built a wall around Thebes by charming the stones into place.

Am·phi·ox′us, *n.* [*amphi-,* and Gr. *oxys,* sharp.] a genus of small, lance-shaped, translucent fishlike animals without bones, representing in structure a very low type of *Vertebrata. Amphioxus lanceolatus,* the lancelet, is the type.

am·phi·plat′y·ăn, *a.* [*amphi-,* and Gr. *platys,* flat, broad.] having the centrum flat at both ends: said of a vertebra.

am′phip·neūst, *n.* [*amphi-,* and Gr. *pnein,* to breathe.] one of a division of amphibians which have both gills and lungs at the same time, as the siren.

am′phi·pod, *a.* relating to the *Amphipoda.*

am′phi·pod, *n.* [*amphi-,* and Gr. *pous, podos,* foot.] an amphipodous animal.

Am·phip′ō·dà, *n.pl.* an order of sessile-eyed crustaceans, having usually seven pairs of legs, with some pairs of feet directed forward and some backward. The sandhopper and shore jumper are examples.

am·phip′ō·dăn, *a.* same as *Amphipod.*

am·phip′ō·dous, *a.* relating to the *Amphipoda;* amphipod; amphipodan.

am·phip′rō·stȳle, *a.* in architecture, having rows of columns in front and back but none on the sides.

am·phip′rō·stȳle, *n.* [Gr. *amphiprostylos,* having a double prostyle; *amphi-,* and *prostylos,* prostyle.] a double prostyle, or an edifice with columns in front and back but none on the sides.

Am·phi·rhī′nà, *n.pl.* [*amphi-,* and Gr. *rhis, rhinos,* nose.] a primary group of vertebrate animals having two nasal openings: opposed to *Monorhina.*

Am·phis·bae′nà, *n.* [Gr. *amphisbaina; amphis, amphi,* at both ends, and *baina,* from *bainein,* to go.]

1. [a–] in mythology, a serpent having a head at each end and capable of moving either way.

2. a genus of snakelike lizards with similar ends and hence seeming to have a head at each end.

am·phis·bae′noid, *a.* resembling the lizards of the genus *Amphisbæna.*

am·phis′ciăns (-fish′anz), **am·phis′ci·ī** (-fish′i-ī), *n.pl.* [L., from Gr. *amphiscios,* pl. *amphiscioi,* throwing a shadow both ways; *amphi,* and *skia,* shadow.] the inhabitants of the tropics: so called because their shadows at noon in one part of the year are cast to the north, and in the other to the south, according as the sun is north or south of their zenith.

am·phis′tō·moid, am·phis′tō·mous, *a.* [*amphi-,* and Gr. *stoma,* mouth, and *-oid.*] pertaining to entozoa of the genus *Amphistomum.*

Am·phis′tō·mum, *n.* a genus of parasitic worms having a minute cup-shaped mouth or sucker at each end of the body, by which they adhere to the intestines of the animals in which they are parasitic.

am″phi·stȳ′lăr, *a.* [from *amphi-,* and Gr. *stylos,* pillar; and *-ar.*] having columns at both front and back or on both sides.

am·phi·stȳ′liç, *a.* [*amphi-,* and Gr. *stylos,* pillar.] having supports for both the upper and lower mandibular arches, as the skulls of certain sharks.

am′phi·thē·à·tēr, am′phi·thē·à·tre (-tēr), *n.* [Gr. *amphitheatron,* from *amphi,* about, and *theatron,* theater, from *theasthai,* to see or look.]

1. an edifice, oval or circular, having a central arena surrounded by rows of seats rising higher as they recede from the arena. The ancient amphitheater at Rome, known as the Colosseum, seated about 90,000 people.

2. in gardening, an arrangement of shrubs, trees, or turf in amphitheatrical form.

3. in a general sense, any arena or place where public contests are held.

4. a sloping theater gallery.

5. a level place surrounded by rising ground; a valley of this form.

am·phi·thē′à·trăl, *a.* same as *amphitheatrical.*

am″phi·thē·at′riç, *a.* same as *amphitheatrical.*

am″phi·thē·at′riç·ăl, *a.* relating to or like an amphitheater; as, an *amphitheatrical* structure; an *amphitheatrical* contest.

am″phi·thē·at′riç·ăl·ly, *adv.* in an amphitheatrical form or manner.

am″phi·thē′ci·um (*or* -shi-um), *n.* [Mod. L., from *amphi-,* and Gr. *thēkion,* dim. of *thēkē,* a case, container.] in botany, the outer layer of cells in the spore case of a moss.

am·phit′ō·ky, *n.* [Gr. *amphitokia; amphi,* on both sides, and *tokia,* from *tiktein,* to produce.] parthenogenetic propagation of both male and female offspring.

Am·phi·trī′tē, *n.* [L., from Gr. *Amphitritē.*] in Greek mythology, one of the Nereids, goddess of the sea and wife of Poseidon.

am·phit′rō·pous, am·phit′rō·păl, *a.* [*amphi-,* and Gr. *tropos,* from *trepein,* to turn.] in botany, applied to an ovule curved upon itself so that the ends are brought near to each other with the hilum in the middle.

Am·phit′ry·ŏn, *n.* [L., from Gr. *Amphitryōn.*] in Greek mythology, a king of Thebes: his wife, Alcmene, became the mother of Hercules by Zeus, who seduced her by appearing in the likeness of Amphitryon.

Am·phi·ū′mà, *n.* [an alteration of Gr. *amphipneuma; amphi,* on both sides, and *pneuma,* breath.] a genus of amphibians, of which the Congo snake is the type, having the form of a snake but with permanent gill openings and four poorly developed limbs. They are found in the southern United States.

am·phō·pep′tōne, *n.* [Gr. *amphō,* both, and *peptone.*] a compound of hemipeptone and antipeptone, produced by gastric digestion.

am·phoph′i·lous, *a.* [Gr. *amphō,* both, and *philein,* to love.] capable of being stained by either acid or basic dyes.

am′phō·rà, *n.*; *pl.* **am′phō·rae,** [L., from Gr. *amphoreus,* a jar with handles.] among the Greeks and Romans, a tall two-handled jar with a narrow neck.

AMPHORAE

am′phō·răl, *a.* pertaining to, or resembling, an amphora.

am·phor′iç, *a.* having a hollow sound, as if produced by blowing across the mouth of a bottle; as, *amphoric* breathing.

am·phō·ter′iç, *a.* [Gr. *amphoteros,* both.] having both acid and basic properties.

am′ple, *a.*; *comp.,* ampler; *superl.,* amplest, [Fr. *ample;* L. *amplus,* prob. from *am, ambi,* around, and *plus, plenus,* full.]

1. large; wide; spacious; extended; great in bulk, size, or capacity; as, an *ample* house.

2. liberal; unrestrained; without parsimony; fully sufficient; as, *ample* provision for the table; *ample* justice.

3. adequate; enough.

Syn.—spacious, capacious, extensive, abundant, sufficient, plenteous, copious, plentiful. —When we mean by *ample* large in extent, we say *spacious* or *extensive;* large in content, *capacious;* large in quantity, *abundant* or *plenteous. Ample* is opposed to *scanty, spacious* to *narrow, capacious* to *small.*

am·pleç′tănt, *a.* [L. *amplectans,* ppr. of *amplecti,* to embrace.] twining about; clasping.

am′ple·ness, *n.* largeness; spaciousness; sufficiency; abundance.

am·plex·i·çau′dāte, *a.* [L. *amplexus,* pp. of *amplecti,* to embrace, and *cauda,* tail.] a term applied to certain bats in which the tail is united to the hind legs by a web.

am·plex′i·çaul, *a.* [L. *amplexus,* pp. of *amplecti,* to embrace, and *caulis,* stem.] in botany, nearly surrounding or embracing the stem, as the base of some leaves.

AMPLEXICAUL LEAVES

am·plex·i·fō′li·āte, *a.* [L. *amplexus,* pp. of *amplecti,* to embrace, and *folium,* leaf.] having stem-embracing leaves.

am′pli·āte, *a.* having an enlarged outer edge, as the wings of some insects.

am′pli·āte, *v.t.* [L. *ampliatus,* pp. of *ampliare,* to enlarge.] to enlarge; to make greater. [Obs.]

am·pli·ā′tion, *n.* 1. enlargement; amplification; diffuseness.

2. in civil law, a delaying to pass sentence; a postponement of a decision to obtain further evidence or hear additional argument.

3. something added; extension.

am′pli·ā·tive, *a.* 1. enlarging. [Rare.]

2. in logic, adding to the primary idea or attributes of a subject.

am″pli·fi·çā′tion, *n.* [L. *amplificatio,* from *amplificare,* to make large.]

1. enlargement; extension; the act of amplifying.

2. additional matter, details, etc.; as, the *amplification* of a report.

3. a statement, etc. with something added.

am′pli·fi·çā·tive, *a.* amplificatory.

am·pli′fi·çà·tō·ry, *a.* of, or having the nature of, amplification, or enlargement.

am′pli·fī·ēr, *n.* 1. a person or thing that amplifies.

2. in electricity and radio, a circuit, electronic tube, apparatus, etc. for increasing the strength of electrical impulses.

am′pli·fȳ, *v.t.*; amplified, *pt., pp.*; amplifying, *ppr.* [Fr. *amplifier;* L. *amplificare,* from *amplus,* large, and *facere,* to make.]

1. to enlarge; to augment; to increase or extend (power, authority, etc.).

2. to make more complete, fuller, etc.; to treat copiously, so as to present the subject in every view.

3. to exaggerate.

4. to strengthen (electrical impulses) by means of electronic tubes, etc.

am′pli·fȳ, *v.i.* to speak or write at length or in great detail; expatiate.

am′pli·tūde, *n.* [L. *amplitudo,* from *amplus,* large.]

1. the quality or state of being ample; extent; size.

2. abundance; fullness; copiousness.

3. scope or breadth, as of mind.

4. in astronomy, the angular distance of a

star from the true east or west point of the horizon, at the moment of its rising or setting.

5. in mathematics and physics, the extreme range of a fluctuating quantity, as an alternating current, pendulum, etc., generally measured from the average or mean to the extreme.

amplitude compass; an azimuth compass for reading amplitudes: its zeros are at the east and west points instead of the north and south.

amplitude of accommodation; in optics, the limit of accommodation.

magnetic amplitude; the arc of the horizon between the sun or a star (at its rising or setting) and the east or west point of the horizon, by the compass. The difference between this and the true amplitude is the variation of the compass.

am′pli·tūde mod·ū·lā′tion, 1. the changing of the amplitude of the transmitting radio wave in accordance with the sound being broadcast.

2. broadcasting that uses this.

Distinguished from *frequency modulation.*

am′ply, *adv.* 1. in an ample manner.

2. to an ample degree.

am·pōule′, am′pūle, *n.* [Fr. *ampoule*, from L. *ampulla*, a kind of vial.] a small hermetically sealed glass vial, for holding one dose of a solution to be used for hypodermic injection; loosely, any similar vial.

am′pul, *n.* 1. a small vial. [Obs.]

2. an ampoule.

3. in the Roman Catholic Church, a cruet used during Mass.

am·pul′là, *n.*; *pl.* **am·pul′làs** or **am·pul′lae,** [L.] 1. a narrow-necked globular vessel used by the ancient Greeks and Romans.

2. a vessel to contain the oil used in church ceremonials, particularly in the consecration of sovereigns.

3. a vessel for the wine or water of the eucharist.

4. in anatomy, a sac or dilated part of a tube or canal, as of a milk duct in a mammary gland.

5. a small membranous float attached to the leaves of some aquatic plants.

am·pul·lā′ceous, *a.* shaped like an ampulla, bottle, or inflated bladder; swelling.

ampullaceous sac; one of the flagellated chambers of sponges.

am′pul·lăr, am′pul·lā·ry, *a.* like an ampulla.

am′pul·lāte, am′pul·lā·ted, *a.* provided with an ampulla; bellied or bottle-shaped.

am·pul′li·fọrm, *a.* shaped like an ampulla; flask-shaped.

am′pū·tāte, *v.t.*; amputated, *pt.*, *pp.*; amputating, *ppr.* [L. *amputatus*, pp. of *amputare*; *amb-*, about, and *putare*, to prune.]

1. to prune; to cut off, as branches of trees.

2. to cut off, as a limb or other part of an animal body, especially by surgery.

am·pū·tā′tion, *n.* [L. *amputatio*.] the act of amputating; especially, the surgical operation of cutting off a limb or other part of the body.

spontaneous amputation; a falling off of a dead limb or part, as in some cases of gangrene.

am′pū·tā·tŏr, *n.* a person or thing that amputates.

am″pū·tee′, *n.* [from *amputate*, and *-ee*.] a person who has had a limb or limbs amputated: one with two limbs amputated is called a *double amputee*, etc.

am′pyx, *n.*; *pl.* **am′pyx·eṣ** or **am′py·cēṣ,** [Gr.] 1. among the ancient Greeks, a band or plate of metal, often enriched with precious stones, worn round the head by ladies of rank, and often having an ornament over the forehead.

2. the headband of a horse.

am·rī′tà, *n.* [Sans. *amrita*; *a* priv., and *mrita*, dead, from the root *mar*, to die.] in Hindu mythology, immortality; also, the ambrosial drink which produced it.

àmt, *n.*; *pl.* **àmt′ẽr** or **àmts,** [Dan. and Norw. *amt*, a district.] a territorial administrative division of the Scandinavian countries.

am′traç, *n.* [from *am*phibious and *trac*tor.] a small, open, armed amphibious vehicle with tractor treads, used in sea-to-shore operations in World War II.

Am′trak″, *n.* [*Am*erican *tr*avel tr*ack*.] a nationwide system of passenger railroad service.

à·muck′, *a.* and *adv.* [Malay *amoq*, engaging furiously in battle.] in a frenzy to kill: also *amok.*

to run amuck; (a) to rush about in a frenzy to kill; hence, (b) to lose control of oneself and do or try to do violent acts.

am′ū·let, *n.* [Fr. *amulette*; Sp. *amuleto*; L. *amuletum*, a charm.] a charm; something worn, often around the neck, as a remedy or protection against evils or mischief. *Amulets* were common in earlier days. They consisted of stones, metals, or plants, and sometimes of words, characters, or sentences, arranged in a particular order.

AMULETS

am·ū·let′iç, *a.* pertaining to an *amulet.*

à·mūr′çous, *a.* foul; full of dregs or lees. [Rare.]

à·mūṣ′à·ble, *a.* able to be amused.

à·mūṣe′, *v.t.*; amused, *pt.*, *pp.*; amusing, *ppr.* [Fr. *amuser*; *a*, L. *ad*, to, and OFr. *muser*, to gaze at, stare fixedly.]

1. to entertain; to occupy or interest the attention of agreeably; to divert.

2. to make laugh, smile, etc. with pleasure; to appeal to the sense of humor of.

3. to delude; to engage the attention of by hope or expectation; as, to *amuse* one by flattering promises. [Rare.]

4. to occupy the attention of; to distract; to bewilder. [Obs.]

Syn.—divert, entertain, beguile, enliven.

à·mūṣed′, *a.* [pp. of *amuse.*]

1. agreeably occupied or interested.

2. caused to laugh, smile, etc. with pleasure.

3. showing amusement.

à·mūṣ′ed·ly, *adv.* in an amused manner.

à·mūṣe′ment, *n.* 1. that which amuses or entertains; an entertainment or pastime.

2. the act of amusing; diversion; recreation; the state of being amused.

Syn.—diversion, pastime, recreation, sport, fun, merriment.

à·mūṣe′ment pärk, an outdoor place where there are various devices for entertainment, as a merry-go-round, roller coaster, etc., and, generally, booths for the sale of things to eat and drink.

à·mūṣe′ment tax, a tax on various forms of entertainment, paid on admissions to theaters, bills in night clubs, etc.

à·mūṣ′ẽr, *n.* one who amuses or entertains.

am·ū·ṣette′, *n.* [Fr., dim. of *amuse*, a toy, from *amuser*, to amuse.] an early type of light field gun.

à·mū′si·à, *n.* [Mod. L., from Gr. *amousos*; *a* priv., and *mousos*, song, music.] in psychology, a disorder characterized by inability to recognize musical sounds or to play or sing them.

à·mūṣ′ing, *a.* entertaining; diverting; exciting mirth; pleasing.

à·mūṣ′ing·ly, *adv.* in an amusing manner.

à·mū′ṣive, *a.* amusing or tending to amuse.

à·mū′ṣive·ness, *n.* the quality of being amusing.

à·myç′tiç, *a.* [Gr. *amyktikos*, lacerating, from *amyssein*, to tear.] abrasive; irritating.

à·mȳ·ē·lin′iç, *a.* devoid of a medullary sheath: applied to nerve fibers.

à·mȳ′e·lous, *a.* [L., from Gr. *amyelos*; *a* priv., and *myelos*, marrow.] without a spinal cord: applied to a fetus.

à·myg′dà·là, *n.*; *pl.* **à·myg′dà·lae,** [L., from Gr. *amygdalē*, almond.]

1. an almond. [Obs.]

2. in anatomy, any almond-shaped organ or part, as a tonsil.

à·myg·dà·lā′ceous, *a.* belonging to a group of shrubs and trees with soft, fleshy fruit that contains a single hard seed or stone, as the peach, almond, cherry, etc.

à·myg′dà·lāte, *a.* made from almonds, or like almonds.

à·myg′dà·lāte, *n.* 1. an emulsion made of almonds; milk of almonds. [Obs.]

2. a salt of amygdalic acid.

am·yg·dal′iç, *a.* 1. of almonds.

2. in chemistry, designating or of a crystalline acid, $C_{20}H_{28}O_{13}$, formed by the decomposition of amygdalin.

à·myg·dà·lif′ẽr·ous, *a.* [L. *amygdala*, almond, and *-ferous*, L. *ferre*, to bear.] bearing almonds; also, yielding almond-shaped bodies or kernels.

à·myg′dà·lin, *n.* [from *amygdala*, and *-in*.] a crystalline glucoside, $C_{20}H_{27}NO_{11}$, existing in bitter almonds.

à·myg′dà·line, *a.* 1. pertaining to or resembling almonds.

2. relating to an almond-shaped part in anatomy, as a tonsil or a lateral lobe of the brain.

à·myg′dà·lō-, a combining form used in anatomy to express relation to an amygdala.

à·myg′dà·loid, *n.* [Gr. *amygdalē*, almond, and *eidos*, form.] a variety of basaltic rock containing small cavities filled, wholly or in part, by nodules or geodes of different minerals, particularly agates, quartz, calcite, and the zeolites. When the imbedded minerals are detached, it is porous, like lava.

à·myg′dà·loid, à·myg·dà·loid′ăl, *a.* 1. pertaining to or consisting of amygdaloid.

2. almond-shaped.

A·myg′dà·lus, *n.* former genus name of the almond which is now listed as *Prunus communis.*

à·myg′dūle, *n.* a nodule occurring in amygdaloid.

am′yl, *n.* [L. *amylum*; Gr. *amylon*, starch, and *-yl*, Gr. *hylē*, matter.] any of various isomeric forms of the monovalent radical C_5H_{11}, found in certain compounds.

amyl acetate; a colorless liquid, $CH_3CO_2C_5H_{11}$; banana oil.

amyl alcohol; a colorless, sharp-smelling alcohol, $C_5H_{11}OH$, obtained by the fermentation of starchy substances and also present in fusel oil.

amyl nitrite; an amber-colored fluid, $C_5H_{11}NO_2$, smelling and tasting like essence of pears, used as a resuscitator in cases of drowning and prolonged fainting.

am′yl-, amylo-.

am·y·lā′ceous, *a.* pertaining to or resembling starch.

am·yl·am′ine (*or* -ēn), *n.* an amine in which one, two, and three hydrogen atoms of ammonia are respectively replaced by one, two, and three molecules of the radical amyl.

am′yl·āse″, *n.* [*amyl-*, and *-ase*.] an enzyme that helps change starch into sugar: it is found in saliva, pancreatic juice, etc.

am′y·lāte, *n.* a salt of the radical amyl.

am′y·lēne, *n.* a hydrocarbon, C_5H_{10}, obtained by the dehydration of amyl alcohol by means of zinc chloride, etc. It is a light, limpid, colorless liquid with a faint odor.

à·myl′iç, *a.* pertaining to amyl; derived from the radical amyl; as, *amylic ether.*

amylic alcohol; amyl alcohol.

amylic fermentation; the process of fermentation in sugar which produces amyl alcohol.

am′y·line, *n.* [L. *amylum*; Gr. *amylon*, neut. of *amylos*, unground; *a* priv., and *mylē*, mill.] the cellulose membrane which constitutes the covering of starch granules.

am′y·lō-, a combining form meaning: (a) *of starch*, as in *amylo*gen; (b) *of amyl*. Also, before a vowel *amyl-.*

am″y·lō·baç′tẽr, *n.* [*amylo-*, and Gr. *bacterion*, a staff.] a bacillus acting on starch.

am″y·lō·dex′trin, *n.* [*amylo-*, and *dextrin*.] a soluble starch.

à·myl′ō·gen, *n.* [*amylo-*, and *-gen*, Gr. *genēs*, born.] the water-soluble part of the starch granule.

am″y·lō·gen′e·sis, *n.* the formation of starch.

am″y·lō·gen′iç, *a.* pertaining to amylogen.

am′y·loid, am·y·loid′ăl, *a.* [*amylo-*, and *-oid*, Gr. *eidos*, form.] resembling or containing starch.

amyloid degeneration; in pathology, a change of structure by which amyloid is formed and deposited in the tissue or organ affected: called also *lardaceous* or *waxy degeneration.*

am′y·loid, *n.* 1. a starchy substance in some seeds, which becomes yellow in water after having been colored blue by iodine.

2. a complex protein deposited or developed in animal tissues in *amyloid* degeneration.

3. a food of nonnitrogenous or starchlike nature; a starchy substance.

am·y·lol′y·sis, *n.* [*amylo-*, and Gr. *lysis*, from *lyein*, to loose.] the process of converting starch into a soluble substance by the action of enzymes.

am″y·lō·lyt′iç, *a.* relating to amylolysis.

am·y·lom′e·tẽr, *n.* [*amylo-*, and Gr. *metron*, measure.] a device for determining the amount of starch in farinaceous substances.

am″y·lō·peç′tin, *n.* a substance that is nearly insoluble and that is obtained from the outer part of starch granules.

am′y·lō·plast, *n.* [*amylo-*, and Gr. *plastos*, verbal adj. of *plassein*, to form.] a starch-forming granule found within the protoplasm of vegetable cells; a leucoplast.

am″y·lō·plas′tid, am″y·lō·plas′tide, *n.* same as *amyloplast.*

am·y·lop′sin, *n.* [*amylo-*, and Gr. *opsis*, appearance.] the amylase in pancreatic juice, capable of converting starch into maltose.

am′y·lōse, *n.* [*amyl-*, and *-ose*.] any of a group of complex carbohydrates, as cellulose or starch, which are converted by hydrolysis into two or more simple sugars: now called *polysaccharide*: formula, $(C_6H_{10}O_5)_n$.

am′y·lum, *n.* [Gr. *amylon.*] starch.

amylum center; a small portion of protoplasm about which starch is formed; a pyrenoid.

am″y·ō·sthē′ni·ȧ, *n.* [L., from Gr. *a* priv., *mys, myos,* muscle, and *sthenos,* strength.] lack of muscular strength; imperfection or deficiency of muscular contraction.

am″y·ō·trōph′iç, *a.* pertaining to amyotrophy.

am·y·ot′rō·phy, *n.* [L., from Gr. *a* priv., and *mys, myos,* muscle, and *trophia,* from *trephein,* to nourish.] atrophy of the muscles.

am′y·ous, *a.* [Gr. *amyos, a* priv., and *mys, myos,* muscle.] lacking muscle or muscular strength.

Am·y·rald′ism, *n.* a moderate form of Calvinism taught by Amyraldus, or Amyrault, of France, in the seventeenth century.

Am·y·rald′ist, *n.* a believer in the doctrine of Amyraldism.

am′y·rin, *n.* a crystalline resin found in various gums, as Mexican gum elemi, etc.

Am′y·ris, *n.* a genus of tropical trees and shrubs yielding resinous products.

am′yss, *n.* almuce. [Obs.]

am′y·tal, *n.* [invented trade-mark based on *amylethyl.*] a colorless crystalline compound, $C_{11}H_{18}O_3N_2$, used as a sedative and hypnotic.

ȧ·myzt′li (-mist′), *n.* [native name.] a large otary or eared seal found on the Pacific coast of North America.

am′zel, am′sel, *n.* [Dan. and G. *amsel.*] the blackbird of Europe; also, the ring ouzel, *Turdus torquatus,* of Europe.

an, *indef. art.* and *a.* [weakened variant of *one* from AS. *an,* the numeral one, which lost stress and shortened its vowel as it came into use as a mere particle; the older and fuller form of *a.*]

1. one; one sort of.
2. each; any one.
3. to each; in each; for each; per; as, two *an* hour.

The chief grammatical function of *an* (*a*) is to contrast with *the.* It connotes a thing not previously noted or recognized; *the* connotes a thing previously noted or recognized. *An* now replaces *a* before all words beginning with a vowel sound or mute *h,* as, *an* orange, *an* honor; older usage also favored *an* before *h* in an unstressed initial syllable, as, *an* hotel, and before the sound (ū), as, *an* union, *an* eulogy (chiefly British usage). See also *a.*

an, an′, *conj.* [from *and*; ME. *an, and,* and, if.]

1. and. [Dial.]
2. if. [Archaic.]

an-, a- (not, without): a prefix used before vowels and *h,* as in *an*androus, *an*hydride.

an-, *ad-*: a prefix used before *n.*

-an, [Fr. *-ain, -en,* from L. *-anus,* of, belong to; also directly from L.] a suffix used in forming adjectives (and nouns derived from them), from nouns, meaning, in general: (a) *of, belonging to, characteristic of,* as in diocesan; (b) *born in, living in,* as in American; (c) *believing in, following,* as in Mohammedan. Also, after a vowel, *-n.*

ā′nȧ, *adv.* [Gr. *ana,* apiece.] in medical prescriptions, of each (ingredient referred to).

an′a-, [L. *ana-*; Gr. *ana-,* from Gr. prep. *ana,* up, upon, throughout.] a prefix meaning *up, upon, back, again, anew, throughout, according to.*

-a′nȧ, [neut. pl. of L. *-anus.*] a suffix used to form collective plurals; as, Johnsoni*ana,* Scaliger*ana,* the sayings, anecdotes, literary gossip, etc., of or pertaining to Johnson or Scaliger.

ā′nȧ, *n.* a collection of anecdotes, reminiscences, etc.

an″ȧ·bae′nȧ, *n.* [Mod. L., from Gr. *anabainein*; see *anabasis.*]

1. a fresh-water alga, often found in reservoirs, which gives a fishy taste and odor to water.
2. a mass of such algae.

ȧ·nab′ȧ·mous, *a.* [Gr. *ana,* up, and *bainein,* to go.] having ability to climb: applied to the climbing fish of India, *Anabas scandens.*

an·ȧ·ban′tid, *n.* a fish belonging to the family *Anabantidæ.*

An·ȧ·ban′ti·dae, An·ȧ·bat′i·dae (-ē), *n.pl.,* a family of fresh-water fishes, of which the genus *Anabas* is the type.

an·ȧ·ban′toid, *a.* of, or pertaining to, the *Anabantidæ.*

an·ȧ·ban′toid, *n.* an anabantid.

An·ȧ·bap′tism, *n.* [Gr. *anabaptismos.*] the doctrine of the Anabaptists.

An·ȧ·bap′tist, *a.* of the Anabaptists.

An·ȧ·bap′tist, *n.* [LL. *anabaptista,* from Gr. *anabaptizein*; *ana,* again, and *baptizein,* to baptize.] a member of a sect that denied the validity of infant baptism and practiced baptism of adults: originated in Switzerland c. 1522.

an″ȧ·bap·tis′tiç, an″ȧ·bap·tis′tiç·ăl, *a.* relating to the Anabaptists, or to their doctrines.

an″ȧ·bap·tis′tiç·ăl·ly, *adv.* in conformity with anabaptistic doctrine or practice.

An·ȧ·bap′tist·ry, *n.* anabaptism. [Rare.]

an″ȧ·bap·tīze′, *v.t.* to rebaptize. [Obs.]

An′ȧ·bas, *n.* [LL., from Gr. *anabas,* second aor. p. of *anabainein,* to go up; *ana,* up, and *bainein,* to go.] a genus of fresh-water fishes resembling the perches in form, but having their respiratory organs so constructed as to enable them to live for a long time out of water. *Anabas scandens* is the climbing fish of India.

ȧ·nab′ȧ·sis, *n.*; *pl.* **ȧ·nab′ȧ·sēs̗,** [Gr. *anabasis,* from *anabainein,* to go up; *ana,* up, and *bainein,* to go.]

1. [A–] the name of a work in which Xenophon gives an account of the expedition of the younger Cyrus into central Asia, 401–400 B.C.
2. [A–] this expedition.
3. any military expedition; as, the *anabasis* of Napoleon; the *anabasis* of Sherman.
4. the course of a disease from beginning to climax. [Obs.]

an·ȧ·basse′, *n.* [Fr.] a coarse blanketing manufactured in Holland and France.

an·ab′ȧ·tȧ, *n.* [LL.] a hooded cape, usually longer than the closed cape, and often worn in ecclesiastical processions.

an·ȧ·bat′iç, *a.* [Gr. *anabatikos.*] relating to an anabasis (sense 4); as, an *anabatic* rash. [Obs.]

an″ȧ·bī·ō′sis, *n.* [Mod. L., from Gr. *anabioein,* to come to life again.] resuscitation.

an″ȧ·bī·ot′iç, *a.* of anabiosis; restoring animation; reviving.

An′ȧ·bleps, *n.* [LL., from Gr. *anablepein,* to look up; *ana,* up, and *blepein,* to look.] a genus of malacopterygian fishes, whose eyes project and have two pupils, each eye appearing as if double, so that the fish apparently has four eyes; but there is only one crystalline humor, one vitreous humor, and one retina. The *Anableps tetraophthalmus* inhabits the rivers of Guiana.

ANABLEPS
Anableps tetraophthalmus

an·ȧ·bol′iç, *a.* pertaining to or promoting anabolism.

an·ab′ō·lism, *n.* [Gr. *anabolē,* a rising up, and *-ism.*] the process in a plant or animal by which food is changed into living tissue; constructive metabolism: opposed to *catabolism.*

an′ȧ·branch, *n.* 1. a river branch which flows back into the main stream.

2. a river branch that becomes absorbed by sandy ground.

an·ȧ·brō′sis, *n.* [LL., from Gr. *anabrōsis,* an eating up, from *ana,* up, and *bibroskein,* to eat.] an ulceration of soft tissues; a wasting away of the body. [Obs.]

an·ȧ·brot′iç, *a.* corrosive. [Obs.]

ä″nä·çä·huï′tẹ (-hwē′), *n.* [Mex.] a boraginaceous shrub, *Cordia Boissieri,* of Mexico, the wood of which was formerly reputed to be a remedy for consumption.

an″ȧ·çȧ·lyp′sis, *n.*; *pl.* **an″ȧ·çȧ·lyp′sēs̗,** [L., from Gr. *anakalypsis,* an uncovering.] revelation; an unveiling. [Rare.]

an·ȧ·çamp′tiç, *a.* [Gr. *anakamptein,* to bend back.] reflecting or reflected: a word formerly applied to that branch of optics or acoustics which treats of reflection.

an·ȧ·çamp′tiç·ăl·ly, *adv.* by reflection; as, echoes are sounds produced *anacamptically.* [Obs.]

an·ȧ·çamp′tiçs, *n.* 1. the study of reflected light. [Obs.]

2. the study of reflected sounds. [Obs.]

an′ȧ·çanth, *n.* one of the *Anacanthini.*

An·ȧ·çan′thī, *n.pl.* Anacanthini. [Obs.]

An·ȧ·çan′thi·nī, *n.pl.* [LL., from Gr. *an* priv., and *akanthinos,* thorny, from *akantha,* thorn.] a group of fishes of the order *Teleostia,* characterized by the absence of spines in the rays of the fins.

an·ȧ·çan′thous, *a.* in botany, having no spines; without thorns.

an′ȧ·çärd, *n.* [Fr. *anacarde*; L. *anacardium,* from Gr. *ana,* according to, resembling, and *kardia,* heart.]

1. the cashew nut.
2. any plant of the genus *Anacardiaceæ.*

An″ȧ·çär″di·ā′cē·ae, *n.pl.* a large and widely distributed order of polypetalous trees or shrubs, natives of tropical America, Africa, and India. There are 450 species, among which the most widely known are the poisonous sumac, the cashew, the pistachio, the mango, and the varnish tree.

an″ȧ·çär″di·ā′ceous, *a.* belonging to, or resembling, the *Anacardiaceæ.*

an·ȧ·çär′diç, *a.* pertaining to the cashew nut or its shell.

anacardic acid; a strong, burning acid obtained from the cashew nut. It is crystalline and white.

An·ȧ·çär′di·um, *n.* a genus of shrubs of the American tropics, including the cashew.

an″ȧ·çȧ·thär′sis, *n.* [LL., from Gr. *anakatharsis,* a clearing away; *ana,* up, away, and *kathairein,* to cleanse.] vomiting; also, a cough accompanied by expectoration.

an″ȧ·çȧ·thär′tiç, *a.* [LL., from Gr. *anakathartikos,* from *anakathairein,* to cleanse upward, vomit.] causing vomiting or spitting.

an″ȧ·çȧ·thär′tiç, *n.* in medicine, an expectorant or emetic.

An·açh′ȧ·ris, *n.* [LL., from Gr. *ana,* up, and *charis,* grace.] a genus of plants of the frogbit family, natives of North America; water thyme or water weeds.

an·açh′ō·ret, *n.* an anchoret.

an·açh′ō·rism, *n.* [Gr. *ana,* up, against, and *chōros,* place.] something foreign to the locality or country.

an·ȧ·çhron′iç, *a.* containing an anachronism; anachronistic.

an·açh′rō·nism, *n.* [Gr. *anachronismos,* from *anachronizein,* to refer to a wrong time; *ana,* against, and *chronos,* time.]

1. the representation of something as existing or occurring at other than its proper time, especially at an earlier time.
2. anything out of its proper historical time.

an·açh′rō·nist, *n.* one who commits an anachronism.

an·açh·rō·nis′tiç, *a.* erroneous in date; characterized by or involving anachronism.

an·açh′rō·nize, *v.t.* to make an anachronism of. [Rare.]

an·açh′rō·nous, *a.* anachronistic.

an·açh′rō·nous·ly, *adv.* erroneously as to time or date.

an·ac′id, *a.* [*an-,* without, and *acid.*] in medicine, without normal acidity.

ȧ·naç′lȧ·sis, *n.* [Gr. *anaklasis,* a bending back, from *anaklan*; *ana-,* back, and *klan,* to bend.] in anatomy, a bending backward; recurvature, as of a joint.

an·ȧ·çlas′tiç, *a.* [Gr. *anaklastos,* reflected, from *anaklan*; *ana,* back, and *klān,* to bend.]

1. in anatomy, bent backward; recurved.
2. in optics, of, caused by, or causing refraction.

an·ȧ·çlas′tiçs, *n.* formerly, that branch of optics which treated of the refraction of light.

an·ȧ·çlī′năl, *a.* [Gr. *ana,* back, and *klinein,* to bend.] in geology, lying across the dip of the rocks; as, an *anaclinal* valley.

an″ȧ·çlit′iç, *a.* [from Gr. *anaklinein,* to lean upon; *ana-,* on, and *klinein,* to lean.]

1. leaning; dependent.
2. in psychoanalysis, having the libido dependent upon another instinct.

an″ȧ·coe·nō′sis, *n.* [L., from Gr. *anakoinōsis,* from *anakoinoun,* to make common.] a figure of rhetoric by which a speaker asks an opinion of the point in debate by appeal to either his opponents or the audience.

an″ȧ·çō·lū′thi·ȧ, *n.* [Gr. *anakolouthia,* inconsequence.] anacoluthon.

an″ȧ·çō·lū′thiç, *a.* pertaining to or using anacoluthon.

an″ȧ·çō·lū′thiç·ăl·ly, *adv.* in a manner lacking sequence.

an″ȧ·çō·lū′thon, *n.*; *pl.* **an″ȧ·çō·lū′thȧ,** [Gr. *anakolouthos,* wanting sequence, not following; *an* priv., and *akolouthos,* following.]

1. a change from one grammatical construction to another within the same sentence, sometimes as a rhetorical device.
2. a sentence in which this occurs.

an·ȧ·çon′dȧ, *n.* [orig., Eng. name for a Ceylonese snake.]

1. a very long, heavy South American snake of the boa family.

2. any similar large snake that crushes its victim in its coils.

A·naç·re·on′tiç, *a.* pertaining to or by Anacreon, a Greek poet of the sixth century B.C., whose odes and epigrams are celebrated for their delicate, easy, and graceful air. They were devoted to the praise of love and wine. Hence, *Anacreontic* sometimes signifies amatory, convivial.

A·naç″re·on′tiç, *n.* 1. a poem by, or like those of, Anacreon.

2. [*pl.*] verses in the stanza form (abab) and rhythm much used by Anacreon.

an·à·çrot′iç, *a.* pertaining to or displaying anacrotism.

à·naç′rō·tism, *n.* [Gr. *ana*, up, again, and *krotos*, a beating, clapping.] in physiology, a notch or a secondary wave in the ascending limb of a pulse curve.

an·à·çrū′sis, *n.* [Gr. *anakrousis*, from *anakrouein*, to strike back; *ana*, up, back, and *krouein*, to strike.] one or more unaccented syllables introducing a line of verse ordinarily beginning with an accented syllable.

an·à·çrus′tiç, *a.* pertaining to an anacrusis.

an·à·çū′si·à, an·à·çū′sis, *n.* [Gr. *anakousis*, from *an* priv., and *akouein*, to hear.] complete deafness.

an′à·dem, *n.* [L. *anadema*; Gr. *anadēma*, from *ana*, up, and *dein*, to find.] a garland or fillet; a chaplet or crown of flowers. [Poetic.]

an″à·di·plō′sis, *n.* [L., from Gr. *anadiplōsis*, from *anadiploun*, to double; *ana*, up, again, and *diploos*, double.] grammatical duplication; the repetition of the last or any important word or words in a clause or sentence, in the beginning of the next; as, "He retained his virtues amidst all his misfortunes—misfortunes which no prudence could foresee or prevent."

an′à·drom, *n.* [Gr. *anadromos*, a running; *ana*, up, and *dromos*, from *dramein*, to run.] a marine fish that ascends rivers to spawn.

à·nad′rō·mous, *a.* ascending; going up: applied to sea fish spawning in rivers, or to ferns branched secondarily above the pinnae.

à·nae′mi·à, *n.* anemia.

à·nae′miç, *a.* anemic.

an·ae·ret′iç, *a.* aneretic.

an·ā′ēr·ōbe, *n.* [Mod. L. *anaerobium*.] a microorganism that can live and grow where there is no air or free oxygen: anaerobes get oxygen by the decomposition of compounds containing it.

an·ā·e·rō′bi·ăn, *a.* anaerobic.

an·ā·e·rō′biç, *a.* 1. of or produced by anaerobes.

2. able to live and grow where there is no air or free oxygen, as certain bacteria.

an·ā′e·rō·bieş (-biz), *n.pl.* anaerobes.

an·ā″e·rō·bi·ot′iç, an·ā·e·rō′bi·ous, *a.* capable of living in the absence of air or free oxygen: applied to microorganisms.

an·ā·e·rō′bi·um, *n.*; *pl.* **an·ā·e·rō′bi·à,** [Mod. L., from Gr. *an-*, without, and *aero-*, air, and *bios*, life.] an anaerobe.

an·ā′e·rō·phȳte, *n.* [Gr. *an* priv., *aēr*, *aeros*, air, and *phyton*, a plant.] in botany, a plant which does not require a direct supply of air.

an·aes·thē′si·à, *n.* anesthesia.

an·aes·thē′sis, *n.* anesthesia. [Obs.]

an·aes·thet′iç, *a.* and *n.* anesthetic.

an·aes′thē·tist, *n.* an anesthetist.

an·aes″thē·ti·zā′tion, *n.* anesthetization.

an·aes′thē·tīze, *v.t.* anesthetize.

An·à·gal′lis, *n.* [LL., from Gr. *ana*, again, and *agallein*, to adorn.] a genus of plants belonging to the family *Primulaceæ*, the pimpernels.

an′à·glyph, *n.* [Gr. *anaglyphon*, embossed work, from *ana*, up, and *glyphein*, to cut out, engrave.] an ornament in low relief chased or embossed in precious metal or stone, as a cameo.

an·à·glyph′iç, an·à·glyph′iç·ăl, *a.* of or relating to anaglyphs or the art of anaglyphy.

à·nag′ly·phy, *n.* 1. the art of sculpturing in low relief.

2. the work thus executed.

an·à·glyp′tiç, *a.* [L. *anaglypticus*; Gr. *anaglyptikos*, from *ana*, up, and *glyptos*, wrought in relief.] wrought in low relief.

an·à·glyp′tiç, *n.* anything wrought in low relief.

an·à·glyp′tiçs, *n.* the art of anaglyphy.

an·à·glyp′tō·gràph, *n.* 1. a device for producing drawings or etchings on a plane surface, so that they have the appearance of relief work.

2. an engraving made by this device.

an·à·glyp·tō·gràph′iç, *a.* pertaining to anaglyptography.

an″à·glyp·tog′rà·phy, *n.* the art or process of producing anaglyptographic drawings or etchings.

an·ag·nor′i·sis, *n.* [Gr. *anagnorisis*, from *ana* and *gnōrizein*, to recognize.] recognition, the unraveling or denouement of a dramatic plot. [Rare.]

an·à·gō′gē, *n.* [Gr. *anagogē*, a leading up; *ana*, up, and *agein*, to lead, drive.]

1. a heavenly or elevated state of the mind. [Obs.]

2. spiritual or mystical interpretation, especially of the Scriptures.

an″à·gō·get′iç·ăl, *a.* anagogical. [Obs.]

an·à·gog′iç, *a.* 1. of or by anagoge.

2. in psychology, relating to the moral or allegorical tendencies of the unconscious: a term used by C. G. Jung.

an·à·gog′iç·ăl, *a.* mysterious; elevated; spiritual; allusive.

an·à·gog′iç·ăl·ly, *adv.* in an anagogic or anagogical manner.

an·à·gog′içs, *n.* the study of hidden or mystical allusions, particularly in the Scriptures.

an′à·gō·gy, *n.* same as *anagoge*.

an′à·gram, *n.* [Fr. *anagramme*; LL. *anagramma*, from Gr. *ana*, back, and *gramma*, from *graphein*, to write.]

1. a word or phrase made from another by rearranging its letters, as *now—won*, *made—dame*.

2. [*pl.*] a game of making words by changing or adding letters.

an″à·gram·mat′iç, an″à·gram·mat′iç·ăl, *a.* of, like, arranged as, or containing an anagram.

an″à·gram·mat′iç·ăl·ly, *adv.* in the manner of an anagram.

an·à·gram′mà·tism, *n.* the act or practice of making anagrams.

an·à·gram′mà·tist, *n.* a maker of anagrams.

an·à·gram′mà·tīze, *v.t.* anagrammatized, *pt.*, *pp.*; anagrammatizing, *ppr.* to make an anagram of.

an·à·gram′mà·tīze, *v.i.* to make an anagram or anagrams.

an′à·gràph, *n.* an inventory; a commentary. [Obs.]

à·nä′guà (-gwà), *n.* the anaqua.

ā′năl, *a.* [LL. *analis*, pertaining to the anus.] pertaining to the anus; situated near the anus.

ā′năl, *n.* in zoology, an anal fin.

à·nal′cīte, à·nal′cim, à·nal′cime, *n.* [Gr. *analkis*, without strength.] a white or fleshred mineral, of the zeolite family, occurring in twenty-four-sided (trapezoidal) crystals and in cubes, and in traprock.

an′à·leçt, *n.*; *pl.* **an·à·leç′tà** or **an′à·leçts,** [Gr. *analecta*, from *analegein*, to collect; *ana*, up, and *legein*, to gather.] a literary fragment; an extract.

the Analects; a collection of the teachings of Confucius.

an·à·leç′tiç, *a.* collecting or selecting; made up of selections; as, an *analectic* magazine.

an·à·lem′mà, *n.* [L. *analemma*, a sundial which showed the latitude and meridian of a place; Gr. *analēmma*, a sundial, support, from *analambanein*, to take up.]

1. in geometry, a projection of the sphere on the plane of the meridian, orthographically made by straight lines, circles, and ellipses, the eye being supposed at an infinite distance, and in the east or west point of the horizon.

2. an instrument of wood or brass, on which such a projection is drawn, with a horizon or cursor fitted to it: formerly used by astronomers.

3. a scale drawn across the Torrid Zone on a terrestrial globe, by which the declination of the sun may be ascertained for every day of the year.

an·à·lep′sis, *n.*; *pl.* **an·à·lep′sēş,** [Gr. *analepsis*, restoration.]

1. the nutrition of an emaciated body; recovery of strength. [Obs.]

2. a kind of epileptic attack. [Obs.]

an′à·lep·sy, *n.* same as *analepsis*.

an·à·lep′tiç, *a.* in medicine, restorative; invigorating.

an·à·lep′tic, *n.* in medicine, a restorative.

an·al·gē′şi·à, *n.* [LL., from Gr. *analgēsia*; *an* priv., and *algēsia*, from *algēsis*, pain.] a state of not being able to feel pain.

an·al·gē′şiç, *a.* of or causing analgesia.

an·al·gē′şiç, *n.* something that produces analgesia.

an·al·get′iç, *a.* and *n.* analgesic.

an″al·lag·mat′iç, *a.* [Gr. *an* priv., and *allagma*, a change, from *allassein*, to change.] in mathematics, remaining unchanged in form by inversion.

an″al·lan·tō′iç, *a.* in anatomy or zoology, without an allantois.

An″al·lan·toid′ē·à, *n.pl.* in zoology, the division of vertebrates having no allantois, including amphibians, fishes, and lower forms.

à·nal′ō·găl, *a.* analogous. [Obs.]

an·à·log′iç·ăl, an·à·log′iç, *a.* [L. *analogicus*; Gr. *analogikos*, proportionate, analogous.] having analogy; founded on analogy.

an·à·log′iç·ăl·ly, *adv.* in an analogical manner; deducibly from some agreement or relation.

an·à·log′iç·ăl·ness, *n.* the quality of being analogical; fitness to be applied as an analogy.

à·nal′ō·gism, *n.* [Gr. *analogismis*, consideration; reasoning; from *analogizesthai*, to calculate, reckon, consider.]

1. an argument from cause to effect.

2. investigation of things by the analogy they bear to each other.

à·nal′ō·gist, *n.* one who uses analogy.

à·nal′ō·gīze, *v.t.*; analogized, *pt.*, *pp.*; analogizing, *ppr.* to demonstrate by analogy.

à·nal′ō·gīze, *v.i.* to use or show analogy.

à·nal′ō·gon, *n.* [Gr.] analogue.

à·nal′ō·gous, *a.* [L. *analogus*; Gr. *analogos*, according to a due ratio, or proportion.]

1. similar or comparable in certain respects.

2. in biology, similar in function but not in origin and structure.

analogous pole; in electricity, that pole of a pyroelectric crystal or other body which becomes positively electrified when subjected to heat.

à·nal′ō·gous·ly, *adv.* in an analogous manner.

à·nal′ō·gous·ness, *n.* the quality of being analogous.

an′à·logue (-log), *n.* [Fr. *analogue*, from L. *analogus*, from Gr. *analogos*, analogous.]

1. a thing or part that is analogous; that which corresponds with something else in construction, function, qualities, etc.

2. in linguistics, a cognate.

3. in biology, an analogous organ or part.

à·nal′ō·gy, *n.* [Gr. *analogia*, proportion, equality of ratios; from *analogos*, analogous.]

1. a similarity or likeness between things in some circumstances or effects, when the things are otherwise entirely different.

2. in mathematics, an equation between ratios; as, Napier's *analogies*.

3. an explaining of something by comparing it point by point with something else.

4. in biology, similarity in function between parts dissimilar in origin and structure: distinguished from *homology*.

5. in logic, the inference that certain admitted resemblances imply probable further similarity.

6. in linguistics, the process by which new or less familiar words, constructions, or pronunciations conform with the pattern of older or more familiar (and often unrelated) ones: as, *energize* is formed from *energy* by *analogy* with *apologize* from *apology*.

Syn.—resemblance, agreement, likeness, similarity, similitude, conformity, relation.

an·al·phà·bet′iç, *a.* and *n.* illiterate.

an′à·lȳse, *v.t.*; analysed, *pt.*, *pp.*; analysing, *ppr.* to analyze.

à·nal′y·sis, *n.*; *pl.* **à·nal′y·sēş,** [Gr. *analysis*, dissolving, a resolution of a whole into parts; *ana*, up, back, and *lysis*, a loosing, from *lyein*, to loose.]

1. a separating or breaking up of any whole into its parts so as to find out their nature, proportion, function, relationship, etc.

2. a statement of the results of this process.

3. in chemistry (a) the separation of compounds and mixtures into their constituent substances for the purpose of determining the nature (*qualitative analysis*) or the proportion (*quantitative analysis*) of the constituents; (b) the determination of the nature or proportion of one or more constituents of a substance, whether separated out or not.

4. in mathematics, (a) the solving of problems by means of equations; (b) examination of the relations of variables, as in differential and integral calculus, etc.

5. psychoanalysis.

6. in logic, the tracing of things to their source; the resolving of knowledge into its original principles.

Syn.—abridgment, digest, dissection.

an′à·lyst, *n.* 1. one who analyzes.

2. a psychoanalyst.

an·à·lyt′iç·ăl, an·à·lyt′iç, *a.* [ML. *analyticus*; Gr. *analytikos*, analytic, from *analytos*, dissoluble, from *analyein*, to loosen, dissolve.]

1. of analysis or analytics.

2. skilled in or using analysis.

3. that separates into constituent parts.
4. in grammar, using two or more words instead of an inflected form, as *more often* instead of *oftener*; expressing the principal grammatical relationships by the use of particles instead of inflections: opposed to *synthetic* or *inflectional*.

an·ȧ·lyt′iç·ăl·ly, *adv.* 1. in the manner of analysis; by analysis.
2. as regards analysis.

an·ȧ·lyt′i·çăl psȳ·chol′ō·gy, 1. psychology using mainly the introspective method.
2. a type of psychoanalysis originated by C. G. Jung, Swiss psychologist (1875–).

an·ȧ·lyt′iç ġē·om′e·try, the branch of geometry in which position is indicated by algebraic symbols and solutions are obtained by algebraic analysis.

an·ȧ·lyt′içs, *n.pl.* [*construed as sing.*] 1. the part of logic having to do with analyzing.
2. mathematical analysis.

an′ȧ·lȳ·zȧ·ble, *a.* capable of being analyzed.

an′ȧ·lȳ·zȧ·ble·ness, *n.* the state of being analyzable.

an·ȧ·ly·zā′tion, *n.* analysis.

an′ȧ·lȳze, *v.t.*; analyzed, *pt., pp.*; analyzing, *ppr.* [Fr. *analyser*, from *analyse*, analysis: see analysis.]
1. to separate or break up (any whole) into its parts so as to find out their nature, proportion, function, relationship, etc.
2. to examine the constituents or parts of; determine the nature or tendencies of.
3. to psychoanalyze.
4. in chemistry, to separate (compounds or mixtures) into their constituent substances in order to determine the nature or the proportion of the constituents.
5. in grammar, to resolve (a sentence) into its grammatical elements.
6. in mathematics, to solve by means of equations.
Also spelled *analyse*.

an′ȧ·lȳ·zẽr, *n.* 1. one who analyzes; that which analyzes or has the power to analyze.
2. in optics, that part of a polariscope which exhibits the properties of polarized light.

An·ȧ·mir′tȧ, *n.* [Mod. L., probably from native name.] a genus of climbing shrubs, native to the East Indies; *Anamirta cocculus* yields cocculus indicus, and is the sole species.

an·am·nē′sis, *n.* [Gr. *anamnēsis*, a calling to mind, from *anamimnēskein*; *ana*, again, and *mimnēskein*, to call to mind.]
1. a remembering, especially of a supposed life before this life.
2. in medicine, the history of a particular case of disease.

an·am·nes′tiç, *a.* aiding the memory.

an·am·ni·ot′iç, *a.* [Gr. *an* priv., and *amnion*, amnion, and *-ic*.] in anatomy, having no amnion, as fishes and amphibians.

an·ȧ·mor′phiṣm, *n.* 1. a distorted image of any object.
2. in biology, a gradual change from one type to another, generally from lower to higher.

an·ȧ·mor′phō·sçōpe, *n.* [Gr. *anamorphōsis*; *ana*, again, *morphē*, form, and *skopos*, a watcher, from *skopein*, to see.] a vertical cylindrical mirror which destroys anamorphosis and gives a correct representation of the object mirrored.

an·ȧ·mor′phō·sis (*or* -mor-phō′), *n.*; *pl.* **an·ȧ·mor′phō·sēṣ,** [Gr. *anamorphōsis*, a forming anew, from *ana*, again, and *morphoun*, to form.]
1. a distorted image which looks normal when viewed with a special device, as with an anamorphoscope.
2. the making of such images.
3. in biology, a gradual change of form by evolution: distinguished from *metamorphosis*.
4. in botany, an abnormal change of form that gives the appearance of a different species.

ANAMORPHOSIS

an·ȧ·mor′phō·sy, *n.* anamorphosis. [Obs.]

ȧ·nan′, *interj.* eh? what? what is it? [Obs.]

ȧ·nā′nas, *n.* [Sp., from native American name.]
1. the pineapple.
2. a wild kind of pineapple, *Bromelia Pinguin*, of the West Indies.

An·an·chȳ′tēs, *n.* [etym. uncertain.] a genus or subdivision of fossil sea urchins belonging to the tribe *Spatangidæ*, called in the south of England shepherds' crowns and fairy loaves, and especially characteristic of the Upper Chalk. They have a raised helmetlike form, simple ambulacra, transverse mouth, and oblong outlet.

ANANCHYTES
1. *A. ovatus* 2. *A. tuberculatus*

an·an′drous, *a.* [Gr. *an* priv., and *anēr*, *andros*, man.] in botany, without stamens: said of female flowers.

an·añ′gū·lăr, *a.* without angles. [Rare.]

An″ȧ·nī′ăs, *n.* 1. a disciple of the first Apostles whom Peter censured for lying and hypocrisy (Acts v.).
2. any liar, cheat, or hypocrite. [Colloq.]

an·an′thẽr·ous, *a.* in botany, without anthers.

an·an′thẽr·um, *n.* in botany, a staminodium.

an·an′thous, *a.* [Gr. *ananthēs*; *an* priv., and *anthos*, flower.] in botany, flowerless.

an′ȧ·paest, *n.* anapest.

an″ȧ·paes′tiç, *a.* anapestic.

an″ȧ·peī·rat′iç, *a.* [Gr. *anapeirasthai*, to try again.] caused by the too frequent or continuous use of the same muscles: applied to affections like writer's cramp.

an′ȧ·pest, an′ȧ·paest, *n.* [L. *anapæstus*; Gr. *anapaistos*, an anapest; from *ana*, back, and *paiein*, to strike.]
1. in poetry, a foot consisting of three syllables, the first two short, or unaccented, the last long, or accented; as, the word *in-tẽr-vēne′*.
2. a line of verse composed of or characterized by such feet. Example:

Can a bo | som so gen | tle remain
Unmoved | when her Cor | ydon sighs?
—Shenstone.

an·ȧ·pes′tiç, an·ȧ·paes′tiç, *n.* an anapestic verse.

an·ȧ·pes′tiç, an·ȧ·pes′tiç·ăl, *a.* pertaining to an anapest; consisting of anapestic feet.

an′ȧ·phāse, *n.* [*ana-*, up, and *phase*.] in biology, the stage in mitosis, after the metaphase and before the telophase, in which the chromosomes move toward the centrosomes.

ȧ·naph′ō·rȧ, *n.* [Gr. *anaphora*, from *anapherein*, to carry up or back.]
1. a figure in rhetoric in which the same word or words are repeated at the beginning of succeeding verses or clauses; as, "*Where* is the wise? *Where* is the scribe? *Where* is the disputer of this world?"
2. the most solemn part of the eucharistic service.
3. in astronomy, the oblique ascension of a star.
4. in linguistics, the device of syntactical cross reference through pronouns, auxiliary verbs, etc.

an·aph·rō·diṣ′i·ȧ, *n.* [Gr. *anaphrodisia*, from *anaphroditos*; *an* priv., and *Aphroditē*, Venus.] a lessening or a lack of sexual desire; impotence.

an·aph·rō·diṣ′i·ac, *a.* tending to lessen sexual desire.

an·aph·rō·diṣ′i·ac, *n.* a drug or treatment tending to lessen sexual desire.

an·aph·rō·dit′iç, *a.* [Gr. *anaphroditos*, without love.] in biology, produced asexually.

an″ȧ·phy·lac′tiç, *a.* of anaphylaxis.

an″ȧ·phy·lax′is, *n.* [Gr. *ana-*, without, and *phylaxis*, watching, guarding.] a condition of hypersensitivity to proteins and other substances in which exposure to or injection of the foreign matter results in attacks, sometimes so severe as to cause collapse and death.

an·ȧ·plas′tiç, *a.* 1. in medicine, characterized by a reversion to a more primitive, imperfectly developed form: said of cells.
2. in surgery, of or by anaplasty.

an′ȧ·plas·ty, *n.* [Gr. *anaplastos*, verbal adj. of *anaplassein*; *ana*, again, and *plassein*, to mold.] plastic surgery; the restoration of injured or deformed parts by the use of healthy tissue from other parts.

an″ȧ·plē·rō′sis, *n.* [LL., from Gr. *anaplērōsis*, from *anaplēroun*, to fill up.] a filling up of tissue to replace lost substance, as in the healing of wounds. [Obs.]

an″ȧ·plē·rot′iç, *a.* filling up; promoting anaplerosis. [Obs.]

an″ȧ·plē·rot′iç, *n.* a medicine which produces anaplerosis. [Obs.]

ȧ·nap′nō·grȧph, *n.* [Gr. *anapnoē*, respiration, and *graphein*, to write.] an automatic apparatus that measures and registers the lung capacity, that is, the greatest volume of air the lungs can expel after the deepest inspiration.

an·ap·nō′iç, *a.* pertaining to respiration.

an·ap·nom′e·tẽr, *n.* a spirometer.

an·ap·ō·diç′tiç, an·ap·ō·deiç′tiç, *a.* [Gr. *anapodeiktos*; *an* priv., and *apodeiktos*, demonstrable.] not demonstrable. [Rare.]

an·ȧ·poph′y·sis, *n.*; *pl.* **an·ȧ·poph′y·sēṣ,** [Gr. *ana*, back, *apophysis*, offshoot.] an auxiliary process found on some lumbar vertebrae.

an·ap·tot′iç, *a.* [Gr. *ana*, again, and *aptōtikos*, indeclinable.] in linguistics, losing or having lost the use of inflections; as, English is an *anaptotic* language: the term is now seldom used.

an·ap′ty·chus, *n.*; *pl.* **an·ap′ti·chī,** [Gr. *anaptychos*; *ana*, back, and *ptyssein*, to fold.] a shell-like, heart-shaped plate found in some fossil cephalopods.

ȧ·nä′quȧ, *n.* [Sp. Am.] a small tree of the borage family, with hard, close-grained wood, found in Texas and Mexico. Also spelled *anagua*.

an′ärch, *n.* [Gr. *anarchos*, without head or chief.] an anarchist.

ȧ·när′chiç, ȧ·när′chiç·ăl, *a.* 1. like, involving, or pertaining to anarchy or anarchism.
2. advocating anarchy.
3. tending to bring about anarchy; lawless.

an′ärch·iṣm, *n.* 1. the theory that formal government of any kind is unnecessary and wrong in principle; the doctrine and practice of anarchists.
2. anarchy; confusion; lawlessness.

an′ärch·ist, *n.* 1. one who believes in or advocates anarchism as a social and political theory.
2. one who promotes anarchy.

an·ärch·is′tiç, an′ärch·ist, *a.* pertaining to or resembling anarchists or anarchism.

an′ärch·īze, *v.t.*; anarchized, *pt., pp.*; anarchizing, *ppr.* to put in a state of anarchy.

an′ärch·y, *n.*; *pl.* **an′ärch·ieṣ,** [Gr. *anarchia*, lack of ruler or government, from *anarchos*, without chief or ruler; *an* priv., and *archos*, ruler.]
1. the complete absence of government and law.
2. political disorder and violence; lawlessness.
3. disorder in any sphere of activity.
Syn.—lawlessness, disorder, tumult, rebellion, riot, insubordination.

An·är′rhi·chas, *n.* [Gr. *anarrhichāsthai*, to clamber up.] a genus of ravenous fishes, including the sea wolf or wolf fish, *Anarrhichas lupus*, found in the northern seas.

An·är·throp′ō·dȧ, *n.pl.* [LL., from Gr. *an* priv., *arthron*, joint, and *pous*, *podos*, foot.] a division of the *Articulata*, having no jointed legs.

an·är·throp′ō·dous, *a.* relating to or resembling the *Anarthropoda*.

an·är′throus, *a.* [Gr. *anarthros*, without joints, without the article; *an* priv., and *arthron*, joint, article.]
1. in Greek grammar, used without the article: applied to a few Greek nouns in certain rare uses.
2. in zoology, really or apparently having no joints.

Ā′nas, *n.* [L. *anas*, a duck.] a genus of swimming birds comprising an indefinite number of species of fresh-water ducks.

an·ȧ·sär′çȧ, *n.* [Mod. L., from Gr. *ana*, up, and *sarka*, acc. of *sarx*, flesh.] generalized edema; generalized dropsy.

an·ȧ·sär′çous, *a.* pertaining to or characteristic of anasarca; dropsical.

an·ȧ·seīs′miç, *a.* [Gr. *anaseisma*, a shaking up and down, from *ana*, up, and *seiein*, to shake.] heaving: applied to an earthquake.

an·ȧ·stal′tiç, *a.* [Gr. *anastaltikos*, fitted for checking, from *anastellein*, to check, send back.] in medicine, astringent; styptic. [Obs.]

an′ȧ·stāte, *n.* [Gr. *ana*, up, and *histanai*, to cause to stand.] in biology, a substance formed in the anabolic processes: opposed to *catastate*.

an·ȧ·stat′iç, *a.* raised; embossed; in relief; also, having raised characters.
anastatic engraving; a process of transferring

an ink design to a metal plate, the uninked portions of which are then etched away by the action of acid, leaving the letters or design raised from the surface.

anastatic printing; the process of printing from anastatic plates.

An·ȧ·stat′i·cȧ, *n.* a genus of cruciferous plants native to the Orient, of which the resurrection plant, or rose of Jericho, is the only species. It is remarkable for the property the dried plant possesses of absorbing water when placed in it and appearing to live.

ANASTATICA
Rose of Jericho (*Anastatica hierochuntina*)
1. the plant 2. the root dried 3. the root expanded after being put in water

an·as′tig·mat, *n.* an anastigmatic lens.

an″as·tig·mat′iç, *a.* 1. not astigmatic.

2. corrected for astigmatism, as a lens.

an″as·tig·mat′iç lens, in photography, a compound lens made up of one converging and one diverging lens so that the astigmatism of one is neutralized by the equal and opposite astigmatism of the other.

ȧ·nas′tō·mōşe, *v.i.* and *v.t.*; anastomosed, *pt., pp.*; anastomosing, *ppr.* [Gr. *ana*, throughout, and *stoma*, mouth.] to connect by anastomosis.

ȧ·nas·tō·mō′sis, *n.*; *pl.* **ȧ·nas·tō·mō′sēş,** [LL., from Gr. *anastomōsis*, opening, from *ana*, again, and *stoma*, mouth.]

1. a connection between blood vessels, veins in a leaf, channels of a river, etc.

2. a surgical joining of one hollow or tubular organ to another, as of the severed ends of the intestine after resection.

ȧ·nas·tō·mot′iç, *a.* pertaining to anastomosis.

ȧ·nas′trō·phē, *n.* [Gr. *anastrophē*, a turning or inversion, from *anastrephein*; *ana*, back, and *strephein*, to turn.] in rhetoric and grammar, an inversion of the usual order of the parts of a sentence; as, *back he came*, for *he came back*.

an′ȧ·tāse, *n.* [Gr. *anatasis*, extension, from *ana*, back, and *teinein*, to stretch.] in mineralogy, an octahedrite.

ȧ·nath′ē·mȧ, *n.*; *pl.* **ȧ·nath′ē·mȧş,** [L., from Gr. *anathema*, anything devoted to evil, a curse; *anathēma*, a votive offering set up in a temple, from *anatithenai*, to set up.]

1. a ban or curse pronounced against an offender; a malediction or imprecation; especially, the solemn ban of excommunication pronounced in the Roman Catholic Church against great offenders.

2. a person or thing considered as accursed or damned.

3. anything greatly detested.

4. any strong curse.

abjuratory anathema; in church history, an anathema pronounced by a proselyte against the faith or church he was leaving for another.

Syn.—curse, ban, denunciation, imprecation.

ȧ·nath·ē·mat′iç, *a.* pertaining to or resembling an anathema.

ȧ·nath·ē·mat′iç·ăl·ly, *adv.* in the manner of an anathema.

ȧ·nath′ē·mȧ·tişm, *n.* the uttering of anathemas; denunciation. [Obs.]

ȧ·nath″ē·mȧ·ti·zā′tion, *n.* the act of anathematizing.

ȧ·nath′ē·mȧ·tīze, *v.t.* and *v.i.*; anathematized, *pt., pp.*; anathematizing, *ppr.* [LL. *anathematizare*; Gr. *anathematizein*, to make accursed, from *anathema*, a curse.] to curse; to pronounce anathemas (against).

ȧ·nath′ē·mȧ·tī·zēr, *n.* one who pronounces an anathema.

ȧ·nat′i·fȧ, *n.*; *pl.* **ȧ·nat′i·fae,** [LL., a contraction of *anatifera*, f. of *anatiferus*, from *anas*, *anatos*, duck, and *ferre*, to bear.] a stalked cirriped of the genus *Lepas*, commonly called goose barnacle.

ȧ·nat′i·fēr, *n.* same as *anatifa*.

an·ȧ·tif′ēr·ous, *a.* [L. *anas*, *anatos*, a duck, and *ferre*, to bear.] producing geese: applied to anatifae, or goose barnacles, and to the trees on which they were thought to grow, from a former belief that they fell into the water and became geese.

an′ȧ·tine, *a.* pertaining to or resembling a duck; ducklike.

ȧ·nat′ō·çişm, *n.* [L. *anatocismus*, from Gr. *anatokismos*, from *ana*, again, and *tokizein*, to lend at interest; *tokos*, interest.] interest upon interest; the taking of compound interest; also, the contract by which such interest is secured. [Archaic.]

an′ȧ·toid, *a.* in zoology, belonging to or resembling the ducks and geese.

An″ȧ·tō′li·ăn, *a.* 1. of Anatolia (the ancient name for Asia Minor) or its people.

2. Anatolia.

An″ȧ·tō′li·ăn, *n.* a native or inhabitant of Anatolia.

An″ȧ·tol′iç, *a.* 1. designating or of a subfamily of Indo-European languages, including the Armenian and extinct Phrygian.

2. Anatolian.

an·ȧ·tom′iç·ăl, an·ȧ·tom′iç, *a.* [Gr. *anatomikos*, from *anatomē*, *anatomia*, anatomy.]

1. pertaining to anatomy.

2. structural.

an·ȧ·tom′iç·ăl·ly, *adv.* 1. with reference to anatomy.

2. from the viewpoint of the science of anatomy.

ȧ·nat′ō·mişm, *n.* 1. the theory that the phenomena of life in organized bodies are the result of anatomical structure.

2. the application of the principles of anatomical structure and the display of anatomical details, as in sculpture, painting, etc.

ȧ·nat′ō·mist, *n.* 1. one who is proficient in the science of anatomy or expert in dissection.

2. one who dissects or analyzes.

ȧ·nat″ō·mi·zā′tion, *n.* the act of dissection; structural analysis.

ȧ·nat′ō·mīze, *v.t.* and *v.i.*; anatomized, *pt., pp.*; anatomizing, *ppr.* 1. to dissect (animal bodies, etc.) for the purpose of examining the structure and relationship of the constituent parts.

2. to analyze; to examine in detail.

ȧ·nat′ō·mī·zēr, *n.* one who anatomizes.

ȧ·nat′ō·my, *n.* [Fr. *anatomie*; L. *anatomia*; Gr. *anatomia*, *anatomē*, a cutting up, from *anatemnein*; *ana*, up, and *temnein*, to cut.]

1. the dissection of an animal or plant in order to determine the position, structure, etc. of its parts.

2. the science of the structure of animals and plants.

3. anatomical structure; the arrangement of parts in an organism.

4. a treatise or textbook on anatomy.

5. any critical analysis of something.

6. a subject for dissection; a result of dissection: variously applied, as to a corpse, a skeleton, an anatomical model, and, figuratively, to an emaciated person or a shadowy and immaterial thing.

comparative anatomy; comparison of higher and lower types, variations, and modifications of organism, in different classes and groups of animals.

Syn.—dissection, division, analysis, dismemberment.

ȧ·nat′ō·pişm, *n.* [Gr. *ana*, back, and *topos*, place, and *-ism*.] faulty arrangement; in art, inharmonious grouping.

an·ȧ·trep′tiç, *a.* [Gr. *anatreptikos*, from *anatrepein*; *ana*, up, and *trepein*, to turn.] refuting; defeating.

an′ȧ·tron, *n.* [Sp., from Ar. *an-natrūn*, from *al*, the, and *natrūn*, natron.]

1. soda; native sodium carbonate. [Obs.]

2. saltpeter. [Obs.]

ȧ·nat′rō·pous, ȧ·nat′rō·păl, *a.* [L. *anatropus*, from Gr. *ana*, up, and *trepein*, to turn.] in botany, inverted early in its development so that the micropyle is turned down toward the funicle: said of an ovule.

ANATROPOUS OVULE

ȧ·nat′tō, *n.* same as *annatto*.

an·ax′i·ăl, *a.* in biology, without a distinct axis; of irregular form.

An·ax·ō′ni·ȧ, *n.pl.* [LL., from Gr. *an* priv., and *axōn*, axle.] organisms lacking a distinct axis, and having consequently an irregular form.

an′bū̆r·y, am′bū̆r·y, *n.* [AS. *ampre*, *ompre*, a crooked, swelling vein, perhaps from *ange*, painful, and *berie*, berry.]

1. a soft tumor, wart, or bloody swelling on horses and cattle.

2. club root, a disease of plants of the cabbage family.

-ance, -an′cy, [Fr. *-ance*; L. *-antia*, *-entia*.] a suffix used in forming nouns from verbs, or from adjectives in *-ant*, and denoting action, quality, state, or result; as, abund*ance*, defi*ance*, forbear*ance*.

an′ces·tŏr, *n.* [OFr. *ancestre*; L. *antecessor*, one who goes before, from *antecedere*; *ante*, before, and *cedere*, to go.]

1. one from whom a person descends, either through the father or the mother, at any distance of time; a forefather.

2. in biology, an early form or type from which a later organism is developed.

3. in law, a predecessor in line of inheritance; a person from whom an estate has descended.

Syn.—progenitor, forefather, forebear.

an·ces·tō′ri·ăl, *a.* ancestral.

an·ces·tō′ri·ăl·ly, *adv.* with reference to one's ancestors.

an·ces′trăl, *a.* relating or belonging to ancestors; also, claimed or descending from ancestors; as, an *ancestral* estate.

an′ces·tress, *n.* a female ancestor.

an′ces·try, *n.* a series of ancestors, or progenitors; lineage, or those who compose the line of natural descent; hence, distinguished descent; as, he is proud of his *ancestry*.

An·çhī′sēş, *n.* [L.; Gr. *Anchisēs*.] in Roman legend, the father of Aeneas.

añ′çhŏr, *n.* [AS. *ancor*; Dan. *ancer*; O.H.G. *anchar*; L. *ancora*; Gr. *ankyra*, an anchor, hook.]

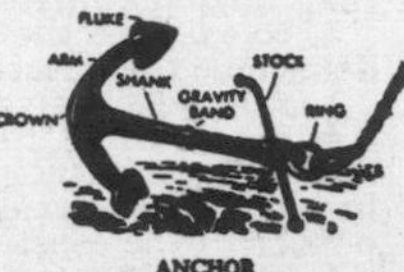

ANCHOR

1. a heavy object, usually a shaped iron weight with hooks, lowered into the water by cable or chain to keep a ship from drifting.

Anchors were named according to their relative importance and varying uses. Formerly, the largest one, and that on which most dependence was placed, was the *sheet anchor*. Then came the *best bower*, the *small bower*, the *stream anchor*, and *kedge anchors*. Today, the sheet anchor and the bower anchors are usually of equal size. A bower anchor for battleships weighs up to 21,000 pounds; kedges weigh from 100 to 900 pounds. A mushroom anchor is mushroom-shaped, capable of fastening wherever it falls, and is used chiefly for permanent moorings.

2. any instrument, device, or contrivance that holds something else secure, keeps it from giving way, etc.

3. in architecture, (a) a metal band holding walls or other parts of a building together; a clamp or brace, often with ornamental visible ends; (b) carved work, resembling anchors, in moldings, cornices, etc.

4. in zoology, an ancora, or one of the anchor-shaped calcareous hooks serving certain holothurians, particularly the *Synaptæ*, as a means of locomotion.

5. in a figurative sense, that which gives or seems to give stability or security.

6. same as *anchorman*.

at anchor; anchored; hence, *to lie* or *ride at anchor*.

foul anchor; (a) an anchor that is hooked or entangled with another anchor, or with a wreck or cable, or with the slack of its own cable; (b) a design showing an anchor with chain or hawser twisted around it.

to cast (or *drop*) *anchor*; (a) to lower an anchor, to keep a ship at rest; (b) to stay or settle in a place.

to drag anchor; (a) to drift inshore because of the failure of the anchor to hold; hence, (b) to lose ground; slip or fail.

to weigh anchor; (a) to heave or raise the anchor; hence, (b) to leave; go away.

añ′çhŏr, *v.t.*; anchored, *pt., pp.*; anchoring, *ppr.* 1. to keep from drifting, giving way, etc. by or as by an anchor.

2. to act as an anchorman on.

añ′çhŏr, *v.i.* 1. to lower the anchor overboard so as to keep from drifting; lie at anchor.

2. to stop; to fix oneself, one's attentions, etc.

añ′çhŏr, *n.* an anchorite. [Obs.]

añ′çhŏr·ȧ·ble, *a.* fit for anchorage.

añ′çhŏr·āġe, *n.* 1. anchor ground; a place where a ship can anchor.

2. a ship's anchor, or set of anchors, and all its necessary tackle.

3. a harbor toll for anchoring.

4. the condition of being at anchor.

5. something which holds like an anchor; as, the *anchorages* of a bridge.

6. that which is steadfast; that upon which one may rely.

añ′çhŏr·āge, *n.* the dwelling place of an anchorite.

añ′çhŏr·āte, *a.* 1. shaped like an anchor.
2. held by or as by an anchor.

añ′çhŏr bōlt, a bolt to hold down or secure a machine, etc.

añ′çhŏr chock, a block on which an anchor rests when stowed.

añ′çhŏr drag, any of various devices towed in the water by a vessel to keep its head to the wind or reduce its speed.

añ′çhŏred, *a.* 1. lying or riding at anchor; fixed in safety.
2. in heraldry, designating a cross with ends like the flukes of an anchor.

ANCHORED CROSS

añ′çhō·ress, *n.* a female anchorite.

añ′çhō·ret, *n.* same as *anchorite.*

añ′çhō·ret′iç, añ·çhō·ret′iç·ăl, *a.* same as *anchoritic, anchoritical.*

añ′çhŏr hōld, the hold of an anchor upon the ground; hence, security.

añ′çhŏr hoy, a lighter for raising anchors and chains in a harbor, etc.

añ′çhō·rīte, *n.* [OFr. *anachorete*; L. *anachoreta*; Gr. *anachōrētēs*, one retired, from *anachōrein*; *ana*, back, and *chōrein*, to retire.] a hermit; a recluse; one who retires to a solitary place, specifically, to devote himself to religious duties.

añ·çhō·rit′iç, añ·çhō·rit′iç·ăl, *a.* of or like an anchorite; solitary.

añ′çhō·rit·işm, *n.* the way of life of an anchorite.

añ′çhŏr·less, *a.* having no anchor; hence, drifting; unstable.

añ′çhŏr lift, a device for raising from the bottom a heavy pointed timber or pile that has served as an anchor.

añ′çhŏr līght, the light required to be shown by a vessel at anchor in a harbor at night.

añ′çhŏr līn′ing, sheathing used to protect the sides of a vessel when weighing anchor

añ′çhŏr·man, *n.*; *pl.* **añ′çhŏr·men,** 1. the end man in a tug of war.
2. the final contestant, as on a relay team or bowling team.
3. in radio and television, that member of a team of newscasters who coordinates the various reports.

añ′çhŏr·pēr″sŏn, *n.* same as *anchorman* (sense 3): used to avoid the masculine implication of *anchorman.*

añ′çhŏr plāte, a fixed metal plate that anchors the end of a cable, as in a suspension bridge.

añ′çhŏr ring, 1. the ring to which a cable is fastened.
2. in geometry, the solid generated by the revolution of a plane curve round an axis external to the revolving plane.

añ′çhŏr rock′et, a rocket with a fluked anchor head, for carrying a line to a wrecked ship: used in the lifesaving service.

añ′çhŏr shot, a shot furnished with anchor like flukes, propelled from a mortar to carry a livesaving line to wrecked ships.

an′çhŏr wätch, the night watch while a vessel is anchored.

añ′çhŏr well, a protecting recess for an anchor: formerly used on battleships to guard the anchor from the enemy's fire.

an′çhŏr·wom″ăn (-woom″), *n.*; *pl.* **an′çhŏr·wom″en** (-wim″), a woman member of a team of newscasters who coordinates the various reports.

an·chō′vy (*or* an′chō-), *n.* [Port. and Sp. *anchova*; Basque, *anchova, anchua*, anchovy, related to *antzua*, dry, dried fish.] a small fish about three inches in length, of the genus *Clupea* or *Engraulis.* Anchovies are found and caught in vast numbers in the Mediterranean, and are usually salted, spiced, and canned in oil, or made into a salty paste.

ANCHOVY

an·chō′vy peār (pār), a fruit of the West Indies, produced by the tree *Grias cauliflora.* It tastes like the mango.

Añ·çhū′să, *n.* [LL., from Gr. *anchousa*, the plant alkanet.]
1. a genus of plants belonging to the family *Boraginaceæ*, with downy, spear-shaped leaves and clusters of small purple or reddish flowers. Alkanet is a well-known species.
2. [a–] a plant of this genus.

añ′çhū·sin, *n.* alkannin.

añ′çhy·lōse, *v.t.* and *v.i.* same as *ankylose.*

añ·çhy·lō′sis, *n.* same as *ankylosis*

an″çhy·los″tō·mī′ȧ·sis, *n.* same as *ancylostomiasis.*

añ·çhy·lot′iç, *a.* same as *ankylotic.*

an·cien ré·gime′ (än″syañ″rā″zhēm′), [Fr., old order.] the former social and governmental system, especially that in France before the Revolution of 1789.

an′cient (-shent), *a.* [ME. *auncient*; OFr. *ancien*; L. *antianus, ancianus*, former, old, from *ante*, before.]
1. of times long past; belonging to the early history of the world, especially before the end of the Western Roman Empire.
2. having existed a long time; very old; antique.
3. aged: said of persons. [Archaic.]
4. having the wisdom, experience, etc. of age; venerable. [Archaic.]
5. in law, having twenty, thirty, or more years' continuous existence: used specifically in cases of defective proof; as, an *ancient* boundary.

ancient demesne; in English law, tenure of manors belonging to the crown in the times of Edward the Confessor or William the Conqueror. These were entered in the Doomsday Book.

Syn.—primitive, pristine, antiquated, obsolete, antique, old, old-fashioned, immemorial. —A thing is *ancient* when it is old; it is *antiquated, antique*, or *obsolete*, when it has gone out of use or fashion.

ān′cient, *n.* 1. a person who lived in ancient times.
2. an aged person.
3. in England, one of the senior members of the Inns of Court or of Chancery. [Obs.]

the Ancient of Days; God; Dan. vii. 9.

the ancients; (a) the people who lived in ancient, especially Graeco-Roman, times; (b) the ancient or classical writers and artists, especially of Graeco-Roman times.

ān′cient, *n.* [confusion of *ensign* with earlier *ancien*, ancient.]
1. a flag or streamer; an ensign. [Archaic.]
2. the bearer of an ensign. [Archaic.]

'Tis one Iago, *ancient* to the general.
—Shak.

ān′cient his′tō·ry, 1. history from the beginning of recorded events to the end of the Roman Empire in the West in 476 A.D.
2. something of the recent past that is well known or no longer important. [Colloq.]

ān′cient·ly, *adv.* 1. in ancient times; in times long since past.
2. in an old or ancient manner. [Rare.]

ān′cient·ness, *n.* the quality or state of being ancient; antiquity; existence from old times.

ān′cient·ry, *n.* 1. the quality or state of being ancient.
2. antiquity; also, that which is ancient.

By gain thereof it could not fail to find
Much proof of *ancientry.* —Jean Ingelow.

3. (a) aged persons collectively; (b) ancestry. [Obs.]

ān′cient·y, *n.* 1. age; antiquity. [Obs.]
2. in some old English statutes and writings, eldership or seniority. [Obs.]

an·cī′lē, *n.* [L.] in Roman antiquity, the sacred shield of Rome, said to have fallen from heaven in the reign of Numa.

an′cil·lā·ry, *a.* [L. *ancillaris*, from *ancilla*, a maidservant.]
1. pertaining to a maidservant, or female service. [Rare.]
2. helping; auxiliary.
3. subservient or subordinate: often used with *to*; as, a court *ancillary* to another jurisdiction.

ancillary administration; in law, a subordinate administration of such assets of a deceased person as are found in a state other than that in which he resided.

ancillary letters; letters issued to give authority for ancillary administration.

an·cip′i·tăl, *a.* [L. *anceps, ancipitis*, two-headed, double, doubtful; *an, amb*, on both sides, and *caput*, head.] in botany, two-edged, as the flat stems of certain grasses.

an·cip′i·tous, *a.* ancipital.

an·cis′troid, *a.* [Gr. *ankistron*, hook, and *eidos*, form.] shaped like a hook.

añ′cle, *n.* same as *ankle.*

añ′çon, *n.*; *pl.* **añ·çō′nēş,** [L. *ancon*; Gr. *ankōn*, the elbow; *ankos*, a bend.]
1. in anatomy, the elbow.
2. in architecture, a bracketlike projection supporting a cornice; a console.

Ancon sheep; a breed of sheep, now extinct, which originated in Massachusetts in 1791: called also *otter sheep.*

añ′çō·năl, añ·çō′nē·ăl, *a.* pertaining to the elbow.

añ′çōne, *n.* same as *ancon.*

añ·çō·nē′us, *n.*; *pl.* **añ·çō·nē′ī,** [L. *ancon*, elbow.] a muscle at the back of the elbow joint, used in extending the forearm.

añ′çō·noid, *a.* elbowlike.

añ′çō·ny, *n.* [prob. from Gr. *ankōn*, elbow, on account of its shape.] a piece of half-wrought iron, in the shape of a bar in the middle, but rude and unwrought at the ends. [Rare.]

añ′çō·rȧ, *n.*; *pl.* **añ′çō·rae,** in zoology an anchor.

-an′cy, see *-ance.*

an·cyl′ō·stōme, *n.* any of a genus of hookworms, parasitic in man and some other mammals.

an″cy·los″tō·mī′ȧ·sis, *n.* [Mod. L., from *Ancylostoma*, hookworm genus, from Gr. *ankylos*, crooked, and *stoma*, the mouth; and *-iasis.*] an infestation by hookworms.

an·cȳ′roid, *a.* [Gr. *ankyra*, anchor, and *eidos*, shape.] in anatomy, anchor-shaped.

and, *conj.* [ME. *and, an*; AS. *and, ond*; akin to G. *und*, O.H.G. *unti*, OS. *endi*, ON. *enn*; the original meaning was "thereupon, then, next."]
1. also; in addition; moreover; as well as.
2. plus; added to; as, six *and* two makes eight.
3. as a consequence or result; as, he told her *and* she wept.
4. if. [Obs.]
5. to; in order to; as, try *and* come tomorrow. [Colloq.]

and so forth; and the rest; and such things; et cetera.

an·dab′ȧ·tişm, *n.* blind struggling; uncertainty. [Obs.]

An·dȧ·lu′siăn, *a.* of Andalusia, its people, etc.

An·dȧ·lu′siăn, *n.* 1. a native or inhabitant of Andalusia.
2. the Spanish dialect of Andalusia.
3. a Mediterranean variety of chicken like the leghorn.

an·dȧ·lū′sīte, *n.* a mineral of different colors, occurring usually in thick lamellar forms and sometimes in rhombic prisms, composed chiefly of silica and alumina. Its name is derived from Andalusia, in Spain, where it was first discovered.

än·dän′tę (*or* an-dan′tē), *a.* and *adv.* [It., ppr. of *andare*, to walk.] in music, moderately slow; faster than larghetto and slower than allegretto.

än·dän′tę (*or* an-dan′tē), *n.* a musical passage or composition in andante time.

än·dän·tī′nō, *a.* and *adv.* [It., dim. of *andante.*] in music, a little faster than andante.

än·dän·tī′nō, *n.* any composition or passage in andantino time.

an′dȧ·raç, *n.* same as *sandarac.*

An·dē′ăn, *n.* pertaining to the Andes Mountains or their inhabitants.

an′dēş·ine, *n.* a triclinic feldspar containing both lime and soda. It was first discovered in the Andes.

an′dēş·īte, *n.* [from the *Andes* Mountains, in which it occurs.] a volcanic rock, the groundmass of which is usually composed of feldspar microliths, containing crystals of plagioclase feldspar.

An′dine, *a.* pertaining to the Andes Mountains; Andean.

An·dī′rȧ, *n.* [LL., from the native name.] a genus of tropical American trees, including the *Andira inermis* of the West Indies, a showy flowering tree yielding building timber and a medicinal bark: called also the *cabbage tree.*

ANDIRONS

and′ī·ron (-ūrn), *n.* [ME. *andyron, aundiren, andyre*; the ending was confused with ME.

iron, yron, yre, iron.] either of a pair of metal supports used to hold up logs in a fireplace: also called *firedog.*

and/or, either *and* or *or,* according to what applies; as, personal *and/or* real property.

an′drȧ·dīte, *n.* [named after the Portuguese mineralogist J. B. de *Andrada* (1763?–1838).] a variety of garnet containing calcium and iron.

an·drȧ·nat′ō·my, *n.* [Gr. *anēr, andros,* a man, and *anatomē,* dissection.] the dissection of a human body, especially of a male. [Obs.]

an′drē·ō·līte, *n.* [named from *Andreas,* in the Hartz Mountains, and *-lite,* Gr. *lithos,* stone.] the mineral harmotome, or cross stone: a former name.

An′drew, *n.* in the Bible, one of the twelve apostles; brother of Simon Peter.

an′drō-, andr-, [Gr. *anēr, andros,* man.] a combining form, denoting *man, male,* and in botany the *anther, stamen.*

an·drō·ceph′ȧ·lous, *a.* [*andro-,* and Gr. *kephalē,* a head.] having a human head and an animal's body, as the sphinx of Egypt.

An′drō·çlēş, *n.* same as *Androclus.*

an·drō·clin′i·um, *n.* same as *clinandrium.*

An′drō·çlus, *n.* [L. *Androclus* or *Androcles;* Gr. *Androklēs.*] a Roman slave who, according to legend, escaped death when thrown into the arena with a lion because the lion recognized him as the man who had once extracted a thorn from his foot.

an·drō·çō′ni·ȧ, *n.pl.* [*andro-,* and Gr. *konia,* dust.] minute scales on certain parts of the wings of some male butterflies.

an″drō·dī·oe′cious, *a.* [*andro-,* and *diœcious;* LL., from Gr. *dis,* twice, and *oikos,* house.] in botany, having hermaphroditic flowers on one plant and male on another plant of the same species, but none with female flowers only.

an·drō·dy̆′nȧ·mous, *a.* [*andro-,* and Gr. *dynamis,* power.] in botany, having stamens of unusual development.

an·droe′ci·um (*or* -shi-um), *n.* [*andr-,* and Gr. *oikos,* house.] in botany, the stamens (and the parts belonging to them) of a flower, taken as a whole.

an′drō·ġen, *n.* [*andro-,* and *-gen.*] a male sex hormone or similar substance that can give rise to masculine characteristics.

an·drŏġ′e·nous, *a.* [*andro-,* and *-genous.*]
1. in biology, producing male offspring.
2. in botany, bearing stamens only.

an″drō·gō·nid′i·um, *n.; pl.* **an″drō·gō·nid′i·ȧ,** same as *androspore.*

an·drŏġ′y·năl, *a.* same as *androgynous.*

an′drō·gyne, *n.* [*andro-,* and Gr. *gynē,* woman.]
1. a hermaphrodite.
2. in botany, an androgynous plant.

an·drŏġ′y·nişm, *n.* same as *androgyny.*

an·drŏġ′y·nous, *a.* [*andro-,* and Gr. *gynē,* woman.]
1. having the characteristics of both sexes; both male and female in one; hermaphroditic.
2. in botany, bearing staminate and pistillate flowers on the same parent stem.

an·drŏġ′y·ny, *n.* hermaphroditism, the state of being androgynous.

an′droid, *n.* [*andro-,* and *-oid.*] in science fiction, an automaton made to resemble a human being.

an·drō·lep′si·ȧ, an′drō·lep·sy, *n.* [*andro-,* and Gr. *lēpsis,* from *lambanein,* to seize.] in international law, the seizure by one nation of a citizen or citizens of another nation to enforce some claim or right: derived from Athenian law.

An·drom′ȧ·çhē, *n.* [L.; Gr. *Andromachē.*] in Greek legend, the faithful wife of Hector.

an·drō·mā′ni·ȧ, *n.* [*andro-,* and Gr. *mania,* madness.] nymphomania.

An·drom′e·dȧ, *n.* [L.; Gr. *Andromedē.*]
1. in Greek legend, the daughter of Cepheus, king of Ethiopia: Perseus rescued her from a sea monster and then married her.
2. a northern constellation.
3. a genus of plants, family *Ericaceæ,* found in northern latitudes and bearing white or rose-colored flowers in masses.

An′drō·mēde, An′drō·med, *n.* one of a stream of meteors which, at intervals of six or seven years, appear to radiate from the constellation of Andromeda.

an″drō·mō·noe′cious, *a.* [*andro-,* and Gr. *monos,* single, alone, and *oikos,* house.] in botany, having male and hermaphroditic flowers on the same plant.

an·drō·mor′phous, *a.* [*andro-,* and Gr. *morphē,* form.] formed like a man; of masculine appearance; as, an *andromorphous* woman.

an′dron, *n.* [Gr. *andrōn,* from *anēr, andros,* man.] in ancient Greece, the men's apartment in a house.

an·drō·pet′ăl·ous, *a.* [*andro-,* and Gr. *petalon,* a leaf or petal.] in botany, designating or of double flowers produced by the conversion of the stamens into petals.

an·droph′ȧ·gous, *a.* man-eating.

an·drō·phō′bi·ȧ, *n.* [*andro-,* and Gr. *phobos,* fear.] abnormal fear of the male sex.

an″drō·phō·nō·mā′ni·ȧ, *n.* [Gr. *androphonos,* man-killing, and *mania,* madness.] homicidal insanity.

an′drō·phōre, *n.* [*andro-,* and Gr. *phoros,* from *pherein,* to bear.]
1. in botany, a stamineal column formed by the union of the filaments, as in a monadelphous plant.
2. in zoology, a part in some pelagic *Hydrozoa* which bears male gonophores.

an·droph′ō·rous, *a.* in zoology, of the nature of an androphore.

an′drō·phyll, *n.* [*andro-,* and Gr. *phyllon,* leaf.] in botany, a microsporophyll.

An·drō·pō′gon, *n.* [*andro-,* and Gr. *pōgōn,* a beard.] a large genus of widely distributed grasses, including the broom sedge.

an′drō·sphinx, *n.* [*andro-,* and Gr. *sphinx,* a sphinx.] a sphinx with the head of a man and the body of a lion.

an′drō·spōre, *n.* [*andro-,* and Gr. *sporē,* seed.] in botany, a spore of some algae, which produces a large number of small bodies having male functions.

an·dros′tēr·ōne″, *n.* [*andro-,* and *sterol,* and *-one.*] a male sex hormone, $C_{19}H_{30}O_2$, found in male urine.

an·drot′ō·mous, *a.* having the filaments of the stamens divided.

an·drot′ō·my, *n.* [*andro-,* and Gr. *tomē,* a cutting, from *temnein,* to cut.] anatomy of the human body. [Obs.]

-an′drous, [Gr. *anēr, andros,* a man, a male.] an adjectival suffix used in botany, meaning *having stamens;* as, mon*androus,* di*androus.*

Än′dvä·ri, *n.* in Norse mythology, a dwarf from whom Loki stole a hoard of gold and a magic ring.

āne, *a.* and *pron.* one. [Dial.]

-āne, [arbitrarily coined.] a suffix denoting a hydrocarbon of the paraffin series; as, meth*ane,* eth*ane,* etc.

ȧ·nēal′, *v.t.* [ME. *anele;* AS. *an,* on, and *elian,* from *ele,* oil.] to anoint; specifically, to give extreme unction to. [Obs.]

ȧ·nēar′, *prep.* and *adv.* near. [Dial. or Poetic.]

ȧ·nēath′, *prep.* and *adv.* beneath. [Scot.]

an′eç·dō·tȧ, *n.* anecdotes (sense 1).

an′eç·dō·tāġe, *n.*
1. anecdotes and anecdotal matter as a whole.
2. the latter part of life, when one is supposed to be garrulous and fond of telling anecdotes: a play on the word *dotage.*

an′eç·dō·tăl, *a.* pertaining to or containing anecdotes.

an′eç·dōte, *n.* [Fr. *anecdote;* L. *anecdota,* from Gr. *anekdota,* neut. pl. of *anekdotos,* unpublished; *an* priv., and *ekdotos,* from *ekdidonai; ek,* out, and *didonai,* to give.]
1. [*pl.*] originally, little-known, entertaining facts of history or biography.
2. a short, entertaining account of some happening, usually personal or biographical.
Syn.—story, incident, tale, narrative, narration.

an·eç·dot′iç, an·eç·dot′iç·ăl, *a.* pertaining to, containing, or given to telling, anecdotes.

an′eç·dō·tist, *n.* a person who tells or collects anecdotes.

an′ē·lāce, *n.* same as *anlace.*

ȧ·nēle′, *v.t.* to aneal. [Archaic.]

an·ē·leç′triç, *a.* not electrifiable by friction.

an·ē·leç′triç, *n.* a substance that friction cannot electrify.

an·ē·leç′trōde, *n.* the positive voltaic pole of an electric battery.

an″ē·leç·trot′ō·nus, *n.* [Gr. *an* priv., *electron,* amber, and *tonos,* strain.] the state of lessened irritability of a nerve or muscle near the anode by the passage of an electric current through it.

an·el′y·trous, *a.* in entomology, without elytra.

ȧ·nē′mi·ȧ, ȧ·nae′mi·ȧ, *n.* [Mod. L., from Gr. *anaimia; an* priv., and *haima,* blood.] a condition in which there is a reduction of the number of red blood corpuscles or of the total amount of hemoglobin in the blood stream or of both.

ȧ·nē·miç, ȧ·nae′miç, *a.* pertaining to or affected with anemia.

an·e·mō-, [Gr. *anemos.*] a combining form meaning *wind,* as in *anemometer.*

ȧ·nem′ō·gram, *n.* [*anemo-,* and Gr. *gramma,* a writing.] the record of an anemograph.

ȧ·nem′ō·grȧph, *n.* [*anemo-,* and Gr. *graphein,* to write.] an instrument that measures and records the velocity and direction of the wind.

ȧ·nem·ō·grȧph′iç, *a.* of or pertaining to anemography; ascertained by the anemograph.

an·ē·mog′rȧ·phy, *n.* [*anemo-,* and Gr. *graphe,* a writing.]
1. the science of measuring and recording the velocity and direction of winds.
2. a treatise on winds.

an·ē·mol′ō·ġy, *n.* [*anemo-,* and Gr. *logos,* a discourse.] the branch of science which deals with the winds and their phenomena.

an·ē·mom′e·tēr, *n.* [*anemo-,* and Gr. *metron,* measure.] an instrument or machine for measuring the force and velocity of the wind. In the simplest form, four hemispherical hollow cups are extended upon metal arms, with their concave surfaces facing the same way, upon a vertical axis, which has at its lower extremity an endless screw. The endless screw is placed in gear with a train of wheelwork, and the indication is given by a needle which moves round a dial.

ANEMOMETER

an″ē·mō·met′riç, an″ē·mō·met′riç·ăl, *a.* relating to anemometry.

an″ē·mō·met′rō·grȧph, *n.* an anemograph.

an·ē·mom′e·try, *n.* the act or process of ascertaining the velocity and force of the wind, as by an anemometer.

A·nem′ō·nē, *n.* [Gr. *anemone,* windflower, from *anemos,* wind.]
1. a genus of plants, natural order *Ranunculaceæ,* having cup-shaped flowers, usually of white, purple, or red.
2. [a–] a plant of the genus *Anemone:* written also *anemony.*
3. [a–] a sea anemone.

VINE-LEAVED ANEMONE (*Anemone vitafolia*)

an·ē·mon′iç, *a.* of, pertaining to, or derived from an anemone, or from anemonin; as, *anemonic* acid.

ȧ·nem′ō·nin, *n.* an acrid, crystallizable substance, obtained from some species of anemone.

ȧ·nem′ō·phīle, *n.* [*anemo-,* and Gr. *philos,* loving.] an anemophilous plant.

an·ē·moph′i·lous, *a.* designating or of a plant in which pollen is conveyed to the stigma by the wind.

ȧ·nem′ō·sçōpe, *n.* [*anemo-,* and Gr. *skopein,* to view.] a device which shows or records the course or direction of the wind.

an·ē·mō′sis, *n.* [Mod. L., from Gr. *anemos,* the wind.] a crack made in young timber by the wind; wind shake.

an·en·cē·phal′iç, an·en·ceph′ȧ·lous, *a.* [L., from Gr. *an* priv., and *enkephalos,* brain.] in zoology, without a brain.

ȧ·nenst′, *prep.* anent. [Rare.]

ȧ·nent′, *prep.* [ME. *anent, anente, onefent;* AS. *on-efen; on,* on, and *efen,* even, on a level with.]
1. with regard to; as to; about; concerning.
2. toward; before; over against. [Obs.]

an·en′tēr·ous, *a.* [Gr. *an* priv., and *enteron,* intestine.] in zoology, without a stomach or intestine.

an·ē·pig′rȧ·phous, *a.* [Gr. *anepigraphos,* from *an* priv., and *epi,* on. and *graphein,* to write. without an inscription: said of coins, medals, etc.

an·ē·ret′iç, *a.* [Gr. *anairetikos*, taking away, destructive, from *anairetēs*, a destroyer.] destructive of animal tissue: also spelled *anaeretic.*

an′ēr·ġy, *n.* [Mod. L. *anergia*, from Gr. *an-*, without, and *ergon*, work.]
 1. a loss of strength; lack of energy.
 2. a condition in which the body fails to respond to the injection of an antigen.

an′ē·roid, *a.* [Gr. *a* priv., *nēros*, wet, liquid, and *eidos*, form.] not using liquid: said of a kind of barometer (*aneroid barometer*) which consists of a metallic box from which the air has been exhausted, the pressure of the atmosphere being shown by the movements of its elastic top, which are registered by a needle.

ANEROID BAROMETER

an′ē·roid, *n.* an aneroid barometer.

ānes, *adv.* once. [Dial.]

an·es·thē′ṣi·ȧ (*or* -thē′zȧ), *n.* [Gr. *anaisthēsia*, from *an-*, without, and *aisthesis*, feeling, from *aisthanein*, to feel.] a partial or total loss of the sense of pain, temperature, touch, etc., produced by disease or an anesthetic; insensibility: also spelled *anaesthesia.*

an″es·thē″ṣi·ol′ō·ġy, *n.* the science of anesthesia and anesthetics.

an·es·thet′iç, *a.* [Gr. *anaisthētos.*]
 1. relating to, with, or characterized by anesthesia.
 2. producing anesthesia.
 Also spelled *anaesthetic.*

an·es·thet′iç, *n.* anything, as a drug, gas, etc., that produces anesthesia: also spelled *anaesthetic.*

an·es′the·tist, *n.* a person trained to administer anesthetics: also spelled *anaesthetist.*

an·es″thē·ti·zā′tion, *n.* an anesthetizing or being anesthetized.

an·es′thē·tīze, *v.t.*; anesthetized, *pt.*, *pp.*; anesthetizing, *ppr.* to cause anesthesia in; give anesthetics to; make insensible: also spelled *anaesthetize.*

an′et, *n.* [Fr. *aneth*; L. *anethum*; Gr. *anethon*, *anisson*, the anise.] the dill or dill seed. [Obs.]

an′ē·thole, an′ē·thōl, *n.* [L. *anethum*, anise, and *-ol.*] a compound obtained from the oils of anise and fennel.

ȧ·net′iç, *a.* [L. *aneticus*; Gr. *anetikos*, relaxing; from *ana*, back, and *ienai*, to send.] in medicine, soothing.

ȧ·neū′ri·ȧ, *n.* [LL., from Gr. *a* priv., and *neuron*, nerve.] lack of nervous energy.

ȧ·neū′riç, *a.* lacking nervous energy; characterized by aneuria.

an′ū·ryṣm, an′eū·riṣm, *n.* [LL., from Gr. *aneurysma*, from *aneurynein*, to widen.] a soft, pulsating tumor formed by the unnatural dilation or rupture of the wall of an artery.

an·ū·ryṣ′măl, an·eū·riṣ′măl, *a.* pertaining to an aneurysm.

ȧ·new′, *adv.* 1. over again; another time.
 2. in a new form or way; as, to create *anew.*

an·fraç′tū·ōse, *a.* same as *anfractuous.*

an·fraç·tū·os′i·ty, *n.* 1. state or quality of being anfractuous.
 2. in anatomy, a sinuous depression or channel like those between the convolutions of the brain.

an·fraç′tū·ous, an·fraç′tū·ōse, *a.* [L. *anfractus*, pp. of *anfringere*; *an*, *ambi*, around, and *frangere*, to break.] winding; full of windings and turnings; roundabout; devious; tortuous.

an·fraç′tū·ous·ness, *n.* the state or quality of being anfractuous.

an·fraç′tūre, *n.* a mazy winding. [Obs.]

an̄·gā′ri·ȧ, *n.* in law, an act made compulsory by a government or feudal lord. [Obs.]

an̄′gȧ·ry, *n.* [L., *en angaros*, a dispatch bearer.] in international law, the right of a belligerent to use or destroy a neutral's property if necessary, subject to full indemnification.

an·ġel·ol′ō·ġy (-ji-), *n.* same as *angiology.*

an̄′ge·kok, *n.* [Esk.] an Eskimo medicine man.

ān′ġel, *a.* resembling angels; angelic; as, *angel* whiteness; *angel* face.

ān′ġel, *n.* [L. *angelus*; Gr. *angelos*, a messenger.]
 1. literally, a messenger. [Rare.]
 2. a spirit, or a spiritual being, employed by God, according to the Scriptures, to communicate his will to man.
 3. a ministering or guiding spirit.
 4. a conventionalized image of a white-robed figure in human form with wings and a halo.
 5. a minister of the gospel, or pastor; as, the *angel* of the church at Ephesus.
 6. a person regarded as beautiful, good, innocent, etc.
 7. an English gold coin current in the fifteenth, sixteenth, and seventeenth centuries: so called from bearing on its obverse a figure of the archangel Michael piercing a dragon.
 8. an angelfish.

ANGEL (sense 7)

 9. a person who provides the money for the production of a play, etc. [Slang.]
 destroying angel; (a) the angel of death; (b) in Mormon church history, a Danite.

ān′ġel, *v.t.* to back financially. [Slang.]

ān′ġel bed, an open bed without posts. [Obs.]

ān′ġel çāke, a light, spongy, white cake made without shortening or egg yolks: also called *angel food.*

ān′ġel·et, *n.* 1. a small gold coin formerly current in England, of half the value of an angel.
 2. a little angel. [Rare.]

ān′ġel·fish, *n.*; *pl.* **ān′ġel·fish, ān′ġel·fish·eṣ,** a species of shark, of the genus *Squatina*. It is from six to eight feet long, and takes its name from its pectoral fins, which are very large and, when spread, extend horizontally like wings.

ANGELFISH (*Squatina angelus*)

ān′ġel food, angel cake.

ān′ġel·hood, *n.* the state of being an angel or angelic.

an·ġel′iç, an·ġel′iç·ăl, *a.* [L. *angelicus.*]
 1. of an angel or the angels; spiritual; heavenly.
 2. like an angel in beauty, goodness, innocence, etc.
 angelic hymn; an ancient hymn of the Christian church, beginning with the song of the angels on the Nativity. Luke ii. 14.

an·ġel′iç, *a.* in chemistry, of or derived from angelica.
 angelic acid; a crystalline compound obtained from the roots of *Archangelica officinalis*, etc.

An·ġel′i·çȧ, *n.* [LL., from *angelicus*, angelic.]
 1. a genus of umbelliferous plants, found in the northern temperate regions and in New Zealand.
 2. [a–] any plant of this genus, including *Archangelica officinalis* or *Angelica Archangelica*, the leafstalks of which are used in confectionery and the roots and seeds in medicine.
 3. [a–] the blanched and candied stems of this plant.
 4. [a–] a liqueur flavored with angelica.
 angelica tree; a thorny shrub, *Aralia spinosa*, the berries of which are used in medicine.

an·ġel′iç·ăl·ly, *adv.* like an angel.

an·ġel′iç·ăl·ness, *n.* the state or quality of being angelic.

an·ġel′i·çō, *n.* a large plant of the parsley family, growing in North America.

an′ġe·lin, *n.* the common name of several tropical timber trees of the genus *Andira.*

ān′ġel·īze, *v.t.*; angelized, *pt.*, *pp.*; angelizing, *ppr.* to make angelic.

ān·ġel·ol′ȧ·try, *n.* [Gr. *angelos*, angel, and *latreia*, worship.] angel worship.

ān·ġel·ol′ō·ġy, *n.* the branch of theology dealing with angels.

ān·ġel·oph′ȧ·ny, *n.* [Gr. *angelos*, angel, and *phania*, from *phainesthai*, to appear.] the supposed manifestation of an angel or angels to man by actual appearance.

an′ġe·lot, *n.* [Fr. *angelot*; LL. *angelotus*, dim. of *angelus*, angel.]
 1. formerly, a musical instrument somewhat resembling a lute.
 2. a French coin of gold, first struck in the fifteenth century, so called because stamped with the figure of St. Michael; also, an English coin, struck at Paris while the city was in the possession of the English under Henry VI, and so called from bearing the figure of an angel supporting the escutcheons of England and France.
 3. a small, rich cheese, formerly made in Normandy and stamped like the French coin.

ān′ġel shot, [Fr. *ange*, an angel, a chain shot; so named from its appearance in the air.] a chain shot, formed of hollow segments, which are fastened by chains to a central disk, and spread winglike when fired.

An′ġe·lus, an′ġe·lus, *n.* 1. in the Roman Catholic Church, a prayer commemorating the Incarnation, offered at morning, noon, and night, at the sound of a bell. It is named from its first word.
 2. the bell rung as a signal for the *angelus* to be said.

ān′ġel wa̤′tẽr, a perfume prepared from angelica or from rose water, musk, etc. [Obs.]

an′ġe·ly wood, same as *angili wood.*

an̄′gẽr, *n.* [ME. *anger*, *angre*, affliction, anger; Ice. *angr*; Dan. *anger*, regret; G. *angst*, anguish, fear; L. *angor*, anguish, a strangling, from *angere*, to strangle; Gr. *anchein*, to strangle.]
 1. a strong feeling excited by a real or supposed injury: often accompanied by a desire to take vengeance, or to obtain satisfaction from the offending party; resentment; wrath; ire.
 2. the pain or smart of a sore or swelling: the original sense of the word. [Obs.]
 3. inflammation of a sore or wound. [Dial.]
 4. pain or trouble. [Obs.]
 Syn.—indignation, resentment, wrath, fury, rage, ire.

an̄′gẽr, *v.t.*; angered, *pt.*, *pp.*; angering, *ppr.*
 1. to excite anger in; to provoke; to enrage.
 2. to make painful; to cause to smart; to inflame; as, to *anger* an ulcer. [Rare.]
 Syn.—enrage, exasperate, inflame, irritate, provoke.

an̄′gẽr·ly, *adv.* angrily. [Obs.]

An′ġe·vin, An′ġe·vine, *a.* 1. of or pertaining to Anjou, an old French province, or to the family that formerly reigned over it.
 2. of or pertaining to the Plantagenet line of English kings (1154–1399).

An′ġe·vin, An′ġe·vine, *n.* 1. a native or inhabitant of Anjou.
 2. a member of the Plantagenet royal line.

an·ġi·eç′tȧ·sis, *n.* [Gr. *angeion* a vessel, and *ektasis*, extension.] in medicine, enlargement of the blood vessels, as in varicose veins.

an·ġi·en′çhy·mȧ, *n.* [L., from Gr. *angeion*, vessel, and *encyhma*, infusion.] the tissue of plants, which is supplied with vessels and ducts for the circulation of the sap.

an′ġi·li wood, an′ġe·ly wood, [Tamil *angili.*] the wood of an evergreen tree of India. *Artocarpus hirsuta.*

an·ġī′nȧ (*or* an′ġi-nȧ), *n.* [LL., from *angere*, to choke.]
 1. in medicine, any inflammatory disease of the throat or fauces, accompanied by spasms of choking or difficulty of breathing, and including quinsy, croup, etc.
 2. angina pectoris.

an·ġī′nȧ (*or* an′ġi-nȧ) **peç′tō·ris,** [L., angina of the breast.] a heart disease in which there are spasms of pain in the chest, with feelings of suffocation, usually due to anemia of the heart muscle.

an′ġi·nous, an′ġi·nōse, *a.* relating to angina or angina pectoris.

an′ġi·ō-, a combining form from Gr. *angeion*, a case, vessel, capsule, and used in compounds relating to seed, blood, or lymph vessels, or to something contained in or covered by such vessels.

an′ġi·ō·blast, *n.* [*angio-*, and Gr. *blastos*, a sprout or shoot.] the embryonic cell of a blood vessel or corpuscle.

an″ġi·ō·blas′tiç, *a.* relating to or resembling an angioblast.

an′ġi·ō·çärp, *n.* [*angio-*, and Gr. *karpos*, fruit.] any fruit that grows encased in an external covering.

an″ġi·ō·çär′pous, *a.* [*angio-*, and Gr. *karpos*, fruit.] having the fruit enclosed in an envelope, as in the case of a chestnut within its husk: also applied to certain lichens and fungi which have their seeds or spores covered.

an·ġi·og′rȧ·phy, *n.* [*angio-*, and Gr. *graphē*, description.]
 1. in anatomy, a description of the vascular system.

2. a treatise on standards of weight and measure, the instruments, and the vessels, used by various nations. [Rare.]

an·ġi·ol′ō·ġy, *n.* [*angio-*, and Gr. *logia*, from *legein*, to speak.] that branch of anatomy which treats of arteries, veins, lymphatics, etc.

an·ġi·ō′mȧ, *n.*; *pl.* **an·ġi·ō′mȧ·tȧ, an·ġi·ō′mȧs̹,** [*angio-*, and *-oma*.] a tumor formed of blood vessels and lymph vessels.

an″ġi·ō·neū·rō′sis, *n.* [*angio-*, and Gr. *neuron*, nerve, and *-osis*.] a disturbance of the vasomotor system.

an″ġi·ō·neū·rot′iç, *a.* pertaining to or afflicted with angioneurosis.

an″ġi·ō·sär·çō′mȧ, *n.*; *pl.* **an″ġi·ō·sär·çō′mȧs̹** or **an″ġi·ō·sär·çō′mȧ·tȧ,** [*angio-*, and *sarcoma*.] a sarcoma containing many dilated blood vessels.

an′ġi·ō·sçōpe, *n.* [*angio-*, and Gr. *skopein*, to view.] in anatomy and botany, an instrument for examining capillary vessels.

an′ġi·ō·spẽrm, *n.* [*angio-*, and Gr. *sperma*, seed.] a plant or tree bearing its seeds in a closed seed vessel, as the apple, the oak, etc.: opposed to *gymnosperm*.

an″ġi·ō·spẽr′mous, an″ġi·ō·spẽr′mȧ·tous, *a.* having seeds in a closed seed vessel: opposed to *gymnospermous*.

An″ġi·ō·stō′mȧ·tȧ, *n.pl.* [*angio-*, and Gr. *stomata*, pl. of *stoma*, mouth.]
1. a suborder of snakes characterized by cloven mouths that do not dilate.
2. a family of gastropods, having shells with contracted apertures.

an″ġi·ō·stom′ȧ·tous, *a*, pertaining to or resembling the *Angiostomata*.

an·ġi·os′tō·mous, *a.* in zoology, having a narrow aperture, as some univalve shells.

an″ġi·ō·ten′sin, *n.* [*angio-*, and *tension*, and *-in*.] a polypeptide that causes a rise in blood pressure by constricting blood vessels, formed by the action of renin on a plasma protein.

an·ġi·ot′ō·my, *n.* [*angio-*, and Gr. *tomē*, a cutting, from *temnein*, to cut.] formerly, in medicine, the anatomy or dissection of the blood vessels.

an̄′gle, *v.i.*; angled, *pt.*, *pp.*; angling, *ppr.* [ME. *angle*; AS. *angel, angul*, a hook, fishhook; Ice. *angi*, a sting, spine, prob. from the same root as Gr. *ongkos*, a hook, barb.]
1. to fish with a hook and line.
2. to try to gain something by some bait or trick; to scheme; as, to *angle* for compliments.

an̄′gle, *v.t.* 1. to fish in with hook or line; as, to *angle* a river. [Rare.]
2. to allure; to entice; as, he *angled* their hearts. [Obs.]

an̄′gle, *n.* 1. a fishhook with or without the line and rod. [Archaic.]
2. a person or thing that ensnares. [Obs.]

an̄′gle, *n.* [Fr. *angle*; Sp. *angulo*, from L. *angulus*, a corner, angle; Gr. *angkylos*, bent, crooked.]
1. the shape made by two straight lines meeting in a point, or by two plane surfaces meeting along a line.
2. the space between such lines or surfaces.
3. the amount of difference in direction between them, measured in degrees.
4. a sharp or projecting corner.
5. an aspect, as of a problem; point of view; as, consider this from all *angles*.
6. in astrology, any of the four houses, the first, fourth, seventh, or tenth, situated at the cardinal points of the compass.
7. in heraldry, a bend or curve in the band or ribbon of an armorial charge.

an̄′gle, *v.t.* and *v.i.*; angled, *pt.*, *pp.*; angling, *ppr.* 1. to move or bend at an angle or by means of angles.
2. to give a specific aspect or point of view to (a story, report, etc.). [Colloq.]
angle of attack; in aeronautics, the acute angle between the line of the normal wind direction and the chord of an airfoil.
angle of incidence; see under *incidence*.
angle of refraction; see under *refraction*.
angle of view; in optics, the angle subtended by two lines drawn from the corners of the objective to the center of a lens.
curvilineal angle; an angle formed by two curved lines.
mixtilineal angle; an angle, one side of which is a right line and the other a curved line.
rectilineal or *right-lined angle*; an angle formed by two straight lines.
spherical angle; an angle made by the meeting of two arcs of great circles, cutting one another on the surface of a globe or sphere.

an̄′gle bär, 1. in carpentry, a vertical bar at the angle made by the meeting of two faces of a bay window.
2. in machinery, same as *angle iron*.

an̄′gle bēad, in architecture, a piece of wood fixed vertically upon an exterior or salient angle, flush with the surface of the plaster.

an̄′gle brāce, 1. a piece of timber fixed as a brace across an interior angle. When it joins opposite corners of a rectangular frame, it is called a *diagonal brace*.
2. an instrument consisting of a rectangular crank frame like the carpenter's brace, used for boring holes in angular positions.

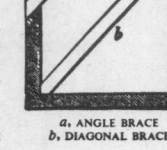

a, ANGLE BRACE
b, DIAGONAL BRACE

an̄′gled (-gld), *a.* 1. having an angle or angles: composed of angles: often used in compounds; as, a many-*angled* figure.
2. in heraldry, designating or of a line, usually straight, which is broken short, as at an angle.
3. set at an angle.

an̄′gle ī″ron (-ũrn), a piece of iron or steel in the shape of the letter L or V, used for joining or reinforcing two beams, girders, etc.

A. ANGLE IRON

an′gle mē′tẽr, [*angle*, and Gr. *metron*, measure.] an instrument for measuring angles; a clinometer.

an̄′gle plāte, two plates of metal set at right angles, having slots for the reception of bolts: used in machine set-up work.

an̄′gle·pod, *n.* a vine of the southern United States, bearing angular pods.

an̄′glẽr, *n.* 1. one who angles; a fisherman.
2. a fish, *Lophius piscatorius*, of Europe and America, having peculiar filaments projecting from its head, with which it is said to entice the fish on which it feeds.
3. a person who schemes or uses tricks to get something.

An̄′gles̹, *n.pl.* [L. *Angli*; AS. *Angle, Engle*, the Angles, from *Angel, Angul*, district in Holstein, lit., hook: so named from its shape.] a Germanic, Anglo-Frisian people that settled in eastern England in the fifth century A.D.: the name *England* is from *Englaland*, land of the Angles, and *English* is from *Englisc*, of the Angles.

an̄′gle·sīte, *n.* [from *Anglesey*, Wales, where it was first found, and *-ite*.] native sulfate of lead. It occurs in white or yellowish prismatic crystals, semitransparent, with a glassy or adamantine luster, and is found associated with other ores of lead.

an̄′gle ståff, an angle bead treated decoratively.

an̄′gle·wīşe, *adv.* angularly.

an̄′gle·wŏrm, *n.* an earthworm: so called because used by fishermen for bait.

An̄′gli·ăn, *a.* of or pertaining to the Angles, or their land, culture, dialect, etc.

An̄′gli·ăn, *n.* 1. one of the Angles.
2. the dialect spoken by the Angles.

An̄′gliç, *n.* a simplified form of the English language for international communication: developed by R. E. Zachrisson (1880–1937), Swedish linguist.

An̄′gli·çăn, *a.* [L. *Anglicanus*, from *Anglicus*, pertaining to the Angles, or to England.]
1. English; pertaining to England, its people, or their culture.
2. of or pertaining to the Church of England, or the churches in accord with it as to doctrines and form, as the Episcopal churches in Ireland, Scotland, Wales, and the British colonies, and the Protestant Episcopal Church of the United States.

An̄′gli·çăn, *n.* a member of the Church of England or any of the churches in accord with it as to doctrines and form; especially, a High-Churchman.

An̄′gli·çăn·iṣm, *n.* 1. belief in the principles and ritual of the established Church of England.
2. the principles and forms of the Church of England: often, in a restricted sense, the doctrines of the High-Church party.
3. devotion to England and things that are English.

An̄′gli·cē, *adv.* [ML.] in English; in the English manner or style; as, Wien, *Anglice* Vienna.

An̄′gli·ciṣm, *n.* 1. a word, idiom, or meaning peculiar to English, especially British English; Briticism.
2. a typically English trait, custom, etc.
3. the quality of being English.

An̄′gli·cist, *n.* a student of or authority on the English language and literature.

An̄″gli·ci·zā′tion, *n.* 1. an Anglicizing or being Anglicized.
2. the result of Anglicizing.

An̄′gli·cize, *v.t.* and *v.i.*; Anglicized, *pt.*, *pp.*; Anglicizing, *ppr.* to change to English idiom, pronunciation, customs, manners, etc.

an′gling, *n.* the act or art of one who angles, or fishes with hook and line.

An̄′glist, *n.* an authority on England.

An̄′glō-, a combining form from Latin *Anglus*, English, and signifying (a) *English, English and*, as in *Anglo*phile, *Anglo*-American; (b) *Anglican*, as in *Anglo*-Catholic.

An̄″glō-Ȧ·mer′i·çăn, *a.* 1. pertaining to Anglo-Americans.
2. of or pertaining to England and America, especially the United States, or to their people jointly.

An̄″glō-Ȧ·mer′i·çăn, *n.* a citizen of America, especially of the United States, who is of English birth or extraction.

An̄″glō-Çath′ō·liç, *n.* a member of the Church of England who believes that its Catholicism is the same as before the Reformation.

An̄″glō-Çath′ō·liç, *a.* of Anglo-Catholics, or their beliefs and practice.

An̄″glō-Çȧ·thol′i·ciṣm, *n.* the principles, practices, or doctrines of Anglo-Catholics.

An̄″glō-French′, *a.* 1. English and French; of or between England and France.
2. of Anglo-French.

An̄″glō-French′, *n.* the medieval French spoken in England by the Norman conquerors: see *Norman French*.

An̄″glō-In′di·ăn, *a.* 1. English and Indian; of or between England and India.
2. of Anglo-Indians or their speech.

An̄″glō-In′di·ăn, *n.* 1. an English citizen living in India.
2. a person of both English and Indian ancestry.
3. the speech of Anglo-Indians, characterized by Anglicization of native words.

An̄″glō-Ī′rish, *a.* 1. pertaining to England and Ireland; as, *Anglo-Irish* relations.
2. of English and Irish parentage.

An̄′glō·măn, *n.*; *pl.* **An̄′glō·men,** 1. a person having Anglomania.
2. a strong partisan of British customs and interests: a term used by Thomas Jefferson.

An̄·glō·mā′ni·ȧ, *n.* [*Anglo-*, and Gr. *mania*, madness.] a mania for English customs, etc., especially by one of another nationality.

An̄″glō-Nor′măn, *a.* 1. English and Norman.
2. of the Anglo-Normans or their language.

An̄″glō-Nor′măn, *n.* 1. a Norman settler in England after the Norman conquest.
2. the French dialect of such settlers.

An̄″glō-Norse′, *n.* Old Norse as spoken by Scandinavian settlers in eastern and northern England before the Norman Conquest.

An̄″glō-Norse′, *a.* of Anglo-Norse.

An̄′glō·phile, *n.* [*Anglo-*, and Gr. *philos*, loving.] a person who admires or is extremely fond of England, its people, customs, etc.

An̄′glō·phīle, *a.* of Anglophiles.

An̄′glō·phōbe, *a.* of Anglophobes.

An̄′glō·phōbe, *n.* [*Anglo-*, and Gr. *phobos*, from *phobein*, to fear.] one who manifests an extreme dislike for or dread of the English people and their customs, etc.

An̄·glō·phō′bi·ȧ, *n.* fear or hatred of England or anything English.

An̄′glō·phōne, *a.* [*Anglo-*, and Gr. *phōnē*, a voice.] of or having to do with speakers of English.

An̄′glō·phōne, *n.* a person who speaks English.

An̄″glō-Sax′ŏn, *n.* 1. a member of the Germanic, Ingwinian peoples (Angles, Saxons, and Jutes) living in England before the Norman Conquest.
2. their West Germanic, Low German language, which they called *Englisc*; Old English.
3. a person of English nationality or descent.

An̄″glō-Sax′ŏn, *a.* 1. of the Anglo-Saxons, their language, or culture.
2. of their descendants; English.

An̄″glō-Sax′ŏn·dŏm, *n.* the entire area throughout which the language, laws, and usages of the Anglo-Saxon people predominate.

An̄″glō-Sax′ŏn·iṣm. *n.* 1. an Anglo-Saxon word, idiom, characteristic, etc.
2. the quality of being Anglo-Saxon.

Añ·gō′lȧ, *n.* Angora.
Añ·gō′lȧ pēa, a species of *Cajanus*: called also *pigeon pea.*
añ′gŏr, *n.* [L.] 1. anguish. [Obs.]
2. in medicine, extreme anxiety, producing constriction in the epigastric region, and often palpitation and oppression.
Añ·gō′rȧ, *n.* [from *Angora*, a city in Asia Minor.] a fine wool fabric made from the hair or the Angora goat; true mohair.
Angora cat; a variety of the domestic cat, distinguished by its size and long silky hair.
Angora goat; a kind of domestic goat, native to the district about Angora, and having long silky hair used in the manufacture of fabrics.
Angora wool; the hair of the Angora goat.
añ·gos·tū′rȧ bärk, [from *Angostura*, former name of a town in Venezuela.] the bitter bark of either of two South American trees, *Galipea officinalis* or *Cusparia trifoliata*, of the rue family, used as a tonic and in bitters.
añ′gri·ly, *adv.* in an angry manner.
añ′gri·ness, *n.* the state or quality of being angry.
añ′gry, *a.*; *comp.* angrier; *superl.* angriest.
1. roused to anger; provoked; indignant.
2. showing or resulting from anger; as, an *angry* countenance, *angry* words.
3. inflamed; red and sore: said of swellings, wounds, etc.
4. raging; furious; tumultuous; as, *angry* waves.
Syn.—enraged, irate, wroth, incensed, choleric, ireful, inflamed, hot, irascible, resentful, irritated, indignant, provoked, raging.
añ′gry yoŭng men, [*often* A- Y- M-] a group of young writers in Great Britain after World War II, bitterly critical of upper-class and middle-class values, practices, etc.
Äñgst, *n.* [G.] [*often* a-] a gloomy, often neurotic feeling of generalized anxiety and depression.
añg′strŏm, Añg′strŏm, *n.* [after A. J. *Ångström.*] one hundred-millionth of a centimeter, a unit used in measuring the length of light waves: symbol, λ: called also *Angstrom unit.*
añ′guid (-gwid), *n.* one of the *Anguidæ.*
Añ′gui·dae (-gwi-), *n.pl.* [L. *anguis*, snake, and *-idæ.*] a family of snakelike lizards, including the blindworms, or slowworms.
añ′gui·fọrm, *a.* [L. *anguis*, snake, and *forma*, shape.] in the form of a snake.
añ·guil′li·fọrm (-gwil′), *a.* [L. *anguilla*, an eel, and *forma*, shape.] in the form of an eel; resembling an eel.
añ·guil′lous, *a.* anguilliform.
añ′guine (-gwin), *a.* pertaining to or resembling a snake.
añ·guin′ē·ăl, *a.* anguineous.
añ·guin′ē·ous, *a.* [L. *anguineus*, from *anguis*, a snake.] resembling a snake.
añ′gui·ped, *a.* [L. *anguis*, snake, and *pes*, *pedis*, a foot.] having serpent-shaped legs.
A winged *anguiped* giant.—A. S Murray.
Añ′guis (-gwis), *n.* [L. *anguis*, serpent.] a genus of reptiles typical of the *Anguidæ*, the best known species being *Anguis fragilis*, the common blindworm.
añ′guish (-gwish), *n.* [ME. *anguisse*; OFr. *anguisse*; It. *angoscia*, anguish, from L. *angustia*, narrowness, straitness; from *angere*, to press tight, to choke.] extreme pain, either of body or of mind; agony.
Syn.—agony, pang, torture, torment, grief, sorrow, distress.
añ′guish, *v.t.* and *v.i.*; anguished, *pt.*, *pp.*; anguishing, *ppr.* to distress or be distressed with extreme pain or grief.
añ′guished (-gwisht), *a.* [pp. of **anguish.**]
1. feeling anguish.
2. showing or resulting from anguish.
añ′gū·lăr, *a.* 1. having an angle, angles, or corners; pointed; as, an *angular* figure.
2. forming an angle; as, an *angular* point.
3. measured by an angle; as, *angular* distance, *angular* velocity.
4. with prominent bones; lean; gaunt.
5. without ease or grace; stiff; as, an *angular* stride.
angular advance; in machinery, the advance of an eccentric from the point where it is perpendicular to the line of its motion to the point it occupies when the crankshaft has reached its dead center.
angular aperture; in a telescope, etc., the angle formed by two lines drawn from the principal focus to the ends of a diameter of the object glass; as, a lens of 60° *aperture.*
angular belting; in machinery, a belt constructed to run over a grooved pulley in such a way as to give it greater tractive capacity.
angular chain belt; a chain belt constructed to bear hard against the grooved sides of a V-shaped pulley.
angular distance; see under *distance.*
angular motion; the motion of a body swinging or moving in an arc, as a pendulum.
angular perspective; in drawing, that kind of perspective in which neither of the sides of the principal object is parallel to the plane of the picture, and therefore, in the representation, the horizontal lines of both converge to vanishing points.
angular velocity; in physics, the rate at which a body revolves round a fixed axis; rate of angular motion.
añ′gū·lăr, *n.* a bone occurring in the lower classes of vertebrates, situated at the base of the lower jaw.
añ·gū·lar′i·ty, *n.* 1. the quality or condition of being angular.
2. [*pl.*] **añ·gū·lar′i·ties**, an angular form or part; sharp corner; angle.
añ′gū·lăr·ly, *adv.* in or with angles or corners; in an angular manner.
añ′gū·lăr·ness, *n.* the quality or condition of being angular.
añ′gū·lāte, añ′gū·lā·ted, *a.* formed with angles or corners; as, *angulate* stems, leaves, petioles, etc.
añ′gū·lāte, *v.t.* and *v.i.*; angulated, *pt.*, *pp.*; angulating, *ppr.* [L. *angulatus*, pp. of *angulare*, to make angled; from *angulus*, an angle.] to make or become angular.
añ·gū·lā′tion, *n.* 1. the act or process of making angular.
2. an angular form, part, or position.
añ·gū·lif′ẽr·ous, *a.* [L. *angulus*, an angle, and *ferre*, to bear.] in conchology, having a whorl, especially the last one, angular in shape.
añ′gū·li·nẽrved, *a.* having the veins branching angularly: said of a leaf.
añ″gū·lō·den′tāte, *a.* [L. *angulus*, angle, and *dentatus*, from *dens*, *dentis*, a tooth.] angularly toothed: said of the margin of a leaf.
añ·gū·lom′e·tẽr, *n.* [L. *angulus*, angle, and *metrum*; Gr. *metron*, measure.] an instrument used in the measurement of external angles.
añ′gū·lōse, *a.* angulous. [Rare.]
añ·gū·los′i·ty, *n.* the state or quality of being angulous or angular. [Rare.]
añ′gū·lous, *a.* angular; having angles or corners.
añ′gū·lus, *n.*; *pl.* **añ′gū·lī**, [L.] in anatomy, an angle of any kind, as of the jawbone or of a rib.
Añ′gus, *n.* [Gael. *Aonghas* and Ir. *Aonghus*, from *aon*, one.] in Celtic mythology, the god of love.
añ·gust′, *a.* [L. *angustus*, narrow.] narrow; strait. [Obs.]
añ·gus′tāte, *a.* narrowed; diminishing rapidly in breadth.
añ·gus·tā′tion, *n.* [L. *angustus*, narrow.] a narrowing or being narrowed.
añ·gus′ti·clāve, *n.* [L. *angustus*, narrow, and *clavus*, a nail, a stripe.] in ancient Rome, a mark of distinction worn by a member of the order of equestrians, consisting of two narrow purple stripes attached to the shoulders of his tunic and extending downward in front and behind.
añ·gus·ti·fō′li·āte, añ·gus·ti·fō′li·ous, *a.* [L. *angustus*, narrow, and *folium*, leaf.] in botany, narrow-leaved.
añ·gus·ti·ros′trāte, *a.* [L. *angustus*, narrow, and *rostratus*, beaked, from *rostrum*, a beak.] in ornithology, having a narrow beak.
añ·gus·tū′rȧ bärk, same as *angostura bark.*
añ·gwän′tĭ·bō, *n.* [native name.] a small animal (*Arctocebus calabarensis*) of western Africa, which bears a strong resemblance to the potto, but has only a rudimentary tail.
an·här·mon′iç, *a.* [Fr. *anharmonique*, from Gr. *anharmonikos*; *an* priv., and *harmonikos*, harmonic.] in mathematics, not harmonic; as, an *anharmonic* ratio.
anharmonic ratio; a kind of ratio introduced into mathematics by the German mathematician Möbius and employed in defining the metrical properties of variables.
an·hē·lā′tion, *n.* [L. *anhelatio*, from *anhelare*, to breathe with difficulty, to pant; *an*, *ambi*, around, and *helare*, to breathe.]
1. shortness of breath; a panting; difficult respiration. [Rare.]
2. breathless anxiety, or panting desire. [Rare.]

These *anhelations* of divine souls after the adorable object of their love.
—Glanville.

an·hēle′, *v.i.* to be eager. [Obs.]
an·hē′lōse, an·hē′lous, *a.* out of breath; panting; breathing with difficulty. [Rare.]
an·hi·drot′iç, *n.* [Gr. *anhidrōs*; *an* priv., and *hidrōs*, perspiration.] a drug that checks perspiration.
an·hi·drot′iç, *a.* tending to check perspiration.
an′hi·mȧ, *n.* [Braz.] a South American aquatic fowl, larger than a swan and somewhat like a crane; the *Palamedea cornuta*, or horned screamer.
an·hiñ′gȧ, *n.* [S. Am. name.] the snakebird, *Plotus anhinga*, an aquatic bird of the southern United States.
an·his′tous, *a.* [Gr. *an* priv., and *histos*, web, tissue.] without a decided structure: said of membranes, etc.
an·huñ′gẽred, *a.* hungry. [Obs.]
an·hȳ′drīde, an·hȳ′drid, *n.* [Gr. *an* priv., and *hydōr*, water.
1. an oxide that becomes an acid or base by the addition of water.
2. any compound formed by the removal of the elements of water, usually from an acid.
an·hȳ′drīte, *n.* anhydrous calcium sulfate, $CaSO_4$. It occurs in rectangular crystals, nearly colorless or of pale shades, and resembles marble.
an·hȳ′drous, *a.* [Gr. *anydros*, dry; *an* priv., and *hydōr*, water.] without water, specifically water of crystallization; as, *anhydrous* salts or acids.
ä′nī, ä′nō, *n.* [Braz.] a tropical American black bird, related to the cuckoo.
an′i·çut, *n.* in India, an irrigation dam.
an·id″i·ō·mat′iç·ăl, *a.* not idiomatical. [Rare].
an·i·ente′, *v.t.* to anientise. [Obs.]
an·i·en′tise, *v.t.* [OFr. *anienter*; Fr. *anéantir*, to destroy.] to frustrate; to make void; to annihilate. [Obs.]
ȧ·nīgh′ (-nī′), *prep.* and *adv.* nigh. [Rare.]
ȧ·nīght′ (-nīt′), *adv.* in the nighttime; by night. [Archaic.]
an′il, *n.* [Port. *anil*; Ar. *an-nīl*; *an*, *al*, the, and *nīl*, from Sans. *nīlī*, indigo, from *nīla*, dark blue.]
1. a shrub from whose leaves and stalks indigo is made; a species of *Indigofera*, or indigo-plant.
2. indigo.
an′īle, *a.* [L. *anilis*, from *anus*, an old woman.] old-womanish; mentally or physically weak.
an′īle·ness, *n.* anility. [Obs.]
an·il′iç, *a.* relating to or obtained from anil.
an·i·līde (*or* -līd), *n.* phenylamide; any one of those amide compounds in which phenyl has replaced the hydrogen of the amido group.
an′i·lin, *n.* and *a.* same as *aniline.*
an′i·line, *a.* made from aniline.
an′i·line (*or* -lēn), *n.* a colorless, poisonous, oily liquid, $C_6H_5NH_2$, formerly made from indigo, but now from nitrobenzene. It is a base from which many dyes are produced.
an′i·line dȳe, 1. any dye made from aniline.
2. any dye like aniline chemically; commonly, any dye produced synthetically from coal-tar products.
ȧ·nil′i·ty, *n.* [L. *anilitas*, from *anilis*, from *anus*, an old woman.] the state of being an old woman; senility.
an′i·mȧ, *n.* [L.] life principle; soul.
an′i·mȧ·ble, *a.* [L. *animare*, to animate.] that can be animated.
an″i·mad·vẽr′săl, *n.* the power of perceiving or noticing. [Obs.]
an″i·mad·vẽr′sion, *n.* [L. *animadversio*, from *animadvertere*, to turn the mind to, criticize, censure.]
1. an unfavorable remark; adverse criticism; reproof; blame.
2. the act or faculty of observing or noticing. [Obs.]
3. a kind of judicial punishment. [Archaic.]
Syn.—blame, censure, chiding, comment, criticism, reproof.
an″i·mad·vẽr′sive, *a.* having the power of perceiving.
an″i·mad·vẽr′sive·ness, *n.* the power of animadverting.
an″i·mad·vẽrt′, *v.i.*; animadverted, *pt.*, *pp.*; animadverting, *ppr.* [L. *animadvertere*, to observe, consider, censure, punish; *animum*, acc. of *animus*, mind, *ad*, to, and *vertere*, to turn.]
1. to take cognizance; to perceive; to notice.
2. to remark by way of criticism or censure (*on* or *upon*).
an″i·mad·vẽrt′ẽr, *n.* one who animadverts.
an′i·măl, *n.* [L. *animal*, from *anima*, air, breath, soul; Gael. *anam*, breath; W. *envil*, *en*, a being, soul, spirit, and *mil*, a beast; Arm. *aneval*; Sans. *ana*, *animi*.]
1. any living being capable of sensation and the power of voluntary motion: distin-

guished from *plants* by its inability to make its own food by photosynthesis.

2. any such organism other than man; especially, any four-footed creature.

3. a brutish, debased, or inhuman person: used as an expression of contempt.

an′i·măl, *a.* [L. *animalis*, living, animate, from *anima*, breath, air, soul.]

1. belonging or relating to animals; as, *animal* habits.

2. relating to the purely physical functions and sensations of men and animals, as opposed in man to mentality, spirituality, etc.; sensual, gross, bestial, etc.; as, *animal* appetites, *animal* pleasures.

3. derived from animals.

animal cracker; a small, sweet cracker shaped like an animal.

animal electricity; the electricity generated in some animal bodies, as in certain eels.

animal kingdom; one of the three great divisions of nature including all animals. It comprises several subkingdoms, and under these are classes, orders, families, genera, and species differently arranged by naturalists. Linnaeus, in his famous system published in 1766, divided animals into the following six primary divisions or classes: 1. Mammalia; 2. Aves; 3. Amphibia; 4. Pisces; 5. Insecta; 6. Vermes. Cuvier in 1817, and Owen in 1860, proposed different divisions, and in 1869 Huxley devised an arrangement of the *animal kingdom* into eight primary classes, as follows: Vertebrata, Mollusca, Molluscoida, Cœlenterata, Annulosa, Annuloida, Infusoria, and Protozoa.

animal magnetism; mesmerism; hypnotism.

animal spirits; vivacity; liveliness.

an·i·mal′çū·lȧ, *n.* plural of **animalculum.**

an·i·mal′çū·lae, *n.pl.* [L. f. pl., formed by assuming *animalcula* to be f. sing.] animalcula.

an·i·mal′çū·lăr, an·i·mal′çū·line, *a.* pertaining to an animalcule or animalcules.

an·i·mal′çūle, *n.* [L. *animalculum*, dim. of *animal*, animal.] a minute animal, especially one that cannot be seen without a microscope.

an·i·mal′çū·lişm, *n.* a former theory in biology that animalcules are the cause of life and disease.

an·i·mal′çū·list, *n.* one who studies animalcules; also, one believing in the theory of animalculism.

an·i·mal′çū·lum, *n.* same as *animalcule.*

an′i·măl flow′ẽr, any of the sea anemones or other animals having some resemblance to flowers.

an′i·măl huş′bănd·ry, the care and raising of domesticated animals, as cattle, horses, sheep, etc.

An·i·mā′li·ȧ, *n.pl.* [L., pl. of *animal.*] the animal kingdom.

an′i·măl·ish, *a.* like an animal. [Rare.]

an′i·măl·işm, *n.* 1. the activity, appetites, nature, etc. of animals.

2. the doctrine that man is a mere animal with no soul or spiritual quality.

an′i·măl·ist, *n.* 1. an animalculist.

2. a believer in the doctrine of animalism.

3. an artist whose chief work is the study and representation of animals.

an″i·măl·is′tiç, *a.* pertaining to animalism.

an·i·mal′i·ty, *n.* 1. animal characteristics or nature.

2. the animal kingdom.

An″i·mȧ·liv′ō·rȧ, *n.pl.* [L., neut. pl. of *animalivorus*, from *animal*, animal, and *vorare*, to devour.]

1. in zoology, a suborder of bats.

2. [a–] any bat of this group.

an″i·mȧ·liv′ō·rous, *a.* pertaining to the *Animalivora.*

an·i·mal·i·zā′tion, *n.* 1. the act of animalizing.

2. conversion into animal matter by the processes of assimilation.

3. the process of being made sensual.

an′i·măl·īze, *v.t.*; animalized, *pt., pp.*; animalizing, *ppr.* 1. to represent in animal form. [Obs.]

2. to convert into animal matter by assimilation.

3. to sensualize; to dehumanize; as, to *animalize* a man.

an′i·măl·ly, *adv.* physically.

a′ni·mȧ mun′dī, [L.] the world soul.

an′i·mănt, *a.* having life and reason. [Obs.]

an′i·mănt, *n.* a living creature. [Obs.]

an·i·mas′tiç, *a.* spiritual.

an·i·mas′tiç, *n.* psychology. [Obs.]

an′i·māte, *v.t.*; animated, *pt., pp.*; animating, *ppr.* [L. *animatus*, pp. of *animare*, to make alive, fill with breath.]

1. to give life to; to make alive.

2. to give motion to, or to put into action; as, the breeze *animated* the leaves.

3. to give spirit or vigor to; to inspire; to stimulate; as, to *animate* dispirited troops.

Syn.—inspire, quicken, exhilarate, revive, inspirit.

an′i·māte, *a.* 1. alive; having life.

2. lively; vigorous; spirited.

an′i·mā·ted, *a.* 1. endowed with life; alive or seeming alive; as, *animated* beings.

2. lively; vigorous; full of spirit; as, an *animated* discourse.

animated cartoon; a kind of motion picture made by photographing a series of thousands of drawings, each showing a stage of movement slightly changed from the one before, so that the figures in them seem to move when the drawings are shown in rapid succession.

an′i·mā·ted·ly, *adv.* vigorously; in a lively manner.

an′i·mā·tẽr, *n.* same as *animator.*

an′i·mā·ting, *a.* giving life; infusing spirit; enlivening; causing animation.

an′i·mā·ting·ly, *adv.* so as to animate or excite feeling.

an·i·mā′tion, *n.* [L. *animatio*, from *animare*, to make alive.]

1. an animating or being animated.

2. the state of being lively; brisk, vigorous quality; as, he recited the story with great *animation.*

3. an animate condition; life.

4. the preparation of animated cartoons.

Syn.—life, vivacity, spirit, buoyancy, gaiety, liveliness.

an′i·mā·tive, *a.* animating.

ä·ni·mä′tọ, *a.* and *adv.* [It.] in music, with animation.

an′i·mā·tŏr, *n.* one who or that which animates.

an′i·mé (-mā *or* -mē), *n.* [Sp.; prob. from native word.] any of various resins; especially, a fossilized copal found in the West Indies and Africa, used in making varnish, etc.

an′i·mé (-mā), *a.* [Fr., animated.] in heraldry, having the eyes of an animal a different color than the animal itself; hence, showing a desire to fight.

an·i·met′tȧ, *n.* [It.] in the Eucharist, the cloth which covers the chalice.

an′i·mine, an′i·min, *n.* a chemical compound derived from bone oil.

an′i·mişm, *n.* [L. *anima*, soul, and *-ism.*]

1. the belief that all life is produced by a spiritual force separate from matter.

2. the belief that natural phenomena and objects, as rocks, trees, the wind, etc., are alive and have souls.

3. the doctrine of the existence of soul as independent of matter.

4. a belief in the existence of spirits, demons, etc.

an′i·mist, *n.* one who believes in animism.

an·i·mis′tiç, *a.* of or pertaining to animism.

an′i·mōse, *a.* animous. [Obs.]

an·i·mōse′ness, *n.* animosity. [Obs.]

an·i·mos′i·ty, *n.* [Fr. *animosité*; It. *animosita*; from L. *animositas*, courage, spirit, from *animus*, courage, life.]

1. strong hatred; active hostility.

2. courage; spiritedness. [Obs.]

Syn.—enmity, hostility, malice, rancor, antipathy, antagonism.

an′i·mous, *a.* full of spirit; hot-tempered; vehement. [Obs.]

an′i·mus, *n.* [L. *animus*, mind.]

1. an animating force.

2. unfriendly spirit; animosity.

an′i·on, *n.* [Gr. *aniōn*, ppr. of *anienai*; *ana*, up, and *ienai*, to go.] a negative ion: in electrolysis, anions go toward the anode: opposed to *cation.*

an′is-, a combining form used in chemistry to denote derivation from anise or anisic acid.

an′ise, *n.* [Sp. *anis*; L. *anisum*; Gr. *anēson*; Ar. *anīsūn*, anise.]

1. a plant of the carrot family, *Pimpinella anisum*. It grows naturally in Egypt, and is cultivated elsewhere for its fragrant seeds.

2. the fruit or seeds of the anise, used for flavoring and in medicine.

an′i·seed, *n.* the ovate, ribbed, aromatic seed of the anise; also, the cordial anisette, prepared from it.

an′ise plant, an Australian herb, *Seseli harveyanum*, with an aroma similar to anise.

an·i·sette′, *n.* [Fr.] a cordial prepared from or flavored with aniseed.

ȧ·nis′iç, *a.* pertaining to or derived from anise.

ȧ·nis′iç ac′id, in chemistry, a crystalline acid obtained by the oxidation of anethole or anisic aldehyde.

ȧ·nis′iç al′de·hȳde, in chemistry, a liquid obtained by oxidizing anethole, and used, under the name *aubepine*, in the manufacture of perfumes.

ȧ·nis′i·dīne, ȧ·nis′i·din, *n.* in chemistry, any one of three isomeric bases, amino derivatives of anisole.

ȧ·nis″i·dī′nō-, in chemistry, the combining form for *anisidine*, designating the univalent radical $CH_3OC_6H_4NH$, of which anisidine is the hydride.

an′i·sil, *n.* in chemistry, a yellow crystalline compound, formed by the action of nitric acid on anisoin.

a·nī′sō-, [Gr. *anisos*, unequal; *an* priv., and *isos*, equal.] a combining form meaning *unequal, dissimilar*, as in *aniso*meric.

a·nī″sō·çär′pŏus, *a.* in botany, having the carpels dissimilar, or having fewer carpels than stamens or floral organs.

a·nī″sō·cẽr′çăl, *a.* [*aniso-*, and Gr. *kerkos*, tail.] having the tail fin unequally lobed: said of fishes.

a·nī″sō·çhrō·mat′iç, *a.* [*aniso-*, and Gr. *chrōma*, color.] not of the same color throughout.

a·nī″sō·çhrō′mi·ȧ, *n.* variation in the color of red blood corpuscles, due to an unequal hemoglobin content.

a·nī″sō·çō′ri·ȧ, *n.* [*aniso-*, and Gr. *korē*, pupil of the eye.] inequality of the diameters of the pupils of the eye.

a·nī″sō·çot·y·lē′dŏ·nous, *a.* in botany, having unequal development of the cotyledons.

a·nī″sō·çrat′iç, *a.* not isocratic; having unequal political power.

a·nī″sō·çȳ′çle, *n.* [*aniso-*, and Gr. *kyklos*, circle.] formerly, a machine used for hurling arrows.

a·nī″sō·çy·tō′sis, *n.* [*aniso-*, and *cyt-*, and *-osis.*] in medicine, inequality in the size of the red blood corpuscles.

a·nī″sō·daç′tyl, a·nī″sō·daç′tyle, *n.* [*aniso-*, and Gr. *daktylos*, finger.]

1. one of an order of birds, *Anisodactyli*, whose toes are of unequal length.

2. one of the *Anisodactyla.*

a·nī″sō·daç′tyl, a·nī″sō·daç′tyle, *a.* same as *anisodactylic.*

A·nī″sō·daç′ty·lȧ, *n.pl.* a group of thick-skinned mammals like the elephant, rhinoceros, etc., having several toes forming a single series, about the bottom of each foot.

A·nī″sō·daç′ty·lī, *n.pl.* a group of birds having one of the four toes on each foot directed backward.

a·nī″sō·daç′tyl·iç, a·nī″sō·daç′ty·lŏus, *a.* 1. pertaining to the *Anisodactyla.*

2. pertaining to the *Anisodactyli.*

a·nī″sō·dȳ′nȧ·mŏus, *a.* [*aniso-*, and Gr. *dynami*, power.] in botany, having greater growth on one side. [Obs.]

a·nī″sō·gȧ·mēte′, *n.* [*aniso-*, and *-gamete.*] a gamete of either sex differing from the other in size and structure.

an″ī·sog′ȧ·mŏus, *a.* [*aniso-*, and *-gamous.*] in biology, characterized by conjugation of unlike gametes.

an″ī·sog′e·ny, *n.* [*aniso-*, and *-geny.*] in botany, production of pollen and ovules that are genetically unlike.

an″ī·sog′nȧ·thŏus, *a.* [*aniso-*, and Gr. *gnathos*, jaw.] having the teeth unlike in form or size in the upper and lower jaws.

an″ī·sog′y·nŏus, *a.* [*aniso-*, and Gr. *gynē*, woman.] having fewer or (sometimes) more carpels than sepals.

ȧ·nis′ō·in, *n.* [from *anise* and *-oin.*] in chemistry, a crystalline ketonic alcohol derived from anisic aldehyde.

an′i·sōle, an′i·sōl, *n.* [from *anise* and *-ole.*] methyl-phenyl ether: used as a solvent and in perfumes.

An″ī·som′e·lēş, *n.* [*aniso-*, and Gr. *melos*, limb.] in botany, a small genus of herbs of the mint family.

a·nī″sō·mer′iç, *a.* [*aniso-*, and Gr. *meros*, part.] not isomeric.

an″ī·som′ẽr·ŏus, *a.* in botany, characterized by an unequal number of parts in the floral whorls.

a·nī″sō·met′riç, *a.* [*aniso-*, and Gr. *metron*, measure.] not isometric.

a·nī″sō·met′rōpe, *n.* one suffering from anisometropia.

a·nī″sō·me·trō′pi·ȧ, *n.* [*aniso-*, and Gr. *metron*, measure, and *-ops*, eye.] a difference in the refractive power of the eyes.

a·nī″sō·me·trop′iç, *a.* unequally refractive; pertaining to anisometropia.

a·nī″sō·mȳ·ăr′i·ăn, *n.* a bivalve mollusk having the anterior adductor muscle more highly developed than the posterior one.

A·nī″sō·mȳ·ō′dī, *n.pl.* same as *Passeres anisomyodi.*

a·nī″sō·mȳ·ō′di·ăn, *a.* [*aniso-*, and Gr. *myōdēs*, muscular.] having the syringeal muscles placed irregularly: said of certain birds.

a·nī″sō·pet′ȧ·lŏus, *a.* [*aniso-*, and Gr. *petalon*, leaf.] with petals unequal.

an″ī·soph′yl·lŏus (*or* -so-phyl′lous), *a.* [*aniso-*, and Gr. *phyllon*, leaf.] with leaves unequal.

A·nī″sō·pleū′rȧ, *n.pl.* [*aniso-*, and Gr. *pleura*, side.] a division of gastropods having unequal sides.

a·nī″sō·pleū′răl, a·nī″sō·pleū′rŏus, *a.* having unequal sides; asymmetrical.

An″ī·sop′tĕr·ȧ, *n.pl.* a suborder of dragonflies.

an″ī·sop′tĕr·ŏus, *a.* [*aniso-*, and Gr. *pteron*, wing.] having wings unequal, as certain flowers.

a·nī″sō·stem′o·nous, *a.* [*aniso-*, and Gr. *stēmōn*, a thread.] having stamens not equal to the petals or the sepals in number.

a·nī″sō·sthen′iç, *a.* [*aniso-*, and Gr. *sthenos*, strength.] of unequal strength: said of paired muscles.

An″ī·sos′ti·ҫhus, *n.* [*aniso-*, and Gr. *stichos*, line, rank.] same as *Bignonia.*

a·nī″sō·trop′iç, an″ī·sot′rō·păl, a·nī′sō·trōpe, an″ī·sot′rō·pŏus, *a.* [*aniso-*, and Gr. *tropos*, a turning, from *trepein*, to turn.]
 1. not isotropic.
 2. in botany, having unequal responses to external stimuli.
 3. in physics, having properties, as conductivity, speed of transmission of light, etc., which vary according to the direction in which they are measured.

an″ī·sot′rō·piṣm, *n.* anisotropy.

an″ī·sot′rō·py, *n.* the state of being anisotropic.

an·ī′sō·yl, *n.* in chemistry, the univalent radical of anisic acid.

ȧ·nī′sum, *n.* in pharmacy, anise.

an′i·syl, *n.* in chemistry, 1. the univalent radical $CH_3OC_6H_4$, of which anisole is the hydride.
 2. the univalent radical p-$CH_3OC_6H_4CH_2$; as, *anisyl* alcohol.
 3. anisoyl.

ā″nī·trog′e·nŏus, *a.* not nitrogenous.

An′jou (-jọọ), *n.* the English royal house of Plantagenet: the name has also been used by several other royal houses.

än″kä·rä′trīte, *n.* [from *Ankaratra* Mountains, Madagascar.] a basalt rock containing feldspar, and some nephelite.

añ′kĕr, *n.* [D.] a measure of wine or alcoholic liquor (particularly the latter), used in some countries of Europe. It is equal to about 10 wine gallons in the United States.

añ′kĕr·īte, *n.* [named after Prof. *Anker* of Austria, and *-ite.*] a mineral resembling dolomite but with iron largely replacing the magnesia.

añkh (ank), *n.* [Egypt. life, soul.] a sacred Egyptian emblem symbolic of life, a cross with a ring at the top.

añ′kle, *n.* [ME. *ankle, ancle, anclowe*; AS. *ancleow*; Dan. *enkel*; O.H.G. *encha, einka*, leg, ankle; L. *angulus*; Gr. *angkylos*, bent, angle; Sans. *anga*, limb.] the joint which connects the foot with the leg; also, the part of the leg between the foot and the calf.

añ′kle·bōne, *n.* the bone of the ankle; the astragalus.

añ′kled (-kld), *a.* having a specified kind of ankles: used in combination; as, thick-*ankled.*

añ′klet, *n.* 1. a little ankle. [Rare.]
 2. anything surrounding the ankle, as an ornament, support, clasp, or fetter.
 3. a short sock.

añ′kus, *n.* [Hind. *ankus*, from Sans. *ankuca.*] an elephant goad.

añ′ky·lōse, añ′ҫhy·lōse, *v.t.* and *v.i.*; ankylosed, *pt.*, *pp.*; ankylosing, *ppr.* to stiffen or join by ankylosis.

añ′ky·lōsed, añ′ҫhy·lōsed, *a.* stiffened or joined by ankylosis.

añ·ky·lō′sis, añ·ҫhy·lō′sis, *n.* [Gr. *ankylōsis*, a stiffening of the joints, from *angkyloein*, to crook, stiffen; *angkylos*, crooked, bent.]
 1. in medicine, a stiffening of a joint, caused by fibrous or bony union.
 2. in zoology, a joining of bones or fibrous parts into a single part.

añ″ky·los″tō·mī′ȧ·sis, *n.* same as *ancylostomiasis.*

añ·ky·lot′iç, añ·ҫhy·lot′iç, *a.* pertaining to ankylosis.

an·kȳ′roid, *a.* same as *ancyroid.*

an′lāce, an′ē·lāce, *n.* [ME. *anlas, anlace*; W. *anglas*, a sword.] a broad, tapering medieval knife or dagger, from eighteen inches to two feet long, worn at the waist.

ANLACES

Än′lä·ge, *n.*; *pl.* **Än′lä·gen,** [G.] the basis of a later development; specifically, in biology, the first stage of growth of an organ or part in an embryo.

än′laut, *n.* [G. *an*, on, the beginning, and *laut*, a sound.] the initial sound of a word.

an′nȧ, *n.* [Hind. *ānā.*] an Indian coin, the sixteenth part of a rupee.

an′nȧ·bĕrg·īte, *n.* [from *Annaberg*, Germany; and *-ite.*] a native arsenate of nickel, $Ni_3As_2O_8 \cdot 8H_2O$, occurring in apple-green, crystalline masses.

an′năl, *n.* singular of *annals.*

an′năl·ist, *n.* a writer of annals.

an·năl·is′tiç, *a.* pertaining to annals or an annalist.

an′năl·īze, *v.t.* to record; to write annals of. [Obs.]

an′năls, *n.pl.* [L. *annalis*, pl. *annales*, from *annus*, year.]
 1. a written account of a series of events arranged in chronological order, year by year.
 2. historical records or chronicles; history.
 3. [*sing.*] the record of a single year or event.
 4. any journal containing reports of discoveries in some field, meetings of a society, etc.
 5. in the Roman Catholic Church, Masses said throughout the period of a year.
 Syn.—history, chronicles, records, registers.

An·nȧ·mēṣe′, *a.* 1. of Annam.
 2. of the Annamese, their culture, or language.

An·nȧ·mēṣe′, *n.*; *pl.* **An·nȧ·mēṣe′,** 1. one of a Mongolian people in Annam and Cochin-China; also, a native or inhabitant of Annam.
 2. the language of the Annamese.

An′nȧ·mīte, *a.* and *n.* Annamese.

an′nātes, an′nats, *n.pl.* [L. *annus*, a year.] in the Roman Catholic Church, a payment to the Pope of the first year's revenue from a bishop's benefice.

än·nät′tō, *n.* [of W. Ind. origin.]
 1. the *Bixa orellana*, a tropical American tree which yields the annatto dye.
 2. a dye of reddish yellow made from pulp around the seeds of this tree: it is used for coloring butter, etc. Also called *arnotto.*

ANNATTO
(*Bixa orellana*)

an·nēal′, *v.t.*; annealed, *pt.*, *pp.*; annealing, *ppr.* [ME. *anelen, onelen*; AS. *anælan, onælan*, to burn; *an, on*, on, and *ælan*, to burn, set on fire; *al, æl*, fire.]
 1. to heat, as glass or metal, in an oven or furnace, and then cool slowly, for the purpose of rendering less brittle; to temper by a gradually diminishing heat.
 2. to strengthen and temper (the mind, will, etc.).
 3. to heat, as glass or tiles, in order to fix colors; to bake. [Archaic.]

an·nēal′ĕr, *n.* one who or that which anneals.

an·nēal′ing, *n.* the process or art of annealing.

an·nēal′ing ŏv′en, a leer (oven).

an·nēal′ing pot, a closed pot in which articles to be annealed are placed to prevent them from being oxidized.

an·neçt′, *v.t.* annex. [Obs.]

an·neç′tent, *a.* connecting; annexing. [Obs.]

an′ne·lid, an′ne·lide, *a.* pertaining to the *Annelida.*

an′ne·lid, an′ne·lide, *n.* an animal belonging to the class *Annelida.*

An·nel′i·dȧ, An·nel′i·dēṣ, *n.pl.* [LL., from *annellus, anellus*, dim. of *anulus*, a ring.] a phylum of animals without jointed legs but with segmented body: it includes the earthworms, similar marine and fresh-water worms, and leeches.

an·nel′i·dăn, *a.* and *n.* same as *annelid.*

an·nel′i·dous, *a.* pertaining to or resembling an annelid.

An·nel·lā′tȧ, *n.pl.* same as *annelida.*

an′ne·loid, *a.* annelidous.

an′ne·loid, *n.* an animal resembling an annelid.

an·nex′, *v.t.*; annexed, *pt.*, *pp.*; annexing, *ppr.* [Fr. *annexer*, from L. *annexus*, pp. of *annectere*; *ad*, to, and *nectere*, to tie, bind.]
 1. to add to the end; as, to *annex* a codicil to a will; to subjoin; to affix.
 2. to unite, as a smaller thing to a greater; as, to *annex* a province to a kingdom.
 3. to unite to something preceding, as the main object; to connect with, as a condition or consequence; as, to *annex* a penalty to a crime.
 4. to join; to connect. [Archaic.]
 Syn.—add, attach, fasten, affix, subjoin, append, connect, unite.

an·nex′, *v.i.* to join; to be united. [Rare.]

an·nex′ (*or* an′nex), *n.* something annexed; as, an *annex* to a building; an appendix; an addition; a supplementary part to a writing, a structure, or a service.

an·nex·ā′tion, *n.* 1. an annexing or being annexed.
 2. something annexed; addition.

an·nex·ā′tion·ăl, *a.* pertaining to annexation.

an·nex·ā′tion·ist, *n.* one who favors annexation of territory by his country.

an·nex′ion (-nek′shun), *n.* the act of annexing; annexation; addition. [Rare.]

an·nex′ion·ist, *n.* [Rare.] same as *annexationist.*

an·nex′ment, *n.* the act of annexing; the thing annexed. [Rare.]

an′ni·çut, *n.* same as *anicut.*

An′nie Oak′ley, [after woman rifle expert (1860–1926) whose small targets resembled punched tickets.] a free ticket; pass. [Slang.]

an·nī′hi·lȧ·ble, *a.* capable of being annihilated.

an·nī′hi·lāte, *v.t.*; annihilated, *pt.*, *pp.*; annihilating, *ppr.* [L. *annihilatus*, pp. of *annihilare*, to reduce to nothing; *ad*, to, and *nihilare*, from *nihil*, nothing.]
 1. to reduce to nothing; to destroy absolutely; to demolish; as, no power can *annihilate* matter.
 2. to destroy the identity, form, or distinctive properties of, so that the specific thing no longer exists; as, to *annihilate* a forest by cutting and carrying away the trees, though the timber may still exist; to *annihilate* a house by demolishing the structure.
 3. to annul or destroy the force of; to abolish; as, to *annihilate* an argument.
 Syn.—abolish, destroy, extinguish, extirpate, nullify.

an·nī′hi·lāte, *a.* annihilated. [Archaic.]

an·nī·hi·lā′tion, *n.* the act of annihilating or state of being annihilated.

an·nī·hi·lā′tion·iṣm, *n.* in theology, the belief that the wicked shall be destroyed after death.

an·nī·hi·lā′tion·ist, *n.* one who believes in annihilationism.

an·nī′hi·lā·tive, *a.* destructive.

an·nī′hi·lā·tŏr, *n.* one who or that which annihilates.

an·nī′hi·lā·tō·ry, *a.* annihilative.

an·ni·vĕr′sȧ·ri·ly, *adv.* annually.

an·ni·vĕr′sȧ·ry, *a.* [L. *anniversarius*; *annus*, year, and *vertere*, to turn; pp. *versum.*]
 1. returning every year at a stated time; annual; yearly; as, an *anniversary* feast.
 2. of or connected with an anniversary.

an·ni·vĕr′sȧ·ry, *n.* 1. the yearly return of the date of some event. The term is usually applied to a day on which some event is annually celebrated or commemorated; as, the *anniversary* of the Declaration of Independence.
 2. in the Roman Catholic Church, an observance on the recurring date of a person's death.
 3. the celebration of a birth, marriage, death, or notable event.

an′ni·vĕrse, *n.* anniversary. [Obs.]

an′nō·dā·ted, *a.* [L. *annodatus*, pp. of *annodare*, to knot; *ad*, to, and *nodare*, from *nodus*, a knot.] in heraldry, shaped or curved in a form resembling that of the letter S.

an′nō Dom′i·nī, [L. *anno*, abl. of *annus*, year, and *Domini*, genit. of *Dominus*, Lord, master.] in the year of the Lord; in the (given) year since the beginning of the Christian era; as, *anno Domini*, or *A.D.*, 1904.

an·nom′i·nāte, *v.t.* to name. [Rare.]

an·nom·i·nā′tion, *n.* [L. *annominatio*; *ad*, to, and *nominatio*, from *nomen*, name.]
 1. paronomasia.
 2. alliteration. [Obs.]

an'nō mun'dī, [L.; abbreviated to A. M.] in the year of the world: used in chronological reckoning with the supposed creation of the world as the starting-point; as, *A. M.* 5908.

an·nō'nȧ, *n.* [L. *annona*, from *annus*, a year.]
1. in ancient Rome, a year's crop production or increase; hence, provisions for a year's subsistence.
2. in the Roman empire, a tax, payable in grain, imposed on some of the more fertile provinces for provisioning the army.

An·nō'nȧ, *n.* [LL., from *menona*, the Malay name.] a genus of plants, the type of the natural order *Annonaceæ*. *Annona squamosa* (sweet sop) grows in the West Indian islands, and yields an edible fruit having a thick, sweet, luscious pulp. *Annona muricata* (sour sop) is cultivated in the West and East Indies: it produces a large, greenish, pear-shaped fruit containing slightly acid pulp. *Annona reticulata* is the custard apple.

An·nō·nā'cē·ae, *n.pl.* in botany, a natural order of polypetalous plants, including the custard apple, sweet sop, sour sop, etc.

an·nō·nā'ceous, *a.* of or relating to the *Annonaceæ*.

an'nō reg'nī, [L.] in the year of the reign.

an'nō·tāte, *v.t.*; annotated, *pt.*, *pp.*; annotating, *ppr.* to make explanatory or critical notes on; to comment upon; as, to *annotate* the works of Shakespeare.

an'nō·tāte, *v.i.* [L. *annotatus*, pp. of *annotare*, to put a note to, write down; *ad*, to, and *notare*, to note, mark; *nota*, a mark, sign.] to comment; to make notes by way of explanation; to make remarks on a writing; as, to *annotate* on the margin of a book.

an·nō·tā'tion, *n.* [L. *annotatio*, from *ad*, to, and *notatio*, a marking, from *notare*, to mark.]
1. a remark, note, or commentary on some passage of a book, intended to illustrate or explain its meaning: generally used in the plural; as, *annotations* on the Scriptures.
2. the act of annotating.
3. in civil law, a judicial reply answering a legal point.
4. the first symptoms of an illness. [Obs.]
Syn.—comment, commentary, remark, criticism, elucidation.

an·nō·tā'tion·ist, *n.* an annotator. [Rare.]

an'nō·tā·tive, *a.* of the nature of or characterized by annotations.

an'nō·tā·tŏr, *n.* one who annotates.

an·nō'tā·tō·ry, *a.* of or pertaining to an annotator; containing annotations.

an'nō·tine, *n.* [L. *annotinus*, a year old.] in zoology, a bird that is one year old, or that has molted once.

an·not'i·nous, *a.* [L. *annotinus*, a year old, from *annus*, year.] in botany, one year old, as branches.

an·nounce', *v.t.*; announced, *pt.*, *pp.*; announcing, *ppr.* [Fr. *annoncer*; It. *annunziare*; L. *annunciare*, *annuntiare*, make known, proclaim; *ad*, to, and *nuntiare*, to report; *nuntius*, a messenger.]
1. to proclaim; to give notice of formally; to make known publicly; as, to *announce* a sale; to *announce* a meeting.
2. to say.
3. to make known the arrival of.
4. to make known through the senses; as, footsteps *announced* his return.
5. in radio and television, to be an announcer for.
Syn.—proclaim, publish, advertise, declare, promulgate.

an·nounce', *v.i.* to act as a radio or television announcer.

an·nounce'ment, *n.* 1. an announcing or being announced.
2. that which is announced; as, he made a startling *announcement*.
3. a written or printed notice.

an·noun'cẽr, *n.* 1. one who announces.
2. in radio and television, the person who introduces the programs, performers, plays, and music, and who also announces the advertisements, identifies the station, etc.

an'nō ūr'bis çon'di·tae, [L.] in the (given) year of the founded city: the ancient Roman way of reckoning dates from Rome's founding, c. 753 B. C.

an·noy', *v.t.*; annoyed, *pt.*, *pp.*; annoying, *ppr.* [OE. *anoyen*, *anoien*; OFr. *anoier*, *ennuyer*, to annoy, weary; It. *inodio*, from L. *in odio*, in hatred.]
1. to irritate; to bother or vex, as by continued or repeated acts.
2. to harm, injure, or molest.
3. to make angry.
Syn.—disturb, worry, plague, harass, discommode, molest, vex, pester.

an·noy', *n.* annoyance. [Archaic.]

an·noy'ănce, *n.* 1. that which annoys.
2. the act of annoying or the state of being annoyed; as, he showed his *annoyance*.

an·noy'ẽr, *n.* one who or that which annoys.

an·noy'ful, *a.* troubled; vexed; full of annoyance. [Obs.]

an·noy'ing, *a.* irritating; vexing; bothersome; as, an *annoying* noise.

an·noy'ing·ly, *adv.* in an annoying manner.

an·noy'ing·ness, *n.* vexatiousness; the quality of being annoying.

an·noy'ous, *a.* troublesome. [Obs.]

an'nū·ăl, *a.* [ME. *annual*; OFr. *annuel*; L. *annualis*, yearly, from *annus*, year.]
1. yearly; returning once every year; coming yearly; as, an *annual* feast.
2. lasting or continuing only one year or season; as, an *annual* plant.
3. performed in a year; as, the *annual* motion of the earth.
4. of or measured by a year.
5. for a year's time, work, etc.; as, an *annual* wage.

an'nū·ăl, *n.* 1. a book or magazine published once a year.
2. a plant that lives but one year, or for a single season.
3. in the Roman Catholic Church, a Mass for the dead or for a special purpose, said daily for a year or once a year.

an'nū·ăl·ist, *n.* one who writes for an annual.

an'nū·ăl·ly, *adv.* yearly; every year; year by year.

an'nū·ăl ring, any of the rings of wood seen in cross sections of the stems of most trees and shrubs: each ring shows a year's growth.

an'nū·ā·ry, *a.* annual. [Obs.]

an'nū·ā·ry, *n.* a yearbook.

an'nū·el·ẽr, *n.* a priest who says anniversary masses for persons deceased. [Obs.]

an'nū·ent, *a.* [L. *annuens*, ppr. of *annuere*, to nod at; *ad*, to, and *nuere*, from Gr. *neuein*, to nod.] nodding: specifically applied to the muscles that bend the head.

an·nū'i·tănt, *n.* one who receives or is entitled to receive an annuity.

an·nū'i·ty, *n.* [Fr. *annuité*; L. *annuitas*, from *annus*, year.]
1. an investment yielding a fixed sum of money, payable yearly, to continue for a given number of years or for life.
2. an annual payment of money.
3. the right to receive such a payment.

an·nul', *v.t.*; annulled, *pt.*, *pp.*; annulling, *ppr.* [Fr. *annuler*, from L. *annullare*, to bring to nothing; *ad*, to, and *nullus*, none, *nullum*, nothing.]
1. to make void; to nullify; to cancel; to abolish: used specifically of laws, decrees, edicts, decisions of courts, or other established rules, permanent usages, and the like, which are made void by competent authority.
2. to reduce to nothing; to obliterate.
Syn.—abolish, repeal, cancel, quash, nullify, revoke, abrogate, reverse, rescind, destroy, set aside, obliterate.

an'nū·lăr, *a.* [L. *annularis*, pertaining to a ring, from *annulus*, *anulus*, a ring.]
1. having the form of a ring; pertaining to a ring; ringed; ring-shaped; as, *annular* ducts.
2. marked with rings or bands.
annular eclipse; an eclipse in which a ring of sunlight can be seen around the edge of the moon.
annular finger; the ring finger.
annular ligament; in anatomy, the ligament surrounding the ankle joint or wrist joint.

An·nū·lā'ri·ȧ, *n.pl.* in botany, a genus of fossiliferous plants: so called from the annuli, or ringlike parts, formed by the whorled leaves when sheathing.

an·nū·lar'i·ty, *n.* the quality or state of being annular.

an'nū·lăr·ly, *adv.* in an annular form or manner.

an'nū·lā·ry, *a.* having the form of a ring; annular.

An·nū·lā'tȧ, *n.pl.* [L., neut. pl. of *annulatus*, furnished with a ring, from *annulus*, a ring.] same as *Annelida*.

an'nū·lāte, an'nū·lā·ted, *a.* [L. *annulatus*, furnished with a ring.] furnished with rings, or circles like rings; surrounded by rings; ringed.

an·nū·lā'tion, *n.* a circular or ringlike formation; a ring.

an'nū·let, *n.* [dim. of L. *annulus*, a ring.]
1. a small ring.
2. in architecture, a fillet or band encircling a column, especially the ringlike molding where the shaft of a column joins the capital: called also *fillet*, *listel*, *cincture*, *taenia*, etc.
3. in heraldry, a little circle borne as a charge in coats of arms.
4. in decorative art, a stripe around a vase or other ornamental vessel.

an'nū·lī, *n.*, pl. of *annulus*.

an·nul'lȧ·ble, *a.* capable of being annulled, repealed, or abrogated.

an·nul'lẽr, *n.* one who or that which annuls.

an·nul'ment, *n.* the act of annulling or the state of being annulled; invalidation.

an'nū·loid, *n.* one of the *Annuloida*.

an'nū·loid, *a.* 1. ringlike.
2. pertaining to or resembling the *Annuloida*.

An·nū·loid'ȧ, *n.pl.* [Mod. L., from L. *annulus*, a ring, and Gr. *eidos*, form.] in zoology, a subkingdom classified by Huxley, including the *Echinodermata* and *Scolecida*.

An·nū·lō'sȧ, *n.pl.* [Mod. L., from L. *annulosus*, from *annulus*, a ring.] in zoology, a division (subkingdom) of animals regarded by some as synonymous with the *Arthropoda* or *Articulata*: according to other systematists, it includes both the *Articulata* and *Annulata*.

an·nū·lō'săn, *n.* one of the *Annulosa*.

an'nū·lōse, *a.* 1. having rings; composed of rings.
2. of or pertaining to the *Annulosa*.

an'nū·lus, *n.*; *pl.* **an'nū·lī,** [L., a ring.]
1. a ringlike figure; a ring.
2. in geometry, the ringlike area between the circumferences of two concentric circles.
3. in botany, (a) the elastic ring which surrounds the spore case in ferns; (b) the slender membrane surrounding the stems of certain agarics (mushrooms) after the spreading of the cap.
4. in zoology, a ring-shaped marking.
5. in astronomy, the visible ring of sunlight in an annular eclipse.

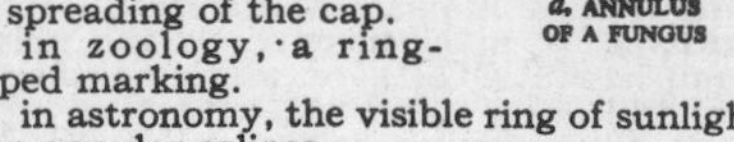
a. ANNULUS OF A FUNGUS

an'num, *n.* [L., acc. of *annus*, year.] a year.

an·nun'ci·ȧ·ble (*or* -shi-ȧ-bl), *a.* that may be announced. [Rare.]

an·nun'ci·āte (*or* -shi-), *v.t.*; annunciated, *pt.*, *pp.*; annunciating, *ppr.* [L. *annunciatus*, *annuntiatus*, pp. of *annuntiare*, to proclaim.] to bring tidings of; to announce.

an·nun'ci·āte (*or* -shi-), *a.* announced; foretold. [Obs.]

an·nun·ci·ā'tion (*or* -shi-), *n.* 1. the act of announcing; promulgation; proclamation; announcement; as, the *annunciation* of a decree.
2. [A–] the announcement of the incarnation of Jesus, made to the Virgin Mary by the angel Gabriel (Luke i. 26–38.).
3. [A–] the festival celebrated in some churches (on March 25) in commemoration of the angel's announcement to Mary.

an·nun'ci·ā·tive (*or* -shi-), *a.* making an announcement; pertaining to annunciation.

an·nun'ci·ā·tŏr (*or* -shi-), *n.* 1. one who or that which announces.
2. formerly, an officer of the Orthodox Eastern Church, whose duty was to announce holy days and festivals.
3. an electric indicator used in hotels, offices, etc. to show the source of calls.

an·nun'ci·ȧ·tō·ry (*or* -shi-), *a.* annunciative.

an'nus mi·ra'bi·lis, [L.] year of wonders.

ā'nō-, [Gr. *anō*, upward, from *ana*, up.] a combining form signifying upward.

An'ō·ȧ, *n.* [native name.] a subgenus of ruminating animals. The typical species is a small forest ox, *Anoa depressicornis*, found on the island of Celebes.

an·ō·çăr'pous, *a.* [*ano-*, and Gr. *karpos*, fruit.] in botany, having the sori, or spore cases, on the upper side of the frond, as ferns.

a·nō''ci·ȧs·sō''ci·ā'tion, *n.* [from *a-*, not, and L. *nocere*, to harm; and *association*.] the prevention of shock in surgery by calming the patient beforehand, handling him gently, and using local anesthetics and sharp dissection, so as to keep pain sensations from reaching the central nervous system.

a·nō·ci·ā'tion, *n.* [contr. of *anociassociation*.] anociassociation.

an'ōde, *n.* [Gr. *anodos*, a way up; *ana*, up, and *hodos*, way.] the positive electrode, as in a battery, radio tube, etc.: opposed to *cathode*.

ȧ·nod'iç, *a.* 1. of or from an anode.
2. in medicine, proceeding in an upward direction; rising.

an'ō·dīze, *v.t.*; anodized, *pt., pp.*; anodizing, *ppr.* to put a protective, often colored, oxide film on (a light metal) by an electrolytic process in which the metal serves as the anode.

An·ō·don'tȧ, *n.* [LL., from Gr. *an* priv., and *odōn, odontos,* tooth.] a genus of fresh-water mollusks without hinge teeth.

an'ō·dȳne, *n.* [Gr. *anōdynos,* without pain; *an* priv., and *odynē,* pain.] any medicine which relieves pain, as an opiate or narcotic; anything that soothes.

an'ō·dȳne, *a.* relieving or assuaging pain; soothing.

ȧ·nod'y·nous, *a.* having the qualities of an anodyne. [Obs.]

ȧ·noint', *v.t.* anointed, *pt., pp.*; anointing, *ppr.* [ME. *anoynten, enoynten*; OFr. *enoindre*; L. *inungere,* to anoint; *in,* on, and *ungere,* to smear.]

1. to pour oil upon; to smear or rub over with oil or ointment.

2. to consecrate by the use of oil: a sacred rite of great antiquity. Monarchs, prelates, and priests were anointed as part of their consecration ceremonies, and the custom still survives, as in the coronation of British monarchs.

Anoint Hazael to be king over Syria.
—1 Kings xix. 15.

A·noint'ed, *n.* 1. the Messiah or Jesus: called the *Lord's Anointed.*

2. [a–] a consecrated person.

ȧ·noint'ēr, *n.* one who anoints.

ȧ·noint'ing, *n.* the act of smearing with oil; a consecrating.

Anointing of the Sick; in the Roman Catholic Church, the sacrament in which a priest prays for and anoints with oil a person dying or in danger of death from sickness or injuries incurred.

ȧ·noint'ment, *n.* the act of anointing or the state of being anointed.

A·nō'lis, *n.* [Mod. L. from *anoli, anoalli,* the native name in the Antilles.] a genus of American lizards of the family *Iguanidæ.*

an'ō·lȳte, *n.* in electricity, that portion of an electrolyte surrounding the anode in an electrolytic cell.

ȧ·nom'ȧ·li·ped, ȧ·nom'ȧ·li·pēde, *a.* [LL. *anomalus,* irregular, and *pes, pedis,* foot.] having webbed feet; syndactylic.

ȧ·nom'ȧ·li·ped, ȧ·nom'ȧ·li·pēde, *n.* in ornithology, a syndactyl; a bird whose toes are joined together, as the kingfisher.

ȧ·nom'ȧ·lişm, *n.* an anomaly; a deviation or departure from rule.

ȧ·nom'ȧ·list, *n.* one who believes that language is arbitrary in its origin. [Rare.]

ȧ·nom·ȧ·lis'tiç, ȧ·nom·ȧ·lis'tiç·ăl, *a.* 1. irregular; departing from common or established rules.

2. in astronomy, pertaining to the anomaly, or angular distance of a planet from its perihelion.

anomalistic month; the time that the moon takes to go from perigee to perigee.

anomalistic revolution; the period in which a planet or satellite passes from any one point in its elliptic orbit to the same point again, completing a cycle of its changes of anomaly.

anomalistic year; the time a planet takes to go from perihelion to perihelion.

ȧ·nom·ȧ·lis'tiç·ăl·ly, *adv.* in an anomalistic manner.

ȧ·nom'ȧ·lous, *a.* [Gr. *anōmalos,* irregular, uneven; *an* priv., and *homalos,* from *homos,* the same, common.] abnormal; irregular; deviating from a general rule, method, or analogy; as, an *anomalous* character. The word is applied, in grammar, to words which deviate from the common rules in inflection; in astronomy, to the seemingly irregular motions of the planets.

ȧ·nom'ȧ·lous·ly, *adv.* abnormally; irregularly; in a manner different from a general rule, method, or analogy.

ȧ·nom'ȧ·lous·ness, *n.* the condition of being anomalous.

ȧ·nom'ȧ·ly, *n.*; *pl.* **ȧ·nom'ȧ·lieş,** [Fr. *anomalie*; L. *anomalia*; Gr. *anōmalia,* inequality.]

1. abnormality; irregularity; deviation from the regular arrangement, general rule, or usual method: thus *oxen,* the plural of *ox,* is an *anomaly* in grammar.

2. anything anomalous.

3. in astronomy, the angular distance of a planet from its perihelion, measured as if seen from the sun: called *true anomaly* when the angle is measured to the real position of the planet, and *mean anomaly* when measured to its mean position.

4. in music, a slight deviation from a perfect interval in tuning instruments with fixed notes or keyboards.

5. in biology, a deviation from the essential characteristics of any given type, as a bird that cannot fly.

Syn.—irregularity, abnormality, exception, peculiarity, eccentricity.

A·nō'mi·ȧ, *n.* [Mod. L., from Gr. *anomoios,* unlike; *an* priv., and *homoios,* like, similar.] in conchology, a genus of bivalve mollusks having unlike valves, the lower being perforated for adhesion to oysters and other shells.

an'ō·mie, an'ō·my, *n.* [Fr., from *ánomia,* lawlessness; *a-,* without, and *nomos,* law.] lack of purpose, identity, or ethical values in a person or in a society; disorganization, rootlessness, etc.

an'ō·mīte, *n.* a variety of biotite.

an'ō·mō-, an'om-, [Gr. *anomos,* irregular; *a* priv., and *nomos,* law.] a combining form signifying unusual or abnormal.

an''ō·mō·çär'pous, *a.* [*anomo-,* and Gr. *karpos,* fruit.] in botany, producing abnormal fruit.

an'ō·mō·dont, *a.* relating to the *Anomodontia.*

an'ō·mō·dont, *n.* one of the *Anomodontia.*

An''ō·mō·don'ti·ȧ, *n.pl.* [*anomo-,* and Gr. *odōn, odontos,* tooth.] an order of extinct reptiles of the Trias, either without teeth or having the premaxillaries sheathed with a horny plate like the turtles, or only one pair of canine tusks in the upper jaw. Also called *Dicynodontia.*

An·ō·moe'ăn, *n.* [LL., from Gr. *anomoios,* dissimilar; *an* priv., and *homoios,* similar.] in church history, one of a sect of extreme Arians of the fourth century. They held the Son to be unlike the Father in his essential nature.

An·ō·mū'rȧ, An·ō·möu'rȧ, *n.pl.* [*anomo-,* and Gr. *oura,* tail.] a suborder of crustaceans, intermediate between the crabs and the lobsters, having the tail unfitted for swimming, as the hermit crab.

an·ō·mū'răl, *a.* of or pertaining to the *Anomura.*

an·ō·mū'răn, *a.* same as *anomural.*

an·ō·mū'răn, *n.* one of the *Anomura.*

an·ō·mū'rous, an·ō·möu'rous, *a.* same as *anomural.*

an'ō·my, *n.* same as *anomie.*

ȧ·non', *adv.* [ME. *anon, anoon, onon, onoon*; AS. *on ān,* acc., in one, together, straightway.]

1. in a little while; soon; with little delay; as, I will be there *anon.*

2. at another time; again.

3. immediately; at once. [Archaic.]

ever and anon; now and then; time after time.

A·nō'nȧ, *n.* same as *Annona.*

An·ō·nā'cē·ae, *n.pl.* same as *Annonaceæ.*

an·ō·nā'ceous, *a.* same as *annonaceous.*

an'ō·nym, an'ō·nyme, *n.* 1. one whose name is unknown; an anonymous person.

2. a pen name; a pseudonym.

3. a book bearing no author's name. [Rare.]

an·ō·nym'i·ty, *n.* 1. the quality or state of being anonymous.

2. that which is anonymous. [Rare.]

ȧ·non'y·mous, *a.* [Fr. *anonyme*; L. *anonymus*; Gr. *anōnymos,* nameless.]

1. nameless; without the real name of the author; as, an *anonymous* pamphlet.

2. of unknown name; as, an *anonymous* author.

3. lacking a name, as an animal not assigned to any species. [Rare.]

Syn.—nameless, authorless, unidentified.

ȧ·non'y·mous·ly, *adv.* without a name; in an anonymous manner.

ȧ·non'y·mous·ness, *n.* the state of being anonymous.

An·oph'e·lēş, *n.* [Mod. L.; Gr. *anōphelēs,* harmful; *an-,* without, and *ōphelēs,* use, help.]

1. a genus of mosquitoes of the family *Culicidæ,* characterized by the long, slender palpi which nearly equal the beak in length. These mosquitoes can carry the malaria parasite and transmit the disease.

2. any mosquito belonging to this genus.

An'ō·plȧ, *n.pl.* [Mod. L., from Gr. *anoplos,* unarmed; *an* priv., and *hoplon,* shield, *hopla,* arms.] a class of nemertean worms, characterized by the absence of stylets on the proboscis.

An·ō·plō·thē'ri·um, *n.* [Mod. L., from Gr. *an* priv., *hoplon,* weapon, and *thērion,* a beast.] a genus of extinct quadrupeds, family *Anoplotheridæ* whose bones were first found in the gypsum quarries near Paris: characterized by their short, weak canine teeth and their long tails.

An·ō·plū'rȧ, *n.pl.* [Mod. L., from Gr. *an* priv., *hoplon,* weapon, and *oura,* tail.] an order of insects parasitic on mammals, and including the true lice.

an'op·sy, ȧ·nop'si·ȧ, *n.* [LL., from Gr. *an* priv., and *opsis,* sight.] deficient sight; blindness.

ä'nō·räk, *n.* [Eskimo (Greenland) *ánoráq.*] a heavy, leather or cloth jacket with a hood, worn in the cold north.

an·ō·reç'tiç, *a.* same as *anorexic.*

an·ō·reç'tiç, *n.* same as *anorexic.*

an·ō·ret'iç, *a.* same as *anorexic.*

an·ō·ret'iç, *n.* same as *anorexic.*

an·ō·rex'i·ȧ, an·ō·rex'y, *n.* [Gr. *anorexia,* want of appetite; *an* priv., and *orexia,* from *oregein,* to desire.] lack of appetite; specifically, anorexia nervosa.

an·ō·rex'i·ȧ nẽr·vō'sȧ, [Mod. L., nervous anorexia.] a personality disorder, chiefly in young women, characterized by aversion to food, obsession with weight loss, etc.

an·ō·rex'iç, *a.* 1. suffering from anorexia.

2. suppressing appetite for food.

an·ō·rex'iç *n.* 1. an anorexic person.

2. an anorexic drug.

ȧ·nor'thiç, *a.* [Gr. *an* priv., and *orthos,* straight.] in crystallography, irregular; triclinic.

ȧ·nor'thīte, *n.* [Gr. *an* priv., *orthos,* straight, and *-ite.*] a mineral of the feldspar family, $CaAl_2(SiO_4)_2$, occurring in basic igneous rocks.

ȧ·nor'thō·çlāse, *n.* [Gr. *an* priv., *orthos,* straight, and *klan,* to break.] a sodium potassium feldspar that is triclinic in crystallization.

an·or·thō'pi·ȧ, *n.* [Gr. *an* priv., *orthos,* straight, and *ops,* eye.] obliquity of vision; squinting.

an·or'thō·site'', *n.* [Fr. *anorthose,* from Gr. *an-,* not, and *orthos,* straight; and *-ite.*] an igneous rock, made up largely of a soda-lime feldspar.

an·os·mat'iç, *a.* without the sense of smell.

an·os'mi·ȧ, *n.* [Mod. L., from Gr. *an-,* without, and *osmē,* smell.] total or partial loss of the sense of smell.

an·ŏth'ẽr, *a.* [ME. *an other, an,* one, the, and *other.*]

1. not the same; different; as, we have one form of government, England *another.*

2. one more, an additional; as, grant one request, they will ask *another* favor.

3. a similar but actually different; some other; as, *another* Caesar.

an·ŏth'ẽr, *pron.* 1. one additional.

2. a different one.

3. one of the same kind.

An·öur'ȧ, *n.* same as *Anura.*

an''ox·ē'mi·ȧ, *n.* [*an-,* not, and *oxygen,* and *-emia.*] a reduction in the normal amount of oxygen in the blood, as at high altitudes.

an·ox'i·ȧ, *n.* [*an-,* not, and *oxygen,* and *-ia.*] in medicine, a condition in which there is not enough oxygen or tissue oxidation.

an'sȧ, *n.*; *pl.* **an'sae,** [L. *ansa,* a handle.]

1. in archaeology, a vase handle.

2. [*pl.*] in astronomy, the projections or arms of the ring on each side of the planet Saturn.

an'sāte, *a.* [L. *ansatus,* from *ansa,* a handle.] having a handle or handlelike part.

an'sāte çross, an ankh.

Än'schluss, *n.* [G.] a union or joining; particularly, the annexation of Austria by Nazi Germany in 1938.

An'sẽr, *n.* [L., a goose.]

1. a genus of geese, family *Anatidæ.*

2. in astronomy, a small star visible in the constellation Fox and Goose.

an'sẽr·ā·ted, *a.* [L. *anser,* a goose, and *-ated.*] in heraldry, with the ends shaped like the heads of lions, eagles, geese, reptiles, etc.: said of a cross.

ANSERATED CROSS

An'sẽr·ēş, *n.pl.* [L., geese.] a suborder of birds, whose characteristics are a broad, smooth, toothed bill, and webbed or palmated toes: it includes the geese, ducks, swans, etc.

An''sẽr·i·fọr'mēş, *n.pl.* [L. *anser,* a goose, and *forma,* form.] an order of birds comprising the ducks, geese, swans, etc.

an'sẽr·ine, *a.* [L. *anserinus,* from *anser,* a goose.]

1. resembling the skin of a goose; uneven, as the surface of the skin after a chill.

2. stupid; foolish.

3. pertaining to the *Anseres.*

an'sẽr·ous, *a.* resembling a goose; stupid, as a goose seems; silly.

an'swẽr (-sẽr), *v.t.*; answered, *pt., pp.*; answering, *ppr.* [ME. *answeren, andsweren*; AS. *andswarian*; Ice. *andsvara*; Sw. *ansvara, and-*, against, in reply, and *svara*, from *swaran*, to swear, affirm.]

1. to reply to in some way; to respond to; as, to *answer* a fool according to his folly; to *answer* a letter.

2. to speak in one's defense against; to refute; as, to *answer* a charge of murder.

3. to comply with, fulfil, pay, or satisfy; as, he *answered* my order; to *answer* a debt.

4. to be equivalent to; to be adequate to, or sufficient for.

5. to agree with; to conform to; to suit; as, he *answers* the description.

6. to atone for.

answer back; to reply forcefully, rudely, or impertinently; talk back. [Colloq.]

an'swẽr, *v.i.* 1. to reply; to speak or write by way of return; to respond; as, there is none to *answer*, he *answered* quickly.

2. to be accountable, liable, or responsible: followed by *to* before the person to whom, and *for* before the thing for which, one is liable; as, the man must *answer to* his employer *for* the money entrusted to his care.

3. to correspond with; to suit: followed by *to*.

As in water face *answereth to* face, so the heart of man *to* man. —Prov. xxvii. 19.

4. to take the place of something; to be sufficient; as, a piece of sail *answered* for clothes.

5. to be in conformity, or agree (with *to*); as, he *answers to* the description.

an'swẽr, *n.* 1. a reply: that which is said in return to a call, a question, an argument, an allegation, or address.

2. in law, a counterstatement of facts, in a course of pleadings; a refutation of what the other party has alleged; the formal reply of one side in a lawsuit to the allegations of the other.

3. a writing, letter, pamphlet, or book, in reply to another.

4. a solution, as of a puzzle, rebus, etc.; the result of a mathematical calculation; as, the *answer* to an equation.

5. an act done in response or return for another; retaliation; as, his *answer* was an immediate assault.

6. in music, a repetition of a theme, made by an instrument or voice other than the original one.

7. in fencing, a return thrust.

Syn.—reply, rejoinder, retort, response, replication, solution.—An *answer* is given to a question; a *reply* is made to an assertion; a *rejoinder* is made to a *reply*; a *response* is made in accordance with the words of another.

an'swẽr·à·ble, *a.* 1. capable of being answered, or satisfied by reply; as, an *answerable* argument.

2. obliged to give an account, or liable to be called to account; responsible; as, an agent is *answerable* to his principal.

3. obliged or liable to pay, indemnify, or make good; as, to be *answerable* for a debt or for damages.

4. correspondent; agreeing with; in conformity with. [Archaic.]

5. suitable; suited; proportionate; commensurate. [Archaic.]

6. equal; equivalent to. [Archaic.]

Syn.—amenable, accountable, responsible, liable.

an'swẽr·à·ble·ness, *n.* the quality of being answerable, liable, or responsible.

an'swẽr·à·bly, *adv.* in an answerable manner.

an'swẽr·ẽr, *n.* one who answers.

an'swẽr·less, *a.* having no answer; unanswerable.

an't, a contraction of *an it*, that is, *if it*. [Obs.]

an't, a contraction of *are not*: the normal contracted form in varieties of English which have lost final and preconsonantal *r*: also variously heard at different levels of usage as an assimilated form for *am not*, and as a contracted form for *is not, have not*, and *has not*: cf. *ain't*. [Chiefly Dial. or Brit. Colloq.]

ant-, same as *anti-*.

-ant, [Fr. *-ant*; L. *-antem* or *-entem*, the ppr. ending.]

1. a suffix used in forming adjectives meaning *performing* (the specified act), as in defi*ant*, radi*ant*.

2. a suffix used in forming nouns meaning *a person or thing that performs* (the specified act), as in occup*ant*, account*ant*.

ȧnt, *n.* [ME. *amte, amete*; AS. *æmete, æmette*; O.H.G. *ameize*; G. *ameise*, ant.] any of a genus of insects (*Formica*) of the order *Hymenoptera*, usually black or red in color, with the body divided into three distinct sections; an emmet; a pismire.

Ants, like bees, live together in colonies. Some raise hillocks of earth, in which they live, propagate and nurture their young, and store their provisions, the nests containing an intricate system of passages and chambers. Others, in rainy climates, build nests on trees. As among bees, there are neuter, or working ants, as well as males and females, the so-called neuter ants being undeveloped, wingless females. They do most of the work of the community, and care for the young. Many of the species are distinguished by names derived from their habits, as *agricultural ants, amazon ants, carpenter ants, honey ants, mason ants*, and *soldier ants*.

an'tȧ, *n.*; *pl.* **an'tae,** [L., from *ante*, before.] in architecture, a pilaster, especially a pilaster on each side of a door or standing opposite a pillar; in Greek and Roman architecture, the pilaster used to terminate the side walls of temples prolonged beyond the face of the end wall. A portico having its columns standing between *antae* is said to be *in antis*.

ANTA
top, portico *in antis*; A, A, antae

ant·ac'id, *n.* in medicine, a substance counteracting or neutralizing acidity, as sodium bicarbonate.

ant·ac'id, *a.* neutralizing acidity.

ant·aç'rid, *a.* having power to correct acridity.

An·tae'ăn, *a.* relating to or like Antaeus.

An·tae'us, *n.* [L.; Gr. *Antaios*.] in Greek mythology, a giant wrestler who was invincible as long as he was touching his mother, the earth.

an·tag'ō·niṣm, *n.* 1. the state of being in active opposition (*to* or *against* someone or something); hostility.

2. an opposing force, principle, etc.

an·tag'ō·nist, *n.* [Gr. *antagōnistēs*, an opponent; from *antagōnizesthai*, to struggle against.]

1. one who struggles for mastery with another; an opponent in a contest of any kind.

2. in anatomy, a muscle which counteracts another; as, a flexor is the *antagonist* of an extensor.

Syn.—adversary, opponent, competitor, enemy, rival, foe.

an·tag'ō·nist, *a.* same as *antagonistic*.

an·tag'ō·nis'tiç, an·tag·ō·nis'tiç·ăl, *a.* counteracting; opposing; combating; antagonistic.

an·tag·ō·nis'tiç·ăl·ly, *adv.* with antagonism; in opposition; adversely.

an·tag'ō·nīze, *v.t.*; antagonized, *pt., pp.*; antagonizing, *ppr.* 1. to contend against; to oppose.

2. to arouse antagonism in; to render antagonistic; as, this subterfuge *antagonized* his associates.

an·tag'ō·nīze, *v.i.* to be in opposition; to act antagonistically.

an·tag'ō·ny, *n.* antagonism; opposition. [Obs.]

ant·al'giç, *a.* [Gr. *anti*, against, and *algos*, pain.] having the tendency to allay pain. [Rare.]

ant·al'giç, *n.* a drug having the power of allaying pain; an anodyne. [Rare.]

ant·al'kȧ·lī, ant·al'kȧ·line (*or* -līn), *n.* in medicine, a substance which neutralizes an alkali, or counteracts an alkaline tendency in the system.

ant·al'kȧ·line (*or* -līn), *a.* neutralizing an alkali or counteracting alkalinity.

ant·am·bū·lā'çrăl, *a.* in zoology, distant from or opposite to the region of the ambulacra.

ant″an·ȧ·çlā'sis, *n.* [Gr. *antanaklasis*, a bending back against; *anti*, against, and *anaklān*, to bend back.]

1. in rhetoric, a figure which consists in repeating the same word in a different sense; as, while we *live*, let us *live*; learn some *craft* when young, that when old you may live without *craft*.

2. in grammar, a repetition of words when resuming a sentence after a long parenthetical phrase or clause.

ant″aph·rō·diṣ'i·aç, *a.* and *n.* same as *anaphrodisiac*.

ant·är'çhiṣm, *n.* [*anti-*, and Gr. *archē*, government.] opposition to all government or to all restraint of individuals by law. [Rare.]

ant·är'çhist, *n.* one who opposes all government. [Rare.]

ant·är·çhis'tiç, ant·är·çhis'tiç·ăl, *a.* opposed to all government. [Rare.]

ant·ärç'tiç, *a.* [*anti-*, and Gr. *arktos*, the Bear, a northern constellation.] opposite to the northern or arctic pole; relating to the South Pole or to the region near it; as, the *Antarctic* Circle, the *Antarctic* Ocean, etc.

Antarctic Circle; an imaginary circle parallel to the equator, 23° 30′ from the South Pole: also written *antarctic circle*.

Antarctic Zone; all of the region south of the Antarctic Circle.

ant·ärç'tiç, *n.* 1. the region around the South Pole.

2. same as *Antarctic Circle*.

An·tā'rēṣ, *n.* [Gr. *Antarēs*; *anti*, against, resembling, and *Arēs*, Mars, so called from its resemblance to Mars in color.] a star of the first magnitude in the constellation Scorpio: also called the *Scorpion's Heart*.

ȧnt beãr, 1. any of the larger species of anteaters: the name is generally restricted to *Myrmecophaga jubata*, found in the warmer parts of South America. Its body is covered with long hair, and the tail is long and bushy. The snout or muzzle is extended and toothless, and the tongue extensile and glutinous. Called also *tamanoir* and *great anteater*.

2. the aardvark, *Orycteropus capensis*, of South Africa.

ANT BEAR
(*Myrmecophaga jubata*)

ȧnt bĩrd, any of several species of birds common in South America, which feed on ants.

ȧnt çat'tle, various aphids kept by ants for the honeydew secreted by them, which forms a source of food for the ants.

ȧnt çow, any individual of the group of insects known as ant cattle.

an'tē-, [L. *ante*, before; Gr. *anti*; Sans. *anti*; Goth. *and-*.] a prefix meaning *before in time, order*, or *position*.

an'tē, *n.* 1. in poker, a stake that must be put into the pool by a player before cards are dealt to him.

2. the amount one must pay as his share. [Slang.]

an'tē, *v.t.* and *v.i.*; anteed, *pt., pp.*; anteing, *ppr.* 1. in poker, to put in (one's stake): often followed by *up*.

2. to pay (one's share). [Slang.]

an'tē·açt, *n.* a preceding act.

an'tē·ăl, *a.* being before or in front. [Rare.]

ȧnt'ēat″ẽr, *n.* any of various animals that live on ants, as the ant bear, the aardvark, etc.

an'tē·bel'lum, *a.* [L.] before the war; specifically, before the American Civil War; as, *ante-bellum* days.

an·tē·braçh'i·ăl, *a.* pertaining to the forearm.

an·tē·braçh'i·um, *n.* [*ante-*, and L. *brachium*, arm.] the forearm.

an″tē·cē·dā'nē·ous, *a.* antecedent; preceding in time.

an·tē·cēde', *v.t.* and *v.i.*; anteceded, *pt., pp.*; anteceding, *ppr.* [*ante-*, and L. *cedere*, to go.] to go before in place, order, or time.

an·tē·cēd'ence, *n.* 1. the act or state of going before in time; precedence.

2. in astronomy, an apparent motion of a planet toward the west, or contrary to the order of the signs of the zodiac.

an·tē·cēd'en·cy, *n.* the condition or quality

of being anterior or prior; antecedence; priority; precedency.

an·tē·cēd′ent, *a.* [L. *antecedens*, ppr. of *antecedere*, to go before.]

1. going before in time; prior; anterior; preceding; as, an event *antecedent* to the war.

2. in logic, presumptive; previous to examination or observation; as, an *antecedent* improbability.

Syn.—prior, preceding, foregoing, previous, anterior, former.—*Antecedent* is specific, referring to something consequent; *foregoing*, *preceding*, and *previous* are more general, being opposed to *subsequent*; *prior*, like priority, implies a preference if there is competition.

an·tē·cēd′ent, *n.* 1. a person or thing that goes before, with reference to time, place, position, etc.

2. in grammar, the word, phrase, or clause to which a pronoun refers: in the sentence "Solomon was the king who built the temple," *king* is the *antecedent* of *who*.

3. in mathematics, the first term of a ratio.

4. in logic, (a) the first of two propositions in an enthymeme, or argument of two propositions; as, *every man is mortal*; therefore every king is mortal; the first proposition being the *antecedent*, the second the *consequent*; (b) the first and conditional part of a hypothetical proposition; as, if the sun is fixed, the earth must move.

5. [*pl.*] the events that have gone before in one's life; facts and circumstances constituting one's previous history; as, his *antecedents* are against him.

an·tē·cēd′ent·ly, *adv.* previously; at a time preceding.

an·tē·ces′sŏr, *n.* [L. *antecessor*, a foregoer, teacher, from *antecedere*, to go before.]

1. one who goes before; a predecessor or a principal.

2. in law, one who possessed land before the present possessor; an ancestor or predecessor. [Obs.]

an′tē·chām″bẽr, *n.* an outer room; a chamber leading to a principal apartment and used as a waiting room.

an′tē·chap″el, *n.* the outer part of a chapel.

an′tē·ç̧hoir (-kwīr), *n.* a space in a church between the choir and the nave, usually partly enclosed.

an′tē Ç̧hris′tum, [L.] before Christ.

an·tē′ciăns, an·toe′ciăns, *n.pl.* [LL. *antœci*, from Gr. pl. *antoikoi*; *anti*, opposite, and *oikein*, to live.] persons living in corresponding latitudes north and south of the equator, and in the same longitude.

an″tē·cŏm·mūn′ion (-yun), *n.* in the Anglican Church, a portion of the liturgy preceding the Communion service.

an·tē·çŭr′sŏr, *n.* [L., a forerunner, from *ante*, before, and *currere*, to run.] one who runs before; a forerunner. [Obs.]

an′tē·dāte, *n.* 1. a prior date; a date antecedent to the actual one. [Rare.]

2. anticipation. [Obs.]

an′tē·dāte, *v.t.*; antedated, *pt.*, *pp.*; antedating, *ppr.* [*ante-*, and L. *datum*, from *dare*, to give.]

1. to precede; to be antecedent to; to belong to an earlier time than; as, folklore *antedates* history.

2. to anticipate; to take before the true time.

And *antedate* the bliss above. —Pope.

3. to make happen earlier; to set an earlier date for.

4. to date too early; as, to *antedate* a deed or note.

an″tē·di·lū′vi·ăn, an″tē·di·lū′vi·ăl, *a.* [*ante-*, and L. *diluvium*, a flood.]

1. before the Flood, or Deluge, in Noah's time; relating to things or times antecedent to the Deluge.

2. apparently antedating the Flood; of great age; antiquated; ancient; primitive; as, *antediluvian* methods, *antediluvian* machinery.

an″tē·di·lū′vi·ăn, *n.* an antediluvian person or thing.

An′tē·don, *n.* [Mod. L., from Gr. *Anthēdōn*, a nymph.]

1. a genus of crinoids, the type of the family *Antedonidæ*.

2. [a–] any comatula belonging to the genus *Antedon*.

An·tē·don′i·dae, *n.pl.* a jointed family of the *Crinoidea* class with five branching arms.

an′tē·façt, *n.* [*ante-*, and L. *factum*, a thing done.] something done before another. [Obs.]

an′tē·fix, *n.*; *pl.* **an·tē·fix′eṣ,** [L. *antefixum*; *ante*, before, and *fixus*, pp. of *figere*, to fasten.] an ornamental tile placed on the cornices and eaves of ancient buildings to conceal the ends of the tiles or to form a spout for the gutter.

an·tē·fleçt′ed, *a.* same as *anteflexed*.

an′tē·flexed, *a.* [L. *ante*, before, and *flexus*, pp. of *flectere*, to bend.] bent or inclined forward; showing anteflexion: applied particularly to the uterus.

an·tē·flex′ion (-flek′shun), *n.* the forward displacement or curvature of an organ, especially of the uterus.

ȧnt eggs, small white cocoons found in the hillocks of ants, usually supposed to be their eggs, but actually the larvae in their first and second states, particularly the latter.

an·tē′li·os, *n.* [Gr. *anti*, opposite, and *hēlios*, sun.] the position of a heavenly body when in front of the sun.

an′tē·lōpe, *n.*; *pl.* **an′tē·lōpes, an′tē·lōpe,** [LL. *antilope*; Gr. *antholops*, deer.] any of a group of ruminant quadrupeds, intermediate between the deer and goat, of which there are a large number of species. Their horns are solid and permanent, straight or curved, sometimes annulated, sometimes surrounded by a spiral, occasionally smooth. They resemble deer in form.

An·tē·lop′i·dae, An·ti·lop′i·dae, *n.pl.* the antelopes regarded as a family.

an′tē·lō·pine, an·tē·lō′pi·ăn, *a.* pertaining to the antelope.

an·tē·lū′căn, *a.* [L. *antelucanus*; *ante*, before, and *lux*, light.] before light: applied, in times of the Roman persecution, to Christian assemblies held before dawn.

an′tē lū′cem, [L. *ante*, before, and *lux*, light.] before dawn or daylight.

an″tē·mē·rid′i·ăn, *a.* [L. *antemeridianus*; *ante*, before, and *meridianus*, pertaining to midday.] before noon; pertaining to the forenoon, or to the time between midnight and the following noon.

an′tē mē·ri′di·em, [L.] before noon.

ant·ē·met′iç, *a.* [Gr. *anti*, against, and *emein*, to vomit.] restraining or reducing vomiting.

ant·ē·met′iç, *n.* a medicine which checks vomiting.

an′tē-mọr′tem, *a.* [L.] before death; as, an *ante-mortem* examination, *ante-mortem* statement.

an′tē-Mō·ṣā′iç, *a.* before the time of Moses.

an·tē·mun′dāne, *a.* [*ante-*, and *mundane*.] before the creation of the world.

an·tē·mū′răl, *n.* [L. *antemurale*; *ante*, before, and *murus*, wall.] a barbican, or outwork, consisting of a strong, high wall with turrets in front of the gate, for defending the entrance to a castle, etc.

an·tē·nā′tăl, *a.* [L. *ante*, before, and *natalis*, pertaining to birth.] before birth; prenatal.

an·tē·nā′tī, *n.pl.* [L. *ante*, before, and *nati*, pl. of *natus*, pp. of *nasci*, to be born.] persons born before a certain event: used particularly in connection with the claiming of political rights, as Americans born before the Declaration of Independence.

an′tē·nāvẹ, *n.* that part of the nave which is farthest from the choir.

an′tē-Nī′cēne, *a.* [*ante-*, and *Nicene*, from *Nice*.] prior to the first council of Nice, 325 A. D.

an·ten′nȧ, *n.*; *pl.* **an·ten′nae,** also, and for sense 2 always, **an·ten′nȧṣ,** [L., from Gr. *anateinein*; *ana*, up, and *teinein*, to stretch.]

1. either of a pair of movable, articulated sense organs attached to the head of an insect, crab, lobster, etc.; a feeler.

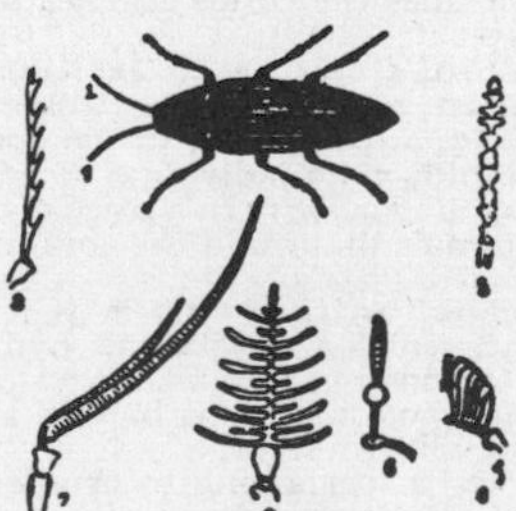

ANTENNAE

1. filiform antennae of Cucujo Firefly of Brazil (*Pyrophorus luminosus*); 2. denticulate antenna; 3. bipinnate; 4. lamellicorn; 5. clavate; 6. geniculate; 7. antenna and antennule of crustacean.

2. in radio and television, a wire or set of wires used in sending and receiving the electromagnetic waves; aerial.

an·ten′năl, *a.* belonging to antennae.

An·ten·nā′ri·ȧ, *n.* a genus of plants belonging to the composite family: commonly called *everlasting*.

an·ten·nif′ẽr·ous, *a.* [L. *antenna*, and *-ferous*, from *ferre*, to bear.] bearing antennae.

an·ten′ni·fọrm, *a.* shaped like antennae.

an·ten′nūle, *n.* a small antenna (feeler); one of the shorter pair of antennae of a crustacean.

an′tē·num·bẽr, *n.* a number that immediately precedes another. [Rare.]

an·tē·nup′tiăl (-shăl), *a.* before marriage; as, an *antenuptial* agreement.

an·tē·ọr′bit·ăl, *a.* [L. *ante*, before, and *orbitus*, orbit.] in anatomy, anterior to the orbit.

an·tē·pag′ment, an″tē·pag·men′tum, *n.* [L. *ante*, before, and *pagmentum*, from *pangere*, to fasten.] an ornamental molding placed on a jamb, post, etc., of a window or doorway.

an·tē·pas′ç̧hăl, *a.* pertaining to the time before Passover, or before Easter.

an′tē·pȧst, *n.* [*ante-*, and L. *pastus*, food.] a foretaste; something taken before the proper time. [Rare.]

an·tē·pen′di·um, *n.*; *pl.* **an·tē·pen′di·ȧ,** [LL., from L. *ante*, before, and *pendere*, to hang.]

1. an altar cloth.

2. a hanging in front of an altar.

an·tē·pē′nult, an″tē·pē·nult′i·mȧ, *n.* [L. *ante*, before, *pæne*, almost, and *ultimus*, last.] the second from the last syllable of a word; as, *-rid-* in *an·te·me·rid·i·an*.

an″tē·pē·nult′i·māte, *a.* pertaining to the antepenult.

an″tē·pē·nult′i·māte, *n.* 1. an antepenult.

2. anything second from the last.

ant·eph·i·al′tiç, an″ti·eph·i·al′tiç, *a.* [Gr. *anti*, against, and *ephialtēs*, nightmare.] preventing nightmare.

ant·eph·i·al′tiç, an″ti·eph·i·al′tiç, *n.* a preventive for nightmare.

an′tē·pōrt, *n.* [*ante-*, and L. *porta*, gate.] an outside door.

an·tē·pōr′ti·cō, *n.* an outer porch or colonnade.

an″tē·pō·ṣi′tion, *n.* [*ante-*, and L. *positio*, from *ponere*, to place.]

1. in grammar, the placing of a word before another, which, in general usage, would follow it.

2. in botany, a change in the arrangement of parts which usually alternate in the circle of flowers.

an·tē·pran′di·ăl, *a.* [*ante-*, and L. *prandium*, early dinner.] before dinner.

an″tē·prē·diç′ȧ·ment, *n.* [*ante-*, and L. *prædicamentum*, that which is predicted, a category.] a term applied in logic to certain previous matters requisite to a clear understanding of the predicaments and categories, as definitions of common terms.

an·tē·pros′tāte, *n.* the gland in front of the prostate gland.

an·tē′ri·ŏr, *a.* [L., from *ante*, before.]

1. before (in time); prior; antecedent; preceding (in time).

2. before or in front (in place); as, the *anterior* lobes of the brain.

3. in botany, opposite to or facing away from the axis; as, the *anterior* side of a flower.

Syn.—previous, former, preceding.

an·tē″ri·or′i·ty, *n.* the state of being anterior, preceding, or in front; the state of being before in time or place.

an·tē′ri·ŏr·ly, *adv.* in an anterior manner; previously.

an′tē·rō-, a combining form used to express *anterior*, *front*; as, *antero*lateral, *antero*posterior.

an″tē·rō·lat′ẽr·ăl, *a.* [*antero-*, and L. *lateralis*, from *latus*, side.] at the front side; anterior.

an′tē·rọọm, *n.* a room, usually small, before or in front of another; a waiting room.

an″tē·rō·pȧ·rī′e·tăl, *a.* [*antero-*, and L. *parietalis*, from *paries*, a wall.] in anatomy, pertaining to the parietal plates of the cranium.

an″tē·rō·pos·tē′ri·ŏr, *a.* reaching from the front to the back; relating to the direction from front to back.

an″tē·stat′ūre, *n.* in fortification, a small retrenchment or work formed of palisades or sacks of earth. [Obs.]

an′tē·stŏm″ach, *n.* a cavity which leads into the stomach, as in birds.

an·tē·tem′ple, *n.* the nave in an ancient church.

an′tē·tȳpe, *n.* an earlier form of something; a prototype.

an·tē·vẽr′sion, *n.* [from L. *anteversus*, pp. of *antevertere*, from *ante*, before, and *vertere*, to turn.] a forward displacement of an organ, as the uterus.

an·tē·vērt′, *v.t.* [L. *antevertere*; *ante*, before, and *vertere*, to turn.]
1. to prevent. [Obs.]
2. in medicine, to cause anteversion of.

an·thē′lȧ, *n.*; *pl.* **an·thē′lae**, [Gr. *anthēlē*, from *anthein*, to bloom.] in botany, a form of cymose inflorescence, in which the lateral branches extend beyond the axis.

ant·hel′i·cine, *a.* pertaining to the antihelix.

ant·hē′li·ŏn, *n.*; *pl.* **ant·hē′li·ȧ** or **ant·hē′li·onş**, [Mod. L., from Gr. *anti*, against, and *hēlios*, sun.] a luminous ring or rings around the shadow of an object, cast by the sun on a cloud or fog bank at high altitudes or in polar regions.

ant·hē′lix, *n.*; *pl.* **ant·hel′i·çeş** or **ant·hē′lix·eş**, same as *antihelix*.

an·thel·min′thiç, *a.* and *n.* same as *anthelmintic*.

an·thel·min′tiç, *a.* [Gr. *anti*, against, and *helmins*, a worm.] destroying or ejecting intestinal worms.

an·thel·min′tiç, *n.* an anthelmintic medicine.

an′them, *n.* [ME. *antem*, *antefne*; AS. *antefen*; L. *antiphona*, an anthem, from Gr. *antiphōnon*; *anti*, in return, and *phōnē*, voice.]
1. formerly, a hymn sung in alternate parts.
2. a religious choral song usually based on words from the Bible.
3. the official national song of a country.
4. any song of praise or reverence.

an′them, *v.t.* to praise with song: usually used poetically.

an·thē′mi·ȧ, *n.* in botany, any flower cluster. [Rare.]

an·thē′mi·ŏn, *n.*; *pl.* **an·thē′mi·ȧ**, [Gr. *anthemion*, a flower or flower ornament.] a flat decoration of floral or leaf forms, used in painting and relief sculpture.

ANTHEMION

An′thē·mis, *n.* [Mod. L., from Gr. *anthemis*, a flower or herb resembling the camomile, from *anthos*, a flower.] in botany, a genus of herbaceous plants belonging to the aster family (*Compositæ*); the camomile.

ant″hem·or·rhaġ′iç (-raj′). *a.* same as *antihemorrhagic*.

an′thẽr, *n.* [L. *anthera*, a flowery plant, from Gr. *antheros*, flowery, from *anthein*, to bloom; *anthos*, a flower.] in botany, the top of the stamen, usually elevated by means of a filament, which contains the pollen.

an′thẽr·ȧl, *a.* pertaining to an anther.

an′thẽr dust, the dust, or pollen, of an anther.

an·thẽr·id′i·ȧl, *a.* pertaining to an antheridium.

an·thẽr·id′i·um, *n.*; *pl.* **an·thẽr·id′i·ȧ**, [Mod. L., from *anthera*, anther, and Gr. dim. *-idion*.] in flowerless and seedless plants (cryptogams), the organ in which the male sex cells are developed.

an·thẽr·if′ẽr·ous, *a.* [L. *anthera*, anther, and *-ferous*, from *ferre*, to bear.] producing anthers.

an·thẽr′i·fọrm, *a.* anther-shaped.

an·thẽr·oġ′e·nous, *a.* [L. *anthera*, and Gr. *genēs*, producing.] produced from an anther.

an′thẽr·oid, *a.* [L. *anthera*, anther, and Gr. *eidos*, form.] having the appearance of an anther.

an″thẽr·ō·zō′id, **an″thẽr·ō·zō′oid**, *n.* [Gr. *antheros*, flowering, *zōon*, animal, and *-oid*.] a spermatozoid developing in the antheridium of a cryptogamic plant.

an·thē′sis, *n.* [Gr. *anthēsis*, bloom, from *anthein*, to bloom.] the state of full bloom in a flower.

ant hill, a mound of dirt carried by ants from their underground nest and heaped around its entrance.

An·thī′nae, *n.pl.* [LL., from Gr. *anthos*, masc., a small bird, and *-inæ*.] a subfamily of singing, passerine birds, including the titlarks or pipits.

an′thō-, [Gr. *anthos*, flower.] a prefix meaning *a flower* or *of flowers*.

an·thō′bi·ăn, *n.* [*antho-*, and Gr. *bios*, life.] a beetle that lives on flowers.

An·thō·brañ′chi·ȧ, *n.pl.* [*antho-*, and Gr. *branchia*, gills.] a suborder of gastropods, including the family *Dorididæ* and allied forms: also called *Pygobranchia*.

an′thō·cărp, *n.* [*antho-*, and Gr. *karpos*, fruit.] a multiple fruit, as the strawberry or pineapple, formed from the ovaries of several blossoms.

an·thō·căr′piç, *a.* anthocarpous.

an·thō·căr′pous, *a.* designating or of an anthocarp, or multiple fruit.

an·thō·çlin′i·um, *n.* same as *clinanthium*.

an·thō·cȳ′ăn, *n.* same as *anthocyanin*.

an·thō·cȳ′ȧ·nin, **an·thō·cy′ȧ·nine**, *n.* [*antho-*, and Gr. *kyanos*, blue, and *-in*.] the reddish-blue pigment in flowers and plants.

an·thō′di·um, *n.*; *pl.* **an·thō′di·ȧ**, [Mod. L., from Gr. *anthos*, flower, and *eidos*, form.] in botany, the head of a compound flower, as the aster.

an·thō·ġen′e·sis, *n.* [*antho-*, and Gr. *genesis*, production.] a kind of reproduction occurring in certain plant lice, the sexual individuals, male and female, arising from pupae furnished by an intervening form.

an″thō·ġē·net′iç, *a.* pertaining to anthogenesis.

an·thog′rȧ·phy, *n.* [*antho-*, and Gr. *graphein*, to write.] the division of botany that describes and treats of flowers.

an′thoid, *a.* flowerlike.

an·thō·kȳ′ăn, *n.* [*antho-*, and Gr. *kyanos*, blue.] same as *anthocyanin*.

an·thō·leū′cin, **an·thō·leū′cine**, *n.* [*antho-*, and Gr. *leukos*, white.] the white pigment in flowers.

an′thō·līte, *n.* [*antho-*, and *-lite*, Gr. *lithos*, stone.] a fossil plant, or a fossil resembling a flower.

an·thō·loġ′iç·ăl, *a.* pertaining to an anthology.

an·thol′ō·ġist, *n.* one who compiles an anthology.

an·thol′ō·ġīze, *v.i.*; anthologized, *pt.*, *pp.*; anthologizing, *ppr.* to make anthologies.

an·thol′ō·ġīze, *v.t.* to make an anthology of.

an·thol′ō·ġy, *n.* [Gr. *anthologia*, a flower-gathering, from *anthologos*; *anthos*, flower, and *legein*, to gather.]
1. a collection of poems, stories, etc.
2. in the Orthodox Eastern Church, a collection of prayers for solemn feasts.

an·thol′y·sis, *n.* [*antho-*, and Gr. *lysis*, from *lyein*, to loose.] in botany, a retrograde transformation of a flower, in which parts that are normally combined become separate.

an·thō·mā′ni·ȧ, *n.* [*antho-*, and Gr. *mania*, madness.] a mania or extravagant fondness for flowers.

An·thoph′i·lȧ, *n.pl.* [*antho-*, and Gr. *philos*, loving.] a division of hymenopterous insects, including the bees.

an·thoph′i·lous, *a.* 1. literally, having a fondness for flowers.
2. living among or feeding upon flowers: said of insects, as bees.

an′thō·phōre, *n.* [*antho-*, and Gr. *phoros*, from *pherein*, to bear.] in botany, a lengthened internode below the receptacle in *Caryophyllaceæ*, which bears the pistils and corolla.

an·thoph′ō·rous, *a.* flower-bearing.

an·thoph′yl·līte, *n.* [*antho-*, and Gr. *phyllon*, leaf.] a brownish-gray mineral of the amphibole group, occurring in brittle fibers, or fibrous or bladed masses, and consisting chiefly of silica, magnesia, and iron oxide.

an″thō·phyl·lit′iç, *a.* pertaining to anthophyllite or containing it.

An·thoph′y·tȧ, *n.pl.* same as *Spermophyta*.

an′thō·tax·y, *n.* [*antho-*, and Gr. *taxis*, order.] the arrangement of flowers on the axis of inflorescence.

-an′thous, [Gr. *anthos*, flower.] a suffix meaning *having flowers* (of a specified kind or number); as, gymn*anthous*, mon*anthous*.

An·thō·zō′ȧ, *n.pl.* [Mod. L., from Gr. *anthos*, flower, and *zōon*, animal.] a class of zoophytes which includes the corals and sea anemones; the polyps.

an·thō·zō′ăn, *a.* relating to the *Anthozoa*.

an·thō·zō′ăn, *n.* one of the *Anthozoa*.

an·thō·zō′iç, *a.* pertaining to the *Anthozoa*.

an·thō·zō′oid, *n.* an individual zooid or polyp in a compound colony. In a piece of coral each of the animals that build the coral mass is an *anthozooid*.

an′thrȧ·cēne, **an′thrȧ·cin**, *n.* [Gr. *anthrax*, coal, and *-ene*.] a crystalline hydrocarbon, $C_{14}H_{10}$, obtained in the last stages of coal-tar distillation, and used as a base in the manufacture of alizarin dyes.

an·thrac′iç, *a.* pertaining to or affected with anthrax.

an·thrȧ·cif′ẽr·ous, *a.* containing anthracite.

an′thrȧ·cin, *n.* same as *anthracene*.

an′thrȧ·cīte, *n.* [Gr. *anthrakitēs*, resembling coal, from *anthrax*, a burning coal.] a hard, compact variety of coal, which gives much heat and little smoke: popularly called *hard coal*.

an·thrȧ·cit′iç, *a.* pertaining to anthracite.

an·thraç′nōse, **an·thraç·nō′sis**, *n.* [Gr. *anthrax*, *anthrakos*, carbuncle, and *nosos*, disease.] a destructive disease, caused by fungi, which attacks the grape, bean, cotton, melon, and other plants.

an′thrȧ·çō-, **an′thraç-**, a combining form from Gr. *anthrax*, meaning *coal* or *carbuncle*.

an′thrȧ·çoid, *a.* [*anthraco-*, and *-oid*.]
1. resembling anthrax (the disease).
2. resembling the carbuncle, a precious stone of deep-red color.

an′thrȧ·çō·man″cy, *n.* [*anthraco-*, and Gr. *manteia*, divination.] divination by observing burning coal.

an·thrȧ·çom′e·tẽr, *n.* [*anthraco-*, and Gr. *metron*, measure.] an instrument for ascertaining the amount of carbonic acid in a gaseous mixture.

an″thrȧ·çō·met′riç, *a.* relating to an anthracometer.

an·thraç′ō·nīte, *n.* [Gr. *anthrakōn*, a pile of coals, from *anthrax*, coal.] a variety of marble of a coal-black luster, giving off a fetid odor when heated or rubbed: also called *stinkstone*.

an·thrȧ·çō′sis, *n.* [*anthrac-*, and *-osis*.] a disease of the lungs caused by inhaling coal dust: called also *black lung*, *collier's lung*, and *miner's phthisis*.

An″thrȧ·çō·thē′ri·um, *n.* [*anthraco-*, and Gr. *thērion*, beast.] a genus of extinct pachydermatous quadrupeds, whose fossils were first found in Italy in Tertiary lignite or brown coal, whence its name.

an·thrȧ·pūr′pū·rin, *n.* an orange-colored dye produced during the conversion of anthracene into alizarin.

an″thrȧ·qui·nōne′, *n.* a yellow crystalline ketone produced by the oxidation of anthracene. It is valued as the source of artificial alizarin.

an′thrax, *n.* [Gr., a burning coal.]
1. a carbuncle or boil.
2. a gem of the ancients, probably identical with the carbuncle.
3. an infectious disease of cattle and sheep, which may be transmitted to man, caused by *Bacillus anthracis*: it is characterized by malignant pustules: also called *splenic fever*.
4. one of these pustules.

An·thrē′nus, *n.* [Mod. L., from Gr. *anthrēnē*, a hornet.] a genus of small beetles, the larvae of which are destructive to woolens, furs, etc.

An·throp′i·dae, *n.pl.* [Mod. L., from Gr. *anthrōpos*, man.] the family of mammals that includes man only.

an′thrō·pō-, a combining form from Gr. *anthrōpos*, man, meaning *man*, *human*; as, *anthropology*.

an″thrō·pō·cen′triç, *a.* [*anthropo-*, and Gr. *kentron*, center.] regarding man as the central fact, or final aim, of the universe.

an″thrō·pō·ġen′e·sis, *n.* [*anthropo-*, and *genesis*.] the study of man's origin and development.

an″thrō·pō·ġen′iç, *a.* relating to anthropogenesis.

an·thrō·poġ′e·ny, *n.* [*anthropo-*, and Gr. *genos*, birth.] anthropogenesis.

an″thrō·pō″ġē·og′rȧ·phy, *n.* [*anthropo-*, and *geography*.] the study of the geographical distribution of man and of his relationship to his physical environment.

an·thrō′pō·glot, *n.* [*anthropo-*, and Gr. *glōtta*, tongue.] an animal having a tongue like that of a man, as the parrot.

an·thrō·pog′rȧ·phy, *n.* [*anthropo-*, and Gr. *graphia*, from *graphein*, to write.] the branch of anthropology that deals with the distribution of man according to his physical characteristics, languages, customs, etc.

an′thrō·poid, *a.* [*anthropo-*, and Gr. *eidos*, resembling.] resembling a human being: applied especially to the most highly developed apes, as the gorilla, orangutan, gibbon, and chimpanzee.

an′thrō·poid, *n.* any anthropoid ape.

an·thrō·poid′ăl, *a.* resembling man.

An·thrō·poid′ē·ȧ, *n.pl.* [Mod. L., from Gr. *anthrōpos*, man, and *eidos*, resembling.] the suborder of primate mammals which includes man, apes, and monkeys.

an·thrō·pol′ȧ·try, *n.* [*anthropo-*, and Gr. *latreia*, worship.] the worship of man; the bestowing of divine honors upon a human being.

an·throp′ō·līte, *n.* [*anthropo-*, and *-lite*, Gr. *lithos*, stone.] a petrifaction of the human body, skeleton, or any bodily part, as by the action of calcareous waters.

an″thrō·pō·loġ′ic·ăl, **an″thrō·pō·loġ′iç**, *a.* pertaining to anthropology, or the study of mankind.

an″thrō·pō·loġ′iç·al·ly, *adv.* from an anthropological point of view.

an·thrō·pol′ō·ġist, *n.* a student of or specialist in the science of anthropology.

an·thrō·pol′ō·ġy, *n.* [*anthropo-*, and Gr. *logia*, from *legein*, to speak.]

1. a discourse upon human nature. [Rare.]

2. a manner of expression in terms of men; anthropomorphic language. [Obs.]

3. the study of the races, physical and mental characteristics, distribution, customs, social relationships, etc. of mankind: often restricted to the study of the institutions, myths, etc. of primitive peoples.

an′thrō·pō·man″cy, *n.* [*anthropo-*, and Gr. *manteia*, divination.] divination by inspecting the entrails of a human being.

an″thrō·pō·met′riç, an″thrō·pō·met′riç·ăl, *a.* relating to anthropometry.

an·thrō·pom′e·try, *n.* [*anthropo-*, and Gr. *metria*, from *metron*, measure.] the part of anthropology having to do with the measurement of the human body to determine differences in races, individuals, etc.

An″thrō·pō·mor′phȧ, *n.pl.* [*anthropo-*, and Gr. *morphē*, form.] the anthropoid apes.

an″thrō·pō·mor′phiç, *a.* relating to or characterized by anthropomorphism.

an″thrō·pō·mor′phiç·ăl·ly, *adv.* in an anthropomorphic manner.

an″thrō·pō·mor′phism, *n.* [*anthropo-*, and Gr. *morphē*, form.] the attributing of human shape or characteristics to gods, objects, animals, etc.

an″thrō·pō·mor′phist, *n.* one who anthropomorphizes.

an″thrō·pō·mor′phīte, *n.* one who believes in anthropomorphism; specifically, one of an ancient religious sect holding such views.

an″thrō·pō·mor′phi·tism, *n.* the doctrines of anthropomorphites.

an″thrō·pō·mor′phīze, *v.t.* and *v.i.*; anthropomorphized, *pt., pp.*; anthropomorphizing, *ppr.* to attribute human shape or characteristics to (gods, objects, etc.).

an″thrō·pō·mor·phol′ō·ġy, *n.* [*anthropo-*, and Gr. *morphē*, form, and *logia*, from *legein*, to speak.] the use of anthropomorphic terms.

an″thrō·pō·mor′phō·sis, *n.* transformation into human form.

an″thrō·pō·mor′phous, *a.* [*anthropo-*, and Gr. *morphos*, from *morphē*, form.] having human shape and appearance.

an″thrō·pō·nom′içs, *n.pl.* [*construed as sing.*] anthroponomy.

an·thrō·pon′ō·my, *n.* [*anthropo-*, and *-nomy.*] the science dealing with the laws of human development in relation to environment and to other organisms.

an″thrō·pō·path′iç, an″thrō·pō·path′iç·ăl, *a.* pertaining to anthropopathy.

an″thrō·pō·path′iç·ăl·ly, *adv.* in an anthropopathic manner.

an·thrō·pop′ȧ·thism, *n.* anthropopathy.

an·thrō·pop′ȧ·thy, *n.* [LL. *anthropopathia*; Gr. *anthrōpopatheia*, humanity, from *anthrōpos*, man, and *pathos*, suffering.] the attributing of human feelings and passions to gods or objects.

an·thrō·poph′ȧ·ġī, *n.pl.*; *sing.* **an·thrō·poph′ȧ·gus,** [*anthropo-*, and Gr. *phagein*, to eat.] man-eaters; cannibals.

an″thrō·pō·phaġ′iç, an″thrō·pō·phaġ′iç·ăl, *a.* pertaining to cannibalism.

an″thrō·pō·phaġ′iç·ăl·ly, *adv.* in the manner of a cannibal.

an″thrō·poph·ȧ·ġin′i·ăn, *n.* a cannibal. [Rare.]

an·thrō·poph′ȧ·ġist, an·thrō·poph′ȧ·ġīte, *n.* a cannibal.

an·thrō·poph′ȧ·gous, *a.* cannibalistic; eating human flesh.

an·thrō·poph′ȧ·gus, *n.* singular of *anthropophagi.*

an·thrō·poph′ȧ·ġy, *n.* cannibalism; the act or practice of eating human flesh.

an″thrō·pō·phō′bi·ȧ, *n.* [*anthropo-*, and Gr. *phobia*, from *phobein*, to fear.] an abnormal fear of human beings.

an·thrō·poph′ū·ism, *n.* [*anthropo-*, and Gr. *phyē*, nature.] the attributing of human nature to God or a god. [Rare.]

an·thrō·poph′y·sīte, *n.* one who attributes human nature to God or a god. [Rare.]

an·thrō·pos′çō·py, *n.* [*anthropo-*, and Gr. *skopia*, from *skopein*, to view.] character reading from the features. [Rare.]

an·thrō·pos′ō·phy, *n.* [*anthropo-*, and Gr. *sophia*, wisdom.] knowledge of the nature of man.

an″thrō·pō·tom′iç·ăl, *a.* relating to anthropotomy.

an·thrō·pot′ō·mist, *n.* one who is skilled in human anatomy.

an·thrō·pot′ō·my, *n.* [*anthropo-*, and Gr. *tomē*, a cutting, from *temnein*, to cut.] the anatomy of the human body.

an″thrō·pō·zō′iç, *a.* [*anthropo-*, and Gr. *zōon*, life.] pertaining to the time during which man has existed; Quaternary.

An·thū′ri·um, *n.* [L., from Gr. *anthos*, flower, and *oura*, tail.] a large genus of tropical American flowering plants belonging to the family *Araceæ*, of which the well-known genus *Arum* is typical. They are largely cultivated in greenhouses.

ant·hyp·not′iç, *a.* and *n.* same as *antihypnotic.*

ant″hyp·ō·çhon′dri·aç, *a.* and *n.* same as *antihypochondriac.*

ant·hys·ter′iç, *a.* and *n.* same as *antihysteric.*

an′ti,- a prefix, from Gr. *anti*, against, used in forming adjectives and nouns derived from them. It means: (a) *against, hostile*; as, *anti*labor, *anti*-Semitism; (b) *that counteracts, that operates against*; as, *anti*aircraft; (c) *that prevents, cures,* or *neutralizes*; as, *anti*toxin; (d) *opposite, reverse*; as, *anti*peristalsis; (e) *rivaling*; as, *anti*pope. Also, before a vowel, sometimes *ant-*; as, *ant*acid.

an′tī, *n.* one who is opposed to some policy, proposal, action, etc. [Colloq.]

an′tī, *a.* opposed; against. [Colloq.]

an″ti·ab·ō·li′tion·ist, *n.* one who opposes abolition; specifically [A–], one who opposed the abolition of slavery: a term used in the United States before and during the Civil War.

an′ti·ae, *n.pl.* [LL. *antiæ*, the forelock, from *ante*, before.] the extensions of the feathers on each side of the bill, seen on some birds.

an″ti·āir′çraft, *a.* used for defense against enemy aircraft; as, an *antiaircraft* gun.

ANTIAIRCRAFT GUN

an″ti·al·bū′mid, *n.* a product of the digestion of albumin by pancreatic and gastric juices.

an″ti-Ȧ·mer′i·çăn, *a.* opposed to America, especially to the government of the United States.

an′ti·är, *n.* [Javanese *antjar.*] a poison extracted from the upas tree, *Antiaris toxicaria*; also, the tree itself.

an′ti·ȧ·rin, *n.* antiar (the poison).

An·ti·ā′ris, *n.* [LL., from *antiar.*] a genus of plants of the nettle family, including the upas tree. They are mostly found in the East Indies.

an″ti·är·thrit′iç, *a.* tending to prevent or cure arthritis.

an″ti·är·thrit′iç, *n.* a remedy for arthritis.

an″ti·at·tri′tion (-trish′un), *n.* a lubricating substance applied to machinery to lessen friction, as black lead mixed with grease.

an″ti·baç·chī′us, *n.*; *pl.* **an″ti·baç·chī′ī,** [L., from Gr. *antibakcheios*; *anti*, against, and *bakcheios*, a bacchius.] in poetry, a foot of three syllables, the first two long, and the last short: opposed to the *bacchius*, in which the first syllable is short and the last two long.

an″ti·baç·tē′ri·ăl, *a.* checking the growth or effect of bacteria.

an·ti·bil′ious (-yus), *a.* counteracting biliousness.

an″ti·bī·ō′sis, *n.* [Mod. L.; *anti-*, and Gr. *biosis*, way of life, from *bios*, life.] in biology, an association between organisms which is harmful to one of them.

an″ti·bī·ot′iç, *a.* 1. of antibiosis.

2. harmful to life; specifically, destroying, or stopping the growth of, bacteria.

an″ti·bī·ot′iç, *n.* an antibiotic substance.

an′ti·bod·y, *n.*; *pl.* **an′ti·bod·ies,** [*anti-*, and *body.*]

1. a protein produced in the body in response to contact of the body with an antigen, and having the specific capacity of neutralizing or reacting with the antigen.

2. in chemistry, a substance that lessens or counteracts another substance.

an·ti·brō′miç, *a.* and *n.* [*anti-*, and Gr. *bromos*, a smell.] deodorant.

An·ti-bŭrgh′ẽr, *n.* a member of a Scottish sect which arose in 1747, in opposition to the so-called burgess oath.

an′tiç, *a.* [It. *antico*, from L. *antiquus*, former, old; *ante*, before.] odd; fantastic; ludicrous.

an′tiç, *n.* 1. a buffoon or merry andrew; a clown. [Archaic.]

2. an odd appearance; a fantastic figure. [Obs.]

3. a piece of buffoonery; a comical trick; a prank; a caper.

an′tiç, *v.i.* to perform or practice antics.

an·tī′çăl, *a.* same as *anticous.*

an·ti·çär′di·um, *n.* [L., from Gr. *antikardion*; *anti*, over against, and *kardia*, heart.] the pit of the stomach; the upper part of the abdomen.

an·ti·çat′ȧ·lyst, *n.* [*anti-*, and *catalyst.*] a substance that slows down a chemical reaction.

an″ti·çȧ·tärrh′ăl, *a.* [*anti-*, and Gr. *katarrhoos*, a catarrh.] beneficial against catarrh.

an″ti·çȧ·tärrh′ăl, *n.* a remedy for catarrh.

an·ti·çath′ōde, *n.* in an X-ray tube, the piece opposite the cathode, serving as the target for the cathode's discharge.

an″ti·çau·sot′iç, *a.* [*anti-*, and Gr. *kausos*, fever, from *kaiein*, to burn.] efficacious against inflammatory fever.

an″ti·çau·sot′iç, *n.* a remedy for inflammatory fever.

an′ti·chăm″bẽr, *n.* antechamber. [Obs.]

an′ti·chlōr, *n.* any substance employed to remove excess chlorine from fabrics, etc., that have been bleached. Sodium thiosulfate is usually the substance used.

an·ti·çhrē′sis, *n.*; *pl.* **an·ti·çhrē′sēs,** [Gr. *antichresis*, from *anti*, in return, and *chresthai*, to use.] in civil law, a mortgage contract in which the borrower gives possession and use of property, the revenues therefrom being applied on account of the principal and interest of the debt.

an′ti·christ, *n.* [ME. *antichrist*; OFr. *antechrist*; L. *antichristus*; Gr. *antichristos*, from *anti-*, against, and *Christos*, Christ.]

1. an opponent of or disbeliever in Christ.

2. [A–] in the Bible, the great antagonist of Christ, expected to spread great evil before the end of the world but finally to be conquered at Christ's second coming. I John ii. 18.

3. a false Christ.

an·ti·çhris′tiăn (-chăn), *a.* opposed to Christians or Christianity.

an·ti·çhris′tiăn, *n.* one opposed to Christians or Christianity.

an·ti·çhris′tiăn·ism, *n.* antichristianity.

an″ti·çhris·ti·an′i·ty, *n.* opposition to Christians or Christianity.

an·ti·çhris′tiăn·ly, *adv.* in an antichristian manner.

an·ti·çhron′iç·ăl, *a.* [*anti-*, and Gr. *chronos*, time.] deviating from the proper order of time. [Rare.]

an·ti·çhron′iç·ăl·ly, *adv.* in an antichronical manner.

an·tiçh′rō·nism, *n.* deviation from the true order of time. [Obs.]

an·tiçh′thon, *n.*; *pl.* **an·tiçh′thō·nēs,** [Gr. *antichthōn*; *anti*, against, opposite, and *chthōn*, the earth.]

1. an imaginary planet similar to the earth, but on the opposite side of the sun; the counter earth of Pythagoras.

2. [*pl.*] the inhabitants of such a planet. [Obs.]

an·tic′i·pănt, *a.* anticipating; expectant: used with *of*; as, *anticipant of* death.

an·tic′i·pāte, *v.t.*; anticipated, *pt., pp.*; anticipating, *ppr.* [L. *anticipatus*, pp. of *anticipare*, to anticipate, take beforehand; *ante*, before, and *capere*, to take.]

1. to take or act before another, so as to forestall him; to take first possession of.

2. to take up before the proper time; as, the advocate has *anticipated* that part of his argument.

3. to foretaste or foresee; to have a previous view or impression of; to consider beforehand; as, to *anticipate* the pleasures of an entertainment.

4. to prevent by acting beforehand; to preclude.

5. to foresee, as a wish, etc., and do in advance (what is desired); as, he *anticipated* our orders.

6. to use or enjoy in advance.

7. in business, to meet (an obligation) before due.

Syn.—foresee, expect, preoccupy, forestall, foretaste, prejudge.—*Expect* is stronger than *anticipate.* We may *anticipate* difficulties when we do not really *expect* them.

an·tic·i·pā′tion, *n.* 1. the act of anticipating; the act of taking up, placing, or considering something before the proper time in natural order.

2. foretaste; foreknowledge; expectation; previous view or impression of what is to happen afterward; as, the *anticipation* of the joys of heaven.

3. expectation.

4. something anticipated.

5. in music, the introduction into a chord of one or more of the component tones of the chord which follows, producing a passing discord.

Syn.—expectation, preconception, foresight, forethought, foretaste, forecast.

an·tic′i·pā·tive, *a.* of or containing anticipation; tending to anticipate.

an·tic′i·pā·tive·ly, *adv.* in an anticipative manner.

an·tic′i·pā·tŏr, *n.* one who anticipates.

an·tic′i·pȧ·tō″ri·ly, *adv.* with anticipation.

an·tic′i·pȧ·tō·ry, *a.* before the time; occurring in advance.

an·ti·çlas′tiç, *a.* [Gr. *antiklān*; *anti*, back, and *klān*, to bend.] in mathematics, curved oppositely in different directions: applied to a surface having concave and convex curvatures transversely opposite, as that of a saddle: opposed to *synclastic*.

an″ti·çler′i·çăl, *a.* opposed to the clergy or church hierarchy, especially to its influence in public affairs.

an″ti·çler′i·çăl·iṣm, *n.* opposition to the clergy or church hierarchy, especially to its influence in public affairs.

an″ti·çlī·maç′tiç, *a.* pertaining to, having, or resembling an anticlimax.

an·ti·çlī′max, *n.* [*anti-*, and Gr. *klimax*, a ladder, climax.]

1. a sudden drop from the dignified or important in thought or expression to the commonplace or trivial, often for humorous effect.

2. a descent, as in a series of events, which is in ludicrous or disappointing contrast to a preceding rise.

an·ti·çlī′năl, *a.* [*anti-*, and Gr. *klinein*, to incline.]

1. inclined in opposite directions.

2. in geology, of or like an anticline.

anticlinal line, or *anticlinal axis*; in geology, the ridge of a wavelike curve, the strata dipping from it on either side as from the ridge of a house: opposed to *synclinal*.

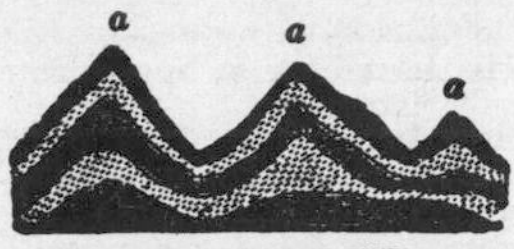

aaa. ANTICLINAL LINE

an·ti·çlī′năl, *n.* in geology, an anticlinal line or axis.

an′ti·çline, *n.* [from *anticlinal*, after *incline*, *decline*.] in geology, a fold of stratified rock from the crest of which the strata slope downward in opposite directions: opposed to *syncline*.

an″ti·çli·nō′ri·um, *n.*; *pl.* **an″ti·çli·nō′ri·ȧ,** [LL., from Gr. *anti*, against, *klinein*, to lean, and *oros*, mountain.] in geology, a succession of anticlines and synclines resembling a row of arches.

an′tiç·ly, *adv.* in an antic manner.

an′tiç mȧsk, *n.* an antimasque. [Obs.]

an′tiç·ness, *n.* the state of being antic.

an″ti-çon·sti·tū′tion·ăl, *a.* opposed to or against the constitution.

an″ti·çon·tā′ġious (-jus), *a.* opposing or destroying contagion.

an″ti·çon·vul′sive, *a.* in medicine, efficacious against convulsions.

an′ti·çor, *n.* [*anti-*, and L. *cor*, the heart.] an inflammation in a horse's breast, opposite the heart; a form of quinsy.

an·tī′çous, *a.* [L. *anticus*, in front, from *ante*, before.] in botany, turned inward toward the axis; introrse.

an′ti·çy·clōne, *n.* 1. an atmospheric condition in which the direction of the outward-spiraling winds and the relations of barometric pressure are opposite to those of a cyclone.

2. the area of high pressure in which this condition is centered.

3. an atmospheric disturbance at the edge of this area.

an″ti·çȳ·çlon′iç, *a.* of or connected with an anticyclone.

an″ti·çȳ·çlon′iç·ăl·ly, *adv.* in the manner of an anticyclone.

an″ti·dem·ō·çrat′iç, *a.* opposing democracy; contrary to government by the people.

An″ti·diç·ō·mā′ri·ăn·īte, *n.* [*antidikos*, opponent; *anti*, against, *dikē*, right, and *Mariaim*, Mary.] one of a sect of Arabian Christians, late in the fourth century, who denied the perpetual virginity of Mary, maintaining that she had children by Joseph after the birth of Jesus: also called *Antidicomarian* and *Antimarian*.

an″ti·dis″es·tab″lish·men·tā′ri·ăn·iṣm, *n.* opposition to the disestablishment of a church or religious body; specifically, strong opposition to the disestablishment of a State Church, as was manifested in Ireland in 1869, when Gladstone disestablished the Irish Church (Protestant) to which all the people, including Roman Catholics, had been compelled to pay tithes.

an·ti·dō′rcn, *n.*; *pl.* **an·ti·dō′rȧ,** see *eulogia*.

an′ti·dō·tăl, *a.* of, like, or serving as an antidote.

an′ti·dō·tăl·ly, *adv.* in an antidotal manner.

an′ti·dō·tȧ·ry, *n.* 1. a pharmacopoeia, or a treatise on antidotes. [Obs.]

2. an antidote. [Obs.]

an′ti·dōte, *n.* [Gr. *antidotos*, an antidote; *anti*, against, and *dotos*, given, from *didonai*, to give.]

1. a remedy to counteract the effects of poison, or of anything noxious taken into the system.

2. anything tending to counteract an evil; as, an *antidote* for poverty.

Syn.—remedy, counteraction, preventive.

an′ti·dōte, *v.t.*; antidoted, *pt.*, *pp.*; antidoting, *ppr.* 1. to counteract the effects of, as a poison.

2. to provide an antidote for, as a disease or condition.

an·ti·dot′iç·ăl, *a.* serving as an antidote. [Rare.]

an·ti·dot′iç·ăl·ly, *adv.* by way of antidote. [Rare.]

an·ti·drom′iç, *a.* [from *anti-*, and Gr. *dromos*, a course; and *-ic*.] in physiology, running or conveying in a direction opposite to the normal, as a nerve fiber, etc.

an·tid′rō·mous, an·tid′rō·măl, *a.* [LL. *antidromus*, from Gr. *antidromein*; *anti*, against, and *dromein*, to run.] of or pertaining to antidromy.

an·tid′rō·my, *n.* in botany, a change in direction of ascending spirals connecting leaf attachments.

an″ti·dys·en·ter′iç, *a.* efficacious against dysentery.

an″ti·dys·en·ter′iç, *n.* a remedy for dysentery.

an″ti·ē·met′iç, *a.* and *n.* same as *antemetic*.

an″ti·en·ẽr·ġis′tiç, *a.* resisting applied energy: opposed to *synergistic*.

an″ti·eph·i·al′tiç, *a.* and *n.* same as *antephialtic*.

an′ti-Fas′ciṣm (-fash′izm), *n.* opposition to Fascism.

an·ti·fē′brile, *a.* reducing fever.

an·ti·fē′brile, *n.* an antifebrile drug.

an·ti·feb′rine, *a.* and *n.* same as *antipyretic*.

an·ti·fed′ẽr·ăl, *a.* opposing federalism.

An·ti·fed′ẽr·ăl·iṣm, *n.* 1. opposition to the ratification of the constitution of the United States, in the early days of the government.

2. [a—] opposition to federalism.

An·ti·fed′ẽr·ăl·ist, *n.* 1. one who, at the formation of the constitution of the United States, opposed its adoption and ratification.

2. [a—] one who is opposed to federalism.

An·ti·fed′ẽr·ăl·ist, *a.* designating or of a former political party led by Thomas Jefferson which opposed the Federalists.

an·ti·fem′i·niṣm, *n.* the theory or practice of those who oppose equal political, economic, and social rights for women.

an·ti·freeze′, *n.* a substance of low freezing point, as alcohol, used especially in the radiators of water-cooled automobile engines in cold weather to prevent freezing.

an·ti·friç′tion, *a.* lessening friction.

an·ti·friç′tion, *n.* a lubricant, device, etc. for reducing friction.

an″ti·gȧ·laç′tiç, *n.* [*anti-*, and Gr. *gala*, *galaktos*, milk.] a drug that tends to diminish the secretion of milk.

an·ti-Gal′li·çăn, *n.* one who is opposed to France or anything French.

an·ti-Gal′li·çăn, *a.* hostile to what is French.

an′ti·gen, *n.* [*anti-*, and *-gen*.] a substance, usually a protein, carbohydrate, or fat-carbohydrate complex which is capable of forming, or inducing the formation of, antibodies when introduced directly into the body, as into the bloodstream.

An·tig′ō·nē, *n.* in Greek legend, the daughter of Oedipus and Jocasta: she defied her uncle, Creon, by performing funeral rites for her brother, Polynices.

an′ti·grȧph, *n.* [Gr. *antigraphon*, a copy; *anti*, corresponding to, and *graphon*, from *graphein*, to write.] a copy. [Obs.]

an·ti·hē′lix, *n.*; *pl.* **an·ti·hē′li·çēṣ, an·ti·hē′lix·eṣ,** the rounded piece of cartilage inside the outer rim (helix) of the ear.

an″ti·hem·or·rhaġ′iç, *n.* a remedy for hemorrhage.

an″ti·hem·or·rhaġ′iç, *a.* checking hemorrhage.

an·ti·his′tȧ·mine (*or* **-min**), *n.* any of several drugs used to minimize the action of histamine in certain allergic conditions: it is variously claimed that they relieve the symptoms in asthma, hay fever, the common cold, etc.

an″ti·hȳ·drō·phōb′iç, *n.* a remedy for hydrophobia.

an″ti·hȳ·drō·phōb′iç, *a.* curing hydrophobia.

an″ti·hȳ·drop′iç, *n.* a medicine to counteract dropsy.

an″ti·hȳ·drop′iç, *a.* efficacious against dropsy.

an″ti·hyp·not′iç, ant·hyp·not′iç, *n.* [*anti-*, and Gr. *hypnotikos*, from *hypnos*, sleep.] a medicine that prevents or tends to prevent sleep.

an″ti·hyp·not′iç, ant·hyp·not′iç, *a.* tending to prevent sleep.

an″ti·hȳp·ō·çhon′dri·aç, *a.* counteracting or tending to eliminate hypochondria.

an″ti·hys·ter′iç, *n.* a medicine for hysteria.

an″ti·hys·ter′iç, *a.* checking hysteria.

an″ti-iç·ter′iç, *n.* [*anti-*, and Gr. *ikterikos*, from *ikteros*, the jaundice.] a medical remedy for jaundice.

an″ti-iç·ter′iç, *a.* checking jaundice.

an″ti-im·pē′ri·ăl·ist, *n.* one opposed to the policy of imperialism; specifically, in United States politics, one opposed to an extension of territory and the consequent colonial policy.

an″ti·kē″tō·gen′e·sis, *n.* [Mod. L.; *anti-*, and *ketone*, and *genesis*.] the use of certain substances, as glucose, to check or prevent ketosis, as in diabetes.

an·ti·knock′, *n.* a substance added to the fuel of internal-combustion engines to do away with noise resulting from too rapid combustion.

an·ti·lā′bŏr, *a.* opposed or harmful to labor unions and the interests, gains, etc. of workers.

an·ti·lā′bŏr·ist, *a.* antilabor.

an·ti·lā′bŏr·ist, *n.* one who is opposed to labor unions.

an″ti·lē·gom′e·nȧ, *n.pl.* [Gr. *antilegomena*, things spoken against, from *antilegein*; *anti*, against, and *legein*, to speak.] those books of the New Testament which were not at first received as canonical: opposed to *homologoumena*.

an·ti·lith′iç, *a.* [*anti-*, and Gr. *lithos*, stone.] in medicine, preventing the formation or development of calculi, as of the urinary tract.

an·ti·lith′iç, *n.* an antilithic drug or other substance.

An·til·lē′ăn, *a.* of the Antilles.

An·til·lē′ăn, *n.* a native or inhabitant of the Antilles.

an·ti·log′ȧ·rithm, *n.* 1. the complement of the logarithm of any sine, tangent, or secant. [Obs.]

2. the number corresponding to any logarithm; as, 100 is the *antilogarithm* of 2.

an″ti·log·ȧ·rith′miç, *a.* pertaining to antilogarithms.

an·til′ō·gous, *a.* of a contrary character; specifically, in electricity, designating that pole of a crystal or like body which exhibits negative electricity when heated.

an·til′ō·ġy, *n.*; *pl.* **an·til′ō·ġieṣ,** [Gr. *antilogia*, from *antilogos*, contradictory; *anti*, against, and *logos*, from *legein*, to speak.] a contradiction in ideas, statements, or terms.

an·ti·loi′miç, *n.* [*anti-*, and Gr. *loimos*, plague.] a remedy for the plague.

an·til′ō·pine, *a.* same as *antelopine*.

an·ti·lys′siç, *a.* [*anti-*, and Gr. *lyssa*, rage, madness,] antihydrophobic.

an″ti·mȧ·ças′săr, *n.* [*anti-*, and *macassar*, a kind of hair oil.] a small cover on the back or arms of a chair, sofa, etc. to prevent soiling.

an″ti·mȧ·lā′ri·ăl, *a.* preventing or relieving malaria.

an″ti·mȧ·lā·ri·ăl, *n.* an antimalarial drug.

An·ti·mā′ri·ăn, *n.* same as *antidicomarianite*.

an·ti·mā′sŏn, *n.* one opposed to freemasonry.

an″ti·mā·son′iç, *a.* opposing freemasonry.

an·ti·mā′sŏn·ry, *n.* opposition to freemasonry.

an′ti·masque, an′ti·mask, *n.* [*anti-*, and

masque.] a comic sketch between the acts of a masque, often a burlesque of the masque.

an′ti·mat″tẽr, *n.* a form of matter in which the electrical charge or other property of each constituent particle is the reverse of that of the usual matter of our universe: an atom of antimatter has a nucleus of antiparticles (called *antiprotons* and *antineutrons*) surrounded by positrons.

an·ti·men′si·um, *n.*; *pl.* **an·ti·men′si·ȧ,** [LL., from Gr. *anti*, in place of, and L. *mensa*, a table.] in the Greek church, an altar cloth used in celebrating the eucharist in churches having no altar.

an″ti·me·phit′iç, *a.* [*anti-*, and L. *mephitis*, a poisonous gas.] efficacious against poisonous gases.

an″ti·me·phit′iç, *n.* a remedy for poisonous gases.

an′ti·mēre, *n.* [*anti-*, and Gr. *meros*, part.] in zoology, either of the corresponding parts opposite each other on both sides of an organism's axis.

an·ti·mer′iç, *a.* relating to an antimere.

an″ti·me·tab′ō·lē, *n.* [L., from Gr. *antimetabolē*, *anti*, against, and *meta*, beyond, and *ballein*, to throw.] a form of speech characterized by a repetition of words or ideas in inverted order.

an″ti·me·tath′e·sis, *n.* [L., from Gr. *antimetathesis*; *anti*, against, and *metathesis*, transposition.] in rhetoric, counter-transposition; a figure of speech by which the position of the elements of an antithesis are changed by inversion.

an′ti·mis″sile, *a.* designed as a defense against ballistic missiles.

an″ti·mō·när′çhiç·ăl, an″ti·mō·när′çhiç, *a.* opposed to monarchy.

an·ti·mon′ärçh·ist, *n.* one opposed to monarchy.

an·ti·mō′nāte, *n.* a salt of antimonic acid.

an·ti·mō′ni·ăl, *a.* of or containing antimony.

antimonial powder; an emetic compound, composed of oxide of antimony and phosphate of calcium in the proportion of one and two.

an·ti·mō′ni·ăl, *n.* an antimonial compound.

an·ti·mō′ni·āte, *n.* antimonate.

an·ti·mō′ni·ā·ted, *a.* in combination with antimony; mixed or prepared with antimony.

an·ti·mon′iç, *a.* 1. relating to or produced from antimony.

2. in chemistry, designating or of compounds of pentavalent antimony.

an·ti·mō′ni·ous, *a.* 1. of or like antimony.

2. in chemistry, designating or of compounds of trivalent antimony.

an′ti·mō·nīte, *n.* 1. a compound of antimonious acid and a base or a radical acting as a base.

2. stibnite.

an·ti·mō′ni·ū·ret″ed, *a.* combined with antimony.

an″ti·mon·soon′, *n.* the air current above and moving oppositely to a monsoon.

an′ti·mō·ny, *n.* [Fr. *antimoine*; L. *antimonium*, antimony.] a silvery-white, brittle, metallic chemical element of crystalline structure, found only in combination: used in alloys with other metals to harden them and increase their resistance to chemical action: compounds of antimony are used in medicines and pigments: symbol, Sb; atomic weight, 121.76; atomic number, 51.

an′ti·mō·ny glance, stibnite.

an′ti·mō·nyl″, *n.* [from *antimony* and *-yl*.] the univalent radical, SbO, found in certain salts, notably antimonyl potassium tartrate.

an′ti·mō·nyl″ pō·tas′si·um tär′trāte, a poisonous, colorless or white crystalline powder, an antimonious tartrate, $KSbOC_4H_4O_6$, used as an emetic and as a mordant in dyeing: called also *tartar emetic*.

an″ti·nē·phrit′iç, *n.* [*anti-*, and Gr. *nephritis*, from *nephros*, kidney.] a remedy for diseases of the kidneys.

an″ti·nē·phrit′iç, *a.* remedial for diseases of the kidneys.

an·tin′i·ăl, *a.* of or pertaining to the antinion.

an·tin′i·on, *n.* [Gr. *anti*, opposite, and *inion*, the back of the head.] the part of the skull between the eyebrows.

an′ti·nōde, *n.* [*anti-*, and L. *nodus*, a knot.] in physics, the point halfway between two adjacent nodes in a vibrating body.

an·ti·nō′mi·ăn, *n.* [from *antinomy*, and *-an*.] [also A-] a member of a Christian sect which held that faith alone, not obedience to the moral law, is necessary for salvation.

an·ti·nō′mi·ăn, *a.* of this sect or doctrine.

an·ti·nō′mi·ăn·işm, *n.* the beliefs and practices of antinomians.

an·tin′ō·my, *n.* [L. *antinomia*, a contradiction between laws, from Gr. *antinomia*; *anti-*, against, and *nomia*, from *nomos*, law.]

1. antagonism between laws; the opposition of one rule, principle, or law to another.

2. the unavoidable contradiction to pure reasoning which human limitations introduce, as formulated by Kant; paradox.

3. a contradiction or inconsistency between two apparently reasonable principles or laws.

An·ti·ō′çhi·ăn, *n.* 1. a resident of Antioch, Syria.

2. a follower of, or a believer in, the school of religious philosophy, founded at Antioch in the fourth century, which propounded a course of scriptural interpretation midway between the literal and allegorical.

an″ti·ō·pel′mous, *a.* [Gr. *antios*, opposite, and *pelma*, sole.] having one of the tendons of the foot trisected and a part running to the first, second, and fourth toes: applied to the foot of a bird, or the bird itself.

an″ti·or·gas′tiç, *a.* [*anti-*, and Gr. *orgaein*, to swell.] having a tendency to repress sexual excitement.

an·ti·pā′păl, *a.* opposed to the pope or papacy.

an·ti·par′ăl·lel, *n.* either of two straight lines or planes which, when joined by a third line or plane form equal but opposite angles.

an·ti·par′ăl·lel, *a.* running parallel in an opposite direction or directions.

an″ti·par·ȧ·lyt′iç, an″ti·par·ȧ·lyt′iç·ăl, *a.* remedial for paralysis.

an″ti·par·ȧ·lyt′iç, *n.* a remedy for paralysis.

an′ti·pär″ti·çle, *n.* any of the constituent particles of antimatter: see *antimatter*.

An′ti·pasçh, *n.* the first Sunday after Easter.

än·ti·päs′tō, [It.] an appetizer or a relish, as a dish of salted fish, meat, olives, etc.

An″ti·pȧ·thā′ri·ȧ, *n.pl.* [LL., from Gr. *antipathēs*, of opposite feelings or properties.] an order of corals having a noncalcareous, hollow, external sclerobase.

an″ti·pȧ·thā′ri·ăn, *a.* of or pertaining to the *Antipatharia*.

an″ti·pȧ·thā′ri·ăn, *n.* one of the *Antipatharia*.

an″ti·pȧ·thet′iç, an″ti·pȧ·thet′iç·ăl, *a.* 1. having antipathy; averse; contrary.

2. opposed or antagonistic in character, tendency, etc.

an·tip′ȧ·thist, *n.* an antagonist. [Rare.]

an·tip′ȧ·thy, *n.*; *pl.* **an·tip′ȧ·thieş,** [Gr. *antipatheia*; *anti*, against, and *patheia*, from *pathein*, to suffer, feel.]

1. inherent aversion or antagonism of feeling; repugnancy; revulsion; as, *antipathy* to snakes; *antipathy* to an offensive person.

2. opposition in character, nature, tendency, etc.

3. any object of strong dislike or repugnancy.

Syn.—abhorrence, aversion, contrariety, detestation, dislike, hatred, opposition.

an·ti·pep′tōne, *n.* a form of peptone unchanged by trypsin.

an″ti·pē·ri·od′iç, *n.* a remedy possessing the property of preventing the return of periodic diseases, as of certain fevers.

an″ti·per·i·stal′sis, *n.* [Gr. *anti*, against, and *peristaltikos*, clasping and compressing.] in physiology, a reversal of the normal downward peristaltic motion of the intestinal system.

an″ti·per·i·stal′tiç, *a.* checking peristalsis; characteristic of antiperistalsis.

an″ti·pe·ris′tȧ·sis, *n.* [Gr. *antiperistasis*; *anti*, against, and *peristasis*, a standing around, from *peristanai*, to stand around; *peri*, around, and *histanai*, to stand.] opposition resulting in the intensification or consequent strength of the thing opposed.

an″ti·per·i·stat′iç, *a.* of antiperistasis.

an″ti·pẽr·sŏn·nel′, *a.* directed against or intended to destroy people rather than material objects; as, *antipersonnel* mines.

an″ti·pẽr′spir·ănt, *n.* an astringent substance applied to the skin to reduce perspiration.

an·ti·pet′ăl·ous, *a.* [*anti-*, and Gr. *petalon*, a leaf.] placed opposite to or in front of a petal.

an·ti·phär′miç, *a.* same as *antidotal*.

an″ti·phlō·ġis′tiăn (-chăn), *n.* an opponent of the theory of phlogiston.

an″ti·phlō·ġis′tiç, *a.* 1. counteracting inflammation.

2. opposed to the doctrine of phlogiston; as, the *antiphlogistic* system.

an″ti·phlō·ġis′tiç, *n.* any medicine or diet which tends to reduce inflammation or fever.

an′ti·phon, an′ti·phōne, *n.* [ML. *antiphona*, from Gr. *antiphōna*; *anti*, in return, and *phonē*, voice, a sound.]

1. a hymn, psalm, etc. chanted or sung in responsive, alternating parts.

2. anything composed for responsive chanting or singing.

3. verses chanted or a piece of plainsong sung before or after a psalm, canticle, etc.

4. an echo or response. [Rare.]

an·tiph′ō·năl, *a.* pertaining to or like an antiphon; sung or chanted in alternation.

an·tiph′ō·năl, *n.* a collection of antiphons.

an·tiph′ō·năl·ly, *adv.* in an antiphonal manner.

an·tiph′ō·nā·ry, *n.*; *pl.* **an·tiph′ō·nā·rieş,** a book of antiphons or anthems; specifically, a book of responsive prayers.

an·ti·phon′iç, an·ti·phon′iç·ăl, *a.* antiphonal.

an·tiph′ō·ny, *n.*; *pl.* **an·tiph′ō·nieş,** 1. the opposition of sounds; also, the harmony produced by this.

2. an antiphon, or antiphonal chanting or singing.

3. any response or echo.

an·tiph′rȧ·sis, *n.*; *pl.* **an·tiph′rȧ·sēş,** [L., from Gr. *antiphrasis*, from *antiphrazein*, to express by antithesis or negation; *anti*, against, and *phrazein*, to speak.] the use of words in a sense opposite to their proper meaning; as when a court of justice is called a court of vengeance.

an·ti·phras′tiç, an·ti·phras′tiç·ăl, *a.* pertaining to antiphrasis.

an·ti·phras′tiç·ăl·ly, *adv.* in the manner of antiphrasis.

an·ti·plas′tiç, *a.* 1. reducing plasticity.

2. in medicine, unfavorable to the healing process.

an″ti·pō·dag′riç, *a.* remedial for gout.

an″ti·pō·dag′riç, *n.* a remedy for gout.

an·tip′ō·dăl, *a.* 1. of or relating to the antipodes; on the other side of the earth.

2. opposed diametrically or directly.

an′ti·pōde, *n.* anything diametrically opposite; an exact opposite.

an·tip·ō·dē′ăn, *a.* 1. antipodal.

2. Australian.

an·tip·ō·dē′ăn, *n.* 1. a person who lives on the other side of the earth.

2. an Australian.

an·tip′ō·dēş, *n.pl.* [Gr. *antipodes*, opposite feet; *anti*, against, opposite, and *pous*, pl. *podes*, feet.]

1. any two places directly opposite each other on the earth.

2. [*construed as pl. or sing.*] a place on the other side of the earth: in British usage, New Zealand and Australia are usually meant.

3. two opposite or contrary things.

4. [*construed as pl. or sing.*] the exact opposite.

5. the people on the other side of the earth. [Obs.]

an′ti·pōle, *n.* the pole opposite; an extreme opposite.

an′ti·pōpe, *n.* a pope set up against the one chosen by church laws, as in a schism.

an·tip·sor′iç, *a.* [Gr. *anti*, against, and *psora*, the itch.] efficacious in curing the itch.

an·tip·sor′iç, *n.* a remedy for the itch.

an·tip·tō′sis, *n.* [Gr. *antiptōsis*; *anti*, against, instead of, and *ptōsis*, a falling, case, from *piptein*, to fall.] in grammar, the putting of one case for another.

an″ti·pū·trē·fac′tive, *a.* checking or preventing putrefaction; antiseptic.

an″ti·pū·tres′cent, *a.* antiputrefactive.

an″ti·pȳ·rē′sis, *n.* [LL., from Gr. *anti-*, against, and *pyressein*, to be feverish; from *pyr*, fire.] treatment of fever by antipyretics.

an″ti·pȳ·ret′iç, *a.* cooling; reducing fever.

an″ti·pȳ·ret′iç, *n.* anything that reduces fever.

an·ti·pȳ′rīne, an·ti·pȳ′rin, *n.* a drug derived from coal tar, used to relieve headaches and neuralgia and to reduce fevers.

an″ti·pȳ·rot′iç, *a.* remedial for burns or pyrosis.

an″ti′pȳ·rot′iç, *n.* a medicine for burns or pyrosis.

an·ti·quā′ri·ăn, *a.* 1. of antiquaries.

2. of antiques or antiquities.

3. of, or dealing in, rare old books.

an·ti·quā′ri·ăn, *n.* an antiquary.

an·ti·quā′ri·ăn·işm, *n.* the study of antiquities.

an·ti·quā′ri·ăn·īze, *v.i.*; antiquarianized, *pt.*, *pp.*; antiquarianizing, *ppr.* to pursue antiquarian reasearches. [Colloq.]

an′ti·quā·ry, *n.*; *pl.* **an′ti·quā·rieş,** [L. *antiquarius*.]

1. one who makes a study of or collects antiquities.

2. one who studies antiquity.

an′ti·quāte, *v.t.*; antiquated, *pt.*, *pp.*; antiquating, *ppr.* [L. *antiquitatus*, pp. of *antiquare*, to restore a thing to its former condition, to make old; *antiquus*, ancient, old.]

1. to make old or obsolete; to cause to become old-fashioned.

2. to make void or abrogate, as laws or customs.

Christianity might introduce new laws and *antiquate* or obrogate old ones. —Hale.

3. to give an antique appearance or style to.

an′ti·quā·ted, *a.* 1. old; obsolete.

2. out-of-date; old-fashioned.

Syn.—old, ancient, antique, old-fashioned, obsolete.

an′ti·quā·ted·ness, *n.* the state or quality of being antiquated.

an·ti·quā′tion, *n.* the act of making, or the state of being, antiquated.

an·tïque′ (-tēk′), *a.* [Fr. *antique*, ancient, old, from L. *antiquus*, former, old, from *ante*, before.]

1. old; ancient; of genuine antiquity; in this sense it usually refers to the flourishing ages of Greece and Rome; as, an *antique* statue.

2. old, as respects the present age, or a modern period of time; old-fashioned; antiquated; as, an *antique* robe.

3. of or in the style of a former period; as, *antique* customs.

Syn.—old, ancient, antiquated, old-fashioned, obsolete, archaic, obsolescent.

an·tïque′, *n.* 1. anything very old; specifically, a term applied to the remains of ancient art, especially to the works of Greek and Roman antiquity.

2. the ancient style, especially of Greek or Roman sculpture, architecture, etc.

3. a piece of furniture, silverware, etc. made in a former period.

4. in printing, a variety of boldface type.

an·tïque′, *v.t.*; antiqued (-tēkt′), *pt.*, *pp.*; antiquing; *ppr.* to make look antique.

an·tïque′ly, *adv.* in an antique manner.

an·tïque′ness, *n.* the quality, condition, or state of being antique.

an′ti·quist (-kwist), *n.* one who collects antiques; an antiquarian. [Obs.]

an·tiq·ui·tā′ri·ăn, *n.* one holding to or admiring antique customs.

an·tiq′ui·ty, *n.*; *pl.* **an·tiq′ui·tieṣ,** [Fr. *antiquité*, from L. *antiquitas*, from *antiquus*, former, old.]

1. the quality of being ancient; ancientness; great age; as, a family of great *antiquity*.

2. the early period of history, especially before the Middle Ages; ancient times; as, Cicero was the most eloquent orator of *antiquity*.

3. the ancients; the people, especially the writers, of ancient times; as, the fact is admitted by all *antiquity*.

4. old age. [Obs.]

5. an old person. [Obs.]

6. the remains of ancient times; ancient relics, institutions, or customs: in this sense usually plural; as, Greek or Egyptian *antiquities*.

an″ti·rȧ·chit′iç, *a.* remedial for rachitis, or rickets.

an″ti·rȧ·chit′iç, *n.* a remedy or preventive for rickets, or rachitis.

an″ti·rē·mon′strănt, *n.* a person opposed to remonstrance or remonstrants; specifically [A–], any of a group of Dutch Calvinists who opposed the Arminian Remonstrants.

an·ti·rent′ẽr, *n.* one opposed to the payment of rent; specifically [A–], one of the Antirent party, an organization which (1839–1848) resisted the payment of rent on certain manorial estates in New York.

an·ti·rent′iṣm, *n.* the policy or principles of the Antirent party.

an″ti·rheū·mat′iç, (-rū-), *a.* efficacious in cases of rheumatism.

An·tir·rhī′num, *n.* [LL. from Gr. *antirrhinon*; *anti*, corresponding to, like, and *rhis*, *rhinos*, nose.]

1. a genus of plants belonging to the figwort or *Scrophulariaceæ* family.

2. [a–] a plant of this genus, as the snapdragon.

an·ti·rust′, *a.* 1. that prevents rust.

2. that cannot rust.

an·ti·rust′, *n.* something that prevents rust.

an″ti·sab·bȧ·tā′ri·ăn, *n.* one who opposes the observance of the Sabbath.

an″ti·saç·ẽr·dō′tăl, *a.* opposed to priests or their power.

An″ti-Sȧ·lo̤on′ Lēague (lēg), an organization founded at Washington, D.C., December 18, 1895, having for its objective the suppression of traffic in alcoholic liquor.

an·tis′ciănṣ, an·tis′ci·ī (-tish′), *n.pl.* [L. *antiscii*, from Gr. *antiskioi*, pl. of *antiskios*, with opposite shadows; *anti*, opposite, and *skios*, from *skia*, shadow.] in geography, the inhabitants of the earth living on the same meridian but on opposite sides of the equator, whose shadows at noon are cast in opposite directions.

an·ti·sçol′iç, *a.* [*anti-*, and Gr. *skolex*, a worm.] anthelmintic.

an″ti·sçor·bū′tiç, an″ti·sçor·bū′tiç·ăl, *a.* counteracting scurvy.

an″ti·sçor·bū′tiç, *n.* a remedy or preventive for scurvy.

an″ti·sçor·bū′tiç ac′id, vitamin C: also called *ascorbic acid*, *cevitamic acid*.

an·ti·sçrip′tūr·ăl, *a.* not accordant with the Scriptures.

an″ti-Sem′īte, *n.* one who is anti-Semitic.

an″ti-Sem·it′iç, *a.* 1. having or showing prejudice against Jews; disliking or fearing Jews and Jewish things.

2. discriminating against or persecuting Jews.

3. of or caused by anti-Semitism.

an″ti-Sem′i·tiṣm, *n.* 1. prejudice against Jews; dislike or fear of Jews and Jewish things.

2. discrimination against or persecution of Jews.

an·ti·sep′ăl·ous, *a.* standing opposite to sepals, as the stamens of some flowers.

an·ti·sep′sis, *n.* [L., from Gr. *antisēpsis*; *anti*, against, and *sēpsis*, putrefaction.]

1. the condition of being antiseptic.

2. the use of antiseptics, etc.; antiseptic method.

an·ti·sep′tiç, an·ti·sep′tiç·ăl, *a.* 1. preventing infection, decay, etc.; inhibiting the action of microorganisms.

2. using antiseptics.

3. free from infection.

an·ti·sep′tiç, *n.* any antiseptic substance, as alcohol, etc.

an·ti·sep′tiç·ăl·ly, *adv.* in an antiseptic manner, or by means of antiseptics.

an·ti·sep′ti·cize, *v.t.*; antisepticized, *pt.*, *pp.*; antisepticizing, *ppr.* to make (something) antiseptic; apply antiseptics to.

an·ti·sē′rum, *n.* [*anti-*, and *serum.*] a serum with antibodies in it.

an·ti·slăv′ẽr·y, *n.* opposition to slavery.

an·ti·slăv′ẽr·y, *a.* opposed to slavery; as, *antislavery* literature.

an·ti·sō′ciăl, *a.* 1. unsociable; averse to society; avoiding social intercourse.

2. hostile to the existence of society, or the principles on which it is founded; against the welfare of the people generally.

an·ti·sō′ciăl·ist, *a.* antagonistic to or tending to undermine the theories and practices of socialism.

an·ti·sō′lăr, *a.* opposite to, or occurring in the heavens at a point 180° from, the sun: used especially as an astronomical term.

an·tis′pȧ·sis, *n.* [Gr. *antispasis*, from *antispān*, to draw in the opposite direction; *anti*, opposite, and *spān*, to draw.] in medicine, the diverting of a disease from one part of the body to another; counterirritation.

an″ti·spaṣ·mod′iç, *a.* preventing or relieving spasms.

an″ti·spaṣ·mod′iç, *n.* a remedy or preventive for spasms.

an′ti·spast, an·ti·spas′tus, *n.* [Gr. *antispastos*, from *antispān*, to draw in the contrary direction; *anti*, opposite, and *spān*, to draw.] in prosody, a tetrasyllabic foot, in which the first and last syllables are short, and the middle syllables long.

an·ti·spas′tiç, *a.* 1. causing a revulsion of fluids or humors; of the nature of antispasis. [Obs.]

2. counteracting spasms; antispasmodic.

an·ti·spas′tiç, *a.* in prosody, pertaining to, of the nature of, or embodying an antispast.

an·ti·spas′tiç, *n.* 1. anything causing antispasis. [Obs.]

2. a remedy which counteracts spasms; an antispasmodic.

an″ti·splē·net′iç, *a.* counteracting or relieving diseases of the spleen.

an·ti·splē·net′iç, *n.* a medicine for disorders of the spleen.

an·tis′tȧ·sis, *n.* [Gr. *antistasis*, a counter-plea, opposition, from *anti*, against, and *stēnai*, to stand.] in oratory, the defense of an action on the ground that if it had been omitted, something worse would have happened.

an·tis′tēṣ, *n.*; *pl.* **an·tis′ti·tēṣ,** [L.] a prelate or chief priest. [Rare.]

an·tis′trō·phē, *n.* [Gr. *antistrophē*, from *antistrephein*, to turn about; *anti*, against, opposite, and *strephein*, to turn.]

1. in rhetoric, the reversal of terms mutually depending on each other; reciprocal conversion; as, the mother of the child, the child of the mother.

2. the construing of an adversary's plea or argument to his disadvantage.

3. the return movement, left to right, made by the chorus of an ancient Greek play in answering the previous strophe.

4. that part of a choric song performed while making this movement.

5. in a Pindaric ode, the stanza, usually in the same or similar form, which follows the strophe.

6. in poems with contrasting or parallel stanza systems, a stanza of the second system.

an·ti·stroph′iç, *a.* of, or having the nature of, antistrophe.

an·ti·stroph′iç·ăl·ly, *adv.* in an antistrophic style.

an·tis′trō·phon, *n.* [neut. of Gr. *antistrophos*, turned against.] in rhetoric, the turning of an opponent's argument against himself.

an″ti·strū·mat′ic, an·ti·strū′mous, *a.* [*anti-*, and L. *struma*, a scrofulous swelling.] remedial for scrofulous disorders.

an″ti·strū·mat′iç, *n.* a remedy for scrofula.

an″ti·syph·i·lit′iç, *a.* remedial in cases of syphilis; antivenereal.

an″ti·syph·i·lit′iç, *n.* a medicine given in cases of syphilis.

An·ti·taç′tēṣ, *n.*; *pl.* **An·ti·taç′tae,** [Gr. *antitactēs*, a heretic, from *antitassein*, to oppose; *anti*, against, and *tassein*, to arrange, draw up.] one of the sect which Clement of Alexandria named Gnostics: they considered that the decalogue originated from the Demiurge, or so-called second Maker, and willfully despised and defied it.

an″ti·tank′, *a.* for use against tanks in war.

an·ti·thā′li·ăn, *a.* [*anti-*, and L. *Thalia*, muse of comedy.] antagonistic to merriment and merrymaking. [Rare.]

an·ti·thē′iṣm, *n.* opposition to belief in a god.

an·ti·thē′ist, *n.* one who opposes the belief in a god.

an″ti·thē·is′tiç, *a.* pertaining to the doctrine of antitheism; opposing the belief in a god.

an·tith′ĕ·sis, *n.*; *pl.* **an·tith′ĕ·sēṣ,** [Gr. *antithesis*, from *antitithenai*; *anti*, against, and *tithenai*, to place, set.]

1. in rhetoric, an opposition or contrast of thoughts, usually in two words, phrases, clauses, or sentences; e.g., the prodigal robs his heir, the miser robs himself; excess of ceremony shows want of breeding.

2. the second part of such an expression.

3. the exact opposite; extreme contrast.

4. an opposition or contrast.

an′ti·thet, *n.* [Gr. *antitheton*, an antithesis, neut. of *antithetos*, opposed.] a statement which partakes of the nature of antithesis. [Rare.]

an·ti·thet′iç, an·ti·thet′iç·ăl, *a.* 1. of antithesis; containing or abounding with antithesis.

2. exactly opposite.

an·ti·thet′iç·ăl·ly, *adv.* by antithesis.

an·ti·tox′iç, *a.* of, containing, or acting as an antitoxin.

an·ti·tox′in, an·ti·tox′ine, *n.* [*anti-*, and *toxin.*]

1. a substance found in blood serum and formed in the body to act against a specific toxin.

2. a serum containing an antitoxin: taken from the blood of an infected animal, such a serum is injected into a person to prevent a specific disease, as diphtheria, tetanus, etc.

an′ti·trādeṣ, *n. pl.* 1. winds moving above the tradewinds and in an opposite direction.

2. prevailing westerly winds of the temperate zone.

an·ti·trag′i·çus, *n.*; *pl.* **an·ti·trăġ′i·cī,** a muscle on the antitragus.

an·tit′rȧ·gus, *n.*; *pl.* **an·tit′rā·ġī,** [LL., from Gr. *antitragos*; *anti*, opposite, and *tragos*, a part of the ear.] the fleshy, cartilaginous protrusion at the rear of the external ear, opposite the tragus.

an″ti·trin·i·tā′ri·ăn, *a.* antagonistic to the doctrine of the Trinity.

an″ti·trin·i·tā′ri·ăn, *n.* a disbeliever or opponent of the doctrine of the Trinity.

an″ti·trin·i·tā′ri·ăn·iṣm, *n.* the opposition

existing against, and the denial of the doctrine of, the Trinity.

an″ti·trō·chan′tēr, *n.* in anatomy, a smooth surface on the ilium against which the great trochanter plays and forms a joint, as in birds.

an″ti·trō·chan·tēr′iç, *n.* pertaining to the antitrochanter.

an·tit′rō·păl, *a.* see *antitropous.*

an′ti·trōpe, *n.* [Fr. *antitrope,* from Gr. *anti,* against, and *tropos,* from *trepein,* to turn.] in anatomy, a part of an organism reversely repeated, so as to form a pair; as, the right and left ears are *antitropes* to each other.

an·ti·trop′iç, an·ti·trop′iç·ăl, *a.* 1. in anatomy, symmetrically related in position, as the two arms.
 2. in botany, same as *sinistrorse.*

an·tit′rō·pous, an·tit′rō·păl, *a.* [L. *antitropus;* Gr. *antitropos; anti,* against, and *tropos,* from *trepein,* to turn.] in botany, having the radicle, in a seed, at the extremity most remote from the hilum, or the embryo inverted with respect to the seed.

an·tit′rō·py, *n.* reversed repetition of a part or organ.

an′ti·trust, *a.* antagonistic to or not in sympathy with trusts; opposed to or regulating business monopolies, cartels, etc.

an·ti·tȳ′păl, *a.* pertaining to an antitype.

an′ti·tȳpe, *n.* [Gr. *antitypos; anti,* against, corresponding to, and *typos,* form, figure.]
 1. the person or thing represented or foreshadowed by an earlier type or symbol.
 2. in anatomy, an antitrope.
 3. an opposite type.

an·ti·typ′iç·ăl, an·ti·typ′iç, *a.* 1. pertaining to an antitype; explaining the type.
 2. in anatomy, same as *antitropic.*

an·ti·typ′iç·ăl·ly, *adv.* by means of an antitype.

an·tit′y·pous, *a.* characterized by antitypy. [Obs.]

an·tit′y·py, *n.* [Gr. *antitypia,* from *antitypos; anti,* against, and *typos,* from *typtein,* to strike.] resistance of matter to the force of penetration.

an″ti·vaç·ci·nā′tion, *n.* opposition to vaccination.

an″ti·vaç·ci·nā′tion·ist, an·ti·vaç′cin·ist, *n.* one who is opposed to vaccination.

an″ti·vā·rī′ō·lous, *a.* preventing or supposed to prevent smallpox contagion.

an″ti·vē·nē′rē·ăl, *a.* used in treating venereal disease.

an·ti·vē′nin, *n.* [*anti-,* and L. *venenum,* poison.]
 1. an antitoxin for venom, as of snakes, formed in the blood by gradually increased injections of the specific venom.
 2. a serum containing this antitoxin.

an″ti·viv·i·seç′tion, *n.* opposition to vivisection.

an″ti·viv·i·seç′tion·ist, *n.* one opposed to vivisection.

an·ti·wạr′, *a.* opposed to war.

an·ti·zym′iç, an″ti·zȳ·mot′iç, *a.* preventing or checking fermentation.

an″ti·zȳ·mot′iç, *n.* that which prevents fermentation.

ant′lēr, *n.* [ME. *anteler;* OFr. *antoiller,* from an assumed L. *antocularis; ante,* before, and *oculus,* eye.]
 1. the branched, deciduous horn of any animal of the deer family.
 2. any branch of such a horn.

ANTLERS
a. brow antler; *b.* bez antler; *c.* antler royal; *d.* sur-royal or crown antler

The first year a stag has only frontal protuberances or *bossets;* the second year, a simple *snag* or *stem;* the third, a longer stem with a branch or *brow antler;* in the fourth, the *bes, bez,* or *bay antler;* in the fifth, the *antler royal* is added; in the sixth, the *crown* or *surroyal* diverges on the top of the horn, forming the cup, which consists of two or three snags or prongs curving upward. To these in future years others are added, the total number of branches often amounting to ten in a stag seven or eight years old.

ant′lēred (-lērd), *a.* 1. furnished with or bearing antlers.
 2. ornamented with antlers.

ant′lēr moth, a European moth, *Charæas graminis,* the larvae of which are ruinous to grass and meadows.

ant′li·ȧ, *n.; pl.* **ant′li·ae,** [L., a pump, from Gr. *antlia,* the hold of a ship, bilgewater.] the haustellum of a lepidopter.

ȧnt lī′ŏn, 1. an insect resembling the dragonfly and belonging to the order *Neuroptera,* the larvae of which build a trap in the earth to catch ants and other small insects.
 2. its larva.

an·toe′ci·ăns, an·toe′cī, *n.pl.* same as *antecians.*

an·tō·nō·mā′și·ȧ (-zhi-ȧ) *n.* [L., from Gr. *antonomasia,* from *antonomazein,* to call by another name; *anti,* instead of, and *onomazein,* to name; *onoma,* name.]
 1. the use of an epithet or title instead of the proper name of a person, as when *his honor* is used for a judge, or when, instead of Aristotle, we say, *the philosopher.*
 2. the use of a proper name instead of a common noun, as when an eminent orator is called *a Demosthenes.*

an·tō·nō·mas′tiç, an·tō·nō·mas′tiç·ăl, *a.* of or pertaining to antonomasia.

an·tō·nō·mas′tiç·ăl·ly, *adv.* by the use of antonomasia.

an·ton′ō·mȧ·sy, *n.* same as *antonomasia.*

an′tō·nym, *n.* [Gr. *antonymia,* a word used instead of another; *anti,* opposite, and *onoma, onyma,* name.] a word whose meaning is the opposite of that of some other word; as, sad is the *antonym* of happy, agreeable of disagreeable, good of bad.

ant·or·gas′tiç, *a.* same as *antiorgastic.*

an′trȧ, *n.,* pl. of *antrum.*

an′trăl, *a.* of or pertaining to an antrum.

an′tre (-tēr), *n.* [Fr. *antre,* L. *antrum;* Gr. *antron,* a cave.] a cavern; a cave. [Archaic or poetic.]

an·trọrse′, *a.* [L. *ante,* before, and *versus,* turned, from *vertere,* to turn.] in biology, forward or upward.

an·trō·vērt′, *v.i.* [L. *ante,* before, and *vertere,* to turn.] to incline or bend forward. [Rare.]

an′trum, *n.; pl.* **an′trums, an′trȧ,** [L., a cave.]
 1. a cavity or cave.
 2. in anatomy, a cavity; especially, either of a pair of sinuses in the upper jaw.

an·trus′tion (-chun), *n.* [Fr.] a follower of the Frankish princes of the seventh century.

ȧnt thrush, a bird of the genus *Pitta,* allied to the *Turdidæ* or thrush family. The name is also given to the ant bird.

A·nū′bis, *n.* [L., from Gr. *Anoubis;* Egypt. *Anepu.*] in Egyptian religion, a god who led the dead to judgment: identified with the Greek Hermes. He is represented as having a human body with a head like that of a jackal.

ANUBIS
from an Egyptian painting

ā·nū′clē·ăr, *a.* in biology, without a nucleus or nuclei.

A·nū′rȧ, *n.pl.* [LL., from Gr. *an* priv., and *oura,* tail.] an order of amphibians which lose the tail when they reach maturity, as the toad and frog. Written also *anoura.*

ȧ·nū′răn, *a.* [Gr. *an* priv., and *oura,* tail; and *-an.*] in zoology, belonging to a group of amphibians that includes the frogs and toads.

ȧ·nū′răn, *n.* any member of the anuran group of amphibians.

an·ū·rē′sis, *n.* same as *anuria.*

an·ū·ret′iç, *a.* pertaining to anuresis.

ȧ·nū′ri·ȧ, *n.* [LL., from Gr. *an* priv., and *ouron,* urine.] inability to excrete urine.

ȧ·nū′riç, *a.* relating to anuria.

ȧ·nū′rous, *a.* tailless, as a frog or toad; relating to the *Anura.* Written also *anourous.*

an′ū·ry, *n.* same as *anuria.*

ā′nus, *n.; pl.* **ā′nus·es, ā′nī,** [L.] the opening at the lower end of the alimentary canal.

an′vil, *n.* [OE. *anvelt, andvell, anvylte;* AS. *anfilt, onfilte,* an anvil; *an,* on, and *fealdan,* to fold.]
 1. an iron or steel block on which metal objects are hammered into shape.
 2. figuratively, anything on which blows are laid.
 3. in anatomy, the incus, one of the three bones of the middle ear.

ANVIL

an′vil, *v.t.* and *v.i.;* anviled *or* anvilled, *pt., pp.;* anviling *or* anvilling, *ppr.* to use an anvil in forming or forging (things).

añx·ī′e·tūde, *n.* anxiety. [Rare.]

añx·ī′e·ty (ang-zī′), *n.; pl.* **anx·ī′e·ties,** [L. *anxietas,* from *anxius,* anxious.]
 1. concern or solicitude respecting some event, future or uncertain, which disturbs the mind and keeps it in a state of painful uneasiness; the state of being anxious.
 2. a thought or thing that causes this.
 3. an eager and often slightly worried desire; as, *anxiety* to do well.
 4. in medicine, a state of restlessness and agitation of the mind, accompanied by a distressing sense of pressure in the vicinity of the heart.
 Syn.—solicitude, care, foreboding, uneasiness, perplexity, disquietude, disquiet, watchfulness, restlessness.

añx′ious (angk′shus), *a.* [L. *anxius,* anxious, troubled, from *angere,* to trouble, choke.]
 1. having anxiety or anxieties; uneasy in mind; apprehensive; worried.
 2. causing anxiety.
 3. eagerly wishing.
 Syn.—solicitous, uneasy, concerned, restless, watchful, disturbed, uneasy, worried.

añx′ious·ly, *adv.* in an anxious manner.

añx′ious·ness, *n.* a being anxious.

añx′ious sēat, at American revival meetings, a bench near the preacher for those with a troubled conscience who seek salvation.

an′y (en′y), *a.* [ME.; AS. *ænig, anig,* from *an,* one; lit., *one,* and *-y.*]
 1. one (no matter which) of more than two; as, *any* boy may go.
 2. some (no matter how much, how many, or what kind); as, do you have *any* apples?
 3. even one; the least amount or number of; as, I haven't *any* money.
 4. every; as, *any* child can tell.

an′y, *pron. sing.* and *pl.* any person or persons (of more than two); any amount or number.

an′y, *adv.* to an indefinite extent; at all; in any degree; as, *any* farther, *any* better, *any* more.

an′y·bod″y, *pron.* 1. any person; anyone.
 2. a person of fame, importance, etc.; as, is he *anybody?*

an′y·how, *adv.* 1. under any circumstances; in any manner or way.
 2. carelessly; haphazardly; as, he performs his work *anyhow.*
 3. at any rate; in any case.

an′y·one, *pron.* any person; anybody.

an′y one, 1. any single.
 2. any single person or thing.

an′y·thing, *pron.* [ME. *ani thing;* AS. *ænige thinga,* somehow.] any thing; any event, fact, etc.
 anything but; not in the least; by no means; as, the movie was *anything but* pleasing.

an′y·thing, *n.* a thing, no matter of what kind.

an′y·thing, *adv.* in any way; at all.

an″y·thing·ā′ri·ăn, *a.* one careless as to creed or belief or indifferent in his views.

an′y·wāy, *adv.* 1. in any manner or way.
 2. at any rate; at least; nevertheless.
 3. haphazardly; carelessly.

an′y·wāys, *adv.* anyway. [Colloq.]

an′y·where (-hwãr), *adv.* 1. in, to, or at any place.
 2. at all; to any extent. [Colloq.]
 anywhere from; any amount, rate, time, etc. between (stated limits); as, *anywhere from* five to ten dollars. [Colloq.]
 to get anywhere; to have any success; to achieve anything. [Colloq.]

an′y·whith·ēr, *adv.* to or toward any place. [Archaic.]

an′y·wīșe, *adv.* in any way or manner; at all.

An′zac̦, *n.* [from the initials of Australian and New Zealand Army Corps.] a soldier in the Australian and New Zealand Army Corps.

An′zac̦, *a.* of the Anzacs.

A-OK (ā″ō-kā′), *a.* [*all* and *OK.*] excellent, fine, in working order, etc.: a generalized term of commendation: also *A-Okay.* [Colloq.]

A one (wun), [orig. a designation of first-class ships, as in Lloyd's Register, *A* indicating the excellent condition of the hull, *1* that of the equipment.] first-class; first-rate; superior; excellent: also *A 1, A number 1.* [Colloq.]

Ā·ō′ni·ȧn, *a.* [L. *Aonius,* from *Aonia,* a part of Boeotia, in Greece.] of the Muses or Aonia in Boeotia, the supposed abode of the Muses.

Aonian fount; the fount of Aganippe at the foot of Mount Helicon, not far from Thebes.

ā′ō·rist, *n.* [Gr. *aoristos,* indefinite, from *a* priv., and *orizein,* to define; *oros,* a limit].
1. a past tense of Greek verbs, denoting an action without indicating whether completed, continued, or repeated.
2. a similar tense in other languages.

ā′ō·rist, *a.* designating or in this tense.

ā·ō·ris′tic̦, *a.* 1. indefinite.
2. pertaining to or in the aorist.

ā·or′tȧ, *n.*; *pl.* **ā·or′tȧs, ā·or′tae,** [Mod. L., from Gr. *aortē,* aorta, from *aeirein,* to raise, heave.] the main artery of the body, carrying blood from the left ventricle of the heart to all organs and parts except the lungs. It rises as the ascending aorta, then curves and gives branches to the head and upper extremities; then it proceeds as the descending aorta, giving branches to the trunk, and finally divides into the two iliacs, which supply the pelvis and lower extremities.

ā·or′tic̦, ā·or′tăl, *a.* of the aorta.

ā·or·tī′tis, *n.* aortic inflammation.

ā·os′mic̦, *a.* [Gr. *aosmos,* odorless; *a* priv., and *osmē,* odor.] without odor.

ä′ou·dad, *n.* [Fr.; Moorish *audad.*] the *Ammotragus tragelaphus,* or bearded argali of North Africa, an ovine quadruped, related to the sheep, distinguished by the heavy growth of hair from the throat to the knees.

AOUDAD
(*Ammotragus tragelaphus*)

ap-, 1. ad-: used before *p.*
2. apo-.

ȧ·pāce′, *adv.* at a quick pace; fast; speedily.

À·pach′ē, *n.*; *pl.* **À·pach′ēs** or **À·pach′ē,** a member of a tribe of fierce, nomadic Athapascan Indians of northern Mexico and the southwestern United States.

ȧ·päche′ (-päsh′, -pash′; Fr. -pȧsh), *n.*; *pl.* **ȧ·päch′es** or **ȧ·päche′,** a gangster or thug of Paris.

ȧ·päche′, *a.* designating a dance, performed as an exhibition in cabarets, etc., which represents an apache handling his girl in a brutal, masterful way.

À·pach′ē plume, a shrub, *Fallucia paradoxa,* found in New Mexico.

ap·ȧ·gō′gē, *n.* [L., from Gr. *apagogē,* a leading away; *apo,* away, and *agein,* to lead, drive.]
1. in logic, the form of proving a proposition by showing that anything else is absurd.
2. in mathematics, a passage from one proposition to another when the first, having been demonstrated, is employed in proving others. [Obs.]

ap·ȧ·gog′ic̦, ap·ȧ·gog′ic̦·ăl, *a.* of apagoge.

ȧ·pāid′, *a.* repaid. [Obs.]

Ap·ȧ·lā′chi·ȧn, *a.* same as *Appalachian.*

ap′ăn·āġe, *n.* an appanage.

ȧ·pan′thrō·py, *n.* [Gr. *apanthrōpia,* from *apanthrōpos,* unsocial, *apo,* away, and *anthrōpos,* man.] an aversion to the company of men; a love of solitude. [Rare.]

ap′ăr, ap′ȧ·rȧ, *n.* same as *mataco.*

ä·pä·re′jō (-hō), *n.*; *pl.* **ä·pä·re′jōs,** [Sp.] a packsaddle made of two pads of leather stuffed with soft material.

ap″ȧ·rith·mē′sis, *n.* [Gr. *aparithmēsis,* from *aparithmein,* to count off, *apo,* off, and *arithmein,* to count.] in rhetoric, enumeration of details.

ȧ·pärt′, *adv.* [ME. *apart;* OFr. *a part;* from L. *ad partem, ad,* to, at, and *partem,* acc. of *pars,* part, side.]
1. to one side; at a little distance; aside.
2. separately or away in place or time.
3. reserved for a particular purpose.
4. separately or independently in function, use, etc.; as, viewed *apart.*
5. in or to pieces.
6. aside; notwithstanding; as, all joking *apart.*

to tell apart; to distinguish one from another.

ȧ·pärt′, *a.* separated; not together: used predicatively.

ȧ·pärt′heid (-hīt), *n.* [S.Afr.D., apartness.] the policy of strict racial segregation and discrimination against the native Negroes and other colored peoples as practiced in South Africa.

ȧ·pärt′ment, *a.* of, in, or for an apartment or apartments.

ȧ·pärt′ment, *n.* [Fr. *appartement;* It. *appartamento,* an apartment, from L. *ad,* to, and *partire,* to separate; from *pars,* a part.]
1. a room.
2. a room or suite of rooms to live in.
3. a compartment. [Obs.]
4. [*pl.*] a suite of rooms to live in. [Brit.]

ȧ·pärt′ment house, a building in which the rooms are arranged and rented as apartments.

ȧ·pärt′ness, *n.* the state of being, or holding oneself, apart.

ap·as′tron, *n.* [L. from Gr. *apo,* from, and *astron,* a star.] in astronomy, the point in the orbit of a double star where the primary and its satellite are farthest apart.

ap·ȧ·tet′ic̦, *a.* [Gr. *apatetikos,* from *apatē,* deceit.] in zoology, resembling the surroundings in color or form.

ap·ȧ·thet′ic̦, ap·ȧ·thet′ic̦·ăl, *a.* 1. devoid of feeling; impassive.
2. listless; indifferent.

ap·ȧ·thet′ic̦·ăl·ly, *adv.* in an apathetic way.

ap′ȧ·thist, *n.* one destitute of feeling.

ap·ȧ·this′tic̦·ăl, *a.* apathetic. [Rare.]

ap′ȧ·thy, *n.*; *pl.* **ap′ȧ·thies,** [L. *apathia;* Gr. *apatheia; a* priv., and *pathos,* from *pathein,* to feel; *paschein,* to suffer.]
1. lack of emotion.
2. lack of interest; listless condition; indifference.

Syn.—impassiveness, lethargy, unconcern.

ap′ȧ·tīte, *n.* [Gr. *apatē,* deceit, and *-ite:* so named from being mistaken for other minerals.] a granular mineral, calcium fluophosphate, in varied colors of white, blue, green, brown, etc.

ȧ·pau·mé′ (ȧ-pō-mā′), *n.* same as *appaumée.*

āpe, *n.* [ME. *ape;* AS. *apa.*]
1. a chimpanzee, gorilla, orangutan, or gibbon; a large, tailless monkey that can stand and walk in an almost erect position.
2. any monkey.
3. a person who imitates; mimic.
4. a person who is uncouth, clumsy, etc.

APE
(*Hylobates cambola*)

āpe, *v.t.*; aped (āpt), *pt., pp.*; aping, *ppr.* to imitate; to mimic as an ape imitates human actions.

Thus while I *ape* the measure wild,
Of tales that charmed me yet a child.
—Scott.

ȧ·pēak′, *adv.* in nautical usage, in a vertical or nearly vertical position. An anchor is apeak when the cable is drawn so as to bring the ship directly over it.

āpe′hood, *n.* the condition of being an ape.

ȧ·pel′lous, *a.* [*a* priv., and L. *pellis,* skin.] in medicine, without skin.

āpe′-man″, *n.* any of several extinct primates, as Pithecanthropus, with structural characteristics intermediate between ape and man.

Ap′en·nīne, *a.* [L. *Apenninus,* from Celt. *pen, ben;* Ir. *benn,* a mountain.] pertaining to the Apennines, mountains in central Italy.

ȧ·pep′si·ȧ, ȧ·pep′sy, *n.* [L., from Gr. *apepsia,* from *apeptos,* undigested; *a* priv., and *peptos,* from *peptein,* to cook, digest.] indigestion.

āp′ẽr, *n.* one who apes.

ȧ·per·çu′ (ȧ-per-sü′), *n.*; *pl.* **ȧ·per·çus′** (ȧ-per-sü′), [Fr. *aperçu,* pp. of *apercevoir,* to perceive.]
1. a quick impression or insight.
2. a brief digest or survey.

ȧ·pe′re·ȧ, *n.* [L.] the restless cavy, *Cavia aperea.*

ȧ·pē′ri·ent, *a.* and *n.* [L. *aperiens,* ppr. of *aperire,* to open, uncover; *ab,* from, and *parire,* to produce.] laxative.

ā·pē·ri·od′ic̦, *a.* 1. not occurring periodically.
2. in physics, without periodic vibrations.

ȧ·pé·ri·tif′ (ȧ-pā-rī-tēf′), *n.* [Fr.] 1. an alcoholic drink taken before meals to stimulate the appetite.
2. an appetizer.

ȧ·per′i·tive, *a.* and *n.* aperient.

ȧ·pẽrt′, *a.* [OFr. *apert,* from L. *apertus,* pp. of *aperire,* to open.] open; evident. [Archaic.]

ȧ·pẽrt′ness, *n.* openness. [Archaic.]

ap·ẽr·tom′e·tẽr, *n.* [*aperture,* and Gr. *metron,* measure.] a measuring instrument used to determine the angular aperture of an object glass.

ap′ẽr·tūre, *n.* [L. *apertura,* an opening; from *apertus,* pp. of *aperire,* to open; *ab,* from, and *perire,* to produce.]
1. an opening; a gap, cleft, or chasm; a passage perforated; a hole.
2. the act of opening. [Obs.]
3. in geometry, the space between two right lines forming an angle.
4. the diameter of the opening in a camera, telescope, etc. through which light passes.

angular aperture; see under *angular.*

Syn.—opening, hole, orifice, perforation, passage, gap, cleft.

āp′ẽr·y, *n.* 1. the practice of aping.
2. a place where apes are kept. [Rare.]
3. an apish act.

À·pet′ȧ·lae, *n.pl.* [L., from Gr. *a* priv., and *petalon,* a leaf.] a subclass of exogenous plants, the flowers of which have no petals.

ā·pet′ăl·ous, *a.* in botany, having flowers without petals; having no corolla; pertaining to the *Apetalæ.*

ā·pet′ăl·ous·ness, *n.* a state of being apetalous.

ā′pex, *n.*; *pl.* **ā′pex·es,** or **ap′i·cēs,** [L. *apex,* a point.]
1. the tip, point, or summit of anything.
2. in botany, the end farthest from the point of attachment, or from the base, of an organ.
3. in geometry, the angular point of a cone or conic section; also, the angular point of a triangle opposite the base.
4. in mining, the edge or outcrop of a vein nearest the surface.
5. the tip and contiguous portion of the blade of the tongue.
6. a climax.

apex of the earth's motion; the orbital point which the earth is nearing.

apex of the sun's way; that point in space which is being approached by the sun and solar system.

Syn.—summit, vertex, acme, top.

aph-, apo-, as in *aphesis.*

ȧ·phaer′e·sis, *n.* [L.; Gr. *aphairesis,* from *aphairein,* to take away, from *apo-,* away, and *hairein,* to take.] elimination of the first letter or syllable of a word (e.g., *bo* for *hobo*): also spelled *apheresis.*

ȧ·phā′gi·ȧ, *n.* in medicine, loss of power to swallow.

ȧ·phā′ki·ȧ, *n.* [Gr. *a* priv., and *phakos,* lentil-seed, lens.] absence of the crystalline lens of the eye.

ȧ·phā′ki·ăl, *a.* relating to aphakia; as, *aphakial* eyes.

Aph·ȧ·nip′te·rȧ, *n.pl.* [L., from Gr. *aphanēs,* unseen; *a* priv., and *phainesthai,* to appear, and *pteron,* wing.] an order of apterous, haustellate insects, having indistinct rudimentary wings. It is composed of the different species of fleas.

aph·ȧ·nip′tẽr·ous, *a.* pertaining to or resembling the *Aphaniptera.*

aph′ȧ·nīte, *n.* [Gr. *aphanēs,* invisible; *a* priv., and *phainesthai,* to appear, and *-ite.*] a very compact rock so closely grained that its individual crystals are visible only under the microscope.

aph·ȧ·nit′ic̦, *a.* relating to or like aphanite.

aph·ȧ·nō·zy′gous, *a.* [Gr. *aphanēs,* indistinct, and *zygon,* for *zygōnia,* a cheekbone.] having the cheekbones invisible when the skull is seen from above.

Aph·ȧ·ryn′ġē·ȧ, *n.pl.* [L., from Gr. *a* priv., and *pharynx,* throat.] an order of planarian worms having no pharynx.

aph·ȧ·ryn′ġē·ăl, *a.* having no pharynx.

ȧ·phā′si·ȧ (-zhȧ), *n.* [L., from Gr. *aphasia,* from *aphatos,* unuttered; *a* priv., and *phatos,* from *phanai,* to speak.] a total or partial loss of the power of using or understanding words, usually caused by brain disease or injury.

motor aphasia; loss of ability to speak.

sensory aphasia; a loss of memory for words.

ȧ·phā′si·ac̦, *n.* a person who has aphasia.

ȧ·phā′sic̦, *a.* of, relating to, or having aphasia.

ȧ·phā′ṣiç, *n.* an aphasiac.

ȧ·phē′li·ŏn, *n.*; *pl.* **ȧ·phē′li·ŏnṣ** or **ȧ·phē′li·ȧ,** [Gr. *apo*, from, and *hēlios*, the sun.] that point of a planet's or comet's orbit which is most distant from the sun; opposed to *perihelion*.

ȧ·phē″li·ō·trop′iç, *a.* [Gr. *apo*, from, *hēlios*, sun, and *tropikos*, from *trepein*, to turn.] in botany, turning away from the sun: said of certain plants.

ȧ·phē·li·ot′rō·piṣm, *n.* [*ap-*, and *heliotropism*.] the tendency of some plants to turn away from the sun.

ȧ·phē′mi·ȧ, *n.* [L., from Gr. *a* priv., and *phēmē*, voice, from *phanai*, to speak.] motor aphasia.

ȧ·pher′e·sis, *n.* same as *aphaeresis*.

aph′e·sis, *n.* [Gr. *aphesis*, a letting go; *apo*, from, and *hienai*, to send.] a form of aphaeresis in which the syllable lost is short and unaccented, as in *down* for *adown*.

aph′e·tȧ, *n.* [L., from Gr. *aphetēs*, one who lets go, from *aphetos*, let go; *aphienai*, to let go; *apo*, away, and *hienai*, to send.] in astrology, the ruling planet; the planet that rules one's life.

ȧ·phet′iç, *a.* of or characterized by aphesis.

ȧ·phet′iç, ȧ·phet′iç·ăl, *a.* of, relating, or pertaining to an apheta.

aph′e·tiṣm, *n.* a word formed by aphesis.

aph′e·tize, *v.t.*; aphetized, *pt., pp.*; aphetizing, *ppr.* to shorten (a word) by aphesis.

ā·phid (*or* **aph′id**), *n.* an insect of the genus *Aphis*; a plant louse.

aph′i·dēṣ, *n.*, pl. of *aphis*.

ȧ·phid′i·ăn, *a.* relating to the genus *Aphis*.

ȧ·phid′i·ăn, *n.* an insect of the genus *Aphis*; an aphid.

aph·i·diph′ȧ·gous, *a.* [L., from *Aphis*, and Gr. *phagein*, to eat.] feeding on insects of the genus *Aphis*.

aph·i·div′ō·rous, *a.* aphidiphagous. [Obs.]

aph·i·lan′thrō·py, *n.* [Gr. *aphilanthrōpos*, not loving man; *a* priv., *philein*, to love, and *anthrōpos*, man.]
1. want of philanthropy.
2. aversion to society.

Ā′phis (*or* **aph′is**), *n.* [L., from Gr. *apheideis*, pl. of *apheidēs*, unsparing.]
1. a genus of insects, belonging to the order *Hemiptera*, that live on plants by sucking their juice. They have an inflected beak and antennae longer than the thorax. In the same species, some males have two pairs of wings while the females are entirely without wings. Many species eject the substance called honeydew.

APHIS (winged and wingless phases, magnified)

2. [a–] *pl.* **aph′i·dēṣ,** any insect of this genus; a plant louse.

ā′phis flȳ, [L., *aphides*, unsparing.] any fly of the genus *Syrphus*, or a related genus, the larvae of which feed on aphids.

ā′phis lī″ŏn, any larva, as that of the lacewing or ladybug, preying upon aphids.

aph·lō·ġis′tiç, *a.* [Gr. *a* priv., and *phlogistos*, on fire.] flameless; as, an *aphlogistic* lamp, in which a coil of wire is kept red-hot by alcohol, without flame.

ȧ·phō′ni·ȧ, *n.* [LL., from Gr. *a* priv., and *phōnē*, sound, tone, voice, from Gr. *phanai*, to speak.] a loss of voice due to organic or psychic causes; dumbness.

ȧ·phon′iç, *a.* 1. of or affected with aphonia.
2. in phonetics, not sounded; not pronounced.

aph′ō·nous, *a.* having the voice lacking; voiceless.

aph′ō·ny, *n.* aphonia.

aph′ō·riṣm, *n.* [Fr. *aphorisme*, from Gr. *aphorismos*, a definition, a short, pithy sentence; from *aphorizein*, to divide, mark off; *apo*, from, and *horizein*, to bound; *horos*, a boundary.]
1. a short, concise statement of a principle.
2. a maxim; a short, pointed sentence containing some important truth or precept.
Syn.—axiom, maxim, adage.

aph·ō·riṣ′mēr, *n.* one who uses aphorisms in speaking or writing. [Obs.]

aph·ō·riṣ′miç, aph″ō·riṣ·mat′ic, *a.* relating to aphorisms; containing an aphorism; aphoristic.

aph′ō·rist, *n.* a speaker or writer of aphorisms.

aph·ō·ris′tiç, aph·ō·ris′tiç·ăl, *a.* in the form of an aphorism; also, full of aphorisms; as, an *aphoristic* style.

aph·ō·ris′tiç·ăl·ly, *adv.* in the form or manner of aphorisms; pithily.

aph′ō·rīze, *v.i.*; aphorized, *pt., pp.*; aphorizing, *ppr.* to make aphorisms.

ā·phō′tiç, *a.* [Gr. *aphōs*, *aphōtos*; *a-*, not, and *phōs*, *phōtos*, light.] without light.

aph′rīte, *n.* [Gr. *aphros*, foam, froth, and *-ite*.] a foliated variety of calcite resembling chalk.

aph·rō·diṣ′i·ȧ, *n.* [Gr. *aphrodisios*, pertaining to Aphrodite.]
1. violent sexual desire.
2. coition.

aph·rō·diṣ′i·aç, aph″rō·di·ṣī′ȧ·çăl, *a.* exciting sexual desire; increasing the appetite for sexual intercourse.

aph·rō·diṣ′i·aç, *n.* a food or drug exciting sexual desire.

aph·rō·diṣ′i·ăn, *a.* relating to Aphrodite; hence, given to sexual gratification.

Aph·rō·dī′tē, *n.* [Gr. *Aphroditē*, the foam-born: so named because she was said to have sprung from the foam of the sea; *aphros*, foam, and *ditē*.]
1. in Greek mythology, the goddess of love, identified by the Romans with Venus.
2. in zoology, a genus of marine annelids; the sea mouse.
3. [a–] a kind of butterfly of the United States, *Argynnis aphrodite*.

aph′thȧ, *n.*; *pl.* **aph′thae,** [Gr. *aphthai*, pl. of *aphtha*, eruption, ulceration, from *aptein*, to set on fire, inflame.]
1. a small ulcer that occurs upon the lips, gums, and palate.
2. a children's disease characterized by these ulcers: commonly called thrush.

Aph·thär″tō·dō·cē′tae, *n.pl.* [Gr. *aphthartos*, incorruptible, and *dokein*, to think.] a religious sect of the sixth century which believed that the body of Christ was incorruptible, his death being an illusion.

aph·thit′ȧ·līte, *n.* [Gr. *aphthitos*, unchangeable, indestructible, *a* priv., and *phthitos*, destructible, from *phthinein*, to destroy, and *alis*, salt, and *lithos*, a stone.] a sulfate of potash and sodium, found in the lava at Vesuvius.

aph′thoid, *a.* like, resembling, or pertaining to aphtha, or thrush.

aph′thong, *n.* [Gr. *aphthongos*, voiceless, without sound, from *a* priv., and *phthongos*, voice.] a letter, or combination of letters, which, in the customary pronunciation of a word, has no sound, as *p* in *pneumonia*. [Rare.]

aph·thoñ′găl, *a.* pertaining to an aphthong. [Rare.]

aph′thous, *a.* aphthoid.

Ȧ·phyl′lon, *n.* [Gr. *aphyllos*, leafless, from *a* priv., and *phyllon*, a leaf.] a genus of leafless plants of North America.

ȧ·phyl′lōse, *a.* same as *aphyllous*.

ȧ·phyl′lous, *a.* [Gr. *a* priv., and *phyllon*, leaf.] in botany, leafless, as the cactus or broomrape.

ā·pi·ā′ceous, *a.* [L. *apium*, parsley, celery.] pertaining to the carrot or parsnip family of plants.

ā·pi·ăn, *a.* [L. *apianus*, belonging to bees, from *apis*, bee.] relating to bees.

ā·pi·ā′ri·ăn, *a.* pertaining to bees or the care of bees.

ā′pi·ā·rist, *n.* one who keeps bees.

ā′pi·ā·ry, *n.* [L. *apiarium*, beehive.] a place where bees are kept; specifically, a number of beehives tended for their honey.

ap′iç·ăl, *a.* [L. *apex*, the tip or top of a thing, the point, summit.]
1. relating to an apex.
2. in phonetics, articulated with the apex of the tongue.

ap′iç·ăl, *n.* a sound so articulated, as *t, d, s, l*.

ap′i·cēṣ, *n.*, pl. of *apex*.

Ȧ·pi′cian (-pish′ăn), *a.* [L. *Apicianus*, from *Apicius*, a celebrated Roman gourmand.] pertaining to cookery or delicate viands; epicurean.

ȧ·piç′ū·lăr, *a.* of or pertaining to a small apex.

ȧ·piç′ū·lāte, ȧ·piç′ū·lā·ted, *a.* [LL., *apiculatus*, *apiculus*, dim. of L. *apex*, point.] in botany, terminated in a small point, as a leaf.

ā′pi·çul·tūre, *n.* [L. *apis*, bee, *cultura*, cultivating, culture.] beekeeping.

ȧ·piç′ū·lus, *n.*; *pl.* **ȧ·piç′ū·lī,** in botany a small point or tip.

ȧ·pièce′, *adv.* [OE. *apeece*, *a piece*; ME. *a pece*.] to or for each; each; as, an orange *apiece*.

ȧ·pièceṣ, *adv.* in pieces. [Obs.]

à pied (à pyā′), *adv.* [Fr.] on foot; afoot.

ā′pi·ŏl, *n.* [L. *apinum*, parsley, and *-ol*.] a crystalline substance obtained by distillation from parsley seeds.

ā·pi·ol′ō·gist, *n.* [L. *apis*, bee; Gr. *ampis*, a gnat, and *logos*, description.] a student of apiology.

ā·pi·ol′ō·ġy, *n.* the branch of science that treats of bees.

Ā′pis, *n.* [L. *apis*, bee.] a genus of insects of the order *Hymenoptera*, including the honeybee.

Ā′pis, *n.* [L. *Apis*; Gr. *Apis*; Egypt. *Hapi*, lit. the hidden.] a bull to which divine honors were paid by the ancient Egyptians because of his supposed connection with the god Ptah.

āp′ish, *a.* apelike; hence, imitative; silly.

āp′ish·ly, *adv.* in an apish manner.

āp′ish·ness, *n.* the quality of being apish.

Ā′pi·um, *n.* [L. *apium*, celery, parsley.] a genus of plants of the carrot family, among which is the common celery, *Apium graveolens*.

ā·piv′ō·rous, *a.* [L. *apis*, bee, and *vorare*, to devour.] making prey of bees; feeding on bees: said of certain birds.

ā·plȧ·cen′tăl, *a.* having no placenta, as the kangaroo.

Ap·lȧ·çoph′ō·rȧ, *n.pl.* [Gr. *a* priv., *plax*, a tablet, or plate, and *pherein*, to bear or carry.] in zoology, an order of *Amphineura* in which the body is without a shell.

ap·lȧ·nat′iç, *a.* [Gr. *aplanētos*, not wandering; *a* priv., and *planētos*, wandering, from *planasthai*, to wander.] in optics, having the quality of correcting for distortion, lack of sharpness, etc.; as, an *aplanatic* lens or telescope.
aplanatic focus; in a lens, the point at which divergent rays of light pass through the lens without spherical aberration.

ȧ·plan′ȧ·tiṣm, *n.* the state of being aplanatic.

ȧ·plā′ṣi·ȧ, *n.* [Gr. *a* priv., and *plasis*, formation, from *plassein*, to form.] incomplete or defective development, as of an organ or tissue.

ȧ·plas′tiç, *a.* [Gr. *aplastos*, not capable of being molded.]
1. not plastic or easily molded.
2. characterized by or pertaining to aplasia.
aplastic anemia; a form of anemia resulting from a failure of the bone marrow to produce adequate quantities of the essential blood components, particularly leukocytes and platelets.

ap′līte, *n.* [Gr. *haplos*, late form of *haploos*, single, simple.] a fine-grained granite, of which quartz and feldspar are the principal constituents.

ȧ·plomb′ (-plom *or* -plọm), *n.* [Fr. *à plomb*, lit. perpendicularity, self-possession, assurance.] self-possession; self-confidence; poise.

ȧ·plus′tre (-tẽr), *n.* [L. *aplustre*, the curved stern of a ship with its ornaments.] in Roman antiquity, an ornament made of wooden planks, rising from the stern of a ship.

APLUSTRE

Ȧ·plys′i·ȧ, *n.* [LL. *aplysiæ*; Gr. *aplysiai*, pl. of *aplysia*, filthiness, from *aplytos*, unwashed.] a genus of marine mollusks. Some of the species discharge a fluid of a deep purple color when in danger.

ap·nē′ȧ, *n.* a temporary suspension of breathing.

ap·neū·mat′iç, *a.* without air; as, an *apneumatic lung*.

Ap·neū′mō·nȧ, *n.pl.* [Gr. *a* priv., and *pneumōn*, lung, from *pnein*, to breathe.] an order of holothurians, without a respiratory system.

ap·neūs′tiç, *a.* [Gr. *apneustos*, without breath; *a* priv., and *pnein*, to breathe.] in zoology, without stigmata.

ap·noe′ȧ, *n.* same as *apnea*.

ap′ō-, [Gr.] a combining form signifying *off, from, away from, separation*, as in *apogamy*, *apocarp*.

ȧ·poç′ȧ·lypse, *n.* [ME. *apocalipse*; L. *apocalypsis*; Gr. *apokalypsis*, an uncovering, revelation, from *apokalyptein*, uncover, reveal; *apo*, from, and *kalyptein*, to cover or conceal.]
1. revelation; discovery; disclosure.
2. [A–] the last book of the New Testament; the book of Revelation.
3. certain Jewish or Christian prophetic writings which appeared between the years 250 B.C. and 150 A.D.

ȧ·poç·ȧ·lyp′tiç, ȧ·poç·ȧ·lyp′tiç·ăl, *a.* 1. containing or pertaining to revelation.
2. pertaining to the Apocalypse.
apocalyptic number; the number 666, spoken of in Rev. xiii. 18.

ȧ·poç·ȧ·lyp′tiç, ȧ·poç·ȧ·lyp′tist, *n.* the writer of the Apocalypse.

ȧ·poç·ȧ·lyp′tiç·ăl·ly, *adv.* in an apocalyptical manner.

ap′ō·çärp, *n.* [*apo-*, and *-carp*.] a group of separate or partially joined carpels, as in the flower of the stonecrop, buttercup, etc.

ap·ō·çär′pous, *a.* [*apo-*, and Gr. *karpos*, fruit.] in botany, having carpels either entirely or partially distinct.

ap″ō·çȧ·tas′tȧ·sis, *n.* [Gr. *apokatastasis*, return, restoration, from *apokathistanai*, to restore, return: *apo*, from, *kata*, down, and *histēmi*, to stand.]
1. in astronomy, the return of a planet to the same position after an orbital revolution.
2. restoration.

ap″ō·chrō·mat′iç, *a.* [*apo-*, and Gr. *chrōma*, color.] in optics, without aberration.

ȧ·poç′ō·pāte, *v.t.*; apocopated, *pt.*, *pp.*; apocopating, *ppr.* [Gr. *apokopē*, a cutting off, from *apokoptein*, to cut off.] to cut off or drop, as the last letter or syllable of a word.

ȧ·poç′ō·pāte, ȧ·poç′ō·pā·ted, *a.* shortened by the omission of the last letter or syllable.

ȧ·poç·ō·pā′tion, *n.* abbreviation by apocope.

ȧ·poç′ō·pē, *n.* [Gr. *apokopē*, a cutting off, from *apokoptein*, to cut off.]
1. the cutting off or omission of the last letter or syllable of a word; e.g., *mos'* for *most.*
2. in surgery, removal by cutting off or out; amputation.

ap·ō·çris′i·ā·ry, ap″ō·çris·i·ā′ri·us, *n.* [Gr. *apokrisis*, an answer, from *apokrinesthai*, to answer.] an official delegated by another; specifically, a legate of the pope at Constantinople.

ap·ō·çrus′tiç, *a.* [Gr. *apokroustikos*, able to drive off; *apo*, off, and *kronein*, to beat.] in medicine, astringent; repellent.

ap·ō·çrus′tiç, *n.* an astringent medicine.

Ȧ·poç′ry·phȧ, *n.pl.* [Gr. *apokryphos*, hidden, concealed, obscure, from *apokryptein*, to hide away; *apo*, away, and *kryptein*, to hide, conceal.]
1. fourteen books of the Septuagint, regarded by Protestants as not canonical: they are not found in Hebrew and are entirely rejected in Judaism, but eleven of them are fully accepted in the Roman Catholic canon.
2. various writings falsely attributed to Biblical characters or kept out of the New Testament as not genuine.
3. [a–] any writings, anecdotes, etc. of doubtful authenticity.

Ȧ·poç′ry·phăl, *a.* 1. of, relating to, or found in the Apocrypha.
2. [a–] of doubtful authorship or authenticity; hence, fictitious; false; spurious.

ȧ·poç′ry·phăl·ist, *n.* a student or advocate of, or believer in, the Apocrypha. [Rare.]

ȧ·poç′ry·phăl·ly, *adv.* so as to be apocryphal.

ȧ·poç′ry·phăl·ness, *n.* the state of being apocryphal.

Ȧ·poc·y·nā′cē·ae, *n.pl.* a family of tropical, dicotyledonous plants, having for its type the dogbane. They have widely varying characteristics, but nearly all yield a milky juice.

ȧ·poc·y·nā′ceous, ap·ō·cyn′ē·ous, *a.* resembling the dogbane, *Apocynum.*

Ȧ·poc′y·num, *n.* [L. *apocynon*, dogbane; Gr. *apokynon*, a plant; *apo*, from, away, and *kyōn*, *kynos*, a dog.] dogbane, a genus of perennial herbs with small, pale, cymose flowers, and a fibrous bark.

ap′od, ap′ō·dăl, *a.* 1. in zoology, having no feet.
2. having no pelvic fins.
3. relating or belonging to the *Apoda.*

ap′od, ap′ōde, *n.* an apodal bird, fish, or reptile.

Ap′ō·dȧ, *n.pl.* [Gr. *apous*, footless; *a*, priv., and *pous*, foot.]
1. a group of fishes without pelvic fins, as the eel, sand eel, etc.
2. the former name of an order of snakelike amphibians without limbs.
3. an order of cirripeds without appendages.

ap′ō·dăl, ap′ō·dăn, *a.* same as *apod.*

ap′ō·dăn, *n.* one of the *Apoda.*

ap·ō·deiç′tiç, *a.* same as *apodictic.*

ap·ō·deix′is, *n.* same as *apodixis.*

ȧ·pod′e·măl, *a.* having an apodeme.

ap′ō·dēme, *n.* [*apo-*, and Gr. *demas*, body.] the plates of chitin which pass inward from the exoskeleton of arthropods and divide as well as support the internal organs.

Ap′ō·dēş, *n.pl.* same as *Apoda* (sense 1).

ap·ō·diç′tiç, *a.* [Gr. *apodeiktikos*, demonstrative, from *apodeiknynai*, to point out, demonstrate.] in philosophy, absolutely certain; evident beyond contradiction; clearly proving: also *apodeictic*, *apodictical.*

ap·ō·diç′tiç·ăl·ly, ap·ō·deiç′tiç·ăl·ly, *adv.* in an apodictic manner.

ap·ō·dix′is, *n.* [L.] absolute demonstration.

ȧ·pod′ō·sis, *n.*; *pl.* **ȧ·pod′ō·sēş,** [Gr. *apodosis*, a giving back; *apo*, back, and *didonai*, to give.] the clause of a conditional sentence which expresses the conclusion or result. Thus in the sentence, if it rains I shall not go, the former clause is the *protasis*, the latter the *apodosis*. By some grammarians the term is not restricted to conditional sentences, but is extended to others similarly constructed.

ap′ō·dous, *a.* apodal.

ȧ·pod·y·tē′ri·um, *n.* [Gr. *apodytērion*, an undressing room, from *apodynai*, to strip, undress; *apo*, off, and *dynai*, to put.] a room in ancient Greek and Roman baths or in the palaestra, where the bathers or those engaged in gymnastic exercises dressed and undressed.

ap·ō·gā′iç, *a.* relating to the apogee.

ap·ō·gam′iç, *a.* relating to apogamy.

ȧ·pog′ȧ·my, *n.* [*apo-*, and Gr. *gamos*, marriage.] the development of a plant without the usual sexual organs, as the development of a sporophyte from a gametophyte without fertilization.

ap·ō·ġē′ăn, ap·ō·ġē′ăl, *a.* relating to the apogee; as, *apogean* tides.

ap′ō·ġee, *n.* [Fr. *apogie*; Gr. *apogaion*; *apo*, from, and *gē*, earth.]
1. in astronomy, that point in the orbit of any heavenly body at its greatest distance from the earth: especially applied to the moon: opposed to *perigee.*
2. the highest or farthest point; culmination; apex.

ap″ō·ġē·ō·trop′iç, *a.* [Gr. *apogaios*, from the earth, and *tropikos*, a turning, from *trepein*, to turn.] characterized by apogeotropism; bending away from the earth.

ap″ō·ġē·ot′rō·pism, *n.* a tendency to grow or move away from the earth, or from the pull of gravity, found in some roots, leaves, etc.

ap′ō·grȧph, *n.* [Gr. *apographē*, a copy; *apo*, from, and *graphein*, to write.] a transcript made from an original; a copy.

ap·ō·hȳ′ăl, *a.* designating a cartilaginous portion of the hyoid bone.

à point′ (ȧ″ pwaṅ′), [Fr., to (the) point.]
1. at the opportune moment; in the nick of time.
2. just sufficiently.

ȧ·poise′ *adv.* in a balanced position; poised.

ā·pō′lăr, *a.* [Gr. *a*, priv., and *polos*, a pivot or axis.] not having a pole: applied specifically to nerve cells not connected with nerve fibers.

ap·ō·laus′tiç, *a.* [Gr. *apolaustikos*, of or for enjoyment, from *apolauein*, to enjoy.]
1. given to enjoyment or pleasure.
2. self-indulgent.

Ȧ·pol·li·nā′ri·ăn, *a.* [L. *Apollinaris*, from Gr. *Apollōn*.] designating, in honor of, or pertaining to Apollo, as the *Apollinarian* games.

Ȧ·pol·li·nā′ri·ăn, *n.* one of a sect deriving their name from *Apollinaris*, bishop of Laodicea in the fourth century, who denied the proper humanity of Christ, maintaining that his body was endowed with a sensitive, not a rational, soul, and that the divine nature took the place of the intellectual principle in man.

Ȧ·pol·li·nā′ri·ăn·işm, *n.* the doctrine of the Apollinarians.

Ȧ·pol·li·nā′ris wạ′tēr, a German alkaline mineral water, having a high percentage of carbonic acid in solution, used in medicine and as a beverage.

Ȧ·pol′lō, *n.* [Gr. *Apollōn*, from *apollynai*, to destroy; *apo*, from, and *ollynai*, to destroy.] in Greek and Roman mythology, the god of archery, prophecy, medicine, poetry, and music, and protector of the Muses, and always represented as the highest type of masculine beauty and grace: later identified with Helios, a sun god.
Apollo Belvedere; a statue of Apollo in the Belvedere gallery of the Vatican palace at Rome.

Ap·ol·lō′ni·ăn, Ap·ol·lon′iç, *a.* Apollinarian.

Ȧ·pol′ly·ŏn (*or* -pol′yun), *n.* [Gr. *apollyon*, destroying, ppr. of *apollynai*, to destroy.] the Devil; Satan: a name used, Revelation ix. 11, for the angel of the bottomless pit.

ȧ·pol′ō·ġēr, *n.* [*apo-*, and Gr. *logos*, description.] a writer or narrator of apologues. [Obs.]

ȧ·pol·ō·ġet′iç, ȧ·pol·ō·ġet′iç·ăl, *a.* [Gr. *apologētikos*, fit for a defense, from *apologeisthai*, to speak in defense; *apo*, from, and *legein*, to speak.]
1. that apologizes; showing realization of and regret for a fault, wrong, etc.; making conciliatory excuses.
2. said or written in defense, or by way of apology; as, an *apologetic* essay.

ȧ·pol·ō·ġet′iç·ăl·ly, *adv.* by way of apology.

ȧ·pol·ō·ġet′içs, *n.pl.* that branch of theology having to do with the defense and proofs of Christianity.

ap·o·lō′ġi·ȧ, *n.* an apology, particularly a formal one to show that some idea, religion, etc. is right.

ȧ·pol′ō·ġist, *n.* one who makes an apology; one who speaks or writes in defense of a doctrine, faith, action, etc.

ȧ·pol′ō·ġīze, *v.i.*; apologized, *pt.*, *pp.*; apologizing, *ppr.* 1. to make an apology.
2. to write or speak in defense of, or to make an excuse for, something: followed by *for*; as, to *apologize for* one's rudeness.
Syn.—defend, justify, exculpate, excuse, plead.

ȧ·pol′ō·ġīze, *v.t.* to offer an apology for (something). [Rare.]

ȧ·pol′ō·ġīz·ēr, *n.* one who makes an apology or defends.

ap′ō·logue (-log), *n.* [Gr. *apologos*, a long speech, a fable.] a moral fable; an allegorical story with a lesson or moral. Aesop's fables are examples of *apologues.*

ȧ·pol′ō·ġy, *n.*; *pl.* **ȧ·pol′o·ġieş,** [Gr. *apologia*, a defense, from *apologeisthai*, to speak in defense.]
1. something said or written in defense; an argument to show that some idea, religion, etc. is right.
2. an acknowledgment of, and expression of regret for, a fault, injury, insult, etc.; the asking of a person's pardon.
3. a makeshift; an inferior substitute, as, a poor *apology* for a building.

ȧ·pol′ō·ġy, *v.i.* to make an apology. [Obs.]

ap″ō·mē·çom′e·tēr, *n.* an instrument for measuring heights of distant objects.

ap″ō·mē·çom′e·try, *n.* [*apo-*, and Gr. *mēkos*, distance, and *metron*, measure.] the art of measuring the height of distant objects.

ap·ō·mix′is, *n.* [Mod. L., from Gr. *apo*, from, and *mixis*, a mingling.] apogamy.

ap·ō·mor′phine, ap·ō·mor′phi·ȧ, *n.* [*apo-*, and Gr. *Morpheus*, the son of sleep, god of dreams.] a crystalline alkaloid produced by synthesis from morphine: used as an emetic.

ap″ō·neū·rō′sis, *n.*; *pl.* **ap″ō·neū·rō′sēş,** [Gr. *aponeurōsis*, the end of a muscle where it becomes tendon; *apo*, from, and *neuron*, a nerve.] a white, shining, fibrous membrane serving to cover certain muscles and connect them with tendons.

ap″ō·neū·rot′iç, *a.* relating to an aponeurosis.

ap″ō·neū·rot′ō·my, *n.* aponeurotic dissection.

ap·ō·pemp′tiç, *a.* [Gr. *apopemptikos*, valedictory, from *apopempein*, to send off, dismiss; *apo*, from, and *pempein*, to send.] valedictory; parting: used especially of a song or hymn sung or addressed to one on his departure.

ap·ō·pemp′tiç, *n.* a valedictory hymn.

ap·ō·pet′ăl·ous, *a.* [*apo-*, and Gr. *petalon*, a leaf.] in botany, polypetalous.

ȧ·poph′ȧ·sis, *n.* [Gr. *apophasis*, a denial, from *apophanai*, to deny.] the act of mentioning something by saying it will not be mentioned; as, "We will not mention his many crimes."

ap″ō·phleg·mat′iç, *a.* [Gr. *apophlegmatikos*, from *apophlegmatizein*, to discharge phlegm; *apo*, from, and *phlegma*, phlegm.] having the quality of producing discharges of phlegm or mucus.

ap″ō·phleg·mat′iç, *n.* a medicine which produces discharges of phlegm or mucus.

ap·ō·phleg′mȧ·tişm, *n.* 1. the action of an apophlegmatic.
2. an apophlegmatic. [Obs.]

ap′ōph·thegm (ap′ō-them), *n.* same as *apothegm.*

ap″ōph·theg·mat′iç, ap″ōph·theg·mat′iç·ăl, *a.* same as *apothegmatic.*

ȧ·poph′y·ġē, *n.* [Gr. *apophygē*, escape from; *apo*, from, and *pheugein*, to flee.] in architecture, the part of a column where it joins its capital or base, usually molded into a concave sweep or cavetto.

ȧ·poph′yl·līte, *n.* [Gr. *apophillizein*, to strip of its leaves; *apo*, from, and *phyllon*, leaf.] a mineral, hydrous potassium calcium silicate, found in square, transparent prisms or grayish-white, layerlike masses.

ȧ·poph′yl·lous, *a.* [*apo*, away, and Gr. *phyllon*, a leaf.] in botany, having the parts distinct: applied to a perianth.

ȧ·poph′y·sis, *n.*; *pl.* **ȧ·poph′y·sēş,** [Gr. *apophysis*, an offshoot, from *apophyesthai*, to grow off from.]
1. a natural process or outgrowth, as of a vertebra or other bone.
2. in botany, a swelling at the base of the capsule of certain mosses.
3. in geology, a lateral offshoot in igneous intrusive rock formations.

ap·ō·pleç'tiç, ap·ō·pleç'tiç·ăl, *a.* [Gr. *apoplēktikos*, from *apoplēktos*, disabled by a stroke, stricken.]

1. pertaining to, having, or symptomatic of apoplexy; as, an *apoplectic* fit.

2. predisposed to apoplexy; as, *apoplectic* with rage.

ap·ō·pleç'tiç, *n.* one having or liable to have apoplexy.

ap·ō·pleç'ti·fọrm, ap·ō·pleç'toid, *a.* resembling apoplexy.

ap'ō·plex, *n.* apoplexy. [Archaic.]

ap'ō·plex·y, *n.* [Fr. *apoplexie*; L. *apoplexia*; Gr. *apoplēxia*, from *apoplēssein*, to strike down; *apo*, from, and *plēssein*, to strike.] sudden paralysis with total or partial loss of consciousness and sensation, usually as a result of hemorrhage causing pressure on the brain tissue: sometimes used of a hemorrhage in some other organ; as, *apoplexy* of the liver.

ap·ō·ret'iç, ap·ō·ret'iç·ăl, *a.* doubting. [Obs.]

ȧ·pō'ri·ȧ, *n.* [Gr. *aporia*, doubt; *apo*, from, and *horos*, boundary.] in rhetoric, an affectation of being at a loss where to begin, or what to say.

Ap·ō·rō'sȧ, *n.pl.* [Gr. *aporos*, without passage.] a group of corals having the corallum solid, and not perforated with minute holes.

ap'ō·rōse, *a.* not porous.

ȧ·pōrt', *adv.* on or toward the left or port side.

ap''ō·sē·mat'iç, *a.* [Gr. *aposēmainein*, to announce by signs; *apo*, from, and *sēma*, sign.] in zoology, furnished with warning colors or some special means of defense or concealment, as the sea anemone.

ap·ō·sep'ȧ·lous, *a.* [*apo-*, and *-sepalous*.] same as *polysepalous*.

ap''ō·si·ō·pē'sis, *n.* [Gr. *aposiōpēsis*, a becoming silent, from *aposiōpān*, to be silent; *apo*, from, and *siōpān*, to be silent.] in rhetoric, the sudden breaking off of a discourse before it is ended and passing over something as if unable or unwilling to tell it.

ap·ō·sit'iç, *a.* [Gr. *apositia*; *apo*, from, and *sitos*, food.] taking away or diminishing the appetite.

ȧ·pos'pō·ry, *n.* a feature of certain ferns and mosses having the prothallium generated directly from the sporangium instead of by spores.

ȧ·pos'tȧ·sis, *n.* [Gr. *apostasis*, a standing away from; *apo*, from, and *histanai*, to stand.] in botany, internodal growth, which separates whorls or other parts of a plant.

ȧ·pos'tȧ·sy, *n.* [ME. *apostasie*; Fr. *apostasie*, Gr. *apostasia*, from *apostasis*, defection, revolt; from *aphistasthai*, to stand away from.] an abandonment or falling away from what one believed in; as, *apostasy* from one's religion, creed, or politics.

ȧ·pos'tāte, *n.* [Gr. *apostatēs*, a runaway, deserter, from *aphistasthai*, to stand away from.] one guilty of apostasy; specifically, one who forsakes his religion for another.

Syn.—convert, proselyte.

ȧ·pos'tāte, *a.* guilty of apostasy.

ȧ·pos'tāte, *v.i.* to apostatize. [Obs.]

ap·ō·stat'iç, ap·ō·stat'iç·ăl, *a.* apostate.

ȧ·pos'tȧ·tīze, *v.i.*; apostatized, *pt.*, *pp.*; apostatizing, *ppr.* to abandon one's belief or church; to forsake one's principles or faith.

ȧ·pos'tē·māte, *v.i.* to form into an abscess; to swell and fill with pus. [Obs.]

ȧ·pos·tē·mā'tion, *n.* the formation of an aposteme; the process of gathering into an abscess.

ap·os·tem'ȧ·tous, *a.* pertaining to an abscess; of the nature of an aposteme.

ap'os·tēme, *n.* [Gr. *apostēma*, interval.] an abscess; a swelling filled with pus: also spelled *apostem*, *apostume*.

ā pos·tē·ri·ō'rī, [L. *a*, or *ab*, from, and *posteriori*, abl. of *posterior*, comp. of *posterius*, subsequent, following.]

1. in logic, reasoning backward from effects, consequences, or facts, to causes; inductive: in opposition to *a priori*.

2. in philosophy, relating to observation or experience; empirical.

ȧ·pos'til, ȧ·pos'tille, *n.* [Fr. *apostille*; L. *ad*, to, in, *post illa*; *post*, after; *illa*, neut. pl. of pron. *ille*, that.] a marginal note or reference.

ȧ·pos'tle (-pos'l), *n.* [AS. *apostol*; ME. *apostle*, *apostel*; L. *apostolus*; Gr. *apostolos*, a messenger; from *apostellein*, to send away; *apo*, from, and *stellein*, to send.]

1. a person sent out on a special mission; specifically [usually A-], a disciple of Jesus commissioned to preach the gospel. Twelve persons were selected by Jesus for this purpose.

2. the person first preaching Christianity in any country or place.

3. in law, a brief statement of a case sent by a court from which an appeal has been taken to a superior court.

4. any early Christian missionary or leader.

5. an early advocate or leader of a new principle or movement, especially one aimed at reform.

6. any of the twelve administrative officials of the Mormon Church.

Apostles' Creed; an old statement of belief in the basic Christian doctrines, formerly supposed to have been composed by the Twelve Apostles: it begins, "I believe in God the Father Almighty . . . and in Jesus Christ his only Son our Lord."

apostle spoon; a spoon of silver gilt, with a handle ending in the figure of an apostle: formerly, one or more were usually presented by sponsors to infants at christenings.

ȧ·pos'tle·ship, *n.* the office of an apostle.

ȧ·pos'tō·lāte, *n.* the duties, office, or period of activity of an apostle.

ap·os·tol'iç, ap·os·tol'iç·ăl, *a.* 1. pertaining or relating to the Apostles; as, the *apostolic* age.

2. according to the doctrines of the Apostles; delivered or taught by the Apostles; as, *apostolic* faith or practice.

3. relating to the Pope; as, the *Apostolic* See.

4. of an apostle.

Apostolic Brothers; a sect of the thirteenth century led by Segarelli, a monk of northern Italy, in opposition to the Pope.

Apostolic Constitutions and Canons; a collection of regulations attributed to the Apostles, but generally supposed to be spurious. They appeared in the fourth century, are divided into eight books, and consist of rules and precepts relating to the duty of Christians, and particularly to the ceremonies and discipline of the church.

Apostolic Fathers; (a) the Christian writers who were contemporary with the Apostles: they are regarded as the fathers of the Christian church; (b) a collection of writings attributed to them.

apostolic king; a title granted by the Pope to the kings of Hungary, first conferred on St. Stephen, the founder of the royal line of Hungary, because of his accomplishments in the spread of Christianity.

Apostolic See; the see of the popes, or bishops of Rome, reputedly founded by Peter.

apostolic succession; the doctrine that the religious authority and mission conferred by Jesus on Saint Peter and the other Apostles have come down through an unbroken succession of bishops (i.e., bishops of Rome, or popes).

ap·os·tol'iç·ăl·ly, *adv.* in the manner of the apostles.

ap·os·tol'iç·ăl·ness, *n.* same as *apostolicity*.

ap·os·tol'i·çiṣm, *n.* a professing of apostolicity.

ȧ·pos·tō·lic'i·ty, *n.* the condition of being apostolic.

ȧ·pos'trō·phē, *n.* [Gr. *apostrophē*, a turning away, from *apostrephein*, to turn away from; *apo*, from, and *strephein*, to turn.]

1. in rhetoric, a digression in a speech or writing; strictly, a turning aside from the course of a speech in order to make a short address to a person or thing, whether present or absent.

> . . . produces at the right moment in parliamentary harangue a pocket crucifix, with the apostrophe, "Will ye crucify him afresh?" —Carlyle.

2. in grammar, (a) the sign (') showing the omission of a letter or letters from a word; as *don't* for *do not*. (b) this sign used to indicate the possessive singular or plural; as, a girl's dress, girls' dresses: it originally showed the omission of the letter *e* in the inflectional ending of the case; (c) this sign used to mark the plural of letters, figures, or other characters; as, mind your p's and q's; several 2's; numerous ¶'s.

ap·os·troph'iç, *a.* pertaining to a rhetorical or grammatical apostrophe.

ȧ·pos'trō·phīze, *v.t.*, and *v.i.* apostrophized *pt.*, *pp.*; apostrophizing, *ppr.* to address by or make use of an apostrophe, as in a speech.

ap'os·tūme, *n.* an aposteme. [Obs.]

Ap·ō·taç'tīte, *n.* [Gr. *apotaktos*, set apart, from *apotassein*, to set apart, or assign specially.] one of a sect of early ascetics, who, in imitation of some primitive Christians, renounced all their effects and possessions.

ȧ·pot'e·leṣm, *n.* [Gr. *apotelesma*, result, effect, the result of certain positions of the stars on human destiny; from *apotelein*, to complete, accomplish; *apo*, from, and *telein*, to end.]

1. fulfillment; result. [Obs.]

2. in astrology, the casting of a horoscope.

ap''ō·tel·eṣ·mat'iç, *a.* relating to apotelesm.

ȧ·poth'ē·çā·ry, *n.*; *pl.* **ȧ·poth'ē·çā·rieṣ,** [ME. *apothecarie*; L. *apotheca*, a repository, from Gr. *apothēkē*, a place where a thing is stored up; *apo*, away, and *tithenai*, to put.] one who prepares and sells drugs and medicines; a druggist or pharmacist.

In England and Ireland the term was formerly applied to a practitioner who was licensed to prescribe as well as dispense drugs.

apothecaries' measure; a system of liquid measure used in pharmacy.

apothecaries' weight; a system of weights used in pharmacy.

ap·ō·thē'ci·um, (-shi-um), *n.*; *pl.* **ap·ō·thē'ci·ȧ** (-shi-a), [Gr. *apothēkē*, a storehouse.] in botany, the receptacle in lichens and certain fungi consisting of the spore cases in which the sexual spores are developed.

ap'ō·thegm (-them), *n.* [Fr. *apophthegme*; Gr. *apophthegma*, a terse, pointed saying; from *apophtheggesthai*, to speak out plainly; *apo*, from, and *phtheggesthai*, to cry out, utter.] a saying; a short, instructive remark: also spelled *apophthegm*.

ap''ō·theg·mat'iç, ap''ō·theg·mat'iç·ăl, *a.* sententious; pertaining to, using, or containing apothegms.

ap·ō·theg'mȧ·tist, *n.* a collector or maker of apothegms.

ap·ō·theg'mȧ·tīze, *v.i.* to utter apothegms, or short, instructive sentences.

ap'ō·them, *n.* [Fr. *apotheme*, from Gr. *apotithenai*, to set off, put aside.]

1. in geometry, a perpendicular dropped from the center of a regular polygon to any one of its sides.

2. in pharmacy, a brown deposit which forms in vegetable extracts exposed to the air. [Rare.]

ȧ·poth·ē·ō'sis, *n.*; *pl.* **ȧ·poth·ē·ō'sēṣ,** [Gr. *apotheōsis*, a deification, from *apotheoein*, *apotheoun*; to deify; *apo*, from, and *theos*, god.]

1. deification; the act of making a god of a person.

2. an honoring or glorification of any kind; as, the *apotheosis* of a career.

3. a glorified ideal.

ap·ō·thē'ō·sīze, *v.t.*; apotheosized, *pt.*, *pp.*; apotheosizing, *ppr.* 1. to consecrate, or elevate to the place of a god; to deify.

2. to glorify; to idealize.

ȧ·poth'e·sis, *n.* [Gr. *apothesis*, a laying up or putting away, from *apotithenai*, to put back or away.]

1. in surgery, the setting of a dislocated bone.

2. a place in early churches furnished with shelves for books, vestments, etc.

ȧ·pot'ō·mē, *n.* [Gr. *apotemnein*, to cut off.]

1. in mathematics, the difference between two quantities commensurable only in power.

2. in music, a major semitone.

ap'ō·zem, *n.* [Gr. *apozema*, a decoction, from *apozein*, to boil off, throw off by fermenting; *apo*, from, and *zein*, to boil.] a decoction. [Obs.]

ap·ō·zem'iç·ăl, *a.* like a decoction. [Obs.]

ap·pāir', *v.t.* and *v.i.* [ME. *apairen*, *apayren*, *empair*.] to impair. [Obs.]

Ap·pȧ·lā'chi·ăn, *a.* of, relating, or pertaining to the system of mountains extending along the eastern coast of North America.

Ap·pȧ·lā'chi·ăn rev·ō·lū'tion, in geology, a late Paleozoic change in the earth's surface by which the Appalachian Mountains were formed.

Ap·pȧ·lā'chi·ăn tēa, a plant with clusters of white flowers, variously colored berries, and finely toothed leaves used for tea: also called *withe rod*.

ap·pạll', ap·pạl', *v.t.*; appalled, *pt.*, *pp.*; appalling, *ppr.* [ME. *appallen*, *apallen*; Fr. *pâle*; L. *ad*, to, and *pallidus*, pale, from *pallere*, to grow pale.]

1. to depress or discourage with fear; to horrify, shock, or dismay; as, the sight *appalled* the stoutest heart.

2. to reduce, weaken, or quell. [Obs.]

3. to cause to turn pale. [Obs.]

Syn.—affright, alarm, terrify, daunt, cow, shock, dishearten, horrify, dismay, astound.

ap·pạll', ap·pạl', *v.i.* 1. to grow faint; to be dismayed. [Obs.]

2. to become stale or weak, as wine. [Obs.]

ap·pall′, ap·pal′, *n.* fright; dismay. [Poet.]

ap·pall′ing, *a.* that appalls or dismays; shocking.

ap·pall′ing·ly, *adv.* in a manner to appall.

ap″pȧ·loo′sȧ, *n.* [altered from *a palouse*: so named after the *Palouse* Indians or the *Palouse* River (in northwest Idaho and southeast Washington), near which the horses were raised.] any of a sturdy breed of Western saddle horses distinguished by black and white spotted markings on the rump and loins.

ap′pȧ·nāge, *n.* [Fr. *apanage*, an estate assigned to a younger son for his maintenance; from L. *ad*, to, *panis*, bread.]

1. the money, land, etc. assigned by a king or prince for the subsistence of his younger sons.

2. a rightful extra gain; a natural endowment; adjunct; perquisite.

3. a territory governed by another country; dependency.

äp″pȧ·rät′, *n.* [Russian, apparatus.] an organization; especially, a political organization.

äp″pȧ·rät′chik, *n.*; *pl.* **äp″pȧ·rät′chiks** or **äp″pȧ·rät′chi·kī,** [Russ., from preceding.]

1. a member, especially an official, of a Communist Party.

2. a member of any political organization; especially, a bureaucrat.

ap·pȧ·rā′tus (*or* -rat′us), *n.*; *pl.* **ap·pȧ·rā′tus** or **ap·pȧ·rā′tus·es,** [L. *apparere*, to prepare; *ad*, to, and *parare*, to prepare.]

1. the instruments, materials, tools, etc. needed for a specific use, experiment, etc.

2. any set of standards or values for judging, measuring, or testing.

3. the notes, indexes, glossaries, etc. of a scholarly edition, especially of an edition of a text.

4. any complex device or machine.

5. in physiology, the system of organs which perform some one special function; as, the *apparatus* of hearing or of digestion.

ap·par′el, *n.* [ME. *aparel*, *apparail*; Fr. *appareil*, preparation; L. *apparere*, to prepare.]

1. clothing; garments; dress.

2. anything that clothes or adorns; external appearance; guise; as, science parading in the *apparel* of mystery.

3. the furnishings or outfit of a ship, as sails, rigging, anchors, etc.

4. an oblong piece of embroidery done in silk and gold, sometimes enriched with pearls and precious stones, worn from the thirteenth to the fourteenth century, attached to the alb and other ecclesiastical vestments.

Syn.—clothes, robes, vesture, vestment, raiment, garniture, habiliments, habit, dress, clothing.

APPAREL (sense 4)

ap·par′el, *v.t.*; appareled *or* apparelled, *pt.*, *pp.*; appareling *or* apparelling, *ppr.* 1. to prepare for. [Obs.]

2. to dress; clothe; adorn.

They which are gorgeously *apparelled* . . . are in kings' courts. —Luke vii. 25.

3. to furnish with equipment or covering; to outfit; as, ships *appareled* for sea.

ap·pâr′ent, *a.* [L. *apparens*, *-entis*, ppr. of *apparere*, to become visible, to appear.]

1. visible; able to be seen; in sight; as, the coast was *apparent* but once.

2. readily understood; obvious; clear; evident; as, the mechanical ingenuity of the American is *apparent* on every side.

3. seeming; appearing (but not necessarily) true: distinguished from *actual* and *real*; as, this *apparent* victory soon demonstrated its own weakness.

apparent horizon; the line where the sky seems to meet the earth.

Syn.—evident, obvious, clear, plain, manifest, visible.

ap·pâr′ent, *n.* an heir apparent. [Obs.]

ap·pâr′ent·ly, *adv.* 1. plainly; openly; clearly.

2. to all appearances; seemingly; in semblance.

ap·pâr′ent·ness, *n.* the quality of being apparent; visibleness; obviousness.

ap·pȧ·ri′tion, *n.* [Fr. *apparition*; L. *apparitio*, in sense of attendance, service, from *apparere*, to attend, to appear.]

1. the act of appearing or becoming apparent, particularly suddenly or unexpectedly.

2. the thing appearing; especially, a strange or extraordinary vision; a ghost; a specter; a phantom.

3. in astronomy, the first appearance of a star or other heavenly body that was previously obscured: opposed to *occultation*.

ap·pȧ·ri′tion·ăl, *a.* relating to apparitions.

ap·par′i·tŏr, *n.* [L. *apparere*, to prepare or make ready.]

1. among the Romans, any officer who attended magistrates and judges to execute their orders.

2. in England, a messenger or officer who serves the summonses of a church court; also, a beadle, in a university.

ap·päs·si·ō·nä′tȧ, *a.* [It.] in music, impassioned.

ap·pau·mée′, a·pau·mée′, (-pō-mā′), *a.* [Fr. *appaumé*, from L. *ad*, to, and *palma*, palm.] in heraldry, with fingers and thumb extended; open, so as to show the palm: applied to a hand.

APPAUMÉE

ap·pāy′, *v.t.* to satisfy. [Obs.]

ap·pēach′, *v.t.* to impeach; to accuse. [Obs.]

ap·pēach′ẽr, *n.* one who impeaches. [Obs.]

ap·pēach′ment, *n.* impeachment; accusation. [Obs.]

ap·pēal′, *v.i.*; appealed, *pt.*, *pp.*; appealing, *ppr.* [ME. *appelen*, *apelen*; Fr. *appeler*; L. *appellare*, to call upon, address; *ad*, to, and *pellere*, to drive.]

1. in law, to apply for an appeal.

2. to make an urgent request (*to* some person, authority, or power) for decision, justification, proof, defense, etc.; as, they *appealed* to the head of the department.

3. to resort; to call upon; as, let us *appeal* to reason.

4. to be attractive, interesting, etc.; to arouse a favorable response: as, his argument *appealed* to me.

ap·pēal′, *v.t.* 1. in law, to make an appeal of (a case, etc.).

2. to accuse; to charge with crime. [Archaic.]

3. to challenge. [Archaic.]

ap·pēal′, *n.* 1. in law, the removal of a case from a lower to a higher court for hearing; also, the right to, or a request for, such action.

2. in old law, (a) an accusation of crime brought by an accomplice; (b) an accusation instituted by a private person for some heinous crime by which he has been injured, when the accused has already been acquitted or pardoned.

3. a summons to answer to a charge; a challenge. [Rare.]

4. a call upon or reference to some authority or power for decision, proof, or assistance; as, an *appeal* to the house; an *appeal* to force.

5. a call for help, sympathy, encouragement, etc.; as, an *appeal* for contributions.

6. a quality that arouses sympathetic response; attraction.

ap·pēal′ȧ·ble, *a.* 1. able to be appealed to a higher court; as, the case is *appealable*.

2. that can be appealed against or to.

ap·pēal′ing, *a.* 1. making or carrying an appeal; imploring.

2. attractive, interesting, etc.

ap·pēal′ing·ly, *adv.* in an appealing or imploring manner.

ap·pēar′, *v.i.*; appeared, *pt.*, *pp.*; appearing, *ppr.* [L. *apparere*, to appear; *ad*, to, and *parere*, to come forth, be visible.]

1. to come or be in sight; to be in view; to be visible.

And God said . . . Let the dry land *appear*. —Gen. i. 9.

2. to become visible to the apprehension of the mind; to be obvious; to be known, as a subject of observation or comprehension; to become manifest; to be clear or made clear by evidence.

It doth not yet *appear* what we shall be. —1 John iii. 2.

3. to come into the light of publicity; to become generally noticed or known; to come before the public; as, a great statesman has *appeared;* this magazine *appears* monthly.

4. to present oneself formally in a court as attorney, plaintiff, etc.

5. to seem; to look; to have the appearance of being; as, the facts *appear* favorable; the man *appears* to be a mile off.

ap·pēar′ance, *n.* 1. The act of coming into sight; the act of becoming visible to the eye; as, his sudden *appearance* surprised me.

2. the thing seen; an apparition; a phenomenon; as, an *appearance* in the sky.

3. external semblance; outward aspect; hence, outward sign, indication, or evidence; as, the *appearance* of the place was altogether pleasing; the writing had every *appearance* of genuineness.

4. a pretense or show; as, the man gave the *appearance* of being busy.

5. a coming into notice; an appearing before the public; as, the *appearance* of an actor, of a new book, etc.

6. probability; likelihood. [Obs.]

7. in law, a being present in court; a coming into court of either party; an appearing in person or by attorney.

to put in an appearance; to appear for a short time.

to save appearances; to maintain a good showing.

Syn.—air, aspect, look, manner, mien, semblance.

ap·pēar′ẽr, *n.* one who or that which appears.

ap·pēar′ing·ly, *adv.* seemingly. [Obs.]

ap·pēaṣ′ȧ·ble, *a.* able to be appeased, quieted, or conciliated.

ap·pēaṣ′ȧ·ble·ness, *n.* the quality of being appeasable.

ap·pēaṣe′, *v.t.*; appeased, *pt.*, *pp.*; appeasing, *ppr.* [ME. *apesen*, *apeisen*; Fr. *apaiser*; L. *ad*, to, and *pax*, peace.]

1. to make quiet; to calm; to still; as, to *appease* the tumult of the ocean, or of the passions; also, to pacify; to soothe; to conciliate, especially by giving in to the demands of; as, to *appease* wrath.

2. to satisfy or relieve, as hunger, thirst, etc.

Syn.—calm, pacify, quiet, still, allay, assuage, compose, conciliate, propitiate, reconcile, soothe, tranquilize.—To *appease* is to allay agitation which demands satisfaction; to *calm* is to bring into a tranquil state. *Appease* respects matters of force or violence, *calm* those of inquietude and distress.

ap·pēaṣe′ment, *n.* 1. the act of appeasing or being appeased.

2. the policy of giving in to the demands of a hostile or dangerous power in an attempt to prevent trouble; as, *appeasement* of fascism proved futile.

ap·pēaṣ′ẽr, *n.* one who appeases or pacifies.

ap·pēa′sive, *a.* having the power to appease; quieting.

ȧp·pel′, *n.* [Fr.] in fencing, a quick tap with the foot, originally to warn one's opponent of a thrust.

ap·pel′lȧ·ble, *a.* same as *appealable*.

ap·pel′lăn·cy, *n.* appeal; capability of appeal.

ap·pel′lănt, *n.* 1. one who makes an appeal.

2. in law, one who appeals, or removes a case from a lower to a higher court.

3. one who accuses another of a crime. [Obs.]

4. one who challenges or summons another to single combat. [Obs.]

ap·pel′lănt, *a.* [Fr. *appelant*, from *appeler*, to call; L. *appellans*, ppr. of *appellare*, to call upon.] pertaining to an appeal; appealing.

ap·pel′lāte, *a.* in law, pertaining to appeals; having cognizance of appeals; as, *appellate* jurisdiction.

appellate court; a court having the power to review appeals and reverse the decisions of lower courts.

appellate judges; judges of appellate courts.

ap·pel·lā′tion, *n.* [L. *appellatio*, an addressing, accosting, from *appellare*, to call upon.]

1. a name; the word by which a person, thing, or class is called and known; a title; as, to give a man his proper *appellation*.

2. the act of appealing; an appeal. [Obs.]

3. the act of naming or calling by name.

Syn.—name, title, cognomen, style, denomination, appellative, epithet.

ap·pel′lȧ·tive, *a.* 1. pertaining to the giving of names; naming.

2. in grammar, relating to a common noun.

ap·pel′lȧ·tive, *n.* 1. in grammar, a common noun.

2. a descriptive name or title; an appellation.

Many a fair flower is burdened with preposterous *appellatives*. —Tupper.

ap·pel′lȧ·tive·ly, *adv.* in an appellative manner; in a manner to express whole classes or species; as, Hercules is sometimes used *appellatively*, that is, as a common name to signify a strong man.

ap·pel′lȧ·tive·ness, *n.* the quality of being appellative.

ap·pel'là·tō·ry, *a.* pertaining to an appeal; containing an appeal; as, an *appellatory* libel. [Obs.]

ap·pel·lee', *n.* in law, the defendant in an appeal; the person appealed against, or prosecuted for a crime.

ap·pel'lŏr (*or* ap-pel-lor'), *n.* in law, a person who carries an appeal to a higher court.

ap'pen·āġe, *n.* same as *appanage.*

ap·pend', *v.t.*; appended, *pt., pp.*; appending, *ppr.* [Fr. *appendre,* to hang up; ME. *appenden;* L. *appendere,* to weigh, consider; *ad,* to, and *pendere,* to hang.]

1. to attach, as by a string, so that the thing is suspended, as a pendant.

2. to affix; to add as an accessory or supplement; as, a glossary is *appended* to this book.

Syn.—affix, supplement, subjoin, attach, add.

ap·pend'āġe, *n.* 1. an adjunct; something added to a principal or greater thing, though not necessary to it, as a portico to a house.

Modesty is the *appendage* of sobriety.
—Jer. Taylor.

2. in biology, any part or organ which is subordinate; an external organ or limb, as an antenna, a tail, a leaf, a hair, etc.

Syn.—appendix, accessory, supplement, concomitant, addition.

ap·pend'āġed, *a.* furnished with an appendage.

ap·pend'ănce, *n.* 1. something annexed. [Obs.]

2. the condition of being appendant.

ap·pend'ănt, ap·pend'ent, *a.* 1. annexed; accompanying; attached; as, a seal *appendant* to a paper.

2. in law, belonging to as a subsidiary right.

common appendant; in English law, a right belonging to the owners or occupiers of land to pasture horses, cows, etc. upon the wasteland of the lord of the manor, or upon the lands of other persons within the same manor.

ap·pend'ănt, *n.* 1. that which belongs to another thing, as incidental or subordinate to it; an appendage.

2. in law, a subsidiary right annexed by prescription to a major one.

ap·pen·deç'tō·my, *n.*; *pl.* **ap·pen·deç'tō·mieṣ,** [L. *appendix,* an appendage, and Gr. *ektemnein,* to cut.] in surgery, the removal, by excision, of the vermiform appendix.

ap·pend'ence, ap·pend'en·cy, *n.* 1. the state of being appendant. [Obs.]

2. something appended. [Obs.]

ap·pend'i·çăl, *a.* pertaining to or of the nature of an appendix.

ap·pend'i·çāte, *v.t.* to append; to add. [Obs.]

ap·pen'di·cēṣ, *n.*, alternative pl. of *appendix.*

ap·pend·i·cī'tis, *n.* inflammation of the vermiform appendix.

ap·pend'i·çle, *n.* a small appendage or appendix.

Ap·pen·diç·ū·lā'ri·à, *n.* [LL. *appendicularius,* from L. *appendicula.*] a genus of minute tunicates, with a taillike appendage like that of a tadpole.

ap·pen·diç·ū·lā'ri·oid, *a.* pertaining to the genus *Appendicularia.*

Ap·pen·diç·ū·lā'tà, *n.pl.* in zoology, an order of annelids, including the marine worms or *Polychæta.*

ap·pen·diç'ū·lāte, *a* 1. in botany, having small appendages.

2. of or pertaining to the *Appendiculata.*

ap·pen'dix, *n.*; *pl.* **ap·pen'dix·eṣ** or **ap·pen'di·cēṣ,** [L. *appendix,* an appendage, from *appendere,* to hang to, or from; *ad,* to, and *pendere,* to hang.]

1. something appended or added; an appendage. [Obs.]

2. additional or supplementary material at the end of a book relating, but not essential, to the main body of the work.

3. in anatomy, an appendage or outgrowth of an organ; especially, the vermiform appendix.

vermiform appendix; a small saclike appendage of the large intestine.

Syn.—addition, supplement, addendum.

ap·pense', *a.* [L. *appensus,* pp. of *appendere,* to hang to.] in botany, hanging from above; pendulous, as an ovule. [Rare.]

ap·pen'sion, *n.* the act of appending. [Obs.]

ap·pen'tis, ap·pen'tice, *n.* [ME. *appentice;* OFr. *apentis;* Fr. *appentis,* a shed; L. *appendere,* to hang to.] an architectural name for a lean-to roof or a kind of open shed supported on columns; its purpose is to afford protection from the weather to a door, window, flight of steps, etc., over which it projects; also, a penthouse. [Obs.]

APPENTIS

ap·pĕr·cēive', *v.t.* [ME. *aperceiven;* OFr. *apercevir;* Fr. *apercevoir,* to perceive; Sp. *apercibir;* L. *ad,* to, and *percipere,* to perceive.]

1. to perceive, or observe. [Obs.]

2. to interpret (new ideas, impressions, etc.) by the help of past experience.

ap·pĕr·cep'tion, *n.* [Fr. *aperception,* perception, from *apercevoir,* to perceive; from L. *ad,* to, and *percipere,* to perceive.]

1. perception.

2. consciousness by the mind of its own consciousness; self-reflective perception applied to metaphysical ends.

Apperception is the essential mental act in the three great stages of mental generalization, perception, conception, and judgment.
—Baldwin.

3. the interpretation of new ideas by past experience.

ap·pĕr·cep'tive, *a.* pertaining to apperception; as, the *apperceptive* function.

ap·per'il, *n.* peril; danger. [Obs.]

ap·pĕr·tāin', *v.i.*; appertained, *pt., pp.*; appertaining, *ppr.* [ME. *apperteinen, aperteinen, apertinen;* OFr. *apartenir;* Fr. *appartenir,* to appertain, belong to; L. *ad,* to, and *pertinere,* to belong to.] to belong as a function, part, etc.; to pertain; to relate; as, give to whom it *appertains.*

ap·pĕr·tāin'ingṣ, *n.pl.* the things which belong to one; appurtenances. [Rare.]

ap·pĕr·tāin'ment, *n.* that which belongs to a person; appurtenance. [Obs.]

ap·pĕr'tē·nence, *n.* appurtenance. [Obs.]

ap·pĕr'ti·nent, *a.* belonging; appertaining.

ap·pĕr'ti·nent, *n.* that which belongs to something else.

ap·pēte', *v.t.* to crave; to desire. [Obs.]

ap'pē·ten·cy, ap'pē·tence, *n.*; *pl.* **ap'pē·ten·cieṣ,** [Fr. *appétence, appetit;* L. *appetentia,* a longing after, appetite, from *appetere,* to strive after.]

1. a strong desire; especially desire for that which gratifies the senses: sensual appetite; as, *appetence* for liquor.

2. an instinctive tendency; propensity.

3. natural attraction or affinity of inanimate objects.

4. the theory that a change of desires or needs produces in an organism a corresponding modification in its structure.

ap'pē·tent, *a.* [L. *appetens,* ppr. of *appetere,* to strive for.] desiring; very desirous. [Rare.]

ap″pē·ti·bil'i·ty, *n.* the quality of being desirable.

ap'pē·ti·ble, *a.* [LL. *appetibilis,* from *appeto.*] desirable; that may be the object of desire.

ap'pē·tīte, *n.* [ME. *appetit, apetite;* Fr. *appétit* appetite; L. *appetitus,* a passionate longing or desire, from *appetere,* to seek for.]

1. a natural or habitual desire for some gratification, either of the body or of the mind; as, sexual *appetite.*

2. a desire for food or drink; as, dining with a good *appetite.*

3. strong desire; longing; as, a vulgar *appetite* for the sensational.

4. the thing desired. [Archaic.]

Power being the natural *appetite* of princes.
—Swift.

5. appetency. [Obs.]

Syn.—passion, desire, propensity, proclivity, inclination, appetency, want, craving.

ap·pē·ti'tion, *n.* desire; craving; a longing for.

ap'pē·ti·tive, *a.* producing appetite; appetizing.

ap'pē·tīze, *v.t.*; appetized, *pt., pp.*; appetizing, *ppr.* to stimulate the appetite of. [Rare.]

ap'pē·tī·zēr, *n.* that which appetizes; a small portion of tasty food or a drink at the beginning of a meal to stimulate the appetite.

ap'pē·tī·zing, *a.* stimulating the appetite.

ap'pē·tī·zing·ly, *adv.* in an appetizing manner.

Ap'pi·ăn, *a.* pertaining to Appius or to any member of the Appii, a Roman family.

Appian Way, or *Via Appia;* a celebrated road from Rome south through Capua to Brundisium (Brindisi), begun by the censor Appius Claudius Caecus, c. 312 B.C. It is more than 365 miles in length, 14 to 18 feet in breadth.

ap'plà·nāte, *a.* [*ad-,* and L. *planus,* flat.] in botany, expanded or flattened out.

ap·plạud', *v.t.*; applauded, *pt., pp.*; applauding, *ppr.* [Fr. *applaudir;* L. *applaudere,* to strike the hands together; *ad,* to, and *plaudere,* to strike.]

1. to praise or show approval of by clapping the hands, acclamation, shouting, etc.

2. to praise by words, actions, or other means; to express approval of; to commend.

I do *applaud* his courage. —Shak.

Syn.—approve, cheer, commend, extol, encore, laud, praise.

ap·plạud', *v.i.* to express praise or approval by clapping the hands, stamping the feet, shouting, or other demonstration; as, the audience *applauded.*

ap·plạud'ẽr, *n.* one who applauds.

ap·plạuṣ'à·ble, *a.* worthy of applause. [Obs.]

ap·plạuṣe', *n.* [Fr. *applaudissement,* applause; L. *applausus,* pp. of *applaudere,* to applaud.]

1. the act of applauding; approval or praise; acclamation; approbation publicly expressed.

2. demonstration of approval by hand clapping, cheering, shouting, etc.

Syn.—commendation, approbation, acclamation, encomium, approval, plaudit, praise.

ap·plạu'sive, *a.* expressive of applause; containing applause.

ap·plạu'sive·ly, *adv.* in a manner expressing applause.

ap'ple (-pl), *n.* [ME. *appel, aple;* AS. *æppl, æpl,* fruit, apple; also, eyeball, anything round.]

1. the firm, fleshy, edible fruit of a tree, *Pyrus Malus,* which is cultivated in almost all the temperate regions of the earth. It is usually round in form, the ends being considerably depressed. Many varieties of *apple* are raised in this country. These are called by distinctive names, some with general, and others with specific, reference. Such terms as *russet, pipin,* etc. are applied to many varieties; while names such as Baldwin, Northern Spy, Winesap, Delicious, Jonathan, etc. are specific.

2. any tree on which the apple grows.

3. any of various plants, fruits, or fruitlike growths resembling the apple; as, the love *apple,* the oak *apple,* etc.

apple brandy; a liquor distilled from apple cider; applejack.

apple of Cain; the strawberry tree, *Arbutus unedo;* also, its fruit.

apple of discord; (a) in Greek mythology, a golden apple marked "For the most beautiful" by Eris, goddess of discord, and claimed by Athena, Hera, and Aphrodite: it was awarded by Paris to Aphrodite and, in return, she helped him to get the beautiful Helen, thus starting the Trojan War; (b) anything which produces dissension among people.

apple of love, or *love apple;* the tomato: former name.

apple of one's eye; the pupil of one's eye; figuratively, any thing or person that one cherishes.

apple of Peru; a Peruvian herb, *Nicandra physaloides.*

apple of Sodom, or *Dead Sea apple;* a plant growing near the Dead Sea, thus described by Josephus. ". . . Which fruits have a color as if they were fit to be eaten; but if you pluck them with your hands they dissolve into smoke and ashes." Hence, anything of promising appearance which disappoints or deceives.

apple-pie bed; a bed made up, as a practical joke, with a sheet so doubled that it prevents one from stretching at full length.

apple-pie order; perfect order. [Colloq.]

bitter apple; see *colocynth.*

ap'ple, *v.i.* to yield or gather apples. [Rare.]

ap'ple blīght (blīt), a species of aphis that attacks apples.

ap'ple bōr″ẽr, a beetle whose larvae bore into the wood of the apple and other trees.

ap'ple but'tẽr, a preserve or sauce made of apples stewed with sugar and spices.

ap'ple çärt, a cart or barrow from which apples are sold or peddled in the street, etc.

to upset the (or *one's*) *apple cart*; to disrupt procedure or upset one's plans or business.

ap′ple çōr′ẽr, a device for cutting out the cores of apples.

ap′ple-fāced, *a.* having a full rosy face like an apple.

ap′ple flȳ, any fly whose larvae bore into apples.

ap′ple green, the yellowish-green color of some apples.

ap′ple·jack, *n.* apple brandy; an alcoholic drink made from apple cider.

ap′ple·john (jon), *n.* a kind of apple which keeps for a long time, but becomes shriveled and dry: called also *John-apple.* [Obs.]

ap′ple midġe (mij), an insect whose larvae bore into apples.

ap′ple moth, a lepidopterous insect, the larvae of which infest apples.

ap′ple pol′ish·ẽr, a person who curries favor by gifts, flattery, etc., as a child bringing his teacher an apple. [Slang.]

ap′ple·sauce, *n.* 1. a dessert or relish made of apples cut into pieces, sweetened, and cooked to a pulp in water.

2. nonsense; hokum. [Slang.]

ap′ple shell, an apple snail.

ap′ple snāil, a gastropod of the genus *Ampullaria.*

ap′ple-squīre (skwīr), *n.* a pimp. [Obs.]

Ap′ple·tŏn lāy′ẽr, [after E. V. *Appleton* (1892–), Eng. scientist.] a stratum of electrically charged air in the Heaviside layer.

ap′ple tree, any tree that yields apples, especially *Pyrus Malus.*

ap′ple wīne, cider made from apples.

ap′ple wŏrm, the larva of a moth, *Carpocapsa pomonella,* which infests apples.

ap·plī′à·ble, *a.* capable of being applied; applicable.

ap·plī′ănce, *n.* 1. the act of applying; application; as, the *appliance* of a theory. [Rare.]

2. pliability; compliance; subservience. [Obs.]

3. something applied to a particular use; a device or machine, especially for household use, an apparatus or instrument; as, a mechanical *appliance.*

Syn.—contrivance, apparatus, device, machine, instrument, tool.

ap″pli·cȧ·bil′i·ty, *n.* the quality of being applicable or fit to be applied.

ap′pli·cȧ·ble, *a.* [Fr. *applicable*; L. *applicare,* to join or fasten to.] capable of being applied; fit to be applied; appropriate; relevant; as, this observation is *applicable* to the case.

Syn.—useful, pertinent, suitable, appropriate, adaptable.

ap′pli·cȧ·ble·ness, *n.* fitness to be applied; the quality of being applicable.

ap′pli·cȧ·bly, *adv.* in an applicable manner.

ap′pli·căn·cy, *n.* the quality of being applicable.

ap′pli·cănt, *n.* [L. *applicans,* ppr. of *applicare,* to join or attach to.] one who applies or makes application, as for employment, help, etc.; a petitioner; as, an *applicant* for charity.

ap′pli·cāte, *a.* applied or put to practical use; as, *applicate* sciences.

applicate number; in mathematics, a number applied in a concrete case.

applicate ordinate; a straight line applied at right angles to the axis of any conic section, and bounded by the curve.

ap′pli·cāte, *n.* an applicate ordinate.

ap′pli·cāte, *v.i.* to apply. [Obs.]

ap·pli·cā′tion, *n.* [Fr. *application*; L. *applicatio,* a binding on, or joining to, from *applicatus,* pp. of *applicare,* to join or fasten to.]

1. the act of applying or laying on; as, the *application* of emollients.

2. the thing applied; as, the pain was abated by the *application.*

3. the act of making request or soliciting; as, he made *application* to a court of chancery.

4. the act of applying as a means; the employment of means; a putting to use; as, children may be governed by a suitable *application* of rewards and punishments.

5. applicability; relevancy; as, a rule of universal *application.*

6. a formal request or solicitation, or the writing embodying such request; as, an *application* for employment.

7. the act of fixing the mind; intensity of thought; close study; diligence.

8. the act of referring something to a particular case; as, I make the remark and leave you to make the *application.*

9. that part of the discourse in which the principles before laid down are applied to practical matters.

10. the act of applying the principles, etc. of one thing to another.

11. in astrology, the approach of a planet to a particular aspect.

ap′pli·cā·tive, *a.* applying or applicable.

ap′pli·cā·tive·ly, *adv.* in an applicative manner.

ap′pli·cā·tŏr, *n.* [from L. *applicatus,* and *-or.*] any device for applying or inserting medicine, etc.

ap′pli·cȧ·tō·ri·ly, *adv.* in an applicatory manner.

ap′pli·cȧ·tō·ry, *a.* applying or suitable for application; applicative.

ap′pli·cȧ·tō·ry, *n.* that which applies. [Rare.]

ap·plīed′, *a.* [pp. of *apply.*] used in actual practice or to work out practical problems; as, *applied* science: distinguished from *pure, abstract, theoretical.*

ap·plī′ed·ly, *adv.* by application. [Rare.]

ap·plī′ẽr, *n.* one who or that which applies.

ap·pli·qué′ (-kā′), *a.* [Fr.] applied or fastened on: said of one material attached by sewing, etc. to another.

ap·pli·qué′ (-kā′), *n.* any appliqué decoration or trimming.

ap·pli·qué′ (-kā′), *v.t.*; appliquéd, *pt., pp.* appliquéing, *ppr.* 1. to decorate with appliqué.

2. to put on as appliqué.

ap·plot′, *v.t.*; applotted, *pt., pp.*; applotting, *ppr.* to allot; to divide into plots. [Rare.]

ap·plot′ment, *n.* allotment. [Rare.]

ap·plȳ′, *v.t.*; applied, *pt., pp.*; applying, *ppr.* [ME. *applyen, applien*; OFr. *aplier*; L. *applicare,* to attach to, apply.]

1. to lay on; to put (one thing) to another; as, to *apply* liniment to a part of the body.

2. to employ for a particular purpose; to use practically or specifically; as, to *apply* a sum of money to the payment of a debt, to *apply* one's knowledge to a problem.

3. to refer to a person or thing with (an epithet or suitable term).

4. to concentrate (one's faculties) on; to employ (oneself) diligently; as, he *applied* himself to the work.

5. to address or direct. [Obs.]

6. to keep busy. [Obs.]

7. to visit. [Obs.]

Syn.—engage, employ, devote, use.

ap·plȳ′, *v.i.* 1. to be appropriate, suitable, or relevant; as, this argument *applies* well to the case.

2. to make request; to solicit; as, to *apply* to the president for an office.

3. to devote or direct one's attention closely. [Rare.]

ȧp·pog·giȧ·tū′rä (ȧp-poj-ä-tū′rä), *n.* [It., from *appogiare,* to prop, lean.] in music, an ornamental and embellishing note, usually written in a smaller character than the regular notes of the piece and sharing the time of the following note: also called *grace note.*

APPOGGIATURA

ap·point′, *v.t.*; appointed, *pt., pp.*; appointing, *ppr.* [ME. *appointen, apointen*; OFr. *apointer*; L. *ad,* to, and *punctum,* a point, from *pungere,* to prick.]

1. to fix; to settle; to establish; to constitute, ordain, or fix by decree or decision; as, to *appoint* a time for the meeting.

2. to designate by authority; to name or select for an office, position, etc.; as, to *appoint* a committee; to *appoint* someone guardian.

3. to ordain, command, or order.

Thy servants are ready to do whatsoever my lord the king shall *appoint.*
—2 Sam. xv. 15.

4. to equip; to furnish and arrange; as, his house is well-*appointed.*

5. to point out by way of censure. [Obs.]

6. in law, (a) to designate, or nominate, as an executor, administrator, or guardian; (b) to allot or divide (an estate) by virtue of a clause, contained in a conveyance, conferring a power on some person to do so.

Syn.—allot, constitute, depute, fix, ordain, designate, name, order, prescribe, nominate.

ap·point′, *v.i.* 1. to ordain; to decree. [Archaic.]

2. to make appointments, as to an office, position, etc.

ap·point′à·ble, *a.* capable of being appointed; as, officers are *appointable* by the executive.

ap·point·ee′, *n.* 1. a person appointed.

2. in law, one receiving appointment from a legally constituted appointor.

ap·point′ẽr, *n.* one who appoints.

ap·point′ive, *a.* filled by or subject to appointment; as, an *appointive* office.

ap·point′ment, *n.* 1. the act of appointing or the state of being appointed.

2. (a) designation to office; (b) the person designated; (c) the office to which one may be appointed.

3. stipulation; assignation; engagement; as, they made an *appointment* to meet at six o'clock.

4. decree; established order or constitution; direction; order; command; as, it is our duty to submit to the divine *appointments.*

5. equipment; furniture: commonly in the plural; as, the *appointments* of a hotel; the *appointments* of an ocean steamer.

6. an allowance to a person; a salary or pension, as to a public officer: properly used only in the plural. [Obs.]

7. in law, the act performed by an appointor in transferring to a person any specific property; also, the deed or conveyance containing the disposition of such property.

Syn.—establishment, order, designation, equipment, position, command.

ap·point′ŏr, *n.* in law, one empowered to allot or divide an estate by virtue of a clause contained in a conveyance previously drawn up.

ap·pōr′tẽr, *n.* [L. *apportare,* bring to; *ad,* to, and *portare,* to bring.] a bringer-in; an introducer. [Obs.]

ap·pōr′tion, *v.t.*; apportioned, *pt., pp.*; apportioning, *ppr.* [*ad-,* and L. *portio,* portion.] to divide and assign in proportion or according to some plan; portion out; as, to *apportion* one's time among various employments.

Syn.—distribute, deal out, divide, share, allot, dispense, dispose.

ap·pōr′tion·āte·ness, *n.* just proportion. [Obs.]

ap·pōr′tion·ẽr, *n.* one who apportions.

ap·pōr′tion·ment, *n.* 1. an apportioning or being apportioned; also, the distribution resulting from this.

2. the allotment or distribution of representatives in Congress, and in the state legislatures. In the former case, a new *apportionment* is made by Congress every ten years, after the census.

ap·pōs′à·ble, *a.* that can be apposed; as, the human thumb is *apposable,* for it can move so as to touch the tip of each of the four fingers.

ap·pōṣe′, *v.t.*; apposed, *pt., pp.*; apposing, *ppr.* [Fr. *apposer*; L. *apponere,* to put or lay at; *ad,* to, and *ponere,* to put.]

1. to put questions to; to examine. [Obs.]

2. to put (something *to* another thing).

3. to put side by side; place opposite or near.

ap·pōṣed′, *a.* arranged in apposition.

ap·pōṣ′ẽr, *n.* an examiner: in the English Court of Exchequer there was, prior to 1833, an officer called the *apposer,* who audited the accounts of the sheriff. [Obs.]

ap′pō·ṣite, *a.* [L. *appositus,* pp. of *apponere,* to put or lay at or near; *ad,* to, and *ponere,* to place.] suitable; fitting; appropriate; pertinent; apt: often followed by *to*; as, his remarks were *apposite to* the subject before us.

ap′pō·ṣite·ly, *adv.* in an apposite manner.

ap′pō·ṣite·ness, *n.* fitness; propriety; suitability.

ap·pō·ṣi′tion (-zish′un), *n.* [Fr. *apposition*; L. *appositus,* pp. of *apponere,* to place against or to.]

1. an apposing or being apposed; putting side by side.

2. the position resulting from this.

3. in grammar, (a) the placing of a word or expression beside another so that the second explains and has the same grammatical construction as the first; (b) the relationship between such words; as, *my cousin* is in *apposition* with *Mary* in "Mary, my cousin, is here."

growth by apposition; in botany, growth in thickness by formation of laminae, as of cellulose in cell walls and of starch in starch grains.

ap·pō·ṣi′tion·ăl, *a.* relating to, or placed in, apposition.

ap·poṣ′i·tive, *n.* a word, phrase, or clause in apposition.

ap·poṣ′i·tive, *a.* of or in apposition.

ap·poṣ′i·tive·ly, *adv.* in an appositive manner.

ap·prāiṣ′à·ble, *a.* capable of appraisal.

ap·prāiṣ′ăl, *n.* 1. an appraising or being appraised.

2. an appraised value or price; estimate.

ap·praise′, *v.t.*; appraised, *pt.*, *pp.*; appraising, *ppr.* [ME. *apraysen*; OFr. *apreiser*, *apretier*, *aprisier*; LL. *appretiare*, to value, esteem.]
1. to set a value on; to estimate the worth of; to value officially.
2. to estimate the quantity of.
3. to judge the quality or worth of.
4. to praise; to speak well of. [Rare.]

ap·praise′ment, *n.* 1. the act of setting the value; the business of an appraiser.
2. an appraised value.

ap·prais′ẽr, *n.* one who appraises; specifically, a person given authority to make a thorough and correct valuation on property of any kind.

ap·prē·cā′tion, *n.* [L. *apprecari*, to worship, pray to, *ad*, to, and *precari*, to pray.] earnest prayer. [Obs.]

ap′prē·cā·tō·ry, *a.* intercessory. [Obs.]

ap′prē′ci·à·ble (-shi-à-bl), *a.* 1. enough to be perceived or estimated; perceptible; as, an *appreciable* amount.
2. that can be appreciated.

ap·prē′ci·à·bly, *adv.* in an appreciable manner; to an appreciable extent.

ap·prē′ci·ȧnt (-shi-), *a.* appreciative. [Rare.]

ap·prē′ci·āte (-shi-), *v.t.*; appreciated, *pt.*, *pp.*; appreciating, *ppr.* [Fr. *apprécier*; L. *appretiare*, to value or estimate, from *ad*, to, and *pretium*, price.]
1. to value; to esteem; to be conscious of the significance, desirability, or worth of; to estimate justly; as, we seldom sufficiently *appreciate* the advantages we enjoy.
2. to recognize gratefully; as, I *appreciate* your kindness.
3. to increase the price set on: opposed to *depreciate*.
4. to be fully or sensitively aware of; to note distinctions in; as, to *appreciate* differences of color.
Syn.—esteem, estimate, value, regard, reckon, prize.—We *estimate* things when we judge by calculation their approximate amount or value; we *appreciate* when we prize them according to their true value or worth; we *esteem* when we regard them with moral approbation.

ap·prē′ci·āte, *v.i.* to rise in value; as, public securities *appreciated* when the debt was funded.

ap·prē′ci·ā·ting·ly, *adv.* with appreciation.

ap·prē·ci·ā′tion (-shi-), *n.* 1. an appreciating; accurate estimate; recognition of good points.
2. grateful recognition, as of benefits.
3. sensitive awareness; discriminating perception or enjoyment, as of art.
4. a rise in value or price: opposed to *depreciation*.

ap·prē′ci·à·tive, *a.* feeling or exhibiting appreciation.

ap·prē′ci·à·tive·ly, *adv.* in an appreciative manner.

ap·prē′ci·à·tive·ness, *n.* the quality of being appreciative.

ap·prē′ci·ā·tŏr, *n.* one who appreciates.

ap·prē′ci·à·tō·ri·ly, *adv.* appreciatively.

ap·prē′ci·à·tō·ry, *a.* appreciative; as, *appreciatory* words.

ap·prē·hend′, *v.t.*; apprehended, *pt.*, *pp.*; apprehending, *ppr.* [Fr. *apprehender*; L. *apprehendere*, to take hold of; *ad*, to, and *prehendere*, to take hold.]
1. to take or seize; to take hold of: in this literal sense, applied chiefly to the arrest of persons by legal process, or with a view to trial; as, to *apprehend* a thief.
2. to take hold of mentally; to perceive with the mind; to understand.
3. to fear; to anticipate with anxiety or dread; as, we *apprehend* calamities.
4. to note; to learn by observation; to discover by experience.

Each man avails him of what worth he *apprehends* in you. —Browning.

5. to become aware of, or have perception of, by the senses; to have a clear impression of; as, if a man sees two distinct persons, he *apprehends* them as different persons.
Syn.—understand, comprehend, anticipate, conceive, arrest, dread.

ap·prē·hend′, *v.i.* 1. to think; to grasp ideas; as, he *apprehends* very thoroughly.
2. to be apprehensive; to expect calamity; to fear.

ap·prē·hend′ẽr, *n.* one who apprehends.

ap·prē·hend′ing·ly, *adv.* with apprehension or perception; understandingly.

ap·prē·hen·si·bil′i·ty, *n.* the state or quality of being apprehensible.

ap·prē·hen′si·ble, *a.* capable of being apprehended.

ap·prē·hen′si·bly, *adv.* so as to be apprehended. [Rare.]

ap·prē·hen′sion, *n.* 1. the act of taking into custody or arresting; as, the felon, after his *apprehension*, escaped.
2. [*often in pl.*] fear; dread; the thought of future evil, accompanied with uneasiness of mind; apprehensiveness.
3. the act of taking in mentally; mental grasp; as, the special charm of Stevenson's works is that, to our *apprehension*, the characters always seem real people.
4. the faculty by which new ideas are conceived; as, a man of dull *apprehension*.
5. opinion; the result of a mental impression; as, in our *apprehension*, the facts prove the issue.
Syn.—arrest, disquietude, alarm, suspicion, comprehension, estimation.

ap·prē·hen′sive, *a.* 1. quick to understand; apt; as, an *apprehensive* scholar.
2. fearful; in expectation of evil; as, we were *apprehensive* of fatal consequences.
3. having to do with perception or understanding.
4. cognizant; aware; conscious. [Archaic.]

ap·prē·hen′sive·ly, *adv.* in an apprehensive manner.

ap·prē·hen′sive·ness, *n.* the quality of being apprehensive.

ap·pren′tice, *n.* [ME. *apprentice*, *aprentis*; OFr. *apprentis*; Fr. *apprenti*, from *apprendre*, to learn; L. *apprehendere*, to seize, take hold of.]
1. a person under legal agreement to work a specified length of time for a master craftsman in a craft or trade in return for instruction and, formerly, support.
2. in old English law, a barrister, considered a learner of law till of sixteen years' standing. [Obs.]
3. one not proficient in a subject; a beginner in a trade, occupation, or profession; novice; as, a literary *apprentice*.

ap·pren′tice, *v.t.*; apprenticed, *pt.*, *pp.*; apprenticing, *ppr.* to place or accept as an apprentice; indenture.

ap·pren′tice·ship, *n.* 1. the term for which an apprentice serves.
2. the service, state, or condition of an apprentice; preliminary practice or training.

ap·pressed′, **ap·prest′**, *a.* [L. *appressus*, pp. of *apprimere*, to press to; *ad*, to, and *premere*, to press.] in botany and zoology, pressed close to or lying flat against a surface.

ap·prīṣe′, **ap·prīze′**, *v.t.*; apprised *or* apprized, *pt.*, *pp.*; apprising *or* apprizing, *ppr.* [Fr. *appris*, pp. of *apprendre*, to teach or inform, from L. *apprehendere*, to lay hold of.] to inform verbally or in writing; notify.

ap·prīṣe′, *n.* notice. [Obs.]

ap·prīz′ăl, *n.* appraisal.

ap·prīze′, **ap·prīṣe′**, *v.t.*; apprized *or* apprised, *pt.*, *pp.*; apprizing *or* apprising, *ppr.* same as *appraise*.

ap·prīze′ment, *n.* appraisement. [Obs.]

ap·prīz′ẽr, *n.* 1. appraiser. [Rare.]
2. in Scots law, a creditor for the benefit of whom an appraisal is made.

ap·prōach′, *v.i.*; approached, *pt.*, *pp.*; approaching, *ppr.* [ME. *aprochen*; OFr. *aprochier*; LL. *appropiare*, from L. *ad*, to, and *propius*, comp. of *prope*, near.]
1. to come or go near or nearer; to draw near; as, to *approach* menacingly; also, to draw near in point of time; as, the dinner hour *approaches*.
2. to draw near, in a figurative sense; to advance near to a point aimed at; to approximate; as, he *approaches* to the character of the ablest statesman.

ap·prōach′, *v.t.* 1. to come near to in character or quality; as, Pope *approaches* Virgil in smoothness of versification.
2. to draw near or nearer to, in place or time; as, to *approach* home.
3. to bring near; to advance; as, the colonel *approached* his troops to the town.
4. to make military approaches to, including the necessary works and fortifications; as, the Prussians *approached* Paris with due care.
5. to make advances, a proposal, or a request to.

ap·prōach′, *n.* 1. the act of drawing near; a coming or advancing near; as, he was apprised of the enemy's *approach*; the *approach* of the holidays.
2. an approximation; resemblance.
3. [*often in pl.*] an advance or overture to someone.
4. a way of coming toward or reaching a person or place; access.
5. in golf, a stroke after the tee shot, meant to knock the ball onto the putting green.
6. an approaching (which see).
7. [*pl.*] in fortification, the works thrown up by besiegers to protect them in their advances toward a fortress or fortified town.

ap·prōach·à·bil′i·ty, *n.* approachableness.

ap·prōach′à·ble, *a.* able to be approached; specifically, (a) easy of access; (b) friendly; informal.

ap·prōach′à·ble·ness, *n.* the state of being approachable.

ap·prōach′ẽr, *n.* one who approaches.

ap·prōach′ing, *n.* in horticulture, the act of ingrafting a sprig or shoot of one tree into another, without cutting it from the parent stock; called also *inarching*, or *grafting by approach*.

ap·prōach′less, *a.* unapproachable; without an approach.

ap·prōach′ment, *n.* approach. [Obs.]

ap′prō·bāte, *a.* approved. [Obs.]

ap′prō·bāte, *v.t.*; approbated, *pt.*, *pp.*; approbating, *ppr.* 1. to express approbation of; to manifest a liking for or degree of satisfaction with; to approve.
2. to sanction.
3. in Scots law, to approve as valid.
to approbate and reprobate; in Scots law, to accept and reject, as when one tries to profit by part of a deed while rejecting the rest.

ap·prō·bā′tion, *n.* [L. *approbatio*, an approving, assenting to, from *approbare*, to approve.]
1. the act of approving; approval; commendation.
2. sanction.
3. a novitiate or probation. [Obs.]
4. attestation; proof. [Obs.]
Syn.—approval, assent, concurrence, commendation, praise, permission, liking, consent.

ap′prō·bā·tive, *a.* approving; implying approbation.

ap′prō·bā·tive·ness, *n.* 1. in phrenology, love of approbation.
2. the quality of being approbative.

ap′prō·bā·tŏr, *n.* one who approves. [Rare.]

ap·prō′bā·tō·ry, *a.* containing approbation, expressing approval or sanction.

ap·prompt′, *v.t.* to prompt; to stimulate. [Obs.]

ap·prooḟ′, *n.* 1. approval. [Archaic.]
2. proof; the act of testing. [Archaic.]

ap·prō·pin′quāte, *v.i.* [L. *appropinquare*, to approach, draw near.] to draw near. [Archaic.]

ap″prō·pin·quā′tion, *n.* a drawing nigh. [Archaic.]

ap·prō·pin′qui·ty, *n.* propinquity; nearness. [Rare.]

ap·prō′pre (-pẽr), *v.t.* to appropriate. [Obs.]

ap·prō′pri·à·ble, *a.* capable of being appropriated, set apart, sequestered, or assigned exclusively to a particular use.

ap·prō′pri·à·ment, *n.* a characteristic peculiar to oneself. [Obs.]

ap·prō′pri·āte, *v.t.*; appropriated, *pt.*, *pp.*; appropriating, *ppr.* [ME. *apropren*; OFr. *aproprier*; Fr. *approprier*; LL. *appropriare*, to appropriate; L. *ad*, to, and *proprius*, one's own.]
1. to set apart for, or assign to, a particular use, in exclusion of all other uses; as, a spot of ground is *appropriated* for a garden; money is *appropriated* by Congress for public buildings.
2. to take to oneself in exclusion of others; to claim or use as by an exclusive right.
3. to make suitable. [Rare.]
4. in ecclesiastical law, to sever (an ecclesiastical benefice) and annex it to a spiritual corporation, for its perpetual use.
Syn.—arrogate, assume, seize, usurp.

ap·prō′pri·āte, *a.* 1. belonging peculiarly; special.
2. set apart for a particular use or person. [Obs.]
3. fit or proper; suitable; as, *appropriate* manners.
Syn.—particular, becoming, congruous, suitable, adapted, peculiar, proper, meet, fit, apt.

ap·prō′pri·āte, *n.* a peculiar characteristic; attribute; property. [Obs.]

ap·prō′pri·āte·ly, *adv.* in an appropriate or proper manner; suitably; fitly.

ap·prō′pri·āte·ness, *n.* the quality of being appropriate, or especially suitable.

ap·prō·pri·ā′tion, *n.* [LL. *appropriatio*, from L. *ad*, to, and *proprius*, one's own.]
1. an appropriating or being appropriated.
2. a sum of money, or any other thing, set apart for a given purpose; as, an *appropria-*

tion for street paving; an *appropriation* for schools.

3. in ecclesiastical law, the severing or sequestering of a benefice to the perpetual use of a spiritual corporation.

appropriation bill; a measure to be approved by a legislative body, authorizing the disbursement of public moneys and specifying the purpose of the various items and the amount of money to be expended for each.

ap·prō′pri·ā·tive, *a.* appropriating; pertaining to appropriation; as, an *appropriative* act of Congress.

ap·prō′pri·ā·tive·ness, *n.* the state or quality of being appropriative.

ap·prō′pri·ā·tŏr, *n.* 1. one who appropriates.

2. in law, one who is possessed of an appropriated benefice.

ap·pröv′ȧ·ble, *a.* that can be approved; meriting approbation.

ap·pröv′ȧ·ble·ness, *n.* the quality of being approvable.

ap·pröv′ăl, *n.* 1. an approving or being approved.

2. favorable attitude or opinion.

3. consent; sanction.

on approval; for the customer to examine and decide whether to buy or return.

ap·pröv′ănce, *n.* approval. [Obs.]

ap·pröve′, *v.t.*; approved, *pt., pp.*; approving, *ppr.* [ME. *aproven*; OFr. *aprover*; Fr. *approuver*; L. *approbare*, to approve, to assent to as good; *ad*, to, and *probare*, to try, test; from *probus*, good.]

1. to like; to be pleased with; to admit the propriety of; to think or declare to be good, satisfactory, etc.; to commend; as, we *approve* the measures of the administration.

2. to prove; to show to be real or true; to justify; to make good. [Obs.]

Wouldst thou *approve* thy constancy? *Approve*
First thy obedience. —Milton.

3. to make or show to be worthy of approbation; as, to *approve* oneself to God by righteousness.

4. to demonstrate; to show by proof; to prove practically.

He had *approved* himself a great warrior. —Macaulay

5. to improve. [Obs.]

6. to sanction officially; to ratify; as, to *approve* the decision of a court martial.

Syn.—commend, sanction, encourage, authorize, support, promote, praise, admire, ratify.

ap·pröve′, *v.i.* to give approval; to have a favorable opinion (*of* someone or something).

ap·pröve′, *v.t.* [OFr. *aproer*, to profit.] in English law, to convert to one's own profit: used particularly of waste or common land formerly appropriated by the lord of a manor.

ap·pröv′ed·ly, *adv.* in an approved manner.

ap·pröve′ment, *n.* 1. approbation; liking. [Obs.]

2. in old English law, the act of a felon who confessed a crime before pleading, and informed on his accomplices in order to obtain his pardon. The confession and accusation were called *approvement* and the person an approver. The term is no longer in use, the act represented by *approvement* being now called, in England, turning king's (or queen's) evidence, and in the United States, turning state's evidence.

ap·pröve′ment, *n.* in old English law, the appropriation of waste or common lands by enclosing and converting them to the uses of husbandry, for the benefit of the lord of the manor.

ap·pröv′ẽr, *n.* 1. one who approves; formerly, one who made proof or trial.

2. in old English law, one who confessed a crime and informed on another: see *approvement*.

3. a bailiff or steward of a manor. [Obs.]

ap·pröv′ing, *a.* yielding, implying, or expressing approval; as, an *approving* conscience.

ap·pröv′ing·ly, *adv.* in an approving manner.

ap·prox′i·măl, *a.* [L. *approximare*; and *-al.*] in anatomy, adjoining; side by side.

ap·prox′i·māte, *a.* 1. near in time, position, or character.

2. approaching; closely resembling.

3. more or less correct or exact.

ap·prox′i·māte, *v.t.*; approximated, *pt., pp.*; approximating, *ppr.* [LL. *approximatus*, pp. of *approximare*, to come near; L. *ad*, to, and *proximus*, superl. of *prope*, near.]

1. to carry or advance near; to cause to approach (*to* something).

To *approximate* the inequality of riches to the level of nature. —Burke.

2. to come near to; to approach; as, this painting *approximates* reality.

ap·prox′i·māte, *v.i.* to come near; to approach; as, they do not *approximate* in style.

Syn.—approach, resemble, border, near.

ap·prox′i·māte·ly, *adv.* nearly; almost; also, by approximation.

ap·prox′i·mā·ting, *a.* close; resembling; near; approaching.

ap·prox·i·mā′tion, *n.* 1. approach; a drawing, moving, or advancing near; the act of approximating.

2. the result of approximating; an approach to correctness in estimating, calculating, or conjecturing; a coming near to a given quantity or quality.

3. in mathematics, a continual approach or coming nearer and nearer to a definite result in the process of finding values; also, a result or value that is approximately correct.

ap·prox′i·mā·tive, *a.* approaching; nearing a correct result; as, *approximative* estimates.

ap·prox′i·mā·tive·ly, *adv.* in an approximative manner.

ap·prox′i·mā·tive·ness, *n.* closeness to correct results; approximation.

ap·prox′i·mā·tŏr, *n.* one who or that which approximates.

ȧp·pui′ (-pwē′), *n.* [Fr. *appui*, a support or prop, from *appuyer*, to prop up.]

1. in horsemanship, the reciprocal feeling of the action of the bridle between the mouth of the horse and the hand of the rider or driver.

2. a prop; a support.

point d'appui; the point of support, as for a battle line; basis; fulcrum.

ap·pulse′, *n.* [L. *appulsus*, pp. of *appellere*, to drive forward; *ad*, to, and *pellere*, to strike.]

1. the act of striking against.

2. an active or energetic approach; a driving or running toward.

3. in astronomy, the approach of any planet to a conjunction with the sun or a star.

ap·pul′sion, *n.* a driving against. [Obs.]

ap·pul′sive, *a.* striking against; driving toward.

ap·pul′sive·ly, *adv.* by appulsion.

ap·pŭr′te·nănce, *n.* [ME. *appertenaunce*; OFr. *apertenance*; from L. *ad*, to, and *pertinere*, to reach, extend.]

1. that which belongs to something else; an adjunct; an appendage. In law, such buildings, rights, and improvements as belong to a house or to land are called the *appurtenances*, as outbuildings, gardens, pasturage, etc. to a house, and a right of way or other easement to land. But land can never properly pass as an *appurtenance* to land.

2. an additional subordinate right or privilege.

ap·pŭr′te·nănt, *a.* 1. belonging to or annexed; pertaining to of right; as, a right of way *appurtenant* to land or buildings.

2. appertaining; pertinent.

ap·pŭr′te·nănt, *n.* an appurtenance.

ȧ·prax′i·ȧ, *n.* [Gr. *apraxia*, inaction, from *a* priv., and *praktos*, from *prassein*, to do, practice.] in pathology, loss or impairment of power to perform purposeful movements, as in handling objects, despite the absence of paralysis: one form is due to a loss of ability to recognize objects or their uses.

ap′ri·cāte, *v.i.* and *v.t.* [L. *apricari.*] to bask in, or to expose to, sunlight. [Rare.]

ap·ri·cā′tion, *n.* the act of basking in the sun. [Rare.]

ā′pri·cot, (*or* ap′) *n.* [OE. *apricock*; Fr. *abricot*; from Sp. *albaricoque*; L. *præcoquus*, early matured fruit, from *præ*, beforehand, and *coquere*, to cook.]

1. the small, yellowish-orange, peachlike fruit of the tree *Prunus Armeniaca*.

2. the tree bearing this fruit, cultivated throughout the Temperate Zone.

3. a yellowish-orange color.

Ā′pril, *n.* [Fr. *avril*; L. *aprilis.*]

1. the fourth month of the year, having 30 days.

2. figuratively, the season of sprouting vegetation, changeable weather, etc.; hence, the early or hopeful period, as of life; also, a period of emotional inconstancy.

The *April's* in her eyes; it is love's spring. —Shak.

April fool; a victim of jokes played on April Fools' Day.

April Fools' Day; the first day of April; All Fools' Day.

ā prī·ō′rī, [*a*, and L. *prior*, comp. of *prius*, first.]

1. from cause to effect; from a generalization to particular instances; deductively.

2. of such reasoning; deductive.

3. based on theory instead of experience or experiment.

4. presumptive; without, or before, examination.

5. in philosophy, prior to, and furnishing the basis of, experience; innate, or based upon innate ideas.

Opposed to *a posteriori*.

ā·prī·ō·rism, *n.* an a priori principle or method of reasoning.

ā·prī·or′i·ty, *n.* 1. the quality or fact of being a priori.

2. the use of a priori reasoning.

À·proc′tȧ, *n.pl.* [L., from Gr. *a* priv., and *prōktos*, anus.] one of the divisions of the *Turbellaria*, including those species which are without an anal opening.

ȧ·proc′tous, *a.* in zoology, having no anal opening.

ā′prŏn (*or* ā′pŭrn), *n.* [by faulty separation of *a napron*; ME. *napron*; OFr. *naperon*, from *nape*, a cloth; L. *mappa*, a cloth.]

1. an article of dress worn by women and men on the front part of the body to keep the clothes clean, to protect them from injury, or as a covering or ornament. It is made of cloth, leather, or fine fabrics, and is usually tied at the waist with strings. Hence, anything like an apron in appearance or use.

2. in gunnery, a cap or lid covering the vent of a muzzle-loading cannon.

3. in shipbuilding, a piece of curved timber just above the foremost end of the keel.

4. a platform or flooring of plank at the entrance of a dock, against which the dock gates are shut.

5. a waterproof protecting shield in an open vehicle.

6. a part of the dress of an Anglican bishop, or of the regalia of Freemasons, etc.

7. a platform placed before a dam or sluiceway to cause the water to fall less precipitously.

8. the wedge holding the cutting tool of a plane.

9. in plumbing, a strip of lead to guide the water from a wall into a gutter.

10. the abdomen of the short-tailed decapod crustaceans, as the crab.

11. a protective work of planking or other material along a river bank.

12. a piece of boarding, leather, etc., used to conduct loose moving material past an opening, as grain in a separator.

13. an endless belt for carrying things.

14. the hard-surfaced area, often paved, in front of an airplane hangar.

15. the part of a stage in front of the curtain.

16. in geology, a sheet of sand or gravel lying in front of a glacial moraine.

ā′prŏn (*or* ā′pŭrn), *v.t.* to put an apron on; provide an apron for.

ā′prŏned (*or* ā′pŭrnd), *a.* wearing an apron.

ā′prŏn·ful, *n.*; *pl.* **ā′prŏn·fuls,** the amount that can be held in an apron.

ā′prŏn·less, *a.* not furnished with an apron.

ā′prŏn man, a man who wears an apron; hence, a laboring man; a mechanic. [Obs.]

ā′prŏn piēce, a horizontal piece of timber supporting the landing of a staircase, against which the slanting pieces bearing the steps are supported.

ā′prŏn string, the tie string of an apron.

to be tied to a woman's apron strings; to be completely under a woman's control, usually as a son or a husband.

ap·rō·pōs′ (-pō′), *adv.* [Fr. *à propos*, to the purpose; *à* (L. *ad*), to, and *propos*, from L. *propositum*, purpose, from *proponere*; *pro*, before, and *ponere*, to place.]

1. opportunely; seasonably; at the right time.

2. by the way: a word used to introduce an incidental observation, suited to the occasion, though not strictly belonging to the subject under consideration: usually with *of*; as, *apropos of* your argument, I will tell a story.

ap·rō·pōs′ (-pō′), *a.* relevant; apt; as, an *apropos* remark.

ap·rō·sex′i·ȧ, *n.* [L., from Gr. *aprosexia*, lack of attention.] a condition characterized by an abnormal lack of the power of mental concentration.

ap·rō·sō′pi·ȧ, *n.* [Gr. *aprosōpos*, without a face; *a* priv., and *prosōpon*, a face.] congenital absence of the face or of a part of the face.

ap·rō·ter′ō·dont, *a.* [Gr. *a* priv., *proteros*, in

front, and *odous, odontos,* tooth.] without front teeth, as some serpents.

apse, *n.* [L. *apsis;* see *apsis.*] 1. in architecture, a portion of any building forming a termination or projection semicircular or polygonal in plan, and having a dome or vaulted roof; especially, the vaulted semicircular or polygonal recess at the east end of the choir or chancel of a church, in which the altar is placed: also called *apsis.*

APSE

2. in ancient churches, the bishop's seat or throne.

3. in astronomy and mathematics, an apsis.

ap'si·dăl, *a.* 1. relating to an architectural apse.

2. pertaining to the apsides of planetary bodies.

ap·sid'i·ōle, *n.* in architecture, a small or secondary apse.

ap'sis, *n.; pl.* **ap'si·dēs,** (L. *apsis,* pl. *apsides,* from Gr. *hapsis,* an arch, bow, vault, a tying, fastening, from *haptein,* to fasten.]

1. in astronomy, that point in the orbit of the moon, a planet, etc. nearest to (*lower apsis*), or that farthest from (*higher apsis*), the center of attraction: also called *apse.* The line connecting the lower apsis and higher apsis is called the *line of the apsides.*

2. in mathematics, a point in a curve with polar coordinates, where the radius vector is either minimum or maximum.

3. in architecture, same as *apse.*

apt, *a.* [Fr. *apte,* L. *aptus,* pp. of *apere,* to fasten, join, from Gr. *haptein,* to fasten.]

1. fitting; suitable; appropriate; as, he used very *apt* metaphors.

2. having a usual tendency; usually liable, used of things; as, wheat on moist land is *apt* to blight.

3. inclined; disposed customarily: used of persons; as, men are too *apt* to slander others.

4. quick of perception; quick to learn; prompt; as, an *apt* scholar, an *apt* wit.

5. ready; prepared. [Archaic.]

All the men of might, strong and *apt* for war.
—2 Kings xxiv. 16.

Syn.—appropriate, suitable, inclined, disposed, dexterous, applicable.

apt, *v.t.* and *v.i.* to fit; to suit or adapt. [Obs.]

apt'ȧ·ble, *a.* that may be adapted. [Obs.]

ap'tāte, *v.t.* to make fit. [Obs.]

Ap'tẽr·ȧ, *n.pl.* [L., from Gr. *aptera,* animals without wings.] a suborder of *Insecta,* embracing the wingless insects.

ap'tẽr·ăl, *a.* 1. in zoology, apterous.

2. in architecture, without lateral columns: applied to buildings which have no series of columns along their sides but are either prostyle or amphiprostyle: opposed to *peripteral.*

ap'tẽr·ăn, *n.* one of the suborder *Aptera.*

ap·te'ri·um, *n.; pl.* **ap·tē'ri·ȧ,** [L., from Gr. *apteros,* wingless, without feathers; *a* priv., and *pteron,* wing.] a space on the skin of a bird where there are no feathers.

ap'tẽr·oid, *a.* having very small or rudimentary wings: said of some birds.

ap'tẽr·ous, *a.* in biology, having no wings or winglike parts.

Ap·tẽr'y·ġēṣ, *n.pl.* [L., from Gr. *apterygos,* wingless; *a* priv., and *pteryx,* from *pteron,* a wing.] a suborder of ratite birds, including the family *Apterygidæ.*

ap·tẽr·yġ'i·ăl, *a.* [from Gr. *apterygos,* from *a-,* without, and *pteryx,* a wing.] in zoology, lacking paired fins or limbs.

Ap·tẽr·yġ'i·dae, *n.pl.* a family of ratite birds made up of the one genus *Apteryx.*

Ap'tẽr·yx, *n.* [Gr. *a* priv., and *pteryx,* wing.]

1. a genus of nearly extinct, tailless ratite birds of New Zealand, with a long slender bill, undeveloped wings, and hairlike feathers.

APTERYX

2. [a–] one of the birds belonging to this genus; a kiwi.

ap'ti·tūde, *n.* [Fr. *aptitude;* L. *aptitudo,* from *aptus,* fit, *apt,* pp. of *apere,* to fit, join; Gr. *haptein,* to fasten; Sans. *āpta,* from *ap,* to reach, attain.]

1. a natural disposition or tendency toward a particular action or effect; as, the *aptitude* of babies to cry when hungry.

2. fitness; suitableness.

3. readiness in learning or understanding.

4. an ability; capacity; talent.

ap'ti·tūde test, a test for determining the probability of a person's success in some activity in which he is not yet trained.

ap·ti·tū'di·năl, *a.* relating to aptitude. [Obs.]

apt'ly, *adv.* in an apt or suitable manner; with proper correspondence of parts; fitly; properly; pertinently; readily.

apt'ness, *n.* 1. fitness; suitableness.

2. disposition of the mind; propensity; as, the *aptness* of men to follow example.

3. quickness in learning.

4. a natural tendency: said of things; as, the *aptness* of iron to rust.

Syn.—fitness, tendency, adaptability, suitableness, propensity, aptitude.

ap·tō″sō·ċhrō'mȧ·tiṣm, *n.* [Gr. *aptōs,* not falling off, from *a* priv., and *piptein,* to fall, and *chrōmatismos,* coloring, from *chrōma,* color.] change of color without change of feathers, as in some species of birds.

ap'tōte, *n.* [L. *aptotum,* pl. *aptota,* from Gr. *aptōton,* neut. of *aptōtos,* not fallen, undeclined; *a* priv., and *ptōtos,* from *piptein,* to fall.] in grammar, a noun which has no variation of termination or distinction of cases; an indeclinable noun.

ap·tot'iç, *a.* containing or characterized by aptotes; without inflection; as, an *aptotic* language.

ap·tȳ'ȧ·liṣm, *n.* [Gr. *a* priv., and *ptyalismos,* from *ptyalizein,* to spit much, from *ptyein,* to spit.] inability, total or partial, to secrete saliva.

ap'ty·ċhus, *n.; pl.* **ap'ty·ċhī,** [Mod. L., from Gr. *a* priv., and *ptychos,* a fold, from *ptyssein,* to fold.] a fossil body regarded as the operculum of an ammonite.

Ā'pus, *n.* [L., from Gr. *apous; a* priv., and *pous,* foot.]

1. a genus of phyllopod crustaceans of the subclass *Entomostraca.*

2. a southern constellation: also called *Bird of Paradise.*

ap·y·ret'ic (*or* ā-pī-), *a.* [Gr. *apyretos,* without fever; *a* priv., and *pyretos,* from *pyr,* fire.] having no fever.

ap·ȳ·rex'i·ȧ (*or* ā-pī-), **ap'ȳ·rex·y,** *n.* [Gr. *apyrexia; a* priv., and *pyressein,* to be feverish; from *pyr,* fire.] the absence or temporary cessation of fever.

ap·ȳ·rex'i·ăl (*or* ā-pī-), *a.* pertaining to apyrexia.

ȧ·pȳ'rō·tȳpe, *n.* [Gr. *apyros,* without fire; *a* priv., and *pyr,* fire, and *typos,* a blow, impress, from *typein,* to strike.] printing type made with dies from cold metal, instead of by casting in molds.

ȧ·pȳ'rous (*or* ap'y-rous) *a.* [Gr. *apyros,* without fire; *a* priv., and *pyr,* fire.] incombustible, or able to sustain intense heat without alteration of form or properties.

aq'uȧ (ak'wȧ *or* ā'kwȧ), *n.* [L.] 1. water.

2. in pharmacy, liquid; solution, especially in water.

aqua ammoniae (or *ammonia*); a water solution of ammonia; ammonium hydroxide.

aqua pura; pure or distilled water.

aqua regia; a mixture of nitric and hydrochloric acids: so called (literally, kingly water) because it can dissolve gold and platinum.

aqua tofana; a liquid poison containing arsenic, prepared, in the seventeenth century, by an Italian woman named Tofana.

aq'uȧ·çāde, *n.* [*aqua,* and *-cade;* coined after *motorcade.*] an aquatic exhibition or entertainment consisting of swimming, diving, etc., often to music.

aq″uae·mȧ·nā'lē, aq″uȧ·mȧ·nā'lē, *n.* [L. *aquæmanalis,* a washbowl, *aqua,* water, and *manus,* hand.]

1. formerly, a basin in which the priest washed his hands before celebrating Mass.

2. a name applied to vessels of the ewer kind, formerly used in ancient Roman houses, and frequently made into grotesque forms representing a real or fabulous animal.

aq'uȧ fọr'tis, [L. strong water.]

1. nitric acid.

2. in art, an etching made by the use of nitric acid.

aq″uȧ·fọr'tist, *n.* an etcher who engraves by means of nitric acid.

aq'uȧ·green″, *n.* a bright yellowish-green color.

aq'uȧ·lung″, *n.* [*aqua* and *lung.*] a kind of self-contained underwater breathing apparatus (see **scuba**): a trade-mark (*Aqua-lung*).

aq″uȧ·mȧ·rīne', *n.* [L. *aqua marina,* sea water.]

1. a variety of beryl: so called because of its pale, bluish-green color.

2. a bluish-green color.

aq″uȧ·mȧ·rīne', *a.* bluish-green.

aq'uȧ nạut″, *n.* [*aqua* and astro*naut.*] a person trained to live and work in a watertight underwater chamber in and from which he can conduct oceanographic experiments.

aq'uȧ·plāne, *n.* [L. *aqua,* water, and *planus,* plane.] a board towed by a motorboat, on which one may ride over the water.

AQUAPLANE

aq'uȧ·plāne, *v.i.;* **aquaplaned,** *pt.,* *pp.* aquaplaning, *ppr.* to ride on an aquaplane.

aq'uȧ·punç″tūre, *n.* [L. *aqua,* water, and *punctura,* from *pungere,* to prick.] in medicine, the subcutaneous injection of water, as for the alleviation of pain.

aq·uȧ·relle' (ak-wȧ-rel'), *n.* [Fr., from It. *acquerella,* water color, from *acqua,* water; L. *aqua,* water.] the process of making pictures by means of transparent water colors; also, a picture made by this process.

aq·uȧ·rel'list, *n.* one who makes pictures in aquarelle.

ȧ·quā'ri·ăn, ȧ·quā'ri·ăl, *a.* relating to an aquarium or aquariums.

Ȧ·quā'ri·ăn, *n.* one of a sect of early Christians who substituted water for wine in the celebration of the Eucharist.

ȧ·quā'ri·um, *n.; pl.* **ȧ·quā'ri·umṣ** or **ȧ·quā'ri·ȧ,** [L., neut. of *aquarius,* pertaining to water, from *aqua,* water.] an artificial pond, tank, glass globe, etc. for the care and exhibition of living specimens of aquatic plants and animals; also, a building containing such collections.

Ȧ·quā'ri·us, *n.* [L., the water carrier, from *aqua,* water.]

1. a large central constellation, supposedly outlining a man pouring water from a container in his right hand.

2. the eleventh sign of the zodiac.

ȧ·quar'tẽr, *adv.* in navigation, in a course 45° abaft the beam; on the quarter.

ȧ·quat'iç, *a.* [L. *aquaticus,* from *aqua,* water.]

1. of or pertaining to water. [Rare.]

2. growing or living in or upon water; as, *aquatic* fowl, *aquatic* plants.

3. done in or upon the water; as, *aquatic* sports.

ȧ·quat'iç, *n.* an aquatic plant or animal.

ȧ·quat'içs, *n.pl.* the exercises and sports practiced in or upon water.

aq'uȧ·tile, *a.* and *n.* aquatic. [Rare.]

aq'uȧ·tint, aq·uȧ·tin'tȧ, *n.* [Fr. *aquatinte;* It. *acqua tinta,* dyed in water; *acqua,* from L. *aqua,* water, and *tinta,* from L. *tintus,* pp. of *tingere,* to dye, tinge.]

1. a method of etching by means of nitric acid, by which an effect is produced resembling a drawing in water colors or India ink.

2. an etching in the aquatint method.

aq'uȧ·tint, *v.t.* to etch in aquatint.

ȧ·quā'tion, *n.* [L. *aquatio, -onis,* watering.] a supplying with or putting in water. [Rare.]

ȧ·quat'ive·ness, *n.* a special interest in the water, particularly water sports.

aq'uȧ·tōne, *n.* 1. a process of photoengraving on a gelatin- and celluloid-coated, sensitized aluminum plate.

2. a print produced in aquatone.

ȧ quatre mains' (ȧ kȧ″tr' maṅ'), [Fr.] in music, a direction indicating a composition for a keyboard instrument, as a piano, is to be played with four hands, that is, as a duet.

aq′uȧ vī′tae, [L., water of life.] formerly, alcohol; hence, brandy or other strong liquor.

aq′uē·duct, *n.* [OFr. *aqueduct*; L. *aquæductus*, a conveyance of water; *aquæ*, genit. of *aqua*, water, and *ductus*, a channel, leading, from *ducere*, to lead.]

1. a large pipe, conduit, canal, or other channel, open or enclosed, for conveying water, especially one for conveying the water supply of a city.

2. an ancient structure raised on one or more series of arches and supporting one or more channels for water, built on a slightly descending plane.

3. a structure, somewhat similar to the ancient aqueducts, for conveying a water channel or conduit over a river or hollow: called also an *aqueduct bridge*.

4. in anatomy, a passage or canal.

ā″quē·ō·ig′ne·ous, *a.* [L. *aqua*, water, and *igneus*, from *ignis*, fire.] in geology, pertaining to or formed by the joint effect of water and heat; as, *aqueoigneous* rocks.

ā′quē·ous, *a.* [L. *aquosus*, watery, from *aqua*, water.]

1. watery; of the nature of water; of water.

2. made with water; as, an *aqueous* solution.

3. formed by the action of water; sedimentary; as, *aqueous* rocks.

4. of the aqueous humor.

aqueous extract; an extract obtained by evaporating an aqueous solution of a vegetable substance.

aqueous humor; a transparent fluid occupying the space between the crystalline lens and the cornea of the eye.

aqueous lava; a kind of muddy lava formed during or after the eruption of a volcano by the mixture of volcanic ashes with the water formed by the condensation of cooling volcanic vapors.

aqueous tint; in painting, a very light, almost colorless, tint.

ā′quē·ous·ness, *n.* the quality of being watery; wateriness.

aq·ui·cul′tūr·ăl, *a.* pertaining to aquiculture.

aq′ui·cul·tūre, *n.* [Fr. *aquiculture*, from L. *aqua*, water, and *cultura*, from *colere*, to cultivate.] the cultivation of things that live in water.

aq′ui·fẽr, *n.* [from *aqui*, and *-fer*.] any water-bearing rock or stratum.

ā·quif′ẽr·ous, *a.* [L. *aqua*, water, and *ferre*, to bear.] conducting or containing water or watery fluid; as, the *aquiferous* system of the sponges.

Aq″ui·fō″li·ā′cē·ae, *n.pl.* [L. *aquifolium*, the holly, from *acus*, needle, and *folium*, leaf.] in botany, an old name for the holly family.

aq″ui·fō″li·ā′ceous, *a.* of or pertaining to the *Aquifoliaceae*.

aq′ui·form, *a.* [L. *aqua*, water, and *forma*, form.] in the form of water; like water; liquid.

Aq′ui·lȧ, *n.* [L., eagle.]

1. in ornithology, a genus of raptorial birds containing the true eagles.

2. in astronomy, a northern constellation in the Milky Way, containing about eighty stars that range from first to sixth magnitude and supposedly outlining an eagle.

Aq·ui·lā′ri·ȧ, *n.* [L. *aquila*, eagle.] a typical genus of evergreen trees belonging to the family *Thymelæaceæ*, found in eastern parts of Asia and the Malay group, and having tough bark, alternate leaves, and pear-shaped fruit in a valved capsule.

aq′ui·lā·ted, *a.* in heraldry, ornamented with eagles' heads.

Aq·ui·lē′ġi·ȧ, *n.* [L. *aquila*, eagle.] in botany, a genus of perennial plants of the crowfoot family (*Ranunculaceæ*), found in the north temperate zone, and characterized by showy flowers with five-spurred petals: called also *columbines*.

aq′ui·līne (*or* -lin), *a.*[L. *aquilinus*, from *aquila*, eagle.]

1. of, like, or belonging to the eagle.

2. like an eagle's: said especially of a curved or hooked nose.

Aq′ui·lon, *n.* [Fr. *aquilon*; L. *aquilo*, the north wind.] the north wind. [Obs.]

ȧ·quip′ȧ·rous, *a.* [L. *aqua*, water, and *parere*, to yield.] in physiology, secreting a watery substance, as certain glands.

Aq·ui·tā′ni·ăn, *a.* pertaining to Aquitania, afterward called Gascony, one of the divisions of Gaul: according to Caesar, it lay between the Garonne River, the Pyrenees, and the ocean.

ȧ·quiv′ẽr, *a.* agitated; tremulous; quivering.

ȧ·quiv′ẽr, *adv.* in an agitated manner; quiveringly.

ā quō, [L.] from which: opposed to *ad quem*.

aq″uō·cap·sū·lī′tis, *n.* [L., *aqua*, water, *capsula*, box, and *-itis*.] in medicine, watery inflammation of the iris of the eye.

ā·quom′e·tẽr, *n.* [L. *aqua*, water, and *metrum*, Gr. *metron*, a measure.] a device in the form of a pump acting both by steam and vacuum, for lifting and forcing water.

ā′quōse, *a.* watery. [Rare.]

ȧ·quos′i·ty, *n.* the state of being watery; moistness.

aq′uū·lȧ (ak′wū-lȧ), *n.* [L., a little stream, dim. of *aqua*, water.]

1. in anatomy, a small collection of watery matter.

2. the crystalline lens of the eye.

är, *conj.* ere; before. [Obs.]

är, *n.* an are (unit of measure).

ar-, ad-: used before *r*, as in *ar*rest.

-ar, [ME. *-er*; OFr. *-er*, *-ier*, *-air*; Fr. *-aire*; L. *-aris*.]

1. a combining form signifying *pertaining to* or *like*, as in singul*ar*, regul*ar*.

2. a variation of *-ary* or *-er*, denoting agency, as in vic*ar*, schol*ar*.

Ā′rȧ, *n.* [L.] in astronomy, the constellation Altar, south of the Scorpion.

Ä′rȧ, *n.* [native Braz. name.] in ornithology, a genus of South American macaws.

Ar′ăb, *n.* [L. *Arabs*; Gr. *Araps*, Ar. *'Arab*, Heb. *arabah*, a desert.]

1. a native or inhabitant of Arabia, or a member of the Arabic division of the Semitic peoples.

2. any of a breed of swift, graceful horses native to Arabia.

3. a waif of the streets; street Arab.

Ar′ăb, *a.* of or pertaining to the Arabs or Arabia; as, an *Arab* steed.

ä·rä′bä, *n.* [Bulg. *araba*; Hind. and Per. *arāba*; Turk. and Ar. *'arabah*, a cart.] a wheeled carriage used in the Near East: called also *aroba*.

ar′ȧ·bä, *n.* same as *araguato*.

ar·ȧ·bä′tȧ, *n.* same as *araguato*.

ar·ȧ·besque′ (-besk′), *a.* [Fr. *arabesque*; It. *arabesco*; Port. *arabesco*, from *Arabo*, an Arab.]

1. Arabian. [Rare.]

2. relating to or exhibiting arabesques (the ornamentations).

ar·ȧ·besque′, *n.* 1. a complex and elaborate design of intertwined flowers, foliage, geometrical patterns, etc. painted or carved in low relief.

2. in ballet dancing, a position in which one leg is extended straight backward and the arms are extended, one forward and one backward.

3. in music, a short, brilliant composition in rondo form.

ARABESQUE

ar·ȧ·besqued′ (-beskt′), *a.* ornamented in arabesque.

ar·ȧ·besque′ly, *adv.* in the manner of arabesque ornamentation.

Ȧ·rā′bi·ăn, *a.* pertaining to Arabia or the Arabs.

Ȧ·rā′bi·ăn, *n.* 1. a native or inhabitant of Arabia; an Arab.

2. any of a breed of swift, graceful horses native to Arabia.

Ȧ·rā′bi·ăn Nīghts, a collection of ancient stories from Arabia, India, Persia, etc.: also called *The Arabian Nights' Entertainment*, or *The Thousand and One Nights*.

Ar′ȧ·biç, *a.* 1. of Arabia.

2. of the Arabs, their language, culture, etc.

3. [a–] designating the gum (*gum arabic*) obtained from certain kinds of acacia.

4. [a–] designating an acid found in gum arabic.

Ar′ȧ·biç, *n.* the Semitic language of the Arabs, used in Arabia, Syria, Trans-Jordan, Iraq, northern Africa, etc. It is the language of the Koran.

Ȧ·rab′iç·ăl, *a.* Arabic. [Obs.]

Ȧ·rab′iç·ăl·ly, *adv.* in an Arabic or Arabian manner. [Obs.]

Ȧ·rab′i·cī, *n.pl.* in church history, a Christian sect of the third century whose members asserted that the body and soul are equally affected by death and resurrection.

Ar′ȧ·biç nū·mẽr·ăls, the figures 1, 2, 3, 4, 5, 6, 7, 8, 9, and 0 (zero).

ar·ȧ·bil′i·ty, *n.* the state of being arable.

ar′ȧ·bin, *n.* in chemistry, a white, soluble substance, the principal constituent of gum arabic.

ȧ·rab′i·nōse, *n.* [*arabic*, and *-in*, and *-ose*.] a pentose sugar, $C_5H_{10}O_5$, obtained especially from certain vegetable gums.

ȧ·rab·i·nō′siç, *a.* pertaining to arabinose.

Ar′ȧ·bis, *n.* [Mod. L., from Gr. *Arabis*, Arabian, from *Arabia*, Arabia.] in botany, a genus of plants of the cruciferous order, found in the north temperate regions of both hemispheres, and having clusters of purple or white flowers: called also *rock cress*.

Ar′ȧ·bism, *n.* an Arabic idiom or peculiarity of language.

Ar′ȧ·bist, *n.* one versed in the Arabic language or literature.

ar′ȧ·ble, *a.* [Fr. *arable*; L. *arabilis*, from *arare*, to plow.] fit for plowing or tillage; cultivable; as, *arable* land.

ar′ȧ·ble, *n.* land suitable for tillage.

Ar′ȧ·by, *n.* Arabia. [Archaic or Poetic.]

Ar″ȧ·çȧ·nēșe′, *a.* and *n.* Arakanese.

ä·rä·çä′rī, *n.* [Port. *aracari*, from the native name.] any of various species of birds of the genus *Pteroglossus*, included in the *Ramphastidæ* or toucan family, but differing from the typical toucans by a smaller bill and smaller size. They are native to the warm parts of South America.

ȧ·rāce′, *v.t.* [ME. *aracen*; OFr. *aracier*, *arachier*, from L. *exradicare*, *eradicare*, to root out; *ex*, out, and *radicare*, from *radix*, *radicis*, root.] to tear up by the roots. [Obs.]

A·rā′cē·ae, *n.pl.* [Mod. L., from *arum*; Gr. *aron*, the wake robin, and *-aceæ*.] a natural order of monocotyledonous plants, having the genus *Arum* as the type. The species are herbaceous, with leaves sheathing at the base; the flowers are unisexual and without a perianth, on a spadix protected, when young, by a spathe; the anthers are nearly sessile, and the fruit succulent. Most of the species have starchy tuberous roots, variously used as a food.

ȧ·rā′ceous, *a.* pertaining to the natural order of plants *Araceae*.

Ar′ȧ·çhis, *n.* [Mod. L., from Gr. *arakis*, name of a plant.] a genus of leguminous food plants much cultivated in warm climates: when the flower falls, the stalk supporting the ovaries lengthens, and, bending downward, pushes the fruit into the ground, where it begins to enlarge and ripen. The best-known species is *Arachis hypogæa*, the common peanut.

ar·ach·nac′tis, *n.* [Mod. L., from Gr. *arachnē*, spider, and *aktis*, ray.] the free-swimming young of certain sea anemones.

Ȧ·rach′nē, *n.* [L.; Gr. *arachnē*, from *arachnē*, spider.] in Greek mythology, a girl turned into a spider by Athena for challenging the goddess to a weaving contest.

ar·ach·nē′ăn, *a.* [Gr. *arachnē*, a spider.] weblike; filmy; gossamery.

ȧ·rach′nid, *n.* any of a large group of arthropods with four pairs of legs, lunglike sacs or breathing tubes, and a body usually divided into two segments: spiders, scorpions, and mites are arachnids.

Ȧ·rach′ni·dȧ, *n.pl.* [Mod. L., from Gr. *arachnē*, spider.] the class of arthropods comprising the arachnids.

ȧ·rach′ni·dăn, *a.* pertaining to the *Arachnida*.

ȧ·rach′ni·dăn, *n.* one of the *Arachnida*; arachnid.

ar·ach·nid′i·ȧ, *n.*; pl. of *arachnidium*.

ar·ach·nid′i·ăl, *a.* relating to the arachnidium.

ar·ach·nid′i·um, *n.*; *pl.* **ar·ach·nid′i·ȧ,** the gland of a spider having for its function the secretion of a sticky, semifluid substance spun into the web.

ar·ach·nī′tis, *n.* inflammation of the arachnoid membrane.

ȧ·rach′noid, *a.* 1. like a cobweb; filmy; gossamery.

2. in botany, covered with or consisting of soft fibers or hairs, so as to appear like a cobweb.

3. in zoology, relating to the *Arachnida*.

4. in anatomy, of or pertaining to the arachnoid membrane.

arachnoid membrane; a very thin and delicate semitransparent membrane spread over the brain and the spinal cord between the *dura mater* and *pia mater*.

ȧ·rach′noid, *n.* 1. in zoology, one of the class *Arachnida*.

2. in anatomy, the arachnoid membrane.

ar·ach·noid′ăl, *a.* arachnoid.

Ar·ach·noid'ē·à, *n.pl.* the *Arachnida.* [Obs.]

à·rach·nō·loġ'iç·ăl, *a.* relating to arachnology.

ar·ach·nol'ō·ġist, *n.* a specialist in arachnology.

ar·ach·nol'ō·ġy, *n.* [Gr. *arachnē*, spider, and *logia*, from *legein*, to speak.] the science of spiders and other *Arachnida.*

ar·ach·noph'à·gous, *a.* [Gr. *arachnē*, spider, and *phagein*, to eat.] in zoology, preying upon arachnids.

ā·rae·om'e·tēr, *n.* an areometer.

ā·rae'ō·style, *a.* and *n.* same as *areostyle.*

ā·rae·ō·sys'tȳle, *a.* and *n.* same as *areosystyle.*

Ar"à·gō·nēşe', *n.*; *pl.* **Ar"à·gō·nēşe',** 1. a native or inhabitant of Aragon, in Spain.

2. the Spanish dialect spoken in Aragon.

Ar"à·gō·nēşe', *a.* relating to Aragon, its people, language, etc.

à·rag'ō·nīte, *n.* [from *Aragon*, in Spain, and *-ite.*] a mineral made up of calcium carbonate in orthorhombic crystals, with less distinct cleavage and greater density than calcite.

är·ä·guä'tō (-gwä'tō), *n.* [S. Am.] a species of monkey found in South America; the ursine howler, *Mycetes ursinus*: also called *araba*, etc.

à·rāişe', *v.t.* to raise. [Obs.]

ar'ak, *n.* arrack. [Obs.]

Ar"ä·kà·nēşe', *n.*; *pl.* **Ar"ä·kà·nēşe',** 1. a native or an inhabitant of Arakan, a province of Burma.

2. the language spoken by the Arakanese.

Ar"ä·kà·nēşe', *a.* of Arakan or the Arakanese language.

À·rā'li·à, *n.* [origin unknown.]

1. a genus of plants, the type of the order *Araliacæ*, eight species of which are found in North America.

2. [a–] any plant of this genus.

À·rā·li·ā'cē·ae, *n.pl.* an order of plants, indigenous to warm climates, akin to the *Umbelliferæ*, but of a more shrubby character. The ginseng and the English ivy are two well-known families of this order.

à·rā·li·ā'ceous, *a.* [from *Aralia*, and *-aceous.*] belonging to the *Araliaceæ*, the plants of which are usually woody and have flat clusters of small, white or greenish flowers and, often, fragrant leaves.

Ar·à·maē'ăn, Ar·à·mē'ăn, *n.* 1. any member of an ancient people who lived in Syria (Aram) and Mesopotamia.

2. their language, Aramaic.

Ar·à·maē'ăn, Ar·à·mē'ăn, *a.* 1. of the Aramaeans.

2. of their language.

Ar·à·mā'iç, *a.* [Gr. *Aramaia*, f. of *Aramaios*, from Heb. *'Arām*, a name given to Syria, and Mesopotamia.]

1. of or pertaining to Aram, or ancient Syria.

2. of the Aramaic language.

Ar·à·mā'iç, *n.* a group of northwest Semitic languages spoken in Biblical times, including the language used in Palestine after the captivity, and spoken by Jesus and his disciples.

Ar·à·mā'işm, *n.* an idiom of the Aramaic language.

Ar·à·nē'i·dà, *n.pl.* [Mod. L., from L. *aranea*, spider.] an order of *Arachnida*, including the spiders. They have the abdomen unsegmented and connected with the thorax by a narrow peduncle. They breathe by means of pulmonary sacs and two stigmata connected with tracheae, and have from four to six spinnerets for making the silken threads from which their webs are spun.

ar·à·nē'i·dăn, *a.* relating to the Araneida, especially to the spiders.

ar·à·nē'i·dăn, *n.* one of the *Araneida.*

ar·à·nē'i·fọrm, *a.* [L. *aranea*, spider, and *forma*, form.] having the shape of a spider.

À·rà·nē·ī'nà, *n.pl.* same as *Araneida.*

Ar·à·nē·oid'e·à, *n.pl.* same as *Araneida.*

à·rā'nē·ōse, à·rā'nē·ous, *a.* [L. *araneosus*, full of or like spider's web, from *aranea*, spider.] resembling the web of a spider; arachnoid.

à·ran'gō, *n.*; *pl.* **à·ran'gōeş,** [native name.] a rough bead made of carnelian, imported from Bombay and used extensively by slave traders in the days of the African slave trade.

À·rap'à·hō, *n.*; *pl.* **À·rap'à·hō** or **À·rap'à·hōeş,** any member of a tribe of Algonquian Indians who lived in the area of the upper Platte and Arkansas Rivers: also spelled *Arapahoe.*

à·rä·paī'mà, *n.* [native name.] one of the largest fresh-water food fishes, found in South America. It frequently measures fifteen feet in length, and sometimes weighs more than 400 pounds.

Ar·à·pun'gà, *n.* [S. Am. native name.] a genus of South American dentirostral insessorial birds, the chatterers, including the white bellbird, or campanero, *Arapunga alba*, remarkable for its clear, far-sounding, bell-like notes and for its peculiar, comblike protuberance which formerly was supposed to have erectile powers and was believed to cause, or contribute to, the bell-like quality of the bird's note by becoming erect; also, a similar species of Australia and New Zealand.

à·rä'rà, *n.* 1. the black macaw.

2. the palm cockatoo of Australia.

ar·à·rō'bà, *n.* [Port., from Braz. native name.]

1. a bitter, yellow powder used in medicine: also called *Goa powder.*

2. the Brazilian tree yielding this powder: it has striped wood.

à·rā'tion, *n.* tillage. [Rare.]

ar'à·tō·ry, *a.* [L. *aratorius*, from *arator*, a plower, from *arare*, to plow.] pertaining to tillage. [Rare.]

A·rau'căn, *n.* 1. the language of the Araucanians.

2. an Araucanian.

Ar·au·cā'ni·ăn, *a.* 1. of the Araucanians.

2. of their language.

Ar·au·cā'ni·ăn, *n.* a member of a linguistic stock of South American Indians of Chile and the Argentine pampas.

Ar·au·cā'ri·à, *n.* [Mod. L., from the *Araucano*, a tribe of Indians in the southern parts of Chile.] a genus of *Coniferæ*, found in South America and Australasia, consisting of large evergreen trees with verticillate spreading branches bearing large cones, each scale having a single large seed.

ar·au·cā'ri·ăn, *a.* pertaining to the *Araucaria.*

ar·au·cā'ri·ăn, *n.* any tree of the genus *Araucaria.*

Ä'rä·wäk, *n.* a member of any branch of the Arawakan Indians.

Ä·rä·wä'kăn, *a.* of a large linguistic family of South American Indian tribes north of the Amazon.

är'bà·lest, är'bà·list, *n.* [ME. *arbaleste*; Port. *arbalesta*, from L. *arcuballista*; *arcus*, bow, and *ballista*, an engine for hurling projectiles; from Gr. *ballein*, to throw.] a crossbow, very common in Europe during the middle ages, consisting of a steel bow set crosswise in a shaft of wood, furnished with a string and a trigger, and bent by a crank windlass. It propelled arrows, balls, or stones.

är'bà·lest·ẽr, är'bà·list·ẽr, *n.* [ME. *arbalester*; OFr. *arbalestier*; L. *arcubalistarius*, one who uses an arcubalist.] a crossbowman. [Obs.]

är'bi·tẽr, *n.* [L. *arbiter*, a witness, judge, from *ar-*, *ad*, to, and *bitere*, *betere*, to come or go.]

1. a person selected to decide a controversy; an arbitrator.

2. one who is fully authorized to judge or decide.

Syn.—adjudicator, arbitrator, umpire, referee, judge.

är'bi·trà·ble, *a.* 1. arbitrary; depending on the will. [Obs.]

2. subject to arbitration.

är'bi·trāġe, *n.* [Fr. *arbitrage*, from *arbitrer*; L. *arbitrari*, to give a decision, from *arbiter*, a witness, judge.]

1. arbitration.

2. a buying of bills of exchange, stocks, etc. in one market and selling them again at a higher price in another market.

är'bi·trăl, *a.* relating to arbiters or arbitration.

är·bit'rà·ment, *n.* 1. arbitration.

2. the final decision of an arbitrator.

3. the power to make an absolute and final decision; as, the *arbitrament* of war.

4. the verdict or award of arbitrators.

är'bi·trā·ri·ly, *adv.* in an arbitrary manner.

är'bi·trā·ri·ness, *n.* the quality or condition of being arbitrary.

är·bi·trā'ri·ous, *a.* arbitrary; despotic. [Obs.]

är·bi·trā'ri·ous·ly, *adv.* arbitrarily. [Obs.]

är'bi·trā·ry, *a.* [L. *arbitrarius*, from *arbiter*, a witness, judge.]

1. not governed by principle; depending on volition; based on one's preference, notion, or whim.

2. capricious.

3. tyrannical; despotic.

> *Arbitrary* power is most easily established on the ruins of liberty abused to licentiousness. —Washington.

4. in law, left to the discretion or judgment of the court; not fixed; not determined by statute; as, *arbitrary* fines.

Syn.—tyrannical, imperious, unlimited, capricious, absolute, positive, despotic, peremptory, tyrannous.

är'bi·trāte, *v.t.*; arbitrated, *pt.*, *pp.*; arbitrating, *ppr.* [L. *arbitratus*, pp. of *arbitrari*, to see, give a decision, from *arbiter*, a witness, judge.]

1. to hear and decide (a dispute) as arbitrator.

2. to decide or determine by arbitration; to give to an arbitrator to decide.

Syn.—settle, adjust, decide, determine, adjudicate.

är'bi·trāte, *v.i.* 1. to submit a dispute to arbitration.

2. to act as arbitrator (*in* a dispute, *between* persons).

är·bi·trā'tion, *n.* an arbitrating or being arbitrated; settlement of a dispute by a person or persons chosen to hear both sides and come to a decision.

a board of *arbitration* usually consists of an odd number of persons chosen equally by the opposing sides, excepting the *umpire* or odd man, who is the choice of the arbitrators before chosen. An award in writing, signed by a majority of the board, is usually binding.

arbitration bond; a bond which is generally entered into by parties wishing to submit their differences to arbitration. It binds them to acquiesce in the award given.

arbitration of exchange; the fixing of the ratio of exchange of the moneys of two countries; also, the changing of money of one country to that of another.

är'bi·trā·tŏr, *n.* [L. *arbitrator*, from *arbitrari*, to see, give judgment, from *arbiter*, a witness, judge.]

1. a person who is chosen by agreement of parties in a controversy, to settle the dispute, or one of two or more persons so chosen.

2. an arbiter; one who is fully authorized to judge or decide.

Syn.—arbiter, judge, umpire.

är'bi·trā·trix, *n.* a woman arbitrator.

är'bi·tress, *n.* a woman arbiter.

är'blȧst, *n.* same as *arbalest.*

är'bŏr, *n.* [ME. *erber*, *herber*; OFr. *erbier*, *herbier*; from L. *herbarium*, a place covered with grass or herbage, from *herba*, grass, an herb.]

1. a place shaded by trees, shrubs, or vines; a frame of latticework, covered with vines, or other plants, for shade; a bower.

2. a plot of grass; garden; orchard. [Obs.]

är'bŏr, *n.*; *pl.* **är'bō·rēş,** [L., a tree, a beam.]

1. in botany, a tree, as distinguished from an shrub.

2. a family tree.

3. *pl.* **är'bŏrş,** in metal casting, the beam or bar in the center of an interior mold or core.

Arbor Day; in many States of the United States, a day appointed by law for the planting of trees, as by the pupils of the public schools, to foster interest in the preservation of forests.

är'bŏr, *n.* [Fr. *arbre*, tree, axis, from L. *arbor*, tree, beam.] in mechanics: (a) a shaft; beam; (b) a spindle; axle; (c) a bar that holds cutting tools.

är'bŏr, *v.t.* to set in an arbor (bar, shaft, etc.).

är·bō·rā'ceous, *a.* [*arbor* (tree), and *-aceous.*]

1. like a tree; treelike.

2. full of trees; wooded.

är'bō·rā·ry, *a.* [L. *arborarius*, from *arbor*, a tree.] arboreal.

är'bō·rā·tŏr, *n.* one who plants or prunes trees. [Obs.]

är·bō'rē·ăl, *a.* 1. pertaining to or like a tree.

2. living in or adapted for living in trees; pertaining to life in woods or among trees; as, *arboreal* animals; *arboreal* pursuits.

är'bŏred, *a.* 1. having an arbor, or bower; as, an *arbored* garden.

2. having trees on both sides or around it.

är·bō'rē·ous, *a.* [L. *arboreus*, from *arbor*, a tree.]

1. arboreal.

2. full of trees; wooded.

3. arborescent.

är·bō·res'cence, *n.* [L. *arborescens*, ppr. of *arborescere*, to become a tree, from *arbor*, a tree.] the state of having the shape or form of a tree; resemblance to a tree, as in minerals.

är·bō·res'cent, *a.* treelike in shape or growth; branching.

är'bō·ret, *n.* [It. *arboreto*, from L. *arbor*, a tree.]

1. a small tree or shrub.

2 a place planted or overgrown with trees. [Obs.]

är·bō·rē'tum, *n.*; *pl.* **är·bō·rē'tumş** or **är·bō·rē'tà,** [L., a place grown with trees, from *arbor*, a tree.]

1. a place where many kinds of trees and shrubs are grown; a botanical or tree garden cultivated for scientific purposes.
2. a wooded public park.

är·bor′i·çōle, *a.* [Fr. *arboricole,* from L. *arbor,* a tree, and *colere,* to dwell, inhabit.] inhabiting trees, as birds of various kinds. [Rare.]

är″bō·ri·çul′tūr·ăl, *a.* relating to arboriculture.

är′bō·ri·çul″tūre, *n.* [Fr. *arboriculture,* from L. *arbor,* tree, and *cultura,* culture.] the scientific cultivation of trees and shrubs.

är″bō·ri·çul′tūr·ist, *n.* one who cultivates trees.

är′bō·ri·form, *a.* having the form of a tree.

är′bŏr·ist, *n.* a specialist in the planting and maintenance of trees.

är″bŏr·i·zā′tion, *n.* 1. the shape or form of a tree or plant, as in minerals or fossils.
2. the formation of such an arrangement.

är′bŏr·ous, *a.* of or consisting of trees.

är′bŏr vī′tae, *n.* [L., tree of life.]
1. any of a number of related trees of the pine family, having soft, fragrant, scalelike leaves; thuja.
2. in anatomy, the treelike structure of the white substance in a longitudinal section of the cerebellum.
Also, especially in sense 2, *arbor vitae.*

är′bŏur, *n.* an arbor (bower): British spelling.

är·bō·vī′rus, *n.* [*ar*thropod, and *bo*rne, and *virus.*] any of a group of viruses, including those that cause yellow fever and viral encephalitis, which are transmitted to man by certain blood-sucking arthropods, especially mosquitos and ticks.

är′bus·cle (-bus-sl), *n.* [L. *arbusculus,* a little tree, dim. of *arbor,* tree.] a dwarf tree, or one in size between a shrub and a tree.

är·bus′çū·lăr, *a.* resembling a shrub; having the shape of a small tree.

är·bus′çūle, *n.* in zoology, a tuft of small, vibratory swimming organs, or hairlike processes; a gill with fine branches.

är′būte, *n.* the arbutus. [Archaic.]

är·bū′tus, *n.* [L. *arbutus,* the wild strawberry tree.]
1. any plant of the genus *Arbutus.*
2. [A–] a genus of evergreen plants belonging to the natural order *Ericaceæ.* It has panicles of large, pale greenish-white flowers, red fruit, and evergreen leaves.
3. the trailing arbutus.
trailing arbutus; a creeping or trailing plant, *Epigæa repens,* with rose-colored blossoms, found chiefly in New England in the spring; the Mayflower, or ground laurel.

ärç, *n.* [Fr. *arc,* from L. *arcus,* a bow, arch.]
1. a bowlike curved line or object.
2. in astronomy, (a) the apparent curved path of a star or planet; (b) the angular measurement of this.
3. in electricity, the band of sparks or incandescent light between two closely placed electrodes when a current leaps the gap from one to the other.
4. in geometry, a part of a curved line, as of a circle.

ärç, *v.i.*; arced *or* arcked (ärçt), *pt., pp.*; arcing *or* arcking, *ppr.* 1. to move in a curved course.
2. in electricity, to form an arc.

är′çȧ, *n.*; *pl.* **är′çae,** [L., a box or coffin.]
1. in the early church, (a) a chest for receiving alms; (b) a box or casket in which the eucharist was carried; (c) a reliquary.
2. [A–] a genus of lamellibranch mollusks, typical of the family *Arcidæ*; the ark shells.

är·çāde′, *n.* [Fr. *arcade*; It. *arcata,* an arcade, from L. *arcata,* from *arcus,* a bow, arch.]
1. in architecture, (a) a series of arches on pillars: used as the screen and roof support of an ambulatory or walk, but in the architecture of the middle ages ornamentally applied to a wall; (b) an arched building.
2. an arched opening in a wall. [Obs.]
3. a passage having an arched roof.
4. any covered passageway, especially one with shops along the sides.
5. an avenue of trees.

är·çāde′, *v.t.*; arcaded, *pt., pp.*; arcading, *ppr.* to make into or provide with an arcade.

Är·çā′di·ȧ, *n.* [L. *Arcadia*; Gr. *Arkadia,* a district of Greece, whose people were noted for simplicity and contentment.] any place where rural simplicity and happiness prevail.

Är·çā′di·ăn, *a.* 1. pertaining to Arcadia.
2. rustic; pastoral; characterized by simplicity and contentment.

Är·çā′di·ăn, *n.* 1. a native or inhabitant of Arcadia.
2. a person of simple manners and tastes.

Är′çā·dy, *n.* Arcadia. [Poetic.]

är·çāne′, *a.* 1. hidden; secret.
2. understood by only a few; esoteric.

är·çā′num, *n.*; *pl.* **är·çā′nums** or **är·çā′nȧ,** [L. *arcanum,* neut. of *arcanus,* shut in, hidden; from *arcere,* to shut up; *arca,* a chest.]
1. secret or hidden knowledge.
2. a mystery; secret.
3. the great secret of nature which the alchemists sought.
4. a secret or mysterious remedy; elixir.

är′çȧ·tūre, *n.* [from ML. *arcata,* arcade; and *-ure.*] in architecture, (a) a small arcade; (b) a closed or false arcade, as for ornament.

ȧrc″-bōu″tänt′ (ȧr″bọọ″täṅ′), *n.*; *pl.* **ȧrcs″-bōu″tänts′** (ȧr″bọọ″täṅ′), [Fr.] in architecture, a flying buttress.

ärç fūr′nāce, an electric furnace in which the heat comes from an arc between an electrode and the material being heated.

ärch, *n.* [Fr. *arche*; L. *arcus,* a bow, an arc.]
1. an archway; any place covered by an arch; as, the *arch* of an arcade.
2. anything shaped like an arch.
3. the form of an arch.
4. in anatomy, an archlike part; as, the dental *arch, arch* of the foot, etc.

ARCH

a, abutments; *v,* voussoirs or archstones; *s,* springers; *p,* piers; *Ex,* extrados; *i,* impost; *In,* intrados; *k,* keystone

5. in mining, a piece of ground left unworked near a shaft.
6. in geometry, an arc. [Obs.]
7. in architecture, a curved structure, as of masonry, used as a support over an open space, as in a bridge, doorway, etc. The separate stones which compose the arch are called voussoirs, or archstones; the extreme, or lowest, voussoirs are termed springers, and the uppermost, or central, one is called the

OGEE EQUILATERAL

keystone. The under or concave side of the voussoirs is called the intrados, and the upper or convex side the extrados of the arch. When the curves of the intrados and extrados are concentric or parallel, the arch is said to be extradosed. The supports which afford resting and resisting points to the arch are called piers and abutments. The upper part of the

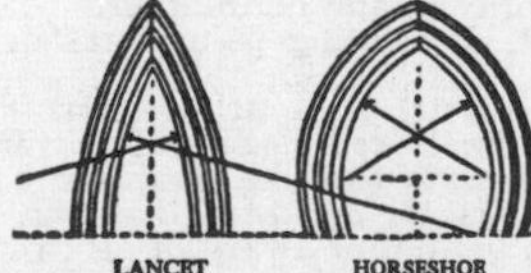

LANCET HORSESHOE

pier or abutment where the arch rests—technically, where it springs from—is the impost. The span of an arch is, in circular arches, the length of its chord; for the span is generally the width between the points of its opposite imposts whence it springs. The rise of an arch is the height of the highest point of its intrados above the line of the impost; this point is sometimes called the under side of the crown, the highest point of the extrados being the crown. Arches are designated in two ways; first, in a general manner, according to their properties, their uses, their position in a building, or their exclusive employment in a particular style of architecture. Thus, there are arches of equilibration, equipollent arches, arches of discharge, skew and reversed arches, Roman, pointed, and Saracenic arches. Second, they are named specifically according to the curve the intrados assumes, when that curve is the section of any of the geometrical solids; as, segmental, semicircular, cycloidal, elliptical

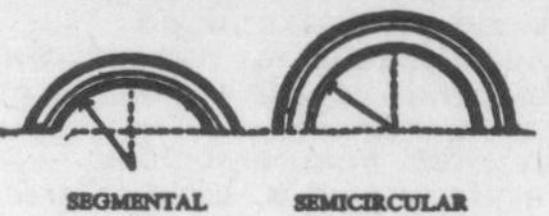

SEGMENTAL SEMICIRCULAR

parabolical, hyperbolical, or catenarian arches; or from the resemblance of the whole contour of the curve to some familiar object, as lancet arch and horseshoe arch; or from the method used in describing the curve, as equilateral,

CYCLOIDAL ELLIPTICAL

three-centered, four-centered, ogee, and the like. When any arch has one of its imposts higher than the other it is said to be rampant.
8. any similar structure, as a monument.
9. a fire chamber, as in a brick kiln and certain kinds of furnaces and ovens; also, the door of an ash pit.

ärch, *v.t.*; arched, *pt., pp.*; arching, *ppr.* 1. to provide with an arch or arches.
2. to cause to take the form of an arch.

ärch, *v.i.* 1. to make an arch or arches.
2. to span as an arch.

ärch, *a.* 1. cunning; sly; shrewd; clever; as, an *arch* villain.
2. pert; waggish; mischievous; mirthful; roguish; as, an *arch* look.
3. chief; of the first class; principal; as, an *arch* deed.

ärch, *n.* a chief. [Obs.]

ärch-, [L. *archi-, arch-*; Gr. *archi-, arch-,* from *archos,* a ruler, *archein,* to rule.] a prefix meaning *main, chief, principal*: used in forming titles of rank; as, *arch*duke, *arch*bishop.

-ärch, [Gr. *archos,* ruler, from *archein,* to rule.] a suffix signifying *ruler,* as in hept*arch.*

Är·çhae′ăn, *a.* [Gr. *archaios,* ancient, from *archē,* beginning.] Archean.

är′çhae·ō-, [Gr. *archaios,* ancient, from *archē,* the beginning, from *archein,* to be first.] a combining form signifying *ancient, original,* as in *archae*ology, *archaeo*zoic: sometimes spelled *archeo-.*

är·çhae·og′rȧ·phy, *n.* [*archæo-,* and Gr. *graphia,* from *graphein,* to write.] a treatise or writing on antiquity or antiques.

är″çhae·ō·lith′iç, *a.* [*archæo-,* and Gr. *lithikos,* from *lithos,* stone.] of, relating to, or designating, the earliest Stone Age.

är″çhae·ō·lō′ġi·ăn, *n.* see *archaeologist.*

är″çhae·ō·loġ′iç·ăl, är″çhae·ō·loġ′iç, *a.* pertaining to archaeology: also spelled *archeological, archeologic.*

är″çhae·ō·loġ′iç·ăl·ly, *adv.* in an archaeological manner.

är·çhae·ol′ō·ġist, *n.* a student of or specialist in archaeology: also spelled *archeologist.*

är·çhae·ol′ō·ġy, *n.* [*archæo-,* and Gr. *logia,* from *legein,* to speak.] the scientific study of the life and culture of ancient peoples, as by excavation of ancient cities, relics, artifacts, etc.: also spelled *archeology.*

är·çhae·op′te·ryx, *n.* [*archæo-,* and Gr. *pteryx,* wing.] one of a family of reptilelike birds of the Jurassic period which had teeth, a lizardlike tail, and well-developed wings.

är·çhae·os′tō·mȧ, *n.* [*archæo-,* and Gr. *stoma,* mouth.] a primitive or elementary blastopore.

Är″çhae·ō·stō′mȧ·tȧ, *n.pl.* [*archæo-,* and Gr. *stoma,* pl. *stomata,* mouth.] in zoology, a group of gastrular animals retaining an elementary mouth during life.

är″çhae·ō·stō·mȧ·tous (*or* -stom′ȧ-tous), *a.* of, relating to, or characteristic of, the *archaeostomata.*

är′çhae·ō·stōme, *n.* same as *archaeostoma.*

Är″çhae·ō·zō′iç, *a.* Archeozoic.

är·çhā′iç, *a.* [Gr. *archaikos,* from *archaios,* old, ancient.]
1. belonging to an earlier period; ancient.
2. antiquated; old-fashioned.
3. that has ceased to be used except in poetry, church ritual, etc.: as, *begat* is the *archaic* past tense of *beget.*

Syn.—ancient, antiquated, obsolescent, obsolete.—*Ancient* denotes merely age; *antiquated*, both age and a passing out of style; *obsolescent* or *archaic*, a passing out of use; *obsolete*, having passed out of use.

är·chā′iç·ăl, *a.* archaic. [Rare.]

är·chā′iç·ăl·ly, *adv.* 1. in an archaic manner.
2. as an archaism.

är′chā·iṣm, *n.* [Fr. *archaisme*, from Gr. *archaismos*, from *archaios*, ancient.]
1. the use or imitation of archaic words, technique, etc.
2. an archaic word, usage, technique, etc.

är′chā·ist, *n.* 1. a student of or expert in archaic things or antiquities.
2. a person who is fond of using archaisms.

är·chā·is′tiç, *a.* 1. using archaisms.
2. characterized by archaism.

är′chā·ize, *v.i.*; archaized (-īzd), *pt., pp.*; archaizing, *ppr.* to make archaistic or archaic.

är′chā·ize, *v.t.* to use archaisms.

ärch′ān″ġel, *n.* [L. *archangelus*; Gr. *archangelos*, chief angel, from *archos*, chief, first, and *angelos*, messenger, angel.]
1. an angel of the highest order; an angel occupying the eighth rank in the celestial hierarchy.
2. any of various labiate plants of different genera; also, the *Angelica archangelica*.

ärch′bish′ŏp, *n.* [ME. *archbisshop, archebiscop*; AS. *arcebiscop*; from L. *archiepiscopus*, from Gr. *archiepiskopos*, an archbishop; *archi*, chief, and *episkopos*, a bishop, overseer.] a chief bishop, who presides over an archbishopric or archdiocese.

ärch″bish′ŏp·riç, *n.* [ME. *archebischopriche*; AS. *arcebiscoprice*; *arcebiscop*, archbishop, and *rice*, jurisdiction.]
1. the office, rank, duties, or term of an archbishop.
2. the church district or province over which an archbishop has jurisdiction.

ärch brick, a brick shaped like a keystone, used in arches.

ärch′but′lẽr, *n.* the chief butler: an officer of the old German empire.

ärch′chām′bẽr·lain (-lin), *n.* the chief chamberlain: an officer of the old German empire whose office was similar to that of the great chamberlain of England.

ärch′chan′cel·lŏr, *n.* a chief chancellor: an officer in the old German empire who presided over the secretaries of the court.

ärch″chem′iç, *a.* of supreme chemical power. [Obs.]

ärch′dēa′çŏn, *n.* [AS. *arcediacon, archidiacon*; L. *archidiaconus*; Gr. *archidiakonos*; *archos*, chief, and *diakonos*, servant, minister.] a chief deacon; church official ranking just below a bishop or an archpriest: in the Anglican Church he has supervisory duties under the bishop.

ärch″dēa′çŏn·ry, *n.*; *pl.* **ärch″dēa′çŏn·rieṣ,**
1. the office, jurisdiction, rank, duties, etc. of an archdeacon.
2. the residence of an archdeacon.

ärch″dēa′çŏn·ship, *n.* the office of an archdeacon.

ärch′dī′ŏ·cēse, *n.* the diocese of an archbishop.

ärch″dū′çăl, *a.* pertaining to an archduke or archduchy.

ärch′duch′ess, *n.* the wife or widow of an archduke; a princess of the former royal family of Austria.

ärch′duch′y, *n.*; *pl.* **ärch″duch′ieṣ,** the territory of an archduke or archduchess.

ärch′dūke′, *n.* a prince of the former royal family of Austria; earlier, either (a) one of various European sovereigns, or (b) the emperor of Austria.

ärch″dūke′dŏm, *n.* an archduchy.

Är·chē′ăn, *a.* [Gr. *archaios*, ancient, from *archē*, a beginning.] in geology, designating or of the oldest known rocks.

är″chē·bī·ō′sis, *n.* [*arche-*, and Gr. *biōsis*, from *bios*, life.] spontaneous generation; abiogenesis.

ärched (ärcht), *a.* 1. made with an arch or curve; covered with an arch.
2. in the form of an arch; curved.

är′chē·gōne, *n.* an archegonium.

är·chē·gō′ni·ăl, *a.* of an archegonium.

är·chē·gō′ni·āte, *a.* having archegonia.

är·chē·gō′ni·um, *n.*; *pl.* **är·chē·gō′ni·ȧ,** [L., from Gr. *archegonos*, first of a race; *archē-*, first, and *gonos*, race.] in botany, the flasklike female organ of reproduction analogous to the pistil in the higher cryptogamous plants (mosses, ferns, etc.)

är·cheg′ō·ny, *n.* abiogenesis; archebiosis.

är·chel′ō·ġy, *n.* [Gr. *archē*, the beginning, and *logia*, from *legein*, to speak.] the science of first principles.

Är·chen·ceph′ȧ·lȧ, *n.pl.* [*archi-*, and Gr. *enkephalos*, the brain; *en*, in, and *kephalē*, head.] in zoology, a subfamily having a single genus, man.

ärch′en′e·my, *n.*; *pl.* **ärch′en′e·mieṣ,** a principal enemy.
the archenemy; Satan.

ärch·en·ter′iç, *a.* pertaining to an archenteron.

ärch·en′tẽr·on, *n.* [*arch-*, and Gr. *enteron*, intestine.] in zoology, the cavity at the center of an embryo in the gastrula stage of development, forming a primitive digestive tract.

ärch″ē·ō·log′iç·ăl, *a.* see *archaeological*.

ärch·ē·ol′ō·ġy, *n.* see *archaeology*.

ärch·ē·os′tō·mȧ, är′chē·ō·stōme, *n.* same as *archaeostoma*.

Ärch″ē·ō·zō′iç, *a.* [*archeo-*, and *zo-*, and *-ic*.] designating or of the earliest known geological era, characterized by thick lava flows, mountain formation, and microscopic plant and animal life.
the Archeozoic; the Archeozoic Era or its rocks.

ärch′ẽr, *n.* [Fr. *archer, archier*; L. *arcarius*, a bowman, from *arcus*, a bow.]
1. one who uses a bow; one who is skilled in the use of the bow and arrow; a bowman.
2. the archerfish.
3. [A–] the constellation Sagittarius.

ärch′ẽr·ess, *n.* a woman or girl archer.

ärch′ẽr·fish, *n.* the *Toxotes jaculator*, a scaly-finned, acanthopterygian fish, about six inches long, inhabiting the sea around Java: it shoots drops of water to a distance of three or four feet at insects, thereby causing them to fall into the water, where it seizes and devours them. The soft, and even the spiny, portions of its dorsal fins are so covered with scales as to be scarcely distinguishable from the rest of the body.

ARCHERFISH (*Toxotes iaculator*)

ärch′ẽr·ship, *n.* an archer's art or skill.

ärch′ẽr·y, *n.* 1. the use of the bow and arrow; the practice, art, or skill of archers; the act of shooting with a bow and arrow.
2. a number of archers; a company of bowmen.
3. an archer's bows, arrows, and other equipment.

ärch′eṣ, *n.*; pl. of *arch*.
Court of Arches; an English ecclesiastical court of appeal, the chief and most ancient consistory court, belonging to the archbishopric of Canterbury: so called from the church in London, known as *St. Mary le Bow* (*de arcubus*), where it was formerly held. The jurisdiction of this court extends over the province of Canterbury.

är′chē·spōre, *n.* the cell or cell group enclosing and productive of the mother cells of pollen or spores.

är′chē·tȳ·păl, *a.* original; constituting a model or pattern; pertaining to an archetype.
archetypal world; the world existing only in the mind of God, antedating the created world.

är′chē·tȳ·păl·ly, *adv.* originally.

är′chē·tȳpe, *n.* [Fr. *archétype*; L. *archetypum*; Gr. *archetypon*, from *archetypos*, stamped first; *archi-*, and *typos*, from *typtein*, to strike.]
1. the original pattern or model of a work; or the model from which all things of the same kind are made.
2. in coinage, the standard weight or coin by which others are adjusted.
3. in biology, the theoretical basic design from which any group of organisms may be said to have sprung.
4. in metaphysics, the idea or essence from which an existent thing has been copied, on the theory that material objects are only the embodiment of ideas.
5. a manuscript, usually no longer in existence, which has served as copy for other manuscripts.
6. in psychology, according to the theory of the psychologist Jung, an idea or way of thinking that has been inherited from the experience of the race and remains in the consciousness of the individual, influencing his perception of the world.

är·chē·typ′iç·ăl, *a.* archetypal.

ärch′fiēnd″, *n.* a chief fiend.
the archfiend; Satan.

är′chi-, [L. *archi-*; Gr. *archi-*, from *archos*, chief, *archein*, to be first, to rule.] a prefix signifying *chief*, *first*, or, in biology, *primitive*.

är″chi·am″phi·as′tẽr, *n.* [*archi-*, and Gr. *amphi*, about, and *astēr*, a star.] in biology, the initial amphiaster produced in an ovum at the time of polar cell expulsion.

Är″chi·an·nel′i·dȧ, *n.pl.* [*archi-*, and *Annelida*.] a small class of *Annelida* of a primitive type.

är′chi·ā·tẽr, *n.* [*archi-*, and Gr. *iatros*, physician.] chief physician: a term formerly applied to the chief physician of princes, and later to the leading physician of some cities.

är′chi·blast, *n.* [*archi-*, and Gr. *blastos*, germ.]
1. egg protoplasm.
2. the outer of the two layers of an embryo in an early stage of development.

är·chi·blas′tiç, *a.* 1. pertaining to the archiblast.
2. having complete and equal cleavage.

är·chi·blas′tū·lȧ, *n.* [*archi-*, and *blastula*, dim. of Gr. *blastos*, sprout.] a hollow, globular blastula.

är′chi·çärp, *n.* [*archi-*, and Gr. *karpos*, fruit.] in botany, the female reproductive organ in an ascomycetous fungus, giving rise to spore sacs (asci) after fertilization: also called *ascogonium*.

är″chi·dī·aç′ō·năl, *a.* 1. pertaining to an archdeacon; as, an *archidiaconal* visitation.
2. of an archdeaconry.

är″chi·ē·pis′çō·pȧ·cy, *n.* 1. the office of an archbishop. [Obs.]
2. church rule by archbishops.

är″chi·ē·pis′çō·păl, *a.* 1. of or pertaining to an archbishop; as, an *archiepiscopal* see.
2. of an archbishopric.

är″chi·ē·pis·çō·pal′i·ty, *n.* archiepiscopacy.

är″chi·ē·pis′çō·pāte, *n.* [*archi-*, and L. *episcopalus*, from *episcopus*; Gr. *episkopos*, a bishop, overseer.] an archbishopric; the tenure of office of an archbishop.

är·chī′e·rey, *n.* [*archi-*, and Gr. *hiereus*, a priest, from *hieros*, holy.] the higher order of the clergy of the Orthodox Eastern Churches, including the metropolitans, archbishops, and bishops.

är·chi·gas′trū·lȧ, *n.* [*archi-*, and L. *gastrula*, dim. of Gr. *gaster*, stomach.] in biology, a bell gastrula of an archiblastic ovum.

är′chil, *n.* [ME. *orchell*; OFr. *orchell*; It. *orchello*; Sp. *orchillo*.]
1. a lichen, especially the *Roccella tinctoria*, which grows on rocks in the Canary and Cape Verde Isles and yields rich dyestuffs and litmus; also spelled *orchal*, *orchil*.
2. a purple-red or violet dye made from this lichen.

ARCHIL (*Roccella tinctoria*)

Är·chi·lō′chi·ăn, *a.* pertaining to the Greek poet Archilochus, who was noted for the severity of his satire, or designating one of the metrical combinations which he first used.

ärch′i·lūte, *n.* same as *archlute*.

är′chi·māġe, är·chi·mā′gus, *n.* [L., from Gr. *archimagos*, chief of the magi; *archi-*, chief, and *magos*, one of the magi.]
1. the high priest of the Persian magi, or worshipers of fire.
2. a great magician or wizard.

är·chi·man′drīte, *n.* [L. *archimandrita*; Gr. *archimandritēs*; *archi-*, chief, and *mandra*, an enclosure, monastery.] in the Orthodox Eastern Church, a chief of a monastery, corresponding to abbot in the Roman Catholic Church; also, a superintendent of several monasteries, corresponding to a superior abbot, or father provincial, in the Roman Catholic Church.

Är″chi·mē·dē′ăn, *a.* pertaining to, or discovered or invented by, Archimedes, a Greek mathematician and physicist, or constructed on the principle of the Archimedean screw; as, an *Archimedean* propeller.
Archimedean screw, or *Archimedes' screw*; an instrument or device for raising water or loose material, as salt, cement, etc., from a lower to a higher level. It is said to have been

invented by Archimedes, and consists of a spiral conduit wound around an inclined axis or of a large screw in a cylinder. After the lower end has been dropped into the liquid or material to be raised, the screw is revolved and the substance rises to the upper level.

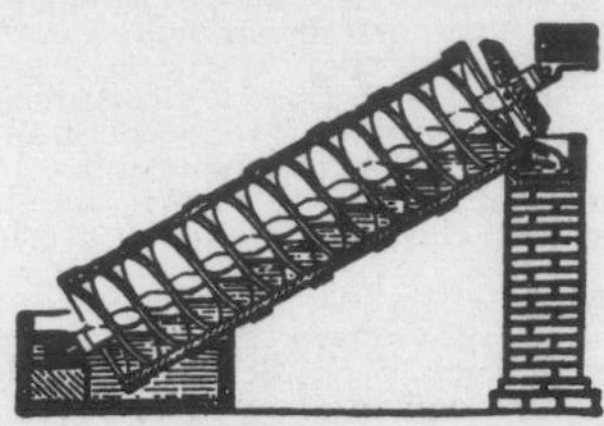

ARCHIMEDEAN SCREW

är·chïne′ (-shin), [Russ.] a Russian unit of linear measure equal to 28 inches: also spelled *arshin*.

är·chi·neph′riç, *a.* relating to the archinephron.

är·chi·neph′ron, *n.* [*archi-*, and Gr. *nephron*, kidney.] in embryology, the primitive kidney.

ärch′ing, *a.* [*pp.* of *arch.*] forming an arch.

ärch′ing, *n.* 1. the arched portion of a structure; any arched work.
2. a series of arches.
3. an archlike form; as, the *arching* of her eyebrows.

är″chi·pe·lag′iç, *a.* relating to, constituting, or resembling an archipelago.

är·chi·pel′a·gō, *n.*; *pl.* **är·chi·pel′a·gōes, är·chi·pel′a·gōs,** [It. *arcipelago*, from Gr. *archi-*, chief, and *pelagos*, sea.]
1. any large body of water studded with islands; also, the islands themselves; a group of islands.
2. [A–] the Grecian Archipelago, or Aegean Sea, abounding with islands and lying between Greece and Asia Minor.

är′chi·plasm, *n.* [*archi-*, and *-plasm.*]
1. the most primitive living matter.
2. archoplasm.

är″chip·te·ryg′i·um, *n.*; *pl.* **är″chip·te·ryg′i·a,** [L., from Gr. *archi-*, first, and *pterygion*, a wing, fin.] the primitive type of limb of the *Vertebrata*; the primitive form of fin.

är′chi·stōme, *n.* [*archi-*, and Gr. *stoma*, mouth.] in embryology, the primitive mouth of bilateral animals.

är′chi·tect, *n.* [L. *architectus*, from Gr. *architektōn*; *archi-*, chief, and *tektōn*, a worker.]
1. one skilled in the art of building; one who designs buildings, draws up plans, and generally supervises the construction.
2. any similar designer.
3. any builder or creator.

är·chi·tec′tive, *a.* used in building; proper for building.

är″chi·tec·ton′iç, är″chi·tec·ton′iç·al, *a.* 1. pertaining to an architect or architecture; having skill in designing or construction.
2. done as though by an architect; showing design.
3. controlling.
4. in logic, pertaining to the scientific arrangement or systematization of knowledge.

är″chi·tec·ton′iç, *n.* architectonics.

är″chi·tec·ton′içs, *n.pl.* [*construed as sing.*]
1. the science of architecture.
2. structural design; as, the *architectonics* of Beethoven's symphonies.
3. in philosophy, the science of systematizing knowledge.

är′chi·tec·tress, *n.* a woman architect.

är·chi·tec′tūr·al, *a.* 1. pertaining to or connected with the art of building.
2. having the qualities of architecture.

är·chi·tec′tūr·al·ly, *adv.* 1. in an architectural manner.
2. from the standpoint of architecture.

är′chi·tec·tūre, *n.* [Fr. *architecture*; L. *architectura*, from *architectus*; Gr. *architektōn*, a chief worker, master builder; *archi-*, chief, and *tektōn*, worker.]
1. the art, profession, or science of designing and constructing buildings.
2. construction; structure; workmanship; as, the *architecture* of that house is defective.
3. a system or style of building, having certain characteristics of structure, decoration, etc.; as, Gothic *architecture*; ecclesiastical *architecture*.
4. architectural productions collectively; as, ancient *architecture*.
5. any framework, system, etc.
military architecture; the art of fortification.
naval architecture; the art of building warships.
marine architecture; shipbuilding of all kinds.

Är·chi·teū′this, *n.* [*archi-*, and Gr. *teuthis*, a kind of squid.] a genus of cephalopods of immense size, the giant squids.

är′chi·trāve, *n.* [Fr. *architrave*; It. *architrave*, from L. *archi-*, and *trabs*, a beam.]
1. in architecture, the lower division of an entablature, or that part which rests immediately on the column; a chief beam.
2. the ornament or molding at the sides of and above a door, window, or other square opening.

är′chi·trāved, *a.* having an architrave.

är′chī·văl, *a.* pertaining to archives or records; contained in records.

är′chīves, *n.pl.* [Fr., pl. of *archif*, from L. *archivum*, *archium*; Gr. *archeion*, a government house; *ta archeia*, archives; *archē*, beginning, government.]
1. a place where public records, documents, etc. are kept.
2. the public records, documents, etc. kept in such a place.

är′chi·vist, *n.* the keeper of archives or records.

är′chi·vōlt, *n.* [Fr. *archivolte*; It. *archivolto*; *archi-*, chief, and *volto*, an arch, vault.]
1. the inner curve of an arch or the structural parts of this.
2. an ornamental molding on the wall side of an arch.

är·chi·zō′iç, *a.* [*archi-*, and Gr. *zōon*, animal.] pertaining to the earliest forms of life.

ärch′lūte, ärch′i·lūte, *n.* [Fr. *archiluth*; It. *arciliuto.*] formerly, a large lute, or theorbo.

ärch′ly, *adv.* in an arch manner.

ärch·mär′shăl, *n.* the grand marshal of the old German empire: an office of the elector of Saxony.

ärch′ness, *n.* sly humor without malice; the quality of being arch.

är′chon, *n.* [Gr. *archōn*, a ruler, from *archein*, to be first, to rule.]
1. in ancient Athens, one of nine chief magistrates, chosen from the most illustrious families to superintend civil and religious matters.
2. a ruler.

är′chon·ship, *n.* the office of an archon.

är′chon·tāte, *n.* the term of office of an archon.

Är·chon′tiç, *n.* one of a fourth century sect who held that the world was not created by God, but by heavenly rulers called archons.

är′chō·plasm, *n.* [Gr. *archē*, beginning, and *plasma*, from *plassein*, to form, mold.] in biology, that part of the cell protoplasm which forms the asters, astral rays, and spindles in mitosis.

är·chō·plas′miç, *a.* containing or relating to archoplasm.

ärch·prel′āte, *n.* a chief prelate.

ärch·pres′by·tēr, *n.* [L. *archipresbyter*; Gr. *archipresbyteros*; *archi-*, chief, and *presbyteros*, elder, comp., from *presbys*, an old man.] a chief presbyter or priest.

ärch′priest′, *n.* 1. formerly, a priest who acted as a bishop's chief assistant; dean.
2. a chief priest.
3. the chief proponent of a school of thought, political theory, etc.

ärch·prī′māte, *n.* the chief primate; an archbishop over other bishops.

ärch′stōne, *n.* the wedge-shaped stone that binds an arch; the keystone.

ärch·treas′ūr·ēr (-trezh′), *n.* the great treasurer of the old German empire; also, any chief treasurer.

ärch′wāy, *n.* a passage under an arch.

ärch′wīfe, *n.* a domineering or masterful wife. [Obs.]

ärch′wīse, *adv.* in the form of an arch.

ärch′y, *a.* having arches; as, *archy* eyebrows.

-är·chy, [Gr. *-archia*, from *archos*, a ruler.] a suffix meaning *ruling, that which is ruled*, as in hept*archy*, mon*archy*.

är′ci·form, *a.* [L. *arcus*, a bow, and *forma*, form.] shaped like a bow; curved.

ärcked (ärkt), alternative past tense and past participle of *arc*.

ärck′ing, alternative present participle of *arc*.

arc lamp, a lamp in which the light is produced by an arc between electrodes.

arc light, 1. an arc lamp.
2. the light of an arc lamp.

är′cō·graph, *n.* [L. *arcus*, bow, and Gr. *graphein*, to write.] an instrument for drawing a circular arc without using a central point.

är·cōse′, *n.* see *arkose*.

Ärc·tā′li·a, *n.* [L., from *arctic*, and Gr. *hals*, sea.] the zoological zone embracing the northern seas southward as far as floating ice descends.

ärc·tā′tion, *n.* [Fr. *arctation*, from L. *arctus*, shut in, narrow, pp. of *arcere*, to shut in.] contraction of a natural opening, as of the anus.

ärc′ti·ăn, *a.* of or pertaining to the *Arctiidæ*, a family of moths having very hairy caterpillars.

ärc′ti·ăn, *n.* a moth of the family *Arctiidæ*.

ärc′tiç, *a.* [Fr. *arctique*; L. *arcticus*; Gr. *arktikos*, from *arktos*, bear.]
1. pertaining to the northern constellations known as Little Bear and Great Bear.
2. pertaining to, characteristic of, or near the North Pole, or the region within the Arctic Circle; hence, cold, frigid.
Arctic Circle; (a) an imaginary circle parallel to the equator, 23° 30′ from the North Pole, marking the southern limit of the north frigid zone; (b) the Arctic Zone.
Arctic Zone; all the region north of the Arctic Circle.

ärc′tiç, *n.* 1. the Arctic Circle.
2. the region around the North Pole.
3. an overshoe: see *arctics*.

ärc′tiçs, *n.pl.* [from *arctic.*] warmly lined, waterproof overshoes.

Ärc·tī′i·dae, *n.pl.* [L., from Gr. *arktos*, bear.] a family of moths belonging to the *Heterocera*. Their larvae are thickly covered with hair, whence they have obtained the name of woolly bears.

Ärc·tis′ça, *n.pl.* [L., from Gr. *arktos*, a bear.] an order of *Arachnida* including the water bears.

Ärc′ti·um, *n.* [L., from Gr. *arktos*, a bear.] a genus of plants of the natural order *Compositæ*, of which several species are weeds. The genus includes *Arctium lappa*, the common burdock.

Ärc·tō·gae′a, *n.* [L., from Gr. *arktos*, north, and *gaia*, land.] a faunal zone comprising the land area of the northern regions.

Ärc·tō·gē′ăl, *a.* of, relating, or pertaining to the zone Arctogaea.

ärc′toid, ärc·toi′dē·ăn, *a.* pertaining to the *Arctoidea*; resembling the bears.

ärc′toid, ärc·toi′dē·ăn, *n.* one of the *Arctoidea*.

Ärc·toi′dē·a, *n.pl.* [L., from Gr. *arktos*, bear, and *eidos*, form.] a subfamily of the *Carnivora*, including the bears, raccoons, weasels, etc.

Ärc·tō·staph′y·los, *n.* [L., from Gr. *arktos*, a bear, and *staphylē*, a bunch of grapes.] a genus of ericaceous plants closely related to *Arbutus*, and including the bearberry and the manzanitas.

Ärc·tū′rus, *n.* [L., from Gr. *Arktouros*; *arktos*, bear, and *ouros*, a guard.] a fixed star of the first magnitude in the constellation Boötes.

ärç′ū·ăl, *a.* relating to an arc.

ärç′ū·āte, ärç′ū·ā·ted, *a.* [L. *arcuatus*, pp. of *arcuare*, to arch, bend like a bow, from *arcus*, a bow.] bent or curved in the form of a bow.

ärç′ū·āte·ly, *adv.* in an arcuate manner.

ärç·ū·ā′tion, *n.* 1. the act of bending; also, the state of being bent.
2. a method of raising trees by layers, by bending branches to the ground and covering the small shoots with earth. [Obs.]
3. the use of arches in building.
4. a row of arches.

ärç′ū·bă·list, *n.* [L. *arcuballista*; *arcus*, a bow, and *ballista*, an engine for hurling missiles.] a crossbow; an arbalest.

ärç·ū·bal′ist·ēr, *n.* a crossbowman; an arbalester.

ärç′ū·bus, *n.* a harquebus. [Obs.]

är′çus, *n.* [L.] in anatomy, a bow or arch.
arcus senilis; a ring of fatty degeneration marginal to the cornea, seen in old persons.

-ard, -art, [OFr.; M.H.G. *-hart*, from *hart*, bold, hardy.] a suffix (originally an intensive) used in forming nouns meaning *one who is too——*, *one who does* (something not admirable) *too much*, as in slugg*ard*, drunk*ard*: also *-art*, as in bragg*art*.

är·das·sïne′, *n.* [Fr., from *ardasse*, a fine silk thread, from Per. *ardan*, raw silk.] a fine Persian silk, used in costly French fabrics.

är′deb, *n.* [Ar. *irdab.*] a unit of dry measure used in Egypt and Moslem countries, varying from 1/5 peck to 7 1/2 bushels.

är′den·cy, *n.* 1. warmth of passion or affection; ardor; eagerness; as, the *ardency* of love or zeal.
2. heat. [Rare.]

är′dent, *a.* [L. *ardens*, ppr. of *ardere*, to burn.]
1. hot; burning; causing a sensation of

great heat; as, *ardent* spirits; an *ardent* fever. [Obs.]

2. having the appearance or quality of fire; glowing; beaming; as, *ardent* eyes.

3. warm, as applied to the passions and affections; passionate; affectionate; zealous; as, *ardent* love or vows; *ardent* zeal.

Syn.—burning, eager, fervent, fiery, hot, intense, passionate, vehement, zealous.

är′dent spir′its, strong alcoholic liquor; whisky, brandy, gin, etc.

Är·dis′i·ȧ, *n.* [L., from Gr. *ardis*, the point of an arrow.] a genus of shrublike trees of the family *Myrsinaceæ*, ornamental plants native to the East and West Indies, cultivated for their evergreen leaves, showy flowers, and strikingly colored berries.

är′dŏr, *n.* [OFr. *ardor, ardour*; L. *ardor*, a burning fire, flame, from *ardere*, to burn.]

1. fire; intense heat; as, the *ardor* of the sun's rays.

2. emotional warmth or heat; eagerness; as, he pursues study with *ardor*; they fought with *ardor*.

3. a bright spirit; brilliancy. [Obs.]

Thousand celestial *ardours*, where he stood.
—Milton.

Syn.—devotion, earnestness, excitement, fervor, intensity, passion, rapture, zeal.

är′dŏur, *n.* ardor: British spelling.

är′dū·ous, *a.* [L. *arduus*, high, steep.]

1. steep, and therefore difficult of ascent; hard to climb.

And pointed out those *arduous* paths they trod.
—Pope.

2. difficult to do; requiring exertion; laborious.

3. energetic; working hard.

Syn.—difficult, hard, laborious.

är′dū·ous·ly, *adv.* in an arduous manner.

är′dū·ous·ness, *n.* the quality of being arduous; difficulty of execution.

äre, *v.* [AS. *aron*.] the plural and second person singular, present indicative, of *be*.

āre (*or* är), *n.* [Fr., from L. *area*, a level piece of ground.] a unit of surface measure in the metric system, containing 100 square meters, or 1076.44 square feet.

ā′rē·ȧ, *n.*; *pl.* **ā′rē·ȧs,** [L. *area*, a level piece of ground.]

1. originally, a level surface or piece of ground.

2. a part of the earth's surface; region; tract.

3. the total outside surface of anything, as measured in square units.

4. a yard of a building; areaway.

5. scope; range; extent.

6. a part of a house, lot, district, city, etc. having a specific use or character; as, dining *area*; slum *area*.

7. *pl.* often **ā′rē·ae,** in biology, a limited part of the surface of an organism.

ā′rē·ȧ cōde, any of the groups of three numerals assigned as a telephone code to each of the more than 120 areas into which the United States and Canada are divided.

ā′rē·ăl, *a.* pertaining to an area.

ȧ·rēar′, *v.t.* and *v.i.* to raise; to exalt; to arouse. [Obs.]

ȧ·rear′, *adv.* to the rear.

ā′rē·ȧ rug, a rug intended to cover only part of a floor.

ā′rē·ȧ·wāy″, *n.* 1. a sunken yard or court leading into a cellar or basement, for entrance or light and air.

2. a passageway between buildings or parts of a building.

A·rē′çȧ, *n.* [Port.] 1. a genus of palm trees, including the betel palm.

2. [a—] any plant of this genus.

ar·ē·fac′tion, *n.* [Fr. *arefaction*, from L. *arefacere*, to make dry; *arere*, to be dry, and *facere*, to make.] the act of drying. [Rare.]

ȧ·rē′nȧ, *n.*; *pl.* **ȧ·rē′nȧs** or **ȧ·rē′nae,** [L. *arena, harena*, sand, a sandy place, arena.]

1. in Roman antiquity, the area in the central part of an amphitheater, in which the gladiators fought and other shows took place: so called because it was covered with sand.

2. any place like this: as, an *arena* for boxing matches.

3. any sphere of struggle or exertion.

4. the central stage in an arena theater.

5. in pathology, "sand" or "gravel" in the kidneys.

ar·ē·nā′ceous, *a.* 1. made up of sand; sandy.

2. growing in sand.

Ar·ē·nā′ri·ȧ, *n.* [L. *arenarius*, sandy.] in botany, the sandworts, a genus of plants belonging to the *Caryophyllaceæ*, or pink family.

ar·ē·nā′ri·ous, *a.* [L. *arenarius*, sandy, from *arena*, sand.] sandy; as, *arenarious* soil.

ȧ·rē′nȧ thē′ȧ·tēr, 1. a theater having a central stage without a proscenium, surrounded by seats.

2. the techniques used in such a theater.

ar·e·nā′tion, *n.* in medicine, a bath of hot sand.

ȧ·reng′, ȧ·reñ′gȧ, *n.* [E. Ind.] a sago palm, *Arenga saccharifera*.

ar·ē·niç′ō·līte, *n.* [L. *arena*, sand, and *colere*, to inhabit.] any of certain holes or markings in rocks, formerly believed to have been caused by marine annelids.

ar·ē·niç′ō·lous, *a.* [from L. *arena*, sand, and *colere*, to dwell.] living in sand, as some burrowing animals.

ȧ·ren·i·lit′iç, *a.* [L. *arena*, sand, and Gr. *lithos*, a stone.] pertaining to or composed of sandstone; as, *arenilitic* mountains.

ar′ē·nōse, *a.* sandy.

äre̤n't (ärnt), are not: also occasionally used as a substitute for a contraction of *am not* in interrogative constructions.

ā′rē·ō-, [from Gr. *areos*, genit. of *Ares*, Mars.] a combining form meaning *of Mars*, as in *areo*logy.

ar″ē·ō·cen′triç, *a.* in astronomy, with the planet Mars regarded as center.

ȧ·rē′ō·lȧ, *n.*; *pl.* **ȧ·rē′ō·lae, ȧ·rē′ō·lȧs,** [L. *areola*, a small open place, dim. of *area*.]

1. in physical science, any small area.

2. in anatomy, (a) the circle surrounding a nipple, varying from pink to brown; (b) the circle surrounding the pustule in vaccination.

3. in entomology, any of the small areas, or veinlets, into which the wings of insects are divided by the nervures.

4. in botany, the minute meshes on the surface of a plant.

5. in biology, a small hollow in a surface.

ȧ·rē′ō·lăr, *a.* 1. like or pertaining to an areola.

2. consisting of areolae.

ȧ·rē′ō·lāte, ȧ·rē′ō·lā·ted, *a.* divided into small spaces or areolations, as the wings of insects, and the leaves of plants.

ā″rē·ō·lā′tion, *n.* 1. any small space, bounded by some part differing in color or structure, as the spaces bounded by the nervures in the wings of insects, or those by the veins in leaves.

2. the division into or space containing areolae.

ā′rē·ōle, *n.* same as *areola*.

ȧ·rē′ō·let, *n.* [dim. of L. *areola*, a small place.] a small areola.

ār″ē·ol′ō·ġy, *n.* [*areo-*, and *-logy*.] the study of the planet Mars.

ā·rē·om′e·tēr, *n.* [Fr. *aréomètre*, from Gr. *araios*, thin, rare, and *metron*, measure.] an instrument for measuring the specific gravity of liquids: also spelled *araeometer*.

ā″rē·ō·met′riç, ā″rē·ō·met′riç·ăl, *a.* pertaining to an areometer.

ā·rē·om′e·try, *n.* [Gr. *araios*, thin, rare, and *metria*, from *metron*, measure.] the process or act of measuring the specific gravity of fluids.

Ar·ē·op′ȧ·ġīte, Ar·ē·op′ȧ·ġist, *n.* any member of the Areopagus in ancient Athens.

ar·ē·op·ȧ·ġit′iç, *a.* pertaining to the Areopagus.

Ar·ē·op′ȧ·gus, *n.* [L., from Gr. *Areiopagos*, from *Areios*, pertaining to Ares, and *pagos*, hill.]

1. a supreme tribunal at Athens, famous for the justice and impartiality of its decisions. It was originally held on the hill of the same name.

2. any final court or tribunal.

ȧ·rē′ō·stȳle, ȧ·rae′ō·stȳle, *a.* [L. *aræostylos*; Gr. *araiostylos*, with columns far apart; *araios*, not dense, thin, and *stylos*, pillar.] pertaining to the style of intercolumnation having the intermediate spaces upward of three columnar diameters in extent.

ā·rē·ot′iç, *a.* [Gr. *araiōtikos*, from *araioun*, to rarefy; *araios*, rare, thin, not dense.] attenuating; making thin, as liquids; rarefying. [Rare.]

Ā′rēs̱, *n.* in Greek mythology, the god of war, corresponding to Mars in Roman mythology.

ȧ·rest′, *n.* 1. a rest for a spear. [Obs.]

2. arrest. [Obs.]

ȧ·re̤t′, ȧ·rette′, *v.t.* [ME. *aretten*; OFr. *areter, aretter*; *a* (L. *ad*, to) and *reter*, from L. *reputare*, to count, reckon again.] to assign; to impute. [Obs.]

ar·ē·tā′iç̱s, *n.* same as *aretology*.

a·rête′ (ȧ-re̤t′), *n.* [Fr., from OFr. *areste*; L. *arista*, an ear of corn, a spine.] a narrow, mountainous crest or sharp ridge.

Ar·ē·thū′s̱a, *n.* [L. *Arethusa*; Gr. *Arethousa*, one of Diana's nymphs, transformed into a fountain.] a genus of orchids of which one species, *Arethusa bulbosa*, is native to New England: the only other known species is found in Japan.

ar·ē·tol′ō·ġy, *n.* [Fr. *aretologie*; Gr. *aretalogia*; *aretē*, virtue, and *logia*, from *legein*, to speak.] that part of ethics which treats particularly of virtue.

ȧ·rew′, *adv.* arow. [Obs.]

är′gal, *n.* same as *argol*.

är′gal, *adv.* a corruption of Latin *ergo*, therefore.

är′gal, *n.* same as *argali*.

är′gȧ·lȧ, *n.* 1. a stork of India; the adjutant.

2. an African stork; the maribou.

är′gȧ·li, *n.*; *pl.* **är′gȧ·lis̱, är′gȧ·li,** [Mongolian.]

1. a species of wild sheep, *Caprovis argali* or *Ovis ammon*, found on the mountains of Siberia, central Asia, and Kamchatka. It is nearly as large as an ox. The horns are nearly four feet in length, and at their base are about nineteen inches in circumference.

2. any of several other wild sheep, as the American bighorn.

Är′gand, *a.* of or pertaining to a lighting system using *Argand* lamps.

Argand burner [after Aimé *Argand*, a Swiss chemist.] an oil burner made up of two concentric tubes separated by a cylindrical wick through which air is passed to increase the rate of combustion.

Argand lamp; a lamp using an Argand burner.

är′gan tree, [Ar. *argān, arjān*.] a low-branched evergreen tree, *Argania sideroxylon*, of Morocco, yielding a compact wood and fruit resembling the olive.

Är′gas, *n.* [L., from Gr. *argos, aergos*; *a* priv., and *ergos*, working.] a genus of ticks, including the chicken tick.

Är·ġē′ăn, *a.* pertaining to the ship or the constellation Argo.

är′gel, *n.* [Syr.] an asclepiadaceous plant, *Solenostemma argel*, the leaves of which are used in Egypt for adulterating senna.

Är·ġe·mō′nē, *n.* [L. *argemone*; Gr. *argemōnē*, from *argema*, a small white speck in the eye, from *argos*, white.] a genus of plants belonging to the family *Papaveraceæ*. The *Argemone mexicana*, believed to have come from Mexico, is now common in other warm countries.

är′ġent, *n.* [Fr. *argent*; L. *argentum*, silver; Gr. *argyros*, silver.]

1. silver. [Archaic or Poetic.]

2. the white color in coats of arms, intended to represent silver, or figuratively, purity, innocence, beauty, or gentleness.

3. silver coin; money; hence, whiteness, or anything white. [Obs.]

är′ġent, *a.* silvery; of silver.

är·ġen′tăl, *a.* pertaining to, consisting of, or combined with silver.

är′ġen·tan, *n.* [L. *argentum*, silver.] an alloy of nickel with copper and zinc; German silver.

är′ġen·tāte, *a.* silvery white: said of certain leaves.

är·ġen·tā′tion, *n.* an overlaying with silver. [Rare.]

är·ġen′tē·ous, *a.* of or like silver; silvery.

är·ġen′tiç, *a.* pertaining to, containing, or derived from silver: applied to compounds of silver with a higher valence than in the corresponding argentous compounds.

är·ġen·tif′ẽr·ous, *a.* [L. *argentum*, silver, and *ferre*, to produce.] containing silver, as ore.

Är·ġen·tī′nȧ, *n.* [L. *argentum*, silver.] a genus of small, smeltlike fishes, belonging to the *Argentinidæ* family: so named from their silvery scales.

är′ġen·tīne, *a.* [Fr. *argentin*, from L. *argentum*, silver.] of, relating, or pertaining to silver.

Är′ġen·tīne, *a.* of Argentina, its people, or culture.

Är′ġen·tīne, *n.* a native or inhabitant of Argentina.

är′ġen·tīne, *n.* 1. silver.

2. any of several metals resembling silver.

3. any of several fishes of the genus *Argentina*.

Är·ġen·tin′ē·ăn, *n.* an Argentine.

är′ġen·tīte, *n.* [L. *argentum*, silver, and *-ite*.] native silver sulfide, Ag_2S, a heavy, dark-gray mineral that is an important ore of silver.

är′ġen·tōl, *n.* [from L. *argentum*, and *-ol*.]

an organic compound of silver, used in powder form as an antiseptic.

är·ġen′tous, *a.* of or containing monovalent silver.

är·ġen′tum, *n.* [L.] silver: symbol, Ag, in chemistry.

är′ġil, *n.* [Fr. *argile*; L. *argilla*, white clay; Gr. *argilla, argillos*, argil, from *argos*, white.] clay, especially that used for pottery.

är·ġil·lā′ceous, *a.* [L. *argillaceus*, from *argilla*, white clay.] of the nature of clay; consisting of clay.

argillaceous sandstone; in geology, sandstone which contains a large percentage of clay.

argillaceous schist or *slate*; argillite.

är·ġil·lif′ẽr·ous, *a.* [L. *argilla*, clay, and *ferre*, to bear.] producing clay: applied to earth that abounds in clay.

är′ġil·līte, *n.* [L. *argilla*, white clay, and *-ite*.] a hardened mudstone showing no slatelike cleavage.

är·ġil·lit′iç, *a.* pertaining to argillite.

är·ġil″lō·ar·ē·nā′ceous, *a.* [L. *argilla*, white clay, and *arena*, sand.] consisting of clay and sand, as a soil.

är·ġil″lō·çal·çā′rē·ous, *a.* consisting of clay and calcareous earth.

är·ġil″lō·fer·rū′ġi·nous, *a.* containing or consisting of iron and clay.

är·ġil′lous, *a.* [ME. *argillous*; OFr. *argillos*; L. *argillosus*, from *argilla*, white clay.] consisting of clay; clayey.

är′ġi·nīne, *n.* [L. *argentum*, silver, and *-in*.] a colorless, soluble amino acid, $C_6H_{14}O_2N_4$, necessary in nutrition, obtained from plant and animal proteins by hydrolysis or by the action of bacteria in digestion.

Är′ġīve, *a.* pertaining to ancient Argolis in Greece, or to its capital, Argos, or to the whole of Greece; Greek.

Är′ġīve, *n.* an inhabitant of Argos or Argolis; also, a poetical designation for any Greek.

Är′gō, *n.* [Gr. *Argō*, from *argos*, swift, bright, glancing.]

1. in Greek mythology, the ship which carried Jason and his companions to Colchis, in quest of the Golden Fleece.

2. in astronomy, a southern constellation between Canis Major and the Southern Cross.

Är·gō′ăn, *a.* pertaining to the ship Argo.

är′gol, är′gal, *n.* unrefined or crude tartar, a substance deposited on the sides of wine casks.

Är·gol′iç, *a.* pertaining to Argolis, a territory or district of the Peloponnesus, between Arcadia and the Aegean Sea; as, the *Argolic* gulf.

är′gon, *n.* [Gr. *argon*, from *aergos*, inactive; *a* priv., and *ergon*, work.] one of the chemical elements, an inert, colorless, odorless gas constituting nearly one per cent of the atmosphere: it is used in incandescent light bulbs, radio tubes, etc.: symbol, A; atomic weight, 39.944; atomic number, 18.

Är′gō·naut, *n.* [L. *Argonauta*; Gr. *Argonautēs*; *Argō*, Jason's ship, and *nautēs*, a sailor, from *naus*, ship.]

1. one who sailed to Colchis with Jason, in the Argo, in quest of the Golden Fleece.

2. one going to California to seek gold, after its discovery in 1849.

3. [a–] any of the mollusks belonging to the genus *Argonauta*.

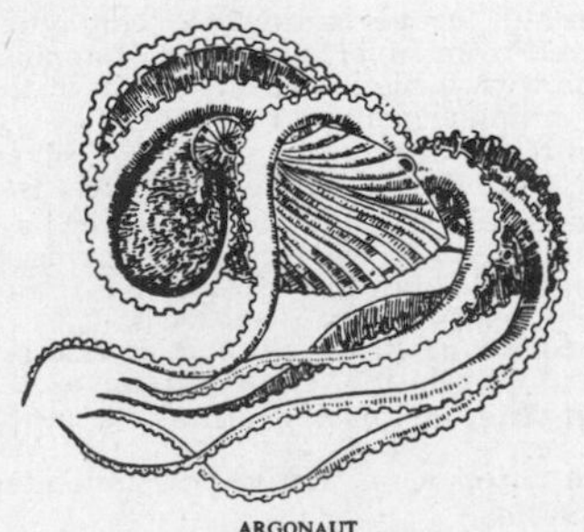

ARGONAUT
(*Argonauta argo*)

Är·gō·nau′tȧ, *n.* [L., an Argonaut.] a genus of the class *Cephalopoda*, related to the octopus. The shell consists of one spiral involuted valve. The species *argo* is the paper nautilus. It propels itself by means of a jet of water, as do other cephalopods.

Är·gō·naut′iç, *a.* pertaining to the Argonauts.

är′gō·sy, *n.*; *pl.* **är′gō·sies,** [ME. *argosie, ragosie, rhaguse, ragusye*; It. *Ragusea*, a vessel of Ragusa.] a large merchant ship; also, a fleet of such ships.

är′got (är′gō *or* är′gŏt), *n.* [Fr.] a jargon or speech used by those in the same work, way of life, etc. to conceal the true import of what is said, as the jargon of tramps or criminals.

är′gū·ȧ·ble, *a.* that may be argued; that can be supported by argument.

är′gūe, *v.i.*; argued, *pt.*, *pp.*; arguing, *ppr.* [ME. *arguen*; OFr. *arguer*; L. *arguere*, to make clear, to prove; from same root as Gr. *argos*, white, clear.]

1. to offer reasons in support of or against a proposition, opinion, or measure.

2. to dispute; to reason: followed by *with*; as, he *argued with* his friend.

3. to present objections.

är′gūe, *v.t.* 1. to debate or discuss; to treat by reasoning; as, the counsel *argued* the cause.

2. to try to prove; contend.

3. to indicate or give evidence of; as, the order visible in the universe *argues* a divine cause.

4. to persuade by giving reasons; as, to *argue* a man into a different opinion.

5. to accuse or charge with: followed by *of*. [Obs.]

Syn.—discuss, debate, dispute, prove, evince.

är′gū·ẽr, *n.* one who argues; a disputer.

är′gū·fȳ, *v.t.* and *v.i.* to argue persistently; to wrangle; to argue for the sake of arguing. [Colloq.]

Är′gū·lus, *n.* [L., dim. of Gr. *argos*; contr. for *aergos*; *a* priv., and *ergon*, work.] a genus of crustaceans. One variety, the *Argulus foliaceus*, is a common parasite upon fresh-water fishes.

är′gū·ment, *v.i.* to argue. [Obs.]

är′gū·ment, *n.* [Fr. *argument*; L. *argumentum*, evidence, proof, from *arguere*, to make clear, prove.]

1. a reason or reasons offered for or against a proposition, opinion, or measure; as, the only *argument* used was force.

2. the offering of such reasons; reasoning.

3. a debate or discussion in which there is disagreement; as, an *argument* was had before the court, in which *argument* all the reasons were urged.

4. the subject of a discourse or writing; an outline of the subject matter; a summary; as, the *argument* of a play.

The abstract or *argument* of the piece is shortly as follows. —Jeffrey.

5. something to make one take action; matter for controversy or dispute. [Obs.]

6. in astronomy, the quantity on which another quantity in a table depends; as, the altitude is the *argument* of the refraction.

7. in logic, the mean or middle term of a syllogism.

8. in mathematics, an independent variable the functional values of which are tabulated.

Syn.—controversy, reasoning, discussion, dispute, topic.

är·gū·men′tȧ·ble, *a.* capable of being argued.

är·gū·men′tăl, *a.* belonging to or consisting of argument.

är″gū·men·tā′tion, *n.* [Fr. *argumentation*; L. *argumentatio*, from *argumentari*, to adduce, as proof.]

1. reasoning; the act of forming reasons, making inductions, drawing conclusions, and applying them to the case under discussion.

2. argument; debate.

3. writing or speaking that argues: conventionally distinguished from *description*, narration, exposition.

är·gū·men′tȧ·tive, *a.* 1. abounding in argument; consisting of argument; as, an *argumentative* discourse.

2. addicted to argument; as, an *argumentative* writer.

3. tending to prove; indicating reasons; as, illustrations *argumentative* of a proposition.

är·gū·men′tȧ·tive·ly, *adv.* in an argumentative manner.

är·gū·men′tȧ·tive·ness, *n.* the state of being argumentative.

är′gū·men·tīze, *v.i.* to engage in discussion; to argue. [Obs.]

är·gū·men′tum, *n.* [L.] an argument: used with various Latin phrases, as *ad hominem*, *ad rem*, etc.

Är′gus, *n.* [L., from Gr. *Argos*; *argos*, bright.]

1. in Greek mythology, a giant with a hundred eyes, who was placed by Hera to guard Io. He was killed by Hermes, and Hera set his eyes into the tail of the peacock.

2. [a–] one noted for watchfulness.

ARGUS PHEASANT
(*Argus giganteus*)

3. a genus of birds, the most common species of which is the *Argus giganteus*, family *Phasianidæ*, a large, beautiful pheasant related to the peacock, found in southeastern Asia.

Är′gus-eyed (-īd), *a.* keenly watchful; vigilant.

är′gus shell, a species of seashell, *Cypræa argus*, distinguished by its many eyelike spots.

är·gū·tā′tion, *n.* frivolous argument; quibble. [Obs.]

är·gūte′, *a.* [L. *argutus*, clear, sharp, pp. of *arguere*, to make clear.] sharp of taste; also, shrill, acute, keen, cunning. [Rare.]

är·gūte′ly, *adv.* in an argute manner; cunningly; wittily. [Rare.]

är′gūte′ness, *n.* wittiness; keenness. [Rare.]

är·ġy·ran′thē·mo̤us, är·ġy·ran′thous, *a.* [Gr. *argyros*, silver, and *anthos*, flower.] having silver-colored flowers.

är·ġyr′i·ȧ, *n.* [Gr. *argyros*, silver.] skin discoloration: an effect produced by the continued use of silver preparations.

är·ġyr′ō·dīte, *n.* [L., from Gr. *argyrōdēs*, like silver; *argyros*, silver, and *eidos*, form.] a lustrous, gray mineral, Ag_8GeS_6, made up of silver, germanium, and sulfur.

Är′ġy·rōl, *n.* a trade-mark for a brand of mild silver-protein, used as a local antiseptic for treating inflamed mucous tissue.

ä′ri·ȧ, *n.* [It., from L. *aer*, air.] an air or melody in an opera, cantata, or oratorio, especially for solo voice with instrumental accompaniment.

-ā′ri·ȧ, [Mod. L., from L. *-arius*.] a plural suffix used, especially in botany and zoology, to form nouns designating groups and genera.

Ar·i·ad′nē, *n.* [L., from Gr. *Ariadnē*.] in Greek legend, King Minos' daughter, who gave Theseus the thread by which he found his way out of the Minotaur's labyrinth: he took her with him, but later deserted her.

-ā′ri·ăn, [L. *-arius*, -ary, and *-anus*, -an.] a suffix used in forming adjectives and nouns, denoting *age*, *sect*, *social belief*, *occupation*, etc.; as antiqu*arian*, nonagen*arian*, Unit*arian*.

Ā′ri·ăn, *a.* and *n.* see *Aryan*.

Ā′ri·ăn, *a.* related to Arius or his doctrines.

Ā′ri·ăn, *n.* a believer in or an advocate of Arianism.

Ā′ri·ăn·iṣm, *n.* the doctrines of Arius, an Alexandrian of the fourth century, who taught that Jesus was not of the same substance as God, but only the best of created beings.

Ā′ri·ăn·īze, *v.i.* to believe in the doctrines of Arianism.

Ā′ri·ăn·īze, *v.t.* to convert to the doctrines of Arius.

ar′i·cīne, ar′i·cin, *n.* [from *Arica*, a seaport in northern Chile.] a crystalline alkaloid obtained from a variety of cinchona bark.

ar′id, *a.* [L. *aridus*, dry, from *arere*, to be dry.]

1. dry; parched; having little rainfall; as, an *arid* waste.

2. barren; unfertile.

3. uninteresting; dull; tedious; as, an *arid* speech.

ȧ·rid′i·ty, *n.* the state or quality of being arid.

ar′id·ness, *n.* aridity.

Ā′ri·el, *n.* [L. *ariel*; Gr. *ariēl*; Heb. *ariēl*, Lioness of God; a name applied to Jerusalem in the Old Testament.]

1. a satellite of the planet Uranus.

2. in Shakespeare's *The Tempest*, the airy spirit, a servant of Prospero.
3. [a–] an Australian flying phalanger.

ā′ri·el, *n.* [Ar. *aryil, ayyil*, a stag.] a kind of gazelle, *Gazella dama*, of Asia and Africa.

Ā′ri·ēs, *n.* [L. *aries*, a ram.]
1. in astronomy, (a) a northern constellation between Pisces and Taurus, supposedly outlining a ram; (b) the first sign of the zodiac.
2. [a–] a battering ram of the ancient Romans.

ar′i·e·tāte, *v.i.* [L. *arietatus*, pp. of *arietare*, to butt like a ram, from *aries*, a ram.] to butt, as a ram. [Obs.]

ar″i·e·tā′tion, *n.* 1. the act of butting like a ram. [Obs.]
2. the act of striking or conflicting. [Rare.]

ȧ·ri·et′tȧ, ar·i·ette′, *n.* [It., dim. of *aria*, from L. *aer*, air.] a short melody or aria.

ȧ·right′ (ȧ-rīt′), *adv.* [*a-* and *right*, AS. *gericht*.] rightly; in a right form; without mistake.
Syn.—appropriately, suitably, properly, justly.

ar′il, *n.* [Fr. *arill*; Sp. *arilla*; L. *arilli*, dried grapes, from *aridus*, dry.] an additional covering that forms on certain seeds after fertilization, developing from the stalk of the ovule.

ar′il·lāte, ar′il·lā·ted, *a.* covered with an aril.

ar′il·lōde, *n.* [from Mod. L. *arillus*; ML., dried grape; and *-ode* (like).] a false aril, developing from an opening in the covering of the ovule instead of its stalk.

ȧ·ril′lus, *n.* same as *aril*.

Ăr′i·măn, *n.* [Per.] same as *Ahriman*.

ar″i·ō·lā′tion, *n.* soothsaying.

ar′i·ōse, *a.* [It. *arioso*, from *aria*; L. *aer*, air.] characterized by melody; songlike: distinguished from *recitative*.

ȧ·ri·ō′sō, *adv.* and *a.* [It., from *aria*; L. *aer*, air.] in the style of an aria; with melodic intonation.

ȧ·ri·ō′sō, *n.* an arioso composition.

-ā′ri·ous, [from L. *-arius*; and *-ous*.] a suffix meaning *relating to, connected with*, as in hil*arious*, vic*arious*.

Ar·i·sae′mȧ, *n.* [L. *aris*; Gr. *aron*, arum, and *haima*, blood.] a genus of perennial herbs of the *Arum* family, including the jack-in-the-pulpit, *Arisæma triphyllum*.

ȧ·rīṣe′, *v.i.*; arose, *pt.*; arising, *ppr.*; arisen, *pp.* [ME. *arisen*; AS. *arisan*; *a*, intensive, and *rīsān*, to rise.]
1. to ascend; to move upward; as, vapors *arise* from humid places.
2. to get up, as from bed.
The king *arose* early and went to the den. —Dan. vi. 19.
3. to come into being; to begin; to originate.
The persecution that *arose* about Stephen. —Acts xi. 19.
4. to begin to act; to exert power; to become active.
Let God *arise*; let his enemies be scattered. —Ps. lxviii. 1.
Syn.—rise, spring, flow, mount, scale, issue, emanate.

ȧ·rīṣe′, *n.* rising. [Obs.]

ȧ·rist′, *n.* a rising. [Obs.]

ȧ·ris′tȧ, *n.* [L.] 1. in botany, the awn; the beardlike part of grain or grasses.
2. in zoology, a bristlelike process, as on the antennae of certain insects.

ar′is·tärch, *n.* [from *Aristarchus*, a critic distinguished among the ancients for severity.] a severe critic.

ar·is·tär′chi·ăn, *a.* severely critical.

ar′is·tär·chy, *n.* severe criticism. [Obs.]

ar′is·tär·chy, *n.* [Gr. *aristarchia*, from *aristarchos*, best ruling; *aristos*, best, and *archos*, from *archein*, to rule.] government by the best men.

ȧ·ris′tāte, *a.* in botany and zoology, awned; having an awn.

ar·is·toc′rȧ·cy, *n.* [Fr. *aristocracie*; Gr. *aristokratia*, the rule of the best born, or nobles; *aristos*, best, and *kratia*, from *kratein*, to be strong, to rule.]
1. originally, government by the best citizens.
2. government by a privileged minority or upper class, usually of inherited wealth and social position.
3. a country with this form of government; oligarchy.
4. a titled ruling class, or nobility of a country.
5. those who rise above the rest and are considered the best in some way, as in knowledge, character, etc.
6. the quality of being an aristocrat; as, his *aristocracy* was in keeping with his education.

ar·is′tō·crat (*or* ar′is-). *n.* 1. a member of the aristocracy.
2. one believing in aristocracy as a form of government.
3. a person with the tastes, manners, beliefs, prejudices, etc. of the upper class.

ar″is·tō·crat′ic, ar″is·tō·crat′ic·ăl, *a.* related in any way to aristocracy; having the qualities (favorable or unfavorable) of an aristocrat.

ar″is·tō·crat′ic·ăl·ly, *adv.* in an aristocratic manner.

ar″is·tō·crat′ic·ăl·ness, *n.* the condition or quality of being aristocratic.

ar·is′tō·crat·ism, *n.* aristocratic principles or rank; the state of being an aristocrat.

Ar″is·tō·lō′chi·ȧ, *n.* [from Gr. *aristolocheia*, an herb promoting childbirth; *aristos*, best, and *locheia*, childbirth.] a genus of tropical herbs and woody climbers, which have flowers of dull color formed to entrap insects.

Ar″is·tō·lō·chi·ā′cē·ae, *n.pl.* a family of tropical climbers and twiners, with dull, heavy-scented, often bad-smelling flowers; the birthwort family.

ar″is·tō·lō·chi·ā′ceous, *a.* relating to the *Aristolochiaceæ*.

ar·is·tol′ō·gy, *n.* [Gr. *ariston*, breakfast, and *logia*, from *legein*, to speak.] the science or art of dining.

Ar″is·tō·phan′ic, *a.* pertaining to the classic Greek poet Aristophanes, or to his comedies.

Ar″is·tō·tē′li·ăn, *a.* pertaining to the classic Greek philosopher Aristotle, or to his philosophy.

Ar″is·tō·tē′li·ăn, *n.* a disciple of Aristotle.

Ar″is·tō·tē′li·ăn·ism, *n.* the philosophical system of Aristotle, the ancient Greek philosopher of the fourth century B.C. maintaining the deductive method in opposition to the inductive, and experimentalism as opposed to intuitionalism.

Ar″is·tō·tē′li·ăn log′ic, 1. Aristotle's method of deductive logic, characterized by the syllogism.
2. the formal logic developed from Aristotle's.

Ar″is·tō·tel′ic, *a.* pertaining to Aristotle or to his philosophy.

ȧ·ris′tō·tȳpe, *n.* [Gr. *aristos*, best, and *typos*, an impression, mark of a blow; from *typtein*, to strike.]
1. any method of printing that uses paper coated with salts of silver in collodion or gelatin.
2. a print made by such a method.

ȧ·ris′tū·lāte, *a.* [L., dim. of *arista*, awn, or beard of grain.] in botany, with a small awn.

ar′ith·man·cy, *n.* [Gr. *arithmos*, number, and *manteia*, divination.] same as *arithmomancy*.

ȧ·rith′me·tic, *n.* [L. *arithmetica*; Gr. *arithmētikē*, from *arithmein*, to reckon, count; *arithmos*, number.]
1. the science or art of computation by positive, real numbers, the fundamental operations of which are performed by addition, subtraction, multiplication, and division.
2. knowledge of or skill in this science; computation; as, my *arithmetic* is poor.
3. a textbook on this science of numbers or their use in computation.
political arithmetic; the statistics relating to the financial condition of a country or state.

ar·ith·met′ic·ăl, ar·ith·met′ic, *a.* pertaining to arithmetic; according to the rules or methods of arithmetic.

ar·ith·met′ic·ăl·ly, *adv.* according to the rules, principles, or methods of arithmetic.

ȧ·rith·me·ti′ciăn (-tish′un), *n.* one skilled in arithmetic.

ar·ith·met′ic mēan, the average obtained by dividing the sum of two or more quantities by the number of quantities.

ar·ith·met′ic prō·gres′sion, a sequence of terms each of which, after the first, is derived by adding to the preceding one a constant quantity (the *common difference*, or *constant*): 5, 9, 13, 17, etc. are in *arithmetic progression*.

ȧ·rith′mō·man·cy, *n.* divination, or the foretelling of future events, by numbers: also called *arithmancy*.

ar·ith·mom′e·tẽr, *n.* [from Gr. *arithmos*, a number, and *metron*, a measure.] a machine for performing the fundamental operations of arithmetic.

ä rï·ve·der′cï (-chē), [It.] until we meet again; good-by: implies temporary parting.

Ar·i·zō′nȧ gōurd (gōrd), a wild squash of California and Mexico, having a large root the pulp of which is used in making soap.

Ar·i·zō′năn, Ar·i·zō′ni·ăn, *a.* of Arizona.

Ar·i·zō′năn, Ar·i·zō′ni·ăn, *n.* a native or inhabitant of Arizona.

Ăr′ju·nȧ, *n.* the hero of the Hindu epic, the Mahabharata.

ärk, *n.* [ME. *ark, arche*; AS. *earc*, arc; L. *arca*, a chest, box, from *arcere*, to shut up, enclose; Gr. *arkein*, to keep off.]
1. a small chest or coffer containing the two stone tablets inscribed with the Ten Commandments, kept in the holiest part of the ancient Jewish Tabernacle. It was made of acacia wood overlaid with gold. Ex. xxv. 10: also called *ark of the covenant*.
2. in the Bible, the huge boat in which Noah, his family, and two of every kind of creature survived the Flood. Gen. vi.
3. any boat like this; big awkward boat.
4. a place of refuge.
5. a chest; coffer. [Obs. or Dial.]

Ăr·kan′săn, *n.* a native or inhabitant of the state of Arkansas.

ärk′īte, *a.* belonging to the ark.

ärk of the cŏv′e·nănt, see *ark*, sense 1.

är·kōse′, är·cōse′, *n.* [Fr.] a sandstone formed from weathered granite with feldspar present.

ärk shell, a bivalve shell of the genus *arca*.

ärleṣ (ärlz), *n.pl.* [Scot. *arles*; Gael. *iarlas*, earnest money; Fr. *arrhes*; L. *arrha*, earnest money.] earnest money; money given in confirmation of a bargain, contract, or agreement. [Scot. or Brit. Dial.]

ärleṣ pen′ny, same as *arles*.

ärm, *n.* [AS. *arm, earm*; L. *armus*, shoulder; Gr. *harmos*, a joining, joint.]
1. in anatomy, either of the two upper limbs, especially the part extending from the shoulder to the hand.
2. in zoology, the corresponding limb of vertebrate animals; also, in general, any limb of an invertebrate animal, as the ray of a starfish.
3. anything resembling an arm; any part projecting from something larger; as, an *arm* of the sea.
4. anything commonly in contact with the human arm; especially, (a) a sleeve of a garment; (b) a support for the arm on a chair, sofa, etc.
5. anything thought of as functioning like an arm; as, the long *arm* of the law, the *arm* of coincidence, etc.
6. any weapon: see *arms*.
7. any combatant branch of the military forces, as the infantry, artillery, etc.
8. the end of the yard of a sailing vessel; also, one of the ends of the bar of an anchor.
arm in arm; with arms intertwined, as two persons walking together.
at arm's length; at a distance, literally or figuratively; beyond familiarity; as, to keep a person *at arm's length*.

ärm, *v.t.*; armed (ärmd), *pt., pp.*; arming, *ppr.* [ME. *armen*; OFr. *armer*; It. *armare*; L. *armare*, to arm, from *arma*, pl., arms.]
1. to equip with weapons, tools, etc.
2. to provide with protective covering; to fortify.
3. to equip or provide with anything advantageous or tending toward greater strength or efficiency; as, he had *armed* himself with proper passports; to *arm* the younger generation with an adequate education.
to arm a magnet; to provide a magnet with an armature.
Syn.—fortify, equip, furnish, attire, array, supply.

ärm, *v.i.* to take to arms; to equip oneself with weapons; as, the nations *arm* for war.

är·mā′dȧ (*or* -mä′), *n.* [Sp. *armada*; It. *armata*, an armed force; L. *armata*, f. of *armatus*, pp. of *armare*, to arm; *arma*, arms.]
1. a fleet of warships; a squadron.
2. [A–] the Spanish fleet, consisting of 130 ships, sent against England, in the reign of Queen Elizabeth I, 1588.
3. a fleet of warplanes.

är·mȧ·dil′lō, *n.*; *pl.* **är·mȧ·dil′loṣ,** [Sp. dim. of *armada*, from L. *armatus*, armed, pp. of *armare*, to arm.]
1. a name given to a species of toothless, burrowing mammals belonging to the genus *Dasypus*, of Texas and Central and South America. They are covered with a hard, bony shell, and some species can roll up like a ball when attacked. They vary in size, the largest being more than three feet in length. They

feed chiefly on fruits, roots, and insects, and their flesh is edible.

2. [A–] a genus of isopod crustaceans, including the pill bugs.

ARMADILLO (*Dasypus encoubert*)

är·mä'dō, *n.* same as *armada.*

Är·mȧ·ged'dŏn, *n.* [LL. *Armagedon*; Gr. *Armageddōn, Harmagedōn*; ? from Heb. *har,* mountain, and *megiddon,* the plain of Megiddo, proverbial scene of decisive battles.]

1. in the Bible, the place where the last, decisive battle between the forces of good and evil will be fought before the Day of Judgment: Rev. xvi. 16.

2. any great, decisive battle.

är'mȧ·ment, *n.* [L. *armamentum,* pl. *armamenta,* implements, tackle of a ship: from *armare,* to arm; *arma,* arms.]

1. [*often pl.*] all the military forces and equipment of a nation.

2. the offensive equipment of a warship, warplane, fortification, or the like, including guns, rifles, etc.; as, the enemy's *armament* was heavier than ours.

3. an arming or being armed for war.

är″mȧ·men·tā'ri·um, *n.* same as *armamentary.*

är·mȧ·men'tȧ·ry, *n.* [L. *armamentarium,* an arsenal, from *armamenta,* arms, equipment.] an armory; a magazine or arsenal. [Rare.]

är'mȧ·tūre, *n.* [Fr. *armature*; L. *armatura,* arms, equipment, from *armatus,* pp. of *armare,* to arm; *arma,* arms.]

1. armor.

2. the natural defenses or armorlike covering of animals and vegetables, as prickles, spines, and horns.

3. in architecture, any means of bracing or stiffening a weak part, as supports for slender columns, etc.

4. flat wire wound around a cable.

5. in magnetism, a piece of iron connecting the two poles of a horseshoe magnet, in order to keep it from losing its magnetic power.

6. in a dynamo electric machine, the part that revolves, consisting of a series of coils of insulated wire wound around a laminated iron core.

7. the vibrating part in an electric relay or bell.

8. in sculpture, a framework for supporting the clay in modeling.

ärm'chāir, *n.* a chair with supports on the sides for the elbows or arms.

ärmed, *a.* [ppr. of *arm.*] 1. equipped with weapons or any means of offense or defense; fortified.

2. having means of strength or efficiency; made powerful or firm.

3. in biology, having defensive parts or weapons, as horns, claws, prickles, thorns, etc.

4. in magnetism, fitted with an armature, as a magnet or dynamo.

5. in heraldry, furnished with beaks, talons, horns, etc. of a different color from the other parts.

armed at all points; completely covered with armor.

ARMED AT ALL POINTS

ärmed, [from *arm* (limb).] having arms; having upper limbs: usually in compounds, as long-*armed.*

ärmed fōr'ceṣ, all the military, naval, and air forces of a country or group of countries.

Är·mē'ni·ăn, *n.* [Fr. *Arménien*; L. *Armenius*; Gr. *Armenios,* from *Armenia.*]

1. a native or inhabitant of Armenia.

2. the language of Armenia.

3. a member of the Armenian Church.

Är·mē'ni·ăn, *a.* pertaining to Armenia, its people, language, etc.

Armenian bole; a bright red clay found in Armenia.

Armenian Church; the church founded in the fourth century by Gregory, the Illuminator. It is independent of the Orthodox Eastern Church, but agrees with it in some doctrines and practices.

Armenian stone; a soft, blue carbonate of copper, used in the preparation of certain blue pigments: also used in medicine.

ärm'et, *n.* [Fr. *armet, armette,* dim. of *armes,* armor.] a medieval steel helmet with a movable visor.

ARMETS
armet grand armet petit

ärm'ful, *n.*; *pl.* **ärm'fuls,** as much as the arm (or arms) can hold.

ärm'gäunt, *a.* slender, as the arm; also, having thin limbs. [Obs.]

ärm'hōle, *n.* 1. the armpit.

2. a hole for the arm in a garment.

är'mi·gēr, *n.* [L. *armiger,* an armor bearer; *arma,* arms, and *gerere,* to carry, bear.] a knight's armor bearer and companion; hence, later, one just below a knight in degree of rank; a person having the right to a coat of arms.

är'mil, *n.* [L. *armilla,* an armlet, bracelet, from *armus,* arm.]

1. an armillary sphere, or a ring in such a sphere.

2. a bracelet. [Obs.]

är·mi·lau'sȧ, *n.* [L., prob. from *armus,* the shoulder, and *clausus,* shut in, pp. of *claudere,* to shut in.] a medieval garment of various forms, worn in Europe. One form, in the fourteenth century, was a kind of short cloak with a hood.

ARMILAUSA

är·mil'lȧ, *n.*; *pl.* **är·mil'lae,** [L., armlet.]

1. a bracelet or ornament for the wrist.

2. an iron ring, hoop, or brace, in which the gudgeons of a wheel move.

3. in anatomy, a circular ligament of the wrist.

4. a ring of feathers around the lower part of the tibia of birds.

är'mil·lā·ry, *a.* [L. *armilla,* an armlet, armring, from *armus,* shoulder.] resembling a bracelet or ring; also, consisting of rings or circles.

armillary sphere; an ancient astronomical instrument consisting of an artificial sphere, composed of a number of metal rings representing the celestial spheres. This artificial sphere revolved upon its axis within a horizon divided into degrees.

ARMILLARY SPHERE

ärm'ing, *n.* 1. the act of taking up, or furnishing with, arms; also, the act of one who arms.

The *arming* was now universal. —Macaulay.

2. in nautical usage, (a) tallow attached to a sounding lead to bring up specimens from the sea bottom; (b) [*pl.*], waistcloths, hung about a ship's upper works.

3. heraldic arms.

4. a part put on something to make it complete or ready for use.

Är·min'i·ăn, *a.* pertaining to Arminius, a sixteenth century, Dutch theologian, or his followers, or designating his principles and doctrines.

Är·min'i·ăn, *n.* a believer in Arminianism.

Är·min'i·ăn·iṣm, *n.* the doctrines of the Arminians. These are: (1) conditional election and reprobation, in opposition to absolute predestination; (2) universal redemption, or that the atonement was made by Christ for all mankind, though none but believers can be partakers of the benefit; (3) that man, in order to exercise true faith, must be regenerated and renewed by the operation of the Holy Spirit, which is the gift of God, but that this grace is not irresistible, and may be lost, so that men may lapse from a state of grace and die in their sins.

är·mip'ō·tence, *n.* [L. *armipotentia,* power in arms; *arma,* arms, and *potens,* ppr. of *posse,* to be able.] power in battle. [Rare.]

är·mip'ō·tent, *a.* powerful in battle.

är'mis·tice, *n.* [Fr. *armistice,* from L. *arma,* arms, and *stare,* to stand still.] a temporary stopping of warfare by mutual agreement, as a truce preliminary to the signing of a peace treaty or agreement.

Är'mis·tice Dāy, November 11, the anniversary of the day on which a general armistice was declared between the Allies and the Central Powers in World War I in 1918.

ärm'less, *a.* 1. without an arm or branch.

2. having no arms or weapons.

ärm'let, *n.* 1. a small arm or inlet of the sea.

2. a small bandlike sleeve.

3. an ornamental band for the upper arm.

ARMLETS

är·moire'(-mwär'), [Fr.; OFr. *armarie*; L. *armarium,* chest for tools, from *arma,* tools.] a large, usually ornate cupboard, cabinet, or clothespress.

är·mō'ni·aç, *a.* ammoniac. [Obs.]

är'mŏr, *n.* [ME. *armour, armure*; OFr. *armure*; It. *armatura*; L. *armatura,* armor, from *armare,* to arm; *arma,* arms.]

1. any covering worn to protect the body against weapons; a coat or suit of mail: often named from the material, as *plate armor, ring armor, chain armor,* etc.

2. the metal plate on warships, warplanes, etc. for protection, as from artillery fire.

3. armored equipment of an army as tanks and motorized artillery.

4. figuratively, any protection or safeguard.

5. any protective covering, as the shells of some animals, the husk of grain, etc.

är'mŏr, *v.t.*; armored, *pt., pp.*; armoring, *ppr.* to put armor on.

är'mŏr beār″ēr, one who carried the armor or weapons of a warrior; a squire; an armiger.

är'mŏr-çlad″, *a.* covered with armor.

är'mŏred (-mērd), *a.* 1. equipped, furnished, or clad with armor; as, an *armored* train, ship, or knight.

2. equipped with armored vehicles; as, an *armored* division.

är'mŏred çā'ble, an electric cable covered with metal tape for mechanical protection.

är'mŏred çär, any of various vehicles covered with armor plate, as a truck for carrying money to or from a bank; specifically, in military usage, a wheeled motor vehicle with such armor plate, usually carrying a mounted machine gun and used especially as a reconnaissance car.

är'mŏred fōrce, a military force consisting of tank units with supporting troops and used primarily as a unit of offense.

är'mŏr·ēr, *n.* [ME. *armurer, armerer*; OFr. *armurier,* from *armure,* armor.]

1. formerly, a maker of armor or arms; a manufacturer of instruments of war.

2. formerly, a servant who cared for a knight's armor and arms and helped him in putting them on.

3. in military usage, an enlisted man in charge of the maintenance and repair of the small arms of his unit, warship, etc.

är·mō'ri·ăl, *a.* belonging to armor or to a coat of arms.

armorial bearings; in a coat of arms, the devices displayed.

Är·mor'iç, Är·mor'i·căn, *a.* [L. *armoricus*; Celtic *ar,* upon, and *mor,* the sea.] of or pertaining to ancient Armorica, a region in northwestern France, or to its people, language, etc.

Är·mor'iç, Är·mor'i·căn, *n.* 1. the Celtic language of the Armoricans.

2. a native of Armorica, or Brittany.

är'mŏr·ist, *n.* [Fr. *armoriste,* from *armoiries,* a coat of arms, arms.] one skilled in heraldry or in the blazoning of arms.

är′mŏr plāte, plates of iron or steel for covering the sides of a ship, tank, etc.
är′mŏr-plāt″ed, *a.* covered with armor plate.
är′mŏr·y, *n.* [Fr. *armoire*; OFr. *armaire, armarie*, from L. *armarium*, a place for keeping arms.]
1. a place where arms and instruments of war are kept; arsenal.
2. armor. [Archaic.]
3. armorial bearings. Archaic.]
4. the art of heraldry.
5. a place where firearms are manufactured.
6. a building containing the drill hall and offices of a unit of the National Guard.
är′mŏur, *n.* and *v.t.* armor: the British spelling.
är′mŏur·ẽr, *n.* armorer: the British spelling.
är′mŏur·y, *n.* armory: the British spelling.
är·mō·zeen′, är·mō·zïne′, *n.* [Fr. *armoisin*; OFr. *armesin*; L. *ermesinus*, taffeta.] a heavy silk, generally black, formerly used in making robes for the clergy.
ärm′pit, *n.* the hollow place or cavity under the arm at the shoulder; the axilla.
ärmṣ, *n.pl.* [ME. *armes*; Fr. *arme*, pl. *armes*, from L. *arma*, arms, equipment.]
1. weapons.
2. military science; warfare; fighting; as, a comrade in *arms*; an assault at *arms*.
3. in heraldry, armorial bearings of a family, consisting of figures and colors borne in shields, banners, etc., as marks of dignity and distinction, and descending from father to son.
4. insignia of countries, corporations, etc.
small arms; firearms of small caliber that can be carried, as rifles, carbines, pistols, etc.
to arms; get ready to fight!: a summoning to war or battle.
to take up arms; to arm for attack or defense; to enter a dispute.
under arms; having arms ready for use; ready for war.
up in arms; prepared to fight; hence, indignant.
är′mūre, *n.* 1. armor. [Obs.]
2. a kind of ribbed woolen cloth woven so that it looks like chain mail.
är′my, *n.* [ME. *armye, armeye*; OFr. *armee*; It. *armata*; L. *armata*, f. of *armatus*, pp. of *armare*, to arm; *arma*, arms.]
1. a large organized body of men armed for war, especially on land: often it includes an air force.
2. a military unit, usually two or more army corps, together with auxiliary troops; field army.
3. the military forces of a nation as distinguished from its navy; the land forces.
4. a great number; a vast multitude.
5. a body of persons organized for some particular cause; as, the Salvation *Army*.
army of occupation; an army sent into a defeated country to ensure compliance with the terms of the peace treaty: the army of occupation exercises military rule of the territory.
standing army; an army maintained in peacetime, as well as in time of war, on a permanent organizational basis.
Är′my Āir Fōr′ceṣ, formerly, the aviation branch of the United States Army.
är′my ȧnt, a foraging ant that travels in large groups, as the driver ant.
är′my cōrps (kōr), a tactical military unit of two or more divisions with auxiliary services, usually commanded by a lieutenant general.
är′my list, an official register of the commissioned officers of an army.
Är′my of the Ū·nīt′ed Stātes, the United States Army, the Organized Reserves, the National Guard, and Selective Service personnel, collectively: organized temporarily during time of war or other national emergency.
är′my wŏrm, the larva of a moth, *Leucania unipuncta*: so called because vast numbers move like an army, destroying all vegetation in their path; also, any related species with similar habits.
är′nȧ, *n.* [Hind. *arnā*.] one of the numerous varieties of wild buffalo, *Bos babulus*, of India.
är′nee, *n.* same as *arna*.
Är′ni·çȧ, *n.* [prob. from *Ptarmica*; Gr. *ptarmikos*, causing to sneeze.]
1. a genus of plants of the order *Compositæ*.
2. [a–] any plant of this genus, especially the perennial *Arnica montana*, or mountain arnica, bearing bright yellow flowers on long stalks with clusters of leaves at the base.
3. [a–] tincture of arnica, applied externally as a treatment for sprains, bruises, and ailments of a similar kind.

är′ni·cin, *n.* in chemistry, a bitter resin that contains the active principle of arnica.
Är′nŏld·ist, *n.* a disciple of Arnold of Brescia, who, in the twelfth century, was executed for insurrection against Roman Catholic corruption.
är·not′tō, *n.* same as *annatto*.
är′nut, *n.* same as *earthnut*.
är·ō·ġi′rȧ (-ā′rȧ), *n.* [native Braz. name.] any one of several South American trees from which a medicinal resin is extracted.
ar′oid, *a.* resembling or belonging to the *Arum* family.
ar′oid, *n.* [L. *arum*; Gr. *aron*, wake robin, and *eidos*, shape, form.] any plant of the *Arum* family.
Ȧ·roi′dē·ae, *n.pl.* [L., from Gr. *aron*, the wake robin, and *eidos*, form.] same as *Araceæ*.
ȧ·roid′ē·ous, *a.* araceous.
ȧ·roint′, ȧ·roynt′, *v.i.* [prob. coined by Shakespeare (*Macbeth* I, iii, 6).] begone; avaunt (usually with *thee*): used in the imperative. [Obs.]
ȧ·rol′lȧ, *n.* [Fr. *arolle*.] a tree of the pine family, *Pinus Cembra*, found in Switzerland.
ȧ·rō′mȧ, *n.* [ME. *aromat*; OFr. *aromat*; L. *aroma*; Gr. *arōma*, a sweet spice, a sweet smell.]
1. the fragrance of plants, or other substances; a pleasant, often spicy odor.
2. a characteristic quality or atmosphere; as, the *aroma* of culture.
Syn.—fragrance, perfume, savor.
ar·ō·mat′iç, ar·ō·mat′iç·ăl, *a.* 1. fragrant; spicy; strong-scented; odoriferous; having an agreeable odor.
2. in chemistry, of or designating any of a series of benzene ring compounds, many of which have an odor or are derived from materials having an odor.
ar·ō·mat′iç, *n.* a plant or chemical characterized by a fragrant smell, and usually by a warm, pungent taste, as ginger.
ar·ō·mat·i·zā′tion, *n.* the act of making aromatic.
ȧ·rō′mȧ·tīze, *v.t.*; aromatized, *pt.*, *pp.*; aromatizing, *ppr.* to make aromatic; to infuse with an aromatic odor; to give a spicy scent or taste; to perfume.
ȧ·rō′mȧ·tī·zẽr, *n.* that which, or one who, aromatizes.
ȧ·rō′mȧ·tous, *a.* aromatic. [Obs.]
ȧ·rōṣe′, past tense of *arise*.
ȧ·round′, *prep.* 1. about; on all sides of; encircling; encompassing; in various places in or on; revolving about (a center or axis).
2. somewhat close to; about; as, *around* five pounds. [Colloq.]
ȧ·round′, *adv.* 1. in a circle; on every side; in circumference; in or to the opposite direction; in various places.
2. to a (specified or understood) place; as, come *around* to see us.
3. in the vicinity; about; near by; as, he visited *around*. [Colloq.]
to have been around; to have had wide experience; to be sophisticated. [Colloq.]
ȧ·rouṣ′ăl, *n.* the act of arousing.
ȧ·rouṣe′, *v.t.*; aroused, *pt.*, *pp.*; arousing, *ppr.* [*a-* and ME. *rowsen, rouzen*.]
1. to wake up; to awaken.
2. to excite into action; to stir up or put in motion; as, to *arouse* the dormant faculties.
Syn.—stimulate, provoke, animate, awaken, excite.
ȧ·rouṣe′, *v.i.* to become aroused.
ȧ·rōw′, *adv.* in a row; successively.
är·peġ′ġiō (-pej′ō), *n.*; *pl.* **är·peġ′ġiōṣ,** [It. *arpeggiare*, to play on a harp.]
1. in music, the sounding of the notes of a chord in rapid succession, as in harp playing, instead of simultaneously.
2. a chord so played.
är′pent, *n.* [Fr. *arpent*; LL. *arapennes*; L. *arepennis*; a word of Celtic origin.] an old measure of land in France, equal to about an acre: retained in Louisiana, and Quebec, Canada.
är·pen·tā′tŏr, *n.* a land surveyor. [Rare.]
är′pine, *n.* arpent. [Obs.]
är′quā·ted, *a.* [L. *arcuare*, to bend like a bow, from *arcus*, bow.] arcuate; curved. [Rare.]
är′quē·bus, *n.* same as *harquebus*.
är″quē·bus·āde′, *n.* same as *harquebusade*.
är″quē·bus·iẽr′, *n.* same as *harquebusier*.
är′qui·fōux (är′ki-fọ̈), *n.* same as *alquifou*.
är·rȧ·çȧ′chȧ, *n.* [Sp.] a Mexican plant, belonging to the genus *Arracacia*.
Är·rȧ·çȧ′ci·ȧ (-shi-ȧ), *n.* [Sp., from a native name.] a genus of umbelliferous plants of the carrot family, growing in Mexico and South America.
ar′răçh, *n.* same as *orach*.

ar′rack, *n.* [Fr. *arac*; Ar. *araq*, sweat, spirit, juice.] in the Orient, a strong alcoholic drink, especially that distilled from rice, molasses, or the sap of the cocoa palm.
ar·rāign′ (-rān′), *v.t.*; arraigned (-rānd), *pt.*, *pp.*; arraigning, *ppr.* [ME. *araynen, arenen*; OFr. *aranier*; L. *ad*, to, and *ratio*, reason.]
1. in law, to call (a prisoner) before a court to stand trial.
2. to accuse; to charge with faults; to call to account or in question.

> They will not *arraign* you for want of knowledge. —Dryden.

Syn.—accuse, attack, censure, impeach, inculpate.
ar·rāign′, *v.t.* in English law, to appeal to; to demand. [Obs.]
ar·rāign′, *n.* arraignment; as, clerk of the *arraigns*.
ar·rāign′ẽr, *n.* one who arraigns.
ar·rāign′ment, *n.* [Norm. *arresnement, araynement*.]
1. the act of arraigning; the act of calling a person before a court to answer to a complaint or indictment and to plead guilty or not guilty.
2. a calling in question for faults; accusation.
ar·rāi′ment, *n.* raiment. [Obs.]
ar·rānġe′, *v.t.*; arranged (-rānjd), *pt.*, *pp.*; arranging, *ppr.* [ME. *arayngen, arengen*; OFr. *arangier*; Fr. *arranger*, from *ad* and *ranger*, to set in order.]
1. to put in proper order; to sort systematically; to classify.
2. to adjust; to settle; to put in order; to prepare; as, to *arrange* details.
3. to adapt (a musical composition) to other instruments or voices than those for which it was written, or to a certain band or orchestra.
Syn.—class, dispose, place, range, group, adjust.
ar·rānġe′, *v.i.* 1. to come to an agreement (*with* a person, *about* a thing).
2. to make plans; provide or prepare (with *for* or an infinitive).
3. in music, to write adaptations, especially as a profession.
ar·rānġe′ment, *n.* 1. the act of putting in proper order; also, the state of being put in order.
2. that which is arranged or the result of arranging.
3. [*usually pl.*] a preparatory measure or plan; as, we have made *arrangements* for receiving company.
4. a settlement or adjustment by agreement; as, the parties have made an *arrangement* between themselves concerning their disputes.
5. a combination of parts; hence, loosely, a contrivance or apparatus.
6. the adaptation of a musical composition to other instruments or voices than those for which it was originally written, or to the style of a certain band or orchestra; also, a composition so adapted.
Syn.—classification, adjustment, agreement, disposition, grouping, disposal, order.
ar·rān′ġẽr, *n.* one who or that which arranges.
ar′rănt, *a.* [a variant of *errant*.]
1. notorious; infamous; vile; as, an *arrant* rogue or coward.
2. wandering. [Obs.]
Syn.—consummate, notorious, flagrant, vile, utter.
ar′rănt·ly, *adv.* notoriously; infamously; shamefully.
ar′răs, *n.* [so called from *Arras*, from L. *Atrebates*, a people of Belgic Gaul.] a tapestry; a wall hanging of tapestry.
ar′răs, *n.* [Sp.] in Spanish law, a marriage settlement.
ar′răs, *v.t.* to hang or furnish with an arras.
ar·răs·ēne′, *n.* a silk or woolen material used for embroidery.
är·răs′trȧ, *n.* same as *arrastre*.
är·răs′tre, *n.* [Sp. *arrastrar*, to drag along the ground; L. *ad*, to, and *radere*, to scrape.] in gold mining, a crude machine formerly used for ore crushing.
ar′răs·wīṣe, *adv.* same as *arriswise*.
ar·rāy′, *n.* [ME. *arayen*; OFr. *areyer, arraier*; L. *ad*, to, and *res*, thing.]
1. regular order or arrangement; specifically, disposition of troops; as, in battle *array*.
2. an impressive collection or assemblage; especially, a body of men in order; hence, military force; troops in order.

> A gallant *array* of nobles and cavaliers. —Prescott.

3. dress; garments arranged in order upon the person; raiment or apparel.

Emily ere day
Arose, and dress'd herself in rich *array*. —Dryden.

4. situation; circumstances; position. [Obs.]

Thou stondest yet (quod sche) in swiche *array*. —Chaucer.

5. in law, (a) the number of persons summoned to serve upon a jury; (b) the act of empaneling a jury; (c) the jury empaneled.

Challenge to the *array*, when exception is taken to the whole number impannelled. —Fonblanque.

ar·rāy′, *v.t.*; arrayed (-rād), *pt., pp.*; arraying, *ppr.* 1. to place in order, as troops for battle.

2. to deck out; to adorn with dress, especially with finery.

Pharaoh *arrayed* him (Joseph) in vestures of fine linen. —Gen. xli. 42.

3. to set (a jury) in order for the trial of a cause; that is, to call (them) man by man.

Syn.—arrange, marshal, dispose, rank, place, deck, adorn, dress.

ar·rāy′ăl, *n.* 1. the act or process of arraying.

2. something arrayed.

ar·rāy′ẽr, *n.* 1. one who arrays.

2. in English history, a commissioner of array, who was charged with putting the soldiers of a county in condition for military service.

ar·rēar′, *adv.* behind; in the rear or toward the back. [Obs.]

ar·rēar′āġe, *n.* 1. the state of being in arrears.

2. arrears.

3. a thing kept in reserve.

ar·rēarṣ, *n.pl.* [Fr. *arriere*, the back part, stern; ME. *arere*; L. *ad*, to, and *retro*, back, backward.]

1. unpaid and overdue debts.

2. any obligation not met on time; unfinished business, work, etc.

in arrears (or *arrear*); behind in paying a debt, doing one's work, etc.

ar·reçt′, ar·reçt′ed, *a.* [L. *arrectus*, pp. of *arrigere*, to set upright.]

1. erect; raised; upright.

2. attentive, as a person listening.

ar·reçt′, *v.t.* to erect; to direct. [Obs.]

ar·reçt′ȧ·ry, *n.* an upright post; a vertical beam. [Obs.]

ar·re·not′ō·kous, *a.* [Gr. *arrēnotokos*, bearing males, from *arrēn*, male, and *tiktein*, to bring forth.] same as *arrhenotokous*.

ar·ren·tā′tion, *n.* [OFr. *arrenter*; L. *ad*, to, and *redditus*, pp. of *reddere*, to return, give back.] in old English law, the act of licensing the owner of land in a forest to enclose it with a small ditch and low hedge for a yearly rent.

ar·rep′tion, *n.* [L. *arripere*, to snatch away.] a removing; the act of taking away. [Obs.]

ar·rep·ti′tious (-tish′us), *a.* snatched away; hence, carried away by dementia; frantic; mad. [Obs.]

ar·rest′, *v.t.*; arrested, *pt., pp.*; arresting, *ppr.* [ME. *arresten*, *aresten*; OFr. *arester*; Fr. *arrêter*; L. *ad*, to, and *restare*, to stay back, remain.]

1. to obstruct; to stop; to check or hinder the motion of; as, to *arrest* the current of a river; to *arrest* the senses; to *arrest* the course of justice.

2. to take, seize, or apprehend by authority of the law; as, to *arrest* one for debt or for a crime.

3. to attract, seize on, and fix; as, to *arrest* the eyes or attention.

4. to rest or fix (the senses, etc.); as, to *arrest* our thoughts upon divine mercy. [Obs.]

Syn.—apprehend, withhold, capture, restrain, detain, seize, take, hold, stop.

ar·rest′, *v.i.* to tarry; to stop; to rest. [Obs.]

ar·rest′, *n.* 1. the act of arresting or state of being arrested; a stop, hindrance, or restraint; any stay, seizure, check, or interruption, as of movement, growth, or development.

2. the taking or apprehending of a person by authority of the law; apprehension; legal custody, or restraint.

3. any seizure, or taking by power, physical or moral.

arrest of judgment; in law, the staying or stopping of a judgment after verdict, for legal causes. The motion for this purpose is called a motion in *arrest of judgment*.

under arrest; in legal custody, as of the police.

ar·res·tā′tion, *n.* arrest.

ar·res·tee′, *n.* in Scots law, the person in whose hands an arrester seizes or attaches property.

ar·rest′ẽr, *n.* 1. one who or that which arrests.

2. in Scots law, the person who arrests a debt or property held by another.

ar·rest′ing, *a.* [ppr. of *arrest*.] attracting attention; interesting; striking.

ar·rest′ive, *a.* having a tendency to arrest.

ar·rest′ment, *n.* 1. the act of arresting or a being arrested; obstruction; stoppage.

2. in Scots law, (a) a process by which a creditor may attach money or movable property which a third party holds on behalf of his debtor; (b) the arrest or detention of a criminal until he gives bail to stand trial, or the securing of a debtor until he pays the debt or gives security for its payment.

ar·rest′ŏr, *n.* one who arrests.

ar·ret′ (*or* -rā′), *n.* [Fr. *arrêt*; OFr. *arest*, to detain, to fix, to determine.]

1. the decision of a court, tribunal, or council; a decree; the edict of a sovereign: applied particularly to the judgments and decisions of courts and tribunals in France.

2. an arrest; a seizure by legal authority.

Ar′re·tine wāre, in ceramics, a red terra cotta pottery made in Italy.

ar′rhȧ (-rȧ), *n.*; *pl.* **ar′rhae,** [L. *arrha*, or *arra*; Gr. *arrabon*, earnest money.] earnest money.

ar·rhȧ·phos′tiç, *a.* [Gr. *arrhaphos*, seamless; *a* priv., and *rhapkē*, a seam.] seamless. [Rare.]

ar·rhe·not′ō·kous, *a.* producing males only, as the females of certain bees and sawflies, by parthenogenesis.

är·rhin′i·ȧ, *n.* congenital absence of the nose.

ar·rhī′zous, ar·rhī′zăl, *a.* [Gr. *arrhizos*, without roots; *a* priv., and *rhiza*, a root.] having no true roots, as certain parasitical plants.

ar·rhyth′mi·ȧ, *n.* [Gr. *arrhythmos*, without rhythm; *a* priv., and *rhythmos*, rhythm.] irregularity in the rhythm of the heartbeat.

ar·rhyth′miç, ar·rhyth′mous, *a.* lacking in rhythm; irregular, as the heartbeat.

ar·rhyth′my, *a.* lack of rhythm or meter. [Rare.]

ar′riāġe (-rāj), *n.* [Scot. contr. of *average*.] in Scots law, a service performed by tenants for their feudal lords: now abolished.

är·rī′bä, *n.* an excellent kind of cacao from Equador. The name comes from an upland district in Guayas, Equador.

är·ric′ciō (-rēt′chō), *n.* [It.] the first coat of plaster used as a base in fresco painting.

ar·rīde′, *v.t.* [L. *arridere*, to laugh at; *ad*, to, *ridere*, to laugh.] to laugh at; also, to please. [Archaic.]

ar′ri·ēre, *n.* [Fr. *arrière*, from OFr. *ariere*, rear.] the rear; that which is behind.

ar·rière-ban′, [Fr. (är-riēr-bän); LL. *aribanum*, *herebannum*, from O.H.G. *heriban*, the summoning of an army to the field.]

1. an edict of the ancient kings of France commanding all their vassals to assemble prepared for war or forfeit their estates.

2. the vassals so assembled.

ar′ri·ēre fee, ar′ri·ēre′ fief, a fee or fief dependent on a superior fee, or a fee held of a feudatory.

ar·rière-pen·sée′ (är-riēr-pän-sā′), *n.* [Fr., lit., a back-thought.] an ulterior motive or mental reservation.

ar′ri·ēre vas′săl, the vassal of a vassal.

ar′ri·ēre-vöus·sūre′, *n.* a rear arch; an arch placed within the opening of a window or door, but of a different form.

ARRIERE-VOUSSURE

ar′ris, *n.* [Fr. *areste*, *arête*; OFr. *areste*; L. *arista*, the awn or beard of an ear of grain.] in architecture, the edge formed by two straight or curved surfaces meeting each other at an angle: applied particularly to the edges in moldings, and to the raised edges which separate the flutings in a Doric column.

ar′ris fil′let, a triangular wooden molding used to raise the slates or shingles of a roof against a chimney or a wall to shed the rain more effectually.

ar′ris gut′tẽr, a wooden eaves gutter having the form of the letter V.

ar′ris·wīṣe, *adv.* diagonally arranged, as certain tiles or slates.

ar·rīv′ăl, *n.* [ME. *aryvaile*, *arrivaile*.]

1. the act of arriving.

2. the attainment or reaching of any object or state by effort or action, or by natural process; as, *arrival* at a just decision.

3. the person or thing arriving; as, news brought by the last *arrival*.

The next *arrivals* here will gladlier build their nests. —Warner.

ar·rīv′ănce, *n.* 1. people arriving. [Obs.]

2. arrival. [Obs.]

ar·rīve′, *v.i.*; arrived, *pt., pp.*; arriving, *ppr.* [Fr. *arriver*; ME. *ariven*, *aryven*; OFr. *ariver*, *arriver*; L. *ad*, to, and *ripa*, bank.]

1. literally, to come to the shore, or bank. [Obs.]

2. to reach one's destination; come to a place.

3. to come; as, the time has *arrived* for action.

4. to attain success, fame, etc.; as, he has *arrived* professionally.

to arrive at; (a) to reach by traveling; (b) to reach by work, thinking, development, etc.; as, to *arrive at* a conclusion.

Syn.—achieve, get to, reach, attain, come.

ar·rīve′, *v.t.* to reach; to come to; also, to bring to shore. [Obs.]

ar·rīv′ẽr, *n.* one who or that which arrives.

är·rō′bä, *n.* [Sp. and Port. *arroba*; Ar. *arrob*; *al*, and *rob*.]

1. a Spanish unit of weight used in Mexico and some South American countries, equal to 25.36 pounds.

2. a Portuguese unit of weight used in Brazil, equal to 32.39 pounds.

3. a unit of liquid measure used in some Spanish-speaking countries, equal to 17.04 quarts (for wine) or 13.28 quarts (for oil).

ar′rō·gănce, *n.* [ME. *arrogance*, *arrogaunce*; OFr. *arrogance*; L. *arrogantia*, arrogance; *arrogare*, to claim.] the act or quality of having unwarranted pride and self-importance; haughtiness.

Supple knees
Feed *arrogance*, and are the proud man's fees. —Shak.

Syn.—assumption, pride, haughtiness, presumption, self-conceit, vanity.

ar′rō·găn·cy, *n.* arrogance.

ar′rō·gănt, *a.* 1. full of or due to unwarranted pride and self-importance; giving oneself an undue degree of importance; haughty; conceited: applied to persons; as, an *arrogant* churchman.

2. containing arrogance; marked with arrogance; proceeding from undue claims of self-importance: applied to things; as, *arrogant* pretensions or behavior.

Syn.—overbearing, domineering, presumptuous, imperious, insolent, stately, haughty, lordly, proud, rude.

ar′rō·gănt·ly, *adv.* in an arrogant manner; with undue pride or self-importance.

ar′rō·gănt·ness, *n.* arrogance. [Rare.]

ar′rō·gāte, *v.t.*; arrogated, *pt., pp.*; arrogating, *ppr.* [L. *arrogare*, to claim; *ad*, to, or for, and *rogare*, to ask.] to claim or demand unduly or presumptuously; to appropriate (*to* oneself) arrogantly; to lay claim to in an overbearing manner; as, to *arrogate* power or dignity to oneself.

Who, not content
With fair equality, fraternal state,
Will *arrogate* dominion undeserved
Over his brethren. —Milton.

Syn.—appropriate, assume, affect, seize.

ar·rō·gā′tion, *n.* 1. the act of arrogating; an unwarranted claim or assumption.

2. in Roman law, the act of adopting an adult person into a family.

ar′rō·gā·tive, *a.* assuming or making undue claims and assumptions. [Rare.]

ȧr·roṇ·disse′ment (-dīs′moṅ), *n.* [Fr., from *arrondir*, to make round.] in France, the largest administrative subdivision of a department; also, a municipal subdivision.

ar·rō′ṣion, *n.* [L. *arrosus*, pp. of *arrodere*, to gnaw at.] a gnawing. [Obs.]

ar′rōw, *n.* [ME. *arow*; AS. *arwa*, *arewe*, arrow; L. *arquus*, *arcus*, a bow.]

1. a slender shaft, usually pointed at one end and feathered at the other, for shooting from a bow.

2. anything like an arrow in form, speed, purpose, etc.

3. a sign (←) used to indicate direction or position.

ar'rōw grȧss, any of various grasslike plants, species of the genus *Triglochin*. Two common species are the marsh arrow grass, *Triglochin palustre*, and the seaside arrow grass, *Triglochin maritimum*.

ar'rōw·head (-hed), *n.* 1. the separable, pointed head of an arrow, formerly made of flint or stone, now usually of steel.
 2. any of various aquatic plants, species of the genus *Sagittaria*; so called from the shape of their leaves.

ar'rōw·head″ed, *a.* shaped like the head of an arrow; cuneiform.

ar'rōw·root, *n.* [so named from use as antidote for poisoned arrows.]
 1. a tropical American plant of the genus *Maranta*, with large leaves, white flowers, and starchy roots.
 2. a digestible starch obtained from the rhizomes or rootstocks of *Maranta arundinacea*, or arrowroot plant.

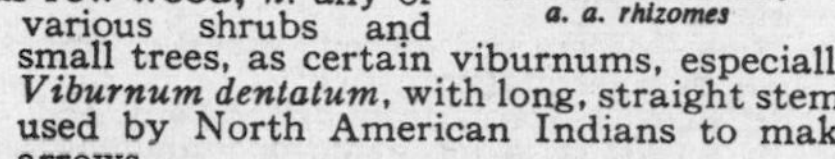

ARROWROOT (*Maranta arundinacea*) a. a. rhizomes

ar'rōw snāke, a snakelike lizard of the genus *Acontias*: also called *dart snake*.

ar'rōw stōne, a belemnite.

ar'rōw·wood, *n.* any of various shrubs and small trees, as certain viburnums, especially *Viburnum dentatum*, with long, straight stems used by North American Indians to make arrows.

ar'rōw·wŏrm (-wẽrm), *n.* one of the phylum *Chaetognatha* of transparent, arrow-shaped marine worms.

ar'rōw·y, *a.* 1. of or full of arrows.
 2. resembling an arrow in form, appearance, or manner of motion; slender; sharp; darting, piercing.

ar·roy'ō, *n.*; *pl.* **ar·roy'ōs,** [Sp.] 1. a dry gully.
 2. a rivulet; a stream.

ärse, *n.* [ME. *ars*; AS. *ears, ærs*; Gr. *orros*, or *orsos*, the rump.] the buttocks: now a vulgar term.

är'se·năl, *n.* [ME. *arcenal, arsinal, archinale*; Sp., Port., Fr., Arm. *arsenal*, a magazine or repository of stores; in It. and Sp., a dock or dockyard; from Ar. *dār aṣ-sinā'ah*, workshop, lit., house of skill or trade.]
 1. a place for making or storing weapons and other munitions.
 2. a store or collection; as, an *arsenal* of facts used in a debate.

är'se·nāte, *n.* a salt or ester of arsenic acid.

är'se·niç, *n.* [ME. *arsenik, arsnek*; OFr. *arcenic*; L. *arsenicum*; Gr. *arsenikon*, from *arsenikos*, strong, masculine.]
 1. a silvery-white, brittle, very poisonous chemical element, compounds of which are used in making insecticides, glass, medicines, etc.: symbol, As; atomic weight, 74.91; atomic number, 33.
 2. loosely, arsenic trioxide, As_2O_3 or As_4O_6, a very poisonous compound of arsenic: it is a white powder and has no taste.

är·sen'iç, *a.* 1. consisting of or containing arsenic.
 2. in chemistry, containing arsenic with a valence of five.

är·sen'iç ac'id, a colorless arsenic compound, H_3AsO_4.

är·sen'iç·ăl, *a.* of or containing arsenic.

är·sen'iç·ăl, *n.* a preparation that contains arsenic.

är·sen'i·çāte, *v.t.*; arsenicated, *pt.*, *pp.*; arsenicating, *ppr.* to combine with arsenic.

är'sen·īde (*or* -id), *n.* in chemistry, a compound of arsenic and an element or a radical, in which arsenic has a negative valence of three.

är·sen·if'ẽr·ous, *a.* yielding arsenic.

är·sē'ni·ous, *a.* same as *arsenous*.

är'sen·īte, *n.* a salt or ester of arsenous acid.

är·sē'niū·ret, *n.* arsenide: former name.

är·sē'niū·ret·ed, är·sē'niū·ret·ted, *a.* [from *arseniuret*, from L. *arsenicum*, arsenic, and *-uret*, Mod. L. *-uretum*, formerly used as equivalent to *-ide*.] combined with arsenic.

är'se·nō-, a combining form meaning *having arsenic as a constituent*; as, *arseno*pyrite.

är″sen·ō·py̆r'īte, *n.* [Gr. *arsen*, male, and *pyritēs*, a flint, from *pyr*, fire.] a hard, brittle, silvery-white mineral, iron arsenic sulfide, FeAsS, the main ore of arsenic.

är'sen·ous, *a.* 1. of or containing arsenic.
 2. in chemistry, containing arsenic with a valence of three.

ärs grā'ti·ȧ är'tis (grā'shi-ȧ), [L.] art for art's sake.

är·shĭn', *n.* same as *archine*.

är·sīne' (*or* är'sēn), *n.* [from *arsenic*, and *-ine*.]
 1. arseniureted hydrogen, AsH_3, a very poisonous, inflammable gas that smells like garlic.
 2. any of its derivatives.

är'sis, *n.*; *pl.* **är'sēs,** [Gr. *arsis*, a raising, omission, from *airein*, to lift up.]
 1. originally, the unaccented part of a foot of verse.
 2. now, the accented part of a foot of verse: this sense resulted from a misunderstanding of the original Greek.
 3. in music, the unaccented part of a measure; upbeat.

ärs lon'gȧ, vī'tȧ bre'vis, [L.] art (is) long, life (is) short.

är'sŏn, *n.* [OFr. *arson, arsoun*; from L. *arsus*, pp. of *ardere*, to burn.] the crime of purposely setting fire to another's building or property, or to one's own so as to collect insurance.

ärs·phen'ȧ·mīne, *n.* a yellowish arsenical powder from which an aqueous, saline solution is prepared for use in the treatment of syphilis and some other diseases: also called *salvarsan*.

ärs pō·e'ti·çȧ, [L.] the art of poetry.

ärt, the archaic second person singular, indicative mood, present tense, of the verb *to be*: used with *thou*.

ärt, *n.* [ME. *art, arte*; OFr. *art*; L. *ars* (*artis*), root *ar*, to join; Gr. *artunein*, to arrange.]
 1. the disposition or modification of things by human skill, to answer the purpose intended. In this sense *art* stands opposed to *nature*.
 2. creative work generally, or its principles; the making or doing of things that have form and beauty: art includes painting, sculpture, architecture, music, literature, drama, the dance, etc. The term *fine arts* usually is restricted to the graphic arts, drawing, painting, sculpture, ceramics, and, sometimes, architecture. The term *arts* is used of any of certain branches of learning, as literature, music, and mathematics: in this sense the *arts* are usually distinguished from the *sciences*.
 3. any branch of this, especially painting, drawing, or work in any other graphic or plastic medium.
 4. products of creative work: paintings, statues, etc.
 5. skill, dexterity, or the power of performing certain actions, acquired by experience, study, or observation; as, he has the *art* of managing his business to advantage.
 6. cunning; artful behavior.
 7. [*usually in pl.*] a trick; wile.
 8. the special skill required by those who practice one of the fine arts; artistic faculty.
 art and part; in Scots law, a term denoting the charge of contriving a criminal design as well as of participating in the perpetration of the criminal act.
 Syn.—aptitude, readiness, skill, dexterity, adroitness, contrivance, cunning, artifice, deceit, duplicity.

-ärt, same as *-ard*.

är'tăl, *n.* plural of *rotl*.

ärt deç'ō, [after the *Exposition Internationale des Arts Décoratifs et Industriels Modernes*, held in Paris (1925).] a decorative style of the late 1920's and the 1930's derived from cubism, based generally on geometric forms, and applied to furnishings, textiles, graphic arts, etc.: revived in the mid-1960's.

är'tē·făçt, *n.* same as *artifact*.

är·tel', *n.* in Soviet Russia, a union of workers who share the income of their collective labor.

Är·tē'mi·ȧ, *n.* [Gr. *Artemis*, the goddess.] a genus of brine shrimp belonging to the subclass *Branchiopoda*.

Är'tē·mis, *n.* [L. and Gr. *Artemis*.] in Greek mythology, the goddess of the moon, wild animals, and hunting, Apollo's twin sister: she is identified with the Roman goddess Diana.

Är·tē·mi'ṣi·ȧ, *n.* [Gr. *Artemisia*.] a genus of plants of numerous species, including the mugwort, southernwood, and wormwood. *Artemisia absinthium* is the common wormwood.

är·tē'ri·ăl, *a.* 1. pertaining to an artery or the arteries; as, *arterial* action.
 2. like an artery; composed of a principal channel and a system of branches; as, an *arterial* river.
 arterial blood; blood that has been arterialized by passing through the lungs. It differs from venous blood particularly in its brighter red color.

är·tē″ri·ăl·i·zā'tion, *n.* the process of changing venous into arterial blood by the absorption of oxygen in the lungs.

är·tē'ri·ăl·īze, *v.t.*; arterialized, *pt.*, *pp.*; arterializing, *ppr.* to change (venous blood) into arterial blood by oxygenation.

är·tē'ri·ō-, [Gr. *artēria*, artery.] a combining form used in anatomy, etc., meaning *artery, of the arteries*.

är·tē'ri·ō·gram, *n.* [*arterio-* and *-gram*.] an X-ray obtained by arteriography.

är·tē·ri·og'rȧ·phy, *n.* [*arterio-* and *-graphy*.] X-ray examination of arteries after injection of radiopaque dyes.

är·tē'ri·ōle, *n.* any of the small arteries.

är·tē·ri·ol'ō·ġy, *n.* [Gr. *artēria*, artery, and *logos*, discourse.] a treatise or discourse on arteries.

är·tē″ri·ō·sçlē·rō'sis, *n.* a thickening and hardening of the walls of the arteries.

är·tē″ri·ō·sçlē·rot'iç, *a.* of or having arteriosclerosis.

är·tē·ri·ot'ō·my, *n.* [Gr. *artēriotomia*, the cutting of an artery; *artēria*, artery, and *temnein*, to cut.]
 1. the opening of an artery by a lancet or other instrument.
 2. that branch of anatomy which treats of the dissection of the arteries.

är·tē·rī'tis, *n.* inflammation occurring in an artery or arteries.

är'tẽr·y, *n.* [ME. *arterie*; OFr. *artere*; L. *arteria*, the windpipe, an artery; Gr. *artēria*, from *aeirein*, to lift up, to heave.]
 1. the trachea, or windpipe. [Obs.]
 2. any one of the system of branching tubes carrying blood from the heart to all parts of the body: distinguished from *vein*.
 3. a main road or channel; as, a railroad *artery*.

Är·tē'ṣiăn, *a.* [Fr. *artésien*, lit., pertaining to *Artois* in France.]
 1. of or belonging to Artois in France.
 2. [a–] of an artesian well, believed to have been first used in Artois.
 artesian well; a perpendicular boring into the ground through which water rises to the surface, due to underground pressure.

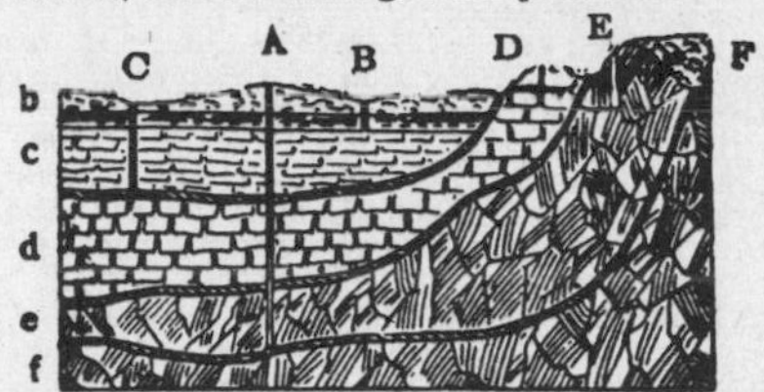

ARTESIAN WELL
Wells *A, B, C* connect through the impermeable strata *b, c, d, e, f,* with the water-bearing strata *D, E, F.*

ärt'fụl, *a.* 1. performed with art or skill. [Archaic.]
 2. artificial; imitative.
 3. cunning; practicing art, or stratagem; crafty; as, an *artful* boy.
 4. proceeding from art or craft; as, an *artful* scheme.
 Syn.—dexterous, designing, cunning, shrewd, crafty, subtle, wily, sly, adroit, deceitful.

ärt'fụl·ly, *adv.* in an artful manner.

ärt'fụl·ness, *n.* art; craft; cunning.

ärthr-, see *arthro-*.

är'thrăl, *a.* [Gr. *arthron*, a joint.] of or pertaining to a joint.

är·thral'ġi·ȧ, *n.* a neuralgic pain in a joint or joints.

är·thral'ġiç, *a.* of or having arthralgia.

är·threç'to·my, *n.* in surgery, the excision of a joint.

är·thrit'iç, är·thrit'iç·ăl, *a.* pertaining to or having arthritis.

är·thrī'tis, *n.* [Gr. *arthritis*, from *arthron*, a joint.] inflammation of a joint or joints.

är'thri·tiṣm, *n.* a tendency to arthritis.

är'thrō-, ärthr-, [L. *artus*; Gr. *arthron*, a joint.] a combining form used to express *relation to* or *connection with a joint*.

är·thrō·brañ'çhi·ȧ, *n.*; *pl.* **är·thrō·brañ'çhi·ae,** [*arthro-*, and Gr. *branchia*, gills.] in crustaceans, a gill attached to the membrane between the body and the first joint of the leg.

är'thrō·dẽrm, *n.* [*arthro-*, and Gr. *derma*, skin.] the horny envelope, or shell, of an arthropod.

är·thrō'di·ȧ, *n.*; *pl.* **är·thrō'di·ae,** [Gr., from *arthron*, joint, and *eidos*, form.] in anatomy, a type of joint in which the head of one bone is received into the shallow socket of another, as that of the humerus into the glenoid cavity of the scapula.

är·thrō′di·ăl, är·throd′iç, *a.* relating to an arthrodia.

är·thrō·dyn′i·ȧ, *n.* [*arthro-*, and Gr. *odynē*, pain.] pain in a joint or joints; arthralgia.

är·thrō·dyn′iç, *a.* pertaining to arthrodynia.

Är·thrō·gas′trȧ, *n.pl.* [*arthro-*, and Gr. *gastēr*, the belly.] an order of *Arachnida* in which the abdomen is distinctly divided into somites, or segments, as in the scorpion.

är·throg′rȧ·phy, *n.* [*arthro-*, and Gr. *graphē*, description.] a scientific description of the joints.

är·throl′ō·ġy, *n.* [*arthro-*, and Gr. *logos*, description.] the branch of anatomy dealing with the joints.

är′thrō·mēre, *n.* [*arthro-*, and Gr. *miros*, a part.] any body segment of a jointed animal.

är′thron, *n.*; *pl.* **är′thrȧ,** a joint.

är·throp′ȧ·thy, *n.* [*arthro-*, and Gr. *pathos*, suffering.] a disease of the joints.

är·thrō·pleū′rȧ, *n.*; *pl.* **är·thrō·pleū′rae,** [*arthro-*, and Gr. *pleura*, side.] the side or limb-bearing part of one of the segments of an arthropod.

är′thrō·pod, *n.* one of the *Arthropoda*.

Är·throp′ō·dȧ, *n.pl.* [*arthro-*, and Gr. *pous*, genitive *podos*, a foot.] one of the two primary divisions (*Anarthropoda* being the other) into which modern scientists have divided the subkingdom *Articulata*, characterized by a segmented body and jointed legs. It includes crustaceans, arachnids, insects, and myriapods.

är·throp′ō·dăl, *a.* of or pertaining to the *Arthropoda*.

Är·thrō·pom′ȧ·tȧ, *n.pl.* one of the two orders of the *Brachiopoda*.

är·throp′tēr·ous, *a.* [*arthro-*, and Gr. *pteron*, a wing.] having the fin rays articulated, as most fishes.

är·thrō′sis, *n.* [Gr. *arthrōsis*, a joining, from *arthron*, a joint.] in anatomy, an articulation; a joint.

är′thrō·spōre, *n.* [*arthro-*, and Gr. *sporos*, seed, from *speirein*, to sow.] in botany, a vegetative resting cell with thick walls, found in certain algae.

är·thrō·spōr′ous, är·thrō·spōr′iç, *a.* of or having arthrospores.

Är·thros′trȧ·çȧ, *n.pl.* [*arthro-*, and Gr. *ostrakon*, a shell.] a division of *Crustacea*, having the thorax and abdomen segmented.

Är·thrō·zō′ȧ, *n.pl.* [*arthro-*, and Gr. *zōon*, an animal, from *zēn*, to live.] a group of invertebrates; one of the divisions of the *Metazoa*.

är·thrō·zō′iç, *a.* of or pertaining to the *Arthrozoa*.

Är′thūr, *n.* a real or legendary king of Britain and hero of the Round Table; supposed to have lived in the sixth century A.D.

Är·thū′ri·ăn, *a.* relating to King Arthur or the knights of the Round Table.

är′ti·ad, *n.* [Gr. *artios*, even.] a chemical element having an even valence. [Obs.]

är′ti·chōke, *n.* [Fr. *artichaut*; It. *articiocco*; Ar. *alkharshuf*.]

1. the *Cynara Scolymus*, a plant somewhat resembling a thistle, with a dilated, imbricated, and prickly calyx.
2. its flower head, cooked as a vegetable.

Jerusalem artichoke; a species of sunflower (*Helianthus tuberosus*), with a tuber that is cooked as a vegetable. The term *Jerusalem* is altered from Italian *girasole*, sunflower.

är′ti·çle, *n.* [ME. *article*; OFr. *article*; L. *articulus*, dim. of *artus*, a joint; Gr. *arthron*, from Indo-Eur. root, *ar*, fit, join.]

1. a single clause in a contract, account, system of regulations, treaty, or other writing: a particular separate charge or item in an account; a term, condition, or stipulation in a contract. In general, a distinct part of a writing, instrument, or discourse, consisting of two or more particulars; as, *articles* of agreement; an account consisting of many *articles*.
2. [*pl.*] the parts of a formal declaration considered as a whole.
3. a point of faith; a doctrinal point or proposition in theology; as, the Thirty-nine *Articles*.
4. a complete piece of writing, as a report or essay, that is part of a newspaper, magazine, or book; as, an *article* on child labor, a series of *articles* on immigration.
5. a distinct part.

Upon each *article* of human duty.
—Paley.

6. a particular commodity; a thing for sale.
7. any one of a group of things; as, an *article* of luggage.

The *articles* which compose the blood.
—Darwin.

8. a point of time. [Obs.]
9. in grammar, any one of the words *a*, *an*, or *the* (and their equivalents in other languages), used as adjectives. In English, *a*, or *an*, is the indefinite article and *the*, the definite article.
10. in zoology, any segment of a jointed part.

Articles of Confederation; the constitution of the thirteen original States of the United States: it was adopted in 1781 and replaced in 1788 by the present Constitution.

articles of impeachment; a formal document in a case of impeachment, similar in function to an indictment filed in a criminal court.

Articles of War; the code of laws governing members of the armed forces of the United States.

Thirty-nine Articles; a statement of the particular points of doctrine, thirty-nine in number, maintained by the Church of England and the Episcopal Church.

är′ti·çle, *v.t.*; articled (-kld), *pt.*, *pp.*; articling, *ppr.* 1. to state (a person's offenses, etc.) in articles.

2. to accuse.
3. to bind by articles of covenant or stipulation; as, to *article* an apprentice to a mechanic.

är′ti·çle, *v.i.* to bring charges (*against*).

är·tiç′ū·lăr, *a.* [L. *articularis*, adj., from *articulus*, joint.] of a joint or joints; as, an *articular* disease.

är·tiç′ū·lăr, är·tiç′ū·lā·ry, *n.* a bone in the lower jaw of some birds, reptiles, and fishes.

Är·tiç·ū·lā′tȧ, *n.pl.* [L. neut. pl. nom. of *articulatus*, pp. of *articulare*, to join.]

1. one of the four subkingdoms of the animal kingdom, according to the arrangement of Cuvier. It includes all the invertebrates with the external skeleton forming a series of rings articulated together and enveloping the body, distinct respiratory organs, and an internal ganglionated nervous system along the middle line of the body. It is divided into five classes, *Crustacea*, *Arachnida*, *Insecta*, *Myriapoda*, and *Annelida*. The first four classes are now commonly included under the term *Arthropoda*.
2. a subdivision of the *Brachiopoda*, having shells united by a hinge.

är·tiç′ū·lāte, *n.* one of the *Articulata*.

är·tiç′ū·lāte, *a.* [L. *articulatus*, jointed, pp. of *articulare*, to join.]

1. having joints; jointed.
2. spoken in distinct syllables or words.
3. expressing oneself clearly; lucid.
4. able to speak.
5. well formulated; clearly presented; as, an *articulate* argument.
6. expressed in articles, or in separate particulars. [Obs.]

är·tiç′ū·lāte, *v.t.*; articulated, *pt.*, *pp.*; articulating, *ppr.* 1. to joint; to put together by joints.

2. to utter distinctly; to pronounce carefully; enunciate.
3. to express clearly.
4. in phonetics, to produce (a speech sound or speech sounds) by moving an articulator; phonate.
5. to draw up or write in separate articles. [Obs.]

är·tiç′ū·lāte, *v.i.* 1. to speak distinctly; pronounce clearly.

2. to be jointed.
3. in phonetics, to produce speech sounds.
4. to treat, stipulate, or make terms. [Obs.]

är·tiç′ū·lā·ted, *a.* 1. uttered distinctly in syllables or words.

2. jointed; having joints, as a plant or animal.

är·tiç′ū·lāte·ly, *adv.* in an articulate manner.

är·tiç′ū·lāte·ness, *n.* the quality of being articulate.

är·tiç·ū·lā′tion, *n.* 1. in anatomy, the joining, or juncture, of the bones. This is of three kinds; (a) diarthrosis, or a movable connection, as the ball and socket joint; (b) synarthrosis, or an immovable connection as by suture, as the teeth in their sockets; (c) amphiarthrosis, or a combination of the first two types, as between vertebrae.

2. in botany, (a) a joint in a stem or between two separable parts, as a branch and leaf; (b) a node or space between two nodes.
3. the forming or words; the distinct utterance of syllables and words by the human voice; the act of articulating; as, he spoke with perfect *articulation*.
4. an articulate sound, especially that of a consonant.
5. an anatomical joint.
6. a jointing or being jointed.
7. in phonetics, a movement of an articulator.

är·tiç′ū·lā·tive, *a.* in phonetics, relating or pertaining to articulation.

är·tiç′ū·lā·tŏr, *n.* 1. a person or thing that articulates.

2. in phonetics, any organ in the mouth or throat which, when moved, gives or helps to give speech sounds their characteristic acoustic properties: in English, the chief articulators are the lips (especially the lower lip), the apex, front, and back of the tongue, and the glottis; the uvula is a minor articulator (co-articulator).

är·tiç′ū·lā·tō·ry, *a.* pertaining to articulation.

är·tiç′ū·lus, *n.*; *pl.* **är·tiç′ū·lī,** [L., dim. of *artus*, a joint.] a joint of the appendage, or stem, of a crinoid.

är′ti·façt, är′tē·façt, *n.* [L. *art* (*artis*), art, and *factus*, pp. of *facere*, to make.]

1. something produced by human work.
2. in archaeology, a simple form of primitive art.
3. a modification of the appearance, or structure, of protoplasm, produced artificially or by death.

är′ti·fice, *n.* [L. *artificium*, a trade or profession, from *ars*, art, and *facere*, to make.]

1. skill; ingenuity.
2. trickery; craft.
3. a clever expedient; trick; artful device.
4. art; trade; skill acquired by science or practice. [Obs.]

Syn.—deception, deceit, finesse, imposition, ruse, stratagem, trick.

är·tif′i·cēr, *n.* [prob. from *artifice*, and *-er*.]

1. an artist; a mechanic or manufacturer; especially, one whose occupation requires skill or knowledge of a particular kind, as a silversmith or saddler.
2. one who makes or contrives; an inventor; as, an *artificer* of fraud or lies.
3. a cunning or artful fellow. [Obs.]
4. a military mechanic.

är·ti·fi′ciăl (-fish′ăl), *a.* [ME. *artificial*; OFr. *artificial*; L. *artificialis*, from *artificium*, a trade or profession.]

1. made or contrived by art, or by human skill and labor: opposed to *natural*; as, *artificial* heat or light; an *artificial* magnet.
2. made in imitation of something natural; simulated; as, *artificial* teeth.
3. contrived with skill or art; artistic. [Obs.]
4. cultivated; not indigenous; not being of spontaneous growth; as, *artificial* grasses.
5. full of affectation; not natural; as, *artificial* manners.

artificial horizon; an instrument on an aircraft, operated by a gyroscope and containing a liquid level, for indicating the position of the craft with reference to the true horizon.

artificial insemination; the impregnation of a female with semen from a male without sexual intercourse.

artificial lines; on a sector or scale, lines so arranged as to represent the logarithmic sines and tangents.

artificial numbers; logarithms.

artificial respiration; the maintenance of breathing by artificial means, usually by creating and relaxing pressure externally on the chest cavity at regular intervals.

Syn.—manufactured, constructed, simulated, pretended, assumed, false.

är·ti·fi·ci·al′i·ty, *n.*; *pl.* **är·ti·fi·ci·al′i·tieṣ,**

1. the quality or state of being artificial.
2. something artificial.

är·ti·fi′ciăl·īze, *v.t.*; artificialized, *pt.*, *pp.*; artificializing, *ppr.* to make artificial.

är·ti·fi′ciăl·ly, *adv.* in an artificial manner.

är·ti·fi′ciăl·ness, *n.* the quality of being artificial.

är·ti·fi′cious, *a.* [L. *artificiosus*, accomplished in an art.] artificial. [Obs.]

ärt′i·līze, *v.t.* to make to resemble art, or to make artificial; as, to *artilize* nature. [Obs.]

är·til′lēr·ist, *n.* 1. a student of gunnery.

2. an artilleryman; gunner.

är·til′lēr·y, *n.* [ME. *artylerye*; OFr. *artillerie*; LL. *artillaria*; from L. *ars*, gen. *artis*, art, skill.]

1. formerly, apparatus for hurling heavy missiles, as catapults, arbalests, etc.
2. now, guns of large caliber, too heavy to carry; mounted guns (excluding machine guns), as cannon: distinguished from *small arms*. Artillery may be mobile, stationary, or mounted on ships, airplanes, tanks, etc.
3. the science which treats of the use and management of guns; gunnery.

the artillery; the military branch specializing in the use of heavy mounted guns.

är·til′lẽr·y·măn, *n.*; *pl.* **är·til′lẽr·y·men,** a soldier in the artillery.

är·til′lẽr·y plant, a South American plant of the nettle family, which discharges its pollen in an explosive manner.

är″ti·ō·daç′tyl, *n.* one of the *Artiodactyla*.

är″ti·ō·daç′tyl, *a.* having an even number of toes or digits, as a camel, hog, etc.

Är″ti·ō·daç′ty·lȧ, *n.pl.* [Gr. *artios*, even, and *daktylos*, a toe.] an order of the *Ungulata*, or hoofed mammals, comprising all those in which the number of the toes is even (two or four), including the ruminants, and also a number of nonruminating animals, as the hippopotamus and the pig.

är″ti·ō·daç′ty·lous, *a.* same as *artiodactyl*.

är′ti·săn, är′ti·zăn, *n.* [Fr. *artisan*; L. *artitus*, skilled in arts; pp. of *artire*.]

1. one who practices an art. [Obs.]

2. a craftsman; a skilled mechanic; an artificer.

ärt′ist, *n.* [Fr. *artiste*; from L. *ars*, art.]

1. one who is skilled in or works in any of the fine, especially graphic, arts.

2. a person who does anything very well, with a feeling for form, effect, etc.; as, his cook is an *artist*.

3. an artiste.

är·tiste′, *n.* [Fr.]

1. a skilled professional entertainer.

2. a person very skilled in some trade or occupation; often humorous or facetious.

är·tis′tiç, är·tis′tiç·ăl, *a.* 1. pertaining to art or an artist.

2. done skillfully; aesthetically satisfying.

3. that appreciates art and beauty; fond of the fine arts.

är·tis′tiç·ăl·ly, *adv.* 1. in an artistic manner.

2. from the standpoint of art.

ärt′ist·ry, *n.* 1. artistic finish or touch; artistic effect.

2. works of art, as a whole.

ärt′ize, *v.t.* and *v.i.*; artized, *pt.*, *pp.*; artizing, *ppr.* to form or live by art; also, to make artificial. [Obs.]

ärt′less, *a.* 1. unskillful; lacking art, knowledge, or skill.

2. free from guile, art, craft, or stratagem; simple; sincere; unaffected; undesigning; as, an *artless* mind.

3. uncultured; ignorant.

Syn.—candid, fair, frank, honest, ingenuous, open, plain.

ärt′less·ly, *adv.* in an artless manner; unaffectedly.

ärt′less·ness, *n.* the quality of being artless; simplicity; sincerity; unaffectedness.

ärt′ly, *adv.* artificially; by human skill or contrivance. [Obs.]

är·tō·çär′pad, *n.* one of the *Artocarpeæ*.

Är·tō·çär′pē·ae, *n.pl.* [Mod. L.; Gr. *artos*, bread, and *karpos*, fruit.] a natural order of plants, the breadfruit order.

är·tō·çär′pous, är·tō·çär′pē·ous, *a.* relating to breadfruit or the breadfruit tree.

Är·tō·çär′pus, *n.* the breadfruit, a genus of plants, natural order *Artocarpeæ*.

är′tō·tȳpe, *n.* an improved form of albertype, or photograph produced by the exposure of a sensitized gelatin plate.

Är·tō·tȳ′rite, *n.* [Gr. *artos*, bread, and *tyros*, cheese.] one of an early religious sect, said to have celebrated the Eucharist with bread and cheese.

ärts′măn, *n.* one skilled in art or in an art. [Obs.]

ärt′y, *a.* pretending to be artistic; ostentatiously artistic. [Colloq.]

Ā′rum, *n.* [L. *arum*; Gr. *aron*, the wake-robin.] a genus of plants, natural order *Araceæ*, bearing flowers on a fleshy spike surrounded by a hoodlike leaf. *Arum maculatum* is the common wake-robin.

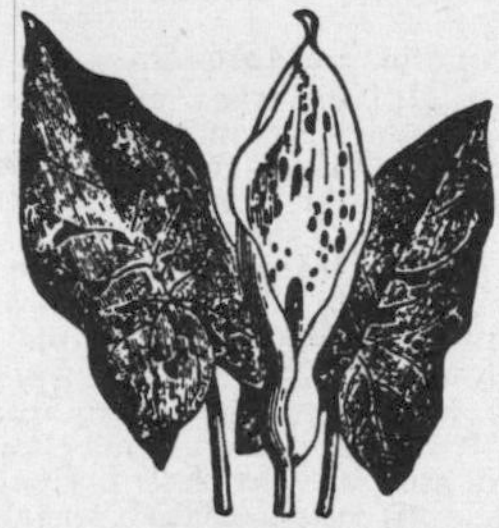

WAKE-ROBIN
(*Arum maculatum*)

Ar·un·dē′li·ăn mär·bleş, a collection of ancient stones, containing a chronological detail of the principal events of Greece from about 1582 B.C. to 264 B.C. The engraving is believed to have been done in Paros, and the chronology is called the Parian Chronicle. The earl of Arundel procured these relics of antiquity in the East, which were later presented to Oxford University. They are also called *Oxford marbles*.

ar·un·dif′ẽr·ous, *a.* [L. *arundo*, reed, and *ferre*, to bear.] bearing canes or reeds.

ȧ·run·di·nā′ceous, *a.* [L. *arundinaceous*, like a reed.] of a reed; like the reed or cane.

Ȧ·run·di·nā′ri·ȧ, *n.* [Mod. L., from L. *arundo*.] a genus of tall, reedlike grasses, native to both Asia and America, and including the cane of the southern United States.

ar·un·din′ē·ous, *a.* full of reeds.

Ȧ·run′dō, *n.* [L., a reed.] a small genus of grasses, with reedy stems and large leaves, which grow in warm climates.

ȧ·rus′pex, ȧ·rus′pice, *n.*; *pl.* **ȧ·rus′pi·çēş,** [L. *aruspex* or *haruspex*, a soothsayer or diviner.] same as *haruspex*.

ȧ·rus′pi·cy, *n.* same as *haruspicy*.

är′văl, *a.* [L. *arvalis*, relating to cultivated land; from *arvum*, a field, neut. of *arvus*, that has been plowed, but not sown, from *arare*, to plow.] pertaining to plowed ground.

Arval Brethren; a group of priests in ancient Rome, who offered sacrifices to the rural goddess Dea Dia.

är′văl, är′vel, *n.* [ME. *arvell*; AS. *erfe*; W. *arwyl*, funeral, from *ar*, over, and *wylo*, to weep.] a funeral feast. [Prov. Eng.]

Är·viç′ō·lȧ, *n.* the typical genus of the subfamily *Arvicolinæ*.

Ȧr·viç·ō·lī′nae, *n.pl.* [from L. *arvum*, plowed land, field, and *colere*, to inhabit.] one of several subfamilies of rodents, which includes the field mice of America, the water rats of Europe, etc.

är·viç′ō·line, är·viç′ō·lous, *a.* 1. living in the fields.

2. relating to the *Arvicolinæ*.

-ary, [L. *-arius*, *-aria*, *-arium*.] a suffix meaning: (a) *relating to*, *connected with*, used in forming adjectives and nouns, as auxili*ary*, diction*ary*; (b) *relating to*, *like*, as in milit*ary*.

Ār′y·ăn, Ār′i·ăn (*or* är′yăn), *a.* [Sans. *arya*, lord, master, *ārya*, a tribal name; akin to OPer. *ariya*, a tribal name; orig. applicable only to the Indo-Iranian tribes, but popularized in a wider sense by Max Müller and less reputable authors; not connected with *Eire*, *Ire*land, *Ir*ish.]

1. formerly, designating or of the family of languages that includes Iranian, Sanskrit, and most of the European languages; Indo-European.

2. designating or of the Indic and Iranian branches of the Indo-European family of languages.

3. of the Aryans.

Ār′y·ăn, Ār′i·ăn, *n.* 1. the hypothetical parent language of the Indo-European family.

2. a person belonging to, or supposed to be a descendant of, the prehistoric people who spoke this language.

Aryan has no validity as a racial term, although it has been so used, notoriously by the Nazis to mean "a Caucasian of non-Jewish descent," etc. The use of the word in connection with race is due to the idea, regarded by most ethnologists as false, that peoples who spoke the same or related languages must have had a common racial origin. Misuse of *Aryan* has led to its replacement in scientific discussion by *Indo-European* (in sense 1 of the *n.* and *a.*).

Ār′y·ăn·işm, *n.* 1. belief in the past existence of an Aryan race.

2. belief that this hypothetical Aryan race possessed a superior civilization.

Ār′y·ăn·ize (*or* är′yăn-īze), *v.t.*; Aryanized, *pt.*, *pp.*; Aryanizing, *ppr.* 1. to make Aryan.

2. in Nazi usage, to rid of (so-called) non-Aryan elements.

See *Aryan*.

ȧ·ry·tē′noid, *a.* [Gr. *arytainoeides*, cup-shaped; *arytēr*, a cup, and *eidos*, form.]

1. ladle-shaped or cup-shaped.

2. designating or of an arytenoid cartilage or muscle.

arytenoid cartilages; two pyramidal bodies articulated by their bases with the oval articular substances which exist on the upper margin of the cricoid cartilage in the human larynx: they help regulate the action of the vocal cords.

arytenoid muscle; a muscle that passes from one of the arytenoid cartilages to the other.

ȧ·ry·tē′noid, *n.* 1. an arytenoid cartilage.

2. an arytenoid muscle.

aş, *adv.* [ME. *as*, *ase*; AS. *alswā*, *ealswā*.]

1. to the same amount or degree; equally; as, I'm *as* tall as he.

2. for instance; for example; thus.

as yet; up to the present time; up to this moment.

aş, *conj.* 1. to the same amount or degree that. "It flew straight *as* an arrow."

2. in the same manner that; according to the way that. "Do *as* you are told."

3. that the consequence was. "The question was so obvious *as* to need no reply."

4. while; during; at the same time. "He trembled *as* he spoke."

5. since; because. "The jury acquitted him, *as* the evidence was insufficient."

6. though; however. "Careful *as* it was, the committee failed in some respects."

7. formerly, equivalent to the relative *that* after *so*. [Obs.]

> The relations are so uncertain *as* they require a great deal of examination.
> —Bacon.

8. formerly, used for *as if*. [Obs.]

> He lies, *as* he his bliss did know.
> —Waller.

as . . . as; a correlative construction used to indicate the equality or sameness of two things; *as large as*, *as heavy as*, *as many as*, etc.

as if, or *as though*; as it (or one) would if.

as it were; as if it were so; so to speak.

aş, *pron.* 1. a fact that. "He is tired, *as* anyone can see."

2. that (preceded by *such* or *the same*). "This is the same color *as* yours (is)."

aş, *prep.* in the role, function, capacity, or sense of. "He poses *as* a friend."

as for, or *as to*; in or with regard or respect to.

ās, *n.* an ace. [Obs.]

as, *n.*; *pl.* **as′seş,** [L.] 1. a Roman unit of weight and measure: as a weight, it was equal to about twelve ounces; as a unit of length, to about twelve inches.

2. a Roman coin of copper alloy, originally weighing a pound, but reduced, after the first Punic war, to two ounces, and subsequently to half an ounce: the most common form had the two-faced head of Janus on one side and the prow of a ship on the other.

AS (coin)

As, *n.* in Norse mythology, one of the Aesir gods.

as-, same as *ad-*: used before *s*, as in *as*similate.

As, in chemistry, arsenic.

Ā′sȧ, *n.* in the Bible, a king of Judah, who opposed idolatry. I Kin. xv. 8–24.

as·ȧ·fet′i·dȧ, as·ȧ·foet′i·dȧ, *n.* [LL. *asa*, gum, and L. *fetida*, *fœtida*, f. of *fetidus* or *fœtidus*, pp. of *fœtere*, to have a disagreeable smell, stink.] a bad-smelling gum resin obtained from various Asiatic plants of the carrot family: it is used in medicine as an antispasmodic. Written also *assafoetida*.

as′ăk, *n.* [Hind. *asok*; Sans. *aśoka*.] a sacred East Indian tree, *Saraca Asoka*: written also *asok*, *asoka*.

as·ȧ′phi·ȧ, *n.* [Mod. L.; Gr. *asaphēs*, not clear; *a* priv., and *saphēs*, distinct.] a condition characterized by indistinct utterance, as in a person who is tongue-tied.

As′ȧ·phus, *n.* [Mod. L.; Gr. *asaphēs*, obscure; *a* priv., and *saphēs*, clear.] a genus of trilobites, characteristic of the lower Paleozoic rocks.

as″ȧ·rȧ·baç′çȧ, *n.* [L. *asarum*, from Gr. *asaron*, and L. *bacca*, berry.] any plant of the genus *Asarum*.

as′ȧ·rōne, as′ȧ·rin, *n.* camphor of asarum, a crystallized substance obtained from the *Asarum Europæum*.

As′ȧ·rum, *n.* [L. *asarum*; Gr. *asaron*; from *a* priv., and *seira*, a cord, string, or band.]

1. a genus of plants belonging to the order *Aristolochiaceæ*, or birthworts. It contains the species *Asarum Europæum*.

2. [a–] any plant of this genus.

as·bes′tiç, as·bes′tous, *a.* same as *asbestine*.

as·bes′ti·fọrm, *a.* having the structure or appearance of asbestos.

as·bes′tine, *a.* pertaining to, or having the properties of, asbestos.

as·bes′tŏs, as·bes′tus, *n.* [ME. *asbeston*; L. *asbestos*; Gr. *asbestos*; inextinguishable; *a* priv., and *sbennynai*, to extinguish.] a grayish mineral, a silicate of calcium and magnesium, which occurs in long, threadlike fibers. It is incombustible and a nonconductor of electricity. It is used as fireproofing material for buildings, safes, etc.; for firemen's clothing and glassworkers' gloves; for roofing and flooring material, and for packing steam joints and pistons.

as·bes′tous, *a.* asbestic.

aṣ′bō·lin, *n.* [Gr. *asbolos*, *aṣbole*.] a yellow, bitter, oily fluid obtained from soot.

as′çăn, *a.* relating to or derived from an ascus.

As·çā′ni·us, *n.* [L.] in Roman legend, the son of Aeneas.

as·çar′i·cīde, *n.* [*ascaris*, and L. *caedere*, to kill.] a vermifuge, used especially to expel ascarids.

as′çȧ·rid, *n.* one of the *Ascaridæ*.

As·çar′i·dae, *n.* a family of worms including several genera of pinworms, roundworms, and other intestinal parasites.

As′çȧ·ris, *n.* [Gr.] in zoology, a genus of intestinal worms.

as·cend′, *v.i.*; ascended, *pt., pp.*; ascending, *ppr.* [ME. *ascenden*; OFr. *ascendre*; L. *ascendere*; from *ad-*, to, and *scandere*, to mount or climb.]

1. to move upward; to mount; to go up; to rise.

2. to proceed from a lower to a higher level or degree, as in rank, pitch, etc.

3. to slope or lead upward.

Syn.—surmount, mount, go up, climb, scale, tower, rise, soar.

as·cend′, *v.t.* to go or move upward along; as, to *ascend* a hill or ladder; to mount; to climb; as, to *ascend* a tree.

as·cend′ȧ·ble, as·cend′i·ble, *a.* that can be ascended.

as·cend′ănce, as·cend′ence, *n.* same as *ascendancy*.

as·cend′ăn·cy, as·cend′en·cy, *n.* the state or quality of being in the ascendant; power; governing or controlling influence.

Custom has an *ascendency* over the understanding. —Watts.

Syn.—superiority, authority, domination, mastery, sway.

as·cend′ănt, as·cend′ent, *a.* 1. superior; predominant; controlling.

2. ascending; rising.

3. in botany, pointing upward.

as·cend′ănt, as·cend′ent, *n.* 1. superiori y, or commanding influence; as, one man has the *ascendant* over another.

2. an ancestor: opposed to *descendant*. [Rare.]

3. in astrology, the sign of the zodiac just above the eastern horizon at any given moment; horoscope.

in the ascendant; at or leading toward the height of power or influence.

as·cend′en·cy, *n.* same as *ascendancy*.

as·cend′ẽr, *n.* 1. a person or thing that ascends.

2. in typography, the extension or upward part of any of the tall lower-case letters, as *b, d, k*, etc.

3. any of these letters.

as·cend′i·ble, *a.* same as *ascendable*.

as·cend′ing, *a.* 1. rising; moving upward; as, an *ascending* star.

2. in botany, rising or curving upward.

ascending latitude; the latitude of a planet when moving upward.

ascending node; that point of a planet's orbit where it passes the ecliptic to proceed upward.

ascending ovule; an ovule which grows from a little above the base of the ovary.

ascending vessels; in anatomy, those vessels which carry the blood upward or toward the higher parts of the body.

as·cend′ing·ly, *adv.* in an ascending manner.

as·cen′sion, *n.* 1. the act of ascending; a rising. Specifically, *the Ascension*, in the Bible, the bodily ascent of Jesus into heaven on the fortieth day after his resurrection. Acts i. 9.

2. the thing rising or ascending. [Obs.]

Ascension Day; the fortieth day after Easter, celebrating the Ascension: called also *Holy Thursday*.

oblique ascension; in astronomy, the arc of the equator intercepted between the first point of Aries and that point of the equator which comes to the horizon with a star.

right ascension; in astronomy, the arc of the equator intercepted between the first point of Aries and that point of the equator which comes to the meridian with the sun or star.

as·cen′sion·ăl, *a.* relating to ascension; ascending or rising up.

ascensional difference; in astronomy, the difference between the right and oblique ascension of the same point on the surface of the sphere.

as·cen′sive, *a.* 1. rising.

2. causing to rise.

3. in grammar, intensive; increasing the force; augmentative. [Rare.]

as·cent′, *n.* [L. *ascensus*, from *ascendere*, to ascend.]

1. the act of rising; rise; a mounting upward; as, the *ascent* of vapors from the earth.

2. a going up; climbing.

3. an eminence, hill, or high place. [Obs.]

4. the amount of upward slope or elevation; as, that road has an *ascent* of five degrees.

5. acclivity; the rise of a hill; as, a steep ascent.

6. an advancement, as in rank, popularity, etc.

7. a going back in time or genealogy.

as·cẽr·tāin′, *v.t.*; ascertained, *pt., pp.*; ascertaining, *ppr.* [OFr. *acertainer*; L. *ad*, to, and *certus*, fixed.]

1. to make certain; to define by removing obscurity or ambiguity; to determine.

The divine law *ascertains* the truth. —Hooker.

2. to make certain by trial, examination, or experiment, so as to know what was before unknown; as, to *ascertain* the purity of a metal.

3. to make certain in the mind. [Archaic.]

4. to fix; to establish with certainty; to render invariable, and not subject to will. [Obs.]

The mildness and precision of their laws *ascertained* the rule and measure of taxation. —Gibbon.

Syn.—find out, discover, determine, detect, discern, learn.

as·cẽr·tāin′ȧ·ble, *a.* capable of being ascertained.

as·cẽr·tāin′ȧ·ble·ness, *n.* the quality or state of being ascertainable.

as·cẽr·tāin′ȧ·bly, *adv.* in an ascertainable manner or condition.

as·cẽr·tāin′ẽr, *n.* one who ascertains, or makes certain.

as·cẽr·tāin′ment, *n.* an ascertaining or being ascertained.

as·ces′săn·cy, *n.* same as *acescency*.

as·ces′sănt, *a.* same as *acescent*.

as·cet′iç, *a.* [Gr. *askētikos*, exercised, from *askein*, to exercise.] of or characteristic of ascetics or asceticism; rigid; severe; austere.

as·cet′iç, *n.* 1. one who lives a life of contemplation and rigorous self-denial for religious purposes.

2. anyone who lives with strict self-discipline and abstinence.

as·cet′i·çal·ly, *adv.* 1. in an ascetic manner.

2. by means of asceticism.

as·cet′i·ciṣm, *n.* 1. the practices or way of life of an ascetic; systematic self-denial for some ideal.

2. the religious doctrine that one can reach a higher spiritual state by rigorous self-discipline and self-denial.

as′çham, *n.* [after Roger *Ascham* (1515–1568), Eng. writer.] a receptacle for archery implements.

as′cī, *n.*, pl. of *ascus*.

as′ciăn (ash′yăn), *n.* [L. *ascius*, shadowless; Gr. *askios*; *a* priv., and *skia*, a shadow.] a person who casts no shadow at noon: said of the inhabitants of the Torrid Zone where the sun is vertical at noon for a few days a year.

As·cid′i·ȧ, *n.pl.* [Gr. *askidion*, a little bottle, from *askos*, a leather bag, a bottle.] an order of *Tunicata*, or sea squirts; ascidians. They are found at low tide on beaches, and are dredged from deep water attached to stones, shells, and fixed objects. They are usually sac-shaped, with a tough outer covering or tunic. A single mass of ganglion represents the nervous system, this mass being placed between the two openings of the body. Male and female reproductive organs exist in each specimen. They may be single or simple, social, or compound. In social ascidians, the peduncles of a number of individuals are united into a common tubular stem, with a partial, common circulation of blood.

as·cid′i·ȧ, *n.*, pl. of *ascidium*.

as·cid′i·ăn, *a.* of or belonging to the *Ascidia*.

as·cid′i·ăn, *n.* one of the *Ascidia*; a sea squirt.

as·cid·i·ā′ri·um, *n.*; *pl.* **as·cid·i·ā′ri·ȧ,** [L.] a compound ascidian.

as·ci·diç′ō·lous, *a.* in zoology, parasitic in or on ascidians.

as·cid′i·form, *a.* resembling an ascidian in shape; bottle-shaped.

as·cid′i·oid, *a.* pertaining to, or of the nature of, an ascidian.

as·cid′i·oid, *n.* an ascidian.

As·cid·i·oi′dȧ, *n.pl.* same as *Ascidia*.

as·cid″i·ō·zō′oid, *n.* [*ascidium*, and Gr. *zōon*, a living being, from *zēn*, to live.] one of the component members of an ascidiarium.

as·cid′i·um, *n.*; *pl.* **as·cid′i·ȧ,** [Mod. L. *ascidium*; Gr. *askidion*, dim. of *askos*, wineskin, bladder.] in botany, a pitcherlike leaf or appendage, as in the pitcher plant or bladderwort.

as·ciġ′ẽr·ous, as·cif′ẽr·ous, *a.* [LL. *ascus*, a bag, and L. *gerere*, to bear, or *ferre*, to bear.] in botany, bearing asci, as lichens and ascomycetous fungi.

As·cī′tăns, *n.pl.* [Gr. *askos*, wineskin.] a sect or branch of Montanists, who appeared in the second century A.D., and introduced bacchanals into their assemblies.

as·cī′tēṣ, *n.* [Gr. *askos*, a bladder.] an accumulation of serous fluid in the abdominal cavity.

as·cit′iç, as·cit′iç·ăl, *a.* pertaining to ascites.

as·ci·ti′tious (-tish′us), *a.* [LL. *ascititius*; L. *ascitus*, pp. of *asciscere*, to approve or adopt.] same as *adscititious*.

as·çlē′pi·ad, *n.* same as *Asclepiadean*.

as·çlē′pi·ad, *n.* a plant of the natural order *Asclepiadaceæ*.

As·çlē′pi·ad, *n.* one of an order of Greek physicians and priests who claimed to be descendants of *Asclepius*.

As·çlē″pi·ȧ·dā′cē·ae, *n.pl.* [from *Asclepias*, the typical genus.] a natural order of monopetalous dicotyledonous plants (the milkweed family), identified by the grains of pollen adhering together in a waxlike mass within the cell of the anther, by the milky juice, and by the pods with tufted seeds.

as·çlē″pi·ȧ·dā′ceous, *a.* of, pertaining to, or resembling plants of the milkweed family.

As·çlē″pi·ȧ·dē′ăn, *a.* [from *Asclepiades*, name of Gr. inventor of the verse.] designating or of a type of classical verse consisting usually of a spondee, two (or three) choriambs, and an iamb.

As·çlē″pi·ȧ·dē′ăn, *n.* an Asclepiadean verse.

As·çlē·pi·ad′iç, *a.* same as *Asclepiadean*.

As·çlē′pi·as, *n.* [Gr. *Asklēpios*.] a genus of plants, the type and the largest genus of the natural order *Asclepiadaceæ*. Most of the species are North American herbs, having opposite, alternate, or verticillate leaves.

As·çlē′pi·us, *n.* [L. *Asclepius*; Gr. *Asklēpios*.] in Greek mythology, the god of healing and medicine, corresponding to the Romans' Aesculapius.

as′çō-, [Gr. *askos*, a wineskin, bladder.] a combining form used especially in botany, as in *asco*carp.

as′çō·cärp, *n.* [*asco-*, and Gr. *karpos*, fruit.] in botany, a structure shaped like a globe, cup, or disk, containing spore sacs; the fruit of ascomycetous fungi.

as·çoġ′e·nous, *a.* [*asco-*, and Gr. *genos*, kind, species.] producing asci.

as·çō·gō′ni·um, *n.*; *pl.* **as·çō·gō′ni·ȧ,** [*asco-*, and Gr. *gonos*, offspring, from *gignesthai*, to be born.] in botany, the female gamete, or archicarp, in an ascomycetous fungus.

as″çō·mȳ·cē′tăl, *a.* same as *ascomycetous*.

as″çō·mȳ·cēte′, *n.* an ascomycetous fungus.

As″çō·mȳ·cē′tēṣ, *n.pl.* [Mod. L., from Gr. *askos*, bladder, and *mykēs*, a mushroom.] a large group of fungi, whose spores are contained within asci. The group includes the mildews, yeasts, knot and wart fungi, cup fungi, etc.

as″çō·mȳ·cē′tous, *a.* belonging to the Ascomycetes.

as′çon, *n.* one of the *Ascones*.

As·çō′nēṣ, *n.pl.* [Gr. *askos*, a bag.] a group of chalk sponges, with thin ventricular walls.

as′çō·phōre, *n.* [*asco-*, and Gr. *pherein*, to bear.] a seed bearer from which asci are produced.

as·çoph′ō·rous, *a.* same as *ascogenous*.

ā·sçor′biç ac′id, [*a-*, not and *scorb*utic, and *-ic*.] vitamin C: called also *cevitamic acid*.

as′çō·spōre, *n.* [*asco-*, and Gr. *spora*, seed.] in botany, a cluster of spores in an ascus.

as′çot, *n.* 1. [A–] a famous horse-racing meet held annually at Ascot Heath, Berkshire, England: it is a British social event.

2. a kind of necktie with very broad ends

hanging from the knot, one upon the other: supposedly developed for wear at the Ascot.

as·çrib'ȧ·ble, *a.* capable of being ascribed.

as·çrībe', *v.t.*; ascribed, *pt.*, *pp.*; ascribing, *ppr.* [ME. *ascriven*; OFr. *ascrire*; L. *ascribere*; *ad*, to, and *scribere*, to write.]
1. to attribute, impute, or assign (*to* a supposed cause or source).
2. to attribute, as a quality or an appurtenance; to consider or allege to belong (*to*).
Syn.—attribute, impute, assign, allege, charge.

as'çript, *a.* enrolled; appointed. [Obs.]

as·çrip'tion, *n.* [L. *ascriptus*, pp. of *ascribere*, to ascribe.]
1. the act of ascribing, imputing, or assigning.
2. a statement that ascribes; specifically, a prayer or text ascribing glory to God.

as·çrip·ti'tious (-tish'us), *a.* 1. ascribed. [Rare.]
2. attached: said of serfs or villains under the feudal system, who were annexed to the freehold and transferable with it. [Obs.]

as'çū·lȧ, *n.* [dim. of LL. *ascus*, sponge.] the stage of a larval sponge in which its cilia have disappeared and it has become fixed.

as'çus, *n.*; *pl.* **as'çī** (as'ī). [Gr. *askos*, a wine-skin, bladder.] a spore sac in an ascomycetous fungus.

as'cy·phous (as'i-fus), *a.* [Gr. *ascyphos*, without a cup; *a* priv., and *scyphos*, a cup.] in botany, without scyphi.

-āse, [after the ending of *diastase*.] a suffix used in forming names of enzymes, usually meaning *that decomposes*, as in amyl*ase*.

ȧ·sēa', *adv.* at sea; in the direction of or toward the sea.

ȧ·sē'i·ty, *n.* [Fr. *aséité*; from L. *a*, *ab*, from, and abl. of reflexive pron, *se*, oneself, of oneself.] in metaphysics, the state or condition of having an independent existence.

ȧ·sē'mi·ȧ, *n.* [Gr. *asēmos*, without sign; *a* priv., and *sēma*, sign.] loss of ability to express or understand thought or ideas by means of signs or symbols, written, uttered, or gesticulated.

ȧ·sep'sis, *n.* [Gr. *a* priv., and *sēpsis*, putrefaction.]
1. the condition of being free from putrefaction; absence of toxic or pathogenic bacteria.
2. aseptic treatment or technique.

ȧ·sep'tiç, *a.* not liable to putrefy; free from septic matter or disease-producing bacteria: distinguished from *antiseptic*.

ȧ·sep'tiç, *n.* any aseptic substance or preparation.

ȧ·sep'ti·çăl·ly, *adv.* by aseptic means; with the use of aseptics.

ȧ·sep'ti·çişm, *n.* treatment by aseptic methods or the theory of aseptic treatment.

ȧ·sep'ti·cīze, *v.t.*; asepticized, *pt.*, *pp.*; asepticizing, *ppr.* to cause to become aseptic.

ā·sex'ū·ăl, *a.* 1. having no distinct sex; sexless.
2. in biology, designating or of reproduction without the union of male and female germ cells.

ā·sex''ū·al'i·ty, *n.* the quality or state of being asexual.

ā·sex'ū·ăl·ly, *adv.* in an asexual manner.

As'gärd, As'gär·dhr (-thr), **As'gärth,** *n.* [ON. *Āsgarthr*; *āss*, god, and *garthr*, yard, court.] in Norse mythology, the home of the gods and slain heroes.

ash, *n.* [ME. *asch, ashe, assh*; AS. *asce, æsc*.]
1. the common name of various species of timber and shade trees of the genus *Fraxinus*, natural order *Oleaceæ*; as, the white *ash*, *Fraxinus Americanus*. They have pinnate leaves, winged fruit, and tough, elastic wood with a straight, close grain.
2. the wood of the ash tree.

ash, *a.* pertaining to or like the ash; made of ash.

ash, *v.t.*; ashed, *pt.*, *pp.*; ashing, *ppr.* to strew or sprinkle with ashes.

ash, *n.* [ME. *ash, ashe, asche*; pl. *ashes, asches, askes*; AS. *asce, æsce*; pl. *ascan, æscan*.]
1. the white or grayish powder left of something after it has been burned.
2. the silvery-gray color of wood ash; pallor. See also *ashes*.

ȧ·shāme', *v.t.* to shame. [Rare.]

ȧ·shāmed', *a.* [ME. *aschamen*; AS. *ascamian*, *gescamian*.]
1. feeling shame, as from doing something bad, wrong, foolish, etc.
2. reluctant because fearing shame beforehand.
Syn.—abashed, confused, mortified, confounded, humiliated.

ȧ·shām'ed·ly, *adv.* bashfully; with shame. [Rare.]

A·shan'tĭ, A·shan'tee, *n.* 1. an inhabitant or native of Ashanti, in western Africa.
2. the language spoken there.

ash bin, a receptacle for ashes and other refuse.

ash çan, 1. a large can for ashes and trash.
2. a depth bomb; depth charge. [Naval Slang.]

ash'en, *a.* 1. pertaining to the ash tree.
2. made of the wood of the ash; as, an *ashen* stick.

ash'en, *a.* resembling or consisting of ashes; pale; as, *ashen* lips.

Ȧ·shē'räh, *n.*; *pl.* **Ȧ·shē'rim,** [Heb.]
1. sacred wood; sometimes a tree or stump of a tree, found beside Canaanitish altars.
2. a Semitic goddess.

ash'ẽr·y, *n.*; *pl.* **ash'ẽr·ieş,** 1. a place where ashes are deposited.
2. a place where potash is made.

ash'eş, *n.pl.* 1. the unburned particles and white or grayish powder remaining after a thing has been burned.
2. the remains of the human body after cremation. Hence, figuratively, a dead body or corpse.
3. fine volcanic lava.
ashes of roses; a bluish-red color, of medium brilliance and medium saturation.

ash fũr'nāce, an oven in which the materials used in glassmaking are fritted.

ȧ·shīne', *a.* shining.

Ash·ke·naz'iç, *a.* of the Ashkenazim or their culture.

Ash·ke·naz'im, *n.pl.* [Heb.]
1. the Jews who settled in middle and northern Europe after the Diaspora.
2. their descendants.
Distinguished from *Sephardim*.

ash'lăr, ash'lẽr, *n.* [ME. *asheler, ascheler*; OFr. *aiseler*, from L. *assula*, a chip; dim. of *assis*, plank.]
1. a square, hewn stone used in building.
2. a facing made of thin slabs, used to cover walls of brick, etc.
3. masonry made of either kind of ashlar.
4. in carpentry, an upright from an attic floor to a rafter.

ash'lăr·ing, ash'lẽr·ing, *n.* 1. the short, upright pieces between the floor beams and rafters in attics for the attachment of lath.
2. ashlar masonry.

ash'man, *n.*; *pl.* **ash'men,** a man who takes away ashes and trash.

ȧ·shōre', *adv.* and *a.* 1. on shore; on the land adjacent to water; to the shore; as, bring the goods *ashore*.
2. on or to land: opposed to *aboard*; as, the captain of the ship remained *ashore*.

ash ŏv'en, same as *ash furnace*.

ash'răm, *n.* [Sans. *āśrama*; *ā*, towards, and *śrama*, fatigue, exhaustion, religious penance.]
1. a secluded place for a community of Hindus leading a life of simplicity and religious meditation.
2. such a religious community.

Ash'tō·reth, *n.* [Heb.] the goddess of love and fertility, Astarte, worshiped by the ancient Syrians and Phoenicians.

ash trāy, a container for smokers' tobacco ashes.

Ä'shur, *n.* in Assyrian mythology, the chief deity, god of war and empire: written also *Asshur, Assur, Asur*.

Ash Wedneş'dāy (wenz'dā), the first day of Lent and seventh Wednesday before Easter: so called from the practice of sprinkling the foreheads of penitents with ashes on that day.

ash'y, *a.*; *comp.* ashier; *superl.* ashiest. 1. belonging to, consisting of, or resembling ashes.
2. ash-colored; pale.

Ā'siăn (-shăn), *a.* and *n.* Asiatic.

Ā'si·ärch (-shi-ärk), *n.* [Gr. *Asia*, and *archōn*, ruler, from *archein*, to rule.] a chief or pontiff in the Roman province of Asia, who had the superintendence of the public games.

Ā·si·at'iç (-shi-at'ik), *a.* pertaining to or characteristic of Asia.

Ā·si·at'iç, *n.* a native or inhabitant of Asia.

Ā·si·at'iç bee'tle, a beetle of Japanese origin, harmful to grasses.

Ā·si·at'iç çhol'ẽr·ȧ, an acute, usually fatal, infectious disease characterized by profuse diarrhea, vomiting, intestinal pain, etc.

Ā·si·at'i·çişm, *n.* something characteristic or imitative of Asia or Asiatics.

ȧ·sīde', *adv.* 1. on or to one side; to or at a short distance off; as, to turn or stand *aside*, to draw a curtain *aside*.
He took him *aside* from the multitude.
—Mark vii. 33.
2. out of one's thoughts, consideration, or regard; away; off; as, to lay *aside* one's animosity, to put one's cares *aside*.
3. away; on reserve; as, put this *aside* for me.
4. apart; notwithstanding; as, joking *aside*, I mean it.
aside from; (a) with the exception of; (b) apart from.

ȧ·sīde', *n.* words spoken aside; a speech or other remark uttered by an actor on the stage, and supposed to be heard only by the audience and not by the other characters on the stage.

ȧ·sid'ẽr·īte, *n.* [Gr. *a* priv., and *sideros*, iron.] a meteorite in which there is no iron.

Ȧ·sil'i·dae, *n.pl.* a family of insects belonging to the order *Diptera*, the hornet flies.

As'i·lus, *n.* [L. *asilus*, a gadfly, a horsefly.] a genus of flies typical of the *Asiladæ*.

Ȧ·sim'i·nȧ, *n.* a genus of shrubby trees, common to temperate North America, of which the papaw, *Asimina triloba*, is a species.

as·i·nē'gō, *n.*; *pl.* **as·i·nē'gōeş,** [Sp. *asnico*, dim. of *asno*, ass; L. *asinus*.] a foolish fellow. [Obs.]

as'i·nīne, *a.* [L. *asininus*, asslike, from *asinus*, ass.] like an ass, regarded as a stupid animal; stupid; silly; unintelligent.

as·i·nin'i·ty, *n.* 1. the state or quality of being asinine.
2. *pl.* **as·i·nin'i·tieş,** an asinine act or remark

Ȧ·sī·phō·nā'tȧ, *n.pl.* [Gr. *a* priv., and *siphōn*, a siphon.] an order of lamellibranchiate bivalve mollusks lacking a siphon, including the oysters, the mussels, etc.

ȧ·sī'phon·āte, *a.* of or pertaining to the *Asiphonata*.

-ȧ·sis, [L.; Gr., ending of nouns derived from verbs with roots ending in *-a-*, and suffix *-sis*, denoting state or process.] a suffix used in forming names of some diseases, meaning *a condition resembling*, *a condition characterized by*, as in elephanti*asis*, psori*asis*.

ȧsk, *v.t.*; asked, *pt.*, *pp.*; asking, *ppr.* [ME. *ashen, esken*; AS. *ascian, acsian*, to ask; originally from Sans. root, *ish*, to seek.]
1. to request; to seek to obtain by words; to petition for: sometimes with *of*, in the sense of *from*, before the person to whom the request is made; as, to ask a favor *of* a person.
2. to require as necessary or useful; to exact; to call for.
3. to interrogate, or inquire of; to put a question to (a person), with a view to an answer.
4. to expect, require, or demand, as the price or value of a commodity; to set (a price); as, what price do you *ask?*
5. to invite; as, to *ask* guests to a wedding or entertainment.
6. to inquire concerning; to seek to be informed about; as, to *ask* the way to the courthouse.
7. to publish (banns); also, to publish the banns of. [Archaic.]
Syn.—demand, entreat, inquire, request, solicit, crave, beg, petition, question, interrogate, invite, require, beseech.

ȧsk, *v.i.* 1. to make a request (*for* something).
2. to inquire, or seek by request; to make inquiry: sometimes followed by *after*, *about*, or *for*; as, to *ask after* one's health.

ȧsk, *n.* the asker, or water newt. [Prov. Eng.]

ȧ·skȧnce', ȧ·skȧnt', *adv.* [origin uncertain.] sideways; obliquely; out of one corner of the eye; hence, distrustfully; with suspicion; as, they regarded us *askance*.

ȧ·skȧnce', *v.t.* to turn aside. [Rare.]

ȧsk'ẽr, *n.* one who asks; a petitioner; an inquirer.

ȧsk'ẽr, *n.* [ME. *aske*; AS. *āthexe*, a lizard or newt.] the water newt. [Prov. Eng.]

ȧ·skew', *adv.* [ME. *askue, ascue*.] to one side; awry; crookedly.

ȧ·skew', *a.* on one side; awry.

ȧsk'ing, *n.* 1. the act of requesting, petitioning, or interrogating; also, the thing requested.
2. the publishing or proclamation of marriage banns.

ȧ·slāke', *v.t.* [ME. *aslaken*; AS. *āslacian*, to slacken.] to remit; to slacken; to diminish. [Obs.]

ȧ·slȧnt', *a.* and *adv.* on a slant; slanting(ly); oblique(ly).
The shaft drove through his neck *aslant*.
—Dryden.

ȧ·slȧnt', *prep.* in a slanting direction over; obliquely across; as, a ray of light *aslant* the room.

ȧ·sleep′, *a.* 1. in a condition of sleep; sleeping.
2. inactive; dull; backward.
3. numb; as, her arm is *asleep.*
4. dead: a euphemism.

ȧ·sleep′, *adv.* into a sleeping condition.

ȧ·slōpe′, *a.* and *adv.* in a leaning, slanting, or inclined position; sloping(ly).

ȧ·slug′, *adv.* in a sluggish manner. [Obs.]

ȧ·smēar′, *a.* and *adv.* smeared.

Aṣ·mō·dē′us, *n.* [L. *Asmodaeus*; Gr. *Asmodaios*; Heb. *ashmadai.*] in Jewish demonology, an evil spirit; chief demon.

ȧ·sōak′, *a.* and *adv.* soaking.

ā·sō′ciăl (-shăl), *a.* [*a*, not, and *social.*] not social; not gregarious; characterized by withdrawal and avoidance of contact with others.

as′ŏk, ȧ·sō′kȧ, *n.* same as *asak.*

ȧ·sō′mȧ·tous, *a.* [Gr. *asōmatos*, without body; *a* priv., and *sōma*, body.] without a material body; incorporeal.

as′ō·nănt, *a.* not sonant.

ȧsp, *n.* [L. *aspis*; Gr. *aspis*, an asp.] any of several small, poisonous snakes of Africa, Arabia, and Europe, as the horned viper, common European viper, etc.

ȧsp, *n.* an aspen. [Poetic.]

As·pal′ȧ·thus, *n.* [Gr. *aspalathos*, a sweet-scented shrub.]
1. the African broom, a large genus of African plants of the bean family, with small heathlike leaves and generally yellow flowers.
2. [a–] a thorny shrub of uncertain species, mentioned in the Bible.

ASP

as·pȧ·raġ′iç, *a.* same as *aspartic.*

as·par′ȧ·ġin, as·par′ȧ·ġine, *n.* an alkaloid found in asparagus, beets, and other vegetables: it is rhombically crystalline.

as·pȧ·raġ′i·nous, *a.* relating or allied to the asparagus; with edible shoots like asparagus.

As·par′ȧ·gus, *n.* [OFr. *esparage*; L. *asparagus*; Gr. *asparagos*, asparagus.]
1. a large genus of perennial plants, of the natural order *Liliaceæ*, with small, scalelike leaves, many flat or needlelike branches, and whitish flowers.
2. [a–] the tender shoots of *Asparagus officinalis*, used as a vegetable.
3. [a–] any plant of this genus.

as·par′ȧ·gus bee′tle, a leaf beetle, as *Crioceris asparagi*, feeding on asparagus plants.

as·par′ȧ·gus stōne, a crystalline form of apatite.

ȧ·spär′kle, *a.* [*a-*, on, and *sparkle.*] sparkling.

as·pär′tiç ac′id, [coined after *asparagus.*] an amino acid, $C_4H_7O_4N$, occurring in proteins in white prisms or colorless leaflets, used in organic synthesis.

as′peçt, *n.* [ME. *aspect*; L. *aspectus*, from *aspicere*, to look at.]
1. look; view; appearance to the eye or the mind as seen from a specific point; as, to present an object or a subject in its true *aspect*, or under a double *aspect.*
2. countenance; look, or particular appearance of the face; as, a mild or severe *aspect.*
3. look; glance; the act of seeing. [Rare.]
4. position with regard to seeing, or that position which enables one to look in a particular direction.
5. position in relation to the points of the compass; exposure; as, a house has a southern *aspect*, that is, a position which faces or looks to the south.
6. in astrology, the position of stars in relation to each other or to the observer.
7. in grammar, the form that a verb takes to indicate duration or completion of action: e.g., he *was eating* (imperfect aspect); he *ate* (perfect aspect).
8. in physics, the position of a plane (flat surface) in relation to a liquid or gaseous substance through which it is moving or which is moving past it.
Syn.—appearance, countenance, complexion, feature, phase, look, view, light.

as′peçt, *v.t.* to behold. [Obs.]

as·peçt′ȧ·ble, *a.* [L. *aspectabilis*, visible.] that may be seen; visible. [Rare.]

as·peçt′ănt, *a.* [L. *aspectans*, ppr. of *aspectare*, to look at repeatedly.] in heraldry and art, facing each other.

as·peçt′ed, *a.* having an aspect. [Rare.]

as·peç′tion, *n.* the act of viewing. [Obs.]

as·peç′tŏr, *n.* a beholder. [Obs.]

asp′en, *n.* [ME. *asp, aspe*; AS. *aespe, aspe*, aspen.] any of several kinds of poplar tree with flattened leafstalks that cause the leaves to flutter in the least breeze.

asp′en, *a.* pertaining to the aspen, or resembling it; fluttering; trembling.

as′pẽr, *a.* rough; rugged. [Obs.]

as′pẽr, *n.* [L. *asper*, rough.] in Greek grammar, the spiritus asper, or rough breathing.

as′pẽr, *n.* [LL. *asprum*; Gr. *aspron*, neut. of *aspros*, white.] a Turkish monetary unit, formerly a coin, equal to $^{1}/_{120}$ of a piaster.

as′pẽr·āte, *v.t.*; asperated, *pt.*, *pp.*; asperating, *ppr.* [L. *asperatus*, pp. of *asperare*, to make rough.] to make rough or uneven.

as′pẽr·āte, *a.* rough; uneven.

as·pẽr·ā′tion, *n.* a making rough.

As·pẽr′ġeṣ, *n.* [L. *aspergere*, to sprinkle; *asperges*, you will sprinkle.]
1. in the Roman Catholic Church, the sprinkling of altar, clergy, and people with holy water before High Mass.
2. a hymn sung during this ceremony, beginning *Asperges me.*

as′pẽr·ġill, *n.* same as *aspergillum.*

as·pẽr·ġil′li·fọrm, *a.* shaped like an aspergillus.

as·pẽr·ġil′lum, *n.*; *pl.* **as·pẽr·ġil′lȧ** or **as·pẽr·ġil′lumṣ**, [ML., from L. *aspergere*, and neut. dim. *-illum.*] a brush or perforated container for sprinkling holy water.

as·pẽr·ġil′lus, *n.*; *pl.* **as·pẽr·ġil′lī**, [L., from *aspergere*, to sprinkle, and dim. *-illus.*]
1. an aspergillum.
2. [A–] a genus of fungi bearing chains of spores attached to stalks on the swollen end of a threadlike branch.
3. any fungus of this genus, as the yellow mildew.

as″pẽr·i·fō′li·āte, as″pẽr·i·fō′li·ous, *a.* [L. *asper*, rough, and *folium*, a leaf.] having rough leaves.

as·per′i·ty, *n.* [ME. *asprete*; OFr. *asprete*; L. *asperitas*, roughness, from *asper*, rough.]
1. roughness of surface; unevenness.
2. roughness of sound; that quality which grates upon the ear. [Archaic.]
3. roughness to the taste; sourness. [Archaic.]
4. roughness or sharpness of temper; crabbedness.
5. difficulty; disagreeableness; as, the pleasures and *asperities* of life.
Syn.—roughness, harshness, sharpness, moroseness, acrimony, acerbity, severity.

ȧ·sper′mȧ·tiṣm, *n.* in medicine, defective secretion of semen or lack of formation of spermatozoa.

ȧ·spẽr′mȧ·tous, ȧ·spẽr′mous, *a.* [Gr. *aspermos*, seedless; *a* priv., and *sperma*, seed.]
1. in botany, having no seeds. [Rare.]
2. characterized by aspermatism.

ȧ·spẽr′mi·ȧ, *n.* same as *aspermatism.*

ȧ·spẽr′mous, *a.* same as *aspermatous.*

as′pẽr·ous, *a.* [L. *asper*, rough.] rough; uneven. [Obs.]

as·pẽrse′, *v.t.*; aspersed, *pt.*, *pp.*; aspersing, *ppr.* [L. *aspersus*, pp. of *aspergere*, to scatter.]
1. to spread false rumors concerning, or damaging charges against; besmirch the reputation of; to slander or calumniate; as, to *asperse* a man's motives.
2. to strew upon or over; to besprinkle. [Rare.]
Syn.—calumniate, scandalize, backbite, slander, traduce, malign, defame, vilify.

as·pẽrsed′, *a.* 1. in heraldry, strewed or powdered with small charges.
2. slandered; vilified.

as·pẽrs′ẽr, *n.* one who asperses or slanders another.

as·pẽr′sion, *n.* 1. a sprinkling, as with water or dust.
2. the spreading of disparaging or damaging reports or charges which tarnish reputation; calumny; false rumor; slander; innuendo.

as·pẽrs′ive, *a.* slanderous.

as·pẽrs′ive·ly, *adv.* in an aspersive manner.

as·pẽr·sō′ri·um, *n.*; *pl.* **as·pẽr·sō′ri·ȧ** or **as·pẽr·sō′ri·umṣ**, [L., from *aspersus*, pp. of *aspergere*, to sprinkle.]
1. a stoup or vessel for holy water, usually of stone and fixed permanently close to the entrance of a church. Sometimes, the aspersorium is portable, of metal, ivory, etc., and highly ornamented with bas-reliefs.
2. an aspergillum.

ASPERSORIUM

as·pẽr′sō·ry, *a.* tending to asperse; defamatory.

as·pẽr′ū·lous, *a.* in botany, slightly rough to the touch.

as′phạlt (*or* -falt), *n.* [Gr. *asphaltos*, asphalt, a word of foreign origin.]
1. a brown or black tarlike substance, a variety of bitumen, found in a natural state or obtained by evaporating petroleum.
2. a mixture of this with sand or gravel, for cementing, paving, roofing, etc.

as′phạlt, *v.t.*; asphalted, *pt.*, *pp.*; asphalting, *ppr.* to spread over with asphalt.

as·phạl′tiç, *a.* pertaining to asphalt, or containing it; bituminous.

as·phạl′tīte, *a.* asphaltic.

as·phạl′tum, *n.* same as *asphalt.*

as′phō·del, *n.* [L. *asphodelus*; Gr. *asphodelos*, a plant like the lily.]
1. any plant of the genus *Asphodelus*, characterized by fleshy roots, narrow leaves, and white or yellow flowers like lilies.
2. a name popularly and poetically applied to plants of other genera, especially to the daffodil or narcissus.

ASPHODEL
(*Asphodelus ramosus*)

As·phod′el·us, *n.* [L.] a genus of hardy perennial plants, of the lily family.

as·phyç′tiç, *a.* in medicine, relating to asphyxia.

as·phyx′i·ȧ, as·phyx′y, *n.* [Gr. *asphyxia*, a stopping of the pulse; *a* priv., and *sphyzein*, to beat violently.] loss of consciousness as a result of too little oxygen and too much carbon dioxide in the blood: suffocation causes asphyxia.

as·phyx′i·ăl, *a.* pertaining to or characterized by asphyxia.

as·phyx′i·ănt, *n.* an agent producing asphyxia.

as·phyx′i·ănt, *a.* producing asphyxia.

as·phyx′i·āte, *v.t.*; asphyxiated, *pt.*, *pp.*; asphyxiating, *ppr.* to cause to suffocate; to produce or cause asphyxia in; as, they were *asphyxiated* by coal gas.

as·phyx′i·āte, *v.i.* to undergo asphyxia.

as·phyx·i·ā′tion, *n.* the act or process of causing suffocation; also, the condition of asphyxia.

as·phyx′i·ā·tŏr, *n.* a person or thing that asphyxiates.

as·phyx′ied (-id), *a.* in a state of asphyxia; asphyxiated.

as·phyx′y, *n.* same as *asphyxia.*

as′piç, *n.* [Fr. *aspic*; L. *aspis*, asp.]
1. the asp (poisonous snake). [Poetic.]
2. formerly, a piece of ordnance carrying a twelve-pound shot.

as′piç, *n.* [Fr. *aspic*; OFr. *espic*; L. *spica*, a spike, an ear of corn.] a European species of lavender (*Lavandula spica*), used in making oil of lavender.

as′piç, *n.* [Fr.] a jelly of meat juice, tomato juice, etc. used as a relish or for a mold of meat, seafood, etc.

ȧ·spiç′ū·lāte, ȧ·spiç′ū·lous, *a.* [Gr. *a* priv., and L. *spiculum*, point.] having no spicules.

as·pi·dis′trȧ, *n.* [Mod. L. from Gr. *aspis*, a shield, and *astron*, a star.] any of a number of related plants of the lily family, with dark, inconspicuous flowers and large, stiff, glossy, evergreen leaves.

As·pid′i·um, *n.* [Gr. *aspidion*, a small round shield, dim. of *aspis*, a round shield.] a genus of ferns including all those which have round sori protected with a roundish covering or indusium; shield fern.

As″pi·dō·brañ′çhi·ȧ, *n.pl.* a group of gastropods having a shieldlike shell.

as″pi·dō·brañ′çhi·āte, *a.* [Gr. *aspis*, shield, and *branchia*, gills.] resembling the *Aspidobranchia.*

as″pi·dō·brañ′çhi·āte, *n.* one of the *Aspidobranchia.*

as·pīr′ănt, *a.* aspiring.

as·pīr′ănt, *n.* [L. *aspirans*, ppr. of *aspirare*, to breathe upon, to endeavor to reach.] one who aspires or seeks with eagerness; as, an *aspirant* to public office.

as′pi·rāte, *v.t.*; aspirated, *pt.*, *pp.*; aspirating, *ppr.* [L. *aspiratus*, pp. of *aspirare*, to breathe; Gr. *aspairein*, to struggle for breath.]
1. to pronounce with a breathing or full emission of breath; as, we *aspirate* the words *horse* and *house.*
2. in medicine, to remove (fluid or gas), as from a body cavity, by suction.

as′pi·rāte, *n.* 1. the speech sound represented by the English *h* or the Greek rough breathing.
2. an expiratory breath puff such as follows initial *p*, *t*, *k* in English.

as′pi·rāte, as′pi·rā·ted, *a.* uttered with an aspirate.

as·pi·rā′tion, *n.* 1. (a) the pronunciation of a letter, etc. with an aspirate; (b) an aspirate.
2. a breathing or breathing in; a breath.
3. the act of aspiring or of ardently desiring; an ardent wish or desire, particularly for advancement, honor, etc.
4. the removal by suction of fluid or gas from a body cavity.
Syn.—ambition, longing, craving, desire, hope, wish.

as′pi·rā·tŏr, *n.* 1. in medicine, an apparatus using suction to remove a fluid or gas from a body cavity.
2. an instrument for creating a vacuum, or for passing a current of air through fluids, gases, etc.: much used in the chemical analysis of gases.

as·pīr′ȧ·tō·ry, *a.* of or suited for breathing or suction.

as·pīre′, *v.i.*; aspired, *pt., pp.*; aspiring, *ppr.* [ME. *aspire*; Fr. *aspirer*; L. *aspirare*, to breathe upon, to aspire to; Gr. *aspairein*, to pant for breath.]
1. to exhale. [Rare.]
2. to desire with eagerness; to long or seek for advancement, honor, etc.: followed by *to* or *after*; as, to *aspire to* the presidency.
3. to rise; to ascend; as, the flames *aspire*. [Archaic.]
Syn.—desire, aim, seek, long, rise, mount, ascend, soar.

as·pīre′, *n.* aspiration. [Obs.]

as·pīre′ment, *n.* aspiration. [Obs.]

as·pīr′ẽr, *n.* one who aspires.

as′pir·in *n.* [G. from *acetyl*, and *spirsäure*, salicylic acid; and *-in*.]
1. a white, crystalline powder, acetylsalicylic acid, $C_9H_8O_4$, used for reducing fever, relieving headaches, etc.
2. a tablet of this.

as·pīr′ing, *a.* ambitious; animated with an ardent desire for power, importance, or excellence; as, an *aspiring* citizen.

as·pīr′ing·ly, *adv.* in an aspiring manner.

as·pīr′ing·ness, *n.* the state of being aspiring.

asp′ish, *a.* resembling an asp.

ā·splañch′niç, *a.* [Gr. *a* priv., and *splanchna*, bowels.] in zoology, lacking an alimentary canal.

As·plē′ni·um, *n.* [Gr. *asplēnion*, the spleenwort, a fern; *a*, euphonic, and *splēn*, spleen.] a large genus of ferns, the spleenworts, belonging to the order *Polypodiaceæ*. Among the best-known species are the *Asplenium Rutamuraria*, or wall rue, and the *Asplenium Trichomanes*, or maidenhair spleenwort.

as·pōr·tā′tion, *n.* [L. *asportatio*, a carrying away; *ab*, from, and *portare*, to carry.]
1. a carrying away.
2. in law, the felonious removal of goods from the place where they were deposited.

ȧ·sprawl′, *a.* and *adv.* sprawling(ly).

ȧ·squăt′, *a.* squatting.

ȧ·squint′, *a.* and *adv.* with a squint; out of the corner of the eye.

ȧss, *n.* [ME. *ass, asse*; OFr. *asne*; AS. *assa*; L. *asinus*, ass.]
1. a quadruped, *Equus asinus*, of the same genus as the horse, but smaller. It has long ears and a short mane. The tame or domestic ass is slow, but very sure-footed, and for this reason very useful on rough, steep ground: also called *donkey, burro*.
2. a dull, stupid fellow; a dolt; a fool: from the fabled obstinancy and stupidity of the animal.
asses' bridge; the fifth proposition of the first book of Euclid, stating that the base angles of an isosceles triangle are equal: so called from the difficulty of learners in grasping it.
to make an ass of oneself; to act or talk foolishly.

ȧss, *n.* arse: vulgar term. [Slang.]

äss, *n.* [Scot.] sing. of *ashes*.

as′sä·çù, as′sȧ·çou, *n.* [Braz.] a euphorbiaceous tree (*Hura crepitans*) of South America, the bark and sap of which contain a poisonous acrid principle.

as·sȧ·fet′i·dȧ, as·sȧ·foet′i·dȧ, *n.* asafetida.

as′sȧ·gaī, as′se·gaī, *n.* [Fr. *archegaie*, from Ar. *az-zaghāyah*, the spear.]
1. a kind of javelin or throwing spear, often with an iron tip, used by some South African tribes.
2. in botany, a tree of the dogwood family, from which the South African natives make their spears.

as′sȧ·gaī, as′se·gaī, *v.t.* to pierce with an assagai.

ȧs·sä′i, *adv.* [It. *assai*, very much; from L. *ad*, to, and *satis*, enough.] in music, very; as in *adagio assai*, very slow; *allegro assai*, very quick.

as·saī′ (as-sī′), *n.* [native name.]
1. a palm tree of Brazil, the *Euterpe edulis*.
2. a beverage made from the fruit of this tree.

as·sāil′, *v.t.*; assailed, *pt., pp.*; assailing, *ppr.* [ME. *assailen*; OFr. *asaillir*; L. *assilire*, to spring upon; *ad*, to, and *salire*, to leap.]
1. to leap or fall upon with violence; to assault; to attack suddenly.
2. to attack with arguments, censure, abuse, criticism, appeals, entreaties, and the like, with a view to injure, bring into disrepute, or overcome mentally or morally.
3. to face or take up (a difficulty, task, etc.) with determination.
Syn.—encounter, assault, fall upon, invade, attack, storm.

as·sāil′ȧ·ble, *a.* that can be assailed or attacked.

as·sāil′ănt, *n.* [Fr. *assaillant*.] one who assails, attacks, or assaults.

as·sāil′ănt, *a.* assaulting; attacking; assailing.

as·sāil′ẽr, *n.* one who assails.

as·sāil′ment, *n.* assault; attack.

as′sȧ·mär, *n.* [L. *assus*, roasted, from *assare*, to roast, and *amarus*, bitter.] the bitter substance formed during the process of roasting meat, bread, starch, sugar, and the like till they are browned: a former designation.

As·săm·ēṣe′, *a.* of or pertaining to Assam, a state of northeastern India, or to its inhabitants, language, etc.

As·săm·ēṣe′, *n.* 1. *pl.* **As·săm·ēṣe′,** a native or inhabitant of Assam.
2. the Indo-European, Indic language of the Assamese.

as·sȧ·pan′, as·sȧ·pan′iç, *n.* [native Am. Indian name.] the flying squirrel of the eastern United States.

as·särt′, *n.* [OFr. *assarter*, to grub up; LL. *exsartare*; from L. *ex*, out, and *sarrire*, to hoe.]
1. in old English law, a grubbing up of trees and bushes so as to make forest land arable.
2. a piece of land cleared in this way.

as·särt′, *v.t.* to grub up (trees and bushes) so as to make forest land arable.

as·sas′sin, *n.* [Fr. *assassin*, from Ar. *hashshāshīn*, hashish eaters, from *hashīsh*, hemp.]
1. [A-], a member of a secret band of hashish-eating Moslems who killed Christian leaders during the Crusades.
2. a murderer who strikes suddenly and without warning: now generally used of the hired or delegated killer of some politically important personage.

as·sas′sin, *v.t.* to assassinate. [Obs.]

as·sas′sin·āte, *v.t.*; assassinated, *pt., pp.*; assassinating, *ppr.* 1. to murder by surprise or secret assault, as an assassin does.
2. to harm or ruin (one's reputation, etc.).
Syn.—kill, murder, slay.

as·sas′sin·āte, *n.* an assassination or an assassin. [Obs.]

as·sas·si·nā′tion, *n.* an assassinating or being assassinated; the act of killing or murdering, by surprise or secret assault.

as·sas′si·nā·tŏr, *n.* one who assassinates; an assassin.

as·sas′sin bug, any of a number of related insects having a curved, sucking beak and living chiefly on the blood of other insects.

as·sas′sin·ous, *a.* murderous. [Obs.]

as·sā′tion, *n.* [L. *assare*, to roast.] a roasting. [Obs.]

as·sąult′, *n.* [ME. *assaut*; OFr. *assaut, assalt*, assault, from L. *ad*, to, *saltare*, to leap.]
1. an attack or violent onset, as with blows or weapons, whether by an individual, a company, or an army.
2. an attack by hostile words or measures; as, an *assault* upon the constitution of a state; also, an attack by argument or appeal.
3. rape: a euphemism.
4. in law, an unlawful threat to harm another physically, or an unsuccessful attempt to do so.
5. in military science, (a) a sudden attack upon a fortified place; (b) the concluding stage of an attack.
Syn.—attack, onset, onslaught, storm, charge.

as·sąult′, *v.t.* and *v.i.*; assaulted, *pt., pp.*; assaulting, *ppr.* to make an assault (upon).
Syn.—encounter, assail, engage, attack, invade, storm, charge.

as·sąult′ȧ·ble, *a.* capable of being assaulted.

as·sąult′ and bat′tẽr·y, in law, the carrying out of threatened physical harm or violence; beating or hitting a person.

as·sąult′ẽr, *n.* one who assaults, or violently attacks.

as·sāy′, *n.* 1. in metallurgy, the determination of the quantity of any particular metal in an ore or alloy; especially, the determination of the quantity of gold or silver in coin or bullion.
2. the substance to be assayed.
3. in law, an examination of weights and measures by a standard: now historical.
4. trial; effort; attempt. [Obs.]
5. ascertained purity or value. [Obs.]
Pearls and precious stones of great *assay*.
—Spenser.
6. an examination or testing, as of quality, fitness, etc.

as·sāy′, *v.t.*; assayed, *pt., pp.*; assaying, *ppr.* [ME. *assayen*; OFr. *asaier, essaier*, to try, from LL. *exagium*, a weighing out, from L. *exigere*, to weigh, try; *ex*, out, and *agere*, to drive.]
1. to make an assay of; test; analyze.
2. to attempt; to try. [Obs.]

as·sāy′, *v.i.* 1. to attempt, try, or endeavor. [Obs.]
2. to be shown by analysis to contain a specified proportion of some precious metal; as, this ore *assays* high in gold.

as·sāy′ȧ·ble, *a.* capable of being assayed.

as·sāy′ bal″ănce, a balance used in the process of assaying.

as·sāy′ẽr, *n.* one who assays.

as·sāy′ fûr′nāce, a furnace used in the process of assaying.

as·sāy′ing, *n.* the determination of the amount of any particular metal in an ore or alloy.

asse, *n.* in zoology, a small African fox, *Vulpes caama*, yielding a valuable fur.

ass ēar, an old name for the common comfrey, *Symphytum officinale*.

as″sē·çū·rā′tion, *n.* assurance; a making sure. [Obs.]

as·sē·çūre′, *v.t.* [L. *ad*. to, and *securus*, secure.] to make sure. [Obs.]

as·sē·çū′tion, *n.* [L. *assequi*, to follow after.] an obtaining or acquiring. [Obs.]

as′se·gaī, *n.* see *assagai*.

as·sem′blāġe, *n.* 1. a collection of individuals or of particular things; as, an *assemblage* of men of note.
2. the act of assembling or the state of being assembled.
3. the act of fitting together, as parts of a machine; also, a whole that results from such fitting together.
Syn.—collection, concourse, convention.

as·sem′blănce, *n.* 1. representation; semblance. [Obs.]
2. an assembling. [Obs.]

as·sem′ble, *v.t.*; assembled, *pt., pp.*; assembling, *ppr.* [ME. *assemblen*; OFr. *assembler, asembler*, to assemble, from L. *ad*, to, and *simul*, together.]
1. to collect (a number of persons or things) into one place or body; to bring or call together; to convene; to congregate; as, to *assemble* an army corps.
2. to put together the parts of; as, to *assemble* a bicycle.
Syn.—collect, convene, convoke, gather, muster.

as·sem′ble, *v.i.* to meet or come together; to convene, as a number of individuals; as, Congress *assembles* every winter.

as·sem′ble, *v.i.* to compare. [Obs.]

as·sem′blẽr, *n.* one who assembles.

as·sem′bling, *n.* 1. a collection or meeting together.
2. the bringing or fitting together of the different parts of an article or machine, as a bicycle, gun, or sewing machine.

as·sem′bly, *n.* [ME. *assemble, assemblaye*; OFr. *assemblee*, an assembly.]
1. an assembling or being assembled.
2. a company or collection of individuals in the same place, usually for the same purpose; an assemblage.
3. in a civil or political sense, a meeting convened by authority for the transaction of public business; as, the *assemblies* of the Roman people; the *assembly* of the states-general, and the national *assembly* in France.
4. [A-] in some States of the United States, the legislature, or the lower branch of it.
5. in the Presbyterian Church, a convocation, convention, or council of ministers and ruling elders, delegated from each presbytery: in full, *General Assembly*.
6. in military tactics, the drumbeat or bugle call summoning a body of troops to form ranks.

7. a fitting together of parts to make a whole, as in making automobiles, etc.

8. the parts to be thus fitted together.

9. the factory in which such assembling is done.

unlawful assembly; in law, a gathering of three or more persons whose actions cause a reasonable doubt of their peaceful intent.

Syn.—assemblage, congregation, convocation, collection, audience, concourse.

as·sem'bly line, in factory production, an arrangement of men and machinery that effects the completion of a manufactured unit in a series of successive specialized operations by sending the work along a slowly moving belt or track from man to man.

as·sem'bly·măn, *n.*; *pl.* **as·sem'bly·men,** 1. a member of an assembly, especially of a legislative assembly.

2. [A-] in some States of the United States, a member of the lower house of the legislature.

as·sem'bly plant, a factory in which parts, as of aircraft, are assembled.

as·sem'bly rọọm, a room in which persons assemble, especially for amusement.

as·sent', *n.* 1. the act of the mind in admitting or agreeing to the truth of a proposition.

Faith is the *assent* to any proposition, on the credit of the proposer. —Locke.

2. concurrence; agreement with a statement, proposal, etc.; also, formal or official sanction.

3. consent; compliance. [Archaic.]

royal assent; formal royal sanction to a legislative act.

Syn.—acquiescence, approbation, concurrence, consent, agreement, compliance.—We *assent* to a statement, but we do not *consent* to it. *Consent* is an agreement to some proposal or measure which affects the rights or interests of the consenter. *Assent* is an act of the understanding; *consent* is an act of the will.

as·sent', *v.i.*; assented, *pt., pp.*; assenting, *ppr.* [ME. *assenten*; OFr. *assenter*; L. *assentari, assentire*, to approve, consent; *ad*, to, and *sentire*, to feel.] to admit something as true; to agree; to yield, or concede; to express an agreement of the mind to what is alleged or proposed; to answer in the affirmative.

as·sen·tā'tion, *n.* [L. *assentatio*, from *assentari*, to comply.] immediate and usually flattering or hypocritical assent.

as'sen·tā·tŏr, *n.* a flatterer. [Rare.]

as·sent'ȧ·tō·ri·ly, *adv.* with flattery. [Rare.]

as·sent'ȧ·tō·ry, *a.* flattering. [Rare.]

as·sent'ẽr, *n.* a person who assents.

as·sen'tient (-shent), *a.* agreeing; assenting.

as·sent'ing, *a.* agreeing to, or admitting as true; yielding to.

as·sent'ing·ly, *adv.* in a manner to express assent; by agreement.

as·sent'ive, *a.* assenting or inclined to assent.

as·sent'ment, *n.* assent; agreement. [Obs.]

as·sent'ŏr, *n.* a person who assents; specifically, in Great Britain, one of the voters whose endorsement must be added to those of the proposer and seconder for the nomination of a political candidate.

as·sẽrt', *v.t.*; asserted, *pt., pp.*; asserting, *ppr.* [L. *assertus*, pp. of *asserere*, to join to; *ad*, to, and *serere*, to join, bind.]

1. to affirm positively; to declare with assurance; to aver.

2. to maintain or defend by words or measures; to vindicate a claim or title to; as, to *assert* our rights and liberties.

to assert oneself; (a) to insist on one's rights, or on being recognized; (b) to thrust oneself forward.

Syn.—asseverate, maintain, declare, affirm, aver, state.

as·sẽrt'ẽr, *n.* one who asserts.

as·sẽr'tion, *n.* 1. the act of asserting.

2. something asserted; a positive declaration or averment; affirmation.

as·sẽr'tion·ăl, *a.* containing an assertion.

as·sẽrt'ive, *a.* 1. characterized by assertion; positive.

2. unduly confident or insistent in stating or claiming.

as·sẽrt'ive·ly, *adv.* in an assertive manner.

as·sẽrt'ive·ness, *n.* the state or quality of being assertive.

as·sẽrt'ŏr, *n.* a person who asserts.

as·sẽr·tō'ri·ăl, *a.* asserting anything to exist; asserting a thing as a fact.

as·sẽrt'ō·ry, *a.* affirming; asserting.

as·sẽrve', *v.t.* to assist; to serve. [Obs.]

as·sẽr'vile, *v.t.* to make servile. [Obs.]

as·sess', *v.t.*; assessed, *pt., pp.*; assessing, *ppr.* [ME. *assesse*; OFr. *assesser*, from L. *assessare*, to impose a tax, set a rate, from *assidere*; *ad*, to, and *sedere*, to sit.]

1. to set or fix a certain sum against, as a tax, fine, or special payment; as, to *assess* each citizen in due proportion; also, to impose (a certain sum) as a tax, fine, etc.

2. to fix the value of (property) for the purpose of being taxed.

3. to set the amount of (damages, a fine, etc.).

as·sess'ȧ·ble, *a.* that can be assessed.

as·sess'ȧ·bly, *adv.* by assessment.

as·ses'sion, *n.* a sitting down beside or together; a session.

as·sess'ment, *n.* 1. an assessing; specifically, a valuation of property for the purpose of taxation.

2. a method or schedule of assessing.

3. an amount assessed.

4. in the United States, (a) payment asked on a stock subscription, usually at stated intervals; (b) a levy for political purposes, called a *political assessment*.

as·sess'ŏr, *n.* [L., an assistant judge, from *assidere*; *ad*, to, by, and *sedere*, to sit.]

1. one appointed to assess income or property for taxation.

2. an inferior officer of justice, who assists the judge.

3. one appointed to advise a committee, etc.

as·ses·sō'ri·ăl, *a.* pertaining to an assessor or assessors.

as·sess'ŏr·ship, *n.* the office of an assessor.

as'set, *n.* [OFr. *assez, asset*; L. *ad satis*; *ad*, to, and *satis*, enough, sufficient.]

1. anything owned that has exchange value.

2. a valuable or desirable thing to have; as, charm is her chief *asset*.

3. [*pl.*] in accounting, all the entries on a balance sheet that shows the entire property or resources of a person or business, as accounts and notes receivable, cash, inventory, equipment, real estate, etc.

4. [*pl.*] in law, property, as of a business, bankrupt, etc., usable to pay debts.

as·sev'ẽr, *v.t.* to asseverate. [Archaic.]

as·sev'ẽr·āte, *v.t.*; asseverated, *pt., pp.*; asseverating, *ppr.* [L. *asseveratus*, pp. of *asseverare*, to assert strongly; *ad*, to, and *severus*, earnest, severe.] to affirm or aver positively or seriously.

Syn.—affirm, aver, avow, avouch, declare, assert.

as·sev·ẽr·ā'tion, *n.* positive affirmation or assertion; a solemn declaration.

as·sev'ẽr·ā·tive, as·sev'ẽr·ā·tō·ry, *a.* asseverating; positively affirming.

ass'head″ (-hed), a blockhead.

Äs'shụr, *n.* same as *Ashur*.

as·sib'i·lāte, *v.t.*; assibilated, *pt., pp.*; assibilating, *ppr.* [L. *assibilatus*, pp. of *assibilare*, to whisper at, or to; *ad*, to, and *sibilare*, to whisper.] to change (a sound) into a sibilant, as in changing the *t* in *position* into *sh*.

as·sib·i·lā'tion, *n.* the change of a nonsibilant letter to a sibilant.

As·si·dē'ăn, *n.* one of a sect of Jews who joined with Mattathias, the father of the Maccabees, to oppose the Hellenistic Jews.

as'si·dent, *a.* [L. *assidens*, ppr. of *assidere*, to sit by; *ad*, to, and *sedere*, to sit.] in medicine, usually, but not always, accompanying a disease: as, *assident* symptoms.

as·sid'ū·āte, *a.* continuous; assiduous. [Obs.]

as·si·dū'i·ty, *n.* 1. diligent application to any enterprise.

2. *pl.* **as·si·dū'i·tieṣ,** an instance of this.

as·sid'ū·ous, *a.* [L. *assiduus*, from *assidere*, to sit by; *ad*, to, and *sedere*, to sit.]

1. constant in application; diligent; as, a person *assiduous* in his occupation.

2. performed with constant diligence or attention; as, *assiduous* labor.

Syn.—industrious, unremitting, sedulous, persevering, zealous, attentive.

as·sid'ū·ous·ly, *adv.* diligently; attentively; with earnestness and care; with regular attendance.

as·sid'ū·ous·ness, *n.* constant or diligent application.

as·siēġe', *v.t.* to besiege. [Obs.]

as·siēġe', *n.* a siege. [Obs.]

as·si·en'tist, *n.* one in any way connected with an assiento.

as·si·en'tō, *n.* [Sp. *assiento, asiento*, a seat, contract, agreement; *a*, L. *ad*, to, and *sentar*, from L. *sedens*, ppr. of *sedere*, to sit.] formerly a contract between Spain and other countries, or between Spain and a company of merchants, for furnishing slaves to the Spanish dominions in America in return for special privileges.

as·sīgn' (-sīn'), *v.t.*; assigned (-sīnd'), *pt., pp.*; assigning, *ppr.* [ME. *assignen*; OFr. *assigner*; L. *assignare*, to mark out, allot; *ad*, to, and *signare*, to mark.]

1. to allot; to appoint or grant by distribution or apportionment; also, to give out as a task.

2. to designate or appoint for a particular purpose, duty, etc.

3. to fix, specify, or designate; as, to *assign* a day for a judicial hearing.

4. in law, to transfer or make over to another, as an estate; in bankruptcy, to transfer (property) to, and vest in certain persons, called assignees, for the benefit of creditors.

5. to ascribe; refer to; as, to *assign* a reason for one's conduct.

Syn.—apportion, appoint, transfer, grant, adduce, convey, give.

as·sīgn', *v.i.* to transfer property, etc. to another, as in trust for the benefit of creditors.

as·sīgn', *n.* 1. [*usually pl.*] an assignee.

2. an asset; a belonging. [Obs.]

as·sīgn·ȧ·bil'i·ty, *n.* the condition or quality of being assignable.

as·sīgn'ȧ·ble, *a.* that may be assigned; as an *assignable* note, motive, etc.

as'sig·nat (*or* ȧ-sē-nyä'), *n.* [Fr., from L. *assignatus*, pp. of *assignare*, to assign, allot.] a form of currency, issued by the Revolutionary government of France, based on the security of lands appropriated by the state.

as·sig·nā'tion, *n.* 1. an appointment for meeting, especially one made secretly by lovers; tryst.

2. in law, a transference of a claim, right, property, etc.

3. the act of apportioning or assigning; also, anything assigned.

house of assignation; a house where meetings for immoral sexual purposes take place.

as·sīgn·ee' (-sī-nē'), *n.* 1. a person to whom property or rights at law have been transferred for the benefit of others or himself; as, an *assignee* in bankruptcy, or the *assignee* of an insolvent debtor. An *assignee* may be created by law, specially appointed, or named in a deed.

2. a person appointed to act for another.

as·sīgn'ẽr, *n.* a person who assigns.

as·sīgn'ment, *n.* 1. an assigning; an allotting, or an appointment to a particular person or use; also, anything assigned or allotted, as a lesson, task, etc.

2. in law, a transfer of a claim, right, property, etc.

3. the writing, as a deed, authorizing such transfer.

assignment in bankruptcy; the transfer of the property of a bankrupt to certain persons called assignees, in whom it is vested for the benefit of creditors.

assignment of dower; the apportionment of the widow's share in an estate.

assignment system; the system which formerly prevailed in Australia of assigning convicts as servants.

as·sīgn·or', *n.* in law, a person who assigns or transfers a claim, right, property, etc.; as, the *assignor* of a bill of exchange.

as·sim″i·lȧ·bil'i·ty, *n.* the state of being assimilable.

as·sim'i·lȧ·ble, *a.* that may be assimilated.

as·sim'i·lāte, *v.t.*; assimilated, *pt., pp.*; assimilating, *ppr.* [L. *assimilatus*, pp. of *assimilare*, to make like; *ad*, to, and *similis*, like.]

1. to make like or alike; to cause to resemble (with *to*).

2. to compare or liken.

3. to take up and make part of itself or oneself; absorb and incorporate; as, the body *assimilates* food.

as·sim'i·lāte, *v.i.* 1. to become similar.

2. to be absorbed and incorporated; as, minority groups often *assimilate* by intermarriage; this food *assimilates* quickly.

as·sim·i·lā'tion, *n.* 1. the act of bringing or coming to a resemblance; also, a state of resemblance.

2. in phonetics, (a) the process whereby a sound, influenced by a contiguous or neighboring sound, tends to become like it in position and type of articulation: thus, in *cupboard, clapboard*, the *p* has been lost by assimilation to *b*; (b) an example of this process.

3. in physiology, the change of digested

food and other material into part of the living organism.

4. in sociology, the merging of diverse cultural elements.

as·sim′i·lā·tive, *a.* assimilating; of or causing assimilation.

as·sim′i·lā·tō·ry, *a.* assimilative.

as·sim′ū·lāte, *v.t.* to simulate. [Obs.]

as·sim·ū·lā′tion, *n.* simulation. [Obs.]

as·si·nē′gō, *n.* same as *asinego.*

ȧss′ish, *a.* stupid; asinine.

as·sist′, *v.t.*; assisted, *pt., pp.*; assisting, *ppr.* [L. *assistere,* to stand by or near; *ad,* to, and *sistere,* to stand.] to help; to aid; to give support to in some undertaking or effort, or in time of distress.

Syn.—cooperate, befriend, relieve, succor, support, second, help, aid.

as·sist′, *v.i.* 1. to lend aid.

2. in euchre, to aid one's partner by ordering up as trumps the card which the partner, as dealer, has turned up.

3. to be present; to attend; as, to *assist* at a public meeting.

as·sist′, *n.* 1. an instance or act of helping.

2. in baseball, a play that helps put a batter or runner out.

as·sist′ănce, *n.* help; aid; succor; support.

writ of assistance; a writ issued to the successful suitor in chancery giving him possession of the property; in the colonial times in America, a judicial writ authorizing officers engaged in searching premises for contraband goods to call upon others to assist them.

as·sist′ănt, *a.* helping; lending aid or support; auxiliary.

as·sist′ănt, *n.* 1. one who assists or serves in a subordinate position; a helper; also, a thing for assisting; aid.

2. an attendant. [Obs.]

3. formerly, in some of the New England colonies, a member of the governor's council.

Syn.—confederate, associate, coadjutor, aid, helper, ally, auxiliary, partner.

as·sist′ănt·ly, *adv.* in a manner to give aid. [Obs.]

as·sis′tănt prō·fes′sŏr, a college teacher ranking above an instructor and below an associate professor.

as·sist′ẽr, *n.* one who lends aid; a helper; an assistant; see *assistor.*

as·sist′fụl, *a.* helpful.

as·sist′ive, *a.* helping.

as·sist′less, *a.* without aid or help. [Rare.]

as·sist′ŏr, *n.* an assister: the usual spelling in law.

as·sith′ment, *n.* same as *assythment.*

as·sīze′, *n.* [ME. *assize*; OFr. *assise, asise,* a sitting, session of a court, judgment, tax, impost, from L. *assidere*; *ad,* to, and *sedere,* to sit.]

1. originally, an assembly or its decree.

2. [*pl.*] in England, the sessions held periodically, by at least one of the judges of the superior courts, in each of the counties, under commissions of assize for civil cases, and of oyer and terminer, and jail delivery, for criminal cases. The commission of assize originally directed the judges to take *assizes,* or the verdicts of a particular jury called the *assize.*

3. a jury. In England the word was formerly used in this sense in the terms *grand assize* and *petty assize,* but is now obsolete. In Scotland at present, the assize exists for the trial of criminal cases.

4. any of certain writs summoning juries, etc.: a former name.

5. the time or place of holding the court of assize: generally in the plural, *assizes.*

6. a statute, or ordinance, generally; as, the *assizes* of the realm; the *assizes of the forest,* rules and regulations for the management of the royal forests; *assize of arms,* a statute of Henry II for arming the kingdom; *assizes of Jerusalem,* a code of feudal laws formed by the crusaders for their kingdom of Jerusalem. [Obs.]

7. formerly, an ordinance regulating the weight, measure, and price of articles sold in market; hence, the weight, measure, or price itself; as, the *assize* of bread.

8. formerly, an ordinance fixing the standard of weights and measures; hence, the standard weights and measures themselves; as, the custody of the *assize.*

9. measure; dimension. [Obs.]

An hundred cubits high by just *assize.*
—Spenser.

as·sīze′, *v.t.* 1. to fix the weight, measure, or price of, by an ordinance or regulation of authority. [Obs.]

2. to fix the rate of; to assess. [Obs.]

as·sīz′ẽr, *n.* 1. an officer who had charge of the inspection of weights and measures.

2. in Scotland, a juror.

as·sīz′ŏr, *n.* an assizer.

as·sō′bẽr, *v.t.* to make or keep sober. [Obs.]

as·sō·ciȧ·bil′i·ty (-shȧ-), *n.* the quality or condition of being associable.

as·sō′ciȧ·ble, *a.* 1. that may be joined or associated.

2. sociable; companionable. [Obs.]

3. in a medical sense, liable to be affected by sympathy with other parts or to receive from other parts correspondent feelings and affections.

as·sō′ciȧ·ble·ness, *n.* associability.

as·sō′ci·āte (-shi-āte), *v.t.*; associated, *pt., pp.*; associating, *ppr.* [L. *associatus,* pp. of *associare,* to join to, unite with; *ad,* to, and *sociare,* to join, or unite with.]

1. to bring (a person) into relationship with oneself or another, as a friend, companion, partner, or confederate.

2. to unite in the same mass; to combine; to join; to connect; as, particles of matter *associated* with other substances.

3. to connect in the mind; as, she *associates* rain with grief.

Syn.—incorporate, combine, couple, unite, link, join.

as·sō′ci·āte, *v.i.* 1. to join (*with* another or others) as a companion, partner, friend, etc.

2. to unite as friends, partners, etc; join for a common purpose; keep company.

as·sō′ci·āte, *a.* 1. joined in interest or purpose; confederate.

2. joined in employment, office, membership, etc., especially with secondary status or privileges; as, an *associate* judge.

3. accompanying; connected.

as·sō′ci·āte, *n.* 1. a person associated; a friend; a partner; a colleague; a fellow worker.

2. a member of a society, institute, etc. without full status or privileges; as, an *associate* of the Royal Academy.

3. anything joined with another thing or things.

4. in some colleges and universities, a degree conferred on one who has completed a course shorter than that required for a degree; as, an *associate* in music.

Syn.—companion, comrade, mate, friend, fellow, coadjutor, partner, accomplice.

as·sō′ci·ā·ted, *a.* united in company or in interest; joined; accompanying.

Associated Press; a newspaper association in the United States for the express purpose of gathering news to be distributed to its members.

as·sō′ci·āte prō·fes′sŏr, a college teacher ranking above an assistant professor and below a full professor.

as·sō′ci·āte·ship, *n.* the state or office of an associate.

as·sō·ci·ā′tion, *n.* 1. the act of associating; union; connection of persons.

2. the state of being associated; companionship; fellowship; partnership.

3. a society formed for transacting or carrying on some business or pursuit for mutual advantage.

4. union of things; apposition, as of particles of matter.

5. union or connection of ideas; also, the use of such connections as a literary device or technique.

6. association football.

association of ideas; in psychology, the conditions under which one idea is able to recall another to consciousness. These conditions may be classified under two general heads, the *law of contiguity,* and the *law of association.* The first states the fact that actions, sensations, emotions, and ideas, which have occurred together, or in close succession, tend to suggest each other when any one of them is afterward presented to the mind. The second indicates that the present actions, sensations, emotions, or ideas tend to recall their like from among previous experiences. On their physical side the principles of association correspond with the physiological facts of reexcitation of the same nervous centers.

association test; in psychology, a test made up of words in which the person tested gives the first associative word that comes to his mind in response to the one given by the person conducting the test: also called *free association test.*

Syn.—community, connection, fellowship, fraternity, alliance, sodality, union, society, club.

as·sō·ci·ā′tion·ăl, *a.* 1. pertaining to or based on association, as of ideas.

2. pertaining to associationism or an association.

as·sō·ci·ā′tion foot′bạll, soccer: so called from the British controlling body, the National Football Association.

as·sō·ci·ā′tion·ism, *n.* 1. in psychology, the theory that mental development is reached through the association of ideas that are formed through the medium of the senses.

2. Fourierism.

as·sō·ci·ā′tion·ist, *n.* one who holds the doctrine of associationism in any of its forms.

as·sō′ci·ā·tive, *a.* of, characterized by, or causing association.

as·sō′ci·ā·tŏr, *n.* a confederate; an associate.

as·soil′, *v.t.* [ME. *assoilen,* from OFr. *assoil,* pres. ind. form of *assoldre*; L. *absolvere*; *ab-,* from, and *solvere,* to loose.]

1. to pardon; absolve. [Archaic.]

2. to atone for. [Archaic.]

as·soil′ment, *n.* the act of assoiling; absolution.

as·soil′ment, *n.* defilement.

as·soil′ziē, *v.t.* in Scots law, to absolve.

as′sō·nănce, *n.* [Fr. *assonance,* from L. *assonans,* ppr. of *assonare,* to sound, to respond to.]

1. likeness to sound.

2. a rough similarity; likeness.

3. a partial rhyme in which the stressed vowel sounds are alike but the consonant sounds are unlike, as in *late* and *make.*

as′sō·nănt, as·sō·nan′tăl, *a.* in prosody, having assonance.

as′sō·nănt, *n.* a word assonant with another.

as′sō·nāte, *v.i.*; assonated, *pt., pp.*; assonating, *ppr.* to correspond in sound.

as·sort′, *v.t.*; assorted, *pt., pp.*; assorting, *ppr.* [ME. *assorte*; Fr. *assortir*; *a,* L. *ad,* to, and *sortir,* from L. *sortiri,* to cast lots, select; *sors,* a lot, condition.]

1. to separate into classes, as similar things, or things which are suited to a like purpose.

2. to supply (a warehouse, etc.) with an assortment of goods.

as·sort′, *v.i.* 1. to be of the same sort; fall into a group or class.

2. to match or harmonize (*with*).

3. to consort or associate (*with*).

as·sort′ed, *a.* 1. in an assortment; various; miscellaneous.

2. fitted or adapted; matched.

They appear no way *assorted* to those with whom they must associate. —Burke.

3. classified.

Syn.—classified, separated, selected, chosen, arranged.

as·sort′ment, *n.* 1. an assorting or being assorted; classification.

2. a mass or quantity separated into kinds, or sorts; an assorted, or miscellaneous, group or collection; a variety; as, an *assortment* of goods.

3. a number of things of the same kind, varied in size, color, quality, price, form, etc.; as, an *assortment* of thread, of silks, or of calicoes; an *assortment* of paintings.

Syn.—collection, selection, miscellany, variety, class, stock, lot.

as·sot′, *v.t.* [Fr. *assoter*; *a,* L. *ad,* to, and *sot,* foolish.] to infatuate; to besot. [Obs.]

ȧss′'ș foot, a medicinal herb, more commonly known as coltsfoot.

as·suāġe′ (-swāj′), *v.t.*; assuaged, *pt., pp.*; assuaging, *ppr.* [ME. *asuagen*; OFr. *asouager, asuager,* from L. *ad,* to, and *suavis,* sweet.]

1. to lessen (pain, distress, etc.); allay; mitigate.

2. to pacify; calm (passion, anger, etc.).

3. to satisfy or quench (thirst, etc.).

Syn.—abate, alleviate, diminish, soothe, pacify, compose, appease, calm, tranquilize.

as·suāġe′, *v.i.* to abate or subside. [Archaic.]

The waters *assuaged.* —Gen. viii. 1.

as·suāġe′ment, *n.* 1. an assuaging or being assuaged.

2. an assuaging thing.

as·suā′ġẽr, *n.* one who or that which assuages.

as·suā′sive, *a.* softening; mitigating; tranquilizing.

as·sub′jū·gāte, *v.t.* to bring into subjection. [Obs.]

as·suē·faç′tion (as-swē-), *n.* [L. *assuefacere,* to accustom to; *assuetus,* pp. of *assuescere,* to accustom, and *facere,* to make.] the act of accustoming. [Obs.]

as′suē·tūde, *n.* [L. *assuetudo,* from *assuetus,*

pp. of *assuescere*, to accustom.] custom; habitual use; habit. [Obs.]

as·sūm′ȧ·ble, *a.* capable of being assumed.

as·sūm′ȧ·bly, *adv.* in an assumable manner; by assumption.

as·sūme′, *v.t.*; assumed, *pt.*, *pp.*; assuming, *ppr.* [L. *assumere*, to take up, claim; *ad*, to, and *sumere*, to take, from *sub*, under, and *emere*, to take, buy.]

1. to take or put on (the appearance, form, role, etc. of).

The god *assumed* his native form again. —Pope.

2. to take (what is not just); to usurp; to arrogate; to seize unjustly; as, to *assume* unwarrantable powers.

3. to take for granted, or without proof; to suppose as a fact; as, to *assume* a principle in reasoning.

4. to appropriate, or take to oneself; to undertake; as, to *assume* the debts of another.

5. to pretend to have; to feign.

6. to receive or adopt; to take into association; to take on; as, *assumed* into that honorable company.

Syn.—appropriate, arrogate, affect, pretend, usurp, claim, feign.

as·sūme′, *v.i.* to be pretentious or presumptuous; to claim more than is due.

as·sūmed′, *a.* 1. supposed; taken for granted.

2. pretended; fictitious; as, an *assumed* character.

as·sūm′ed·ly, *adv.* by or according to assumption.

as·sūm′ent, *n.* an addition. [Obs.]

as·sūm′ẽr, *n.* one who assumes.

as·sūm′ing, *a.* taking or disposed to take upon oneself more than is just; presumptuous.

as·sūm′ing, *n.* presumption.

as·sump′sit, *n.* [L., he undertook, perf. tense of *assumere*, to assume.]

1. in law, a promise or undertaking, not under seal. This promise may be verbal or written. An assumpsit is express or implied; express, when made in words or writing; implied, when, in consequence of some benefit or consideration accruing to one person from the acts of another, the law presumes that person has promised to make compensation. In this case, the law, upon a principle of justice, implies or raises a promise, on which an action may be brought to recover the compensation. Thus, if A contracts with B to build a house for him, by implication and intendment of law, A promises to pay B for the same, without any express words to that effect.

2. an action to recover damages for the nonfulfillment of such an agreement. When this action is brought on a debt, it is called *indebitatus assumpsit*.

as·sumpt′, *v.t.* to assume. [Obs.]

as·sumpt′, *n.* that which is assumed. [Obs.]

as·sump′tion, *n.* [ME. *assumpcioun*, *assumptioun*; L. *assumptio*, from *assumere*, to take up.]

1. an assuming or being assumed.

2. anything taken for granted; supposition.

3. presumption.

4. a postulate, or proposition assumed. In logic, the minor or second proposition in a categorical syllogism.

5. a supposed taking up of a person into heaven.

6. [A–] in the Roman Catholic and Orthodox Eastern Churches, (a) the ascent of the Virgin Mary into heaven; (b) the festival celebrating this (August 15).

Syn.—supposition, postulate, appropriation, undertaking, arrogance.

as·sump′tive, *a.* 1. assumed.

2. of, or having the character of, an assumption.

3. assuming; presumptuous.

assumptive arms; in heraldry, formerly, such arms as a person had a right, with the approbation of his sovereign and of the heralds, to assume in consequence of an exploit; armorial bearings not inherited.

as·sump′tive·ly, *adv.* by way of assumption.

Äs′sụr, *n.* Ashur.

as·sūr′ănce (-shūr′), *n.* [ME. *assuraunce*; OFr. *asseurance*, from L. *assecurantia*, from *assecurare*, to assure.]

1. an assuring or being assured.

2. full confidence or trust; freedom from doubt; certain expectation; the utmost certainty.

3. firmness of mind; undoubting steadiness; intrepidity; self-reliance; self-confidence.

Brave men meet danger with *assurance*. —Knolles.

4. excess of boldness; impudence; as, his *assurance* is intolerable.

5. anything that inspires confidence, as a promise, positive statement, etc.; guarantee.

6. insurance; a contract for the payment of a sum on occasion of a certain event, as loss or death. [Brit.] The word *assurance* has been used in England in relation to life contingencies, and *insurance* in relation to other contingencies.

7. any written or other legal evidence of the conveyance of property. In England, such evidences are called the *common assurances* of the kingdom.

Syn.—confidence, conviction, impudence, promise, certainty, effrontery, presumption.

as·sūre′, *v.t.*; assured, *pt.*, *pp.*; assuring, *ppr.* [ME. *assuren*, from L. *assecurare*, to assure; *ad*, to, and *securus*; *se*, without, and *cura*, care.]

1. to make (a person) sure of something; to give confidence by a promise, declaration, or other evidence; as, he *assured* me of his sincerity.

2. to make (a doubtful thing) certain or secure; to guarantee.

3. to embolden; to make confident.

4. to affiance; to betroth. [Obs.]

5. to insure.

6. to make secure. [Obs.]

as·sūred′, *a.* 1. sure; guaranteed.

2. confident; bold.

3. insured.

as·sūred′, *n.* one who has his life or property insured.

as·sūr′ed·ly, *adv.* certainly; indubitably.

as·sūr′ed·ness, *n.* the state of being assured; certainty; full confidence.

as·sūr′ẽr, *n.* 1. one who or that which assures.

2. an underwriter of insurance policies. [Brit.]

as·sūr′ġen·cy, *n.* the tendency to rise.

as·sūr′ġent, *a.* [L. *assurgens*, ppr. of *assurgere*, to rise up.]

1. rising.

2. in botany, rising at an oblique angle, as some stems.

3. in heraldry, rising from the ocean, as the sun: applied to a bearing.

as·sūr′ing·ly, *adv.* in a way to create assurance.

as·swāġe′, *v.t.* and *v.i.* same as *assuage*.

As·syr′i·ăn, *a.* 1. of Assyria, its people, language, or culture.

2. designating or of the ancient architecture of Assyria, characterized by low, massive brick walls, carved slabs, and rich ornamentation.

As·syr′i·ăn, *n.* 1. a native or inhabitant of Assyria.

2. the Semitic language of the Assyrians.

As·syr″i·ō·log′iç·ăl, *a.* relating to Assyriology.

As·syr·i·ol′ō·gist, *n.* one who makes Assyriology his special study.

As·syr·i·ol′ō·ġy, *n.* [Gr. *Assyria*, and *logia*, from *legein*, to speak.] the study of the civilization, history, language, etc. of ancient Assyria.

as·sȳth′ment, *n.* [Scot., from *assyth*; OFr. *asset*, from L. *ad satis facere*; *ad*, to, *satis*, enough, and *facere*, to make.] in Scots law, an indemnification due to the heirs of a person murdered, from the person guilty of the crime. Where the penalty of the law is suffered by the criminal no claim for indemnity is allowed.

as·tā′ciăn, *n.* an animal belonging to the genus *Astacus*, or the family *Astacidæ*.

As·tac′i·dae, *n.pl.* a family of crustaceans belonging to the order *Decapoda* and the suborder *Macrura*.

as′tȧ·cīte, *n.* [L., from Gr. *astakos*, and *-ite*.] any fossil crustacean resembling a lobster or crawfish.

As·tȧ·çoi′dē·ȧ, *n.pl.* a group or series of crustaceans that includes the crawfish and the lobster.

as·taç′ō·līte, *n.* [Gr. *astakos*, a lobster, and *lithos*, stone.] same as *astacite*.

As′tȧ·çus, *n.* [L., from Gr. *astakos*, a lobster, crawfish.] a genus of decapod, long-tailed crustaceans, the typical one of the family *Astacidæ*. It includes the *Astacus marinus*, or lobster, and the *Astacus fluviatilis*, or crawfish.

ȧ·stär′bōard, *adv.* on the starboard side, as a rudder.

ȧ·stärt′, ȧ·stẽrt′, *v.i.* to start off; to escape; to flee, to get free. [Obs.]

ȧ·stärt′, *v.t.* to cause to start; to startle; to terrify; to affright; to release; to avoid. [Obs.]

As·tär′tē, *n.* [Gr. *Astartē*.]

1. in Phoenician mythology, the goddess of the moon, fertility, and sexual love, corresponding to the *Ashtoreth* of Scripture.

2. in zoology, a genus of bivalve mollusks.

3. [a–] any species of this genus.

as·tā′si·ȧ, *n.* [L., from Gr. *astasia*, unsteadiness, from *astatos*; *a* priv., and *statos*, from *histanai*, to stand.] in medicine, inability to stand erect due to motor inco-ordination.

ȧ·stāte′, *n.* estate. [Obs.]

ȧ·stat′iç, *a.* [Gr. *astatos*, unstable, uncertain; *a* priv., and *statos*, from *histanai*, to stand.]

1. unstable; unsteady.

2. in physics, not taking a definite position or direction; as, an *astatic* needle is not affected by the earth's magnetism.

astatic needle; a needle movable about an axis in the plane of the magnetic meridian, and parallel to the inclination. When so situated, the terrestrial magnetic couple acting in the direction of the axis cannot impart to the needle any determinate direction, and therefore it is *astatic*.

astatic system; a combination of two needles of equal force joined parallel to each other, with the poles in contrary directions.

ȧ·stat′iç·ăl·ly, *adv.* in an astatic manner.

ȧ·stat′i·çişm, *n.* the state or quality of being astatic.

as′tȧ·tine, *n.* [from Gr. *astatos*, unstable; and *-ine*.] an unstable chemical element formed from bismuth when it is bombarded by alpha particles: symbol, At; atomic weight, 211 (?); atomic number, 85 (formerly designated as *alabamine*).

as′tȧ·tīze, *v.t.*; astatized, *pt.*, *pp.*; astatizing, *ppr.* to make astatic.

ȧ·stāy′, *adv.* a term used in regard to an anchor which, on being hauled up, takes such a position that the cable or chain from which it hangs forms an acute angle with the surface of the water, appearing to be in line with the ship's stays.

ȧ·stē·ȧ·tō′sis, *n.* [L., from Gr. *a* priv., and *stear*, *steatos*, fat, tallow.] faulty secretion by the sebaceous glands.

as′tē·işm, *n.* [Gr. *asteismos*, from *asteizesthai*, to be witty, talk cleverly, from *asteios*, witty, clever, from *asty*, city.] in rhetoric, genteel irony; a polite and ingenious manner of deriding another.

as′tel, *n.* [ME. *astelle*; OFr. *astelle*; L. *astula*, dim. of *assis*, a board.] an arch or ceiling in a mine.

-as′tẽr, [L. *-aster*, a dim. suffix.] a suffix denoting *diminution*, *slight resemblance*, *inferiority*, or *worthlessness*, as in medic*aster*, a quack; poet*aster*, a dabbler in poetry.

as′tẽr-, as′tẽr·ī-, as′tẽr·ō-, combining forms from Gr. *astēr*, a star.

As′tẽr, *n.* [Gr. *astēr*, star.]

1. a genus of plants of the composite family, with spear-shaped leaves and purplish, blue, pink, or white flowers like daisies.

2. [a–] any plant of the genus *Aster*.

3. [a–] the China aster.

4. [a–] in biology, a structure shaped like a star, formed in cytoplasm of a cell during mitosis.

As·tẽr·ā′cē·ae, *n.pl.* [L., from Gr. *astēr*, star, and *-aceæ*.] an order of plants of which the genus *Aster* is the type.

as·tẽr·ā′ceous, *a.* in botany, of the aster or thistle family.

as·tē′ri·ȧ, *n.* [L., from Gr. *astēr*, a star.] a variety of sapphire, not perfectly transparent, but showing a starlike opalescence in the direction of the axis of the crystal if cut round.

As·tē′ri·as, *n.* [L., from Gr. *asterias*, starred, a fish, from *astēr*, star.] a genus of common starfishes of the family *Asteriidæ*.

as·tē′ri·ā·ted, *a.* [Gr. *asterios*, radiated.]

1. radiated; presenting diverging rays, like a star.

2. in mineralogy, having asterism.

as′tẽr·id, *n.* a starfish; one of the *Asterias*.

As·tẽr·id′ē·ȧ, *n.pl.* an order of *Echinodermata* which includes the true starfishes: called also *Asteroidea*.

As·tē·rī′i·dae, *n.pl.* [L., from Gr. *asterias*, radiated, starred, and *-idæ*.] a family of radiated animals belonging to the class *Echinodermata*, order *Stellerida*. It contains the starfishes.

as·tē′ri·on, *n.* the point on the skull where the sutures formed by the union of the occipital, temporal, and parietal bones intersect one another.

as·tẽr·is′çus, *n.* [L., from Gr. *asteriskos*, a little star.] a small bone found in the inner ear of certain fishes.

as'tẽr·isk, *n.* [Gr. *asteriskos*, a little star, from *astēr*, a star.]
1. a starlike sign (*) used in printing and writing as a reference to a passage or a note in the margin, or to fill the space where words are omitted.

ASTERISK (sense 2)

2. in the Greek church, an appliance in the form of a star or cross, with the ends bent to serve as supports, placed during the liturgy over the paten so as to keep the cover of the latter from touching the sacred bread.

as'tẽr·isk, *v.t.* to mark with an asterisk.

as'tẽr·ișm, *n.* [Gr. *asterismos*, a marking with stars, from *asterizein*, to mark with stars; *astēr*, a star.]
1. in astronomy, (a) a constellation; (b) a small cluster of stars.
2. in printing, (a) an asterisk, or mark of reference: a rare use; (b) three asterisks placed in triangular form (⁂ or ⁂) to call attention to a special passage.
3. the property possessed by cleft sapphires, mica, and other stones, of exhibiting a starlike reflection.

ȧ·stẽrn', *adv.* 1. at or toward the rear; as, to go *astern*.
2. backward.
3. behind a ship, at any indefinite distance. Distinguished from *aft*.
to back astern; to move with the stern foremost.
to be astern of the reckoning; to fail to make the distance required by the schedule, or reckoning.
to drop astern; to fall behind.
to go astern; to go backward.

ȧ·stẽr'năl, *a.* [Gr. *a* priv., and *sternon*, breastbone.]
1. not joined to or proceeding from the sternum, or breastbone, as the floating ribs.
2. without a sternum.

as'tẽr·oid, *n.* [*aster-*, and Gr. *eidos*, form.]
1. in astronomy, any of the small planets, or planetoids, between the orbits of Mars and Jupiter.
2. in zoology, a starfish.

as'tẽr·oid, *a.* starlike; specifically, (a) in zoology, belonging to the *Alcyonaria*, or *asteroid* polyps; (b) in botany, resembling the aster.

as·tẽr·oid'ăl, *a.* 1. resembling a star.
2. pertaining to the asteroids.
3. pertaining to the starfishes.

As·tẽr·oid'ē·ȧ, *n.pl.* a term sometimes used as the equivalent of *Asteridea*, formerly including, along with that order, the *Ophiuroidea*, or starfishes with discoid bodies; the *Alcyonaria*.

As·te·rol'ē·pis, *n.* [*aster-*, and Gr. *lepis*, a scale.] a genus of gigantic ganoid fishes, now found only in fossil state. These fishes sometimes attained the length of eighteen or twenty feet. The illustration shows one of their most characteristic bones, the hyoid plate, with its central strengthening ridge. The stellate markings from which the genus derives its name seem to have been restricted to the dermal plates of the head.

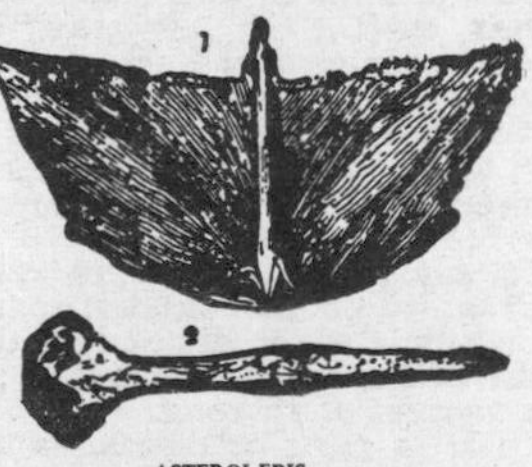

ASTEROLEPIS
1. hyoid plate of *Asterolepis*
2. internal ridge of hyoid plate

as''tẽr·ō·phyl'līte, *n.* one of the genus *Asterophyllites*.

As''tẽr·ō·phyl·lī'tēs, *n.* [*aster-*, and Gr. *phyllon*, a leaf.] star leaf, a genus of fossil plants (horsetail family), so called from the stellated arrangement of the leaves around the branches. They abound in the coal measures, and are believed to be the foliage of the *Calamites*.

ȧ·stẽrt', *v.i.* astart. [Obs.]

as'tẽr·wŏrt, *n.* any composite plant of the aster family.

as·thē'ni·ȧ, as'the·ny, *n.* [L., from Gr. *astheneia*, weakness, from *asthenēs*, weak.] a debilitated condition of body; lack or loss of bodily strength.

as·then'iç, *a.* [Gr. *a* priv., and *sthenos*, strength.] weak; characterized by debility.

as·then'iç, *n.* in psychology, a person of slender physique.

as·the·nol'ō·ġy, *n.* [Gr. *asthenēs*, without strength, and *logia*, from *legein*, to speak.] the science which treats of debility and of the diseases connected with it.

as·the·nō'pi·ȧ, *n.* [Mod. L., from Gr. *asthenēs*, weak, and *ōps*, *opis*, eye.] a strained condition of the eyes, often with headache, dizziness, etc.

as·the·nop'iç, *a.* relating to asthenopia.

as'the·ny, *n.* same as *asthenia*.

asth'mȧ (az'mȧ *or* as'mȧ), *n.* [L. *asthma*; Gr. *asthma*, a panting, asthma, from *azein*, to breathe hard; Sans. root *vā*, blow.] a chronic disorder characterized by paroxysms of the bronchi, shortness of breath, wheezing, a suffocating feeling, and labored coughing to remove tenacious mucus from the air passages.
asthma herb; *Euphorbia pilulifera*, a weed used as a remedy for asthma.
asthma weed; *Lobelia inflata*, a plant containing properties which are supposed to give it value as a remedy for asthma.

asth·mat'iç, *n.* a person who suffers from asthma.

asth·mat'iç, asth·mat'iç·ăl, *a.* pertaining to or having asthma.

asth·mat'iç·ăl·ly, *adv.* in an asthmatic manner.

as·tig·mat'iç, *a.* 1. pertaining to or characterized by astigmatism.
2. correcting astigmatism.

ȧ·stig'mȧ·tism, *n.* [Gr. *a* priv., and *stigma*, *stigmatos*, a mark, spot.] a structural defect of a lens or the eyes that prevents light rays from an object from meeting in a single focal point, so that indistinct images are formed.

as·tip'ū·lāte, *v.i.* to agree. [Obs.]

as·tip·ū·lā'tion, *n.* agreement; concurrence. [Obs.]

ȧ·stīr', *adv.* and *a.* 1. on the stir; on the move; stirring; active; as, the people are *astir*.
2. out of bed.

A·stō'mȧ·tȧ, *n.pl.* [L., from Gr. *a* priv., and *stoma*, *stomatos*, mouth.] one of the two groups into which the *Protozoa* are divided with regard to the presence or absence of a mouth, of which organ the *Astomata* are destitute. The group comprises two classes, *Gregarinida* and *Rhizopoda*.

ȧ·stom'ȧ·tous, *a.* without a stoma; without stomata; specifically, belonging or pertaining to the *Astomata*.

as'tō·mous, *a.* astomatous; specifically applied in botany to a division of mosses the capsules of which have no aperture.

as·ton', as·tōne', *v.t.* to astound. [Obs.]

as·ton'ied, *a.* bewildered; dazed. [Archaic.]

as·ton'ied·ness, *n.* the state of being astonished. [Obs.]

as·ton'ish, *v.t.*; astonished, *pt.*, *pp.*; astonishing, *ppr.* [ME. *astonien*, *astunian*; OFr. *estoner*, *estuner*, *estonner*, from L. *attonare*, to thunder at, astonish, stun; *ad*, to, at, and *tonare*, to thunder.] to stun, or strike dumb with sudden fear, terror, surprise, or wonder; to amaze; to fill with sudden wonder; to surprise exceedingly.

as·ton'ish·ȧ·ble, *a.* astonishing. [Rare.]

as·ton'ished, *a.* amazed; confounded with fear, surprise, or admiration.
Syn.—appalled, dismayed, astounded, overwhelmed, surprised, amazed, dumfounded, thunderstruck.

as·ton'ished·ly, *adv.* in an astonished manner. [Rare.]

as·ton'ish·ing, *a.* calculated to astonish; amazing; wonderful; as, with *astonishing* celerity.

as·ton'ish·ing·ly, *adv.* in an astonishing manner.

as·ton'ish·ing·ness, *n.* the quality of exciting astonishment.

as·ton'ish·ment, *n.* 1. an astonishing; sudden surprise; amazement.
2. anything that astonishes.
Thou shalt become an *astonishment*, a proverb, and a byword among all nations.
—Deut. xxviii. 37.

as·ton'y, *v.t.* 1. to astonish; to amaze. [Obs.]
2. to stun, as with a blow. [Obs.]

ȧ·stoop', *adv.* in a stooping posture.

as·tound', *a.* astounded. [Obs.]

as·tound', *v.t.*; astounded, *pt.*, *pp.*; astounding, *ppr.* [ME. *astouned*, *astoned*, pp. of *astounen*, *astonen*, to astonish.] to astonish greatly; to amaze; to bewilder with sudden surprise.

as·tound'ed, *a.* astonished; stunned; confounded; amazed.

as·tound'ing, *a.* astonishing; amazing.

as·tound'ing·ly, *adv.* in an amazing manner.

as·tound'ment, *n.* amazement. [Rare.]

as'trȧ·çhan, *n.* 1. astrakan.
2. [A–] a variety of apple, originally from Russia.

ȧ·strad'dle, *adv.* and *a.* in a straddling position; with one leg on either side; astride; as, to sit *astraddle*.

As·trae'ȧ, As·trē'ȧ, *n.* [L., from Gr. *Astraia*, goddess of justice, f. of *astraios*, starry, from *astron*, a star.]
1. in Greek and Roman mythology, the goddess of justice, who was the last deity to leave the earth after the fabled golden age and finally became the constellation Virgo.
2. an asteroid, or planetoid, discovered in December, 1845.
3. a genus of coral zoophytes, the typical one of the family *Astræidæ*.

as·trae'ăn, as·trē'ăn, *a.* pertaining to the genus *Astræa*.

as·trae'ăn, *n.* a coral of the family *Astræidæ*; a star coral.

As·trae'i·dae, *n.pl.* a family of radiated animals belonging to the class *Actinozoa* and the order *Sclerodermata*. It is specially to this family that the formation of coral reefs is to be attributed. Among others it contains the genera *Astræa* and *Meandrina*.

as'trȧ·găl, *n.* [L. *astragalus*, from Gr. *astragalos*, a turning joint, vertebra, an architectural molding.]
1. in architecture, a small, convex molding, sometimes cut into the form of a string of beads.
2. in gunnery, a round molding on a cannon near the mouth.
3. in anatomy, the astragalus.
4. [*pl.*] dice: hucklebones were used as dice by the ancient Greeks.

as·trag'ȧ·lăr, *a.* relating to the astragulus.

as·trag'ȧ·lō-, a combining form from Gr. *astragalos*, meaning *connection with* or *relation to the astragalus*; as, *astragalo*navicular.

as·trag'ȧ·loid, *a.* [*astragalo-*, and Gr. *eidos*, form.] like the astragalus in shape.

as·trag'ȧ·lō·man''cy, *n.* [Gr. *astragalos*, in the pl., dice, and *manteia*, divination.] pretended divination performed by throwing down hucklebones (called astragals) or dice with marks corresponding to letters of the alphabet, and observing what words they form.

as·trag'ȧ·lus, *n.*; *pl.* **as·trag'ȧ·lī,** [L., from Gr. *astragalos*, a vertebra, anklebone, a die, an architectural molding.]
1. in anatomy, the anklebone; talus; the upper bone of that part of the foot called the tarsus, supporting the tibia; the astragal.
2. [A–] a genus of papilionaceous plants, of the natural order *Fabaceæ*, containing numerous species, including milk vetch and licorice vetch. Gum tragacanth is obtained from different species, particularly the *Astragalus verus*.
3. in architecture, same as *astragal*.

as'trȧ·khan, *n.* 1. the pelt of very young lambs from Astrakhan, in the U.S.S.R., with tightly curled wool.
2. a woolly cloth made in imitation of this.

as'trȧ·khan, *a.* made of or resembling astrakhan.

as'trăl, *a.* [L. *astralis*, from *astrum*, a star.]
1. of, from, or like the stars; starry.
2. in biology, of or pertaining to an aster.
3. in theosophy, designating or of an alleged supernatural substance.
astral body; (a) a supposed spirit or ghostlike double of the human body, able to leave it at will; (b) loosely, a star or planet.
astral lamp; an Argand lamp in which the oil is contained in a vessel in the form of a flattened ring, obliquely inclined outward and downward, and surmounted by a flattened hemispherical ground glass, the whole being designed to throw no shadow downward.

ȧ·strand', *adv.* stranded; aground; as, a boat washed *astrand*.

ȧ·strāy', *adv.* and *a.* [ME. *astray*, *astraei*; OFr. *estraié*, *estrayé*, from *estraier*, to stray; Pr. *estraguar*, from L. *extravagare*; *extra*, out, and *vagare*, to wander.] off the right way or path.

As·trē'ȧ, *n.* see *Astræa*.

as·trē'ăn, *a.* see *Astræan*.

as·trict′, *v.t.* [L. *astrictus*, pp. of *astringere*, to draw close; *ad*, to, and *stringere*, draw.]
 1. to bind; constrict; limit. [Rare.]
 2. to restrict legally or morally. [Rare.]

as·trict′, *a.* concise; contracted. [Obs.]

as·tric′tion, *n.* 1. the act of binding fast, or confining.
 2. a contraction of parts by applications.
 3. astringency. [Obs.]
 4. constipation. [Obs.]
 5. in Scotland, an obligation to have corn raised on certain land ground at a specified mill, paying a toll called multure: also called *thirlage*.

as·tric′tive, *a.* and *n.* astringent.

as·tric′tive·ly, *adv.* in an astrictive manner.

ȧ·strīde′, *adv.* and *a.* 1. with legs stretched far apart.
 2. with a leg on each side; as, to ride horseback *astride*.

ȧ·strīde′, *prep.* with a leg on either side of (a horse, etc.).

as·trif′ėr·ous, *a.* [L. *astrifer*, from *astrum*, a star, and *ferre*, to bear.] bearing or containing stars. [Rare.]

as·tringe′, *v.t.*; astringed, *pt.*, *pp.*; astringing, *ppr.* [L. *astringere*, to draw close, contract; *ad*, to, and *stringere*, to bind, strain.]
 1. to bind fast; to constrict; to contract; to cause (parts) to draw together. [Rare.]
 2. to bind by obligation. [Obs.]

as·trin′gen·cy, *n.*; *pl.* **as·trin′gen·cies**, the quality of being astringent; that quality in medicines by which soft or relaxed parts of the body are contracted; as, the *astringency* of acids or bitters; hence, also, harshness or austerity in disposition; as, the *astringencies* of character or human nature.

as·trin′gent, *a.* [L. *astringens*, ppr. of *astringere*, to contract, draw close; *ad*, to, and *stringere*, to draw, bind.]
 1. that contracts body tissue and blood vessels, checking the flow of blood; styptic.
 2. causing to shrink or contract.
 3. austere, harsh, or stern.

as·trin′gent, *n.* an astringent substance, drug, etc.

as·trin′gent·ly, *adv.* in an astringent manner.

as′trīte, *n.* [L. *astroites*, a precious stone; Gr. *astron*, a star.] a radiated or starlike fossil, as one of the detached articulations of fossil encrinites; star stone; also, a precious stone valued by the ancients, probably the sapphire. Written also *astroite* and *astrion*. [Obs.]

as′trō-, a combining form from Gr. *astron*, a star, meaning (a) in astronomy, *of a star* or *stars*, as in *astro*physics; (b) in biology, *of an aster*, as in *astro*sphere.

as″trō·bī·ol′ō·ġy, *n.* the branch of biology that investigates the existence of living organisms on planets other than the earth.

as′trō·dōme, *n.* a domelike transparent structure for housing astronomical or navigational instruments; specifically, one mounted on top of an aircraft fuselage for the navigator.

as″trō·dy·nam′ics, *n.pl.* [*construed as sing.*] the branch of dynamics dealing with the motion and gravitation of natural and artificial objects in space.

as′trō·fel, as′trō·phel, *n.* [L. *astrum*, star, and *fel*, gall, bitter.] a bitter herb; supposed to be identical with the aster, or starwort.

as·trog′e·ny, *n.* [*astro-*, and Gr. *gennaein*, to produce.] the theory or doctrine of the creation or evolution of the heavenly bodies.

as·trog′nō·sy, *n.* [*astro-*, and Gr. *gnōsis*, knowledge.] knowledge of the stars, especially the fixed stars, in respect to their names, magnitudes, positions, and the like.

as·trō·gon′ic, *a.* relating to the genesis or evolution of the stars.

as·trog′ō·ny, *n.* same as *astrogeny*.

as·trog′rȧ·phy, *n.* [*astro-*, and Gr. *graphia*, from *graphein*, to describe.] the science of describing or mapping the stars.

as′trō·īte, *n.* same as *astrite*.

as′trō·lābe, *n.* [Fr. *astrolabe*; LL. *astrolabium*; Gr. *astrolabon*, an astrolabe, from *astron*, star, and *lambanein*, *labein*, to take.]
 1. an instrument formerly used for taking the altitude of the sun or stars, now superseded by the sextant.
 2. a stereographic projection of the sphere, on the plane of a great circle, usually either upon the plane of the equator, or upon the plane of the meridian; a planisphere.

as·trol′ȧ·tėr, *n.* one who worships the stars.

as·trol′ȧ·try, *n.* [Fr. *astrolatrie*, from Gr. *astron*, star, and *latreia*, worship.] the worship of the stars.

as″trō·li·thol′ō·ġy, *n.* [*astro-*, and Gr. *lithos*, stone, and *logia*, from *legein*, to speak.] the science of aerolites or meteoritic stones.

as·trol′ō·ġėr, *n.* [ME. *astrologer*; L. *astrologus*; Gr. *astrologos*, an astronomer, astrologer; *astron*, star, and *logos*, from *legein*, to speak.]
 1. one who professes to interpret or determine the supposed influence of the stars on events, qualities, or the destinies of men; one who practices astrology or foretells events by the positions and aspects of the stars.
 2. an astronomer. [Obs.]

as·trō·log′ic·ăl, as·trō·log′ic, *a.* pertaining to astrology; professing or practicing astrology.

as·trō·log′ic·ăl·ly, *adv.* by means of or in accordance with astrology.

as·trol′ō·ġīze, *v.t.*; astrologized, *pt.*, *pp.*; astrologizing, *ppr.* to interpret by means of astrology; to apply astrology to.

as·trol′ō·ġīze, *v.i.* to study or practice astrology.

as·trol′ō·ġy, *n.* [ME. *astrology*; L. *astrologia*; Gr. *astrologia*, astronomy, astrology; *astron*, star, and *logia*, from *legein*, to speak.] literally, the science or doctrine of the stars, and formerly often used as equivalent to *astronomy*, but now restricted in meaning to the pseudo science which claims to foretell the future by studying the supposed influence of the relative positions of the moon, sun, and stars on human affairs.
 judicial astrology; that branch of astrology which professes to foretell events connected with the life of men or nations.
 natural astrology; that branch of astrology which dealt with the prediction of natural effects, as changes of the weather, winds, and storms. [Obs.]

as′trō·man·cy, *n.* [*astro-*, and Gr. *manteia*, divination.] astrology. [Rare.]

as·trō·man′tic, *a.* of or pertaining to astromancy.

as″trō·mē″tē·or·ō·log′ic·ăl, *a.* of or pertaining to astrometeorology.

as″trō·mē″tē·or·ol′ō·ġist, *n.* one who studies or practices astrometeorology.

as″trō·mē″tē·or·ol′ō·ġy, *n.* [*astro-*, and Gr. *meteōrologia*, meteorology; *meteōron*, meteor, and *logia*, from *legein*, to speak.] the pseudo science claiming to foretell the weather and its changes from the appearance of the moon and stars; or, a scientific investigation of the supposed influence of the heavenly bodies upon atmospheric conditions.

as·trom′e·tėr, *n.* [*astro-*, and Gr. *metron*, measure.] an instrument for measuring the apparent relative magnitude of the stars.

as·trom′e·try, *n.* that branch of astronomy dealing with the measurement of planets, stars, etc., their apparent positions, and their movements.

as′trō·naut, *n.* [Fr. *astronaute*.] a person trained to make rocket flights in outer space.

as·trō·nau′tics, *n.pl.* [*construed as sing.*] [Fr. *astronautique* (coined 1927).] the science that deals with the problems of travel in outer space, especially to the moon and to other planets.

as″trō·nav″i·gā′tion, *n.* same as *celestial navigation*.

as·tron′ō·mėr, *n.* [ME. *astronomer*; L. *astronomia*; Gr. *astronomia*, from *astronomos*, an astronomer; *astron*, star, and *nemein*, to distribute, arrange.]
 1. a student of or an authority on astronomy.
 2. an astrologer. [Obs.]

as·trō·nō′mi·ăn, *n.* an astrologer. [Obs.]

as·trō·nom′ic·ăl, as·trō·nom′ic, *a.* 1. pertaining to astronomy.
 2. very large, as the numbers or quantities used in astronomy.
 astronomical day; the mean solar day, from noon to noon.
 astronomical unit; a unit of length equal to the mean radius of the earth's orbit (c. 93 million miles).
 astronomical year; the period in which the earth makes a complete revolution around the sun (365 days, 5 hours, 48 minutes, 45.51 seconds); time from one equinox to the next corresponding equinox; solar year.

as·trō·nom′ic·ăl·ly, *adv.* 1. from the viewpoint of astronomy.
 2. by means of astronomy.
 3. as in astronomy; as, *astronomically* large numbers.

as·tron′ō·mīze, *v.i.*; astronomized, *pt.*, *pp.*; astronomizing, *ppr.* to study or discourse upon astronomy. [Rare.]
 They *astronomized* in caves.
 —Sir T. Browne.

as·tron′ō·my, *n.* [Gr. *astronomia*, from *astronomos*, an astronomer; *astron*, star, and *nomos*, from *nemein*, to arrange, distribute.]
 1. the science which treats of the heavenly bodies—fixed stars, planets, satellites, and comets—their nature, distribution, magnitudes, motions, distances, periods of revolution, eclipses, etc.
 2. *pl.* **as·tron′ō·mies**, a book or treatise on astronomy.
 3. astrology. [Obs.]

as′trō·phel, *n.* see *astrofel*.

as″trō·phō·tog′rȧ·phy, *n.* [*astro-*, and Gr. *phōs*, *phōtos*, light, and *graphia*, from *graphein*, to write, describe.] photography as used in investigating astronomical phenomena.

as″trō·phō·tom′e·tėr, *n.* [*astro-*, and Gr. *phōs*, *phōtos*, light, and *metron*, measure.] an instrument fitted to a telescope and used to determine the brightness of stars, the standard of comparison being an artificial light.

as″trō·phō″tō·met′ric·ăl, *a.* of or pertaining to an astrophotometer or to astrophotometry.

as″trō·phō·tom′e·try, *n.* the science of determining the brightness of the heavenly bodies.

as·trō·phys′ic·ăl, *a.* of astrophysics.

as·trō·phys′ics, *n.pl.* [*construed as sing.*], [*astro-*, and *physics*.] the science of the physical properties and phenomena of the stars, planets, etc.

As·troph′y·ton, *n.* [*astro-*, and Gr. *phyton*, plant.] a genus of ophiurans including the basket fish or sea basket.

as′trō·scope, *n.* [*astro-*, and Gr. *skopein*, to view.] an old astronomical instrument, composed of two cones, on whose surface the constellations were delineated.

as·tros′cō·py, *n.* observation of the stars by means of the astroscope. [Obs.]

as′trō·sphēre, *n.* [*astro-* and *sphere*.] in biology, (a) the central body of an aster; centrosphere; (b) all of an aster except the centrosome.

as″trō·thē·ol′ō·ġy, *n.* [*astro-*, and Gr. *theologia*, theology.] theology based upon observation of the stars, planets, etc.

ȧ·struc′tive, *a.* [L. *astructus*, pp. of *astruere*, to build in addition, add; *ad*, to, and *struere*, to heap up.] constructive. [Obs.]

ȧ·strut′, *a.* strutting; pompous.

ȧ·strut′, *adv.* in a swelling or strutting manner, as in walking.

as·tū′cious, as·tū′tious, *a.* [Fr. *astucieux*, astute.] crafty; subtle; astute.

as·tū′cious·ly, *adv.* astutely.

as·tū′ci·ty, *n.* astuteness.

As′tūr, *n.* [L. *astur*, *astor*, a goshawk.] a genus of rapacious birds including the goshawk, *Astur palumbarius*.

As·tū′ri·ăn, *a.* of Asturias, a region of northern Spain, or its people, language, etc.

As·tū′ri·ăn, *n.* 1. a native or inhabitant of Asturias.
 2. the Spanish dialect of the Asturians.

as·tūte′, *a.* [L. *astutus*, from *astus*, craft, cunning.] of a shrewd and penetrating mind; cunning; crafty; sagacious.
 That *astute* little lady of Curzon street.
 —Thackeray.
 Syn.—penetrating, sagacious, discerning, critical, shrewd, subtle, keen.

as·tūte′ly, *adv.* in an astute manner; shrewdly.

as·tūte′ness, *n.* the quality of being astute.

as·tū′tious, *a.* same as *astucious*.

As·ty′ȧ·nax, *n.* [L.; Gr. *Astyanax*.] in Greek legend, the young son of Hector and Andromache: he was killed when thrown from the walls of Troy by the Greek conquerors.

ȧ·sty′lăr, *a.* [Gr. *a* priv., and *stylos*, a column.] in architecture, having no columns or pilasters.

ȧ·sun′dėr, *adv.* [ME. *a sundir*, *on sunder*; AS. *on sundran*; *on*, on, and *sunder*, apart.]
 1. in a sundered or divided state; in different directions; apart; separately; as, wide *asunder* as right and wrong.
 2. into or in parts or pieces, as by an explosion.

ȧ·sun′dėr, *a.* separated; not close; apart.

Ā·sur′, *n.* same as *Ashur*.

ȧ·su′rȧ, *n.* [Sans. *asura*, spiritual, a spirit.] in Hindu mythology, an antagonist of the gods; especially one of a race of Titans or demons.

as′wāil, *n.* [native name.] the sloth bear, *Ursus labiatus*, of the mountains of India.

ȧ·swēve′, *v.t.* to stupefy. [Obs.]

ȧ·swing′, *adv.* in a state of swinging.

ȧ·swoon′, *adv.* in a swoon.

ȧ·swooned′, *adv.* aswoon.

ā·syl·lab′ic, *a.* not syllabic.

ȧ·sy′lum, *n.* [L. *asylum*; Gr. *asylon*, an asylum, from *a* priv., and *sylē*, right of seizure.]

1. formerly, a sanctuary or inviolable place of protection, as a church, where criminals and debtors sheltered themselves from capture and punishment, and from which they could not be forcibly taken without sacrilege. Temples and altars were anciently considered asylums, as were tombs, statues of the gods, and monuments.

2. any place of retreat and security.

3. an institution for the protection or relief of unfortunate, afflicted, destitute, or defective persons; as, an *asylum* for the poor, for the insane, for orphans, or for the aged.

4. the protection given by a sanctuary or refuge.

right of asylum; in modern usage, the right of one state to receive, shelter, and protect those accused of offenses in another.

Syn.—refuge, retreat, sanctuary, shelter.

ā·sym′me·trăl, ā·sym′me·trous, *a.* asymmetrical. [Obs.]

ā·sym·met′riç·ăl, ā·sym·met′riç, *a.* 1. not symmetrical.

2. in crystallography, relating to the triclinic system, crystals belonging to this classification having three unequal axes or being without a plane of symmetry.

ā·sym′me·try, *n.* [Gr. *asymmetria*, disproportion; *a* priv., and *symmetros*; *syn*, with, and *metron*, measure.]

1. the want of proportion between the parts of a thing; lack of symmetry.

2. in mathematics, incommensurability, as when there is no common measure between two quantities. [Obs.]

as′ymp·tōte (as′im-tōt), *n.* [Gr. *a* priv., and *sympiptein*, to fall together; *syn*, with, together, and *ptōtos*, from *piptein*, to fall.] a line which continually approaches nearer to some curve, but, though infinitely extended, would never meet it. This may be conceived as a tangent to a curve at an infinite distance.

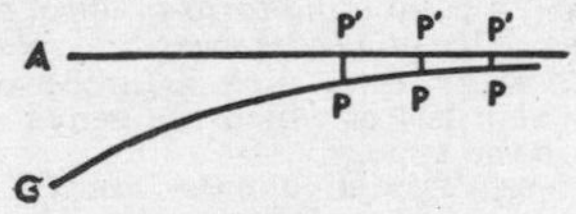

ASYMPTOTE
A, asymptote of curve *c*
(PP′ becomes smaller but does not disappear)

as·ymp·tot′iç, as·ymp·tot′iç·ăl, *a.* of, or of the nature of, an asymptote.

as·ymp·tot′iç·ăl·ly, *adv.* in an asymptotic manner.

à·syn′är·tēte, à·syn″är·tet′iç, *a.* [Gr. *asynartētos*, disconnected; *a* priv., *syn*, with, and *artein*, to join, fasten.] literally, disconnected; not fitted or adjusted.

asynartete sentence; a sentence in which the members are not united by connective particles; as, I came, I saw, I conquered.

asynartete verse; in prosody, a verse consisting of two members, having different rhythms; as when the first consists of iambuses and the second of trochees, or the first of dactyls and the second of iambuses.

à·syn′çhrō·niṣm, *n.* lack of synchronism; failure to occur at the same time.

à·syn′çhrō·nous, *a.* [Gr. *a* priv., and *syn*, with, and *chronos*, time.] without coincidence in time; not synchronous.

as·yn·det′iç, *a.* using or involving asyndeton.

as·yn·det′iç·ăl·ly, *adv.* in an asyndetic manner.

à·syn′de·ton, *n.* [Gr. *asyndeton*, asyndeton, neut. of *asyndetos*; *a* priv., and *syndetos*, from *syndein*, to bind together.] in rhetoric, the practice of leaving out the conjunctions between co-ordinate sentence elements, e.g., *veni, vidi, vici*; I came, I saw, I conquered.

as·y·nēr′ġi·à, à·syn′ēr·ġy, *n.* [Gr. *a* priv., and *synergein*, to work together.] in medicine, lack of co-ordination of muscles normally acting in unison.

ā·syn·taç′tiç, *a.* [*a* priv., and *syntactic*.] not syntactical.

à·sys′tō·lē, à·sys′tō·liṣm, *n.* [Gr. *a* priv., and *systole*, contracting, from *syn*, with, and *stellein*, to set, arrange.] in medicine, imperfect contraction of the ventricles of the heart.

at, *prep.* [ME. *at*; AS. *æt*; akin to Goth., OS., *at*; L. *ad*.]

1. on; in; near; by; as, *at* the office, *at* heart.

2. to or toward; as, gaze *at*, throw *at*.

3. through; as, come in *at* the front door.

4. from; as, get the facts *at* their source.

5. attending; as, *at* the party.

6. occupied in; busy with; as, *at* work.

7. in a condition or state of; as, *at* war.

8. in the manner of; as, *at* a trot.

9. because of; as, terrified *at* the sight.

10. according to; as, *at* his discretion.

11. in the amount, degree, number, price, etc. of; as, *at* twenty miles per hour, *at* five cents each.

12. on or close to the age or time of; as, *at* five o'clock, *at* once, *at* sixty-five. Basically, *at* is the preposition of general (usually static) location, answering the question "Where?" It is replaced by *in, on, over, under, near, by* when more precise indications of locality are needed. The meanings of all these, together with more idiomatic meanings roughly paraphrased above, are latent in *at* but not emphasized or actually expressed by it.

at′à·bal, *n.* [Sp. *atabal*, from Ar. *at-tabl*; *al*, the, and *tabl*, drum.] a kind of kettledrum or tabor used by the Moors: also spelled *attabal*.

at′à·brine, at′à·brin, at′e·brin, *n.* [G. *atebrin*; perhaps from *antifebrine*.] quinacrine hydrochloride, a synthetic drug used in treating malaria: a trade-mark (*Atabrine*).

à·taç′à·mīte, *n.* a native chloride of copper, originally found in the desert of Atacama, between Chile and Peru.

à·taç′tiç, *a.* [Gr. *ataktos*, without order; *a* priv., and *taktos*, from *tassein*, to order.]

1. without order or arrangement; irregular.

2. in grammar, not syntactic.

3. in medicine, ataxic; in-co-ordinate.

at′à·ghan, *n.* a Moslem sword: see *yataghan*.

At·à·lan′tà, *n.* [L. *Atalanta*; Gr. *Atalantē*.] in Greek legend, a beautiful, swift-footed maiden who offered to marry any man able to defeat her in a race, death being the penalty for failure: Hippomenes won from her by dropping three golden apples, which she stopped to pick up, along the way.

at′à·man, *n.* [Russ. *ataman*; Pol. *ataman*, a chief, headman.] a Cossack chief.

at·à·màs′çō, *n.* [Am. Ind.] a plant, *Zephyranthes Atamasco*, of the amaryllis family, found in southern United States: also called *atamasco lily*.

at·à·rax′i·à, at′à·rax·y, *n.* [Gr. *ataraxia*, calmness, from *a* priv., and *taraktos*, from *tarassein*, to disturb.] calmness of mind: a term used by the Stoics and Skeptics to denote a freedom from the emotions which proceed from vanity and self-conceit.

à·taunt′, *adv.* [ME. *ataunt*; OFr. *ataunt*, *altant*; *al*, L. *alius*, other, and *tant*, L. *tantus*, so much.] in nautical usage, fully rigged; set on end; set right: commonly applied to the masts of a ship.

all ataunt; fully rigged, with the upper masts and yards aloft; hence, all right; all in good order or in readiness.

à·tav′iç, *a.* of a remote ancestor.

at′à·viṣm, *n.* [Fr. *atavisme*, from L. *atavus*, the father of a great-grandfather, from *avus*, a grandfather.]

1. resemblance to a remote ancestor in some characteristic which nearer ancestors do not have.

2. reversion to a primitive type.

3. in medicine, the recurrence in a descendant of any abnormality or disease of an ancestor.

at′à·vist, *n.* a person or thing characterized by atavism.

at·à·vis′tiç, *a.* 1. of or due to atavism.

2. tending to atavism.

à·tax′i·à, à·tax′y, *n.* [Gr. *ataxia*, disorder, from *ataktos*; *a* priv., and *taktos*, from *tassein*, to order, arrange.]

1. lack of order; disturbance; irregularity.

2. total or partial inability to co-ordinate voluntary bodily movements, especially muscular movements.

3. locomotor ataxia.

à·tax′iç, *a.* of or due to ataxia.

ataxic fever; malignant typhus fever.

à·tax′iç, *n.* a person who has ataxia.

at·à·zir′, *n.* [Sp., from Ar. *attasīr*, influence.] in astrology, the influence of a star upon other stars, or upon man. [Obs.]

āte, past tense of *eat*.

-āte, [L. *-atus*, the pp. ending of verbs belonging to the first conjugation.]

1. a suffix used to form verbs, originally from stems containing the Latin pp. ending *-atus*, but now from various other stems, and meaning: (a) *to become*, as in evapor*ate*, matur*ate*; (b) *to cause to become*, as in invalid*ate*, sublim*ate*; (c) *to form* or *produce*, as in ulcer*ate*, saliv*ate*; (d) *to provide* or *treat with*, as in vaccin*ate*, refriger*ate*; (e) *to put in the form of* or *form by means of*, as in delin*eate*, triangul*ate*; (f) *to arrange for*, as in orchestr*ate*; (g) *to combine, infuse*, or *treat with*, as in chlorin*ate*, oxygen*ate*.

2. a suffix used to form adjectives from nouns, and meaning: (a) *of* or *characteristic of*, as in collegi*ate*, rose*ate*; (b) *having* or *filled with*, as in proportion*ate*, passion*ate*; (c) in botany and zoology, *having* or *characterized by*, as in spatul*ate*, caud*ate*.

3. a suffix used to form adjectives, either from verbs of the same form or, more rarely, from verbs of another form, and roughly equivalent to the *-ed* of the English past participle, as anim*ate* (*animated*), determin*ate* (*determined*).

-āte, [L. *-atus*, a noun ending.]

a noun suffix denoting: (a) *an office, function, official, group of officials*, or *agent*, as in episcop*ate*, potent*ate*, director*ate*; (b) *a person* or *thing that is the object of* (an action), as in leg*ate*, mand*ate*; (c) [L. *-atum*, neut. of *-atus*.] in chemistry, *a salt made from* (an acid with a name ending in *-ic*), as in acet*ate*, nitr*ate*.

at′e·brin, *n.* in pharmacy, atabrine.

à·teçh′niç, *a.* [Gr. *atechnos*, without art; *a* priv., and *technē*, art.] not having technical knowledge.

à·teçh′niç, *n.* one who lacks technical knowledge.

at′el-, see *atelo-*.

at′e·lēne, *a.* [Gr. *atelēs*, imperfect.] in mineralogy, imperfect; lacking regular forms in the genus.

At′e·lēṣ, *n.* [L., from Gr. *atelēs*, incomplete; *a* priv., and *telos*, end, completion.] a genus of American monkeys, the spider monkeys, having attenuated bodies, long slender limbs, and a prehensile tail: so called because the thumbs are but rudimentary.

à·te·lier′ (à-te-lyā′), *n.* [Fr.] a studio or workshop.

À·tel′lăn, *a.* relating to the dramas at Atella, in ancient Italy.

À·tel′lăn, *n.* one of the plays given at Atella: later, applied to any dramatic representation which was satirical or licentious.

at′e·lō-, [Gr. *atelēs*, imperfect.] a combining form denoting *incomplete* or *undeveloped structure*, as in *atelo*cardia.

at″e·lō·cär′di·à, *n.* [*atelo-*, and Gr. *kardia*, heart.] an imperfect or undeveloped state of the heart.

at″e·lō·chī′li·à, *n.* [*atelo-*, and Gr. *cheilos*, lip.] imperfect development of a lip: also written *atelocheilia*.

at″e·lō·glos′si·à, *n.* [*atelo-*, and Gr. *glōssa*, tongue.] imperfect development of the tongue.

at″e·log·nā′thi·à, *n.* [*atelo-*, and Gr. *gnathos*, jaw.] imperfect development of a jaw, especially of the lower jaw.

at″e·lō·stō′mi·à, *n.* [*atelo-*, and Gr. *stoma*, mouth.] incomplete development of the mouth.

ä tem′pō, [It.] in music, in time: a direction to the performer to return to the rate of speed immediately preceding the movement.

Ath·à·bas′căn, *a.* and *n.* same as *Athapascan*.

à·thal′à·mous, *a.* [Gr. *a* priv., and *thalamos*, bed.] in botany, lacking thalami: applied to certain lichens.

à·thal′line, *a.* [Gr. *a* priv., and *thalos*, a shoot, branch.] without a thallus.

ath′à·maunt, *n.* adamant. [Obs.]

ath·à·nā′ṣi·à (-zhi-à), **à·than′à·sy,** *n.* [Gr. *athanasia*, from *a* priv., and *thanatos*, death.] immortality.

Ath·à·nā′ṣiăn, (-zhăn), *a.* pertaining to Athanasius, patriarch of Alexandria in the fourth century.

Athanasian Creed; a creed, confession, or exposition of faith of unknown authorship, supposed formerly to have been drawn up by Athanasius. It is an explicit avowal of the doctrines of the Trinity, as opposed to Arianism.

Ath·à·nā′ṣiăn, *n.* a follower of Athanasius, or a believer in the Athanasian Creed.

ath′à·nor, *n.* [ME. *athanor*; Sp. *atanor*, from Ar. *at-tannūr*; *al*, the, and *tannūr*, from Heb. *tannūr*, an oven; *nūr*, fire.] a digesting furnace, formerly used in alchemy, so constructed as to maintain a uniform and constant heat.

Ath·à·pas′căn, *a.* designating or of the most

widely scattered linguistic family of North American Indians, ranging from Alaska to northern Mexico and including the Navajo and Apache tribes.

Ath·ȧ·pas′căn, *n.* 1. an Indian of this family.
 2. a language of this family, as the Hupa of California.

Ath·ē·çā′tȧ, *n.* [L., from Gr. *a* priv., and *thēkē*, a box, chest.] a division of the *Hydroidea* in which the zooids are not sheathed.

ath′ē·çāte, *a.* resembling the *Athecata*.

ā′thē·iṣm, *n.* [Fr. *athéisme*, from Gr. *atheos*, without a god; *a* priv., and *theos*, god.] the belief that there is no God.
 A little philosophy inclineth men's minds to *atheism*, but depth in philosophy bringeth men's minds to religion. —Bacon.

ā′thē·ist, *n.* one who believes that there is no God.
 By night an *atheist* half believes a God. —Young.

ā′thē·ist, *a.* atheistic.

ā·thē·is′tiç, ā·thē·is′tiç·ăl, *a.* 1. pertaining to atheism or atheists.
 2. inclined to atheism; impious.

ā·thē·is′tiç·ăl·ly, *adv.* 1. in an atheistic manner.
 2. from an atheistic point of view.

ā·thē·is′tiç·ăl·ness, *n.* the quality of being atheistic.

ā′thē·īze, *v.i.*; atheized, *pt.*, *pp.*; atheizing, *ppr.* to discourse as an atheist. [Rare.]

ā′thē·īze, *v.t.* to render atheistic. [Rare.]

ā′thē·ī·zẽr, *n.* one who atheizes. [Rare.]

ath′el·ing, ad′el·ing, *n.* [ME. *atheling*; AS. *ætheling*; O.H.G. *adaling*, from *athele*, noble.] in Anglo-Saxon times, a prince or nobleman.

À·thē′nȧ, *n.* [Gr. *Athēnē*.] in Greek mythology, the goddess of wisdom, skills, and warfare: identified by the Romans with Minerva.

ath·e·nae′um, ath·e·nē′um, *n.* [L., from Gr. *Athēnaion*, a temple of Athene.]
 1. [A–] in ancient Athens, the temple of Athena, where poets, philosophers, and rhetoricians met.
 2. a school of law, literature, etc. founded at Rome by Hadrian.
 3. a literary or scientific club.
 4. any building or hall used as a library or reading room.

A·thē′nē, *n.* Athena.

A·thē′ni·ăn, *a.* of Athens, its people, or culture.

A·thē′ni·ăn, *n.* 1. a native or inhabitant of Athens.
 2. a citizen of ancient Athens.

ā″thē·ō·log′iç·ăl, *a.* opposed to theology.

ā·thē·ol′ō·ġy, *n.* opposition to theology.

ā′thē·ous, *a.* 1. atheistic; impious. [Obs.]
 The hypocrite or *atheous* priest.—Milton.
 2. not taking God into account; neither accepting nor denying God. [Rare.]

Ath·e·rī′nȧ, *n.* [L., from Gr. *atherinē*, a kind of smelt.] a genus of abdominal fishes, characterized by a rather flat upper jaw, six rays in the gill membrane, and a silvery side belt or line. It includes the sand smelts.

ath′ẽr·ine, *n.* any of the fishes belonging to the genus *Atherina*.

ȧ·thẽr′măn·cy, *n.* [Gr. *athermantos*, not heated; *a* priv., and *thermainein*, to heat, from *thermē*, heat.] the quality of being athermanous.

ȧ·thẽr′mȧ·nous, ȧ·thẽr′mous, *a.* impervious to heat rays: opposed to *diathermanous*.

ath′ẽr·oid, *a.* [Gr. *atheros*, an ear of grain.] formed like an ear of grain.

ath·e·rō′mȧ, *n.* [L., from Gr. *athērōma*, from *atharē*, porridge.]
 1. a kind of wen or encysted tumor, containing cheesy matter.
 2. the fatty degeneration of the walls of the arteries in arteriosclerosis.

ath″e·rō·mā′ṣi·ȧ (-zhi-a), *n.* an atheromatous condition.

ath·e·rom′ȧ·tous, *a.* characterized by or affected with atheroma.

Ath″e·rō·spẽr′mȧ, *n.* [Gr. *athēr*, *atheros*, the beard, or spike, of an ear of corn, and *sperma*, a seed.] a genus of plants, of Australia and Tasmania, containing but one species, the plume nutmeg, *Atherosperma moschatum*.

ath′e·tīze, *v.t.*; athetized, *pt.*, *pp.*; athetizing, *ppr.* [Gr. *athetein*, to set aside; *a* priv., and *thetos*, from *tithenai*, to set.] to reject; to set aside.

ath′e·toid, *a.* of or characteristic of athetosis.

ath·e·tō′sis, *n.* [L., from Gr. *athetos*, without place; *a* priv., and *thetos*, from *tithenai*, to place.] in medicine, a condition characterized by involuntary twitchings and tremors of hands and feet.

ȧ·thīrst′, *a.* 1. thirsty; wanting drink. [Archaic and Poetic.]
 2. eager (for a thing).

ath′lēte, *n.* [L. *athleta*; Gr. *athlētēs*, a contestant in the games; from *athlein*, to contest for a prize; *athlos*, a contest; *athlon*, a prize.]
 1. among the ancient Greeks and Romans, one who contended for a prize in the public games.
 2. one trained to engage or compete in exercises, games, and contests requiring physical strength, endurance, agility, speed, etc.
 3. figuratively, one fitted or trained for mental contests; as, *athletes* of debate.

ath′lēte's foot, ringworm of the feet, a contagious skin disease caused by a tiny fungus often found in gymnasiums, shower rooms, etc.

ath′lēte's heärt, a heart condition in which there is some enlargement, caused by continued physical exertion and strain.

ath·let′iç, *a.* 1. of, like, or proper to athletes or athletics.
 2. strong; lusty; robust; vigorous; fitted for vigorous exertions; as, an *athletic* boy.

ath·let′iç·ăl·ly, *adv.* in an athletic manner.

ath·let′i·ciṣm, *n.* 1. addiction to athletics.
 2. an athletic quality; as, the *athleticism* of her dancing.

ath·let′içs, *n.pl.* [*sometimes construed as sing.*] art of physical training; athletic games, sports, exercises, etc.

ath′lē·tiṣm, *n.* the state or characteristics of an athlete.

ath′ō·dyd, *n.* [contr., from *a*ero-*th*ermo-*dy*namic *d*uct.] a ramjet, a type of jet engine.

at-hōme′, *n.* an informal reception at one's home, usually in the afternoon.

ȧ·threp′si·ȧ, *n.* [L., from Gr. *a* priv., and *threpsis*, nourishment, from *trephein*, to nourish.] lack of nourishment; extreme weakness or debility, especially among children, resulting from lack of food and neglect of hygiene.

ȧ·thwạrt′, *prep.* 1. across; from side to side of; as, *athwart* the path.
 2. against; in opposition to.
 3. in nautical usage, across the course or length of.
 athwart hawse: said of a ship when it lies across the stem of another, whether in contact or at a small distance.

ȧ·thwạrt′, *adv.* 1. obliquely; crosswise; transversely.
 2. so as to block or thwart.

ȧ·thwạrt′ships, *adv.* athwart or across the ship from side to side, or in that direction.

ȧ·thy′mi·ȧ, *n.* [Gr. *athymia*, faint-heartedness; *a* priv., and *thymos*, soul, courage.] in medicine, despondency; melancholia.

-at′iç, [a compound L. suffix composed of a pp. stem in *-at* and *-icus*; Gr. *-atikos*, in which *ikos* is added to a noun stem in *-at*.] a suffix used in adjectives of Greek and Latin origin and signifying *of, of the kind of*.

ȧ·tilt′, *adv.* 1. tilting, as with a spear; in the position or with the action of a man making a thrust; as, to stand or run *atilt*.
 2. in an inclined position; tilted.

at′i·my, *n.* [Gr. *atimia*, from *a* priv., and *timē*, honor.] in ancient Greece, public disgrace; exclusion from office or magistracy, by some disqualifying act or decree.

ȧ·tin′gle, *a.* [*a-*, on, and *tingle*.] tingling; excited.

-ā′tion, [Fr. *-ation*, from L. *atio(n)*; a suffix added to verbs of the first conjugation.] a suffix used in forming nouns of action often equivalent to abstract nouns in *-ing*, and explaining the state resulting from the action. These nouns are usually formed from verbs in *-ate*, as transl*ation*, and *-ize*, as realiz*ation*, or verbs without a suffix, as fix, fix*ation*, quote, quot*ation*.

ȧ·tip′tōe, *adv.* 1. on tiptoe.
 2. figuratively, in a state of high expectation or eagerness.

-ā′tive, [from Fr. or L.; Fr. *-atif*, f. *-ative*; L. *-ativus*.] a suffix meaning *of the nature of, relating to*: used in forming adjectives generally from *-ate* verbs, as demonstr*ative*, correl*ative*.

At′kins, Tom′my, see *Tommy Atkins*.

At·lan′tȧ, *n.* [L., from Gr. *Atlas*, *Atlantos*.] a genus of pelagic gastropodous mollusks typical of the family *Atlantidæ*.

at·lan′tăl, *a.* in anatomy, relating to the atlas.

At·lan·tē′ăn, *a.* 1. of or like Atlas.
 2. pertaining to the island Atlantis.

at·lan′tēṣ, *n.pl.* [Gr. *Atlantes*, pl. of *Atlas*.] in architecture, standing or kneeling figures or half figures of men, used in the place of columns or pilasters to support an entablature: called by the Romans *telamones*. Female figures so used are called *caryatides*.

ATLANTES

At·lan′tiç, *a.* [L. *Atlanticus*, from Gr. *Atlas*, *Atlantos*, a mountain in west Africa: so named because fabled to be the pillar of heaven.]
 1. pertaining to or descended from Atlas. [Obs.]
 2. pertaining to, designating, in, on, or near the Atlantic Ocean.
 3. pertaining to the island Atlantis. [Obs.]

At·lan′tiç Chär′tẽr, a declaration of peace aims in World War II, made by Roosevelt and Churchill at a meeting on the Atlantic, August, 1941.

At·lan′tiç plāin, one of the chief physiographic divisions of the United States, including all the plains on the eastern seacoast.

At·lan′ti·dae, *n.pl.* [L., from Gr. *Atlas*, *Atlantos*, Mt. Atlas.] in zoology, a family of gastropodous mollusks of the order *Nucleobranchiata*, with a small shell resembling that of the nautilus.

At·lan′ti·dēṣ, *n.pl.* the Pleiades or seven stars, fabled to be the daughters of Atlas.

At·lan′tis, *n.* [L.; Gr.] a legendary island or continent supposed to have existed in the Atlantic west of Gibraltar and to have been sunk by an earthquake.

at·lan′tō-, a combining form of *atlas*, *atlantos*, meaning *of the atlas of the vertebral column*.

At·lan·tō·sạu′ri·dae, *n.pl.* a family of dinosaurian reptiles, of which the genus *Atlantosaurus* is the type.

At·lan·tō·sạu′rus, *n.* [*atlanto-*, and Gr. *sauros*, a reptile.] a genus of gigantic dinosaurian reptiles, remains of which have been found in the Jurassic strata of Colorado.

at′lăs, *n.* [Gr. *Atlas*.]
 1. [A–] in Greek legend, (a) a giant compelled to support the heavens on his shoulders; (b) in Homer, a god in charge of the pillars of heaven; (c) a king changed into a mountain.
 2. [A–] one who bears a great burden.
 3. a collection of maps in a volume: supposed to be so called from a picture of Atlas supporting the globe, which often appeared on the front page of early atlases.
 4. a book of tables, charts, illustrations, etc. of a specific subject or subjects; as, an anatomical *atlas*.
 5. a large, square folio, resembling a volume of maps: called also *atlas folio*.
 6. the top vertebra of the neck, articulating immediately with the occipital bone, and thus supporting the head, whence the name.
 7. a size of drawing paper, 26 by 33 or 34 inches.
 8. a collection or volume of plates or engravings explanatory of some subject.
 9. the atlas beetle, *Chalcosoma atlas*.
 10. *pl.* **at·lan′tēṣ,** in architecture, any of the atlantes.
 Atlas powder; a compound of nitroglycerin used in blasting.

at′lăs, *n.* [Ar., smooth, bare, satin.] a fine fabric of silk and satin, manufactured in the East Indies.

at′lăs fōl′iō, a large, square folio size of books.

at′lăs grid, a system of parallel and perpendicular lines on an aerial photograph, dividing it into small squares for locating points on the photograph quickly.

at′lee, *n.* [native name.] the East Indian tamarisk salt tree, *Tamarix orientalis*.

Ät′li, *n.* [ON., from Goth. *Attila*, lit., little father.] in Norse mythology, a king of the Huns, killed by his wife, Gudrun, because he had killed her brothers for the treasure of Sigurd.

at′lō-, at·loid′ō-, a combining form used in anatomy, signifying *pertaining* or *referring to the atlas*.

at′loid, *a.* [*atlo-*, and Gr. *eidos*, form.] in anatomy, pertaining to the atlas.

ät′măn, *n.* [Sans., breath, soul, Supreme

Spirit.] in Hinduism: (a) the individual soul or ego; (b) [A–] the universal soul; source of all individual souls; oversoul.

at·mi·dom'e·tẽr, *n.* [Gr. *atmis, atmidos,* vapor, and *metron,* a measure.] an atmometer.

at·mi·dom'e·try, *n.* the science of ascertaining and measuring evaporation in the atmosphere.

at·mō·loġ'iç, at·mō·loġ'iç·ăl, *a.* pertaining to atmology.

at·mol'ō·ġist, *n.* one skilled in atmology; a student of atmology.

at·mol'ō·ġy, *n.* [Gr. *atmos,* vapor, and *logia,* from *legein,* to speak.] that branch of science which treats of the laws and phenomena of aqueous vapor.

at·mol'y·sis, *n.* [Gr. *atmos,* vapor, and *lysis,* a loosing, from *lyein,* to loose.] a method of separating mingled gases by causing them to pass through a vessel of porous material, such as graphite.

at″mol·y·zā'tion, *n.* the separation of mingled gases by atmolysis.

at'mō·lȳze, *v.t.*; atmolyzed, *pt., pp.*; atmolyzing, *ppr.* to separate by atmolysis.

at'mō·lȳ·zẽr, *n.* an instrument for atmolyzing.

at·mom'e·tẽr, *n.* [Gr. *atmos,* vapor, and *metron,* a measure.] an instrument used in measuring the evaporation from a humid surface in a given time; an evaporometer.

at'mŏs·phēre, *n.* [Gr. *atmos,* vapor, and *sphaira,* a sphere.]

1. all the air surrounding the earth.
2. the gaseous mass surrounding any star, planet, etc.
3. the air in any given place.
4. a pervading or surrounding mental or social influence; social environment.
5. the general tone of a work of art; as, a play with a fateful *atmosphere.*
6. the general effect, often exotic, produced by decoration, furnishings, etc.; as, the food is good but there's no *atmosphere.* [Colloq.]
7. in physics, a unit of pressure equal to 14.69 pounds per square inch.

at·mŏs·pher'iç, at·mŏs·pher'iç·ăl, *a.* 1. pertaining to, characteristic of, or existing in the atmosphere; as, *atmospheric* air or vapors, *atmospheric* currents.

2. dependent on the atmosphere. [Rare.]
 I am an *atmospheric* creature. —Pope.
3. caused, produced, or acted upon by the atmosphere; as, an *atmospheric* effect.
4. of, having, or giving atmosphere or an atmosphere; as, *atmospheric* lighting.

atmospheric engine; a steam engine in which the steam is admitted only to the under side of the piston and for the up stroke, the steam being then condensed and a vacuum thereby created under the piston, which in consequence descends by the pressure of the atmosphere acting on its upper surface.

atmospheric line; in a steam pressure diagram, a line drawn by the pencil when the steam is shut off from the piston of the indicator and it is acted on by the pressure of the atmosphere alone. The height of the steam line above this shows the pressure of the steam, and the depth of the vacuum line below shows the degree of condensation which is then taking place in the engine.

atmospheric pressure; the weight of the atmosphere per square inch of surface; the pressure of 14.69 pounds per square inch exerted in all directions, at the sea level, by the atmosphere.

at·mŏs·pher'iç·ăl·ly, *adv.* 1. with regard to atmosphere.

2. by atmospheric pressure or influence.

at·mŏs·pher'içs, *n.pl.* in radio, (a) disturbances in reception, produced by natural electric discharges, as in a storm; static; (b) the phenomena producing these disturbances.

at·mŏs·phē·rol'ō·ġy, *n.* [Gr. *atmos,* vapor, *sphaira,* sphere, and *logia,* from *legein,* to speak.] the science which treats of the atmosphere.

at·mos'tē·ăl, *a.* relating to or of the nature of an atmosteon.

at·mos'tē·on, *n.*; *pl.* **at·mos'tē·ȧ,** [Gr. *atmos,* air, and *osteon,* bone.] in ornithology, an airbone; an ossified tube that conveys air into the interior of a bone.

at'ō·kous, *a.* [Gr. *atokos,* barren; *a* priv., and *tokos,* offspring.]

1. in zoology, producing only asexual offspring, as the eggs of certain species of the *Annelida.*
2. asexual: applied to certain worms.

at'oll, *n.* [from Maldive Is. term; perhaps from Malayalam *adal,* closing, uniting.] a coral island consisting of a ring of coral surrounding a central lagoon, very common in the Indian and Pacific Oceans.

ATOLL

at'ŏm, *n.* [Fr. *atome*; L. *atomus*; Gr. *atomos,* an atom, indivisible; *a* priv., and *tomos,* from *temnein,* to cut.]

1. a tiny particle; an extremely small bit of anything; a jot.
2. in chemistry and physics, any of the smallest particles of an element that combine with similar particles of other elements to produce compounds: atoms combine to form molecules, and consist of a complex arrangement of electrons revolving about a positively charged nucleus containing protons and neutrons; the fission of a nucleus by bombardment either with neutrons (as in atomic bombs), or with certain other very small particles, releases energy.

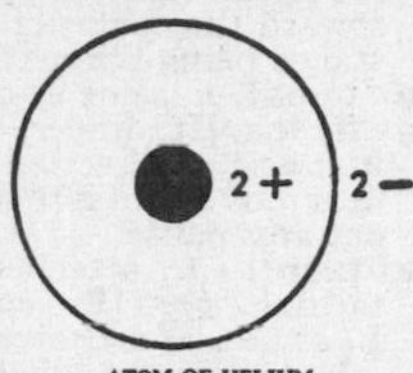

ATOM OF HELIUM

3. according to the theory of atomism, one of the extremely small particles which are not capable of division, out of which the entire universe is composed.

at'ŏm·bomb″ (-bom″), *n.* an atomic bomb: also *atom bomb.*

at'ŏm·bomb″, *v.t* to attack or destroy with atomic bombs.

ȧ·tom'iç, ȧ·tom'iç·ăl, *a.* 1. pertaining to an atom or atoms, atomic bombs, the energy in the atom, etc.

2. separated into atoms.
3. very small; tiny; minute.

Ȧ·tom'iç Āġe, the period characterized by the use of atomic energy: regarded as beginning with the creation of the first self-maintaining nuclear chain reaction on December 2, 1942.

ȧ·tom'i·căl·ly, *adv.* in an atomic way; specifically, (a) into atoms or very small particles; (b) by atomic energy.

ȧ·tom'iç bomb (bom), an extremely destructive type of bomb, the power of which results from the immense quantity of energy suddenly released when a chain reaction of nuclear fission is set off by neutron bombardment in the atoms of a charge of plutonium or of the uranium isotope which has an atomic weight of 235 (U235): first used in warfare (1945) by the United States against the Japanese cities of Hiroshima and Nagasaki.

ȧ·tom'iç en'ẽr·ġy, the energy released from an atom in nuclear reactions; especially, the energy released in nuclear fission.

at·ō·mic'i·ty, *n.* 1. the condition of being made up of atoms.

2. in chemistry, (a) the number of atoms in a molecule; (b) the number of replaceable atoms or groups of atoms in the molecule of a compound; (c) valence.

ȧ·tom'iç num'bẽr, in chemistry, a number representing the relative position of an element in the periodic table, in which the elements are arranged in the order of either their atomic weights or their nuclear charges; a number representing the positive charge or the number of protons in the nucleus of the atom of an element: isotopes have the same atomic numbers but different atomic weights.

ȧ·tom'iç struç'tūre, in physics, a conventionalized, hypothetical concept of an atom, regarded as consisting of a central, positively charged nucleus and a number of negatively charged electrons revolving about it in various orbits: the number and arrangement of the electrons vary in the different elements.

ȧ·tom'iç thē'ō·ry, the theory that all material objects and substances are composed of atoms: see *atom.*

ȧ·tom'iç vol'ūme, in chemistry, the quotient obtained by dividing the atomic weight of an element by its specific gravity.

ȧ·tom'iç weight, in chemistry, a number representing the weight of one atom of an element as compared with an arbitrarily selected number representing the weight of one atom of another element taken as the standard (usually oxygen at 16).

at'ŏm·işm, *n.* [*atom,* and *-ism.*] the theory that the universe is made up of tiny, simple particles that cannot be destroyed or divided.

at'ŏm·ist, at″ŏm·is'tiç, *a.* of atomism or atomists.

at'ŏm·ist, *n.* one who believes in atomism.

at″ŏm·i·zā'tion, *n.* an atomizing or being atomized.

at'ŏm·īze, *v.t.*; atomized, *pt., pp.*; atomizing, *ppr.* 1. to separate into atoms.

2. to reduce a liquid to a fine spray.

at'ŏm·ī·zẽr, *n.* 1. one who atomizes.

2. a device for breaking a liquid, especially a medicine or perfume, into very small particles and spraying these out.

ATOMIZER

at·ŏm·ol'ō·ġy, *n.* the doctrine of atoms.

at'ŏm·y, *n.*; *pl.* **at'ŏm·ieş,** 1. an atom.

2. a pygmy.

at'ŏm·y, *n.*; *pl.* **at'ŏm·ieş,** [*anatomy,* separated into *an atomy.*] a skeleton. [Archaic.]

ȧ·tōn'ȧ·ble, *a.* capable of being atoned for.

ā·tōn'ăl, *a.* [*a-,* priv., and *tonal.*] having atonality; lacking tone.

ā·tōn'ăl·işm, *n.* the use or theory of atonality in composing music.

ā·tō·nal'i·ty, *n.* [*a-,* priv., and *tonality.*] in music, lack of tonality through intentional disregard of key.

ȧ·tōne', *v.i.*; atoned, *pt., pp.*; atoning, *ppr.* [ME. *attone, atoon, aton, at one,* at one, agreed.]

1. to make amends or reparation (*for* wrongdoing, a wrongdoer, etc.).
2. to be in agreement. [Obs.]

ȧ·tōne', *v.t.* 1. to expiate. [Obs.]

2. to harmonize. [Obs.]

ȧ·tōne'ment, *n.* 1. agreement; concord; reconciliation after enmity or controversy. [Obs.]

2. an atoning.
3. expiation; satisfaction or reparation given for an offense, injury, etc.: with *for.*
4. [A–] in theology, (a) the effect of Jesus' sufferings and death in redeeming mankind and bringing about the reconciliation of God to man; (b) this reconciliation.

ȧ·tōn'ẽr, *n.* one who makes atonement.

ȧ·ton'iç, *a.* [Gr. *atonos,* not stretched; *a* priv., and *tonos,* from *teinein,* to stretch.]

1. caused by or characteristic of atony.
2. unaccented: said of a word or syllable.
3. in phonetics, lenis. [Rare.]

ȧ·ton'iç, *n.* 1. an unaccented word or syllable.

2. in phonetics, a lenis consonant. [Rare.]

at'ō·ny, *n.* [Fr. *atonie*; L. *atonia*; Gr. *atonia,* languor; *a* priv., and *teinein,* to stretch.]

1. lack of bodily tone; weakness of the body or of a muscle or an organ.
2. in phonetics, lack of accent or stress.

ȧ·top', *prep.* on the top of.

ȧ·top', *adv.* and *a.* on or at the top.

-ā·tor, [L. *-ator,* in which *-tor,* an agency suffix is added to stems in *-a* of the first conjugation.] a suffix signifying the doer, agent, actor, as in cre*ator,* liber*ator,* educ*ator.*

-ȧ·to·ry, [L. *-atorius,* a compound suffix in which *-ius* is added to nouns in *-ator.*] a suffix signifying *of* or *pertaining to, of the nature of, produced by,* as in accus*atory,* exclam*atory,* declam*atory.*

à toute force (á tọọt), [Fr., with all force.] certainly; by all means.

at″rȧ·bi·lā'ri·ăn, *n.* a melancholy person.

at″rȧ·bi·lā'ri·ous, at″rȧ·bi·lā'ri·ăn, *a.* [L. *atrabilarius,* from *atra bilis,* black bile.] affected with melancholy, which the ancients attributed to the black bile; atrabilious.

at″rȧ·bi·lā'ri·ous·ness, *n.* the state of being melancholy, or atrabilious.

at·rȧ·bil'iăr (-yăr), *a.* atrabilious.

at·rȧ·bil'iȧ·ry (-yȧ-ry), *a.* in medicine, (a) of or relating to black bile; (b) pertaining to or designating certain renal organs; as, the *atrabiliary* capsules or blood vessels.

at·rȧ·bil'ious (-yus), *a.* 1. melancholy or morose: from the supposed preponderance of black bile.

2. hypochondriac.

at·raç·teñ′çhy·må, *n.* [L., from Gr. *atraktos*, a spindle, and *enchyma*, infusion.] vegetable tissue consisting of spindle-shaped cells.

at·rå·men′tăl, at·rå·men′tous, *a.* [L. *atramentum*, black ink, from *ater*, black.] inky; black, like ink.

at·rēde′, *v.t.* to excel in council. [Obs.]

å·trem′ble, *a.* trembling.

at·ren′, *v.t.* to outrun. [Obs.]

å·trē′si·å, (-shi-å), *n.* [L., from Gr. *atrētos*, not perforated; *a* priv., and *trētos*, from *tetrainein*, to perforate.] absence or abnormal constriction of any natural passage of the body.

Ā′treus (-troos), *n.* [L.; Gr. *Atreus*.] in Greek legend, a king of Mycenae, son of Pelops and father of Agamemnon and Menelaus: to avenge the treachery of his brother, Thyestes, who seduced his wife and planned his murder, Atreus killed Thyestes' sons and served their flesh to him at a banquet.

ā′tri·å, *n.*, pl. of *atrium*.

ā′tri·ăl, *a.* in anatomy, of or pertaining to an atrium.

å·triçh′i·å, *n.* loss of the hair, especially of the head; baldness.

ā′tri·ō-, a combining form used in anatomical and medical terms to denote some relation to an atrium, as in *atrio*ventricular.

ā·tri·op′ō·răl, *a.* pertaining to the atrial pore.

ā′tri·ō·pōre, *n.* [*atrio-*, and Gr. *poros*, a passage.] the atrial pore.

å·trip′, *adv.* in nautical language, said of an anchor just raised clear of the bottom. Sails are *atrip* when they are sheeted home, and ready for trimming. Yards are *atrip* when hoisted up, ready to have the stops cut for crossing; an upper mast is said to be *atrip* when the fid is loosed.

At′ri·plex, *n.* [L., from Gr. *atraphaxys*, an orach.] a genus of plants, order *Chenopodiaceæ*. They are mealy or scaly herbs or shrubs, with small unisexual flowers.

ā′tri·um, *n.*; *pl.* **ā′tri·å, ā′tri·umș,** [L.]
1. the central court or main room of an ancient Roman house, generally ornamented with statues and pictures.
2. a hall or court in front of the entrance of certain ancient temples.
3. in anatomy, a chamber or cavity, especially an auricle of the heart.
4. in zoology, the large chamber into which the intestine opens in the *Tunicata*.

at′rō·çhå, *n.* [L., from Gr. *a* priv., and *trochos*, a wheel, from *trechein*, to run.] the larva, or embryo, of a chaetopod worm, in which the cilia are spread over the body and do not appear in distinct rings.

at′rō·çhous, at′rō·çhăl, *a.* pertaining to or like the atrocha.

å·trō′cious, *a.* [L. *atrox*, fierce, cruel, from *ater*, black.]
1. extremely brutal or cruel; outrageously wicked; evil.
2. very bad; in bad taste; abominable; as, an *atrocious* dress. [Colloq.]
3. very grievous; violent; as, *atrocious* symptoms. [Obs.]

Syn.—outrageous, flagitious, monstrous, villainous, flagrant, heinous, wicked, cruel.

å·trō′cious·ly, *adv.* in an atrocious manner.

å·trō′cious·ness, *n.* the state or quality of being atrocious; atrocity.

å·troc′i·ty, *n.* [Fr. *atrocité*; L. *atrocitas*, from *atrox*, *atrocis*, cruel; *ater*, black.]
1. enormous wickedness; extreme cruelty.
2. a specific act of extreme cruelty.

The *atrocities* committed in that holy name. —De Quincey.

3. a thing in very bad taste; a very displeasing thing; as, that picture's an *atrocity*. [Colloq.]

At′rō·på, *n.* [L., from Gr. *Atropos*, one of the Fates, who cut the thread of life, unchangeable; from *a* priv., and *trepein*, to turn.] a genus of poisonous plants, of the order *Solanaceæ*. *Atropa belladonna*, or deadly nightshade, has a shining black berry like a cherry enclosed in the permanent calyx.

at′rō·păl, *a.* in botany, erect; orthotropous: said of an ovule.

å·troph′iç, *a.* pertaining to or affected with atrophy.

at′rō·phied (-fid), *a.* affected with atrophy; wasting or wasted away.

at′rō·phy, *n.* [Fr. *atrophie*; L. *atrophia*; Gr. *atrophia*, a wasting away; *a* priv., and *trephein*, to nourish.] a wasting away, especially of body tissue, an organ, etc., or the failure of an organ or part to grow because of insufficient nourishment.

at′rō·phy, *v.t.*; atrophied, *pt.*, *pp.*; atrophying, *ppr.* to cause to be wasted away.

at′rō·phy, *v.i.* to waste away; to fail to grow.

å·trō′pi·å, *n.* same as *atropin*.

at′rō·pine, at′rō·pin, *n.* [Gr. *atropos*, inflexible; *a* priv., and *trepein*, to turn.] a crystalline alkaloid, $C_{17}H_{23}NO_3$, obtained from the deadly nightshade, *Atropa belladonna*. It is very poisonous and is used to dilate the pupil of the eye and to relieve spasms.

at′rō·pișm *n.* poisoning resulting from the improper use of atropine.

At′rŏ·pos, *n.* [L.; Gr. *Atropos*, lit., not to be turned, from *a-*, not, and *trepein*, to turn.] in Greek mythology, that one of the three Fates who is represented as cutting the thread of life.

at′rō·pous, *a.* same as *atropal*.

ā′trous, *a.* [L. *ater*, black.] intensely black.

A·trȳ′på, *n.* [L., from Gr. *a* priv., and *trypa*, a hole.] an extinct genus of brachiopods, having rigid branchial appendages spirally coiled toward the center of the shell, the shell substance being fibrous and impunctate.

at′tå·bal, *n.* same as *atabal*.

åt·tăç′çå, [It., imper. of *attaccare*, to tie, bind.] in music, a direction which denotes that the next movement is to follow immediately, without any pause.

at·tach′, *v.t.*; attached (-tacht′), *pt.*, *pp.*; attaching, *ppr.* [Fr. *attacher*, to tie, fasten; *a*, L. *ad*, to, and Breton *tach*, a nail.]
1. to cause to adhere; to tie, bind, or fasten; as, to *attach* one thing to another by a string, by glue, etc.
2. to connect; to associate; as, to *attach* great importance to a particular circumstance.
3. to lay hold of; to seize. [Obs.]

Then, homeward, every man *attach* the hand
Of his fair mistress. —Shak.

4. to add (*to*) or affix, as a signature.
5. to ascribe (with *to*); as, I attach great significance to the news.
6. to appoint by authority or order.
7. in law, to take (property, etc.) by legal authority; also, to arrest (a person).
8. to take, seize, and lay hold of, by ties of affection, attraction, etc.; as, his kindness *attached* us all to him.
9. in military usage, to join (troops, a unit, etc.) temporarily to some other unit.

Syn.—add, affix, append, annex, connect, fasten, fix, stick, tack.

at·tach′, *v.i.* to be attached or connected; to be joined or fastened; to belong.

at·tach′, *n.* attachment. [Obs.]

at·tach′å·ble, *a.* capable of being attached, legally or otherwise.

at·tȧ·ché′ (å-tå-shā′), *n.* [Fr., pp. of *attacher*, to attach.] one attached to another, as attendant or a part of his suite; specifically, a member of the diplomatic staff of an ambassador or minister to another country.

at·tach′ment, *n.* 1. the act of attaching or the state of being attached.
2. close affection; devotion; regard; as, an *attachment* to a friend, or to a party.
3. that by which one thing or person is attached to another; as, to cut the *attachments* of a muscle.
4. anything added or attached.
5. some accessory for an instrument, machine, or other object; as, attachments for a vacuum cleaner.
6. in law, (a) the taking of a person, goods, or estate into custody; (b) the writ directing such action.

foreign attachment; the taking of the money or goods of a debtor in the hands of a third person, considered in law as the agent, attorney, factor, or trustee of the debtor, as when the debtor is not within the jurisdiction of the court.

Syn.—adherence, fondness, affection, inclination, bond, tie, adjunct, appendage.

at·tack′, *v.t.*; attacked (-takt′), *pt.*, *pp.*; attacking, *ppr.* [Fr. *attaquer*, to attack; another form of *attacher*, to fasten, join; *a*, L. *ad*, to, and Breton *tach*, a nail.]
1. to use force against in order to harm; to start a fight or quarrel with; to take the offensive against; to assault.
2. to begin a fight against with unfriendly words or writing; to begin a controversy with; to attempt to bring into disrepute, by satire or criticism; as, to *attack* a man or his opinions in the newspapers.
3. to begin to perform energetically; to undertake vigorously; as, to *attack* a piece of work.
4. to begin to destroy or affect injuriously; as, he was *attacked* by malaria; restlessness *attacked* the community; sulfuric acid *attacks* zinc vigorously.

Syn.—encounter, assail, assault, charge, invade, fall upon.

at·tack′, *v.i.* to make an assault; as, to *attack* methodically.

at·tack′, *n.* 1. the act of attacking.
2. any hostile offensive action, especially with armed forces; also, a body of troops making such action.
3. the beginning of any action or undertaking; the start; the entering upon a piece of work.
4. the act or manner of such beginning.
5. an onset or occurrence of a disease.
6. destructive action, as by a chemical agent.

Syn.—assault, invasion, onset, inroad, charge.

at·tack′å·ble, *a.* open to attack; assailable.

at·tack′ĕr, *n.* one who attacks.

at′tȧ·gen, at′tȧ·gas, *n.* [L. *attagena*, from Gr. *attagen*, *attagas*, a bird.] any of various European birds, as the common partridge.

at′tȧ·ghan, *n.* same as *yataghan*.

at·tāin′, *v.i.*; attained (-tānd′), *pt.*, *pp.*; attaining, *ppr.* [ME. *attainen*, *atteinen*; OFr. *ataindre*; L. *attingere*, to touch upon, attain; *ad*, to, and *tangere*, to touch.] to come or arrive by motion, bodily exertion, or effort toward a place, object, etc.; also, to reach a goal: usually with *to*.

at·tāin′, *v.t.* 1. to gain through effort; to achieve or accomplish.

Is he wise who hopes to *attain* the end without the means! —Tillotson.

2. to reach or come to; to arrive at.

But ere such tidings shall his ears *attain*. —Hoole's Tasso.

3. to reach in excellence or degree; to equal. [Obs.]
4. to ascertain; to get possession of. [Obs.]
5. to overtake. [Obs.]

Syn.—accomplish, acquire, compass, procure, achieve, reach, gain, get, earn, win.

at·tāin′, *n.* attainment. [Obs.]

at·tāin·å·bil′i·ty, *n.* attainableness.

at·tāin′å·ble, *a.* capable of being attained.

at·tāin′å·ble·ness, *n.* the quality of being attainable.

at·tāin′dĕr, *n.* [ME. *attayndere*; OFr. *ataindre*, *ateindre*, to accuse, convict, from L. *attingere*; *ad*, to, and *tangere*, to touch, attain.]
1. the act of attainting or state of being attainted; the legal consequences of judgment of death or outlawry pronounced for being sentenced for a treason or felony. By English common law, the attainder formerly brought the consequences of forfeiture of lands, tenements, and hereditary rights, and loss of civil rights generally: see *bill of attainder*.
2. a disgracing; a state of being in dishonor. [Obs.]

at·tāin′ment, *n.* 1. the act of attaining; the act of arriving at or reaching by effort; as, the *attainment* of excellence.
2. that which is attained, as an acquired skill or accomplishment; as, a man of great *attainments*.

at·tāint′, *v.t.*; attainted, *pt.*, *pp.*; attainting, *ppr.* [ME. *atayntеn*, *atteinten*, to convict; OFr. *ateint*, pp. of *ateindre*, from L. *attingere*; *ad*, to, and *tangere*, to touch, fasten.]
1. to condemn to attainder; to find guilty of a crime, as of felony or treason, involving forfeiture of civil privileges.
2. to convict; to prove guilty. [Obs.]
3. to disgrace; to taint or stain.
4. to infect, as with some noxious quality. [Rare.]
5. to make a charge of crime or misconduct against; to accuse. [Archaic.]
6. to touch. [Obs.]

at·tāint′, *n.* 1. a taint; dishonor; especially some mark of personal dishonor or social corruption.
2. an attainder.
3. a blow or wound on the legs or feet of a horse, from overreaching.
4. the conviction of a jury for the rendering of a false verdict; also, a writ issued after such conviction, reversing the original verdict.

at·tāint′ment, *n.* the state of being attainted, or the act of attainting; conviction; attainder.

at·tāin′tūre, *n.* attaintment; attainder.

At·tā′lē·å, *n.* [L., from Gr. *Attalos*, a king of Pergamum.] a genus of palms allied to the coconut palm, found in tropical America. One species, *Attalea funifera*, yields a valuable fiber, the piassava.

at·tāme′, *v.t.* 1. to begin. [Obs.]
2. to make an incision into. [Obs.]

at·tam′i·nāte, *v.t.* to contaminate. [Obs.]
at′tap, *n.* [Malay.] the nipa palm.
at′tăr, *n.* [Pers. *'atar,* fragrance, from Ar. *'atara,* to smell sweet.] a highly fragrant essential oil or perfume obtained from flowers, especially from the petals of roses; also called *ottar,* or *otto.*
attar of roses; a fragrant oil made from the petals of roses, especially damask roses.
at·tȧsk′, *v.t.* to take to task; to reprove. [Obs.]
at·tāste′, *v.t.* to taste. [Obs.]
at′tē, at the: an obsolete contraction.
at·tem′pẽr, *v.t.;* attempered, *pt., pp.;* attempering, *ppr.* [ME. *attempren;* OFr. *atemprer;* L. *attemperare,* to fit, adjust; *ad,* to, and *temperare,* to control, moderate.]
1. to reduce, modify, or moderate by mixture; as, to *attemper* heat by a cooling mixture, or liquors by diluting with water.
2. to control the temperature of.
3. to soften, mollify, or moderate; to temper; as, to *attemper* rigid justice with clemency.
4. to mix in just proportion; to regulate; as, a mind well *attempered* with kindness and justice.
5. to accommodate; to fit or make suitable (*to*).
Acts *attempered* to the lyre. —Pope.
at·tem′pẽr·ȧ·ment, *n.* a regulating or mixing in proper proportion.
at·tem′pẽr·ănce, *n.* temperance. [Obs.]
at·tem′pẽr·āte, *a.* temperate; moderate. [Obs.]
Hope must be proportioned and *attemperate* to the promise. —Hammond.
at·tem′pẽr·āte, *v.t.* to attemper. [Obs.]
at·tem·pẽr·ā′tion, *n.* the act of attemperating, adjusting, or accommodating. [Obs.]
at·tem′pẽr·ly, *adv.* in a temperate manner. [Obs.]
at·tem′pẽr·ment, *n.* attemperament.
at·tempt′, *v.t.;* attempted, *pt., pp.;* attempting, *ppr.* [OFr. *atempter, atenter;* It. *attentare;* L. *attemptare, attentare,* to try, solicit; *ad,* to, and *temptare, tentare,* to try, attack.]
1. to try to do; to try to get; to try; to endeavor; to undertake; as, to *attempt* to sing; to *attempt* a bold flight.
2. to attack; to try to take by force; as, to *attempt* the enemy's camp.
3. to make a trial or experiment of; to venture upon; as, to *attempt* the wilderness.
4. to make an assault upon the feelings or passions of; to try to win or seduce; to tempt. [Archaic.]
He will never *attempt* us again. —Shak.
Syn.—try, endeavor, essay, undertake, strive.
at·tempt′, *v.i.* to make an attack; to make an attempt. [Obs.]
at·tempt′, *n.* 1. a try, trial, or endeavor; an effort to gain a point.
The *attempt,* and not the deed, confounds us. —Shak.
2. an attack or assault; an endeavor to gain a point by force or violence; as, an *attempt* upon one's life.
Syn.—effort, endeavor, essay, trial, enterprise, undertaking.
at·tempt′ȧ·ble, *a.* able to be attempted, tried, or attacked; liable to an attempt, or attack.
at·tempt′ẽr, *n.* one who attempts or attacks.
at·tempt′ive, *a.* inclined to make attempts; willing to venture. [Obs.]
at·tend′, *v.t.;* attended, *pt., pp.;* attending, *ppr.* [OFr. *atendre,* to wait, expect; It. *attendere;* L. *attendere,* to stretch toward, give heed to; *ad,* to, and *tendere,* to stretch.]
1. to go with or accompany, as a companion or servant.
2. to serve professionally; to wait on; to watch over or care for; as, a physician *attends* the sick.
3. to accompany as a circumstance or result; to be consequent to, from connection of cause; as, fever *attends* a cold; a measure *attended* with ill effects.
4. to be present at; as, lawyers or spectators *attend* a court.
5. to await; to remain, abide, or be in store for; as, happiness or misery *attends* us after death. [Archaic.]
6. to listen to; to give attention to. [Archaic.]
7. to wait for; to expect. [Obs.]
Syn.—accompany, escort, serve, wait upon.
at·tend′, *v.i.* 1. to exercise attention; to pay heed.
Attend to the voice of my supplications. —Ps. lxxxvi. 6.
2. to be present; to be in readiness; to wait: followed by *on* or *upon;* as, to *attend upon* a committee.
3. to stay; to wait; to delay. [Obs.]
For this perfection she must yet *attend,*
Till to her Maker she espoused be. —Davies.
Syn.—heed, listen, give regard to, observe.
at·tend′ănce, *n.* [ME. *attendaunce;* OFr. *atendance;* L. *attendantia,* from *attendens(-entis),* ppr. of *attendere,* to stretch toward, give heed; *ad,* to, and *tendere,* to stretch.]
1. the act of attending.
2. a being present on business of any kind; presence; as, the *attendance* of witnesses in court.
3. the number of persons attending a meeting, game, etc.
4. a train; a retinue.
5. attention; regard. [Obs.]
6. expectation. [Obs.]
at·tend′ăn·cy, *n.* attendance. [Obs.]
at·tend′ănt, *a.* [Fr. *attendant,* ppr. of *attendre,* to wait, from L. *attendere,* to give heed; *ad,* to, and *tendere,* to stretch.]
1. being present on a given occasion.
2. attending or serving; as, an *attendant* nurse.
3. accompanying, connected with, or immediately following; consequential; as, intemperance with all its *attendant* evils.
4. in law, depending on or owing duty or service to.
at·tend′ănt, *n.* 1. one who attends or accompanies, as a friend, companion, or servant.
2. one who is present; as, an *attendant* at or upon a meeting.
3. in law, one who owes duty or service to, or depends on another.
4. that which accompanies.
A love of fame, the *attendant* of noble spirits. —Pope.
at·tend′ẽr, *n.* one who attends.
at·tend′ment, *n.* an accompanying circumstance. [Obs.]
at·tent′, *a.* attentive. [Archaic.]
at·tent′, *n.* attention; as, due *attent.* [Obs.]
at·ten′tāte, at·ten′tat, *n.* [Fr. *attentat;* L. *attentatum,* a crime, from *attentare,* to attempt; *ad,* to, and *tentare,* to try, attack.]
1. an assault. [Obs.]
2. in law, an improper proceeding in a court of justice, pending appeal.
at·ten′tion, *n.* 1. the act of attending or heeding.
They say, the tongues of dying men
Enforce *attention* like deep harmony. —Shak.
2. the ability to give heed or observe carefully.
3. careful observation; heed; notice.
4. thoughtful consideration for others.
5. an act of civility, courtesy, or consideration; as, he paid her very marked *attention.*
6. in military science, (a) the erect, motionless posture of soldiers in readiness for another command; (b) a command to assume this posture.
7. in psychology, a readiness to respond to stimuli.
Syn.—application, heed, consideration, study, watchfulness.
at·ten′tive, *a.* 1. heedful; intent; observant; regarding with care.
2. characterized by thoughtful regard or attention; courteous; polite.
Syn.—careful, thoughtful, heedful, mindful, intent, observant, watchful.
at·ten′tive·ly, *adv.* heedfully; carefully; with attention.
at·ten′tive·ness, *n.* the state of being attentive; heed; attention.
at·tent′ly, *adv.* attentively. [Obs.]
at·ten′ū·ȧ·ble, *a.* that can be attenuated.
at·ten′ū·ănt, *a.* [Fr. *atténuant;* L. *attenuans,* ppr. of *attenuare,* to make thin.] making thin, as liquid; diluting.
at·ten′ū·ănt, *n.* in medicine, a substance that thins liquids.
at·ten′ū·āte, *v.t.;* attenuated, *pt., pp.;* attenuating, *ppr.* [L. *attenuatus,* pp. of *attenuare,* to make thin; *ad,* to, and *tenuare,* from *tenuis,* thin.]
1. to make thin or slender.
2. to dilute; to rarefy.
3. to lessen or weaken in severity, value, etc.
4. in bacteriology, to make (a virus, etc.) less deadly.
at·ten′ū·āte, *v.i.* to become thin, slender, or fine; to diminish; to weaken.
at·ten′ū·āte, at·ten′ū·ā·ted, *a.* 1. made thin or less viscid; also, made slender.
2. in botany, growing slender toward an extremity.
at·ten·ū·ā′tion, *n.* [L. *attenuatio,* from *attenuare,* to make thin.]
1. the act of making thin, as fluids or gases.
2. the act of making fine by pulverization, as of rocks.
3. the act or process of making slender, thin, or lean.
4. the act or process of lessening in intensity or virulence, as of a virus.
5. in brewing, the change which takes place in the worts during fermentation.
at·ten′ū·ā·tŏr, a person or thing that attenuates.
at′tẽr, *n.* [AS. *ættor,* poison.] poison; venom. [Obs.]
at′tẽr·çop, *n.* [ME. *attercop;* AS. *attercoppe; ator,* poison, and *cop,* head, lungs.]
1. a spider. [Obs.]
2. an ill-natured person. [Prov. Eng.]
at·tẽr′mi·năl, *a.* same as *adterminal.*
at′tẽr·rāte, *v.t.;* atterrated, *pt., pp.;* atterrating, *ppr.* [L. *atterratus,* pp. of *atterrare,* to carry earth to another place; *ad,* to, and *terra,* earth.] to form or fill up with alluvial earth. [Obs.]
at·tẽr·rā′tion, *n.* the act of atterrating. [Obs.]
at·test′, *v.t.;* attested, *pt., pp.;* attesting, *ppr.* [Fr. *attester,* from L. *attestari,* to bear witness to; *ad,* to, and *testis,* a witness.]
1. to bear witness to; to certify; to declare to be true or genuine; to make a solemn declaration, in speech or writing, for the support of; as, to *attest* the truth of a writing; to *attest* a copy of record.
2. to support the truth of; to demonstrate; to make clear; as, the ruins of Palmyra *attest* its ancient magnificence.
3. to place (a person) on oath.
Streams which heaven's imperial state
Attests in oaths, and fears to violate. —Dryden.
at·test′, *n.* witness; testimony; attestation.
at·test′ănt, *a.* that attests; attesting.
at·test′ănt, *n.* one who attests.
at·tes·tā′tion, *n.* testimony; a solemn or official declaration, oral or written, in support of a fact; evidence.
at·test′ȧ·tive, *a.* serving to attest or corroborate.
at·test′ẽr, at·test′ŏr, *n.* one who attests.
at·test′ive, *a.* giving attestation; attesting.
At′tiç, *a.* [L. *Atticus;* Gr. *Attikos.*]
1. pertaining to Attica, in Greece, or to its principal city, Athens.
2. marked by such qualities as were characteristic of the Athenians; hence, classical, simple, etc.
Attic base; a style of base used by the ancient architects in the Ionic and Corinthian orders.
Attic faith; inviolable faith.
Attic order; an order of small square pillars placed by Athenian architects at the uppermost parts of a building.
Attic wit, Attic salt; graceful, piercing wit.
At′tiç, *n.* 1. the Greek dialect of Attica, a state of ancient Greece.
2. an Athenian.
at′tiç, *n.* [Fr. *attique;* It. *attico,* an attic; from L. *Atticus,* Attic.]
1. a low story or wall erected over the cornice of a classical façade, generally decorated with pilasters and a cornice, but having neither capital nor base.
2. a room or rooms in the upper part of a house, immediately beneath the roof; a garret.

ATTIC
A, attic in classical architecture

At′tiç·ăl, *a.* same as *Attic.*
At′ti·çism, at′ti·çism, *n.* [Gr. *Attikismos,* from *Attikos,* Attic.]
1. anything typical of Attic Greek.
2. refined and elegant speech; concise and elegant expression.
3. a particular attachment to or taking the part of the Athenians: specifically applied to

the act of siding with the Athenians during the Peloponnesian War.

At′ti·cīze, *v.t.*; Atticized, *pt., pp.*; Atticizing, *ppr.* to make conform to the language, style, idiom, customs, etc. of Attica: written also *atticize.*

At′ti·cīze, at′ti·cīze, *v.i.* 1. to use Attic dialect or literary style.
 2. to side with the Athenians.

at·tig′ū·ous, *a.* [L. *attiguus,* from *attingere,* to touch.] near; adjoining; contiguous. [Obs.]

at·tig′ū·ous·ness, *n.* the state of being attiguous. [Obs.]

at·tinġe′, *v.t.* [L. *attingere,* to touch.] to touch lightly. [Obs.]

at·tīre′, *v.t.*; attired, *pt., pp.*; attiring, *ppr.* [ME. *atiren*; OFr. *atirer,* put in order, arrange, from *a tire,* in a row, in order; *a,* L. *ad,* to, and *tire,* order, row, dress.] to dress; to array; to adorn; especially, to adorn with elegant or splendid garments.
 With the linen mitre shall he be *attired.*
 —Lev. xvi. 4.

at·tīre′, *n.* 1. dress; clothes; especially, rich, ornamental dress.
 Can a bride forget her *attire?* —Jer. ii. 32.
 2. in heraldry, the antlers of stags and similar animals.
 3. in botany, the stamens of a flower. [Obs.]

at·tīred′, *a.* in heraldry, provided with antlers.

at·tīre′ment, *n.* attire.

at·tīr′ẽr, *n.* one who attires, or dresses.

at′ti·tūde, *n.* [Fr. *attitude*; It. *attitudine,* attitude, aptness; L. *aptitudo,* from *aptus,* fitted, from *apere,* to fasten, join.]
 1. the posture or position of a person showing or meant to show a mental state, emotion, or mood.
 2. the manner of acting, feeling, or thinking that shows one's disposition, opinion, etc.; as, a threatening *attitude,* an *attitude* of entreaty.
 3. one's disposition, opinion, etc.
 4. in aeronautics, the position of an aircraft in relation to a given point of reference, usually on the ground level.
 5. in painting and sculpture, the posture, disposition, or action in which a figure is placed.
 to strike an attitude; to assume a posture or pose, often an affected or theatrical one.
 Syn.—situation, standing, position, posture, pose.

at·ti·tū′di·năl, *a.* pertaining to attitude.

at·ti·tū·di·nā′ri·ăn, *n.* one who gives particular attention to attitudes.

at·ti·tū·di·nā′ri·ăn·ism, *n.* the practice of using studied or affected attitudes.

at·ti·tū′di·nīze, *v.i.*; attitudinized, *pt., pp.*; attitudinizing, *ppr.* to practice or assume attitudes.
 They had the air of figurantes, *attitudinizing* for effect. —De Quincey.

at·ti·tū′di·nī·zẽr, *n.* one who poses.

at′tle, *n.* [Corn., refuse, waste.] in mining, refuse containing no ore worth extraction.

at·tŏnce′, *adv.* at once; at the same time. [Obs.]

at·tŏrn′, *v.t.*; attorned, *pt., pp.*; attorning, *ppr.* [OFr. *attorner*; L. *attornare,* to commit business to another; *ad,* to, and *tornare,* to turn.] in law, to turn over; to assign to another; to transfer.

at·tŏrn′, *v.i.* 1. in feudal law, to transfer homage or service to a new possessor.
 2. to continue as tenant under a new landlord.

at·tŏr′ney, *n.* [ME. *atturny*; OFr. *attorne, atorne*; L. *attornatus,* pp. of *attornare,* to commit business to another.] one who is legally appointed by another to act for him; especially, a lawyer. An *attorney* is either public or private. A *private attorney* is a person appointed by another, by a letter or power of attorney, to transact any business for him out of court. A *public attorney,* or attorney at law, is an officer of a court of law, legally qualified to prosecute and defend actions in such court, on the retainer of clients or order of the court. In Great Britain, attorneys are not admitted to plead at the bar, this being the duty of barristers.
 power or *letter of attorney*; a written authority from one person empowering another to act for him.

at·tŏr′ney, *v.t.* to perform by proxy; to employ as a proxy. [Obs.]

at·tŏr′ney at law, a lawyer.

at·tŏr′ney ġen′ẽr·ăl; *pl.* **at·tŏr′ney ġen′ẽr·ăls** or **at·tŏr′neys ġen′ẽr·ăl,** 1. the highest officer of the law of a State or national government: he is the legal adviser of the chief executive.
 2. [A—G—] the head of the United States Department of Justice.

at·tŏr′ney·ism, *n.* shrewdness or unscrupulousness sometimes ascribed to attorneys.

at·tŏr′ney·ship, *n.* the office or duties of an attorney; agency for another.

at·tŏrn′ment, *n.* [OFr. *attornment,* from *attorner*; L. *attornare,* to commit business to another.] the act of a feudatory, vassal, or tenant, by which he consents, upon the alienation of an estate, to receive a new lord or superior, and transfers to him his homage and service.

at·tract′, *v.t.*; attracted, *pt., pp.*; attracting, *ppr.* [L. *attractus,* pp. of *attrahere,* to draw to; *ad,* to, and *trahere,* to draw.]
 1. to draw to or toward; to exert the power of attraction on; to make approach or adhere; as, a magnet *attracts* iron filings.
 2. to get the admiration, attention, etc. of; to invite or allure; to engage; as, beauty *attracts* people.
 Syn.—draw, allure, invite, entice.

at·tract′, *v.i.* to be attractive.

at·tract′, *n.* attraction. [Obs.]

at·tract·ȧ·bil′i·ty, *n.* the quality of being attractable or of being subject to the law of attraction. [Rare.]

at·tract′ȧ·ble, *a.* that may be attracted; subject to attraction. [Rare.]

at·tract′ȧ·ble·ness, *n.* the state or quality of being attractable. [Rare.]

at·tract′ẽr, *n.* same as *attractor.*

at·tract′ile, *a.* having the power to attract, or make approach.

at·tract′ing·ly, *adv.* in an attracting manner.

at·trac′tion, *n.* [L. *attractio,* from *attrahere,* to draw to; *ad,* to, and *trahere,* to draw.]
 1. in physics, the tendency, force, or forces through which particles, bodies, etc. are attracted or drawn toward each other; the inherent tendency in bodies to approach each other, to unite, and to resist separation: opposed to *repulsion.*
 2. the act of attracting; the effect of the principle of attraction.
 3. the power of alluring, drawing to, inviting, or engaging; as, the *attraction* of beauty or eloquence.
 4. charm; fascination.
 5. anything that attracts; as, plays and motion pictures are sometimes called *attractions.*
 chemical attraction or *affinity*; the force which is exerted between molecules not of the same kind, as when two molecules of hydrogen unite with one molecule of oxygen to form water.
 cohesive attraction; the force uniting adjacent molecules of the same nature; cohesion.
 magnetic, diamagnetic, and *electrical attraction*; similar attractive polar forces dependent upon certain conditions of matter.
 Syn.—allurement, charm, fascination, inclination, tendency.

at·trac′tion sphēre, in biology, the central area of an aster, including the centrosome: called also *centrosphere.*

at·tract′ive, *a.* [Fr. *attractif.*]
 1. having the power or quality of attracting; drawing to; as, the *attractive* force of bodies.
 2. pleasing; alluring; inviting; engaging; as, the *attractive* graces.

at·tract′ive, *n.* an attraction. [Obs.]

at·tract′ive·ly, *adv.* in an attractive manner.

at·tract′ive·ness, *n.* the quality of being attractive or engaging.

at·trac·tiv′i·ty, *n.* the attractive power of an object.

at·tract′ŏr, *n.* a person or thing that attracts.

at′tră·hent, *a.* [L. *attrahens,* ppr. of *attrahere,* to draw to; *ad,* to, and *trahere,* to draw.] drawing to; attracting.

at′tră·hent, *n.* 1. that which draws to or attracts, as a magnet.
 2. in medicine, a surface application that attracts action to the part where it is applied, as a rubefacient.

at·trap′, *v.t.* to clothe; to dress; to adorn with trappings. [Obs.]

at·trap′, *v.t.* [Fr. *attraper,* to trap, ensnare; *a,* L. *ad,* to, and *trappe,* trap.] to catch in a trap. [Obs.]

at·trec·tā′tion, *n.* [L. *attrectatio,* from *ad,* to, and *tractare,* to handle.] touching; handling. [Obs.]

at·trib′ū·tȧ·ble, *a.* capable of attribution.

at·trib′ūte, *v.t.*; attributed, *pt., pp.*; attributing, *ppr.* [L. *attributus,* pp. of *attribuere,* to assign; *ad,* to, and *tribuere,* to assign, give.] to consider as belonging to, produced by, or resulting from; to assign or ascribe (*to*).
 Faulty men use oftentimes
 To *attribute* their folly unto fate.
 —Spenser.
 Syn.—ascribe, impute, assign, refer, charge.

at′tri·būte, *n.* [L. *attributum,* attribute, predicate, from *attribuere,* to assign, ascribe.]
 1. any property, quality, or characteristic that can be ascribed to a person or thing; as, strength and bravery are two of his *attributes.*
 But mercy is above this sceptered sway; . . .
 It is an *attribute* to God himself. —Shak.
 2. in grammar, a word or phrase used as an adjective.
 3. an object used in literature or art as a symbol for a position, person, etc.; as, the eagle is the *attribute* of Jupiter, a club of Hercules, the bow and arrow of Love.
 The ladder is a striking *attribute* for the patriarch Jacob, and the harp for King David. —Fairholt.
 4. reputation; honor. [Obs.]
 Much *attribute* he hath; and much the reason
 Why we ascribe it to him. —Shak.
 Syn.—property, quality, characteristic.

at·tri·bū′tion, *n.* 1. the act of attributing.
 2. that which is attributed; attribute.
 3. commendation; praise. [Obs.]

at·trib′ū·tive, *a.* 1. pertaining to or expressing an attribute; as, an *attributive* word.
 2. in grammar, expressing a quality meant to apply to a following substantive: said of adjectives, and distinguished from *predicate* and *predicative.*

at·trib′ū·tive, *n.* in grammar, a modifier; an attributive word.

at·trib′ū·tive·ly, *adv.* in an attributive manner.

at·trīte′, *a.* [L. *attritus,* pp. of *atterere,* to wear, rub away; *ad,* to, and *terere,* to rub.]
 1. worn away by rubbing or friction. [Rare.]
 2. in theology, repentant only from fear of punishment.

at·tri′tion, (-trish′un), *n.* [Fr. *attrition*; L. *attritio,* a rubbing; from *attritus,* pp. of *atterere,* to rub, wear away.]
 1. abrasion; the act of wearing away by friction, or by rubbing substances together; as, the *attrition* of rocks.
 2. the state or process of being gradually worn down.
 3. any gradual wearing or weakening.
 4. in theology, grief for sin, arising only from fear of punishment; the lowest degree of repentance: distinguished from *contrition.*

at·trī′tus, *n.* finely ground or powdered matter resulting from attrition.

at·tūne′, *v.t.*; attuned, *pt., pp.*; attuning, *ppr.*
 1. to tune, or put in tune; as, to *attune* the voice to a harp.
 2. to make musical. [Obs.]
 Vernal airs *attune* the trembling leaves.
 —Milton.
 3. to bring into harmony or agreement.

ATV (ā′tē′vē′), *n.*; *pl.* **ATVs,** [*A*ll-*T*errain *V*ehicle.] a small, amphibious motor vehicle with wheels or tractor treads for traveling over rough ground, snow, ice, and water.

ȧ·twāin′, *adv.* in two; asunder. [Archaic or Poetic.]

ȧ·tween′, *adv.* and *prep.* between. [Archaic or Dial.]

ȧ·twirl′, *a.* and *adv.* twirling; in a twirl.

ȧ·twist′, *a.* and *adv.* awry; twisted.

ȧ·twixt′, *adv.* and *prep.* betwixt. [Dial.]

ā·typ′iç, ā·typ′iç·ăl, *a.* [Gr. *atypos*; *a* priv., and *typos,* type.] having no type; not typical; not characteristic; abnormal.

au (ō), [Fr., contr. of *à le*; *à,* to, and *le,* masc. form of def. art., the.] see *à la.*

Au, *aurum,* [L.] in chemistry, gold.

au·bȧde′ (ō-bȧd′), *n.* [Fr., from *aube,* dawn.] music suitable for performance in the morning: distinguished from *serenade.*

au·bāin′ (ō-bān′), *n.* [Fr., from L. *albanus,* an alien; *alibi,* elsewhere, and *-anus.*] an alien liable to *droit d'aubaine.*

au·bāine′ (ō-bān′), *n.* in French law, the disposition of the goods of a deceased alien.
 droit d'aubaine; in France prior to 1819, the king's right to the personal property of a deceased alien.

ạube, *n.* an alb. [Obs.]

au·berġe′ (ō-berzh′), *n.* [Fr.] an inn.

au′bẽr·ġine (*or* ō-ber-zhēn′), *n.* [Fr.] the eggplant or its fruit.

ạu′bŭrn, *a.* [ME. *auburne*; OFr. *auborne, alborne*; L. *alburnus,* from *albus,* white.] originally, whitish or flaxen-colored; now, reddish brown.

ạu·chē′ni·um, *n.* [L., from Gr. *auchēn*, neck.] in ornithology, the part of the neck nearest the back. [Rare.]

au çȯn·trāire′ (ō), [Fr.] on the contrary.

au çou·ränt′ (ō ko͞o-rän′), [Fr., lit., with the current.] fully informed; well acquainted with current matters; up-to-date.

ạuç′tā·ry, *n.* augmentation. [Obs.]

ạuç′tion, *n.* [L. *auctio*, an increasing, a public sale, from *augere*, to increase.]
1. a public sale of items, one by one, to the highest bidder, usually by a person licensed and authorized for the purpose.
2. the property sold or offered for sale at auction. [Obs.]
3. auction bridge.
4. the bidding in bridge.
auction bridge; a variety of the game of bridge in which the players bid for the privilege of naming the suit to be played as trump, or of playing "no trump." The declarer of the highest bid then plays with the dummy for a partner and scores toward game.
auction pinochle; a variety of pinochle in which the players bid for the privilege of naming the trump.
auction pitch; a game of cards in which the players bid for the privilege of pitching, or leading, trump.
Dutch auction; an auction in which a certain price is set and gradually lowered by the auctioneer until a bid is received, the first bidder becoming the buyer.

ạuç′tion, *v.t.* to sell at auction.
to put up at auction; to offer for sale at an auction.

ạuç′tion·ā·ry, *a.* pertaining to an auction or public sale. [Rare.]

ạuç·tion·eer′, *n.* one whose business it is to auction things; one licensed to sell property at public sale.

ạuç·tion·eer′, *v.t.*; auctioneered, *pt.*, *pp.*; auctioneering, *ppr.* to sell at auction.

Ạu′çū·bȧ, *n.* [Mod. L., from Japan. *aoki*, green, and *ba*, leaf.] a genus of plants of the dogwood family, natural order *Cornaceæ*, native to eastern Asia. They are branching shrubs, with smooth opposite leaves and small unisexual flowers. *Aucuba Japonica* is cultivated for its mass of glossy, leathery, green leaves mottled with yellow, and its coral-red berries.

ạu·dā′cious, *a.* [Fr. *audacieux*; L. *audacia*, from *audax*, bold, from *audere*, to be bold, to dare.]
1. bold; daring; reckless.
2. bold or daring; impudent; insolent.
3. committed with, or proceeding from, daring effrontery or contempt of law; as, an *audacious* crime.
Syn.—impudent, insolent, shameless, unabashed, daring, bold.

ạu·dā′cious·ly, *adv.* in an impudent manner; with excess of boldness.

ạu·dā′cious·ness, *n.* the quality of being audacious; impudence; audacity..

ạu·dac′i·ty, *n.* [L. *audax*, bold, from *audere*, to be bold, dare.]
1. boldness; daring spirit; venturesomeness.
The freedom and *audacity* necessary in the commerce of men. —Tatler.
2. audaciousness; presumptuous impudence; effrontery; as, arrogant *audacity*.
3. *pl.* **ạu·dac′i·tieṣ,** an audacious act or remark.
Syn.—boldness, effrontery, impudence, hardihood.

Ạu′de·ăn, Ạu′di·ăn, *n.* a follower of Audius, a Syrian of the fourth century A.D., who held that God had a body and that man was created in its image.

ạu′di-, same as *audio-*.

ạu·di·bil′i·ty, *n.* the capacity or condition of being audible.

ạu′di·ble, *a.* [L. *audibilis*, from *audire*, to hear.] that may be heard; loud enough to be heard; as, an *audible* voice.

ạu′di·ble·ness, *n.* the capacity or condition of being audible.

ạu′di·bly, *adv.* so as to be audible.

ạu′di·ence, *n.* [ME. *audience*; OFr. *audience*; L. *audientia*, a hearing, listening, from *audiens*, ppr. of *audire*, to hear.]
1. those assembled to hear and see a concert, play, etc.
2. those who listen to a radio program or view a televised program.
3. those who pay attention to what one writes or says; one's public.
4. the act or state of hearing.
5. an opportunity to have one's ideas heard; a hearing.
6. a formal interview with a person in high position, especially with a sovereign or the head of a government.
court of audience; an English ecclesiastical court formerly held before an archbishop: also written *audience court*.
in general audience; in public.
to give audience; to grant an interview.

ạu′di·ence çōurt, see *court of audience*, under *audience*.

ạu′di·ence ro͝om, a room in which formal interviews are held.

ạu′di·ent, *a.* [L. *audiens*, ppr. of *audire*, to hear.] listening; attentive; hearing.

ạu′dile, *a.* [from L. *audire*, to hear; and *-ile*.] auditory.

ạu′dile, *n.* in psychology, a person who relies mainly on his sense of hearing or whose imagery is chiefly in terms of sound.

ạu′di·ō, *a.* [from L. *audire*, to hear.]
1. in electricity, of frequencies corresponding to sound waves that can normally be heard by the human ear.
2. in television, designating or of the sound phase of a broadcast, as distinguished from the *video* (or picture) portion.

ạu′di·o-, ạu′di-, a combining form meaning *relating to hearing*, as in *audio*meter.

ạu′di·ō-frē′quen·cy, *a.* of the band of audible sound frequencies or corresponding electric current frequencies, about 20 to 20,000 cycles per second.

ạu′di·ō·gram″, *n.* a graph showing the percentage of hearing loss in a particular ear, as indicated by an audiometer.

ạu″di·ol′ō·ġy, *n.* the science of hearing; especially, the evaluation of hearing defects and the rehabilitation of those who have such defects.

ạu″di·om′e·tẽr, *n.* [L. *audire*, to hear, and *metrum*; Gr. *metron*, measure.] an instrument for determining the acuteness of hearing or the intensity of sounds.

ạu′di·on, *n.* in radio, an early type of three-electrode electron tube: a trade-mark (*Audion*).

ạu′di·ō-viṣ′ū·ăl āidṣ, motion pictures, lantern slides, phonograph records, and other materials except books, used in teaching.

ạu′di·phōne, *n.* [from L. *audire*, to hear; and *-phone*, after *telephone*.] a device for the hard of hearing that transmits sound to the auditory nerves through the bones of the head.

ạu′dit, *n.* [L. *auditus*, a hearing, from *audire*, to hear.]
1. an examination of an account or of accounts by proper officers or persons appointed for that purpose, who compare the charges with the vouchers, examine witnesses, and report the result.
2. the result of such an examination, or an account as adjusted by auditors.
3. a final statement of account.

ạu′dit, *v.t.* and *v.i.* 1. to examine and check (accounts, claims, etc.).
2. to attend (a college class or classes) as a listener receiving no credits.

ạu·di′tion (-dish′un), *n.* 1. the sense of hearing; something heard.
2. a hearing; particularly, a hearing to test the abilities, voice, etc. of a speaker, actor, or musician.

au·di′tion, *v.t.* to give an audition to.

au·di′tion, *v.i.* to perform in an audition.

au′di·tive, *a.* auditory. [Rare.]

ạu′di·tŏr, *n.* [L. *auditor*, a hearer, from *audire*, to hear.]
1. a hearer; one who listens, as to a lecture, concert, etc.
2. a person appointed and authorized to audit an account or accounts.
3. a person who audits classes.
4. a judicial hearer in an audience court.

ạu·di·tō′ri·ăl, *a.* auditory; also, relating to an auditor.

ạu·di·tō′ri·ly, *adv.* by means of hearing; through the sense of hearing.

ạu·di·tō′ri·um, *n.*; *pl.* **ạu·di·tō′ri·umṣ, ạu·di·tō′ri·ȧ,** [L. *auditorium*, neut. of *auditorius*, of or for hearing.]
1. in a church, public hall, and the like, the room where the audience sits.
2. an apartment in ancient monasteries for the reception of strangers.
3. a building or hall used for speeches, concerts, etc.

ạu′di·tŏr·ship, *n.* the position or office of an auditor.

ạu′di·tō·ry, *a.* [L. *auditorius*, from *auditor*, a hearer; *audire*, to hear.] relating to hearing or to the sense or organs of hearing.
auditory nerve; the eighth cranial nerve, supplying the internal ear.

ạu′di·tō·ry, *n.* 1. an assembly of hearers; audience.
2. an auditorium; especially, in ancient churches, the nave where the hearers stood to be instructed.
When Agrippa and Bernice entered into the *auditory*. —Acts xxv. 23, Wyclif's Trans.

ạu′di·tress, *n.* a woman auditor or hearer.

ạu·dit′ū·ăl, *a.* auditory. [Rare.]

au fāit (ō fā), [Fr., lit., to the fact; *au*, to the, and *fait*, from L. *factum*, fact.] skilled; accomplished; equal to the mastery of anything.

Auf′klä·rung (ouf′klăr-oong), *n.* [G., from *aufklären*, to enlighten; *auf-*, up, and *klären*, to clear.] the Enlightenment, an eighteenth century philosophical movement.

au fond (ō fōṅ), [Fr., at the bottom.] basically; essentially; at heart.

au frō·mäġe′ (-mäzh′), [Fr.] with cheese.

auf Wie′dẽr·se·hen (vē′dẽr-zā-en), [G.] till we see each other again; good-by: implies temporary parting.

Ạu·ġē′ăn, *a.* 1. in Greek legend, of or relating to Augeas, king of Elis.
2. resembling the stable of Augeas; hence, extremely filthy; foul; corrupt.
Augean stable; the stable of Augeas, containing 3,000 oxen and uncleaned for thirty years, but cleaned by Hercules in a day by diverting two rivers through it.

au′ġend, *n.* [L. *augendum*, from *augere*, to increase.] a number having another number (the addend) added to it.

ạu′gẽr, *n.* [ME. *nauger*, *naugor*, *navegor*; AS. *nafegār*; *nafa*, *nafu*, the nave of a wheel, and *gār*, a spear, bore.]

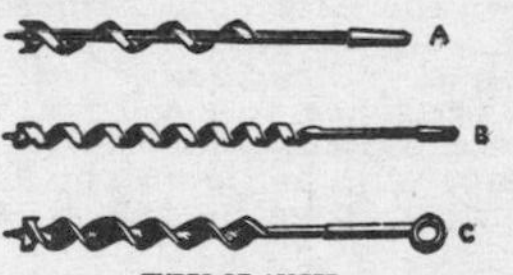

TYPES OF AUGER
A, screw auger; B, ship auger; C, lip-ring auger

1. a tool for boring holes in wood or other soft substances. It is used for making holes larger than those made by a gimlet.
2. a similar tool, used for boring in the earth.

ạu′gẽr bit, a bit with a blade like that of an auger.

ạught (ạt), *n.* [ME. *aught*; AS, *awiht*; *a*, *an*, one, and *wiht*, a creature, thing.]
1. anything whatever; any little part.
But go, my son, and see if *aught* be wanting. —Addison.
2. a zero.

ạught, *adv.* at all; in any manner.

ạught (ạt), **ạucht** (ạt), *n.* [ME. *aught*, *auhte*, *ahte*; AS. *æht*, from *agān*, to own.] property; possession. [Scot.]

ạu′ġīte, *n.* [L. *augites*; Gr. *augitēs*, a precious stone, from *augē*, bright, shining.] a black complex silicate mineral of vitreous luster and granular structure, occurring in igneous rocks; a kind of pyroxene.

ạu·ġit′iç, *a.* of, relating to, or containing augite.

ạug·ment′, *v.t.*; augmented, *pt.*, *pp.*; augmenting, *ppr.* [Fr. *augmenter*; L. *augmentare*, from *augmentum*, increase; *augere*, to increase.]
1. to increase; to enlarge in size or extent; to swell; to make bigger; as, to *augment* an army by reinforcement.
2. in grammar, to add an argument to; as, the Greek language *augments* certain tenses of the indicative.

ạug·ment′, *v.i.* to increase; to grow larger; as, a stream *augments* by rain.

ạug′ment, *n.* 1. an increase.
2. in grammar, a prefixed vowel or lengthening of the initial vowel to show past time in Greek and Sanskrit verbs.

ạug·ment′ȧ·ble, *a.* that can be increased; capable of augmentation.

ạug·men·tā′tion, *n.* 1. the act of increasing, or making larger, by addition, expansion, or dilatation.
2. the state of being increased or enlarged.
3. a thing that augments; addition.
4. in music, a variation of a theme by doubling the time value of the notes.
5. in heraldry, an additional charge on a coat of arms, often as a mark of honor, and generally borne on the escutcheon or a canton.
6. in medicine, the period of a fever between its commencement and its height.

7. in botany, a number of parts greater than normal, as of petals or sepals; multiplication.

Syn.—accession, expansion, enlargement, extension, increase, addition.

aug·ment'ā·tive, *a.* 1. augmenting; capable of augmenting.

2. in grammar, increasing the force of an idea expressed by a word; as, an *augmentative* prefix.

aug·ment'ā·tive, *n.* an augmentative prefix, suffix, word, etc.; intensifier: as, *per*durable, eat *up*.

aug·ment'ā·tive·ly, *adv.* in an augmentative manner.

aug·ment'ed in'tēr·văl, in music, an interval that is a half step greater than the corresponding major interval.

aug·ment'ēr, *n.* one who or that which augments.

au grä'tin (ō grä'tin *or* gra'tin), [Fr., with scrapings.] made with a lightly browned crust of bread crumbs or grated cheese.

au'gūr, *n.* [L. *augur*, perhaps from *avis*, a bird, and *gar*; Sans. *gār*, to call.]

1. among the Romans, a priest who foretold future events by interpreting omens, as the motion of birds in flight or the appearance of the entrails of sacrificial animals. *Augurs* carried a staff or wand, and were held in great respect.

2. a fortuneteller; prophet; soothsayer.

We all know that *augur* cannot look at *augur* without laughing. —Buckminster.

au'gūr, *v.i.*; augured (-gūrd), *pt., pp.*; auguring, *ppr.* to guess; to conjecture by signs or omens; to prognosticate.

au'gūr, *v.t.* 1. to predict or foretell.

2. to be an omen of; as, to *augur* ill success.

Syn.—predict, forebode, betoken, portend, presage.

au'gū·răl, *a.* [L. *auguralis*, from *augur*, an augur.] pertaining to augurs or to augury; as, *augural* consultations.

au'gū·rāte, *v.i.* [L. *auguratus*, pp. of *augurare*, to augur.] to judge by augury; to predict. [Obs.]

au'gū·rāte, *n.* an augurship.

au·gū·rā'tion, *n.* the practice of augury. [Obs.]

au'gūr·ēr, *n.* an augur. [Obs.]

au·gū'ri·ăl, *a.* relating to augurs or to augury.

au·gū·rist, *n.* an augur. [Obs.]

au'gūr·ize, *v.t.* to augur. [Obs.]

au'gū·rous, *a.* predicting; foretelling; foreboding. [Obs.]

au'gūr·ship, *n.* the office, or period of office, of an augur.

au'gū·ry, *n.*; *pl.* **au'gū·ries,** [L. *augurium*, divination, from *augur*, an augur.]

1. the art or practice of foretelling events by signs or omens.

She knew by *augury* divine. —Swift.

2. that which forebodes; that from which a prediction is drawn; an omen; portent.

Sad *auguries* of winter thence she drew. —Dryden.

3. a formal ceremony conducted by an augur.

au·gust', *a.* grand; magnificent; majestic; inspiring awe or reverence; as, *august* in visage.

Au'gust, *n.* [ME. *August*, *Augst*; L. *Augustus*; named from Emperor Octavius Augustus Caesar; name originally from *augere*, to increase.] the eighth month of the year, containing thirty-one days. The old Roman name was *Sextilis*, the sixth month from March, which was reckoned as the first of the year.

Au·gus'tăn, *a.* 1. pertaining to Augustus Caesar; as, the *Augustan* age.

2. pertaining to the city of Augsburg, in Bavaria, Germany; as, the *Augustan* Confession.

Augustan age; the period in Latin literature during the reign of Augustus Caesar, when elegance and correctness were highly valued; hence, in any national literature, the supposed period of its highest state of purity and refinement. The reign of Louis XIV has been called the *Augustan age* of French literature, and that of Queen Anne, the *Augustan age* of English literature.

Augustan Confession; the confession drawn up at Augsburg in 1530 by Martin Luther and Philipp Melanchthon, and containing the principles of the Protestants and their reasons for separating from the Roman Catholic Church.

Au·gus'tăn, *n.* a writer living in an Augustan age.

Au·gus'tin, Au·gus'tine, Au·gus·tin'i·ăn, *n.* a member of an order of monks, named after St. Augustine, bishop of Hippo.

Au·gus·tin'i·ăn, *a.* pertaining to St. Augustine or his doctrines.

Augustinian canons; an order of monks formerly numerous and popular in England and Ireland.

Augustinian hermits; an order of austere mendicant friars originally hermits, who were congregated into a body in 1265: also called *Austin friars*.

Augustinian nuns; an order of nuns who follow the rules of St. Augustine.

Augustinian rules; a set of rules governing religious orders, based on the letters of St. Augustine.

Au·gus·tin'i·ăn, *n.* [L. *Augustinus*, pertaining to Augustus.]

1. a person who believes in Augustinianism.

2. a member of an Augustinian religious order.

Au·gus·tin'i·ăn·ism, Au·gus'tin·ism, *n.* the doctrines of St. Augustine, who taught absolute predestination and the immediate efficacy of grace.

au·gust'ly, *adv.* in an august manner.

au·gust'ness, *n.* dignity of mien; grandeur; magnificence.

au jus (ō zhü), [Fr., with the juice.] served in its natural juice or gravy: said of meat.

auk, *n.* [Prov. Eng. *alk*, from Ice. *alka.*] any of a number of related diving birds of northern seas (genus *Alca*, order *Anseres*), with a heavy body, webbed feet, a short tail, and short wings used as paddles.

AUK

auk'let, *n.* one of several species of small auks, among them the sea dove or little auk, *Mergulus alle.*

auk'wărd, *a.* awkward. [Obs.]

au'là, *n.* [L. *aula*; Gr. *aulē*, a hall or court.] the anterior portion of the third ventricle of the cerebrum.

au lait (ō lā), [Fr.] with milk.

au·lā'ri·ăn, *a.* [LL. *aularis*, pertaining to a hall.] pertaining to a hall.

au·lā'ri·ăn, *n.* in certain English universities, a member of a hall, or minor college.

auld, *a.* old. [Dial. and Scot.]

Take thine *auld* cloak about thee. —Shak.

auld lang syne; literally, old long since: a Scotch phrase referring to the good old days or times (of one's youth, etc.).

au·let'iç, *a.* [Gr. *aulētēs*, a flute player, from *aulein*, to play a flute.] pertaining to pipes or instruments of the flute family. [Rare.]

au'liç, *a.* [L. *aulicus*; Gr. *aulikos*, pertaining to a court; from *aulē*, court.]

1. pertaining to a court; courtly.

2. in anatomy, relating to the aula.

Aulic Council; in the Holy Roman Empire, a personal council of the emperor that served as a supreme court: it was dissolved in 1806.

au'liç, *n.* the ceremony formerly observed in conferring the degree of doctor of divinity at the University of Paris: so called because it took place in the great hall (L. *aula*) of the archbishopric.

aul'nāge, *n.* same as *alnage.*

aul'nā·gēr, *n.* same as *alnager.*

au'lō·phȳte (-fīt), *n.* [Gr. *aulos*, pipe, and *phyton*, plant.] a nonparasitic plant living inside another, as some of the algae.

Au·los'tō·mà, *n.* [Gr. *aulos*, pipe, and *stoma*, mouth.] a genus of fishes, family *Aulostomidæ*, having an elongated, pipe-shaped mouth.

Au·lō·stom'i·dae, *n.pl.* a family of fishes that includes the *Aulostoma.*

aum, *n.* same as *aam.*

au·māil', *v.t.* and *n.* (to) enamel. [Obs.]

aum'bry, au'mē·ry, *n.* an ambry. [Archaic.]

au'mil, au'mil·dăr, *n.* [Anglo-Ind.] in India, a revenue collector.

au na·tu·rel' (ō nà-tū-rel'), [Fr.] 1. in the natural state; hence, naked.

2. prepared or served simply: said of food.

aun'cel, *n.* [ME. *auncel*, *aunselle*; It. *lancelle*, a balance; L. *lanx*, genit. *lancis*, a plate.] a kind of balance formerly used in England for weighing.

aune (ōn), *n.* [Fr. *aune*; OFr. *alne*, ell, from L. *ulna*; Gr. *ōlenē*, the elbow.] an old French cloth measure, corresponding to the English ell.

ȧunt (ȧnt), *n.* [ME. *aunte*; OFr. *ante*, *aunte*; L. *amita*, aunt.]

1. the sister of one's father or mother.

2. the wife of one's uncle.

3. an elderly woman; an old woman. [Obs.]

4. a prostitute. [Obs.]

Aunt Sally; a game which consists of throwing sticks or balls at a clay pipe stuck in the mouth of a wooden figure of a woman's head; also, the figure itself.

aun'tēr, *n.* [ME.] adventure. [Obs.]

aun'tēr, aun'tre, *v.t.* to venture. [Obs.]

ȧunt'ie, ȧunt'y, *n.* aunt: a familiar or affectionate form.

aun'trous, *a.* venturesome. [Obs.]

au'rà, *n.*; *pl.* **au'ràs, au'rae,** [L. *aura*; Gr. *aura*, air, from *aēnai*, to breathe, blow.]

1. an invisible emanation or vapor, as the aroma of flowers.

2. an invisible atmosphere supposedly arising from and surrounding a person or thing; as, he was enveloped in an *aura* of grandeur.

3. in electricity, an air current caused by an electric discharge from a sharp metallic point.

epileptic aura; a sensation as of a current of air, rising from some part of the body to the head, preceding an attack of epilepsy.

hysteric aura; a similar sensation preceding an attack of hysterics.

au'răl, *a.* pertaining to the air or to an aura.

au'răl, *a.* [L. *auris*, the ear.] relating to the ear; as, the *aural* orifice, *aural* surgery.

au'răm·ine, *n.* [L. *aurum*, gold, and *amine*, from L. *ammoniacum*, ammonia.] an artificial yellow dye.

Au·ran·ti·ā'cē·ae, *n.pl.* [Mod. L. *aurantium*, an orange, from L. *aurum*, gold.] the citrus plants, formerly a natural order of plants, now classified as a genus of the natural order *Rutaceæ*.

au·ran·ti·ā'ceous, *a.* pertaining to or like the *Aurantiaceæ*.

au'rāte, *n.* [L. *auratus*, pp. of *aurare*, to overlay with gold.] a combination of auric acid with a base; as, *aurate* of potash.

au'rā·ted, *a.* resembling gold; gold-colored; gilded.

au'rā·ted, *a.* [L. *auris*, the ear.] eared; having ears like the scallop shell.

au'rē·āte, *a.* [LL. *aureatus*, from L. *aureus*, golden, from *aurum*, gold.]

1. golden; gilded.

2. splendid; ornate.

au·rē'li·à, *n.* [It., from L. *aureolus*, golden, dim. of *aureus*, golden.]

1. in zoology, the chrysalis of a lepidopterous insect.

2. [A–] a genus of *Acalephæ*, or medusiform *Hydrozoa*, which passes through several changes of form in its development.

au·rē'li·ăn, *a.* like or pertaining to the aurelia; as, the *aurelian* form of an insect.

au·rē'li·ăn, *n.* an entomologist who specializes in the study of lepidopterous insects; a lepidopterist.

au·rē'ō·là, au'rē·ōle, *n.* [L. *aureolus*, dim. of *aureus*, golden, from *aurum*, gold.]

1. a halo; a radiance encircling the head or body as in religious paintings, etc.: also called *glory*.

2. anything resembling this; specifically, (a) in astronomy, the ring of light seen round the moon in total eclipses of the sun; (b) in meteorology, a kind of halo surrounding a shadow cast upon a cloud, a fog bank, or dew-covered grass.

3. in Roman Catholic theology, a reward given after death to those who have been spiritually victorious on earth.

AUREOLA

 fāte, fār, fȧst, fall, finăl, cāre, at; mēte, prey, hēr, met; pīne, marīne, bīrd, pin; nōte, mōve, fọr, atŏm, not; mọọn, book;

ạu·rē′ō·lin, *n.* [L. *aureolus.*] cobalt yellow.

ạu·rē·ō·mȳ′cin, *n.* [from L. *aureus*, golden, Gr. *mykēs*, fungus, and *-in.*] an antibiotic drug similar to penicillin, effective against certain viruses and against both Gram-positive and Gram-negative bacteria.

au re·voir′ (ō rē-vwär′). [Fr., from L. *revidere*, to see again; *re*, again; and *videre*, to see.] until we meet again; good-by: implies temporary parting.

ạu′ri-, [from L. *auris*, ear.] a combining form meaning *ear*, as in *auri*form.

ạu′riç, *a.* [L. *aurum*, gold.] 1. pertaining to or containing gold.

2. designating or of compounds in which gold has a valence of three.

ạu·ri·çhal′cē·ous, *a.* brass-colored.

ạu·ri·çhal′cīte, *n.* [L. *aurichalcum*; Gr. *oreichalkon*, from *oros*, mountain, and *chalkos*, brass or copper.] a mineral occurring in transparent verdigris-green, needle-shaped crystals, which when reduced yields a gold-colored alloy of copper and zinc.

ạu·ri·çhal′çum, *n.* same as *orichalch.*

ạu′ri·çle, *n.* [L. *auricula*; dim. of *auris*, ear.]

1. the external ear, or that part which projects from the head.

2. either of two chambers in the heart, placed above the two cavities called ventricles, and resembling in shape the external ear. It receives the blood from the veins, and communicates it to the ventricles.

3. formerly, an instrument applied to the ears to assist the hard of hearing; a kind of ear trumpet.

4. one of the internal processes curving over the ambulacra near the mouth, as in sea-urchins: also called *auricula.*

5. in botany and zoology, an earlike part or organ.

ạu′ri·çled (-kld), *a.* 1. having ears or auricles; having appendages resembling ears.

2. in botany, furnished with a pair of leaflets: said of some leaves.

ạu·riç′ō·mous, *a.* [L. *auricomus*, from *aurum*, gold, and *coma*, hair; Gr. *komē*, hair.] golden-haired.

ạu·riç′ū·lȧ, *n.*; *pl.* **ạu·riç′ū·lȧṣ,** or **ạu·riç′ū·lae,** [L., the external ear, dim. of *auris*, an ear.]

1. in botany, a garden flower derived from the yellow *Primula Auricula*, found native in the Swiss Alps: sometimes called *bear's-ear* from the shape of its leaves.

2. [A–] in zoology, a genus of phytophagous or plant-eating gastropodous mollusks, whose organs of respiration are formed for breathing air.

AURICULA
(*Primula Auricula*)

3. in echinology, same as *auricle.*

ạu·riç′ū·lăr, *a.* 1. pertaining to the ear or to the sense of hearing; as, the *auricular* nerves.

2. spoken directly into or confided to one's ear; especially, privately confided to the ear of a priest; as, *auricular* confession.

3. perceived by the ear; known or obtained by the sense of hearing; as, *auricular* evidence.

> You shall by an *auricular* assurance have your satisfaction. —Shak.

4. communicated or known by report.

> *Auricular* traditions and feigned testimonies. —Bacon.

5. shaped like an ear.

6. in anatomy, of an auricle.

auricular finger; the little finger, so called from its being most easily introduced into the ear passage.

ạu·riç′ū·lăr, *n.* [*usually in pl.*] any of the feathers covering the opening of a bird's ear.

ạu·riç·ū·lā′ri·ȧ, *n.* in zoology, an early stage in the development of certain holothurians.

ạu·riç′ū·lăr·ly, *adv.* in an auricular manner; specifically, in a secret manner; by whispering; by words addressed to the ear.

ạu·riç′ū·lāte, ạu·riç′ū·lā·ted, *a.* 1. having ears.

2. having auricles.

3. in botany, having a pair of small earlike projections at the base: said of a leaf.

ạu·riç′ū·lō-, [L. *auricula.*] a combining form used in medical and anatomical terms, meaning *of* or *pertaining to an auricle.*

ạu·rif′ẽr·ous, *a.* [L. *aurifer*, gold-producing; from *aurum*, gold, and *ferre*, to bring forth.] yielding or producing gold; containing gold; as, *auriferous* quartz; *auriferous* strata.

ạu·rif′iç, *a.* [L. *aurum*, gold, and *facere*, to make.] yielding gold.

ạu·ri·flam′mȧ, ạu′ri·flamme, *n.* [L. *aurum*, gold, and *flamma*, flame.] same as *oriflamme.*

ạu′ri·form, *a.* [L. *auris*, the ear, and *forma*, form.] shaped like the human ear; as, an *auriform* shell.

Ạu·rī′gȧ, *n.* [L. *auriga*, a charioteer.] in astronomy, the Wagoner, a constellation in the Northern Hemisphere between Perseus and Gemini, including Capella, a star of the first magnitude.

ạu·rī′găl, *a.* pertaining to a chariot or carriage. [Rare.]

ạu·ri·gā′tion, *n.* [L. *aurigatio*, the act of chariot-driving.] the act or practice of driving horses harnessed to carriages. [Rare.]

Ạu·rig·nā′ciăn, *a.* [from *Aurignac*, France, where remains were found.] designating or of a people of the last part of the Paleolithic Age, noted for stone carving.

ạu·rig′rȧ·phy, *n.* [L. *aurum*, gold, and *graphium*, style, from Gr. *graphein*, to write.] the art or practice of writing in golden characters.

ạu′ri·lāve, *n.* [L. *auris*, the ear, and *lavare*, to wash.] an ear brush, or ear sponge.

ạu′rin, ạu′rine, *n.* [L. *aurum*, gold.] an aromatic compound obtained from coal tar, used as a dye under the name of corallin or rosalic acid.

ạu·ri·phrӯġ′i·āte (-frij′), *a.* [L. *aurum*, gold, and *phrygius*, embroidered with Phrygian needlework.] ornamented with embroidery in gold. [Rare.]

> Nor wore he mitre here, precious or *auriphrygiate.* —Southey.

ạu′ri·sçalp, *n.* [L. *auris*, ear, and *scalpere*, to scrape.] an instrument to clean the ears.

ạu′ri·sçōpe, *n.* [L. *auris*, ear, and Gr. *skopein*, to view.] an instrument for examining the ear.

ạu·ris′çō·py, *n.* the act or practice of using the auriscope.

ạu′rist, *n.* a doctor specializing in disorders of the ear; otologist.

ạu′ri·ted, *a.* [L. *auritus*, furnished with ears, from *auris*, ear.] in botany and zoology, eared; having any part resembling an ear; auriculate.

ạu·riv′ō·rous, *a.* [L. *aurum*, gold, and *vorare*, to devour.] eating gold. [Rare.]

ạu·rō·ceph′ȧ·lous (-sef′), *a.* [L. *aurum*, gold, and Gr. *kephalē*, the head.] in zoology, characterized by a head of golden color.

ạu′roçhs, *n.*; *pl.* **ạu′roçhs,** [G. *auerochs*, from O.H.G. *urohso*; L. *urus*; Gr. *ouros*, wild ox.]

1. originally, the wild ox of Europe, now extinct, once roaming over the plains and through the forests of northern Europe, and resembling the bison of the American plains, but having a less shaggy head and neck, a lighter thorax, a heavier pelvic development, and a longer tail.

2. now, the European bison.

AUROCHS
(*Bison bonasus*)

ạu·rō·cȳ′ȧ·nīde, *n.* [L. *aurum*, gold, and Gr. *kyanos*, a dark blue substance used in the heroic age to adorn works in metal.] a double cyanide in which gold and some other metal are combined.

ạu·rō′rȧ, *n.*; *pl.* **ạu·rō′raṣ** or **ạu·rō′rae,** [L.]

1. [A–] in Roman mythology, the goddess of dawn: identified with the Greek Eos.

2. the dawn.

3. the beginning or early period of anything.

4. the aurora australis or aurora borealis.

aurora glory; the corona of the aurora borealis.

ạu·rō′rȧ ạus·trā′lis, [L., lit., southern aurora, from *auster*, south wind, south.] luminous bands or streamers of light sometimes appearing in the night sky of the Southern Hemisphere.

ạu·rō′rȧ bō·rē·al′is, [L., lit., northern aurora, from *boreas*, from Gr. *boreas*, *borras*, north wind, north.] luminous bands or streamers of light sometimes appearing in the night sky of the Northern Hemisphere; northern lights.

ạu·rō′răl, *a.* 1. of or like the dawn; rosy; dawning.

2. of or like the aurora (borealis or australis).

3. bright; radiant.

ạu·rō′rē·ăn, *a.* of or like the dawn; auroral.

ạu′rous, *a.* 1. containing gold.

2. in chemistry, designating or of compounds in which gold has a valence of one.

ạu′rum, *n.* [L.] gold: symbol, Au (no period).

ạus·çult′, *v.i.* and *v.t.* to auscultate.

ạus′çul·tāte, *v.i.* and *v.t.*; auscultated, *pt.*, *pp.*; auscultating, *ppr.* [L. *auscultare*, to listen.] to examine by auscultation.

ạus·çul·tā′tion, *n.* [L. *auscultatio*, a listening, from *auscultare*, to listen.]

1. the act of listening.

2. a listening to sounds in the chest, abdomen, etc., so as to determine the condition of the heart, lungs, etc. It is called *immediate* when the ear is directly applied to the part, and *mediate* if practiced with the aid of a stethoscope.

ạus′çul·tā·tŏr, *n.* an expert in auscultation.

ạus·çul′tȧ·tō·ry, *a.* pertaining to or determined by auscultation.

aus′laut, *n.* [G. *aus*, denoting completion, from, and *laut*, loud.] a final sound, as of a syllable or word.

Ạu·sō′ni·ăn, *a.* [L. *Ausonia*, a name given to middle and lower Italy.] of or relating to Italy or to the inhabitants of Italy. [Poet.]

ạus′pex, *n.*; *pl.* **ạus′pi·cēṣ,** [L., contr. of *avispex*, from *avis*, bird, and *spicere*, to see.] a Roman priest who found omens in the flight of birds, etc.; augur.

ạus′pi·çāte, *v.t.*; auspicated, *pt.*, *pp.*; auspicating, *ppr.* [L. *auspicari*, to take the auspices.]

1. to begin formally or auspiciously; inaugurate: a sense derived from the practice of the Romans of taking the *auspicium*, or inspection of birds, before they undertook any enterprise.

2. to foreshow. [Obs.]

ạus′pi·çāte, *a.* giving promise of a favorable issue; auspicious. [Obs.]

ạus′pice, *n.* [L. *auspicium*, an omen, from *auspicari*, to take the auspices.]

1. an augury from birds; an omen or sign in general; as, to take the *auspices*; an *auspice* of a good fortune.

2. any prophecy, especially when favorable.

3. [*usually pl.*] patronage; protection; as, under his *auspices* the war was soon brought to a successful termination; an entertainment under the *auspices* of a church.

ạus·pi′ciăl (-pish′ăl), *a.* 1. of augury.

2. auspicious.

ạus·pi′cious, *a.* [L. *auspicium*, auspice, from *auspicari*, to take the auspices.]

1. having omens of success, or favorable appearances; as, an *auspicious* beginning.

2. prosperous; fortunate; as, *auspicious* chief.

3. favorable; kind; propitious; as, an *auspicious* mistress; *auspicious* gales.

Syn.—favorable, propitious, promising, encouraging, advantageous, lucky.

ạus·pi′cious·ly, *adv.* in an auspicious manner.

ạus·pi′cious·ness, *n.* a state of fair promise; prosperity.

Ạus′sie, *n.*, an Australian, especially one in the armed forces. [Colloq.]

Ạus′tẽr, *n.* [L.] the south wind: a personification. [Poetic.]

ạus·tēre′, *a.* [ME. *austere*; OFr. *austere*; L. *austerus*, harsh; Gr. *austēros*, dry, harsh.]

1. severe; harsh; rigid; stern; as, an *austere* master; an *austere* look.

2. sour with astringency; harsh to the taste; as, *austere* fruit or wine.

3. simple; plain; without adornment or embellishment.

4. morally strict; abstinent; ascetic.

5. grave; sober; as, an *austere* face.

ạus·tēre′ly, *adv.* in an austere manner.

ạus·tēre′ness, *n.* 1. severity in manners; harshness; austerity.

2. pungency or bitterness as to taste.

ạus·ter′i·ty, *n.*; *pl.* **ạus·ter′i·tieṣ,** 1. [*usually in pl.*] severity of manners or life; rigor; strictness; harsh discipline.

2. sourness; harshness as to taste. [Obs.]

3. the absence of adornment or embellishment; severe plainness.

ạus'trăl, *a.* [L. *australis*, southern, from *auster*, the south wind, or south.]

1. southern; lying or being in the south; as, *austral* land, *austral* ocean.

2. [A–] Australian.

austral signs; the last six signs of the zodiac, or those south of the equator.

Ạus·trăl·ā'siăn, *a.* pertaining to Australasia or its peoples.

Ạus·trăl·ā'siăn, *n.* a native or inhabitant of Australasia.

Ạus·trăl'iȧ an'ti·ġen, [after its first discovery "in an Australian aborigine.] an antigen present in the blood of some persons with one form of hepatitis.

Ạus·trăl'iăn, *a.* relating to Australia, its people, languages, or culture.

Ạus·trăl'iăn, *n.* a native or inhabitant of Australia.

Australian ballot; a type of secret ballot originating in Australia and widely used in the United States. It is prepared by a legally constituted board of election officers and is furnished to voters when they appear at the proper place for voting. It contains the names of all candidates for election to public office, and it is marked by the voter in a secluded stall or booth.

Ạus·trăl'iăn çrạwl, a modified crawl stroke in which alternate arm and leg action causes the swimmer's body to roll slightly as it is propelled forward.

Ạus'tri·ăn, *a.* of or relating to Austria, its people, dialect, or culture.

Ạus'tri·ăn, *n.* 1. a native or inhabitant of Austria.

2. the German dialect of Austria.

Ạus'trō-, a combining form meaning *Austria*, as in *Austro*-Hungarian.

ạus'trō-, [L. *auster*, the south, south wind.] a combining form meaning, (a) *south wind*; (b) [A–] *South*; (c) [A–] *Australian*.

Ạus"trō-Huñ·gā'ri·ăn, *a.* relating to the former kingdom of Austria-Hungary.

ạus'trō·man·cy, *n.* [L. *auster*, the south wind, and Gr. *manteia*, divination.] soothsaying, or prediction of future events, from observations of the winds.

Ạus·trō·nē'siăn, *a.* 1. of Austronesia (the islands in the central and south Pacific), its people, etc.

2. designating or of a family of languages spoken there, comprising the Indonesian, Melanesian, Micronesian, and Polynesian subfamilies; Malayo-Polynesian.

Ạus·trō·nē'siăn, *n.* the Austronesian languages.

ạut-, same as *auto-*.

ạu'tă·çoid, *n.* [from *aut-*, and Gr. *akos*, cure, remedy; and *-oid*.] an organic substance, such as a hormone, carried by the blood stream or other body fluids from a part of the body where it is formed to another part on which it has activating effects, like those of drugs: spelled also *autocoid*.

ạu·tär'çhiç, ạu·tär'çhi·căl, *a.* of or characteristic of an autarchy.

ạu'tär·çhy, *n.* [Gr. *autarchia*, absolute power; *autos*, self, and *archein*, to rule.]

1. unlimited sovereignty; autocracy.

2. a country under such rule.

3. loosely, autarky.

ạu·tär'kiç, *a.* of or characterized by autarky.

ạu·tär'ky, *n.* [Gr. *autarkeia*, independence, self-sufficiency, from *autos*, self, and *arkeein*, to achieve, endure, suffice.] economic self-sufficiency as a national policy; getting along without goods from other countries.

ạut Cae'săr ạut nī'hil, [L.] either (a) Caesar or nothing; hence, either everything or nothing.

ạu·tē'cious, *a.* same as *autoecious*.

ạu·tē'cism, *n.* same as *autoecism*.

ạu·then'tiç, *a.* [ME. *autentike*; OFr. *autentique*; LL. *autenticus*; Gr. *authentikos*, warranted, authentic, from *autos*, self, and *entea*, instruments, tools.]

1. having a genuine original or authority, in opposition to that which is false, fictitious, or counterfeit; being what it purports to be; genuine; true: applied to things; as, an *authentic* paper or register.

2. of approved authority; trustworthy; reliable; as, an *authentic* writer.

3. in law, vested with all due formalities, and legally attested.

4. in music, having an immediate relation to the keynote or tonic: in distinction from *plagal*, having a corresponding relation to the fifth or dominant, in the octave below the keynote.

Syn.—genuine, true, certain, faithful, credible, reliable, official, authorized.—A distinction is made between *authentic* and *genuine*, the former being opposed to *false*, and the latter to *spurious*; as, an *authentic* history, a *genuine* manuscript.

ạu·then'tiç·ăl, *a.* authentic.

ạu·then'tiç·ăl·ly, *adv.* in an authentic manner; with the requisite or genuine authority.

ạu·then'tiç·ăl·ness, *n.* authenticity. [Rare.]

ạu·then'ti·çāte, *v.t.*; authenticated, *pt.*, *pp.*; authenticating, *ppr.* 1. to render authentic or valid.

2. to determine as genuine; to prove the authenticity of; to verify.

3. to prove (a painting, book, etc.) to be the product of a certain person.

ạu·then·ti·çā'tion, *n.* an authenticating or being authenticated.

ạu·then'ti·çā·tŏr, *n.* a person or thing that authenticates.

ạu·then·tic'i·ty, *n.* the quality or state of being authentic; genuineness.

ạu·then'tiç·ly, *adv.* authentically.

ạu·then'tiç·ness, *n.* authenticity. [Rare.]

Ạu·then'tiçṣ, *n.* a Latin translation from the Greek of the Novels (new constitutions) of Justinian, made by an anonymous author.

ạu·thi·ġen'iç, ạu"thi·ġē·net'iç, ạu·thiġ'e·nous, *a.* [Gr. *authi*, on the spot, and *gignesthai*, to be born.] in geology, formed where found, as rock crystals.

ạu'thŏr, *n.* [ME. *autour*; OFr. *autor*; L. *auctor*, author, from *augere*, to cause to grow, increase.]

1. one who produces, creates, or brings into being; the beginner, creator, or first mover of anything.

2. one who composes or writes a book, or whose occupation is to compose and write books.

3. an author's writings.

4. an editor. [Obs.]

ạu'thŏr, *v.t.* to occasion; to be the author of. [Obs.]

ạu'thŏr·ess, *n.* a woman author. [Now Rare.]

ạu·thō'ri·ăl, *a.* pertaining to an author.

ạu'thŏr·iṣm, *n.* authorship. [Rare.]

ạu·thor·i·tăr'i·ăn, *a.* [from *authority*, and *-arian*.] believing in, relating to, or characterized by unquestioning obedience to authority rather than individual freedom of judgment and action.

ạu·thor·i·tăr'i·ăn, *n.* a person who believes in, advocates, practices, or enforces such obedience.

ạu·thor·i·tăr'i·ăn·iṣm, *n.* authoritarian principles; the policy or practice of unquestioning obedience to the authority of a dictator or a small dictatorial group.

ạu·thor'i·tā·tive, *a.* 1. having due authority; official.

2. asserting authority; fond of giving orders; dictatorial.

3. based on competent authority; reliable because coming from recognized experts; as, an *authoritative* dictionary.

ạu·thor'i·tā·tive·ly, *adv.* in an authoritative manner.

ạu·thor'i·tā·tive·ness, *n.* the quality of being authoritative.

ạu·thor'i·ty, *n.*; *pl.* **ạu·thor'i·tieṣ,** [ME. *autorite*, *auctorite*; OFr. *autorite*; L. *auctoritas*, authority, from *auctor*, author.]

1. the power or a right to command, act, enforce obedience, or make final decisions; jurisdiction.

By what *authority* doest thou these things?
—Matt. xxi. 23.

2. this power as delegated to another; authorization; as, he has my *authority* to do it.

3. the power derived from opinion, respect, or esteem; influence of character or office.

4. testimony; witness.

5. weight of testimony; credibility; as, a historian of no *authority*.

6. a person or thing that may be appealed to for support of an opinion or act.

7. warrant; justification.

8. in law, a precedent or decision of a court; an official declaration, an eminent opinion or saying.

9. the author of an authoritative statement, or one commanding the respect of others; also, a book containing the writings of such an author.

10. [*usually in pl.*] the officers of government; the persons or the body exercising power or command.

Syn.—ascendancy, dominion, rule, influence, force, power, command, sway, control.

ạu'thŏr·i·zā·ble, *a.* capable of being authorized.

ạu·thŏr·i·zā'tion, *n.* 1. an authorizing or being authorized.

2. legal power or right; sanction.

ạu'thor·īze, *v.t.*; authorized, *pt.*, *pp.*; authorizing, *ppr.* 1. to give official approval or legal power to; to give a right to act; to empower; as, to *authorize* commissioners to settle the boundary of the State.

2. to make legal; as, to *authorize* a marriage.

3. to establish by authority, as by usage or public opinion; as, idioms *authorized* by usage.

4. to give authority to; to sanction; as, to *authorize* a report.

5. to justify; to support as right; as, suppress desires which reason does not *authorize*.

ạu'thŏr·īzed, *a.* warranted by right; supported or established by authority; derived from legal or proper authority; having power or authority.

Authorized Version; the revised English translation of the Bible prepared at the suggestion of James I. It was first published in England in 1611. Also called *King James Version*.

ạu'thŏr·ī·zēr, *n.* one who authorizes.

ạu'thŏr·less, *a.* without a known author or authors; anonymous.

ạu'thŏr·ship, *n.* 1. the profession or occupation of a writer.

2. origin; source; as, the *authorship* of a book, a deed, or a condition.

ạu'thō·tȳpe, *n.* [Gr. *autos*, self, and *typos*, a stamp or imprint.] a type or block bearing the facsimile of an autograph.

ạu'tiṣm, *n.* [*aut-*, and *-ism*.] in psychology, a state of mind characterized by daydreaming, hallucinations, and disregard of external reality.

ạu·tis'tiç, *a.* of or having autism.

ạu'tō-, [Gr. *autos*, self.]

1. a combining form meaning *self*, as in *auto*graph, *auto*biography: also *aut-*.

2. a combining form from *automobile*, meaning *self-moving*, as in *auto*car, *auto*truck.

ạu'tō, *n.*; *pl.* **ạu'tōṣ,** an automobile. [Colloq.]

ạu'tō, *v.i.* to go by automobile. [Colloq.]

ạu"tō·an'ti·bod·y, *n.* an antibody that acts against a component substance of the body in which it is produced.

Ạu'tō·bähn, *n.*; *pl.* **Ạu'tō·bähn·en, Ạu'tō·bähnṣ,** [G.; *auto* (contr. of *automobil*, automobile) and *bahn*, a course, highway.] in Germany, a four-lane highway for fast driving, with a strip of grass, etc. down the middle to separate traffic bound in opposite directions.

ạu"tō·bī·og'rȧ·phēr, *n.* [*auto-*, and Gr. *bios*, life, and *graphein*, to write.] a person who writes his own life.

ạu"tō·bī·ō·graph'iç, ạu"tō·bī·ō·graph'iç·ăl, *a.* 1. of or containing autobiography.

2. characteristic of autobiography or autobiographers; as, *autobiographic* touches.

ạu"tō·bī·ō·graph'i·căl·ly, *adv.* 1. in an autobiographic manner or form.

2. by means of autobiography.

ạu"tō·bī·og'rȧ·phy, *n.*; *pl.* **ạu'tō·bī·og'rȧ·phieṣ,** [*auto-*, and Gr. *bios*, life, and *graphein*, to write.]

1. the art or practice of writing the story of one's own life.

2. a biography or narrative of one's life, written by oneself.

ạu'tō·bōat, *n.* a type of motorboat.

ạu'tō·bus, *n.* a motor omnibus; any self-propelled four-wheeled vehicle.

ạu'tō·çär, *n.* an automobile.

ạu·tō·çär'pous, ạu·tō·çär'pi·ăn, *a.* [*auto-*, and Gr. *karpos*, fruit.] in botany, consisting of the pericarp without any organ, such as the calyx, outwardly adhering: said of fruit.

ạu·tō·ceph'ȧ·lous, ạu·tō·ceph'ȧ·liç (-sef'), *a.* [*auto-*, and Gr. *kephalē*, head.] in church history, having a head of its own; ecclesiastically independent.

ạu'tō·çhrōme, *n.* a specially prepared panchromatic plate used in the Lumière process of color photography; a positive plate or print obtained from such negative.

ạu·tō·çhron'ō·grȧph, *n.* [*auto-*, and Gr. *chronos*, time, and *graphein*, to write.] an instrument for the recording of time instantaneously and automatically.

ạu·toçh'thon, *n.*; *pl.* **ạu·toçh'thonṣ, ạu·toçh'thō·nēṣ,** [Gr. *autochthōn*, sprung from the land itself; *autos*, self, and *chthōn*, the earth, the ground.]

1. a person who was born where he lives; a native.
2. [*pl.*] the earliest known inhabitants of a place; aborigines.
3. any indigenous animal or plant.

ạu·toch'thō·năl, ạu·toch·thon'iç, ạu·toch'thō·nous, *a.* aboriginal; indigenous; native.

ạu·toch'thō·nişm, ạu·toch'thō·ny, *n.* the state of being autochthonal.

ạu'tō·clāve, *n.* [Fr., from *auto-*, and L. *clavis*, key, from *claudere*, to shut.] a container for sterilizing, cooking, etc. by superheated steam under pressure.

ạu'tō·clāve, *v.t.*; autoclaved, *pt.*, *pp.*; autoclaving, *ppr.* to sterilize or cook by means of an autoclave.

ạu'tō·çoid, *n.* same as *autacoid*.

ạu·toç'rȧ·cy, *n.*; *pl.* **ạu·toç'rȧ·cieş,** [Fr. *autocratie*; Gr. *autokrateia*, absolute power, from *autos*, self, and *kratein*, to rule.]
1. absolute power or authority of one person over others.
2. supreme, uncontrolled, unlimited authority or right of governing, held by one person; dictatorship; despotism.
3. a country with this kind of government.

ạu'tō·çrat, *n.* [Gr. *autokratēs*, an absolute ruler.]
1. a ruler who holds and exercises supreme power; despot; dictator.
2. one who is invested with or assumes absolute independent power over others.
3. any domineering, self-willed person.

ạu·tō·çrat'iç, ạu·tō·çrat'iç·ăl, *a.* pertaining to autocracy; absolute; holding independent and unlimited powers of government.

ạu·tō·çrat'iç·ăl·ly, *adv.* in an autocratic manner.

ạu·toç'rȧ·trix, *n.* a woman autocrat: title given formerly to empresses of Russia.

ạu'tō·çrat·ship, *n.* the office, position, or rank of an autocrat.

au"to-da-fé' (ạu"tō-dä-fẹ'), *n.*; *pl.* **au"tos-da-fé'** (ạu"tōş-dä-fẹ'), [Port. *auto de fé*; *auto*, from L. *actum*, act; *de*, from L. *de*, from, and *fé*, from L. *fides*, faith.]
1. in the Inquisition, the ceremony connected with trying and sentencing a heretic.
2. the execution by the secular power of the sentence thus passed.
3. a public burning of a heretic.

ạu'tō de fẹ', *n.*; *pl.* **ạu'tōş de fẹ',** same as *auto-da-fé*.

ạu"tō·dī·ag·nō'sis, *n.* self-diagnosis.

ạu'tō·di·daçt", *n.* [Gr. *autodidaktos*, self-taught; *autos*, self, and *didaskein*, to teach.] a person who is self-taught.

ạu"tō·di·ġes'tion (-chun), *n.* [*auto-*, and *digestion.*] same as *autolysis*.

ạu"tō·dȳ·nam'iç, *a.* [*auto-*, and *dynamic.*] operating by its own power or force.

ạu'tō·dȳne, *a.* [*auto-*, and *dyne.*] designating or of a system of heterodyne radio reception in which a single tube serves both as oscillator and first detector.

ạu'tō·dȳne, *n.* 1. an autodyne system.
2. an autodyne receiver.

ạu·toe'cious (-tē'), *a.* [*auto-*, and Gr. *oikos*, a dwelling.] in biology, passing the entire life cycle on one host, as certain parasites do, especially rust fungi.

ạu·toe'cişm (-tē'), *n.* the state of being autoecious.

ạu"tō·e·rot'iç, *a.* of or indulging in autoerotism.

ạu"tō·e·rot'i·cişm, *n.* same as *autoerotism*.

ạu"tō·er'o·tişm, *n.* [*auto-*, and *erotism*; term coined by Havelock Ellis.]
1. sexual sensation arising without external stimulus, direct or indirect, from another person.
2. self-generated sexual activity directed toward oneself, as masturbation.

ạu"tō·feç·un·dā'tion, *n.* [*auto-*, and L. *fecundare*, to make fruitful.] in biology, the act of self-impregnation.

ạu·tog'ȧ·mous, *a.* in botany, fertilized by its own pollen.

ạu·tog'ȧ·my, *n.* [*auto-*, and Gr. *gamos*, marriage.] in botany, self-fertilization, as in a flower receiving pollen from its own stamens.

ạu·tō·ġē'nē·ăl, *a.* same as *autogenous*.

ạu·tō·ġē'nē·ous, *a.* same as *autogenous*.

ạu·tō·ġen'e·sis, *n.* [*auto-*, and *genesis.*] spontaneous generation.

ạu"tō·ġē·net'iç, *a.* of or resulting from autogenesis.

ạu"tō·ġē·net'iç·ăl·ly, *adv.* by autogenesis.

ạu·toġ'e·nous, *a.* [Gr. *autogenēs*, self-produced; from *autos*, self, and *genesis*, origin, or birth.]
1. self-engendered; self-produced.
2. in anatomy, proceeding from distinct and separate centers of ossification, as in the knitting together of fractured bones.
autogenous soldering; a method of uniting metals by fusion of the parts to be joined.
autogenous vaccine; in medicine, a vaccine prepared from bacteria from a patient's own body as an immunizing agent for him.

ạu·toġ'e·nous·ly, *adv.* in an autogenous manner; autogenetically.

ạu·toġ'e·ny, *n.* autogenesis.

ạu·tō·ġī'rō, *n.*; *pl.* **ạu·tō·ġī'rōş,** [from *auto-*, and Gr. *gyros*, a circle.] a kind of aircraft that moves forward by means of a propeller and is supported in the air mainly by means of another large propeller mounted horizontally above the fuselage and turned by air pressure rather than motor power.

ạu'tō·grȧph, *n.* [Fr. *autographe*; from Gr *autos*, self, and *graphein*, to write.]
1. anything written with one's own hand, as a letter or a signature.
2. an original manuscript.
3. a copy made by autography.

ạu'tō·grȧph, *a.* written by one's own hand.

ạu'tō·grȧph, *v.t.* 1. to write (something) with one's own hand.
2. to write one's signature on or in.
3. to reproduce by means of autography.

ạu·tō·grȧph'iç, ạu·tō·grȧph'iç·ăl, *a.* 1. written by one's own hand.
2. pertaining to an autograph.
3. of or produced by autography (sense 4).

ạu·tog'rȧ·phy, *n.* 1. a person's own handwriting; an autograph.
2. the writing of something with one's own hand.
3. autographs in general.
4. in lithography, a process for transferring a writing or drawing from paper to stone.

ạu·tō·ġȳ'rō, *n.*; *pl.* **ạu·tō·ġȳ'rōş,** same as *autogiro*.

ạu'tō·härp, *n.* [*auto-*, and *harp.*] a musical instrument resembling the zither.

ạu"tō·hyp·nō'sis, *n.* [*auto-*, and *hypnosis.*]
1. the act of hypnotizing oneself.
2. the hypnosis resulting from this.

ạu"tō·hyp·not'iç, *a.* self-hypnotizing.

ạu"tō·hyp·not'iç, *n.* one who hypnotizes himself.

ạu·tō·hyp'nō·tişm, *n.* [*auto-*, and *hypnotism.*] autohypnosis.

ạu·toi'çous, *a.* same as *autoecious*.

ạu"tō·in·feç'tion, *n.* [*auto-*, and *infection.*] infection from a source within the organism itself, as from harmful bacteria previously present but heretofore away from vulnerable areas.

ạu"tō·in·oç·ū·lā'tion, *n.* [*auto-*, and *inoculation.*]
1. in medicine, the inoculation of a healthy part of a body with virus from a diseased part.
2. a spreading of infection from one part to others in the body.

ạu"tō·in·tox·i·çā'tion, *n.* [*auto-*, and *intoxication.*] poisoning by toxic substances generated within the body.

au'tō·ist, *n.* same as *motorist*.

au"tō·ki·net'iç, *a.* moving automatically; as, an *autokinetic* fire alarm system.

ạu·tol'ȧ·try, *n.* [*auto-*, and Gr. *latreia*, worship.] self-worship.

ạu·tol'ō·gous, *a.* [*auto-*, and homo*logous.*] derived from the same organism or from one of its parts; as, an *autologous* graft.

ạu·tol'ō·ġy, *n.* [*auto-*, and Gr. *logos*, description.] the study of self.

ạu·tō·lȳ'sin, *n.* [*autolysis*, and *-in.*] a substance that can destroy the cells or tissues of the organism in which it is produced.

ạu·tol'y·sis, *n.* [*auto-*, and *-lysis.*] the destruction of cells or tissues by substances within them, as after death or in some diseases.

ạu·tō·lyt'iç, *a.* of or by autolysis.

ạu'tō·lȳze, *v.t.* and *v.i.*; autolyzed, *pt.*, *pp.*; autolyzing, *ppr.* to affect with or undergo autolysis.

ạu'tō·mat, *n.* [Gr. *automatos*, self-acting.]
1. an apparatus for serving foods mechanically when a coin is dropped in a slot.
2. a restaurant having such an apparatus.

ạu·tom'ȧ·tȧ, *n.*, alt. pl. of *automaton*.

ạu'tō·māte, *v.t.*; automated, *pt.*, *pp.*; automating, *ppr.* [backformation from *automation.*]
1. to convert (a factory, process, etc.) to automation.
2. to use the techniques of automation in; as, *automated* teaching.

ạu'tō·māte, *n.* [Fr.; Gr. *automatos*, self-acting.] an automaton. [Obs.]

ạu'tō·math, *n.* [*auto-*, and Gr. *manthanein*, to learn.] a self-taught person. [Rare.]

ạu·tō·mat'iç, ạu·tō·mat'iç·ăl, *a.* [Gr. *automatos*, self-moving; *autos*, self, and *matenein*, to strive to do.]
1. conducted or carried on by self-acting machinery; as, *automatic* operations.
2. mechanical; done without conscious effort.
3. in physiology, not voluntary; not depending on the will; instinctive.

ạu·tō·mat'iç, *n.* 1. an automatic rifle or pistol.
2. any automatic machine.

ạu·tō·mat'iç·ăl·ly, *adv.* in an automatic manner; involuntarily; mechanically.

ạu·tō·mat'iç pī'lŏt, same as *gyropilot*.

ạu·tō·mat'iç pis'tŏl, ạu·tō·mat'iç rī'fle, etc. a pistol, rifle, etc. that uses the force of the explosion of a shell to eject the empty cartridge case and place the next cartridge into the breech so that shots are fired in rapid succession until the trigger is released.

ạu"tō·mā'tion, *n.* 1. in manufacturing, a system or method in which many or all of the processes are automatically performed or controlled by machinery, electronic devices, etc.
2. any system or method that uses self-operating equipment, electronic devices, etc. to replace human beings in doing routine or repetitive work; as, *automation* in teaching.
3. the condition of being automated.

ạu·tom'ȧ·tişm, *n.* 1. the state of being automatic; also, involuntary action.
2. in metaphysics, a theory that animals lack consciousness, that their actions are governed only by physical laws, and that they are automata.
3. in physiology, (a) action independent of outside stimulus; (b) action not controlled by the will; (c) the power of such action.
4. in psychology, an automatic or unconscious action, as a tic.
5. in surrealism, free expression of the unconscious mind without control by the conscious.

ạu·tom'ȧ·tīze, *v.t.*; automatized, *pt.*, *pp.*; automatizing, *ppr.* 1. to make automatic.
2. same as *automate*.

ạu·tom'ȧ·ton, *n.*; *pl.* **ạu·tom'ȧ·tons, ạu·tom'ȧ·tȧ,** [Gr. *automatos*, self-moving.]
1. anything that can move or act of itself.
2. an apparatus that automatically performs certain actions by responding to preset controls or encoded instructions.
3. an electronic machine, control device, etc. equipped with a computer and designed to operate automatically in response to instructions previously fed into the computer.
4. a person or animal acting in an automatic or mechanical way.

ạu·tom'ȧ·tous, *a.* having in itself the power of motion; automatic.

ạu·tō·mō'bile, *a.* 1. self-moving; as, an *automobile* carriage, an *automobile* bicycle.
2. of or for an automobile or automobiles.

ạu'tō·mō·bīle" (*or* ạ·tō·mō'bil), *n.* [*auto-*, and L. *mobilis*, movable.] a car, usually four-wheeled, propelled by an engine or motor that is part of it, and meant for traveling on streets or roads; a motorcar.

ạu'tō·mō·bīle", *v.i.*; automobiled, *pt.*, *pp.*; automobiling, *ppr.* to drive or ride in an automobile. [Now Rare.]

ạu·tō·mō'bil·işm, *n.* the act or practice of using an automobile. [Now Rare.]

ạu·tō·mō'bil·ist, *n.* one who drives an automobile. [Now Rare.]

ạu·tom'ō·līte, *n.* [Gr. *automolos*, a deserter.] a variety of gahnite.

ạu·tō·mọr'phiç, *a.* [*auto-*, and Gr. *morphē*, form.]
1. made similar in form to oneself, or drawn after the pattern of oneself.
2. in mineralogy, idiomorphic.

ạu·tō·mọr'phişm, *n.* the attribution of one's own traits to another.

ạu·tō·mō'tive, *a.* [*auto-*, and *-motive.*]
1. self-propelling.
2. having to do with automobiles.

ạu·tō·mō'tŏr, *n.* [*auto-*, and L. *motus*, motion, from *movere*, to move.] any automobile vehicle. [Rare.]

ạu·tō·nom'iç, ạu·tō·nom'iç·ăl, *a.* 1. relating to autonomy; having self-government.
2. of the autonomic nervous system.
3. in botany, resulting from internal causes.

ạu·tō·nom'iç nẽrv'ous sys'tem, the sympathetic and parasympathetic divisions of the nervous system, innervating glands as well as smooth and cardiac muscle.

ạu·ton'ō·mous, *a.* 1. independent in government; having the right of self-government.

2. in biology, functioning independently of other parts.

3. in botany, autonomic.

au·ton′ō·my, *n.*; *pl.* **au·ton′ō·mies,** [Gr. *autonomia*, independence, from *autos*, self, and *nemein*, to hold sway.]

1. the quality or condition of being autonomous; self-government.

2. any state that governs itself.

3. in the philosophy of Kant, the right of reason to dominate in matters of ethics; the right of the individual to govern himself according to his own reason.

4. in biology, an autonomous organism.

au′tō·nym, *n.* [*auto-*, and Gr. *onoma*, name.]

1. one's real name: opposed to *pseudonym.*

2. a production bearing the originator's real name.

au·tō·path′ic, *a.* [Gr. *autopatheia*, one's own feelings or experience; *autos*, self, and *pathos*, feeling.] in pathology, caused by or influenced by the peculiar structure and characteristics of the diseased organism.

Au·toph′a·gi, *n.pl.* [*auto-*, and Gr. *phagein*, to eat.] a division of birds that can run about and feed themselves as soon as hatched.

au·toph′a·gous, *a.* 1. pertaining to or resembling the *Autophagi.*

2. in medicine, of the nature of autophagy.

au·toph′a·gy, *n.* [*auto-*, and Gr. *phagein*, to eat.] the drawing of nourishment by the body from its own tissues, as in fasting; self-consumption.

au·toph′ō·by, *n.* [*auto-*, and Gr. *phobos*, fear.] a shrinking from reference to oneself. [Rare.]

au′tō·phōn, *n.* [*auto-*, and Gr. *phōnein*, to make a sound.] a musical instrument, the sounds of which are determined by perforations, corresponding to notes, in a band or ribbon of material which unreels within the instrument.

au·toph′ō·ny, *n.* [*auto-*, and Gr. *phōnē*, sound.]

1. a form of auscultation in which the examiner speaks close to the patient's chest and notes the modification of his own voice as affected by the conditions of the patient's chest.

2. a form of deafness in which the patient's voice seems very loud to himself.

au″tō·phyl·log′e·ny, *n.* [*auto-*, and Gr. *phyllon*, leaf, and *genea*, offspring.] in botany, the abnormal growth of one leaf from another.

au′tō·phȳte, *n.* [*auto-*, and *-phyte.*] in botany, any plant that can make its own food: opposed to *saprophyte.*

au′tō·plast, *n.* [*auto-*, and Gr. *plastos*, formed, from *plassein*, to form.] same as *chloroplast.*

au·tō·plas′tic, *a.* 1. relating to autoplasty.

2. adaptable to the environment.

au′tō·plas·ty, *n.* in surgery, the repairing of injuries with the living tissue of some other part of the same body.

au·top′sic, au·top′sic·ăl, *a.* pertaining to autopsy.

au′top·sy, *n.* [Gr. *autopsia*, a seeing with one's own eyes; *autos*, self, and *opsis*, a sight, appearance.]

1. personal inspection; ocular view. [Rare.]

2. post-mortem examination; examination and dissection of the body after death to discover the cause of death, damage done by disease, etc.

au·top′tic, au·top′tic·ăl, *a.* relating to or based on autopsy, or personal observation; as, *autoptic* evidence. [Rare.]

au·top′tic·ăl·ly, *adv.* by means of ocular view or one's own observation.

au·tō·sche·di·as′tic, au·tō·sche·di·as′tic·ăl, *a.* [Gr. *autoschediazein*, to do a thing offhand; *autos*, self, and *schediazein*, to do a thing suddenly.] impromptu; offhand; slight; hasty; not fully considered.

au′tō·scōpe, *n.* [*auto-*, and Gr. *skopein*, to look at, examine.] an instrument whereby one is enabled to examine his own eye, throat, etc.

au·tos′cō·py, *n.* the examination of oneself, particularly of the eyes or throat, by instruments designed for the purpose.

au′tō·sīte, *n.* [*auto-*, and Gr. *sitos*, food.] part of a twin fetal monster which supplies nourishment to the other, which is called the *parasite.*

au·tō·sit′ic, *a.* pertaining to or having the characteristics of an autosite.

au′tō·sōme, *n.* [*auto-*, and chromo*some.*] any chromosome other than the sex chromosomes.

au″tō·stă·bil′i·ty, *n.* [*auto-*, and *stability.*] in mechanics, (a) stability due to a thing's qualities; (b) stability due to an automatic stabilizing mechanism, as a gyroscope.

au·tō·sty̆l′ic, *a.* [*auto-*, and Gr. *stylos*, column.] in anatomy, lacking a regular suspensorium; having the jaws attached directly to the cranium.

au′tō·sug·ges′tion (-chun), *n.* [*auto-*, and L. *suggestio*, a suggestion, from *suggerere*, to put under.] suggestion to oneself arising within one's own mind and having effects on one's thinking and bodily functions.

au·tō·tem′nous, *a.* [*auto-*, and Gr. *temnein*, to cut.] in biology, capable of self-division, as tissue cells, etc.

au′tō·thē·ism, *n.* [*auto-*, and Gr. *theos*, God.]

1. the doctrine of the self-existence of the Deity: used particularly with reference to Christ, or the second person of the Trinity. [Rare.]

2. self-worship; excessive vanity.

au′tō·thē·ist, *n.* 1. a believer in autotheism.

2. a worshiper of self.

au·tot′ō·mic, *a.* self-intersecting.

au″tō·tox·ē′mi·a, au″tō·tox·ae′mi·a, *n.* autointoxication.

au·tō·tox′ic, *a.* of or producing autotoxemia.

au·tō·tox′in, *n.* [*auto-*, and *toxin.*] any toxin or poison produced inside the body.

au″tō·trans·fọrm′ẽr, *n.* [*auto-*, and L. *transformare*, to change in shape.] in electricity, a transformer with part of the winding common to both primary and secondary circuits.

au·tō·troph′ic, *a.* [*auto-*, and *trophic.*] in botany, making its own food: said of a plant in which photosynthesis can occur.

au′tō·truck, *n.* [*auto-*, and *truck.*] a truck driven by a motor.

au′tō·type, *n.* [*auto-*, and Gr. *typos*, a stamp.]

1. in photography, (a) a process of reproducing works of art in one color or different shades of one color by a carbon pigment; (b) a picture produced by this process.

2. a facsimile.

au″tō·ty·pog′ra·phy, *n.* [*auto-*, and Gr. *typos*, an impression, stamp, and *graphein*, to write.] a process of printing in which relief drawings in gelatin are transferred to a soft metal plate, from which copies may be printed.

au·tot′y·py, *n.* the art of reproducing by the autotype process.

au·tox″i·dā′tion, *n.* [*aut-*, and *oxidation.*] in chemistry, the oxidation of a substance by its exposure to air.

au·tre·fois′ (ō-tr-fwä′), *adv.* [Fr.] in law, formerly; at a former time, as in *autrefois acquit* (or *attaint*, or *convict*), formally acquitted (or attainted, or convicted): used in a plea that is entered in order to prevent a second prosecution for the same offense.

au′tumn, *n.* [ME. *autumpne*; OFr. *autompne*; L. *autumnus*, autumn; prob. of Etruscan origin.]

1. the third season of the year, or that between summer and winter: also called *fall.* Astronomically, it dates in the northern temperate zone from the autumnal equinox, September 23, to the winter solstice, December 21. Popularly, however, *autumn* in the United States comprises the months of September, October, and November.

2. any period of ripeness; maturity; the beginning of old age and decline; as, life's *autumn.*

au′tumn, *a.* of, in, characteristic of, or like autumn: also called *fall.*

au·tum′năl, *a.* 1. of, in, or characteristic of autumn.

2. blooming or maturing in autumn.

3. of or in the later period of life.

autumnal equinox; the time when the sun crosses the equator as it proceeds southward, the equinox occurring about September 23.

autumnal point; the point of the equator intersected by the ecliptic, as the sun proceeds southward; the first point of Libra.

autumnal signs; the signs Libra, Scorpio, and Sagittarius, through which the sun passes between the autumnal equinox and winter solstice.

au·tum′năl, *n.* a plant that blossoms in autumn.

au·tum′năl·ly, *adv.* in or as in autumn.

au′tumn bells, the European plant *Gentiana Pneumonanthe*, whose bell-shaped flowers appear in autumn.

au′tumn crō′cus, any of various related plants of the lily family, with large, white, pink, or purplish flowers in autumn; colchicum: not related to the true crocus.

au′tun·īte, *n.* [*Autun*, name of a French city, and *-ite.*] a yellowish uranium calcium phosphate: it is radioactive and occurs in the form of crystals or scales.

aux (ō; before vowel sounds, ōz), [Fr. contr. of *à les*; *à*, to, and *les*, pl. def. art., the.] see *à la.*

aux·a·nom′e·tẽr, *n.* [Gr. *auxein*, to increase, and *metron*, measure.] an instrument for measuring and recording the growth of plants.

aux·ē′sis, *n.* [Gr. *auxēsis*, increase.]

1. in rhetoric, a figure by which anything is exaggerated; the use of a more unusual and high-sounding word for the ordinary and proper word; hyperbole; exaggeration.

2. in mathematics, the ratio in which an element in one figure must be increased to conform to the corresponding element in a conformable figure.

3. increase in magnitude or extent.

aux·et′ic, *a.* relating to auxesis; amplifying; increasing.

aux·il′iăr (agz-), *n.* an auxiliary. [Rare.]

aux·il′iăr, *a.* auxiliary. [Rare.]

aux·il′iăr·ly, *adv.* by means of aid or help.

aux·il′ia·ry, *a.* [L. *auxiliaris*, helpful, from *auxilium*, aid, from *augere*, to increase; Gr. *auxanein*, to grow.]

1. helping; aiding; assisting; giving aid or support by joint exertion, influence, or use; as, *auxiliary* troops.

2. subsidiary.

3. additional; supplementary.

auxiliary notes; in music, notes representing tones subsidiary to harmony but inserted for variety.

auxiliary quantity; in mathematics, a quantity employed to elucidate an equation or trigonometrical problem.

auxiliary scales; in music, the six keys or scales, consisting of any key major, with its relative minor, and the attendant keys of each.

auxiliary ship; (a) a ship that tends and supplies warships; (b) a naval vessel not used for combat, as a mine layer or hospital ship.

auxiliary verb; a verb that helps form tenses, aspects, moods, or voices of other verbs, as *have, be, may, can, must, do, shall, will.* Examples: *has* and *been* in "He has been working."

aux·il′ia·ry, *n.*; *pl.* **aux·il′ia·ries,** 1. an auxiliary person or thing.

2. foreign or allied armed forces aiding those of a country at war.

3. an assisting or supplementary group or organization; as, this club has a women's *auxiliary.*

4. an auxiliary verb.

5. in mathematics, an auxiliary quantity.

aux·il′ia·tō·ry, *n.* help; aid. [Rare.]

aux·il′ia·tō·ry, *a.* helping; aiding. [Rare.]

aux′in (aks′), *n.* [from Gr. *auxein*, to increase, grow; and *-in.*] any of several related substances found in plant sprouts, human urine, etc., which can stimulate cell growth in plant tissues, promote root formation, etc.

aux′ō·chrōme, *n.* [from Gr. *auxanein*, to increase; and *chrome.*] in chemistry, any group of atoms, as the -OH radical, which, when added to a chromogen, converts it into a pigment or dye.

aux·ol′ō·gy, *n.* [Gr. *auxanein*, to increase, and *logos*, description.] a division of zoology that includes embryology.

aux·om′e·tẽr, *n.* [Gr. *auxanein*, to increase, and *metron*, a measure.] an instrument for measuring the magnifying power of an optical apparatus.

aux·ō·ton′ic, *a.* [Gr. *auxanein*, to grow, and *tonos*, a strain, tension.] in botany, determined or induced by growth: applied to movements of the organs in plants.

ä·va′, *adv.* of all; at all. [Scot.]

ä′vä, *n.* kava.

av″a·da·vat′, *n.* amadavat.

a·vāil′, *v.i.* and *v.t.*; availed, *pt., pp.*; availing; *ppr.* [ME. *availen*; OFr. *avaler*; from L. *ad*, to, or for, and *valere*, to be strong.] to be of use, help, worth, or advantage (to), as in accomplishing an end; as, will force alone *avail* us?

to avail oneself of; to take advantage of (an opportunity, etc.); utilize.

a·vāil′, *n.* 1. profit; advantage; use or help; benefit; as, labor, without economy, is of little *avail*; I doubt whether it will be of much *avail.*

2. [*pl.*] profits or proceeds; as, the *avails* of a year's trade. [Rare.]

Syn.—benefit, profit, service, use, utility.

a·vāil′, *v.t.* and *v.i.* avale. [Obs.]

a·vāil·a·bil′i·ty, *n.* 1. availableness; the state or quality of being available.

2. *pl.* **a·vāil·a·bil′i·ties,** an available person or thing.

a·vāil′a·ble, *a.* 1. capable of being used; usable; as, *available* resources.

2. that can be got, had, or reached; handy; accessible.

3. that can avail. [Obs.]
4. in law, valid.

à·vāil'à·ble·ness, *n.* 1. the quality of being available.
2. competent power; legal force; validity; as, the *availableness* of a title.

à·vāil'à·bly, *adv.* in an available manner.

à·vāil'ment, *n.* profit; efficacy; successful issue. [Rare.]

ā'văl, *a.* [L. *avus,* grandfather.] relating to a grandparent or grandparents.

à·văl', *n.* [Fr. *à val,* at the bottom.] an endorsement on a bill, etc., guaranteeing that it will be paid.

av'à·lanche, *n.* [Fr. (altered by association with *avaler,* to descend) from *lavanche,* from LL. *labina,* slippery place, from L. *labes,* a falling down, from *labi,* to slip, glide down.]
1. a mass of loosened snow, earth, etc. suddenly and swiftly sliding down a mountain and often growing as it descends.
2. anything regarded as like an avalanche; as, an *avalanche* of mail, of blows, etc.

av'à·lanche, *v.i.* and *v.t.*; avalanched, *pt., pp.*; avalanching, *ppr.* to come down (on) like an avalanche.

à·vāle', *v.t.* [ME. *avalen;* OFr. *avaler,* to let down; from L. *ad vallem,* to the valley.]
1. to let down; to lower; to cause to descend; as, to *avale* a sail. [Obs.]
2. to depress; to make abject; as, to *avale* the sovereignty. [Obs.]

à·vāle', *v.i.* to fall, as rain or the tide; to descend; to dismount. [Obs.]

Av'à·lon, Av'ăl·lon, *n.* [Fr., from ML. *Avallonis* (*insula*), from Celt.] in Celtic legend, the isle of the dead, an island paradise in the west where King Arthur and other heroes supposedly went after death: also *Avilion.*

à·vänt'-çöu''ri·ẽr, [Fr. *avant,* before, and *courir,* to run, from L. *currere,* to run.] a person dispatched before another person or company, to give notice of his or their approach.

à·vänt-gärde', *n.* [Fr., lit., advance guard.] the leaders in new or unconventional movements, esp. in the arts; vanguard.

av'à·rice, *n.* [ME. *avarice;* OFr. *avarice;* L. *avaritia,* avarice, from *avarus,* greedy, from *avere,* to wish, desire.] an inordinate desire of gaining and possessing wealth; covetousness; greediness or insatiable desire of gain; cupidity; also, in a figurative sense, an excessive desire for some benefit or advantage.

Syn.—covetousness, greediness, cupidity.

av·à·ri'cious, *a.* covetous; greedy of gain; immoderately desirous of accumulating property; characterized by avarice.

Syn.—covetous, parsimonious, penurious, miserly, niggardly.—The *covetous* eagerly desire wealth, even at the expense of others; the *avaricious* hoard it; the *penurious, parsimonious,* and *miserly* save it by disgraceful self-denial; and the *niggardly,* by meanness in their dealings with others.

av·à·ri'cious·ly, *adv.* covetously; with inordinate desire of gaining wealth.

av·à·ri'cious·ness, *n.* the quality of being avaricious; insatiable or inordinate desire for property.

av'à·rous, *a.* greedy of gain. [Obs.]

à·väst', *interj.* [corrupted from D. *hou'vast, houd vast,* hold fast.] in nautical usage, stop! cease!

av·à·tär', *n.* [Sans. *avatâra,* from *ava,* down, and *tarati,* he goes, passes beyond.]
1. in Hindu religion, a god's coming down in bodily form to the earth; incarnation.
2. an embodiment; bodily manifestation.

à·vaunce', *v.t.* and *v.i.* to advance. [Obs.]

à·vaunt', *interj.* [ME. *avaunt;* OFr. *avant,* forward; LL. *abante,* from L. *ab,* from, and *ante,* before.] begone! depart! go away! [Archaic.]

à·vaunt', *v.t.* and *v.i.* to advance; also, to boast. [Obs.]

à·vaunt', *n.* a boast. [Obs.]

à·vaunt'ẽr, à·vaunt'öur, *n.* a boaster. [Obs.]

Ā'vē (*or* ä'vē), *n.* [L., imper. of *avere,* to be well.]
1. the prayer *Ave Maria.*
2. the time when this prayer is said.
3. [a–] the salutation *ave.*

ā'vē, *interj.* 1. hail!
2. farewell!

à''veç'' plāi''șir', [Fr.] with pleasure; gladly.

av'el, *n.* [ME. *aile, eile;* AS. *egl,* the beard of grain.] the beard or awn of barley, oats, and some other grains. [Dial.]

à·vel', à·vell', *v.t.* to pull or tear away. [Obs.]

av'el·ẽr, av'el·lẽr, *n.* a machine for avelling grain.

à·vel'lāne, à·vel'lan, *a.* [OFr. *avelane,* the filbert nut; name derived from L. *Avellana,* or *Abellana,* a town in Campania.] in heraldry, pertaining to a cross whose quarters resemble filbert nuts (the fruit of *Corylus Avellana*), as in the accompanying figure.

AVELLANE CROSS

Ä'vę Mä·ri'ä, Ā'vē Mā'ry, [from the first words of the Roman Catholic prayer to the Virgin Mary; L. *ave, Maria,* hail, Mary.]
1. a prayer to the Virgin Mary used in the Roman Catholic Church, chaplets and rosaries being divided into a certain number of *Ave Marias* and paternosters.
2. any of several musical settings of this prayer.
3. a particular time, in Roman Catholic countries, as in Italy, about half an hour after sunset, and also at early dawn, when the bells ring and the people repeat the *Ave Maria,* or Hail Mary.

A·vē'nȧ, *n.* [L., oats.] a genus of plants belonging to the family *Gramineæ.* The most important species is the cultivated oat, *Avena sativa.*

av·ē·nā'ceous, *a.* [L. *avenaceus,* from *avena,* oats.] belonging to, or having the nature of, oats or the oat grasses.

av'ē·nāge, *n.* [OFr. *avenage,* from L. *avena,* oats.] in old English law, a certain quantity of oats paid by a tenant to a landlord in lieu of rent or other duty.

av'ē·nẽr, av'ē·nor, *n.* [Fr.] in English feudal law, an officer attached to the king's stables, whose duty was to provide oats, etc. for the horses.

à·venġe', *v.i.* and *v.t.*; avenged, *pt., pp.*; avenging, *ppr.* [ME. *avengen;* OFr. *avengier,* to avenge; *a-,* and *vengier,* to avenge; from L *ad,* to, and *vindicare,* to punish.]
1. to get revenge for (a wrong, injury, etc.) by punishing the injuring party.
2. to take vengeance on behalf of, as for a wrong.

à·venġe', *n.* vengeance. [Obs.]

à·venġe'ănce, *n.* vengeance. [Obs.]

à·venġe'fụl, *a.* vengeful.

à·venġe'ment, *n.* vengeance; punishment; the act of taking satisfaction for an injury by inflicting pain or evil on the offender; satisfaction taken; revenge.

à·ven'ġẽr, *n.* one who avenges or vindicates; a vindicator; a revenger.

à·ven'ġẽr·ess, *n.* a woman avenger. [Rare.]

à·vē'nin, *n.* [L. *avena,* oats.] a proteid substance found in oats.

à·vē'nous, à·vē'ni·ous, *a.* [Gr. *a* priv., and L. *vena,* vein.] in botany, lacking veins or nerves.

av'ens, *n.* [ME. *avans;* OFr. *avence.*] a plant belonging to the genus *Geum.* Common *avens,* or herb bennet, is *Geum urbanum,* and water *avens* is *Geum rivale.*

av'en·tāil, av'en·tāyle, *n.* [ME. *aventayle;* OFr. *esventail,* lit. air hole, from L. *ex,* out of, and *ventus,* wind.] the movable part of the front of a helmet.

Av'en·tine (*or* -tīn), *n.* [L. *Aventinus* (*mons*), Aventine (hill).]
1. one of the seven hills on which Rome stood.
2. a post of safety. [Obs.]

Av'en·tine, *a.* of the Aventine hill.

à·ven'tre (-tẽr), *v.t.* to hurl, as a spear. [Obs.]

à·ven'tūre, *n.* [Fr. *aventure,* from L. *advenire,* to come to.] in old law, a mischance causing a person's death without felony, as by drowning or falling from a house. [Obs.]

à·ven'tū·rine, à·ven'tū·rin, *n.* [Fr. *aventure,* adventure.]
1. a variety of translucent quartz, spangled throughout with scales of yellow mica.
2. an ornamental glass, brown with gold specks, now made in Venice. Also written *avanturin(e).*

av'e·nūe, *n.* [Fr. *avenue,* avenue, from *avenir,* to happen, to come, from L. *advenire,* to come to.]
1. a passage; a way or opening for approach or departure.
2. an alley or walk planted on each side with trees, and leading to a house, gate, wood, etc.; hence, any wide walk or driveway bordered by trees.
3. a street, especially a wide one; thoroughfare.
4. figuratively, means of access or attainment; as, the *avenues* to public office.

à·vẽr', *v.t.*; averred, *pt., pp.*; averring, *ppr.* [ME. *averren;* OFr. *averrer,* to confirm; from L. *ad,* to, and *verus,* true.]
1. to affirm with confidence; to declare to be true.
2. in law, to prove; to justify.

Syn.—affirm, declare, assert, asseverate, allege, avow.

ā'vẽr, *n.* [OFr., from L. *habere,* to have.] in England, a horse or ox when used as a beast of burden. [Obs.]

av'ẽr·āġe, *n.* [Fr. *avaris,* decay of wares or merchandise; OFr. *average;* LL. *averagium,* property, prob. from L. *habere,* to have.]
1. in feudal law, a duty or service which a tenant was bound to render to his lord, by his horses, carts, etc., such as the carrying of grain.
2. the numerical result obtained by dividing the sum of two or more quantities by the number of quantities; an arithmetical mean.
3. an approximation to this; usual or normal kind, amount, quality, rate, etc.; as, his opinion is *average.*
4. in marine law, (a) a loss incurred by damage to a ship at sea or to its cargo; (b) an incurring of such loss; (c) the equitable division of such loss among interested parties; (d) a charge arising from such loss.
5. a small duty payable by the shippers of goods to the master of a ship, over and above the freight, for his care of the goods. Hence, the expression in bills of lading, "paying so much freight, with primage and *average* accustomed." [Obs.]

on the average; as an average quantity, rate, etc.; as, he works eight hours a day, *on the average.*

av'ẽr·āġe, *a.* 1. constituting a numerical average; as, his *average* speed is high.
2. usual; normal; ordinary.
3. in marine law, assessed in accordance with the laws of average.

av'ẽr·āġe, *v.t.*; averaged, *pt., pp.*; averaging, *ppr.* 1. to calculate the average or mean of.
2. to do, take, etc. on an average; as, he *averages* eight hours of work a day.
3. to divide proportionately among more than two; as, they *averaged* the loss among themselves.

av'ẽr·āġe, *v.i.* 1. to come to an average; to amount to on an average; as, the results *average* well.
2. to buy or sell more shares, goods, etc. so as to get a better average price.

av'ẽr·āġe·ly, *adv.* in an average manner; on the average.

à·vẽr'ment, *n.* [ME. *averren;* OFr. *averrer,* to confirm; from L. *ad,* to, and *verus,* true, and *-ment.*]
1. an averring or being averred.
2. something averred; assertion.
3. in law, formerly, an offer of either party to justify or prove what he alleged.

A·vẽr'năl, A·vẽr'ni·ăn, *a.* [L. *Avernus,* from Gr. *aornos,* without birds; *a* priv., and *ornos,* bird.] pertaining to *Avernus,* a lake near Naples, Italy, represented by classical poets as the entrance to hell. From its waters mephitic vapors arose which are said to have killed the birds that attempted to fly over it.

A·vẽr'nus, *n.* in Roman mythology, Hades; hell.

av'ẽr·pen''ny, *n.* in old English law, money paid by a tenant instead of the service of average.

A·ver'rō·ișm, A·ver'rhō·ișm, *n.* the doctrines of the Averroists, especially that the soul is mortal.

A·ver'rō·ist, A·ver'rhō·ist, *n.* one of the followers of Averr(h)oës (1126–1198), a Moslem philosopher and physician.

av·ẽr·ruñ'çāte, *v.t.* [L. *averruncare,* to avert, or turn away; *a,* or *ab,* from, and *verruncare,* to turn about.]
1. to root up; to scrape or tear away by the roots. [Obs.]
2. to prune.
3. to avert; to turn aside; to ward off. [Obs.]

av''ẽr·ruñ·çā'tion, *n.* 1. the act of tearing up or raking away the roots. [Obs.]
2. the act of pruning, or cutting off superfluous branches.
3. the act of turning aside or averting. [Obs.]

av·ẽr·ruñ'çā·tŏr, *n.* in arboriculture, an instrument for pruning trees, consisting of two blades fixed on the end of a rod, and so constructed as to operate like a pair of shears.

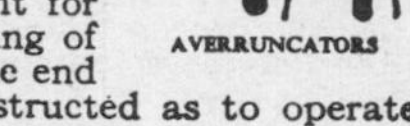

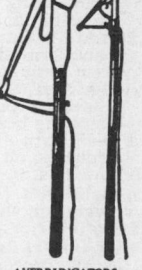

AVERRUNCATORS

ȧ·vẽr′sănt, *a.* [L. *aversans*, turning away, ppr. of *aversari*, to turn away.] in heraldry, turned to show the back: said of a right hand.

av·ẽr·sā′tion, *n.* a turning from with disgust or dislike; aversion; hatred; disinclination. [Obs.]

ȧ·vẽrse′, *a.* [L. *aversus*, pp. of *avertere*, to turn away.]

1. turned away or backward. [Archaic.]

2. disliking; unwilling; set against; reluctant.

And Pallas, now *averse*, refused her aid. —Dryden.

3. in botany, turned away from the axis or main stem: opposed to *adverse*.

This word and its derivatives are now regularly followed by *to*, and not by *from*.

Syn.—backward, loath, reluctant, repugnant, unwilling, disinclined, hostile, opposed. —*Averse* implies habitual dislike or unwillingness, though not of a very strong character, and is nearly synonymous with *disinclined*; as, *averse* to study, to active pursuits. *Reluctant* implies some degree of struggle, either with others who are inciting us on, or between our own inclination and some compelling motive, as sense of duty.

ȧ·vẽrse′, *v.t* and *v.i.* to avert. [Obs.]

ȧ·vẽrse′ly, *adv.* 1. with repugnance; unwillingly.

2. backward; behind; as, an arm stretched *aversely*. [Rare.]

ȧ·vẽrse′ness, *n.* opposition of mind; dislike; unwillingness; backwardness.

ȧ·vẽr′sion, *n.* [L. *aversus*, pp. of *avertere*, to turn away; *a*, or *ab*, from, and *vertere*, to turn.]

1. an averting; a turning away.

2. intense or definite dislike; antipathy; repugnance.

3. the object arousing such dislike; as, snobs are his chief *aversion*.

4. reluctance.

Syn.—antipathy, disgust, reluctance, repugnance, abhorrence, contrariety, detestation, dislike, hatred, opposition.

ȧ·vẽrt′, *v.t.*; averted, *pt.*, *pp.*; averting, *ppr.* [L. *avertere*, to turn away; *a*, or *ab*, from, and *vertere*, to turn.]

1. to turn from; to turn off or away; as, to *avert* the eyes from an object.

2. to ward off, divert, or prevent; as, to *avert* an approaching calamity.

3. to dislike; to oppose. [Obs.]

ȧ·vẽrt′, *v.i.* to turn away. [Obs.]

ȧ·vẽrt′ed, *a.* turned from or away; unfavorable; unpropitious.

ȧ·vẽrt′ẽr, *n.* a person or thing that averts.

ȧ·vẽrt′i·ble, *a.* capable of being averted or prevented.

ȧ·vẽr′ti·ment, *n.* advertisement. [Obs.]

Ā′vēş, *n.pl.* [L., pl. of *avis*, bird.] the class of vertebrates comprising the birds: they breathe by lungs, have warm, red blood and a double circulation, are produced from eggs, and covered with feathers, and have a prominent naked toothless bill and four limbs, the two anterior being adapted for flight and called wings.

Ȧ·ves′tȧ, *n.* [from Per.] the sacred writings of the ancient Zoroastrian religion and of its present-day form among the Parsees.

Ȧ·ves′tăn, *a.* 1. of or pertaining to the Avesta.

2. of the Indo-European, Iranic language in which the Avesta was written.

Ȧ·ves′tăn, *n.* the Indo-European, Iranic language in which the Avesta was written, sometimes identified as that of the Medes.

ä″vi·ä·dôr′, *n.* [Sp. Am.] a person who supplies funds and materials for working a mine.

ā′vi·ăn, *a.* of or pertaining to birds; of Aves.

ā′vi·ā·ry, *n.*; *pl.* **ā′vi·ā·rieş,** [L. *aviarium*, an aviary, from *avis*, a bird.] a large cage or enclosure for the breeding, rearing, and keeping of birds.

ā′vi·āte, *v.i.*; aviated, *pt.*, *pp.*; aviating, *ppr.* [back-formation from *aviation*.] to fly in, especially to operate, an aircraft.

ā·vi·ā′tion, *n.* [Fr., from L. *avis*, bird.] the art or science of flying airplanes; making and operating heavier-than-air craft.

ā′vi·ā·tŏr, *n.* [L. *avis*, bird.] a person who flies airplanes; airplane pilot; airman; flier.

ā″vi·ā′trix, *n.* a woman aviator.

Ȧ·viç′ū·lȧ, *n.* [L., dim. of *avis*, bird.] a genus of bivalve mollusks, including the wing shells.

ȧ·viç′ū·lăr, *a.* of or pertaining to birds.

ȧ·viç·ū·lā′ri·um, *n.*; *pl.* **ȧ·viç·ū·lā′ri·ȧ,** a prehensile process found in the cells of many of the *Polyzoa*, resembling a bird's head in shape.

ā′vi·çul·tūre, *n.* [L. *avis*, bird, and *cultura*, culture.] the raising and care of birds.

av′id, *a.* [L. *avidus*, covetous.] very eager; greedy.

av′i·din, *n.* [*avid*, and *-in*; so named because of its peculiar biotin-binding capacity.] a substance, protein in nature, found in egg white and neutralized in action by biotin, which forms a compound with it.

ȧ·vid′i·ous, *a.* avid.

ȧ·vid′i·ous·ly, *adv.* eagerly; with greediness.

ȧ·vid′i·ty, *n.* [Fr. *avidité*; L. *aviditas*, greed, from *avere*, to desire.]

1. greediness; great eagerness.

2. in chemistry, (a) the strength of a base or acid in terms of its dissociation; (b) the degree of affinity. [Rare.]

Syn.—greediness, eagerness, gluttony, cupidity, graspingness.

ā·vi·fau′nȧ, *n.* [L. *avis*, bird, and *faunus*, faun, from *favere*, to favor.] all the birds of a district.

av″i·gā′tion, *n.* the science or art of piloting aircraft by means of instruments, the position of the stars, or by landmarks.

A·vi·gnon′ ber′ry (ȧ-vēn-yaṅ′), the fruit of *Rhamnus infectorius*, so called from the city Avignon, in France. It is used by dyers and painters as a yellow stain: also called *buckthorn berry*, *yellow berry*.

Ȧ·vil′iŏn, *n.* [Fr.] Avalon.

ā·vir′ū·lent, *a.* not virulent or no longer virulent, as certain bacteria, etc.

ȧ·vīşe′, *v.t.* and *v.i.* [Fr. *aviser*, to advise.] to advise. [Obs.]

ȧ·vi′şion, *n.* vision. [Obs.]

ȧ·vī′şō, *n.*; *pl.* **ȧ·vī′şōş,** [Sp.] 1. advice; information; intelligence.

2. a dispatch boat.

ā·vī″tȧ·min·ō′sis, *n.* a pathological condition caused by insufficient vitamins in the food eaten.

av·i·zan′dum, *n.* [Fr. *aviser*, to advise; L. *avisandum*, gerund of *avisare*, to advise; a term used in Law Latin.] in Scots law, private consideration. A judge makes *avizandum* with a case when he removes it from court and takes it into his private consideration.

av·ō·çä′dō, *n.*; *pl.* **av·ō·çä′dōş,** [corrupted from Mex. *ahuacatl*.]

1. a thick-skinned, pear-shaped tropical fruit, *Persea gratissima*, yellowish-green to purplish-black, with a single large seed and yellow, buttery flesh, used in salads: also called *alligator pear*.

2. the tree that bears this fruit.

AVOCADO

av′ō·çat, *n.* [Fr., from L. *avocatus*, pp. of *avocare*, to call away.] an advocate.

av′ō·çāte, *v.t.* [L. *avocare*, from *a*, from, and *vocare*, to call.] to call off or away. [Obs.]

av·ō·çā′tion, *n.* [L. *avocatio*, a calling off; from *avocare*, to call away.]

1. the act of calling away or diverting from something. [Obs.]

2. a person's regular business or occupation; vocation; employment. [This use of the word is generally avoided to prevent confusion with sense 3.]

The ancient *avocation* of picking pockets. —Sydney Smith.

The wandering *avocation* of a shepherd. —Buckle.

3. something one does in addition to his vocation or regular work, and usually for fun; hobby: the current sense.

Syn.—employment, occupation, business, vocation, calling.

ȧ·voç′ȧ·tive, *a.* same as *avocatory*.

av·ō·çä′tō, *n.* same as *avocado*.

ȧ·voç′ȧ·tō·ry, *a.* calling away or aside; recalling.

letters avocatory; letters from a ruler recalling subjects from another country or directing them to discontinue certain illegal acts.

av′ō·cet, *n.* [Fr. *avocette*; It. *avocetta*.] any of a number of related long-legged wading birds with webbed feet and a slender bill that curves upward: also spelled *avoset*.

Ä·vō·gä′drō′s law, the theory, formulated by Avogadro, that equal volumes of all gases under identical conditions of temperature and pressure contain equal numbers of molecules.

ȧ·void′, *v.t.*; avoided, *pt.*, *pp.*; avoiding, *ppr.* [ME. *avoiden*, to avoid; OFr. *esvuidier*, *esveudier*, to empty out, from L. *ex*, out, and *viduare*, to deprive of.]

1. to shun; to keep at a distance from; to keep clear of; to abstain from; as, to *avoid* the company of gamesters, to *avoid* expense.

2. to void; to make empty; also, to quit; to evacuate; to shun by leaving. [Obs.]

3. to make void; to annul or invalidate; as, to *avoid* a deed or grant.

4. in pleading, to defeat or evade (the allegation of the other party) by setting up some new matter.

Syn.—shun, elude, eschew, avert, escape, evade, keep away from, keep clear of.

ȧ·void′, *v.i.* 1. to retire; to withdraw. [Obs.]

2. to become void, vacant, or empty, as a benefice. [Obs.]

ȧ·void′ȧ·ble, *a.* 1. that may be avoided, shunned, or escaped.

2. that may become void or invalid. [Rare.]

ȧ·void′ănce, *n.* 1. the act of avoiding or the state of being avoided.

2. the act of becoming vacant, or the state of being vacant: said of a church benefice.

3. the act of annulling.

4. the act of emptying; removal. [Obs.]

5. a means of emptying; an outlet. [Obs.]

ȧ·void′ẽr, *n.* 1. one who avoids, shuns, or escapes.

2. one who or that which empties or carries things away. [Obs.]

ȧ·void′less, *a.* that cannot be avoided; inevitable.

av″oir·dū·poiş′ (-ẽr-dū-), *n.* [ME. *aver de poiz*; OFr. *aver de peis*; *aver*, goods, from L. *habere*, to have; *de*, from, L. *de*, from; *peis*, from L. *pensum*, weight.]

1. a system of weights commonly used in the United States and England for commodities of all kinds except precious metals, precious stones, and drugs: also called *avoirdupois weight*. The pound, the unit weight, contains 16 ounces instead of 12 ounces, as in troy weight; 2,000 pounds constitute the common or "short" ton, while the "long" ton contains 2,240 pounds. The pound *avoirdupois* contains 7,000 troy grains, and is equivalent to $1^{31}/_{144}$ pound troy.

2. commodities sold by weight. [Obs.]

3. weight; heaviness; as, *avoirdupois* counts in football. [Colloq.]

ȧ·vōke′, *v.t.* [L. *avocare*, to call away.] to call back or away. [Rare.]

av′ō·lāte, *v.i.* [L. *avolare*, to fly away.] to fly off; to escape; to evaporate. [Obs.]

av·ō·lā′tion, *n.* the act of flying away; flight; escape; evaporation. [Obs.]

ȧ vo·lon·té′ (ȧ vō-lōṅ-tā′), [Fr.] at will: at pleasure.

av′ō·set, *n.* same as *avocet*.

ȧ vo·tre san·té′ (ȧ vō-tr säṅ-tā′), [Fr.] to your health: a toast in drinking.

ȧ·vouch′, *v.t.*; avouched, *pt.*, *pp.* avouching, *ppr.* [ME. *avouchen*; OFr. *avochier*, to affirm positively; from L. *advocare*, to summon.]

1. to affirm openly; to declare or assert with positiveness; to avow; also, to acknowledge openly; as, to *avouch* one's guilt; to *avouch* the Lord to be thy God.

2. to maintain, vindicate, or justify; to make good; to answer for; to establish; to substantiate; to guarantee.

3. to appeal to; to cite as authority. [Obs.]

ȧ·vouch′, *v.i.* to give assurance or guarantee; as, to *avouch* for another's character or reputation.

ȧ·vouch′, *n.* avouchment. [Archaic.]

ȧ·vouch′ȧ·ble, *a.* capable of being avouched.

ȧ·vouch′ẽr, *n.* one who avouches.

ȧ·vouch′ment, *n.* the act of avouching; affirmation; guarantee.

ȧ·vou·é′ (ä-vö-ā′), *n.* [Fr., from OFr. *avoue*, pp. of *avouer*, to avow, from L. *advocare*, to call upon or summon.]

1. in France, formerly, a patron of a church or religious community.

2. a French attorney.

ȧ·vow′, *v.t.*; avowed, *pt.*, *pp.*; avowing, *ppr.* [ME. *avowen*; OFr. *avouer*, to avow, or confess; from L. *advocare*, to call upon.]

1. to declare openly; to own, acknowledge, or confess frankly.

2. to acknowledge (oneself) to be; as, he *avowed* himself a patriot.

3. in law, to acknowledge and justify.

Syn.—acknowledge, profess, declare, confess, admit, aver, own.

ȧ·vow′, *n.* an avowal; acknowledgment. [Obs.]

ȧ·vow′, *v.t.* and *v.i.* to devote; to promise; to bind. [Obs.]

ȧ·vow′ȧ·ble, *a.* capable of being avowed.

ȧ·vow′ăl, *n.* an open declaration; frank acknowledgment.

a·vow'ănce, *n.* 1. avowal.
2. defense or vindication. [Obs.]
a·vow'ănt, *n.* in law, the defendant in replevin, who admits the distraining of goods, and maintains his right to do so.
a·vowed', *a.* openly declared; known; frankly acknowledged.
a·vow'ed·ly, *adv.* in an open manner; with frank acknowledgment.
a·vow'ẽr, *n.* one who avows.
a·vow'ry, *n.* 1. in law, the act of the distrainer of goods, who, in an action avows and justifies the taking by maintaining that he took them in his own right.
2. justification. [Obs.]
a·voy'ẽr, *n.* [Fr. *avoyer.*] formerly, the chief magistrate of an imperial city or canton of French Switzerland.
á vues'tra sa·lud' (á vwes'trä sä-lud'), [Sp.] to your health: a toast in drinking.
a·vulse', *v.t.* [L. *avulsus,* pp. of *avellere,* to pluck off.] to pull off; to pluck.
a·vul'sion, *n.* [L. *avulsio,* from *avello; a,* from, and *vello,* to pull.]
1. a pulling or tearing away; a rending or forcible separation.
2. that part which is torn away.
3. in law, a sudden removal of part of the land of one person and its addition to the land of another without change in ownership, as by a change in the course of a stream.
a·vun'çū·lăr, *a.* [L. *avunculus,* uncle.] of, pertaining to, or like an uncle.
aw, *interj.* a sound of protest, dislike, disgust, etc.
a·wä', *adv.* [Scot.] away.
a·wāit', *v.t.*; awaited, *pt., pp.*; awaiting, *ppr.* [ME. *awaiten*; OFr. *awaiter,* to wait for; *a,* to, and *waiter*; later *guaitier,* Fr. *guetter,* to watch.]
1. to lie in wait for. [Obs.]
2. to wait for; to look for or expect.
Betwixt these rocky pillars Gabriel sat,
Chief of the angelic guards, *awaiting* night.
—Milton.
3. to be in store for; to be ready for; as, a glorious reward *awaits* the good.
4. to wait upon; to serve. [Obs.]
a·wāit', *v.i.* 1. to watch. [Obs.]
2. to remain in waiting; to wait.
a·wāit', *n.* ambush; a state of waiting. [Obs.]
a·wāke', *v.t.*; awoke *or* awaked, *pt.*; awaked *or* awoke, *pp.*; awaking, *ppr.*; awoken *or* awaken, *obs. pp.* [ME. *awecchen*; AS. *aweccan,* to awaken.]
1. to rouse from sleep.
I go, that I may *awake* him out of sleep.
—John xi. 11.
2. to excite or rouse from a state resembling sleep, as from death, stupor, or inaction; to put into action or new life; as, to *awake* the dead; to *awake* the dormant faculties.
3. to call forth (memories, fears, etc.)
Syn.—arouse, excite, provoke, stimulate, incite, animate.
a·wāke', *v.i.* [ME. *awaken,* awake; AS. *āwacian,* to be awake.]
1. to cease to sleep; to come out of sleep.
Jacob *awaked* out of his sleep.
—Gen. xxviii. 16.
2. to be roused from a state of inaction; to become active; to be invigorated with new life; as, the mind *awakes* from its stupidity; he *awoke* to life's higher significance.
a·wāke', *a.* 1. not sleeping.
2. in a state of vigilance or action; active; alert.
a·wāk'en, *v.t.* and *v.i.*; awakened, *pt., pp.*; awakening, *ppr.* to rouse from inactivity; to stir into life and energy; to awake; wake up.
a·wāk'en·ẽr, *n.* one who or that which awakens.
a·wāk'en·ing, *n.* the act of rousing from sleep or inactivity; specifically, a revival of religion, impulses, etc.
a·wāk'en·ing·ly, *adv.* in an awakening manner.
a·wāk'en·ment, *n.* an awakening.
a·want'ing, *a.* wanting; lacking.
a·ward', *v.t.*; awarded, *pt., pp.*; awarding, *ppr.* [ME. *awarden*; OFr. *eswarder,* to award; *es,* out, and *warder,* to guard, from O.H.G. *warten,* to guard.]
1. to adjudge; to give by sentence or judicial decision; to assign as the result of careful consideration, as to competitors in any contest.
2. to grant; to allot; to bestow.
The child had many more luxuries and indulgences than had been *awarded* to his father. —Thackeray.
a·ward', *v.i.* to judge; to determine; to make an award. [Obs.]
a·ward', *n.* 1. a judgment, sentence, or decision; as, the *award* of Providence; the *award* of posterity.
2. the paper containing the decision of arbitrators, etc.; as, a sealed *award.*
3. something awarded; a prize.
a·ward'ẽr, *n.* one who awards.
a·wāre', *a.* [ME. *aware, iwar*; AS. *gewær* aware, from *wær,* cautious.]
1. watchful; vigilant; guarded. [Obs.]
2. knowing; cognizant; informed; conscious; as, the general was *aware* of the enemy's designs.
Syn.—cognizant, conscious, apprised, informed, sensible, acquainted.
a·warn', *v.t.* to warn. [Obs.]
a·wash', *a.* and *adv.* 1. just above the surface of the water, as a rock just above the waves.
2. floating on the water.
3. washed about by the water.
a·wāy', *adv.* [ME. *away, awey*; AS. *aweg, on weg,* on way.]
1. literally, on the way; along; as, come *away.*
2. at a distance; distant; as, *away* back home.
3. from here or there; from proximity; off; as, to go *away*; to clear *away* rubbish.
4. separate; detached; out of one's possession; as, to give *away* a secret; to put *away* a temptation.
5. in another direction; off; aside; as, to turn *away.*
6. out of existence; to another condition or state; to an end; as, to pass *away*; to fade *away.*
7. on; without intermission; steadily; continuously; as, sing *away.*
8. far; as, *away* behind.
9. at once; as, fire *away.*
10. begone; as, *away,* slight man!: used as a command.
away with; (a) take away; as, *away with* him; (b) go or come away.
far and away; greatly; by far; beyond doubt.
to do away with; to discard or destroy.
to make away with; to kill or destroy; also, to steal or get rid of.
a·wāy', *a.* 1. not present; absent; gone; as, he is *away.*
2. at a distance; as, a mile *away.*
a·wāy'-gō"ing, *a.* departing; leaving; going away from.
away-going crops; in law, crops sown during the last year of a tenancy, but not ripe until after the expiration of it. The right which an outgoing tenant has to take an *away-going crop* is sometimes given to him by the express terms of the contract, but where this is not the case he is generally entitled to do so by the custom of the district.
a·wāy'wărd, *adv.* away. [Obs.]
awe (ạ), *n.* [ME. *aw, awe,* from Ice. *agi,* awe, fear; same root as in Gr. *achos,* fear.]
1. fear mingled with admiration or reverence; a feeling produced by something majestic, sublime, etc.
Stand in *awe,* and sin not. —Ps. iv. 4.
2. fear; dread; as of something evil. [Obs.]
to stand in awe of; to have great fear, dread, or respect for.
Syn.—dread, veneration, reverence.
awe, *v.t.*; awed, *pt., pp.*; awing, *ppr.* to inspire awe in; to influence by fear or respect; as, his majesty *awed* them into silence.
a·wēa'ry, *a.* same as *weary.*
a·weath'ẽr (-weth'), *adv.* and *a.* in nautical usage, to windward or toward the wind; as, the helm is *aweather*: opposed to *alee.*
a·weigh' (-wā'), *a.* in nautical usage, clearing the bottom; being weighed: said of an anchor.
awe'less, *a.* [ME. *awles*; AS. *egeleas,* aweless; *ege,* awe, and *-leas,* less.] lacking awe; also, lacking the ability to inspire awe.
awe'less·ness, *n.* the quality or condition of being aweless.
awe'sōme, *a.* inspiring awe; indicating awe.
awe'sōme·ness, *n.* the quality of causing awe.
awe'-strick"en, *a.* filled with awe.
awe'-strīke, *v.t.* to fill or strike with awe.
awe'-struck, *a.* filled or struck with awe; awe-stricken.
aw'ful, *a.* [ME. *awful, agheful*; AS. *egeful,* awful.]
1. inspiring awe; filling with profound reverence; impressive; as, the *awful* majesty of Jehovah.
2. filling with terror and dread; frightful; dreadful; as, the *awful* approach of death.
3. worthy of reverence and solemn respect.
4. frightful; ugly; detestable; as, an *awful* bonnet; also, excessive; great; remarkable; as, an *awful* lie. [Colloq.]
Syn.—dreadful, fearful, solemn, direful, impressive, appalling.
aw'ful·ly, *adv.* 1. in a manner to fill with awe; in a reverential manner.
2. very; exceedingly; as, *awfully* bad taste. [Colloq.]
aw'ful·ness, *n.* 1. the quality of striking with awe or reverence; solemnity; as, the *awfulness* of this sacred place.
2. the state of being struck with awe. [Obs.]
A help to prayer, producing in us reverence and *awfulness.* —Taylor.
a·whāpe' (-hwāp'), *v.t.* [ME. *awhaped.*] to strike with amazement; to confound. [Obs.]
a·whīle' (-hwīl'), *adv.* for a while; for a short time.
a·wing', *a.* or *adv.* on the wing; in flight.
awk, *n.* an auk. [Obs.]
awk, *a.* [ME. *awke, auke,* from Ice. *öfigr, öfugr,* contrary; root *af,* off, away.]
1. contrary; backward; hence, perverse, wrong, erroneous. [Obs.]
2. not dexterous; unhandy; awkward; clumsy. [Obs.]
awk, awk'ly, *adv.* 1. awkwardly. [Obs.]
2. perversely; in the wrong way. [Obs.]
awk'wărd, *a.* [ME. *awkwarde,* from *awk-,* off, and *-ward*; AS. *-weard*; same root as L. *vertere,* to turn.]
1. hard to handle; inconvenient to use; unwieldy.
2. ungainly; ungraceful in manners; clumsy.
3. inopportune; embarrassing; as, an *awkward* situation.
4. inconvenient; uncomfortable; cramped; as, an *awkward* position.
5. unfavorable; untoward; adverse; unfortunate. [Obs.]
Syn.—clumsy, uncouth, unhandy, bungling, ungainly, unskillful, rough.
awk'wărd āġe, early adolescence, characterized by rapid growth, awkward behavior, and emotional instability.
awk'wărd·ly, *adv.* clumsily; in a bungling manner; inelegantly; badly; uneasily.
awk'wărd·ness, *n.* clumsiness; ungracefulness in manners; want of dexterity in the use of the hands or instruments; unsuitableness; embarrassment.
awl, *n.* [ME. *aul, awel*; AS. *æl,* awel, an awl.] a small, pointed tool for piercing holes in leather, wood, and other soft materials. It is made in various shapes for special uses.

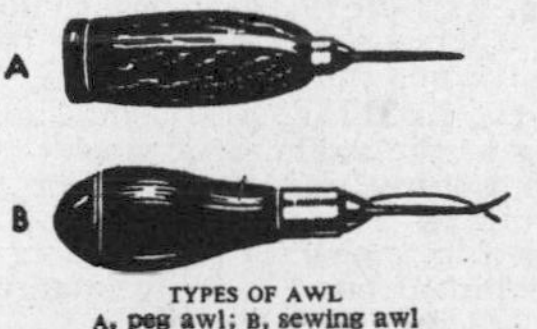

TYPES OF AWL
A, peg awl; B, sewing awl

aw'less, *a.* same as *aweless.*
aw'less·ness, *n.* same as *awelessness.*
awl'-shāped (-shāpt), *a.* 1. having the shape of an awl.
2. in botany, subulate; tapering to a point.
awl'wŏrt, *n.* a small water plant of the mustard family, *Subularia aquatica*: so called from its awl-shaped leaves, which grow in clusters around the root.
awm, aum, *n.* same as *aam.*
awn, *n.* [ME. *awne, agun,* from Ice. *ōgn,* chaff.] the beard of grain or grass; slender, sharp bristles on the head of barley, oats, etc.
awned, *a.* in botany, furnished with awns.
awn'ing, *n.* [Fr. *auvent,* a penthouse; Per. *āwan,* anything suspended; origin uncertain.]
1. a piece of canvas stretched over a frame to shelter from the sun's rays, the rain, and the wind: originally employed as a shelter to a vessel's deck, or a boat, but now used for various other purposes, as before windows.
2. that part of the poop deck which is continued forward, beyond the bulkhead of the cabin.
awn'inged, *a.* equipped with an awning.
awn'less, *a.* without awn or beard.
awn'y, *a.* having awns.
a·wōke', *v.,* alternative past tense and occasional past participle of *awake.*
a·wōk'en, obsolete past participle of *awake.*
A. W. O. L., a. w. o. l., absent without leave: often pronounced (ā'wol).
a·wŏrk', *adv.* [ME. *awerke.*] at work.

ȧ·wrēak′, *v.t.* [ME. *awreken*; AS. *awrecan*, to take vengeance on.] to avenge; to take vengeance on. [Obs.]

ȧ·wrọng′ (-rọng′), *adv.* in a wrong manner.

ȧ·wrȳ′ (-rī′), *a.* or *adv.* [ME. *awry*, *awrye*, *on wry*, turned or twisted.]
1. turned or twisted toward one side: not in a straight or true direction or position; askew; as, to glance *awry*; the lady's cap is *awry*.
2. turned aside from the line of truth or reason; wrong; amiss.

ąw′sōme, *a.* same as *awesome*.

ax, axe, *v.t.* to ask. [Dial.]

ax, axe, *n.*; *pl.* **ax′eṣ,** [ME. *ax*, *axe*; AS. *æx*, *eax*, ax; L. *ascia*; Gr. *axinē*, an ax, mattock.]
1. a tool for hewing or chopping wood, etc., consisting of a head of iron or steel with a cutting edge, and a long handle.
2. any similar tool or weapon, as a battle-ax, headsman's ax, etc.

ax, axe, *v.t.*; axed, *pt.*, *pp.*; axing, *ppr.* to trim with an ax.

ax′ăl, *a.* same as *axial*.

axed (axt), *a.* having a surface dressed smooth with an ax.

axe′măn, *n.* same as *axman*.

ax′ēṣ, *n.*, pl. of *axis*.

ax′eṣ, *n.* pl. of *ax*.

ax′fitch, *n.* [O.D. *akes*, ax, and *vitsche*, fitch.] a leguminous plant having the pods ax-shaped.

ax′i·ăl, *a.* 1. of, pertaining to, or like an axis.
2. moving about an axis.
3. constituting an axis.

ax′i·ăl·ly, *adv.* in the direction or line of the axis.

ax′i·fọrm, *a.* [L. *axis* and *forma*.] in the form of an axis.

ax′il, *n.* [L. *axilla*, shoulder joint, from *ala*, wing.] in botany, the angle between an axis and the upper side of any organ growing from it, as between a branch and the stem of a leaf.

aa. AXILS

ax′ile, *a.* [L. *axis*, an axle.] belonging to, occupying, or lying in the direction of an axis.

ax·il′lȧ, *n.*; *pl.* **ax·il′lae** or **ax·il′lȧṣ,** [L. *axilla*, the armpit.]
1. the hollow underneath the shoulder; the armpit.
2. in botany, an axil.

ax·il′lănt, *a.* in botany, enclosing an axil; forming an axil.

ax′il·lăr, ax′il·lă·ry, *n.* in ornithology, one of the feathers on the under side of the wing where it joins the body.

ax′il·lă·ry, ax′il·lăr, *a.* 1. in anatomy, pertaining to the axilla, or armpit.
2. in botany, pertaining to or proceeding from an axil.

ax′in, *n.* [Sp. *axina*.] a secretion of the Mexican cochineal: used in the preparation of certain medicines and varnishes.

ax′i·nīte, *n.* [Gr. *axinē*, an ax.] a dark-brown mineral, occurring in sharply edged crystals. It consists chiefly of silica, alumina, lime, and oxide of iron.

ax·in′ō·man·cy, *n.* [Gr. *axinē*, an ax, and *manteia*, divination.] an ancient kind of divination by means of an ax. Thus, an ax might be placed on a bar, and the names of suspect persons called out; if the ax appeared to move at the name of any one, he was pronounced guilty.

ax′i·ō·līte, *n.* [L. *axis*; Gr. *axōn*, an axle, and *lithos*, stone.] a collection of crystal fibers, grouped about an axis: found in certain rocks.

ax″i·ō·lit′iç, *a.* pertaining to or resembling axiolites.

ax·i·ol′ō·ġy, *n.* [from Gr. *axios*, worthy; and *-logy*.] the branch of philosophy dealing with the nature of value and the types of value, as in morals, aesthetics, religion, and metaphysics.

ax′i·ŏm, *n.* [Gr. *axiōma*, authority, an authoritative sentence, from *axioun*, to think worthy.]
1. a self-evident truth or a proposition whose truth is so evident at first sight that no process of reasoning or demonstration can make it plainer; as, the whole is greater than a part.
2. an established principle in some art or science; a principle received without new proof.
3. a statement universally accepted as true; a maxim.

Syn.—maxim, aphorism, adage.

ax″i·ō·mat′iç, ax″i·ō·mat′iç·ăl, *a.* 1. pertaining to or like an axiom; of obvious truth; self-evident.
2. full of maxims; aphoristic.

ax″i·ō·mat′iç·ăl·ly, *adv.* by the use of or in accordance with axioms; self-evidently.

ax′i·ō·pis·ty, *n.* [Gr. *axiopistos*, trustworthy; *axios*, worthy, and *pistos*, trusty.] the quality which renders a thing worthy of belief; trustworthiness. [Rare.]

ax′is, *n.*; *pl.* **ax′ēs,** [L. *axis*; Gr. *axōn*, axis, axle.]
1. the straight line, real or imaginary, passing through a body, on which it revolves, or may be imagined to revolve; as, the *axis* of the earth.

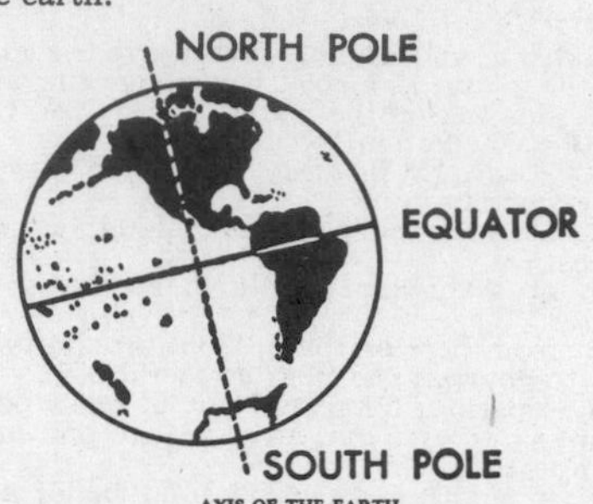

AXIS OF THE EARTH

2. in mechanics, the support for any rotating body; a shaft, axle, or spindle.
3. in geometry, (a) the imaginary line passing through the center of a plane or solid; the central line with reference to which the parts are symmetrically arranged; (b) any straight line for measurement or reference, as in a graph.
4. in anatomy, (a) the second cervical vertebra, which has a toothlike process passing upward through the central foramen of the first vertebra or atlas, thus serving as a pivot on which the latter turns; (b) any of several axial parts; especially, the spinal column.
5. in botany, (a) the main stem of a plant; (b) the central system of a cluster.
6. in crystallography, an imaginary line assumed through a crystal, with reference to its different faces and angles.
7. in physical geography and geology, the main line of direction of ranges, valleys, etc. The axis running along a crest is an *anticlinal axis*; the axis running along a valley is a *synclinal axis*.
8. in art and architecture, one of the main central lines of design.
9. figuratively, a turning point or condition.
10. in aeronautics, any of three straight lines, the first running through the center of the fuselage lengthwise, the second at right angles to this and parallel to the horizontal airfoils, and the third perpendicular to the first two at their point of intersection.
11. a state of diplomatic accord between two or more nations for the furtherance of their mutual aims: now usually a derogatory term.
12. in optics, (a) a straight line through the centers of both surfaces of a lens (*optic axis*); (b) a straight line from the object of vision to the fovea of the eye (*visual axis*).

axis of a curve; a straight line dividing a curve into two symmetrical parts, so that the part on one side exactly corresponds to that on the other, as in a parabola, ellipse, or hyperbola.

axis of a lens; a straight line drawn through the optical center of the lens and joining both its surfaces.

axis of oscillation; a straight line parallel to the horizon, passing through the center about which a pendulum vibrates.

axis of refraction; a straight line drawn perpendicular to the surface of the refracting medium at the point of incidence.

axis of symmetry of a body; a line on both or all sides of which the parts of a body are symmetrically arranged.

conjugate or *minor axis*; in conic sections, the straight line perpendicular to the transverse axis.

neutral axis (*of a beam*, etc.); in mechanics, the line or plane along which neither tension nor compression is operative.

spiral axis; in architecture, the axis of a twisted column or shaft drawn spirally so that the circumvolutions may be traced externally.

the Axis. the countries aligned against the United Nations in World War II: originally applied to Nazi Germany and Fascist Italy (Rome-Berlin Axis), later extended to include Japan, etc. (Rome-Berlin-Tokyo Axis).

transverse or *major axis*; in conic sections, the straight line which passes through the foci.

ax′is, *n.* in zoology, the white-spotted deer of India and southern Asia (*Cervus axis*), with slender, sparsely branched antlers: also called *hog deer*.

ax′is cyl′in·dẽr, the essential core of white tissue in the center of a nerve fiber.

ax′le (ax′l), *n.* [ME. *axel*, *exel*, shoulder; AS. *æx*, *eax*, axle; L. *axilla*, the armpit.]
1. a shaft on or with which a wheel revolves.
2. an axletree.
3. the spindle at either end of an axletree.
4. an axis, as of the earth or sun. [Archaic.]

ax′le box, a box enclosing the end of an axle that rotates in a bearing.

ax′led (ax′ld), *a.* equipped with an axle or with axles.

ax′le hook, a hook on an axle, to which the doubletree is attached.

ax′le pin, a pin inserted through the end of an axletree to keep the wheel in place; a linchpin.

ax′le·tree, *n.* the bar connecting two opposite wheels of a carriage, wagon, etc.

ax′măn, axe′măn, *n.*; *pl.* **ax′men, axe′men,**
1. one who uses an ax.
2. in civil engineering, one who cuts away obstructions and sets stakes for the rodman.
3. formerly, one who carried a battle-ax.

Ax′min·stẽr, *n.* a kind of carpet having a long, soft pile: so called from Axminster, England, where it was formerly made by hand.

ax′oid, ax·oid′ē·ăn, *a.* [L. *axis*, axle.] in anatomy, pertaining to the axis.

ax′ō·lotl, *n.* [Mex.] a salamander of the genus *Amblystoma*, found in the lakes of Mexico and the western United States: it matures sexually and breeds in the larval stage: used for food in Mexico.

ax·om′e·tẽr, *n.* [L. *axis*; Gr. *axōn*, an axle, and *metron*, a measure.] in optics, an instrument for adjusting the axes of lenses.

ax′on, ax′ōne, *n.* [Gr. *axōn*, axis.] that part of a nerve cell through which impulses travel away from the cell body.

Ax·ō′ni·ȧ, *n.pl.* [Gr. *axōn*, axle.] organisms, animal or vegetable, which have definite axes: opposed to *Anaxonia*.

ax·ot′ō·mous, *a.* [Gr. *axōn*, axis, and *tomos*, cut; from *temnein*, to cut.] in mineralogy, having a cleavage with a single face, perpendicular to the axis.

ax′seed, *n.* [*ax*, and *seed*; so named from the shape of the pods.] any of a group of European plants of the bean family, now cultivated in the United States, having pinnate leaves and pink or white flowers.

ax′stōne, *n.* a light green or greenish-gray variety of jade or nephrite. It is used, because of its toughness, by the natives of the South Sea Islands for making axes or hatchets.

ax′tree, *n.* an axletree. [Obs. or Dial.]

ax′unġe, *n.* [Fr., from L. *axis*, axle, and *ungere*, to grease.] animal fat; especially, in pharmacy, hog's lard or goose grease.

aȳ (ī), *interj.* ah; alas: a sound expressing sorrow, distress, etc.

aȳ (ī), *adv.* same as *aye* (yes).

āy (ā), *adv.* same as *aye* (always).

ä′yȧh, *n.* [Anglo-Ind., from Hindu *āya*, from Port. *aia*, nurse, governess.] a native nursemaid or lady's maid in India.

ä·yȧ·tōl′lȧh, *n.* [Ar., lit., sign of God.] a leader of the Shiite sect of the Moslem religion, serving as teacher, judge, and administrator.

aȳe (ī), *adv.* [ME. *ay*; Ice. *ei*, ever.] yes; yea.

aȳe (ī), *n.* one who votes in the affirmative; an affirmative vote; as, the *ayes* have it.

āye, (ā), *adv.* [ME. *ay*, *aye*, *ai*, ever, from Ice. *ei*, *ey*, ever, from AS. *awa*, *awi*, ever.] always; ever; continually. [Archaic.]

for aye; forever.

aȳe′-aȳe (ī′ī), [the native name, from its peculiar cry.] a nocturnal rodentlike lemur, found in Madagascar, the *Chiromys madagascariensis*: it has shaggy, generally brown, fur, large ears, pointed claws, and a long, bushy tail.

ȧ·yen′, ȧ·yein′ (-yen′), *adv.* and *prep.* again. [Obs.]

ȧ·yen′wărd, *adv.* backward. [Obs.]

āy′green, āye′green (ā′), *n.* the houseleek.

ä′yin, *n.* the sixteenth letter of the Hebrew alphabet, representing originally a voiced velar fricative, but now used only with diacritical marks to indicate vowel sounds.

āyle, *n.* [ME. *aiel*; Fr. *aieul*: OFr. *aiel*, grand

father, from L. *avus*, grandfather.] in law, a grandfather. [Obs.]

Ay·mä·rä′ (ī-), *n.*; *pl.* **Ay·mä·räs′, Ay·mä·rä′,** 1. a member of a South American Indian tribe living largely in Bolivia and Peru and believed to have been the builders of a great ancient culture, later supplanted by the Incan.

2. their language.

Ay·mä·rän′ (ī-), *a.* of the Aymaras or their language.

Ay·mä·rän′ (ī-), *n.* Aymara, the language.

à·yont′, à·yond′, *prep.* and *adv.* beyond; past; farther. [Brit. Dial.]

Āyr′shire (âr′), *a.* relating to the county of Ayr, Scotland, and designating a breed of cattle (brown or red with white markings) originating there; as, an *Ayrshire* bull.

Āyr′shire (âr′), *n.* one of the Ayrshire breed of cattle.

ä·yun″tä·mi·en′tō, *n.* [Sp. and Sp. Am.] a municipal government; also, the place where it is located.

A·zā′lē·à, *n.* [Gr. *azaleos*, dry, the allusion being to the arid habitation of the plant.]

1. a genus of plants, natural order *Ericaceæ*, resembling the rhododendron and having deciduous leaves and fragrant flowers. The species are principally native to North America and Asia.

AZALEA (*Azalea Indica*)

2. [a-] any plant belonging to the genus *Azalea.*

alpine azalea; a small shrub, *Loiseleuria procumbens*, with trailing branches, growing in mountainous districts of the eastern United States and Canada and in the Scottish Highlands.

ä·zän′, *n.* [from Ar. *ādhan.*] the Moslem summons to prayer: it is usually called five times a day by the muezzin, from a minaret on the mosque.

az′à·rōle, *n.* [Fr. *azerole.*] the *Cratægus azarolus*, a fruit-bearing shrub allied to the hawthorn; also, the fruit from this shrub.

A·zā′zel, *n.* [Heb. *'azāzēl*, lit., removal.] in Milton's *Paradise Lost*, one of the angels who rebelled with Satan.

à·zed′à·rach, *n.* [Fr. *azédarac*, from Per. *azaddirakht*, noble tree.]

1. a beautiful oriental tree (*Melia Azedarach*), extensively cultivated in the southern United States.

2. the fruit of this tree.

3. the bark of the *azedarach*, used in medicine as a cathartic, emetic, etc.

az·ē·lā′iç, *a.* [Gr. *a* priv., and *zōē*, life, and *elaion*, oil.] of, pertaining to, or containing a substance derived from the action of nitric acid on an oil, oleic acid, etc.; as, *azelaic* acid.

Ä″zēr·baī·jä′ni, *n.*; *pl.* **Ä″zēr·baī·jä′nis** or **Ä″zēr·baī·jä′ni,** 1. a native or inhabitant of Azerbaijan.

2. one of a Turkic people of Azerbaijan.

3. the Turkic dialect spoken there.

az′i·muth, *n.* [ME. *azymuth*; OFr. *azimut*, from Ar. *as-sumut*; *as*, from *al*, the, and *sumut*, pl. of *samt*, way or path.] in astronomy, angular distance measured on a horizon circle in a clockwise direction, from either the north or the south point in the horizon.

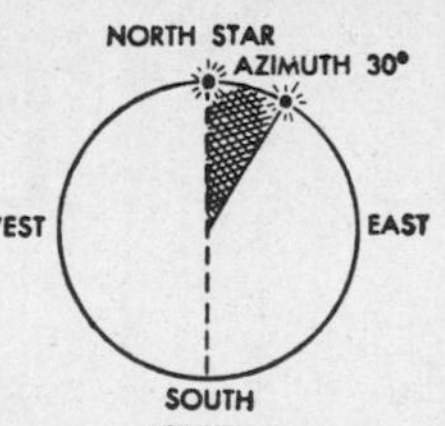

AZIMUTH

azimuth circle; any great circle which passes through the zenith and the nadir, and cuts the horizon at right angles.

azimuth compass; an instrument resembling the ordinary mariner's compass, so fitted as to ascertain the magnetic azimuth of a heavenly body.

magnetic azimuth; angular distance of any heavenly body, east or west, from the magnetic meridian. This is found by observing the object with an *azimuth* compass.

az′i·muth·ăl (*or* -mū-thăl), *a.* pertaining to the azimuth.

azimuthal error; any error arising out of a deviation in azimuth from the vertical plane.

az′i·muth·ăl·ly (*or* -mū-thăl-), *adv.* in the manner or direction of the azimuth.

az′i·muth dī″ăl, a dial whose pointer or gnomon is at right angles to the plane of the horizon. The shadow marks the sun's azimuth.

az′in, *n.* an azine.

az′ine, *n.* [*az-*, and *-ine.*] any of a group of chemical compounds with a six-membered ring containing one or more nitrogen atoms: the group consists of the diazines, triazines, etc.

az′ō-, [Gr. *azōos*, lifeless; *a* priv., and *zōē*, life.] a combining form meaning *nitrogen*, used in chemistry to form the names of certain chemical compounds.

az·ō·ben′zēne, *n.* [*azo-*, and Fr. *benjoin*, benzene.] a chemical compound derived from nitrobenzene in an alkaline solution.

az″ō·ben·zō′iç, *a.* pertaining to azobenzene.

az′ō dȳes, in chemistry, a large group of dyes containing the divalent radical –N:N–.

ä·zō′gue (ä-thō′gā), *n.* a Spanish-American name for quicksilver.

à·zō′iç, *a.* [Gr. *azōos*, lifeless; from *a* priv., and *zōē*, life.] without life; formed previous to the existence of life on the earth: applied to rocks in which no fossils have been found.

azoic age; in geology, the age preceding the beginning of life on the earth.

az′ōle, *n.* [*az-*, and *-ole.*] any of a group of chemical compounds with a five-membered ring containing one or more nitrogen atoms: the group consists of the diazoles, triazoles, etc.

A·zol′là, *n.* [Gr. *azein*, to dry, and *ollynai*, to kill.] a genus of minute cryptogamous plants of the *Salvinia* family.

ā·zon′iç, *a.* [Gr. *a* priv., and *zōnē*, region.] not restricted to any particular zone or region; not local.

A·zō′ri·ăn, *a.* [Sp. *Azores*, the Azores, from *azor*, a hawk.] of or pertaining to the Azores.

A·zō′ri·ăn, *n.* an inhabitant of the Azores.

az′ōte (*or* à-zōte′), *n.* [Gr. *a* priv., and *zōē*, life.] nitrogen: so called by Lavoisier from its inability to sustain life.

ä·zọ·tẹ′ä (ä-thọ-), *n.* [Sp.] a flat roof on a house or building of Spanish-Mexican architecture.

az′oth, *n.* [Ar. *az-zaug*, mercury.]

1. the metal mercury; quicksilver.

2. the universal remedy of Paracelsus.

à·zot′iç, *a.* pertaining to azote; formed or consisting of azote; nitric. [Rare.]

az′ō·tīte, *n.* [Gr. *a* priv., and *zōein*, to live.] a salt of nitrous acid; a nitrite.

az′ō·tīze, *v.t.*; azotized, *pt., pp.*; azotizing, *ppr.* to impregnate with nitrogen or azote; to nitrogenize.

az·ō·tom′e·tẽr, *n.* [*azo-*, and Gr. *metron*, a measure.] an instrument for measuring the proportion of nitrogen in a substance; a nitrometer.

à·zō′tous, *a.* same as *nitrous.*

az·ō·tū′ri·à, *n.* [*azo-*, and L. *urina*, urine.] a pathological condition characterized by an excess of nitrogenous matter in the urine.

Az′rà·el, *n.* [Heb. *Azraēl*, help of God.] the angel of death, who, in ancient Jewish and Moslem belief, parts the soul from the body.

Az′teç, *a.* [a native name.]

1. of or pertaining to the Aztecs, a people with an advanced civilization living in Mexico at the time of the Spanish invasion under Cortes in 1519.

2. their language.

Az′teç, *n.* a member of the Aztec people.

Az′teç·ăn, *a.* 1. Aztec.

2. Nahautlan.

ä·zu·lẹ′jō (ä-thu-lā′hō), *n.* [Sp.] a kind of richly decorated tile.

ä·zum′brẹ (ä-thum′brā), *n.* [Sp.] a Spanish liquid measure of between two and three quarts.

az′ūre (*or* ā′zūre), *a.* [ME. *azure*; OFr. *azur*; LL. *azura*; Ar. *lazward*; Per. *lazhward*, azure; the initial *l* lost through confusion with the definite article, Fr. *l'*, *le*, etc.]

1. sky-blue; resembling the color of the clear blue sky.

2. cloudless; like the clear sky.

az′ūre (*or* ā′zūre), *n.* 1. the clear blue color of the sky.

Her eyes a bashful *azure.* —Tennyson.

2. any of various blue pigments, as that made of lapis lazuli.

3. the clear sky. [Poet.]

4. the lapis lazuli. [Obs.]

5. in heraldry, blue: in engraving it is represented by parallel horizontal lines.

az′ūre, *v.t.* to color blue.

à·zū′rē·ous, *a.* of a clear blue color.

az′ūre stōne, lazulite or azurite.

az′ū·rine, *a.* azure.

az′ū·rine, *n.* 1. the blue roach, a fish common in Europe.

2. the blue wren of Australia.

az′ū·rīte, *n.* 1. a blue ore of copper, basic copper carbonate, $2CuCO_3 \cdot Cu(OH)_2$.

2. a semiprecious gem made from this ore.

az′ūrn (*or* ā′zūrn), *a.* of a blue color. [Obs.]

az·y·gom′à·tous, *a.* [Gr. *a* priv., and *zygoun*, to yoke.] without zygomatic arches.

az′y·gos, *n.* in anatomy, an azygous part.

à·zȳ′gō·spōre, *n.* [Gr. *a* priv., and *zygon*, a yoke, and *sporos*, a sowing.] in botany, a parthenogenetic spore resembling a zygospore.

az′y·gous, *a.* [Gr. *azygos*, unmatched; *a* priv., and *zygoun*, to yoke.] in anatomy, a term applied to certain parts or organs which have no mates or are not found in pairs, as certain muscles, veins, bones, etc.

az′yme, az′ym, *n.* [Gr. *azymos*, unleavened; *a* priv., and *zymē*, leaven.] unleavened bread.

à·zym′iç, *a.* pertaining to unleavened bread.

Az′y·mīte, *n.* in church history, one of a sect of Christians who administered the Eucharist with unleavened bread; also, a term applied by the Greeks in the eleventh century to the Latins.

az′y·mous, *a.* [Gr. *azymos*, unleavened; *a* priv., and *zymē*, leaven.] unleavened; unfermented.

B

B, b (bē), *n.*; *pl.* **B's, b's, Bs, bs** (bēz), 1. the second letter of the English alphabet: from the Greek *beta*, a borrowing from the Phoenician.
2. a sound of B or b.
3. a type or impression for B or b.
4. *a symbol for* the second in a sequence or group.

B, b (bē), *a.* 1. of B or b.
2. second in a sequence or group.

B (bē), *n.* 1. an object shaped like B.
2. a Roman numeral for 300: with a superior bar (B̄), 300,000.
3. the second party in a given case.
4. a large size of shot.
5. in chemistry, *the symbol for* boron.
6. in education, a grade second in quality; as, a *B* in history.
7. in music, (a) the seventh tone or note in the scale of C major, or the second in the scale of A minor; (b) a key, string, etc. producing this tone; (c) the scale having B as the keynote.
8. in physics, *a symbol for* magnetic induction.

B (bē), *a.* 1. shaped like B.
2. secondary; inferior to the best; as, a class *B* motion picture.

B-, bomber: followed by a number to designate a specific model of United States Air Force bombing airplane.

b, in algebra, a symbol representing a known quantity or a constant.

bä, *n.* in Egyptian mythology, the soul, symbolized by a bird with a human head.

ba, *v.t.* [OFr. *baer*, to open the mouth.] to kiss. [Obs.]

Ba, in chemistry, barium.

bäa, *n.* the cry or bleating of a sheep.

bäa, *v.i.* to cry or bleat as sheep.

bäa'ing, *n.* the bleating of sheep.

Bā'ăl, *n.*; *pl.* **Bā'ăl·im**, [Gr. *Baal*, from Heb. *Ba'al*, lord, or owner.]
1. the supreme male deity among some ancient Semitic peoples; the sun god, or the god of fertility. The name is used in Scripture in combinations designating other deities, as *Baal zebub*, literally the god of flies.
2. a false god; idol.

Bā'ăl·ish, *a.* 1. of or like Baal.
2. idolatrous.

Bā'ăl·ism, *n.* 1. the worship of Baal.
2. idolatry.

Bā'ăl·ist, Bā'ăl·īte, *n.* 1. one who worships Baal.
2. an idolater.

Bäb, *n.* [a shortening of *Bāb-ud-Dīn* (literally, Gate of the Faith).] a Persian title taken by the founder of Babism.

bä'bä, *n.* [Fr.] a kind of fruit cake.

bab'bitt, *v.t.*; babbitted, *pt.*, *pp.*; babbitting, *ppr.* to apply Babbitt metal to; to line with Babbitt metal.

bab'bitt, *n.* Babbitt metal.

bab'bitt, Bab'bitt, *n.* [after George *Babbitt*, the title character of a satirical novel by Sinclair Lewis (1922).] an uncultivated, conventional businessman; philistine; person characterized by babbittry.

Bab'bitt met'ăl, [after Isaac *Babbitt* (1799–1862), Am. inventor.]
1. a soft, silver-colored alloy of tin, copper, and antimony, used to reduce friction in bearings, etc.
2. loosely, any antifriction alloy.

bab'bitt·ry, Bab'bitt·ry, *n.* the behavior, attitudes, etc. of babbitts as a class, characterized by a striving for business and social success, conventionality, smugness, and a lack of interest in cultural matters; philistinism.

bab'ble, *v.i.*; babbled (-bld), *pt.*, *pp.*; babbling, *ppr.* [ME. *babelen*; Fr. *babiller*, to babble; of echoic origin.]
1. to utter words imperfectly or indistinctly, as children.
2. to talk idly or irrationally; to talk thoughtlessly.
3. to talk too much; to prate; to chatter; to tell secrets.
4. to make a continuous low sound; as, a *babbling* echo; a *babbling* stream.
Syn.—chatter, chat, prattle, prate, gabble, twaddle.

bab'ble, *v.t.* 1. to say indistinctly or incoherently.
2. to tell a secret or secrets; to blab.

bab'ble, *n.* 1. idle or senseless talk; as, gossipy *babble*.
2. confused incoherent talk or vocal sounds.
3. a continuous murmur; as, the *babble* of the stream.

bab'ble·ment, *n.* same as *babble*.

bab'blẽr, *n.* 1. one who or that which babbles; specifically, a hunting dog that yelps or bays noisily after having struck the scent.
2. in zoology, a bird of the family *Timalinæ*, a subfamily of thrushes of the East Indies.

bab'ble·ry (-bl-), *n.* babble. [Obs.]

bābe, *n.* [ME. *babe*; earlier form *baban*, babe, prob. so called from saying *ba-ba*.]
1. an infant; a young child of either sex.
2. a naive, gullible, or helpless person.
3. a girl or young woman, especially a pretty one. [Slang.]
4. a child's doll. [Obs.]

bābe'hood, *n.* babyhood. [Rare.]

Bā'bel, *n.* [Heb. *bābel*, Babylon.]
1. in the Bible, a city in Shinar in which Noah's descendants tried to build a tower intended to reach to heaven: God punished its builders for this presumption and prevented them from finishing by causing them all suddenly to speak in different languages so that they could not understand one another. Gen. xi. 1–9.
2. any impossibly high tower or building.
3. an impracticable scheme.
4. [*also* b–], (a) a confusion of voices, languages, etc.; tumult; (b) a place where there is such a confusion.
Syn.—hubbub, confusion, clamor, jargon, din, discord, clang.

bāb'ẽr·y, *n.* grotesque ornamentation, as in architecture or in book illustrations. [Obs.]

Ba'bi, *n.* 1. Babism.
2. a Babist.

Ba'bi, *a.* Babist.

bā'bi·ăn, bā'bi·ŏn, *n.* a baboon. [Obs.]

bā'bies'-breath'' (-breth''), *n.* 1. a fairly tall plant of the pink family, with small, fragrant, white or pink flowers.
2. any of several similar plants, as the wild madder, grape hyacinth, etc.

bab'il·lärd, *n.* [Fr. *babiller*, to chatter.] the lesser whitethroat or chatterer, *Sylvia curruca*, of Europe.

bab'ing·tŏn·īte, *n.* [named after Wm. *Babington*, English mineralogist.] a greenish-black mineral of the pyroxene subgroup, characterized by triclinic crystallization.

Bab'ing·tŏn's cũrse, an aquatic plant, *Elodea Canadensis*, troublesome to navigation and fisheries. It was falsely supposed to have been introduced into England by Charles Babington (1808–1895), English botanist.

bab·i·rú'sȧ, bab·i·rus'sȧ, bab·i·röus'sȧ, *n.* [from Malay. *babi*, hog, and *rusa*, deer.] a species of wild hog, sometimes called *horned hog* or *hog deer* from the fact that its upper tusks, which are of great length, curve backward from each jaw so as to resemble horns. It is a native of southeast Asia and East India.

bāb'ish, *a.* like a babe; childish. [Obs.]

bāb'ish·ly, *adv.* childishly. [Obs.]

bāb'ish·ness, *n.* childishness. [Obs.]

Bäb'ism, *n.* [Per. *bab*, a gate; so called because the founder claimed that no one could know God except through him.] the pantheistic doctrine and principles of a religious sect founded in Persia in 1843: it forbids begging, drinking alcoholic liquors, buying and selling slaves, having more than one wife, etc.

Bäb'ist, *n.* one who believes in Babism.

Bäb'ist, *a.* of Babism.

Bäb'īte, *a.* and *n.* Babist.

bab'lȧh, *n.* [Hind.] a pod of several species of *Acacia*, which comes from the East under the name of *neb-neb*. It contains gallic acid and tannin and is used in dyeing and tanning.

bä'boo, *n.* 1. a Hindu title equivalent to *Mr.*, *Sir*, or *Esq.*
2. a native clerk in India who can write English.
3. a native of India who has a little English education: derogatory term.

bä·bool', *n.* same as *bablah*.

bab·oon', *n.* [ME. *babewyne*; OFr. *babuin*, baboon, origin of name unknown.] the dog-faced ape of various genera, including the *Cynocephalus* and *Mandrilla*. They have an elongated abrupt muzzle like that of a dog, strong tusks or canine teeth, a short tail, cheekpouches, small, deep eyes with huge eyebrows, and naked callosities on the buttocks.

BABOON (*Cynocephalus maimon*)

bab·oon'ẽr·y, *n.* 1. baboons collectively.
2. baboonish behavior.

bab·oon'ish, *a.* like a baboon; stupid; uncouth.

bȧ·bouche', bȧ·boosh' (-boosh'), *n.* [Fr. *babouche*; Ar. *babush*; Per. *paposh*, a slipper, from *pa*, foot, and *posh*, covering.] a heelless slipper, consisting of a vamp and sole, worn in Eastern countries.

bä·bú', *n.* same as *baboo*.

bȧ·búl', *n.* same as *bablah*.

bȧ·bush'kȧ, *n.* [Russ., grandmother.] a kerchief or scarf worn on the head by a woman or girl.

bā'by, *n.*; *pl.* **bā'bies**, [dim. of *babe*.]
1. an infant or young child of either sex; a babe.
2. a person who behaves like an infant; helpless or cowardly person.
3. the youngest or smallest in a group.
4. a girl or young woman, especially a pretty one. [Slang.]
baby bunting; an infant's sleeping bag with an attached hood.

bā'by, *a.* 1. babyish; infantile or childish.
2. small of its kind.
3. of or for an infant.

bā'by, *v.t.*; babied, *pt.*, *pp.*; babying, *ppr.* to treat like a baby; pamper; coddle.

bā'by beef, meat from a prime heifer or steer fattened for butchering when one to two years old.

bā'by blüe, light blue.

bā'by blüe-eyes, a California plant with dark-spotted blue flowers.

bā'by bug'gy, a light carriage for wheeling a baby about; perambulator.

bā'by färm, a place where young children can

be boarded. The term now generally implies mistreatment and neglect.
bā′by grand, a small grand piano.
bā′by·hood, *n.* 1. the state of being a baby; infancy.
2. babies collectively.
bā′by house, a place for children's dolls; dollhouse.
bā′by·ish, *a.* 1. like a baby; very childish.
2. timid, silly, etc.
bā′by·ish·ly, *adv.* in a babyish manner.
bā′by·ish·ness, *n.* the quality of being like a baby; extreme childishness.
bā′by·ism, *n.* 1. the state of being a baby; babyhood.
2. a childish mode of speech.
Bab·y·lō′ni·ăn, Bab·y·lō′nish, *a.* [Gr. *Babylōnia*; Heb. *bābel.*]
1. pertaining to Babylon, the capital of the ancient kingdom of Babylonia, or to Babylonia.
2. resembling or having the characteristics of ancient Babylon, famed as a center of luxury and vice; as, *Babylonian* splendors; *Babylonish* orgies.
3. mixed; confused.
Bab·y·lō′ni·ăn, *n.* 1. an inhabitant or native of Babylonia or Babylon.
2. the Semitic language of the Babylonians.
3. an astrologer.
Bab·y·lō′ni·ăn Çap·tiv′i·ty, 1. the exile of the Jews, deported by Nebuchadnezzar into Babylonia in 597 B. C.
2. the period of forced residence of the Popes at Avignon, France (1309–1377): so called after the exile of the Jews.
Bab·y·lon′iç, Bab·y·lon′iç·ăl, *a.* same as *Babylonian.*
Bab·y·lō′nish, *a.* same as *Babylonian.*
bā′by pin, a safety pin.
bab·y·rŭs′sȧ, bab·y·roŭs′sȧ, *n.* same as *babirussa.*
bā′by's-breath″ (-breth″), *n.* same as *babies'-breath.*
bā′by·ship, *n.* the state of being an infant; babyhood.
baç, *n.* a vat used by brewers, etc.; a back.
bä·çä′bȧ, *n.* [S. Am. name.] a Brazilian palm, *Œnocarpus distichus,* or *bacaba,* from the fruit of which the natives make a refreshing beverage or a thin oil.
bä·çȧ·lä′ō, *n.* [Cuban.] a West Indian fish, called the *scamp.*
Bȧ·cär′di, *n.* [after *Bacardi,* the original distiller.] a variety of Cuban rum.
Bȧ·cär′di, *a.* made with Bacardi rum.
baç′çȧ, *n.* [L. *baca,* or *bacca,* berry.] in botany, a berry; more precisely, a fruit, with many cells and seeds, indehiscent, in which, when ripe, the seeds lose their attachment and scatter throughout the flesh, as the gooseberry.
baç·çȧ·lau′rē·āte, *n.* [ML. *baccalaureatus*; as if from L. *bacca laureus,* laurel berry, but actually from hyp. L. *baccalaris* or *baccalarius,* vassal farmer, young man, from *bacca,* a cow.]
1. the degree of bachelor of arts, bachelor of science, etc.
2. an address or sermon delivered to a graduating class at commencement: also *baccalaureate sermon.*
baç·çȧ·lau′rē·āte, *a.* pertaining to the degree of bachelor or to the conferring of it; as, a *baccalaureate* sermon.
Baç·çȧ·när′ist, *n.* a member of a religious order founded in Italy in the last decade of the eighteenth century by *Baccanari.*
baç·çȧ·rät′ (-rä′), **baç·çȧ·rä′,** *n.* [Fr., origin unknown.]
1. a gambling game played with cards.
2. in this game, the ten, which counts zero.
baç·çā′rē, *interj.* backare. [Obs.]
baç′çāte, *a.* [L. *bacca,* berry.]
1. having a pulpy texture like a berry.
2. having or bearing berries; berried.
baç′çā·ted, *a.* [L. *baccatus,* garnished with berries or pearls, from *bacca,* a berry.]
1. having many berries.
2. set or adorned with pearls. [Obs.]
Baç′chae (baç′ē), *n.pl.* [L.; Gr. *Bakchai,* from *Bakchos,* Bacchus.]
1. women companions of Bacchus.
2. women worshipers or priestesses of Bacchus.
baç′chȧ·năl, *a.* [L. *bacchanal,* a place devoted to *Bacchus,* the god of wine.]
1. reveling in intemperate drinking; riotous; noisy.
2. relating to Bacchus or his worship; bacchanalian.
baç′chȧ·năl, *n.* 1. a votary of Bacchus; a bacchant or bacchante.
2. one who indulges in drunken revels; one who is noisy and riotous when intoxicated; a drunkard.
3. any orgy of drunkenness and debauchery.
4. [*pl.*] the Bacchanalia.
5. a dance or song after the bacchanalian style.

Then Genius danced a *bacchanal.*
—Cowper.

Baç·chȧ·nā′li·ȧ, *n.pl.* [L.]
1. in classical antiquity, feasts in honor of Bacchus, the god of wine, which were celebrated in spring and autumn, with games and shows.
2. [b–] a drunken feast; an orgy.
baç·chȧ·nā′li·ăn, *n.* a drunken carouser.
baç·chȧ·nā′li·ăn, *a.* 1. of or like bacchanals or the Bacchanalia.
2. noisily drunken; carousing; orgiastic.
baç·chȧ·nā′li·ăn·işm, *n.* the practice of bacchanalian rites; drunken revelry; riotous festivity.
baç·chȧ·nā′li·ăn·ly, *adv.* in a bacchanalian manner.
baç′chănt, *n.*; *pl.* **baç′chănts** or **baç·chan′tēş,** [L. *bacchans,* ppr. of *bacchari,* to celebrate the feast of Bacchus.]
1. a priest, priestess, or devotee of Bacchus.
2. a bacchanal; one given to intemperate reveling.

They appear in a state of intoxication and are the *bacchants* in a delirium. —Rees.

3. formerly, in Germany, a wandering student.
baç′chănt, *a.* bacchanalian; wine-loving; reveling; carousing.
baç·chan′tē (*or* baç-çant′), *n.*; *pl.* **baç·chan′tēş,** a priestess of Bacchus, or one who joined in the celebration of the feasts of Bacchus; one in a state of bacchanal frenzy; hence, a woman addicted to intemperance or bacchanalian revelry.

BACCHANTE

baç·chan′tiç, *a.* of or like bacchants or bacchantes.
baç′chȧ·riç, *n.* same as *Bacharach.*
Baç′chȧ·ris, *n.* [name of a shrub dedicated to Bacchus.] a large genus of plants, natural order *Compositæ.* They are shrubs or herbs, the genus containing more than two hundred species, all natives of America.
Baç′chiç, Baç′chiç·ăl, *a.* 1. relating to Bacchus, the god of wine, or his worship; as, a *Bacchic* feast or song, *Bacchic* mysteries.
2. [*often* b–] bacchanalian; carousing; drunken; mad with intoxication.
baç·chī′us, *n.*; *pl.* **baç·chī′ī,** [Gr. *Bakcheios,* a metrical foot.] in ancient prosody, a foot composed of a short syllable and two long ones.
Baç′chus, *n.* [L.; Gr. *Bakchos.*] in Greek and Roman mythology, the god of wine and revelry, son of Zeus (Jupiter) and Semele: earlier called *Dionysus* by the Greeks. He is said first to have taught the cultivation of the grape, and the preparation of wine and other intoxicating liquors.
baç′ci-, [from L. *bacca,* berry.] a combining form meaning berry, as in *baccivorous.*
baç·cif′ẽr·ous, *a.* [L. *bacifer,* berry-bearing.] bearing or producing berries.
baç′ci·form, *a.* [L. *bacca,* berry, and *forma,* shape.] of the shape of a berry.
baç·civ′ō·rous, *a.* [L. *bacca,* berry, and *vorare,* to devour.] eating berries; subsisting on berries; as, *baccivorous* birds.
bach, *v.i.* [from *bachelor.*] to live alone or keep house for oneself, as a bachelor. [Slang.]

BACCHUS

bach′e·lŏr, *n.* [ME. *bacheler, bachiler,* bachelor; LL *baccalarius,* the vassal or holder of a farm.]
1. a man of any age who has not been married.
2. a person who has received the baccalaureate from a college or university.
3. a knight of the lowest order, or novice in arms, who fought under another's banner: styled a *knight bachelor.*
4. a fresh-water fish, resembling the bass; the crappie.
bach′e·lŏr, *a.* of or for a bachelor.
bach′e·lŏr-at-ärmş, *n.* a young knight serving under another's banners.
bach′e·lŏr·dŏm, *n.* 1. the state or condition of bachelorhood.
2. bachelors collectively.
bach′e·lŏr girl, an unmarried girl or young woman who works and lives independently. [Colloq.]
bach′e·lŏr·hood, *n.* the state or period of being a bachelor; way of life of an unmarried man.
bach′e·lŏr·işm, *n.* the state of a bachelor; a bachelor's mannerism.
Bach′e·lŏr of Ärts, 1. a degree given by a college or university to a person who has completed a four-year course or its equivalent in the humanities, social sciences, etc.
2. a person who has this degree.
Bach′e·lŏr of Scī′ence, 1. a degree given by a college or university to a person who has completed a four-year college course or its equivalent, with a major in science rather than the humanities.
2. a person who has this degree.
bach′e·lŏr's-but′tŏn, *n.* any of several plants with button-shaped flowers, including the cornflower, knapweed, and tansy.
bach′e·lŏr·ship, *n.* bachelorhood.
bach′el·ry, *n.* the whole company of young candidates for knighthood. [Obs.]
bac′il·lăr (*or* bȧ-cil′lăr), *a.* [Mod. L. *bacillarius,* from L. *bacillum,* small staff.]
1. rod-shaped; bacilliform.
2. consisting of rodlike structures.
3. of, like, characterized by, or caused by bacilli.
Bac·il·lā′ri·ȧ, *n.* a former genus of microscopic *Algæ,* belonging to the class *Diatomaceæ.*
bac′il·lā·ry, *a.* bacillar.
bȧ·cil′lī, *n.* plural of *bacillus.*
bȧ·cil′li·cīde, *n.* [L. *bacilli,* and *cædere,* to kill.] a substance intended to kill bacilli.
bȧ·cil′li·form, *a.* having the form of a bacillus; rod-shaped.
bȧ·cil′lus, *n.*; *pl.* **bȧ·cil′lī,** [Mod. L., from L. *bacillum,* a small staff; dim. of *baculus,* a stick, from Gr. *baktron,* a staff.]
1. any of a genus of rod-shaped bacteria which occur in chains, produce spores, and are active only in the presence of oxygen.
2. any rod-shaped bacterium: distinguished from *coccus, spirillum.*
3. [*usually pl.*] loosely, any of the bacteria, especially those causing disease.
bac″i·trā′cin, *n.* [arbitrary blend, from *bacillus* and Margaret *Tracy,* name of an Am. girl (b. 1936) from whose wounds the strain was isolated and *-ine.*] an antibiotic obtained from a particular strain of bacteria and used in the treatment of certain bacterial infections, especially of the body surface.
back, *n.* [Fr. *bac,* trough, ferryboat.]
1. a vat used by brewers, dyers, and others, for mixing, holding water, etc.
2. a ferryboat, hauled by rope or chain, especially one adapted to carry vehicles.
3. a wooden trough for fuel. [Scot.]

Narrowly escaping breaking my shins on a turf *back.* —Scott.

back, *n.* [ME. *bak, bac*; AS. *baec,* back.]
1. the part of the body opposite to the front; in man and many other animals, the part to the rear or top, opposite the chest, breast, or belly, and reaching from the base of the neck to the end of the spine.
2. the backbone.
3. a support for the human back; as, the *back* of a chair.
4. the part of a garment or harness associated with the back of a person or an animal.
5. physical strength.
6. the rear or hinder part of anything.
7. the farther or other side of something; the reverse.
8. the part of anything opposite the part that is used; as, the *back* of the hand.

9. the part of a tool or weapon opposite the useful edge.
10. the unexposed face of a fabric; the wrong side.
11. the part of a book that holds it together; the part showing when the book is shelved.
12. in football, a player in a position behind the front line; the quarterback, halfback, or fullback.
13. the keel and keelson of a ship.
14. by synecdoche, the whole body; as, he has no clothes to his *back*.
15. a reserve or secondary resource: now supplanted by *backing*.
behind one's back; without one's knowledge or consent.
to be on one's back; to be ill, unable to help oneself, etc.
to bow the back; to submit to oppression.
to cast behind the back; (a) to forget and forgive; (b) to treat with contempt.
to get (or *put*) *one's back up*; (a) to make or become angry, as a cat arching its back; (b) to be obstinate.
to plow the back; to oppress and persecute.
to turn one's back on; (a) to show anger, contempt, etc. toward by turning away from; (b) to ignore the plight of; to desert; to fail.
to turn one's back to; to dismiss contemptuously.

back, *a.* 1. at the rear; behind; opposite to the front.
2. remote in place or condition; as, a *back* district.
3. in a backward direction; returning; reversed; as, *back* action, *back* course.
4. of or for a time in the past; as, *back* dues, *back* work, the *back* issues of a paper.
5. in phonetics, made at the rear of the mouth; velar; guttural.
back page; in printing, the left-hand page of a book; a verso.

back, *adv.* [formed from *aback*, by apheresis; from ME. *abak*; AS. *on bæc*, backward.]
1. at the rear; behind; as, the sun passed *back* of the cloud.
2. backward; to the rear; as, the men fell *back*.
3. backward to a previously occupied point, whether of state, condition, or place; as, *back* to the old home; he gave *back* the gift; *back* to his old duties; *back* to civilization.
4. in a manner so as to impede; as, the blockade held him *back*.
5. toward times or things past; as, to look *back* on former ages.
6. in return or as a reward; as, how shall I pay you *back?*
7. for the purpose of reserve or concealment; as, to keep *back* the truth.
back and forth; to and fro; from side to side.
to go back on; to forsake; desert; fail. [Colloq.]

back, *v.t.*; backed, *pt.*, *pp.*; backing, *ppr.* 1. to mount; to get upon the back of; to sit (a horse); sometimes, to place or carry upon the back; as, to *back* a load.
2. to support; to second or strengthen by encouragement or financial aid (often with *up*); as, the court was *backed* by justice and public sentiment; he *backed* his agent up without limit.
3. to put backward; to cause to move backward or to the rear (sometimes with *up*); as, to *back* oxen.
4. to adjoin behind; to lie back of; to form the back of; as, the orchard *backs* the garden.
5. to strengthen or support at the back; to furnish with a back or backing; as, to *back a* book.
6. to endorse or sign on the back, as a document, note, etc.; to write on the back of, as a letter.
7. to gamble on; to make a wager in support of; as, to *back* a horse or a pugilist.
to back an anchor; in seamanship, to lay down a small anchor ahead of a large one, the cable of the small one being fastened to the crown of the large one, to prevent its coming home.
to back an engine; to reverse the action of the engine.
to back a rope; to put on a preventer so as to reduce the strain upon the rope.
to back astern; in rowing, to manage the oars in a direction contrary to the usual method, so as to move a boat stern foremost.
to back the field; in horse racing, to bet that some one of all the other horses in a race will beat a specified horse.
to back the oars; to row backward.
to back the sails; to put the sails in such a position that the wind acts upon their forward surfaces, thus arresting or reversing the motion of the ship.
to back water; (a) to reverse the power so as to force the boat or ship backward; (b) to retract something said.

back, *v.i.* 1. to move or go backward (often with *up*).
2. to move in the reverse direction; to shift counterclockwise: said of the wind, and opposed to *veer*.
to back and fill; (a) to handle sails so that they repeatedly spill wind and fill with wind; (b) to zigzag; (c) to take first one position and then another; continually change one's mind.
to back down; to retreat from a position or attitude; to give in. [Colloq.]
to back out; (a) to retreat from a difficulty or engagement; (b) to refuse to keep a promise or an engagement. [Colloq.]

back'āche (-āk), *n.* a continuous ache, or pain, in the back.

back'āche brāke, a fern supposed to possess medicinal qualities, the *Asplenium filix-fœmina*, or lady fern.

back'āche root, a variety of button snakeroot.

Back'a·rack, *n.* see *Bacharach.*

baç·kā'rē, baç·çā'rē, *interj.* [a humorously formed pseudo-Latin word, perhaps from the Eng. *back* with a Latin termination, apparently that of the infinitive of the first conjugation.] stand back! go back! [Obs.]

back'band, *n.* the strap worn over the back of a horse to support the shafts of a carriage.

back'bīte, *v.t.* and *v.i.*; backbit, *pt.*; backbit or backbitten, *pp.*; backbiting, *ppr.* [ME. *bakbiten, bacbiten.*] to slander; speak evil of (an absent person or persons).

back'bīte, *n.* a backbiting.

back'bīt"ẽr, *n.* one who backbites.

back'bīt"ing, *n.* the act of a backbiter; calumny.

back'bōard, *n.* [AS. *bæcbord.*]
1. a board for the support or rest of the back.
2. a board across the stern of a boat for the passengers to lean against.
3. a board attached to the rim of a water wheel to prevent the water running off the floats or paddles into the interior of the wheel.
4. a thin sheet of wood, veneering, or pasteboard, to sustain and protect the back of a picture or a mirror in a frame.
5. in basketball, a board or flat surface, as of glass, just behind the basket.

back'bond, *n.* in Scots law, a deed attaching a qualification or condition to the terms of a conveyance, or other instrument.

back'bōne, *n.* [ME. *bakbone, bakbon, bacbon,* backbone.]
1. the column of bones along the center of the back of man and many animals; the spine; the vertebral column.
2. something resembling a backbone in appearance, position, or function.
3. courage; determination; firmness; stability of purpose; as, he has no *backbone* in him.
to the backbone; to the utmost extent of one's power or nature; out and out; thoroughly.

back·bōned', *a.* having a backbone.

back'break·ing, *a.* requiring great physical exertion; very tiring.

back'çȧst, 1. a cast or throwback.
2. a backward stroke, or a stroke driving one back; hence, figuratively, any discouragement or cause of relapse or failure. [Scot.]

back'chat, *n.* back talk. [Colloq.]

back'çōurt, *n.* the back part of a tennis court, basketball court, etc.

back'crȯss, *v.t.* and *v.i.* to cross or breed (a hybrid) with one of its parents.

back'crȯss, *n.* a breeding of a hybrid with one of its parents.

back'dōor, *a.* 1. relating to a rear entrance.
2. secret; underhand; surreptitious.

back'down, *n.* a yielding or surrender. [Colloq.]

back'drop, *n.* a painted cloth hung at the back of a scene or at the rear of the stage; a drop curtain at the back of the stage.

backed (bakt), *a.* 1. having a back or backing: often used in hyphenated compounds meaning *having a* (specified kind of) *back*; as, broad-*backed*, canvas-*backed*.
2. mounted; placed on the back.

back'ẽr, *n.* one who backs another person or a project or that which backs something else; specifically, (a) a supporter of, or better for, a party in a contest; (b) in architecture, a narrow slate laid on the back of a broad square-headed one, where the slates begin to diminish in width.

back'fąll, *n.* 1. (a) a falling back; (b) that which falls back.
2. in wrestling, a throw in which one contestant lands on his back.

back'fiēld, *n.* in football, the four players (quarterback, two halfbacks, and fullback) whose regular position is behind the line of scrimmage; also, their positions regarded as a unit.

back'fill"ing, *n.* any substance, as mortar, small stone, etc., used in filling a space between walls or parts of a wall.

back'fīre, *v.i.*; backfired, *pt.*, *pp.*; backfiring, *ppr.* 1. to set or use a backfire.
2. to explode as a backfire.
3. to light from the inner rather than the outer jet, as in a Bunsen burner.
4. to have an unexpected or unwelcome result; to go awry; as, his plan *backfired*.

back'fīre, *n.* 1. a fire purposely started in front of an advancing forest or prairie fire in order to stop it by creating a burned area in its path.
2. an explosion occurring too soon in a cylinder of a gasoline or oil engine, thereby tending to reverse the motion of the piston.
3. an explosion in an intake or exhaust pipe.
4. an explosion in the back part of a gun.

back'-fọr·mā"tion, *n.* a word actually formed from, but looking as if it were the base of, another word; e.g., *burgle* (from *burglar*).

back'friend (-frend), *n.* 1. an enemy in secret.
2. one who stands behind, or supports, another as a friend. [Rare.]

back'fũr"rōw, *v.t.* and *v.i.*; backfurrowed, *pt.*, *pp.*; backfurrowing, *ppr.* to plow (land) so as to leave a ridge between two furrows.

back"gam'mŏn, *v.t.* to win at backgammon.

back"gam'mŏn, *n.* [ME. *bak*; AS. *bæc*, back, and AS. *gamen*, sport, game.] a game played by two persons on a special board, with box and dice. The board is in two parts, on which are twenty-four black and white spaces, called points. Each player has fifteen pieces, and the advance of the pieces is determined by the throw of the dice.

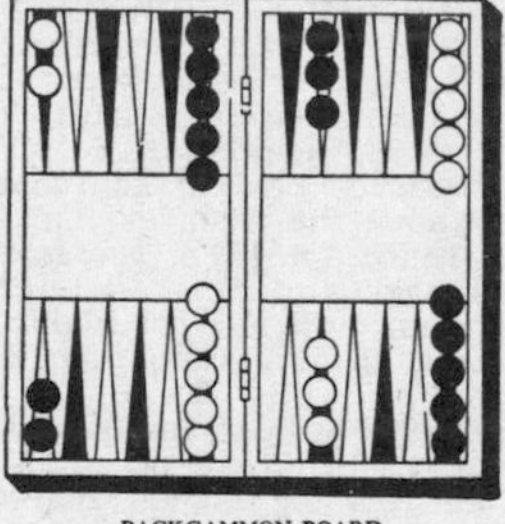

BACKGAMMON BOARD

back gēar, an arrangement of toothed wheels by which the power of a driving belt is proportionately increased.

back'ground, *n.* 1. the distant part of a landscape, picture, etc.
2. surroundings, especially those behind something and providing harmony or contrast; surrounding area or surface.
3. an unimportant or seemingly unimportant place or position; as, he stays in the *background*.
4. the whole of one's study, training, and experience; as, she has the right *background* for this job.
5. the events leading up to something; causes.
6. information which will help to explain something; as, give me the *background* of the problem.
7. in motion pictures, radio, etc., music or sound effects used as a subordinated accompaniment to dialogue or action.

back'hand, *n.* 1. handwriting in which the letters slope backward, up to the left.

Backhand writing

2. a method of stroking, as in tennis, with the back of the hand turned forward, the

arm being brought forward from across the body.

3. a stroke so made.

BACKHAND STROKE

back'hand, *a.* backhanded.

back'hand, *adv.* with a backhanded stroke.

back'hand″ed, *a.* 1. made or performed with the back of the hand, or with the back of the hand turned forward, as some strokes in tennis.

2. with the letters slanting backward, up to the left.

3. not direct; equivocal; insincere; sarcastic: said of a compliment that contains a rebuke, etc.

4. turned in a direction opposite to the normal; as, a *backhanded* cable.

5. clumsy; awkward.

back'hand″ed·ly, *adv.* in a backhanded manner.

back'hand″ed·ness, *n.* the state of being backhanded.

back'hand″ẽr, *n.* a backhanded blow.

back'house, *n.* a small building behind the main one; especially, a privy.

back'ing, *n.* 1. the act of supporting at the back or strengthening with a back.

2. support or aid given to a person or cause; endorsement.

3. those giving such support or aid.

4. a going backward.

5. something put at or attached to the back of something else by way of support or finish, or the act of putting it there; as, (a) a layer or layers of timber, generally teak, on which the iron plates of armor-clad ships are bolted; (b) in bookbinding, the preparing of the back of a book with glue, etc., before putting on the cover; (c) in weaving, the web of coarser or stronger material at the back of such piled fabrics as velvet, plush, etc.

6. a musical accompaniment. [Slang.]

back'joint, *n.* in masonry, a rabbet such as that made on the inner side of a chimneypiece to receive a slip.

back'lash, *n.* 1. a quick, sharp recoil.

2. a snarl in a reeled fishing line.

3. in mechanics, the jarring reaction of loose or worn parts; play.

back'less, *a.* having no back.

back liṅk, in engines, one of the links in a parallel motion which connect the air-pump rod to the beam.

back'list, *n.* all the books of a publisher that are kept in print over a relatively long period of time.

back'list, *v.t.* to include in a backlist.

back'log, *n.* 1. a log of wood against which a fire is made on a hearth or in a fireplace.

2. reserve resources, as of a business house, especially an accumulation of unfilled orders.

back'log, *v.i.* and *v.t.*; backlogged, *pt., pp.*; backlogging, *ppr.* to accumulate in reserve.

back num'bẽr, 1. an old issue of a periodical.

2. an old-fashioned or passé person or thing. [Colloq.]

back ọr'dẽr, an order not yet filled.

back'pack, *n.* 1. a kind of knapsack, often attached to a lightweight frame, worn by campers or hikers.

2. a piece of equipment, as a radio transmitter, used while being carried on the back.

back'pack, *v.i.* to hike wearing a backpack.

back'pack, *v.t.* to carry in a backpack.

back pāint'ing, the method of painting mezzotint prints pasted on glass to produce the effect of painted glass.

back pāy, overdue or retroactive wages.

back'ped·ăl, *v.i.*; backpedaled *or* backpedalled, *pt., pp.*; backpedaling *or* backpedalling, *ppr.* 1. to press backward on the pedals of a bicycle in braking.

2. to move backward quickly, as in boxing to avoid a blow.

3. to retreat from a previously held opinion.

back'pïēce, *n.* the piece or plate, in a suit of armor, covering the back.

back'plāte, *n.* same as *backpiece.*

back pres'sūre (presh'ũr), the resistance of the atmosphere or waste steam to the action of the piston of a steam engine on its return stroke.

back'rest, *n.* a rest or support for or at the back.

back rōad, a road that is away from the main road; a country road, usually in poor condition.

back'rōpe, in nautical language, the rope or wire stay running from the end of the dolphin striker to the ship's bows.

back'sa̤w, *n.* a saw having a blade stiffened by a metallic back, such as a tenon saw.

back'-sçratch″ẽr, *n.* 1. a device for scratching the back.

2. a person who scratches another's back.

3. a toady. [Colloq.]

back seat, 1. a seat at the back.

2. a secondary or inconspicuous position. [Colloq.]

back'-sēat drīv'ẽr, a passenger in an automobile who offers advice and directions for driving.

back'set, *n.* 1. one who or that which checks; a relapse.

2. an eddy or backwater.

back'set, *v.t.* to give a second plowing in the fall to (sod ground broken in the spring). [Western U. S.]

back'set″tlẽr, *n.* one who lives in a district remote from a settled part of the country.

back'sheesh, *n.* baksheesh.

back'sīde, *n.* 1. the rear part.

2. the buttocks.

back'sīght (-sīt), *n.* in surveying, (a) a sight taken from a located point back to the point from which the location was originally made; (b) a sight taken on a point of known elevation in order to determine the elevation of the instrument.

back slang, a kind of slang in which the words are pronounced or written backward, or as nearly so as possible; thus, penny becomes *ynnep,* woman *namow.*

back'slap″pẽr, *n.* a person who slaps others on the back; effusively friendly, too hearty person. [Colloq.]

back'slīde, *v.i.*; backslid, *pt.*; backslidden or backslid, *pp.*; backsliding, *ppr.* to slide backward in morals or religious enthusiasm; to become less virtuous, less pious, etc.

back'slīd·ẽr, *n.* one who backslides.

back'slīd·ing, *n.* apostasy; a falling away from a faith.

back'spāce, *v.i.*; backspaced, *pt., pp.*; backspacing, *ppr.* to move a typewriter carriage back along the same line one space at a time by depressing a special key.

back'spin, *n.* the backward rotation of a ball, wheel, etc. that is moving forward.

back'stȧff, *n.* [so called from its being used with the observer's back toward the sun.] an instrument formerly used for taking altitudes at sea.

back'stāġe', *adv.* 1. in the dressing rooms behind the stage; behind the curtain.

2. upstage; at or to the rear of the stage.

back'stāġe″, *a.* 1. situated backstage.

2. covert; concealed.

back'stāirs̹, back'stāir, *a.* indirect; secret; underhanded; involving intrigue.

back stāirs̹, 1. stairs in the back part of a house; private stairs.

2. a way or method of intrigue.

back'stāy, *n.* 1. a long rope or stay extending from the masthead to the side of a ship, slanting a little aft, to assist the shrouds in supporting the mast: often called *running backstay.*

2. a rope or shroud extending from the mast to the stern: often called *permanent backstay.*

3. a support for the back.

4. in printing, a strap used to check the carriage of a press.

5. a spring used to maintain the contact of the cutting edges of shears.

6. in a lathe, a backrest.

back step, rearward movement, as of a body of troops, while maintaining the same front.

back'stitch (-stich), *v.t.* and *v.i.*; backstitched (-sticht), *pt., pp.*; backstitching, *ppr.* to sew with stitches overlapping each other.

back'stitch, *n.* a stitch made by doubling the thread back on part of the stitch before.

back'stop, *n.* a fence, screen, etc. serving to stop balls that go too far: in baseball the backstop is behind the catcher.

back'-strapped (-strapt), *a.* compelled to sail to leeward by head winds or adverse currents.

back'stress, *n.* a woman baker. [Obs.]

back'stretch, *n.* the part of a race track farthest from the grandstand and opposite and parallel to the homestretch.

back'strōke, *n.* 1. a stroke backward; backhanded stroke.

2. a stroke made by a swimmer lying face upward.

back'strōke, *v.i.* to perform a backstroke.

back'strōke, *v.t.* to hit with a backstroke.

back'swept, *a.* formed so as to extend or slope away from the front.

back swim'mẽr, a hemipterous water bug, family *Notonectidæ,* that swims rapidly on its back by use of its long, oarlike legs.

back'swōrd (-sōrd), *n.* 1. a sword with one sharp edge; broadsword.

2. in England, a stick with a basket handle used in fencing; also, the game of singlestick.

3. a person who fences with the backsword.

back talk, a talking back; saucy or insolent answers or retorts. [Colloq.]

back'track, *v.i.* to return by the same path; to retreat.

back'up, back'-up, *a.* 1. standing by as an alternate or auxiliary.

2. supporting.

back'up, back'-up, *n.* 1. an accumulation because of a stoppage.

2. a support or help.

back'wărd, back'wărds̹, *adv.* 1. with the back in advance or to the front; reversely; as, to ride *backward.*

2. toward the back or rear; behind; as, to throw the arms *backward*; to move *backward* and forward.

3. on the back, or with the back downward; as, to fall *backward.*

4. toward past times or events; as, to look *backward* on the history of man.

5. by way of reflection; reflexively; as, the mind turns *backward* on itself.

6. from a better to a worse state; as, public affairs go *backward.*

7. reversely; toward the beginning.

8. in a way contrary to the normal or usual way.

9. in an opposite direction; as, to drive the enemy *backward.*

back'wărd, *a.* [ME. *bakward, bacward,* from *aback*; AS. *on bæc,* back, and *-weard,* toward.]

1. retiring; bashful; unwilling; averse; reluctant; hesitating.

2. slow; sluggish; dilatory.

3. dull; not quick of apprehension; unprogressive; as, a *backward* youth.

4. late; behind in time; coming after something else, or after the usual time; as, *backward* fruits; the season is *backward.*

5. retrogressive; reversed; turned or directed toward the rear or in the opposite way; as, a *backward* look, a *backward* course.

Syn.—averse, bashful, retiring, reluctant.

back'wărd, *n.* the things or state behind or past. [Obs.]

back'wărd·ly, *adv.* unwillingly; reluctantly; aversely; perversely.

back'wărd·ness, *n.* 1. unwillingness; reluctance; bashfulness; shyness.

2. the state of being behind in progress; slowness; tardiness; as, the *backwardness* of spring.

back'wäsh, *v.t.* to cleanse from oil, as wool after being combed.

back'wäsh, *n.* 1. water moved backward, as by a ship in motion, an oar, etc.

2. a backward current or flow, as of air from an airplane propeller.

3. a reaction or commotion caused by some event.

back'wa̤″tẽr, *n.* 1. water thrown back by the turning of a water wheel or similar movement.

2. water held or forced back, as in a millrace, or in a tributary of a stream, in consequence of some obstruction, as a dam or the swelling of the river below.

3. a water reserve obtained at high tide and to be discharged at low tide for clearing off deposits in channel beds and tideways.

4. a creek or arm of the sea near to and parallel to the coast, and communicating with the sea by barred entrances.

5. stagnant water in a small stream or inlet.

6. a place or condition regarded as stagnant, backward, etc.; as, he lives in a cultural *backwater.*

back'wa̤″tẽr, *a.* like a backwater; stagnant; backward.

back'woods̹, back'wood, *a.* in, from, or characteristic of backwoods.

back'woods̹, *n.pl.* 1. heavily wooded districts in thinly settled regions remote from population centers; any wild region of country with vegetation.

2. any remote, thinly populated place. [Colloq.]

back·woods̹'măn, *n.*; *pl.* **back·woods̹'men,** an inhabitant of the backwoods; a pioneer.

bā′çŏn, *n.* [ME. *bacon*; OFr. *bacon*; O.H.G. *bahho, bacho,* a side of bacon.] hog's flesh, especially the back and sides, salted or pickled and dried, usually in smoke.

to bring home the bacon; (a) to earn a living; (b) to succeed; to win. [Colloq.]

to save one's bacon; to preserve oneself or one's property from harm. [Colloq.]

Bā·çō′ni·ăn, *a.* 1. pertaining to Francis Bacon, his system of philosophy, or his style of writing.

2. designating or of the theory that Francis Bacon was the author of Shakespeare's works.

Bā·çō′ni·ăn, *n.* 1. a believer in the philosophy of Francis Bacon.

2. one holding to the theory that Francis Bacon was the author of Shakespeare's works.

Bā′çŏn·ism, *n.* the essence or the philosophy of Bacon's writings; the philosophy or scientific method propounded by Bacon in his Novum Organum, a revolt against ancient authority and an advocacy of induction from facts as the basis for scientific investigation.

baç″te·rē′mi·ȧ, *n.* presence of bacteria in the blood stream.

baç·tē′ri·ȧ, *n.pl.*; *sing.* **baç·tē′ri·um,** [Mod. L., pl. of *bacterium*, from Gr. *baktērion*, dim. of *baktron*, a staff.] typically one-celled microorganisms which have no chlorophyll, multiply by simple division, and can be seen only with a microscope: they occur in three main forms, spherical (cocci), rod-shaped (bacilli), and spiral (spirilla); some bacteria cause diseases such as pneumonia, tuberculosis, and syphilis, but others are necessary for fermentation, nitrogen fixation, etc.

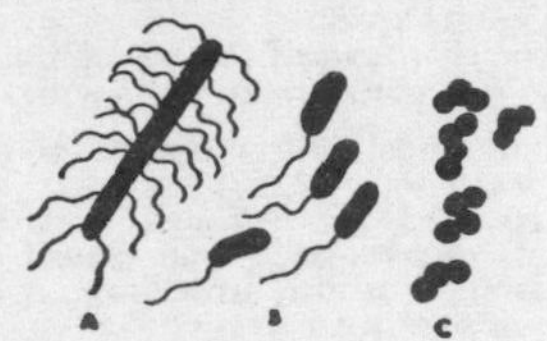

TYPES OF BACTERIA
A, rod (bacillus); B, spiral (spirillum); C, sphere (coccus)

baç·tē′ri·ăl, *a.* of or caused by bacteria.

baç·tē′ri·ăl·ly, *adv.* 1. by the action of bacteria.

2. in the manner of bacteria.

baç·tē′ri·cī″dăl, *a.* destructive to bacteria.

baç·tē′ri·cīde, *n.* [L. *bacterium*, bacterium, and *cædere*, to kill.] an agent or substance that destroys bacteria.

baç′te·rin, *n.* [from *bacteri-*, and *-in*.] a vaccine that contains specific bacteria and is injected into a person's body to increase his immunity to them.

baç·tē′ri·ō-, baç·tē′ri-, [from *bacterium*.] a combining form meaning *of bacteria*, as in *bacterio*logy, *bacteri*cide.

baç′tē″ri·ō·loġ′iç·ăl, *a.* of bacteriology.

baç′tē″ri·ol′ō·ġist, *n.* a student of or specialist in bacteriology.

baç′tē″ri·ol′ō·ġy, *n.* [*bacterio-*, and Gr. *logos*, a description.] that science that treats of bacteria.

baç′tē″ri·ol′y·sis, *n.* [*bacterio-*, and *-lysis*.]

1. chemical decomposition caused by bacteria.

2. the dissolution or destruction of bacteria.

baç·tē′ri·ō·lyt″iç, *a.* of, producing, or characterized by bacteriolysis.

baç·tē′ri·ō·phāġe″, *n.* [*bacterio-*, and *-phage*.] a microscopic agent that destroys disease-producing bacteria in a living organism.

baç·tē″ri·ō·sçop′iç, *a.* of bacterioscopy.

baç′tē″ri·os′çō·pist, *n.* a person skilled in bacterioscopy.

baç′tē″ri·os′çō·py, *n.* [*bacterio-*, and Gr. *skopein*, to see.] the study of bacteria by means of the microscope.

baç·tē″ri·ō·stā′sis, *n.* [Mod. L., from *bacterio-*, and *stasis*.] prevention of the growth or multiplication of bacteria.

baç·tē″ri·ō·stat′iç, *a.* preventing the growth or multiplication of bacteria.

baç·tē″ri·ō·stat′iç, *n.* a bacteriostatic substance.

baç·tē′ri·um, *n.* singular of *bacteria*.

baç·tē″ri·ū′ri·ȧ, *n.* existence of bacteria in the urine.

baç′tēr·īze, *v.t.*; bacterized, *pt., pp.*; bacterizing, *ppr.* to cause a change in by bacterial action.

baç′tē·roid, baç·tē·roid′ăl, *a.* resembling bacteria.

baç′tē·roid, *n.* a structurally modified form of bacterium, as that forming nodules on the roots of leguminous plants.

Bac′tri·ăn, *a.* relating to Bactria.

Bac′tri·ăn, *n.* 1. a native or inhabitant of Bactria.

2. the language of Bactria.

Bactrian camel; a two-humped camel, native to southwestern Asia: it is shorter and hairier than the Arabian camel.

baç′ūle, *n.* [Fr. *bascule*.] a bascule.

ba·cū′li·fọrm, *a.* [from L. *baculum*, a stick; and *-form*.] shaped like a rod.

baç′ū line, *a.* relating to the rod, or punishment with the rod.

Baç·ū·lī′tēs̹, *n.pl.* [L. *baculum*; Gr. *baktron*, a staff, and *lithos*, a stone.] a genus of polythalamous or many-chambered cephalopods belonging to the family *Ammonitidæ*. The species are only known in a fossil state, having become extinct at the close of the Cretaceous period.

baç·ū·lom′e·try, *n.* [L. *baculum*, a staff, and Gr. *metron*, measure.] the act of measuring distance or altitude by a staff or staves.

bad, *a.*; *comp.* worse; *superl.* worst. [ME. *bad*, *badde*, bad, worthless.]

1. not good; not as it should be; defective in quality; below standard; lacking in worth; inadequate.

2. unfit; unskilled.

3. unfavorable; unpleasant; disagreeable; as, *bad* news.

4. rotted; decomposed; spoiled.

5. incorrect; faulty; erroneous; as, *bad* spelling.

6. wicked; immoral.

7. harmful; injurious; dangerous.

8. severe; as, a *bad* storm.

9. ill; in poor health; in pain.

10. bothered; sorry; distressed; as, he feels *bad* about it.

11. offensive; disgusting; as, a *bad* smell.

12. in law, defective; not valid; void.

not bad; good; fairly good; not unsatisfactory: also *not half bad, not so bad*. [Colloq.]

13. very good, stylish, effective, etc. [Slang.]

bad, *adv.* badly. [Colloq.]

Syn.—wicked, evil, ill, vile, wrong, corrupt, vicious, abandoned, base, unsound, abominable.

bad, *n.* 1. anything that is bad; a bad quality or state.

2. wickedness.

3. those who are wicked (preceded by *the*).

in bad; (a) in trouble; (b) in disfavor. [Colloq.]

bad, *v.* 1. archaic past tense of *bid*.

2. obsolete past tense of *bide*.

bad blood, a feeling of enmity, especially mutual enmity.

bad′dēr, *a.* obs. comp. of *bad*, now superseded by *worse*.

bad′dēr·locks, *n.* [perhaps for *Balder's locks*, from *Balder*, the hero of Scandinavian mythology.] a seaweed, *Alaria esculenta*, found on the shores of the north of Europe. It is sometimes eaten by the people of Scotland, Ireland, Denmark, etc. Called also *henware* and *murlins*.

bad′dest, *a.*, obs. superl. of *bad*, now superseded by *worst*.

bad′die, bad′dy, *n.*; *pl.* **bad′dies̹,** a bad or wicked person, especially such a character in a play, movie, etc. [Slang.]

bad′dish, *a.* somewhat bad; indifferently bad.

bade, *v.* 1. alternative past tense of *bid*.

2. alternative past tense of *bide*.

bad egg, a worthless, dishonest, or vicious person. [Slang.]

badġe (baj), *n.* [ME. *badge*, *bagge*; LL. *bagea*, *bagia*, a badge; origin unknown.]

1. (a) a mark, sign, or token worn on the person, by which one's relation to a particular occupation, society, or superior is distinguished; (b) an honorable decoration; a mark of rank or of service.

2. any distinctive sign or symbol; as, the *badge* of bitterness.

3. an ornament or carving formerly placed on ships near the stern, decorated with figures and containing a window or a resemblance of one.

Syn.—mark, sign, insignia, token, emblem.

badġe, *v.t.*; badged, *pt., pp.*; badging, *ppr.* to mark or distinguish with a badge.

badġ′ēr, *n.* a licensed porter, carrier, or hawker required to wear a badge. [Brit. Dial.]

badġ′ēr, *n.*; *pl.* **badġ′ērs̹** or **badġ′ēr,** [16th-c. term for earlier *brock*.]

1. a plantigrade quadruped of the genus *Meles* or some allied genus, characterized by

BADGER (2 ft. long)

a broad back, short, thick legs, and long claws on the forefeet. It inhabits the northern parts of Europe, Asia, and North America. *Taxidea taxus* is the American *badger*.

2. the fur of this animal.

3. a brush of badger's hair.

4. in Australia, (a) a wombat; (b) a bandicoot.

5. [B–] a native or inhabitant of Wisconsin, called the *Badger State*. [Colloq.]

badġ′ēr, *v.t.*; badgered, *pt., pp.*; badgering, *ppr.* 1. to torment as if baiting a badger; to pester or worry.

2. to beat down in price; to cheapen; to bargain. [Dial.]

badġ′ēr dog, the dachshund.

badġ′ēr·ēr, *n.* 1. a person who badgers.

2. a dog trained for badger baiting.

badġ′ēr·ing, *n.* the act of pestering or worrying.

badġ′ēr-legged, *a.* having a leg or legs shorter on one side than on the other, as the badger was erroneously supposed to have.

Badġ′ēr Stāte, the nickname for Wisconsin.

bā′di·ăn, bā′di·āne, *n.* [Fr. *badiane*; L. *badius*, bay-colored, from the color of the capsules.] the Chinese anise tree, *Illicium verum*, or its fruit. The fruit abounds in a volatile oil, giving it an aromatic flavor and odor: it is much used in China and India as a condiment, and is imported into France for flavoring.

bȧ·di′ġeŏn (-jun), *n.* [Fr.] a mixture of plaster and freestone, ground together and sifted, and used by sculptors to fill the small holes and repair the defects of the stones of which they make their statues.

bȧ·di·näġe′ (-näzh′, *or* bad′i-nāge), *n.* [Fr. *badiner*, to jest or make merry; Pr. *badar*, to gape, from LL. *badare*, to gape, to trifle.] light or playful discourse; banter.

> He seems most to have indulged himself only in an elegant *badinage*.
> —Warburton.

bȧ·di·näġe′, *v.t.*; badinaged, *pt., pp.*; badinaging, *ppr.* to banter; tease with playful talk.

bȧ·di′ne·riē, *n.* [Fr., from *badiner*, to jest.] light or playful discourse; nonsense; badinage. [Rare.]

> The fund of sensible discourse is limited; that of *badinerie* is infinite.—Shenstone.

bad·i·neūr, *n.* [Fr.] one who indulges in badinage; a banterer; a trifler.

bad′lands̹, *n.pl.* any section of barren land where rapid erosion has cut the loose, dry soil or soft rocks into strange shapes.

bad′ly, *adv.* [ME. *badly, baddeliche*.] in a bad manner; not well; unskillfully; grievously; unfortunately; imperfectly. Colloquially it is used, in connection with *want* or *need*, etc., for *very much*; as, help is *badly* needed.

bad′mash, *n.* same as *budmash*.

bad′min·tŏn, *n.* [from *Badminton*, an English countryseat.]

1. a game, similar to lawn tennis, but played with a feathered cork (shuttlecock) and light rackets (battledores), the net being narrow and suspended at some height above the ground.

2. a drink made with claret, soda, etc.

bad′-mouth′, *v.t.* and *v.i.* to find fault (with); criticize or disparage. [Slang.]

bad′ness, *n.* the state of being bad, vicious, evil, or depraved; want of good qualities, physical or moral.

bad′-tem′pēred, *a.* having a bad temper or cranky disposition; irritable.

Bāe′de·kēr, *n.* 1. a guidebook, one of a series first published in Germany by Karl Baedeker (1801–1859).

2. loosely, any guidebook.

bae′ty·lus, *n.*; *pl.* **bae′ty·lī,** [Gr. *baitylos*, a sacred stone.] in classical antiquity, a sacred meteoric stone, or any stone shaped so as to serve as a symbol of divinity.

baff, *n.* [Scot.] 1. a blow; a heavy thump.

2. in golf, a loft stroke made by hitting the

ground with the sole of the club in striking the ball.

baff, *v.i.*; baffed (baft), *pt., pp.*; baffing, *ppr.* in golf, to strike the ground with the club-head in playing, and so loft the ball.

baf'fe·tȧ, *n.* same as *baft.*

baf'fle (baf'l), *v.t.*; baffled, *pt., pp.*; baffling, *ppr.* [16th-c. Scot.; prob. respelling of obs. Scot. *bauchle.*]

1. to mock or elude by artifice; to elude by shifts and turns; hence, to defeat, or confound; as, to *baffle* the enemy.

2. to frustrate or balk by puzzling or bewildering; to thwart; to defeat.

3. to hinder, impede; interfere with.

4. to force submission to disgraceful public punishment, as a recreant or perjured knight. [Obs.]

Syn.—defeat, disconcert, confound.

baf'fle, *v.i.* 1. to practice deceit. [Obs.]

2. to struggle ineffectually; as, to *baffle* with the wind.

baf'fle, *n.* 1. a baffling or being baffled.

2. an obstructing device, as a wall or screen to hold back or turn aside the flow of liquids, gases, etc.

3. in radio, a mounting for the loudspeaker, designed to improve reproduction of low frequencies.

baf'fle·ment, *n.* the act of baffling or state of being baffled.

baf'fle·plāte, *n.* a baffle (sense 2).

baf'flẽr, *n.* one who or that which baffles.

baf'fling, *a.* 1. puzzling; bewildering.

2. inscrutable; as, a *baffling* person.

3. obstructing; hindering.

baffling wind; among seamen, one that frequently shifts from one point to another.

baf'fling·ly, *adv.* in a baffling manner.

baf'fling·ness, *n.* the quality of baffling.

baf'fy, *n.* [from Scot. *baff*, a blow; of echoic origin.] a golf club with a wooden head and backward-slanting face for giving the ball high loft: now called *spoon* or *number three wood.* [Obs.]

baft, baf'tȧ, *n.* [Per.] a fine cotton fabric, originally made in India. The name is now applied to similar fabrics of British manufacture.

baft, *adv.* same as *abaft.*

bag, *n.* [ME. *bagge*; Ice. *baggi*, a bag, from *belgr*, skin, bellows.]

1. a sack; a pouch, usually of cloth, paper, or leather, used to hold, preserve, or carry anything; as, a *bag* of money, a *bag* of grain.

2. a sac, inside an animal, containing some fluid or other substance; also, the udder of a female mammal.

3. formerly, a sort of silken pouch in which the back hair of the wig was worn. [Obs.]

4. a bagful; a certain quantity of a commodity, such as is customarily sold in a sack; as, a *bag* of coffee or hops, a *bag* of oats.

5. a piece of hand luggage; satchel; suitcase.

6. a woman's small container for money, cosmetics, etc.; handbag; purse.

7. a container for game.

8. the quantity of game killed in one day or during a hunting expedition; as, our trip to the woods resulted in a good *bag.*

9. anything shaped like a bag.

10. the swelling or bagging part of something.

11. a woman. [Slang.]

12. in mining, a hole or cavity filled with water or gas.

13. [*pl.*] garments, especially when they fit badly; more specifically, in England, a man's trousers; as, a pair of flannel *bags.* [Colloq.]

14. in baseball, any one of the bases.

bag and baggage; (a) with all of one's belongings; (b) completely; entirely. [Colloq.]

to be in the bag; to have its successful outcome assured. [Slang.]

to give one the bag; to dismiss (a person) from employment. [Colloq.]

bag, *v.t.*; bagged, *pt., pp.*; bagging, *ppr.* 1. to put into a bag; as, to *bag* oats.

2. to make bulge.

3. to entrap; to capture; to snare; also, to kill; as, to *bag* game.

4. to steal. [Slang.]

5. to obtain or collect. [Slang.]

bag, *v.i.* 1. to swell like a full bag, as sails when filled with wind.

2. to hang loosely.

bag'ȧ·rȧ, *n.* [Port. *bagre*, a fish.] a sciaenoid fish, *Menticirrhus undulatus*, of the Pacific coast.

bȧ·gasse', *n.* [Fr. *bagasse*, or *bagace*; Mod. Pr. *bagasso*, the refuse of sugar cane.] the refuse of sugar cane and sugar beets after the juice has been taken out: it is used for fuel and in the manufacture of insulation.

bag·ȧ·telle', *n.* [Fr.; It. *bagatella*, a trifle.]

1. a trifle; a thing of no importance.

2. a game played on a board having numbered cups, arches, or holes, into which balls are to be struck with a rod, or cue, held in the hand of the player.

3. a short musical composition, especially for the piano.

bag'gāġe, *n.* [ME. *baggage, bagage*; OFr. *bagage, baggage*, baggage, from *baguer*, to tie up.]

1. the tents, clothing, provisions, utensils, and other supplies and gear of an army.

2. the trunks, valises, satchels, bags, or cases, containing clothing and other conveniences, which a traveler carries with him on a journey; luggage.

3. rubbish; a worthless thing; an incumbrance. [Obs.]

4. [by transference of sense "army baggage" to "camp follower."] formerly, a prostitute or wanton.

5. a saucy, impudent, or lively girl.

bag'gāġe cär, the car of a railroad train used for carrying the baggage of passengers.

bag'gāġe·man, a man who handles the baggage of passengers on a railroad or steamship line.

bag'gāġe más'tẽr, an officer of a railroad or steamship company who is in charge of receiving and dispatching baggage.

bag'ga·ġẽr, *n.* one who carries baggage.

bag'gȧ·lȧ, bag'lō, *n.* [Ar. *baggala*, a female mule.] a two-masted boat used for trading in the Indian Ocean, generally from two hundred to two hundred and fifty tons burden.

BAGGALA

bäg'gie, *n.* [dim. of *bag.*] 1. a little bag. [Scot.]

2. the belly or stomach. [Scot.]

bag'gi·ly, *adv.* in a baggy manner.

bag'gi·ness, *n.* the state of being baggy.

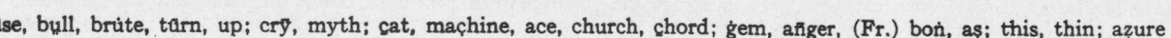

bag'ging, *n.* 1. any coarse fabric out of which bags are made, or with which bales are covered.

2. the act of putting into bags.

3. the act of swelling, or becoming baggy.

4. filtration through canvas bags.

bag'git, *n.* [Scot.] an adult female salmon that has lately spawned.

bag'gy, *a. comp.* baggier; *superl.* baggiest.

1. puffed or swelling in a baglike way.

2. hanging loosely; unpressed; as, *baggy* trousers.

bag'lō, *n.* see *baggala.*

bag'măn, *n.*; *pl.* **bag'men,** 1. a traveling salesman. [British.]

2. a go-between in offering bribes, collecting money as for the numbers racket, etc. [Slang.]

bag'net, *n.* a net in the form of a bag for catching fish.

bagn'iō (ban'yō), *n.* [It. *bagno*, from L. *balneum*, a bath.]

1. a Turkish or Italian bathhouse.

2. a brothel; a house of prostitution.

3. in the Orient, a prison for slaves.

Bag·nō'li·ăn, *n.* [from *Bagnoles*, in France, where the heresy had its rise.] one of a sect of French heretics of the eighth century, who rejected the whole of the Old and part of the New Testament.

bag'ō·net, *n.* bayonet. [Dial.]

bag'pīpe, *n.* [*sometimes pl.*] a musical wind instrument, now played chiefly in Scotland, consisting of a leather bag, which receives the air from the mouth, or from bellows, and of pipes, into which the air is pressed from the bag by the performer's elbow. One pipe (called the chanter) plays the melody, others (called drones) sound respectively the keynote (an octave lower) and the fifth of the scale, the sound being produced by means of reeds. The chanter has eight holes, or stops. There are several kinds of bagpipes, as the soft and melodious Irish *bagpipe*, the more martial Scottish Highland *bagpipe*, and the Italian *bagpipe.*

BAGPIPE

bag'pīpe, *v.t.* to cause (a sail) to resemble a bagpipe.

to bagpipe the mizzen; in nautical language, to lay the mizzen aback by carrying the sheet to the mizzen shrouds.

bag'pīp"ẽr, *n.* one who plays the bagpipe: often called a *piper.*

bag' pụd·ding, a pudding cooked in a bag. [Obs.]

bag'reef, *n.* in nautical usage, the lowest reef of a fore-and-aft sail.

bag'room, *n.* in a ship, a room for storing the clothing bags of the crew.

bȧ·guette', bȧ·guet' (-get'), *n.* [Fr. *baguette*, a rod, wand; It. *baccheta*, dim. of *bacchio*, from L. *baculum*, a rod, stick.]

1. a thing with the shape of a convex oblong, as a gem, watch, etc.

2. a convex, oblong shape.

3. in architecture, a small, convex molding.

bag'wig, *n.* an eighteenth century wig with the back hair enclosed in a bag.

bag'wŏrm, *n.* the larva of any of several moths, family *Psychidæ*, which encloses itself in a protecting case or bag, as *Thyridopteryx ephemeræformis*: called also the *basket worm.*

bäh, *interj.* an exclamation expressive of contempt, disgust, or scorn.

bȧ·hạ·dụr, bȧ·hau'dụr, *n.* [Hind. *bāhadur*, brave, hero.] a Hindu title of respect, used especially of foreign officers and officials.

Bȧ·hä'ī, *n.*; *pl.* **Bȧ·hä'īs,** 1. a believer in Bahaism.

2. Bahaism.

Bȧ·hä'ism, *n.* [Ar. *ba-ha*, splendor; and *-ism.*] a religious sect developed out of Babism: begun in 1863 by Mirza Husayn Ali.

Bȧ·hä'ist, *n.* one who professes Bahaism.

Bȧ·hä'ist, *a.* of Bahaism or Bahaists.

bȧ·här', *n.* [Ar. *bahār.*] an East Indian measure of weight, varying, according to the locality and the substances weighed.

bȧ·hī'ȧ (-ē'), *n.* [Sp.] a bay.

bäht, *n.*; *pl.* **bähts** or **bäht,** [from Thai.]

1. the monetary unit of Thailand.

2. a coin of this value.

bȧ·hụt', *n.* [Fr.] 1. a richly carved or ornamented chest or cabinet of a medieval type.

2. an extra wall built above the cornice proper in convex form and supporting the roof.

baī'där, *n.* [native name.] a canoe used in the Aleutian and Kurile islands.

bāigne (bān), *v.t.* [Fr. *baigner*, to bathe.] to soak or drench. [Obs.]

bāi·gnoire' (-nwär'), *n.* [Fr.] a lower box in a theater.

baī'käl·ite, *n.* [from *Baikal*, a lake in northern Asia.] a greenish variety of augite, occurring in grouped or radiated needlelike prisms.

bāil, *v.t.*; bailed (bāld), *pt., pp.*; bailing, *ppr.* [OFr. *bailler*, to keep in custody, to deliver, from L. *bajulare*, to bear a burden, from *bajulus*, a bearer, carrier.]

1. to set (an arrested person) free on bail (often with *out*).

2. to have (an arrested person) set free by giving bail (often with *out*).

3. to deliver (goods) in trust for a special purpose.

4. to release from imprisonment. [Obs.]

5. to secure or protect. [Obs.]

bāil, *n.* [OFr. *bail*, power, control, jurisdiction, from *bailler*, to control, keep in custody.]

1. the person or persons who procure the release of a prisoner from custody, by becoming surety for his appearance in court.

2. money or credit deposited with the court to get an arrested person temporarily released on the assurance that he will come back for trial, etc. at the proper time.

3. the release thus brought about.

common bail; imaginary bondsmen offered as surety for the appearance of defendant; as, John Doe and Richard Roe. [Obs.]

out on bail; under bond for trial, but at large.

special bail; bail secured by responsible bondsmen.

to go bail for; to furnish bail for.

to hold to bail; to oblige to find bail.

to stand bail; to act as bail or surety.

bāil, *v.t.* and *v.i.* [Fr. *baille*, a bucket, pail, from L. *bacula*, dim. of *bacca*, a vessel.]

1. to remove water from (a boat) with or as with a bail.

2. to dip out (water, etc.) with or as with a bail.

to bail out; to make a parachute jump from an airplane.

bāil, *v.t.* [OFr. *baillier*, to shut in, bar, from *baille*, a bar, crossbar.]

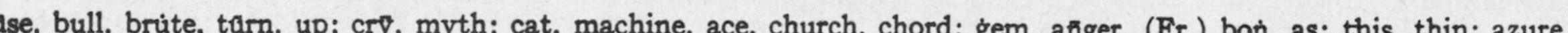

1. to confine by means of a bail, or bar.
2. to furnish with a bail or hoop.

bāil, *n.* [ME. *bayle, baile;* OFr. *bail, baille,* barrier, palisade; from *bajulus,* a porter, carrier.]
1. [*pl.*] an outer fortification made of stakes; palisades.
2. the outer wall or the outer court of a medieval castle.
3. a bar or pole to keep animals separate in a barn.
4. in cricket, either of two pieces of wood laid across the three stumps to form a wicket.

bāil, *n.* [ME. *bayle;* Dan. *beugel,* a hoop, ring, handle; G. *biegel, bügel,* a bow, ring.]
1. a hoop-shaped support for holding up the cloth of a canopy, etc.
2. a hoop-shaped handle on a bucket, kettle, etc.
3. an iron yoke by which to lift or suspend heavy objects, as guns.

bāil'a ble, *a.* 1. able to be bailed.
2. allowing payment of bail; as, a *bailable* offense.

bāil bond, a bond (money or property) offered or deposited as bail.

bāil·ee', *n.* [*bail* (to deliver in trust), and *-ee.*] a person who receives property from another under contract of bailment.

bāil'ẽr, *n.* one who bails or frees from water; anything used to bail out water, especially a small, shallow vessel made for the purpose.

bāil'ẽr, *n.* a bailor.

bāi'ley, *n.* [ME. *baily, bailie;* OFr. *bail, baille,* a palisade, from *baillier,* to enclose.] the outside wall of a medieval fortress or castle: also, the space enclosed by the outer wall: still in some proper names, as *Old Bailey.*

Bāi'ley bridġe, [after the Eng. inventor, D. C. *Bailey.*] in military engineering, a portable bridge consisting of a series of prefabricated steel sections in the form of lattices.

bāil'ie, *n.* in Scotland, a municipal officer corresponding to an alderman in England.

bāil'iff, *n.* [ME. *bailif, baillif;* OFr. *bailif,* from L.*bajulus,* a guardian, administrator.]
1. a sheriff's deputy who serves warrants, writs, and other court papers.
2. an officer of a court when in session into whose care prisoners are committed during trial and who guards the jurors in court and preserves order.
3. an overseer or steward of an estate.
4. in England, an administrative official of a district, with power to collect taxes, serve as magistrate, etc. *Bailiffs* of hundreds collect fines, summon juries, attend assizes, and execute writs and processes; *bailiffs* of forests and of manors direct husbandry, collect rents, etc.; *water bailiffs* protect rivers from fish poachers and illegal fishing.

bāil'i·wick, *n.* [ME. *bailie,* a bailiff, and *wick;* AS. *wic,* a village.]
1. the district within which a bailiff has jurisdiction.
2. one's special field of interest or authority.

bāil'ment, *n.* [OFr. *baillement,* from *bailler,* to deliver, bail.]
1. the providing of bail for an arrested person.
2. the delivering of goods to be held in trust for a specific purpose and returned when that purpose is ended.

bāil'ŏr, *n.* in law, one who delivers property to another under contract of bailment.

bāil'out, *n.* [see *bail* (to set free).] a helping out of one in difficulty; specifically, a providing of government financial aid to a failing company, city, etc.

bāil'piēce, *n.* a judicial certificate containing a recognizance of bail.

bāilṣ'man, *n.;* *pl.* **bāilṣ'men,** a person who gives bail for someone.

Bāi'ly'ṣ bēadṣ, [after the 19th-c. Eng. astronomer, F. *Baily.*] bright spots visible along the rim of the moon, caused by sunlight passing through its valleys and clefts just before and after a total eclipse of the sun.

bāin, *n.* [Fr.] a bath. [Obs.]

bain-mȧ·rie' (ban-mȧ-rē'), *n.;* *pl.* **bains-mȧ·rie'** (ban-), [Fr.; L. *balneum Mariæ,* bath of Mary.] a large pan or bath of water, in which food, etc. contained in another vessel may be heated without burning.

Baī'răm, *n.* [Turk. *bairām.*] either of two Moslem religious festivals following the fast of Ramadan.

bâirn, *n.* [ME. *barn;* AS. *bearn,* from *beran,* to bear.] a child; a son or daughter. [Scot.]

bäiṣe'māin, *n.* [Fr.] act of kissing the hands; in plural, respects or compliments. [Obs.]

bāit, *n.* [ME. *baiten, beiten;* ON. *beita,* to make bite; caus., from *bīta,* to bite.]
1. any substance, such as a grub, a grasshopper, or a piece of meat, used to catch fish, or other animals, by luring them to swallow a hook, or to be caught in snares, or in an enclosure or net.
2. a portion of food and drink, or a hasty luncheon taken on a journey.
3. a stop for food and rest during a journey.
4. anything used as a lure; enticement.

bāit, *v.t.;* baited, *pt., pp.;* baiting, *ppr.* 1. to put food on (a hook), or in (an enclosure), or among (snares), as a lure for fish, fowls, and other animals.
2. to give a portion of food and drink, as a beast upon the road; as, to *bait* horses. [Rare.]
3. to provoke and harass with dogs; as, to *bait* a bull.
4. to attack with violence: to torment or goad, especially by insulting remarks.
5. to lure; tempt; entice.

bāit, *v.i.* 1. to stop for food and drink for refreshment on a journey.
2. to act in a manner calculated to torment. [Obs.]

bāit'-and-switch', *a.* of, related to, or employing an illegal or unethical sales technique in which a seller lures customers by advertising an often nonexistent item at a bargain price and then attempts to switch their attention to more expensive items.

bāit'ẽr, *n.* a person who baits; a tormenter.

bāit'ing, *n.* 1. the act of baiting.
2. refreshment at an inn; also, food given to a horse, etc., especially on a journey.
3. the act of teasing or tormenting bears, bulls, and other animals.

bāize, *n.* [OFr. *baie,* pl. *baies,* baize.]
1. a coarse woolen stuff, with a long nap, sometimes frizzed on one side, without wale, now often dyed green and used to cover tables, etc.
2. a drape, table cover, etc. made of this.

bāke, *v.t.;* baked, *pt., pp.;* baking, *ppr.* [ME. *baken;* AS. *bacan,* to bake.]
1. to cook (food) by dry heat, especially in an oven.
2. to make dry and hard by heat; to fire, as glazed stoneware.
3. to expose (oneself) to the rays of the sun, a lamp, etc.
4. to harden or cake. [Obs.]

bāke, *v.i.* 1. to do the work of baking; as, she cooks and *bakes.*
2. to be baked; hence, to dry and harden in heat; as, the bread *bakes;* the ground *bakes* in a hot sun.

bāke, *n.* 1. the process of baking, or the results of it; also, the amount baked.
2. a cracker. [Scot.]

bāked (bākt), *a.* cooked by dry heat, in an oven; hence, dried and hardened by heat, as pottery.
baked beans; beans baked, usually with salt pork, after they have been soaked and boiled.

bāked-ap'ple, *n.* the cloudberry, especially its dried fruit.

bāke'house, *n.* a house or building for baking.

bāk'e·līte, *n.* a synthetic resin made from formaldehyde and phenol, and used for the same purposes as hard rubber, celluloid, etc.: a trade-mark (*Bakelite*): named after L. H. Baekeland, Belgian chemist.

bāke'mēat, *n.* meat which is baked, especially in the form of a pie: also *baked meat.* [Obs.]

bāk'en, *v.,* archaic past participle of *bake.*

bāk'ẽr, *n.* [ME. *baker;* AS. *bæcere,* from *bacan,* to bake.]
1. one whose occupation is baking bread, biscuits, pastry, etc.
2. a small, portable oven in which baking is performed.
baker's dozen; thirteen; a generous measure.
baker's itch; a skin disease of the hands sometimes affecting bakers.
baker's knee or *leg;* knock-knee.

bāk'ẽr·y, *n.* 1. the trade of a baker. [Rare.]
2. a place devoted to the business of baking or selling bread, biscuits, rolls, pies, cakes, cookies, etc.

bāk'ing, *n.* 1. a drying or hardening by heat.
2. a cooking by dry heat, in an oven, etc.
3. the quantity baked at once; as, a *baking* of bread.
baking powder; a powder used in baking for raising dough. It usually consists of starch or flour mixed with bicarbonate of soda, and some cream of tartar, calcium acid phosphate, or sodium aluminum sulfate.
baking soda; sodium bicarbonate, $NaHCO_3$, used in baking as a leavening agent and in medicine to counteract acidity.

bak'sheesh, bak'shīsh, *n.* [Hind. and Per. *bakhshīsh,* from *bakhshidan,* to give.] in Turkey, Egypt, and some other Eastern countries, a tip; gratuity.

bȧl, *n.* [Fr.] a dance; a ball.

Bā'laam (-lăm), *n.* in the Bible, a prophet hired to curse the Israelites: when he beat his donkey, the animal rebuked him: Num. xxii–xxiv.

bal'ȧ·chong, *n.* [Malay.] a condiment made of fishes and shrimps pounded up with salt and spices, and dried: it is much used on rice and other food eaten in the Far East.

Bȧ·lae'ni·ceps, *n.* [L. *balæna,* a whale, and *-ceps,* from *caput,* head.] a genus of birds embracing the *Balæniceps rex,* or whale-headed stork, a large wading bird about three and one-half feet in height, with a large beak.

Balæniceps rex

Bȧ·lae'ni·dae, *n.pl.* L. *balæna,* a whale, and *-idæ.*] a family of whalebone whales, including the bowhead, or Greenland right whale.

bȧ·lae'noid, *a.* pertaining to the *Balænoidea.*

bȧ·lae'noid, *n.* a right whale which yields baleen, or whalebone; the whalebone whale.

Bal·ae·noi'dē·ȧ, *n.pl.* [L. *balæna,* whale, and Gr. *eidos,* form.] one of the divisions of *Cetacea,* including the whalebone whales.

Bal″ae·nop·ter'i·dae, *n.pl.* a family of whalebone whales, including the finbacks (*Balænoptera*) and humpbacks.

bä·lȧ·gän', *n.* 1. a hut of branches used as a shelter by the Tartars.
2. a hut on stilts used by some Kamchatkan tribes.

bä·lȧ·ghät', [Anglo-Ind.] tableland above mountain passes.

bäl·ȧ·laī'kȧ, *n.* a stringed musical instrument used chiefly in Russia: it is triangular, has two to four strings, and is plucked like a guitar.

BALALAIKA

bal'ănce, *n.* [ME. *balance;* OFr. *balance,* from L. *bilanx, bilancis;* *bis,* twice, and *lanx,* a dish, scale.]
1. an instrument for ascertaining the weight of something. In its original and simplest form it consists of a beam or lever suspended exactly in the middle on a pivot as its center of gravity, with a scale or pan of precisely equal weight hung from each extremity.
2. figuratively, the act of mentally comparing or estimating two things, one against the other.

> Upon a fair *balance* of the advantages on either side. —Atterbury.

3. the weight or sum necessary to make two unequal weights or sums equal; that which is necessary to bring them to a balance or equipoise; the excess by which one thing is greater than another.
4. an equality of weight, power, advantage, and the like; equipoise or just proportion; as, *balance* of force.
5. that which renders power or authority equal; a counterpoise; as, the *balance* between the executive, legislative, and judicial bodies of the United States government should be carefully maintained.
6. the imaginary scales of fortune or fate, as an emblem of justice or the power to decide.
7. the power to decide human fate, value, etc.
8. bodily equilibrium; as, he kept his *balance* on the tightrope.
9. mental or emotional equilibrium.
10. the equilibrium of various elements in a design, painting, musical composition, etc.; harmonious proportion.
11. equality of debits and credits in an account.
12. the excess of credits over debits or of debits over credits.
13. the amount still owed after a partial settlement.

14. a balancing.
15. [B–] the constellation Libra, or the seventh sign of the zodiac.
16. a balance wheel.
17. whatever is left over; remainder. [Colloq.]
alloy balance; a balance for weighing metals which are to be combined in definite proportions.
assay balance; a sensitive balance used in experimental or testing operations for weighing minute bodies. Such balances, besides being made with extraordinary care, are always placed under glass cases to protect them from currents of air.
balance of power; (a) a distribution of military and economic power among nations that is sufficiently even to keep any one of them from being too strong or dangerous; (b) the power of a minority to give control to a larger group by allying with it.
balance of trade; the difference between the amount or value of the commodities exported and imported by a particular country.
bent-lever balance; a weighing scale in which the scale pan is attached to the short arm of a bent lever, the long arm indicating the weight in the pan by traversing a graduated arc.
hydrostatic balance; a balance for weighing a substance in water to determine its specific gravity.
in the balance; not yet settled; not yet determined.
torsion balance; an appliance for measuring small amounts of electricity and magnetism by the torsion of a wire.
to strike a balance; in bookkeeping, to write up the final accounts, so that the debits and credits balance; figuratively, to finally adjust matters in an equitable way.

bal'ănce, *v.t.*; balanced, *pt.*, *pp.*; balancing, *ppr.* 1. to adjust, as weights in the scales of a balance, so as to bring them to an equipoise; to weigh in a pair of scales or balance.
2. to poise on a point or small base; to bring into or keep in equilibrium; as, to *balance* oneself on a tightrope; the juggler *balanced* a plate on his nose.
3. to compare by estimating the relative force, importance, or value of different things; as, to *balance* good and evil.
4. to regulate so as to keep in a state of just proportion; as, to *balance* the powers of Europe.
5. to counterpoise; to make of equal weight or force; also, to be equal to in weight, force, etc.; to neutralize or offset; as, one kind of attraction *balances* another.
6. to find any difference which may exist between the debit and credit sides of (an account).
7. to equalize the debit and credit sides of (an account).
8. to settle (an account) by paying what is due.
9. in seamanship, to reef (a fore-and-aft sail) by taking it in at the peak.
10. in dancing, to move toward, and then away from (one another); as, to *balance* partners.
Syn.—adjust, counterpoise, equalize.

bal'ănce, *v.i.* 1. to be in equilibrium.
2. to be equal in value, weight, force, etc.
3. to have the credit and debit sides equal to each other.
4. to waver slightly; to tilt and return to equilibrium.
5. in dancing, to move toward a person or couple opposite, and then back.

bal'ănce·ȧ·ble, *a.* capable of being balanced.

bal'ănce bēam, 1. the beam of a balance.
2. a beam serving as a counterpoise for lowering a drawbridge: when it moves upward, it causes the bridge to descend.
3. a long, horizontal wooden beam raised about four feet above the floor, on which women gymnasts perform balancing exercises consisting of jumps, turns, leaps, running steps, etc.

bal'ănced dī'et, a diet with the right amount, proportion, and variety of the foods needed for health.

bal'ance ē·leç·trom'e·tēr, an instrument constructed on the principle of the common balance and weights, used to estimate the mutual attraction of oppositely electrified surfaces.

bal'ănce fish, the hammerhead shark.

bal'ănce knīfe (nīf), a table or carving knife, which, when laid on the table, rests wholly on the handle, without the blade touching the cloth: so called because the weight of the handle counterbalances that of the blade.

bal'ăn·cēr, *n.* 1. a person or thing that balances.
2. an acrobat.
3. either of the halteres (balancing organs) of a fly, mosquito, etc.
4. in radio, a device used with a direction finder to increase its accuracy.

bal'ănce rud'dēr, a rudder supported on a projection from the keel so that part of it is forward of its vertical axis of motion: also called *equipoise rudder*.

bal'ănce sheet, in bookkeeping, a statement of the assets, liabilities, net worth, etc. of an individual, firm, or corporation, usually figured at the close of a fiscal year.

bal'ănce step, in military drill, a goose step.

bal'ănce valve, a valve in which steam is admitted to both sides so as to render it more readily operated, by relieving the pressure on the seat.

bal'ănce wheel, a wheel that regulates the movement of a mechanism, as in a watch, clock, music box, etc.

bal'ăn·cing, *n.* the art or act of maintaining balance or equipoise, either of one's own body or of an object.

bȧ·lan'drȧ, *n.* [Sp., from Dan. *bijlander*; *bij*, by, and *land*, land.] a coasting vessel used along the South American coasts.

bal·an'drȧ·nȧ, *n.* [OFr. *balandran*.] a wide cloak or mantle, worn in the twelfth and thirteenth centuries.

bal·an·i-, bal·an·ō-, combining forms from Gr. *balanos*, an acorn, a gland.

bal'ȧ·nid, *n.* a cirriped of the family *Balanidæ*, the acorn barnacle.

Bal·an'i·dae, *n.pl.* [L., from Gr. *balanos*, acorn.] a family of cirripeds, of which the genus *Balanus* is the type. The animals of this family are frequently called *acorn shells* or *acorn barnacles*.

bal·ȧ·nif'ēr·ous, *a.* [*balani-*, and L. *ferre*, to bear.] acorn-bearing.

bal'ȧ·nīte, *n.* 1. a cirriped fossil similar to a balanid.
2. a kind of precious stone.

Bal·ȧ·nī'tēs̹, *n.* [L., from Gr. *balanitēs*, acorn-shaped; *balanos*, an acorn.] a genus of plants containing two species, which are small spiny trees found in desert places in Asia and Africa. The oval fruits are purgative.

bal·ȧ·nī'tis, *n.* [L., from Gr. *balanos*, a gland, an acorn.] inflammation of the glans penis or the glans clitoridis.

Bal''ȧ·nō·glos'si·dae, *n.pl.* [*balano-*, and Gr. *glossa*, tongue.] a family of *Enteropneusta*, having a system of gill-like structures at the side of the alimentary canal.

Bal''ȧ·nō·glos'sus, *n.* [*balano-*, and Gr. *glōssa*, tongue.] a genus of soft-bodied, marine, wormlike animals, related to the vertebrates and having gill-like openings along the alimentary canal.

bal'ȧ·noid, *a.* [Gr. *balanos*, acorn, and *eidos*, like.] like an acorn: applied, in zoology, to certain barnacles with acorn-shaped shells.

Bal''ȧ·nō·phō·rā'cē·ae, *n.pl.* [*balano-*, and Gr. *phoros*, from *pherein*, to bear.] a family of parasitic, leafless, flowering plants. They are generally of a bright yellow or red color. Their small flowers, in most cases unisexual, are clustered into dense masses. The fruit is one-celled, with a single seed.

bal''ȧ·nō·phō·rā'ceous, *a.* related to the family *Balanophoraceæ*.

Bal'ȧ·nus, *n.* [L., from Gr. *balanos*, a gland or acorn.] a genus of sessile cirripeds, family *Balanidæ*, the acorn barnacles. Colonies are found on rocks left dry at low water. They differ from the goose barnacles (genus *Lepas*) in having a symmetrical shell and in lacking a flexible stalk. They pass through a larval stage of existence, at which period they are not fixed, but move about by means of swimming feet, and possess large stalked eyes, both feet and eyes disappearing when they attach themselves to rocks, etc. Often called *acorn shells*.

bä·lä'ō, *n.* the halfbeak, a marine fish.

bal'ās, *n.* [ME. *balas*; OFr. *balais*; Port. *balache*; from Ar. *balakhsh*, from Per. *Badakhshan*, name of a Persian Province where the gem occurs.] a variety of the spinel ruby, of a pale rose-red or orange color. Its crystals are usually octahedrons, composed of two four-sided pyramids lying base to base. Called also *balas* ruby.

bal'ȧ·tȧ, *n.* [Sp., from native name.]
1. a sapotaceous tree (*Mimusops globosa*) of tropical America, from the inspissated juice of which a gum somewhat similar to gutta-percha is made; the bully tree.
2. the dried juice or gum of the *balata*, used in the insulation of wires and the manufacture of golf balls, etc.

bȧ·lau̧s'tȧ, *n.* [L. *balaustium*; Gr. *balaustion*, the flower of the wild pomegranate.] any fruit (of which the pomegranate is a type) whose ovary is many-seeded and pulpy and whose tough skin is surmounted by the adnate or united calyx.

bȧ·lau̧s'tine, *n.* 1. the wild pomegranate tree.
2. the flower of this tree, used, when dried, as an astringent.

Bȧ·lau̧s'ti·on, *n.* [Gr. *balaustion*, the flower of the wild pomegranate.] a genus of plants, order *Myrtaceæ*, containing one known species, *Balaustion pulcherrimum*, a shrub of southwestern Australia, with numerous flowers resembling in shape and color those of the dwarf pomegranate.

bȧ·lȧ·yeūs̹e', *n.* [Fr., f. of *balayeur*, sweeper, from *balayer*, to sweep.] a ruffle placed on the inside of the bottom of a woman's dress to protect it.

bäl·bō'ȧ, *n.* [Sp., after Vasco de *Balboa*.] a silver coin, the monetary unit of Panama.

bal·brig'găn, *n.* [after *Balbriggan*, Ireland.]
1. a knitted cotton material used for hosiery, underwear, etc.
2. a similar woolen material.
3. [*pl.*] garments made of balbriggan.

bal'bū·s̹ärd, *n.* the bald buzzard, or osprey. [Obs.]

bal·bū'ti·āte (-shi-), *v.i.* [L. *balbutire*, from *balbus*, stammering.] to stammer in speaking. [Obs.]

bal·bū'ti·ēs̹ (-shi-), *n.* stammering; also, a kind of defective pronunciation.

bal·çon', *n.* a balcony or gallery. [Obs.]

bal'çō·net, *n.* [Fr., dim. of *balcon*, balcony.] a low ornamental railing to a door or window, projecting but slightly beyond the threshold or sill.

bal'çō·nied (-nid), *a.* having a balcony or balconies.

bal'çō·ny, *n.* [Fr. *balcon*; It. *balcone*, from *balcon*, a beam, scaffold.]
1. a platform projecting from the wall of a building, supported by pillars, brackets, or consoles, and enclosed by a balustrade, railing, or parapet. Balconies usually open onto an upper story.

BALCONY

2. the projecting gallery in the interior of a building, as of a theater.
3. a stern gallery in a ship of war.

bäld, *a.* [ME. *balde*, *belde*, *ballede*, pp. of *ball*, to reduce to roundness like a ball, as when the hair is removed.]
1. lacking hair on the head.
2. lacking the natural covering; as, a *bald* oak, a *bald* mountain.
3. figuratively, without attempt to conceal; naked; bold; as, *bald* blasphemy, egotism, sophistry.
4. unadorned; inelegant; as, a *bald* literary style.
5. in biology, having white on the head, as some animals and birds.
bald acacia; a small Australian shrub.
bald brant; the blue goose.
bald buzzard; the osprey.
bald cypress; a tree growing in swamps in the southern United States: it yields a hard red wood much used for making shingles.
bald eagle; the common North American eagle: so called because of the white head feathers which give it a bald appearance. It is represented on the seal of the United States.

bąld, *n.* a bare mountain top.

bal'dȧ·çhin, bal'dȧ·quin (-kin), *n.* [It. *baldacchino*; Sp. *baldaquino*, from *Baldacco*, the Italian form of *Bagdad*, where the cloth was manufactured.]

1. a rich brocade, formerly made of silk and gold.

2. a canopy of this or other material, carried in church processions or placed over an altar or throne.

3. a marble or stone structure like a canopy, built over an altar.

bald coot, same as *baldicoot*.

Bal'dẽr, *n.* [Ice. *Baldr*, from *baldor*, bold, a hero.] in Norse mythology, the son of Odin and Frigg, the young and beautiful god of light and peace, killed by the trickery of Loki: written also *Baldr*.

bal'dẽr·dash, *n.* [Dan. *balder*, noise, and *dask*, a dash, a slap.]

1. senseless talk or writing; nonsense; as, his speech was nothing but *balderdash*.

2. a senseless mixture of liquors, as of milk and beer. [Obs.]

To drink such *balderdash* or bonnyclabber. —B. Jonson.

bal'dẽr·dash, *v.t.* to mix or adulterate. [Rare.]

bald'-fāced, *a.* white-faced, or with white on the face: said of animals; as, a *bald-faced* horse.

bald'head (-hed), *n.* 1. a person who has a bald head.

2. a kind of pigeon, so called from its white head; also, the widgeon, or fresh-water duck, the top of whose head is white.

bald'head″ed, *a.* having little or no hair on the top of the head.

bal'di·coot, *n.* 1. the common European coot, *Fulica atra*: also called *bald coot*.

2. a monk: so called from his shaven head.

bald'ing, *a.* becoming bald.

bald'ly, *adv.* in a bald manner; barely; nakedly; inelegantly; openly.

bald'mŏn″ey, *n.* [ME. *baldmony*, from *baldemoin*, a name given the gentian.] the mew, or *Meum athamanticum*, a European umbelliferous plant: called also *spicknel*.

bald'ness, *n.* the state or quality of being bald.

bald'pāte, *n.* 1. a person with a bald head.

Come hither, goodman *baldpate*. —Shak.

2. the American widgeon, *Anas americana*.

bald'pāte, bald'pāt″ed, *a.* bald-headed.

bald'rib, *n.* 1. a lean cut of pork from a section nearer the rump than the sparerib.

2. a very lean person: a jocular usage.

bal'dric, bal'drick, *n.* [ME. *baudrik*; OFr. *baudrei, baldrei*; G. *balderich*, a girdle; O.H.G. *balz*, a belt.]

1. a belt worn round the waist, as the Roman cingulum or military belt. [Rare.]

2. a jeweled ornament worn round the neck by both ladies and gentlemen in the sixteenth century. [Obs.]

3. a broad belt, worn over the right or left shoulder, diagonally across the body, to the waist or below it, either simply as an ornament or to suspend a sword, dagger, or horn. Some were magnificently decorated, as with bells and precious stones. The baldric was worn in feudal times, partly as a military and partly as a heraldic symbol, and its style served to indicate the rank of the wearer.

A radiant *baldric* o'er his shoulder tied. —Pope's *Iliad*.

bal'dric·wīse, *adv.* after the manner of a baldric; over one shoulder and hanging diagonally across the body.

Bald'win, *n.* a large winter apple of a reddish color and a somewhat tart flavor, grown in the United States.

bāle, *n.* [ME. *bale*; OFr. *bale, balle*; L. *bala, balla*, a package, ball.] a large package of compressed material, usually a standardized quantity, bound and sometimes wrapped; as, a *bale* of hay or cotton.

bāle, *v.t.*; baled, *pt., pp.*; baling, *ppr.* to make into a bale or bales.

bāle, *v.t.* and *v.i.* to bail (water, a boat, etc.).

bāle, *n.* [ME. *bale, balw*; AS. *balw*, evil, calamity.]

1. calamity; evil; disaster. [Poetic.]

2. sorrow; misery. [Poetic.]

bāle, *n.* a balefire. [Archaic.]

bȧ·leen', *n.* [ME. *balene*; OFr. *balene*; L. *balæna*, a whale.] the narrow, elastic plates extending in a fringe from the upper jaw of certain whales, *Mysticeti*, serving to strain and retain their food; the whalebone of commerce.

bāle'fīre, *n.* [ME. *balefyre*; AS. *bælfȳr*; *bæl*, bale, and *fȳr*, fire.]

1. a signal fire; an alarm fire.

2. an outdoor fire; bonfire.

3. a funeral pyre. [Obs.]

bāle'ful, *a.* [ME. *baleful, baluful*; AS. *bealufuil*; *bealu*, bale, and *-full*, full.]

1. evil; destructive; pernicious; calamitous; deadly; as, *baleful* enemies; *baleful* war.

2. sorrowful; woeful; sad. [Archaic.]

bāle'ful·ly, *adv.* in a baleful manner.

bāle'ful·ness, *n.* the state or quality of being baleful.

Bä·li·nēṣe', *a.* of or pertaining to the island of Bali, or its inhabitants, language, etc.

Bä·li·nēṣe', *n.* 1. *pl.* **Bä·li·nēṣe'**, a native or inhabitant of Bali.

2. the language of the Balinese.

bal'i·sä·ūr, *n.* [Hind. *bālusūr*, a sandhog.] an East Indian mammal, *Arctonyx collaris*, related to the badger.

bal'is·tẽr, *n.* [ME. *balester*, from L. *ballista*, a *crossbow*.] a crossbow or a crossbowman. [Obs.]

Bȧ·lis'tēṣ, *n.* the typical genus of the family of fishes known as *Balistidæ*: called also the *triggerfish* because the large first ray of the dorsal fin cannot be pressed down until the second ray is depressed, when the first snaps down like the hammer of a gun.

Bȧ·lis'ti·dae, *n.pl.* [L., from *balista*, a military engine.] a family of hard-scaled, bright-colored fishes of the order *Plectognathi*, frequenting coral beds for their food. They have no ventral fins or spines.

bal'is·toid, *a.* of, relating to, or pertaining to the triggerfishes, genus *Balistes*.

bal·is·trā'ri·ȧ, *n.* [L., from *balistra*, a form of *ballista*, a crossbow.] a cross-shaped opening in the walls of a fortress, for the discharge of arrows; also, a storeroom for crossbows.

bȧ·līze', *n.* [Fr. *balise*, a beacon.] a pole with a barrel or similar object mounted on top, raised at sea as a beacon.

balk (bak), *n.* [ME. *balk*; AS. *balka*, a ridge; G. *balke*, a beam, a bar.]

1. anything acting as a hindrance or interference; a temporary or complete check; a delay or thwarting; a stop; failure; as, a *balk* in negotiations.

2. anything left untouched, as a ridge between furrows in plowing.

3. in baseball, an uncompleted pitch, entitling the base runners to advance one base.

4. in billiards, the space bounded by the cushion and balkline, from which a player must cue off or resume playing when his ball has left the table.

5. a beam or piece of timber of considerable length and thickness; as, (a) a crossbeam or tiebeam in a roof; (b) any squared timber or square log; (c) a connecting beam for the supports of a trestle or bateau bridge.

6. a blunder; an error.

balk, *v.t.*; balked (bakt), *pt., pp.*; balking, *ppr.*

1. to leave untouched in plowing. [Obs.]

2. to leave untouched generally; to omit; to pass over; to neglect; to let slip.

3. to frustrate; to thwart; to foil; to obstruct.

4. to heap up so as to form a balk or ridge. [Rare.]

Syn.—estop, bar, thwart, frustrate, foil, stop, prevent, hinder, neutralize, nullify, mar, counteract, disappoint, defeat, baffle.

balk, *v.i.* 1. to stop in one's course and obstinately refuse to move or act; as, the horse *balked*.

2. to deal at cross-purposes; to talk contradictorily. [Obs.]

balk, *v.i.* [ME. *balken, belken*; AS. *bælcian*; Dan. *balken*, to brawl, brag.] to indicate by calls or signs from shore, to fishermen at sea, the direction of schools of herring.

Bal'kăn, *a.* 1. of the Balkan Peninsula.

2. of the Balkans, their people, etc.

3. of the Balkan Mountains.

Bal'kăn·īze, *v.t.* and *v.i.*; Balkanized, *pt., pp.*; Balkanizing, *ppr.* to break up into small, mutually hostile political units, as the Balkan States after World War I.

balk'ẽr, *n.* one who or that which balks.

balk'ẽr, *n.* one who signals fishermen by balking.

balk'ing·ly, *adv.* in a manner to balk or frustrate.

balk'ish, *a.* uneven; furrowy; ridged. [Obs.]

balk line, 1. in billiards, one of four lines drawn parallel to and usually fourteen or eighteen inches from each side and end of the table for restricting the play; also, the line at the end of the table marking the position of the cue balls at the opening of the game.

2. a line on the take-off run in the high jump, pole vault, etc., the crossing of which by a contestant is counted as one of the specified number of trials allowed.

balk'y, *a.* obstinate; inclined to balk; as, a *balky* horse.

ball, *n.* [ME. *ball, bal*; M.H.G. *bal, balle*, a ball.]

1. a round body; a spherical object; a sphere; a globe; also, a body nearly round; as, a *ball* of thread.

2. (a) any part of a thing, especially of the human body, that is rounded or protuberant; as, the eye*ball*, the *ball* of the thumb; (b) [*pl.*] the testicles: a vulgar usage. [Slang.]; (c) [*pl.*] daring, courage, etc. [Slang.]

3. a planet or star, especially the earth.

4. in veterinary medicine, a large pill; a bolus.

5. a round, solid missile of a gun; a cannon ball or rifle ball: also used collectively; as, to supply a regiment with powder and *ball*.

6. in printing, formerly, a cushionlike dauber, attached to a handle, for inking the type.

7. in pyrotechnics, a round case filled with combustible materials.

8. in athletics, a round or egg-shaped object used in various games; also, any game in which a ball is used, particularly baseball.

9. in baseball, (a) the style of delivery of a pitcher; as, a high *ball*; specifically, a delivery by the pitcher to the batter, not passing over the plate and between the knee and shoulder limits and not struck at by the batter; (b) any strike or throw; as, a foul *ball*; a wild *ball*.

10. in horticulture, the roots of a plant, bound and packed for shipping.

to play ball; (a) to begin or resume playing a ball game; (b) to begin or resume any activity; (c) [Colloq.] to cooperate.

ball, *n.* [Fr. *bal*, a dance, from *baler*, to dance; L. *ballare*; Gr. *ballizein*, to dance, jump about; *ballein*, to throw.] a formal social dance.

ball, *v.i.* and *v.t.* balled (bald), *pt., pp.*; balling, *ppr.* 1. to form into a ball or balls.

2. to have sexual intercourse (with). [Slang.]

to ball up; to muddle; to confuse. [Slang.]

ball, *interj.* [*pl.*] nonsense! [Slang.]

bal'lăd, *n.* [Fr. *ballade*, a dancing song, from L. *ballare*, to dance.]

1. a romantic or sentimental song with the same melody for each stanza.

2. a song or poem that tells a story in short stanzas and simple words, with repetition, refrain, etc.: most old ballads are of unknown authorship and have been handed down orally, usually with additions and changes.

bal·lȧde', *n.* [Fr.] a verse form having three stanzas of eight or ten lines each and an envoy of four or five lines.

bal·lăd·eer', *n.* a singer of ballads.

bal'lăd·ẽr, *n.* a writer of ballads.

bal'lăd·iṣm, *n.* the quality in a literary or musical composition which fixes its character as a ballad.

bal'lăd·mŏn″gẽr, *n.* 1. a dealer in ballads.

2. an inferior poet; poetaster.

bal'lăd·ry, *n.* compositions of the ballad kind; also, the art of composing ballads.

bal'lăd stan'zȧ, the four-line stanza commonly used in ballads, generally rhymed *abcb*.

bal'lȧ·hōu, bal'lȧ·hoo, *n.* [native name.] a two-masted sailing vessel, rigged with high fore-and-aft sails, used in West Indies.

ball and chāin, 1. a heavy metal ball on a chain which can be fastened to a prisoner's body to keep him from escaping.

2. one's wife, or rarely, husband. [Slang.]

ball'-and-sock'et joint, a joint, as that of the hip or shoulder, formed by a ball in a socket, allowing limited movement in any direction.

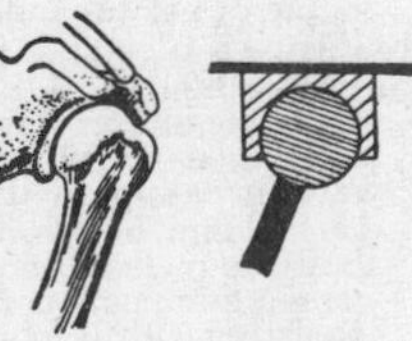

BALL-AND-SOCKET JOINTS

bal'lăn wrasse, [Gael. and Ir. *ballach*, spotted, and *wrasse*.] a fish, of little food value (*Labrus maculatus*), found on the British coast: called also *ballan*.

bal'lȧst, *n.* [G. *ballast*; D. *barlast*; *bar*, bare, waste, and *last*, a load.]

1. any weighty, compact substance, as stone, sand, or iron, placed in the hold of a ship to give it stability, or in an aircraft to help control altitude.

2. any material, as gravel, cinders, or crushed stone, placed on the roadbed of a railway to make the track firm and lasting; also, similar material used as a base for concrete.

3. that which gives firmness to the mind or steadiness to the character.

in ballast; without a commercial cargo, carrying only ballast: said of a ship.

bal'lăst, *v.t.*; ballasted, *pt., pp.*; ballasting, *ppr.*
1. to provide with ballast; stabilize.
2. to fill in (a railroad bed, etc.) with ballast.

bal'lăst·āġe, *n.* a toll paid for the privilege of taking up ballast in a port or harbor.

bal'lăst·ing, *n.* that which is used for ballast.

bal'lăst līne, the water line of a ship in ballast.

bal'lăst plant, a plant whose seeds have been introduced to a country by being carried in ballast.

bal'lăst tañk, a tank in a ship's hold, into or out of which water for ballast can be pumped.

bal'lȧ·try, *n.* balladry. [Obs.]

ball bēar'ing, 1. in mechanics, a bearing in which freely rolling metal balls turn in a socket round the shaft, thus reducing friction.
2. a metal ball for such a bearing.

ball çock, a device consisting of a valve connected by a lever with a floating ball which shuts the valve when raised and opens it when lowered, as in most flush toilets.

bal·le·ri'nȧ, *n.* [It.] a woman ballet dancer.

bal'let (ba'lā *or* ba-lā'), *n.* [Fr. *ballet*; dim. of *bal*, a dance.]
1. an intricate group dance using pantomime and conventionalized movements to tell a story.
2. dancing of this kind.
3. collectively, the entire number of dancers so performing.

ballet dancer; one who dances in ballets.

ballet divertissement; an ensemble dance with music and pantomime, performed as an interlude in an opera.

ballet russe; the Russian ballet.

ballet slipper; a slipper of kid or fabric, with no heel and a reinforced toe, used for toe dancing.

bal'let, *n.* [Fr. *ballette*, dim. of *bal*, *balle*, a ball.] in heraldry, a small ball.

bal''let·ō·māne', *n.* [Fr. coinage; *balleto-* (from It. *balleto*, ballet), and *-mane*, from *manie*, lit., mania.] a person enthusiastic about the ballet.

ball-flow''ẽr, *n.* in architecture, an ornament resembling a ball placed in a circular flower, the three petals of which form a cup round it. This ornament is usually found inserted in a hollow molding, and is characteristic of the decorative style of the fourteenth century.

bal'li·bun''tl hat, or **bal'li·bun''tl,** *n.* [prob. from *Baliuag*, Luzon, where it is manufactured, and *buntal*.] a hat woven of lightweight Japanese straw.

bal·lis'mus, *n.* [L., from Gr. *ballismos*, from *ballizein*, to dance, jump about.] St. Vitus's dance.

bal·lis'tȧ, *n.*; *pl.* **bal·lis'tae,** [L. *ballista*, from Gr. *ballein*, to throw.] a machine or engine shaped like a crossbow and used by the ancients in war, for throwing heavy stones, etc.

bal·lis'tiç, *a.* 1. of or connected with ballistics.
2. relating to the motion and force of projectiles.

ballistic curve; the path actually traveled by a projectile, as distinguished from its theoretical parabolic path if gravity were the only force acting on it.

ballistic pendulum; formerly, a device consisting of a heavy, suspended mass against which a shot was fired and the deflection of the mass noted. From the laws of impact and those of the pendulum the initial velocity of the projectile could be calculated.

bal''lis·ti'ciăn (-shun), *n.* one skilled in the science of ballistics.

bal·lis'tiç mis'sile, a long-range missile that is guided by preset mechanisms in the first part of its flight, but is a free-falling object as it approaches its target.

bal·lis'tiçs, *n.pl.* 1. the science or art of throwing missiles by the use of an engine.
2. the modern science dealing with the motion and impact of projectiles, especially those discharged from firearms.

bal·lis''tō·çär'di·ō·gram, *n.* a tracing made by a ballistocardiograph.

bal·lis''tō·çär'di·ō·grȧph, *n.* [from *ballistic*, and *cardiograph*.] an instrument for measuring the pumping power of the heart by recording the movements of the body in repose that are caused by the contractions of the heart.

bal'li·um, *n.* same as *bailey*.

bal·lon·et', bal·lọọn·et', *n.* [Fr. *ballonnet*, dim. of *ballon*.] any of several auxiliary air or gas containers within a balloon or airship, which are inflated or deflated to compensate for changes in the volume of the gas in the main gas chamber.

bal·lọọn', *n.* [Fr. *ballon*, a balloon, football.]
1. a large, airtight bag filled with hot air, helium, hydrogen, or any other gas lighter than air, the contained gas causing it to rise and float in the atmosphere; also, a bag of this sort with an attached basket or car for carrying passengers or instruments.
2. in chemistry, a round vessel with a short neck to receive whatever is distilled; a glass receiver of a spherical form.
3. in architecture, a ball or globe on the top of a pillar.
4. in pyrotechnics, a king of bomb stuffed with combustibles. [Obs.]

BALLOON
(see *captive balloon* below)

5. in weaving, a cylindrical reel on which sized woolen yarn for warp is wound in order to be dried by rapid revolution in a heated chamber.
6. in a cartoon, the outline enclosing words supposed to be spoken by a figure or character.
7. a large inflated leather ball; also, the game played with it, a kind of football. [Obs.]
8. a small, inflatable rubber bag, used as a toy.

captive balloon; a balloon held in place in the air by a rope or ropes leading to the ground.

dirigible balloon; a balloon which can be steered.

kite balloon; a captive balloon, elongated in form, which is so constructed that it may be held against the wind, somewhat like a kite.

bal·lọọn', *v.t.*; ballooned, *pt., pp.*; ballooning, *ppr.* 1. to carry up in a balloon. [Rare.]
2. to cause to swell like a balloon; to inflate.

bal·lọọn', *v.i.* 1. to go up or travel in a balloon.
2. to puff up; to swell; to expand.

bal·lọọn' băr·rāġe' (-räzh'), a line of anchored balloons holding up nets and cables to disable attacking aircraft or keep them away.

bal·lọọned', *a.* inflated like a balloon.

bal·lọọn'ẽr, *n.* an aeronaut.

bal·lọọn'et, *n.* same as *ballonet*.

bal·lọọn' fab'riç, rubberized cotton or other cloth from which a balloon gasbag is made.

bal·lọọn' fish, a tropical malacopterygian or soft-spined fish of the order *Plectognathi*: the *Tetraodon lineatus* or striped spinebelly. It has the power of distending itself by swallowing air.

bal·lọọn'ing, *n.* 1. the art or practice of managing balloons.
2. inflation of values; also, extravagant praise, especially of a political candidate. [Colloq.]

ballooning spider; a spider that floats through the air on its web.

bal·lọọn'ist, *n.* one who ascends in a balloon.

bal·lọọn' jib, a triangular sail used by yachts in light winds, set between the foretop masthead and the end of the jib boom.

bal·lọọn'ry, *n.* the art or practice of ascending in a balloon.

bal·lọọn' sāil, a large, light sail used on yachts together with or instead of the customary working sails.

bal·lọọn' tīre, a pneumatic cord tire containing a large volume of air at low pressure: it has a large flexible frame with a wide cross section.

bal·lọọn' vīne, a tropical climbing plant belonging to the soapberry family (*Sapindaceæ*).

bal'lŏt, *n.* [It. *ballotta*; Fr. *ballotte*, a little ball.]
1. originally, a ball used in voting. Ballots were usually of two colors, white and black, the former being used for an affirmative and the latter for a negative vote.
2. a printed or written ticket, paper, etc., by which a vote is registered.
3. the act or method of voting, especially secret voting by the use of ballots or voting machines.
4. the entire number of votes cast at an election.
5. a list of people running for office; a ticket.

Australian ballot; see *Australian*.

bal'lŏt, *v.i.*; balloted, *pt., pp.*; ballotting, *ppr.* to vote by ballot.

bal'lŏt, *v.t.* to vote for or against by ballot; to choose or elect by ballot. [Obs.]

bal'lō·tāde, bal'lŏt·tāde (*or* -täd'), *n.* [Fr. *ballottade*, from *ballotter*, to toss; *ballotte*, a little ball, from *bal*, a ball.] a leap of a horse made so that he exposes only the shoes of his hind feet while all four feet are elevated.

bal·lō·tā'tion, *n.* a voting by ballot. [Obs.]

bal'lŏt box, a box for receiving ballots.

bal'lŏt·ẽr, *n.* one who votes by ballot.

bal'lŏt·ing, *n.* the act of voting by ballot.

bal·lotte'ment, *n.* [Fr., from *ballotter*, to toss.]
1. a method of determining pregnancy by pushing against the uterus with the finger, either through the abdominal wall (*abdominal ballottement*) or through the vagina, so as to feel the impact of the embryo if there is one.
2. a similar method of diagnosing floating kidney.

bal'lōw, *n.* a cudgel. [Rare.]

ball'pärk, *n.* a stadium for playing baseball.

ball'pärk, *a.* designating an estimate, figure, etc. that is thought to be reasonably accurate. [Colloq.]

in the ballpark; (a) reasonably accurate; (b) fairly close to what is required. [Colloq.]

ball'plāy''ẽr, *n.* a person who plays ball games, especially baseball.

ball point pen, a type of fountain pen having instead of a point a small ball bearing that rolls over an ink reservoir and deposits the ink on the writing surface.

ball'rọọm, *n.* a large room or hall in which balls and dances are given.

ball'rọọm'' dăn'cing, a kind of dancing in which two people dance as partners to a waltz, foxtrot, etc.: distinguished from *folk dancing*, *square dancing*, *ballet*, etc.

ball valve, a valve that works by the action of a ball resting on an outlet hole: pressure applied externally raises the ball and opens the hole; when the pressure is removed, the ball drops and closes the hole.

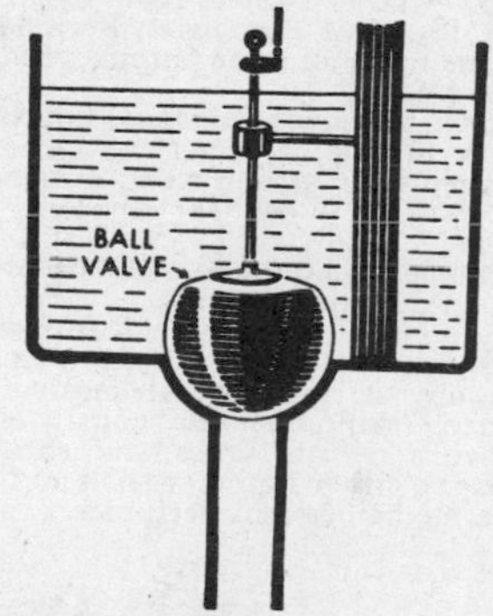

BALL VALVE

bal'ly·hoo'', *n.* [after *Ballyhooly*, village in County Cork, Ireland.]
1. loud talk; noisy uproar. [Colloq.]
2. loud, exaggerated, or sensational advertising or propaganda. [Colloq.]

bal'ly·hoo'', *v.t.* and *v.i.* ballyhooed, *pt., pp.*; ballyhooing, *ppr.* to advertise or promote by sensational, showy methods. [Colloq.]

băl'ly·rag, *v.t.* to bullyrag. [Obs.]

bälm (bäm), *n.* [ME. *baume*; OFr. *basme*; L. *balsamum*, from Gr. *balsamon*, balsam.]
1. an aromatic gum resin obtained from certain trees and used as a medicine; balsam.
2. any fragrant ointment or aromatic oil for healing or anointing.
3. anything which heals, soothes, or mitigates pain or mental distress.
4. in botany, the name of several aromatic plants, as the herb *Melissa officinalis*.

bälm, *v.t.* 1. to anoint with balm, or with anything medicinal. [Obs.]
2. to soothe; to assuage. [Archaic.]

bal·mȧ·çaan' (-kan'), *n.* [after *Balmacaan*, Inverness, Scotland.] a loose overcoat with raglan sleeves.

bälm' ap'ple, same as *balsam apple*.

bälm'i·ly, *adv.* in a balmy manner.

bälm'i·ness, *n.* the quality or state of being balmy.

bälm of Gil'ē·ăd, 1. a small evergreen tree of the myrrh family, native to Asia and Africa.
2. an aromatic ointment prepared from its resin.
3. the American balsam fir.
4. a resin-bearing American poplar.

bal′mō·ny, *n.* the turtlehead, a plant of the figwort family.

Bal·mor′ăl, *n.* [after the English royal residence at Deeside, Aberdeenshire, Scotland.]
1. a heavy, serviceable, striped or figured woolen cloth.
2. [*usually* b–] a heavy, laced shoe.
3. a striped or figured woolen petticoat worn under a skirt which is looped up in front.
4. a round, brimless, flat cap worn in Scotland.

Bäl′mung (-moong), *n.* the sword of Seigfried in the *Nibelungenlied*, used to slay Fafner, the dragon.

bälm′y, *a.* 1. having the qualities of balm; aromatic; fragrant.
2. producing balm; as, the *balmy* tree.
3. soothing; soft; mild; assuaging.
4. [variant of *barmy*.] mildly crazy; idiotic; foolish. [British Slang.]

bal′nē·ăl, *a.* [L. *balneum*, a bath.] pertaining to a bath or bathing.

bal′nē·ā·ry, *n.* a bathing place.

bal·nē·ā′tion, *n.* the act of bathing. [Rare.]

bal′nē·ō-, [L. *balneum*, a bath.] a combining form designating relation to baths or bathing.

bal·nē·og′rȧ·phy, *n.* [*balneo-*, and Gr. *graphia*, from *graphein*, to write.] a description of baths, especially from the medical standpoint.

bal·nē·ol′ō·ġy, *n.* [*balneo-*, and Gr. *logia*, from *legein*, to write.] the science of the therapeutic use of various sorts of bathing.

bal″nē·ō·ther′ȧ·py, *n.* [*balneo-*, and Gr. *therapeuein*, to heal.] the treatment of diseases by means of baths or water cure.

bȧ·lō′nē·ȧ, *n.* [Gr. *balania*, the holm oak; *balanos*, an acorn.] same as *valonia*.

bȧ·lō′nēy, *n.* [altered from *bologna*, sausage.]
1. bologna.
2. nonsense; buncombe. [Slang.]
Also spelled *boloney*.

bȧ·lō′nēy, *interj.* nonsense! [Slang.]

bal′sȧ, *n.* [Sp. and Port. from Peruvian *balza*, the native name of light porous wood used in Peru for rafts.]
1. a tree (*Ochroma Lagopus*) flourishing on the coasts of tropical America; the corkwood.
2. a very light strong wood obtained from the balsa tree, used for airplane models, rafts, etc.
3. a raft, especially one made up of a frame resting on cylindrical floats.

bal′săm, *n.* [AS. *balsam*; L. *balsamum*, from Gr. *balsamon*, *balsamos*, a balsam tree.]
1. an oily or gummy, aromatic, resinous substance, flowing spontaneously or by incision from certain trees and shrubs. The balsams are either liquid or solid and are used in some medicines and perfumes.

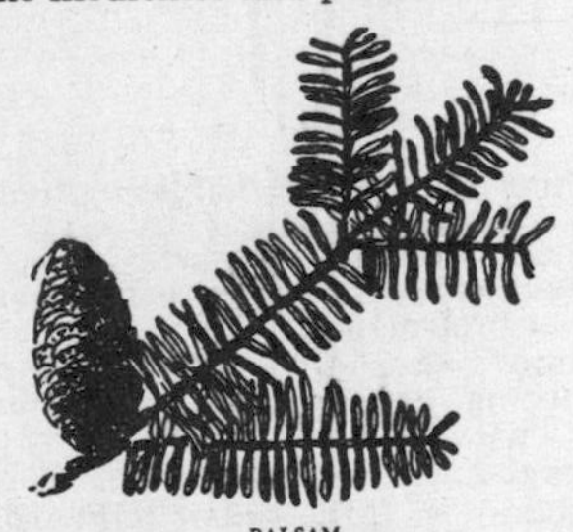
BALSAM
needles and cone

2. a preparation for preservative purposes, as embalming. [Obs.]
3. any of various aromatic, resinous oils or fluids.
4. figuratively, anything that heals, soothes, mitigates suffering, or ministers to the mind.
5. in botany, (a) a tree that exudes aromatic resin, especially one of the genus *Abies*; as, *Abies balsamea*, the balsam fir, from which Canada balsam is produced; (b) an ornamental flowering plant of the genus *Impatiens*, as the garden balsam, lady's slipper, or touch-me-not.
balsam of copaiba; same as *copaiba*.
balsam of Mecca; the balm of Gilead (sense 1).
balsam of Peru; a product of a tree grown in tropical America (*Myroxylon Perieræ*), used as an expectorant and stomachic.
balsam of Saturn; an ointment compounded of acetate of lead dissolved in turpentine and mixed with camphor.
balsam of Tolu; the product of *Myroxylon toluiferum*, the tolu tree of Colombia and Venezuela. It is of a yellowish- or reddish-brown color, semisolid, turning brittle with age. It is very fragrant, allied to balsam of Peru, and used as a stomachic and expectorant.
Canada balsam; the liquid resin of *Abies balsamea*, used to cement and preserve the objects mounted on microscopic slides.

bal′săm, *v.t.*; balsamed, *pt.*, *pp.*; balsaming, *ppr.* to treat with balsam.

bal′săm ap′ple, an East Indian plant of the gourd family, genus *Momordica*, that bears a small gherkin-shaped fruit, yellowish red in color.
wild balsam apple; a climbing vine, *Echinocystis lobata*, of the gourd family.

bal·săm·ā′tion, *n.* the art or act of embalming.

bal″săm·ē·ā′ceous, *a.* [from *balsam*, and *-aceous*.] of a family of plants and trees yielding balsams and resins.

bal′săm fir, an evergreen timber tree, native to Canada and the northern United States, the source of balsam lumber and turpentine: also called *balm of Gilead*, *fir pine*.

bal·sam′iç, bal·sam′iç·ăl, *a.* 1. having the qualities of balsam; soothing; unctuous; soft; mitigating; mild.
2. containing or yielding balsam.

bal·sam′iç, *n.* a soothing or demulcent medicine, of a smooth and oily consistency.

bal·sam′iç·ăl·ly, *adv.* in a balsamic manner.

bal·săm·if′ēr·ous, *a.* [L. *balsamum*, balsam, and *ferre*, to bear.] producing balsam.

Bal″săm·i·nā′cē·ae, *n.pl.* [L. *balsamina*, the balsam plant, and *-aceæ*.] the balsam family of plants, bearing irregular flowers with a spur or nectar sac formed by one of the sepals.

bal″săm·i·nā′ceous, *a.* of the *Balsaminaceæ*.

bal′sam·ine, *n.* the garden balsam, *Impatiens balsamina*.

Bal″săm·ō·den′drŏn, *n.* [Gr. *balsamon*, balsam, and *dendron*, a tree.] a genus of trees yielding a balsamic resin. They have compound leaves, small green flowers, and, in season, small oval nuts.

bal′săm·ous, *a.* balsamic.

bal′săm pop′lăr, a North American poplar whose buds are coated with a fragrant, sticky substance.

bal′săm sprüce, a North American evergreen tree with silvery bark, drooping cones, and blue-green needles.

bal′tēr, *v.t.* 1. to tangle. [Dial.]
2. to walk on clumsily. [Dial.]

bal′tēr, *v.i.* 1. to become tangled. [Dial.]
2. to dance clumsily. [Obs.]

Bal′tiç, *a.* 1. pertaining to the Baltic Sea, which separates Norway and Sweden from Denmark, Germany, and Russia.
2. situated on the Baltic Sea.
3. of the Baltic States.

Bal′tiç, *n.* the western branch of the Balto-Slavic languages, including Lithuanian and Lettish.

Bal′ti·more ō′ri·ōle, [so named from having the colors of the coat of arms of Lord *Baltimore*, in colonial times proprietor of Maryland.] a North American oriole that has an orange body with black on the head, wings, and tail: also called *hangbird*, *hangnest*, *golden robin*.

Bal′tō-, a combining form meaning *Baltic*.

Bal″tō-Slȧv′iç, *a.* denoting a subfamily of the Indo-European languages, including the Baltic and Slavic groups.

Bȧ·lü′chi, *n.* 1. a native or inhabitant of Baluchistan.
2. the langauge of the Baluchis.

bal′us·tēr, *n.* [Fr. *balustre*, It. *balaustra*, a pillar, from *balausto*; L. *balaustium*, Gr. *balaustion*, the flower of the wild pomegranate: from the resemblance in shape.] any of the small posts that support the upper rail of a railing, as on a staircase.

bal′us·tēred, *a.* having balusters.

bal′us·trāde, *n.* [Fr. *balustrade*; It. *balaustrata*, from *balaustro*, a baluster.] a row of balusters, joined by a rail, serving as an enclosure for balconies, staircases, terraces, etc.

BALUSTRADE

bam·bi′nō, *n.*; *pl.* **bām·bi′nī,** [It., a child, dim. of *bambo*, childish.]
1. a child; a baby.
2. any image of the infant Jesus.

bam·boc′ci·āde (-boch′i-), *n.* [It. *bambocciata*, a grotesque painting, from *bamboccio*, a little child, simpleton, a nickname given to Pieter Van Laer, the painter.] in painting, a grotesque scene from common life, as one depicting rustic games, tavern scenes, and weddings.

bam·bo͝o′, *n.* [Malay. *bambu*.]
1. a treelike tropical plant of the reed kind, sometimes reaching a height of more than a hundred feet. The best-known species is *Bambusa arundinacea*. From the main root, which is long, thick, and jointed, spring several round, jointed stalks. At a distance of ten or twelve feet from the ground, these, in turn, send out shoots from their joints. The offshoots are united at their base, spinose at the joints, with one or two sharp, rigid spines, and furnished with oblong, oval leaves, eight or nine inches long, on short footstalks. The flowers are arranged in pyramidal form, growing from the joints, three in a group. The mature stalk, which often attains a diameter of half a foot, is so durable as to be used for house frames, furniture, ship masts, palanquin poles, etc. The smaller stalks are used for fishing poles, canes, and reed musical instruments, and the young shoots are used for food.

1. BAMBOO TREE (*Bambusa arundinacea*)
2. FLOWERS, LEAVES, AND STEM

2. a stalk or cane of bamboo.
3. an Oriental measure of length, about eleven feet; also, an Oriental measure of capacity.
Bamboo Books; ancient Chinese writings inscribed on bamboo tablets, discovered about A.D. 279.

bam·bo͝o′, *a.* of bamboo; also, made of bamboo stems.

bam·bo͝o′, *v.t.* to flog or beat with a bamboo stick.

bam·bo͝o′ rat, a molelike rodent of Asia, found chiefly in bamboo jungles.

bam·bo͝o′zle, *v.t.*; bamboozled, *pt.*, *pp.*; bamboozling, *ppr.* [c. 1700; cant form, with reversed vowels, of *bumbazzle*, from *bombace*, *bombast*.] to trick or cheat; also, to confuse or puzzle. [Colloq.]

bam·bo͝o′zlēr, *n.* a person who bamboozles. [Colloq.]

Bam·bū′sȧ, *n.* [L., from Malay. *bambu*, bamboo.] a genus of gigantic tropical grasses, including the two species which furnish commercial bamboo, i.e., *Bambusa vulgaris* and *Bambusa arundinacea*.

ban, *n.* [ME. *ban*; AS. *bann*, an edict, decree; Ice. *bann*; Dan. *band*; G. *bann*, a proclamation; L. *fari*, to speak; Gr. *phanai*, to say; Sans. *bhan*, to speak.]
1. in medieval times, a public proclamation or edict; a public order or notice, especially an official call to arms.
2. [*pl.*] same as *banns*.
3. an edict of interdiction, prohibition, or proscription. In the Holy Roman Empire, to put a prince under the *ban of the empire* was to divest him of his dignities, and to interdict all intercourse and all offices of humanity with the offender. Sometimes cities or districts were put under the *ban of the empire*, that is, deprived of their rights and privileges.

4. interdiction; prohibition; also, a sentence or decree of outlawry.
5. in ecclesiastical usage, excommunication; anathema.
6. a curse; imprecation.
7. (bän), in France, the younger group of army reserves.
8. (bän), formerly, in Prussia, a division of the Landwehr.

ban, *n.* [from *banana*, from the stalk fiber of which it is made.] a smooth, fine muslin, imported from the East Indies.

ban, *v.t.*; banned, *pt., pp.*; banning, *ppr.* 1. (a) to curse; to execrate; (b) to place under ban. [Archaic.]
2. to prohibit (a thing); to forbid.
3. to prohibit (a person) from doing something.

ban, *v.i.* to curse. [Archaic.]

ban, *n.* [Per. *bān*, master, lord.] formerly, a title of the chief of the eastern marches of Hungary and, later, of the governor of Slavonia and Croatia. The territory over which he ruled was called a banat.

bā′năl, *a.* [Fr. *banal*; L. *bannalis*, from *bannum*, a proclamation, decree.] commonplace; trivial; trite; hackneyed.

ban′ăl, *a.* pertaining to a ban or a banat.

bȧ·nal′i·ty, *n.* [Fr. *banalité*, from *banal*; L. *bannum*, a decree, proclamation.]
1. the state of being banal; triteness or triviality; also, anything trite or trivial; a commonplace.
2. in French law, the authority by which a landed proprietor required his tenants to use his agricultural machinery; also, the district over which such authority extended.

bȧ·nan′ȧ, *n.* [Sp.] a large tropical perennial plant or tree, *Musa sapientum*, akin to the plantain; also, its fruit, which is narrow and somewhat curved, and has a sweet, creamy flesh covered by a yellowish or reddish skin. The plant grows fifteen to twenty feet high and has a soft stalk and leaves that are six feet long and a foot broad. Bananas grow in large bunches, which weigh as much as 80 pounds, and are picked green for shipment.
banana oil; (a) amyl acetate, a colorless liquid with a bananalike odor: it is used in flavorings, in making lacquers, etc.; (b) [Slang.] insincere or foolish talk; nonsense.

bȧ·nan′ȧ bīrd, a bird (*Icterus leucopteryx*) of the West Indies and the warmer parts of America. It eats the ripe fruit of the banana.

BANANA BIRD (*Icterus leucopteryx*)

bȧ·nan′ȧ quit, a bird of the genus *Certhiola*, commonly known as *honey creeper*, found in tropical America.

ban′at, ban′āte, *n.* [Fr. and G. *banat*; Per. *bān*, a master, lord.] the territory or jurisdiction of a ban.

Ban′bur·y tärts (-ber-i), [after *Banbury*, in Oxfordshire, England, noted for its cakes.] small baked pastries filled with mincemeat.

banç, *n.* [Fr. *banc*; L. *bancus*, a bench.] a bench; a seat of justice; a court.
in banc or *in banco*; in full session; as, sitting *in banc*, i.e., all the judges of a court being present, or, before a full bench.

bäñ′cȧ, *n.* [Sp., from native name.] a boat resembling a canoe, used by the natives in the Philippine islands.

bañ′căl, *n.* [Fr., bowlegged.] a curved saber formerly in use in France.

bäñ·cäl′, *n.*; *pl.* **bäñ·cä′leṣ,** [Sp., from *banca*, a bench.] a cover for a bench or seat, made of ornamented carpet, leather, or similar material.

bañ′cō, *n.* [It.]
1. a bank, particularly, the bank of Venice.
2. in commerce, bank money of account, as distinguished from the current depreciated money of a particular place.

band, *n.* [ME. *band*; Ice., G., Sw., Dan., *band*; Sans. *bandha*, a binding; *bandh*, to bind.]
1. a fillet; a cord; a tie; a chain; anything by which a thing is bound, tied, or fastened, or by which a number of things are bound together.
2. in architecture, (a) any flat, thin strip or molding; specifically, the round molding, or series of moldings, which encircles the middle of the shaft in the early English style; (b) the tablet or stringcourse around a tower or other part of a building.
3. figuratively, any fetter or chain; any means of restraint; that which draws or confines. [Archaic.]
4. means of union or connection between persons; as, Hymen's *band*.
5. a contrasting strip or stripe running across or along the edge of material, or separating different sorts of material.
6. [*pl.*] a pair of linen strips hanging in front from the neck, as part of certain academic, legal, or clerical dress.
7. a slip of canvas sewn across a sail to strengthen it.
8. a narrow strip of cloth sewn upon a garment to strengthen and complete it, or as a means of fastening it together; as, a neck*band*, wrist*band*, etc.
9. in zoology, a stripe around, or partly around, the body of an animal.
10. in mechanics, a driving belt.
11. a bond; an agreement; security. [Obs.]
Thy oath and *band*. —Shak.
12. a metal ring around the axle, hub, or circumference of a wheel.
13. in botany, the space between the ribs or lines of umbelliferous fruits.
14. a kind of ruff or collar worn in the sixteenth and seventeenth centuries.
15. in mining, a thin layer of ore or metal.
16. in radio, a continuous sequence of broadcasting frequencies within given limits; as, a *band* from 830 to 870 kilocycles.

band, *n.* [Fr. *bande*, a troupe, division; orig., prob., those following the same sign, from Goth. *bandwa*, a sign.]
1. a group of people gathered or united for a common purpose.
2. a group of musicians playing together, especially upon wind and percussion instruments; as, a brass *band*, a dance *band*.

band, *v.t.*; banded, *pt., pp.*; banding, *ppr.* 1. to bind together; to tie with a band.
2. to mark with a band or stripe, as a flag.

band, *v.i.* and *v.t.* to gather or unite for a common purpose (usually with *together*).

band, *v.t.* to beat to and fro; to bandy. [Obs.]

band, *v.*, past tense of *bind*. [Obs.]

band′āġe, *n.* [Fr., from *bande*, a band, strip.]
1. a fillet, roll, or strip of cloth, used in dressing and binding up wounds.
2. something resembling a bandage; that which is bound over something.

band′āġe, *v.t.*; bandaged, *pt., pp.*; bandaging, *ppr.* to bind or cover with a bandage; to put a bandage on; as, to *bandage* a wound.

ban·dä′lȧ, *n.* [native name.] cloth or cordage (especially white rope) woven in Manila, from the outer fiber of the abacá.

ban·dan′nȧ, ban·dan′ȧ, *n.* [Hind. *bāndhnū*, a mode of dyeing.]
1. a large, silk or cotton handkerchief, originally made by the Hindus, having a uniformly dyed ground, usually of red or blue, with white figures of a circular or lozenge form.
2. a style of calico printing, in which white or bright spots are produced on a red or dark ground.

band′box, *n.* a light paper box for collars, caps, hats, muffs, or other light articles.

ban′deau (-dō), *n.*; *pl.* **ban′deaux** (-dōz), [Fr., a fillet, diadem.]
1. a narrow band or fillet, especially one worn around the head to confine the hair.
2. a narrow brassiere.

band′ed, *a.* being encircled, bound, or marked by a band; as, the *banded* serpent, the *banded* sheaves of grain.
banded architrave, column, pier, shaft, etc.; any of these architectural forms whose outline is broken by bands or projections running across it at right angles.
banded mail; a style of medieval armor in which the rings were arranged in bands around the body.

bän·de̤·rïl′lä (bän-dā-rēl′yä), *n.* [Sp.] a small dart having a barbed head and bearing a banderole, which is stuck into the neck and shoulders of the bull by a banderillero during a bullfight.

bän″de̤·rïl·le̤′rō (-lyā′rō), *n.* one who sticks banderillas into the neck and shoulders of the bull during a bullfight.

ban′de·rōle, ban′de·rōl, *n.* [Fr. *banderole*; It. *banderuola*, dim. of *bandiera*, a banner.]
1. a narrow banner or flag, especially one attached to a lance or carried at the masthead of a ship; a streamer. Written also *bannerol*.
2. in heraldry, a streamer attached to the head of a bishop's staff or crozier, folding over it.
3. a painted or sculptured ribbon bearing an inscription.

BANDEROLE

4. in bullfighting, the small flag forming part of the banderilla.

band fish, a small fish, the *Cepola rubescens*: also called the *ribbon fish*.

ban′di·cọọt, *n.* [corruption of native *pandikokku*, pig rat.]
1. a name given to *Mus giganteus*, a very large rat of India and Ceylon. It is as large as a rabbit, and very destructive to growing crops.
2. an Australasian marsupial of the genus *Perameles*, resembling the *bandicoot* of India.

band′ing plāne, a plane for making grooves and inlaying bands and strings.

band′ing ring, in hatmaking, a ring which keeps the hat in place upon the block, slipped around it at the position of the hatband.

ban′dit, *n.*; *pl.* **ban′dits** or **ban·dit′ti,** [It. *bandito*, from *bandire*; L. *bandire*, to banish, outlaw.] an outlaw; a brigand; a robber; a highwayman.

ban′dit·ry, *n.* a bandit's work; highway robbery; brigandage.

band′let, band′e·let, *n.* [Fr. *bandelette*, dim. of *bandel*, a band.] any little band or flat molding, as that which crowns the Doric architrave.

band′mȧs″tẽr, *n.* the leader or conductor of a band of musicians.

ban′dog, *n.* [*band* (something that binds), and *dog*.]
1. a dog kept tied up as a watchdog or because he is ferocious.
2. a mastiff or bloodhound.

ban·dō·leer′, *n.* [Fr. *bandoulière*; It. *bandoliera*, from *banda*, band.] a large leather belt worn over one shoulder, and across the chest, and containing receptacles for cartridges, etc. The term was also applied to the small leather cases attached to the belt. Also spelled *bandolier, bandileer*.

ban′dō·līne, *n.* a sticky, perfumed dressing for the hair.

ban′dō·līne, *v.t.*; bandolined, *pt., pp.*; bandolining, *ppr.* to use bandoline upon, as the hair, for the purpose of glossing or keeping in shape.

ban′dŏn, *n.* disposal; license. [Obs.]

ban′dōre, *n.* [Sp. *bandurria*; L. *pandura*; Gr. *pandoura*, a musical instrument.] an ancient musical stringed instrument resembling a guitar; a pandore.

band′-pȧss′ fil′tẽr, in electricity, a combination of filters which will pass frequencies within a desired range but will virtually cut out other frequencies.

band pụl′ley, a flat-faced wheel or pulley fixed on a shaft, driven by a band and used in the transmission of power.

band sa̤w, a saw in the form of a narrow, endless steel band on pulleys.

band shell, an outdoor platform for concerts, having a concave, nearly hemispherical back serving as a sounding board.

bandṣ′măn, *n.*; *pl.* **bandṣ′men,** a member of a band, especially of musicians.

band′stand, *n.* an outdoor stand or platform for the use of a band or orchestra, usually with a roof.

band′string, *n.* a string or lace in former times attached to a neckband.

band′wag″ŏn, *n.* a high, elaborately decorated wagon intended for the use of a band of musicians.
to get on the bandwagon; to go with the crowd; to side with a successful candidate or cause. [Colloq.]

band wheel, a wheel with a face nearly flat or grooved to hold the band that drives it, as in the lathe; a band pulley.

ban′dy, *n.* [Anglo-Ind.] a cart or conveyance, used in India.

ban′dy, *n.*; *pl.* **ban′dieṣ,** [Fr. *bander*, to bend.]
1. a club bent at the lower part for striking a ball at play; a hockey stick.
2. a game played with such a club; a variety of field hockey.

ban′dy, *v.t.*; bandied, *pt., pp.*; bandying, *ppr.* [Fr. *bander*, to bandy at tennis, from *bande*, a band, side, party.]
1. to toss to and fro, as a ball when playing at bandy.
2. to exchange; to give and receive reciprocally; as, to *bandy* words.
3. to agitate; toss about, as from man to man.
4. to pass (gossip, rumor, etc.) about freely and carelessly.

ban′dy, *v.i.* 1. to drive the ball, as in a return stroke at tennis.
2. to form into a band or union. [Obs.]

3. to contend, either in a friendly or hostile spirit.

ban′dy, *a.* bent or curved outward; bowed.

ban′dy-leg′ged, *a.* having bandy legs; bow-legged.

bāne, *v.t.* to poison; to ruin. [Obs.]

bāne, *n.* [ME. *bane*; AS. *bana*, a slayer, murderer; O.H.G. *bana*, murder, *bano*, murderer.]

1. poison of a deadly quality: now obsolete except in *ratsbane*, etc.
2. the cause of mischief, injury, or destruction; as, vice is the *bane* of society.
3. a disease in sheep, more commonly termed the *rot*.
4. death; destruction. [Obs.]

bāne′ber″ry, *n.*; *pl.* **bāne′ber″ries,** 1. any of a number of related plants with poisonous berries colored white, red, or purplish black, and clusters of small, white flowers.

2. the berry of any of these plants.

bāne′fụl, *a.* poisonous; pernicious; destructive; deadly.

bāne′fụl·ly, *adv.* in a baneful manner; dangerously.

bāne′fụl′ness, *n.* the state or quality of being baneful or pernicious.

bāne′wŏrt, *n.* a poisonous plant, of the crowfoot family, especially the deadly nightshade and the lesser spearwort, the latter being particularly baneful to sheep.

bang, *v.t.*; banged (bangd), *pt., pp.*; banging, *ppr.* [ON. *banga*, to hammer.]

1. to beat, as with a club or cudgel; to thump; to strike hard and noisily.
2. to close (a door, etc.) noisily.
3. to handle roughly; to treat with violence; as, to *bang* a drum.

bang, *v.i.* 1. to make a great noise, as by striking a series of blows; to slam.

2. to move noisily or with a violent impact (*against* something).

bang, *v.t.* to cut short and straight across, as a horse's tail, or hair over the human forehead; to dock.

bang, *n.* 1. a hard blow, as with a club; a resounding thump.

2. an explosive noise; as, the *bang* of a door.
3. pleasure; enjoyment; stimulation. [Slang.]

bang, *n.* 1. the front hair cut squarely across the forehead; a curl of the front hair or a false front brought down low upon the forehead.

2. [*pl.*] banged hair worn across the forehead.

bang, *n.* [Per. *bang*; Sans. *bhangā*, hemp.] see *bhang*.

bang, *adv.* 1. hard and noisily.

2. loudly and abruptly.

bang, *interj.* a sound imitating that of a shot or explosion.

bañ′gȧ·lọre tọr·pē′dō, [from *Bangalore*, a city in India.] in military usage, a piece of metal tubing filled with high explosive, used especially to blast a path through a barbed-wire entanglement or to detonate buried mines.

bang′bọard, *n.* [*bang*, v., and *board*.] a large board mounted along one side of a wagon, against which corn huskers toss the ears of corn, causing them to rebound into the wagon.

bañ′gle (-gl), *v.t.*; bangled (-gld), *pt., pp.*; bangling, *ppr.* to waste gradually; to squander in bits. [Obs.]

bañ′gle, *v.i.* to bang loosely; to flutter. [Dial.]

bañ′gle, *n.* [Hind. *bangrī*, glass bracelet.] a form of bracelet or armlet; a circlet of gold, silver, glass, or other material, worn by the women of eastern countries; also, an ornament worn on the ankle in India and Africa.

bañ′gle ēar, an ear that hangs loosely, like that of a spaniel or bloodhound.

bang′ling, *n.* trivial disputation; wrangling. [Obs.]

Bang's dis·ēase′, [after B. L. F. *Bang*, 19th-c. Danish physician.] an infectious disease of cattle, caused by a bacterium and often resulting in abortion.

bang′-up′, *a.* very good; excellent. [Slang.]

ban′iăn, *n.* a banyan.

ban′iăn, *n.* [Port., from Hind. *vaniyo*, trader; Sans. *vanỹ*, merchant.]

1. a Hindu trader or merchant, one of a class or caste that abstains from eating meat.
2. a loose-fitting gown or shirt worn in India.

ban′ish, *v.t.*; banished, *pt., pp.*; banishing, *ppr.* [ME. *banishen*; OFr. *banir*, *bannir*; L. *bandire*, to proclaim, banish; *bannum*, a ban.]

1. to condemn to leave one's country, by authority of the sovereign or government, either temporarily or for life; to exile.
2. to drive away; to forcibly dismiss; as, to *banish* sorrow.
3. to put out of one's thoughts; as, security *banishes* fear.

Syn.—exile, expel.

ban′ish·ẽr, *n.* one who compels another to quit his country; one who banishes.

ban′ish·ment, *n.* 1. the action of a monarch or a government, compelling a citizen to leave his country.

2. the state of being banished.
3. the act of driving away or dispelling; as, the *banishment* of care.

ban′is·tẽr, *n.* 1. a baluster.

2. [*pl.*] a balustrade.

Also spelled *bannister*.

ban′jō, *n.*; *pl.* **ban′jōs, ban′jōes,** [altered from *bandore*.] a stringed musical instrument having a long neck and a circular body covered on top with tightly stretched skin: the strings are plucked with the fingers or a plectrum.

ban′jō·ist, *n.* a player of the banjo.

bañk, *n.* [ME. *bank*; Ice. *bakki*, a bank of a river, ridge; Dan. *bakke*, a hill.]

1. a long mound or heap, as of ground or clouds; a ridge.
2. a steep rise or slope, as of a hill.
3. a stretch of rising land at the edge of a body of water, especially a stream.
4. a shoal or shallow place, as in a sea or lake.
5. the sloping of an airplane laterally to avoid slipping sideways on a turn.
6. a cushion of a billiard table.
7. in mining, the face or top end of the body of ore.

bañk, *n.* [ME. *banck*; OFr. *banc*, a bench, from O.H.G. *bank*, a bench.]

1. a bench for rowers in a galley.
2. a row or tier of oars.
3. a row or series of objects; a tier.
4. in electricity, a group of pieces of similar equipment placed near each other and operating in conjunction.
5. a table or sloping shelved rack used by printers.
6. the track of the moving carriage of a printing press.
7. in billiards, the cushion; as, along the *bank*.
8. a row of keys in a keyboard or console.

bañk, *n.* [Fr. *banque*; It. *banca* from O.H.G. *bank*, a bench, money-changer's bench.]

1. an establishment for the deposit, custody, and issue of money, for making loans and discounts, and for making easier the exchange of funds by checks, notes, etc.: banks make profit by lending money at interest.
2. a company or association carrying on such a business.
3. the building or office in which the transactions of a banker or banking company are conducted.
4. the funds of a gambling establishment; the fund or pool held by the banker or dealer in some gambling games; as, to break the *bank*; a faro *bank*.
5. a joint stock or capital. [Obs.]

bank discount; interest deducted by a bank from a loan when the loan is made and equal to the normal interest for the period from the date of the loan to the date of the final payment.

bank of deposit; a bank whose operations are limited to receiving the money of its customers, and circulating it in loans, etc.

Bank of England; the great national bank closely connected with the government of England, custodian of the public funds and manager of the public debt.

bank of issue; a bank duly authorized by law to issue its own bank notes, which circulate as currency.

to break the bank; in gambling, to win all of the amount which has been designated as the limit which the bank is willing to lose in a single day.

bañk, *v.t.*; banked, *pt., pp.*; banking, *ppr.* 1. to heap dirt around for protection from cold, light, etc.; to embank.

2. to arrange (a fire) by covering with ashes, adding fuel, etc., so that it will burn low and keep longer.
3. to heap or pile up so as to form a bank.
4. to give a rising slope to (a curve in a road, etc.).
5. to slope (an airplane) laterally on a turn, with the inside wing low and the outside wing high so as to prevent slipping sideways.
6. in billiards, (a) to stroke (a ball) so that it recoils from a cushion; (b) to make (a shot) in this way.

bañk, *v.t.* to arrange in a bank, or row.

bañk, *v.i.* 1. to take the form of a bank (ridge, steep slope, etc.) or banks.

2. to bank an airplane; to fly with lateral slope on a turn.

bañk, *v.t.* and *v.i.* to deposit (money) in a bank.

bañk, *v.i.* 1. to engage in banking; to operate or manage a bank.

2. to keep the bank, as in some gambling games.

to bank on; to depend on; rely on. [Colloq.]

bañk′ȧ·ble, *a.* acceptable to a bank.

bañk aç·çount′, money deposited in a bank and subject to withdrawal by the depositor.

bañk an·nū′i·tieṣ, bonds of the British government; consols.

bañk bill, 1. a bank note.

2. a bill of exchange issued or accepted by a bank.

bañk′book, *n.* a book in which the account of a depositor in a bank is recorded: also called *passbook*.

bañk çred′it, a specified sum up to which one will be allowed to draw money from a bank upon the deposit of security.

bañk dråft, a draft or bill of exchange drawn by a bank on another bank.

bañk′ẽr, *n.* 1. a person or company that owns or manages a bank or is engaged in the business of banking.

2. one who keeps the bank, or handles the money, in a gambling house or private game of chance; the dealer.
3. the backer of any individual or enterprise; one who furnishes funds.
4. a vessel engaged in cod fishing on the banks of Newfoundland.
5. a money changer. [Obs.]
6. a sculptor's modeling table, provided with a circular revolving platform.
7. a bench used by masons or bricklayers in cutting or squaring stone or brick; a banket.
8. one who makes banks or mounds.
9. one who digs ditches or drains; a ditcher. [Brit. Dial.]
10. a cushion or covering for a seat. [Obs.]

bañk′ẽr·ess, *n.* a woman banker, or the wife of a banker.

bañk′et, *n.* [AS. *benc*, bench, and E. dim. *-et*.] the workbench of a mason or bricklayer, used for trimming and squaring.

bañk hol′i·dāy, 1. in Great Britain, any of six legal holidays on which banks are closed.

2. any weekday on which banks are closed.

The term also designates a period when banks are closed throughout the country: specifically, the period from March 4 to 14, in 1933, when President Roosevelt proclaimed the banks closed, pending measures to restore public confidence.

bañk′ing, *n.* the business of a bank or employment of a banker; the business or study of operating a bank.

bañk′ing, *n.* the act of one who or that which banks (in various senses).

bañk′ing, *a.* relating to a bank or banker.

bañk′ing house, any establishment engaged in a banking business.

bañk′man, *n.* in printing, a compositor who attends to the proving of galleys on the bank.

bañk mär′tin, same as *bank swallow*.

bañk nīght, an evening when cash prizes are given away at a motion-picture theater. [Colloq.]

bañk nōte, a promissory note issued by a bank, payable on demand: it is a form of paper money.

bañk pā′pẽr, 1. bank notes collectively.

2. any bankable notes, bills, etc.

bañk pōst, letter paper of large size, varying in weight from $5^1/_2$ to 10 pounds per ream.

bañk rāte, a standard rate of discount set by a central bank or banks.

bañk′rupt, *n.* [Fr. *banqueroute*, a bankrupt, from It. *banca rotta*, lit., broken-benched; *banca*, bench, and *rotta*, f. of *rotto*, broken, from L. *ruptus*, pp. of *rumpere*, to break.]

1. one who fails in business, or becomes unable to pay his debts; insolvent individual.
2. in old English law, a trader who defrauded or sought to defraud his creditors by secreting himself or his property. In England, prior to Bankruptcy Act of 1861, only insolvent traders were termed *bankrupts*, all others unable to pay their debts being styled insolvents; but since passage of that act, insolvent traders and non-traders alike are called *bankrupts*.
3. in law, a person who has been declared by legal authority unable to pay his debts and adjudged to be discharged from his indebtedness under the provisions of the bank-

ruptcy laws, either on showing that he has no assets to meet his liabilities or on surrender of his property for distribution among his creditors or for administration for their benefit.

4. a person who lacks a certain quality; as, a mental *bankrupt*.

bañk'rupt, *a.* 1. in the condition of having been legally declared insolvent; as, a *bankrupt* firm.

2. out of funds; depleted of means; having no money to meet liabilities; as, a *bankrupt* treasury.

3. lacking in some quality; as, *bankrupt* in health, in gratitude, etc.

4. pertaining to bankruptcy.

5. hopelessly discredited, as in resources or character.

bankrupt law, bankruptcy law; a law formed with the view of protecting a person who cannot pay his debts from unduly harsh proceedings by his creditors, and those creditors from any fraudulent conduct on the part of their debtor. Bankrupt laws have the double object of enforcing a complete discovery and equitable distribution of the property and effects of an insolvent, and of conferring on the bankrupt the advantage of security of person, and a relief from all future annoyance or claims on the part of his creditors.

bañk'rupt, *v.t.*; bankrupted, *pt., pp.*; bankrupting, *ppr.* to make insolvent; to cause to become bankrupt.

bañk'rupt·cy, *n.*; *pl.* **bañk'rupt·cieṣ,** 1. the state of being bankrupt or insolvent; inability to pay just or legal debts.

2. the act of becoming a bankrupt; the act of rendering oneself a bankrupt; failure in trade or commerce.

3. in law, the condition of being judicially declared bankrupt.

4. the legal act or process of applying for relief from debts under the bankruptcy law; as, to go into *bankruptcy*.

5. serious or complete loss, as of faith, belief, reputation, etc.

bañk shot, in billiards, a shot which rebounds from the cushion, or bank.

Bañk'si·ȧ, *n.* [from Sir Joseph *Banks*, Eng. botanist (1743–1820).]

1. a genus of evergreen shrubs with clusters of showy yellow flowers, natives of Australia and Tasmania.

2. [b–] any plant belonging to this genus.

Bañk'sīde, *n.* a district along the south bank of the Thames in London, formerly the site of many theaters, including the Shakespearean Globe Theater.

bañk'sīde, *n.* the side of a bank: applied to a brook or river.

bañk stock, a share or shares in the capital stock of a bank.

bañk swäl'lōw, a name for the sand martin, *Clivicola riparia*, which makes its nest by burrowing in banks: also called *bank martin*.

bañ'li·eūe (bañ'li-ū), *n.* [Fr., from *ban*, a command, and *lieue*, league.] the territory outside the walls, but within the legal limits, of a town or city.

ban'nẽr, *n.* [ME. *banere*; OFr. *banere, baniere*; LL. *bandum*, from Goth. *bandwa*, a sign.]

1. a flag; a military ensign or standard; an official emblem; as, the Star-Spangled *Banner*; an army with *banners*.

2. a streamer, formerly borne at the end of a lance or spear, as the standard of a military chief, to mark a rallying point.

3. in botany, the upper petal of a papilionaceous flower; the vexillum.

4. formerly, one of the divisions of the Chinese imperial or Manchu army, each having its distinctive flag.

5. a large square or piece of heavy silk or other material inscribed with the emblem, name, motto, slogan, etc. of a society, union, or other organization, borne at the end of a staff or staves, often attached to a crosspiece, and displayed in parades, processions, or public assemblies.

6. a form of sign or advertisement for outdoor display, usually consisting of a large square or rectangular piece of cloth, netting, etc., duly inscribed and suspended in public view, as across a street, in front of a building, or along the sides of a railroad car or other vehicle.

7. in heraldry, a little flag or banneret of various forms, used as the emblem of a knight.

8. a headline extending across a newspaper page.

ban'nẽr cr̄y, a rallying cry; as, the *banner cry* of freedom.

ban'nẽred, *a.* equipped with or carrying banners; as, a *bannered* host.

ban·nẽr·et', ban·nẽr·ette', *n.* a small banner.

ban'nẽr·et, *n.* [ME. and OF. *baneret*, dim. of *banere*, banner.]

1. originally, an independent knight or feudal lord; a knight *banneret*; one of a middle grade of knights between barons and simple knights, in the Middle Ages, having his own battle flag.

2. a title or dignity earned by heroic deeds upon the battlefield; hence, an order of knighthood above that of knight bachelor; also, the person elevated to this order. The dignity of knight *banneret* was conferred in the field by removing the points of the pennant on the lance or spear of the person knighted, thus changing the emblem to the square form of a *banneret* or little banner.

3. formerly, a magisterial officer of the second rank in some Swiss cantons; also, a civil officer in certain Italian republics.

ban'nẽr-fish, a large salt-water fish of the swordfish family, having a large, erect dorsal fin like a banner: also called *sailfish* and *spikefish*.

ban'nẽr·man, *n.*; *pl.* **ban'nẽr·men,** 1. a standard bearer.

2. one who was a member of a banner in the Manchu army.

ban'nẽr·ōl, *n.* same as *banderole*.

ban'nẽr plant, a plant of the genus *Anthurium*, having bright scarlet spathes or modified leaves of bannerlike appearance.

ban'nẽr stōne, in archaeology, a stone ornament resembling a two-edged ax with a hole for a handle or staff, supposed to have been a symbol of authority among aboriginal tribes in North America, many having been found in various parts of the United States.

ban'nis·tẽr, *n.* a banister.

ban·ni'tion (-nish'un), *n.* the act of expulsion. [Obs.]

ban'nŏck, *n.* [ME. *bannok*; from AS. *bannuc*; from Gael. *bannach*, a cake.] a cake made of coarse meal, usually oatmeal, pease meal, or barley meal, common in Scotland and northern England. It is baked on an iron or stone griddle.

ban'nŏck flūke, the turbot. [Scot.]

bannṣ, *n.pl.* [ME. *bannen*, from AS. *bannan*, to summon.] proclamation or notice of a proposed marriage, especially in a church by a priest or minister, such notice being given that anyone may object who is aware that there is just impediment to the union of the parties concerned: also spelled *bans*.

The publication of banns is not essential to a valid civil marriage in the United States, England, or Scotland, though it occurs, as a matter of form, in several churches, as the Anglican or Protestant Episcopal. In the Roman Catholic Church it is regarded as highly reprehensible to omit such public notice of a marriage, though the omission does not invalidate a marriage ceremony. Banns are proclaimed three times, usually on three successive Sundays or festival days.

to forbid the banns; to make public or formal objection to a proposed marriage, an opportunity for such objection being offered during the proclamation of the banns.

bañ'quet, *n.* [Fr. *banquet*, a feast, from dim. of *banc*, a table.]

1. a feast; an elaborate meal.

2. a formal or ceremonious dinner in honor of some particular person or occasion, and usually followed by speeches, music, etc.; as, a *banquet* in honor of the president, the St. Patrick's day *banquet*.

3. dessert; sweets to be eaten after meat. [Obs.]

Syn.—feast, festivity, entertainment.

bañ'quet, *v.t.*; banqueted, *pt., pp.*; banqueting, *ppr.* to honor with or entertain at a feast, or sumptuous entertainment.

bañ'quet, *v.i.* to feast; to regale oneself with good eating and drinking; to attend a banquet.

bañ'quet·ẽr, *n.* 1. a feaster; one who banquets.

2. formerly, one who gives banquets or sumptuous entertainments.

bañ'quet hąll, a hall, either public or private, provided for the giving of banquets.

bañ·quette' (-ket'), *n.* [Fr., dim. of *banc*, a bench.]

1. in fortification, an elevated earthen footbank running along the inside of a parapet or trench, on which soldiers stand to fire upon the enemy; also, an outer earthwork.

2. an upholstered bench, especially one along a wall in a restaurant.

3. a raised way; a sidewalk.

4. a small window seat; a narrow shelf.

Bañ'quō, *n.* a character in Shakespeare's Macbeth: the ghost of Banquo disrupts a banquet by appearing only to Macbeth, who had ordered his murder.

banṣ, *n.pl.* banns.

ban'shee, ban'shïe, *n.* [Gael. *ban-sīth*; Ir. *beansīdhe*; from *ban*, woman, and *sīth*, fairy; lit. woman of the fairies.] in Irish and Scottish folklore, a supernatural being, commonly supposed by the superstitious to take the shape of an old woman and to foretell death by mournful singing or wailing outside a dwelling: written also *benshi*.

ban'stiç·kle, *n.* [ME. *banstickle*, lit. prickle bone, from AS. *bān*, bone, and *sticels*, prickle.] the three-spined stickleback, a small fish of the genus *Gasterosteus*.

ban'tăm, *n.* [after *Bantam*, a province in Java.]

1. [B–] any of several breeds of small fowl: the male often is a good fighter.

2. a small but aggressive or pugnacious person.

3. a bantamweight.

ban'tăm, *a.* like a bantam; small, aggressive, etc.

ban'tam·wēight (-wāt), *n.* in sports, a boxer or wrestler who weighs between 113 and 118 pounds.

ban'tam·wēight, *a.* of bantamweights.

ban'teng, *n.* a species of small wild ox, *Bos banteng* or *Banteng sondaicus*, native to the Malay Archipelago.

ban'tẽr, *v.t.*; bantered (-tẽrd), *pt., pp.*; bantering, *ppr.* [17th-c. slang; prob. influenced by *bandy, v.*]

1. to tease or make fun of in a playful, good-natured way.

2. to ridicule; to joke or jest about. [Rare.]

3. to trick; to impose upon; to befool. [Archaic.]

4. to provoke to a trial or contest; to challenge. [Colloq. Southern and Western U.S.]

Syn.—deride, jest, rally, mock, chaff, make game of.

ban'tẽr, *v.i.* to exchange banter (*with* someone).

ban'tẽr, *n.* 1. a joking or jesting; good-humored raillery; pleasantry.

2. a challenge to a match or contest. [Colloq. Southern and Western U.S.]

Syn.—badinage, chaff, mockery, derision, ridicule, irony, jeering, raillery.

ban'tẽr·ẽr, *n.* one who banters or jests.

ban'tẽr·ing, *n.* the act of joking, teasing, or jesting.

ban'tẽr·ing·ly, *adv.* in a bantering manner.

Ban'ting·ism, *n.* a course of diet for reducing weight, adopted and recommended in 1864 by William Banting, of London. The method recommended was the use of lean meat principally, and abstinence from liquids and fat-producing foods, especially those containing a large percentage of starch, sugar, or fat.

bant'ling, *n.* [altered from G. *bänkling*, a bastard.]

1. a young child; a brat.

2. a foundling; a bastard. [Obs.]

3. figuratively, an immature product, as of an author or artist.

Ban'tū, *n.* [Bantu *ba-ntu*, mankind, men; *ba*, var. of *aba*, pl. personal prefix, and *-ntu*, a person.]

1. *pl.* **Ban'tū** or **Ban'tūṣ,** a member of a large group of Negroid tribes in central and southern Africa.

2. the family of languages of these tribes.

Ban'tū, *a.* pertaining to the Bantu or their languages.

bañx'ring, *n.* the native name of a small insectivorous mammal resembling the squirrel, found in the East Indies, *Tupaia javanica*.

ban'yăn, *n.* [so called (orig. by Europeans) in allusion to a tree of this kind at Gambroon on the Persian Gulf, under which the *banians* had built a pagoda.] an East Indian fig tree from whose branches grow shoots that take root and become new trunks: also spelled *banian*.

ban'zaī', *interj.* [Jap., lit., ten thousand years.] a Japanese greeting, battle cry, and cheer, meaning "May you live ten thousand years!"

ban'zaī' chärġe, a suicidal charge by Japanese troops, especially as a diversionary action.

bā'ō·bab, *n.* [prob. E. Afr. native name.] a tall tree (*Adansonia digitata*) with a thick trunk, found in Africa and India: fiber from its bark is used in making rope, paper, etc., and the gourdlike fruit has an edible pulp.

Baph'ō·met, *n.* [Fr., derived from Mahomet, or Mohammed.] an idol or spiritual symbol which the medieval Knights Templars were accused of worshiping in their secret ceremonies.

Bap·ti′ṣi·ȧ (-tizh′ȧ), *n.* [Gr. *baptein*, to dye.] a genus of leguminous plants, ornamental as border flowers: some of the species, which are found mainly in the eastern parts of North America, are used in dyeing: called also *wild indigo*.

bap′tiṣm, *n.* [OFr. *baptesme*, from LL. *baptisma*, from Gr. *baptismos*, that which is dipped; from *baptizein*, to dip.]
1. a baptizing or being baptized; specifically, the ceremony or sacrament of admitting a person into Christianity or a specific Christian church by dipping him in water or sprinkling water on him, as a symbol of washing away sin.
2. any experience or ordeal that initiates, tests, or purifies.
baptism of blood; (a) in Christian church history, martyrdom before baptism, regarded as a valid substitute for the baptismal rite; (b) the first actual experience of the horrors of war, as by a regiment of soldiers, a state, nation, or people.
baptism of fire; (a) in theology, the baptism of the Spirit, as distinguished from the rite of baptism: variously interpreted among theologians; (b) in early church history, martyrdom; (c) the first experience of a soldier or regiment, etc. under fire or in combat; (d) any experience that tests one's courage, strength, etc. for the first time.

bap·tiṣ′măl, *a.* relating to baptism; taken or used at baptism; as, a *baptismal* vow.
baptismal name; the Christian name bestowed at baptism; as, his *baptismal name* is Henry.

bap·tiṣ′măl·ly, *adv.* by means of baptism; in a baptismal manner.

Bap′tist, *n.* [ME. *baptiste*, baptizer; OFr.; L. *baptista*; Gr. *baptistēs*, from *baptizein*, to plunge, immerse.]
1. [b–] originally, a person who baptizes.
2. John the Baptist.
3. a member of a Protestant denomination holding that baptism should be given only to adult believers and by immersion rather than sprinkling.
Freewill Baptist; one of a sect of Baptists who are Arminians and believe in open communion.
German Baptist; see *Dunkard*.
Hard-Shell Baptist; same as *Primitive Baptist*.
Primitive Baptist; one of a sect of Baptists who are rigid Calvinists, opposed to foreign missionary work and to special education for their ministers: popularly styled *Hard-Shell Baptist*.
Seventh-Day Baptist; one of a sect of Baptists who observe Saturday as the Sabbath.

Bap′tist, *a.* of or pertaining to the Baptists of their beliefs.

bap′tis·tēr·y, bap′tis·try, *n.*; *pl.* **bap′tis·tēr·ieṣ,** or **-trieṣ,** [L. *baptisterium*, a place for bathing, from Gr. *baptizein*, to dip.]
1. a place where the rite of baptism is administered.
2. a building or a portion of a building in which is administered the rite of baptism. In the early Christian church the *baptistery* was distinct from the basilica or church, but was situated near its west end, and was generally circular or octagonal in form, and domeroofed. About the end of the sixth century the *baptistery* began to be absorbed into the church, the font being placed within and not far from the western door.
3. part of a church furnished with a font and used only for baptisms.
4. in Baptist churches, the tank used for baptism by immersion, usually concealed beneath removable flooring of the pulpit or auditorium.

bap·tis′tiç, *a.* [Gr. *baptistikos.*] relating to baptism or the doctrines of the Baptist Church.

bap·tis′tiç·ăl, *a.* baptistic. [Rare.]

bap·tis′tiç·ăl·ly, *adv.* in a baptistic manner.

bap′tis·try, *n.* see *baptistery*.

bap·tīz′ȧ·ble, *a.* capable of being or fit to be baptized. [Rare.]

bap·ti·zā′tion, *n.* the act of baptizing; the state of being baptized. [Obs.]

bap·tīze′, *v.t.*; baptized (-tīzd), *pt., pp.*; baptizing, *ppr.* [Gr. *baptizein*, to dip under water.]
1. to administer the sacrament of baptism to.
2. to christen; to name; to give a first name to (a person) as part of the baptismal ceremony; as, to *baptize* a child Thomas.
3. to consecrate to special purposes; as, to *baptize* a ship.
4. to purify; to cleanse; to sanctify; as, *baptized* with the Spirit.

bap·tīze′, *v.i.* to administer the sacrament of baptism.

bap·tīzed′, *a.* having received baptism; christened.

bap·tīze′ment, *n.* baptism; the act of baptizing. [Rare.]

bap·tīz′ẽr, *n.* one who christens, or administers baptism.

bȧ·quet′ (-kā′), *n.* [Fr.] a small tub.

bär, *n.* [ME. *barr*, *barre*, from OFr. *barre*, from LL. *barra*, a bar.]
1. a piece of wood, iron, or other solid substance longer than it is wide or thick, used for various purposes, but especially for a hindrance or obstruction; as, the *bars* of a fence; the *bar* of a door.
2. [*pl.*] in athletics, various forms of gymnastic apparatus in the shape of bars; as, parallel *bars* and horizontal *bars*.
3. any obstacle which obstructs, hinders, or prevents; an obstruction.

Must I new *bars* to my own joy create?
—Dryden.

4. (a) an oblong piece or mass of a substance; as, a *bar* of chocolate; (b) a unit of quantity based on such a piece; as, this gun barrel contains four *bars* of copper.
5. the railing that encloses the place (or the place so enclosed) where the judges or lawyers sit, or where prisoners are brought to trial.
6. a law court or system of law courts.
7. lawyers collectively.
8. the legal profession.
9. figuratively, any tribunal; as, the *bar* of public opinion; the *bar* of God, or the final judgment.
10. an establishment or room with a counter at which alcoholic drinks and sometimes food are served to customers; also, the counter over which the articles are served.
11. a bank of sand, gravel, or earth, forming a shoal at the mouth of a river or harbor, obstructing entrance, or rendering it difficult; as, crossing the *bar*.
12. a rock or other obstruction in the sea.
13. a strip, stripe, band, or broad line, as of light or color.
14. the part of the jaw of a horse between the tusks and grinders, which bears no teeth, and to which the bit is applied; also, the mouthpiece of the bit.

BAR (sense 15)

15. in heraldry, a horizontal stripe or stripes on a shield or bearing.
16. in law, (a) the nullifying of a claim or action; (b) the process of bringing this about.
17. in music, (a) a vertical line across a staff, dividing it into measures; (b) a measure; (c) two vertical lines across a staff; double **bar.**

18. in zoology, either of the ends of the wall of a horse's hoof, curving into the sole.
19. an ingot, lump, or wedge of gold or silver from the mines, run in a mold, and unwrought. A *bar* of iron is wrought and hammered from a pig or block.
20. in architecture, a strip of wood dividing and supporting the glass of a window; as, a sash *bar*.
21. a barrier across a city gateway; as, old *Temple Bar* in London.
22. a place in the United States Senate, the House of Representatives, the State legislatures, and deliberative bodies, usually near the speaker or presiding officer, where persons, not members, stand when they are permitted to address those assemblies, or are called before them for any reason.
to cross the bar; to die.
trial at bar; in English law, a trial before the full bench of a superior court.

bär, *n.* [Fr.] the maigre; a European fish whose flesh is white and bloodless.

bär, *v.t.*; barred (bärd), *pt., pp.*; barring, *ppr.* [ME. *barren*, from OFr. *barrer*, to fasten with a bar.]
1. to fasten with a bar or as with a bar; as, to *bar* a door or gate.
2. to obstruct by means of a bar; shut off; close.
3. to prevent; to oppose; to exclude; to hinder; to make impracticable.
4. in law, to prevent or stop (an action) by legal objection.
5. to except; to exclude; to keep (a person) out of; as, he was *barred* from the contest.
6. to cross with stripes of a different color.
7. in mechanics, to operate by using a bar as a lever.
to bar a vein; in veterinary surgery, to operate upon a horse by disengaging a vein, tying it above and below, and then striking between the two ligatures.

bär, *prep.* leaving out; excluding; except; as, this is the best hotel in town, *bar* none.

Bȧ·rab′bȧs, *n.* in the Bible, the prisoner whom the people wanted freed instead of Jesus: Matt. xxvii. 16–21.

bar′ad, *n.* [Gr. *barys*, weighty, and Eng. *farad.*] an electrical unit of pressure; the pressure of one dyne per square centimeter.

Bar·ȧ·lip′ton, *n.* [composed of symbolical letters, especially the vowels. *A* is equivalent to a universal affirmative. *I* is equivalent to a particular affirmative, and *ton* is a termination given for euphony.] in logic, the first indirect mood of the first figure of syllogisms. A syllogism in *Baralipton* is one in which the first two propositions are universal affirmatives, and the third a particular affirmative.

bar·ȧ·mun′dȧ, *n.* same as *barramunda*.

bar·ȧ·thē′ȧ, *n.* a soft fabric made of a mixture of silk and wool or silk and cotton.

bar′ȧ·thrum, *n.*; *pl.* **bar′ȧ·thrȧ,** [Gr. *barathron*, a gulf.]
1. a pit; an abyss.
2. a rocky pit outside the walls of Athens, into which criminals, dead or alive, were cast.
3. the fathomless pit; Hades.
4. in figurative use, a relentless devourer; a glutton; an extortioner.

bärb, bärbe, *n.* [OFr. *barbe*; L. *barba*, beard.]
1. (a) [Obs.] the beard of a man; (b) a thin, somewhat beardlike growth near the mouth of certain animals.
2. a sharp point turning backward from the main point, as in a fishhook or arrow, making withdrawal difficult.
3. in botany, a bristle or hair that has a double hook at its end.
4. a lateral branch growing from the shaft of a feather.
5. [*pl.*] projections of the mucous membrane under the tongues of horses and cattle: called also *paps*.
6. a roughness or imperfection occurring in the process of metal working; a bur.
7. in heraldry, one of the five green leaves that appear around the outer edge of a rose and extend beyond the petals.

BARB (sense 8)

8. a scarf or muffler worn by women, particularly nuns.

bärb, *v.t.*; barbed, *pt., pp.*; barbing, *ppr.* **1.** to shave, as the beard. [Obs.]
2. to furnish with barbs, as an arrow, fishhook, spear, or other implement.

bärb, *n.* [Fr. *barbe*, a Barbary horse, from *Barbarie*; Ar. *Barbar*, the Berbers.]
1. a horse of a breed native to Barbary, noted for speed, strength, and gentle behavior.
2. the Barbary pigeon, a bird of a black or grayish-brown color.
3. a kingfish of the eastern coast of the United States.

bärb, *n.* armor for a horse; bard. [Obs.]

bär′bȧ·çăn, *n.* same as *barbican*.

bär′bȧ·çūe, *n.* and *v.t.* same as *barbecue*.

Bär·bā′di·ăn, *a.* [Port. *barbadas*, the bearded, from L. *barbatus*, bearded.] relating to Barbados.

Bär·bā′di·ăn, *n.* an inhabitant of Barbados.

Bär·bā′dōṣ prīde, 1. a low, spiny shrub, *Poinciana pulcherrima*, with an odor like savin. In the tropics it is used for fences, and hence is called *flower fence*.
2. an East Indian tree bearing yellow blossoms and now cultivated for ornamental purposes in the West Indies.

bär′bȧ·rȧ, *n.* a mnemonic word in logic, being the first word in the mnemonic verses intended to represent the various forms of syllogism. It indicates a syllogism, the three propositions of which are universal affirmatives.

Bär·bȧ·resque′ (-resk′). *a.* 1. relating to Barbary.
2. barbarous in style: said especially of architecture.

bär·bā′ri·ăn, *n.* [L. *barbarus*; Gr. *barbaros*, foreign; so called by the Greeks because the talk of a foreigner sounded like *bar-bar*.]
1. a member of a people or group with a civilization regarded as primitive, savage, etc.
2. an insensitive, coarse, or unmannerly person; boor.
3. a cruel, savage, brutal person.
4. a foreigner. The Greeks and Romans called other peoples *barbarians*.

bär·bā′ri·ăn, *a.* 1. relating to a barbarian or barbarians.
2. cruel; inhuman.

bär·bar′iç, *a.* [L. *barbaricus*, from Gr. *barbarikos*, barbaric, foreign.]
1. of, like, or characteristic of barbarians; primitive or lacking in civilization.
2. exhibiting the characteristics of a barbarian, as in taste and dress; unrefined; barbarous.

bär′bȧ·riṣm, *n.* 1. the use of words and expressions not standard in a language.
2. a word or expression of this sort (e.g., "youse" for "you").
3. the state of being primitive or lacking civilization.
4. a barbarous action, custom, etc.
5. brutal behavior; barbarity.

bär·bar′i·ty, *n.* 1. the manners of a barbarian; savageness; cruelty; ferocity; inhumanity.
2. an act of cruelty.
3. a barbaric taste, manner, form, etc.
4. a word or expression that is substandard in usage.

bär′bȧ·rīze, *v.t.*; barbarized, *pt., pp.*; barbarizing, *ppr.* to make barbarous.

bär′bȧ·rīze, *v.i.* to become barbarous.

bär′bȧ·rīzed, *a.* made barbarous.

bär′bȧ·rīz·ing, *a.* making barbarous.

bär′bȧ·rous, *a.* 1. originally, different from one's own language or customs; foreign; alien: in the ancient world, any person or thing that was non-Greek, non-Roman, or non-Christian was called barbarous.
2. characterized by words and phrases that are substandard in usage; also, not classical: said of language.
3. crude, coarse, rough, etc.
4. harsh in sound; raucous.
5. uncivilized; savage; primitive.
6. cruel; ferocious; inhuman.

bär′bȧ·rous·ly, *adv.* in a barbarous manner.

bär′bȧ·rous·ness, *n.* the state, quality, or fact of being barbarous.

Bär′bȧ·ry, *n.* a Barbary horse; a barb.
Barbary ape; a tailless ape, easily trained, found in northern Africa and on the Rock of Gibraltar.

bär′bȧ·stel, *n.* [Fr. *barbastelle*; L. *barba*, beard.] a species of bat with hairy or bearded cheeks.

bär′bāte, bär′bā·ted, *a.* [L. *barbatus*, bearded, from *barba*, beard.]
1. in botany, bearded; having hairlike tufts, or awns, as oats, barley, etc.
2. in zoology, fringed with hair; having hair or feathers.

bär′bē·cūe, *n.* [Sp. *barbacoa*, from Haitian *barbacoa*, a framework of sticks.]
1. originally, a framework to hold meat over a fire to be smoked, dried, or broiled.
2. any meat broiled or roasted on a spit over an open fire.
3. an entertainment, usually outdoors, at which such meat is prepared and eaten.
4. a restaurant that makes a specialty of barbecuing.
5. a smooth floor, or other space, exposed to the sun for the drying of coffee beans.

bär′bē·çūe, *v.t.*; barbecued (-kūd), *pt., pp.*; barbecuing, *ppr.* 1. to cure by drying or smoking on a framework.
2. to roast or broil whole, as an animal after it has been properly prepared.
3. to cut (meat or fish) in thin slices and cook in a highly seasoned vinegar sauce.
4. to prepare (meat or fish) by cooking over an open fire on a spit, cutting into thin slices, and putting into a highly seasoned sauce made from the drippings.

bär′bē·çūe, *a.* (a) barbecued; (b) of barbecued meat.

bär′bē·çūe sauce, a highly seasoned sauce made chiefly of vinegar, vegetables, sugar, and spices.

bärbed, *a.* 1. stinging; cutting.
2. having a barb or barbs.
3. in heraldry, (a) having barbs or green leaves; as, a rose *barbed*; (b) having wattles, as a cock.
4. furnished with armor; applied to a horse.
barbed shot; a shot fired from a mortar, carrying a lifeline and provided with barbs to hold it wherever it strikes.
barbed wire; wire for fences, barriers, etc., having sharp barbs or points of metal twisted into the strands at regular intervals.

bär′bel, *n.* [Fr. *barbeau*, from OFr. *barbel*, a barbel fish, from L. *barba*, beard.]
1. a fish of the genus *Barbus*, especially the *Barbus vulgaris*, having four beardlike appendages on the upper jaw.
2. a slender, threadlike growth on the mouths or nostrils of certain fishes: it is an organ of touch.
3. an inflamed swelling in the mouths of cattle and horses, usually under the tongue: also written *barble* and *barb*.

bär′bell, *n.* [*bar*, a piece of metal, and *dumbbell*.] a metal bar or rod to which disks of varying weights are attached at each end, used for weight-lifting exercises: also *bar bell*.

bär′bel·lāte, *a.* having bristles or short stiff barbed hairs, as some kinds of plants.

bär·bel′lū·lāte, *a.* having barbules.

bär′bẽr, *n.* [ME. *barbour, barbor*, from OFr *barbeor*, from L. *barba*, a beard.] a person whose occupation is that of shaving, trimming, and dressing the hair, etc.
barber college; a school for teaching the trade of barbering.
barber pole; a pole symbolizing the barber's trade, striped spirally with red and white.
barber's basin; a rimmed basin for lather, formerly fitted to the neck and used while shaving.
barber's itch; an infectious inflammation of the hair follicles of the face and neck, caused by a fungus: so called because it can be contracted in unsanitary barbershops.

bär′bẽr, *v.t.*; barbered, *pt., pp.*; barbering, *ppr.* to shave the beard of, cut or dress the hair of, etc.

bär′bẽr fish, the surgeonfish.

bär′ber·ry, bẽr′ber·ry, *n.* [ME. *barbere*, from OFr. *berbere*; LL. *berberis*, the barberry.] a plant of the genus *Berberis*; specifically, *Berberis vulgaris*, a spiny shrub with yellow flowers, native in Europe and naturalized in the United States: it bears sour red berries.

bär′bẽr·shop, *a.* designating or characterized by the close harmony of male voices, especially in sentimental songs; as, a *barbershop* quartet. [Colloq.]

bär′bẽr·shop, *n.* the shop in which a barber has his business.

bär′bẽr·y, *n.* 1. a barber's shop. [Obs.]
2. the barber's trade. [Obs.]

bär′bet, *n.* [Fr., from L. *barba*, a beard.] a small beard. [Obs.]

bär′bet, *n.* [Fr., from L. *barbatus*, bearded.]
1. a variety of curly-haired poodle.
2. a species of larva that feeds on aphides.
3. in ornithology, a bird resembling the cuckoo: their conical beaks are bearded with stiff bristles.

AFRICAN BARBET (*Pogonias hirsutus*)

bär·bette′ (-bet′), *n.* [Fr., from L. *barbatus*, bearded.]
1. a platform or elevation of earth from which cannon may be fired over a parapet.
2. the protective armored structure around a gun platform on a warship.
barbette battery; a battery of guns placed on a barbette.
barbette carriage; a carriage to raise a gun for firing over a parapet.
barbette gun; a gun placed on a barbette.
barbette ship; a ship on which the guns are mounted to fire over the bulwarks.
en or *in barbette*; mounted on a barbette: applied to guns.

bär′bi·çăn, bär′bȧ·çăn, *n.* [ME. *barbican*, from OFr. *barbicane*, a barbican; a word of Arabic or Portuguese origin, introduced into Europe by the crusaders; perhaps from Ar. *babh-khānah*, a gate house, or house on a wall.]
1. a fort at a gate or bridge leading into a city or castle.
2. an opening in a fortress wall through which guns can be fired. [Obs.]

bär′bi·çăn, *n.* [L. *barba*, beard.] a climbing barbet of Africa, genus *Pogonias*.

bär′bi·çăn·āġe, bär′bȧ·çăn·āġe, *n.* money paid to maintain a barbican. [Obs.]

bär′bi·cel, *n.* [L. *barba*, beard.] one of the minute projections on the barbule of a feather.

bär′biẽrṣ, *n.* [Cingalese *beri*, weakness.] a paralytic disease common in India, closely resembling *beriberi*.

bär·biġ′ẽr·ous, *a.* [L. *barba*, beard, and *gerere*, to carry.] having hair, as a petal; bearded.

bär′bi·ŏn, *n.* [L. *barba*, beard.] an African barbet of the genus *Pogoniulus*.

bär′bi·tal, *n.* a white, crystalline powder, diethylbarbituric acid, which is used as a drug to induce sleep. It is habit-forming.

bär′bi·ton, bär′bi·tos, *n.*; *pl.* **bär′bi·tȧ,** [Gr. *barbiton*, a lyre.] a musical instrument of ancient Greece resembling a lyre.

bär″bi·tū′rate (-rit), *n.* [*barbituric*, and *-ate*.] any salt of barbituric acid, used as a sedative or to deaden pain.

bär″bi·tū′riç, *a.* [Mod. L. *Usnea barbata*, lit., bearded moss, and *uric* acid.] designating or of a crystalline acid, $CH_2CONHCONHCO$, derivatives of which are used to induce sleep or deaden pain.

bär′ble, *n.* same as *barbel*.

bär′bō·tine, *n.* [Fr. *barbotine*, wormwood, from *barboter*, to dabble.]
1. thin potter's clay used for relief design.
2. any of the various species of wormseed.

Bär′bū·lȧ, *n.* [L.] a large genus of the true mosses.

bär′būle, *n.* [L. *barbula*, a little beard.]
1. a very small barb; barbel.
2. one of the finely divided hairlike processes forming the fringe along the barbs of a feather.

bärb wīre, barbed wire.

bär′çȧ·rōle, bär′çȧ·rōlle (-rōl), *n.* [It. *barcarolo*, boatman.]
1. an Italian boatman.
2. typical boat song of a Venetian gondolier.
3. any piece of music imitating such a song.

bär″ce·lō′nȧ, *n.* a neckerchief or handkerchief of silk twill said to have originated in Barcelona, Spain. [Obs.]

Bär″ce·lō′nȧ nut, a Spanish variety of hazel nut.

bär′çŏn, bär′çō·ne, *n.* [It. *barcone*, a bark.] a Mediterranean freight boat.

bär çut′tẽr, a machine for cutting bars of metal into lengths.

bärd, *n.* [Gael. and Ir. *bard*, of Celtic origin.]
1. a poet. [Poetic.]
2. among the ancient Celts, a poet who sang or recited verses of his own composition, usually to the accompaniment of the harp.
3. formerly, a minstrel or wandering musician of Scotland.

bärd, bärde, *n.* [Fr. *barde*, horse armor.]
1. a piece of horse armor: it generally consists of leather studded with metal points.
2. [*pl.*] the ornamental trappings of a horse in medieval tournaments.
3. [*pl.*] in late medieval times, plate armor worn by a man-at-arms.

bärd, *n.* a slice of bacon used to cover game or meat while cooking.

bärd, *v.t.*; barded, *pt., pp.*; barding, *ppr.* 1. to equip (a man or horse) with defensive armor.
2. to harness (a horse) with rich ornaments.

bärd, *v.t.* to cover (meat) with slices of bacon for cooking.

Bär·des′ȧ·nist, *n.* one of that branch of Gnostics of the second century A.D. who were followers of Bardesanes of Edessa, in Mesopotamia. They believed in two original self-existent beings, one good, the other evil; that human souls originally had no material bodies; that Christ had only the semblance of a body, and did not die on the cross, nor rise from the dead; and that redemption consists in being divested of our material bodies and being clothed again in ethereal or spiritual bodies.

bärd′iç, *a.* pertaining to bards, or having the characteristics of bardism.
bärd′ish, *a.* having the characteristics of a bard or of bardism.
bärd′işm, *n.* the principles, system, poetry, etc. of bards.
bärd′ling, *n.* an immature or would-be poet.
Bärd of Ā′von, William Shakespeare: so called from his birthplace, Stratford-on-Avon.
bärd′ship, *n.* the condition of being a bard; the office or rank of a bard.
bāre, *a.* [ME. *bare, bar*; AS. *bær*, without covering.]
1. naked; stripped; without covering, as a body unclothed.
2. with the head uncovered, from respect. [Rare.]
3. plain; simple; unadorned; as, *bare* facts.
4. exposed; laid open to view; detected; no longer concealed.
5. empty; unfurnished; as, *bare* rooms.
6. mere; alone; unaccompanied by more than absolutely necessary; as, *bare* expenses.
7. threadbare; much worn.
under bare poles; in nautical language, having no sail set.
Syn.—destitute, naked, nude, uncovered, stripped, unadorned, undressed, unclothed.
bāre, *v.t.*; bared, *pt., pp.*; baring, *ppr.* [ME. *baren*, from AS. *barian*, to make bare.] to strip of the covering; to make bare; to expose; to reveal.
bāre, alternative past tense of *bear*. [Archaic.]
bāre′back, *adv.* and *a.* on a horse without a saddle.
bāre′backed, *a.* 1. with the back uncovered.
2. having no saddle.
bāre′bōne, *n.* a very lean person. [Rare.]
bāre′bōned, *a.* lean, so that the bones show through the skin.
bāre′fāced, *a.* 1. with the face uncovered; not masked.
2. undisguised; without concealment; hence, shameless; impudent; audacious; as, a *barefaced* falsehood.
bāre′fāced·ly, *adv.* without disguise or reserve; openly; impudently.
bāre′fāced·ness, *n.* effrontery; shamelessness; audaciousness.
bāre′foot, *a.* and *adv.* with the feet bare.
bāre′foot″ed, *a.* having the feet bare.
ba·rège′ (bȧ-rāzh′), *n.* [Fr. *barège*, from *Barèges*, a town famous as a watering place in the Pyrenees.] a gauzy dress fabric woven from worsted and silk or cotton.
bāre′hand″ed, *a.* 1. with hands bare or unprotected.
2. in unquestionable guilt; in the act. [Colloq.]
bāre′head″ed, *a.* having the head uncovered; without a hat, etc. on.
bāre′head″ed·ness, *n.* the state of being bareheaded.
bāre′leg·ged, *a.* and *adv.* having the legs bare.
bāre′ly, *adv.* 1. nakedly; without clothing or covering.
2. hardly; scarcely; only; without anything to spare.
3. openly.
4. meagerly; scantily.
5. merely. [Archaic.]
bāre′ness, *n.* the state of being bare.
bāre′särk, *n.* [Ice. *berserkr*, without a shirt; *bera*, bare, and *serkr*, shirt.] a frenzied warrior; a berserker.
bāre′särk, *adv.* without armor on; with only a shirt on.
bar′et, *n.* same as *barret*.
bär′fish, *n.* same as *calico bass*.
bär′flȳ, *n.* a person who spends much time in barrooms. [Slang.]
bär′gain (bär′gen), *n.* [ME. *bargain, bargayne*; OFr. *bargaine*, a bargain.]
1. an agreement to exchange, sell, or buy goods.
2. the terms of such an agreement.
3. such an agreement considered in relation to one of the parties; as, he made a bad *bargain*.
4. a mutual agreement or contract.
5. something offered, bought, or sold at a price favorable to the buyer.
bargain and sale; in law, a kind of conveyance, by which the bargainer contracts to convey the lands to the bargainee, and becomes by such contract a trustee for and seized to the use of the bargainee. The statute then completes the purchase; that is, the bargain vests the use, and the statute vests the possession.
into the bargain; in addition to what is agreed on; furthermore.
to strike a bargain; (a) to make an agreement; (b) to come upon a bargain.
Syn.—agreement, contract, stipulation, purchase, pledge, compact.
bär′gain, *v.i.*; bargained, *pt., pp.*; bargaining, *ppr.* [ME. *bargainen*, from OFr. *bargaigner*, to traffic.]
1. to discuss or dispute terms for selling, buying, etc.; to haggle.
2. to make a contract or conclusive agreement for the transfer of property, etc.: often with *for*.
bär′gain, *v.t.* to trade; to barter.
to bargain away; to part with a thing in a bargain, usually at a loss.
bär′gain bāse′ment, that part of a department store, usually in the basement, where goods are sold at lower prices than in the main part.
bär′gain çoun′tẽr, a counter on which are goods for sale at special or reduced prices.
bär′gain dāy, a day on which certain goods are sold by a business house at special or reduced prices.
bär·gain·ee′, *n.* the party to a contract who stands as the recipient of the property.
bär′gain·ẽr, *n.* one who bargains or makes a bargain.
bär′gain·ŏr, bär′gain·ẽr, *n.* in law, the party to a contract who agrees to sell property to another.
bärġe, *n.* [OFr. *barge*; LL. *barca*, a bark; L. *baris*, an Egyptian rowboat; Gr. *baris*, a skiff, raft.]
1. a large, flat-bottomed freight boat used on inland waters.
2. a pleasure boat, especially one handsomely furnished and used for state ceremonies, pageants, etc.
3. the official launch of a flagship.
4. a houseboat.
5. any clumsy boat. [Slang.]
bärġe, *v.t.*; barged, *pt., pp.*; barging, *ppr.* to transport by barge.
bärġe, *v.i.* 1. to move clumsily and slowly.
2. to enter, especially in a rude, abrupt, clumsy way (with *in* or *into*). [Colloq.]
3. to collide with (with *into*). [Colloq.]
bärġe′bōard, *n.* [see *barge couple*]. a board, often ornate, attached along the barge couples of a gabled roof, as in Tudor and Gothic architecture.

BARGEBOARD

bärġe′ çoup′le, [perh. from base of Fr. *barge*, slope (of a river).] in architecture, (a) either of the pair of outside rafters forming the projection of a gabled roof; (b) two beams fitted together to strengthen a building.
bärġe′çōurse, *n.* in architecture, (a) a part of the tiling which projects beyond the principal rafters of a gable roof; (b) a course of bricks, laid on end, capping a gable wall.
bär·ġee′, *n.* a bargeman. [Brit.]
bärġe′măn, *n.*; *pl.* **bärġe′men,** a man who operates a barge or is one of the crew on a barge.
bärġe′mȧs″tẽr, *n.* the proprietor or master of a barge, especially of one conveying goods for hire.
bär′ġẽr, *n.* a bargemaster or bargeman.
bär′ghest, bär′guest (-gest), *n.* [perh. from ON. *bjarg, berg*, mountain, and *gastr* or AS. *geist*, stranger; akin to G. *berg geist*, mountain demon.] an imaginary goblin or spirit, generally in the shape of a dog, supposed to mean death or bad fortune to the person to whom it appears.
bär gown, a gown of a lawyer.
bā′ri·ȧ, *n.* same as *baryta*.
bar′iç, *a.* pertaining to barium. [Rare.]
bar′iç, *a.* [Gr. *barys*, weighty.] in physics, relating to weight or pressure, especially to that of the air; barometric.
bȧ·ril′lȧ, *n.* [from Sp. *barrilla*, impure soda.]
1. a plant cultivated in Spain for its ashes, from which soda ash is obtained.
2. the soda ash procured from this plant and other varieties of the genus *Salsola*, or saltworts, used in making glass and soap, and in bleaching linen.
3. any soda ash obtained by burning seaweed, etc.
bā′rīte, *n.* [Gr. *barytēs*, weight.] a native form of barium sulfate, occurring usually in white tabular crystals; heavy spar: it is the principal source of barium and its compounds, and is used in the manufacture of paint.
bar′i·tōne, bar′y·tōne, *n.* [It. *baritono*; Gr. *barytonos*, deep-toned; *barys*, deep, and *tonos*, tone.]
1. in music, a male voice with a range between bass and tenor, from the second A below middle C to the first F above.
2. this range.
3. a singer who possesses a baritone voice.
4. a brass-wind instrument with a similar range.
5. a musical part for a baritone voice.
6. in Greek grammar, a word not having the acute accent on the final syllable.
bar′i·tōne, bar′y·tōne, *a.* 1. ranging between tenor and bass; as, a *baritone* voice.
2. suited to a baritone; as, a *baritone* solo.
3. in Greek grammar, not having the acute accent on the final syllable.
bā′ri·um, *n.* [Mod. L., from Gr. *barys*, heavy.] a silver-white, slightly malleable, metallic chemical element, found as a carbonate or sulfate and used in alloys: symbol, Ba; atomic weight, 137.36; atomic number, 56.
bärk, *n.* [ME. *barke*; AS. *barc*, bark or rind.]
1. the outermost covering of trees and some plants. This is composed of the cuticle or epidermis, the outer bark or cortex, and the inner bark or fiber.
2. such material used in tanning, dyeing, etc.
3. cinchona, a medicinal bark.
bärk, *v.t.*; barked, *pt., pp.*; barking, *ppr.* 1. to strip bark off (a tree or log).
2. to take the skin off. [Colloq.]
3. to cover or enclose with bark.
4. to color or tan by means of bark.
bärk, bärque (bärk), *n.* [Fr. *barque*; It. *barca*; L. *barca*, small boat.]
1. any sailing boat, especially a small one. [Poetic.]
2. a sailing vessel with its two forward masts square-rigged and its rear mast rigged fore-and-aft.

BARK

bärk, *v.i.* [ME. *barken, berken*; AS. *beorcan*, to bark.]
1. to make the typical sound that a dog makes; to make a sharp, abrupt outcry.
2. to make a similar sound; as, the engine *barked*.
3. to clamor; to pursue with unreasonable reproach.
To *bark* at sleeping fame. —Spenser.
4. to speak sharply; to snap.
5. to cough. [Colloq.]
6. to advertise a show, sale, etc. by shouting in public. [Slang.]
to bark at the moon; to make futile outcries or protests.
to bark up the wrong tree; (a) to attack the wrong thing; (b) to direct one's energies in the wrong direction.
bärk, *v.t.* to say or advertise with a bark or shout.
bärk, *n.* the sharp, abrupt noise made by a dog; also, any sharp, abrupt noise like this.
bärk′ăn·tīne, *n.* same as *barkentine*.
bärk bee′tle, a beetle of the *Scolytidæ* family, that injures trees by boring under the bark.
bärk′bound, *a.* having the bark too firm or close, as trees.
bär′keep, *n.* a barkeeper.
bär′keep″ẽr, *n.* 1. a proprietor or manager of a bar where alcoholic drinks are sold.

2. one who sells liquor over a bar; a bartender.

bärk′en, *a.* made from bark. [Rare.]

bärk′en·tīne, *n.* a vessel having three masts, the forward one square-rigged, the other two schooner-rigged: spelled also *barquantine.*

bärk′ẽr, *n.* 1. one who or that which barks; one who clamors or cries out.

2. in zoology, the spotted redshank.

3. a person who stands before a shop, theater, side show, etc. and attracts passing people with loud, animated talking.

4. a pistol. [Slang.]

bärk′ẽr, *n.* 1. a person or machine that strips bark from trees.

2. a person or machine that prepares bark.

Bärk′ẽr's mill, a machine, moved by the centrifugal force of water, invented in the seventeenth century by Dr. *Barker*: it is one of the simplest water mills constructed. It has a vertical axis C D, moving on a pivot at D, and carrying the upper millstone *m*, after passing through an opening in the fixed millstone *n*. Round this axis is a tube T T, connecting with a horizontal tube A B, with two apertures in opposite directions A and B. When water from the mill course M N is introduced into the tube T T, it flows out of the apertures A and B, and by pressure the arm A B (and the whole machine) is put in motion. The bridge tree *a b* is raised or lowered by turning the nut *c* at the end of the lever *c b*. The grain is passed into the hopper H, and thence to the grindstones.

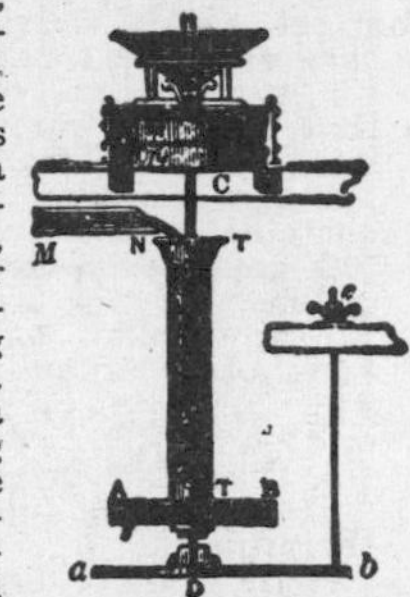
BARKER'S MILL

bärk′ẽr·y, *n.* a tanhouse.

bärk′ing ī′rons (ī′ũrnz), instruments used in taking off the bark of trees.

Bär′kis, *n.* a character in Dickens' *David Copperfield*, whose proposal of marriage took the form of "Barkis is willin'."

bärk′less, *a.* without bark.

bärk louse, a coccid insect which lives on the bark of vines and trees.

bärk pit, a pit filled with bark and water, in which hides are steeped in tanning.

bärk′y, *a.*; *compar.* barkier; *superl.* barkiest, like bark; consisting of bark; containing bark.

bär′ley, *n.*; *pl.* **bär′ley, bär′leys,** [ME. *barly*, from AS. *bærlic*, barley.]

1. a hardy, widely cultivated species of cereal grass, of the genus *Hordeum*, having bearded spikes of flowers.

2. its seed or grain, used especially for making malt, from which are prepared liquors of extensive use, as beer, ale, and porter.

bär′ley bîrd, 1. a European finch: called also the *siskin*.

2. the nightingale.

bär′ley·brāke, bär′ley·break, *n.* an ancient game similar to the game of tag, usually played around stacks of barley or in other grain fields.

bär′ley-bree, bär′ley-broo, *n.* a strong liquor made from barley; ale or whisky. [Scot.]

bär′ley broth, a strong ale. [Scot.]

bär′ley·corn, *n.* 1. barley or a grain of barley.

2. a unit of length equal to one-third of an inch: an old linear measure.

John Barleycorn; any strong alcoholic liquor, especially whisky: a humorous personification.

bär′ley sug′ăr (shug′ẽr), sugar boiled till it is brittle (formerly with an extract of barley), and candied.

bär′ley wa′tẽr, a drink made by boiling barley in water, given to invalids, etc.

bär′ley wine, a kind of beer made from barley.

bärm, *n.* [ME. *barme, berme*, from AS. *beorma*, yeast.] a foamy yeast forming on beer or other malt liquors when fermenting, and used as leaven in bread to make it rise and in alcoholic liquors to make them ferment: also called *brewers' yeast.*

bärm, *n.* [AS. *bearm.*] the bosom or lap. [Obs.]

bär mag′net, a magnet in the form of a bar.

bär′māid, *n.* a woman who serves alcoholic drinks in a bar.

bär′măn, *n.*; *pl.* **bär′men,** a barkeeper or bartender.

bär′mas″tẽr, *n.* [perh. from G. *bergmeister*, a surveyor of mines; *berg*, a hill, a mine, and *meister*, a master or overseer.]

1. formerly, in mining, a surveyor or local judge who looked after the interests of the owner and the rights of the miners.

2. a magistrate of the barmote. [Brit.]

bärm′brack, *n.* [Ir. *bairin*, cake, and *breac*, speckled.] a currant bun. [Ir. and Prov. Eng.]

bärm′cloth, *n.* an apron. [Obs.]

Bär′mē·cī·dăl, *a.* like Barmecide or Barmecide's entertainment; illusive; unreal.

Bär′mē·cīde, *n.* a person who offers a pretended pleasure or spurious gift: a reference to the imaginary food given by *Barmecide*, in *The Arabian Nights.*

Bär′mē·cīde, *a.* Barmecidal; unreal.

Bär′mē·cīde fēast, 1. a pretended feast with no food.

2. any pretended or illusory generosity or hospitality.

bär mitz′väh, bär miz′väh, [Heb. *bar mitzwāh*, a son of duty or enjoinder.] in Judaism, (a) the ceremony, occurring on the thirteenth birthday, by which a male is accepted into the congregation of men; (b) a youth so accepted.

bär′mōte, *n.* [G. *berg*, a hill, and AS. *mote*, meeting.] in Derbyshire, England, a court established to adjudicate among the miners.

bärm′y, *a.* 1. containing barm; yeasty.

2. silly; idiotic: often confused with *balmy*. [Brit. Slang.]

bärn, *n.* [ME. *barn, bern*; AS. *bern*, contr. from *berern*; *bere*, barley, and *ern*, a place for storing.]

1. a building for storing farm produce, stabling livestock, etc.

2. a large building for streetcars, etc.

3. any room or building like a barn in size, temperature, etc. [Colloq.]

barn dance; (a) a dance held in a barn, with square dances, etc.; (b) any party characterized by rural dancing, dress, music, etc.; (c) a country dance resembling the schottische.

bärn, *n.* a bairn.

Bär′nȧ·bīte, *n.* a member of a Roman Catholic religious order named after St. Barnabas.

bär′nȧ·cle, *n.* [ME. *barnakylle*, dim. of *bernak*, a goose.]

1. a barnacle goose: written also *bernacle, bernicle.*

2. any of several species of the *Cirripedia*, especially the sessile and stalked species (*Lepas anatifera*). They are found adhering to submerged bottoms of vessels or to rocks.

3. any person or thing that resembles a barnacle in clinging persistently, as to some office or support; a hanger-on. [Colloq.]

BARNACLE (*Lepas anatifera*)

bär′nȧ·cled, *a.* covered with barnacles.

bär′nȧ·cle ēat′ẽr, a fish of the *Alutera* genus: the New England filefish.

bär′nȧ·cle goose, a species of European wild goose, *Anser bernicla.*

bär′nȧ·cles (-klz), *n.pl.* [OFr. *bernac*, a kind of bit.]

1. an instrument consisting of two branches joined at one end with a hinge, to put upon a horse's nose, to confine or control him.

2. an instrument of torture resembling this.

3. spectacles. [Brit. Colloq.]

bär′nȧ·cle scāle, a barnacle-shaped louse infesting the bark of orange and quince trees.

Bärn′bũrn″ẽr, *n.* a member of a section of the Democratic Party in New York State, that in 1846 opposed the extension of slavery to the territories. The name was bestowed by its opponents, the Hunkers, who likened the group to the man who burned down his barn to clear it of rats.

bärn owl, an owl, usually brown and gray with a spotted white breast, that frequents buildings, especially barns, in search of mice: zoologically known as *Strix flammea.*

bärn′storm, *v.i.* [*barn*, and *storm*, *v.*]

1. to go about the country performing plays, giving lectures, etc., using barns or any available places in small towns and rural districts.

2. to tour the country giving short airplane rides, exhibitions of stunt flying, etc.: so called from the use of barns as hangars.

bärn′storm″ẽr, *n.* 1. a traveling actor who gives performances in barns or any available building; an actor who plays in country districts.

2. an inferior actor.

3. a free-lance aviator.

bärn′storm″ing, *n.* the act of one who barnstorms.

bärn swäl′lōw, a swallow which frequents barns, attaching its mud nest to the rafters, especially the American variety (*Hirundo horreorum*).

bärn′yärd, *n.* the yard or ground near a barn, often enclosed.

bärn′yärd, *a.* 1. of a barnyard.

2. like or fit for a barnyard; earthy, smutty, etc.

bar′ō-, [from Gr. *baros*, weight.] a prefix meaning *of atmospheric pressure*, as in *barograph.*

bȧ·rō′cō, bȧ·rō′kō, *n.* [a mnemonic word the vowels of which represent the premises and conclusion of the syllogism.] in logic, the fourth mode of the second figure of syllogisms, in which the first proposition (A) is a universal affirmative, the second and third (O) particular negatives, and the middle term the predicate in the first two propositions. Written also *baroque*. Example:

All scholars of the first rank have, as one essential characteristic, intense love of knowledge.

But the mass of mankind does not possess this.

Therefore the mass of mankind cannot reach the first rank of scholarship.

bar″ō·cȳ″clon·om′e·tẽr, *n.* [from *baro-*, and *cyclone*, and *-meter.*] a barometric instrument used to locate cyclones and follow their movement.

bar′ō·gram, *n.* [*baro-*, and *gram.*] the tracings of a barograph.

bar′ō·grȧph, *n.* [*baro-*, and *-graph.*] an instrument for recording, by automatic tracings, variations in the pressure of the atmosphere.

bȧ·rol′ō·gy, *n.* [Gr. *baros*, weight, and *logos*, description.] the science of weight or of gravity.

bar″ō·mȧ·crom′e·tẽr, *n.* [Gr. *baros*, weight, *macros*, long, and *metron*, measure.] an instrument for determining the weight and length of infants at birth.

bȧ·rom′e·tẽr, *n.* [Gr. *baros*, weight, and *metron*, measure.]

1. an instrument for measuring atmospheric pressure and thus for forecasting the weather or finding height above sea level.

2. anything that reflects or indicates change; as, the newspaper is a *barometer* of public opinion.

aneroid barometer; see under *aneroid, a.*

marine barometer; a barometer whose tube is contracted at the neck to avoid oscillations of the mercury. It is hung in gimbals so as to remain upright regardless of the vessel's motion.

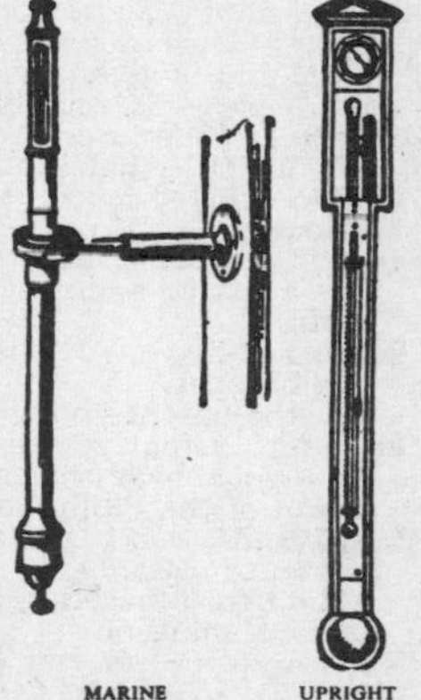
MARINE BAROMETER UPRIGHT BAROMETER

mountain barometer; a mercurial barometer, with a tripod attachment, used for measuring altitudes.

bȧ·rom′e·tẽr flow′ẽr, an artificial flower, tinted with chloride of cobalt, which turns blue when dry and pink when wet.

bȧ·rom′e·tẽr gauge, a gauge attached to a steam chamber for indicating the degree of vacuum therein.

bar·ō·met′riç, bar·ō·met′riç·ăl, *a.* pertaining to a barometer; measured or shown by a barometer.

barometric gradient; the variation of atmospheric pressure; also, a diagram of such variation.

bar·ō·met′riç·ăl·ly, *adv.* by means of a barometer; according to barometric observations.

bar·ō·met′rō·grȧph, *n.* [Gr. *baros*, weight, *metron*, measure, and *graphein*, to write.] a self-recording barometer; a barograph.

bȧ·rom′e·try, *n.* the science of measuring atmospheric pressure through use of barometers.

bar′ō·metz (-mets), *n.* [Russ. *baranetsu*, club moss.] in botany, the Scythian lamb, the hairy rootstock of the fern *Dicksonia barometz*, which somewhat resembles a recumbent lamb in form.

bar′ŏn, *n.* [ME. *baron, barun*, a baron; OFr. *baron, barun*; O.H.G. *baro*, a man.]

1. a member of the lowest rank of British nobility; one who holds the rank of nobility next below that of a viscount. Originally, the barons were the proprietors of land held by

honorable service. Hence, in ancient records, the word *barons* comprehends all the nobility.

In the Middle Ages, *barons* were feudal tenants of the king (called *greater barons*) or of any higher-ranking lord (called *lesser barons*).

2. this rank or its title. The title is no longer attached to the possession of a manor, but given by the king's letters patent, or writ of summons to parliament.

3. a European or Japanese nobleman of like rank.

4. a title of certain British officers: as, *barons of the exchequer*, formerly the four judges who tried cases between the king and his subjects relating to the revenue. *Barons of the Cinque Ports* were, before the Reform Act of 1832, members of the House of Commons, elected by the seven Cinque Ports, two for each port. These ports were Dover, Sandwich, Romney, Hastings, Hythe, Winchelsea, and Rye.

5. in old law, a husband: as, *baron and feme*, husband and wife.

6. in cookery, two sirloins of beef not cut entirely apart.

7. a powerful capitalist; a magnate; as, a coal *baron*.

bar'ŏn·ā̤ge, *n.* [ME. *baronage*, from OFr. *barnage*, baronage.]

1. the whole body of barons or peers as a class; peerage.

2. the rank, title, status, or domain of a baron.

3. the nobility in general.

4. a list or annotated account of the barons.

bar'ŏn·ess, *n.* 1. a baron's wife, widow, or (in some European countries) daughter.

2. a woman who holds a barony in her own right.

bar'ŏn·et, *n.* [Fr., dim. of *baron*.]

1. a man holding the lowest hereditary British rank, next below a baron and above a knight. The rank has precedence over all degrees of knighthood except that of the Garter. The order was founded by James I, in 1611, and is given by patent. In the official title *baronet* is usually abbreviated; as, Sir Thomas Jones, *Bart.*

2. the title that shows this rank.

bar'ŏn·et·ā̤ge, *n.* 1. the collective body of baronets.

2. the state or rank of a baronet.

3. a list or annotated account of the baronets.

bar'ŏn·et·cy, *n.* 1. the rank, status, or title of a baronet.

2. the patent giving such rank.

bȧ·rong', *n.* [native name; prob. akin to Malay. *parang*.] a heavy sheath knife used by the Moros of the Philippines.

bȧ·rō'ni·ăl, *a.* 1. pertaining to a baron, his estate, or class.

2. fit for a baron; grand, showy, etc.; as, a *baronial* mansion.

bar'ŏn·y, *n.*; *pl.* **bar'ŏn·ieṣ**, [ME. *baronie*, from OFr. *baronie*, barony.]

1. the rank, title, or domain of a baron.

2. in Ireland, a territorial division, corresponding nearly to the English hundred, and supposed to have been originally the district of a native chief.

3. any extensive freehold estate in Scotland, which may be held by a commoner.

bȧ·rōque' (-rōk'), *a.* [Fr. *baroque*, odd, irregular, from Port. *barroco*, rough, uneven.]

1. having unusual formation; distorted; as, a *baroque* pearl.

2. of, characteristic of, or like a style of art and architecture characterized by much ornamentation and curved rather than straight lines.

3. designating or of the period in which this flourished (c. 1550–1750).

4. of the late or decadent baroque period style; rococo.

5. fantastically overdecorated; gaudily ornate.

bȧ·rōque', *n.* in the fine arts, especially architecture, any baroque form or ornamentation.

bar'ō·sçōpe, *n.* [Gr. *baros*, weight, and *skopein*, to view.]

1. an instrument to show the approximate weight of the atmosphere.

2. an instrument that measures the weight lost by an object in the air and shows that this weight equals that of the air displaced.

bar·ō·sçop'iç, **bar·ō·sçop'iç·ăl**, *a.* pertaining to a baroscope.

bar·ō·sel'ē·nīte, *n.* [Gr. *baros*, weight, and *selēnē*, the moon.] barite. [Obs.]

Ba·ros'mȧ, *n.* see *buchu*.

bȧ·rouche', *n.* [Gr. *barutsche*; It. *baroccio*, from LL. *birota*, a two-wheeled vehicle, from L. *bis*, two, and *rota*, a wheel.] a four-wheeled carriage having a collapsible top, with a driver's seat on the outside and two inside seats facing each other.

bȧ·rou·çhet' (-shā'), *n.* a variety of small barouche.

bȧ·rox'y·ton, *n.* [Gr. *barys*, heavy, and *oxytonos*, sharp sounding.] a large brass-wind instrument sometimes used in military bands.

bär pin, a long, bar-shaped, ornamental brooch or pin.

bär'pōst, *n.* one of the side posts of a field gate.

bärque (bärk), *n.* a bark (sailing vessel).

bär'quen·tīne (-ken-), **bär'quăn·tīne** (-kăn-), *n.* same as *barkentine*.

bärr, *v.i.* [Fr. *barrir*, from L. *barrire*, to cry like an elephant, from *barrus*, an elephant.] to imitate the cry of an elephant. [Obs.]

bär'rȧ·ble, *a.* in law, capable of being barred.

bar'rȧ·çan, *n.* [Fr. *barracan*; Turk. *barrakan*; Ar. *barrakān*, a sort of black gown; from Per. *barak*, a stuff made of camel's hair.] a thick, strong fabric, somewhat like camlet: used in the Levant for cloaks and other outer garments.

bar'răck, *n.* [Fr. *baraque*, from It. *barraca*, a tent or soldier's hut.]

1. an improvised hut. [Rare.]

2. [*pl.*] a building or group of buildings for soldiers, especially in garrison.

3. [*pl.*] a large, plain, often temporary building for housing workmen, etc.

4. a detachable roof, on posts, used to cover hay, etc.

bar'răck, *v.t.* to furnish with barracks; to put (soldiers) in barracks.

bar'răck, *v.i.* to occupy barracks.

bar'răcks bag, a cloth bag to hold a soldier's equipment and personal possessions.

bar'rȧ·clāde, *n.* [D. *baare*, bare, and *kleed*, cloth.] a homemade woolen blanket without nap originally made by the Dutch of New Amsterdam (New York).

bar'rȧ·çoon, *n.* [Sp. *barracon*, a stronghold, from *barraca*, a barrack.] a temporary barrack, pen, or enclosure for slaves, sometimes fortified.

bar·rȧ·çū'dȧ, **bar·rȧ·çōu'tȧ**, *n.* [native name.] a large, ferocious, pikelike sea fish, attaining ten feet in length, found in the West Indian and Mediterranean seas.

bar'rad, *n.* a conical cap worn by the Irish before the seventeenth century.

bär'rā̤ge, *n.* [Fr. *barrage*, a dam, from *barrer*, to stop.]

1. a barring.

2. an artificial dam placed in a watercourse to increase the depth of water.

băr·räge' (-räzh'), *n.* [Fr.]

1. a wall of artillery fire which is thrown against an advancing enemy with such regularity that the troops are unable to pierce it: used to prevent an enemy's advance or retreat, and also to protect troops as they advance for an attack.

2. a heavy, prolonged attack of words, blows, etc.

rolling barrage; a barrage which moves ahead of attacking troops at a predetermined rate.

băr·räge', *v.t.* and *v.i.*; barraged, *pt.*, *pp.*; barraging, *ppr.* to lay down a barrage (against).

băr·räge' bal·loon', an anchored balloon, often one of a series, with cables or nets attached to it for entangling attacking airplanes.

bar·rȧ·mun'dȧ, *n.*; *pl.* **bar·rȧ·mun'dȧ**, **bar·rȧ·mun'dȧṣ**, [native name.] (a) an Australian fresh-water fish of the genus *Ceratodotus*, having both gills and lungs; (b) an Australian river fish having large scales.

bar·rȧ·mun'di, *n.*; *pl.* **bar·rȧ·mun'di**, **bar·rȧ·mun'diṣ**, **bar·rȧ·mun'dieṣ**, a barramunda.

bar·rañ'çȧ, **bar·rañ'çō**, *n.* [Sp.] a ravine caused by rain, or a watercourse.

bar'rȧ·tŏr, **bar'rȧ·tĕr**, *n.* [ME. *barator*, from OFr. *barateor*, a trader, from *barater*, to barter, cheat.]

1. in law, one guilty of barratry.

2. in maritime law, any officer or crew member of a ship who commits fraud in the management of the ship, or in relation to his duties, by which the owner or insurers are injured.

bar'rȧ·trous, *a.* having the nature of barratry.

bar'rȧ·trous·ly, *adv.* in a barratrous manner.

bar'rȧ·try, *n.* [ME. *barratrie*; OFr. *baraterie*, barratry, from *barater*, to barter, cheat.]

1. in law, the practice of exciting and encouraging lawsuits and quarrels.

2. in maritime law, cheating or fraud committed by a ship's officers or crew, by which owners or insurers are injured as by the sinking or deserting of the ship or the embezzling of cargo.

3. in Scottish law, the acceptance by a judge of a bribe designed to influence his decision.

4. the buying or selling of ecclesiastical or civil positions.

bärred (bärd), *a.* 1. fastened with a bar; hindered; restrained; excluded; forbidden.

2. striped; checkered.

barred owl; a large American species of owl, *Syrnium nebulosum*, having broad, brown stripes or bars across the breast.

bar'rel, *n.* [ME. *barel*, *barayl*, OFr. *bareil*, LL. *barillus*, *barile*, a barrel.]

1. a cylindrical vessel or cask with sides that bulge outward and flat ends, made of staves and heading, and bound with hoops.

2. the quantity which a standard barrel contains: in the United States it is usually $31\frac{1}{2}$ gallons; in Great Britain, 36 imperial gallons.

3. any hollow or solid cylinder; as, the *barrel* of a fountain pen.

4. a revolving cylinder, wound with a chain or rope; as, the *barrel* of a windlass.

5. the hollow or quill part of a feather.

6. the straight tube of a gun, which directs the projectile.

7. the body of a horse, cow, etc.

8. a great amount; as, a *barrel* of fun. [Colloq.]

bar'rel, *v.t.*; barreled *or* barrelled (-reld), *pt.*, *pp.*; barreling *or* barrelling, *ppr.* 1. to put in a barrel; to pack in a barrel.

2. to store away.

bar'rel, *v.i.* to go at high speed. [Slang.]

bar'rel-bel″lied (-lid), *a.* having a large belly.

bar'rel bulk, a measure for estimating the freight capacity of a ship, being 5 cubic feet in space, holding $^1/_8$ of a ton weight.

bar'rel chāir, a kind of upholstered chair with an upright, rounded back.

bar'reled, *a.* 1. put or packed in a barrel.

2. having a barrel or tube.

bar'rel-house, *a.* in jazz music, of or in the unrestrained style of playing associated with a barrel house.

bar'rel house, formerly, a small, disreputable saloon with a row of racked barrels along the wall.

bar'rel or'găn, a mechanical musical instrument having a cylinder studded with pins which open pipe valves or strike metal tongues when the cylinder is revolved, producing a tune; a hand organ.

bar'rel rōll, a complete revolution made by an airplane around its longitudinal axis while in flight.

bar'rel vạult, see phrase under *vault* (arched roof).

bar'ren, *a.* [ME. *barein*, *barain*; OFr. *baraigne*, barren.]

1. not producing young or offspring; sterile.

2. not bearing or pregnant at the regular time: said of plants or animals.

3. unfruitful; not fertile; without vegetation; as, *barren* fields.

4. unproductive; not inventive; dull.

5. empty; fruitless; unprofitable.

barren flower; a flower without stamens and pistils, or having only stamens.

Barren Grounds, *Barren Lands*; a vast region of bare tundras in Canada, north of the forest line.

bar'ren, *n.* [ME. *barein*; OFr. *brahain*, barren.]

1. [*usually pl.*] a tract of slightly elevated land with shrubs, brush, etc. and sandy soil.

2. any unproductive tract of land.

bar'ren·ly, *adv.* unfruitfully.

bar'ren·ness, *n.* 1. the quality of not producing its kind; want of the power of conception.

2. unfruitfulness; sterility; infertility; the quality of not producing at all, or only in small quantities; as, the *barrenness* of soil.

3. lack of inventiveness; dullness: applied to the mind.

4. lack; scantiness.

5. lack of emotion, sensibility, or fervency; as, the *barrenness* of devotion.

bar'ren·wŏrt, *n.* a low-growing, herbaceous plant, *Epimedium alpinum*, with a creeping root and having many stalks, each with three flowers.

bar'ret, *n.* [Fr. *barrette*; LL. *barretum*, a cap.]

1. a cap formerly worn by soldiers: called also *barret cap*.

2. the flat cap worn by priests of the Roman Catholic Church; biretta.

bär·rette′, *n.* [Fr. *barette*, dim. of *barre*, a bar.] a small bar or clasp worn by a girl or woman for holding the hair in place.

bar·ri·çāde′, *n.* [Fr. *barricade*; Sp. *barricada*, a barricade; literally, made of barrels, from *barrica*, a barrel.]

1. any barrier made hastily that will obstruct the progress of an enemy, or serve for defense or security, usually erected in streets; as, a *barricade* of rubble.

2. any bar or obstruction; that which defends.

3. in horse racing, a gate that keeps the horses in line before the start of a race.

bar·ri·çāde′, *v.t.*; barricaded, *pt.*, *pp.*; barricading, *ppr.* 1. to stop up a passage; to obstruct.

2. to fortify with any hasty or slight work that hinders the approach of an enemy.

bar·ri·çād′ēr, *n.* one who builds barricades.

bar·ri·çā′dō, *n.*; *pl.* **bar·ri·çā′does** (-dōz), a barricade.

bar·ri·çā′dō, *v.t.*; barricadoed, *pt.*, *pp.*; barricadoing, *ppr.* to barricade.

bar·rī′çō, *n.*; *pl.* **bar·rī′çōs**, **bar·rī′çōes**, [Sp. *barrica*, a cask.] a small cask.

bar′ri·ēr, *n.* [ME. *barrere*; OFr. *barriere*, a barrier; LL. *barra*, a bar.]

1. a kind of fence to obstruct the advance of persons or things; an enemy's advance.

2. a wall for defense.

3. a fortress or fortified town on the frontier of a country.

4. any obstruction; anything which confines, or which hinders approach or attack; as, constitutional *barriers*.

5. anything that marks the limits of a place; any limit or boundary; a line of separation.

6. a customs gate on a country's border.

7. [*sometimes* B–] the part of the south polar ice sheet that extends into the sea.

barrier beach; a ridge of sand and gravel thrown up along a coast line by the waves.

barrier reef; a reef of rock or coral which parallels a coast, usually serving as a breakwater.

Syn.—bar, barricade, bulwark, hindrance, obstacle, obstruction, prohibition, rampart, restraint, restriction.

bar′ri·ēr gāte, a strong, heavy barrier to a stockade or palisade.

bar·ri·gū′dō, *n.* [Sp., big-bellied.] any of several South American monkeys of the genus *Lagothrix*, having a long prehensile tail.

bär′ring, *prep.* [ppr. of *bar*.] excepting; excluding; as, *barring* accident, I shall be there.

bär′ri·ō, *n.* [Sp., from *barra*; LL. *barra*, a bar.] in Spanish-speaking countries, a political subdivision of a city; a suburb.

bar′ris·tēr, *n.* [from *bar* (court of justice).] in England, a counselor or advocate learned in the law, qualified and admitted to plead at the bar and to undertake the defense of clients: formally called in full, a *barrister-at-law*.

bar·ris·tē′ri·ăl, *a.* pertaining to a barrister.

bär′rọom, *n.* a room in which alcoholic drinks are sold over a bar or counter.

bar′rōw, *n.* [ME. *barrow*, *barow*, *barowe*, a barrow, from AS. *beran*, to bear, carry.]

1. a frame or box having handles or shafts, and with or without a wheel, used in transporting small, heavy loads; a handbarrow or wheelbarrow.

2. the capacity or contents of a barrow.

3. a wicker case in a saltworks, where the salt is put to drain.

bar′rōw, *n.* [ME. *barow*, *barowe*; AS. *bearg*, *bearh*, a castrated boar.] a castrated hog.

bar′rōw, *n.* [ME. *berw*; AS. *beorg*, a grove.]

1. a hillock or mound of earth or rocks, marking a grave, especially an ancient one.

2. a mountain; hill. [Dial.]

bar′rōw, *n.* a flannel swaddling cloth: also called *barrow coat*. [Prov. Eng.]

Bar′rōw·ist, *n.* a disciple of Henry Barrowe (executed in 1593), one of the founders of Congregationalism in England.

bar′rụ·let, *n.* [dim. of OFr. *barre*, a bar.] in heraldry, a stripe one fourth the width of a bar.

bar′rụ·ly, *a.* in heraldry, traversed by barrulets: said of the field.

BARRY

bär′ry, *a.* [Fr. *barré*, pp. of *barrer*, to bar, hinder.] in heraldry, divided into bars: said of the field.

bärse, *n.* [ME. *barse*; AS. *bærs*, *bears*, perch.] the common perch (fish). [Eng. Dial.]

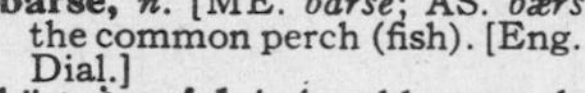

BARS GEMEL

bärs ġem′el, in heraldry, parallel barrulets placed in couples.

bär shōe, a kind of horseshoe having a bar across the open part of the heel, to protect the tender frog of the foot from injury.

bär shot, two cannon balls, or half balls, joined together by an iron bar, and formerly used in sea fights to cut the masts or rigging of an enemy's ship.

BAR SHOT

bär sīght (sīt), a rifle sight, consisting of a bar placed across a ring.

bär sin′is·tēr, in heraldry, erroneously, a baton or bend sinister.

bär′tend″ēr, *n.* a man who mixes and serves alcoholic drinks at a bar.

bär′tēr, *v.i.*; bartered, *pt.*, *pp.*; bartering, *ppr.* [ME. *bartren*; OFr. *bareter*, to barter, trick, cheat.] to trade by exchanging one commodity for another, in distinction from a sale and purchase, in which money is paid for the commodities transferred.

bär′tēr, *v.t.* to give (goods or services) in return for other goods or services; to trade.

to barter away; to give or trade for too small a return.

bär′tēr, *n.* 1. the act or practice of trading by exchanging commodities or services; exchange.

2. anything bartered.

Syn.—exchange, dealing, traffic, trade.

bär′tēr·ēr, *n.* one who barters.

bärth, *n.* a place of shelter for cattle. [Eng. Dial.]

Bär·thol′ō·mew, *n.* in the Bible, one of the twelve Apostles.

Bär·thol′ō·mew fāir, a fair at West Smithfield, England, held annually at Bartholomewtide from 1133 to 1855.

Bär·thol′ō·mew·tīde″, *n.* the time of the festival of St. Bartholomew, August 24.

bär′ti·zăn, **bär′ti·săn**, *n.* [a corrupted Scot. spelling of *bratticing*.] a small, overhanging turret on a tower, parapet, etc., used originally for defense or as a lookout.

Bärt′lett peār, a large, juicy variety of English pear: named after Enoch *Bartlett*, of Dorchester, Mass., who introduced it in the United States.

bär′trăm, *n.* same as *bertram*.

Bär′uçh, *n.* [Heb., lit., blessed.]

1. in the Bible, Jeremiah's scribe: Jer. xxxii. 12–14.

2. a book of the Old Testament Apocrypha attributed to him.

BARTIZAN
aa. balistraria

bär′wāy, *n.* a passage into a field or yard, closed by bars.

bär′wīse, *adv.* in heraldry, horizontally across the field.

bär′wood, *n.* a strong, flexible, red dyewood, obtained from a tree that grows in Africa.

bar·y-, a combining form from Gr. *barys*, meaning *heavy*, *difficult*.

bar·y·cen′triç, *a.* [*bary-*, and Gr. *kentron*, center.] pertaining to the center of gravity.

bar′y·on, *n.* [from Gr. *barys*, heavy, and elec*tron*.] one of a class of heavy atomic particles, including the proton, neutron, and the hyperons.

bar·y·phō′ni·ȧ, **bȧ·ryph′ō·ny**, *n.* [*bary-*, and Gr. *phōnē*, voice.] difficulty of speech.

bȧ·ry̅′tȧ, *n.* [Gr. *barytēs*, weight, from *barys*, heavy.]

1. barium oxide.

2. loosely, barium hydroxide.

bȧ·ry̅′tēs, *n.* [Gr. *barytēs*, weight.] native sulfate of barium; barite.

bȧ·ryt′iç, *a.* pertaining to baryta; formed of baryta or containing it.

bȧ·ry̅·tō·çal′cīte, *n.* [LL. *baryta*, barium, from Gr. *barytēs*, weight, and L. *calx*, *calcis*, lime.] a compound of carbonate of lime and carbonate of barium, of a dark or light gray color, occurring massive or crystallized.

bar′y·tōne, *a.* and *n.* see *baritone*.

bar′y·tron, *n.* [Gr. *bary-*, from *barys*, heavy, and *-tron*, particle.] same as *mesotron*.

bäs (bä), *n.* [Fr., bottom.] in roulette, a bet placed at the bottom of a column.

bā′săl, *a.* 1. of or constituting the base.

2. basic; fundamental.

bā′săl an·es·thē′si·ȧ, in medicine, anesthesia induced as a preliminary to further and deeper anesthesia.

bā′săl bod′y, in biology, an embryonic stage.

bā′săl cell, in anatomy, a cell of the deepest layer of the skin.

bȧ·sā′lē, *n.*; *pl.* **bȧ·sā′li·ȧ**, [L. *basis*, base.] a cartilage at the base of the fins of certain fishes.

bā′săl me·tab′ō·lism, the quantity of energy used by any organism at rest; amount of heat produced by the human organism fourteen to eighteen hours after eating and when at rest for thirty to sixty minutes but not asleep: it is measured by the rate (*basal metabolic rate*) at which heat is given off, and is expressed in calories per hour per square meter of skin surface.

bā′săl-nērved, *a.* in botany, having the nerves starting from the base: said of leaves.

bā′săl plāne, in crystallography, a plane parallel to the horizontal axis.

bā′săl point, a starting point.

bā′săl rā′tion (-shun), in physiology, sufficient food to produce energy but lacking in other vital elements which may be added singly to study the effects of their addition.

bȧ·sạlt′, *n.* [L. *basaltes*, dark, hard marble.]

1. a fine-grained, heavy, crystalline, igneous rock, consisting of labradorite, augite, magnetite, and sometimes a little olivine. It is amorphous, columnar, tabular, or globular. It is usually of a greenish-black color, but sometimes dull brown or black. Fingal's Cave, on the island of Staffa, and the Giant's Causeway, Ireland, contain examples of basaltic columns.

2. a kind of glassy, black pottery designed by Josiah Wedgwood.

bȧ·sạlt′iç, *a.* pertaining to basalt; formed of or containing basalt.

bȧ·sạlt′i·fọrm, *a.* in the form of basalt; columnar.

bȧ·sạlt′ine, *n.* a variety of common hornblende, found in basalt and lavas. [Obs.]

bȧ·sạlt′oid, *a.* formed like basalt; basaltiform.

bas′ăn, *n.* same as *basil* (sheepskin).

bas′ȧ·nīte, *n.* [Gr. *basanos*, the touchstone.] a grayish or bluish-black igneous rock often interspersed with veins of quartz: formerly employed to test the purity of gold.

bäs bleu (bä blü), [Fr., blue stocking; *bas*, stocking, *bleu*, blue.] a literary woman; a blue-stocking.

bas′ci·net, *n.* same as *basinet*.

bas′cūle, *n.* [Fr., a seesaw.] a mechanical device based on the principle of a seesaw, one end rising as the other falls.

bascule bridge; a balanced drawbridge, so counterbalanced that it may be raised in whole or in halves to a vertical position when not in use or to let vessels pass.

BASCULE BRIDGE

bāse, *a.*; *comp.* baser; *superl.* basest. [ME. *base*, *bass*; OFr. *bas*, base, low; L. *basis*, a base or pedestal.]

1. low in place. [Obs.]

2. mean; worthless; inferior in value or estimation: used of things.

3. of low station; menial; without rank or dignity: used of persons.

4. morally low; low-minded; disgraceful; vile; as, it is *base* to betray a friend.

5. of little comparative value: applied to metals, in distinction from the *precious* metals, as gold and silver.

6. debased; counterfeit.

7. deep; grave: applied to sound; as, the *base* sounds of a viol.

8. of illegitimate, servile, or humble birth. [Archaic.]

9. in old English law, servile: a base estate was an estate held by villienage and not by fixed services. Such a tenure was called *base*, or low, and the tenant, a *base* tenant.

Syn.—mean, vile, low, dishonorable, worthless, ignoble, low-minded, shameful, inferior.

bāse, *n.* 1. a deep, low sound; bass tone.
2. a bass voice, bass part, etc.

bāse, *n.*; *pl.* **bās'eṣ,** [ME. *base, bas, baas*; OFr. *base*; L. *basis*, a base or pedestal; Gr. *basis*, a pedestal, step; from *bainein*, to go, to walk.]
1. the bottom of a thing, considered as its support, or the part of a thing on which it rests; foundation; as, the *base* of a column.
2. the foundation or most important element, as of a system or set of ideas.
3. anything from which a start is made; basis.
4. the principal or essential ingredient, or the one serving as a vehicle; as, paint with an oil *base*.
5. the point of attachment of a part of the body; as, the *base* of the thumb.
6. a goal, starting place, or safety point in certain games, as baseball.
7. a center of operations or source of supply; headquarters.
8. (*a*) the bottommost layer or coat, as of paint; (*b*) a makeup cream to give a desired color to the skin, especially in the theater.
9. in geometry, the lowest side of the perimeter of a figure, on which it is thought of as resting.
10. in chemistry, a substance which forms a salt when it reacts with an acid; in terms of the theory of the dissociation of electrolytes, a compound, such as sodium hydroxide or ammonium hydroxide, which liberates hydroxyl ions in aqueous solutions; in terms of the modern theory of acids and bases, a substance that removes hydrogen ions (protons) from an acid and combines with them in a chemical reaction.
11. in pharmacy, the principal ingredient of a compound.
12. in botany, the part of fruit where it is united with the peduncle; the part of a leaf next to the stem: opposed to the *apex*.
13. in linguistics, any morpheme to which prefixes, suffixes, etc. are added.
14. in dyeing, a substance used for fixing colors.
15. in heraldry, the lower portion of a shield.
16. in mathematics, a constant figure upon which a mathematical table is computed, as in logarithms.
off base; (*a*) in baseball, not touching the base; (*b*) taking a position, attitude, etc. that is unsound or in error. [Slang.]
to get to first base; (*a*) in baseball, to reach first base safely; (*b*) to succeed in the first step of anything. [Slang.]

bāse, *a.* forming a base.

bāse, *v.t.*; based (bāst), *pt., pp.*; basing, *ppr.*
1. to lay the base or foundation of.
2. to put (a thing) on a base or foundation: often used figuratively; as, he *based* his argument on authority.
3. to establish or found.
4. to debase; to reduce the value of, by the admixture of meaner metals. [Obs.]

bāse'ball, *n.* 1. a game played with a hard, rawhide-covered ball and wooden bat by two opposing teams, properly of nine players each: it is played on a field with four bases forming a diamond-shaped circuit which a runner must complete to score a run.
2. the ball used in this game.

bāse'bōard, *n.* 1. a board or molding covering a wall of a room where it meets the floor and furnishing protection to the plastering.
2. any board serving as a base.

bāse'bọrn, *a.* 1. born out of wedlock.
2. born of low or humble parentage.
3. vile; mean.

bāse broom, in botany, the woadwaxen, *Genista tinctoria*.

bāse bụl'liŏn (-yun), crude lead, containing silver, antimony, etc.

bāse'bũrn'ẽr, bāse'-bũrn'ẽr, *n.* a stove or furnace with a fire box and grate at the bottom and supplied with fuel through a tube projected from above.

bāse çōurse, the first or lowest layer, as of stone in a wall.

bāse'-çōurt, *n.* in law, an inferior court.

Bä'ṣe·dōw'ṣ diṣ·ēaṣe', exophthalmic goiter: named after Karl von *Basedow* (1799–1854), a German physician.

bāse'heärt''ed, *a.* vile in heart.

bāse hit, in baseball, a hit which allows a batter to reach first base safely, without benefit of any error by an opponent and without forcing out a runner already on base.

bāse hos'pi·tăl, a military hospital far from the battle front: distinguished from *field hospital*.

bas'e·lärd, *n.* a baslard. [Obs.]

bāse'less, *a.* without a base; having no foundation or support.

bāse lev'el, 1. in geology, the lowest level to which erosion can be carried.
2. in surveying, the elevation to which other elevations are referred.

bāse līne, 1. an established line from which to measure and to which all other lines are secondary; the principal line, as in engineering.
2. in baseball, the straight line between any two consecutive bases.

Bȧ·sel'lȧ, *n.* [native name in Malabar.] a typical genus of East Indian herbs, some species being eaten like spinach.

bāse'ly, *adv.* in a base manner; meanly; dishonorably; illegitimately.

bāse'măn, *n.*; *pl.* **bāse'men,** in baseball, any of the three infielders stationed at first, second, and third base, respectively.

bāse'ment, *n.* [Fr. *soubassement*, base.]
1. the foundation or lower part of a wall or walls.
2. the lowest story of a building or the one just below the main floor, usually wholly or partially lower than the surface of the ground.
basement membrane; in anatomy, a delicate membrane found beneath the epidermis or epithelium on all the free surfaces of the body, both external and internal: also called *primary membrane*.

bāse met'ăl, 1. any of the common, nonprecious metals: distinguished from *precious metal*.
2. the metal under a coating or plating.
3. the main metal in an alloy.

bāse'-mīnd''ed, *a.* morally low; low-minded.

bāse mōld'ing, a projecting molding at the base of any architectural feature, as a wall or column.

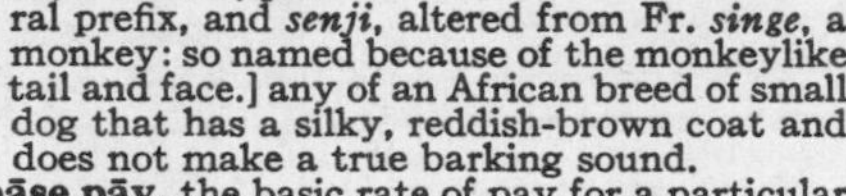
BASE MOLDINGS

bāse'ness, *n.* 1. the quality or state of being morally base.
2. a dishonorable act or trait.

bas'ĕ·net, *n.* same as *basinet*.

bȧ·sen'jī, *n.* [Bantu, from *ba-*, plural prefix, and *senji*, altered from Fr. *singe*, a monkey: so named because of the monkeylike tail and face.] any of an African breed of small dog that has a silky, reddish-brown coat and does not make a true barking sound.

bāse pāy, the basic rate of pay for a particular job exclusive of overtime pay, bonuses, etc.

bāse run'nẽr, in baseball, any member of the team at bat who is on base.

bās'eṣ, *n.*, pl. of *base*.

bā'sēṣ, *n.*, pl. of *basis*.

bāse'-spir''it·ed, *a.* low in courage; mean; cowardly.

bash, *v.t.*; bashed, *pt., pp.*; bashing, *ppr.* [ME. *basshen, baschen*, for *abashen*, abash.] to make ashamed. [Obs.]

bash, *v.i.* to be ashamed. [Obs.]

bash, *v.t.* [echoic; akin to (perh. from) hyp. ON. *basca*, to strike.] to strike with a violent blow; to smash (*in*). [Colloq.]

bash, *n.* 1. a heavy, crushing blow. [Colloq.]
2. a gala event or party. [Slang.]

bȧ·shąw', *n.* [Turk. *bāshā*, head, ruler; Per. *pādshāh*, a governor, king.]
1. same as *pasha*.
2. an important or self-important person.

bash'fụl, *a.* [*abash*, and *-ful*.]
1. modest to excess; sheepish; shy.
2. showing an embarrassed timidity.
Syn.—modest, diffident, reserved, shy, timid, unassuming, unobtrusive.

bash'fụl·ly, *adv.* in a bashful manner.

bash'fụl·ness, *n.* excessive or extreme modesty; the quality or state of being bashful.

bash'i-bȧ·zōuk', *n.* [Turk. *bashi-bozuq*, one in no special dress; *bashi*, headdress, and *bozuq*, disorderly, unkempt.] a member of the Turkish irregulars, troops notorious in the nineteenth century for their brutality.

Bȧsh·kir', *n.* 1. a member of a Turko-Tartar tribe of Moslems of the Bashkir A.S.S.R.
2. their language.

bash'lyk, bash'lik, *n.* [Russ. *bashluik*.] a cloth hood covering the ears, worn in Russia as a protection against the cold.

bā'si-, [from L. *basis*; Gr. *basis*, base.] a combining form, used in biology to denote *the base, position at* or *near a base*, as in *basi*fugal.

bā'siç, *a.* [L. *basis*, base.]
1. of or at the base; forming a base or basis; fundamental; essential.
2. in chemistry, of, having the nature of, or containing a base; alkaline.
3. of or resulting from a process for eliminating phosphorus in the manufacture of some steels, during which the phosphorus combines with the basic substance lining the converters to form basic slag.
4. in mineralogy, having less than 52 per cent silica: said of crystalline rocks.
basic slag; a slag, especially of steel, useful as a fertilizer because of its low silica (and high alkaline) content.

bās'i·căl·ly, *adv.* at basis; at bottom; fundamentally; primarily.

bā'siç dress, a simple, dark dress that can be worn with changes of accessories.

Bā'siç Eng'lish, a simplified vocabulary of 850 elementary English words, promoted especially as a possible medium for international communication, and for instruction in fundamental English: it was invented by Charles K. Ogden (1889–1957) and is copyrighted.

bȧ·sic'ẽr·īte, *n.* [*basi-*, and Gr. *keras*, horn.] in zoology, the part of the long feeler of a crustacean next to the coxocerite, or first joint.

bȧ·sic'i·ty, *n.* in chemistry, (a) the quality or condition of being a base; (b) the capacity of an acid to react with a base, measured by the number of chemical equivalents of a base with which one gram molecular weight of the acid reacts.

bā''si·diġ·i·tā'lē, *n.*; *pl.* **bā''si·diġ·i·tā'li·ȧ,** [*basi-*, and L. *digitus*, finger.] a cartilage or bone at the base of a finger or a toe.

bȧ·sid''i·ō·ġē·net'iç, *a.* [Gr. *basis*, base, and *genesis*, origin.] originating from basidia.

bȧ·sid''i·ō·mȳ·cēte', *n.* [from *basidium*, and *mycete*.] in botany, a basidiomycetous fungus, as a mushroom, rust, smut, puffball, etc.

Bȧ·sid''i·ō·mȳ·cē'tēṣ, *n.pl.* [Gr. *basis*, base, and *mykes*, a mushroom.] a large subdivision of fungi named from and characterized by spore-bearing basidia, including the common mushrooms and toadstools.

bȧ·sid''i·ō·mȳ·cē'tous, *a.* of *Basidiomycetes*.

bȧ·sid'i·ō·phōre, *n.* [Gr. *basis*, base, and *phoros*, something brought, from *pherein*, to bear.] a part of a fungus which bears basidia.

bȧ·sid'i·ō·spōre, *n.* [Gr. *basis*, base, and *spora*, seed.] a spore produced by a basidium.

bȧ·sid''i·ō·spōr'ous, *a.* relating to or having the characteristics of basidiospores.

bȧ·sid'i·um, *n.*; *pl.* **bȧ·sid'i·ȧ,** [L., from Gr. *basis*, a base.] in botany, any of a number of club-shaped cells on which are borne the spores in basidiomycetous fungi.

bā'si·fī·ẽr, *n.* [*basi-*, and L. *fieri*, to be made.] in chemistry, that which converts a compound into a base.

bȧ·sif'ū·găl, *a.* [*basi-*, and L. *fugere*, to flee.] in botany, tending away from the base.

bā'si·fȳ, *v.t.*; basified, *pt., pp.*; basifying, *ppr.* in chemistry, to convert into a base.

bȧ·sig'nȧ·thīte, *n.* the second joint in a mouth appendage of an arthropod.

bȧ·si·ġyn'i·um, *n.* [*basi-*, and Gr. *gynē*, a female.] the pedicel on which the ovary of certain flowers is situated.

bȧ·si·hȳ'ăl, *a.* [*basi-*, and the Gr. letter upsilon, Υ; from its arch-shaped appearance.] of the components of the hyoid arch.

bȧ·si·hȳ'ăl, *n.* the body or middle part of the hyoid bone.

bȧ·si·hȳ'oid, *a.* and *n.* same as *basihyal*.

baṣ'il, *n.* same as *bezel*.

baṣ'il, *n.* [ME. *basile*; OFr. *basile*, the basil plant; name from Gr. *basilikos*, royal; *basileus*, king.] any of various species of plants of the mint family, all native to warm climates. They are fragrant and aromatic. The sweet basil, *Ocymum basilicum*, is used in cookery.
holy basil; a kind of tropical basil of the Eastern Hemisphere (*Ocymum sanctum*), held sacred to Vishnu in India.
wild basil; an aromatic herb, *Calamintha clinopodium*.

bas'il, *n.* the tanned skin of a sheep.

bas'i·lär, bas'i·lȧ·ry, *a.* 1. relating to the base; situated at the base.
2. in anatomy, designating or of (a) the sphenoid bone, and the cuneiform process of the occipital bone, at the base of the cranium; (b) an artery of the brain, resting on the cuneiform process of the occipital bone.
3. fundamental; basic; basal; as, *basilar* instincts.

Bȧ·sil′i·ăn, *a.* pertaining to the order of St. Basil, who founded it in Cappadocia.

Basilian rule; a set of rules established by St. Basil, a father of the church in the fourth century, to which monasteries of the Orthodox Eastern Church adhere.

Bȧ·sil′i·ăn, *n.* a member of a religious order under the Basilian rule; a Basilian monk.

bȧ·sil′iç, *n.* same as *basilica.*

bȧ·sil′iç, bȧ·sil′iç·ăl, *a.* 1. pertaining to a basilica.

2. pertaining to the middle vein of the upper arm and the interior branch of the axillary vein.

3. kingly. [Obs.]

bȧ·sil′i·cȧ, *n.* [Gr. *basilikē* (*stoa*), royal (portico), from *basilikos*, royal.]

1. anciently, a public hall or courtroom of rectangular shape, with a broad nave ending in an apse, and flanked by colonnaded aisles. The same ground plan was generally followed in the early Christian churches, which were also called *basilicas*. The term is still applied to some Roman Catholic Churches by way of distinction.

2. in the Middle Ages, a large structure erected over the tomb of a person of distinction.

3. a basilisk, a large piece of ordnance. [Obs.]

Bȧ·sil′i·cȧ, *n.pl.* an abridgment, in Greek, of the Justinian code, made in the ninth century, under Basil I.

bȧ·sil′i·căn, *a.* pertaining to or like a basilica.

bȧ·sil′i·çok, *n.* a basilisk, a mythical lizardlike monster. [Obs.]

bȧ·sil′i·çon, *n.* [Gr. *basilikos*, royal.]

1. originally, any of several ancient medical compounds.

2. an ointment consisting largely of pitch, resin, wax, and some fat, as olive oil or lard.

Bas·i·lid′i·ăn, *a.* pertaining to Basilides, an Alexandrian Gnostic of the second century, or to the doctrines taught by him.

Bas·i·lid′i·ăn, *n.* one of the followers of Basilides.

bas′i·lisk, *n.* [ME. *basilisk*, from Gr. *basiliskos*, dim. of *basileus*, king.]

1. a mythical lizardlike monster with supposedly fatal breath and glance, fabled to have been hatched by a serpent from a cock's egg: also called *cockatrice*.

2. one of a genus of lizards (*Basiliscus*) characterized by their ability to distend the skin on the head to form a baglike protrusion, and by an erectile crest or ridge along the back.

3. an obsolete cannon decorated with lizards.

baș′il thȳme (tīm), either of two fragrant species of *Calamintha*, *Calamintha nepeta* of North America and *Calamintha acinos* of Europe.

baș′il·weed, *n.* the wild basil, an aromatic herb: also called *stone basil.*

bā′sin (bā′sn), *n.* [ME. *basin*, *bacin*; OFr. *bacin*; LL. *bachinus*, a bowl; from L. *bacca*, a water vessel.]

1. a circular, broad, shallow vessel or dish, used to hold liquids and for various other purposes; a pan.

A silver *basin* full of rose water. —Shak.

2. the contents of a basin; the quantity it will contain.

3. a wash bowl or sink.

4. any reservoir for water, natural or artificial, as a pond, bay, or dock for ships.

5. in glass grinding, a concave piece of metal with which convex glasses are formed.

6. a large shell or case, usually of iron, on which felt hats were formerly molded into shape.

7. any hollow vessel, as the scale of a balance: applied to various forms used in the arts and industry.

8. in physical geography, (a) a circular or oval valley or surface depression, the lowest part of which is generally occupied by a lake, or traversed by a river; (b) the region drained by a river and its tributaries; (c) a great hollow in the earth's surface filled by an ocean: called *ocean basin*.

9. in geology, any dipping or inclination of strata toward a common axis or center, due to upheaval and subsidence.

10. in anatomy, a round cavity between the anterior ventricles of the brain; the third ventricle of the brain.

bā′sined (bā′snd), *a.* situated or confined in a basin, or valley.

bas′i·net, bas′net, *n.* [ME. *basinet*; OFr. *bacinet*, dim. of *bacin*, a basin; a helmet basin-shaped.] a small, round, steel cap or helmet, often with a visor, used in the Middle Ages: also written *bascinet*, *basenet*, *bassinet*.

BASINETS
1. unvisored basinet
2. visored basinet
3. coroneted basinet with camail

bā′si·oç·cip′i·tăl, *a.* [*basi-*, and L. *occiput*, pl. *occipita*, the occipital bone, from *ob*, against, and *caput*, head.] pertaining to the base, or basilar process, of the occipital bone.

bā′si·oç·cip′i·tăl, *n.* the bone, separate in infants, forming in adults the lower part of the occipital.

bā′si·on, *n.* [L. *basis*, a base.] the middle point of that part of the basioccipital bone which forms the anterior border of the great foramen of the human skull.

bā·sip′e·tăl, *a.* [L. *basis*, a base, and *petere*, to seek.] in botany, developing from the apex downward, as in compound leaves or in certain inflorescence.

bā·sip′ō·dīte, *n.* [*basi-*, and Gr. *pous*, genit. *podos*, foot.] the joint connecting the limb of a crustacean with its body.

bā·sip·te·ryġ′i·ăl, *a.* pertaining to the basipterygium; lying near the base of a fin.

bā·sip·te·ryġ′i·um, *n.*; *pl.* **bā·sip·te·ryġ′i·ȧ,** [*basi-*, and Gr. *pteryx*, *pterygos*, wing, fin.] in some fishes, one of the main basal cartilages of an embryonic fin, which later forms the metapterygium.

bā·sip·ter′y·goid, *a.* [*basi-*, and Gr. *pterygion*, dim. of *pteryx*, a wing, or fin.] pertaining to the base of the sphenoid bone, or the pterygoid process in some birds.

bā·sip·ter′y·goid, *n.* the base of the pterygoid bone or the pterygoid process of the sphenoid bone.

bā′sis, *n.*; *pl.* **bā′sēș,** [L. *basis*; Gr. *basis*, a base or pedestal, from *bainein*, to go.]

1. the base or foundation of anything; that on which a thing stands or lies; the bottom or foot of a thing.

2. the groundwork or first principle; that which supports; foundation; as, the charge is without *basis*.

The *basis* of public credit is good faith. —Hamilton.

3. the chief ingredient or component; as, oil constitutes the *basis* of the preparation.

4. in prosody, (a) an introductory foot preceding a logaoedic verse; (b) the portion of a metrical foot receiving the stress.

5. in military science, a starting point; a base.

Syn.—foundation, ground, support, footing, base.

bā·sis′ō·lūte, *a.* [*basi-*, and L. *solutus*, free.] in botany, extended at the base below the point of origin: applied to some leaves.

bā·si·sphē′noid, bā″si·sphē·noid′ăl (-sfē-), *a.* of or situated near the basisphenoid bone.

bā·si·sphē′noid, *n.* [*basi-*, and Gr. *sphēn*, a wedge, and *eidos*, form.] the posterior part or main body of the sphenoid bone, as distinct from its processes.

bȧsk, *v.i.*; basked, *pt.*, *pp.*; basking, *ppr.* [coinage due to Shakespeare's misunderstanding of Lydgate; ME. *basken*, to beat, strike (cf. *bash*); only in Gower & Lydgate.] to lie in warmth; to be exposed to genial heat; figuratively, to be at ease and thriving under benign influences; as, to *bask* in the blaze of day; to *bask* in one's favor.

bȧsk, *v.t.* to warm by continued exposure to heat; to warm with genial heat.

bȧs′ket, *n.* [ME. *basket*; W. *basged*, a basket; of Celtic origin.]

1. a container made of interwoven twigs, rushes, thin strips of wood, or other flexible material. The forms and sizes of baskets are various, as well as the uses to which they are applied; as, corn *baskets*, clothes *baskets*.

2. the contents of a basket; as much as a basket will contain; as, a *basket* of grapes.

3. in old English stagecoaches, the two outside seats facing one another behind.

4. in architecture, the central portion of a Corinthian capital.

5. in military defenses, a gabion.

6. a basket hilt.

7. a wickerwork or wire screen of an oval shape, formerly used in making hats.

8. a passenger cabin hung from a balloon.

9. in basketball, (a) the goal, a net shaped like a basket open at the bottom; (b) a toss of the ball through this net, counted as a score when properly made.

bȧs′ket, *v.t.*; basketed, *pt.*, *pp.*; basketing, *ppr.* to put in a basket.

bȧs′ket·ball, *n.* 1. a game between two opposing teams of five players each, the object of the play being to toss a large inflated ball into a raised basket or goal at either of the two opposite ends of the floor area, which is usually zoned.

2. the large, round, inflated, leather-covered ball used in this game.

bȧs′ket çāse, 1. a person lacking all four limbs. [Slang]

2. a person unable to function, especially because of emotional disturbance. [Slang]

3. Anything that does not function properly. [Slang]

bȧs′ket fish, a species of sea star, or starfish, of the genus *Astrophyton*, having five rays, divided into many branches, issuing from an angular body.

bȧs′ket·fųl, *n.*; *pl.* **bȧs′ket·fųlș,** the amount a basket will hold.

bȧs′ket hilt, a hilt, as of a sword, with a covering wrought like basketwork, to protect the hand.

bȧs′ket hoop, a shrub, *Croton lucidus*, native to the West Indies, the bark of which has medicinal properties.

bȧs′ket pälm (päm), the talipot, a palm tree native to Ceylon and India.

bȧs′ket·ry, *n.* 1. the making of baskets.

2. baskets collectively; basketware.

bȧs′ket wēave, a weave of fabrics resembling the weave used in basketmaking.

bȧs′ket·wood, *n.* a climbing shrub, *Serjania polyphylla*, having pliable stems used in the making of baskets: found in the West Indies.

bȧs′ket·wŏrk, *n.* anything made of woven twigs, osiers, or other material, to resemble a basket; wickerwork.

bȧs′ket wŏrm, any of various lepidopterous insects which weave a basket or bag of silk together with bits of leaves and twigs, for protection during the pupal stage; a bagworm.

bȧsk′ing shärk, a species of shark, the *Cetorhinus maximus*. It grows from ten to forty feet in length, is viviparous, and frequents the northern seas: so called from its habit of lying on the surface of the water basking in the sun.

bas′lärd, bas′e·lärd, *n.* [ME. *baselard*; OFr. *basalart*, from *base*, a short knife or saber.] a fifteenth-century ornamental dagger worn hanging at the waist.

bas′net, *n.* same as *basinet.*

Bā·som·mȧ·toph′ō·rȧ, *n.pl.* [Gr. *basis*, base, *omma*, eye, and *pherein*, to bear.] a group or division of gastropods of the order *Pulmonifera*, in which the eyes are situated at the base of the tentacles, as in the pond snail.

bā′sŏn, *n.* a basin (sense 6). [Obs.]

bā′sō·phīle, *n.* [from *basic*, and *-phile.*] in biology, a cell or tissue that is readily stained with basic dyes.

bā·sō·phil′iç, bā·soph′i·lous, *a.* [Gr. *basis*, base, and *philos*, friendly.] readily stained by means of basic dyes: said of cells or tissues.

Bȧsque (bȧsk), *a.* [Fr.] pertaining to the Basques, their country, or language.

Bȧsque, *n.* [Fr.] 1. any of a certain people occupying a district of the western Pyrenees contiguous to the Bay of Biscay.

2. the language of the Basques.

bȧsque, *n.* a woman's blouse with a tight-fitting waist, and made with or without a short skirt attached.

bȧs·quïne′ (-kēn′), **bȧs·quï′nä** (-kē′nyä), *n.* [Fr., from Sp. *basquina.*] an elaborate outer petticoat worn by Basque women on great occasions. It is also worn in the Spanish provinces adjacent to the Basque district.

bäs-rē·liēf′ (bä-rē-leef′), **bȧss-rē·liēf′,** *n.* [Fr. *bas-relief*; It. *basso-relievo*; *basso*, low, and *rilievare*, to raise up.] low relief; a manner of sculpturing with figures nearly flat; sculpture in which the figures stand out only a little from the background.

In *alto-rilievo*, high relief, the figures project boldly and strongly; in *demi-relief*, half relief, they are given a medium prominence; while in *bas-relief*, low relief, the projection is less than half of the real proportion. Called also *basso-rilievo*.

BAS-RELIEF

bȧss, *n.*; *pl.* **bȧss** or **bȧss'eṣ,** [ME. *base, bace,* bass, from *bars*; AS. *bears, bærs*.]

1. any of many species of valuable food fishes of the perch family, found in fresh or salt water. The varieties include the striped bass, *Roccus lineatus*; the black bass, *Micropterus salmoides*; the sea bass, *Centropristis atrarius*; the white or silver bass, *Roccus chrysops*; the rock bass or redeye; and the calico bass.

2. a European food fish, *Labrax lupus*: called also *sea dace*, and from its voracity *sea wolf*.

bȧss, *n.* [from ME. *bast*; AS. *bæst*, the strong inner bark of various trees.]

1. the American linden or lime tree: called also *basswood*.

2. bast.

3. a coarse mat, a hassock, etc. made of bast or a material resembling bast.

bāss, *n.* in mining, a dark-colored shale containing considerable carbon.

bāss, *n.* [ME. *base, bace, bas*; OFr. masc. *bas*, f. *basse*, low, from L. *basis*, a base, a pedestal.]

1. the lowest male singing voice.

2. a low, deep sound or tone of or as of such a voice.

3. the lowest part in vocal or instrumental music.

4. a singer or instrument having a very low range; specifically, a bass viol.

bāss, *a.* 1. having a very low musical pitch or range.

2. for the bass or basses.

3. able to sing or play bass.

bass string; the string of a musical instrument which produces the lowest note.

bāss, *v.t.* to sound in a deep tone. [Rare.]

Bas·sā'li·ȧ, *n.* [LL. *bassus*, low, from L. *basis*, base, from Gr. *basis*, a base, and *halia*, an assembly.] the faunal realm of the deep sea.

Bas·sā'li·ăn, *a.* of or found in Bassalia.

bāss'-bär, *n.* a strip of wood running lengthwise inside instruments of the viol group to support the pressure of the bridge.

bāss çlef, in music, (a) a sign on a staff indicating that the notes on the staff are below middle C: symbol, F; (b) the range so shown. Also called *F clef*, distinguished from *G* (or *treble*) *clef*.

bāss drum, the largest and lowest-toned of the double-headed drums.

bas'set, *n.* [Fr. *bassette*, from It. *bassetta*, basset, f. adj., dim. of *basso*, low.] a game at cards, resembling modern faro, popular in Europe during the seventeenth and eighteenth centuries.

bas'set, *n.* [Fr., from *bas*, small, low.] a kind of hound with a long body, short legs, and long, drooping ears, used in hunting: also called *basset hound*.

bas'set, *n.* [OFr. *basset*, dim. of *bas*, low.] in geology and mining, the outcrop of strata.

bas'set, *v.i.*; basseted, *pt., pp.*; basseting, *ppr.* in geology and mining, to appear at or emerge above the surface.

bas'set, *a.* inclined upward; as, the *basset* edge of strata.

bas'set hǫrn, a clarinet in F: in size it is between a clarinet proper and a bass clarinet.

bas'set·ing, *n.* the upward direction of a vein or a stratum.

bas·set'tō, *n.* [It. *bassetto*, somewhat low, dim. of *basso*, low.] a small bass viol.

bāss hǫrn, a tuba.

Bas'si·ȧ, *n.* [named after Ferdinando *Bassi*, an Italian botanist of the eighteenth century.] a genus of valuable sapotaceous trees, native to Africa, India, and the Malay peninsula, including the gutta percha and mahwa.

bas'si·net, *n.* [OFr. *bacinet*, a basinet, dim. of *bacin*, a basin.]

1. a wicker basket with a covering or hood over one end, in which young children are placed, as in a cradle; also, a child's carriage with a wicker top or hood.

2. a basinet.

bȧs'sō, *n.*; *pl.* **bȧs'sōṣ;** It. **bäs'sī,** [It., from L. *bassus*, low.] a bass voice, voice part, or singer.

bȧs'sō bụf'fō, a bass singer of comic opera.

bas'sŏck, *n.* a thick mat; a hassock.

bȧs'sō çon·ti'nụ·ō, figured bass; thorough bass.

bas·sọọn', *n.* [Fr. *basson*; It. *bassone*, a bassoon; *basso*, low.]

1. a double-reed bass musical instrument of the wood-wind class, with a long, curved mouthpiece. Its compass includes three octaves. It serves for the bass in a section of oboes, clarinets, etc.

2. an organ stop with a deep tone like that of a bassoon.

BASSOON

bas·sọọn'ist, *n.* a performer on the bassoon.

bȧs'sō os·ti·nä'tō, [It. *basso*, bass, *ostinato*, obstinate; lit. obstinate bass.] fundamental bass; ground bass.

bȧs'sō prō·fun'dō, [It. *basso*, low, bass, and *profondo*, deep; L. *profundus*, deep.]

1. a very deep bass voice.

2. a man with such a voice.

bȧs'sō-rï·liẹ'vō (-rē-lyā'vō), *n.*; *pl.* **bȧs'sō-rï·liẹ'vōṣ,** bas-relief.

bas'sō·rin, *n.* a constituent part of a species of gum from Bassora, Iraq, as also of gum tragacanth, and some gum resins.

bȧss-rē·liēf', *n.* see *bas-relief*.

bāss stȧff, in music, a staff marked with the bass clef.

bāss vīŏl, the largest and deepest-toned musical instrument of the viol group, resembling a huge violin: called also *double bass, contrabass, string bass*.

bȧss'wood, *n.* 1. any of a number of related trees of the genus *Tilia*, with fragrant, yellowish flowers and light, soft, durable wood; linden.

2. its wood.

The word is also loosely used of the tulip tree or its wood.

bast, *n.* [ME. *bast*, from AS. *bæst*.]

1. phloem.

2. fiber obtained from phloem, used in making ropes, mats, etc.

Bȧs'täard, *n.* one of the Griquas, or mulattoes of South Africa, of Dutch and native ancestry.

bas'tärd, *n.* [ME. *bastard*; OFr. *bastard, bastart*, from Goth. *bansts*, a stable, barn; and *-ard*.]

1. a person born of parents not married to each other; a child begotten and born out of lawful wedlock; an illegitimate child. By the civil and canon laws, and by the statutes of many of the United States, a bastard becomes a legitimate child by the marriage of the parents at any future time. But by the laws of some of the states of the United States, as by those of England, a child, to be legitimate, must at least be born after the lawful marriage.

2. anything of inferior quality or varying from standard.

3. a counterfeit; sham.

4. a refuse brown sugar obtained from thin syrups.

5. a large mold for draining sugar.

6. a large, valuable food fish of Australasia: also called *trumpeter* or *bastard trumpeter*.

bas'tärd, *a.* 1. of illegitimate birth or origin; of uncertain origin.

2. spurious; not genuine; false; sham; inferior; adulterate; as, a *bastard* hope; *bastard* honors.

3. of unusual size; not conforming to standard measure; as, a *bastard* bolt.

bastard bar; in heraldry, the baton or bar of bastardy.

bastard file; a medium file, neither coarse not fine.

bastard title; not the full title of a book, but a short title on a preceding page; a half title.

bastard type; in printing, a typeface cast on a body larger or smaller than that which properly belongs to it.

bastard wing; in ornithology, a structure consisting of from three to five quill-like feathers placed on a small joint rising from the middle part of the wing, and corresponding to the thumb in some mammals.

bas'tärd, *v.t.*; bastarded, *pt., pp.*; bastarding, *ppr.* to bastardize. [Obs.]

bas'tärd·iṣm, *n.* the state of a bastard.

bas"tärd·i·zā'tion, *n.* 1. a bastardizing or being bastardized.

2. a corruption; misuse.

bas'tärd·īze, *v.t.*; bastardized, *pt., pp.*; bastardizing, *ppr.* 1. to make or prove to be a bastard; to declare, legally, illegitimate.

> The law is so indulgent as not to *bastardize* the child, if born, though not begotten, in lawful wedlock. —Blackstone.

2. to beget illegitimately. [Rare.]

3. to misuse; to corrupt; as, he *bastardized* the language.

bas'tärd·īze, *v.i.* to become inferior.

bas'tärd·ly, *adv.* like a bastard; of illegitimate or uncertain origin, counterfeit, etc.

bas'tär·dy, *n.* 1. the state of being a bastard, or being begotten and born out of lawful wedlock; illegitimacy.

2. the offense of begetting an illegitimate child.

3. a legal proceeding to determine the paternity of a bastard child and compel its father to support it.

bāste, *v.t.*; basted, *pt., pp.*; basting, *ppr.* [from OFr. *basser*, to moisten, from *bassiner*, to moisten, from *bassin*.] to moisten (meat) with melted butter, drippings, etc. while roasting.

bāste, *v.t.* [ON. *beysta*, to beat.]

1. to strike; beat; thrash.

2. to attack with words; abuse.

bāste, *v.t.* [ME. *basten*, from OFr. *bastir*, from O.H.G. *bestan*, to sew, from *bast*; AS. *bæst*, bast, the fibers of which were used for sewing.] to sew with long, loose stitches so as to keep the parts together until properly sewed.

bas·tīde', *n.* a small fort or a fortified house or tower. [Obs.]

bas·tīlle', bas·tīle', *n.* [ME. *bastile*; Fr. *bastille*; OFr. *bastir*, to build.]

1. a tower or elevated work used for the defense or in the siege of a fortified place. [Obs.]

2. [B–] an old castle in Paris, built in the fourteenth century and long used as a state prison: demolished by the populace July 14, 1789, the anniversary of that date being now observed as a national holiday.

3. a prison.

bas·ti·nāde', *n.* same as *bastinado*.

bas·ti·nā'dō, *n.*; *pl.* **bas·ti·nā'dōeṣ,** [Fr. *bastonnade*.]

1. a beating with a stick or cudgel; the blows given with a stick; specifically, an Oriental punishment consisting of beating an offender on the soles of his feet.

2. a rod, stick, or cudgel.

bas·ti·nā'dō, *v.t.*; bastinadoed, *pt., pp.*; bastinadoing, *ppr.* to inflict the bastinado on.

bāst'ing, *n.* 1. the act of sewing with loose, temporary stitches.

2. [*pl.*] loose, temporary stitches.

3. a thread used for basting.

bas'tion (-chun), *n.* [Fr. *bastion*; OFr. *bastir*, to build.]

BASTION

1. in fortification, a work of earth, brick, or stones, standing out from a fortified work to protect the wall. It usually consists of two flanks, and two faces. Each flank commands and defends the adjacent curtain, or that portion of the wall extending from one bastion to another. The two faces form an acute angle called the salient angle, and command the outworks and ground before the fortification. The distance between the two flanks is the gorge, or entrance into the bastion.

2. any strong defense or bulwark: often used figuratively.

bas'tioned (-chund), *a.* provided with a bastion or bastions.

bast'nā·sīte, *n.* a fluocarbonate of the cerium metals, named from Bastnas, Sweden.

bas'tō, *n.* [Sp.] the ace of clubs in the games of quadrille and omber.

bas'tŏn, *n.* [ME. *baston*; OFr. *baston*, a stick.]

BASTON

1. a staff: sometimes written *batoon*. [Obs.]

2. formerly, a royal court officer who bore a painted staff. [Obs.]

3. in heraldry, a staff borne sinister, as a badge of bastardy.

4. in architecture, a round molding at the base of a column: called also *torus*.

Bȧ·sū'tō, *n.* any of a Bantu people living in the region of Basutoland (Lesotho).

bat, *n.* [ME. *batte*; AS. *batt*, cudgel, from Celt.; influenced in some senses by OFr. *batre*.]
1. any stout club, stick, or cudgel.
2. a club used in striking the ball in baseball and cricket.
3. a tennis racket, ping-pong paddle, etc.
4. the process of batting.
5. a turn or chance at batting.
6. a batsman at cricket. [Brit.]
7. a chunk, wad, or lump, as of clay.
8. [*usually pl.*] cotton batting, especially of an inferior quality; batt.
9. a blow or hit. [Colloq.]
10. speed; fast pace. [Colloq.]
11. a drinking bout; spree. [Slang.]
12. in mining, shale or bituminous shale.
13. a piece of a brick with one whole end; hence, any part of a brick; a brickbat.
14. a wooden tool used in dressing and flattening sheet lead.
15. in hat making, a felted mass of fur or wool: also spelled *batt*.
at bat; having a turn at batting, as in baseball.
to go on a bat; to go on a protracted spree or drinking bout. [Slang.]

bat, *v.t.*; batted, *pt., pp.*; batting, *ppr.* to strike or hit with or as with a bat.

bat, *v.t.* batted, *pt., pp.*; batting, *ppr.* [var. of obs. *bate*, from OFr. *batre*, to batter.] to wink or flutter; as, to *bat* the eyes; the bird *bats* its wings.

bat, *v.i.* 1. to use a bat, as in games.
2. to take a turn at batting.

bat, *n.* [altered from ME. *bakke*, from ON.] one of the *Chiroptera*, an order of flying mammalia, divided into several distinct genera. The forefeet have the toes connected by membranes, expanded into elongated wings, by means of which the animals fly. The species are numerous.

GREATER HORSESHOE BAT

bāt'ȧ·ble, *a.* debatable. [Obs.]

bȧt'āiled, *a.* having embrasures like a battlement. [Obs.]

bä·tä'rȧ, *n.* [S. Am.] a species of bush shrike.

bȧ·tär·deau' (-dō'), *n.* [Fr. *battre*, to repel, and *eau*, water.] a cofferdam; a defensive wall built across a ditch, and having a sluice gate.

bȧ·tä'tȧ, *n.* the sweet potato.

Bȧ·tā'vi·ăn, *a.* [L. *Batavi*, the people who inhabited the isle by that name.] pertaining to ancient Batavia, an island in Holland, between the Rhine and the Waal; hence, pertaining to the Netherlands or the Dutch; also, pertaining to Batavia (now Jakarta), chief city of Java.

Bȧ·tā'vi·ăn, *n.* a native of Batavia, or of the Netherlands. [Rare.]

bat bōlt, a bolt barbed or jagged at its butt or tang to give it a firmer hold.

batch (bach), *n.* [ME. *bacche, batche*, from AS. *bacan*, to bake.]
1. the amount (of bread, etc.) produced at one baking.
2. the amount of material, as dough, needed for one operation.
3. the quantity of anything made in one operation or lot.
4. a number of things or persons taken as a group; lot; set.

bāte, *n.* strife; contention; debate. [Obs.]

bāte, *v.t.*; bated, *pt., pp.*; bating, *ppr.* [ME. *baten*; OFr. *batre*, to beat; L. *batuere*, to beat, strike.]
1. to reduce; diminish; to beat down; to lessen; to abate; as, to *bate* the laborer's wages.
2. to deduct in abatement; as, to *bate* the price.
3. to hold in.
4. to deprive (*of*). [Archaic.]
with bated breath; with the breath held in because of fear, excitement, etc.

bāte, *v.i.* to grow or become less; to be or become reduced.

Abate thy speed, and I will *bate* of mine.
—Dryden.

bāte, *n.* in tanning, an alkaline solution of chemicals or, formerly, of manure, for softening hides.

bāte, *v.t.* in tanning, to soak or steep in bate, as hides in the process of making leather.

bȧ·teau' (bȧ-tō'), *n.*; *pl.* **bȧ·teaux'** (-tōz'), [Fr. *bateau*; OFr. *batel*, boat.] a lightweight, flat-bottomed river boat used chiefly in Canada and Louisiana.

bāt'ed, *a.* restrained; checked; lowered: used especially in the phrase, *with bated breath*.

bāte'fụl, *a.* contentious; given to strife; exciting contention. [Obs.]

bāte'less, *a.* not to be abated. [Obs.]

bāte'ment, *n.* abatement; deduction; diminution.

bāte'ment līght, a window, or part of a window, with the lower edge cut to fit a staircase, an arch, etc.

bat'fish, *n.*; *pl.* **bat'fish** or **bat'fish·es,** 1. a fish, family *Ogcocephalidæ*, especially *Ogcocephalus vespertilio* of the Atlantic coast.
2. the flying gurnard, *Dactylopterus volitans* of the Atlantic.
3. a California sting ray *Myliobatis californicus*.

bat'fowl, *v.i.* to catch birds by batfowling.

bat'fowl″ẽr, *n.* one who practices batfowling.

bat'fowl″ing, *n.* a method of catching birds at night by blinding them with a light, and netting or hitting them.

bȧth, *n.*; *pl.* **bȧthṣ,** [AS. *bæth*, a bath.]
1. [*often pl.*] a resort where bathing is part of the medical treatment; spa.
2. a building or set of rooms for bathing.
3. a bathtub.
4. a bathroom.
5. the act of immersing or showering and washing the body or part of the body in water for the sake of cleanliness, health, and comfort; also, the act of exposing the body, as a medical or hygienic measure, to steam, vapor, hot air, etc.; as, to take a hot *bath*, a medicated *bath*.
6. exposure of the body to action of the sun; as, I sat beside my cottage door taking a sun *bath*.
7. in photography, the solution used in developing and fixing.
8. in metallurgy, molten metal in a furnace.
9. in chemistry, any material that acts as a medium for regulating the temperature of things put in or on it; also, the container for this.
10. water or other liquid prepared for bathing, or for dipping or soaking anything; as, your *bath* is ready.
11. a container for such liquid.
take a bath; to suffer a heavy financial loss. [Slang.]

bȧth, *v.t.* and *v.i.* to soak or steep in a bath.

bath, *n.* [Heb.] a measure of the ancient Hebrews, containing the tenth of a homer, if used for liquids, and less if for a dry measure.

Bȧth brick, [after *Bath*, England, where it was made.] a brick-shaped piece of earth containing carbonate of lime or of calcium, used for cleaning polished metal, etc.

Bȧth chȧir, a hooded wheelchair: first used at Bath, England.

bāthe, *v.t.*; bathed, *pt., pp.*; bathing, *ppr.* [ME. *bathien, bathen*; AS. *bathian*, to bathe.]
1. to wash by immersion, as in a bath.
2. to wash or moisten, for the purpose of making soft and supple, or for cleansing, as a wound.
3. to moisten or suffuse with a liquid.
4. to apply water or other liquid to, for healing or soothing; as, to *bathe* the hands with oil.
5. to lave; to wash; as, waters *bathing* the foot of a mountain.
6. to suffuse or envelop, as with a liquid; as, the moonlight *bathed* the plain.

bāthe, *v.i.* 1. to take a bath; to bathe oneself.
2. to go into or be in a body of water so as to swim, cool oneself, etc.
3. to soak oneself in some substance or influence, as sunlight.

bāthe, *n.* a bathing in a sea, a pool, etc.; a swim. [Brit.]

bāth'ẽr, *n.* one who bathes or swims.

bāth'ẽr, *v.i.* to bathe or rub in dust, as some birds do. [Brit. Dial.]

bȧ·thet'iç, *a.* of the nature of bathos.

bȧth'house, *n.* 1. a house or building equipped for bathing.
2. a building used by bathers for changing clothes.

bath'iç, *a.* [Gr. *bathys*, deep.] deep; pertaining to the depths of the sea.

bȧth'i·nette, *n.* a portable folding bathtub for babies, made of rubberized cloth, etc.: a trade-mark (*Bathinette*).

bāth'ing, *n.* the act of taking a bath, or washing oneself or another.
bathing beauty; a beautiful woman wearing a bathing suit, especially one who competes in a beauty contest. [Slang.]
bathing cap; a tight-fitting cap of rubber, etc. worn to keep the hair from getting wet in swimming.
bathing suit; a garment designed for swimming.

bȧth'mat, *n.* a mat used in or next to a bathtub, as to prevent slipping.

Bȧth met'ăl, [from *Bath*, England.] a variety of brass which is an alloy of zinc and copper, consisting of four and one-half ounces of the former to one pound of the latter.

bath'miṣm, *n.* [Gr. *bathmos*, a step or stair, from *bainein*, to go, to step.] the power of growth as one of the vital forces; growth force.

bath'mō·dont, *a.* [Gr. *bathmos*, step, and *odous*, tooth.] having the upper molars ranged obliquely.

Bȧth nōte, a kind of folio writing paper measuring, when opened, eight and one-half by fourteen inches.

bath'ō-, [Gr. *bathos*, depth.] a combining form meaning *depth*, as in *batho*meter.

bath'ō·lith, bath'ō·līte, *n.* [*batho-*, and *-lith* (or *-lite*)], a large, deep-seated igneous rock intrusion, usually granite, often forming the base of a mountain range, and uncovered only by erosion.

bȧ·thom'e·tẽr, *n.* [Gr. *bathos*, depth, and *metron*, a measure.] an instrument for taking depths or soundings, consisting of a specially constructed spring balance, instead of a sounding line.

bat'hợrse, *n.* a horse employed to carry an officer's baggage; a packhorse.

bā'thos, *n.* [Gr. *bathos*, depth.]
1. change from the exalted to the trite and commonplace, in writing or speech; an anticlimax.
2. false or overdone pathos.
3. hackneyed quality; triteness.

bȧth'rōbe, *n.* a long, loose-fitting garment with sleeves, used either as a dressing gown or as a robe before and after the bath.

bȧth'rợọm, *n.* 1. a room where baths are taken.
2. a toilet.
3. a dressing room for bathers.

Bath·shē'bȧ, *n.* [Heb. *Bathsheba'*, lit., daughter of Sheba, daughter of the oath.] in the Bible, the mother of Solomon by King David, whom she married after he had sent her first husband, Uriah, to death in battle. II Sam. xi.

Bȧth stōne, a creamy limestone found near Bath, very easily quarried and used in England for building since the twelfth century.

bȧth'tub, *n.* 1. originally, any tub used to take a bath in.
2. a bathroom fixture designed for this purpose.

bath'y-, a combining form from Greek *bathys*, deep, and signifying *deep, of the sea depths*, as in *bathy*sphere.

bȧ·thyb'iç, *a.* pertaining to, native to, or living in the deep waters.

bȧ·thyb'i·us, *n.* [*bathy-*, and Gr. *bios*, life.] a gelatinous substance found in deep-sea mud: once supposed by Huxley to be living protoplasm.

bath'y·lith, bath'y·līte, *n.* batholith, batholite.

bath·y·lith'iç, bath·y·lit'iç, *a.* pertaining to bathylith or bathylite.

bȧ·thym'e·tẽr, *n.* same as *bathometer*.

bath·y·met'riç, bath·y·met'riç·ăl, *a.* pertaining to bathymetry.

bȧ·thym'e·try, *n.* [*bathy-*, and Gr. *metron*, measure.] the science of measuring depths: the art of deep-sea sounding.

bath'y·sphēre, *n.* [Gr. *bathy-*, from *bathys*, deep, and *sphaira*, a ball.] a round, watertight chamber with windows, in which men can be lowered into the sea depths to observe and study the plants and animals there.

bȧ·tĭk', *n.* [Malay.]
1. a process for coloring fabrics, originating among Dutch East-Indian natives, in which the design is covered with melted wax and the uncovered portions dyed, the wax then being dissolved in boiling water.
2. cloth thus decorated.
3. a design thus made. Also spelled *battik*.

bȧ·tĭk', *a.* of or like batik. Also spelled *battik*.

bȧ·tĭk', *v.t.* to dye or design by means of batik. Also spelled *battik*.

bāt′ing, *prep.* a bating; taking away; deducting; excepting. [Archaic.]

Bā′tis, *n.* [Gr. *batis*, the prickly roach, a kind of plant.] a monotypic genus of saline plants containing a single species.

bȧ·tiste′, *n.* [Fr. *batiste*; OFr. *baptiste*, so called from its alleged first maker, *Baptiste* of Cambrai.] a kind of cambric, lawn, or fine linen: also applied to cotton cloth of fine texture, and sometimes to a thin, fine woolen cloth.

bat′lēr, bat′let, *n.* a small bat, or square piece of wood with a handle, for beating clothes in washing them.

bat′măn, *n.* [Turk.] a weight used in Smyrna and other places in the East, varying according to the locality.

bat′măn, *n.*; *pl.* **bat′men,** [Fr. *bât*, a pack saddle.] the servant of an officer in the British army.

Bȧ·toi′dē·ī, *n.pl.* [Gr. *batos*, a kind of ray, and *eidos*, form.] a suborder of the division *Selachii*, which includes flatfishes such as rays and skates.

ba·ton′ (*or* bat′un *or Fr.* bȧ-tọṅ′), *n.* [Fr.]

1. a staff serving as a symbol of office.

2. the staff used by the conductor of an orchestra, band, or choir, to direct the musicians or singers and mark the time.

3. in heraldry, a short, narrow, diagonal band on a coat of arms, running from the upper right corner to the lower left (as seen by the observer) to indicate bastardy in the family line.

bat print′ing, the process of printing on glazed ware with a gelatinous pad upon which the pattern has been stamped.

Bȧ·trā′chi·ȧ, *n.pl.* [Gr. *batrachos*, a frog.]

1. an order of amphibians without tails, including frogs and toads.

2. loosely, all amphibians.

bȧ·trā′chi·ăn, *a.* pertaining to animals of the order *Batrachia*.

bȧ·trā′chi·ăn, *n.* an animal of the order *Batrachia*.

bat′rȧ·chīte, *n.* [Gr. *batrachos*, a frog.] a stone resembling a frog in color.

bat′rȧ·choid, *a.* [Gr. *batrachos*, a frog, and *eidos*, form.] having the form of a frog or toad.

Bat″rȧ·chō·mȳ·om′ȧ·chy, *n.* [Gr. *batrachos*, frog; *mys*, mouse; and *machē*, battle.] an ancient Greek parody on the Iliad, of uncertain authorship and describing a battle between the frogs and mice.

bat·rȧ·choph′ȧ·gous, *a.* [Gr. *batrachos*, frog, and *phagein*, to eat.] feeding on frogs.

bats′măn, *n.*; *pl.* **bats′men,** in baseball and cricket, the batter.

batt, *n.* [*usually pl.*] cotton batting.

bat′tä, *n.* [Anglo-Ind., from Hind. *batta*, *bhata*, allowance for maintenance.] extra allowance, as that formerly given to English troops serving in India.

bat′tāil·ănt, *n.* a combatant. [Obs.]

bat′tāil·ous, *a.* warlike; having the form or appearance of an army arrayed for battle; marshaled, as for an attack. [Obs.]

bat·tāl′iȧ (-yȧ), *n.* [It. *battaglia*, battle.]

1. order of battle; troops arrayed in their proper brigades, regiments, battalions, etc., as for action. [Archaic.]

2. the main body of an army in array. [Obs.]

bat·tal′ion (-yun), *n.* [Fr. *bataillon*; It. *battaglione*, battalion.]

1. a large group of soldiers in battle array.

2. a large group somewhat like this; as, a *battalion* of strikers.

3. [*pl.*] military forces.

4. a tactical unit now usually made up of four infantry companies and a headquarters company, or four artillery batteries and a headquarters battery: three battalions form a regiment.

bat′tel (bat′tl), *n.* battle. [Obs.]

bat′tel, *v.i.* to stand indebted on the college books at Oxford University for provisions and drink from the buttery.

bat′tel·ēr, bat′tlēr, *n.* at Oxford University, one who battels.

bat′ten (bat′tn), *v.i.*; battened, *pt.*, *pp.*; battening, *ppr.* [Ice. *batha*, to improve.]

1. to grow fat; to thrive.

2. to be well fed or wealthy at another's expense.

3. to become fruitful, fertile, or rank.

bat′ten, *v.t.* to fatten up; to overfeed.

bat′ten, *n.* [Fr. *baton*, a stick.]

1. a sawed strip of wood, flooring, etc.

2. a strip of wood put over a seam between boards as a fastening or covering.

3. a short, flexible strip of wood inserted in a horizontal pocket at the outer edge of a jib-headed sail to prevent it from cupping.

4. a strip used to fasten canvas over a ship's hatchways.

batten door; a door of boards held in position by cleats of battens.

bat′ten, *v.t.* to furnish or fasten with battens (with *up* or *down*); as, to *batten down* the hatches of a ship during a storm.

bat′ten·ing, *n.* the operation of fixing battens to a wall for nailing laths upon.

bat′tēr, *v.t.*; battered, *pt.*, *pp.*; battering, *ppr.* [ME. *bateren*; from OFr. *batre*, from LL. *battere*, from L. *batuere*, to beat.]

1. to beat with successive blows; to beat repeatedly with violence; as, to *batter* a wall.

2. to break to bits by pounding.

3. to wear or impair, as by beating or by use; as, *battered* furniture.

4. in welding, to beat in order to widen, as a piece of metal.

bat′tēr, *n.* 1. in printing, a defect in a form of type or a plate, caused by bruising.

2. type thus damaged.

bat′tēr, *n.* [ME. *bature*; OFr. *bature*; prob. from *batre*.] a thin mixture of flour, milk, etc., used in making cakes, waffles, etc.

bat′tēr, *n.* a backward slope in the face of a wall.

batter rule; an instrument for determining the slope of a wall.

bat′tēr, *v.i.* in architecture, to slope gently backward.

bat′tēr, *n.* in baseball and cricket, the player whose turn it is to bat; a batsman.

bat′tēr·ēr, *n.* one who batters or beats.

bat′tēr·ing-ram, 1. in ancient times, a military machine used to beat down walls, gates, etc. It was generally a large beam, with a head of iron somewhat resembling the head of a ram.

BATTERING-RAM

2. anything used like this to force entrance.

3. a blacksmith's hammer, swinging horizontally, used for heavy work.

bat′tēr·ing trāin, a train of artillery for siege purposes.

bat′tēr·y, *n.* [Fr. *batterie*, battery, from *battre*, to beat; L. *batuere*, to beat.]

1. the act of battering; attack or assault, with the view of beating down.

2. in law, the beating or illegal touching of another's person either directly or with an object.

3. the instrument or agency employed in battering or attacking; as, a *battery* of guns.

4. in military affairs, (a) a body of artillery for field operations; (b) the armament, or part of the armament of a warship.

5. the men attached to a battery of artillery.

6. in fortification, a parapet thrown up to cover the gunners and the artillery.

7. in baseball, the pitcher and catcher.

8. in manufacturing or the arts, any series of similar devices arranged, connected, or used together; as, a *battery* of ore-crushers.

9. metal objects or utensils collectively.

10. a hunting boat showing little above the water.

11. in mining, (a) a working platform; (b) a brace.

12. in electricity, a cell or connected group of cells storing an electrical charge and capable of furnishing a current.

13. in music, the percussion instruments of an orchestra.

14. in optics, a series of lenses or prisms.

bunsen battery; an electrical battery of one or more cells in which the carbon of gas coke is used with zinc.

ANODE + CATHODE −
GLASS JAR
BATTERY SOLUTION
METAL PLATES

BATTERY (wet cell)

in battery; placed in position and ready for firing: said of a gun.

masked battery; a concealed artillery battery.

out of battery or *from battery*; withdrawn from action, as for loading: said of a gun.

storage battery; see under *storage*.

bat′tick, *n.*, *a.*, *v.t.* batik.

bat′ting, *n.* 1. the action of a batter, as in baseball.

2. cotton in sheets, prepared for use in making quilts, etc.

bat′ting av′ēr·āġe, 1. a number expressing the average effectiveness of a baseball player's batting, figured by dividing the number of hits by the number of times at bat.

2. the average level of competence or success reached by a person in any activity. [Colloq.]

bat′tle (-tl), *n.* [ME. *batel*, *batelle*, from OFr. *bataille*, battle, from LL. *battere*; L. *batuere*, to beat, to fight.]

1. a fight, especially a large-scale engagement, between armed forces on land, at sea, or in the air.

2. armed fighting; combat or war.

3. any fight or fighting; conflict; struggle.

4. a division of an army or the main body itself. [Obs.]

battle royal; (a) a battle in which more than two are engaged; a melée; free-for-all: the term is also applied to a fight of gamecocks, in which more than two are engaged; (b) a long, bitterly fought battle; (c) a heated dispute.

drawn battle; one in which neither party gains the victory.

pitched battle; one in which the arrangement of troops and the line of combat have been planned beforehand.

to give battle; to engage in battle.

to join battle; to meet in battle.

Syn.—fight, combat, engagement, conflict.

bat′tle, *v.t.* and *v.i.*; battled, *pt.*, *pp.*; battling, *ppr.* [ME. *batailen*, *bataillen*; OFr. *batailler*, to join battle; from L. *batuere*, to strike.] to join battle; to fight.

bat′tle, *v.t.* to build battlements on (a fort, etc.). [Archaic or Poetic.]

bat′tle ar·rāy′, 1. order or formation of troops, etc. for battle.

2. battle equipment.

bat′tle-ax, bat′tle-axe, 1. a heavy ax with a broad blade, used in ancient times as a weapon of war.

2. a woman who is harsh, domineering, etc. [Slang.]

bat′tle çruis′ēr, a large, fast warship less heavily armed than a battleship.

bat′tle çrȳ, 1. a shout used by troops in battle.

2. a slogan or motto for any kind of struggle, contest, etc.

bat′tled (-tld), *a.* 1. furnished or strengthened with battlements.

2. in heraldry, having the chevron, fesse, etc. borne in the form of the battlements of a castle.

bat′tle·dōre, bat′tle·dōor, *n.* [OE. *batyldoure*, a wooden bat used in washing clothes.]

1. a flat, wooden paddle used to hit a shuttlecock back and forth in the game of battledore and shuttlecock.

2. the game of battledore and shuttlecock.

3. a child's hornbook; so called from its shape. [Obs.]

bat′tle fȧ·tīgue′, combat fatigue.

bat′tle·fiēld, *n.* 1. the place where a battle takes place or took place; the site of a battle.

2. any area of conflict.

bat′tle frŏnt, the sector where actual combat is taking place between armed forces.

bat′tle·ground, *n.* a battlefield.

bat′tle·ment, *n.* [ME. *batelment*; OFr. *bastiller*, to fortify.] a low wall formed by a series of rising parts called cops or merlons, separated by openings for shooting called crenelles or embrasures. Battlements were originally built on top of castle walls, towers, or forts, but were afterward used freely in ecclesiastical and civil buildings by way of ornament, on parapets, cornices, tabernacle work, etc.

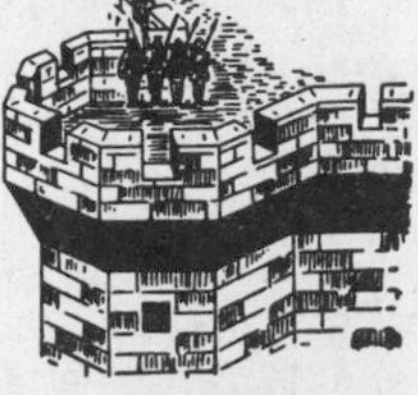

BATTLEMENT

bat′tle·ment·ed, *a.* having battlements.

bat′tle·plāne, *n.* a warplane.

bat'tle rānge, the effective firing distance for small arms.

bat'tle·ship, *n.* a warship of the largest class carrying the heaviest armor and guns: i usually displaces over 25,000 tons.

bat'tle stā'tions, the places to which soldiers, sailors, warships, etc. are assigned for a battle or an emergency.

bat'tle·wag"ŏn, *n.* a battleship. [Slang.]

bat·tol'ō·ġy, *n.* [Gr. *battologein,* to stammer, from *battos,* a stammerer, and *legein,* to speak.] a needless repetition of words in speaking or writing.

bat'tŏn, *n.* a baton or a batten. [Obs.]

bat'tūe, *n.* [Fr., pp. f. of *battre,* to beat.]
1. a hunt conducted by driving game from cover to a place near waiting hunters.
2. a hunt of this kind.
3. the game thus killed.
4. any kind of mass slaughter of the weak or unresisting.

bat·tūre', *n.* [Fr., from *battre,* to beat.] an elevated portion of a river or sea bottom.

bat·tū'tä, *n.* [It., from *battere,* to beat.] in music, the measuring of time by beating; a measure; a bar.

bat'ty, *a.* 1. insane; crazy. [Slang.]
2. odd; eccentric. [Slang.]

bat'ūle, *n.* a springboard used by acrobats in leaping and vaulting.

batz, *n.*; *pl.* **bat'zen,** [G., a coin having the image of a bear, from *bätz,* a bear.] a small copper coin with a mixture of silver, formerly current in some parts of Germany and Switzerland.

bau·bee', *n.* same as *bawbee.*

bau'ble, *n.* [ME. *bable*; OFr. *babel, baubel,* a toy.]
1. a short stick with a fool's head, frequently ornamented with asses' ears: carried by the jesters attached to courts and great houses. [Archaic.]

The kynges foole
Sate by the fire upon a stoole,
As he that with his *bauble* plaide.
—Gower.

2. a trifling piece of finery; that which is gay or showy; a gewgaw, a trifle.
3. a baby's toy.

BAUBLE (sense 1)

bau'bling, *a.* bawbling. [Obs.]

bauch, *a.* poor; weak; without strength; distasteful: also spelled *baugh.* [Scot. and Prov. Eng.]

Bau'cis, *n.* in Greek legend, an old woman, the devoted wife of Philemon: although poor, the old couple showed such genuine hospitality to Zeus and Hermes disguised as mortals that the grateful gods made Baucis a priestess.

baud, *n.* [after J. M. E. *Baudot,* 19th-century French inventor.]
1. a unit of signaling speed in telegraphic code.
2. the number of bits per second that can be transmitted in a given computer system.

bau'dē·kin, baud'kin, *n.* [ME. *baudkin*; OFr. *baudekin*; It. *baldacchino.*] baldachin (kind of brocade).

bau'drŏns, *n.* a cat: an epithet used without an article. [Scot.]

Bau'haus (bow'hous), *n.* [G., from *bauen,* to build, and *haus,* a house.] the architectural school of Walter Gropius, founded in Germany, 1919: it became known for its adaptation of science and technology to art, and for experimental use of metal, glass, etc. in buildings.

Bau·hin'i·à, *n.* [from Jean and Gaspard *Bauhin,* noted Swiss botanists.] a genus of leguminous tropical plants.

baulk, *n.* and *v.* same as *balk.*

Bau·mé' (bō-mā'), *a.* [after Antoine *Baumé* (1728–1805), Fr. chemist.] designating or of a scale used in hydrometers.

Baumes laws (bowmz), a series of amendments to the criminal code of New York, drafted by a joint committee of the legislature headed by State Senator Caleb H. Baumes, and put into effect July 1, 1926: their object was to check the crime wave by prompt prosecution and stricter punishment. Under these laws, persons convicted of a felony for the fourth time are automatically sentenced to life imprisonment, and are not subject to pardon or executive clemency.

baum mär'ten (bowm), [from G. *baummarder*; *baum,* tree, and *marder,* marten.] the brown fur of the European marten.

bau'sŏn, *n.* a badger. [Archaic.]

baux'īte, *n.* [Fr., from *Baux* or *Beaux,* near Arles.] a hydrated oxide of aluminum, the principal ore from which aluminum is obtained.

Bà·vā'ri·ăn, *a.* of or pertaining to Bavaria.

Bà·vā'ri·ăn, *n.* 1. a native or inhabitant of Bavaria.
2. the High German dialect of the Bavarians.

Bà·vā'ri·ăn çrēam, a gelatin dessert made with whipped cream, eggs, and fruit flavoring.

bā'vi·ăn, *n.* [OE. *babewin,* baboon.] a baboon.

bav'in, *n.* limestone containing impurities. [Prov. Eng.]

baw·bee', *n.* a halfpenny or any small coin. [Scot.]

baw'ble, *n.* same as *bauble.*

bawb'ling, *a.* trifling; contemptible. [Obs.]

baw'çock, *n.* a fine fellow. [Archaic.]

bawd, *n.* [ME. *baude,* a lewd person; OFr. *baud,* from O.H.G. *bald,* bold.]
1. a procuress; a person who keeps a house of prostitution.
2. a prostitute. [Rare.]

bawd, *v.i.* 1. to procure; to provide women for prostitution. [Archaic.]
2. to befoul or dirty. [Obs.]

bawd'i·ly, *adv.* obscenely; lewdly.

bawd'i·ness, *n.* obscenity; lewdness.

bawd'rick, *n.* a baldric. [Obs.]

bawd'ry, *n.* 1. the acts or practice of a procurer or bawd. [Archaic.]
2. obscenity; indecent language.
3. illicit intercourse; fornication. [Obs.]

bawd'y, *a.*; *comp.* bawdier; *superl.* bawdiest, characteristic of a bawd; indecent; obscene.

bawd'y·house, *n.* a house of prostitution.

bawl, *v.t.* and *v.i.*; bawled, *pt., pp.*; bawling, *ppr.* [ME. *baul*; Ice. *baula,* to low, as a cow.]
1. to cry out with a loud sound; to howl.
2. to cry noisily, as a child from pain or vexation. [Colloq.]

Syn.—shout, vociferate, roar, bellow.

bawl, *n.* a loud, prolonged cry; an outcry.

bawl'ēr, *n.* one who bawls.

bawn, *n.* an enclosure with mud or stone walls for keeping cattle; a fortification. [Obs.]

baw'rel, *n.* a kind of hawk. [Obs.]

baw'sin, baw'sŏn, *n.* a bauson. [Obs.]

bax'tēr, *n.* [ME. *baxter, bakestre*; AS. *bæcestre,* a baker.] a baker; formerly, a female baker. [Now Dial.]

Bax·tē'ri·ăn, *a.* pertaining to Richard Baxter, an English minister and writer; as, the *Baxterian* doctrines.

bāy, *a.* [Fr. *bai*; L. *badius,* bay.] reddish-brown; chestnut: applied to horses.

bāy, *n.* 1. a horse (or other animal) of reddish-brown color.
2. reddish brown.

bāy, *n.* [Fr. *baie*; LL. *baia,* bay.]
1. a part of a sea or lake indenting the shore line: the word is often applied to very large tracts of water around which the land forms a curve, as Hudson's *Bay.*
2. a small body of water formed by a dam for the purpose of driving mill wheels.
3. any level land area making an indentation, as into a woods, range of hills, etc.

bāy, *n.* [ME. *bai*; OFr. *baée* (Fr. *baie*), from *baer, bayer,* to gape, yawn; LL. *badare,* to gape.]
1. an opening or alcove marked off by pillars, columns, etc.
2. a part of a building projecting from the main part; wing.
3. a compartment, as in a barn, for storing hay or grain.
4. a place for the sick and wounded on a ship: usually *sick bay.*
5. a recess in the wall line of a building, as for a window.
6. any opening in a wall.

bāy, *v.t.* to dam up, as water.

bāy, *n.* [OFr. *baie, baye,* a berry; L. *baca,* a berry.]
1. the laurel tree, *Laurus nobilis.*
2. [*pl.*] an honorary garland or crown, anciently bestowed as a prize for victory or excellence, made or consisting of bay leaves.

Beneath his reign shall Eusden wear the *bays.* —Pope.

3. [*pl.*] honor; fame.
4. any of various trees or shrubs like the laurel.

bāy, *v.i.*; bayed, *pt., pp.*; baying, *ppr.* [ME. *bayen*; OFr. *bayer,* to bark.] to bark excitedly and continually, as a dog at his game; especially, to bark in long, deep tones.

bāy, *v.t.* 1. to bark at.
2. to bring to bay; as, to *bay* the wolf.
3. to chase with yelps and barks.

'Tis sweet to hear the watchdog's honest bark
Bay deep-mouthed welcome as we draw near home. Byron.

bāy, *n.* [ME. *bay, abay*; OFr. *abai*; Fr. *aboi,* a barking.]
1. a long, deep cry or bark; a baying.
2. the turning of a hunted animal when it is forced to fight its foe; as, the stag stood at *bay.*
3. the state of one who is forced to fight an opponent or face a problem when escape has been cut off.

bāy, *v.t.* to bathe. [Obs.]

bä'yä, *n.* [native name.] the East Indian weaverbird, *Ploceus philippinus.*

bä·yà·dēre', bä·yà·deer, *n.* [Fr. *bayadère*; Port. *bailadeira,* a dancer.]
1. a female dancer in India, especially one in a temple.
2. a fabric or design with crosswise stripes.

bä·yà·derē', *a.* striped crosswise.

bä·yä'mō, *n.* [Cuban.] a storm peculiar to the vicinity of Bayamo, on the south coast of Cuba, consisting of violent gusts of wind accompanied by thunder, lightning, and rain.

bāy ant'lēr, the second prong of a stag's antler.

bāy'ărd, *n.* [OFr. *bayard, baiard,* a bay horse.]
1. a bay horse.
2. [B–] in medieval romances, a magic horse given to Rinaldo by Charlemagne.
3. any horse: humorous term.

bāy'ărd·ly, *a.* blind; stupid. [Obs.]

bāy'ber"ry, *n.* 1. the fruit of the bay tree or *Laurus nobilis.*
2. the fruit of *Myrica cerifera* (wax myrtle), or the plant itself.
3. a tropical tree yielding an oil used in bay rum.

bāy'ber·ry tal'lōw, a waxy substance obtained from the bayberry, or wax myrtle: called also *myrtle wax.*

bāy'bōlt, *n.* a bolt having a sharp-pointed, barbed shank.

bāyed (bād), *a.* having bays, as a building.

Bā·yeux' Tap'es·try (-yoo', Fr. bà-yü'), an eleventh-century tapestry, over 200 feet long and 1½ feet wide, in the museum of Bayeux, northern France, picturing incidents that led to the Norman Conquest: the work is traditionally ascribed to the wife of William the Conqueror.

bāy gall, in the southern states, a kind of swamp overspread with soft earth and fibrous matter.

bāy lēaf, the aromatic leaf of the bay tree, dried and used as a seasoning.

bāy'măn, *n.*; *pl.* **bāy'men,** in the U. S. Navy, a nurse in the sick bay; specifically, a hospital apprentice or pharmacist's mate.

bāy'ō·net, *n.* [Fr. *bayonnette*; so called because the first bayonets were made at *Bayonne.*]
1. a detachable daggerlike blade put on the muzzle end of a rifle, for hand-to-hand fighting.
2. a part like a bayonet in shape or function.
3. a pin which plays in and out of holes made to receive it, and which thus serves to engage or disengage parts of the machinery.

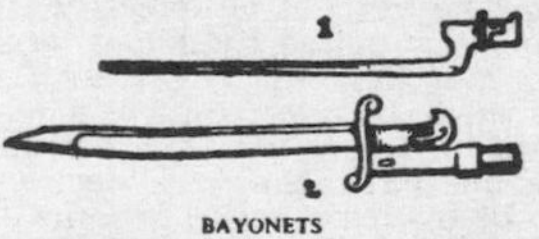

BAYONETS
1. common bayonet 2. sword bayonet

bāy'ō·net, *v.t.*; bayoneted, *pt., pp.*; bayoneting, *ppr.* 1. to stab, prod, or kill with a bayonet.
2. to compel or drive by the bayonet.

bāy'ō·net, *v.i.* to use a bayonet.

bāy'ō·net çlutch (kluch), in machinery, a form of clutch having two prongs, *a a,* which, in gear, act on the ends or lugs of a friction strap *b,* fitted on a side boss of the wheel to be driven, and which is loose on the same shaft. The clutch is attached to the shaft by a feather key, and when drawn back or out of gear with the strap the wheel remains at rest, and the clutch continues to revolve with the shaft. When it is required to set the machinery again in motion, the clutch is thrown forward by the fork *c,* and its prongs, engaging with the strap, gradually put the wheel in motion.

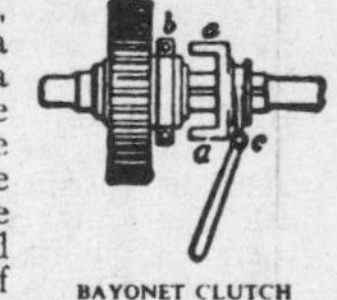

BAYONET CLUTCH

bāy'ou (bȳ'ö), *n.* [corruption of Fr. *boyau*, a gut, a long, narrow passage.] in some parts of the southern United States, a marshy inlet or outlet of a lake, river, etc.; also, a backwater.

bāy rum, a liquid formerly obtained by distilling the leaves of the West Indian bayberry tree and now made by combining certain oils, water, and alcohol: used as a cosmetic and in medicine.

bāy salt, a coarse-grained salt obtained by evaporation of sea water.

bāy tree, the bay, a species of laurel; the *Laurus nobilis.*

bāy win'dōw, 1. a window or series of windows usually rising from the ground and projecting from the wall, forming an alcove or recess within.

2. a large, protruding belly. [Slang.]

bāy wood, a kind of mahogany, particularly that from Campeche Bay and Honduras.

bāy yärn, woolen yarn. [Obs.]

bȧ·zäar', bȧ·zär', *n.* [Per. *bazar*, a market.]

1. in the Orient, an exchange, market place, or street of shops.

2. a shop or department fitted with counters or stands for the sale of various kinds of goods.

3. a sale, lasting usually for a few days, at which all manner of articles are sold for the benefit of some hospital, church, etc.

bȧ·zoo', *n.* 1. a kazoo.

2. (a) the mouth; (b) loud talk. [Slang.]

bȧ·zook'ȧ, *n.* [extension of *bazoo*: name applied by Bob Burns (189?–1956), U.S. comedian, to a comic horn consisting of two gas pipes and a whiskey funnel.] a weapon of metal tubing, for aiming and launching electrically fired, armor-piercing rockets.

B bat'tēr·y, an electric battery used in the plate circuit and the screen-grid circuit of certain radio tubes: it is usually made up of a number of dry cells in series.

BCG (vaç'cine), [bacillus *C*almette-*G*uérin, after A.L.C. *Calmette* (1863–1933) and A.F.M. *Guérin* (1816–95), Fr. physicians who developed it.] a vaccine prepared from an attenuated strain of the tubercle bacillus and used for immunization against tuberculosis.

bdel'li·um (del'), *n.* [L., from Gr. *bdellion.*] a fragrant, bitter-tasting gum resin from the East Indies, Arabia, etc. It is used as incense, in perfumes, and in medicines.

bdel'loid (del'), *a.* [Gr. *bdella*, a leech, and *eidos*, form.] pertaining to leeches.

bdel'loid (del'), *n.* any leech.

Bdel·loi'dē·ȧ (del-), *n.pl.* the order of *Annulata* to which the leeches belong.

bdel·lom'e·tēr (del-), *n.* [Gr. *bdella*, a leech, from *bdellein*, to suck, and *metron*, measure.] in medicine, an instrument used to take the place of a leech, consisting of a cupping glass, a scarificator, and an exhausting syringe.

Bdel·lō·mor'phȧ (del-), *n.pl.* [L., from Gr. *bdella*, leech, and *morphē*, form.] an order of *Nemertina*, to which the sucking worms found in clams belong.

bē, *v.i.*; was, were, *pt.*; been, *pp.*; being, *ppr.* [AS. *beon*, to be, *beom*, I am; O.H.G. *bim*; G. *bin*. The verb *be* is defective, its missing parts being supplied by *am, is, are, was,* and *were*, and archaically by *art, wast,* and *wert.*]

1. to exist; to live; to have a real state or existence for a longer or shorter time.

To *be*, contents his natural desire.—Pope.

2. to be made to be; to become.

3. to remain; to continue; as, let the garment *be* as it was made.

4. to be present in a place; as, where *was* I at the time? When will you *be* at my house?

5. to happen or occur; as, when will the wedding *be?*

6. to come to; to belong; as, peace *be* with you.

As a copula, *be* links its subject to a predicate nominative, adjective, or pronoun so as to express attribution or identity, and, by extension, value, cause, signification, etc.; e.g., he *is* an actor, she *is* pretty, the hat *is* five dollars, let x *be* y. As an auxiliary, *be* is used in forming the tenses of other verbs, and particularly in giving to them the passive form; as, he has *been* disturbed. It forms, with the infinitive, a particular future tense, which often expresses duty, necessity, or purpose; as, government *is to be* supported; we *are to pay* our just debts.

Be is conjugated, in the present indicative: (I) *am*, (he, she, it) *is*, (we, you, they) *are*; in the past indicative: (I, he, she, it) *was*, (we, you, they) *were*. Archaic forms are (thou) *art, wert, wast.* The present subjunctive is *be*, the past subjunctive *were.*

to be off; to go away.

bē-, [AS. *bi-, be-* (G. *be-*; Goth. *bi-*); weakened from AS. prep. *be, bi*, by, about.] a prefix of various uses and meanings:

1. prefixed to verbs: (a) with the general meaning of *around*, as in *be*sprinkle, *be*set; (b) as an intensifier, with the general meanings of *completely, thoroughly, excessively*, as in *be*deck, *be*smear; (c) as a deprivative, with the general meaning of *away*, as in *be*reave, *be*take; (d) as a transitive prefix, with the general meaning of *about*, as in *be*think, *be*moan.

2. prefixed to nouns (sometimes adjectives) to form transitive verbs: (a) with the general sense of *make*, as in *be*sot, *be*pretty, *be*dirty; (b) with the general senses of *furnish with, cover with, affect by*, as in *be*friend, *be*cloud.

3. prefixed to past participles in *-ed* used as adjectives, with the general senses of *covered with, furnished with, furnished with to excess*, as in *be*medaled, *be*whiskered.

Be, in chemistry, beryllium.

bēach, *n.* [perhaps from Ice. *bakki*, a bank, shore, with *k* softened to *ch*, as in *kirk*, church.] the pebbly or sandy shore of the sea, or of a lake, which is washed by the tide or waves; the strand.

Syn.—shore, coast, seacoast, seashore.

bēach, *v.t.* and *v.i.*; beached, *pt., pp.*; beaching, *ppr.* to run or haul (a boat) onto the beach.

bēach'-cōmb"ẽr (-kōm"ẽr), *n.* 1. a long wave that rolls up on a beach; a comber.

2. a man who loafs about wharves and beaches in seaports: the word is especially applied to vagabonds living on Pacific islands.

bēached, *a.* having a beach; also, driven onto a beach; stranded; as, the ship is *beached.*

bēach flēa, in zoology, a small crustacean infesting seashores and hopping like a flea.

bēach'head, *n.* a position on a beach secured by an invading force and used to land troops for further operations inland against the enemy.

bēach-lä-mär', *n.* bêche-de-mer (mixed language).

bēach um·brel'lȧ, a large umbrella used as a sunshade on beaches, in gardens, etc.

bēach wag'ŏn, a station wagon.

bēach'y, *a.* covered with pebbles.

bēa'çŏn, *n.* [AS. *beácen, bēcen, bēcn*, a signal.]

1. a signal fire.

2. any light for warning or guiding.

3. a lighthouse.

4. a hill, station, or tower from which signals are given.

5. something serving as a signal, summons, etc.

6. a guiding signal given by radio to airplanes.

bēa'çŏn, *v.t.*; beaconed, *pt., pp.*; beaconing, *ppr.* to furnish, mark, light up, guide, etc. with a beacon.

bēa'çŏn, *v.i.* 1. to shine brightly, as a beacon.

2. to serve as a summons or guide.

bēa'çŏn·āġe, *n.* money paid for the maintenance of a beacon.

bēa'çŏn·less, *a.* having no beacon.

bēad, *n.* [ME. *bede*, a prayer; AS. *bedu*, from *biddan*, to pray.]

1. a small, usually round piece of glass, wood, metal, etc. pierced for stringing.

2. [*pl.*] a string of beads for counting off prayers; rosary.

3. [*pl.*] a string of beads; necklace.

4. any small, round object, as the sight at the muzzle end of a gun barrel.

5. a drop or bubble.

6. foam or head on beer, etc.

7. a small quantity of metal, as gold or silver, obtained by refining.

8. in architecture, (a) a narrow, half-round molding; (b) a molding composed of small rounded ornaments, like a string of beads.

9. in chemistry, a beadlike mass usually formed inside the loop of a platinum wire by the action of a flux, such as borax, upon the oxide or salt of certain metals: used in identifying certain metals in their compounds since the color of the bead depends upon the metal involved.

to count (or *tell* or *say*) *one's beads*; to say prayers with a rosary.

to draw a bead on; to take careful aim at.

to put a bead on; to pour (liquor) in such manner that the top is covered with beads.

bēad, *v.t.*; beaded, *pt., pp.*; beading, *ppr.* 1. to ornament or string with beads.

2. to string like beads.

bēad, *v.i.* to form beads, as champagne.

bēad'ed, *a.* 1. decorated with beads.

2. having a bead or beads.

3. formed into or like beads.

bēad'house, bēde'house, *n.* in England, formerly, a refuge for the sick and poor, where inmates were expected to pray daily for their benefactors.

bēad'ing, *n.* 1. beadwork or molding in imitation of beadwork.

2. a narrow, half-round molding.

3. a narrow trimming, as on a half-round molding.

4. a beadlike openwork.

5. bubbles or froth on beer, wine, etc.

bēa'dle, *n.* [ME. *bedel, bidel, budel*; confused with AS. *bydel*, a messenger, from *beodan*, to bid; OFr. *bedel.*]

1. a messenger or crier of a court; a servitor; one who cites persons to appear and answer: called also an *apparitor* or *summoner.*

2. in England, an officer in a university whose duty is to walk with a mace at the head of public processions; a bedel.

3. formerly, in the Church of England, a parish officer with various subordinate duties, as waiting on the clergyman, keeping order in church, attending meetings of vestry or session, etc.

4. a similar minor official, as in a synagogue.

bēa'dle·dŏm, *n.* beadles as a class, and their characteristics; hence, petty and officious stupidity.

bēa'dle·ry, *n.* the jurisdiction of a beadle.

bēa'dle·ship, *n.* the office of a beadle.

bēad'prọof, *a.* designating or of alcoholic liquors which, after being shaken, form a crown of bubbles that will stand for some time.

bēad'rōll, *n.* 1. in the Roman Catholic Church, a list or catalogue of persons for the repose of whose souls a certain number of prayers is to be said or counted off on the beads of a chaplet or rosary; a roll of prayers or hymns. [Archaic.]

2. any list or catalogue.

The *beadroll* of her vicious tricks. —Prior.

bēad'-rụ·by, *n.*; *pl.* **bēad'-rụ·bieṣ,** any of a group of small North American plants with white flowers and red berries shaped like beads.

bēadṣ'măn, *n.*; *pl.* **bēadṣ'men,** 1. a man employed in praying for another.

2. a resident of an almshouse in England.

3. a licensed beggar in Scotland.

Also spelled *bedesman.*

bēad'snāke, *n.* a small venomous snake of North America, marked with yellow, black, and red bands.

bēadṣ'wom"ăn (-woom"ăn), *n.*; *pl.* **bēadṣ'wom"en** (-wim"en), a woman, especially one in a poorhouse, who prays for a benefactor: also spelled *bedeswoman.*

bēad tree, the *Melia Azedarach*, a native tree of the East Indies, growing about twenty feet high. Its nuts are used in Spain and Portugal for the beads of rosaries.

bēad'wŏrk, *n.* ornamental work with beads; also, beaded molding; beading.

bēad'y, *a.* 1. resembling beads; small, round, and glittering like a bead; as, *beady* eyes.

2. decorated with beads.

3. full of or covered with drops or bubbles; as, *beady* wine.

bēa'gle, *n.* [OE. *begele*, small dog.]

1. a small hound, or hunting dog, with a smooth coat, short legs, and drooping ears.

2. figuratively, a detective or constable.

BEAGLE
(13–15 in. high at shoulder)

bēa'gling, *n.* the sport of hunting with beagles.

bēak, *n.* [ME. *beeke, beke, bek*; OFr. *bec*; L. *beccus*, a beak.]

1. the bill or nib of a bird, consisting of a horny substance, either straight or curving,

and usually ending in a point: the form varies much, according to the food and habits of the bird.

2. the prolongation of the mouth or mandibles of some fishes, reptiles, and insects, in form analogous to the beak of a bird.

3. a pointed piece of wood fortified with metal, fastened to the prow of ancient galleys and intended to pierce the vessels of an enemy.

4. in farriery, a little clip at the toe of a horseshoe, about an inch long, turned up and fastened in upon the forepart of the hoof; a toe clip.

5. anything ending in a point, like a beak.

6. in botany, a process, like the beak of a bird, terminating the fruit and other parts in certain plants.

7. in architecture, a slight, continuous projection ending in a narrow fillet; that portion of a drip which casts off the water.

8. the lip or spout of a vessel, like a pitcher, through which the contents are poured.

9. a magistrate, judge, or policeman. [Brit. Slang.]

10. the horn of an anvil.

11. the nose, especially if large and hooked. [Slang.]

beak, *v.t.* to take hold of or strike with the beak.

bēaked (bēkt), *a.* 1. having a beak or beaklike process.

2. beaklike; curved, hooked, etc.

bēak'ēr, *n.* [ME. *biker*; Ice. *bikarr*, a cup, from L. *bicarium*, a wine cup; Gr. *bikos*, a wine jar.]

1. a large drinking cup with a wide mouth, sometimes supported on a standard; a goblet.

2. an open-mouthed, jarlike glass vessel having a lip or spout for pouring: used by chemists and druggists.

bēak'head (-hed), *n.* 1. in architecture, an ornament resembling the head and beak of a bird, or, as used over a Romanesque doorway, a grotesque human head terminating in a beak.

2. in marine architecture, a platform in the forepart of a ship.

bēak'ī″ron (-ī″ūrn), *n.* a bickern; an anvil ending in a point; also, the horn of an anvil.

bēal, *n.* [ME. *beele, bele, bile, bule*, a boil.] a pimple; a small inflammatory tumor; a pustule. [Now only Dial.]

bēal, *v.i.*; bealed, *pt., pp.*; bealing, *ppr.* to gather matter; to swell and come to a head, as a pimple. [Now only Dial.]

bēal, biēl, *n.* [Scot., from Gael. *bealach*, a mountain pass.] the mouth of a narrow pass or valley between hills. [Scot.]

bē'-ąll, *n.* the whole; all that will ever be.

bēam, *n.* [AS. *beam*, a tree, beam, ray of light; O.H.G. *baum*; Goth. *bagms*; Gr. *phyma*, a growth; Sans. root *bhū*, to grow.]

1. any one of the principal pieces of timber, metal, etc. in a building, that lie across the walls, and serve to support the principal rafters.

2. any large piece of timber, long in proportion to its thickness, and finished for use.

3. the part of a balance from the ends of which the scales are suspended; also, the balance itself.

4. (a) any of the heavy, horizontal crosspieces of a ship; (b) a ship's breadth at its widest; (c) the side of a ship or the direction out sidewise from a ship.

5. in zoology, (a) the main stem bearing the antlers or branches on a stag's head; (b) a long, stiff feather in the wing of a hawk, etc.

6. the pole of a carriage. [Obs.]

7. a wooden cylinder forming that portion of a weaver's loom on which the warp is wound before weaving; also, the cylinder on which the cloth is wound during weaving.

8. the straight part or shank of an anchor.

9. any one of the main cross timbers or pieces of iron or steel which span the sides of a ship horizontally and support the decks.

10. the main piece of a plow, to which are attached the handles and colter; a plow beam.

11. the oscillating lever of a steam engine, reciprocating upon a center and forming the connection between the piston rod and the crankshaft: called also *working beam* or *walking beam.*

12. a ray or aggregation of parallel rays of light; a slender shaft of light.

13. figuratively, anything analogous to a ray of light; as, a *beam* of hope; *beams* of majesty.

14. a radiant look, smile, etc.

15. in radio, (a) a signal sent continuously in one direction from a landing field, harbor, etc. as a guide for incoming aircraft or ships; (b) the angle at which a microphone receives or a loud-speaker transmits most effectively; (c) the maximum effective range of a microphone or loud-speaker.

on the beam; (a) in a line with the beams, or at right angles with the keel of the ship; (b) accurately following a radio directional signal; hence, (c) [Slang.] on a correct or direct course; (d) [Slang.] doing well; working well; alert, keen, etc.

on her beam-ends; inclined so far on one side that the beams almost stand on end: said of a ship.

bēam, *v.t.*; beamed, *pt., pp.*; beaming, *ppr.*

1. to give out (shafts of light); radiate.

2. to guide or communicate with (aircraft, etc.) by a beam.

3. to direct or aim (a radio signal, program, etc.).

bēam, *v.i.* 1. to emit rays of light, or beams; to shine.

2. to smile warmly.

bēam'bīrd, *n.* a small European bird, *Muscicapa grisola*, so called because it often builds its nest on the projecting end of a beam or in a building: also called *spotted fly-catcher.*

bēam çal'i·pēr, same as *caliper square.*

bēam çŏm'păss, an instrument consisting of a beam having sliding sockets that carry steel or pencil points: used for describing large circles and laying off distances.

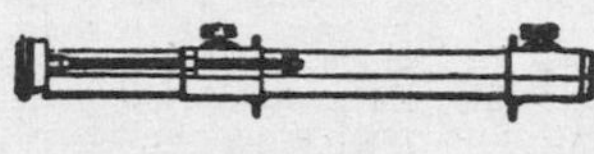

BEAM COMPASS

bēamed, *a.* [pp. of *beam.*] 1. having beams, especially exposed and sometimes false ones; as, a *beamed* ceiling.

2. in radio, directed toward a certain place; as, a *beamed* program.

bēam'-endṣ', *n.pl.* the ends of a ship's beams.

on the beam-ends (or *beam's ends*); (a) tipping so far to the side as to be in danger of overturning; (b) at the end of one's resources, money, strength, etc.

bēam en'ġine, a steam engine having a working beam to transmit power.

bēam feath'ēr (feth'ēr), one of the long feathers in the wing of a hawk.

bēam fill'ing, the filling in of mason work between beams or joists, its height being equal to the depth of the timbers filled in.

bēam'fụl, *a.* having many rays of light; radiant.

bēam'i·ly, *adv.* in a radiant manner.

bēam'i·ness, *n.* the state of being radiant.

bēam'ing, *a.* 1. emitting rays of light or beams; shining.

2. smiling warmly; happy.

bēam'ing, *n.* 1. radiation; emission or darting of light in rays.

2. the use of a beam, as in weaving.

bēam'ing·ly, *adv.* radiantly.

bẹam'ish, *a.* [*beam*, and *-ish*; used by Lewis Carroll in *Through the Looking Glass*, apparently with the sense of happy, fine, etc.] beaming; radiant.

bēam'less, *a.* emitting no rays of light.

bēam'let, *n.* a thin shaft of light.

bēam tree, a tree of the pear kind, *Pyrus Aria*, the wood of which is hard, compact, and tough, and used in making axletrees, hubs of wheels, and cogs of machinery: called also *whitebeam tree.*

bēam'y, *a.*; *comp.* beamier; *superl.* beamiest,

1. emitting rays of light; radiant; shining.

2. resembling a beam in size and weight; broad; massive.

3. having horns, or antlers.

4. in nautical usage, having a broad beam; of more than adequate width as compared with over-all length.

bēan, *n.* [ME. *bene*; AS. *bean*, bean.]

1. the edible, smooth, kidney-shaped seed of any one of various leguminous plants or herbs, the most important of which belong to the genera *Phaseolus, Faba*, and *Dolichos*; also, the plant itself.

2. a pod with such seeds.

3. a plant bearing such pods.

4. the bean-shaped seed of some other plants.

5. any of these plants.

6. head; brain; mind. [Slang.]

bēan, *v.t.* to hit on the head. [Slang.]

bēan ā'phis, a parasite of the bean plant: called also *bean dolphin.*

bēan'bag, *n.* 1. a small cloth bag filled with beans, for throwing in certain games.

2. any of these games.

bēan bee'tle, a small, tan insect with eight black spots on each wing cover: it is harmful to bean plants.

bēan çā'pēr, any plant whose buds are used as capers, especially a Levantine species, *Zygophyllum Fabago.*

bēan çod, 1. a small fishing vessel or pilot boat, used in the rivers of Portugal.

2. a bean pod.

bēan'ēr·y, *n.*; *pl.* **bēan'ēr·ieṣ,** a cheap restaurant: beans are frequently served in a restaurant of this sort. [Slang.]

bēan'fēast, *n.* a rustic dinner given by an employer to his workmen. [Brit.]

bēan flȳ, a fly found on bean flowers.

bēan gọọse, a small wild goose, *Anser segetum*, of northern Europe, which migrates to England and other temperate regions in the fall and returns to the north in summer: so called from the likeness of the nail of the bill to a horse bean.

bēan'ō, *n.* [from the *beans* used as counters, by analogy with *lotto*, etc.] bingo.

bēan'pōle, *n.* 1. a long stick put upright in the ground for bean plants to grow on.

2. a tall, lanky person. [Colloq.]

bēan'shọọt·ēr, *n.* a device for shooting beans; a peashooter.

bēan shot, small copper shot formed by pouring molten metal through a sieve into water.

bēan'stạlk, *n.* the main stem of a bean plant.

bēan tree, any one of various trees bearing podlike fruit, as the catalpa, carob, etc.

bēan trē'foil, the laburnum.

bēan wee'vil, a small weevil whose larva is injurious to beans.

bēar, bēre, *n.* [ME. *bere*; AS. *bere*, barley.] a kind of barley, cultivated in Scotland and the north of England; the common four-rowed barley, *Hordeum vulgare*; also the six-rowed barley, *Hordeum hexastichon.* [Dial.]

beār, *v.t.*; bore *or archaic* bare, *pt.*; bearing, *ppr.*; borne, born, *pp.* [ME. *beren*; AS. *beran*; akin to Goth. *bairan*, to bear; L. *ferre*; Gr. *pherein*; Sans. *bhar*, to bear, carry.]

1. to carry; to transport.

2. to carry with one or on it; to show; to wear: as, the letter *bore* his signature.

3. to carry and bring forth; to give birth to.

4. to support or hold up; sustain.

5. to sustain the burden of; to undergo; as, let him *bear* the expenses.

6. to undergo the torture.

7. to be capable of withstanding; to allow; to permit of; as, this will *bear* investigation.

8. to carry or conduct (oneself); as, he *bears* himself well.

9. to carry over or hold (a sentiment); as, *bear* a grudge.

10. to move or push as if carrying; as, the crowd *bore* us along.

11. to give, offer, or supply; as, he will *bear* witness.

12. to possess and use, as power; to exercise; as, to *bear* sway.

13. to carry on, or maintain; to have; as, to *bear* a part in conversation.

14. to be the object of; as, let me *bear* your love. [Rare.]

15. to gain or win. [Obs.]

Some think to *bear* it by speaking a great word. —Bacon.

16. to conduct; to take; as, *bear* the prisoner away.

to bear a hand; in seamanship, to make haste; to be quick.

to bear a price; to have a certain price; often, to bear a good or high price.

to bear date; to have the mark of time when written or executed; as, a letter or bond *bears date* January 1, 1953.

to bear down; to crush; to overwhelm, as an enemy.

to bear in hand; to amuse with false pretenses; to deceive. [Obs.]

to bear in mind; to remember.

to bear off; to remove; also, to gain or win, as a prize.

to bear on; to press against; also, to carry forward, to press, incite, or animate; as, confidence shall *bear* him *on.*

to bear one company; to furnish companionship to.

to bear out; to support; to confirm; as, his statement *bears* me *out.*

to bear through; to maintain or support to

the end; as, religion will *bear* us *through* the evils of life.

to bear up; to support; to keep from falling; as, religious hope *bears up* the mind.

to bear with; to put up patiently with; to tolerate.

Bear, signifying *to bring forth*, has the past participle, when used passively, spelled *born*, but when used after the verb *to have*, it is spelled *borne*. Thus, a child was *born*; but, she has *borne* a child. In all the other senses, the past participle is spelled *borne*; as, I have *borne* the expenses; the expenses must be *borne*.

beãr, *v.i.* 1. to carry or sustain a heavy burden.

But man is born to *bear*. —Pope.

2. to endure; to be patient; as, my burden is greater than I can *bear*.

3. to produce fruit; to be fruitful; as, the tree *bears* well.

This age to blossom, and the next to *bear*. —Dryden.

4. to press (with *on* or *upon*); as, to *bear* hard *upon* an opponent.

5. to take effect; to succeed; to have an influence; as, to bring matters to *bear*.

6. to be situated, as to the point of compass, with respect to something else; as, the land *bore* southeast by east from the ship.

7. to relate or refer (to): with *on* or *upon*; as, his argument *bears upon* the subject with force.

8. to extend, point, lie, or move in a given direction; as, the road *bore* left: bring the guns to *bear*.

9. to be capable of sustaining weight; as. the ice will *bear*.

10. to be oppressive; weigh; as, grief *bears* heavily on her.

to bear away; in nautical language, to keep or change a ship's course away from the wind.

to bear back; to retire in retreat.

to bear in; to tend toward, as a ship approaching the land: opposed to *bear off*.

to bear off; to remove to a greater distance.

to bear up; to tend or move toward; as, to *bear up* to one another; also, to endure, as under a strain; to have fortitude; to be firm; as, to *bear up* under afflictions.

Syn.—suffer, endure, support, maintain, uphold, sustain, undergo, tolerate, carry, convey, waft, produce, yield.

beãr, *n.*; *pl.* **beãrs** or **beãr,** [ME. *bere*; AS. *bera*, orig. sense, "the brown one."]

1. a plantigrade carnivorous mammal of the genus *Ursus*, family *Ursidæ*. There are many species, of which the grizzly bear and polar bear are the most formidable. Bears, while belonging to the *Carnivora*, live, to a large extent, on insects, fruits, roots, etc. They have stout, heavy bodies, usually thickly covered with fur, and very short tails. They are native to temperate and arctic zones. The brown or black bear of Europe and Asia is the *Ursus arctos*. The American black bear, *Ursus americanus*, of which the brown or cinnamon bear is a variant, has black shining hair, and is rarely more than five feet in length. The grizzly bear (*Ursus ferox* or

POLAR BEAR
(*Ursus maritimus*)

horribilis) is a ferocious animal, and has a bulky and unwieldy form, but is nevertheless capable of great rapidity of motion. The polar or white bear, *Ursus maritimus*, is an animal possessed of great strength and fierceness. It lives in the polar regions, chiefly on the ice, feeds on fish, seals, etc., and usually is seven to eight feet in length. The only South American species of bear is the *Ursus ornatus*, or spectacled bear, so called because of a peculiar marking about the eye suggesting spectacles. The Syrian bear, *Ursus syriacus*, and the sloth bear, *Ursus* or *Melursus labiatus*, the latter a native of India and Ceylon, are among the notable species. *Ursus torquatus* and *Ursus japonicus* are the black bears of the Himalayas and Japan, respectively.

2. in zoology, any one of several animals allied to the true bears by resemblance in form or habits, as the ant *bear*, the woolly *bear*, the sea *bear*, the water *bear*, and the sand *bear*.

BROWN BEAR
(*Ursus arctos*)

3. [B–] in astronomy, either of two constellations in the northern hemisphere, called the *Great* and *Little Bear*, or Ursa Major and Ursa Minor. In the tail of the *Little Bear* is the polestar.

4. in nautical usage, a scouring block used in cleaning decks.

5. in mechanics, a press for punching holes.

6. in metallurgy, a rough, conglomerate mass found in blast furnaces after long use.

7. a bearlike person; anyone who is clumsy, ill-mannered, etc.; a person of coarse, rough habits or speech.

8. in the stock exchange, etc. a speculator who sells and promises to deliver shares, commodities, etc. which he does not yet own, hoping to buy them at a lower price before the date of delivery; a manipulator who sells short: opposed to *bull*.

beãr, *a.* of or favorable to bears (sense 8) and their manipulations for lowering prices of stocks, etc.

beãr, *v.t.*; beared (bãrd), *pt.*, *pp.*; bearing, *ppr.* in the stock exchange, etc., to reduce or try to reduce the price of, or prices in, for speculative purposes; as, to *bear* a railroad stock; to *bear* oats.

beãr′ȧ·ble, *a.* capable of being borne; tolerable; endurable.

beãr′ȧ·bly, *adv.* in a bearable manner.

beãr bāit′ing, the act of harassing, tormenting, badgering, or worrying a chained bear, as by setting on dogs, for the entertainment of spectators.

beãr′bāne, *n.* a poisonous plant, of the aconite family.

beãr′ber″ry, *n.*; *pl.* **beãr′ber″ries,** 1. a medicinal plant, *Arctostaphylos uva-ursi*, of the heath family, having small bright-green leaves, white or pinkish flowers, and red berries.

2. a related shrub with black berries.

3. a variety of holly.

beãr′bīne, *n.* in botany, the bindweed, *Convolvulus arvensis*.

beãr′cat, *n.* 1. an Asiatic variety of civet with a prehensile tail.

2. a panda.

3. a strong, brave, fierce fighter.

beãr cat′ẽr·pil·lãr, a larval tiger moth, especially of the genus *Euprepia*; a woolly bear.

bēard, *n.* [ME. *berde*; AS. *beard*; O.H.G. *bart*; Dan. *baard*; L. *barba*, beard.]

1. (a) the hair that grows on the chin and cheeks and around the lips, especially of a man; hence, a mark of virility; (b) this hair, especially on the chin and cheek, when worn long or trimmed in various shapes.

2. the awn or sharp prickles on the ears of some kinds of grain; also, parallel hairs, or a tuft of stiff hairs, terminating the leaves of plants.

3. a barb or sharp process of an arrow, or other instrument, bent backward from the point to prevent its being easily drawn out.

4. the part of a horse's lower jaw which bears the curb of a bridle, underneath the lower mandible and above the chin.

5. the rays of a comet, emitted toward that part of the heaven to which its proper motion seems to direct it. [Archaic.]

6. (a) the byssus of certain kinds of mollusks, consisting of fine threads or hairs, by which they fasten themselves to rocks, etc.; (b) the gills or respiratory organs of the oyster and other bivalves.

7. in insects, two small, oblong, fleshy bodies, placed just above the trunk, as in gnats, moths, and butterflies.

8. the long hairs around the face or chin of some animals, as the goat, the cat, etc.

9. in printing, the outside, beardlike shading of some kinds of ornamental type, formerly much used.

bēard, *v.t.*; bearded, *pt.*, *pp.*; bearding, *ppr.*

1. to take by the beard; to seize, pluck, or pull the beard of, in contempt or anger.

2. to oppose or face courageously; to defy.

I have been *bearded* by boys. —More.

3. to provide with a beard.

bēard′ed, *a.* 1. having a beard, as a man.

Bearded like the pard. —Shak.

2. in botany, having an awn or awns, as ears or heads of grain.

3. barbed or jagged, as an arrow.

bēard grȧss, any one of several species of coarse grass of the genus *Andropogon*.

bēard′ie (-i), *n.* [dim. of *beard*.] the loach, *Nemachilus barbatus*. [Scot.]

bēard′less, *a.* 1. without a beard; young; not having arrived at manhood.

2. in botany, having no awn or awns.

bēard′less·ness, *n.* the state or quality of being beardless.

bēard moss, a grayish moss, *Usnea barbata*, growing on trees.

bēard′tŏngue (-tung), *n.* a plant of the genus *Pentstemon*, so called from its tongue-shaped bearded stamen.

beãr′ẽr, *n.* 1. in a general sense, one who or that which bears, sustains, or carries.

2. one who carries packages, letters, or news; as, a *bearer* of good news; a *bearer* of dispatches.

3. one who carries a body to the grave, at a funeral; a pallbearer.

4. one who wears or carries anything officially, or as a duty; a sword bearer; an armor bearer.

5. a tree or plant that bears fruit or blooms; as, a good *bearer*.

6. in architecture, a post or brick wall between the ends of a piece of timber, to support it; often, any support.

7. in heraldry, a figure in an achievement, placed by the side of a shield, and seeming to support it: generally the figure of a beast. The figure of a human being, used for a like purpose, is called a *tenant*.

8. in India, (a) a house servant similar to a valet; (b) one of the carriers of a palanquin.

9. in commercial language, any person having, holding, or presenting a note, check, draft, etc.; as, pay to *bearer*.

10. in printing, (a) a type-high metal support for the sides of matter that is to be cast into a plate, to prevent the spreading of or damage to the type on the edges; (b) a piece of wood or metal locked into a platen press, or built onto the bed of a cylinder press, to sustain the impression.

beãr gär′den, 1. a place for bear baiting or similar pastimes.

2. a scene of disorderly conduct or riot; as, the meeting of the city council degenerated into a *bear garden*.

beãr grȧss, 1. any of a group of plants of the lily family, with grasslike leaves and small, white flowers.

2. any of various similar plants, as a kind of camass.

beãr′hẽrd, *n.* a bear's keeper; an attendant on bears.

beãr′hound, *n.* a dog of the hound variety, used in hunting bears.

beãr′ing, *n.* 1. the manner in which a person bears or conducts himself; gesture; mien; behavior.

I know him by his *bearing*. —Shak.

2. the situation of an object, with respect to another object, by which it is supposed to have a connection with it or influence upon it, or to be influenced by it; relation.

But of this frame, the *bearings* and the ties. —Pope.

3. in architecture, the portion of a piece of timber which rests upon, or is inserted into a wall; also, the wall that supports it.

4. in navigation, the position of a distant object with regard to a ship's position, as on the bow, on the lee quarter, etc.; the direction or point of the compass in which an object is seen.

5. [*pl.*] in heraldry, any figure on the field.

A carriage covered with armorial *bearings*. —Thackeray.

6. the act, capacity, or time of producing or giving birth; as, the *bearing* of a child.

7. anything borne or produced, as crop, fruit, etc.

8. in machinery, any part of a machine in or on which another part revolves, slides, etc.
9. endurance; patience under affliction; as, my trials are past *bearing*.
10. relevant; meaning; significance; relation; connection; application; as, your remarks have no *bearing* upon the subject.
11. [*pl.*] in shipbuilding, (a) the widest part of a ship below the gunwale; (b) a ship's water line when she is perfectly trimmed.
to lose one's bearings; to become lost or bewildered as to direction.
to take bearings; to ascertain one's position, as by the compass; hence, figuratively, to discover how matters stand; to ascertain the conditions.
Syn.—deportment, demeanor, carriage, behavior, conduct, manner, mien.

bēar′ing clo̤th, the cloth in which a child is wrapped when carried to be baptized.

bēar′ing re̤in, a short rein for keeping or pulling a horse's head up; a checkrein.

bēar′ish, *a.* 1. bearlike; rude, rough, cross, surly, etc.
2. directed toward or causing a lowering of prices in the stock exchange, etc.

bēar′ish·ness, *n.* the manner of a bear; rude behavior.

bēar-lēad′ẽr, *n.* 1. one who leads a bear, or travels with a bear, as for exhibition purposes.
2. a tutor; especially, one who conducts a young man on educational travels.

bēar′līke, *a.* resembling a bear in appearance or behavior.

bēarn, *n.* a bairn. [Obs.]

bēar′s̱′-breech, *n.* 1. any of various species of plants of the genus *Acanthus*.
2. the cow parsnip, *Heracleum Sphondylium*, common in England.

bēar′s̱′-ēar, *n.* the *Primula auricula*, a variety of primrose with yellow flowers and leaves shaped like a bear's ear.

bēar′s′-foot, *n.* a bad-smelling variety of hellebore, with toothed leaves and clusters of five-petaled, cup-shaped flowers.

bēar′skin, *n.* 1. the skin or fur of a bear.
2. a rough, shaggy cloth for overcoats.
3. anything made from bearskin, as a rug, coat, etc.
4. a large headdress, made of bear's fur, especially one worn by a drum major or by the soldiers of certain British regiments.

bēar′s′-pa̤w, *n.* an ornamental East Indian bivalve shell.

Bēar Stāte (bãr), Arkansas: a nickname.

bēar′wa̤rd, *n.* a keeper of bears; a bearherd. [Rare.]

bēar′wood, *n.* a small tree of the western United States, the bark of which is used as a laxative: also called *cascara buckthorn*.

bēar′wŏrt, *n.* a European herb, spicknel or mew, *Meum athamanticum*.

bēast, *n.* [ME. *beeste, beste*; OFr. *beste*; L. *bestia*, a beast.]
1. any four-footed animal, which may be used for labor, food, or sport: distinguished from birds, insects, fishes, and man, and applied especially to large animals; as, *beasts* of burden; *beasts* of the chase.
2. any irrational animal, as opposed to *man*; as in the phrase, *man and beast*.
3. a brutal man; a person brutal, coarse, filthy, or acting in a manner unworthy of a rational creature.
4. qualities or impulses like an animal's; as, it's the *beast* in him.
5. a game at cards similar to loo; also, a forfeit at this game. [Obs.]
beast of burden; any animal used for carrying things.
beast of prey; any animal that hunts or kills other animals for food.
beast royal; the lion. [Obs.]

bēast′hood, *n.* the state of being, or the nature of, a beast.

bēast′ing̱s, *n.pl.* beestings.

bēast′ish, *a.* like a beast; brutal.

bēast′li·head (-hed), *n.* beastliness. [Obs.]

bēast′līke, *a.* like a beast; brutal.

bēast′li·ness, *n.* 1. the quality or state of being beastly; bestiality.
2. a beastly act.
3. disagreeable or unpleasant quality. [Colloq.]

bēast′ly, *a.*; *comp.* beastlier; *superl.* beastliest.
1. like a beast; brutal; coarse; filthy; contrary to the nature and dignity of man.
2. having the form and nature of a beast.
3. nasty; unpleasant; as, *beastly* weather. [Slang.]
Syn.—brutish, base, bestial, carnal, coarse, sensual, swinish, vile, irrational, degrading.

bēast′ly, *adv.* very; as, *beastly* bad news. [Brit.]

bēat, *v.t.*: beat, *pt.*; beating, *ppr.*; beaten, beat, *pp.* [ME. *beten*; AS. *beātan*, to beat.]
1. to strike or hit repeatedly; to pound.
2. to punish by striking repeatedly and hard; to flog; to spank; to whip.
3. to mark (time or rhythm) by tapping, etc.
4. to break, bruise, or pulverize by beating or pounding, as pepper or spices.
5. to shape or flatten by hammering, as gold or other malleable substance; to hammer into any form; to forge: often followed by *out*; as, to *beat out* gold.
6. to hunt through; to search; specifically, to shake by beating, or to make a noise in, to rouse game; as, to *beat* the woods.
7. to mix by stirring or striking repeatedly with a utensil; to whip (cream, etc.).
8. to strike or dash repeatedly against, as water or wind.
9. to make flat or smooth by walking or riding; to form by treading; as, we *beat* a path to the road.
10. to cheat; to swindle; to defraud; to trick: often followed by *out*; as, he *beat* me *out* of the money. [Colloq.]
11. to overcome in a battle, contest, etc.; to defeat; as, he always *beats* her at tennis.
12. to harass; to exercise severely; to perplex; as, to *beat* the brains about logic.
13. to flutter or flap; to move (wings, etc.) up and down.
14. to signal or give notice of, by beat of drum; as, to *beat* an alarm, the reveille, etc.
15. to puzzle; to perplex; to pass (one's) understanding; as, his actions *beat* me. [Colloq.]
16. to make, force, or drive by or as by flailing; as, he *beat* his way through the crowd.
to beat back; to compel to retire or return.
to beat down; (a) [Colloq.] to lower the price by importunity or argument; (b) to quell or crush; as, to *beat down* opposition.
to beat into; to teach or instill by repetition of instruction.
to beat off; to repel or drive back.
to beat up(*on*); to give a beating to in a fight; to maul; to thrash. [Slang.]
Syn.—hit, strike, belabor, drub, maul, pummel, thump, bang, thwack, defeat, vanquish, conquer, overcome.

bēat, *v.i.* 1. to strike, hit, or dash repeatedly and, usually, hard.
2. to move or sound rhythmically; to throb.
3. to hunt through underbrush, woods, etc., for game.
4. to take beating or stirring; as, this cream doesn't *beat* well.
5. to have a beat or rhythm; to pulsate, vibrate, etc.; as, the heart *beats*.
6. to make a sound by being struck, as a drum.
7. to win. [Colloq.]
8. in nautical usage, to progress by tacking into the wind.
9. in radio, to combine two waves of different frequencies, thus producing additional frequencies equal to the difference between these.
to beat about; (a) to hunt or look through or around; (b) in nautical usage, to tack into the wind.

bēat, *n.* 1. a stroke; a striking; a blow.
2. a recurring stroke; a pulsation; as, the *beat* of the pulse.
3. the unit of musical rhythm; as, four *beats* to a measure.
4. the rise or fall of the hand or foot, in marking the divisions of time in music.
5. a grace note in music, struck immediately before the note it is intended to ornament.
6. in acoustics and music, the regularly recurring amplification of sound produced by two simultaneous sounds having different rates of vibration.
7. a round or course which is frequently gone over; as, a policeman's *beat*.
8. a person or thing that surpasses; as, you never saw the *beat* of it. [Colloq.]
9. a cheat or swindler; one who does not pay his debts; a sponge; a dead beat. [Colloq.]
10. in journalism, the act of obtaining and publishing a piece of news before rival newspapers; also, the news itself; as, the story was a *beat*.
11. in hunting, a diligent search for game, as by striking bushes to drive it forth.
12. in fencing, a quick blow on the adversary's blade.
13. in radio, one cycle of a frequency formed by beating.

bēat, *n.* the heavy, matted growth of vegetation from moorland or fallow land, which is burned off to enrich the land for plowing. [Brit. Dial.]

bēat, *v.t.* to remove the sod or surface vegetation from. [Brit. Dial.]

bēat, *n.* flax or hemp bound in small bundles ready for macerating: written also *beet* and *bait*. [Brit. Dial.]

bēat, *a.* 1. weary; tired; worn out. [Slang.]
2. of or belonging to a group of young people in the United States who reject conventional attitudes, dress, etc. and affect extreme slang speech and an interest in jazz music and some other forms of art expression. [Slang.]

bēat′en, *a.* 1. conquered; vanquished.
2. made smooth by treading; worn by use; as, a *beaten* path.
3. shaped or formed by beating or hammering; as, *beaten* brass.
4. exhausted; tired out.
5. struck with repeated blows; whipped.
6. searched through for game.
7. mixed, as ingredients in cooking.
8. puzzled; confused. [Colloq.]

bēat′ẽr, *n.* 1. one who or that which beats.
2. an instrument for beating.
3. in hunting, one who strikes bushes, etc. to drive game from cover.

bēat′ẽr-up, *n.* one who beats for game.

bē·ȧ·tif′iç, bē·ȧ·tif′iç·ăl, *a.* [L. *beatificus*, from *beatus*, happy, and *facere*, to make.]
1. having the power to bless or make happy; making blessed or blissful.
2. showing happiness or delight; blissful; joyful; as, a *beatific* smile.

bē·ȧ·tif′iç·ăl·ly, *adv.* in a beatific manner.

bē·ȧ·tif′i·çāte, *v.t.* to beatify. [Obs.]

bē·at″i·fi·çā′tion, *n.* the act of beatifying, or the state of being beatified; especially, in the Roman Catholic Church, the act or process of declaring a dead person to be among the blessed in heaven: he is then entitled to public worship and is usually, but not necessarily, canonized.

bē·at′i·fȳ, *v.t.*; beatified, *pt.*, *pp.*; beatifying, *ppr.* 1. to make happy; to bless.
2. in the Roman Catholic Church, to declare by a papal decree (a deceased person) to be one of the blessed in heaven, and, though not necessarily canonized, to be worthy of public worship.
3. to ascribe extraordinary virtue or excellence to; to regard as saintly or blessed.

bēat′ing, *n.* 1. the act of a person or thing that beats.
2. the act of conquering or the state of being conquered; a defeat.
3. in nautical language, the act of sailing against the wind, by tacking.
4. a pulsation or throbbing; as, the *beating* of the heart.
5. a beat (sense 6).

bē·at′i·tūde, *n.* [Fr. *béatitude*; L. *beatitudo*, from *beatus*, happy, blessed.]
1. perfect blessedness or happiness.
2. in the Roman Catholic Church, same as *beatification*.
3. a blessing.
the Beatitudes; the pronouncements in the Sermon on the Mount, which begin "Blessed are the poor in spirit": Matt. v. 3–12.

bēat′nik, *n.* [*beat, a.*2, and Russ. *-nik*, equivalent to Eng. *-er*.] a member of the beat group. [Slang.]

beau (bō), *n.*; *pl.* **beau̱s, beaux** (bōz), [Fr. *beau, bel*, f. *belle*, from L. *bellus*, pretty, fair.]
1. a man greatly concerned with his personal appearance and with fashion; a dandy.
2. a man who devotes himself to a lady; a sweetheart; a lover. [Colloq.]
Syn.—gallant, sweetheart, lover, suitor.

Beau Brum′mell (bō), [after George Bryan *Brummell*, 1778–1840, Englishman famous for his fashionable dress and manners.] a dandy or fop.

beau′fin (bō′), *n.* a biffin.

Beau′fŏrt sçāle (bō′), [after Sir Francis *Beaufort* (1774–1857), Brit. naval officer who invented it in 1805.] in meteorology, a scale of wind velocities ranging from 0 for velocities of less than one mile per hour (a calm) to 12 for velocities of more than 75 miles per hour (a hurricane).

beau ġeste (zhest), [Fr.]
1. a fine or graceful gesture.

2. an act or an offer, especially in politics or diplomacy, that is of a conciliatory nature, or that seems fine or noble, but is in reality empty.

beau ī·dē′ăl, [Fr.]
1. a perfect conception or image; a standard of excellence; a model.
2. ideal beauty.

beau′ish (bō′), *a.* like a beau; foppish.

beau monde (bō′ mōnd′), [Fr., lit., elegant world.] fashionable society.

beau′pere (bō′pâr), *n.* [Fr., lit., good father.]
1. a companion or friend. [Obs.]
2. a father, especially a priest; good father. [Obs.]

beau′pot (bō′], *n.* a vase of large size to contain cut flowers.

beau·sę·ȧnt′ (bō-sā-äṅ′), *n.* [Fr. *beaucéant*, a flag, black-and-white-spotted.] the Knights Templars' standard, half black and half white.

beau′ship (bō′), *n.* the state or quality of being a beau.

beaū′tē·ous (bū′), *a.* beautiful.

beaū′tē·ous·ly (bū′), *adv.* in a beauteous manner.

beaū′tē·ous·ness (bū′), *n.* the state or quality of being beauteous; beauty.

beaū·ti′cian (-shun), *n.* one skilled in hairdressing, manicuring, massaging, etc.; a manager of, or operator in, a beauty parlor.

beaū′tied, *a.* full of beauty.

beaū″ti·fi·ca′tion (bū″), *n.* 1. a beautifying.
2. the fact or state of being beautified.

beaū′ti·fied, *a.* adorned; made beautiful.

beaū′ti·fi·ēr (bū′), *n.* one who or that which makes beautiful.

beaū′ti·fụl (bū′), *a.* full of beauty; having the qualities which constitute beauty.

A circle is more *beautiful* than a square; a square is more *beautiful* than a parallelogram. —Kames.

Syn.—fine, handsome, pretty, elegant, fair, lovely.

beaū′ti·fụl·ly (bū′), *adv.* in a beautiful manner.

beaū′ti·fụl·ness (bū′), *n.* beauty.

beaū′ti·fȳ (bū′-), *v.t.*; beautified (-fīd), *pt.*, *pp.*; beautifying, *ppr.* to make beautiful; to adorn; to deck; to grace; to add beauty to; to embellish.

Syn.—adorn, decorate, embellish, deck, ornament.

beaū′ti·fȳ (bū′), *v.i.* to become beautiful.

beaū′ti·less (bū′), *a.* without beauty.

beaū′ty (bū′), *n.* [ME. *bewty*, *beute*; OFr. *biaute*, *bealtet*, *beltet*; L. *bellitas*, beauty, from *bellus*, fair, pretty.]
1. the quality which makes an object seem pleasing or satisfying in a certain way; those qualities which give pleasure to the esthetic sense, as by line, color, form, texture, proportion, rhythmic motion, tone, etc., or by behavior, attitude, etc.
2. a particular grace, feature, or ornament; any particular thing having this quality; as, the *beauties* of nature.
3. any very attractive feature.
4. a beautiful person, especially a beautiful woman; collectively, beautiful women.
5. good looks.
6. fashion. [Obs.]

Syn.—loveliness, grace, fairness, seemliness, picturesqueness, exquisiteness, adornment, embellishment.

beaū′ty pär′lŏr (or **shop** or **sȧ·lon′**), a shop or place where women and girls can go for hair-waving, facial treatment, massage, manicuring, etc.

beaū′ty sleep (bū′), 1. sleep before midnight, popularly thought to be the most healthful. [Colloq.]
2. any extra sleep. [Colloq.]

beaū′ty spot (bū′), 1. a piece of black paper, cloth, etc. that a woman sometimes puts on her face or back to emphasize the beauty or whiteness of the skin; patch.
2. a natural mark or mole on the skin.
3. any place noted for its beauty.

beaux (bōz), *n.*, alternative pl. of *beau*.

beaux-arts′ (bō-zär′), *n.pl.* [Fr., the beautiful arts.]
1. the fine arts.
2. [B–A–] short for École des beaux-arts.

beaux-es·prits′ (bō-zes-prē′), pl. of *bel-esprit*.

beaux′īte (bōx′), *n.* same as *bauxite*.

bēa′vēr, *n.* [ME. *baviere*; OFr. *baviere*, the beaver of a helmet, a bib, from *bave*, foam, saliva.]
1. the movable face shield of a helmet, so constructed that it could be raised and lowered.
2. later, the visor of a helmet.

BEAVERS
1. beaver raised 2. beaver closed

bēa′vēr, *n.* [ME. *bever*; AS. *beofer*; D. *bæver*.]
1. an amphibious animal of the genus *Castor*. It has short ears, a blunt nose, chisellike teeth, small forefeet, large, webbed hind feet, with a flat, broad tail. It furnishes castor, or castoreum, taken from its preputial glands and used formerly as a medicine and now as a perfume.
2. the fur of the beaver.

BEAVER
(*Castor fiber*)

3. a man's high silk hat, originally made of this fur.
4. a heavy cloth of felted wool, used for overcoats, etc.

bēa′vēr·bōard, *n.* an artificial board made of pressed and chemically treated fibers and used in building for partitions, etc.: a trademark (*Beaverboard*).

bēa′vēr ēat′ēr, the wolverine.

bēa′vēr poi′sŏn, the water hemlock.

bēa′vēr rat, a member of the genus *Hydromys*, a Tasmanian rodent inhabiting banks of salt and fresh waters.

bēa′vēr tree, the sweet bay, *Magnolia glauca*, a tree with fragrant white flowers: so called because beavers eat its bark.

bē·bee′rụ, *n.* [native name.] a tropical South American evergreen tree, *Nectandria Rodiæi*.

bē·bi′rīne, bē·bee′rin, *n.* a drug used as a substitute for quinine, obtained from the bark of the bebeeru.

bē·bleed′, *v.t.* to make bloody. [Obs.]

bē·blood′ (-blud′), *v.t.* to make bloody. [Obs.]

bē·blot′, *v.t.* to blot; to stain. [Obs.]

bē·blub′bēr, *v.t.*; beblubbered, *pt.*, *pp.*; beblubbering, *ppr.* to disfigure by weeping.

bē′bop″, *n.* [perh. from sound made on trumpet.] a modification of jazz music, characterized by much improvisation, lack of restraint, deviation from key, and, often, meaningless lyrics.

bę′bụng, *n.*; *pl.* **bę′bụng·en,** [G., a trembling, from *beben*, to tremble.] in music, a sustained note, as on a clavichord, having a pulsating or trembling effect.

bē′çall, *v.t.* to call; to summon; to challenge. [Obs.]

bē·çälm′ (-käm′), *v.t.*; becalmed, *pt.*, *pp.*; becalming, *ppr.* 1. to still; to make quiet; to appease.
2. to keep (a sailing vessel) motionless from lack of wind.

bē·çāme′, *v.*, past tense of *become*.

beç′ärd, *n.* [Fr. *bec*, a beak.] any of a number of South American birds having hooked bills, particularly those of the genus *Tityra*.

bē·çaụse′, *conj.* [ME. *because*, *bi cause*, *by cause*; *by*, by, and *cause*, cause.] by cause; on this account; for the reason or cause that; since.

because of; by reason of; on account of.

The spirit is life, *because of* righteousness. —Rom. viii. 10.

Syn.—for, as, since, inasmuch as.

beç·çȧ·fi′çō, *n.* [It., from *beccare*, to peck, and *fico*, L. *ficus*, a fig.] a small songbird (*Sylvia hortensis*), family *Sylviadæ*, which feeds on fruits: they are eaten as a delicacy in Italy: known also as the *garden warbler*.

beçh′ȧ·mel, *n.* [Fr., from *Béchamel*, steward to Louis XIV.] a fine, white sauce, made of cream, butter, flour, etc.

bē·chȧnce′, *v.t.* and *v.i.* to befall; to happen (*to*).

bē·chȧnce′, *adv.* accidentally; by chance. [Obs.]

bē·chärm′, *v.t.*; becharmed (-chärmd′), *pt.*, *pp.*; becharming, *ppr.* to charm; to captivate.

bĕche (bāsh), *n.* [Fr., a spade.] a device to grasp and remove an obstruction in a bore hole.

bĕche-de-mer′ (bāsh-dē-mer′), *n.* [Fr., spade of the sea.]
1. the trepang, *Holothuria edulis*.
2. a mixed trade language, combining elements from English and Malay, spoken by both natives and whites in island areas of the central western Pacific: also *beach-la-mar*.

bē′çhiç, *a.* [L. *bechicus*; Gr. *bēchikos*, from *bēx*, cough, *bēssein*, to cough.] relieving or tending to relieve a cough.

bē′çhiç, *n.* a remedy or treatment for a cough.

Bech·ū·ä′nä (*also* bek-), *n.* 1. [*pl.* **Bech·ū·ä′nä** or **Bech·ū·ä′näs.**] a member of a Bantu-speaking people living in Bechuanaland, in South Africa.
2. their language.

beck, *n.* [ME. *bek*; AS. *becc*; Ice. *bekkr*, a brook.] a small brook, especially one with a rocky bottom.

beck, *n.* [ME. *becken*, *bekken*, *becknen*, to beckon.] a nod of the head; a gesture of the hand, etc. meant to summon.

at the beck and call of; at the service of; obedient to the wishes of.

beck, *v.t.* and *v.i.*; becked (bekt), *pt.*, *pp.*; becking, *ppr.* to nod or gesture with the head or hand.

beck, *n.* a tank or vat.

beck′ēr, *n.* [Eng. Dial.] a fish of the genus *Pagrus*: also called *braize* or *seabream*.

beck′et, *n.* a device used on ships to confine loose ropes, tackles, or spars, as a large hook, a rope with an eye at one end, or a wooden cleat; a grommet.

beck′et bend, a kind of knot; sheet bend.

beck′ŏn, *v.t.* and *v.i.*; beckoned (-ŏnd), *pt.*, *pp.*; beckoning, *ppr.* [ME. *beknen*, *becnen*; AS. *bēcnian*, from *beácen*, a sign, beacon.] to call or summon by a sign or silent gesture, as a nod, wink, or motion of the hand or finger: often used figuratively; as, the woods *beckon*.

beck′ŏn, *n.* a summoning gesture.

bē·çlap′, *v.t.* to grab; to seize. [Obs.]

bē·çlip′, *v.t.* [AS. *beclyppan*, to embrace.] to embrace. [Obs.]

bē·çloud′, *v.t.*; beclouded, *pt.*, *pp.*; beclouding, *ppr.* 1. to cloud; to obscure; to dim.
2. to confuse; to muddle.

bē·çŏme′, *v.i.*; became, *pt.*; becoming, *ppr.*; become, *pp.* [ME. *becumen*; AS. *becuman*, to come, happen; *be*, by, about, and *cuman*, to come.]
1. to pass from one state to another; to enter into some state or condition, by a change from another state or condition, or by assuming or receiving new properties or qualities, additional matter, or a new character; as, a scion *becomes* a tree.
2. to come into being.
3. to happen. [Obs.]

to become of; to happen to; to be the fate of; to be the end of; to be the final or subsequent condition of; as, what will *become of* our commerce?

bē·çŏme′, *v.t.* to suit or to be suitable to; to befit; to accord with, in character or circumstances; to be worthy of, or proper to; to grace; to adorn.

If I *become* not a cart as well as another man, a plague on my bringing up! —Shak.

Nothing in his life *became* him like the leaving it. —Shak.

bē·çŏm′ed, *a.* becoming. [Obs.]

bē·çŏm′ing, *a.* fit; suitable; congruous; befitting; proper; graceful; belonging to the character, or adapted to the circumstances; as, he speaks with *becoming* boldness; that dress is very *becoming*.

bē·çŏm′ing, *n.* 1. anything suitable or appropriate.
2. the change from nonbeing to being; a coming into existence.

bē·çŏm′ing·ly, *adv.* in a becoming manner.

bē·çŏm′ing·ness, *n.* fitness; congruity; propriety; the quality of being appropriate or becoming.

Beçque′rel rays, see under *ray*.

bē·çrip′ple, *v.t.* to make lame; to cripple.

bē·çui′bȧ (-kwē′), *n.* [native name.] a tree growing in Brazil, which produces a nut yielding a balsam: it is the *Myriscati Bicuhyba*.

bē·çū′nȧ, *n.* [LL.] a ferocious fish of the Mediterranean, *Sphyræna vulgaris*, resembling the pike. From its scales and air bladder is obtained a substance useful in the manufacture of artificial pearls.

bē·cûrl′, *v.t.* to curl.

bed, *n.* [AS. *bed*; D. *bed*, bed; G. *bett*, or *beet*, a bed, plat of ground.]

1. an article of furniture to sleep or rest on: it usually includes a bedstead, spring, mattress, and bedding.

2. a bedstead.

3. any place used for sleeping or reclining.

4. such a place regarded as the scene of sexual intercourse or procreation.

5. the grave.

6. a plot of soil where plants are raised.

7. the flowers or vegetables growing in this.

8. lodging; a convenient place for sleep.

9. marriage; matrimonial connection.

George, the eldest son of his second *bed*.
—Clarendon.

10. the channel of a river, the bottom of a lake, etc.

11. in geology, a layer; a stratum; an extended mass of anything; as, a *bed* of coal or iron.

12. any flat surface used as a foundation or support for a piece of machinery; as, the *bed* of a lathe.

13. in a printing press, the part against which the form rests.

14. in building, (a) either of the horizontal surfaces of a building stone in position; (b) the under surface of a brick, shingle, slate, or tile in position; (c) the mortar in which a brick or stone is to be laid; (d) a single horizontal course of brick or stone in a wall.

15. an enclosing substance, as rock in which shells, minerals, etc. are lodged.

16. a pile or heap resembling a bed, especially in softness or shape; as, a *bed* of leaves.

bed and board; (a) sleeping quarters and meals; (b) home; the marriage relationship; as, she has left her husband's *bed and board*.

bed curtain; hangings suspended around a bed so as to screen the occupant from the room.

bed joint; in architecture, a joint running horizontally in ordinary masonry.

bed of roses; a situation, a position, or a place that is favorable or pleasant; a life of ease.

to be brought to bed; to give birth to a child.

to make a bed; to put a bed in order after it has been used.

bed, *v.t.*; bedded, *pt.*, *pp.*; bedding, *ppr.* 1. to place in a bed. [Obs.]

2. to have sexual intercourse with.

3. to furnish with a bed or bedding.

4. to plant in a bed or beds of earth; as, to *bed* the roots of a plant in soft mold.

5. to fix or place firmly; to embed; as, to *bed* a stone.

6. to lay in a place of rest or security, covered, surrounded, or enclosed; as, a fish *bedded* in sand.

7. to lay in a stratum; to stratify; to arrange in layers; as, *bedded* clay; *bedded* hairs.

8. in masonry, to trim up (a stone or boulder) preparatory to laying.

bed, *v.i.* 1. to go to bed; rest; sleep.

2. to form in layers; to stratify.

bē·dab′ble, *v.t.*; bedabbled (-bld), *pt.*, *pp.*; bedabbling, *ppr.* to wet; to sprinkle.

bē·dag′gle, *v.t.*; bedaggled (-gld), *pt.*, *pp.*; bedaggling, *ppr.* to soil, as clothes.

bē·dash′, *v.t.* to wet, as by throwing water.

bē·daub′, *v.t.*; bedaubed, *pt.*, *pp.*; bedaubing, *ppr.* 1. to daub over; to smear; to soil with anything thick and dirty.

2. to overdecorate; to ornament showily.

bē·dāze′, *v.t.* to daze thoroughly; bewilder; stupefy.

bē·daz′zle, *v.t.*; bedazzled (-zld), *pt.*, *pp.*; bedazzling, *ppr.* to blind by too strong a light; to dazzle; to confuse thoroughly.

bed′bug, *n.* the *Cimex lectularius*, a wingless insect having an unpleasant smell: it infests beds, furniture, etc.

BEDBUG (3/16 in. long)

bed′chāir (-chãr), *n.* an adjustable chairlike frame for supporting an invalid unable to leave his bed.

bed′chăm″bẽr, *n.* a bedroom.

bed′clothes, *n.pl.* blankets, sheets, coverlets, etc. for beds.

bed′cord, *n.* a cord or rope woven across a bedstead so as to support the mattress or bed.

bed′cŏv·ẽr, *n.* a cover for a bed; coverlet; bedspread.

bed′ded, *a.* laid in a bed; enclosed as in a bed; stratified.

bed′dẽr, *n.* 1. the lower stone of an oil mill.

2. in gardening, a plant used for bedding.

bed′ding, *n.* 1. a bed and its materials.

2. mattresses and bedclothes.

3. straw, hay, etc. used to bed animals.

4. the act of putting to bed.

5. in geology, the stratification or position of beds and layers.

6. a foundation or bottom layer of some kind.

7. a growing of plants in a mass for a showy effect.

Bē·deaux′ sys′tem (bē-dō′), [after Chas. *Bedeaux* (1887–1944) American industrial engineer.] a method of measuring industrial work done by individuals, involving a point system of wage payments.

bē·deck′, *v.t.* to deck; to adorn; to grace.

bed′ē·guär (-gär), **bed′ē·gär**, *n.* [Fr. *bédegar*; Per. *badawar*, a white thorn, literally, windbrought, from *bād*, wind, and *āwar*, pp. of *āwardan*, to bring.] a hairy or spongy gall on rose bushes, produced by certain insects, and once supposed to have medicinal properties.

bēde′house, *n.* same as *beadhouse*.

bē′del, bē′dell (bē′dl), *n.* a beadle: archaic spelling.

bed′en, *n.* [Ar. *baden*.] an ibex.

bēdes′măn, *n.* same as *beadsman*.

bēdes′wom″ăn (-woom″), *n.* same as *beadswoman*.

bē·dev′il, *v.t.*; bedeviled *or* bedevilled (-ld), *pt.*, *pp.*; bedeviling *or* bedevilling, *ppr.* 1. to throw into utter disorder and confusion.

2. to plague diabolically; torment.

3. to bewitch.

4. to corrupt; spoil.

bē·dev′il·ment, *n.* 1. a bedeviling.

2. the fact or state of being bedeviled.

bē·dew′, *v.t.*; bedewed (-dewd), *pt.*, *pp.*; bedewing, *ppr.* [ME. *bedewen*; G. *bethauen*.] to moisten with or as with dew; to moisten in a gentle manner with any liquid; as, tears *bedew* her face.

bē·dew′ẽr, *n.* one who or that which bedews.

bed′fȧst, *a.* having to stay in bed; bedridden.

bed′fel″lōw, *n.* 1. one who shares the same bed with another.

2. any associate, co-worker, etc.

bed′fēre, bed′phēre, *n.* a bedfellow. [Obs.]

bed′gown, *n.* 1. a sleeping gown.

2. in northern England, a woman's short, loose jacket.

bē·dīght′ (-dīt′), *v.t.*; bedight *or* bedighted, *pt.*, *pp.*; bedighting, *ppr.* to adorn; to dress; to array. [Archaic.]

bē·dīght′ (-dīt′), *a.* bedecked; arrayed. [Archaic.]

bē·dim′, *v.t.*; bedimmed (-dimd), *pt.*, *pp.*; bedimming, *ppr.* to make dim; to obscure or darken: said especially of the eyes or the vision.

Bed′i·vēre, in Arthurian legend, the loyal knight who was with the dying King Arthur and saw him go away to Avalon.

bē·diz′en (*or* -dīz′n), *v.t.*; bedizened, *pt.*, *pp.*; bedizening, *ppr.* to adorn; to deck; especially, to adorn in a cheap, showy manner.

bē·diz′en·ment, *n.* that which bedizens; also, the state of being bedizened.

bed jack′et, a woman's short, loose upper garment, sometimes worn over a nightgown.

bed′kēy, *n.* a kind of wrench formerly used for assembling or disassembling bedsteads.

bed′lăm, *n.* [ME. *bedlem*, *bedleem*, *bethlem*, from *Bethlehem*, a religious house in London, converted into a hospital.]

1. a madhouse; a hospital for the mentally ill.

2. a madman; a lunatic; one who lives in bedlam. [Obs.]

3. any scene of uproar and confusion.

A division of possessions would make the country a *bedlam* for one short season and a charnel house ever after.
—Brougham.

bed′lăm, *a.* full of noise and confusion.

bed′lăm·ism, *n.* action or speech suggesting insanity; madness and disorder.

bed′lăm·ite, *n.* a patient in a mental hospital; a lunatic.

bed lin′en, bed sheets, pillowcases, etc., whether of linen or not.

Bed′ling·tŏn ter′ri·ẽr, [after *Bedlington*, Northumberland, England.] a blue or livercolored, woolly-coated terrier, about 15 or 16 inches high, that looks like a small lamb.

bed′măk″ẽr, *n.* 1. one who puts a bed in order, usually involving care of the bedroom, as in English universities and hotels.

2. one who manufactures beds.

bed′māte, *n.* 1. a person who shares one's bed.

2. one's wife or husband.

bed mōld′ing, in architecture, the moldings of a cornice which are placed below the corona and above the frieze.

bē·dōte′, *v.t.* to make to dote. [Obs.]

Bed′ou·in, *n.* [Fr. *Bédouin*; Ar. *bedâwî*, dwellers in the desert.]

1. an Arab of any of the wandering desert tribes of Arabia, Syria, and North Africa.

2. a nomad; also, a street vagabond.

Bed′ou·in, *a.* of, resembling, or pertaining to the Bedouins; nomadic.

bed′pan, *n.* 1. a covered pan for holding hot coals, used to warm a bed.

2. a shallow pan serving as a toilet for a person who is ill and has to stay in bed.

bed′plāte, bed′piēce, *n.* a plate forming the base or support, as for a piece of machinery or a stove.

bed′pōst, *n.* any of the vertical supporting posts at the corners of some beds.

bed′quilt, *n.* a quilted spread or cover for a bed.

bē·drab′ble, *v.t.*; bedrabbled (-bld), *pt.*, *pp.*; bedrabbling, *ppr.* to soil with slush, mud, or rain.

bē·drag′gle, *v.t.*; bedraggled (-gld), *pt.*, *pp.*; bedraggling, *ppr.* to make wet, limp, and dirty, as by dragging through mire.

bē·drag′gled, *a.* [pp. of *bedraggle*.] soiled and wet; unkempt; as, a *bedraggled* dress.

bed′rāil, *n.* a rail along the side of a bed.

bē·drench′, *v.t.*; bedrenched (-drencht′), *pt.*, *pp.*; bedrenching, *ppr.* to drench; to soak; to saturate with moisture.

bed rest, 1. a resting in bed.

2. a metal or wooden device used to prop patients up in bed.

bed′rid″den, bed′rid, *a.* [ME. *bedred*; AS. *bedreda*, bedridden, from *bed*, bed, and *rida*, *ridda*, a rider.] confined to the bed, usually for a long period, because of illness, age, or infirmity.

bed′rīght, bed′rīte, *n.* the privilege of the marriage bed. [Obs.]

bē·driz′zle, *v.t.* to rain upon.

bed′rock, *n.* 1. solid rock beneath the soil and superficial rock.

2. a secure foundation.

3. the very bottom.

4. basic principles.

bed′rōll, *n.* a portable roll of bedding, generally for sleeping outdoors.

bed′room, *n.* 1. a room to sleep in; a lodging room.

2. room in a bed. [Rare.]

bē·drop′, *v.t.* [ME. *bedroppen*.] to sprinkle, as with drops.

bē·drug′, *v.t.* to drug to excess.

bed′sīde, *n.* the side of a bed; space beside a bed; as, the nurse was at his *bedside* constantly.

bed′sīde, *a.* 1. near a bed; as, a *bedside* table.

2. with a patient or patients; as, a doctor's *bedside* manner.

bed′sīte, *n.* a recess where a bed is to stand.

bed′sore, *n.* a sore on the body of a bedridden person, caused by chafing or pressure.

bed′spread (-spred), *n.* an outer covering for bedclothes, mainly for ornament.

bed′spring, *n.* 1. a framework of springs placed in a bedstead to support the mattress and make the bed softer.

2. any of these springs.

bed′stȧff, *n.*; *pl.* **bed′stāves**, a stick formerly used about a bed, sometimes as a means of keeping the bedclothes in place: sometimes used as a defensive weapon.

bed′stead, *n.* [ME. *bedstede*, from AS. *bed*, bed, and *stede*, place.] a framework for supporting the spring and mattress of a bed.

bed′steps, *n.pl.* steps used to mount a bed.

bed′stock, *n.* part of the frame of a bed, generally considered the front or back. [Dial.]

bed′strąw, *n.* [ME. *beddestrawe*.]

1. formerly, straw put into a bed to make it soft.

2. any plant of the genus *Galium*, a number of related plants with clusters of small, yellow or white flowers and stalkless leaves.

white bedstraw; a wild summer flower, *Galium Mollugo*.

bed′swẽrv″ẽr, *n.* an adulterer or adulteress. [Obs.]

bed′tick, *n.* a case of strong linen or cotton cloth, used for enclosing the hair, kapok, etc. in a mattress.

bed′tīme, *n.* the time to go to rest; the usual hour of going to bed.

bed′tīme stō′rieṣ, 1. stories told to children at bedtime.

2. pleasant but unconvincing accounts or explanations.

bed′wărd, bed′wărdṣ, *adv.* toward bed; on the way to bed.

bē·dwarf′, *v.t.*; bedwarfed, *pt., pp.*; bedwarfing, *ppr.* to make little; to stunt or hinder the growth of; to dwarf.

bed′wet·ting, *n.* urinating in bed.

bed′wrench (-rench), *n.* same as *bedkey.*

bē·dȳe′, *v.t.* to dye; to stain.

bee, *n.* [ME. *bee*; from AS. *beo.*]

1. a four-winged, hairy insect of the genus *Apis*; specifically, the common hive bee, which has been cultivated from the earliest periods for its wax and honey. It lives in swarms containing three classes of bees: the females or queen bees, of which there is only one in each swarm; the males or drones, and the neuters or working bees. The queen bee propagates the species, the drones serve to impregnate the queen, after which they are destroyed by the neuters, who are the laborers of the hive, collecting the honey from the nectar of flowers, and conveying it to the hive. The pollen of flowers, also collected by the neuters and called *beebread*, is the food of the larvae or young. The wax is formed from the honey by a digestive process. The females and neuters have a barbed sting.

2. any insect related to the common hive bee, as the ***mason bee***, the ***bumblebee***, etc.

3. a gathering of neighbors or friends who work together to help out some individual or family; as, a husking *bee*, a raising *bee*, a quilting *bee*. Also, a gathering for friendly competition; as, a spelling ***bee***.

bee larkspur; a plant, *Delphinium elatum.*

to have a bee in one's bonnet; (a) to be a crank on some subject, especially in regard to one's ambition; (b) to be not quite sane.

to have a bee in the head; to be full of fancies; to be restless or uneasy.

bee, *n.* [ME. *beah*; AS. *beah, beag*, a ring, armlet, from *bugan*, to bend, turn.] in nautical usage, (a) a metal ring; (b) a bee block.

bee bälm (-bäm), 1. Oswego tea, a plant with red flowers and a mintlike scent.

2. the garden balm, a plant whose leaves have the odor and flavor of lemons.

bee bee′tle, a parasitic beetle, *Trichodes apiarius*, which invades beehives.

bee bīrd, an American flycatcher or kingbird: so called because it lives on insects caught in flight.

bee block, a piece of wood on each side of the bowsprit of a ship, used for fastening stays from the mast or foremast.

bee′bread (-bred), *n.* a brown, bitter mixture of pollen and honey, made and eaten by some bees.

beech, *n.* [ME. *beche*; AS. *bēce*, beech.]

1. a tree, arranged by Linnaeus under the genus *Fagus*, which grows to a large size, with hard wood, dark-green leaves, and edible three-cornered nuts. The bark is smooth and was formerly used for writing upon.

2. the wood of any of these trees.

copper beech; the European beech, *Fagus sylvatica.*

beech, *a.* of any of the beech trees; beechen.

beech′drops, *n.* a parasitic plant, *Epifagus virginiana*, growing upon the roots of the beech.

beech′en, *a.* 1. of the beech tree.

2. made of beechwood.

beech mȧst, beechnuts.

beech′nut, *n.* the nut of the beech tree.

beech oil, the oil of beech mast or beechnuts.

beech′wood, *n.* the wood of the beech tree.

beech′y, *a.* of or pertaining to beeches.

bee ēat′ẽr, a bird that feeds on bees and other insects: a name applied to various species of birds, family *Meropidæ*, of which the *Merops apiaster* of Europe is remarkable for the brilliancy of its plumage.

beef, *v.i.* to complain; to protest. [Slang.]

beef, *v.t.* to fatten or slaughter (a beef animal) for food.

beef, *n.*; *pl.* **beeveṣ** or **beefs,** [ME. *beef, befe*; Fr. *boef, buef*, beef; L. *bos*, genit. *bovis*; Gr. *bous*, an ox.]

1. an animal of the bovine genus, whether ox, bull, steer, or cow, in the full grown state.

A herd of *beeves*, fair oxen, and fair kine.
—Milton.

Flesh of muttons, *beefs*, or goats.
—Shak.

2. meat from such animals.

3. human flesh or muscle. [Colloq.]

4. strength; brawn. [Colloq.]

5. a complaint. [Slang.]

BEEF CUTS

beef tea; a beverage extracted from finely cut lean beef by pouring hot water over the beef; also, a beverage prepared by dissolving beef extract in boiling water.

beef′ȧ·lō, *n.*; *pl.* **beef′ȧ·lōeṣ, beef′ȧ·lōṣ, beef′ȧ·lō,** [*beef* + buff*alo.*] an animal developed by crossing the American buffalo, or bison, with beef cattle.

beef cat′tle, cattle bred and fattened for meat.

beef′ēat″ẽr, *n.* 1. one who eats beef; one who looks well-fed or beefy.

2. in England, any of the yeomen of the king's guard, who attend the sovereign at state banquets and on other ceremonial occasions.

3. a guard at the Tower of London.

4. the *Buphaga africana*, an African bird that feeds on the larvae encysted under the hides of cattle.

5. an Englishman. [Slang.]

BEEFEATER

beef′i·ness, *n.* the state of being beefy; fleshiness; brawn; strength.

bee′flow·ẽr, *n.* see *bee orchis.*

bee flȳ, any of various flies that look like bees.

beef′steāk, *n.* a steak or slice of beef to be broiled or fried.

beef Wel′ling·tŏn, a lightly roasted beef fillet covered with pâté de foie gras, wrapped in pastry, and then baked.

beef′-wit″ted, *a.* dull in intellect; stupid.

beef′wood, *n.* the timber of some species of Australian trees belonging to the genus *Casuarina*, of a reddish color, hard, and close-grained, with dark and whitish streaks, and used chiefly in fine ornamental work.

beef′y, *a.*; *comp.* beefier; *superl.* beefiest; beeflike; fleshy and solid; brawny; of a heavy build; thickset.

bee gär′den, a garden or enclosure to set beehives in.

bee glūe, a soft, adhesive matter with which bees cement the honeycombs to the hives, and close up the cells: called also *propolis.*

bee gum, 1. a hollow gum tree used as a hive by bees.

2. a beehive, especially one made from such a tree.

bee′hīve, *n.* 1. a box or other shelter for a colony of domestic bees, in which they make and store honey.

2. a place of great activity.

beehive houses; ancient houses, or remains of houses, found in Scotland and Ireland, and so called from their shape, which is that of the old style beehive.

bee′house, *n.* an apiary.

bee′keep·ẽr, *n.* a person who keeps bees for producing honey; apiarist.

bee kill′ẽr, any of various large flies that kill bees with their piercing beaks; robber fly.

bee′līne, *n.* the shortest distance between two points or localities.

Bē·el′zē·bub, *n.* [L. *Beelzebub*; Gr. *Beelzeboub*; Heb. *Baalzebub*; literally meaning the god of insects; *baal*, lord, and *zebub*, a fly, insect.]

1. the chief devil; Satan.

2. any devil.

3. in Milton's *Paradise Lost*, Satan's chief lieutenant among the fallen angels.

Bē·el′zē·bul, *n.* Beelzebub.

bee mär′tin, the kingbird, *Tyrannus tyrannus*: so called because it supposedly eats bees.

bee′mȧs″tẽr, *n.* a beekeeper.

bee moth, a kind of moth whose larvae, hatched in beehives, eat the wax of the honeycomb.

been (bin *or* bēn), *v.*, past participle of *be.*

been (bēn), *n.* [Hind. *bīn*, a lute or guitar.] a stringed musical instrument of the guitar family, having nineteen frets: long used in India.

bee or′chis, a European orchid, *Listera apifera*, having flowers formed somewhat like a bee: called also *bee flower.*

beep, *n.* [echoic.]

1. the brief, high-pitched sound of a horn, as on an automobile or bicycle.

2. a brief, high-pitched electronic signal, used in warning, direction-finding, etc.

beep, *v.i.* to make a beep.

beep, *v.t.* to cause to make a beep.

bee plant, any plant that especially attracts bees, as the white clover, spiderflower, etc.

beer, *n.* [ME. *bere*; AS. *beōr*, beer.]

1. a mildly alcoholic drink made from any farinaceous grain, but generally from barley, which is first malted and ground, and its fermentable substance then extracted by hot water. This extract or infusion is boiled in caldrons, and hops or some other substance of an agreeable bitterness added. The liquor is then allowed to ferment in vats.

2. any undistilled, fermented malt beverage, as ale, porter, or stout.

3. any of several soft drinks made from extracts of the roots and other parts of various plants, as ginger ***beer***, root ***beer***, etc.

bitter beer; ale or beer containing a large percentage of hops.

green beer; beer that has been recently fermented.

near beer; malt liquor with a very low alcoholic content.

small beer; (a) weak beer; (b) figuratively, matters of little or no importance.

To suckle fools, and chronicle *small beer.*
—Shak.

weiss beer; a variety of German beer, brewed from wheat and very light in color.

beer and skit′tles, anything comfortable; pleasure or enjoyment, as that of drinking beer while playing the old game of skittles.

beer gär′den, any enclosed outdoor place where beer and other refreshments are sold.

beer′house, *n.* a house where malt liquors are sold; an alehouse.

beer′i·ness, *n.* beery condition or quality.

beer mŏn′ey, an allowance to servants, etc., in lieu of beer.

beer′y, *a.*; *comp.* beerier; *superl.* beeriest, 1. of, pertaining to, or resembling beer.

2. drunken; tipsy; in a maudlin condition.

beest′ingṣ, *n.* [ME. *bestinge*; AS. *bysting*, from *beost*, beestings.] the first milk of a cow after having a calf: its chemical composition is different from that of later milk: also spelled *biestings.*

beeṣ′wax, *n.* a tallowlike substance secreted by honeybees and used by them in making their honeycomb: it is used in candles, polishes, etc.

beeṣ′wax, *v.t.* and *v.i.* to polish, etc., with beeswax.

beeṣ′wing, *n.* 1. a gauzy film forming in old wines.

2. any wine so crusted over.

beet, *n.* [ME. *bete*; AS. *bēte*; from L. *beta*, beet.]

1. a plant of the genus *Beta*, with edible leaves and a thick, fleshy root. The species cultivated in gardens usually is *Beta vulgaris*, naturally a perennial. There are many varieties, some with long tapering roots, and others with flat roots, like turnips.

2. the roots of plants of this genus: some varieties are eaten as a vegetable, and some serve as a source of sugar.

bee′tle (-tl), *n.* [AS. (Anglian) *betel*, mallet, hammer.]

1. a heavy wooden mallet, used to drive wedges, tamp earth, etc.

2. a household mallet or pestle for mashing or beating.

3. a club used in finishing handmade linen.

4. a machine for finishing cloth by beating it over or between rollers.

bee′tle, *v.t.*; beetled (-tld), *pt., pp.*; beetling, *ppr.* 1. to use a beetle on; to beat with a heavy wooden mallet, as linen or cotton cloth, as a substitute for mangling.

2. to put a glossy finish on (cloth) by flattening the fibers.

bee′tle, *n.* [ME. *bitle, bityl*; from AS. *bitela, bitel*, beetle, from *bitan*, to bite.]

1. any insect belonging to the order *Coleoptera.* Sometimes the term is used in a more restricted sense, as equivalent to *Scarabæidæ*, a family of this order embracing more than 3,000 species, characterized by clavated antennae, fissile longitudinally, legs frequently dentated, biting mouth parts, and hard front

wings used to cover the membranous hind wings when the latter are folded.

2. any insect resembling a coleopterous insect.

Colorado beetle or *potato bug*; a coleopterous insect, *Doryphora decemlineata*, somewhat larger than a pea, nearly oval, convex, of a yellowish color, marked with black spots, and having ten black longitudinal stripes on the hard front wings. It destroys potato crops.

bee′tle, *v.i.* to jut; to be prominent; to overhang; as, a cliff that *beetles* over its base.

bee′tle, *a.* jutting; overhanging.

bee′tle brow, a prominent or overhanging brow.

bee′tle-browed, *a.* 1. having bushy or overhanging eyebrows.

2. frowning; scowling.

bee′tle·head (-hed), *n.* a stupid fellow.

bee′tle·head·ed, *a.* having a head like a beetle; dull; stupid.

bee′tle stock, a beetle handle.

bee′tling, *a.* jutting out; prominent; as, *beetling* brows.

beet rad′ish, beet′rāve, *n.* [Fr. *bette-rave*; *bette*, beet, and *rave*, radish; from L. *beta*, beet, and *rapa*, a turnip.] the common beet.

bee tree, 1. a hollow tree used as a hive by bees.

2. the basswood: so called because its flowers have much nectar.

beet sug′ăr (shug′ăr), sugar extracted from certain beets.

beeveș, *n.*, alternative pl. of *beef*.

bee wolf (wulf), a bee beetle in the larval stage.

bē·fall′, *v.t.*; befell, *pt.*; befalling, *ppr.*; befallen, *pp.* [ME. *befallen*, fall, happen; AS. *befællan*, to fall.]

1. to happen to; to occur to; as, the worst that can *befall* one.

2. (a) to be fitting to; (b) to pertain to. [Archaic.]

bē·fall′, *v.i.* 1. to happen; to come to pass; to occur.

I have revealed this discord which *befell*.
—Milton.

2. to be fitting; also, to pertain. [Archaic.]

bē·fit′, *v.t.*; befitted, *pt.*, *pp.*; befitting, *ppr.* to be suitable or proper for; to be suited or becoming to.

That name best *befits* thee. —Milton.

bē·fit′ting, *a.* appropriate; suitable; proper; right.

bē·fit′ting·ly, *adv.* becomingly; in a suitable or befitting manner.

bē·flat′tẽr, *v.t.* to flatter effusively.

bē·flow′ẽr, *v.t.* to scatter with flowers.

bē·fōam′, *v.t.* to cover with foam. [Rare.]

bē·fog′, *v.t.*, befogged, *pt.*, *pp.*; befogging, *ppr.*

1. to cover with or envelop in fog; make foggy.

2. to make hard to see or understand; blur; obscure; confuse.

bē·fool′, *v.t.*; befooled, *pt.*, *pp.*; befooling, *ppr.*

1. to fool or deceive; to trick; to dupe; to delude or lead into error.

Men *befool* themselves. —South.

2. to call (a person) a fool.

3. to treat as a fool.

bē·fōre′, *prep.* [ME. *beforen*, *biforen*, from AS. *beforan*, *biforan*, from *be*, by, and *foran*, adv., before.]

1. in front of; at the forepart of; in advance of in space; as, *before* the house; *before* the fire.

2. in the presence of; in the sight of.

Abraham bowed down himself *before* the people of the land. —Gen. xxiii. 12.

3. under the cognizance, jurisdiction, or consideration of.

The cause of both parties shall come *before* the judges. —Ex. xxii. 9.

4. earlier than; preceding in time; as, I will return *before* six o'clock.

5. in preference to; rather than; having precedence of in rank, dignity, or the like.

We think poverty to be infinitely desirable *before* the torments of covetousness.
—Taylor.

6. still to be reached, accomplished, etc. by; as, the hardest task was *before* them.

before the mast; in or into the condition of a common sailor, the portion of a ship behind the mainmast being reserved for the officers.

before the wind; nautically, in the direction of the wind by its impulse.

bē·fōre′, *adv.* 1. ahead; in advance; in front; in the forepart.

Reaching forth unto those things which are *before*. —Phil. iii. 13.

The battle was *before* and behind.
—2 Chron. xiii. 14.

2. in the past; up to now; previously; formerly; already.

You tell me what I knew *before*.
—Dryden.

3. ahead (of a given time); earlier; sooner.

bē·fōre′, conj. 1. in advance of the time that; as, see me *before* you leave.

2. sooner than; rather than; as, I'd die *before* I'd tell.

bē·fōre′hand, *adv.* and *a.* 1. in a state of anticipation or preoccupation: often followed by *with*; as, you are *beforehand with* me.

2. antecedently; early; ahead of time; betimes; as, I got ready *beforehand*.

bē·fōre′hand, *a.* in good pecuniary circumstances. [Archaic.]

bē·fōre′tīme, *adv.* formerly; of old time. [Archaic.]

bē·forc′tūne, *v.t.* to happen to; to betide.

bē·foul′, *v.t.*; befouled, *pt.*, *pp.*; befouling, *ppr.* [ME. *befoulen*; from AS. *befylan*, to befoul.]

1. to make foul; to soil.

2. to fall foul of; to entangle with; to run against.

3. to cast aspersions on.

bē·friend′ (-frend′), *v.t.*; befriended, *pt.*, *pp.*; befriending, *ppr.* to favor; to act as a friend to; to countenance, aid, or benefit.

bē·friend′ment, *n.* the act of befriending. [Rare.]

bē·frill′, *v.t.* to adorn with a frill or frills.

bē·fringe′, *v.t.* to furnish with a fringe; to adorn as with a fringe.

bē·fud′dle (-dl), *v.t.*; befuddled, *pt.*, *pp.*; befuddling, *ppr.* to mystify; to confuse; to muddle, as with drink.

beg (*or* bāg), *n.* a bey.

beg, *v.t.*; begged, *pt.*, *pp.*; begging, *ppr.* [ME. *beggin*, from Anglo-Fr. *begger*; OFr. *begard*, beggar; MD. *beggaert*; perh. from *beggen*, to request urgently.]

1. to ask earnestly; to beseech; to entreat or supplicate with humility.

2. to ask for as charity; as, to *beg* bread.

3. to ask as a kindness or favor.

4. to ask respectfully or deferentially; as, to *beg* pardon; to *beg* leave.

to beg off; to ask to be released from.

to beg the question; (a) to use an argument that assumes as proved the very thing one is trying to prove; (b) loosely, to evade the issue.

Syn.—beseech, solicit, entreat, supplicate, implore, crave, ask, pray, petition.—To *beg* denotes a state of want; to *beseech*, *entreat*, and *solicit*, a state of urgent necessity; *supplicate* and *implore* a state of abject distress; *crave*, the lowest state of physical want.

beg, *v.i.* 1. to ask for alms or charity; to practice begging; to live by asking alms.

2. to ask humbly; to entreat.

3. in card games, as seven-up, to ask for a point or new trump.

to go begging; to be valueless or not wanted; to fail to find a taker.

bē·gan′, *v.*; past tense of *begin*.

bē·gat′, *v.*, past tense of *beget*. [Archaic.]

bē·gem′, *v.t.*; begemmed (-jemd), *pt.*, *pp.*; begemming, *ppr.* to decorate with jewels or gems.

bē·get′, *v.t.*; begot *or archaic* begat, *pt.*; begetting, *ppr.*; begot *or* begotten, *pp.* [ME. *begeten*, to obtain; AS. *begitan*, to acquire; *bi*, be-, and *gitan*, to get.]

1. to procreate, as a father or sire; to generate; as, to *beget* a son.

2. to produce, as an effect; to cause to exist; to generate; as, luxuries *beget* vice.

bē·get′tẽr, *n.* one who begets or procreates.

beg′gȧ·ble, *a.* capable of being begged.

beg′găr, *n.* [ME. *beggar*, *beggere*; OFr. *begard*; see *beg*, *v.t.*]

1. one who lives by asking alms, or makes it his business to beg for charity.

2. one who assumes in argument what he does not prove. [Obs.]

3. a person who is very poor.

4. a rascal; scoundrel: in this sense, often used humorously.

beg′găr, *v.t.*; beggared (-gărd), *pt.*, *pp.*; beggaring, *ppr.* 1. to reduce to beggary; to impoverish; as, to *beggar* one's family.

2. to make appear poor or useless; as, to *beggar* description.

beg′găr·dŏm, *n.* 1. beggars collectively.

2. the state of being a beggar.

beg′găr·hood, *n.* beggardom.

beg′găr·iṣm, *n.* the state of beggary. [Rare.]

beg′găr-līce, *n.*; *pl.* **beg′găr-līce,** beggar's-lice.

beg′găr·li·ness, *n.* 1. extreme poverty.

2. shabbiness.

3. inadequacy.

beg′găr·ly, *a.* like or fit for a beggar; very poor, worthless, inadequate, etc.

beg′găr·ly, *adv.* meanly; indigently; despicably.

beg′găr's-līce, *n.*; *pl.* **beg′găr's-līce,** 1. any of a number of plants, as the tick trefoil, cleavers, etc., with prickly fruit or seeds that stick to one's clothes.

2. the fruit or seed of any of these plants.

beg′găr's-ticks, beg′găr-ticks; *pl.* **beg′găr's-ticks, beg′găr-ticks,** 1. the prickly, one-seeded fruit, or achene, of a bur marigold.

2. a bur marigold.

3. beggar's-lice.

beg′găr·weed, *n.* 1. any of a number of plants that grow in wasteland, as some tickseeds and knotweed.

2. a West Indian plant of the pea family, with purple or blue flowers and twisted pods: it is grown for fodder in the southern United States.

beg′găr·y, *n.*; *pl.* **beg′găr·ieș,** [ME. *beggerie*; from *beggere*, a beggar.]

1. a state of extreme indigence.

2. beggardom.

3. a beggarly aspect or appearance. [Rare.]

4. a place where beggars live.

Syn.—indigence, poverty, want.

beg′găr·y, *a.* 1. beggarly; mean. [Rare.]

2. run to weeds; weedy. [Brit. Dial.]

Beg′härd (beg′ärd *or* bi-gärd′), *n.* [ML. *beghardus*, *begardus*; from OFr. *begard*; see *beg*, *v.t.*] a member of any of several lay brotherhoods in Belgium, Holland, etc. in the thirteenth century.

bē·gild′, *v.t.*; begilded *or* begilt, *pt.*, *pp.*; begilding, *ppr.* to gild.

bē·gilt′, *a.* gilded.

bē·gin′, *v.i.*; began, *pt.*; beginning, *ppr.*; begun, *pp.* [ME. *beginnen*, from AS. *beginnan*, *onginnan*, to begin.]

1. to start.

2. to come into being.

3. to be or do in the slightest degree (with an infinitive); as, they don't *begin* to compare.

bē·gin′, *v.t.* 1. to cause to start; to commence.

2. to cause to come into being; to lay the foundation of; originate.

Syn.—commence, enter upon, originate, inaugurate, institute, start.

bē·gin′, *n.* beginning. [Obs.]

bē·gin′nẽr, *n.* 1. a person who begins anything.

2. a person just beginning to do or learn something; inexperienced, unskilled person; novice.

beginner's luck; the proverbial good fortune, met by a beginner, especially at gambling.

bē·gin′ning, *n.* 1. a starting or commencing.

2. the time or place of starting; birth; origin; source; as, English democracy had its *beginning* in the Magna Charta.

3. the first part; as, the *beginning* of this book is dull.

4. [*usually pl.*] an early stage or example; as, the *beginnings* of scientific agriculture.

bē·gird′, *v.t.*; begirt *or* begirded, *pt.*, *pp.* begirding, *ppr.* [ME. *begirden*, from AS. *begyrdan*, to gird.]

1. to bind around, as with a girdle.

2. to surround; to encompass.

bē·gir′dle, *v.t.*; begirdled (-girdld), *pt.*, *pp.*; begirdling, *ppr.* to encompass or bind as with a girdle.

bē·girt′, *v.t.* to begird.

beg′lẽr·beg, *n.* [Turk.] formerly, the governor of a province in the Turkish empire, next in dignity to the grand vizier.

bē·gnaw′ (-naw′), *v.t.* [AS. *begnagan.*] to bite or gnaw; to eat away; to corrode.

bē·god′, *v.t.* to deify. [Obs.]

beg′ōhm″, *n.* [*b*illion, and m*egohm*.] in electricity, a unit of resistance equivalent to a billion ohms.

bē·gone′, *interj.* and *v.i.* (to) go away; depart; be gone: usually in the imperative.

Bē·gō′ni·ȧ, *n.* [named after Michel *Begon* (1638–1710), a French botanist.]

1. a genus of herbaceous plants, native to the tropical regions of America. They have showy white, pink, or red flowers and ornamental leaves.

2. [b–] any plant of this genus.

Bē·gō·ni·ā′cē·ae, *n.pl.* a family of dicotyledonous plants including the Begonia: they occur mostly in the tropical parts of Asia and America.

bē·gō·ni·ā′ceous, *a.* of the family *Begoniaceæ.*

bē·gōre′, *v.t.* to spatter with gore.

bē·got′, *v.,* past tense and alternative past participle of *beget.*

bē·got′ten, alternative past participle of *beget.*

bē·grīme′, *v.t.,* begrimed, *pt., pp.;* begriming, *ppr.* to make dirty; to soil.

bē·grudġe′ (-gruj′), *v.t.;* begrudged, *pt., pp.;* begrudging, *ppr.* 1. to grumble at.
2. to envy (another) the possession of.
3. to give with ill will or reluctance; as, he *begrudges* her every cent.

bē·guīle′ (-gīl′), *v.t.;* beguiled (-gīld′), *pt., pp.;* beguiling, *ppr.* 1. to deceive; to mislead by deceit.
2. to deprive (*of* or *out of*) by deceit; cheat; as, he was *beguiled* of his money.
3. to relieve weariness in, by amusement; to pass (time) pleasingly.
4. to charm or delight.
Syn.—deceive, delude, mislead, divert, entertain.

bē·guīle′ment, *n.* the act of beguiling; the state of being beguiled.

bē·guīl′ēr, *n.* one who beguiles or deceives.

bē·guīl′ing·ly, *adv.* in a manner that beguiles.

bẹ·guï·nāge′ (bā-gi-näzh′), *n.* [Fr.] a convent or community of Beguines.

Bẹ·guïne′ (bā-gēn′), *n.* [OFr. *beguine;* LL. *beguina,* from Lambert le *Begue,* the Stammerer, who founded the order.]
1. one of an order of lay sisterhoods founded in the twelfth century in the Low Countries; it was composed of women who united for devotion and charity, and lived together without monastic vows.
2. [b–] (bi-gēn′), a native dance of Martinique: its music and rhythm have been popularized in the United States by Negroes.

BEGUINE

bē′gum (*or* bā′gum), *n.* [Anglo-Ind. word, from Hind. *begam,* a lady, from Turk. *bgim,* a princess.]
1. in India, a Moslem princess or lady of high rank.
2. in England, a wealthy Anglo-Indian woman.

bē·gun′, *v.* past participle of *begin.*

bē·hälf′ (-häf′), *n.* [ME. *behalve,* in the phrase *on behalve,* on my side; AS. *on healve, on healfe; on,* on, and *healve,* dat. of *healf,* half.] favor; profit; support; defense; vindication; as, in *behalf* of the prisoner. *Behalf* is always preceded by the prepositions *in, on,* or *upon.*

bē·hap′pen, *v.i.* to happen to. [Obs.]

bē·hāve′, *v.i.;* behaved, *pt., pp.;* behaving, *ppr.*
1. to act in a specified way; to conduct oneself or itself; as, to *behave* badly or well; the ship *behaved* admirably.
2. to conduct oneself well; do the right things.
3. to act or react.

bē·hāve′, *v.t.* [ME. *behaven;* AS. *behabban,* to hold, restrain; *be,* about, and *habban,* to have.]
1. to restrain; to govern; to subdue. [Obs.]
2. to conduct; to carry: used reflexively; as, to *behave* oneself.
Syn.—conduct, carry, deport, comport, manage, act.

bē·hāv′iŏr (-yūr), *n.* manner of behaving; conduct; manners; carriage of oneself, with respect to propriety or morals; deportment. It expresses external appearance or action. In this sense it is used also of inanimate objects; as, the *behavior* of a ship; the *behavior* of a magnetic needle.
2. an organism's muscular or glandular response or responses to stimulation, especially those that can be observed.
behavior modification; in psychology, a technique that seeks to modify animal and human behavior, in which rewards and reinforcements, or punishments, are used to establish desired habits, or patterns of behavior: also called *behavioral modification.*
Syn.—conduct, deportment, demeanor, bearing, carriage, manner.

bē·hāv′iŏr·iṣm (-yūr-izm), *n.* in psychology, the theory that all investigation of behavior must be objective or observed as introspection is considered invalid.

bē·hāv′iŏr·ist (-yūr-ist), *n.* one who accepts the theory of behaviorism.

bē·hāv′iŏr·ist (-yūr-ist), *a.* of or connected with behaviorism.

bē·hāv·iŏr·is′tiç (-yūr-is′tik), *a.* of or connected with behaviorism.

bē·hāv′iour (-yūr), *n.* behavior: British spelling.

bē·head′ (-hed′), *v.t.;* beheaded, *pt., pp.;* beheading, *ppr.* to cut off the head of; to decapitate.

bē·head′ăl, *n.* the act of beheading.

bē·held′, past tense and past participle of *behold.*

bē·hē′mŏth, *n.* [Heb. *b'hemoth,* huge beast, supposedly from Egyptian *p-ehe-mau,* water ox.]
1. a huge animal described in Job xi. 15–24, assumed to be the hippopotamus.
2. any huge animal.

bē′hen, ben, *n.* [Per. and Ar. *bahman, behmen,* the name of a flower.] the bladder campion, *Silene inflata.*

bē·hest′, *n.* [ME. *behest, bihest,* from AS. *behæse,* a command.]
1. an order; command; precept; mandate.
2. a pledge or solemn vow. [Obs.]

bē·hest′, *v.t.* to swear; to vow. [Obs.]

bē·hēte′, *v.t.* to behight. [Obs.]

bē·hīght (-hīt′), *v.t.* [AS. *behatan,* to promise.] to promise; to entrust; to call or name; to command; to adjudge; to address; to inform; to mean; to reckon. [Obs.]

bē·hīght′, *n.* a promise or vow. [Obs.]

bē·hīnd′, *prep.* [ME. *behinde, behinden,* from AS. *behindan,* behind; *be,* by, and *hindan,* adv., behind.]
1. on the side opposite the front or nearest part of; on the other side of; as, *behind* a bed; *behind* a hill; *behind* a house, tree, or rock.
2. at the back of; in the rear of; as, to walk or ride *behind* some one.
3. remaining after; as, a man leaves *behind* him his estate.
4. at a point less advanced in progress or improvement than; as, one student is *behind* another in mathematics; hence, inferior to in position, achievement, etc.
For I suppose I was not a whit *behind* the very chiefest apostles. —2 Cor. xi. 5.
5. later than; as, the train was *behind* schedule.
6. supporting or advocating; as, Congress is *behind* the plan.
7. hidden by; not yet revealed about; as, there's something *behind* this news.
behind the times; out of date; old-fashioned.
behind time; late; not up to the proper or appointed time.

bē·hīnd′, *adv.* 1. backward; in the rear; as, to look *behind;* to walk *behind.*
2. past; at an earlier time.
Forgetting those things which are *behind.* —Philip. iii. 13.
3. in a former place, condition, etc.; as, the girl he left *behind.*
4. yet to come; as, there is greater news *behind.*
5. below standard; in or into a retarded state; as, he dropped *behind* in his studies.
6. into arrears; as, he fell *behind* in his dues.
7. slow in time; late; as, the train was running *behind.*
8. to or toward the back; as, looking *behind.*

bē·hīnd′, *n.* the buttocks. [Colloq.]

bē·hīnd′hand, *adv.* and *a.* 1. in a state of arrears; behind in paying debts; as, *behindhand* with payments.
2. in a backward state; not equally advanced; slow in progress; as, *behindhand* in studies.
3. late; behind time; as, government expeditions are generally *behindhand.*

bē·hith′ēr, *prep.* on this side of. [Obs.]

bē·hōld′, *v.t.;* beheld, *pt., pp.;* beholding, *ppr.* [ME. *beholden, biholden;* AS. *behealdan,* to hold, keep; *be,* be-, intensive force, and *healdan,* to hold, keep.] to fix the eyes upon; to hold in attention; to observe; to look at; to see.
Behold the Lamb of God, which taketh away the sin of the world.—John i. 29.
When he *beheld* the serpent of brass, he lived. —Num. xxi. 9.
Syn.—see, regard, view, discern, observe, descry, eye, survey.

bē·hōld′, *v.i.* to look; to direct attention to an object: often used in the imperative as an interjection.
And I *beheld,* and, lo, in the midst of the throne, a Lamb. —Rev. v. 6.
Behold, I stand at the door, and knock. —Rev. iii. 20.

bē·hōld′en, *a.* [past participle of *behold.*] obliged; bound in gratitude; indebted.
Little are we *beholden* to your love. —Shak.

bē·hōld′ēr, *n.* one who beholds; a spectator.

bē·hōld′ing, *a.* beholden. [Obs.]

bē·hōld′ing, *n.* the act of beholding; also, that which is beheld.

bē·hōld′ing·ness, *n.* the state of being obliged. [Obs.]

bē·hoof′, *n.* [ME. *behof,* advantage; AS. *behofic,* advantageous, from *behofiane,* to need, be necessary.] that which is advantageous; advantage; profit; benefit; interest; behalf.
No mean recompense it brings to your *behoof.* —Milton.

bē·hoov′ă·ble, *a.* needful; profitable. [Obs.]

bē·hoove′, *v.t.* and *v.i.;* behooved, *pt., pp.;* behooving, *ppr.* [ME. *behoven, behofen;* AS. *behōfian,* to need.]
1. to be necessary (for).
2. to be fitting (for).
And thus it *behoved* Christ to suffer. —Luke xxiv. 46.
Also written *behove.*

bē·hoove′, *n.* behoof. [Obs.]

bē·hoove′ful, *a.* needful; useful; profitable; advantageous. [Archaic.]

bē·hoove′ful·ly, *adv.* usefully; profitably. [Obs.]

bē·hoove′ful·ness, *n.* advantageousness. [Obs.]

bē·hōve′, *v.t.* and *v.i.* same as *behoove.*

beiġe (bāzh), *n.* 1. a dress fabric of soft wool, originally of unbleached and undyed wool.
2. its characteristic sandy color; grayish tan.

beiġe, *a.* grayish-tan.

bē′ing, *v.,* present participle of *be.*

bē′ing, *n.* 1. existence; the state of existing; living; life.
2. one's fundamental nature; as, she responds to music with her whole *being.*
3. a creature that lives or exists, or is assumed to do so; as, a human *being,* a divine *being.*
4. [B–] God; usually with a qualifying term; as, the *Supreme Being.*
5. fulfillment of possibilities; essential completeness.
6. in philosophy, that which is, is possible, or can be logically conceived.

bē′ing, *a.* at hand; immediate; as, for the time *being* I'll stay.

bē·jāde′, *v.t.* to tire. [Obs.]

bē′jăn, bē′jănt, *n.* [Scot., from Fr. *béjaune;* from OFr. *becjaune,* a novice; literally, a yellow beak.] formerly, a freshman at certain Scottish universities. [Obs.]

bē·jāpe′, *v.t.* to laugh at; to deceive. [Obs.]

bē·jew′el, *v.t.;* bejeweled *or* bejewelled, *pt., pp.;* bejeweling *or* bejewelling, *ppr.* to adorn with gems or jewels.

bẹ·jú′ço (bā-hú′kō), *n.* [Sp.] any of various species of woody vines of tropical America.

bē′käh, *n.* [Heb.] one half a shekel.

bē·knāve′ (-nāv′), *v.t.* to call knave.

bē·knōw′ (-nō′), *v.t.* to acknowledge. [Obs.]

Bel, *n.* [the Chaldaic form of the Hebrew *Baal.*] the Babylonian god of heaven and earth.

bel, *n.* [Hind., from Sans. *bilva,* the name of a thorn tree.] the *Ægle marmelos,* a tree of India, producing an orangelike fruit, which has a medicinal use. From its rind a perfume and yellow dye are obtained. Called also *Bengal quince, wood apple, golden apple.*

bel, *n.* [after Alexander Graham *Bell,* the inventor.] in radio or wireless, the unit for the logarithmic expression of the ratios of current or of power.

bē·lā′bŏr, *v.t.;* belabored, *pt., pp.;* belaboring, *ppr.* 1. to work diligently at or upon. [Obs.]
2. to beat soundly; to thump; to hit or whip.
Ajax *belabours* there a harmless ox. —Dryden.
3. to beat with words; to attack verbally.
Syn.—toil, work, cudgel, flog, pommel, thrash, beat.

bel-aç·çoil′, bel-aç·çoyle′, [Fr. *bel,* beautiful, *accueil,* reception.] a kind salutation and reception. [Obs.]

bē·lāce′, *v.t.* 1. to adorn with lace. [Obs.]
2. to beat; to whip. [Obs.]

bē·lam′, *v.t.* to beat; to thrash. [Obs.]

bel′ă·mōur, *n.* [Fr. *bel,* fair, *amour,* love.]
1. a lover. [Obs.]
2. an old, unidentified flower. [Obs.]

bel′ȧ·my, *n.* [Fr. *bel*, good, *ami*, friend.] a good friend; an intimate. [Obs.]

bē·lāte′, *v.t.*; belated, *pt., pp.*; belating, *ppr.* to detain or make late.

bē·lāt′ed, *a.* 1. abroad late at night. [Archaic.]
2. too late; as, a *belated* traveler.

bē·lāt′ed·ness, *n.* the state of being belated.

bē·laud′, *v.t.* to laud; to praise highly.

bē·lāy′, *v.t.*; belayed, *pt., pp.*; belaying, *ppr.*
1. to await in ambush; to lie in wait for. [Obs.]
2. to adorn, surround, or cover. [Obs.]
3. in nautical usage, to fasten, or make fast, by winding a rope round a cleat or belaying pin.
4. to hold; to stop; as, *belay* there! [Colloq.]

bē·lāy′ing pin, in nautical usage, a strong pin in the side of a vessel, or by the mast, around which ropes are fastened.

bel çăn′tō, [It., lit., beautiful song]. a style of singing characterized by brilliant vocal display and purity of tone.

belch, *v.t.* and *v.i.*; belched, *pt., pp.*; belching, *ppr.* [ME. *belkan*; AS. *bealcan*, to belch, to swell or heave.]
1. to throw up or eject (gas) from the stomach; eructate.
2. to eject violently from within; to emit; as, a volcano *belches* flames and lava.
3. to speak (curses, etc.) violently (often with *forth*.)
4. to vomit.

belch, *n.* 1. the act of belching or ejecting gas from the stomach; eructation.
2. a thing belched.
3. malt liquor; bad beer: a vulgar usage.

belch′ẽr, *n.* one who or that which belches.

bel′dăm, bel′dāme, *n.* [Fr. *bel*; L. *bellus*, grand, and Fr. *dame*, lady.]
1. a hideous old woman; a hag.
2. a grandmother. [Obs.]
3. any old woman.

bē·lēa′gũer, *v.t.*; beleaguered, *pt., pp.*; beleaguering, *ppr.* [D. *belegeren*, to besiege.]
1. to besiege; to block up; to surround with an army.
2. to surround, as with denunciations.

bē·lēa′gũer·ẽr, *n.* one who besieges.

bē·lēave′, *v.t.* to leave. [Obs.]

bē·leç′tūre, *v.t.* to weary with lectures; to lecture too frequently.

bē·lee′, *v.t.* to place (a ship) on the lee, or in a position so that the wind cannot fill the sails.

bē·lem′nīte, *n.* [Gr. *belemnon*, a dart, or arrow; from *ballein*, to throw.]
1. the cigar-shaped fossil shell of an extinct kind of cuttlefish, belonging to the class *Cephalopoda* and found in Jurassic and Cretaceous formations: also called *thunderstone*.
2. the animal itself.

bel·em·nit′iç, *a.* of the nature of a belemnite.

Bē·lem·nit′i·dae, *n.pl.* a family of cephalopods including the belemnites.

bē·lep′ẽr, *v.t.* to infect with leprosy. [Obs.]

bel-es·prit′ (-prē′), *n.*; *pl.* **beaux-es·prits′** (bōz-es-prē′), [Fr. *bel*, fine, *esprit*, spirit, genius.] a wit; a clever, cultivated person.

bel′fry, *n.* [ME. *belfray*, a watch tower; OFr. *belfroi*; LL. *berefredus*, a watch tower; from G. *bercvrit*, *bercfrit*, literally a protecting shelter; *berc*, from *bergen*, to protect, and *frit*, for *vride*, an enclosed place.]
1. in ancient warfare, a movable tower for attacking walled positions.
2. that part of a tower or steeple in which a bell or bells are hung.
3. a bell tower.
4. any tower.
5. in nautical usage, the framing on which a ship's bell is suspended.

bel′gȧ, *n.* [L., a Belgian.] a Belgian unit of currency; money of account equivalent to $.139 when established in 1926.

Bel′ġae, *n.pl.* [L.] a former Gallic people of northern France and Belgium.

bel·gärd′, *n.* [It. *bel guardo*, a lovely look.] a loving look or glance. [Obs.]

Bel′ġi·ăn, *a.* pertaining to Belgium or its people.

Bel′ġi·ăn, *n.* a native or inhabitant of Belgium.

Bel′ġi·ăn hāre, a large, reddish-brown domestic rabbit.

Bel′ġiç, *a.* [L. *Belgicus*, from *Belgæ*, the Belgians.]
1. pertaining to the Belgae.
2. pertaining to Belgium or to its language, customs, or productions.
3. pertaining to the Netherlands.

Bel′ġic, *n.* the Gallic language of the Belgae.

Bel·grā′vi·ȧ, *n.* 1. in Victorian London, a residential area surrounding Belgrave Square, home of the newly rich, upper middle class.
2. this social class, its life, tastes, etc.

Bel·grā′vi·ăn, *a.* pertaining to Belgravia; hence, of a fashionable or exclusive character.

Bel·grā′vi·ăn, *n.* 1. an inhabitant of Belgravia.
2. a member of the Belgravian social class.

Bē′li·ăl, *n.* [Heb. *b′līya′al*, wickedness.]
1. in the Old Testament, the personification of wickedness as an evil force.
2. one of the fallen angels in Milton's *Paradise Lost*.
3. in the New Testament, Satan.
son of Belial; a very wicked and depraved person.

> The sons of Eli were *sons of Belial*.
> —I Sam. ii. 12.

bē·lī′bel, *v.t.* to libel or traduce.

bē·līe′, *v.t.*; belied, *pt., pp.*; belying, *ppr.* [ME. *belyen*, from AS. *beleogan*, to give the lie to; be, be-, and *leogan*, to lie.]
1. to lie about.
2. to disguise; as, the heart *belies* the tongue: used of appearances which are false or misrepresentative.
3. to leave unfulfilled; disappoint.
4. to show to be mistaken; to prove false.

bē·lief′, *n.* [ME. *beleve*, *beleafe*; AS. *geleāfa*, belief, from *gelēfan*, to believe.]
1. an acceptance of something as true.
2. in theology, faith, or a firm persuasion of the truths of a religion.

> No man can attain [to] *belief* by the bare contemplation of heaven and earth.
> —Hooker.

3. the body of religious doctrine held by the professors of a faith; a creed.

> In the heat of persecution, to which Christian *belief* was subject upon its first promulgation.
> —Hooker.

4. anything believed; the object of believing.

> Superstitious prophecies are the *belief* of fools.
> —Bacon.

5. trust; confidence; as, I have *belief* in his ability.
6. an opinion; expectation; judgment; as, my *belief* is that he'll come.

Syn.—conviction, faith, opinion, credence, creed, trust, persuasion, confidence.

bē·lief′fu̧l, *a.* possessing belief or faith. [Rare.]

bē·liēv′ȧ·ble, *a.* capable of being believed; credible.

bē·liēv·ȧ·bil′i·ty, *n.* the condition of being believable; credibility.

bē·liēv′ȧ·ble·ness, *n.* credibility.

bē·liēve′, *v.t.*; believed, *pt., pp.*; believing, *ppr.*
1. to accept as the truth; to take as true, real, etc.
2. to expect or hope for with confidence; to assume.

> I had fainted, unless I had *believed* to see the goodness of the Lord in the land of the living.
> —Ps. xxvii. 13.

3. to have confidence in a promise or statement of (another person).

bē·liēve′, *v.i.* 1. to have trust or confidence.
2. in theology, to have faith.
3. to think or suppose; to hold views or opinions.
to believe in; to trust; to have the utmost confidence in the existence of; also, to trust implicitly in the ability of.

bē·liēv′ẽr, *n.* 1. one who believes.
2. in theology, one who has a specific religious faith.

bē·liēv′ing·ly, *adv.* in a believing manner.

bē·līght′ (bē-līt′), *v.t.* to light or illuminate. [Obs.]

bē·līke′, *adv.* probably; likely; perhaps. [Archaic.]

bē·līke′ly, *adv.* probably. [Obs.]

bē·līme′, *v.t.* to smear with birdlime.

bē·lit′tle, *v.t.*; belittled, *pt., pp.*; belittling, *ppr.*
1. to disparage; to lower in character; to depreciate.
2. to make (a thing) little or smaller.

bē·līve′, *adv.* speedily; quickly. [Obs.]

belk, *v.t.* to belch. [Obs.]

bell, *n.* [ME. *bel*, *belle*; AS. *belle*, a bell.]
1. a hollow, metallic object which rings when struck. It may be cup-shaped, with a wide mouth, saucer-shaped, as a gong, or spherical, as a sleighbell. A bell produces sound when struck with a hammer of some kind, either outside or in. In some, a clapper or tongue is the hammer; in the spherical bell, a metal ball.
2. anything in the form of a bell, as the cup or calyx of a flower.
3. a bell rung to mark the hours at the beginning and end of a period of time.
4. the sound made by a bell.
5. [*pl.*] a musical instrument made up of a series of metal bars or hollow tubes that sound like bells.
6. in nautical usage, (a) a bell rung every half hour to mark the periods of the watch, which begin at one bell (12:30, 4:30, and 8:30 o'clock) and end at eight bells (4:00, 8:00, and 12:00 o'clock); (b) any of these periods.
Liberty Bell; the bell of Independence Hall in Philadelphia, which was rung when the Continental Congress announced the Declaration of Independence in 1776. It is a symbol of American liberty. It was cast in 1753, and bears the inscription, "Proclaim liberty throughout all the land, to all the inhabitants thereof." It cracked in 1835.
to bear the bell; to be the first or leader; to be the best.
to curse by bell, book, and candle; in the Roman Catholic Church, to excommunicate by means of a formal ceremony.

bell, *v.t.*; belled, *pt., pp.*; belling, *ppr.* 1. To attach a bell or bells to; to furnish or equip with a bell or bells.
2. to make into the form of a bell; as, to *bell* the mouth of a horn.
to bell the cat; to undertake a hazardous task: from the fable of the mice resolving to put a bell on the cat, to guard them against his attack.

bell, *v.i.* to grow in the form of bells; to become bell-shaped.

bell, *v.i.* [ME. *belle*, from AS. *bellan*, to roar.] to call or make a peculiar sound, as that of the deer in the rutting season.

> The wild buck *bells* from ferny brake.
> —Scott.

bell, *n.* [D. *bel*, a bubble.] a bubble formed by gas in a liquid; as, an air *bell* in a photographic plate.

bel·lȧ·don′nȧ, *n.* [It. *bella donna*, beautiful lady; from L. *bella*, f. of *bellus*, beautiful, and *domina*, lady.] a European poisonous plant of the nightshade family (*Atropa belladonna*), with purplish or reddish bell-shaped flowers and black berries. It is a perennial herb, containing the alkaloid atropine. The extracts of its root and leaf are largely used medicinally to relieve pain and, in optical surgery, to dilate the pupil of the eye. Also called *deadly nightshade*.

bel·lȧ·don′nȧ lil′y, an ornamental plant, with large rose-tinted bell-shaped flowers that look like lilies: a native of South Africa. The *Amaryllis belladonna*.

BELLADONNA LILY
(*Amaryllis belladonna*)

bell an·i·mal′çūle, [L. *bellus*, fine, and *animal*, a living being.] one of the species of the genus *Vorticella*.

bell beăr′ẽr, a leaf hopper of Brazil (*Bocydium tintinnabuliferum*), distinguished for having four bell-shaped appendages on its thorax.

bell′bīrd, *n.* one of several species of birds named from the bell-like character of their songs, including *Chasmorhynchus niveus* of South America and *Manorhina melanophrys* of Australia.

bell′boy, *n.* a boy or man employed by a hotel, club, etc. to carry luggage and do errands.

bell buoy (boy, bö′i), a buoy with a warning bell rung by the motion of the waves.

bell çrañk, a lever whose two arms meet the fulcrum at right angles or nearly so. It is used for changing the direction of motion in the wires of bell pulls, etc.

BELL CRANK

belle (bel), *n.* [Fr., f. of *beau*, beautiful; OFr. *bel*; L. *bellus*, beautiful, fine.]
1. a very attractive woman or girl.
2. the most attractive or most popular woman or girl of a certain place or on a given occasion; as, the *belle* of the ball.

belled (beld), *a.* furnished with bells.

Bel·leek′, *n.* [after *Belleek*, County Donegal, Ireland, where it was made.] a fine, glossy, often iridescent pottery resembling porcelain: also *Belleek ware*.

Bel·ler′ō·phon, *n.* [L.; Gr. *Bellerephōn*.]
1. in Greek mythology, the hero who killed the monster Chimera with the help of the winged horse Pegasus.
2. a genus of fossil shells, of the Paleozoic Era.

belles-let′tres (bel-let′tr), *n.pl.* [Fr., lit., beautiful letters, fine literature.] literature as one of the fine arts; fiction, poetry, drama, etc. as distinguished from technical and scientific writings.

bel·let′rist, belle-let′trist, *n.* one devoted to belles-lettres.

bel·le·tris′tiç, bel·le·tris′ti·çăl, *a.* characteristic of belles-lettres.

bell′-fāced, *a.* having a convex striking surface, as a hammer.

bell′flow″ẽr, *n.* 1. any one of a number of different species of plants of the genus *Campanula*, with showy, bell-shaped flowers, usually of blue, white, or pink.

2. a large winter apple.

bell gā′ble, a gable-shaped structure for hanging a bell.

bell glȧss, a bell jar.

bell′hop, *n.* a bellboy. [Slang.]

bell′i·bōne, *n.* [Fr. *belle et bonne*, beautiful and good.] a woman excelling both in beauty and goodness. [Obs.]

bel′liç, bel′liç·ăl, *a.* [Fr. *bellique*; L. *bellicus*, warlike; *bellum*, war.] concerning war; characteristic of war. [Obs.]

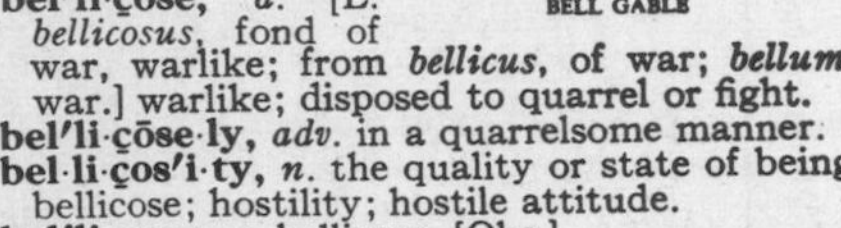

BELL GABLE

bel′li·çōse, *a.* [L. *bellicosus*, fond of war, warlike; from *bellicus*, of war; *bellum*, war.] warlike; disposed to quarrel or fight.

bel′li·çōse·ly, *adv.* in a quarrelsome manner.

bel·li·ços′i·ty, *n.* the quality or state of being bellicose; hostility; hostile attitude.

bel′li·çous, *a.* bellicose. [Obs.]

bel′lied, *a.* 1. swelled or prominent like the belly: used chiefly in combination; as, a big-*bellied* bottle.

2. in botany, ventricose; swelling out in the middle, as a monopetalous corolla.

bel·liġ′ẽr·ence, *n.* [from belligerent.] the state or quality of being belligerent.

2. war.

bel·liġ′ẽr·en·cy, *n.* 1. the state of being a belligerent.

2. belligerence.

bel·liġ′ẽr·ent, *n.* [Fr. *belligérant*, waging war, from L. *belligerans*, ppr. of *belligerare*, to wage war.] any person, group, or nation engaged in war or fighting.

bel·liġ′ẽr·ent, *a.* 1. hostile; addicted to war; bellicose; warlike in attitude or intention; threatening war.

2. pertaining to warfare or fighting; pertaining to belligerents, or those at war with one another.

3. at war.

bel·liġ′ẽr·ent·ly, *adv.* in a hostile or warlike manner; bellicosely.

bel·liġ′ẽr·ous, *a.* belligerent. [Obs.]

bell′ing, *n.* [AS. *bellan*, to bellow.] (a) the noise of deer in rutting time; (b) the baying of hounds in a fox chase.

bel·lip′ō·tent, *a.* [L. *bellipotens*, powerful in war, from *bellum*, war, and *potens*, powerful.] powerful or mighty in war. [Rare.]

bel′lis, *n.* [L., from *bellus*, beautiful.] the daisy, a small genus of annual or perennial flowering plants found in great profusion in North America and Europe.

bell jär, a bell-shaped container or cover made of glass: also called *bell glass, cloche*.

bell′măn, *n.*; *pl.* **bell′men,** 1. a town crier.

2. same as *bellboy*.

bell met′ăl, an alloy of copper and tin, used for making bells.

bell-metal ore; same as *stannite* (sense 1).

bell′mouthed, *a.* with a bell-like opening at the mouth, as a cornet.

bel′lŏn, *n.* [origin unknown.] lead or painter's colic.

Bel·lō′nȧ, *n.* [L.] in Roman mythology, the goddess of war, sister of Mars.

bel′lōw, *v.i.*; bellowed, *pt., pp.*; bellowing, *ppr.* [ME. *belwen*; AS. *bylgean*, to bellow.]

1. to roar with a powerful, reverberating sound, as a bull, elephant, etc.

2. to make a sound like this.

3. to cry out loudly, as in anger or pain.

bel′lōw, *v.t.* to utter loudly or powerfully.

bel′lōw, *n.* 1. the roar of a bull, elephant, etc.

2. any loud, powerful sound made by bellowing.

bel′lōw·ẽr, *n.* one who bellows.

bel′lōw·ing, *n.* a loud, hollow sound or roar, like that of a bull.

bel′lōwṣ, *n. sing.* and *pl.* [ME. *belowes, belwes*; AS. *bælg, bælig*, a bellows.]

1. a device for producing a stream of air under pressure, used for blowing fires, in pipe organs, etc. It is so formed that by being expanded, it draws in air by an orifice which is opened and closed with a valve, and by contraction expels a stream of air.

2. anything like a bellows, as the folding part of a camera, the lungs, etc.

bel′lōwṣ çam′e·rȧ, a photographic camera that can be drawn out like a bellows.

bel′lōwṣ fish, the trumpet fish, *Centriscus scolopax*, which has a long tubular snout, like the pipe of a pair of bellows: called also *snipe-fish*.

BELLOWS FISH
(*Centriscus scolopax*)

bell pep′pẽr, the common garden red pepper.

bell pụll, a cord to ring a bell with; the handle by which to pull a wire to ring a bell.

bell punch, an instrument used to cancel tickets on railroad trains, streetcars, etc. It rings a small bell when a perforation is made.

bell ring′ẽr, one whose business is to ring a church bell or chimes, or hand bells.

bell rọof, a roof having the contour of a bell.

bell′-shāped, *a.* having the form of a bell.

bel′lū·ine, *a.* [L. *belluinus*, beastlike; from *bellua*, a beast.] beastly; brutal. [Rare.]

bell′weth″ẽr, *n.* a wether or male sheep which leads the flock, with a bell on his neck; hence, any leader, especially of a foolish, sheeplike crowd.

bell′wŏrt, *n.* 1. any one of the species of plants of the genus *Uvularia*, with yellow, bell-shaped flowers and drooping leaves.

2. a bellflower; campanula.

bel′ly, *n.*; *pl.* **bel′lieṣ,** [ME. *bely, beli*, the belly, stomach; AS. *belg, baelg, bielg*, a bag.]

1. the lower front part of the human body between the chest and thighs; the abdomen.

2. the underside of an animal's body.

3. the abdominal cavity, especially as a center of pain or receptacle of food.

4. the stomach.

5. the capacity of the stomach.

6. the deep interior (of a thing); as, the *belly* of a ship.

7. an enlarged or bulging part or section.

8. any curved surface or area, especially if hollow.

9. the front part or underside of anything: opposed to *back*.

10. the upper plate or front of a musical instrument of the viol group.

11. the womb. [Obs.]

bel′ly, *v.t.*; bellied, *pt., pp.*; bellying, *ppr.* to fill; to swell out.

bel′ly, *v.i.* to swell and become protuberant, like the belly; to bulge.

bel′ly·āçhe (-āk), *n.* pain in the abdomen; colic. [Colloq.]

bel′ly·āçhe (-āk), *v.i.*; bellyached, *pt., pp.*; bellyaching, *ppr.* to complain clamorously; to complain whiningly. [Slang.]

bel′ly·band, 1. a band that encompasses the belly of a horse and fastens the saddle; a girth.

2. a cloth band worn about the belly; specifically, one that is put about a baby's abdomen to reinforce the weak muscles.

3. in seamanship, a strengthening band of canvas on a sail.

bel′ly bōard, the sounding board of a musical instrument.

bel′ly-bound, *a.* constipated.

bel′ly·but·tŏn, *n.* the navel: also *belly button*. [Colloq.]

bel′ly chēat, an apron. [Obs.]

bel′ly cheer, good cheer. [Obs.]

bel′ly dȧnce, a dance of eastern Mediterranean origin characterized by a twisting of the abdomen, sinuous movements, etc.

bel′ly flop, 1. to dive awkwardly so that the belly strikes flat against the water. [Colloq.]

2. to throw oneself on a sled, with the belly downward, and coast, as down a hill. [Colloq.]

bel′ly fret′ting, 1. the chafing of a horse's belly with a girth.

2. a violent pain in a horse's belly, caused by worms.

bel′ly·fụl, *n.* 1. enough or more than enough to eat.

2. enough or more than enough of anything. [Slang.]

bel′ly god, one who takes great pleasure in eating, a gluttonous person.

bel′ly läugh (läf), 1. a hearty laugh. [Slang.]

2. anything that produces such a laugh, as a line or situation in a play. [Slang.]

bel′ly-pinched, *a.* starved; pinched with hunger.

bel′ly rōll, a barrel-shaped roller, to roll plowed land between ridges, or in hollows.

bel′ly slāve, a slave to the appetite.

bel′ly wŏrm, a worm that breeds in the belly or stomach.

bē·lock′, *v.t.* [AS. *belucan*, to lock.] to lock, or fasten as with a lock. [Obs.]

bel′ō·man·cy, *n.* [Gr. *belos*, an arrow, and *manteia*, divination.] a kind of divination practiced with arrows, in former times. A number of arrows, being marked, were put into a bag or quiver, and drawn out at random, and the marks or words on the arrow drawn signified what was to happen.

bē·lọng′, *v.i.*; belonged, *pt., pp.*; belonging, *ppr.* [ME. *belongen*, to be the property of, from *be-*, and AS. *langian*, to go along with.] to have a proper or suitable place; have the proper qualities to be; as, she *belongs* in the movies.

belong to; (a) to be part of; to be related to or connected with; (b) to be owned by; to be the possession of; (c) to be associated with; to be a member of; (d) to be the owner; as, who *belongs* to this toothbrush? [Slang.]

bē·lọng′ing, *n.* 1. that which belongs to a person or thing.

2. [*pl.*] possessions or property, such as clothes, household goods, etc.

3. close relationship; affinity; rapport; as, a feeling of *belonging*.

bel′ō·nīte, *n.* [Gr. *belonē*, a needle.] a small crystalline formation sometimes found in glassy volcanic rocks.

Bel·ọọ′chē, *n.* see *Baluchi*.

bē·lord′, *v.t.* 1. to treat in a manner characteristic of a lord.

2. to address as "my lord."

Bel·os′tō·mȧ, *n.* [Gr. *belos*, a dart, and *stoma*, mouth.] the typical genus of the water bug family *Belostomidæ*. The largest species, *Belostoma grandis*, reaches four inches in length and is found in South America. It preys upon fish and other animals of considerable size: called also the *great water bug*.

bē·lōve′, *v.t.* to love. [Obs.]

bē·lŏv′ed (*or* bē-luvd′) *n.* one greatly loved.

bē·lŏv′ed, *a.* loved; greatly loved.

bē·lōw′, *prep.* [ME. *bilooghe*, from *bi*, be, and *logh*, low.]

1. under in place; beneath; not so high as; as, *below* the moon; *below* the knee.

2. lower than, as in rank, excellence, worth, price, etc.

3. unworthy of; unbefitting.

bē·lōw′, *adv.* and *a.* 1. in or to a lower place; beneath.

2. in a lower place on a page.

3. in a following part (of a book, etc.).

4. in hell.

5. on earth.

6. on or to a lower floor or deck.

7. in a lesser rank, function, etc.

8. in music, in a lower pitch.

Syn.—beneath, under, underneath.

Bel·shaz′zăr, *n.* [Heb. *bēlshatstsar*; from Bab. *bel-sharra-uṣur*, lit., may Bel protect the king.] in the Bible, the last king of Babylon, who was warned of defeat by the handwriting on the wall: Dan. v.

bel′sīre, *n.* a grandsire or any ancestor. [Obs.]

bel′swag″gẽr, *n.* a lewd man; a bully. [Obs.]

belt, *n.* [ME. *belt*, from AS. *belt*, from L. *balteus*, a belt.]

1. a girdle, band, or cincture, of leather or any other material, worn around the waist or body to hold clothing up, support tools, etc., or as an ornament or sign of rank; as, a lady's *belt*; a sword *belt*.

2. anything having resemblance to a *belt*; a stripe; a strip; as, a *belt* of woods.

3. an area or zone characterized by some peculiarity or natural phenomenon; as, the cotton *belt*; a *belt* of calms; a heat *belt*.

4. [B–] a narrow passage of water; a strait; specifically, the Great and Lesser *Belt* in the Baltic Sea.

5. in mechanics, a wide, endless strap or band around two or more wheels, pulleys,

etc., transferring motion from one to the other; also, a similar band used to carry things.

6. in architecture, a course of stone marking a band across the wall of a building.

7. a blow; as, a *belt* with a club. [Slang.]

8. a series of armored plates around a ship at the water line.

9. an encircling or beltlike road, highway, or route; belt line.

below the belt; (a) unfair; foul; (b) unfairly: originally said of a blow to the groin in boxing.

belt, *v.t.*; belted, *pt., pp.*, belting, *ppr.* 1. to surround or encircle with or as with a belt; to girdle.

2. to fasten or attach with a belt.

3. to strike with a belt.

4. to strike with force. [Slang.]

Bel'tāne, *n.* [Scot., from Gael. *Bealltainn.*]

1. an ancient Scottish festival, formerly celebrated on May 1, Old Style. It marked the beginning of summer.

2. the ancient Celtic May Day.

belt'ed, *a.* 1. wearing a belt, especially as a mark of distinction; as, a *belted* knight.

2. marked or adorned by a band or stripe.

3. worn at or hanging from the belt.

belted cattle; a breed of black-and-white cattle originally from Holland, the white being in the form of a wide belt about the body.

Bel'tein, Bel'tin, *n.* Beltane.

belt'ing, *n.* 1. belts, collectively.

2. the material used in making belts.

3. a beating. [Slang.]

belt lā'cing, strong, pliable leather thongs used in uniting machine belts.

belt līne, a railroad, trolley line, etc. that makes a circuit.

belt'wāy", *n.* an expressway passing around an urban area.

bē·lū'gȧ, *n.*; *pl.* **bē·lū'gȧ** or **bē·lū'gȧṣ,** [Russ., from *byeli*, white.]

1. a large cetacean, *Delphinapterus leucas*, of the northern seas, twelve feet and upwards in length: called also *white whale* or *whitefish*.

2. a large, white sturgeon of the Black Sea and the Caspian Sea, *Acipenser huso*.

bel·ve·dēre', *n.* [It. *belvedere*, a beautiful view; *bel*, beautiful, and *vedere*, a view, from L. *bellus*, fine, and *videre*, to see.]

1. the uppermost story of a building, open to the air, at least on one side, and frequently on all, for the purpose of giving a view of the country.

AA, BELVEDERE

2. a summerhouse on an eminence in a park or garden.

bel'zē·buth, *n.* [from *Beelzebub.*] a spider monkey of Brazil, *Ateles belzebuth*.

bē'mȧ, *n.*; *pl.* **bē'mȧ·tȧ,** [Gr. *bēma*, a step.]

1. in the early Christian church and Orthodox Eastern Church, a low enclosure surrounding the altar.

2. in ancient Greece, a stage or platform, on which speakers stood when addressing an assembly.

bē·maṅ'gle, *v.t.* to mangle; to tear asunder. [Rare.]

bē·mȧsk', *v.t.* to mask; to conceal.

bē·mȧs'tēr, *v.t.* to master with thoroughness.

bē'mȧ·tȧ, *n.*, pl. of *bema*.

bē·maul', *v.t.* to beat severely; to bruise.

bē·māzed', *a.* [MD. *bemased*, pp. of *bemasen*, to confuse.] muddled; confused; dazed.

Bem'bȧ, *n.* 1. *pl.* **Bem'bȧṣ, Bem'bȧ,** any member of a people of northern Zambia.

2. their Bantu language.

bē·mēan', *v.t.*; bemeaned, *pt., pp.*; bemeaning, *ppr.* to render mean; to degrade.

bē·miṅ'gle, *v.t.* to mingle; to mix. [Rare.]

bē·mīre', *v.t.* 1. to drag or encumber in the mire; to soil by passing through mud or dirt.

2. to stick or bog down in mud.

bē·mist', *v.t.* to cover or envelop in mist.

bē·mōan', *v.t.* and *v.i.*; bemoaned, *pt., pp.*; bemoaning, *ppr.* [ME. *bemenen*; AS. *bemænan*; *be*, be-, with intensive force, and *mænen*, to moan.] to lament; to bewail; to moan or wail about (a loss, grief, etc.).

Syn.—grieve, lament, mourn, sorrow.

bē·mōan'ēr, *n.* one who laments.

bē·mock', *v.t.*; bemocked, *pt., pp.*; bemocking, *ppr.* to treat with mockery; to ridicule.

bē·moil', *v.t.* [Fr. *mouiller*, to wet.] to bedraggle; to soil or encumber with dirt. [Obs.]

bē·mon'stēr, *v.t.* to make monstrous.

bē·mōurn', *v.t.* to mourn over. [Obs.]

bē·mud'dle, *v.t.*; bemuddled, *pt., pp.*; bemuddling, *ppr.* to muddle; to stupefy or confuse.

bē·muf'fle, *v.t.* to cover; to wrap up; to muffle. [Rare.]

bē·mūṣe', *v.t.* 1. to muddle; confuse; stupefy.

2. to plunge in thought; preoccupy: usually in the passive voice.

bē·mūṣed', 1. stupefied; confused.

2. plunged in thought; preoccupied.

ben, ben nut, [Ar. *bān*, the name of the ben nut tree.] the seed of an East Indian tree of the genus *Moringa*, which yields an oil used in some perfumes.

ben, *adv.* and *prep.* within. [Scot.]

Wi' kindly welcome Jenny brings him *ben*.
—Burns.

ben, *n.* the inner room or parlor. [Scot.]

ben, *n.* [Heb. *bēn*, son.] son (of); as, Rabbi *Ben* Ezra.

ben, *n.* [Scot.; from Gael. *beann*, a peak.] a mountain peak; as, *Ben* Nevis. [Scot. and Irish.]

ben, obsolete plural indicative present of *be*.

ben'ȧ·dryl, *n.* a drug used in the treatment of certain allergic conditions, as hives, hay fever, and asthma: a trade-mark (*Benadryl*).

bē·nāme', *v.t.*; benamed, *pt.*; benamed, benempt, *or* benempted, *pp.*; benaming, *ppr.* to give a name to; to call. [Archaic.]

bench, *n.* [ME. *benk, bynk*; AS. *benc*, bench.]

1. a long seat made of wood, stone, etc., often without a back.

2. a worktable.

3. a seat between the two sides of a boat.

4. a terrace along the bank of a body of water, often marking a former shore line.

5. a stand upon which dogs are exhibited at shows.

6. a level, narrow, high area.

7. the place where judges sit in a court.

8. [*sometimes* B–] the status or office of a judge.

9. judges collectively.

10. a law court.

bench, *v.t.* 1. to provide with benches.

2. to place on a bench, especially an official one.

3. to exhibit on a platform at a dog show.

4. in sports, to take (a player) out of a game.

bench, *v.i.* to sit on a seat of justice. [Obs.]

bench dog, any dog exhibited at a dog show.

bench'ēr, *n.* 1. a person who sits on or works at a bench.

2. [*often* B–] in English law, one of the senior members of an Inn of Court who have the government of the society.

3. an alderman of a corporation. [Eng.]

4. a judge. [Rare.]

5. an idler; one who frequents the benches of a tavern. [Obs.]

bench'-māde", *a.* made on a bench; hence, hand-made.

bench märk, 1. a surveyor's mark made on a permanent landmark that has a known position and altitude: bench marks are used as reference points in determining other altitudes within a given line of levels.

2. a standard or point of reference in measuring or judging quality, value, etc.

Also *benchmark*.

bench plāne, any hand plane used for working a flat surface on wood, as a jack plane.

bench shōw, a dog show.

bench tā'ble, in architecture, a projection, as of masonry, from an interior wall, of such height as to furnish a seat.

bench wär'rȧnt, an order issued by a judge or law court for the arrest of a person charged with contempt of court or a criminal offense: distinguished from *magistrate's warrant*.

bend, *v.t.*, bent *or archaic* bended, *pt., pp.*, bending, *ppr.* [ME. *benden*, from AS. *bendan*, to bend.]

1. originally, to cause tension in (a bow, etc.), as by drawing with a string.

2. to make (an object) curved or crooked.

3. to turn from a straight line; to cause to swerve; as, he *bent* his steps from the path.

4. to make stoop, bow, or give in; as, he *bent* the prisoner's will to his wishes.

5. to turn or direct (one's eyes, attention, energy, etc. *to*).

6. in nautical usage, to fasten into position: said of sails and ropes.

bend, *v.i.* 1. to turn or be turned from a straight line or from some direction or position; swerve; curve.

2. to yield by curving or crooking, as from pressure.

3. to crook or curve the body from a standing position; stoop; bow (often with *over*).

4. to give in; yield: as, he *bent* to her wishes.

5. to move from a given line or direction; to incline away.

6. to direct one's attention, energy, etc. (*to* something).

bend, *n.* 1. a bending or being bent.

2. a bent or curving part; a curve; a crook; as, a *bend* in a stream.

3. any of various knots by which one part of a rope is fastened to another, or to a post, spar, or anchor.

4. in a ship, one of the strongest planks in its sides, more generally called a *wale*.

5. in tanning, one half of a trimmed hide or butt.

6. in mining, indurated clay.

bend, *n.* 1. a band. [Obs.]

2. in heraldry, a stripe or band from the upper left to the lower right corner of a coat of arms.

BEND

bend sinister; a band or stripe from the upper right to the lower left corner of a coat of arms: it has come to signify bastardy in the family line.

bend'ȧ·ble, *a.* capable of being bent or curved.

Ben Dā'vis, a variety of large winter apple.

Ben Dāy proc'ess, [named for the American inventor, Benjamin Day.] a mechanical process for stippling, shading, or tinting line engravings.

bend'ēr, *n.* 1. one who or that which bends.

2. a drinking bout; a spree. [Slang.]

bend'let, *n.* [early modern Eng. *bendlet.*] in heraldry, a narrow bend which occupies a sixth part of a shield.

bendṣ, *n.* cramps that often attack a person who goes too quickly from a place of abnormal atmospheric pressure to one of normal pressure, as in deep-sea diving or high-altitude flying: used with *the*: also called *caisson disease*. [Colloq.]

bend'wīṣe, bend'wāyṣ, *adv.* in heraldry, diagonally; in the direction of a bend.

ben'dy, *n.* [Hind. *bhiṇdi.*] the okra plant: its pods are used as a vegetable.

ben'dy, *a.* [Fr. *bandé*, from OFr. *bende*, a band or fillet.] in heraldry, divided into four, six, or more bends and varying in metal and color: said of the field.

A SWORD BENDWISE

ben'dy tree, a naturalized West Indian tree, *Thespesia populnea*: called also *portia* and *umbrella tree*. It is a native of Eastern Asia, and Polynesia. It produces portia seeds, from which an oil is made, and a dye is made from the flowers.

bē'nē, *n.* [AS. *ben.*] a prayer; a boon. [Obs.]

ben'e, ben, *n.* [native name.] the *Sus papuensis*, a wild hog of New Guinea.

bē·nēaped' (-nēpt'), *a.* neaped.

bē·nēath', *prep.* [ME. *benethe, binethe*; AS. *beneothan*, beneath; *be-*, intensive be-, and *neothan*, below.]

1. below; lower than.

2. directly under; underneath.

3. covered by; as, *beneath* blankets.

4. under the influence of (something powerful, oppressive, etc.); as, living *beneath* a tyranny.

5. inferior to or lower than in rank, quality, worth, etc.

6. unworthy of; as, it is *beneath* him to cheat.

bē·nēath', *adv.* and *a.* 1. in a lower place; below.

2. just below something; underneath.

ben·ē·dic'i·tē, *n.* 1. the invocation of a blessing, as in asking grace at meals.

2. [B–] the canticle that begins *Benedicite, omnia opera Domini Domino* (Bless the Lord, all ye works of the Lord).

ben·ē·dic'i·tē, *interj.* bless you.

Ben'ē·dick, *n.* [from L. *Benedictus*, lit., blessed.]

1. in Shakespeare's *Much Ado About Nothing*, a bachelor who finally falls in love with the clever Beatrice.
2. [b–] a benedict.

ben'ē·dịct, *n.* [from *Benedick*.]
1. a man newly married: applied especially to one who has previously scoffed at marriage.
2. any married man.

ben'ē·dịct, *a.* [L. *benedictus*, pp. of *benedicere*, to speak well of.] mild; blessed. [Obs.]

Ben·ē·dic'tine (*or* -tēn), *a.* [Fr. *bénédictin*.]
1. of Saint Benedict.
2. designating the monastic order based on his teachings, founded c. 529 A.D.
3. of this order or its members.

Ben·ē·dic'tine, *n.* 1. a Benedictine monk or nun.
2. [b–] (-tēn), a liqueur, originally made by Benedictine monks.

Ben·ē·dic'tine rụle, the rules governing life in Benedictine monasteries.

Ben·ē·dic'tin·ịsm, *n.* the practices and organization of the Benedictines

ben·ē·dic'tion, *n.* [LL. *benedictio*, from L. *benedicere*, to speak well of.]
1. the act of blessing.
2. a blessing pronounced in favor of any person or thing; a solemn invocation of divine blessing, especially at the end of a church service.
3. a giving of thanks; grace.
4. the form of instituting an abbot, answering to the consecration of a bishop
5. blessedness.
6. [B–] in the Roman Catholic Church, a solemn ecclesiastical ceremony by which the ceremonial appurtenances, as bells, candles, etc., are rendered sacred or venerable and dedicated to God.

Syn.—blessing, commendation, approval, benison.

BENEDICTINE

ben·ē·dic'tion·ăl, *n.* in ecclesiastical usage, a book containing benedictions or blessings.

ben·ē·dic'tion·ā·ry, *n.* a benedictional.

ben·ē·dic'tive, *a.* tending to bless; giving a blessing.

ben·ē·dic'tō·ry, *a.* of or giving a benediction.

Ben·ē·dic'tus, *n.* [L. *benedicere*, to speak well of; later, to bless.]
1. a canticle beginning, "Blessed be the Lord God of Israel" (Luke i. 68), the song of Zacharias at the birth of John the Baptist.
2. a short hymn of praise used in the Mass, beginning *Benedictus qui venit in nomine Domini* (Blessed is He that cometh in the name of the Lord): Matt. xxi. 9.
3. music for either of these.

ben·ē·fac'tion, *n.* [LL. *benefactio*, a kindness, from L. *benefacere*, to do well; *bene*, well, and *facere*, to do.]
1. the act of conferring a benefit, especially as an act of charity or generosity.
2. a benefit conferred, especially a charitable donation.
3. in metallurgy, the preliminary conditioning of an ore for refinement.

Syn.—alms, bequest, boon, bounty, charity, donation, gift, grant, gratuity; present.

ben'ē·fac·tŏr, *n.* [LL. *benefactor*, from L. *benefacere*, to do well, or to do a kindness.] one who confers a benefit, especially one who makes financial contributions or gives help; a patron.

Syn.—friend, supporter, contributor, upholder, well-wisher, favorer, well-doer, patron, protector, guardian.

ben'ē·fac·tress, *n.* a woman benefactor.

bē·nef'ịc, *a.* 1. beneficent, favorable, or kindly.
2. in astrology, of favorable influence: said of a star or planet.

ben'ē·fice, *n.* [OFr. *benefice*; L. *beneficium*, a favor; *bene*, well, and *facere*, to do.]
1. a benefit; a kindness. [Obs.]
2. an endowed church office, as in the Church of England, providing a living for a vicar, rector, etc.
3. the income provided by such a church office.
4. land held by a feudal tenant for services rendered the owner.

ben'ē·fice, *v.t.*; beneficed, *pt.*, *pp.*, beneficing, *ppr.*, to provide with a benefice.

ben'ē·ficed, *a.* possessed of or provided with a benefice.

ben'ē·fice·less, *a.* having no benefice.

bē·nef'i·cence, *n.* [L. *beneficentia*, active kindness, from *benefacere*, to do a kindness.]
1. the practice of doing good.
2. a kindly action or gift.

Syn.—benevolence, munificence.

bē·nef'i·cent, *a.* 1. bringing about or doing acts of kindness and charity.
2. resulting in benefit.

bē·nef·i·cen'tiăl (-shăl), *a.* pertaining to beneficence.

bē·nef'i·cent·ly, *adv.* in a beneficent manner.

ben·ē·fi'ciăl (-fish'ăl), *a.* [LL. *beneficialis*, beneficial, from *beneficium*, a benefit.]
1. advantageous; conferring benefits; useful; profitable; helpful; contributing to a valuable end.
2. receiving or entitled to have or receive benefit; as, the *beneficial* owner of an estate.
3. in law, for one's own benefit; as, a *beneficial* interest.

Syn.—profitable, salutary, advantageous, wholesome, salubrious, useful, good, helpful.

ben·ē·fi'ciăl·ly, *adv.* advantageously; profitably; helpfully.

ben·ē·fi'ciăl·ness, *n.* the quality of being useful or helpful.

ben·ē·fi'ci·ā·ry, *a.* [L. *beneficiarius*, one receiving a favor.] of or holding a benefice.

ben·ē·fi'ci·ā·ry, *n.*; *pl.* **ben·ē·fi'ci·ā·ries** [L. *beneficiarii*, pl. of *beneficiarius*, a name given to soldiers who had received some honor or special exemption from duty.]
1. one who holds a church benefice.
2. in the middle ages, a feudatory or vassal.
3. one who receives anything as a gift or benefit
4. a person named to receive the income or inheritance from a will, insurance policy, etc.

ben·ē·fi'ci·āte (-fish'i-āt), *v.t.* 1. to work or improve, as a mine.
2. to reduce (ores).

ben·ē·fi·ci·ā'tion (-fish-i-ā'shun), *n.* 1. improvement, as of a mine.
2. the process of reducing ores.

ben·ē·fi'cien·cy, *n.* the practice of doing good. [Obs.]

ben·ē·fi'cient, *a.* doing good. [Obs.]

ben'ē·fit, *n.* [ME. *benefet*, *bienfet*, from OFr. *bienfait*, a kindness; from L. *benefacere*, to do a kindness.]
1. an act of kindness; a favor conferred.

> Bless the Lord, O my soul, and forget not all his *benefits*. Ps. ciii. 2.

2. advantage; profit; anything contributing to an improvement in condition.

> Men have no right to what is not for their *benefit*. —Burke.

3. a public performance at a theater, a dance, a bazaar, etc., the proceeds of which are given in aid of some individual, group, or cause.
4. [*often pl.*] payments made by an insurance company, public agency, welfare society, etc.

benefit of clergy; (a) the exemption which the medieval clergy had from trial or punishment except in a church court; (b) an administering or sanctioning by the church; as, their marriage was without *benefit of clergy*.

benefit society (or *association*); a co-operative association in which the members, by the regular payment of dues become entitled to financial aid in case of sickness, old age, or injury: life insurance and burial expenses are also sometimes provided.

Syn.—boon, behoof, service, utility, avail, use, good, advantage, profit, favor, blessing.

ben'ē·fit, *v.t.*; benefited, *pt.*, *pp.*; benefiting, *ppr.* to do good to or for; to aid; as, exercise *benefits* health; trade *benefits* a nation.

ben'ē·fit, *v.i.* to gain advantage; to receive profit; as, he *benefited* by advice.

ben'ē·fit·ẽr, *n.* one who bestows a benefit; also, one upon whom a benefit is bestowed.

Be'ne·lux, *n.* [from *Be*lgium, *Ne*therlands, *Lux*emburg.] in political science, Belgium, the Netherlands, and Luxemburg.

bē·nēme', *v.t.* [AS. *benæman*.] to deprive (of); to take away (from). [Obs.]

bē·nempt', alternative pp. of *bename*.

bē·nempt'ed, alternative pp. of *bename*.

bē·net', *v.t.* to catch in a net; to ensnare. [Obs.]

be'nē vā'lē, [L.] farewell.

bē·nev'ō·lence, *n.* [ME. *benivolence*; OFr. *benivolence*; L. *benevolentia*, good feeling; *bene*, well, and *volens*, ppr. of *velle*, to wish.]
1. any inclination to do good; good will; kindness; charitableness.
2. an act of kindness; good done; charity given; gift.
3. a forced loan formerly levied by some English kings on their subjects.

Syn.—kindness, benignity, tenderness, alms-giving, beneficence, bounty, charity, generosity, good will, humanity, kindheartedness, kindliness, liberality, munificence, philanthropy.

bē·nev'ō·lent, *a.* having a disposition to do good; kind; charitable

bē·nev'ō·lent·ly, *adv.* in a benevolent manner.

bē·nev'ō·lous, *a.* kind; benevolent. [Obs.]

Ben·gạl', *n.* [from *Bengal*, a province of India.]
1. a fabric of silk and hair.
2. striped gingham, originally brought from Bengal: sometimes called *Bengal stripes*.

Ben'gạl, *a.* of or from Bengal, in India.

Ben·găl·ēse' (*or* -ēz'), *n. sing.* and *pl.* a native of Bengal.

Ben·găl·ēse', *a.* pertaining to Bengal, its inhabitants, or their language.

Ben'gạl gràss, a forage plant, *Setaria Italica*: also called *Italian millet*.

Ben·gạl'ī, Ben·gạl'ee (*or* -găl'), *n.* 1. a native of Bengal.
2. the Indo-European, Indic language of Bengal.

Ben·gạl'ī, Ben·gạl'ee, *a.* pertaining to Bengal, its inhabitants, or their language.

ben'găl·ine, *n.* a fabric corded like poplin, the cords running across the material, which is made of silk, silk and wool, or silk and cotton.

Ben'găl light, a colored light used in fireworks, as a signal, etc.; specifically, a blue light made of potassium nitrate, sulfur, and antimony sulfide.

Ben'găl lil·y, an herb of South Africa resembling a lily.

Ben'găl mŏn'key, the rhesus monkey.

Ben'găl rọọt, the root of certain plants belonging to the ginger family, as the *Curcuma Zedoaria* and *Curcuma Zenembel*.

Ben'găl silk, any of various fabrics from Bengal; especially, a cloth made from hair and silk.

Ben'găl tī'gẽr, the short-haired tiger.

Ben Hũr, the Jewish hero in General Lew Wallace's novel *Ben Hur*.

bē·nīght' (-nīt'), *v.t.*; benighted, *pt.*, *pp.*; benighting, *ppr.* 1. to involve in darkness; to make obscure. [Archaic.]

> The clouds *benight* the sky. —Garth.

2. to overtake with night, or with darkness; as, the traveler was *benighted*.
3. to involve in moral darkness or ignorance; to exclude from intellectual light; as, absorption in routine *benights* the mind.

bē·nīght'ed, *a.* 1. involved in darkness, physical or moral; unenlightened.
2. overtaken by the night.

bē·nīght'ment, *n.* the condition of being benighted.

bē·nīgn' (-nīn'), *a.* [ME. *benigne*; OFr. *benigne*; L. *benignus*, good, kind.]
1. kind; of a kind disposition; gracious; showing favor; kindly; agreeable.

> Our Creator, bounteous and *benign*. —Milton.

2. generous; liberal; as, a *benign* benefactor.
3. favorable; beneficial; as, the *benign* aspect of the seasons
4. gentle in effect: said of medicines. [Obs.]
5. in medicine, doing little or no harm; not malignant; as, a *benign* disease.

bē·nig'năn·cy, *n.* [L. *benignitas*, kindness.] kindliness; graciousness; the quality or manner of being benignant.

bē·nig'nănt, *a.* 1. kindly or gracious, especially to inferiors.
2. benign; beneficial.

bē·nig'nănt·ly, *adv.* in a generous, kindly manner.

bē·nig'ni·ty, *n.* [L. *benignitas*, kindness.]
1. goodness of disposition or heart; kindness of nature; graciousness.
2. a kind act; a favor.
3. healthful, wholesome quality: said of climate, etc.

bē·nīgn'ly (-nīn'ly), *adv.* favorably; kindly; graciously.

bē·nim', *v.t.* [AS. *beniman*.] to take away; to rob; to spoil. [Obs.]

ben'i·ṣŏn, *n.* [ME. *benisoun*; OFr. *beneison*, a blessing, from LL. *benedictio*, a blessing, from L. *benedicere*, to speak well of.] blessing; benediction.

> God's *benison* go with you. —Shak.

bé·ni′tier (bā-nē′tyā), *n.* [Fr., from *bénir*, to bless.] in Roman Catholic Churches, a stoup or font for holy water, into which worshipers dip the fingers of the right hand, and bless themselves by making the sign of the cross.

BÉNITIER

Ben′jȧ·min, *n.* [Heb. *binyāmīn*, lit., son of the right hand; hence, favorite son.]
 1. in the Bible, Jacob's youngest son and his favorite.
 2. the tribe of Israel descended from him.

ben′jȧ·min, *n.* a style of overcoat originally made by an English tailor named Benjamin, and once fashionable.

ben′jȧ·min, *n.* [altered from Fr. *benjoin.*]
 1. gum benzoin.
 2. a tree or shrub, *Lindera benzoin*, native to North America: called also *spicebush*.

ben′jȧ·min tree, 1. the *Styrax benzoin*, a tree from which benzoin is obtained.
 2. the East Indian *Ficus benjamina.*
 3. the benjamin or spicebush.

Ben′jȧ·mīte, *n.* a descendant of Benjamin; one of the tribe of Benjamin.

ben′nē, ben′ē, *n.* [Malay *bijen.*] the sesame, an East Indian plant whose seeds yield an oil (*benne*, or *sesame, oil*) used in the manufacture of soap and as a substitute for olive oil.

BENNE
(*Sesamum orientale*)

ben′net, *n.* [ME. *benet*, from Fr. *benoite*, from LL. *benedictus*, pp. of *benedicere*, to bless. Called the *herba benedicta*, or blessed herb.]
 1. a yellow-flowered plant, *Geum urbanum*, of the rose family: also called *herb bennet*.
 2. poison hemlock.
 3. common valerian.

ben′ny, *n.*; *pl.* **ben′nies̹,** an amphetamine pill, especially benzedrine, used as a stimulant. [Slang.]

ben′sel, *n.* impetus; violence; a blow. [Prov. Eng. and Scot.]

ben′sel, *v.t.* [Ice. *benzl*, a bending, tension, from *benda*, to bend.] to drive; to beat. [Prov. Eng. and Scot.]

ben′shī, same as *banshee.*

bent, *a.* 1. not straight; curved; crooked; as, a *bent* bow, a *bent* knee, a *bent* pin.
 2. strongly inclined; determined: used with *on* or *upon*; as, *bent* on war.
 3. set in a course; bound; as, travelers westward *bent.*

bent, *n.* 1. inclination; disposition; tendency; also, a mental leaning or bias; propensity; as, the *bent* of the mind or will; the *bent* of a people toward greater tolerance.
 2. flexure; curvature; state of being bent; as, lowly *bent* of knee; a rod at a *bent.* [Obs.]
 3. a framework transverse to the length of a structure, for supporting lateral as well as vertical loads.
 4. a bent or curved part. [Obs.]
 Syn.—bias, inclination, prepossession, tendency, propensity, disposition.

bent, *n.* [ME. *bent*; AS. *beonet*, bent, a rush.]
 1. *pl.* **bent,** the stiff flower stalk of certain grasses.
 2. any of various reedy grasses.
 3. any of a number of related grasses, chiefly low-growing and spreading: also called *bent grass.*
 4. a heath; a moor. [Archaic.]

ben′thăl, *a.* [Gr. *benthos*, the depth of the sea.] pertaining to the greatest depths of the ocean.

Ben·tham′iç, *a.* relating to Benthamism.

Ben′thăm·is̹m, *n.* a moral doctrine promulgated by Jeremy Bentham (1748–1832), English philosopher of utilitarianism, which holds that the greatest happiness of the greatest number should be the ultimate goal of society and of the individual.

Ben′thăm·īte, *n.* a believer in the doctrine of Benthamism.

ben′thiç, *a.* of the benthos; benthonic.

ben·thon′iç, *a.* of the benthos; benthic.

ben′thos, *n.* [Gr. *benthos*, depth of the sea.] the bottom or depths of the ocean; also, the fauna and flora found there.

bent′ing tīme, the time when pigeons, etc. have to feed on bent for lack of other food.

ben′tŏn·īte, *n.* [from Fort *Benton* (after Thomas Hart *Benton*, Am. statesman) in Montana, where it is found.] a soft, porous clay formed as a weathering product from volcanic ash.

ben trō·vä′tō, [It., lit., well found.] well thought up; artfully invented.

bent′wood, *a.* designating furniture made of wood permanently bent into various forms by heat, moisture, and pressure.

bent′y, *a.* 1. having many bents, or stalks of coarse grass.
 2. like bent.

bē·numb′ (-num′), *v.t.*; benumbed, *pt.*, *pp.*; benumbing, *ppr.* [AS. *benumen*, pp. of *beniman*, to deprive; *be-*, and *niman*, to take; with unhistoric *-b.*] to make numb physically or emotionally; to deaden the mind, will, or feelings of; to stupefy; as, fingers *benumbed* by cold; to *benumb* the senses.

bē·numbed′ (-numd′), *a.* deprived of sensation; stupefied.

bē·numbed′ness (-numd′), *n.* the state of being benumbed.

bē·numb′ment, *n.* the process of benumbing, or condition of being benumbed.

benz-, same as *benzo-.*

ben′zal, *n.* the compound organic radical C_6H_5CH.

ben·zal′dē·hȳde, *n.* in chemistry, a clear, pleasant-smelling liquid, C_6H_5CHO, found in the oil of the bitter almond and used in making dyes, perfumes, flavorings, etc.

ben′zȧ·mide (*or* -mīd), *n.* an amide of benzoic acid, $C_6H_5CO{\cdot}NH_2$, obtained by subjecting chloride of benzoyl to the action of ammonia.

ben′ze·drīne, *n.* a derivative of ephedrine, $C_6H_5CH_2CH(NH_2)CH_3$, used to overcome fatigue or nervous exhaustion: also used in nasal and sinus disorders to relieve congestion: a trade-mark (*Benzedrine.*)

ben′zēne, *n.* an extremely inflammable colorless liquid, C_6H_6, obtained commercially by the fractional distillation of coal tar: it is used as a solvent for fats and in making lacquers, varnishes, many dyes, and other organic compounds: also called *benzol, benzole.*
 benzene ring or *benzene nucleus*; a structural unit believed to exist in the molecules of aromatic organic compounds, consisting of a ring of six atoms of carbon: in the molecule of benzene six atoms of hydrogen are believed to be attached to the ring, one to each atom of carbon, but in derivatives of benzene one or more atoms of hydrogen are replaced by atoms of other elements or by groups of atoms.

ben′zi·dine, *n.* a white, crystalline basic substance, $NH_2C_6H_4C_6H_4NH_2$, used in preparing certain dyes.

ben′zil, ben′zile, *n.* a compound, $C_{14}H_{10}O_2$, resulting from the oxidization of benzoin.

ben′zīne, ben′zin, *n.* a colorless, inflammable liquid obtained from petroleum by fractional distillation: it is used as a motor fuel and as a solvent for fats and oils in dry cleaning, etc.

ben′zō-, a combining form meaning *relating to benzene*: also *benz-.*

ben′zō·āte, *n.* a salt or ester of benzoic acid.

ben′zō·āte of sō′dȧ, same as *sodium benzoate.*

ben′zō·çāine, *n.* [*benzo-*, and *cocaine.*] a white, crystalline, odorless powder, $C_6H_4NH_2{\cdot}COOC_2H_5$, used in ointments as a local anesthetic and to protect against sunburn.

ben·zō′iç, *a.* of or derived from benzoin.
 benzoic acid; a white, crystalline organic acid, C_6H_5COOH, produced commercially from toluene and used as an antiseptic and preservative.

ben′zō·in (*or* ben-zō′in, *or* ben′zoin), *n.* [G. *benzoe, benzoin*; Fr. *benjoin*; Ar. *lubān jāwā*, incense of Java.]
 1. a balsamic resin obtained from certain tropical Asiatic trees (genus *Styrax*) and used in medicine and perfumery and as incense.
 2. any of a genus (*Lindera*) of aromatic plants of the laurel family; especially, the spicebush of eastern North America.
 3. in chemistry, a white, crystalline substance, $C_{14}H_{12}O_2$, used in making antiseptic ointments.

ben·zoin′ā·ted, *a.* filled with benzoin.

ben′zōl, ben′zōle, *n.* benzene: as used in the chemical industry, the term sometimes denotes a mixture distilling below 100°C., 70 per cent of which is benzene.

ben″zō·phē′nōne, *n.* [*benzo-*, and *phen*ol, and *-one.*] a white, crystalline organic compound, $C_6H_5COC_6H_5$, classified as a ketone: it is produced by the distillation of calcium benzoate and is used as an intermediate compound in the formation of certain other organic compounds.

ben′zoyl, *n.* the univalent radical, C_6H_5CO, found in benzoic acid and certain other compounds.

ben′zyl, *n.* a univalent radical, $C_6H_5CH_2$, found in organic compounds derived from toluene.

Be̤′ō·wụlf, *n.* the hero of the Anglo-Saxon folk epic of that name, an Anglian poem probably composed c. 700 A.D.: Beowulf slays Grendel and Grendel's mother, eventually reigns over the Geats, and dies after a fight with a dragon that is ravaging his kingdom.

bē·pāint′, *v.t.* 1. to cover with paint.
 2. to color.

bē·plūmed′, *a.* decorated with feathers.

bē·pow′dẽr, *v.t.* to powder; to sprinkle or cover with powder.

bē·prāis̹e′, *v.t.* 1. to praise greatly.
 2. to praise too highly; to flatter.

bē·puff′, *v.t.* to puff; to bepraise.

bē·pũr′ple, *v.t.* to tinge or dye with a purple color.

bē·quēath′, *v.t.*; bequeathed, *pt.*, *pp.*; bequeathing, *ppr.* [ME. *bequethen, bicwethen*; AS. *becwethan*, to declare, give by will; *be-*, and *cwethan*, to say.]
 1. to give or leave to another by last will and testament; as, to *bequeath* an estate.
 2. to hand down; to give by inheritance.
 3. to offer; to give, as services. [Obs.]
 Syn.—devise, give, bestow, confer, consign.

bē·quēath′ȧ·ble, *a.* that can be bequeathed.

bē′quēath′ăl, *n.* same as *bequest.*

bē·quēath′ẽr, *n.* one who bequeaths.

bē·quēath′ment, *n.* the act of bequeathing; a bequest.

bē·quest′, *n.* 1. a bequeathing.
 2. something left by will; a legacy.

bē·quōte′, *v.t.* to quote with great frequency.

bē·rāte′, *v.t.*; berated, *pt.*, *pp.*; berating, *ppr.* to chide vehemently; to scold.

bē·rat′tle, *v.t.* to rattle; also, to scold. [Obs.]

bē·rāy′, *v.t.* to make foul; to soil. [Archaic.]

bẽrbe, *n.* a small African animal, *Genetta pardina*, a kind of genet.

Bẽr′bẽr, *n.* [Ar.] 1. any of a Moslem people living in northern Africa.
 2. the Hamitic language spoken by the Berbers.

Bẽr′bẽr, *a.* of the Berbers, their culture, or their language.

Bẽr″be·ri·dā′cē·ae, *n.pl.* [L., from *berberis*, and *-aceæ.*] the barberry family of plants, bearing fruit in the form of either a berry or a capsule. There are about twenty genera and over one hundred species, including some American varieties, as *Podophyllum.*

bẽr·bẽr·i·dā′ceous, *a.* belonging to the *Berberidaceæ.*

bẽr′bẽr·ine, bẽr′bẽr·in, *n.* a bitter yellowish substance, obtained as an alkaloid from the root of the barberry, etc.: it is used in dyeing and as a drug.

Bẽr′be·ris, *n.* [L.] a widely distributed genus of shrubs, type of the family *Berberidaceæ. Berberis vulgaris*, the barberry, is the best-known species.

bẽr′ber·ry, *n.* same as *barberry.*

bẽr·ceūs̹e′, *n.* [Fr., a rocker, from *bercer*, to rock, to lull to sleep.] a musical composition having a soothing or lulling effect, as a cradle song.

Bē·rē′ăn, *n.* 1. an inhabitant of the ancient city of Berea, in Asia Minor.
 2. a member of a Scottish religious sect founded toward the end of the eighteenth century by John Barclay, who taught that religion should be derived from the Scriptures alone, according to Acts xvii. 11.

bē·rēave′, *v.t.*; bereaved *or* bereft, *pt.*, *pp.*; bereaving, *ppr.* [ME. *bereven*; AS. *bereafian*, to rob, bereave; *be-*, and *reafian*, to rob, plunder.]
 1. to deprive; to strip; to leave destitute; to deprive, as by death: with *of* before the person or thing taken away; as, *bereaved of* a father or mother; *bereft of* hope.

 Me have ye *bereaved* of my children.
 —Gen. xlii. 36.

 2. to take away from. [Obs.]
 Syn.—strip, divest, dispossess.

bē·rēaved′, *a.* deprived; stripped and left destitute; having lost a friend or relative by death; as, a *bereaved* parent.

bē·rēave′ment, *n.* the state of being bereaved; deprivation, particularly by the loss of a friend by death.

Syn.—destitution, affliction, deprivation, loss.

bē·rēav′ẽr, *n.* one who bereaves.

bē·reft′, alternative past tense and past participle of *bereave.*

bē·reft′, *a.* 1. deprived.

2. left sad and lonely, as by loss of someone dear.

Ber·en·gā′ri·ȧns, *n.pl.* a sect of the eleventh century which followed Berengarius, archdeacon of Angers (998–1088), who denied the doctrine of transubstantiation.

be·rẹt′ (-rā′), *n.* [Fr., from L. *berretta*, dim. of *birrus*, a cloak.]

1. a flat, round cap of wool or other material.

2. same as *biretta.*

bē·ret′tȧ, *n.* same as *biretta.*

bẽrg, *n.* [AS. and G. *berg*, a hill.]

1. a hill or mountain.

2. a large mass or floating island of ice; an iceberg.

Glittering *bergs* of ice. —Tennyson.

Bẽr′gȧ·mȧsk, *n.* a rustic dance, named after the inhabitants of *Bergamo*, Italy, once proverbial for their awkwardness.

bẽr′gȧ·mot, *n.* [from *Bergamo*, a town in Italy.]

1. a variety of pear.

2. a plant of the mint family.

3. a species of citron whose fruit has a fine taste and smell: its oil is used as a perfume. This oil is extracted from the yellow rind of the fruit. The tree is the *Citrus bergamia*, a distinct species, with a pear-shaped fruit.

4. the perfume produced from the bergamot citron.

5. a kind of snuff perfumed with bergamot.

6. a coarse tapestry, manufactured out of flock of wool, silk, cotton, hemp, and ox or goat's hair: said to have been first made at Bergamo, in Italy.

bẽr′gan·dẽr, *n.* [ME. *bergander*; *berg*, a burrow, and *gander*, a male goose.] the sheldrake or burrow duck of England (*Anas tadorna*).

Ber′ġe·raç, Cy′rȧ·nō de (Fr. bār″zhȧ·räk′), the hero of a poetic drama, by Edmond Rostand; based on the life of the French playwright, author, and soldier (1619–1655) of the same name: he was famous for his large nose.

bẽr′ġẽr·et, *n.* [OFr., from *berger*, a shepherd.] a pastoral song. [Obs.]

bẽrg′măn·nīte, *n.* [named after *Bergmann*, a mineralogist.] a variety of natrolite found in Norway.

bẽrg′mẹhl, *n.* [G., from *berg*, a mountain, and *mehl*, meal.] in mineralogy, an earthy material of the fineness of flour or meal, consisting of the shells of *Infusoria.*

Bẽr′gō·mȧsk, *n.* Bergamask.

Berg·sō′ni·ăn, *a.* of Henri Bergson or his philosophy.

Berg·sō′ni·ăn, *n.* a believer in Bergson's philosophy.

Berg′sŏn·iṣm, *n.* the philosophy of Bergson, which maintains that there is an original life force carried through all successive generations.

bẽrg′stock, *n.* [G., from *berg*, a mountain, and *stock*, a stick.] a spiked pole used in mountain climbing; a kind of alpenstock.

bẽr′gylt, *n.* [Norw.] the Norwegian haddock, or rosefish, *Sebastes marinus.*

bē·rhȳme′, bē·rīme′, *v.t.* 1. to make rhymes about.

2. to satirize in verse.

bē·rib′bŏned, *a.* covered with ribbons.

ber′i·ber′i, *n.* [Singhalese *beri*, weakness.] a deficiency disease, occurring mainly in Asia, caused by lack of vitamin B_1 in the diet: it is characterized by extreme weakness, paralysis, anemia, and wasting away.

ber″i·ber′ic, *a.* of or resulting from beriberi.

ber·i·gor′ȧ, *n.* [native name.] an Australian falcon, *Hieracidea berigora.*

bē·rīme′, to berhyme.

Bẽrke·lē′iăn, *a.* of or pertaining to George Berkeley, bishop of Cloyne (1685–1753), or his system of philosophical idealism.

Bẽrke·lē′iăn, *n.* a follower of Bishop Berkeley, or an adherent of Berkeleianism.

Bẽrke·lē′iăn·iṣm, Bẽrke′ley·iṣm, *n.* the philosophy of Bishop Berkeley, who held that material things exist only in so far as they are perceived, and that the mind is conscious of subjective impressions only and therefore cannot know external things.

Bẽrke′ley·īte, *n.* a Berkeleian.

bẽr·kē′li·um, *n.* [from University of California at *Berkeley*, where first isolated.] a radioactive chemical element produced by bombarding americium with alpha particles having a high energy level: it does not occur naturally on earth: symbol, Bk; atomic weight, 243 (?); atomic number, 97.

Bẽrk′shire, *n.* one of a breed of swine, originally from Berkshire, England, characterized by medium size, hair mostly black, short legs and head, and broad, straight back.

bẽr·lin′, *n.* 1. a large four-wheeled vehicle with two interior seats and a footman's platform behind, separate from the body: so called from Berlin, where it was first made in the seventeenth century.

2. fine dyed worsted used for knitting, embroidery, tapestry, and other kinds of fancywork; zephyr wool: called also *Berlin wool.*

3. a knitted glove.

4. a dance belonging to the polka class.

5. a berline.

Berlin black; black varnish, used in coating ironware, which dries with a dead black surface.

Berlin blue; Prussian blue.

Berlin iron; a fusible kind of soft iron, largely used in making delicate or ornamental articles, as jewelry and fine smooth castings, which are sometimes stained or lacquered in imitation of bronze.

Berlin shop; a store selling embroidery, Berlin wools, patterns, knitting needles, etc.

Berlin ware; a kind of pottery of such quality as to resist the action of almost all chemical reagents.

Berlin work; embroidery or fancywork made of Berlin or zephyr wool.

bẽr·line′, *n.* an automobile body with a glass partition between the front seat and the rear seat: also *berlin.*

bẽrm, bẽrme, *n.* [Fr. *berme*; D. *berme*; M.D. *baerm.*]

1. a narrow ledge; specifically, in fortification, a space of ground, from three to five feet in width, left between the rampart and the moat or foss, designed to receive the earth from the rampart and prevent it from filling the ditch.

2. in engineering, a horizontal ledge or bench at the bottom of or part way up a bank or cutting, to catch earth that may roll down the slope, or to strengthen the bank.

3. a ledge or shoulder along the side of a paved road.

4. the bank or side of a canal which is opposite to the towpath.

Bẽr·mū′dȧ grȧss, a kind of pasture grass; *Cynodon Dactylon*, which is widespread in warm countries. Called also *Bermuda devil grass*, *Bahama grass*, and *scutch grass.*

Bẽr·mū′dȧ ŏn′iŏn, a large onion with a mild flavor, grown in Texas and California as well as in Bermuda.

Bẽr·mū′di·ăn, *n.* a native or inhabitant of Bermuda.

Bẽr·mū′di·ăn, *a.* of Bermuda.

bẽr′nȧ·çle, *n.* same as *barnacle* (sense 1).

Bẽr′năr·dine (*or* -dēn), *n.* one of the order of Cistercian monks founded by St. Bernard in the twelfth century.

Bẽr′năr·dine, *a.* of St. Bernard of Clairvaux (1091–1153) or the monastic order founded by him.

Bẽr·nēṣe′, *a.* pertaining to the canton or city of Bern, Switzerland, or to its people.

Bẽr·nēṣe′, *n.*; *pl.* **Bẽr·nēṣe′,** a native or inhabitant of Bern.

bẽr′ni·çle, *n.* same as *barnacle* (sense 1).

bẽr′ni·çle goose, a barnacle goose.

bẽr·nöus′, *n.* same as *burnoose.*

bē·rob′, *v.t.* to plunder; to rob. [Obs.]

Ber′ō·ē, *n.* [L., from Gr. *Beroē*, one of the ocean nymphs.]

1. the typical genus of ctenophorans of the family *Beroidæ.*

2. [b–] a small jellyfish or ctenophoran of this genus. These marine invertebrates, which are transparent and gelatinous, are either oval or globular, and float in the ocean, where they are widely distributed. They are phosphoric, and shine at night.

ber′ret, *n.* same as *beret.*

ber·ret′tȧ, *n.* see *biretta.*

ber′ried (-rid), *a.* 1. having or yielding berries.

2. consisting of or resembling berries.

3. bearing eggs: said of lobsters, crayfish, etc.

ber′ry, *n.*; *pl.* **ber′rieṣ,** [ME. *bery*, *berie*; AS. *berie*; O.H.G. *beri*; Ice. *ber*, berry.]

1. in botany, any fleshy simple fruit with one or more seeds and a skin, as a tomato, cranberry, banana, grape, etc.

2. any of the small, juicy, fleshy fruits having numerous small seeds, as the gooseberry, blackberry, strawberry, mulberry, huckleberry, etc.

BERRY
1. fruit of currant
2. section of same

3. the dry seed or kernel of various plants, as a coffee bean.

4. one of the ova or eggs of a lobster, crayfish, etc.

5. a dollar. [Slang.]

in berry; containing spawn: said of lobster, etc.

ber′ry, *v.i.*; berried, *pt.*, *pp.*; berrying, *ppr.* to bear or produce berries; also, to seek for or gather berries.

ber′ry, *n.* [AS. *beorh*, a hill.] a mound or hillock: a corruption of *barrow.*

ber′ry·ing, *n.* the act of seeking for berries.

bẽr′seem, *n.* [Ar. *barsim*; ult. from *birshīm*, clover.] a kind of clover, grown for fodder; Egyptian clover.

bẽr′sẽrk, *a.* and *adv.* in or into a state of violent rage or frenzy.

bẽr′sẽrk·ẽr, bẽr′sẽrk, *n.* [ON. *berserkr*, warrior clothed in bearskin, from *ber*, a bear, and *serkr*, a coat.]

1. in Norse legends, a warrior who fought with peculiar frenzy, called the "berserker rage."

2. one given to fury and violence.

bẽrs′tle, *n.* a bristle. [Obs.]

bẽrth, *n.* [from the root of *bear*, to carry.]

1. enough space at sea; hence, any space or place where a vessel lies, or can lie, whether at anchor or at a wharf.

2. a room in a vessel in which officers or men eat and sleep; also, a storage place in a vessel for sailors' chests.

3. a sleeping place or bunk in a ship's cabin, a Pullman car, or elsewhere.

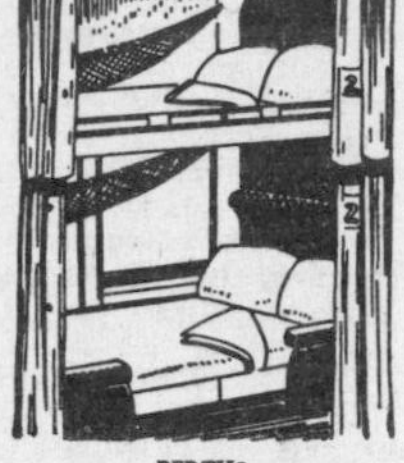
BERTHS

4. an allotted place; a position, office, appointment, or employment; as, a snug *berth* in the civil service.

to give a wide berth to; to keep at a safe distance from.

bẽrth, *v.t.*; berthed, *pt.*, *pp.*; berthing, *ppr.* 1. in nautical usage, to give anchorage ground to; to give space to lie in, as a ship in a dock, or at a wharf.

2. to allot a berth or berths to; as, to *berth* a ship's company; to *berth* a traveler in a railway sleeping car.

3. to furnish with employment.

bẽrth, *v.i.* 1. to have a berth.

2. to occupy a berth.

bẽr′thȧ, *n.* [Fr. *berthe*, from *Berthe*, Bertha, a feminine name.] a wide collar or cape, usually of lace, for feminine wear.

bẽrth′āġe, *n.* 1. the place allotted to a vessel at a dock or in a harbor.

2. fees for a berth at a dock or a place for anchorage.

bẽrth deck, the deck of a vessel on which the berths are located; in war vessels, the deck next below the gun deck.

bẽr′thi·ẽr·īte, *n.* an ore of antimony, consisting of a sulfide of antimony and iron. It has a metallic luster, a dark steel-gray color, and occurs massive or in elongated prisms: so called from Pierre *Berthier*, a French mineralogist.

bẽrth′ing, *n.* 1. the exterior planking of the sides of a vessel, above the sheer strake; the bulwark.

2. the displacement, from rising or working up, of the planks in the side of a vessel.

bẽrth′ing, *n.* 1. the disposal of accommodations for sleeping in a sleeping car or on a vessel.

2. the act of placing a vessel in a dock or berth.

Bẽr·thol·lē′ti·ȧ (-shi-ȧ), *n.* a genus of South American trees which grow to great size and yield the Brazil nut: so called from C.L. *Berthollet*, a French chemist.

Bẽr′til·lon sys′tem (Fr. bār·tē·yoṅ′), a system of personal identification devised by the French anthropologist, Alphonse *Bertillon*. It records those dimensions of the human body which are least subject to change, confining the principal measurements to the bones, as the skull, ulna, radius, femur, and to proportional meaurement from the coccyx to top of cranium, and to the calcaneum or heel bone, and from point to point of the shoulder; it also notes external physical peculiarities, such as deformities, color, fingerprints, etc. A distinguishing feature of the system is the classification, by which the anthropometric indices are tabulated to facilitate a prompt identification regardless of change of name or appearance. The system is generally employed by police authorities for the purpose of identifying criminals.

bẽr'trăm, *n.* [corrupted from L. *pyrethrum*; Gr. *pyrethron*, a spicy plant; *pyr*, fire.] the pellitory, *Pyrethrum Parthenium*, or feverfew, and *Anacyclus Pyrethrum* or Spanish pellitory, both of which plants belong to the aster family. Written also *bartram.*

bē·ruf'fled, *a.* with ruffles.

ber'y·çoid, *a.* [L. *Beryx*, the name of the typical genus, and Gr. *eidos*, form.] pertaining to the *Berycidæ*, a family of marine fishes.

ber'yl, *n.* [L. *beryllus*; Gr. *bēryllos*, a gem, *beryl*.] beryllium aluminum silicate, $Be_3Al_2(SiO_3)_6$, a very hard, lustrous mineral that is a source of beryllium: emerald and aquamarine are two of several different varieties of beryl.

be·ryl'li·ȧ, *n.* same as *glucina.*

ber'yl·line, *a.* like a beryl as to color; light green, or bluish green.

be·ryl'li·um, *n.* a hard, rare, metallic chemical element, found only in combination with other elements: it forms a very tough, light alloy with copper or nickel: symbol Be; atomic weight, 9.02; atomic number, 4: former name, *glucinum.*

ber'yl·loid, *n.* [*beryl*, and Gr. *eidos*, form.] a solid, consisting of two twelve-sided pyramids put base to base, as in beryl crystals.

Bes, *n.* [Egypt. *besa.*] an Egyptian god of pleasure.

bes'ȧ·bol, *n.* [Ar.] a fragrant balsam resin, formerly called Indian myrrh, and differing from the real myrrh principally in color. It is obtained from a tree in eastern Africa.

bē·ṣant', *n.* same as *bezant.*

beṣ ant'lẽr, same as *bez antler.*

bē·sāyle', bē·sāiel', *n.* [ME. *besayle*, OFr. *besayel*, a great-grandfather: *bes* (L. *bis*), twice, and *ayel*, grandfather.]

1. a great-grandfather. [Obs.]

2. in old English law, a writ of abatement, by which a great-grandchild, illegally excluded from lands of which either of his great-grandfathers died seized, vindicated his claim to it. Written also *besaille.*

bē·sçat'tẽr, *v.t.* to scatter over; also, to strew or cover sparsely, as with flowers.

bē·sçorn', *v.t.* to treat with scorn.

bē·sçratch', *v.t.* to scratch; to tear with the nails.

bē·sçrawl', *v.t.* to scribble over.

bē·sçreen', *v.t.* to cover with a screen; to shelter; to conceal.

bē·scrib'ble, *v.t.* to scribble over.

bē·sçum'bẽr, bē·sçum'mẽr, *v.t.* to befoul with ordure. [Obs.]

bē·seech', *v.t.*; besought *or* beseeched, *pt., pp.*; beseeching, *ppr.* [ME. *besechen, bisechen, beseken*; *be-*, and *sechen*, to seek.]

1. to entreat; to supplicate; to implore; to ask or pray with urgency; as, I *beseech* you to come with us.

2. to beg eagerly for; to solicit: followed by the thing solicited.

> But Eve fell humble, and *besought* his peace. —Milton.

Syn.—beg, entreat, solicit, supplicate, implore, crave, appeal to, invoke, request, pray. —*Beg* supposes simply a state of want; to *beseech, entreat*, and *solicit*, a state of urgent necessity; to *implore* and *supplicate*, a state of overwhelming distress.

bē·seech', *n.* a request; a supplication. [Obs. or Poet.]

bē·seech'ẽr, *n.* one who beseeches.

bē·seech'ing·ly, *adv.* in a beseeching manner.

bē·seech'ing·ness, *n.* same as *beseechment.*

bē·seech'ment, *n.* the act of beseeching, supplicating, or earnestly entreating. [Rare.]

bē·seek', *v.t.* to beseech. [Obs.]

bē·seem', *v.i.* 1. to be suitable or appropriate (to): what appears to be the direct object of the verb (e.g., *him* in "it ill beseems him") is really the indirect object.

2. to be seemly; to be meet.

3. to seem. [Obs.]

bē·seem'ing, *n.* 1. appearance. [Obs.]

2. comeliness.

bē·seem'ing, *a.* becoming; fit; worthy of. [Rare.]

bē·seem'ing·ly, *adv.* in a beseeming manner.

bē·seem'ing·ness, *n.* the quality of being meet, or suitable.

bē·seem'ly, *a.* becoming; suitable. [Rare.]

bē·seen', *a.* 1. seen. [Obs.]

2. arrayed; equipped. [Rare.]

bē·sen'nȧ, *n.* same as *mesenna.*

bē·set', *v.t.*; beset, *pt., pp.*; besetting, *ppr.* [ME. *besetten, bisetten*; AS. *besettan*; *be*, about, and *settan*, to set.]

1. to surround; to enclose; to hem in; to besiege; as, we are *beset* with enemies; the city is *beset* with troops.

2. to press on all sides, so as to perplex; to press hard, or to press hard upon; to harass, obstruct, or embarrass.

3. to ornament; to set or stud, as with gems.

4. (a) to employ; (b) to set or place; (c) to become or suit. [Obs.]

Syn.—surround, enclose, environ, hem in, besiege, encircle, encompass, embarrass, urge, press.

bē·set'ment, *n.* the condition of being beset; also, that by which one is beset, as a sin or failing.

bē·set'tẽr, *n.* one who or that which besets.

bē·set'ting, *a.* habitually attending; constantly attacking, troubling, or pressing; as, a *besetting* sin.

bē·shine', *v.t.*; beshone, *pt., pp.*; beshining, *ppr.* to shine upon.

bē·shōw', *n.* [native name.] the black candlefish, *Anoplopoma fimbria*, of the north Pacific Coast, which grows to a large size and is edible.

bē·shrew', *v.t.* [ME. *bischrewen*, from *be-*, and *schrewen*, to curse.] to curse: now used only as a literary archaism in mild imprecations; as, *beshrew* you. [Archaic.]

bē·shroud', *v.t.* to cover with a shroud; to screen.

bē·shut', *v.t.* to shut up; to shut out. [Obs.]

bē·sīde', *adv.* 1. close by; near; at hand. [Obs.]

2. besides; in addition.

bē·sīde', *prep.* [ME. *beside, biside, byside*; AS. *be sīdan*; *be*, by, and *sīdan*, dat. of *sīde*, side.]

1. at the side of; near; as, he sat *beside* me; *beside* the stream.

> *Beside* him hung his bow. —Milton.

2. over and above, distinct from; in addition to; besides.

3. in comparison with; as, my writing is poor *beside* yours.

4. out of the regular course or order; other than; aside from.

> It is *beside* my present business to enlarge upon this speculation. —Locke.

beside oneself; mad, as with fear, rage, etc.

> Paul, thou art *beside* thyself. —Acts. xxvi. 24.

bē·sīdeṣ', *adv.* [ME., from *beside*, and adv. genit. -(e)s.]

1. in addition; as well.

2. except for that mentioned; else.

3. moreover; furthermore.

bē·sīdeṣ', *prep.* 1. in addition to; as well as.

2. other than; except.

bē·siēġe', *v.t.*; besieged, *pt., pp.*; besieging, *ppr.* [ME. *besegen, bisegen*; *be-*, and *segen*, to siege; OFr. *siége*, a seat, a siege.]

1. to lay siege to; to beleaguer; as, to *besiege* a fort or city.

2. to beset; to throng round; as, *besieged* with cares.

3. to overwhelm; as, they *besieged* us with invitations.

Syn.—encompass, surround, hem in, invest, engird, enclose.

bē·siēġe'ment, *n.* the act of besieging or state of being besieged.

bē·siē'ġẽr, *n.* one who lays siege or is employed in a siege.

bē·siē'ġing, *a.* surrounding in a hostile manner; laying siege to.

bē·siē'ġing·ly, *adv.* in a besieging manner.

bē·sit', *v.t.* to suit; to become. [Obs.]

bē·slab'bẽr, *v.t.* to beslobber.

bē·slāve', *v.t.* to enslave; to make a slave of.

bē·slāv'ẽr, *v.t.*; beslavered, *pt., pp.*; beslavering, *ppr.* to befoul or defile with slaver; to slobber over.

bē·slīme', *v.t.* to daub with slime; to soil. [Obs.]

bē·slob'bẽr, *v.t.* to soil or smear with spittle; to bedaub, as with spittle; to slobber over, as with kisses.

bē·slub'bẽr, *v.t.* same as *beslobber.*

bē·smēar', *v.t.*; besmeared, *pt., pp.*; besmearing, *ppr.* to bedaub; to overspread with any viscous, glutinous matter, or with any soft substance that adheres; to befoul; to soil.

bē·smēar'ẽr, *n.* one who besmears.

bē·smīrch', *v.t.*; besmirched, *pt., pp.*; besmirching, *ppr.* to soil; to befoul; to discolor; hence, to dishonor; to sully.

bē·smōke', *v.t.*; besmoked, *pt., pp.*; besmoking, *ppr.* to foul with smoke; also, to harden or dry in smoke.

bē·smut', *v.t.*; besmutted, *pt., pp.*; besmutting, *ppr.* to blacken with smut; to foul with soot.

bē·snōw', *v.t.*; besnowed, *pt., pp.*; besnowing, *ppr.* 1. to scatter like snow. [Rare.]

2. to whiten with or as with snow.

bē'ṣọm, *n.* [ME. *besum, besem, besma*, a broom, rod; AS. *besema*, a rod, pl., a bundle of twigs.]

1. a broom, especially one consisting of twigs tied to a handle.

2. anything that cleanses: used figuratively.

3. the broom (plant).

bē'ṣọm, *v.t.* to sweep, as with a besom. [Rare.]

bē'ṣọm·ẽr, *n.* one who uses a besom. [Rare.]

bē·sọrt', *v.t.* to suit; to fit; to become. [Obs.]

bē·sọrt', *n.* company; attendance; train. [Obs.]

bē·sot', *v.t.*; besotted, *pt., pp.*; besotting, *ppr.*

1. to make sottish; to make drunk.

2. to make silly or foolish.

bē·sot'ted, *a.* 1. silly; foolish; infatuated.

2. stupefied, as with liquor.

bē·sot'ted·ly, *adv.* in a besotted manner.

bē·sot'ted·ness, *n.* the state or quality of being besotted.

bē·sot'ting·ly, *adv.* in a besotting manner.

bē·sọught', alternative past tense and past participle of *beseech.*

bē·spāke', archaic past tense of *bespeak.*

bē·spañ'gle, *v.t.*; bespangled, *pt., pp.*; bespangling, *ppr.* to adorn with spangles; to dot or sprinkle with something brilliant; as, the heavens are *bespangled* with stars.

bē·spat'tẽr, *v.t.*; bespattered, *pt., pp.*; bespattering, *ppr.* 1. to soil by spattering; to sprinkle with water, or with dirt and water.

2. to asperse with calumny or reproach.

bē·spạwl', *v.t.* to soil or make foul with spittle. [Obs.]

bē·spēak', *v.t.*; bespoke, *or archaic* bespake, *pt.*; bespeaking, *ppr.* bespoken, bespoke, *pp.*

1. to speak for beforehand; to order or engage in advance; as, to *bespeak* a favor.

2. to speak to; to address. [Archaic or Poetic.]

3. to be indicative of; to show; as, his words *bespeak* the fiend.

4. to foreshadow; to point to; as, today's events *bespeak* future tragedy.

Syn.—betoken, foreorder, forestall, prearrange, indicate, evidence.

bē·spēak', *v.i.* to speak out; to exclaim. [Obs.]

bē·spēak', *n.* among actors, a benefit. [Eng.]

bē·spēak'ẽr, *n.* one who bespeaks.

bē·speç'kle, *v.t.* to mark with speckles or spots.

bē·speç'ta·çled (-çld), *a.* wearing spectacles; having glasses on.

bē·spew', *v.t.* to soil with spew; to cover with vomit.

bē·spīce', *v.t.* to season or flavor with spices.

bē·spīrt', *v.t.* to bespurt. [Obs.]

bē·spit', *v.t.* to daub or soil with spittle.

bē·spōke', past tense and alternative past participle of *bespeak.*

bē·spōke', *a.* 1. ordered in advance. [Brit.]

2. made to special order; custom-made. [Brit.]

bē·spō'ken, alternative past participle of *bespeak.*

bē·spot', *v.t.*; bespotted, *pt., pp.*; bespotting, *ppr.* to mark with spots; to dapple.

bē·spread' (-spred'), *v.t.*; bespread, *pt., pp.*; bespreading, *ppr.* to spread over; to cover over; as, to *bespread* with flowers.

bē·sprent', *a.* [ME. *bespreynt*, pp. of *besprengen*; AS. *besprengan*; *be-*, and *sprengan*, caus., from *springan*, to spring.] sprinkled; strewed. [Poetic.]

bē·sprin'kle, *v.t.*; besprinkled, *pt., pp.*; besprinkling, *ppr.* to sprinkle over (*with* something); as, to *besprinkle* with dust.

bē·sprin'klẽr, *n.* one who sprinkles over.

bē·sprin'kling, *n.* the act of sprinkling or the state of being besprinkled.

bē·spūrt', *v.t.* to spurt over or on. [Obs.]

Bes·sȧ·rā'bi·ăn, *a.* of Bessarabia.

Bes·sȧ·rā'bi·ăn, *n.* a native or inhabitant of Bessarabia.

Bes·sel'iăn, *a.* in mathematics, of or pertaining to F. W. Bessel, Prussian astronomer, or to Bessel's functions.

Bes'se·mẽr, *a.* [named from Sir Henry *Bessemer*, an English engineer.] pertaining to the process of making Bessemer steel.

Bes′se·mẽr, *n.* 1. a Bessemer converter.

2. steel produced by the Bessemer process.

Bessemer converter; a large steel retort in which Bessemer steel is made.

Bessemer process; a method of making steel by forcing a blast of air through molten iron to remove carbon and impurities.

Bessemer steel; steel produced by the Bessemer process.

best, *a.*, superl. of *good.* [AS. *best*, contr. from *betest, betsta, betst*, best. The word has no connection in origin with *good*, of which it is the superlative.]

1. most excellent; of the most excellent sort; surpassing all others.

2. most suitable, most desirable, most favorable, most profitable, etc.

3. largest; as, it took the *best* part of an hour to do this.

4. most healthy; least indisposed; as, he feels *best* in the morning.

best work; in mining, the richest part of the ore.

best, *n.* 1. people of the highest worth, ability, or reputation; as, he is among the *best* in his profession.

2. the most excellent thing, condition, circumstance, action, etc.

3. the most one can do; utmost.

4. advantage; as, she got the *best* of her opponent.

5. finest clothes; as, dressed in her *best*.

at best; at most; under the most favorable conditions or interpretation; as, life is *at best* very short.

to get the best of; to best; to defeat; to gain an advantage over, by fair or foul means; as, *to get the best of* a bargain or of an enemy.

to make the best of; (a) to carry to its greatest perfection; to improve to the utmost; (b) to utilize or adapt oneself to, as well as possible; as, *to make the best of* ill fortune.

best, *adv.*, superl. of *well.* 1. in the highest degree; beyond all other; as, to love one *best*.

2. to the most advantage; with the most ease; in the most suitable way; as, which instrument can you *best* use?

3. with most profit or success.

4. most intimately or particularly; most correctly; as, it is *best* known to himself.

best, *v.t.*; bested, *pt., pp.*; besting, *ppr.* to get the better of; to overcome; to defeat; to excel.

bē·stead′ (-sted′), *v.t.*; besteaded, bested, *pt., pp.*; besteading, *ppr.* 1. to aid; to assist.

2. to avail; to benefit; to profit; to serve.

bē·stead′, *a.* situated; placed.

bes′tiăl (bes′chăl), *a.* [L. *bestialis*, from *bestia*, beast.]

1. of a beast, or the class of beasts.

2. having the qualities of a beast; brutal, coarse, vile, etc.; as, a *bestial* appetite.

Syn.—beastly, depraved, low, vile, sensual, carnal.

bes′tiăl, *n.* in Scots law, the cattle on a farm taken collectively.

bes·tial′i·ty (-chal′), *n.* 1. the quality of beasts; the state or quality of being bestial.

2. a bestial act or practice.

bes′tiăl·īze, *v.t.*; bestialized, *pt., pp.*; bestializing, *ppr.* to make bestial; to degrade to a bestial condition.

bes′tiăl·ly, *adv.* brutally; in a bestial manner.

bes′ti·ā·ry, *n.*; *pl.* **bes′ti·ā·rieṣ,** [L. *bestiarium*, neut. of *bestiarius*, pertaining to wild beasts; *bestia*, a beast.] a medieval collection of fables, allegories, and fanciful, often moralistic, stories about animals.

bē·still′, *v.t.* to make still; to quiet.

bē·stir′, *v.t.*; bestirred, *pt., pp.*; bestirring, *ppr.* to put into brisk or vigorous action; to move with life and vigor: usually used reflexively.

best man, the principal attendant of the bridegroom at a wedding.

best′ness, *n.* the state of being best. [Rare.]

bē·stōw′, *v.t.*; bestowed, *pt., pp.*; bestowing, *ppr.* [ME. *bestowen*; *be-*, and *stowen*, from *stowe*, a place. Literally, to set or place.]

1. to give as a gift; to confer; to impart: often followed by *on* or *upon*.

2. to give in marriage.

3. to apply; to devote; as, to *bestow* our whole force upon an object.

4. to lay out, or dispose of; to give in payment for. [Obs.]

5. to lay up in store; to deposit for safekeeping; to stow; to place. [Archaic.]

6. to behave: followed by the reflexive pronoun. [Obs.]

7. to house. [Archaic.]

Syn.—give, grant, confer, present, lodge, arrange, pack.

bē·stōw′ăl, *n.* the act of bestowing; disposal.

bē·stōw′ẽr, *n.* one who bestows; a giver.

bē·stōw′ment, *n.* the act of giving; also, that which is given.

bē·strad′dle (-dl), *v.t.* to bestride.

bē·straught′ (-strạt′), *a.* distracted; mad. [Obs.]

bē·strēak′, *v.t.* to mark with streaks.

bē·strew′, *v.t.*; bestrewed, *pt.*; bestrewed, bestrewn, *pp.*; bestrewing, *ppr.* to scatter over; to besprinkle; to strew.

bē·strīde′, *v.t.*; bestrode, bestrid, *pt.*; bestridden, bestrid; bestrode, *pp.*; bestriding, *ppr.* [ME. *bestriden*; AS. *bestridan*; *be-*, and *stridan*, to stride.]

1. to stride over; to stand or sit with a leg on each side.

2. to step over or across; as, to *bestride* a threshold.

best′-sell′ẽr, *n.* a book, phonograph record, etc. currently outselling most others.

bē·stud′, *v.t.*; bestudded, *pt., pp.*; bestudding, *ppr.* to set with studs; to adorn with bosses; as, to *bestud* with stars.

bet, *n.* [prob. by apheresis from *abet.*]

1. an agreement between two persons or sides that the one proved wrong about an outcome or fact will do or give a stipulated thing or pay a stipulated sum of money to the other; a wager.

2. the terms of such an agreement; the thing or sum thus staked.

3. the proposition about which such an agreement is made.

4. the thing or person that something is or may be thus staked on; as, this team is a good *bet*.

bet, *v.i.*; bet, betted, *pt., pp.*; betting, *ppr.* to lay a bet or bets (*on, against, with*); to lay a wager; to stake or pledge something upon the event of a contest.

bet, *v.t.* 1. to declare in or as in a bet; as, I *bet* he'll be late.

2. to stake (money, etc.) in a bet.

bẹ′tȧ (*or* bē′tȧ), *n.* the second letter in the Greek alphabet, corresponding to English *B, b*: used specifically to designate the second of a series, as, in astronomy, the star that is the second brightest in a constellation.

bẹ′tȧ (*or* bē′tȧ), *a.* in chemistry, designating the relative position of the carbon atom to which a substituting atom or group of atoms is attached in one of two or more isomerous organic compounds

beta blocker; any of a class of drugs used to control heartbeat, relieve angina pectoris, reduce anxiety, etc. by inhibiting the activity of nerves that stimulate adrenal gland secretions.

beta decay; radioactive disintegration of a nucleus with the accompanying emission of a beta particle: the residual nucleus has one more unit of positive charge after electron emission and one less after positron emission.

beta emitter; a radioactive element, either natural or artificial, which transforms into another element by emitting a beta particle.

beta particle; an electron: so called from its presence in beta rays.

beta rays; rays given off by radioactive substances, consisting of electrons that move with velocities varying from 30,000 to 180,000 miles per second.

beta test; in psychology, an intelligence test for people who cannot read or write, first used during World War I by the United States Army.

Bē′tȧ, *n.* [L. a beet.] a genus of apetalous plants of the family *Chenopodiaceæ*, having large succulent roots and a green calyx: *Beta vulgaris* is the common beet.

bē′tȧ·ine, bē′tȧ·in, *n.* [L. *beta*, beet, and *-in.*] a crystalline basic organic compound found in the common beet.

bē·tāke′, *v.t.*; betook, *pt.*; betaken, *pp.*; betaking, *ppr.* [ME. *betaken*; Sw. *betaka*, *be-*, and *taka*, to take, seize.]

1. to take to; to have recourse to; to apply; to resort: used reflexively; as, let us *betake* ourselves to arms.

2. to go (used reflexively); as, he *betook* himself to his home.

3. to take or seize. [Obs.]

bẹ·tȧ·naph′thōl (*or* bē-), *n.* a colorless, crystalline isomer of naphthol, used in medicine as an antiseptic and parasiticide.

bẹ′tȧ·tron, *n.* [*beta* rays, and elec*tron*.] a device used to accelerate the velocities of electrons.

bête (bet), *n.* [Fr., from OFr. *beste.*] a beast or beastlike person.

bete noire (lit., black beast); a bugbear; a person or thing particularly disliked, feared, and avoided.

bē·teem′, *v.t.* (a) to bring forth; to produce; (b) to shed; (c) to bestow. [Obs.]

bē′tel (bē′tl), *n.* [Fr. *bétel*; Port. *betel, betelhe, vitele*; Malay. *vettila*, betel.] a species of pepper, *Piper betle*, a creeping or climbing plant native to the East Indies.

Bē′tel·ġeuṣe, Bē′tel·ġeux (-jọọz, -jooz), *n.* [Fr. *Bételgeuse*, from the Arabic.] a star of the first magnitude, the largest in the constellation Orion: written also *Betelguese* and *Betelgueze*.

bē′tel nut, the nut of the betel palm, *Areca catechu*, chewed in the East with a little lime and leaves of the betel (pepper) plant.

bē′tel pälm (päm), any of a number of related tropical palms with a smooth trunk, a feathery crown of leaves, fragrant white flowers, and orange-colored, nutlike fruit: also called *areca palm*.

BETEL PALM (*Areca catechu*) leaf, flowers, and nut

beth (*or* bāth, bāz), *n.* [Heb.] the second letter of the Hebrew alphabet, corresponding to English *B, b*.

beth′el, *n.* [Heb. *bēth-ēl*, house of God.]

1. a worshiping place; any sacred spot.

2. a house of worship for sailors.

3. in England, a place of worship for Protestants belonging to any church except the Anglican.

Be·theṣ′dȧ, *n.* [L. Gr. *Bethesda*; Aram. *bēth'esda*, lit., house of mercy.]

1. in the Bible, a pool at Jerusalem, supposed to have healing properties: John v.2.

2. a chapel or holy place.

bē·thiñk′, *v.t.*; bethought, *pt., pp.*; bethinking, *ppr.* to call to mind; to recall or bring to recollection, reflection, or consideration: always used with a reflexive pronoun, with *of* or *that* before the subject of thought.

I have *bethought* me *of* another fault. —Shak.

Syn.—recollect, remember.

bē·thiñk′, *v.i.* to think; to ponder. [Archaic.]

Beth′lē·hem, *n.* 1. a hospital for the mentally ill: so called from the hospital of St. Mary of Bethlehem, in London, England: see *bedlam*.

2. in architecture, a small building attached to some Oriental church edifices, in which the communion bread is baked.

Beth′lē·hem·īte, Beth′lem·īte, *n.* 1. an inhabitant of Bethlehem in Judea.

2. [*pl.*] in church history, an order of monks, introduced into England in the year 1257, who dressed like the Dominicans, except that they wore a star with five rays, in memory of the star of Bethlehem. There was an order of Bethlehemites also in Spanish America.

bē·thought′ (-thọt′), past tense and past participle of *bethink*.

bē·thumb′ (-thum′), *v.t.*; bethumbed, *pt., pp.*; bethumbing, *ppr.* to handle or mark with the thumbs; as, his books are well *bethumbed*.

bē·thump′, *v.t.* to beat or thump soundly.

bē·tīde′, *v.t.*; betided, *pt., pp.*; betiding, *ppr.* [ME. *betiden*; *be-*, and AS. *tīdan*, to happen.] to happen to; to befall; to come to.

What will *betide* the few? —Milton.

bē·tīde′, *v.i.* to come to pass; to happen.

What news else *betideth* here? —Shak.

bē·tīmeṣ′, bē·tīme′, *adv.* 1. seasonably; in good season or time; before it is late.

2. soon; in a short time; speedily.

3. occasionally; at times. [Scot.]

Syn.—early, soon.

bê·tise′ (be-tēs′), *n.* [Fr. from *bete*, beast; LL. *besta*; L. *bestia*.] a foolish act, remark, suggestion, etc.; stupidity; absurdity; folly.

bē·tī′tle (-tl), *v.t.* to supply with a title or titles; to entitle. [Obs.]

bē·tō′ken, *v.t.*; betokened, *pt., pp.*; betokening,

ppr. [ME. *betokenen*, from AS. *be-*, and *tācn*, *tācen*, a token.]
1. to foreshow by present signs; to be a sign or token of.
2. to indicate; denote.

bé·ton′ (bā-tọṅ′), *n.* [Fr., concrete; Pr., *beton*; Sp. *betun*, from L. *bitumen*, bitumen.] concrete made of gravel, sand, and hydraulic cement.

bē·tŏngue′ (-tung′), *v.t.* to attack with the tongue; to abuse; to scold.

bet′ō·ny, *n.* [ME. *betony*; OFr. *beteine*; L. *betonica*, a corruption of *vettonica*, called after the Vettones, an ancient tribe in Gaul.] the *Stachys Betonica*, a plant which grows in woods. It was formerly much employed in medicine, and is sometimes used to dye wool a dark-yellow color.

bē·took′, past tense of *betake*.

bē·tọrn′, *a.* torn. [Obs.]

bē·toss′, *v.t.* to toss; to agitate; to disturb; to put in violent motion.

bē·trap′, *v.t.* 1. to entrap; to ensnare.
2. to put trappings on; to clothe. [Obs.]

bē·trāy′, *v.t.*; betrayed, *pt.*, *pp.*; betraying, *ppr.* [ME. *betrayen*, *betrain*; *be-*, and *traien*, betray; OFr. *trair*, L. *tradere*, to hand over, deliver.]
1. (a) to deliver into the hands of an enemy by treachery or fraud, in violation of trust; as, an officer *betrayed* the city; (b) to help the enemy of (one's country, cause, etc.); to be a traitor to.
2. to violate by fraud or unfaithfulness; as, to *betray* a trust.
3. to break faith with by disclosing a secret or that which was entrusted; to expose: followed by the person or the thing; as, my friend *betrayed* me, or *betrayed* the secret.
4. to disclose, as something intended to be kept secret or that which prudence would conceal; to disclose unintentionally; as, to *betray* one's ignorance.
5. to mislead; to lead astray; to victimize; as, great confidence *betrays* a man into errors.
6. to show; to disclose; to indicate: used of that which is not obvious at first view, or would otherwise be concealed; as, all the names in the country *betray* great antiquity.
7. to fail, or deceive; as, my legs *betray* me.
8. to seduce and fail to marry.
Syn.—deceive, delude, dupe, ensnare, dishonor, reveal.

bē·trāy′ăl, *n.* the act of betraying; a breach of trust; also, the fact or state of being betrayed.

bē·trāy′ẽr, *n.* one who betrays; a traitor.

bē·trāy′ment, *n.* betrayal. [Rare.]

bē·trim′, *v.i.*; betrimmed, *pt.*, *pp.*; betrimming, *ppr.* to adorn; to embellish.

bē·trọth′ (*or* -trōth′), *v.t.*; betrothed, *pt.*, *pp.*; betrothing, *ppr.* [ME. *betrouthen*, to betroth; *be-*, and *treuthe*; AS. *treowth*, troth, truth.]
1. to promise or pledge in marriage; to affiance; as, the father *betroths* his daughter.
2. to plight one's troth to; to engage oneself to; as, a man *betroths* a lady. [Archaic.]

bē·trọth′ăl (*or*-trōth′al), *n.* the act of betrothing, or the state of being betrothed; a promise or engagement between two persons for a future marriage; betrothment; engagement.

bē·trọthed′ (*or* -trōthd′), *a.* engaged to be married.

bē·trọthed′, *n.* a person engaged to be married.

bē·trọth′ment (*or* -trōth′), *n.* betrothal.

bē·trust′, *v.t.* to entrust; to commit to another in confidence or fidelity; to trust. [Obs.]

bē·trust′ment, *n.* the act of entrusting; also, the thing entrusted. [Obs.]

bet′sō, *n.* [It. *pezzo*, a piece; a piece of money.] a small Venetian coin. [Obs.]

bet′tȧ, *n.* [Mod.L.] any of a genus (*Betta*) of brightly colored, tropical, fresh-water fishes of southeastern Asia, especially an aquarium species (*Betta splendens*).

bet′ted, alternative past tense and past participle of *bet*.

bet′tẽr, *a.*, comp. of *good*. [ME. *bettere*, *betere*; AS. *betera*, better, from a positive not in use, but which appears in the adv. *bet*; D. *beter*; M.H.G. *bezzer*; G. *besser*; Sw. *battre*; Sans. *bhadra*, excellent.]
1. having good qualities in a greater degree than another; surpassing another or others; as, *better* soil, a *better* man, a *better* house, *better* air, a *better* harvest.
2. more advantageous, acceptable, safe, useful, or to be preferred for any other reason.
Better is a dinner of herbs where love is, than a stalled ox and hatred therewith.
—Prov. xv. 17.
3. improved in health; less affected by disease; as, the patient is *better*.
4. larger in amount or size; as, he gave me the *better* part of the cake.
5. more nearly perfect or complete; as, *better* acquaintance; to have a *better* understanding; a *better* knowledge of a subject.
better half; a wife or, occasionally, a husband. [Colloq.]
to be better off; to be in better circumstances.

bet′tẽr, *adv.*, comp. of *well*. 1. in a more excellent manner; in a more suitable way; as, to perform work *better*; to plan a scheme *better*; land *better* cultivated.
2. more correctly or fully; as, to understand a subject *better* than another.
3. in a higher degree; to a greater extent; more.
to think better of; to reconsider and change, as an opinion or decision.

bet′tẽr, *v.t.*; bettered, *pt.*, *pp.*; bettering, *ppr.* 1. to improve; to meliorate; to increase the good qualities of; as, manure *betters* land; discipline may *better* the morals.
2. to surpass; to exceed.
The works of nature do always aim at that which cannot be *bettered*. —Hooker.
3. to advance; to support; to give advantage to; as, to *better* a cause. [Obs.]
4. to improve; to increase; to enhance in value; as, to *better* one's station in life.
Syn.—amend, improve, advance, meliorate.

bet′tẽr, *v.i.* to become better; to improve.

bet′tẽr, *n.* 1. one of superior rank or standing; one entitled to precedence: generally in the plural; as, he stood in the way of his *betters*.
2. a more excellent thing, condition, circumstance, action, etc.
3. advantage: used with *of*; as, he got the *better* of me.
all the better; wholly better; better by all the difference.
for the better; so as to improve; as, a change *for the better*.
to get or *gain the better of*; to obtain advantage, superiority, or victory over.
to have the better of; to have the advantage or superiority over.

bet′tẽr, bet′tŏr, *n.* a person who bets or lays a wager.

bet′tẽr·ment, *n.* 1. a making better; improvement.
2. in law, an improvement of an estate which makes it better than mere repairs would and increases its value.

bet′tẽr·mōst, *a.* best; as, the *bettermost* classes. [Rare.]

bet′tẽr·ness, *n.* 1. superiority.
2. the excess of fineness of a precious metal above the standard.

bet′ting, *n.* the act or practice of making bets; wagering.

bet′tŏng, *n.* [native name.] the kangaroo rat, a marsupial of the genus *Bettongia*, about the size of a common hare. It is nocturnal in its habits and is found in Australia.

bet′tŏr, *n.* see *better*.

bet′ty, *n.* 1. a small instrument used by thieves in entering houses, etc.; a short bar or wrench: now called a *jimmy*. [Slang.]
2. a man who engages in woman's work: a contemptuous term.
3. a pear-shaped Italian flask or bottle for wine or olive oil; a Florence flask.

Bet′ū·lȧ, *n.* [L., the birch.] a genus of hardy trees or shrubs, natives of the north temperate and arctic regions, the birches.

Bet·ū·lā′ce·ae, *n.pl.* a natural order of apetalous dicotyledonous plants, of which *Betula* is the typical genus.

bet·ū·lā′ceous, *a.* relating to the *Betulaceæ*.

bet′ū·lin, bet′ū·line, *n.* a substance extracted from the bark of the common or white birch. It is of a white color, crystallized in the form of long needles, volatile and inflammable.

bē·tum′ble (-bl), *v.t.* to tumble. [Rare.]

bē·tween′, *n.* an interval. [Rare.]

bē·tween′, *prep.* [ME. *betwene*, *bitwenen*; AS. *betweonum*, *betwynum*; *be*, by, and *tweonum*, from *twa*, two.]
1. in or through the space that separates (two things).
2. in or of the time, amount, or degree that separates (two things); intermediate to; as, *between* blue and green.
3. separating.
5. connecting; relating; as, a bond *between* friends.
6. by the action of both of; as, *between* them they landed the fish.
7. in the combined possession of; as, the men had fifty dollars *between* them.
8. to the exclusion of all but both of; as, they divided it *between* them.
9. one or the other of; as, choose *between* love and duty.
10. as a consequence of the combined effect of; as, *between* her job and her studies she has little time for reading.
between ourselves, between you and me; in confidence.

bē·tween′, *adv.* 1. in an intermediate space, position, or function.
2. in an intermediate time; in the interval.

bē·tween′ decks, in the space between the decks of a ship.

bē·twixt′, *prep.* [ME. *betwixt*, *bytwyxte*; AS. *betwyxt*, *betwyx*; from *be*, by, and *twa*, two.] between: now archaic except in the following phrase.
betwixt and between; in an intermediate position; not definitely one thing nor altogether another.

beur·ré′ (bũr-rā′), *n.* [Fr., from *beurre*, butter.] a pear, the succulent part of which is luscious and melting; used with a distinguishing word; as, *beurré* d'Anjou.

bev, Bev, *n.*; *pl.* **bev, Bev**, [*b*illion, and *e*lectron, and *v*olts.] a unit of energy equal to one billion electron-volts.

bev′ȧ·tron, *n.* [from *bev*, and *-tron*, as in cyclotron.] a synchrotron for accelerating protons and other atomic particles to an energy level of six or more billion electron-volts.

bev′el, *n.* [Fr. *biveau*, a bevel.]
1. an instrument used by mechanics for drawing angles and in fixing surfaces at an angle: it consists of two limbs joined together, the stock and the blade, movable on a pivot at the joint, and adjustable so as to include any angle between it and the stock; a bevel square.

BEVEL

2. an angle other than a right angle.
3. a sloping part or surface, as the angled edge of plate glass.

bev′el, *a.* sloped; beveled.

bev′el, *v.t.*; beveled, bevelled, *pt.*, *pp.*; beveling, bevelling, *ppr.* to cut to an angle other than a right angle.

bev′el, *v.i.* to slant; to slope at an angle.

bev′el-aṅ′gle, *n.* an angle not a right angle.

bev′eled, bev′elled, *a.* 1. formed with a bevel-angle.
2. in mineralogy, replaced by two planes inclining equally upon the adjacent planes, as an edge; having its edges replaced by inclining planes, as a cube or other solid.

bev′el gēar, a gear wheel meshed with another so that their shafts are at an angle of less than 180°. Such wheels are frequently called conical wheels, as they resemble the frustums of fluted cones.

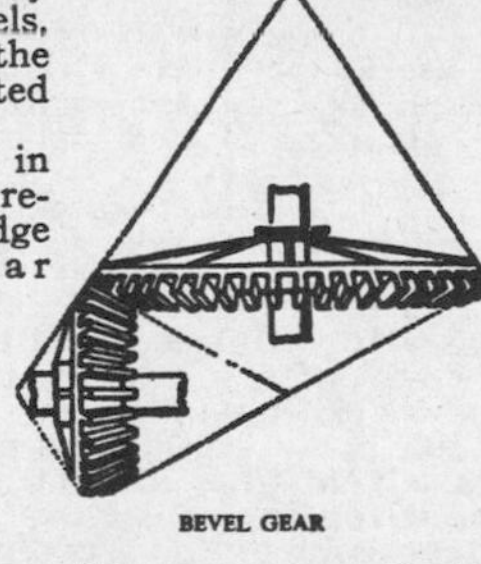

BEVEL GEAR

bev′el·ment, *n.* in mineralogy, the replacement of an edge by two similar planes, equally inclined to the including faces or adjacent planes.

bev′el squāre, see *bevel*, *n.* sense 1.

bev′el wheel, same as *bevel gear*.

bē′vẽr, *n.* [ME. *bever*; OFr. *bevre*, from L. *bibere*, to drink.] a collation or small repast between meals. [Obs.]

bē′vẽr, *v.i.* to take a small repast between meals. [Obs.]

bev′ẽr·āge, *n.* [ME. *beverage*; OFr. *bevrage*, from *bevre*, L. *bibere*, to drink.]
1. any drink, as milk, coffee, lemonade, etc.
2. drink money; a treat. [Prov. Eng.]

bē·vūe′, *n.* [Fr. *bévue*; OFr. *besvue*; *bes* (L. *bis*), double, and *vue*, view.] an error; a slip.

bev′y, *n.* [ME. *bevy*, *bevey*; OFr. *beveye*, from *bevre*, L. *bibere*, to drink.]
1. a flock of birds; especially, a flock of quail.
2. a company of girls or women.

A lovely *bevy* of fair ladies sat,
Courted of many a jolly paramour.
—Spenser.

3. a collection of objects. [Colloq.]

bē·wāil′, *v.t.*; bewailed, *pt.*, *pp.*; bewailing, *ppr.* [ME. *bewailen*; *be-*, and *wailen*, to wail; Ice. *væla*, from *væ*, woe.] to bemoan; to lament; to express deep sorrow for; as, to *bewail* the loss of a child.

Syn.—lament, bemoan, sorrow, deplore.

bē·wāil′, *v.i.* to express grief; mourn; weep.

bē·wāil′ȧ·ble, *a.* lamentable.

bē·wāil′ẽr, *n.* one who laments.

bē·wāil′ing, *n.* lamentation.

bē·wāil′ing·ly, *adv.* in a mournful manner.

bē·wāil′ment, *n.* the act of bewailing.

bē·wāre′, *v.i.* [ME. *beware*; *be*, AS. *beo*, second pers. imper. of v. *be*, and *ware*; AS. *wær*; O.H.G. *wara*, notice, attention.]

1. to be wary, guarded, or careful; to be watchful; to look out: often with *of*; as, let him *beware*; *beware of* him.

Beware of all, but most *beware of* man.
—Pope.

2. to take heed; to be heedful or attentive; to pay special attention. [Obs.]

Beware of him, and obey his voice.
—Ex. xxiii. 21.

bē·wāre′, *v.t.* to guard against; to be wary of; as, *beware* the flatterer.

bē·wash′, *v.t.*; bewashed, *pt.*, *pp.*; bewashing, *ppr.* to soak with water; to drench.

bē·weep′, *v.t.*; bewept, *pt.*, *pp.*; beweeping, *ppr.* to weep over; to bedew with tears. [Rare.]

bē·weep′, *v.i.* to make lamentation. [Rare.]

bē·wet′, *v.t.* to wet; to moisten. [Obs.]

bew′et, bew′it, *n.* [ME. *bewette*, dim. of OFr. *beue*, *bue*, a chain, collar; L. *boja*, a collar.] in falconry, the strap for attaching a bell to the leg of a hawk.

bē·whōre′ (-hōr′), *v.t.* to corrupt with regard to chastity; also, to denounce as unchaste. [Obs.]

bē·wig′, *v.t.* to put a wig on.

bē·wigged′, *a.* wearing a wig.

bē·wil′dẽr, *v.t.*; bewildered, *pt.*, *pp.*; bewildering, *ppr.* [Dan. *forvilde*, to bewilder; G. *verwildern*; AS. *wilde*, wild.]

1. to confuse hopelessly; befuddle; puzzle.

2. to cause (a person) to be lost in a wilderness. [Archaic.]

Syn.—daze, dazzle, confound, mystify, puzzle, astonish, perplex, confuse, mislead.

bē·wil′dẽred, *a.* lost as in a maze; perplexed with disorder, confusion, or intricacy.

Lost and *bewildered* in the fruitless search.
—Addison.

Syn.—confused, amazed, mystified, puzzled, perplexed.

bē·wil′dẽred·ness, *n.* bewilderment. [Rare.]

bē·wil′dẽr·ing·ly, *adv.* in a bewildering manner.

bē·wil′dẽr·ment, *n.* 1. the fact or state of being bewildered; a chaotic state of the mental forces; perplexity.

2. a confusion or jumble.

bew′it, *n.* see *bewet*, n.

bē·witch′ (-wich′), *v.t.*; bewitched (-witcht), *pt.*, *pp.*; bewitching, *ppr.* [ME. *bewicchen*; *be-*, and *wicchen*, a witch; AS. *wilga*, *wiliga*, a witch.]

1. to use witchcraft or magic on; to gain an ascendancy over by charms or incantation.

Look, how I am *bewitched*; behold, mine arm
Is like a blasted sapling, withered up.
—Shak.

2. to charm; to fascinate; to please to such a degree as to take away the power of resistance.

Syn.—enchant, fascinate, charm, captivate.

bē·witch′ed·ness, *n.* state of being bewitched.

bē·witch′ẽr, *n.* one who bewitches.

bē·witch′ẽr·y, *n.* fascination; charm; irresistible power exerted in a pleasing manner.

bē·witch′ful, *a.* alluring; fascinating. [Rare.]

bē·witch′ing, *a.* having power to bewitch or captivate by the arts of pleasing.

bē·witch′ing·ly, *adv.* in a fascinating manner.

bē·witch′ing·ness, *n.* the quality of bewitching.

bē·witch′ment, *n.* fascination; power of charming; the act of bewitching or state of being bewitched.

bē·wrap′ (-rap′), *v.t.* to wrap up.

bē·wrāy′ (-rā′), *v.t.* [AS. *wregan*, to accuse.] to disclose perfidiously; to betray; to show or reveal. [Archaic.]

Thy speech *bewrayeth* thee.
—Matt. xxvi. 73.

bē·wrāy′ẽr, *n.* a divulger of secrets. [Archaic.]

bē·wrāy′ment, *n.* the act of bewraying. [Archaic.]

bē·wreck′ (-rek′), *v.t.* to ruin.

bē·wrought′ (-rọt′), *a.* worked; wrought. [Obs.]

bey, *n.* [Turk. *bey*, *beg*; Per. *baig*, a lord.]

1. the governor of a minor Turkish district or province.

2. a Turkish title of respect.

3. the former native ruler of Tunis.

bey′liç, bey′lik, *n.* the jurisdiction of a bey.

bē·yond′, *prep.* [ME. *beyonde*, *beyende*; AS. *begeondan*; *be*, by, and *geondan*, from *geond*, across, beyond, over.]

1. on or to the further side of; as, *beyond* the sea.

2. past; later than; as, *beyond* the hour of welcome.

3. above; in a degree to exceed or excel; as, one man is great or good *beyond* another.

4. out of reach or understanding of; further than; as, *beyond* the power of evil; *beyond* belief.

to go beyond; to exceed in any action or scheme; hence, to deceive or circumvent.

bē·yond′, *adv.* 1. at a distance; yonder; farther off.

2. in addition; besides.

bē·yond′, *n.* 1. whatever is beyond or far away.

2. whatever follows death; afterlife: also *the great beyond*.

Usually with *the*.

bez′ăn, *n.* [E. Ind.] a cotton cloth from Bengal.

bez′ănt, bez′zant (*or* bē-zant′), *n.* [Fr. *besant*; L. *Besantius*, from *Byzantium*, Gr. *Byzantion*, Byzantium.]

1. a gold coin of Byzantium: properly called *solidus*; also, any of various gold and silver coins used in Europe c. 450–1450 A.D.

2. in architecture and heraldry, a circle representing such a coin.

bez·an·tée′ (-tā′), *n.* [OFr. *besanté*, from *besant*, a gold coin.] an ornamental design, representing a series of bezants, found on Norman moldings.

bez ant′lẽr, [OFr. *bes*, from L. *bis*, twice, and *antler*.] the second branch of a deer's horn, next above the brow antler: also called *bay antler*.

bez′el, bez′il, *n.* [Fr. *biseau*, sloping edge, from OFr. *bisel*.]

1. (a) the upper part of the collet of a ring, which encompasses and fastens the stone; (b) the rim which fastens the crystal of a watch in the cavity in which it is set; (c) a movable rim on a watch or clock that can be rotated so that marks on it can record certain kinds of data.

2. the slanting faces of a cut jewel, especially those of the upper half.

3. the bevel or beveled edge of any cutting tool.

be·zique′ (-zēk′), *n.* [Fr.] 1. a card game resembling pinochle, but using a double, triple, or quadruple deck of all the cards above the six.

2. a combination, the queen of spades and jack of diamonds, counting forty points in the game of bezique.

bē′zōar, *n.* [Sp. *bezoar*; Ar. *bāzarh*; Per. *bādzarh*, *pādzahr*; *pād*, expelling, and *zāhr*, poison.]

1. any of certain calculi or concretions found in the stomach or intestines of some animals (especially ruminants), formerly supposed to be a remedy for poisoning.

2. any antidotal remedy. [Obs.]

bē′zōar gōat, the wild goat of Persia, one of the animals from which bezoars are obtained.

bē·zō′ni·ăn, *n.* [Fr. *besoin*; It. *bisogno*, need, want.] a beggar; also, a scoundrel. [Obs.]

bez′zle, *v.t.* to waste in riot. [Obs.]

bez′zle, *v.i.* to carouse; to revel. [Obs.]

B′-gïrl″ (bē′gïrl″), *n.* [from *bar girl*.] a woman employed by a bar to entice men into buying drinks freely.

Bha′gȧ·vȧd-Gī′tä (bug′), *n.* [Sans.] in the Mahabharata, the philosophical poem relating a discourse between Krishna and his pupil Arjun in the midst of a battle: it is a sacred Hindu text.

bhang (bang), *n.* [Hind., from Sans. *bhangā*, hemp.] an Indian variety of the common hemp; also, its dried leaves and seed capsules, which have narcotic and intoxicating qualities: also spelled *bang*, *beng*.

bhär′al, *n.* the blue sheep of Tibet.

bhees′ty, bhees′tie (bēs′), *n.* [Anglo-Ind.] in India, a water carrier for a household or in military service.

bī-, [L. *bi-*, from *bis*, twice.] a prefix used to form adjectives, adverbs, verbs, and nouns, and meaning: (a) *having two*, as in *bi*angular, *bi*capsular; (b) *doubly, on both sides, in two ways* or *directions*, as in *bi*convex, *bi*lingual; (c) *coming, happening*, or *issued every two*, as in *bi*ennial, *bi*weekly; (d) *coming, happening*, or *issued twice during every*, as in *bi*monthly, *bi*yearly: often replaced by *semi-* or *half-*, to avoid confusion with sense c; (e) *using two* or *both*, as in *bi*labial, *bi*manual; (f) *joining two, combining* or *involving two*, as in *bi*lateral, *bi*partisan; (g) in botany and zoology, *twice, doubly, in pairs*, as in *bi*furcate, *bi*pinnate; (h) in chemistry, *having twice as many atoms or chemical equivalents for a definite weight of the other constituent of the compound*, as in sodium *bi*carbonate ($NaHCO_3$, as distinguished from sodium carbonate, Na_2CO_3); also, in organic compounds, *having a combination of two radicals of the same composition*, as in *bi*phenyl, $(C_6H_5)_2$: usually replaced by *di-* except in the names of acid salts, such as sodium *bi*sulfate, etc.

Also, before a vowel, *bin-* as in *bin*ary; before *c* or *s*, *bis-*, as in *bis*sextile.

Bi, in chemistry, bismuth.

bī′ȧ, *n.* a species of cowry shell formerly used in the East Indies as a medium of exchange.

bī·ac′id, *a.* in chemistry, capable of combining with an acid in two different proportions: said of a base.

bī·ȧ·çū′mi·nāte, *a.* in botany, having two diverging points.

biä′ly, *n.*; *pl.* **biä′lys**, [Yid., from *Bialystok*, Poland, where originally made.] a flat bread roll made with gluten flour and topped with chopped onions, etc.: also spelled *biali*.

bī·an′gū·lăr, *a.* having two angles.

bī·an′gū·lāte, bī·an′gū·lā·ted, bī·an′gū·lous, *a.* same as *biangular*.

bī·an′nū·ăl, *a.* occurring or appearing twice a year; semiannual.

bī·an′nū·ăl·ly, *adv.* twice a year.

bī·an′nū·lāte, *a.* in zoology, having two rings or bands of color, etc.

bī·är·tiç′ū·lāte, *a.* consisting of two joints.

bī′ăs, *n.*; *pl.* **bī′ăs·es**, [Fr. *biais*, a slope, slant.]

1. in bowling, (a) a weight in the side of a ball which causes it to curve in its course; (b) this curve or tendency to curve; (c) the force causing this.

2. a mental leaning or inclination; prepossession; propensity toward an object, not leaving the mind indifferent; as, a *bias* resulting from misinformation.

3. that which causes the mind to lean or incline from a state of indifference. [Rare.]

4. a slanting or diagonal line, cut or sewn in cloth.

5. in radio, the fixed voltage applied to an electrode, usually with the cathode voltage as reference.

Syn.—tendency, inclination, propensity, disposition, bent, prepossession, prejudice.

bī′ăs, *a.* slanting; diagonal.

bī′ăs, *adv.* 1. in a bias manner; diagonally; as, a seam sewed *bias*.

2. awry.

bī′ăs, *v.t.*; biased or biassed (-ăst), *pt.*, *pp.*; biasing or biassing, *ppr.* 1. to warp; to prejudice; to prepossess; as, judgment is often *biased* by interest.

2. in radio, to apply a bias to (an electrode).

bī′ăs·ness, *n.* inclination to some side.

bī·ath′lŏn, *n.* [from *bi-*, and Gr. *athlon*, a contest.] in the winter Olympic games, an event combining a ski run and marksmanship.

bī·au′răl, *a.* same as *binaural*.

bī·au·riç′ū·lăr, *a.* in anatomy, (a) biauriculate; (b) of the external opening of both ears.

bī·au·riç′ū·lāte, *a.* 1. having two auricles, as the heart in all reptiles, birds, and mammals.

2. in botany, having two projections the shape of an ear, as some leaves.

bī·ax′i·ăl, bī·ax′ăl, *a.* having two axes.

bī·ax′i·ăl·ly, *adv.* in a biaxial manner.

bib, *n.* 1. a small piece of linen or other cloth worn by children around the neck at meals.

2. a similar piece of cloth attached to the upper part of an apron.

3. the whiting pout, an arctic fish.

bib and tucker; clothes. [Colloq.]

bib, *v.t.* and *v.i.*; bibbed, *pt.*, *pp.*; bibbing, *ppr.* [ME. *bibben*; L. *bibere*, to drink.] to sip; to tipple; to drink.

bī·bā′cious, *a.* [L. *bibax*, from *bibere*, to drink.] addicted to drinking.

bī·bac′i·ty, *n.* the habit of drinking much or frequently.

bī·bā′siç, *a.* in chemistry, dibasic. [Rare.]

bibb, *n.* 1. a faucet; a bibcock.

2. a bracket of timber supporting the trestletrees of a mast.

bib′bẽr, *n.* a tippler; a man given to drinking.

bib′ble-bab′ble, idle talk. [Rare.]

bib′çock, *n.* a faucet having a turned-down nozzle.

bibe′lot (bib′lō), *n.* [Fr.] a small object whose value lies in its beauty or rarity.

bi·bī′rine, *n.* same as *bebeerine.*

bi·bī′rū, *n.* same as *bebeeru.*

bib′i·tō·ry, *a.* [L. *bibitor,* a drinker, from *bibere,* to drink.] pertaining to drinking.

bī″bī·vā′lent, *a.* in chemistry, separating into two bivalent ions: said of electrolytes.

Bī′ble (-bl), *n.* [ME. *bible;* OFr. *bible,* from L. *biblia,* neut. pl., from Gr. *biblia,* pl. of *biblion,* a little book; *biblos,* a book.]

1. the sacred book of Christianity; the Old Testament and New Testament: the Roman Catholic (Douay) Bible also includes the Apocrypha.

2. the sacred book of Judaism; the Old Testament.

3. any collection or book of writings sacred to a religion; as, the Koran is the Moslem *Bible.*

4. [b–] any book regarded as authoritative or official.

See also *Authorized Version, Revised Standard Version, Douay Bible, Vulgate, Septuagint, Apocrypha.*

BOOKS OF THE BIBLE

(Names used in the Douay Bible, when different, are in parentheses.)

Old Testament

Genesis	Proverbs
Exodus	Ecclesiastes
Leviticus	Song of Solomon (Canticle of Canticles)
Numbers	
Deuteronomy	Isaiah (Isaias)
Joshua (Josue)	Jeremiah (Jeremias)
Judges	Lamentations
Ruth	Ezekiel (Ezechiel)
I Samuel (I Kings)	Daniel
II Samuel (II Kings)	Hosea (Osee)
I Kings (III Kings)	Joel
II Kings (IV Kings)	Amos
I Chronicles (I Paralipomenon)	Obadiah (Abdias)
	Jonah (Jonas)
II Chronicles (II Paralipomenon)	Micah (Micheas)
	Nahum
Ezra (I Esdras)	Habakkuk (Habacuc)
Nehemiah (II Esdras)	Zephaniah (Sophonias)
Esther	Haggai (Aggeus)
Job	Zechariah (Zacharias)
Psalms	Malachi (Malachias)

Old Testament Apocrypha

I Esdras (III Esdras)	Additions to Daniel, including the Song of the Three Holy Children, the Story of Susanna, and the Idol Bel and the Dragon
II Esdras (IV Esdras)	
Tobit (Tobias)	
Judith	
Additions to Esther	
Wisdom of Solomon	Prayer of Manasses
Ecclesiasticus	I Maccabees (I Machabees)
Baruch	II Maccabees (II Machabees)
Epistle of Jeremy	

New Testament

Matthew	Ephesians	Hebrews
Mark	Philippians	James
Luke	Colossians	I Peter
John	I Thessalonians	II Peter
The Acts	II Thessalonians	I John
Romans	I Timothy	II John
I Corinthians	II Timothy	III John
II Corinthians	Titus	Jude
Galatians	Philemon	Revelation

Bī′ble Çhris′tiăn, a Bryanite, or member of an English Methodist sect started by William Bryan in 1816.

bī′ble pā′pẽr, a thin, strong, opaque paper used for many Bibles, dictionaries, etc.

bib′lẽr, *n.* [L. *bibere,* to drink.] a tippler; a man given to drinking.

Bib′li·çăl, bib′li·çăl, *a.* pertaining to or in harmony with the Bible; as, *Biblical* criticism.

Bib·li·çal′i·ty, bib·li·çal′i·ty, *n.* the quality of being Biblical; that which is Biblical.

Bib′li·çăl·ly, bib′li·çăl·ly, *adv.* according to the Bible.

Bib′li·ciṣm, *n.* strict adherence to Biblical teachings.

Bib′li·cist, *n.* 1. one skilled in the knowledge and interpretation of the Bible.

2. one who strictly adheres to Bible teachings.

bib′li·ō-, [from Gr. *biblion,* a book.] a combining form meaning: (a) *book, of books;* (b) *of the Bible.*

bib′li·ō·film, *n.* a type of microfilm used especially in photographing rare or fragile books in libraries, etc.

bib′li·og·nost, *n.* [*biblio-,* and Gr. *gnōstēs,* from *gignōskein,* to know.] a well-read lover of books; one learned in bibliography.

bib·li·og′rȧ·phẽr, bib′li·ō·graph, *n.* [Gr. *bibliographos,* a writer of books, *biblion,* a book, and *graphos,* from *graphein,* to write.] an expert in bibliography.

bib″li·ō·graph′iç·ăl, bib″li·ō·graph′iç, *a.* pertaining to bibliography.

bib″li·ō·graph′iç·ăl·ly, *adv.* 1. in the manner of a bibliographer.

2. through the use or in the style of a bibliography.

bib·li·og′rȧ·phy, *n.* 1. the study of the editions, dates, authorship, etc. of books and other writings.

2. a book containing such information.

3. a list of an author's writings or the literature dealing with a certain subject or author; as, the *bibliography* of Omar Khayyam.

bib·li·ol′ȧ·tẽr, bib·li·ol′ȧ·trist, *n.* 1. a worshiper of the Bible and devout believer in its literal interpretation.

2. one who loves books exceedingly.

bib·li·ol′ȧ·try, *n.* [*biblio-,* and Gr. *latreia,* from *latreuein,* to worship.] worship or homage paid to books, especially to the Bible.

bib′li·ō·līte, *n.* [*biblio-,* and Gr. *lithos,* stone.] a laminated schistose rock: called also *book stone.*

bib·li·ō·loġ′ic·ăl, *a.* pertaining to bibliology.

bib·li·ol′ō·ġist, *n.* one who is well informed or interested in bibliology.

bib·li·ol′ō·ġy, *n.* [*biblio-,* and Gr. *logia,* from *legein,* to speak.]

1. the literature of the Bible or its doctrine.

2. bibliography.

bib′li·ō·man″cy, *n.* [*biblio-,* and Gr. *manteia,* prophecy.] a kind of divination by means of the Bible, consisting of selecting passages of Scripture at random and predicting from them future events.

bib′li·ō·māne, *n.* one having a mania for acquiring books.

bib″li·ō·mā′ni·ȧ, *n.* [*biblio-,* and Gr. *mania,* madness.] a craze for collecting books, especially rare ones.

bib″li·ō·mā′ni·aç, *n.* one who has bibliomania.

bib″li·ō·mȧ·nī′aç·ăl, *a.* pertaining to bibliomania.

bib″li·ō·peġ′iç, *a.* relating to the binding of books. [Rare.]

bib·li·op′e·ġist, *n.* one who binds books.

bib″li·op·e·ġis′tiç, *a.* relating to bookbinders or the bookbinding art.

bib·li·op′e·ġy, *n.* [*biblio-,* and Gr. *pēgia,* from *pēgnynai,* to fasten, bind.] the bookbinding art.

bib′li·ō·phīle, bib′li·ō·phil, *n.* [*biblio-,* and Gr. *philos,* loving.] a book lover or book collector.

bib·li·oph′i·liṣm, *n.* love for or collecting of books.

bib·li·oph′i·list, *n.* a bibliophile.

bib″li·ō·phō′bi·ȧ, *n.* [*biblio-,* and Gr. *phobia,* fear.] a dread of or distaste for books.

bib′li·ō·pōle, *n.* same as *bibliopolist.*

bib″li·ō·pol′iç, bib·li·op′ō·lăr, *a.* pertaining to bookselling.

bib·li·op′ō·liṣm, *n.* the business of buying and selling books.

bib·li·op′ō·list, *n.* [L. *bibliopola,* Gr. *bibliopōlēs; biblion,* a book, and *polein,* to sell.] a bookseller, especially one who deals in rare or curious books.

bib·li·op·ō·lis′tiç, *a.* relating to bibliopolism.

bib·li·op′ō·ly, *n.* bookselling.

bib′li·ō·taph, bib·li·ot′ȧ·phist, *n.* [*biblio-,* and Gr. *taphos,* from *taphein,* to bury.] one who stows away or hides books.

bib′li·ō·theç, *n.* one who has charge of a collection of books; a librarian; also, a library.

bib″li·ō·thē′çȧ, *n.* [L. *bibliotheca;* Gr. *bibliothēkē,* a library, bookcase; *biblion,* a book, and *thēkē,* from *tithenai,* to place.]

1. a collection of books; a library.

2. a bookseller's catalogue.

3. the Bible. [Obs.]

bib″li·ō·thē′çăl, *a.* belonging to a library.

bib·li·oth′ē·çā·ry, *n.* a librarian.

bib′li·ō·thēke, *n.* a library. [Obs.]

Bib′list, *n.* 1. a Biblicist.

2. a person who believes that the Bible presents the only true religious faith.

bī·braç′tē·āte, *a.* doubly bracteate.

bib′ū·lous, *a.* [L. *bibulus,* from *bibere,* to drink.]

1. highly absorbent; spongy.

2. fond of or in the habit of drinking alcoholic liquor.

3. drunk.

bib′ū·lous·ly, *adv.* in a bibulous manner.

bī·cal′çȧ·rāte, *a.* in zoology, having two spurs.

bī·cal′lōse, bī·cal′lous, *a.* in botany, having two calluses.

bī·cam′ẽr·ăl, *a.* [*bi-,* and L. *camera,* a vault, chamber.] consisting of two houses or chambers: applied to a legislative body.

bī·çap′sū·lăr, *a.* [*bi-,* and L. *capsula,* a little chest, from *capsa,* a chest.] in botany, (a) having two capsules; as, a *bicapsular* pericarp; (b) having a capsule with two cells.

bī·cär′bŏn·āte, *n.* an acid salt of carbonic acid containing the radical HCO_3.

bī·cär′bŏn·āte of sō′dȧ, sodium bicarbonate; baking soda.

bī·cär′bū·ret·ed, bī·cär′bū·ret·ted, *a.* combined with or containing two atoms of carbon; as, *bicarbureted* hydrogen, C_2H_4. [Obs.]

bī·car′i·nāte, *a.* in biology, having two ridge-like parts.

bī·çau′dăl, bī·çau′dāte, *a.* having two tails.

bicch′ed (bich′), *a.* [origin unknown.] cursed. [Obs.]

bicched bones; dice. [Obs.]

bīce, bīse, *n.* [ME. *bise, bys;* OFr. *bis, bise,* dusky, dark.]

1. a pale blue color, prepared from azurite or smalt: called also *blue bice.*

2. a grayish blue, duller than azure.

3. loosely, a green color or pigment.

bī·cen′te·nā·ry, *a.* consisting of or pertaining to two hundred, usually two hundred years; as, a *bicentenary* celebration.

bī·cen′te·nā·ry, *n.; pl.* **bī·cen′te·nā·rieṣ,** *n.* that which consists of two hundred, usually two hundred years; also, the two hundredth anniversary or the celebration of it.

bī·cen·ten′ni·ăl, *a.* consisting of or lasting two hundred years; also, occurring every two hundred years.

bī·cen·ten′ni·ăl, *n.* 1. the two hundredth anniversary of an event.

2. the celebration of this.

bī·ceph′ȧ·lous, *a.* having two heads.

bī′ceps, *n.; pl.* **bī′ceps·eṣ,** [L. *biceps; bi-,* two, and *caput,* head.]

1. a muscle which has two heads or points of origin: specifically applied to the *biceps brachii* or *humeri* of the upper arm and the *biceps femoris* of the thigh.

2. figuratively, strength or muscular development, especially of the arm.

bich′ĭr, *n.* [native name.] any fish of the genus *Polypterus;* specifically, *Polypterus bichir* of the Nile.

bī·çhlō′rīde, bī·çhlō′rid, *n.* 1. a compound made up of two atoms of chlorine for each atom of another element.

2. bichloride of mercury.

bī·çhlō′rīde of mẽr′çū·ry, a poisonous compound, $HgCl_2$, used as a disinfectant: called also *corrosive sublimate.*

bī′chō, *n.* same as *chigoe.*

bī·çhrō′māte, *n.* a dichromate.

bī·çhrō′māte, *v.t.* bichromated, *pt., pp.;* bichromating, *ppr.* to treat or mix with a bichromate.

bī·çhrō·mat′iç, *a.* dichromatic.

bī·çhrō′mȧ·tīze, *v.t.* to combine or treat chemically with a bichromate.

bī·cip′i·tăl, bī·cip′i·tous, *a.* [L. *biceps,* from *bis,* twice, and *caput, capitis,* head.]

1. having two heads; two-headed. [Rare.]

2. in anatomy, having two heads or points of origin, as a biceps muscle.

3. of a biceps.

4. in botany, dividing into two parts at the top or bottom.

bick′ẽr, *n.* 1. a petty dispute; wrangle; quarrel.

2. a short, jerky run.

bick′ẽr, *v.i.;* bickered, *pt., pp.;* bickering, *ppr.* [ME. *bicheren, bikkeren;* W. *bicra,* fight.]

1. to skirmish; to fight intermittently; to exchange blows. [Rare.]

2. to quarrel; wrangle.

3. to move quickly and unsteadily, as flame or water.

4. to make quick, rippling noises or movements; gurgle; patter.

bick′ẽr·ẽr, *n.* one who bickers.

bick′ẽr·ing, *n.* 1. a fight or skirmish.

2. quarreling; wrangling.

bick′ẽrn, *n.* [ME. *bickhorn, bicorn;* OFr. *bicorne;* L. *bicorna,* a two-handled cup, from *bicornus,* two-horned; *bis,* two, and *cornu,* horn.] an anvil with two tapering ends; also, one of the ends.

Bī′çōl, *n.* same as *Bikol.*

bī·col′li·gāte, *a.* [*bi-,* and L. *colligatus,* pp. of *colligare; con,* together, and *ligare,* to bind.] in ornithology, having the anterior toes connected by a web.

bī·çŏl′ŏr, bī·çŏl′ŏred, *a.* of two colors.

bī·con′çāve, *a.* concave on both surfaces.

bī·con′iç·ăl, *a.* similar in form to two cones placed base to base.

bī·con′jū·gāte, *a.* [*bi-,* and L. *conjugatus,* pp.

of *conjugare*; *con*, together, and *jugare*, to join.] in botany, twice-paired.
bī-çon′vex, *a.* convex on both surfaces.
bī′çọrn, bī-çọr′nous, bī′çọrned, *a.* [L. *bicornis*; *bis*, twice, and *cornu*, horn.] having two horns; shaped like a crescent.
bī-çọr′nū-āte, *a.* same as *bicorn*.
bī-çọr′pō-răl, *a.* having two bodies or main parts.
bī-çọr′pō-rāte, *a.* [*bi-*, and L. *corporatus*, pp. of *corporare*, to shape into a body; from *corpus*, body.] in heraldry, having two bodies.
bī-çọr-pō′rē-ăl, *a.* same as *bicorporal*.
bī-ços′tāte, *a.* in botany, having two longitudinal ribs, as a leaf.
bī-çrē′nāte, *a.* in botany, twice scalloped.
bī-çres-cen′tiç, *a.* formed as a double crescent.
bī′çron, *n.* [*bi*llion, and mi*cron*.] one billionth (.000,000,001) of a meter: symbol, $\mu\mu$.
bī-çrū′răl, *a.* having two legs.
bī-çus′pid, bī-çus′pid-āte, *a.* [L. *bicuspis*; *bis*, twice, and *cuspis*, *cuspidis*, a point.] having two points; applied to teeth, leaves, etc.
bicuspid valve; same as *mitral valve*.
bī-çus′pid, *n.* any of eight adult teeth with two-pointed crowns; a premolar tooth.
bī-çȳ′à-nide, *n.* same as *dicyanide*.
bī′cy-çle, *n.* [*bi-*, and L. *cyclus*; Gr. *kyklos*, a wheel.] a vehicle consisting of two wheels, one behind the other, connected by a simple framework of steel tubing: it is equipped with handle bars and a saddlelike seat, and is propelled by the feet of the rider or, if it is a motor bicycle, by a small gasoline motor.

BICYCLE

bī′cy-çle, *v.i.* and *v.t.*; bicycled, *pt.*, *pp.*; bicycling, *ppr.* to ride or travel on a bicycle.
bī′cy-çlẽr, *n.* a bicyclist.
bī-cyç′liç, *a.* pertaining to or resembling bicycles.
bī-cȳ′cliç, *a.* 1. of or forming two circles, cycles, etc.
2. in chemistry, containing two fused rings in the molecule.
Also **bī-cy′çli-çăl.**
bī′cy-çling, *n.* the art or practice of riding a bicycle.
bī′cy-çlist, *n.* a person who rides a bicycle.
bī-cyç′ū-lăr, *a.* pertaining to bicycling; bicyclic.
bid, *v.t.*; bade, bid, *or archaic* bad, *pt.*; bidden, bid, *pp.*; bidding, *ppr.* [ME. *bidden*; AS. *biddan*, to ask, pray, invite, and confused with AS. *beódan*, to offer, command, threaten.]
1. to ask or command; as, do as you are *bidden*.
2. to say to by way of greeting or benediction; as, to *bid* good day, farewell, etc.
Neither *bid* him God speed.—2 John 10.
3. [*pt.* and *pp.* bid.] to offer; to propose; specifically, (a) to offer (a certain amount) as the price or fee for; (b) to offer (to do something specified) for a given sum.
4. to declare; to say; to tell; as, *bid* defiance to your enemies.
5. to express in greeting or taking leave; as, *bid* farewell to your friends.
6. to invite. [Archaic or Dial.]
7. to offer membership to; as, the fraternity may *bid* five new men. [Colloq.]
8. [*pt.* and *pp.* bid.] in card games, to state (the number of tricks or points one expects to take) and declare (a suit or no trump).
to bid fair; to appear likely.
Syn.—tell, request, instruct, direct, order, proffer, charge, command, propose, offer.
bid, *n.* 1. an offer; a proposal; a bidding.
2. in card games, (a) a bidding; (b) the number of tricks or points stated; (c) a player's turn to bid.
3. an amount, etc. offered or proposed.
4. an attempt or try (*for* something.)
5. an invitation, especially to become a member. [Colloq.]
bid, *v.i* 1. to pray. [Obs.]
2. [*pt.* and *pp.* bid.] to make a bid.
bid, obsolete past participle of *bide*.
bī-daç′tyl, bī-daç′tyle, *a.* same as *didactyl*.
bid′āle, *n.* in England, a feast for the benefit of someone in need. [Obs.]
bi-där′kȧ, bi-där′kee, *n.* [native name.] a light Aleutian boat made of sealskins.
bid′dȧ-ble, *a.* 1. tractable; willing; obedient.
2. worth bidding on; as, a *biddable* bridge hand.
bid′den, alternative past participle of *bid*.
bid′den, *a.* invited.
bid′den, obsolete past participle of *bide*.
bid′dẽr, *n.* one who bids or offers a price.
bid′dẽr-y, *n.* same as *bidri*.
bid′ding, *n.* 1. command; order.
2. an invitation or summons.
3. the bids or the making of bids in a card game or auction.
bid′ding prāyer (prãr), in Roman Catholic and Anglican churches, the prayer offered before the sermon, in which special persons, living or dead, are prayed for.
bid′dy, *n.*; *pl.* **bid′dieṣ,** a chicken, especially a hen.
bid′dy, *n.* [dim. of *Bridget*, Ir. *Brighid*, from *brigh*, strength.]
1. female domestic servant. [Colloq.]
2. a woman, especially an elderly woman regarded contemptuously as eccentric, gossipy, etc. [Slang.]
bīde, *v.i.*; bode *or* bided *or* bade, *pt.*; bided, *pp.*; biding, *ppr.*; *obs. pt.* bad; *obs. pp.* bid, biden, bidden, [ME. *biden*; AS. *bidan*, to wait.]
1. to dwell; to inhabit. [Archaic or Dial.]
2. to remain; to continue. [Archaic or Dial.]
3. to wait. [Archaic or Dial.]
bīde, *v.t.* 1. to endure; to suffer.
2. to wait for; as, I *bide* my time.
Syn.—wait, remain, tarry, stay.
Bī′denṣ, *n.* [L. *bidens*; *bis*, twice, and *dens*, tooth.] a genus of composite plants of the thistle family; the beggar's lice. The achenes of these plants have barbed awns.
bī′dent, *n.* [L. *bidens*, having two prongs; *bis*, twice, and *dens*, *dentis*, a tooth.] a two-pronged weapon or instrument.
bī-den′tăl, *a.* bidentate.
bī-den′tăl, *n.*; *pl.* **bī-den-tā′li-ȧ,** a place in ancient Rome that had been struck by lightning and was consecrated.
bī-den′tāte, *a.* having two teeth, or two toothlike parts.
bi-det′, *n.* [Fr.] 1. a small horse, formerly allowed to each trooper or dragoon for carrying his baggage.
2. a low, bowl-shaped, porcelain bathroom fixture equipped with running water, used for bathing the crotch.
bī-dig′i-tāte, *a.* having two fingers or parts similar to fingers.
bīd′ing, *n.* residence; habitation.
bid′ri, bid′ry, *n.* [from *Bidar*, a town in India.] an alloy, primarily composed of copper, lead, and tin, to which zinc is added; also, the Indian ware made from it, being generally inlaid with silver or gold and polished: also written *bidree*, *biddery*, *beder*, etc.
bid′ū-ous, *a.* [L. *biduus*, *bis*, and *dies*, day.] lasting two days, as certain flowers.
Biē′dẽr-meī-ẽr, *a.* [G., from (*Gottlieb*) *Biedermeier*, fictitious author of stodgy poems published (1855–57, and later) by Adolf Kussmaul and Ludwig Eichrodt to satirize German bourgeois tastes.] designating or of a style of mid-19th-century German furniture design, essentially a heavy, stolid variation of French Empire.
biēld, *n.* a shelter; a place of refuge. [Scot.]
biēld, *v.t.* to shelter. [Scot.]
bī-en′ni-ăl, *a.* [L. *biennialis*, from *biennis*; *bis*, twice, and *annus*, year.]
1. continuing for two years.
2. happening, or taking place, once in two years; as, a *biennial* election.
3. in botany, continuing for two years and then perishing, as plants whose roots and leaves are formed the first year, and which produce fruit and flowers the second.
bī-en′ni-ăl, *n.* 1. anything that occurs once in two years.
2. a plant which lives for two years.
bī-en′ni-ăl-ly, *adv.* once in two years; every two years.
bien-ve-nüe′, (byaṅ-), *n.* [Fr., lit., well come.] a welcome.
biẽr, *n.* [ME. *beere*, *bere*; AS. *bær*, a bier; from *beran*, to bear.]
1. a frame of wood, with handles at each end, on which a coffin or corpse is placed.
2. a coffin.
biẽr′bąlk (-bąk), *n.* a path through fields, left for funerals. [Obs.]
biēst′ingṣ, *n.pl.* [ME. *beestynge*, AS. *bȳsting*, from *beoast*, biest.] the first milk given by a cow after calving: also *beestings*, *biest*.
bī-fā′ciăl, *a.* 1. having two faces or surfaces.
2. in botany, having two unlike opposite surfaces.
bī-fā′ri-ous, *a.* [L. *bifarius*, twofold, *bis*, twice, and *fari*, to speak.] in botany, pointing two ways, or arranged in two opposite rows, as leaves that grow only on opposite sides of a branch.
bī-fā′ri-ous-ly, *adv.* in a bifarious manner.
bī-fer′ous, *a.* [L. *biferus*, *bis*, twice, and *ferre*, to bear.] bearing fruit or flowering twice a year.
biff, *n.* a blow; a cuff. [Slang.]
biff, *v.t.* to strike or punch. [Slang.]
bif′fin, *n.* [a corruption of *beefing*, from *beef* and *-ing*, so called from the color of the apple.]
1. a baked apple crushed down into a flat, round cake.
2. a deep-red cooking apple of England.
bī′fid, *a.* [L. *bifidus*, forked; from *bis*, twice, and *findere*, to cleave, divide.] in botany, forked; divided by a cleft.
bif′i-dāte, *a.* forked; bifid.
bī-fī′lăr, *a.* [*bi-*, and *filar*, from L. *filum*, thread.] having or requiring the use of two threads, as certain measuring instruments.
bī-fis′tū-lăr, *a.* having two ducts or channels.
bī-flā-bel′lāte, *a.* [*bi-*, and L. *flabellum*, a fan.] fan-shaped on both sides.
bī-flā-ģel′lāte, *a.* in biology, having two flagella.
bī-fleç′nōde, *n.* [*bi-*, and L. *flectere*, to bend, and *nodus*, node.] in geometry, the crossing point of a curve, simultaneously a point of inflection or change of direction.
bī′flex, *a.* [*bi-*, and L. *flexus*, pp. of *flectere*, to bend.] bending in two directions; having two bends or curves; as, a *biflex* tube.
bī-flō′rāte, bī-flō′rous, *a.* [*bi-*, and L. *flos*, *floris*, flower.] bearing two flowers.
bī-fō′çăl, *a.* adjusted or ground to two different focal lengths, as certain eyeglasses.
bī′fō-çăl, *n.* a lens with one part ground to adjust the eye for close focus, as for reading, and the other ground for distant focus.
bī-fō′çălṣ, *n.pl.* a pair of glasses with bifocal lenses.
bī′foil, *n.* [*bi-*, and ME. *foil*, from L. *folium*, a leaf.] the twayblade, *Listera ovata*.
bī′fōld, *a.* twofold; double.
bī-fō′li-āte, *a.* having two leaves.
bī-fō′li-ō-lāte, *a.* [*bi-*, and L. *foliatus*, from *folium*, leaf.] in botany, bearing two leaflets.
bif′ō-rāte, *a.* in botany, having two perforations, as the anthers of the rhododendron.
bif′ō-rine, *n.* [L. *biforis*, two-doored; *bis*, twice, and *foris*, a door.] a minute oval sac found in the interior of the green pulpy part of the leaves of some plants: it discharges its contents by an opening at each end.
bī′fọrked (-fọrkt), *a.* bifurcate.
bī′fọrm, *a.* [L. *biformis*; *bis*, twice, and *forma*, form.]
1. having two forms, bodies, or shapes.
2. incorporating the features of two forms.
bī′fọrmed, *a.* same as *biform*.
bī-fọrm′i-ty, *n.* a double form.
bī′fọrn, *prep.* and *adv.* before. [Obs.]
bī-frŏnt′ed, *a.* having two fronts.
Bif′rost, *n.* [ON. *bifröst*, lit., the tremulous way; *bif-*, from *bifask*, and *furca*, two-pronged fork.] in Norse mythology, the rainbow bridge from Midgard, the earth, to Asgard, home of the gods: only the gods could travel on it.
bī′fũr-çāte, bī′fũr-çā-ted, *a.* [L. *bifurcatus*, from *bifurcus*; *bis*, twice, and *furca*, a two-pronged fork.] forked; divided into two branches or parts.
bī′fũr-çāte, *v.i.* and *v.t.*; bifurcated, *pt.*, *pp.*; bifurcating, *ppr.* to separate into two branches.
bī-fũr-çā′tion, *n.* 1. a forking, or division into two branches.
2. the place where this occurs.
bī-fũr′çous, *a.* forked. [Rare.]
big, *a.*; *comp.* bigger; *superl.* biggest. [ME. *big*, *bigg*, *byg*, strong, powerful.]
1. of great size, extent, or capacity; large.
2. full-grown.
3. swollen, pregnant, or filled (*with*).
4. loud.
5. important; prominent; impressive; as, he does *big* things.
6. extravagant; pompous; as, *big* talk.
7. magnanimous; noble; as, he has a *big* heart.
Big is much used in combination to form adjectives (*big*-bodied, *big*-headed, *big*-souled, *big*-talking, etc.).
Syn.—large, great, wide, huge, bulky, arrogant, pompous, fat, massive, gross.
big, *adv.* 1. pompously; boastfully; extravagantly; as, he talks *big*. [Colloq.]
2. impressively. [Colloq.]
3. in a broad way; showing imagination; as, think *big!* [Colloq.]
big, bigg, *n.* [ME. *byge*; Ice. *bygg*; Dan. *byg*, barley.] a kind of barley.

big, bigg, *v.t.* [ME. *biggen, byggen*; Ice. *byggja*, to build, to dwell in.] to construct. [Prov. Scot. and Eng.]

bī′gȧ, *n.* [L.] in ancient Rome, a chariot drawn by two horses.

big′ăm, *n.* a bigamist. [Obs.]

big′a·mist, *n.* one who has committed bigamy.

big′ȧ·mous, *a.* 1. involving bigamy.
2. guilty of bigamy.

big′ȧ·my, *n.* [ME. *bigamie*; OFr. *bigamie*; LL. *bigamus*; *bis*, twice, and Gr. *gamos*, marriage.] the statutory crime of entering into a second marriage while a previous marriage is still legally in effect.

big′ȧ·rāde, *n.* [Fr.] the bitter orange.

big·ȧ·ro͞on′, *n.* same as *bigarreau*.

big·ăr·reau′ (-rō′), [Fr., from *bigarré*, flecked, from *bigarrer*, to fleck.] a variety of sweet cherry, heart-shaped and firm-fleshed.

big′-bel″lied, *a.* having a large belly.

Big Ben, 1. the large deep-toned bell of the famous Westminster clock in the tower of Parliament, in London.
2. the clock itself.

Big Bẽr′thȧ, [in allusion to Frau *Bertha* Krupp von Bohlen und Halbach: the Krupp steelworks made most of the German artillery.]
1. a very large cannon used by the Germans to bombard Paris in World War I. [Slang.]
2. any very large cannon. [Slang.]

Big Dip′pẽr, a dipper-shaped group of stars in the constellation Ursa Major (Great Bear).

bī·ġem′i·nāte, *a.* [*bi-*, and L. *geminatus*, pp. of *geminare*, to double; *geminus*, double.] in botany, designating or of a decompound leaf having a forked petiole with leaflets at the end of each division; biconjugate.

bī′ġē·nẽr, *n.* [L., a hybrid, from *bis*, twice, and *genus*, kind, family.] a cross from species of different genera; a mongrel; a hybrid.

bī·ġē·ner′iç, *a.* of a hybrid nature.

bī·ġen′tiăl (-shăl), *a.* [L. *bigens* (*-entis*); *bi-*, *bis*, two, and *gens*, a nation, race.] including two tribes or races of man.

big′eȳe, *n.* a fish of the genus *Priacanthus*, named from its prominent eyes.

Big Five, 1. after World War I, the United States, Great Britain, France, Italy, and Japan.
2. after World War II, the United States, the Soviet Union, Great Britain, China, and France.

big gāme, 1. large wild animals hunted for sport, as lions, tigers, moose, etc.
2. the object of any important or dangerous undertaking. [Colloq.]

big′gẽr, *a.*, comparative of *big*.

big′gest, *a.*, superlative of *big*.

big′gin, *n.* [Fr. *béguin*, a cap, from a cap worn by the nuns called *Beguines*.]
1. a child's bonnet; a head covering varied in form. [Brit.]
2. a white cap worn by a sergeant-at-law. [Brit.]

big′gin, *n.* a coffeepot containing a metal strainer to hold ground coffee: boiling water is poured through in making coffee. Named after the inventor.

big′gish, *a.* somewhat big.

big′gō·net, *n.* [Fr. *beguinet*, dim. of *beguin*, a cap.] a woman's cap or hood with ear flaps.

BIGGONET

bī′ghȧ, bē′gȧ, *n.* an East Indian measure of land, containing an acre or less.

big′head, *n.* conceit; egotism: also *big head*. [Colloq.]

big′-heärt·ed, *a.* quick to give or forgive; generous; magnanimous.

big′horn, *n.*; *pl.* **big′hornṣ** or **big′horn,** a wild sheep with long, curved horns, found in the Rocky Mountains.

big house, penitentiary. [Slang.]

bight (bīt), *n.* [ME. *bycht*; AS. *byht*, a bend, a corner, from *būgan*, to bend, to bow.]
1. a bend or small bay between two points of land.
2. a round bend or coil in a rope anywhere except at the ends; a loop in a rope.
3. a bending, corner, hollow, or fork, especially in the human or animal body.
4. a curve in a river, coast line, etc.

bī·glan′dū·lăr, *a.* having two glands.

big lēague (lēg), American League or National League of professional baseball clubs.

big′-lēague″ (lēg″), *a.* of the big leagues.

big′ly, *adv.* in a bragging, boasting style.

big′ness, *n.* bulk; size; largeness.

Big·nō′ni·ȧ, *n.* [named for the Abbe *Bignon*.]
1. a genus of tropical American climbing vines of the order *Bignoniaceæ*, the trumpet flowers.
2. [b–] any plant of this genus.

Big·nō·ni·ā′cē·ae, *n.pl.* a natural order of monopetalous, dicotyledonous plants with irregular flowers, a podlike fruit, and winged seeds. They are trees or twining or climbing shrubs, inhabiting the hotter parts of Asia, Africa, and America.

big·nō·ni·ā′ceous, *a.* of the *Bignoniaceæ*.

big′ŏt, *n.* [OFr.; prob. from Sp. *hombre de bigote*, lit., man with a mustache (*bigote*, mustache, ult. from L. *biga*, span of horses), hence man of spirit, firm character, obstinate person.]
1. a person who holds blindly and intolerantly to a particular creed, opinion, etc.
2. a narrow-minded, intolerant person.

big′ŏt·ed, *a.* having the characteristics of a bigot; narrow-minded; prejudiced.

big′ŏt·ed·ly, *adv.* in a bigoted manner.

big′ŏt·ry, *n.* [Fr. *bigoterie*, from *bigot*, a bigot, hypocrite.]
1. obstinate or blind attachment to a particular creed; unreasonable zeal in favor of a party, sect, or opinion; excessive prejudice; intolerance.
2. the beliefs or practices of a bigot.

big′ro͞ot, *n.* a plant of the gourd family, having a large root.

big shot, a person regarded as important or influential; a bigwig. [Slang.]

big tīme, 1. vaudeville performed only in the larger cities, paying the actors better and requiring fewer daily appearances. [Slang.]
2. the level regarded as highest or best in any given profession, occupation, etc. [Slang.]
3. a very enjoyable time. [Slang.]

big top, the canvas roof of a circus tent; hence, a circus. [Colloq.]

big tree, the giant sequoia or redwood tree.

bī·gut′tāte, *a.* [*bi-*, and L. *guttatus*, from *gutta*, a spot, drop.] in biology, marked with two spots of color resembling drops.

big′wig, *n.* an important or influential person; one high in authority or rank; as, the *bigwigs* of society. [Colloq.]

bī·hour′ly, *a.* and *adv.* once every two hours.

bī·il′i·aç, *a.* same as *bisiliac*.

bi′jöu (-zhö), *n.*; *pl.* **bi′jöux** (-zhöz), [Fr.] a jewel; something small and very pretty; a trinket.

bi·jöu′teriē (-trē), *n.* [Fr., from *bijou*, a jewel.] jewelry; trinkets.

bi·jöu′try, *n.* same as *bijouterie*.

bī′jū·gāte, *a.* [*bi-*, and L. *jugatus*, pp. of *jugare*, to join; *jugum*, a yoke.] having two pairs of leaflets, as some pinnate leaves.

bī′jū·gous, *a.* same as *bijugate*.

bīke, *n.*, *v.t.* and *v.i.* bicycle. [Colloq.]

bīke, *n.* 1. a wild bee's nest; a concealed store of anything. [Scot.]
2. a swarm of bees, ants, etc.; a crowd. [Scot.]

bikh (bik), *n.* [Hind.] any one of several plants of the aconite group, especially *Aconitum ferox*; also, a medicinal poison obtained from its roots.

Bi·kōl′, *n.* 1. a member of a Christianized Malayan people of southeastern Luzon and neighboring islands.
2. their language.

bī·lā′bi·ăl, *a.* 1. having two lips; bilabiate.
2. in phonetics, made by stopping or constricting the air stream between the lips, as the English consonants *p*, *b*, and *m*, Spanish intervocalic *b*, etc.

bī·lā′bi·ăl, *n.* a bilabial sound.

bī·lā′bi·āte, *a.* [*bi-*, and L. *labium*, a lip.] in botany, having two lips or lobes: applied to certain forms of calyx and corolla.

bī·lā·cin′i·āte, *a.* in botany, doubly laciniate or fringed.

bi·lä′lō, *n.* [native name.] a passenger boat about sixty-five feet long and ten feet broad, used in the Bay of Manila, combining local characteristics with European forms. Behind the mainmast is a large cabin. It carries an outrigger for use in fresh winds.

bī·lam′el·lāte, bī·lam′el·lā·ted, *a.* [*bi-*, and L. *lamella*, a thin plate.] doubly lamellate; having two lamellae; specifically, in botany, (a) composed of two plates, as many stigmas and placentas; (b) bearing two plates, as in the lip of the flowers of some orchids.

bī·lam′i·năr, bī·lam′i·nāte, *a.* [*bi-*, and L. *lamina*, a plate, scale.] having two laminae; consisting of two plates, scales, or layers.

bī′land, *n.* a peninsula; a byland. [Obs.]

bil′ăn·dẽr, *n.* [D. *bijlander*, from *bij*, by, and *land*, land.] a small vessel with two masts, distinguished by the form of the mainsail, the gaff or yard of which hangs fore and aft and is inclined at an angle of about forty-five degrees. The bilander is used chiefly in the canals of the Low Countries.

BILANDER

bī·lat′ẽr·ăl, *a.* [L. *bilateralis*; *bi-*, two, and *latus*, a side.]
1. of, having, or involving two sides, halves, factions, etc.
2. on two or both sides.
3. affecting both sides equally; reciprocal.
4. having bilateral symmetry.

Bī·lat·e·rā′li·ȧ, *n.pl.* animals that are bilaterally symmetrical.

bī·lat·ẽr·al′i·ty, *n.* the state or quality of being bilateral.

bī·lat′ẽr·ăl·ly, *adv.* in a bilateral manner; with reference to two sides.

bil′ber″ry, *n.*; *pl.* **bil′ber″rieṣ,** [probably from Dan. *böllebær*, bilberry.]
1. a shrub of the heath family, with small, egg-shaped leaves, rose-colored flowers, and dark-blue berries.
2. its fruit.
Also called *whortleberry*.

bil′bō, *n.*; *pl.* **bil′bōeṣ,** [after *Bilbao*, Spain, once famous for its ironworks.]
1. a rapier; a sword. [Archaic.]
2. a long bar or bolt of iron with shackles sliding on it and a lock at the end, formerly used to confine the feet of prisoners or offenders, especially on board ships.

BILBO

bil·bō·quet′ (-ket′), *n.* [Fr.] the toy called cup and ball.

bil′çock, *n.* in zoology, the common European water rail, *Rallus aquaticus*.

bild′stein, *n.* [G. *bild*, shape, image, and *stein*, stone.] agalmatolite, figure stone, or pagodite: often cut into grotesque ornaments by the Chinese.

bīle, *n.* [Fr. *bile*; L. *bilis*, bile, anger.]
1. a yellow or greenish fluid, slightly alkaline, separated from the blood in the liver, collected in the branches of the hepatic duct, and thence discharged by the common bile duct into the duodenum. It aids in the digestive process.
2. ill nature; bitterness of feeling; irritability: a meaning derived from the old idea that the bile was the humor that produced ill temper.
bile duct; a canal to convey bile: a term applied, in anatomy, to the duct through which the secretions of the gall bladder and the liver, after passing through the cystic and hepatic ducts respectively, flow into the duodenum.

bīle, *n.* an inflamed tumor; a boil. [Obs.]

bi·leç′tion, *n.* same as *bolection*.

bīle′stōne, *n.* a gallstone.

bilġe, *n.* [a variant of *bulge*, a protuberance.]
1. the protuberant part of a cask, which is usually in the middle.
2. the rounded, lower part of a ship's hull or hold.
3. bilge water.
4. something silly or distasteful; nonsense. [Slang.]

bilġe, *v.i* and *v.t.*; bilged, *pt.*, *pp.*; bilging, *ppr.*
1. to break open in the bilge; to spring a leak by a fracture in the bilge: said of a vessel.
2. to bulge out.

bilġe′-free, *a.* so stowed as to rest entirely on its beds, the bilge being free from pressure or contact: a nautical term applied to a barrel, cask, etc.

bilge keel (or **piece**), a beam fastened lengthwise on either side of a ship's bottom to prevent heavy rolling, damage to the bilges, etc.

bilge pump, a pump for drawing bilge water from a ship.

bilge wa'ter, water which has collected in the bilge of a ship and become foul.

bilge'ways, *n.pl.* planks of timber placed under a vessel's bilge on the building slip to support her while launching: also termed *launching ways*.

bil'gy, *a.* having the properties (as smell, etc.) of bilge water.

Bil·här'zi·à, *n.* [named after Theodor *Bilharz.*] a genus of parasitic worms found in the veins of the human body, and especially those of the bladder and mesentery.

bil'i·ăr·y, *a.* [L. *bilis*, bile.]
1. pertaining to the bile; conveying the bile; as, a *biliary* duct.
2. bilious.
biliary calculus; a gallstone, or concretion formed in the gall bladder or its ducts.

bil·i·ā'tion, *n.* the act or process of secreting and discharging bile.

bil'iç, *a.* pertaining to or obtained from the bile.
bilic acid; a compound obtained in the form of white crystals from the oxidation of cholic acid.

bī·lif'ẽr·ous, *a.* [L. *bilis*, bile, and *ferre*, to bear.] producing bile.

bil·i·fus'cin, *n.* [L. *bilis*, bile, and *fuscus*, dark.] a dark brown pigment present in gallstones and bile.

bi·lim'bi, bi·lim'bing, *n.* the fruit of the *Averrhoa Bilimbi*, which is very acid but edible after cooking, and the juice of which has some medicinal properties.

bil'i·ment, *n.* part of a woman's attire, particularly an ornament for the head or neck. [Obs.]

bī·lin'ē·ăr, *a.* of or bounded by two straight lines.

bī·lin'ē·āte, *a.* in zoology, marked with two parallel lines; striped.

bī·lin'guăl (-gwăl), **bī·lin'guăr** (-gwăr), *a.* [*bi-*, and L. *lingua*, tongue.]
1. of two languages.
2. using or capable of using two languages.

bī·lin'guăl·ism, *n.* the quality of being bilingual; the use of two languages.

bī·lin'guăl·ly, *adv.* in a bilingual manner; in two languages.

bī·lin'guăr, *a.* see *bilingual.*

bī·lin'guist, *n.* a person able to speak two languages.

bī·lin'guous (-gwus), *a.* using or capable of using two languages. [Obs.]

bil'ious (-yus), *a.* [L. *biliosus*, from *bilis*, bile.]
1. pertaining to bile; consisting of bile.
2. having or resulting from some ailment of the bile or the liver; affected with, or characterized by, headache, indigestion, nausea, and related disorders, supposed to be due to an abnormal condition of the liver.
3. ill-tempered; cross; out of humor.

bil'ious·ness, *n.* the state or quality of being bilious, in a physical or figurative sense.

bil·i·prā'sin, *n.* [L. *bilis*, bile, and *prasinus*, leek-green.] a pigment of a green color present in human gallstones, icteric urine, and bile.

bil·i·rū'bin, *n.* [from L. *bilis*, bile, and *ruber*, red.] the principal pigment of the bile, orange-red in color.

bī·lit'ẽr·ăl, *a.* [*bi-*, and L. *littera*, a letter.] consisting of two letters; as, a *biliteral* root in language.

bī·lit'ẽr·ăl, *n.* any two-letter linguistic element.

bī·lit'ẽr·ăl·ism, *n.* the state or quality of being biliteral.

-bil'i·ty, -ability: used to form nouns corresponding to adjectives ending in *-ble*, as responsibility.

bil·i·vẽr'din, *n.* [L. *bilis*, bile, and *viridis*, green.] a green pigment of the bile produced by oxidation of bilirubin.

bilk, *v.t.*; bilked, *pt.*, *pp.*; bilking, *ppr.* [origin doubtful; probably a form of *balk.*]
1. to frustrate or disappoint; to deceive or defraud, by nonfulfillment of engagement; as, to *bilk* a creditor.
2. to get away without paying (a debt, etc.).
3. in the game of cribbage, to balk an adversary's crib-score.
4. to steal away from; to elude.

bilk, *n.* 1. a tricky person; a cheat; a swindler.
2. a bilking or being bilked; a hoax; a deception; a trick.
3. meaningless words; nonsense. [Obs.]
4. in cribbage, the spoiling of an adversary's score.

bill, *n.* [ME. *bill*, *bil*; AS. *bil*; G. *bille*, an ax.]
1. a mattock, pickax, or other implement for digging. [Obs.]
2. a variously shaped tool used for pruning, etc.; a billhook. In general, the head consists of a blade, hook-shaped toward the point, and with a concave cutting edge.
3. an ancient military weapon consisting of a broad hook-shaped blade with a pike at the end and the back, and fitted to a long handle or staff; a halberd: used especially by the English infantry of the fourteenth and fifteenth centuries.
4. a person armed with such a weapon.
5. formerly, a broadsword.

BILL (sense 3)

bill, *n.* [ME. *bille*, a letter, writing; ML. *billa*, *bulla*, a writing, edict; L. *bulla*, knob, bubble.]
1. in law, a declaration in writing, expressing some wrong the complainant has suffered from the defendant, or a fault committed by some person against a law. It contains the fact complained of, the damage sustained, and a petition or process against the defendant for redress. It is used both in civil and criminal cases. In Scots law, every summary application in writing, by way of petition to the court of session, is called a *bill.*
2. an acknowledgment of debt given in writing by one person to another, the sum due and the time of payment, as well as the place and date of signing, being set down; in the United States, more usually known as a note, note of hand, or promissory note.
3. a form or draft of a law, presented to a legislature, but not yet enacted; also, rarely, an enacted law or statute.
4. a paper written or printed, and intended to give public notice of something, especially by being exhibited in some public place; a poster; a placard; as, the *bill* of an auction or of a show.
5. the entertainment offered in a theater.
6. an account of goods sold or delivered, services rendered, or work done, with the price or value noted for each article; a statement of money due; as, a butcher's *bill.*
7. any written statement of particulars; as, a *bill* of fare; a *bill* of the play.
8. a bank note or piece of paper money; as, a five-dollar *bill.*
9. a bill of exchange.
10. a written document, especially one with a seal. [Obs.]
bill of attainder; a legislative bill making certain crimes, especially treason and outlawry, punishable by forfeiture of property and loss of all civil rights: prohibited in the United States by the Constitution.
bill of costs; an itemized statement of the costs of a legal action as charged against the parties to the suit.
bill of credit; (a) a bill or note for raising money on the mere credit of a State (prohibited by the Constitution of the United States); (b) a written request that the receiver thereof shall credit the bearer as specified, on the security of the writer.
bill of divorce; in old Jewish law, a writing given by the husband to the wife, by which the marriage relation was dissolved.
bill of entry; a written account of goods entered at the customhouse, whether imported or intended for exportation.
bill of exchange; an order drawn by one person on another, directing him to pay money to some third specified person or to his account, and charge the amount to the drawer; a draft. The drawer makes the order; the drawee is directed to make payment; and the payee receives the money.
bill of fare; a menu; a printed or written list of the articles of food to be served at a meal, or to be obtained at a public eating house, hotel, or restaurant.
bill of health; a certificate stating whether there is infectious disease aboard a ship or in the port which the ship is leaving: it is given to the captain for him to show at the next port: a *clean bill of health* certifies the absence of infectious disease.
bill of indictment; a formal statement of an accusation of criminal offense presented by a public prosecutor to a grand jury. If the jury sanctions the bill by reason of evidence submitted, it is marked *a true bill.*
bill of lading; (a) originally, a cargo list; (b) a contract issued to a shipper by a transportation agency, listing the goods shipped, acknowledging their receipt, and promising delivery to the person named.
bill of mortality; formerly, in London, an official register of the number and causes of deaths in a district, in a given time.
bill of parcels; an invoice; a statement giving the different items of purchase, with the value of each.
bill of particulars; in a law, a written statement detailing the various points of a pleading.
bill of rights; (a) a list of the rights and freedoms assumed to be essential to a group of people; (b) [B– R–] an act of the British Parliament passed in 1689 to prevent a restoration of royal absolutism; (c) [B– R–] the first ten amendments to the Constitution of the United States, which guarantee certain rights to the people, as freedom of speech, assembly, and worship.
bill of sale; a written statement certifying that the ownership of something has been transferred by sale.
bill of sight; in England, a form of entry at the customhouse by which goods, respecting which the importer is not possessed of full information, may be provisionally landed for examination.
bill of store; a license from the customhouse to permit stores required for a voyage to be carried on a merchant vessel without duty.
bill payable; a promissory note, bill of exchange, or other commercial paper, by which money is to be paid to another.
bill receivable; a promissory note, bill of exchange, or other commercial paper, by which money is to be received from another.

bill, *v.t.* 1. to make out a bill of (items); to list.
2. to present a statement of charges to.
3. to advertise or announce by bills or posters.
4. to post bills or placards throughout (a town, etc.).
5. to ship (goods).

bill, *n.* [ME. *bill*, *bile*; AS. *bile*, a beak.]
1. a bird's beak.
2. a beaklike mouth part, as of a turtle.
3. the point of an anchor fluke.

bill, *v.i.*; billed, *pt.*, *pp.*; billing, *ppr.* to join bills, as doves; to indulge, like doves, in demonstrative caresses.
to bill and coo; to kiss, talk softly, etc., as in love-making.

bill, *n.* the cry, or boom, of the bittern.

bill'à·ble, *a.* that can be billed; subject to billing.

bil'là·bong, *n.* in Australia, a lagoon; a backwater.

bil'lāge, *n.*, *v.t.*, and *v.i.* bilge. [Obs.]

bil'lărd, *n.* the coal-fish. [Brit. Dial.]

bill'bee"tle (-tl), *n.* one of a large group of beetles; a weevil; a curculio: also called *billbug.*

Bill·bẽr'gi·à, *n.* [named after J. G. *Billberg*, a Swedish botanist.] a tropical American genus of air plants belonging to the *Bromeliaceæ.* The species are cultivated in greenhouses and are crossed into many varieties.

bill'bōard, *n.* 1. a plank or other projection at the bow of a vessel, on which the bill of the anchor rests.
2. a signboard, usually outdoors, for announcements and advertising posters.

bill book, a book in which is kept an account of notes, bills, bills of exchange, etc., issued and received.

bill brō'kẽr, one who negotiates bills, promissory notes, etc. at a discount.

bill'bug, *n.* see *billbeetle.*

billed, *a.* having a bill.

bil'let, *n.* [Fr. *billet*, dim. of *bille*, a bill.]
1. a small paper or note in writing; a short letter; a note. [Archaic.]
2. a written order to provide quarters or lodging for military personnel.
3. lodging; quarters.
4. a position, job, or situation.

bil'let, *v.t.*; billeted, *pt.*, *pp.*; billeting, *ppr.*
1. to assign (soldiers, etc.) to lodging by billet.
2. to assign (a person) to a post.
3. to serve a billet on.

bil'let, *v.i.* to lodge; as, I *billeted* across the street from my comrade.

bil'let, *n.* [ME. *billette*; OFr. *billette*, dim. of *bille*; L. *billus*, a log.]

1. a small log; a stick of firewood.
2. a wooden club.
3. in architecture, an ornament in a Norman molding, resembling a billet of wood.
4. a short bar of iron or steel.
5. in harness, etc., (a) a loop receiving the end of a buckled strap; (b) that part of a belt or strap which fits into a buckle.
6. in heraldry, a charge in the form of an oblong figure.

BILLETS

bil'let-doux' (bil'ā-dö'), *n.*; *pl.* **bil'lets-doux'** (bil'ā-döz'), [Fr. *billet*, a note, and *doux*, L. *dulcis*, sweet.] a love note or love letter.

bil'let·head (-hed), *n.* 1. a post at the bow of a whaleboat, around which the harpoon line is paid out.
2. a scroll or ornamental carving taking the place of a figurehead on a ship.

bil'let mōld'ing, a molding ornamented with a design of spaced billets, either end to end or upright.

BILLET MOLDING

bill'fish, *n.*; *pl.* **bill'fish** or **bill'fish·es**, 1. any of various fishes with long, narrow jaws that resemble a beak, as many gars, the needlefish, the skipper, etc.
2. a sailfish; spearfish.

bill'fōld, *n.* a folding, pocket-size case, usually of leather, for carrying bank notes and papers; a wallet.

bill'head (-hed), *n.* 1. a sheet of paper at the top of which a name and business address are printed, used for statements of charges.
2. a name and business address printed on such a sheet; a letterhead.

bill'hōld''ēr, *n.* 1. the holder of a bill of acceptance or note.
2. a device for holding bills.

bill'hook, *n.* a thick knife having a hooked point, used to prune shrubs, etc.

bil'liărd (bil'yărd), *a.* of or for the game of billiards.

bil'liărd (bil'yărd), *n.* a point scored in billiards by causing the cue ball to touch the other two balls; a carom.

BILLHOOK

bil'liărds (-yărdz), *n.* [Fr. *billard*, billiards, a billiard cue, or stick with a curved end, from *bille*, a log, stock of a tree; L. *billus*, a log.] a game played on a table with balls and a cue. The standard size of table used in the United States has a level surface 5x10 feet, composed of solid slate, covered with green cloth. This surface is bounded by rubber cushions set in a solid hardwood frame. The balls are ivory, standard size 2³/₈ inches in diameter. The cue is heavy at the butt, and diminishes gradually in size to the slender end. The point is furnished with a leather tip. The French or American game is played with three balls on a pocketless table. The English game is played upon a larger table, 6x12 feet, furnished with six pockets.

bill'ing, *n.* 1. the listing of the actors' names on a playbill or theater marquee.
2. the order in which the names are listed.

bil'lings·gāte, *n.* [from a fish market of this name in London, celebrated for the foul language of its dealers.] foul, vulgar, abusive talk; ribaldry.

bil'liŏn, *n.* [Fr. contr. of L. *bis*, twice, and *million*, a million.]
1. in the United States and France, a thousand millions (1,000,000,000).
2. in Great Britain and Germany, a million millions (1,000,000,000,000).
3. a billion (unspecified but understood) monetary units, as dollars, pounds, francs, etc.; as, he has made a *billion*.

bil'liŏn, *a.* amounting to one billion in number.

bil'liŏn·āire, *n.* a person whose wealth comes to at least a billion dollars, pounds, francs, etc.; a multimillionaire.

bil'liŏnth, *a.* 1. coming last in a series of a billion.
2. designating any of the billion equal parts of something.

bil'liŏnth, *n.* 1. the last in a series of a billion.
2. any of the billion equal parts of something.

bill'măn, *n.* one who uses a bill or hooked ax; formerly, a soldier armed with a bill.

bil'lon, *n.* [Fr.] an alloy of gold or silver with a greater proportion of a baser metal, as copper: used in metals, tokens, etc.

bil'lot, *n.* [Fr., dim. of *bille*, a stick.] bullion previous to being coined.

bil'lōw, *n.* [ON. *bylgja*.] a great wave or surge of the sea or other large body of water, occasioned usually by violent wind; figuratively, a wave of anything; as, a *billow* of laughter.

bil'lōw, *v.i.*; billowed, *pt.*, *pp.*; billowing, *ppr.* to swell; to rise and roll in large waves or surges.

bil'lōw·y, *a.*; *comp.* billowier; *superl.* billowiest, swelling in or as in a billow or billows.

bill'pōst''ēr, *n.* one who is hired to put up advertisements or posters in public places.

bill'stick''ēr, *n.* a billposter.

bil'ly, *n.*; *pl.* **bil'lies**, 1. a short club; a truncheon, especially one carried by a policeman.
2. a slubbing machine formerly used in wool manufacture.

bil'ly, *n.*; *pl.* **bil'lies**, [from dial. *billycan*.] a can or kettle used in outdoor cooking.

bil'ly-, [from the nickname *Billy*, from *Willie*, from *William*.] a formative element denoting: (a) *masculinity*, as in *billy goat*; (b) [British Dial.] *intimacy* or *intimate use*, as in *billycan* (Dial.), a billy.

bil'ly·boy, *n.* a river barge or coasting vessel with a flat bottom. [Brit.]

BILLYBOY

bil'ly·çock, *n.* a stiff, low-crowned felt hat, like a derby. [Brit. Colloq.]

bil'ly gōat, a male goat. [Colloq.]

bī·lō'bāte, bī·lō'bāt·ed, *a.* [*bi-*, and Gr. *lobos*, a lobe.] separated into two lobes; as, a *bilobate* leaf.

bī'lōbed, *a.* bilobate.

bī·lō·çā'tion, *n.* the ability to be in two places at once.

bī·lō·cel'lāte, *a.* [*bi-*, and L. *locellus*, dim. of *locus*, a place.] having two locelli, or secondary cells, as an ovary or an anther.

bī·loç'ū·lăr, bī·loç'ū·lāte, *a.* [*bi-*, and L. *locularis*, from *locus*, a place.] in biology, divided into two cells or containing two cells; as, a *bilocular* pericarp.

bī·loph'ō·dont, *a.* [*bi-*, and Gr. *lophos*, a hill, and *odous*, *odontos*, tooth.] having two transverse ridges or crests, as the molar teeth of tapirs.

bil'säh, *n.* a fine quality of tobacco grown in central India.

bil'sted, *n.* [18th c.; early sp. *boilsted* suggests orig. *bilested*; perhaps from *bile*, and dial. *stead*, aid, remedy (with reference to medicinal use of the balsam).] a tree with maplelike leaves and spiny fruit: also called *sweet gum*.

bil'tong, *n.* [S.Afr. D.; *bil*, rump (from which it is cut), and *tong*, tongue (from the shape).] lean meat, as of deer or buffalo, cut into strips and dried in the sun.

bī·maç'ū·lāte, *a.* [*bi-*, and L. *maculatus*, from *macula*, a spot.] having two spots.

Bim'ȧ·nȧ (*or* bī-mā'nȧ), *n.pl.* [L., neut. pl. of *bimanus*, two-handed.] two-handed animals: a term applied to the highest order of *Mammalia*, of which man is the type and sole genus.

bī'māne, *n.* [Fr., from Mod. L. *bimanus*.] a bimanous animal.

bī·mā'nous, *a.* [Mod. L. *bimanus*; L. *bi-*, bi-, and *manus*, hand.] having two hands.

bī·măn'ū·ăl, *a.* done with two hands; requiring the use of both hands; as, *bimanual* turning.

bī·mär'ġin·āte, *a.* in conchology, having a double margin: said of shells.

bī·mas'tiç, *a.* [*bi-*, and Gr. *mastos*, a breast.] in anatomy, having two mammae or teats.

bī·mas'tişm, *n.* the state of having two mammae.

bī·mas'toid, *a.* in anatomy, relating to the two mastoid formations.

bī'mas·ty, *n.* same as *bimastism*.

bim·bash'i, *n.* same as *binbashi*.

bī·mē'di·ăl, *a.* [*bi-*, and L. *medialis*, from *medius*, middle.] in geometry, designating a line composed of two mean proportional lines or medials.

bī·mem'brăl, *a.* [L. *bimembris*, from *bi-*, two, and *membrum*, a member.] having two members.

bī·mes'tri·ăl, *a.* [L. *bimestris*, from *bi-*, two, and *mensis*, a month.]
1. lasting two months.
2. bimonthly.

bī·mē·tal'liç, *a.* [*bi-*, and L. *metallum*, metal.]
1. pertaining to or using bimetallism.
2. of, using, or formed of two metals; as, a *bimetallic* chain.

bī·met'ăl·lişm, *n.* the legalized concurrent use of a double metallic standard (as gold and silver) in the coinage or currency of a country, at a fixed ratio of value; also, the doctrine, actions, or policies supporting such use, as opposed to monometalism.

bī·met'ăl·list, *n.* a believer in or advocate of bimetallism.

bī·mŏnth'ly, *a.* and *adv.* 1. once every two months; as, *bimonthly* visits.
2. twice a month: loosely, so used.

bī·mŏnth'ly, *n.*; *pl.* **bī·mŏnth'lies**, a publication issued once every two months.

bī·mō'tōred, *a.* having two motors, as some airplanes.

bī·mus'çū·lăr, *a.* having two adductor muscles which close the shell, as a bivalve mollusk.

bin, *n.* [AS. *binn* or *binne*, a manger or crib.]
1. a wooden compartment, box, chest, frame, or enclosed place, used as a repository for wheat, corn, coal, and other commodities; as, the *bins* of a grain elevator or a coalyard; the *bins* of a wine cellar; a corn *bin*.
2. a receptacle, especially for ashes or trash.

bin, *v.t.*; binned, *pt.*, *pp.*; binning, *ppr.* to place or store in a bin; as, to *bin* corn.

bin, dialectal form of *been*.

bin-, bi-: used before a vowel, as in *binary*.

bī'năl, *a.* twofold.

bī'nȧ·ry, *a.* [L. *binarius*, from *bini*, two by two, from *bis*, double.]
1. compounded or consisting of two things or parts; double; twofold.
2. in chemistry, composed of two elements, as *binary* compounds.

binary arithmetic; a system of arithmetic in which two figures only, 0 and 1, are used, in place of ten, the cipher multiplying everything by 2, as in common arithmetic by 10. Thus, 1 is one; 10 is two; 11 is three; 100 is four; 101 is five; 110 is six; 111 is seven; 1000 is eight; 1001 is nine; 1010 is ten. It is said this species of arithmetic has been used by the Chinese for 4000 years.

binary logarithms; an arrangement of logarithms having 2 for its base.

binary measure; in music, a measure having two beats to a bar.

binary scale; in arithmetic, a consistent scale of notation with 2 as the ratio.

binary star; a double star, whose members have a revolution round their common center of gravity.

binary theory; in chemistry, the theory that all chemical compounds are formed of two constituents of contrary and different qualities.

bī'nȧ·ry, *n.*; *pl.* **bī'nȧ·ries**, 1. that which is made up of two figures or parts; a couple; a pair.
2. a binary star.

bī'nāte, *a.* [L. *binatus*, from *bini*, two by two; *bis*, double.] in botany, composed of or almost divided into two parts: said of a leaf.

bī·na'tion·ăl, *a.* composed of or involving two nations or two nationalities.

BINATE LEAVES

bin·au'răl, *a.* [*bin-*, and L. *auris*, ear.]
1. having two ears.
2. of or involving the use of both ears.

bin·bash'i, *n.* [Turk. chief of a thousand; *bin*, a thousand, and *bash*, a head.] an officer in the Turkish army having the rank of major.

bīnd, *v.t.*; bound, *pt.*, *pp.*; binding, *ppr.* [ME. *binden*; AS. *bindan*; akin to ON. *binda*.]
1. to tie; to secure; to fasten, as with a band or rope.
2. to hold; to make prisoner; to restrain.
3. to gird or encircle with (a belt, girdle, etc.); to wrap around.
4. to wrap; to cover, as with a bandage: frequently followed by *up*; as, to *bind up* a wound.
5. to make stick together; to make coalesce into a mass.

6. to make costive or constipated; as, certain kinds of food *bind* the bowels.
7. to strengthen, secure, or ornament along the edges with stitching; to protect with a band on the edges; as, to *bind* a skirt.
8. to sew together and cover; to cover with anything firm; as, to *bind* the pages of a book.
9. to secure by moral force, as a promise, duty, or authority.
10. to hold or attract, as by affection or personal qualities.
11. to put under oath, legal restraint, or contract.
bound up in; engrossed in; absorbed in.
to bind over; to oblige by bond to appear at a court.
to bind to; to contract; as, *to bind* oneself *to* a wife.
Syn.—tie, fasten, secure, fetter, oblige, restrain, restrict.

bind, *v.i.* 1. to contract; to grow hard or stiff; as, clay *binds* by heat.
2. to stick, owing to friction or pressure; as, the wheel *binds*.
3. to be obligatory.
4. to do the act of binding.

bind, *n.* 1. a twining stem.
2. any quantity forming a specific count; as, a *bind* of eels. [Eng.]
3. anything that binds.
4. in music, a line to indicate that the sound of certain notes is to be sustained; a slur.

bind'ĕr, *n.* [ME. *byndere*, from AS. *bindere*, binder, from *bindan*, to bind.]
1. a person who binds.
2. one whose occupation is to bind books.
3. anything that binds.
4. a fillet, cord, rope, or band.
5. a binding substance, as tar.
6. a detachable cover, used for magazines, etc.
7. in agriculture, (a) a device attached to a reaper, for tying grain in bundles; (b) a machine that both reaps and binds grain.
8. in law, a temporary contract, in effect pending execution of the final contract.

bind'ĕr·y, *n.*; *pl.* **bind'ĕr·ies,** a place where books are bound.

bind'ing, *a.* causing to be bound; obligatory, from a legal or moral standpoint; as, the *binding* force of a moral duty or of a command.

bind'ing, *n.* 1. the action of a person or thing that binds.
2. the state of being bound.
3. anything that binds; a bandage.
4. the covers and backing of a book.
5. a band of masonry, brick, etc.
6. a braid or strip of cloth sewed over an edge, seam, etc. for strengthening or protecting it; as, the *binding* of a dress skirt.
7. a cohesive substance for holding a mixture together.
8. [*pl.*] the principal timbers used in building and giving stability to a ship.

bind'ing joists, in architecture, the joists of a floor into which the trimmers of staircases and chimney ways are framed.

bind'ing·ly, *adv.* so as to bind.

bind'ing·ness, *n.* the state of having force to bind.

bind'ing pōst, a metallic post connected with electrical apparatus to serve as a convenience in making connections with wires, etc.

bin'dle, *n.* [prob. from *bundle*.] a bundle of bedding carried by a hobo. [Slang.]

bind'weed, any of a number of related plants belonging to the genus *Convolvulus*, usually twining, with funnel-shaped flowers.

bine, *n.* [a dialectic form of *bind*.] the winding stem of a climbing plant, as of the hop, woodbine, etc.

bi·nĕrv'āte, *a.* [*bi-*, and L. *nerva*, nerve.] having two nerves: said of some leaves or the wings of some insects.

Bi·net'-Si'mŏn test (bi·nā' sī'mŏn; Fr. bē″ne'sē″mōṅ'), [after the French psychologists who devised it, Alfred *Binet* (1857–1911) and Theodore *Simon* (1873–1961).] a Binet test.

Bi·net' (-nā') test, an intelligence test consisting of questions, problems, and things to do, graded in terms of mental age (*Binet age*).

bing, *n.* [ME. *bing*, *binge*, from Ice. *bingr*, a heap.] a heap; specifically, a heap of grain.

binge, *n.* [perhaps from dial. *binge*, to soak.] a drunken celebration or spree. [Slang.]

biñ'gle (-gl), *n.* in baseball, a base hit.

biñ'gō, *n.* [origin uncertain.] a gambling game, resembling lotto, usually with many players.

bin·i'ō·dide, *n.* a salt with two iodine atoms.

bin'nȧ·cle, *n.* [formerly *bittacle*, from Port. *bitacola*; L. *habitaculum*, a dwelling place; *habitare*, to inhabit.] the case in which the compass and a light are kept on board ship for use by the steersman.

BINNACLE

bin'ny, *n.*; *pl.* **bin'nies,** [native name.] a species of edible barbel (*Barbus bynni*), found in the Nile.

bin'ō·cle, *n.* [L. *bini*, double, and *oculus*, an eye.] a binocular telescope, opera glass, or field glass.

bin·oc'ū·lăr, *a.* 1. of or pertaining to both eyes at once.
2. having two apertures or tubes so joined that one may use both eyes at once in viewing a distant object; as, a *binocular* telescope.

bin·oc'ū·lăr, *n.* [L. *bini*, double, and *oculus*, eye.] a binocular instrument.

bin·oc'ū·lăr·ly, *adv.* in a binocular manner.

bin·oc'ū·lărs, *n.pl.* 1. field glasses.
2. opera glasses.

bi·nōd'ăl, *a.* having two joints or nodes.

bi·nō'mi·ăl, *n.* [*bi-*, and L. *nomen*, name.]
1. a mathematical equation or expression consisting of two terms connected by a plus or minus sign.
2. the scientific name of a plant or animal, consisting of the genus name followed by that of the species.

bi·nō'mi·ăl, *a.* 1. pertaining to binomials.
2. composed of two terms.
binomial nomenclature (or *system*); the scientific system of giving a double name to each plant and animal, consisting of the name of the genus followed by that of the species: e.g., *Ananas comosus* (pineapple).
binomial theorem; in algebra, the theorem, first demonstrated by Sir Isaac Newton, for raising a binomial to any power. Example: $(a+b)^2=a^2+2ab+b^2$.

bi·nor'măl, *n.* [*bi-*, and L. *norma*, a square.] in geometry, a normal perpendicular to the osculating plane.

bin·ox'ide, *n.* same as *dioxide*.

bin'tū·rong, *n.* [native name.] a small carnivorous animal of southern Asia and the East Indies, *Arctictis binturong*.

bi·nū'clē·āte, bi·nū'clē·ăr, *a.* of or having two nuclei or centers.

bi·nū'clē·ō·lāte, *a.* [*bi-*, and L. *nucleus*, a nut.] having two nucleoli: applied to cells.

bi'ō, *n.*; *pl.* **bi'ōs,** a biography, often a very brief one. [Colloq.]

bi'ō-, [Gr. *bios*, life.] a combining form meaning *life, of living things, biological*, as in *bio*graphy, *bio*chemistry: also *bi-*.

bi″ō·as″trō·nau'tics, *n.pl.* [*construed as sing.*], the science that deals with the physical responses of living things to the environment of space and space travel.

bi'ō·cat'ȧ·lyst, *n.* [*bio-*, and *catalyst*.] a substance, as an enzyme or hormone, that activates or speeds up a biochemical reaction.

bi·oc'el·lāte, *a.* [*bi-*, and L. *ocellus*, dim. of *oculus*, eye.] in zoology, having two simple eyes or eyelike markings.

bi·ō·chem'i·căl, bi·ō·chem'ic, *a.* pertaining to biochemistry.

bi·ō·chem'ist, *n.* a student of or specialist in biochemistry.

bi·ō·chem'is·try, *n.* [*bio-*, and Fr. *chemique*, chemistry.] the branch of chemistry that deals with plants and animals and their life processes; biological chemistry.

bi'ō·cide″, *n.* [*bio-*, and *-cide*.] a poisonous chemical substance that can kill living organisms.

bi″ō·dē·grād'a·ble, *a.* [*bio-*, and *degrade*, and *-able*.] capable of being readily decomposed by biological means, especially by bacterial action: said of some detergents with reference to disposal in sewage.

bi″ō·dy·nam'ic, bi″ō·dy·nam'i·căl, *a.* relating to biodynamics.

bi″ō·dy·nam'ics, *n.pl.* [*construed as sing.*], [*bio-*, and *dynamics*.] the branch of physiology that deals with the life processes of plants and animals: opposed to *biostatics*.

bi″ō·eth'ics, *n.pl.* [*construed as sing.*], the study of the ethical problems arising from scientific advances, especially in biology and medicine.

bi″ō·feed'back, *n.* a technique of seeking to control certain emotional states, such as anxiety or depression, by training oneself, with the aid of electronic devices, to modify involuntary body functions, such as blood pressure or heartbeat.

bi″ō·flā'vō·noid *n.* [*bio-*, and *flavone*, and *-oid*.] a derivative of a flavone compound, as vitamin P.

bi'ō·gen, *n.* [*bio-*, and *gen*.] the hypothetical smallest unit of protoplasm.

bi·ō·gen'e·sis, bi·og'e·ny, *n.* [*bio-*, and Gr. *genesis*, origin, from *gignesthai*, to become.]
1. the development of living organisms from other living organisms.
2. the principle that living organisms come only from other living organisms.

bi″ō·gē·net'ic, bi″ō·gē·net'i·căl, *a.* pertaining to or connected with biogenesis.

bi·ō·gē·og'rȧ·phy, *n.* the branch of biology that deals with the geographical distribution of plants and animals.

bi·og·nō'sis, *n.* [*bio-*, and Gr. *gnōsis*, inquiry, from *gnōnai*, to know.] the inquiry into or study of life; that branch of science which treats of living organisms.

bi·og'rȧ·phĕr, *n.* one who writes a biography or biographies.

bi·ō·graph'ic·ăl, bi·ō·graph'ic, *a.* 1. connected with or pertaining to biography.
2. about a person's life.

bi·ō·graph'ic·ăl·ly, *adv.* in the manner of a biography.

bi·og'rȧ·phy, *n.*; *pl.* **bi·og'rȧ·phies,** [Fr. *biographie*, biography, from Gr. *bios*, life, and *graphein*, to write.]
1. the histories of individual lives, considered as a branch of literature.
2. an account of a person's life, written or told by another; life story.

bi'ō·haz″ărd, *n.* [*bio-* and *hazard*.] a risk or danger to life or health, especially that resulting from biological experimentation.

bi'ō·haz″ărd, *a.* having to do with biohazards, especially their prevention or control.

bi″ō·in·stru·men·tā'tion, *n.* the use of instruments, as sensors, to detect and measure certain body functions, as of persons in spaceflight, and transmit the data to a point where it is evaluated.

bi·ō·log'ic·ăl, bi·ō·log'ic, *a.* 1. of or connected with biology; of plants and animals.
2. of the nature of living matter.
3. used in or produced by practical biology.

bi·ō·log'ic·ăl, *n.* a biological product.

bi·ō·log'ic·ăl clock, any of various rhythm patterns in organisms, associated with recurrent natural cycles, as of tides, days and nights, seasons, etc.

bi·ō·log'ic·ăl·ly, *adv.* 1. in a biological way.
2. by means of biology.

bi·ō·log'ic·ăl wạr'fāre, the use of disease-spreading microorganisms, toxins, etc. against enemy armed forces or civilians.

bi·ol'ō·gist, *n.* one having a thorough knowledge of biology; also, a student of biology.

bi·ol'ō·gy, *n.* [Fr. *biologie*, biology, from Gr. *bios*, life, and *logos*, description.]
1. the science of life; the branch of science which treats of the phenomena of animals and plants with regard to their morphology, physiology, origin, development, distribution, habits, etc.: it includes botany, zoology, and their subdivisions.
2. animal and plant life, as of a given area.
3. biological history, principles, etc.

bi″ō·lu·mi·nes'cence, *n.* [*bio-*, and *luminescence*.] a giving off of light from living matter, caused by internal oxidation.

bi·ol'y·sis, *n.* [*bio-*, and Gr. *ollynai*, to destroy.] the destruction of life, as by bacteria or other microorganisms.

bi·ō·lyt'ic, *a.* of or produced by biolysis.

bi'ō·mass, *n.* the total mass or amount of living organisms in a particular area or volume.

bi″ō·math·ē·mat'ics, *n.pl.* [*construed as sing.*], the science that deals with the application of mathematical methods to the structure and functions of living organisms.

bi″ō·med'i·cine, *n.* a branch of medicine that is combined with research in biology.

bi·ō·met'rics, *n.pl.* [*construed as sing.*], [from *bio-*, and *metric*.] that branch of biology which deals with its data statistically and by quantitative analysis.

bi·om'e·try, *n.* [*bio-*, and Gr. *metron*, a measure.]
1. measurement of the probable duration of the life of human beings.
2. biometrics.

bi'on, *n.* [Gr. *biōn*, living, ppr. of *bioun*, to live.] in biology, the physiological person, characterized by self-reliant function and definiteness: opposed to *morphon*.

bī·on′iç, *a.* 1. of, like, or having to do with bionics.

2. designating an artificial replacement for a bodily part.

3. furnished with such a replacement part or parts, specifically in science fiction, so that strength, abilities, etc. are greatly enhanced.

4. exceptionally strong, skillful, etc.

bī·on′içs, *n.pl.* [*construed as sing.*], [Gr. *bion*, living, and *-ics.*] the science of designing instruments or systems modeled after living organisms.

bī·ō·nom′içs, *n.pl.* [*construed as sing.*], [from *bionomy*, and *-ics.*] the branch of biology that deals with the adaptation of living things to their environment; ecology.

bī·on′ō·my, *n.* [*bio-*, and Gr. *nomos*, law.]

1. the science that deals with the natural laws controlling life processes.

2. bionomics.

bī·oph′ȧ·gous, *a.* [*bio-*, and Gr. *phagein*, to eat.] subsisting upon living organisms, as insectivorous plants such as Venus's flytrap.

bī′ō·phōr, bī′ō·phōre, *n.* [*bio-*, and Gr. *phoros*, something brought, from *pherein*, to bear.] in biology, one of the hypothetical fundamental units of germ plasm.

bī·ō·phyș′i·çal, *a.* of biophysics.

bī·ō·phyș′içs, *n.pl.* [*construed as sing.*] the branch of physics that deals with living matter.

bī′ō·plașm, *n.* [*bio-*, and Gr. *plasma*, something molded, as an image, from *plassein*, to mold.] living matter; protoplasm.

bī·ō·plaș′miç, *a.* of or composed of bioplasm.

bī·ō·plas′tiç, *a.* bioplasmic.

bī·op′siç, *a.* pertaining to biopsy.

bī′op·sy, *n.* in medicine, the microscopic examination of a piece of excised tissue from a live body for purposes of diagnosis.

bī″ō·psȳ′çhiç, *a.* pertaining to biopsychology.

bī″ō·psȳ·çhol′ō·ġy, *n.* psychology in its relation to biology.

bī·ọr′găn, *n.* [*bi-*, and L. *organum*, an organ or instrument.] a physiological organ possessing a function: opposed to *idorgan.*

bī′ō·rhythm, *n.* [*bio-*, and *rhythm.*] any of three separate biological cycles in terms of which, according to a theory, a person's physical, emotional, and intellectual energy levels regularly and predictably rise and fall.

bī′ō·sçōpe, *n.* [*bio-*, and Gr. *skopein*, to view.] a motion-picture projector.

bī·os′çō·py, *n.* [*bio-*, and *-scopy.*] in medicine, examination to find out whether life is present.

-bī·ō′sis [from Gr. *biōsis*, way of life, from *bios*, life.] a combining form meaning *a* (specified) *way of living*, as in *symbiosis.*

bī·ō·sō′cial (-shul), *a.* of the communal or family relationships of animals, as bees, apes, etc.

bī·ō·stat′i·çal, *a.* of biostatics.

bī·ō·stat′içs, *n.pl.* [*construed as sing.*], [*bio-*, and Gr. *statikē* (supply *technē*) statics, the science that treats of bodies at rest.] the branch of physiology that deals with the relation of structure to function in plants and animals: opposed to *biodynamics.*

bī·ō′tȧ, *n.* [from Gr. *bios*, life.] the plant and animal life of a region.

bī·ō·ther′ȧ·py, *n.* [*bio-*, and *therapy.*] the treatment of disease by means of substances secreted by or derived from living organisms, as serums, vaccines, bile, penicillin, etc.

bī·ot′iç, bī·ot′iç·ăl, *a.* of life; of living things.

bī·ot′içs, *n.* [Gr. *biōtikos*, pertaining to life.] that branch of science treating of the functions and phenomena of living organisms.

bī′ō·tin, *n.* [*biotic*, and *-in.*] a bacterial growth factor found in liver, egg yolk, and yeast; vitamin H: the lack of it may cause dermatitis.

bī′ō·tīte, *n.* [after J. B. *Biot* (1774–1862), French naturalist.] a dark-brown or black mineral of the mica family, occurring in igneous and metamorphic rocks.

bī′ō·tȳpe, *n.* [*bio-*, and *-type.*] a group of plants or animals with similar hereditary characteristics.

bī·pal′māte, *a.* [*bi-*, and L. *palma*, the palm of the hand.] in botany, having a palmate arrangement on secondary petioles which are palmately arranged on the primary petiole.

bī·par·ȧ·sit′iç, *a.* [*bi-*, and L. *parasitus*, from Gr. *parasitos*, one who eats off another, a diner-out, from *para*, beside, and *sitos*, food.] in botany, parasitic upon or deriving subsistence from another parasite.

bī·pȧ·ren′tăl, *a.* derived from both parents.

bī·pȧ·rī′e·tăl, *a.* of or connected with the prominent rounded part of the two parietal bones.

bip′ȧ·rous, *a.* [*bi-*, and L. *parere*, to bring forth, to bear.]

1. bringing forth two offspring at a birth.

2. in botany, dividing into two branches.

bī·pär′tient (-shent), *a.* [*bi-*, and L. *partire*, to divide.] dividing into two parts.

bī·pär′tient, *n.* a number which divides another number into two exactly equal parts.

bī·pär′tile, *a.* same as *bipartible.*

bī·pär′ti·șăn, *a.* of, having members from, or representing two parties.

bī·pär′tīte, *a.* [*bi-*, and L. *partitus*, divided.]

1. having two parts.

2. having two corresponding parts, as a legal contract or writing, one for each party.

3. in botany, divided into two parts nearly to the base, as a leaf.

bī·pär·ti′tion, *n.* partition, or division, into two parts.

bī·peç′ti·nāte, bī·peç′ti·nā·ted, *a.* [*bi-*, and L. *pecten*, a comb.] having two margins toothed like a comb.

bī′ped, *n.* [*bi-*, and L. *pes* (*pedis*), a foot.] an animal having only two feet, as man.

bī′ped, *a.* two-footed; bipedal.

bī′pe·dăl (*or* bip′ē-dăl), *a.* 1. of bipeds.

2. having two feet.

bī·pen′ni·fọrm, *a.* in biology, having a median line with parts on both sides symmetrically disposed with reference to it.

bī·pen′nis, *n.* [L. *bipennis*, having two edges, a two-edged ax.] an ax with two blades or heads, one on each side of the handle.

BIPENNIS

bī·pet′ăl·ous, *a.* [*bi-*, and Gr. *petalon*, a leaf.] in botany, having two petals.

bī·phen′yl, *n.* [*bi-*, and *-phenyl.*] a white, crystalline hydrocarbon whose molecule consists of a double phenyl group, $C_6H_5 \cdot C_6H_5$.

Bī·pin·nā′ri·ȧ, *n.* [*bi-*, and *pinna*, wing.] in zoology, the larvae of certain echinoderms, as a starfish, developed to the stage of free-swimming: a generic name for such forms.

bī·pin′nāte, bī·pin′nā·ted, *a.* [*bi-*, and L. *pinnatus*, feathered, from *pinna*, a feather.] in botany, having pinnate leaflets on stems that grow opposite each other on a main stem.

bī·pin·nat′i·fid, *a.* [*bi-*, and L. *pinnatus*, feathered, and *findere*, to split.] in botany, having both pinnae and pinnulae pinnatifid.

BIPINNATE LEAF

bī′plāne, *n.* an airplane with two main planes, typically one above the other.

bī′pod, *n.* [*bi-*, and *tripod.*] a two-legged stand for instruments, weapons, etc.

bī·pō′lăr, *a.* [*bi-*, and L. *polus*; Gr. *polos*, the end of an axis.]

1. of or having two poles.

2. of or involving both of the earth's poles or polar regions.

bī·pō·lar′i·ty, *n.* the state of being bipolar.

Bī′pont, Bī·pont′ine, *a.* relating to certain editions of classic authors, famous as products of the bookprinter's art, made at Zweibrücken (Latin *Bipontium*), Bavaria, in the latter part of the eighteenth century.

bī·punç′tāte, *a.* having two holes or punctures.

bī·punç′tū·ăl, *a.* having two points.

bī·pū′pil·lāte, *a.* in entomology, having an eyelike spot on the wing, with two pupillike dots within it of a different color, as in some butterflies.

bī·py·ram′i·dăl, *a.* having two pyramids placed with their bases facing each other, as in the crystal of quartz.

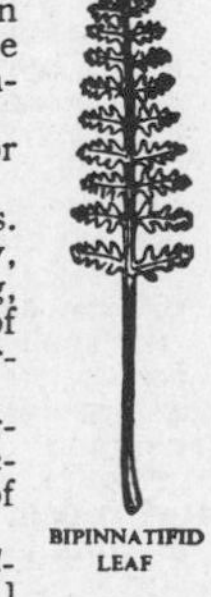

BIPINNATIFID LEAF

bī·quäd′rāte, *n.* [*bi-*, and L. *quadratus*, pp. of *quadrare*, to square.] in mathematics, the fourth power of a number or quantity, or its square squared: also called *quartic.*

bī·quäd·rat′iç, *n.* 1. a biquadrate.

2. an algebraic equation of the fourth power.

bī·quäd·rat′iç, *a.* pertaining to the fourth power; quartic.

biquadratic equation; in algebra, an equation of the fourth degree, or one which involves the fourth power of the unknown quantity or quantities.

biquadratic root of a number; the square root of the square root of that number. Thus the square root of 81 is 9, and the square root of 9 is 3, which is the *biquadratic root* of 81.

bī·quạr′tẽr·ly, *a.* happening or appearing twice in every three-month period.

bī′quạrtz, *n.* two wedge-shaped pieces of quartz placed together, forming a plate, one half of which will tend to rotate the plane of polarization to the right and the other half to the left, so that by adjustment of the wedges the deviation of the plane of polarization may be overcome. It is used with a polariscope.

bī″quā·tẽr′ni·ŏn, *n.* [*bi-*, and L. *quaterni*, four each, by fours.] in mathematics, a quaternion with imaginary coefficients.

bī·quin′tile, *n.* [*bi-*, and L. *quintus*, fifth.] an aspect of the planets, when they are distant from each other by twice the fifth part of a great circle, that is, 144 degrees, or twice 72 degrees.

bī·rā′di·ăl, *a.* in biology, having both bilateral and radial symmetry.

bī·rā′di·ăl·ly, *adv.* in a biradial manner.

bī·rā′di·āte, bī·rā′di·ā·ted, *a.* having two rays; as, a *biradiate* fin.

bī·rā′mous, *a.* [*bi-*, and L. *ramus*, a branch.] in biology, having two branches: said of any organ or appendage.

birch, *n.* [ME. *birche, birke*; AS. *beorc*, birch.]

1. any tree of the genus *Betula*; as, the white *birch*, the dwarf *birch*, the Canada *birch*, of which there are several varieties, and the black *birch*. Birches generally have slender branches, hard, close-grained wood, and smooth bark easily stripped off in layers.

2. the wood of a birch tree, valuable in furniture-making, etc.

3. a bundle of birch twigs or a birch rod, used for chastisement.

4. a very light canoe made of birch bark.

5. any of several birchlike trees of New Zealand.

birch of Jamaica; a tree, *Bursera gummifera*, which yields a kind of turpentine; the turpentine tree.

birch wine; a beverage made from the juice or sap of the birch.

oil of birch; see *birch oil.*

birch, *v.t.*; birched, *pt., pp.*; birching, *ppr.* to beat with a rod of birch; to flog.

birch, bïrch′en, *a.* made of birch; consisting of birch.

birch çam′phŏr, same as *betulin.*

birch oil, 1. an oil obtained from either *Betula alba*, the white birch, or *Betula lenta*, the black birch. The former is used in the manufacture of Russia leather, to which it gives its distinguishing odor, and the latter as a substitute for oil of wintergreen.

birch pärt′ridġe (-rij), the ruffed grouse.

bird, *n.* [ME. *bird, berd, byrde*; AS. *brid*, pl. *briddas*, a bird, especially a young bird.]

1. originally, the young of fowls or other feathered vertebrates; a nestling. [Rare.]

2. any animal belonging to a class of warm-blooded vertebrates (*Aves*) with wings and feathers.

3. a small game bird, as a partridge or quail.

4. a maiden; a girl.

5. a clay pigeon.

6. a person; as, he's a queer *bird.* [Slang.]

7. a sound of disapproval made by the lips fluttering. [Slang.]

8. in badminton, the round, feather-tipped cork struck with the racket; a shuttlecock.

Arabian bird; the phoenix: a symbol of immortality.

bird of freedom; the bald eagle: an emblem

BIRD

A, bill; B, chin; C, throat; D, breast; E, abdomen; F, heel; G, tarsus; H, tibia; I, tail coverts; J, tail feathers; K, flanks; L, secondaries; M, primaries; N, wing coverts; O, nape; P, crown; Q, auriculars

of freedom in the coat of arms of the United States.

bird of ill omen; (a) a bearer of bad news; (b) an unlucky person.

bird of Jove; the eagle.

bird of Juno; the peacock.

bird of Minerva or *bird of night*; the owl.

bird of paradise; (a) a beautiful bird of the genus *Paradisea*, native in the Orient and New Guinea. One of the better known species has the head and back part of the neck lemon-colored, the throat emerald green, the breast black, and the wings of a chestnut color. (b) in Australia, the lyrebird, so named by early settlers; (c) in astronomy, a small constellation of the southern heavens.

bird of passage; a bird that migrates at the changes of season in spring and autumn; hence, anyone who roams about constantly.

bird of peace; the dove.

bird of prey; any of a number of flesh-eating birds, as the eagle, hawk, owl, vulture, etc.

birds of a feather; persons having like tastes or characteristics.

early bird; one who arrives or rises early. [Colloq.]

man-of-war bird; a raptorial sea bird, *Fregata aquila*, with a strong hooked bill and small webbed feet.

bird, *v.i.* to catch or shoot birds.

bird'bȧth, *n.* a basinlike garden ornament for birds to bathe in.

bird'bōlt, *n.* an arrow, broad and blunt at the end, for killing birds by concussion, without injuring the plumage.

bird çāġe, a cage made of wires, small sticks, or wicker, for confining birds.

bird'çall, *n.* 1. the sound or song of a bird.

2. an imitation of this.

3. a device for imitating bird sounds.

bird cher'ry, a European tree or shrub, *Prunus Padus*, bearing small black fruit; also, the fruit of this tree.

bird dog, any dog trained to hunt birds, as a pointer, setter, or retriever.

bird duf'fẽr, one who alters the color or form of living or stuffed birds by artificial processes, usually with intent to deceive.

bird'-eyed, *a.* quick-sighted; catching a glance as one goes.

bird fan'ci·ẽr, one who is interested in birds; particularly, one who keeps, breeds, or trains birds, especially cage birds.

bird'-foot, *n.* bird's-foot.

bird grȧss, a weed of the buckwheat family, with jointed stems, narrow leaves, and spikes of tiny, greenish flowers; knotgrass.

bird'house″, *n.* 1. a small box, often resembling a house, for birds to live in.

2. a building for exhibiting birds.

bird'ie, *n.* 1. a small bird: a child's word.

2. in golf, a score of one stroke under par for any hole.

bird'i·kin, *n.* one of the young of a bird.

bird'ing, *n.* the hunting of birds.

bird'let, *n.* a small or very young bird.

bird'līke, *a.* resembling a bird.

bird'līme, *n.* 1. a sticky substance, usually made of the juice of holly bark or mistletoe berries, extracted by boiling. It is used to catch birds by smearing it on the twigs of a bush.

2. anything that ensnares or prevents escape.

bird'līme, *v.t.* to ensnare and capture by the use of birdlime.

bird'ling, *n.* same as *birdlet*.

bird louse, a parasitic wingless insect infesting birds and some mammals.

bird'măn, *n.*; *pl.* **bird'men**, 1. a person whose work deals with birds, as an ornithologist or taxidermist.

2. an aviator. [Colloq.]

bird mīte, a small parasitic mite, occurring in numerous species and mainly infesting birds.

bird pep'pẽr, a species of *Capsicum* (*Capsicum baccatum*), a pepper bearing small red fruit.

bird plant, a plant flourishing in Mexico, which bears a yellow flower suggestive of a bird.

bird'ş bēak, a form of molding, a section of which somewhat resembles a bird's beak.

bird'seed, *n.* a mixture of seeds used for feeding birds, as the seeds of hemp, millet, and canary grass.

bird'ş'-eȳe, *n.* 1. a genus of plants, called also *pheasant's eye*, known in botany by the generic term *Adonis*. There are several species, some of which have small bright flowers.

2. a kind of smoking tobacco containing sections of stalk resembling a bird's eye.

3. a pattern of small diamond-shaped figures, each with a dot like a bird's eye in the center, woven into cotton and linens.

4. a cotton or linen cloth with such a pattern: used for diapers, napkins, etc.

bird'ş'-eȳe, *a.* 1. seen from above or a distance, as if by a flying bird; hence, general; not minute, or entering into details; as, a *bird's-eye* view of a city; a *bird's-eye* view of a subject or proposition.

2. having spots looking like birds' eyes.

bird's-eye maple; a kind of curly-grained maple, the wood of which when dressed and polished has many eyelike markings.

bird's-eye rot; same as *anthracnose*.

bird's-eye spot; in plant pathology, a fungus, *Cercospora theae*, which attacks the leaves of the tea plant.

bird'ş'-foot, *n.* any of various plants of the genus *Ornithopus*, whose leaves resemble a bird's claw.

bird's-foot fern; a kind of fern with small, wiry leaves in groups of three.

bird's-foot trefoil; a species of *Lotus* with pods resembling claws and having small yellow flowers.

bird's-foot violet; a kind of violet bearing large, purple flowers with dark upper petals and pale lower ones.

bird shot, small shot for shooting birds.

bird'ş mouth, in architecture, an interior angle or notch cut across a piece of timber, for its reception on the edge of another, as that on a rafter to be laid on a plate.

bird'ş nest, the nest in which a bird lays eggs and hatches her young.

bird'ş'-nest, *n.* 1. a British orchid, *Neottia nidus-avis*.

2. in cookery, the nest of a small swallow of the Malay Archipelago, much prized in China as an article of food, being mixed with soups. It is of a gelatinous consistency, and formed of a marine plant partly digested by the bird.

3. the wild carrot.

4. same as *crow's-nest*.

bird's-nest pudding; an apple pudding in which the apples are cored and the hollows filled with sugar; also, a plain pudding with a fresh fruit dressing.

bird'ş nest'ing, the act of searching for and taking bird's nests or their eggs.

bird spī'dẽr, a large hairy South American spider that sometimes preys on small birds.

bird'ş tŏngue (tung), same as *bird weed*.

bird this'tle (this'l), the bull thistle.

bird tick, an insect, usually winged, that is parasitic on birds.

bird weed, the knotgrass, *Polygonum aviculare*.

bird'-wit″ted, *a.* flighty; passing rapidly from one subject to another; not having the faculty of attention.

bird'wom″ăn (-woom″), *n.*; *pl.* **bird'wom″en** (-wim″), a female aviator. [Colloq.]

bī·reç·tañ'gū·lăr, *a.* [*bi-*, and L. *rectus*, right, and *angulus*, angle.] having two right angles; as, a *birectangular* spherical triangle.

bī·rē·frin'ġence, *n.* [*bi-*, and L. *refringere*, to break open.] in optics, the power of double refraction.

bī·rē·frin'ġent, *a.* having the quality of birefringence.

bī'rēme, *n.* [L. *biremis*, a two-oared boat.] an ancient galley with two banks or tiers of oars on each side, one under the other.

bi·ret'tȧ, bir·ret'tȧ, *n.* [It. *birretta*; LL. *birrettum*, dim. of *birrus*, a hood or cloak.] a square cap with three projections and a tassel on top, worn by prelates and priests of the Roman Catholic Church. The *biretta* of a cardinal is scarlet; a bishop's is purple; those of priests are black. Also spelled *baretta*, *beretta*, etc.

BIRETTA

bir'gan·dẽr, *n.* a bergander. [Obs.]

bī·rī·bī'rī, *n.* same as *beriberi*.

bī·rī'mōse, *a.* [*bi-*, and L. *rimosus*, from *rima*, a chink.] in botany, having two slits or fissures.

birk, *n.* and *a.* [Prov. Eng.] birch.

birk'en, *v.t.* to beat with a birch rod. [Obs.]

birk'en, *a.* relating to the birch; birchen. [Scot.]

bir'kie, *n.* [Scot.] 1. a pert or lively young fellow.

2. a game of cards.

birl, *v.t.* and *v.i.* [Scot.] to twirl or spin; to make a humming noise by spinning.

bir'lạw, *n.* same as *byrlaw*.

birle, *v.t.* and *v.i.* [ME. *birlen*; AS. *byrlian*, *byrelian*, to pour out drink; *byrele*, a cupbearer, from *beran*, to bear.] to ply or furnish with drink; to pour out (drink). [Obs.]

birl'ing, *n.* a competitive game among lumberjacks in which each tries to keep his balance while revolving a floating log with his feet.

bī·ros'trāte, bī·ros'trā·ted, *a.* [*bi-*, and L. *rostrum*, a beak.] having a double beak or a process resembling two beaks.

birr, *v.i.*; birred, *pt.*, *pp.*; birring, *ppr.* to make a whirring noise, as of wheels in motion; also, to move with a whirring sound.

birr, *n.* 1. a whirring or buzzing sound.

2. force or energy; a rushing, as of wind.

3. emphatic speech or statement.

bir·ret'tȧ, *n.* same as *biretta*.

bir'rus, *n.*; *pl.* **bir'rī**, [L., a kind of cloak originally of a red color, from Gr. *pyrros*, *pyrsos*, red, flame-colored, from *pyr*, fire.]

1. in Roman antiquity, a cloak or cape with a hood worn over the head as a cowl.

2. a coarse, thick woolen cloth used by the poorer classes in the Middle Ages, for cloaks and other clothing.

BIRRUS

birse, *n.* [Scot.] a bristle or bristles; short hair.

birt, *n.* the brill or the turbot. [Prov. Eng.]

birth, *n.* [ME. *birth*, *byrthe*, *byrde*; AS. *gebyrde*, from *beran*, to bear; O.H.G. *giburt*; Goth. *gabaurths*; Gael. *breith*; Sans. *bhriti*, birth.]

1. the act or fact of coming into life, or of being born; nativity; as, the *birth* of a son.

2. lineage; extraction; descent; as, of Grecian *birth*: often used by way of distinction for a descent from noble or honorable parents and ancestors; as, a man of *birth*.

3. the condition to which a person is born; natural state or position; inherited inclination to act in certain ways; as, an actor by *birth*.

4. a person or thing that is born or produced.

5. the act of bringing forth offspring; as, she had two children at a *birth*.

6. origin; beginning; as, an empire's *birth*.

birth stone; a precious or semiprecious stone which symbolizes the month of one's birth. The usual list is as follows: January, garnet; February, amethyst; March, bloodstone; April, diamond; May, emerald; June, pearl; July, ruby; August, sardonyx; September, sapphire; October, opal; November, topaz; December, turquoise.

Syn.—parentage, extraction, nativity, family, race, origin, source, rise, lineage, nobility.

birth çŏn·trōl', the act of regulation of childbearing, especially by contraceptives.

birth çŏn·trōl'lẽr, an advocate of birth control.

birth'dāy, *n.* 1. the day on which any person is born or anything begun.

2. the anniversary of a person's birth or a thing's beginning.

birth'dāy, *a.* of or pertaining to the day of one's birth, or its anniversary; as, *birthday* gifts or festivities.

birth'dŏm, *n.* inheritance by birth; birthright. [Obs.]

birth'ing, *n.* same as *berthing*.

birth'less, *a.* of inferior extraction or birth. [Rare.]

birth'märk, *n.* a mark or blemish found on the body at birth.

birth'night (-nīt), *n.* the night in which a person is born; also, the anniversary of that night.

birth'plāce, *n.* the place where a person is born; also, a place of origin or birth, in its more general sense; as, the *birthplace* of freedom.

birth rāte, *n.* the number of births per year per thousand of population in a given district, group, etc.: sometimes other units of time or population are used in giving the birth rate.

birth'rīght (-rīt), *n.* 1. any right, privilege, or possession into which a person is born, such as an estate descendible by law to an heir, or civil liberty under a free constitution.

2. the rights or inheritance of the firstborn.

bĩrth'rọọt, *n.* in botany, a herbaceous plant (*Trillium erectum*) of the lily family with an astringent rootstock, leaves in groups of three, and three-parted flowers; trillium; birthwort: so called because formerly supposed to be of help in childbirth.

bĩrth'wŏrt, *n.* 1. any plant of the genus *Aristolochia*.

2. same as *birthroot*.

bis, *adv.* [L. *bis*, twice, from *duo*, two.] twice: used to indicate repetition, especially in music.

bis-, bi-: used before a vowel.

bī'sȧ, *n.* 1. an African antelope, *Oryx beisa*; the oryx.

2. a South American monkey, with hairy, non-prehensile tail; the black saki.

bī·saç'çāte, *a.* in botany, having two small sacs, or pouches.

Bi·sä'yȧn, *n.* Visayan.

bis·çä'chȧ, *n.* same as *viscacha*.

Bis·çāy'ăn, *a.* of or pertaining to the province of Biscay, Spain.

Bis·çāy'ăn, *n.* a native or inhabitant of the Spanish province of Biscay.

bis'çō·tin, *n.* [Fr.] a biscuit made of flour, sugar, marmalade, and eggs. [Obs.]

bis'çuit (-kit), *n.* [ME. *bysket, biscute*; OFr. *bescoit, bescuit*; It. *biscotto*, twice-cooked; L. *bis*, twice, and *coctus*, pp. of *coquere*, to cook.]

1. (a) a kind of unleavened bread, of many varieties, plain, sweet, or fancy, formed into flat thin cakes and baked until crisp; (b) any of these cakes or wafers; a cracker or cooky. [Chiefly Brit.]

2. (a) bread, raised and shortened or made light with soda or baking powder, and baked in small pieces; (b) any of these pieces.

3. earthenware or porcelain which has undergone the first baking, before glazing.

4. light-brown; tan.

bis'çuit rọọt, the root of various plants, used as food by the Indians of British Columbia.

bī·sçū'tāte, *a.* [*bi-*, and L. *scutum*, shield.] in botany, resembling two bucklers or shields placed side by side.

bīşe, *n.* [Fr. *bise, bis*, dark brown.] a cold northerly wind prevailing in Switzerland and parts of France.

bīse, *n.* same as *bice*.

bī·seçt', *v.t.*; bisected, *pt., pp.*; bisecting, *ppr.* [*bi-*, and L. *sectus*, pp. of *secare*, to cut.] 1. to cut or divide into two parts.

2. in geometry, to divide into two equal parts.

bī·seçt', *v.i.* to divide; to fork.

bī·seç'tion, *n.* 1. the act of cutting into two parts; the division of any line or quantity into two equal parts.

2. a line or point of bisecting.

3. either of two equal sections.

BISCUTATE LEAF (*Dionæa muscipula*)

bī·seç'tŏr, *n.* 1. one who or that which bisects.

2. in geometry, a straight line which divides an angle or another line into two equal parts.

bī·seç'trix, *n.* in crystallography, the line bisecting the angles formed by the optic axes in a biaxial crystal.

bī·seg'ment, *n.* one of the parts of a line divided into two equal parts.

bī·sep'tāte, *a.* [*bi-*, and L. *sæptum*, a partition.] having two partitions or septa.

bī·sē'ri·ăl, bī·sē'ri·āte, *a.* existing in two series or rows.

bī·ser'rāte, *a.* [*bi-*, and L. *serratus*, from *serra*, a saw.]

1. in botany, doubly serrate, or having notched teeth along the margins, as some leaves.

2. in zoology, notched on both sides, as some antennae.

bī·sē'tōse, bī·sē'tous, *a.* [*bi-*, and L. *setosus*, from *seta*, a bristle.] having two bristles.

bī·sette' (-zet'), *n.* [Fr.] a cheap narrow French lace.

bī·sex'ous, *a.* bisexual. [Obs.]

bī·sex'ū·ăl, *a.* 1. in botany, being of both sexes, as a flower containing both stamens and pistils within the same envelope.

2. in zoology, hermaphrodite.

bī·sex'ū·ăl, *n.* 1. a hermaphrodite.

2. a person who is sexually attracted by both sexes.

bī·sex'ū·ous, *a.* bisexual.

bish, *n.* same as *bikh*.

bish'ŏp, *n.* [ME. *bishop*; AS. *biscop, bisceop*; LL. *episcopus*; Gr. *episkopos*, a bishop, an overseer; *epi*, upon, and *skopos*, from *skopein*, to look.]

1. in the early Christian church, a spiritual overseer.

2. in the churches maintaining apostolic succession, a prelate superior to the priesthood, consecrated for the spiritual government and direction of a diocese, bishopric, or see: he admits priests to holy orders, and is himself under the rule of an archbishop.

3. in certain Protestant churches, a high-ranking clergyman with authority over a church district.

4. one of the pieces in a game of chess, placed next to the royal pieces and usually made to resemble a bishop's miter: these pieces can move in a diagonal direction across any number of squares.

5. a sweet drink of port wine, oranges, and sugar, served hot.

6. in the United States, a woman's bustle. [Obs.]

bishop sleeve; a wide sleeve sometimes worn by women.

bishop's length; a canvas measuring fifty-eight by ninety-four inches, used in painting portraits.

bish'ŏp, *v.t.*; bishoped, *pt., pp.*; bishoping, *ppr.* to confirm; to admit solemnly into the church.

bish'ŏp, *v.t.* [from the name of the man who first practiced it.] to change the appearance of the teeth of (a horse) in order to deceive purchasers as to its age. [Eng.]

bish'ŏp·dŏm, *n.* jurisdiction of a bishop.

bish'ŏp·ly, *adv.* in the manner of a bishop. [Obs.]

bish'ŏp·ly, *a.* episcopal; bishoplike. [Obs.]

bish'ŏp rāy, same as *obispo*.

bish'ŏp·riç, *n.* [ME. *bisshoprike, bisshopriche*; AS. *bisceoprīce*; *bisceop*, a bishop, and *rīce*, jurisdiction, kingdom.]

1. a diocese; the district over which the jurisdiction of a bishop extends.

2. the position, authority, or rank of a bishop.

bish'ŏp's-çap, *n.* any of a group of small woodland herbs with heart-shaped leaves and white or greenish flowers; miterwort.

bish'ŏp's eld'ẽr, the bishopweed.

bish'ŏp's mī'tẽr, 1. a fetid bug injurious to fruit.

2. a miter shell.

bish'ŏp's stọọl, the see or seat of a bishop.

bish'ŏp's-weed, *n.* any of various species of plants of the parsley family; bishop's elder; goutweed.

bish'ŏp's wŏrt, 1. the wood betony.

2. fennel flower.

bis·il'i·aç, *a.* in anatomy, relating to the two crests of the iliac bones: also *bi-iliac*.

bī·sil'i·çāte, *n.* a salt of metasilicic acid, the oxygen of the silica being in the ratio of two to one to the oxygen of the base.

bisk, *n.* same as *bisque*.

bis'ket, *n.* a biscuit. [Obs.]

bis'mȧr, *n.* a kind of steelyard. [Scot.]

bis'mẽr, bis'mȧr, *n.* disgrace; shame; abuse. [Obs.]

biş'mīte, *n.* a yellow earthy bismuth trioxide.

biş'muth, *n.* a hard, brittle metallic element that is grayish-white with a tinge of red: it is often found in a native state, crystallized in rhombs or octahedrons, or in the form of dendrites, or in thin laminae investing the ores of other metals, particularly cobalt. It is used chiefly in making alloys of low melting point: symbol, Bi; atomic weight, 209.00; atomic number, 83.

bismuth ocher; bismite.

biş'muth·ăl, *a.* consisting of bismuth, or containing it.

biş·mū'thiç, *a.* of or containing bismuth with a valence of five; as, *bismuthic* acid.

biş·muth·if'ẽr·ous, *a.* yielding bismuth.

biş'muth·ine, *n.* same as *bismuthinite*.

biş·muth'in·īte, *n.* bismuth sulfide.

biş'muth·ous, *a.* of, pertaining to, or containing bismuth with a valence of three.

biş'muth·yl, *n.* the bismuthal radical BiO.

biş'mū·tīte, *n.* an uncrystallized brownish or greenish carbonate of bismuth: also written *bismuthite*.

bī'sŏn, *n.* [Fr. *bison*; L. *bison*, a wild ox.] either of two four-legged mammals: (a) *Bos* or *Bonassus bison*, the European *bison* or aurochs; (b) *Bison americanus*, the American *bison*, popularly called *buffalo*, now nearly extinct, formerly roaming the plains of central and western United States in herds. The fore parts are massive and shaggy, the hair being rust-colored, the horns black and curving upward, and the back humped.

AMERICAN BISON

bī·spī'nōse, *a.* [*bi-*, and L. *spina*, the spine.] having two spines.

bī'spōre, *n.* [*bi-*, and Gr. *sporos*, a sowing.] one of a pair of spores produced by cell division in certain algae.

bī·spōr'ous, *a.* having the qualities of a bispore.

bisque (bisk), *n.* in ceramics, same as *biscuit*.

bisque, *n.* [Fr.] in tennis, golf, croquet, etc., a handicap of one point, stroke, turn, etc. per game.

bisque, *n.* [Fr.] 1. a thick rich soup made from meat or shellfish, especially crabs and lobsters.

2. a thick, strained, creamed vegetable soup.

3. an ice cream containing ground macaroons or nuts.

bis·sex'tile, *n.* [L. *bissextilis*, leap year, from *bissextus* (*bis* and *sextus*), the *sixth* day before the calends of March, or twenty-fourth day of February, which was reckoned *twice* every fourth year, by the intercalation of a day.] leap year: see *leap year*.

bis·sex'tile, *a.* pertaining to leap year or the extra day (February 29) of a leap year.

bis'sŏn, *a.* purblind. [Obs.]

bis'tẽr, bis'tre (-tẽr), *n.* [Fr. *bistre*, a dark brown color.]

1. a dark-brown pigment extracted from soot.

2. dark brown.

bis'tẽr, bis'tre (-tẽr), *a.* dark-brown.

bī·stip'ūled, *a.* having two stipules.

bis'tort, *n.* [*bi-*, and L. *tortus*, pp. of *torquere*, to twist.] a plant, *Polygonum Bistorta*, with spikes of pink or white flowers: so called because of its twisted root, which is used as an astringent: also called *snakeweed*.

bis'tou·ry, *n.* [Fr. *bistouri*, a bistoury; OFr. *bistorie*, a dagger.] a small, slender surgical knife with a straight or curved blade and a very sharp point.

bis'trō, *n.* [Fr. (Parisian) slang, wine seller.]

1. a small wine shop or restaurant where wine is served.

2. a small night club or bar.

bī·sul'çāte, *a.* [*bi-*, and L. *sulcatus*, pp. of *sulcare*, to furrow.]

1. having two grooves.

2. in zoology, clovenhoofed.

bī·sul'çous, *a.* bisulcate. [Obs.]

bī·sul'fāte, *n.* [*bi-*, and L. *sulfur*, brimstone.] an acid sulfate; compound of an element or radical which, in water solutions, produces hydrogen ions as well as sulfate ions.

bī·sul'fīde (*or* -fid), *n.* 1. hydrosulfide.

2. erroneously, a disulfide.

bī·sul'fīte, *n.* an acid sulfite; the compound of an element or radical which, in water solutions, produces hydrogen ions as well as sulfite ions.

bī·sym·met'riç, bī·sym·met'ri·çăl, *a.* having double symmetry.

bī·sym'mē·try, *n.* the quality or condition of being bisymmetrical.

bit, *n.* [ME. *bite*, a bit, morsel; AS. *bita*, a bit, something bitten off; *bītan*, to bite.]

1. a small piece or amount of anything.

Power to grant a patent for stamping round *bits* of copper. —Swift.

2. somewhat. The word is often used in certain phrases expressive of extent or degree; thus, a *bit* older means somewhat older; not a *bit*, not a whit, not in any degree; a *bit* of a humorist, somewhat of a humorist.

Your case is not a *bit* clearer than it was seven years ago. —Arbuthnot.

3. an amount equal to twelve and one-half cents, a quarter being two *bits*. [Colloq.]

4. a short time; a moment. [Colloq.]

5. a very small role in a play or motion picture.

bit by bit; little by little; gradually.

to do one's bit; to do one's share.

Syn.—piece, part, fragment, morsel.

bit, *a.* very small; as, a *bit* part in a play.

bit, *n.* [ME. *bit*, *bitt*, from AS. *bite*, a bite, from *bītan*, to bite.]

1. the metal part of a bridle which is inserted in the mouth of a horse, and is used as a control.

We have strict statutes and most biting laws,
The needful *bits* and curbs to headstrong steeds. —Shak.

2. anything that curbs or controls.

3. any of various boring tools for wood or metal applied by means of a brace. The typical form is the *shell bit* (fig. *a*), which is shaped like a gouge, for shearing the fibers around the circumference of the hole. The *center bit* (fig. *b*) is another typical form, of which there are many modifications. The *half round bit* (fig. *c*) is employed for enlarging holes in metal. The *rose bit* (fig. *d*) is cylindrical, and terminates in a truncated cone, the oblique surface of which is cut into teeth like the rose countersink. It is also used for enlarging holes of considerable depth in metals and hard woods.

4. any of several similar tools or parts of tools; specifically, (a) the wedge-shaped portion or edge of an ax, hatchet, etc.; (b) a plane blade; (c) the bladelike portion of a key that is inserted in a lock and engages the bolt; the web.

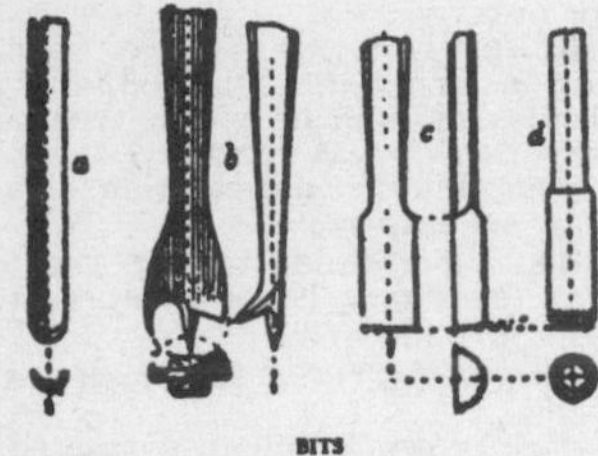

BITS

to take (or *get*) *the bit in one's teeth*; (a) to get the bit between the teeth, so that it fails to restrain: said of horses; (b) to be beyond control: said of persons.

bit, *v.t.*; bitted, *pt.*, *pp.*; bitting, *ppr.* 1. to put a bit in the mouth of (a horse); to train to the bit.

2. to check or curb.

3. to make the bit on (a key).

bit, *n.* [*b*inary dig*it*.] a single digit in a binary number system; specifically, a unit of information equal to the amount of information obtained by learning which of two equally likely events occurred.

bit, past tense and alternative past participle of *bite*.

bī·tan′gent, *a.* pertaining to or possessing the qualities of a bitangent.

bī·tan′gent, *n.* a straight line that touches a curve at two points.

bī·tär′trāte, *n.* an acid tartrate; the compound of an element or radical which, in water solutions, produces hydrogen ions as well as tartrate ions.

bitch (bich), *n.* [ME. *bicche*; AS. *bicce*, bitch.]

1. the female of the dog, wolf, fox, etc.

2. a bad or bad-tempered woman: used as a strong term of contempt or hostility.

bitch, *v.i.* to complain. [Slang.]

bitch, *v.t.* [from *botch*.] to botch; spoil by bungling (usually with *up*). [Slang.]

bitch′y, *a.* of or like a bitch.

bīte, *v.t.*; bit, *pt.*; biting, *ppr.*; bitten *or* bit, *pp.* [ME. *biten*; AS. *bītan*, to bite.]

1. to break or crush with the teeth, as in eating; to pierce with or as with the teeth; to seize with the teeth.

2. to cause to smart; to pinch or nip, as with frost; to blast, blight, or injure in various ways; as, pepper *bites* the mouth.

3. to take fast hold of; to grip or catch into or on; as, the anchor *bites* the ground; the file *bites* the iron; the wheels *bite* the rails.

4. to cheat; to trick.

5. to corrode or eat into, by nitric or other acid; as, to *bite* a steel plate.

to bite off more than one can chew; to attempt more than one is capable of.

to bite the bullet; to confront a painful situation with fortitude or stoicism: from an earlier practice of having the patient bite on a bullet during battlefield surgery when no anesthetic was available.

to bite the dust or *the ground*; (a) to fall dead or dying, as in combat; (b) to be thrown or struck down; to be vanquished or humbled.

to bite the thumb at; to insult so as to provoke a quarrel.

to bite the tongue; to maintain fixed silence.

bīte, *v.i.* 1. (a) to press or snap the teeth (*into*, *at*, etc.); (b) to have a tendency to do this.

2. to cause a biting sensation or have a biting effect.

3. to swallow a bait.

4. to be caught, as by a trick.

bīte, *n.* [ME. *byte*, *bite*; AS. *bītan*, to bite.]

1. the seizure of anything by the teeth or with the mouth; specifically, the seizure of a bait; as, the *bite* of a dog, the *bite* of a fish.

2. the wound, bruise, or sting made by biting; as, a mosquito *bite*.

3. as much as is taken at once by biting; a mouthful; a bit; as, a *bite* of bread.

4. a cheat; a trick; a fraud.

5. a sharper; one who cheats. [Rare.]

6. in printing, that part of the impression which is improperly printed, owing to the frisket not being sufficiently cut away.

7. the grip or hold that one object or part of an apparatus has on another; as, the *bite* of an anchor on the ground; the *bite* of the wheels of a locomotive on the rails.

8. a small lunch; a snack. [Colloq.]

9. in dentistry, the way the upper and lower teeth meet.

10. in etching, the corrosion of the metal plate by the acid.

bī·tem′pō·răl, *a.* [*bi-*, and L. *tempora*, the temples.] pertaining to the two temporal bones.

bīt′ẽr, *n.* 1. one who or that which bites.

2. one who cheats or defrauds. [Obs.]

bī·tẽr′nāte, *a.* [*bi-*, and L. *terni*, thrice.] in botany, doubly ternate, as when a petiole has three ternate leaflets.

bī·tẽr′nāte·ly, *adv.* in a biternate manner.

bī′thē·ism, *n.* [*bi-*, and Gr. *theos*, god.] belief in the existence of two gods.

bīt′ing, *a.* sharp; severe; sarcastic; as, a *biting* affliction, a *biting* jest.

bīt′ing·ly, *adv.* in a sarcastic or caustic manner.

bit′less, *a.* not having a bit or bridle.

bī′tō, bī′tō tree, *n.* [native name.] a small tree, *Balanites ægyptiaca*, found in dry tropical regions of Asia and Africa: it has valuable wood and bark and an edible fruit.

bit plāy′ẽr, an actor with a small role.

bit′stock, *n.* the handle or stock by which a boring bit is held and rotated; a brace.

bitt, *n.* [perh. from ON. *biti*, a beam.] in nautical usage, any of the deck posts, often in pairs, around which ropes or cables are wound and held fast.

bitt, *v.t.* to wind around a bitt; as, to *bitt* the cable in order to fasten or slacken it.

bit′te, *interj.* G., lit., (I) request (of you).]

1. please.

2. I beg your pardon.

3. you're welcome; don't mention it: said in answer to thanks.

bit′ten, alternative past participle of *bite*.

bit′tẽr, *n.* in nautical usage, a turn of the cable which is around the bitts.

bit′tẽr, *a.* [ME. *biter*; AS. *biter*, *bitor*, bitter, from *bītan*, to bite.]

1. sharp or biting to the taste; acrid.

2. sharp; cruel; severe; as, *bitter* enmity.

3. caustic; reproachful; sarcastic; as, *bitter* words.

4. sharp to the feeling; piercing; painful; as, a *bitter* cold day, a *bitter* wind.

5. painful to the mind; calamitous; poignant; as, a *bitter* fate.

6. mournful; distressing; expressive of misery; as, a *bitter* complaint.

bitter apple, *cucumber*, or *gourd*; same as *colocynth*.

bitter cassava; a kind of cassava from whose roots tapioca is made.

bitter cress; any plant of the genus *Cardamine*.

bitter earth; magnesia.

bitter principle; any of various bitter substances found in plants, as lupulin, aloin, etc.

bitter salt; Epsom salts; magnesium sulfate.

bitter vetch; (a) *Vicia ervilia*, a plant cultivated for fodder; (b) all the species of the genus *Orobus*, now frequently included in the genus *Lathyrus*.

Syn.—harsh, sour, sharp, tart, acrimonious, sarcastic, severe, sad, afflictive, intense, stinging, pungent, acrid, cutting.

bit′tẽr, *adv.* bitterly.

bit′tẽr, *n.* 1. anything bitter; bitterness; as, the *bitter* and the sweet of life.

2. same as *bitters*.

bit′tẽr, *v.t.* and *v.i.* to make or become bitter.

bit′tẽr·blāin, *n.* *Vandellia diffusa*, an herb of tropical America possessing medicinal properties.

bit′tẽr·blo͞om, *n.* the North American centaury.

bit′tẽr·bump, *n.* the European bittern; the butterbump. [Eng. Dial.]

bit′tẽr end, in nautical usage, (a) that end of a rope or cable that is wound around a bitt; (b) that part of a cable which is abaft the bitts, and therefore within board, when the ship rides at anchor.

to the bitter end; (a) until the end, however uncomfortable; (b) until death.

bit′tẽr-end′ẽr, *n.* a person who persists beyond reason; one who will not give in. [Colloq.]

bit′tẽr hẽrb (ẽrb), the European centaury.

bit′tẽr·ing, *n.* bittern, a bitter compound employed in the adulteration of beer.

bit′tẽr·ish, *a.* bitter in a moderate degree.

bit′tẽr·ish·ness, *n.* the quality of being somewhat bitter.

bit′tẽr king, a shrub belonging to the quassia family, found in the East Indies.

bit′tẽr·ling, *n.* a fresh-water fish, *Rhodeus amarus*, of Europe.

bit′tẽr·ly, *adv.* in a bitter manner.

bit′tẽrn, *n.*; *pl.* **bit′tẽrns, bit′tẽrn,** [ME. *bitter*, *bitoure*; OFr. *butor*, the bittern bird.] a heronlike wading bird of the genus *Botaurus*, a native of Europe. It has long legs and neck, and a booming cry. *Botaurus lentiginosus* is the American species.

EUROPEAN BITTERN (*Botaurus stellaris*)

bit′tẽrn, *n.* 1. the bitter liquid remaining after the crystallization of salt from brine.

2. a very bitter compound of quassia, used in adulterating beer.

bit′tẽr·ness, *n.* [ME. *bitternesse*, from AS. *biternys*, bitterness.] the state or quality of being bitter; figuratively, extreme enmity; sharpness; severity of temper; biting sarcasm; painful affliction; deep distress of mind.

Syn.—acrimony, asperity, harshness, spite, grief, malignity, distress.

bit′tẽr·nut, *n.* the swamp hickory, *Carya cordiformis*, bearing small, bitter nuts with a thin shell.

bit′tẽr ōak, the *Quercus cerris*, a common European oak tree.

bit′tẽr·ro͞ot, *n.* a plant with nutritious roots, flourishing in the mountainous regions of Montana and Idaho.

bit′tẽrs, *n.pl.* a liquor in which bitter herbs or roots are steeped; generally an alcoholic liquor.

bit′tẽr spär, see *dolomite*.

bit′tẽr·sweet, *a.* both sweet and bitter; figuratively, pleasant but painful.

bit′tẽr·sweet, *n.* 1. anything bittersweet in character.

2. a kind of apple.

3. in botany, (a) *Solanum dulcamara*, the woody nightshade, a poisonous vine with purple flowers and red berries that taste bitter and sweet; (b) *Celastrus scandens*, an American climbing plant with clusters of greenish flowers, yellow fruit, and red seeds.

bit′tẽr·weed, *n.* a variety of ragweed, *Ambrosia artemisiifolia*, growing in America.

bit′tẽr·wood, *n.* a tree of the West Indies which yields Jamaica quassia; also, the wood of the tree.

bit′tŏck, *n.* a little piece of anything. [Scot.]
bit′tŏr, bit′tŏur, *n.* the bittern (bird). [Obs.]
bi·tūme′, *n.* bitumen. [Rare.]
bi·tūmed′, *a.* smeared with bitumen. [Rare.]
bi·tū′men, *n.* [L.] 1. originally, mineral pitch.
2. any of several hard or semisolid materials obtained as asphaltic residue in the distillation of coal tar, wood tar, petroleum, etc., or occurring as natural asphalt.
bi·tū′mi·nāte, *v.t.*; bituminated, *pt., pp.*; bituminating, *ppr.* to impregnate or coat with bitumen; to bituminize.
bi·tū·mi·nif′ẽr·ous, *a.* [L. *bitumen*, bitumen, and *ferre*, to produce.] producing bitumen.
bi·tū″mi·ni·zā′tion, *n.* the process of forming bitumen.
bi·tū′mi·nīze, *v.t.*; bituminized, *pt.; pp.*; bituminizing, *ppr.* to form into, coat, or impregnate with bitumen.
bi·tū′mi·noid, *a.* like bitumen.
bi·tū′mi·nous, *a.* having the qualities of bitumen; compounded with bitumen; containing bitumen.
bituminous cement or *bituminous mastic*; a cement composed chiefly of asphalt, used for roofing, paving, etc.
bituminous coal; coal that yields pitch or tar when it burns; soft coal.
bituminous limestone; limestone of a lamellar structure, brown or black in color, and, when rubbed, emitting an unpleasant smell.
bī′ū·ret, *n.* [*bi-*, and L. *urina*, urine.] in chemistry, a crystalline product of urea.
bī·vā′lence (*or* biv′å-lence), *n.* [*bi-*, and L. *valens*, ppr. of *valere*, to be strong.] the quality or state of being bivalent.
bī·vā′len·cy (*or* biv′å-len-si), *n.* bivalence.
bī·vā′lent (*or* biv′å-lent), *a.* 1. having two valences.
2. having a valence of two.
3. in biology, double: said of a chromosome formed by two similar chromosomes that lie close together or appear to join completely.
Also, for sense 1 and especially for sense 2, *divalent.*
bī·vā′lent (*or* biv′å-lent), *n.* a double chromosome.
bī′valve, *n.* [Fr. *bivalve*, from L. *bis*, two, and *valva*, door.]
1. any mollusk having a shell consisting of two parts or valves, hinged together by an elastic ligament, or a shell consisting of two parts, which open and shut. The clam closes its shell by contracting two transverse muscles attached to the shell inside; the oyster has but one such muscle.
2. in botany, a separable, two-part seedcase, as in the common pea.
bī′valve, *a.* 1. having two shells or valves which open and shut, as the oyster.
2. having two parts or valves which open at maturity, as the seed vessels of certain plants.
bī′valved, *a.* same as *bivalve.*
Bī·val′vi·ȧ, *n. pl.* in zoology, a former term for the class *Lamellibranchiata.*
bī·val′vous, *a.* having two valves.
bī·val′vū·lăr, *a.* bivalve.
bī·vault′ed, *a.* having two vaults or arches.
bī·ven′trăl, *a.* having two bellies or belly-shaped parts; as, a *biventral* muscle.
biv′i·ăl, *a.* of or pertaining to the bivium.
biv′i·ous, *a.* [L. *bivius*, having two passages, from *bis*, two, and *via*, passage.] having two ways, or leading two ways.
biv′i·um, *n.* [L. *bivius*, having two passages.] in zoology, the two posterior ambulacra of echinoderms, the three anterior ones being known as the *trivium.*
biv′ouac (biv′oo-ak *or* biv′wak), *n.* [Fr. *bivouac*; prob. from G. dial. *beiwacht*, lit., a by-watch; *bei*, by, and *wacht*, a guard.] a temporary encampment of soldiers in the open with or without shelter; hence, figuratively, a position or situation demanding extreme watchfulness.
The *bivouac* of life. —Longfellow.
biv′ouaç, *v.i.*; bivouacked (-akt), *pt., pp.*; bivouacking, *ppr.* to watch; to encamp in the open.
bī·week′ly, *a.* 1. occurring or appearing at intervals of two weeks; fortnightly.
2. semiweekly.
bī·week′ly, *n.*; *pl.* **bī·week′lies,** a periodical issued fortnightly or semiweekly.
bī·week′ly, *adv.* 1. once every two weeks.
2. semiweekly.
bi·wreye′ (-rā′), *v.t.* to bewray. [Obs.]
Bix′ȧ, *n.* a genus of plants of the Indian plum family, containing a few species of small trees native to tropical America. The pulp of the fruit of the *Bixa Orellana* yields annatto.
Bix·ā′cē·ae, *n.pl.* the Indian plum family, tropical trees and shrubs having simple leaves and showy axillary or terminal flowers.
bix·ā′ceous, *a.* of or pertaining to the *Bixa* or the *Bixaceæ.*
bix′in, *n.* the orange coloring principle, $C_{16}H_{20}O_5$, of annatto, occurring in small, yellowish crystals.
bī·yēar′ly, *a.* and *adv.* twice a year.
Bi·zan′tine, *a.* and *n.* same as *Byzantine.*
bi·zärre′, *a.* [Fr., from Sp. or Port. *bizarro*, bold, handsome, knightly, from Basque *bizar*, a beard.]
1. odd in manner, appearance, etc.; grotesque; queer; eccentric.
2. marked by extreme contrasts and incongruities of color, design, or style.
bi·zet′, *n.* [Fr. *biseau*, a sloping edge.] a bezel, or slanting face of a cut jewel.
Bk, in chemistry, berkelium.
blab, *v.t.* and *v.i.*; blabbed, *pt., pp.*; blabbing, *ppr.* [Dan. *blabbre*, babble; echoic.]
1. to utter or tell in a thoughtless manner; to give away (secrets) without discretion.
2. to chatter; to prattle.
blab, *n.* [ME. *blabbe.*]
1. loose chatter; gossip.
2. a babbler; one who betrays secrets.
blab′bẽr, *n.* [from ME. *blaberen*, to stammer; echoic.] a person who blabs.
blab′bẽr, *v.t.* and *v.i.* to blab; to babble. [Obs. or Dial.]
black, *a.* [ME. *blak, blek*, from AS. *blæc*, black.]
1. of the darkest color; the opposite of white. A surface perfectly black cannot reflect light.
2. dark in skin or complexion.
Black men are pearls in beauteous ladies' eyes. —Shak.
3. Negro.
4. destitute of light; in complete darkness; dark.
In the twilight, in the evening, in the *black* and dark night. —Prov. vii. 9.
5. figuratively, dismal, gloomy, sullen, forbidding, or the like; destitute of moral light or goodness; mournful; calamitous; evil; wicked; atrocious; thus Shakespeare speaks of *black* deeds, thoughts, envy, tidings, despair, etc.
6. soiled; dirty.
7. wearing black clothing.
8. disgraceful.
9. without hope; as, a *black* future.
10. inveterate; confirmed; deep-dyed; as, a *black* villain.
11. humorous or satirical in a morbid, cynical, or savage way; as, *black* comedy.
Black Act; in English history, statute 9 of George I's reign, which decreed that to appear armed in any park or warren, etc., or to hunt or steal deer, etc., with the face blacked or disguised, was felony: repealed in 1827.
black angelfish; a dark-colored fish of the family *Chætodontidæ.*
black antimony; the mineral stibnite, Sb_2S_3, the principal ore of antimony.
black art; necromancy; black magic.
black bass; (a) an eastern North American game and food fish, *Micropterus dolomieu.* The name is also given to the large-mouthed or straw bass, *Micropterus salmoides*; (b) the sea bass or blackfish.
black bear; see *bear* (sense 1).
black belt; (a) [often B– B–] that territory in the southern part of the U. S. where Negroes predominate; (b) any district, as of a city, in which Negroes predominate; (c) an area of very rich soil in the coastal plain of Alabama and Mississippi.
black bonnet; the European reed bunting.
black bur; the yellow avens, *Geum strictum.*
black cattle; beef cattle, regardless of their color, raised for slaughter, as distinguished from dairy animals. [Eng. Dial.]
Black Death; a deadly disease, probably bubonic plague, which spread over Asia and Europe in the fourteenth century and greatly reduced the population: so called from the black spots caused on the skin.
black earth; common black dirt or mold.
black flag; the flag of a pirate, usually with a white skull and crossbones on a black background; Jolly Roger.
black flux; a mixture of carbonate of potash and charcoal.
Black Friar; a friar of the Dominican order.
black hole; any subterranean or dark prison; used in reference to the Black Hole of Calcutta, an unventilated room about 18 feet square, in which 146 prisoners were confined on June 20, 1756, and only 23 were said to have survived.
black horse; a fish, the Missouri sucker, *Cycleptus elongatus.*
black manganese; pyrolusite, native manganese dioxide, MnO_2.
Black Maria; a vehicle, formerly painted black, used to take arrested persons to and from jail; patrol wagon.
Black Monday; Easter Monday, April 14, 1360, recorded in history as being so cold that many men of Edward III's army at Paris died from exposure.
Black Monk; a monk of the Benedictine order.
black oak; (a) the black-barked oak, *Quercus tinctoria*; (b) its wood.
black ocher; a variety of mineral black, combined with iron and alluvial clay; wad.
black pigment; a very fine, light, carbonaceous substance, or lampblack, prepared chiefly for the manufacture of printers' ink, and obtained by burning common coal tar.
black plate; sheet iron before tinning.
black pudding; a kind of pudding made of blood, suet, etc.; blood pudding.
black quarter; splenic fever; anthrax.
black rent; formerly, in England, rent paid in produce or copper coin.
Black Rod; (a) in England, the chief usher to the Order of the Garter and the House of Lords: so called from the black rod which he carries; (b) a similar official in British colonial parliaments.
black rust; grain blight, a dark-colored fungus attacking cereals, especially wheat.
black sheep; (a) a sheep with black fleece; (b) a member of a family or society regarded as undesirable, disgraceful, etc. by the other members.
black shirt, Black Shirt; formerly a member of the Italian Fascist Party or of the German Nazi Elite Guard: so called from their custom of wearing black shirts.
black silver; the mineral stephanite.
black tea; tea fermented and withered before being dried by heating.
black tin; tin ore made ready for smelting, having been finely powdered.
black turpeth; mercurous oxide. [Archaic.]
black vomit; (a) vomit characteristic of yellow fever, dark because of the blood in it; (b) yellow fever.
black walnut; (a) the American walnut, *Juglans nigra*, a tall tree with edible, oily nuts and hard, heavy dark-brown wood, much used in making furniture; (b) its wood; (c) its nut.
Black Watch; a famous Scottish regiment formed in the eighteenth century: so called because of their dark tartans.
black, *n.* [ME. *blak, blek*, from AS. *blæc*, black.]
1. the darkest color.
2. a black dye or pigment or a hue produced by such; as, this cloth has a good *black.*
3. the pupil of the eye. [Obs.]
4. black clothing, as for mourning; as, to be clothed in *black*: formerly used in the plural; as, to put on *blacks.*
5. a small flake of soot.
A fog that tastes of *blacks* and smells of decomposed frost. —Young.
6. one with the face blacked or disguised; specifically, a deer stealer. [Obs.]
7. a person of dark complexion.
8. a Negro.
black and white; (a) writing or print; as, a statement in *black and white*; (b) a sketch, drawing, or any picture done in black and white.
Brunswick black; see *Japan black.*
black, *v.t.* and *v.i.*; blacked, *pt., pp.*; blacking, *ppr.* 1. to make or become black; to blacken; to soil.
2. to put blacking on (shoes, etc.).
black ạl′dẽr, a shrub with glossy leaves and bright red berries; winterberry.
black′a·mọọr, *n.* 1. a Negro, especially an African Negro.
2. any dark-skinned person.
black′-and-blūe′, *a.* discolored from congestion of blood under the skin; bruised.
black′-and-tan′, *n.* a dog having a smooth, black coat and tan markings: also called *Manchester terrier, rat terrier.*
Black and Tan, a member of the British troops sent to Ireland to help put down disturbances during the Sinn Fein rebellion (1919–1921).
black ash, crude carbonate of soda.
black′-ȧ-vīsed (-vīst), *a.* of dark complexion; swarthy. [Dial.]
black′bạll, *n.* 1. a composition used by engravers, shoemakers, etc.: called also *heelball.*

2. originally, a small, black ball used as a vote against a person or thing.

3. a secret ballot or vote against a person or thing.

black′ball, *v.t.*; blackballed, *pt., pp.*; blackballing, *ppr.* 1. to vote against.

2. to exclude from social life, etc.; to ostracize.

black′band, *n.* a carbonate of iron, valuable as an iron ore.

black bee′tle, a cockroach.

black′bel″ly, *n.* the blueback, a kind of herring.

black belt, a black-colored belt or sash awarded to an expert in judo or karate: a beginner wears a *white belt*, and increasing degrees of skill are symbolized by belts of other colors, culminating in the black belt.

black′ber″ry, *n.* one of several species of fruit-bearing plants of the genus *Rubus*; also, the small, edible, dark purple or black fruit.

black′ber″ry lil′y, a plant of the iris family, bearing orange flowers with red spots, and fruit like a blackberry.

black bīnd′weed, 1. a European twining vine with long-stemmed leaves and small red berries.

2. a European twining plant now found in America as a tenacious weed.

black′bird, *n.* 1. any of several species of birds of the family *Icteridæ*, common throughout North America. The marsh or red-winged *blackbird* is *Agelaius phœniceus*; the crow *blackbird*, *Quiscalus quiscula*, etc.

2. in England, the European thrush, *Turdus merula*.

BLACKBIRD (*Turdus merula*)

black′bōard, *n.* a smooth surface of slate or other material, used in schools, lecture rooms, etc. for displaying writing and diagrams.

black′bod′y, *n.* an ideal surface or body that can absorb totally all radiation striking it.

black book, 1. a book for recording names of those black-listed.

2. a book dealing with black magic.

little black book; an address book for listing available women companions. [Colloq.]

to be in one's black book; to be regarded unfavorably by one.

black box, an intricate, compact assemblage of electronic equipment. [Slang.]

black′boy, *n.* an Australian plant with long, wiry leaves and long spikes of flowers.

black bread (bred), a dark, coarse bread, usually of rye flour.

black′-browed, *a.* having black eyebrows; hence, threatening; as, a *black-browed* look.

black buck, 1. a long-horned antelope of India, brownish-black above and white below.

2. the sable antelope of Africa.

black′çap, *n.* 1. the chickadee; also, the mock nightingale, *Sylvia atricapilla*, of Europe.

2. the black raspberry plant or its fruit.

black çat, a marten, the fisher.

black′çoat, *n.* a clergyman: a familiar name.

black′çock, *n.* the male of the black grouse, *Lyrurus tetrix*, a gallinaceous fowl of Europe and Asia. The female and young are called *gray hen* and *poults*, respectively.

BLACKCOCK (*Lyrurus tetrix*)

black çof′fee, coffee without cream or sugar.

black çoun′try, [often B– C–], a mining and industrial district in the English Midlands around Birmingham: so called from the prevailing soot and grime.

black′damp, *n.* same as *chokedamp*.

black dī′ȧ·mŏnds, coal.

black drȧft, a cathartic composed of senna, magnesia, fennel, etc.

black drop, a liquid preparation of opium in vinegar.

black′en, *v.t.*; blackened, *pt., pp.*; blackening, *ppr.* 1. to make black; to cloud.

2. to sully; as, vices *blacken* character.

Syn.—befoul, defame, calumniate, dishonor, asperse, traduce, malign.

black′en, *v.i.* to grow black or dark.

black′en·ẽr, *n.* one who or that which blackens.

black eȳe, 1. an eye with a very dark iris.

2. a discoloration of the skin or flesh surrounding an eye, resulting from a contusion.

3. (a) shame; dishonor; bad reputation; (b) a cause or source of this. [Colloq.]

black′-eȳed (-īd), *a.* having black eyes.

black′-eȳed pēaṣ, the seeds of the cowpea.

black′-eȳed Sū′ṣȧn, 1. a hairy plant bearing yellow, daisylike flowers with a purple-brown, cone-shaped center: also called *yellow daisy*.

2. the bladder ketmie.

black′fāce, *a.* 1. having a black or blackened face.

2. in printing, bold-faced.

black′fāce, *n.* 1. a Negro in a minstrel show.

2. a person made up as a Negro.

3. make-up used by performers of Negro roles, usually exaggerated for comic effect.

4. in printing, boldface.

Black′feet, *n.pl.*; *sing.* **Black′foot,** members of three tribes of North American Indians of the Algonquian stock, formerly living in Montana and Saskatchewan, east of the Rocky Mountains.

black′fel″lōw, *n.* a member of any dark-skinned native tribe of Australia: patronizing term.

black′fin, *n.* a food fish found in the Great Lakes, a kind of cisco.

black′fish, *n.*; *pl.* **black′fish, black′fish·eṣ,** 1. a small, black whale.

2. any of various black-colored fishes, as (a) the New England tautog; (b) the common sea bass or an allied fish; (c) *Centrolophus niger*, of Europe; (d) an Alaskan food fish, *Dallia pectoralis*; (e) a female salmon immediately after spawning.

black flēa, a coleopterous insect, *Haltica nemorum*, the turnip flea.

black flȳ, 1. the bean plant louse, *Aphis fabæ*.

2. any of a number of related small, biting flies of North American forests.

Black′foot, *n.*; *pl.* **Black′feet**; *collectively*, **Black′foot,** one of the Blackfeet.

Black′foot, *a.* of the Blackfeet.

Black Frī′dāy, Good Friday: so called because the clergy wear black vestments on that day.

black frost, a severe frost.

black gāme, the black grouse.

black grȧss, 1. a rush, *Juncus gerardi*, found in salt marshes in the United States.

2. an English grass, *Alopecurus agrestis*.

black grouse, the European grouse, *Lyrurus tetrix*.

black′guȧrd (blag′gärd), *n.* 1. originally, the lowest servants of a large household, in charge of pots and pans.

2. (a) one who uses scurrilous language; (b) a scoundrel; a villain.

black′guȧrd, *a.* scurrilous; abusive; vicious.

black′guȧrd, *v.t.* to revile; to abuse scurrilously.

black′guȧrd, *v.i.* to behave as a blackguard.

black′guȧrd·iṣm, *n.* the conduct of a blackguard.

black′guȧrd·ly, *a.* of or characteristic of a blackguard; scurrilous; abusive; rascally.

black′guȧrd·ly, *adv.* in the manner of a blackguard.

black gum, the pepperidge, *Nyssa sylvatica*, a tall tree with crooked branches, greenish-white flowers, and blue or purple fruit.

Black Hand, 1. originally, a nineteenth-century anarchist society in Spain.

2. a group of Sicilian immigrant blackmailers who operated in New York in the early twentieth century.

3. any similar secret society.

black haw, 1. a hawthorn common in the western United States.

2. a kind of viburnum with clusters of white flowers and blue-black berries.

3. the sheepberry, a related shrub.

black′head (-hed), *n.* 1. the scaup duck.

2. a black-tipped plug of dried fatty matter in a pore of the skin; comedo.

3. a disease of turkeys that affects the intestine, liver, and comb.

black′heȧrt, *n.* a dark-colored, heart-shaped cherry.

black′-heȧrt″ed, *a.* wicked; malevolent.

Black Hōle, 1. a small dungeon at Calcutta, India: on the night of June 20, 1756, 123 of the 146 Europeans reputedly confined there were said to have died from heat and lack of air. 2. any dungeon: also *black hole*.

black hōle, a hypothetical body in space, supposed to be an invisible collapsed star so condensed that neither light nor matter can escape from its gravitational field.

black hore′hound, a bad-smelling weed of the mint family, with purple flowers.

black′ing, *n.* that which makes black; specifically, a preparation for polishing shoes.

black′ish, *a.* somewhat black or dark.

black′jack, *n.* 1. a large leather vessel in which beer was formerly served.

2. a card game in which the object is to get a combination of cards adding to twenty-one.

3. in mining, zinc sulfide.

4. an oak, *Quercus marilandica*, of the eastern United States.

5. a pirate's flag; the black flag.

6. a small bludgeon-like weapon.

LEATHER BLACKJACKS

black′knot, *n.* a fungoid growth, *Dibotryon morbosa*, or the wartlike mass it produces on cherry and plum trees.

black′-lead (-led), *v.t.* to cover or polish with black lead, or graphite.

black lead, graphite: it is used in lead pencils, and as a polish or lubricant.

black′leg, *n.* 1. a professional gambler who cheats; a sharper. [Colloq.]

2. an infectious disease of cattle and sheep.

3. a fungous disease of cabbage, etc.

4. a strikebreaker or scab. [Brit.]

black let′tẽr, a kind of type, the Old English or Gothic, in which the early English manuscripts were written and the first English books were printed.

This line is set in black letter.

black′-list, *v.t.* to put on a black list.

black list, a list of persons debarred from employment, credit, etc. or to be punished.

black lung, a pneumoconiosis caused by the inhalation of coal dust.

black′ly, *adv.* 1. darkly; gloomily.

2. angrily; threateningly.

black maġ′iç, magic with an evil purpose; sorcery.

black′māil, *n.* [lit., black rent; from ME. *maille*; OFr. *maille*, a coin.]

1. formerly, a tribute paid in the north of England to freebooters and bandits to assure protection from pillage.

2. anything, as money, extorted by means of threats of exposure or danger.

3. the act of blackmailing.

black′māil, *v.t.* 1. to get or try to get blackmail from.

2. to coerce (*into* doing something) as by threats.

black′māil″ẽr, *n.* one who blackmails.

black märk, a mark indicating something unfavorable in one's record.

black mär′ket, illegal dealing in commodities; sale and purchase of goods at higher than legal prices; outlaw trading, as in rationed goods; also, the place where this is done.

black mass, 1. a religious service or mass at which the clergy are dressed in black.

2. a blasphemous imitation of the mass.

black mēa′sleṣ, see under *measles*.

black mōld, bread mold.

black mŏn′ey, income not reported to the government to avoid paying taxes on it; especially, such income derived from illegal activities.

Black Muṣ′lim, a member of a militant Islamic sect of American Negroes that advocates asceticism, racial separation, and the establishment of Negro States: members of the sect call themselves simply "Muslims."

black na′tion·ăl·iṣm, a movement advocating the establishment of a separate Negro nation within the United States.

black′ness, *n.* the quality or state of being black; black color; darkness.

black nīght′shāde, 1. a weedy plant of the nightshade family, with white flowers, poisonous leaves, and black berries.

2. the deadly nightshade.

black′out, *n.* 1. the extinguishing of all stage lights to end a play or scene.

2. the act of plunging a city or district into darkness as air-raid protection during war.
3. a momentary lapse of consciousness or vision.
4. a loss of memory of an event or fact.
5. suppression, censorship, concealment, etc., as of news.

black'out, *a.* pertaining to or for a blackout; as, a *blackout* curtain.

black pep'pẽr, 1. a hot seasoning made by grinding the dried, black berries of a kind of pepper plant.
2. the plant.

black'pōll, *n.* the wood warbler, the male of which has a black crown.

black'pōll wạr'blẽr, same as *blackpoll*.

black pow'ẽr, political and economic power as sought by black Americans in the struggle for civil rights.

black race, see *race* (sense 1).

black'ro͝ot, *n.* 1. a figwort.
2. a plant of the aster family.

black rot, see under *rot*.

black'smith, *n.* [AS. *blæc*, black, and *smid*, a smith.]
1. a man who works, repairs, and shapes iron with a forge, anvil, hammer, etc.; specifically, one who prepares and fits horseshoes.
2. a fish, *Chromis punctipinnis*, having a black back and spotted blue-black fins.

black'snāke, *n.* 1. an ophidian reptile, the *Coluber constrictor*, a common, harmless snake found in the United States. It is one of the largest North American snakes, reaching a length of five or six feet.

BLACKSNAKE (*Coluber constrictor*)

2. a Jamaican snake, *Natrix atra*.
3. a flexible, braided whip of leather or rawhide.
Also written *black snake*.

black spruce, see under *spruce*.

black'strap, *n.* 1. a mixture of molasses and rum, vinegar, etc.
2. among sailors, any of the dark-red wines of the Mediterranean region.
blackstrap molasses; crude, dark, thick molasses.

black'tāil, *n.* 1. a kind of perch; the pope.
2. the black-tailed deer, *Cariacus columbianus*, native to California, Washington, and British Columbia; also, the mule deer.

black'thorn, *n.* 1. the sloe, *Prunus spinosa*, a thorny, white-flowered shrub with purple or black, plumlike fruit.
2. the hedge hawthorn, *Cratægus tomentosa*, of America.
3. a walking stick made of the stem of the sloe.

black tie, 1. a black bow tie, properly worn with a dinner jacket.
2. a dinner jacket and the proper accessories.

black'top, *n.* a bituminous mixture, usually asphalt, used as a surface for roads, etc.

black'top, *v.t.*; blacktopped, *pt., pp.*; blacktopping, *ppr.* to cover with blacktop.

Black'wall hitch, a kind of knot: see *knot*, illus.

black'wăsh, *n.* 1. a mixture of calomel and limewater, used medicinally.
2. any preparation used as a black stain: opposed to *whitewash*.

black'wạ·tẽr fē'vẽr, an acute fever due to infection with malignant tertiary malaria.

black wi'dōw, a poisonous spider of the genus *Latrodectus*, especially, the female, which devours its mate.

black'wood, *n.* 1. the West Indian black mangrove, *Avicennia nitida*.
2. the wood of various trees; as (a) a papilionaceous East Indian tree, *Dalbergia latifolia*; (b) *Melharica melanoxylon*, of Australia.

black'wŏrk, *n.* unpolished parts of a machine, as those left rough from casting.

blad, *n.* a sharp blow. [Scot.]

blad'dẽr, *n.* [ME. *bladder, bleddre*, from AS. *blæddre*, a bladder.]
1. a bag or sac in animals, which serves as the receptacle of some secreted fluid; as, the urinary *bladder*, the gall *bladder*.
2. a thing resembling such a bag; as, a football *bladder*.
3. in botany, (a) a distended membranaceous pericarp; (b) an air sac, as in some water plants.
4. anything having marked distention; something empty or illogical; as, mere *bladders* of argument.

blad'dẽr, *v.t.* and *v.i.* 1. to put (something) into a bladder or bladders.
2. to puff up; to fill with wind. [Obs.]

blad'dẽr çam'pi·ŏn, a plant of the pink family, with an inflated calyx.

blad'dẽr hẽrb (ẽrb), the winter cherry.

blad'dẽr kelp, the bladder wrack; also, a laminarian North Pacific seaweed bearing an air bladder.

blad'dẽr ket'mie, a plant of the mallow family, having yellow flowers with dark centers.

blad'dẽr·nōṣe, *n.* a variety of seal, the male of which has on its head a hoodlike sac that can be inflated: also called *hooded seal*.

blad'dẽr·nut, *n.* 1. any of a number of related plants of the genus *Staphylea*, having inflated seed pods; also called *bladder tree*.
2. the seed pod of any of these plants.

blad'dẽr·pod, *n.* 1. a papilionaceous plant, genus *Physolobium*.
2. a genus of plants, *Vesicaria*, having bladderlike pods.

blad'dẽr·seed, *n.* any plant of the genus *Physospermum*, having inflated seeds.

blad'dẽr sen'nȧ, any shrub of the genus *Colutea*; specifically, *Colutea arborescens*.

blad'dẽr tree, a bladdernut.

blad'dẽr wŏrm, any encysted worm in its larval stage, as a tapeworm or trichina.

blad'dẽr·wŏrt, *n.* a genus of slender aquatic plants, *Utricularia*, the leaves of which have floating bladders.

blad'der wrack (rak), a seaweed, *Fucus vesiculosus*, having floating vesicles in its fronds.

blad'dẽr·y, *a.* resembling a bladder; containing a bladder or bladders.

blāde, *n.* [ME. *blad, blade*, from AS. *blæd*, a leaf.]
1. in botany, (a) the leaf of a plant, especially grass; (b) the broad part of a leaf; the lamina.
2. a thing resembling a blade in shape, etc.; (a) the cutting part of an instrument; as, the *blade* of a knife or sword; (b) the broad part of an oar; (c) the scapula or scapular bone; (d) [*pl.*] the four large plates of shell on the sides, and the five large plates in the middle, of the carapace of the turtle, which yield the best tortoise shell.
3. a dashing or rollicking fellow; a swaggerer; a rakish fellow.
He saw a turnkey in a trice
Fetter a troublesome *blade*. —Coleridge.
4. one of the main rafters of a roof.
5. a swordsman.
6. a flat bone; as, a shoulder *blade*.
7. in phonetics, the flat part of the tongue, behind the tip.

blāde, *v.t.*; bladed, *pt., pp.*; blading, *ppr.* to furnish with a blade.

blāde, *v.i.* to come into blade; to grow with blades.

blāde'bōne, *n.* the scapula, or upper bone in the shoulder.

blād'ed, *a.* 1. having a blade or blades; as, (a) an instrument; (b) a plant.
2. in mineralogy, composed of long, narrow plates like the blade of a knife.

blāde'fish, *n.*; *pl.* **blāde'fish, blāde'fish·eṣ,** an acanthopterygious fish, *Trichiurus lepturus*: so called from its flatness and resemblance to a sword blade.

blāde'smith, *n.* a sword cutler. [Obs.]

blād'y, *a.* like or having a blade or blades. [Rare.]

blae (blā *or* blē), *a.* [Scot., from ME. *bla, blaa*, blue, from Ice. *blār*, dark blue, livid; AS. *blænen*, bluish.] of a dark-blue or bluish-gray color. [Scot.]

blāe'ber″ry, *n.* [Ice. *blāber.*] the bilberry. [Scot.]

blȧgue (blȧg), *n.* [Fr. *blaguer*, to humbug.] arrant jesting; humbug.

blăh, *interj.* and *n.* nonsense. [Slang.]

blāin, *n.* [ME. *blane, blayn*; AS. *blegen*, a blister, from same root as *blāwan*, to blow.]
1. a pustule; a blister.
2. in cattle, a bladder growing on the root of the tongue against the windpipe, which swells so as to stop the breath.

blām'ȧ·ble, blāme'ȧ·ble, *a.* faulty; culpable; reprehensible; deserving of censure.

blām'ȧ·ble·ness, blāme'ȧ·ble·ness, *n.* culpableness; fault; the state of being deserving of censure.

blām'ȧ·bly, blāme'ȧ·bly, *adv.* culpably; in a manner deserving of censure.

blāme, *v.t.*; blamed, *pt., pp.*; blaming, *ppr.* [ME. *blamen*; OFr. *blasmer*, to speak evil of; LL. *blasphemare*; Gr. *blasphēmein*, to speak ill of.]
1. to censure; to accuse (a person, etc.) of being at fault; condemn (*for* something.)
2. to find fault with (*for* something).
3. to put the responsibility of, as an error, fault, etc. (*on* someone or something).
4. to bring reproach upon; to blemish. [Obs.]
She had *blamed* her noble blood. —Spenser.
to be to blame; to be blamable; to be at fault; as, inattention *is to blame* for that.
Syn.—censure, condemn, reprehend, reproach, reprove, upbraid.

blāme, *n.* 1. censure; reprehension; accusation; condemnation.
Let me bear the *blame* forever. —Gen. xliii. 9.
2. responsibility for a fault or wrong.
3. fault; crime; sin; that which is deserving of censure or disapprobation. [Archaic.]
That we should be holy and without *blame* before him in love. —Eph. i. 4.
4. hurt; injury. [Obs.]
And glancing down his shield, from *blame* him fairly blest. —Spenser.

blāmed, *a.* and *adv.* [pp. of *blame.*] a mild expletive, used as a substitute for *damned*. [Colloq.]

blāme'fụl, *a.* meriting blame; giving blame; reprehensible; faulty; guilty; criminal.
Thy mother took into her *blameful* bed
Some stern, untutored churl. —Shak.

blāme'fụl·ly, *adv.* in a blameful manner.

blāme'fụl·ness, *n.* the state of being blameful.

blāme'less, *a.* without fault; innocent; guiltless; not meriting censure: sometimes followed by *of*.
We will be *blameless of* this thine oath. —Josh. ii. 17.
Syn.—faultless, guiltless, innocent, irreproachable, spotless, unblemished.

blāme'less·ly, *adv.* in a blameless manner.

blāme'less·ness, *n.* the state of being blameless.

blām'ẽr, *n.* one who blames or censures.

blāme'wŏr″thi·ness, *n.* the quality of being blameworthy.

blāme'wŏr″thy, *a.* deserving blame; censurable; culpable; reprehensible.

blanç (*Fr. pron.* blän), *n.* [Fr. *blanc*, white.]
1. a base silver coin of the reign of Henry V of England. It was so called from its color, and to distinguish it from the gold coins which were then coined. Also spelled *blank, blanck*.
2. a small silver coin of France, first coined by Philip of Valois.
3. white paint; a cosmetic.
4. a rich gravy used in serving entrees.

blañ'çärd, *n.* [Fr. *blanc*, white.] a kind of linen cloth manufactured in Normandy: so called because the thread is half blanched before it is woven.

blȧnch, *v.t.*; blanched, *pt., pp.*; blanching, *ppr.* [ME. *blaunchen*; OFr. *blanchir*, to whiten.]
1. to whiten; to remove the color of and make white; to bleach.
2. to make pale.
3. in horticulture, to bleach (endive, celery, etc.) by keeping the leaves of a plant from the light, to improve the flavor and texture.
4. to palliate; to pass over. [Rare.]
5. in cookery, (a) to remove the skin of by scalding; (b) to soak (meat or vegetables) in hot water, or to scald in order to make firm or white.
6. in metallurgy, (a) to whiten or make lustrous, as metals, by acids or other means; (b) to cover with a thin coating of tin.

blȧnch, *v.i.* to whiten; to turn pale; as, his cheeks *blanched* with fear.

blȧnch, *v.t.* to evade; to pass by or avoid, as from fear; to shrink from. [Obs.]

blȧnch, *v.i.* to practice evasion; to fail; to be reserved; to remain blank or silent. [Obs.]
Books will speak plain, when counsellors *blanch*. —Bacon.

blȧnch, *v.t.* [var. of *blench.*] to turn aside or head off (a deer, etc.).

blȧnch, *a.* [OFr. *blanche*, f. of *blanc*, white.] white. [Obs.]

blȧnch, *n.* 1. in mining, lead ore found together with other minerals.
2. a cosmetic. [Obs.]

blȧnch′ẽr, *n.* one who or that which blanches, or whitens.

blȧnch hōld′ing, [Scot.] in law, a tenure by which the tenant is bound to pay only a nominal yearly duty to his superior, as an acknowledgment of his right, and only if demanded.

blȧnch·im′e·tẽr, *n.* [*blanch*, and Gr. *metron*, measure.] an instrument for measuring the bleaching power of chloride of lime and potash.

blȧnch′ing liq′uŏr (lik′ũr), a solution of chloride of lime for bleaching.

blanc·mange′ (blȧ-mäṅzh′), *n.* [Fr. *blanc*, white, and *manger*, to eat.] a sweet, molded, jellylike dessert made of a starchy substance and milk.

blanc·man′ger (blȧ-mäṅ′zhā), *n.* blancmange. [Obs.]

bland, *a.* [L. *blandus*, mild.]
1. mild; soft; gentle; balmy.
Like the bountiful season *bland*.
—Tennyson.
2. affable; suave; kindly; as, *bland* manners.
3. soothing: said of drugs.

blan·dā′tion, *n.* gross flattery. [Obs.]

blan·dil′ō·quence, *n.* [L. *blandus*, mild, and *loqui*, to speak.] fair, mild, flattering speech. [Rare.]

blan·dil′ō·quous (-kwus), *a.* flattering; smooth of speech. [Rare.]

blan′dise, *v.t.* same as *blandish*. [Obs.]

blan′dish, *v.t.*; blandished, *pt., pp.*; blandishing, *ppr.* [ME. *blaundishen*; OFr. *blandir*; L. *blandiri*, to flatter.]
1. to soften; to coax; to cajole; to flatter by using kind words or affectionate actions.
2. to render pleasing, alluring, or enticing.
In former days a country life
Was *blandish'd* by perpetual spring.
—Cooper.

blan′dish·ẽr, *n.* one who or that which flatters.

blan′dish·ment, *n.* [OFr. *blandissement*, from *blandir*, to flatter; L. *blandiri*, to flatter.] the act of blandishing; soft words; kind speeches; caresses; expressions of kindness; words or actions expressive of affection or kindness, and tending to win the heart; enticement; flattery.

bland′ly, *adv.* in a bland manner.

bland′ness, *n.* the state of being bland.

blaṅk, *a.* 1. white or pale; colorless. [Rare.]
Blank as death in marble. —Tennyson.
2. not written on; not marked; empty; as, a *blank* sheet of paper.
3. having an empty, vacant, or monotonous look or character.
4. without interest or expression; as, *blank* looks.
5. empty of thought; lacking ideas; as, my mind is *blank*.
6. unproductive; barren; as, *blank* years.
7. pale from fear or terror; hence, confused; confounded; dispirited; dejected.
Adam astonished stood, and *blank*.
—Milton.
8. pure; unmingled; entire; complete; as, *blank* stupidity.
9. lacking certain elements or characteristics.
blank bar; in law, a common bar, or a plea in bar, which, in an action of trespass, is put in to oblige the plaintiff to assign the place where the trespass was committed.
blank cartridge; a powder-filled cartridge without a bullet.
blank door, or *blank window*; in architecture, an imitation door or window.
blank line; in printing, a blank space, as wide as a line, on a printed page.
blank verse; (a) rarely, unrhymed verse; (b) unrhymed verse typically having five iambic feet per line, as in Elizabethan drama.

blaṅk, *n.* [ME. *blank*; OFr. *blanc*, f. *blanche*; O.H.G. *blanch*, white, lustrous.]
1. an empty space, especially one to be filled out in a printed form or document.
2. a printed form or document with such empty spaces; as, a mortgage *blank*, a notary's *blank*.
3. an emptiness; a void; a vacancy; as, a *blank* in one's memory.
4. a ticket in a lottery on which no prize is won; a lot by which nothing is gained.
5. in archery, the white mark in the center of a target; hence, a thing aimed at or pointed at.
6. a coin, the blanc.
7. a small copper coin formerly current in France.
8. a manufactured article yet to be cut to a pattern or marked with a design.
9. a blank cartridge.
10. a mark, usually a dash (—), indicating an omitted word, especially an oath or curse.
11. a blank verse. [Obs.]
to draw a blank; 1. to draw a lottery ticket that fails to win.
2. to be unsuccessful or unlucky in any attempt. [Colloq.]

blaṅk, *v.t.*; blanked, *pt., pp.*; blanking, *ppr.*
1. to conceal or obscure by covering over (usually with *out*).
2. in games, to hold (an opponent) scoreless.
3. to make void; to annul. [Obs.]
4. to deprive of color; to blanch; as, to *blank* the face of joy. [Obs.]

blaṅk′book″, a book of blank pages used for keeping notes, records, etc.

blaṅk check, 1. a check form that has not been filled in.
2. a check carrying a signature only and allowing the bearer to fill in any amount; hence, permission to use an unlimited amount of money, authority, etc.

blaṅk en·dorse′ment, an endorsement naming no payee, making the endorsed amount payable to the bearer.

blaṅ′ket, *n.* [ME. *blanket*; OFr. *blanquete*, a blanket; dim. of *blanc*, white.]
1. a cover for a bed, often made of soft woolen cloth; also, a similar fabric used as a robe or as a cover for a horse, etc.
2. anything used as or resembling a blanket; as, a *blanket* of leaves.
3. in printing, woolen cloth, felt, rubber, or other material used to cover the impression surface, to prevent damage to the type.
4. a layer of blubber in whales.

blaṅ′ket, *a.* covering a group of conditions or requirements; including many items; as, a *blanket* insurance policy.
blanket ballot; a large ballot sheet containing the names of the candidates for many offices, to be voted for at the same time.
blanket mortgage; a mortgage given to secure various items of indebtedness or to cover numerous items and various forms of property.
blanket policy; in fire insurance, a policy written on several risks to cover any one of them for the face of the policy in case of loss.

blaṅ′ket, *v.t.*; blanketed, *pt., pp.*; blanketing, *ppr.* 1. to cover with or as with a blanket.
2. to toss in a blanket, as for punishment.
3. to take the wind out of the sails of (a sailboat, etc.), by passing close to windward, as in yacht racing.
4. to apply uniformly to, as regulations or rates.
5. to overspread; to overlie.
6. to suppress; to hinder; to obscure; as, a powerful radio station *blankets* a weaker one.

blaṅ′ket·ing, *n.* 1. the punishment or act of tossing in a blanket.
2. cloth for blankets.

blaṅ′ket sheet, a large folio newspaper.

blaṅ′ke·ty·blaṅk, *a.* and *adv.* humorous euphemism for damned, etc. [Slang.]

blaṅk′ly, *adv.* 1. in a blank manner; without expression.
2. directly; positively; point-blank.

blaṅk′ness, *n.* the state of being blank.

blaṅ·quette′ (-ket′), *n.* [Fr. dim. of *blanc*, white.] in cookery, a white fricassee.

blaṅ·quil′lō (-kēl′yo), *n.* [Sp. *blanquillo*, whitish, dim. of *blanco*, white.] any of several large fishes of the genus *Caulolatilus*, especially a species which is found off the coast of Florida and in the West Indies, and the Pacific whitefish.

blāre, *v.i.*; blared, *pt., pp.*; blaring, *ppr.* [ME. *bleren*, to cry, weep; echoic.] to roar; to sound loudly.

blāre, *v.t.* to proclaim noisily; to tell abroad as with a trumpet; as, he *blared* the news.

blāre, *n.* 1. a roar; a noise; a blast, as of a trumpet.
2. brilliance or glare, as of color.

blär′ney, *n.* [see *Blarney stone*.] smooth, deceitful talk; flattery.

blär′ney, *v.t.* and *v.i.*; blarneyed, *pt., pp.*; blarneying, *ppr.* to influence or wheedle with smooth talk; to flatter.

Blär′ney stōne, a stone in Blarney Castle in the county of Cork, Eire, said to impart skill in blarney to those who kiss it.

bla·sé′ (blȧ-zā′), *a.* [Fr., pp. of *blaser*, to satiate.] satiated and bored by excess of entertainment or enjoyment; having the appetite for physical or social pleasures deadened by indulgence.

blȧs·phēme′, *v.t.*; blasphemed, *pt., pp.*; blaspheming, *ppr.* [ME. *blasfemen*; OFr. *blasfemer*; LL. *blasphemare*; Gr. *blasphēmein*, to speak evil of.]
1. to speak of (sacred things) in terms of irreverence; to revile or speak reproachfully of (God or anything sacred).
2. to speak evil of; to utter abuse or calumny against; to curse or revile (another).

blȧs·phēme′, *v.i.* to utter blasphemy.

blȧs·phēm′ẽr, *n.* one who blasphemes.

blȧs′phē·mous, *a.* characterized by blasphemy; calumnious; irreverent; profane.

blȧs′phē·mous·ly, *adv.* in a blasphemous manner.

blȧs′phē·my, *n.*; *pl.* **blȧs′phē·mieṣ,** 1. profane or mocking speech, writing, or action concerning God or anything regarded as sacred.
In law, blasphemy is an indictable offense defined as wanton and malicious revilement of God and the Christian religion. In English law, according to Blackstone, blasphemy is an offense against God and religion, by impiously denying the existence or providence of God, by contumelious reproaches of Jesus Christ, or by profanely scoffing at Holy Scripture or exposing it to contempt and ridicule.
2. contempt for God.
3. vilification; malicious detraction; abuse; used figuratively in regard to things held in high esteem; as, *blasphemy* against the theory of equality. [Obs.]

-blast, [Gr. *blastos*, a sprout.] a combining form meaning *formative, germinative, embryonic*, as in meso*blast*, osteo*blast*.

blȧst, *n.* [ME. *blast*, *blest*; AS. *blæst*, a puff of wind.]
1. a gust or violent puff of wind; a sudden rush of air.
2. the sound made by a sudden rush of air or gas; as, he blew a *blast* upon the bugle.
3. an abrupt and destructive influence upon animals or plants; a blight.
4. a disease of sheep, in which the stomach and bowels are distended with air.
5. a forcible, artificially created stream of air.
6. a violent explosion of gunpowder, etc.
7. a charge of explosive causing this.
8. in smelting, the steady stream of air forced into a blast furnace to aid combustion.
9. the exhaust steam from an engine, used to create an intense draft through the fire by driving air out of a boiler chimney.
hot blast, cold blast; the state (heated or unheated) of a current of air on its entrance to the blast furnace.
in full blast, or *at full blast*; at full speed or capacity.
Syn.—explosion, blight, burst, blaze, destruction, squall, gale, tempest, hurricane.

blȧst, *v.t.*; blasted, *pt., pp.*; blasting, *ppr.* 1. to damage or destroy by or as by a blight; to wither; to shrivel; to ruin.
2. to blow up or move with or as with an explosive; to explode.
3. to confound, or strike with force, by a loud blast or din. [Obs.]
Syn.—blight, shrivel, destroy, wither, desolate.

blȧst, *v.i.* 1. to be withered or blighted.
2. to blow, as on a trumpet. [Obs.]

blȧst′ed, *a.* 1. affected by some cause that checks growth; blighted; withered; destroyed.
2. damned; confounded; accursed: used as a mild form of oath.

blas·tē′mȧ, *n.*; *pl.* **blas·tē′mȧ·tȧ,** [Gr. *blastēma*, a bud, from *blastanein*, to bud or sprout.] the undifferentiated embryonic tissue from which cells, tissues, and organs are developed.

blas·tē′măl, *a.* pertaining to the blastema.

blas·te·mat′iç, *a.* pertaining to or proceeding from the blastema.

blȧst′ẽr, *n.* one who or that which blasts.

blȧst fŭr′nȧce, a towerlike furnace for separating metal from the impurities in the ore: a blast of air is forced into the furnace from below to produce the intense heat needed.

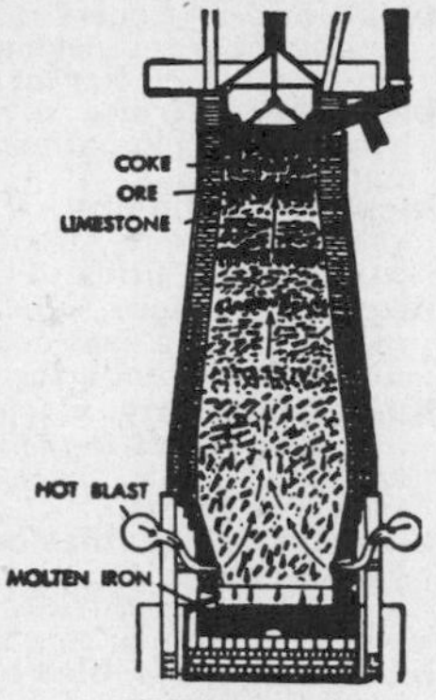

COKE
ORE
LIMESTONE
HOT BLAST
MOLTEN IRON

BLAST FURNACE

blas′tī, *n.* plural of *blastus.*

-blas′tiç, a combining form containing *-blast,* from the Greek *blastos,* a sprout, and *-ic:* used to signify *germinating.*

blas′tid, *n.* one of the *Blastoidea.*

blas′tide (*or* -tīd), *n.* [Gr. *blastos,* sprout, germ.] the first indication of the nucleus in a fertilized ovum.

blȧs′tie, *n.* a dwarf. [Scot.]

blȧst′ing, *n.* 1. a blast; a blight.
2. the act of splitting rock, etc., as by an explosion of gunpowder.
3. the occupation of a blaster.

blȧst′ment, *n.* a blast; a sudden stroke of some destructive cause. [Obs.]

blas′tō-, [Gr. *blastos,* a sprout.] a combining form used in biology to signify *connection with the embryo, relation to germination,* as in *blasto*derm, *blasto*genesis: also, before a vowel, *blast-.*

blas·tō·çăr′pous, *a.* [*blasto-,* and Gr. *karpos,* fruit.] in botany, germinating inside the pericarp, as the mangrove.

blas′tō·çhēme, *n.* [*blasto-,* and Gr. *ochema,* a support, from *ochein,* to carry.] a special sexual bud in hydroid medusas.

blas′tō·çhȳle, *n.* [*blasto-,* and Gr. *chylos,* juice.] the fluid substance that fills the segmentation cavity.

blas′tō·coele, *n.* [*blasto-,* and Gr. *koilos,* hollow.] the segmentation cavity of a developing ovum or of the blastula.

blas·tō·çol′lȧ, *n.* [*blasto-,* and Gr. *kolla,* glue.] a balsamic gum that protects the buds of certain plants from the weather.

blas′tō·cyst, *n.* [*blasto-,* and Gr. *kystis,* bladder.] a blastula.

blas′tō·dẽrm, *n.* [*blasto-,* and Gr. *derma,* skin.] the portion of the fertilized ovum that gives rise to the germinal disk from which the embryo develops.

blas·tō·dẽr′miç, blas″tō·dẽr·mat′iç, *a.* relating to the blastoderm.
blastodermic vesicle; the blastula.

blas′tō·disk, *n.* [*blasto-,* and Gr. *diskos,* a disk.] in embryology, the germinal disk.

blas·tō·ġen′e·sis, *n.* [*blasto-,* and Gr. *genesis,* origin.]
1. reproduction by budding, as in coral.
2. the theory that the germ plasm transmits hereditary characteristics: opposed to *pangenesis.*

blas′toid, *n.* a budlike fossil; one of the *Blastoidea.*

blas′toid, *a.* of or pertaining to the *Blastoidea.*

Blas·toid′ē·ȧ, *n.pl.* [*blasto-,* and Gr. *eidos,* form, shape.] a division of budlike fossils found in Paleozoic rocks.

blas′tō·mēre, *n.* [*blasto-,* and Gr. *meros,* a part.] in embryology, any of the first segments formed by the division of the ovum after fertilization.

Blas″tō·mȳ·cē′tēs, *n. pl.* a genus of pathogenic yeasts: formerly called *Saccharomycetaceæ.*

blas·toph′ō·răl, blas·tō·phor′iç, *a.* pertaining to the blastophore.

blas·toph′y·ly, *n.* [Gr. *blastos,* germ, and *phylē,* tribe.] the tribal history of persons.

blas′tō·pōre, *n.* [*blasto-,* and Gr. *poros,* a passage.] the duct leading into the gastrula cavity, or archenteron.

blas′tō·sphēre, *n.* [*blasto-,* and Gr. *sphaira,* a sphere.] a blastula.

blas′tō·stȳle, *n.* [*blasto-,* and Gr. *stylos,* a pillar.] a simple zooid which produces generative buds.

blȧst pīpe, a pipe, as in a locomotive engine, to carry the exhaust steam up the stack so as to create a strong draft.

blas′tū·lȧ, *n.*; *pl.* **blas′tū·lae,** [L., from Gr. *blastos,* a sprout, germ.]
1. the stage of development at which an embryo consists of one or several layers of cells around a central cavity, forming a hollow sphere.
2. an embryo at this stage.

blas′tū·lăr, *a.* of, or having the nature of, a blastula.

blas′tūle, *n.* same as *blastula.*

blas′tus, *n.*; *pl.* **blas′tī,** the plumule, or rudimentary bud, of grasses.

blȧst′y, *a.* 1. affected by sudden puffs of wind; gusty.
2. causing blights. [Obs.]

blat, *v.t.*; blatted, *pt., pp.*; blatting, *ppr.* to utter heedlessly; to blurt out; to blab; as, he *blatted* the news. [Colloq.]

blat, *v.i.* to make a sound like that of a sheep or calf; to bleat. [Colloq.]

blā′tăn·cy, *n.*; *pl.* **blā′tăn·cieş,** a blatant quality or thing.

blā′tănt, *a.* 1. bellowing, as a calf.
2. loud-mouthed; offensively noisy.
3. too conspicuous; obtrusive.
4. very showy; gaudy; flashy.

blā′tănt·ly, *adv.* in a blatant manner.

blāte, *a.* 1. bashful; naturally diffident. [Scot. and Prov. Eng.]
2. dull or spiritless. [Obs.]

blath′ẽr, *v.i.* and *v.t.* to talk nonsensically.

blath′ẽr, *n.* foolish or nonsensical talk.

blath′ẽr·skīte, *n.* 1. balderdash; nonsense. [Colloq.]
2. a talkative, foolish person. [Colloq.]

Blat′tȧ, *n.* [L., a beetle, or cockroach.]
1. a genus of insects of the family *Blattidæ,* including the cockroach.
2. [b-] a cockroach; an insect of the genus *Blatta.*

blat′tȧ, *n.* an interwoven silk of purple and gold used in the Middle Ages.

blat′tẽr, *v.i.* and *v.t.* [L. *blaterare,* to prate, babble.] to talk or utter volubly; to rattle; to patter; as, the hail *blatters.* [Rare.]

blat′tẽr, *n.* a continuous clattering noise; as, the *blatter* of hail. [Rare.]

blat·tẽr·ā′tion, *n.* the act of blustering; blattering. [Obs.]

blat′tẽr·ẽr, *n.* a noisy, blustering boaster. [Obs.]

blat′tẽr·ing, *n.* senseless blustering or boasting. [Obs.]

blat·tẽr·ọọn′, *n.* a blatterer. [Obs.]

blau′bok, *n.*; *pl.* **blau′bok, blau′boks,** [D., bluebuck.] a large, bluish-gray antelope of South Africa, now extinct; the bluebuck: also spelled *blauwbok.*

blạw, *v.t.* and *v.i.* to blow. [Brit. Dial. or Scot.]

blā′wŏrt, *n.* [Scot. *bla, blae,* blue, and *wort,* an herb.]
1. the harebell.
2. the bluebottle (plant).

blāy, *n.* a river fish, the bleak.

blāze, *n.* [ME. *blase,* a flame; AS. *blæse, blase,* a flame, torch.]
1. the brilliant mass or burst of flame from any substance when burning; fire.
2. an outburst of any quality or emotion; a sudden, spectacular occurrence; as, a *blaze* of anger.
3. any bright light or glare; as, the *blaze* of searchlights.
4. a brightness; vivid display; flash.
5. [*pl.*] hell: a euphemism, especially in the phrase *go to blazes!*

blāze, *v.i.*; blazed, *pt., pp.*; blazing, *ppr.* 1. to burn rapidly or brightly; to flame; as, the fire *blazes.*
2. to send forth or show a strong, bright light; to glare.
3. to be deeply stirred or excited, as with anger.

blāze, *v.t.* 1. to cause to flame or burn.
2. to shine with (light, etc.).
to blaze away; (a) to fire guns; to shoot; (b) to speak rapidly or heatedly.

blāze, *v.t.* [ME. *blasen,* to blow as a trumpet; D. *blazen;* O.H.G. *blāsan;* Ice. *blāsa;* Goth. *blēsan,* from *blāwan,* to blow, breathe.] to make public far and wide; to spread the news of; to proclaim.

To *blaze* those virtues which the good would hide. —Pope.

blāze, *n.* [prob. D., *blaze,* from *bles,* white spot, from ON *blesi,* from same ult. source as *blaze* (flame).]
1. a white or light-colored spot on the face of a horse or other animal.
2. a mark made on a tree by cutting off a piece of bark.

blāze, *v.t.* 1. to make a mark on (a tree) by paring off a part of the bark.
2. to indicate (a trail, path, etc.) by cutting the bark of trees so as to show a succession of white spots.

blāz′ẽr, *n.* 1. that which blazes or flames.
2. a light sports jacket, usually of a bright color.
3. a dish used for cooking over a chafing-dish lamp, or coals of a brazier.

blāz′ing, *a.* emitting flame or light.

blāz′ing stär, 1. a comet. [Obs.]
2. in heraldry, a star having six points and a comet's tail.
3. any of a number of unrelated American plants bearing showy, colorful flowers, as the button snakeroot, torch lily, fairy wand, etc.
4. a person or thing that attracts great attention.

blā′zŏn, *v.t.*; blazoned, *pt., pp.*; blazoning, *ppr.* [Fr. *blasonner,* to blazon; It. *blasonare,* from *blason,* a shield, coat of arms; confused with O.H.G. *blāsan,* to blow, to sound a trumpet, proclaim.]
1. to explain in technical terms, as the figures on armorial bearings or heraldic devices.
2. to deck; to embellish; to adorn.

She *blazons* in dread smiles her hideous form. —Garth.

3. to display; to celebrate by words or writing; to make known far and wide; to proclaim (often with *forth, out,* or *abroad.*)

There pride sits *blazoned* on th' unmeaning brow. —Trumbull.

4. to paint (coats of arms); to emblazon.

blā′zŏn, *n.* 1. a technical description or illustration of a coat of arms.
2. a coat of arms; an armorial shield; heraldic bearing.
3. show; pompous display, either by words or by other means.

blā′zŏn, *v.i.* to be conspicuous, shining, or prominent. [Rare.]

blā′zŏn·ẽr, *n.* one who blazons coats of arms; also, one who proclaims loudly or extravagantly.

blā′zŏn·ment, *n.* 1. a blazoning.
2. a thing blazoned.

blā′zŏn·ry, *n.*; *pl.* **blā′zŏn·rieş,** 1. the art of properly describing or illustrating coats of arms.
2. emblems or bearings of heraldry; coats of arms.
3. any brilliant display.

-ble, same as *-able.*

blēa, *n.* the part of a tree which lies immediately under the bark. [Rare.]

blēa′ber″ry, *n.* same as *blaeberry.*

blēach, *v.t.*; bleached, *pt., pp.*; bleaching, *ppr.* [ME. *bleche;* AS. *blæcan,* from *blac,* pale, bleak.]
1. to whiten; blanch.
2. to make colorless, as by means of chemicals or by exposure to the sun's rays.

blēach, *v.i.* to become white, colorless, or pale.

blēach, *n.* 1. a bleaching or whitening.
2. any chemical used to bleach something.
3. the degree of whiteness resulting from bleaching.

blēach′ẽr, *n.* 1. one who whitens, or whose occupation is to whiten cloth.
2. any utensil or apparatus used for bleaching.

blēach′ẽrs, *n.pl.* [from *bleacher;* in reference to the effects of exposure.] seats for spectators at outdoor baseball games, sporting events, etc.: most bleachers are roofless and are made of planks laid lengthwise.

blēach′ẽr·y, *n.*; *pl.* **blēach′ẽr·ieş,** a place where bleaching is done; as, a wax *bleachery.*

blēach fiēld, a field where cloth or yarn is bleached.

blēach′ing, *n.* the act or art of whitening, especially cloth.

blēach′ing pow′dẽr, a powder used in bleaching, usually chloride of lime.

blēak, *a.* [ME. *bleke, blake, blak;* AS. *blac, blæc,* pale, wan, from *blican,* to shine.]
1. pale; wan; of sickly color.
2. open; desolate; exposed to wind and cold; unsheltered; as, a *bleak* hill.
3. cold; piercing; as, *bleak* winds.
4. cheerless; gloomy; desolate; depressing.
Syn.—cold, cutting, harsh, bare, stormy, nipping.

blēak, *n.* [ME. *bleke;* AS. *blæga,* pale, from the color of its scales.] a small, slender, European river fish of the carp family, five or six inches long, so named from its whiteness. It belongs to the genus *Alburnus.* Its silvery scales are used in the manufacture of artificial pearls.

blēak′ish, *a.* of a bleak, cheerless nature.

blēak′ly, *adv.* in a bleak, desolate manner.

blēak′ness, *n.* the state or quality of being bleak.

blēak′y, *a.* somewhat bleak.

blēar, *a.* 1. made dim by tears, mucous film, etc.: applied to the eye.
2. indistinct; blurred; misty; dim; obscure.

blēar, *v.t.*; bleared, *pt., pp.*; blearing, *ppr.* [ME. *bleren,* to make dim; Dan. *blire,* to blink; G. *blerr,* an ailment of the eyes.]
1. to dim (the eyes) with tears, film, etc.
2. to obscure (the face) with tears, etc.
3. to blur (a surface or an outline.)

blēar'ed·ness, *n.* the state of being bleared, or dimmed with tears, etc.

blēar'eȳe, *n.* a chronic disease of the eyelids, causing inflammation of the margins with gummy secretions.

blēar'-eȳed (-īd), *a.* 1. having blear eyes; dim-sighted.
2. dull-witted.

blēar'eȳed·ness, *n.* the condition of being blear-eyed.

blēar'i·ly, *adv.* in a bleary manner.

blēar'i·ness, *n.* a bleary state or quality.

blēar'y, *a.*; *comp.* blearier; *superl.* bleariest.
1. somewhat blear or blurred.
2. having blear eyes.

blēat, *v.i.*; bleated, *pt., pp.*; bleating, *ppr.* [ME. *bleten*; AS. *blætan,* to bleat; L. *balare*; Gr. *blēchē,* a bleating.]
1. to make the cry of a sheep, lamb, goat, or calf.
2. to make a sound like this cry.
3. to speak foolishly, whine, etc.

blēat, *v.t.* to say in a weak, trembling voice.

blēat, *n.* 1. the cry of a sheep, goat, or calf.
2. any noise like this.

blēat'ẽr, *n.* an animal that bleats, as a sheep.

blēat'ing, *a.* crying like a sheep, goat, or calf.

blēat'ing, *n.* the cry of a sheep, goat, or calf.

bleb, *n.* [from ME. *bleb, blob* from sound produced in forming a bubble with the lips.]
1. a small swelling on the skin or on plants; blister; vesicle.
2. an air bubble, as in water or glass.

bleb'by, *a.* full of blebs.

bleck, *v.t.* to pollute; to defile; to blacken. [Obs.]

bled, *v.,* past tense and past participle of *bleed.*

bleed, *v.i.*; bled, *pt., pp.*; bleeding, *ppr.* [ME. *bleden*; AS. *blēdan,* to bleed, from *blōd,* blood.]
1. to lose blood; to emit blood; as, his arm is *bleeding.*
2. to suffer wounds or die from loss of blood.
3. to suffer; feel pain, grief, or sympathy.
4. to ooze.
5. to ooze sap, juice, etc., as bruised plants.
6. to run together, as dyes in wet cloth.
7. to come through a covering coat of paint, as certain stains.
8. in printing and bookbinding, to have a small part at the edge cut off when the paper is trimmed: said of pictures, designs, etc.
to bleed white; (a) to bleed until all the blood is out; (b) to take all the money or resources from.

bleed, *v.t.* 1. to let blood from; to take blood from by opening a vein; to leech.
2. to lose or exude (sap, etc.).
3. to extort valuables from; to cheat; to sponge on. [Colloq.]
4. to draw sap or juice from.
5. to empty of liquid or gas.
6. in printing and bookbinding, to print (a picture, design, etc.) so that a small part at the edge is cut off when the paper is trimmed.

bleed, *n.* in bookbinding and printing, that part of the printed or engraved matter which overlaps the margin to be trimmed; a page or picture having such a margin.

bleed, *a.* pertaining to a bleed or bleed page.

bleed'ẽr, *n.* 1. in medicine, a person in whom the loss of blood from even slight wounds is extremely difficult to control; a hemophiliac.
2. one who draws blood from another.
3. one who takes undue advantage of another's generosity or hospitality. [Colloq.]
4. in engineering, a device which controls the loss of steam from a turbine.

bleed'ing, *n.* 1. a running or issuing of blood, as from the nose; a hemorrhage.
2. the operation of letting blood, as in old surgery.
3. the drawing of sap from a tree or plant.

bleed'ing heärt, 1. a garden plant, *Dicentra spectabilis,* a native of China. It has fernlike leaves and drooping clusters of pink or reddish heart-shaped flowers.
2. the English wallflower, *Cheiranthus Cheiri.*

bleed'ing tooth, a neritoid shell, having small reddish projections along the border of its mouth, resembling bleeding teeth.

bleit, blāte, *a.* [ME. *blate*; AS. *blāt,* pale, diffident.] bashful; blunt; dull. [Scot.]

blek, *v.t.* to bleck. [Obs.]

blel'lum, *n.* an idle senseless fellow; a blab. [Scot.]

blem'ish, *v.t.*; blemished, *pt., pp.*; blemishing, *ppr.* [ME. *blemisshen,* to wound, spoil; OFr. *blemir, blesmir,* from *bleme, blesme,* pale, wan.] to mark with deformity; to injure or impair; to mar, either in body or mind; to sully.

blem'ish, *n.* 1. any mark of deformity; any flaw, as a stain, spot, scar, etc.
2. a defect or shortcoming; a fault.
Syn.—stain, spot, speck, flaw, defect, fault, imperfection.

blem'ish·less, *a.* without blemish; spotless.

blem'ish·ment, *n.* disgrace. [Rare.]

blench, *v.i.*; blenched, *pt., pp.*; blenching, *ppr.* [ME. *blenchen,* to evade, shrink back, give way; AS. *blencan,* to deceive.] to shrink back; to shy away; to flinch; to quail.

blench, *v.t.* to baffle; to foil. [Obs.]

blench, *n.* 1. a start or shrinking back.
2. a side glance. [Obs.]

blench, *v.i.* and *v.t.* to blanch; to become or make pale.

blench'ẽr, *n.* 1. a guard at a deer hunt stationed to prevent the escape of the game. [Obs.]
2. one who draws back in fear.

blend, *v.t.*; blended *or* blent, *pt., pp.*; blending, *ppr.* [ME. *blenden*; AS. *blandan* and ON. *blanda,* to mix.]
1. to mix together; to combine, so that the separate things mixed cannot be distinguished.
2. to pollute by mixture; to spoil or corrupt. [Obs.]
3. to mix or mingle (varieties of tea, tobacco, etc.), especially so as to produce a desired quality.

blend, *v.i.* 1. to mix; merge; unite.
2. to pass gradually or imperceptibly into each other, as colors.
3. to go well together; harmonize.
Syn.—mix, harmonize, unite, combine, fuse, merge, amalgamate, mingle, commingle, coalesce.

blend, *n.* 1. a thorough mixture of two things, as colors or liquids, so that the various constituents can no longer be distinguished; a shading or merging as of one color into another.
2. the result of blending; a mixture of varieties, as a *blend* of coffee.

blende, *n.* [G. *blende,* from *blenden,* to blind, dazzle.]
1. sphalerite, an ore of zinc or zinc sulfide.
2. any of certain other sulfides, especially metallic sulfides, having a fairly bright luster.

blend'ed whis'ky, whisky blended with neutral spirits, as of grain or potatoes.

blend'ẽr, *n.* one who blends; also, an object used to blend.

blend'ing, *n.* the act of intermixing or shading, as of colors in painting.

blend'ing in·her'it·ȧnce, the blending of characteristics of the parents in the offspring, as in a pink flower that results from the mating of a red flower with a white one.

blend'ous, *a.* pertaining to blende.

blend wa'tẽr, a cattle distemper affecting the liver.

Blen'heim span'iel (blen'um), [after *Blenheim* Palace, seat of the Duke of Marlborough, where the dogs were bred.] a variety of toy spaniel that is white with reddish-brown spots.

blenk, *v.i.* to look; to blink. [Obs.]

blen'nies, *n.* pl. of *blenny.*

blen'ni·oid, blen'ni·id, *a.* [L. *blennius,* blenny, and Gr. *eidos,* form.] in zoology, pertaining to or like the blennies.

blen·nog'e·nous, *a.* [Gr. *blennos,* mucus, and *genēs,* producing.] producing mucus.

blen'noid, *a.* mucous.

blen·nor·rhē'ȧ, blen·nor·rhoe'ȧ, *n.* [L., from Gr. *blennos,* mucus, and *rhoia,* from *rhein,* to flow.] an abnormal discharge or secretion of mucus.

blen'ny, *n.*; *pl.* **blen'nies,** [L. *blennius*; Gr. *blennos,* a blenny, from *blennos, blenna,* mucus.] any of a number of related spiny-finned fishes, usually of small size, of the genus *Blennius,* so called from their covering of mucus.

blent, *v.,* past tense and past participle of *blend.*

bleph'ȧ·rism (blef'), *n.* spasmodic twitching of the eyelids.

bleph·ȧr·ī'tis, *n.* [Gr. *blepharon,* eyelid, and *-itis.*] inflammation of the eyelids.

bleph'är·ō-, [from Gr. *blepharon,* eyelid.] a combining form meaning *eyelid, eyelids*: also, before a vowel, *blephar-.*

bleph″är·op·tō'sis, *n.* [*blepharo-,* and Gr. *ptōsis,* a fall.] in pathology, a drooping of the upper eyelid.

bleph·är·or'rhȧ·phy, *n.* [*blepharo-,* and Gr. *rhaphē,* a sewing, from *rhaptein,* to sew.] in surgery, a suturing of the eyelids.

bleph'är·ō·spaşm, *n.* [*blepharo-,* and Gr. *spasmos,* spasm.] a spasmodic twitching of orbicular muscle, producing continuous winking.

bleph·är·ot'ō·my, *n.* [*blepharo-,* and Gr. *tomē,* a cutting, from *temnein,* to cut.] in surgery, an incision into the eyelid to correct some muscular defect.

bles'bok, *n.*; *pl.* **bles'bok** or **bles'boks,** [D. *blesbok*; *bles,* blaze, and *bok,* a buck.] an antelope of South Africa, *Alcelaphus albifrons,* with a white mark on its face.

bles'buck, *n.*; *pl.* **bles'buck** or **bles'bucks,** a blesbok.

bless, *v.t.*; blessed *or* blest, *pt., pp.*; blessing, *ppr.* [ME. *blessen, blessien*; AS. *blētsian, blēdsian,* to bless, from *blōd,* blood; from the consecration by sprinkling the altar with blood.]
1. to set apart or consecrate to holy purposes; to make and pronounce holy.
2. to make happy; to make successful; to make prosperous in temporal concerns; as, he *blessed* us with his leadership.
3. to wish happiness to.
4. to consecrate by prayer; to invoke a blessing upon; as, he *blessed* the eucharist.
5. to praise; to magnify; to extol.
6. to think (oneself) happy; congratulate (oneself).
7. to make the sign of the cross upon (oneself).
8. to curse: used ironically or euphemistically.
9. to keep; guard; preserve: now obsolete, except in prayers, exclamations, etc.
bless me (or *you, him,* etc.)!; an exclamation of astonishment, surprise, pleasure, dismay, etc.
Syn.—felicitate, endow, enrich, gladden, rejoice, cheer, thank.

bless'ed, *a.* 1. hallowed; sacred; consecrated; holy; beatified.
2. bringing comfort or joy.
3. enjoying great happiness; joyful; blissful.
4. confounded; cursed; worthless: used ironically as a mild oath; as, that *blessed* rascal; he hasn't a *blessed* cent.
blessed bread; see *eulogia.*
blessed thistle; an annual, *Centaurea benedicta* or *Cnicus benedictus,* once reputed to be an antidote for poisons.
the blessed; (a) people who are blessed; (b) in the Roman Catholic Church, those dead who have been beatified and are thereby entitled to receive veneration from the living.

bless'ed ē·vent', the birth of a child: now chiefly jocular.

bless'ed·ly, *adv.* happily; in a fortunate manner.

bless'ed·ness, *n.* 1. happiness; felicity; heavenly joy.
2 sanctity.
single blessedness; the state of being unmarried.

Bless'ed Sac'rȧ·ment, the Eucharist.

Bless'ed Vir'gin, the Virgin Mary.

bless'ẽr, *n.* one who blesses.

bless'ing, *n.* [ME. *blessinge, blessunge*; AS. *bletsung,* from *blētsian,* to bless.]
1. a statement of divine favor; benediction.
2. an invoking of divine favor.
3. a grace said before or after eating.
4. the gift of divine favor.
5. a wish for prosperity, success, etc.; as, they send us their *blessing.*
6. approval; as, this method has his *blessing.*
7. anything that gives happiness or prevents misfortune.
8. a cursing or scolding: used ironically.

blest, *a.* blessed.
While these *blest* sounds my ravished ear assail. —Trumbull.

blest, *v.,* alternative past tense and past participle of *bless.*

blet, *n.* [Fr. *blettir,* from *blet, blette,* overripe, soft.] a kind of rot that takes place in overripe fruit.

blet, *v.i.*; bletted, *pt., pp.*; bletting, *ppr.* to decay within, as fruit when overripe.

bleth'ẽr, *v.* and *n.* same as *blather.*
bleu cheese (bloo), [Fr. *bleu,* blue.] same as *blue cheese,* under *blue.*
blew, *v.,* past tense of *blow.*
blē'wȧrt, *n.* [Scot.] the germander speedwell.
blew'its, *n.* [Fr. *bluet,* dim. of *bleu,* blue.] an edible mushroom of Europe, of a purplish color.
blick, *n.* a fish; same as *bleak.*
blick, *n.* same as *fulguration.*
blick'ey, *n.* [G. *blech,* tin.] a tin dinner pail. [Local U. S.]
blīght (blīt), *n.* [origin unknown.]
1. any atmospheric or soil condition, parasite, or insect that kills, withers, or checks the growth of plants.
2. any of several plant diseases, as rust, mildew, or smut.
3. anything that destroys, prevents growth, etc.
4. a person or thing that withers the hopes or ambitions of another person.
5. the condition or result of being blighted.
6. either of two eruptive diseases: (a) in the United States, a kind of rash; (b) in Australia, a disease of the eye in which the eyelids become pustular, inflamed, swollen, and mucous.
blīght, *v.t.;* blighted, *pt., pp.;* blighting, *ppr.*
1. to affect with blight; to blast; to prevent the growth of.
2. to destroy.
3. to frustrate, as hopes or plans; to blast the happiness of.
blīght, *v.i.* to suffer blight.
blīght'bird, *n.* a bird that clears trees of blight, especially that produced by insects.
blīght'ẽr, *n.* 1. a person or thing that blights.
2. (a) a low or contemptible fellow; rascal; (b) a fellow; chap. [Slang, chiefly British.]
blīght'ing, *a.* producing blight.
blīght'ing·ly, *adv.* in such a manner as to blight.
blīghts, *n.pl.* a form of eruptive skin disease; nettle rash. [Local U. S.]
blīght'y, Blīght'y, *n.;* *pl.* **blīght'ies, Blīght'ies,** [Hind. bilāyatī, foreign country; Ar. *wilāyatī,* from *wilāyat,* government, from *wālī,* governor.]
1. England; home. [Brit. Slang.]
2. a wound permitting a soldier to be sent home from the front. [Brit. Slang.]
blī'mey, *interj.* [from (*God*) *blind me.*] a British exclamation of surprise, wonder, etc.
blimp, *n.* [echoic coinage.] a small, nonrigid or semirigid airship. [Colloq.]
blin, *v.t.* and *v.i.* [AS. *blinnan,* to cease.] to stop or cease. [Obs.]
blin, *n.* cessation. [Obs.]
blīnd, *a.* [ME. *blind;* AS. *blind,* blind.]
1. destitute of the sense of seeing, either by natural defect or by deprivation; sightless.
2. lacking insight; unable to understand or judge; ignorant; as, some authors are *blind* to their own defects.
3. unseen; out of public view; private; dark; obscure; not easily found; not easily discernible; as, a *blind* path, a *blind* corner.
4. heedless; inconsiderate; reckless.
This plan is recommended neither to *blind* approbation nor to *blind* reprobation. —Jay.
5. complicated; winding; difficult to follow or trace; as, the *blind* mazes of the dance.
6. not bearing flowers or fruits; unproductive; as, *blind* buds.
7. without openings for or impervious to light; as, a *blind* wall.
8. closed at one end; having no outlet; as, the *blind* gut or caecum; a *blind* alley.
9. not clear or comprehensible; not legible; as, a *blind* stanza in a poem.
10. done without adequate directions or knowledge; as, a *blind* search.
11. not controlled by intelligence; as, *blind* destiny.
12. insensible.
13. drunk.
14. in aeronautics, by the use of instruments only; as, *blind* flying.
15. in architecture, (a) false; (b) walled up; as, a *blind* window.
16. in bookbinding, without gilding or coloring; as, *blind* tooling.
blind area; a covered space outside the wall of a building to keep it dry.
blind axle; an axle which turns without communicating motion.
blind coal; flameless or anthracite coal.
Syn.—sightless, unseeing, undiscerning, ignorant, prejudiced, uninformed, unaware.
blīnd, *v.t.;* blinded, *pt., pp.;* blinding, *ppr.* 1. to make blind; to deprive of sight.
2. to darken; to obscure to the eye.
3. to deprive of the power of insight or judgment; as, to *blind* the mind.
4. to confuse; to dazzle by great brilliancy.
5. in paving, to cover with a layer of fine sand or gravel, so that the spaces between paving blocks, etc. will be filled.
6. to cover or conceal.
7. to outshine or eclipse.
blīnd, blīnde, *n.* same as *blende.*
blīnd, *n.* 1. something to obscure vision or obstruct the passage of light; particularly, a shade for a window.
2. a person or thing used to deceive or mislead; a decoy.
3. in fortification, a blindage.
4. a place of concealment for hunters.
the blind; people who are blind.
blīnd, *adv.* 1. blindly; specifically, so as to be blind, insensible, etc.
2. recklessly.
3. in aeronautics, by the use of instruments alone; as, to fly *blind.*
4. sight unseen; as, to buy a thing *blind.*
blīnd'āġe, *n.* in earlier military usage, a screen or cover for a trench, protecting those in the trench from the enemy's fire; a mantelet.
blīnd al'ley, 1. a passage shut off at one end.
2. anything offering no opportunity for progress or advancement.
blīnd'ball, *n.* in botany, a puffball.
blīnd bee'tle, any one of the large bugs that fly blindly at night.
blīnd dāte, 1. a social engagement arranged by a third person for a man and a woman who are strangers to each other. [Slang.]
2. either person involved.
blīnd'ẽr, *n.* 1. a person or thing that blinds.
2. either of two leather flaps on a horse's bridle that shut out the side view.
blīnd'fish, *n.;* *pl.* **blīnd'fish** or **blīnd'fish·es,** any of a number of small fishes with functionless eyes, found in underground streams, waters of caves, etc.
blīnd'fōld, *a.* 1. having the eyes covered.
2. careless, rash, or unconcerned; as, *blindfold* rage.
blīnd'fōld, *v.t.;* blindfolded, *pt., pp.;* blindfolding, *ppr.* 1. to cover the eyes of with a cloth or bandage.
2. to hinder from seeing.
3. to delude; to mislead.
blīnd'fōld, *n.* 1. something used to cover the eyes.
2. anything that hinders the sight or understanding.
blīnd'fōld, *adv.* 1. blindly.
2. recklessly; heedlessly.
blīnd'ing, *n.* 1. the act of destroying sight.
2. sand or gravel used to blind a road.
blīnd'ing, *a.* producing blindness or hindering vision; as, *blinding* sleet.
blīnd'ly, *adv.* without sight or understanding; implicitly; without examination; without judgment; as, to be *blindly* led by another.
blīnd'man, *n.* 1. one who is blind or blinded.
2. same as *blind reader.*
blindman's-ball; same as **blindball.**
blindman's buff; a game in which a blindfolded person must catch a player and identify him.
blindman's holiday; the part of the evening between daylight and dark. [Humorous.]
blīnd'ness, *n.* the state of being without sight; also, a lack of discernment.
blīnd net'tle, the dead nettle or hemp nettle.
blīnd pig, same as *speakeasy.* [Old Slang.]
blīnd rēad'ẽr, a person in a post office whose duty it is to decipher addresses which are doubtful or illegible.
blīnd spot, 1. the small area, insensitive to light, in the retina of the eye where the optic nerve enters.
2. a person's lack of sensitivity to a particular thing; a prejudice or ignorance that one has but is often unaware of.
3. an area where radio reception is difficult.
blīnd stag'gẽrs, a disease of horses or cattle characterized by staggering.
blīnd'stitch, *v.t.* to stitch so that the stitches show on only one side of the material, or do not show at all.
blīnd'stō″ry, *n.;* *pl.* **blīnd'stō″ries,** in architecture, (a) a windowless story; (b) in Gothic churches, a gallery (triforium) without windows, above the main arches.
blīnd tī'gẽr, same as *speakeasy.* [Old Slang.]
blīnd tool'ing, impressions made on leather by heated tools: used in bookbinding.
blīnd trust, an agreement whereby a person, as a public official, in an effort to avoid conflicts of interest, places certain personal assets under the control of an independent trustee with the provision that the person is to have no knowledge of how those assets are managed.
blīnd'wŏrm, *n.* a small, legless lizard, *Anguis fragilis,* having a dark, snakelike body with greenish or yellow spots or stripes, a small head, very small eyes, and a brittle tail.
blin'ī, *n.pl.;* *sing.* **blin,** [Russ.] small, thin pancakes, commonly served with caviar and sour cream.
bliñk, *v.t.;* blinked, *pt., pp.;* blinking, *ppr.* 1. to wink (the eyes) rapidly.
2. to cause (eyes, light, etc.) to wink or blink.
3. to close the eyes to (a fact or situation); evade or avoid.
4. to signal (a message) by flashing a light, etc.
5. to cheat; to delude. [Scot.]
bliñk, *v.i.* [ME. *blinken;* Dan. *blinke;* D. *blinken;* Sw. *blinka,* to blink, shine, twinkle; AS. *blican,* to shine.]
1. to wink rapidly.
2. to look with the eyes half shut, winking, as in a glare.
3. to shine fitfully; to flicker, as a lamp.
4. to become sour: said of milk or beer.
5. to look (*at*) as if not seeing; disregard; ignore; as, she *blinked* at my mistake.
Syn.—wink, ignore, connive, overlook.
bliñk, *n.* 1. a glimpse or glance.
2. a fitful gleam or flicker.
3. a moment; the time that it takes to wink.
4. a winking.
5. a shining reflection on the horizon caused by ice masses at sea.
on the blink; not working right; out of order. [Slang.]
bliñk'ȧrd, *n.* 1. a person who chronically or habitually blinks his eyes.
2. a person who fails to perceive or understand; stupid person.
bliñk'ẽr, *n.* 1. a flap to shut off a horse's side view; blinder.
2. a flashing warning light at crossings.
3. an eye. [Slang.]
bliñk'ẽr, *v.t.,* to put blinkers or blinders on.
bliñk'ẽrs, *n.pl.* [from *blinker.*] a sort of goggles.
bliñk'-eyed (-īd), *a.* habitually blinking.
bliñk'ing, *a.* winking; twinkling.
bliñk'ing, *n.* the act of twinkling or winking; as, the *blinking* of an eye.
bliñk'ing chick'weed, a marsh herb of the order *Portulacaceæ:* called also *blinks.*
bliñks, *n.* same as *blinking chickweed.*
blintz (blints), *n.* [Yid. *blintze,* from Russ. *blinyets,* dim. of *blin,* pancake.] a thin pancake rolled with a filling of cottage cheese, fruit, etc.
blip, *n.* [echoic of a brief sound.]
1. a luminous image on an oscilloscope, as in a radar set.
2. a quick, sharp sound.
blip, *v.i.;* blipped, *pt., pp.;* blipping, *ppr.* to make a blip or series of blips.
blirt, *n.* a burst of tears. [Scot.]
bliss, *n.* [AS. *blis, blisse,* from *blīds, blīths,* joy, from *blīthe,* joyful.]
1. extreme joy; felicity; heavenly joy.
2. any cause of bliss.
Syn.—blessedness, joy, ecstasy, rapture.
bliss'fụl, *a.* full of joy and felicity; causing or characterized by great happiness.
bliss'fụl·ly, *adv.* in a blissful manner.
bliss'fụl·ness, *n.* exalted happiness; felicity.
bliss'less, *a.* destitute of bliss.
blis'sŏm, *v.i.* [Ice. *blæsma,* in heat, as a goat.] to be lustful; to be in heat; said of a ewe.
blis'sŏm, *a.* in heat: said of a ewe.
blis'tẽr, *n.* [ME. *blister;* D. *bluyster;* OFr. *blestre,* a blister, swelling.]
1. a little swelling of the skin, filled with watery matter and caused by burning or rubbing.
2. any similar swelling on the surface of other substances, as plants or metals.
3. a gun turret shield on an airplane.
4. any substance applied to cause a blister.
blis'tẽr, *v.t.;* blistered, *pt., pp.;* blistering, *ppr.*
1. to raise a blister upon (the skin).
2. to raise blisters on (iron) in a furnace, in the process of converting iron into steel.
3. to beat severely.
4. to lash with words.
blis'tẽr, *v.i.* to form a blister or blisters.
blis'tẽr çop″pẽr, a kind of copper obtained by calcining the variety known as pimple metal.
blis'tẽr flȳ, blis'tẽr bee'tle, 1. the Spanish

fly, *Cantharis vesicatoria*, used in raising blisters.

2. any of a number of beetles related to this insect: some are harmful to plants.

blis′tēr plȧs′tēr, a plaster, generally of Spanish flies, designed to raise a blister.

blis′tēr rust, a disease of pine trees caused by certain fungi: it causes blisters on the bark.

blis′tēr·y, *a.* characterized by or full of blisters.

blīte, *n.* [L. *blitum*; Gr. *bliton*, a plant.] any of various plants, mostly of the goosefoot family, with succulent leaves, frequently used as pot herbs.

blīthe, *a.* [ME. *blithe, blythe*; AS. *blīthe*, joyful.] gay; joyous; sprightly; mirthful.

Syn.—light, merry, happy, bright, buoyant, gladsome, bonny, vivacious, lively, cheerful, blithesome.

blīthe′ly, *adv.* in a gay, joyful manner.

blīthe′ness, *n.* the quality of being blithe.

blith′ēr, *v.i.* to talk at random; speak foolishly or nonsensically. [Dial.]

blith′ēr·ing, *a.* [ppr. of *blither*.] jabbering; talking without sense.

blīthe′sōme, *a.* gay; merry; cheerful.

blīthe′sōme·ly, *adv.* in a blithesome manner.

blīthe′sōme·ness, *n.* the quality of being blithesome.

blitz, *n.* [a shortened form of *blitzkrieg*.] a sudden, savage attack, as from the air, causing great devastation; as, the *blitz* of London by the Nazis. [Colloq.]

blitz, *v.t.* 1. to attack suddenly with great force and resulting devastation; as, the planes *blitzed* the city. [Colloq.]

2. in gin rummy, to defeat (one's opponent) without allowing him to score a point. [Colloq.]

blitz′krieg, *n.* [G. *blitz*, lightning, and *krieg*, war.]

1. a quick or short war; specifically, one waged with great fury and intensity in order to win a quick victory.

2. any swift, sudden, overwhelming attack.

bliz′zărd, *n.* [dial. *bliz*, violent blow, and *-ard*.]

1. originally, an effective shot or blow.

2. a severe snowstorm with high wind.

3. a violent windstorm.

blōak, *n.* see *bloke*.

blōat, *v.t.*; bloated, *pt., pp.*; bloating, *ppr.* [ME. *blout*, soft; ON. *blautr*, soaked.]

1. to cause to swell or make turgid with water, air, or other means.

2. to inflate; to puff up; to make vain.

blōat, *v.i.* 1. to grow turgid; to swell; to dilate.

2. to puff up; to inflate.

blōat, *a.* bloated.

blōat, *n.* 1. a bloated person or thing.

2. a drunkard. [Slang.]

3. in veterinary medicine, a swelling of the abdomen caused by watery foods or eating too fast.

blōat, *v.t.* [from ME. *blote*, soft with moisture, from ON. *blautr*, soaked.] to cure or preserve (herring, etc.) by soaking in salt water, smoking, and half-drying.

blōat, *n.* a bloater.

blōat′ed, *a.* [pp. of *bloat* (to swell).]

1. swollen; distended; too large.

2. puffed up, as with pride.

3. unhealthily fat from overeating.

blōat′ed·ness, *n.* a bloated condition or state.

blōat′ēr, *n.* [orig. *bloat herring*, soft herring (as opposed to dried): the curing process has been altered.] a fat herring or mackerel that has been bloated (cured).

blōat′ing, *n.* a state of being swelled or bloated.

blob, *n.* [Prov. Eng., from Scot. *bleb, bleib, blab*, a bubble.]

1. a drop or lump of something viscid or thick; a bubble; a blister.

2. a small mass or splash of color.

blob, *v.t.*; blobbed, *pt., pp.*; blobbing, *ppr.* to splash or splotch, as with blobs.

blob′bēr, *n.* blubber. [Obs.]

blob′bēr lip, *n.* a thick lip.

blob′bēr·lipped, *a.* having thick lips.

bloc, *n.* in politics, a coalition of parties, or a combination of members of various parties, formed for a common cause or purpose.

blō·çage′ (-kȧzh′), *n.* [Fr.] a rough, cheap kind of rubblework in masonry.

block, *n.* [ME. *blok*; Fr. *bloc*, of Germanic origin; M.H.G. *bloch*; L.G. *blok*.]

1. any mass of matter with an extended surface; as, a *block* of marble.

2. a solid body of wood, metal, or stone, with surfaces more or less plane; as, a butcher's *block*.

3. a continuous row of buildings; as, a *block* of houses.

4. a city section or square, whether vacant or built upon; the distance between streets; also, one side of a city square.

5. the piece of wood upon which persons expose the neck when beheaded; as, he was brought to the *block*.

6. any obstruction or cause of obstruction; a stop; hindrance; obstacle.

7. a pulley, or a system of pulleys, mounted in its frame or shell, with its band or strap.

8. a blockhead; a stupid fellow.

9. in printing, (a) a form of hard wood, on which figures are cut in relief with knives, chisels, etc.; (b) a piece of hard wood used by engravers and printers for the mounting of electrotypes or stereotypes.

10. in falconry, the perch on which a bird of prey was kept.

11. in commerce, a number of shares of stock to be sold in a series or lump.

12. in cricket, the position of the batter when defending his wicket.

13. an auctioneer's platform.

14. a mold upon which things are shaped, as hats.

15. the shape of a hat.

16. any solid piece of material used to strengthen or support.

17. a large, hollow building brick.

18. a child's toy brick, usually wooden.

19 any number of persons or things regarded as a unit; bloc.

20. a person's head. [Slang.]

21. in medicine, a blocking; interruption of the passage of impulses through a nerve by means of pressure or anesthetics.

22. in psychiatry, a sudden interruption in speech or thought processes, resulting from deep emotional conflict, repression, etc.

23. in radio, the sudden cessation of oscillations of an oscillator, accompanied by a high plate current.

24. in railroading, a length of track governed by signals.

25. in sports, an interception or thwarting of an opponent's play or movement.

26. in stamp collecting, a set of four or more undetached stamps forming a rectangle.

on the block; up for sale or auction.

block, *v.t.*; blocked, *pt., pp.*; blocking, *ppr.* [Fr. *bloquer*, to block up, from *bloc*, a block.]

1. to impede the passage or progress of; to stop up; to obstruct by placing obstacles in the way; often followed by *up*; as, to *block up* a town, or a road.

2. to shape or form by using a block.

3. to support or secure by means of blocks.

4. to stop, as a blow.

5. in athletics, (a) to impede the progress of (an opponent or his play), as in football; (b) stop (a ball) with the bat, as in cricket.

6. to blot out or deface, as in photography, when part of a picture may be removed by erasing it from the plate or by covering it with some opaque substance before printing.

7. to blockade.

8. to create difficulties for; stand in the way of; hinder.

9. to form into blocks.

10. in chemistry, to render inactive.

11. in medicine, to prevent the transmission of impulses in; deaden (a nerve), especially by anesthetizing.

12. in psychiatry, to withold or forget, as the result of a block.

13. in radio, to stop (the output of alternating current from an electron tube) by overloading the input.

14. in railroading, to run (trains) by the block system.

block, *v.i.* to behave so as to hinder.

block, *a.* 1. made or taken in the form of blocks; as, *block* coal.

2. block-shaped.

3. set out like or belonging to a city square.

4. in aggregate.

5. in stenography, having no indentation in address, heading, or paragraphs.

to block in (or *out*); to roughly sketch or diagram, omitting details.

block·āde′, *n.* [*block*, and *-ade*.]

1. a shutting off of a place or region by hostile troops or ships in order to prevent passage.

2. any blocking action designed to isolate an enemy and cut off communication and commerce with him.

3. the force that maintains a blockade.

4. any strategic barrier.

to raise a blockade; either to withdraw or to drive away the forces which make a blockade effective.

block·āde′, *v.t.*; blockaded, *pt., pp.*; blockading, *ppr.* to subject to a blockade.

block·ād′ēr, *n.* 1. a vessel stationed to blockade a port.

2. one employed in blockading.

block·āde′ run′nēr, a ship or person that tries to go through or past a blockade.

block′āġe, *n.* [from OFr. *bloc*, a barrier, and *-age*.] a blocking or being blocked.

block and tack′le, an arrangement of one or more pulley blocks, with rope or cables, for pulling or hoisting large, heavy objects.

block′book, *n.* a book printed from engraved wooden blocks instead of movable type.

block book′ing, a method of leasing motion pictures by the lot, without letting the exhibitors select only those that they wish to exhibit.

block′bus·tēr, *n.* 1. a very large destructive bomb that can devastate a considerable area, as a city block. [Colloq.]

2. a particularly powerful or effective person or thing; specifically, an expensive or pretentious movie, novel, etc. intended to have wide popular appeal. [Colloq.]

block grant, a grant of Federal funds to a State or local government for discretionary use in funding a block of programs, with or without guidelines.

block′head (-hed), *n.* 1. a block of wood shaped like a head, used for shaping or displaying hats or wigs.

2. a stupid or foolish person; nitwit.

Syn.—dolt, dunderhead, dunce, ninny, numbskull, dullard, simpleton, booby, loggerhead, ignoramus.

block′head·ed, *a.* stupid; dull.

block′head·ism, *n.* stupidity; that which is characteristic of a blockhead.

block′head·ly, *a.* stupid. [Obs.]

block′house, *n.* 1. a strong wooden fort with a projecting second story and openings in the walls for the defenders to shoot from.

2. any building of squared timber or logs.

BLOCKHOUSE
a, a, a, a, loopholes

block′ing, *n.* 1. material used to support or prop.

2. the act of obstructing.

3. the act of shaping, stamping, or supporting with blocks.

block′ing çourse, the final course of a wall above the cornice.

block′ish, *a.* 1. blocklike.

2. stupid; dull; deficient in understanding.

block′ish·ly, *adv.* in a stupid manner.

block′ish·ness, *n.* stupidity; dullness.

block lä′vȧ, lava formed in sharp, angular, rough-surfaced blocks.

block let′tēr, in printing, (a) a type cut from wood; (b) a style of letter that is simple in form, as sans-serif.

block′līke, *a.* like a block; stupid.

BLOCKING COURSE
a, blocking course; *b*, cornice; *c*, front of wall

block līne, a rope or cable used in a block and tackle.

block plāne, a carpenter's plane for cutting across the grain on board ends.

block print′ing, 1. the act or process of printing from engraved blocks coated with ink or dyes.

2. a mode of printing on paper and cotton with colors from a design cut in relief upon a block.

block′ship, *n.* a ship used to block the entrance to a port or harbor; an old hulk.

block sig′năl, any of the signals used in a block system.

block sys′tem, a system of dividing a railroad track into several sections and regulating the trains by automatic signals so that there is usually no more than one train in one section.

block′y, *a.*; *comp.* blockier; *superl.* blockiest.

1. having contrasting blocks or patches.

2. stocky; chunky.
3. tending to break apart into large chunks or masses.

blo'dīte, bloe'dīte (blũ'), *n.* [named after the chemist C. A. *Blöde.*] a hydrous compound of magnesium, sodium, and sulfur.

blōke, blōak, *n.* [word found in Shelta, Irish tinkers' argot.]
1. a fellow; a man. [Slang.]
2. a contemptible fellow. [Slang.]

blond, *a.* [Fr. *blond,* f. *blonde,* light, from LL. *blondus,* yellow.]
1. possessing a fair or light complexion, light (usually blue) eyes, and hair of a golden or flaxen hue.
2. straw-colored; flaxen: said of hair.
3. light-colored; as, *blond* furniture.

blond, *n.* 1. a blond man or boy.
2. blonde (lace).

blonde, *a.* blond.

blonde, *n.* 1. a blonde woman or girl.
2. a type of silk bobbin lace: so called because of its original resemblance to flaxen hair: also called *blonde* (or *blond*) *lace.*

blond met'ăl, a clay ironstone used for making tools, and found in Staffordshire, England.

blond'ness, blonde'ness, *n.* the quality or condition of being blond.

blood (blud), *n.* [ME. *blood, bloud;* AS. *blōd,* blood, from *blōwan,* to flourish, bloom.]
1. the fluid circulating through the heart, arteries, and veins of people and many animals.
2. a similar fluid in lower animals.
3. family line; parental heritage; lineage.
4. descent from nobility; royal or honorable lineage; as, a prince of the *blood;* a gentleman of *blood.*
5. slaughter, murder, or bloodshed; as, his *blood* shall be avenged.
6. guilt of shedding blood.
7. the essence of life; life: often *lifeblood.*
8. the life fluid, sap, or juice of a plant.
9. passion, temperament, or disposition.
10. racial heritage; race: loosely and unscientifically so used, for blood is not one of the ethnic differentia.
11. kinship; family relation.
12. an animal of pure breed or stock.
13. a dandy.
bad blood; anger; hatred.
blood is thicker than water; family ties are stronger than other ties.
in cold blood; (a) with cruelty; unfeelingly; (b) dispassionately; deliberately.

blood, *v.t.;* blooded, *pt., pp.;* blooding, *ppr.* 1. to let blood from; to bleed. [Archaic.]
2. to stain with blood. [Archaic.]
3. to train or inure to blood, as a hound or a soldier.
4. to heat the blood of; to exasperate. [Obs.]

blood a·ven'ġẽr, one who devotes himself to pursuing and killing the murderer of his relative or friend.

blood bank, 1. a place where whole blood or plasma is typed, processed, and stored for future use.
2. any reserve of blood for use in transfusion.

blood bap'tiṣm, see *baptism of blood.*

blood bȧth, the killing of many people; massacre.

blood'bīrd, *n.* a honey-sucking bird of Australia, the male bird being of a bright-red color.

blood blis'tẽr, a blister full of blood or serum mixed with blood.

blood brŏth'ẽr, 1. a brother by birth.
2. a person bound to one by the ceremony of mingling his blood with one's own.

blood'-çŏl·ŏred, *a.* having the color of blood.

blood çor'pus·cle, see *corpuscle.*

blood çount, the examination of a specimen of blood of standard volume for the purpose of determining the number of red corpuscles and white corpuscles it contains.

blood çups, in botany, cup-shaped fungi of the genus *Peziza,* of fleshy, waxy, brilliant-red appearance, with naked spores on a fructifying surface, and gills covered with a delicate membrane.

blood'çur"dling, *a.* very frightening; causing terror or horror.

blood'ed, *a.* 1. having (a specific kind of) blood; as, hot-*blooded.*
2. of fine stock or breed; pedigreed; thoroughbred.

blood'flow"ẽr, *n.* any plant bearing red flowers of the genus *Hæmanthus.*

blood group, any of several (usually four) groups into which any person's blood is classified with reference to the type of agglutinogen of its corpuscles.

blood'guilt"i·ness (-gilt"), *n.* the guilt or crime of shedding blood.

blood'guilt"less, *a.* not guilty of shedding blood or of murder.

blood'guilt"y, *a.* guilty of murder or bloodshed.

blood hēat, the normal temperature of human blood, 98.6°F.

blood'-hŏrse, *n.* a horse of the purest blood or best lineage.

blood'-hot, *a.* as warm as blood at its normal temperature.

blood'hound, *n.* a variety of large, keen-scented dog, with long, smooth, drooping ears and a wrinkled face. It is often employed for hunting escaped prisoners.

BLOODHOUND (25 in. high)

blood'i·ly, *adv.* in a bloody manner; also, cruelly; savagely.

blood'i·ness, *n.* the state of being bloody.

blood is'lăndṣ (ī'lăndz), blood-colored patches or spots dotted over the vascular embryonic tissues, denoting the development of blood vessels and corpuscles.

blood'less, *a.* 1. without or appearing to be without blood; lifeless.
2. without shedding of blood; as, a *bloodless* victory.
3. without spirit or activity.
4. not having enough blood; anemic or pale.
5. unfeeling; cruel.

blood'less·ly, *adv.* in a bloodless manner.

blood'less·ness, *n.* the state of being bloodless.

blood'let, *v.t.* to draw blood from; to bleed. [Rare.]

blood'let"tẽr, *n.* one who lets blood; a phlebotomist.

blood'let"ting, *n.* 1. the act of letting blood, or bleeding by opening a vein.
2. bloodshed.

blood'līne, *n.* a direct line of descent; pedigree; strain: usually of animals.

blood mŏn'ey, 1. money paid in compensation to the next of kin of a murdered person.
2. money paid as the reward for having committed, or as the inducement to commit, a murder.

blood piç'tūre, an analysis of the blood in respect to the relative proportions of red and white corpuscles, etc.

blood plaṣ'mȧ, see *plasma* (blood).

blood plāte'let, blood plāte, blood plaque (-plak), see *platelet* (blood constituent).

blood poi'ṣŏn·ing, a diseased condition of the blood, caused by certain microorganisms, their toxins, or other poisonous matter.

blood pres'sūre, pressure of blood on the walls of its vessels, especially the arteries: it varies with health, age, emotional tension, physical exercise, etc.

blood pụd'ding, 1. a dish made of pig's blood, suet, etc.: also called *black pudding.*
2. a kind of sausage that is dark from the blood in it; blood sausage.

blood pũrġe, the murder of those people not in sympathy with the policies of, or suspected of subversive actions against, a party or government.

blood rāin, rain colored red by falling through red dust.

blood'-red, *a.* 1. stained red with blood.
2. having the deep-red color of blood.

blood rē·lā'tion, a person related by birth.

blood rē·venġe', a form of revenge in which either the next of kin of a murdered person or some member of his clan must undertake to kill the murderer or a relative of the murderer.

blood'rọọt, *n.* a North American plant of the poppy family, so named from its red root and red sap; a species of *Sanguinaria* (*Sanguinaria Canadensis*): called also *red puccoon, turmeric,* and *redroot.*

blood'shed, *n.* the shedding or spilling of blood; slaughter.

blood'shed"dẽr, *n.* one who sheds blood; a murderer.

blood'shed"ding, *n.* the shedding of blood.

blood'shot, *a.* red and inflamed; suffused or tinged with blood; as, the eyes become *bloodshot* when small blood vessels break in them.

blood'shot"ten, *a.* bloodshot. [Obs.]

blood spav'in, a swelling of the parts about the hock joint of a horse, caused by bleeding within the joint.

blood'stāin, *n.* a dark discoloration caused by a blot or smear of blood.

blood'stāin, *v.t.* to discolor with blood.

blood'stāined, *a.* stained with blood; hence, guilty of murder.

blood'stick, *n.* a piece of wood weighted with lead, used in veterinary surgery to force a lancet into a vein.

blood'stōne, *n.* 1. a semiprecious, dark-green variety of quartz spotted with red jasper, used as a gem: the usual birthstone for March: often called *heliotrope.*
2. hematite, a valuable iron ore.

blood strēam, the blood flowing through the body.

blood'strōke, *n.* apoplexy.

blood'suck"ẽr, *n.* 1. any animal that sucks blood; specifically, the leech.
2. a cruel man; a murderer. [Obs.]
3. a person who extorts or takes from others as much as he can get; an extortioner.

blood sụg'ăr (shụg'), sugar in the blood; also, its relative percentage in the blood, a percentage of more than 0.15 usually indicating a pathological condition.

blood test, an analysis of a small amount of a person's blood, for the purpose of determining the relative proportions of its constituent elements, the presence in it of abnormal contents, etc.

blood'thīrst"i·ness, *n.* the desire to shed blood.

blood'thīrst"y, *a.* eager to shed blood; murderous; cruel.

blood trans·fū'ṣiŏn (-zhun), in medicine, the transference of blood from one person to another.

blood tree, a small West Indian tree, named from the color of its juice: also called *dragon's blood.*

blood tȳpe, in physiology, one of the four general kinds of blood.

blood tȳp'ing, the examination of a person's blood for the purpose of determining his blood type: compatible types are used in blood transfusion.

blood'ulf, *n.* the European species of bullfinch.

blood'-vas"çū·lăr, *a.* relating to blood vessels.

blood ves'sel, any vessel in which blood circulates in the body; an artery, a vein, or a capillary.

blood'wīte, *n.* in ancient law, a fine paid as a compensation for the shedding of blood; also, a riot in which blood was shed: sometimes spelled *bloodwit.*

blood'wood, *n.* any of several trees with red wood or sap; especially, the logwood.

blood'wŏrm, *n.* 1. the active red larva of a fly of the dipterous genus *Chironomus.*
2. a parasite living in the blood.

blood'wŏrt, *n.* any of a species of *Rumex* with red roots or leaves, as the bloodroot.

blood'y, *a.;* *comp.* bloodier; *superl.* bloodiest.
1. stained with blood.
2. cruel; murderous; given to the shedding of blood; having a cruel, savage disposition.
3. attended with bloodshed; marked by cruelty: applied to things; as, a *bloody* battle.
4. full of or like blood; as, *bloody* sweat.
5. cursed; damned. [Brit. Slang.]
6. having the color of blood.
bloody flux; a form of dysentery in which the discharges from the bowels have a mixture of blood.
bloody hand; a hand stained with deer's blood, which, under the old English forest laws, was sufficient evidence of trespass; also, a red hand used as the distinctive ensign of the order of baronets.
bloody man's finger; the foxglove.

blood'y, *v.t.* bloodied *pt., pp.;* bloodying, *ppr.*
1. to cover or stain with blood.
2. to draw blood from.

blood'y, *adv.* very; as, *bloody* sick; *bloody* drunk. [Brit. Slang.]

blood'y·bōneṣ, *n.* a bugbear.

blood'y-eȳed, *a.* having bloody or cruel eyes.

blood'y-fāced, *a.* having a bloody face or appearance.

blood'y-fluxed, *a.* afflicted with the bloody flux.

blood'y-mīnd"ed, *a.* having a fierce, evil disposition; barbarous; inclined to murder.

blood'y-scep"tēred, *a.* having a scepter obtained by blood or slaughter.

blood'y wạr"riŏr (-yēr), the wallflower, or bleeding heart [*Cheiranthus Cheiri*).

blọọm, *n.* [ME. *blome*, a blossom; AS. *blōstma*, a blossom, from *blōwan*, to blow, bloom.]

1. a blossom; the flower of a plant; an expanded bud.

While opening *blooms* diffuse their sweets around. —Pope.

2. the opening of flowers in general; state or time of blossoming.

3. a state or time of most beauty, vigor, health, or freshness; as, the *bloom* of youth.

4. the fine gray dust found upon plums and grapes newly gathered; also, figuratively, anything lending freshness to the appearance; a youthful, healthy glow; as, the *bloom* on her cheeks.

5. any fine gray coating, as on new coins.

6. the appearance of cloudiness sometimes given to a picture by varnish.

7. the yellow powder found on leather after a complete tanning.

8. any of several minerals of a bright color, usually found in a powdery state.

blọọm, *v.i.*; bloomed, *pt.*, *pp.*; blooming, *ppr.* 1. to produce or yield blossoms; to flower.

2. to be in a state of healthful, growing youth and vigor; to be in one's prime.

3. to glow with color, health, etc.

blọọm, *v.t.* to make flower; to give a bloom to; to cause to flourish.

Charitable affection *bloomed* them. —Hooker.

blọọm, *n.* [AS. *blōma*, a lump of metal, in a deflected sense from *blōwan*, to blow.]

1. in metallurgy, a rough, heavy, and relatively short bar of wrought iron made from the puddling balls. It is the form in which the metal is handled prior to its being formed into bars.

2. a thick bar of iron or steel obtained by rolling or hammering an ingot.

blọọm'ȧ·ry, *n.* same as *bloomery*.

blọọm'ēr, *n.* [named for Mrs. Amelia *Bloomer*, of New York, who in 1849–50 attempted to introduce this type of dress for general use.]

1. a costume for women, consisting of a short skirt extending to the knees, loose trousers fastened about the ankles, and, usually, a large, low hat.

2. a woman dressed in a bloomer costume.

3. a slip of the tongue; a mistake. [Slang.]

blọọm'ērs̗, *n.pl.* [see *bloomer*, 1.] 1. loose, baggy trousers worn by women or girls for athletics: usually they reach to the knee.

2. an undergarment, worn by women, made of silk, cotton, or wool, fitting tightly at the waist and knee.

blọọm'ēr·y, *n.* in iron working, a puddling furnace or forge in which the ore is made directly into wrought-iron blooms.

blọọm'ing, *a.* 1. opening in blossoms; flowering.

2. thriving in health, beauty, and vigor; showing the freshness and beauties of youth; flourishing.

3. utter; confounded; extreme; as, a *blooming* fool. [Colloq.]

Syn.—flourishing, fair, flowering, blossoming, young, beautiful.

blọọm'ing, *n.* in metallurgy, the process of making blooms.

blọọm'ing, *n.* 1. the clouded appearance, like the bloom of grapes or plums, sometimes assumed by varnish, as on the surface of a picture.

2. in dyeing, the bright appearance of goods due to the addition of some substance after the dyeing proper is completed.

blọọm'ing·ly, *adv.* in a flourishing or thriving manner.

blọọm'ing·ness, *n.* a flourishing condition; thriving state.

blọọm'ing sal'ly, the willow herb, *Epilobium angustifolium*.

blọọm'less, *a.* lacking bloom or flowers.

blọọm'y, *a.*; *comp.* bloomier; *superl.* bloomiest, 1. full of bloom; flowery; flourishing with the vigor of youth; as, a *bloomy* spray, *bloomy* beauties.

2. covered with bloom, as ripe plums.

blọọp, *v.i.* [onomatopoeic.] in radio, to howl, as a receiving set.

blọọp'ēr, *n.* a radio set that bloops.

blọọp'ing, *n.* a howling sound produced by a radio receiving set when under the influence of radiation from the antenna of a near-by set.

blọọth, *n.* the process of blooming or blossoming. [Prov. Eng.]

blōre, *n.* the act of blowing: a blast. [Obs.]

blos'sŏm, *n.* [ME. *blossome*; AS. *blōstma*, *blōsthma*, a blossom, flower, from *blowan*, to blow.]

1. a flower or bloom, especially of a fruit-bearing plant.

2. a state or time of flowering, literally and figuratively.

3. the peculiar color of a horse, when bay or sorrel hairs are mixed freely with white; a kind of peach color.

in blossom; in the period of blossoming; applied to plants or trees.

blos'sŏm, *v.i.*; blossomed, *pt.*, *pp.*; blossoming, *ppr.* 1. to have or open into blossoms or flowers; to bloom; to flower.

2. to flourish and prosper.

The desert shall rejoice, and *blossom* as the rose. —Isa. xxxv. 1.

blos'sŏm·less, *a.* without blossoms.

blos'sŏm·y, *a.* 1. having many blossoms.

2. like a blossom.

blot, *v.t.*; blotted, *pt.*, *pp.*; blotting, *ppr.* [ME. *blotten*, to blot, from Ice. *blettr*, a blot, spot.]

1. to spot; to stain or bespatter; to blur; as, to *blot* a paper.

2. to obliterate; to cancel or efface (usually with *out*); as, to *blot out* a sentence; to *blot out* a crime.

3. to dry with or as with blotting paper, as manuscript.

4. to stain (a reputation); to tarnish; to disgrace; to disfigure; to impair; to damage.

Blot not thy innocence with guiltless blood. —Rowe.

5. to darken; to eclipse; to obscure (with *out*).

Syn.—expunge, erase, efface, cancel, obliterate.

blot, *v.i.* 1. to make blots, as of ink.

2. to absorb or diffuse, as ink; as, this paper *blots* nicely.

3. to become blotted.

blot, *n.* [ME. *blot*, *blotte*, a blot, probably from Ice. *blettr*, a stain.]

1. a spot or stain: usually applied to ink.

2. an obliteration of something written or printed; an erasure.

3. a spot on the reputation; a stain; a disgrace; a reproach; blemish.

4. a disgraceful person.

5. an unsightly thing, especially one out of place; as, that building is a *blot* on the landscape.

blot, *n.* [prob. from D. *bloot*, bare, naked, exposed.]

1. in backgammon, (a) an exposure of an unprotected piece; (b) a single man so exposed.

2. an unprotected point; a weak spot; a place inviting attack; a failing.

blotch (bloch), *v.t.*; blotched, *pt.*, *pp.*; blotching, *ppr.* to disfigure with blotches; to put blotches on.

blotch, *n.* 1. a discolored or broken-out patch on the skin, an eruption.

2. any large, irregular blot or spot, as an ink *blotch*, or a paint *blotch*; hence, a disfiguring stain or blemish; as, a moral *blotch*.

blotched, *a.* covered with blotches.

blotch'y, *a.*; *comp.* blotchier; *superl.* blotchiest. 1. marked with blotches.

2. like a blotch.

blōte, *v.t.* to bloat. [Obs.]

blot'less, *a.* having no blot.

blot'tēr, *n.* 1. a piece of blotting paper; a means of removing an excess of liquid ink from the surface of paper by absorption.

2. a book for recording events or transactions as they occur; as, a police *blotter* is a record of arrests and charges.

blot·tesque' (-tesk'), *a.* in painting, characterized by blots or heavy touches; blotchy.

blot·tesque' (-tesk'), *n.* a blurred or dauby piece of work.

blot'ting, *n.* the making of blots; a staining or obliterating; also, the act of absorbing blots.

blot'ting pā'pēr, a kind of thick, soft paper serving to absorb wet ink.

blot'tō, *a.* [perhaps from *blot* (to absorb).] very drunk; unconscious because of drinking too much. [Slang.]

blouse (*or* blouz), *n.* [Fr. (18th c.) workman's or peasant's smock.]

1. a loose upper garment worn by certain European peasants and workmen.

2. a loose outer garment extending to the waistline or just below, worn by women and children; a kind of shirtwaist.

3. a coat or tunic worn by soldiers, marines, and navy officers.

4. a sailor's jumper.

blouse (*or* blouz), *v.t.* and *v.i.*; bloused, *pt.*, *pp.*; blousing, *ppr.* to gather in at the waistline; to drape loosely.

blōw, *n.* [ME. *blaw*, a blow.]

1. a hit or stroke; a sudden and violent impact of the hand, fist, or an instrument, against an object or person.

2. an act of hostility; a sudden attack or forcible effort; as, the nation which strikes the first *blow*.

3. a sudden calamity or misfortune; sudden or severe evil; as, the *blows* of fortune were too hard for him.

at a blow; in a single act; with a single effort; in one sweep; as, to gain a kingdom *at a blow*.

to come to blows; to engage in combat.

Syn.—stroke, infliction, disappointment, affliction, knock, shock, calamity, misfortune.

blōw, *v.i.*; blew, *pt.*; blown, *pp.*; blowing, *ppr.* [ME. *blowen*, *blawen*; AS. *blawan*, to blow.]

1. to stir or speed up a current of air; to move, as air; particularly, to move with appreciable force or speed; as, the wind *blows*.

2. to send forth air with or as with the mouth; hence, to pant; to puff; to breathe hard or quick.

3. to give forth sounds or tones by blowing or being blown, as a horn or trumpet.

4. to eject a stream of water or other fluid and air, as a whale or geyser.

5. to be carried about or along by the wind; as, the dust *blows* throughout August in that region.

6. to talk loudly or boastingly. [Colloq.]

7. to storm.

8. to lay eggs: said of flies.

9. to go away; to leave. [Slang.]

to blow hot and cold; to act inconsistently; to be favorable toward and then opposed to.

to blow in; (a) to squander; (b) to arrive. [Slang.]

to blow off; (a) to emit a stream of water or steam; to let off pressure, as a boiler; (b) [Colloq.] to let one's emotions or thoughts out, as by loud or long talking.

to blow out; (a) to burst suddenly, as a tire; (b) in electricity, to be melted or burned by too much electric current, as a fuse; hence, to fail, as an electrical apparatus; (c) to come out suddenly or violently, as steam or air.

to blow over; to pass away; to cease or be dissipated; as, the clouds have *blown over*; the scandal will *blow over*.

to blow up; (a) to be disrupted by an explosion; as, a powder magazine *blows up*; (b) to arise and become more intense, as a storm. (c) [Colloq.] to lose one's temper.

blōw, *v.t.* 1. to throw or drive a current of air upon; also, to fan.

2. to drive by a current of air; as, the tempest *blew* the ship ashore.

3. to breathe upon; as, to *blow* the fingers on a cold day.

4. to sound (a wind instrument) by blowing; as, *blow* the trumpet.

5. to make (a sound or signal) by blowing.

6. to cool, warm, dry, or soothe by blowing on or toward.

7. to intensify (a fire) by blowing.

8. to inflame.

9. to spread by report.

And through the court his courtesy was *blown*. —Dryden.

10. to deposit eggs on, as flies do on meat.

11. to form by inflating, as glass in the plastic state is formed into a desired shape by the breath, or as soap bubbles are formed.

12. to put out of breath from fatigue; to cause to pant; as, to *blow* a horse.

13. to clean or clear by forcing air or fluid through; as, to *blow* the nose; to *blow* boiler tubes.

14. to destroy; to explode; usually followed by *up*, *down*; as, the wind *blew* the house *down*; the steam *blew* the boiler *up*.

15. to melt (a fuse, etc.).

16. to spend (money) freely. [Colloq.]

17. to treat (*to* something). [Slang.]

18. to go away from; to leave. [Slang.]

to blow away; to dissipate; to scatter with wind.

to blow off; (a) to remove, as by wind; as, to *blow off* fruit, from trees; (b) to cause the whole or a part of a fluid under pressure to escape from (a receptacle) by rising through an opening; as, to *blow off* a boiler.

to blow one's own trumpet; to resort to fulsome self-praise.

to blow out; (a) to extinguish by a current of air, as a candle; (b) in electricity, to cause to be melted or burned by the current.

to blow out the brains of; to kill by shooting through the head.

to blow through; to admit live steam into the condenser of (a steam engine) in order to drive out the air, preliminary to starting the engine.

to blow up; (a) to fill with air; to swell; as, to *blow up* a bladder or a bubble; (b) to inflate; to puff up; as, to *blow* one *up* with flattery; (c) to burst, to raise into the air, or to scatter, by explosion; (c) [Colloq.] to scold severely; (d) in photography, to enlarge (a picture).

to blow upon; to betray. [Slang.]

blōw, *n.* 1. a strong or violent air movement; a strong wind; a gale; as, the great *blow* of '99.

2. the act of forcing air through anything, as the mouth or an instrument.

3. the stream of water and air emitted by a whale.

4. in metallurgy, the time consumed in one operation of the Bessemer process, or the mass of metal acted on at one time.

5. an egg deposited by a fly on flesh or other substance; also called a *fly blow.*

6. (a) inflated speech; boastfulness; brag; (b) [Slang.] a braggart.

blōw, *v.i.*; blew, *pt.*, blown, *pp.*; blowing, *ppr.* [AS. *blowan*, to bloom.] to bloom; to flower.

blōw, *v.t.* 1. to cause to bloom.

2. to put forth (blossoms), as plants.

blōw, *n.* 1. a profusion of blossoms.

2. any splendid display.

blōw'ball, *n.* a downy head, as of the dandelion, formed by the pappus, after the blossom has fallen.

blōw'çock, *n.* a cock for blowing off pressure in a steam boiler.

blōw'-drȳ", *v.t.;* blow-dried, *pt., pp.;* blow-drying, ppr. to dry (wet hair) with an electric device that sends out a stream of heated air.

blōw'-drȳ", *n.* the act of blow-drying the hair.

blōw'-drȳ"ẽr, *n.* an electric device for blow-drying the hair.

blōw'ẽr, *n.* 1. one who blows; one who is employed in smelting tin or blowing glass.

2. a machine for ventilating a building or shaft, for blowing air into a furnace, for cleaning grain, etc.; a mechanical fan.

3. a blowing out of gas from a hole in a coal mine.

4. the whale.

5. the swellfish, or puffer, *Spheroides maculatus*, found along the Atlantic coast.

6. a loud or boastful talker. [Slang.]

blōw'fish, *n.; pl.* **blōw'fish** or **blōw'fish·eṣ,** 1. any fish which can blow up or inflate its body.

2. the walleyed pike, a fresh-water fish.

blōw'flȳ, *n.; pl.* **blōw'flieṣ,** a species of dipterous insect, *Musca carnaria*, that deposits its eggs in meat or in the wounds of living animals.

blōw'gun, *n.* 1. a tube-shaped weapon, of cane or reed, directing and propelling a missile ejected by a strong puff of breath: used by various savage tribes.

2. a device using compressed air for spraying paint, oil, etc.

blōw'härd, *n.* a person who talks much and foolishly or boastfully. [Slang.]

blōw'hōle, *n.* 1. a hole through which gas or air can escape.

2. a hole in the ice giving seals and the like access to air.

3. the hole in the top of the head through which the whale, dolphin, and similar mammals breathe.

4. a flaw in a casting made by a gas or air bubble.

blōw'ing, *n.* 1. the sound of a blast of air or gas.

2. noisy breathing, as of a horse.

blōw'ing ad'dẽr, same as *puff adder.*

blōwn, past participle of *blow* (to make a current of air).

blōwn, *a.* 1. swollen with gas.

2. out of breath, as with effort.

3. flyblown.

4. made by blowing or by using a blowpipe, etc.

blōwn, past participle of *blow* (to bloom).

blōwn, *a.* opened, as a flower; unfolded; having blossomed; as, a full-*blown* rose.

blōw'ọff", *n.* 1. a blowing off, as of steam; also, the device causing it.

2. a boaster. [Slang.]

blōw'ọff", *a.* pertaining to a blowoff; as, a *blowoff* cock.

blōw'out, *n.* 1. the act or state of blowing out or having blown out.

2. the bursting of a tire.

3. the melting of an electric fuse from too much current.

4. an entertainment; a festive occasion or celebration. [Slang.]

blōw'pīpe, *n.* 1. a tube by which a current of air is driven into a flame to intensify and concentrate its heat.

2. a blowgun.

3. a blowtube.

blowpipe analysis; a method of rapid qualitative analysis of mineral substances which utilizes the heat of the blowpipe to facilitate the reactions.

BLOWPIPE
a, ball for catching the moisture of the mouth; *b*, nozzle

blōw'point, *n.* a game for children, in which arrows or small pins were blown through a tube at certain numbers. [Obs.]

blowṣe, *n.* same as *blowze.*

blōwth, *n.* a bloom or blossom; the state of blossoming; blossoms collectively. [Obs. or Dial.]

blōw'tọrch, *n.* a small gasoline torch that shoots out a hot flame intensified by a blast of air: it is used to melt metal, remove old paint, etc.

blōw'tūbe, *n.* 1. a blowgun.

2. a metal tube for discharging light missiles; a pea shooter: usually used by children.

3. in glass making, a hollow metal tube with which the blower gathers up the semifluid glass and by blowing through which he expands the molten material while shaping it on the marver.

blōw valve, the snifting valve of a condensing engine.

blōw'y, *a.; comp.* blowier; *superl.* blowiest, windy; breezy; gusty; as, *blowy* weather.

blowze, *n.* [AS. *blyscan, bliscan*, to blush, shine.] a ruddy, fat-faced woman; a blowzy woman; a wench. [Obs.]

blowzed, *a.* blowzy; ruddy; flushed; coarse-complexioned, as from exposure to weather.

Huge women *blowzed* with health and wind and rain. —Tennyson.

blowz'y, *a.; comp.* blowzier; *superl.* blowziest. 1. ruddy-faced; fat and flushed; course-complexioned.

A face made *blowzy* by cold and damp. —George Eliot.

2. unkempt; slatternly; disheveled; as, *blowzy* hair.

blub, *v.t.* to swell; to inflate, to blubber, as with weeping. [Obs.]

blub'bẽr, *n.* [ME. *blubber*, a bubble, formed from the verb.]

1. a bubble.

2. the fat of whales and other large sea mammals, from which oil is extracted. The blubber lies immediately under the skin and over the muscular flesh.

3. the sea nettle, or sea blubber; a jellyfish or medusa.

4. the act of blubbering.

blub'bẽr, *v.i.*; blubbered, *pt., pp.*; blubbering, *ppr.* [ME. *blubren*; G. dial. *blubbern*, to blubber; an onomatopoeic word.] to weep loudly, especially in such a manner as to puff out the cheeks or disfigure the face.

She wept, she *blubbered*, and she tore her hair. —Swift.

blub'bẽr, *v.t.* 1. to swell, wet, or disfigure (the face) with weeping.

2. to utter while blubbering; as, he *blubbered* his confession.

blub'bẽr, *a.* swollen, as from weeping.

blub'bẽred, *a.* swollen; marred; turgid; disfigured by or as by weeping; as, a *blubbered* lip.

blub'bẽr·ing, *n.* the act of weeping in a noisy, childish manner.

blub'bẽr·y, *a.* 1. swollen or disfigured, as by blubbering.

2. resembling blubber; fat.

3. of or full of blubber.

blū'chẽr (*or* blọọ'kẽr), *n.* [after Field Marshal von *Blücher* (1742–1819), Prussian general.]

1. a heavy half boot.

2. a kind of shoe in which the upper laps over the vamp, which is of one piece with the tongue.

bludġ'eŏn (bluj'ŏn), *n.* [origin unknown; perhaps from D. *bludsen, blutsen*, to bruise.] a short club with one end loaded or thicker and heavier than the other.

bludġ'eŏn, *v.t.* and *v.i.* 1. to strike with or as with a bludgeon.

2. to threaten; to coerce; to bully.

blūe, *n.* [ME. *blew, blewe*; Fr. *bleu*; O.H.G. *blao*, blue; AS. *blæw*, in deriv. as *blæwen*, bluish.]

1. any color between green and violet in the spectrum; the color of the clear sky or deep sea.

2. a dye or pigment of this hue or color.

3. the sky; the atmosphere: from its blue tint; as, a bolt from the *blue.*

4. the sea.

5. a pedantic literary woman: a contraction of *bluestocking.* [Colloq.]

6. a small blue butterfly.

7. bluing.

8. a member of a party or any organization of persons which has adopted blue as its color; as, the buffs and the *blues.*

9. a sailor.

10. [*pl.*] a sailor's blue uniform. [Slang.]

11. anything colored blue, as the second ring of an archer's target.

the blues; (a) [short for *blue devils.*], [Colloq.] a depressed, unhappy feeling; (b) a type of Negro folk song, characterized by minor harmony, slow jazz rhythm, and melancholy words; (c) any imitation of this.

blūe, *a.*; *comp.* bluer; *superl.* bluest. 1. having the color of the clear sky, or the deep sea.

2. despondent; melancholy; low or depressed in spirits; as, she looked a bit *blue* last night.

3. tending or suited to cause low spirits; dismal; dreary; lacking cheerfulness; as, a *blue* outlook, a *blue* day.

4. austere or puritanical in morals or religion; overstrict; as, a *blue* Covenanter; also, inculcating or prescribing a severe code of conduct; rigorous; as, *blue* laws.

5. genuine; faithful; unwavering; as, his friend was true *blue.*

6. having a purplish color; livid, as the skin from a bruise or from extreme cold or fear.

7. pedantic; learned: said of women, especially those with literary inclinations: an abbreviation of *bluestocking.*

8. pale, without glare or redness, as a flame; of the color of burning brimstone; hence, suggestive of the flames of hell; baleful; as, the air was *blue* with oaths.

9. indecent; obscene; as, *blue* stories. [Slang.]

blue asbestos; same as *crocidolite.*

blue cheese; a cheese similar to Roquefort, but made of cow's milk.

blue cod; the buffalo cod.

blue crab; the common edible crab found along the Atlantic coast of the United States.

blue devils; (a) low spirits; melancholy; (b) delirium tremens or its hallucinations.

blue flag; any iris with blue flowers.

blue fox; (a) an arctic fox during the period when its fur has a bluish cast; (b) its fur; (c) the fur of the white fox when dyed blue.

blue jaundice; same as *cyanosis.*

blue light; a composition burning with a brilliant blue flame, and used as a night signal at sea and in fireworks displays.

blue mantle; one of the pursuivants of the British College of Heralds: named from the color of his official dress.

blue mass; in pharmacology, a preparation containing powdered mercury, from which blue pills are formed.

blue mold; any mold or fungus of the genus *Penicillium*, which appears on cheese, bread, etc.

blue Monday; any Monday: so called because considered depressing as the beginning of a week of work contrasted with the pleasures of the weekend. [Colloq.]

blue ointment; in medicine, mercurial ointment for killing certain varieties of body lice.

blue peter; (a) a blue flag with a white square in the center, used as a signal to announce a ship's sailing, etc.; (b) the call for trumps in the game of whist.

blue pill; (a) a pill containing mercury, glycerin, honey, etc.; (b) blue mass.

blue racer; a harmless, long, blue-green North American snake that moves rapidly: also called *hoop snake, black snake.*

blue ribbon; (a) a member of the British Order of the Garter: so called from the ribbon worn as a badge; (b) first place in a competition; first prize; as, his horse won the *blue ribbon* at the fair; (c) a badge of temperance workers and total abstainers in America and

England. In colloquial usage, the term is applied attributively to a jury (*blue-ribbon jury*) whose members have been selected with special care.

blue ruin; (a) complete ruin; (b) gin. [Slang.]
blue spar; azure spar; lazulite.
blue vitriol; crystalline cupric sulfate, $CuSO_4 \cdot 5H_2O$.
blue water; the open sea.

blūe, *v.t.*; blued, *pt., pp.*; bluing *or* blueing, *ppr.* 1. to make blue; to dye blue.
2. to use bluing on or in.
3. to cause to become blue by a heating process; as, to *blue* steel.

blūe bā'by, a baby born with cyanosis as a result of a congenital heart lesion or incomplete expansion of the lungs.

blūe'back, *n.* 1. a trout found in some of the lakes of Maine.
2. a species of salmon found in the Columbia River and in rivers to the northward.
3. a river herring, *Clupea æstivalis.*

blūe' bạll, the nilgau, the dominant color of which is blue.

Blūe'bēard, *n.* a character in an old story who, when about to leave home, forbade his young wife to enter a certain room in his castle. Her curiosity being thus aroused, she disobeyed him, entered the forbidden chamber, and in it found the heads of several previous wives whom he had murdered.

blūe'bell, *n.* any one of various plants having blue, bell-shaped flowers; specifically, (a) in the United States, the grape hyacinth, *Muscari botryoides*, and the Virginia lungwort; (b) in England, the wild hyacinth, *Scilla nutans*; (c) in Scotland, the *Campanula rotundifolia*, or harebell.

blūe'ber"ry, *n.*; *pl.* **blūe'ber"rieṣ,** 1. an edible berry containing many tiny seeds, produced by any one of several varieties of *Vaccinium*. It differs from the American huckleberry, which contains ten nutlets instead of many seeds.
2. the shrub on which the blueberry grows.
3. the edible berry of an Australian tree, sometimes called the native currant.

blūe'bill, *n.* a duck of the genus *Fuligula*, especially the scaup.

blūe'bīrd, *n.* 1. a small song bird, *Sialia sialis*, very common in the United States. The upper part of the body is blue, and the throat and breast reddish.
2. any one of a number of other birds, as the slate-colored snowbird, *Junco hyemalis*, and the fairy bluebird of the East Indies.

blūe'-black, *a.* intensely black; so black as to have a bluish cast in bright light.

blūe black, a blue-black color or pigment.

blūe blood (blud), 1. descent from nobility or royalty.
2. a person of such descent; an aristocrat.

blūe'-blood·ed, *a.* 1. of royal or noble descent; aristocratic.
2. of pure breed.

blūe'bon"net, *n.* 1. (a) a bluebottle; (b) the blue flowering lupine.
2. the European blue titmouse; the bluecap, *Parus Cæruleus*.
3. a broad, flat cap of blue woolen, worn in Scotland; also, one wearing such a cap; a Scotsman.
Also written *blue bonnet*.

blūe'book, *n.* a blue book (in senses 3 and 4).

blūe book, 1. a British parliamentary publication: so called from its blue cover.
2. the official United States list of governmental officeholders.
3. a book listing people who are socially prominent.
4. a booklet with a blue paper cover, used in many colleges for students to write examination answers in.

blūe'bot"tle, *n.* 1. a plant, the *Centaurea cyanus*, which grows among grain, having white, pink, or purple flowers with bottle-shaped rays.
2. a large blowfly with a steel-blue abdomen and a hairy body.
3. any of several similar flies.

blūe'breast (-brest), *n.* a small European bird; the bluethroat.

blūe'buck, *n.* a South African antelope; the blaubok.

blūe'buṣh, *n.* a Mexican shrub, *Ceanothus azureus*, yielding abundant blue flowers and belonging to the buckthorn family.

blūe'but"tŏnṣ, *n.* in botany, some species of *Scabiosa*, having blue flowers.

blūe'çap, *n.* 1. a one-year-old salmon, with blue spots on its head. [Eng.]
2. the blue titmouse, or tomtit, of Europe.
3. a Scot or Scotsman; so called from wearing a blue bonnet.

blūe'-chip', *a.* [after the high-value *blue chips* of poker.]
1. designating any high-priced stock with a good record of earnings and price stability.
2. excellent, valuable, etc. [Colloq.]

blūe'çōat, *n.* any one dressed in a blue uniform, as a policeman or sailor.
bluecoat boy; a pupil of Christ's Hospital school, London; so named from the dress worn by the boys of this institution.

blūe'-çol'lar, *a.* [from the color of many work shirts.] designating or of industrial workers, especially the semiskilled and unskilled.

Blūe Cross, 1. a society organized in England in 1912 to promote humane treatment of horses, dogs, and other animals.
2. a similar society organized in New York in 1914.
3. any of a number of non-profit hospitalization plans in the United States and Canada.

blūe çurlṣ, any one of several herbs of the genus *Trichostema*, belonging to the mint family and having narrow leaves and blue flowers with blue or purple fuzz: sometimes called bastard pennyroyal.

blūe eȳe, in zoology, the blue-faced honeysucker of New South Wales.

blūe'-eȳed (-īd), *a.* having blue eyes.

blūe'-eȳed grȧss, any of a number of related plants of the iris family, with blue flowers and grasslike leaves.

blūe'fish, *n.*; *pl.* **blūe'fish** or **blūe'fish·eṣ,** 1. a food fish, *Pomatomus saltatrix*, common along the Atlantic coast of the United States. It is bluish in color, large, and voracious.
2. a marine fish of Florida and the West Indies, belonging to the family *Labridæ*.
3. any of various other fishes, as the bluegill, blue bass, etc.

blūe flụ, [from the traditional color of police uniforms.] a sickout, especially by police officers.

blūe'gill, *n.* a fresh-water sunfish of a bluish color.

blūe'gown, *n.* one of a class of licensed beggars or paupers in Scotland, called also the *king's beadsmen*, to whom formerly the kings annually distributed certain alms on condition of their praying for the royal welfare. The alms included a blue gown or cloak.

blūe'grȧss, in botany, any of several species of *Poa*, having bluish-green stems and adapted to light, gravelly soils; wire grass.
Bluegrass Region (or *Country*); a region in central Kentucky where there is much bluegrass: also *the Bluegrass*.

blūe'-green' al'ġae, a kind of algae that are typically bluish green.

blūe gum, a large, tall gum tree, *Eucalyptus globulus*, native to Australia, valuable for its timber, gums, and oil.

blūe'heärts, *n.*; *pl.* **blūe'heärts,** an American herb, *Buchnera americana*, of the figwort genus, having a terminal spike of dark-blue flowers and hairy leaves.

blūe'ing, *n.* bluing.

blūe'ish, *a.* bluish.

blūe'jack, *n.* 1. blue vitriol.
2. a small oak tree of the southern United States.

blūe'jack"et, *n.* an enlisted man in the United States or British navy.

blūe'jāy, *n.* any of a number of related noisy, crested birds with a blue back: also *blue jay*.

blūe john, a kind of blue fluor spar, found in the mines of Derbyshire, England, and made into vases and ornamental figures.

blūe lạw, 1. any of the strict puritanical laws prevalent in colonial New England.
2. a law prohibiting dancing, shows, sports, business, etc. on Sunday.

blūe'ly, *adv.* with a blue color.

blūe'ness, *n.* the quality of being blue; a blue color.

blūe'nōṣe, *n.* 1. [B–] a Nova Scotian: so called because of the cold climate. [Colloq.]
2. a puritanical person. [Colloq.]

blūe'-pen'cil, *v.t.* to edit, cut, or correct (a manuscript, etc.): from the blue marking made by the pencils generally used by editors.

blūe'point, *n.* an oyster much in favor for eating raw because of its small size; originally, an oyster found at Blue Point, Long Island.

blūe'point"ēr, *n.* a shark, *Lamna glauca*, of the Pacific Ocean.

blūe'print, *n.* 1. a photographic reproduction in white on a blue background, as of architectural or engineering plans.
2. any exact or detailed plan or outline.

blūe'print, *v.t.* to make a blueprint of.

blūe proc'ess, the making of blueprints.

blūe'-skȳ', *a.* [see next entry.] of no value; worthless.

blūe'-skȳ' lạw, a law designed to regulate the selling of stocks and bonds, in the interest of protecting the public from fraud. [Colloq.]

blūe'stärt, *n.* [G. *blausterz*, the blue tail.] the blue-tailed warbler, *Ianthia cyanura*.

blūe'stock"ing, *n.* 1. [from the unconventional blue worsted stockings worn by a leading figure at literary meetings in 18th-c. London.] a learned, bookish, or pedantic woman.
2. in zoology, the American avocet, *Recurvirostra americana*.

blūe'stock"ing·iṣm, *n.* a taste for the literary, or for pedantry, as shown by a woman.

blūe'stōne, *n.* 1. blue vitriol.
2. any building stone of a bluish color; specifically, a blue-gray sandstone.

blūe strēak, anything regarded as like a streak of lightning in speed, vividness, etc. [Colloq.]
talk a blue streak; to talk much and rapidly.

blū'et, *n.* [Fr. *bluet*, the cornflower; dim. of *bleu*, blue.] a blue-flowered plant, growing in small, rounded tufts, as *Houstonia cærulea*.

blūe'thrōat, *n.* a singing bird, with a tawny breast marked with a sky-blue crescent, inhabiting northern Europe and Asia.

blūe'weed, *n.* a bristly weed with blue flowers and pink buds.

blūe'wing, *n.* the blue-winged teal.

blūe'-winged tēal, any of a group of small North American ducks found on ponds and rivers and having bluish markings on the wings.

blūe'wood, *n.* a compact shrub, *Condalia obovata*, found in southwestern United States and adjacent parts of Mexico.

blūe'y, *n.*; *pl.* **blūe'yṣ,** in Australia, a bushman's bundle, or the blue blanket in which it is generally wrapped.

blūe'y, *a.* somewhat blue; bluish.

bluff, *a.* [orig. a nautical term from D. *blaf*, flat, broad; L.G. *blaffen*, to frighten.]
1. having, or ascending steeply with, a broad, flat front.
2. rough and hearty; plain and frank; somewhat boisterous and unconventional.

Bluff Harry broke into the spence,
And turn'd the cowls adrift.
—Tennyson.

3. pompous; surly; churlish. [Obs.]
Syn.—open, bold, abrupt, frank, plain-spoken, blunt, brusque, rough.

bluff, *n.* a high, steep, broad-faced bank or cliff.

bluff, *v.t.* and *v.i.* [17th c.; prob. from D. *bluffen* or *verbluffen*, to baffle, mislead.]
1. to mislead (a person) by a false, bold front.
2. to frighten (a person) by threats that cannot be made good.
3. in poker, to try to mislead (other players) by betting or raising the bet while holding poor cards.

bluff, *n.* 1. a bluffing.
2. a person who bluffs.

bluff'-bowed, *a.* having broad and flat bows, as a boat or ship.

bluff'ēr, *n.* one who bluffs.

bluff'-head"ed (-hed"), *a.* in nautical language, bluff-bowed.

bluff'ness, *n.* the state or quality of being bluff.

bluff'y, *a.* 1. having bluffs, or bold projecting points of land.
2. inclined to bluffness in speech or action.

blū'ing, *n.* 1. the act of making or rendering blue; as, the *bluing* of steel; the *bluing* of clothes in a laundry.
2. any preparation as indigo or other blue coloring matter used in rinsing white fabrics to prevent yellowing: also spelled *blueing*.

blū'ish, *a.* somewhat blue.

blū'ish·ly, *adv.* in a bluish manner.

blū'ish·ness, *n.* a small degree of blue color.

blun'dēr, *v.i.*; blundered, *pt. pp.*, blundering, *ppr.* [ME. *blondren*, *blunderen*, to blunder; from ON. *blunda*, to shut the eyes.]
1. to be grossly mistaken; to err foolishly or stupidly; as, some one had *blundered*.
2. to move clumsily or carelessly; flounder, stumble.

blun'dēr, *v.t.* 1. to do (something) blunderingly; to botch; as, to *blunder* an example.
2. to say stupidly, clumsily, or confusedly; to blurt (with *out*).

blun'dēr, *n.* a foolish or stupid mistake; a gross error.
Syn.—error, mistake, oversight.

blun'dēr·buss, *n.* [*blunder*, on account of its

random action, and D. *bus*, box, gunbarrel; or D. *donderbus*, a thunderbox.]

1. an obsolete short gun with a broad muzzle.

2. a stupid blundering fellow.

BLUNDERBUSS

blun′dẽr·ẽr, *n.* one who is apt to blunder, or to make gross mistakes; a careless person.

blun′dẽr·head (-hed), *n.* a stupid fellow; one who blunders.

blun′dẽr·ing, *a.* making blunders; as, a *blundering* idiot.

blun′dẽr·ing·ly, *adv.* in a blundering manner.

blunġe, *v.t.*; blunged, *pt., pp.*; blunging, *ppr.* [perhaps from *plunge.*] in ceramics, to mix (clay, etc.) with water.

blun′ġẽr, *n.* 1. in ceramics, an instrument having a straight, flat, wooden blade, used for mixing clay with water.

2. a blunging apparatus.

3. a person who blunges.

blun′ġing, *n.* the process of mixing clay and water with a blunger.

blunt, *a.*; *comp.* blunter; *superl.* bluntest [ME. *blunt, blont*, blunt, sluggish; prob. from ON.]

1. having a dull edge or point, as an instrument; not sharp.

2. dull in understanding; slow to perceive; obtuse.

3. abrupt in address; plain-spoken; unceremonious; wanting the forms of civility; rough in manners or speech.

Syn.—dull, thick, edgeless, obtuse, pointless, coarse, rude, uncivil.

blunt, *v.t.*; blunted, *pt., pp.*; blunting, *ppr.* 1. to dull, as an edge of point, by making thicker.

2. to repress or weaken, as an appetite, desire, or power of the mind; to impair the force of; as, to *blunt* the edge of love; to *blunt* the stings of pain.

blunt, *v.i.* to become dull or insensitive.

blunt, *n.* 1. a kind of needle used for heavy work.

2. a fencing foil having a blunt point. [Obs.]

blunt′ish, *a.* somewhat dull or blunt.

blunt′ish·ness, *n.* the state of being bluntish.

blunt′ly, *adv.* in a blunt manner; abruptly.

blunt′ness, *n.* the state or quality of being blunt.

blunt′-wit″ted, *a.* dull; stupid.

blũr, *n.* 1. a confused, ill-defined, or dim figure, outline, or representation; an indistinct appearance.

2. a dark spot; a stain; a blot, whether upon paper or other substance, or upon reputation.

3. the state of being blurred or dim.

blũr, *v.t.* and *v.i.*; blurred, *pt., pp.*; blurring, *ppr.* 1. to smear; stain; blot; smudge.

2. to make or become hazy or indistinct in outline or shape.

3. to dim.

blũrb, *n.* [arbitrary coinage (c. 1914) by Gelett Burgess, "to sound like a publisher."] an exaggerated or fulsome advertisement or announcement, as on a book jacket. [Colloq.]

blũr′ry, *a.* 1. somewhat blurred; hazy in outline; dim.

2. full of blurs; smeary; stained.

blũrt, *v.t.*; blurted, *pt., pp.*; blurting, *ppr.* [16th–17th c.; perhaps from *bl*ow, *bl*ast, etc., and *spurt*, *squirt*.] to say thoughtlessly, suddenly, or impulsively (with *out*).

blush, *v.i.*; blushed, *pt., pp.*; blushing, *ppr.* [ME. *bluschen, blyschen*, to glow, glance; AS. *blyscan, bliscan*, to shine.]

1. to redden in the cheeks or over the face, as from a sense of guilt, shame, confusion, or modesty; as, *blush* at your vices; *blush* for your degraded country; hence, to be ashamed (usually with *at* or *for*).

2. to exhibit a red or rosy color; to be red.

Made the western welkin *blush*. —Shak.

3. to bloom; to blossom.

Full many a flower is born to *blush* unseen. —Gray.

blush, *v.t.* 1. to make red by blushing; as, to *blush* the cheek.

2. to express by blushing.

blush, *n.* 1. a red color suffusing the cheeks only, or the face generally, and excited by confusion, which may spring from shame, guilt, modesty, diffidence, or surprise.

2. a red or reddish color; a rosy tint.

at first blush; at first glance; at first sight; without further consideration.

to put to the blush; to cause shame, confusion, or embarrassment to.

blush, *a.* having the color of a blush.

blush′ẽr, *n.* 1. a person who blushes, especially one who blushes readily.

2. any of various cosmetic powders, gels, creams, etc. applied to the face to give it color.

blush′ful, *a.* full of blushes.

blush′ful·ly, *adv.* with many blushes.

blush′ing, *n.* the act of turning red; the appearance of color on the cheeks.

blush′ing·ly, *adv.* in a blushing manner.

blush′wŏrt, *n.* in botany, a cultivated plant of the gentian family.

blush′y, *a.* like a blush; having the color of a blush. [Rare.]

blus′tẽr, *v.i.*; blustered, *pt., pp.*; blustering, *ppr.* [ME. *blostren, blustren*, to rush violently.]

1. to threaten noisily without the intention or power to make good the threat.

2. to be loud, noisy, or swaggering; to bully; to puff; to swagger, as a turbulent or boasting person.

3. to roar and be tumultuous, as wind; to be windy.

blus′tẽr, *v.t.* 1. to utter in a blustering manner; as, to *bluster* out blasphemy.

2. to force by blustering; to bully.

blus′tẽr, *n.* 1. a blustering threat.

2. noise; tumult; boisterousness.

3. roar of a tempest; violent wind; any stormy noise and tumult from wind.

Syn.—boasting, bragging, bullying, raging, storming, swaggering.

blus′tẽr·ẽr, *n.* one who blusters; that which blusters; specifically, a braggart or bully.

blus′tẽr·ing, *a.* 1. stormy; windy; as, *blustering* weather.

2. noisy; tumultuous; swaggering; as, a *blustering* fellow.

blus′tẽr·ing·ly, *adv.* in a blustering manner.

blus′tẽr·ous, blus′trous, *a.* blustery.

blus′tẽr·y, *a.* blustering.

-bly, -ably: used to form adverbs corresponding to adjectives ending in *-ble*, as possi*bly*.

B′nāi B′rith, a Jewish fraternity founded in New York in 1843, now international in membership.

bō, *n.* a hobo. [Slang.]

bō, *interj.* a sound that one makes in order to frighten, startle, etc. Written also *boh* and *boo*.

not able to say bo! to a goose; very timid.

Bō′a, *n.* [L. *boa*, also *bova*, a water serpent.]

1. a genus of ophidian reptiles, family *Boidæ*, distinguished from allied families by having a prehensile tail.

2. [b–] any snake of this genus.

3. [b–] a long, ornamental scarf of fur, feathers, or other material, worn by women around the neck or shoulders.

boa constrictor; a large and powerful species of boa, pale brown with dark crossbars, which attains a length of ten to fifteen feet. The name has also been loosely applied to other large serpents, particularly of the genus *Python*, found in Asia and Africa.

BOA CONSTRICTOR

Bō·ȧ·nẽr′ġēs, *n.pl.* [Gr. *Boanerges*, from Heb. *benōi regesh*, sons of wrath: interpreted in Greek as "sons of thunder."]

1. sons of thunder: an appellation given by Jesus to two of his disciples, James and John: Mark iii. 17.

2. [*construed as sing.*] a loudmouthed, declamatory preacher or speaker.

bōar, *n.* [ME. *boor, bore*; AS. *bār*, boar.]

1. an uncastrated hog.

2. a wild hog of Europe, Asia, and Africa, with a hairy coat and a long snout.

bōard, *n.* [ME. *bord*; AS. *bord, bred*, a plank, shield, flat surface.]

1. a long piece of timber sawed thin, used for building and other purposes; a thin plank.

2. a table at which food is eaten; hence, food served at a table.

3. meals provided regularly for pay.

4. a table at which a council or court is held; hence, a council convened for business, or any group of administrators; as, a *board* of directors; a school *board*.

5. a tablet of wood, pasteboard, or other material adapted for a particular use; as, a chess*board*, a mortar*board*, a bulletin *board*, etc.

6. a heavy pasteboard; paper made stiff and thick, to be used for book covers, etc.

7. [*pl.*] the stage (of a theater): with *the*: used especially in the phrase *to tread the boards*, to be an actor.

bed and board; food and lodging regularly supplied; as, to work for *bed and board*.

board of directors; the body of directors controlling a corporation.

board of education; the board directing and supervising the schools of a district or municipality; a school board.

board of health; a government department that supervises public health.

board of pardon; a body of commissioners appointed to act on pardons.

board of trade; (a) in the United States, an association of businessmen for the promotion and furtherance of their business interests; (b) [B–T–] in England, a committee of the privy council with control over industry and commerce.

to sweep the board; to win all the tricks at a game of cards; also, to win all the prizes in a contest.

bōard, *v.t.*; boarded, *pt., pp.*; boarding, *ppr.* 1. to lay or spread with boards; to cover with boards (often with *up*).

2. to furnish with food, or food and lodging, regularly for pay; as, she *boards* ten students.

3. to put where board is supplied; as, I board my horse at a livery stable.

bōard, *v.i.* to receive table board or board and lodging at a price; as, he *boards* at a private house.

to board out; to board elsewhere than at home.

to board round; to live in rotation at different houses in the community, as formerly in the case of country school teachers.

bōard, *n.* [ME. and AS. *bord*, side of a ship, shield; akin to ON. *borth*, edge, border, ship's side.]

1. the side of a ship, as in over*board*.

2. a rim, border, or coast, as in sea*board*.

3. in nautical usage, (a) a tack; (b) the distance made in a single tack.

on board; on or in a ship, aircraft, bus, etc.

to go by the board; (a) to fall or be swept overboard; (b) to be got rid of, lost, ruined, etc.

bōard, *v.t.* 1. to come alongside (a ship) especially with hostile purpose.

2. to come over the rail and onto the deck of (a ship).

3. to get on (a train, bus, etc.).

4. to accost.

bōard, *v.i.* in nautical usage, to tack.

bōard′ȧ·ble, *a.* capable of being boarded, as a ship.

bōard′ẽr, *n.* one who pays for food and lodging in another's house; a paying guest.

bōard′ẽr, *n.* one who boards a ship, aircraft, etc.; one who is selected to board a hostile ship; as, *boarders*, away!

bōard foot; *pl.* **bōard feet,** a unit of measure of lumber, equal to a board one foot square and one inch thick.

bōard′ing, *n.* 1. the act of covering with boards; also, the covering itself.

2. boards collectively.

3. the act or practice of obtaining one's food, or food and lodging, in the house of another for a fixed price.

bōard′ing, *n.* 1. a coming or going aboard (a ship, train, etc.).

2. an attack on or capture of a ship by boarders.

bōard′ing·house, a house where meals, or lodging and meals, can be had for pay: also written *boarding house*.

bōard′ing net′ting, a netting formerly rigged up above the rail of a ship to prevent an enemy from boarding.

bōard′ing of′fi·cẽr, a naval or revenue officer who is sent or appointed to board vessels on their arrival from foreign ports.

bōard′ing pīke, a long pike formerly used by seamen in boarding a ship or repelling boarders.

bōard′ing sçhool, a school providing lodging and meals for the pupils.

bōard meaṣ′ūre (mezh′), 1. the measurement of lumber in board feet.

2. a measure or scale used for this purpose.

bōard rūle, a figured scale for finding the number of board feet in a quantity of lumber.

bōard wā′ġeṣ, 1. bed and board in return for services rendered.
 2. wages hardly sufficient to pay for food and lodging.
 3. special wages for board and lodging.

bōard′wạlk, *n.* 1. a walk made of thick boards.
 2. a walk placed along a beach or sea front.

bōar′fish, *n.*; *pl.* **bōar′fish** or **bōar′fish·eṣ,** 1. a fish found in the Mediterranean, belonging to the family *Caproidæ*: so named from the shape of its snout.
 2. a species of perch found in Australia and used for food.
 3. a New Zealand fish: also called *bastard dory*.

bōar′hound, *n.* a great Dane or other large dog used in hunting wild boar.

bōar′ish, *a.* swinish; brutal; coarse.

bōar's′-foot, an herb of the crowfoot family; hellebore.

bōar spēar, a short spear with a stout shaft, used in hunting boars.

bōar stag, a castrated boar.

bōart, *n.* same as *bort*.

bōast, *v.i.*; boasted, *pt., pp.*; boasting, *ppr.* [ME. *boosten, bosten,* from *bost,* a boast.]
 1. to brag; to make an ostentatious display, in speech, of one's own or another's worth, property, or actions.
 2. to glory; to exult; to be vainly proud.
 I *boast of* you to them of Macedonia.
 —2 Cor. ix. 2.

bōast, *v.t.* 1. to speak of in ostentatious language; to speak of with pride, vanity, or exultation; to brag about.
 2. to possess, as something of which one may be proud; as, the town *boasts* not less than five churches.
 Syn.—vaunt, brag, swagger, swell, bluster, triumph, glory.

bōast, *n.* 1. an expression of ostentation, pride, or vanity; a bragging.
 Thou that makest thy *boast* of the law.
 —Rom. ii. 23.
 2. the cause of boasting; the occasion of pride, vanity, or laudable exultation; as, Shakespeare, the *boast* of English literature.

bōast, *v.t.* 1. to dress or trim (a stone, etc.) with a broad-faced chisel.
 2. in sculpture, to dress or to form roughly; to roughhew to the approximate outline preparatory to elaborating the details.

bōast′ẽr, *n.* one who boasts, glories, or vaunts.
 Syn.—braggadocio, braggart.

bōast′ẽr, *n.* a mason's or stonecutter's broad-faced chisel.

bōast′fụl, *a.* given to boasting; ostentatious.

bōast′fụl·ly, *adv.* in a boastful manner.

bōast′fụl·ness, *n.* the state of being boastful.

bōast′ing, *n.* ostentatious display of one's own or another's worth or actions; a glorying or vaunting.

bōast′ing·ly, *adv.* in a boasting manner.

bōast′ive, *a.* boastful. [Obs.]

bōast′less, *a.* without ostentation. [Rare.]

bōat, *n.* [ME. *boot, bote, bot*; AS. *bāt,* a boat; Sw. *bat*; Ice. *bātr,* a boat.]
 1. a small open vessel, or water craft, moved by oars, sails, or engine.
 2. a large vessel; ship: landsman's term applied especially to river steamers.
 3. any similar craft; as, a flying *boat*.
 4. a deep, narrow dish or utensil having a form like a boat; as, a sauce *boat*.
 5. a receptacle for holding incense, used in Catholic churches.
 in the same boat; in the same situation; involved in a similar predicament.

bōat, *v.i.* to go in a boat.

bōat, *v.t.*; boated, *pt., pp.*; boating, *ppr.* to transport in a boat; as, to *boat* goods across a lake.

bōat′ȧ·ble, *a.* navigable by boats, or small river craft.

bōat′āġe, *n.* the charge for conveying by boat; also, a carrying by boat.

bōat′bill, *n.* a species of wading bird, *Cancroma cochlearia,* a native of the tropical parts of South America. It has a bill four inches long resembling an inverted boat.

bōat bug, same as *boat fly*.

bōat′build″ẽr (-bild″ẽr), *n.* a builder of boats.

bōat′build″ing, *n.* the building of boats.

bōat flȳ, any of a species of hemipterous insects, which swim on the back, and somewhat resemble small boats.

bōat′fụl, *n.* the quantity or number that a boat can hold.

bōat hook, an iron hook with a point on the back, fixed to a long pole, with which to pull or push a boat.

bōat′house, *n.* a building primarily for storing a boat or boats, but often equipped with recreational facilities.

bōat′ing, *n.* 1. the act or practice of rowing, sailing, or cruising.
 2. the act or practice of transporting in boats.
 3. boats collectively.

bō·ā′tion, *n.* [L. *boatus,* from *boare*; Gr. *boān,* to cry out.] a reverberation; a roar; loud noise. [Obs.]

bōat′lōad, *n.* 1. all the freight or passengers that a boat can carry or contain.
 2. the load carried by a boat.

bōat′măn, *n.*; *pl.* **bōat′men,** a man who operates, takes care of, works on, buys, or sells boats.

bōat′măn·ship, *n.* the art or skill of handling a boat.

bōat′-shāped, *a.* having the shape of a boat.

bōat shell, a marine shell of the genus *Cymba,* so called from its form.

bōats′măn, *n.*; *pl.* **bōats′men,** a boatman.

bōat′swain (bō′sn *or* bōt′swān), *n.* 1. a warrant officer or petty officer of a ship who has charge of the deck crew, the rigging, etc.
 2. the tropic bird; also, the jaeger gull.
 boatswain's chair; a seat used by sailors while at work aloft, or to transport sailors and passengers from another ship. It is made of a short board or seat with ropes run through holes at each end.
 boatswain's mate; an assistant to the boatswain.

bōat tāil, a species of blackbird found in the southern part of the United States.

bōat trāin, a train timed to reach or leave a port at the convenience of ship's passengers.

bōat′wom″ăn (-woom″), *n.*; *pl.* **bōat′wom″en** (-wim″), a woman who has charge of a boat.

bōat′wrīght (-rīt), *n.* a boat builder.

Bō′az, *n.* [Heb. *bo'az,* lit., swiftness.] in the Bible, Ruth's husband: Ruth iv. 13.

bob, *n.* [ME. *bob, bobbe,* a cluster; Ice. *bobbi,* a cluster; OFr. *bober,* to mock.]
 1. a short, jerking action; as, a *bob* of the head.
 2. any little round thing that hangs loosely at the end of a string, cord, or chain; a little ornament or pendant that hangs loosely.
 3. the words repeated at the end of a stanza; the refrain of a song.
 4. a light blow or tap.
 5. the ball of a short pendulum.
 6. a mode of ringing bells.
 7. a bob wig, or short curl of hair; also, a woman's or girl's short haircut.
 8. a docked tail, as of a horse.
 9. a float used in angling to show when a fish bites.
 10. a spherical leather tool used for polishing metal, as spoons, etc.
 11. the working beam of a steam engine.
 12. a shilling. [Brit. Slang.]
 13. a suckling calf.
 14. a type of Scottish dance.
 15. a quick curtsy.
 16. a bobsled or bob skate.

bob, *v.t.*; bobbed, *pt., pp.*; bobbing, *ppr.* 1. to make move in a short, jerking manner; as, to *bob* one's head.
 2. to do jerkily.
 3. to knock against; to cause to knock against; to rap.
 4. to cut short; as, to *bob* a horse's tail.

bob, *v.i.* 1. to play backward and forward; to move or act in a bobbing manner.
 2. to angle or fish with a bob.
 3. to dance athletically or awkwardly.
 4. to curtsy quickly.
 5. to try to catch suspended or floating fruit with the teeth (usually with *for*).

bō′baç, *n.* [Pol. *bobak.*] the Polish marmot, resembling the American woodchuck.

bō·bance′, *n.* a boasting. [Obs.]

bob′bẽr, *n.* that which bobs; also, one who bobs.

bob′bẽr·y, *n.* [slang, from Hind. *bāp re,* O father.] a disturbance; a noisy quarrel.

bob′bin, *n.* [Fr. *bobine,* a bobbin.]
 1. a small pin or cylindrical piece of wood, bone, or other material, with a head, on which thread is wound for making bobbin lace; also, a similar reel or spool used in spinning, weaving, machine sewing, etc. to wind thread or silk on.
 2. round tape or narrow braid.
 3. an insulated coil of wire for an electromagnet.
 4. a piece of wood at the end of a latch-string.

Bob′bin and Jōan, a European wild flower of the arum family, the cuckoopint.

bob·bi·net′, *n.* [a contr. of *bobbin* and *net.*] a kind of machine-made bobbin lace which has an open mesh.

bob′bin lāce, a lace whose design is laid out with pins around which thread is drawn and interlaced by means of bobbins.

bob′bin·wŏrk, *n.* work woven with bobbins.

bob′by, *n.*; *pl.* **bob′bies,** a policeman: so called from Sir Robert (*Bobby*) Peel (1788–1850) who remodeled the police force of London. [Brit. Slang.]

bob′by pin, a small metal hairpin with the ends pressing close together.

bob′by socks, [from *bob,* to cut (hair, etc.) short.] ankle socks worn by girls and women. [Colloq.]

bob′by sox′ẽr, [from the *bobby socks* worn by many of them.] a girl in her teens, especially one regarded as conforming to current fads. [Colloq.]

bob′cat, *n.* the lynx of America; a wildcat.

bob′flȳ, *n.* in angling, a drop fly.

bob′ō·liñk, *n.* the *Dolichonyx oryzivorus,* an American migratory song bird of fields and meadows.

bob skāte, a skate with two runners.

bob′sled, *n.* 1. a sled made up of two short sleds, one before the other, connected by a coupling.
 2. either of the sleds thus joined.
 3. a long toboggan, equipped with steering apparatus and brakes, often ridden by a four-man team in races.

bob′sled, *v.i.* to ride on a bobsled.

bob′sleigh (-slā), *n.* and *v.i.* bobsled.

bob′stāy, *n.* a chain or rope used to keep a vessel's bowsprit down and counteract the upward strain of the stays.

bob′tāil, *n.* 1. a short tail, or a tail cut short.
 2. a short-tailed animal.

bob′tāil, *a.* bobtailed; having a bobtail.

bob′tāil, *v.t.* 1. to dock the tail of.
 2. to cut short; to curtail.

bob′tāiled, *a.* having the hair of tail cut short.

bob′tāil wig, same as *bob wig*.

bob′whīte, *n.*; *pl.* **bob′whītes** or **bob′whīte,** the North American quail, having markings of brown and white on a gray body: so named from its call.

bob wig, a short wig, having the bottom locks curled in small ringlets or bobs: also called *bobtail wig*.

bō·çăc′ciō (-kä′chō), *n.* [It. *boccaccio,* from *boccaccia,* large mouth, from *bocca,* mouth.] a large-mouthed rockfish, found near California.

bō′çăl, *n.* [Fr. *bocal,* a bottle with a short, wide neck; L. *bucalis*; Gr. *baukalis,* a vessel in which wine was cooled.]
 1. a glass vessel of a cylindrical form, having a short, wide neck.
 2. the mouthpiece of a brass musical instrument, as a horn or trombone.

bō·çăr′dō, *n.* a mood in logic.

boç′ȧ·sīne, *n.* [Fr. *boccasin*; Turk. *bōhāsi,* a sort of cotton cloth.] a sort of fine linen or buckram.

boç′çȧ, *n.* [It., the mouth.] the round hole of a glass furnace, for use in taking out the melted glass.

bōce, *n.* a fish found in European waters: also called *bogue, boga,* and *box*.

Boçhe, *n.* [prob. shortened from Fr. *caboche,* hard head; hence a thick-headed person; a stupid man.] a German; especially, a German soldier: hostile term.

bock, bock beer.

bock beer, [from G. *Eimbockbier,* from *Eimbock* or *Eimbeck,* a town in Prussia, famous for its beer.] a dark beer, usually brewed in the spring.

bock′e·rel, bock′e·let, *n.* a kind of long-winged hawk. [Obs.]

bock′ey, *n.* [D. *bokaal, bakje,* a small bowl or vessel.] a cup or bowl made from a gourd.

bock′ing, *n.* [from *Bocking,* England.] a sort of coarse cloth, like baize or drugget, used for covering floors, stairways, etc.

bock′ing, *n.* [Dan. *bokking.*] a red herring.

bock′land, *n.* same as *bookland*.

bō·därk′, *n.* the Osage orange: also called *bodock*.

bod′dice, *n.* same as *bodice*.

bōde, *v.t.*; boded, *pt., pp.*; boding, *ppr.* [ME. *boden, bodien*; AS. *bodian,* to foretell.] to portend; to foreshow; to presage; to indicate (future events) by signs; to be the omen of.

bōde, *v.i.* to foreshow or presage something.
 Syn.—forebode, foreshadow, augur.

bōde, *n.* 1. an omen. [Obs.]
2. a bid; an offer. [Obs.]
bōde, *n.* [ME. *bode, bod*, from AS. *bod, gebod*, a command, from *beodan*, to command.] a messenger; one who proclaims; a herald. [Obs.]
bōde, *n.* a stop; a halting. [Obs.]
bōde, *v.* alternative past tense of *bide*.
bōde′fụl, *a.* full of portent; ominous.
bō·dē′gȧ, *n.* [Sp.] a wine cellar; a place where wine is sold or kept.
bōde′ment, *n.* an omen; a portent; a foreshowing. [Obs.]
bodġe, *n.* a clumsy patch. [Dial.]
bodġe, *v.t.* to mend clumsily; to patch; to botch. [Obs.]
bod′ice, *n.* [corruption of *bodies*, pl. of *body*.]
1. stays; a corset; a sort of underwaist, stiffened with whalebone, worn by women. [Obs.]
2. the close-fitting upper portion of a woman's dress.
3. a woman's wide, sleeveless vest tightly laced in front, worn over a blouse or dress.
bod′iced (-ist), *a.* wearing a bodice.
bod′ied (-id), *a.* 1. having a specified kind of body; as, able-*bodied*.
2. having a body, substance, or form.
bō·di·ē′rŏn, *n.* [local name.] the California or Pacific rock trout.
bod′i·less, *a.* 1. having no body.
2. having no material form; incorporeal.
3. without a torso.
bod′i·li·ness, *n.* the state of having bodily existence.
bod′i·ly, *a.* 1. of, in, or for the body; corporeal; as, *bodily* dimensions.
2. of or pertaining to the body; physical; as, *bodily* defects; *bodily* pain.
3. real; actual; as, *bodily* act. [Obs.]
Syn.—corporeal, corporal, physical.
bod′i·ly, *adv.* 1. corporeally; in person; in the flesh.

It is his human nature, in which the Godhead dwells *bodily*. —Watts.

2. in entirety; as a single body; entirely; completely; as, to carry away *bodily*.
3. as a single group.
bōd′ing, *n.* [ME. *bodynge, bodunge*, an omen; AS. *bodung*, foretelling, verbal noun from *bodian*, to announce.] prediction, particularly of evil; a foreshadowing; an omen.
bōd′ing, *a.* predicting evil; fearful; ominous.
bōd′ing·ly, *adv.* in a fearful or ominous manner.
bod′kin, *n.* [ME. *bodekyn*, a bodkin; of Celtic origin.]
1. an instrument of steel, bone, ivory, etc. with a sharp point, for making holes in cloth.
2. a thick, blunt needle.
3. a dagger. [Obs.]
4. a long, ornamental hairpin.
5. in printing, a sharp-pointed tool used for picking out letters from set type.
bō′dle, *n.* [name said to have come from *Bothwell*, the name of a mint master.] an old Scottish coin worth about one-sixth of an English penny; hence, the smallest particle; the least bit.
Bod′lēi·ăn, *a.* pertaining to Sir Thomas *Bodley*, or to the library founded by him at Oxford, England, in the sixteenth century.
bō·dock′, *n.* same as *bodark*.
Bō·dō′nï, *n.* a style of type designed by Giambattista *Bodoni* (1740–1813), an Italian printer.
bod′rāġe, *n.* a raid. [Obs.]
bod′y, *n.*; *pl.* **bod′ieṣ,** [ME. *body, bodi*; AS. *bodig*, body.]
1. the frame or physical part of a man, animal, or plant; the material organism, living or dead: also, specifically, a dead person; corpse.
2. the trunk or torso of a human being or animal, in distinction from the head and extremities.
3. flesh or material substance, as opposed to spirit.
4. a person; a human being. [Colloq.]
5. reality, as opposed to representation.
6. a collective mass; a number of individuals or particulars regarded as a unit; as, the *body* of mankind.
7. the main or central part of anything; the bulk; as, the *body* of an army; the *body* of a tree.
8. in law, a corporation; a number of men, united by a common tie, by one form of government, or by occupation; something regarded as a person; as, the legislative *body*; the *body* of the clergy; *body* corporate; *body* politic.
9. in physics, any portion of matter; mass; separate part; as, a *body* of water.
10. in geometry, a solid figure.
11. the stem of a plant.
12. the part of an automobile, truck, etc. that holds the load of passengers; the part of a vehicle that is not the chassis.
13. strength or concentration; as, wine of a good *body*.
14. opacity; consistency; as, the *body* of paint.
15. that portion of a garment which covers the trunk; as, the *body* of a dress or a coat.
16. in printing, the shank of a type or the width of the shank, by which the size is indicated; as, a nonpareil *body*.
body of a law; the operative part of a law.
the bodies seven; in alchemy, the metals supposed to correspond to the planets. [Obs.]
Syn.—substance, mass, whole, substantiality, collectiveness, assemblage, collection, matter, association, organization, carcass, clay, corpse, dust, form, frame, remains.
bod′y, *v.t.*; bodied, *pt.*, *pp.*; bodying, *ppr.* 1. to furnish with a body; to make substantial.
2. to make part of; to embody.

Imagination *bodies* forth the forms of things unknown. —Shak.

bod′y bōl′stẽr, a crossbeam over the center of the truck of a railway car, supporting the car and transmitting its weight to the truck.
bod′y brāce, an inclined timber to brace the panels of a frame.
bod′y ça̤v′i·ty, the space between the viscera and the body wall.
bod′y clock, the body mechanism by which a person's physiological rhythms are automatically established, maintained, or, as after jet travel, readjusted.
bod′y çloth, a horse blanket.
bod′y çlōtheṣ, clothing or covering for the body; especially, underwear.
bod′y çōat, a close-fitting dress coat.
bod′y çŏl′ŏr, *n.* 1. a pigment that has substance and gives opacity to paint.
2. an opaque coat of paint.
bod′y çor′pō·rāte, in law, a corporation.
bod′y çount, a count made of persons killed in battle.
bod′y·guärd, a person or persons, usually armed, assigned to guard someone.
bod′y lan̄′guāġe, gestures, unconscious bodily movements, facial expressions, etc. which serve as nonverbal communications or as accompaniments to speech.
bod′y louse, a louse, *Pediculus vestimenti*, which sometimes infests the human body and clothing.
bod′y mē·çhan′içs, body exercises that are intended to improve one's posture, stamina, poise, etc.
bod′y plan, in shipbuilding, an end plan of a ship showing her contour at various points.
bod′y pol′i·tiç, people constituting a political unit with a government; a state.
bod′y sẽr′vănt, a servant who attends to the personal wants of his employer; a valet.
bod′y shop, a garage where repair work on the body and chassis of automotive vehicles is done.
bod′y snatch′ẽr, one who steals corpses from graves; a grave robber; a resurrectionist.
bod′y snatch′ing, the act of robbing a grave, as for the purpose of dissection or the exaction of a ransom.
bod′y stock′ing, a tightfitting garment, usually of one piece, that covers the torso and, sometimes, the legs.
bod′y·sūit″, *n.* a one-piece, tightfitting, sleeved or sleeveless garment that covers the torso, usually worn with slacks, a skirt, etc.: also called *body shirt*.
bod′y·sûrf″, *v.i.* to engage in the sport of surfing, lying prone on the wave without the use of a surfboard.
bod′y vär′nish, a thick copal varnish used in carriage making, etc.
bod′y wa̤ll, in anatomy and zoology, the envelope or walls of the body.
Bœh·mē′ri·ȧ, *n.* [named after G. R. *Boehmer*, 18th-c. German botanist.] a widely distributed genus of shrubs and herbs of the nettle family, some of which furnish valuable fibers used for making rope, twine, and thread.
Boe·ō′tiăn (bē-), *a.* 1. of or pertaining to Boeotia, a state in ancient Greece, or its people, who were reputed to be dull and stupid.
2. dull; ignorant; stupid.
Boe·ō′tiăn, *n.* [L. *Bœotia*; Gr. *Boiōtia*, Boeotia.] a native of Boeotia; hence, one who is dull, ignorant, and stupid.
Bōer (*or* bọr, bör), *n.* [D. *boer*, a peasant or farmer.] a descendant of Dutch colonists in South Africa.
Bōer *a.* of the Boers.
Bōer Wa̤r, a war (1899–1902) in which Great Britain defeated the Boers of South Africa.
bog, *n.* [Ir. *bogach*, a bog, from Gael. *bog*, soft, moist.] a quagmire covered with grass or other plants; wet, spongy ground; a small marsh.
bog, *v.t.* and *v.i.*; bogged, *pt.*, *pp.*; bogging, *ppr.* to sink or submerge in mud or mire; to become stuck or cause to become stuck in or as in a bog (often with *down*).
bō′gä, *n.* same as *boce*.
bog as′phō·del, a North American plant, *Narthecium americanum*, that grows in bogs.
bog bēan, the buck bean, *Menyanthes trifoliata*, also called the marsh trefoil, which grows in moist and marshy places and bears white or reddish flowers and bitter leaves.
bog ēarth, a soil composed for the most part of siliceous sand and partially decomposed vegetable matter.
bō′gey, bō′gie, *n.* 1. in golf, (a) a fixed number of strokes for each hole, used as a standard of skill; par; (b) one stroke more than par.
2. same as *bogy*.
bog′gi·ness, *n.* the quality or state of being boggy.
bog′gle, *v.i.*; boggled, *pt.*, *pp.*; boggling, *ppr.* [Scot. *bogle, bogill*, a specter.]
1. to be startled; to shy away (with *at*).
2. to doubt; to hesitate; to have scruples (with *at*).
3. to dissemble; to equivocate; to shuffle (with *at*).
4. to perform awkwardly; to bungle.
5. to be or become confused or overwhelmed as by something very difficult, surprising, vast, etc.; as, the mind *boggles* at the infinite universe.
bog′gle, *v.t.* 1. to embarrass with difficulties. [Dial.]
2. to make a botch of.
3. to confuse or overwhelm (the mind, imagination, etc.).
bog′glẽr, *n.* a person who boggles.
bog′gy, *a.* containing bogs; full of bogs.
bō′gie, *n.* 1. a low, swiveled undercarriage at either end of a railroad car.
2. one wheel of the several pairs supporting the tread of an armored tank or tractor.
3. a low, heavy cart or truck. [North British Dial.]
4. same as *bogey*.
bō′gle, bog′gle, *n.* [Eng. dial. *boggle*; Scot. *bogle*, a specter.] a bugbear; a specter; a bogy.
bog mo̤ss, any aquatic moss plant or peat moss of the genus *Sphagnum*.
bog ōak, see *bogwood*.
Bog′ō·mile, *n.* a member of a Bulgarian sect, of the eleventh and twelfth centuries, who believed that God had two sons, one Jesus and the other Satanaël.
bog ōre, a variety of brown iron ore, or limonite, found in swamps; also, hydrated peroxide of manganese.
bog rush, a rush or sedge that grows in bogs.
bog spav′in, in horses, an encysted tumor on the inside of the hock, containing gelatinous matter.
bog′suck″ẽr, *n.* the American woodcock.
bog′trot″tẽr, *n.* one who lives in a boggy country: formerly applied to the Irish peasantry in boggy districts.
bōgue (bōg), *v.i.* [Sp. *bogar*, to row.] to edge to leeward.
bōgue, *n.* same as *boce*.
bō′gus, *a.* [origin uncertain.] false; sham; counterfeit.
bō′gus, *n.* a mixture of rum and molasses.
bog′wood, *n.* trunks and large branches of oak, pine, etc., found preserved in bogs and frequently used for making ornamental pieces of furniture and small ornaments.
bō′gy, *n.*; *pl.* **bō′gieṣ,** 1. a bugbear; a hobgoblin.
2. [B-] the devil; as, *Old Bogy*.
bō′gy, *n.*; *pl.* **bō′gieṣ,** a bogie (undercarriage).
bō·hēa′, *n.* [Chinese *Woo-ye*, hills in Fukien, China, where the tea is grown; *w* being sounded like *b*.] a coarse, black, low-priced tea from China.
Bō·hē′mi·ȧ, *n.* the community or sphere of those called Bohemians (sense 4).
Bō·hē′mi·ăn, *a.* 1. pertaining to Bohemia, a province of Czechoslovakia, its people, or their language.
2. roving; easy-going; unconventional: especially applied to artists, dilettantes, etc.
Bohemian Brethren; a sect formed from the remnants of the Hussites in the fifteenth cen-

tury: they were the forerunners of the Moravians.

Bō·hē′mi·ăn, *n.* 1. a native or inhabitant of Bohemia.

2. the West Slavic language of the Bohemians: also called *Czech.*

3. a gypsy; a vagabond.

4. one who is unconventional in life and habits; especially, an artist, writer, or musician who leads a free-and-easy or irregular life.

Bō·hē′mi·ăn·işm, *n.* the life or habits of Bohemians (sense 4).

Bōhr thē′ō·ry, a theory suggesting that the transfer of electrons from one orbit to another accounts for the absorption and radiation of energy by the hydrogen atom: proposed by Niels *Bohr,* Danish physicist, in 1913.

bō′hunk, *n.* [prob. from *Bo*hemian and *Hung*arian.]

1. a person from east central Europe. [Slang.]

2. any unskilled laborer; especially, one from east central Europe. [Slang.]

Vulgar term of prejudice and contempt.

bō′hun ū′pȧs, same as *upas.*

bō·iär′ (bō-yär′), *n.* same as *boyar.*

Boi′dae, *n.pl.* a family of nonvenomous ophidian reptiles, of which the type genus is *Boa.*

boil, *v.i.*; boiled, *pt., pp.*; boiling, *ppr.* [ME. *boilen, boylen*; OFr. *boillir*; Sp. *bullir,* to boil, move, be active; L. *bullire,* to bubble, boil; *bulla,* a bubble, stud.]

1. to swell, heave, or be agitated by the action of heat; to bubble; to rise in bubbles; as, the water *boils.*

2. to pass from a liquid to a vaporous state at the boiling point.

3. to simulate the agitation of a boiling liquid; as, the *boiling* waves which roll and foam.

4. to be hot or fervid; to be emotionally agitated; as, his blood *boils* with anger.

5. to be in boiling water; to cook by boiling; as, the meat is *boiling.*

6. to bubble; to effervesce, as a mixture of an acid and a carbonate.

to boil away; to evaporate by boiling.

to boil over; to come to a boil and spill over the top of a vessel.

to keep the pot boiling; to provide the means of living.

boil, *v.t.* 1. to heat to the boiling point; as, to *boil* a liquid.

2. to cook, make, clean, etc. by boiling; as, to *boil* food, salt, etc.

to boil down; to reduce in bulk by boiling; hence, to condense or summarize.

boil, *n.* the act or state of boiling.

boil, *n.* [ME. *byle, bule*; AS. *b̄yle, b̄yl*; G. *beule*; D. *buele,* a boil; Ice. *bola,* a blister, blain.] an inflamed, painful, pus-filled swelling on the skin, with a hard center: it is caused by infection.

boil′ȧ·ry, *n.* same as *boilery.*

boiled, *a.* prepared by boiling; as, *boiled* beef.

boiled oil; oil that has been boiled to give it better drying qualities for use in paints, etc.

boiled shirt; a man's dress shirt; hence, a pompous man.

boil′ẽr, *n.* 1. a container in which things are boiled or heated.

2. specifically, a steam boiler; a vessel constructed to hold and sustain an internal pressure, in which, by the application of heat, steam is generated and raised to or above the pressure of the atmosphere, for the purpose of utilizing its expansive energy for the production of mechanical work, for supplying heat by conduction of the steam, and for a number of applications in the industrial arts, as for cleaning, bleaching, etc.

3. a tank to hold hot water.

4. one who boils.

boil′ẽr çlamp, a clamp used by riveters to hold boiler plates in place.

boil′ẽr flōat, an attachment to a steam boiler that regulates the water feed or acts as an alarm for low water.

boil′ẽr ī′ron (-ŭrn), boiler plate.

boil′ẽr mē′tẽr, an instrument to measure the water consumed by a steam boiler.

boil′ẽr plāte, iron or steel plate from which boilers are made.

boil′ẽr shell, the outside case of a cylinder boiler.

boil′ẽr shop, a shop where boilers are made.

boil′ẽr·smith, *n.* a workman engaged in forging the parts of boilers.

boil′ẽr·y, *n.* a place or apparatus for boiling something, as one for evaporating salt or refining sugar.

boil′ing, *a.* 1. bubbling; heaving in bubbles; being agitated; as, *boiling* liquid.

2. swelling with heat, ardor, or passion.

boiling spring; a spring which gives out hot water and steam, often ejecting it with great force.

boil′ing, *n.* 1. the act or state of bubbling; agitation by heat; ebullition.

2. the act of cooking by hot water.

3. the act of preparing by hot water, or of evaporating by heat.

boil′ing·ly, *adv.* in a boiling manner; with ebullition.

boil′ing point, the degree of heat at which a fluid is converted into vapor with boiling. This point varies for different liquids and for the same liquid at different atmospheric pressures, being higher when the pressure of the atmosphere is increased, and lower when it is diminished. When the barometer stands at 30 inches, water boils at 212° Fahrenheit (100° Centigrade).

bois d′ärç′ (bwȧ dȧrk′), [Fr., bowwood: so called because used for bows by the Indians in the western part of the United States.] the Osage orange.

bois dur·ci′ (bwȧ dür-sē′), [Fr., hardened wood.] an artificial wood made by compressing a paste of blood and hardwood sawdust: it takes a high polish.

boist, *n.* [OFr. *boiste,* a box.] a box. [Obs.]

bois′tẽr·ous, *a.* [ME. *boistous, buystous*; W. *bwystus,* wild, ferocious.]

1. rough; violent; turbulent; as, a *boisterous* wind.

2. loud and exuberant; noisily good-natured; as, a *boisterous* man.

3. large; unwieldy; huge; clumsily violent; as, a *boisterous* club. [Obs.]

4. vehement; intense; as, a *boisterous* heat. [Rare.]

Syn.—furious, impetuous, noisy, vehement, violent.

bois′tẽr·ous·ly, *adv.* in a boisterous manner; violently; furiously; noisily; tumultuously.

bois′tẽr·ous·ness, *n.* the state or quality of being boisterous; turbulence; disorder; tumultuousness.

bois′tous, *a.* boisterous. [Obs.]

bo′ka·dăm, *n.* an East Indian snake of the genus *Cerberus.*

bō′kärk, *n.* a birch-bark basket for maple sugar, used by the Lake Superior Indians.

bok choy, [Cantonese, white vegetable.] a variety of Chinese cabbage: see *Chinese cabbage.*

bōke, *v.t.* and *v.i.* to poke. [Obs.]

bō′lȧ, *n.* [Sp. a ball; L. *bulla,* a bubble, ball.] a weapon made of a long cord or thong with heavy balls at the end, used for throwing at and entangling cattle, etc.: also *bolas.*

bō′lăr, *a.* of, or having the nature of, bole; clayey.

bō′lȧ·ry, *a.* bolar. [Obs.]

bō′lȧs, *n.* [Sp., pl. of *bola.*] a bola.

bōld, *a.* [ME. *bold, bald*; AS. *beald, bald*; O.H.G. *bald,* bold.]

1. daring; courageous; brave; intrepid; fearless.

2. requiring courage in the execution; executed with spirit or boldness; planned with courage and spirit; as, a *bold* enterprise.

3. confident; not timorous. [Obs.]

4. rude; forward; impudent.

5. unconventional; showing great liberty of style or expression; very free in behavior or manner.

6. standing out to view; striking to the eye; as, *bold* figures in painting, sculpture, and architecture.

7. steep; abrupt; prominent; as, a *bold* cliff.

to make bold; to take the liberty; to presume; to venture.

Syn.—courageous, daring, brave, intrepid, fearless, dauntless, valiant, manful, audacious, stouthearted, high-spirited, adventurous, confident, forward, impudent.—One may be *fearless* where there is no apprehension of danger or no cause for apprehension, but he is *bold* only when he is conscious or apprehensive of danger, and prepared to encounter it. A man may be *fearless* in a state of inaction; he is *bold* only in action, or when in a frame of mind for action; he is *intrepid* who has no fear where the most *fearless* might tremble; he is *undaunted* whose spirit is not discouraged by that which would make the stoutest heart yield.

bōld, *v.t.* to make bold. [Obs.]

bōld, *v.i.* to be bold; to become bold. [Obs.]

bōld′en, *v.t.* to make bold; to give confidence. [Obs.]

bōld′fāce, *n.* 1. a person who is impudent, saucy, or bold.

2. in printing a type with a heavy face: the words listed in this dictionary are in boldface.

bōld′-faced, *a.* 1. impudent; saucy.

2. printed in boldface.

bōld′ly, *adv.* [ME. *boldly, boldliche*; AS. *beald-līche,* from *beald,* bold.] in a bold manner.

bōld′ness, *n.* 1. the quality of being bold.

2. a bold act, remark, etc.

Syn.—intrepidity, assurance, audacity, effrontery, presumption, confidence, daring, bravery.

bol′dō, *n.* [native Chilean name.] in botany, a small, aromatic, evergreen tree growing in Chile and bearing edible fruit; the *Boldoa fragrans* or *Peumus Boldus.* The leaves have medicinal value; the bark is used in tanning and the wood, in making charcoal.

bōle, *n.* [ME. *bole*; Ice. *bolr,* the trunk of a tree.]

1. the trunk of a tree.

2. anything having cylindrical shape.

bōle, *n.* same as *boll* (a measure).

bōle, *n.* [ME. *bole*; OFr. *bol*; L. *bolus,* clay; Gr. *bōlos,* a lump of earth.]

1. any friable clayey shale or earth, generally yellow or yellowish-red, consisting of hydrous bisilicate of alumina, with iron oxide in various proportions, and with a little magnesia when soapy or greasy.

2. a bolus or dose. [Obs.]

bōle, *n.* an opening in a wall to let in light and air; also, a small recess in a wall. [Scot.]

bō·leç′tion, *n.* in architecture, a kind of molding which projects beyond the surface of the work which it decorates.

bō·le′rō, *n.* [Sp.] 1. a Spanish dance done to castanets and lively music in 3/4 time; also, the music of the dance.

2. a short, open vest, with or without sleeves, worn by men and women.

bō·let′iç, *a.* pertaining to or obtained from the *Boletus*; as, *boletic* acid. [Obs.]

Bō·lē′tus, *n.* [L. *Boletus*; Gr. *bōlitēs,* a species of mushroom; *bōlos,* a lump of earth.] in botany, a genus of mushrooms containing many species.

bō′lide (*or* lid), *n.* a bright, shooting meteor, especially one that explodes.

bol′i·văr, *n.* [named after Simón *Bolívar,* Bolivian and Venezuelan liberator.] the monetary unit of Venezuela, a silver coin.

Bō·liv′i·ăn, *n.* a native or inhabitant of Bolivia.

Bō·liv′i·ăn, *a.* pertaining to Bolivia or its people.

bō·lï·vï·ä′nō, *n.* the Bolivian monetary unit.

bōll, *n.* [AS. *bolla,* a bowl.]

1. the pod or capsule of a plant, as of flax or cotton; a globular pericarp.

2. an ancient dry measure used in Scotland and the north of England, varying from two bushels for salt to six bushels for potatoes.

bōll, *v.i.* to form into a pericarp or seed vessel.

Bol′lănd·ist, *n.* any of the Jesuits who edited the *Acta Sanctorum,* begun by John *Bolland* in 1643.

bol′lărd, *n.* [from LG. *poller, polder,* from OFr. *poldre, poltre,* orig., colt, horse; then, supporting beam, from ML. *pulletrum,* from L. *pullus,* colt, young horse.] a strong post on a ship or dock, for holding a hawser fast.

bōll′en, *a.* boln. [Obs.]

bōll′ing, *n.* a tree divested of top and branches; a pollard.

bol′lix, *v.t.*; bollixed, *pt. pp.*; bollixing, *ppr.* [euphemistic respelling of nautical slang, from ME. *ballokes*; AS. *beallucas,* testicles (dim. of *ball*), used as an extension of *ball, v.i.*] to make a muddle of; bungle; botch (usually with *up*). [Slang.]

bōll rot, a disease which destroys the boll of the cotton plant before maturity.

bōll wee′vil, a weevil very destructive to cotton bolls: its larvae are hatched in the bolls.

bōll′wŏrm, *n.* the larva of the moth *Heliothis armigera,* which ravages the immature bolls of the cotton plant.

bōln, bōll′en, *a.* puffed out; swelled out, as a sail filled with wind; swollen. [Obs.]

bōln, *v.i.* to swell; to enlarge. [Obs.]

bō′lō, *n.* [Sp.] a large, single-edged knife used in the Philippine Islands as a weapon or utensil: it is of varied form and size.

bō·lō′gnȧ (-lō′nyȧ, -nȧ, *or* -nē), *n.* [from *Bologna,* Italy.] a large, smoked sausage made of bacon, veal, pork, etc., chopped fine and highly seasoned.

bologna stone; radiated sulfate of barium, found in roundish masses, composed of radiating fibers: discovered near Bologna. It is phosphorescent when calcined.

bologna vial; a wide-mouthed vial or bottle of unannealed glass so brittle that it will break into pieces when it is scratched.

Bō·lō·gnēṣe′ (bō-lōn-yēz′), *n.* a native or inhabitant of Bologna.

Bō·lō·gnēṣe′, *a.* pertaining to Bologna, its people, or their dialect.

Bolognese school; a school of painting established at Bologna by Carracci: called also *Eclectic school* and *Lombard school*.

Bō·lō′gniăn (bō-lōn′yăn *or* bō-lō′ni-ăn), *n.* and *a.* Bolognese.

bō′lō·grȧph, *n.*, [*bolo-* (see *bolometer*), and *-graph*.]

1. a record of variations registered by a bolometer.

2. a bolometer.

bō′lō·măn, *n.*; *pl.* **bō′lō·men,** a man armed with a bolo.

bō·lom′e·tẽr, *n.* [Gr. *bole*, a ray, lit. something thrown, from *ballein*, to throw, and *metron*, a measure.] an instrument for measuring minute quantities of radiant energy used especially in radio for detection of ultrahigh frequencies.

Bol′she·vik, bol′she·vik (*or* bōl′), *n.*; *pl.* **Bol′she·viks** or **Bol·she·vī′kī,** [Russ., lit., the larger.]

1. originally, a member of the radical branch of the Socialist Democratic Party in Russia, favoring the rule of the proletariat: so called because this was originally the larger group of the party, the Mensheviki being the smaller. The Bolsheviks came into power in 1917 and formed the Communist Party.

2. a member of a Communist party, especially that of the Soviet Union.

3. a person who has communist views and traits but is not a member of a Communist party.

4. loosely, any radical: hostile usage.

Bol′she·vik, bol′she·vik, *a.* of, characteristic of, or like the Bolsheviks or Bolshevism.

Bol′she·viṣm, bol′she·viṣm, *n.* the policies and practices of the Bolsheviks.

Bol′she·vist, bol′she·vist, *n.* and *a.* Bolshevik.

Bol·she·vis′tiç, bol·she·vis′tiç, *a.* Bolshevik.

Bol′she·vīze, bol′she·vīze, *v.t.*; Bolshevized, *pt. pp.*; Bolshevizing, *ppr.* to make Bolshevik; indoctrinate with Bolshevism.

Bōl′sŏn, *n.* [Sp., lit., big purse.] a flat desert valley surrounded by mountains draining into a shallow lake in the center.

bōl′stẽr, *n.* [ME. *bolstre*; AS. *bolster*, a headrest, bolster.]

1. a long, narrow cushion or pillow, used to support the head of persons lying on a bed: generally laid under the pillows.

2. anything resembling a bolster in shape or manner of usage.

3. a pad or quilt used to support or relieve pressure on any part of the body; a compress.

4. the part of a bridge between a truss or girder and the masonry.

5. in architecture, the lateral part of the volute of the Ionic capital: also called *baluster*.

6. in saddlery, a part of a saddle raised upon the bows or hinder part, to hold the rider's thigh.

7. a wooden block on the carriage of a cannon upon which the breech rests when it is moved.

8. the part of a knife, chisel, etc. which joins the end of the handle; also, a metallic plate on the end of a pocketknife handle.

9. in ships, a cushion or bag, filled with tarred canvas, used to preserve the stays from being worn or chafed by the masts.

10. a piece of timber placed on various parts of a ship to prevent the works or ropes from being abraded.

11. in railroad cars, the principal crossbeam of a truck, or the transverse beam bearing the body of a car; a truck bolster.

12. the perforated block of a punching machine.

13. the crossbar, supported by the axle, upon which the body or bed of a vehicle rests.

14. the raised ridge which holds the tuning pins of a piano.

bōl′stẽr, *v.t.*; bolstered, *pt., pp.*; bolstering, *ppr.* 1. to support with a bolster or pillow.

2. to support; to hold up; to maintain with difficulty or great effort: often followed by *up*; as, he tried to *bolster up* his ridiculous theory.

bōl′stẽr, *v.i.* to lie together, as on the same bolster. [Rare.]

bōl′stẽred, *a.* supported with or as with a bolster.

bōl′stẽr·ẽr, *n.* a supporter.

bōlt, *n.* [ME. *bolt*, a shaft or arrow; AS. *bolt*, a catapult for throwing bolts.]

1. an arrow; a dart; a short, heavy shaft with a thick, blunt head, intended to be shot from a crossbow or catapult.

2. a strong cylindrical pin of iron or other metal, used to hold something in place, often having a head at one end and a screw thread at the other to receive a nut.

3. a sudden stream of lightning; a thunderbolt; as, a *bolt* from the blue.

4. the quantity of cloth, as of cotton, silk, or canvas, contained in an original roll or package; usually about forty yards.

5. a shackle; a fetter for the legs. [Obs.]

6. (a) that portion of a lock which forms the fastening and is moved back and forth by the key; (b) any movable or sliding catch, bar, or other fastening for a door, window, gate, etc.

7. a bundle, as of osiers or straw.

8. withdrawal from one's party or group; refusal to support the nominee or platform of one's political party.

9. (a) precipitate departure or flight; as, the *bolt* of a horse; (b) any sudden, unforeseen occurrence, often an unfortunate one.

10. in firearms, a sliding bar that pushes the cartridge into place, closes the breech, and extracts the empty cartridge case after firing.

bōlt, *v.t.*; bolted, *pt., pp.*; bolting, *ppr.* [ME. *bolten, bulten*, to spring off suddenly, to bolt; AS. *bolt*, a catapult.]

1. to shoot or discharge (an arrow, etc.).

2. to fasten or secure with or as with a bolt.

3. to blurt out; to utter or throw out precipitately.

4. to swallow unmasticated; to gulp down; as, to *bolt* food.

5. to roll (cloth, etc.) into bolts.

6. among sportsmen, to start or dislodge, as game.

7. in politics, to break from; to withdraw support from; as, he *bolted* his party and its candidates.

bōlt, *v.i.* 1. to shoot forth suddenly; to spring out with speed (commonly followed by *out*); as, to *bolt out* of the house.

2. to start suddenly and run away, as a horse.

3. to make a sudden flight or escape; as, he *bolted* to avoid his creditors.

4. in horticulture, to produce seed before the natural time.

5. to refuse to support the candidate of one's party; to break away from or abandon a group, political party, etc.

6. to swallow food hurriedly.

bōlt, *v.t.* [ME. *bulten*; OFr. *bulter, buleter*, to bolt, to sift.]

1. to sift or separate, as bran from flour, by passing through a bolter.

2. figuratively, to examine as if by sifting; to find the truth of.

Time and nature will *bolt* out the truth of things. —L'Estrange.

bōlt, *n.* a fine sieve for sifting flour or meal; a bolter.

bōlt, *adv.* in the manner of a bolt; stiffly; suddenly.

bolt upright; in an erect posture; straight up.

bōlt ạu′gẽr, a large auger used in shipbuilding to bore holes for bolts.

bōlt bōat, a strong boat that will endure a rough sea.

bōl′tel, *n.* [ME. *boltel, bowtell*, prob. from *bolt*, with reference to its shaftlike shape.] in architecture, a shaft of a clustered column, or any plain round molding.

bōlt′ẽr, *n.* [ME. *bulter, bulture*, one who bolts, from *bulten*, to bolt.]

1. an instrument or machine for separating bran from flour, or the coarser part of meal from the finer; a milling sieve.

2. one who sifts flour or meal.

bōlt′ẽr, *n.* one who bolts; specifically, one who bolts his party platform or candidates, or a horse given to running away.

bōlt′ẽr, *n.* a fishing line; boulter.

bōlt′head (-hed), *n.* 1. a long, straight-necked glass flask, used by early chemists.

2. the end of a bolt opposite the threaded end.

bōl′ti, *n.* [Ar. *boltuiy*.] an edible fish of the rivers of Egypt and Palestine, belonging to the genus *Chromis*: written also *bolty, bulti*.

bōlt′ing, *n.* [ME. *bultinge*, verbal noun of *bulten*, to bolt.] the act of fleeing; a darting off or aside.

bōlt′ing, *n.* the act of sifting flour or meal.

bōlt′ing çloth, a silk, linen, hair, or wire cloth of which bolters are made for sifting meal.

bōlt′ing hutch, a bin or tub in which to keep bolted flour or meal.

bōlt′ing mill, a machine or apparatus for sifting meal.

bōl·tō′ni·ȧ, *n.* [Mod. L., after the Eng. botanist James *Bolton*.] any of several plants of the composite family, with white or purplish, asterlike flowers.

bōl′tŏn·īte, *n.* a granular mineral of a grayish or yellowish color, found in *Bolton*, Mass.

bōlt′rōpe, *n.* a rope to which the edges of sails are sewed to strengthen them.

bōlt′sprit, *n.* bowsprit. [Obs.]

bō′lus, *n.*; *pl.* **bō′lus·eṣ,** [L. *bolus*; Gr. *bolos*, a throw, a mass, from *ballein*, to throw.]

1. in veterinary medicine, a large pill.

2. a small, round lump or mass of something.

bom, *n.* a large South American ringed serpent or boa, the *Epicrates cenchris*.

bō′mȧh nut, the fruit of a tropical African plant, *Pycnocoma macrophylla*. It is used in tanning, and its oil in cooking.

Bō·mā′rē·ȧ, *n.* [named after Valmont de *Bomare*, 18th-c. French naturalist.] a large genus of climbing plants, family *Amaryllis*, having showy flowers: chiefly found in the American tropics. The roots of some species are used as food, especially the *Bomarea salsilla*.

bomb (bom), *n.* [Fr. *bombe*, a bomb, from L. *bombus*, Gr. *bombos*, a deep, hollow sound.]

1. an explosive, incendiary, or gas-filled container, for dropping, hurling, or setting in place to be exploded by a timing mechanism.

2. a sudden, surprising occurrence, especially an unpleasant one.

3. a mass of lava and scoria, generally spherical in form and varying in size, which has been ejected from a volcano.

bomb, *v.t.* and *v.i.* to attack, damage, or destroy (anything) with a bomb or bombs.

bombs away; bombs have been released: said by the bombardier to the pilot of a bomber.

bom·bȧ·çā′ceous, *a.* [LL. *bombax*, and *-aceous*.] belonging to the family of silk-cotton trees, which bear fruit with woolly seeds.

bom′bāce, *n.* cotton; padding. [Obs.]

Bom·bā′cē·ae, *n.pl.* [L. *bombyx*, from Gr. *bombyx*, the silkworm.] a family of tropical plants allied to the *Malvaceæ*; the silk-cotton family.

bom′bärd, *n.* [Fr. *bombarde*, cannon, from *bombe*; from L. *bombus*, Gr. *bombos*, a deep, hollow sound.]

1. formerly, a piece of short, thick ordnance, with a large mouth. It was called also *basilisk*, and was the earliest type of cannon, hurling stones or other large missiles.

2. an attack with bombs; bombardment. [Rare.]

3. a barrel; a drinking vessel or leather bottle for carrying liquors. [Obs.]

4. [*pl.*] breeches heavily padded. [Obs.]

bom·bärd′, *v.t.*; bombarded, *pt., pp.*; bombarding, *ppr.* [Fr. *bombarder*, to batter with a cannon.]

1. formerly, to attack with bombs thrown from bombards. Now, to attack with or as with bombs or artillery; to shell; to fire shot or shells at; as, the fleet *bombarded* the forts.

2. to attack with words or speech; as, he *bombarded* me with questions.

3. to assail with missiles of any kind; as, the rioters *bombarded* the police with stones.

bom·bärd′ẽr, *n.* one who bombards.

bom·băr·diẽr′, *n.* [Fr. *bombardier*, from *bombarde*, a bombard.]

1. a ship firing bombards. [Archaic.]

2. a noncommissioned artillery officer in the British army.

3. the person who operates the bombsight and releases the bombs in a bomber.

bombardier beetle; one of several varieties of beetle, which, when irritated, discharge a pungent vapor from the anal glands.

bom′bärd·măn, *n.* one who carried beer or liquor in a bombard. [Obs.]

bom·bärd′ment, *n.* a bombarding or being bombarded.

bom·bär′dō, *n.* the bombardon. [Obs.]

bom·bär′dŏn, *n.* [It. *bombardone*, a musical instrument.]

1. formerly, a musical instrument of the wind family, an early type of bassoon.

2. a bass reed stop of the organ.

3. a bass or contrabass tuba.

bom·bȧ·ṣine′, *n.* same as *bombazine*.

bom′bast, *n.* [OFr. *bombace*; LL. *bombax*, cotton, *bombasium*, a doublet of cotton, from L.

bombyx, Gr. *bombyx*, the silkworm, a garment of silk.]

1. originally, a material of soft, loose texture, used to pad garments; also, any kind of stuffing or padding. [Obs.]

2. high-sounding words; an inflated style; fustian; a grandiloquent attempt to elevate something which in reality is unimportant.

Syn.—rodomontade, braggadocio, gasconade, bluster, inflatedness, pomposity, fustian.

bom′bast, *a.* high-sounding without meaning; bombastic.

bom·bast′, *v.t.* to swell; to pad. [Obs.]

bom·bas′tiç, bom·bas′tiç·ăl, *a.* using, characterized by, or fond of high-sounding but unimportant or silly language; pompous; grandiloquent.

bom·bas′tiç·ăl·ly, *adv.* in a bombastic manner; grandiloquently.

bom′bast·ry, *n.* grandiloquent words without much meaning; bombastic language. [Obs.]

Bom′bax, *n.* [L. *bombyx*; Gr. *bombyx*, the silkworm.] a genus of trees of the mallow family; the silk-cotton tree.

bom·bȧ·zet′, bom·bȧ·zette′, *n.* a thin woolen cloth, either plain or twilled.

bom·bȧ·zïne′, *n.* [Fr. *bombasin*; LL. *bombacinium*, a silk texture; from L. *bombyx*, Gr. *bombyx*, the silkworm.] a twilled fabric of which the warp is silk and the weft worsted or cotton: much used for mourning garments. Also spelled *bombasine*.

bomb bāy, a compartment for the bombs in a bomber, made so that it can be opened when they are to be dropped.

bomb çal·ŏ·rim′e·tẽr, a special form of calorimeter to measure the heat of combustion, as of coal.

bomb chest, in military mining, a chest filled with explosives, which is to be buried and exploded near the enemy's works.

bombe (bōṅb), *n.* [Fr.; see *bomb*.] a frozen dessert consisting of a melon or a mold with an inner coating of one kind of ice cream and a center of another.

bomb′ẽr, *n.* 1. one who bombs.

2. an airplane designed for dropping bombs.

bomb här·pọọn′, a harpoon carrying an explosive head: used chiefly in whale fishing.

bom′biç, *a.* [L. *bombyx*, from Gr. *bombyx*, the silkworm.] pertaining to or derived from the silkworm; as, *bombic* acid.

bombic acid; an acid compound secreted by the silkworm.

bom′bi·lāte, *v.i.* [L. *bombus*; Gr. *bombos*, any deep, hollow sound.] to buzz, or hum; to boom. [Rare.]

bom·bi·lā′tion, *n.* sound; report; noise; as, the *bombilation* of guns. [Rare.]

bom′bi·nāte, *v.i.* same as *bombilate*.

bom·bi·nā′tion, *n.* [from L. *bombus*; Gr. *bombos*, a deep, hollow sound.] a buzzing or humming. [Rare.]

bomb′ing run, a flight by a bombing crew over the target for the release of bombs.

bomb ketch, a small ship or vessel formerly used for shelling a fortress from the sea.

bom′bō·lō, *n.* [It. *bombola*, a bottle.] a spheroidal retort of flint glass used in the condensation of sublimated camphor: written also *bumbelo* and *bumbolo*.

bomb′prọọf, *a.* secured against the force of bombs; able to withstand or resist bombardment.

bomb′prọọf, *n.* a bombproof shelter, often underground.

bomb rack, a device underneath or within an aircraft for transporting and releasing aerial bombs.

bomb′shell, *n.* 1. a bomb.

2. any sudden unforeseen occurrence, especially an unpleasant one.

bomb sīght, an instrument for aiming bombs dropped from aircraft.

bom′by·cid, *a.* pertaining to the genus *Bombyx*, or to any of a certain family of moths found chiefly in tropical regions, as the silkworm moth.

bom·byc′i·nous, *a.* [L. *bombycinus*, silken, from *bombyx*, a silkworm.]

1. silken; made of silk. [Obs.]

2. having the color of the silkworm; transparent, with a yellow tint.

Bom′byx, *n.* [L., from Gr. *bombyx*, the silkworm.] a genus of moths, including the silkworm moth.

Bŏn, *n.* [Japan.] a religious festival observed by Japanese Buddhists from July 13 to 16, when the spirits of dead ancestors are supposed to come back.

bōṅ, *a.* [Fr., from L. *bonus*, good.] good.

bō′nä, *n.pl.* [L., neuter pl. of *bonus*, good.] in law, goods or property, movable and immovable.

bona notabilia; formerly, in English law, goods belonging to one deceased and at the time of his death not situated in the same diocese as that in which he died.

bona peritura; in law, perishable goods.

bona vacantia; goods without an apparent owner, as shipwrecks, etc.

bōṅ-aç·çord′, *n.* [Fr. *bon*, good, and *accord*, fellowship, agreement.] good fellowship; agreement; good will. [Scot.]

bon′āce tree, a small West Indian tree, *Daphnopsis tinifolia*, the fibrous inner bark of which is used for making cordage.

bō·nä·cï′, *n.* any of certain groupers important as food fishes, found near Florida, the West Indies, etc.

bō′nȧ fī′dē, [L., ablative of *bona fides*, good faith.] with good faith; without fraud or deception; genuine; as, a *bona fide* purchase of a *bona fide* picture.

bō′nȧ fī′dēş, [L.] good faith; honesty.

bō·nāir′, *a.* [ME. *bonair*, from Fr. *debonnaire*, easy-tempered, kind.] complaisant; yielding; gentle; debonair. [Obs.]

bōṅ ȧ·mï′, [Fr.] good friend: said of a man or boy.

bō·nan′zä, *n.* [Sp. *bonanza*, fair weather at sea, prosperity; from L. *bonus*, good.]

1. a rich vein, mine, or pocket of ore; a rich find in mining or prospecting.

2. anything which yields a large income; as, his patent proved to be a *bonanza*. [Colloq.]

Bō·nȧ·pär′tē·ăn, *a.* pertaining to Napoleon Bonaparte or the Bonaparte family.

Bō′nȧ·pärt·işm, *n.* 1. belief in and support of Napoleon Bonaparte and his actions, methods, and doctrines.

2. the methods, doctrines, etc. of any political dictator like Napoleon Bonaparte.

Bō′nȧ·pärt·ist, *n.* one who practices or advocates Bonapartism.

bō′nȧ rō′bȧ, [It.] a gay wanton. [Obs.]

bō·nā′sus, bō·nas′sus, *n.* [L. *bonasus*, Gr. *bonasos*, the wild ox, from *bous*, an ox.] a species of *Bos*, or wild ox; the aurochs.

bon′bon, *n.* [Fr. *bon*, good, emphasized by repetition.] a small piece of candy, often with creamy filling.

bon·bon·nière′ (bọṅ-bọṅ-yãr′), *n.* [Fr.] a container for bonbons; a candy box or dish.

bonce, *n.* [origin uncertain.] a boys' game played with large marbles.

bon chré·tien′ (bọṅ krā-tyaṅ′), [Fr., literally, good Christian.] formerly, in England, the Bartlett pear.

bond, *n.* [ME. *bond*; AS. *bindan*, to bind.]

1. anything that binds or fastens, as a cord, a chain, or a rope; a band.

2. a substance or device, as glue, solder, or a chain which holds things together or unites them.

3. union; connection; a binding.

> Let walls be so constructed as to make a good *bond*. —Mortimer.

4. [*pl.*] chains; fetters; hence, imprisonment; captivity.

> This man doeth nothing worthy of death or of *bonds*. —Acts xxvi. 31.

5. cause of union; a tie which unites; link of connection; as, the *bonds* of affection.

6. an obligation imposing a moral duty, as by a vow or promise, by law, or other means.

7. a binding agreement; a covenant.

8. bond paper.

9. in chemistry, (a) a unit of combining capacity equivalent to one atom of hydrogen; (b) the means or mechanism by which atoms or groups of atoms are combined in molecules.

10. in commerce, (a) an agreement by an agency holding taxable goods that taxes on them will be paid before they are sold; (b) the condition of goods kept in a warehouse until taxes are paid; (c) an insurance contract by which a bonding agency guarantees payment of a specified sum to an employer, etc., in the event of a financial loss caused him by the act of a specified employee or by some contingency over which the payee has no control.

11. in finance, an interest-bearing certificate issued by a government or business promising to pay the holder a specified sum on a specified date: it is a common means of raising capital.

12. in law, (a) a written obligation under seal to pay specified sums, or to do or not do specified things; (b) a person acting as surety for another's action; payer of bail; (c) an amount paid as surety or bail.

13. in masonry, any arrangement of bricks, etc. in a wall, which binds them into a compact whole; as, *English bond*, where one course consists of bricks with their ends toward the face of the wall, called headers, and the next course of bricks with their lengths parallel to the face of the wall, called stretchers; *Flemish bond*, where each course consists of headers and stretchers alternately.

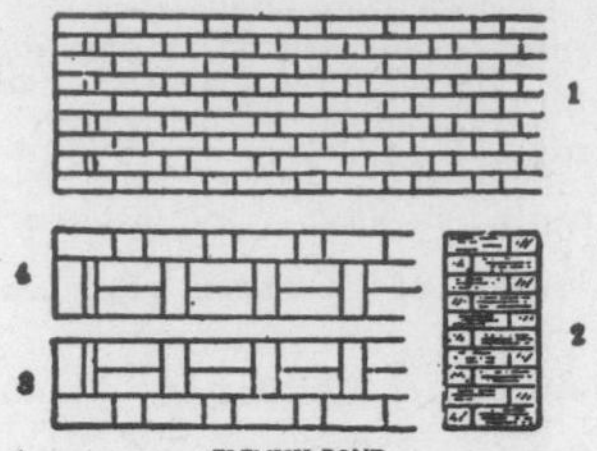

FLEMISH BOND
1. face of wall; 2. end of wall; 3. first course bed; 4. second course bed

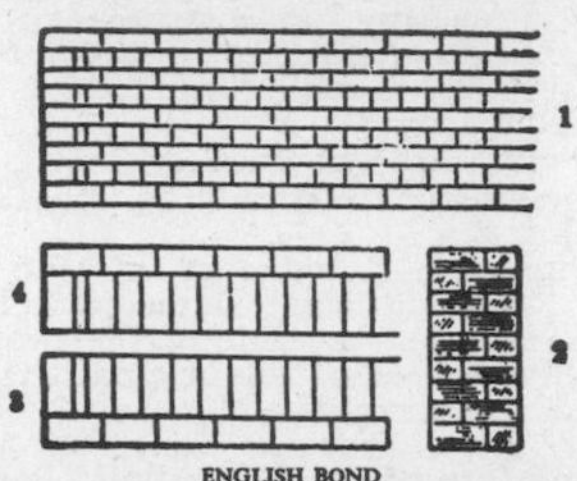

ENGLISH BOND
1. face of wall; 2. end of wall; 3. first course bed; 4. second course bed

14. a circuit connection of copper, used between the rails in an electric railway line.

15. (a) [*pl.*] in building, all the timbers employed in constructing the walls of a building; (b) the jointing together of timbers, etc.

average bond; a bond given to the captain of a ship by the consignees of a cargo, to secure the payment of their share of a general average, their goods having been delivered to them.

convertible bond; a bond that may be converted into stock at the option of the holder.

income bond; a bond guaranteeing the payment of certain sums at stipulated times, and pledging the income of a corporation to do so.

penal bond; a bond by which a sum of money is forfeited in case of failure to do a thing specified.

straw bond; a fraudulent bond; a bond by which worthless or nonexistent property is pledged as security.

Syn.—tie, fastening, chain, manacle, fetter, compact, obligation, security.

bond, *v.t.*; bonded, *pt., pp.*; bonding, *ppr.* 1. to connect with or as with a bond; to bind.

2. to furnish a bond (sense 12, (*a*) and thus become a surety for (another).

3. to place or hold (goods) in or under bond.

4. to issue interest-bearing certificates on; to mortgage.

5. to put under bonded debt.

6. to arrange (timbers, bricks, etc.) in a pattern that gives strength.

bond, *v.i.* to connect, hold together, or solidify by or as by a bond.

bond, *n.* [OE. *bond, bonde*, serf.] a serf or slave. [Obs.]

bond, *a.* in slavery or serfdom; captive.

> Whether we be *bond* or free. —1 Cor. xii. 13.

bond′āġe, *n.* [ME. *bondage*; OFr. *bondage*, the condition of being bound; AS. *bonda, bunda*, husbandman, servant; ON. *bondi*.]

1. slavery or involuntary servitude; serfdom; captivity; imprisonment; restraint of a person's liberty by compulsion.

2. in ancient English law, villeinage.

3. obligation; tie of duty. [Obs.]

> Brought under the *bondage* of observing oaths. —South.

4. voluntary or involuntary subjection to some force, compulsion, or influence; as, the *bondage* of sin; the *bondage* of fashion; the *bondage* of orthodoxy.

Syn.—servitude, captivity, slavery.

bond′ā·ġẽr, *n.* one who works in the field, in payment of rent. [Scot.]

bon′där, *n.* [native name.] a small animal, *Paradoxurus bondar*, found in southern Asia; a palm civet.

bond çọọp′ẽr, one who has charge of bonded liquor.

bond çred′i·tŏr, in law, a creditor who has a bond to secure his claim.

bond debt (det), in law, a debt secured by a bond or bonds; a bonded debt.

bond'ed, *a.* 1. subject to or secured by bond, as duties; under bond for the faithful performance of a contract.

2. placed in a warehouse pending payment of taxes.

bonded debt; a debt secured by a bond or bonds; a bond debt.

bonded warehouse; a warehouse, certified by the Department of Internal Revenue and guaranteed by a bonding agency, where goods may be stored until necessary duties or taxes are paid.

bond'ẽr, *n.* 1. one who stores goods under bond.

2. in building, a bondstone.

bond'ẽr, *n.* in Norway, one having a small freehold.

bond'hōld"ẽr, *n.* one who holds or owns the bonds issued by a company, government, or person.

bond'māid, *n.* a girl or woman bond servant or slave.

bond'măn, *n.*; *pl.* **bond'men,** 1. a man or boy slave. [Archaic.]

2. in old English law, a villein, or tenant in villeinage; a feudal serf.

bond pā'pẽr, 1. rag paper used for bonds.

2. a strong, superior stock of paper with a hard surface, used for letterheads, etc.

bond'-sẽr·vȧnt, *n.* 1. a person bound to service without pay.

2. a slave.

Also written *bond servant.*

bond'-sẽrv·ice, the condition of a bond-servant; slavery; service without pay.

bondṣ'măn, *n.*; *pl.* **bondṣ'men,** 1. a bondman.

2. a surety; one who is bound, or who gives security, for another.

bond'stōne, *n.* a stone that binds or holds a wall together, by running through from face to face, thereby strengthening it.

bondṣ'wom"ăn, *n.*; *pl.* **bondṣ'wom"en,** same as *bondwoman.*

bond tim'bẽr, a strengthening timber inserted in building a wall, etc.

bon'duç, *n.* [Fr., from Arm. *bondug*, the filbert; Per. *funduq*, the hazel or filbert.] a climbing plant, *Cæsalpinia* or *Guilandina Bonduc*, the nicker tree or yellow nicker, native in the tropics and bearing a pod containing two hard seeds.

bond'wom"ăn (-woom"), *n.*; *pl.* **bond'wom"en** (-wim"). a woman slave.

bōne, *n.* [ME. *boon, ban*; AS. *bān*, a bone.]

1. a firm, hard substance, of a dull white color, composing the skeleton of most full-grown vertebrate animals. The bones of an animal support all the softer parts, as the flesh and vessels. In a fetus they are soft and cartilaginous, but they gradually harden with age. They are covered with a thin, strong membrane, called the *periosteum*, and their cells and cavities contain a fatty substance called the *medulla* or *marrow*.

2. [*pl.*] the skeleton; hence, the body, living or dead.

3. any part or piece of a skeleton, especially a piece between two joints; as, the collar *bone*, a *bone* of the wrist, a ham *bone*.

4. a thin layer of slaty substance found in coal beds.

5. [*pl.*] dice. [Colloq.]

6. a bonelike substance or thing.

7. a thing made of bone or bonelike material.

8. [*pl.*] flat sticks used as clappers by end men in minstrel shows, for keeping time to music, etc.

9. *pl.* [*construed as sing.*] an end man in a minstrel show.

10. a student who studies hard. [Slang.]

bone in the mouth; in nautical usage, the foam dashing up a vessel's bows.

bone of contention; a subject of dispute.

bone to pick; a dispute to be settled.

to make no bones about; (a) to make no attempt to hide; to admit freely; (b) to have no objection to or qualms about. [Colloq.]

to pick a bone with; to quarrel or dispute with.

bōne, *v.t.*; boned, *pt., pp.*; boning, *ppr.* 1. to take out the bones from, as fish.

2. to put whalebone or other stiffening into, as corsets.

3. to steal; to pilfer. [Slang.]

4. to cover with bone for fertilizing.

5. to importune. (Slang.)

bōne, *v.i.* to study diligently (often with *up*). [Slang.]

bōne, *v.t.* [Fr. *bornoyer*, to sight with one eye, from *borgnē*, one-eyed.] to look with one eye along (a set of objects) in order to find whether they are level or in line; also written *born, bourn*, etc.

bōne āce, a game at cards, in which he who has the highest third card turned up to him wins the bone, that is, one-half the stake.

bōne ash, a white porous ash prepared by burning bones in the open air and consisting chiefly of calcium phosphate: used in making bone china: also *bone earth.*

bōne'black, *n.* a fine charcoal made by roasting animal bones in closed containers and used as a coloring, in refining sugar, etc.: also *bone black.*

bōne'breāk"ẽr, *n.* 1. an individual or thing that breaks bones; especially, a wrestler. [Slang.]

2. the osprey.

bōne chī'nȧ, a kind of china made with clay to which bone ash or calcium phosphate has been added.

bōned, *a.* 1. having (a specific kind of) bone; as, high-*boned*; strong-*boned.*

2. having the bones taken out; as, *boned* turkey.

3. fertilized with bones.

4. having stays of whalebone, etc.

bōne'dog, *n.* the dogfish.

bōne'drȳ', *a.* as dry as bone; very dry.

bōne dust, ground or pulverized bones, used as fertilizer.

bōne ẽarth, bone ash.

bōne'fish, *n.* the ladyfish (sense 1).

bōne'head (-hed), *n.* a stupid or ignorant person. [Slang.]

bōne' lāce, a lace made of linen thread, woven with bobbins of bone. [Obs.]

bōne'less, *a.* without bones; specifically, with the bones removed; as, *boneless* sardines.

bōne mēal, crushed or finely ground bones, used as feed or fertilizer.

bōne oil, a thick, black oil obtained by the dry distillation of bones.

bōn'ẽr, *n.* a stupid or silly blunder. [Slang.]

bōne'set, *n.* a plant of the composite family, the thoroughwort, *Eupatorium perfoliatum*, with flat clusters of white or bluish-purple flowers: used in medicine as a drug to increase perspiration, as a tonic, etc.

bōne'set"tẽr, *n.* one who sets broken bones.

bōne'set"ting, *n.* the practice of setting bones.

bōne'shaw, *n.* sciatica. [Obs.]

bōne spav'in, a bony excrescence on the inside of the hock of a horse's leg.

bōne whāle (hwāl), a right whale.

bōne whīte, an off shade of white varying from grayish white to beige-white.

bon'fīre, *n.* [ME. *bonefire, bonefyre*, originally a fire of bones.]

1. a fire made in the open air for any purpose, as for amusement, for warmth, or as an expression of public joy or celebration.

2. a funeral pyre. [Obs.]

boṅ'gō, *n.*; *pl.* **boṅ'gōṣ,** [native African name.] a large African antelope of the genus *Boöcercus*, reddish-brown with white stripes.

boṅ'gō, *n.*; *pl.* **boṅ'gōṣ,** [Am.Sp.] either of a pair of small joined drums, each of different pitch, struck with the fingers: in full *bongo drum.*

bon'grāce, *n.* [Fr., from *bonne*, f. of *bon*, good, and *grâce*, beauty, charm.] a covering for the forehead: a projecting bonnet or hat. [Obs.]

bon·ho·miē', bon·hom·miē' (bon-o-mē'), *n.* [Fr. *bon*, good, and *homme*, man.] pleasing manner; cheerful disposition.

bon'i·fāce, *n.* [from *Boniface*, the kind-hearted landlord in Farquhar's comedy, "Beaux' Stratagem."] a hotel proprietor; innkeeper.

bon'i·form, *a.* [L. *bonus*, good, and *forma*, form.] of a good form or nature. [Rare.]

bon'i·fȳ, *v.t.* [Fr. *bonifier*, to improve; L. *bonus* good, and *facere*, to do.] to convert into good. [Rare.]

bōn'i·ness, *n.* the quality or condition of being bony.

bōn'ing, *n.* 1. the treatment of soil with bones as fertilizer.

2. the removing of bones from animal bodies.

bon·i·tā'ri·ăn, *a.* [L. *bonitas*, goodness.] reasonable; just; honest; bonitary.

bon'i·tā·ry, *a.* having a beneficiary enjoyment of property without legal title.

bō·nī'tō, *n.*; *pl.* **bō·nī'tōṣ, bō·nī'tōeṣ,** [Sp. *bonito*, dim. of *bueno*, good.]

1. any of several saltwater food fishes of the mackerel family, specifically, a large, active fish of the genus *Sarda*, found on both the Atlantic and Pacific coasts of the United States. There are numerous related species which are important food fishes.

2. the crabeater or cobia, *Elacate canada.*

3. the madregal, *Seriola fasciata*, of the West Indies.

boṅ" jöur' (zhör'), [Fr.] good day; good morning.

boṅ" mōt' (mō'), *n.*; *pl.* **boṅs" mōts'** (boṅ" mōz'; Fr. mō'), [Fr. *bon*, good, and *mot*, a word.] a jest; a witty, clever, or apt saying.

bonne (bon), *n.* [Fr., f. of *bon*, good.]

1. a maidservant.

2. a nursemaid.

bonne ȧ·miē' (ȧ-mē'), [Fr., f. of *bon ami.*] good friend: said of a woman or girl.

bonne" böuçhe', [Fr., from *bonne*, f. of *bon*, good, and *bouche*, mouth.] a delicious morsel or mouthful.

bonne" foi' (fwȧ'), [Fr., lit., good faith.] honesty; sincerity.

bon'net, *n.* [ME. *bonet, bonette*; OFr. *bonet, bonnet*, bonnet or cap.]

1. a hat, usually brimless, with a chin ribbon, worn by women or children.

2. in fortification, a small work with two faces, having only a parapet, with two rows of palisades about ten or twelve feet distant.

3. in nautical language, an addition to a sail, or an additional part laced to the foot of a jib, in small vessels.

4. a flat, brimless woolen cap worn by men and boys in Scotland.

5. an Indian headdress; as, a Sioux war-*bonnet.*

6. the second stomach of a cud-chewing animal.

7. a decoy; a confederate.

8. anything used as a bonnet or protective covering, as the top casting of a valve, a covering over an elevator cage, the wire netting that covers a locomotive smokestack, an automobile hood, or the projection over a fireplace to increase the draft.

bon'net, *v.t.*; bonneted, *pt., pp.*; bonneting, *ppr.* 1. to put a bonnet on.

2. to push the hat down over the eyes of.

bon'net, *v.i.* to uncover the head as a mark of respect. [Obs.]

bon'net·ed, *a.* wearing or provided with a bonnet.

bon'net grȧss, white bent grass, *Agrostis alba.*

bon'net·head (-hed), *n.* a shark, *Reniceps tiburo*, native in the West Indies.

bon'net·less, *a.* not having a bonnet.

bon'net lim'pet, a name given to various species of shells of the family *Calyptræidæ*, which are found adhering to stones and shells.

bon'net moṅ'key, the macaque or munga, *Macacus sinicus*, an East Indian monkey distinguished by the bonnetlike arrangement of the hair on its head.

bon'net piēce, an old Scottish gold coin on which the head of James V appears, wearing a bonnet.

bon·net röuge (bon-nā rözh'); *pl.* **bon·net röuges** (rözh'), [Fr.] a red cap worn by the French revolutionists of 1793 as a sign of their patriotism; hence, a revolutionist.

bon'ni·bel, *n.* [Fr. *bonne et belle*, good and beautiful.] a handsome girl. [Obs.]

bon'nie, *a.* same as *bonny.*

bon'ni·lȧsse, *n.* a beautiful girl. [Obs.]

bon'ni·ly, *adv.* gaily; handsomely.

bon'ni·ness, *n.* a bonny quality or state.

bon'ny, bon'nie, *a.*; *comp.* bonnier; *superl.* bonniest, [Fr. *bon, bonne*, good; L. *bonus*, good.]

1. handsome; beautiful; comely; sweetly attractive: used especially in Scotland and the northern part of England.

2. gay; merry; frolicsome; blithe. [Obs.]

3. healthy-looking; robust.

4. fine; pleasant.

Syn.—fair, pretty, pleasant, cheerful.

bon'ny, *n.* [origin unknown.] among miners, a distinct bed of ore that communicates with no vein.

bon'ny·çlab"bẽr, *n.* [Ir. *bainne*, milk, and *claba*, thick mud.]

1. milk that has become thick in the process of souring; clabber; curd.

2. a drink made of beer and buttermilk or sour cream.

bon·sāī', *n.* [Japan., lit., tray arrangement.]

1. the art of dwarfing and shaping trees and shrubs in shallow pots by pruning, controlled fertilization, etc.

2. *pl.* **bon·sāī',** such a tree or shrub.

boṅ" soir' (swȧr'), [Fr.] good evening.

bon'spiēl, *n.* formerly, in sports, any match game; now generally restricted to a curling match between two clubs, towns, etc. [Scot.]

bon'tē·bok, *n.*; *pl.* **bon'tē·bok, bon'tē·boks,** [D. *bont*, spotted, and *bok*, buck.] a species of purplish-red antelope, *Alcelaphus pygargus*, of South Africa, white on the face and rump.

bŏn″ tŏn′, [Fr., good tone, manner.]
1. the style of fashionable people; good style.
2. fashionable society.
3. good breeding; fine manners.

bō′nus, *n.*; *pl.* **bō′nus·eṣ**, [L. *bonus*, good.]
1. a premium given for a loan, a charter or other privilege granted to a company.
2. an extra dividend to shareholders of a joint stock company, out of accumulated profits.
3. extra compensation beyond an amount agreed upon; an extra payment or consideration given as a reward or an inducement, or as a means of avoiding loss, in many contracts and business transactions; an honorarium.
4. a payment made by a government to discharged members of the armed forces.

bō′nus, *v.t.*; bonused, *pt.*, *pp.*; bonusing, *ppr.* to promote by giving a bonus to; to add a bonus to [Rare.]

bŏn vi·vänt′ (vē-vän′); *pl.* **bŏn vi·vänts′** (vē-vän′), [Fr.] one who enjoys good food and other pleasant things.

bŏn voy·ȧge′ (vwȧ-yȧzh′), [Fr., lit., good voyage.] pleasant journey.

bōn′y, *a.*; *comp.* bonier; *superl.* boniest. 1. of or like bone.
2. consisting of bones; full of bones.
3. having large or prominent bones; hence, thin; gaunt; lean.

bōn′y-fish, the menhaden, *Brevoortia tyrannus*.

bōn′y-pīke, a gar pike.

bonze, *n.* [Fr., from Port. *bonzo*; Japanese *bozu*, a Buddhist priest.] a Chinese or Japanese Buddhist monk.

bon′zẽr, *a.* extraordinarily good or fine. [Australian Slang.]

bo̤o, bo̤oh, *interj.* and *n.* [echoic.] a sound that one makes to express disapproval, scorn, etc., or to startle.

bo̤o, *v.i.*; booed, *pt.*, *pp.*; booing, *ppr.* to make the sound "boo."

bo̤o, *v.t.* to shout "boo" at.

bo̤ob, *n.* [from booby.] a stupid or foolish person. [Slang.]

bo̤o′by, *n.* [Sp. *bobo*, a dunce or idiot.]
1. a dunce; a stupid fellow; a nitwit.
2. any of several birds of the genus *Sula*, the gannet family, as *Sula leucogastra*, the common *booby* of the South Atlantic coast; a booby gannet.
3. the player who gets the poorest score in a game, or does worst in a contest.
4. the dunce of a class or school.

bo̤o′by, *a.* having the characteristics of a booby; dull; stupid.

bo̤o′by gan′net, a large, tropical sea bird related to the gannets, with eyes near the base of the bill.

bo̤o′by hatch (hach), 1. a hatchway leading to storage space under the poop deck of a ship.
2. a hospital for the mentally ill. [Slang.]

bo̤o′by hut, a sleigh with a hooded cover.

bo̤o′by hutch (huch), a roughly built covered carriage used in the east of England.

bo̤o′by·ish, *a.* like a booby; silly; stupid.

bo̤o′by prīze, a prize, usually a ridiculous one, given to whoever has done worst in a game, race, etc.

bo̤o′by trap, 1. any scheme or device for tricking a person unawares.
2. an antipersonnel mine made to be exploded by some action of the intended victim, as by picking up an innocent-looking object to which the detonator is attached.

Bo̤odh, Bo̤odh′ȧ, *n.* see *Buddha*.

Bo̤odh′iṣm, *n.* see *Buddhism*.

Bo̤odh′ist, *n.* see *Buddhist*.

bo̤o′dle, *n.* [perhaps from D. *boedel*, possession, property, estate.]
1. the whole crowd; mob; caboodle. [Slang.]
2. money disbursed or received for bribery or corruption in politics or the public service. [Slang.]
3. counterfeit money. [Slang.]
4. the loot taken in a robbery.

bo̤o′dlẽr, *n.* one who accepts boodle; one who aids, abets, or participates in corruption involving public funds.

boo′gie-woo′gie, *n.* [echoic.] 1. a style of jazz piano playing in which repeated bass figures in 8-8 rhythm accompany melodic variations in the treble.
2. any jazz music in this style.

bo̤o·ho̤o′, *v.i.*; boohooed, *pt.*, *pp.*; boohooing, *ppr.* to cry noisily; to bawl; to blubber.

bo̤o·ho̤o′, *n.*; *pl.* **bo̤o·ho̤oṣ′**, noisy weeping.

bo̤o′ho̤o, *n.* the *Histiophorus americanus*, or sailfish: also called *woohoo*.

book, *n.* [ME. *book, boke, bok*; AS. *boc*, pl. *bēc*, a writing, record, book, from *boc, bece*, a beech (beech bark probably formed the original writing material of the Teutonic nations); Ice. *bok*, a book, and a beech tree; D. *boek*, a book, a beech; G. *buch*, a book, *buche*, a beech.]
1. any literary or scientific composition or treatise which is printed, distinguished by length and form from a magazine, tract, etc.
2. any number of written or printed sheets when bound or sewed together along one edge, usually between protective covers.
3. a volume of blank paper, or of printed blank forms, intended for any kind of writing, as for memorandums, accounts, or receipts.
4. a particular part of a literary composition; a division of a subject in the same volume; as, the *books* of the Bible.
5. a volume or collection of sheets in which accounts are kept; a register of debts and credits, receipts and expenditures, etc.; as, to keep a set of *books*; hence, a record; an account.
6. a writing; a written charter; a deed. [Obs.]

By that time will our *book*, I think, be drawn. —Shak.

7. the Bible: commonly written *the Book*.
8. any formal composition of length, whether printed or in manuscript; as, she has written a *book*.
9. in whist, six tricks taken by one side; in bridge and some other card games, a specified number of cards or tricks forming a set.
10. anything considered as a subject for study; as, the *book* of nature.
11. the words of a play; the libretto of an opera; as, A wrote the music and B the *book*.
12. in betting, the list of bets made by a bookmaker; an individual's bets upon any sporting event.
13. a booklike package, as of matches, tickets, gold leaf, etc.

book of account; (a) a book to keep accounts in; (b) [*pl.*] the records needed for auditing the accounts of a business.

Book of Books; the Bible.

Book of Common Prayer; the official book of services and prayers for the Church of England or, with some minor modifications, for the Episcopal Church.

Book of Mormon; the sacred book of the Mormon Church, first published in 1830.

Book of the Dead; the priestly and prophetic rules and sacred directions buried in the tombs of the favored Egyptian dead, as an assurance of immortality.

by the book; according to the rules; in the prescribed or usual way.

to be in one's bad or *black books*; to be out of favor with one.

to be in one's good books; to be in favor with one.

to bring to book; to make give an account.

to make a book; in betting, to lay the odds.

without book; impromptu; spontaneously; by memory; also, without authority.

book, *v.t.*; booked, *pt.*, *pp.*; booking, *ppr.* 1. to enter, write, or register in a book.
2. to engage ahead of time, as lectures, rooms, performances, performers, transportation, etc.
3. to make up in the form of a book, as gold leaf or tobacco.
4. to record charges against on a police record.

book, *v.i.* to book (sense 2) persons or things.

book aç·count′, an account or register of debt or credit in a book.

book ā′ġent, one who solicits orders for books, most frequently for books published in parts or numbers, or sold on the installment plan.

book′bīnd″ẽr, *n.* one whose occupation is to bind books.

book′bīnd″ẽr·y, *n.* a place for binding books.

book′bīnd″ing, *n.* the art, trade, or business of binding books.

book′çāse, *n.* a set of shelves or a cabinet to hold books.

book çlamp, a device to hold books firm in the process of binding.

book club, 1. a lending library supported by members who pay a fixed price for the privilege of borrowing books.
2. an organization that sells books, usually at reduced prices, to members who undertake to buy a minimum number of them annually.

book debt (det), a debt for goods delivered, and charged by the seller in an account book.

book end, an ornamental weight or bracket put at the end of a row of books to keep them upright.

book′ẽr, *n.* 1. one who enters accounts in a book. [Rare.]
2. a person whose work is making bookings.

book′ẽr·y, *n.* 1. a love of books; bookishness. [Obs.]
2. a library or collection of books. [Rare.]

book fōld, book muslin.

book′ful, *a.* full of notions gleaned from books; stuffed with book learning. [Obs.]

book′ful *n.* as much as fills a book.

book′hōld″ẽr, *n.* 1. one who holds the prompt book at a theater. [Obs.]
2. a device for supporting a book and holding it open while in use.

book′ie, *n.* in horse racing, a bookmaker. [Slang.]

book′ing, *n.* an engagement, as for a lecture, performance, etc.

book′ing çlẽrk, a clerk who sells tickets at a booking office or who registers passengers, baggage, etc., for conveyance by rail, steamship, etc. [Brit.]

book′ing of′fice, 1. an office where passage or theater tickets are sold. [Brit.]
2. an office where passengers, baggage, etc. are registered for conveyance by transportation lines. [Brit.]

book′ish, *a.* 1. of or connected with books.
2. inclined to read and study; literary; scholarly.
3. having book learning; erudite.
4. pedantic; characterized by formality of expression; as, a *bookish* manner of speech.

book′ish·ly, *adv.* in a bookish manner.

book′ish·ness, *n.* attachment to books; fondness for study; quality of being bookish.

book jack′et, a detachable cover of paper, etc. for protecting the binding of a book, usually with colored illustrations and designs for advertising or calling attention to the book.

book′keep″ẽr, *n.* a person whose profession is bookkeeping.

book′keep″ing, *n.* the art or profession of recording business transactions in a regular, systematic manner.

There are two systems of *bookkeeping* in common use, known as single entry and double entry. In single entry *bookkeeping*, the record of each transaction is carried either to the debit or the credit side of a single account. In double entry, two entries of every transaction are made and carried to the ledger, one balancing and checking the other.

book knowl′edġe (nol′ej), knowledge gained by reading books, as distinguished from practical knowledge.

book′land, *n.* [AS. *bocland*; *boc*, a charter, writing, and *land*, land.] in old English law, charter land, held by deed under certain rents and free services.

book′-lẽarn″ed, *a.* 1. having knowledge gained from books; learned.
2. having book knowledge as opposed to knowledge of life and things from practical experience and observation; bookish: a somewhat contemptuous term.

book lẽarn′ing, knowledge of books and literature; knowledge derived from reading or studying.

book′less, *a.* without books; unlearned.

book′let, *n.* a small book, often paper covered.

book′lōre, *n.* knowledge acquired from books.

book louse, one of various species of tiny, wingless insects that destroy books, papers, botanical collections, etc., especially *Atropus pulsatorius*.

book mad′ness, a rage for possessing books; bibliomania.

book′māk″ẽr, *n.* 1. a maker, compiler, or publisher of books.
2. a person in the business of taking bets on race horses.

book′māk″ing, *n.* 1. the practice of making, compiling, or publishing books.
2. the business of taking bets on race horses.

book′măn, *n.*; *pl.* **book′men**, 1. a student of books; a scholar; a studious or learned man.
2. a man whose business is making, publishing, or selling books.

book′märk, *n.* 1. anything placed in a book to mark a place or passage.
2. a label designating the owner of a book; a bookplate.

book match′eṣ, safety matches made of paper and fastened into a small cardboard folder.

book′māte, *n.* a schoolfellow or associate in study.

book′mō·bīle, *n.* [*book*, and auto*mobile*.] a

traveling lending library transported in a truck, trailer, etc. to small towns or rural areas lacking permanent libraries.

book′mōn̄·gẽr, *n.* a bookseller.

book mus′lin, 1. a kind of muslin used in covering books.

2. a thin, white muslin used for women's dresses.

book nāme, in zoology and botany, a name, other than the technical one, found in scientific works only.

book nō′tice, a brief description of a new book in any publication.

book ōath, an oath taken on the Bible.

I put thee now to thy *book oath.* —Shak.

book′plāte, *n.* 1. in printing, an electrotype plate, mounted or unmounted, of a book page, from which impressions are printed.

2. a label with the owner's name or some identifying design, for pasting in a book.

book pōst, an arrangement granting the use of the mails for sending books and kindred matter at a special low rate. [Brit.]

book′rack, *n.* 1. an open set of shelves for holding books and similar articles.

2. a support for a single book.

book rē·view′ (-vū′), a critical résumé, usually of a newly published book.

book sçor′pi·ŏn, a small arachnid infesting old books, and bearing some resemblance to a scorpion without a tail.

book′sell″ẽr, *n.* one whose occupation is selling books.

book′sell″ing, *n.* the business of selling books.

book′shop, *n.* a bookstore. [Brit.]

book′stack, *n.* a series of bookshelves, one over the other, as in a library.

book′stall, *n.* 1. a stand or stall, commonly in the open air, for retailing books.

2. a newsstand [Brit.]

book′stamp, *n.* a brass or electrotype plate that stamps the cover of a book with title, etc.

book′stand, *n.* 1. a stand or frame for containing books offered for sale in the streets.

2. a stand or support for books; a bookcase.

3. a bookstall.

book stōne, same as *bibliolite.*

book′stōre, *n.* a store where books, and often stationery, office supplies, etc., are sold.

book′truck, *n.* a set of low, open shelves mounted on wheels and used for moving books from one part of a building to another.

book val′ūe, 1. the value of any of the assets of a business as shown on its account books.

2. (a) the net worth of a business, or the value of its capital stock, as shown by the excess of assets over liabilities; (b) the value, on this basis, of a single share of stock.

book′wŏrk, *n.* 1. in printing, the process, or any part of the process, of making books, in distinction from printed matter not bound, as job or newspaper work.

2. work that involves reading or studying.

book′wŏrm, *n.* 1. any of several species of larvae which harm books by eating the binding, paste, etc.

2. a student of books; one who absorbs himself in reading or studying.

book′y, *a.* bookish.

book′y, *n.* in horse racing, a bookmaker. [Slang.]

Bool′ē·ȧn al′ġe·brȧ, [after George *Boole* (1815-64), Eng. mathematician.] a mathematical system, originally devised for the analysis of symbolic logic, in which all variables have the value of either zero or one: widely used in digital computers.

bǫǫ′ly, bǫǫ′ley, *n.*; *pl.* **bǫǫ′lieṣ,** [Ir. *buaile,* a fold, place for milking cows.] in Ireland, one who wandered from place to place with his flocks and herds in search of pasture. [Obs.]

bǫǫm, *n.* [D. *boom,* a tree, a pole.]

1. in ships, a long pole or spar extending from the bottom of a mast to keep a sail outstretched; as, the jib *boom.*

2. a strong iron chain cable, or barrier of logs extended across a river, etc., to hinder navigation.

3. a pole set up as a mark to direct seamen how to keep the channel in shallow water.

4. a beam which projects from the mast of a derrick to lift and guide anything lifted.

5. (a) a line of connected floating timbers used to keep sawlogs from floating away; (b) the area in which logs are thus confined.

6. in aeronautics, a retractable metal tube for transferring fuel from one plane to another in flight.

lower the boom; to act suddenly and forcefully in dealing out punishment or criticism, in defeating, etc. [Colloq.]

the booms; in sailing vessels, the space on the deck amidships formerly used for stowage of extra spars and booms and boats.

bǫǫm, *v.t.* 1. to stretch out (sails) on, with, or as with a boom.

2. to stretch out (sails) so as to take maximum advantage of a wind abaft the beam and hence make speed.

bǫǫm, *v.i.* 1. to sail with or as with studding-sails boomed out.

2. to sail with maximum speed (usually with *along.*).

3. to go rapidly along; to move with speed or vigor.

bǫǫm, *n.* [imitative word.]

1. a deep hollow sound, as of thunder or cannon.

2. a resonant cry like that of the bittern.

bǫǫm, *v.i.* 1. to make a deep, hollow, resonant sound.

2. to roll and roar, as waves.

The hoarse waves *booming* to the ocean shore. —Hillhouse.

bǫǫm, *v.t.* to speak or indicate with a deep, hollow, resonant sound; as, the clock *boomed* the hour.

bǫǫm, *n.* [from *boom, v.i.* (to sail); later associated with *boom* (noise).]

1. a sudden favorable turn in business or political prospects: applied to stocks, commodities, real estate, political chances of candidates, etc.

2. a period of business prosperity, industrial expansion, etc.

bǫǫm, *a.* of, characteristic of, or resulting from a boom in industry.

a boom town; a town whose sudden growth or prosperity is caused by a business boom.

bǫǫm, *v.i.* to increase suddenly or grow swiftly; to make a favorable turn; to flourish; as, business *boomed.*

bǫǫm, *v.t.* 1. to cause to increase suddenly or grow swiftly; to make flourish; as, they *boomed* the aircraft industry.

2. to try to make favorable prospects for; to popularize; to support; as, they *boomed* him for mayor.

bǫǫm′-and-bust′, *n.* a period of prosperity followed by a depression. [Colloq.]

bǫǫm′däs, *n.* [D. *boom,* tree, and *das,* badger.] a small African animal, *Dendrohyrax arboreus,* resembling the rock rabbit.

bǫǫm′ẽr, *n.* 1. one who or that which booms; one who assists in working up a boom.

2. a North American beaver, *Haplodon rufus*; so named because of its booming noise.

3. in Australia, a large male kangaroo.

4. a migratory worker. [Slang.]

bǫǫm′ẽr·ang, *n.* [Australian *bumarin, wo-murrang,* names of clubs.] a weapon used in hunting and in war by the aborigines of Australia. It is in the form of a flat, curved stick of hard wood: when thrown it spins and curves, and returns to a point near the thrower.

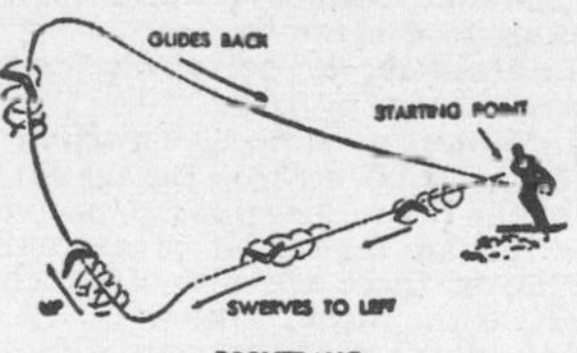

BOOMERANG

2. something which recoils upon the person using or doing it; as, gossip is a *boomerang,* injuring him who spreads it.

bǫǫm′ẽr·ang, *v.i.* to act as a boomerang; to result in harm to the user or doer.

Bǫǫm′ẽr Stāte, Oklahoma: a nickname.

bǫǫm′ing, *a.* 1. making a loud, hollow, resonant sound.

2. advancing in price or in favor suddenly; as, a *booming* market; *booming* stocks.

bǫǫm′ing, *n.* 1. a reverberating, roaring sound; as, the *booming* of surf on the shore.

2. a deep sound, like the cry of the bittern.

bǫǫm ī′ron (-ũrn), an iron ring on a ship's yard through which the studding-sail boom passes.

bǫǫm′kin, *n.* same as *bumkin.*

bǫǫm′let, *n.* a small boom, as in business.

bŏŏ′mō·räh, *n.* [native name.] a small ruminant (genus *Tragulus*) of western Africa.

bǫǫm′slang, *n.* [D. *boom,* a tree, and *slang,* a snake.] a large African tree snake, *Bucephalus capensis.*

bǫǫn, *n.* [Fr. *bon,* from L. *bonus,* good; Ice. *bon,* a petition.]

1. a favor or request. [Archaic.]

2. a prayer or petition. [Obs.]

3. a benefit; a thing to be thankful for; as, the *boon* of good health.

bǫǫn, *a.* 1. kind; generous; pleasant. [Archaic.]

2. gay; merry; convivial; as, a *boon* companion.

bǫǫn, *n.* [Gael. *bunach,* coarse tow, refuse of flax; *bun,* stump, stock.] the refuse or useless vegetable matter from dressed flax.

bǫǫn′docks, *n.pl.* [orig. World War II military slang, from Tag. *bundok,* mountain.]

1. a jungle or a wild, heavily wooded area; wilderness. [Colloq.]

2. any remote rural or provincial region; hinterland. [Colloq.]

bǫǫn′dog·gle, *n.* 1. originally, a looped or braided cord made by Boy Scouts as a slide for their neckerchiefs or as an ornament.

2. trifling, valueless work. [Slang.]

bǫǫn′dog·gle, *v.i.*; boondoggled, *pt., pp.*; boondoggling, *ppr.* to engage in trifling, valueless work; to engage in useless occupation. [Slang.]

bō′ops, *n.* [L., from Gr. *boōpis,* ox-eyed; *bous,* ox, and *ōps, opis,* eye.] a fish, *Box boöps,* found mostly in the Mediterranean.

bǫǫr, *n.* [D. *boer,* a farmer, boor, from *bouwen,* to build, cultivate.] a peasant or farm worker; hence, one who has manners attributed to a peasant; a rude ill-mannered person.

bǫǫr′ish, *a.* rude; ill-mannered; awkward.

bǫǫr′ish·ly, *adv.* in a boorish manner.

bǫǫr′ish·ness, *n.* the quality of being boorish.

bǫǫrt, *n.* same as *bort.*

bǫǫṣe, a stall or enclosure for an ox, cow, or other animal. [Brit. Dial.]

bǫǫṣe, *n.* and *v.i.* same as *booze.*

bǫǫṣ′ẽr, *n.* same as *boozer.*

bǫǫst, *v.t.*; boosted, *pt., pp.*; boosting, *ppr.*

1. to lift or raise by pushing; to assist upward by a push from behind or below. [Colloq.]

2. to urge the merits of; to speak in favor of. [Colloq.]

bǫǫst, *n.* 1. a helping lift; a push upward; hence, commendation; recommendation; as, he gave me a good *boost.* [Colloq.]

2. a raising or increase. [Colloq.]

bǫǫst′ẽr, *n.* 1. one who boosts; one who speaks or writes in favor of any particular individual or thing. [Colloq.]

2. a device for the regulation or control of electromotive force in an electric circuit.

3. in radio, an amplifier.

bǫǫst′ẽr shot, an injection of a vaccine or other antigen some time after the initial series of injections, for maintaining immunity.

bǫǫ′sy, *a.* same as *boozy.*

bǫǫt, *v.t.* and *v.i.*; booted, *pt., pp.*; booting, *ppr.* [ME. *boote, bote*; AS. *bot,* advantage, reparation.

1. to profit; to benefit. [Obs.]

2. to remedy.

bǫǫt, *n.* 1. profit; gain; advantage. [Obs.]

2. remedy; relief; reparation. [Obs.]

3. that which is given to make an exchange equal, or to supply the deficiency of value in one of the things exchanged. [Dial.]

to boot; in addition to; besides.

bǫǫt, *n.* [ME. *boote, bote,* OFr. *bote*; LL. *botta,* a boot.]

1. a protective covering, of leather, rubber, cloth, etc., for wearing on the foot and part or all of the leg: in England, shoes are called boots.

2. a kind of rack for the leg, formerly used as an instrument of torture. It was made of boards bound fast to the legs by cords, or was a boot or buskin, made wet and drawn upon the legs, and then dried by a fire so as to contract and squeeze the legs.

TORTURE WITH THE BOOT

3. a compartment either in front or at the back of a vehicle, for carrying baggage, parcels, etc.

4. a place at the side of old-fashioned coaches where attendants or passengers might ride.

5. a protective covering for a horse's foot.

6. in aeronautics, a rubber strip, operated pneumatically, used for deicing the leading edge of an airfoil.

7. in ornithology, a tarsal envelope occurring in thrushes and warblers.

8. a patch for the inner surface of an

automobile tire to protect a break or weak spot in the casing.

9. a box that holds the reed in a reed pipe of an organ.

10. a kick.

11. discharge, as from employment; dismissal: used with *the*; as, to get *the boot.* [Slang.]

12. a recent recruit to the navy. [Slang.]

to die with one's boots on; to die in action.

to lick the boots of; to be servile toward; to fawn on.

bọọt, *v.t.*; booted, *pt., pp.*; booting, *ppr.* 1. to put boots on, especially for hunting or riding.

2. to subject to the torture of the boot (*n.* sense 2).

3. to kick.

4. to put (a person) out of a place or job; to dismiss. [Slang.]

bọọt, *v.i.* to put on one's boots.

bọọt, *n.* spoil; plunder; booty. [Obs.]

bọọt′black, *n.* one whose work is shining boots or shoes.

bọọt çlōs′ẽr, a workman who sews the uppers of boots: also applied to a machine used for that purpose.

bọọt çrimp, a machine that crimps boot uppers by successive operations.

bọọt′ed, *a.* 1. wearing boots, especially long-topped riding boots.

2. in ornithology, having a boot, or tarsal envelope, as thrushes, warblers, etc.

3. kicked.

4. discharged; dismissed.

bọọt·ee′, *n.* [dim. of *boot.*] 1. a baby's soft, knitted shoe.

2. a short boot or light overboot worn by women and children.

Bō·ō′tēṣ, *n.* [L., from Gr. *boōtēs*, a plowman, from *bous*, an ox.] a northern constellation, including the bright star Arcturus.

bọọth, *n.* [ME. *bothe*; Ice. *budh*; Sw. *bod*; G. *bude*, a booth, house; AS. *buan*, to dwell.]

1. a house or shed built of boards, boughs of trees, or other slight materials, for a temporary residence; a shack.

2. a compartment in a fair or market building, partitioned off for temporary purposes; a market stand.

3. a voting compartment at a polling place.

4. a small permanent structure or enclosure to house a sentry, public telephone, etc.

5. a small, partially enclosed compartment with a table and seats, as in some restaurants.

bọọt′hāle, *v.t.* and *v.i.* to plunder; to pillage. [Obs.]

bọọt′hōṣe, *n.* leggings; spatterdashes.

bọọth′y, *n.* same as *bothy.*

bọọt′i·kin, *n.* a small boot.

bọọt′ing, *n.* booty; advantage. [Obs.]

bọọt′ing, *n.* 1. torture with the boot (*n.* sense 2).

2. a kicking.

bọọt′jack, *n.* a device for use in pulling off boots.

bọọt′lȧst, *n.* an implement for shaping boots.

bọọt′leg, *n.* 1. the part of a boot above the upper.

2. bootlegged liquor.

bọọt′leg, *v.t.* and *v.i.*; bootlegged, *pt., pp.*; bootlegging, *ppr.* [in allusion to concealing objects in the leg of a high boot.] to make, carry, or sell (liquor, etc.) illegally.

bọọt′leg, *a.* 1. bootlegged.

2. of bootlegging.

bọọt′leg·gẽr, *n.* one who sells, transports, or imports illegally, especially alcoholic liquor.

bọọt′less, *a.* unavailing; unprofitable; useless; without advantage or success.

bọọt′less·ly, *adv.* without use or profit.

bọọt′less·ness, *n.* the state of being unavailing.

bọọt′lick, *v.t.* and *v.i.* to try to gain favor with (someone) by fawning, flattery, servility, etc. [Slang.]

bọọt′lick, *n.* a bootlicker. [Slang.]

bọọt′lick·ẽr, *n.* a servile or fawning person; a toady; a flatterer. [Slang.]

bọọt′māk″ẽr, *n.* a maker of boots.

bọọt′māk″ing, *n.* the making of boots; the trade of a bootmaker.

bọọt pat′tẽrn, an apparatus for marking out patterns of various parts of boots.

bọọts, *n.* a hotel servant who cleans and blacks boots and shoes, and performs minor errands for guests. [Brit.]

bọọts and sad′dleṣ, [? confusion of Fr. *boute-selle!*, lit., put saddle!] a cavalry bugle call used as the first signal for mounted drill or other mounted formation.

bọọt stock′ing, an overstocking to protect the booted foot and leg in cold weather.

bọọt′-top″ping, *n.* 1. the operation of cleansing a ship's bottom near the surface of the water, by scraping off the slime, shells, etc., and daubing it with a protective mixture of tallow, sulfur, and resin.

2. the act of painting the portion of a ship's hull which is above the water line.

3. the operation of sheathing a vessel with planking over felt.

bọọt tree, a wooden or metal form put into a boot or shoe to keep its shape; shoe tree.

bọọ′ty, *n.* [ME. *botye*, *buty*; G. *beute*, booty, exchange, barter; Ice. *byte*, give out, distribute, exchange.]

1. spoil taken from an enemy in war; plunder; pillage.

2. that which is seized by violence and robbery; swag.

3. any valuable gain; a prize.

bọọze, *v.i.*; boozed, *pt., pp.*; boozing, *ppr.* [D. *buizen*; G. *bausen*, to drink.] to drink alcoholic liquor to excess. [Colloq.]

bọọze, *n.* 1. a carouse; a drinking bout. [Colloq.]

2. liquor; alcoholic drink. [Colloq.]

bọọz′ẽr, *n.* one who is excessively addicted to alcoholic liquor. [Colloq.]

bọọz′i·ly, *adv.* in a boozy manner. [Colloq.]

bọọz′y, *a.* drunk, especially habitually so. [Colloq.]

bō·peep′, *n.* the act of looking out quickly from behind something and drawing back, as children in play, for the purpose of surprising each other; the game of peekaboo.

bō′rȧ, *n.* [It.] in meteorology, a northeast wind, very cold and dry, that blows along the Adriatic coasts.

bōr′ȧ·ble, *a.* capable of being bored. [Rare.]

bō·rach′i·ō, *n.* [Sp. *borracha*, a leather bottle for wine; *borracho*, drunk; *borra*, a lamb.] a leather bottle or wineskin; figuratively, a winebibber. [Obs.]

bō·rac′iç, *a.* same as *boric.*

boracic acid; same as *boric acid.*

bō′rȧ·cīte, *n.* a native borate and chloride of magnesium.

bō′rȧ·çous, *a.* obtained from borax; relating to or containing borax.

bŏr′āġe (bũr′), *n.* [ME. *borage*, *burage*; LL. *borrago*, *borago*, from *borra*, the hair of beasts.] a plant of the genus *Borago*, used medicinally for its soothing and perspiratory properties and sometimes used in salads: written also *burridge.*

bŏr′āġe·wŏrt, *n.* any plant belonging to the borage family.

Bō·raġ·i·nā′cē·ae, *n.pl.* [L., from *borago*, *boraginis*, borage, and *-aceæ.*] a natural order of plants, with cup-shaped blossoms, known as the borage family, chiefly found in the northern temperate regions. All the species have a demulcent, mucilaginous juice and their surfaces are covered over with white hairs. Alkanet, comfrey, and the forget-me-not belong to this family.

bō·raġ·i·nā′ceous, *a.* pertaining to the *Boraginaceæ.*

bōr·ȧ·ġin′ē·ous, *a.* same as *boraginaceous.*

Bō·rā′gō, *n.* [LL. *borago*, borage.] the type genus of the order *Boraginaceæ*, natives of the Mediterranean region. It is a small genus, consisting of three species, of which *Borago officinalis* is the most common.

bor′ȧ·mez, *n.* same as *barometz.*

bō·ras′çō, *n.* [Sp. *borrasca*; It. *burasca*, from *bora*, *borea*, the north wind.] a squall of wind sometimes accompanied by thunder and lightning, occurring especially in the Mediterranean.

Bō·ras′sus, *n.* [L., from Gr. *borassos*, the palm fruit.] a genus of palms having but one species, *palmyra*, found in the tropics of Asia and Africa.

bō′rāte, *n.* a salt or ester of boric acid.

bō′rāte, *v.t.*; borated, *pt., pp.*; borating, *ppr.* to treat or mix with borax or boric acid.

bō′rāt·ed, *a.* treated or mixed with borax or boric acid.

bō′rax, *n.* [LL. *borax*; Ar. *boraq*, *buraq*; Per. *burah*, borax.] a white, crystalline salt, $Na_2B_4O_7$, with an alkaline taste. California is now the most important natural source of supply for the United States. It is also made in large quantities from the boric acid found in hot springs. It is especially valuable, (a) as a reagent in blowpipe analysis; (b) for making colored glazes and enamels for pottery and porcelain; (c) as a flux in soldering metals; and (d) in modified forms in various medicinal and toilet preparations.

bō′rax bēad, in chemistry, a glassy drop of borax, used in blowpipe analysis as a solvent and color test for certain mineral earths and oxides.

bọr′bō·rygm (-rim), *n.* [Gr. *borborygmos*, a rumbling; *borboryzein*, to have a rumbling in the bowels.] the noise produced by wind in the bowels.

bōrd, *n.* 1. a board or a table. [Obs.]

2. in mining, the lateral face of a coal deposit.

bōrd′āġe, *n.* [OFr. *bordage*; *borde*, a hut, cot, and *-age.*] in feudal law, the terms under which a bordar held his dwelling.

bōrd′āġe, *n.* [Fr. *bordage*, from *bord*, side of a ship.] the side planking of a ship.

bōrd′ȧr, *n.* [LL. *bordarius*, a cottager, from *borda*, a cottage, hut.] a feudal tenant who gave his services for his cottage; a cottier; a villein.

Bọr·deaux′ (-dō′), *n.* a red or white wine from near Bordeaux, France: the red wine is generally called *claret.*

Bọr′deaux mix′tūre, a preparation of copper sulfate, lime, and water, used as a spray on trees and plants to kill insects and fungi.

bọr′del, bọr·del′lō, *n.* [OFr. *bordel*; It. *bordello.*] a brothel; a house of prostitution.

Bọr·dē·lais′ (bọr-dē-le′), *a.* pertaining to Bordeaux or the surrounding district.

bọr′dẽr, *n.* [ME. *border*, *bordure*; OFr. *bordure*; LL. *bordatura*, border, edging; *bordus*, edge, side.] the outer edge of anything; the extreme part or surrounding line; specifically, (a) the confine or exterior limit of a country, or of any region or tract of land; (b) the exterior part or edge of a garment; (c) the rim or brim of a vessel; (d) an ornamental strip of flowers or shrubs along the edge of a garden, walk, etc.; (e) the outer edge of an armorial bearing, with a tincture distinct from the field; (f) an overhead piece of scenery in a theater; (g) a limit or boundary; a margin.

the Border; the district on and near the boundary between Scotland and England.

bọr′dẽr, *a.* pertaining to that which adjoins, or to outlying districts; as, a *border* country or district.

border States; a name applied before the Civil War to Maryland, Virginia, Delaware, Kentucky, and Missouri, the five slave states which bordered upon the northern free states.

Syn.—edge, rim, brim, brink, margin, verge. —Whatever is wide enough to admit of any space around its circumference may have a *border*; whatever comes to a narrow extended surface has an *edge.* A *rim* is the *edge* of any vessel; the *brim* is the exterior edge of a cup; a *brink* is the *edge* of any precipice or deep place; a *margin* is the *border* as of a book or a piece of water; a *verge* is the extreme *border* of a place.

bọr′dẽr, *v.i.*; bordered, *pt., pp.*; bordering, *ppr.* [ME. *borduren*, *bourduren*, to border, from LL. *bordatura*, from *bordus*, edge, side.]

1. to touch at the edge, side, or end; to be contiguous or adjacent: with *on* or *upon*; as, Connecticut, on the north, *borders on* or *upon* Massachusetts.

2. to approach; to be like: followed by *on* or *upon.*

bọr′dẽr, *v.t.* 1. to make a border for; to adorn with a border; as, to *border* a garment or a garden.

2. to reach to; to extend along the edge of; to bound.

bọr·de·reau′ (bọr-d′rō′), *n.*; *pl.* **bọr·de·reaux′** (-rō′), [Fr.] in marine insurance, a document in which a description of reinsured risks is detailed by an original underwriter; hence, any memorandum of account, especially one containing a listing of documents.

bọr′dẽred, *a.* having a border; as, a *bordered* handkerchief.

bọr′dẽr·ẽr, *n.* one who dwells on a border or at the extreme part or confines of a country, region, or tract of land.

bọr′dẽr·ing, *a.* lying adjacent; forming a border.

bọr′dẽr·ing, *n.* material for a border; also, the act of making a border.

bọr′dẽr·land, *n.* 1. land on the frontiers of adjoining countries; land constituting a border.

2. a vague or undetermined situation, condition, place, etc.

bọr′dẽr·līne, *n.* a boundary; a dividing line.

bọr′dẽr·līne, *a.* 1. on a boundary; as, a *borderline* fence.

2. falling between two classifications; indefinite; doubtful.

bōrd′land, *n.* in old English law, land held by a bordar.

bōrd′lōde, bōrd′lōad, *n.* [ME. *bord*, board,

and *lode*, a load, way.] the service required of a bordar, as the carrying of timber from the woods to the lord's house.
bōrd′măn, *n.* a bordar.
bọrd′rāġe, bọrd′rā·ġing, *n.* a raid. [Obs.]
bōrd sẽrv′ice, the tenure by which bordland was held.
bọr′dūre, *n.* [OFr. *bordure*, border, edge.] in heraldry, a border of metal, color, or fur, within the escutcheon and around it.

BORDURE

bōre, *v.t.*; bored, *pt., pp.*; boring, *ppr.* [ME. *boren, borien*; AS. *borian*, to bore, from *bor*, an auger.]
1. to perforate or penetrate, and make a hole in, by turning an auger, gimlet, or other instrument; hence, to make hollow; to form a round hole in; as, to *bore* a cannon.
2. to make (a hole, tunnel, etc.) by drilling, burrowing, digging, etc.
3. to force (one's way), as through a crowd.
4. to tire by annoying repetition; to weary by being dull, uninteresting, or monotonous.
5. to delude; to befool. [Obs.]
Syn.—penetrate, perforate, pierce, weary, fatigue.
bōre, *v.i.* 1. to make a hole or perforation with a boring device, as an auger or gimlet; especially, to penetrate the earth for water, oil, or minerals.
2. to be pierced or penetrated by an instrument that cuts as it turns; as, this timber does not *bore* well, or is hard to *bore*.
3. to push forward or advance by persistent action.
4. to thrust out the head or jerk it in the air: said of a horse.
bōre, past tense of *bear*.
bōre, *n.* [ME. *bore*; AS. *bor*, an auger, gimlet; Ice. *bora*, a hole.]
1. the hole made by boring; hence, the cavity or hollow of a gun, cannon, pistol, or other firearm, or of any pipe or tube.
2. the diameter of the cavity of a gun barrel or tube; the caliber.
3. any instrument for making holes by boring or turning, as an auger or gimlet.
4. a person or thing that wearies by being dull, uninteresting, or monotonous.
bōre, *n.* [ME. *bare*, a wave, billow; Ice. *bara*, a billow.] in physical geography, (a) a roaring, high-crested, and destructive wave or flood caused by the rushing of a floodtide up the estuaries of certain rivers, as the Amazon in South America, the Hooghly, Ganges, and Indus in India, and the Tsientang in China: also called *eagre*; (b) loosely, a high, swift tidal flow such as occurs in the Bay of Fundy and the Bristol Channel.
bō′rē·ȧl, *a.* [LL. *borealis*, from *Boreas*, Boreas.] northern; pertaining to the north, especially the north wind.
Bō′rē·as, *n.* [L., from Gr. *Boreas*.]
1. in Greek mythology, the god of the north wind.
2. the north wind; a cold, northerly wind.
bōre′çōle, *n.* [D. *boerenkool*, from *boer*, farmer, and *kool*, cabbage.] a variety of cabbage (*Brassica oleracea*) whose leaves are not formed into a compact head, but are loose, and generally curled or wrinkled: called also *kale*.
bōre′dŏm, *n.* 1. the state of being wearied or annoyed by a bore; a condition of ennui.
2. bores, in a collective sense.
bō·ree′, *n.* [Fr. *bourrée*, a rustic dance.] a French dance or movement in common time; a bourrée. [Obs.]
bō·reen′, *n.* a lane leading from a main road. [Anglo-Irish.]
bor′ē·gat, *n.* the rock trout (*Hexagrammus*) of California.
bor′e·le, *n.* the smaller of the double-horned rhinoceroses found in South Africa.
bōr′ẽr, *n.* 1. one who bores; also, a tool for boring or drilling.
2. in zoology, (a) a bivalve mollusk that burrows into wood, as a shipworm; (b) a gastropod that bores through the shells of oysters, etc.; (c) a beetle, moth, or other insect that bores into trees, usually in the larval state; (d) the hagfish, an eellike marine fish allied to the lamprey.
bōre′sŏme, *a.* boring; tiresome.
bō′riç, *a.* in chemistry, of, derived from, or containing boron.
bō′riç ac′id, a white, crystalline compound, H_3BO_3, with the properties of a weak acid, used as a mild antiseptic and in the manufacture of cements, enamels, etc.: also called *boracic acid*.
bō′rīde (*or* -rid), *n.* a compound consisting of boron and one other, more positive, element or radical.
bōr′ing, *n.* 1. the action of a person or thing that bores.
2. the hole made by boring.
3. [*pl.*] the shavings or material removed by boring.
bōr′ing, *a.* 1. for making holes.
2. wearying by being dull, uninteresting, etc.
bōr′ing bär, a bar that rotates in a boring machine and carries the cutting tools.
bōr′ing head (hed), the head of a diamond drill.
bōr′ing spŏnġe, a species of sponge of the genus *Cliona* that bores into the shells of mollusks and into limestone.
bōr′ing tọọl, a tool which rotates and is used for dressing or finishing holes previously made in metal.
bọrn, *a.* [pp. of *bear* (to give birth): now used only in passive constructions not followed by *by*.]
1. brought into life or existence.
2. by birth or nature; as, a *born* musician.
in all one's born days; during one's lifetime. [Colloq.]
bọrn′-ȧ·gain′ (ȧ-gen′), *a.* 1. professing a new or renewed faith in evangelical Christianity.
2. having a new, strong belief in some principle, movement, etc.; as, a *born-again* romantic.
bōrne, past participle of *bear* (to carry): see *born*.
bọr′nē·ōl, *n.* [from *Borneo*.] a white, crystalline terpene alcohol, $C_{10}H_{18}O$, somewhat like the common camphor of commerce. It is found in the camphor tree of Borneo and Sumatra (*Dryobalanops camphora*). Also called *Borneo camphor*, *Malay camphor*, and *camphol*.
bọr′nīte, *n.* [after Dr. Ignatius von *Born*, Austrian metallurgist.] copper iron sulfide, Cu_5FeS_4, a lustrous bronze-blue ore of copper: called also *purple copper ore* and *horseflesh ore*.
bō·rō·flū′ō·rīde (*or* -rid), *n.* a salt of fluoboric acid.
bō·rō·glyc′ẽr·īde (*or* -id), *n.* a compound of boric acid and glycerin: used as an antiseptic.
bō′ron, *n.* [*bor*ax and *-on*.] a nonmetallic, chemical element occurring only in combination, as with sodium and oxygen in borax, and produced in the form either of a brown amorphous powder or very hard, brilliant crystals: its compounds are used in the preparation of boric acid, water softeners, soaps, enamels, glass, pottery, etc.: symbol, B; atomic weight, 10.82; atomic number, 5.
bō·rō·sil′i·çāte, *n.* a compound of silicic and boric acids, found in natural minerals, as in tourmaline.
bŏr′ōugh (bũr′ō), *n.* [ME. *borwe, borgh*, burgh; AS. *burh*, a town, fortified place; from *beorgan*, to protect.]
1. originally, a fortified city or town.
2. in Connecticut, New Jersey, Minnesota, and Pennsylvania, a municipality smaller than a city and incorporated with distinctive privileges.
3. in Scotland, an incorporated municipality; a burgh.
4. any one of the administrative districts into which New York City is divided.
5. in England, (a) a town with a municipal corporation and rights to self-government granted by royal charter; (b) a town that sends one or more representatives to Parliament.
close or *pocket borough*; in Great Britain, a borough whose parliamentary representation, before 1832, was controlled by one family or person.
rotten borough; (a) in England (before the Reform Act of 1832), a borough in which there were few voters, but which claimed the right to send a member to Parliament; (b) any electoral district or political unit with greater representation than its population warrants.
bŏr′ōugh Eng′lish, formerly, in England, a descent of lands and tenements to the youngest son, instead of to the eldest, or if the owner left no son, to the youngest brother.
bŏr′ōugh·hōld″ẽr, *n.* a headborough; a borsholder.
bŏr′ōugh·mŏn″gẽr, *n.* one who bought or sold the parliamentary representation of a borough.
bor·rag·i·nā′ceous, *a.* same as *boraginaceous*.
bor′rel, *a.* rustic; rude; ignorant. [Archaic.]
bor′rōw, *v.t.*; borrowed, *pt., pp.*; borrowing, *ppr.* [ME. *borowen, borwen*; AS. *borgian*, to borrow, give a pledge; *borh, borg*, a pledge, security.]
1. to take from another by request and consent, with a view to use the thing taken and return it or its equivalent; as, to *borrow* a book, a sum of money, or a loaf of bread: opposed to *lend*.
2. to adopt or take over (something) as one's own; as, to *borrow* a passage from a printed book; to *borrow* another's manners.
3. in arithmetic, to take (a unit of ten) from the next higher denomination in the minuend and add it to the next lower so that a subtraction may be made.
4. to derive; to receive; to take.
to borrow trouble; to be unnecessarily worried or apprehensive.
bor′rōw, *v.i.* 1. to get, take, or receive anything, as a loan; to borrow anything.
2. to knock a ball up a hill so that it will roll back toward a hole, as in golf.
3. in nautical language, to come close to land or to the wind.
bor′rōw, *n.* [ME. *borowe, borwe*; AS. *borh, borg*, a security, pledge, from *beorgan*, to protect, secure.]
1. any place from which earth is taken for use elsewhere.
2. (a) a surety; a pledge; anything deposited as security; (b) a person who acts as surety. [Obs.]
3. a borrowing; the act of borrowing. [Rare.]
Yet of your royal presence I'll adventure
The *borrow* of a week. —Shak.
bor′rōw·ẽr, *n.* one who borrows.
bor′rōw·ing dāyṣ, the last three days in March, Old Style, which, according to Scottish folklore, were borrowed from April, because, being often stormy days, they rightfully belonged to March, the stormy month.
bọrsch (bọrsh; Russ. bọrshch), *n.* [Russ. *borshch*.] a Russian beet soup, served usually with sour cream.
bọrsch (or **bọrsht**) **circuit**, [humorously so called from the characteristic cuisine.] summer camps in the Catskills and White Mountains, where entertainment is provided for the guests. [Slang.]
bọrs′hōld″ẽr, *n.* same as *headborough*.
bọrsht, *n.* borsch.
bọrt, *n.* [origin unknown.] defective diamonds or fragments of diamonds, used for industrial purposes as an abrasive.
bọrtz, *n.* bort.
bọr′zoi, *n.* [Russ. *borzoy*, swift.] any of a breed of large dog with a narrow head, long legs, and silky coat; Russian wolfhound.
Bos, *n.* [L.] in zoology, a genus of quadrupeds characterized by horns hollow within and turned outward in the form of crescents, eight fore-teeth in the under jaw but none in the upper, and no dogteeth. It includes the common ox, the bison, the buffalo, and other species.
bō′ṣȧ, *n.* same as *boza*.
bos′çāġe, bos′kāġe, *n.* [OFr. *boscage*, a grove; LL. *boscus*; from O.H.G. *busc*, a thicket.]
1. wood; underwood; lands covered with underwood; also, a thicket.
2. in old law, food or sustenance for cattle, yielded by bushes and trees; also, a tax levied on wood brought into a city.
bosçh′bok, bosh′bok, *n.* same as *bushbuck*.
bosçh′värk, bosh′värk, *n.* [D.; *bosch*, bush, and *vark*, pig.] a wild hog of South Africa.
bosh, *n.* [G. *böschen*, to slope.]
1. the lower part of the sides forming an obtuse angle at the bottom of a blast furnace.
2. a cooling trough for ingots and tools, used in forging and smelting.
bosh, *n.* [from Fr. *ébauche*, a rough sketch.] a mere sketch or rough outline. [Obs.]
bosh, *n.* and *interj.* [Turk.] nonsense. [Colloq.]
Bos′jes·man (-yes-), *n.*; *pl.* **Bos′jes·men**, same as *Bushman*.
bosk, *n.* [ME. *bosc, busk*, from O.H.G. *busc*, a bush.] an area covered by a thick growth of shrubbery or small trees.
bos′kāġe, *n.* same as *boscage*.
bos′ket, *n.* [Fr. *bosquet*, dim. of *bos*, a thicket.] in gardening, a grove.
bosk′i·ness, *n.* the quality of being bosky.
bosk′y, *a.* 1. woody; covered with thickets.
2. shaded with trees, bushes, etc.
bō′s′n, *n.* a boatswain.
Bos′ni·ȧn, *a.* of Bosnia, in Yugoslavia, or its people.
Bos′ni·ȧn, *n.* a native or inhabitant of Bosnia.
bọṣ′ŏm (booz′ *or* booz′), *a.* 1. of or pertaining to the bosom.
2. held close; intimate; cherished; dear; as, a *bosom* friend.

bos'ŏm, *n.* [ME. *bosom*; AS. *bosum, bosm*; from *bog, boh*, the shoulder, arm.]
1. (a) the breast of a human being; (b) a thing like this; as, the *bosom* of a hill.
2. the part of a dress, shirt, etc. that covers the breast.
3. embrace with or as with the arms; enclosure; compass: often implying friendship or affection; as, to live in the *bosom* of a church or a family.
4. the breast regarded as the seat of the emotions or secret thoughts.
5. any enclosed place; the interior; as, the *bosom* of the earth or of the deep.
6. inclination; desire. [Obs.]
7. the smooth, shallow, depressed area around the center of a millstone.
in Abraham's bosom; in paradise; in a state of heavenly bliss, peace, etc.
to take to one's bosom; to take to heart; to cherish; also, to wed.

bos'ŏm, *v.t.*; bosomed, *pt., pp.*; bosoming, *ppr.*
1. to enclose in the bosom; to keep with care.
Bosom up my counsel. —Shak.
2. to conceal; to hide from view.
To happy convents, *bosomed* deep in vines. —Pope.
3. to embrace, as a child.

bos'ŏmed, *a.* 1. having a bosom, or the semblance of a bosom.
2. held or cherished in the bosom; concealed.
3. having a (specified kind of) bosom; as, big-*bosomed*.

bos'ŏm·y, *a.* having hollows or recesses.

bōs'on, *n.* [after S. N. *Bose* (1894–1974), a physicist of India, and *-on.*] a subatomic particle, as a photon or any of certain mesons, any number of which, in obedience to statistical rules, can occupy a specified quantum state.

Bos·pō'ri·ăn, *a.* pertaining to the Bosporus, a strait between the Sea of Marmara and the Black Sea.

bos'pō·rus, bos'phō·rus, *n.* [L., from Gr. *bosporos, boos poros*, ox's ford; *boos*, genit. of *bous*, ox, and *poros*, a ford, from *perān*, to cross.] a narrow sea or a strait between two seas, or between a sea and a lake.

bos'quet (-ket), *n.* same as *bosket.*

boss, *n.* [ME. *bos, boce*; OFr. *boce*, the boss of a buckler, a botch; O.H.G. *bozo*, a bundle; *boz*, a blow, from *bozan*, to strike, beat.]
1. a stud or knob; a protuberant ornament of silver, ivory, or other material, used on bridles, harness, etc.
2. a protuberant part; a prominence; as, the *boss* of a buckler.
3. in architecture, a projecting ornament at the intersections of the ribs of ceilings, etc.

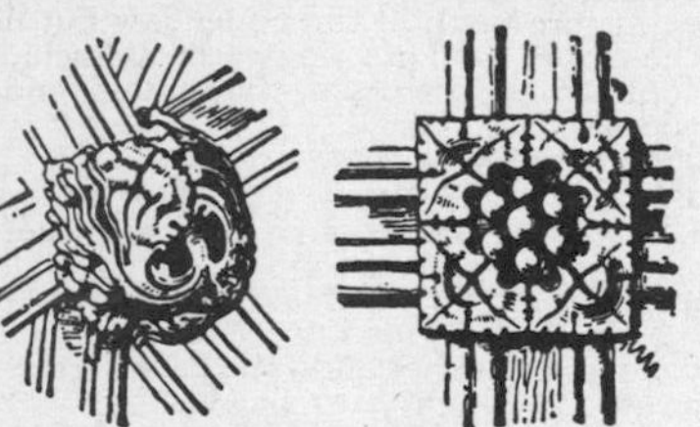
ARCHITECTURAL BOSSES

4. a water conduit swelled out at the middle. [Obs.]
5. a receptacle for mortar, made of wood and hung by means of a hook.
6. a die used for stamping metals into shape.
7. a leather pad used to make the color on pottery uniform.
8. the enlarged part of a shaft or of a hub at the part where a joining is made.
9. in geology, a protuberant body of igneous rock laid bare by erosion.

boss, *v.t.*; bossed, *pt., pp.*; bossing, *ppr.* to furnish or adorn with bosses.

boss, *n.* [D. *baas*, a master.]
1. a person in authority over employees; an employer, foreman, supervisor, director, etc. [Colloq.]
2. a person who controls a political machine or organization, usually within a certain place: often *political boss.* [Colloq.]

boss, *v.i.* to act the boss. [Colloq.]

boss, *v.t.* to act as boss of; to exercise authority or undue authority over. [Colloq.]

boss, *n.* [cf. dial. *boss, buss*, calf.] a cow or calf.

boss'āge, *n.* [Fr. *bossage*, from *bosse*, a knob, boss.]
1. in building, an undressed stone projecting beyond the plane of the walls, to be afterward adorned by carving.
2. rustic finish in a stone wall, the stones being dressed only along the edges of their joinings and at the corners of the building, leaving their rough surfaces projecting beyond the plane of the wall proper.

bossed, *a.* studded; ornamented with bosses; embossed.

bos'sē·lā·ted, *a.* [Fr. *bosseler*, to ornament with bosses, from *bosse*, a boss, knob.] studded or covered with bosses or small prominences.

bos'set, *n.* a small bump or boss; specifically, the bump on the head of a young male red deer produced by the underlying rudimentary horn.

boss'ism, *n.* the domination or methods of bosses, particularly political bosses. [Colloq.]

boss'y, *a.* containing a boss; ornamented with bosses.
His head reclining on his *bossy* shield. —Pope.

boss'y, *a.* [from *boss* (employer).] domineering. [Colloq.]

bos'sy, *n.* a cow or a calf. [Colloq.]

bos·tan'ji, *n.* [Turk.] formerly, any of the gardeners of the sultan of Turkey; also, any of his bargemen, guards, or other attendants about the palace.

bos'tŏn, *n.* a game of cards, played by four persons with two packs of cards, said to have been originated by French army officers in this country during the siege of Boston in the Revolutionary War.

Bos'tŏn brown bread (bred), a dark steamed bread made of corn meal, rye, wheat, etc. and molasses.

Bos'tŏn bull, a Boston terrier.

Bos'tŏn crēam pīe, a cake of two layers with icing and a creamy filling.

Bos·tō'ni·ăn, *a.* of Boston, Massachusetts.

Bos·tō'ni·ăn, *n.* a native or inhabitant of Boston.

Bos'tŏn Mas'sȧ·cre (-kẽr), an outbreak (1770) in Boston against British troops, in which several citizens were killed.

Bos'tŏn rock'ẽr, a type of nineteenth century American rocking chair, having a curved wooden seat and a high back formed of spindles held in place by a broad headpiece at the top.

Bos'tŏn Tēa Pär'ty, a protest (1773) against the British duty on tea imported by the American colonies: colonists disguised as Indians boarded British ships in Boston harbor and dumped the tea overboard.

Bos'tŏn ter'ri·ẽr, any of a breed of small dog having a smooth coat of brindle or black with white markings: it originated as a cross between a bulldog and a bull terrier.

BOSTON TERRIER
(14–20 in. high)

bos'try·choid, bos·try·choid'ăl, *a.* having the characteristics of a bostryx.

bos'tryx, *n.* [L., from Gr. *bostrychos*, a curl, lock of hair.] an inflorescence with the flowers in a cyme, or flattish cluster, developed on one side only of the axis and curved at the end.

bō'sun, *n.* a boatswain.

Bos·wel'li·ȧ, *n.* [named after Dr. John *Boswell*, of Edinburgh.] a genus of trees belonging to the family *Burseraceæ*, found in eastern Africa and parts of Asia: various species yield fragrant gums used for making incense or perfumery, such as myrrh and frankincense, also gums and resins of value in the arts, such as gum elemi, an Oriental masticatory.

Bos·well'i·ăn, *a.* pertaining to or characteristic of James Boswell, the biographer of Dr. Johnson.

bot, bott, *n.* [perh. from Gael. *botus*, belly worm, from *boiteag*, maggot.] a botfly larva.

bō·tan'iç·ăl, bō·tan'iç, *a.* [LL. *botanicus*; Gr. *botanikos*, from *botanē*, a plant, herb.]
1. (a) pertaining to botany; (b) relating to plants and plant life.
2. of vegetable drugs.
botanical garden; a place where collections of living and preserved plants and trees are kept and exhibited.

bō·tan'iç·ăl, *n.* a vegetable drug prepared from bark, roots, herbs, etc.

bō·tan'iç·ăl·ly, *adv.* according to the system of botany; from the viewpoint of botany.

bot'ȧ·nist, *n.* one skilled in botany; one versed in the knowledge of plants.

bot'ȧ·nīze, *v.i.*; botanized, *pt., pp.*; botanizing, *ppr.* 1. to gather plants for the purpose of botanical investigation.
2. to study plant growth; to examine or classify plants.

bot'ȧ·nīze, *v.t.* to examine or survey for specimens of plants or for botanical investigation, as a region or district.

bot'ȧ·nī·zẽr, *n.* one who botanizes.

bot'ȧ·nō·man″cy, *n.* [Gr. *botanē*, a plant, and *manteia*, divination.] an ancient method of divination by means of plants.

bot'ȧ·ny, *n.* [Gr. *botanē*, a plant, from *boskein*, to feed, graze.
1. the science which treats of the structure of plants, the functions of their parts, their places of growth, their classification, and the terms which are employed in their description and denomination.
2. a book expounding the science of botany.
3. the plant life of an area.
4. the life cycle of a plant or plant group.
paleontological botany; the department of botany dealing with plants known only from their fossil remains or impressions.
physiological botany; the department of botany dealing with the organic functions of plants.
structural botany; the department of botany which deals with the structure and composition of plants.
systematic botany; the department of botany relating to the nomenclature and classified arrangement of plants.

Bot'ȧ·ny wool, [from *Botany* Bay, orig. source of export.] a kind of merino wool.

bō·tär'gō, bō·tär'gȧ, *n.* [Sp.] a relish made of the roes of the mullet or tunny strongly salted.

botch (boch), *n.*; *pl.* **botch'es**, 1. a patch, or the part of a garment patched or mended in a clumsy manner.
2. work which is botched; work done clumsily or unsuitably; a bungle; as, he made a *botch* of the job.
3. one who botches; a bungler. [Dial.]
Syn.—patch, jumble, mess, bungle.

botch, *v.t.*; botched, *pt., pp.*; botching, *ppr.* [ME. *bocchen*, to repair; D. *botsen, butsen*, to patch, knock together.]
1. to mend or repair awkwardly; to put together unsuitably, or unskillfully.
For treason *botched* in rhyme will be thy bane. —Dryden.
2. to spoil or injure by bungling work.

botch, *n.* [ME. *botche, bocche*; OFr. *boche*, a botch, swelling.] a swelling on the skin; a large ulcerous affection; a boil. [Obs.]

botch, *v.t.* to mark with botches. [Obs.]

botch'ed·ly, *adv.* in a clumsy or botchy manner.

botch'ẽr, *n.* one who botches; specifically, (a) a clumsy workman; a bungler; (b) a mender of old clothes.
Let the *botcher* mend him. —Shak.

botch'ẽr·ly, *a.* bungling. [Rare.]

botch'ẽr·y, *n.* a botching; awkwardness of performance. [Rare.]

botch'y, *a.* full of botches; botched; badly done.

bōte, *n.* [the old form of *boot*, but retained in compounding legal terms.]
1. in old law, compensation; amends; satisfaction; as, man *bote*, a compensation for a man slain; also, payment of any kind. [Rare.]
2. a privilege or allowance of necessaries: used in compounds as equivalent to *estovers*, supplies, necessaries; as, house*bote*, a sufficiency of wood to repair a house, or for fuel, sometimes called fire*bote*; plow*bote*, cart*bote*, wood for making or repairing instruments of husbandry; hay*bote* or hedge*bote*, wood for hedges or fences, etc. These were privileges enjoyed by tenants under the feudal system. [Rare.]

bōte'less, *a.* bootless. [Obs.]

bot'flȳ, *n.* [Gael. *botus*, a belly worm; *boiteag*, a maggot.] a two-winged insect of the family *Œstridæ*, resembling a small bumblebee: the larvae are parasitic in horses, sheep, etc.

bōth, *a.* and *pron.* [ME. *bothe*; Ice. *bathir, badhir*; Dan. *baad*, both; Goth. *bai*; AS. *bā*; L. *ambo*; Gr. *ampho*; Sans. *ubhāu*, both.] the one and the other; as, here are two books, take them *both*; the two; the pair or the couple. In such a sentence as "*both* men were there," it is an adjective; in "he invited James and John, and *both* went," it is a pronoun.

bōth, *conj.* and *adv.* as well; equally; not only; together; alike: used correlatively with *and*; as, I am *both* tired *and* hungry.

both'ēr, *v.t.* and *v.i.* bothered, *pt., pp.*; bothering, *ppr.* [Ir. *buaidhirt*, trouble; *buaidhrim*, I vex.]

1. to annoy; worry; trouble; harass.

2. to bewilder; fluster; as, a big city *bothers* him.

3. to concern or trouble (oneself): as, she *bothers* too much about everything.

both'ēr, *n.* 1. a cause or condition of worry, anxiety, or irritation; trouble; fuss.

2. a person who gives trouble.

Syn.—worry, excitement, stir, plague, confusion, vexation, flurry, trouble.

both'ēr, *interj.* a mild expression of annoyance, etc.; as, Oh, *bother!*

both·ēr·ā'tion, *n.* the state of being bothered or the act of bothering; perplexity; bother. [Colloq.]

both·ēr·ā'tion, *interj.* bother. [Colloq.]

both'ēr·ēr, *n.* anyone who bothers.

both'ēr·sŏme, *a.* producing or giving bother; perplexing.

bōth'-hands, *n.* a handy man. [Rare.]

both'ie, *n.* same as *bothy*.

Both'ni·ăn, Both'niç, *a.* pertaining to Bothnia, a region (formerly so called) bordering on the Gulf of Bothnia, or to the Gulf itself.

Both'ni·ăn, Both'niç, *n.* an inhabitant of Bothnia.

both·reñ'çhy·mȧ, *n.* [L., from Gr. *bothros*, a trench, and *enchyma*, an infusion; *en*, in, and *cheein*, to pour.] in botany, tissue composed of pitted ducts.

both'ri·um, *n.*; *pl.* **both'ri·ȧ**, [L., from Gr. *bothrion*, dim. of *bothros*, a pit, trench.] a small suctorial organ such as that on the head of the tapeworm.

Both"rō·den'drŏn, *n.* [Mod. L., from Gr. *bothros*, a pit, trench; and *-dendron*.] in paleontology, a plant of the Paleozoic times between the genus *Lepidodendron* and the genus *Sigillaria*. It has a slight resemblance to the modern *Lycopodium*.

Bō'throps, *n.* [Mod.L., from Gr. *bothros*, a pit, trench, and *-ops*.] in zoology, a genus of pit vipers which are extremely poisonous. One species, the fer de lance (*B. atroz*), is found in Central and South America. Their venom causes death by internal hemorrhages.

both'rŏs, *n.* [Gr.] in Greek antiquity, a hole dug in the ground into which were poured drink offerings to certain gods.

both'y, *n.* a small wooden hut or cottage, particularly a hut for farm servants to live in.

bō tree, [Cingalese *bo*, a shortened form of Pali *bodhi*, the bo tree, from *bodhi-taru*; *bodhi*, wisdom, enlightenment, and *taru*, tree.]

1. a fig tree of India: also called *pipal*.

2. [B—T—] the sacred tree of Buddhism: Gautama supposedly got heavenly inspiration under a bo tree at Buddh Gaya.

Bō·tryçh'i·um, *n.* [L., from Gr. *botrychos*, curl: so named from the resemblance the spore cases bear to bunches of grapes.] a genus of cryptogamous ferns of the family *Ophioglossaceæ*: also called *grape ferns*.

bot'ry·ō·ġen, *n.* [Gr. *botrys*, a bunch of grapes, and *-genes*, producing.] a ferro-ferric sulfate occurring in botryoid form and having a deep-red color.

bot'ry·oid, bot·ry·oid'ăl, *a.* [Gr. *botrys*, a bunch of grapes, and *eidos*, form.] resembling a grape cluster in form, as the crystallizations of a mineral.

bot'ry·ō·līte, *n.* [Gr. *botrys*, a bunch of grapes, and *lithos*, a stone.] a variety of datolite, occurring in botryoid forms, and consisting of silica, boric acid, and lime.

bot"ry·ō·mȳ·çō'sis, *n.* [from Gr. *botrys*, bunch of grapes, and *mycosis*.] a disease of horses caused by a micrococcus producing a tumerous growth especially in the shoulder, or at the cut end of the spermatic cord after castration.

bot'ry·ōse, *a.* [Gr. *botrys*, a bunch of grapes, and *-ose*.] in botany, (a) resembling a grape cluster in form; (b) having the buds branching from the stem; racemose.

bots, *n.pl.* [Gael. *botus*, belly worm; *boiteag*, a maggot.] a disease caused by the larvae of the botfly in the intestines of horses, under the hides of cattle, in the nostrils of sheep, etc.

bott, *n.* in metal casting, a clay stopper for the hole through which the molten metal runs from a cupola into the pouring ladles.

bott, *n.* a bot.

bott ham'mēr, [ME. *botte*, from *batte*, a stick, club, and *hammer*.] a heavy mallet for breaking flax stalks in order to remove the woody parts from the fiber.

bŏt·tïne', *n.* [Fr., dim. of *botte*, a boot.]

1. a low boot; a woman's boot.

2. a supporting and constraining appliance formed like a boot with adjustable tops and ankle straps: used for correcting deformities of the legs.

bot'tle (-tl), *n.* [ME. *botel*; OFr. *botel*, *boutelle*; LL. *buticula*, dim. of *butis*, *butta*, a flask.]

1. a hollow vessel of glass, earthenware, or other material, with a narrow mouth and no handles, for holding and carrying liquids.

2. the contents of a bottle; as much as a bottle contains.

3. intoxicating drink or the use of intoxicants; as, he took to the *bottle*.

bot'tle, *v.t.*; bottled, *pt., pp.*; bottling, *ppr.* 1. to put into bottles and seal; as, to *bottle* wine.

2. to confine or restrain as if placed in a bottle: with *up*; as, the Spanish fleet was *bottled up* in Santiago harbor; to *bottle up* one's anger.

bot'tle, *n.* [ME. and OFr. *botel*, dim. of *botte*, from MD. *bote*, a bundle.] a bundle, as of hay. [Obs.]

bot'tle·bīrd, *n.* a bird that builds a nest shaped like a bottle: called also the *weaverbird*.

bot'tle brush, 1. a brush used for cleaning out bottles.

2. in botany, a number of common plants, having the shape of a *bottle brush*, as the mare's tail, the horsetail, etc.

bot'tle çod, a shrub found in the West Indies: so called from the shape of its pods; the *Capparis cynophallophora*.

bot'tled, *a.* 1. put into bottles; enclosed in bottles.

2. like a bottle; protuberant.

bot'tle·fish, *n.* a deep-sea eel with a body which it can inflate, giving it the shape of a bottle. The ability to inflate enables it to swallow fish much larger than its normal self.

bot'tle·flow"ēr, *n.* a plant, the *Centaurea cyanus*, growing in fields of grain: also called the *bluebottle* from the color and shape of its flowers.

bot'tle glȧss, a coarse, green glass, used in the manufacture of bottles.

bot'tle gōurd, in botany, the common gourd (*Lagenaria vulgaris*), from the fruit of which cups, dippers, bottles, etc. are made.

bot'tle grȧss, popular name of the *Setaria glauca* or *Setaria viridis*, a meadow grass: also known as *foxtail* or *pigeon grass*.

bot'tle green, a shade of very dark green similar to that of the glass used in many bottles.

bot'tle-green, *a.* having a very dark-green color.

bot'tle·head (-hed), *n.* the bottlenose whale.

bot'tle·hōld"ēr, *n.* 1. the ringside attendant of a boxer in a prize fight: he keeps a bottle of water in readiness to refresh the fighter.

2. a supporter in any contention; a backer. [Colloq.]

3. a stand or rack for a bottle.

bot'tle imp, a Cartesian devil.

bot'tle·neck, *n.* 1. a narrow passage.

2. a condition or situation that impedes progress.

3. the neck of a bottle.

bot'tle·nōse, *n.* 1. any of several small whales, especially the *Hyperoödon edentulus* and the *Globicephalus deductor*, usually from twenty to thirty feet long, and characterized by a peculiar formation of the snout: also called *bottlehead*.

2. any one of a number of bottle-nosed varieties of the dolphin, as the *Tursiops tursio*.

3. the puffin, a sea bird having the beak short and very thick. [Obs.]

4. a bottle-shaped nose; also, a nose discolored or bulbous from drink.

bot'tle-nōsed, *a.* having a bottlenose.

bot'tle ōre, any one of several coarse varieties of North Atlantic seaweed, especially the *Fucus vesiculosus*, or bladder wrack, and the *Fucus nodosus*.

bot'tlēr, *n.* one engaged in the bottling of beverages, liquors, medicines, etc.

bot'tle·sçrew, *n.* a screw to draw corks out of bottles; a corkscrew.

bot'tle tit, in zoology, the European titmouse, *Acredula caudata*, which builds a nest shaped like a bottle.

bot'tle tree, a tree native to Australia, belonging to the family *Sterculiaceæ*, so named from the bottlelike swelling of its trunk.

bot'tling, *n.* the act, process, or business of putting anything into bottles and corking them for preservation and future use.

bot'tŏm, *a.* pertaining to the bottom; situated at the bottom; lowest; fundamental; last.

bot'tŏm, *v.t.*; bottomed *pt., pp.*; bottoming, *ppr.* 1. to found or build upon; to fix upon as a support: usually with *on* or *upon*; as, sound reasoning is *bottomed on* just premises.

2. to furnish with a seat or bottom; as, to *bottom* a chair.

3. to find the meaning of; to understand; to fathom; as, to *bottom* a mystery.

4. in mining, to make a channel under for drainage, as in hydraulic gold-mining.

5. to wind, as a ball or skein of thread. [Obs.]

bot'tŏm, *v.i.* 1. to reach or rest upon the bottom.

2. to be based or established: usually with *on* or *upon*.

3. in machinery, to strike against the bottom so as to prevent further movement.

bot'tŏm, *n.* [ME. *bottom*, *botme*; AS. *botm*; D. *bodem*; Ice. *botn*; Sw. *botten*; Dan. *bund*; L. *fundus*; Gr. *pythmēn*, bottom; Sans. *budhna*, depth, ground.]

1. the lowest part of anything; as, the *bottom* of a well, vat, or ship; the *bottom* of a hill.

2. the underside.

3. whichever end is underneath; as, the *bottom* of a barrel.

4. the ground under any body of water; the bed; as, a sandy *bottom*.

5. the foundation or groundwork of anything; the base; that which supports.

6. the seat of a chair.

7. the buttocks. [Colloq.]

8. [*often pl.*] low ground; a dale; a valley; alluvial land adjoining rivers, etc.

9. the fundamental element or quality; cause, spring, or origin; the first moving cause.

10. the place farthest away from the head; the least honorable place; as, the *bottom* of the list of eligibles; the *bottom* of the class.

11. the hull of a vessel normally below the water; the keel; hence, a ship.

12. the lees or dregs; as, the *bottom* of beer.

13. stamina; endurance; as, an animal of good *bottom*.

14. that on which thread is wound; a ball of thread; the cocoon of a silkworm. [Obs.]

15. in painting or in dyeing, the base color; the color used as a foundation for other colors.

16. in mining, the floor of a seam or vein; also, the channel of a former river in which gold deposits are to be found.

at bottom, at the bottom; in fact or reality; fundamentally; actually.

to be at the bottom of; to be the real source or cause of; to be the real reason for.

to go to the bottom; to become submerged; to sink out of sight; specifically, to sink, as a ship at sea.

to stand on one's own bottom; to rely on oneself; to be independent.

bot'tŏm grȧss, 1. a rich grass, excellent for pasturage, growing on bottom lands.

2. any low-growing grass used to form turf or sod.

bot'tŏm hēat, heat artificially applied to plants through the soil, as by electricity, steam pipes, fermenting manure, etc.

bot'tŏm land, land lying low, bordering on a river and rich in alluvial soil.

bot'tŏm·less, *a.* 1. without a bottom; ungrounded; as, a *bottomless* rumor.

2. seeming to have no bottom; very deep, inexhaustible, etc.; as, a *bottomless* abyss; a *bottomless* supply.

bot'tŏm·less pit, the underworld; hell.

bot'tŏm līne, 1. the bottom line of the earnings report of a company, on which net profit per share of stock is shown.

2. profits or losses, as of a business. [Colloq.]

3. (a) the basic or most important factor, consideration, meaning, etc. [Slang.]; (b) the final or ultimate statement, decision, etc. [Slang.]

bot'tŏm·ry, *n.* [ME. *bottomery*, *bodomery*; D. *bodomerij*, bottomry.] in maritime law, the act of borrowing money, and pledging the ship itself as security for the payment of the debt. The contract of *bottomry* is in the nature of a mortgage. If the ship is lost the debt is canceled.

bot'tŏn·y, bot'to·né (-tō-nā), *a.* [OFr. *botonné*,

pp. of *botonner*, to ornament with buds or buttons; *boton*, bud, button.] in heraldry, having knobs or buttons at the end.

botts, *n.pl.* same as *bots.*

bot'ū·li·form, *a.* [L. *botulus*, sausage, and *forma*, form.] resembling a sausage in shape.

bot'ū·lin, *n.* the toxin causing botulism.

bot·ū·lī'nus, *n.* the bacillus producing botulin.

bot'ū·lism, *n.* poisoning caused by meats, fish, vegetables, etc. improperly preserved and containing a toxin produced by a certain bacillus: it is characterized by nausea, vomiting, muscular weakness, and, sometimes, disturbance of vision.

bouche, *n.* [Fr. *bouche*, mouth, food.]
1. the portion of food formerly allowed servants, or inferior officers, at court or in a feudal lord's household. [Obs.]
2. a notch or hole in a shield, to hold a weapon, as a sword blade.
3. the mouth of a firearm. [Obs.]

bouche, *v.t.*; bouched, *pt., pp.*; bouching, *ppr.* to form or drill a new mouth or vent in, as in a gun which has been spiked.

bou·chée' (bö̇u-shā'), *n.* [Fr. *bouche*, mouth.] a small, baked pastry shell; a small tart.

bou'chẽr·ize, *v.t.*; boucherized, *pt., pp.*; boucherizing, *ppr.* [from *Boucherie*, a French chemist.] to preserve (timber, etc.) by treating with a solution of copper sulfate.

bou·clé' (bö̇u-klā'), [Fr.] 1. a kind of yarn having a loose thread that gives the cloth made from it a tufted or knotted texture.
2. cloth made from this yarn.

boud, *n.* an insect that breeds in malt or grain; a weevil. [Obs.]

bou'doir (-dwär), *n.* [Fr., from *bouder*, to pout, sulk.] a woman's private sitting room or dressing room.

bouf·fant', bouf·fante', *a.* [Fr.] puffed out; full: said of a skirt.

bouffe, *n.* [Fr., a buffoon.] comic or light opera; opera bouffe.

Bou·gain·vil'lē·à, *n.* a genus of tropical South American plants, climbing shrubs of the family *Nyctaginaceæ*, the flowers of which are nearly enclosed by large colored bracts; named after Louis Antoine de *Bougainville* (1729–1811), a French explorer.

bouge, *v.i.* [Fr.] to swell out; to bulge; also, to spring a leak in the bottom. [Obs.]

bouge, *v.t.* to bilge; to break a hole in. [Obs.]

bouge, *n.* a bouche. [Obs.]

bou'get, *n.* [Fr. *bougette*, a little bag.] in heraldry, a representation of a water vessel, used as a charge.

bough (bou), *n.* [ME. *bog, boh*; AS. *bog, boh*, the shoulder, arm; Ice. *bogr*; Sw. *bog*; O.H.G. *buog*; Gr. *pēchys*; Sans. *bahu*, the arm.]
1. the branch of a tree, usually a large branch.
2. the hangman's gallows. [Obs.]

bough'pot, bow'pot, beau'pot (bō'), *n.* 1. a bouquet or vase of flowers used as a conventional design in decoration.
2. a vase for flowers, or a large pot for boughs or shrubs.
3. a bouquet. [Brit.]

bought (bout), *n.* a twist; a link; a bend. [Obs.]

bought (bọt), past tense and past participle of *buy.*

bought'en, *a.* obtained by purchase; not homemade. [Dial.]

bought'y (bout'), *a.* bending. [Obs.]

bou·gie' (-zhē'), *n.* [Fr., a wax candle; *bugia*, from *Bugia*, in North Africa, whence wax candles were imported.]
1. in medicine, (a) a long, slender instrument, introduced into the urethra and other canals of the body to stretch or dilate them. It was originally made of slips of waxed linen, coiled into a cylindrical or slightly conical form by rolling. Bougies are also made of catgut, rubber, and metal; (b) a thin stick of gelatin or other material impregnated with medicine, to be introduced into the urethra, rectum, etc., where it is melted by the heat of the body.
2. a wax candle.

bouil·là·baisse' (bọọl-yȧ-bās'; Fr. bọọ''yȧ''-bes'), [Fr., from Pr. *boulh-abaisso*, lit., boils and settles, from *bouli* (Fr. *bouiller*), to boil, and *abaissa* (Fr. *abaisser*), humble.] a chowder made of two or more kinds of fish and sometimes seasoned with wine.

bouil·li' (bö-yē'), *n.* [Fr., from *bouillir*, to boil.] beef or other meat that has been boiled, particularly that from which soup or bouillon has been made.

bouil·lon' (bool'yon; Fr. bö-yōṅ'), *n.* [Fr., from *bouillir*, to boil.] a clear broth, usually of beef.

bouil·lon' çūbe, a small cube of concentrated stock for making bouillon.

bouk, *n.* [AS. *buc*, the belly.]
1. magnitude; volume; bulk. [Scot.]
2. the body; the trunk. [Obs.]

boul, *n.* a kind of semicircular handle, or handle like a loop. [Scot.]

bou·lan'gẽr·ite, *n.* [named after *Boulanger*, a French mineralogist.] a sulfide of antimony and lead, occurring in bluish-gray masses.

bōul'dẽr, *n.* [ME. *bulderston*, a boulder; Sw. *bullersten*; *bullra, buldre*, to thunder, roar, and *sten*, a stone.] any large rock worn and rounded by weather and water; specifically, in geology, a rock lying on the surface of the soil, or embedded in the clays and gravels of a drift formation, generally differing in composition from the rocks in its vicinity, a fact which shows that it has probably been transported from a distance: also spelled *bowlder.*

bōul'dẽr çlāy, unstratified material left by a glacier, consisting of boulders and rocks embedded in a hard clay matrix.

bōul'dẽr·head (-hed), *n.* a row of piles in front of a breakwater or dike to resist the force of the waves.

bōul'dẽr·ing stōne, hard flint pebbles obtained in gravel pits, used for dressing the faces of emery wheels and glazers.

bōul'dẽr·y, *a.* having many boulders; resembling a boulder.

boule, *n.* same as *buhl.*

Bou'lē, *n.* 1. the lower branch of the legislative assembly of modern Greece.
2. [b–] an ancient Greek senate, or legislative assembly of elders.

bou·let' (*or* -lā'), *n.* [Fr.] a horse whose fetlock or pastern-joint bends forward out of its natural position.

bou'le·värd, *n.* [Fr., from G. *bollwerk*, a bulwark.]
1. originally, the top surface of a rampart or fortification.
2. a wide street or avenue, well-paved, usually ornamented with trees and grass plots.

bou'le·vär·diẽr (*Fr. pron.* böl-vär-dyā'), *n.* [Fr.] in Europe, one who frequents the boulevards, particularly those of Paris; a man about town.

bou·le·vẽrse'ment (*Fr. pron.* böl-vers-mäṅ'), *n.* [Fr. *bouleverser*, to overthrow.] turmoil; a complete overthrow; disorder; revolution.

bou·lim'i·à, *n.* same as *bulimia.*

boult, *n.* same as *bolt.*

boul'tel, *n.* same as *boltel.*

boul'tẽr, *n.* a long, strong line for deep-sea fishing, having many hooks attached; a trawl: also spelled *bolter.*

boun, *a.* [ME. *boun*; Ice. *buinn*, ready, prepared, pp. of *bna*, to till, prepare.] ready; prepared. [Obs.]

boun, *v.t.* and *v.i.* to prepare (oneself); to get ready. [Archaic.]

bounce, *v.i.*; bounced, *pt., pp.*; bouncing, *ppr.* [ME. *bounsen, bunsen*; D. *bonzen*, to bounce, throw.]
1. to leap or spring; to rush out suddenly.
Out *bounced* the mastiff. —Swift.
2. to spring or leap against anything, so as to rebound; to bound or rebound, as a ball.
3. to boast; to brag. [Brit.]
4. to move in a sudden or noisy rush.

bounce, *v.t.* 1. to cause to bound or rebound; as, to *bounce* a ball.
2. to bump; to thump.
3. to discharge from employment. [Slang.]
4. to put (a person) out by force. [Slang.]

bounce, *n.* 1. a sudden spring or bound; a rebound.
2. a heavy blow, thrust, or thump, with a large, solid body.
The *bounce* burst open the door. —Dryden.
3. a loud or heavy sound. [Obs.]
4. a boast; a bluster; a bold lie. [Brit.]
5. dismissal; discharge; as, he received the *bounce.* [Slang.]
6. great energy; spirit; dash. [Slang.]

bounce, *adv.* suddenly.

boun'cẽr, *n.* 1. a boaster; a bully; a bold liar; also, an impudent lie. [Rare.]
2. one who or that which bounces.
3. one who is employed to eject very disorderly people from a night club, restaurant, etc.
4. anything very big.

boun'cing, *a.* 1. stout; buxom; large; heavy; as, a *bouncing* lass.
2. healthy; strong; lusty.

boun'cing Bet, *Saponaria officinalis*, a species of soapwort with dense clusters of white or pinkish flowers.

boun'cing·ly, *adv.* 1. boastingly.
2. with a bounce.

bound, past tense and past participle of *bind.*

bound, *n.* [ME. *bounde, bunne*; OFr. *bunne, bonde*; LL. *bodina, butina*, a bound, limit.]
1. a limit; anything that limits the whole of any given object or space; a boundary or confine.
2. [*pl.*] an area near, alongside, or enclosed by a boundary.
out of bounds; (a) beyond the boundaries or limits, as of a playing field; (b) prohibited; forbidden.
to keep within bounds; to keep within the limits; to act with regard to propriety.

bound, *v.t.*; bounded, *pt., pp.*; bounding, *ppr.*
1. to limit; to terminate; to restrain or confine; as, to *bound* our wishes.
2. to name the boundaries of, as a state.
3. to be a limit or boundary to.

bound, *v.i.* to have a boundary (*on* another country, etc.).

bound, *v.i.* [Fr. *bondir*, to leap, make a noise; LL. *bombitare*, to buzz, hum; L. *bombus*, a humming, buzzing.]
1. to leap; to jump; to spring; to move forward by leaps.
Before his lord the ready spaniel *bounds.* —Pope.
2. to rebound; to recoil, as a ball when thrown against anything.

bound, *v.t.* to cause to rebound; to bounce; as, to *bound* a ball against a wall.

bound, *n.* 1. a leap; a jump; a spring.
2. a rebound, as of a ball.

bound, *a.* 1. made fast by a band, or by chains or fetters, etc.; confined; restrained.
2. under obligation or compulsion; as, he is legally *bound* to do it.
3. constipated.
4. provided with a binding or cover, as a book.
5. sure; destined; certain; as, *bound* to lose.
6. determined; resolved; as, I am *bound* to go there. [Colloq.]
7. closely connected or related.
bound bailiff; in England, an officer appointed by a sheriff to execute the law: so named from the bond given for the faithful discharge of his trust: contemptuously called *bumbailiff.*
bound up in; absorbingly attached or devoted to; inseparable from.
Syn.—restrained, confined, obliged, destined, compelled, determined, resolved.

bound, *a.* destined; on the way; going, or intending to go; headed: often with *to* or *for*; as, the ship is *bound to* New Orleans, or *for* New Orleans; homeward *bound.*

-bound, a combining form used in hyphenated compounds, meaning *going*, or *headed in* (a specified direction) or *to* (a specified place), as in *south-bound, Chicago-bound.*

bound'à·ry, *n.*; *pl.* **bound'à·ries** (-riz), [from *bound*, a limit; LL. *bunnarium, bonnarium*, a field with limits.] a limit; a bound; anything marking a limit.
Sensation and reflection are the *boundaries* of our thoughts. —Locke.
Syn.—limit, border, bound, confine, extent, termination, margin, edge, verge.

bound'en, *a.* [obs. pp. of *bind.*]
1. under obligation; obliged; beholden.
I am much *bounden* to your majesty.—Shak.
2. obligatory; binding; as, our *bounden* duty.

bound'ẽr, *n.* 1. a boundary. [Now Dial.]
2. an ill-mannered, rude, pushing person; a cad. [Colloq.]

bound'ing, *a.* leaping; springing; rebounding; advancing with leaps; as, a *bounding* deer.

bound'less, *a.* unlimited; unconfined; immeasurable; illimitable; as, *boundless* space; *boundless* power; *boundless* love.
Syn.—illimitable, infinite, unbounded, unlimited, immeasurable, vast.

bound'less·ly, *adv.* without bound or limit.

bound'less·ness, *n.* the quality of being boundless.

boun'tē·ous, *a.* [ME. *bountevous*; OFr. *bontif, bontive*, from *bonte*, goodness, bounty.]
1. liberal in charity; disposed to give freely; generous; munificent; beneficent; free in bestowing gifts; as, *bounteous* nature.
2. abundant; plentiful; ample.

boun'tē·ous·ly, *adv.* liberally; generously; largely; freely.

boun'tē·ous·ness, *n.* liberality in bestowing gifts or favors; munificence; kindness.

boun'ti·fụl, *a.* 1. free to give; liberal in be-

stowing gifts and favors; munificent; generous.
God, the *bountiful* author of our being. —Locke.
2. liberal; abundant; plentiful; as, a *bountiful* harvest.
boun'ti·ful·ly, *adv.* liberally; largely; in a bountiful manner.
boun'ti·ful·ness, *n.* the quality of being bountiful.
boun'ti·head (-hed), *n.* goodness; liberality. [Obs.]
boun'ty, *n.*; *pl.* **boun'ties,** [ME. *bounte*; OFr. *bonte*; L. *bonitas*, goodness, from *bonus*, good.]
1. liberality in bestowing gifts and favors; generosity; munificence; lack of restraint in giving.
2. something given freely; generous gift.
3. a reward, premium, or allowance, especially one given by a government for killing certain animals, raising certain crops, enlisting in the military service, emigrating, etc.
4. goodness; kindness. [Obs.]
Queen Anne's bounty; a provision made in Queen Anne's reign for augmenting poor clerical livings.
Syn.—liberality, bounteousness, benevolence, munificence, donation, gift, generosity, charity, benignity.
boun'ty jump'ẽr, one who receives a bounty on enlistment and then deserts, as in the United States during the latter part of the Civil War.
bou·quet' (-kā'), *n.* [Fr., a plume, a nosegay; OFr. *bosquet*, dim. of *bos*, a wood, thicket.]
1. a nosegay; a bunch of flowers.
2. an aroma; fragrance, especially of a wine or brandy.
bou·que·tiẽr', *n.* a device for holding cut flowers, especially one carried in the hand.
bou·que·tin' (bō-ke-taṅ'), *n.* [Fr.] in zoology, an animal of the genus *Ibex*.
bour, *n.* a chamber; a bower. [Obs.]
Bour'bŏn (*or* boor'bŏn), 1. the ruling family of France (1589–1793; 1814–1830); of Spain (1700–1808; 1814–1833; 1874–1931); of Naples (1735–1805; 1815–1860); and of Parma (1748–1859).
2. a political and social reactionary.
bour'bŏn (*or* bũr'bŏn), *n.* [from Bourbon County, Kentucky, where it has been produced.] a whisky made from corn, sometimes with added rye or malt.
bour'bŏn, *a.* designating, of, or made with bourbon.
Bour'bŏn·ism, *n.* advocacy or support of conservative government, like that of the Bourbons; extreme political and social reaction.
Bour'bŏn·ist, *n.* one who practices or advocates Bourbonism.
bourd, *v.i.* to jest. [Obs.]
bourd, *n.* a jest. [Obs.]
bourd'ẽr, *n.* a jester. [Obs.]
bour'dŏn, *n.* [OFr. *bourdon*, a staff; LL. *burdo*, *burdonis*, an ass, mule.] a pilgrim's staff. [Obs.]
bour'dŏn, *n.* [Fr.] in music, (a) the drone of the bagpipe; (b) a bass stop on the organ, usually of the sixteen-foot pipes.
bourg, *n.* [Fr.] 1. a medieval town or village, especially one near a castle.
2. a market town.
bour·gāde', *n.* [Fr., from *bourg*, a town, market town.] an unprotected village or unfortified town.
bour·geois' (bũr-jois'), *n.* [so called after a French type founder, *Bourgeois*.] a kind of type, 9 point, in size between long primer and brevier.
This line is set in bourgeois.
bour·geois' (bōr-zhwä'), *n.*; *pl.* **bour·geois',** [Fr.; OFr. *burgeis*, from *bourg*.]
1. originally, a freeman of medieval town.
2. a shopkeeper.
3. a member of the bourgeoisie.
4. a person with the characteristic traits or viewpoint of the bourgeoisie.
5. [*pl.*] the bourgeoisie.
bour·geois' (bōr-zhwä'), *a.* of or characteristic of a bourgeois or the bourgeoisie; middle-class: used variously to mean commonplace, conventional, respectable, thrifty, smug, greedy, etc.
bour·geoise' (bōr-zhwäz'), *n.*; *pl.* **bour·geoises'** (bōr-zhwäz'), feminine of bourgeois.
bour·geoi·sie' (bōr-zhwä-zē'), *n.* [*construed as sing.* or *pl.*], [Fr.]
1. the social class between the aristocracy or very wealthy and the working class, or proletariat; the middle class.
2. in Marxist doctrine, capitalists as a social class antithetical to the proletariat.
bour'ġeŏn, *n.*, *v.t.*, and *v.i.* burgeon.
bou'ri, *n.* [native name.] in zoology, a gray mullet (*Mugil capito*) of Europe and Africa.
Bou·rign'iăn (-rin'yăn), *a.* in ecclesiastical history, pertaining to Antoinette *Bourignon* (1616–1680), who taught in Great Britain and the Low Countries a religious creed independent of a Bible or church.
Bou·rign'iăn, *n.* a member of the Bourignian sect.
Bou·rign'iăn·ism, *n.* the creed of the Bourignians.
bōurn, bōurne (*or* bōrn), *n.* [Fr. *borne*; OFr. *bonne*, *bodne*; LL. *bodina*, *bonna*, a boundary, limit.]
1. a bound; a limit; a boundary. [Archaic.]
The undiscovered country, from whose *bourn*
No traveler returns. —Shak.
2. a goal; objective.
3. loosely, a domain. [Poetic.]
bōurn, bōurne, *n.* [ME. *bourne*, *burne*; AS. *burne*, *burna*, a stream.] a brook; a stream; a rivulet: retained in many names of towns situated on the banks of streams. Also *burn*.
bourn'less, *a.* without limits.
bour'nŏn·īte, *n.* [named after Count de *Bournon*, a French mineralogist.] an ore consisting of lead, antimony, copper, and sulfur, occurring in steel-gray crystals, often aggregated into shapes like small cog wheels.
bour·nous', *n.* same as *burnoose*.
bour·rée' (bou-rā'), *n.* Fr., from *bourrir*, to beat wings, whir; OFr. *burir*, to dart forth, from O.H.G. dial., *burjan*.]
1. a lively French or Spanish dance similar to a gavotte.
2. a piece of music for this dance or in a similar rapid tempo.
bourse, *n.* [Fr., a purse, exchange; OFr. *borse*; LL. *bursa*, a purse, bag.]
1. a stock exchange or place of meeting for business.
2. [B–] the stock exchange of Paris or any of a number of other European cities.
bouse, *n.* [ME. *bous*; MD. *buse*, a drink, cup.] same as *booze*. [Archaic.]
bouse, *v.t.* and *v.i.*; boused, *pt.*, *pp.*; bousing, *ppr.* same as *booze*. [Archaic.]
bouse, *v.t.* and *v.i.*; boused, *pt.*, *pp.*; bousing, *ppr.* [from D.; see *boost*.] in nautical usage, to pull up by means of a tackle; to hoist.
bous'ẽr, *n.* a drinker; a carouser.
bou·strō·phē'dŏn, *n.* [Gr. *boustrophēdon*; *bous*, an ox, and *strephein*, to turn.] an ancient mode of writing in alternate lines, one from right to left, and the next from left to right, as fields are plowed.
bou·stroph·ē·don'iç, *a.* pertaining to the method of writing known as boustrophedon.
bou·stroph'iç, *a.* [Gr. *boustrophos*, ox guiding.] boustrophedonic.
bous'y, *a.* drunk.
bout, *n.* [ME. *bout*, *bowt*; AS. *byht*, a bend, from *bugan*, to bend.]
1. a turn; a single part of an action carried on at successive intervals; essay; attempt.
2. a contest; a match; as, a fencing *bout*.
3. a period of time spent in some activity; spell or term; as, a *bout* of floor scrubbing.
4. a twist; a bend; a bight. [Obs.]
bou·tāde', *n.* [Fr., from *bouter*, to thrust, butt.] a sudden outbreak; hence, a whim. [Obs.]
boute'fēu, *n.* [Fr.] an incendiary; a firebrand. [Obs.]
Bou·tē·lou'ȧ, *n.* [named after Claudius *Boutelou*, a Spanish botanist.] an important genus of grasses, abundant in Mexico and southwestern United States, and including the mesquite grasses.
bou·tique' (-tēk'), *n.* [Fr., from Gr. *apothēkē*, storehouse.] a small shop, or a small department in a store, where fashionable, usually expensive, clothes and other articles are sold.
bou·ton·niere', bou·ton·nière' (bou-tŏn-nyâr'), *n.* [Fr., a buttonhole.] a flower or a small bouquet worn in a buttonhole, as of a lapel.
bouts ri·més' (bō rē-mā'), [Fr. *bout*, end; *rime*, pp. of *rimer*, to rime; *rime*, a rime.] words to be placed at the ends of verses and rhymed.
Bou·vär'di·ȧ, *n.* [named after Dr. Charles *Bouvard*, a French botanist.] a genus of herbs and shrubs with showy flowers, natives of tropical America, and widely cultivated in greenhouses. They belong to the madder family, *Rubiaceæ*.
bō'vāte, *n.* [LL. *bovata*, from L. *bos*, *bovis*, an ox.] in old English law, an oxgang, or as much land as an ox could plow in a year; an ancient land measure, from 10 to 18 acres.
bō'vid, *a.* [from L. *Bovidæ*, name of the family, from *bos*, *bovis*, ox.] of the ox family of ruminants, having, characteristically, a pair of hollow, unbranched horns, and including cattle, sheep, goats, antelopes, etc.
bō'vi·form, *a.* [L. *bos*, *bovis*, an ox, and *forma*, form.] oxlike in form.
bō'vīne (*or* -vin), *a.* [LL. *bovinus*, from L. *bos*, *bovis*, an ox.]
1. pertaining to oxen and cows, or the quadrupeds of the genus *Bos*.
2. oxlike or cowlike.
3. sluggish, dull, stolid, patient, etc.
bō'vīne, *n.* an ox, cow, or similar animal.
bow, *v.t.*; bowed, *pt.*, *pp.*; bowing, *ppr.* [ME. *bowen*, *buwen*, *bogen*; AS. *bugan*, to bend, flee.]
1. to cause to bend; as, to *bow* vines. [Dial.]
2. to bend (the head or body) in token of respect, civility, or condescension.
3. to cause to turn or incline. [Obs.]
4. to weigh down; to overwhelm; to crush; to subdue.
His heavy hand hath *bowed* you to the grave. —Shak.
5. to express (agreement, thanks, etc.) by bowing.
bow, *v.i.* 1. to bend; to curve; to bend, in token of respect; often with *down*; as, money is the idol to which the world *bows down*.
2. to stoop; to fall upon the knees. [Dial.]
3. to bend the head or body forward as a mark of assent or salutation.
4. to yield or submit, as to authority.
bow, *n.* an inclination of the head, or a bending of the body, in token of respect, civility, or submission.
bow, *n.* [16th-c., from LG. or Scand.; cf. LG. *būg*, D. *boeg*, Sw. *bog*, shoulder, bows.]
1. the front part of a ship, boat, or airship; the prow.
2. the oarsman nearest the bow.
bows on; head first.
bows under; making difficult progress; overwhelmed.
bow, *a.* of or near the bow; fore: opposed to *stern*.
bōw, *n.* [ME. *bowe*, *boge*; AS. *boga*, from *bugan*, to bend.]
1. a curve; a bend.
2. a device for shooting arrows: it is a flexible, curved strip of wood, metal, etc. with a cord connecting the two ends.
3. [*pl.*] bowmen; archers.
4. a slender stick, originally curved, strung along its length with horsehairs and drawn across the strings of a violin, etc. to play it.
5. anything bent, or in the form of a curve, as the rainbow, the doubling of a string in a knot, an ornamental tie or piece of neckwear, a knot of ribbon worn in the hair, etc.
6. a primitive quadrant.
7. an instrument for turning a drill; also, one for turning wood; also, in hat-making, for breaking fur and wool.
8. in architecture, any circular or polygonal projection. A *bow window* is a window of circular construction: more commonly termed a *bay window*.
9. [*pl.*] in saddle-making, two pieces of wood, etc. forming the arch in front of a saddle.
10. one of the curved ends of a pair of spectacles, passing over the ear: also called a *riding bow*.
11. the curved piece of metal forming a guard for the trigger of a firearm; a metal guard about a sword hilt.
12. an arcograph, or appliance for drawing an arc.
to draw the long bow; to lie; to exaggerate.
to have two strings, or *more than one string, to one's bow*; to have more than one resource.
bōw, *v.t.*; bowed, *pt.*, *pp.*; bowing, *ppr.* 1. in music, to play with the bow; as, to *bow* a difficult passage well.
2. to bend in the form of a bow.
bōw, *v.i.* in music, to play with or handle the bow.
bow'ȧ·ble, *a.* of a flexible nature or disposition; yielding. [Obs.]
bōw ärm, the arm used in manipulating a bow in archery or in playing the violin and similar instruments.
bōw'-backed (-bakt), *a.* having a bent or humped back.
bōw beär'ẽr, in Old English law, an under-officer of the English forests, whose duty was to arrest trespassers.
Bōw'bells, *n.* the bells of St. Mary-le-Bow, a church situated in the heart of London, or cockneydom. Bowbells is therefore another name for cockneydom.

bō̆w'bent, *a.* bent like a bow.

bow chās'ẽr, a gun so situated in the bow of a ship that it can be fired at a vessel being chased.

bōw çŏm'păss, bōw çŏm'păss·eṣ, 1. a pair of small compasses having a bow-shaped piece of metal riveted to one of the legs, upon which the other slides.

2. a pair of compasses connected by a bow-shaped spring.

bōwd'lẽr·iṣm, *n.* the practice of omitting passages considered to be indelicate or offensive from an author's published works.

bōwd"lẽr·i·zā'tion, *n.* editorial expurgation.

bōwd'lẽr·īze, *v.t.*; bowdlerized, *pt., pp.*; bowdlerizing, *ppr.* [after Dr. Thomas *Bowdler*, who in 1818 published an edition of Shakespeare with all indelicate passages omitted.] to remove supposedly offensive passages from (a book, etc.); to expurgate.

bōw drill, a drill worked by a bow and string.

bōwed (bōd), *a.* bent like a bow.

bow'el, *n.* [ME. *bowel, boel*; OFr. *boel, buel*; LL. *botellus*, an intestine; L. *botellus*, dim. of *botulus*, a sausage.]

1. an intestine; an entrail; especially, a human entrail: generally used in the plural.

2. [*pl.*] the interior part of anything; as, the *bowels* of the earth.

3. [*pl.*] the seat of compassion, pity, or kindness, or the attributes themselves; as, *bowels* of compassion; hast thou no *bowels?* [Archaic.]

4. [*pl.*] children; offspring. [Obs.]

bow'el, *v.t.*; boweled *or* bowelled, *pt., pp.*; boweling *or* bowelling, *ppr.* to take or remove the bowels from; to disembowel.

bow'eled, bow'elled, *a.* possessed of bowels; hollow; as, the *boweled* cavern.

bow'el·less, *a.* without tenderness or pity.

bow'el mōve'ment, 1. the passing of waste matter from the large intestine.

2. the waste matter thus passed; feces.

bō̆w'en·īte, *n.* [from G. T. *Bowen*, who analyzed it.] a variety of serpentine that is hard and compact in quality and of a light green color, resembling jade.

bow'ẽr, *n.* an anchor carried near the bows of a ship. There are generally two *bowers*, on the starboard and port sides, called respectively, first and second, great and little, or best and small.

bow'ẽr, *n.* [G. *bauer*, a peasant. So called from the figure sometimes designating the jack in a pack of cards.] one of the two best or highest cards in the game of euchre.

best bower; an extra card sometimes added to the pack in euchre and other games, and taking precedence over all others; the joker.

left bower; the jack of the same color as the trump but of a different suit: it is next in value to the right bower.

right bower; the jack of the trump suit; the highest card in a pack without the joker: used colloquially to describe a trusty friend or valuable assistant.

bow'ẽr, *n.* [ME. *bour*; AS. *bur*, a dwelling, room, chamber, from *buan*, to build; Ice. *bua*, to dwell.]

1. a recess sheltered or covered with foliage; an arbor.

2. a country seat; a cottage. [Poetic.]

3. a bedchamber; boudoir. [Archaic.]

bow'ẽr, *v.t.*; bowered, *pt., pp.*; bowering, *ppr.* to embower; to enclose; to form into a bower.

bow'ẽr, *v.i.* to lodge. [Obs.]

bow'ẽr, *n.* [ME. *bough, bogh*; AS. *bog, boh*, the arm, a branch of a tree.] in falconry, a young hawk before it is fairly on the wing.

bow'ẽr·bird, *n.* an Australian bird, related to the crow: the males construct bowers or runs which are used to attract the females of the species.

SPOTTED BOWERBIRD (*Chlamydera maculata*)

bow'ẽr·y, *n.*; *pl.* **bow'ẽr·ieṣ,** [D. *bouwerij*, farm, from *bouer*, a farm.]

1. a farm or plantation: so called by the early Dutch settlers in New York.

2. [B–] a New York street, or the district around this street, characterized by cheap hotels, saloons, etc.: the street originally traversed the plantation, or bowery, of Governor Peter Stuyvesant.

bow'ẽr·y, *a.* 1. covering; shading, as a bower.

2. containing bowers.

A *bowery* maze that shades the purple streams. —Trumbull.

bō̆w'fin, *n.* a voracious fresh-water fish, *Amia calva*, the mudfish, with a rounded tail fin and a long, narrow fin on its back.

bow'grāce, *n.* a frame of timber or junk used to protect the bows or sides of a ship from injury; a kind of ship's fender.

bōw hand, the hand that draws a bow: in archery, usually the left hand; in violin-playing, usually the right.

bō̆w'head (-hed), *n.* a kind of whale with a very large, arched head that yields whalebone; right whale.

bō̆w'iē knīfe (nīf), [after Colonel James *Bowie* (d. 1836), its inventor.] a steel hunting knife about fifteen inches long, with a single edge: it is usually carried in a sheath.

BOWIE KNIFE

bō̆w'ing, *n.* 1. the manner or technique of using the bow in playing a violin, etc.

2. in hat-making, the process of preparing hair and fur for felting by means of an instrument called a bow.

bow'ing·ly, *adv.* in a bending manner; with many bows and bends.

bō̆w'knot (-not), *n.* a knot having either one loop and one end or two loops and two ends: it is untied by pulling the end or ends.

bōwl, *n.* [ME. *bolle*; AS. *bolla*, a bowl, round vessel; Ice. *bolli*; O.H.G. *bolla*, a bowl.]

1. a hollow, rounded, cup-shaped container or dish, open at the top.

2. the bowllike part of anything; as, the *bowl* of a spoon; the *bowl* of a pipe.

3. a large drinking cup.

4. any intoxicating drink.

5. (a) an amphitheater; stadium; (b) any of various football games played annually after the regular season between teams selected because of their superior records: in full *bowl game*.

6. the quantity a bowl will hold; a bowlful; as, a *bowl* of soup.

bōwl, *n.* [ME. *bowle*; OFr. *boule*; L. *bulla*, a bubble, stud.]

1. a heavy ball rolled on a level surface in bowling, especially that used in the game of bowls: often weighted on one side to give it a bias in rolling.

2. a turn or delivery of the ball in bowling or bowls.

3. a roller, drum, or wheel, as in some machines.

bōwl, *v.t.*; bowled, *pt., pp.*; bowling, *ppr.* 1. to roll; to throw so as to make roll.

2. to bear or convey smoothly; to roll as on wheels; as, the bus *bowled* us rapidly along.

3. to strike with anything rolled; hence, to strike down; as, the storm of bullets *bowled* them down.

4. in cricket, to put out (a batsman) by bowling the bails off the wicket (often with *out*).

bowl over; (a) to knock over with something rolled; (b) [Colloq.] to astonish and confuse; to stagger.

bōwl, *v.i.* 1. to participate in bowling; to play the game of bowls.

2. to throw a bowl, usually underhand, so as to make it roll.

3. to move swiftly and smoothly (usually with *along*); as, the car *bowled* steadily along.

4. in cricket, to deliver a ball to the batsman.

bōwl'dẽr, *n.* a boulder.

bō̆w'leg, *n.* 1. a leg with outward curvature.

2. the condition or degree of such curvature.

bō̆w'leg·ged (*or* -legd), *a.* having bowlegs.

bōwl'ẽr, *n.* [from *bowl* (ball), because of its shape.] a derby hat. [Brit.]

bōwl'ẽr, *n.* one who bowls.

bō̆w'line (*or* -lĭn), *n.* [ME. *boweline, bouline*; from ON. *boglina*; *bog*, a shoulder, bow of a ship, and *lina*, a line.] a rope fastened near the middle of the leech or perpendicular edge of a ship's square sails, by subordinate parts, called bridles, and used to keep the weather edge of the sail tight forward, when the ship is sailing into the wind.

on a bowline; close-hauled; with sails set so as to go as nearly against the wind as possible.

bō̆w'line brī'dle, in nautical usage, a rope by which the bowline is attached to the side of the sail.

bō̆w'line knot (not), a knot used to tie off a loop.

bōwl'ing, *n.* 1. a game in which a heavy ball is bowled along a wooden lane (bowling alley) in an attempt to knock over ten wooden pins set upright at the far end; tenpins.

2. the game of bowls.

3. the playing of either of these games.

bōwl'ing, *a.* of or for bowling.

bōwl'ing al'ley, 1. a long, narrow, enclosed wooden lane used in bowling: the player rolls a ball down it so as to knock down the pins placed upright at the far end.

2. [*often pl.*] a building for bowling.

bōwl'ing green, a smooth, level lawn for playing the game of bowls.

bōwlṣ, *n.* 1. an old game played on a smooth lawn (bowling green) with a weighted wooden ball (bowl) which is rolled in an attempt to make it stop near another, stationary ball (jack).

2. ninepins or tenpins.

3. skittles.

bō̆w'măn, *n.*; *pl.* **bō̆w'men,** an archer.

bow'măn, *n.*; *pl.* **bow'men,** the oarsman nearest to the bow of the boat; the bow oar.

bown, bowne, *v.t.* and *v.i.* to boun.

bōw net, 1. a trap of wickerwork, etc., for catching lobsters and crawfish.

2. a kind of bird net.

bow ōar, the foremost oar used in a boat, except in a whaleboat, where it is sometimes the second oar; also, the person who pulls it.

bōw pen, a metallic ruling pen having the part which holds the ink bowed out toward the middle; also, a bow compass carrying such a pen.

bōw pen'cil, a bow compass, on one leg of which there is a pencil.

bōw pin, the pin which secures the bows of an ox yoke.

bow'pot, *n.* a boughpot.

bōw saw, a saw with a narrow blade set in a strong frame resembling a bow.

bowṣe (*or* bouz), *n., v.t.*, and *v.i.*; bowsed, *pt., pp.*; bowsing, *ppr.* bouse (drink).

bō̆w'shot, *n.* the distance marked by the flight of an arrow.

bow'sprit (*or* bō'sprit), *n.* [ME. *bowsprit*; D *boegspriet*; *boeg*, bow of a ship, and *spriet*, a sprit.] a large, tapered pole or plank extending forward from the bow of a sailing vessel: the foremost stays are fastened to it.

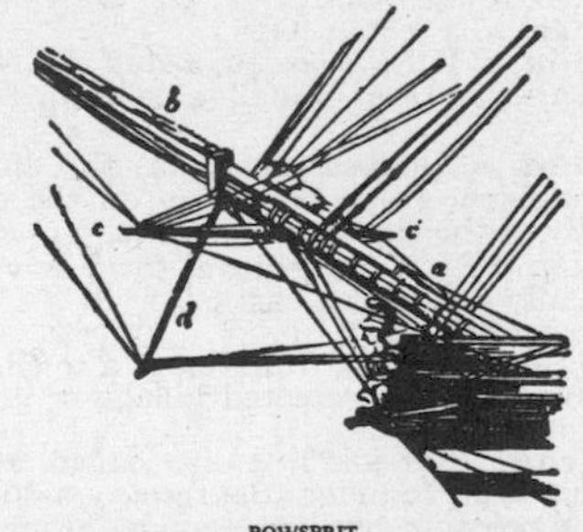

BOWSPRIT
a, bowsprit; *b*, jib boom; *cc*, spritsailyard; *d*, martingale

bows'sen, *v.t.* to drench in water; especially, to dip in water supposed to have healing properties for mental disorders. [Obs.]

bō̆w'string, *n.* 1. the string of a bow.

2. formerly, a string used by the Turks in strangling offenders.

3. any strong, light cord.

bowstring bridge; a bridge of timber or iron having an arched frame with a strong horizontal tie like a *bowstring*.

bowstring girder; an arched beam, the two ends of which are connected and strengthened by a horizontal tie or tie rod.

bowstring hemp; any of a group of plants of the lily family, with stiff, thick leaves that yield a fiber used in making bowstrings.

bō̆w'string, *v.t.*; bowstringed (-stringd) *or* bowstrung, *pt., pp.*; bowstringing, *ppr.* to strangle by means of a bowstring; to garrote.

bōw tie, a necktie tied in a small bowknot.

bōw win'dōw, a bay window built in a curve.

bōw′wood, *n.* the Osage orange of the Mississippi valley, a wood much favored by the Indians in the making of their bows.

bow′wow′, *n.* [echoic.] a sound imitating a dog's bark.

bow′wow′, *v.i.* to make a sound imitative of a dog's bark; to bark.

bōw′yẽr, *n.* [*bow* (the weapon), and *-yer*.]
1. a person who makes or deals in bows.
2. a bowman. [Rare.]

box, *n.* [AS. *box*; L. *buxus*; Gr. *pyxos*, the box tree.]
1. an evergreen tree or shrub, the *Buxus sempervirens*, with small, leathery leaves and inconspicuous flowers. It is used for bordering flower beds. The name is also given to other species of the genus. The African *box* is the *Myrsine Africana*. The wood of the tree varieties is very hard and is extensively used in the manufacture of fine furniture and scientific and musical instruments.
2. any Australian tree of the various genera *Eucalyptus*, *Murraya*, and *Tristania*: their timber is like boxwood.
3. the hard, close-grained wood of any of these plants.

box, *n.* [AS. *box*, a box, chest; L. *buxus*, anything made of boxwood; Gr. *pyxos*, the box tree.]
1. any of many kinds of containers, usually with lids, and of various sizes, shapes, and materials; case; carton.
2. the contents or capacity of a box.
3. a boxlike thing.
4. the case which contains the mariner's compass.
5. a receptacle for money or other valuables; as, a contribution *box*; a *box* in a safety deposit vault.
6. formerly, the tool box on a coach or carriage, on which the driver sat.
7. the driver's seat in a vehicle.
8. a small, enclosed group of seats, as in a theater, stadium, etc.
9. a small booth or shelter for men on outdoor duty.
10. a small country house used by sportsmen; as, a grouse *box*.
11. a horse stall.
12. a space or section for a certain person or group; as, a press *box*, jury *box*.
13. a short, newspaper article enclosed in borders.
14. in baseball, (a) the place where a player must stand while at bat; (b) the place where the pitcher stands.
15. in mechanics, a protective casing for a part; as, a journal *box*.
16. a gift which is contained in a box; as, a Christmas *box*.
17. a compartment of a printer's case; as, the comma *box*.

box, *a.* 1. shaped or made like a box.
2. packaged in a box.
box beam; in architecture, a hollow beam composed of metal and similar to a box.
box calf; a type of tanned calf leather characterized by square markings.
box camera; a relatively inexpensive camera shaped like a box and having a fixed focus and, generally, a single shutter speed.
box drain; an underground drain boxed up on the sides and top and covered with earth.
box pleat (or *plait*); a double pleat with the under edges folded toward each other.
box score; a statistical summary of a baseball game, showing the number of hits, runs, errors, etc.: it is printed in boxlike form.
box seat; a seat in a box at a theater, stadium, etc.
box stall; a large, enclosed, more or less square stall, as for a horse or cow.

box, *v.t.*; boxed (bokst), *pt., pp.*; boxing, *ppr.*
1. to enclose in a box; often followed by *up*; as, to *box up* cloth.
2. to supply with a box, as a wheel.
3. to make an incision into (a tree) to procure the sap; as, to *box* a maple.
4. to boxhaul.
to box off; (a) to divide into boxes; (b) in nautical language, to turn the head of a vessel either way by bracing the headyards aback.
to box the compass; to name the thirty-two points of the compass in the proper order; hence, to make a complete circuit, returning to the starting point.
to box up; to keep in; to confine.

box, *n.* [ME. *box*, a blow, slap; Dan. *bask*, a blow, slap.] a blow with the hand, especially on the ear or the side of the head.

box, *v.t.* to strike with the hand or fist, especially on the ear.

box, *v.i.* to use the fists; to spar with boxing gloves; also, to be a boxer.

box′ber″ry, *n.*; *pl.* **box′ber·rieṣ,** 1. a creeping evergreen plant with small flowers and red fruit; wintergreen.
2. a trailing plant with pinkish-white flowers and red berries; partridgeberry.

box′çär, *n.* 1. a fully enclosed railroad freight car.
2. [*pl.*] in dice, a throw of twelve. [Slang.]

box chrō·nom′e·tẽr, a ship's chronometer suspended in gimbals.

box çōat, 1. a thick overcoat, formerly worn by coachmen.
2. an outer coat that fits somewhat loosely and hangs straight from the shoulders.

box çoup′ling (kup′), a metal collar which unites such parts of machinery as shafts.

box çrab, a crab of the genus *Calappa*, which, with its pincers folded, resembles a box.

box el′dẽr, the ash-leaved maple (*Acer negundo*), a native of North America: it grows rapidly and drops its leaves early.

box′en, *a.* made of boxwood or box trees, or pertaining to either. [Archaic.]

box′ẽr, *n.* 1. one who boxes, spars, or fights, whether with gloves or bare hands; a pugilist; a prize fighter.
2. any of a breed of medium-sized dog with a sturdy body and a smooth fawn or brindle coat: it is related to the bulldog.

box′ẽr, *n.* one who packs or puts things in boxes.

Box′ẽr, *n.* [from *box* (a blow); Eng. trans. of Chin. *I-He-Chuan*, "righteous-uniting-band," misunderstood as "righteous-uniting-fists."] a member of a Chinese society that led an unsuccessful uprising (the *Boxer Rebellion*, 1900) against foreign powers and foreigners in China, as a result of which China was forced to make economic and territorial concessions.

box′fish, *n.* a trunkfish of the genus *Ostracion*.

box′fụl, *n.* the contents or capacity of a box.

box′hạul, *v.t.*; boxhauled (-hạld), *pt., pp.*; boxhauling, *ppr.* 1. in seamanship, to veer (a vessel) sharply around on her heel when it is not practicable to tack.
2. to haul (the yards) so as to meet slight shifts in wind direction.

box′hạul″ing, *n.* a method of changing (a vessel) from one tack to another.

box hol′ly, butcher's-broom, *Ruscus aculeatus*.

box′ing, *n.* 1. the act of enclosing in a box, or confining in any way; as, *boxing* for storage or shipment.
2. material suitable for making boxes or used for that purpose.
3. one of the cases on either side of a window frame into which inside shutters fold back.
4. in shipbuilding, a kind of notched or scarfed diagonal joint used for connecting the stem to the keel.
5. the process of mortising a piece of wood to receive a tenon.
6. [*pl.*] coarse flour from a reel, separated in the process of bolting.

box′ing, *n.* the act or practice of fighting with the fists, especially in special padded mittens.

Box′ing Dāy, in England, the first weekday after Christmas, a legal holiday: so called from the custom of giving Christmas boxes to employees, letter carriers, etc. on that day. The night succeeding is called *Boxing Night*.

box′ing glŏves, padded leather mittens worn for boxing.

box′ing match, a prize fight.

box ī′ron (-ũrn), a hollow smoothing-iron which may be heated by inserting hot coals, metal, etc.

box′keep″ẽr, *n.* an attendant in a theater who supervises and regulates admissions to boxes.

box kēy, a socket key or wrench for turning nuts.

box kīte, a kite with an oblong, box-shaped framework, covered with paper or fabric except at the ends and the middle.

box lock, a lock made to screw to a surface and not to be mortised in the wood.

box met′ăl, an alloy of copper and tin, or of zinc, lead, and antimony, for making journal bearings.

box of′fice, an office for the sale of admission tickets, as in a theater.

box oys′tẽr, a large oyster of fine quality.

box spring, a bedspring consisting of a boxlike, cloth-enclosed frame containing rows of coil springs.

box′thorn, *n.* any of a group of shrubs of the nightshade family, with small, inconspicuous flowers and red or orange-red berries, particularly *Lycium barbarum*.

box tree, same as *box* (a tree).

box tũr′tle, a land turtle or tortoise of the genera *Cistudo*: so named because it is able to shut itself up completely within its shell, as in a box, by means of hinged joints.

box′wood, *n.* 1. the wood of the box (*Buxus sempervirens*), a yellowish, fine, close-grained wood used in engraving, instrument-making, and in fine woodwork.
2. any of several species of hardwood trees that yield boxwood, particularly *Cornus florida* of southern United States and *Bignonia Leucoxylon* of the West Indies.

boy, *n.* [ME. *boy*, *boi*; East Friesic, *boi*, a boy, young man; related to D. *boef*, a boy, knave.]
1. a male child, from birth to the age of puberty; a lad; a youth.
2. any man; fellow: familiar term.
3. a young servant; a page; a bellboy.
4. in some countries, a male servant.
5. one who displays boyish traits or immaturity; as, he is a mere *boy* in judgment.
6. a son; as, he's my *boy*. [Colloq.]
boy bishop; formerly, a choirboy elected mock bishop by his comrades on St. Nicholas' day (December 6), and permitted to serve with some authority over the other boys of the choir until the 28th of the same month. The name is sometimes given to St. Nicholas himself, because of his reputed piety as a boy.

boy, *interj.* an exclamation of pleasure, surprise, etc.: often *oh boy!* [Slang.]

boy, *v.t.* 1. to treat as a boy, or as something belonging to or befitting a boy. [Obs.]
2. to act or represent in the manner of a boy: in allusion to the practice of boys acting women's parts on the stage. [Obs.]

bō·yär′, bō·yärd, *n.* [Russ. *boyarīn′*, pl. *boyare*.] a member of an old Russian aristocratic order or class, next in rank to the ruling princess, which was abolished by Peter the Great; also, formerly, in Romania, a privileged person holding a large landed estate.

boy·au′ (bwä-yō′), *n.*; *pl.* **boy·aux′** (bwä-yōz′), [Fr., a gut.] in fortification, a trench of zigzag form, which protects against an enfilading fire, leading from one parallel of attack to another, or to a magazine or other point: also called *zigzag*.

boy′çott, *n.* [from Captain *Boycott*, an Irish land agent who was put under the ban of ostracism by his neighbors during the Land League agitation in Ireland in 1880, the term being first applied by Charles Stewart Parnell in that year.]
1. originally, a concerted social ostracism or ban openly directed by a community against one of its own members as a mark of disapproval.
2. a joining together in refusal to deal with a landlord, businessman, organization, nation, etc., so as to punish, cause to do something, etc.; as, a *boycott* of a company by the labor unions.
3. a refusal to buy, sell, or use something; as, there was a *boycott* of the newspaper.

boy′çott, *v.t.*; boycotted, *pt., pp.*; boycotting, *ppr.* 1. to engage in a boycott against, so as to punish, cause to do something, etc.
2. to place under a ban, as any particular business, products, or commodities.

boy′çott·ẽr, *n.* one who boycotts.

boy′çott·ing, *n.* the act of taking part in a boycott.

boy′çott·iṣm, *n.* the principles and methods of a boycott.

boy′de·kin, *n.* a bodkin. [Obs.]

boy′ẽr, *n.* [Fr. *boyer*, from Fl. *boeyer*, a vessel used for laying buoys; *boey*, a buoy.] a Flemish sloop with a small tower at each end.

boy friend, a boy or man who is a friend, escort, or sweetheart of a girl or woman. [Colloq.]

boy′hood, *n.* 1. the state of being a boy, or the period during which one is a boy.
2. boys collectively.

boy′ish, *a.* belonging to a boy; childish; resembling a boy in manners, opinions, etc.

boy′ish·ly, *adv.* childishly; in a boyish manner.

boy′ish·ness, *n.* childishness; the manners or behavior of a boy.

boy sçout, 1. a member of the Boy Scouts.
2. a man regarded as being very naive or idealistic: disparaging term. [Slang.]

Boy Sçouts, a world-wide organization for the physical and moral development of boys: founded in England, 1908, by Sir Robert S. S. Baden-Powell.

boy′sen·ber″ry (*or* -zen-), *n.* [after Rudolph *Boysen*, American horticulturist who developed it.] a berry, dark red or almost black when ripe, resulting from crossing varieties of raspberry, loganberry, and blackberry.

bō·yū′nȧ, *n.* 1. a large South American snake, black and slender.
2. a harmless snake common in Ceylon.

bō′zȧ, *n.* [Ar. *buze*; Per. *buza*; Hind. *buza, boza*; Turk. *boza.*] an Egyptian and Turkish fermented beverage made from millet seed by adding various astringents; also, an intoxicant made from a mixture of darnel meal, hemp seed, and water: written also *bosa, boosa, booza, bozah, bouzah.*

B piç′tūre, a motion picture made quickly and inexpensively. [Slang.]

Br, in chemistry, bromine.

brä, *n.* [from *brassiere.*] a brassiere.

brab, brab tree, [Anglo-Ind.] the palmyra palm, *Borassus flabelliformis.*

Brȧ·bant′ine, *a.* pertaining to Brabant.

brab′ble, *n.* quarrelsome chatter; a wrangle.

brab′ble, *v.i.*; brabbled, *pt., pp.*; brabbling, *ppr.* [D. *brabbelen,* to talk confusedly, to stammer.] to quarrel noisily over trifles. [Dial.]

brab′ble·ment, *n.* a noisy dispute; a brabble. [Dial.]

brab′blẽr, *n.* a clamorous, quarrelsome, noisy fellow; a wrangler.

braç′çāte, *a.* [L. *bracatus,* from *bracæ,* breeches.] in ornithology, having feathers which conceal the feet and legs.

bràc′ciō (brȧt′shō), *n.*; *pl.* **bràc′ciȧ** (-shȧ), [It.] an Italian measure of length, varying from fifteen to thirty-nine inches.

brāce, *n.* [OFr. *brace,* an armful, a fathom; L. *brachia,* pl. of *brachium,* the arm.]
1. in architecture, a diagonal piece of timber with bevel joints, placed near and across the angles in the frame of a building in order to strengthen it.
2. that which holds anything tightly; a thing that clasps or connects; a fastener.
3. a pair; a couple; as, a *brace* of ducks.
4. in printing or writing, either of the signs { }, used for connecting or enclosing words, lines, or staves of music.
5. in nautical language, a rope reeved through a block at the end of a yard, by which the yard is swung from the deck.
6. a device for setting up or maintaining tension.
7. [*pl.*] suspenders. [Brit.]
8. an instrument with a crank motion for holding and rotating drilling bits, to bore or drill holes, drive screws, etc.
9. a defense for the arm, especially in archery; a piece of armor for the protection of the forearm.
10. a support for any weak part of the body or for correcting deformed bone structure.
11. in English mining, the mouth of a shaft.
12. a leather slide upon the cords of a drum, used for raising or lowering the tone by tightening or loosening the head.

brāce, *v.t.*; braced (brāst), *pt., pp.*; bracing, *ppr.* [ME. *bracen*; OFr. *bracer,* to brace, embrace; L. *brachia,* pl. of *brachium,* an arm.]
1. to make tight and firm with or as with bandages.
2. to tie or bind on firmly.
3. to strengthen or make firm by supporting the weight of, resisting the pressure of, etc.; to prop up.
4. to make ready for an impact, shock, etc.
5. to give vigor or energy to; stimulate; invigorate.
6. to ask a loan from. [Slang.]
7. in nautical language, to bring (the yards) to either side.
8. to furnish with braces; as, to *brace* a building.
to brace aback; to brace so as to lay the sails aback.
to brace about; to turn the yards round for the contrary tack.
to brace a yard; to trim a yard, or shift it horizontally, with a brace.
to brace by; to brace the yards in contrary directions on the different masts so as to stop the vessel's progress.
to brace in; to let out the lee braces and haul in the weather braces.
to brace up; (a) to lay the yards more fore-and-aft to cause the ship to sail closer to the wind; (b) to brace oneself; to call forth one's courage, resolution, etc. [Colloq.]

brāce and bit, a tool for boring, consisting of a removable drill (bit) in a rotating handle (brace).

brāced (brāst), **brāzed,** *a.* in heraldry, interlaced or linked together.

THREE CHEVRONS BRACED

brāce′let, *n.* [Fr. *bracelet,* dim. of OFr. *bracel, brachel,* an armlet, defense for the arm.]
1. an ornamental band, ring, or chain for the wrist or arm.
I decked thee also with ornaments, and I put *bracelets* upon thy hands, and a chain on thy neck.
—Ezek. xvi. 11.
2. a piece of defensive armor for the arm.
3. a handcuff. [Colloq.]

BRACELETS

brā′cẽr, *n.* 1. that which braces, binds, or makes firm; a band or bandage; also, a protection band worn about the wrist or arm in archery or fencing.
2. one who braces.
3. a drink taken as a stimulant. [Slang.]

brä·çe′rō, *n.*; *pl.* **brä·çe′rōs,** [Sp., from *brazo,* an arm, from L. *brachium,* an arm.] a Mexican farm laborer brought into the United States temporarily for migrant work in harvesting crops.

brach, *n.* [OFr. *brache*; O.H.G. *bracho,* a dog that hunts by the scent.] a bitch; a female hound. [Archaic.]

Brȧ·çhel′y·trȧ, *n.pl.* [L., from Gr. *brachys,* short, and *elytron,* a covering.] a group of beetles with short wing sheaths or elytra.

brȧ·çhel′y·trous, braçh·y·el′y·trous, *a.* distinguished by short wing sheaths or elytra.

brāch′et, *n.* [OFr., dim. of *brache,* a brach.] a brach.

braçh′i- (*or* brā′çhi-), brachio-.

braçh′i·ȧ, *n.,* pl. of *brachium.*

braçh′i·ăl, *a.* [L. *bracchialis,* from *bracchium,* the arm.]
1. of or like an arm.
2. of an armlike part.

braçh″i·al′ġi·ȧ, *n.* pain in the arm or arms.

Braçh·i·ā′tȧ, *n.pl.* [L. *bracchiatus,* from *bracchium,* the arm.] in zoology, a branch of the *Crinoidea* having arms.

braçh′i·āte, *a.* in botany, furnished with branches in pairs, arranged alternately, all nearly horizontal and each pair at right angles with the next pair on the stem or trunk, as the maple.

braçh′i·ō- (*or* brā′çhi-ō-), a combining form meaning *of an arm* or *the arms.*

braçh″i·ō·gan′oid, *n.* one of the *Brachioganoidei.*

Braçh″i·ō·gan·oid′ē·ī, *n.pl.* an order of fishes such as the gar, the sturgeon, and the bichir of the river Nile. Their scales are ganoid, that is, have a bony tissue overlaid by enamel.

braçh″i·ō·lā′ri·ȧ, *n.* [L., from *bracchiolum,* dim. of *bracchium,* an arm.] an early larval stage of certain starfishes, in which they swim by the vibration of ciliated bands.

braçh′i·ō·pod, *n.* any of the Brachiopoda.

Braçh·i·op′ō·dȧ, *n.pl.* [L., from Gr. *brachiōn,* the arm, and *poda,* feet.] a class of bivalve mollusks characterized by two armlike parts, one on each side of the mouth, which they can protrude and withdraw.

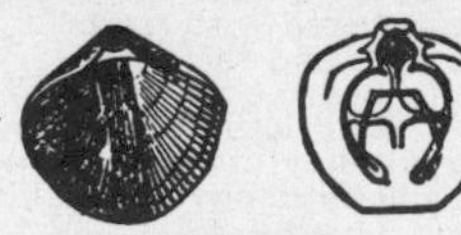

BRACHIOPOD
1. dorsal valve, with perforated summit of ventral valve; 2. interior of dorsal valve, showing the shelly loop which supports the arms

braçh″i·ot′ō·my, *n.* amputation of an arm.

brȧ·çhis″tō·cē·phal′iç, brȧ·çhis·tō·ceph′ȧ·lous, *a.* [Gr. *brachistos,* superl. of *brachys,* short, and *kephalē,* head.] having a wide head; having the breadth of the cranium greater than the length, according to the cephalic index.

brȧ·çhis′tō·çhrōne, *n.* [Gr. *brachistos,* superl. of *brachys,* short, and *chronos,* time.] in mathematics, the curve in which a body moves most swiftly.

braçh′i·um, *n.*; *pl.* **braçh′i·ȧ,** [L.]
1. the arm from shoulder to elbow.
2. in biology, a part that is armlike.
3. in zoology, a limb corresponding to a human arm.

Braçh′man, *n.* Brahman. [Obs.]

braçh′y-, a combining form meaning *short.*

braçh·y·çär′di·ȧ, *n.* [*brachy-,* and Gr. *kardia,* the heart.] in medicine, slow or retarded heart action: also called *bradycardia.*

braçh″y·çat·ȧ·leç′tiç, *a.* [L. *brachycatalecticum*; Gr. *brachykatalēkton*; *brachys,* short, and *katalēgein,* to leave off; *katalektikos,* deficient.] in prosody, too short by two syllables.

braçh″y·çat·ȧ·leç′tiç, *n.* in Greek and Latin prosody, a verse wanting two syllables to complete its length.

braçh″y·cē·phal′iç, braçh·y·ceph′ȧ·lous, *a.* [*brachy-,* and Gr. *kephalē,* head.] short-headed; having a skull very short in proportion to its width.

braçh·y·ceph′ȧ·ly, braçh·y·ceph′ȧ·lişm, *n.* the state or condition of being brachycephalic.

brȧ·çhyc′ẽr·ous, brȧ·çhyc′ẽr·ăl, *a.* [*brachy-,* and Gr. *keras,* a horn.] possessing short antennae.

braçh″y·daç·tyl′i·ȧ, braçh″y·daç′tyl·işm, *n.* abnormal shortness of fingers or toes.

braçh″y·daç·tyl′iç, *a.* having abnormally short fingers or toes.

braçh″·y·dī·ag′ō·năl, *a.* pertaining to the short diagonal or lateral axis.

braçh″·y·dī·ag′ō·năl, *n.* the shorter diagonal or lateral axis in a rhombic prism.

braçh′y·dōme, *n.* [*brachy-,* and Gr. *dōma,* a house, chamber.] a plane parallel to the brachydiagonal of a prism, as in crystals.

braçh′y·dont, *a.* [*brachy-,* and Gr. *odous, odontos,* a tooth.] having short-crowned molar teeth, as deer.

Braçh·y·el′y·trȧ, *n.pl.* same as *Brachelytra.*

braçh·y·el′y·trous, *a.* same as *brachelytrous.*

brȧ·çhyg′rȧ·phẽr, *n.* a shorthand writer.

brȧ·çhyg′rȧ·phy, *n.* [*brachy-,* and Gr. *-graphia,* from *graphein,* to write.] the art or practice of writing in shorthand; stenography.

brȧ·çhyl′ō·ġy, *n.* [Gr. *brachylogia,* from *brachylogos,* short in speech; *brachys,* short, and *logos,* from *legein,* to speak.]
1. in rhetoric, the expressing of anything in the most concise manner; brevity.
2. *pl.* **brȧ·çhyl′ō·ġieş,** an abridged expression.

braçh·y·pin′ȧ·çoid, *n.* in an orthorhombic crystal, a plane parallel to the vertical and the brachydiagonal axes.

brȧ·çhyp′ō·dous, *a.* [*brachy-,* and Gr. *pous, podos,* foot.]
1. in zoology, having short legs.
2. in botany, having short stalks.

braçh′y·prişm, *n.* [*brachy-,* and *prism.*] a prism lying between the brachypinacoid of an orthorhombic crystal and its unit prism.

Brȧ·çhyp′te·rȧ, *n.pl.* [L., from Gr. *brachys,* short, and *pteron,* a wing.] a group of beetles of the order *Coleoptera.*

Brȧ·çhyp′te·rī, *n.pl.* a group of short-winged diving birds, as auks, divers, or penguins.

brȧ·çhyp′tẽr·ous, *a.* [Gr. *brachypteros*; *brachys,* short, and *pteron,* a wing.] short-winged.

braçh·y·pyr′ȧ·mid, *n.* [*brachy-,* and Gr. *pyramis,* a pyramid.] an orthorhombic pyramid between the brachydomes and the zone of unit pyramids.

brāçh′yşm, *n.* a state or condition of dwarfishness, in which the limbs are extremely short.

brȧ·çhys′tō·çhrōne, *n.* same as *brachistochrone.*

brȧ·çhyt′y·pous, *a.* [*brachy-,* and Gr. *typos,* form.] in mineralogy, of a short form.

Braçh·y·ū′rȧ, Braçh·y·ōu′rȧ, *n.pl.* [L., from Gr. *brachys,* short, and *oura,* tail.] a class of decapodous *Crustacea,* as the ordinary crab, with short tail or abdomen folding beneath the cephalothorax.

braçh·y·ū′ran, *n.* one of the Brachyura.

braçh·y·ū′ran, *a.* designating or of any of the Brachyura.

braçh·y·ū′rous, braçh·y·ū′răl, *a.* pertaining to the *Brachyura.*

brā′cing, *n.* 1. the act of bracing, or state of being braced.
2. a device that braces.
3. braces; suspenders.

brā′cing, *a.* having the quality of giving strength or tone; invigorating.

brack, *n.* [Ice. *brak*; Dan. *bræk,* a break, fissure; AS. *brecan,* to break.] an opening caused by the parting of any solid body; a breach; a broken part; a flaw. [Obs.]

brack, *n.* [D. *brak*, salt.] brackish water. [Obs.]

brack′en, *n.* [ME. *braken*, from ON.; cf. Sw. *brakan*, Dan. *bregne*, fern.]
 1. any of a number of large, coarse ferns, as the brake.
 2. a growth of such ferns.

brack′et, *n.* [OFr. *braguette*; Sp. *bragueta*, a projecting molding, a codpiece, from *bragas*; L. *bracæ*, breeches.]
 1. in architecture, a projection from the face of a wall to support a statue or other weight, or appearing to do so: in the latter case, often of an ornamental nature.
 2. an angular stay to support shelves, scaffolds, and the like; also, a wall shelf or shelves held up by brackets.
 3. the cheek of a gun carriage, made of strong plank.
 4. in printing, either of the signs used to enclose explanatory or interpolated matter; thus, [ ].
 5. a list or group contained within brackets or braces.
 6. a classification: as, there are several income *brackets*.
 7. in military usage, the interval between the ranges of two rounds of artillery fire, one over and the other short of the target, used to find the correct range.
 8. a gas or electric wall fixture

ORNAMENTAL BRACKET

brack′et, *v.t.*; bracketed, *pt.*, *pp.*; bracketing, *ppr.* 1. to enclose within brackets; to place brackets upon or between.
 2. to provide or support with brackets.
 3. to group or classify.
 4. in military usage, to fire both beyond and short of (a target) so as to find the correct range.

brack′et·ing, *n.* 1. a series of brackets.
 2. the use of brackets.

brack′ish, *a.* 1. mixed with salt; briny.
 2. distasteful; nauseous.

brack′ish·ness, *n.* the state or quality of being brackish.

brack′y, *a.* brackish.

braç′ō·nid, *n.* one of the *Braconidæ*.

Brȧ·çon′i·dae, *n.pl.* [origin unknown.] a family of ichneumon flies of which there are many species. Some prey on caterpillars, others on plant lice.

braçt, braç′tē·ȧ, *n.* [L. *bractea*, a thin metal plate.] in botany, a modified leaf, growing at the base or on the stalk of a flower. It usually differs from other leaves in shape or color.

braç′tē·ăl, *a.* resembling a bract in nature and appearance.

brac′tē·āte, braçt′ed, *a.* having bracts.

braç·tē′i·form, *a.* resembling a bract in form.

braç′tē·ō·lāte, *a.* furnished with bractlets.

braç′tē·ōle, *n.* same as *bractlet*.

braçt′less, *a.* without bracts.

braçt′let, *n.* a small or secondary bract at the base of a flower.

brad, *n.* [ME. *brad*; Ice. *broddr*, a spike; Dan. *braad*, a prick, a sting; AS. *brord*, a point, spire of grass.] a small slender flat nail made with a small or off-center head.

brad′ąwl, a chisellike awl for making holes for brads, etc.

brad′ded, *a.* fastened or decorated with brads.

brȧ·doon′, *n.* same as *bridoon*.

brad′y-, a combining form meaning *slow*, *delayed*, *tardy*.

brad·y·är′thri·ȧ, *n.* [*brady-*, and Gr. *arthria*, a joint.] slowness in speaking.

brad·y·çär′di·ȧ, *n.* [*brady-*, and Gr. *kardia*, heart.] abnormally slow beating of the heart.

brad·y·pep′si·ȧ, brad′y·pep·sy, *n.* [*brady-*, and Gr. *pepsis*, from *peptein*, to digest.] slow digestion.

Brad·y·pod′i·dae, *n.pl.* [L., from Gr. *bradypoda*, neut. pl. of *bradypous*, slow of foot; *bradys*, slow, and *pous*, *podos*, foot.] a family of edentates, the sloths.

Brad′y·pus, *n.* the typical genus of the family *Bradypodidæ*.

brāe, *n.* [ME. *bra*, *bro*; ON. *bra*, eyelid, brow, river bank.] a hillside; a sloping bank or hill. [Scot.]

brag, *v.i.*; bragged, *pt.*, *pp.*; bragging, *ppr.* [ME. *braggen*; OFr. *braguer*, to flaunt, brag; *brague*, pleasure, fun; Ice. *braga*, to creak; *braka*, a noise.] to boast; to tell boastful stories: followed by *of* or *about*; as, to *brag of* a feat.
 Syn.—boast, swagger, vaunt.

brag, *v.t.* to boast of. [Obs.]

brag, *n.* 1. a boast or boasting.
 2. a person who boasts; braggart.
 3. a person or thing of which one boasts.
 4. an old game of cards, similar to poker.

brag, *a.* 1. courageous; lively. [Obs.]
 2. worthy of a boast. [Obs.]

brag, *adv.* proudly. [Obs.]

Brä′ge, *n.* Bragi.

brag·gȧ·dō′ci·ō (-shi-), *n.*; *pl.* **brag·gȧ·dō′ci·ōs,** [from a bragging character of that name in Spenser's "Faerie Queene"; *brag*, with an Italian ending.]
 1. vain boasting; ostentatious pretension.
 2. a boasting fellow; a braggart.

brag′gärd·işm, *n.* boastfulness; vain ostentation.

brag′gärt, *n.* [OFr. *bragard*, from *braguer*, to flaunt, brag; *brague*, amusement, pleasure.] a boaster; a vain fellow.

brag′gärt, *a.* boastful; vainly ostentatious.

brag′gärt·ly, *adv.* in a vain, ostentatious manner; boastfully.

brag′gẽr, *n.* one who brags; a boaster.

brag′get, *n.* [ME. *braket*, *bragot*; W. *bragawd*, *bragot*, *brag*, malt.] a liquor made by fermenting the wort of ale and mead. [Obs.]

brag′ging·ly, *adv.* boastingly.

Brä′gi, *n.* in Norse mythology, the god of poetry and eloquence, son of Odin and Frigga.

brag′less, *a.* without bragging or ostentation. [Rare.]

brag′ly, *adv.* finely; in such a way that it may be bragged of. [Obs.]

Bräh′mȧ, Brähm, *n.* [Hind. *brahm*, *brahma*; from Sans. *brahman* (neut.), devotion, divine science, impersonal divinity.] in Hindu theology, the absolute, self-existent, eternal essence or spirit of the universe, the source of all things, the ultimate of all things; the impersonal, ineffable sacredness, the object of the loftiest philosophic adoration.

Bräh′mȧ, *n.* [Hind. *Brah′mā*, from Sans. *brahman′* (masc.), worshiper, overseer of sacred things, personal divinity.] in Hindu theology, the creator, divine essence, or personified Brahm. Brahma was unknown to the older Hindu religion, but became the object of adoration by the Brahmans, and the first person in the trinity with Vishnu, redeemer, and Siva, destroyer. Brahma is represented by a red figure with four heads and four arms.

BRAHMA

Bräh′mȧ, bräh′mȧ, *n.* [contr. of *Brahmaputra*.] any of an Asiatic breed of large domestic fowl with feathered legs and small tail and wings.

Bräh′măn, *n.*; *pl.* **Bräh′mănş,** [Hind. *brāhman*; Sans. *brāhmana′*, from *brah′man*, prayer, devotion.] one belonging to the highest or sacerdotal caste among the Hindus. In the beginning the Brahmans were individuals or families distinguished for mental or spiritual superiority; but they gradually gathered to themselves powers over public worship, and became a strictly hereditary class, zealously holding in their hands the ministry of holy things. In later times, however, the relations of the castes have greatly changed and Brahmans are now found in many different walks of life, though retaining much of their former dignity and exclusiveness.

Bräh′măn, *a.* Brahmanic.

Bräh′măn·ess, *n.* a Brahmani.

Bräh′măn·ï, Bräh′măn·ee, *n.* any Brahman woman.

Bräh·man′iç, Bräh·man′iç·ăl, *a.* pertaining to the Brahmans or Brahmanism.

Bräh′măn·işm, *n.* 1. the religious doctrines and system of the Brahmans.
 2. the Hindu caste system.

Bräh′măn·ist, *n.* a follower of the Brahmans; an adherent to the religion of Brahma.

Bräh′min, *n.* 1. a Brahman.
 2. a cultured person from a long-established upper-class family, especially one regarded as haughty or conservative.

Bräh·min′iç, Bräh·min′iç·ăl, *a.* of or characteristic of a Brahmin or Brahmins.

Bräh′min·işm, *n.* 1. Brahmanism.
 2. the characteristic spirit, attitude, etc. of Brahmins.

Bräh′mō·işm, *n.* the combined religious tenets of the Brahmo Somaj.

Bräh′mō Sō·mäj′, [Hind. *brahma*, Brahma, prayer, and *samaj*, society, assembly.] a modern sect among the Hindus, having reformed and monotheistic views: established by Ram Mohun Roy. Also written *Brahma Samaj*.

brāid, *v.t.*; braided, *pt.*, *pp.*; braiding, *ppr.* [ME. *braiden*, *breyden*; AS. *bregdan*, *bredan*, to move to and fro, to weave, braid.]
 1. to interweave three or more strands of (hair, straw, etc.).
 2. to tie up (the hair) in a ribbon or band.
 3. to mingle by rubbing in some fluid or soft substance; as, to *braid* starch.
 4. to bind or decorate with braid.

brāid, *v.t.* to reproach. [Obs.]

brāid, *n.* 1. a string, cord, band, or plait, formed by weaving together different strands of any material.
 2. a woven tape or band of various materials, as cotton, wool, or silk, for binding or for trimming wearing apparel.
 3. a strip of braided hair.
 4. a ribbon or band for tying up the hair.

brāid, *a.*, *adv.*, and *n.* broad. [Scot.]

brāid, *v.i.* to start; to awake. [Obs.]

brāid, *a.* deceitful. [Obs.]

brāid′ing, *n.* 1. braids, collectively.
 2. trimming with or of braids.
 3. the act of plaiting or making braids.

brāid′işm, *n.* the theories of Dr. James *Braid*, of England, in regard to the phenomena of mesmerism, hypnotism, etc.; also, a method of producing hypnotism similar to that suggested by him.

brāil, *n.* [ME. *brayle*; OFr. *braiel*, *braiol*, a cincture, from *braie*; L. *bracæ*, breeches.]
 1. in falconry, a piece of soft leather to bind up a hawk's wing.
 2. in nautical language, one of the ropes passing through pulleys and employed to haul up the foot and leeches of a fore-and-aft sail, preparatory to furling.
 3. a staff at the end of a seine upon which to stretch the lines.

brāil, *v.t.* to haul in or to fasten by the brails: usually used with *up*; as, to *brail up* a sail.

Brāille, brāille, *n.* [after Louis *Braille* (1809–1852), Frenchman who invented the system.]
 1. a system of printing and writing for the blind, in which letters, numerals, and punctuation are made of raised dots distinguishable by the fingers.
 2. the characters used in this system.

Brāille, brāille, *v.t.*; Brailled *or* brailled, *pt.*, *pp.*; Brailling *or* brailling, *ppr.* to print or write in Braille characters.

brāin, *n.* [ME. *brain*, *brayne*; AS. *brægan*, *bregen*; D. *brein*; L.G. *brägen*, *bregen*, the brain.]

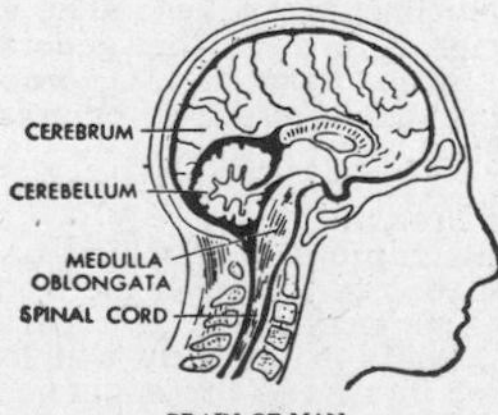

BRAIN OF MAN

 1. the mass of nerve tissue in the cranium of vertebrate animals: it is the main part of the nervous system, and is made up of gray matter (the outer cortex of nerve cells) and white matter (the inner mass of nerve fibers); the human brain comprises the cerebrum, the cerebellum, the pons, and the medulla oblongata.
 2. a corresponding organ in invertebrate animals.
 3. [*often pl.*] intelligence; mental ability.
 brain coral, *brainstone coral*; a large reef-

building coral, so called because it is so ridged as to resemble the surface of the brain.

to have on the brain; to think of continually; to be obsessed by.

brāin, *v.t.*; brained, *pt., pp.*; braining, *ppr.* 1. to dash out the brains of; to kill by beating out the brains; figuratively, to destroy; to put an end to.

2. to conceive; to understand. [Obs.]

brāin cell, any nerve cell of the brain.

brāin chīld, an idea, plan, etc. regarded as produced by a person's mental labor. [Colloq.]

brāin death, a condition in which all functions of the brain are determined to have irreversibly ceased: this condition satisfies some legal definitions of death.

brāin drāin, depletion of the intellectual or professional resources of a country, region, etc., especially through emigration.

brāin fag, weariness of the brain.

brāin fē'vēr, encephalitis.

brāin'ish, *a.* hotheaded; furious. [Rare.]

brāin'less, *a.* 1. having no brain.

2. silly; thoughtless; witless.

brāin'less·ness, *n.* the state of being without brains or wit.

brāin'pan, *n.* the part of the skull containing the brain; the cranium.

brāin'sand, *n.* particles of calcareous matter found either in the pineal gland or the pia mater folds of the brain.

brāin'sick, *a.* having or caused by a mental disorder.

brāin'sick·ly, *adv.* weakly; with a disordered understanding.

brāin'sick·ness, *n.* disorder of the understanding.

brāin stọrm, 1. a series of sudden, violent cerebral disturbances.

2. a sudden inspiration, idea, or plan: humorous term. [Colloq.]

brāin trust, a group of advisers with expert or special knowledge: term applied originally to the advisers surrounding President Franklin D. Roosevelt. [Slang.]

brāin'wăsh, *v.t.*; brainwashed, *pt., pp.*; brainwashing, *ppr.* to indoctrinate so intensively and thoroughly as to effect a radical transformation of beliefs and mental attitudes. [Colloq.]

brāin wāve, 1. a sudden inspiration; brain storm. [Colloq.]

2. in physiology, rhythmic electric impulses given off by nerve centers in the brain and spinal cord during sleep.

brāin'y, *a.*; *comp.* brainier; *superl.* brainiest, intelligent; mentally acute. [Colloq.]

brāird, *n.* [from AS. *brord*, blade (of grass) and *brerd*, edge.] the first shoots or sprouts of grass and grain. [Scot.]

brāird, *v.i.* to sprout; to germinate. [Scot.]

brāiṣe, brāize, *n.* 1. in zoology, an iridescent marine fish of Europe, *Pagrus vulgaris*: called also *becker*.

2. in Scotland, the roach.

brāiṣe, brāize, *n.* meat that is braised.

brāiṣe, brāize, *v.t.*; braised, *pt., pp.*; braising, *ppr.* [Fr. *braiser*, to cook over live coals, from *braise*, live coals, embers.] to cook (meat) by browning in fat and then simmering in a covered pan with only a little liquid.

brāiṣ'ēr, *n.* a covered vessel for braising.

brāke, archaic past tense of *break*.

brāke, *n.* a break (carriage).

brāke, *n.* [ME.] a large, coarse fern of the genus *Pteris*, particularly the large fern *Pteris aquilina*; a bracken; also, any of various species of fern of other genera.

brāke, *n.* [prob. from M.L.G. *brake*, stumps, broken branches.] a clump or area of brushwood, briars, etc.; a thicket.

brāke, *n.* [ME. *brake*; L.G. *brake*, an instrument for breaking flax.]

1. an instrument or machine to break flax or hemp; that is, to bruise the woody part so that the fiber may easily be separated.

2. the handle or lever by which a pump is worked, as in a hand fire engine.

3. a baker's kneading device.

4. a sharp bit, or snaffle. [Obs.]

5. a device for confining horses while the smith is shoeing them; also, an enclosure for cattle, horses, etc.

6. the fore part of a carriage or engine, which enables it to turn.

7. a large, heavy harrow for breaking clods after plowing; a drag.

8. an ancient engine of war for hurling missiles at the enemy; a ballista.

9. any device for slowing or stopping the motion of a vehicle or machine, as by causing a block or band to press against a moving part: many brakes are operated by compressed air, hydraulic pressure, or electromagnetic force.

10. a former instrument of torture.

11. a tool used by basket makers for stripping the bark from willow wands.

continuous brake; a series of car brakes controllable from a single point, as an atmospheric brake.

vacuum brake; a continuous brake operated by the exhaustion of air from chambers situated under the cars.

brāke'ăġe, *n.* 1. the action or application of a brake.

2. braking capacity.

brāke band, a band that serves as a braking force by creating friction when applied to the drum of a brake, as in an automobile.

brāke bär, the beam on the underside of a carriage or railway car to which the brake shoes are attached: called also *brake beam*.

brāke block, the solid backing of a brake shoe, or the part which holds the shoe.

brāke drum, the metal cylinder, as on the hub of an automobile wheel, to which the brake band is applied in braking.

brāke head (hed), the brake block and shoe combined in one piece or detachable.

brāke họrse'pow"ēr, the actual horsepower of an engine, measured by a brake attached to the driving shaft and recorded on a dynamometer.

brāke līn'ing, a material woven of cotton, asbestos, fine copper wire, etc., and fastened to the brake band to create the friction necessary for braking.

brāke'măn, *n.*; *pl.* **brāke'men,** 1. the man in a train crew on railroads, whose business is to take care of the brakes and couplings, to signal and flag trains, and generally to oversee the cars under the direction of the conductor.

2. the person in charge of a hoisting machine in a mine.

brāke shōe, the curved part or face of a brake, which presses against a wheel to retard or stop its rotation.

brāke sieve (siv), in mining, a coarse sieve for sifting ores, worked by a lever.

brākes'măn, *n.*; *pl.* **brākes'men,** a brakeman. [Brit.]

brāke valve, a valve used in the operation of power brakes.

brāke wheel, 1. a small hand wheel used in the operation of a brake.

2. a cam wheel governing the action of a trip hammer.

brāk'y, *a.* full of brakes; abounding with brambles or shrubs; rough; thorny.

Brä'mȧ, *n.* same as first *Brahma*.

bram'ble, *n.* [ME. *brembel*; AS. *bræmbel*, *bremble*, a bramble.]

1. any of a number of related shrubs of the genus *Rubus*, as the raspberry, dewberry, blackberry, etc.: they are usually prickly.

2. any rough, prickly shrub.

bram'ble·bụsh, *n.* the bramble, or a collection of brambles growing together.

bram'bled (-bld), *a.* overgrown with brambles.

bram'ble finch, the brambling.

bram'ble net, a hallier, or a net with which to catch birds.

bram'bling, *n.* a bright-colored finch, a species of *Fringilla*, found in Europe and Asia.

bram'bly, *a.* 1. full of or covered with brambles.

2. like brambles; prickly.

brāme, *n.* earnest desire; sharp passion; longing. [Obs.]

Brä'min·ess, Brä'min·ee, *n.* same as *Brahmanee*.

Bran, *n.* [perhaps from Ir. *bran*, raven.]

1. a mythical king of Britain.

2. in Celtic mythology, a god of the underworld.

bran, *n.* [ME. *bran, bren*; OFr. *bren*, bran.] the skin or husk of grains of wheat, rye, oats, etc., separated from the flour, as by sifting.

bran, *n.* the common crow. [Brit. Dial.]

brañ'çärd, *n.* [Fr.] a horse litter. [Obs.]

brȧnch, *v.i.*; branched, *pt., pp.*; branching, *ppr.* 1. to shoot or spread in branches; to ramify; as a plant, or as horns.

2. to separate into different parts or subdivisions, as a stream, or a subject of discourse.

to branch off; (a) to separate into branches; to fork; (b) to go off in another direction; to diverge.

to branch out; (a) to put forth branches; (b) to extend the scope of interests, activities, etc.

brȧnch, *v.t.* 1. to divide, as into branches; to make subordinate divisions in.

2. to adorn with needlework representing branches, flowers, foliage.

brȧnch, *n.* [ME. *branche*; OFr. *branche, brance*; LL. *branca*, the claw of a bird or beast.]

1. any woody extension growing from the trunk, main stem, or bough of a tree, bush, or shrub, especially an offshoot from a main limb; bough; limb; twig.

2. anything like a branch; ramification.

3. a tributary stream running out of or into a larger stream.

4. any stream smaller than a creek: a brook, rivulet, etc.

5. a separately located unit of a business; as, a suburban *branch* of a department store.

6. any arm or part extending from the main body of a thing; as, the *branch* of a candlestick or of an artery; the *branch* of a trunk railroad line; the *branch* of a stag's horn, etc.

7. any member or part of a body, or system; a section or subdivision; as, chemistry is a *branch* of learning.

8. a division of a family.

9. one of the two pieces of bent iron in a bridle, which bear the bit, the cross chains, and the curb.

10. in nautical usage, a warrant or commission given to a pilot.

11. in geometry, a portion of a curve that may extend outward for an unlimited distance.

12. in mining, a vein separating from the main lode.

Syn.—bifurcation, bough, member, limb, offspring, offshoot, spray, sprig, shoot, ramification, twig.

brȧnch chuck, an attachment to a lathe for holding tools or work, and carrying four branches or jaws.

brȧnched wọrk, the sculptured leaves and branches in monuments and friezes.

brȧnch'ēr, *n.* 1. one who or that which shoots forth branches.

2. a young hawk when it begins to leave the nest and take to the branches.

brañ'çhi·ae, *n.pl.*; *sing.* **brañ'çhi·ȧ,** [L., from Gr. *branchia*, gills.] in zoology, gills; organs for breathing the air contained in water, as those of crustaceans, mollusks, fishes, and amphibians.

brañ'çhi·ăl, *a.* 1. relating to the branchiae; or gills.

2. possessed of gills; as, the *branchial* pouch.

branchial aperture; an outlet for water behind the gill of a fish.

branchial arch; one of the bony arches supporting the gills, or branchiae.

branchial cleft; an aperture found behind the head in the embryo of a vertebrate: it corresponds to the branchial aperture of a fish.

Brañ·çhi·ā'tȧ, *n.pl.* [L., from Gr. *branchia*, gills.] in zoology, animals having gills.

brañ'çhi·āte, *a.* 1. provided with branchiae, or gills.

2. of or pertaining to the *Branchiata*.

brȧnch'i·ness, *n.* fullness of branches.

brȧnch'ing, *a.* dividing into branches; shooting out branches.

brañ'çhi·ō-, brañ'çhi-, a combining form from Gr. *branchia*, gills.

Brañ"çhi·ō·gas·trop'ō·dȧ, *n.pl.* [*branchio-*, and Gr. *gastēr*, *gastros*, stomach, and *pous*, *podos*, foot.] a division of gastropodous mollusks, so constructed that they can breathe the air contained in water. They are distinct in sex or hermaphroditic, have the gills exposed or enclosed, and are sessile or free-swimming. The whelks are well-known types.

brañ'çhi·ō·pod, *n.* a member of the *Branchiopoda*.

Brañ·çhi·op'ō·dȧ, *n.pl.* [*branchio-*, and Gr. *pous*, *podos*, foot.] an order of *Crustaceæ* having many pairs of flattened, leaflike limbs: called also *Phyllopoda*.

brañ·çhi·os'tē·găl, *a.* [*branchio-*, and Gr. *stegein*, to cover.] pertaining to the tissue which covers the branchiae of fishes.

brañ·çhi·os'tē·găl, *n.* one of the radiating spines, or rays, which support the branchiostege.

brañ·çhi·os'tēġe, *n.* the branchiostegal tissue or membrane.

brañ·çhi·os'tē·gous, *a.* same as *branchiostegal*.

Brañ·çhi·os'tō·mȧ, *n.* same as *Amphioxus*.

brañ'çhi·rēme, *n.* [*branchi-*, and L. *remus*, an oar.] any one of the legs of a branchiopod.

Brañ·çhi·ū'rȧ, *n.pl.* [*branchi-*, and Gr. *oura*, a tail.] a genus of *Entomostraca*, including fish parasites, such as carp lice, with mouths adapted for sucking, and having four pairs of legs.

brȧnch lēaf, a leaf growing on a branch.
brȧnch'less, *a.* without branches or shoots; without any valuable product; barren; naked.
brȧnch'let, *n.* a little branch; a twig: the subdivision of a branch.
brȧnch'y, *a.* full of branches; having widespreading branches.
brand, *n.* [AS. *brand, brond,* a burning sword, from *byrnan, beornan,* to burn; Ice. *brandr,* a firebrand, sword; D. *brand,* burning fuel.]
1. a burning stick of wood, or a piece partly burned.
2. a sword; a thunderbolt. [Rare.]
3. formerly, a mark made upon a criminal, by burning with a hot iron; hence, a stigma; a mark of disgrace.
4. a fungous disease in plants by which their leaves and tender bark are partially destroyed, as if burned: called also *burn.*
5. any fungus causing this disease.
6. a device to brand with; a branding iron.
7. a mark or label of identification, grade, etc. on merchandise; trade-mark; hence, the kind or make of a commodity; as, a *brand* of cigarettes.
8. a mark burned into anything by its owner, as a means of identification, as upon a cask or cattle.
brand, *v.t.*; branded, *pt., pp.*; branding, *ppr.*
1. to burn or impress a mark upon, with a hot iron; as, to *brand* a steer.
2. to fix a mark or character of infamy upon; to stigmatize as infamous; as, to *brand* a vice.
3. to mark with a stencil, as a box, cask, etc., in order to give a description of the contents, or the name of the manufacturer.
4. to impress indelibly, as with a brand; as, the date is *branded* on my memory.
Bran'den·bŭrg, *n.* [named after *Brandenburg,* a district and town of Prussia.] a sort of trimming for the front of a coat; an ornamental facing on the breasts of the coats worn by military men.
brand'ẽr, *n.* 1. one who or that brands; a branding iron.
2. a gridiron. [Scot.]
brand'ẽr, *v.t.*; brandered, *pt., pp.*; brandering, *ppr.* to broil on a gridiron; to grill. [Scot.]
brand'ẽr, *v.i.* to be broiled. [Scot.]
brand goose, a brant.
bran'died (-did), *a.* 1. mingled with brandy; made stronger by the addition of brandy; preserved in brandy; as, *brandied* cherries.
2. containing brandy.
brand'ing ī'ron (-ũrn) see *brand iron.*
brand ī'ron (-ũrn), 1. an iron plate containing the device, trade-mark, or letters to be branded on an object.
2. a trivet to set a pot on. [Now Dial.]
3. the arm of an andiron. [Now Dial.]
4. a gridiron. [Now Dial.]
bran'dish, *v.t.*; brandished, *pt., pp.*; brandishing, *ppr.* [ME. *braundishen, braundisen;* OFr. *brandir,* to brandish; *brand,* a sword.]
1. to move or wave, as a weapon; to raise and move in various directions; to shake or flourish: often with the meaning of threatening; as, to *brandish* a sword or a cane belligerently.
2. figuratively, to play with; to flourish; as, to *brandish* syllogisms.
bran'dish, *n.* a motion or flourish, as with a sword, whip, etc.
bran'dle, *v.t.* and *v.i.* to shake; to reel. [Obs.]
brand'ling, bran'lin, *n.* 1. a small red worm, allied to the earthworm, used as fish bait.
2. a salmon in its parr stage.
brand'-new', bran'-new', *a.* 1. recently made; not secondhand; quite new.
2. loosely, recently acquired.
bränd'schätz (bränt'shäts), *v.t.* [G. *brandschatzen; brand,* burning, and *schatzen,* from *schatz,* a tax, contribution.] to levy tribute upon in time of war by threat of burning. [Rare.]
bran'dy, *n.*; *pl.* **bran'dies,** [D. *brandewijn,* from *branden,* to burn, and *wijn,* wine.] an alcoholic liquor obtained by the distillation of wine, or of the refuse of the wine press, and containing an average of from 48 to 54 per cent of alcohol. In France, the finest brandy is called *cognac,* an inferior sort, distilled from dark red wines, lees, grape refuse, etc., being called *eau-de-vie.* The name *brandy* is sometimes given to spirit distilled from other liquors, or from cider, peaches, etc. Inferior brandies are distilled from grain and malt liquors and given the flavor and color of French brandy by artificial means.
brandy pawnee; brandy and water. [Anglo-Ind.]
bran'dy·wīne, *n.* brandy.
brañ'gle, *n.* [Scot., to shake.] a wrangle; a squabble; a noisy contest or dispute. [Rare.]
brañ'gle, *v.i.* to wrangle; to dispute contentiously; to squabble. [Rare.]
brañ'gle·ment, *n.* a quarrel. [Rare.]
brañ'glẽr, *n.* one who brangles. [Rare.]
brañk, *n.* buckwheat. [Brit. Dial.]
brañk, *v.i.* 1. to caper; to prance, like a horse. [Scot. and Dial.]
2. to toss the head, as a horse.
brañks, *n.pl.* [Norm. Fr. *branques;* OFr. *branches,* pl. of *branche;* LL. *branca,* a claw, paw.]
1. an iron curb for the tongue, held in place by a frame around the head: formerly used to punish noisy, quarrelsome women.
2. a kind of bridle, having wooden side pieces, joined to a halter to which a bit or muzzle is attached. [Scot.]
3. in medicine, mumps.

BRANKS

brañk'ŭr·sine, *n.* [Fr. *brankursine;* LL. *branca,* a claw, and L. *ursinus,* from *ursus,* a bear.] in botany, bear's breech, a plant of the genus *Acanthus.*
bran'lin, *n.* see *brandling.*
bran'-new', *a.* brand-new.
bran'ny, *a.* having the appearance of bran; consisting of bran.
brant, *n.*; *pl.* **brants** or **brant,** [perhaps from *brand,* because of the burnt color of the bird.] any of a number of related small, dark wild geese of Europe and North America.
brant, *a.* steep. [Brit. Dial.]
bran'tāil, *n.* a small bird with a bright red tail; the redstart of Europe.
brant fox, [for *brand fox,* so called from its dark color.] in zoology, a Swedish fox, *Vulpes alopex,* smaller than the common fox.
bran'ū·lăr, *a.* pertaining to the brain; cerebral. [Rare.]
Brȧ·sē'ni·ȧ, *n.* [origin unknown.] a genus of plants having only one species, the watershield.
brȧ·se̤'rō, *n.* [Sp.] a brazier.
brash, *a.* [orig., dial. and Scot.; prob. from *break,* and *dash, crash, rash,* etc.]
1. brittle or fragile, as some wood.
2. rash; too hasty.
3. insolent; impudent.
brash, *n.* 1. an eruption or rash.
2. pyrosis, a temporary stomach disorder with acid belching: usually *water brash.*
3. a sudden shower of rain.
brash, *n.* [Fr. *brèche,* from O.H.G. *brecha,* fragment, from *brehhan,* to break.]
1. broken pieces or fragments, as of rock or ice.
2. fragments or debris of hedge or tree prunings.
brash'y, *a.*; *comp.* brashier; *superl.* brashiest,
1. broken; crumbling; resembling brash; fragmentary.
2. showery. [Scot.]
brā'siẽr (-zhẽr), *n.* same as *brazier.*
brȧ·s̤il'ē·in, *n.* same as *brazilein.*
bras̤'il·in, *n.* same as *brazilin.*
brasque (brask), *n.* [Fr.] a paste of coke dust or charcoal and clay, used in lining crucibles, etc.
brȧss, *n.* [ME. *bras, bres;* AS. *bræs,* brass; Ice. *bras,* cement, solder; *brasa,* to harden by fire.]
1. a yellowish metal that is essentially an alloy of copper and zinc.
2. [*pl.*] ornaments, utensils, etc. made of brass.
3. [*pl.*] brass-wind musical instruments.
4. a plate of brass or a slab of stone inlaid with brass, engraved or stamped with a device; especially, one intended as a memorial to the dead.
5. hardness, durability, or obduracy.
6. impudence; forwardness; rudeness. [Colloq.]
7. money. [Slang.]
8. military officers of high rank. [Slang.]
9. in machinery, the lining or bushing of a bearing.
10. in mining, iron pyrites occurring in small, bright particles in coal.
brȧss, *a.* brazen; made of or containing brass; as, a *brass* bedstead.
brȧss, *v.t.* to coat with brass.
brȧs'sāġe, *n.* [OFr. *brassage, brassaige,* brassage, coinage, mintage.] a charge made by a government to defray the expense of coinage: the face value of a coin is the worth of the bullion plus brassage.
bras'särd, *n.* [Fr., from *bras,* arm.]
1. a badge or emblem, generally worn on the arm, denoting some particular duty, office, or distinction.
2. armor for the upper part of the arm, from the elbow to the shoulder: also applied to armor for the entire arm.
bras'särt, *n.* same as *brassard.*

BRASSARDS

brȧss band, a band in which the instruments played are mainly brasses.
brasse, *n.* [G. *brassen,* the bream.]
1. a pale, spotted European pike perch.
2. the European bass.
bras'set, *n.* same as *brassard.*
brȧss'ey, *n.* same as *brassie.*
brȧss foil, Dutch metal; foil formed by beating plates of brass into very thin sheets.
brȧss hat, 1. a staff officer in the British army; so called from the gold braid on his cap. [Slang.]
2. any military officer of high rank. [Slang.]
Bras'si·çȧ, *n.* [L., cabbage.] in botany, a genus of plants including the cabbage, *Brassica oleracea,* the cauliflower, turnip, broccoli, kohlrabi, kale, Brussels sprouts, etc.
bras·si·çā'ceous, *a.* [L. *brassica,* cabbage.] pertaining to the plants of the cabbage family.
brȧss'ie, *n.* [from *brass;* so called because orig. made with a brass plate on the bottom of the head.] a golf club with a wooden head and a loft between that of a driver and a spoon, used for long fairway play: also spelled *brassy, brassey.*
bras·sière', bras·sière, (brȧ-zēr' *or* brȧs-i-ēr'), *n.* [Fr., from *bras,* an arm.] an undergarment worn by women to support the breasts or give a desired contour to the bust.
brȧss'i·ly, *adv.* in a brassy manner.
brȧss'i·ness, *n.* 1. the quality or condition of being brassy.
2. impudence. [Colloq.]
brȧss knuç'kles (nuk'lz), linked metal rings or a metal bar with holes for the fingers, worn for rough fighting.
brȧss tacks, basic facts; really important matters. [Colloq.]
to get (or *to come*) *down to brass tacks;* to discuss basic facts or really important matters. [Colloq.]
brȧss'wāre, *n.* articles made of brass.
brȧss'-wind, *a.* of the brass winds.
brȧss winds̤, musical instruments made of coiled metal tubes, through which tones are made by blowing into a cup-shaped mouth piece.
brȧss'y, *a.* 1. pertaining to brass; containing brass; hard as brass; having the color of brass.
2. impudent; impudently bold.
3. cheap and showy.
4. loud; blaring.
brȧss'y, *n.*; *pl.* **brȧss'ies̤,** same as *brassie.*
brat, *n.* [ME. *brat,* a coarse cloak; Gael. *brat,* a cloak, mantle, rag.] a child, especially an impudent, unruly child; scornful or playful term.
brat, *n.* an apron of coarse fabric; a kind of bib. [Dial.]
brat, *n.* in mining, a thin bed of coal containing pyrites or carbonate of lime.
brät'sche, *n.* [G.] a viola.
brat'tach, *n.* a banner or standard. [Scot.]
brat'tice, *n.* [ME. *bretasce,* a parapet; OFr. *breteche, bretesche,* a wooden tower; O.H.G. *bret,* a board.]
1. in mining, (a) planking used as a roof or wall support; (b) any partition in a level or shaft, especially one designed to control ventilation; (c) a cloth impregnated with creosote for ventilation.
2. an improvised wooden parapet put up during a siege. [Obs.]
brat'tice, *v.t.*; bratticed, *pt., pp.*; bratticing, *ppr.* to provide with a brattice.
brat'ti·cing, brat'tish·ing, *n.* [ME. *bretasynge,* an outwork, from *bretasce,* an outwork, brattice.]
1. a fence of boards in a mine or around dangerous machinery; brattice work.
2. in architecture, any open or carved work, as on a shrine or parapet.
brat'tle, *v.i.*; brattled, *pt., pp.*; brattling, *ppr.* [echoic.]
1. to make a rattling or clattering noise. [Scot.]

2. to run with a clatter; to scamper noisily. [Scot.]

brat'tle, *n.* any clattering or rattling noise. [Scot.]

Brät'wŭrst (-vūrsht), *n.* [G.] a small pork sausage for frying.

brąu'nȧ, *n.* [Braz.] a leguminous tree, *Melanoxylon brauna,* found in Brazil: it furnishes a valuable reddish-brown, hard, fine-grained wood.

brąun'īte, *n.* [named after Herr *Braun* of Gotha.] in mineralogy, a native oxide of manganese, having a small percentage of silica, and varying from brownish-black to steel-gray in color.

brȧ·vä'dō, *n.*; *pl.* **brȧ·vä'dōes, brȧ·vä'dōs,** [Sp.] pretended courage or defiant confidence when there is really little or none.

brāve, *a.* [Fr. *brave*; Sp., Port., It. *bravo,* brave, fine; MD. *brave,* fierce, gallant; Dan. *brav,* brave, worthy.]

1. courageous; bold; daring; intrepid; fearless of danger; as, a *brave* warrior.

2. showing to good effect; having a fine appearance.

3. excellent; admirable. [Archaic.]

Syn.—valiant, gallant, valorous, fearless, undaunted, bold, heroic, intrepid, daring.

brāve, *n.* 1. a bully. [Archaic.]

Hot *braves* like thee may fight.—Dryden.

2. a boast; a challenge; a defiance. [Obs.]

3. a North American Indian warrior: a term first applied by the French.

4. any brave man; one who is daring; also, brave people collectively; as, the home of the *brave.*

brāve, *v.t.*; braved, *pt., pp.*; braving, *ppr.* [Fr. *braver,* to brave, defy, from *brave,* brave.]

1. to defy; to challenge; to set at defiance; to dare.

2. to meet or undergo with courage.

3. to make brave. [Obs.]

4. to make showy; to adorn. [Obs.]

Syn.—dare, defy, encounter, challenge.

brāve'ly, *adv.* 1. courageously; gallantly; heroically; splendidly; in a brave manner.

2. finely; gaudily.

3. thrivingly; in a prosperous manner. [Colloq.]

brāve'ness, *n.* the quality of being brave.

brāv'ẽr·y, *n.* [Fr. *braverie,* gallantry, splendor, from *brave,* brave.]

1. courage; valor; fearlessness of danger.

2. splendor; magnificence; showy appearance; ostentation; fine dress.

The *bravery* of their tinkling ornaments. —Isa. iii. 18.

3. bravado; boast. [Obs.]

4. a showy person. [Obs.]

Syn.—courage, intrepidity, heroism, audacity, valor, fearlessness, hardihood, dauntlessness.—*Courage* is that firmness of spirit which meets danger without fear; *bravery* defies or braves it, and shows itself in outward acts; *audacity* is *bravery* with a quality of rashness.

brāv'ing, *n.* defiance; challenge or bravado.

brāv'ing·ly, *adv.* in an undaunted or defiant manner.

brä·vis'si·mō, *interj.* [It., superl. of *bravo.*] very well done! splendid!

brä'vō, *n.*; *pl.* **brä'vōes, brä'vōs;** It. **brä'vi,** [It. and Sp.] a hired killer; assassin; desperado.

brä'vō, *interj.* [It.] well done! very good! excellent!: an exclamation of approval or applause.

brä'vō, *n.*; *pl.* **brä'vōs,** a shout of "bravo!"

brȧ·vō'rȧ, *n.* [It., bravery, spirit.]

1. a bold attempt or display of daring; dash.

2. in music, (a) a brilliant passage or piece that displays the performer's skill and technique; (b) brilliant technique in performance.

brąw, *a.* [from *brane, a.*]

1. well-groomed; smart; brave. [Scot.]

2. fine; pleasant; as, a *braw* day. [Scot.]

brąwl, *v.i.*; brawled, *pt., pp.*; brawling, *ppr.* [ME. *brallen,* to cry out, vociferate; *braulen,* to quarrel; D. *brallen,* to boast; Dan. *bralle,* to jabber, chatter.]

1. to quarrel or speak noisily; to create a disturbance by quarreling or fighting.

2. to roar; to move or flow noisily over rapids, falls, etc.: said of water.

brąwl, *n.* 1. a noisy quarrel; uproar; loud or angry contention.

2. a noisy party. [Slang.]

brąwl, *n.* [Fr. *branle,* from *branler,* to sway, toss about, swing.]

1. an old French country dance.

2. the music for this.

brąwl'ẽr, *n.* a noisy fellow; a wrangler.

brąwl'ing, *n.* the act of quarreling.

brąwl'ing, *a.* quarreling; quarrelsome.

brąwl'ing·ly, *adv.* in a quarrelsome manner.

brąwn, *n.* [ME. *braun, brawn,* muscle, boar's flesh; OFr. *braon,* a piece of flesh; O.H.G. *brato,* a piece of flesh for roasting.]

1. the fleshy, muscular part of the body, especially of the arm or leg; hence, bulk; muscular strength.

2. the flesh of a boar or hog, especially prepared by being pressed, boiled, spiced, and pickled.

3. headcheese.

4. a boar. [Dial.]

brąwned, *a.* brawny; strong.

brąwn'ẽr, *n.* a boar killed for use as food.

brąwn'i·ness, *n.* the quality of being brawny; strength; hardiness.

brąwn'y, *a.*; *comp.* brawnier; *superl.* brawniest, muscular; strong.

Syn.—athletic, bulky, muscular, powerful, robust, sinewy, stalwart, strong, vigorous.

brax'y, *n.*; *pl.* **brax'ies,** [prob. from *break, v.*; compare AS. *broc,* disease, misery; G. *brechen,* vomiting, and *brechen,* to break].

1. any of various intestinal disorders of sheep, especially one resembling anthrax.

2. a sheep affected with this disease, or mutton from such a sheep.

brax'y, *a.* having braxy.

brāy, *v.t.*; brayed, *pt., pp.*; braying, *ppr.* [ME. *brayen*; OFr. *breier,* to pound, bray; M.H.G. *brechen,* to break.]

1. to pound, beat, or grind into a powder, as in a mortar.

2. to spread thin, as ink.

brāy, *v.i.* [ME. *brayen*; OFr. *braire*; LL. *bragire, bragare,* to cry, squall.]

1. to make a loud, harsh sound, as an ass.

2. to make a harsh, disagreeable, grating sound.

brāy, *v.t.* to utter loudly and harshly; as, to *bray* discords.

brāy, *n.* 1. the loud, harsh cry of an ass.

2. a harsh, grating sound like this.

brāy, *n.* see *brae.*

brāy'ẽr, *n.* one who brays like an ass.

brāy'ẽr, *n.* in printing, a hand roller to spread ink.

brāy'ing, *n.* 1. the noise of an ass.

2. roar; noise; clamor.

brä'zä (-thä *or* -sä), *n.* [Sp. from *brazo,* an arm.] a Spanish measure of length equal to 5.48 feet in Spain and 5.68 feet in Argentina.

brāze, *v.t.* [AS. *bræsian,* from *bræs,* brass.]

1. to make, cover, or ornament with brass or a brasslike substance.

2. to make hard like brass.

brāze, *v.t.*; brazed, *pt., pp.*; brazing, *ppr.* [ME. *brasen*; OFr. *braser,* to solder; Ice. *brasa,* to harden by fire.] to solder with a metal having a high melting point, especially with an alloy of copper and zinc.

brāzed, *a.* see *braced.*

brā'zen, *a.* [ME. *brasen*; AS. *bræsen,* from *bræs,* brass.]

1. of brass; as, a *brazen* helmet.

2. like brass in color or other qualities.

3. impudent; shameless; having no shame; as, he put on a *brazen* face.

4. having the ringing sound of brass; harsh and piercing.

brazen age; in mythology, the age which succeeded the silver age, when men had degenerated from primitive purity.

brā'zen, *v.t.*; brazened, *pt., pp.*; brazening, *ppr.* to make impudent or bold and shameless.

to brazen out (or *through*); to behave as if unashamed of.

brā'zen-browed, *a.* shamelessly bold.

brā'zen·fāce, *n.* an impudent person.

brā'zen·fāced (-fāst), *a.* having, or uttered with, a brazen expression; impudent; shameless.

brā'zen·ly, *adv.* in a bold, impudent manner.

brā'zen·ness, *n.* the quality of being brazen.

brā'ziẽr, *n.* a metal container to hold burning coals or charcoal.

brā'ziẽr, *n.* a person who does brasswork.

brȧ·zil', *n.* [ME. *brasil, brasyle*; OFr. *bresil*; Sp. and Port. *brasil*; LL. *brasilium, bresillum.*]

1. same as *brazilwood.*

2. a red dye obtained from brazilwood.

3. originally, the wood of *Cæsalpinia Sappan*; sapanwood.

brȧ·zil'ē·in, *n.* [from *brazil,* and *-in.*] a bright-red compound, $C_{16}H_{12}O_5$, obtained by oxidizing brazilin and used as a dye: also spelled *brasilein.*

braz·i·let'tō, *n.* [Port. *brazilete*; It. *brasiletto,* dim. of *brasil,* brazilwood.] a kind of red dyewood, inferior to brazilwood, found in Jamaica: it is obtained from two trees, *Cæsalpinia Brasiliensis* and *Cæsalpinia crista.*

Brȧ·zil'iăn (-yăn), *n.* pertaining to Brazil, its people, or culture.

Brȧ·zil'iăn, *n.* a native or inhabitant of Brazil.

braz'i·lin, *n.* a bright-yellow crystalline substance extracted from brazilwood: also written *brasilin, breziline.*

Brȧ·zil' nut, the seed, or nut, of *Bertholletia excelsa,* the Brazil-nut tree, of the family *Myrtaceæ.* The fruit is nearly round and about six inches in diameter, having a hard shell about one-half inch thick. It contains the edible, oily, three-sided seeds.

Brȧ·zil'-nut tree, a very tall tree of tropical America, bearing round, hard-shelled fruit with edible seeds.

brȧ·zil'wood, *n.* the reddish wood of certain trees of South America and the East and West Indies, yielding a red dye.

brēach, *n.* [ME. *breke, breche*; AS. *brice, bryce, gebrece,* from *brecan,* to break.]

1. the act of breaking, or state of being broken; a rupture; a break; a gap; as, a *breach* in stonework or in a fortification.

2. a failure to observe the terms, as of a law, promise, etc.

Every *breach* of the public engagements is hurtful to public credit. —Hamilton.

3. a break or interruption in friendly relations.

4. an inrush or surging of waters, as over a pier, ship, etc.; also, the waves themselves.

5. a contusion or wound.

6. in medicine, a hernia.

breach of arrest; the offense committed by a military officer under technical arrest, of leaving without permission the limits within which he has been ordered to remain.

breach of faith; a failure to keep faith; the breaking of a promise.

breach of privilege; an act in violation of the rules, order, privileges, or dignity of a legislative body.

breach of promise; failure to fulfill one's word; especially, failure to keep a promise to marry.

breach of the peace; a violation of the public peace, as by a riot, affray, or any tumult which is contrary to law, and destructive to the public tranquillity; disorderly conduct.

breach of trust; violation by fraud or omission of any duty or confidence lawfully imposed on a trustee, executor, or other person in a position of trust.

clean breach; the rolling of waves over a vessel which sweeps away everything movable on deck.

clear breach; the rolling of waves over a vessel without breaking.

Syn.—break, chasm, gap, opening, rent.—A *breach* and a *gap* are the consequence of a violent removal, which destroys the connection; a *break* and a *chasm* may arise from the absence of that which would form a connection. A *breach* and a *chasm* always imply a larger opening than a *break* or *gap.*

brēach, *v.t.*; breached, *pt., pp.*; breaching, *ppr.* to make a breach, gap, or opening in; as, to *breach* the gate of the citadel.

brēach, *v.i.* to break the surface of water by leaping out: said of a whale or porpoise.

brēach'y, *a.* inclined to break out of fenced-in fields; as, *breachy* cattle.

bread (bred), *n.* [ME. *breed, bred*; AS. *bread*; D. *brood*; Ice. *braudh,* bread; from the root of *breowan,* to brew.]

1. a food made by moistening, kneading, and raising or fermenting the flour or meal of some species of grain, and baking it in an oven, usually in the form of loaves, or as biscuits, rolls, etc.

2. food in general, regarded as a source of life; as, give us this day our daily *bread.*

3. support of life in general; maintenance; a livelihood; a living.

bread and butter; figuratively, means of livelihood; as, he earns his *bread and butter.*

to break bread; (a) to partake of a meal; (b) to partake of the sacrament of the Holy Eucharist; to attend a communion service.

to cast one's bread upon the waters; to be generous or do good deeds without expecting something in return.

to know on which side one's bread is buttered; to be aware and careful of one's own economic interests.

to take the bread out of (a person's) mouth; to deprive (a person) of his means of living.

bread, *v.t.* in cookery, to cover (meat, fish, etc.) with bread crumbs before cooking; as, to *bread* veal.

bread'-and-but'tẽr, *a.* 1. youthful; immature.
2. commonplace; everyday.
3. prompted by necessity.
4. for the purpose of thanking, as a letter sent to one's host after a visit.

bread'bȧs"ket, *n.* 1. a region that supplies much grain.
2. the stomach. [Slang.]
3. an aerial bomb which combines explosives and incendiaries. [Slang.]

bread'bōard, *n.* 1. a board on which bread is kneaded, shaped, or rolled.
2. a board on which bread is sliced.

bread box, a box in which bread, pastry, etc. is put to help keep it fresh.

bread çorn, any grain or cereal of which bread in some form is made, as wheat, rye, etc.

bread çrumb (krum), 1. bread crumbled for use in cookery.
2. the soft part of bread within the crust.

bread'en, *a.* made of bread. [Rare.]

bread'fruit, *n.* 1. the edible fruit of a tree, *Artocarpus altilis,* found especially on South Pacific islands. The fruit is a large, round, starchy mass and when baked is thought to resemble fresh bread, whence its name.
2. the tree that bears it: called also *bread tree.*

BREADFRUIT
(*Artocarpus altilis*)

bread knīfe (nīf), a knife for cutting bread.

bread'less, *a.* without bread; destitute of food.

bread line, a line of people waiting to be given food as government relief or private charity.

bread mōld, a kind of fungus that grows on decaying bread: also called *black mold.*

bread'nut, *n.* the nut of a moraceous tree, *Brosimum alicastrum,* found in the West Indies and Mexico: it is roasted, ground into a flour, and made into bread.

bread'root, *n.* the starchy, edible root of a leguminous plant, *Psoralea esculenta,* found on the western plains near the Rocky Mountains: called also *prairie turnip.*

bread'stuff, *n.* 1. any grain, flour, or meal of which bread is made.
2. bread.

breadth (bredth), *n.* [ME. *bredthe, bredethe, brede;* AS. *brædu,* breadth, from *brad,* broad.]
1. the measure or extent of any surface or thing from side to side; width.
2. spaciousness; magnitude; scope; extent.
3. liberality of thought or sentiment; fredom from narrowness in opinion; as, a man of intellectual *breadth.*
4. a piece of a given and regular width; as, two *breadths* of silk.

breadth'less, *a.* having no breadth.

breadth'wāys, *adv.* in the direction of the breadth.

breadth'wīse, *adv.* breadthways.

bread'win"nẽr, *n.* that member of a family by whose earnings it is supported; a provider or producer.

break, *v.t.*; broke (brake, *archaic*), *pt.*; broken (broke, *archaic*), *pp.*; breaking, *ppr.* [ME. *breken;* AS. *brecan;* D. *breken;* L.G. *breken, bræken;* G. *brechen;* Goth. *brikan,* to break.]
1. to cause to part or divide by force, as a solid substance; to separate into pieces by shattering; to crack; to smash; to burst; as, to *break* a dish; to *break* a thread or a cable.
2. to cut open the surface of (soil, the skin, etc.).
3. to bring to an end by force; to overwhelm; as, the strike was *broken.*
4. to make unusable or inoperative by cracking or disrupting.
5. to tame; to train to obedience; to make tractable; as, to *break* a horse.
6. to reduce to poverty or bankruptcy.
7. to lower in rank or grade; to demote; as, to *break* an officer.
8. to surpass (a record).
9. to fail to follow the terms of; to violate; as, he *broke* his agreement.
10. to escape from suddenly; as, they cannot *break* prison.
11. to lessen the force of by interrupting; as, to *break* a fall.
12. to lay open, as a purpose; to propound, as something new; to make a disclosure of, as information or opinions; as, to *break* the news.
13. to destroy the order or completeness of; to make irregular; as, the troops *broke* formation.
14. to cut through or penetrate (silence, darkness, etc.)
15. to begin; to open; to start.
16. to exchange (coins or currency) for smaller denominations; as, to *break* a ten-dollar bill.
17. to interrupt (a journey, electric circuit, etc.).

to break a lance; to engage in a tilt; figuratively, to engage in a contest of any kind.

to break down; (a) to crush or overcome (opposition, etc.); (b) to separate into parts; to analyze.

to break from; to disengage from; to depart abruptly or with vehemence.

to break in; (a) to force in; as, *to break in* a window or door; (b) to interrupt; (c) to train; to tame; as, *to break in* a horse.

to break in on (or *upon*); (a) to approach violently or unexpectedly; to enter abruptly; (b) to interrupt.

to break into; (a) to enter by force; as, *to break into* a house; (b) to interrupt; (c) to begin suddenly to utter, perform, etc.

to break of; to make give up (a habit).

to break off; (a) to put a sudden stop to; to discontinue; (b) to stop being friendly or intimate.

to break the back; (a) to strain or dislocate the vertebrae with too heavy a burden; to disable totally; (b) to get through the worst part of; as, *to break the back* of an undertaking.

to break up; (a) to separate; to disperse; (b) to take apart; to dismantle and scrap; (c) to dissolve or put an end to; as, *to break up* housekeeping; (d) [Colloq.] to distress; to upset; to grieve.

to break with; (a) to stop being friendly or intimate with; (b) to stop conforming to.

Syn.—batter, burst, demolish, crack, rend, split, fracture, rupture, shatter, shiver, destroy, tame, curb, tear asunder, sever, smash, subdue, violate, infringe.

break, *v.i.* 1. to part; to separate; to divide into separate pieces; to burst; as, a rope *breaks.*
2. to scatter; disperse; as, let's *break* and run.
3. to become unusable or inoperative; break down; weaken.
4. to come into being, evidence, or general knowledge; to appear; to dawn; as, the day begins to *break.*
5. to change suddenly; as, his voice *broke.*
6. to move away suddenly; burst forth; escape.
7. to begin suddenly to utter, perform, etc. (with *into, forth in,* or *out in*).
8. to become poverty-stricken or bankrupt.
9. to terminate friendship; to quarrel (often with *up* or *with*).

Be not afraid to *break* with traitors.
—B. Jonson.

10. to appear suddenly above water, as a periscope, fish, etc.
11. to fall apart slowly; to disintegrate.
12. to change into a diphthong: said of vowels.
13. to curve near the plate: said of a pitched baseball.
14. to happen in a certain way; as, things were *breaking* badly. [Colloq.]

to break away; (a) to disengage oneself abruptly; to escape; (b) to start too soon, as in a race.

to break down; (a) to go out of working order; (b) to give way to tears or emotion; (c) to have a physical or nervous collapse.

to break in; to enter by force; to enter unexpectedly; to intrude.

to break off; (a) to become parted or divided; (b) to desist suddenly.

to break out; (a) to begin suddenly; to arise or spring up; as, a fire or a fever *breaks out;* (b) to appear in eruptions, as pustules; to have pustules or an efflorescence on the skin; as, a child *breaks out* with measles; (c) to escape; (d) to loosen the ship's anchor from the bottom before weighing.

to break up; to dissolve and separate; to disperse; as, a company *breaks up,* a fog *breaks up.*

break, *n.* 1. a breaking; breach; fracture.
2. a breaking in, out, or forth.
3. the result of a breaking; broken place; separation; crack.
4. a beginning to appear; as, the *break* of day.
5. an interrupting or discontinuing of regularity.
6. the result of this; a pause; an interruption; as, a *break* in the conversation.
7. [*pl.*] a series of dots used as punctuation; suspension points; e.g., came the dawn . . . .
8. a sudden change or deviation.
9. a sudden decline, as in price.
10. an imperfection; flaw.
11. an unbroken series or sequence, as of points in billiards.
12. in music, (a) the point where one register changes to another; (b) this change; (c) a transitional or ornamental phrase played during the pause between regular divisions of a jazz melody.
13. in telegraphy, (a) an instrument for changing the direction of an electrical current; a commutator; (b) an opening in the circuit interrupting the current; as, a *break* in the circuit.
14. an unfortunate remark or ill-advised action; as, he made a bad *break.* [Colloq.]
15. a chance piece of luck, especially good luck. [Slang.]

brea̤k, *n.* a large, four-wheeled carriage for six or more passengers: also spelled *brake.*

brea̤k'ȧ·ble, *a.* capable of being broken.

brea̤k'ȧ·ble, *n.* a thing easily broken; fragile article.

brea̤k'ăge, *n.* 1. the act of breaking; also, that which is broken.
2. loss or damage due to breaking.
3. an allowance for things broken in transportation or use.

brea̤k'ax, brea̤k'axe, *n.* any one of several kinds of extremely hard wood found in Jamaica and Mexico, especially *Sloanea jamaicensis.*

brea̤k'bōne fē'vẽr, same as *dengue.*

brea̤k'down, *n.* 1. the act or result of breaking down or failing to work, as machinery.
2. a failure of health; physical collapse; as, he had a nervous *breakdown.*
3. decomposition.
4. an analysis.
5. a spirited, shuffling dance originated by American Negroes.

brea̤k'down, *a.* in electricity, causing the failure of an insulator: said of an excessive voltage.

brea̤k'ẽr, *n.* 1. one who or that which breaks.
2. a machine for crushing rocks or coal.
3. a wave which breaks into foam.
4. a circuit breaker.

brea̤k'ẽr, *n.* [Sp. *barrica.*] a small water cask suitable for use in small boats.

brea̤k"-ē'ven, *a.* designating that point, as in a commercial venture, at which profits and losses are equal.

break'fȧst (brek'), *n.* [ME. *brekefast; breke;* AS. *brecan,* to break; *fast,* from *fasten,* to observe, fast.]
1. the first meal in the day, or the food eaten at the first meal.
2. any meal with which a fast is broken.

break'fȧst, *v.t.* breakfasted, *pt., pp.*; breakfasting, *ppr.* to furnish with the first meal in the morning; to give breakfast to.

break'fȧst, *v.i.* to eat breakfast.

break'fȧst food, any prepared cereal for eating at breakfast.

brea̤k'-frŏnt, *a.* having a break front.

brea̤k'frŏnt, *n.* a large cabinet with a break front.

brea̤k frŏnt, a front, as of a cabinet, with the continuity of the main surface broken.

brea̤k'-in, *n.* the act of forcibly entering a building, apartment, etc., especially in order to rob.

brea̤k'-in, *a.* designating or of the period of first use of something new, intended to work the stiffness out.

brea̤k'ing, *n.* in phonetics, a sound resulting from the change of a simple vowel to a diphthong before certain consonants, as in Anglo-Saxon *earm,* Old Saxon *arm;* Friesic *earm,* Old Friesic *arm, erm,* an arm; AS. *eorthe,* Old Saxon *ertha,* earth.

brea̤k'măn, *n.* see *brakeman.*

brea̤k'neck, *a.* endangering the neck or likely to break it; dangerous to life and limb; as, *breakneck* speed.

brea̤k'neck, *n.* 1. a fall that breaks the neck. [Obs.]
2. a steep place endangering the neck. [Obs.]

brea̤k'stōne, *n.* any of various plants growing in stony places, as saxifrage, parsley, piert, the dewcup, or the pimpernel.

brea̤k'through (-thrū), *n.* the act, result, or place of gaining by force against set resistance, as of a flood through a dike or of armed forces through a defense line.

brea̤k'up, *n.* 1. a breaking up; dispersion.
2. a disintegration or decay.
3. a collapse.
4. a stopping or ending.

breāk′wa̤″tẽr, *n.* any barrier placed at the mouth of a river, estuary, etc. to form a harbor or to break the force of waves and protect shipping, docks, etc.

brēam, *n.* [ME. *breem, breme*; OFr. *bresme*; O.H.G. *brahsima, brahsina*; D. *brasem*; Dan. *brasen*, a bream.]
1. a fresh-water cyprinoid fish, *Abramis brama*, the carp bream of Europe, or the *Abramis blicca*, the white bream.
2. any of a number of fresh-water sunfishes of the genus *Lepomis* or any allied genus, as the blue bream, *Lepomis pallidus*.
3. any of various marine sparoid food fishes of the genera *Diplodus* and *Pagellus*, or any species of the genus *Labrus*, family *Labridæ*. The common sea bream is *Pagellus centrodontus*.

brēam, *v.t.*; breamed, *pt., pp.*; breaming, *ppr.* [D. *brem*, furze.] to clean a ship's bottom, originally by scraping or applying burning reeds or furze.

breast (brest), *n.* [ME. *brest, breest*; AS. *breost*; Ice. *brjost*, the breast.]
1. either of two milk-secreting glands protruding from the upper, front part of a woman's body.
2. a corresponding gland in a female primate.
3. a corresponding undeveloped gland in the male.
4. figuratively, a source of nourishment.
5. the upper, front part of the body, between the shoulders, neck, and abdomen.
6. the part of a garment, etc. that is over the breast.
7. figuratively, the seat of the affections and emotions; the affections; the heart.
Each in his *breast* his secret sorrow kept. —Rowe.
8. one's feelings.
9. anything resembling the breast in position or form; as, (a) the front of a moldboard; (b) the part of a wall between a window and the floor; (c) the undersurface of a handrail, rafter, or beam; (d) in mining, the face of an excavation or tunnel.
10. the power of singing. [Obs.]
to make a clean breast of; to disclose (one's secrets, especially guilty secrets) fully; to confess.

breast, *v.t.*; breasted, *pt., pp.*; breasting, *ppr.*
1. to oppose the breast to; to face.
2. to meet in front boldly or openly; to oppose; to contend with.
(Who) *breasts* the blows of circumstance,
And grapples with his evil star. —Tennyson.
3. to move forward against.
to breast up; to trim (a hedge) on one side, baring the stalks.

breast′band, *n.* in nautical usage, a strap, rope, or band, especially a band of canvas, passed round the body of the man who heaves the lead in sounding, and fastened to the rigging to prevent his falling: called also *breastrope*.

breast′bēam, *n.* 1. the cloth beam of a loom.
2. the forward connecting rod of a locomotive. [Brit.]

breast′bōne, *n.* a thin, flat bone extending down the front of the chest and attached to the ends of the upper ribs by cartilages; sternum.

breast′-deep, *a.* as deep as the breast is high; up to the breast; as, a stream is *breast-deep*.

breast drill, a drillstock with a breastplate, held up to the work by the driller's breast.

breast′ed, *a.* having (a specified kind of breast): used especially in hyphenated compounds; as, a double-*breasted* coat.

breast fȧst, a line or hawser used to hold a ship alongside a wharf or another vessel; a line which passes from the waist of the ship, as distinguished from bow and stern fasts. Called also *breast line*.

breast′-feed, *v.t.*; breast-fed, *pt., pp.*; breast-feeding, *ppr.* to feed (a baby) milk from the breast; to suckle; to nurse.

breast′heīght (-hīt), *n.* a sloping bank on the inner side of a parapet in a fortification.

breast′-hīgh (-hī), *a.* as high as the breast.

breast′hook, *n.* a thick, V-shaped timber so placed as to strengthen and connect the sides of the hull of a ship.

breast′ing, *n.* the closely fitting channel of a water wheel, confining the water so as to take advantage of its momentum and weight.

breast′knot (-not), *n.* a knot of ribbons worn on the breast.

breast līne, same as *breast fast*.

breast′pin, *n.* a pin worn for a fastening, or for ornament, on a dress, near the throat.

breast′plāte, *n.* 1. a piece of armor for the breast.
2. a strap across the breast of a saddled horse.
3. in ancient times, a part of the vestment of a Jewish high priest, consisting of an embroidered cloth set with twelve precious stones, which represented the twelve tribes of Israel.
4. a plate on a drillstock or similar tool, to allow the driller to press the tool up to the work with his breast.
5. the abdominal part of a turtle's shell; plastron.

breast′plow, *n.* a plow, driven by the breast, used to cut turf.

breast′rāil, *n.* a top rail about breast-high, as the upper rail of the breastwork on a ship's quarter-deck.

breast′rōpe, *n.* same as *breastband*.

breast strōke, 1. a stroke in which the swimmer faces the water and brings both arms outward and sideways from a position close to the chest, at the same time drawing up the legs and then extending them quickly backward.
2. a variation of this in which the arms are stretched forward and brought back to the sides.

breast′sum″mẽr, *n.* a beam or girder set over an opening, as a doorway, for supporting the superstructure: also written *brestsummer*.

breast′weed, *n.* the lizard's-tail, *Saururus cernuus*.

breast wheel (hwēl), a water wheel on which the stream of water strikes at about the mid point of the wheel.

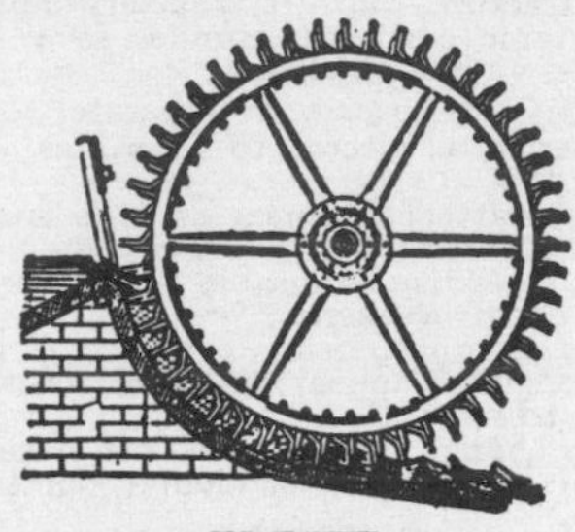

BREAST WHEEL

breast′wood, *n.* shoots branching from fruit trees trained against a wall.

breast′wŏrk, *n.* 1. a low, quickly constructed barrier to protect gunners.
2. a railing on a ship, either as a division or a guard.

breath (breth), *n.* [ME. *breeth, breth*; AS. *bræth*, breath, odor; O.H.G. *bradam*; G. *brodem*, vapor, exhalation.]
1. the air inhaled and exhaled in the respiration of animals.
2. breathing; respiration.
3. air or vapor given off from anything.
4. spirit; life.
No man has more contempt than I of *breath*. —Dryden.
5. the power of breathing freely; the capacity to breathe.
6. a slight respite or pause; as, let me take *breath*, give me some *breath*.
7. a slight breeze; air in gentle motion.
Calm and unruffled as a summer's sea.
When not a *breath* of wind flies o'er its surface. —Addison.
8. an instant; the time taken by a single respiration.
He smiles and he frowns in a *breath*. —Dryden.
9. a whisper; a murmur; a word or words; as, a *breath* of suspicion.
A *breath* can make them, as a *breath* has made. —Goldsmith.
10. air carrying fragrance; odor; as, the *breath* of the violet.
11. something produced by a breath, as moisture on a mirror.
12. in phonetics, a voiceless exhalation of air producing a hiss or puff, as in pronouncing *s* or *p*.
below one's breath; in a very low tone; in a whisper.
in the same breath; almost simultaneously.
out of breath; breathless from or as from exertion.
to catch one's breath; (a) to gasp or pant; (b) to pause or rest so as to regain a normal rhythm of breathing.
to save one's breath; to refrain from talking: said when talk would be useless.
under one's breath; in a very low tone; in a whisper.
Syn.—respiration, inspiration, expiration, inhalation, exhalation.

brēath′ȧ·ble, *a.* capable of being breathed; fit to be breathed.

brēath′ȧ·ble·ness, *n.* the state of being breathable.

brēathe, *v.t.* and *v.i.*; breathed, *pt., pp.*; breathing, *ppr.* [ME. *brethen*, to breathe, blow, from *breth*; AS. *bræth*, breath, odor.]
1. to inhale (air) into the lungs, and expel it; to respire.
2. to inject by or as by breathing; to infuse: followed by *into*.
And the Lord God *breathed into* his nostrils the breath of life. —Gen. ii. 7.
3. to inhale.
4. to exhale.
5. to live.
6. to give out (an odor).
7. to utter softly or in private; to whisper; to murmur; as, to *breathe* a vow.
8. to express; to manifest.
Other articles *breathe* the same severe spirit. —Milner.
9. to blow softly.
10. to give an opportunity to recover normal breathing; to give rest to.
11. to pant (with *hard*) or cause to pant, as from exertion.
12. in phonetics, to produce an unvoiced sound.
not breathe a word; to say nothing; to keep a secret.
to breathe again; *to breathe freely*; to feel a sense of relief, as from care or danger.
to breathe one's last; to die.

breathed (breṭht), *a.* 1. having a (specified kind of) breath: usually in hyphenated compounds, as, foul-*breathed*.
2. (*or* brēthd) in phonetics, voiceless.

brēath′ẽr, *n.* 1. one who breathes in a certain way.
2. that which makes one breathless, as brisk exercise. [Colloq.]
3. a rest to regain one's breath. [Colloq.]

breath′ful, *a.* full of breath; full of odor; pleasing to the sense of smell. [Obs.]

brēath′ing, *a.* 1. that breathes; living; alive.
2. lifelike.

brēath′ing, *n.* 1. respiration; the act of inhaling and exhaling air.
2. a single respiration.
3. the time taken by a single respiration; a moment.
4. air in gentle motion: applied also, figuratively, to a gentle influence or operation; as, the *breathings* of the Spirit.
5. aspiration; yearning.
6. exercise to assist or improve the respiration.
7. communication by speech.
8. a breathing place; a vent. [Obs.]
9. the sound of the letter *h* in English; an aspirate.
10. the mark indicating the aspiration, or the aspirate (ʽ), as before some initial vowels in Greek.

brēath′ing märk, in music, a mark in the score indicating where the vocalist is to draw breath.

brēath′ing plāce, 1. a pause.
2. a vent.

brēath′ing spāce, 1. enough space or time to breathe freely.
2. a chance or pause to rest or consider a situation.

brēath′ing tīme, pause; relaxation; time to recover one's breath.

breath′less (breth′), *a.* 1. without breath.
2. out of breath; spent with labor or violent action.
3. no longer breathing; dead; as, a *breathless* body.
4. tense with expectation, fear, or interest; intensely eager, as if so wrought up as to refrain from breathing.
5. having no breeze; stifling.

breath′less·ly, *adv.* in a breathless or intent manner.

breath′less·ness, *n.* the state of being breathless.

breath′-tāk″ing, *a.* 1. that takes one's breath away.
2. very exciting; thrilling.

breath′y, *a.* 1. pertaining to breath; like breath.

2. characterized by an excessive and audible emission of breath: said of the voice, speech, a speaker, etc.

brec′cià (bret′chȧ), *n.* [It., a breach, fragments of stone.] in geology, an aggregate composed of angular fragments of the same rock or of different rocks united by a matrix or cement.

osseous breccia; a breccia composed largely of bones.

brec′ci·ā·ted (bret′chi-ā-ted), *a.* consisting of angular fragments cemented together.

bred, past tense and past participle of *breed*.

brēde, *n.* a braid; a design or piece of embroidery. [Archaic.]

Spoilt all her silver mail and golden *brede*. —Keats.

brēde, breede, *n.* breadth. [Obs.]

bree, *n.* [ME. *bre*; AS. *briw*.] broth. [Scot.]

breech, *n.* [ME. *breech, breche*; AS. *broc*, breech, pl. *brec, brœc*, breeches.]

1. the buttocks; the rump.

2. breeches. [Obs.]

3. the under or back part of a thing.

4. the large, thick end of a cannon or other firearm; in breech-loading artillery, the metal part behind the entrance to the chamber; the part of a gun behind the barrel.

5. in shipbuilding, the outer angle of a knee timber.

breech, *v.t.*; breeched, *pt., pp.*; breeching, *ppr.*

1. to put into breeches.

2. to whip on the breech. [Obs.]

3. to fasten with a breeching.

4. to equip with a breech, as a gun.

breech′block, *n.* a strong metal block, bolt, or wedge in a breechloading firearm which when open permits loading and when closed receives the force of the combustion of the charge.

breech′çloth, breech′çlout, *n.* a cloth worn about the loins to cover the buttocks.

breech dē·liv′ẽr·y, the delivery of a fetus presenting itself with its breech at the head of the birth canal.

breech′eṣ (brich′ez), *n.pl.* [AS. *brec*, breeches.] trousers reaching to the knee: colloquially used in the sense of any trousers.

Breeches Bible; an English translation of the Bible printed in Geneva, Switzerland (1557–1560) in which a part of Genesis 3:7 was translated as "they sewed figge tree leaves together and made themselves breeches."

breech′eṣ buoy (boi), an apparatus used in rescuing persons at sea, consisting of a pair of canvas breeches, secured to a ring of buoyantmaterial, in which the person is conveyed to the shore or other place of safety by means of a line run from the ship to shore or to another ship.

BREECHES BUOY

breech′eṣ pīpe, a pipe branching out into two, usually parallel, pipes.

breech′ing (brich′ing), *n.* 1. a harness strap put around the hindquarters of a horse to help him hold back on a down grade.

2. a flogging administered on the breech; the act of administering it. [Obs.]

3. formerly, a stout, short length of hawser passing through a knob at the back of a broadside gun and shackled to the ship's side, to stop the movement of the gun inboard upon recoil, and also used to secure the gun at sea.

4. the sheet-iron smoke box fitted to the ends of boilers to carry off smoke from the flues.

5. the parts of a gun that make up the breech.

breech′less, *a.* 1. without a breech.

2. without breeches.

breech′lōad″ẽr, *n.* a gun or cannon that is loaded at the breech.

breech′-lōad″ing, *a.* fitted for being loaded at the breech instead of the muzzle; as, a *breech-loading* rifle.

breech pin, a strong plug or screw used to close the bottom of the bore of a muzzle-loading firearm, or forming the bottom of the chamber in a breechloader.

breech sçrew, a breech pin.

breech sīght (sīt), the rear sight of a gun, mounted near the breech.

breed, *v.t.*; bred, *pt., pp.*; breeding, *ppr.* [ME. *breden*; AS. *bredan*, to nourish, cherish, keep warm, from *brod*, brood; D. *broeden*; O.H.G. *bruoten*; G. *brüten*, to brood, hatch.]

1. to hatch from the egg; to bring forth (offspring) from the womb.

2. to produce within or upon the body; as, to *breed* teeth. [Obs.]

3. to be the source of; to produce; to originate.

4. to educate; to train; to form by education; as, to *breed* a son to an occupation; a man *bred* at a university.

5. to bring up; to nurse and foster; to take care of in infancy, and through the age of youth; to provide for and train; to rear.

To bring thee forth with pain, with care to *breed*. —Dryden.

6. to cause to produce; to raise; as, to *breed* cattle for the market.

to breed in and in; to breed from animals of the same stock that are closely related; to inbreed.

breed, *v.i.* 1. to bring forth offspring; to reproduce.

2. to be formed in the parent or dam; to be generated, or to grow, as young before birth; as, children or young *breed* in the matrix.

3. to originate; to be produced; as, crime *breeds* in slums.

4. to raise a breed; as, to choose the best species of cattle to *breed* from.

breed, *n.* 1. a race or stock, especially one with certain inherited characteristics; as, there are many *breeds* of dog.

2. a kind; a sort; a type; as, men of the same *breed*: also applied to inanimate things or attributes.

3. a number produced at once; a hatch; a brood. [Obs.]

breed′bāte, *n.* one who breeds or starts quarrels. [Obs.]

breede, *n.* breadth. [Obs.]

breed′ẽr, *n.* 1. an animal or plant that breeds, procreates, or reproduces offspring.

2. a cause; a source; an originator.

3. a person who raises a particular breed or breeds of animals or plants.

breed′ing, *n.* 1. the producing of young.

2. the rearing of young; upbringing; formation of manners.

She had her *breeding* at my father's charge. —Shak.

3. good upbringing; good manners and intelligent social behavior; as, tolerance is a sign of *breeding*.

4. the raising of animals or plants, especially for the purpose of improving the stock.

5. extraction; descent. [Obs.]

close breeding; breeding from closely related parents.

Syn.—education, air, decorum, demeanor, manners, discipline, instruction, training.

breeks, *n.pl.* breeches. [Dial.]

breeze, *n.* [ME. *brese*; AS. *breosa, briosa*, a gadfly; named from the sound it makes in flying.] one of certain buzzing insects of the family *Tabanidæ*; a gadfly or horsefly: also called *breeze fly*.

breeze, *n.* [ME. *brize*; Fr. *brize, brise*, a breeze; Port. *briza*, a northeast wind.]

1. a light, gentle wind.

From land a gentle *breeze* arose at night. —Dryden.

2. a flurried state of feeling; excitement; a slight disturbance. [Colloq.]

3. a vague intimation; a rumor. [Colloq.]

4. in meteorology, any wind ranging in velocity from 7 to 38 miles per hour.

breeze, *v.i.* 1. to blow.

2. to move or go briskly or jauntily. [Slang.]

breeze, *n.* [Fr. *braise*, live coals, embers.] a substance left when coke or charcoal is burned, used as a filler for concrete, etc.

breeze′less, *a.* motionless; lacking breezes.

breeze ŏv′en, a furnace in which breeze is used as fuel; also, an oven in which coke is manufactured.

breeze′wāy, *n.* a covered passageway between a house and garage, sometimes enclosed on the sides.

breez′i·ly, *adv.* in a breezy manner; briskly; jauntily.

breez′i·ness, *n.* a breezy quality or state.

breez′y, *a.*; *comp.* breezier; *superl.* breeziest.

1. fanned with gentle winds or breezes; as, the *breezy* shore.

2. subject to frequent breezes.

3. brisk; carefree; lively. [Colloq.]

breg′mȧ, *n.*; *pl.* **breg′mȧ·tȧ,** [Gr. *bregma*, the front of the head.] the point where the coronal and sagittal sutures of the skull unite.

breg·mat′iç, *a.* relating to the bregma.

brē′hŏn, *n.* [Ir. *breitheamh*, from *brath*, a decision.] an ancient Irish judge.

Brehon Laws; in ancient Ireland, the general laws, which were unwritten, like the common law of England.

bre·loque′ (-lok′), *n.* [Fr.] a seal or locket worn on a watch chain or necklace.

brēme, *a.* same as *brim*.

bren, *v.t.* and *v.i.*. [AS. *bærnan*, to burn.] to burn. [Obs.]

bren, *n.* bran (grain). [Obs.]

Bren gun, [from *Br*no, Czechoslovakia, where they were first made, and *En*field, England, where they were manufactured for the Brit. army.] a light, fast, gas-operated machine gun used by the British army in World War II.

bren′nāġe, *n.* [OFr. *brenage*, from *bren*, bran.] in the Middle Ages, a tribute which tenants paid to their lord, in or in lieu of bran, which they were obliged to furnish for his hounds.

brenne, *v.t.* and *v.i.* to burn. [Obs.]

bren′ning·ly, *adv.* ardently; zealously. [Obs.]

brent, *a.* 1. steep; high. [Obs.]

2. smooth; void of wrinkles. [Scot.]

brent, *n.* same as *brant*.

brent, obsolete past tense and past participle of *burn*.

br′ẽr, brother: used before a name. [Southern Dial.]

brēre, *n.* a brier. [Obs.]

brest, breste, *v.t.* and *v.i.* to burst. [Obs.]

brest′sum″mẽr, *n.* same as *breastsummer*.

bret, *n.* the turbot or the brill. [Brit. Dial.]

bret·esse′, *n.* [OFr. *bretesse*, the battlements of a wall.] same as *brattice* (parapet).

bret′ful, *a.* brimful. [Obs.]

breth′ren, *n.pl.* [ME. *brether, bretheren*, pl. of *brother*, brother.] brothers: now used only of fellow members of a fraternity, religious group, etc. [Archaic.]

Bret′ŏn, *a.* [Fr.] pertaining to Brittany in France, or its people or language.

Bret′ŏn, *n.* a native or inhabitant of Brittany.

2. the Celtic language of the Bretons.

3. a kind of hat with the brim turned upward evenly all around, worn by girls and women: so called from the hat worn by Breton peasants.

Bret′ŏn lāce, a delicate lace with a design of heavy thread embroidered on net.

brett, *n.* same as *britska*.

bret′tice, *n.* same as *brattice*.

Bret′wal·dȧ, *n.* [AS. *bretwalda, bryten walda*, a powerful ruler.] the name or title sometimes given to an Anglo-Saxon chieftain or king of acknowledged power or supremacy.

bret′zel, *n.* same as *pretzel*.

brēve, *n.* [It. *breve*, from L. *brevis*, short.]

1. a letter of authority, as from a pope.

2. in music, (a) a note equivalent to two whole notes; (b) the sign for this (◯).

3. in law, a writ or brief.

4. a curved sign (˘) to mark the short quality of a vowel or syllable.

5. in zoology, the Sumatra ant thrush, *Pitta gigas*, a tropical bird, that somewhat resembles the American ground thrush, but has a very short tail, whence the name.

brē·vet′, *n.* [ME. *brevet*; OFr. *brievet*, a commission, license; dim. of *brief*, a writing.]

1. formerly, in France, a document without seal or a warrant by which the king granted a favor, privilege, title, or dignity.

2. in military usage, a commission to an officer which entitles him to a higher rank without higher pay.

brē·vet′, *v.t.*; brevetted *or* breveted, *pt., pp.*; brevetting *or* breveting, *ppr.* to confer brevet rank upon.

brē·vet′, *a.* holding or giving rank by brevet; as, a *brevet* captain.

brē·vet′cy, *n.*; *pl.* **brē·vet′cieṣ,** any rank conferred by brevet; honorary rank.

brev′i-, a combining form from L. *brevis*, short, and meaning *brief, short, little*.

brē′vi·ā·ry, *n.*; *pl.* **brē′vi·ā·rieṣ,** [L. *breviarium*, an abridgment, from *brevis*, short.]

1. an abridgment; a compendium; an epitome. [Now Rare.]

2. a book containing the daily service of the Roman Catholic Church. It consists of prayers and offices to be used at the canonical hours.

3. a similar book used in the Orthodox Eastern Church.

brē′vi·āte, brē′vi·at, *n.* [L. *breviatum*, from *breviare*, to shorten; *brevis*, short.]

1. a short compendium; a summary.

2. the brief of a lawyer. [Rare.]

brē′vi·āte, *v.t.* to abbreviate. [Obs.]

brē′vi·ȧ·tūre, *n.* an abbreviature. [Obs.]

brev·i·çau′dāte, *a.* [*brevi-*, and L. *cauda*, a tail.] having a short caudal appendage.

brē·viēr′, *n.* [so called from being used in printing breviaries; G. *brevier*; L. *breviarium*, a breviary; *brevis*, short.] a size of type, eight-point.

This line is set in brevier.

brev·i·lin′guăl (-gwăl), *a.* [*brevi-*, and L. *lingua*, tongue.] having a short tongue; as, a *brevilingual* bird.

bre·vil′ō·quence, *n.* [L. *breviloquentia*, from *breviloquens* (*-entis*), short speaking; *brevis*, short, and *loquens*, ppr. of *loqui*, to speak.] a brief way of speaking.

brev′i·ped, *a.* [*brevi-*, and L. *pes*, *pedis*, foot.] having short legs, as certain birds.

brev′i·ped, *n.* a bird having short legs.

brev′i·pen, *n.* [*brevi-*, and L. *penna*, a wing.] a short-winged bird.

brev·i·pen′nāte, *a.* [*brevi-*, and L. *pennatus*, from *penna*, a wing.] having short wings: a term applied to a family of grallatory birds, *Brevipennes*, which are unable to fly, as the cassowary.

brev·i·ros′trāte, brev·i·ros′trăl, *a.* [*brevi-*, and L. *rostratus*, beaked, from *rostrum*, a beak.] short-beaked; having a short bill: said of a bird.

brev′i·ty, *n.*; *pl.* **brev′i·tieṣ,** [L. *brevitas*, from *brevis*, short.]

1. shortness of time; as, the *brevity* of human life.

2. shortness; conciseness; contraction into few words: applied to discourses or writings.

Brevity is the soul of wit. —Shak.

Syn.—conciseness, pointedness, shortness, succinctness, terseness, pithiness, laconism.

brew, *v.t.*; brewed, *pt.*, *pp.*; brewing, *ppr.* [ME. *brewen*; AS. *breówan*, to brew; D. *brouwen*; O.H.G. *briuwan*; Ice. *brugga*, to brew.]

1. to prepare from malt and hops by steeping, boiling, and fermentation, as ale, beer, or other similar liquor.

2. to prepare for use by steeping, boiling, or mixing; as, to *brew* a pot of tea.

3. to contrive; to plot; as, to *brew* mischief.

brew, *v.i.* 1. to be in a state of preparation; to begin to form; to gather; as, a storm *brews* in the west.

2. to perform the business of brewing or making beer.

brew, *n.* 1. the mixture formed by brewing; that which is brewed.

2. an amount brewed.

brew′āġe, *n.* 1. malt liquor; anything which has been brewed.

2. brewing.

brew′ẽr, *n.* one whose occupation is to prepare malt liquors; one who brews.

brew′ẽr·y, *n.*; *pl.* **brew′ẽr·ieṣ,** an establishment where beer, ale, etc. are brewed.

brew′house, *n.* a brewery.

brew′ing, *n.* 1. the preparation of a brew.

2. the quantity brewed at once; a brew.

3. in nautical usage, a collection of black clouds portending a storm.

brew′is, *n.* [ME. *brewes*; OFr. *broues*; LL. *brodum*, gravy, broth; O.H.G. *brod*, broth.]

1. bread soaked in gravy, broth, or pottage of any kind. [Dial.]

2. broth; pottage. [Dial.]

brew′stẽr·īte, *n.* [named after Sir David *Brewster* (1781–1868).] in mineralogy, a rare hydrous zeolite having monoclinic crystals of pearllike luster.

brez′i·lin, *n.* same as *brazilin*.

brī′ăr, *n.* same as *brier*.

Brī·ăr′ē·ăn, *a.* 1. of Briareus.

2. like Briareus; many-handed; reaching in many directions.

Brī·ăr′ē·us, *n.* [L.; Gr. *Briareōs*, from *briaros*, strong.] in Greek mythology, a hundred-handed giant who fought with the Olympians against the Titans.

brī′ăr·root, *n.* same as *brierroot*.

brī′ăr·wood, *n.* same as *brierwood*.

brī′ăr·y, *n.* same as *briery*.

brīb′ȧ·ble, capable of being bribed.

brībe, *n.* [OFr. *bribe*, a piece of bread, usually that given to beggars; a gift, present; LL. *briba*, a scrap of bread.]

1. a price, reward, gift, or favor bestowed or promised to induce one to commit a wrong or illegal act.

2. anything given or promised to induce a person to do something against his wishes.

brībe, *v.t.*; bribed, *pt.*, *pp.*; bribing, *ppr.* [ME. *briben*, to steal; OFr. *briber*, to beg.]

1. to give or promise a bribe to.

2. to gain or influence by bribing.

brībe, *v.i.* to offer or give a bribe or bribes.

The bard may supplicate, but cannot *bribe*. —Goldsmith.

brībe′less, *a.* not to be bribed; not bribed.

brīb′ẽr, *n.* one who bribes, especially for corrupt purposes.

brīb′ẽr·y, *n.*; *pl.* **brīb′ẽr·ieṣ,** [OFr. *briberie*, theft, robbery.] the act or practice of giving, offering, or taking rewards for corrupt practices; the act of paying or receiving a reward for a false judgment or testimony, or for the performance of that which is known to be illegal or unjust. It is applied both to the one who gives and to the one who receives the bribe, but especially to the giver.

brīb′ẽr·y ōath, an oath sometimes required to be taken by a voter, declaring that he was not bribed. [Brit.]

briç′-ȧ-braç, briç′-ȧ-braç, *n.* [Fr.] small, rare, or artistic objects of miscellaneous pattern and assortment, used for decorating and as shelf ornaments.

brick, *n.* [ME. *bryke*; OFr. *brique*, a brick, plate, wedge of metal; D. *bricke*, *brigke*, a tile, brick.]

1. a substance made from clay molded into oblong blocks and baked or burned in a kiln or by the sun: used in buildings and walls.

2. one of these blocks, usually 2¼ x 4 x 8 inches.

3. bricks collectively.

4. anything in the form of a rectangular solid; as, a *brick* of ice cream.

5. a fine fellow; a trustworthy friend. [Colloq.]

brick tea; a small brick made of refuse tea, tea leaves, and twigs, mixed with fat, steamed, and pressed into shape.

to make bricks without straw; to do something without the necessary materials.

brick, *a.* 1. built or paved with brick.

2. like brick, as *brick* red.

brick, *v.t.* 1. to build or pave with brick.

2. to close or wall in with brick (with *up* or *in*).

brick′bat, *n.* 1. a piece of a brick, especially one used as a missile.

2. an unfavorable remark.

brick cheese, a semihard, elastic American cheese with a strong, sweetish taste, shaped like a brick and containing many small holes.

brick′fiēld, *n.* a yard where bricks are made.

brick′kiln (-kil), *n.* a kiln, or furnace, in which bricks are baked or burned; also, a pile of loose bricks with arches underneath to receive the fuel for burning them.

brick′lāy″ẽr, *n.* one whose occupation is to build or pave with bricks.

brick′lāy″ing, *n.* the art or trade of constructing walls, roads, etc. with bricks and mortar or cement; the act of laying bricks.

briç′kle, *a.* [ME. *brekil*, from AS. *brecan*, to break.] brittle; easily broken. [Dial.]

briç′kle·ness, *n.* brittleness. [Obs.]

brick′māk″ẽr, *n.* one whose occupation is to make bricks.

brick′māk″ing, *n.* the art or act of making bricks.

brick′nog″ging, *n.* a filling of brickwork between the wooden framework of a building.

brick′-red′, *a.* of the color brick red.

brick red, a yellowish or brownish red.

brick trim′mẽr, in architecture, a brick arch abutting against a wooden trimmer in front of a fireplace to guard against accidents by fire.

brick′wŏrk, *n.* work done with bricks.

brick′y, *a.* 1. full of bricks, or formed of bricks.

2. like a brick, especially in color.

brick′yärd, *n.* a place where bricks are made or sold.

bri·çōle′, *n.* [Fr.] 1. a medieval machine for throwing missiles and darts against an enemy.

2. a kind of harness for men who move guns in places where the use of horses is impossible.

3. in court tennis, a side stroke; also, the rebound of the ball.

4. in billiards, a stroke by which the cue ball is driven against the cushion before striking an object ball; a bank shot.

brid, *n.* a bird. [Obs.]

brīd′ăl, *a.* belonging to a bride, or to a wedding; nuptial; connubial; as, *bridal* ornaments.

brīd′ăl, *n.* [ME. *bridale*; AS. *brydealo*, bridal, bride-ale, bride feast; *bryd*, bride, and *ealo*, ale.] a wedding.

brīd′ăl·ty, *n.* a wedding. [Obs.]

brīd′ăl wrēath (rēth), a plant, *Spiræa hypericifolia*, having long slender branches, dark leaves, and clusters of white blossoms: also called *St. Peter's wreath*.

brīde, *v.t.* to take a woman in marriage. [Obs.]

brīde, *n.* [ME. *bride*, *bryde*; AS. *bryd*, a bride.] a woman newly married; also, a woman espoused or about to be married.

brīde, *n.* [Fr.; OFr. *bridle*; ME. *bridel*, a bridle.]

1. a loop that connects or ties in lace or needlework.

2. a bridle. [Obs.]

brīde′-āle, *n.* 1. a bridal. [Obs.]

2. mulled ale sometimes served to guests at a wedding. [Brit.]

brīde′bed, *n.* the marriage bed. [Archaic.]

brīde′çāke, *n.* the cake which is made for a wedding: commonly called *wedding cake*.

brīde′chăm″bẽr, *n.* the nuptial apartment.

brīde′groom, *n.* [ME. *bridegome*, *bridgume*; AS. *brydguma*, *brydiguma*; *bryde*, genit. of *bryd*, bride, and *guma*, man.] a man newly married or a man about to be married.

brīde′knot (-not), *n.* a wedding ornament of ribbons.

brīde′pot, *n.* the adjustable socket or bearing in which the spindle of a millstone rests.

brīde′ṣ′-lāc″eṣ, *n.* the common dodder or ribbon grass, *Phalaris arundinacea*.

brīdeṣ′māid, brīde′māid, *n.* an unmarried woman who attends a bride just before and during her wedding.

brīdeṣ′măn, brīde′măn, *n.* a man who attends a bridegroom at a wedding: generally called *best man*.

brīde′stāke, *n.* a stake or post set in the ground to dance round, especially at a wedding.

brīde′well, *n.* a prison or house of correction for minor offenses; a jail: so called from the palace built near St. Bride's (or Bridget's) well in London, which was turned into a workhouse.

brīde′wŏrt, *n.* the common meadowsweet, *Spiræa salicifolia*.

bridġe (brij), *n.* [ME. *brigge*, *brugge*; AS. *brycg*, *bricg*; D. *brug*; O.H.G. *brucca*; G. *brücke*, a bridge; Ice. *bryggja*; Sw. *brygga*, a pier, landing place.]

1. any structure of wood, stone, brick, or iron raised to afford convenient passage over a river, pond, lake, railroad, ravine, or any other obstacle.

2. the upper, bony part of the nose.

3. the thin, removable arch of a stringed musical instrument over which the strings are stretched and their vibrations transmitted.

4. an elevated platform on a ship, upon which the commanding officer stands to control the ship; a hurricane deck; a bridge deck.

5. in gunnery, the two pieces of timber which go between the two transoms of a gun carriage.

6. any one of a variety of structures or objects resembling a bridge.

7. in electricity, a device employed to measure resistances, frequencies, etc., by comparing the effect of the unknown element with that of a known or standard element in the circuit.

8. the curved bow of a pair of glasses fitting over the nose.

9. a reef or ridge in a channel.

10. a dividing partition for keeping fuel in place in a furnace or boiler.

11. in billiards and pool, a cue rest, a notched piece of wood at the end of a rod.

12. in dancing, a bending backward to touch the floor.

13. in dentistry, a fixed or removable mounting for false teeth, attached to a real tooth or teeth.

14. in music, a connecting passage between two subjects, as in a composition in sonata form.

bridge crane; a crane which is movable upon a bridge, or tramway.

Bridge of Sighs; (a) an elevated passageway from a palace in Venice to a prison on the opposite side of the street; (b) a passageway formerly joining the Tombs prison and the criminal court in New York City.

bridge train; in military usage, the trucking equipment and men for moving the materials needed for the construction of bridges.

flying bridge; (a) a bridge constructed for temporary use, as one rapidly built for the passage of troops and then removed or destroyed; (b) a kind of ferry anchored by a strong cable upstream and so placed and handled as to be carried across the stream by the force of the current.

lattice bridge; a bridge of wood or iron constructed with cross framing, like latticework.

skew bridge; a bridge by which a road or railway is carried over an opening at some angle other than a right angle; an oblique bridge.

tubular bridge; a bridge built in the form of a rectangular tube, through which the roadway or railway passes.

Wheatstone's bridge; an electric apparatus, invented by Sir Charles *Wheatstone* (1802–1875), English physicist, for measuring resistance by means of a bridge, or wire carrying a current between two points, and including a galvanometer whose needle indicates no current when the resistances in the two arms of the instrument are equal. The resistance in one of these arms is known by means of the resistance box of which it mainly consists, while that in the other is the resistance sought.

bridġe, *v.t.*; bridged, *pt., pp.*; bridging, *ppr.* 1. to build a bridge over.
2. to make a passage over or through; to get across; as, to *bridge* a river.

bridġe, *n.* [earlier (1886) *biritch*, "Russian whist," altered after *bridge*; game (and prob. its name) of Russ. origin.] a card game similar to whist: see *auction bridge, contract bridge.*

bridġe′bōard, *n.* a notched board supporting the steps and risers of a wooden staircase.

bridġe′head (-hed), *n.* a fortified place or position established by an attacking force on the enemy's side of a bridge, river, or gap.

bridġe′less, *a.* having no bridge.

bridġe rāil, a railroad rail with an arched tread and lateral foot flanges.

bridġe′tree, *n.* in a grinding mill, the beam supporting the shaft of the rotating millstone.

bridġe′wŏrk, *n.* 1. the building of bridges.
2. a fixed or removable mounting for a false tooth or teeth, fastened to a real tooth or teeth.

bridġ′ing, *n.* braces used between floor joists or other beams for reinforcement and distribution of strain.

bridġ′ing joist, in architecture, a joist in a double-framed floor which is laid transverse to the girder, and to which the flooring boards are nailed.

bridġ′y, *a.* having many bridges. [Rare.]

brī′dle, *n.* [AS. *bridel*; OFr. *bridel*; D. *breidel*; O.H.G. *bridel, britel*, a bridle.]
1. the head harness with which a horse is guided by a rider or driver, consisting of a headstall, a bit, and reins.
2. a restraint; a curb; a check.
3. that part of a gunlock which covers and holds in place the tumbler and sear, being itself held by the screws on which they turn.
4. in seamanship, a Y-shaped arrangement of two lines, cables, hawsers, or the like, meeting in a point and so fixed at each end that another line, etc. can be attached between the ends.
scolding bridle; a device like a gag formerly used for the correction of scolding women; branks.

brī′dle, *v.i.*; bridled, *pt., pp.*; bridling, *ppr.* [ME. *bridlen, bridelen*; AS. *gebridlian*, to bridle, restrain, from *bridel*, a bridle.]
1. to put a bridle on; as, to *bridle* a horse.
2. to restrain, guide, or govern; to check, curb, or control; as, to *bridle* the passions; to *bridle* a muse.

brī′dle, *v.i.* 1. to throw up the head, and hold in the chin, as from vexation, indignation, pride, or disdain.
2. to become angry, scornful, etc.; as, she *bridled* at the insinuation.

brī′dle hand, the hand in which the bridle is usually held while riding, i.e., the left hand.

brī′dle ī′ron (-ūrn), a metal strap bent into the shape of a stirrup and used to hold the end of a horizontal beam.

brī′dle pȧth, brī′dle wāy, a path used by or set apart for saddle horses or pack animals.

brī′dle pōrt, in a ship, the foremost porthole on each side of the bow, generally on the main deck: so called because the legs of a towing bridle may be passed through them.

brī′dlẽr, *n.* one who bridles; one who restrains and governs.

brī′dle-wīşe, *a.* trained to obey the pressure of the reins on the neck instead of the pull on the bit.

bri·dọọn′, *n.* [Fr. *bridon*, from *bride*, a bridle, check.] in a military bridle, the light snaffle bit and reins, used with or without curbs.

Brie cheese (brē chēz), a soft, white cheese, originally made in *Brie*, France, matured by mold; also, a similar American variety matured by bacteria.

brief, *a.*; *comp.* briefer; *superl.* briefest, [OFr. *bref, brief*; It. *breve*; Sp. *breve*; L. *brevis*; Gr. *brachys*, short.]
1. short; not lasting; ending quickly; as, a *brief* respite from work.
2. concise; of few words; compact in expression; as, a *brief* letter.
3. short in manner; curt; abrupt; somewhat rude.
4. of limited length or extent; short in length; as, a *brief* stretch of ground.
5. prevalent; widespread. [Brit. Dial.]
in brief; briefly; in a few words.
Syn.—condensed, concise, laconic, short, succinct, curt, transitory.

brief, *adv.* in brief; in short; soon; in a short time. [Obs.]

brief, *n.* 1. an epitome; a short or concise writing; any summary or brief statement.
2. a letter patent, from proper authority, sanctioning the collection of money in the churches for some particular purpose. [Brit.]
3. in music, a breve. [Obs.]
4. in the Roman Catholic Church, a letter or communication from the pope to an individual or community. It differs from a bull in contents, being less formal (consisting often of merely a friendly message or congratulatory letter to a person of high rank), and in form, being shorter, written on paper in Roman letters, and sealed in red wax with the ring of the fisherman.
5. in law, (a) an abridgment of a client's case made out for the instruction of counsel in a trial at law; (b) a statement in writing of the points of an argument and the authorities cited; (c) a writ; a breve.
6. in Scots law, same as *brieve*.
brief of title; a summary of the deeds and all other instruments bearing upon the ownership of property; an abstract of title.

brief, *v.t.* 1. to make a summary of; to shorten or condense.
2. in military usage, to tell about the detailed plan of action about to be carried out; as, to *brief* the pilots before an air attack.
3. to furnish with a legal brief. [Brit.]
4. to hire as counsel. [Brit.]
5. to tell about. [Colloq.]

brief çāse, a flat case or bag, usually of leather, for carrying papers, books, etc.

brief′less, *a.* without a brief; hence, lacking clients: applied to lawyers.

brief′ly, *adv.* concisely; in a few words.

brief′măn, *n.* one who makes a brief; also, one who makes a transcript of a manuscript.

brief′ness, *n.* the state or quality of being brief.

briefs, *n.pl.* legless undershorts.

brī′ẽr, brī′ăr, *n.* [ME. *brere*; AS. *brer, brær*, a bramble; Ir. *briar*, a prickle, thorn, pin.]
1. any shrub or bush having prickles or little thorns along its stems; in particular, a plant of genera *Rosa*, *Rubus*, or others of the rose family; as, the sweet*brier* and wild *brier*; hence, the thorny twig of such a bush.
2. a growth of shrubs or bushes having prickles or thorns.

brī′ẽr, brī′ăr, *n.* [Fr. *bruyère*, white heath.]
1. the tree heath, bearing a root from which tobacco pipes are made.
2. this root.
3. a pipe made from this root.

brī′ẽr bam′bọọ, the greenbrier, common to southern U. S.

brī′ẽr·ber″ry, brī′ăr·ber″ry, *n.* the purple-black fruit of a brier bush (*Rubus cuneifolius*): also, the bush itself.

brī′ẽr bird, the American goldfinch.

brī′ẽred, brī′ăred, *a.* set with briers.

brī′ẽr·rọọt, brī′ăr·rọọt, *n.* same as *brierwood*.

brī′ẽr stitch, an embroidery stitch similar to featherstitching.

brī′ẽr·wood, brī′ăr·wood, *n.* 1. the root wood, especially the root burl, of the brier (white heath).
2. a tobacco pipe made of this.

brī′ẽr·y, brī′ăr·y, *a.* full of briers; rough; thorny.

brī′ẽr·y, brī′ăr·y, *n.* a place where briers grow.

brieve, *n.* [a Scot. form of *brief*; Fr. *bref*, a writing.] in Scots law, a writ issuing from the chancery directed to any judge ordinary, commanding and authorizing that judge to call a jury to inquire into the case and, upon their verdict, to pronounce sentence.

brig, *n.* [contr. of *brigantine*.] a vessel with two masts, square-rigged, or rigged nearly like a full-rigged ship's mainmast and foremast.
hermaphrodite brig; a brig having the mainmast rigged fore and aft.

BRIG

brig, *n.* [origin unknown.] 1. the prison on a United States warship.
2. the guardhouse. [Military Slang.]

bri·gāde′, *n.* [Fr. *brigade*; It. *brigata*, a troop, company, from *brigare*, to contend; *briga*, strife, quarrel.]
1. formerly, in the United States Army, a unit comprising two or more regiments and commanded by a brigadier general.
2. any organized body of persons acting under authority; as, a fire *brigade*.
3. a large unit of soldiers.

bri·gāde′, *v.t.*; brigaded, *pt., pp.*; brigading, *ppr.* 1. to form into a brigade or brigades.
2. to sort into groups; to classify.

bri·gāde′ mā′jŏr, in the United States Army, formerly, an officer appointed by a brigadier general to assist him in the management and ordering of his brigade.

brig·ȧ·dier′, *n.* [Fr. *brigadier*, from *brigade*, a brigade.]
1. a person commanding a brigade.
2. in the United States armed forces, a brigadier general.
3. in the British armed forces, an officer temporarily commanding a brigade.
4. in the French army, a cavalry corporal.

brig·ȧ·dier′ ġen′ẽr·ăl; *pl.* **brig·ȧ·dier′ ġen′ẽr·ălş,** a military officer ranking above a colonel and below a major general: now normally an assistant divisional commander.

brig′ănd, *n.* [Fr. *brigand*; It. *brigante*, a brigand, pirate, from *brigare*, to strive for, contend; *briga*, quarrel, trouble.]
1. a robber; a freebooter; a bandit; a lawless fellow who lives by plunder.
2. a soldier of some irregular band. [Obs.]

brig′ănd·āġe, *n.* [Fr., from *brigand*, a brigand, robber.]
1. theft; robbery; organized plundering.
2. brigands collectively.

brig′ăn·dīne, brig′ăn·tīne, *n.* [OFr. *brigandine*, from *brigand*, a foot soldier.] formerly, a coat of mail, consisting of thin, jointed scales of plate fastened to leather or cloth, making the coat flexible.

brig′ănd·ish, *a.* like a brigand, or robber.

brig′ănd·işm, *n.* robbery; plunder; brigandage.

brig′ăn·tīne (*or* -tīn), *n.* [Fr. *brigantin*; It. *brigantino*, a brigantine, pirate vessel; *brigante*, a brigand, pirate; from *brigare*, to contend for, struggle; *briga*, trouble, quarrel.]
1. a two-masted vessel, square-rigged like a brig, excepting the mainmast, which is fore-and-aft rigged; a hermaphrodite brig.
2. a light sailing vessel formerly much used by pirates. [Obs.]

brigge, *n.* a bridge. [Obs.]

bright (brīt), *a.* [ME. *bright, briht*; AS. *bryht, briht, beorht*; O.H.G. *beraht, bereht*; Goth. *bairhts*, bright; Sans. root *bhraj*, to shine.]
1. giving forth, shedding, or reflecting much light; radiant; shining; as, a *bright* sun or star; a *bright* metal.
2. clear; transparent, as liquors.
3. of active mind; discerning; clever; keen-witted; as, a *bright* scholar.
4. characterized by cheerfulness and gaiety; lively; pleasant; as, *bright* memories.
5. giving promise of prosperity or happiness; favorable; auspicious; as, a *bright* outlook.
6. illustrious; glorious; famous; as, the *brightest* period of a kingdom.
7. sparkling; animated; as, *bright* eyes.
8. of brilliant hue or color; vivid; as, a *bright* blue; the *bright* poppy.

9. resplendent with charms; having attractive qualities; as, a *bright* beauty.

10. evident; clear; manifest to the mind, as light is to the eyes.

The evidence of this truth is *bright*. —Watts.

Syn.—sparkling, shining, clear, luminous, gleaming, radiant, brilliant, clever, witty, sunny, limpid, pellucid, resplendent, translucent, lustrous, glittering.

brīght, *v.i.* to brite. [Obs.]

brīght, *n.* brightness; brilliancy. [Poet.]

Dark with excessive *bright* thy skirts appear. —Milton.

brīght, *adv.* brightly; with brightness. [Poet.]

The moon shines *bright*. —Shak.

brīght'en (brīt'), *v.t.* and *v.i.*; brightened, *pt.*, *pp.*; brightening, *ppr.* 1. to make or become bright or brighter; to add to the color or luster of.

2. to cheer; to make or become gay or cheerful; to make or become happy; as, to *brighten* sorrow.

brīght'ly, *adv.* 1. splendidly; with luster.

2. intelligently; sharply; alertly; keenly.

brīght'ness, *n.* 1. the condition or quality of being bright.

2. the luminous aspect of a color (as distinct from its hue) by which it is regarded as approaching the maximum luminosity of pure white or the lack of luminosity of pure black.

Brīght's dis·ēase', [from Dr. Richard *Bright* (1789–1858), the London physician who first diagnosed it.] a kidney inflammation characterized by the presence of albumin in the urine; nephritis.

brīght'sŏme, *a.* bright; shining; cheerful.

bri·gōse', *a.* contentious. [Obs.]

brīgue (brēg), *n.* [Fr.] a cabal; intrigue; faction; contention. [Obs.]

brīgue, *v.i.* to intrigue. [Obs.]

brīke, *n.* [AS. *brice*, a fracture, breaking.] a trap; snare; peril; ruin. [Obs.]

brill, *n.* [Corn. *brilli*, mackerel, contr. of *brithelli*, from *brith*, spotted, speckled.] one of the flatfishes, in general form resembling the turbot, but inferior in food value.

brīl·lăn'te, *adv.* [It.] in music, in a gay and lively style.

bril'liănce (-yăns), **bril'liăn·cy** (-yăn-), *n.* 1. splendor; glitter; great brightness.

2. intensity or vividness, as of a color or musical tone.

3. splendor; magnificence.

4. keen intelligence; quickness of mind.

bril'liănt, *a.* [Fr. *brillant*, sparkling, ppr. of *briller*, to glitter, sparkle; from L. *beryllus*, *berillus*, a precious stone, beryl.]

1. sparkling; shining brightly; glittering; as, a *brilliant* gem; a *brilliant* dress.

2. splendid; remarkable; illustrious; as, a *brilliant* achievement.

3. vivid.

4. very able; keenly intelligent; talented; as, a *brilliant* orator; a *brilliant* writer.

Syn.—beaming, effulgent, flashing, glorious, luminous, lustrous, radiant, shining, sparkling.

bril'liănt, *n.* 1. a diamond of the finest cut; formed into facets so as to reflect the light, by which it is made more glittering.

2. in horsemanship, a brisk, high-spirited horse, with a stately carriage.

3. the smallest size of type in common use, 3½ point.

4. a figured cotton fabric.

bril'liăn·tīne, *n.* [Fr.] 1. an oily preparation for the hair to make it smooth and glossy.

2. a dress material of mohair and cotton somewhat resembling, but superior to, alpaca: both sides have a hard and smooth finish.

bril'liănt·ly, *adv.* splendidly; with brilliance, in a brilliant manner.

bril'liănt·ness, *n.* brilliance.

brills, *n.pl.* [G. *brille*, spectacles.] the hair on the eyelids of a horse. [Obs.]

brim, *n.* [AS. *brim*; Ice. *brim*, the surf, sea; Dan. *bræmme*; G. *bräme*, the edge, border; AS. *bremman*, to roar; Gr. *bremein*, to roar, especially as the waves; Sans. *bhram*, to whirl, wander.]

1. the rim, lip, border, or upper edge of a cup, glass, bowl, etc.

2. the edge or brink of any body of water; the verge.

3. the top or surface of any liquid near the edge; that part next to the border at the top.

4. the projecting rim of anything; as, the *brim* of a hat.

Syn.—border, brink, edge, margin, rim, verge.

brim, *a.* [AS. *bryme*, celebrated, famous.]

1. well known; celebrated. [Obs.]

2. fierce; cruel. [Obs.]

brim, *v.t.*; brimmed, *pt.*, *pp.*; brimming, *ppr.* to fill to the brim.

brim, *v.i.* to be full to the brim.

brim'ful, brim'full, *a.* full to the brim; completely full; as, a glass *brimful*; a heart *brimful* of sorrow.

brim'ful·ness, *n.* fullness to the brim.

brim'ing, brim'ming, *n.* [AS. *bryme*.] a condition of the sea at night characterized by a phosphorescent glow. [Brit.]

brim'less, *a.* having no brim.

brimmed, *a.* 1. with a brim.

2. full to or level with the brim.

brim'mēr, *n.* a bowl or cup full to the brim.

brim'ming, *a.* full to the top or brim; as, a *brimming* pail.

brim'stōne, *n.* [ME. *brimston*, *brinston*, *bernston*, from *brin-*, *bren-*, from *brinnen*, *brennen*, to burn, and *ston*, stone.]

1. sulfur.

2. in zoology, a species of butterfly, *Gonopteryx rhamni*.

brim'stōne·wŏrt, *n.* same as *sulfurwort*.

brim'stō·ny, *a.* full of brimstone, or sulfur; also, resembling brimstone.

brin, *n.* [Fr.] one of the smaller sticks forming the frame of a fan.

brin'ded, *a.* [a variant of *branded*, from AS. *brinnen*, *byrnan*, to burn.] marked with spots; having different colors; brindled. [Archaic.]

brin'dle, *n.* 1. the state of being brindled; spottedness.

2. a brindled color.

3. a brindled animal.

brin'dle, *a.* brindled; as, a *brindle* cow.

brin'dled (-dld), *a.* [a dim. of *brinded*, brindled.] streaked or spotted with a darker color: said especially of a gray or tawny cow, dog, etc.

brīne, *n.* [AS. *bryne*, a burning, salt liquor, from *brinnan*, *byrnan*, to burn.]

1. water containing much salt; any heavily saturated salt solution.

2. the ocean or sea.

3. tears: so called from their saltiness.

brīne, *v.t.*; brined, *pt.*, *pp.*; brining, *ppr.* to steep in brine, as in pickling; also, to treat with brine.

brīne fly̆, a fly of the genus *Ephydra*: so called because its larvae are found in brine.

brīne gāuge, an instrument which measures the amount of salt in a liquid.

Bri·nell' test, [after 19th-c. Swed. metallurgist, J. A. *Brinell*.] a test for determining the relative hardness of a metal by measuring the diameter of the indentation made when a hardened steel ball is forced into the metal under a given pressure.

brīne pan, a pit of salt water, where brine is evaporated to form salt.

brīne pit, a salt spring or well, from which water may be taken to be boiled or evaporated for making salt.

brīne pump, a pump for cleaning the brine from the boilers of a steamship.

brīne shrimp, a minute crustacean, *Artemia salina*, which lives in the strong brines of salt works and in salt lakes.

brīne spring, a spring of salt water.

brīne wŏrm, same as *brine shrimp*.

bring, *v.t.*; brought, *pt.*, *pp.*; bringing, *ppr.* [ME. *bringer*; AS. *bringan*; Sw. *bringa*; Dan. *bringe*; D. *bringen*; G. *bringen*; Goth. *briggan*, to bring.]

1. to fetch; to bear, convey, or lead from a distant to a nearer place or to a person; as, *bring* me a book from the shelf; *bring* me a morsel of bread.

2. to cause to come about; to make happen; as, nothing *brings* a man more honor than to be invariably just.

3. to cause to have; as, rest *brings* health.

4. to obtain in exchange; to sell for; as, what does coal *bring?*

5. to cause to come to a point; to lead, persuade, or influence along a course of action or belief; as, to *bring* the mind to assent to a proposition; to *bring* a man to terms by persuasion or argument.

6. in law, (a) to present in a law court; as, *bring* charges; (b) to advance (evidence, etc.).

to bring about; to bring to pass; to effect; to accomplish; to make happen.

to bring by the lee; to turn (a ship) so rapidly to leeward as to bring the lee side suddenly to the windward, and, by laying the sails aback, expose her to the danger of capsizing.

to bring down; (a) to cause to come down; (b) in hunting or warfare, to kill or wound; as, *to bring down* a bird.

to bring forth; (a) to produce, as young or fruit; (b) to bring to light; to make manifest; to disclose.

to bring in; (a) to import; to introduce; to bear from a remote place; (b) to produce, as income, rent, or revenue; (c) to cause (an oil well, etc.) to produce; (d) to give; to render, as a verdict, or a report.

to bring off; (a) to bear or convey from a distant place; as, *to bring off* men from an isle; (b) to accomplish.

to bring on; (a) to cause to begin; as, *to bring on* an action; also, to originate or cause to exist; as, *to bring on* a disease; (b) to aid in advancing; as, *to bring* one *on* his way.

to bring out; (a) to expose; to detect; as, *to bring out* an accomplice or his crimes; the place of concealment was *brought out* at the trial; (b) to bring (a play, person, etc.) before the public; publish (a book, magazine, etc.); (c) to cause to appear; (d) to introduce (a girl) formally to society.

to bring over; (a) to persuade; to cause to change an opinion; (b) to bring on a visit.

to bring to; (a) in navigation, to check the course of a ship; (b) to restore to consciousness, as a half-drowned or fainting person.

to bring under; to subdue; to repress.

to bring up; (a) to nurse; to educate; to instruct; to take care of during infancy and childhood; (b) to introduce, as in a discussion; (c) to stop abruptly; (d) to cough up; (e) to vomit.

to bring up the rear; to be at the end.

Syn.—fetch, procure, convey, carry, bear, adduce, import, produce, cause, induce.

bring'ēr, *n.* one who brings or conveys.

bring'ing-up', *n.* 1. care during infancy and childhood; rearing.

2. education, especially in how to behave.

brīn'i·ness, *n.* the quality of being briny; saltiness.

brīn'ish, *a.* like brine; somewhat salty.

brīn'ish·ness, *n.* saltiness; the quality of being salty.

brin'jal, brin'jaul, *n.* [Anglo-Ind. name.] the fruit of the eggplant, *Solanum Melongena*.

brin·jär'ree, brin·jär'ry, *n.* [Anglo-Ind.]

1. in India, a traveling dealer in grain, etc.

2. a kind of East Indian hound.

brink, *n.* [ME. *brink*, edge; LG. *brink*, brink, margin, edge; Sw. *brink*, a declivity, hill; Ice. *brekka*, a slope.] the edge, margin, or border of a steep place, as of a precipice, or the bank of a river: also used figuratively; as, to be on the *brink* of failure.

brink'măn·ship, *n.* [*brink*, and *-manship*, as in *statesmanship*.] the policy of pursuing a hazardous course of action to the brink of catastrophe. Also **brinks'măn·ship.**

brīn'y, *a.*; *comp.* brinier; *superl.* briniest, pertaining to brine, or to the sea; partaking of the nature of brine; salty; as, a *briny* taste.

bri'ō, *n.* [It.] animation; vivacity; zest.

brī·ōche', *n.*; *pl.* **brī·ōch'es** (Fr. brē-ōsh'), [Fr.] a light roll made with butter, eggs, and yeast.

brī·ō·lette', *n.* [Fr., from *brilliant*, a brilliant.] a pearlike shape given to a diamond or other precious stone; also, the stone so shaped.

brī'ō·ny, *n.*; *pl.* **brī'ō·nies,** see *bryony*.

brī·quette', brī·quet' (-ket'), *n.* [Fr. *briquette*, dim. of *brique*, brick.]

1. a molded, bricklike block of compressed coal dust, peat, etc., used for fuel.

2. a brick-shaped piece of artificial stone.

brī·sānce, *n.* [Fr., lit. breaking, ppr. of *briser*, to break; OFr. *bruiser*.] the shattering effect of the sudden release of energy, as in an explosion of nitroglycerine or in nuclear fission.

bri·sé' (brī-zā'), *a.* [Fr.] broken; in music, broken off short, as a chord.

Brī·sē'is, *n.* in Greek legend, a pretty woman seized by Agamemnon from Achilles, her captor.

brisk, *a.* [prob. from Fr. *brusque*, brusque.]

1. lively; active; nimble; gay; sprightly; vivacious; as, a *brisk* young man; a *brisk* movement.

2. stimulating; keen; sharp; invigorating; as, *brisk* air.

Syn.—animated, spirited, vivacious, sprightly, alert, active, nimble, quick.

brisk, *v.t.* and *v.i.*; brisked, *pt.*, *pp.*; brisking, *ppr.* to make lively; to enliven; to animate; to come up with life and speed; to take an erect or bold attitude: generally with *up*; as, to *brisk up* a horse, or a servant.

bris'ket, *n.* [ME. *bruskette*; OFr. *bruschet*; Bret. *bruched*, *brusk*, the breast, chest, of a bird; W. *brysced*, the breast of a slain animal.]

1. the breast of an animal or that part of

the breast that lies next to the ribs; also, a joint cut from this portion of the animal.
2. the forepart or breast of a horse, from the shoulder down to the forelegs.
brisk'ly, *adv.* actively; vigorously; with life and spirit.
brisk'ness, *n.* liveliness; vigor in action; quickness; gaiety; vivacity; also, effervescence of liquors.
bris'ling, *n.* [Norm. dial., from older Dan. *bretling*, from LG. *bretling*, lit., the broad one.] a small, edible European fish packed as a sardine.
bris'tle (bris'sl), *n.* [OE. *bristel, brustel*; AS. *bristl, byrst*, a bristle; O.H.G. *burst*; G. *borste*, a bristle, brush; Sans. *bhrshti*, an edge, point.]
1. a stiff, glossy hair of swine, especially one of those growing on the back, used for making brushes; also, a similar hair on other animals.
2. a species of pubescence on plants, in the shape of a stiff, roundish hair.
3. any of the hairs of a brush.
bris'tle, *v.t.*; bristled, *pt., pp.*; bristling, *ppr.* 1. to stiffen the bristles of; to erect in defiance or anger, like the bristles of a hog; as, to *bristle* the crest.
2. to attach a bristle to; as, to *bristle* a piece of cotton thread.
bris'tle, *v.i.* 1. to rise or stand erect; as, the hair *bristles*.
2. to raise the head and show anger or defiance.
3. to seem as though hidden by bristles; as, the hill *bristled* with bayonets.
4. to have one's hair stand up.
bris'tle-bear''ing, *a.* having bristles.
bris'tle·līke, *a.* stiff as a bristle.
bris'tle-point''ed, *a.* needle-pointed, as some leaves; terminating in a bristle.
bris'tle rat, the hedgehog rat.
bris'tle-shāped (-shāpt), *a.* of the thickness and length of a bristle, as a leaf.
bris'tle·tāil, *n.* an insect belonging to the *Thysanura*, particularly one which has bristle-like abdominal appendages.
bris'tli·ness (bris'sli-), *n.* the state of having bristles.
bris'tling (bris'sling), *n.* same as *brisling*.
bris'tly (bris'sli), *a.* thickset with bristles, or with hairs like bristles; rough.
Bris'tŏl bōard (or **paper**), [named after the city of *Bristol*, Eng.] a fine calendered pasteboard, usually not glazed, used in drawing, in printing, etc.
bris'ūre (*or* bri-sụr'), *n.* [Fr., from *briser*, to break.]
1. any part of a parapet or rampart out of line with the general direction of a fortification.
2. in heraldry, a mark of cadency; a device designating the son by whom a paternal shield is borne.
brit, britt, *n. sing.* and *pl.* 1. the young of the herring, found, at some seasons, in immense numbers on the coast of New England; the sprat.
2. the minute animals upon which the right or whalebone whale feeds.
Bri·tan'ni·ȧ, *n.* [from L. *Britannia*, Great Britain.]
1. the female figure symbolizing Britain or the British Empire. [Poetic.]
2. [b–] Britannia metal.
Bri·tan'ni·ȧ met'ăl, bri·tan'ni·ȧ met'ăl, an alloy of tin, copper, and antimony, used in making tableware.
Bri·tan'niç, *a.* [L. *Britannicus*, from *Britannia*, Great Britain.] pertaining to Great Britain; British: applied almost exclusively to the title of the king; as, His *Britannic* Majesty.
brīte, brīght (brīt), *v.i.* to be or become overripe, as wheat, barley, or hops. [Brit. Dial.]
Brit'i·çism, *n.* a British characteristic or mode of speech, or a word, phrase, idiom, etc. peculiar to British English; as, his speech was full of *Briticisms*.
Brit'ish, *n. sing.* and *pl.* [ME. *Britissh, Brytisc*; AS. *Bryttisc*, from *Bryttas, Brettas*, the Britons.]
1. British English.
2. the language of the ancient Britons; Cymric.
the British; the people of Great Britain: sometimes broadly applied to all the people of the British Commonwealth of Nations.
Brit'ish, *a.* 1. of Great Britain, etc., or its people.
2. of the British Commonwealth of Nations.
British gum; dextrin: a commercial name.
Brit'ish Eng'lish, the English language as spoken and written in England: usually distinguished from *American English*.
Brit'ish·ẽr, *n.* an Englishman; a subject of Great Britain: sometimes broadly applied to any British subject.
Brit'ish·ism, *n.* a Briticism.
Brit'ish thẽr'măl ū'nit, a unit of heat equal to 252 calories; quantity of heat required to raise the temperature of one pound of water from 62° F. to 63° F.
Brit'ŏn, *n.* [ME. and OFr. *Briton*; L. *Brito, Britto*; of Celt. origin.]
1. a native or inhabitant of Great Britain or the British Commonwealth of Nations.
2. a member of an early Celtic people living in the southern part of Britain at the time of the Roman invasion.
brits'ka, *n.* [Pol. *bryczka*, dim. of *bryka*, freight wagon.] a long spacious carriage with a folding top: also spelled *britzka, britzska*.
britt, *n.* see *brit*.
brit'tle, *a.* [ME. *britel, brutel*, from AS. *breotan*, to break.] easily broken or shattered; crisp; fragile; as, *brittle* stone or glass.
brit'tle, *n.* a crisp, breakable candy; as, peanut *brittle*.
brit'tle·ly, *adv.* in a brittle manner.
brit'tle·ness, *n.* aptness to break; fragility.
brit'tle·stär, *n.* any species of sand star: so called from its fragility.
brīze, *n.* same as *breeze*, the gadfly. [Obs.]
brōach, *n.* [ME. *broche*, a pin, peg, spit; OFr. *broche*; LL. *brocca*, a spit, sharp stake; Gael. *brog*, a shoemaker's awl, from *brog*, to spur, goad.]
1. a sharp-pointed rod for holding roasting meat; spit; skewer.
2. a narrow, pointed mason's chisel.
3. a hole made by a broach.
4. an awl; a bodkin. [Brit. Dial.]
5. same as *brooch*.
6. a start of an antler, like the end of a spit, on the head of a young stag.
7. a rod used in candle-making to dip the wicks.
8. in architecture, a spire built on a tower without an intermediate parapet.
9. the pin or projection in a lock that enters the barrel of a key.
10. a reamer, or tapering tool for enlarging and smoothing holes in metal.
11. a borer for sampling casks of wine, etc.
12. a metal worker's tool with file teeth, used for dressing holes where rotating tools cannot reach.

BROACH (sense 8)

brōach, *v.t.*; broached (brōcht), *pt., pp.*; broaching, *ppr.* [ME. *brochen*; OFr. *brocher*, from *broche*, a spur, spit.]
1. to spit; to pierce as with a spit. [Obs.]
2. to tap; to pierce, as a cask in order to draw the liquor; hence, to shed, as blood.
3. to open, as a storehouse or a case of goods.
4. to utter; to bring up; to introduce in conversation; as, he *broached* the subject at dinner.
5. in masonry, to chisel roughly into shape, as a block of stone.
6. to use a broach in enlarging or dressing (a hole).
to broach to; in navigation, to incline suddenly to windward so as to lay the sails aback and expose the vessel to the danger of upsetting.
brōach'ẽr, *n.* 1. a spit. [Obs.]
2. one who broaches, opens, or introduces.
brọad, *a.*; *comp.* broader; *superl.* broadest, [ME. *brood, brod*; AS. *brad*; Ice. *breidhr*; D. *breed*; Sw. *bred*; Dan. *bred*; Goth. *braids*, broad.]
1. wide; extended in breadth, or from side to side, as distinguished from long: opposed to *narrow*.
2. wide; extensive; as, the *broad* ocean.
3. liberal; not limited; as, *broad* statesmanship.
4. open; clear; as, in *broad* sunshine.
5. coarse; gross; ribald; as, a *broad* comment.
6. comprehensive; liberal; tolerant; as, he was too *broad* to be orthodox.
7. evident; plain; as, a *broad* hint.
8. strongly marked; very noticeable; as, he has a *broad* accent.
9. extensive; general; as, in a *broad* sense that's true.
10. main; essential; as, in *broad* outline.
11. spoken with the tongue held flat and low in the mouth and the oral passage wide open, as *a* in *father*: the current phonetic term is *open*.
as broad as it is long; equal upon the whole; amounting to the same thing in the end.
Syn.—ample, extensive, large, wide.
brọad, *n.* 1. the broad part of anything.
2. a turning lathe for cylinders.
3. a broadened fen at flood. [Brit. Dial.]
4. an English gold coin of the time of James I, worth twenty shillings.
5. a woman or girl: a vulgar term. [Slang.]
brọad, *adv.* broadly; completely; as, to be *broad* awake.
brọad ar'rōw, 1. an arrow with a broad head.
2. an identification mark that the British government puts on its property and on prisoners' uniforms.

BROAD ARROW

brọad'ax, brọad'axe, *n.* an ax with a broad blade, used as a weapon or for cutting timber.
brọad bēan, a plant bearing thick, broad pods with flat seeds, used chiefly for fodder.
brọad'bill, *n.* 1. a wild duck frequenting the eastern coast of the United States in autumn; the scaup duck.
2. the shoveler duck, *Spatula clypeata*.
3. one of several species of birds belonging to the family *Eurylæmidæ*, and found in the East Indies.
brọad'brim, *n.* 1. a hat with a very wide brim, like that worn by Quakers.
2. ⌊*often* B–⌋ a Friend; a Quaker. [Colloq.]
brọad'-brimmed, *a.* having a wide brim.
brọad'çast, *v.t.*; broadcast or, in radio, broadcasted, *pt., pp.*; broadcasting, *ppr.* 1. to scatter (something) over a broad area.
2. to spread (information, etc.); inform many people of.
3. to transmit widely by radio.
brọad'çast, *v.i.* to broadcast radio programs.
brọad'çast, *n.* 1. a sowing by broadcasting.
2. a radio program.
brọad'çast, *adv.* far and wide.
brọad'çast, *a.* 1. widely scattered.
2. of or for radio broadcasting.
brọad'çast·ẽr, *n.* 1. a person, organization, etc. that prepares, makes, or transmits radio broadcasts.
2. equipment for radio broadcasting; transmitter.
brọad'çast·ing stā'tion, 1. an organization for broadcasting radio programs: it is often part of a network.
2. the studios, offices, or building of such an organization.
Brọad'-chũrch, *a.* in the Church of England, (a) designating a group (*Broad Church*) with liberal views as to doctrine and communion; (b) of this group or its views.
brọad'çloth, *n.* 1. a fine, smooth woolen cloth, used in making tailored garments: so called because it was originally made of greater width than ordinary woolens.
2. a fine, smooth cotton or silk cloth, used for shirts, etc.
brọad'en, *v.i.* to grow or become broad or broader.
brọad'en, *v.t.*; broadened, *pt., pp.*; broadening, *ppr.* to make broad or broader; to widen; to expand.
brọad'-gāuġe, *a.* 1. for or having a broad gauge.
2. broad-minded. [Colloq.]
brọad gāuġe, 1. a width (between the rails) of more than 56½ inches (standard gauge).
2. a railroad having such a gauge.
3. a locomotive for such a railroad.
brọad'-gāuġed, *a.* broad-gauge.
brọad'họrn, *n.* a flat-bottomed river freight boat.
brọad'-họrned, *a.* having widespread horns.
brọad'ish, *a.* rather broad.
brọad jump, a jump for distance rather than height, made either from a stationary position (*standing broad jump*) or with a running start (*running broad jump*).
brọad'lēaf, *n.* 1. a Jamaican tree, *Terminalia latifolia*, which furnishes wood for building purposes: also called *almond tree*.
2. any of various tobaccos with broad leaves used for making cigars.
brọad'lọọm, *a.* woven on a wide loom: said of rugs and carpets.
brọad'ly, *adv.* in a broad manner; liberally.

broad′-mīnd′ed, *a.* tolerant of other people's opinions and behavior; not bigoted; liberal.

broad′mouth, *n.* a passerine bird of the East Indies, family *Eurylæmidæ*; a broadbill.

broad′ness, *n.* the state or condition of being broad.

broad′piēce, *n.* a broad (sense 4).

broad sēal, the public seal of a nation or state.

broad′-sēal, *v.t.* to stamp with a broad seal; to set the stamp of authority upon. [Obs.]

broad′sheet, *n.* a broadside (sense 6).

broad′sīde, *n.* 1. the simultaneous discharge of all the guns on one side of a ship.
 2. all the guns so placed.
 3. the whole of a vessel's side above the water line from bow to quarter.
 4. a vigorous, effective attack in words, especially in a newspaper.
 5. the broad surface of any large object.
 6. a large sheet of paper printed on one side, as with advertising or a political message.
 7. violent abuse. [Colloq.]

broad′sīde, *adv.* 1. with the length turned (*to* an object); as, the ship came *broadside* to the dock.
 2. directly in the side; as, the train rammed the car *broadside*.
 3. indiscriminately; as, to level charges *broadside*.

broad′-spec′trum, *a.* effective against a wide variety of microorganisms; as, a *broad-spectrum* antibiotic.

broad′spread (-spred), *a.* widespread.

broad′spread″ing, *a.* spreading widely.

broad′stōne, *n.* same as *ashler*.

broad′swōrd (-sōrd), *n.* a sword with a broad blade and a cutting edge.

broad′tāil, *n.* 1. a thick-tailed sheep of Asia Minor; karakul.
 2. the flat, wavy pelt of its lamb; astrakhan.
 3. any parrot of the genus *Platycercus*, with broad tail feathers.

broad′thrōat, *n.* a broadbill (sense 3).

broad′-tread (-tred), *a.* having a wide face; as, a *broad-tread* car wheel.

Broad′wāy, *n.* [from *Broadway*, a street in New York City, known for its theaters, etc.] the New York commercial theater or entertainment industry, or its life, world, etc.

broad′wīse, *adv.* in the direction of the breadth.

brob, *n.* a specially shaped spike used to hold an abutting timber in place.

Brob·ding·nag′i·ăn, *a.* [from *Brobdingnag*, a country of giants, in Swift's *Gulliver's Travels*.] gigantic; of great height.

Brob·ding·nag′i·ăn, *n.* a giant.

brō·cāde′, *n.* [Sp. *brocado*, from LL. *brocare*, to embroider, stitch.] a rich cloth with a raised design woven into it, as of silk, velvet, gold, or silver.

brō·cāde′, *v.t.*; brocaded, *pt.*, *pp.*; brocading, *ppr.* to weave a raised design into (cloth).

brō·cād′ed, *a.* 1. woven like or into brocade.
 2. decorated or covered with brocade.

brō·cāde′ shell, a parti-colored cone shell, *Conus geographicus*.

brō′cāge, *n.* see *brokerage*.

broc′ărd, *n.* [OFr., from *Brocard*, French for *Burchhard*, bishop of Worms, who published a collection of ecclesiastical canons.] a brief maxim, rule, or proverb in philosophy, ethics, or law.

Brō′cärd cir′cle, in mathematics, a circle plotted around a triangle: named after H. *Brocard*, 1845–1922, a French mathematician.

Brō′cärd el·lipse′, in mathematics, a derivation of the Brocard circle. The ellipse uses as foci two of the points of the Brocard circle.

Brō′cȧ's ȧ·phā′si·ȧ, the inability to speak or use the vocal organs although they are not actually paralyzed.

Brō′cȧ's scāle, in anthropology, a chart for rating skin color: named for P. *Broca*, 1824–1880, a French surgeon.

broc·ȧ·tel′, broc·ȧ·telle′, *n.* [Fr. *brocatelle*; It. *broccatello*, dim. of *broccato*, brocaded.]
 1. a calcareous stone or marble, having a yellow ground flecked with white, gray, and red.
 2. a heavy, figured cloth like brocade, used chiefly for upholstery.

broc′cō·li, *n.* [It. *broccoli*, sprouts; pl. of *broccolo*, a sprout, cabbage sprout; dim. of *brocco*, LL. *brocca*, a spit, sharp-pointed thing.]
 1. a variety of the common cabbage, *Brassica oleracea*, resembling the cauliflower.
 2. a related vegetable with small, loose, white or green heads; sprouting broccoli.

broch, *n.* [Scot.] a circular stone tower of ancient and unknown origin, found in ruins in the Orkney and Shetland islands and the northern part of Scotland.

broch′ăn·tīte, *n.* [after *Brochant* de Villiers, French mineralogist.] a basic sulfate of copper, occurring in emerald-green crystals.

brōche, *n.* a broach. [Obs.]

bro·ché′ (brō-shā′), *a.* [Fr., from *brocher*, to stitch, sew.]
 1. ornamentally woven; brocaded.
 2. stitched, as a pamphlet or unbound book.

brō·chette′ (-shet′), *n.* [Fr., dim. of *broche*, a spit.] a skewer; a small spit.

brō·chid′ō·drōme, *a.* [Gr. *brochis*, dim. of *brochos*, a loop, and *dromos*, a running.] having loops: applied to nervation in leaves, where loops are formed within the blade.

brō·chure′, *n.* [Fr., from *brocher*, to stitch.] a brief treatise or essay, in pamphlet form.

brock, *n.* [AS. *broc*; Ir. *broc*; W. *broch*, a badger.] a badger.

brock, *n.* a broken portion; a fragment. [Brit. Dial. and Scot.]

brock, *n.* a cart horse; sometimes, a cow. [Brit. Dial.]

brock, *v.t.* [ME. *brokken*, from *brekken*, to break.] to break in pieces; to crumble. [Scot.]

brock, *v.i.* to complain. [Rare.]

brock′āge, *n.* 1. coin rejected as having been imperfectly minted.
 2. articles broken or damaged.

brock′et, *n.* [ME. *broket*; Fr. *brocart*, *broquart*, a brocket; OFr. *broc*, a tine of a stag's horn.]
 1. a male deer two years old; a pricket.
 2. any South American deer of the genus *Cariacus*, with short, unbranched horns.

brōde′kin, brōde′quin (-kin), *n.* [Fr.] a buskin or half boot. [Obs.]

brog, *n.* a sharpened prodding instrument, as a needle, pin, or awl. [Scot. and Brit. Dial.]

brog, *v.t.* to pierce or prick with or as with a brog. [Scot. and Brit. Dial.]

brō′găn, *n.* [Gael.] a brogue (shoe).

brög′ger·ite (brŭg′gẽr-īte), *n.* named after W. C. *Brögger*.] a rare mineral of the nature of uraninite or pitchblende.

brog′gle, *v.i.* to fish for eels with a brog. [Brit. Dial. and Scot.]

brōgue (brōg), *n.* [Gael. and Ir. *brog*, a shoe.]
 1. a coarse shoe of untanned leather, formerly worn in Ireland.
 2. a man's heavy, comfortable oxford shoe, usually with decorative perforations.

IRISH BROGUES

brōgue (brōg), *n.* [apparently from *brogger* (Anglo-Fr. *brogour*, var. of *broker*).] a trick; a deception. [Scot.]

brōgue (brōg), *n.* [prob. from Ir. *barroq*, a hold, a grip (especially on the tongue).] the pronunciation peculiar to a dialect, especially that of English as spoken by the Irish.

broid, *v.t.* to braid. [Obs.]

broi′dẽr, *v.t.* [ME. *broiden*, *brouden*; Fr. *broder*; *border*, from *bord*, a border, edge, welt.] to embroider. [Archaic.]

 A robe, a *broidered* coat, and a girdle.
 —Ex. xxviii. 4.

broi′dẽr·ẽr, *n.* one who embroiders. [Archaic.]

broi′dẽr·y, *n.* [ME. *broiderie*; OFr. *broderie*, from *broder*, *border*, to border, edge.] embroidery. [Archaic.]

broil, *n.* [Fr. *brouiller*, to mix, confuse, quarrel; LL. *brogilus*, *broilus*, a thicket, wood.] a tumult; a noisy quarrel; contention.

 Syn.—affray, altercation, feud, fray, quarrel, contest, uproar.

broil, *v.i.* to take part in a broil, or quarrel.

broil, *v.t.*; broiled, *pt.*, *pp.*; broiling, *ppr.* [ME. *broilen*; OFr. *bruiller*, to broil, roast; from *bruir*; M.H.G. *brüen*, to scald, burn.]
 1. to cook over coals, especially upon a gridiron; to cook by exposing to direct, intense heat of any kind.
 2. to expose directly to intense heat.

broil, *v.i.* 1. to cook by broiling.
 2. to be exposed directly to great heat.
 3. to become heated or angry.

broil, *n.* 1. a broiling; a great heat.
 2. anything broiled.

broil′ẽr, *n.* one who engages in brawls or quarrels.

broil′ẽr, *n.* 1. one who cooks by broiling.
 2. a pan, gridiron, etc. for broiling.
 3. the part of a stove designed for broiling.
 4. a chicken suitable for broiling.

broil′ing, *a.* extremely hot.

broil′ing, *n.* the operation of cooking by direct application of heat.

brō′kāge, *n.* the business or fee of a broker, especially a marriage broker.

brōke, *v.i.*; broked, *pt.*, *pp.*; broking, *ppr.* to transact business for another in trade; to act as agent in buying and selling. [Rare.]

brōke, *v.* past tense and archaic past participle of *break*.

brōke, *a.* broken; bankrupt; without money or resources; penniless. [Slang.]
 to go broke; to lose one's money or property; to exhaust one's resources; to become bankrupt. [Slang.]
 to go for broke; to risk everything on an uncertain undertaking. [Slang.]

brō′ken, *v.* past participle of *break*.

brō′ken, *a.* [pp. of *break*; ME. *broken*; AS. *brocen*, from *brecan*, to break.]
 1. parted by violence into two or more pieces or fragments; splintered, fractured, burst, etc.; as, a *broken* beam; a *broken* dish.
 2. uneven; rough; as, a *broken* surface; opened up with the plow; as, *broken* ground.
 3. intersected with hills and valleys; as, *broken* country.
 4. uttered disjointedly; ejaculated; faltering; as, *broken* speech caused by emotion.
 5. not fluent; imperfectly spoken, especially with reference to grammar and syntax; as, *broken* English.
 6. interrupted; discontinuous; incomplete; as, *broken* sleep.
 7. violated; unfulfilled; as, *broken* laws; *broken* promises.
 8. unsettled; as, *broken* weather.
 9. ruined in resources; bankrupt.
 10. weakened; enfeebled; made infirm; as, *broken* health; a *broken* constitution.
 11. crushed; humbled; as, a *broken* spirit.
 12. subdued; tamed; trained; as, a *broken* colt.
 13. in music, arranged for several instruments, or in parts.
 14. in painting, reduced in tone by the admixture of gray: said of a color.
 15. demoted. [Colloq.]

brō′ken-backed, *a.* 1. having a broken back.
 2. in nautical language, hogged; so weakened in the frame as to droop at each end: said of a ship.

brō′ken-down, *a.* 1. worn out; shattered; disheartened; broken in health or spirit.
 2. ruined; useless.

brō′ken·heärt″ed, *a.* having the spirits depressed or crushed by grief or despair; heartbroken.

brō′ken·ly, *adv.* in a broken, interrupted manner.

brō′ken·ness, *n.* 1. the state of being broken.
 2. the state of being crushed by grief or despair; as, *brokenness* of heart.

brō′ken wind, in veterinary medicine, the heaves.

brō′ken-wind″ed, *a.* having the heaves, as a horse.

brō′kẽr, *n.* [ME. *broker*, *brokour*, from AS. *brucan*, to use, possess, enjoy.]
 1. a person paid a fee or commission for acting as an agent in making contracts or sales.
 2. one who deals in money, notes, bills of exchange, etc.; a money lender; a pawnbroker.
 3. one who deals in old household goods. [Brit.]
 4. a stockbroker.
 broker's note; a memorandum of particulars of a contract existing between a broker and his client.
 curbstone broker or *street broker*; a broker, not a member of an exchange, who transacts his business on the street or by calling at various offices.
 exchange broker; a broker who makes a specialty of dealing in foreign bills of exchange and currencies.
 insurance broker; a person whose business is to write insurance.
 ship broker; a broker who buys and sells ships, procures cargoes, etc.

brō′kẽr·āge, *n.* 1. the business or employment of a broker.
 2. a broker's fee or commission.

brō′kẽr·ly, *a.* like, or having the nature of, a broker. [Obs.]

brō′kẽr·y, *n.* the business of a broker. [Obs.]

brō′king, *n.* the business or occupation of a broker. [Obs.]

brō′mȧ, *n.* [Gr. *broma*, food, from *bibrōskein*, to eat.]
 1. in medicine, any solid food that is chewed.
 2. a preparation made from cacao seeds or beans by removing the oil.

brō′măl, *n.* [*brom*ine and *al*cohol.] an oily, colorless fluid obtained by passing bromine through alcohol.

brō'māte, *n.* a salt of bromic acid.

brō'māte, *v.t.*; bromated, *pt.*, *pp.*; bromating, *ppr.* to impregnate or saturate with bromine; also, to combine with bromine.

brō·mȧ·tol'ō·ġist, *n.* a student of or expert in bromatology.

brō·mȧ·tol'ō·ġy, *n.* [Gr. *broma* (*-atos*), food, and *-logia*, from *legein*, to speak.] the science of nutrition.

brōme, *n.* same as *bromine*.

brōme gráss, a species of coarse forage grass belonging to the genus *Bromus*.

Brō·mē'li·ȧ, *n.* [named after Olaf *Bromel* (1639–1705), Swedish botanist.] a genus of tropical American plants, including the wild pineapple, *Bromelia Pinguin*, belonging to the family *Bromeliaceæ*; also, [b–], a plant of this genus.

Brō·mē·li·ā'cē·ae, *n.pl.* a family of plants remarkable for the hardness and dryness of their gray foliage. They abound in tropical America, commonly growing on trees or rocks.

brō·mē·li·ā'ceous, *a.* belonging to or resembling the *Bromeliaceæ*.

brō'mē·lin, *n.* a digestive enzyme present in the juice of the pineapple.

brō'miç, *a.* of or containing bromine, especially bromine with a valence of five.

bromic acid; an acid, $HBrO_3$, of which bromates are salts: it cannot be prepared in the pure state, and is found only in dilute aqueous solutions.

brō'mīde (*or* -mid), **brō'mid,** *n.* 1. a compound formed by the union of bromine with another element or radical.

2. potassium bromide, KBr, used in medicine as a sedative.

3. a trite saying or statement; platitude.

4. a person who says trite things. [Slang.]

bromide paper; a paper sensitized with bromide of silver, used in printing photographs.

brō·mid'iç, *a.* using or containing a trite remark or remarks.

brō·mi·drō'sis, *n.* [L., from Gr. *brōmos*, a stench, and *hidrōs*, sweat.] a disease of the sweat glands, characterized by an offensive odor; osmidrosis.

brō'mi·nāte, *v.t.*; brominated, *pt.*, *pp.*; brominating, *ppr.* in chemistry, to combine with bromine.

brō'mīne (*or* -min), **brō'min,** *n.* [L. *brominium*, from Gr. *brōmos*, stench.] a chemical element, usually in the form of a reddish-brown, corrosive liquid, volatilizing to form a vapor that has an unpleasant odor and is very irritating to mucous membranes: used in making dyes, in photography, and, in the form of certain compounds, in antiknock motor fuel: symbol, Br; atomic weight, 79.916; atomic number, 35.

brō'miṣm, brō'min·iṣm, *n.* in medicine, a disorder produced by the excessive use of bromine or bromides.

brō'mīte, *n.* same as *bromyrite*.

brō'mīze, *v.t.*; bromized, *pt.*, *pp.*; bromizing, *ppr.* to treat or impregnate with bromine or a bromide, as chemicals and plates used in photography.

brom'līte, *n.* [from *Bromley* Hill, Alston, Eng.] a carbonate of barium and calcium occurring in white, gray, and pink crystals: also called *alstonite*.

brō'mō-, a combining form used in chemical compounds in which bromine is a principal ingredient.

brō'mō·form, *n.* a liquid similar to chloroform in composition and producing similar effects, made by bromine acting upon wood spirits or alcohol.

brō·mō·ġel'ȧ·tin, *n.* [*bromo-*, and Fr. *gelatine*, from L. *gelare*, to congeal.] an emulsion formed of bromides, silver nitrate, and gelatin, used for preparing photographic dry plates.

brō·mog'rȧ·phy, *n.* same as *bromatography*.

brōm'ū·ret, *n.* a bromide. [Obs.]

Brō'mus, *n.* [L., from Gr. *brōmos*, oats.] a genus of coarse grasses similar to oats; the brome grasses.

brōm'y·rīte, *n.* [*bromine*, from Gr. *brōmos*, a stench, and *argyros*, silver.] native silver bromide, yellowish-green in color.

broñch-, broncho-.

broñ'chī, *n.*, pl. of *bronchus*.

broñ'chi·ȧ, *n.pl.* [LL., from Gr. *bronchia*, the bronchial tubes.] bronchial tubes smaller than the bronchi but larger than the bronchioles.

broñ'chi·ȧl, *a.* of the bronchia, bronchi, or bronchioles.

bronchial arteries; branches from the superior part of the descending aorta, accompanying the bronchi and supplying the lungs with blood.

bronchial glands; lymphatic glands lying along the bronchi.

bronchial membrane; the mucous membrane which lines the bronchi.

bronchial tubes; the bronchi and the minute branches of the bronchi, terminating in the air cells of the lungs.

broñ'chiç, *a.* same as *bronchial*.

broñ'chi·ōle, *n.* a small subdivision of the bronchia.

broñ·chit'iç, *a.* relating to or having bronchitis.

broñ·chī'tis, *n.* [Gr. *bronchia*, the bronchia, and *-itis*.] an inflammation, acute or chronic, of any part of the bronchial membrane.

broñ'chō, *n.*; *pl.* **broñ'chōs,** a bronco.

broñ'chō-, a combining form meaning *having to do with the bronchi*; as, *broncho*pneumonia.

broñ'chō·bust·ẽr, *n.* a broncobuster.

broñ'chō·cēle, *n.* [Gr. *bronchokēlē*; *bronchos*, the windpipe, and *kēlē*, a tumor.] an enlarged thyroid gland; goiter.

broñ·choph'ō·ny (-kof'), *n.* [*broncho-*, and Gr. *phōnē*, voice.] the sound of the voice as heard normally in the bronchi through the stethoscope, or abnormally in other parts of the chest.

broñ''chō·pneū·mō'ni·ȧ, *n.* [*broncho-*, and Gr. *pneumonia*, from *pneumōn*, pl. *pneumones*, the lungs.] inflammation of the bronchia accompanied by inflamed, pus-forming patches in the near-by lobules of the lungs: it generally occurs as a secondary disease following an infection of the upper respiratory tract.

broñ'chō·sçōpe, *n.* an instrument with a small electric light which gives a view of the bronchia and lungs, enabling a surgeon to perform operations on those organs or remove an obstruction from them.

broñ'chō·tōme, *n.* [*broncho-*, and Gr. *tomos*, from *temnein*, to cut.] a surgical instrument used in making a bronchotomy.

broñ·chot'ō·my, *n.* [*broncho-*, and Gr. *tomia*, from *temnein*, to cut.] an incision into the windpipe or larynx, between the rings: called also *tracheotomy*, or *laryngotomy*.

broñ'chus, *n.*; *pl.* **broñ'chī,** [L., from Gr. *bronchos*, the windpipe.] either of the two primary branches of the windpipe.

broñ'cō, *n.*; *pl.* **broñ'cōṣ,** [Sp. *bronco*, rough, rude, crabbed, morose.] a small horse, broken or unbroken, native to the plains of the western United States; a mustang.

broñ'cō·bust·ẽr, *n.* a person who tames broncos; also, a cowboy. [Slang.]

brond, *n.* a brand. [Obs.]

bron'tō-, a combining form meaning: (a) thunder; (b) in paleontology, hugeness.

bron'tō·grȧph, *n.* [*bronto-*, and Gr. *graphein*, to write.] an instrument that makes a record of thunderstorms; also, the record made.

bron'tō·lith, bron'tō·līte, *n.* [*bronto-*, and Gr. *lithos*, a stone.] a meteoric rock or stone; an aerolite; a thunderstone.

bron·tol'ō·ġy, *n.* [*bronto-*, and Gr. *-logia*, from *legein*, to speak.] the scientific study of, or a discourse upon, thunder.

bron·tom'e·tẽr, *n.* same as *brontograph*.

bron·tō·sau'rus, *n.* [*bronto-*, and Gr. *sauros*, a lizard.] a huge, extinct American dinosaur of the Jurassic Period, which had a long, slender neck, a small head, and a thick tapering tail.

BRONTOSAURUS

Bron·tō·thē'ri·um, *n.* [*bronto-*, and Gr. *thērion*, a wild beast.] a genus of extinct rhinoceros-like animals that grew to the size of the elephant and at one time inhabited North America.

bron·tō·zō'um, *n.* [*bronto-*, and Gr. *zōon*, an animal.] a huge, extinct, three-toed dinosaur, the tracks of which are found in Mesozoic sandstone in the Connecticut valley.

Bronx cheer (broñks), a derisive cheer; a sound of contempt made by noisily vibrating the lips. [Slang.]

bronze, *n.* [Fr. *bronze*; It. *bronzo*; from *bruno*; O.H.G. *brūn*; AS. *brun*, brown.]

1. an alloy of copper and tin, to which other metallic substances, especially zinc, are sometimes added. It is hard, sonorous, and sometimes brittle: used for statues, bells, and cannon, the proportions of the respective ingredients being varied to meet the particular requirements.

2. a reddish-brown color.

3. a prepared pigment imitating the typical bronze color; also, various pigments, similar to bronze, having a gold or silver effect; as, aluminum *bronze*, which is compounded of aluminum and copper and is of a pale gold color.

4. anything, as a work of art, made of bronze.

5. effrontery; boldness; brass. [Rare.]

Bronze Age; the prehistoric period which followed the Stone Age, characterized by bronze tools and weapons.

Bronze Star; a United States Army military decoration awarded for heroic or meritorious achievement not involving participation in aerial flight: instituted in 1942.

bronze, *v.t.*; bronzed, *pt.*, *pp.*; bronzing, *ppr.* 1. to give the color of bronze to; to make look like bronze.

2. to make hard-hearted or unsympathetic; to brazen.

bronze liq'uŏr (lik'ẽr), a solution of chloride of antimony and sulfate of copper, used for bronzing.

bronze pow'dẽr, a metallic powder, mixed with oil paint, for coloring objects in imitation of bronze.

bronze'wing, *n.* any of several species of Australian pigeons, chiefly of the genus *Phaps*, distinguished by the bronze color of their plumage.

bronz'ine, *a.* having the appearance of bronze. [Rare.]

bronz'ing, *n.* 1. the act or art of imparting to any substance the appearance of bronze.

2. any preparation for giving a bronze color.

bronz'ist, *n.* a worker in bronze.

bronz'īte, *n.* a ferriferous variety of enstatite, having nearly the luster of bronze.

bronz'y, *a.* resembling bronze, especially in color.

brọo, *n.* [probably from OFr. *breu*.] broth. [Scot. and N. Eng. Dial.]

brōoch (*or* brōch), *n.* [ME. *broche*, a pin, peg, spit; OFr. *broche*; LL. *brocca*, a spit, sharp stake.] an ornamental pin or clasp worn by women at the bosom or neck, used for fastening the dress or merely for display.

brōoch, *v.t.* to adorn or furnish with or as with a brooch. [Rare.]

brọod, *n.* [ME. *brood*; AS. *brod*; D. *broed*; O.H.G. *bruot*, a brood.]

1. the offspring of animals, especially of birds or fowl.

2. (a) the young birds hatched at one time and cared for together; as, a *brood* of chickens or of ducks; (b) the young of bees before they issue from the brood cells; (c) the pupae of ants.

3. the children in a family.

4. a breed or kind; as, a *brood* of minor poets.

5. in mining, any heterogeneous waste mixture found in copper and tin ores.

brọod, *v.t.*; brooded, *pt.*, *pp.*; brooding, *ppr.* 1. to sit on and cover (eggs) for the purpose of warming and hatching them.

2. to hover over or protect (offspring, etc.) with or as with the wings.

3. to think moodily on (a subject).

brọod, *v.i.* 1. to brood eggs or offspring.

2. to sit on or spread over anything; as, darkness is *brooding* over the vast abyss.

3. to meditate moodily on a subject; as, to *brood* over one's failure.

brọod, *a.* 1. kept for breeding; as, a *brood* mare.

2. brooding on eggs; as, a *brood* hen.

brọod bud, 1. in botany, same as *bulbil*.

2. a soredium.

brọod'ẽr, *n.* 1. a covered apparatus or structure, artificially heated, for raising young fowl without a hen.

2. a person or animal that broods.

brọod gem'ma, in botany, a gemma or leaf-bud.

brọod'i·ness, *n.* the state or quality of being broody.

brọod'ing, *a.* 1. sitting on and hatching eggs.

2. deeply thoughtful; pondering; meditating; as, *brooding* eyes; a *brooding* look.

brọod'ing·ly, *adv.* in a brooding manner.

brọod māre, a mare kept for breeding purposes.

brọod pouch, a pouch or sac in which eggs are carried during the hatching process, as in many species of crustaceans.

brood'y, *a.* 1. having an inclination to brood, or dwell on one's own thoughts.
2. ready to brood: said of chickens.

brook, *n.* [ME. *brook, brok*; AS. *broc*, a stream; D. *brock*; LG. *brook*, a marsh; G. *bruch*, a marsh; from the root to break, in the sense of a stream bursting forth.] a small stream, usually smaller than a river.

brook, *v.t.*; brooked (brookt), *pt., pp.*; brooking, *ppr.* [ME. *brook, brok*; AS. *brucan*, to use, enjoy, as food; LG. *bruken*, to use; O.H.G. *bruhhan*, to use, need; Goth. *brukjan*; Sans. root *bhuj*, to enjoy, especially food.]
1. to bear; to endure; to tolerate: usually in the negative; as, young men cannot *brook* restraint.
2. to make use of. [Obs.]
3. to enjoy; to be in possession of. [Obs.]

Brook Färm, a farm near West Roxbury, Massachusetts, where a group of American writers and scholars experimented in setting up a model communist community from 1841 to 1847.

brook'ite, *n.* [named after H. J. *Brooke* (1771–1857), English mineralogist.] a yellowish or reddish-brown mineral, titanium dioxide. It crystallizes in the orthorhombic system.

brook'let, *n.* a small brook.

brook'lime, *n.* a plant (*Veronica beccabunga*) with blue flowers in loose lateral spikes; also, the European speedwell, the water speedwell or lesser brooklime, and the American brooklime (*Veronica americana*).

brook mint, the water mint, *Mentha aquatica*.

brook'side, *n.* the side or bank of a brook.

brook trout, the common speckled trout found in the rivers of eastern North America.

brook'weed, *n.* either of two plants related to the primrose, one European and the other North American, that grow in moist places and have small white flowers.

brook'y, *a.* abounding with brooks.

broom, *n.* [AS. *brōm*; LG. *bram*, broom; D. *brem*, broom, furze; closely allied to *bramble*, both being, according to Max Müller, from same root as Sans. *bhram*, to whirl, to be confused.]
1. any of various plants of the pea family. The common broom (*Cytisus scoparius*) is a leguminous shrub growing abundantly on sandy pastures and heaths in Britain and throughout Europe. It is distinguished by having large, yellow flowers, small leaves, and angular branches.
2. a brush with a long handle, for sweeping floors, etc.: so called because originally made of the twigs of the broom plant.

broom, *v.t.*; broomed, *pt., pp.*; brooming, *ppr.* to sweep with a broom.

broom, *v.t.* same as *bream*.

broom'corn, *n.* a variety of grass, *Sorghum vulgare*, resembling corn: the long, stiff stems of the flower clusters are used in brooms and brushes.

broom gràss, same as *broom sedge*.

broom'rāpe, *n.* [*broom*, and *rape* (the vegetable); used as a trans. of ML. *rapum genistae*, lit., broom tuber.] any of a number of related leafless plants of the genus *Orobanche*, with yellow, purplish, or reddish-brown flowers: they are parasitic on the roots of other plants.

broom sedge (sej), any one of several species of grass of the genus *Andropogon*, as *Andropogon scoparius*.

broom'stick, *n.* the handle of a broom.

broom tree, a shrub of Jamaica, *Baccharis scoparia*, having thickly clustered branches almost devoid of leaves.

broom'y, *a.* pertaining to or resembling broom; covered with broom; as, *broomy* land.

brōse, *n.* a thick porridge made by mixing boiling liquid with meal: called water *brose*, milk *brose*, chicken *brose*, beef *brose*, etc., according to the kind of liquid used. [Scot.]

brot'an, *n.* *Artemisia abrotanum*, a variety of wormwood.

broth, *n.* [AS. *broth*; Ice. *brodh*; O.H.G. *brot*, *brod*, broth.] a thin watery soup; water in which meat and, sometimes, vegetables or cereals have been boiled.

broth'el, *n.* [ME. *brothel, brethel*, a prostitute, worthless fellow; AS. *breothan*, to ruin, frustrate; confused with *bordel*.] a house of prostitution.

brŏth'ẽr, *n.*; *pl.* **brŏth'ẽrs** or *archaic* **breth'ren,** [ME. *brother*; AS. *brothor, brother*, brother; D. *broeder*; G. *bruder*; Ice. *brodhir*; Sw. *broder*; Goth. *brothar*; L. *frater*; Gr. *phratēr*; Sans. *bhrātar*, brother.]
1. a man or boy in his relation to another person born of the same father and mother. He is a *half brother* if there is but one parent in common.
2. any person closely united to another by some common bond or interest, as of occupation, class, profession, organization, etc.
3. one who resembles another in manners or disposition.

He also that is slothful in his work is *brother* to him that is a great waster. —Prov. xviii. 9.

4. a stepbrother.
5. a foster brother.
6. a friend who is like a brother.
7. a lay member of a men's religious order.
8. in Scripture, a kinsman by blood more remote than a son of the same parents, as in the case of Abraham and Lot, Jacob and Laban.
Brother Jonathan; the citizens of the United States collectively, or the government: probably originating from Washington's frequent jocular reference to Jonathan Trumbull, governor of Connecticut. [Colloq.]

brŏth'ẽr, *v.t.* to make a brother of; to designate as a brother; to admit to brotherhood.

brŏth'ẽr-ġẽr'măn, *n.* a full brother; a brother through both parents.

brŏth'ẽr·hood, *n.* 1. the state or quality of being a brother or brothers.
2. an association of men for any purpose, as a society of monks; a fraternity.
3. a class of men of the same kind, profession, or occupation; as, the legal *brotherhood*; the *brotherhood* of iron workers.
4. a class of similar individuals or objects.

A *brotherhood* of lofty elms. —Wordsworth.

Syn.—fraternity, association, fellowship, society, sodality.

brŏth'ẽr-in-lạw, *n.*; *pl.* **brŏth'ẽrs-in-lạw,**
1. the brother of one's husband or wife.
2. the husband of one's sister.
3. occasionally, the husband of the sister of one's wife or husband.

brŏth'ẽr·less, a. without a brother.

brŏth'ẽr·līke, *a.* characteristic of or befitting a brother.

brŏth'ẽr·li·ness, *n.* the quality of being brotherly.

brŏth'ẽr·ly, *a.* 1. pertaining to brothers; such as is natural for brothers; befitting brothers.
2. kind; affectionate; as, *brotherly* love.
Syn.—kind, affectionate, fraternal, loving, tender, devoted.

brŏth'ẽr·ly, *adv.* in a brotherly manner.

I speak but *brotherly* of him. —Shak.

brŏth'ẽr·wŏrt, *n.* wild thyme.

brough (brok), *n.* same as *broch*.

brough'ăm (brö'am *or* bröm), *n.* [named after the first Lord *Brougham* (1778–1868).]
1. a four-wheeled closed carriage for either two or four persons, having a curved opening underneath the driver's open seat in front enabling the wheels to turn within a narrow space.

BROUGHAM

2. an electrically powered automobile, between a coupe and a sedan in size.
3. a gasoline-powered limousine with the driver's seat unenclosed.

brought (brạt), past tense and past participle of *bring*.

bröu'hä''hä'', *n.* [Fr.] a noisy stir or wrangle; hubbub; uproar; commotion.

Bröus·sō·nē'ti·ȧ (-shi-ȧ), *n.* [from *Broussonet*, a French naturalist.] a genus of trees, family *Moraceae*, including the paper mulberry.

brow, *n.* [ME. *browe, bruwe*; AS. *bru*, brow, *bræw, breaw*, the eyelid; G. *braue*, the eyebrow; Ice. *bra*; Sans. *bhru*, the eyebrow.]
1. the eyebrow.
2. the forehead; hence, a person's facial expression; the general air of the countenance; as, his *brow* was sad.
3. the edge of a steep cliff; the projecting upper part of a hill; as, the *brow* of a hill.
to knit the brow; to frown.

brow, *v.t.* to bound; to limit; to form the edge or border of. [Rare.]

brow'bēat, *v.t.*; browbeat, *pt.*; browbeaten, *pp.*; browbeating, *ppr.* to subdue or silence with stern looks, or arrogant speech; to intimidate by abusive treatment; to bully; as, to *browbeat* a witness.

brow'bēat''ẽr, *n.* one who browbeats.

brow'bēat''ing, *n.* a subduing by harsh, stern speech or manners.

brow'bound, *a.* crowned. [Poet.]

browed, *a.* possessing a brow (of a specified kind); as, low-*browed*, dark-*browed*.

brow'less, *a.* without shame. [Rare.]

brown, *a.* [ME. *brown, brun*; AS. *brun*; O.H.G. *brun*; Ice. *brunn*; Sw. *brun*; Dan. *brun*; Lith. *brunas*; Sans. *bhru*, brown.]
1. having the color of chocolate or coffee, a combination of red, black, and yellow.
2. tanned by or as by the sun; dark-skinned.
brown algae; a kind of algae in which the green of the chlorophyll is somewhat obscured by brown pigmentation.
brown bear; a bear with brown fur, found in Europe, North America, etc.
brown Betty; a baked pudding made of bread crumbs, apples, and sugar.
brown bread; (a). any bread made of dark flour; (b). a dark, sweetened, steamed bread.
brown coal; same as *lignite*.
brown hematite; same as *limonite*.
brown paper; coarse, dark wrapping paper, made of unbleached stock.
Brown Shirt; a person who belonged to the Nazi Sturmabteilung (S.A.) in Germany or to some similar organization in other countries: so called because of the uniforms.
brown thrasher; a common songbird of America, related to the mocking bird, brownish-red above and whitish below.
brown thrush; the brown thrasher.
to do up brown; to accomplish in a thorough manner; to do to perfection.

brown, *n.* 1. a brown color.
2. any pigment or dye that makes things brown.

brown, *v.t.*; browned, *pt., pp.*; browning, *ppr.*
1. to make brown or dusky.
2. to give a bright brown color, as to articles of iron, such as gun barrels, by forming a thin, uniform coat of oxide on their surface.
3. to make brown by subjecting to heat, either natural or artificial; as, to *brown* bread; to *brown* the skin.
to brown out; to cause a brownout in.

brown, *v.i.* to become brown, as bread in the oven.

brown'back, *n.* same as *dowitcher*.

brown'-bag', *v.t.*; brown-bagged, *pt., pp.*; brown-bagging, *ppr.* 1. to carry one's lunch to work or school, as in a brown paper bag.
2. to bring one's own liquor into a restaurant, nightclub, etc. which is not permitted to sell liquor but may furnish setups.
Often used with *it*.

brown Bess, a smoothbore, bronzed flintlock musket, formerly the regulation arm of the British service.

brown fat, a heat-producing tissue stored in certain areas of the body by a hibernating animal: it prevents freezing and helps to warm the awakening animal.

Brown'i·ăn, *a.* relating to Dr. Robert Brown or to the Brownian movement.

Brown'i·ăn möve'ment, [after Robert *Brown* (1773–1858), who first demonstrated it.] the constant zigzag movement of colloidal dispersions in a liquid medium, caused by collision with molecules of the liquid.

brown'ie, *n.* [dim. of *brown*: from its supposed color.]
1. a small, helpful elf or goblin in stories, who does housework and other good deeds for people at night.
2. [B–] a girl scout between the ages of eight and eleven.
3. an unfrosted, chocolate cake with nuts in it, generally cut into small bars.

Brown'ie point, [perh. from the erroneous notion that merit points are awarded to Brownies in the Girl Scouts.] favor gained, as with a superior, for a meritorious, but relatively unimportant act.

brown'ing, *n.* 1. the act or operation of giving a brown color to articles of iron, as gun barrels, etc.
2. in masonry, a coat of brown mortar forming the foundation for the last coat of plaster.
3. a preparation of sugar, port wine, spices, etc., for coloring and flavoring meat and made dishes.

brown'ish, *a.* somewhat brown; inclined to brown.

Brown'ism, *n.* 1. the doctrines or religious

creed of the Brownists, or followers of Robert Brown, a Puritan dissenter, who, in the sixteenth century, maintained that any body of professing Christians united under one pastor, or communing together, constituted a church independent of any other. The Independent or Congregational sect of English dissenters was developed from Brownism.

2. the Brunonian theory of medicine.

Brown'ist, *n.* a follower of Robert Brown: cf. *Brownism.*

brown'ness, *n.* the quality of being brown.

brown'out, *n.* a partial elimination or dimming of lights in a city to prevent observation by enemy air raiders at night or to save fuel.

brown rīce, unpolished grains of rice.

brown rot, 1. a disease of stone fruits and pome fruits, marked by blight of flowers and twigs, rotting, etc.

2. any fungus causing this disease.

brown spär, a sparry or crystallized variety of dolomite, colored a reddish-brown from the presence of a small portion of oxide of iron and manganese.

brown'stōne, *n.* a brownish-red variety of sandstone, used for building.

brown'stōne front, 1. a façade of brownstone.

2. a house with such a façade.

brown stud'y, [orig., somber thought, from early sense of *brown*, somber, gloomy.] a condition of being deeply absorbed in thought; reverie.

brown sug'ăr (shug'), sugar that is wholly or partly unrefined.

Brown Swiss, a hardy breed of dairy cattle, first raised in Switzerland.

brown'tāil, *n.* a white moth with a tuft of reddish-brown hairs at the posterior end: its hairy larvae are harmful to trees.

brown'wŏrt, *n.* the *Scrophularia vernalis*, or yellow figwort, with brown stalks.

brown'y, *a.* brown or brownish; as, *browny* locks.

brow'pōst, *n.* a crossbeam.

browse, *v.t.*; browsed, *pt., pp.*; browsing, *ppr.* [OFr. *brouster*, to browse, from *broust*, a sprout, shoot.]

1. to feed on, as the ends or branches of trees and shrubs, or the young shoots: said of cattle, deer, and some other animals.

2. to pasture on; to nibble off; to graze on.

browse, *v.i.* 1. to feed on the tender branches or shoots of shrubs and trees, as cattle, sheep, etc.

2. to nibble; to graze.

3. to glance through a book, library, etc. in a leisurely way.

browse, *n.* [OFr. *broust*, a bud, shoot; M.H.G. *broz*, a bud.] the tender branches or twigs of trees and shrubs, fit for the food of cattle and other animals.

browse, *n.* [origin unknown.] an imperfectly smelted mass of metallic ore, slag, etc.

brows'ĕr, *n.* any animal that browses or feeds on green vegetation.

browse'wood, *n.* shrubs and bushes upon which animals browse.]Rare.]

brows'ing, *n.* 1. tender green growths on which animals browse.

2. a place where such growths abound.

brow'spot, *n.* the intercular gland of a toad or frog; a round organ between the eyes of toads.

brū'ang, *n.* [native name.] the sun bear of the Malayan archipelago.

brū·cel·lō'sis, *n.* [after Sir David *Bruce* (1855–1931), Scot. physician; and *-osis.*] undulant fever.

Brū'chi·dae, *n.pl.* a family of herbivorous beetles.

Brū'chus, *n.* [LL., a field cricket, from Gr. *brouchos*, a locust without wings.]

1. in entomology, a genus typical of *Bruchidæ.*

Bruchus pisi
(natural size and magnified)

2. [b–] a weevillike beetle; a locust without wings.

brū·cī'nȧ, *n.* same as *brucine.*

brūc'īne, brūc'in, *n.* [from James *Bruce* (1730–1794), Scottish traveler.] a bitter, poisonous, white alkaloid, found in the seeds of various species of *Strychnos*, chiefly in the nux vomica.

brū'cīte, *n.* native hydrate of magnesium; a white, pearly mineral, having a thin, foliated structure, like talc. It was named in honor of Dr. A. Bruce, of New York. The name *brucite* has also been given, by American mineralogists, to chondrodite. [Rare.]

bruck'eled, *a.* draggled; grimy. [Obs.]

brū'in, *n.* [D. *bruin*; O.H.G. *brun*, brown.] a bear, especially a brown bear: name used in fairy tales.

brūise, *v.t.*; bruised, *pt., pp.*; bruising, *ppr.* [ME. *broosen, brisen*, from AS. *brysan*, to break, bruise, and influenced by OFr. *bruser, bruiser*, to break.]

1. to injure the surface of (the skin) without breaking it but causing discoloration.

2. to injure the surface or outside of.

3. to crush with or as with mortar and pestle.

4. to hurt slightly, as feelings.

brūise, *v.i.* to be or become bruised.

brūise, *n.* 1. a discoloration of the skin caused by a blow.

2. an injury to the outside of fruit, plants, etc.

brūis'ĕr, *n.* 1. a concave tool for grinding lenses or specula.

2. a pugilist; a professional boxer.

3. a strong, pugnacious man; a bully.

4. a machine for crushing or bruising grain, as for fodder.

brūise'wŏrt, *n.* any plant whose preparations are considered healing in case of bruises, as soapwort, the comfrey, the daisy, etc.

brūis'ing, *n.* a beating; also, boxing, or prize fighting.

brūit, *n.* [Fr. *bruit*, noise, uproar, rumor, from *bruire*, rustle, roar.]

1. clamor. [Archaic.]

2. report; rumor; fame. [Archaic.]

brūit (*Fr. pron.* brwē), *n.* in medicine, an abnormal sound, varying in kind and pathological significance, and detected by auscultation.

brūit, *v.t.*; bruited, *pt., pp.*; bruiting, *ppr.* to make known to the public; to tell abroad.

Brū·māire', [Fr., from L. *bruma*, winter.] the second month (October 22–November 20) of the French Revolutionary Calendar, adopted by the First Republic in 1793.

brū'măl, *a.* [L. *brumalis*, from *bruma*, winter.] of winter; wintry.

brūme, *n.* [Fr., mist, fog, from L. *bruma*, winter.] mist; fog; vapors.

brum'mȧ·ġem, *a.* from *Birmingham*, formerly *Bromwycham*, Eng., where much cheap jewelry and gilt toys were manufactured.] not genuine; cheap and gaudy. [Colloq.]

brum'mȧ·ġem, *n.* anything cheap and gaudy, especially imitation jewelry. [Colloq.]

brū'mous, *a.* characterized by fog or mist.

brun, *n.* [Scot.] a brook or small stream. [Rare.]

brunch, *n.* [*b*reakfast, and *l*unch.] a combined breakfast and lunch. [Colloq.]

brū·net', *a.* [Fr.; OFr. *brunet, brunette*, dim. of *brun*, brown; O.H.G. *brun.*]

1. having a dark or olive color.

2. having black or dark-brown hair and eyes, and a dark complexion.

brū·net', *n.* a man or boy with brunet hair, eyes, and complexion.

brū·nette', *n.* [Fr. f. dim. of *brun*, brown.] a girl or woman with dark hair, eyes, and complexion.

brū·nette', *a.* brunet.

Brün'hild (*or* G. brün'hilt), *n.* in the Nibelungenlied, a queen of Iceland whom Gunther, king of Burgundy, gets as his bride with the help of Siegfried's magic.

brun'iōn (-yun), *n.* [Fr. *brugnon*, from L. *prunum*, a plum.] a nectarine. [Obs.]

Brün·ne·hil'de, *n.* in Richard Wagner's *Die Walküre*, a Valkyrie whom Siegfried releases from enchantment.

Brū·nō'ni·ăn, *a.* 1. pertaining to any individual by the name of Brown; Brownian.

2. designating or of a system of medicine founded by Dr. John Brown of Edinburgh (1735–1788), who classified and treated diseases according to his theory as to whether they were caused by too much or too little excitement.

Brū·nō'ni·ăn, *n.* 1. an adherent of the Brunonian medical theory.

2. a Brownist.

brunt, *n.* [ME. *brunt, bront*, a shock, impetus, from Ice. *bruna*, to rush.]

1. shock (of an attack); impact (of a blow).

2. the main part of the shock or impact: as, he bore the *brunt* of the argument.

brush, *n.* [ME. *brusshe*; OFr. *broche, broce, brosse*, a bush, brushwood; LL. *brustia, bruscia*, perhaps from O.H.G. *brusta, burst*, a bristle.]

1. a device having bristles, hairs, or wires fastened in a back of some sort, with or without a handle attached: brushes are used for cleaning, polishing, painting, smoothing the hair, etc.

2. brushwork.

3. any bushy tail, especially that of a fox.

4. the act of brushing.

5. a motion that barely touches; a light touch in passing.

6. in electricity, a piece, plate, rod, or bundle of carbon, copper, etc., used as a conductor between an outside circuit and a revolving part, as in a motor.

7. in optics, divergent rays of a brushlike appearance, (a) from an electrical ball serving as a conductor, or (b) as seen in the polarized light of certain crystals.

brush, *v.t.*; brushed (brusht), *pt., pp.*; brushing, *ppr.* [ME. *bruschen*; OFr. *brosser*, to beat the brush for game; from *brosse*, a brush, thicket.]

1. to sweep or rub with a brush; as, to *brush* a hat.

2. to strike as with a brush; to strike lightly, by passing over the surface without injury or impression; as, to *brush* the arm in passing.

3. to paint, clean, polish, smooth, etc. with a brush.

4. to remove by or as by brushing: usually followed by *off*; as, to *brush off* dust; also, to carry away by an act like that of brushing, or by passing over lightly, as by wind.

to brush aside; (a) to sweep from one's way; (b) to dismiss from consideration.

to brush away; to remove or drive away by brushing.

to brush up; (a) to clean up; to make presentable; (b) to refresh one's memory.

brush, *v.i.* to move nimbly in haste; to move so lightly as scarcely to be perceived; to move or skim over, with a slight contact, or without much impression; as, to *brush* by.

brush, *n.* [ME. *brusche*; OFr. *brosse*, a bush, brushwood.]

1. brushwood.

2. sparsely settled country, covered with brush.

brush, *n.* [from ME. *bruschen*, rush.] a short quick fight or quarrel; skirmish.

brush, *v.i.* [ME. *bruschen*, rush.] to go fast; to hurry.

brush būrn, an injury to the flesh similar to a burn or scald, resulting from great friction, as from sliding down a pole, rope, or the like.

brush dis'chärġe, a visible, brushlike electric discharge, as in the air surrounding a wire at high potential; corona.

brush'ĕr, *n.* one who or that which brushes.

brush'i·ness, *n.* a condition or appearance characteristic of a brush.

brush'ing, *n.* a rubbing or sweeping.

brush'ing, *a.* 1. brisk; light; as, a *brushing* gallop.

2. used or made to brush with.

brush'īte, *n.* a colorless, white, or gray monoclinic crystal formed by calcium phosphate: named after George J. Brush, an American mineralogist.

brush'līke, *a.* resembling a brush.

brush'-off, *n.* dismissal. [Slang.]

to give the brush-off; to dismiss; to get rid of. [Slang.]

BRUSH TURKEY
(*Talegalla lathami*)

brush tūr'key, a large bird found in Australia and New Guinea, making its habitat in the brush: several species are known by this name, but it is especially applied to the *Talegalla lathami.*

brush wheel (hwēl), a revolving circular brush used for polishing by silversmiths, lapidaries, turners, etc.; a cogless wheel which, in light machinery, turns a like wheel by the friction of a rubbing surface of bristles, rubber, buff leather, etc.

brush'wood, *n.* brush; a thicket or coppice of small trees and shrubs; also, branches of trees cut off.

brush'wŏrk, *n.* 1. work done with a brush; painting.
2. a characteristic way of putting on paint with a brush; as, Renoir's *brushwork*.

brush'y, *a.*; *comp.* brushier; *superl.* brushiest. 1. resembling a brush; rough; shaggy; having long hair.
2. characterized by brushwood.

brusque, brusk (brusk *or* broosk), *a.* [Fr. *brusque*, from It. *brusco*, tart, sour, rude.] abrupt, blunt, or short in manner or speech; bluff; as, he had a *brusque* way of speaking.

brusque'ness, brusk'ness, *n.* bluntness; the quality of being brusque.

brus·que·rie' (-ke-rē'), *n.* [Fr.] brusqueness.

Brus'sels cär'pet, [after *Brussels*, Belgium, where it was made.] a patterned carpeting made of small loops of colored woolen yarn in a linen warp.

Brus'sels grif'fŏn, any of a breed of lap dogs, reddish-brown in color, with large eyes, a turned-up nose, and a protruding lower jaw.

Brus'sels lāce, a machine-made lace with an appliquéd design.

Brus'sels sprouts, 1. a kind of cabbage with a tuft of leaves at the top and a stem covered with edible, small, cabbagelike buds or heads.
2. the heads of this plant.

brus'tle (-sl), *v.i.*; brustled, *pt.*, *pp.*; brustling, *ppr.* [ME. *brustlien*; AS. *brastlian*, *bærstlian*, to crackle, burst.] to crackle; to make a small, crackling noise; to rustle, as a silk garment; also, to bristle up. [Obs.]

brus'tle, *n.* a bristle. [Obs.]

brut, *a.* [Fr.; see *brute*.]
1. dry: said of wines.
2. with the minimum (1 per cent or less) of liqueur added: said of champagne.

brut, *v.i.* [Fr. *brouter*, to browse.] to browse. [Obs.]

Brū'tà, *n.* same as *Edentata*.

brū'tăl, *a.* [LL. *brutalis*, from L. *brutus*, heavy, dull, irrational.]
1. pertaining to a brute; as, *brutal* acts.
2. savage; cruel; inhuman; brutish; unfeeling, like a brute; merciless; as, *brutal* courage; *brutal* manners.
Syn.—savage, inhuman, rude, unfeeling, merciless, ruthless, brutish, barbarous, sensual, beastly, ignorant, stolid, dense, cruel, violent, bloodthirsty, intemperate.

brū'tăl·işm, *n.* a brutal state or quality; brutality.

brū·tăl'i·ty, *n.* 1. inhumanity; savageness; churlishness; insensibility to pity or shame.
2. *pl.* **brū·tăl'i·tieş,** an act of brutal character.

brū"tăl·i·zā'tion, *n.* the act or process of making inhuman or brutal.

brū'tăl·īze, *v.t.*; brutalized, *pt.*, *pp.*; brutalizing, *ppr.* 1. to make brutal, churlish, or inhuman; to deaden the humane feelings or sensibilities of.
2. to treat with brutality.

brū'tăl·īze, *v.i.* to become brutal, inhuman, or coarse and beastly.

brū'tăl·ly, *adv.* cruelly; inhumanly; in a coarse, churlish, or brutal manner.

brūte, *a.* [Fr. *brut*, from L. *brutus*, senseless, irrational.]
1. unconscious; insensate; as, the *brute* earth.
2. irrational; senseless; not gifted with reason; as, a *brute* beast.
3. bestial; resembling an animal; having the nature or characteristics of an animal; brutal; ferocious; also, gross or carnal; as, *brute* violence.
4. uncivilized; insensible; as, a *brute* philosopher. [Rare.]
5. rough; coarse; unrefined.

brūte, *n.* 1. a beast; any animal: the word is applied mostly to the larger quadrupeds.
2. a brutal person; a savage in heart or manners; an inhuman person; also, a sensual, gross person.
3. the animal impulses in man; sensuality; as, it's the *brute* in him that makes him act like that.

brūte, *v.t.* to bruit. [Obs.]

brūte'ly, *adv.* in a rude manner.

brūte'ness, *n.* 1. brutality. [Obs.]
2. insensibility.

brū'ti·fȳ, *v.t.* and *v.i.*; brutified, *pt.*, *pp.*; brutifying, *ppr.* [Fr. *brutifier*, from L. *brutus*, senseless, irrational, and *-ficare*, from *facere*, to make.] to brutalize.

brū'tish, *a.* of or like a brute or beast in qualities and attributes; as, *brutish* men.
Syn.—savage, ferocious, brutal, gross, carnal, bestial, base, beastly, animal, coarse, sensual, swinish, vile.

brū'tish·ly, *adv.* in the manner of a brute; grossly; irrationally; stupidly; savagely.

brū'tish·ness, *n.* stupidity; insensibility; brutality; savageness; the qualities of a brute.

brū'tişm, *n.* the characteristic qualities or actions of a brute; extreme stupidity, or beastly vulgarity.

Brū'tus, *n.* a style of hair dressing supposed to be in imitation of Lucius Brutus, and consisting chiefly of a rough cropping of the hair.

Brȳ·ā'cē·ae, *n.pl.* [L., from Gr. *bryon*, moss, lichen, and *-aceæ*.] the principal family of small cryptogams; the true mosses.

brȳ·ā'ceous, *a.* belonging to the *Bryaceæ*.

Brȳ'ăn·īte, *n.* see *Bible Christians*, under *Bible*.

Bryn'hild, *n.* in Norse legend, a Valkyrie awakened from an enchanted sleep by Sigurd: when she is deceived by him into marrying Gunnar, she brings about Sigurd's death and then kills herself.

brȳ·ō·log'iç·ăl, *a.* relating to bryology.

brȳ·ol'ō·ġist, *n.* a student of or specialist in bryology.

brȳ·ol'ō·ġy, *n.* [Gr. *bryon*, moss, lichen, and *-logia*, from *legein*, to speak.] in botany, the study of mosses and liverworts (bryophytes).

brȳ'ō·nin, *n.* an alkaloid obtained from the root of the white bryony, *Bryonia alba.* It is a yellowish-brown, bitter substance, and is emetic and cathartic.

brȳ'ō·ny, brī'ō·ny, *n.*; *pl.* **brȳ'ō·nieş, brī'ō·nieş,** [L. *bryonia*; Gr. *bryōnia*, from *bryein*, to swell.] any of a number of related vines of the gourd family, with large, fleshy roots, five-lobed leaves, and clusters of greenish-white flowers.

Brȳ·oph'y·tà, *n.pl.* [L., from Gr. *bryon*, moss, and *phyton*, plant.] in botany, a subdivision of the *Cryptogamia*, or plants which propagate from spores, comprising the mosses, the scale mosses, and the liverworts.

brȳ'ō·phȳte, *n.* any member of the *Bryophyta*.

brȳ·ō·phyt'iç, *a.* of a bryophyte.

Brȳ·ō·zō'à, *n.pl.* [L. from Gr. *bryon*, moss, the *zōon*, an animal.] in zoology, a class of minute mollusks, mostly marine, which propagate by budding: called also the *Polyzoa*.

brȳ·ō·zō'ăn, *a.* pertaining to the *Bryozoa*.

brȳ·ō·zō'ăn, *n.* any member of the *Bryozoa*.

brȳ·ō·zō'um, *n.* an individual of a bryozoan colony.

Bryth'ŏn, *n.* [W., from Celt. base of L. *Brito*, *Britto*.] a Briton of Cornwall, Wales, or ancient Cumbria.

Bry·thon'iç, *a.* of the Brythons or their language.

Bry·thon'iç, *n.* the Celtic language of the Brythons: Brythonic and Goidelic (Gaelic) are the two great divisions of Celtic.

bū·an·sū'àh, *n.* the *Cyon primævus*, the wild dog of northern India, thought to be the prototype of the domestic dog; also, the dhole.

bū'at, *n.* a hand lantern. [Scot.]

bū'āze, *n.* the fiber of an African climbing shrub of the milkwort family; also, the shrub itself.

bub, *n.* a familiar term of address to a small boy or young brother. [Colloq.]

bub, *v.t.* to throw out in bubbles. [Obs.]

bū'băl, bū'bāle, *n.* same as *bubalis*.

bū'bà·līne, *a.* [L. *bubalinus*, from *bubalus*, the buffalo.] a group of large, horned antelopes, including the hartebeests, bonteboks, etc.
bubaline antelope; same as *bubalis*.

bū'bà·lis, *n.* [Gr. *boubalis*, the antelope.] a large antelope found in northern Africa.

bub'ble, *n.* 1. a film of liquid enveloping air or gas; as, a soap *bubble*.
2. a space filled with air or gas in a liquid or a transparent solid; as, the *bubbles* in glass or champagne.
3. the act or state of bubbling; also, the sound made by bubbles, as in boiling a liquid.
4. anything that lacks firmness or solidity; a vain project; that which is more specious than real. Hence, a false show; a cheat or fraud; similarly, a delusive scheme or speculation; an empty project to raise money on imaginary grounds; as, the South Sea *bubble*.
5. a person deceived by an empty project. [Obs.]
the South Sea bubble; a stock company organized in England to monopolize the British South Sea trade. The shares had an immense sale at greatly inflated values, which caused financial distress throughout England when the company failed in 1720.

bub'ble, *v.i.*; bubbled, *pt.*, *pp.*; bubbling, *ppr.* 1. to rise in bubbles, as liquids when boiling or agitated; to contain bubbles.
2. to run with a gurgling noise; as, a *bubbling* stream.
3. to warble in singing, as a nightingale.
4. to be in a ferment; to be unable to contain news, excitement, or good spirits; to effervesce: usually followed by *over*; as, she *bubbled over* with joy.

bub'ble, *v.t.* 1. to cause to effervesce; to produce bubbles in.
2. to utter with a bubbling sound.
3. to cheat; to deceive or impose on. [Archaic.]

bub'ble båth, 1. a bath perfumed and softened by a solution, crystals, or powder that forms surface bubbles.
2. such a solution, etc.

bub'ble gum, a kind of chewing gum that can be blown into large bubbles.

bub'blẽr, *n.* 1. one who cheats. [Obs.]
2. a drumfish.
3. a drinking fountain in which water comes up out of a vent so that it can be drunk without a cup.

bub'ble shell, a univalve sea shell of the genus *Bulla*: so called from its general resemblance in form to a bubble.

bub'bling jock, the wild turkey cock: it makes a gurgling or gobbling sound; hence, also called the *gobbler*.

bub'bly, *a.* full of bubbles; bubbling.

bub'by, *n.* a familiar term of address to a small boy. [Colloq.]

bū'bō, *n.*; *pl.* **bū'bōeş,** [L. *bubo*, a swelling in the groin, from Gr. *boubōn*, the groin.] an inflammation, with enlargement of a lymph gland, particularly in the armpit or groin.

Bū'bō, *n.* [L., an owl.] a genus of large owls, including the great owl or eagle owl of Europe, the largest of the nocturnal birds, and the horned owl of America.

BUBO

bū·bon'iç, *a.* pertaining to a bubo; accompanied by buboes.
bubonic plague; a contagious disease, usually fatal, characterized by buboes, chills and fever, prostration, and delirium: fleas from infected rats are the carriers.

Bū·bō·nī'nae, *n.pl.* [L., from *bubo*, *bubonis*, and *-inæ*.] a subfamily of *Strigidæ*, of which *Bubo* is the type.

bū·bon'ō·cēle, *n.* [Gr. *boubōnokēlē*; *boubon*, the groin, and *kēlē*, a tumor.] an incomplete or partial inguinal hernia forming a swelling in the groin.

bū'bu·kle, *n.* a red pimple. [Rare.]

bu'bū·lin, *n.* [L. *bubulus*, pertaining to cattle; from *bos*, *bovis*, an ox.] a compound obtained from the excrement of cattle, used in calico printing.

buç'ăn, buç'çăn, *n.* [Fr. *boucan*, from a native Carib word.] a gridiron for smoking meat, or a place for drying coffee or cocoa.

buç'ăn, buç'çăn, *v.t.* to prepare and smoke (meat), after the manner of the Caribs of the West Indies.

bū'çà·rō, *n.* [Sp.] a water jug of rough, porous earthenware.

buç'çăl, *a.* [L. *bucca*, the cheek.] 1. pertaining to the cheek or cheeks.
2. of the mouth or mouth cavity.

buç·çà·neer', *n.* [Fr. *boucanier*, user of a *boucan* (Braz.), grill for roasting meat; orig. applied to Fr. hunters of wild oxen in Haiti.] a pirate, or sea robber, especially one who raided along the Spanish coasts of America in the seventeenth and eighteenth centuries.

buç·çà·neer', *v.i.* to live or behave as a buccaneer.

buç'çāte, *a.* [L. *bucca*, the cheek.] in zoology, having distended cheeks, as certain flies.

buç·çhe'rō, *n.* [It.] an ancient variety of rough earthenware, most frequently found as jugs or bottles, rudely fashioned and of a dark color, without glazing or painting, but often ornamented with figures in relief, representing an early stage of Etruscan ceramic art.

buç′ci·năl, *a.* [L., a trumpet.] having a shape or sound like a trumpet.

buç′ci·nā·tŏr, *n.* [L., from *buccinare*, to blow a trumpet; *buccina*, a trumpet.] the thin, flat muscle in the cheek which retracts the corners of the mouth.

buç′ci·nīte, *n.* a fossil or petrifaction of the shells called *Buccinum.*

buç′ci·noid, *a.* [L. *buccinum*, shellfish, from *buccina*, a trumpet, and Gr. *eidos*, form.] pertaining to or bearing a resemblance to the genus *Buccinum*, a family of marine mollusks.

Buç′ci·num, *n.* [L.] a genus of large univalve mollusks, of which the common whelk is a species.

Buç′çō, *n.* [L. *bucco*, one with distended cheeks, a babbler, blockhead.] a genus of birds typical of the family *Bucconidæ*, whose distinguishing feature is a very broad bill, giving the appearance of distended cheeks.

buç·cō·lā′bi·ăl, *a.* relating to both the cheek and lip; as, the *buccolabial* nerve.

Buç·çon′i·dae, *n.pl.* the puff birds; a family of picarian birds allied to the jacamars. The group is small and confined to America.

bū·cen′taur, *n.* [Gr. *bous*, ox, and *kentauros*, centaur.]

1. a mythical beast, half ox and half man.
2. a state barge of ancient Venice.

Bū·ceph′ȧ·lus, *n.* the war horse of Alexander the Great.

Bū′cē·ros, *n.* [L., from Gr. *boukerōs*, *boukeraos*, horned like an ox; *bous*, ox, and *keras*, horn.] a genus of birds inhabiting the warmer countries of Africa and Asia. The name *hornbill* is common to the different species.

Buçh′măn·iṣm, a religious movement which emphasizes the personal confession of sins and inculcates a return to the faith and practices of the early Christians: after Frank Buchman (1878–1961), its founder: often called *Oxford Group Movement.*

Buçh′măn·īte, *n.* a follower of Buchmanism.

buçh′ōl·zīte, *n.* [from *Bucholz*, a German chemist.] a fibrous silicate of aluminum, the structure of which sometimes consists of irregular columns. It is of a gray or pale yellow color and is also called *fibrolite* or *sillimanite.*

bū′çhū, *n.* [native name.] any one of several species of shrubs or plants found chiefly in Cape Colony, of the genus *Barosma.* The leaves have an aromatic taste and spicy odor and are medicinally used in diseases of the stomach and kidneys.

buck, *n.* 1. lye or soapsuds in which clothes are soaked in bleaching and washing; also, the liquid in which clothes are washed. [Archaic or Dial.]

2. the clothes soaked or washed in this. [Archaic or Dial.]

buck, *v.t.*; bucked (bukt), *pt., pp.*; bucking, *ppr.* [ME. *boucken*; L.G. *büken*; M.H.G. *buchen*; G. *bauchen*; Sw. *byka*, to wash in lye.]

1. to soak, steep, or boil (clothes) in lye or soapsuds, as in the process of bleaching or washing.

2. to wash or cleanse by beating in water, with a bat, especially on stones in running water.

buck, *v.t.* to break into small bits or pulverize, as ore with a hammer.

buck, *n.* [ME. *bucke*, *buk*; AS. *bucca*, *buc*, a he-goat; D. *bok*; G. *bock*; Ir. *boc*; W. *bwch*; Sans. *bukka*, a goat.]

1. the male of the deer, the goat, the sheep, the rabbit, etc.

BUCK OF FALLOW DEER

2. a gay, dashing young fellow; a young blood; a dandy.

3. the act of bucking.

4. a young male: used contemptuously or patronizingly of a young male Negro or Indian. [Colloq.]

5. a dollar. [Slang.]

The word *buck* is often used in connection with the names of antelopes; as, bush*buck*, spring *buck*, etc.

buck, *a.* male.

buck, *v.i.* 1. to copulate, as bucks and does.

2. to leap from the ground, as an unruly horse or mule, while keeping the forelegs stiff, the back arched, and the head as low as possible, the object being to throw off a pack or unseat a rider.

3. to plunge forward with lowered head, as a goat.

4. to resist something as if plunging against it. [Colloq.]

5. to move jerkily, as a car. [Colloq.]

buck, *v.t.* 1. formerly, to inflict punishment on (a person) by tying the wrists together, putting the arms over the bended knees, and forcing a stick under the knees and across the elbow joints.

2. to throw or attempt to throw (a rider) by bucking; as, the bronco *bucked* him out of the saddle.

3. to charge against, especially with the head down, as in football.

4. to resist. [Colloq.]

to buck for; to work eagerly, sometimes too obviously, for (a promotion, etc.). [Slang.]

to buck up; to cheer up; to brace up. [Colloq.]

buck, *n.* 1. a sawhorse or framework upon which wood is sawed; sawbuck.

2. a somewhat similar gymnastic apparatus with a padded, leather-covered top, for vaulting over, etc.

3. the beech tree.

buck, *n.* in poker, a counter, etc. placed before a player to remind him that the next turn to deal is his or of his obligation, after he has won the jackpot, to order a new jackpot when his next turn to deal comes.

to pass the buck; to evade blame, responsibility, etc. by passing it to someone else. [Colloq.]

buck and wing, a complicated, fast tap dance.

buck′ȧ·roo, *n.*; *pl.* **buck′ȧ·roos,** [altered from Sp. *vaquero.*] a cowboy.

buck·āy′rō, *n.* a buckaroo.

buck bȧs′ket, a basket in which clothes are carried to the wash.

buck bēan, [after D. *boksboon*, lit., goat's bean.] a bog plant with white or pink flowers and leaves made up of three leaflets.

buck′bōard, *n.* a four-wheeled open carriage in which flexible boards or slats, extending from axle to axle and upon which the seat rests, take the place of the ordinary springs: called also *buck-wagon.*

BUCKBOARD

buck·een′, *n.* [from *buck* (a dandy).] in Ireland, a young man who pretends to be aristocratic or wealthy.

buck′ẽr, *n.* 1. one who bucks or pulverizes ore.

2. a hammer with a broad face used in bucking ore.

3. a bucking horse or mule.

buck′et, *n.* [ME. *boket*; AS. *buc*, a bucket, water pot.]

1. a deep, rounded, flat-bottomed container hung from a curved handle, for holding or carrying water, coal, etc.; a pail.

2. a bucketful.

3. a thing like a bucket; specifically, (a) one of the V-shaped troughs of a water wheel; (b) a tub or scoop for hoisting coal, grain, earth, etc.; (c) the piston of a lifting pump, with a valve opening upward.

to kick the bucket; to die. [Slang.]

buck′et, *v.t.*; bucketed, *pt.,pp.*; bucketing, *ppr.*

1. to draw, dip, catch, or carry (water, etc.) in a bucket or as in a bucket.

2. to saturate from a bucket.

3. to ride (a horse) furiously or cruelly. [Colloq.]

buck′et, *v.i.* 1. to move fast, as the body in the swinging motion incident to rowing or horseback riding.

He sprang into the saddle, and *bucketed* back
at a hand gallop. —Dickens.

2. to draw, dip, catch, or carry water, etc. in a bucket or as in a bucket.

buck′et·ful, *n.* as much as a bucket will hold; contents of a full bucket.

buck′et sēat, a single seat with a rounded back, as in some automobiles and airplanes, often made so that it can be tipped forward.

buck′et shop, an establishment ostensibly accepting orders to buy and sell stocks, bonds, and commodities but actually engaged in gambling on the rise and fall of their prices, or in betting secretly against its customers, speculating with funds entrusted to it, etc.

buck′et·y, *n.* [a corrupted form of *buckwheat.*] paste used for dressing webs in weaving. [Scot.]

buck′eȳe, *n.* [*buck* (male deer), and *eye*: from the appearance of the seed.]

1. any one of several species of American trees and shrubs of the genus *Æsculus*, including the horse chestnut; as, the Ohio or fetid *buckeye*, *Æsculus glabra.*

BUCKEYE

2. a native or inhabitant of Ohio. [Colloq.]

3. a small schooner used chiefly for oyster fishing, and peculiar to Chesapeake Bay.

4. a species of butterfly, *Junonia cœnia.*

Buckeye State; Ohio: so named because of the many buckeye trees growing there.

buck′-eȳed (-īd), *a.* having bad or speckled eyes.

buck fē′vẽr, nervous agitation such as beginning hunters experience when they first see game. [Colloq.]

buck′finch, *n.* the chaffinch.

buck flȳ, a buck moth.

buck′horn, *n.* the prepared horn of the deer: used for cane heads, knife handles, buttons, etc.

buck′hound, *n.* a small hound used in hunting deer.

buck′ie, *n.* any of certain species of marine shells, as the common whelk. [Scot.]

buck′ing, *n.* 1. the act or process of soaking cloth in lye for bleaching; also, the lye or liquid used.

2. a wash or washing.

3. the act of crushing or pulverizing ores.

Buck′ing·ham Pal′ȧce, the official residence in London of British sovereigns.

buck′ing ī′ron (-ũrn), a hammer used in bucking ores.

buck′ing kiẽr, a large bleaching boiler.

buck′ing stool, a washing block.

buck′ish, *a.* pertaining to a buck, or gay young fellow; foppish.

buck′jump, *v.i.* same as *buck*, v.i., 2.

buck′jump″ẽr, *n.* a horse or mule that bucks.

buck′le (-l), *n.* [ME. *bocle*, a buckle, boss of a shield; OFr. *bocle*, *bucle*, the boss of a shield, a ring, a buckle; LL. *bucula*, *buccula*, a beaver, a shield; L. *buccula*, a little cheek, a beaver, dim. of *bucca*, a cheek.]

1. a device, usually made of some kind of metal, and consisting of a ring or rim with a chape and tongue, used for fastening the ends of a strap, belt, etc.

2. a curl, or a state of being curled or crisped, as hair. [Archaic.]

3. a clasplike ornament for shoes, the hair, etc.

buck′le, *v.t.*; buckled, *pt., pp.*; buckling, *ppr.* [ME. *buclen*, *boclen*; OFr. *boucler*, to buckle; from *bocle*, *bucle*, the boss of a shield, ring, buckle.]

1. to fasten with a buckle or buckles.

2. to prepare for action: usually followed by the reflexive pronoun; as, he *buckled himself* to his task.

3. to join in battle. [Obs.]

4. to confine or limit. [Rare.]

A span *buckles* in his sum of age. —Shak.

5. to bring together; to join.

buck′le, *v.i.* 1. to be fastened or joined by a buckle.

2. to engage in a struggle; to grapple.

buck′le, *v.i.* and *v.t.* [D. *bukken*, to bow.]

1. to bend; to bow; as, to *buckle* under life.
2. to give way; to yield.
3. to bend out of original form or position; to warp; to crumple; as, a beam *buckles.*

to buckle down; to apply oneself earnestly, as to hard work.

to buckle to; to bend to; to apply with vigor; to engage with zeal.

to buckle under; to yield; submit. [Colloq.]

to buckle up; to marry. [Scot.]

buck'le, *n.* a distortion caused by buckling; bend, bulge, kink, etc.

buck'lẽr, *n.* [OFr. *bocler*, so named from the *bocle* or boss in its center.]

1. a small, round shield, a piece of defensive armor anciently used in war, and worn on the arm or held in the hand. Bucklers varied considerably in size, form, and materials in different ages and nations. In early times they were of wickerwork, or of wood covered with leather, and ornamented with metal plates, and during the Middle Ages they were made entirely of metal.

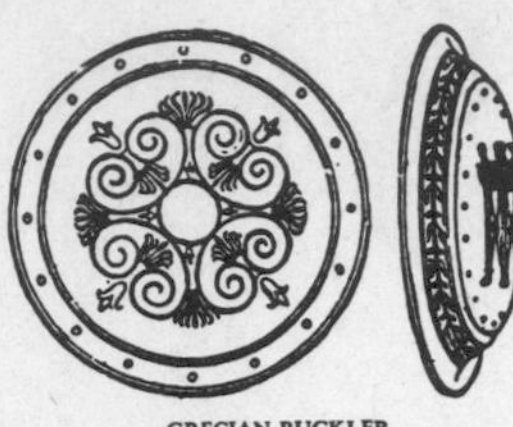

GRECIAN BUCKLER

2. a block of wood or piece of steel to fit into the portholes in a vessel's side, or the holes through which the ropes pass, to keep the water out when the vessel pitches or rolls.

3. a shell-like plate found on many ganoid fishes.

4. the anterior segment of the carapace or shell in trilobites.

5. a peron or thing serving as a protection or defense.

blind buckler; a buckler with no opening.

riding buckler; a buckler with an opening for a rope or cable.

buck'lẽr, *v.t.* to shield; to defend.

buck'lẽr-head"ed (-hed"), *a.* having a head like a buckler.

buck'ling, *n.* a bending or warping, usually from pressure; a tendency to bend or warp.

buck mack'ẽr·el, the scad (*Trachurus trachurus*). [Scot.]

buck måst, the nuts of the beech tree.

buck mọth, a moth appearing in the fall, belonging to the genus *Bombyx*.

buck'ō, *n.*; *pl.* **buck'ōes,** [from buck (he-goat).] a bully.

buck prī'vāte, an enlisted man of the lowest grade in the army. [Slang.]

buck'rä, *n.* [from Nigerian *mbākara*, a master.] a white man: term originating in Africa, also used in the West Indies, etc.

buck'rȧ, *a.* white; belonging or pertaining to the white man; hence, good and strong.

buck'răm, *n.* [ME. *bokeram*, *bockrom*; OFr. *boqueran*; perhaps from *Bokhara*, in Asia Minor.]

1. a coarse cotton, hemp, or linen cloth, stiffened with glue or a gluelike substance, used in garments to keep them in the form intended, for wrappers to cover cloths and other merchandise, and in bookbinding.

2. the ramson or wild garlic, *Allium ursinum*.

3. formality or stiffness of manner.

buck'răm, *a.* made of buckram, or resembling buckram; hence, stiff; precise; formal.

buck'răm, *v.t.* to stiffen or strengthen with buckram; hence, figuratively, to make stiff or formal.

buck'sạw, *n.* a framed saw used for sawing wood on a sawhorse.

BUCKSAW

buck's họrn, a species of plantain, *Plantago Coronopus*, having forked or branched leaves; also, *Lobelia coronopifolia*.

buck'shot, *n.* a coarse grade of lead shot used in killing large game.

buck'skin, *n.* 1. the skin of a buck.

2. a soft, strong, yellowish-gray leather, originally made from deerskins, but later chiefly from sheepskins.

3. one clad in buckskin; especially, [B–] an American soldier of the American Revolution.

4. [*pl.*] trousers or shoes made of buckskin.

buck'skin, *a.* made of buckskin.

buck'stạll, *n.* a toil or net to take deer.

Buck'tāil, *n.* one of a political faction formed in New York State about 1815, which opposed the administration of Governor DeWitt Clinton. They were given this name because some of the Tammany Society, which held the same political views, wore the tails of bucks in their hats.

buck'thọrn, *n.* any shrub or small tree of the genus *Rhamnus*. The common buckthorn grows to the height of twelve or fourteen feet and bears a black berry.

buck'thọrn bẽr'ry, same as *Avignon berry*.

buck'tọọth, *n.*; *pl.* **buck'teeth,** a tooth that protrudes noticeably.

buck'tọọthed, *a.* having buckteeth.

buck'whēat (-hwēt), *n.* [Scot. from AS. *boc*, beech, and *whæt*, wheat; so called from the resemblance of the fruit to beechnuts.]

1. a plant, *Fagopyrum esculentum*, or *Polygonum fagopyrum*, natural order *Polygonaceæ*, grown for its triangular seeds. It is a native of central Asia, but is naturalized both in Europe and the United States. It is cultivated as food for horses, cattle, and poultry, but is also much used for human food, especially in the form of flour for griddlecakes.

2. the seed of this plant from which a dark flour is made.

3. this flour.

false buckwheat; a North American plant that has seeds resembling buckwheat.

buck'whēat çāke, a pancake made of buckwheat flour.

buck'whēat tree, a small evergreen shrub, *Cliftonia nitida*.

bū·çol'iç, bū·çol'iç·ăl, *a.* [L. *bucolicus*; Gr. *boukolikos*; from *boukolos*, a herdsman; *bous*, an ox.]

1. of shepherds; pastoral.

2. of the countryside; rural; rustic.

bū·çol'iç, *n.* 1. a pastoral poem: usually in the plural; as, the *bucolics* of Virgil.

2. a writer of pastorals. [Rare.]

3. a rustic; a countrified person: humorously so called.

bū'çrāne, *n.* [Fr.] same as *bucranium*. [Rare.]

bū·çrā'ni·um, *n.*; *pl.* **bū·çrā'ni·ȧ,** [LL., from Gr. *boukranion*, an ox head; *bous*, an ox, and *kranion*, head, skull.] a sculptured ornament representing an ox skull adorned with wreaths or other ornaments, which was used to decorate the frieze of the entablature in the Ionic and Corinthian orders of architecture.

bud, *n.* [ME. *budde*; AS. *budda*, beetle.]

1. a small swelling or projection on a plant, from which a shoot, cluster of leaves, or flower develops.

2. an unexpanded flower.

3. a small protuberance on the body of some lower animals that expands into a new organism.

4. an undeveloped thing or person; as, a *bud* of a girl.

in the bud; (a) in the time of budding; (b) in a budding condition.

to nip in the bud; to stop before fully developed; to check at the earliest stage.

bud, *n.* buddy; fellow; used in addressing a man or boy. [Slang.]

bud, *v.i.*; budded, *pt.*, *pp.*; budding, *ppr.* 1. to put forth or produce buds.

2. to be in the condition of a bud; to sprout; to begin to grow or to issue from a stock in the manner of a bud, as a horn.

3. to be young and undeveloped, as a bud, or a young girl.

Syn.— germinate, sprout, shoot.

bud, *v.t.* 1. to put forth as a bud or buds.

2. to cause to bud.

3. to insert a bud of (a plant) into the bark of another sort of plant.

Bụd'dhȧ (-dȧ), *n.* [Sans., the enlightened, wise, sage, from *budh*, to know.] Gautama Siddhartha (563?–483? B.C.), a religious philosopher and teacher who lived in India and was the founder of Buddhism: the name is a title given by Buddhists to someone regarded as having divine wisdom and virtue and has been applied to other religious leaders of Asia.

IMAGE OF BUDDHA

Bụd'dhism, *n.* a religion and philosophic system of central and eastern Asia, founded in India in the sixth century B.C. by Buddha. It teaches that right living, right thinking, and self-denial will enable the soul to reach Nirvana, a divine state of release from earthly and bodily pain, sorrow, and desire.

Bụd'dhist, *n.* a follower of Buddha or a believer in his doctrine.

Bụd'dhist, *a.* pertaining to Buddhism, Buddha, or the Buddhists.

Bụd·dhis'tiç, *a.* same as *Buddhist*.

bud'ding, *n.* 1. bud production.

2. asexual reproduction, as when part of the parent animal or plant develops into a new organism.

3. the insertion of a bud of one tree under the bark of another, for propagation: a form of grafting.

BUDDING

bud'ding knīfe (nīf), a knife used by gardeners in budding.

bud'ding·ness, *n.* state of budding.

bud'dle, *n.* in mining, a shallow, inclined trough or drain used in washing ore.

bud'dle, *v.i.*; buddled, *pt.*, *pp.*; buddling, *ppr.* [origin unknown.] in mining, to wash ore.

bud·dlē'iȧ, *n.* [Mod. L., Adam *Buddle*, Eng. botanist.] any of a number of related shrubs or trees growing in warm climates and bearing clusters of small flowers that are purplish, yellow, or white.

bud'dy, *n.*; *pl.* **bud'dieș,** [c. 1852; perhaps from Brit. dial. *butty*, companion, with weakening of the stop consonant.]

1. a comrade; companion; pal. [Colloq.]

2. a fellow soldier. [Colloq.]

3. little boy: so used in direct address. [Colloq.]

budġe (buj), *v.i.* and *v.t.*; budged, *pt.*, *pp.*; budging, *ppr.* [Fr. *bouger*, to stir, move; Pr. *bolegar*; It. *bulicare*, from L. *bullire*, to boil.] to move a little; as, the boy couldn't *budge* the door.

budġe, *n.* [ME. *bowge*, a bag; OFr. *bouge*, from L. *bulga*, a leather bag.]

1. the dressed skin or fur of lambs, with the wool worn outward.

2. intoxicating liquor; spirits; booze. [Slang.]

budġe, *a.* 1. trimmed with budge in scholastic fashion; as, *budge* robes.

2. pompous; solemn; formal.

budge bachelors; a company of men clothed in long gowns lined with budge fur, the members of which formerly accompanied the lord mayor of London at his inaugural procession.

budġe, *a.* brisk; stirring; jocund. [Obs.]

budġe bar'rel, a kind of powder barrel, having at one end a leather covering drawn close by strings, like a purse.

budġ'ẽr, *n.* one who moves from his place.

budġ"ẽr·i·gär', *n.* [native name.] an Australian parakeet having a greenish-yellow body, marked with bright blue on the cheeks and tail, and wings striped with brown.

budġe'rō, budġe'rōw, *n.* [Anglo-Ind.] a barge without a keel, used by travelers on the Ganges.

budġ'et, *n.* [Fr. *bougette*, dim. of OFr. *bouge*, a bag.]

1. originally, a pouch or small bag with its contents; hence, a collection or supply; as, a *budget* of news.

2. a plan or schedule adjusting expenses during a certain period to the estimated or fixed income for that period.

3. the cost or estimated cost of living, operating, etc.
4. the annual statement of the probable revenues and expenditures of a country for the following year.

budg'et, *v.t.* 1. to put into or on a budget; to plan or arrange in accordance with a budget.
2. to plan or arrange for; to schedule; as, *budget* your time.

budg'et·ăr·y, *a.* of a budget.

budg'et plan, an installment plan.

budg'y, *a.* consisting of fur. [Obs.]

bud'let, *n.* a little bud springing from a parent bud.

bud'mash, *n.* [Hind. *badm'āsh*; Per. *bad*, evil, and Ar. *m'āsh*, means of living; *'āsh*, to live.] a disreputable character; a worthless fellow. [India.]

bue'näs nō'ches (bwe'), [Sp.] good night.

bue'nō (bwe'), *interj.* [Sp.] good; correct; very well.

bue'nōs dï'äs (bwe'), [Sp.] good day; good morning.

buff, *n.* [ME. *buff, buffle*; Fr. *buffle*, a buffalo.]
1. a heavy, soft, brownish-yellow leather, prepared from the skin of the buffalo or ox, dressed with oil, like chamois; also called *buff leather*.
2. a military coat made of buff or similar leather.
3. the color of buff; a light or brownish yellow.
4. in medicine, a yellow, viscid substance, formed on the surface of the buffy coat.
5. a polishing stick or spindle covered with leather or cloth.
6. a buffing wheel.
7. the naked skin. [Colloq.]
8. a buffalo. [Obs.]

buff, *a.* 1. made of buff.
2. of the color of buff; brownish-yellow.

buff, *v.t.*; buffed (buft), *pt., pp.*; buffing, *ppr.* 1. to polish with a buff stick or wheel.
2. to make smooth or soft like buff.

buff, *n.* [ME. and OFr. *buffe*, a blow.] a blow: now only in *blindman's buff*.

buff, *v.t.* to lessen the force of.

buff, *v.i.* to serve as a buffer.

buff, *a.* [origin unknown.] steady; firm; as, to stand *buff* against a shock or collision.

bŭf'fä, *n.* [It.] a woman opera singer who plays a comic role.

buf'fȧ·lō, *n.* [Sp. *bufalo*; It. *bufalo, bubalo*; LL. *bufalus, buffalus*; L. *bubalus*, the wild ox; Gr. *boubalos*, an African species of antelope; *bous*, an ox.]
1. a species of wild oxen (*Bubalus bubalis*), originally from India, but now found in the warmer countries of the Eastern Hemisphere. It is larger and not as docile as the common ox.

BUFFALOES
(top) Cape buffalo; (bottom) Indian buffalo

2. a large, black, very fierce buffalo (*Syncerus caffer*), found in South Africa and commonly called the Cape *buffalo*: it is savage and of large size.
3. popularly but unscientifically, the bison of North America.
4. a robe made of buffalo skin.
5. the buffalo fish.

buf'fȧ·lō, *v.t.* to intimidate; overawe; bamboozle; as, she's got him *buffaloed*. [Slang.]

buf'fȧ·lō ber'ry, either of two shrubs of the oleaster family, bearing sour red berries; also, the berries of either shrub.

buf'fȧ·lō bird, any of several birds that perch on buffalo and cattle to eat the insects on them; cowbird.

buf'fȧ·lō bug, a small, black beetle with white spots; carpet beetle.

buf'fȧ·lō çlō'vẽr, a kind of clover (*Trifolium reflexum*) found in the old herding grounds of the American bison.

buf'fȧ·lō cod, a large marine fish (*Ophiodon elongatus*) used as food on the north Pacific coast: also called *blue cod*.

buf'fȧ·lō fish, a large, hump-backed, fresh-water fish of the sucker family, genus *Ictiobus*, found in the Mississippi Valley.

buf'fȧ·lō flȳ, a small, biting, two-winged insect, which infests the lower sections of the Mississippi Valley, often causing heavy losses among horses and cattle.

buf'fȧ·lō gnat, same as *buffalo fly*.

buf'fȧ·lō grȧss, a kind of grass which grows on the prairies east of the Rocky Mountains, where bison used to graze.

buf'fȧ·lō moth, the hairy larva of the carpet beetle, harmful to furs and woolens.

buf'fȧ·lō nut, the oily fruit of a shrub of the sandalwood family, *Pyrularia pubera*; also, the bush itself.

buf'fȧ·lō pẽrch, 1. the fresh-water drumfish.
2. a buffalo fish.

buf'fȧ·lō rōbe, the skin of the North American bison, prepared with the hair on.

buf'fel duck, same as *buffle duck*.

buff'ẽr, *n.* [*buff* (to lessen force), and *-er*.]
1. a cushion, fender, or apparatus with strong springs, to deaden the concussion or absorb the shock of an impact or collision.
2. anything or anyone serving to lessen and absorb shock.

buff'ẽr, *n.* [*buff* (to polish), and *-er*.]
1. a wheel for buffing; a buff.
2. one who uses a buff in polishing.
3. a rather dull, but good-tempered person; as, a good old *buffer*. [Colloq.]

buff'ẽr stāte, a small, independent state located between two large, antagonistic powers and regarded as lessening the possibility of conflict between these.

buf·fet' (bȧ-fā' *or* boo-fā'), *n.* [Fr. *buffet*, a sideboard, refreshment room.]
1. a piece of furniture with drawers and cupboards for dishes, silver, table linen, etc.
2. a counter or table where refreshments are served, or a restaurant with such a counter or table.
3. the part of an organ in which the pipes are placed.

buf'fet, *n.* [OFr. *buffet*, a blow in the face, a pair of bellows; from *buffe, bufe*, a blow.]
1. a blow with the hand or fist.
2. a blow, or anything producing an effect like a blow; anything that harasses.
Fortune's *buffets* and rewards. —Shak.
3. a low stool or footstool.

buf'fet, *v.t.*; buffeted, *pt., pp.*; buffeting, *ppr.* [from Fr. *buffe, bufe*, a blow, a box.]
1. to strike with hand or fist; to box; to beat.
2. to beat back; as, the waves *buffeted* the boat.

buf'fet, *v.i.* 1. to struggle; to fight.
2. to progress by blows; to force a way by struggling or hitting.
Strove to *buffet* to land in vain.—Tennyson.

buf·fet' çär (boo-fā'), a railroad lounge car, usually with a bar and sandwich counter.

buf'fet·ẽr, *n.* a boxer; one who buffets.

buf'fet·ing, *n.* 1. a striking with the hands.
2. a succession of blows.

buf·fet' sup'pẽr (or **lunch**) (boo-fā'), a meal at which guests help themselves to food set out on a buffet or table.

buf'fin, *n.* a sort of coarse cloth; as, *buffin* gowns. [Obs.]

buff'ing, *n.* 1. in leather manufacturing, the cutting away or trimming of a hide; also, the portion so removed.
2. the process of polishing metal goods, such as cutlery, with a buffing wheel.

buff'ing ap·pȧ·rā'tus, same as *buffer* (cushion) sense 1.

buff'ing wheel (hwēl), a wheel with a covering of leather, cloth, etc., used in metal polishing.

buf'fle, *n.* [Fr.] the buffalo. [Obs.]

buf'fle, *v.i.* to puzzle; to be at a loss. [Obs.]

buf'fle duck, the buffle-headed duck (*Bucephala albeola*), a small North American duck with a short, blue bill and a head whose size is apparently increased by the fullness of its feathers.

buf'fle·head (-hed), *n.* 1. the buffle duck.
2. a foolish person; a blockhead.

buf'fle-head"ed, *a.* dull; stupid; foolish.

buf'fle·horn, *n.* a small, rubiaceous South African tree with a strong, tough wood.

bŭf'fō, *n.* [It.] an opera singer, generally a bass, who plays a comic role.

buf'font, *n.* [Fr. *bouffant*, ppr. of *bouffer*, to puff out.] a puffed-out, gauzy covering, sometimes made of linen, worn over the breast by women in the eighteenth century.

BUFFONT

buf·fo͞on', *n.* [Fr. *bouffon*; It. *buffone*, a jester; *buffa*, a jest, a mocking.] one who tries to amuse others by tricks and jokes; a clown.

buf·fo͞on', *a.* characteristic of a buffoon.

buf·fo͞on', *v.t.* to make ridiculous.

buf·fo͞on', *v.i.* to indulge in buffoonery.

buf·fo͞on'ẽr·y, *n.*; *pl.* **buf·fo͞on'ẽr·ieṣ,** the arts and practices of a buffoon.

buf·fo͞on'ish, *a.* like a buffoon.

buf·fo͞on'iṣm, *n.* same as *buffoonery*.

buf·fo͞on'ly, *a.* buffoonish. [Obs.]

buff stick, a stick covered with leather, cloth, etc., used in polishing.

buff wheel (hwēl), a buffing wheel.

buf'fy, *a.* 1. resembling the buff of the blood in color and texture.
2. relating to the buffy coat.
buffy coat; the coagulated fluid of the blood, after the red corpuscles have settled.

Bū'fō, *n.* [L. *bufo*, a toad.] a genus of toads including the common American and European toads.

bū'fŏn·īte, *n.* same as toadstone.

bū"fō·ten'ïne, *n.* a poisonous hallucinogen, $C_{12}H_{16}ON_2$, extracted from the skin glands of the common toad, (*Bufo vulgaris*).

bug, *n.* [ME. *bugge*; W. *bwg, bwgan*, a specter.]
1. any crawling insect with sucking mouth parts and forewings thickened toward the base, as a water bug, squash bug, etc.
2. any insect or similar animal.
3. any microscopic organism, especially one causing disease; germ; bacterium. [Colloq.]
4. a tiny microphone hidden to record conversation secretly. [Slang.]
5. a defect, as in a machine. [Slang.]
6. (a) an enthusiast or devotee; (b) a particular enthusiasm or obsession. [Slang.]
7. a small, compact automobile. [Slang.]

bug, *v.t.*; bugged, *pt., pp.*; bugging, *ppr.* 1. to hide a microphone in (a room, etc.), as for recording conversation secretly. [Slang.]
2. (a) to annoy, bother, anger, etc.; (b) to confuse or puzzle. [Slang.]

bug, *v.i.* to bulge or open wide, as in amazement: said of the eyes. [Slang.]

bug, *n.* [ME. *bugge*, from W. *bwg, bwgan*.] a bugbear; a hobgoblin. [Obs.]

bug·ȧ·bo͞o', *n.*; *pl.* **bug·ȧ·bo͞oṣ',** a bugbear.

bug'bāne, *n.* [*bug*, and ME. *bane*, destruction; AS. *bana*, murderer.] a tall plant, *Cimicifuga americana*, flowering in long spikes; also, any related plant, as *Cimicifuga racemosa*: their odor is supposed to repel insects.

bug'beȧr, *n.* [W. *bwg, bwgan*, a specter.]
1. an imaginary hobgoblin or terror described to frighten children into good conduct.
2. something that causes needless fear.
Syn.—hobgoblin, goblin, gorgon, ghoul, spirit, spook, specter, ogre, scarecrow.

bug'-eyed, *a.* with eyes bulging. [Slang.]

bug'fish, *n.* the menhaden, an American fish belonging to the herring family.

bug'gȧ·lōw, *n.* same as *baggala*.

bug'gẽr, *n.* 1. a sodomite.
2. a contemptible person.
3. a fellow; chap: used humorously or affectionately.

bug'gẽr, *v.t.* to commit sodomy with.

bug'gẽr·y, *n.* sodomy: legal term in England.

bug'gi·ness, *n.* the state of being infested with bugs.

bug'gy, *a.*; *comp.* buggier; *superl.* buggiest, infested or swarming with insects.

bug'gy, *n.*; *pl.* **bug'gieṣ,** [18th cent.; origin uncertain.]
1. a light vehicle with two or four wheels,

with or without a top, generally with one seat, and usually drawn by one horse.

2. in England, a light one-horse, two-wheeled vehicle without a hood.

3. a small perambulator or carriage for a baby; a baby buggy.

buggy cultivator; a riding cultivator.

buggy plow; a sulky plow.

bug′house, *n.* a hospital for the mentally ill; an insane asylum. [Slang.]

bug′house, *a.* insane; crazy. [Slang.]

bū′gle, *n.* [OFr. *bugle*, a wild ox; L. *buculus*, dim. of *bos*, an ox.]

1. a hunting horn.

2. a wind instrument, usually without keys or valves, consisting of a seamless tube of metal, generally in one coil, ending in a flared bell, used for sounding military signals, in military bands, etc.

3. a wild ox. [Obs.]

bū′gle, *v.i.* and *v.t.*; bugled, *pt., pp.*; bugling, *ppr.* to blow on a bugle; to call or signal by or as by blowing a bugle.

bū′gle, *n.* [LL. *bugulus*, an ornament; G. *bugel*, a bent piece of metal.] a long glass bead, of various colors, though more commonly black for trimming dresses, etc.

bū′gle, *a.* having the color of a glass bugle; jet-black; also, trimmed with bugles.

bū′gle, *n.* [Fr. *bugle*, from LL. *bugillo*, a plant.] any of a number of plants of the mint family, with spikes of blue, rose, purple, or white flowers.

bū′gled, *a.* ornamented with bugles (beads).

bū′gle hǫrn, 1. a musical instrument, the bugle.

2. a drinking vessel of horn. [Obs.]

bū′glẽr, *n.* one who plays a bugle; specifically, a soldier whose duty is to blow signals on a bugle.

bū′gle·weed, *n.* a plant of the mint family *Lycopus virginicus*, with tiny, bell-shaped flowers of white or blue.

bū′gloss, *n.* [Fr. *buglosse*; *L. buglossa, buglossus*; Gr. *buglōssos, bugloss*, oxtongue; *bous*, an ox, and *glōssa*, a tongue.] a plant, *Anchusa officinalis*, with small blue or white flowers and hairy stems and leaves, used in dyeing and coloring. The small wild bugloss is *Asperugo procumbens*, and the viper's bugloss, *Echium vulgare*.

bugs̱, *a.* crazy; insane. [Slang.]

bug′seed, *n.* a low, branching herb of the goose foot family, native to north temperate regions: so called from having oval seeds.

bu̇hl (bu̇l), *n.* [named after André Charles *Boulle* (1642–1732), a French woodworker.] a decoration of brass, unburnished gold, tortoise shell, etc. set into surfaces of ebony or other dark wood: called also *buhlwork*.

bu̧hl′bu̧hl, *n.* same as *bulbul*.

bũhr′stōne (bũr′), *n.* [*buhr*, var. of *bur*, burr, and *stone*.]

1. a very hard siliceous rock used to make grinding stones.

2. a stone made of this rock. Also spelled *burrstone*.

build (bild), *v.t.*; built *or archaic* builded, *pt., pp.*; building, *ppr.* [ME. *bilden, bylden*; AS. *byldan*, to build, from *bold*, a house; *buan*, to dwell.]

1. to construct or erect, as a house, ship, or wall; to unite into a structure.

2. to raise on a support or foundation; to make a basis for; to establish; as, to *build* our hopes on air.

3. to increase and strengthen; to establish and preserve: usually followed by *up*; as, to *build up* a reputation.

4. to create.

Syn.—construct, erect, establish, found, frame.

build (bild), *v.i.* 1. (a) to put up a building; have a house, etc. built; (b) to be in the business of building.

2. to construct, rest, rely, or depend (with *on* or *upon*); as, to *build on* the opinions of others.

3. in card games, to form a sequence according to suit, number, etc.

build, *n.* style of construction; general figure; as, a person of large *build*.

build′ẽr, *n.* 1. one who builds; that which builds.

2. one whose business is the erection or supervision of the erection of buildings.

3. an ingredient or substance that makes soap work better.

build′ẽr's knot (not), a clove hitch, a type of knot.

build′ing, *n.* 1. the act, art, or business of constructing, erecting, or establishing.

2. anything that is built, as a house, a church, etc.

Syn.—edifice, architecture, construction, erection, fabric, structure.

build′ing and lōan as·sō·ci·ā′tion, an organization that helps its members to build or buy homes, either by investing their savings or by loans.

build′-up, *n.* favorable publicity or praise, especially when systematic and intended to make something popular, well-known, etc. [Slang.]

built, past tense and past participle of *build*.

built, *a.* 1. constructed; made; formed.

2. built-up.

built′-in′, *a.* constructed as an integral, permanent part, as a *built-in* cupboard.

built′-up, *a.* consisting of a number of parts so fitted as to give strength or solidity; as, a *built-up* spar.

buïs·sǫn′, *n.* [Fr.] a closely pruned fruit tree trained on a low stem.

buk′shish, *n.* same as *backsheesh*.

Bu̧l, *n.* [Heb.] Cheshvan: the early Hebrew name.

bū′lau, *n.* [native name.] a ratlike insectivorous animal, *Gymnura rafflesi*, resembling a hedgehog: found in the East Indies.

bulb, *n.* [Fr. *bulbe*; L. *bulbus*; Gr. *bolbos*, a bulbous root.]

1. an underground bud that sends down roots and consists of a very short stem covered with leafy scales or layers, as in a lily, onion, hyacinth, etc.

2. anything resembling a bulb, especially an expansion at the end of a stalk or long and slender body; as, the *bulb* of a thermometer; the *bulb* of a hair; the *bulb* of the aorta.

3. a corm, tuber, or rhizome resembling a bulb, as in a crocus, dahlia, etc.

4. any plant that grows from a bulb.

5. in anatomy, (a) an enlargement on some tissues and organs, as at the root of a hair; (b) the medulla oblongata.

bulb of a hair; the thickened portion at the root of a hair.

bulb of a tooth; the enlargement of a tooth filling the pulp cavity.

bulb of the eye; the eyeball.

bulb of the spinal cord; the medulla oblongata.

bulb, *v.i.* to swell; to be protuberant.

bul·bā′ceous, *a.* bulbous.

bulb′ăr, *a.* [L. *bulbus*, a bulb.] pertaining to a bulb; as, in pathology, *bulbar* paralysis, affecting the medulla oblongata.

bulbed, *a.* having a bulb or bulbs.

bul·bif′ẽr·ous, *a.* [L. *bulbus*, a bulb, and *ferre*, to bear.] producing bulbs; as, *bulbiferous* stems.

bulb′il, bulb′el, *n.* [dim. from L. *bulbus*, a bulb.] a bulblet.

bul·bil′lȧ, *n.*; *pl.* **bul·bil′lae,** [from L. *bulbus*, a bulb.] in zoology, a hydroid bud capable of reproduction.

bulb′let, *n.* a small bulb or fleshy bud formed above ground on some plants, as on the lily or onion.

bul′bōse, *a.* bulbous.

bul′bō tū′bẽr, a corm, as a turnip.

bulb′ous, *a.* [L. *bulbosus*, from *bulbus*, a bulb.]

1. growing from bulbs.

2. of or having a bulb or bulbs.

3. shaped like a bulb.

bu̧l′bu̧l, *n.* [Per. *bulbul*, a nightingale.]

1. the Persian nightingale, *Pycnonotus jocosus*: made familiar in English poetry by Moore, Byron, and others.

2. any of various small, bright-colored birds related to the thrush, found in Asia and Africa.

bul′būle, *n.* [LL. *bulbulus*, dim. of L. *bulbus*, a bulb.] a bulblet, or small bulb.

bu̧l′chin, *n.* [ME. *bulchin*, dim. of *bul*, a bull.] a bull calf: used contemptuously. [Obs.]

Bul′gär, *n.* and *a.* Bulgarian.

Bul·gãr′i·ăn, *a.* of Bulgaria, its people, or their language.

Bul·gãr′i·ăn, *n.* 1. a native or inhabitant of Bulgaria.

2. the Slavic language of the Bulgarians.

bulġe, *n.* [ME. *bulge*, a swelling, lump; Sw. *bulgja*, to swell; AS. *belgan*, to swell.]

1. the protuberant or most convex portion of a thing; a part that swells out; as, the *bulge* of a cask; the *bulge* of a shield.

2. in a ship, the bilge.

to get the bulge on; to get the better of; to obtain an advantage. [Slang.]

bulġe, *v.i.* and *v.t.*; bulged, *pt., pp.*; bulging, *ppr.* to swell out; to bend outward; to protrude.

Bulġe, Bat′tle of the, the last major German counteroffensive of World War II (December 16, 1944–January, 1945), an unsuccessful attempt to push the Allies back through Belgium to Paris.

bulġ′ẽr, *n.* in golf, a driving club having a convex face.

bu̧l′gũr (*or* bul′-), *n.* [Turk.] wheat that has been cooked, dried, and coarsely ground: often cooked as a dish like pilau: in full *bulgar wheat*.

bul′ġy, *a.* swollen; unduly protuberant; bending, or having a tendency to bend, outward.

bū·lim′i·ȧ, *n.* [Gr. *boulimia*; *bous*, ox, and *limos*, hunger.] in medicine, a voracious appetite; a disease in which the patient has an insatiable appetite for food: also written *bulimy*.

Bū′li·mus, *n.* [L. *bulimus*; Gr. *boulimos*, great hunger; *bous*, ox, and *limos*, hunger, famine.] an extensive genus of pulmoniferous snails allied to the genus *Helix*.

bulk, *n.* [ME. *bulke, bolke*, a heap; Ice. *bulki*, a cargo of a ship.]

1. magnitude; dimension; size; mass; as, an ox or ship of great *bulk*.

2. the main mass; the largest part or portion; as, the *bulk* of a debt; the *bulk* of a nation.

3. a ship's hold or cargo.

4. the body. [Obs.]

in bulk; (a) in a mass; in a large amount; in great volume; (b) not packaged.

to break bulk; to make (a package, shipment, etc.) incomplete by removing a part.

Syn.—size, magnitude, greatness, largeness, extent, majority.

bulk, *v.i.*; bulked (bulkt), *pt., pp.*; bulking, *ppr.* 1. to grow large; to swell.

2. to appear large or important; as, the question *bulked* large in his sight.

3. to form into a mass.

bulk, *v.t.* to make (something) form into a mass.

bulk, *a.* 1. total; aggregate.

2. not packaged.

bulk, *n.* a part of a building protruding from the rest. [Archaic.]

bulk′ẽr, *n.* in nautical usage, one who measures goods for shipment to ascertain the proper freightage.

bulk′head (-hed), *n.* 1. an upright partition separating parts of a ship, airplane, etc. for protection against fire, leakage, etc.

2. a wall or embankment to confine or restrain something pressing from without, as water or earth.

3. a boxlike structure built over an opening, as a stairway, elevator shaft, etc.

bulkhead line; a line along a coast marking the limit to which wharves may be built.

bulk′i·ness, *n.* the quality or state of being bulky.

bulk′y, *a.*; *comp.* bulkier; *superl.* bulkiest, 1. large; of great bulk; massive.

2. awkwardly large; big and clumsy.

Syn.—massive, massy.

bu̧ll, *n.* [ME. *bul, bole*; G. *bulle*; D. *bul*, a bull.]

1. the male of any bovine animal, or of the different species of the genus *Bos*; also, the male of other large animals, as the whale, moose, etc.

2. [B–] Taurus, one of the twelve signs of the zodiac; also, the constellation Taurus.

3. a person who buys stocks or securities and tries to raise, or anticipates a rise in, their market price, in order to sell at a profit.

4. a very large, noisy, or strong person.

5. a policeman. [Slang.]

6. foolish, empty, or insincere talk; nonsense. [Slang.]

bull in a china shop; one who, from total lack of judgment, commits great havoc, presumably in a delicate situation.

to take the bull by the horns; to grapple boldly with a difficulty.

bu̧ll, *n.* [ME. *bulle*; OFr. *bulle*; It. *bulla*; LL. *bulla*, a papal edict; L. *bulla*, a stud, knob, boss.]

1. a letter, edict, or official document from the Pope.

2. a seal affixed to a document, especially to one from the Pope: it is impressed on one side with the heads of St. Peter and St. Paul, on the other with the name of the Pope and the year of his pontificate: also called *bulla*.

The Golden Bull; an edict or imperial constitution, made by the Emperor Charles IV (1356), containing the fundamental law of the Holy Roman Empire: so called from its golden seal.

bu̧ll, *n.* [early Mod. Eng., a jest; ME. *bul*, a lie; OFr. *boule*, a lie; L. *bulla*, a bubble.] an absurd and illogical mistake in statement.

bull, *v.t.*; bulled, *pt.*, *pp.* bulling, *ppr.* to try to raise the price of (stocks) or prices in (a stock market).

bull, *v.i.* 1. to go up in price, as stocks.
2. to show sexual desire, as a cow in heat.

bull, *a.* 1. male.
2. like a bull in size, strength, etc.
3. rising in price; as, a *bull* market.

bull-, [from *bull* (ox).] a combining form meaning: (a) *of a bull* or *bulls*, as in *bull*fight; (b) *like a bull* or *bull's* as in *bull*head; (c) *large* or *male*, as in *bull*frog, *bull*finch.

Bull, John, [first used by Arbuthnot (1712).] England, the English people, etc.: a personification.

bul'lȧ, *n.*; *pl.* **bul'lae**, [L. *bulla*, bubble.]
1. in medicine, a large blister or vesicle.
2. in anatomy, the egg-shaped inflated part of the bony external meatus of the ear. Also called *bulla ossea*.
3. a leaden seal for a document: used especially in reference to the round, leaden seal used by the Pope and attached to the papal bulls.

BULLA

4. [B–] a genus of univalvular hard-shelled *Mollusca*.

bul'lāce, *n.* [ME. *bolas*, *bolace*; OFr. *beloce*.]
1. the wild plum, a species of *Prunus* (*Prunus insititia*) from Asia Minor.
2. a West Indian tree, *Melicocca bijuga*, which bears an egg-shaped fruit of pungent flavor, known as the *bullace plum*.

bul'lȧ·hoo, *n.* same as *ballahoo*.

bul·lan'tiç, *a.* [LL. *bullans* (*-antis*), ppr. of *bullare*, to attach the seal; *bulla*, a seal.] designating certain Gothic letters, used in apostolic bulls.

bul'lȧ·ry, *n.* [LL. *bullarium*, from *bulla*, a papal bull.] a collection of papal bulls.

bul'lȧ·ry, *n.* a place for the preparation or boiling of salt; a salt house; a boilery.

bul'lāte, *a.* [L. *bullatus*, from *bulla*, bubble.] having elevations like blisters; inflated; puckered. In botany, a bullate leaf is one the membranous part of which rises between the veins in elevations like blisters.

bull bāit'ing, an old English sport, now prohibited, of tormenting bulls by setting dogs to attack them.

bull'bat, *n.* a nighthawk: also *bull bat*.

bull bee, the bullfly; the gadfly.

bull beef, the flesh of a bull; coarse, sinewy beef. [Colloq.]

bull'beg″gär, *n.* a hobgoblin; a bugbear; something terrible or frightful. [Obs.]

bull'ber″ry, *n.* the buffalo berry.

bull'brī″ēr, *n.* a species of greenbrier or smilax, with very stout thorns, growing on the Atlantic coast, from New Jersey to the Gulf of Mexico, and in southern portions of the United States: called also *China brier* and *bamboo brier*.

bull'çomb″ēr, (-kōm″ẽr), *n.* a scaraboid beetle, or one whose antennae terminate in scales called lamellae; especially, the English beetle, *Typhœus vulgaris*.

bull'dog, *n.* 1. one of a breed of short-haired, square-jawed dogs of great courage, ferocity, and tenacity of grip: so named, probably, from being formerly employed in baiting bulls, or from the size of the head.

BULLDOG

2. a heat-resisting material used as a lining for puddling furnaces and converters: produced by calcining slag from the furnace of a rolling mill.
3. a short, powerful pistol of large caliber: often called a *bulldog revolver*.
4. a large Australian ant, which is both aggressive and venomous: also called *bull ant*.
5. (a) a sheriff's officer; (b) a university attendant employed to enforce the rules of behavior for students. [Brit.]

bull'dog, *v.t.* to throw (a steer) by taking hold of its horns and twisting its neck.

bull'dog, *a.* having the characteristics of a bulldog; as, *bulldog* courage.
bulldog bat; a bat of the genus *Nyctinomus*: so named because the shape of its face is similar to that of a bulldog.

bull'dog e·di'tion, the early edition of a morning newspaper, chiefly for out-of-town distribution.

bull'dōze, *v.t.*; bulldozed, *pt.*, *pp.*; bulldozing, *ppr.* [perhaps from *bull*-whip, and *dose*, hence, lit., to give a dose of the whip.] to restrain or coerce by intimidation or violence: originally used in the southern part of the United States in connection with the intimidation of Negro voters. [Colloq.]

bull'dō·zēr, *n.* 1. one who bulldozes.
2. a large tractor with a heavy blade across the front for moving or pushing heavy masses of material: used in clearing debris, leveling air fields, etc.

BULLDOZER

bul'len·bul″len, *n.* [from the native Australian name] the lyrebird: so named because of its cry.

bul'len nāil, a short lacquered nail with a large round head, used chiefly by upholsterers.

bul·les'cence, *n.* [L. *bullescens*, from *bulla*, a bubble.] in botany, the state of being bullate.

bul'let, *n.* [Fr. *boulet*, dim. of *boule*, a ball.]
1. a small ball.
2. a small piece of lead, steel, or other metal formed into a ball or cone-shaped missile with a round or pointed end, to be shot from a firearm: bullets are now usually set in a metal casing.
3. loosely, a bullet with its casing; a cartridge.
4. a cannon ball; a sling missile. [Obs.]
5. a fetlock.
6. in heraldry, a black circle, representing a bullet or cannon ball.

bul'let-head″ed, *a.* round-headed.

bul'le·tin, *n.* [Fr. *bulletin*, a ballot, news; It. *bulletino*, *bulleta*, dim. of LL. *bulla*, a papal edict.]
1. a brief official statement about a matter of public concern, as of military operations, political events, or of the health of some distinguished personage.
2. any public notice or announcement, especially of news recently received.
3. a publication issued periodically, especially one which chronicles the proceedings of a society.

bul'le·tin, *v.t.* to announce or publish in a bulletin or bulletins.

bul'le·tin bōard, a wall area or a board conspicuously placed on which announcements are posted, as in offices, clubs, etc.

bul'let·proof, *v.t.*, to make bulletproof.

bul'let·proof, *a.* that bullets cannot pierce.

bul'let tree, same as *bully tree*.

bull'-fāced (-fāst), *a.* having a large, threatening face.

bull fid'dle, a bass viol. [Slang.]

bull'fight, *n.* an entertainment in which a bull is first provoked by men on horseback and afoot, who stick lances and darts into it, and is then maneuvered into position for the kill by the matador, who must run his sword skillfully down into its neck: popular in Spain and Spanish America.

bull'fight″ēr, *n.* one who fights with a bull to furnish sport for spectators, especially a matador.

bull'fight″ing, *n.* 1. the performance of a bullfight.
2. the art or profession of a bullfighter.

bull'finch, *n.* any of a number of small, variously colored songbirds of Europe and Asia, with a short, rounded beak: they are related to the grosbeaks.

BULLFINCH

bull'finch, *n.* [perhaps from *bull fence*.] a hedge with a ditch on one side, too high for a horse and rider to jump.

bull'fist, bull'fīce, *n.* [*bull*, and Prov. Eng. *feist*, *foist*, wind from the anus.] a variety of fungus filled with dustlike spores: called also *puffball*.

bull'flȳ, *n.* a gadfly; a breeze fly; any large fly troublesome to cattle or horses.

bull'frog, *n.* the *Rana catesbiana*, a large species of frog, found in North America, of a dusky-brown color, mixed with a yellowish-green, and spotted with black. These frogs utter a loud, croaking sound, from which they receive their name.

BULLFROG
(*Rana catesbiana*)

bull'head (-hed), *n.* 1. any one of several varieties of fish having a broad, massive, bull-like head; specifically, (a) the American catfish (*Amiurus melas*), found chiefly in the eastern sections of the United States; (b) the miller's thumb of the United States and England; (c) the sculpin, or cottoid, a river bullhead of Great Britain; (d) the kingfish of Florida; (e) the goby of New Zealand; (f) the Tasmanian shark.
2. a stupid fellow; a blockhead.
3. a small, black water vermin.
4. the black-bellied plover (*Squatarola helvetica*): sometimes called *beetlehead*; also, the golden plover, *Charadrius dominicus*.
bullhead kelp; in botany, the bladder kelp, a large seaweed, or wrack.

bull'head″ed (-hed″ed), *a.* 1. having a head like a bull's.
2. blindly stubborn; headstrong.

bull'horn, *n.* a portable electronic voice amplifier.

bull'ing, *n.* the process of blasting rock by exploding gunpowder or dynamite in its fissures.

bul'liŏn, *n.* [D. *bulioen*; Fr. *billon*, small coin.]
1. uncoined gold or silver in the mass; the precious metals when smelted and not perfectly refined, or when refined, but in bars, ingots, or in any form uncoined, as in plate.
2. gold and silver regarded as raw material.
3. coin which is base or uncurrent, and therefore of only metallic value. [Obs.]

bul'liŏn, *n.* [Fr. *bouillon*, from L. *bulla*, a bubble.]
1. a boss or bright ornament of metal used to decorate bridles, saddles, etc. [Obs.]
2. a thick, heavy fringe, sometimes of gold or silver thread and used for epaulets, etc.

bul'liŏn·işm, *n.* the doctrine that all currency should be metallic, or, if paper, at all times convertible into gold or silver.

bul'liŏn·ist, *n.* one who advocates or is a believer in bullionism.

bul'li·rag, *v.t.* same as *bullyrag*.

bull'ish, *a.* 1. like a bull in nature and characteristics.
2. having a tendency to rise in price or to make rise in price on the stock exchange; as, a *bullish* market.

bull'ist, *n.* a writer of papal bulls. [Rare.]

bul·li′tion, *n.* ebullition. [Obs.]

Bull Moose, a member of the Progressive Party led by Theodore Roosevelt in the presidential campaign of 1912: so called from the symbol of the party.

bull′-necked (-nekt), *a.* having a short, thick, coarse neck resembling that of a bull.

bull nōse, a contagious disease of pigs, caused by infection with a bacillus and characterized by a swelling of the snout and a sloughing off of the infected tissues.

bull′nut, *n.* the mocker nut, a species of hickory.

bul′lŏck, *n.* [ME. *bullok*; AS. *bulluc*, a young bull.]
 1. a young bull. [Obs.]
 2. a castrated bull; ox; steer.

bul′lŏck, *v.t.* to abuse or bully. [Obs.]

bul′lŏck's-eȳe, *n.* 1. a small, thick glass or skylight, in a covering or roof.
 2. a garden plant, *Sempervivum tectorum*, of the houseleek family.

bul′lŏck's heärt, the custard apple, *Anona reticulata*.

bul′lon, *n.* [W. Ind.] the *Scarus croicensis*, or West Indian parrot fish.

bul′lous, *a.* [L. *bulla*, a bubble, boss.] characterized by or partaking of the nature of bullae, or vesicles; vesicular.

bull pen, 1. a fenced enclosure for bulls.
 2. a large room or enclosure in a penitentiary, where prisoners are herded during riots. [Colloq.]
 3. in baseball, an area alongside the playing field, where relief pitchers practice and warm up.

bull pōll, a kind of hair grass, *Aira cæspitosa*, with very slender leaves or branches.

bull′pout, *n.* a bullhead, or species of *Amiurus*.

bull ring, an enclosed arena for bullfighting.

bull′-rōar′ẽr, a long, narrow piece of wood attached to a string, which produces a roaring noise when whirled in the air. Among some tribes, a similar instrument is used in religious rites.

bull′s eȳe, 1. [B–] in astronomy, Aldebaran, a star in the constellation Taurus, the Bull.
 2. in nautical usage, (a) a small wooden pulley; (b) a small, obscure cloud, ruddy in the middle, supposed to portend a storm; hence, a severe storm.
 3. a small circular or elliptical opening or window for light or air.
 4. a small, thick disk of glass inserted in various parts of a ship to admit light.
 5. a lantern provided with a convex lens on one side for focusing light on any object; also, the lens itself.
 6. in archery or marksmanship, the center of a target; also, a shot which hits this.
 7. any direct hit.
 8. a successful act.
 9. a thick protuberance left on crown glass by the end of the blowpipe.
 10. a hard, round candy.

bull snāke, a gopher snake.

bull's nōse, in joinery, the external angle of a polygon, or of two lines which meet at an obtuse angle.

bull ter′ri·ẽr, one of a breed of strong, lean, active dog with a smooth, white coat: it is a cross between the bulldog and the terrier.

bull′-tŏngue (-tung), *v.t.* and *v.i.* to plow with a bull tongue.

bull tŏngue, [so called from its shape.] a simple, heavy plow, usually with a single shovel, used especially in cotton growing.

bull trout, 1. a large species of European salmon trout, either *Salmo cambricus* or *Salmo trutta*; the sea trout, which, like the salmon, ascends rivers periodically to spawn.
 2. the Dolly Varden trout, *Salvelinus malma*, found on the Pacific coast of North America.
 3. the huso, *Acipenser huso*, or Danube salmon.

bull′weed, *n.* knapweed.

bull′-whip (-hwip), *n.* a long, heavy whip, formerly used by cattle drivers and teamsters.

bull′wŏrt, *n.* bishop's-weed, *Ammi majus*.

bul′ly, *n.*; *pl.* **bul′lies**, [orig. sweetheart; D. *boel*, lover, brother, from M.H.G. *buole* (G. *buhle*), lover; later influenced by *bull* (ox).]
 1. a person who hurts, frightens, threatens, or tyrannizes over those who are smaller or weaker.
 2. a pimp.
 3. a hired cutthroat or thug. [Archaic.]
 4. a fine fellow. [Archaic.]

bul′ly, *a.* 1. dashing; gallant; as, my *bully* boy.
 2. first-rate; fine. [Colloq.]

bul′ly, *v.t.*; bullied, *pt.*, *pp.*; bullying, *ppr.* to act the bully toward; to force (a person) into doing something by threatening loudly; browbeat; bulldoze.

bul′ly, *v.i.* to be a bully.

bul′ly, *n.* [Fr. *bouilli*, boiled meat, from Fr. *bouillir*, to boil.] pickled beef; canned beef: also called *bully beef*.

bul′ly·rag, *v.t.*; bullyragged, *pt.*, *pp.*; bullyragging, *ppr.* to bully; to insult; to intimidate with noisy threats.

bul′ly·rook, *n.* a bully. [Rare.]

bul′ly tree, [corruption of *balata*, the native name.] any one of several sapotaceous trees native to the West Indies and the American tropics, especially the balata.

bul′rush, *n.* [ME. *bulryshe*, *bolroysche*, *bole*, stem of a tree, and AS. *risc*, a rush; L. *ruscum*, a butcher's broom.]
 1. a large kind of rush growing in wet land or water. The name *bulrush* is applied, in England, to the *Scirpus lacustris* and also to the cattail, *Typha latifolia* and *Typha angustifolia*; in America, to the *Juncus effusus*, etc.
 2. in the Bible, the papyrus

bulse, *n.* [Anglo-Ind.]
 1. a certain quantity of diamonds, gold dust, etc.
 2. a purse or jewel bag.

bul′ti, *n.* bolti.

bul′tōw, *n.* [*bull*, large, and *tow*, from AS. *teon*, to draw.] a manner of trawling with many hooks strung on one line: used by fishermen on the banks of Newfoundland; also, the line and hooks used.

bul′wärk, *n.* [ME. *bulwerk*; D. *bolwerk*; G. *bollwerk*, Sw. *bolverk*; Dan. *bulvark*, a rampart.]
 1. in fortification, a bastion; a rampart; an earthwork or defensive wall, capable of resisting cannon shot, and formed with bastions, curtains, etc.
 2. a protection; defense; as, a navy is the *bulwark* of a nation.
 3. a breakwater.
 4. [*usually pl.*] the sides of a vessel above the upper deck.
 Syn.—rampart, defense, barrier.

bul′wärk, *v.t.*; bulwarked, *pt.*, *pp.*; bulwarking, *ppr.* 1. to fortify with a rampart; to secure by a fortification.
 2. to be a bulwark to; to protect.

bum, *n.* a buzzing sound; a hum. [Obs.]

bum, *v.i.* to make a buzzing or humming noise. [Obs.]

bum, *n.* [ME. bom.] the buttocks. [Brit. Slang.]

bum, *a.*; *comp.* bummer; *superl.* bummest, inferior or poor in quality. [Slang.]

bum, *n.* [from *bummer*; prob. from G. *bummler*, loafer, from *bummeln*, to waste time.]
 1. a loafer; idler; vagrant: sometimes used jokingly. [Colloq.]
 2. a dissolute or worthless person. [Slang.]
 3. a spree. [Slang.]
 on the bum; (a) living the life of a vagrant; (b) out of repair; broken [Colloq.]

bum, *v.i.*; bummed, *pt.*, *pp.*; bumming, *ppr.* 1. to loaf; to idle away time in a somewhat dissolute way. [Colloq.]
 2. to live by begging or sponging on people. [Colloq.]
 3. to drink heavily. [Slang.]

bum, *v.t.* to get by begging or sponging on people. [Slang.]

bum·bāil′iff, *n.* [*bum* (buttocks), and *bailiff*.] a bailiff or sheriff's officer: a term of contempt. [Brit.]

bum′bast, *n.* bombast. [Obs.]

bum·bāze′, *v.t.* to amaze; to confuse; to perplex. [Scot.]

bum′ble, *n.* 1. a bittern. [Dial.]
 2. a bungle. [Dial.]
 3. a bumblebee. [Scot.]

bum′ble, *v.i.* [ME. *bumblen*, freq. of *bummen*, to hum; L.G. *bummeln*; D. *bommelen*, to hum.]
 1. to make a humming sound, as a bee. [Dial.]
 2. to cry out, as a bittern. [Dial.]

bum′ble·bee, *n.* a large, hairy, yellow-and-black bee of the genus *Bombus*, that makes a loud, humming sound in flight: there are more than sixty species in America: also called *humblebee*.

bum′ble·foot, *n.* 1. a suppurative disease of the feet of domestic fowls.
 2. a clubfoot.

bum′ble·pup″py, *n.* 1. whist played regardless of rules.
 2. the game of nineholes.

bum′bling, *a.* [ppr. of *bumble*, to buzz, or of *bumble*, to blunder, bustle about; prob. influenced by Mr. *Bumble*, officious beadle in Dickens' *Oliver Twist*.] noisily and blunderingly self-important.

bum′bōat, *n.* [*bum* (buttocks), and *boat*.] a small boat for carrying provisions to a ship at a distance from shore.

Bū·mē′li·ȧ, *n.* [L., from Gr. *boumelia*, a large kind of ash; *bous*, ox, large, and *melia*, ash tree.] a genus of trees and shrubs of the natural order *Sapotaceæ*, native in eastern United States, the West Indies, and Central America, and including the southern buckthorn, bastard bully tree, etc.

bum′kin, bōom′kin, *n.* [D. *boomkin*, dim. of *boom*, a tree, bar.]
 1. a short boom projecting from each side of the bow of a ship, to extend the clew of the foresail to windward.
 2. a small outrigger over the stern of a boat, to extend the mizzen.
 3. a projecting spar on each quarter of a ship, to which the brace blocks are fastened.

bum′mȧ·lō, *n.* [E. Ind.] a small, ravenous, teleostean fish of the size of a smelt, abounding on the southern coast of Asia: when dried and salted, it is relished as a food in Europe and India: humorously called *Bombay duck*.

bum′mẽr, *n.* 1. a dissolute sponger. [Old Slang.]
 2. an unpleasant experience, especially one resulting from taking drugs. [Slang.]

bum′me·ry, *n.* bottomry. [Obs.]

bump, *n.* 1. a swelling or protuberance, especially one caused by a blow.
 2. a thump; a blow.
 3. a collision; a jolt.
 4. one of the protuberant lumps on the skull which are associated by phrenologists with distinct traits of character.

bump, *v.t.*; bumped (bumpt), *pt.*, *pp.*; bumping, *ppr.* 1. to strike, as with or against anything large or solid; to thump; as, to *bump* the head against a wall.
 2. to take the place of; to displace, as from a job, airplane seat, etc. [Slang.]
 bump off; (a) to bump so as to cause to fall off (a table, etc.); (b) [Slang.] to murder; kill.

bump, *v.i.* 1. to hit or collide with a bump (often with *into* or *against*).
 2. to move with bumps or jolts.

bump, *n.* [imitative of the sound.] a booming, hollow noise; as, the bittern's *bump*.

bump, *v.i.* to make a loud, heavy, or hollow noise, as the bittern; to boom.

bump′ẽr, *n.* [corruption of *bumbard*, a drinking vessel.]
 1. a cup or glass filled to the brim, or till the liquor runs over.
 2. a crowded house at a theater, etc., in honor of some favorite performer.

bump′ẽr, *n.* 1. a buffer; anything that modifies the force of a bump or shock; as, a *bumper* on a car or ship.
 2. anything or anyone that bumps or causes a bump.

bump′ẽr stick′ẽr, a slogan, witticism, etc. printed on gummed paper for sticking on an automobile bumper.

bump′i·ly, *adv.* in a bumpy manner.

bump′i·ness, *n.* the quality or state of being bumpy.

bump′kin, *n.* [D. *boomkin*, a short tree; dim. of *boom*, a tree.]
 1. a short, projecting beam or spar on a ship, as at the stern of a yacht for securing a permanent backstay; a boom: also spelled *bumkin*.
 2. [perhaps in allusion to the characteristic short, blocky build.] an awkward or loutish person from the country; a clumsy yokel.

bump′tious, (-shus), *a.* impertinent; conceited; self-assertive.

bump′tious·ly, *adv.* in a bumptious manner.

bump′tious·ness, *n.* the quality of being bumptious.

bum′wood, *n.* same as *burnwood*.

bun, bunn, *n.* [ME. *bunne*, small loaf.]
 1. a kind of cake or sweetened roll; a raised biscuit glazed and sugared on top.
 2. hair worn in a roll or knot on a woman's head or neck.

bun, *n.* [Gael. *bun*, stock, stump, root.]
 1. a pet name for a rabbit or squirrel; a bunny.
 2. a rabbit's or hare's tail. [Obs.]

bū′nȧ, *n.* [G., from *butadiene*, and *Na*, the

symbol for sodium (natrium).] a synthetic rubber made by polymerizing butadiene; a trade-mark (*Buna*).

bunch, *n.* [ME. *bunche*, a hump; Ice. *bunki*; Sw. *bunke*, a heap, pile.]
1. a protuberance; a knob or hump; as, the *bunch* on a camel's back. [Rare.]
2. a cluster; a number of the same kind growing together; as, a *bunch* of grapes.
3. a number of things tied together; as, a *bunch* of keys; a *bunch* of rods.
4. a collection of things; a knot; as, a *bunch* of hair; a *bunch* of trees.
5. in mining, a small mass of ore.
6. a group (of people). [Colloq.]

bunch, *v.i.* bunched (buncht), *pt.*, *pp.*; bunching, *ppr.* 1. to swell out in a protuberance; to be protuberant or round. [Rare.]
2. to gather in a bunch or bunches.

bunch, *v.t.* to form or tie in a bunch or bunches.

bunch'-backed, *a.* having a bunch on the back; crooked. [Rare.]

bunch'ber"ry, *n.*; *pl.* **bunch'ber"ries**, in botany, the dwarf cornel, *Cornus canadensis*, bearing clusters or bunches of edible berries; dwarf dogwood.

bunch'flow"ẽr, *n.* a plant, *Melanthium virginicum*, of the lily family, bearing a panicle of greenish flowers: found in the eastern and southern parts of the United States.

bunch grȧss, any of various pasture grasses that usually grow in clumps.

bunch'i·ness, *n.* the quality of being bunchy, or growing in bunches.

bunch'y, *a.*; *comp.* bunchier; *superl.* bunchiest. 1. growing or swelling out in bunches; like a bunch; having knobs or protuberances.
2. in mining, yielding irregularly: said of a mine where the vein is not continuous.

buñ'ço, *n.*; *pl.* **buñ'ços**, [from Sp. *banca*, card game (c. 1875).] a swindle, especially one carried out with confederates, as at a card game, lottery, etc.; confidence game; also spelled *bunko*. [Colloq.]

buñ'ço, *v.t.* to swindle, to cheat: also spelled *bunko*. [Colloq.]

buñ'çombe (-kum), **buñ'kum**, *n.* 1. anything said for mere show; inflated or bombastic speechmaking for the gratification of constituents or to gain applause; empty talk. [Colloq.]
2. anything said or done merely for effect; humbug. [Colloq.]
The word originated near close of the debate on the Missouri Question in Sixteenth Congress (1819–1821). Felix Walker, an old North Carolina mountaineer, whose district included the county of Buncombe, rose to speak. Several members begged him to desist, but he persevered, declaring that his constituents expected it and that he was bound to talk "for *Buncombe*."

Bund (boont), *n.*; *pl.* **Bun'de** or **Bunds**, [G.]
1. a league; association.
2. a league of North German states established in 1867.
3. an organized group of people, especially one for political purposes.
4. the German-American Bund, a former pro-Nazi organization in the United States.

bund, *n.* [Anglo-Ind.] an embankment or dike to prevent inundation.

bun'dẽr, *n.* [Per. *bandar*, a landing place.] a landing place; a dock.

bun'dẽr, bhun'dẽr, *n.* [Hind. *bandar*, a monkey, ape.] an East Indian monkey of various species, as the rhesus, etc.

Bun'des·rät, Bun'des·räth (-rät), *n.* [G. *bundes*, genit. of *bund*, a league, and *rath*, a council.]
1. the federal council of the German Empire, which shared with the Reichstag the legislative power. It consisted primarily of two members from each state in the empire, and was presided over by the imperial chancellor.
2. the federal council of Switzerland, composed of seven members, who exercise executive and administrative functions. They are chosen by the united congress and headed by the president of the republic.

bun'dle (-dl), *n.* [ME. *bundel*; AS. *byndel*, from *bindan*, to bind.]
1. a number of things fastened or tied together.
2. a roll; anything bound or rolled into a convenient form for carrying; package; parcel; as, a *bundle* of lace; a *bundle* of hay.
3. a bunch; a collection; a group.
4. in botany, any of the bunches of specialized cells that conduct fluids in higher plants.
5. a definite quantity of certain things; as, a *bundle* of linen thread, or twenty hanks of 3,000 yards each; a *bundle* of paper, or two reams.

bun'dle, *v.t.*; bundled, *pt.*, *pp.*; bundling, *ppr.* 1. to tie or bind in a bundle or roll; often followed by *up*; as, to *bundle up* clothes.
2. to send off in a hurry, or without ceremony (with *away*, *off*, *out*, or *into*); as, they *bundled* me *into* a car.
to bundle off; to send away abruptly; as, to *bundle* a boy *off* to school.
to bundle oneself up; to wrap oneself up warmly, or in cumbrous garments.

bun'dle, *v.i.* 1. to set off hurriedly or without ceremony; to make ready for departure.
2. to lie in the same bed with one's sweetheart without undressing: formerly a courting custom, especially in New England.

bun'dle pil'lăr, in architecture, a column having other columns of smaller dimensions clustering about it.

bun'dō·bust, *n.* [Anglo-Ind.] systematic regulation of one's affairs; discipline.

bung, *n.* [ME. *bunge*; W. *bwnge*, an orifice, a bung; Ir. *buinne*, a tap, spigot.]
1. a cork or other stopper of the orifice in the side or end of a cask, keg, etc.
2. a bunghole.
3. a pickpocket or sharper. [Obs.]
4. one who serves out grog on board ship.

bung, *v.t.*; bunged, *pt.*, *pp.*; bunging, *ppr.* 1. to stop up or close with a bung.
2. to close up.
3. [prob. influenced by *bang*.] to bruise or damage, as in a fight (with *up*). [Slang.]

buñ'gȧ·lōw, *n.* [Anglo-Ind.]
1. in India, a house or cottage, thatched or tiled, consisting of one story and surrounded by a wide veranda.
2. a small house or cottage, usually of one story or one and a half stories.

buñ'gȧ·rum, *n.* [from native name, *bungar*.] a venomous snake of India, related to the cobra, but having no hood.

bung'hōle, *n.* the hole or orifice in the side or end of a cask, barrel, or keg by means of which it is filled or emptied: sometimes shortened to *bung*.

buñ'gle (-gl), *v.i.*; bungled, *pt.*, *pp.*; bungling, *ppr.* to perform in a clumsy, awkward manner; as, to *bungle* in making shoes.

buñ'gle, *v.t.* [echoic; akin to Sw. *bangla*, to work ineffectually.] to make or mend clumsily; to botch; to manage awkwardly.

buñ'gle, *n.* a botch; a gross blunder; a clumsy performance.

buñ'glẽr, *n.* a clumsy, awkward workman; one who bungles.

buñ'gling, *a.* clumsy; awkwardly done; as, a *bungling* workman; a *bungling* job.

buñ'gling·ly, *adv.* clumsily; awkwardly.

buñ'gō, *n.* a Central or South American canoe.

bung sēat, a metal bushing around a bunghole: it is usually screwed in.

bung stärt'ẽr, a wooden mallet for starting the bung out of a cask.

bung stāve, the stave of a barrel which contains the bunghole.

bung vent, a small hole in a bung, to allow gases to escape during fermentation, or to admit air to increase the flow of liquid through the faucet.

bun'iŏn, bun'yŏn, *n.* [It. *bugnone*, a knob, boil; OFr. *bugne*, *bune*; Ice. *bunga*, an elevation.] an inflammation and swelling of the bursa at the base of the big toe, with a thickening of the skin.

buñk, *n.* buncombe; nonsense; twaddle. [Slang.]

buñk, *n.* [Ice. *bunki*, a heap, pile; Dan. *bunke*, a cargo stowed in the hold of a ship.]
1. a case, shelf, or box of boards used for a bed, especially in crowded quarters, as in a car or ship.
2. one of a number of berths or bed places arranged one above another.
3. a bed or anything used for a bed.
4. a piece of lumber so arranged across a lumber sled as to support the ends of logs; also, the sled so arranged.

buñk, *v.i.*; bunked (bunkt), *pt.*, *pp.*; bunking, *ppr.* 1. to go to bed; to sleep; especially, to go to bed or to sleep in a bunk. [Colloq.]
2. to be off; as, I must *bunk* now. [Brit. Slang.]

buñk'ẽr, *n.* 1. a large bin or receptacle for various things, as coal, etc.
2. a sort of box or chest, the lid forming a seat, as in a window. [Scot.]
3. a sand trap or mound of earth serving as a hazard or obstacle on a golf course.
4. a unit of a modern underground steel-and-concrete fortification system.

buñk'ẽr, *v.t.* in golf, to hit (a ball) into a bunker.

buñk'ẽr, *n.* in zoology, the mossbunker; the menhaden.

buñ'kō, *n.*; *pl.* **buñ'kos**, and *v.t.*; bunkoed, *pt.*, *pp.*; bunkoing, *ppr.* bunco.

buñ'kum, *n.* see *buncombe*.

bunn, *n.* see *bun*.

bun'niăn (-yun), *n.* bunion. [Obs.]

bun'ny, *n.* in mining, a mass of ore, as distinguished from a vein.

bun'ny, *n.* [dim. of *bun*; Gael. *bun*, a stock, a short, thick person or animal.] a rabbit: pet name used by children.

bū'nō·dont, *a.* [Gr. *bounos*, hill, mound, and *odous*, *odontos*, a tooth.] in zoology, having tuberculated molar teeth; pertaining to the *Bunodonta*.

bū'nō·dont, *n.* any of the *Bunodonta*.

Bū·nō·don'tȧ, *n.pl.* a group of nonruminant artiodactyl mammals, including the hogs and hippopotamuses: so called because the teeth are tuberculated.

Bun'sen bũrn'ẽr, see under *burner*.

bunt, *n.* [Sw. *bunt*; Dan. *bundt*; G. *bund*, a bundle.]
1. the middle part, cavity, or belly of a sail.
2. the sagging part of a fish net.

bunt, *v.i.* and *v.t.*; bunted, *pt.*, *pp.*; bunting, *ppr.* 1. to strike or butt with or as with horns. [Brit. Dial.]
2. in baseball, to bat (a pitched ball) lightly so that it does not go beyond the infield: usually done as a sacrifice play.

bunt, *n.* 1. a push or shove; a butt.
2. in baseball, (a) the act of bunting the ball, especially to advance a runner on base at a sacrifice; (b) a hit made by bunting.

bunt, *n.* 1. a disease of wheat in which the grains are destroyed.
2. the smut fungus, *Tilletia caries*, causing this disease.

bunt, *n.* the tail of a hare or rabbit.

bun'tẽr, *n.* a female ragpicker; a low, vulgar woman. [Dial.]

bun'tine, *n.* bunting (cloth).

bun'ting, *n.* [ME. *bounting*, *bunting*, pet name applied to bird, from ME. *Bunetun*, OFr. *Bonneton*, double dim. of *bon*, good.] any of various fringilline birds of the genus *Emberiza* and related genera; as, the English or common *bunting*, the snow *bunting*, and the rice *bunting*, or bobolink, etc.

bun'ting, bun'tine, *n.* [perhaps from ME. *bunten*, to sift; hence, cloth used for sifting.]
1. a thin cloth used in making flags, etc.
2. flags collectively.
3. strips of cloth in patriotic colors, used as holiday decorations for halls, automobiles, etc.
4. a baby's garment of soft, warm cloth made into a kind of hooded blanket that can be closed so that only the face is exposed.

bun'ting ī'ron (ī'ũrn), in glass-making, a blower's rod for handling hot glass; a pontil.

bunt'line (*or* -lin), *n.* [ME. *bunt*, the middle part of a sail, and *line*, a rope.] a rope fastened to a cringle on the bottom of a square sail to prevent the sail from bellying when drawn up to be furled.

bun'tŏns, *n.pl.* [origin unknown.] in mining, horizontal timbers in a shaft, dividing it into compartments and supporting the guides.

bun'yȧ, *n.* [Anglo-Ind.] in India, especially in Bengal, a grain dealer.

bun'yȧ-bun"yȧ, [native name.] a tall Australian evergreen tree, *Araucaria Bidwillii*, bearing edible seeds.

Bun'yăn, Paul, see *Paul Bunyan*.

bun'yŏn, *n.* bunion.

buoy (boy *or* bȯi), *n.* [D. *boei*; OFr. *buie*, a chain, fetter; L. *boia*, a leather collar for the neck; Gr. *boeios*, made of leather; *bous*, an ox.]
1. a floating object anchored in a position to indicate channels or dangerous rocks, bars, etc.
2. any apparatus or buoyant object which keeps a person or thing afloat in the water; a life buoy: it may be in the form of a jacket, belt, or ring.
anchor buoy; a buoy fastened to an anchor and marking its position.
bell buoy; a large buoy supporting a bell, to be rung in warning by the action of the waves.
cable buoy; a buoy consisting of an empty

cask, used to support a cable in rocky anchorage.

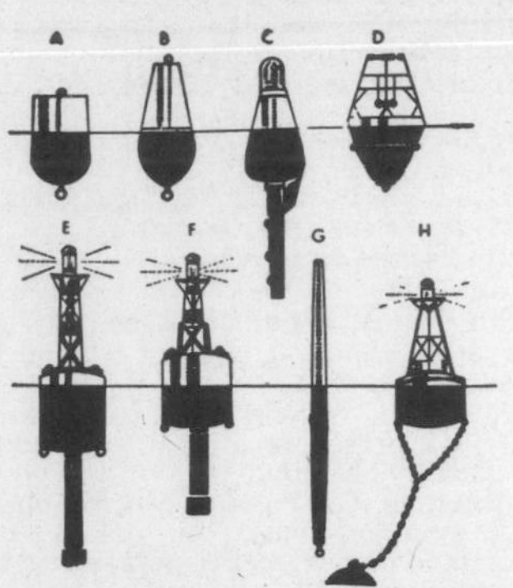

TYPES OF BUOY
A, can; B, nun; C, whistle; D, bell; E, lighted whistle; F, lighted bell; G, spar; H, lighted with mooring

whistling buoy; a buoy supporting a whistle to be sounded by the action of the waves.

buoy, *v.t.*; buoyed, *pt., pp.*; buoying, *ppr.* 1. to keep afloat in a fluid; to bear up, or keep from sinking in a fluid, as in water or air: with *up*.
 2. to support or sustain; to keep from sinking into ruin or despondency.
 3. to fix buoys in, as a direction to mariners; as, to *buoy* a channel.
 4. to indicate the position of with a buoy; as, to *buoy* an anchor.

buoy, *v.i.* to float; to rise by specific lightness.

buoy'ăge, *n.* 1. a series of buoys to indicate a channel or course for ships or boats.
 2. the providing of such buoys.
 3. buoys collectively.

buoy'ănce, *n.* buoyancy. [Rare.]

buoy'ăn·cy, *n.* 1. the quality of floating on the surface of water or in the atmosphere; specific lightness.
 2. in physics, the upward pressure by any fluid on a body partly or wholly immersed therein: it is equal to the weight of the fluid displaced.
 3. the power or tendency of any fluid, etc. to support or buoy up a body.
 4. ability to withstand or overcome depression of any kind; gaiety; cheerfulness; as, *buoyancy* of temperament.
 Syn.—animation, resilience, cheerfulness, life, vivacity, liveliness, sprightliness.

buoy'ănt, *a.* 1. floating; light; having the quality of rising or floating in a fluid.
 2. bearing up, as a fluid; sustaining another body.
 3. cheerful; gay; light-hearted.
 4. rising, or tending to rise; as, a *buoyant* market.
 Syn.—sprightly, spirited, vivacious, lively, light, floating, hopeful, cheerful, joyous.

buoy'ănt·ly, *adv.* in a buoyant manner.

bū·pres'tid, bū·pres'ti·dăn, *n.* a coleopterous insect, or beetle, distinguished by its bright metallic coloring; an individual of the genus *Buprestis*.

Bū·pres'tis, *n.* [L., from Gr. *bouprestis*, a poisonous beetle causing swelling in cattle; *bous*, an ox, and *prethein*, to blow up, swell up.] the typical genus of the *Buprestidæ*, a family of beetles distinguished by their brilliant colors and metallic luster. The larvae bore into the bark and timber of trees, often doing great damage.

bũr, *n.* [ME. *burre*; from ON.]
 1. the rough, prickly seedcase or fruit of certain plants, as of the sticktight, cocklebur, etc.
 2. a weed or other plant with burs.
 3. a person who clings like a bur.
 4. a burr.

bũr, *v.t.*; burred, *pt., pp.*; burring, *ppr.* 1. to remove burs from.
 2. to burr.

bũr, *n., v.i.*, and *v.t.* same as *burr* (the sound).

bu̇·rän', *n.* [Turk.] a strong windstorm of the steppes of Russia and Siberia, accompanied in winter with driving snow and in summer with hot dust.

bũr'bärk, *n.* the fibrous bark of certain shrubs found in India, Ceylon, the West Indies, etc.

bũr'ble, *v.i.*; burbled, *pt., pp.*; burbling, *ppr.* [ME. *burbelen*, to bubble; echoic.] to make a gurgling or bubbling sound.

bũr'bōlt, *n.* a birdbolt. [Obs.]

bũr'bŏt, *n.*; *pl.* **bũr'bŏt** or **bũr'bŏts,** [a corruption of Fr. *barbote*, a burbot, from *barbe*, L. *barba*, a beard.] a fish, *Lota maculosa*, shaped like an eel, but shorter and thicker, with a flat head: it has two small barbels on the nose and another on the chin: called also *eelpout, ling*, etc.

bũrd, *n.* [ME. *burde, bird, berde*, dial. var., by metathesis, from AS. *bryd*, bride.] a lady; a young lady. [Obs.]

bũr·dē·lāis' (-lā'), *n.* [Fr. *bourdelais*.] a sort of grape. [Obs.]

bũr'den, *n.* [ME. *burden, birden, birthen*; AS. *byrthen*; O.H.G. *burdin, burthin*, a burden, load.]
 1. that which is borne or carried; a load.
 2. that which is borne with labor or difficulty; that which is grievous, wearisome, or oppressive; as, my *burden* is greater than I can bear.
 3. a birth. [Obs.]
 4. a fixed quantity of certain commodities; as, a *burden* of gad steel, i.e., 120 or 180 pounds.
 5. the contents of a ship; the quantity or number of tons a vessel will carry; as, a ship of a thousand tons *burden*.
 6. in metallurgy, the charge of a blast furnace.
 7. a customary or prescribed load. [Obs.]
 8. the carrying of loads; as, a beast of *burden*.
 burden of proof; the obligation to prove an assertion, especially to prove the plaintiff's case in a court of law.
 Syn.—weight, load, encumbrance, impediment, cargo.

bũr'den, *n.* [ME. *burdoun*, the bass in music, the refrain; *bourdon*, a humming, buzzing; LL. *burdo, burdonis*, a drone, an organ pipe.]
 1. a bass accompaniment in music.
 2. the verse repeated in a song, or the return of the theme at the end of each verse; the chorus; the refrain.
 3. that which is often repeated; a subject on which one dwells; as, the *burden* of a speech.
 4. the drone of certain musical instruments, as the bagpipe. [Obs.]

bũr'den, *v.t.*; burdened, *pt., pp.*; burdening, *ppr.* 1. to load; to lay a heavy load on; to encumber with weight.
 2. to oppress with anything grievous; as, to *burden* a nation with taxes.

bũr'den·ẽr, *n.* one who loads; an oppressor.

bũr'den·ous, *a.* 1. grievous; heavy to be borne; oppressive. [Obs.]
 2. cumbersome; useless. [Obs.]

bũr'den·sŏme, *a.* heavy; grievous to be borne; causing uneasiness or fatigue; oppressive.

bũr'den·sŏme·ly, *adv.* in a burdensome manner.

bũr'den·sŏme·ness, *n.* the quality of being burdensome; heaviness; oppressiveness.

bũr'dock, *n.* [ME. *bur*, a bur, and AS. *docce*, a dock.] the *Arctium lappa*, a coarse, troublesome weed, bearing burs that adhere tenaciously to clothing and to the hair of cattle, horses, dogs, etc.

bū'reau (-rō), *n.*; *pl.* **bū'reaus, bū'reaux** (-rōs), [Fr. *bureau*, a writing table or desk, an office, the people engaged in an office; OFr. *bureau*, a coarse brown cloth with which writing tables were covered, from *burel*, a coarse cloth.]
 1. a desk or table for writing, having drawers to hold papers, etc. [Brit.]
 2. a chest of drawers, with or without a mirror, for keeping clothing, etc.
 3. a government department, or a subdivision of a government department. On the continent of Europe, the highest departments, in most countries, have the name of bureau; as, the *bureau* of the minister of foreign affairs. In the United States, the term is usually confined to subordinate departments.
 4. an office, especially one for a specific part of a business; as, an information *bureau*.
 Bureau of Engraving and Printing; the bureau of the United States Department of the Treasury in charge of making all money, stamps, etc. of the government.
 Bureau of Internal Revenue; the bureau of the United States Department of the Treasury in charge of collecting Federal taxes.
 Bureau of Standards; the bureau of the United States Department of Commerce in charge of testing weights, measures, materials, etc.
 Bureau Veritas; an institution for the uniform inspection and rating of ships of all nationalities, in the interest of marine underwriters. It was established in Brussels in 1828, moved to Paris in 1830, and returned to Brussels in 1870.

bū·reauç'rȧ·cy (-rok'rȧ- *or* -rō'krȧ-), *n.*; *pl.* **bū·reauç'rȧ·cieṣ,** [Fr. *bureaucratie*, from *bureau*, and Gr. *kratia*, from *kratein*, to be strong.]
 1. the administration of government through departments and subdivisions managed by sets of officials following an inflexible routine.
 2. the officials collectively.
 3. governmental officialism or inflexible routine.
 4. the concentration of authority in administrative bureaus.

bū'reau·ċrat (-rō-), *n.* [from *bureaucracy*.]
 1. an official in a bureaucracy.
 2. an official who follows and insists on an inflexible routine, proper forms, rules, etc.

bū·reau·ċrat'iç, bū·reau·ċrat'iç·ăl, *a.* 1. of or characterized by bureaucracy.
 2. of, like, or characteristic of a bureaucrat or bureaucrats.

bū·reau·ċrat'i·căl·ly, *adv.* in a bureaucratic manner.

bū·reauç'rȧ·tist (-rok'rȧ-), *n.* one who advocates or supports bureaucracy; a bureaucrat.

bũr'el, *n.* same as *burrel*.

bu·rẹ'ō, *n.* [Sp., from Fr. *bureau*, a bureau.] in Spanish law, a court in which persons belonging to the royal household are tried.

bū·rette', bū·ret', *n.* [Fr., dim. of OFr. *buire*, a flagon, from *buire*, to drink.]
 1. in chemistry or physics, a graduated glass tube for measuring small quantities of liquid or gas. It is of even bore, stands vertically, with a small aperture below, and is fitted with a stopcock.
 2. a decorated cruet.

bũr'fish, *n.* a fish found along the Atlantic coast of North America, capable of expanding its body, which, being covered with spines, presents the appearance of a chestnut bur, whence the name: called also *balloon fish, swell fish*, and *porcupine fish*.

bũrg, *n.* [ME. *burgh*; AS. *burh, burg*, a fortified town.]
 1. originally, a fortified town.
 2. a city, town, or village. [Colloq.]

-bũrg, a suffix meaning *burg* or *borough*, as in Vicks*burg*: also *-burgh*, as in Pitts*burgh*.

bũr·găde', *n.* a bourgade. [Obs.]

bũrg'ăge, *n.* [ME. *burgage*, from *burg*, a town.] in law, a former system of tenure of real estate, held at a fixed rate of rent payable in money or in services; socage.

bũr'gall, *n.* a small sea fish, the cunner, blue perch, or nibbler. [Dial.]

bũr'gȧ·mot, *n.* same as *bergamot*.

bũr'gȧ·net, *n.* a burgonet.

bũr'ġee, *n.* [origin unknown.]
 1. a sort of small coal for firing furnaces. [Brit.]
 2. an identifying flag on a ship, triangular or swallow-tailed in shape.

bũr·ġeois' (-jois'), *n.* same as *bourgeois*.

bũr'ġeŏn, *n.* [ME. *burgen, burgeon*; OFr. *borjon*, a bud; O.H.G. *burjan*, to raise, lift up.] a bud; a sprout.

bũr'ġeŏn, *v.i.* and *v.t.* burgeoned, *pt., pp.*; burgeoning, *ppr.* to put forth (buds, etc.); to sprout.

-bũr'gẽr, [from ham*burger*.] a combining form meaning *sandwich of ground meat (and)*, as in steak*burger*, cheese*burger*, etc. [Slang.]

bũr'ġess, *n.* [OFr. *burgeis*; LL. *burgensis*, a citizen; *burgus*, a borough, town; O.H.G. *burc*, a fortified town.]
 1. a citizen or freeman of a borough.
 2. in England, a representative of a borough, corporate town, or university in the British Parliament.
 3. a magistrate of certain corporate towns.
 4. before the American Revolution, a representative in the lower house of the legislature of Maryland or Virginia, which bore the title *House of Burgesses*.
 burgess oath; a solemn oath of allegiance formerly taken by the burgesses of Scotland.

bũr'ġess·ship, *n.* the state or office of a burgess.

bũrg'grāve, *n.* a burgrave.

bũrgh (bũrg), *n.* 1. a borough. [Brit.]
 2. in Scotland, an incorporated or chartered town.
 Also burh.

-bũrgh, -burg.

bũrgh'ăl, *a.* pertaining to a burgh.

bũrgh'bōte, *n.* [AS. *burgbōte*; *burg*, *burh*, a borough, and *bōt*, compensation, boot.] in old law, a contribution toward the building or repairing of castles or walls for the defense of a city or town.

bũrgh'brĕch, *n.* in old English law, a fine imposed on a burgh, for a breach of the peace.

bũrgh'ẽr, *n.* [D. *burger*; M.H.G. *burgære*, *burger*; G. *bürger*, a citizen; *burgh*, a town.]
1. an inhabitant of a burgh or borough who enjoys the privileges of the borough of which he is a free citizen; a citizen of a town.
2. [B–] a member of that section of the Scotch Seceders which recognized the legality of the burgess oath, the opposing parties being called *Antiburghers*.

bũrgh'ẽr·mȧs''tẽr, *n.* same as *burgomaster*.

bũrgh'ẽr·ship, *n.* the state or privileges of a burgher.

bũrgh'mȧs''tẽr, *n.* 1. a burgomaster.
2. an officer in tin mines who directs and lays out the boundaries for the workmen: called also *bailiff* and *barmaster*. [Brit.]

bũrgh'mōte, *n.* the court of a burgh or borough.

bũr'glăr, *n.* [OFr. *burg*, from LL. *burgus*, a town, and OFr. *lere*, from L. *latro*, a thief.] one who commits burglary.

bũr'glăr ȧ·lärm', a contrivance designed to give an alarm, as by ringing a bell, if a building is entered by an intruder.

bũr·glā'ri·ăn, *n.* a person guilty of burglary. [Obs.]

bũr·glā'ri·ous, *a.* pertaining to, involving, constituting, or inclined to burglary.
To come down a chimney is held a *burglarious* entry. —Blackstone.

bũr·glā'ri·ous·ly, *adv.* with an intent to commit burglary; in the manner of a burglar.

bũr'glăr·ize, *v.t.*; burglarized, *pt.*, *pp.*; burglarizing, *ppr.* to commit burglary in or upon. [Colloq.]

bũr'glăr·proof, *a.* constructed so as to be safe against burglary.

bũr'glȧ·ry, *n.* 1. the act or crime of breaking into a house at night, with an intent to commit theft or other felony. In many States of the United States, the term has been amplified to include the breaking and entering of any building by day as well as by night, with the intention of committing crime. Many degrees of the crime are defined by law. Raising a latch or obtaining entrance by trick or threat is construed as a breaking-in.
2. loosely, theft; robbery.

bũr'gle, *v.i.* and *v.t.*; burgled, *pt.*, *pp.*; burgling, *ppr.* to burglarize or commit burglary. [Colloq. and Humor.]

bũr'gō·mȧs''tẽr, *n.* [D. *burgemeester*; *burg*, borough, and *meester*, master.]
1. the mayor or head magistrate of a city or town in the Netherlands, Flanders, Austria, or Germany.
2. an aquatic bird, the glaucous gull (*Larus glaucus*), common in arctic regions.

bũr'gō·net, *n.* [Fr. *bourguignotte*, orig. fem. of *Bourguignot*, Burgundian, from *Bourgogne*, Burgundy.] a lightweight helmet or cap made of steel, worn in the sixteenth century: also spelled *burganet*.

BURGONETS

bũr'goo, bũr'gout (-gö), *n.* [18th-c. nautical slang.]
1. oatmeal porridge or thick gruel.
2. (a) a highly seasoned soup of meat and vegetables; (b) a barbecue, or feast, at which this is served. [Dial.]

bũr'grȧss, *n.* a kind of grass that grows in sand and bears burs: it is a species of *Cenchrus*.

bũr'grāve, *n.* [G. *burggraf*; *burg*, borough, and *graf*, a count.] in German history, the lord of a burg and its environs, originally appointed, later hereditary: also spelled *burggrave*.

Bũr·gun'di·ăn, *a.* of Burgundy, its people, etc.

Bũr·gun'di·ăn, *n.* a native or inhabitant of Burgundy.

Bũr'gun·dy, *n.*; *pl.* **Bũr'gun·dies,** a full-bodied red or white wine, originally produced in Burgundy, a province of France.
Burgundy pitch; a resinous product of the Norway spruce, *Abies excelsa*, and other pines. It is in reality turpentine from which the essential oil has been distilled, with the addition of water. It is used in medicine as a stimulating plaster.

bũrh, *n.* a burg or burgh.

bũr'hel, bũrr'hel, *n.* [E. Ind.] the wild sheep of the Himalayas, *Ovis burrhel*; the blue sheep.

bur'i·ăl (ber'), *n.* [ME. *burial*, *beriel*; AS. *byrgel*, a tomb, a grave, from *byrgan*, to bury.]
1. the act of burying a deceased person; sepulture; interment; the act of depositing a dead body in the earth, in a tomb or vault, or in the water.
2. the act of placing anything under earth or water.
3. a grave or tomb. [Obs.]
burial service; the service performed at the interment of the dead, or that portion of a liturgy read at a burial.

bur'i·ăl çāse, a casket or coffin.

bur'i·ăl ground, a tract of land set apart for a cemetery or graveyard.

bur'i·ẽr (ber'), *n.* one who buries a deceased person; also, that which covers or buries.

bū'rin, *n.* [Fr. *burin*, a graver's chisel.]
1. a graver; an instrument for engraving on metal. It is made of hard steel, the cutting end being ground to a diamond-shaped point.

BURIN

2. the style of an engraver's work; as, a soft *burin*; a brilliant *burin*.
3. a tool for engraving on stone.

bū'rin·ist, *n.* one who uses the burin; an engraver.

bū'ri·ŏn, *n.* [origin unknown.] the red-breasted sparrow or house finch, native to California (*Carpodacus frontalis*).

bũrke, *v.t.*; burked, *pt.*, *pp.*; burking, *ppr.* [from the name of a criminal executed for the act, Edinburgh, 1829.]
1. to murder (a person) in such a way as to produce no incriminating marks, usually by suffocation, and with the intention of selling the body for dissection.
2. to get rid of in a hidden or disguised manner; to suppress or postpone; as, to *burke* a legislative measure or inquiry.

bũrk'ing, *n.* the crime of murdering persons in order to sell their bodies for dissection.

bũrl, *n.* [ME. *burle*; OFr. *bouril*, *bourril*, flocks or ends of threads, from *bourre*; LL. *burra*, coarse hair.]
1. a kink in thread or a knot in a woven fabric.
2. a knot overgrown by bark, or a similar projection on a tree; also, the veneer made from such a knot.

bũrl, *v.t.*; burled, *pt.*, *pp.*; burling, *ppr.* to finish (cloth) by taking out the burls, loose threads, etc.
burling iron; a kind of nippers used for picking the knots from woolen cloth.

bũr'lap, *n.* [origin unknown.] a cloth of coarse texture made of jute, flax, or hemp, and used for making bags or wrappings. A finer variety of the same material is used for wall hangings, curtains, and in upholstery.

bũr'laps, *n.pl.* [*construed as sing.*] burlap.

bũrled, *a.* having burls.

bũrl'ẽr, *n.* a dresser of cloth.

bũr·lesque' (-lesk'), *a.* [Fr. *burlesque*; It. *burlesco*, from *burla*, a jest, mockery.]
1. parodying; jocular; tending to excite laughter by ludicrous images, or by a contrast between the subject and the manner of treating it, as when a trifling subject is treated with mock gravity.
2. of or connected with the kind of vaudeville called burlesque.

bũr·lesque', *n.* 1. ludicrous representation; a contrast between the subject and the manner of treating it, which tends to excite laughter or ridicule; satirical exaggeration; derisive caricature; parody.
2. a literary or dramatic composition in which a trifling subject or low incident is treated with much gravity, as a subject of great dignity or importance; or one in which the contrast between the subject and the manner of considering it makes it ludicrous or ridiculous; specifically, in theatrical parlance, an extravaganza; a travesty of a serious play or subject, usually interspersed with music.
3. any gross or ludicrous copy, travesty, or caricature.
4. a kind of vaudeville characterized by low comedy and a display of nudity.
Syn.—farce, mimicry, mockery, travesty, extravaganza.

bũr·lesque', *v.t.* and *v.i.*; burlesqued, *pt.*, *pp.*; burlesquing, *ppr.* to imitate derisively or comically; to parody.

bũr·les'quẽr (-kẽr), *n.* 1. one who burlesques.
2. a burlesque actor or actress.

bũr·let'tȧ, *n.* [It.] a comic opera.

bũr'ley, Bũr'ley, *n.* a thin-bodied, light-colored tobacco, grown chiefly in Kentucky: used in cigarettes, pipe tobacco, etc.

bũr'li·ness, *n.* the quality of being burly.

bũr'ly, *a.* [O.H.G. *burlih*, high, elevated; *bor*, an elevation.]
1. big and strong; heavy and muscular.
2. overbearing; coarse; boisterous. [Archaic.]

Bũr'măn, *n.*; *pl.* **Bũr'măns,** an inhabitant of Burma; also, the language of the Burmese.

Bũr'măn, *a.* Burmese.

Bũr·man·ni·ā'cē·ae, *n.pl.* [named after Johannes *Burmann*, a Dutch botanist.] a family of monocotyledonous plants containing ten genera and about sixty species. They grow chiefly in the tropics and bear regular flowers.

bũr·man·ni·ā'ceous, *a.* pertaining to the *Burmanniaceæ*.

bũr mar'i·gōld, any of a number of weedy plants of the composite family, with yellow flowers and burs; sticktight.

Bũr·mēse', *a.* of or relating to Burma or its people.

Bũr·mēse', *n. sing.* and *pl.* a native or inhabitant of Burma; also, the language of the Burmese.

bũrn, *v.t.*; burned *or* burnt, *pt.*, *pp.*; burning, *ppr.* [ME. *bernen*, *bærnan*, *brennan*; AS. *bærnan*, *beornan*; L.G. *brennen*; Ice. *brenna*, to burn.]
1. to consume with fire; to reduce to ashes by the action of fire; as, to *burn* wood.
2. to subject to the action of fire: (a) in surgery, to apply a cautery to; to cauterize; (b) to brand; (c) to expel the volatile parts and reduce to charcoal; as, to *burn* wood into charcoal; (d) in chemistry, to calcine; to make undergo combustion; (e) to harden or glaze by fire; as, to *burn* bricks.
3. to injure by fire or something with the effect of fire, as friction or acid; (a) to scorch; as, to *burn* the clothes by the fire; to *burn* meat or bread in cookery; (b) to dry excessively; to cause to wither by heat; as, the sun *burns* the grass or plants; (c) to sunburn.
4. to produce or effect by burning; to cause by fire or heat; as, to *burn* a name on a box; to *burn* a hole in a blanket.
5. to produce a sensation or effect in or upon, similar to that of heat; (a) to inflame with anger, desire, etc.; (b) to affect with excess of heat; as, fever *burns* a patient; (c) to impair, or to destroy partially the tissue of, as if by burning; as, to *burn* with lye or acid.
6. to consume or use as a heating or illuminating agent; as, to *burn* coke; to *burn* kerosene.
7. to put to death by fire.
8. to electrocute. [Slang.]
9. to use (candles, light, heaters, etc.).
to burn a hole in one's pocket; to be on one's mind until spent: said of money.
to burn daylight; to illuminate artificially before it is dark; hence, to do that which is unnecessary or useless.
to burn one's bridges behind one; to destroy all means of retreat.
to burn one's fingers; to get into trouble, as by meddling or taking part in any matter not concerning one.
to burn the candle at both ends; to be extravagant; especially, to use one's energies extravagantly.
to burn together; to unite two pieces of like metal by pouring on them around the place of juncture a quantity of molten metal of the same kind.

bũrn, *v.i.* 1. to be on fire; to flame; as, the mount *burned* with fire.
2. to give out light or heat; to shine; to sparkle.
O prince! O wherefore *burn* your eyes? —Rowe.
3. to be inflamed with passion or desire; as, to *burn* with anger or love.
4. to be injured by fire or heat; to be scorched, singed, etc.
The groan still deepens and the combat *burns*. —Pope.
5. to be affected with a sensation of heat, pain, or acidity; as, the heart *burns*.
6. to feel excess of heat; to be in a glow; as, her face *burns*; the patient *burned* with a fever.
7. in chemistry, to undergo combustion.

8. in certain games, to come close to the truth or the solution of anything; to be warm. [Colloq.]
9. to die by fire.
10. to be electrocuted. [Slang.]
to burn down; to burn to the ground.
to burn out; to burn till the fuel is exhausted, and the fire ceases.
to burn up; to be consumed.
Syn.—ignite, kindle, brand, consume, cauterize, cremate, incinerate, rage, glow, smolder, blaze, flash.

bŭrn, *n.* 1. a hurt or injury of any part of the body, caused by burning; the result of burning or of undue exposure to heat.
2. a mark made by branding.
3. a sunburn.

bŭrn, *n.* a small stream; a brook. [Scot.]

bŭrn'a·ble, *a.* capable of being burned.

bŭrned, *a.* same as *burnt.*

bŭrn'ẽr, *n.* 1. one who or that which burns.
2. the part of an apparatus for illuminating, heating, or cooking from which the flame comes.
3. an apparatus for burning; furnace, stove, etc.; as, an oil *burner.*
4. a person whose work consists in burning something; as, he is a charcoal *burner.*
Bude burner; a burner of two or more concentric Argand lamps fitted with a tube by which air or oxygen is supplied.
Bunsen burner; a kind of gas burner invented by Professor R. W. Bunsen (1811–1899), German chemist, and consisting of a short, straight tube provided with air holes, through which air is drawn to be mixed with the gas. It produces a hot blue flame.

bŭr'net, *n.* [ME. *burnet*; OFr. *brunete, brunette,* the name of a plant.] any of several plants, all perennial, of the rose family, specifically *Poterium Sanguisorba,* the common or garden *burnet.*

bŭr'net moth, any moth of the genera *Zygæna* or *Anthrocera*; specifically, a European moth, *Zygæna filipendulæ,* having crimson spots on its wings.

bŭr'net sax'i·frāge, any of several different species of herbs of the genus *Pimpinella.*

bŭr'nett·ize, *v.t.*; burnettized, *pt., pp.*; burnettizing, *ppr.* [named after Sir William *Burnett,* the inventor of the process.] to preserve (wood, etc.) from decay by saturating with Burnett's liquid, a solution of chloride of zinc.

bŭrn'ie, *n.* a burn or small brook. [Scot.]

bŭrn'ing, *a.* 1. being on fire; scorching.
2. causing excitement or strong emotion; intense; vehement; exciting; as, a *burning* shame; a *burning* question.
Syn.—ardent, earnest, fervent, impassioned, intense, glowing, hot, fiery, consuming.

bŭrn'ing, *n.* 1. combustion; a fire; inflammation; also, the heat or raging of passion.
2. in surgery, cauterization.
3. in ceramics, the act of baking or firing pottery, etc.

bŭrn'ing bush, 1. any one of several shrubs or plants bearing crimson foliage or flowers; as, (a) the wahoo, *Euonymus atropurpureus,* a large shrub or tree with inconspicuous flowers and red fruit; (b) the fraxinella, *Dictamnus Fraxinella,* a strong-smelling bushy plant with loose spires of white flowers that give off an inflammable vapor; (c) the artillery plant, *Pilea serpyllifolia.*
2. the emblem adopted by the Presbyterian churches of Scotland in memory of the persecutions of the seventeenth century, and in allusion to the appearance of God to Moses in the blazing bush (Ex. iii. 2). The legend is *Nec tamen consumebatur,* "yet not consumed."

bŭrn'ing flu̇'id, any inflammable fluid, especially one composed of oil of turpentine and alcohol, formerly used in lamps.

bŭrn'ing glȧss, a convex lens for focusing the direct rays of the sun to produce heat or set fire to something.

bŭrn'ing mir'rŏr, a concave mirror, or a combination of plane mirrors, of much greater power than a burning glass.

bŭr'nish, *v.t.* and *v.i.*; burnished (burnisht), *pt., pp.*; burnishing, *ppr.* [OFr. *brunir, burnir,* to make brown, to polish.] to make or become smooth, bright, and glossy; to polish, especially by friction; as, to *burnish* steel.

bŭr'nish, *n.* gloss; brightness; luster.

bŭr'nish·ẽr, *n.* 1. one who burnishes or polishes.
2. anything which burnishes or polishes; specifically, a tool of metal or bone, with a smooth surface, used in polishing by rubbing.

bŭr·nọọse', bŭr·nöus' (*or* bŭr'nös), *n.* [Fr. *burnous*; Sp. *albornoz,* a Moorish cloak; Ar. *burnus,* a high-crowned cap.]
1. an outer cloak or garment, worn by the Arabs, having a hood attached and usually made in one piece.
2. a similar cloak formerly worn by women.

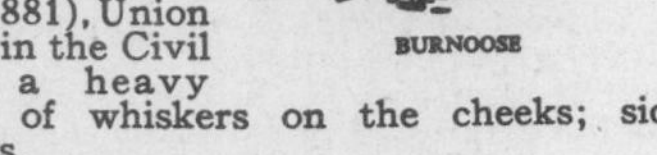
BURNOOSE

bŭrn'sīdeṣ, *n.pl.* [after A. E. *Burnside* (1824–1881), Union general in the Civil War.] a heavy growth of whiskers on the cheeks; side whiskers.

bŭrn'stiç·kle, *n.* same as *stickleback.*

bŭrnt, *v.* alternative past tense and past participle of *burn.*

bŭrnt, *a.* affected by fire or heat; parched; charred.
burnt offering; an animal, food, etc. burned on an altar as an offering or sacrifice to a god.

bŭrnt ēar, a disease in grain in which the seed is partly developed and its coat covered with a black powder.

bŭrnt si·en'nȧ, 1. a dark brown.
2. paint of this color.

bŭrnt um'bẽr, 1. a reddish brown.
2. paint of this color.

bŭrn'wood, *n.* coral sumac, *Rhus Metopium,* of Florida and the West Indies: called also *bumwood.*

bŭr ōak, 1. a North American oak tree bearing acorns in prickly cups.
2. its hard wood.

bŭrp, *n.* and *v.i.* [echoic.] belch. [Slang.]

bŭrr, *n.* 1. a prickly seedcase; bur.
2. a plant with burs.
3. a person who clings like a bur.
4. a rough edge or ridge left on metal or other material by cutting or drilling.
5. a washer on the small end of a rivet.
6. a dentist's drill.
Also spelled *bur,* especially in senses 1, 2, and 3.

bŭrr, *v.t.* 1. to form a rough edge on.
2. to remove burs from.

bŭrr, *n.* [prob. echoic.] 1. the trilling of *r* with uvula or tongue.
2. any rough pronunciation; as, a Scottish *burr.*
3. a whirring sound.
Also spelled *bur.*

bŭrr, *v.i.* 1. to speak with a burr.
2. to make a whirring sound.
Also spelled *bur.*

bŭrr, *v.t.* to pronounce with a burr: also spelled *bur.*

bŭrr, *n.* 1. buhr.
2. buhrstone.
Also spelled *bur.*

bŭr·rȧ·mun'di, *n.* same as *barramunda.*

bŭr'rȧ·wang, *n.* [native name.] in botany, one of the species of the nut-bearing Australian *Macrozamia.*

bŭr reed, any of various related plants with narrow leaves and rounded, burlike fruit.

bŭr'rel, *n.* [Fr. *beurré,* butter pear, from *beurre,* butter; OFr. *burel,* reddish.] a variety of pear, called also the *red butter pear,* from its smooth, soft pulp.

bŭr'rel, *n.* [OFr. *burel,* reddish, a kind of coarse, reddish cloth; LL. *burra,* a shaggy garment; L. *burras,* red; Gr. *pyrros,* red, flame-colored; *pyr,* fire.] a coarsely woven cloth of brownish or russet color; also, a garment made of this cloth. Also written *borrel, borel, burel.*

bŭr'rel flȳ, the gadfly. [Rare.]

bŭr'rel shot, [Fr. *bourreler,* to torment, and *shot.*] small shot, nails, stones, pieces of old iron, etc., put into cases, to be discharged at short range. [Obs.]

bŭrr'hel, *n.* [E. Ind.] in zoology, a species of wild sheep peculiar to the Himalayas (*Ovis burrhel*): also written *burhel, burrel.*

bŭrr'ing mȧ·ċhïne', a machine for turning edges on metal cylinders or disks.

bŭrr'ing rēam'ẽr, 1. a tapered reamer for removing burrs caused by cutting metal.
2. a tool for countersinking.

bŭr'rō, *n.*; *pl.* **bŭr'rōṣ,** [Sp.] a donkey.

bŭr'rŏck, *n.* [AS. *beorg, burg,* a hill, and dim. *-ock.*] a small weir or dam laid in a river to aid in catching fish.

bŭr'rōw, *n.* [ME. *borow, borur,* a hole for shelter, a mound; AS. *beorh,* a mound, *burh,* a fortified place.]
1. a hollow place in the earth dug by an animal.
2. any hole or tunnel in the ground for shelter, refuge, etc.
3. in mining, a heap of dirt or rubbish; a mound.

bŭr'rōw, *v.i.*; burrowed, *pt., pp.*; burrowing, *ppr.* 1. to make a burrow or burrows, especially one to lodge in.
2. to live or hide in a hole excavated in the earth, as rabbits. In a more general sense, to lodge in any deep or concealed place.
3. to search, as if by digging.
4. to dig.

bŭr'rōw, *v.t.* 1. to dig holes in.
2. to make by burrowing.
3. to hide in or as in a burrow.

bŭr'rōw duck, a sheldrake.

bŭr'rōw·ẽr, *n.* one who or that which burrows.

bŭr'rōw·ing owl, a ground owl of North and South America having long legs and a small head: it makes its nest in burrows dug in the ground.

bŭrr'stōne, *n.* same as *buhrstone.*

bŭr'ry, *a.*; *comp.* burrier; *superl.* burriest, 1. full of burs.
2. resembling burs.

bŭr'ry, *a.*; *comp.* burrier; *superl.* burriest, having a burr or burrs.

bŭr'sȧ, *n.*; *pl.* **bŭr'sae** or **bŭr'sȧṣ,** [LL., a purse, sac.] in anatomy, a sac, especially one situated at a joint.

bŭr'săl, *a.* 1. having to do with public revenue and disbursement; fiscal.
2. of or functioning as a bursa.

bŭr'săr, *n.* [LL. *bursarius,* a treasurer, from *bursa,* a purse.]
1. a treasurer, or keeper of cash; as, the *bursar* of a college, or of a monastery; a purser.
2. in Scotland, a student to whom a scholarship is given.

bŭr·săr'i·ăl, *a.* of a bursar or bursary.

bŭr'săr·ship, *n.* the office of a bursar.

bŭr'sȧ·ry, *n.* 1. the treasury of a college or monastery.
2. in Scotland, a university scholarship; also, a grant or fund established in a college or university for scholarships.

bu̇rsch, *n.*; *pl.* **bu̇rsch'en,** [G., from M.H.G. *bürse,* a society of students; a common purse; LL. *bursa,* a purse.] a youth; especially, a student in a German university.

Bu̇r'schen·schăft, *n.*; *pl.* **Bu̇r'schen·schăft-en,** [G., from *bursch,* student, young fellow.] any of various social fraternities at German universities.

bŭrse, *n.* [Fr. *bourse,* a purse, exchange; LL. *bursa,* a purse.]
1. a purse.
2. in Scotland, a bursary.
3. in the Roman Catholic Church, a receptacle for the chalice cover. It is square and flat, made of cardboard covered with rich silk or cloth of gold, embroidered and studded with jewels, open on one side only, and placed over the chalice veil when the sacred vessels are carried to the altar.

bŭr'seed, *n.* a weedy plant with spikes of flowers and bristly fruit.

Bŭr'sē·rȧ, *n.* [named after Joachim *Burser,* a German botanist.] a genus of tropical trees or shrubs, exuding aromatic gums, resins, and balsams, and typical of the family *Burseraceæ.*

Bŭr·sē·rā'cē·ae, *n.pl.* [LL.] a family of tropical trees and shrubs, usually with small flowers and alternate compound leaves, and furnishing many valuable balsams and aromatic gums.

bŭr·sē·rā'ceous, *a.* in botany, pertaining to the *Burseraceæ.*

bŭr·siç'ū·lāte, *a.* same as *bursiform.*

bŭr'si·fọrm, *a.* [from ML. *bursa,* pouch, and *-form.*] in anatomy and zoology, shaped like a bursa or sac; pouchlike.

bŭr·sī'tis, *n.* [LL. *bursa,* a purse, bag, and *-itis.*] in medicine, inflammation of a bursa.

bŭrst, *v.i.*; burst, *pt., pp.*; bursting, *ppr.* [ME. *bersten, bristen*; AS. *berstan*; D. *bersten*; O.H.G. *brestan*; Ice. *bresta,* to burst, break asunder.]
1. to fly or break open with force, or with sudden violence, as under internal pressure; to explode; to be suddenly liberated; also, to be surcharged with emotions; as, the heart *bursts* with grief.
2. to come or fall upon suddenly or with violence; to rush upon unexpectedly; as, a sound *bursts* upon our ears.
3. to break forth into action suddenly; as, to *burst* into tears.

4. to break or rush in suddenly or violently; as, to *burst* into a house or a room.
5. to be full beyond normal capacity; be blown up to the bursting point; bulge.

bũrst, *v.t.* 1. to puncture or rupture by force or violence; to open suddenly; as, to *burst* a chain or a door; to *burst* a cannon.
2. to make (a thing) swell or fill up to the bursting point.
Syn.—break, split, explode, rend, fracture, rive, disrupt, crack, separate.

bũrst, *n.* 1. a sudden breaking forth; an outbreak; an explosion; as, a *burst* of thunder; a *burst* of applause; a *burst* of passion.
2. a brief, intense effort; a spurt; as, a *burst* of speed.
3. the result of a bursting; a break; a breach.
4. the series of shots fired from an automatic firearm by a single pull on the trigger.

bũrst′en, *v.*, obsolete past participle of *burst.*

bũrst′ẽr, *n.* one who or that which bursts.

bũrst′ing chärġe, in gunnery, a quantity of powder placed in a shell to cause it to burst upon impact.

bũr′stōne, *n.* same as *buhrstone.*

bũrst′wŏrt, *n.* the *Herniaria glabra*, a plant which, in former times, was supposed to be effective in the cure of rupture or hernia.

bũr′then, *n.* and *v.* burden. [Archaic.]

bũr′tŏn, *n.* a small tackle formed by two blocks or pulleys, used to set up or tighten the rigging, or for various other purposes.

bũr′weed, *n.* any of various plants with burs, as the burdock, bur marigold, cocklebur, etc.

bur′y (ber′i), *n.* [variant of *burg, burh, borough.*] a manor or castle: now obsolete except in many names of places, as in Shrews*bury*, Dan*bury*, Aldermanb*ury*, etc.

bur′y (ber′i), *v.t.*; buried, *pt.*, *pp.*; burying, *ppr.* [ME. *beryen, buryen, byrien*; AS. *byrgan*, to bury, inter; *beorgan*, to protect, shelter, save.]
1. to inter; to place (a deceased person) in the earth or in the sea, usually in a ceremonial manner; to entomb; also, to perform funeral services for.
2. to cover from sight by placing anything on; to hide; to conceal.
3. to sink; to immerse; to cause to be wholly absorbed in; as, he is *buried* in thought.
4. to put away from one's life, social life, etc.
to bury the hatchet; to stop fighting; to make peace.
Syn.—entomb, inter, conceal, inhume, hush, repress, compose, cancel, obliterate, suppress.

Bụr·yät′, *n.*; *pl.* **Bụr·yät′** or **Bụr·yäts′,** 1. a member of one of the Mongolian tribes living in south central Siberia.
2. the language of the Buryats.

bur′y·ing bee′tle, a beetle belonging to the genus *Necrophorus*: also called *sexton beetle.*

bur′y·ing ground, a place for burying the dead; a graveyard; a cemetery.

bus, *n.*; *pl.* **bus′eṣ** or **bus′seṣ,** [contr. of *omnibus.*]
1. an omnibus; a large motor coach that can carry many passengers, generally following a regular route.
2. an automobile. [Colloq.]
3. in electricity, a conductor or group of conductors serving as a common connection for three or more circuits: in the form of a bar, also called *busbar.*

bus, *v.t.*; bused *or* bussed, *pt.*, *pp.*; busing *or* bussing, *ppr.* to transport by bus.

bus, *v.i.* 1. to go by bus.
2. to do the work of a bus boy.

bus boy, one who sets and clears tables, brings water, etc. in a restaurant; a waiter's assistant.

buṣ′by, *n.*; *pl.* **buṣ′bieṣ** (-biz), a tall, fur hat worn by hussars, artillerymen, etc. in the British army, and sometimes having a bag marked with the distinguishing colors of the regiment hanging from the top over the right side.

BUSBY

bus′ċärl, *n.* a mariner; a sailor. [Obs.]

bus′ċŏn, *n.* [Sp. *buscon*, from *buscar*, to search.] a miner who works for a certain percentage of extracted ore.

bụsh, *n.* [ME. *bussh, bosch, bosk*, a bush, thicket; O.H.G. *busc*; Dan. *busk*, a bush, shrub.]
1. a shrub; particularly, a shrub with branches rising from or near the root; a thick shrub; a cluster of shrubs.
2. a thicket of shrubs or bushes.
3. a tavern sign; hence, the tavern itself.
Good wine needs no *bush*. —Old proverb.
4. a shrub or shrubby branch of a tree, used as a prop; as, a *bush* for pease.
5. shrubby woodland; wild or uncleared country.
6. a thick tail or anything else resembling a bush.
7. in hunting, a fox's tail or brush.
the bushes; rural or small-town districts. [Slang.]
to beat about the bush; to suggest or hint at anything; to approach a subject indirectly.

bụsh, *v.i.* to grow thick or bushy.

bụsh, *v.t.*; bushed, *pt.*, *pp.*; bushing, *ppr.* 1. to decorate, support, etc. by setting bushes.
2. to cover (seeds) with earth by means of a bush harrow; as, to *bush* a garden.

bụsh, *n.* [G. *büsshe*; D. *bos*, a box.] a bushing (metal lining).

bụsh, *v.t.* to line with a bushing.

bụsh bēan, a variety of bean growing in bushlike form; a dwarf bean.

bụsh′boy, *n.* same as *bushman.*

bụsh′buck, *n.*; *pl.* **bụsh′buck** or **bụsh′bucks,** [D. *boschbok*; *bosch*, a bush, and *bok*, a buck.] a small, striped antelope, *Tragelaphus sylvaticus*, found in the South African bush.

bụsh′ċat, *n.* an African wildcat; the serval.

bụsh′chat, *n.* a bird of the thrush family, as the whinchat or stonechat.

bụsh ċlō′vẽr, Japan clover.

bụsh ċran′ber·ry, a shrub or tree of the honeysuckle family, with clusters of white flowers and red, cranberrylike fruit; cranberry tree.

bụsh dog, 1. a small wild dog of South America, *Icticyon venaticus.*
2. the lemuroid potto of West Africa.

bụshed, *a.* 1. lost in the bush.
2. very tired; fatigued. [Colloq.]

bụsh′el, *n.* [ME. *busshel, buschel*; OFr. *bussel, boissel*; LL. *bussula*, a little box, dim. of *bustia*, from L. *pyxis*, a box.]
1. a unit of dry measure for grain, fruit, etc., containing eight gallons or four pecks.
2. a measure or vessel with the capacity of a bushel.
3. a quantity that would fill a bushel measure; as, a *bushel* of potatoes.
4. loosely, a large quantity; as, a *bushel* of money.

bụsh′el, *v.t.* and *v.i.*; busheled, *pt.*, *pp.*; busheling, *ppr.* in tailoring, to alter or mend (men's clothes).

bụsh′el·āġe, *n.* a duty payable on commodities by the bushel.

bụsh′el·bȧs·ket, *n.* a rounded basket with a capacity of one bushel.

bụsh′el·ẽr, *n.* a bushelman.

bụsh′el·măn, *n.* a tailor's assistant who repairs or alters men's clothes; a busheler.

bụsh′et, *n.* a thicket; also, a small bush. [Obs.]

bụsh′fight″ẽr (-fīt″ẽr), *n.* one skilled in bush-fighting.

bụsh′fight″ing, *n.* a mode of fighting in which the combatants fight in the bush or from behind the shelter of trees and bushes.

bụsh′gōat, *n.* same as *bushbuck.*

bụsh′ham″mẽr, *n.* any of various hammers used by masons for shaping and dressing stone. It commonly consists of a solid head with a face cut into rows having projecting points.

bụsh′ham″mẽr, *v.t.*; bushhammered, *pt.*, *pp.*; bushhammering, *ppr.* to trim or dress (stone) with a bushhammer.

bụsh har′rōw, a frame to which is attached brush and branches, used to cover grass seed.

bụsh hog, a wild hog of South Africa, *Potamochœrus africanus*; the boschvark.

bụ′shï·dō, Bụ′shï·dō, *n.* the code of conduct for the samurai of feudal Japan, emphasizing loyalty, courage, and plain living, and preferring suicide (hara-kiri) to dishonor.

bụsh′i·ness, *n.* the state or quality of being bushy.

bụsh′ing, *n.* 1. the removable metal lining of a pivot hole, axle bearing, etc., for reducing friction or securing a tighter fit.
2. a hollow, circular block fitted into the bore of a breech-loading cannon, and forming the foundation of the breechblock.
3. in electricity, an insulating lining or part.

bụsh lạw′yẽr, the *Rubus australis*, a blackberry of New Zealand.

bụsh lēague, in baseball, a small or second-rate minor league. [Slang.]

bụsh lēa′guẽr, 1. a baseball player in a bush league. [Slang.]
2. an unimportant or second-rate performer in any sphere of activity. [Slang.]

bụsh′less, *a.* devoid of bushes; bare.

bụsh′măn, *n.*; *pl.* **bụsh′men,** 1. in Australia, one who dwells in the bush or interior; hence, a backwoodsman.
2. [B–] any member of a nomadic tribe in southwestern Africa in the region of the Kalahari Desert; also, their language.

bụsh′mȧs″tẽr, *n.* a large, poisonous snake, *Lachesis mutus*, of the family *Crotalidæ*, related to the rattlesnake, and found in Central and South America.

bụsh′ment, *n.* 1. a thicket; a cluster of bushes. [Obs.]
2. an ambush or ambuscade. [Obs.]

bụsh′răn″ġẽr, *n.* 1. one who lives in the bush.
2. in Australia, a fugitive from justice taking refuge in the bush.

bụsh′răn″ġing, *n.* the act or practice of living as a bushranger.

bụsh shrīke, a bird of the family *Formicariidæ*, and subfamily *Thamnophilinæ*; especially, the tropical American ant thrush of the genus *Thamnophilus.*

bụsh tit, a small passerine bird belonging to the genus *Psaltriparus*, of which a species is found in western North America.

bụsh′whack, *v.i.* [prob. from *bush* (shrub), and *whack.*]
1. to beat or cut one's way through bushes.
2. to move a boat along a stream by pulling at the bushes on the bank.
3. to engage in guerrilla fighting, attacking from ambush.

bụsh′whack, *v.t.* to ambush.

bụsh′whack″ẽr, *n.* 1. one who is accustomed to beating or cutting his way through bushes; a backwoodsman.
2. a guerrilla fighter, especially one on the Confederate side in the Civil War: so called by the Northern soldiers.
3. a country clown; an awkward fellow.
4. a kind of scythe for cutting down or trimming bushes; also, one who wields it.

bụsh′y, *a.*; *comp.* bushier; *superl.* bushiest, 1. overgrown or covered with bushes.
2. having many close twigs and branches; low and shrubby.
3. resembling a bush or bushes; thick and spreading; shaggy; as, a *bushy* tree, a *bushy* beard, *bushy* eyebrows.

buṣ′i·ly (biz′), *adv.* in a busy manner; earnestly; steadily; unceasingly.

buṣi′ness (biz′nes), *n.* [ME. *business, bysiness*, labor, diligence, from *busy*, busy.]
1. employment; occupation; profession; calling; vocation; means of livelihood; that which occupies the time, attention, and labor of men, for the purpose of profit or improvement; as, his *business* was that of a merchant; the *business* of a banker.
2. commerce or trade in general; as, a good knowledge of *business.*
3. in a theatrical sense, the work determined upon and arranged by the director for the action of a play.
Consider what scope the *business* of the scene gives to the actor's purpose. —Irving.
4. concern; right or power of interference; as, it was none of his *business.*
5. anxiety; care. [Obs.]
6. the state of being busy or actively employed. [Obs.]
7. a matter or affair; also, serious engagement; important occupation, as distinguished from trivial affairs; as, *business* before pleasure; life is a serious *business.*
8. a commercial or industrial establishment; store, factory, etc.
9. commercial practice or policy; as, it is poor *business* to insult the customers.
business is business; sentiment, friendship, etc. cannot be allowed to interfere with profit-making.
to do business with; (a) to engage in commerce with; (b) to have dealings with.
to give (or *get*) *the business*; to subject (or be subjected) to rough treatment, practical joking, etc. [Slang.]
to have no business; to have no right (to do something).
to make it one's business; to take the management of; to consider and act upon as a personal affair.
to mean business; to be determined; to be in earnest. [Colloq.]
to mind one's own business; to confine oneself to one's own affairs; to refrain from interference with the affairs of others.
Syn.—employment, calling, vocation, occupation, trade, profession, office, affair, matter, transaction.

bus̤i′ness, *a.* of or for business.

bus̤i′ness çol′lege (or **sçhool**), a school offering instruction in stenography, bookkeeping, office routine, etc.

bus̤i′ness cȳ′çle, the continual alternation between periods of prosperity (booms) and periods of depression (slumps) as characteristic of business and industry.

bus̤i′ness en′vel·ōpe, an envelope into which standard-size (8½″ x 11″) letterhead stationery can be put with only two folds: also called *business-size envelope.*

bus̤i′ness·līke, *a.* practical; systematic; efficient; methodical; as, to do a thing in a *businesslike* manner.

bus̤i′ness·man, *n.*; *pl.* **bus̤i′ness·men,** a man in business, especially as an owner or executive.

bus̤i′ness·wom·ăn (-woom-), *n.*; *pl.* **bus̤i′ness·wom·en** (-wim-), a woman in business, especially as an owner or executive.

bus′ing, bus′sing, *n.* the act of transporting children by bus to a school outside of their neighborhood, especially in order to desegregate the school.

busk, *n.* [Fr. *busc, busque,* busk.]
 1. a strip of steel, whalebone, or other material, that strengthens and shapes the front of a woman's corset; a corset stay.
 2. the entire corset when made of stiffened material. [Dial.]

busk, *v.t.*; busked, *pt., pp.*; busking, *ppr.* [ME. *busken*; Ice. *buask,* to get oneself ready; *bua,* to prepare, live, dwell, and *sik,* self.]
 1. to prepare; to equip; to fit out. [Scot.]
 2. to dress; to array; to apparel. [Scot.]
 Busk ye, *busk* ye, my bonny, bonny bride.
 —Hamilton.
 3. to employ; to use or make use of. [Obs.]

busk, *v.i.* 1. to go; to hurry; to guide or direct one's course. [Obs.]
 2. to dress; to get ready. [Scot.]
 3. in nautical usage, (a) to tack or beat about; to stand off and on shore; (b) to cruise, as a pirate. [Obs.]

busk, *n.* a harvest feast, or feast of first fruits, among the Creek Indians.

busked (buskt), *a.* wearing a busk.

bus′ket, *n.* 1. a small bush; a bouquet. [Obs.]
 2. a shrubbery in a garden. [Rare.]

bus′kin, *n.* [D. *brooskin,* a buskin, dim. of *broos,* a buskin, a purse.]
 1. a half boot or high shoe, worn for protection against thorns, mud, etc., which reaches halfway to the knee, being laced or strapped to the ankle and calf of the leg.
 The hunted red deer's
 undressed hide
 Their hairy *buskins* well
 supplied. —Scott.

BUSKINS (sense 2)

 2. a similar covering worn by actors in tragedy among the ancients in contradistinction to the *sock* worn by comedians. The stage *buskins* had very thick soles to give an appearance of elevation to the stature of the actor.
 3. hence, tragedy or the tragic drama, as opposed to comedy.
 He was a critic upon operas, too,
 And knew all niceties of the sock and *buskin.*
 —Byron.
 4. a woman's laced shoe or half boot.
 5. in the Roman Catholic Church, a kind of stocking of rich stuff, as satin, cloth of gold, or silk embroidered, worn by bishops when celebrating Mass.

bus′kined, *a.* 1. dressed in buskins.
 2. relating to tragedy; tragic.

busk′y, *a.* same as *bosky.*

bus′măn, *n.*; *pl.* **bus′men,** the driver or conductor of a bus.

bus′măn's hol′i·dāy, a holiday in which one does for recreation much the same thing that he does as his daily work.

buss, *n.* [G. *bus,* a kiss; Ir. and Gael. *bus,* a mouth, a lip.] a smacking kiss. [Archaic or Dial.]

buss, *v.t.* and *v.i.*; bussed, *pt., pp.*; bussing, *ppr.* to kiss; to smack with the lips. [Archaic or Dial.]
 We *buss* our wantons, but our wives we kiss.
 —Herrick.

buss, *n.* [OFr. *busse*; LL. *bussa, buscia,* a small boat, a box; L. *buxus,* a box.] a small vessel of from fifty to seventy tons, long used in herring fishery.

bus′seṣ, *n.* alternative plural of *bus.*

bus̤′sū, *n.* [native name.] a short palm, *Manicaria saccifera,* with leaves longer than the trunk or stem, and spreading spathes used in making a coarse cloth. It thrives in the swamps of the Amazon. Also called *bussu palm.*

bust, *n.* [Fr. *buste*; It. *busto*; LL. *bustum,* the trunk of the body.]
 1. a piece of sculpture showing only the head, shoulders, and breast.
 Can storied urn or animated *bust,*
 Back to its mansion call the fleeting breath?
 —Gray.
 2. the bosom, especially of a woman.

bust, *v.t.* and *v.i.* [orig., dial. var. of *burst.*]
 1. to burst; break. [Slang.]
 2. to make or become bankrupt. [Slang.]
 3. to demote or become demoted. [Slang.]
 4. to tame: said of broncos, etc. [Slang.]
 5. to hit or punch. [Slang.]

bust, *n.* 1. a failure. [Slang.]
 2. a blow or punch. [Slang.]
 3. a spree. [Slang.]

bus′tărd, *n.* [OFr. *bistard, oustarde*; Pr. *aus tarda*; L. *avis tarda,* slow bird.] a large bird of the genus *Otis,* related to the crane and plover. The great bustard, *Otis tarda,* is the largest European bird, the male often weighing thirty pounds, with a breadth of wing of six or seven feet. It inhabits regions of Europe, Asia, and Africa.

GREAT BUSTARD (*Otis tarda*)

bus′ted, *a.* without funds; bankrupt. [Slang.]

bus′tẽr, *n.* 1. something remarkable or great. [Slang.]
 2. a drunken carousal; a spree. [Slang.]
 3. in Australia and New Zealand, a cutting, violent wind; a gale. [Slang.]
 4. a person who breaks up (trusts, etc.). [Slang.]
 5. [B–] little boy: used in direct address. [Slang.]

bus′tiç, *n.* [perh. altered from native name.] a tree of the sapodilla family, found in Florida.

bus′tle (bus′sl), *v.i.* and *v.t.*; bustled, *pt., pp.*; bustling, *ppr.* [Ice. *bustla,* to bustle, splash; *bustl,* a splashing, turmoil.] to move quickly, busily, fussily, as with rudeness, noise, etc.

bus′tle, *n.* hurry; noise; fuss; tumult.

bus′tle, *n.* 1. a pad or framework formerly worn by women on the back part of the body below the waist, to fill out the figure.
 2. a large bow or gathered material worn over the back of the skirt below the waist.

bus′tlẽr (bus′lẽr), *n.* an active, fussy, bustling person.

bus′tling (bus′ling), *a.* stirring; moving actively, with noise or agitation; as, a *bustling* throng.

bus′tō, *n.* [It.] a bust. [Obs.]

bust′y, *a.* having a large bust, or bosom.

bus̤′y (biz′i), *a.* [ME. *bisy, bysy, busi*; AS. *bysig,* busy, occupied; D. *bezig*; L.G. *besig,* active, busy.]
 1. employed with constant attention; active; at work; not idle.
 My mistress is *busy,* and
 cannot come. —Shak.

BUSTLE

 2. filled with business; characterized by much activity; as, a *busy* town; a *busy* day.
 3. continually active or at work; as, the *busy* bee; *busy* thoughts; *busy* feet.
 4. officiously or foolishly active; meddling; as, a *busy* gossiper.
 5. solicitous; cautious. [Obs.]
 6. being used: said especially of a telephone.

bus̤′y (biz′i), *v.t.*; busied, *pt., pp.*; busying, *ppr.* to employ with attention; to keep engaged; to make busy: often used reflexively; as, to *busy* oneself with books.
 To be *busied* with genus and species.
 —Locke.

bus̤′y·bod″y, *n.* a meddling person; one who officiously concerns himself with the affairs of others.

bus̤′y·ness (biz′i-), *n.* the state of being busy. [Rare.]

but, *n.* the outer room, especially the kitchen, of a cottage. [Scot.]
 but and ben; (a) the outer and inner parts of a dwelling; (b) the whole house. [Scot.]

but, *a.* [AS. *butan,* outside, without.] outside, outer. [Scot.]

but, *n.* a butt (especially, a flatfish).

but, *n.* the conjunction *but*; hence, a condition, objection, or exception; as, there are too many ifs and *buts* in this contract.

but, *v.i.* and *v.t.* to abut.

but, *prep.* [ME. *but, bote, bute, buten*; AS. *butan, buton,* without, outside; *be,* by, and *utan,* out, from without; *ut,* out; *butan* is primarily an adverb.]
 1. except; barring; besides; save.
 Who can it be, *but* perjured Lycon?
 —Smith.
 2. otherwise than; other than; as, we cannot choose *but* stay.
 3. without; unless with. [Obs.]
 but for; if it were not for.

but, *adv.* 1. only; as, if I had *but* known.
 2. merely; no more than; not otherwise than; as, he is *but* a child.
 3. just; as, I heard it *but* now.
 4. on the other hand; yet.
 5. in the outer apartment, or to the outer room of a cottage having a but and a ben; as, to gae (go) *but.* [Scot.]
 6. outside; without. [Dial.]

but, *conj.* 1. except; with exception of the fact that; excepting that; as, most people joined in the demonstrations, *but* the students refrained.
 2. however; yet; still; as, he is a villain, *but* he has some virtues.
 3. unless; if not; as, it never rains *but* it pours.
 4. that; as, I don't question *but* you're correct.
 5. that . . . not; as, I never think of summer *but* I think of childhood.
 6. who . . . not; which . . . not; as, not a man *but* felt it.
 7. than; as, I had not left the room *but* he commenced to betray me; no sooner conceived, *but* done.
 8. otherwise than; other than; more than; as, we cannot *but* believe that death does not end all; I cannot *but* try.
 9. on the contrary; on the other hand; as, the spirit is willing, *but* the flesh is weak.
 But always functions as an adversative correlator; it is often indistinguishable, therefore, as a preposition, conjunction, or adverb.
 Syn.—except, excepting, however, nevertheless, notwithstanding, save, still, yet.

bū·tȧ·dī′ēne, *n.* a hydrocarbon, C_4H_6, obtained from petroleum or alcohol, and used in making synthetic rubber.

bū′tāne, *n.* [L. *butyrum,* butter.] an inflammable gaseous hydrocarbon, C_4H_{10}, belonging to the methane series, and having two isomeric forms.

bū′tȧ·nōne, *n.* [*butane* and *-one.*] a highly inflammable liquid, $CH_3COCH_2CH_3$, that is a by-product of acetone, used as a solvent.

bu̇tch′ẽr, *n.* [ME. *bocher*; OFr. *bochier, bouchier,* one who kills and sells he-goats; OFr. *boc,* a he-goat.]
 1. one who slaughters animals for market; one whose occupation is to kill and dress animals for the table.
 2. one who cuts up and sells meat.
 3. one who kills men, or commands troops to kill them; one who sheds human blood in abundance.
 4. a mutilator of any good work; hence, a poor workman; a poor performer; a bungler.
 5. a person who sells candy, magazines, etc. in railroad cars or theaters; a candy butcher.

bu̇tch′ẽr, *v.t.*; butchered, *pt., pp.*; butchering, *ppr.* 1. to kill or slaughter (animals) for food or for market.
 2. to murder; specifically, to murder with unusual cruelty, or under circumstances of uncommon barbarity; to kill (people, game, etc.) in large numbers senselessly.
 3. to spoil; to mess up; to mutilate; to bungle.

bu̇tch′ẽr·bīrd, *n.* the shrike: a name common to different birds of the genus *Lanius.* They derive the name from their habit of suspending the uneaten portions of their prey upon thorns, as a butcher hangs meat upon hooks, for consumption at their leisure. The great northern shrike, *Lanius borealis,* and the white-rumped shrike or loggerhead, *Lanius ludovicianus*, are common in America.

butch'ẽr block, [because made like a butcher's chopping block.] designating or of a thick slab made by gluing together strips of hardwood, as maple or oak, used for counter and table tops, etc.

butch'ẽr·ing, *n.* 1. the act of needless and cruel killing; wanton slaughtering.
 2. the business of slaughtering animals for food, or selling meat.

butch'ẽr knīfe (nīf), a large, sharp knife for cutting meat, etc.

butch'ẽr·ly, *a.* and *adv.* 1. cruel; savage; murderous; grossly and clumsily barbarous.
 2. like a butcher.

butch'ẽr's-broom', *n.* [said to be so named because once used by butchers for sweeping their shops.] a plant with glossy, leaflike branches, clusters of small white flowers, and large, red berries.

butch'ẽr shop, a store where meat, poultry, etc. are sold.

butch'ẽr·y, *n.*; *pl.* **butch'ẽr·ies,** 1. the business of slaughtering cattle for the table or for market.
 2. murder, especially murder committed with unusual barbarity; great slaughter.
 3. the place where animals are killed for market; a shambles, or slaughterhouse.
 4. a butcher shop.
 5. the act or result of butchering.
 Syn.—slaughter, murder, carnage, massacre.

Bū'tē·ä, *n.* a genus of East Indian leguminous trees, named after the Earl of Bute (1713-1792). *Butea frondosa* yields butea gum.

bū'tēne, *n.* [from *butyl* and *-ene.*] one of the three hydrocarbons of the butylene series having the general formula C_4H_8.

bū'te·sin, *n.* a local anesthetic for application to the skin, wounds, mucous membranes, etc.

bū'te·sin piç'rāte, a local anesthetic obtained by combining butesin with picric acid: used in the treatment of burns and lesions.

but'lẽr, *n.* [Fr. *bouteillier*, from *bouteille*, a bottle, i.e., the bottler.]
 1. a manservant employed to take charge of the wine cellar, tableware, and dining-room arrangements and generally to have supervision of other servants.
 2. formerly, an officer attached to a royal court, usually entrusted with the supply of wine for the royal table.

but'lẽr·äġe, *n.* a duty of two shillings formerly levied on every tun of wine imported into England: so called because originally paid to the king's butler for the king.

but'lẽr·ship, *n.* the office or duties of a butler.

but'lẽr's pan'try, a serving pantry between the kitchen and the dining room.

but'lẽr·y, *n.*; *pl.* **but'lẽr·ies,** [re-formed from *butler* and *-y*; orig. ME. *botelerie*, from OFr. *bouteillerie.*] the butler's pantry; buttery.

but'ment cheek, one of the sides of a mortise.

Bū·tō·mā'cē·ae, *n.pl.* [L., from Gr. *boutomos*, a kind of water plant.] a small family of herbs, including the flowering rush.

bū·tō·mā'ceous, *a.* relating to the *Butomaceæ.*

butt, but, *n.* [ME. *but, butte*, a goal, mark; OFr. *but, butte*, a goal, mark to shoot at; from *buter, boter*, to push, butt, strike; O.H.G. *bozen*, to beat, strike.]
 1. literally, end; furthest point; hence, a mark to be shot at; a target; the point where a mark is set or fixed to be shot at.
 2. the point to which a purpose or effort is directed. [Obs.]
 3. the object of aim; the thing against which an attack is directed. [Archaic.]
 4. the person at whom ridicule, jest, or contempt is directed; as, the *butt* of ridicule.
 5. a push or thrust given by the head of an animal; as, the *butt* of a ram; also, a thrust in fencing.
 6. the larger or thicker end of anything; as, the *butt* of a rifle or of a fishing rod.
 7. the end of a plank in a ship's side or bottom.
 8. a particular kind of double hinge for doors: called also *butt-hinge.*
 9. a small portion of unplowed land at the sides or end of a field.
 10. a joint where two ends meet without being grooved into each other.
 11. the square end of a shaft or connecting rod to which a boxing or bushing is attached.
 12. the thickest part of tanned hides, used for sole leather: also called *back.*
 13. the end of a hose where a nozzle or another length of hose may be attached.
 14. a shelter for the target attendant at a rifle range.
 15. (a) a pile of earth, etc. behind a target, to stop the projectiles that miss or go through the target; (b) [*pl.*] a target range.
 16. a bound; a limit; as, the *butts* and bounds of an estate. [Obs.]
 17. the remaining end of anything; stub.
 18. the stub of a partially smoked cigarette or cigar.
 19. a cigarette. [Slang.]
 20. the buttocks. [Slang.]
 butt and butt; end to end, as timbers joined without overlapping.
 butts and bounds; [contraction of *abuttals and boundaries.*] in ordinary rectangular lands, the ends and the sides, as they were once termed in conveyancing.
 butt's length; the ordinary distance from the place of shooting to the butt, or mark.
 full butt; headfirst with much force, or without warning; full tilt.

butt, *v.t.* and *v.i.*, to join end to end.

butt, but, *n.* [ME. *butte, but* (also in tur*bot*, hali*but*); prob. from M.L.G. *butte, a.*, lumpy.] any of various flatfishes, as the halibut, turbot, etc.

butt, *n.* [AS. *butte, butt.*]
 1. a large cask for wine or beer.
 2. a measure of liquid capacity equal to 126 gallons or two hogsheads: called also a *pipe.*

butt, *v.i.*; butted, *pt., pp.*; butting, *ppr.* [ME. *butten*, to push, throw; OFr. *buter, boter*, to push, strike.]
 1. to thrust the head forward.
 2. to move or drive headfirst.
 3. to stick out; project.
 4. to abut.

butt, *v.t.* 1. to bump or push with the head or horns; ram with the head.
 2. to strike or bump against.
 3. to abut on.
 4. to make abut (*on, upon*, or *against*).
 to butt in; (a) to interfere; meddle; (b) to intrude. [Slang.]
 to butt into; (a) to bump into; collide with; (b) [Slang.] to interfere or meddle in.

butt chāin, a chain attached to the end of a tug, in a harness.

būtte, *n.* [Fr.] a high detached hill or ridge rising steeply from a plain, especially in the Rocky Mountains and vicinity; a small mesa.

but'ted, *a.* having a butt; as, heavy-*butted.*

butt end, the stouter or blunt end of any object; as, the *butt end* of a rifle or of a log.

but'tẽr, *n.* [ME. *butter, butere*; AS. *butere*; D. *boter*; L.G. *botter*; O.H.G. *butra*; It. *burro, butiro*; L. *butyrum*; Gr. *boutyron*, butter; *bous*, ox, cow, and *tyros*, cheese.]
 1. an oily, thick, yellowish substance obtained by churning the fatty part of milk.
 2. any substance resembling butter in consistency, etc.; as, apple *butter*; also, one of the fat, solid vegetable oils: sometimes called *vegetable butter*; as, cacao *butter.*
 3. in old chemistry, any of certain metallic chlorides; as, *butter* of antimony.
 4. flattery [Colloq.]
 butter and eggs; one of many species of plants which have flowers in different shades of yellow, as the toadflax, *Linaria vulgaris.*
 to know which side one's bread is buttered on; to be prudently aware of what one's material security or comfort depends on.
 to look as if butter would not melt in one's mouth; to look innocent or demure.

but'tẽr, *v.t.*; buttered, *pt., pp.*; buttering, *ppr.*
 1. to spread or cover with butter.
 2. in gambling, to raise (the stakes) at every throw or every game. [Obs. Slang.]
 3. to flatter (often with *up*). [Colloq.]

butt'ẽr, *n.* one who or that which butts.

but'tẽr·ball, 1. the bufflehead.
 2. a fat person. [Colloq.]

but'tẽr bēan, 1. a variety of bean with yellow pods; wax bean.
 2. the lima bean: so called in the southern United States.

but'tẽr·bīrd, *n.* the bobolink: the Jamaican name.

but'tẽr bōat, a small dish for serving melted butter, etc., often boat-shaped.

but'tẽr·bump, *n.* [*butter*, a dial. form of *bittern*, and *bump*, the sound made by the bittern.] the bittern. [Dial.]

but'tẽr·būr, but'tẽr·būrr, *n.* [so called from the leaves being used to wrap butter.] any of several related plants with clusters of white or purplish flowers.

but'tẽr çŏl'ŏr, a preparation used to color butter, butterine, or similar products yellow.

but'tẽr·çup, *n.* 1. any of several plants of the genus *Ranunculus*, which have bright yellow, cup-shaped flowers: called also *butterflower, kingcup*, and *goldcup.*
 2. its flower.

but'tẽr dish, a dish used for holding butter.

but'tẽr·fat, *n.* the fatty part of milk, from which butter is made.

but'tẽr·fin"gẽred, *a.* liable to let things slip through one's fingers, or to let things fall; careless. [Colloq.]

but'tẽr·fin"gẽrs, *n.* one who lets drop anything he should hold; specifically, in games, one who drops the ball. [Colloq.]

but'tẽr·fish, *n.*; *pl.* **but'tẽr·fish** or **but'tẽr·fish·es,** any of various fishes with a slippery coating, as *Stromateus triacanthus*, the dollarfish.

but'tẽr·flow"ẽr, *n.* the buttercup.

but'tẽr·flȳ, *n.*; *pl.* **but'tẽr·flies,** [ME. *butturflye, boterflye*; AS. *buttorfleoge, buturflege*, a butterfly, white moth; *butere*, butter, *fleoge*, a fly; probably first applied to the yellow variety.]
 1. any of certain diurnal lepidopterous insects, having a sucking mouth part, slender body, and four broad, membranous wings covered with tiny scales, usually bright-colored.
 2. figuratively, one who leads an idle, gay life; an idler; a trifler; also, a person, especially a woman, who is brightly dressed.
 3. a kind of breaststroke in which the swimmer brings both arms out of the water and, while bringing them forward, lunges before beginning the next stroke.
 butterfly damper; a type of butterfly valve consisting of a disk which turns on its diametrical axis across a pipe.
 butterfly valve; a pair of clack valves consisting of two hinged plates, back to back, that somewhat resemble the wings of a butterfly: used in pumps: also *butterfly cock.*

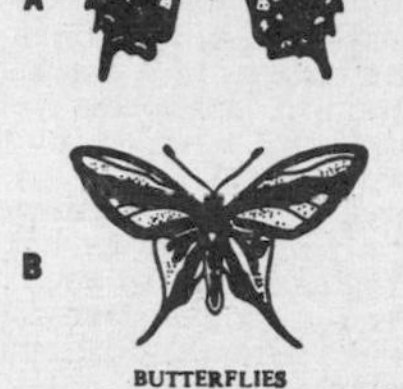

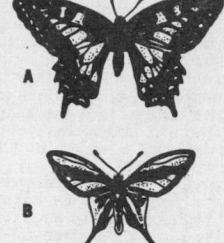

BUTTERFLIES
A, swallowtail (3 ¼ in. wide); B, New Guinea golden (2 ¼ in. wide)

but'tẽr·fly fish, any of various fishes resembling butterflies in coloring or in having winglike fins, as the blenny, the angelfish, etc.

but'tẽr·flȳ plant, a West Indian orchid, having flowers resembling butterflies; also, an East Indian orchid having similar flowers.

but'tẽr·flȳ-shell, *n.* a shell belonging to the genus *Voluta*; also, a pteropod.

but'tẽr·fly tā'ble, a small drop-leaf table with leaf supports shaped like a butterfly's wings.

but'tẽr·flȳ weed, a common weed, *Asclepias tuberosa*, of the milkweed family, used in medicine, as a cathartic, for increasing perspiration, etc.; the pleurisy root.

but'tẽr·ine (*or* -in), *n.* [*butter*, and *-ine.*]
 1. a substitute for butter made from oleomargarine, or animal fat, with milk, coloring matter, etc.
 2. such a substance with a little butter mixed into it.

but'tẽr·is, *n.* [form of *buttress*, from Fr. *bouter*, to push.] an instrument of steel set in wood, used for paring the hoof of a horse.

but'tẽr knīfe (nīf), a small, dull-edged knife for cutting or spreading butter.

but'tẽr·milk, *n.* 1. a sour liquid, that part of milk which remains after the butter is extracted.
 2. artificially curdled milk.

but'tẽr·nut, *n.* 1. the edible fruit of an American tree, *Juglans cinerea*, so called from the oil it contains; also, the tree itself: called also *white walnut.*
 2. the nut of the *Caryocar nuciferum*, a native of South America: called also *souari nut.*
 3. the brown color from the dye of the butternut.
 4. [*pl.*] brown homespun overalls.
 5. a Confederate soldier in the Civil War: from the color of their clothing which resembled that of butternuts.

but'tẽr print, a block of carved wood for molding butter: also called *butter stamp.*

but'tẽr·sçotch, *n.* a kind of crisp, sticky candy made of butter and brown sugar.

but'tẽr·sçotch, *a.* made of, or having the flavor of, butterscotch.

but'tẽr tooth, a broad front tooth.

but'tẽr tree, any of various trees yielding a butterlike substance.

but'tẽr-trī'ẽr, *n.* an instrument used in sampling butter from a firkin.

but'tẽr·weed, *n.* any of various plants with yellow flowers, as a kind of ragwort, etc.

but'tẽr weight (wāt), overweight: from the former practice of selling eighteen ounces of butter to the pound.

but'tẽr·wŏrt, *n.* any of a number of small plants of the bladderwort family, with flat, sticky leaves on which insects are caught; especially the *Pinguicula vulgaris*, growing on bogs or soft ground.

but'tẽr·y, *a.* 1. having the qualities or appearance of butter.

2. containing or spread with butter.

but'tẽr·y (*or* but'ry), *n.*; *pl.* **but'tẽr·ies,** 1. a room in a house, originally for the keeping of liquor; now, also, a pantry.

2. in some English colleges, a room where liquors, fruit, and refreshments are kept for sale to the students.

3. a cellar or underground place where butts of wine are stored.

but'tẽr·y hatch, a hatch or half-door giving entrance to a buttery.

butt-hinge, *n.* a butt (sense 8).

but'thorn, *n.* a starfish, *Asterias rubens*, common in European waters.

but'ting, *n.* anything that abuts; a boundary; an abuttal.

butt joint, in engineering, any joint made by putting plates or bars together end to end: it is sometimes strengthened with an additional plate or plates.

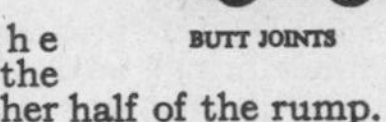

BUTT JOINTS

but'tŏck, *n.* [ME. *buttok, bottok*; *butt*, limit, extremity, and dim. *-ock*.]

1. either of the rounded parts at the back of the hips; either half of the rump.

2. [*pl.*] the rump.

3. [*sometimes pl.*] the round part of a ship's stern above the water line.

but'tŏn, *n.* [ME. *boton, botoun*; OFr. *boton*, a button, bud; from *boter*, to push out, butt.]

1. a knob or flattened piece of some substance, such as metal, bone, china, etc., with or without a covering of cloth: it is attached to material by means of holes or a shank on the underside and is commonly fitted into a buttonhole or slit in a corresponding part of the material as a fastening. Buttons are made in various forms and often used for ornamental purposes only.

2. any small knob.

3. (a) a bud; (b) a knoblike swelling on a plant; (c) a small, immature mushroom.

4. a flat, usually oblong, piece of wood or metal, turning on a pivot, used to fasten a door, window, etc.

5. a small, round mass of metal found at the bottom of a crucible, after fusion, or which remains in the cupel in the process of assaying.

6. formerly, an ornamental knob worn on the hat in China, indicating rank; as, a red-*button* mandarin.

7. [*pl., construed as sing.*] a page or bellboy: so called from the rows of buttons which adorn his jacket. [Colloq.]

8. a small emblem of membership, distinction, etc., generally worn in the lapel.

9. a small knob for operating a doorbell, electric lamp, etc.

10. a guard on the tip of a fencing foil.

11. the point of the jaw. [Slang.]

to hold by the button; to persist in conversation; to bore with talk.

but'tŏn, *v.t.*; buttoned, *pt., pp.*; buttoning, *ppr.* [ME. *botonen*, to button, from *boton*, a button.] to fasten with a button or buttons; to enclose or make secure with buttons: often followed by *up*; as, to *button up* a coat.

but'tŏn, *v.i.* to be capable of being buttoned; as, the glove *buttons* with difficulty.

but'tŏn·ball, *n.* same as *buttonwood*.

but'tŏn·bush, any of a number of shrubs of the madder family, with dense, round clusters of small, white flowers; especially, the *Cephalanthus occidentalis*.

but'tŏn·hōle, *n.* the hole or loop into which a button is inserted.

but'tŏn·hōle, *v.t.*; buttonholed, *pt., pp.*; buttonholing, *ppr.* 1. to make buttonholes in.

2. to make with a buttonhole stitch.

3. to hold (a person) by or as by a buttonhole; detain in conversation.

but'tŏn·hōle stitch, a closely worked loop stitch making a reinforced edge, as around a buttonhole.

but'tŏn·hook, *n.* a small metal hook for pulling a button through a buttonhole, as in fastening some shoes.

but'tŏn·mōld, *n.* a knob or disk of hard material to be covered with leather or cloth to make a button.

but'tŏn-shell, *n.* a marine mollusk of the genus *Rotella*, the shell of which is small and polished.

but'tŏn snāke'root, any of a number of plants of the composite family, with narrow leaves and, usually, a globe-shaped tuber and purple flowers; especially, a plant of the genus *Liatris*; also, a perennial plant of southern and western United States, the leaves of which are bristly along the margins, and the flowers white and spherical.

but'tŏn tree, the *Conocarpus*, a genus of trees native to tropical America and western Africa; also, a buttonwood.

but'tŏn·weed, *n.* any of various plants of the genera *Spermacoce* and *Diodia*.

but'tŏn·wood, *n.* 1. the *Platanus occidentalis*, or western plane tree, a large tree producing rough balls, from which it is named.

2. the wood of this tree.

but'tŏn·y, *a.* 1. trimmed with numerous buttons.

2. of or like a button.

but'tress, *n.* [ME. *buttrace, butterasse*; OFr. *bouterets*, a buttress, from *bouter*, to thrust.]

1. a structure, generally of brick or stone, serving to support a wall which is very high or loaded with a heavy superstructure: used also for decorative purposes, especially to produce symmetrical effects.

2. any prop or support, material or figurative; as, the *buttress* of a good cause.

flying buttress; see under *flying*.

BUTTRESS

but'tress, *v.t.*; buttressed, *pt., pp.*; buttressing, *ppr.* 1. to strengthen or brace by means of a buttress.

2. to bolster; to support; to uphold.

butt shäft, a blunt-headed arrow often used in shooting at a target.

butt'-strap, *v.t.*; butt-strapped, *pt., pp.*; butt-strapping, *ppr.* to weld (the ends of two pieces of metal) to form a butt.

butt weld, a joint made by the abutting of two pieces of metal, welded into a butt joint.

butt'-weld, *v.t.*; butt-welded, *pt., pp.*; butt-welding, *ppr.* to join by means of a butt weld.

but'ty, *n.* [shortened form of Early Modern Eng. *boty felowe*, a partner; *boty*, property shared, and *felowe*, a fellow.]

1. in mining, one who takes a contract for mining coal or ore at a specified price per ton.

2. a chum or associate. [Brit. Dial.]

but'ty gang, a number of men working together as a body, on contract, and sharing the profits jointly.

bū'tyl, *n.* [*butyric*, and *-yl*.] any of the four organic radicals (normal butyl, secondary butyl, tertiary butyl, isobutyl) combined from the same elements in the same proportion by weight and having a valence number of one, but differing in properties and structure; C_4H_9.

bū'tyl al'cō·hol, an alcohol, C_4H_9OH, formed by the combination of hydroxyl with butyl: there are four types corresponding to the four types of butyl.

bū'tyl·am·ine, *n.* [*butyl*, and *amine*.] the hydrocarbon $C_4H_9NH_2$, a colorless fluid.

bū'ty·lēne, *n.* any of the three isomeric modifications of the gaseous hydrocarbon of the ethylene series, C_4H_8.

bū'tyl (rub'bẽr), a synthetic rubber prepared as the copolymer of butylene with isoprene, etc., and vulcanized to form a substance that is especially impermeable to gases: a trademark (*Butyl*).

bū'tyn, *n.* a colorless crystalline substance, $(C_{18}H_{30}N_2)_2H_2SO_4$, used as an anesthetic, especially for surface anesthesia of mucous membranes and in the eye: a trade-mark (*Butyn*).

bū·ty·rā'ceous, *a.* having the qualities of butter; resembling butter; also, producing butter.

bū'ty·rāte, *n.* a salt or ester of butyric acid.

bū·tyr'iç, *a.* [from L. *butyrum*, butter.] of, pertaining to, or obtained from butter.

bū·tyr'iç ac'id, a colorless acid, $C_3H_7CO_2H$, with an unpleasant odor, found in rancid butter, perspiration, etc.

bū'ty·rin, *n.* a glyceryl ester of butyric acid.

bū·ty·rom'e·tẽr, *n.* [L. *butyrum*, butter, and *metrum*, Gr. *metron*, measure.] an instrument by which the amount of butterfat in milk can be measured.

bū'ty·rōne, *n.* the colorless liquid ketone of the butyric series: produced by distilling calcium butyrate.

bū'ty·rous, *a.* same as *butyraceous*.

bux'ē·ous, *a.* [L. *buxeus*, from *buxus*, a box tree.] of, pertaining to, or like the box tree.

bux'in, bux'ine, *n.* an alkaloid obtained from the leaves of the common box tree.

bux'ŏm, *a.* [ME. *buxom, boxom*, pliable, obedient, from *bugan*, to bend, and *-sum*.]

1. obedient; pliable; ready to obey; meek; humble. [Archaic.]

2. gay; lively; brisk; large and hearty; evidencing good health and spirits; comely and plump: said of a woman or girl.

bux'ŏm·ly, *adv.* in a buxom manner.

bux'ŏm·ness, *n.* the state or quality of being buxom.

Bux'us, *n.* [L., box tree.] a genus of trees of the family *Buxaceæ*, the various species of which yield the valuable hardwood called boxwood. The best-known specimen is the common box tree, the *Buxus sempervirens*.

buy̆ (bī), *v.t.*; bought, *pt., pp.*; buying, *ppr.* [ME. *buyen, byen, biggen*; AS. *bycgan*, to buy.]

1. to acquire the ownership, right, or title to (anything) by paying or agreeing to pay money.

2. to procure by a consideration given, or by something that is deemed worth the thing bought; to get by an exchange or sacrifice; as, to *buy* pleasure with pain; to *buy* favor with flattery.

3. to bribe; to obtain by illegal or dishonorable means; as, to *buy* a seat in the legislature.

4. to be the means of purchasing; as, all that money can *buy*.

to buy in; to buy back (a commodity) for its owner at an auction; also, to buy stock in any corporation.

to buy off; to influence; to bribe; to cause to bend or yield by some consideration; as, to *buy off* conscience.

to buy on credit; to purchase on a promise to make payment at a future day.

to buy out; (a) to buy off; (b) to purchase the share or shares of (a person) in a stock, fund, or association.

Syn.—purchase, acquire, obtain, secure, procure.

buy̆, *v.i.* to negotiate about a purchase; be a buyer.

I will *buy* with you and sell with you.
—Shak.

buy̆, *n.* 1. a buying.

2. anything bought or buyable.

3. something bought or buyable that is worth the price. [Colloq.]

bad buy; something bought or buyable that is not worth the price [Colloq.]

good buy; something bought or buyable that is worth the price [Colloq.]

buy̆'à·ble, *a.* that can be bought.

buy̆'ẽr, *n.* 1. one who purchases anything for money.

2. a purchasing agent who buys goods for his employer.

buy̆'ẽr's strīke, an organized boycott (by consumers) of certain goods or merchants in an attempt to bring down prices.

buzz, *v.i.*; buzzed, *pt., pp.*; buzzing, *ppr.* [an onomatopoeic word.]

1. to make a low, humming sound, as bees; to make the sound of a prolonged *z*.

2. to speak with a low, humming voice, excitedly or incessantly.

3. to gossip.

4. to move with a buzzing sound.

to buzz about (or *around*); to scurry about.

buzz, *v.t.* 1. to whisper; to spread (gossip, rumors, etc.) by whispers or secretly.

2. to make (wings, etc.) buzz.

3. to fly an airplane low over (a building, etc.).

4. to signal (someone) with a buzzer.

5. to telephone. [Colloq.]

buzz, *n.* 1. the noise of bees.

2. anything of a buzzing character, as the confused sound of many excited voices.

to give (a person) a buzz; to telephone (a person). [Slang.]

buz'zärd, *n.* [ME. *busard, bosarde, busart*;

OFr. *busart, buzart,* from *buse, buze,* a buzzard.]
1. a large raptorial bird, genus *Buteo,* of the falcon family, marked by a short curved bill hooked at the tip, long wings, long tarsi, and short, weak toes. *Buteo borealis,* from feeding upon poultry, is commonly called the *hen hawk,* as is *Buteo lineatus. Buteo vulgaris* is the common buzzard of Europe.
2. a blockhead; a dunce. [Dial.]
3. the turkey buzzard.

buz'zărd, *n.* [*buzz,* and *-ard.*] any insect that makes a buzzing noise, as a cockchafer. [Dial.]

buz'zărd, *a.* senseless; stupid.

buzz bomb (bom), a self-propelled bomb characterized by a loud buzzing sound in flight, used by Nazi Germany in World War II: also called *V-1.* [Colloq.]

buzz'ĕr, *n.* 1. a person or thing that buzzes; especially, a whisperer or bearer of tales. [Obs.]
2. an electrical device making a buzzing sound, used for signaling, as a certain type of doorbell.

buzz'ing·ly, *adv.* in a buzzing manner.

buzz saw, a circular saw rotated by a machine: so named because of the sound it makes when in rapid motion.

buzz'wig, *n.* 1. a large, bushy wig.
2. a person who wears a buzzwig; hence, an important person; a bigwig.

bȳ, *prep.* [ME. *by, bi, be;* AS. *bi, big, be,* near to, by, of, from, according to; G. *bei;* O.H.G. *bi;* Goth. *bi,* by, about.]
1. near; at; beside; as, stand *by* the door.
2. in or during; as, he travels *by* night.
3. for a fixed time; as, she works *by* the hour.
4. not later than; as, be back *by* ten o'clock.
5. through; as, we went *by* way of New York.
6. past; beyond; as, he walked right *by* me.
7. toward; as, the region lies north *by* west of this point.
8. in behalf of; as, he did well *by* his children.
9. through the means, work, or operations of; as, things made *by* human labor; poems *by* Dryden.
10. according to; as, he fights *by* the book.
11. in; as, it grows dark *by* degrees.
12. with the authority or sanction of; as, yes, *by* heaven.
13. in or to the amount or degree of; as, apples *by* the peck.
14. in another dimension; as, two *by* four.
15. against. [Obs.]
by all means; certainly; most assuredly.
by and by; in a short time; after a while; presently; soon.

When persecution ariseth because of the word, *by and by* he is offended.
—Matt. xiii. 21.

by the by; in passing; before proceeding; incidentally.
by the head; in nautical usage, drawing most water forward.
by the way; (a) along the way; as, they conversed *by the way;* (b) incidentally; by the by.
by the wind; sailing with the yards all drawn in so as to go as near into the wind as possible; close-hauled.
to come by; to obtain; to get possession of.
to do by; to behave toward; to do for.
to stand by; to stand near; to support; approve; defend.

bȳ, *adv.* 1. near; in the vicinity.
2. aside; as, to lay *by.*
3. beyond; over; close in passing; past; as, a bird flying *by.*
by and large; (a) from all standpoints; in every way; (b) on and off the wind, as a ship sails.

bȳ, *a.* same as *bye.*

bȳ, *n.* same as *bye.*

bȳ, *n.* [ME. *by, bi;* AS. *by,* from *buan,* to dwell; Dan. *by,* a town, village.] a dwelling place; a town: now used only terminally in names of places; as, Rug*by.*

bȳ-, [from *by.*] a prefix meaning (a) *close by, near,* as in *by*stander; (b) *side,* as in *by*street; (c) *on the side, secondary, incidental to the main,* as in *by*-product.

bȳ'-and-bȳ, *n.* future time.

bȳ'ărd, *n.* a piece of leather crossing the breast, used by men who drag cars in coal mines.

bȳ'-bid''dĕr, *n.* a confederate who bids in behalf of an owner or auctioneer at an auction, not to purchase, but simply to raise the prices.

bȳ'-bid''ding, *n.* bidding by prearrangement with the auctioneer or owner so as to raise the price of the thing being sold at auction.

bȳ'-blōw, *n.* 1. an indirect blow.
2. a child born out of wedlock.

bȳ'-book, *n.* a book for memoranda; a notebook.

bȳ'-çor''nĕr, *n.* a private corner.

bȳ'-dē·pend''ence, *n.* an appendage; accessory. [Obs.]

bȳ'-drink''ing, *n.* a drinking outside of regular meal hours. [Obs.]

bȳe, *n.* 1. that which is not of primary importance: now only in *by the by,* incidentally.
2. a run made on a passed ball in the game of cricket.
3. in sports tournaments in which competitors are paired, the position of the odd man, who advances automatically to the next round without having to play.
4. in golf, any hole or holes left unplayed at the end of a match.
Also spelled *by.*

bȳe, *a.* aside from the main consideration; incidental: also spelled *by.*

bȳe, *n.* same as *by* (a place name).

bȳe-, same as *by-.*

bȳe'-bȳe', *n.* and *interj.* good-by: a child's word.

bȳ'e·lec''tion, *n.* an election held at a time apart from the regular one, generally to fill a vacancy.

Bye·lō·rus'siăn (-rush'ăn), *a.* of Byelorussia, its people, or their dialect.

Bye·lō·rus'siăn, *n.* 1. a native or inhabitant of Byelorussia.
2. the dialect of Russian spoken in Byelorussia.

bȳe'-lōw, *adv.* and *interj.* hush: used in lullabies.

bȳ'-end, *n.* private end; secret purpose or advantage.

bȳ'fel''lōw, *n.* a student of an English university not elected to full fellowship.

bȳ'form, *n.* a related or parallel but secondary form of a word.

bȳ'gone, *n.* something past, or gone by.
let bygones be bygones; let the past be forgotten.

bȳ'gone, *a.* past; gone by.

bȳ'-in''tĕr·est, *n.* private advantage.

bȳ'land, *n.* a point or peninsula. [Obs.]

bȳ'lănd·ĕr, *n.* a bilander. [Obs.]

bȳ'-lāne, *n.* a private lane, or one branching off the main road.

bȳ'law'', *n.* [Dan. *bylov;* Sw. and Dan. *bylag;* Ice. *bæjar-lög,* a town law; *byjar,* genit. of *by,* a town, and *lög,* a law.]
1. a town law; the local or subordinate law of a city, town, or private corporation.
2. one of a number of subordinate laws usually drawn up by societies or corporations for the government of their members or stockholders.
3. a secondary law or rule.

bȳ'-line, *n.* a line printed above a newspaper or magazine article, telling who wrote it.

bȳ'-mat''tĕr, *n.* something incidental.

bȳ'nāme, *n.* 1. a nickname; an epithet.
2. a second name; a surname.

bȳ'nāme, *v.t.* to give a nickname to. [Obs.]

bȳ'-pȧss, *n.* 1. an auxiliary pipe leading around a valve or chamber, preventing a complete cessation of the flow when the valve or chamber is closed.
2. a way, path, etc. between two points that avoids or is auxiliary to the main way; detour.
3. in electricity, a shunt.

bȳ'-pȧss, *v.t.* 1. to go around instead of through.
2. to furnish with a by-pass.

bȳ'-pas''sāġe, *n.* a passage aside from the main one; a byway.

bȳ'-pȧss çŏn·dens'ĕr, in radio, a low-impedance condenser which provides an alternate path for alternating current while not passing any direct current.

bȳ'-pȧssed, *a.* [pp. of *by-pass.*] avoided by means of a by-pass.

bȳ'-pȧst, *a.* past; gone by.

bȳ'pȧth, bȳ'-pȧth, *n.* a private path; a little-used way.

bȳ'plāy, *n.* on the stage, a scene which is carried on aside from the main action; hence, anything accessory to the main action.

bȳ'-prod''uçt, *n.* something produced in the process of making another thing; secondary or incidental product or result.

bȳre, *n.* a cow barn.

bȳ'-rē·speçt', *n.* private end or view. [Obs.]

byr'law, *n.* [Ice. *bæjar-lög,* a town law.] a local system of government in northern England and Scotland according to which disputes involving property boundaries, rights of pasture, etc. are settled out of law court by the landowners in the district concerned; also, the district in which such a court has jurisdiction.

byr'nie (-ni), *n.* [AS. *byrne;* O.H.G. *brunna;* Ice. *brynja;* Dan. *brynje,* a corselet, coat of mail.] a coat of chain mail used in the Middle Ages by Norwegians, Icelanders, and others.

bȳ'rōad, *n.* a private road; a road not a main road.

Bȳ·ron'iç, *a.* pertaining to Lord Byron, or to the literary style characteristic of his writings; romantic, proud, cynical, etc.

bȳ'-room, *n.* a private room or apartment.

bȳ'-speech, *n.* an incidental or casual speech.

bȳ'-spell, *n.* [ME. *bispel;* AS. *bispell, bigspell,* a parable, example, story; *bi,* by, and *spell,* a story.] a proverb; a parable.

bys·sā'ceous, *a.* [L. *byssus;* Gr. *byssos,* a fine flax or linen.] resembling a byssus; consisting of fine silky filaments.

bys'săl, *a.* relating to a byssus.

bys·sif'ĕr·ous, *a.* [L. *byssus,* byssus, and *ferre,* to bear.] bearing a byssus or tuft.

bys'sin, *n.* same as *byssus* (a cloth).

bys'sine, *a.* [L. *byssinus;* Gr. *byssinos,* from *byssos,* byssus.] made of silk; having a silky or flaxlike appearance.

bys'soid, *a.* byssaceous.

bys'sō·līte, *n.* [Gr. *byssos,* fine flax, and *lithos,* stone: so called from its resemblance to flax.] a variety of hornblende having short silky fibers and an olive-green color.

bys'sus, *n.;* *pl.* **bys'sī,** [L. *byssus;* Gr. *byssos,* fine linen, or cotton.]
1. among the ancients, a linen, silk, or cotton cloth of exceedingly fine texture: used by the Egyptians in mummy wrapping.
2. a fine, yellow flax grown in ancient times, from which a linen cloth was made.
3. in zoology, a long, lustrous, silky bunch of filaments, secreted by certain bivalve mollusks, serving to attach them to fixed objects.

bȳ'stand''ĕr, *n.* one who stands near but does not participate; a spectator.
Syn.—looker-on, spectator, observer, beholder, gazer, witness.

bȳ'street, *n.* a private or side street; a street off a main street.

bȳ'-strōke, *n.* an incidental or indirect stroke.

bȳ'talk (-tok), *n.* incidental or irrelevant talk; small talk.

bȳ'-tũrn''ing, *n.* a turning or leading aside.

bȳ'-view (-vū), *n.* private view; self-interested purpose.

bȳ'walk'', *n.* a secluded or private walk.

bȳ'wăsh, *n.* a conduit or by-pass to carry off surplus water from a reservoir or dam.

bȳ'wāy, *n.* a secluded path; a private or little-traveled road.

bȳ'-wīpe, *n.* a sly gibe or stroke of sarcasm.

bȳ'word (-wũrd), *n.* 1. a common saying; a proverb; a saying that has a general currency.
2. a nickname.
3. a person or thing proverbial as being contemptible or ridiculous.

bȳ'work (-wũrk), *n.* a secondary business; employment aside from regular work in one's leisure time.

byz'ănt, *n.* same as *bezant.*

By·zan'tine (*or* biz'ăn-tēn), *a.* [LL. *Byzantinus,* from *Byzantium;* Gr. *Byzantion, Byzantium,* from *Byzas,* said to have been its founder.] relating to Byzantium or the Byzantine Empire, its culture, etc.

BYZANTINE CAPITALS

By·zan'tine, *n.* one native to or residing in Byzantium.
Byzantine architecture; the style of architecture developed in Byzantium between the fourth and fifteenth centuries: it is characterized by domes over square areas, round arches, elaborate mosaics, etc.
Byzantine church; the Greek church.

C

C, c (sē), *n.*; *pl.* **C's, c's, Cs, cs** (sēz), 1. the third letter of the English alphabet: from the Greek *gamma*, a borrowing from the Phoenician.
2. a sound of C or c.
3. a type or impression for C or c.
4. *a symbol for* the third in a sequence or group.

C, c (sē), *a.* 1. of C or c.
2. third in a sequence or group.

C (sē), *n.* 1. an object shaped like C.
2. a Roman numeral for 100: with a superior bar (C̄), 100,000.
3. in chemistry, *the symbol for* carbon.
4. in education, a grade third in quality; as, a *C* in biology.
5. in mathematics, *a symbol for* constant.
6. in music, (a) the first tone or note in the scale of C major, or the third in the scale of A minor; (b) a key, string, etc. producing this tone; (c) the scale having C as the keynote; (d) the sign for 4/4 time; (e) contralto.
7. in physics, *the symbol for* coulomb.

C (sē), *a.* shaped like C.

C-, cargo transport: followed by a number to designate a specific model of United States Army airplane designed to carry cargo or troops.

Ca, in chemistry, calcium.

ça, çaa, *v.t.* to drive; impel; knock. [Scot.]
But *ca* them out to park or hill. —Burns.

çaa'ing whāle, [Scot. *caa*, to drive, and *whale*; so called from their being driven in herds.] a porpoiselike cetacean, *Globicephalus svineval*, frequenting the shores of the Orkney, Shetland, and Faeroe islands, and Iceland, appearing in large herds.

çäa'mȧ, *n.* the hartebeest; also a South African fox, *Vulpes chama*.

çab, *n.* [abbrev. of *cabriolet*.]
1. an automobile or horse-drawn carriage for public hire; taxicab.
2. the place in a locomotive, motor truck, crane, derrick, steam shovel, etc. where the operator sits.

çab, *n.* [Heb. *qab*, a hollow, from *qābab*, to hollow out.] a Hebrew dry measure, variously estimated to contain from one to two quarts: also spelled *kab*.

çȧ·bal', *n.* [Fr. *cabale*, an intrigue, club, society; LL. *cabbala*, a cabala; Heb. *qabbālāh*, reception, mysterious doctrine; *qābal*, to take, receive.]
1. a small group of persons united in some secret design or scheme, usually to promote their interests in church or state by intrigue; a junto. This name was given to the ministry of Charles II, Clifford, Ashley, Buckingham, Arlington, and Lauderdale, the initials of whose names compose the word.
2. the intrigues of a cabal; a plot.
3. something hidden or secret. [Obs.]
4. the cabala. [Obs.]
Syn.—party, faction, combination, conspiracy, intrigue, junto, plot.

çȧ·bal', *v.i.*; caballed, *pt.*, *pp.*; caballing, *ppr.* to unite in a small party to promote private views by intrigue; to intrigue or plot; to unite in secret artifices to effect some design.

çab'ȧ·lȧ, *n.* [LL. *cabbala*; Heb. *qabbālāh*, a reception, mysterious doctrine, from *qābal*, to receive, take.]
1. an occult religious philosophy developed by certain Jewish rabbis, based on a mystical interpretation of the Scriptures.
2. occultism; mystical or secret doctrine.
Also spelled *cabbala, kabala*.

çȧ·bal'iç, *a.* cabalistic.

çab'ȧ·lişm, *n.* occult doctrine.

çab'ȧ·list, *n.* 1. one who professes faith in the cabala.
2. a mystic.

çab·ȧ·lis'tiç, çab·ȧ·lis'tiç·ăl, *a.* 1. pertaining to the cabala.
2. mystic; occult.

çab·ȧ·lis'tiç·ăl·ly, *adv.* in the manner of the cabalists.

çab'ȧ·līze, *v.i.* to use the manner or language of the cabalists. [Rare.]

çȧ·bal'lẽr, *n.* one who cabals.

çä·bäl·lẹ·rï'ȧ (-lyā-rē'ȧ), *n.* [Sp., from *caballo*; L. *caballus*, a horse.] a Spanish land measure, now varying, in Spanish-speaking countries, from thirty-three to one hundred and ninety-four acres.

çä·bäl·lẹ'rō (-lyā'rō), *n.*; *pl.* **çä·bäl·lẹ'rōş,** [Sp., from *caballo*; L. *caballus*, a horse.]
1. a Spanish cavalier or gentleman.
2. in the southwestern United States, (a) a horseman; (b) a lady's escort or admirer.

çab'ăl·line, *a.* [L. *caballinus*, from *caballus*, a horse.] pertaining to a horse.
caballine aloes; horse aloes, *Aloe caballina*.
caballine spring; same as *Hippocrene*.

çä·bäl'lō (-lyō), *n.* a horse. [Sp. Am.]

çȧ·bä'nȧ (*or* -nyä), *n.* [Sp.]
1. a small house or cabin.
2. a small shelter used as a bathhouse.

çȧ·bàne' (-bȧn'), *n.* [Fr., cabin.] an arrangement of struts supporting the wings of an airplane.

çab·ȧ·rẹt' (-rā'; also esp. for senses 1 and 2, kab'ȧ-rā), *n.* [Fr.]
1. a tavern; a house where liquors are retailed.
2. a set or service, as for tea or coffee.
3. a restaurant or barroom with dancing and singing as entertainment; hence, entertainment of this type.

çä'bȧs (-bȧ), *n.* [Fr.] a fig basket; also, a lady's flat workbasket or handbag.

çȧ·bas'söu, *n.* same as *kabassou*.

çab'bāġe, *v.t.* and *v.i.*; cabbaged, *pt.*, *pp.*; cabbaging, *ppr.* [Fr. *cabasser*, to put into a basket; OFr. *cabas*, a basket.] to steal, as pieces of cloth after cutting out a garment.

çab'bāġe, *n.* cloth appropriated by one who cuts out garments; hence, anything stolen.

çab'bāġe, *n.* [ME. *cabbish*; OFr. *cabus*, *caboche*, cabbage; It. *capuccio*, a little head, from *capo*, L. *caput*, head.]
1. a common vegetable of the mustard family, *Brassica*, especially any of the thick-leaved, hearting, garden varieties of *Brassica oleracea*, cultivated for food. The kinds most cultivated are the common cabbage, the savoy, the broccoli, and the cauliflower.
2. an esculent terminal bud occurring in certain palms: also called *palm cabbage*.

çab'bāġe, *v.i.*; cabbaged, *pt.*, *pp.*; cabbaging, *ppr.* to form a cabbagelike head in growing.

çab'bāġe ā'phis, çab'bāġe ā'phid, [*cabbage*, and Mod. L. *aphis*, a louse, insect.] the cabbage plant louse.

çab'bāġe bug, a bright-colored insect, *Murgantia histrionica*, destructive to cabbages, that has invaded the United States from Central America: called also *calicoback*, *calico bug*, and *harlequin cabbage bug*.

çab'bāġe but'tẽr·flȳ, a butterfly of the genus *Pieris*, the larvae of which destroy cabbage and other plants.

çab'bāġe flēa, a beetle, as *Haltica consobrina*, having larvae subsisting upon cabbages.

çab'bāġe flȳ, a fly, *Anthomyia brassica*, the larvae of which feed upon cabbage roots.

çab'bāġe·head (-hed), *n.* 1. the compact leaves of a cabbage, forming a head.
2. a stupid or foolish person. [Colloq.]
3. a disease caused in rutabagas by the larvae of a midge.

çab'bāġe mag'gŏt, the larva of the cabbage fly.

çab'bāġe moth, the *Mamestra* or *Noctua brassicæ*, whose larva eats through cabbages.

çab'bāġe pälm (päm), any of several palms with terminal buds used as a vegetable; palmetto.

çab'bāġe pal·met'tō, a palm tree with fan-shaped leaves, native to the southern United States and to the Bahamas: also called *fan palm*.

çab'bāġe rōşe, a species of rose, *Rosa centifolia*, of many varieties, used in the manufacture of rose water and attar: it has large, compact flowers.

çab'bāġe tree, 1. any of a number of palms having an edible, succulent bud terminally on the stem, as *Sabal Palmetto*, of southern United States, *Oreodoxa* or *Areca oleracea*, the cabbage palm of the West Indies, and the Australian fan leaf palm, *Livistona australis*.
2. any tree of the genus *Andira*, the bark of which is used as a vermifuge.

çab'bāġe wŏrm, the cabbage butterfly, fly, or moth when in the larval stage.

çab'bȧ·lȧ, *n.* cabala.

çab'ble, *v.t.*; cabbled, *pt.*, *pp.*; cabbling, *ppr.* [origin unknown.] in metallurgy, to break flat masses of partially finished iron into pieces, to be again heated in a furnace and wrought or hammered into bar iron.

çab'blẽr, *n.* one employed at cabbling.

çab'by, *n.* a cabman. [Colloq.]

çȧ·bẹ'zä (-sä), *n.* [Sp.] in the southwestern United States, head or head man; chief.

çab'e·zon, *n.* [Sp., from *cabeza*, head.] any of several fishes; especially a large Californian fish, *Scorpænichthys marmoratus*.

çȧ·bï'aī, *n.* same as *capybara*.

çab'in, *n.* [ME. *caban*; OFr. *cabane*; LL. *capanna*, a cabin.]
1. a small room; an enclosed place. [Obs.]
2. a cottage; a hut or small house.
3. any covered place for a temporary residence. [Obs.]
4. an officer's quarters, originally in the deckhouse of a ship; hence, any enclosed office, bedroom, or living quarters on a ship, or quarters under the cabin trunk of a smaller vessel.
5. an enclosed space for passengers in an aircraft.

çab'in, *v.i.*; cabined, *pt.*, *pp.*; cabining, *ppr.* to live in a cabin; to lodge.

çab'in, *v.t.* to confine in a cabin.

çab'in boy, a boy who serves and runs errands for the officers and cabin passengers of a ship.

çab'in çlass, a class of accommodations in a passenger ship, formerly the best (*first class*), now the second-best (lower than *first class* and higher than *tourist class*).

çab'in çrui̇ş'ẽr, a powerboat with a cabin and the necessary equipment for living on board.

çab'ined, *a.* enclosed in or furnished with a cabin. [Rare.]

çab'i·net, *n.* [Fr. *cabinet*, dim. of *cabine*, *cabane*, a cabin, hut.]
1. a closet; a small room or apartment. [Archaic.]
2. a private room in which consultations are held; hence, a meeting held in such a room.
3. [often C-] a body of official advisers to the chief executive of a government; specifically, (a) in the United States, the heads (taken collectively) of the executive departments, being the Secretaries of State, Treasury, Defense, Interior, Agriculture, Commerce, Labor, the Postmaster General, and the Attorney General; (b) in Great Britain, the committee of ministers, from twelve to seventeen in number, under the leadership of the Prime Minister, who take charge of the government.
4. a case for foods, medicines, supplies, etc.
5. a case with drawers or shelves where things of value are deposited for safekeeping.

6. a hut; a cottage; a small house. [Obs.]
7. in printing, a closed stand for job type, leads, cuts, etc., with or without a galley top.
kitchen cabinet; an epithet applied to certain friends of President Jackson who were supposed to have influenced his official actions to a large extent.

çab′i·net, *a.* 1. of a cabinet, or private room.
2. private; secret; confidential.
3. suitable for a cabinet; valuable or beautiful enough to keep in a case or a private room.
4. of a political cabinet.
cabinet photograph; a standard size photograph printed from a plate 4½ x 6½ inches.

çab′i·net, *v.t.* to shut in or enclose. [Rare.]

çab′i·net·māk″ẽr, *n.* one whose occupation is to make cabinets, tables, bureaus, bedsteads, and similar furniture.

çab′i·net·māk″ing, *n.* the business or trade of a cabinetmaker.

çab′i·net·work″ (-wẽrk″), *n.* fine joinery or woodwork.

Çȧ·bī′rī, *n.pl.* [L., from Gr. *Kabeiroi.*] divinities worshiped in the ancient Greek islands of Lemnos, Imbros, and Samothrace, and also on the neighboring coast of Troy in Asia Minor.

çā′ble (-bl), *n.* [ME. *cable, cabel*; OFr. *cable*; LL. *capulum*, a cable, rope, from *capere*, to take hold.]
1. any large, strong rope or chain designed to support a heavy weight or stand a powerful strain; specifically, (a) a ship's hawser; (b) a wire rope, as of a *cable* railway, suspension bridge, or gravel plow of a construction train.
2. a bundle of insulated and protected wires through which an electric current can be passed: telegraph or telephone cables are often laid under the ground or on the ocean floor.
3. a cablegram.
4. in architecture, (a) a kind of wreathed convex molding in the form of a rope; (b) a molding representing a spiral scroll.
to pay out, or *to veer out the cable*; to slacken the cable so that it may run out of the ship.
to slip the cable; to let the cable run out end for end; colloquially, to die.

çā′ble, *v.t.*; cabled, *pt., pp.*; cabling, *ppr.* 1. to fasten with a cable.
2. to furnish with a cable or cables.
3. to transmit by a cable under the sea.
4. to send a cablegram to.

çā′ble, *v.i.* to send a cablegram.

çā′ble ad·dress′, an address that has been condensed into a code word, for use in cablegrams.

çā′ble çär, a car drawn by a moving cable, as across a canyon, up a steeply inclined street, etc.

çā′bled (-bld), *a.* 1. fastened with a cable.
2. having the architectural ornament called a cable.

çā′ble·gram, *n.* [*cable*, and *-gram.*] a message sent across the sea by telegraphic cable.

çā′ble-lāid, *a.* 1. formed of three three-stranded ropes twisted into one.
2. twisted in the manner of a cable; as, a gold chain.

çā′ble mōld′ing, *n.* see *cable* (molding).

çā′ble rāil′wāy, a street railway on which the cars are pulled by a continuously moving underground cable to which they are attached by a grip that can be released to halt the car.

çā′ble's leṅgth, a unit of nautical measure, either 120 fathoms, 720 feet, or, in the British navy, one-tenth of a nautical mile, 608 feet.

çā′blet, *n.* a little cable; specifically, one having a circumference of less than ten inches.

çā′ble tel′ē·vi·ṣiŏn, same as *community antenna television*.

çā′ble tiẽr, the place in a vessel where the cables are coiled away.

çā′ble tooḷṣ, a set of tools, including a heavy steel bit, attached to a cable in one system of drilling wells and alternately raised and dropped to cut through rock.

çā′bling, *n.* 1. the cables used in decorating; any cable molding, or moldings.
2. transmission by cable.

çab′măn, *n.*; *pl.* **çab′men,** the driver of a cab.

çȧ·bob′, *n.* [Ar. *kabāb.*]
1. [*pl.*] (a) an Oriental dish, consisting generally of a neck or loin of mutton cut in pieces and roasted on a skewer, and dressed with onions, eggs, spices, and sauce; (b) in India, roast meat.
2. roast leg of mutton with stuffing of herbs and herrings.
Also spelled *kabob*.

çȧ·bob′, *v.t.* to roast or prepare (meat) for a cabob. [Rare.]

çȧ·boched′, *a.* caboshed.

çȧ·bō·çhoṅ′, *n.* [Fr.]
1. a precious stone cut in such a manner as to leave a convex surface instead of the usual facets.
2. the style in which such a stone is prepared: often *en cabochon*.

Çȧ·bom′bȧ, *n.* [native Guiana name.] a small genus of the water-lily family, nearly identical with the water shields, found in the still waters of southern United States, having the submerged leaves dissected and those at the surface peltate.

çȧ·boo′dle, *n.* [a corruption of *kit and boodle*; *kit, kith*, family, relations, and *boodle*, D. *boedel*, property, possessions.] lot; group; number: used mostly in the phrase *the whole caboodle*. [Slang.]

çȧ·boose′, *n.* [M.D. *kabuis, kombuis*, a ship's galley, booth, hut.]
1. the cook room of a merchant vessel; a ship's galley or kitchen.
2. the trainmen's car, usually having a lookout, attached to a freight or construction train, usually at the rear.

çȧ·boshed′ (-bosht′), *a.* [OFr. *caboche*, the head; It. *capocchia*, from *capo*, L. *caput*, head.] in heraldry, showing full-faced, with none of the neck visible: said of an animal's head used as a bearing.

çab′ō·tāġe, *n.* [Fr. *cabotage*, from *caboter*, to coast, go from cape to cape; Sp. *cabo*, a cape.] navigation along a coast; coasting trade.

çȧ·brer′īte, *n.* [named from the Sierra *Cabreras*, in Spain, where it was first found.] a green hydrous arsenate of cobalt, nickel, and magnesium, found native in fibrous masses.

çȧ·bril′lȧ (*or* kä-brē′yä), *n.* [Sp.] any of various edible, perchlike fishes of Florida and the West Indies, as the groupers.

çab′ri·ōle, *n.* [Fr.; see *cabriolet.*] in furniture, a leg that curves outward and then tapers inward down to a clawlike foot grasping a ball: characteristic of Queen Anne and Chippendale furniture.

çab·ri·ō·leṭ′ (-lā′), *n.* [Fr. dim. of *cabriole*, a leap, caper; It. *capriola*, from L. *caper*, a he-goat.]
1. a two-wheeled, one-horse carriage, usually with a hood that folds.

CABRIOLET

2. an automobile somewhat like a coupe, with a folding top.

çab′rit, *n.* a North American antelope, the pronghorn: also written *cabree, cabret*, etc.

çab′stand, *n.* a place where cabs are stationed for hire.

Çȧ′bul çlō′vẽr, sweet white clover.

çab′ŭrnṣ, *n.pl.* [origin unknown.] in nautical usage, small lines made of spun yarn, to bind cables, seize tackles, and the like.

çȧ·bu′yȧ, *n.* [Sp., from Taino *cabuya.*] the sissal hemp; the cajun.

çaç″ȧ·fue′gō (-fwe′), *n.* [Sp. *cagar*, to cack, or L. *cacare.*] a braggart. [Obs.]

çȧ·çā′in, *n.* theobromine.

Çaç″ȧ·jā′ō, *n.* [Mod. L., from Port. *cacjão.*] in zoology, the genus comprising the ouakaris.

çä′ çan′ny, see *canny*.

çȧ·çā′ō, *n.* [Sp., from Mex. *cacauatl*, the cacao.] the chocolate tree, *Theobroma cacao*, grown in tropical America for its seeds; also, the seeds (also called *cacao beans*). The tree grows about twenty feet high, bearing pods which are oval and pointed. The nuts or seeds are numerous, lodged in a white, pithy substance, and furnish the cocoa and chocolate of commerce.

CACAO
(*Theobroma cacao*)

çȧ·çā′ō but′tẽr, a yellowish fat obtained from cacao seeds, used in cosmetics, pharmacy, etc.: also *cocoa butter*.

çäc″cia·tō′re (kät″chä-tō′rā; Eng. kach″ȧ-tō′rē), *a.* [It., lit., a hunter, from *cacciare*, to hunt.] cooked in a casserole with olive oil and tomatoes, onions, spices, etc.; as, chicken *cacciatore*.

çaçh′ȧ·lot, *n.* [Fr.] the sperm whale.

çaçhe (kash), *n.* [Fr., from *cacher*, to hide.]
1. a place in which stores of food, supplies, etc. are hidden.
2. a place for hiding anything.
3. anything stored or hidden in such a place.

çaçhe, *v.t.* and *v.i.*; cached, *pt., pp.*; caching, *ppr.* to hide or store (things) in a cache.

çaçhe′pot, *n.* [Fr., from *cacher*, to hide, and *pot.*] a casing of ornamental design to hide an ordinary flowerpot.

çaçh·eṭ′ (kash-ā′), *n.* [Fr., from *cacher*, to hide.]
1. originally, a seal or stamp on an official letter, indicating the confidential nature of the contents.
2. a mark by which quality or authenticity can be distinguished.
3. a mark stamped or imprinted on mail.
4. a kind of capsule, etc. for enclosing disagreeable medicine.

çȧ·çhex′i·ȧ, çȧ·çhex′y, *n.* [Gr. *kachexia*, from *kakos*, bad, and *hexis*, habit, from *echein*, to have.] general poor health, with weakness and malnutrition: applied sometimes to mental health.

çaçh′i·bōu, *n.* [Fr., from a native West Indian name.] a tree of the myrrh family, growing in tropical North America; also, the aromatic resin obtained from it.

çaçh′in·nāte, *v.i.*; cachinnated, *pt., pp.*; cachinnating, *ppr.* [from L. *cachinnatus*, pp. of *cachinnare*, of echoic origin.] to laugh loudly or too much.

çaçh·in·nā′tion, *n.* [L. *cachinnatio*, from *cachinnare.*] loud or unrestrained laughter.

çȧ·çhin′nȧ·tō·ry, *a.* of or pertaining to cachinnation or immoderate laughter.

çȧ·çhī′rī, *n.* an intoxicant manufactured in Cayenne from the root of the manioc.

çaçh′ō·long, *n.* [Fr. *cacholong*; *Cach*, the name of a river in Bokhara, and *cholon*, a Kalmuck word for stone.] a variety of opal, often called *pearl-opal*, usually milk-white, sometimes grayish- or yellowish-white, opaque or slightly translucent at the edges.

çȧ·çhōu′, *n.* [Fr.; Malay *kachu.*]
1. catechu.
2. an aromatic pill or tablet for perfuming the breath.

çȧ·chu′chȧ, *n.* [Sp.]
1. an Andalusian dance or piece of dance music in three-four time, similar to the bolero.
2. music for this dance.

çȧ·çique′ (kȧ-sēk′), *n.* [Sp., from a Haitian word.]
1. in Latin America and the West Indies, a native chief.
2. any of several kinds of tropical American oriole.
3. in the Philippines, an owner of much land.
Also spelled *cassique*.

çack, *v.i.* [ME. *cakken*; D. *kakken*; L. *cacare*; Gr. *kakkān*, from *kakkē*, ordure, dung.] to void excrement. [Now Dial.]

çaç′kle, *v.i.*; cackled, *pt., pp.*; cackling, *ppr.* [ME. *cakelen*; G. *kakeln*, to cackle. Imitative word.]
1. to utter a noisy, broken cry such as that made by a hen or goose.
2. to laugh or talk in a shrill, noisy manner; to giggle.
3. to prate; to prattle; to tattle; to talk in a silly manner.

çaç′kle, *v.t.* to say or utter in a cackling manner.

çaç′kle, *n.* 1. the cackling of a goose or hen.
2. idle talk; silly prattle.
3. shrill, noisy, broken laughter.

çaç′klẽr, *n.* one who or that which cackles; sometimes, a telltale.

çaç′kling, *n.* the act or sound of one that cackles.

çaç′ō-, a combining form from Gr. *kakos*, bad, evil, meaning *bad, poor, harsh*, as in *cacography, cacophony*: also, before a vowel, *cac-*: opposed to *eu-*.

çaç·ō·çhym′i·ȧ, çaç′ō·çhym·y, *n.* [*caco-*, and Gr. *chymos*, juice.] a vitiated state of the fluids of the body, especially of the blood.

çaç·ō·çhym′iç, çaç·ō·çhym′iç·ăl, *a.* having the fluids of the body vitiated, especially the blood.

çaç·ō·dē′mŏn, *n.* [Gr. *kakodaimōn*; *kakos*, bad, evil, and *daimōn*, spirit.]

1. an evil spirit.
2. in medicine, formerly, a nightmare.

çaç·ō·dox′iç·ăl, *a.* heretical; heterodox.

çaç′ō·dox·y, *n.* [*caco-*, and Gr. *doxa*, opinion.] heresy. [Rare.]

çaç′ō·dyl, *n.* [Gr. *kakōdēs*, ill-smelling; *kakos*, bad, and *ozein*, to smell, and *-yl.*] in chemistry, (a) the radical $As(CH_3)_2$, composed of arsenic and methyl: its compounds are poisonous and bad-smelling; (b) a poisonous, colorless liquid, $As_2(CH_3)_4$, with a bad smell: it is a polymer of this radical.

çaç·ō·dyl′iç, *a.* pertaining to cacodyl.
cacodylic acid; a colorless crystalline compound, obtained by the oxidation of cacodyl.

çaç′ō·e·py, *n.* [Gr. *kakoepeia*, incorrect language; *kakos*, bad, and *epos*, word.] faulty pronunciation.

çaç·ō·ē′thēş, *n.* [L., from Gr. *kakoēthēs*, a bad habit; *kakos*, bad, and *ēthos*, habit, custom.]
1. a bad custom or habit.
2. an itch (to do something); a mania.
cacoethes loquendi; a propensity for talking or making speeches.
cacoethes scribendi; an itch for writing.

çaç·ō·gas′triç, *a.* [*caco-*, and Gr. *gastēr*, *gastros*, stomach.] dyspeptic. [Rare.]

çaç·ō·ġen′içs, *n.pl.* [*construed as sing.*], [*caco-*, and *eugenics.*] dysgenics.

çaç·ō·graph′iç, *a.* pertaining to cacography; written or spelled incorrectly.

cȧ·çog′rȧ·phy, *n.* [*caco-*, and Gr. *-graphia*, from *graphein*, to write.]
1. illegible writing.
2. incorrect spelling.

ça′çō·let (-lā), *n.* [Fr.] a pack saddle fitted with folding chairs or a litter, by means of which travelers or feeble persons may be carried on a mule's back in the mountains.

CACOLET

cȧ·çol′ō·ġy, *n.* [Gr. *kakologia*, evil speaking, abuse; *kakos*, bad, and *legein*, to speak.] substandard pronunciation or diction.

çaç′ō·mis·tle (-mis-l), *n.* [Sp., from native Mex. *tlacomiztli.*] a slender, long-tailed, racoonlike animal, *Bassaris astuta*, of the United States and Mexico.

çaç′ō·mix·le, çaç′ō·mixl, *n.* a cacomistle.

çaç′ō·nym, *n.* [*caco-*, and Gr. *onyma*, name.] in zoology, an undesirable name.

çaç·ō·nym′iç, *a.* relating to a caconym.

cȧ·çoon′, *n.* [African name.] the bean of a tropical shrub, *Entada scandens*, used for making snuffboxes, purses, etc.

çaç·ō·phon′iç, çaç·ō·phon′iç·ăl, *a.* cacophonous.

cȧ·çoph′ō·nous (-nus), *a.* having a harsh sound; discordant; unmelodious.

cȧ·çoph′ō·ny, *n.* [Gr. *kakophōnia*, from *kakophōnos*, harsh-sounding; *kakos*, bad, evil, and *phōnē*, voice.]
1. in rhetoric, a jarring or disagreeable sound of words, proceeding from the meeting of harsh letters or syllables.
2. in medicine, a discordant or harsh state of the voice.
3. in music, a combination of discordant sounds.
4. harsh, jarring sound; discord.

çaç·ō·plas′tiç, *a.* [*caco-*, and Gr. *plastikos*, from *plassein*, to form.] in pathology, susceptible of only a low degree of organization, as the indurations resulting from low or chronic inflammation, cirrhosis, etc.

çaç′ō·teçh·ny, *n.* [*caco-*, and Gr. *technē*, art.] a corrupt state of art.

cȧ·çox′ēne, cȧ·çox′e·nīte, *n.* [Gr. *kakoxenos*, unfriendly to strangers; *kakos*, bad, and *xenos*, stranger, guest.] hydrous phosphate of iron, a mineral occurring in yellowish, radiating tufts.

Çaç·tā′cē·ae, *n.pl.* [L., from *cactus*, a prickly plant, and *-aceæ.*] a family of dicotyledonous plants, the cactus family.

çaç·tā′ceous, *a.* belonging to or resembling the *Cactaceæ.*

çaç′tus, *n.*; *pl.* **çaç′tus·eş, çaç′tī,** [L., from Gr. *kaktos*, prickly.] any of various plants of the family *Cactaceæ*, with fleshy stems, branches bearing spines or scales instead of leaves, and, sometimes, showy flowers: cactuses grow in hot, arid parts of North and South America.

CACTUS (*Echinocactus oxygonus*)

çaç′tus bîrd, any oscine bird of the genus *Cactornis.*

çaç′tus wren (ren), any one of the genus of birds, *Campylorhynchus.*

cȧ·çū′mi·năl, *a.* [L. *cacumen* (*-inis*), the top or summit, and *-al.*]
1. pertaining to a top or summit.
2. in phonetics, pronounced with the tip of the tongue turned backward and upward against or toward the hard palate, as Swedish *d* or *t* following an *r*; retroflex; cerebral.

cȧ·çū′mi·năl, *n.* a cacuminal consonant.

cȧ·çū′mi·nāte, *v.t.* to make sharp or pointed. [Obs.]

çad, *n.* [an abbrev. of *cadet.*] a man or boy whose behavior is not gentlemanly; an ill-mannered fellow: word originally applied to servants, then to town boys, by students at British universities and public schools.

cȧ·das′trăl, *a.* [Fr.] relating to a cadastre.

cȧ·das′tre (-tēr), **cȧ·das′tēr,** *n.* [Fr. *cadastre*; LL. *capitastrum*, a poll-tax register, from L. *caput*, head.] a public record of the extent, value, and ownership of land for purposes of taxation.

cȧ·dav′ēr, *n.* [L., from *cadere*, to fall.] a corpse, as for dissection; a dead body, especially of a person.

cȧ·dav′ēr·iç, *a.* resembling or pertaining to a cadaver.

cȧ·dav′ēr·ine, *n.* [*cadaver*, and *-ine.*] a colorless, bad-smelling, liquid ptomaine, $C_5H_{14}N_2$, produced by the hydrolysis of proteins, as in putrefying flesh.

cȧ·dav′ēr·ous, *a.* [L. *cadaverosus*, corpselike; *cadaver*, a corpse.]
1. having the appearance or color of a dead human body; pale; hollow; wan; gaunt; ghastly; as, a *cadaverous* look.
2. having the qualities of a dead body.

cȧ·dav′ēr·ous·ly, *adv.* in a cadaverous form.

cȧ·dav′ēr·ous·ness, *n.* the quality of being cadaverous.

çad′bāit, *n.* the larva of the caddis fly.

çad′die, *n.* [Scot. form of Fr. *cadet.*]
1. originally, a boy employed to run errands.
2. a person who attends a golfer, carrying his clubs, etc.: also spelled *caddy.*

çad′die, *v.i.*; caddied, *pt.*, *pp.*; caddying, *ppr.* to act as a caddy: also spelled *caddy.*

çad′dis, çad′dice, *n.* [ME. and OFr. *cadas*, floss silk; confused with Fr. *cadis*, coarse serge.]
1. a coarse woolen material; worsted yarn.
2. a worsted ribbon.

çad′dis, çad′dice, *n.* a caddis worm.

çad′dis flȳ, çad′dice flȳ, a small, mothlike fly of the order *Neuroptera*, commonly called the May fly, the larva or grub of which forms a case of small stones, grass roots, shells, etc., and lives under water till ready to emerge from the pupa state.

çad′dish, *a.* like a cad; ill-bred; vulgar.

çad′dis wŏrm, cad′dice wŏrm, the wormlike larva of the caddis fly, used as bait by anglers.

Çad′dō, *n.*; *pl.* **Çad′dō** or **Çad′dōeş,** a member of a confederacy of North American Indians formerly living in Louisiana, Arkansas, and eastern Texas, of Caddoan linguistic stock.

Çad′dō·ăn, *a.* designating or of a family of North American Indian languages spoken by the Caddo and other tribes in southwestern Arkansas and near-by parts of Louisiana, Texas, and Oklahoma, by the Pawnee in Nebraska and Kansas, and by some other tribes in North Dakota.

Çad′dō·ăn, *n.* the Caddoan family of languages.

çad′dōw, *n.* a jackdaw. [Brit. Dial.]

çad′dy, *n.* [corruption of *catty*, from Malay *kati*, a weight equivalent to one and one-half pounds.] a small box for keeping tea; a tea canister.

çad′dy, *n.*; *pl.* **cad′dieş,** and *v.i.*; caddied, *pt.*, *pp.*; caddying, *ppr.* caddie.

çāde, *a.* [of doubtful origin, perhaps from Ice. *kād*, a new-born child.] tame; bred by hand; domesticated; as, a *cade* lamb.

çāde, *v.t.* [ME. *cade*, *cad*, a lamb.] to bring up or nourish by hand, or with tenderness. [Obs.]

çāde, *n.* [ME. *cade*; L. *cadus*; Gr. *kados*, a jar, liquid measure.] a barrel or cask; hence, a measure containing five hundred herrings or a thousand sprats.

çāde, *n.* [Fr.; Pr., from L. dial. *catanus.*] a large, bushy European juniper whose wood yields a thick, brown oil used in medicine.
oil of cade; cade oil.

-çāde, [from *cavalcade.*] a suffix meaning *procession*, *parade*, as in aqua*cade*, motor*cade.*

cȧ·delle′, *n.* [Fr.] the larva or adult of a horny-headed beetle, *Trogosita mauritanica*, very destructive to grain in the bin.

çā′dence, *n.* [ME. *cadence*; L. *cadentia*, a falling, from *cadere*, to fall.]
1. a fall; a decline; a state of sinking.
2. a fall of the voice in reading or speaking, as at the end of a sentence.
3. inflection or modulation in tone.
4. flow of rhythm.
5. any regularity and uniformity of beat or measure, as in marching or dancing.
6. in horsemanship, an equal measure or proportion in all the motions of a horse.
7. in music, (a) in general, the close of a musical passage or phrase; (b) specifically, a vocal or instrumental trill, run, or division, introduced as an ending or as a means of return to the first subject; (c) a cadenza.

çā′dence, *v.t.*; cadenced, *pt.*, *pp.*; cadencing, *ppr.* to impose a cadence on.

çā′denced, *a.* having cadence; rhythmical.

çā′den·cy, *n.*; *pl.* **çā′den·cieş,** 1. cadence.
2. descent of a younger son or of the younger branch of a family.
marks of cadency; in heraldry, marks intended to show the descent of a younger branch of a family from the main stock.

çā′dent, *a.* [L. *cadens* (*-entis*), ppr. of *cadere*, to fall.]
1. falling; sinking: applied specifically in astrology to planets.
2. having cadence; cadenced.

cȧ·den′zȧ, *n.* [It., from L.; see *cadence.*]
1. an elaborate, often improvised musical passage played by an unaccompanied instrument in a concerto, usually toward the end of the first movement.
2. any brilliant flourish put into an aria or a solo passage.

çāde oil, a thick, brown oil from the cade, or European juniper, used in medicine.

cȧ·det′, *n.* [Fr. *cadet*, a younger brother; a dim. from L. *caput*, head.]
1. a younger son or brother in a gentleman's family.
2. formerly, a younger son who became a gentleman volunteer in the army to offset his lack of patrimony.
3. a young man in training for the rank of an officer in the armed forces; as, a West Point *cadet*, an air-force *cadet.*

cȧ·det′cy, *n.*; *pl.* **cȧ·det′cieş,** a cadetship.

cȧ·det′ship, *n.* 1. the position or rank of a cadet.
2. the period of time during which one is a cadet.

cȧ·det′ tēach′ēr, 1. an upper-class college student who does practice teaching.
2. a public school teacher assigned to a regular position but without its customary benefits, such as pension, etc., and paid at a daily rate.

cȧ·dew′, çāde′wŏrm, *n.* a caddis worm.

çadġe (kaj), *n.* a round frame on which to carry hawks for sale.

çadġe, *v.t.* and *v.i.*; cadged, *pt.*, *pp.*; cadging, *ppr.* [ME. *caggen.*]
1. to carry, especially to carry for sale; to hawk or peddle. [Dial.]
2. to sponge on another or get by sponging or begging. [Colloq.]

çadġ′ēr, *n.* [OFr. *cagier*, one who carried about falcons or other birds in a cage for sale.]
1. an itinerant huckster; a truck peddler. [Dial.]
2. one who gets his living by trickery; a beggar; a sponger. [Colloq.]

çadġ′ēr, *n.* one who carries hawks.

çadġ′y, *a.* [from *cadge*, and *-y.*] lively; frolicsome; cheerful; also, loose; lustful; lewd; wanton. [Scot. and Brit. Dial.]

çä′di, *n.* [Ar. *qādi.*] a minor Moslem magistrate or judge: also spelled *kadi.*

çad′ie, *n.* same as *caddie.*

cȧ·di·les′kēr, *n.* a chief judge in the Turkish

Empire, whose jurisdiction was originally military as well as civil.

çad′is, *n.* caddis.

Çad·mē′ăn, *a.* of, like, or relating to Cadmus.
Cadmean victory; a victory won at great sacrifice and destructive to the victors.

çad′mi·ȧ, *n.* [L. *cadmia*; Gr. *kadmeia*, calamine.]
1. calamine. [Obs.]
2. an oxide of zinc which collects on the sides of furnaces where zinc happens to be present in an ore and is sublimed. [Obs.]

çad′miç, *a.* containing, relating to, or derived from cadmium.

çad′mi·um, *n.* [Mod. L.; named by Strohmeyer (1817); L. *cadmia*, zinc ore, calamine, from *Cadmus*.] a blue-white, malleable, ductile, metallic chemical element occurring as a sulfide or carbonate in zinc ores: it is used in some alloys, electroplating, pigment, etc.: symbol; Cd; atomic weight, 112.41; atomic number, 48.

çad′mi·um sul′fīde, a pigment, CdS, varying from lemon yellow (*cadmium yellow*) to yellowish orange (*cadmium orange*).

Çad′mus, *n.* in Greek legend, a Phoenician prince who founded Thebes and killed a dragon sacred to Mars: from the dragon's teeth, which he sowed in the earth, armed men sprang up and proceeded to fight one another until only five were left, who then helped Cadmus build the city.

çad′răns, *n.* [Fr. *cadran*, a quadrant.] an instrument for measuring the angles in cutting and polishing gems, and keeping the gems at the proper angle during the process.

çä′dre (-dr), *n.* [Fr. *cadre*, a frame; L. *quadrum*, a square.]
1. a framework; the skeleton of a thing.
2. a nucleus around which an expanded organization, as a military unit, can be built.
3. staff officers.

çȧ·dū′çȧ·ry, *a.* [L. *caducarius*, from *caducum*, property without a master, from *cadere*, to fall.] in old law, of, relating, or pertaining to escheat.

çȧ·dū′cē·ăn, *a.* of the caduceus.

çȧ·dū′cē·us, *n.*; *pl.* **çȧ·dū′cē·ī,** [L.] 1. the staff of an ancient herald; especially, the winged staff with two serpents twined about it, carried by Mercury.
2. Mercury's staff as a symbol of the medical profession.

CADUCEUS

çȧ·dū′ci·ā·ry (-shi-), *a.* 1. caducary.
2. in Scots law, not acquired by succession.

çȧ·dū·ci·brañ′chi·āte, *a.* [L. *caducus*, falling, and *branchiae*, gills.] in zoology, of, belonging to, or pertaining to tailed amphibians, such as the newts, which lose the gills before attaining maturity.

çȧ·dū′ci·ty, *n.* [LL. *caducitas*, from L. *cadere*, to fall.]
1. the quality or state of being perishable.
2. senility; decrepitude.

çȧ·dū′çous, *a.* [L. *caducus*, falling, from *cadere*, to fall.]
1. dropping off.
2. fleeting; unenduring.
3. in botany, falling off early, as some leaves.

çȧ·dūke′, *a.* transitory; fleeting; short-lived. [Obs.]

çad′y, *n.* same as *caddie*.

cae′çȧ (sē′kȧ), *n.*, pl. of *caecum*.

cae′çăl, *a.* of, relating to, or pertaining to the caecum; specifically, bag-shaped; as, the *caecal* extremity of a duct.

cae′ci·äs, *n.* [L. *cæcias*; Gr. *kaikias*, the northeast wind.] a wind from the northeast.

cae·cil′i·ăn, *n.* [from L. *cæcilia*, variety of lizard.] any of a group of legless, tropical amphibians resembling worms.

cae′çum, *n.*; *pl.* **cae′çȧ,** [L., from *intestinum cæcum*, blind intestine, from *cæcus*, blind.]
1. the pouch which is the beginning of the large intestine.
2. in zoology, a cavity open at one end.
Also spelled *cecum*.

Cae′li·ăn, *n.* one of the seven hills on which Rome was built.

cae·lom′e·tẽr, *n.* [L. *cælum*, *cœlum*, heaven, and *metrum*, Gr. *metron*, a measure.] an instrument employed in illustrating the positions of heavenly bodies.

cae′nō-, same as *coeno-*.

Cae·nō·ġae′ȧ (sē-nō-jē′ȧ), *n.* [L., from Gr. *kainos*, new, and *gaia*, land.] one of several proposed primary zoogeographical divisions, including the Nearctic, Palearctic, and Oriental regions, its complement being *Eogæa*.

Cae·nō·ġae′ăn, *a.* pertaining to the *Caenogaea*.

cae·nō·ġen′e·sis, *n.* same as *cenogenesis*.

cae″nō·ġē·net′iç, *a.* same as *cenogenetic*.

Cae·nō·zō′iç, *a.* same as *Cenozoic*.

Caes·al·pin′i·ȧ (ses-), *n.* [named after Andreas *Cæsalpinus*, an Italian botanist.] a genus of trees of the bean family bearing showy flowers, and found in the tropics of both hemispheres. Brazilwood comes from *Cæsalpinia echinata*.

Cae′ṣăr, *n.* [L., the hairy one.]
1. Julius Caesar's family name.
2. the title of the emperor of Rome from Augustus to Hadrian, or of the emperor of the Holy Roman Empire.
3. any powerful ruler or autocrat; an emperor or dictator.

Cae·ṣā′rē·ăn, Cae·ṣā′ri·ăn (sē-), *a.* pertaining to or characteristic of Caesar or the Caesars; imperial; autocratic.
Caesarean section or *operation*; a surgical operation for delivering a baby by cutting through the mother's abdominal and uterine walls: so called because Julius Caesar was supposedly born in this manner.

Cae′ṣăr·iṣm, cae′ṣăr·iṣm, *n.* a system of government in which the power rests with a single person; autocracy; imperialism.

cae′ṣi·ous, *a.* [L. *cæsius*, bluish-gray.] pale blue, bluish-gray, or lavender.

cae′ṣi·um, *n.* same as *cesium*.

caes′pi·tōse (ses′), *a.* same as *cespitose*.

caes′pi·tōse·ly, *adv.* same as *cespitosely*.

cae·ṣū′rȧ, *n.*; *pl.* **cae·ṣū′rȧṣ, cae·ṣū′rae,** [L., a cutting, felling, from *caedere*, to cut.]
1. a break or pause in a line of verse: in Greek and Latin verse, the caesura falls within the metrical foot; in English verse, it is usually about the middle of the line: shown in scanning by the sign ||, as, "Loveliest of trees, || the cherry now."
2. a pause showing rhythmic division of a melody.

cae·ṣū′răl, *a.* of a caesura.

ca·fé′ (kȧ-fā′), *n.* [Fr., coffee, a coffeehouse.]
1. coffee.
2. a coffeehouse or restaurant.
3. a restaurant serving alcoholic drinks and sometimes providing entertainment.
café au lait; [Fr.] (a) coffee with milk; (b) pale brown.
café noir; [Fr.] strong, black coffee; coffee without milk: usually served at the close of a meal.

çaf′e·net, çä′fe·neh (-nā), *n.* [Turk. *qahveh-khāneh*, a coffeehouse.] a Turkish coffeehouse and resting place for travelers; an inn.

ca·fé′ sō·ci′e·ty, (kȧ-fā′) 1. a well-publicized set of habitual frequenters of cafés or night clubs in New York City.
2. any similar set elsewhere.

çȧ′fe·tăl, çȧ·fe·tȧ′le, *n.* [Sp. Am.] a coffee plantation.

çaf·e·tē′ri·ȧ, *n.* a restaurant in which food is displayed on counters and customers serve themselves.

çaf′fȧ, *n.* [native name.]
1. a rich cloth, probably silk, in use during the sixteenth century.
2. a cotton cloth, ornamented with painting, formerly made in India.

çaf·fē′iç, *a.* [Fr. *caféique*, from *café*, coffee.] obtained from or pertaining to coffee.
caffeic acid; a vegetable acid, $C_9H_8O_4$, found in coffee tannin.

çaf′fē·ine, çaf′fē·in (*or* kaf′ēn), *n.* [Fr. *caféine*, from *café*, coffee.] the alkaloid $C_8H_{10}N_4O_2$, present in coffee, tea, and kola: it is a stimulant to the heart and central nervous system: the methyl derivative of theobromine.

çaf·fē·in′iç, *a.* pertaining to or derived from caffeine.

çaf′fē·in·iṣm, *n.* a diseased condition characterized by nervousness, sleeplessness, etc., brought on by the excessive use of coffee.

çaf·fē·tan′niç, *a.* obtained from or pertaining to tannin and caffeine.
caffetannic acid; caffeic acid.

çaf′fi·lȧ, çä′fi·lȧh, *n.* [Ar. *qāfila*, a caravan.] a pack train of camels; a caravan: also spelled *kafila*.

Çaf′fre (-fẽr), *n.* see *Kafir*.

çaf′tăn, kaf′tăn, *n.* [Ar. *qaftān*, a kind of garment.] a garment consisting of a long, wide-sleeved robe usually fastened by a belt or sash, worn in eastern Mediterranean countries.

çag, *n.* a keg. [Obs.]

çāġe, *n.* [ME. *cage*; OFr. *caige*; O.H.G. *chevia*; Port. and Sp. *gavia*; L. *cavea*, a hollow place.]
1. a box or enclosure made of boards, or with latticework of wood, wicker, wire, etc., for confining animals or birds.
2. a fenced-in area for confining prisoners of war.
3. any cagelike contrivance or framework, as, in machinery, the frame used to confine a ball valve; also, a wire guard used in pumps and pipes to prevent the passage of solids.
4. an elevator car.
5. a jail. [Archaic.]
6. in baseball, a partially enclosed backstop used for batting practice, etc.
7. in basketball, the basket.
8. in hockey, the network frame used as a goal.
9. in mining, the trundle wheel or drum on which the rope winds in a hoisting apparatus.

çāġe, *v.t.*; caged, *pt.*, *pp.*; caging, *ppr.* to confine in a cage; to shut up or confine.

çāġe′ling, *n.* a bird confined in a cage, especially a young bird. [Poetic.]

çāġ′ẽr, *n.* a basketball player. [Colloq.]

çāġe′y, çāġ′y, *a.* [prob. from *cage*, a jail.] sly; tricky; cunning. [Slang.]

çȧ′ġit, *n.* a green parrot of the Philippine Islands.

çag′mag, *n.* 1. a tough, old goose; hence, poor food, offal. [Brit. Dial.]
2. a kind of inferior sheep. [Brit. Dial.]

çag′mag, *a.* inferior. [Brit. Dial.]

Çȧ·gou·lärd′ (kȧ-gọọ-lär′), *n.* [Fr.] a member of a secret French fascist society, whose plot for the overthrow of the republic was uncovered in 1937.

Çȧ·hens′ly·iṣm, *n.* a plan to regulate the policy of the Roman Catholic Church in the appointment of its bishops and priests, and especially those in America, suggested to Pope Leo XIII, in 1891, by P. P. Cahensly, a member of the German parliament. Its main provision was that every bishop and pastor should be of the same nationality as the majority of his flock. Other measures were suggested for the continuance, among the various races represented in the United States, of the use of their mother tongues, and for the preservation of their national traditions.

çȧ·hiẽr′ (*or* kä-yā′), *n.* [Fr. *cahier*; OFr. *caier*, *quayer*; It. *quaderno*; LL. *quaternus*, four each.]
1. a book of loose leaves held together; notebook.
2. a report of the proceedings of any body, as a legislature.

çȧ·hiñ′çȧ rọọt, the root of a shrub, *Chiococca racemosa*, found in tropical America: also written *cainca root*.

çȧ·hin′ciç, *a.* pertaining to the cahinca root.

çȧ·họọts′, *n.* [perh. from Fr. *cahute*, a cabin.] partnership. [Slang.]
in cahoots; in partnership: usually applied to shady dealing. [Slang.]
to go cahoots; to share alike. [Slang.]

Çāi′ȧ·phȧs, *n.* in the Bible, the high priest who presided at the trial that led to the condemnation of Jesus. Matt. xxvi. 57–66.

Çāi′jăn, *n.* same as *Cajun*.

çāi·mȧ·kam′, *n.* see *kaimakam*.

çāi′măn, *n.* see *cayman*.

Çāin, *n.* 1. in the Bible, the oldest son of Adam and Eve: he killed his brother Abel. Gen. iv.
2. a murderer.
to raise Cain; see phrase under *raise*.

çȧ·iñ′çȧ rọọt, same as *cahinca root*.

çȧ′ing whāle, same as *caaing whale*.

Çāin′īte, *n.* 1. a descendant of Cain.
2. one of a sect of fanatical heretics of the second century, who professed to venerate Cain, Korah, Dathan, Abiram, and the Sodomites.

Çāi·nō·zō′iç, (*or* kī-), *a.* same as *Cenozoic*.

çä·ïque′ (kä-ēk′), *n.* [Fr. *caique*, from Turk. *qayik*, a boat.] a small skiff or rowboat; especially a light skiff used in the Bosporus; also, a sailboat used especially in the eastern Mediterranean.

çȧ ï·rȧ′, [Fr.; lit., "It (the revolution) shall go (on)."] the refrain of a popular French Revolutionary song.

çāird, *n.* [Gael. *ceard*, a tinker, smith.] an itinerant tinker, vagrant, gypsy, etc. [Brit. Dial.]

çāirn, *n.* [Scot., from Gael. *carn*, a heap.] a heap of stones; specifically, (a) certain piles of stones of a rounded or conical form, erected by the early inhabitants of the British Isles, apparently as sepulchral monuments; (b) a stone mound for a landmark, or to indicate a specified site.

çairn′gorm, *n.* [name of Scot. mountain and mountain range; Gael. *carngorm,* blue cairn.] a yellow or brown variety of quartz, used as a gem: also called *Cairngorm stone*

çairn ter′ri·ẽr, [said to be so named from burrowing in or around cairns.] a small, shaggy Scottish terrier.

çāis′sŏn, *n.* [Fr., from *caisse,* a chest, box.]
1. an ammunition chest.
2. a two-wheeled wagon for transporting ammunition.
3. a subterranean box containing explosives to be fired as a mine.
4. in architecture, the sunken panels in flat or vaulted ceilings, or in soffits generally.
5. a vessel in the form of a boat used as a floodgate at a dock or basin.
6. a watertight box inside which men can do construction work under water.
7. a watertight box for raising and floating sunken ships, etc.: after the box is sunk and attached, the water is forced out of it so that it floats and raises the ship.

çāis′sŏn dis·ēase′, decompression sickness.

çāi′tiff, *n.* [OFr. *caitif,* a captive, wretched man; L. *captivus,* a captive, from *capere,* to take.]
1. a mean, evil, or cowardly person.
2. a miserable or unfortunate person. [Obs.]
3. one held captive. [Obs.]

çāi′tiff, *a.* 1. characteristic of a caitiff; base; vile.
2. wretched; enslaved. [Obs.]

Çȧ·jā′nus, *n.* [Malay *kachany.*] a genus of East Indian leguminous shrubs. *Cajanus Indicus,* or angola pea, is the most extensively cultivated species.

çaj′ē·put, *n.* 1. same as *cajuput.*
2. a California laurel.

çȧ·jōle′, *v.t.* and *v.i.*; cajoled, *pt., pp.*; cajoling, *ppr.* [Fr. *cajoler,* to coax, to wheedle.] to flatter; to coax; to deceive or delude by flattery.
Syn.—coax, flatter, wheedle.

çȧ·jōle′ment, *n.* cajolery; the act of cajoling.

çȧ·jōl′ẽr, *n.* a flatterer; a wheedler.

çȧ·jōl′ẽr·y, *n.*; *pl.* **çȧ·jōl′ẽr·ies,** [Fr. *cajolerie,* from *cajoler,* to coax, wheedle.] flattery; a wheedling to delude.

Çā′jun, *n.* [from *Acadian.*]
1. a native of Louisiana supposed to be of Acadian French descent: sometimes used contemptuously.
2. the dialect of the Cajuns.
Also spelled *Caijan.*

çaj′u·put, *n.* [Malay *kāyūputīh,* from *kāyū,* tree, and *putīh,* white.] an East Indian tree of the myrtle family, yielding a greenish oil used externally in some skin diseases: also spelled *cajeput.*

çaj′u·put·ēne, *n.* an aromatic compound obtained from cajuput.

çāke, *n.* [ME. *cake*; Sw. *kaka,* a cake.]
1. a small, flat mass of baked or fried dough or batter.
2. a mixture of flour, butter, sugar, or other ingredients, baked in a mass and often covered with icing.
3. a small, flat mass of fish, vegetables, etc. fried on both sides.
4. something made or concreted in the form of a cake; a mass of matter in a solid form; as, a *cake* of soap.
one's cake is dough; one's undertaking has met with disappointment or failure.
to take the cake; (a) to win the prize; (b) to excel; to outdo. [Slang.]

çāke, *v.t.* and *v.i.*; caked, *pt., pp.*; caking, *ppr.* to form into a hard mass.

çāke flour, finely ground and well-sifted wheat flour for baking.

çākes and āle, the good things of life; worldly pleasures.

çāke ŭr′chin, a sea urchin having a discoid shape.

çāke′wąlk (-wąk), *n.* 1. an elaborate step or walk formerly performed by Negroes in the South competing for the prize of a cake.
2. a strutting dance developed from this.

çāke′wąlk, *v.i.* to perform a cakewalk.

çal, *n.* wolframite: the Cornish name.

çal′ȧ·bȧ, *n.* [native name.] a tree, *Calophyllum calaba,* of the West Indies, furnishing resin and valuable timber.

çal′ȧ·bär, *n.* same as *calaber.*

Çal′ȧ·bär bēan, [prob. after *Calabar,* name of a river, town, and district in Southern Nigeria.] the poisonous brown seed of an African climbing plant, used in medicine for various nervous disorders, to contract the pupil of the eye, etc.

çal′ȧ·bär·in, çal′ȧ·bär·ine (*or* -ĭn), *n.* an alkaloid found in the Calabar bean.

çal′ȧ·bash, *n.* [Fr. *calebasse*; Port. *calabaca,* a calabash; Ar. *qar,* a gourd, and *yābis, aybas,* dry.]

CALABASHES

1. a vessel made of a dried gourd shell, or of the shell of a calabash tree, used as a bowl, pipe, etc.
2. the calabash tree.
3. the gourdlike fruit of the calabash tree.
4. any of various gourds.

çal′ȧ·bash tree, 1. a tropical American tree belonging to the genus *Crescentia.*
2. *Adansonia digitata,* the baobab of Africa.

çal″ȧ·bä·zĭl′lȧ (-sēl′yȧ), *n.* [Mex., from Sp. *calabaza,* gourd.] a large-rooted, California squash, *Cucurbita perennis,* yielding a soaplike substance.

çal′ȧ·bẽr, çal′ȧ·bär, *n.* [from Fr. *Calabre,* Calabria, city in France.]
1. a gray Siberian squirrel.
2. its fur.

çal·ȧ·bọose′, *n.* [Sp. *calabozo,* prison.] a prison; a jail. [Slang.]

çal′ȧ·bŭr tree, a tropical American tree, *Muntingia calabura,* yielding a cordage fiber.

çȧ·lāde′, *n.* [Fr.] the slope on a manège ground down which a horse is ridden in training him.

Çȧ·lā′di·um, *n.* 1. a genus of tropical American plants of the order *Araceæ,* having tuberous roots and sagittate leaves of a brilliant color, sometimes spotted or variegated.
2. [c–] any plant of this genus.

çal′ā·ite, *n.* [L. *callais*; Gr. *kallais, kalais,* a sea-green stone.] turquoise. [Obs.]

Çal″ȧ·mȧ·gros′tis, *n.* [L., from Gr. *kalamos,* a reed, and *agrōstis,* a sort of grass.] a genus of grasses allied to *Arundo.*

çal·ȧ·mañ′çō, *n.* [LL. *calamancus,* from Gr. *kamelaukion,* a headdress.]
1. a woolen cloth of a fine gloss and checkered in the warp.
2. clothing made of this.

çal′ȧ·man·dẽr, *n.* the hard wood of any of certain East Indian trees related to the ebony: it is striped alternately hazel-brown and black and is used in making furniture: also *calamander wood.*

Çal·ȧ·mā′ri·ae, *n.pl.* [L., from *calamarius,* pertaining to a reed; *calamus,* a reed.] one of the principal families of plant life of the Carboniferous Period.

çal·ȧ·mā′ri·ăn, *a.* pertaining to the *Calamariæ.*

çal′ȧ·mā·ry, çal′ȧ·mär, *n.* [L. *calamarius,* from *calamus,* a reed, pen; Gr. *kalamos,* a reed.] any of various decapod cuttlefishes, or squids, of the order *Dibranchiata,* especially those of the genus *Loligo.* They have pen-shaped skeletons.

çal′ăm·baç, *n.* [Fr., from Per. *kalambak,* a fragrant wood.] see *agalloch.*

çal′ăm·böur, *n.* [Fr. *calambour*; Sp. *calambuco*; Per. *kalambak.*] see *agalloch.*

çal·ȧ·mif′ẽr·ous, *a.* [L. *calamus,* reed, and *ferre,* to bear.] bearing reeds; reedy.

çȧ·lam′i·fọrm, *a.* [L. *calamus,* a reed, and *forma,* form.] reedlike in form.

çal′ȧ·mīne, çal′ȧ·min, *n.* [Fr. *calamine*; LL. *calamina,* from L. *cadmia,* calamine.]
1. hydrous zinc silicate, $(ZnOH)_2SiO_3$, a zinc ore.
2. native zinc carbonate, $ZnCO_3$: variously used in skin ointments and lotions: also called *smithsonite.*

çal′ȧ·mint, *n.* a plant of the genus *Calamintha*: also called *calamint balm.*

Çal·ȧ·min′thȧ, *n.* [LL. *calamintha*; L. *calaminthe*; Gr. *kalaminthē,* a kind of mint; *kalos,* beautiful, and *mintha,* mint.] a genus of plants of the mint family.

çal′ȧ·mist, *n.* [L. *calamus,* a reed.] a player upon a pipe or reed. [Obs.]

çal·ȧ·mis′trāte, *v.t.* to curl (the hair). [Obs.]

çal·ȧ·mis′trum, *n.*; *pl.* **çal·ȧ·mis′trȧ,** [L., a curling iron, from *calamus,* a reed.] any of the short, curved, spiny bristles along the upper surface of the sixth joint of the hind legs of certain spiders: used in forming the thread of the web.

çal′ȧ·mīte, *n.* [L. *calamus,* a reed.]
1. a variety of tremolite, occurring in imperfect or rounded prismatic crystals, of a vitreous luster, longitudinally striated, and sometimes resembling a reed.
2. any fossil plant of the genus *Calamites.*

Çal·ȧ·mī′tēs, *n.* [Gr. *kalamitēs,* reedlike, from *kalamos,* a reed.] a genus of fossil plants, found in coal deposits in the form of jointed fragments, having a stem and branch marked with ribs and furrows: referred by some to the order *Equisetaceæ.*

çȧ·lam′i·tous, *a.* 1. very miserable; involved in deep distress; wretched from misfortune. [Obs.]
2. producing distress and misery; making wretched; bringing calamity with it; as, a *calamitous* event.
3. full of misery; distressful; wretched.

çȧ·lam′i·tous·ly, *adv.* in a calamitous manner.

çȧ·lam′i·tous·ness, *n.* deep distress; wretchedness; misery; the quality of being in misery.

çȧ·lam′i·ty, *n.*; *pl.* **çȧ·lam′i·ties,** [Fr. *calamité*; L. *calamitas,* damage, misfortune.]
1. any great misfortune; disaster.
2. a condition of distress; a time of adversity; misery.

The deliberations of *calamity* are rarely wise.
—Burke.

Syn.—disaster, misfortune, mischance, mishap.

çal′ȧ·mus, *n.*; *pl.* **çal′ȧ·mī,** [L., from Gr. *kalamos,* a stalk, a reed, stubble; Sans. *kalamas,* a stalk, stem, straw.]
1. the sweet flag or sweet rush, *Acorus calamus,* the pungent and aromatic root of which is used medicinally.
2. in the Bible, an aromatic plant, probably Indian lemon grass, or sweet flag.
3. [C–] a genus of tropical East Indian palms, of which the stems of the different species form canes.
4. the quill or horny part of a feather.
5. a reed; a cane.
6. a flute made of a reed.
7. in ancient Greece and Rome, (a) a split reed used as an instrument for writing; (b) a Pan's pipe.
8. an ancient Greek measure of length, equal to ten feet.

çȧ·lan′dō, *a.* and *adv.* [It., ppr. of *calare,* to decrease.] in music, more slowly and decreasing in volume of tone: a direction to the performer.

çȧ·lan′drȧ, *n.* [Fr. *calandre*; LL. *calandra*; Gr. *kalandra,* a kind of lark.]
1. a thick-billed lark, *Melanocorypha calandra,* a habitant of the Mediterranean countries.
2. [C–] a genus of weevils, as the corn weevil, *Calandra granaria.*

çȧ·lañ′gāy, *n.* [native name.] a hook-billed cockatoo of the Philippine Islands.

çȧ·lash′, *n.* [Fr. *calèche*; G. *kelesche*; Bohem. *kalesha*; Russ. *kolyaska,* a calash; Russ. *koleso,* a wheel.]
1. a light, low-wheeled carriage, usually having an adjustable top or hood: also spelled *calèche.*
2. an adjustable top of a carriage.
3. a folding hood or bonnet, worn by women in the eighteenth century.

çal·ȧ·thid′i·um, *n.*; *pl.* **çal·ȧ·thid′i·ȧ,** [L., dim. of *calathus,* a basket.] in botany, the flower head of a composite plant.

çȧ·lath′i·fọrm, *a.* [L. *calathus,* a basket, and *forma,* form.] concave; cup-shaped.

çȧ·lā′thi·um, *n.* same as *calathidium.*

çal′ȧ·thus, *n.*; *pl.* **çal′ȧ·thī,** [L., from Gr. *kalathos,* a basket.] in ancient Greece, a lily-shaped basket for fruits: it is often represented on monuments as a symbol of abundance.

çȧ·lȧ·ve′rīte, *n.* a native telluride of gold, $AuTe_2$, discovered in Calaveras County, California. It contains some silver.

çalç-, [G. *kalk,* lime, from L. *calx,* lime.] a combining form meaning *calcareous,* as in *calc*spar.

çal·çā′nē·ăl, *a.* in anatomy, pertaining to the calcaneus, or heel bone.

çal·çā′nē·ō-, a combining form from L. *calcaneum,* the heel, used in anatomy to denote relation to the calcaneus; as, *calcaneo*-fibular, pertaining to the calcaneus and the fibula.

çal·çā′nē·um, *n.* [L., the heel.] same as *calcaneus.*

çal·çā′nē·us, *n.* [LL.] the heel bone; one of the tarsal bones.

çal′çär, *n.*; *pl.* **çal·çā′ri·ȧ,** [L. *calcar*, a spur, from *calx*, the heel.]
1. in botany, a basal spur or spurlike projection from a petal or sepal.
2. in anatomy, the smaller of the two projections on the floor of the lateral ventricles of the brain, the hippocampus minor or *calcar* avis.
3. in zoology, (a) the spur of a bird; (b) an eminence on the tarsus of a bat, acting as a support to the interfemoral web.

çal′çär, *n.* [L. *calcaria*, a lime kiln.]
1. in glassmaking, a kind of oven or reverberatory furnace, used to calcinate sand and potash and convert them into frit.
2. an oven for annealing metals.

çal′çȧ·rāte, çal′çȧ·rā·ted, *a.* [L. *calcar*, a spur.] in biology, provided with a spur; as, a *calcarate* corolla.

çal·çā′rē·ō-, a combining form from L. *calcarius*, pertaining to lime, and meaning *calcareous and*.

çal·çā″rē·ō·är·ġil·lā′ceous, *a.* having or containing lime and clay: said of earths.

çal·çā″rē·ō·bi·tū′mi·nous, *a.* having lime and bitumen in combination.

çal·çā″rē·ō·si·li′ceous (-lish′us), *a.* containing lime and silica.

çal·çā″rē·ō·sul′fūr·ous, *a.* containing lime and sulfur.

çal·çā′rē·ous, *a.* [L. *calcarius*, pertaining to lime, from *calx*, *calcis*, lime.] of, like, or containing calcium carbonate, calcium, or lime.
calcareous spar; see *calcite*.

çal·çā′rē·ous·ness, *n.* the quality of being calcareous.

çal·çā′ri·ȧ, *n.* pl. of *calcar*.

çal·çȧ·rif′ẽr·ous, *a.* [from L. *calcar*, spur, and *-ferous*.] in botany and zoology, bearing a spur or spurs.

çal·çar′i·fọrm, *a.* [L. *calcar*, a spur, and *forma*, form.] spur-shaped.

çal′çȧ·rine, *a.* 1. calcaneal.
2. pertaining to the calcar avis.

çal·çȧ·vel′lȧ, *n.* [named from *Carcavelhos*, the district in Portugal where it is made.] a sweet wine from Portugal: written also *carcavelhos*, *calcavellos*.

çal′cē·ā·ted, *a.* [L. *calceatus*, pp. of *calceare*, to shoe; *calceus*, a shoe.] shod; wearing shoes. [Obs.]

çalced (kalst), *a.* [L.] shod; wearing shoes; as, a *calced* Carmelite.

çal′cē·dŏn, *n.* same as *chalcedony*.

çal·cē·don′iç, çal·cē·dō′ni·ăn, *a.* same as *chalcedonic*.

çal·ced′ō·ny, *n.* same as *chalcedony*.

çal′cē·i·fọrm, *a.* [L. *calceus*, a shoe, and *forma*, form.] in botany, having the form of a shoe or slipper, as the corolla of *Calceolaria*; calceolate.

Çal″cē·ō·lā′ri·ȧ, *n.* [L. *calceolarius*, from *calceolus*, a slipper, dim. of *calceus*, a shoe; so called from the shape of the corolla.]
1. a genus of ornamental herbaceous or shrubby plants of South America, belonging to the family *Scrophulariaceæ*.
2. [c–] any plant of this genus.

CALCEOLARIA

çal′cē·ō·lāte, *a.* same as *calceiform*.

çal′cēṣ, *n.* alternative pl. of *calx*.

Çal′chȧs, *n.* [L.; Gr. *kalchas*.] in Greek legend, a priest of Apollo who accompanied the Greeks during the Trojan War.

çal′ci-, [from L. *calx*, *calcis*, lime.] a combining form meaning *calcium* or *lime*, as in *calci*ferous, *calci*fy.

çal′ciç, *a.* [L. *calx*, *calcis*, lime.] from or containing lime or calcium; as, *calcic* chloride.

çal·cif′ẽr·ōl, *n.* [*calci*ferous, and ergoster*ol*.] vitamin D_2: it is a crystalline alcohol, $C_{28}H_{43}OH$.

çal·cif′ẽr·ous, *a.* [L. *calx*, *calcis*, lime, and *ferre*, to bear.] producing or containing calcite; as, *calciferous* sandstone.
Calciferous Epoch; that epoch in the Lower Silurian System following the Cambrian Period.

çal·cif′iç, *a.* [L. *calx*, *calcis*, lime, and *ficus*, from *facere*, to make.] calciferous.

çal″cif·i·çā′tion, *n.* 1. a calcifying; deposition of calcium salts in the tissues.
2. a calcified substance or structure.

çal′ci·fọrm, *a.* [L. *calx*, *calcis*, lime, and *forma*, form.] in the form of chalk or lime.

çal·cif′ū·gous, *a.* [L. *calx*, *calcis*, lime, and *fugere*, to flee.] in botany, avoiding calcareous soils: said of certain lichens.

çal′ci·fȳ, *v.t.* and *v.i.*; calcified, *pt.*, *pp.*; calcifying, *ppr.* [L. *calx*, *calcis*, lime, and *ficare*, from *facere*, to make.] to change into a hard, stony condition by the deposit of lime, as in the formation of teeth.

çal·ciġ′e·nous, *a.* [L. *calx*, *calcis*, lime, and *-genus*, producing.] yielding calx on oxidation, as certain metals.

çal·ciġ′e·rous, *a.* [L. *calx*, *calcis*, lime, and *gerere*, to bear.] lime-producing, as certain cells of the teeth.

çal′ci·mīne, *n.* [L. *calx*, *calcis*, lime.] a white or colored liquid used as a wash for plastered walls and ceilings: also spelled *kalsomine*.

çal′ci·mīne, *v.t.*; calcimined, *pt.*, *pp.*; calcimining, *ppr.* to apply calcimine to: also spelled *kalsomine*.

çal′ci·mī·nẽr, *n.* a person who calcimines.

çal·cīn′ȧ·ble, *a.* capable of calcination.

çal′ci·nāte, *v.t.* to calcine. [Obs.]

çal·ci·nā′tion, *n.* [LL. *calcinatio*, from *calcinare*, to calcine.]
1. the act or process of calcining.
2. a calcined substance.

çal·cin′ȧ·tō·ry, *a.* for calcining.

çal·cin′ȧ·tō·ry, *n.* a vessel or furnace for calcining.

çal′cīne (*or* kal-sīn′), *v.t.* and *v.i.*; calcined, *pt.*, *pp.*; calcining, *ppr.* [Fr. *calciner*; ML. *calcinare*, to reduce to lime or calx; L. *calx*, *calcis*, lime.]
1. to reduce to calx or powder by the action of heat.
2. to burn to ashes or powder.
3. to oxidize, as a metal.

çal′ci·nẽr, *n.* 1. one who calcines.
2. a calcining furnace.

Çal·ci·spon′ġi·ae, *n.pl.* [L. *calx*, *calcis*, lime, and *spongia*, a sponge.] a division of the sponges having three-rayed calcareous needles or spicules.

çal′cīte, *n.* [L. *calx*, *calcis*, lime.] calcium carbonate, $CaCO_3$, with hexagonal crystallization, a mineral found in limestone, marble, chalk, Iceland spar, etc.

çal′ci·trănt, *a.* kicking; obstinate.

çal′ci·trāte, *v.t.* [L. *calcitratus*, pp. of *calcitrare*, to kick, be stubborn; *calx*, a heel.] to kick.

çal·ci·trā′tion, *n.* the act of kicking.

çal′ci·um, *n.* [Mod. L., from L. *calx*, *calcis*, lime.] a soft, silver-white metallic chemical element found in limestone, marble, chalk, etc., always in combination: symbol, Ca; atomic weight, 40.08; atomic number, 20.

çal′ci·um är′se·nāte, a white compound, $Ca_3(AsO_4)_2$, used as an insecticide in the form of a spray or dust.

çal′ci·um çär′bīde, a dark-gray crystalline compound, CaC_2, used in making acetylene and calcium cyanamide.

çal′ci·um çär′bŏn·āte, a white powder or colorless, crystalline compound, $CaCO_3$, found mainly in limestone, marble, and chalk, as calcite, aragonite, etc., and in bones, teeth, shells, and plant ash: used in making lime.

çal′ci·um çhlō′rīde, a white crystalline compound, $CaCl_2$, used in making ice, as a dehydrating agent, etc.

çal′ci·um çȳ·an·am′īde, a white, crystalline compound, $CaCN_2$, used as a fertilizer: also called *lime nitrogen*.

çal′ci·um hȳ·drox′īde, a white, crystalline compound, $Ca(OH)_2$, prepared by the action of water on calcium oxide, used in making alkalies, bleaching powder, plaster, etc.: also called *slaked lime*.

çal′ci·um līght, a brilliant white light produced when a very hot flame is played on a piece of lime; limelight.

çal′ci·um ox′īde, a white, soft, caustic solid, CaO, prepared by heating calcium carbonate; quicklime.

çal′ci·um phos′phāte, any of a number of phosphates of calcium found in bones, teeth, and other animal tissues and used in medicine and in the manufacture of enamels, glass, cleaning agents, etc.

çal·civ′ō·rous, *a.* [L. *calx*, lime, and *vorare*, to devour.] eating into or living on limestone; as, *calcivorous* plants.

çal·çog′rȧ·phẽr, *n.* one who draws with crayons.

çal·çō·graph′iç·ăl, *a.* pertaining to calcography.

çal·çog′rȧ·phy, *n.* [L. *calx*, lime, chalk, and Gr. *-graphia*, from *graphein*, to write.] the art of drawing with crayons.

çalc′-sin″tẽr, *n.* [G. *kalksinter*; *kalk*, from L. *calx*, *calcis*, lime, and *sinter*, a stalactite.] travertine.

çalç′-spär, *n.* [L. *calx*, *calcis*, lime, and AS. *spær*, spar.] calcite.

çalç′-tū′fȧ, *n.* [L. *calx*, lime, and It. *tufa*, L. *tofus*, tuff-cone.] in mineralogy, porous lime carbonate deposited by the waters of calcareous springs; calcareous tufa.

çal″çū·lȧ·bil′i·ty, *n.* the quality or state of being calculable.

çal′çū·lȧ·ble, *a.* that can be calculated or ascertained by calculation.

çal′çū·lā·ry, *n.* [L. *calcularius*, pertaining to calculation, from *calculus*, a pebble, a reckoning.] a congeries of little stony knots dispersed through the soft portion of the pear and other fruits.

çal′çū·lȧ·ry, *a.* relating to calculi, or stones, in the bladder.

çal′çū·lāte, *v.t.*; calculated, *pt.*, *pp.*; calculating, *ppr.* [L. *calculatus*, pp. of *calculare*, to reckon; *calculus*, a pebble, a reckoning.]
1. to ascertain by computation; to compute; to reckon; as, to *calculate* distances.
2. to ascertain or determine by reasoning; to estimate.
3. to fit or prepare by the adaptation of means to an end; to make suitable: generally in the past participle.

> This letter was admirably *calculated* to work on those to whom it was addressed.
> —Macaulay.

4. to intend; to plan: used in the passive.
5. to think; to suppose; to guess; as, I *calculate* it will rain. [Colloq.]
Syn.—compute, estimate, reckon, count.

çal′çū·lāte, *v.i.* 1. to make a computation; to arrive at a conclusion after weighing all the circumstances; to estimate by calculation; to deliberate.

> The strong passions, whether good or bad, never *calculate*. —Robertson.

2. to rely or depend (*on*).

çal′çū·lā·ted, *a.* 1. relating to something which may be or has been subjected to calculation; as, a *calculated* plot.
2. designed or suitable for; as, a machine *calculated* for rapid work. [Colloq.]

çal′çū·lā·ting, *a.* 1. given to forethought and calculation; especially given to looking ahead with thoughtful regard to self-interest; deliberate and selfish; scheming.

> With his cool *calculating* disposition he easily got the better of his rival.
> —Godwin.

2. shrewd; cautious.

çal′çū·lā·ting, *n.* the act of estimating or computing.

çal′çū·lā·ting mȧ·chïne′, any machine by which mathematical calculations may be made rapidly.

çal·çū·lā′tion, *n.* 1. the act or practice of calculating or computing; as, geometrical *calculation*.
2. something deduced by calculating; inference; plan.
3. forethought; prudence.
Syn.—estimation, consideration, reckoning, computation, anticipation, forethought, regard, circumspection, watchfulness, vigilance, caution, care.

çal′çū·lā·tive, *a.* pertaining to calculation; tending to calculate.

çal′çū·lā·tŏr, *n.* [L., from *calculare*, to calculate.]
1. one who calculates.
2. a book of tables for calculating.
3. a calculating machine.

çal′çū·lā·tō·ry, *a.* belonging to calculation.

çal′çūle, *n.* a reckoning; computation. [Obs.]

çal′çūle, *v.t.* to calculate. [Obs.]

çal′çū·lī, *n.* alternative pl. of *calculus*.

çal′çū·lous, *a.* caused by or having a calculus or calculi.

çal′çū·lus, *n.*; *pl.* **çal′çū·lī, çal′çū·lus·eṣ,** [L. *calculus*, a small stone or pebble; dim. of *calx*, *calcis*, a stone.]
1. a small stone or pebble.
2. any hard, solid concretion or deposit in any part of the body; as, a urinary *calculus*, biliary *calculus*.
3. in higher mathematics, (a) a method of calculation; (b) the use of symbols; (c) a method of analysis: see phrases below; (d) a textbook of calculus; (e) a school course or class in calculus.
calculus of finite differences; that branch of mathematics dealing with the changes of

functions due to finite changes in the variables involved, without the assumption of continuity: E, Δ, and Σ are the chief symbols.

calculus of functions; that branch of mathematical analysis which investigates the form of a function and not its value in any particular case, nor the conditions under which it may have a particular value.

calculus of imaginaries; a method of investigating the nature of imaginary quantities required to fulfill apparently impossible conditions, using $\sqrt{-1}$ as a unit.

calculus of operations; a systematic method of treating problems by operating algebraically upon symbols of operation.

calculus of probability; the science of calculating the mathematical likelihood of probability of events or chances.

calculus of variations; that branch of analysis which seeks the laws of changes attending a slight alteration in the form of the function, or in the transformation of one function into another.

differential calculus; the branch of mathematics that deals with the infinitely small differences between consecutive values of a variable quantity, and with their relation to the constant on which they depend.

integral calculus; the branch of calculus dealing with the theory, application, functions, etc. of integrals.

çal·dā·ri·um, *n.; pl.* **çal·dā′ri·ȧ,** [L.] one of the rooms in the Roman thermae, in which the hot baths were taken.

çäl·dẹ′rä, *n.* [Sp.] a deep, caldronlike cavity found at the summit of a volcano, formed by an explosion or by collapse of the cone.

Çäl·dẹ·rä′ī, *n.pl.* [It., coppersmiths.] a politico-religious sect in Italy during the reign of Murat, opposed to the Carbonari.

çal′drŏn, çaul′drŏn, *n.* [ME. *caldron, caudron*; OFr. *caudron, chaudron*; L. *caldaria*, a kettle for hot water, from *calidus*, hot, *calere*, to be hot, warm.] a large kettle or boiler.

Çā′leb, *n.* [Heb. *kālēb*, lit., dog; hence, faithful.] in the Bible, one of the only two men who survived after the forty years' wanderings of the Israelites.

çāle çan·nŏn, *n.* [AS. *caul*; L. *caulis*, cabbage.] same as *colcannon*.

ca·lèche′, (kȧ-lesh′), *n.* [Fr.; see *calash*.]

1. in Quebec, a two-wheeled carriage with a folding top.

2. a calash.

Çal·ē·dō′ni·ȧ, *n* [L.] Scotland. [Obs. or Poetic.]

Çal·ē·dō′ni·ăn, *a.* 1. of or pertaining to ancient Caledonia.

2. Scottish: humorous or poetic term.

Çal·ē·dō′ni ăn, *n.* a native or inhabitant of ancient Caledonia, or Scotland.

çal′ē·dō·nīte, *n.* [named from *Caledonia*.] a green mineral, a basic copper lead sulfate.

çal·e·fā′cient (-shunt), *a.* [L. *calefaciens* (-*entis*), ppr. of *calefacere*, to make warm; *calere*, to be warm, and *facere*, to make.] warming; heating.

çal·e·fā′cient, *n.* a remedy that warms or heats, as a mustard plaster.

çal·e·faç′tion, *n.* [L. *calefactio*, from *calefacere*, to make warm.]

1. the act or operation of heating.

2. the state of being heated.

çal·e·faç′tive, çal·e·faç tō·ry, *a.* having the quality of producing or communicating heat.

çal·e·faç′tō·ry, *n.*; *pl.* **çal·e·faç′tō·rieş,** 1. a heated room in a monastery.

2. a warming pan.

çal′e·fȳ, *v.i.*; calefied, *pt., pp.*; calefying, *ppr.* [L. *calefio*, to become warm or hot; *calere*, to be warm, and *fieri*, to become.] to grow hot or warm. [Obs.]

çal′e·fȳ, *v.t.* to make warm or hot. [Obs.]

çal′em·bour (-boor *or* Fr. kȧ-läṅ-bo͝or′), *n.* [Fr.] a pun.

Çal′e·mēş, *n.* same as *Camenes*.

çal′en·dăr, *n.* [ME. *calendar*; L. *calendarium*, an account book; from *calendæ, kalendæ*, the calends.]

1. a series of tables giving in tabulated form the days, weeks, and months of the year, sometimes with certain astronomical information.

2. any concise and systematic arrangement of facts, observances, etc.; a register; a list; a schedule, as of pending court cases.

3. a system of determining the beginning, length, and divisions of a year; as, the Julian *calendar*.

calendar day; see under *day*.
calendar month; see under *month*.
calendar year; see under *year*.
Gregorian calendar; see under *Gregorian*.
Julian calendar; see under *Julian*.
perpetual calendar; a calendar that is mathematically so arranged that the correct day of the week can be determined for any given date over a wide range of years.

çal′en·dăr, *v.t.*; calendared, *pt., pp.*; calendaring, *ppr.* 1. to enter or write in a calendar.

2. to schedule.

çal′en·dăr çlock, a clock showing the day of the week and month as well as the hour of the day.

çal·en·dăr′i·ăl, *a.* of or pertaining to a calendar.

çal′en·dăr·y, *a.* [L. *calendarius, kalendarius*, from *calendarium*, a calendar.] calendarial.

çal′en·dẽr, *n.* [Fr. *calendre*; LL. *calendra*; L. *cylindrus*; Gr. *kylindros*, a roller, cylinder.]

1. a machine consisting of two or more cylinders revolving so nearly in contact with each other that cloth or paper passing between them is smoothed and given a glossy finish by their pressure.

2. a place where calendering is done.

3. one who calenders.

çal′en·dẽr, *v.t.*; calendered, *pt., pp.*; calendering, *ppr.* to press (paper, cloth, etc.) between rollers, for the purpose of making smooth, glossy, and wavy.

çal′en·dẽr, *n.* [Per. *qalandar*.] a member of an order of wandering dervishes among the Sufis.

çal·en·dog′rȧ·phẽr, *n.* [L. *calendarium*, a calendar, and Gr. *graphein*, to write.] a calendar maker. [Rare.]

çal′en·drẽr, *n.* a person who calenders cloth.

çȧ·len′driç, çȧ·len′driç·ăl, *a.* pertaining to a calendar. [Rare.]

çal′endş, kal′endş, *n.pl.* [AS. *calend*, a month; L. *calendæ, kalendæ*, the first of the month; from *calare*, Gr. *kalein*, to call.] the first day of each month in the ancient Roman calendar.

Çȧ·len′dū·lȧ, *n.* [dim. from L. *calendæ*, the first day of the month; so called from its producing flowers during almost the entire year.]

1. a genus of plants, family *Compositæ*, with yellow or orange flowers, as the pot marigold.

2. [c-] any plant of this genus.

3. [c-] the dried florets of such a plant, used as a remedy for wounds, etc.

çȧ·len′dū·lin, *n.* a mucilaginous substance derived from the marigold.

çal′en·tūre, *n.* [Fr. *calenture*; Sp. *calentura*, heat, a calenture, from *calentar*; L. *calere*, to be warm, hot.] a tropical fever with delirium.

çal′en·tūre, *v.i.* to have illusions like those of the delirium of calenture. [Poet.]

çä·le′sä, *n.* [Sp.] a kind of calash; cab.

çȧ·les′cence, *n.* [L. *calescens*, ppr. of *calescere*, to grow warm or hot; *calere*, to be warm or hot.] an intensifying heat.

çȧ·les′cent, *a.* increasing in warmth; getting hot.

çȧlf (kȧf), *n.*; *pl.* **çȧlveş** (kȧvz) [ME. *calf*; AS. *cealf*; Ice. *kalfr*; Dan. *kalv*; O.H.G. *calb*; D. *kalf*, a calf.]

1. the young of the cow, or of the bovine genus of quadrupeds; also, the young of other mammals, as the elephant, whale, etc.

2. leather prepared from the hide of a calf, used in making shoes, in bookbinding, etc.

3. a small island situated near a larger one.

4. a fragment of ice detached from an iceberg or coast glacier.

5. an awkward, callow, or silly young person. [Colloq.]

calf love; the immature love that boys and girls may feel for each other; puppy love. [Colloq.]

to kill the fatted calf; to make a feast of celebration or welcome.

çȧlf, *n.*; *pl.* **çȧlveş,** the thick, fleshy back part of the leg between the knee and the ankle.

çȧlf′ş′-foot (kȧvz′), *n.* in botany, the common wakerobin, *Arum maculatum*, of Europe.

çȧlf′s-foot jel′ly, a jelly made by sweetening and flavoring the gelatinous matter obtained by boiling calves' feet.

çȧlf′s′-head (kȧfs′hed), *n.* the pitcher plant of California.

çȧlf′skin, *n.* the hide or skin of a calf, or leather made of the skin.

Çal′i·ban, *n.* [form of *canibal*, cannibal, with interchanged *n* and *l*.] a deformed, savage creature, the slave of Prospero in Shakespeare's *The Tempest*.

çal′i·bẽr, çal′i·bre, *n.* [Fr. *calibre*, perh. from L. *qua libra*, what pound, weight, size.]

1. the size of a bullet or shell as measured by its diameter.

2. the diameter of the bore of a gun.

3. the diameter of a cylindrical body or of its hollowed interior.

4. figuratively, quality; ability.

çal′i·bẽr çŏm′pȧss, same as *calipers*.

çal′i·bẽr rūle, gunner's calipers, an instrument used to determine the caliber of a ball from its weight.

çal′i·brāte, *v.t.*; calibrated, *pt., pp.*; calibrating, *ppr.* 1. to determine the caliber of.

2. to fix, check, or correct the graduations of (a measuring instrument, as a thermometer).

3. to find for (a firearm) by actual use the ways in which it must be corrected or adjusted for uniformity in firing.

çal·i·brā′tion (-shun), *n.* the act or process of calibrating.

çal′i·brā·tŏr, *n.* a person or thing that calibrates.

çal′i·cēş, *n.* pl. of *calix*.

çä·lī′chẹ, *n.* [Sp., from *cal*, L. *calx*, lime.]

1. impure native nitrate of soda, $NaNO_3$, found in Chile.

2. crusted calcium carbonate formed on certain soils in dry regions.

çal′i·çle (-kl), *n.* [L. *caliculus*, a small cup; dim. of *calix, calicis*, a cup.] in zoology, a small, cuplike cavity in coral; a calyculus.

çal′i·çō, *n.*; *pl.* **çal′i·çōeş** or **çal′i·çōş,** [from *Calicut*, India, whence it was first imported.] any of several kinds of cotton cloth. In the United States, it is a coarse cotton cloth printed with a figured design on one side. In England it is any plain or unprinted white cotton cloth. Originally, it was a cotton cloth from India.

çal′i·çō, *a.* 1. of calico.

2. resembling calico; spotted; as, a *calico* pony.

çal′i·çō ash, wood of the white ash.

çal′i·çō as′tẽr, *Aster lateriflorus*, an American variety of aster.

çal′i·çō·back, *n.* 1. the calico bass.

2. the calico bug.

3. the turnstone, a bird allied to the plover: so called from its spotted plumage.

çal′i·çō bȧss, a common variety of fresh-water fish, the *Pomoxis sparoides*, found in the central and eastern United States: also called *calicoback, strawberry bass, grass bass*, etc.

çal′i·çō bug, a black beetle, *Murgantia histrionica*, with red, orange, and yellow markings, destructive to cabbage, radishes, etc.

çal′i·çō bụsh, the mountain laurel, *Kalmia latifolia*, an evergreen bush of the eastern United States: also called *calico flower, calico tree*.

çal′i·çō print′ing, the process of printing colored designs on calico.

çal′i·çō wood, a small American tree, *Halesia tetraptera*, yielding a soft, light-brown wood: called also *silverbell tree*.

çȧ·liç′ū·lȧ, *n.*; *pl.* **çȧ·liç′ū·lae,** in botany, same as *calycle*.

çȧ·liç′ū·lăr, çȧ·liç′ū·lāte, *a.* [L. *caliculus*, dim. of *calix*, a cup.] shaped like a cup.

çal′id, *a.* [L. *calidus*, from *calere*, to be hot.] hot; burning; ardent. [Obs.]

çȧ·lid′i·ty, *n.* heat. [Obs.]

çal′i·duçt, *n.* [L. *calere*, to be warm, and *ductus*, from *ducere*, to lead, conduct.] a pipe to convey hot air or steam. [Rare.]

çā′lif, *n.* same as *caliph*.

çal′i·fāte, *n.* same as *caliphate*.

Çal·i·fọr′ni·ăn, *a.* pertaining to California; as, *Californian* wines.

Çal·i·fọr′ni·ăn, *n.* an inhabitant or native of California.

Çal·i·fọr′ni·ȧ or′anġe, an orange, especially a navel orange, grown in California.

Çal·i·fọr′ni·ȧ pop′py, a variety of poppy with small flowers varying in color from pale cream to deep orange.

çal·i·fọr′ni·um, *n.* [from University of *California*, and *-ium*.] a radioactive chemical element produced by the atomic bombardment of curium; symbol, Cf; atomic weight, 244 (?); atomic number, 98.

çal′i·gā·ted, *a.* see *laminiplantar*.

çal·i·gā′tion, *n.* [L. *caligatio*, from *caligare*, to be dark, *caligo*, dark.] darkness; dimness of sight. [Obs.]

çȧ·liġ·i·nos′i·ty, *n.* darkness; dimness of sight. [Archaic.]

çȧ·liġ′i·nous, *a.* dim; obscure; dark. [Archaic.]

çȧ·liġ′i·nous·ly, *adv.* obscurely. [Archaic.]

çȧ·liġ′i·nous·ness, *n.* dimness; obscurity. [Archaic.]

çȧ·lī′gō, *n.* [L., darkness.] impairment of sight.

çal·i·graph′iç, *a.* see *calligraphic*.

ca·lig′ra·phy, *n.* see *calligraphy.*

cā′lin, *n.* [Fr., prob. from Malay *kelang*, tin.] an alloy, probably composed of lead and tin, of which the Chinese make tea canisters, etc.

cal·i·pash′, *n.* [a form of *calabash*, with sense of *carapace*; Fr. *carapace*, the shell of a turtle.] a greenish, jellylike, edible substance adhering to the upper shell of a turtle.

cal·i·pee′, *n.* a yellowish, jellylike, edible substance adhering to the lower shell of a turtle.

cal′i·pēr, *n.* [var. of *caliber.*]
 1. [*usually pl.*] an instrument consisting of a pair of movable curved legs fastened together at one end with a screw or rivet, used to measure the thickness or diameter of something: there are *inside calipers* and *outside calipers.*
 2. a caliper rule.
 Also spelled *calliper.*

CALIPERS

cal′i·pēr, *v.t.* and *v.i.* to measure with calipers: also spelled *calliper.*

cal′i·pēr rule, a graduated rule with one sliding jaw and one that is stationary.

cal′i·pēr square, a square used like calipers, having a graduated scale and adjustable jaws.

cā′liph, *n.* [ME. *caliphe*; OFr. *calife*; Ar. *khalīfa*, a caliph, successor, from *khalafa*, to succeed.] in a Moslem state, supreme ruler; successor; the title taken by Mohammed's successors as secular and religious heads of Islam: also spelled *calif, kalif, kaliph, khalif.*

cal′i·phāte, *n.* 1. the office, reign, or rank of a caliph.
 2. the land ruled by a caliph.

cā′liph·ship, *n.* a caliphate.

cal·i·sā′ya bärk, [S. Am.] cinchona bark, especially *Cinchona Calisaya*, from which quinine is obtained.

cal·is·thē′nē·um, *n.* a hall or gymnasium for calisthenics: also spelled *callisthenium.*

cal·is·then′iç, cal·is·then′iç·ăl, *a.* relating to calisthenics: also spelled *callisthenic, callisthenical.*

cal·is·then′içs, *n.pl.* [Gr. *kallos*, beauty, and *sthenos*, strength.]
 1. athletic exercises; simple gymnastics.
 2. [*construed as sing.*] the art of developing bodily strength and gracefulness by such exercises.
 Also spelled *callisthenics.*

cal′i·vēr, *n.* [a corruption of *caliber.*] a kind of hand gun, musket, or harquebus. [Obs.]

cā′lix, *n.*; *pl.* **cal′i·çēs**, a cup; a chalice.

Ca·lix′tine, *n.* [LL. *Calixtini*, from L. *calix* (*-icis*), a cup.] one of a Hussite sect, established in the fifteenth century, who maintained that the laity should receive the cup as well as the bread in the Eucharist: called also *Utraquist.*

calk (kak), *v.t.*; calked, *pt., pp.*; calking, *ppr.* [ME. *cauken*, to tread; OFr. *cauquer*, to tread, tread in; L. *calcare*, to tread; from *calx*, a heel.]
 1. to drive tar, oakum, etc. into the seams of (a boat, etc.) to prevent its admitting water; also, to stop up (cracks of windows, pipes, etc.) with filler.
 2. to force the edge of (one metal plate against the edge of another) in order to make a tight seam, as in boilermaking, shipbuilding, etc.
 Also spelled *caulk.*

calk, *v.t.* [Fr. *calquer*, to chalk, trace; It. *calcare*; from L. *calx, calcis*, chalk.] to copy, as a design or drawing, by tracing with a stylus on the print itself, the back of which has been treated with chalk.

calk (kak), *n.* [AS. *calc*, shoe, hoof; L. *calx, calcis*, a heel; *calcar*, a spur.]
 1. a sharp-pointed piece of iron projecting downward on a horseshoe to prevent slipping.
 2. a metal plate worn on the sole of a shoe or boot to give it longer wear or to prevent slipping.

calk, *v.t.* 1. to fit or furnish with calks; as, to *calk* a horse or shoe.
 2. to injure or wound (a horse's leg) with a calk.

calk′ēr, *n.* 1. a person who calks boats, ships, etc.
 2. a tool used in calking.
 Also spelled *caulker.*

calk′ēr, *n.* a calk on a shoe.

calk′in, *n.* a calk on a horseshoe.

calk′ing ī′ron (-ūrn), an instrument resembling a chisel, used in calking ships.

call, *v.t.*; called, *pt., pp.*; calling, *ppr.* [ME. *callen, kallen*; AS. *ceallian*, to call, speak; D. *kallen*, to speak, say; Ice. *kalla*, to say, call, name.]
 1. to name; to give a name to.
 And God *called* the light Day, and the darkness he *called* Night. —Gen. i. 5.
 2. to say in a loud voice; to shout; to announce.
 3. to designate or characterize as; to affirm to be.
 Call you that backing of your friends? A plague upon such backing. —Shak.
 4. to summon; as, to *call* a messenger, to *call* a meeting.
 5. to convoke judicially or officially, as a court or legislative body (often with *together*); as, the president *called* the cabinet *together.*
 6. to select or appoint for a specific office, duty, or employment.
 Paul, *called* to be an apostle. —Rom. i. 1.
 7. to address an invocation or appeal to.
 I *call* God for a record upon my soul. —2 Cor. i. 23.
 8. to arouse, as from sleep; to awaken (a person).
 You must wake, and *call* me early, *call* me early, mother dear. —Tennyson.
 9. to lure (an animal or bird) by uttering a call imitative of its own.
 10. to give a signal to.
 11. to telephone.
 12. to stop; call a halt to (a baseball game, etc.).
 13. to demand or order payment of (a loan or a bond issue).
 14. in games, to tell the aim, etc. of (a shot) before making it.
 15. in poker, to require a show of cards by equaling the bet of (another player).
 to call attention to; to direct attention to (something definite and important).
 to call back; (a) to direct the return of; to recall; (b) to revoke or retract; (c) to telephone again or in return.
 to call down; (a) to invoke; to pray for; (b) [Slang.] to take to task; to rebuke.
 to call for; (a) to demand; (b) to come and get; to stop for.
 to call forth; to bring into play; as, to *call forth* one's entire resources.
 to call in; (a) to collect, as debts; (b) to withdraw from circulation, as coin or bonds; (c) to request the co-operation or assistance of; as, *to call in* a physician for consultation.
 to call in question; to challenge as to truthfulness, soundness, or veracity.
 to call into play; to employ in an active way.
 to call off; (a) to divert; to summon away; (b) [Colloq.] to cancel a proposed or promised event or function; to revoke; (c) to read aloud from a list or enumeration; as, *to call off* the names of the eligible candidates.
 to call on; (a) to visit briefly; (b) to ask (a person) to speak.
 to call out; (a) to speak aloud; to shout; (b) to challenge, as to a fight; (c) to summon into action, as the militia.
 to call to account; (a) to demand an explanation or examination of; (b) to reprimand.
 to call to the bar; to admit as a practitioner of law.
 to call up; (a) to revive the memory of; (b) to take necessary steps to bring up for action or discussion, as in a meeting or council; to demand the consideration of; (c) to telephone.
 Syn.—invite, convoke, summon, name, designate, term, denominate, assemble.—*Call* is generic; *summon* and *convoke* imply some right or authority; as, to *summon* a witness or *convoke* an assembly.

call, *v.i.* 1. to speak in a loud tone; to shout.
 The angel *called* to Hagar. —Gen. xxi. 17.
 2. to visit for a short while; to make a short stop; as, to *call* at the inn.
 3. to telephone.
 4. in poker, to require a show of cards by equaling the bet of another player.
 to call out; to make an outcry, as of one in distress.

call, *n.* 1. a calling; as, I did not hear your *call*; the *call* of the bugle.
 2. a loud utterance.
 3. a summons; invitation.
 4. a signaling; signal.
 5. a demand; as, a *call* for low-priced books.
 6. a sound uttered to attract an animal or bird.
 7. the distinctive cry or sound of an animal or bird.
 8. religious duty or vocation regarded as divinely inspired.
 9. a formal invitation to a minister to accept a pastorate.
 10. need; occasion; as, no *call* for laughter.
 11. in commerce, a demand that grain or stock be delivered within a certain time and at a stated price.
 12. a short visit, especially a formal or professional visit.
 13. in law, a reference to some natural mark, object, line, or direction, in the descriptive part of a deed, grant, or survey.
 14. in poker, a demand for a show of cards.
 15. a demand for payment.
 at call or *on call*; (a) available when called for or summoned; (b) payable on demand without previous notice; as, a sum of money deposited in a bank *at call.*
 close call; a narrow escape from disaster or death. [Colloq.]
 within call; close enough to be called or spoken to.

Cal′la, *n.* [L. *calla*, a plant mentioned by Pliny.]
 1. a genus of plants, family *Orontiaceæ.*
 2. [c—] any plant of this genus, with a large, white leaf surrounding a yellow flower spike: also called *calla lily.*
 3. its flower: also called *calla lily.*

call′a·ble, *a.* that can be called; specifically, (a) that must be paid upon demand, as a loan; (b) that must be presented for payment upon notice, as a bond.

call bell, a bell by which attendants are called or signals given.

call bird, a bird trained to decoy other birds by sounding its call.

call′bōard, *n.* in the theater, a bulletin board backstage for posting instructions, time of rehearsals, etc.

call′boy, *n.* 1. a boy whose duty it is to call actors when it is time for them to go on the stage.
 2. the boy who repeats the orders of the captain of a steamboat to the steward.
 3. a bellboy.

call but′tŏn, a button for closing the circuit of an electric current, which causes a call bell to ring.

call duck, a decoy duck.

call′ēr, *n.* 1. one who or that which calls.
 2. a person who makes a short visit.

cal′lēr, *a.* refreshing; cool; reviving; as, *caller* breezes; also, fresh; not decayed or tainted; as, *caller* fish. [Scot.]

cal′let, cal′lat, *n.* a trull; a strumpet; a scolding or gossiping woman. [Obs.]

cal′let, *v.i.* to rail; to scold. [Obs.]

call girl, a prostitute sent out to a man who telephones for an appointment. [Slang.]

cal′lid, *a.* [L. *callidus*, expert, shrewd.] skillful; cunning; crafty. [Rare.]

cal·lid′i·ty, *n.* skill; shrewdness. [Rare.]

cal·lig′ra·phēr, ca·lig′ra·phēr, *n.* one skilled in calligraphy; an excellent penman.

cal·li·graph′iç, cal·i·graph′iç, *a.* pertaining to calligraphy.

cal·li·graph′iç·ăl, cal·i·graph′iç·ăl, *a.* same as *calligraphic.*

cal·lig′ra·phist, ca·lig′ra·phist, *n.* a calligrapher.

cal·lig′ra·phy, ca·lig′ra·phy, *n.* [Gr. *kalligraphia*, from *kalligraphos*; *kalos*, beautiful, and *graphein*, to write.]
 1. beautiful or expert handwriting.
 My *calligraphy*, a fair hand
 Fit for a secretary. —B. Jonson.
 2. handwriting.

call′ing, *n.* 1. the act of one who or that which calls.
 A *calling* of the sea. —Tennyson.
 2. divine summons; state of being divinely called; call.
 3. a vocation; profession; trade; occupation.
 4. a body of persons following any profession.
 Not to impose celibacy on whole *callings.* —Hammond.
 5. one's name, title, or designation. [Obs.]
 Syn.—business, vocation, pursuit, function, occupation, concern, employment, office, duty, work.

call′ing çärd, a small card with one's name and, sometimes, one's address on it, used in making visits, etc.

call′ing hāre, see *pika.*

Cal·lī′ō·pē, *n.* [L., from Gr. *Kalliopē*, the beautiful-voiced; *kalos*, beautiful, and *ops*, *opos*, voice.]
1. in Greek and Roman mythology, the Muse of eloquence and heroic poetry.
2. [c–] a musical instrument consisting of a number of steam-whistles toned to different notes and played like an organ.
3. [c–] a California hummingbird of the genus *Stellula*.

CALLIOPE

cal′li·op·sis, *n.* [Mod. L., from Gr. *kallos*, beauty, and *opsis*, appearance.] the coreopsis.
cal·li·pash′, *n.* same as *calipash*.
cal·li·pee′, *n.* same as *calipee*.
cal′li·pēr, *n.* and *v.t.* same as *caliper*.
cal·li·pyg′i·ăn, *a.* [Gr. *kallipygos*, from *kalos*, beautiful, and *pygē*, buttocks.] having shapely buttocks.
cal·li·sec′tion, *n.* [L. *callere*, to be insensible, and *sectio*, from *secare*, to cut.] vivisection made painless by use of an anesthetic: opposed to *sentisection*.
cal·lis·then′iç, *a.* same as *calisthenic*.
cal·lis·then′içs, *n.pl.* same as *calisthenics*.
cal·lis·thē′ni·um, *n.* same as *calistheneum*.
Cal·lis′tō, *n.* [L.; Gr. *Kallistō*.] in Greek and Roman mythology, a nymph who, because she was loved by Zeus (Jupiter), was changed into a bear by Hera (Juno): Zeus placed her among the stars as the constellation of the Bear.
cal′li·thump, cal′i·thump, *n.* a noisy and boisterous mock serenade; a charivari.
cal·li·thump′i·ăn, *a.* pertaining to a callithump.
cal·li·thump′i·ăn, *n.* a callithump; sometimes, a participant in such a demonstration.
Cal′li·tris, *n.* [L., from Gr. *kalos*, beautiful.] a genus of conifers, including *Calitris quadrivalvis*, the sandarac tree.
call let′tērs, the letters, and sometimes the numbers, that identify a radio sending station, whether on land or on a ship.
call lōan, a loan of money that must be paid on demand.
call mŏn′ey, money borrowed as a call loan.
call nōte, the note used by a bird or animal to call its mate or young.
call num′bēr, the number given a library book to show the division, case, and shelf to which it is assigned.
cal·lō′săl, *a.* in anatomy, pertaining to the corpus callosum.
cal′lōse, *a.* [L. *callosus*, hard-skinned, from *callum*, *callus*, hardened skin.] in botany, having hard, protuberant spots.
cal·los′i·ty, *n.*; *pl.* **cal·los′i·ties**, 1. the state or quality of being hardened or indurated.
2. any thickened or hardened part on the skin of an animal or the bark of a tree; a callus.
3. the quality of being hardhearted.
cal·lō′sum, *n.* same as *corpus callosum*.
cal′lot, *n.* same as *calotte*.
cal′lous, *a.* [L. *callosus*, from *callum*, *callus*, hard skin.]
1. having a callus or calluses; thick-skinned.
The patient rustic came, whose *callous* hand. —Goldsmith.
2. hardened in mind or feelings; insensitive; unfeeling.
And *callous*, save to crime. —Byron.
Syn.—hard, hardened, indurated, insensitive, unfeeling, obdurate.
cal′lous, *v.t.* and *v.i.* to make or become callous.
cal′lous·ly, *adv.* in a callous or unfeeling manner.
cal′lous·ness, *n.* the quality of being callous.
cal′lōw, *a.* [ME. *calowe*, *calu*; AS. *calu*; O.H.G. *calo*; D. *kaal*, bald, bare.]
1. unfledged.
2. without feathers, as a young bird not yet able to fly.
3. immature; without experience; as, *callow* love.
cal′lōw, *n.* a species of duck, the old squaw.
call rāte, the rate of interest on call loans.
call slip, in libraries, a form on which the patron lists the title and call number of a desired book which is then procured for him by the librarian.
call tö quar′tērs, in military usage, a signal by bugle or drums a short time before taps, notifying soldiers to retire to their quarters.
cal′lus, *n.*; *pl.* **cal′lus·es**, [L. *callus*, *callum*, hard skin.]
1. a hardened, thickened place on the skin.
2. a hard substance formed around the ends of a broken bone that helps them to knit.
3. a growth that forms over a cut or wounded area on a plant stem; callosity.
cal′lus, *v.i.* to develop a callus.
çälm (käm), *n.* [Fr. *calme*; LL. *cauma*, the heat of the sun; Gr. *kauma*, from *kaiein*, to burn; probably from the period of rest, during midday.] lack of motion, agitation, or disturbance; stillness; tranquillity; quiet.
The soul as even as a *calm*. —Shak.
çälm, *a.*; *comp.* calmer; *superl.* calmest, 1. still; quiet; at rest; undisturbed; not agitated; not stormy.
Calm is the morn without a sound. —Tennyson.
2. undisturbed by passion; not agitated or excited; quiet; tranquil, as the mind, temper, or attention.
People are generally *calm* at the misfortunes of others. —Goldsmith.
Syn.—tranquil, placid, quiet.—*Calm*, when applied to the mind, implies that the person remains unagitated, even though there may be considerable care and anxiety; *tranquil* implies that the mind is serene and free from anxiety. *Quiet*, when applied to the disposition, implies that the person is naturally silent and undemonstrative. *Placid* is nearly allied in sense to *tranquil*, but denotes a more cheerful and settled state.
çälm, *v.t.* and *v.i.*; calmed, *pt.*, *pp.*; calming, *ppr.* to make or become calm (often with *down*).
cal′mȧ·tive, *a.* calming; soothing; sedative.
cal′mȧ·tive, *n.* a calmative medicine.
çälm′ēr, *n.* one who or that which calms.
çälm′ly, *adv.* in a calm manner; quietly.
çälm′ness, *n.* the state of being calm; repose.
Cal′muck, *n.* same as *Kalmuck*.
çälm′y, *a.* calm; quiet; peaceful; tranquil. [Poetic or Archaic.]
Cal·ō·chor′tus, *n.* [L., from Gr. *kalos*, beautiful, and *chortos*, grass.] a genus of bulbous plants of Mexico and California, family *Liliaceæ*.
cal′ō·mel, *n.* [Gr. *kalos*, beautiful, and *melas*, black.] mercurous chloride, HgCl, a white, tasteless powder, used as a cathartic, for intestinal worms, etc.
Cal·ō·phyl′lum, *n.* [L., from Gr. *kalos*, beautiful, and *phyllon*, leaf.] a genus of tropical, guttiferous timber trees, including *Calophyllum calaba*, the calaba tree.
cal·ō·res′cence, *n.* [L. *calor*, heat.] the change of infrared radiant energy into visible light.
cȧ·lor′iç, *n.* [L. *calor*, heat.]
1. a substance formerly thought to exist, to which the sensation and other phenomena of heat were formerly attributed.
2. heat.
cȧ·lor′iç, *a.* pertaining to heat.
caloric engine; a hot-air engine.
caloric paradox; same as *thermal paradox*.
cal·ō·ric′i·ty, *n.* the ability of living animals to produce the heat necessary for the maintenance of life, and to control this heat so as to maintain an almost constant temperature of the body.
cȧ·lor′i·duçt, *n.* [L. *calor*, heat, and *ductus*, from *ducere*, to lead.] a tube or passage for conveying heat.
cal′ō·rie, *n.* [Fr. *calorie*, from L. *calor*, heat.]
1. the amount of heat needed to raise the temperature of one gram of water one degree centigrade: called *small calorie*.
2. [*usually* C–] the amount of heat needed to raise the temperature of one kilogram of water one degree centigrade: called *large calorie*, *great calorie*: used as the unit for measuring the energy produced by food when oxidized in the body.
Also spelled *calory*.
cȧ·lor·i·fā′cient (-shent), *a.* [L. *calor*, heat, and *faciens*, ppr. of *facere*, to make.] heat-producing: also *calorificient*, *calorifiant*, *calorifient*.
cȧ·lor·i·fī′ănt, *a.* same as *calorifacient*.
cal·ō·rif′iç, *a.* capable of producing heat; causing heat; heating.
cȧ·lor″i·fi·cā′tion, *n.* the production of heat, especially animal heat.
cȧ·lor·i·fi′cient (-fish′ent), *a.* same as *calorifacient*.
cal·ō·rif′içs, *n.* the science treating of heat and heating appliances.
cȧ·lor·i·fī′ent, *a.* same as *calorifacient*.
cal·ō·rim′e·tēr, *n.* [L. *calor*, heat, and *metrum*; Gr. *metron*, a measure.] an apparatus for measuring amounts of heat, as in chemical combination, friction, etc.
cal″or·i·met′riç, cal″or·i·met′riç·ăl, *a.* of or pertaining to calorimetry.
cal″or·i·met′riç·ăl·ly, *adv.* by means of a calorimeter; according to calorimetry.
cal·ō·rim′e·try, *n.* the science and practice of measuring quantities of heat.
cȧ·lor·i·mō′tŏr, *n.* [L. *calor*, heat, and *motor*, from *movere*, to move.] an electric battery having very large contact surfaces in the electrodes, low internal resistance, and producing a current of high heating effect.
cal′ō·rīte, *n.* [L. *calor*, heat.] an alloy of nickel, iron, and chromium, used in wiring electrical resistance heating units: a trade-mark (*Calorite*).
cal′ō·rīze, *v.t.*; calorized, *pt.*, *pp.*; calorizing, *ppr.* to coat or alloy (a metal) with aluminum by heating in a closed retort containing an aluminum mixture.
cal′ŏ·ry, *n.*; *pl.* **cal′ŏ·ries**, see *calorie*.
Cȧ·lot′rō·pis, *n.* [L., from Gr. *kalos*, beautiful, and *tropis*, a ship's keel.] a genus of tropical fiber-producing plants of the milkweed family.
cȧ·lotte′, cal′lot, *n.* [Fr. *calotte*, dim. of OFr. *cale*, a kind of cap.]
1. a small, brimless cap: also spelled *calot*.
2. a skullcap worn by Roman Catholic clergymen.
3. in architecture, a round cavity or depression in the form of a cup, used to lessen the height of a chapel, alcove, etc.
4. in ornithology, a colored, hoodlike eminence on the head of a bird.
cal′ō·tȳpe, *n.* [Gr. *kalos*; beautiful, and *typos*, impression, type.] an early process of photography.
cȧ·loy′ēr, *n.* [Fr., from Gr. *kalogeros*, a monk; *kalos*, beautiful, good, and *gēras*, old age.] a monk of the Eastern Orthodox Church, especially one belonging to the order of St. Basil.
cal′paç, cal′pack, *n.* [Turk. *qālpāk*.] a large, caplike headgear worn in some parts of the Near East: also spelled *kalpak*.
calque, *v.t.* same as *calk* (to copy).
cal′sŏns, *n.pl.* hose; drawers. [Obs.]
cal′trŏp, cal′trăp, *n.* [ME. *caltrap*, *calletrappe*, a caltrop, star thistle; AS. *coltræppe*, *calcatrippe*, a star-thistle, caltrop; LL. *calcatrippa*; *calx*, heel, and *trappa*, a snare.]
1. a device with four iron points arranged in a triangular form, so that, three of them being on the ground, the other points upward: used formerly to impede the progress of advancing enemy cavalry.

CALTROP

2. a similar device with hollow spikes that puncture pneumatic tires passing over them.
3. in botany, any of several herbaceous plants, so called because their stout spines resemble the military *caltrop*; as, (a) the star thistle, *Centaurea Calcitrapa*; (b) the water caltrop, *Trapa natans*; (c) the land caltrop, *Tribulus terrestris*.
cȧ·lum′bȧ, *n.* same as *columbo*.
cȧ·lum′bin, *n.* same as *columbin*.
cal′ū·met, *n.* [Fr. *calumet*, a reed pipe; dim. of OFr. *chalemel*; LL. *calamellus*, dim. of L. *calamus*, a reed.] among American Indians, a tobacco pipe having a bowl made of soft red stone and a long reed for the stem, usually ornamented with many feathers. It was smoked as a symbol of peace, as a mark of welcome to strangers, etc.

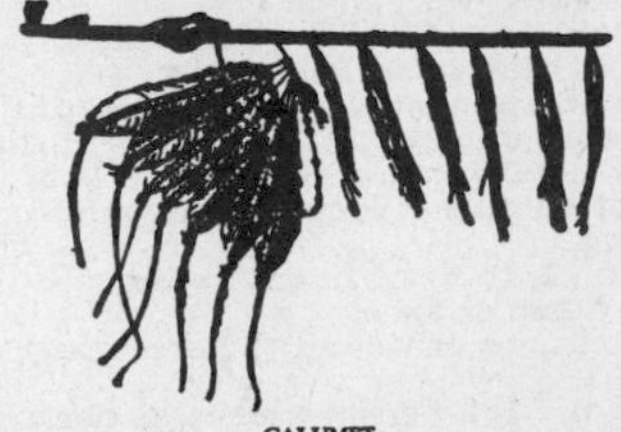
CALUMET

cȧ·lum′ni·āte, *v.t.* and *v.i.*; calumniated, *pt.*, *pp.*; calumniating, *ppr.* [L. *calumniatus*, pp. of *calumniari*, to slander; *calumnia*, slander.] to accuse or charge (a person) falsely and knowingly with some crime or offense; to slander.

ca·lum·ni·ā'tion, *n.* 1. a false accusation of a crime or offense; a calumny.
2. a calumniating; slandering.
ca·lum'ni·ā·tŏr, *n.* one who calumniates.
ca·lum'ni·ā·tō"ry, *a.* slanderous.
ca·lum'ni·ous, *a.* slanderous; bearing or implying calumny; injurious to reputation.
ca·lum'ni·ous·ly, *adv.* slanderously.
ca·lum'ni·ous·ness, *n.* slanderousness.
cal'um·ny, *n.* [Fr. *calomnie*; L. *calumnia*, trickery, slander; from *calvi*, to deceive.]
1. slander; a false accusation of a crime or offense, knowingly or maliciously made to hurt someone's reputation.
Neglected *calumny* soon expires.
—Tacitus.
2. slander.
Syn.—traducement, aspersion, slander, defamation, detraction, libel, backbiting, opprobrium.
cal·vā'ri·ȧ, *n.* [L.] the upper, domed part of the skull.
cal·vā'ri·ăn, *a.* of or pertaining to the calvaria.
cal·vā'ri·um, *n.* same as *calvaria*.
Cal'vȧ·ry, *n.* [L. *calvaria*, a skull, from *calva*, a scalp without hair.]
1. in the Bible, the place where Jesus was crucified, on a small hill west of Jerusalem; Golgotha: Luke xxiii. 33; Matt. xxvii. 33.
2. [c–]; *pl.* **cal'vȧ·ries,** a series of pictures or statues, representing the fourteen stations of the cross, placed in a church or chapel; also, the church or chapel containing such a representation.
3. [c–]; *pl.* **cal'vȧ·ries,** a representation of the crucifixion of Jesus, consisting of the three crosses erected in the open air, often upon an elevation.
calve (kȧv), *v.i.* and *v.t.*; calved, *pt.*, *pp.*; calving, *ppr.* [ME. *calven*; AS. *cealfian*, from *cealf*, a calf.]
1. to give birth to (a calf).
2. to release or throw off from itself; as, a glacier *calves* in producing an iceberg.
cal'vĕr, *v.t.* 1. to cut in slices. [Obs.]
2. to prepare (fish) as by crimping or by spicing and pickling. [Obs.]
calves (kȧvz), *n.* pl. of *calf*.
calves' snout, the snapdragon, *Antirrhinum majus*: so called from the appearance of its seed vessels.
Cal'vin·ism, *n.* the religious system of John Calvin (1509–1564), French Protestant reformer. The distinguishing doctrines of this system are predestination, particular redemption, total depravity, irresistible grace, and the certain perseverance of the saints.
Cal'vin·ist, *n.* 1. a follower of Calvin; one who believes in the theological doctrines of Calvin.
2. a dogmatist.
Cal'vin·ist, *a.* of or like Calvin, Calvinism, or Calvinists.
Cal·vin·is'tic, Cal·vin·is'tic·ăl, *a.* 1. pertaining to Calvin or Calvinism.
2. like a Calvinist; dogmatic.
Cal'vin·ize, *v.t.* to convert to Calvinism.
calv'ish (kȧv'), *a.* like a calf.
cal·vi'ti·ēs (-vish'i-ēz), *n.* [L., from *calvus*, bald.] baldness.
cal'vi·ty, *n.* baldness. [Rare.]
calx, *n.*; *pl.* **calx'ēs** or **cal'cēs,** [L. *calx*, a small stone, lime.]
1. lime or chalk. [Obs.]
2. the ashy powder which remains after calcination of a mineral by heat, or solution by acid. Metallic *calxes* are now called oxides.
3. glass fragments or refuse, returned to the melting pot.
Cal"y·can·thā'cē·ae, *n.pl.* [L., from Gr. *kalyx*, *kalykos*, a cup, and *anthos*, a flower.] a family including two genera of shrublike plants, having two seed lobes, with large sweet-scented blossoms. These plants grow in eastern Asia and the United States.
cal"y·can·thā'ceous, *a.* of or pertaining to the family *Calycanthaceæ*.
cal·y·can'thē·mous, *a.* [Gr. *kalyx* (*-ykos*), a calyx, and *anthemon*, a flower.] having petal-like sepals.
cal·y·can'thē·my, *n.* the conversion, wholly or partially, of sepals into petals.
Cal·y·can'thus, *n.* 1. a genus of North American shrubs having two species, *Calycanthus floridus* being the Carolina allspice.
2. [c–] any plant of this genus.
cal'y·cāte, *a.* [L. *calyx*, *calycis*, a calyx.] provided with a calyx.
cal'y·cēs, *n.* alternative plural of *calyx*.
cal·y·cif'ĕr·ous, *a.* calyx-bearing.
ca·lyc·i·flō'răl, ca·lyc·i·flō'rous, *a.* calyciflorate.
ca·lyc·i·flō'rāte, *a.* [L. *calyx* (*-ycis*), a calyx, and *flos*, *floris*, a flower.] having the calyx bearing the petals and stamens.
ca·lyc'i·form, *a.* in biology, calyx-shaped; resembling a calyx.
cal'y·cine, ca·lyc'i·năl, *a.* relating to a calyx; situated on, adjacent to, or having a resemblance to a calyx.
cal'y·cle (-kl), *n.* [L. *calyculus*, dim. of *calyx*, a calyx.]
1. in botany, an outer accessory calyx, or set of leaflets or bracts looking like a calyx, as in the pink.
2. in zoology, a calyculus.
cal'y·coid, cal·y·coid'ē·ous, *a.* [L. *calyx*; Gr. *kalyx* (*-ykos*), a calyx, cup, and Gr. *eidos*, form.] in biology, resembling a calyx in any manner.
Cal"y·cō·zō'ȧ, *n.pl.* [L., from Gr. *kalyx* (*-ykos*), a calyx, cup, and *zōon*, an animal.] a group of animals, the *Lucernaria*, characterized by cup-shaped bodies, having little differentiation of the digestive system.
ca·lyc'ū·lăr, *a.* pertaining to a calycle.
ca·lyc'ū·lāte, ca·lyc'ū·lā·ted, *a.* having calyx-shaped bracts.
cal'y·cūle, *n.* same as *calycle*.
ca·lyc'ū·lus, *n.*; *pl.* **ca·lyc'ū·lī,** in anatomy and zoology, a small, cuplike part, as a taste bud.
Cal·y·dō'ni·ăn, *a.* of Calydon, an ancient Greek city.
Cal·y·dō'ni·ăn bōar, in Greek mythology, a boar sent by Artemis to scourge the fields of Calydon: it was finally killed by Meleager.
Ca·lym'e·nē, *n.* [Gr. *kekalymmenē*, concealed; pp. of *kalyptein*, to conceal.] a genus of trilobites found in the Silurian rocks.
ca·lym'nȧ, *n.* [Gr. *kalymma*, a covering, from *kalyptein*, to hide.] the adhering, jellylike covering of the protoplasmic body of radiolarians.
cal'yŏn, *n.* a pebble or flint. [Obs.]
Ca·lyp'sō, *n.* [L., from Gr. *Kalypsō*, a nymph in Greek mythology.]
1. a genus of orchids found in bogs, bearing on each stem a single white flower with purple or yellow markings. It has one species, *Calypso borealis*, a small tuberous plant found in high latitudes throughout the northern hemisphere.
2. [c–] any plant of this genus.
3. in Homer's *Odyssey*, a sea nymph who detained Odysseus for seven years on an island.
ca·lyp'sō, *n.* a song or music on any of several themes, improvised and sung by the natives of Trinidad: they are lively ballads, often on political, sexual, or humorous themes, characterized by wrenched syllabic stress, loose rhyme, and journalistic language.
ca·lyp'sō, *a.* designating or of calypso songs or calypso music.
ca·lyp'trȧ, *n.* [Gr. *kalyptra*, a veil, from *kalyptein*, to cover.] a hoodlike covering; specifically, in botany, the remains of the female sex organ, archegonium, of a moss, forming the caplike covering of a spore case.
ca·lyp'tri·form, *a.* [L. *calyptra*, a hood, and *forma*, form.] having the form of a calyptra.
ca·lyp'trō·gen, *n.* [Gr. *kalyptra*, a veil, covering, and *genēs*, producing.] in botany, the layer of cells from which the rootcap develops.
cā'lyx, *n.*; *pl.* **cā'lyx·es** or **cal'y·cēs,** [L. *calyx*; Gr. *kalyx*, a calyx, cup.]
1. the outer covering of a flower external to the corolla, which it encloses, and consisting of a whorl of leaves, or sepals, usually of a green color and less delicate texture than the corolla.
2. in anatomy, a membranous sac, enclosing each papilla of the kidney, opening at its apex into the pelvis of the kidney.
cal'zoons, cal'sounds, *n.pl.* calsons. [Obs.]
cam, *n.* [ME. *camb*; AS. *camb*; D. *kam*; G. *kamm*, a comb, ridge.]
1. a ridge or long elevation of earth. [Brit. Dial.]
2. a moving piece of machinery, such as a wheel, the projecting part of a wheel or curved plate, etc., so shaped as to cause an eccentric or alternating motion of any required velocity or direction in another piece engaging or meeting it.

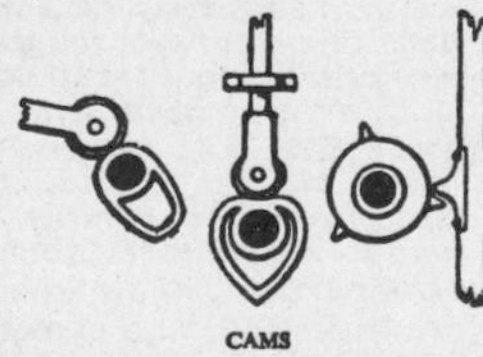
CAMS

cam, kam, *a.* [Gael. and Ir. *cam*, crooked.] awry; bent; crooked. [Obs.]
ca·māi'eu, *n.* [Fr., from ML. *cammaeus*.]
1. a cameo.
2. in the fine arts, monochrome painting, or painting with a single color, varied only by the effect of chiaroscuro.
3. a method of printing pictures to make them resemble drawings.
ca·māil', *n.* [Fr.]
1. in ancient armor, a guard for the neck, hanging from the headpiece and made of chain mail.
2. a furred tippet formerly worn by the Roman Catholic clergy.
Ca·mal'dō·līte, *n.* a member of a fraternity of monks founded in Camaldoli in the Apennines in the eleventh century by St. Romuald, a Benedictine monk.
Cam·al·dū'li·ăn, Ca·mal·dūle', *n.* same as *Camaldolite*.
cam'ȧ·rȧ, *n.* [from native Guiana name.] a durable wood obtained from the tonka-bean tree or others of the same genus.
ca·mȧ·rȧ·de·riē', *n.* [Fr., from *camarade*, a comrade.] intimate, loyal, and good-spirited comradeship; good-fellowship.
Cam"ȧ·rȧ·sau'rus, *n.* [L., from Gr. *kamara*, a vaulted chamber, and *sauros*, a lizard.] a genus of huge American Jurassic dinosaurs, characterized by cavities in the vertebrae.
cam·ȧ·ril'lȧ (*or* -rēl'yȧ), *n.* [Sp.]
1. a small meeting room; private chamber.
2. any of various, notorious groups of confidential advisers to former Spanish monarchs.
3. a group of secret or confidential advisers to anyone in authority; cabal; clique.
cam'ăss, cam'ăs, *n.* the *Camassia esculenta*, a blue-flowered lily of the northwestern United States; also, its sweet, edible bulb.
Ca·mas'si·ȧ, *n.* a genus of North American plants, resembling the lily and having edible bulbed roots: called also *Quamasia*.
ca·ma'tȧ, *n.* the half-grown acorns of a species of oak tree, which are used for tanning.
cam·bāye', *n.* [named from *Cambay*, India.] a kind of Indian cotton cloth.
cam'bĕr, *n.* [Fr. *cambrer*, to arch, to vault, to bend; L. *camerare*, from *camera*, an arch, vault.]
1. in architecture, the convexity of a beam on its upper surface.
2. a slight convex curve of a surface, as of a road.
3. in aeronautics, the slight arch in the surface of a wing or other airfoil.
cam'bĕr, *v.t.* and *v.i.* to arch slightly; to curve convexly.
cam'bĕr bēam, a beam arched or curved upward.
cam'bĕr deck, a deck which is higher in the middle, or arched.
cam'bĕr-keeled, *a.* having the keel slightly arched, but not hogged.
cam'bĕr win'dōw, a window arched or curved at the top.
cam'bi·ăl, *a.* [LL. *cambialis*, from *cambire*, to exchange.] pertaining to cambium.
cam'bi·form, *a.* [LL. *cambium*, exchange, and *forma*, form.] resembling cambium cells in shape.
cam"bi·ō·ġe·net'ic, *a.* [LL. *cambium*, exchange, cambium, and L. *genesis*, from Gr. *gignesthai*, to beget.] yielding or forming cambium cells.
cam'bist, *n.* [Fr. *cambiste*; It. *cambista*, from L. *cambire*, to exchange.]
1. one who deals in bills of exchange, or is skilled in the science of exchange or finance.
2. a book that gives the rates of foreign exchange and equivalents of measures, weights, etc.
cam'bist·ry, *n.* the science of exchange in finance.
cam'bi·um, *n.* [LL., change.]
1. in botany, the layer of tissue between the bark and wood in woody plants, from which new wood and bark develop.
2. exchange of property. [Obs.]
3. a body fluid formerly supposed to repair waste of tissue. [Obs.]
cam'blet, *n.* came as *camlet*.
cam·bōge', *n.* same as *gamboge*.
cam·bō'ġi·ȧ, *n.* [from *Cambodia*, a state of French Indo-China.] gamboge, a yellow gum resin extracted from certain Asiatic trees.
cam·boose', *n.* same as *caboose*.
cam'brȧ·sine, *n.* [Fr.] a fine linen made in Egypt.
cam'brel, *n.* same as *gambrel*.
Cam'bri·ȧ, *n.* [ML.; var. of ML. *Cumbria*, from base of O.Celt. *Combroges*, lit., co-land-

ers, whence Celt. *Cymry*, Britons of the West, Welshmen.] Wales. [Poetic.]

Çam′bri·ăn, *a.* 1. pertaining to Wales.
2. designating or of the first geological period in the Paleozoic Era, marked by the appearance of the first simple marine animal and plant life, as shown by fossils found in Wales and Cumberland.

Çam′bri·ăn, *n.* 1. a native or inhabitant of Wales.
2. in geology, the Cambrian period.

çām′briç, *n.* [from *Cambrai*, a town in France.]
1. a kind of fine white linen cloth.
2. a cotton imitation of such a cloth.

çām′briç gràss, the ramie plant.

çām′briç tēa, a hot drink made of weak tea, milk, and sugar.

Çam′brō Brit′ŏn, a native of Wales.

çam·bū′çà, *n.* [LL.] a pastoral staff; also, a golf club.

çāme, past tense of *come*.

çāme, *n.* [Scot. *came*, *caim*, comb.] a slender grooved rod of lead, used to fasten together panes of glass, tile, etc.

çam′el, *n.* [OFr. *camel*; L. *camelus*; Gr. *kamēlos*; Heb. *gāmāl*, a camel.]
1. a large, domesticated, four-footed animal with a humped back: there are two species, the *Camelus dromedarius*, the dromedary, or Arabian camel (with one hump), and *Camelus bactrianus*, or Bactrian camel (with two humps). Both species are long-necked and have broad, cushioned feet and pouches in the paunch to store up water. The camel is valuable as a beast of burden especially in Asian and African deserts.
2. a watertight cylinder used for raising sunken ships.

çam′el-backed (-bakt), *a.* having a back like a camel; humpbacked.

çam′el bĩrd, the African ostrich.

çam′el·çāde, *n.* a group of persons mounted on camels.

çam′el çōrps (kōr), a military cavalcade mounted on camels.

çam′el çrick′et, the camel insect.

çam·el·eer′, *n.* the driver of a camel.

çam′el gràss, a sweet-scented grass or hay, *Andropogon schœnanthus*, or an allied species.

çam′el-hãir, *a.* camel's-hair.

Çam·e·lī′nà, *n.* [L., irregularly formed from Gr. *chamai*, on the ground, and *linon*, flax.] a genus of plants of the mustard family: the species *sativa* is the gold-of-pleasure.

çam′e·line, *n.* a plant belonging to the genus *Camelina*.

çam′el in′seçt, the mantis.

Çà·mel′li·à, *n.* [after George Joseph *Kamel* (d. 1706), a Moravian Jesuit missionary.]
1. a genus of trees or shrubs, family *Ternstrœmiaceæ*, with red or white, rose-shaped flowers and laurellike leaves, allied to the plants which yield tea.
2. (*or* kà-mēl′yà), [c–] any plant of this genus; specifically, *Camellia japonica*; also, its flower.

CAMELLIA (*Camellia japonica*)

çà·mel′ō·pärd (*or* kam′el-ō-pärd), *n.* [LL. *camelopardus*; L. *camelopardalus*; Gr. *kamēlopardalis*; *kamēlos*, a camel, and *pardalis*, a pard, leopard.]
1. the giraffe.
2. [C–] a northern constellation situated between Ursa Major and Cassiopeia.

Çam′e·lot, *n.* the legendary English town where King Arthur had his court and Round Table.

çam′el·ry, *n.* 1. troops having camels for mounts.
2. a depot for the handling of goods to be transported by camels.

çam′el's hãir, 1. the hair of the camel.
2. cloth made of this hair, sometimes mixed with wool or other fiber: it is usually light tan and very soft.

çam′el's-hãir, *a.* made of camel's hair or a similar material.
camel's-hair brush or *pencil*; a small, fine brush for artists, made of the tail hairs of the squirrel.
camel's-hair shawl; a cashmere shawl.

çam′el's thorn, a spiny leguminous shrub, *Alhagi camelorum*, on which the camel feeds, and which yields a sweet, gummy juice from its leaves and branches.

Çam′em·bert cheese (-ber), [from district near *Camembert*, France.] a soft, creamy kind of cheese.

Çà·mē′nae, *n.pl.* in Roman mythology, nymphs having prophetic powers who inhabited springs and fountains: later identified with the Greek Muses.

çam′en·ēs, *n.* in logic, a mnemonic word to express a syllogism in the fourth figure having one universal affirmative and one universal negative premise and a universal negative conclusion.

çam′ē·ō, *n.* [It. *cameo*, *cammeo*, from LL. *cammæus*, a cameo; a word of uncertain origin.]
1. a gem having two layers, with a figure carved in one layer so that it is raised on a background of the other.
2. a carving made in this way: opposed to *intaglio*.

çam′ē·ō çonch, any marine shell used in cameos, as the queen conch.

çam′ẽr·à, *n.*; *pl.* **çam′ẽr·às, çam′ẽr·ae,** [L. *camera*, *camara*, a vault; Gr. *kamara*, a vaulted chamber.]
1. a chamber; specifically, the private office of a judge.
2. a device for taking photographs, the essentials of which are a closed box, a lens, or combination of lenses, and means for holding a sensitized plate or film so as to receive and record rays of light passing through the lens, thus fixing an image of the object in focus.

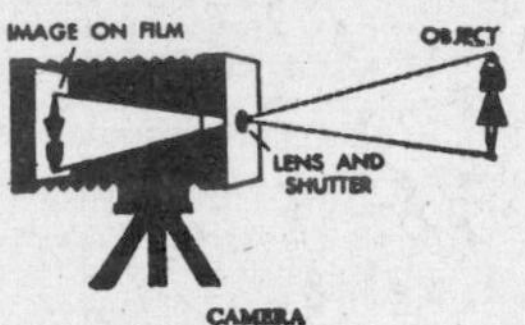

CAMERA

3. a camera obscura.
4. in television, that part of the transmitter which consists of a lens and a special cathode-ray tube containing a plate on which the image to be televised is projected for transformation into a flow of electrons.
in camera; (a) in a judge's private office; (b) privately.

çame′rade, *n.* a comrade. [Obs.]

çam′ẽr·ȧl, *a.* [G. *kameral*, from ML. *cameralis*; L. *camera*, a camera.]
1. of a chamber.
2. of a council that manages public business.

çam″ẽr·ȧl·is′tiç, *a.* [Fr. *cameralistique*, from It. *camerale*; LL. *camera*, a chamber; L. *camera*, a vault.] pertaining to finance and public revenue.

çam″ẽr·ȧl·is′tiçs, *n.* the science of public finance.

çam′ẽr·à lū′ci·dà, [L., light chamber.] an apparatus containing a prism or an arrangement of mirrors for reflecting an object on a surface so that its outline may be traced: often used with a microscope.

çam′ẽr·à·man″, *n.*; *pl.* **çam′ẽr·à·men″,** one who operates a motion-picture camera, or any other camera.

çam′ẽr·à ob·sçū′rà, [L., dark chamber.] a camera consisting of a dark chamber with a lens or opening through which an image is projected in natural colors onto an opposite surface: used in drawing, exhibits, etc.

çam′ẽr·āte, *v.t.*; camerated, *pt.*, *pp.*; camerating, *ppr.* [L. *cameratus*, pp. of *camerare*, to arch over; from *camera*, a vault.] to build in vaults or chambers; to arch. [Rare.]

çam·ẽr·ā′tion, *n.* an arching, or vaulting.

çam·ẽr·leñ′gō, *n.* a camerlingo.

çam·ẽr·liñ′gō, *n.* [It., a chamberlain, from L. *camera*, a chamber.] in the Roman Catholic Church, a cardinal who has charge of the papal treasury and accounts: the papal chamberlain.

Çam·ẽr·ō′ni·ȧn, *a.* of Richard Cameron, Scottish Covenanter (?–1680), his beliefs, or his followers.

Çam·ẽr·ō′ni·ȧn, *n.* any of the followers of Richard Cameron; a member of the Reformed Presbyterian Church.

çà·mes′trēs, *n.* in logic, a mnemonic word to express a syllogism in the second figure, its special nature being indicated by each letter of the word.

çam gēar, a gear not centered on the shaft, used where discontinuous action is required.

çà·mioṅ′, *n.* [Fr. *camion*, dray or truck.]
1. a truck for the transportation of heavy artillery.
2. a dray.

çam·i·sā′dō, çam·i·sāde′, *n.* [Fr. *camisade*, from OFr. *camise*, a shirt.]
1. a shirt worn by soldiers over their armor in a night attack to enable them to recognize each other. [Archaic.]
2. a surprise attack at night, originally one in which shirts were worn over armor. [Archaic.]

Çam′i·särd, *n.* [Fr.] one of the French Calvinists of the Cevennes in revolt, 1688–1705.

çam′i·sā·ted, *a.* wearing an outer shirt. [Obs.]

çà·mīse′, çam′is, çà·mēse′, *n.* [OFr. *camise*; LL. *camisia*, a shirt, tunic.] a loose-fitting shirt or tunic; a dressing gown.

çam′i·sōle, *n.* 1. a short light garment worn by women as a dressing gown.
2. a woman's loose underwaist or corset cover.
3. formerly, a kind of jacket for men.
4. a straitjacket.

çam′let, *n.* [Fr. *camelot*; LL. *camelotum*; Ar. *khamlat*, camlet, from *khaml*, pile, plush.]
1. an Oriental cloth made of camel's hair and silk.
2. a similar fabric of silk and wool.
3. clothing made of either of these fabrics.

çam′mȧs, *n.* the camass.

çam′mŏck, *n.* [AS. *cammoc*, a plant.] a plant, *Ononis arvensis*, the rest-harrow.

çam′ō·mīle, çham′ō·mīle, *n.* [OFr. *camamille*; L. *chamomilla*; Gr. *chamaimēlon*, earth apple; *chamai*, ground, and *mēlon*, an apple.] any of several plants of the aster family, having flowers of a strong fragrance and a bitter taste. The dried leaves, flowers, and buds of the common camomile, *Anthemis nobilis*, are used in medicine.

CAMOMILE (*Anthemis nobilis*)

Çà·mor′rȧ, *n.* [It., assault with violence.]
1. an Italian secret society. organized in Naples, c. 1820, ostensibly for political purposes: it later became notorious for extortion and violence.
2. [c–] any secret society like this.

Çà·mor′rist, *n.* 1. a member of the Camorra.
2. [c–] a member of a secret society.

çam′ou·flāge (-flązh), *n.* [Fr. *camoufler*, to disguise.]
1. the process of disguising or changing the appearance of troops, ships, guns, etc. by paint, nets, leaves, etc. to conceal them from the enemy.
2. a disguise of this sort.
3. any device used to conceal; a deception.

çam′ou·flāge, *v.t* and *v.i.* camouflaged, *pt.*, *pp.*; camouflaging, *ppr.* to disguise or conceal (a thing or person) by changing the appearance.

çà·mou·flet′ (-flā′), *n.* [Fr.] a mine with a small charge that will cause damage but not produce any crater: also called a *stifler*.

çà·mou·fleur′ (-flũr′), *n.* one employed or skilled in camouflage.

çamp, *v.i.*; camped, *pt.*, *pp.*; camping, *ppr.*
1. to rest or lodge, as an army; to pitch tents, or to live in them.
2. to live as if in a camp, without conveniences or comforts.

çamp, *v.t.* 1. to supply with lodging accommodations, as travelers or an army.
2. to put into camp.

çamp, *n.* [Fr. *camp,* a camp; L. *campus,* a field.]
1. the ground upon which tents or other temporary structures are put up for the lodging of an army, or a smaller body of people, such as lumbermen, miners, etc.
2. the persons lodging in such a place.
3. a scene of preparation for war.
4. (a) a group of tents, huts, etc. used for temporary lodging; (b) a tent, cabin, or the like, used for outings or vacations.
5. a place in the country for vacationers or children, with facilities for recreation, as swimming, riding, etc., often organized and supervised.
6. (a) a group of people who support or advance a common opinion, cause, etc.; (b) the position taken by such a group.
7. [orig., homosexual jargon.] banality, mediocrity, artifice, ostentation, etc. so extreme as to amuse or have a perversely sophisticated appeal. [Slang.]
in the same camp; in agreement.
to break camp; to dismantle a camp; to pack up camping equipment and go away.
to pitch camp; to erect the tents for an army, or other body of men.

çamp, *a.* characterized by camp (sense 7). [Slang.]

Çam·pä′gnä (-nyä), *n.* [It., from L. *campus,* field.]
1. the plain around Rome.
2. [c–] a level plain.

çȧm·pȧ·gnol′ (-nyol′), *n.* [Fr., from *campagne,* field.] a species of field rat or vole, the *Arvicola arvalis* or *agrestis.*

çam·pāign′ (-pān′), *n.* [Fr. *campaigne, campagne,* an open field, military expedition; LL. *campania,* level country; L. *campus,* a field.]
1. a series of military operations with a particular objective.
2. a series of organized, planned actions for a particular purpose, as for electing a candidate.
3. the time during which a blast furnace is continuously operated.

çam·pāign′, *v.i.*; campaigned, *pt., pp.*; campaigning, *ppr.* to serve in a campaign.

çam·pāign′ẽr, *n.* one who campaigns or has served in several campaigns.

çam·pä′nȧ, *n.* [LL. and It. *campana,* a bell.]
1. a church bell.
2. in botany, the pasqueflower.
3. in archaeology, one of the drops, or guttae, of the Doric architrave.

çam·pāne′, *n.* [Fr. *campane*; LL. *campana,* a bell.] in heraldry, a bell.

çam·pāned′, *a.* in heraldry, bearing bells.

çam·pȧ·nē′rō, *n.* [Sp., a bellman, from *campana,* a bell.] the South American bellbird.

çam·pan′i·form, *a.* [LL. *campana,* a bell, and *forma,* form.] shaped like a bell.

çam·pȧ·nī′lē, *n.*; *pl.* **çam·pȧ·nī′lēs, çam·pȧ·nī′li,** [It. *campanile,* from LL. *campana,* a bell.] a bell tower: a term applied especially to a detached building near a church, erected for the purpose of containing bells.

CAMPANILE

çam·pȧ·nil′i·form, *a.* campaniform.

çam·pȧ·nol′ō·ġist, *n.* a bell ringer; one practiced in campanology.

çam·pȧ·nol′ō·ġy, *n.* [LL. *campana,* a bell, and Gr. *logia,* from *legein,* to speak.]
1. the art of ringing bells.
2. the study of bells.

Çam·pan′ū·lȧ, *n.* [LL. *campanula,* dim. of *campana,* a bell.]
1. a genus of plants bearing bell-shaped flowers.
2. [c–] any plant of this genus.

Çam·pan·ū·lā′cē·ae, *n.pl.* the bellflower family of monopetalous, dicotyledonous plants, having bell-shaped flowers of blue, pink, or white.

çam·pan·ū·lā′ceous, *a.* pertaining to the *Campanulaceæ.*

Çam·pan·ū·lā′ri·ȧ, *n.pl.* a genus of zoophytes in which the polyp is protected by a bell-shaped footstalk.

çam·pan·ū·lā′ri·ăn, *n.* one of the *Campanulariidæ.*

Çam·pan″ū·lȧ·rī′i·dae, *n.pl.* a family of hydroids having the polyps protected by a campanulate calycle.

çam·pan′ū·lāte, *a.* [L. *campanula,* dim. of *campana,* a bell.] having the form of a bell.

çamp bed, a bed having a light folding frame.

Çamp′bell·īte (kam′), *n.* 1. a member of the denomination more properly called Disciples of Christ, founded by Alexander Campbell (1788–1866), of Virginia.
2. a follower of Rev. John McLeod Campbell, deposed from the ministry in 1831 for teaching universal atonement. [Scot.]

çamp cēil′ing, in architecture, a ceiling formed by an inclination of the wall on each side toward the plane surface in the middle.

çamp chāir, a lightweight folding chair, often with canvas seat and back.

çamp′çrȧft, *n.* the art or practice of camping outdoors.

çam·pēa′chy wood, [after *Campeche,* Mexico.] logwood.

çamp′ẽr, *n.* one who camps.

çäm″pe·sī′nō, *n.*; pl. **çäm″pe·sī′nōs,** [Sp.] a peasant or farm worker.

çam·pes′trăl, çam·pes′tri·ăn, *a.* [L. *campestris,* from *campus,* a field.]
1. pertaining to an open field.
2. growing in a field, or on open ground.

çamp′fīght, *n.* in English law, a duel fought to decide a case. [Obs.]

çamp′fīre, *n.* 1. an outdoor fire used for cooking, etc., in a camp.
2. a gathering around such a fire for social purposes.

çamp′fīre gīrl, a member of the Camp Fire Girls of America.

Çamp Fīre Gīrls of A·mer′i·çȧ, an organization of girls between the ages of ten and eighteen, founded in 1912 for the purpose of building character and health by co-operation, outdoor activities, etc.

çamp fol′lōw·ẽr, 1. a civilian who goes along with an army to sell goods or services.
2. a prostitute with an army.
3. the wife of a serviceman who follows him in his transfers from post to post.

çamp′ground, *n.* 1. a place where a camp is set up.
2. a place where a camp meeting or religious revival is held.

çam′phēne (*or* kam-fēn′), *n.* [*camph*or, and *-ene.*]
1. a colorless, crystalline compound, $C_{10}H_{16}$, prepared synthetically from pinene and used like camphor.
2. a purified oil of turpentine, obtained by distilling the oil over quicklime to free it from resin.

çam′phīre, *n.* camphor. [Obs.]

çam′phō·ġen, *n.* [LL. *camphora,* camphor, and *-genus,* producing.] a colorless hydrocarbon, $C_{10}H_{14}$, produced by distilling camphor with phosphorous pentoxide; cymene.

çam′phōl, *n.* [*camph*or, and *-ol.*] a kind of camphor obtained from a tree native to Borneo: also called *borneol.*

çam·phol′iç, *a.* relating to camphol.
campholic acid; a volatile substance, white in color, obtained from camphor.

çam′phŏr, *n.* [ME. *camfere*; Fr. *camphre*; Sp. *canfor*; LL. *canfora, camphora*; Ar. *kāfūr*; Sans. *karpūra,* camphor.]
1. a volatile crystalline substance, $C_{10}H_{16}O$, with a strong, characteristic odor, derived chiefly from the wood of the camphor tree: used to protect fabrics from moths, in manufacturing celluloid, and in medicine as an irritant and stimulant.
2. any one of a number of substances resembling camphor; as, borneol.

çam·phō·rā′ceous, *a.* of the nature of camphor.

çam′phŏr·āte, *v.t.*; camphorated, *pt., pp.*; camphorating, *ppr.* to put camphor in or on.

çam′phŏr·āte, *n.* a salt formed by the combination of camphoric acid with a base.

çam′phŏr·āte, *a.* pertaining to camphor, or impregnated with it. [Obs.]

çam′phŏr·ā·ted oil, a solution of camphor in cottonseed oil, used as a liniment.

çam′phŏr ball, a small ball impregnated with camphor, used to protect fabrics from moths.

çam·phor′iç, *a.* of or containing camphor.

çam·phor′iç ac′id, a crystallized acid, produced by the action of hot nitric acid on camphor.

çam′phŏr īce, an ointment made of white wax, camphor, spermaceti, and castor oil.

çam′phŏr lau′rel, the camphor tree.

çam′phŏr oil, any one of various oily products of the camphor tree.

çam′phŏr tree, a large laurel tree, *Cinnamomum camphora,* native to the Far East and Oceania, which yields camphor.

çam′phŏr wood, the wood of the camphor tree.

çam′pi·ŏn, *n.* [prob. from L. *campus,* a plain, a field.] any of various plants of the pink family belonging to the genera *Lychnis* and *Silene.* Bladder campion, having a bladderlike calyx, is *Silene inflata*; red campion or adder's flower, *Lychnis dioica*; rose campion, a handsome garden flower, *Lychnis coronaria.*

çamp meet′ing, a religious outdoor gathering or series of meetings, for preaching, public worship, and revival work.

çam′pō, *n.* [Sp. and It. from L. *campus,* a field.]
1. *pl.* **çam′pōs,** a level, grassy plain in South America, often with scattered plants and small trees.
2. *pl.* **çam′pi,** a small square, or open place, in a town.

çamp·ō·ree′, *n.* [*camp,* and jamb*oree.*] a gathering or assembly of Boy Scouts on the regional or district level: distinguished from *jamboree.*

çam′pō sän′tō, [It., sacred field.] a cemetery.

çamp′stool, *n.* a folding seat or stool.

çamp′tō·drōme, *a.* [Gr. *kamptos,* from *kamptein,* to bend, and *dromos,* course.] pertaining to a system of venation in which the veinlets join after curving near the margin of the leaf.

çam pump, a pump in which a cam imparts motion to the valves.

çam′pus, *n.*; *pl.* **çam′pus·eṣ,** [L. *campus,* a field.]
1. the space or grounds belonging to or enclosed by the buildings of a college or school.
2. an open place or field used by the ancient Romans for military exercises, public assemblies, etc.

çam′pus, *a.* 1. on or of the campus.
2. of the student body; as, *campus* activities.

çam′py·lō·drōme, *a.* [Gr. *kampylos,* curved, and *dromos,* course.] in botany, having a nerve-curvature which terminates at the apex of a leaf.

çam″py·lō·spẽr′mous, *a.* [Gr. *kampylos,* curved, and *sperma,* a seed.] in botany, having the albumen of the seed curved at the margin so as to form a longitudinal furrow, as in the sweet cicely.

çam·py·lot′rō·pous, çam·py·lot′rō·păl, *a.* [Gr. *kampylos,* curved, and *trope,* a turning.] in botany, designating or of curved ovules in which the nucleus is folded over upon itself in the form of the letter U.

çam′shȧft, a shaft of which a cam is an essential part, or to which a cam is fastened.

çam wheel, a wheel formed so as to move eccentrically and produce a reciprocating rectilinear and interrupted motion in some other part of machinery connected with it.

çam′wood, *n.* same as *barwood.*

çan, an obsolete form of *began,* past tense of *begin,* occasionally found in old poetry.
With gentle words he *can* her fairly greet.
—Spenser.

çan, *n.* [AS. *canne*; D. *kan*; G. *kanne,* a can, mug.]
1. a container, usually made of metal, for liquids.
2. a container made of tinned iron or other metal, in which liquids, foods, etc. are sealed for preservation.
3. the contents of a can; a canful.
4. (a) prison; (b) buttocks; (c) toilet. [Slang.]

çan, *v.t.*; canned, *pt., pp.*; canning, *ppr.* 1. to put into a can or cans; to put up in airtight cans or jars for preservation; as, to *can* meat.
2. to make a phonograph record of. [Slang.]
3. to dismiss; to discharge. [Slang.]
4. to dispense with. [Slang.]

çan, *v.i.*; could, *pt.* [AS. *can, cann,* pres. ind. of *cunnan,* to know, be able; D. *kunnen*; G. *können,* to know.]
1. to be able to; to possess the qualities, qualifications, or resources necessary for the attainment of an end or the accomplishment of a purpose.
2. to know how to.
3. to have the right to.
4. to be permitted to; may. [Colloq.]
Can is used both as an auxiliary verb and

as a substitution verb, and is followed by an infinitive without *to*.

Çā'năan·īte, *n.* 1. an inhabitant of the land of Canaan; specifically, one of the inhabitants before the return of the Israelites from Egypt.

2. in the Bible, any person descended from Canaan, the son of Ham.

3. an anti-Roman Jewish zealot.

Çā'năan·it·iç, *a.* of Canaan, its inhabitants, or their language.

Çā'năan·ī·tish, *a.* pertaining to or characteristic of the country or people of Canaan.

Çan'ȧ·dȧ, *a.* 1. of or from Canada.

2. of, from, or connected with the northern parts of North America.

ca·ña'da (kȧ-nyä'dȧ), *n.* [Sp.] a small or narrow canyon; a valley resembling a canyon.

Çan'ȧ·dȧ goose, the largest variety of wild goose of Canada and the northern United States: it is brownish-gray, with black head and neck and a white patch on each side of the face.

Çan'ȧ·dȧ jāy, a North American jay with gray and black feathers and no crest.

Çan'ȧ·dȧ lil'y, a wild lily with small, funnel-shaped, orange-yellow or reddish flowers.

Çan'ȧ·dȧ lynx, a North American lynx, related to but larger than the bobcat.

Çȧ·nā'di·ăn, *a.* pertaining to Canada.

Canadian bacon; cured, smoked pork cut from the loin and back of a pig in a boneless strip: it has a hamlike flavor.

Canadian French; French as spoken by French Canadians, mainly in Quebec and the Maritime Provinces.

Çȧ·nā'di·ăn, *n.* an inhabitant or native of Canada.

çȧ·nāi'gre (-gẽr), *n.* a species of Texan dock, *Rumex hymenosepalus*, the root of which yields an acid used in tanning.

çȧ·nāille' (-nāl'), *n.* [Fr. *canaille*, a mob, pack of dogs; from L. *canis*, a dog.]

1. the lowest class of people; the rabble.

2. shorts, or coarse flour.

çan'ȧ·kin, *n.* a little can or cup.

And let me the *canakin* clink. —Shak.

çȧ·nal', *n.* [Fr. *canal*, from L. *canalis*, a channel, from the same root as Sans. *khan*, to dig.]

1. an artificial watercourse for transportation and irrigation.

2. in architecture, a channel; a groove or a flute.

3. in anatomy and zoology, any cylindrical or tubular structure in the body; a tube; a duct; as, the alimentary *canal*.

4. a river artificially improved by locks, levees, etc. to permit navigation.

5. any of the long, narrow markings on the planet Mars.

çȧ·nal', *v.t.*; canalled *or* canaled, *pt.*, *pp.*; canalling *or* canaling, *ppr.* to build a canal through or across.

çȧ·nal'bōat, *n.* a boat used on canals for carrying freight: it is usually long and narrow.

çan'ăl çōal, same as *cannel coal*.

çan·ȧ·liç'ū·lăr, *a.* [L. *canaliculus*, dim. of *canalis*, a channel, canal.] in anatomy, canaliculate.

çan·ȧ·liç'ū·lāte, çan·ȧ·liç'ū·lā·ted, *a.* [L. *canaliculatus*, from *canaliculus*, little pipe, dim. of *canalis*, a channel, pipe.] channeled; furrowed; specifically, relating to a canaliculus or canaliculi.

çan·ȧ·liç'ū·lus, *n.*; *pl.* **çan·ȧ·liç'ū·lī,** [L., dim. of *canalis*, a channel, pipe.] in anatomy, botany, and zoology, a minute canal or tube.

çan·ȧ·lif'ẽr·ous, *a.* grooved; furrowed.

çȧ·nal''i·zā'tion, *n.* 1. a canalizing.

2. a system or network of canals or channels.

3. the formation of canals in the body tissues, effected naturally or artificially, as sometimes to drain wounds.

4. direction (*of* thought, etc.) into a specific channel or channels.

çȧ·nal'īze, *v.t.*; canalized, *pt.*, *pp.*; canalizing, *ppr.* 1. to make a canal through.

2. to change into a canal; to make resemble a canal.

3. to direct into a specific channel or channels.

4. to give an outlet to.

çȧ·nal' rāyṣ, in physics, rays consisting of positive ions passing through openings in the cathode of a vacuum tube.

ca·na·pé' (kȧ-nȧ-pā'; *Eng.* kan'ȧ-pi), *n.* [Fr.] a toasted piece of bread or a cracker spread with anchovies, spiced meat, cheese, etc., served as an appetizer, often with drinks.

çȧ·närd' (*or* kȧ-när'), *n.* [Fr., a duck, a false newspaper report.]

1. a hoax; especially, an untruthful report; a false statement or rumor.

2. an obsolete type of airplane having the controlling surfaces in front of the main planes and the propeller behind them.

Çan·ȧ·rēse' (*or* -rēz'), *n.* and *a.* same as *Kanarese*.

çan'ȧ·rin, çan'ȧ·rine, *n.* a dye for imparting a permanent bright yellow to various fabrics, prepared by the oxidation of potassium sulfocyanide and potassium sulfate while subjected to hydrochloric and sulfuric acids.

Çȧ·nā'ri·um, *n.* [L., from *canari*, an E. Ind. name.] a genus of plants of the *Amyridaceæ* family, consisting of lofty trees which yield resin or balsam.

çȧ·nā'ry, *n.*; *pl.* **çȧ·nā'rieṣ,** [Sp. *canario*, a bird, a dance; from L. *Canaria insula*, Canary island, so called from its large dogs; L. *canis*, a dog.]

1. wine made in the Canary Islands, resembling madeira.

2. an old Spanish dance.

3. the canary bird.

4. canary yellow.

çȧ·nā'ry, *a.* of or pertaining to the color of a canary; of a light yellow color.

çȧ·nā'ry, *v.i.* to dance; to frolic; to perform the old dance called the canary. [Obs.]

çȧ·nā'ry bīrd, a small, yellow singing bird of the finch family, from the Canary Islands, Madeira, and the Azores, the *Carduelis canaria*, or *Fringilla canaria*: it is one of the most common cage birds.

canary-bird flower; same as *canary vine*.

çȧ·nā'ry finch, same as *canary bird*.

çȧ·nā'ry grȧss, a plant, *Phalaris canariensis*, native to the Canary Islands, the seeds of which are used as food for birds.

çȧ·nā'ry mȯss, any of various lichens from which a rich violet dye is obtained: also called *canary weed*.

çȧ·nā'ry seed, grass seed used as food for canary birds.

çȧ·nā'ry stōne, a rare variety of carnelian: so named from its yellow color.

çȧ·nā'ry vīne, a tropical climbing or trailing plant, *Tropæolum peregrinum*, bearing yellow flowers: called also *canary-bird flower*.

çȧ·nā'ry wood, the wood of the trees *Persea indica* and *Persea canariensis*, light orange in color and having a straight, coarse grain.

çȧ·nā'ry yel'lōw, a light yellow.

çȧ·nas'tȧ, *n.* [Sp., basket.] a card game for two to six players, using a double deck of cards.

çȧ·nas'tẽr, *n.* [Fr. *canastre*; L. *canastrum*; Gr. *kanastron*, a wicker basket.]

1. the rush basket in which tobacco is packed in South America.

2. a tobacco for smoking, formerly imported in rush baskets, consisting of the dried leaves, coarsely broken.

çan'çan, *n.* [Fr.] a gay, wild dance, originating in France and characterized by much high kicking.

çan'cel, *v.t.*; canceled *or* cancelled, *pt.*, *pp.*; canceling *or* cancelling, *ppr.* [Fr. *canceller*; L. *cancellare*, to make like a lattice; to strike out a writing by drawing lines across.]

1. to draw lines across so as to deface; to blot out or obliterate.

2. to annul or make invalid; to throw aside; as, to *cancel* an obligation or a debt.

Know then, I here forget all former griefs,
Cancel all grudge. —Shak.

3. to do away with; to abolish.

4. to neutralize; to balance (often with *out*).

5. in mathematics, to strike out (a common factor), as from the numerator and denominator of a fraction; as, by *canceling* 2 in the fraction $^4/_6$ we obtain the equivalent fraction $^2/_3$.

6. in printing, to delete or omit.

Syn.—to blot out, obliterate, deface, erase, efface, expunge, annul, abolish, revoke, abrogate, repeal, destroy, set aside.

çan'cel, *v.i.* to balance (with *out*).

çan'cel, *n.* [Sp. *cancel*; L. *cancelli* (pl.), latticework, grating.]

1. latticework, or one of the crossbars in latticework; hence, a barrier; a limit. [Obs.]

2. in printing, (a) the deletion or omission of matter; (b) the matter so deleted or omitted; (c) the replacement for this.

çan·cel·eer', çan·cel·iẽr', *v.i.* [OFr. *canceler*, to waver, to cross the legs so as not to fall.] in falconry, to turn two or three times on the wing before seizing, as a hawk, especially when it misses.

çan·cel·eer', çan·cel·iẽr', *n.* the canceleering of a hawk.

çan'cel·ẽr, çan'cel·lẽr, *n.* a person or thing that cancels.

çan·cel·lā'rē·ăn, *a.* [LL. *cancellarius*, a chancellor, an officer in charge of records.] relating to a chancellor, or his position. [Rare.]

çan·cel·lā'rē·āte, *a.* same as *cancellarean*.

çan'cel·lāte, *a.* [L. *cancellatus*, pp. of *cancellare*, to make like a lattice.]

1. consisting of a network of veins, without intermediate tissue, as the leaves of certain plants.

2. in anatomy, cancellous.

çan'cel·lā·ted, *a.* cancellate.

çan·cel·lā'tion, *n.* 1. a canceling or being canceled.

2. something canceled.

3. the mark showing that something is canceled.

çan·cel'lī, *n.pl.* [L., a lattice.] latticework; specifically, (a) in churches, the latticework partition between the choir and the nave of the church; (b) in anatomy, the latticelike cellular or spongy texture of bones.

çan'cel·lous, *a.* in anatomy, having a latticelike structure: said of the spongy part of bones.

Çan'cẽr, *n.* [L. *cancer*, *cancri*, a crab, an ulcer; Gr. *karkinos*, a crab.]

1. the crab genus.

2. a northern constellation between Gemini and Leo, supposedly resembling a crab in shape.

3. in astronomy, the fourth sign of the zodiac, entered by the sun about June 22.

4. [c-] in medicine, a malignant new growth anywhere in the body of a person or animal; a malignant tumor: cancers tend to spread and ulcerate.

5. anything bad or harmful that spreads and destroys.

çan'cẽr·āte, *v.i.* to grow into a cancer; to become cancerous.

çan·cẽr·ā'tion, *n.* a growing cancerous, or into a cancer.

çan'cẽr·īte, *n.* [L. *cancer*, a crab.] a fossil crab.

çan'cẽr·ous, *a.* [LL. *cancerosus*, from *cancer*, a crab.] of, like, or having cancer.

çan'cẽr·ous·ly, *adv.* in the manner of a cancer.

çan'cẽr·ous·ness, *n.* the state of being cancerous.

çan'cẽr·rȯȯt, *n.* a species of herbs of the broomrape family, parasitic on the roots of trees.

çan'cẽr·weed, *n.* same as *rattlesnake root*.

çan'cẽr·wŏrt, *n.* the toadflax.

çan·chȧ·lä'guä, *n.* [Sp.] the herbaceous plant *Erythræa Chilensis*, of Chile; also, a plant of the species *venusta*, of the same genus.

çañ'çri·fọrm, *a.* [L. *cancer*, *cancri*, a crab, cancer, and *forma*, form.]

1. cancerous.

2. having the form of a cancer or crab.

çañ'çrine, *a.* having the qualities of a crab.

çañ'çri·nīte, *n.* [named after Count *Cancrin*, a Russian minister of finance.] a silicate closely resembling nephelite.

çañ·çri·sō'ciăl, *a.* [L. *cancer*, *cancri*, a crab, cancer, and *socialis*, from *socius*, a companion.] associated as a commensal with crabs, as the sea anemone.

çañ·çriv'ō·rous, *a.* [L. *cancer*, *cancri*, a crab, and *vorare*, to eat.] feeding on crabs or similar crustaceans.

çañ'çroid, *a.* [L. *cancer*, *cancri*, a crab, and Gr. *eidos*, form.]

1. pertaining to the crab family; also, like a crab.

2. like cancer.

çañ·çroph'ȧ·gous, *a.* same as *cancrivorous*.

çand, *n.* [Corn.] in mineralogy, fluor spar.

çan·dȧ·reen', *n.* a Chinese monetary unit; also, a weight equal to about 5.8 grains troy.

çan·de·lā'brȧ, (*or*-lä'), *n.*; *pl.* **çan·de·lā'brȧṣ,** a candelabrum (sense 2).

çan·de·lā'brum, (*or*-lä'), *n.*; *pl.* **çan·de·lā'brȧ** or **çan·de·lā'brumṣ,** [L. *candelabrum*, from *candela*, a candle, torch.]

1. in antiquity, (a) a tall candlestick often highly ornamented; (b) a stand for supporting lamps.

2. a large, branched candlestick.

çan'dent, *a.* [L. *candens* (*-entis*), ppr. of *candere*, to be white-hot.] very hot; heated to whiteness; glowing with heat.

çan'de·ros, *n.* [E. Ind.] an East Indian gum, of the appearance of amber, but white and clear.

çan·des'cence, *n.* incandescence.

çan·des'cent, *a.* [L. *candescens* (*-entis*), ppr. of *candescere*, to become white or hot.] incandescent.

çan'di·çȧnt, *a.* growing white. [Obs.]

çan'did, *a.* [L. *candidus*, white, pure, sincere, from *candere*, to be white or hot.]

1. white. [Obs.]
2. open; frank; outspoken; honest.
3. free from bias; disposed to think without partiality or prejudice; unbiased; impartial.

A *candid* judge will read each piece of wit
With the same spirit that its author writ.
—Pope.

çan′di·dȧ·cy, *n.*; *pl.* **çan′di·dȧ·cieṣ,** the state of being a candidate.

çan′di·dāte, *n.* [L. *candidatus,* a candidate, white robed, from *candidus,* white; those who sought office in Rome wore white gowns.] a person who aspires or is put forward by others as an aspirant to an office or honor; one who offers himself, or is proposed for preferment, by election or appointment.

çan′di·dāte, *v.i.* to be an aspirant or candidate.

çan′di·dāte·ship, *n.* same as *candidacy.*

çan′di·dȧ·tūre, *n.* same as *candidacy.*

çan′did çam′ẽr·ȧ, any small camera with a fast lens, used to take informal pictures of unposed subjects.

çan′did·ly, *adv.* openly; frankly; impartially; ingenuously.

çan′did·ness, *n.* the state or quality of being candid.

çan′died (kan′did), *a.* 1. preserved with sugar, or encrusted with it; covered with crystals of sugar or with matter resembling them; as, *candied* raisins.
2. wholly or partially converted into sugar; as, *candied* honey.
3. figuratively, honeyed; flattering; blandishing; as, a *candied* tongue.

çan′di·fȳ, *v.t.* and *v.i.* to make or become white. [Rare.]

çan′di·fȳ, *v.t.* and *v.i.* to make or become candied. [Rare.]

Çan′di·ot, Çan′di·ōte, *a.* pertaining to Candia or Crete.

Çan′di·ot, Çan′di·ōte, *n.* an inhabitant or native of Candia; a Cretan.

çan′dīte, *n.* a kind of spinel found at Candy, Ceylon: called also *ceylonite.*

çan′dle, *n.* [ME. *candel, candele*; AS. *candel*; L. *candela,* a light, torch, from *candere,* to shine, be bright.]
1. a taper; a cylindrical body of tallow, wax, spermaceti, or other fatty material, formed on a wick composed of linen or cotton threads woven or twisted loosely, and used for a portable light.
2. anything like a candle in form or use.
3. a unit of luminous intensity, based on a standard candle.
excommunication by inch of candle; an old form of excommunication which gives the offender the length of time it takes a candle to burn out to repent or be excommunicated.
not worth the candle; not worth doing.
sale by inch of candle; an auction sale in which persons are allowed to bid only till a small piece of candle burns out.
to burn the candle at both ends; to work or play too much so that one's energy is quickly dissipated.

çan′dle, *v.t.*; candled, *pt., pp.*; candling, *ppr.* to examine (eggs) by holding in front of a light, originally that of a candle: light shining through the egg shows how fresh it is, whether it has been fertilized, etc.

çan′dle·ber″ry, *n.*; *pl.* **çan′dle·ber″rieṣ,** 1. the fruit of the candlenut or of the wax myrtle tree.
2. either of these trees.

çan′dle·ber″ry tree, 1. the *Myrica cerifera,* or wax myrtle; a shrub, common in North America, the drupes of which are covered with a greenish-white wax (popularly called bayberry tallow), of which candles are made. The wax is collected by boiling the drupes in water and skimming off the surface. It is afterward melted and refined, a bushel of berries yielding from four to five pounds of wax.

CANDLEBERRY, OR WAX MYRTLE (*Myrica cerifera*)

2. the *Aleurites triloba,* or candlenut, found in the Pacific islands, the nuts of which are dried and used for candles.

çan′dle·bomb (-bom *or* -bum), *n.* a small glass bubble, filled with water, which, when placed in the flame of a candle, bursts with a report.

çan′dle çōal, see *cannel coal.*

çan′dle·fish, *n.*; *pl.* **çan′dle·fish** or **çan′dle·fish·eṣ,** 1. a large, edible fish, the *Anoplopoma fimbria,* somewhat resembling the pollack.
2. an oily sea fish of the salmon family, the *Thaleicthys pacificus,* frequenting the northwestern shores of North America, of about the size of the smelt. When it is dried, a wick may be passed through it and ignited, the whole acting as a candle.

çan′dle flȳ, 1. the lantern fly.
2. a moth. [Obs.]

çan′dle-foot, *n.* a foot-candle.

çan′dle·hōld″ẽr, *n.* 1. one who or that which holds a candle; specifically, a menial.
2. a candlestick.

çan′dle·līght (-līt), *n.* 1. the light of a candle.
2. the time for lighting candles; twilight; evening.

Çan′dle·mȧs, *n.* [ME. *candelmasse*; AS. *candelmæsse*; *candel,* a candle, and *mæsse,* a mass.] an ecclesiastical festival held on the second day of February in honor of the purification of the Virgin Mary. This feast in the medieval church was remarkable for the number of lighted candles borne about in processions and placed in churches.

çan′dle·nut, *n.* 1. the fruit of the candleberry tree, *Aleurites triloba.*
2. the *Aleurites triloba*: also called *candleberry.*

çan′dle·pin, *n.* a pin shaped like a candle, used in a game of tenpins called *candlepins.*

çan′dle pow′ẽr, 1. the luminous intensity or illuminating capacity of a standard candle.
2. luminous intensity or illuminating capacity, as of a lamp, measured in candles.

çan′dlẽr, *n.* a person who candles eggs.

çan′dle·stick, *n.* a cupped or spiked holder for a candle or candles.

çan′dle tree, 1. a tree, *Parmentiera cerifera,* growing on the Isthmus of Panama and bearing fruit resembling a candle.
2. a catalpa tree of the United States, bearing long, round pods.

çan′dle·wāst″ẽr, *n.* one who wastes or consumes candles, as by late study.

çan′dle·wick, *n.* 1. the wick of a candle.
2. the cattail plant.
candlewick bedspread; a spread for a bed, made of unbleached cotton material: the pattern on the spread is hooked in with wicking.

çan′dle·wood, *n.* [so called prob. because of the bright flame that the wood produces.]
1. any of a number of related spiny desert plants with slender stems and clusters of brightly colored flowers.
2. the wood of these plants.
3. any resinous wood cut for kindling or used for torches, etc.

çan′dock, *n.* any of various species of *Equisetum,* or horsetails: some species are employed in polishing tin cans and other vessels.

çan·dōl′lē·ȧ, *n.* [Mod. L., from the Swiss botanist, Augustin Pyramus de *Candolle.*] a plant belonging to the genus *Stylidium.*

çan′dŏr, çan′dŏur, *n.* [L. *candor,* whiteness, radiance, openness, from *candere,* to be white, to shine.]
1. openness of heart; frankness; sincerity; honesty in expressing oneself.
2. a disposition to treat others with fairness; freedom from prejudice or disguise.
3. clearness; purity. [Obs.]
4. kindliness. [Obs.]
Syn.—fairness, ingenuousness, frankness, openness, sincerity, impartiality.

çan′droy, *n.* [origin unknown.] a machine used in preparing cotton cloths for printing.

çan′dy, *v.t.*; candied, *pt., pp.*; candying, *ppr.* [Fr. *candir*; It. *candire,* from *candi.*]
1. to preserve by cooking with sugar.
2. to crystallize into sugar.
3. to cover with or as with crystallized sugar.
4. to sweeten; make pleasant.

çan′dy, *v.i.* [Fr. *candir*; It. *candire,* to candy; from *candi,* candy.] to form into crystals or become congealed; to take on the form of candied sugar.

çan′dy, *n.*; *pl.* **çan′dieṣ,** [Fr. *candi*; It. *candi,* from Ar. *qandi,* made of sugar; from Sans. *khanda,* a piece, sugar in pieces, from *khand,* to break.]
1. crystallized sugar made by boiling and evaporating cane sugar, sirup, etc.
2. a solid confection of sugar or sirup, flavored, colored, and often enriched with nuts or fruits.

çan′dy, kan′dy, *n.* [Tamil *kandi,* a measure of weight; Sans. *khanda,* a portion, piece, from *khand,* to break.]
1. an Eastern measure of weight, averaging 500 pounds.
2. in Malabar, a measure of length equivalent to 28¹/₄ inches.

çan′dy pull, a party, or social gathering, especially of young people, at which the guests entertain themselves by making taffy or similar candy.

çan′dy·tuft, *n.* [from *Candia,* the ancient name of Crete.] any of several plants of the genus *Iberis,* especially *Iberis umbellata,* a tufted flower brought from the island of Candia.

çāne, *n.* [ME. *cane, canne*; OFr. *cane, canne*; It. *canna*; L. *canna,* a reed, cane; Gr. *kanna*; Heb. *qāneh,* a reed.]
1. the slender, hollow, jointed, usually flexible stem of any of certain plants, as bamboo, rattan, etc.
2. any plant with such a stem.
3. the stem of a small fruit plant, as the blackberry, raspberry, etc.
4. a stem used as a walking stick or for beating.
5. any walking stick.
6. a stick used for beating.
7. sugar cane.
8. split rattan, used in making chair seats, wickerwork, etc.

çāne, *v.t.*; caned, *pt., pp.*; caning, *ppr.* 1. to beat with a cane or walking stick.
2. to make or furnish (chairs, etc.) with cane.
cane apple; the strawberry tree.
cane borer; a beetle whose larva destroys the woody stalks of plants such as raspberry and blackberry.
canebrake rattler; banded rattlesnake.
cane cactus; a cylindrical-stemmed cactus of the genus *Opuntia.*
cane chair; a chair made with cane or split cane in the seat and in the back panel.
cane gun; a gun constructed like a cane.
cane osier; the common osier.
cane rat; ground pig (*Thryonomys swinderianus*) of western and southern Africa.
cane reed; the giant reed, *Arundinaria.*
cane rust; in plant pathology, diseases attacking the stalks of berry bushes or rose bushes.
cane sugar; sucrose; the sugar from sugar cane.

çāne′brāke, *n.* a dense thicket of cane plants.

çāned, *a.* mothery: said of vinegar. [Brit. Dial.]

Çȧ·nel′lȧ, *n.* [Mod. L. *canella,* dim. of *canna,* a cane, reed.]
1. one of the genera of the order *Canellaceæ,* ornamental aromatic trees.
2. [c–] any tree of this genus, particularly *Canella alba,* the wild cinnamon of the West Indies and Florida.
3. [c–] the bark of *Canella alba,* used as a spice and a tonic.

çāne mill, a mill in which sugar cane is ground.

çan′e·phōr, çan′e·phōre, *n.* a canephoros.

çȧ·neph′ō·ros, *n.*; *pl.* **çȧ·neph′ō·roi,** [L. *canephora*; Gr. *kanēphoros,* a basket-bearer; *kaneon,* a wicker basket, and *-phoros,* from *pherein,* to bear.]
1. in ancient Greece, a basket bearer; specifically, any of the girls who carried on their heads the baskets containing the implements of sacrifice, in the processions of the Dionysia, Panathenaea, and other ancient Grecian festivals.
2. in architecture, a figure bearing a basket on the head, sometimes used as a caryatid.

CANEPHOROS

çȧ·nes′cent, *a.* [L. *canescens* (*-entis*), ppr. of *canescere,* to become white or hoary; *canus,* white or hoary.] growing white or hoary.

çāne trash, the refuse after grinding sugar cane.

çan′fiēld, *n.* [after Richard A. *Canfield,* Am. who invented the game.] in card games, a form of solitaire used for gambling.

çangue (kang), *n.* [Port. *cangue*, a wooden collar, from Chinese *kang*, to bear on the shoulders, and *kia*, a wooden collar.] a wooden collar formerly worn by Chinese criminals as a penalty.

çan hook, a rope with hooks at each end for raising casks by the projecting ends of the staves.

Ça·niç'ū·lȧ, *n.* [L. *canicula*, a little dog, dim. of *canis*, a dog.] the Dog Star, or Sirius.

çȧ·niç'ū·lăr, *a.* [L. *canicularis*, from *canicula*, a little dog, the Dog Star.]
 1. pertaining to the star Canicula, in the constellation Canis Major.
 2. of Procyon, a star in the constellation of Canis Minor.
 3. measured by the rising of either of these stars.
 4. of the dog days in July and August.
 canicular days; same as *dog days.*
 canicular year; the Egyptian natural year, which was reckoned from one heliacal rising of Canicula to the next.

Çan'i·çūle, *n.* same as *Canicula.*

çȧ·nī'năl, *a.* canine. [Obs.]

çā'nīne, *a.* [L. *caninus*, from *canis*, a dog.]
 1. pertaining to dogs; having the properties or qualities of a dog.
 2. of the family of animals that includes dogs, wolves, jackals, and foxes.
 3. of a canine tooth.

çā'nīne, *n.* 1. a dog.
 2. a canine tooth.
 3. one of the genus *Canis.*

çā'nīne mad'ness, hydrophobia.

çā'nīne tooth, one of the four sharp-pointed teeth between the incisors and bicuspids: also called *cuspid* or, in the upper jaw, *eyetooth.*

çȧ·nin'i·fo̤rm, *a.* [L. *caninus* (supply *dens*, a tooth), canine, and *forma*, form.] formed like a canine tooth.

çan'iŏn (-yun), *n.* same as *cannon* (*n.* sense 9).

Çā'nis, *n.* [L.] 1. a genus of digitigrade carnivorous mammals, including the dog, wolf, fox, and jackal.
 2. Canis Major.
 Canis Major; the Greater Dog, a constellation of the Southern Hemisphere southeast of Orion, including Sirius, or the Dog Star.
 Canis Minor; the Lesser Dog, a constellation of the Northern Hemisphere, near Gemini, including Procyon, a star of the first magnitude.

çan'is·tẽr, *n.* [L. *canistrum*, a wicker basket; Gr. *kanistron*, from *kanna*, a reed.]
 1. a small basket made of reeds, twigs, or the like. [Obs.]
 2. a box or can for tea, coffee, spices, etc.
 3. canister shot.
 4. the part of a gas mask that contains the chemicals for filtering the air to be breathed.

çan'is·tẽr shot, metal cases containing bullets which scatter after leaving the gun: also called *case shot.*

çȧ·ni'ti·ēṣ (-nish'i-ēz), *n.* [L., from *canus*, hoary, white.] the condition of having gray or white hair.

çañ'kẽr, *n.* [ME. *canker, kankir*; AS. *cancer*; D. *kanker*; from L. *cancer*, a crab, cancer.]
 1. an ulcerlike sore that spreads, usually in the mouth.
 2. a cankerworm.
 3. a disease of plants that causes decay of bark and wood.
 4. anything causing decay or rot.
 Sacrilege may prove an eating *canker.* —Atterbury.
 5. a kind of rose, the dog rose.
 6. in farriery, a disease in horses' feet, discharging a fetid matter from the cleft in the frog.

çañ'kẽr, *v.t.*; cankered, *pt., pp.*; cankering, *ppr.*
 1. to attack, infect, corrupt, or consume with canker.
 2. to cause to decay or rot.

çañ'kẽr, *v.i.* 1. to grow corrupt; to be or become infected with canker.
 And as with age his body uglier grows,
 So his mind *cankers.* —Shak.
 2. to grow rusty or discolored by oxidation, as a metal. [Obs.]

çañ'kẽr·ber''ry, *n.* 1. the fruit of the wild dog rose of England, *Rosa canina.*
 2. the berry of a Jamaican nightshade, *Solanum bahamense.*

çañ'kẽr·bīrd, *n.* the cedarbird.

çañ'kẽr bloom, the flower of the dog rose.

çañ'kẽr blos'sŏm, a cankerworm or plant canker. [Rare.]

çañ'kẽred, *a.* infected with or as with canker, either literally or figuratively; as, a *cankered* tree; a *cankered* temper.

çañ'kẽred·ly, *adv.* in a cankered or cross manner.

çañ'kẽr·flȳ, *n.* any fly preying on fruit.

çañ'kẽr·ous, *a.* 1. of, having, or like a canker or cankers.
 2. causing canker.
 3. corrupting.

çañ'kẽr-rash, *n.* scarlet fever.

çañ'kẽr·ro͞ot, *n.* a name given to a number of plants having astringent roots, as the marsh rosemary, the three-leaved goldthread, the common sorrel, etc.

çañ'kẽr·weed, *n.* ragwort. [Obs.]

çañ'kẽr·wŏrm, *n.* a worm or larva destructive to trees or plants; specifically, the fall worm, *Anisopteryx pometaria*, and the spring species, *Anisopteryx vernata.* These geometrid spanworms attack the foliage of shade and fruit trees, consuming the leaves for food, and are found throughout the United States generally.

çañ'kẽr·y, *a.* 1. cankered; corroded; rusty.
 2. ill-natured; crabbed; venomous; vexing.

Çan'nȧ, *n.* [L., a cane, reed.]
 1. a genus of tropical plants with thick roots, large leaves, and brilliant flowers.
 2. [c–] any plant of this genus; also, its flower.
 Canna indica; a common garden plant having red, yellow, or variegated flowers: it is valued for foliage and summer flowering.

CANNA
(*Canna indica*)

çan'nȧ·bēne, *n.* [L. *cannabis*, hemp, and *-ene.*] a white, volatile oil obtained from Indian hemp.

çan'nȧ·biç, *a.* [L. *cannabis*, hemp.] relating to hemp; obtained from hemp.

çan'nȧ·bin, çan'nȧ·bine, *n.* a poisonous, white crystalline resin extracted from Cannabis and believed to be its active narcotic principle.

çan'nȧ·bīne (*or* -bin), *a.* [L. *cannabinus*, from *cannabis*, hemp.] pertaining to hemp; hempen.

Çan'nȧ·bis, *n.* [L., hemp.]
 1. a genus of plants of the nettle family, having the single species *Cannabis sativa*, which yields hemp and hashish.
 2. [c–] hashish.
 Cannabis indica; the variety of hemp obtained from India: in full, *Cannabis sativa indica*; also, hashish from this plant.

çanned (kand), *a.* 1. sealed in cans; preserved by canning.
 2. recorded to be reproduced by mechanical means, such as a phonograph; as, *canned* music. [Slang.]
 3. drunken or intoxicated. [Slang.]
 4. discharged from a position. [Slang.]

çan'nel çōal [from *candle coal.*] a variety of bituminous coal that burns with a bright flame and has a high volatile content: often shortened to *cannel.*

çan'ne·lūre, *n.* [Fr., from *canneler*, to groove, flute.] a groove or channel on the surface of anything, as the fluting on Doric columns, or on a conical bullet or projectile.

çan'ne·lūred, *a.* grooved; fluted.

çan'e·quin (-kin), *n.* [Fr.] white cotton cloth from the East Indies.

çan'nẽr, *n.* a person whose work or business is canning foods.

çan'nẽr·y, *n.*; *pl.* **çan'nẽr·ieṣ,** a factory for canning food products for the market.

çan'ni·băl, *n.* [Fr. *cannibale*; G. *canibale*; Sp. *canibal*, a savage, cannibal; a corruption of *Caribal*, a Carib, a word used by Columbus but later changed to *canibal*, as if from L. *canis*, a dog.]
 1. a human being that eats human flesh; an anthropophagite.
 2. an animal that eats other animals of its own kind.

çan'ni·băl, *a.* of or resembling cannibals; having the habits of cannibals.

çan'ni·băl·iṣm, *n.* 1. the act or habit of eating others of one's own kind.

çan'ni·băl·ly, *adv.* in the manner of a cannibal.

çan'ni·kin, *n.* a small cup or can.

çan'ni·ly, *adv.* in a canny manner. [Scot.]

çan'ni·ness, *n.* the quality of being canny. [Scot.]

çan'ning, *n.* 1. the process of preserving food by sealing it in cans or jars.
 2. the business or industry of manufacturing canned goods.

çan'nŏn, *n.*; *pl.* **çan'nŏnṣ, can'nŏn,** [Fr. *canon*, a gun, barrel of a gun; LL. *canon*, a tube, pipe, gun; L. *canna*; Gr. *kanōn*, from *kanē, kannē*, a reed.]
 1. a large, mounted piece of artillery too heavy to be carried by a soldier.
 2. any large gun with a relatively short barrel, as a howitzer.
 3. a miniature gun like a cannon.
 4. a cannon bit.
 5. a part on a bell by which it is hung.
 6. the cannon bone.
 7. in billiards, a carom. [Brit.]
 8. in mechanics, a hollow tube within which a shaft revolves independently of the outer tube.
 9. an ornamental bottom of a breeches leg, in style in the sixteenth and seventeenth centuries. [Obs.]

çan'nŏn, *v.i.*; cannoned, *pt., pp.*; cannoning, *ppr.* 1. to fire cannon.
 2. to make a carom. [Brit.]

çan'nŏn, *v.t.* 1. to attack with cannon.
 2. to cause to carom. [Brit.]

çan·nŏn·āde', *n.* [Fr. *canonnade*, from *canon*, a cannon.]
 1. a continuous firing of artillery.
 2. an attack with artillery.

çan·nŏn·āde', *v.t.*; cannonaded, *pt., pp.*; cannonading, *ppr.* to attack with cannon.

çan·nŏn·āde', *v.i.* to fire cannon.

çan'nŏn ba̤ll, a heavy ball of iron or other metal, formerly used as a projectile in cannon.

çan'nŏn bit, a smooth, round bit for a horse: also *canon bit.*

çan'nŏn bōne, the bone between hock or knee and fetlock in four-legged, hoofed animals: also spelled *canon bone.*

çan'nŏn çrack'ẽr, a large firecracker that explodes with a loud noise.

çan'nŏned, *a.* supplied with cannon.

çan·nŏn·eer', çan·nŏn·ier', *n.* [Fr. *canonnier*, from *canon*, a cannon.] an artilleryman; a gunner.

çan·nŏn·eer'ing, *n.* the act of using cannon.

çan'nŏn fod'dẽr, soldiers, sailors, etc. thought of as being expended, i.e., killed or maimed, in war.

çan'nŏn met'ăl, same as *gun metal.*

çan'nŏn pin'iŏn (-yun), in watchmaking, a squared tubular piece on the arbor of the center wheel, to hold the minute hand and enable it to be turned by means of the watch key.

çan'nŏn-pro͞of, *a.* able to resist cannon shot.

çan'nŏn·ry, *n.*; *pl.* **çan'nŏn·rieṣ,** cannon, collectively; also, cannon fire.

çan'nŏn shot, 1. a shot from a cannon.
 2. projectiles for firing from a cannon.
 3. the range or distance a cannon will throw a ball.

çan'not, can not.
 cannot but; must; have no choice but to.

çan'nū·lȧ, *n.*; *pl.* **çan'nū·lae,** [L., dim. of *canna*, a reed, pipe.] in surgery, a tube used for withdrawing fluids from the body, generally fitted with a pointed rod for puncturing the skin.

çan'nū·lăr, *a.* [L. *cannula*, dim. of *canna*, a reed.] tubular; having the form of a tube.

çan'nū·lāte, *a.* cannular.

çan'nū·lāte, *v.t.*; cannulated, *pt., pp.*; cannulating, *ppr.* [L. *cannula*, dim. of *canna*, a reed, pipe.] to make cannular.

çan'ny, çan'nie, *a.*; *comp.* cannier; *superl.* canniest, [from *can* (to know, be able).]
 1. cautious; prudent; knowing; wary; watchful.
 Whate'er he wins I'll guide with *canny* care. —Ramsay.
 2. skilled; expert.
 His wife was a *cannie* body, and could dress things very well. —Scott.
 3. moderate, as in charges, exactions, treatment, and the like; not extortionate or severe.
 4. gentle; quiet in disposition; tractable.
 5. easy; comfortable.
 6. possessed of supernatural power; skilled in magic.
 7. thrifty.
 8. shrewd.
 [Scot. or N. Eng. Dial. in all senses.]
 ca'canny; (a) [Scot.] to call "canny"; hence, to go warily; (b) [Brit.] cautious; slow; hesitating.

çan'ny, çan'nie, *adv.* in a canny manner. [Scot. and N. Eng. Dial.]

çà·nöe', *n.*; *pl.* **çà·nöes',** [Sp. *canoa*, from the Carib name.] any light boat, narrow in the beam, and propelled by paddles. The name was originally given to boats used in primitive societies, especially to such as are formed of the body or trunk of a tree, excavated by cutting or burning into a suitable shape; but canoes are also constructed of bark—as among the North American Indians—and similar boats are now commonly used for pleasure boats, being of light construction and often equipped for sailing.

CANOE OF CARIB INDIANS

çà·nöe', *v.i.*; canoed, *pt., pp.*; canoeing, *ppr.*
1. to paddle a canoe.
2. to go in a canoe.

çà·nöe', *v.t.* to transport by canoe.

çà·nöe'ing, *n.* the act or sport of managing or riding in a canoe.

çà·nöe'ist, *n.* one who manages or rides in a canoe.

çà·nöe'măn, *n.*; *pl.* **çà·nöe'men,** a canoeist.

çan'ŏn, *n.* [AS. *canon*, a rule; OFr. *canone*; LL. *canon*, from L. *canon*, a measuring line, rule; Gr. *kanōn*, from *kanē*, *kannē*, a reed, rod.]
1. a law or rule in general.
2. a law or body of laws of a church; as, the Roman Catholic *canon*, the Anglican *canon*, etc.
3. a list of the books of the Holy Scriptures officially accepted by a church as genuine.
4. the rules of a religious order, or of persons devoted to a strictly religious life, as monks and nuns; also, the book in which such rules are written.
5. a standard used in judging something; a criterion.
6. a catalogue of saints acknowledged and canonized in the Roman Catholic Church.
7. an official list or catalogue.
8. [C–] a part of the Mass from the Preface to the Pater, in the middle of which the priest consecrates the Host.
9. in music, a round; a composition in which there are exact repetitions of a preceding part in the same or related keys.
10. in geometry and algebra, a general rule for the solution of cases of a like nature. [Obs.]
11. in surgery, an instrument used in sewing up wounds.
12. in printing, one of the largest kinds of type, forty-eight point: supposed to be so named because it was used in the printing of canons.
13. a device for supporting a bell.
14. in billiards, a carom.

çan'ŏn, *n.* [ME. *canon*, *canoun*; AS. *canonic*; L. *canonicus*, from *canon*; see *canon* (law).]
1. a member of a clerical group living according to a canon, or rule.
2. a clergyman serving in a cathedral or collegiate church.
honorary canon; a canon not obliged to keep the canonical hours and serving without emolument.
minor canon; in the Church of England, a canon of a lower rank assisting in the performance of the daily choral service in a cathedral.
regular canon; in the Roman Catholic Church, a canon living an ascetic life, in monasteries or in community, and who, to the practice of the rules, has added the profession of vows.
secular or *lay canon*; in the Roman Catholic Church, a layman living outside a monastery, but keeping the canonical hours.

çañ'on, (kan'yun), *n.* same as *canyon*.

çan'ŏn bit, a cannon bit.

çan'ŏn bōne, see *cannon bone*.

çan'ŏn·ess, *n.*, 1. a woman member of a religious group living according to a canon, or rule, but not under an everlasting vow such as a nun takes.
2. a woman holding a canonry.
regular canoness; a canoness who has taken all the vows.
secular canoness; a woman living after the manner of a secular canon.

çà·non'iç, *a.* same as *canonical*.

çà·non'iç·ăl, *a.* [LL. *canonicalis*; L. *canonicus*, from *canon*, a rule.]
1. of, according to, or ordered by church law.
2. authoritative; accepted.
3. belonging to the canon of the Bible.
canonical books or *canonical Scriptures*; those books of the Bible which are admitted by the canons of a church to be of divine origin.
canonical epistles; see *Catholic epistles*.
canonical hours; certain stated times of the day, fixed by the ecclesiastical laws and appropriated to the offices of prayer and devotion; in the Roman Catholic Church there are seven periods of daily prayer, viz., matins with lauds, prime, tierce, sext, nones, vespers, and complin.
canonical life; the method or rule of living prescribed by the ancient clergy who lived in community; a course of living prescribed for the clergy less rigid than the monastic.
canonical obedience; submission to the canons of a church, especially the submission of the inferior clergy to their bishops, and of religious orders to their superiors.
canonical punishments; such punishments as the church may inflict, as excommunication, degradation, penance, etc.
canonical sins; in the ancient church, those sins for which excommunication or penance was inflicted, as idolatry, murder, adultery, heresy, etc.

çà·non'iç·ăl·ly, *adv.* in a manner agreeable to the canons.

çà·non'iç·ăl·ness, *n.* the quality of being canonical.

çà·non'iç·ăls, *n.pl.* the full dress of the clergy, worn when they officiate.

çà·non'i·çāte, *n.* [LL. *canonicatus*, canonical, from L. *canon*, a rule.] the benefice or position of a canon; canonry.

çan·ŏn·ic'i·ty, *n.* 1. the state of belonging to the Biblical canon.
2. the quality of being genuine.
3. conformity to church law.

çà·non'iças, *n.* in theology, the scientific analysis of the canon of the Scriptures.

çan'ŏn·ist, *n.* 1. an expert in canon law.
2. a skilled composer of musical canons.

çan·ŏn·is'tiç, çan·ŏn·is'tiç·ăl, *a.* pertaining to a canonist.

çan″ŏn·i·zā'tion, *n.* 1. in the Roman Catholic Church, the act of declaring a dead person a saint. This act is preceded by beatification, and by an examination into the life and miracles of the person.
2. the state or fact of being canonized.

çan'ŏn·ize, *v.t.*; canonized, *pt., pp.*; canonizing, *ppr.* [LL. *canonizare*, to put into the catalogue of saints, from *canon*, a canon.]
1. to enroll (a deceased person) in the canon or list of saints; to declare one a saint.
2. to sanction as canonical.
3. to raise to the highest rank of honor and glory, as if enrolled in the canon.
4. to put in the Biblical canon.

çan'on ląw, those laws governing a Christian church and its members; particularly the ecclesiastical laws of the Corpus Juris Canonici. This set of laws governed the Roman Catholic Church until the Codex Juris Canonici, published in 1917, was put into effect. During the latter part of the Middle Ages the law of the church was legally binding in all countries under the influence of the church. In countries where the state religion is Catholic, this legal enforcement of canon law still holds. A few traces of its influence remain in the laws of the United States and England, such as the exemption of church property from taxation.

çan'ŏn·ry, *n.*; *pl.* **çan'ŏn·ries,** 1. the office held by a canon; in England, the benefice filled by a canon.
2. canons collectively.

çan'ŏn·ship, *n.* the position or term of office of a canon.

çan ō'pen·ēr, a special tool for cutting open cans and tins.

çà·nō'piç ūrn, [from L. *Canopic*, of *Canopus*, an ancient city of Egypt.] an urn used in ancient Egypt to preserve and bury the internal organs of the dead.

Çà·nō'pus, *n.* [L., from Gr. *Kanōpos*, *Kanōbos*, a town in Egypt.]
1. a star of the first magnitude in the rudder of the constellation Argo; the brightest star in southern skies.
2. *pl.* **Çà·nō'pī,** an Egyptian jar.

çan'ō·py, *n.*; *pl.* **çan'ō·pies,** [OFr. *conopée*; L. *conopeum*; Gr. *kōnōpeion*, a pavilion, or net spread over a bed to keep off gnats; *kōnōps*, a gnat.]
1. a drapery, awning, or other rooflike covering fastened above a bed, throne, etc., or on poles over a person or sacred thing.
2. a high covering; overhanging shelter; as, the *canopy* of the sky.
3. in architecture, a decoration serving as a hood or cover suspended over an altar, throne, door, pulpit, and the like; also, the ornamented projecting head of a niche or tabernacle.

CANOPY (sense 3)

çan'ō·py, *v.t.*; canopied, *pt., pp.*; canopying, *ppr.* to cover with or as with a canopy; also, to form a canopy over.

çà·nō'rous, *a.* [L. *canorus*, from *canere*, to sing.] musical; tuneful.

çà·nō'rous·ness, *n.* state of being melodious.

çanst, *v.* archaic second person singular, present indicative, of *can*: used with *thou*.

çan'stick, *n.* a candlestick. [Obs.]

çant, *n.* [OFr. *cant*, a corner, angle, edge; LL. *cantus*, a side, corner; L. *canthus*, the tire of a wheel; Gr. *kanthos*, the corner of the eye, the felly of a wheel.]
1. a corner or niche; an angle. [Obs.]
2. an external or salient angle.
3. one of the segments forming a sidepiece in the head of a cask.
4. a segment of the rim of a wooden cogwheel.
5. an inclination from a horizontal line; as, to be on the *cant*.
6. a wooden block attached to a vessel's deck for any purpose, as for a bulkhead support.
7. a sloping or slanting surface; beveled edge.
8. a sudden movement, toss, or pitch that causes tilting, turning, or overturning.
9. the tilt, turn, or slant of direction or position thus caused.

çant, *v.t.*; canted, *pt., pp.*; canting, *ppr.* 1. to turn about or over by a sudden push or thrust; as, to *cant* over a pail or cask.
2. to toss; to throw with a jerk; pitch; as, to *cant* a ball.
3. to give a sloping edge to; to bevel.
4. to throw off or out by tilting.

çant, *v.i.* 1. to tilt or turn over.
2. to slant.
3. in nautical usage, to turn; change direction.

çant, *a.* 1. with oblique sides or corners.
2. slanting.

çant, *n.* [OFr. *cant*, singing, in allusion to the tone of voice assumed by beggars; L. *cantus*, pp. of *canere*, to sing.]
1. a whining or singsong manner of speech; specifically, the whining speech of beggars.
2. the secret slang spoken by thieves, beggars, and the like; argot.
3. the words and phrases peculiar to or characteristic of a sect, party, or profession; jargon.

> Of all the *cants* which are canted in this canting world, though the *cant* of hypocrisy may be the worst, the *cant* of criticism is the most tormenting.
> —Sterne.

4. insincere or almost meaningless talk used merely from convention or habit.
5. religious phraseology used hypocritically; insincere, pious talk.

çant, *v.i.* [L. *cantare*, freq. of *canere*, to sing.]
1. to speak with a whining voice or in an affected tone, as in begging.
2. to make a hypocritical pretense of great goodness.
3. to talk in a certain special jargon; to use

the words and phraseology peculiar to a particular sect, party, profession, and the like.

çant, *a.* 1. used only by a certain group: said of words or phrases.
2. trite; platitudinous.
3. hypocritical; insincere: said of words or phrases.

çant, *n.* an auction. [Chiefly Irish.]

çant, *v.t.* to bid or sell at auction. [Chiefly Irish.]

çȧn't, cannot.

cän·tä'bi·le, *a.* and *adv.* [It.] in music, executed in an easy, flowing style.

cän·tä'bi·le, *n.* music characterized by an easy, flowing, singing style.

Çan·tā'bri·ăn, *a.* pertaining to the Cantabri, an ancient, warlike people of northern Spain.

Çan·tȧ·brig'i·ăn, *n.* [LL. *Cantabrigiensis*, pertaining to Cambridge; *Cantabrigia*, Cambridge.] a native or inhabitant of Cambridge, England; also, a student or graduate of the University of Cambridge: often shortened to *Cantab.*

çan'tȧ·lev·ẽr, *n.* same as *cantilever.*

çan'tȧ·liv·ẽr, same as *cantilever.*

çan'tȧ·lōupe, çan'tȧ·lōup (-lōp), *n.* [from *Cantalupo*, near Rome, where they were first grown in Europe.] a small round variety of melon, with a ribbed, pale-green or yellow rind and sweet, juicy, orange-colored flesh; also, loosely, any muskmelon: written also *cantaleup*, etc.

çan·tañ'kẽr·ous, *a.* [ME. *conteck, contak*, contention, quarreling.] ill-natured; cross; contentious; disputatious.

çan·tañ'kẽr·ous·ly, *adv.* in a cantankerous manner.

çan·tañ'kẽr·ous·ness, *n.* the state or quality of being cantankerous.

çan'tär, çan·tä'rō, *n.* [It. *cantaro*; Turk. *qantār*; Ar. *qintār*; L. *centenarius*, consisting of a hundred, from *centum*, a hundred.] a varying measure of weight and capacity used in certain Mediterranean countries.

çȧn·tä'tȧ, *n.* [It., from *cantare*, L. *cantare*, to sing.] a musical composition in the form of an oratorio, but shorter; a story or poem set to music.

Çan·tā'tē, *n.* [L., 2d pers. pl. imper. of *cantare*, to sing.] the 98th Psalm: so called from the first words of the Latin version, *Cantate Domino.*

çan·tā'tion, *n.* a singing. [Obs.]

çant'ȧ·tō·ry, *a.* [L. *cantator*, a singer, from *cantare*, to sing.] having a singsong, whining, or canting manner. [Rare.]

çan·tȧ·trī'ce (-che), *n.*; *pl.* **çan·tȧ·trī'cī** (-chē), [It.] a woman professional singer.

çant dog, same as *cant hook.*

çant'ed, *a.* 1. sloping; slanting; tilted up.
2. having cants or angles; as, a *canted* ornament.
canted column; a polygonal column, or one whose flutes are formed in cants instead of curves.

çan·teen', *n.* [Fr. *cantine*, from It. *cantina*, a wine cellar, a vault, from *canto*, an angle, a corner.]
1. a military shop where soldiers can buy refreshments and provisions; post exchange.
2. a place outside a military camp where refreshments and entertainment are provided for members of the armed forces.
3. a small flask for carrying drinking water.
4. formerly, a military kit containing cooking equipment.

çan·teen' çup, in military usage, a drinking cup of metal or plastic shaped as a carrying case for a canteen.

çan'tel, *n.* same as *cantle.*

çan'te·leup, çan'te·lōup, *n.* same as *cantaloupe.*

çan'tẽr, *n.* [abbrev. of *Canterbury gallop.*]
1. a moderate gallop; a Canterbury gallop.
The *canter* is to the gallop very much what the walk is to the trot, though probably a more artificial pace. —Youatt.
2. a hasty skimming or passing over.
A rapid *canter* in the Times over all the topics of the day. —Stephen.

çan'tẽr, *v.i.*; cantered, *pt., pp.*; cantering, *ppr.* to move or ride at a moderate gallop, raising the two forefeet nearly at the same time, with a leap or spring.

çan'tẽr, *v.t.* to cause (a horse or other animal) to move at a gentle gallop.

çant'ẽr, *n.* 1. one who cants or whines.
2. one who talks cant.

Çan'tẽr·bur·y (-ber-i), *n.*; *pl.* **Çan'tẽr·bur·ieș,** [named from *Canterbury*, England, where it is made.] a stand with divisions for music, portfolios, loose papers, etc.

Çan'tẽr·bur·y bell, the bellflower, *Campanula trachelium*; also, other flowers of the same genus.

Çan'tẽr·bur·y gal'lop, the moderate gallop of a horse, commonly abbreviated to *canter*: said to be derived from the pilgrims riding to Canterbury at this pace.

Çan'tẽr·bur·y Tāleș, an unfinished literary work (1387–1400) by Chaucer, consisting of a prologue, connecting passages, and twenty-four stories told to one another by an imaginary company of pilgrims on their way to Thomas à Becket's shrine at Canterbury: it is largely in verse.

çant frāmeș, in a ship, those ribs situated at the ends of the vessel; cant timbers.

çan·thar'i·dăl, *a.* relating to or obtained from cantharides.

Çan·thar'i·dēș, *n.pl.*; *sing.* **Çan'thȧ·ris,** 1. the genus of beetles to which the Spanish fly belongs: see *Cantharis.*
2. [c–] in pharmacy, a preparation of Spanish flies, used internally as a diuretic or genitourinary stimulant, and externally as a skin irritant.

çan·thȧ·rid'iç, çan·thar'iç, *a.* pertaining to or derived from cantharidin.

çan·thar'i·din, çan·thar'i·dine, *n.* a substance which causes blistering, existing in the Spanish fly.

Çan'thȧ·ris, *n.*; *pl.* **Çan·thar'i·dēș,** [L., from Gr. *kantharis*, a blistering fly, from *kantharos*, a kind of beetle.] a genus of coleopterous insects having the head separated from the thorax by a neck. The best-known species is that which is sold under the name of Spanish fly, *Cantharis vesicatoria.* It is of a shining green color mixed with azure, has a nauseous smell, and is powdered and used as the active element in blistering plasters.

CANTHARIS VESICATORIA

çan'thȧ·rus, *n.*; *pl.* **çan'thȧ·rī,** [L., from Gr. *kantharos*, a tankard, pot.]
1. in classical antiquity, a large wide-mouthed drinking cup, having two handles rising above the brim.
2. a fountain or basin in the courtyard before ancient churches, where persons could wash before entering the church.

çant hook, a wooden lever with a movable hook at the end, for canting or turning over heavy logs.

CANT HOOK

çan'thō·plas·ty, *n.* [Gr. *kanthos*, a corner of the eye, and *plastos*, from *plassein*, to form, mold.] the operation of enlarging the opening between the eyelids by slitting the canthus.

çan'thus, *n.*; *pl.* **çan'thī,** [Gr. *kanthos*, corner of the eye.] an angle of the eye; a corner at the extremities of the eyelids.

çan'ti·çle (-kl), *n.* [ME. *canticle*; L. *canticulum*, dim. of *canticum*, a song; from *cantus*, a singing, *canere*, to sing.]
1. a hymn taken from the Bible and used in church service.
2. a canto; a division of a song or poem. [Obs.]
3. a song or chant.

Çan'ti·çleș (-klz), *n.pl.* a book of the Old Testament: also called *The Song of Solomon, Song of Songs*, and (in the Douay Bible) *Canticle of Canticles.*

çan'tile, *v.t.* to cantle. [Obs.]

çan'ti·lev·ẽr, *n.* [as if from *cant* (an angle) plus *lever*, perh. in obs. sense "bar, beam"; earlier *candiliver, cantinglivre* suggest Sp. hyp. *can de llevar*, lit., raising-dog, hence supporting bracket.]
1. a bracket or block, projecting from a wall to support a balcony, cornice, etc.
2. a projecting beam or structure anchored at one end to a pier and extending over a space to be bridged: it is usually joined to a similar structure extending from an opposite pier.

çan'ti·lev·ẽr bridġe, *n.* a bridge whose span is formed by the projecting ends of two cantilevers, the opposite ends of which are supported on piers.

CANTILEVER BRIDGE

çan'til·lāte, *v.t.* [L. *cantillare*, to sing, hum; dim. of *cantare*, to sing.] to chant; to recite with musical tones.

çan·til·lā'tion, *n.* a chanting; recitation with musical modulations.

çan·tī'nȧ, *n.* [Sp.] in the southwestern United States, a place where liquor is sold; saloon.

çant'ing, *n.* 1. the use of cant.
2. the language of cant.

çant'ing, *a.* 1. affectedly pious; as, a *canting* hypocrite.
2. whining; as, a *canting* tone of voice.

çant'ing·ly, *adv.* in a canting manner.

çan·ti·nière' (kȧn-tī-nyâr'), *n.* [Fr.] a woman sutler; a vivandière.

çan'tion, *n.* a song. [Obs.]

çan'tle, *n.* [OFr. *cantel*, a corner, piece; LL. *cantellus*, dim. of *cantus*, a side, corner.]
1. a fragment; a piece or part.
2. the upward-curving rear part of a saddle: also spelled *cantel.*
3. a corner.

çan'tle, *v.t.* to cut into pieces. [Obs.]

çant'let, *n.* a small piece; a fragment.

çan'tō, *n.*; *pl.* **çan'tōș,** [It. *canto*; L. *cantus*, a song, from *canere*, to sing.]
1. a part or division of a long poem, corresponding to a chapter of a book.
2. in music, the highest voice part; soprano; the melody or air.
3. a song or ballad. [Obs.]
canto fermo; same as *cantus firmus* under *cantus.*

çan'ton, *n.* same as *canto.* [Obs.]

çan'tŏn, *n.* [Fr. *canton*; LL. *canto*, a region, district; from L. *cantus*, a corner.]
1. one of the political divisions of a country or territory; in Switzerland, a state; in France, a subdivision containing a group of communes.
2. in heraldry, a part of the design on a shield usually occupying the upper right corner.
3. the part of a flag occupying the upper corner next to the staff, as the blue field studded with stars in the flag of the United States.
4. in architecture, a corner with a pilaster, or any projection.

çan·ton' (*or* kan-tōn'), *v.t.*; cantoned, *pt., pp.*; cantoning, *ppr.* 1. to divide into cantons.
2. to allot quarters to (troops, etc.).

çan'tŏn·ăl, *a.* pertaining to a canton or cantons.

Çan'tŏn çrepe, a kind of fragile, soft silk fabric.

çan'tŏned, *a.* having a canton or cantons: used specifically in heraldry and architecture; as, a *cantoned* shield; a *cantoned* corner.

Çan·tŏn·ēșe', *a.* 1. of Canton, a province of China, or its people.
2. of the Chinese dialect spoken in and around Canton.

Çan·tŏn·ēșe', *n.* 1. *pl.* **Çan·tŏn·ēșe',** a native or inhabitant of Canton.
2. the Chinese dialect spoken by the Cantonese.

Çan'tŏn flan'nel, a heavy twilled cotton fabric with a long, fleecy nap on one side: called also *cotton flannel.*

çan'tŏn·ize, *v.t.*; cantonized, *pt., pp.*; cantonizing, *ppr.* to canton, or divide into districts. [Obs.]

çan·ton'ment, *n.* [Fr. *cantonnement.*]
1. the assignment of troops to temporary quarters, especially winter or training quarters.
2. the quarters assigned.
3. in India, a military post.

çan·tọọn', *n.* [origin unknown.] a cotton fabric with a satinlike surface on one side and finely corded on the other.

çan'tŏr, *n.* [L., a singer, from *canere*, to sing.]
1. the leader of a choir in church.
2. a singer of liturgical solos in a synagogue.

çan′tŏr·ăl, *a.* relating to a cantor.
çan·tō′ris, *a.* [L., genit. of *cantor*, a singer.] of or relating to a cantor; specifically, designating the stall on the left side of the choir as one faces the altar.
çan′trip, çan′trap, *n.* [Scot.] 1. a magic spell.
2. a prank.
çant tim′bẽr, 1. in shipbuilding, one of the timbers at the ends of a ship, which rise obliquely from the keel.
2. [*pl.*] same as *cant frames*.
çan′tus, *n. sing.* and *pl.* [L., a song.] 1. a church song or chant.
2. the melody; the principal part, usually the soprano, of a polyphonic work.
cantus firmus; (a) a liturgical chant or plain song: see *plain song*; (b) a simple melody serving as the main theme of a contrapuntal work.
çăn′ty, *a.* full of cheer; characterized by liveliness and good feeling: applied to persons and things. [Scot. and Brit. Dial.]
Çă·nuck′, *n.* 1. a Canadian. [Slang.]
2. a French Canadian. [Slang.]
3. a kind of Canadian pony or sinewy small horse. [Colloq.]
çan′văs, *n.* [ME. *canvas*; OFr. *canevas*; LL. *canabacius*, hempen cloth, canvas; L. *cannabis*; Gr. *kannabis*, hemp.]
1. a coarse cloth made of hemp, cotton, or flax, used for tents, sails of ships, painting, and other purposes.
2. a clear, unbleached cloth, loosely woven in little squares, used for needlework.
3. the rough draft of a piece of music given to the librettist as a guide. [Rare.]
4. nautically, cloth in sails, or sails in general; as, to spread as much *canvas* as the ship will bear.
5. by metonymy, anything wholly or partly made of *canvas*, as a painting or paintings, a ship, tents, etc.
Touched by the glowing *canvas*, into life. —Addison.
under canvas; (a) in tents, especially army or circus tents; (b) with sails unfurled; (c) by means of sails.
under light canvas; with all additional sails (studding sails, spinnaker, etc.) set.
çan′văs, *a.* made of canvas; as, a *canvas* sack.
çan′văs·back, *n.*; *pl.* **çan′văs·backs** or **çan′văs·back,** a kind of duck, the *Aythya vallisneria*, highly esteemed for the delicacy of its flesh, and deriving its name from the color of its back.
çan′văss, *v.t.*; canvassed, *pt.*, *pp.*; canvassing, *ppr.* [OFr. *canabasser*, to beat out, shake, examine; from LL. *canabacius*, hempen cloth, canvas.]
1. to discuss in detail; to examine carefully; as, to *canvass* a subject, or the policy of a measure.
2. to go through soliciting for votes, opinions, orders, etc.; as, to *canvass* a district.
çan′văss, *v.i.* to go about soliciting votes, orders, etc.
çan′văss, *n.* 1. examination; close inspection to know the state of; as, a *canvass* of votes.
2. discussion; debate.
3. a seeking or soliciting, as of votes, orders, etc.
çan′văss·ẽr, *n.* one who canvasses or solicits; also, an examiner of voting returns.
çān′y, *a.* 1. consisting of cane, or abounding in a growth of canes; as, a *cany marsh*.
2. made of cane or canes; as, *cany* wagons.
çan′yŏn, *n.* [Sp. *cañon* from *caña*, a tube, funnel; L. *canna*, a reed, cane.] a long, narrow valley between high cliffs, usually with a stream flowing through it: also spelled *cañon*.
çăn·zō′nä (-tsō′), *n.* same as *canzone*.
çăn·zō′ne (-tsō′ne), *n.*; *pl.*, **çăn·zō′nī,** [It., from L. *cantio*, *cantionis*, a singing, from pp. of *canere*, to sing.]
1. a lyric poem of Provençal or early Italian origin, often set to music, somewhat like a madrigal.
2. a similar instrumental composition.
çan·zō·net′, *n.* [It. *canzonetta*, dim. of *canzona*, from L. *cantio*, a singing.] in music, (a) a short song, less elaborate than the aria of oratorio or opera; (b) a short, sprightly concerted air.
çaout′chin (kö′), *n.* a distillation of caoutchouc isomeric with the terpenes.
çaöut′chöuç (ko̤o̤′cho̤o̤k), *n.* [Fr. *caoutchouc*, from native S. Am. name, *cahuchu*.]
1. India rubber, an elastic gum, the dried juice of numerous tropical plants of the dogbane, spurge, and nettle families, as *Siphonia elastica*, *Ficus elastica*, etc. It is extremely elastic and is impervious to water and to nearly all other fluids.

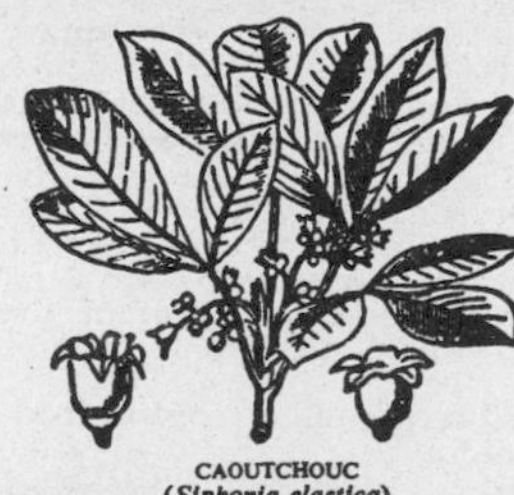
CAOUTCHOUC
(*Siphonia elastica*)

2. pure rubber.
çaöut′chöu·cin, *n.* an oil obtained by distilling caoutchouc.
Çap, *n.* Captain: a term of address. [Slang.]
çap, *n.* [ME. *cappe*, *coppe*; AS. *cæppe*, a cap, cape, hood; LL. *cappa*, *capa*, a cape, hooded cloak.]
1. an article of clothing made to cover the head: generally applied to a head covering of softer material and less definite form than a hat, and without a brim.
2. the badge or ensign of some office, rank, etc.; as, a cardinal's *cap*, a fool's *cap*.
He'll make his *cap* coequal with the crown. —Shak.
3. the top or chief; the acme.
Thou art the *cap* of all the fools alive. —Shak.
4. an act of respect made by uncovering the head.
Give a *cap* and make a leg in thanks. —Fuller.
5. a certain size of paper. *Full cap* is 14 x 17 inches; *double cap*, 17 x 28; *legal cap* is 13 x 16: see *foolscap*.
6. anything resembling a *cap* in appearance, position, or use; as, (a) in architecture, the capital of a column; (b) in botany, the cap-shaped part of a mushroom; (c) in carpentry, the uppermost of any assemblage of parts; (d) in heraldry, the figure of a cap used in charges, and as part of a crest or an accessory in a coat of arms; (e) the inner case which covers the movement of some kinds of watches, etc.; (f) a percussion cap; hence, a little paper percussion cap for toy guns; (g) nautically, a tarred canvas cover for the end of a rope; (h) in mining, a streak of poor matter overlying good ore; (i) a cover for a jar, lens, etc.; (j) a kneecap; (k) a metal reinforcement on a shoe toe.
cap and bells; the bauble carried by a professional fool or jester, denoting his calling.
cap and gown; a costume consisting of a flat cap (called *mortarboard*) and a long, dark-colored robe, worn at some academic ceremonies, as commencement, by teachers, students receiving degrees, etc.: often used to symbolize the academic life.
cap in hand; cringingly obedient; in a servile manner.
cap of liberty; see *liberty cap*.
cap of maintenance; an ornament of state, carried before the sovereigns of England at their coronation. It is also carried before the mayors of some cities.
to set one's cap for; to try to win (a man) in marriage. [Colloq.]
çap, *v.t.*; capped, *pt.*, *pp.*; capping, *ppr.* 1. to put a cap on; to cover with or as with a cap; as, to *cap* a dunce at school; to *cap* a gun.
The cloud-*capped* towers. —Shak.
2. to complete; to crown; to follow up with something more remarkable than what has previously been done; to equal or match; as, he *capped* this exploit by another still more audacious.
3. to deprive of the cap. [Obs.]
to cap the climax; to exceed the limit; be or do more than could be expected or believed.
çap, *v.i.* to uncover the head in reverence or civility.
çä′pä, *n.* [Sp., a cape, cloak.]
1. an overgarment.
2. a fine quality of tobacco used in making wrappers for Cuban cigars.
çā·pȧ·bil′i·ty, *n.* 1. the quality of being capable; capacity; capableness.
2. the capacity of being used or developed.
3. [*pl.*] undeveloped abilities, features, etc.; as, a theme possessing great *capabilities*.
çā′pȧ·ble, *a.* [Fr. *capable*; LL. *capabilis*, from L. *capere*, to take, seize.]
1. able to hold or contain; able to receive; sufficiently capacious. [Archaic.]
2. endued with physical power sufficient for an act; as, that man is *capable* of lifting over 300 pounds.
3. possessing mental powers; intelligent; able to understand, or to receive into the mind; having a capacious mind; as, a *capable* judge.
4. susceptible; as, *capable* of pain or grief. [Archaic.]
5. having legal power or capacity; as, a minor is not *capable* of voting. [Obs.]
Syn.—able, adequate, competent, equal, qualified, suitable, fitted, efficient, clever, gifted, skillful, susceptible.
çā′pȧ·ble·ness, *n.* the state or quality of being capable.
çā′pȧ·bly, *adv.* in a capable manner.
çȧ·pac′i·fȳ, *v.t.*, to qualify. [Obs.]
çȧ·pā′cious, *a.* [L. *capax*, *capacis*, from *capere*, to take, hold, contain.]
1. wide; large; capable of holding much; as, a *capacious* vessel.
2. extensive; comprehensive; able to take a wide view; as, a *capacious* mind.
Syn.—commodious, extensive, spacious, ample, roomy, large, broad, wide, great.
çȧ·pā′cious·ly, *adv.* in a capacious manner or degree.
çȧ·pā′cious·ness, *n.* the state or quality of being capacious.
çȧ·pac′i·tănce, *n.* 1. the ratio between the charging current and the rate of change of voltage with time: if one ampere of current flows when the voltage changes at the rate of one volt per second, a circuit is said to have unit *capacitance*.
2. that property of a condenser which determines how much charge can be stored in it for a given potential difference across its terminals.
çȧ·pac′i·tāte, *v.t.*; capacitated, *pt.*, *pp.*; capacitating, *ppr.* to make capable; specifically, in law, to furnish with legal powers; as, to *capacitate* one for an office.
çȧ·pac·i·tā′tion, *n.* the act of making capable. [Rare.]
çȧ·pac′i·tive, *a.* of electrical capacitance.
çȧ·pac′i·tive çoup′ling, in radio, the coupling of two circuits by means of a condenser or other capacitance.
çȧ·pac′i·tŏr, *n.* in electricity, a condenser.
çȧ·pac′i·ty, *n.* [L. *capacitas*, from *capax* (*-acis*), from *capere*, to take, hold, contain.]
1. (a) the power of receiving or containing; (b) all that can be contained; content or volume.
2. the extent or comprehensiveness of the mind; the power of receiving ideas or knowledge; mental ability; as, instruction should be adapted to the *capacity* of the pupil.
3. active power; ability; productive amount; output; as, a factory having a *capacity* of a thousand pieces a day.
4. ability in a moral or legal sense; legal qualification; legal power or right; as, a corporation may have a *capacity* to hold estate.
He had been restored to his *capacity* of governing by renouncing the errors of Popery. —Brougham.
5. character; profession; occupation; as, in the *capacity* of teacher.
6. in electricity, (a) the amount of electrical current that can be obtained under set conditions from a battery; (b) the total maximum power which a generator can deliver; (c) capacitance.
Syn.—capability, power, faculty, skill, ability, function.
çap-ȧ-pïe′, çap-ȧ-pē′, *adv.* [OFr. *de cap a pie*, from head to foot.] from head to foot; all over; as, armed *cap-a-pie*.
çȧ·par′i·sŏn, *n.* [OFr. *caparason*; Sp. *caparazon*, a cover for a saddle or coach; from LL. *cappa*, *capa*, a cape, hooded cloak.]
1. a cloth or covering laid over the saddle of a horse, especially a horse equipped for a state occasion.
2. figuratively, clothing, especially gay clothing.
çȧ·par′i·sŏn, *v.t.*; caparisoned, *pt.*, *pp.*; caparisoning, *ppr.* 1. to cover with a cloth, as a horse.
2. to adorn with rich dress; to deck out.
çȧ·pär′rō, *n.* [native name.] a large South American monkey, *Lagothrix humboldti*.
çap′çāse, *n.* a kind of covered case for carrying clothing. [Obs.]
çāpe, *n.* [Fr. *cap*, a cape, headland, from L. *caput*, a head.]
1. a piece of land jutting into a body of

water beyond the rest of the coast line; a headland; a promontory.

2. [C–] a kind of wine from the Cape of Good Hope.

Cape jasmine; see under *jasmine*.

Cape pigeon; a small sea bird, *Daption capense*, common about the Cape of Good Hope.

çāpe, *v.i.*; caped, *pt.*, *pp.*; caping, *ppr.* [Fr. *cap*, a cape, head of a ship.] nautically, to keep in a certain direction or course; as, she *capes* north by northeast. [Obs.]

çāpe, *n.* [OFr. *cape*; LL. *capa*, *cappa*, a cape, hooded cloak.] a garment without sleeves, fastened at the neck and hanging over the back and shoulders, sometimes attachable to a coat.

çāpe, *n.* capeskin.

çāpe, *v.i.* to gape. [Obs.]

Çāpe Dutch (duch), Afrikaans, the Dutch dialect spoken in South Africa.

çā'pel, çā'ple, *n.* in mining, a composite rock occurring in the walls of tin and copper lodes.

çap'e·lin, *n.*; *pl.* **çap'e·lin** or **çap'e·lins**, [Fr., *caplan*, *capelan*.] a variety of smelt found in North Atlantic waters, used as food and especially as bait for cod fishing.

çap'e·line, çap'el·line, *n.* [Fr., from LL. *capella*, dim. of *capa*, *cappa*, a cape, hooded cloak.] in the Middle Ages, a kind of iron skullcap worn by archers.

Çȧ·pel'lȧ, *n.* [L., dim. of *capra*, a goat.] a bright fixed star in the left shoulder of the constellation Auriga.

çȧ·pel'lāne, *n.* one having the care of a chapel. [Obs.]

çap'el·let, *n.* [Fr. *capelet*; LL. *capelletum*, a little cape, dim. of *capella*, from *capa*, *cappa*, a cape.] a kind of swelling, like a wen, growing on the heel of the hock of a horse.

Çȧ·pell'meis"tẽr, *n.* same as *Kapellmeister*.

çā'pẽr, *v.i.*; capered, *pt.*, *pp.*; capering, *ppr.* [Fr. *cabriole*; It. *capriola*, from L. *caper*, *capra*, a goat.] to leap; to skip or jump about in a gay, playful manner; to gambol; to prance; to spring.

çā'pẽr, *n.* 1. a leap; a skip; a spring; as in dancing or mirth, or in the frolic of a goat or lamb.

2. a wild, foolish action; a prank.

to cut a caper (or *capers*); to leap and dance in a frolicsome manner; to do something ridiculous.

çā'pẽr, *n.* [D. *kaper*, from *kapen*, to take, seize.] a privateer of the seventeenth century. [Obs.]

çā'pẽr, *n.* [Fr. *capre*; L. *capparis*; Gr. *kapparis*, a caper.]

1. a prickly, trailing bush, *Capparis spinosa*, generally growing from the joints of old walls and from fissures in rocks in the southern part of Europe.

CAPER
(*Capparis spinosa*)

2. [*pl.*] the flower buds of the caperbush, pickled and used for flavoring sauces, etc.

caper sauce; a kind of sauce flavored or seasoned with capers.

wild caper; the caper spurge.

çā'pẽr ber'ry, the fruit of the caperbush.

çā'pẽr·bush, *n.* the caper.

çap·ẽr·çāil'lie (-kāl'yi), **çap·ẽr·çāil'zie**, *n.* [Scot.] the Scotch wood grouse, *Tetrao urogallus*, the largest grouse of Europe, found in the northern part of the continent, especially in Norway and Sweden. It had become extinct in the British Isles, but has been reintroduced: also called *cock of the woods*.

CAPERCAILLIE
(*Tetrao urogallus*)

çā'pẽr·çlaw, *v.t.* to clapperclaw. [Obs.]

çā'pẽr·ẽr, *n.* one who or that which capers.

Çȧ·pẽr'nȧ·īte, *n.* a native or an inhabitant of Capernaum, an ancient city in Palestine; by extension, a believer in transubstantiation: see John vi. 24.

Çȧ·pẽr·nȧ·it'iç, *a.* of or pertaining to the Capernaites.

çā'pẽr spurge, a poisonous weed, *Euphorbia Lathyris*, sometimes called *wild caper*.

çāpe'skin, *n.* [originally made from the skin of goats from the *Cape* of Good Hope.] leather made from the skin of certain goats, used especially for gloves.

Çȧ·pē'tiȧn, *a.* designating or of the French dynasty (987–1328 A.D.) founded by Hugh Capet.

çȧ·pe·ú'nȧ, *n.* [Braz.] a tropical food fish, the white grunt.

çāpe'weed, *n.* 1. a lichen, *Roccella tinctoria*, of the Cape Verde Islands.

2. an Australian composite plant resembling the marigold.

çap'ful, *n.*; *pl.* **çap'fuls**, as much as fills a cap; a small quantity; specifically, in nautical language, a light puff of wind which suddenly careens a vessel and passes off.

çäph, *n.* kaph, the eleventh letter of the Hebrew alphabet.

çā'pi·ȧs, *n.* [L. *capias*, you take; 2d pers. sing. pres. subj. of *capere*, to take.] in law, a document issued by a court commanding an officer to arrest a person.

çap·i·bä'rȧ, *n.* same as *capybara*.

çap·il·lā'ceous, *a.* [L. *capillaceus*, hairy.] having long, hairlike filaments; also, resembling a hair.

çap·il·lāire', *n.* [Fr. *capillaire*, the maidenhair fern, and a sirup from it, from L. *capillaris*, capillary.] originally, a kind of sirup prepared from the maidenhair fern, but now applied to any simple sirup, as of sugar or honey, flavored with orange flowers.

çȧ·pil'lȧ·ment, *n.* [L. *capillamentum*, from *capillus*, the hair.] a filament or threadlike fiber. [Obs.]

çap"il·lȧ·rim'e·tẽr, *n.* [L. *capillaris*, from *capillus*, hair, and *metrum*, Gr. *metron*, a measure.] a tester for liquids used in determining their properties by means of capillary attraction.

çap'il·lā·ri·ness, *n.* the state of being capillary.

çap·il·lar'i·ty, *n.* 1. the state or condition of being capillary.

2. capillary attraction or repulsion.

3. the property of having capillary attraction or repulsion.

çap'il·lā·ry, *a.* [L. *capillaris*, from *capillus*, hair, from *caput*, head.]

1. resembling a hair, especially in being fine and slender; filiform; as, a *capillary* tube or pipe; a *capillary* vessel in animals.

2. in botany, resembling hair in the manner of growth: applied in this sense to ferns.

3. pertaining to capillary tubes, or to the capillaries in animals; as, *capillary* action.

capillary action; capillary attraction or repulsion.

capillary attraction (or *repulsion*); a force that is the resultant of adhesion, cohesion, and surface tension in liquids which are in contact with solids, as in a capillary tube: when the cohesive force is greater, the surface of the liquid tends to rise in the tube (resulting in apparent attraction); when the adhesive force is greater, the surface tends to be depressed in the tube (resulting in apparent repulsion).

capillary tube; a tube with a very small bore. If a tube of this sort has an end immersed in water, the water will rise within the tube to a height above the surface of the water in the vessel, as a result of capillary attraction.

capillary vessels; in anatomy, the capillaries.

çap'il·lā·ry, *n.*; *pl.* **çap'il·lā·ries**, 1. a tube with a very small bore.

2. a minute blood vessel constituting the termination of an artery or vein; one of the minute vessels which connect the terminal arteries and veins.

3. in botany, a fern: especially applied to ferns that grow like hair. [Obs.]

çap·il·lā'tion, *n.* a capillary (sense 2). [Obs.]

çȧ·pil'lȧ·tūre, *n.* the act of dressing the hair. [Obs.]

çȧ·pil'li·form, *a.* in the shape or form of a hair or hairs.

çap·il·li'ti·um (-lish'i-um), *n.* [L. *capillus*, a hair.] in botany, a network of hairlike filaments in which the sporules of some fungi are retained.

çap'il·lōse, *a.* hairy; having abundant hair. [Rare.]

çȧ·pis'trāte, *a.* [L. *capistratus*, pp. of *capistrare*, to halter; *capistrum*, a halter.] in ornithology, having a hood of distinct color.

çap'i·tȧ, *n.* [L.] plural of *caput*.

çap'i·tāine, *n.* [Fr.] the Florida hogfish.

çap'i·tăl, *a.* [OFr. *capital*; L. *capitalis*, relating to the head, chief, pre-eminent, from *caput*, head.]

1. relating to the head; on the head. [Obs.]

Needs must the serpent now his *capital* bruise
Expect with mortal pain. —Milton.

2. first in importance; chief; principal; notable; as, a *capital* requisite; a *capital* instance.

3. affecting the head or life; incurring the forfeiture of life; punishable with death; as, treason and murder are *capital* offenses or crimes.

4. very good; excellent; first-class; as, a *capital* singer or player; a *capital* dinner.

When the reading was over, nobody said *capital*, or even good, or even tolerable. —Hook.

5. in writing and printing, designating such letters as are used to begin sentences, proper names, etc., distinguished from lowercase letters by different form and larger size; as, a *capital* A.

6. of most political importance, as being the seat of government; as, a *capital* city.

7. of or having to do with capital.

small capitals; in printing, letters having the form of capitals and the height of lowercase letters.

Syn.—chief, principal, leading, prominent, notable, essential, important, excellent, first-class, splendid.

çap'i·tăl, *n.* [ME. *capital*; It. *capitello*; LL. *capitellum*, the head of a column or pillar; dim. of *caput* (*-itis*), head.]

1. the head or uppermost member of any part of a building; specifically, the uppermost part of a column, pillar, or pilaster, serving as the head or crowning, and placed immediately over the shaft, and under the entablature.

EGYPTIAN CAPITAL

2. in fortification, the line which bisects the salient angle of a ravelin.

MOORISH CAPITAL

GOTHIC CAPITAL

çap'i·tăl, *n.* a city or town that is the official seat of government of a state, nation, etc.; as, Washington is the *capital* of the United States.

çap'i·tăl, *n.* 1. money or wealth used in trade, in manufacture, or in any business.

2. stock in trade; specifically, in political economy, the product of industry which remains either in the shape of national or of individual wealth, after a portion of what is produced is consumed, and which is still available for further production.

This accumulated stock of the product of former labor is termed *capital*. —Mill.

3. figuratively, stock of any kind, whether physical or moral; any source of profit or benefit; assets; resources; as, energy and education are his only *capital*.

4. a capital letter.

5. [often C–] capitalists collectively: distinguished from *labor*.

6. in accounting, (a) the net worth of a business; amount by which the assets exceed the liabilities; (b) the face value of all the stock issued or authorized by a corporation.

active capital; any property immediately convertible into money; ready cash.

capital stock; (a) the capital of a corporation, divided into negotiable shares; (b) the face value of all such shares.

fixed capital; wealth in a permanent form

which is used in the course of production and exchange, as lands and buildings.

to make capital of; to take advantage of, as for personal profit or power; make the most of; exploit.

çap′i·tăl aç·çount′, 1. an account of the total capital invested in fixed assets by the owners of a business, including real estate, machinery, etc., but excluding current or operating expenses.

2. in accounting, a summary of the assets and liabilities of a business on any given date.

çap′i·tăl ex·pend′i·tūre, money spent for expanding and improving a business: it does not include operating expenses.

çap′i·tăl gāinș, profit resulting from the sale of capital investments, as stock, etc.

çap′i·tăl goodș, commodities for use in production, as raw materials, machinery, buildings, etc.; producers' goods: distinguished from *consumers' goods*.

çap′i·tăl-in·ten′sive, *a.* requiring a large investment in capital goods and a relatively small labor force; as, a *capital-intensive* industry or plant.

çap′i·tăl·ișm, *n.* 1. the economic system in which all or most of the means of production and distribution, as land, factories, railroads, etc., are privately owned and operated for profit, originally under fully competitive conditions: it has been generally characterized by a tendency toward concentration of wealth, and, in its later phase, by the growth of great corporations, increased governmental control, etc.

2. the principles, methods, interests, power, influence, etc. of capitalists, especially of those with large holdings.

çap′i·tăl·ist, *n.* 1. a man who has capital which is or may be employed in business.

2. an upholder of capitalism.

3. loosely, a wealthy person.

çap″i·tăl·is′tiç, *a.* 1. of, relating, or pertaining to capital, capitalism, or capitalists.

2. upholding, preferring, or practicing capitalism.

capitalistic system; the economic system of capitalism.

çap″i·tăl·is′ti·căl·ly, *adv.* 1. in a capitalistic manner.

2. toward capitalism; as, he is *capitalistically* inclined.

çap″i·tăl·i·zā′tion, *n.* the use of capital letters.

çap″i·tăl·i·zā′tion, *n.* 1. (a) a capitalizing or being capitalized; (b) the amount or sum resulting from this.

2. the total capital funds of a corporation, represented by stock, bonds, etc.

3. in accounting, (a) the total invested in a business by the owner or owners; (b) the total corporate liability; (c) the total reached after adding liabilities.

çap′i·tăl·īze, *v.t.*; capitalized, *pt., pp.*; capitalizing, *ppr.* 1. to write or set with capital letters.

2. to begin (a word) with a capital letter.

çap′i·tăl·īze, *v.t.* 1. to use as capital; convert into capital.

2. to use to one's advantage or profit (often with *on*).

3. to calculate the present value of (a periodical payment, annuity, income, etc.); convert (an income, etc.) into one payment or sum equivalent to the computed present value.

4. to establish the capital stock of (a business firm) at a certain figure.

5. to convert (floating debt) into stock or shares.

6. to supply capital to or for (an enterprise).

7. in accounting, to set up (expenditures) as assets.

çap′i·tăl let′tẽr, any letter written or printed in a form larger than, and often different from, that of the corresponding small letter, as A, B, C, etc.; upper-case letter.

çap′i·tăl lev′y, a tax levied on all capital, whether individual or corporate, other than income.

çap′i·tăl·ly, *adv.* 1. in a capital or excellent manner; nobly; finely.

2. in a way involving the loss of life; as, to punish *capitally*.

çap′i·tăl·ness, *n.* the state or quality of being capital. [Rare.]

çap′i·tăl pun′ish·ment, execution as punishment for a crime; the death penalty.

çap′i·tăl ship, any armored vessel, other than an aircraft carrier, of over 10,000 tons displacement and with 8-inch guns or larger; battleship or battle cruiser.

çap′i·tăl sūr′plus, any surplus of a business firm not derived from direct earnings or profits.

çap′i·tāte, *a.* [L. *capitatus*, from *caput*, a head.] in botany, growing in a head; having an enlarged head or tip: applied to a flower or stigma.

çap·i·tā′tim, *a.* of a certain sum per head; as, a *capitatim* assessment.

çap·i·tā′tion, *n.* 1. numeration by the head; a counting of persons.

2. a tax or fee upon each head or person.

çap′i·tē, *n.* see *tenant in capite*, under *tenant*.

çap·i·tel′lāte, *a.* [L. *capitellum*, dim. of *caput*, a head.] in botany, growing in small heads; capitular.

çap·i·tel′lum, *n.*; *pl.* **çap·i·tel′lȧ,** [L.] see *capitulum* (sense 1).

Çap″i·ti·brañ·chi·ā′tȧ, *n.pl.* [L. *caput* (*-itis*), a head, and *branchia*, gills.] the *Cephalobranchia*.

Çap′i·tŏl, *n.* [Fr. *capitole*; L. *capitolium*, from *caput*, the head.]

1. the temple of Jupiter, in Rome, and a fort or castle, on the Capitoline Hill, in which the senate of Rome anciently assembled.

2. the hill itself.

3. the edifice occupied by the Congress of the United States.

4. [*usually* c–] a statehouse, or house in which a State legislature holds its sessions.

Çap′i·tō·līne, Çap·i·tō′li·ȧn, *a.* [L. *Capitolinus*, from *Capitolium*, the Capitol.] pertaining to the Capitol (buildings or hill) in Rome.

Capitoline games; in ancient Rome, annual games instituted by Camillus in honor of Jupiter, and in commemoration of the preservation of the Capitol from the Gauls, and other games instituted by Domitian, celebrated every five years.

Çap′i·tō·līne, *n.* one of the seven hills on which Rome was built.

çȧ·pit′ū·lȧ, *n.*, pl. of *capitulum*.

çȧ·pit′ū·lȧr, *n.* 1. a member of a chapter.

2. a capitulary (sense 2).

çȧ·pit′ū·lȧr, *a.* [LL. *capitularis*, pertaining to a chapter, from L. *capitulum*, a chapter, dim. of *caput*, a head.]

1. pertaining to a chapter, as of a religious order.

2. in botany, growing in a head or capitulum.

3. in anatomy, relating to a capitulum; as, the *capitular* process of a bone.

çȧ·pit′ū·lȧ·ry, *a.* relating to the chapter of a religious order; capitular (sense 1).

çȧ·pit′ū·lȧ·ry, *n.*; *pl.* **çȧ·pit′ū·lȧ·rieș,** 1. a capitular (sense 1).

2. [*pl.*] ordinances, especially those made formerly by Frankish kings or those made now by cathedral chapters.

çȧ·pit′ū·lāte, *a.* capitular; arranged in heads. [Obs.]

çȧ·pit′ū·lāte, *v.i.*; capitulated, *pt., pp.*; capitulating, *ppr.* [LL. *capitulatus*, pp. of *capitulare*, to draw up in heads or chapters, to arrange conditions, from L. *capitulum*, a chapter, from *caput*, a head.]

1. to draw up a writing in chapters, heads, or articles. [Obs.]

2. to surrender, as an army or garrison, (*to* an enemy) by treaty, in which the terms of surrender are specified and agreed to by the parties.

3. to give up; stop resisting.

çȧ·pit′ū·lāte, *v.t.* to surrender (an army or garrison) conditionally. [Rare.]

çȧ·pit·ū·lā′tion, *n.* 1. the act of capitulating, or surrendering to an enemy, upon stipulated terms or conditions.

2. a document containing terms of surrender, conditions of office, articles of concession, etc.; treaty; covenant; convention.

3. [*pl.*] such terms, conditions, concessions, etc.

4. a statement of the main parts of a subject.

çȧ·pit′ū·lā·tŏr, *n.* one who capitulates.

çȧ·pit′u·lum, *n.*; *pl.* **çȧ·pit′ū·lȧ,** [L. *capitulum*, dim. of *caput*, a head.]

1. in anatomy, the head of a bone.

2. in botany, a close head of flowers all attached directly to the same stem, as in the *Compositæ*.

çȧ·pī′vi, *n.* see *copaiba*.

çā′ple, çā′pel, *n.* a horse. [Obs.]

çap′lin, *n.* a capelin.

çap′lin, *n.* the end of the handle of a flail, where the swingle is attached.

Çap′n, *n.* Captain. [Dial.]

çap′nō·man·cy, *n.* [Gr. *kapnos*, smoke, and *manteia*, divination.] divination by the ascent or motion of smoke.

çap′nō·mor, *n.* [Gr. *kapnos*, smoke, and *moira*, a part, from *meiresthai*, to divide.] a transparent, colorless, oillike fluid, obtained from the smoke of organic bodies or wood tar.

çā′poç, *n.* see *kapok*.

çā′pŏn, *n.* [ME. *capon*; AS. *capun*; It. *cappone*; L. *capo*; Gr. *kapōn*, a capon, from *koptein*, to cut.]

1. a castrated cock; a rooster castrated for the purpose of improving the flesh for table.

2. a love letter. [Obs.]

çā′pŏn, *v.t.*; caponed, *pt., pp.*; caponing, *ppr.* to castrate, as a cock.

çā′pŏn·et, *n.* a small capon. [Obs.]

çap·ō·nière′, *n.* [Fr., from Sp. *caponera*, a coop for capons, a covered lodge; *capon*, a capon.] in fortification, (a) a defensive work constructed in or across a ditch, generally in the form of a single or double row of palisades, sometimes covered overhead, serving as a kind of blockhouse or lodgment for soldiers. When there is a stockade on one side only, it is called a *demi-caponiere*. A *double caponiere* is arranged for firing in two directions. (b) a passageway, covered or otherwise, protected by walls or parapets on each side, between two parts of a work.

çā′pŏn·īze, *v.t.* to castrate (a fowl).

çap·ō·ral′, *n.* [Fr. from *tabac du caporal*, lit., corporal's tobacco: so named because it is better than *tabac du soldat* (soldier's tobacco); It. *caporale*.] a kind of tobacco.

çȧ·pot′, *n.* [Fr.] a winning of all the tricks at the game of piquet.

çȧ·pot′, *v.t.* to win all the tricks from at piquet.

çȧ·pōte′, *n.* [Fr. *capote*, from LL. *cappa*, a cape.]

1. a kind of long, coarse cloak, especially one with a hood, but of various forms and for both sexes.

2. a woman's bonnet tying under the chin.

3. a movable hood or top for a vehicle.

çȧ·pouçh′, *n.* same as *capuche*.

çap′pȧ·dine, *n.* [origin unknown.] waste silk flock sheared from the silkworm's cocoon after the good silk has been reeled off.

çap pā′pẽr, 1. a coarse paper: so called from being used to wrap commodities.

2. a kind of writing paper: usually called *foolscap*.

Çap″pȧ·ri·dā′cē·ae, *n.pl.* [from L. *capparis* (*-idos*), the caperbush, caper, and *-aceæ*.] a family of dicotyledonous, polypetalous, herbaceous plants, sometimes shrubs or trees; the caper family, found in tropical and subtropical regions.

çap·pȧ·ri·dā′ceous, *a.* pertaining or belonging to the *Capparidaceæ*.

Çap′pȧ·ris, *n.* [L., the caperbush, caper.] a large genus of plants and shrubs, typical of the family *Capparidaceæ*, including the *Capparis spinosa*, which yields the common caper.

çap′pẽr, *n.* 1. one who makes or sells caps.

2. a device for fitting percussion caps to cartridges or shells.

3. one employed as a stool pigeon or decoy for gamblers; also, a by-bidder. [Slang.]

çap′ping plāne, a plane for slightly rounding the upper surface of hand rails, as of staircases.

Çā′prȧ, *n.* [L., a she-goat.] a genus of ruminants having hollow horns, belonging to the family *Bovidæ*, typified by the common goat.

çap′rāte, *n.* [*capric* and *-ate*.] a salt of capric acid.

çap′rē·ō·lȧ·ry, *a.* in anatomy, capreolate.

çap′rē·ō·lāte (*or* kȧ-prē′ō-lāt), *a.* [from L. *capreolus*, a wild goat, tendril, and *-ate*.]

1. in botany, having tendrils.

2. in anatomy, resembling a tendril.

çap′rē·ō·līne, *a.* of or pertaining to the genus *Capreolus*.

çȧ·prē′ō·lus, *n.*; *pl.* **çȧ·prē′ō·lī,** [L., dim. from *caper*, a goat.]

1. the tendril of a plant. [Obs.]

2. [C–] a genus of *Cervidæ*, comprising the roebucks.

çap′riç, *a.* [L. *caper*, a goat.] of or pertaining to a goat; resembling or derived from a goat.

capric acid; an acid, $C_{10}H_{20}O_2$, occurring in small quantities in butter, coconut oil, fusel oil, etc.

çȧ·prĭc′ciō (-prĭt′chō), *n.* [It. freak, whim.]

1. a loose, irregular musical composition, usually lively and whimsical in spirit.

2. any caprice, whim, or expression of fancy.

çȧ·prĭc·ciō′sō (-prĭt-chō′sō), *a.* and *adv.* [It.] in music, in a free, whimsical style.

çȧ·prīce′, *n.* [Fr. *caprice*; It. *capriccio*, whim,

freak, fancy, originally a fantastical goat leap, from L. *caper*, f. *capra*, a goat.]

1. a sudden start of the mind; a sudden change of opinion or humor; a whim, freak, or particular fancy.

2. capriciousness.

Everywhere I observe in the feminine mind something of beautiful *caprice*. —De Quincey.

3. in music, a capriccio.

Syn.—vagary, whim, freak, fancy, humor, conceit, inclination, crotchet.

cȧ·prich′iō, *n.* capriccio. [Obs.]

cȧ·pri′cious (-prish′us), *a.* 1. governed by or showing caprice; unsteady; changeable; fickle; fanciful; as, a man of a *capricious* temper.

2. fantastic; playful. [Obs.]

Syn.—wayward, whimsical, changeable, fanciful, fickle, fitful, unsteady, crotchety, inconstant.

cȧ·pri′cious·ly, *adv.* in a capricious manner; whimsically.

cȧ·pri′cious·ness, *n.* the quality of being capricious.

Ca̤p′ri·co̤rn, *n.* [L. *capricornus*, from *caper*, a goat, and *cornu*, a horn.]

1. the tenth sign of the zodiac, which the sun enters at the winter solstice, about December 22: represented by the figure of a goat, or a figure having the fore part like a goat, and the hind part like a fish.

2. a southern constellation between Sagittarius and Aquarius, anciently represented by the figure of a goat.

capricorn beetles; long-horned beetles of the family *Cerambycidæ*, the larvae of which are destructive to trees and shrubbery.

ca̤p′rid, *a.* of the genus *Capra*.

ca̤p″ri·fi·ca̤′tion, *n.* [L. *caprificatio*, from *caprificare*, to ripen figs by caprification; *caprificus*, a fig tree.] a process intended to hasten the ripening of cultivated figs and to improve the quality of the fruit, by suspending above the tree branches of the caprifig containing a species of wasps, which spread themselves over the whole tree, distributing the pollen of the male flowers.

ca̤p′ri·fig, *n.* [from L. *caprificus*, wild fig; L. *caper*, goat, and *ficus*, fig.] the wild fig, growing mainly in southern Europe and the Near East.

ca̤p′ri·foil, *n.* a plant of the honeysuckle family.

ca̤p′ri·fōle, *n.* the caprifoil. [Obs.]

Ca̤p·ri·fō·li·ā′cē·ae, *n.pl.* [LL. *caprifolium*, the honeysuckle, woodbine, and *-aceæ*.] a family of monopetalous dicotyledons, allied to the *Rubiaceæ*, including a number of erect or twining shrubs and herbaceous plants, among which are the honeysuckle, elder, viburnum, and snowberry. The characteristics of the order are opposite leaves without stipules, free anthers, epipetalous stamens, and fruit not splitting open when ripe.

ca̤p·ri·fō·li·ā′ceous, *a.* of, pertaining to, or resembling the family *Caprifoliaceæ*.

ca̤p·ri·fō′li·um, *n.* [LL., the honeysuckle.] honeysuckle; woodbine.

ca̤p′ri·fo̤rm, *a.* [L. *caper*, *capri*, a goat, and *forma*, form.] having the form of a goat.

cȧ·prig′e·nous, *a.* [L. *caper*, *capri*, a goat, and *genus*, producing.] produced by or formed like a goat.

ca̤p′rin, *n.* a substance found in butter, which, with butyrin and caprone, gives it its peculiar taste and odor. It is a compound of capric acid and glycerin, or a salt of glycerin.

ca̤p′rine, *a.* [L. *caprinus*, from *caper*, a goat.] of or pertaining to goats; goatlike.

ca̤p′ri·ōle, *n.* [Fr., from It. *capriola*; L. *capreolus*, a wild goat; from *caper*, a goat.]

1. in horsemanship, an upward leap made by a horse in which he does not advance.

2. a frolicsome leap or caper.

ca̤p′ri·ōle, *v.i.*; caprioled, *pt.*, *pp.*; caprioling, *ppr.* to leap; to caper; to execute a capriole.

Far over the billowy sea of heads may be seen Rascality *caprioling* on horses from the royal stud. —Carlyle.

ca̤p′ri·ped, *a.* [L. *caper*, *capri*, a goat, and *pes*, *pedis*, a foot.] having feet like those of a goat.

ca̤p′ri·zănt, *a.* [Fr. *caprisant*; LL. *caprizans* (*-antis*), from L. *caper*, a goat.] literally, leaping: applied to an uneven pulse beat.

ca̤p′rō·āte, *n.* a salt of caproic acid.

cȧ·prō′ic ac′id, a fatty acid, $C_6H_{12}O_2$, found in butter, coconut oil, etc. It is fluid, colorless, inflammable, and has a penetrating taste: used in the manufacture of esters.

ca̤p′rōne, *n.* [*capric* and *-one*.] a volatile ketone, $C_{11}H_{22}O$, found in butter.

ca̤p′ryl, *n.* same as *octyl*.

ca̤p′ry·lāte, *n.* a salt of caprylic acid.

cȧ·pryl′ic, *a.* 1. of, pertaining to, or derived from capryl, or octyl.

2. designating or of a fatty acid, $C_8H_{16}O_2$, found in butter.

ca̤p·sā′i·cin, *n.* [L. *capsicum*, Cayenne pepper; *capsa*, a box.] a colorless, active irritant, $C_9H_{14}O_2$, obtained from Cayenne pepper.

ca̤p sc̤rew (skrụ), a bolt with a long thread and, usually, a square head, used with or without a nut for securing cylinder covers, etc.

ca̤p′shēaf, *n.* 1. the top bundle of a shock of grain.

2. the summit or finishing part.

ca̤p′si·cin, *n.* an alkaloid, the active principle of the capsules of *Capsicum*. It is resinous, has a burning taste, is soluble in alcohol, and forms crystallizable salts with acetic, nitric, and sulfuric acids.

CAPSICUM (*Capsicum annuum*)

Ca̤p′si·cum, *n.* [L. *capsa*, a box: so named from the shape of the seed pods.]

1. a genus of South American and Asiatic annual subshrubby plants, of the nightshade family. Many of the species are cultivated for their fruit, which in some reaches the size of an orange, is fleshy and variously colored, and contains capsicin, present also in the seed. The fruit or pod is used for pickles, sauces, etc., and also in medicine. Cayenne pepper consists of the ground pods of various species, especially *Capsicum fastigiatum*, the African or Guinea pepper, or spur pepper, and of the common red pepper of the garden, *Capsicum annuum*.

2. [c—] a plant of this genus.

ca̤p·sīze′, *v.t.* and *v.i.*; capsized, *pt.*, *pp.*; capsizing, *ppr.* [perhaps a corruption of Sp. *capuzar*, to sink a vessel by the head, from L. *caput*, a head.] to upset; to overturn, as a boat.

ca̤p·sīze′, *n.* the act of capsizing; an overturn.

ca̤p squāre (skwār), in gunnery, one of the strong plates of iron which pass over the trunnions of a cannon and keep it in the carriage.

ca̤p′stan, *n.* [Fr. *cabestan*; Sp. *cabestrante*, *cabrestante*, *cabra*, a goat, a machine for throwing stones, and *estante*, a shelf, crossbeam; from L. *stans*, ppr. of *stare*, to stand.] an apparatus consisting of a spool-shaped cylinder adjusted on an upright axis, which is turned around by means of horizontal bars or levers, so that a rope is thus wound around it and a weight raised or moved. It is chiefly used for weighing anchor, hauling in hawsers, etc. Sometimes written *capstern*.

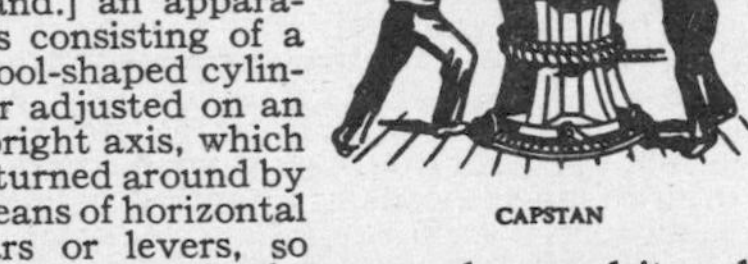
CAPSTAN

to heave in at the capstan; to go around with the capstan by pushing with the breast against the bars.

to surge the capstan; to slacken the rope wound around the capstan.

ca̤p′stan bär, a lever or bar used in turning a capstan.

ca̤p′stōne, *n.* 1. a crowning stone at the summit of a wall, turret, tower, or other structure.

2. any of a series of flat slabs placed on top of a wall to protect its joints.

3. a fossil sea urchin of the genus *Conulus*: so called from its resemblance to a cap.

ca̤p′sū·lăr, ca̤p′sū·lă·ry, *a.* pertaining to, resembling, or of the nature of a capsule.

capsular ligament; in anatomy, the ligament which surrounds every movable joint and contains the synovia like a bag.

ca̤p′sū·lāte, ca̤p′sū·lā·ted, *a.* in botany, enclosed in a capsule.

ca̤p′sūle, *n.* [Fr. *capsule*; L. *capsula*, a little chest, dim. of *capsa*, a chest, from *capere*, to take, contain.]

1. in botany, a case, pod, or fruit, containing seeds, spores, or carpels: it usually bursts when ripe.

2. in chemistry, (a) a small saucer made of clay for roasting samples of ores, or for melting them; (b) a small, shallow vessel for evaporating liquids.

3. in anatomy, a membranous envelope enclosing a part like a bag; as, the *capsule* of the crystalline lens.

4. a small, soluble gelatinous shell or envelope for a dose of medicine.

5. the thin metallic seal or cover for closing a bottle.

6. a small case or sheath.

7. (a) an ejectable airplane cockpit; (b) a detachable, closed compartment designed to hold and protect men, instruments, etc. in a rocket: in full, *space capsule*.

atrabiliary capsule; a suprarenal gland.

Bowman's capsule; the membrane forming the beginning of uriniferous tubules and surrounding a tuft of blood vessels in the kidney; the cap of a Malpighian body of the kidney.

Glisson's capsule; a fibrous envelope which protects the portal vessels in their course through the liver.

ca̤p′sūl·īze, *v.t.*; capsulized, *pt.*, *pp.*; capsulizing, *ppr.* 1. to enclose in a capsule.

2. to express in a concise form; condense.

ca̤p′tain (-tin), *n.* [ME. *captain*; OFr. *capitaine*; LL. *capitaneus*, pertaining to the head; L. *caput*, the head.]

1. one who is at the head of or has authority over others; a chief; a leader.

2. an army officer who commands a company, troop, etc., whether of infantry, cavalry, or artillery; the officer next in rank above a first lieutenant and below a major.

3. in the United States Navy, an officer who ranks next below a commodore and above a commander, and who is equal in rank to a colonel in the army.

4. the commander or master of a merchant ship or other vessel.

5. in some occupations, the title given to an overseer, foreman, or superintendent; as, the *captain* of a mine.

6. a man skilled in war, or military affairs; as, Napoleon was a great *captain*.

7. a leader; an organizer; one having authority over persons acting in concert; as, the *captain* of a football team.

8. a precinct commander in a police or fire department.

9. the district leader of a political party.

ca̤p′tain, *a.* chief; head. [Obs.]

ca̤p′tain, *v.t.*; captained, *pt.*, *pp.*; captaining, *ppr.* to act as a leader of; to conduct as a captain of; to manage; to control.

ca̤p′tain·cy, *n.*; *pl.* **ca̤p′tain·cieṣ,** 1. the rank, post, or commission of a captain.

2. the jurisdiction of a captain, or commander, as in Spanish colonial government.

ca̤p′tain·cy ġen′ẽr·ăl, the office, rank, or jurisdiction of a captain general.

ca̤p′tain ġen′ẽr·ăl, 1. the commander in chief of an army, or of the militia.

2. in Spain, formerly, the governor of a colony, or of one of the chief military divisions.

ca̤p′tain pȧ·shä′, in Turkey, the high admiral of the fleet.

ca̤p′tain·ry, *n.* power or command over a certain district; captaincy. [Obs.]

ca̤p′tain·ship, *n.* 1. the condition or post of a captain; captaincy.

2. a district under control of a captain.

3. leadership.

ca̤p·tā′tion, *n.* [L. *captatio*, from *captare*, to reach after, desire.] the act or practice of seeking favor or applause, as by flattery.

ca̤p′tion, *n.* [L. *captio*, a taking, seizing, fraud, from *capere*, to seize, take.]

1. seizure. [Rare.]

2. caviling; cavil. [Obs.]

3. in British law, the act of taking or apprehending by a judicial process; legal arrest.

4. in law, (a) the certificate of execution of a warrant, commission, or indictment stating the time and place of execution and such other particulars as are necessary to make it legal and valid; (b) a heading showing the names of the parties, court, and docket number in a pleading or deposition.

5. the heading of a chapter, section, or page in a book or document; a title or subtitle, as of a picture.

ca̤p′tion, *v.t.* to supply a caption for.

ca̤p′tious, *a.* [L. *captiosus*, from *captio*, a seizing, fraud, deceit, from *capere*, to take.]

1. disposed to find fault or raise objections; quibbling; carping; as, a *captious* man.

2. made for the sake of argument or faultfinding, as a question, objection, etc.; sophistical; tricky.

ca̤p′tious·ly, *adv.* in a captious manner.

ca̤p′tious·ness, *n.* disposition to find fault; the quality of being captious.

çap′ti·vāte, *v.t.*; captivated, *pt., pp.*; captivating, *ppr.* [L. *captivatus*, pp. of *captivare*, to take captive; *captivus*, a captive; from *captus*, pp. of *capere*, to take.]
1. to take prisoner; to seize by force; to subdue, as an enemy in war. [Obs.]
2. to capture the attention or affection of, as by beauty, excellence, etc.; to charm; to fascinate.
Syn.—entrance, enchant, charm, overpower, bewitch, enslave.

çap′ti·vāte, *a.* captivated. [Archaic.]

çap′ti·vā·ting, *a.* having power to engage the attention or affection; charming; enchanting.

çap′ti·vā·ting·ly, *adv.* in a captivating manner.

çap·ti·vā′tion, *n.* 1. the act of captivating or the state of being captivated.
2. the ability to captivate; charm.

çap′tive, *n.* [L. *captivus*, from *captus*, pp. of *capere*, to take.]
1. a prisoner; one held in confinement or subjection.
2. one who is charmed or overcome by beauty or excellence; one who is captivated.

çap′tive, *a.* 1. taken or held prisoner.
2. of captives or captivity.
3. captivated.

çap′tive, *v.t.*; captived, *pt., pp.*; captiving, *ppr.* to take prisoner; to bring into subjection. [Rare.]

çap′tive au′di·ence, any group of people forced against their will to listen to something, as passengers on a bus equipped with a radio loudspeaker.

çap′tive bal·loon′, see under *balloon*.

çap·tiv′i·ty, *n.* [Fr. *captivité*; L. *captivitas*, from *captivus*, a captive.] the state of being a captive; imprisonment; bondage.
Syn.—bondage, enthrallment, confinement, subjection, imprisonment, slavery, servitude, thralldom.

çap′tŏr, *n.* [L. *captor*, from *capere*, to take.] one who captures.

çap′tūre, *n.* [Fr. *capture*; L. *captura*, from *capere*, to take.]
1. a taking or being taken by force, surprise, stratagem, etc.; seizure; as, the *capture* of an enemy ship.
2. the thing taken or seized.

çap′tūre, *v.t.*; captured, *pt., pp.*; capturing, *ppr.* to take or seize by force, surprise, or stratagem, as an enemy or his property; to make a prisoner of.

çȧ·puç′ciō (-put′chō), *n.* [It.] a capuche. [Obs.]

çȧ·pūche′, *n.* [Fr.; It. *capuccio*; LL. *capuccium*, *caputium*, a cowl, from *capa*, *cappa*, cape, hood.] the long, pointed hood worn by the Capuchins: also spelled *capouch*.

Çap′ū·chin (*or* -shin), *n.* [Fr. *capucin*, a monk who wears a cowl, from *capuce*, It. *cappuccio*, a cowl.]
1. a monk of a certain Franciscan order whose members all wear the capuche. The order, which is most austere, was founded by Matteo di Bassi, in 1526 or 1528.
2. [c—] a garment worn by women, consisting of a cloak and hood, made in imitation of the dress of Capuchin monks.
3. [c—] a kind of pigeon with a range of inverted feathers on the back part of the head, like the cowl of a monk.
4. [c—] a South American monkey, *Cebus capucinus*, having a bare, wrinkled, whitish face and black hair growing like a monk's cowl.
Capuchin nun; one of the Franciscan nuns, whose order, established by Maria Longa, adopted the Capuchin rule in 1538.

çap′ū·cine, *n.* a monkey, the capuchin.

Çap′ū·let, the family name of Juliet in Shakespeare's *Romeo and Juliet*.

çap′ū·let, *n.* same as *capellet*.

çā′put, *n.*; *pl.* **çap′i·tȧ,** [L., the head.]
1. in anatomy, the head or any headlike protuberance.
2. the council of Cambridge University, England, previous to 1856.
caput mortuum; in old chemistry, the residue after distillation or sublimation; therefore, any worthless residue.

çap·y·bā′rȧ, *n.* [Sp. *capibara*, from the Braz. native name.] a tailless, partially web-footed animal that lives in and around lakes and streams in South America: it is the largest extant rodent, over 48 inches in length and 24 inches in height: also spelled *capibara*.

çär, *n.* [OFr. *car*; LL. *carrus*, a two-wheeled vehicle; L. *carrus*, *currus*, from *currere*, to run.]
1. an automobile.
2. a vehicle for running on rails or tracks, as a streetcar.
3. any vehicle on wheels.
4. in poetical language, any vehicle of dignity or splendor; a chariot.
5. the cage of an elevator.
6. the basket of a balloon, for carrying crew and equipment.
7. a perforated box floating in water for keeping live fish.
8. [C—] the constellation called Charles's Wain, the Great Bear, or the Big Dipper.

çä″rȧ·bä′ō, *n.*; *pl.* **çä″rȧ·bä′ōṣ, çä″rȧ·bä′ō,** [Sp., from Malay *karbau*.] in the Philippines, a water buffalo.

Çar·ab′i·dae, *n.pl.* [L., from Gr. *karabos*, a horned beetle.] a family of beetles of which there are more than 6,000 known species. The bombardier beetle, *Brachinus crepitans*, belongs to this family.

çar′ȧ·bin, çar′ȧ·bīne, *n.* same as *carbine*.

çar″ȧ·bi·neer′, çar″ȧ·bi·nïer′, *n.* [Fr. *carabinier*.] a cavalryman armed with a carbine: also *carbineer*.

çä″rä·bi·nie′rï (-nye′), *n.pl.*; *sing.* **çä″rä·bi·nie′re,** [It., from Fr. *carabinier*, carabineer.] the Italian police.

çar′ȧ·boid, *a.* pertaining to or resembling the genus *Carabus*.

Çar′ȧ·bus, *n.* [L., from Gr. *karabos*, a horned beetle.]
1. the type genus of the family *Carabidæ*.
2. [c—] a beetle belonging to this genus.

çar′ăç, *n.* a carrack. [Obs.]

çar′ȧ·çal, *n.* [Fr. *caracal*; Turk. *qara qulaq*; *qara*, black, and *qulaq*, ear.]
1. a lynx, the *Lynx caracal*, a native of northern Africa and southwestern Asia. Its color is a uniform reddish-brown; its ears black externally, and tipped with long, black hairs.
2. the fur of the caracal.

çä·rȧ·çä′rȧ, *n.* [named in imitation of their cry.] any one of the birds of the subfamily *Polyborinæ*. They resemble the vultures in appearance, are habitants of tropical America, and subsist on carrion.

çär′ăck, *n.* same as *carrack*.

çar′ȧ·çōle, *n.* [Fr. *caracole*, a snail, winding staircase, a caracole.]
1. in horsemanship, a half turn, to the right or left.
2. in architecture, a staircase in a spiral form.

çar′ȧ·çōle, *v.i.*; caracoled, *pt., pp.*; caracoling, *ppr.* to move in a caracole; to make a caracole.

çar′ȧ·çol·i, çar′ȧ·çol·y, *n.* [origin unknown.] an alloy of gold, silver, and copper, of which jewelry and ornaments are made.

çar·ȧ·çō′rȧ, *n.* [Malay *karakura*, a kind of boat.] a long, narrow, sailing boat or canoe, used by the inhabitants of Borneo and by the East Indian Dutch.

çar′ȧ·çul, *n.* 1. a sheep of central Asia.
2. the loosely curled fur made from the hide of its newborn lambs.
Also spelled *karakul*.

çȧ·rafe′, çȧ·raffe′, *n.* [Fr. *carafe*; It. *caraffa*, a vessel for liquids; Ar. *ghirāf*, a vessel.] a glass bottle or decanter used for water.

Çar·ȧ·gā′nȧ, *n.* [L., from *caragan*, the Mogul name.] a genus of leguminous Asiatic trees, several species of which are cultivated for ornament: commonly called *pea trees*.

çar′ȧ·geen, çar′ȧ·gheen, *n.* same as *carrageen*.

çä·rȧ·ï′pï, *n.* [S. Am.] the pottery tree, *Moquilea utilis*, of South America. Its pulverized bark is valuable as an ingredient in clay mixtures in the manufacture of pottery.

Çā′rȧ·īte, *n.* same as *Karaite*.

çȧ·ram′bō·lȧ, *n.* [E. Ind.] an East Indian tree, *Averrhoa carambola*, of the geranium family; also, the acid fruit of this tree, eaten by the natives.

çar′ȧ·mel (*or* kär′mel), *n.* [Fr. *caramel*, burnt sugar.]
1. burnt sugar used to color or flavor food, spirits, etc.
2. a kind of sweet, chewy candy, usually made in small cubes; also, a piece of this.

çar′ȧ·mel·īze (*or* kär′mel-īz), *v.t.* and *v.i.*; caramelized, *pt., pp.*; caramelizing, *ppr.* to turn into caramel.

çȧ·rañ′goid, *a.* of or pertaining to the *Carangidæ*, a family of spiny-finned fishes represented by the genus *Caranx*, related to the mackerels, and embracing numerous species of tropical fishes, as the cavallies, pompanos, and pilot fish.

çȧ·rañ′goid, *n.* a fish of the carangoid family.

çȧ·ran′nȧ, *n.* same as *carauna*.

Çar′añx, *n.* [Sp. *carangue*, *caranga*, a W. Ind. flatfish.]
1. a genus of fishes of the family *Carangidæ*, found along the Atlantic coast and including the yellow or golden mackerel and the horse mackerel.
2. [c—] a fish of this genus.

Çar′ȧ·pȧ, *n.* [Fr. *caraipi*, a native Guiana name.] a small genus of tropical trees of the bead tree family, species of which are found in Africa and South America. The wood of these trees is valuable and their nuts yield a bitter oil having medicinal properties, which sometimes is also used for illuminating purposes.

çar′ȧ·pāce, *n.* [Fr. *carapace*; Sp. *carapacho*, a gourd.] the upper shell or bonelike covering of the turtle, armadillo, crab, etc.

çä·rȧ·pä′tō, *n.* [from *carrapato*, the Port. name.] a tick of the genus *Amblyomma*, common to South America.

çar′ȧ·pax, *n.* same as *carapace*.

çar′ăt, *n.* [Fr. *carat*; Ar. *qirat*, a pod, husk, the weight of four grains; Gr. *keration*, the fruit of the locust tree, a weight; dim. of *keras*, a horn.]
1. the unit of weight used by jewelers, etc. in weighing precious stones and pearls: it is equal to about 3.17 grains troy or .2 of a gram.
2. one 24th part (of pure gold): 20-*carat* gold is 20 parts pure gold and 4 parts alloy.

çȧ·rau′nȧ, *n.* [from native name.] a resinous gum having an aromatic flavor, the product of various South American trees, used sometimes as a medicine.

çar′ȧ·van, *n.* [Fr. *caravane*; Sp. *caravana*; Ar. *kairawan*; Per. *kārwān*, a caravan.]
1. a company of travelers, pilgrims, or merchants, traveling in a body for safety, as over deserts.
2. a number of vehicles traveling together.
3. a large closed vehicle for conveying passengers, circus animals, gypsies, etc.; a van.

çar″ȧ·van·eer′, *n.* [Fr. *caravanier*, from *caravane*, a caravan.] the leader or driver of a caravan.

çar·ȧ·van′sȧ·ry, *n.* [Fr. *caravanserai*; Turk. *kerwānseray*; Per. *kārwānserāī*; from *kārwān*, a caravan, and *serāī*, a place, an inn.] a place for loading caravans; a kind of Oriental inn, with a large central court, where caravans stop for the night.

CARAVANSARY

çar·ȧ·van′se·raī, çar·ȧ·van′se·rȧ, *n.* a caravansary.

çar′ȧ·vel, çar′ȧ·velle, *n.* [Sp. *caravela*, *carabela*, dim. of *caraba*, a small vessel; LL. *carabus*, from Gr. *karabos*, a kind of light ship, a beetle, crawfish.]
1. a fifteenth-century sailing ship, having its origin in Spain and Portugal. It had broad bows, a high poop, and lateen sails.

CARAVEL

2. a later sailing ship of the same type.
3. a frigate or man-of-war belonging to the Turkish navy.
4. a small French boat used in the fisheries.

çar'ȧ·wāy, *n.* [from Sp. *alcarahueyā*, caraway; *al*, the, and *karwiya*, from Gr. *karon*, caraway.]
1. a biennial plant, *Carum carui*, a native of Europe, having a tapered root like a parsnip and spicy, strong-smelling seeds.
2. the seeds of the plant, having an aromatic smell and semipungent taste. They are used in cookery and confectionery, and as a carminative.
3. a pastry in which caraway is an ingredient.

çärb-, carbo-.

çär·bam'iç, *a.* [*carb-* and *amide* and *-ic.*] designating or of the simple amino acid, NH_2COOH.

çär·bam'ide (*or* -īd), *n.* [*carb-* and *amide.*] in chemistry, urea.

çär·bam'ine, *n.* a liquid compound of cyanogen with a hydrocarbon radical.

çär'bȧ·zōle, çär'bȧ·zōl, *n.* [*carb-* and *azote* and *-ole.*] a white, crystalline substance, $C_{12}H_9N$, occurring in crude anthracene: certain dyes are made from it.

çär·baz'ō·tāte, *n.* picrate, a salt derived from picric acid.

çär·bȧ·zot'iç, *a.* [*carb-* and *azote* and *-ic.*] relating or allied to carbon and nitrogen. [Obs.]
carbazotic acid; picric acid. [Obs.]

çär'bide (*or* -bīd), *n.* [*carb-* and *-ide.*] a compound of an element, usually a metal, with carbon; especially, calcium carbide.

çär'bi·mide (*or* -mīd), *n.* [*carb-* and *-imide.*] in chemistry, isocyanic acid or any of the salts formed from it.

çär'bīne (*in military usage, now often* kär'bēn), *n.* [Fr. *carabine*, from *carabin*, mounted rifleman, from *escarrabin*, corpse bearer, from *scarabée*, a beetle.]
1. a rifle with a short barrel, chiefly for use by cavalry: also spelled *carabin, carabine*.
2. in the United States Army, a light semiautomatic, 30-caliber rifle of relatively great fire power and limited range.

çär·bi·neer', *n.* same as *carabineer*.

çär'bi·nōl, *n.* [*carbin* (name used by Kolbe for the methyl radical), and *-ol.*] methanol (wood alcohol), or any alcohol derived from it, as diethyl carbinol, $(CH_3{\cdot}CH_2)_2CHOH$.

çär'bo-, a combining form meaning *carbon*, as in *carbo*hydrate: also, before a vowel, *carb-*.

çär·bō·hȳ'drāse, *n.* in chemistry, an enzyme acting on carbohydrates.

çär·bō·hȳ'drāte, *n.* [*carbo-* and *hydrate.*] any of certain organic compounds composed of carbon, hydrogen, and oxygen, including the sugars, starches, and celluloses.

çär·bō·hȳ'drīde (*or* -drid), *n.* same as *hydrocarbon*.

çär'bō·lāt·ed, *a.* containing or treated with carbolic acid.

çär·bol'iç, *a.* [L. *carbo*, coal, and *oleum*, oil, and *-ic.*] designating or of a poisonous acid, C_6H_6O, obtained from coal or coal tar by distillation, and used, in various solutions, as an antiseptic, disinfectant, etc.: also called *phenol*.

çär'bō·līze, *v.t.*; carbolized, *pt., pp.*; carbolizing, *ppr.* 1. to use carbolic acid in the treatment of; to apply carbolic acid to as a wash or disinfectant.
2. to add carbolic acid to.

çär'bō·loy, *n.* [*carb*ide, and *o*, and al*loy*.] tungsten carbide, an extremely hard alloy used in the machine-tool industry for its high abrasive quality: a trade-mark (*Carboloy*).

çär'bŏn, *n.* [Fr. *carbone*, from L. *carbo*, coal.]
1. a nonmetallic chemical element found in many inorganic compounds and all organic compounds: diamond and graphite are pure carbon; carbon is also present, with other substances, in coal, coke, charcoal, soot, etc.: symbol, C; atomic weight, 12.01; atomic number, 6.
2. a sheet of carbon paper.
3. a carbon copy.
4. in electricity, (a) a stick of carbon used in an arc lamp; (b) a carbon plate or rod used in a battery.

çär'bŏn, *a.* 1. of, containing, or treated with carbon.
2. like carbon.

çär·bō·nā'ceous, *a.* 1. pertaining to, containing, or composed of carbon; as, *carbonaceous* matter.
2. containing or like coal.

çär'bō·nāde, *n.* same as *carbonado* (a piece of meat).

çär·bō·nāde', *v.t.* same as *carbonado*.

çär·bō·nā'dō, *n.*; *pl.* **çär·bō·nā'dōeş** or **çär·bō·nā'dōş**, [Sp. *carbonada*, from L. *carbo*, coal.]
1. a piece of meat, often fish or fowl, scored and broiled.
2. a massive form of diamond characterized by opacity and dark color, used for drills: also called *black diamond*.

çär·bō·nā'dō, *v.t.*; carbonadoed, *pt., pp.*; carbonadoing, *ppr.* 1. to score and then broil (meat).
2. to cut gashes in; slash; hack.

Çär·bō·nä'rī, *n.pl.*; *sing.* **Çär·bō·nä'rō**, [It., charcoal burners.] an Italian revolutionary group organized about 1811 to establish a united republican Italy.

Çär·bō·nä'rişm, *n.* anything pertaining or relating to the Carbonari.

çär″bŏn·ȧ·tā'tion, *n.* carbonation (sense 1): the preferred form in chemistry.

çär'bŏn·āte, *n.* a salt or ester of carbonic acid.

çär'bŏn·āte, *v.t.*; carbonated, *pt., pp.*; carbonating, *ppr.* 1. to burn to carbon; to carbonize.
2. to charge with carbon dioxide.
3. in chemistry, to change into a carbonate.

çär'bŏn·ā·ted, *a.* combined with carbonic acid.
carbonated water; water impregnated with carbon dioxide

çär·bŏn·ā'tion, *n.* 1. the saturation of water with carbon dioxide, as in the manufacture of soda water: cf. *carbonatation*.
2. a purifying process in sugar-making in which the lime salts are precipitated from the juice by means of carbon dioxide.
3. carbonization.

çär'bŏn bī·sul'fīde, carbon disulfide.

çär'bŏn çop'y, 1. a copy, as of a letter, made with carbon paper.
2. any person or thing very much like another. [Colloq.]

çär'bŏn dī·ox'īde, a colorless, odorless gas, CO_2, somewhat heavier than air: it passes out of the lungs in respiration and is absorbed by plants, which convert the carbon into certain carbohydrates and release the oxygen into the air.

çär'bŏn dī·ox'īde snōw, carbon dioxide made solid by great pressure and used as a refrigerant; dry ice.

çär'bŏn dī·sul'fīde, a heavy, volatile, colorless liquid, CS_2, highly inflammable and poisonous, used as a solvent, preservative, insecticide, etc.

çär'bōne, *v.t.* to cook over coals. [Obs.]

çär·bō·ne'rō, *n.* [Sp., a charcoal burner.] a fish of the family *Carangidæ*, having markings of a dark color, common to West Indian waters.

çär·bon'iç, *a.* 1. of or containing carbon.
2. obtained from carbon.

çär·bon'iç ac'id, a weak, colorless acid, H_2CO_3, formed by the solution of carbon dioxide in water and existing only in solution.

çär·bon'iç-ac'id gas, carbon dioxide.

çär·bon'iç ox'īde, carbon monoxide.

çär'bŏn·īde, *n.* a carbide. [Rare.]

çär·bŏn·if'ēr·ous, *a.* [L. *carbo* (*-onis*), coal, and *ferre*, to bear.]
1. producing or containing carbon or coal.
2. [C—] designating or of a great coal-making period of the Paleozoic Era: the warm, damp climate produced great forests, which later formed rich coal seams.
the Carboniferous; (a) the Carboniferous Period; (b) the rock and coal strata during this period.
Carboniferous formation; the collective formation of rocks embracing the strata of the Carboniferous Period.

çär″bŏn·i·zā'tion, *n.* the act or process of carbonizing.

çär'bŏn·īze, *v.t.*; carbonized, *pt., pp.*; carbonizing, *ppr.* 1. to convert into carbon, as by partial burning.
2. to treat, cover, or combine with carbon.
3. to prepare with carbon; as, to *carbonize* a battery by adding carbon plates.

çär'bŏn mon·ox'īde, a colorless, odorless, highly poisonous gas, CO, produced by the incomplete combustion of any carbonaceous material: it burns with a pale-blue flame.

çär″bŏn·ō·hȳ'drous, *a.* composed of carbon and hydrogen.

çär'bŏn·om'e·tēr, *n.* [L. *carbo* (*-onis*), coal, and *metrum*, Gr. *metron*, a measure.] an instrument for determining the presence of carbon or carbon dioxide, and measuring the amount.

çär'bŏn pā'pēr, 1. very thin paper coated on one side with a carbon preparation or similar dark-colored substance: it is placed between two sheets of paper so that the pressure of writing, drawing, etc. on the upper sheet makes a copy on the lower.
2. paper used in the carbon process.

çär'bŏn point, a pencil of carbon used in the arc light.

çär'bŏn proc'ess, a method of printing light-resisting photographs on paper coated with gelatin and pigment.

çär'bŏn tet·rȧ·çhlō'rīde, a noninflammable, colorless liquid, CCl_4, used in fire extinguishers, as a solvent for fats (in cleaning mixtures), etc.

çär'bŏn tis'sūe (tish'ū), a gelatin-coated paper having suitable coloring material, for use in the carbon process.

çär'bŏn·yl, *n.* [*carbon*, and *-yl.*] in chemistry, (a) the bivalent radical CO; (b) any of a series of metal compounds containing this radical.

çär'bŏn·yl çhlō'rīde, a colorless, volatile, highly poisonous gas, $COCl_2$, prepared by the reaction of carbon monoxide and chlorine in the presence of activated carbon: also called *phosgene*.

çär·bŏn·yl'iç, *a.* of or containing carbonyl.

çär·bō·run'dum, *n.* a very hard abrasive substance, a compound of carbon and silicon, SiC, made into grindstones, etc.: a trade-mark (*Carborundum*).

çär·box'īde (*or* -id), *n.* carbon and oxygen in combination with some radical; as, potassium *carboxide*.

çär·box'yl, *n.* [*carb*on and *ox*ygen, and *-yl.*] the univalent radical CO_2H, occurring in the fatty acids and most other organic acids.

çär·box·yl'iç, *a.* of or containing carboxyl.

çär'boy, *n.* [Per. *qarāba*, a large bottle.] a large bottle of green glass, enclosed in basketwork or securely boxed for protection: used especially for carrying corrosive liquids, as sulfuric acid.

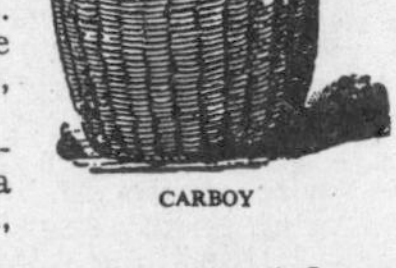
CARBOY

çär'buñ·çle (-buñk-l), *n.* [L. *carbunculus*, a little coal, a gem, from *carbo*, coal.]
1. any of certain deep-red gems, especially a garnet with a smooth, convex surface.
2. a painful, localized, pus-bearing inflammation of the tissue beneath the skin, more severe than a boil and having several openings.
3. any pimple.
4. in heraldry, a charge or bearing consisting of eight radii, four of which make a common cross, and the other four, a saltier.

çär'buñ·çled (-buñk-ld), *a.* set with or having carbuncles.

çär·buñ'çū·lăr, *a.* belonging to a carbuncle; resembling a carbuncle; red; inflamed.

çär·buñ·çū·lā'tion, *n.* the blasting of the young buds of trees or plants, by excessive heat or cold.

çär'bū·ret, *n.* a carbide.

çär'bū·ret (*or* -ret), *v.t.*; carbureted *or* carburetted, *pt., pp.*; carbureting *or* carburetting, *ppr.* 1. to combine chemically with carbon.
2. to mix or charge (gas or air) with volatile compounds of carbon in order to increase the potential heat energy.

çär'bū·re·tănt (*or* -ret-ănt), *n.* a substance, as gasoline or benzene, added to air or gas to carburet it.

çär'bū·re·ted, çär'bū·ret·ted (*or* -ret-ed), *a.* combined with carbon in the manner of a carburet; as, *carbureted* hydrogen gas.
carbureted hydrogen gas; any of various gaseous compounds of carbon and hydrogen.
heavy carbureted hydrogen; a colorless inflammable gas, C_2H_4, one of the constituents of coal gas; ethylene.
light carbureted hydrogen; a compound of carbon and hydrogen, CH_4, formed in stagnant pools and mines; marsh gas; methane.

çär·bū·re'tion (*or* -resh'ŏn), *n.* a carbureting or being carbureted.

çär'bū·re·tŏr, çär'bū·ret·tŏr (*or* -ret-), *n.* an apparatus for carbureting air or gas; especially, a device in which air is mixed with gasoline spray to make an explosive mixture in an internal-combustion engine.

çär″bū·ri·zā'tion, *n.* a carburizing or being carburized.

çär'bū·rīze, *v.t.*; carburized, *pt., pp.*; carburizing, *ppr.* [from Fr. *carbure*, carbide, hydrocarbon; and *-ize.*] to treat or combine with carbon; especially, to treat (iron) by heating in contact with carbon in making case-hardened steel.

çär″byl·ȧ·mīne' (*or* -am'in), [from *carbyl.*] any

of a group of organic cyanides, containing the radical NC.

çär′çȧ·jöu, *n.* [Fr., from native Ind. name.]

1. the wolverine.

2. loosely, the cougar, the Canadian lynx, or the American badger.

çär′çȧ·net, *n.* [a dim. from Fr. *carcan*, the collar of a criminal, a carcanet; LL. *carcannum*, the throat.] an ornamental collar, band, or necklace, usually of gold and often jeweled.

çär′çȧss, çär′çāse, *n.* [Fr. *carcasse*; It. *carcassa*, a bomb, shell; OFr. *carquais*.]

1. the dead body of an animal. The word is applied to the living or dead body of the human species in scornful or humorous usage.

2. the worthless remains of something, especially its outer shell or semblance.

3. the framework, skeleton, or base structure, as of a ship, building, tire, etc.

4. in military usage, formerly, an iron case or hollow vessel, about the size of a bomb, of an oval figure, filled with combustibles and other substances, as saltpeter, gunpowder, sulfur, broken glass, turpentine, etc., to be thrown from a mortar.

çär·çȧ·vel′hōs (-yōs), *n.* [Port., from *Carcavelhos*, a village in Portugal.] a sweet wine produced in Portugal.

çär′cel, *n.* [named after *Carcel*, a French inventor.] a standard of luminous intensity used in France, equal to nine and one-half candle power, or the light of a *Carcel* lamp.

Carcel lamp; a lamp in which the oil is raised through tubes by clockwork, producing a very brilliant light.

çär′cel·āġe, *n.* [L. *carcer*, a prison.] prison fees. [Obs.]

çär′cẽr, *n.* [L.] in ancient Rome, (a) a starting post; (b) a prison.

çär′cẽr·ăl, *a.* belonging to a prison.

Çär·çhar′ō·don, *n.* [L., from Gr. *karcharodōn*, with sharp, jagged teeth; *karcharos*, sharp, and *odous, odontos*, tooth.] a genus of nearly extinct man-eating sharks of great size; the only living species is *Carcharodon rondeleti*.

çär·çhar′ō·dont, *a.* 1. pertaining to the genus *Carcharodon*.

2. having pointed teeth, as a serpent.

çär·cin′ō·ġen, *n.* [*carcinoma*, and *-gen*.] any substance that produces cancer.

çär′ci·noid, *a.* [Gr. *karkinos*, crab, and *eidos*, form.] resembling a carcinoma: usually applied to certain benign tumors.

çär″ci·nō·loġ′iç·ăl, *a.* pertaining to carcinology.

çär·ci·nol′ō·ġy, *n.* [Gr. *karkinos*, a crab, and *-logia*, from *legein*, to speak.] the branch of zoology relating to lobsters and crabs, or the crustaceans: called also *crustaceology*.

çär·ci·nō′mȧ, *n.*; *pl.* **çär·ci·nō′mȧş** or **çär·ci·nō′mȧ·tȧ,** [Gr. *karkinōma*, a cancer, from *karkinoun*, to affect with a cancer, from *karkinos*, a crab, cancer.] any of several kinds of epithelial cancer.

çär″ci·nō″mȧ·tō′sis, *n.* a condition in which cancers are spread extensively throughout the body.

çär·ci·nom′ȧ·tous, *a.* of, having the nature of, or affected by cancer.

Çar″ci·nō·mor′phȧ, *n.pl.* [Gr. *karkinos*, a crab, and *morphē*, form.] a group of crustaceans including the common crab: called also *Brachyura*.

çär″ci·nō·mor′phiç, *a.* pertaining to or resembling the crab.

çär·ci·nō′sis, *n.* [Gr. *karkinos*, cancer.] any form or development of carcinoma.

çärd, *n.* [ME. *carde*; OFr. *carte*; LL. *carta, charta*, a card, paper; L. *charta*, a leaf of paper, tablet; Gr. *chartē*, a leaf of paper, layer of papyrus.]

1. a piece of thick paper or thin pasteboard, usually rectangular, prepared for various purposes; specifically, (a) a card bearing figures, a picture, or printed matter; as, a club membership *card*; a playing *card* in games; (b) a card with one's name, etc. written, engraved, or printed on it, used in making visits, etc.; as, a calling *card*; a business *card*, etc.; (c) the chart on which the points of the compass are printed; the dial of a compass; (d) a card on which is written, printed, or engraved an invitation or announcement; as, a wedding *card*; (e) a post card; (f) a card bearing a message or greeting, and, sometimes, appropriate pictures, etc., for some occasion; as, a birthday *card*; (g) a card to advertise or announce an event, product, etc.; as, a window *card*; (h) the printed program or record form for sporting events, etc.; as, a race *card*.

2. an event or attraction as described in a printed program; as, a drawing *card*.

3. a note published by someone in a newspaper, containing a brief statement, explanation, or request.

4. that part of a Jacquard loom which guides the threads.

5. a person who attracts attention by his wit, eccentricity, etc. [Colloq.]

card up one's sleeve; a plan or resource kept secret or held in reserve.

in (or *on*) *the cards*; possible or probable; likely to occur: from the use of cards in fortune-telling.

to have the cards in one's own hands; to be in possession of the means for successful accomplishment in any matter; to be master of the situation.

to play one's cards well; so to employ one's abilities and control one's circumstances as to gain a desired end.

to show one's cards; to expose one's plans; to divulge that which has previously been guarded as a secret.

to speak by the card; to speak accurately and from exact knowledge.

çärd, *v.i.* to play at cards; to game. [Obs.]

çärd, *v.t.* 1. to provide with a card.

2. to put on a card.

3. to list on cards for filing, cataloguing, etc.

çärd, *n.* [ME. *carde*; Fr. *carde*; Sp. *carda*; It. *carda*; LL. *cardus*, a card, thistle, from L. *carere*, to card.] a metal comb or wire brush for raising the nap on cloth or disentangling the fibers of wool, cotton, flax, etc.

çärd, *v.t.*; carded, *pt., pp.*; carding, *ppr.* 1. to comb or open, as wool, flax, cotton, etc., with a card, for the purpose of cleansing it of extraneous matter, separating the coarser parts, and making it fine and soft for spinning.

2. to clean out, as with a card. [Obs.]

3. to mix, mingle, or unite (one quality) with another, as a good grade with a poor one. [Obs.]

Çär′dȧ·mīne, *n.* [L. *cardamina*, Gr. *kardaminē*, from *kardamon*, a kind of cress.] a genus of herbs including lady's smock, cuckooflower, and meadow cress.

çär′dȧ·mŏm, çär′dȧ·mum, *n.* [L. *cardamomum*; Gr. *kardamōmon*, cress.]

1. the Asiatic plant *Elettaria cardamomum*; also, any of various species of *Amomum*.

2. its seed capsule or seed, used in medicine and as a spice.

çär′dȧ·mŏn, *n.* same as *cardamom*.

Çär·dan′iç, *a.* relating to or named after Cardan, a celebrated mathematician and physician of Italy, living in the sixteenth century.

Cardanic suspension; a manner of suspending an object by which it may move freely in any direction, as by expanding the limitations of ordinary gimbals.

çärd′bōard, *n.* a more or less stiff variety of pasteboard, smooth or unglazed, used in making boxes, tickets, price cards, and the like.

çärd′çāse, *n.* a case for holding calling cards, made of leather or other material; also, a case in which any kind of cards are held.

çärd çat′ȧ·logue (-log), a card file.

çärd′çlōth′ing, *n.* a covering for the main cylinder and doffers of a carding machine, formed of wire teeth of varying size set on a card back and cut in convenient strips.

çär′de·çū, *n.* [a corruption of Fr. *quart d'écu*.] a former French coin of silver. [Obs.]

çärd′ed, *a.* combed; opened; cleansed with cards, as wool or cotton.

çärd′ẽr, *n.* a person or machine that cards wool, cotton, or any other fibrous material; also, formerly, one who plays much at cards.

çärd′ẽr bee, a name applied to a bee of the genus *Bombus*, which has a habit of carding or smoothing out certain mosses for use in building a nest.

çärd file, a collection of cards containing data or records, arranged systematically, as in alphabetical order, in boxes or drawers: also called *card catalogue*.

çär′di-, cardio-.

çär′di·ȧ, *n.* [Gr. *kardia*, the heart.] the cardiac orifice of the stomach, the point where it is entered by the esophagus, being to the left and in the vicinity of the heart.

çär′di·aç, *a.* [L. *cardiacus*; Gr. *kardiakos*, pertaining to the heart; *kardia*, the heart.]

1. pertaining to the heart.

2. near the heart.

3. relating to the upper part of the stomach.

çär′di·aç, *n.*, a medicine which stimulates action of the stomach.

çär·dī′ȧ·çăl, *a.* cardiac.

çär′di·ȧ·graph, *n.* cardiograph.

çär·di·al′ġi·ȧ, çär′di·al·ġy, *n.* [Gr. *kardialgia*, heartburn; *kardia*, heart, and *algos*, pain.] a feeling of pain or discomfort in the esophagus or stomach, resulting from certain digestive disorders; heartburn.

çär′di·fŏrm, *a.* [LL. *cardus*, a card, and L. *forma*, shape.] resembling a wool card in appearance, as the teeth of certain fishes.

çär′di·găn, *n.* [after 7th Earl of *Cardigan* (1797–1868).] a knitted woolen jacket; a sweater that opens down the front: also *cardigan jacket* (or *sweater*).

Çär·dī′i·dae, *n.pl.* [from L. *cardia*, heart, and *-idæ*.] the family of mollusks, including the cockles, shaped like a heart and having two central or cardinal teeth in each valve.

çär′di·năl, *a.* [L. *cardinalis*, from *cardo*, hinge, that on which something turns or depends.]

1. chief, principal, pre-eminent, or fundamental; as, the *cardinal* virtues.

2. bright-red, like the robe of a cardinal.

cardinal numbers (or *numerals*); the numbers *one, two, three*, etc., in distinction from *first, second, third*, etc., which are called *ordinal numbers*.

cardinal points; the four principal points of the compass: north, south, east, and west. In astrology, the *cardinal points* are the rising and setting of the sun, the zenith, and nadir.

cardinal signs; in astronomy, Aries, Libra, Cancer, and Capricorn.

cardinal teeth; the teeth in the center of a bivalve shell.

cardinal veins; the two veins which in embryos traverse each side of the vertebral column, sending the blood back to the heart. Certain fishes retain them through life.

cardinal virtues; in theology, the basic virtues: prudence, justice, temperance, and fortitude.

cardinal winds; winds which blow from the cardinal points of the compass: north, south, east, and west.

çär′di·năl, *n.* [Fr. *cardinal*; It. *cardinale*; LL. *cardinalis*, a cardinal, from L. *cardo*, a hinge, that on which something important depends.]

1. an ecclesiastical prince in the Roman Catholic Church, who has a voice in the conclave at the election of a pope, the latter being chosen from among the cardinals. The cardinals are divided into three classes or orders, containing six cardinal bishops, fifty cardinal priests, and fourteen cardinal deacons, making seventy. These constitute the Sacred College, and compose the Pope's council. The dress of a cardinal is a red soutane or cassock, a rochet, a short purple mantle, and a red hat.

2. a deep red color, something between scarlet and crimson, the color of a cardinal's vestments.

3. a mulled drink made chiefly of claret.

4. a woman's short cloak, originally red and usually hooded.

5. the cardinal bird.

6. a cardinal number.

cardinal's hat; a red hat with a low crown and broad brim, forming a part of a cardinal's state dress. From each side hangs a cord, and at the end of each cord are fifteen tassels. The figure is used as a cardinal's heraldic charge.

CARDINAL'S HAT

çär′di·năl·āte, *n.* 1. the office, rank, or dignity of a cardinal.

2. the Pope's council of cardinals.

çär′di·năl bird, an American songbird, *Cardinalis cardinalis*, or *Cardinalis virginianus*, belonging to the finch family. It has a brilliant red plumage and a pointed crest. The male birds have a clear, musical whistle. Also called *redbird, cardinal, cardinal grosbeak*.

çär′di·năl flow′ẽr, 1. a plant, native to North America, the *Lobelia cardinalis*: so called from its brilliant red flowers.

2. the flower of this plant

çär′di·năl·īze, *v.t.* to make a cardinal, or give anything the distinctive color of his vestments. [Obs.]

çär′di·năl·ship, *n.* 1. the state of being a cardinal.

2. the position, rank, or term of office of a cardinal.

çärd in′dex, a card file.

çärd′ing, *n.* 1. the combing and disentangling

of fibers of wool, cotton, etc., to prepare them for spinning.

2. carded fibers.

3. a spool of combed material taken direct from the carding machine.

çärd′ing mȧ·çhine′, çärd′ing en′ġine, a machine for combing, breaking, and cleansing wool and cotton. It consists of cylinders, set with teeth, and is moved by water, steam, etc.

çär′di·ō-, a combining form from Gr. *kardia,* the heart, meaning *of the heart,* as in *cardi*ometer, *cardio*logy.

çär′di·ō·gram, *n.* [*cardio-,* and Gr. *gramma,* a writing.] the record traced by a cardiograph.

çär′di·ō·gräph, *n.* [*cardio-,* and Gr. *graphein,* to write.] an instrument for making a graph of the heart's action.

çär″di·ō·graph′iç, *a.* pertaining to or recorded by a cardiograph.

çär·di·og′rȧ·phy, *n.* the use of a cardiograph; recording the action of the heart.

çär′di·oid, *n.* [Gr. *kardioeidēs,* heart-shaped; *kardia,* heart, and *eidos,* form.] in mathematics, a curve more or less in the shape of a heart, traced by a point on the circumference of a circle that rolls around the circumference of another equal circle.

çär′di·oid, *a.* heart-shaped; characteristic of the *Cardiidæ.*

çär″di·ō·in·hib′i·tō·ry, *a.* [*cardio-,* and LL. *inhibitorius*; *in,* in, and *habere,* to have, hold.] curbing or stopping the heart's action.

çär·di·ol′ō·ġy, *n.* [*cardio-,* and Gr. *-logia,* from *legein,* to speak.] the study of the heart, its functions, and its diseases.

çär·di·om′e·tẽr, *n.* [*cardio-,* and Gr. *metron,* measure.] an instrument for ascertaining and measuring the strength of the heart's action.

çär·di·om′e·try, *n.* [*cardio-,* and Gr. *-metria,* from *metron,* a measure.] measurement of the heart, as by sounding or tapping on the chest.

çär·di·op′ȧ·thy, *n.* [*cardio-,* and Gr. *-patheia,* from *pathein,* to suffer.] any disease of the heart.

çär″di·ō·phō′bi·ȧ, *n.* in medicine, a morbid fear of heart disease.

çär″di·ō·pul′mō·nãr·y, *a.* of or involving the heart and lungs as they function interdependently.

çär″di·ō·sphyg′mō·gräph, *n.* a cardiograph and a sphygmograph combined.

çär″di·ō·vas′çū·lãr, *a.* of the heart and the blood vessels as a unified body system.

çär·dī′tis, *n.* [from Gr. *kardia,* the heart, and *-itis.*] inflammation of the heart.

Çär′di·um, *n.* [L., from Gr. *kardia,* heart.] the true cockles, the type genus of the family *Cardiidæ.*

çär′dō, *n.*; *pl.* **çär′di·nēş,** [L., a hinge.] the connecting joint of an insect's maxilla; also, the connecting hinge of a double shell.

çär′dol, *n.* an oil obtained from the shell of the cashew nut.

çär·dōōn′, *n.* [ME. *cardoun*; OFr. *cardon*; Sp. *cardon,* a cardoon, thistle; LL. *cardo*; L. *carduus,* a thistle.] a species of *Cynara,* a plant with edible stalks, related to the artichoke.

çärdş, *n.pl.* 1. a game or games played with a deck of cards, as bridge, rummy, poker, pinochle, etc.

2. the playing of such games; card playing.

çärd shärk, 1. an expert card player. [Colloq.]

2. a cardsharp. [Colloq.]

çärd′shärp, *n.* a professional swindler at cards.

çärd′shärp·er, *n.* a cardsharp.

çärd tā′ble, a table for card playing; especially, a small square table with folding legs.

çär·dū·ā′ceous, *a.* [from L. *carduus,* thistle; and *-aceous.*] of a family of thistlelike plants (called *thistle family* or *aster family*) with heavy heads of purple, tubular flowers.

Çär′dū·us, *n.* [L., a thistle.] in botany, a genus of carduaceous plants containing numerous species, freely distributed over the northern portions of the globe.

Carduus benedictus; the herb *blessed thistle.*

çâre, *n.* [ME. *care*; AS. *cearu, caru,* sorrow, anxiety; O.H.G. *kara, chara,* a lament.]

1. (a) [Obs.] grief; mental pain; hence, (b) worry; anxiety; solicitude; as, oppressed with the *care* of many things.

2. caution; watchfulness; heed; close attention; as, to take *care* of yourself.

3. charge; protection; custody; as, he was under the *care* of a physician.

4. the object of *care,* or watchful regard and attention; as, she is his constant *care.*

5. a liking or regard (*for*); inclination (*to* do something).

care of; in the charge of; at the address of: abbreviated *c/o, c.o.* (on mail).

to have a care; to be careful; to be cautious: also *to take care.*

Syn.—anxiety, solicitude, concern, attention, caution, trouble, precaution, forethought, heed, regard.—*Care* belongs primarily to the intellect, and becomes painful from overburdening thought; *anxiety* is a state of painful uneasiness from the dread of evil; *concern* expresses the same feeling in diminished degrees.

çâre, *v.i.*; cared, *pt., pp.*; caring, *ppr.* [ME. *carien, caren*; AS. *cearian,* to be anxious, from *cearin,* anxiety, sorrow.]

1. to be anxious or solicitous; to be concerned about.

Master, *carest* thou not that we perish?
—Mark iv. 38.

2. to have objection, worry, regret, etc.; mind; as, do you *care* if I go?

3. to feel love or liking (*for*).

4. to take charge of; to look after; to provide (*for*).

5. to wish (*for*); to want; as, do you *care* for more pie?

çâre, *v.t.* 1. to feel concern about or interest in; as, I don't *care* what you did.

2. to wish or desire; as, do you *care* to eat now?

could care less; [corruption of phr. *couldn't care less.*] feel or feels the least possible degree of interest, sympathy, etc. [Colloq.]

çȧ·reen′, *v.t.*; careened, *pt., pp.*; careening, *ppr.* [Fr. *carener,* to careen, from *carene, carine*; L. *carina,* the keel of a ship.] in nautical language, to cause (a ship) to lie on one side, for the purpose of calking, repairing, or cleaning.

2. to calk, clean, or repair (a ship in this position).

3. to cause to lean sideways; tip; tilt.

çȧ·reen′, *v.i.* 1. to incline to one side, as a ship under press of sail.

2. to lurch or toss from side to side.

çȧ·reen′, *n.* 1. the act of careening.

2. the position of being inclined to one side.

çȧ·reen′āġe, *n.* 1. cost of careening vessels.

2. a place where vessels are careened.

çȧ·reer′, *n.* [early modern Eng. *careere, carreer*; Fr. *carriere,* a road, race-course; OFr. *carier,* to carry by wagon; L. *carrus,* a wagon.]

1. originally, a racing course.

2. a swift course, as of the sun through the sky.

3. full speed.

4. one's progress through life.

5. one's advancement or achievement in a particular vocation.

6. a lifework; profession; occupation.

çȧ·reer′, *v.i.*; careered, *pt., pp.*; careering, *ppr.* to move or run rapidly, as a sailing vessel.

çȧ·reer′ *a.* pursuing a normally temporary activity as a lifework; as, a *career* soldier.

çȧ·reer′işm, *n.* the behavior of a careerist; exclusive or selfish devotion to professional ambitions.

çȧ·reer′ist, *n.* a person interested chiefly in achieving his own professional ambitions, to the neglect of other things.

çȧ·reer′ wom′ȧn (woom′), a woman who follows a professional or business career, often to the exclusion of marriage. [Colloq.]

çâre′free, *a.* free from anxiety, worry, etc

çâre′fụl, *a.* [ME. *careful*; AS. *cearful, carful,* from *cearu,* anxiety, and *full,* full.]

1. caring (*for*) or taking care (*of*).

2. watchful; cautious; wary; dealing thoughtfully or cautiously (*with*).

3. accurately or thoroughly done or made; painstaking; as, a *careful* analysis.

4. feeling or causing sorrow, worry, etc.; anxious. [Archaic.]

Syn.—attentive, solicitous, thoughtful, heedful, anxious, watchful, prudent, wary.

çâre′fụl·ly, *adv.* 1. with care, anxiety, or solicitude.

2. heedfully; attentively; cautiously.

çâre′fụl·ness, *n.* 1. anxiety, solicitude.

Drink thy water with trembling and with *carefulness.* —Ezek. xii. 18.

2. heedfulness; caution; vigilance in guarding against evil and providing for safety.

çâre′less, *a.* 1. having no care; heedless; negligent; unthinking; inattentive; regardless; unmindful; followed by *of* or *about*; as, a mother *careless of* or *about* her children is an unnatural parent.

2. free from care or anxiety; hence, undisturbed; cheerful.

Thus wisely *careless,* innocently gay.—Pope

3. done or said without care; unconsidered; negligent; not thorough; as, a *careless* throw.

4. not regarding with care; unmoved by; unconcerned for: with *of*; as, *careless of* money; *careless of* consequences.

5. artless; unstudied; spontaneous; easy; also untidy; as, *careless* attire; *careless* habits.

Syn.—heedless, inattentive, incautious, inconsiderate, negligent, thoughtless, unconcerned, unmindful.

çâre′less·ly, *adv.* in a careless manner; negligently; heedlessly; inattentively.

çâre′less·ness, *n.* heedlessness; inattention; negligence.

çȧ·rēne′, *n.* [LL. *carena,* a corruption of *quarentena,* from L. *quadraginta,* forty.] a fast lasting forty days. [Obs.]

çȧ·ress′, *v.t.*; caressed *or archaic* carest, *pt., pp.*; caressing, *ppr.* [Fr. *caresser,* from *caresse,* a caress.]

1. to touch, stroke, or pat lovingly or gently; also, to embrace or kiss: often used figuratively, as of a voice, music, etc.

2. to flatter; cajole.

çȧ·ress′, *n.* [Fr. *caresse*; L. *carus,* dear, precious; from Sans. root *kam,* to love, desire.] an affectionate touch or gesture, as a kiss, embrace, etc.; as, conjugal *caresses*; his very words were *caresses.*

çȧ·ress′ing·ly, *adv.* in a caressing manner.

çȧ·res′sive, *a.* caressing; like a caress.

çȧ·rest′, archaic past tense and past participle of *caress.*

çar′et, *n.* [L. *caret,* there is wanting; from *carere,* to want.] in writing and proofreading, this mark, ^, which shows that something, omitted in the line, is interlined above or inserted in the margin, and should be read in the place thus indicated.

çā′ret, *n.* [Sp. *careta,* a pasteboard mask; dim. of *cara,* the face.] the hawkbill, a sea turtle.

çâre′tāk·ẽr, *n.* 1. a person hired to take care of something or someone, especially of a house, estate, etc. for an owner who is not always in residence; custodian.

2. a person temporarily carrying out the duties as of an office.

çâre′-tūned, *a.* tuned by care; mournful.

çâre′wōrn, *a.* harassed, tired, or burdened with care; having the appearance caused by worry.

Çā′rex, *n.* [L., a sedge, rush.]

1. a widespread genus of perennial herbaceous plants of which the sedge is the type, and *Cyperaceæ* the order.

2. [c–] *pl.* **çā′ri·cēş,** a grass of this order.

çär′fâre, *n.* the price of a ride on a public conveyance, as a streetcar or bus.

çär′gō, *n.*; *pl.* **çär′gōeş** or **çär′gōş,** [Sp. *cargo, carga,* burden, load, from *cargar,* to load, charge, impose taxes.]

1. the lading or freight of a ship; the goods, merchandise, or whatever is conveyed in a ship or other merchant vessel.

2. load.

çär′goose, *n.* [Gael. and Ir. *cir, cior,* a crest, comb, and *goose.*] a fowl belonging to the genus *Colymbus.* [Brit. Dial.]

çar′hop, *n.* [*car* and bell*hop.*] a waiter or, especially, a waitress who serves food to customers in cars at a drive-in restaurant.

çar′i·ȧ·çöu, çar′jȧ·çöu, *n.* [S. Am.] a deer of the genus *Cariacus.*

Çȧ·rī′ȧ·çus, *n.* [L., from *cariacou.*] a genus of deer smaller than animals of the genus *Cervus,* including the white-tailed or Virginia deer.

çȧ·rï·ä′mȧ, *n.* [native name.] a South American bird of large size having remarkably long legs. It is the *Cariama cristata* which lives on small reptiles.

Çar′ib, *n.* [see *cannibal.*]

1. a member of a tribe of Indians who inhabited the southern West Indies and the northern coast of South America.

2. a family of related South and Central American languages.

Çar·ib·bē′ȧn (*or* çȧ-rib′i-), *a.* 1. of the Caribs, their language, culture, etc.

2. of the Caribbean Sea, its islands, etc.

Çar·ib·bē′ȧn, *n.* a Carib.

Çar′ib·bee, *n.* a Carib.

çar′i·bē, *n.* [Sp., a cannibal.] a voracious freshwater fish of South America, belonging to the genus *Serrasalmo,* having a scaly body and a naked head: in schools, they will even attack a human being.

çar′i·böu, çar′i·bōō, *n.*; *pl.* **çar′i·böus** or **çar′i·böu, çar′i·bōōş** or **çar′i·bōō,** [Canadian Fr.] any of several varieties of reindeer of North America, including those found in wild woodlands, *Rangifer caribou,* also those of the barren lands of the Arctic regions, the *barren-ground caribou.*

Çar'i·çȧ, *n.* [L., a fig.] a genus of American trees found for the most part in the tropics, one species of which is popularly called *pawpaw*: it is the type of the family *Caricaceæ*.

Çar·i·çā'cē·ae, *n.pl.* [from L. *carica*, a fig, and *-aceæ*.] a family of dicotyledonous trees found in the tropics of America and Africa.

çar'i·çȧ·tūre, *n.* [Fr. *caricature*; It. *caricatura*, a satirical picture, from *caricare*, to load, exaggerate.]
1. the deliberately distorted picturing or imitating of a person, literary style, etc. by exaggerating features or mannerisms for satirical effect.
2. a picture, literary work, performance, etc. in which this is done.
3. a bad likeness; poor imitation; something so distorted, ugly, or inferior as to seem a ludicrous imitation.
Syn.—burlesque, exaggeration, farce, imitation, mimicry, parody, travesty.

çar'i·çȧ·tūre, *v.t.*; caricatured, *pt., pp.*; caricaturing, *ppr.* to make or draw a caricature of; to represent, as by a caricature.

çar'i·çȧ·tūr·ist, *n.* one who makes caricatures or is skilled in caricature.

çar·i·çog'rȧ·phy, *n.* [L. *carex* (*-icis*), a sedge, and Gr. *graphein*, to write.] a description of the plants of the genus *Carex*, or sedge.

çar·i·çol'ō·ġist, *n.* in botany, a specialist in the study of the sedges.

çar'i·çous, *a.* [L. *carica*, a fig.] resembling a fig; as, *caricous* tumors.

çâr'ieṣ, *n.* [L. *caries*, decay.] decay of teeth or bones, or, sometimes, of tissue.

çar'il·lŏn, *n.* [Fr., a chime of bells, originally composed of four.]
1. a set of stationary bells, each producing one tone of the chromatic scale, sounded by means of a keyboard or by a clockwork mechanism.
2. a melody played on such bells.
3. an organ stop producing a sound like that of such bells.

çar'il·lŏn, *v.i.* to play a carillon.

çar''il·lŏn·neūr', *n.* [Fr.] a carillon player.

çȧ·rī'nȧ, *n.*; *pl.* **çȧ·rī'nae,** [L., the keel of a ship.]
1. in botany, the keel of the blossom, or the united petals of certain leguminous plants, which envelops the stamens and pistil; also, a keellike ridge on the glumes or husks of grass-seeds.
2. in zoology, the keel or ridge of a bird's breastbone.
3. [C–] one of the divisions of the constellation Argo, containing the bright star Canopus.

çȧ·rī'năl, *a.* of a carina.

Çar·i·nā'ri·ȧ, *n.* [L. *carina*, the keel of a ship, and *-aria*; so called from their shape.] a genus of marine heteropods, the nucleus and gills of which are covered with a thin glassy shell resembling a bonnet in shape.

Çar·i·nā'tae, *n.pl.* in zoology, formerly, a division of birds which includes all the living varieties except those belonging to the ostrich family, whose breasts are flat rather than keellike.

çar'i·nāte, çar'i·nā·ted, *a.* [L. *carinatus*, from *carina*, a keel.] in botany, shaped like the keel of a ship; having a longitudinal prominence on the back, like a keel: applied to a calyx, corol, or leaf.

çar·i·ō'çȧ, *n.* [Braz. Port., native of Rio de Janeiro, where the dance originated.]
1. a variety of South American dance.
2. music for this.

çar'i·ōle, *n.* [Fr.] a small open carriage; a covered cart; a kind of calash: also spelled *carriole*.

çar·i·op'sis, *n.* see *caryopsis*.

çā·ri·os'i·ty, *n.* [L. *cariosus*, from *caries*, decay, and *-ity*.] the quality or state of being carious.

çā'ri·ous, *a.* [L. *cariosus*, from *caries*, decay.]
1. having caries; decayed.
2. corroded.

çärk, *n.* [ME. *cark*, care, anxiety; AS. *carc*; W. *carc*, care, anxiety.] care; anxiety; concern; solicitude; distress. [Obs.]

çärk, *v.i.* to be careful or anxious. [Obs.]

çärk, *v.t.* to annoy, worry, burden, make anxious, or vex. [Obs.]

çärk'ing, *a.* distressing; perplexing; oppressive; troublesome; as, *carking* care. [Archaic or Poetic.]

çärl, çärle, *n.* [ME. *carl*, *carle*; AS. *ceorl*, a man, a churl.]
1. a peasant, bondman, or villein. [Archaic or Obs.]
2. an ill-bred fellow; churl. [Scot. or Archaic.]
3. a sturdy fellow. [Scot.]
4. a seed-bearing hemp plant: called also *carl hemp*.

çär'line, çär'lin, *n.* [ON. *kerling*, wife, old woman, from *karl*, man, male, and fem. suffix.]
1. a woman; especially, an old woman. [Scot.]
2. a hag; witch. [Scot.]

çär'line, *n.* a thistlelike plant of the genus *Carlina*: also called *carline thistle*.

çär'ling, çär'line, *n.* [Fr. *carlingue*.] any of the pieces of timber running fore and aft between two of the transverse beams supporting the deck of a ship.
carline knees; timbers in a ship, lying across from the sides to the hatchway and serving to sustain the deck.

çär'lish, *a.* rude; boorish; churlish.

Çär'liṣm, *n.* the principles, activities, or claims of Carlists.

Çär'list, *n.* an adherent to the claims of Don Carlos of Spain, or of his heirs, or of Charles X of France.

çär'lōad, *n.* 1. a load that fills or can fill a car.
2. the minimum weight of a carload lot.

çär'lōad lot, a freight shipment large enough to be shipped at a special rate (called *carload rate*).

çär'lock, *n.* [Fr., from Russ. *karlukŭ*.] a sort of isinglass from Russia, made of the sturgeon's bladder.

çär'lot, *n.* a peasant; a carl. [Obs.]

Çär·lō·vin'ġi·ăn, *a.* and *n.* Carolingian.

çär'mȧ·gnōle (-măn-yōl), *n.* [Fr., from *Carmagnola*, in Piedmont.]
1. the short jacket with wide lapels and metal buttons adopted by French revolutionaries (1792) as part of their costume.
2. this costume, including wide black trousers, a red cap, and a tricolored girdle.
3. a soldier of the French Revolution.
4. a lively song and round dance popular during the French Revolution.

çär'măn, *n.*; *pl.* **çär'men,** 1. a streetcar conductor or motorman.
2. a man who drives a wagon or cart; especially, one hired to haul goods; a carter. [Obs.]

Çär'mel·in, *a.* and *n.* same as *Carmelite*.

Çär'mel·īte, *n.* a monk or a nun of the order established on Mount Carmel, Syria, in the twelfth century, and known as the Order of Our Lady of Mount Carmel.

CARMELITE

Çär'mel·īte, *a.* belonging to the order of Carmelites.

çär·min'ȧ·tive, *a.* [from L. *carminatus*, pp. of *carminare*, to card, cleanse, from *carere*, to card; and *-ive*.] expelling gas from the stomach and intestines.

çär·min'ȧ·tive, *n.* a carminative medicine.

çär'mine (*or* -mīn), *n.* [Fr. *carmin*; Sp. *carmin*; LL. *carmesinus*, purple color, crimson; from *kermes*; Ar. *qirmizī*, *qirmiz*, crimson.]
1. a red or purplish-red pigment obtained mainly from cochineal.
2. a red or purplish-red color.
burnt carmine; a pigment, reddish purple in color, obtained by burning cochineal carmine.

çär'mine (*or* -mīn), *a.* red or purplish-red; crimson.

çär·min'iç, *a.* pertaining to carmine.

çär'mot, *n.* in alchemy, the supposed material of the philosopher's stone.

çär'nāġe, *n.* [Fr. *carnage*; It. *carnaggio*; LL. *carnaticum*, a tribute of animals; L. *caro*, *carnis*, flesh.]
1. slaughter; great destruction of men, especially in battle; massacre; bloodshed.
2. [Fr.; Pr. *carnatge*, flesh, carrion, from *carn*, flesh, from L. *caro*.] dead bodies, especially on a battlefield.

çär'năl, *a.* [L. *carnalis*, from *caro*, *carnis*, flesh.]
1. in or of the flesh; bodily; material or worldly, not spiritual.
2. sensual; sexual.
3. related by natural descent or blood. [Obs.]
carnal knowledge; sexual intercourse.

çär'năl·iṣm, *n.* the indulgence of carnal appetites.

çär'năl·ist, *n.* one given to the indulgence of sensual appetites. [Obs.]

çär·nal'i·ty, *n.*; *pl.* **çär·nal'i·tieṣ,** a carnal condition, nature, act, or manner; sensuality.

çär'năl·īze, *v.t.*; carnalized, *pt., pp.*; carnalizing, *ppr.* to make carnal.

çär'năll·īte, *n.* [after Rudolf von *Carnall* (1804–1874), G. mineralogist.] a hydrous chloride of magnesium and potassium, $MgCl_2 \cdot KCl \cdot 6H_2O$.

çär'năl·ly, *adv.* in a carnal manner; in a manner to gratify the flesh or sensual desire.

çär'năl-mīnd'ed, *a.* worldly minded.

çär''năl-mīnd'ed·ness, *n.* grossness of mind.

çär'nȧ·ry, *n.* [L. *carnarium*, from *caro*, *carnis*, flesh.] a charnel house or vault used for keeping human bones which have been disinterred. [Obs.]

çär·nas'si·ăl, *a.* [Fr. *carnassier*, carnivorous; from L. *caro*, flesh.] designating or of the last premolar on either side of the upper jaw and the first molar on either side of the lower jaw in flesh-eating animals.

çär·nas'si·ăl, *n.* a carnassial tooth.

çär'nāte, *a.* [L. *carnatus*, from *caro*, *carnis*, flesh.] having flesh.

çär·nā'tion, *n.* [L. *carnatio*, fleshiness, from *caro*, *carnis*, flesh.]
1. formerly, flesh color or rosy pink; now, deep red.
2. any of the cultivated varieties of the clove pink, *Dianthus caryophyllus*.
3. its fragrant flower of pink, white, or red.
4. [*pl.*] those parts of a painting that represent flesh.

çär·nā'tioned, *a.* having a carnation, flesh, or pink color.

çär·nau'bȧ, *n.* [Braz.] the wax palm, a Brazilian palm that yields a wax used to make candles.

çär·nēl'iăn, *n.* [altered (after L. *caro*, *carnis*, flesh: because of its color) from *cornelian*.] a variety of chalcedony, of a deep-red, flesh-red, or reddish-white color. It is fairly hard, capable of a good polish, and used for seals. Formerly called *cornelian*.

çär'nē·ous, *a.* [L. *carneus*, from *caro*, *carnis*, flesh.] fleshy; having the qualities of flesh.

çär'ney, *n.* [L. *carneus*, fleshy, from *caro*, *carnis*, flesh.] a disease of horses, in which the mouth is so furred that they cannot eat.

çär'niç, *a.* [L. *caro*, flesh.] pertaining to flesh.

çär'ni·fex, *n.* [L. *caro*, *carnis*, flesh, and *facere*, to make.] an executioner; particularly, the public executioner of the lowest criminals in ancient Rome.

çär''ni·fi·çā'tion, *n.* a turning to flesh, as the tissues of the vital organs in certain diseases.

çär'ni·fȳ, *v.t.*; carnified, *pt., pp.*; carnifying, *ppr.* [L. *carnificare*; *caro*, *carnis*, flesh, and *facere*, to make.] to form into flesh.

çär'ni·fȳ, *v.i.* 1. to form or become flesh.
2. to become fleshlike.

çär'nin, çär'nine, *n.* [L. *caro*, *carnis*, flesh.] an alkaloid found in meat extract; it is white, crystalline, and contains nitrogen.

çär'ni·văl, *n.* [Fr. *carnaval*; It. *carnevale*; from LL. *carnelevarium*, from hyp. *carnem levare*, to remove meat; associated by folk etym. with ML. *carne vale*, "Flesh, farewell!" from L. *caro*, *carnis*, flesh, and *vale*, farewell, from *valere*, to be strong.]
1. the period of feasting and revelry just before Lent: Mardi gras is the last day of this festival.
2. a reveling or time of revelry; festivity; merrymaking.
3. an entertainment with side shows, rides, games, and refreshments, usually operated as a commercial enterprise, sometimes by a social or charitable organization.
Syn.—revel, festivity, masquerade.

Çär·niv'ō·rȧ, *n.pl.* [Mod. L., neut. pl. of L. *carnivorus*; *caro*, *carnis*, flesh, and *vorare*, to eat.] in zoology, an order of mammals including the dog, wolf, cat, lion, bear, seal, etc., having large, sharp teeth and powerful jaws, adapted to flesh-eating. Some, however, such as bears, live also on vegetable food.

çär''niv·ō·rac'i·ty, *n.* greediness of appetite for flesh: a nonce word used by Pope.

çär'ni·vōre, *n.* a flesh-eating animal or an insect-eating plant.

çär·niv'ō·rous, *a.* 1. flesh-eating: opposed to *herbivorous*.
2. of the Carnivora.

çär·nos'i·ty, *n.* [Fr. *carnosité*; LL. *carnositas*, from *caro*, *carnis*, flesh.]
1. fleshiness. [Obs.]

2. an abnormal growth of flesh upon any portion of the body.

çär′nō·tīte, *n.* [after the Fr. official, A. *Carnot.*] a radioactive mineral containing hydrous potassium uranium vanadate.

çär′nous, çär·nōse′, *a.* 1. fleshy; pertaining to flesh.

2. in botany, of a fleshy character; as, *carnous* leaves.

çar′ŏb, *n.* [Fr. *caroube*, from It. *carrubo*, from Ar. *kharrūb*, bean pods.]

1. an evergreen tree, *Ceratonia siliqua*, native to southern Europe and northern Africa.

2. the long, flat pods which grow on this tree, fed to animals and sometimes eaten by people: often called *St. John's bread, carob bean*, and *algarroba*.

çȧ·rōche′, *n.* [MFr. *carroche*; It. *carroccia*, from ML. hyp. *carrautium*, from *carracutium*, from L. *carrus*, orig., two-wheeled Celtic war chariot.] in the seventeenth century, a coach or carriage used for state occasions.

çȧ·rōched′ (-rōcht′), *a.* placed in a caroche. [Obs.]

çar′oigne (-oin), *n.* [OFr. *caroigne*; LL. *caronia*, a carcass, from L. *caro*, flesh.] a dead body; carrion. [Obs.]

çar′ŏl, *n.* [ME. *carol, carole*; OFr. *carole*, a kind of dance, a Christmas song; ML. *choraula*, a dance to the flute, from L. *choraules*; Gr. *choraulēs*, flute player who accompanied the choral dance, from *choros*, dance, and *aulein*, to play on the flute, from *aulos*, flute.]

1. a song of joy, rapture, or gladness; as, the *carol* of birds.

2. a hymn of praise, especially in honor of the Nativity; as, a Christmas *carol*.

çar′ŏl, *v.t.*; caroled *or* carolled, *pt., pp.*; caroling *or* carolling, *ppr.* 1. to celebrate or praise in song.

2. to sing (a tune, etc.).

çar′ŏl, *v.i.* to sing with joy; to warble.

çar′ŏl, çar′rŏl, *n.* [OFr. *carole*, a circular space.]

1. a study in a cloister. [Archaic.]

2. a ring, as of stones. [Obs.]

Çar·ō·lē′ȧn, *a.* of Charles I or Charles II of England, or their period; Carolinian.

çar′ō·lī, *n.*, pl. of *carolus*.

çar′ō·lin, *n.* [LL. *Carolinus*, from *Carolus*, Charles.] any of various gold coins of Sweden.

Çar′ō·līne (*or* -lin), *a.* [LL. *Carolinus*, from *Carolus*, Charles.]

1. relating to Charles I or Charles II of England or their times; as, the *Caroline* age of England.

2. of Charlemagne or his period.

çar′ŏl·ing, *n.* a song of praise or devotion.

Çar·ō·lin′ġi·ăn, *a.* designating or of the second Frankish dynasty, founded (751 A.D.) by Pepin the Short, son of Charles Martel: also called *Carlovingian*.

Çar·ō·lin′ġi·ăn, *n.* a member of the Carolingian dynasty: also called *Carlovingian*.

Çar·ō·lin′i·ăn, *a.* 1. of Charlemagne or his period.

2. of Charles I or Charles II of England, or the period in which they lived: also *Carolean*.

3. of North Carolina or South Carolina.

Çar·ō·lin′i·ăn, *n.* a native or inhabitant of North Carolina or South Carolina.

çar·ō·lit′iç, *a.* in architecture, decorated with branches and leaves.

çar′ō·lus, *n.*; *pl.* **çar′ō·lus·eş, çar′ō·lī,** [LL. *Carolus*, Charles.] an English gold coin, first issued during the reign of Charles I, worth originally about twenty shillings.

çar′ŏm, *n.* [corruption of Fr. *caramboler*, to carom; *carambolage*, a carom; *carambole*, the red billiard ball.]

1. a shot in billiards in which the cue ball strikes successively two other balls; also, the stroke used in making such a shot.

2. in curling, etc., a shot like this.

3. a hitting and rebounding.

Also spelled *carrom*.

çar′ŏm, *v.i.*; caromed, *pt., pp.*; caroming, *ppr.*

1. to make a carom, as in billiards.

2. to hit and rebound.

çar′ō·mel, *n.* same as *caramel*.

çar′ŏmş, *n.pl.* [*construed as sing.*] a game for two or four players, played with 24 round counters on a large, square board with corner pockets.

çar·ō·tel′, çar·ō·teel′, *n.* [E. Ind.] a bundle, tierce, or cask of dried fruits weighing about 700 pounds.

çar′ō·tēne, *n.* a red- or orange-colored compound, $C_{40}H_{56}$, found in carrots and certain other vegetables, and changed into vitamin A in the body: spelled also *carotin*.

çȧ·rot′e·noid, *n.* any of several red and yellow pigments related to carotene: spelled also *carotinoid*.

çȧ·rot′e·noid, *a.* 1. of or like carotene.

2. of the carotenoids.

Spelled also *carotinoid*.

çȧ·rot′iç, *a.* [Sp. *carótico*; Gr. *karōtikos*, stupefying; from *karoun*, to stupefy; *karos*, stupor, heavy sleep.]

1. characterized by or pertaining to stupor.

2. in anatomy, carotid.

çȧ·rot′id, çȧ·rot′id·ăl, *a.* pertaining or adjacent to the carotids; as, a *carotid* canal.

çȧ·rot′id, *n.* [Gr. *karōtis*, pl. *karōtides*, the two great arteries of the neck; from *karoun*, to plunge into sleep or stupor: so called because compression of these causes unconsciousness.] either of two principal arteries which convey blood from the aorta to the head: one is on each side of the neck.

çar′ō·tin, *n.* same as *carotene*.

çar·ō·ti·nē′mi·ȧ, çar·ō·ti·naē′mi·ȧ, *n.* in medicine, a condition due to carotene in the blood.

çȧ·rot′i·noid, *n.* and *a.* same as *carotenoid*.

çȧ·rouş′ăl, *n.* [Fr. *carrousel*, a tilting match; It. *carosello*, from *garosello*, dim. of *garoso*, quarrelsome, from *gara*, strife, contention.] a rough, noisy feast or drinking party; a carousing.

Syn.—banquet, feast, festival, orgy, revel, festivity, wassail.

çȧ·rouşe′, *v.i.*; caroused, *pt., pp.*; carousing, *ppr.* to drink heartily and heavily; to participate in a carousal.

çȧ·rouşe′, *n.* [OFr. *carous, carousse*, a drinking bout; G. *garaus*, all out, a finishing stroke; *gar*, quite, completely, and *aus*, out.]

1. a drinking party.

2. a glassful drunk all at once, especially as a toast. [Obs.]

çar′ou·şel (*or* kar-ụ-sel′), *n.* a carrousel.

çȧ·rouş′ẽr, *n.* a drinker; a toper; a noisy reveler.

çȧ·rouş′ing·ly, *adv.* in a carousing manner.

çärp, *v.i.*; carped, *pt., pp.*; carping, *ppr.* 1. to censure, cavil, or find fault, particularly without reason, or petulantly.

2. to prattle; to talk. [Obs.]

çärp, *v.t.* [ME. *carpen*, to tell, say; Ice. *karpa*, to boast, brag; associated with L. *carpere*, to snatch, envy, slander.]

1. to tell; to say. [Obs.]

2. to censure; to find fault with. [Obs.]

çärp, *n.*; *pl.* **çärp** or **çärps,** [Fr. *carpe*; LL. *carpa*, a carp.]

1. a large-scaled fresh-water fish, genus *Cyprinus*, that is largely used as food and lives in ponds or other tranquil waters. It breeds rapidly, grows to a large size, and lives to a great age. Several varieties have been developed by breeding, including the *leather carp* and the *mirror carp*.

2. any of various other similar or related fishes, as the goldfish, dace, etc.

-çärp, [from Gr. *karpos*, fruit.] a terminal combining form meaning *fruit*, as in endo*carp*, peri*carp*.

çär′păl, *a.* [L. *carpus*, the wrist.] pertaining to the carpus, or wrist.

carpal angle; the angle at the joint nearest the body in the folded wing of a bird.

çär′păl, *n.* a bone of the carpus; carpale.

çär·pā′lē, *n.*; *pl.* **çär·pā′li·ȧ,** a bone of the carpus, or wrist, particularly one joining with the metacarpals.

Çär·pā′thi·ăn, *a.* pertaining to a range of mountains between Poland and Czechoslovakia.

çär′pel, *n.* [from Gr. *karpos*, fruit.] in botany, a simple pistil, regarded as a modified leaf; also, any of the two or more carpels that unite to form a compound pistil.

çär′pel·lăr·y, *a.* belonging to carpels, or containing them.

çär′pel·lāte, *a.* having carpels.

çär′pen·tẽr, *n.* [ME. *carpenter*; OFr. *carpentier*; LL. *carpentarius*, a carpenter, wagonmaker, from L. *carpentum*, a two-wheeled carriage, a cart.] a workman who builds and repairs wooden articles or the wooden parts of buildings, etc.

çär′pen·tẽr, *v.i.* to do a carpenter's work.

çär′pen·tẽr, *v.t.* to make or repair by or as if by carpentry.

çär′pen·tẽr ȧnt, any ant that gnaws holes in the wood of dead trees, in which it builds its nest; specifically, *Formica pennsylvanica*.

çär′pen·tẽr bee, any bee of the genus *Xylocopa*, which makes its nest by boring elongated chambers in dry, sound wood.

çär′pen·tẽr bïrd, a bird that makes holes or openings in the wood of dead trees; specifically, the *Melanerpes formicivorus* of California, which picks holes in trees and deposits acorns in them.

çär′pen·tẽr·ing, *n.* the art, trade, or work of a carpenter.

çär′pen·tẽr mọth, a moth of the *Cossinæ* family, whose larvae, called *carpenter worms*, subsist by boring beneath the bark of trees.

çär′pen·tẽr′ş hẽrb (ẽrb), an herb whose application was formerly supposed to heal wounds; specifically, the *Brunella vulgaris*.

çär′pen·tẽr wọ̈rm, see *carpenter moth*.

çär′pen·try, *n.* the art, work, or trade of a carpenter.

çärp′ẽr, *n.* one who carps; a caviler.

çär′pet, *n.* [ME. *carpette*; OFr. *carpite*, a carpet, a kind of cloth; LL. *carpita, carpeta*, a kind of thick woolen cloth, from L. *carpere*, to card, to pluck.]

1. a thick, heavy fabric of wool, jute, etc. for covering a floor, originally woven or felted, now often piled like a rug.

2. a strip, or several joined strips, of such fabric, used for covering a floor, stairs, etc.

3. any covering resembling or suggesting a carpet.

on the carpet; (a) under consideration; (b) in the position of, or into the place for, being reprimanded.

çär′pet, *v.t.*; carpeted, *pt., pp.*; carpeting, *ppr.* to cover with or as with a carpet; as, nature *carpets* the lawn with green.

çär′pet·bag, *n.* an old-fashioned traveler's bag made of carpet; also, any bag for holding one's personal belongings while traveling.

çär′pet·bag″gẽr, *n.* a Northern officeholder in the South during the period of reconstruction after the Civil War who took advantage of the unsettled conditions: contemptuous term, referring to the fact that such men usually carried all their belongings in a single carpetbag.

2. any wandering or irresponsible politician, promoter, etc.

3. in England, a candidate for or member of Parliament who does not actually live in the district he represents, or who moved there for political reasons.

çär′pet bee′tle, çär′pet bug, the *Anthrenus scrophulariæ*, a beetle whose larvae feed upon carpets and other woolen fabrics.

çär′pet·ing, *n.* carpets or the material of which carpets are made

çär′pet knīght (nīt), a knight or soldier who has never been in battle and has an easy, comfortable position: a disparaging term.

çär′pet·mŏn″gẽr, *n.* a gallant who frequents ladies' boudoirs.

çär′pet mọth, a carpet beetle in its larval stage.

çär′pet snāke, same as *diamond snake*.

çär′pet sweep′ẽr, a mechanical device for sweeping carpets, consisting essentially of rotating brushes which pick up the dirt.

çär′pet·wāy, *n.* a grassy strip left unplowed around the margin of a field.

çär′pet·weed, *n.* a low, prostrate, herbaceous weed which makes a carpetlike covering on the ground in southern climates, belonging to the pink family; specifically, *Mollugo verticillata*.

çär·phō·lō′ġi·ȧ, çär·phol′ō·ġy, *n.* same as *floccillation*.

çär′pī, *n.* pl. of *carpus*.

-çär′piç, -carpous.

çärp′ing, *n.* the act of caviling; a finding fault; unreasonable censure.

çärp′ing, *a.* caviling; captious; censorious.

çärp′ing·ly, *adv.* captiously; in a carping manner.

çär·pin·te′rō, *n.* same as *carpenter bird*.

çärp louse; *pl.* **çärp līce,** a crustacean of the family *Argulidæ*, which is parasitic upon the carp and other species of fish.

çär′pō-, [from L. *carpus*, wrist.] a combining form used in medicine and anatomy to indicate relation to the wrist.

çär′pō-, [from Gr. *karpos*, fruit.] a combining form meaning *fruit* or *seeds*, as in *carpo*phore, *Carpo*phaga.

çär·pō·bal′sȧ·mum, *n.* [*carpo-*, and Gr. *balsamon*, balsam.] the dried fruit of the *Balsamodendron gileadense*, or balm-of-Gilead tree of the Orient; also, the fragrant oil yielded by that fruit.

Çär·pō·crā′tiăn, *n.* a believer in the doctrines of Carpocrates, a Gnostic of Alexandria living in the second century.

Çär·pō·çrā′tiăn, *a.* related in any way to Carpocrates or to his teachings; specifically, believing in the doctrines of Carpocrates, i.e., the transmigration of the soul and the humanity of Christ, the latter purified, elevated, and strengthened in a superlative degree by his recollection of past experience.

çär·pō·gen′iç, çär·pog′e·nous, *a.* [*carpo-*, and Gr. *genesis*, origin, birth.] producing fruit.

çär·pō·gō′ni·um, *n.*; *pl.* **çär·pō·gō′ni·ȧ,** [*carpo-*, and Gr. *-gonos*, from *gignesthai*, to beget, produce.] the female reproductive organ of certain algae which, after fertilization, develops a sporocarp.

çär′pō·līte, *n.* [*carpo-*, and Gr. *lithos*, a stone.] the fossil of any kind of fruit, usually of a nut or hard seed: written also *carpolith*.

çär·pō·log′iç·ăl, *a.* relating in any way to carpology.

çär·pol′ō·ġist, *n.* a specialist in carpology.

çär·pol′ō·ġy, *n.* [*carpo-*, and Gr. *-logia*, from *legein*, to produce.] the study of the structure of seeds and seed vessels, or of fruits.

Çär·poph′ȧ·gȧ, *n.pl.* [Gr. *karpophagos*, fruit-eating; *karpos*, fruit, and *phagein*, to eat.] the genus comprising the fruit pigeons.

çär·poph′ȧ·gous, *a.* fruit-eating.

çär′pō·phōre, *n.* [Gr. *karpophoros*, bearing fruit; *karpos*, fruit, and *pherein*, to bear.] in botany, generally, the organ that supports the carpels; specifically, a very much elongated axis to which the carpels are attached.

çär′pō·phyl, *n.* [*carpo-*, and Gr. *phyllon*, a leaf.] in botany, a carpel or modified leaf.

çär′pō·phȳte, *n.* [*carpo-*, and Gr. *phyton*, a plant.] a cryptogamous plant, as the red algae, which upon fertilization bears spores and true fruit.

çär·pop′ō·dīte, *n.* [*carpo-*, and Gr. *pous*, *podos*, a foot.] the fifth segment of the leg of certain crustaceans.

çär′pos, *n.* same as *carpopodite*.

çär′pō·spẽrm, *n.* [*carpo-*, and Gr. *sperma*, seed.] the oösphere of the red algae changed by fertilization.

çär′pō·spōre, *n.* [*carpo-*, and *spora*, a sowing, generation.] a spore developed from the fertilized carpogonium of the red algae.

çär·pō·spōr′iç, *a.* of or relating to a carpospore.

çär′pō·stōme, *n.* [*carpo-*, and Gr. *stoma*, a mouth.] the opening through which the carpospores are discharged from the cystocarp of the red algae.

-çär′pous, [from Gr. *karpos*, fruit.] a terminal combining form meaning *fruited*; *having* (a certain number of) *fruits* or (a certain kind of) *fruit*, as in mono*carpous*, apo*carpous*.

çärp suck′ẽr, any one of several varieties of North American fresh-water fishes belonging to the genus *Carpiodes* and related genera: called also *quillback* and *buffalo fish*.

çär′pus, *n.* [L.] 1. in anatomy, (a) the wrist; (b) the wrist bones.

2. in crustaceans, the carpopodite.

çar′răck, *n.* [OFr. *carraque*, *caraque*; Sp. *carraca*; Ar. *quaraqir*, pl. of *qurqur*, merchant ship, from Gr. *kerkouros*, light vessel with a long stern, from *kerkos*, tail, and *oura*, tail, rear.] a galleon: also spelled *carack*.

çar′rȧ·geen, çar′rȧ·gheen (-gēn), *n.* [from *Carrageen*, near Waterford, Ireland.] a purplish, edible seaweed, *Chondrus crispus*, found along rocky coasts: when dried known as *Irish moss*.

çär·rän′chä, *n.* the Brazilian caracara, *Polyborus plancus*.

çar′rȧ·wāy, *n.* same as *caraway*.

çar′rel, *n.* [OFr. *carrel*, *quarrel*; LL. *quadrellus*, a square tile, a dart; L. *quadrum*, a square.] a fabric of the seventeenth century composed of silk and worsted.

çar′re·lȧġe′ (-läzh′), *n.* [Fr., from OFr. *carrel*, *quarrel*, a square tile, dart.] tiling; especially, patterned and variegated tiling laid in a floor.

çar′rell, *n.* [var. of *carol*, *n.*] a small enclosure or space in the stack room of a library, designed for study or reading by individual patrons.

çär·re̤′tȧ, *n.* [Sp. Am.] a two-wheeled cart: used chiefly in the southwestern United States.

çar′ri·ȧ·ble, *a.* capable of being carried.

çar′riaġe (-rij), *n.* [ME. *cariage*, baggage, transport; OFr. *cariage*, a cart, carriage, from *carier*, to carry.]

1. the act of carrying, bearing, transporting, or conveying; as, the *carriage* of goods.

2. the act of taking, as by an enemy; conquest; acquisition. [Obs.]

3. a four-wheeled passenger vehicle, usually horse-drawn and often private.

4. a wheeled frame or support for something heavy; as, a gun *carriage*.

5. manner of carrying the head and body; posture; poise; bearing.

6. in mechanics, any solid, parallel portion of a machine which carries another part; as, the *carriage* of a typewriter.

7. (çar′ri-ij), the price or expense of carrying; transportation charge.

8. that which is carried; burden; baggage; tonnage. [Rare.]

9. behavior; conduct; deportment; personal manners.

10. measures; practices; management.

Syn.—bearing, behavior, demeanor, deportment, conduct, gait, manner, mien, pace, walk.

çar′riaġe dog, a coach dog; Dalmatian.

çar′riaġe pōrch, a roofed structure over a driveway of a house, for the protection of a carriage and its occupants.

çar′riaġe trāde, the wealthy customers or patrons of a theater, store, etc.: so called because they arrived, formerly, in private carriages.

çar′ri·bo̤o̤, *n.* same as *caribou*.

çar′rick, *n.* [Scot.] the game of shinny; also, the ball used in the game.

çar′rick, *n.* same as *carack*.

çar′rick bend, a particular kind of knot used for joining two ropes.

çar′rick bitt, in nautical usage, one of the posts which support the windlass.

çar′ri·ẽr, *n.* 1. one who or that which carries; a messenger, porter, etc.

2. a person or company employed to transport goods or passengers.

3. a person or animal that carries and transmits disease germs but remains immune to that disease.

4. a carrier pigeon.

5. an aircraft carrier.

6. a container, support, or course in or on which something is carried or conducted, as a mechanical part or device, a water conduit, etc.

7. in chemistry, a catalytic agent that causes an element or radical to be transferred from one compound to another.

8. in electricity and radio, the steady transmitted wave whose amplitude, frequency, or phase is modulated by the signal.

common carrier; a person or company in the business of transporting passengers or goods for a fee, at uniform rates available to all persons.

çar′ri·ẽr piġ′eŏn, a pigeon trained to fly between points which it has previously visited, carrying written messages attached to its leg.

çar′ri·ẽr shell, in zoology, a snail, the *Xenophora conchylophora*, that conceals its shell by encrusting it with bits of shell, coral, and stones.

çar′ri·ōle, *n.* a cariole.

çar′ri·ŏn, *n.* [ME. *carion*, *caryon*, *caraigne*; OFr. *caroigne*; LL. *coronia*, a carcass, from L. *caro*, flesh.] the decaying flesh of a dead body.

çar′ri·ŏn, *a.* 1. relating to carrion.

2. feeding on carrion; as, a *carrion* crow.

3. like carrion; decaying, rotten, etc.

çar′ri·ŏn bee′tle, a beetle that feeds on, or deposits its eggs in, decaying flesh.

çar′ri·ŏn buz′zărd, any of various birds of prey, as the vulture, representing several genera and species.

çar′ri·ŏn çrōw, 1. the European crow.

2. the black vulture, *Catharista atrata*.

çar′ri·ŏn flow′ẽr, any plant of the genus *Stapelia*, whose flowers have a putrid odor.

çar′ritch, car′ritch·e̤s, *n.* [Scot.] in Scotland, a catechism.

çar·ro̤ç′ciō (-rōch′ ō), *n.* [It.] a war chariot on which was borne the standard of a medieval Italian state.

çar′rŏl, *n.* same as *carol*.

çar′rŏm, *n.* same as *carom*.

çär·rō·mä′tȧ, *n.* [Sp. *carromato*; It. *carromatto*, dray, truck, cannon truck, from *carro*, car, and *matto*, lit., mate.] a long, narrow, two-wheeled cart used in the Philippines for transporting goods.

çar·rŏn·āde′, *n.* [named from *Carron*, in Scotland, where it was first made.] an obsolete type of short, light cannon of large caliber: carried on the upper deck of a ship for us short range.

CARRONADE

çar′rŏn oil, a liniment for burns and scal made of linseed oil and limewater: first us at the iron works in Carron, Scotland.

çar′rŏt, *n.* [Fr. *carotte*; L. *carota*; Gr. *karōt* a carrot.]

1. the edible, orange-red root of the *Dauc carota*, a plant of the celery family.

2. any plant of the genus *Daucus*.

3. any one of several other umbellifero plants, some of them poisonous; as, the *Tha sia garganica*, or *deadly carrot* of northe Africa.

4. anything resembling a carrot in shap as a twist or roll of tobacco leaves.

çar′rŏt·y, *a.* 1. like a carrot in color, as orang red hair.

2. red-haired.

çar′roṳ·s̤el (*or* kar-ṳ-sel′), *n.* [Fr., from It *carosello*, from *carro*, a cart.]

1. a merry-go-round.

2. something that revolves like a merry go-round, as a revolving tray from whic slides are fed one at a time into a projecto or a circular conveyor in an airport fro which arriving passengers pick up thei luggage.

Also spelled *carousel*.

çar′rōw, *n.* in Ireland, a gambler.

çar′ry, *v.t.*; carried, *pt.*, *pp.*; carrying, *ppr.* [ME. *carien*; OFr. *carier*, from *car*; L. *carrus*, a car, cart.]

1. to convey or transport, especially in a vehicle; as, a car *carries* the mail.

2. to effect; to accomplish; to achieve; to influence; as, to *carry* a point, measure, or resolution.

3. to hold, and direct the motion of; as, a pipe *carries* water.

4. to urge, impel, lead, or draw; as, passion *carries* a man too far.

5. to keep with one; as, he *carries* a wound in his arm; she *carries* sunshine wherever she goes.

6. to be the means of moving or accomplishing; as, sound is *carried* by the atmosphere; the audience was *carried* by his eloquence.

7. to endure; to bear the weight of or responsibility for; as, to *carry* a great sorrow.

8. to prolong or to extend in space or in time; as, to *carry* an edifice higher; to *carry* a reader along in a narrative.

9. to hold or poise (oneself, etc.) in a specified way; as, he *carries* himself well.

10. to bring with it; to indicate; as, your arguments *carry* conviction.

11. to transfer (a figure, entry, account, etc.) from one column, page, time, etc. to the next in order.

12. to capture (a fortress, etc.).

13. to win (an election, argument, etc.).

14. to hold or support (something) while moving; as, she is *carrying* the child in her arms.

15. to be pregnant with.

16. to accompany; escort. [Archaic or Southern Dial.]

17. in golf, to go past or beyond (an object or expanse) or cover (a distance) with one stroke.

18. in farming, (a) to bear as a crop; produce; (b) to support (livestock).

19. in hunting, to keep and follow (a scent).

20. in music, to bear or sustain (a melody or part), as in singing.

21. in commerce, (a) to keep on one's account books, etc.; as, to *carry* for one his indebtedness until he becomes able to pay; (b) to keep in stock; as, the shop *carries* leather goods.

to carry all before one; to overcome all resistance in any undertaking; to meet with success after success.

to carry a (or *the*) *torch for*; to be in love with. [Slang.]

to carry away; (a) in nautical usage, to break off; as, our foretopmast was *carried away*;

(b) to excite great or unreasoning emotion or enthusiasm in.

to carry coals to Newcastle; to take things to a place where they already abound.

to carry off; (a) to remove to a distance; (b) to kill; as, the epidemic *carried off* thousands; (c) to win (a prize, etc.); (d) to handle (a situation), especially with success.

to carry on; (a) to do; to engage in; to conduct; (b) to go on with; to continue as before.

to carry out; (a) to put (plans, instructions, etc.) into practice; (b) to get done; to bring to completion.

to carry over; (a) to have remaining; (b) to transfer to a new place, time, etc.; (c) to continue from one time to another; as, habits that *carry over* to adulthood.

to carry through; to support to the end; to succeed in; to sustain, or keep from failing; as, he *carried* his project *through* in spite of opposition.

Syn.—convey, transport, transfer, transmit, move, support, sustain, bear, deport.

çar′ry, *v.i.* 1. to act as a bearer; as, the horse was *carrying* double, that is, had two persons mounted on it.

2. to bear the head in a particular manner, as a horse.

3. in falconry, to escape with the quarry: said of a hawk.

4. to have or cover a range; as, a gun or mortar *carries* well.

to carry on; to conduct oneself in a wild, reckless manner; to frolic. [Colloq.]

çar′ry, *n.*; *pl.* **çar′rieș** (-riz), 1. a transportation, as of boats or stores, from one navigable water to another; a portage.

2. the distance covered by, or the range of, a gun, golf ball, etc.

3. a carrying.

çar′ry·all, *n.* [corrupted from *cariole.*]

1. a light vehicle drawn by one horse, having usually four wheels, and designed to carry a number of persons.

2. an enclosed automobile having two long seats placed lengthwise and facing each other.

çar′ry·all, *n.* a large bag, basket, etc.

çar′ry·ing, *n.* the act of a person or thing that carries.

çar′ry·ing chärġe, interest charged by brokers, merchants, etc. on the balance owed on a purchase.

çar′ry·ing plāce, a portage.

çar′ry·ingș-on′, *n.pl.* wild, silly, or childish behavior. [Colloq.]

çar′ry·ing trāde, freightage, especially by water.

çar′ryk, *n.* a carrack. [Obs.]

çar′ry-ō·vẽr, *n.* 1. something carried over; extension; remainder.

2. a remainder, as of crops, goods, etc., held for future sale.

3. an amount carried forward in an account.

çar′ry-tāle, *n.* a talebearer. [Obs.]

çärse, *n.* [Scot.] low, fertile land, adjacent to a river.

çär′-sick, *a.* nauseated from riding in a streetcar, railroad car, automobile, etc.

çärt, *n.* [ME. *cart, kart*; AS. *cræt*; Ir. *cairt*, dim. of *car*, a car.]

1. (a) a heavy vehicle for rough work, usually two-wheeled and drawn by horses or oxen; (b) a light, two-wheeled pleasure carriage, with or without a top; (c) a small, wheeled vehicle, drawn or pushed by hand.

2. a cart load; as, two *carts* of sand.

to put the cart before the horse; to make a mistake by inverting facts or ideas logically dependent.

çärt, *v.t.*; carted, *pt., pp.*; carting, *ppr.* 1. to carry or convey on a cart; as, to *cart* hay.

2. formerly, to expose in a cart, by way of punishment.

çärt, *v.i.* to carry anything in a cart; to be engaged in the business of a carter.

çärt′āġe, *n.* 1. the act of carrying in a cart.

2. the price paid for carting.

çärt′bōte, *n.* in old English law, wood to which a tenant was entitled for making and repairing carts and other farm implements.

çärte, *n.* [Fr., a card.]

1. a bill of fare; as, a dinner ordered *à la carte* is one ordered from the bill of fare.

2. a carte de visite.

3. (a) a playing card; (b) [*pl.*] a card game or games. [Scot.]

4. a chart or map [Archaic.]

carte blanche; a paper duly authenticated with signature, etc., and allowing the bearer to fill in such conditions as he pleases; hence, unconditional terms; unlimited power to decide.

çärte, *n.* [Fr. *quarte*, from L. *quartus*, fourth.] a position of thrust or parry in fencing, consisting of turning the hand palm up, with the point of the sword toward the adversary's breast: written also *quart, quarte.*

çärte de vi·șite′, *pl.* **çärtes de vi·șite′** (kärt), [Fr.] 1. literally, a visiting card.

2. a photograph of a person, mounted on a small card.

çär·tel′, *n.* [Fr. *cartel*; It. *cartello*; LL. *cartellus*, a dim. from L. *carta, charta*, a piece of paper or papyrus; a writing.]

1. a writing or agreement between nations at war, especially for the exchange of prisoners.

2. a letter of challenge, as to a duel.

3. [often C–] a political bloc in certain European countries.

çär·tel′, *n.* [G. *kartell.*] an association between financial or industrial interests for establishing a national or international monopoly by the fixing of prices and the ownership of controlling stock; a trust.

çär·tel′, *v.t.* to combine in a cartel; to pool.

çär·tel′, *v.i.* 1. to agree upon or carry out the terms of a cartel.

2. to form a cartel.

çär′tel, *v.t.* to defy. [Obs.]

çär·tel′ ship, a ship employed in the exchange of prisoners, or in carrying propositions to an enemy.

çärt′ẽr, *n.* 1. one whose work or trade is driving a cart.

2. in zoology, (a) the daddy longlegs; (b) a flatfish, the whiff.

Çär·tē′șiăn (-zhăn), *a.* [from Renatus *Cartesius*, a Latinized form of René *Descartes.*] pertaining to the philosopher René Descartes (1596–1650), or to his philosophy.

Cartesian co-ordinates; in geometry, numbers used to locate a point in relation to two intersecting straight lines.

Cartesian devil; a hydrostatic toy consisting of a hollow figure partly filled with air, which may be induced to float at various depths in a tube of water by compression of the air in the tube: called also *bottle imp.*

Cartesian oval; the locus of a describing point having a distance from two fixed points equal to a given constant.

Çär·tē′șiăn, *n.* a follower of the philosophy of Descartes.

Çär·tē′șiăn·ism, *n.* the philosophy of Descartes: a belief in the duality of mind and body.

Çär·thȧ·ġin′i·ăn, *a.* pertaining to ancient Carthage, a city in northern Africa.

Çär·thȧ·ġin′i·ăn, *n.* an inhabitant or native of Carthage.

çär′thȧ·min, çär′thȧ·mine, *n.* a red pigment obtained from the flowers of the *Carthamus tinctorius*, or safflower. It is used in dyeing and making rouge.

çärt horse, a large, strong horse for drawing heavily loaded carts; work horse.

Çär·thū′șiăn (-zhăn), *n.* one of a very strict order of monks or nuns, founded at Chartreuse, France, in 1086, under Benedictine rule, by St. Bruno.

Çär·thū′șiăn, *a.* pertaining to the Carthusians.

çär′ti·lāġe, *n.* [Fr. *cartilage*; L. *cartilago*, gristle.]

1. a tough, elastic, whitish tissue occurring in vertebrate animals, and forming the tissue from which bone is formed by a process of calcification. In some parts of the body it remains permanent. *True cartilage*, or *hyaline*, consists of a clear matrix with nucleated cells; *articular cartilage* coats the ends of bones; *yellow* or *reticular cartilage* is any cartilage having a matrix that consists mainly of a network of yellow fibers.

2. any part of the body consisting of cartilage.

çär′ti·lāġe bōne, ossified cartilage.

Çär″ti·lȧ·ġin′e·ī, *n.pl.* [from L. *cartilago* (*-inis*), gristle.] the cartilaginous fishes: also called *Chondropterygii.*

çär″ti·lȧ·ġin′e·ous, *a.* cartilaginous. [Obs.]

çär″ti·lȧ·ġin″i·fi·çā′tion, *n.* [L. *cartilago* (*-inis*), gristle, and *facere*, to make.] the process of converting into cartilage.

çär·ti·laġ′i·nous, *a.* 1. pertaining to or resembling cartilage; gristly.

2. having a skeleton consisting mainly of cartilage; as, *cartilaginous* fishes.

Çär′tist, *n.* [Sp. and Port. *carta*, a charter.] a Spanish or Portuguese supporter of the constitutional charter.

çärt′lōad, *n.* 1. as much as a cart will hold.

2. a large quantity. [Colloq.]

çärt′măn, *n.*; *pl.* **çärt′men,** a driver of a cart; a teamster.

çär′tō·gram, *n.* [Fr. *cartogramme.*] a map showing geographical statistics by means of lines, dots, shaded areas, etc.

çär·tog′rȧ·phẽr, *n.* a person whose work is making charts or maps.

çär·tō·graph′iç, çär·tō·graph′iç·ăl, *a.* pertaining to cartography.

çär·tō·graph′iç·ăl·ly, *adv.* according to cartography.

çär·tog′rȧ·phy, *n.* [Fr. *cartographie*, from L. *charta*, Gr. *chartēs*, a leaf of paper; and *-graphy.*] the art or practice of making charts or maps.

çär′tō·man·cy, *n.* [LL. *carta*, a card, and Gr. *manteia*, divination.] the use of playing cards to tell fortunes; divination by cards.

çär′tŏn, *n.* [Fr.] 1. a thin kind of pasteboard.

2. a cardboard box, especially a large one.

3. a full carton or its contents.

4. a cartoon, or design.

5. in rifle practice, (a) a white disk fixed on the bull's-eye of a target; (b) a shot that hits this disk.

çär′tŏn·nāġe, *n.* [Fr., from *carton*, pasteboard.]

1. pasteboard.

2. a kind of material used by the ancient Egyptians for mummy casings, consisting of layers of linen cloth fixed together with glue, stucco being often added as a coating.

çär·toṇ pierre′ (pyãr), [Fr., lit., stone paper.] a substance resembling papier-mâché, largely used in making statuettes, moldings, etc.

çär·tōōn′, *n.* [Fr. *carton*; It. *cartone*, pasteboard, a cartoon; L. *charta*, a paper, writing.]

1. in painting, a design drawn on strong paper, afterward copied on the fresh plaster of a wall to be painted in fresco; also, a design colored for working in mosaic, tapestry, etc.; as Raphael's famous *cartoons*, which were designs for tapestry to be made in Flanders.

2. a pictorial representation or caricature, often satirical, showing some action, situation, or person of topical interest.

3. a comic strip.

4. an animated cartoon.

çär·tōōn′, *v.t.* to draw a cartoon of.

çär·tōōn′, *v.i.* to draw cartoons.

çär·tōōn′ist, *n.* a person who draws cartoons.

çär·tōuçhe′, çär·touçh′, *n.* [Fr. *cartouche*; OFr. *cartoche*, from It. *cartoccio*, a cartridge, a roll of paper, from *carta*, paper; L. *charta*, paper; Gr. *chartēs*, a leaf of paper.]

CARTOUCHE OF PTOLEMY

1. an oval figure on ancient Egyptian monuments and in papyri, containing groups of characters expressing the name or title of a king or deity.

2. in architecture, (a) a sculptured ornament in the form of a scroll unrolled, often appearing on the cornices of columns and sometimes inscribed; (b) a kind of ornamental block used in the cornices of house interiors.

3. formerly, a cartridge or cartridge box.

4. a case for holding cannon balls. [Obs.]

5. in some fireworks, a case holding the combustible materials.

6. in heraldry, the oval escutcheon of a churchman.

çär′tridġe (-trij), *n.* [formerly also *cartrage*, altered from *cartouche.*]

1. a cylindrical case of cardboard, metal, or other material, containing the charge, and usually the projectile, for a firearm.

CARTRIDGE

2. any somewhat similar small container, as for recharging a siphon, refilling a razor, etc.

3. a protected roll of camera film.

center-fire cartridge; a cartridge having the primer in the center of the shell base, as opposed to a *rim-fire cartridge*, in which the primer is contained in the rim of the shell base.

çär′tridġe bag, in gunnery, a cloth bag in which the charge of cannon is contained.

çär′tridġe belt, a belt for the waist or to go over the shoulder, for carrying cartridges or equipment, as a water canteen, compass, etc.

çär′tridġe box, a portable case or box for carrying cartridges.

çär′tridġe çāse, 1. a cartridge box.
2. the tube in which the powder of a cartridge is contained.

çär′tridġe çlip, a metal container for cartridges, inserted in certain types of firearms.

çär′tridġe pā′pẽr, 1. a thick paper for making cartridge cases.
2. a kind of drawing paper.

çär′tū·lăr·y, *n.*; *pl.* **çär′tū·lăr·ieṣ,** same *chartulary.*

çärt′wāy, *n.* a roadway for carts or other vehicles.

çärt wheel (hwēl), 1. the wheel of a cart.
2. a large coin, especially a silver dollar. [Slang.]
3. a kind of handspring performed sidewise.

çärt′wrīght (-rīt), *n.* an artisan whose business is making or repairing carts.

çar′ū·çāġe, *n.* [LL. *carrucagium,* from LL. *carruca,* a plow; L. *carruca,* a coach.]
1. act of plowing.
2. a duty or tax on a plow: also written *carrucage.* [Obs.]

Çā′rum, *n.* [from Gr. *karon,* caraway.] a large genus of plants, family *Umbelliferæ,* including *Carum carui,* the caraway plant.

çar′uñ·çle, çȧ·ruñ′çū·lȧ, *n.* [L. *caruncula,* dim. from *caro,* flesh.]
1. a small fleshy excrescence; specifically, a fleshy excrescence on the head of a fowl, as the comb of a cock, the wattles of a turkey.
2. in botany, a protuberance surrounding the hilum of a seed.

çȧ·ruñ′çū·lăr, çȧ·ruñ′çū·lous, *a.* resembling or pertaining to a caruncle; having caruncles.

çȧ·ruñ′çū·lāte, çȧ·ruñ′çū·lā·ted, *a.* caruncular.

çȧ·rū′tō, *n.* [S. Am. name.]
1. a dye of a deep blue-black obtained from genipap.
2. the genip tree, *Genipa americana.*

çär′vȧ·çrōl, *n.* [Fr. *carvi,* caraway, and L. *acer, acris,* sharp, and *oleum,* oil.] a derivative of oil of mint and other essential oils, being a thick, oily liquid used as an antiseptic and anesthetic.

çär′vȧ·çryl, *n.* in chemistry, the univalent radical $C_{10}H_{13}$, of which carvacrol is the hydroxide.

çärve, *v.t.*; carved, *pt., pp.*; carven, *archaic pp.*; carving, *ppr.* [ME. *kerven*; AS. *ceorfan,* to carve, cut; G. *kerben*; Gr. *graphein,* to inscribe.]
1. to make (an object, design, etc.) by or as by cutting; to hew; as, to *carve* an image out of wood or stone; to *carve* a career.
2. to shape or decorate by cutting; to decorate the surface of with cut figures, etc.; as, the chest is finely *carved.*
3. to divide by cutting; to slice, as meat at the table.

çärve, *v.i.* 1. to cut up meat.
2. to carve statues or designs.

çärved, *a.* cut or divided; engraved; formed by carving.

çär′vel, *n.* a caravel; a small ship.

çär′vel-built (-bilt), *a.* in shipbuilding, with the hull planks flush at the seams: distinguished from *clinker-built,* in which the joints lap.

çär′ven, *a.* carved; made by carving; embellished by carvings, as fine woodwork or objects of art. [Archaic or Poetic.]

çär′ven, archaic past participle of *carve.*

çär′vēne, *n.* [Fr. *carvi,* caraway.] an oily, odorless, tasteless substance, obtained from oil of caraway.

çärv′ẽr, *n.* 1. one who cuts meat at the table.
2. a sculptor.
3. a carving knife.

çärv′ing, *n.* 1. the act or art of cutting figures in wood or stone.
2. a piece of decorative work designed and cut in stone, wood, marble, ivory, or other material.

çärv′ing fork, a fork with a metal guard to protect the hand, used to hold meat being carved.

çärv′ing knife (nīf), a large knife for carving meat.

çär′vist, *n.* in falconry, a hawk which is of proper age and training to be carried on the hand.

çär wheel (hwēl), a wheel of iron, steel, or other material, with a flange on the inside to keep it on a track: used on railway cars, etc.

çar·y·at′ic, *a.* pertaining to a caryatid or characterized by caryatids.

çar·y·at′id, *n.*; *pl.* **çar·y·at′idṣ, çar·y·at′i·dēṣ,** [from L. pl. *caryatides*; Gr. *karyatides,* priestesses of the temple of Diana at Karyai.] in architecture, a sculptured female figure, fully draped, which takes the place of a column or pilaster in supporting an entablature.

CARYATID

çar·y·at′i·dēṣ, *n.,* alternative pl. of *caryatid.*

çar′y·ō-, same as *karyo-.*

Çȧ·rȳ′ō·çär, *n.* [Gr. *karyon,* a nut, and *kara,* a head.] a genus of tropical American trees, family *Rhizobolaceæ,* having valuable wood and large, edible, kidney-shaped seeds (called *souari*).

Çar″y·ō·phyl·lā′cē·ae, *n.pl.* [from Gr. *karyophyllon,* the clove tree; *karyon,* a nut, and *phyllon,* a leaf.] the pink family of plants, including the chickweed, spurrey, sandwort, pink, carnation, sweet William, etc. They are characterized by bright-colored flowers, opposite or whorled leaves, and stems usually swollen at the joints.

çar″y·ō·phyl·lā′ceous, *a.* 1. pertaining to the *Caryophyllaceæ.*
2. having five petals with long claws in a tubular calyx.

çar″y·ō·phyl′liç, *a.* pertaining to caryophyllin.

çar″y·ō·phyl′lin, *n.* a crystalline substance obtained from cloves.

çar·y·oph′yl·lous, *a.* same as *caryophyllaceous.*

çar·y·op′sis, *n.* [Gr. *karyon,* a nut, and *opsis,* an appearance.] in botany, a small one-seeded, dry, indehiscent fruit, in which the seed adheres to the thin pericarp, so that the fruit and seed are incorporated into one body, as in wheat and other kinds of grain.

çar·y·ō′tin, *n.* karyotin; chromatin.

çȧ·sä′bȧ, *n.* [from *Kassaba,* town near Smyrna, Asia Minor, whence the melon was introduced.] any of several kinds of winter muskmelon, having a yellow rind and a sweetish, white, watery flesh: also called *casaba melon, cassaba, winter melon.*

çāṣ′ăl, *a.* in grammar, pertaining to case.

ças′çȧ·bel, *n.* [Sp., a small bell, rattle, rattlesnake.] a knob behind the base ring or breech of some muzzle-loading cannons.

cas·çāde′, *n.* [Fr. *cascade*; It. *cascata,* from *cascare,* to fall.]
1. a small, steep waterfall, especially one of a series.
2. a thing like this; rippling or showering fall, as of sparks, lace, drapery, etc.
3. in electricity, the charging of a number of connected Leyden jars.
cascade amplification; in electricity, the use of several electron tubes, each in turn amplifying the sound and passing it on to the next tube.

cas·çāde′, *v.t.* and *v.i.* 1. to fall or cause to fall in a cascade.
2. to vomit. [Rare Colloq.]

çȧs·çäl′hō (-yō), *n.* [Port.] in Brazil, a deposit of pebbles, gravel, and ferruginous sand, in which the diamond is usually found.

cas·çä′r′ȧ, *n.* [Sp.] the cascara buckthorn, or its bark.
cascara buckthorn; bearwood growing on the Pacific coast of the United States.
cascara sagrada; bark from the cascara buckthorn: used as a mild laxative.

cas·çȧ·ril′lȧ, *n.* [Sp. dim. of *cascara,* peel, bark.] the aromatic, bitter bark of *Croton eleuteria,* a small tree closely allied to cinchona, cultivated chiefly in the Bahamas: used as a tonic: usually called *cascarilla bark.*

cas·çȧ·ril′lin, *n.* a white, crystalline, bitter substance obtained from cascarilla bark.

çaṣ′çō, *n.* [Sp.] a flat boat of the Philippines, almost of rectangular form, used for conveying freight.

CASCARILLA PLANT
(*Croton eleuteria*)

çāse, *n.* [ME. *case*; OFr. *casse*; L. *capsa,* a box, chest, from *capere,* to take, contain, hold.]
1. a covering, box, sheath, crate, folder, etc.; that which encloses or contains; as, a *case* for knives.
2. a protective cover or covering part; as, a watch *case.*
3. the skin of an animal. [Obs.]
4. the exterior portion of a building; an outer framework for walls. [Rare.]
5. a full box or its contents; as, a *case* of wine.
6. a set or pair; as, a *case* of pistols.
7. a frame for a window, door, or stairs.
8. in printing, one of the shallow compartmented trays in which type is kept: the *upper case* is used for capitals and special characters, the *lower case* for small letters, figures, etc.
9. in mining, a small fissure which lets water into the workings.

çāse, *v.t.*; cased, *pt., pp.*; casing, *ppr.* 1. to cover with a case; to surround with any material that encloses or protects.
2. to put in a case or box.
3. to fuse (glass) with an overlay of another color.
4. to remove the skin of. [Obs.]

çāse, *n.* [ME. *cas, case*; OFr. *cas,* an event, chance; L. *casus,* a falling, accident, from *cadere,* to fall.]
1. literally, that which falls, comes, or happens; an event; hence, a state of affairs or set of circumstances; condition; situation.
2. an example, occurrence, or instance; as, a *case* of fever.
3. a person in whom a disease occurs; a patient.
4. a statement of facts involving a question for discussion or decision; as, the lawyer for the defendant stated the *case.*
5. convincing arguments or evidence; just cause or grounds for a statement or action; as, he has no *case.*
6. a legal action or investigation, especially one studied or cited as a precedent.
7. a question or problem; as, this child is a difficult *case.*
8. a peculiar person; queer type; as, he's a *case.* [Slang.]
9. in grammar, (a) a form taken by a noun, pronoun, or adjective to show its relation to neighboring words; (b) any such relation, whether expressed by inflection or otherwise; (c) such forms or relations collectively.
case lawyer; a lawyer well-versed in previous court decisions.
in any case; anyhow; anyway.
in case; in the event or contingency that; if.
in case of; in the event of; if there is; in order to be prepared for.
in no case; by no means; not under any circumstances.
to put a case; to suppose an event or a certain state of things.
Syn.—situation, condition, state, circumstance, plight, predicament.

çāse, *v.t.* to examine carefully; to look over; as, the thief *cased* the house before the robbery. [Slang.]

çāse, *v.i.* to put cases; to give illustrations. [Obs.]

çā′sē·āse, *n.* [*case*in, and *-ase.*] an enzyme made from bacterial cultures, which dissolves casein and albumin: used in the process of ripening cheese.

çā′sē·āte, *n.* a salt of caseic acid.

çā′sē·āte, *v.i.*; caseated, *pt., pp.*; caseating, *ppr.* in medicine, to undergo caseation.

çā·sē·ā′tion, *n.* 1. precipitation of casein during the coagulation of milk to form cheese.
2. in medicine, a degenerative process in which tissue changes into a dry, crumbly, cheeselike substance.

çāse bāy, 1. the space between two girders.
2. a joist framed between two girders.

çāse bīnd′ing, a method of bookbinding in which the cover is finished separately before being fastened to the book.

çā′sē·fȳ, *v.t.* and *v.i.*; casefied, *pt., pp.*; casefying, *ppr.* [from L. *caseus,* cheese, and *-fy.*] to make or become cheeselike.

çāse′härd″en, *v.t.*; casehardened, *pt., pp.*; casehardening, *ppr.* 1. to form a hard, thin surface on (iron or steel).
2. to make callous or unfeeling.

çāse′härd″ened, *a.* having the outside surface hardened, as tools; hence, callous; unfeeling.

çāse′härd″en·ing, *n.* the process of forming a hard, thin surface on iron or steel, while the interior retains the softness and toughness of malleable iron.

çāse his′tō·ry, collected information about an individual or group, for use especially in sociological, medical, or psychiatric studies.

çā'sē·iç, *a.* [L. *caseus*, cheese.] of or pertaining to cheese.

çā'sē·in, *n.* a phosphoprotein that is one of the chief constituents of milk and the basis of cheese.

çā·sē·in'ō·ġen, *n.* [from *casein*, and *-gen*.] that protein of milk which produces casein when acted upon by rennin.

çāse knīfe (nīf), 1. a knife carried in a case or sheath.
 2. a table knife.

çāse lạw, law based on previous judicial decisions, or precedents: distinguished from *statute law*.

çāse'lōad, *n.* the number of cases being handled as by a court, social agency, or welfare department, or by a social worker, probation officer, etc.

çāse'māte, *n.* [Fr. *casemate*, from It. *casamatta*, a casemate, from Gr. *chasmate*, pl. of *chasma*, a gulf; confused with It. *casa*, a house, and *matto*, foolish, dull, dim, dark.]
 1. in fortifications, (a) a vault of stone or brickwork, as in the rampart of a fortress or on a warship, and pierced in front with embrasures, through which artillery may be fired; (b) a shellproof vault of stone or brick to protect the troops, ammunition, etc.
 2. in architecture, a hollow molding, chiefly used in cornices: called also *cavetto*.

çāse'māt·ed, *a.* furnished with or as with a casemate or casemates.

çāse'ment, *n.* 1. a glass frame or sash forming a window or part of a window, hinged so as to open outward.
 2. a casing; a covering.
 3. a deep, hollow molding. [Archaic.]

çāse'ment·ed, *a.* 1. having casements.
 2. encased; covered.

çā'sē·ōse, *n.* [*casein*, and *-ose*.] a soluble protein derivative formed during the digestion of casein.

çā'sē·ous, *a.* [L. *caseus*, cheese.] pertaining to, like, or having the qualities of cheese.
 caseous degeneration; in medicine, caseation.

çà·ṣẽrn', çà·ṣẽrne', *n.* [Fr. *caserne*; Port. *caserna*, from L. *casa*, a hut, cottage, barrack.] [*usually in pl.*] any of a series of barracks for soldiers in garrison towns.

çāse shot, any projectile made of an enclosing case and small balls, as a shrapnel shell: called also *canister shot*.

çāse sys'tem, a method of training law students by analyzing and discussing selected cases and decisions rather than by systematic study of textbooks on law.

çā'sē·um, *n.* same as *casein*.

çāse'weed, *n.* the shepherd's-purse, a flower.

çāse wŏrk, social work in which the worker investigates a case of personal or family maladjustment, and gives advice and guidance.

çāse'wŏrm, *n.* any of various insect larvae that build protective cases about their bodies; especially, the caddis worm.

çash, *n.* [Fr. *caisse*, a box, case, money box, cash; OFr. *casse*; from L. *capsa*, a box, chest, from *capere*, to take, contain.]
 1. a money box. [Obs.]
 2. money that a person actually has, including money on deposit; ready money.
 3. bills and coins; currency.
 4. money, a check, etc., paid at the time of purchase; as, he paid *cash* for the house.

çash, *v.t.*; cashed, *pt., pp.*; cashing, *ppr.* 1. to turn into money, or to get money for; as, to *cash* a note or an order.
 2. to pay money for; as, the clerks of a bank *cash* notes when presented.
 to cash in; (a) to turn into cash; to get money for; (b) [Slang.] to die.
 to cash in on; (a) to make a profit from; (b) to make profitable use of.

çash, *a.* of, for, requiring, made with, or using cash; as, a *cash* sale.

çash, *n.*; *pl.* **çash,** [Port. *caixa*, from Tamil *kasu*.]
 1. any of several East Indian or Chinese coins of small value.
 2. a Chinese copper-alloy coin based on the tael: it has a square perforation in the center so that it can be carried on a string.

çash, *v.t.* to discard. [Obs.]

çash'à, *n.* [perh. from *cashmere*.] soft cloth made of wool and cashmere, used for dresses, coats, etc.

çash aç·çount', that part of bookkeeping which constitutes a record of cash received and paid out.

çash-and-çar'ry, *a.* 1. with cash payments and no deliveries.
 2. operated on a cash-and-carry system.

çà·shạw', *n.* same as *cushaw*.

çash'book, *n.* a book in which a register or account of money received or paid is kept.

çash'boy, *n.* formerly, a boy who carried money received from a customer by a salesman to the cashier, and brought back change.

çash çred'it, in Scottish banking, an account with a bank by which, security having been given for repayment, the bank may be drawn upon to an agreed amount: called also *bank credit*.

çash dis'çount, a discount from the purchase price allowed to the purchaser if he pays within a specified period.

çash'ew, (*or* kà-shö'), *n.* [from Fr. *acajou*, *cajou*, from Hind. *kaju*, the cashew nut.]
 1. a tree of the West Indies, *Anacardium occidentale*, bearing kidney-shaped nuts, each at the end of an edible, pear-shaped receptacle.
 2. the nut.

çash'ew nut, the nut of the cashew tree.

çash flōw, the pattern of receipts and expenditures of a company, government, etc., resulting in the availability or nonavailability of cash.

çash·iēr', *n.* [Fr. *caissier*, from *caisse*, a money box, money.] one who has charge of the cash payments and receipts of a bank, store, restaurant, etc.

çash·iēr', *v.t.*; cashiered, *pt., pp.*; cashiering, *ppr.* [OFr. *casser*, to discharge, cashier, from LL. *cassare*, to bring to naught, destroy; *cassus*, empty, void.]
 1. to dismiss from an office or place of trust; to break, as for malconduct, and therefore with disgrace; as, to *cashier* an army officer.
 2. to discard or reject.

CASHEW (*Anacardium occidentale*) 1, 1, 1, cashew nuts

çash'iēr's check, a check drawn by a bank on its own funds and signed by the cashier.

çash'keep·ēr, *n.* one entrusted with the keeping of money; a cashier.

çash'mēre, *n.* 1. a fine, soft wool obtained from goats native to Kashmir and Tibet.
 2. a soft, twilled fabric made from this or similar wool.
 3. a cashmere shawl.

çash·mē·rette', *n.* [dim. of *cashmere*.] a dress fabric having a fine, glossy surface, made in imitation of cashmere.

çash on dē·liv'ẽr·y, payment in cash when a purchase or shipment is delivered.

çash reġ'is·tẽr, a machine for containing and registering the amounts of cash received.

çash sāle, a sale of goods made for cash and immediate delivery.

ças'i·mēre, ças'i·mïre, *n.* same as *cassimere*.

çās'ing, *n.* 1. the act or process of encasing.
 2. a covering or protective outside part; specifically, (a) the frame, as of a window or door; (b) the shoe of an automobile tire; (c) the cleaned intestines, usually of pigs or cattle, used as a sausage container.

çā'sings, *n.pl.* cattle manure dried and used as fuel. [Brit. Dial.]

çà·sï'nō, *n.* [It., dim. of *casa*; L. *casa*, a house, cottage.]
 1. a clubhouse or building used for social meetings, having rooms for public amusement, gambling, dancing, etc.
 2. in Italy, a small country dwelling; summerhouse.
 3. same as *cassino*.

çȧsk, *n.* [Fr. *casque*; Sp. *casco*, a cask, helmet, from *cascar*, to break in pieces, burst.]
 1. a barrel of any size, especially one for containing liquids.
 2. a casque. [Obs.]
 3. the quantity held by a cask.
 4. a jewel box; a casket. [Obs.]

çȧsk, *v.t.* to enclose in a cask.

çȧs'ket, *n.* [ME. *casket*; OFr. *cassette*, dim. of *casse*, a box, chest.]
 1. a small chest or box, for jewels or other small articles.
 2. anything intended as a receptacle for something highly prized or of great value, as a book containing choice selections.
 3. a coffin, especially a costly one.

çȧs'ket, *v.t.*; casketed, *pt., pp.*; casketing, *ppr.* to put into a casket.

Ças'pi·ăn, *a.* of or near the Caspian Sea.

çȧsque, *n.* [from Fr. *casque*; It. *casco*; Sp. *casco*, a helmet, skull.]
 1. a headpiece; a helmet; a piece of defensive armor to cover and protect the head and neck in battle.
 2. in zoology, (a) the cone or helmet-shaped protuberance or shield on the upper bill of certain birds of the *Icteridæ* family, as the cassowary; (b) a process on the upper jaw of certain insects, as beetles.

çasqued (kaskt), *a.* wearing a casque, or helmet.

çȧs·quet·el' (-ket-), *n.* a small cap of steel or an open, visorless helmet, resembling a casque and provided with a jointed neckpiece.

CASQUETEL
side and back views

çass, *v.t.* [Fr. *casser*; L. *quassare*, to break, to quash.] to quash; to defeat; to annul. [Obs.]

ças·sä'bȧ, *n.* same as *casaba*.

ças''sa·bȧ·nä'nȧ, *n.* a decorative vine of the tropics: called also *curuba* and *musk cucumber*.

ças'sȧ·bụl''ly, *n.* winter cress. [Brit. Dial.]

ças·sä'dȧ, ças·sä'dō, *n.* same as *cassava*.

Ças·san'drȧ, *n.* in Greek legend, the daughter of Priam, King of Troy, and Hecuba. She was given the gift of prophecy by Apollo, who loved her, but becoming angry with her, he made the gift worthless by causing people to disbelieve her prophecies. The name is hence applied to any person whose prophecies of evil are not believed.

ças'sȧ·reep, *n.* [S. Am. name.] a seasoning obtained from the juice of the cassava root.

ças'sāte, *v.t.* [L. *cassatus*, pp. of *cassare*, to annul.] to vacate, annul, or make void. [Obs.]

ças·sā'tion, *n.* the act of annulling or abrogating, as of a court decision, an election, etc.

ças·sä'vȧ, *n.* [Fr. *cassave*; Sp. *casabe*, from the Haitian *kasabi*.]
 1. a tropical shrub or plant belonging to the genus *Manihot*, producing large thick roots from which an edible starch is obtained: also called *manioc*.
 2. the edible starch obtained from the cassava, which by drying is used in making tapioca and bread.
 3. bread made from this starch.

CASSAVA (*Manihot utilissima*)

ças·sä'vȧ-wood, *n.* the drumwood; the *Turpinia occidentalis*, a tree belonging to the soapberry family, found in the West Indies.

ças·sē'nȧ, *n.* [of N. Am. Ind. origin.] the yaupon, an evergreen shrub, *Ilex cassine*.

ças'se pā'pẽr, [Fr. *cassé*, pp. of *casser*, to break, and *paper*.] spoiled paper, wrinkled or injured in the making and not sold as perfect.

ças'se·rōle, *n.* [Fr. *casserole*, a saucepan, dim. of OFr. *casse*, a basin.]
 1. a vessel of earthenware, porcelain, or the like, usually with a cover, and either a handle or a separate holder of metal, in which food may be baked and served; also, food served in such a dish.
 2. in chemistry, a small dish of porcelain, with a handle attached, used for heating or evaporating a substance.
 3. in cookery, a hollow form or shell made of pastry, rice, potatoes, or the like, baked with a filling made of meat or vegetables.

çasse-tête' (kȧs-tāt'), *n.* [Fr., from *casser*, to break, and *tête*, head.] a bludgeon; a club; specifically, a war club having a stone fastened to a wooden handle.

çȧs·sette' (-set'), *n.* [Fr., dim. of *casse*, a case.]
 1. a casket.
 2. same as *sagger* (sense 1).
 3. a case with roll film in it, for loading a camera quickly and easily.
 4. a similar case with magnetic tape, for use in a tape recorder.

Ças'si·ȧ (kash'i-ȧ *or* kash'ȧ), *n.* [L., from Gr. *kasia*, *kassia*, cassia.]

1. a genus of plants belonging to the *Leguminosæ*, containing many species, from some of which is extracted the cathartic drug senna.

2. [c–] cassia bark.

3. [c–] in medicine, the pulp from the pods of the *Cassia fistula*, found in tropical countries, especially in the East Indies, and used as a mild laxative.

ças′siȧ bärk, the bark of certain tropical evergreen trees, used in adulterating cinnamon: also called *Chinese cinnamon.*

ças′siȧ buds, the dried buds of *Cinnamomum cassia* and several related species.

ças′siȧ oil, an aromatic oil obtained from cassia buds and cassia bark.

ças′si·çăn, *n.* [from L. *cassis*, a helmet.] a species of oriole belonging to the genus *Cassicus*, found in North America: also called *cacique* or *crested oriole.*

ças·sid′ē·ous, *a.* [L. *cassis* (*-idis*), a helmet.] in botany, helmet-shaped.

ças′si·dō·ny, *n.* [Fr. *cassidoine*; LL. *cacedonius, chalcedonius*, from *Chalcedon*, a town in Bithynia.] in botany, (a) a species of *Gnaphalium*, cottonweed, cudweed, or goldilocks; (b) *Lavandula stœchas*, or French lavender.

ças′si·mēre, *n.* [Fr. *casimir*; Sp. *casimiro*; Turk. *qāzmir*, cassimere.] a thin, twilled, woolen cloth: also spelled *casimere, casimire.*

ças·si·nette′, *n.* [from *cassimere.*] a cloth made of a cotton warp, and a woof of very fine wool, or wool and silk.

Ças·sin′i·ăn, *a.* pertaining to or named from the Cassini family, which included many French astronomers and mathematicians.

cassinian oval; a closed plane curve forming the locus of a point the sum of whose distances from two fixed points does not vary.

ças·sï′nō, *n.* a type of card game for two or four players: also spelled *casino.*

ças′si·ō·ber″ry, *n.*; *pl.* **ças′si·ō·ber″ries,** [Am. Ind. origin.] the black, edible fruit of the shrub *Viburnum obovatum*, growing in the southeastern United States.

Ças″si·ō·pē′iȧ (-pē′yȧ), *n.* 1. in Greek legend, the wife of Cepheus and mother of Andromeda.

2. a northern constellation between Andromeda and Cepheus.

Ças″si·ō·pē′iȧ's Chāir, the five brightest stars in the constellation Cassiopeia; their outline suggests the shape of a chair.

ças·sique′, (kȧ-sēk′), *n.* same as *cacique.*

ças·sit′ēr·īte, *n.* [L. *cassiterum*; Gr. *kassiteros*, tin.] dioxide of tin in the natural state, SnO_2: it is the chief natural tin compound and usually occurs as a brown or black lustrous crystal.

Ças′si·us pŭr′ple, see under *purple.*

ças′sŏck, *n.* [Fr. *casaque*, a cassock; It. *casacca*, a greatcoat, a house; L. *casa*, a house.]

1. a long, close-fitting garment, generally black, worn as an outer garment or under the surplice or gown by clergymen, choristers, etc.

2. the position of a clergyman.

3. a clergyman.

ças′sŏcked, *a.* clothed with a cassock; as, the *cassocked* priest.

ças·sō·lette′, *n.* [Fr.] a vase or box, with small holes in the lid for the diffusion of perfumes; an incense burner.

ças·sŏn·āde′, *n.* [Fr., from OFr. *casson*, a large chest: the sugar was shipped in casks.] cask sugar; sugar not refined.

ças′sō·wăr·y, *n.*; *pl.* **ças′sō·wăr·ies** (-riz), [Malay *kassuwaris*, cassowary.] a large fleet-footed East Indian bird of the genus *Casuarius*, much resembling an ostrich, though not so tall, and having a brightly colored neck and head: it is unable to fly. Species are found in Australia and New Guinea.

CASSOWARY
(*Casuarius galeatus*)

ças·sū·mū′năr, ças·sū·mū′ni·ăr, *n.* [E. Ind.] a tonic and stimulant obtained from an East Indian aromatic root, *Zingiber cassumunar*, having a bitter, pungent taste.

çȧst, *v.t.*; cast, *pt., pp.*; casting, *ppr.* [ME. *casten*; Ice. *kasta*; Dan. *kaste*, to throw.]

1. to project; to fling, throw, or thrust; as, to *cast* a stone.

2. to deposit (a ballot or vote).

3. to cause to fall or turn; project; direct; as, this evidence may *cast* some light on the crime.

4. to shed or throw off; as, the snake *casts* its skin.

5. to drop or let fall; as, to *cast* anchor.

6. to throw out (a fly, etc.) at the end of a fishing line.

7. to distribute (the parts of a play) among the actors; as, the play is *cast*; also, to assign (an actor) to a part; as, I am *cast* for Lear.

8. to draw (lots) or shake (dice) out of a container.

9. to throw down; to defeat (a wrestler).

10. to add up (accounts), originally by means of counters.

11. to calculate (a horoscope, tides, etc.).

12. to arrange in some system; formulate; distribute.

13. (a) to form (molten metal, etc.) into a particular shape by pouring or pressing into a mold; as, to *cast* cannon; (b) to make by such a method.

14. to twist; to turn; to warp.

15. to bring forth (young), especially prematurely.

16. in printing, to electrotype or stereotype.

to cast aside; to reject as useless or undesirable.

to cast away; to throw aside.

to cast down; (a) to turn downward; (b) to deject or depress.

to cast in one's lot with; to risk one's fortune with that of (another).

to cast in the teeth of; to upbraid face to face; to charge with something.

to cast off; (a) to disburden; (b) to drive away.

to cast out; to force to get out or go away; to expel.

to cast the lead; to take a sounding of the depth of water by dropping a lead at the end of a line.

to cast up; (a) to compute; to calculate; (b) to vomit; (c) to remind in an accusing way; (d) to turn upward.

çȧst, *v.i.* 1. to throw dice.

2. to throw out a fly or artificial bait at the end of a fishing line.

3. to warp; to twist; to veer.

4. to throw up food; to vomit.

5. to add up figures; to calculate.

6. to calculate horoscopes, tides, etc.

7. to make a forecast, diagnosis, estimate, etc.; to conjecture.

8. to consider; to deliberate; to plan.

9. in hunting, to scatter in all directions in search for a lost scent.

to cast about; (a) to search; to look (*for*); (b) to make plans; to devise.

to cast off; (a) to free a ship from a dock, quay, etc., as by releasing the lines; (b) in knitting, to make the last row of stitches.

to cast on; in knitting, to make the first row of stitches.

çȧst, *n.* 1. a throw; a throwing; a casting.

2. the distance which a thing is thrown; also, the way of casting; as, a stone's *cast.*

3. a motion or turn of the eye.

4. a throw of dice; also, the number thus thrown; hence, a stroke of fortune.

> It is an even *cast*, whether the army should march this way or that way. —South.

5. a throw of a fishing line, net, etc.

6. an overthrow, as in wrestling.

7. an adding up; calculation; hence, a conjecture; forecast.

8. a sample or sign, as of one's abilities, views, etc.

9. something thrown up, off, or out, as bait on a line, a pair (of hawks), produce, vomit, excrement, etc.

10. among founders, a tube of wax, fitted into a mold, to give shape to metal.

11. a cylindrical piece of brass or copper, slit in two lengthwise, to form a canal or conduit, in a mold, for conveying metal.

12. something formed in a mold, as a statue; also, the mold itself.

13. a plaster form for immobilizing a broken arm, leg, etc.

14. the set of actors in a play.

15. a plot or design. [Obs.]

16. the form or direction in which a thing is cast; specifically, (a) an arrangement; (b) an appearance or stamp, as of features; (c) kind; quality; (d) a tinge; shade; (e) a turn or twist to one side; tendency; bent; (f) a slight error of focus (*in, to*, or *of* the eye).

17. in brewing, the quantity of water necessary to make a given quantity of beer.

18. an afterswarm of bees.

19. in hunting, a scattering of the hounds to find a lost scent.

20. in medicine, a plastic substance formed in the cavities of some diseased organs: as, renal *casts.*

Syn.—mold, stamp, kind, figure, form, aspect, mien, air, style, manner, character.

Ças·tā′li·ȧ, *n.* a genus of aquatic plants of the water lily family, including the common lily of the United States.

Ças·tā′li·ăn, *a.* pertaining to Castalia, a mythical spring on Mount Parnassus, sacred to the Muses and considered a source of poetic inspiration; hence, poetic.

Ças·tā′nē·ȧ, *n.* [L., a chestnut, from Gr. *kastanon.*] a genus of trees typified by the common chestnut.

ças·tā′nē·ous, *a.* relating to or having the color of a chestnut.

ças′tȧ·nets, *n.pl.* [Sp. *castañeta*, L. *castanea*, chestnut.] small, concave shells of ivory or hard wood, used in pairs to beat time to music, especially in Spanish dances: they are held in the hand by a connecting cord or ribbon over the thumb, and struck with the fingers.

CASTANETS

çȧst′ȧ·wāy, *n.* 1. a person or thing cast out or off; especially, an outcast from home or society.

2. one who is shipwrecked.

çȧst′ȧ·wāy, *a.* 1. thrown away; rejected.

2. shipwrecked; stranded; cast adrift.

çȧste, *n.* [Fr. *caste*; Port. *casta*, breed, race, caste, from L. *castus*, pure, chaste.]

1. any of the distinct, hereditary Hindu social classes (*Brahman, Kshatriya, Vaisya, Sudra*), each formerly excluded from social dealings with the others.

2. any exclusive social or occupational class or group.

3. rigid class distinction based on birth, wealth, etc., operating as a social system or principle.

4. the diversity in form or type of classes of certain social insects, as bees.

to lose caste; to suffer loss of social standing.

Syn.—order, class, rank, lineage.

çȧs′tel·lăn, *n.* [ME. *castellain*; OFr. *castellain*; LL. *castellanus*, keeper of a castle; from L. *castellum*, a castle.] a governor or constable of a castle.

çȧs′tel·lā·ny, *n.* 1. the office or position belonging to a castellan.

2. the extent of the land of a castle.

çȧs′tel·lā·ted, *a.* 1. enclosed in a building, as a fountain or cistern. [Obs.]

2. adorned with turrets and battlements, like a castle.

3. having many castles, as a district, river, etc.

çȧs·tel·lā′tion, *n.* the act of making castellated; the building of a castle or a castlelike structure.

çȧs′tel·let, *n.* a small castle: also written *castlet.*

çȧst′ẽr, *n.* 1. one who that which casts.

2. a small bottle or other container for serving vinegar, mustard, salt, or other condiments at the table.

3. a stand for holding such small bottles or cruets for the table.

4. a small wheel on a swivel, for supporting furniture or other heavy articles.

Also written *castor* (in senses 2, 3, 4).

ças′ti·gāte, *v.t.*; castigated, *pt., pp.*; castigating, *ppr.* [L. *castigatus*, pp. of *castigare*, to purify, chastise, from *castus*, pure.] to chastise; to correct or subdue by punishing; to chasten; to rebuke.

ças·ti·gā′tion, *n.* 1. severe punishment, criticism, or rebuke.

2. correction; emendation; alteration. [Obs.]

ças′ti·gā·tŏr, *n.* one who castigates.

ças′ti·gȧ·tō·ry, *a.* tending to castigate; corrective; punitive.

ças′ti·gȧ·tō·ry, *n.* a device formerly used to punish and correct arrant scolds: called also *ducking stool* or *trebucket.*

Ças′tïle sōap, ças′tïle sōap, [from *Castile*, Spain, where first made.] a fine, hard soap prepared from olive oil and sodium hydroxide.

Ças·til′iăn, *a.* pertaining to Castile (in Spain), its people, language, or culture.

Ças·til′iăn, *n.* 1. an inhabitant or native of Castile.

2. the Castilian form of Spanish, now the standard form of the language.

çast′ing, *n.* 1. the act of throwing, as a line in fishing or dice in gambling.

2. that which is cast in a mold; anything formed by pouring a liquid in a hollow form and allowing it to harden or solidify; especially, a metal piece so formed.

3. computation, especially of an arithmetical sum.

4. assignment or distribution, as of parts in a play.

5. the warping of a board.

6. in zoology, anything thrown off or ejected, as vomit, dirt thrown up by worms, etc.

çast′ing bot′tle, an atomizer.

çast′ing box, a box used in throwing dice.

çast′ing līne, the leader at the end of a fishing line to which the fly and hook are attached; also, the unreeled part of a line.

çast′ing net, a fishing net which is cast and drawn, in distinction from a net that is set and left.

çast′ing vōte, çast′ing voice, the vote of a presiding officer which decides a question when the votes are equally divided between the affirmative and negative.

çast′ing weight (wāt), a weight that tips the beam of a balance.

çast′-ī″ron (-ŭrn), *a.* 1. formed of iron that has been cast.

2. rigid; set; strong.

çast ī′ron (-ŭrn), a hard, unmalleable pig iron made by casting: it contains between 6 and 8 per cent impurities, including a high proportion of carbon, and is very fluid and fusible when molten.

çȧs′tle (kȧs′l), *n.* [ME. *castle, castel,* a castle; AS. *castel,* a village; OFr. *castel,* from L. *castellum,* dim. of *castrum,* a fort.]

1. a large building fortified with thick walls, battlements, and, often, a moat; a fortress. The term often includes the building and the walls or other works around it.

2. any dwelling characterized by size, imposing structure, and resemblance to an ancient castle.

3. any place of security or structure of defense; as, a floating *castle* (a heavily armed warship).

4. a small tower, especially one on an elephant's back or on the deck of a ship.

5. a helmet. [Obs.]

6. in chess, either of the two corner pieces shaped like a castle tower: it can move only in a vertical or horizontal direction: also called *rook.*

castle in the air, castle in Spain; a visionary project; a scheme having no solid foundation; a daydream.

çȧs′tle, *v.t.*; castled, *pt., pp.*; castling, *ppr.* 1. to put into, or furnish with, a castle.

2. in chess, to move (a king) two squares to either side and then, in the same move, set the castle in the square skipped by the king: permitted only when neither piece has been moved before and the spaces between them are not occupied.

çȧs′tle, *v.i.* in chess, (a) to castle a king; (b) to be castled.

çȧs′tle-build″ẽr (-bild″ẽr), one who forms visionary schemes.

çȧs′tle-build″ing, *n.* indulgence in daydreams; a reverie.

çȧs′tled (-ld), *a.* 1. having a castle or castles.

2. castellated.

çȧs′tle-guärd, çȧs′tle-wa̤rd, *n.* 1. a feudal tenure, or knight service, which obliged the tenant to perform service within the realm, without limitation of time.

2. those upon whom the defense of a castle devolved.

3. in old English law, a levy on buildings within a certain radius of a castle.

çȧs′tle·ry, *n.* the government of a castle.

çȧs′tlet, *n.* same as *castellet.*

çȧs′tle-wa̤rd, *n.* same as *castle-guard.*

çȧst′ling, *n.* an abortion. [Obs.]

çȧst′ling, *n.* in chess, a combined move in which the king and castle take part.

çȧst′o̤ff, *a.* no longer in use or no longer wanted; as, *castoff* garments.

çȧst′o̤ff, *n.* 1. a useless or rejected article or person.

2. in printing, the computation in type of any manuscript.

3. the offset of a gunstock.

4. in nautical usage, a casting off.

çȧs′tŏr, *n.* [L. *castor*; Gr. *kastōr,* a beaver.]

1. same as *castoreum.*

2. [C—] a genus of rodents characterized by a resemblance to the beaver.

3. a hat made of the fur of the beaver or rabbit.

4. a heavy, wool cloth used especially for men's overcoats.

5. a wooden tablet, serving as money, formerly used by the Hudson Bay Company in their trade with the Indians.

6. a light-brown color.

çȧs′tŏr, *a.* of a light-brown color.

çȧs′tŏr, *n.* 1. see *castorite.*

2. [C—] in Greek and Roman legend, one of the twin sons of Jupiter and Leda.

Castor and Pollux; (a) a globular electric glow (St. Elmo's fire) which is sometimes seen on some parts of the rigging of a ship: so called when a double flame; (b) the two most luminous stars in the constellation Gemini; (c) in Greek and Roman legend, the twin sons of Jupiter and Leda.

çȧs′tŏr, *n.* same as *caster.*

çȧs′tŏr bēan, 1. the oily seed of the castor-oil plant.

2. the plant.

çȧs·tō′rē·um, *n.* [L.] a substance having a strong, penetrating smell, obtained from the sex glands of the beaver: used in medicine as a stimulant and in making perfumes.

çȧs′tō·rin, *n.* a white, crystalline constituent of castoreum.

çȧs′tŏr·īte, *n.* a mineral, silicate of aluminum and lithium, which is a variety of petalite: also called *castor.*

çȧs′tŏr oil, a colorless or yellowish oil obtained from the castor bean, used as a cathartic and as a lubricant.

çȧs′tŏr-oil plant, the tropical plant, *Ricinus communis,* or palma Christi, with large, beanlike seeds from which castor oil is extracted.

çȧs″trȧ·mē·tā′tion, *n.* [LL. *castrametari,* to pitch a camp; L. *castra,* a camp, and *metari,* to measure, lay out.] the marking or laying out of a military camp.

çȧs′trāte, *v.t.*; castrated, *pt., pp.*; castrating, *ppr.* [L. *castratus,* pp. of *castrare,* to castrate, to prune.]

1. to geld; to remove the testicles of; to emasculate.

2. to cut out or revise, thereby depriving of essential vigor or significance.

3. in botany, to take away the stamens from (a flower).

çȧs′trāte, *a.* 1. in botany, destitute of anthers, or deprived of them.

2. gelded; emasculated. [Obs.]

çȧs·trā′tion, *n.* the act of castrating, in any of its senses.

çȧs·trä′tō, *n.*; *pl.* **çȧs·trä′tī,** [It.] a man castrated when young so as to retain his soprano voice for singing.

çȧs′trel, *n.* same as *kestrel.*

çȧs·tren′siăn, çȧs·tren′siăl, *a.* [L. *castrensis,* from *castra,* a camp.] belonging to a camp.

çaṣ′ū·ăl (*or* kaẓ′), *a.* [Fr. *casuel*; Sp. *casual*; LL. *casualis,* by chance, from L. *casus,* chance, event.]

1. falling, happening, or coming to pass without volition and without being foreseen or expected; accidental; fortuitous; coming by chance; as, the parties had a *casual* meeting.

2. occasional; coming at certain times, without regularity, in distinction from stated or regular; as a *casual* worker is one without regular employment.

3. taking place, or beginning to exist, without method or design.

> Atheists assert that the existence of things is *casual.* —Dwight.

4. careless; cursory.

5. nonchalant; indifferent.

6. of, for, affected by, or resulting from accidents; as, the *casual* ward in a hospital.

Syn.—accidental, fortuitous, incidental, occasional.—*Casual* and *fortuitous* are substantially the same; a thing is *accidental* when not planned or sought, as a meeting; *incidental* when it falls in as secondary, or out of the regular course of things, as a remark; *occasional* when it occurs only now and then.

çaṣ′ū·ăl, *n.* 1. a person who does something or is in some place only occasionally or temporarily; especially, a casual worker or occasional recipient of charity.

2. in military usage, a person temporarily attached to a unit, awaiting a permanent assignment.

çaṣ′ū·ăl·iṣm, *n.* the theory that all things occur by chance.

çaṣ′ū·ăl·ist, *n.* a believer in casualism.

çaṣ′ū·ăl·ly, *adv.* accidentally; fortuitously; without design; by chance.

çaṣ′ū·ăl·ness, *n.* accidentalness; the quality of being casual.

çaṣ′ū·ăl·ty, *n.* 1. accident; that which comes by chance or without design, or without being foreseen; contingency.

2. any injury of the body from accident, whether resulting in death or not; also, anyone hurt or killed in an accident.

3. in military usage, (a) a member of the armed forces who is lost to active service, especially through being killed, wounded, or captured; (b) [*pl.*] losses of personnel resulting from death, injury, etc.

4. in Scots law, an amount due from a tenant to his superior, beyond the stated yearly duties, upon certain casual events.

casualty ward; a hospital ward for the treatment of persons injured accidentally; an emergency ward.

Çaṣ″ū·ȧ·rī′nȧ, *n.* [from L. *casuarius,* the cassowary: so called from the resemblance of the twigs to the feathers of the cassowary.] a genus of trees chiefly found in Australia, having no leaves and with drooping, reedlike branches. Some furnish a heavy, hard timber known as beefwood and she-oak.

Çaṣ·ū·ar·i·nā′cē·ae, *n.* a small family of trees, growing mostly in Australia, and having but one genus, *Casuarina.*

çaṣ·ū·ar·i·nā′ceous, *a.* relating to or like the *Casuarinaceæ.*

çaṣ′ū·ist, *n.* [Fr. *casuiste,* from L. *casus,* a case, fall.] one who studies and resolves questions of right and wrong in conduct; an expert in casuistry: often used disparagingly of one who quibbles, rationalizes, or reasons falsely.

çaṣ′ū·ist, *v.i.* to play the part of a casuist.

çaṣ·ū·is′tiç, çaṣ·ū·is′tiç·ăl, *a.* 1. relating to questions of right or wrong in conduct.

2. of or for casuists.

3. quibbling; sophistical; specious.

çaṣ′ū·ist·ry, *n.*; *pl.* **çaṣ′ū·ist·rieṣ,** the solving of special cases of right and wrong in conduct by applying general principles of ethics, and deciding how far circumstances alter cases: often used disparagingly of subtle but evasive reasoning in questions of duty.

çaṣ′ū·lȧ, çaṣ′ūle, *n.* same as *chasuble.*

çā′sus, *n.* [L.] a case; an occurrence; an event.

casus belli; the cause of war, real or alleged.

casus fœderis; whatever comes under the terms of a treaty.

casus fortuitus; an unpreventable accident.

casus omissus; a case for which the statutes make no provision.

çat, *n.* [AS. *cat*; D. *kat*; LL. *catus*; Hind. *katās*; Turk. *qadi,* a cat.]

1. a species of carnivorous quadrupeds, of the genus *Felis.* It has been domesticated since ancient times and includes many distinct varieties, such as the *Angora cat,* the *Maltese* (or *blue*) *cat,* the *Manx cat,* and the *Persian cat.* It is a small, lithe, soft-furred animal and is often kept as a pet or for killing mice.

2. any of various flesh-eating mammals related to this, as the lion, tiger, cougar, leopard, etc.

3. a person regarded as like a cat in some way; especially, a woman who makes spiteful remarks.

4. a cat-o'-nine-tails.

5. a tripod having six feet: so called because it always lands on three feet, however placed.

6. a catfish.

7. the game of tipcat; also, the thick, short stick pointed at each end, used in playing the game.

8. a caterpillar tractor. [Military Slang.]

9. in military history, a movable shelter used in besieging.

10. in nautical usage, (a) a cathead; (b) a strong tackle or combination of pulleys, to hook and draw an anchor perpendicularly up to the cathead of a ship; (c) a catboat.

to let the cat out of the bag; to tell a secret before the time is ripe.

çat, *v.t.*; catted, *pt., pp.*; catting, *ppr.* 1. to hoist (an anchor) to the cathead.

2. to flog with a cat-o'-nine-tails.

çat′ȧ-, a prefix from Gr. *kata,* and signifying *down, downward, against, away, completely, through, throughout, backward, in regression*; the final *a* is sometimes dropped, and, before an aspirate, the form becomes *cath-,* as in *cat*opter, *cath*artic, *cath*ode. Also spelled *kata-.*

çat·ȧ·bap′tist, *n.* [Late Gr. *katabaptistēs,* from *katabaptizein,* to dip down or into; *kata,* down, *baptizein*, to dip.] one who opposes baptism.

çat·à·bā′sion, *n.* [Gr. *katabasion*; *kata*, downward, and *bainein*, to go.] a chamber in a Greek church, under the altar, where relics are kept.

çà·tab′à·sis, *n.*; *pl.* **çà·tab′à·sēș,** [Gr. *katabasis*, a going down; *kata*, down, and *bainein*, to go.] the act of descending; hence, in medicine, the abating of a disease.

çat·à·bat′iç, *a.* [Gr. *katabatikos*, from *katabainein*, to go down; *kata*, down, and *bainein*, to go.] slowly yielding; abating.

çat″à·bī·ot′iç, *a.* [*cata-*, and Gr. *bios*, life.] pertaining to energy used up in catabolic processes.

çat·à·bol′iç, *a.* relating to or caused by catabolism.

çà·tab′ō·lism, *n.* [Gr. *katabolē*, a throwing down; from *kata*, down, and *ballein*, to throw.] destructive metabolism, in which living tissue is changed into waste products of a simpler chemical composition: opposed to *anabolism*: also spelled *katabolism*.

çà·tab′ō·līte, *n.* a waste product of catabolism.

çat·à·çaus′tiç, *a.* [*cata-*, and Gr. *kaustikos*, from *kaiein*, to burn.] designating or of a caustic curve or surface produced by reflection.

çat·à·çaus′tiç, *n.* a caustic curve or surface resulting from the reflection of rays of light.

çat·à·çhrē′sis, *n.*; *pl.* **çat·à·çhrē′sēș,** [L., from Gr. *katachrēsis*, the misuse of a word, from *katachrēsthai*; *kata*, against, and *chrēsthai*, to use.]

1. incorrect use of a word or words, as by misapplication of terminology or by strained or mixed metaphor.

2. a change in the form of a word resulting from a misunderstanding of its etymology.

çat·à·çhres′tiç, çat·à·çhres′tiç·ăl, *a.* [Gr. *katachrēstikos*, misused, misapplied.] of the nature of a catachresis; forced; far-fetched.

çat·à·çhres′tiç·ăl·ly, *adv.* in a forced manner.

çat′à·clașm, *n.* [Gr. *kataklasma*, from *kata*, down, and *klaein*, to break.] disruption; a breaking down or apart on a large scale.

çat·à·clī′năl, *a.* [Gr. *kataklinēs*, sloping, from *kata*, down, and *klinein*, to bend.] in geology, descending in the same direction as the incline of the strata; as, a *cataclinal* valley: opposed to *anaclinal*.

çat′à·clyșm, *n.* [L. *cataclysmos*; Gr. *kataklysmos*; from *kataklyzein*; *kata*, down, and *klyzein*, to wash.]

1. a deluge, or overflowing of water: also used figuratively; as, *cataclysms* of blood.

2. any extraordinary and violent change, as an earthquake, war, etc.

çat·à·clyș′măl, *a.* same as *cataclysmic*.

çat·à·clyș′măl thē′ō·ry, the theory that the shaping of the earth's crust was caused by sudden and violent upheavals rather than by slow action of air, water, etc.

çat·à·clyș′miç, *a.* 1. of or caused by a cataclysm.

2. having the nature or effect of a cataclysm.

çat·à·clyș′mist, *n.* a believer in the cataclysmal theory.

çat′à·cōmb (-kōm), *n.* [It. *catacomba*; LL. *catacumba*; a sepulchral vault; Gr. *kata*, down, and *kymbē*, a hollow, a cavity.] [*usually in pl.*] a cave, grotto, or subterranean place for the burial of the dead: originally applied to a vast number of subterranean sepulchers; about three miles from Rome, on the Appian Way, in which were deposited the bodies of the early Christian martyrs. Catacombs are found also at Naples, and in other places.

çat″à·çō·rol′là, *n.* [*cata-*, and L. *corolla*, dim. of *corona*, a crown.] in botany, a second corolla within or outside the true one; also, an abnormal growth of petals inside the true corolla.

çat·à·çöus′tiçs, *n.* [*cata-*, and Gr. *akoustikos*, from *akouein*, to hear.] that part of the science of acoustics which treats of reflected sounds; cataphonics.

çat·à·çrot′iç, *a.* [*cata-*, and Gr. *krotos*, a beating, knocking.] pertaining to a kind of sphygmogram, or pulse tracing, in which the descending part of the curve shows secondary elevations.

çat″à·dī·op′triç, çat″à·dī·op′triç·ăl, *a.* reflecting light.

çat″à·dī·op′triçs, *n.* [*cata-*, and Gr. *dioptrika*; *dia*, through, and the root of *opsomai*, I shall see.] the science of the reflection of light, and of the use of instruments for observing its phenomena.

çat′à·drōme, *n.* [Gr. *katadromos*, a race course.]

1. a race track. [Obs.]

2. a crane for lifting great weights. [Rare.]

çà·tad′rō·mous, *a.* [Gr. *katadromos*, overrun; *kata*, down, and *dramein*, to run.]

1. in botany, having the inferior fronds rise from the posterior of the pinnae: said of ferns: opposed to *anadromous*.

2. going back to or toward the sea to spawn: said of certain fresh-water fishes.

Çà·tad′y·săs, *n.* [Gr. *katadysis*, a dipping under water; *kata*, down, and *dyein*, to enter, dive.] the type genus of the family *Catadysidæ*.

Çat·à·dys′i·dae, *n.pl.* a North American family of spiders with only two pulmonary sacs and the fangs directed in a vertical direction.

çat′à·falque (-falk), **çat·à·fal′çō,** *n.* [Fr. *catafalque*; It. *catafalco*, a funeral canopy, stage.] a temporary resting place or platform, usually draped and canopied, used for supporting the coffin in which a dead person lies in state during an elaborate funeral.

çat·ag·mat′iç, *a.* [Gr. *katagma* (-*atos*), a breakage; from *kata*, intens., and *agnynai*, to break.] having the quality of consolidating broken parts; promoting the union of fractured bones.

Çà·tāi′ăn, Çà·thāi′ăn, *n.* a native of China, formerly called *Cathay*: used by early writers in the sense of a villian, a blackguard, etc. [Obs.]

Çat′à·lan, *n.* a native of Catalonia, an old province of Spain, or one of Catalonian descent; also, the language of Catalonia.

Çat′à·lan, *a.* of Catalonia, its people, or their language.

çat′à·lāse, *n.* an enzyme which liberates free oxygen by decomposing hydrogen peroxide.

çat·à·leç′tiç, *a.* [LL. *catalecticus*; Gr. *katalēktikos*, a leaving off, incomplete; from *katalēgein*; *kata*, intens., and *lēgein*, to leave off, cease.] in prosody, lacking a syllable at the end, or terminating in an imperfect foot; as, a *catalectic* verse.

çat′à·lep·sy, çat·à·lep′sis, *n.* [LL. *catalepsis*; Gr. *katalēpsis*, a seizing, grasping, from *katalambanein*; *kata*, down, and *lambanein*, to take, seize.] a sudden loss of motion and sensation, in which the patient is speechless, senseless, and fixed in one posture, with his eyes open, without seeing or understanding. It may occur in epilepsy, schizophrenia, etc.

çat·à·lep′tiç, *a.* pertaining to catalepsy; as, a *cataleptic fit*.

çat·à·lep′tiç, *n.* a person subject to catalepsy.

çat·à·lep′ti·form, *a.* having the nature of catalepsy.

çat·à·lex′is, *n.* [Gr. *katalēxis*, an ending, termination, from *katalēgein*, to leave off, cease; *kata*, down, and *lēgein*, to cease.] in prosody, the state of being catalectic; incompleteness of a foot at the end of a verse, or, more generally, incompleteness of any foot.

çat″à·lī′nà, *n.* a fish, *Anisotremus tæniatus*, very gaily colored, related to the porkfish.

Çat″à·lī′nà cher′ry, [from Santa *Catalina* Island.] a small evergreen bush or tree found on the islands off the coast of California.

çat″à·li·neț′tà, *n.* the porkfish.

Çat·al·laç′tà, *n.pl.* [from Gr. *katallassein*, to exchange, change.] a class or division of Protozoa, with pear-shaped cells and with stems meeting in the center of spherical colonies.

çat·al·laç′tiçs, *n.* [Gr. *katallaktikos*, changeable, easy to reconcile, from *katallassein*, to exchange, reconcile; *kata*, down, and *allassein*, to exchange, from *allos*, other.] in political economy, the science of commercial exchanges.

çat′à·lō, *n.*; *pl.* **çat′à·lōeș** or **çat′à·lōș,** [*cat*tle, and buff*alo*.] an animal developed from crossing the American buffalo, or bison, with domestic cattle: also spelled *cattalo*.

çat′à·log·īze, *v.t.* to insert in a catalogue. [Obs.]

çat′à·logue (-log), **çat′à·log,** *n.* [Fr. *catalogue*; LL. *catalogus*; Gr. *katalogos*, a list, register, from *katalegein*, to reckon, count up; *kata*, down, completely, and *legein*, to say.]

1. a list or enumeration of names, titles, articles, etc., arranged in a certain order, often alphabetically; as, a *catalogue* of books, of merchandise, etc.

2. a card file, book, pamphlet, etc. containing such a list.

çat′à·logue, çat′à·log, *v.t.* and *v.i.*; catalogued, *pt.*, *pp.*; cataloguing, *ppr.* to enter or arrange (items) in a catalogue.

çat′à·log·uēr, *n.* one who makes or compiles catalogues.

çà·tà·lōgue′ rai·son·né′ (re-zō-nā′), [Fr., lit., reasoned catalogue.] a catalogue arranged by subjects; a classified list, often with explanatory notes.

çat′à·log·uist (-ist), *n.* a cataloguer.

Çat″à·lō′ni·ăn, *n.* same as *Catalan*.

Çat″à·lō′ni·ăn ass, a Spanish ass of high breeding: in color it is black or brown with lighter spots.

çat″à·lōwne′ (-lōn′), [F., *catalogne*.] a woolen fabric, similar to buffin.

Çà·tal′pà, *n.* [Am. Ind.]

1. a genus of hardy trees, having large, heart-shaped leaves, showy clusters of trumpet-shaped flowers, and long cylindrical pods. They are found in many parts of North America, notably in the Mississippi valley, and in Japan, China, and the East Indies.

2. [c-] any tree belonging to this genus.

çà·tal′y·sis, *n.*; *pl.* **çà·tal′y·sēș,** [Gr. *katalysis*, dissolution; *kata*, down, and *lyein*, to loose.]

1. dissolution; decay; deterioration. [Rare.]

2. in chemistry, the action of a catalyst in a chemical reaction.

çat′à·lyst, *n.* a substance which either speeds up or slows down a chemical reaction, but which itself undergoes no permanent chemical change thereby.

çat·à·lyt′iç, *a.* of, in, or causing catalysis.

çat·à·lyt′iç, *n.* 1. in medicine, a counteracting agent employed to arrest pathogenic processes in an organism.

2. a catalyst.

çat·à·lyt′iç çŏn·vērt′ēr, a device that is part of the exhaust system of an automotive vehicle and contains a chemical catalyst to reduce polluting emissions.

çat′à·lyze, *v.t.*; catalyzed, *pt.*, *pp.*; catalyzing, *ppr.* to change by catalysis.

çat″à·mà·ran′, *n.* [E. Ind.]

1. a kind of long, narrow raft made of logs or floats fastened together, and propelled by sails or paddles: used on the coasts of India and South America, and in the waters of the East and West Indies.

CATAMARAN

2. a vessel having twin hulls; particularly, a pleasure boat so built, which is noted for its speed and safety.

3. a kind of raft used to send fire or torpedoes into an enemy's fleet. [Obs.]

4. a petulant or scolding woman; a vixen. [Colloq.]

çat·à·mē′ni·à, *n.pl.* [Gr. *katamēnia*, neut. pl. of *katamēnios*, monthly; *kata*, according to, and *mēn*, a month.] menstruation; menstrual discharge.

çat·à·mē′ni·ăl, *a.* pertaining to the catamenia.

çat′à·mīte, *n.* [L. *Catamitus*, altered from *Ganymedes*, from Gr. *Ganymēdēs*, Ganymede.] a boy used in pederasty.

çat′à·mount, *n.* [*cat*, and *a*, of, and *mount*.]

1. a catamountain.

2. a puma; cougar.

3. a lynx.

çat·à·moun′tain (-tin), *n.* any of several wild animals of the cat family, especially a leopard or a European wildcat: also *cat-o'-mountain*.

çat·à·nad′rō·mous, *a.* [Gr. *kata*, down, *ana*, up, and *dromos*, a course, a running.] in ichthyology, passing annually from salt water to fresh water, to spawn. [Obs.]

çat·à·pet′ăl·ous, *a.* [*cata-*, and Gr. *petalon*, a leaf.] having petals held together by stamens, which grow to their bases, as in the mallow.

çat·à·phā′și·à, *n.* a mental disorder which shows itself in a derangement of the speech, one or more words being repeated continuously in reply to a question.

çat·à·phon′iç, *a.* pertaining to cataphonics. [Obs.]

çat·à·phon′içs, *n.* [*cata-*, and Gr. *phōnē*, sound.] the science of reflected sounds, a branch of acoustics; catacoustics. [Obs.]

çat″à·phō·rē′sis, *n.* [Gr. *kataphora*, a lethargic attack, a bringing down, from *katapherein*; *kata*, down, and *pherein*, to bring.]

1. in physical chemistry, the movement, under the influence of an electrical field, of electrically charged particles suspended in a fluid: also called *electrophoresis*.

2. in medicine, the introduction of a liquid, usually medicinal, into body tissue by means of an electric current.

çat′à·phraçt (-frakt), *n.* [L. *cataphracta*; Gr. *kataphraktēs*, a coat of mail, from *kataphras-*

sein, to cover with mail; *kata*, against, and *phrassein*, to fence.]

1. in ancient Greece and Rome, a piece of heavy, defensive armor, formed of cloth or leather, strengthened with metal scales or links, used to protect the body of a man or horse.

2. a horseman in complete armor.

3. the natural armor or covering of certain fishes.

çat′ȧ·phraçt·ed, *a.* in zoology, covered with a hard, callous skin, or with horny or bony plates or scales, closely joined together.

çat·ȧ·phraç′tī, *n.pl.* [L., from Gr. *kataphraktos*, mailed.]

1. the body of soldiers introduced into the Roman army in the fourth century armored with the cataphract, or any soldiers thus protected.

2. [C–] a group of spiny-finned fishes whose faces or cheeks are covered with large, strong plates.

çat·ȧ·phraç′tiç, *a.* pertaining to or resembling a cataphract.

çat′ȧ·phyll, *n.* [from *cata-* and *-phyll*.] in botany, any rudimentary leaf, as a bud scale, preceding the true foliage leaves.

çat·ȧ·phyl′lum, *n.*; *pl.* **çat·ȧ·phyl′lȧ,** [*cata-*, and Gr. *phyllon*, a leaf.] a cataphyll.

çat·ȧ·phyṣ′iç, çat·ȧ·phyṣ′iç·ȧl, *a.* [*cata-*, and Gr. *physis*, nature.] unnatural; not according to nature. [Rare.]

çat·ȧ·plā′ṣi·ȧ, *n.*; *pl.* **çat·ȧ·plā′ṣi·ae,** [Mod. L.] in biology, a change in cells or tissues, characterized by reversion to an earlier stage.

çȧ·tap′lȧ·sis, *n.* [Gr. *kataplassis*; *kata*, down, and *plassein*, to form.] the natural period of decline in organic or germ development.

çat′ȧ·plaṣm, *n.* [Gr. *kataplasma*, from *kataplassein*, to anoint, spread over.] a poultice.

çat·ȧ·pleç′tiç, *a.* pertaining to cataplexy.

çat′ȧ·plex·y, *n.* [Gr. *kataplēx*, stricken; *kata*, down, and *plessein*, to strike.] a sudden nervous shock resulting in muscular rigidity.

çat′ȧ·pūce, *n.* [Fr.] the herb spurge. [Obs.]

çat′ȧ·pult, *n.* [L. *catapulta*; Gr. *katapeltēs*, an engine for throwing stones, from *kata*, down, and *pallein*, to toss, whirl.]

1. a military contrivance used by the ancient Greeks and Romans for throwing stones, spears, arrows, etc.

CATAPULT

2. a toy consisting of a forked stick to which is attached an elastic band, used for shooting small missiles: popularly known as a *slingshot*.

3. a device for launching an airplane from the deck of a ship.

çat′ȧ·pult, *v.t.* to shoot from or as from a catapult; to hurl.

çat·ȧ·pul′tiç, *a.* pertaining to a catapult.

çat′ȧ·raçt, *n.* [L. *cataracta*; Gr. *katarraktēs*, a waterfall, portcullis, from *katarrēgnynai*; *kata*, down, and *rēgnynai*, to break.]

1. a large waterfall; a cascade upon a great scale.

2. any downpour like a cataract; a deluge.

3. in medicine and surgery, an opacity of the crystalline lens of the eye, or its capsule, causing partial or total blindness; also, the opaque area.

4. in mechanics, a hydraulic brake which regulates or modifies the action of pumping engines and other machines.

çat·ȧ·raç′tine, *a.* pertaining to a cataract (waterfall), or similar to it.

çat·ȧ·raç′tous, *a.* of the nature of a cataract in the eye.

çȧ·tärrh′ (-tär′), *n.* [L. *catarrhus*; Gr. *katarrhoos*, from *katarrhein*, to flow down; *kata*, down, and *rhein*, to flow.] an inflammation of a mucous membrane, more particularly of the throat and nose, accompanied by an increased secretion of mucus; as, nasal *catarrh*; *catarrh* of the stomach.

çȧ·tärrh′ȧl, *a.* pertaining to catarrh, produced by it, or attending it; as, a *catarrhal* fever.

Çat·ăr·rhī′nȧ, *n.pl.* a division of Primates with narrow heads and nostrils, the latter being turned downward.

çat′ăr·rhīne (*or* -rin), *n.* [Gr. *katarrhis*; *kata*, down, and *rhis*, *rhinos*, nose.] one of the *Catarrhina*.

çȧ·tärrh′ous, *a.* catarrhal.

çat·ȧ·stal′tiç, *a.* [Gr. *katastaltikos*, fitted for checking, from *katastellein*, to keep down, to check; *kata*, down, and *stellein*, to send.] in medicine, astringent or styptic; effective in checking evacuations.

çȧ·tas′tȧ·sis, *n.*; *pl.* **çȧ·tas′tȧ·sēṣ,** [Gr. *katastasis*, an arranging, setting forth, from *kathistanai*; *kata*, down, and *histanai*, to set up, cause to stand.]

1. in ancient times, the heightened part of the action in Greek drama, which prepared for the catastrophe.

2. in rhetoric, the narrative part of a speech.

çat′ȧ·stāte, *n.* [Gr. *kathistanai*, to settle down.] any of the series of substances produced by a catabolic process: written also *katastate*.

çȧ·tas′tēr·iṣm, *n.* [Gr. *katasterismos*, from *katasterizein*, to place among the stars; *kata*, down, and *asterizein*, to make into a star, from *astēr*, a star.] (a) a constellation; (b) a placing of a mythical person, etc. among the stars.

çȧ·tas′tō·mid, *a.* and *n.* same as *catostomid*.

çȧ·tas′tō·moid, *a.* same as *catostomoid*.

çȧ·tas′trō·phē, *n.* [L. *catastropha*; Gr. *katastrophē*, an overthrowing, from *katastrephein*, to overturn; *kata*, down, and *strephein*, to turn.]

1. the culminating event of a drama, especially of a tragedy, by which the plot is resolved; denouement. The ancients divided a play into the protasis, epitasis, catastasis, and catastrophe—the introduction, continuance, heightening, and development or conclusion.

2. a disastrous overthrow or ruin.

3. any great and sudden calamity, disaster, or misfortune.

4. any event that disturbs or overthrows the existing order of things.

5. in geology, a cataclysm.

çat·ȧ·stroph′iç, *a.* pertaining to a catastrophe; disastrous; calamitous.

çȧ·tas′trō·phiṣm, *n.* the theory that geological changes are the result of sudden and violent physical causes.

çȧ·tas′trō·phist, *n.* a believer in the theory of catastrophism.

çat·ȧ·tō′ni·ȧ, *n.* [Gr. *kata*, down, and *tonos*, tension.] in psychiatry, any of various schizophrenic syndromes characterized by phases of stupor, often alternating with phases of excitement and marked muscular rigidity, and often accompanied with stereotypy of posture or activity.

çat·ȧ·ton′iç, *a.* of or having catatonia.

çat·ȧ·ton′iç, *n.* a catatonic person.

Çȧ·tạw′bȧ, *n.* [named from the Catawba River in South Carolina, where it was first raised.]

1. a reddish variety of American grape.

2. a light-colored wine made from the Catawba grape.

çat back, a small rope which helps in hooking the cat block to the anchor.

çat bēam, the longest beam of the boat, terminating in the cathead, which, in turn, supports the anchor.

çat′bĩrd, *n.* (a) an American mimic bird, *Galeoscoptes carolinensis*, allied to the thrush, and less perfect in its imitative qualities than the mockingbird; (b) an Australian bird, *Ptilonorhynchus smithii*. In both varieties the cry of alarm resembles the mewing of a cat.

çat block, the block by which the anchor is hoisted to the cathead.

çat′bōat, *n.* a one-masted sailboat which has its mast placed far forward.

çat brī′ẽr, any of several plants with prickly stems, oval leaves, and black berries; a kind of smilax.

çat′çall, *n.* a shrill noise or whistle expressing derision or disapproval, as of speakers, actors, etc.; also, an instrument for imitating such a noise.

çat′çall, *v.t.* to deride by making the sounds known as catcalls.

çat′çall, *v.i.* to make catcalls.

çatch (kach), *v.t.*; caught (kạt), *pt.*, *pp.*; catching, *ppr.* [ME. *catchen*, *cachen*; OFr. *cacher*, *cachier*; LL. *captiare*, from L. *captare*, intens. of *capere*, to take.]

1. to seize and hold, as after a chase; to capture.

2. to seize, in a general sense; to lay hold of; to grab; as, to *catch* a ball.

3. to seize, as in a snare or trap; to ensnare; to entangle.

4. to deceive.

5. to seize the affections of; to charm; fascinate.

6. to take or receive passively; to incur or contract without effort or intention, as by contagion or infection; as, to *catch* the measles.

7. to snatch; to take suddenly; as, to *catch* a book out of the hand.

8. to be acted upon by; as, the sails *catch* the breeze.

9. to seize with the senses or mind; to apprehend; to get; as, to *catch* a melody; to *catch* the meaning of a remark; to *catch* a glimpse of a person.

10. to get possession of; to attain. [Obs.]

11. to come upon unexpectedly; to surprise; as, to *catch* one in the act of stealing.

12. to reach in time; as, to *catch* a train.

13. to strike suddenly; to hit; as, the blow *caught* him in the abdomen.

to catch at; (a) to try to catch; (b) to reach for eagerly; to seize desperately.

to catch fire; to become ignited.

to catch it; to receive a scolding or other punishment. [Colloq.]

to catch one's eye; to attract one's attention.

to catch up; (a) to take or lift up suddenly; seize; snatch; (b) to show to be in error; (c) to heckle; (d) to come up and not be behind; overtake; (e) to fasten in loops.

Syn.—grasp, clutch, capture, entrap, ensnare, discover, apprehend.

çatch, *v.i.* 1. to attain possession. [Obs.]

2. to become caught; to become held, fastened, or entangled; as, her stocking *caught* on a nail.

3. to take hold or spread, as fire.

4. to take fire; to burn.

5. to take and keep hold, as a lock.

6. to act as a catcher.

catch as catch can; with any hold or approach: originally said of a style of wrestling.

to catch on; (a) to grasp the situation; to understand; (b) to become fashionable, popular, etc. [Colloq.]

çatch, *n.* 1. seizure; the act of catching.

2. anything that seizes or catches.

3. a state of preparation to catch, or of watching an opportunity to seize; as, to lie upon the *catch*. [Obs.]

4. (a) the person or thing caught; (b) a person or thing worth catching, especially as a husband or wife; as, that bachelor is a good *catch*.

5. a snatch; fragment; scrap.

It has been writ by *catches*. —Locke.

6. an artful plan to entrap; as, there is a *catch* in your query.

7. in music, a round for three or more unaccompanied voices.

8. the quantity of anything caught.

9. a sudden stoppage of the breath or voice.

10. a simple game of throwing and catching a ball.

11. in sports, a catching of a ball in a specified manner.

12. a hidden qualification; a tricky condition. [Colloq.]

çatch, *a.* 1. tricky.

2. attracting attention; meant to arouse interest.

çatch′ȧ·ble, *a.* that can be caught.

çatch′all, *n.* a receptacle for various articles, as a basket, attic, etc.

çatch bā′sin, a sievelike device at the entrance to the intersection of a sewer, for retaining solid matter likely to clog the sewer.

çatch çrop, a supplementary crop grown at a time when the ground would ordinarily lie fallow, as between the plantings of two principal crops.

çatch drāin, a ditch or drain on the side of a hill to catch the surface water; also, a ditch on the side of a canal to catch the surplus water.

çatch′ẽr, *n.* one who catches; that which catches, or in which anything is caught; also, in baseball, the player behind homeplate.

çatch′flȳ, *n.* a plant of the genus *Lychnis*, of the pink family. The joints of the stem, and sometimes other portions, give out a sticky discharge to which insects adhere: called also *campion*.

çatch′ing, *a.* 1. communicating, or that can be communicated, by contagion; infectious; as, a disease is *catching*.

2. captivating; attractive.

catching bargain; a bargain made with an heir expectant for the purchase of his expectancy, at an inadequate price.

çatch līne, a line of fine type between two lines of large type; or, in manuscript, any line at the bottom or the top of the page, which directs attention to what follows.

catch mead′ōw (med′dō), a meadow which is irrigated by water from a spring or rivulet on the slope of a hill.

catch′ment, *n.* 1. a catching.
2. a reservoir or other basin for catching.
3. anything caught in or as in a catchment.

catch′ment ā′rē·ȧ (or **bā′sin**), the area draining into a catchment.

catch′pen″ny, *a.* made merely to sell; cheap and flashy; worthless.

catch′pen″ny, *n.*; *pl.* **catch′pen″nies,** a catchpenny commodity.

catch phrāse, a phrase that catches or is meant to catch the popular attention.

catch′pōle, catch′pōll, *n.* [ME. *catchepoll*, a bailiff, taxgatherer; OFr. *chacepol*, a taxgatherer.] formerly, a sheriff's officer whose usual duty was to arrest nonpaying debtors.

catch stitch, a stitch that catches up the one before it so as to give the appearance of a herringbone pattern.

catch′up, *n.* [E. Ind. *kitjap*.] catsup; ketchup.

catch′wa″tẽr, *n.* same as *catch drain*.

catch′weed, *n.* any one of various herbaceous plants, distinguished by stiff spines on the stems and fruits: also called *cleavers*.

catch′weight (-wāt), *n.* in certain sports or competitions, as horse racing, the weight of a contestant as it happens to be, as distinguished from weight fixed by rule or agreement.

catch′weight (-wāt), *adv.* without a weight handicap.

catch′wŏrd, *n.* 1. originally, the first word of the following page, printed in the lower right-hand corner of each page so as to catch the reader's eye.
2. a word placed so that it will catch attention, as the first or last word of a page in a dictionary, etc., printed at the top of the page as a guide.
3. among actors, the last word of the preceding speaker, which reminds one that he is to speak next; cue.
4. a word or phrase repeated so often that it becomes a slogan, as "Remember the Maine."

catch′wŏrk, *n.* a system of irrigation for hilly and meadow land, for catching water and distributing it from the higher to lower levels.

catch′y, *a.* 1. catching attention; arousing interest.
2. easily caught up and remembered; as, a *catchy* tune.
3. tricky; deceiving.
4. spasmodic; fitful.

cāte, *n.* [from OFr. *acat*, a purchase.] rich or delicate food: usually used in the plural; as, he fed on *cates*. [Archaic.]

cat·ē·chē′sis, *n.*; *pl.* **cat·ē·chē′sēs,** [L.; Gr. *katēchēsis*, from *katēchein*.] oral instruction, especially for catechumens, by the method of question and answer.

cat·ē·chet′i·căl, cat·ē·chet′ic, *a.* [Gr. *katēchētikos*, from *katēchētēs*, an instructor; *katēchein*, to instruct, teach by word of mouth.]
1. relating to catechesis or a catechism.
2. consisting of, or teaching by the method of questions and answers.

cat·ē·chet′ic·ăl·ly, *adv.* by question and answer.

cat·ē·chet′ics, *n.* the art of instruction by questions and answers.

cat′ē·chin (*or* -kin), *n.* a yellow, powdery, acid compound, $C_{15}H_{14}O_6$, used in tanning, textile printing, etc.

cat″ē·chi·sā′tion, *n.* same as *catechization*.

cat′ē·chīse, *v.t.* same as *catechize*.

cat′ē·chīs·ẽr, *n.* same as *catechizer*.

cat′ē·chism, *n.* [LL. *catechismus*, from Gr. *katēchizein*, to catechize.]
1. a form of oral instruction by means of questions and answers, particularly in the principles of religion. [Obs.]
2. a handbook for instruction containing a summary of the principles of a religion or the fundamentals of a subject, reduced to the form of questions and answers.
3. a formal series of questions; close questioning.

cat·ē·chis′măl, *a.* having an arrangement of questions and answers, like a catechism.

cat′ē·chist, *n.* one who instructs by question and answer; a catechizer; one appointed by the church to instruct in the principles of religion.

cat·ē·chis′tic, cat·ē·chis′tic·ăl, *a.* pertaining to a catechist or catechism.

cat″ē·chi·zā′tion, *n.* the act of examining by the putting of questions: also spelled *catechisation*.

cat′ē·chīze, cat′ē·chīse, *v.t.*; catechized, *pt.*, *pp.*; catechizing, *ppr.* 1. to instruct by asking questions, receiving answers, and offering explanations and corrections.
2. to question; to interrogate; to examine or try by questions, sometimes with a view to elicit condemnatory answers.
3. to question concerning the doctrines of a religion; to examine (pupils) and give instruction in the principles of religion.

cat′ē·chīz·ẽr, *n.* one who catechizes; one who instructs by question and answer, particularly in the principles of a religion.

cat′ē·chōl, *n.* a colorless crystalline compound, $C_6H_6O_2$, used in medicine as an antiseptic and in photography as a developer.

cat″ē·chōl′ȧ·mīne, *n.* any of various compounds that are secretions, or by-products of secretions, of the medulla of the adrenal gland and affect the sympathetic nervous system.

cat′ē·chū, *n.* a dry, brown, astringent extract, obtained by boiling and evaporation from the *Acacia catechu* and other Asiatic trees and shrubs. It contains a large portion of tannin or tannic acid.

cat·ē·chū′ic, *a.* pertaining to catechu.

cat·ē·chū′men, *n.* [LL. *catechumenus*; Gr. *katēchoumenos*, one instructed, ppr. of *katēchein*, to instruct.]
1. a person, especially an adult, receiving instruction in the fundamentals of Christianity after conversion and before confirmation.
2. a person receiving instruction in the fundamentals of any subject.

cat·ē·chū′men·āte, *n.* the condition of a catechumen, or the period during which one is a catechumen.

cat″ē·chū·men′i·căl, *a.* pertaining to a catechumen or catechumens.

cat·ē·chū′men·ist, *n.* a catechumen. [Obs.]

cat·ē·gor·ē·mat′ic, *a.* [Gr. *katēgorēma* (-*atos*), a predicate.] in logic, designating or of a word which can be employed by itself as the subject or predicate of a proposition.

cat·ē·gor′ic·ăl, *a.* [LL. *categoricus*; Gr. *katēgorikos*, from *katēgoria*, a category.]
1. pertaining to a category.
2. absolute; positive; express; unqualified; not relative or hypothetical; as, a *categorical* answer is requested.

cat·ē·gor′ic·ăl im·per′ȧ·tive, the Kantian doctrine that one's behavior should be governed by principles which one would have govern the behavior of all people.

cat·ē·gor′ic·ăl·ly, *adv.* absolutely; directly; expressly; positively; as, to affirm *categorically*.

cat·ē·gor′ic·ăl·ness, *n.* the quality of being categorical, absolute, or positive.

cat′ē·gō·rist, *n.* one who compiles or classifies a category.

cat′ē·gō·rīze, *v.t.*; categorized, *pt.*, *pp.*; categorizing, *ppr.* to classify in a category; to catalogue.

cat′ē·gō·ry, *n.*; *pl.* **cat′ē·gō·ries,** [L. *categoria*; Gr. *katēgoria*, from *katēgorein*, to accuse, assert, predicate; *kata*, against, and *agoreuein*, to declaim, address an assembly; *agora*, an assembly.]
1. in logic, any of the various basic concepts into which all knowledge can be classified. Aristotle made ten categories, viz., substance, quantity, quality, relation, action, passivity, time, place, position, and condition.
2. a class or division in a scheme of classification; as, to put a person in the same *category* with another.

cat′el, *n.* [ME. *catel*; OFr. *catel*; LL. *captale*, *capitale*, property, goods.] cattle. [Obs.]

cat·ē·lec·trō·ton′ic, *a.* pertaining to or distinguished by catelectrotonus.

cat″ē·lec·trot′ō·nus, *n.* [*cata-*, and Gr. *ēlektron*, amber, and *tonos*, tension.] in physiology, the increased tension produced in a nerve near the cathode or negative pole, when an electric current passes through it.

cȧ·tē′nȧ, *n.*; *pl.* **cȧ·tē′nae,** [L. *catena*, a chain.] a chain of connected things or subjects, specifically relating to theology.

cat′ē·nā·ry, cat·ē·nā′ri·ăn, *a.* [L. *catenarius*, from *catena*, a chain.]
1. relating to a chain; like a chain.
2. designating the curve of a catenary.

cat′ē·nā·ry, *n.*; *pl.* **cat′ē·nā·ries,** the curve formed by a perfectly flexible cord or chain, of uniform density, hanging freely between two points at the same level.

cat′ē·nāte, *v.t.*, catenated, *pt.*, *pp.*; catenating, *ppr.* to link; to connect in a series of links or ties.

cat′ē·nāte, cat′ē·nā·ted, *a.* connected, as links in a chain.

cat·ē·nā′tion, *n.* 1. connection of links or union of parts, as in a chain.
2. a catenating; a linking.

cȧ·ten′ū·lāte, *a.* [L. *catenula*, dim. of *catena*, a chain.]
1. consisting of little links or chains.
2. in zoology, having on the surface a series of oblong swellings resembling a chain.

cā′tẽr, *v.i.*; catered, *pt.*, *pp.*; catering, *ppr.* [ME. *catour*, a purchaser, caterer; OFr. *acator*, from *acater*, to buy, provide; from LL. *accaptare*; *ad*, to, and *captare*, to strive, seize; intens. of L. *capere*, to take.]
1. to provide food; to serve as a caterer; as, to *cater* for a large company.
2. to give what is wanted or required, especially as a means of pleasure: followed by *for* or *to*; as, to *cater to* public ideas.

cā′tẽr (*or* kat′), *v.t.* to cut in a diagonal direction. [Obs.]

cā′tẽr, *n.* a provider; a caterer. [Obs.]

cā′tẽr, *n.* [Fr. *quatre*, from L. *quattuor*, four.] the four of cards or dice. [Obs.]

cat′e·ran, *n.* a Scottish Highlands robber or freebooter.

cat′ẽr-cor″nẽr, *a.* cater-cornered.

cat′ẽr-cor″nẽred, *a.* [from Fr. *quatre*, four; and *cornered*.] diagonal.

cat′ẽr-cor″nẽred, *adv.* diagonally.

cā′tẽr-cous′in (-kuz′n), *n.* [Fr. *quatre*; L. *quattuor*, four, and *cousin*.] a close friend. [Archaic.]

cā′tẽr·ẽr, *n.* one who caters; one whose work is providing food and service for parties, etc.

cā′tẽr·ess, *n.* a woman who caters.

cat′ẽr·pil·lăr, *n.* [ME. *catyrpel*, a corruption of OFr. *chatepelouse*, *catepelue*, from *chate*, a she-cat, and *pelouse*, hairy; LL. *catus*, a cat, and *pilosus*, from *pilus*, a hair.]
1. the wormlike, often hairy larva of lepidopterous insects; also, the larva of other insects, such as the *Tenthredo*, or sawfly. Caterpillars are produced immediately from the egg. They contain the embryo of the adult insect, enclosed within a muscular envelope, which is thrown off when the insect enters the nymph or chrysalis state, in which it remains for some time. It then throws off its last envelope and emerges as an adult.
2. a plant belonging to the genus *Scorpiurus*, having pods similar to caterpillars in appearance.

caterpillar tractor; a tractor used for hauling or pulling, and having a continuous, hinged series of metal strips, or two endless belts, over cogged wheels, running the length of the machine on either side: a trademark (*Caterpillar Tractor*).

CATERPILLAR TRACTOR

cat′ẽr·pil·lăr catch′ẽr, a bird of the shrike family, which devours caterpillars.

cat′ẽr·pil·lăr ēat′ẽr, 1. a caterpillar catcher.
2. a worm bred in the body of a caterpillar, which eats its way out.

cat′ẽr·pil·lăr fun′gus, a fungus of the genus *Cordyceps*, which infests caterpillars; especially, the *Cordyceps robertsii* of New Zealand.

cat′ẽr·pil·lăr hunt′ẽr, one of several species of beetles which feed upon caterpillars.

cat′ẽr·waul, *v.i.* caterwauled, *pt.*, *pp.*; caterwauling, *ppr.* to cry or waul, as cats in rutting time; to screech; to wail; to scream.

cat′ẽr·waul, *n.* a caterwauling.

cat′ẽr·waul·ing, *n.* the cry of cats at rutting time or any cry resembling this.

cā′tẽr·y, *n.* the place where provisions are deposited in a royal household. [Obs.]

cātes (kāts), *n.pl.* [ME. *acates*, provisions, from OFr. *acater*, to buy provisions, from LL. *accaptare*, to buy, provide; L. *ad*, to, and *captare*, to take, seize.] provisions bought; hence, food; viands. [Obs.]

cat′-eyed (-īd), *a.* having eyes like a cat; able to see well in dim light.

cat′fall, *n.* in nautical usage, a rope used in hoisting the anchor to the cathead.

cat′fish, *n.* 1. the wolf fish.
2. any of a large group of scaleless fishes especially the family *Ictaluridae*, characterized by long feelers (called *barbels*), somewhat like a cat's whiskers, about the mouth.
3. any fish resembling the catfish.

çat′foot, *n.* a stubby foot, with arched toes, like that of a cat.

çat′foot·ed, *a.* having feet like a cat; hence, sly; stealthy.

çat′gut, *n.* 1. the intestines of sheep and other animals, dried and twisted, used for strings of violins and other instruments, for surgical sutures, etc.
2. a sort of linen or canvas, with wide spaces between the threads.

çath-, cata-.

Çath′à·rī, *n.pl.* [from Gr. *katharos*, pure.] the pure; hence, the members of such Medieval religious sects as protested against corruption in life or doctrine.

Çath′à·rine wheel, [so called from St. *Catharine* of Alexandria, who is represented with a *wheel* in connection with her martyrdom.]
1. an ornamented window, or compartment of a window, of a circular form, with rosettes arranged as the spokes of a wheel: known also as *rose window* or *wheel window*.
2. a revolving piece of fireworks similar in form to the rose window.
3. in heraldry, the figure of a hooked wheel symbolic of St. Catharine's martyrdom.

çath′à·rism, *n.* 1. the act or process of making a surface chemically clean.
2. [C–] the doctrine or principles of the Cathari.

Çath′à·rist, *n.* [Gr. *katharos*, pure.] one who pretends to more purity than others possess; specifically, one of the Cathari.

çath′à·rize, *v.t.*; catharized, *pt., pp.*; catharizing, *ppr.* [Gr. *katharizein*, to cleanse, from *katharos*, pure.] to make clean, as a surface, by the use of chemicals.

çat′härp·in, çat′härp·ing, [origin unknown.] a rope serving to brace in the shrouds of the lower masts behind their respective yards, to tighten the shrouds, and give more room to draw in the yards, when the ship is close-hauled.

çà·thär′sis, *n.* [Gr. *katharsis*, purification, from *kathairein*, to purify.]
1. purgation, especially of the bowels.
2. the purifying or relieving of the emotions by art: an Aristotelian concept, applied originally to the effects of tragic drama.
3. in psychiatry, the alleviation of fears, problems, and complexes by bringing them to consciousness and giving them expression.
Also spelled *katharsis*.

Çà·thär′tēs, *n.* [Gr. *kathartēs*, a cleanser, from *kathairein*, to purify.] a genus of vultures of the family *Cathartidæ*, comprising the turkey buzzards.

çà·thär′tiç, çà·thär′tiç·ăl, *a.* [Gr. *kathartikos*, from *kathairein*, to purify; *katharos*, pure.] having to do with catharsis; purging.

çà·thär′tiç, *n.* a medicine that stimulates evacuation of the bowels; a purgative or laxative.

çà·thär′tiç·ăl·ly, *adv.* in the manner of a cathartic.

çà·thär′tiç·ăl·ness, *n.* the quality of stimulating discharges from the bowels.

Çà·thär′ti·dae, *n.pl.* in zoology, an American family of birds of prey, different from true vultures. The group includes the condors, turkey buzzards, etc.

çà·thär′tin, *n.* the active purgative principle of different species of *Cassia*, popularly known as *senna*: it is a glucoside, having the nature of a weak acid.

çat haw, the berry of the hawthorn. [Brit. Dial.]

çat′head (-hed), *n.* a strong beam projecting horizontally over a ship's bow, carrying two or three sheaves, about which a rope, called the catfall, passes, and connects with the cat block.

çat′head stop′pēr, the chain or rope running between the cathead and the anchor ring.

çath′ē·drà (*or* cà·thē′drà), *n.* [L. *cathedra*; Gr. *kathedra*, a seat, bench; *kata*, down, and *hedra*, from *hezesthai*, to sit.] a chair; especially, the official chair or throne of a bishop, or the professional chair of anyone entitled to teach with authority or possessed of high dignity; hence, *ex cathedra*, from or with official authority; as, he speaks *ex cathedra*.

çà·thē′drăl, *n.* [LL. *cathedralis* (supply *ecclesia*), from L. *cathedra*; Gr. *kathedra*, a seat, bench.]
1. the main church of a bishop's see, containing the cathedra.
2. loosely, any large imposing church.

çà·thē′drăl, *a.* 1. pertaining to the church which is the bishop's seat, or head church of a diocese; containing the see of a bishop; as, a *cathedral* church; *cathedral* service.
2. like or characteristic of a cathedral.
3. of, like, or containing a cathedra.
4. emanating from the official chair, as of a pope or bishop; authoritative.

çath·ē·dral′iç, *a.* cathedral. [Rare.]

çath′ē·drā·ted, *a.* relating to the authority of a bishop. [Obs.]

çath·ē·ret′iç, *n.* [Gr. *kathairetikos*, from *kathairein*, to destroy.] a caustic of mild nature used to treat warts, moles, and similar growths.

Çath′ēr·ine wheel, same as *Catharine wheel*.

çath′e·tăl, *a.* [Gr. *kathetos*, a perpendicular line.] of or pertaining to a cathetus.

çath′e·tēr, *n.* [LL. *catheter*; Gr. *kathetēr*, a catheter, a plug; from *kathienai*, to let down, thrust in; *kata*, down, and *hienai*, to send.] in surgery, a tubular metal or rubber instrument inserted into the bladder, to draw off the urine, when the natural discharge is stopped; also, a similar instrument designed to pass through other canals.
Eustachian catheter; a catheter introduced into the Eustachian tube in order to reach the middle ear.

çath′e·tēr·ism, çath″e·tēr·i·zā′tion, *n.* the operation of inserting a catheter.

çath′e·tēr·ize, *v.t.*; catheterized, *pt., pp.*; catheterizing, *ppr.* to insert a catheter into.

çath·e·tom′e·tēr, *n.* [Gr. *kathetos*, perpendicular, and *metron*, a measure.] an instrument for determining with precision small differences in the height of the same column of mercury or other fluid at various moments and under different conditions, or the difference in height of two such columns. It consists of a telescope, or telescopes, sliding on a graduated rod.

çath′e·tus, *n.*; *pl.* **çath′e·tī,** [L., from Gr. *kathetos*, perpendicular, a perpendicular line.] in geometry, a line falling perpendicularly on another line or surface. Thus, the catheti of a right-angled triangle are the two sides that include the right angle.

çà·thex′is, *n.* [from Gr. *kathexis*, a holding, a transl. of G. *besetzung*, as used by Freud.] in psychoanalysis, concentration of the psychic energy on some particular person, thing, or idea.

çath′ō·dăl, *a.* [Gr. *kathodos*, a descent; *kata*, down, and *hodos*, a way.] pertaining to a cathode.

çath′ōde, *n.* [Gr. *kathodos*, going down; *kata*, *down*, and *hodos*, way.] a negatively charged electrode, as of a vacuum tube, electrolytic cell, etc.: also spelled *kathode*.
cathode current; the entire amount of current going to, or coming from, the cathode in an electron tube.
cathode drop; in arc welding, the drop or decrease in voltage that occurs between the stream of the arc and the negative electrode.
cathode particle; an electron.
cathode rays; the stream of electrons projected from the surface of a cathode: cathode rays produce X rays when they strike solids.
cathode-ray tube; a vacuum tube in which cathode rays are produced.

çà·thod′iç, *a.* [Gr. *kathodos*, going down.] pertaining to a cathode; emanating from or having its origin in a cathode.

çà·thod′ō·grȧph, *n.* [Gr. *kathodos*, going down, and *graphein*, to write.] a picture showing the internal appearance of an opaque body, usually produced by X rays: called also a *radiograph*.

çat′hōle, a hole in the stern of a ship for the passage of a hawser or cable. [Rare.]

çath′ō·liç, *a.* [L. *catholicus*, universal, general; Gr. *katholikos*; *kata*, down, completely, and *holos*, whole.]
1. universal; general; all-inclusive.
2. liberal; not narrow-minded, partial, or bigoted; as, a *catholic* man; *catholic* principles.
3. [C–] pertaining to or affecting the Roman Catholics; as, *Catholic* emancipation.
4. of the universal Christian church; of the Christian church as a whole.
5. [C–] of the Western (Roman) Christian Church as distinguished from the Eastern (Orthodox) Christian Church.
6. [C–] of any of the orthodox Christian churches, including the Roman, Greek, Orthodox, and Anglo-Catholic, as distinguished from the Reformed or Protestant churches.
Catholic Epistles; the epistles of the Apostles, which are not addressed to a particular church; as, James, Peter, and Jude, and usually the three epistles of John.
Catholic Majesty; the former title of Spanish monarchs in recognition of their devotion to the Roman Catholic Church.

Çath′ō·liç, *n.* 1. a member of any of the Catholic churches, especially the Roman Catholic Church.
2. [c–] one who accepts the creeds received in common by all sects of the universal Christian Church.
Old Catholics; those Roman Catholics who seceded from the Church of Rome in 1870. In that year, Pope Pius IX promulgated the doctrine of papal infallibility, which they declined to accept as an article of faith. The *Old Catholics* in the United States refuse to recognize that the decisions of the Vatican council are binding on the whole Roman Catholic Church.

çà·thol′i·çăl, *a.* catholic. [Obs.]

çà·thol′i·çăl·ly, *adv.* in a catholic manner; universally.

Çath′ō̆l·iç Chŭrch, the Roman Catholic Church.

Çà·thol′i·çīse, *v.t.* and *v.i.* same as *Catholicize*.

Çà·thol′i·çism, *n.* 1. the doctrine, faith, practice, and organization of a Catholic church, especially of the Roman Catholic Church.
2. [c–] liberality; universality; catholicity; as, his *catholicism* was a marked trait.

Çath·ō·liç′i·ty, *n.* 1. Catholicism.
2. the system of doctrine, discipline, and worship held in common by all denominations of the universal Christian church.
3. [c–] universality; as, the *catholicity* of a doctrine.
4. [c–] the quality of being catholic; freedom from prejudice; liberality, as of ideas.

Çà·thol′i·çīze, *v.i.* and *v.t.* 1. to become or cause to become a Catholic, or convert to Catholicism.
2. [c–] to make or become catholic.

çath′ō·liç·ly, *adv.* generally; in a catholic manner.

çath′ō·liç·ness, *n.* universality.

çà·thol′i·çon, *n.* [Gr. *katholikon*, neut. of *katholikos*, universal.]
1. a remedy for all diseases; a universal remedy; a panacea.
2. anything all-inclusive.

çà·thol′i·ços, *n.* the spiritual head of the Armenian church.

çat hook, a strong hook fitted to the cat block.

Çat″i·li·nā′ri·ăn, *a.* of, pertaining to, or resembling Catiline, the noted Roman conspirator, or his conspiracy.

Çat″i·li·nā′ri·ăn, *n.* one who acts like Catiline.

Çat′i·lin·ism, *n.* the practices of Catiline; conspiracy. [Obs.]

çat′i·on, *n.* [coined by Faraday from Gr. *katiōn*, going down, ppr. of *katienai*; *kata*, down, and *ienai*, to go.] a positively charged ion: cations move toward the cathode in an electrolized solution: also spelled *kation*.

çat′kin, *n.* [a dim. of *cat*, from its resemblance to a cat's tail.] a scaly spike, the flowers of which are unisexual and petalless, as on a willow or birch: called also *ament*.

HAZEL CATKIN

çat′līke, *a.* like a cat; vigilant; watchful; stealthy.

çat′ling, *n.* 1. a long, straight, double-edged surgical knife, used in amputating.
2. a little cat; a kitten. [Rare.]
3. catgut; the string of a lute, violin, etc. [Rare.]

çat′lin·ite, *n.* [named after George *Catlin*, an American traveler.] a red clay stone used by the North American Indians for making pipes, etc.

çat′mint, *n.* catnip.

çat nap, a very brief sleep or nap.

çat′nip, *n.* a plant of the mint family with downy leaves and spikes of bluish flowers: cats are fond of its odor.

çat″ō·çà·thär′tiç, *a.* [Gr. *katō*, downward, and *kathartikos*, purging.] stimulating evacuation of the bowels.

çat″ō·çà·thär′tiç, *n.* a medicine that purges; a cathartic.

Çat′ō·don, *n.* [Gr. *katō*, down, and *odons*, *odontos*, tooth.] a genus of cetaceans, including the sperm whale, *Physeter macrocephalus*: so called from the fact of its having teeth in the lower jaw only.

çat′ō·dont, *a.* 1. having teeth in the lower jaw only; as, a *catodont* serpent or cetacean.
2. pertaining to whales of the genus *Catodon*.

Çat·ō·don′tà, *n.pl.* a suborder of the *Ophidia*, including the family *Stenostomidæ*.

Çat·ō·don′ti·dae, *n.pl.* a family of whales, the typical genus of which is *Catodon*.

çat-ō′-moun′tain (-tin), *n.* catamountain.

Ça·tō′ni·ăn, *a.* pertaining to either of the two Romans, Cato the Censor or Cato Uticensis, both noted for severity of manners; hence, grave; severe; inflexible.

çat-ō′-nīne′-tāils, *n.*; *pl.* **çat-ō′-nīne′-tāils,** 1. a whip consisting of nine knotted pieces of line or cord fastened to a piece of thick rope: formerly used for flogging.
2. same as *cattail.*

çȧ·top′triç, *n.* catoptrics.

çȧ·top′triç, çȧ·top′triç·ăl, *a.* relating to catoptrics, or the reflection of light; as, a *catoptric* telescope.

çȧ·top′triçs, *n.pl.* [Gr. *katoptrikos,* from *katoptron,* a mirror.] [*construed as sing.*] the branch of optics which deals with the properties of incident and reflected light, and particularly that which is reflected from mirrors or polished bodies.

çȧ·top′trō·man·cy, *n.* [Gr. *katoptron,* a mirror, and *manteia,* divination.] divination by means of mirrors.

çȧ·tos′tō·mid, *a.* of or pertaining to the *Catostomidæ.*

çȧ·tos′tō·mid, *n.* one of the *Catostomidæ.*

Çā·tos·tom′i·dae, *n.pl.* [from Gr. *katō,* down, and *stoma,* mouth, and *-idæ.*] a family of fresh-water fishes, including the suckers and buffalo fish of North America.

çȧ·tos′tō·moid, *a.* and *n.* same as *catostomid.*

çat rig, a rig consisting of a single large sail on a mast well forward in the bow; rig of a catboat.

çat′-rigged, *a.* having the sails and rigging of a catboat.

ÇAT sçan, [*c*omputerized *a*xial *t*omography.]
1. a method for diagnosing disorders of the soft tissues of the brain: it uses a computerized combination of many X-ray photographs taken by tomography to form an image.
2. the image so formed.

çat's çrā′dle, a child's game played by looping a string on the fingers, and sometimes transferring it to the hand of another player so as to form designs.

CAT'S CRADLE

çat's′-eȳe, *n.* 1. a variety of quartz used as a gem, and having yellowish, opalescent reflections from within, especially apparent when cut with a convex surface. These reflections resemble those observable in the eye of a cat.
2. a small reflector device on road signs, bicycles, etc., used to indicate their presence at night.

çat's′-foot, *n.* a plant of the genus *Nepeta,* ground ivy: also called *cat's-paw.*

çat's′-head (-hed), *n.* a kind of large apple.

çat′sō, *n.* [It. *cazzo.*] a rogue; a cheat; a base fellow. [Obs.]

çat's′-pa̤w, *n.* 1. a dupe; a person used by another to accomplish his designs and protect himself: so called from the story of the monkey which, to save its own paw, used the paw of the cat to draw the roasting chestnuts out of the fire. Also written *catspaw.*
2. in nautical usage, (a) a light breeze rippling the surface of the water; (b) the ripple so made; (c) a turn in the bight of a rope, to hook a tackle on.
3. same as *cat's-foot.*

çat's′-tāil, *n.* same as *cattail.*

çat′stick, *n.* a stick or bat used in playing tipcat.

çat′stitch, *v.t.* in needlework, (a) to join (two edges) with a cross stitch; (b) to turn down the edge of and sew with a zigzag stitch.

çat′sup, *n.* [var. of *ketchup.*] a sauce for meat, fish, etc.; especially, a thick sauce (*tomato catsup*) made of tomatoes, flavored with onion, salt, sugar, and spice: also *ketchup, catchup.*

çat's whisk′ẽr, same as *cat whisker.*

çat′tāil, *n.* 1. a tall marsh plant with long, flat, reedlike leaves and long, brown, fuzzy, cylindrical flower spikes.
2. any grass of the genus *Phleum.*
3. a catkin.

çat′tȧ·lō, *n.*; *pl.* **çat′tȧ·lōes, çat′tȧ·lōs,** a catalo.

çat·ti·man′do̤o, *n.* [native E. Ind. name.] a resinous cement obtained from the juice of the East Indian plant, *Euphorbia cattimandoo*: written also *kattimundoo.*

çat′ti·ness, *n.* the quality of being catty; spitefulness.

çat′tish, *a.* resembling a cat; feline.

çat′tle, *n.pl.* [ME. *catel, katel*; OFr. *catel*; LL. *captale, capitale,* property, goods, stock; L. *capitalis,* principal, chief, from *caput* (*-itis*), head.]
1. farm animals collectively; livestock.
2. domesticated bovine animals collectively; cows, bulls, steers, or oxen: the term is usually not applied to calves and heifers.
3. human beings in the mass: used in contempt or reproach.

çat′tle guärd, a device at a railroad crossing, so constructed as to prevent cattle from straying upon the track.

çat′tle louse, any of several species of parasites that infest cattle.

çat′tle·măn, *n.*; *pl.* **çat′tle·men,** one who raises or cares for cattle.

çat′tle plāgue (plāg), a contagious disease of cattle: also called *rinderpest.*

çat′tle ranch, a cattle range.

çat′tle rānġe, çat′tle run, a large tract of land used for the grazing and breeding of cattle.

Çat′tlē·yȧ, *n.* 1. a genus of orchids consisting of many-colored flowers: named after William Cattley, an English botanist.
2. [c–] a plant of this genus.

çat′ty, *n.* [Malay *kati,* a pound.] an Asiatic unit of weight varying from place to place, but generally equivalent to 1.33 pounds avoirdupois.

çat′ty, *a.*; *comp.* cattier; *superl.* cattiest, 1. of or pertaining to cats; like a cat.
2. malicious; sly; spiteful.

çat′ty, *n.* 1. tipcat.
2. a catstick.

çat′wa̤lk, *n.* 1. originally, a narrow bridge connecting the elevated midship section of a ship with the bow or stern.
2. a narrow pathway or platform, as along a bridge, over an engine room, or inside a dirigible along the keel.

çat whisk′ẽr, 1. in electronics, a sharply pointed wire for making contact with a semiconductor crystal.
2. in radio, a thin wire that makes contact with a sensitive spot on the crystal of a crystal detector.

çat′-whis″tleṣ (-lz), *n.* the horsetail *Equisetum palustre.*

çat′wŏrt, *n.* catnip.

çau·been′, *n.* [Ir. caipin.] a battered old hat.

Çau·çā′siăn (*or*-zhun), *a.* 1. of the Caucasus, its people, or their culture.
2. [so named in 1795 by the G. anthropologist Johann Blumenbach, who erroneously thought that the original home of the hypothetical Indo-Europeans was the Caucasus; although the following senses are now not scientific and often tinged with racism, the word is used in this dictionary in default of a better.] designating or of one of the main ethnic divisions of the human race: it includes the Mediterranean, Alpine, and Nordic subdivisions, and is loosely called the *white race.*
3. designating or of all languages in the area of the Caucasus which are neither Indo-European nor Turkic.

Çau·çā′siăn, *n.* 1. any native or inhabitant of the Caucasus.
2. a member of the Caucasian division of mankind: loosely called *white person.*
3. the Caucasian languages, including Circassian, Georgian, etc.

Çau·ças′iç, *a.* Caucasian.

çau′çus, *n.* [etymology uncertain; prob. from Algonquian *cau-cau-a-su,* adviser.]
1. in a general sense, a private or secret meeting of members of a political or other organization for the purpose of choosing candidates for election to office, deciding upon joint action on pending public measures, or discussing and deciding questions of policy.
2. formerly, a meeting of local members of a particular party, to select delegates to a nominating convention or candidates for office: now generally superseded by the direct primary election.
3. a private meeting of members of a particular party in a legislative body; as, to abide by the decision of the Democratic *caucus.*
4. a secret meeting of any persons associated in a common cause or by common interests; as, a *caucus* of bank presidents.
5. in English politics, a local party committee having power to select candidates, settle questions of local policy, etc., and conduct election campaigns.

çau′çus, *v.i.*; caucused, *pt., pp.*; caucusing, *ppr.* to hold a caucus.

çau′dȧ, *n.*; *pl.* **çau′dae,** [L., a tail.] in anatomy and zoology, a tail or taillike appendage.
cauda galli; a plume-shaped fossil of the Devonian Period, supposed to have been a seaweed.

çau′dad, *adv.* [L. *cauda,* a tail, and *ad,* to.] in anatomy and zoology, toward the tail or the caudal part of the body; posteriorly: opposed to *cephalad.*

çau′dăl, *a.* [L. *cauda,* a tail.]
1. pertaining to or resembling a tail.
2. at or near the tail.
caudal fin; the tail fin of a fish.

Çau·dā′tȧ, *n.pl.* [L. *cauda,* tail.] an order of amphibians having a long caudal appendage: called also the *Urodela.*

çau′dāte, çau′dā·ted, *a.* [L. *cauda,* a tail.] having a tail or taillike part.

çau′dex, *n.*; *pl.* **çau′di·çēṣ** or **çau′dex·eṣ,** [L., stem of a tree.] in botany, (a) the base of a perennial plant; (b) the axis or stem of a woody plant, especially of a palm or tree fern.

çau′di·çle, çau·diç′ū·lȧ, *n.* [dim. of L. *caudex,* stem.] the thin pliable stalk in orchids, on which the mass of pollen accumulates.

çau·dil′lō (-yō), *n.* [Sp., from Ar.] leader; commander.

çau′dle, *n.* [ME. *caudel*; OFr. *caudel,* from L. *calidus, caldus,* warm.] a warm drink for invalids; especially, a spiced and sugared gruel with wine or ale added.

çau′dle, *v.t.*; caudled, *pt., pp.*; caudling, *ppr.* to make into caudle; also, to serve a caudle to.

çau′fle, *n.* same as *coffle.*

çaught (ka̤t), *v.* past tense and past participle of *catch.*

çaul, *n.* [ME. *calle, kalle*; OFr. *cale,* a kind of cap; Ir. *calla,* a veil, hood.]
1. the membrane enclosing a fetus, or a part of this membrane sometimes enveloping the head of a child at birth: formerly believed to bring good luck.
2. the part of the peritoneum that extends from the stomach to the large intestine: also called *great omentum.*
3. a kind of net in which women sometimes enclosed their hair. [Obs.]
4. any kind of net or thin membrane. [Obs.]

çaul, *n.* [Fr. *cale,* wedge; G. *keil*; O.H.G. *chil,* a wedge.] a wooden clamp used to hold veneers together until the glue has set.

çauld, *a.* [Northumbrian AS. *cald.*] cold. [Scot. and North Eng. Dial.]

çaul′drŏn, *n.* same as *caldron.*

Çau·lẽr′pȧ, *n.* [L. *caulis*; Gr. *kaulos,* a stem, and *herpein,* to creep.] a large genus of single-celled algae found in tropical seas.

çau·les′cent, *a.* [L. *carlis,* a stem, and *-escent.*] in botany, having an obvious stem above the ground.

çau′li·çle, *n.* [L. *cauliculus,* dim. of *caulis,* a stem.] in botany, a little stem or rudimentary stem: applied to the neck of the embryo to distinguish it from the cotyledons or seed leaves.

çau′li·çōle, *n.* same as *cauliculus.*

çau·liç′ō·lous, *a.* [L. *caulis,* stem, and *colere,* to inhabit.] in botany, parasitic on the stem or stalk, as certain fungi.

çau′li·çūle, *n.* a caulicle.

çau·liç′ū·lus, *n.*; *pl.* **çau·liç′ū·lī,** [L., dim. of *caulis,* a stem.]
1. in architecture, the smaller stalks in the Corinthian capital, representing the twisted tops of the larger acanthus stalks, or caules: also written *caulicole.*
2. in botany, same as *caulicle.*

çau·lif′ẽr·ous, *a.* same as *caulescent.*

çau′li·flow·ẽr, *n.* [earlier *cole florye,* from Fr. *chou flori* (now *chou-fleur*), cauliflower; mod. sp. after L. *caulis,* a cabbage.]
1. a variety of *Brassica oleracea,* a cabbage with a compact white head of fleshy stalks bearing small flowers and buds.
2. the head of this plant, used as a vegetable.

çau′li·flow·ẽr ēar, an ear permanently deformed as a result of being injured in boxing, etc.

çau′li·fo̤rm, *a.* [L. *caulis,* a stem, and *forma,* form.] having the form of a caulis or stem, either in architectural decoration or botany.

çau·liġ′e·nous, *a.* carried on a stem.

çau′line, *a.* [L. *caulis,* a stalk.] in botany, of or growing on a stem, especially the upper part of a stem.

çau′lis, *n.*; *pl.* **çau′lēṣ,** [L., from Gr. *kaulos,* a stock, stem.]
1. in botany, the main stem or stalk of a plant.
2. in architecture, one of the main stems or leaves which spring from the angle of a Corinthian capital.

çaulk, *n.* and *v.t.* see *calk.*

çau·lō·cär′pous, *a.* [Gr. *kaulos,* a stem, and *karpos,* fruit.] in botany, having stems that produce flowers and fruit annually.

çau′lōme, *n.* [Gr. *kaulos,* a stem, and *-ome.*] the stem of a plant, or its axial portion.

çau·lom′iç, *a.* pertaining to the caulome.

çau′mȧ, *n.* [Gr. *kauma,* heat.] in medicine, burning heat; febrile heat. [Rare.]

çau′pō·nāte, *v.t.* [L. *cauponatus,* pp. of *cauponari,* to traffic.] to trade or traffic in. [Obs.]

çau·pō·nā′tion, *n.* huckstering. [Obs.]

çau′pō·nīze, *v.t.* to cauponate. [Obs.]

çauş′ȧ·ble, *a.* that can be caused, produced, or effected.

çauş′ăl, *a.* [L. *causalis,* from *causa,* cause, reason.]
1. of a cause or causes.
2. like or constituting a cause.
3. relating to cause and effect.
4. expressing a cause or reason.

çauş′ăl, *n.* in grammar, a causal connective, as *since, therefore, for.*

çau·sal′ġi·ȧ, *n.* [Mod. L., from Gr. *kausos,* fever, heat, and *algos,* pain.] neuralgia characterized by a burning sensation.

çau·şal′i·ty, *n.*; *pl.* **çau·şal′i·tieş,** 1. causal quality or agency.
2. the interrelation of cause and effect; principle that nothing can exist or happen without a cause.
3. in phrenology, the faculty of tracing effects to their causes.

çauş′ăl·ly, *adv.* 1. as a cause.
2. by the operation of cause and effect.

çau·şā′tion, *n.* 1. a causing or being caused.
2. a causal agency; anything producing an effect.
3. causality.
law of causation; the law that every event or phenomenon results from an antecedent cause.

çau·şā′tion·ist, *n.* a believer in universal causation.

çauş′ȧ·tive, *a.* [L. *causativus,* from *causa,* a cause, reason.]
1. producing an effect; causing.
2. expressing causation, as certain verbs: *fell* is a *causative* verb meaning "to cause to fall."

çauş′ȧ·tive, *n.* a causative word or form.

çauş′ȧ·tive·ly, *adv.* in a causative manner.

çau·şā′tŏr, *n.* [LL. *causator,* from L. *causare,* to cause.] one who causes or produces an effect. [Obs.]

çauşe, *n.* [ME. *cause;* OFr. *cause;* L. *causa,* a cause, reason.]
1. a suit or action in court; any legal process which a party institutes to obtain his demand, or by which he seeks to realize his claim, lawsuit, case.
The *cause* of both parties shall come before the judges. —Ex. xxii. 9.
2. that which produces an effect or result; that from which anything proceeds, and without which it would not exist.
Cause is a substance exerting its power into act, to make a thing begin to be. —Locke.
3. a person or thing acting voluntarily or involuntarily as the agent that brings about an effect or result; as, a woman was the *cause* of his downfall.
4. a reason, motive, or ground for producing or trying to produce a given effect; as, *cause* for joy; *cause* for anger.
5. reason enough; as, *cause* for divorce.
6. any activity or movement that a number of people are interested in and support; as, slum clearance is a good *cause.*
7. any matter as a subject of discussion.
efficient cause; the power or agent that effects a result.
final cause; the purpose or end for which anything is produced.
formal cause; the ideal form according to which any thing or event is produced or brought about, as the form of a painting in the mind of an artist.
material cause; the means employed to produce a formal cause, as the oils, water colors, etc. used in a painting.
to make common cause with; to work together with toward the same objective; to form an alliance with.
Syn.—incitement, inducement, motive, origin, reason, source, purpose, object.

çauşe, *conj.* contraction of *because.* [Dial.]

çauşe, *v.t.,* caused, *pt., pp.;* causing, *ppr.* [Fr. *causer,* from *cause,* L. *causa,* a cause, reason.] to be the cause of; bring about; make happen; effect; induce; produce.
I will *cause* it to rain on the earth forty days. —Gen. vii. 4.

çauşe, *v.i.* to assign cause; to give reasons. [Obs.]

cause cé·lèbre′ (kōz sā-lebr′), [Fr.] a celebrated law case, trial, or controversy.

çauşe′fųl, *a.* having a sufficient cause. [Rare.]

çauşe′less, *a.* 1. having no apparent cause.
2. without adequate ground, reason, or motive; as, *causeless* hatred; *causeless* fear.

çauşe′less·ly, *adv.* without cause or reason.

çauşe′less·ness, *n.* the state of being causeless.

çauş′ēr, *n.* one who or that which causes; the agent by which an effect is produced.

çau·şe·rie′ (kō-), *n.* [Fr., from *causer,* to chat, from L. *causari,* to plead, debate, from *causa,* a cause, lawsuit.]
1. an informal talk or discussion; chat.
2. a short piece of writing in a conversational style.

çau·şeūşe′ (kō-zūz′), *n.* [Fr.] a seat for two persons.

çauşe′wāy, *n.* [from *causey,* and *way.*]
1. a road or path raised above the natural level of the ground by stones, earth, timber, etc., serving as a dry passage over wet or marshy ground.
2. a paved way or road; highway.

çauşe′wāy, *v.t.* to make a causeway over or through; furnish with a causeway.

çau′şey, *n.*; *pl.* **çau′şeys,** [ME. *cauce;* ONorm.-Fr. *caucie,* from LL. *calciare,* to make a road, from L. *calx, calcis,* lime.] a causeway. [Brit. Dial.]

çau·sid′i·çăl, *a.* [L. *causidicalis,* pertaining to an advocate or pleader, *causidicus,* a pleader; *causa,* a cause, and *dicere,* to say.] pertaining to an advocate or to the pleading of lawsuits.

çaus′son, *n.* see *cavezon.*

çaus′tiç, *a.* [L. *causticus,* Gr. *kaustikos,* from *kaustos,* burning, from *kaiein,* to burn.]
1. that can burn, eat away, or destroy living tissue by chemical action; corrosive.
2. cutting; biting; stinging; sardonic; sarcastic.
3. designating or of the curved radial surface, or a plane curve in this surface, formed by the reflection or refraction of rays from a curved solid surface.

çaus′tiç, *n.* [L. *causticum,* from the *a.*]
1. any caustic substance.
2. a caustic surface or curve.

çaus′tiç·ăl, *a.* caustic.

çaus′tiç·ăl·ly, *adv.* in a caustic manner.

çaus·tiç′i·ty, *n.* caustic quality.

çaus′tiç·ness, *n.* causticity.

çaus′tiç pot′ash, potassium hydroxide, KOH.

çaus′tiç sō′dȧ, sodium hydroxide, NaOH.

çau′tel, *n.* [L. *cautela,* from *cavere,* to take care.]
1. caution. [Obs.]
2. duplicity; deceit; craft. [Obs.]

çau′te·lous, *a.* 1. cautious; wary; provident. [Obs.]
2. cunning; treacherous; wily. [Obs.]

çau′te·lous·ly, *adv.* 1. cunningly; slyly; treacherously. [Obs.]
2. cautiously; warily. [Obs.]

çau′te·lous·ness, *n.* cautiousness. [Obs.]

çau′tēr, *n.* [LL., from Gr. *kautēr,* a burner, *kaiein,* to burn.] a cauterizing iron.

çau′tēr·ănt, *a.* cauterizing.

çau′tēr·ănt, *n.* a substance or instrument which cauterizes.

çau′tēr·işm, *n.* cauterization. [Obs.]

çau″tēr·i·zā′tion, *n.* 1. in surgery, the act of cauterizing or searing some part, by the application of a cautery or of caustics, etc.
2. the effect of the application of a cautery or caustic.

çau′tēr·īze, *v.t.;* cauterized, *pt., pp.;* cauterizing, *ppr.* [LL. *cauterizare,* from Gr. *kautēriazein,* from *kautērion, kautēr,* a burning or branding iron, from *kaiein,* to burn.]
1. to burn or sear with a hot iron or needle, or with a caustic substance, so as to destroy dead tissue, prevent the spread of infection, etc.
2. to sear, in a figurative sense.
The more *cauterized* our conscience is, the less is the fear of hell. —Jer. Taylor.

çau′tēr·y, *n.*; *pl.* **çau′tēr·ieş,** [L. *cauterium;* Gr. *kautērion,* dim. of *kautēr,* a branding iron.]
1. a burning or searing, as of dead tissue, by a hot iron or needle, or by caustic substances that burn, corrode, or destroy any solid part of an animal body. The burning by a hot iron or needle is called *actual cautery;* that by caustic medicines, *potential cautery.*
2. the instrument or substance employed in cauterizing.

çau′tion, *n.* [L. *cautio (-onis),* from *cavere,* to be on one's guard, to take care.]
1. provident care; prudence in regard to danger; wariness, consisting in a careful attention to the probable effects of a measure, and a judicious course of conduct to avoid failure or disaster.
2. security for the performance of an obligation, as bail; a guarantee. [Rare.]
3. provision or security against; measures taken for security; as, the rules and *cautions* of government. [Obs.]
4. precept; advice; injunction; warning; admonition, intended as security or guard against evil.
5. a word, sign, etc. by which warning is given.
6. an extraordinary person or thing. [Colloq.]
Syn.—care, forethought, forecast, heed, prudence, vigilance, watchfulness, circumspection, warning, admonition.

çau′tion, *v.t.;* cautioned, *pt., pp.;* cautioning, *ppr.* to give notice of danger; to warn; to exhort to take heed.
You *cautioned* me against their charms. —Swift.

çau′tion·ā·ry, *a.* 1. urging caution; admonishing; as, *cautionary* advice.
2. given as a pledge or in security; as, a *cautionary* town. [Now Chiefly Scot.]
3. cautious. [Obs.]

çau′tion·ēr, *n.* 1. one who cautions or advises.
2. in Scots law, the person who is bound for another to the performance of an obligation.

çau′tion·ry, *n.* in Scots law, the position of a cautioner; suretyship.

çau′tious, *a.* wary; watchful; examining probable effects and consequences of measures with a view to avoiding danger or misfortune; prudent; circumspect.
Syn.—wary, circumspect, careful, watchful, prudent.

çau′tious·ly, *adv.* with caution.

çau′tious·ness, *n.* the quality of being cautious.

çav′ăl·çāde, *n.* [Fr. *cavalcade;* It. *cavalcata,* a troop of horsemen, from *cavalcare,* to ride; *cavallo,* L. *caballus,* a horse.] a procession of persons on horseback; a ceremonial parade of horsemen, carriages, etc., as in triumph.

çav·ȧ·lẹ′rō, çav·ȧ·lie′rō (-lyẹ′), *n.* [Sp. *cavallero, caballero,* a cavalier, knight.] a cavalier.

çav·ȧ·liēr′, *n.* [Fr., from LL. *caballarius,* a knight, horseman, from L. *caballus,* a horse.]
1. a horseman, especially an armed horseman; a knight.
2. a gay, sprightly, military man; a gallant or courteous gentleman, especially one serving as a lady's escort.
3. [C–] a partisan of Charles I of England in his struggles with Parliament (1641–1649); Royalist: opposed to *Roundhead.*
4. in fortification, an elevation of earth, situated ordinarily in the gorge of a bastion, bordered with a parapet. [Rare.]

çav·ȧ·liēr′, *a.* 1. gay; free and easy; offhand; brave; generous.
2. haughty; disdainful.
3. [C–] pertaining to the Cavaliers.

çav·ȧ·liēr′ish, *a.* pertaining to a cavalier.

çav·ȧ·liēr′işm, *n.* the practice or principles of cavaliers.

çav·ȧ·liēr′ly, *adv.* haughtily; arrogantly; disdainfully.

çav·ȧ·liēr′ness, *n.* haughtiness; a disdainful manner.

çȧ·val′lȧ, *n.*; *pl.* **çȧ·val′lȧ** or **çȧ·val′lȧş,** [Port., from *cavallo,* a horse, from L. *caballus,* a horse.]
1. the cero, a fish like the mackerel.
2. any of several fishes of the carangoid group, especially an edible fish found off the coasts of tropical America.

çȧ·val′ly, çȧ·val′li, *n.* [Port. *cavalla,* from *cavallo,* a horse.] the cavalla.

çav′ăl·ry, *n.*; *pl.* **çav′ăl·rieş,** [Fr. *cavalerie;* It. *cavalleria,* cavalry, from *cavaliere,* a horseman, knight.] combat troops mounted originally on horses but now often on motorized armored vehicles: distinguished from *infantry.*

çav′ăl·ry·măn, *n.*; *pl.* **çav′ăl·ry·men,** a member of the cavalry.

çȧ·vȧ·sī′nȧ, *n.* [origin unknown.] a fish of California, *Seriola dorsalis:* called also *yellow tail.*

çȧ·vass′, *n.* in Turkey, a police officer or an official military attendant: also spelled *kavass.*

çā′vāte, *v.t.* [L. *cavatus,* pp. of *cavare,* to make hollow; *cavus,* hollow.] to dig out; to make hollow. [Rare.]

çȧ·vȧ·tī′nȧ, *n.* [It.] 1. a short, simple solo

song or melody that is part of a larger composition, such as an opera or oratorio.

2. loosely, any instrumental composition of lyric quality.

ça·vā'tion, *n.* [It. *cavazione*; L. *cavatio (-onis)*, from *cavare*, to make hollow, excavate; *cavus*, hollow.] the underdigging or hollowing of the earth, for the foundation of a building, or for cellarage. [Obs.]

çāve, *n.* [ME.; Fr. *cave*; L. *cava*, cavity, from *cavus*, hollow.]

1. a hollow place in the earth; a subterranean cavern extending back horizontally.

2. any hollow. [Obs.]

3. secession from a political party over an issue; also, those seceding. [Brit. Slang.]

çāve, *v.t.*; caved, *pt.*, *pp.*; caving, *ppr.* [from the *n.*] to hollow out; make a hollow in.

çāve, *v.i.* 1. to cave in. [Colloq.]

2. to dwell in a cave. [Obs.]

to cave in; (a) to collapse; fall or sink in or down; (b) to make collapse; cause to fall or sink in or down; (c) [Colloq.] to give way; give in; submit; yield.

çāve, *v.t.* to toss up or pitch; especially to winnow (grain) from chaff by tossing with a rake or by threshing. [Brit. Dial.]

çā'vē·ȧ, *n.*; *pl.* **çā'vē·ae,** [L., a cave, cage.] in ancient architecture, a den or stable for wild beasts, under the seats and around the arches of an amphitheater; also, the amphitheater itself.

çȧ·vēach', *n.* [W. Ind.] West Indian fish, especially mackerel, seasoned and pickled.

çȧ·vēach', *v.t.* to prepare (mackerel) after the West Indian method.

çā'vē·at, *n.* [L. *caveat*, let him beware, 3d pers. sing. pres. subj. of *cavere*, to beware, take heed.]

1. in law, a notice that an interested party (called the *caveator*) files with the proper legal authorities directing them to stop or refrain from an action until he can be heard.

2. a warning; admonition.

3. in the patent laws of the United States, formerly, a description of some invention, designed to be patented, lodged in the office before the patent right is taken out. It operated as a bar to other applications respecting the same invention. It was abolished in 1910.

caveat emptor; let the purchaser beware, that is, buy at his own risk.

çā'vē·at, *v.i.* 1. to file a caveat.

2. in fencing, to disengage.

çā'vē·ā·tŏr, *n.* one who files a caveat.

çāve beär, a fossil bear of the Quaternary Epoch contemporaneous with the cave dwellers.

çā'vē çā'nem, [L.] beware the dog.

çāve hȳ·ē'nȧ, a species of fossil hyena found in the caves of Great Britain.

çāve'-in, *n.* 1. a caving in.

2. a place where the ground, etc. has caved in.

çav'el, çav'il, kev'el, *n.* 1. a part or share; especially, an allotment of land. [North Eng. and Scot.]

2. a gag or a horse's bit.

3. a ship's cleat.

4. an ax for trimming stone.

çāve lī'ŏn, a fossil lion found in European caves.

çāve man, a prehistoric human being of the Stone Age who lived in caves; cave dweller: sometimes applied to men who are rough and crudely direct, especially toward women.

çav'en·dish, *n.* [from the proper name *Cavendish*.] leaf tobacco which has been softened, sweetened, and pressed into plugs.

cut cavendish; cavendish tobacco cut into small shreds.

çav'ẽrn, *n.* [L. *caverna*, from *cavus*, hollow.] a cave, especially a large cave.

çav'ẽrn, *v.t.* 1. to enclose in or as in a cavern.

2. to hollow out.

çav'ẽrned, *a.* 1. full of caverns or deep chasms; having caverns.

2. inhabiting a cavern.

çav·ẽr·niç'ō·lous, *a.* [L. *caverna*, cave, and *colere*, to live in.] living in caves.

çav'ẽrn·ous, *a.* 1. hollow; full of caverns; filled with small cavities.

2. deep and hollow in sound.

3. deep-set, as eyes.

cavernous body; a body made up of erectile tissue, as in the penis and clitoris.

cavernous respiration; an unnatural respiratory sound heard distinctly in auscultation over diseased interspaces in the lungs.

ça·vẽr'nū·lous, *a.* full of little cavities; as, *cavernulous* metal.

çav'es·sŏn, *n.* same as *cavezon*.

çȧ·vet'tō, *n.*; *pl.* **çȧ·vet'tī** or **çȧ·vet'tōş,** [It., dim. of *cavo*; L. *cavus*, hollow.]

1. a concave molding, as in the cornices of classic structures.

2. in decorative art, a pattern which is sunken: opposed to *relief*.

çav'e·zŏn, *n.* [Fr. *cavesson*; It. *cavezzone*, from *cavezza*, a halter; from L. *caput*, head.] a noseband used to facilitate the breaking of a horse.

çav'i·är, çav'i·äre, *n.* [Fr. *caviar*; It. *caviale*, from Turk. *havyār*, caviar.] a salty relish prepared from the eggs of sturgeon, salmon, or certain other fish.

çav'i·çorn, *a.* [L. *cavus*, hollow, and *cornu*, horn.] hollow-horned, or relating to the *Cavicornia*.

çav'i·çorn, *n.* one of the cavicorn ruminants.

Çav·i·çor'ni·ȧ, *n.pl.* [L. *cavus*, hollow, and *cornu*, a horn.] a family of ruminants, characterized by hollow horns.

çav'il, *v.i.*; caviled *or* cavilled, *pt.*, *pp.*; caviling *or* cavilling, *ppr.* [OFr. *caviller*; L. *cavillari*, to jeer, mock, quibble; *cavilla*, a jeering, mocking.] to raise captious and frivolous objections; to find fault without good reason; to carp; to quibble (with *at* or *about*).

çav'il, *v.t.* to cavil at.

çav'il, *n.* a false or frivolous objection; a quibble.

çav'il, *n.* see *cavel*.

çav'il·ẽr, çav'il·lẽr, *n.* one who cavils.

çav'il·ing, *a.* having a disposition to cavil.

çav'il·ing·ly, *adv.* in a caviling manner.

çav·il·lā'tion, *n.* the act of caviling. [Archaic.]

çav'il·ous, çav'il·lous, *a.* [L. *cavillosus*, from *cavilla*, a mocking, jeering.] captious; caviling. [Rare.]

çav'il·ous·ly, *adv.* in a cavilous manner. [Rare.]

çav'il·ous·ness, *n.* captiousness. [Rare.]

çav'in, *n.* [Fr., from L. *cavus*, hollow.] in early military usage, a natural hollow adapted to cover troops and facilitate their approach to a place.

çāv'ings, *n.* chaff, screenings, etc. [Brit. Dial.]

çav'i·tā·ry, *a.* in zoology, containing a cavity: specifically applied to a class of entozoic worms.

çav·i·tā'tion, *n.* [from L. *cavitas*, a hollow, cavity; and *-tion*.] the formation of partial vacuums in a flowing liquid as a result of the separation of its parts.

çav'i·ty, *n.*; *pl.* **çav'i·tieş** (-tiz), [Fr. *cavité*, from L. *cavus*, hollow.]

1. a hole; a hollow place.

2. a natural hollow place within the body; as, the abdominal *cavity*.

3. a hollow place in a tooth, usually caused by decay.

çä'vō ri·liē'vō, çä'vō rē·liē'vō (-lyä'vō), [It.] in sculpture, relief made by cutting into a flat surface, so that no part of the design stands above the plane of the original stone.

çȧ·vọrt', *v.i.*; cavorted, *pt.*, *pp.*; cavorting, *ppr.* [Americanism; earlier *cauvaut*, *cavault*; perhaps a blend of *curvet* and *gavotte*.] to prance; leap about; caper; as, the horse *cavorted*.

çā'vy, *n.*; *pl.* **çā'vieş,** [from Braz. name *cabiai*.] any of several short-tailed South American rodents of the family *Caviidæ*, as the guinea pig.

giant or *water cavy*; the capybara.

çaw, *v.i.*; cawed, *pt.*, *pp.*; cawing, *ppr.* [imitative.] to cry like a crow, rook, or raven: also written *kaw*.

çaw, *n.* the harsh, strident sound made by the crow, raven, or rook.

çawk, *n.* same as *chalk*.

çax'ŏn, *n.* [Sp. *caxa*, from L. *capsa*, a chest.]

1. in mining, a chest of ores of any metal that has been burnt, ground, and washed, and is ready to be refined.

2. a wig used in the eighteenth century. [Obs.]

Çax'tŏn, *n.* 1. any book printed by William Caxton, who introduced the printer's art into England in the latter half of the fifteenth century.

2. a black-letter type like that used by Caxton.

çāy, *n.* [Sp. *cayo*, a shoal, rock.] a coral reef or sand bank off a mainland.

çāy·enne' (*or* kī'), *n.* [named from *Cayenne*, a town in Fr. Guiana.]

1. a very hot red pepper made from the dried seeds or fruit of a pepper plant, especially of the capsicum: also *cayenne pepper*.

2. the fruit of a capsicum.

Çāy'lēy·ăn, *n.* a complex curve in higher mathematics, named from Arthur Cayley, an English mathematician.

çāy'măn, *n.*; *pl.* **çāy'men,** [Sp. *caiman*, from the native Guiana name.] any of several large alligators common to tropical America, especially *Caiman palpebrosus* and *Caiman trigonatus*.

çāy'närd, *n.* a sluggard: written also *kaynard*. [Obs.]

Çā·yū'gȧ, *n.*; *pl.* **Çā·yū'gȧ** or **Çā·yū'gȧş,** a member of a tribe of Iroquoian Indians originally located in western New York.

Çāy·ūse', *n.* [Am. Ind.]

1. a member of a tribe of Oregonian Indians who lived in the Blue Mountains section of northeastern Oregon.

2. [c–] an Indian pony.

çȧ·zïque', çȧ·ziç', *n.* same as *cacique*.

Cb, in chemistry, columbium.

CB (sē'bē'), *n.*; *pl.* **CBş** or **CB'ş,** same as *citizens' band*.

C bat'tẽr·y, in radio, a battery that sets the grid of a vacuum tube at some desired potential.

C çlef, in music, a sign on a staff indicating that C is the note on the third line (*alto clef*) or on the fourth line (*tenor clef*): distinguished from *treble clef* and *bass clef*.

Cd, in chemistry, cadmium.

Ce, in chemistry, cerium.

Cē·ȧ·nō'thus, *n.* [from Gr. *keanōthos*, a kind of thistle.]

1. a genus of large shrubs of the buckthorn family, common to North America and bearing various colored flowers.

2. [c–] a plant belonging to this genus.

cēase, *v.i.*; ceased, *pt.*, *pp.*; ceasing, *ppr.* [ME. *ceesen*, *cessen*; OFr. *cesser*; L. *cessare*, to loiter, cease, give way; freq. of *cedere*, to go away, yield, withdraw.]

1. to stop moving, acting, or speaking; to leave off; to give over.

2. to fail to be; to become extinct. [Obs.]

cēase, *v.t.* to end; to stop; to discontinue.

Cease this impious rage. —Milton.

Syn.—desist, discontinue, leave off, quit.

cēase, *n.* [OFr. *ces*, from the *v.*] a ceasing: seldom used except in *without cease*.

cēase'fīre', *n.* a temporary cessation of warfare by mutual agreement of the participants; truce.

cēase'less, *a.* without a stop or pause; incessant; continual; unceasing.

cēase'less·ly, *adv.* incessantly; continually.

ceb·ȧ·dil'lȧ, *n.* same as *cevadilla*.

Cē·bī'nae, *n.pl.* a subfamily of South American monkeys, with broad noses and prehensile tails, including the spider monkey and the squirrel monkey.

cē'bīne, *a.* [Gr. *kēbos*, a monkey.] relating to the *Cebinæ*, a family of monkeys.

Cec''i·dō·mȳ'i·ȧ, *n.* [from Gr. *kekis (-idos)*, a gallnut, and *myia*, a fly.] a genus of flies, producing galls for the protection and food of the larvae or laying its eggs in various grains. The Hessian fly is a well-known variety.

cec''i·dō·mȳ'i·ăn, *a.* pertaining to the genus *Cecidomyia*.

cec''i·dō·mȳ'i·id, *n.* a member of the genus *Cecidomyia*.

cē'ci·ty, *n.* [L. *cæcitas*, from *cæcus*, blind.] blindness. [Rare.]

Cē·crō'pi·ȧ, *n.* [named after *Cecrops*, first king of Athens.]

1. in botany, a large genus of moraceous tropical trees, the products of which find numerous uses in the arts and manufactures.

2. [c–] in zoology, a moth of the family *Bombycidæ*, or silkworm family.

ce'çum, *n.* same as *caecum*.

cē·çū'tien·cy (-shen-cy), *n.* tendency to blindness. [Rare.]

cē'dăr, *n.* [ME. *cedar*, *cedre*; OFr. *cedre*; L. *cedrus*; Gr. *kedros*, a cedar tree.]

1. any of various evergreen trees of the genus *Cedrus*, that grow to a large size and are remarkable for the durability and fragrance of their wood. The name is also given to the *deodar* and to many trees which have no relation to the true cedar, as the Bermuda cedar, *Juniperus bermudiana*, used for making pencils, the red cedar, *Juniperus virginiana*, the Honduras, or bastard Barbados cedar, *Cedrela odorata*, and the red cedar of Australia, *Cedrela australis*, used in making cigar boxes.

2. the wood of any variety of cedar.

cē'dăr ap'ple, a parasitic outgrowth forming on twigs of the red cedar tree. When fully grown it presents a number of slim arms extending from a central mass, the whole being of a bright orange color.

cē′dăr·bīrd″, *n.* the cedar waxwing.

cē′dăr chest, a large box made of cedar, in which woolens, furs, etc. are stored for protection against damage by moths.

cē′dăred, *a.* covered or furnished with cedars.

cē′dărn, *a.* pertaining to cedar or cedars. [Poetic.]

cē′dăr wax′wing, a brownish-gray, crested American bird with red, waxlike tips on its secondary wing feathers: also *cedarbird*.

cēde, *v.t.*; ceded, *pt.*, *pp.*; ceding, *ppr.* [Fr. *ceder*, from L. *cedere*, to withdraw, yield.]
1. to yield; to surrender; to give up; to resign; as, to *cede* a fortress, a province, or country, by treaty.
2. to admit; to grant, as a point in debate.

cē′dent, *n.* [L. *cedens* (*-entis*), ppr. of *cedere*, to yield, withdraw.] an assignor in a lawsuit.

cē·dil′lȧ, *n.* [Fr. *cédille*; Sp. *cedilla*, dim. of *zeda*; Gr. *zēta*, the Greek name of the letter *z*; so called because *z* was written after *c*, to give the sound of the letter *s*.] a hooklike mark put under *c* in some French words (e.g., *garçon*) to show that it is to be sounded like a voiceless *s* or, formerly, in some Spanish words (e.g., *direcçion*) to show that it is to be sounded like a voiceless *th*.

cē′drāte, cē′drat, *n.* [Fr.] a species of citron tree.

Cē·drē′lȧ, *n.* [Mod. L., from Sp. *cedrela*, dim. of *cedro*, a cedar.]
1. a genus of large tropical trees of both hemispheres; *Cedrela toona*, an East Indian species, and *Cedrela odorata*, of Honduras and the West Indies, are examples.
2. [c–] a tree belonging to this genus.

cē′drēne, *n.* [L. *cedrus*, cedar, and *-ene*.] any hydrocarbon expressed by the general formula $C_{15}H_{24}$, especially that obtained from the oil of red cedar.

cē′drin, *n.* the bitter active principle of cedron.

cē′drine, *a.* [L. *cedrinus*; Gr. *kedrinos*, from *kedros*, cedar.] pertaining to cedar.

ced′ri·ret, *n.* same as *cerulignone*.

cē′drŏn, *n.* [from L. *cedrus*, cedar.] a tree, *Simaba cedron*, or its fruit. It grows in tropical America, and the seeds are employed as a remedy for serpent bites, hydrophobia, and intermittent fever.

Cē′drus, *n.* [L., from Gr. *kedros*, cedar.] a genus of trees closely allied to the genus *Larix*. It includes only three species or varieties, the *Cedrus libani*, or cedar of Lebanon; *Cedrus deodara*, or deodar, and *Cedrus atlantica*, or Mount Atlas cedar.

ced′ū·lȧ, *n.* [Sp. *cédula*; LL. *scedula*, a schedule].
1. in Spanish-speaking countries, a certificate or permit.
2. in the Philippines, a certificate of personal registration.
3. the tax for this.

ced′ū·ous, *a.* fit to be felled. [Obs.]

cee, *n.* C; c.

cee, *a.* shaped like C.

çē′i·bä (Sp. the′ē-), *n.* [Sp., from native name in South America.]
1. a tropical tree whose seed pods contain kapok; silk-cotton tree.
2. (*also* sī′bȧ), kapok; silk-cotton.

cēil, *v.t.*; ceiled, *pt.*, *pp.*; ceiling, *ppr.* [Fr. *ciel*, heaven, canopy, from L. *cælum*, heaven, vault, covering; Gr. *koilos*, hollow.]
1. to build a ceiling in or over.
2. to cover (the ceiling or walls of a room), as with plaster.
3. to cover the ceiling or walls of (a room).

cēil′ing, *n.* 1. the inside top part or covering of a room, opposite the floor.
2. any overhanging expanse seen from below.
3. in nautical usage, the inner planking of a ship.
4. an upper limit set on anything; as, a *ceiling* on prices.
5. in aeronautics, (a) the upper limit of visibility; (b) the highest that an aircraft can go under certain conditions.
service ceiling; under standard air conditions, the altitude above sea level at which an airplane can no longer climb faster than a given set rate (in the United States, 100 feet per minute).
to hit the ceiling; to become suddenly very angry; lose one's temper. [Slang.]

ceiǹ·tūre′ (saǹ-), *n.* [Fr.] a cincture, a girdle.

cel′ȧ·don, *n.* [Fr.]
1. the color sea-green.
2. fine pottery or porcelain of a sea-green color.

cel′ăn·dīne, *n.* [ME. *celidoine*, *celydon*; OFr. *celidoine*; L. *chelidonia*; Gr. *chelidonion*, swallow wort, from *chelidōn*, a swallow.]
1. a weedy plant, *Chelidonium majus*, of the poppy family, with deeply divided leaves and yellow flowers and juice.
2. the pilewort, *Ficaria verna*.

Cel′ȧ·nēṣe, *n.* [coined from *cel*lulose *a*cetate, and *-ese* by Dr. Henri Dreyfus, Eng. pioneer in the development of the fiber.] rayon made of cellulose acetate: a trade-mark.

cē·lā′rent, *n.* a mnemonic name given to one of the moods in logic.

Cel·as·trā′cē·ae, *n.pl.* [*celastrus*, and *-aceæ*.] an order of polypetalous exogens, consisting of shrubs or trees, sometimes spinous or climbing, having seeds with scarlet arils. They are found principally in warm latitudes.

cel·as·trā′ceous, *a.* of or pertaining to the order *Celastraceæ*.

Cē·las′trus, *n.* [Gr. *kēlastros*, an evergreen.] a small genus of low shrubs or climbing vines of the family *Celastraceæ*. *Celastrus paniculatus* of the East Indies is an example of this genus. Called also *staff tree* and *climbing bittersweet*.

cē·lā′tion, *n.* [L. *celatio* (*-onis*), from *celare*, to conceal.] the concealment of pregnancy.

cel′ȧ·tive, *a.* [L. *celatio*, concealment.] adapted for partial or complete concealment.

cel′ȧ·tūre, *n.* [L. *cælatura*, from *cælare*, to engrave, carve.]
1. the act or art of engraving or embossing.
2. that which is engraved.

-cēle, [from Gr. *kēlē*.]
1. a combining form meaning *tumor* or *swelling*.
2. -coele.

cel′ē·brănt, *n.* [L. *celebrans* (*-antis*), ppr. of *celebrare*, to frequent, celebrate.]
1. one who performs a religious rite.
2. the officiating priest at Mass.

cel′ē·brāte, *v.t.*; celebrated, *pt.*, *pp.*; celebrating, *ppr.* [L. *celebratus*, pp. of *celebrare*, to frequent, go in great numbers, honor, from *celeber*, frequented, populous.]
1. to praise or honor publicly; to extol.
2. to commemorate (an anniversary, holiday, etc.) with ceremony or festivity.
3. to proclaim.
4. to perform or solemnize with reverence or veneration, as a religious ceremony.
Syn.—praise, extol, commemorate, glorify, honor.

cel′ē·brāte, *v.i.* 1. to observe a holiday, anniversary, etc. with festivities.
2. to perform a religious ceremony.
3. to have a convivial good time. [Colloq.]

cel′ē·brā·ted, *a.* having celebrity; distinguished; well-known.

cel·ē·brā′tion, *n.* [L. *celebratio*.]
1. a celebrating; formal commemoration.
2. that which is done to celebrate.

cel′ē·brā·tŏr, cel′ē·brā·tēr, *n.* one who celebrates.

cē·lē′bri·ous, *a.* famous; renowned. [Obs.]

cē·leb′ri·ty, *n.* [L. *celebritas*, a multitude, fame, from *celeber*, frequented, populous, famous.]
1. fame; renown; the distinction or honor publicly bestowed on one because of noted character or exploits.
2. a famous or well-publicized person.
3. celebration. [Obs.]
Syn.—fame, honor, glory, reputation, distinction, renown.

cel′ē·ō·mọrph, *n.* [Gr. *keleos*, woodpecker, and *morphē*, form.] one of the family of woodpeckers.

cel″ē·ō·mọr′phiç, *a.* of or relating to the woodpeckers.

cē·lē′ri·aç, *n.* [from *celery*.] a variety of celery: called also the *turnip-rooted celery*.

cē·ler′i·ty, *n.* [L. *celeritas*, from *celer*, swift, quick.] rapidity of motion; swiftness; speed.
Syn.—quickness, rapidity, speed, speediness, swiftness, fleetness, velocity.

cel′ēr·y, *n.* [Fr. *céleri*; It. *seleri*; L. *selinon*, parsley; Gr. *selinon*, parsley.] a plant, *Apium graveolens*, whose crisp, blanched stalks are used as a vegetable.

cel′ēr·y çab′bāġe, same as *Chinese cabbage*.

cel′ēr·y salt, a seasoning made of celery seed and salt.

ce·les′tȧ, *n.* [Fr. *célesta*.] a small keyboard instrument whose bell-like tones are produced by the striking of hammers against small metal plates.

cē·les′tiăl, *a.* [OFr. *celestial*; L. *cælestis*, from *cælum*, heaven.]
1. heavenly; belonging or relating to heaven; dwelling in heaven; as, *celestial* spirits; *celestial* joys.
2. of the heavens; of the sky; as, *celestial* signs; the *celestial* globe.
3. [C–] pertaining to the Chinese empire or its inhabitants.
Syn.—heavenly, ethereal, atmospheric, supernal, angelic, radiant, eternal, immortal, seraphic, divine, godlike, Elysian.

cē·les′tiăl, *n.* 1. any being regarded as living in heaven.
2. [C–] a Chinese.

Cē·les′tiăl Cit′y, in Bunyan's *Pilgrim's Progress* (1678), the heavenly New Jerusalem toward which Christian makes his pilgrimage.

Cē·les′tiăl Em′pīre, China or the Chinese Empire: translation of a former Chinese name for China.

cē·les′tiăl glōbe, a globe representing the celestial sphere, with all the stars, planets, etc. placed in their proper relative positions.

cē·les′tiăl·īze, *v.t.* to make celestial. [Rare.]

cē·les′tiăl·ly, *adv.* in a heavenly or transporting manner.

cē·les′tiăl nav·i·gā′tion, a determination of position and course, as at sea or in an airplane, by observing the sun, moon, and stars.

cē·les′tiăl pōle, either of the two points in the celestial sphere where the earth's axis of rotation, if extended, would intersect.

cē·les′tiăl sphēre, 1. the infinite sphere of the heavens hypothecated from the half visible from a point on the earth.
2. the rounded ceiling of a planetarium, upon which is projected a chart of the stars, planets, etc.

cē·les′ti·fȳ, *v.t.* to communicate something of a heavenly nature to; to make heavenly. [Obs.]

Cel′es·tine, Cel·es·tin′i·ăn, *n.* 1. a member of a Benedictine order founded by Pope Celestine in the thirteenth century.
2. a Pelagian, especially a supporter of Caelestius, an early adherent of Pelagianism.

cel′es·tīte, *n.* [altered (by J. D. Dana, Am. mineralogist) from *celestine*.] in mineralogy, strontium sulfate, $SrSO_4$, which occurs usually in white, crystalline form, but is sometimes blue: most strontium compounds are produced from it.

cē′li·aç, *a.* same as *coeliac*.

cel′i·bȧ·cy, *n.* [L. *cælibatus*, from *cælebs* (*-itis*), a single life.] an unmarried state; single life, particularly that of a person bound by solemn vows to remain single.

cel′i·bāte, *n.* 1. state of celibacy; order of celibates. [Archaic.]
2. a person who is unmarried, particularly one who has taken a vow not to marry.

cel′i·bāte, *a.* [L. *cælibatus*, from *cælebs*, a single life.]
1. unmarried; single.
2. bound by a vow to remain unmarried.

cel′i·bȧ·tist, *n.* an advocate of celibacy.

cel·i·dog′rȧ·phy, *n.* [Gr. *kelis* (*-idos*), a spot, and *graphia*, from *graphein*, to write.] the description of apparent spots on the disk of the sun, or on planets.

cel·i·ot′ŏ·my, *n.* incision into the abdominal cavity.

cell, *n.* [ME. *celle*; OFr. *celle*; L. *cella*, a small room, hut.]
1. a small room; cubicle, as in a convent or prison.
2. a small convent or monastery attached to a larger one.
3. a hermit's hut.
4. a very small hollow, cavity, or compartment.
5. any very small natural cavity in the body.
6. in architecture, the hollow space between the ribs of a vaulted roof.
7. in biology, a very small unit of protoplasm, usually with a nucleus and an enclosing membrane: all plants and animals are made up of one or more cells.

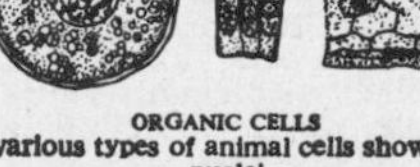

ORGANIC CELLS
various types of animal cells showing nuclei

8. in botany, (a) any compartment of an ovary; (b) a pollen sac or spore sac.
9. in zoology, (a) a cuplike cavity enclosing the zooids of certain hydroids, as in corals; (b) a protective covering for the eggs or young of insects; (c) one of the spaces

outlined by the veins in the wing of an insect.

10. in electricity, (a) a receptacle containing electrodes and an electrolyte, used either for generating electricity by chemical reactions or for decomposing compounds by electrolysis; (b) any compartment of a storage battery.

11. in sociology, any group within a large organization whose purpose is to propagandize, proselytize, etc.

Bunsen cell; a cell in which carbon forms the negative electrode, zinc the positive, and nitric acid is used in a porous cup with the carbon, while sulfuric acid is in the outer vessel with the zinc.

Daniell cell; a cell in which the anode is zinc, the cathode copper. The zinc plate is surrounded by a porous cup filled with dilute sulfuric acid, or a zinc sulfate solution; the copper electrode is immersed in a solution of copper sulfate.

gravity cell; a modification of the Daniell cell, in which the two fluids are separated by their difference in specific gravity, so that the porous septum is dispensed with.

Grove cell; a cell in which platinum replaces the carbon of the Bunsen cell.

primary cell; see *primary cell*.

cell, *v.t.*; celled, *pt.*, *pp.*; celling, *ppr.* to shut up in a cell. [Rare.]

cel'là, *n.*; *pl.* **cel'lae,** [L. *cella*, a small room, hut.] the inner part of an ancient Greek or Roman temple, exclusive of the porticoes.

cel'lăr, *n.* [ME. *celler*; OFr. *celier*; L. *cellarium*, a pantry, storeroom, from *cella*, a small room, hut.]

1. a room or group of rooms below the ground level and usually under a building, often used for storing fuel, provisions, etc.

2. a cellar for wines.

3. a stock of wines; as, he keeps a good *cellar*.

the cellar; the lowest position, as in the relative standings of competing teams. [Colloq.]

cel'lăr, *v.t.* to store in a cellar.

cel'lăr·āġe, *n.* 1. space of or in a cellar.

2. cellars collectively.

3. charge for storage in a cellar.

cel'lăr·ẽr, cel'lăr·ist, *n.* [L. *cellarius*, a steward, butler, from *cellarium*, a pantry.] an officer in a monastery who has the care of the cellar, or the charge of procuring and keeping the provisions.

cel'lăr·et, *n.* a cabinet for bottles of wine or liquor, glasses, etc.

celled (seld), *a.* furnished with a cell or cells: commonly used in hyphenated compounds; as, single-*celled*.

Cel·lep'ō·rà, Cel·lip'ō·rà, *n.* [L. *cella*, a cell, and *porus*, Gr. *poros*, a passage.] a genus of molluscoid animals, phylum *Bryozoa*, composed of minute distinct cells arranged like fringes in longitudinal rows.

cel·lif'ẽr·ous, *a.* [L. *cella*, a cell, and *ferre*, to bear.] bearing or producing cells.

cel'list, 'cel'list (chel'), *n.* a person who plays the cello; violoncellist.

cel'lō, 'cel'lō (chel'), *n.*; *pl.* **cel'lōṣ** or **'cel'lōṣ, cel'lï** or **'cel'lï** (chel'), [from *violoncello*.] an instrument of the violin family, between the viola and the double bass in size and pitch; violoncello.

CELLO

cel·loi'din, *n.* [*cell*, and *-oid*, and *-in*.] a concentrated solution of pyroxylin used in microscopy for embedding specimens that are to be cut into thin cross sections.

cel'lō·phāne, *n.* [from *cellulose*, and Gr. *phanein*, to appear, seem.] a thin, transparent material made from cellulose, used as moisture-proof wrapping for foods, tobacco, etc., or to make packages look more attractive: formerly a trade-mark (*Cellophane*).

Cel'lū·çot″tŏn, *n.* the trade name of a very absorbent surgical dressing; also, [c–] the dressing itself.

cel'lū·là, *n.* [L. *cellula*, dim. of *cella*, a room, hut.] a small cell.

cel'lū·lăr, *a.* 1. of or like a cell.

2. consisting of or containing cells.

cellular or *cell theory*; the theory that all animal and vegetable bodies consist of either a cell or cells, and that all cells develop from other cells.

cellular plants; plants having no spiral vessels, as mosses, lichens, etc.

cellular tissue; (a) in anatomy, the ordinary connective tissue made up of cells with large interspaces; (b) in botany, parenchyma, or vegetable pulp.

cel'lū·lăr, *n.* a plant having no spiral vessels, and bearing no flowers, as lichens and mosses.

cel'lū·lāte, *a.* cellular.

cel'lū·lāte, *v.t.*; cellulated, *pt.*, *pp.*; cellulating, *ppr.* to make cellular; to form into cells.

CELLULAR TISSUE IN PLANTS

cel'lū·lā·ted, *a.* cellular.

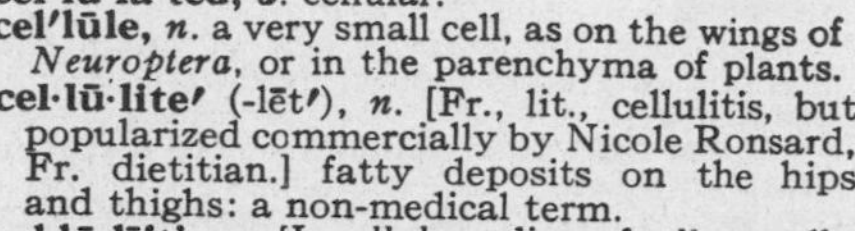

cel'lūle, *n.* a very small cell, as on the wings of *Neuroptera*, or in the parenchyma of plants.

cel·lū·lite' (-lēt'), *n.* [Fr., lit., cellulitis, but popularized commercially by Nicole Ronsard, Fr. dietitian.] fatty deposits on the hips and thighs: a non-medical term.

cel·lū·lī'tis, *n.* [L. *cellula*, a dim. of *cella*, a cell, and *-itis*.] an inflammation of a cellular tissue, especially of subcutaneous tissue.

cel'lū·loid, *n.* [*cellulose*, and *-oid*.] a thin, inflammable substance made from pyroxylin and camphor, used for photographic films, toilet articles, etc.: a trade-mark (*Celluloid*).

cel'lū·lōse, *a.* [L. *cellula*, dim. of *cella*, a room, hut.] containing or made up of cells.

cel'lū·lōse, *n.* [Fr., from L. *cellula*, dim. of *cella*, a small room, hut.] the chief substance composing the cell walls or woody part of plants, a carbohydrate of unknown molecular structure but having the composition represented by the empirical formula $(C_6H_{10}O_5)_x$: it is used in the manufacture of paper, rayon, explosives, etc.

cellulose acetate; any of several compounds produced by the action of acetic acid or acetic anhydride upon cellulose in the presence of concentrated sulfuric acid: used in making artificial silks, photographic films, etc.

cellulose nitrate; an ester of nitric acid and cellulose obtained by the action of nitric acid upon wood, cotton, or some other form of cellulose in the presence of concentrated sulfuric acid: it is used in the manufacture of guncotton and other explosives, rayon, varnishes, etc.

cel'lū·lōse, *v.t.*; cellulosed, *pt.*, *pp.*; cellulosing, *ppr.* to treat or cover with a cellulose compound.

cel'lū·lōsed, *a.* made or consisting of cellulose.

cel·lū·lōs'iç, *n.* a product or material made from cellulose.

cel'lū·lous, *a.* 1. full of cells.

2. consisting of cells.

cell wall, in biology, the covering or separating wall of a cell; especially, the relatively rigid covering of a plant cell.

cē'lom, *n.* the coelom.

Cē·lō'si·à, *n.* [Gr. *kēlos*, dry, burned, from the burned-like appearance of the flowers of some species.] a genus of annual plants, generally native to the tropics, order *Amaranthaceæ*. The cockscomb, *Celosia argentea*, common in cultivation, is perhaps the best known variety.

cel'ō·tex, *n.* [cf. *cellulose* and *texture*.] a composition board made of sugar-cane residue, used for insulation in buildings: a trade-mark (*Celotex*).

cel'si·tūde, *n.* [L. *celsitudo*, from *celsus*, high.] height; elevation of rank; excellency. [Obs.]

Cel'si·us, *a.* [after Anders *Celsius* (1701–1744), Swed. astronomer, the inventor.] designating or of a thermometer on which, under laboratory conditions, 0° is the freezing point and 100° is the boiling point of water; centigrade: the formula for converting a Celsius temperature to Fahrenheit is $C° = 5/9(F° - 32)$.

Celt, (*or* kelt), *n.* [L. *Celtæ*, pl.; Gr. *Keltoi*, Celts; W. *celt*, a covert, *celtiad*, one that dwells in a covert, from *celu*, to hide.]

1. a Celtic-speaking person: the Bretons, Irish, Welsh, and Highland Scots are Celts.

2. one of an ancient people in central and western Europe, reputedly including the Gauls and Britons.

celt, *n.* [LL. *celtis*, a chisel, a celt.] a prehistoric tool of stone or bronze, resembling a chisel or ax head.

Celt·i·bē'ri·ăn, *a.* [L. *Celtiberi*, compounded of *Celtæ*, Celts, and *Iberi*, Iberians, the supposed original inhabitants of Spain.] pertaining to Celtiberia and its inhabitants, the Celtiberi, an ancient people of Spain.

Celt·i·bē'ri·ăn, *n.* an inhabitant of Celtiberia, the name given in ancient times to central Spain.

CELTS

Celt'iç (*or* kelt'ik), *a.* [L. *Celticus*; Gr. *Keltikos*, from *Keltoi*, Celts.] of the Celts, their languages, culture, characteristics, etc.

Celtic cross; a Latin cross having a wheellike circle around the intersection of the limbs.

Celt'iç, *n.* a subfamily of the Indo-European family of languages with a *Goidelic* branch (Irish Gaelic, Scottish Gaelic, and Manx) and a *Brythonic* branch (Breton, Cornish, and Welsh.)

Celt'i·ciṣm, *n.* 1. the manners and customs of the Celts.

2. a Celtic idiom, as in Irish English.

3. fondness for Celtic customs.

Celt'i·cīze, *v.t.* to render Celtic.

Celt'i·cīze, *v.i.* to become Celtic.

Celt'is, *n.* [L., an African species of lotus.] a genus of trees of several species, family *Ulmaceæ*; the nettle trees. *Celtis occidentalis*, the hackberry, is the principal North American species.

cem'bà·lō, *n.* [It.] (a) the harpsichord; (b) the dulcimer.

cē·ment', *n.* [ME. *ciment*; OFr. *cement*, *ciment*; L. *cæmentum*, rough stone, chippings, from *cædere*, to cut.]

1. a substance made of powdered lime and clay, mixed with water and used to fasten stones and bricks together, or as paving: the mixture (mortar) hardens like stone when it dries.

2. any soft substance that fastens things together firmly when it hardens, as paste or glue.

3. a cementlike substance used in filling cavities, as in teeth.

4. anything that joins together or unites; a bond.

5. the bony outer crust of the root of a tooth.

6. in metallurgy, a dust or powder, as of charcoal or sand, or a finely divided metal, used in cementation.

7. in placer and hydraulic mining, a firml compacted mass of gravel, held together b clay or silica.

Portland cement; see under *Portland*.

rubber cement; a cement made of pure rubber mechanically mixed with sulfur and dissolved in some such hydrocarbon as benzene, gasoline, etc.

cē·ment', *v.t.*; cemented, *pt.*, *pp.*; cementing, *ppr.* 1. to unite or join with or as with cement.

2. to unite firmly or closely; as, to *cement* friendship.

3. to spread or cover with cement.

cē·ment', *v.i.* to become cemented; to stick; to cohere.

cē·ment'ăl, *a.* pertaining to cement, as of a tooth.

cē″men·tā'tion, *n.* 1. a cementing or being cemented.

2. in chemistry, the process by which a solid substance is caused to enter into or combine with another at a high temperature without fusion of either; specifically, the conversion of iron into steel by heating the iron in a mass of ground charcoal, and thus causing it to absorb a certain quantity of the charcoal.

cē·ment'à·tō·ry, *a.* cementing; having the quality of uniting firmly.

cē·ment'ẽr, *n.* one who or that which cements.

cē·ment'īte, *n.* [*cement*, and *-ite*.] the carbide of iron, Fe_3C, occurring in steel, cast iron, and most other alloys of iron and carbon.

cē″men·ti'tious (-tish'us), *a.* [L. *cæmentitius*, pertaining to quarried stones; from *cæmentum*, rough stone, stone chippings.] pertaining to cement; having the quality of cementing; of the nature of cement.

cē·men'tum, *n.* [L.; cf. *cement*.] the hard, bony tissue forming the outer layer of the root of a tooth: also *cement*.

cem·ē·tē'ri·ăl *a.* pertaining to a cemetery or burial. [Rare.]

cem'ē·ter·y, *n.*; *pl.* **cem'ē·ter·ieṣ,** [LL. *cæmeterium*; Gr. *koimētērion*, a sleeping place, cemetery, from *koiman*, to put to sleep.] a place set apart for burial or interment; a graveyard; a necropolis.

cen'à·çle, *n.* [Fr. *cénacle*, from L. *cenaculum*, a dining room, from *cena*, dinner.]

1. [C-] the room in which Jesus and his disciples ate the Last Supper.

2. a coterie, as of writers.

cē·nā'tion, *n.* [L. *cenatio*, from *cenare*, to dine, eat.] the act of dining or supping. [Obs.]

cen'ȧ·tō·ry, *a.* pertaining to dinner or supper. [Rare.]

The Romans washed, were anointed, and wore a *cenatory* garment. —Browne.

ceñ'chrus, *n.*; *pl.* **ceñ'chrī,** [Gr. *kenchros*, millet.]

1. an insect of the family *Tenthredinidæ*; a kind of sawfly.

2. in entomology, one of the two pale marks on the mesothorax of sawflies.

3. [C-] a small genus of grasses, including the species commonly known as *burgrass* and *hedgehog grass*.

cen'dal, *n.* same as *sendal*.

-cēne, [from Gr. *kainos*, recent.] a combining form meaning *recent, new*, or especially, *designating a* (specified) *epoch in the Cenozoic Era of geological time*, as Mio*cene*.

cē·nes·thē'sia (-zȧ), *n.* coenesthesia.

cē·nes·thē'sis, *n.* coenesthesis.

cē'nō-, coeno-.

cen'ō·bīte, *n.* [LL. *cœnobita*, from *cœnobium*; Gr. *koinobion*, a convent, neut. of *koinobios*; *koinos*, common, and *bios*, life.] a member of a religious order living in a convent or monastery: in opposition to an *anchorite*, or hermit, who lives in solitude.

cen·ō·bit'iç, cen·ō·bit'iç·ăl, *a.* of or like a cenobite; living the life of a cenobite; not anchoritic: also spelled *coenobitic*.

cen'ō·bī·tism, *n.* 1. the state of being a cenobite.

2. the principles or practice of a cenobite. Also spelled *coenobitism*.

ce·nō'bi·um, *n.*; *pl.* **ce·nō'bi·ȧ,** 1. same as cenoby.

2. same as *coenobium*.

cen'ō·by, *n.*; *pl.* **cen'ō·bieṣ,** a monastery or conventual abode.

cē·nō·ġen'e·sis, *n.* [from Gr. *kainos*, new; and *-genesis*.] that form of the development of an individual plant or animal which does not repeat the evolutional history of its group: opposed to *palingenesis*: also spelled *caenogenesis, kenogenesis*

cē″nō·ġē·net'iç, *a.* of or relating to cenogenesis: also spelled *caenogenetic, kenogenetic*.

cē·nos'i·ty, *n.* [L. *cænositas*, from *cænosus*, filthy.] uncleanness; filthiness; squalor.

cē'nō·spē·cieṣ, *n.* [*ceno-*, and *species*.] separate species of organisms that are related through their capability of interbreeding, as dogs and wolves.

cen'ō·taph, *n.* [L. *cenotaphium*; Gr. *kenotaphion*, an empty tomb; *kenos*, empty, and *taphos*, a tomb.] an empty tomb erected in honor of some deceased person; a monument erected to one who is buried elsewhere; as, a *cenotaph* in Westminster Abbey.

CENOTAPH

cen'ō·taph·y, *n.*; *pl.* **cen'ō·taph·ieṣ,** same as *cenotaph*.

ce·nō'tē, *n.* [Am. Sp., from Maya *tzonot*.] a deep natural well carved out of friable limestone.

Cē·nō·zō'iç, *a.* [from Gr. *kainos*, new, recent, and *zōē*, life; and *-ic*.] designating or of the geological era following the Mesozoic and including the present: it began about 60 million years ago and is characterized by the appearance and development of the mammals: also *Cainozoic*.

the Cenozoic; the Cenozoic Era or its rocks.

cens (säṅs), *n.* [Fr.] in French-Canadian law, the annual payment, apart from rent, exacted from a tenant by the owner of an estate, as a formal acknowledgment of his title.

cense, *n.* [OFr. *cens, cense*; L. *census*, a registering, rating of property, tax.]

1. a public rate or tax. [Obs.]

2. condition; rank. [Obs.]

3. a census. [Obs.]

cense, *v.t.*; censed, *pt., pp.*; censing, *ppr.* [abbrev. from *incense*.]

1. to perfume (a room, person, etc.) by burning incense.

The Salii sing, and *cense* his altars round. —Dryden.

2. to burn incense to (a god).

cense, *v.i.* to burn or offer incense; as, *censing* about the altar.

cen'sẽr, *n.* [a shortened form for *incenser*.] an ornamental container in which incense is burned; a thurible.

cen'sō (*or Sp.* then'sō), *n.* [Sp.]

1. in Spanish American law, a ground rent; an annual ground rent charged upon specific property.

2. the right to an annuity out of a specific fund or estate.

cen'sŏr, *n.* [L. *censor*, from *censere*, to tax, value, judge.]

1. one of two magistrates in ancient Rome whose business was to draw up a register of the citizens and the amount of their property, for the purposes of taxation, and to keep watch over the morals of the citizens, for which purpose they had power to censure vice and immorality by inflicting a public mark of ignominy on the offender.

2. any supervisor of public morals; a person who tells people how to behave.

3. a person whose task is to examine literature, motion pictures, etc., and to remove or prohibit anything considered unsuitable.

4. an official or military officer who reads publications, mail, etc. to remove any information that might be useful to the enemy.

5. one who censures, blames, or reproves; one who is given to censure; any faultfinder or adverse critic.

6. in English colleges and universities, an official appointed to keep the register of all who attend, to mark those who are absent each day on meeting, to report faults, etc.

7. in psychoanalysis, censorship.

cen'sŏr, *v.t.* to examine, review, expurgate, or change (literature, mail, etc.) as a censor; to subject to censorship.

cen'sŏr·āte, *n.* a body or board of censors.

cen·sō'ri·ăl, cen·sō'ri·ăn, *a.* 1. of, like, or characteristic of a censor.

2. full of censure; censorious. [Obs.]

cen·sō'ri·ous, *a.* [L. *censorius*, from *censor*, a magistrate, judge.]

1. addicted to censure; apt to blame or condemn; severe in making remarks on others, or on their writings or manners; as, a *censorious* critic.

2. implying or expressing censure; as, *censorious* remarks.

Syn.—faultfinding, hypercritical, captious, severe, carping, caviling.

cen·sō'ri·ous·ly, *adv.* in a censorious manner.

cen·sō'ri·ous·ness, *n.* the quality of being censorious; disposition to blame and condemn; the habit of censuring or reproaching.

cen'sŏr·ship, *n.* [*censor*, and *-ship*.]

1. a censoring.

2. a system of censoring.

3. the work or position of a censor.

4. in psychoanalysis, the agency that prevents unpleasant ideas, memories, etc. from entering the consciousness in their original form.

cen'sụ·ăl (-shụ-ăl), *a.* [L. *censualis*, from *census*, a census.] relating to or containing a census.

cen'sụr·ȧ·ble (-shụr-), *a.* deserving of censure; blamable; culpable; reprehensible; faulty; as, a *censurable* person, *censurable* conduct.

cen'sụr·ȧ·ble·ness, *n.* blamableness; fitness to be censured.

cen'sụr·ȧ·bly, *adv.* in a manner deserving of blame.

cen'sụre (-shụr), *n.* [L. *censura*, the office of a censor, judgment, opinion, from *censere*, to judge, tax.]

1. an estimate or judgment without implying disapproval. [Obs.]

2. the act of blaming or finding fault and condemning as wrong; blame; reproof; reprehension: reprimand; adverse criticism.

3. a judgment or resolution condemning a person for misconduct; specifically, an official expression of disapproval passed by a legislature.

4. (a) [Archaic.] judicial sentence; judgment that condemns; (b) an ecclesiastical sentence of condemnation or penalty inflicted on a member of a church for malconduct, by which he is deprived of the communion of the church, or debarred from the sacerdotal office.

Syn.—blame, condemnation, invective, rebuke, reproach, remonstrance, reprimand, stricture, reproof.

cen'sụre (-shụr), *v.t.*; censured, *pt., pp.*; censuring, *ppr.* 1. to find fault with and condemn as wrong; to criticize adversely; to blame; to express disapproval of; as, to *censure* a man.

2. to condemn by a judicial sentence, as in ecclesiastical affairs. [Obs.]

3. to estimate; to form or express an opinion of. [Obs.]

Syn.—accuse, blame, carp, cavil, condemn, reproach, reprove, upbraid.

cen'sụre, *v.i.* to judge; to form or express an opinion. [Obs.]

cen'sụr·ẽr, *n.* one who criticizes or censures.

cen'sus, *n.* [L., from *censere*, to enroll, tax, assess.]

1. in ancient Rome, an official enumeration of the people, with special reference to the value of their property and estates, for the purpose of determining the rate of taxation.

2. an official enumeration of the people of a nation, state, district, or city, together with the collecting of statistics concerning their property, nativity, age, sex, occupation, etc. In the United States, a general federal census has been taken at the end of every ten years since 1790, an intermediate census being taken by some of the states and cities.

cent, *n.* [OFr. *cent*; L. *centum*, a hundred.]

1. a hundred: only in *per cent*, etc.

2. a 100th part of a dollar or of certain other monetary units.

3. in the United States, a coin formerly made of copper, but later of copper with a five per cent alloy of tin and zinc, the value of which is a 100th part of a dollar; a penny.

4. an old game of cards, resembling piquet, in which 100 was the game.

cent'āġe, *n.* rate by the hundred; percentage. [Rare.]

cen'tăl, *n.* a hundredweight; a unit of weight equal to 100 pounds avoirdupois.

cen'tāre, *n.* a centiare.

cen'tạur, *n.* [L. *Centaurus*; Gr. *Kentauros*.]

1. in Greek mythology, a monster with a man's head, trunk, and arms, and a horse's body and legs: the centaurs were supposed to have been the offspring of Ixion.

2. [C-] Centaurus.

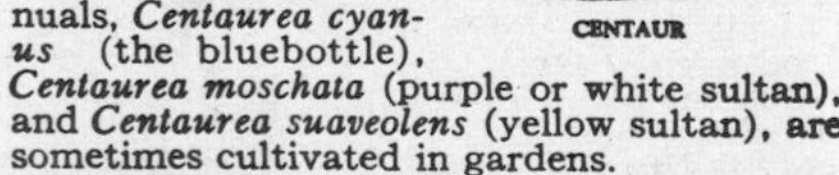

CENTAUR

Cen·tạu·rē'ȧ, *n.* [L. *centauria*; Gr. *kentaureion*, centaury, from *kentauros*, a centaur.] an extensive genus of herbaceous plants, members of the *Compositæ*. The species are annual or perennial herbs. They are found in Europe, western Asia, and north Africa. The annuals, *Centaurea cyanus* (the bluebottle), *Centaurea moschata* (purple or white sultan), and *Centaurea suaveolens* (yellow sultan), are sometimes cultivated in gardens.

cen'tạur·īze, *v.i.* to perform the acts of or to be like a centaur. [Rare.]

cen·tạu·rom'ȧ·chy, *n.*; *pl.* **cen·tạu·rom'ȧ·chieṣ,** [L. *centauromachia*; Gr. *kentauromachia*; *kentauros*, a centaur, and *machē*, battle.] a fight between centaurs, or between centaurs and men: a theme much used for relief sculpture.

Cen·tạu'rus, *n.* [L.; see *centaur*.] a southern constellation between Hydra and the Southern Cross: its brightest star, *alpha Centauri*, is nearer the earth than any other known star.

cen'tạu·ry, *n.*; *pl.* **cen'tạu·rieṣ,** [L. *centauria*; Gr. *kentaureion*, centaury, from *Kentauros*, a centaur.] any of a genus *Centaurium* of low-growing plants of the gentian family, with flat clusters of red or rose flowers.

cen·tä'vō, *n.*; *pl.* **cen·tä'vōṣ,** [Sp. from L. *centum*, hundred.]

1. a unit of currency in the Philippines, Mexico, and certain South American countries, equal to one-hundredth peso.

2. a unit of currency equal to one-hundreth of a Portuguese escudo, Brazilian cruzeiro, etc.

3. a coin of certain of these units.

fāte, fär, fȧst, fạll, finăl, cāre, at; mēte, prẹy, hẽr, met; pīne, marīne, bīrd, pin; nōte, mōve, fọr, atŏm, not; mọọn, book;

cen·te·när'i·ăn, *a.* [from *centenary.*]
1. of one hundred years; of a centenary.
2. of a centenarian; at least one hundred years old.

cen·te·när'i·ăn, *n.* a person at least one hundred years old.

cen'te·nā·ry, *n.*; *pl.* **cen'te·nā'ries,** [L. *centenarius*, from *centum*, a hundred.]
1. a century; a period of a hundred years.
2. a centennial; as, the *centenary* of Burns; the *centenary* of Emerson.

cen'te·nā·ry, *a.* 1. relating to a century; of a period of a hundred years.
2. of a centennial.

cen·ten'ni·ăl, *a.* [L. *centum*, a hundred, and *annus*, a year.]
1. of a hundred years.
2. a hundred years old.
That opened through long lines
Of sacred ilex and *centennial* pines.
—Longfellow.
3. happening once every hundred years.
4. lasting a hundred years.
5. of a hundredth anniversary.

cen·ten'ni·ăl, *n.* 1. a hundredth year of existence or duration; a hundredth anniversary.
2. the commemoration or celebration of any event which occurred a hundred years before; as, the *centennial* of American Independence; the *centennial* of the Louisiana Purchase.

cen·ten'ni·ăl·ly, *adv.* once in every hundred years; as, to celebrate an event *centennially*.

cen'tẽr, *n.* [OFr. *centre*; L. *centrum*; Gr. *kentron*, a sharp point, goad, spur, the point around which a circle is described; from *kentein*, to prick, goad.]
1. a point equally distant from all points of the circumference of a circle or surface of a sphere.
2. the point around which anything revolves; pivot.
3. a place considered as the middle or central point of activity; headquarters.
4. the approximate middle point, place, or part of anything.
5. a thing at the middle point.
6. the ring around the bull's-eye of a target, or a shot that hits this.
7. a point or place that actions, forces, people, etc. go to or come from; focal point; as, Broadway is the theatrical *center* for the whole country.
8. in biology, a group of cells having a common function.
9. in football, basketball, hockey, etc., a player assigned to the center of a floor, field, or line: the center often puts the ball or puck into play.
10. in mechanics, one of two tapered or conical pins or rods, as on a lathe, for holding a revolving object in position.
11. a temporary structure which supports the materials of a vault or arch while the work is in process of construction; centering.
12. in military usage, (a) that portion of an army situated between the flanks; (b) that portion of a fleet between the van and the rear, or (when sailing) between the weather and the lee.
13. [often C-] in politics, a position, party, or group between left (radicals and liberals) and right (conservatives and reactionaries): so called from the position of the seats occupied in some European legislatures.
Also spelled *centre.*
center of a conic section; that point which bisects any diameter of a conic section, or that point in which all the diameters intersect each other.
center of attraction of a body; the point to which bodies tend in consequence of the action of gravity.
center of buoyancy; the center of mass of the volume of water displaced by a floating body: also called the *center of cavity*, *center of immersion*, and *center of displacement*.
center of conversion; a point in a body about which it turns, or tends to turn, when a force is applied to any part of it.
center of gravity; that point in a thing around which its weight is evenly distributed or balanced; center of mass; point of equilibrium.
center of gyration; the point at which, if the whole mass of a revolving body were collected, the rotary effect would remain unaltered.
center of inertia; same as *center of mass*.
center of mass; the point in a body, or in a system of bodies, so situated that any plane drawn through it divides the body or system into parts having exactly equal masses: for bodies near the earth, this coincides with, and is used as a synonym for, *center of gravity*.
center of motion; the point which remains at rest, while all the other parts of a body move round it.
center of oscillation; the point of a body suspended by an axis at which, if all the matter were concentrated, the oscillations would be performed in the same time.
center of percussion; the point at which, if a moving body encountered an immovable obstacle, the motion would be arrested without producing any strain on the axis. It coincides with the center of oscillation when the percutient body moves about a fixed point and with the center of gravity when the body moves in a straight line.
center of population; the geographical point about which the entire population of a country or district is supposed to balance.
center of pressure; in hydrostatics, that point on the surface of a body subjected to pressure which would be in equilibrium if an equal counter pressure were exerted in the same line.
center of vision; the point in the retina from which the radial line in perspective starts.

cen'tẽr, *v.i.*; centered, centred, *pt., pp.*; centering, centring, *ppr.* 1. to be placed in a center or in the middle.
2. to be collected to one point; to be concentrated or united in one; as, our hopes must *center* in ourselves alone.
Life's choicest blessings *center* all in home.
—Cowper.
Also spelled *centre.*

cen'tẽr, *v.t.* 1. to place in, at, near, or toward the center; to fix on a central point.
2. to collect to a point; to draw to one place.
Thy joys are *centered* all in me alone.
—Prior.
3. in mechanics, to form an indentation or supply with a center.
4. in football, to pass (the ball) from the line to a player in the backfield.
Also spelled *centre.*

cen'tẽr bär, an arbor, or mandrel of a circular saw or turning lathe.

cen'tẽr bit, a bit with a sharp, projecting center point and cutting wings on either side.

cen'tẽr·bōard, *n.* a movable or shifting keel passing through a slot in the bottom of a vessel and swinging on a pin at the forward lower corner. It consists of a broad slab of wood or metal, and can be raised in shallow water; when lowered it acts as a projecting keel, increasing the area of lateral resistance, and when raised is completely housed in the boat, reducing her draft to that of the keel proper.

cen'tẽred, *a.* 1. being at the center.
2. having (a specified thing) as the focus of interest or activity: used in hyphenated compounds; as, consumer-*centered*.

cen'tẽr fïeld, in baseball, the middle part of the outfield.

cen'tẽr-fīre, *a.* having the fulminating charge of powder in the center of the base: said of cartridges.

cen'tẽr·ing, *n.* 1. a placing at, aiming at, or drawing toward a center.
2. the framing of timber by which the arch of a bridge or other structure is supported during its erection. The same name is given to the woodwork or framing on which any vaulted work is constructed. The centering of a bridge has to keep the stones or voussoirs in position till they are keyed in.

CENTERING

cen'tẽr·piēce, *n.* a central ornament, as of a table, ceiling, etc., or a decorative article or figure between other ornaments.

cen'tẽr punch, a steel punch for marking a spot where a hole is to be drilled.

cen·tes'i·măl, *a.* 1. hundredth.
2. of or divided into hundredths.

cen·tes'i·măl, *n.* a hundredth part.

cen·tes·i·mā'tion, *n.* [L. *centesimare*, to take out every hundredth, from *centesimus*, hundredth; *centum*, a hundred.] a military punishment for desertion, mutiny, or the like, where one person in every hundred is selected for execution, as in ancient Rome.

cen·tes'i·mō, *n.*; *pl.* **cen·tes'i·mōs** or It. **cen·tes'i·mī.** [It. and Sp., from L. *centesimus*, hundredth.]
1. a unit of currency equal to 100th part of an Italian lira, Uruguayan peso, Panamanian balboa, etc.
2. a coin of certain of these units.

cen'tesm, *n.* [L. *centesimus*, hundredth.] a hundredth part. [Obs.]

Cen·tet'i·dae, *n.pl.* [Gr. *kentētēs*, one who pierces, from *kentein*, to pierce.] a family of insectivores, of which there are several species, including the little tenrecs of Madagascar.

cen'ti-, a combining form from L. *centum*, hundred, and meaning: (a) *hundred* or *hundredfold*, as in *centi*pede; (b) *a hundredth part of*, as in *centi*gram, *centi*meter.

cen'ti·äre, *n.* [Fr.; see *centi-* and *are* (unit of area).] a 1/100 part of an are; a unit of land measure, equal to one square meter.

cen·ti·cip'i·tous, *a.* [L. *centiceps* (*-ipitis*); *centum*, hundred, and *caput*, head.] having a hundred heads. [Rare.]

cen·tif'i·dous, *a.* [L. *centifidus*; *centum*, hundred, and *findere*, to split.] divided into a hundred parts. [Rare.]

cen·ti·fō'li·ous, *a.* [L. *centifolius*; *centum*, hundred, and *folium*, leaf.] having a hundred leaves.

cen'ti·grāde, *a.* [Fr., from L. *centum*, hundred, and *gradus*, a degree.]
1. consisting of a hundred degrees; graduated into a hundred divisions or equal parts.
2. same as *Celsius*: the preferred term in English until the adoption of *Celsius* in 1948 by an international conference on weights and measures.

cen'ti·gram, cen'ti·gramme, *n.* [*centi-*, and Fr. *gramme*, a weight; Gr. *gramma*, a writing.] in the metric system, a unit of weight, equal to 1/100 gram.

cen'tïle (*or* -til), *n.* same as *percentile*.

cen'ti·lï·tẽr, cen'ti·lï·tre, *n.* [*centi-*, and Fr. *litre*; Gr. *litra*, a silver coin.] a unit of capacity, equal to 1/100 liter (.6102 cubic inch).

Cen·til'ō·quy, *n.* [L. *centum*, a hundred, and *loqui*, to speak.] a collection of a hundred aphorisms of astrology, attributed to Ptolemy.

cen·tïme' (sän-teem'), *n.* [Fr.; OFr. *centisme*, the hundredth, from L. *centisimus*, from *centum*, a hundred.]
1. the 100th part of a franc, the Haitian gourde, etc.
2. a coin of this value.

cen'ti·mē·tẽr, cen'ti·mē'tre, *n.* [*centi-*, and Fr. *mètre*, Gr. *metron*, a measure.] in the metric system, a unit of measure, equal to 1/100 meter (.3937 inch).

cen'ti·mē·tẽr-gram'-seç'ŏnd, *a.* in physics, designating or of a system of measurement in which the centimeter, gram, and second are used as the units of length, mass, and time, respectively.

cen'ti·mō, *n.*; *pl.* **cen'ti·mōs,** [see *centime.*]
1. the 100th part of a Spanish peseta, a Venezuelan bolivar, a Costa Rican colon, etc.
2. a coin of certain of these units.

cen'ti·nel, *n.* sentinel. [Obs.]

cen·tin'ō·dy, *n.* [L. *centinodia*; *centum*, hundred, and *nodus*, a knot.] knotgrass. [Obs.]

cen'ti·pēde, *n.* [L. *centipeda*; *centum*, a hundred, and *pes*, *pedis*, a foot.] any of a group of related wormlike animals of the class *Chilopoda*, with a pair of legs for each body segment: the two front legs are modified into poison fangs.

cen'ti·stēre, *n.* [*centi-*, and Fr. *stere*, from Gr. *stereos*, solid.] a unit of volume, equal to 1/100 cubic meter (.353 cubic foot).

cent märk (or **sīgn**), the symbol ¢, meaning *cent* or *cents*: it is placed after the numeral (e.g., 40¢).

cent'nẽr, *n.* [G. *centner*, *zentner*; L. *centenarius*, from *centum*, a hundred.]
1. a European commercial weight equal to 50 kilograms (110.23 pounds).
2. a metric weight equal to 100 kilograms (220.46 pounds).
3. the cental; 100 pounds.
4. in assaying, one dram.

cen'tō, *n.*; *pl.* **cen'tōs,** [L. *cento*, patchwork.]
1. a literary or musical work made up of passages from other compositions.
2. anything made up of badly matched parts.
3. a patchwork. [Obs.]

cen'tō·niṣm, *n.* the act or practice of arranging borrowed literary, artistic, or musical features in a new order, thus forming a patchwork composition.

cen'tr-, centro-.

cen'trȧ, *n.* alternative plural of *centrum.*

cen'trad, *adv.* [L. *centrum*, center, and *ad*, to.] toward the middle, the center, or the interior of a body or organ.

cen'trăl, *a.* [L. *centralis*, from *centrum*, center.]
1. in, at, or near the center.
2. of or forming the center.
3. from the center.
4. equally distant or accessible from various points.
5. main; principal; chief; basic.
6. in anatomy and physiology, (a) denoting that part of the nervous system consisting of the brain and spinal cord (of a vertebrate); (b) of the centrum of a vertebra.
7. in phonetics, pronounced with the tongue in center position; mixed: said of vowels.
central forces; in mechanics, the two antagonistic forces, the centripetal and centrifugal.
central particle; same as *centrosome.*
Central Powers; during World War I, Germany and Austria-Hungary: sometimes used to include their allies, Bulgaria and Turkey.

cen'trăl, *n.* 1. a telephone exchange, especially the main one.
2. [sometimes C–] a telephone operator.

Cen'trăl A·mer'i·căn, 1. of Central America, its people, etc.
2. a native or inhabitant of Central America.

cen·trā'lē, cen'trăl, *n.* [L. *centralis*, central.] one of the middle bones of the eight composing the wrist of man, or of the seven forming his ankle. In animals, one of the bones between the antibrachium and the forefoot or between the tibia and metatarsus.

cen'trăl·iṣm, *n.* the system or principle of centralizing power or authority, as in government; centralization.

cen'trăl·ist, *n.* a person who believes in centralism.

cen'trăl·ist, *a.* of or believing in centralism.

cen·tral'i·ty, *n.*; *pl.* **cen·tral'i·tieṣ**, 1. the quality, state, or fact of being central; center position.
2. the tendency to remain at or near the center.

cen″trăl·i·zā'tion, *n.* 1. the act or process of centralizing, or the state of being centralized; the combining or concentrating of several parts into a whole.
2. a concentration of power or authority; systematization under one control.

cen'trăl·īze, *v.t.*; centralized (-īzd), *pt., pp.*; centralizing, *ppr.* 1. to make central; to gather together; to draw to a central point; to bring to a center.
2. to organize or systematize under one authority or control.

cen'trăl·īze, *v.i.* to become centralized.

cen'trăl·ly, *adv.* 1. in, at, or near the center; from a center.
2. with reference to the center.

Cen'trăl Stan'dărd Tīme, one of the four standard times in the United States, corresponding to the mean local time of the 90th meridian west of Greenwich, England: it is six hours behind Greenwich time and one hour behind Eastern Standard Time.

cen'tre (-tẽr), *n., v.t.*, and *v.i.*; centred, *pt., pp.*; centring, *ppr.* center: chiefly British spelling.

cen'tri-, centro-, as in *centri*petal.

cen'triç, cen'triç·ăl, *a.* [Gr. *kentrikos*, from *kentron*, center.]
1. in, at, or near the center; central.
2. of or having a center.
3. in physiology, of a nerve center.

cen'triç·ăl·ly, *adv.* in a central position.

cen'triç·ăl·ness, *n.* situation in the center.

cen·tric'i·ty, *n.* the state or quality of being centric.

cen·trif'ū·găl, *a.* [Mod.L. *centrifugus* (coined by Newton from *centri-*, and L. *fugere*, to flee); and *-al.*]
1. moving or tending to move away from the center.
2. using or acted on by centrifugal force.
3. in botany, developing from the center outward, as certain flower clusters.
4. in physiology, conveying away from a center; efferent.
centrifugal force; the force which tends to make a rotating body move away from the center of rotation: it is due to inertia.
centrifugal machine; a machine using or causing centrifugal movement, designed to drive moisture out of damp articles, separate fluids of different densities, raise water, ventilate mines, etc.

cen·trif'ū·găl, *n.* a machine that uses or causes centrifugal movement, as a milk separator.

cen·trif'ū·găl·īze″, *v.t.*; centrifugalized, *pt., pp.*; centrifugalizing, *ppr.* to subject to the action of a centrifuge; to separate by whirling in a centrifuge.

cen'tri·fūġe, *a.* [Fr.] centrifugal.

cen'tri·fūġe, *n.* a machine using centrifugal force to separate particles of varying density, as cream from milk.

cen'tri·fūġe, *v.t.*; centrifuged, *pt., pp.*; centrifuging, *ppr.* to centrifugalize.

cen·trif'ū·ġence, *n.* centrifugal force or tendency.

cen'tring, *n.* same as *centering.*

cen·trip'e·tăl, *a.* [Mod.L. *centripetus* (coined by Newton from *centri-*, and L. *petere*, to seek, move toward); and *-al.*]
1. moving or tending to move toward the center.
2. using or acted on by centripetal force.
3. in botany, developing inward toward the center, as certain flower clusters.
4. in physiology, conveying toward a center; afferent.

cen·trip'e·tăl fōrce, the force tending to make rotating bodies move toward the center of rotation.

cen·trip'e·tence, cen·trip'e·ten·cy, *n.* [L. *centrum*, center, and *petens* (*-entis*), ppr. of *petere*, to seek.] centripetal force or tendency.

cen·tris'çoid, *a.* [Gr. *kentriskos*, a kind of fish, and *eidos*, form.] pertaining to the genus *Centriscus.*

Cen·tris'çus, *n.* [Gr. *kentriskos*, a kind of fish, dim. of *kentron*, a spine.] a genus of fishes including the bellows fish, trumpet fish, etc.

cen'trist, *n.* [Fr. *centriste*, from *centre.*] a person whose political position is neither leftist nor rightist; a member of the center, as in some European legislatures.

cen'trō-, a combining form from L. *centrum*, center; Gr. *kentron*, a horn, point, center, meaning *center*, as in *centro*some: also *centri-* or, before a vowel, *centr-.*

cen·trō·bar'iç, *a.* [*centro-*, and Gr. *baros*, weight.] pertaining to the center of gravity, or to the means of finding it.

cen'troid, *n.* [Gr. *kentron*, center, and *eidos*, form.] center of mass.

cen·trō·lec'i·thăl, *a.* [*centro-*, and Gr. *lekithos*, yolk of an egg.] having the food yolk in the center of the ovum, with regular or unequal segmentation.

cen·trō·lin'ē·ad, *n.* [*centro-*, and L. *linea*, a line.] an instrument used in perspective drawing, for drawing lines converging toward a point.

cen·trō·lin'ē·ăl, *a.* [*centro-*, and L. *linea*, a line.] converging to a center: said of lines.

cen'trō·sōme, *n.* [*centro-*, and Gr. *sōma*, the body.] a very small body near or, sometimes, in the nucleus in most animal cells and some plant cells: in mitosis it divides into two parts, toward each of which a group of the divided chromosomes moves.

cen·trō·som'iç, *a.* of a centrosome.

cen'trō·sphēre, *n.* [*centro-*, and *sphere.*]
1. in biology, the central mass of protoplasm about the centrosome; the central mass of an aster.
2. in geology, the central part of the earth.

cen'trum, *n.*; *pl.* **cen'trumṣ** or **cen'trȧ**, [L., from Gr. *kentron*, center.]
1. a center.
2. in anatomy, the body of a vertebra.
3. in geology, the focus or place of origin of an earthquake shock.

cen·tum'vir, *n.*; *pl.* **cen·tum'vi·rī**, [L. *centumvir*; *centum*, hundred, and *vir*, a man.] one of a group of judges in ancient Rome, appointed by the praetor, to decide common causes among the people. At first, three were taken from each of the thirty-five tribes, making 105, though, for the sake of the round number, they were called *centumviri.* The number was afterward increased to 180, without a change of their title.

cen·tum'vi·răl, *a.* pertaining to the centumvir.

cen·tum'vi·rāte, *n.* the office of a centumvir.

cen·tum'vi·rī, *n.* Latin plural of *centumvir.*

cen'tū·ple, *a.* [Fr., from L. *centuplex*, hundredfold; *centum*, hundred, and *plicare*, to fold.] a hundred times as much or as many; a hundredfold.

cen'tū·ple, *v.t.*; centupled, *pt., pp.*; centupling, *ppr.* to multiply a hundredfold.

cen·tū'pli·çāte, *v.t.*; centuplicated, *pt., pp.*; centuplicating, *ppr.* to increase a hundredfold; to centuple.

cen·tū'pli·çāte, *a.* hundredfold; centuple.

cen·tū'pli·çāte, *n.* a centuple quantity.

cen·tū'ri·ăl, *a.* relating to a century (in all senses).

cen·tū'ri·āte, *v.t.* [L. *centuriatus*, pp. of *centuriare*, to divide into hundreds; *centuria*, a hundred.] to divide into hundreds. [Obs.]

cen·tū'ri·āte, *a.* pertaining to centuries or divided into hundreds. [Rare.]

cen·tū'ri·ā·tŏr, cen'tū·rist, *n.* [from L. *centuriare*, to divide into hundreds.] a historian who distinguishes time by centuries, as in the Universal Church History of Magdeburg.

cen·tū'ri·ŏn, *n.* [L. *centurio* (*-onis*), from *centuria*, a company of a hundred.] among the Romans, a military officer who commanded a century, or a unit of a hundred men.

cen'tū·ry, *n.*; *pl.* **cen'tū·rieṣ**, [L. *centuria*, from *centum*, a hundred.]
1. in a general sense, a hundred; a series or group of a hundred persons or things.
2. in antiquity, a division of the Roman people for the purpose of electing magistrates and enacting laws, the people voting by *centuries*; also, a military company consisting of a hundred men; one of the sixty companies composing a legion of the army.
3. a period of a hundred years reckoned from a certain time, especially from the beginning of the Christian Era; as, the *first century*, A.D. 1–100; the *nineteenth century*, A.D. 1801–1900, both inclusive.
4. any period of a hundred years, as from 1620 to 1720.
5. in sports, a hundred; in cricket, a hundred runs; in bicycling, a hundred miles.
The Centuries of Magdeburg; an ecclesiastical history, arranged in thirteen centuries, compiled by a great number of Protestants at Magdeburg.

cen'tū·ry plant, a tropical American agave having fleshy leaves and a tall stalk with greenish flowers: so called because mistakenly thought to bloom only once a century.

ceorl (cheọrl), *n.* [AS.] in early English history, a freeman of the lowest class, ranking above a slave and below a thane; a churl.

cē·pā'ceous, *a.* [L. *cepa*, *cæpa*, the onion.] characteristic of an onion; smelling like an onion; alliaceous.

cē·pev'ō·rous, *a.* [L. *cepa*, an onion, and *vorare*, to devour.] feeding or subsisting upon onions. [Rare.]

Ceph·ȧ·ē'lis, *n.* [*cephal-*, and Gr. *eilein*, to compress.] a large genus of herbs or shrubs, natural order *Rubiaceæ*, found in the tropical parts of America.

ceph'ăl-, ceph'ȧ·lō-, combining forms from Gr. *kephalē*, head, and meaning *head*, *skull*, or *brain*, as in *cephalo*pod.

ceph'ȧ·lad, *adv.* [from Gr. *kephalē*, head, and L. *ad*, toward.] in anatomy and zoology, toward the head, or anterior part of the body: opposed to *caudad.*

ceph·ȧ·lal'ġi·ȧ, ceph'ȧ·lal·ġy, *n.* [Gr. *kephalalgia*, headache; *kephalē*, head, and *algos*, pain.] headache.

ceph·ȧ·lal'ġiç, *a.* pertaining to or afflicted with headache.

ceph·ȧ·lal'ġiç, *n.* a cure for headache; also, one who suffers from headache.

ceph·ȧ·lan'thi·um, *n.* same as *anthodium.*

Ceph·ȧ·las'pis, *n.* [*cephal-*, and Gr. *aspis*, a shield.] a genus of fossil fishes found in the Devonian formation. The head, which is very large, is covered by a protecting plate shaped like a buckler, and prolonged backward into a point on either side.

Ceph·ȧ·lā'tȧ, *n.pl.* [from Gr. *kephalē*, head.] an order of mollusks with specially developed head, comprising the pteropods, gastropods, and scaphopods, but not the bivalves.

ceph'ȧ·lāte, *a.* possessing a head: applied to certain mollusks.

ceph·ȧ·lē'tron, *n.* [*cephal-*, and Gr. *ētron*, abdomen.] the head or anterior division of the body of some crustaceans, as the king crab.

cē·phal'iç, *a.* [L. *cephalicus*; Gr. *kephalikos*, from *kephalē*, head.]
1. of the head, skull, or cranium.
2. in, on, near, or toward the head.

cē·phal'iç, *n.* a medicine for headache, or other disorder in the head.

-cē·phal'iç, a combining form meaning head or skull, as in dolicho*cephalic.*

cē·phal'iç in'dex, a measure of the human

skull computed by dividing its maximum breadth by its maximum length and multiplying by 100: if an individual's index is 80 or more, he is short-headed (*brachycephalic*); if less than 80, he is long-headed (*dolichocephalic*). Sometimes an intermediate category (*mesocephalic*) is recognized, indexes of 81 or more then being criteria of brachycephaly, and those under 76 of dolichocephaly.

cē·phal′iç vein, a large vein which runs along the arm: so named because the ancients used to open it for disorders of the head.

ceph′ȧ·liṣm, *n.* [Gr. *kephalē*, head.] the development of the skull, as characteristic of the different races of mankind.

ceph·ȧ·lī′tis, *n.* inflammation of the brain.

ceph″ȧ·li·zā′tion, *n.* [from *cephal-*, and *-ize*, and *-ation*.]
1. the increasing importance of the head or anterior end in the development of animal life.
2. the concentration of important organs or functions in or near the head.

ceph′ȧ·lō-, see *cephal-*.

Ceph″ȧ·lō·brañ′çhi·ȧ, *n.* [*cephalo-*, and Gr. *branchia*, gills.] a subdivision of *Annelida*, characterized by gills on or near the head.

ceph″ȧ·lō·cẽr′çăl, *a.* [*cephalo-*, and Gr. *kerkos*, tail.] in anatomy, extending from head to tail.

Ceph″ȧ·lō·çhor′dȧ, *n.pl.* [*cephalo-*, and Gr. *chordē*, a string, cord.] the lancelets, *Amphioxus*, small, fishlike animals that have a permanent notochord extending from the anterior to the posterior end.

ceph″ȧ·lō·çhor′dăl, *a.* relating to the *Cephalochorda*.

ceph″ȧ·lō·çhor′dāte, *a.* of the Cephalochorda.

ceph″ȧ·lō·çhor′dāte, *n.* any animal belonging to the Cephalochorda.

ceph′ȧ·lō·çōne, *n.* [*cephalo-*, and Gr. *kōnos*, a cone.] a cone-shaped organ, somewhat like a tentacle, on the head of a pteropod.

ceph″ȧ·lō·çon′iç, *a.* pertaining to a cephalocone.

ceph·ȧ·lō′di·um, *n.*; *pl.* **ceph·ȧ·lō′di·ȧ,** [Gr. *kephalōdēs*, like a head; *kephalē*, head, and *eidos*, form.] a convex development on the thallus of a lichen, containing algal cells.

ceph′ȧ·loid, *a.* [Gr. *kephalē*, head, and *eidos*, form.] having the shape of a head; spherical.

ceph·ȧ·lol′ō·ġy, *n.* [*cephalo-*, and Gr. *-logia*, from *legein*, to speak.] the scientific study of the head; a treatise on the head.

ceph′ȧ·lō·man″cy, *n.* [*cephalo-*, and Gr. *manteia*, divination.] divination by means of a head.

ceph′ȧ·lō·mēre, *n.* [*cephalo-*, and Gr. *meros*, part.] a somite, or segment, of the head of arthropods.

ceph·ȧ·lom′e·tẽr, *n.* [*cephalo-*, and Gr. *metron*, measure.] an instrument for measuring the head or skull; craniometer.

ceph″ȧ·lō·met′riç, *a.* pertaining to cephalometry or craniometry; craniometric.

ceph·ȧ·lom′e·try, *n.* the art of measuring skulls; craniometry.

ceph′ȧ·lon, *n.* [Gr. *kephalē*, the head.] in zoology, the head.

Ceph·ȧ·loph′ō·rȧ, *n.pl.* same as *Cephalata*.

ceph′ȧ·lō·pod, *n.* one of the *Cephalopoda*.

Ceph·ȧ·lop′ō·dȧ, *n.pl.* [*cephalo-*, and Gr. *pous*, *podos*, a foot.] the highest class of mollusks (*Mollusca*), having a distinct head with two large eyes, a beak, and muscular tentacles about the mouth, often with suckers on them. They are divided into two sections, *Tetrabranchiata* and *Dibranchiata*. The nautilus and several fossil genera belong to the *Tetrabranchiata*, in which the animal has an external shell. The dibranchiate group includes the argonaut, the octopus or eight-armed cuttlefishes, and the ten-armed forms, as the calamaries, the fossil belemnites, etc. The shell is in all these internal, in some rudimentary. The fossil *Cephalopoda* are multitudinous.

ceph·ȧ·lop′ō·dăn, *n.* a cephalopod.

ceph·ȧ·lop′ō·dous, ceph″ȧ·lō·pod′iç, *a.* belonging to the cephalopods.

ceph′ȧ·lō·sōme, *n.* [*cephalo-*, and Gr. *sōma*, body.] the anterior part or head of insects, crustaceans, etc.

ceph′ȧ·lō·stȳle, *n.* [*cephalo-*, and Gr. *stylos*, a pillar.] the anterior part of the notochord, or that part of it which is situated in the head.

ceph″ȧ·lō·thē′çȧ, *n.* [*cephalo-*, and Gr. *thēkē*, a case.] in entomology, the head case of an insect pupa.

ceph″ȧ·lō·thē′çăl, *a.* pertaining to a cephalotheca.

ceph″ȧ·lō·thō′rax, *n.* [*cephalo-*, and Gr. *thōrax*, a breastplate.] a united head and thorax, such as is found in the higher crustaceans.

ceph′ȧ·lō·tōme, *n.* [*cephalo-*, and Gr. *tomē*, a cutting.] an instrument used in obstetrics for dividing the head of a fetus so as to make delivery possible.

ceph·ȧ·lot′ō·my, *n.* 1. in anatomy, dissection of the head.
2. in obstetrics, the act or practice of operating with the cephalotome.

ceph′ȧ·lō·trip·sy, *n.* the operation of crushing the fetal head to make delivery possible. [Obs.]

ceph′ȧ·lō·troçh, *n.* [*cephalo-*, and Gr. *trochos*, a wheel.] the ciliated band on the head of the larvae of certain annelids, as the marine worms.

Ceph·ȧ·lot′rō·çhȧ, *n.* [*cephalo-*, and Gr. *trochos*, a wheel.] a group of annelids whose larvae have a ciliated band on the head.

ceph·ȧ·lot′rō·çhăl, *a.* relating to the *Cephalotrocha*.

ceph′ȧ·lous, *a.* [Gr. *kephalē*, the head.] possessing a head; cephalate.

-ceph′ȧ·lous, [Gr. *kephalē*.] a combining form meaning *-headed*, as in micro*cephalous*.

Ceph′ē·id vãr′i·ȧ·ble, [from *Cepheus*, and *-id*.] in astronomy, any of a class of stars whose light periodically varies in brightness.

Cē′pheūs (-fūs), *n.* [L., from Gr. *Kepheus*, in Greek mythology, a king of Ethiopia, and husband of Cassiopeia, placed among the stars after his death.] in astronomy, a constellation in the Northern Hemisphere, surrounded by Cassiopeia, Ursa Major, Draco, and Cygnus.

cē·rā′ceous, *a.* [L. *cera*, wax.] waxlike; partaking of the nature of wax.

cē·rā′gō, *n.* [L. *cera*, wax.] beebread, a mixture of pollen and honey made and eaten by bees.

cē′răl, *a.* in ornithology, pertaining to a cere.

Cē·rā·mi·ā′cē·ae, *n.pl.* [Gr. *keramion*, a jar, pitcher: so called from the shape of the filaments.] the rose tangles, a natural order of cellular seaweeds, *Algæ*, consisting of threadlike jointed plants of a red or brown-red hue.

cē·rā·mi·ā′ceous, *a.* pertaining to or belonging to the *Ceramiaceæ*.

cē·ram′iç, *a.* [Gr. *keramikos*, from *keramos*, potter's clay, a jar.]
1. of pottery, earthenware, tile, porcelain, etc.
2. of ceramics.
Also *keramic*.

cē·ram′içs, *n.pl.* 1. [*construed as sing.*] the art or work of making pottery, earthenware, tile, porcelain, etc.
2. objects made of these materials.
3. [*construed as sing.*] a course of study in pottery or pottery making.
Also *keramics*.

cer·ȧ·mid′i·um, *n.*; *pl.* **cer·ȧ·mid′i·ȧ,** [Gr. *keramidion*, dim. of *keramos*, potter's clay, pottery, a jar.] one of the conical or ovate capsules of the *Ceramiaceæ* or rose-spored algae. They generally open by a terminal pore for the escape of the spores.

cer′ȧ·mist, *n.* an expert in ceramics; a ceramic artist.

Cē·rā′mi·um, *n.* [Gr. *keramion*, dim. of *keramos*, potter's clay, an earthen vessel.] the typical genus of the rose tangle family of seaweeds, *Ceramiaceæ*.

cē·rär′ġy·rīte, *n.* [Gr. *keras*, a horn, and *argyritēs*, of silver; *argyros*, silver.] silver chloride, AgCl, a native ore of silver, nearly white when fresh, but changing to brown when exposed to light. It crystallizes in the isometric system and is found both massive and in cubic crystals. It looks somewhat like wax, and is easily cut: also called *horn silver*.

cer′ȧs, *n.* singular of *cerata*.

cer′a·sin, *n.* [L. *cerasus*, a cherry tree.]
1. a kind of gum which exudes from cherry and plum trees. It is distinguished from gum arabic by being insoluble in cold water.
2. a crude precipitate from tincture of chokecherry.

cer′ȧ·sine, *a.* [Gr. *keras*, horn.] corneous.

cē·ras′i·nous, *a.* [L. *cerasinus*, from *cerasus*; Gr. *kerasos*, a cherry.]
1. of, pertaining to, or containing cerasin.
2. having the color of a cherry; deep-red. [Rare.]

cer′ȧ·sīte, *n.* [L. *serasus*, cherry tree, and *-ite*.]
1. a petrifaction resembling a cherry.
2. a variety of Japanese iolite.

Cē·ras′tēṣ, *n.* [L. *cerastes*; Gr. *kerastēs*, a horned serpent, from *keras*, a horn.] in zoology, a genus of poisonous African snakes having two little horns formed by the scales above the eyes; horned vipers.

Cē·ras′ti·um, *n.* [from Gr. *keras*, a horn, so called from the horn-shaped capsules of many of the species.] mouse-ear chickweed, a genus of plants, natural order *Caryophyllaceæ*, consisting of many pubescent herbs with small leaves and white flowers. The plants are common weeds in all temperate and cold regions.

WATER MOUSE-EAR CHICKWEED (*Cerastium aquaticum*)

cer′at-, cerato-.

cer′ȧ·tȧ, *n.pl.*; *sing.* **cer′as,** [Gr. *keras*, *keratos*, a horn.] in zoology, the notal projections or papillae of the *Ceratobranchia*.

cē′rāte, *n.* [L. *ceratus*, pp. of *cerare*, to wax; *cera*, wax.] a thick kind of ointment composed of a fat, as oil, lard, etc., mixed with wax, resin, and other ingredients, applied externally in various diseases.

cē′rāte, *a.* in zoology, possessing a cere.

cē′rā·ted, *a.* [L. *ceratus*, pp. of *cerare*, to cover with wax; *cera*, wax.]
1. covered with wax.
2. having a cere.

cer′ȧ·tin, *n.* keratin.

cer·ȧ·tī′tis, *n.* keratitis.

cē·rā′ti·um (-shi-um), *n.*; *pl.* **cē·rā′ti·ȧ,** [Gr. *keration*, dim. of *keras*, *keratos*, a horn.] in botany, a pod or capsule resembling a silique, but having no dividing wall.

cer′ȧ·tō-, [from Gr. *keras*, *keratos*, a horn.] a combining form meaning *horn*, *hornlike*: also, before a vowel, *cerat-*, as in *Cerat*odus.

Cer″ȧ·tō·brañ′çhi·ȧ, *n.pl.* [*cerato-*, and Gr. *branchia*, gills.] a group of mollusks, having gills situated on the back or sides and without protecting shell or covering.

cer″ȧ·tō·brañ′çhi·ăl, *a.* pertaining to the lower of the two bony pieces which form the branchial arches in fishes.

Cer·ȧ·tō′dȧ, *n.pl.* same as *Ceratospongiæ*.

cer′ȧ·tōde, *n.* keratode.

cē·rat′ō·dont, *a.* pertaining to *Ceratodus*.

Cē·rat′ō·dus, *n.* [Gr. *keras*, *keratos*, a horn, and *odous*, *odontos*, a tooth.]
1. a genus of dipnoan fishes (with gills and lungs) of which the Australian salmon or barramunda is typical.
2. [c—] a fish of this genus.

cer·ȧ·tog′e·nous, *a.* keratogenous.

cer″ȧ·tō·hȳ′ăl, *a.* [*cerato-*, and Gr. *hyoeidēs*, from the letter ϒ, and *eidos*, form.] in anatomy, pertaining to the smaller and anterior cornu of the hyoid arch.

cer″ȧ·tō·hȳ′ăl, *n.* the lesser cornu of the hyoid arch.

cer′ȧ·toid, *a.* [Gr. *keratoeidēs*, hornlike; *keras*, a horn, and *eidos*, form.] horny.

Cer·ȧ·toi′dē·ȧ, *n.pl.* same as *Ceratospongiæ*.

cer′ȧ·tōme, *n.* same as *keratome*.

Cer″ȧ·tō·phyl·lā′cē·ae, *n.pl.* [*cerato-*, and Gr. *phyllon*, a leaf.] a family of plants, containing a single genus with only one species, *Ceratophyllum demersum* (hornwort). It is common in pools and streams.

cer·ȧ·toph′yl·lous, *a.* having linear leaves resembling horns; pertaining to the *Ceratophyllum*.

Cer″ȧ·tō·phyl′lum, *n.* [*cerato-*, and Gr. *phyllon*, a leaf.] a genus of aquatic plants belonging to the family *Ceratophyllaceæ*.

cer′ȧ·tō·phȳte, *n.* [*cerato-*, and Gr. *phyton*, a plant.] in zoology, a coral having an interior axis of horny fibers.

Cer·ȧ·tō′sȧ, *n.pl.* same as *Ceratospongiæ*.

cer″ȧ·tō·sau′rus, *n.* [*cerato-*, and Gr. *sauros*, a lizard.] an American species of dinosaur whose skull exhibits a bony horn core.

cer′ȧ·tōse, *a.* [Gr. *keras*, *keratos*, a horn.]
1. horny.
2. pertaining to the *Ceratosa*.

Cer″ȧ·tō·spon′ġi·ae, *n.pl.* [*cerato-*, and Gr. *spongos*, a sponge.] an order of sponges, distinguished by their soft flexible skeleton, of which the bath sponge is the type.

cer·ȧ·tos′tō·mȧ, *n.*; *pl.* **cer″ȧ·tō·stom′ȧ·tȧ,** [*cerato-*, and Gr. *stoma* (*-atos*), mouth.] in botany, the long-necked and narrow-mouthed receptacle containing the fruit in certain fungi.

cer′ȧ·tō·stōme, *n.* same as *ceratostoma*.

cē·rau′niçs, *n.* [Gr. *keraunos*, a thunderbolt, thunder and lightning.] that branch of physics which deals with heat and electricity, and their phenomena. [Rare.]

cē·rau′nō·sçōpe, *n.* [Gr. *keraunos,* thunder and lightning, and *skopein,* to view.] an apparatus used in the ancient mysteries for the purpose of imitating thunder and lightning.

Cẽr·bē′rē·ăn, Cẽr·bē′ri·ăn, *a.* relating to or resembling Cerberus.

Cẽr′bẽr·us, *n.* [L.]
1. in Greek and Roman mythology, a monster in the shape of a dog, the offspring of the giant Typhaon and the serpent-woman Echidna, guarding the entrance into Hades, and described by different ancient writers as having three, fifty, and even a hundred heads: usually portrayed with three heads and a serpent's tail, and with serpents around his neck.
2. any rough vigilant guardian; as, a *Cerberus* of the stage door.
3. a subgenus of serpents (ophidians) which have nearly the whole of the head covered with small scales, as the bokadam of the East Indies.

CERBERUS

cẽr′çăl, *a.* [Gr. *kerkos,* tail.] pertaining to the tail.

cẽr·çā′ri·ȧ, *n.*; *pl.* **cẽr·çā′ri·ae,** [Gr. *kerkos,* a tail.] in zoology, the second larval stage of a trematode worm or fluke, characterized by a tadpolelike body, which becomes encysted, and gives rise to the sexual forms. The larvae are chiefly found in the bodies of mollusks, the adults in vertebrate animals.

cẽr·çā′ri·ăn, *a.* pertaining to or resembling a cercaria.

cẽr′çō·pod, *n.* [Gr. *kerkos,* tail, and *pous, podos,* a foot.] in zoology, one of the jointed anal appendages of certain insects and crustaceans, as those of the genus *Apus.*

cẽr′çus, *n.*; *pl.* **cẽr′cī,** same as *cercopod.*

cēre, *n.* [L. *cera,* wax, from its appearance.] a soft, waxlike membrane at the base of the beak of some birds, as the parrot, eagle, etc.

cēre, *v.t.*; cered, *pt., pp.*; cering, *ppr.* [L. *cerare,* from *cera,* wax.]
1. to wax or cover with wax. [Obs.]
2. to wrap in a cerecloth.

cē′rē·ăl, *a.* [L. *Cerealis,* pertaining to *Ceres,* goddess of agriculture.] of grain or the grasses producing grain.

cē′rē·ăl, *n.* 1. any edible grain, as wheat, oats, barley, rye, etc.
2. any grass producing such grain.
3. food made from grain, especially breakfast food, as oatmeal, etc.

Cē·rē·ā′li·ȧ, *n.pl.* 1. that group of the *Gramineæ,* or grasses, which comprises the edible grains or cereals.
2. in Roman antiquities, festivals in honor of Ceres, the goddess of agriculture.

cē′rē·ȧ·lin, *n.* same as *aleurone.*

cer′ē·bel, *n.* the cerebellum. [Obs.]

cer·ē·bel′lăr, cer·ē·bel′lous, *a.* relating to the cerebellum.

cer·ē·bel′lum, *n.* [L. *cerebellum,* dim. of *cerebrum,* the brain.] the part of the brain which is behind and below the cerebrum: it is regarded as the co-ordinating center for muscular movement.

cer′ē·brăl, *a.* [L. *cerebrum,* brain.]
1. pertaining to the cerebrum or the brain.
2. of, appealing to, or conceived by the intellect rather than the emotions.

cer′ē·brăl, *n.* [a mistranslation of Sans. *mūrdhanya,* head sounds.] in Sanskrit, one of the lingual consonants: called in English philology, a *cerebral letter.*

cer′ē·brăl·iṣm, *n.* the theory that consciousness results solely from the activity of the brain.

cer′ē·brăl·ist, *n.* one who believes in the theory or doctrine of cerebralism.

cer′ē·brăl pąl′ṣy, paralysis due to a lesion of the brain, usually one suffered at birth, and characterized chiefly by spasms: see *spastic.*

cer′ē·brāte, *v.i.*; cerebrated, *pt., pp.*; cerebrating, *ppr.* to use one's brain; to think.

cer′ē·brāte, *v.t.* to perform by means of the action of the brain.

cer·ē·brā′tion, *n.* exertion or action of the brain, conscious or unconscious; thinking.

cer′ē·briç, *a.* relating to or obtained from the brain.

cer·ē·bric′i·ty, *n.* the power of the brain. [Rare.]

ce·reb′ri·fọrm, *a.* [L. *cerebrum,* brain, and *forma,* form.] brain-shaped.

cer·ē·brif′ū·găl, *a.* [L. *cerebrum,* brain, and *fugere,* to flee.] transmitting cerebral impulses outward: applied to nerve fibers passing from the brain to the spinal cord.

cer′ē·brin, *n.* [L. *cerebrum,* the brain, and *-in.*] any of several nitrogenous substances obtained chemically from the brain.

cer·ē·brip′e·tăl, *a.* [L. *cerebrum,* the brain, and *petere,* to seek.] transmitting sensations to the brain: applied to nerve fibers passing from the spinal cord to the brain.

cer·ē·brī′tis, *n.* [L. *cerebrum,* the brain, and *-itis.*] an inflamed condition of the cerebrum.

cer′e·bro-, cer′e·br-, [from L. *cerebrum,* the brain.]
1. *the brain* or *cerebrum,* as in *cerebr*itis.
2. *the brain and* or *cerebrum and,* as in *cerebro*spinal.

cer′ē·broid, *a.* [L. *cerebrum,* brain, and Gr. *eidos,* form.] resembling the brain.

cer·ē·brol′ō·ġy, *n.* [*cerebro-,* and Gr. *-logia,* from *legein,* to speak.] the science or study of the brain.

cer·ē·brop′ȧ·thy, *n.* [*cerebro-,* and Gr. *pathos,* suffering.] a diseased condition, usually accompanied by melancholia, caused by anxiety or overwork.

cer·ē·bros′çō·py, *n.* [*cerebro-,* and Gr. *-skopia,* from *skopein,* to view.] the examination of the condition of the brain, especially by means of ophthalmoscopy, in the diagnosis of brain disease.

cer′ē·brōse, *n.* a substance resembling sugar, obtained by the decomposition of cerebrin.

cer′ē·brōse, *a.* [L. *cerebrosus,* from *cerebrum,* the brain.] brainsick; mad; willful. [Rare.]

cer″ē·brō·spī′năl, *a.* [*cerebro-,* and L. *spina,* the spine.]
1. pertaining to the brain and spinal cord together with their cranial and spinal nerves; as, the *cerebrospinal* axis or system.
2. of or affecting the brain and spinal cord.
cerebrospinal fever, cerebrospinal meningitis; an acute, infectious disease characterized by inflammation of the meninges of the brain and spinal cord.
cerebrospinal fluid; a fluid between the arachnoid and the pia mater membranes of the brain and spinal cord.

cer′ē·brum, *n.*; *pl.* **cer′ē·brumṣ** or **cer′ē·brȧ,** [L.] the upper, main part of the brain of vertebrate animals, consisting of two equal hemispheres: in man it is the largest part of the brain and is believed to control conscious and voluntary processes.

cēre′çlọth, *n.* [L. *cera,* wax, and *cloth.*]
1. a cloth treated with melted wax, or with some gummy or glutinous matter.
2. such a cloth used to wrap a dead person for burial.

cēre′ment, *n.* [L. *cera,* wax.]
1. a cerecloth with which a dead body is wrapped for burial.
2. [*pl.*] any burial clothes.

cer·ē·mō′ni·ăl, *a.* [LL. *cærimonialis,* from L. *cærimonia,* ceremony.]
1. relating to ceremony, or ritual; according to the forms of established rites; as, *ceremonial* exactness.
2. formal; exact; precise in manners; ceremonious.

cer·ē·mō′ni·ăl, *n.* 1. an established system of rites connected with an occasion, including all the forms prescribed; a system of rules and ceremonies, enjoined by law, or established by custom, as in religious worship, court procedure, etc.
2. the order for rites and forms in the Roman Catholic Church, or the book containing the rules prescribed to be observed on solemn occasions.
3. a rite.

cer·ē·mō′ni·ăl·iṣm, *n.* esteem for ceremonial forms; adherence to ritualism.

cer·ē·mō′ni·ăl·ly, *adv.* according to rites and ceremonies; as, a person *ceremonially* unclean; an act *ceremonially* unlawful.

cer·ē·mō′ni·ăl·ness, *n.* the quality of being ceremonial.

cer·ē·mō′ni·ous, *a.* 1. ceremonial.
2. full of ceremony.
3. according to the rules and forms prescribed or customary; characterized by ceremony or formality; punctilious.

cer·ē·mō′ni·ous·ly, *adv.* in a ceremonious manner; formally.

cer·ē·mō′ni·ous·ness, *n.* the condition of being ceremonious; great formality in manners.

cer′ē·mō·ny, *n.*; *pl.* **cer′ē·mō·nieṣ,** [L. *cærimonia,* sacredness, a sacred rite.]
1. a formal act or set of formal acts established by custom or authority as proper to a special occasion, such as a wedding, religious rite, etc.
2. the service or function at which such acts are used.
3. a conventional social act.
4. formality or formalities.
5. empty or meaningless formality.
6. rules established by custom for governing social behavior; also, behavior governed by strict etiquette.
7. a crown, scepter, or other symbol of ceremony. [Obs.]
8. an omen. [Obs.]
to stand on ceremony; to behave with or insist on formality.

cē′rē·ous, *a.* [L. *cereus,* from *cera,* wax.] waxen; like wax.

Cē′rēṣ, *n.* [L.]
1. in Roman mythology, the goddess of agriculture, the daughter of Saturn and Ops, sister of Jupiter, and mother of Proserpine: identified with the Greek Demeter.
2. one of the asteroids revolving between the orbits of Mars and Jupiter. It was discovered by G. Piazzi (1746–1826), Italian astronomer, at Palermo, in Sicily, in 1801, and was the first of the asteroids to be observed.

cer′ē·sin, *n.* [L. *cera,* wax.] a white wax used as a substitute for beeswax: made from ozocerite by a bleaching and purifying process.

CERES

Cē′rē·us, *n.* [L., a wax candle.]
1. a large genus of plants of the cactus family, chiefly tropical, but found growing from California to Chile: several species produce large tubular nocturnal blossoms, especially *Cereus grandiflorus,* which is extensively cultivated for its beautiful, short-lived flowers. *Cereus giganteus,* native to Arizona, New Mexico, and Texas, has a columnar trunk which often rises to a height of sixty feet.
2. [c–] any plant of this genus.

cẽrġe, *n.* a wax candle used in religious rites: written also *cierge.*

cē·ri′ȧ, *n.* [from *cerium.*] cerium dioxide, CeO_2, a white compound.

cer′i·ăl, *a.* cerrial. [Obs.]

cē′riç, *a.* pertaining to cerium; as, *ceric* compounds.

cer′if, cer′iph, *n.* a serif: British spelling.

cē·rif′ẽr·ous, *a.* [L. *cera,* wax, and *ferre,* to produce.] yielding wax.

cē′rin, *n.* [L. *cera,* wax, and *-in.*]
1. a waxy substance which has been evaporated from cork by the action of alcohol.
2. cerotic acid.
3. a variety of the mineral allanite.

Cē·rin′thi·ăn, *n.* one of a sect of heretics, the earliest of the Gnostic sects: so called from Cerinthus, the founder of this sect in the first century A.D.

ce·riṣe′, *a.* [Fr., a cherry.] of a bright red; cherry-red.

ce·riṣe′, *n.* a bright red color; cherry red.

cē′rite, *n.* the silicious oxide of cerium, a mineral of a brownish color.

cē′ri·um, *n.* a gray, metallic chemical element of the rare-earth group: symbol Ce; atomic weight, 140.13; atomic number, 58.

cē′ri·um met′ălṣ, a series of closely related metals belonging to the rare-earth group and having atomic numbers from 57 to 62: lanthanum, cerium, praseodymium, neodymium, illinium, and samarium.

cẽr′nū·ous, *a.* [L. *cernuus,* stooping.] in botany, having the top curved downward; pendulous; drooping: said of a bud, flower, or fruit.

cē′rō, *n.*; *pl.* **cē′rō** or **cē′rōṣ,** [Sp. *sierra*; L. *serra,* a saw.] a large food fish of the genus *Scomberomorus,* related to the Spanish mackerel, but much larger. Two species are found in the West Indies and on the Atlantic coast.

cē′rō-, [from L. *cera*; Gr. *kēros*, wax.] a combining form meaning *wax*: also, before a vowel, *cer-*.

cē′rō·gráph, *n.* [Gr. *kēros*, wax, and *graphein*, to write.] a representation of any kind made on wax; anything written or engraved on wax.

cē·rō·graph′iç, cē·rō·graph′iç·ăl, *a.* pertaining to the art of making cerographs.

cē·rog′rà·phist, *n.* one who is skilled in, or who practices, cerography.

cē·rog′rà·phy, *n.* 1. a writing on wax.
2. the art of engraving on wax spread on a sheet of copper, from which a stereotype plate is taken.

cē′rō·līte, *n.* [Gr. *kēros*, wax, and *lithos*, stone.] silicated magnesium occurring in waxlike masses of a greenish-yellow color: also spelled *kerolite*.

cē·rō′mȧ, *n.* [L., from Gr. *kērōma*, a wax tablet, salve, from *kēros*, wax.]
1. in ancient Roman baths, the room in which wrestlers used to anoint themselves with an ointment of oil and wax.
2. this ointment of oil and wax.
3. in ornithology, the cere of a bird's bill.

cē′rō·man·cy, *n.* [Gr. *kēros*, wax, and *manteia*, divination.] divination from forms produced by dropping melted wax in water.

cē·roon′, *n.* same as *seroon*.

cē·rō·plas′tiç, *a.* [Gr. *kēroplastikos*, from *kēros*, wax, and *plassein*, to mold.] pertaining to the art of wax modeling; as, a *ceroplastic* statuette.

cē·rō·plas′tiçs, cē′rō·plas·ty, *n.pl.* [*construed as sing.*] the art of making models in wax.

cē′rō·sin, *n.* [L. *cera*, wax.] a delicate crystalline wax extracted from sugar-cane bark, having a lamellar crystallization.

cē′rōte, *n.* cerate. [Obs]

cē′rō·tēne, *n.* [L. *cerotum*, a pomade.] a solid white wax similar to paraffin: obtained from Chinese wax by distillation.

cē·rot′iç, *a.* [Gr. *kērotē*, a salve, cerate, from *kēros*, wax.] designating or of either of two fatty acids, $C_{26}H_{52}O_2$ or $C_{27}H_{54}O_2$, esters of which are found in beeswax and other waxes and oils.

cē′rō·tin, *n.* a crystalline substance derived from Chinese wax and regarded as belonging to the marsh gas series of alcohols: called also *cerotic alcohol* and *ceryl alcohol*.

cē′rō·tyl, *n.* same as *ceryl*.

cē·rō′tȳpe, *n.* [*cero-*, and *type*.] the process of engraving on a wax-covered metal plate from which a printing surface is prepared by electrotyping.

cē′rous, *a.* of or containing cerium with a valence of three.

cē′rous, *a.* in zoology, pertaining to a cere.

cer′ri·ăl, *a.* pertaining to the cerris, or bitter oak.

cer′ris, *n.* [L. *cerrus*, a kind of oak.] the bitter oak, *Quercus cerris*.

cẽr′tain (-tin), *a.* [Fr. *certain*, from L. *certus*, determined, fixed, settled, pp. of *cernere*, to distinguish, decide, resolve.]
1. sure; true; undoubted; unquestionable; that cannot be denied; existing in fact and truth.
2. assured; having no doubts.
To make her *certain* of the sad event.
—Dryden.
3. unfailing; always producing the intended effect; reliable; dependable; as, we have no *certain* remedy for that disease.
4. stated; fixed; determinate; regular; as, a *certain* rate of interest.
5. particular, but not specified; as, a *certain* man whom I shall not mention.
6. sure (to happen, etc.); inevitable.
7. controlled; unerring; as, his aim was *certain*.
8. some; appreciable; as, success to a *certain* degree.
for certain; most surely; without any doubt.
Syn.—sure, undeniable, unquestionable, indisputable, indubitable, incontrovertible, unfailing.

cẽr′tain, *n.* 1. certainty. [Obs.]
2. one or more; some.
Certain of your own poets have said.
—Acts xvii. 28.

cẽr′tain, *adv.* certainly. [Obs.]

cẽr′tain·ly, *adv.* 1. without doubt or question; in truth and fact; surely; as, *certainly* he was a good man.
2. without failure; as, he will *certainly* return.

cẽr′tain·ness, *n.* same as *certainty*.

cẽr′tain·ty, *n.*; *pl.* **cẽr′tain·ties,** 1. a fixed or real state; truth; fact.
2. full assurance of mind; exemption from doubt.
of a certainty; assuredly; without doubt. [Archaic.]

cẽr′tēş, *adv.* certainly; in truth. [Archaic.]

cẽr′ti·fī·à·ble, *a.* that can be certified.

cẽr·tif′i·çāte, *n.* [LL. *certificatus*, pp. of *certificare*, to certify; L. *certus*, certain, and *facere*, to make.] a written or printed statement testifying to a fact, qualification, or promise.
certificate of deposit; a bank's written acknowledgment that a stated sum has been deposited to the credit of the person named.
certificate of disability discharge; a discharge from the United States Army because of physical unfitness for further military service.
certificate of incorporation; a legal document stating the name and purpose of a proposed corporation, the names of its incorporators, the nature and amount of stock to be issued, etc.
certificate of origin; a certificate submitted by an exporter to those countries requiring it, listing goods to be imported and stating their place of origin.
certificate of stock; a certificate issued by a corporation showing that a specified person owns a specified amount of capital stock in the corporation, and is subject to the rights and liabilities of a stockholder.

cẽr·tif′i·çāte, *v.t.*; certificated, *pt.*, *pp.*; certificating, *ppr.* 1. to give a certificate to.
2. to verify or attest by certificate.

cẽr″ti·fi·çā′tion, *n.* 1. the act of certifying.
2. a certified statement.

cẽr′ti·fied, *a.* [past participle of *certify*.]
1. vouched for; guaranteed.
2. having a certificate.

cẽr′ti·fied check, a check that a bank guarantees to be good.

cẽr′ti·fied māil, 1. a postal service which provides, for a fee, a receipt to the sender of first-class mail and a record of its delivery.
2. mail sent by this service: it is not insurable.

cẽr′ti·fied milk, milk guaranteed to have been produced according to certain regulations of an authorized medical milk commission, but not pasteurized.

cẽr′ti·fied pub′liç aç·çount′ănt, an accountant who has received a certificate stating that he has met the requirements of State law.

cẽr′ti·fī·ẽr, *n.* one who certifies.

cẽr′ti·fȳ, *v.t.*; certified, *pt.*, *pp.*; certifying, *ppr.* [OFr. *certifier*; LL. *certificare*; L. *certus*, certain, and *facere*, to make.]
1. to testify by formal declaration, often in writing; to make known or establish (a fact).
2. to declare officially insane; send to an asylum or similar institution.
3. to guarantee the quality or worth of; vouch for; as, the bank must *certify* your check.
4. to assure; make certain. [Archaic.]
Syn.—acknowledge, aver, attest, vouch, avow, avouch, testify, declare, demonstrate.

cẽr′ti·fȳ, *v.i.* to testify (*to*).

cẽr″ti·ō·rā′rī (sẽr″shi-ō-rā′rī), *n.* [LL. *certiorari*, from L. *certior*, comp. of *certus*, certain.] a writ issuing out of a higher court, to call up the records of a lower court, or remove a case there pending to a higher court. This writ is obtained upon complaint of a party, that he has not received justice, or that he cannot have an impartial trial in the lower court.

cẽr′ti·tūde, *n.* [LL. *certitudo*, from L. *certus*, certain.] certainty; assurance; freedom from doubt.

cer′ūle, *a.* [L. *cæruleus*, dark blue.] blue. [Obs.]

cē·rū′lē·ăn, *a.* of a deep, clear blue; sky-blue.

cē·rū′lē·in, *n.* a dye product of coal tar used in dyeing fabrics a brownish-green color: written also *coerulein*.

cē·rū′lē·ous, *a.* sky-colored; blue.

cer·ū·les′cent, *a.* [L. *cæruleus*, dark blue.] approximating a sky-blue color; light blue.

cer·ū·lif′iç, *a.* producing a blue color. [Rare.]

cē·rū·lig′nōne, *n.* [L. *cæruleus*, sky-blue, and *lignum*, wood, and Eng. *quinone*.] a blue compound crystalline substance obtained from wood tar: written also *coerulignone*.

cē·rū′men, *n.* [L. *cera*, wax.] the wax or yellow matter secreted by the glands of the external ear.

cē·rū′mi·nous, *a.* relating to cerumen; secreting cerumen.

cē′ruse, *n.* [L. *cerussa*, white lead, from *cera*, wax.]
1. white lead, $2PbCO_3·Pb(OH)_2$.
2. a cosmetic made chiefly of white lead.

cē′ruse, *v.t.*; cerused, *pt.*, *pp.*; cerusing, *ppr.* to wash with a cosmetic of white lead.

cē′rus·sīte, cer′ū·sīte, *n.* [L. *cerussa*, white lead, and *-ite*.] a massive, compact mineral, white or yellowish; native carbonate of lead.

cẽr′và·lat, cẽr′vē·lat, *n.* [Fr. *cervelat*, a kind of sausage.] an old-fashioned wind instrument with a tone like that of a bassoon.

cẽr′van·tīte, *n.* [named from *Cervantes*, a town in Spain.] the gray ore of antimony.

cer·ve·lière′ (sẽr-ve-lyãr′), *n.* [Fr., from *cervelle*, brain.] a close-fitting steel cap for protecting the head, worn in medieval times.

cẽr′vi·căl, *a.* [L. *cervix* (*-icis*), the neck.] of or belonging to the neck; as, the *cervical* nerves.

cẽr·vī′çēş, *n.* alternative pl. of *cervix*.

cẽr′vi·cīde, *n.* [L. *cervus*, deer, and *cædere*, to kill.] deer-killing. [Rare.]

cẽr·vi·cī′tis, *n.* inflammation of the cervix of the uterus.

cẽr′vi·çō-, [from L. *cervix*, *cervicis*, the neck.] a combining form meaning *cervical* or *cervical and*, as in *cervico*dorsal: also, before a vowel, *cervic-*.

cẽr″vi·çō·braçh′i·ăl, *a.* [*cervico-*, and L. *brachium*, the arm.] relating to both the neck and the arm.

Cẽr″vi·çō·brañ′çhi·ȧ, *n.* [*cervico-*, and Gr. *branchia*, gills.] a suborder of gastropods with a conical shell and cervical gills.

cẽr″vi·çō·brañ′çhi·āte, *a.* pertaining to the *Cervicobranchia*.

cẽr″vi·çō·dọr′săl, *a.* [*cervico-*, and *dorsal*.] in anatomy, of the neck and the back.

cẽr′vi·çorn, *a.* [L. *cervus*, deer, and *cornu*, horn.] having horns like the antlers of a deer; also, having the appearance of antlers.

cẽr·viç′ū·lāte, *a.* [L. *cervicula*, dim. of *cervix*, neck.] having a small or slim neck. [Rare.]

Cẽr′vi·dae, *n.pl.* [from L. *cervus*, a deer.] a family of ruminants, the males generally being antlered.

cẽr′vīne, *a.* [L. *cervinus*, from *cervus*, a deer.]
1. pertaining to the deer, or to animals of the family *Cervidæ*.
2. like a deer.

cẽr′vix, *n.*; *pl.* **cẽr·vī′çēş, cẽr′vix·eş,** [L., neck.]
1. the part between the thorax and the head; the neck, especially the back of the neck.
2. any necklike part or appendage, as of the uterus, urinary bladder, etc.

Cẽr′vus, *n.* [L., a deer.] a genus of ruminants, formerly including all species of deer, now confined to the red deer and related species.

cē′ryl, *n.* [L. *cera*, wax, and *-yl*.] the hypothetical radical of cerotin.
ceryl alcohol; same as *cerotin*.

cē′ṣȧ·rē, *n.* in logic, a mnemonic word designating a syllogism with a universal negative major premise, a universal affirmative minor premise, and a universal negative conclusion; as, x is not y; y is z; therefore x is not z.

Cē·ṣā′rē·ăn, Cē·ṣā′ri·ăn, *a.* and *n.* same as *Caesarean*.

cē′ṣi·ous, *a.* same as *caesious*.

cē′ṣi·um, *n.* [neut. of L. *caesius*, bluish-gray.] a soft, bluish-gray, ductile, metallic chemical element, the most electropositive of all the elements: used in photoelectric cells: symbol, Cs; atomic weight, 132.91; atomic number, 55: also spelled *caesium*.

ces′pi·tine, *n.* [L. *cæspes* (*-itis*), a turf.] an oil distilled from peat.

ces·pi·ti′tious (-tish′us), *a.* [L. *cæspes* (*-itis*), a turf.] pertaining to turf; made of turf.

ces′pi·tōse, *a.* in botany, growing in tufts or clumps; matted.

ces′pi·tōse·ly, *adv.* in a cespitose manner.

ces′pi·tous, *a.* pertaining to turf; turfy; as, a *cespitous* plant.

ces·pit′ū·lōse, *a.* growing in little bunches, as the tufted grasses.

cess, *n.* [for *sess*, from *assess*.] in Ireland, an assessment; a tax on land: now used only in *bad cess to*, meaning "bad luck to."

cess, *v.t.*; cessed (sest), *pt.*, *pp.*; cessing, *ppr.* to levy a tax; to make an assessment: contraction of *assess*. [Obs.]

cess, *v.i.* [ME. *cessen*; OFr. *cesser*; L. *cessare*, to cease.] to relinquish a legal duty. [Obs.]

ces′sănt, *a.* [L. *cessans* (*-antis*), ppr. of *cessare*, to cease.] ceasing; intermittent. [Obs.]

ces·sā′tion, *n.* [L. *cessatio*, from *cessare*, to cease.] a ceasing; a stop; the act of discontinuing motion or action of any kind, whether temporary or final.
a cessation of arms; an armistice or truce agreed to by the commanders of armies.

Syn.—stop, rest, pause, intermission.—*Stop* is the general term; *cessation* is a ceasing from action, either temporary or final; *pause* is a temporary stopping; *rest* is a stopping for the sake of relief or repose; *intermission* is a stopping at intervals to recommence.

ces·sā′vit, *n.* [L., he has ceased; third person sing. perf. ind. act. of *cessare*, to cease.] in law, formerly a writ given by statute, to cover lands, when the tenant or occupier had ceased for two years to perform the service which constituted the condition of his tenure.

ces′sẽr, *n.* [OFr. *cesser*, a ceasing.] a ceasing; a neglect to perform services or make payment for two years.

ces·si·bil′i·ty, *n.* the act of giving way or receding. [Obs.]

ces′si·ble, *a.* giving way; yielding; ready to give way. [Obs.]

ces′sion (sesh′un), *n.* [L. *cessio* (-*onis*), from *cessare*, to yield.]
1. the act of giving way; a yielding to force or impulse. [Obs.]
2. a yielding or surrender, as of property or rights, to another person; particularly, a ceding of territory to another sovereign by treaty.
3. in the civil law, a voluntary surrender of a person's effects to his creditors to avoid imprisonment.
4. in ecclesiastical law, the leaving of a benefice without dispensation.

ces′sion·ā·ry, *a.* having surrendered effects; as, a *cessionary* bankrupt.

ces′sion·ā·ry, *n.*; *pl.* **ces′sion·ā·ries,** the person to whom a cession is made; assignee.

cess′ment, *n.* an assessment or tax. [Obs.]

ces′sŏr, *n.* [L. *cessare*, to cease.]
1. in law, a tenant who neglected, for two years, to perform the service by which he held lands, so that he became liable to the writ of cessavit.
2. an assessor or taxer. [Obs.]

cess′pīpe, *n.* a pipe for draining water from a cesspool or sink.

cess′pit, *n.* [*cess-* (from *cesspool*), and *pit*.] a pit for garbage, excrement, etc.

cess′pool, *n.* 1. a cavity sunk in the earth to receive and retain the drainage and sewage from sinks, toilets, etc.
2. a filthy, smelly place.

cest, *n.* [L. *cestus*, a girdle.] a cestus; the girdle of Venus.

Ces′ti·dae, *n.pl.* an invertebrate family with ribbonlike bodies, the type and only genus of which is *Cestum*.

Ces·tō′dȧ, *n.pl.* [Gr. *kestos*, girdle.] a group of worms of the phylum *Platyhelmintha*, having a flat body containing numerous joints. They have neither mouth nor intestinal canal and are parasitic.

ces′tōde, *a.* having reference to the group of worms *Cestoda*.

ces′tōde, *n.* a member of the *Cestoda*.

ces′toid, *a.* and *n.* same as *cestode*.

Ces·toid′ē·ȧ, *n.pl.* [Gr. *kestos*, girdle, and *eidos*, form.] same as *Cestoda*.

ces·toid′ē·ăn, *n.* same as *cestode*.

Ces·trā′ci·on, *n.* [from Gr. *kestra*, a poleax, a kind of fish.] a genus of heterodont sharks.

ces·trā′ci·ont, *n.* [Gr. *kestra*, a hammer or weapon.] a shark of the now nearly extinct genus *Cestracion* and similar genera, the back teeth of which form a series of plates for crushing the shellfish on which they feed.

ces·trā′ci·ont, *a.* characteristic of the genus *Cestracion*.

ces′trum, *n.*; *pl.* **ces′trȧ,** [L., from Gr. *kestron* from *kentein*, to prick.] in encaustic painting, a metal tool for fusing the wax and fixing the colors.

ces′tui, ces′tuy (ses′twi *or* set′i), *n.* [OFr.] in law, a person; the one; as, *cestui que trust*, one who is a beneficiary of a trust; *cestui que use*, one who has a right to use.

Ces′tum, *n.* [L. *cestus*, a girdle.] in zoology, a genus of *Ctenophora*, the only genus of the family *Cestidæ*. Venus's girdle, *Cestum veneris*, a typical Mediterranean species, is ribbonlike in form and several feet long.

ces′tus, *n.* [L. *caestus*, *cestus*; Gr. *kestos*, a girdle.]
1. a girdle; belt.
2. in Greek and Roman mythology, the girdle of Venus, or marriage girdle, which gave whoever wore it the power to excite love.
3. [C–] in zoology, same as *Cestum*.

ces′tus, caes′tus, *n. sing.* and *pl.* [L. *caestus*, from *caedere*, to strike, beat.] in ancient Rome, a kind of leather band worn on the hands of boxers and often loaded with lead or other metal to give effect to the blows.

VARIOUS FORMS OF CESTUS

ces′tuy (-twi), *n.* same as *cestui*.

cē·ṣū′rȧ (*or* -zū′rȧ), *n.*; *pl.* **cē·ṣū′rȧṣ** or **cē·ṣū′rae,** [L. *cæsura*, from *cædere*, to cut off.] a caesura.

cē·ṣū′răl, *a.* same as *caesural*.

Cē′tȧ, *n.pl.* same as *Cete*.

Cē·tā′cē·ȧ, *n.pl.* [L. *cetus*; Gr. *ketos*, a whale.] an order of mammals of fishlike form, including the whales of the suborders *Mysticete*, or whalebone whales, *Denticete*, embracing the sperm whale and dolphin, and the extinct *Zeuglodontia*.

cē·tā′ceăn (-shăn), *n.* a member of the *Cetacea*.

cē·tā′ceăn, *a.* [from L. *cetus*, large sea animal, whale; Gr. *ketos*.] of a group of hairless, fishlike water mammals with paddlelike forelimbs: whales, porpoises, and dolphins are cetaceans.

cē·tā′ceous, *a.* cetacean.

cē′tāne, *n.* [from L. *cetus*, whale; and *-ane*.] a saturated hydrocarbon of the methane series, $C_{16}H_{34}$, found as a colorless oil in petroleum.

cē′tāne num′bẽr, a number representing the ignition properties of Diesel engine fuel oils, determined by the percentage of cetane that must be mixed with *a*-methylnaphthalene to produce the ignition quality of the fuel being tested: the higher the number, the better the ignition quality.

Cē′tē, *n.pl.* [Gr. *kētē*, *kētea*, pl. of *kētos*, any sea-monster, especially a whale.] the *Cetacea*.

cēte, *n.* a whale. [Obs.]

cē′tēne, *n.* a hydrocarbon product of spermaceti: also called *cetylene*.

cet′e·rach, *n.* [Fr. *ceterac*; It. *cetracca*.] a species of fern found in Europe and western Asia.

ce′te·ris pa′ri·bus, [L.] other things being equal.

cē′tic, *a.* pertaining to whales.
cetic acid; a pearly substance in the form of starlike crystals obtained from spermaceti.

cē′tin, *n.* the main component of spermaceti.

cē·tō·log′ic·ăl, *a.* pertaining to cetology.

cē·tol′ō·gist, *n.* one who studies the whale and related animals.

cē·tol′ō·gy, *n.* [Gr. *kētos*, a whale, and *-logia*, from *legein*, to speak.] the branch of zoology having to do with whales.

cē·trar′ic, *a.* [L. *cetra*, *cætra*, a Spanish shield.] obtained from or pertaining to *Cetraria islandica*, or Iceland moss.

cē·trăr′in, *n.* a compound extracted from several lichens, as *Cetraria islandica* and *Sticta pulmonacea*. It forms a white crystal very bitter to the taste.

Cē′tus, *n.* [L., the whale.] an equatorial constellation south of Pisces and Aries.

cē′tyl, *n.* [L. *cetus*, a whale, and *-yl*.] in chemistry, a radical corresponding in structure to the ethyl compounds. It is formulated as $C_{16}H_{33}$, and is derived from spermaceti.

cē·tyl′ic, *a.* [*cetyl*, and *-ic*.] relating to cetyl; as, *cetylic* acid.
cetylic alcohol; a solid crystalline form of alcohol derived from spermaceti: often called *cetyl alcohol*.

cev·ȧ·dil′lȧ, ceb·ȧ·dil′lȧ, *n.* same as *sabadilla*.

cē·vi·tam′ic ac′id (*or* sē-vi-), in biochemistry, ascorbic acid, $C_6H_8O_6$, or vitamin C: it prevents scurvy.

Cēy·lon·ēṣe′, *a.* relating to the island of Ceylon or its people.

Cēy·lon·ēṣe′, *n. sing.* and *pl.* an inhabitant or the inhabitants of Ceylon.

cēy′lon·īte, *n.* a dingy blue variety of spinel: also called *pleonaste*.

Cēy·lon′ moss, an East Indian seaweed from which agar-agar is made.

chab′ȧ·zīte, chab′ȧ·sīte, *n.* [Fr. *chabazie*, missp. of Gr. *chalazie*, vocative of *chalaza*, hailstone.] a mineral classed with the zeolites, occurring in oblique, glassy crystals (rhombohedrons), having nearly the form of the cube. It is either colorless or tinged with red or a shade of yellow.

Chȧ·blis′ (-blē′), *n.* [Fr.] a very dry, white Burgundy wine: so named because made near Chablis, France.

chä′bouk, chä′buk, *n.* [Hind. *chābuk*, a whip.] a long horsewhip, used in Oriental countries for the infliction of corporal punishment.

Chā′çȧ, *n.* 1. a genus of East Indian catfishes, family *Chacidæ*.
2. [c–] a fish of this genus: also spelled *chaka*.

chāce, *v.* and *n.* chase. [Obs.]

chä·chä·lä′çȧ, *n.* [imitative of the bird's cry.] a gallinaceous bird, the guan, of Texas: also written *chiacalaca*.

chack, *v.t.*; chacked, *pt.*, *pp.*; chacking, *ppr.*
1. to toss or jerk (the head), as a horse does to relieve the strain of the reins. [Obs.]
2. to pinch; bite; crush. [Scot.]

chaç′mȧ, *n.* [native name.] a large species of South African baboon, *Cynocephalus porcarius*: called also the *ursine baboon*.

chȧ·çonne′, *n.* [Fr., from Sp. *chacona*, a dance.]
1. a slow, stately dance of the eighteenth century, similar to the passacaglia and derived from an early Spanish dance.
2. music for this dance, in 3/4 time.
3. a similar movement in various musical compositions.

cha·cun′ à son goût′ (shȧ-kun′ ȧ sōṅ gọọ′), [Fr.] everyone to his own taste.

çhad, *n.* a kind of fish; the shad. [Obs.]

çhaet-, çhae′to-, [from Gr. *chaitē*, long, flowing hair, a mane.] a combining form meaning *hair, a bristle, seta*, as in *chaetognatha*, *chaetiferous*.

çhae′tȧ (kē′tȧ), *n.*; *pl.* **çhae′tae,** [Gr. *chaitē*, hair.] in biology, a bristle, spine, or stiff hair: called also a *seta*.

çhae·tif′ẽr·ous, *a.* [*chæto-*, and L. *ferre*, to bear.] bearing bristles or stiff hairs.

çhae′tō·dont, *n.* [*chæt-*, and Gr. *odous*, *odontose*, a tooth.] a salt-water fish of the family *Chætodontidæ*, having a wide, thin, and brightly colored body.

çhae′tō·dont, *a.* having relation to a chaetodont.

çhae′tog·nath, *n.* one of the *Chætognatha*.

çhae′tog·nath, *a.* having relation to the *Chætognatha*.

Çhae·tog′nȧ·thȧ, *n.pl.* [*chæto-*, and Gr. *gnathos*, jaw.] an order of transparent marine worms of bright color, having cephalic setae. The genus *Sagitta* belongs to this order.

çhae·toph′ō·rous, *a.* [*chæto-*, and Gr. *pherein*, to bear.] bearing stiff hairs, or setae.

çhae′tō·pod, *a.* having relation to the *Chætopoda*.

çhae′tō·pod, *n.* an individual of the *Chætopoda*.

Çhae·top′ō·dȧ, *n.pl.* [*chæto-*, and Gr. *pous*, *podos*, foot.] a large order of earth and marine worms, *Annelida*, having spines on most of their segments. The principal groups are the *Oligochæta* and the *Polychæta*.

çhae′tō·tax·y, *n.* [*chæto-*, and Gr. *taxis*, arrangement.] the arrangement of the bristles of an insect.

chāfe, *v.t.*; chafed, *pt.*, *pp.*; chafing, *ppr.* [ME. *chaufen*; OFr. *chauffer*, to warm; L. *calefacere*, to make warm; *calere*, to be warm, and *facere*, to make.]
1. to heat or stimulate by rubbing; as, to *chafe* the skin.
2. to wear away by rubbing; as, to *chafe* a cable.
3. to excite heat in the mind of; to excite passion in; to inflame; to make angry; to provoke or incense; to annoy; as, her words sorely *chafed* him.
4. to excite violent action in; as, the wind *chafes* the ocean.
5. to irritate or make sore by rubbing.

chāfe, *v.i.* 1. to be excited or heated; to rage; to fret; to be in violent action.

The troubled Tiber *chafing* with his shores.
—Shak.

2. to be worn by rubbing; to rub (often with *on* or *against*; as, a cable *chafes*.
to chafe at the bit; to be impatient; to become angry or irritable because of delay: originally said of horses.

chāfe, *n.* 1. a chafing.
2. violent agitation of the mind or passions; fret; annoyance.
3. wear or damage caused by rubbing.

chāfed (chāft), *a.* heated or irritated by rubbing; worn by friction.

chāf′ẽr, *n.* 1. one who chafes.
2. a small furnace or water heater.
3. a chafing dish. [Obs.]

chāf'ẽr, *n.* [AS. *ceafor, ceafer*; D. *kever,* a beetle, chafer.] any of a group of related beetles that feed on plants, as the cockchafer, scarab, rose bug, etc.

chāf'ẽr·y, *n.* [from *chafe.*] in ironworking, a forge in which the metal is reheated.

chāfe'wax, chaff'wax, *n.* in England, formerly, a chancery officer who prepared the wax for the sealing of documents.

chāfe'weed, *n.* a weed, a species of Gnaphalium: called also *cudweed.*

chȧff, *n.* [ME. *chaf, caffe*; AS. *ceaf,* chaff.]
1. the husk or dry calyx of wheat or other grain: usually applied to the husks when separated from the grain by threshing or winnowing.
2. hay or straw cut small for the food of cattle.
3. refuse; worthless matter, especially that which is light.
4. banter; jesting; good-natured teasing.
5. in botany, dry scales or bracts, as those on the receptacle subtending the flowers in the heads of certain *Compositæ.*

chȧff, *v.i.*; chaffed, *pt., pp.*; chaffing, *ppr.* to banter or jest.

chȧff, *v.t.* to tease or make fun of in a good-natured manner.

chȧff'çut"tẽr, *n.* same as *straw-cutter.*

chȧf'fẽr, *v.i.*; chaffered, *pt., pp.*; chaffering, *ppr.* [ME. *chaffaren, cheffaren,* to bargain, negotiate, from *chaffare, chapfare, cheapfare,* a bargaining, merchandise; *cheap, chep,* a bargain, trade, and *fare,* a going, journey.]
1. to bargain; to haggle; to negotiate; as, to *chaffer* over pennies.
2. to talk idly; to chatter lightly.

chȧf'fẽr, *v.t.* 1. to buy; to exchange; to sell. [Obs.]
2. to bandy (words).

chȧf'fẽr, *n.* 1. merchandise. [Obs.]
2. buying and selling. [Obs.]
3. a haggling over price; a bargaining.

chȧf'fẽr·ẽr, *n.* one who chaffers; a bargainer.

chȧf'fẽr·y, *n.* traffic; buying and selling. [Obs.]

chȧf'finch, *n.* [so called on account of eating *chaff* or grain.] a common European finch (*Fringilla cœlebs*) belonging to the *Fringillidæ,* which is admired for its singing and is often kept in a cage as a pet.

chȧff'ing, *n.* raillery; banter; talk of a jesting character.

chȧff'seed, *n.* a perennial herb, *Schwalbea americana,* bearing seeds with loose seed coverings like chaff: found along the Atlantic coast.

chȧff'weed, *n.* a plant of the genus *Centunculus,* a low annual, common in America and Europe.

chȧff'y, *a.* 1. like chaff; full of chaff; light; as, *chaffy* straws; *chaffy* opinions.
2. in botany, covered with light, dry scales; resembling chaff.
3. worthless.

chāf'ing, *n.* 1. the state of being irritated.
2. the act of rubbing to produce heat, restore circulation, etc.

chāf'ing dish, 1. a dish or vessel for the cooking of food at the table, or for keeping food warm: it is usually set upon a stand furnished with a small heating apparatus.
2. a portable grate for coals.

chāf'ing gēar, among seamen, anything used to protect sails, ropes, etc. from friction.

çhȧ·green', *n.* shagreen. [Obs.]

çhȧ·grin', *n.* [Fr. *chagrin,* grief, sorrow, vexation, from *chagrin,* a kind of roughened leather used for rasping wood.] mortification, disappointment, humiliation, embarrassment, etc. caused by failure or discomfiture.

Syn. — vexation, mortification. — *Vexation* springs from a sense of loss, disappointment, etc.; *mortification* from wounded pride; *chagrin* may spring from either, and is not usually so keen or lasting.

çhȧ·grin', *v.t.*; chagrined, *pt., pp.*; chagrining, *ppr.* to vex; to mortify; to cause to feel chagrin: used chiefly in the passive.

çhȧ·grin', *v.i.* to be vexed or mortified. [Rare.]

çhȧ·grin', *a.* chagrined. [Obs.]

chāin, *n.* [ME. *chaine, cheine*; OFr. *chaine, chæne,* from L. *catena,* a chain.]
1. a flexible series of joined links or rings, usually of some kind of metal; as, a *chain* of gold or of iron. Chains are used often for an ornament about the person; as, a watch *chain.*
2. [*pl.*] that which binds; that which restrains, confines, or fetters; as, a prisoner held in *chains.*
3. bondage; slavery; also, affliction; as, my *chain* is heavy.

In despotism the people sleep soundly in their *chains.* —Ames.

4. a series of things linked together; a series of things connected or following in succession; as, a *chain* of causes, of ideas, or events; a *chain* of mountains.
5. in surveying, an instrument formed of a series of links and used in measuring land. The chain in general use is *Gunter's chain,* which has 100 links, each 7.92 inches in length, making the total length of the chain 66 feet or 4 rods.
6. a land measure of length, etc.: a *linear chain* is 66 feet long, a *square chain* is 16 square rods or one-tenth of an acre.
7. in weaving, the warp.
8. [*pl.*] in shipbuilding and nautical usage, strong links or plates of iron, bolted at the lower end to the ship's side, used to hold the blocks called *dead eyes,* by which the shrouds of the mast are extended: also called the *channel plates* or the *chain plates.*
9. in bacteriology, four or more cells joined end to end.
10. in chemistry, a linkage of atoms in a molecule.

chain cable; a cable made like a chain, usually of iron.

endless chain; a chain having its ends united by a link so as to form a belt usually called a *chain belt*: also applied figuratively to any succession of actions, circumstances, or events without end.

chāin, *v.t.*; chained, *pt., pp.*; chaining, *ppr.*
1. to fasten, bind, or connect with or as with a chain.
2. to enslave; to keep in bondage.
3. to guard with a chain, as a harbor.
4. to unite closely and strongly; to attach.

O Warwick, I do bend my knee with thine,
and in this vow do *chain* my soul to thine. —Shak.

5. in surveying, to measure with a chain.

chāin bear'ẽr, same as *chainman.*

chāin belt, in mechanics, a chain used for transmitting power.

chāin bōat, same as *anchor hoy.*

chāin bōlt, 1. the bolt which fastens the chain plate to the side of the ship.
2. a bolt with a chain attached for withdrawing the bolt.

chāin bond, a chain, bar, or timber, built into masonry to bind it together.

chāin bridġe, a suspension bridge held by chains.

chāin çor'ăl, a fossil coral whose parts are so placed as to resemble the uniformly joined links of a chain.

chāin çoup'ling (kup'), a chain used for a supplementary coupling of railroad cars.

chāin gang, a number of prisoners chained together while working.

chāin hook, a hook for moving chain cables about the deck of a ship.

chāin'less, *a.* 1. having no chain; as, a *chainless* bicycle.
2. incapable of being chained; unfettered.

chāin'let, *n.* a little chain.

chāin let'tẽr, a letter to be circulated among many people by being copied and passed from one to another after it has been read.

chāin līght'ning, lightning that zigzags rapidly across the sky.

chāin māil, flexible armor made of joined metal links.

chāin'măn, *n.*; *pl.* **chāin'men,** 1. a man whose work is to carry or take care of metal chains.
2. either of the two workers needed to use a surveyor's chain.

chāin meaṣ'ūre (mezh'), a system of linear measurement used in surveying, in which 7.92 inches equal one link, 100 links equal one chain, and 80 chains equal one mile.

chāin mōld'ing, a Norman style of architectural molding resembling a chain.

chāin piẽr, a pier extending into the sea and suspended by chains in the manner of a suspension bridge.

chāin plāte, one of the iron plates on the ship's side to which the shrouds are fastened.

chāin pụl'ley, a pulley with depressions and projections on its rim to fit the links of a chain: called also a *sprocket wheel.*

chāin pump, a pump with an endless chain passing over a wheel at the top and entering below the level of the water. It is fitted with disks or buckets by means of which the water is raised.

chāin'-rē·aċt', *v.i.* to be involved in or subjected to a chain reaction.

chāin rē·aç'tion, 1. a series of chemical reactions in which the products of each reaction activate additional molecules of the reactants, thus causing new reactions: it can be started by light, an electric spark, sodium vapor, bombardment with alpha particles from radium, etc.
2. any sequence of events, each of which results in, or has an effect on, the following.

chāin rüle, an arithmetical process used to find the equivalent value of two items of different denominations by means of a chain of equivalent intermediates.

chāin sạw, a portable power saw with an endless chain that carries cutting teeth.

chāin shot, a projectile consisting of two cannon balls or two halves of a cannon ball, connected by a short chain, formerly used in firing into an enemy ship's rigging.

chāin stitch, an ornamental stitch in which the loops are connected in a chainlike way, used in crocheting, etc.; also, a similar stitch made by a sewing machine.

chāin'stitch, *v.t.* to ornament, crochet, or sew with chain stitches.

chāin stōre, any of a group of retail stores owned and controlled by one company, usually with the same merchandise and policy.

chāin tim'bẽr, see *chain bond.*

chāin wāle, a channel (of a ship).

chāin wheel, a sprocket wheel; a chain pulley.

chāin'wŏrk, *n.* 1. work linked together in the fashion of a chain.
2. in sewing, chain-stitch work.

chāir, *n.* [ME. *chaire, chaere*; OFr. *chaiere, chaere,* from L. *cathedra,* Gr. *kathedra,* a seat.]
1. a seat, usually movable, for a single person, with a back and with or without arms.
2. a seat of justice or of authority; as, a *chair* of state.
3. an office or position of authority, as a professorship or a judgeship.
4. the seat for a speaker or presiding officer of a public council or assembly; as, the speaker's *chair*; also, by metonymy, the speaker himself; as, to address the *chair.*
5. the electric chair; also, execution by this means.
6. a sedan; a covered chair on poles borne by men.
7. a two-wheeled carriage; a gig. [Obs.]
8. an iron block used to support and secure the rails of a railway track.

curule chair; an ivory seat used by the highest magistrates of ancient Rome.

chāir, *v.t.*; chaired, *pt., pp.*; chairing, *ppr.* 1. to place in a chair; to seat.
2. to carry publicly in a chair in triumph. [Chiefly Brit.]
3. to place in authority.

chāir çär, a railroad car with individual chairs; parlor car; distinguished from *coach, sleeping car,* etc.

chāir'lift, *n.* a number of seats suspended from a power-driven endless cable, used especially to carry skiers up a mountain slope.

chāir'măn, *n.*; *pl.* **chāir'men,** 1. the presiding officer of an assembly, committee, etc.
2. one who carries or wheels people in a chair.

chāir'măn·ship, *n.* 1. the office of a chairman or presiding officer.
2. the term of office of a chairman.

chāir'pẽr"sŏn, *n.* [*chair* and *person.*] a person who presides at a meeting or heads a committee, board, etc.

chāir'wom"ăn (-woom"), *n.*; *pl.* **chāir'wom"en** (-wim"), a woman who presides at a meeting or heads a committee, board, etc.

çhāiṣe (shāz), *n.* [Fr. *chaise,* a seat or chair.]
1. any of several kinds of lightweight carriage, some with a collapsible top, having two or four wheels and drawn by one or two horses.
2. a gold coin current in France from 1346 to 1430, varying in value at different periods.

çhāiṣe lọngue (shāz lọng), *n.* [Fr., lit., long chair.] an elongated seat or couch with a support for the back at one end and a seat long enough for the outstretched legs.

chä'jä (chä'hä), *n.* [Braz.] the crested screamer.

çhä'kȧ, *n.* same as *chaca.*

çhȧ·lā'zȧ, *n.*; *pl.* **çhȧ·lā'zȧṣ, çhȧ·lā'zae,** [Gr. *chalaza,* hail, pimple.]
1. in botany, that part of the ovule or seed where the outer coverings join with each other and with the nucleus.
2. in zoology, either of the two membranous twisted cords which bind the yolk bag of an egg to the lining membrane at the two end of the shell.

çhȧ·lā′zăl, *a.* of a chalaza; as, the *chalazal* end of an ovule.

çhȧ·lā′zi·ȧ, *n.* pl. of *chalazion.*

çhal·ȧ·zif′ẽr·ous, *a.* chalaza-bearing; as, the *chalaziferous* membrane.

çhȧ·lā′zi·on, çhȧ·lā′zi·um, *n.*; *pl.* **çhȧ·lā′zi·ȧ,** [Gr. *chalazion*, dim. of *chalaza*, hail, a pimple.] a small tumor on the eyelid.

çhal·çan′thīte, *n.* [L. *chalcanthum*; Gr. *chalkanthon*, a solution of blue vitriol; *chalkos*, bronze, and *anthos*, flower.] copper sulfate, or blue vitriol.

çhal·cē·don′iç, *a.* pertaining to chalcedony.

çhal·ced′ō·ny (*or* kal′se-dō-ny), *n.* [L. *chalcedonius*; Gr. *chalkēdōn*, a precious stone found at *Chalkēdōn*, a Greek town in Asia Minor.] a cryptocrystalline, translucent variety of quartz, having a luster nearly like wax. It is usually grayish or milky colored and comprises onyx, agate, sard, cat's eye, jasper, carnelian, and chrysoprase: also written *calcedony.*

çhal·ced′ō·nyx, *n.* a variety of agate in which white and gray layers alternate.

chal·chi·huītl′ (-wētl′), *n.* [Mex.] turquoise.

çhal′cid, *n.* [from Mod. L. *Chalcis*, name of the typical genus of the family *Chalcididæ*, from Gr. *chalkos*, copper: so named because of their metallic color.] any of a large group of very small insects, either four-winged or wingless, whose larvae are parasitic on the eggs, larvae, or pupae of other insects: also *chalcid fly.*

çhal′cid, *n.* a chalcidian.

çhal′cid, *a.* of the chalcids.

çhal·cid′i·ăn, *n.* [L. *chalcis*; Gr. *chalkis*, a lizard.] a lizard of the tropical family *Chalcididæ*, characterized by rudimentary legs and a snakelike body.

çhal·cid′i·ăn, *a.* 1. relating to the *Chalcididæ*.
2. [C–] relating to the city Chalcis or to its inhabitants.

çhal·cid′i·ăn, *n.* 1. an individual of the *Chalcididæ*.
2. [C–] a native or resident of the Greek city Chalcis, in Euboea.
Chalcidian alphabet; the alphabet from which the Roman alphabet is derived, being that of the Chalcidians, who came from Chalcis, in Euboea, and formed colonies in Sicily and adjacent parts of Italy.

çhal·cid′i·çum, *n.*; *pl.* **çhal·cid′i·çȧ,** [L. *chalcidicum*; Gr. *chalkidikos*, from *Chalkis*, a Greek city.] in ancient Rome, an entrance in the form of a room or porch; also, a vestibule to a basilica or to a modern church.

Çhal·cid′i·dae, *n.pl.* [Gr. *chalkis*, a kind of lizard, from *chalkos*, bronze.]
1. a parasitic family of insects, the members of which attach themselves chiefly to the larvae or eggs of insects. Their bodies are hard and have brilliant metallic colors.
2. a family of lizards found chiefly in tropical America, including various species.

çhal′çō-, [from Gr. *chalkos*, copper, brass.] a combining form meaning *copper* or *brass*, as in *chalc*ocite.

çhal′çō·cīte, *n.* [Gr. *chalkos*, bronze.] a vitreous crystalline mineral copper sulfide, Cu_2S.

çhal·çog′rȧ·phẽr, çhal·çog′rȧ·phist, *n.* an engraver on copper and brass.

çhal·çō·graph′iç, *a.* of or having the nature of chalcography.

çhal·çog′rȧ·phy, *n.* [Gr. *chalkos*, bronze, and *-graphia*, from *graphein*, to write, engrave.] the act or art of engraving on copper or brass, particularly for printing purposes.

çhal·çō·pyr′īte, *n.* [Gr. *chalkos*, bronze, and *pyritēs*, from *pyr*, fire.] a yellow crystalline compound of copper, iron, and sulfur, $CuFeS_2$; copper pyrites.

çhal·çō·stib′īte, *n.* [Gr. *chalkos*, bronze, and *stibi*, antimony.] a lead-gray mineral compound of sulfur, antimony, and copper: called also *wolfsbergite* from its occurrence at Wolfsberg in the Harz mountains.

Çhal·dā′iç, *a.* and *n.* Chaldean.

Çhal′dā·ism, *n.* an idiom or peculiarity of Chaldean.

Çhal·dē′ăn, *n.* [L. *Chaldaeus*; Gr. *Chaldaios*.]
1. a native or inhabitant of Chaldea; a member of a Semitic people related to the Babylonians.
2. an astrologer or sorcerer.
3. the Semitic language of the Chaldeans.

Çhal·dē′ăn, *a.* 1. of Chaldea, its people, their language, or culture: astrology and magic flourished in Chaldea.
2. having to do with astrology or occult lore.

Çhal′dee, *a.* and *n.* 1. Chaldean.
2. formerly and erroneously, Biblical Aramaic.

chal′dẽr, *n.* 1. a dry measure of capacity, formerly used in Scotland.
2. a chaldron. [Brit.]

chal′drick, *n.* a bird with red feet and bill and black-and-white plumage, called *oyster catcher* from its feeding upon small mollusks.

chal′drŏn, *n.* [OFr. *chaldron*; L. *caldaria*, a pot for boiling, from *caldus*, hot.] a unit of dry measure variously equal to 32, 36, or more bushels, formerly used in England for measuring coal, coke, etc.

çhȧ·let′ (-lā′), *n.* 1. a Swiss herdsman's summer hut in the mountains.
2. a Swiss summer cottage with overhanging eaves.
3. any country cottage built in the Swiss style.

chal′ice, *n.* [OFr. *chalice, calice*; L. *calix* (*-icis*), a cup.]
1. a drinking cup; goblet; particularly, a communion cup.
2. a cup-shaped flower.

chal′ice cell, same as *goblet cell.*

chal′iced, *a.* 1. held in a chalice.
2. cup-shaped: said of a flower.

chal′ice veil, a covering for the communion chalice, made of silk or other fine material, and of a different color for each of the ecclesiastical seasons.

CHALICE

çhal·i·çō′sis, *n.* a disease of the lungs, caused by inhaling stone dust.

chalk (chąk), *n.* [ME. *chalk*; AS. *cealc*, chalk, lime; L. *calx, calcis*, limestone, chalk.]
1. a calcareous earthy substance, of an opaque white color, soft, and easily pulverized. It is a variety of limestone, calcium carbonate ($CaCO_3$), and composed mainly of small sea shells.
2. a piece of chalk, often colored, used for writing or drawing on a blackboard, etc.
3. any chalklike substance.
4. a score; tally; reckoning, as of credit.
French chalk; soapstone or steatite, a soft magnesian mineral used by tailors, etc. for marking on cloth, or for removing grease stains.
to walk a chalk line; to prove one's sobriety by walking straight along a chalk mark without staggering; hence, to keep in the line of strict discipline or propriety.

chalk, *v.t.*; chalked (chąkt), *pt., pp.*; chalking, *ppr.* 1. to rub with chalk; to smear with chalk.
2. to fertilize (soil) with chalk; to lime.
3. to bleach; to make white or pale by the use of chalk.
4. to write or draw with chalk.
to chalk out; to lay out, draw out, or describe, as with chalk; as, *to chalk out* a plan of procedure.

chalk′cut″tẽr, *n.* one who digs chalk.

chalk′i·ness, *n.* the state or quality of being chalky.

chalk līne, a cord covered or rubbed with chalk so that when held taut and snapped against any surface it will leave a straight line on it; also, the mark so made.

chalk pit, a pit in which chalk is dug.

chalk′stōne, *n.* 1. in medicine, a chalklike concretion in the joints of persons with gout.
2. a lump of chalk.

chalk tąlk, a lecture accompanied with explanatory diagrams, etc. drawn in chalk on a blackboard.

chalk′y, *a.* 1. resembling chalk; as, a *chalky* texture.
2. white with chalk; consisting of chalk; as, *chalky* cliffs.
3. impregnated with chalk; as, *chalky* water.

chal′lenġe, *n.* [ME. *chalenge*; OFr. *chalenge, chalonge, calenge, calonge*, an accusation, claim, dispute; L. *calumnia*, a false accusation.]
1. a calling upon one to take part in a fight, contest, etc.; an invitation or summons, verbal or written, to decide a controversy, as by a duel.
2. a calling into question, as of a claim.
3. a demand for identification; as, the sentry gave the *challenge.*
4. an exception to a vote or to someone's right to vote.
5. a claim or demand.
6. among hunters, the opening and crying of hounds at first finding the scent of their game.
7. in law, a formal objection or exception; the claim of a party that certain jurors shall be disqualified, as for bias, from sitting in trial upon him or his cause.

chal′lenġe, *v.t.*; challenged, *pt., pp.*; challenging, *ppr.* [ME. *chalengen*; OFr. *chalengier*; L. *calumniari*, to attack with false accusations.]
1. to call, invite, or summon to a contest, controversy, debate, or similar affair; especially, to invite to a duel.
2. to claim; to demand; as, truth *challenges* our admiration.
3. to accuse; to call to answer; to censure. [Obs.]
4. in military usage, to demand the identification of.
5. to object to (a person or thing); to take exception to; to question; as, to *challenge* the accuracy of a solution or demonstration.
6. in law, to take formal exception to; as, to *challenge* a juror.
7. to take exception to (a vote) as not being valid or (a person at the polls) as not being legally qualified to vote.

chal′lenġe, *v.i.* 1. to make known a right. [Obs.]
2. to make, utter, or issue a challenge.
3. in hunting, to cry when the scent of game is first discovered: said of a hound.
Syn.—defy, summon, dare, question, brave.

chal′lenġe·ȧ·ble, *a.* liable or subject to challenge.

chal′len·ġẽr, *n.* one who challenges.

çhal′lis, çhal′lie, çhal′ly (shal′ly), *n.* [Fr.] a fine fabric of wool, woolen mixture, or cotton and rayon, used for dresses.

çhä′lon, *n.* a coverlet; a blanket. [Obs.]

çhal′ōne, *n.* [Gr. *chalōn*, ppr. of *chalein*, to slacken, relax.] an internal secretion that reduces, restrains, or arrests the activity of various organs of the body.

çhȧ·lụ·meau′ (-mō′), *n.* [Fr.]
1. (a) an obsolete double-reed wind instrument of the oboe family; (b) an obsolete single-reed wind instrument, forerunner of the clarinet.
2. the lowest register of the modern clarinet.

chä·lụtz′ (khä-), *n.*; *pl.* **chä·lụtz·īm′,** [Heb.] a halutz.

Çhȧ·lyb′ē·ăn, *a.* pertaining to the Chalybes, an ancient people of Asia noted as workers in iron and steel.

çhȧ·lyb′ē·āte, *a.* [L. *chalybs*; Gr. *chalyps* (*-ybos*), steel: so called from the *Chalybes*.]
1. containing salts of iron; as, *chalybeate* waters.
2. tasting like iron.

çhȧ·lyb′ē·āte, *n.* any medicine or liquid in which iron is contained in solution.

çhȧ·lyb′ē·ous, *a.* looking like tempered steel; steel-blue.

çhal′y·bīte, *n.* an iron ore consisting chiefly of carbonate of iron; siderite.

çham, *n.* a sovereign of Tartary; a khan. [Archaic.]

cham, *v.t.* and *v.i.* champ. [Obs.]

çhȧ·māde′, *n.* [Fr., from It. *chiamata*, from *chiamare*; L. *clamare*, to call out.] in military usage, a signal for an armistice or retreat, sounded on a trumpet or drum. [Archaic.]

Çham·ae·cyp′ȧ·ris, *n.* [Gr. *chamai*, on the ground, and *kyparissos*, cypress.] a genus of trees of the pine family, valuable for their wood: *Chamæcyparis thyoides*, the common white cedar, and *Chamæcyparis nutkaensis*, the yellow or Alaska cedar, are species of the genus.

Çhȧ·mae′rops, *n.* [L., from Gr. *chamairhōps*; *chamai*, on the ground, and *rhōps*, a bush, shrub.] a genus of palms consisting of dwarf trees with fan-shaped leaves borne on prickly petioles. They are natives of the northern hemisphere. The leaves are used in making hats, baskets, etc.

çhä′măl, *n.* [native name.] the angora goat.

chām′bẽr, *n.* [ME. *chamber*; OFr. *chambre, cambre*; LL. *camera*, a chamber, room; L. *camera*; Gr. *kamara*, anything with an arched cover, a vault.]
1. a room in a house, especially a sleeping room; a bedroom.
2. [*pl.*] furnished rooms hired for residence in the house of another; lodgings. [Brit.]
A bachelor life in *chambers.* —Thackeray.
3. the place where an assembly meets; an assembly hall; also, a legislative or judicial body; as, the senate *chamber.*
4. a compartment or enclosed space; a hol-

low or cavity in the body of an animal or plant; as, the *chamber* of the eye; the *chamber* of a flower.

And all the secret of the Spring
Moved in the *chambers* of the blood.
—Tennyson.

5. [*pl.*] a room where professional men, as lawyers, conduct their business; especially, the judge's office located near the courtroom.

6. an airtight room or a hollow part of an instrument or mechanism, as, (a) the space between the gates of a canal lock; (b) the part of a pump in which the bucket or plunger works; (c) that part of a firearm which holds the charge; (d) a receiver for cartridges in a revolver; (e) a fixing room for printed fabrics.

7. a cavity in a mine, generally of a cubical form, where the powder is confined.

8. a chamber pot.

chamber of commerce; an association to protect the interests of business, chosen from among the merchants and business men of a city.

to sit at chambers; to transact business in chambers: said of a judge.

chām'bẽr, *v.i.*; chambered, *pt., pp.*; chambering, *ppr.* 1. to reside in or occupy a chamber. [Obs.]

2. to be wanton; to indulge in lewdness or licentiousness. [Obs.]

chām'bẽr, *v.t.* 1. to shut up in, or as in, a chamber. [Archaic.]

2. to make chambers in, as a gun.

chām'bẽr çon'cẽrt, a concert of chamber music.

chām'bẽr çoun'cil, private or secret council.

chām'bẽr çoun'sel·ŏr, chām'bẽr çoun'sel, a counsel or person learned in the law who gives his opinion in private, but does not plead cases in court. [Brit.]

chām'bẽred, *a.* provided with a chamber or chambers; as, a *chambered* shell.

chām'bẽr·ẽr, *n.* 1. a gallant. [Rare.]

2. a chambermaid. [Obs.]

chām'bẽr fel'lōw, one who sleeps in the same apartment as another; a roommate.

chām'bẽr hang'ings, tapestry or hangings for a chamber.

chām'bẽr·ing, *n.* wanton behavior; lewdness. [Obs.]

chām'bẽr·lain (-lin), *n.* [OFr. *chamberlain*; LL. *camarlingus, camerlengus*; O.H.G. *chamarlinc, chamarling*, from *chamara*, a chamber; L. *camera*, a vault.]

1. a person charged with the direction and management of the household of a ruler or lord; a steward.

2. a chambermaid at an inn. [Obs.]

3. a high officer in certain royal courts.

4. a treasurer; as, the *chamberlain* of a municipality.

chām'bẽr·lain·ship, *n.* the position of a chamberlain.

chām'bẽr lȳe, *n.* urine. [Obs.]

chām'bẽr·māid, *n.* 1. a woman who has the care of chambers, making the beds, and cleaning the rooms, as in a hotel.

2. a lady's attendant. [Obs.]

chām'bẽr mū'şiç, musical compositions suitable for performance in a room or small hall, as opposed to a concert hall.

chām'bẽr pot, a portable container kept in a bedroom and used as a toilet.

Çhām·ber·tin' (shäṅ-ber-taṅ'), *n.* a red Burgundy wine, named after the place where the grapes from which it is made grow.

çham'brāy, *n.* [Fr., from *Cambray*, a town in France where it was made.] a kind of gingham or plain-colored dress goods, made by weaving white cotton threads across a colored warp.

çham'brel, *n.* same as *gambrel*.

çhȧ·mē'lē·ŏn, *n.* [L. *chamæleon*; Gr. *chamaileōn*; *chamai*, on the ground, and *leōn*, lion.]

1. a lizard of the genus *Chamæleo*, having a

CHAMELEON

prehensile tail, four feet suited for grasping branches, and the eyes covered by a single circular eyelid with an aperture in the center. The best known species is *Chamæleo africanus* or *Chamæleo vulgaris*, a native of Africa. The faculty which the chameleon possesses of changing its color is due to the presence of clear or pigment-bearing contractile cells placed at various depths in the skin, their contractions and dilatations being controlled by the nervous system.

2. a changeable or fickle person.

chameleon mineral; potassium manganate, produced by fusing oxide of manganese with niter or potash. When dissolved in water it assumes a variety of colors, changing from green to blue, purple, and red.

çhȧ·mē·lē·on'iç, *a.* like a chameleon; changeable; fickle.

çhȧ·mē'lē·ŏn·īze, *v.t.* to change into various colors. [Rare.]

cham'fẽr, *n.* [Fr. *chanfrein*, a chamfer.]

1. in carpentry, a small groove or furrow cut in wood or other hard material.

2. a bevel or slope; the flat surface created by slicing off the square edge or corner of a block of wood, stone, etc.

cham'fẽr, *v.t.*; chamfered, *pt., pp.*; chamfering, *ppr.* 1. in carpentry, to cut a groove in; to flute; to channel.

2. to cut or grind in a sloping manner, as the edge of anything square, so as to form a chamfer or bevel.

cham'frain (-frin), *n.* same as *chamfron*.

cham'fret, *n.* and *v.* chamfer. [Obs.]

cham'frŏn, *n.* [OFr. *chamfrein*, chamfron.] in medieval times, defensive armor for the forepart of the head of a war horse: written also *chamfrain*.

chä·mi·sal', *n.* [Sp. Am.] a thicket of chamiso.

chȧ·mi'sō, *n.* [Sp. Am.] a small, close, densely growing shrub, *Adenostoma fasciculatum*, of the rose family.

cham'let, *n.* camlet. [Obs.]

çham'ois (sham'i), *n.*; *pl.* **çham'ois,** [Fr. *chamois*; Sp. *camuza, gamuza*; from O.H.G. *gamz*, chamois.]

1. a species of small, goatlike antelope, *Antilope rupicapra* or *Rupricapra tragus*, inhabiting mountains in Europe and the west of Asia. Its size is about that of a goat, and it is so agile that it can clear at a bound crevices sixteen or eighteen feet wide.

2. a soft leather made from various skins dressed with fish oil: so called because first prepared from the skin of the *chamois*: spelled also *chammy, shammy*.

çham'ois, *v.t.*; chamoised, *pt., pp.*; chamoising, *ppr.* 1. to prepare like a chamois skin.

2. to dry or polish with a chamois skin.

çham'ois, *a.* 1. made of chamois.

2. fawn-colored.

çham·oi·sette' (sham-i-zet'), *n.* [from *chamois*.] a close-woven cotton cloth used for gloves: a trade-mark (*Chamoisette*).

çham'ō·mīle, *n.* same as *camomile*.

Chä·mor'rō, *n.* 1. *pl.* **Chä·mor'rōş,** a member of one of the native tribes of Guam and the Marianas Islands.

2. the Indonesian language spoken by the Chamorros.

champ, *v.t.* and *v.i.*; champed, *pt., pp.*; champing, *ppr.* [OE. *cham*, to chew; connected with Sw. dial. *kämsa*, to chew.]

1. to bite down hard and restlessly; as, a horse *champs* the bit.

2. to bite into small pieces; to chew; to masticate; to munch.

champ, *n.* the act of champing; noisy chewing.

champ, *n.* a champion. [Slang.]

champ, champe, *n.* [Fr. *champ*, from L. *campus*, a field.] the field or ground, as of a shield, on which carving is raised.

cham'paç, *n.* [Hind. *campak*, from Sans. *campaka*.] an Indian tree of the magnolia family, with fragrant, yellow flowers: also spelled *champak*.

çham·pāgne' (-pān'), *n.* [from *Champagne*, an old province of France.]

1. originally, any of various wines, sparkling or still, white or red, produced in Champagne, France.

2. now, any highly effervescent, white wine, the effervescence being caused by fermentation in the bottle and the consequent generation of carbon dioxide: regarded as a symbol of luxurious living.

çham·pāign' (-pān'), *a.* [OFr. *champaigne*, from *campaigne*, from L. *campus*, a field.]

1. flat; open; level.

2. having to do with flat, open country.

çham·pāign', *n.* 1. a broad expanse of plain.

2. flat, open country.

cham'pak, *n.* same as *champac*.

cham'pȧr·ty, *a.* same as *champerty*.

champ'ẽr, *n.* one who champs, or bites.

cham'pẽr·tŏr, *n.* one who is guilty of champerty.

cham'pẽr·tŏus, *a.* in law, of the nature of, or having to do with, champerty.

cham'pẽr·ty, *n.* [Fr. *champart*, field rent, from L. *campi pars*; *campi*, genit. of *campus*, a field, and *pars, partis*, a part.]

1. in law, an illegal agreement with a litigating party to meet the expense of a suit for a share in the proceeds.

2. joint power; partnership in authority. [Obs.]

çham·pi'gnŏn (-pin'yŏn), *n.* [Fr., from L. *campus*, a field.] the common edible mushroom.

cham'pi·ŏn, *n.* [OFr. *champion*; LL. *campio* (-*onis*), a gladiator; from L. *campus*, a field, place for games.]

1. one who comes forward in defense of another or for a cause; one who defends or maintains; a protector or vindicator.

2. the victor having acknowledged superiority in certain matters; a winner of first place or first prize in a competition.

3. a valiant fighter.

cham'pi·ŏn, *a.* holding superiority or first prize over all competitors.

cham'pi·ŏn, *v.t.*; championed, *pt., pp.*; championing, *ppr.* 1. to challenge to a combat. [Obs.]

2. to maintain or support, as a cause or individual; to protect; to defend.

cham'pi·ŏn·ship, *n.* 1. a championing; defending or supporting.

2. the position or title of a champion.

3. the period of time that a champion keeps his title.

Çham·plāin', *n.* [named from the beds near Lake *Champlain*.] the epoch that followed the glacial epoch; also, the deposits made at that time.

champ·le·vé' (shamp-le-vā'), *n.* [Fr., pp. of *champlever*; *champ*, a surface, and *lever*, to lift.] a style of enamel having part or all of the pattern cut out of the surface; also, the process of so enameling.

chȧnce, *n.* [ME. *chance, chaunce*; OFr. *cheance*, a chance, risk; LL. *cadentia*, that which falls out; L. *cadens* (-*entis*), ppr. of *cadere*, to fall.]

1. apparent absence of cause or design; destiny; fortune: often personified; as, *chance* could not rule the world.

2. a happening; fortuitous event; accident; as, to meet a person by *chance*.

That power
Which erring men call *chance*. —Milton.

3. the way things turn out.

4. possibility of an occurrence; uncertainty; hazard; risk; gamble.

I would set my life on any *chance*. —Shak.

5. possibility; the ratio of probability of a thing happening to its not happening; as, in drawing from a pack of cards there is one *chance* in fifty-two of drawing a given card.

6. opportunity; favorable circumstances; as, now is my *chance*.

7. a share in a lottery.

8. a mishap; a mischance. [Archaic.]

Syn.—accident, fortuity, hazard, fortune, casualty, luck.

chȧnce *v.i.*; chanced, *pt., pp.*; chancing, *ppr.* to happen; to come or arrive without design or cause.

Ah, Casca, tell us what hath *chanced* to-day.
—Shak.

chȧnce, *v.t.* to risk or hazard.

chȧnce, *a.* happening by chance; accidental, as, a *chance* comer.

chȧnce, *adv.* by chance.

chȧnce'ȧ·ble, *a.* accidental; fortuitous. [Obs.]

chȧnce'ȧ·bly, *adv.* casually; by chance. [Obs.]

chȧnce'fụl, *a.* 1. eventful.

2. dependent on chance. [Archaic.]

3. risky. [Archaic.]

chȧn'cel, *n.* [OFr. *chancel, cancel*; LL. *cancellus*, a chance; L. *cancelli*, pl., lattices, crossbars.] the part of a church between the altar and the railing that usually encloses it, or the portion where the altar is placed, reserved for the clergy; sometimes enclosed with lattices or rails.

chancel aisle; the aisle on either side of or around the chancel.

chancel arch; the arch spanning the main opening leading to the chancel.

chancel casement; the main window in a chancel.

chancel table; the communion table.

chȧn'cel·lẽr·y, *n.*; *pl.* **chȧn'cel·lẽr·ieş,** chancellorship; the rank or position of a chancellor.

chȧn′cel·lŏr, *n.* [OFr. *chanceler*; LL. *cancellarius*, a chancellor, an officer in charge of records who stood behind latticework; L. *cancelli*, latticework.]

1. a chief judge of a court of chancery or equity in some States of the United States.

2. originally, a chief secretary under the Roman emperors; but, in later times, a high official invested with judicial powers, and particularly with the superintendence of all letters and other official writings of a monarch, as in Great Britain.

3. the chief secretary of an embassy, consulate, etc.

4. the title of the head or president in some universities.

5. the prime minister in certain countries; as, Bismarck was *chancellor* of Germany.

chancellor of a bishop or *of a diocese*; the vicar general to the bishop, who holds his courts and directs and assists him in matters of ecclesiastical law.

chancellor of a cathedral; an officer who arranges the celebration of religious services, hears lessons, lectures in the church, keeps the books, etc.

Chancellor of the Exchequer; the highest finance minister of the British government and a member of the Cabinet.

The Lord High Chancellor of Great Britain, or *Keeper of the Great Seal*; the highest officer of the crown, and after the princes of the blood royal the first lay subject. He is a cabinet minister and privy councilor and presiding officer of the House of Lords. He appoints all justices of the peace and is judge of the High Court of Chancery.

chan′cel·lŏr·ship, *n.* the office of a chancellor; also, the time during which one is chancellor.

chȧnce′-med·ley, *n.* [from *chance* and *medley*; OFr. *meslee*, a fray, a melee or mellay.]

1. in law, originally, a casual affray or riot, accompanied with violence, and without deliberate or preconceived malice; now, accidental homicide; unpremeditated manslaughter, as in self-defense.

2. haphazard action.

chȧn′cẽr, *v.t.*; chancered, *pt., pp.*; chancering, *ppr.* to judge or settle equitably, as in a court of chancery. [Obs.]

chȧn′cẽr·y, *n.* [contr. from *chancelery*; OFr. *chancellerie*; LL. *cancellaria*, a chancery court, record office of a chancellor.]

1. in the United States, a court of equity, as distinguished from a common-law court; a court having jurisdiction in cases of rights, recognized and protected by municipal jurisprudence, where a plain and adequate remedy cannot be obtained in courts of common law; also, equity or proceedings in equity.

2. in England, formerly the highest court of justice next to Parliament, but since 1873 a division of the High Court of Justice, presided over by the Lord High Chancellor of England.

3. a court of record; office of public archives.

4. a chancellery.

in chancery; (a) in process of litigation in a court of equity; (b) in wrestling, having the head of an opponent under one's arm and against one's chest.

Inns of Chancery; see under *inn*.

çhañ′çre (-kẽr), *n.* [Fr.] a venereal sore or ulcer; an initial syphilitic lesion.

hard chancre; a venereal ulcer that is the primary lesion of syphilis.

soft chancre; a chancroid.

çhañ′çroid, *n.* a non-syphilitic venereal ulcer characterized by local glandular involvement, and often suppuration.

çhañ′çrous, *a.* ulcerous; having the qualities of a chancre.

chȧn′cy, *a.*; *comp.* chancier; *superl.* chanciest,

1. lucky. [Scot.]

2. risky; uncertain. [Colloq.]

chan·de·liēr′, *n.* [Fr. *chandelier*; Pr. *candelier*; LL. *candelarius*; L. *candela*, a candle.]

1. a branching fixture, often ornamental in design, suspended from a ceiling to support lights: it may be equipped to hold candles or lamps, or have fixtures for the burning of gas or for electric lights.

2. in fortification, a movable parapet, serving to support fascines to cover pioneers. [Obs.]

chȧn·delle′, *n.* [Fr., lit. Roman candle.] in aviation, a very sudden and steep climb and turn executed simultaneously.

chan′dlẽr, *n.* [ME. *chandeler*; OFr. *chandelier*; LL. *candelarius*, a candle maker; a candlestick; L. *candela*, a candle.]

1. one who makes or sells candles.

2. a retailer of supplies and groceries; as, a ship *chandler* sells provisions for ships.

chan′dlẽr·ly, *adv.* like a chandler. [Obs.]

chan′dlẽr·y, *n.* 1. a warehouse or storeroom for candles and other small wares.

2. the merchandise, business, or warehouse of a chandler.

chan·dọọ′, *n.* [Malay.] a preparation of opium used by the Chinese for smoking.

chan′dry, *n.* a place where candles are kept.

chan′frin, *n.* 1. the fore part of a horse's head.

2. chamfron.

chānġe, *v.t.*; changed, *pt., pp.*; changing, *ppr.* [ME. *changen*; OFr. *changier*; LL. *cambiare*, from L. *cambire*, to exchange, barter.]

1. to cause to turn or pass from one state to another; to alter or make different; to vary in external form or in essence; as, to *change* the shape of a thing.

2. to substitute another thing or things for; to shift; as, to *change* one suit of clothes for another.

3. to give or receive the equivalent of (a coin or banknote) in currency of other, especially lower, denominations.

4. to give and take reciprocally; to barter; to exchange.

> Those thousands with whom thou would'st not *change* thy fortune and condition.
> —Jer. Taylor.

to change hands; to change ownership.

to change one's tune; to change one's attitude or manner. [Colloq.]

chānġe, *v.i.* 1. to be altered; to become different; to undergo variation; to be partially or wholly transformed; as, men sometimes *change* for the better.

2. to pass from one phase to another, as the moon.

3. to leave one train, bus, etc. and board another.

4. to put on other clothes.

5. to make an exchange.

Syn.—alter, vary, innovate, diversify, shift.

chānġe, *n.* 1. any variation or alteration in form, state, quality, or essence; or, a passing from one state or form to another; as, a *change* of countenance; a *change* of habits.

> The sky is changed! And such a *change!*
> —Byron.

2. variety.

3. a succession of one thing in the place of another; as, a *change* of seasons.

4. the beginning of a new monthly revolution; the passing from one phase to another; as, a *change* of the moon.

5. [*pl.*] in mathematics, alteration in the order of a series; permutations.

6. that which is or may be substituted for another; as, a *change* of clothing.

7. small coins; also, any equivalent sum in smaller denominations, given for money of larger denominations.

8. money given to a purchaser as the difference between the price of what he is buying and the larger amount of money that he has given in payment.

9. a place where merchants and others meet to transact business; a building appropriated for mercantile transactions; an exchange: sometimes erroneously written *'change.*

10. exchange. [Obs.]

> Give us a prince of the blood in *change* of him.
> —Shak.

11. a public house; a change house. [Scot.]

> They call an ale house a *change.* —Burt.

12. a round in dancing; as, the first *change* of a quadrille.

13. [*usually pl.*] in bell ringing, any pattern or order in which the bells are rung.

14. in music, modulation; shift of key.

change of life; the time in a woman's life when menstruation permanently ceases; the menopause.

to ring the changes on; to present (a subject) with variations, and in a prolix manner.

Syn.—variety, variation, alteration, modification, deviation, transformation, mutation, transition, vicissitude, innovation, novelty, transmutation, revolution, reverse.

chānġe·ȧ·bil′i·ty, *n.* changeableness.

chānġe′ȧ·ble, *a.* 1. liable to change; subject to alteration; fickle; inconstant; mutable; variable; as, a person of a *changeable* mind.

2. having the quality of undergoing alteration of external appearance; as, *changeable* silk.

Syn.—fickle, inconsistent, mutable, uncertain, unstable, unsteady, variable, wavering, whimsical.

chānġe′ȧ·ble·ness, *n.* the quality of being changeable; fickleness; inconstancy.

chānġe′ȧ·bly, *adv.* inconstantly.

chānġe′fụl, *a.* full of change; changing or tending to change; inconstant; mutable.

chānġe′fụl·ly, *adv.* in a changeful manner.

chānġe′fụl·ness, *n.* the state of being changeful.

chānġe′less, *a.* unchanging; constant; not admitting alteration.

chānġe′less·ness, *n.* the state of being changeless.

chānġe′ling, *n.* 1. a child secretly put in the place of another.

2. any ugly, queer, idiotic, or bad-tempered child, superstitiously explained away as being a substitute left by the fairies for a child stolen by them.

3. an idiot; a fool. [Archaic.]

4. one apt to change; a waverer. [Archaic.]

chānġe′ling, *a.* subject to change; fickle. [Obs.]

chānġe′-ō″vẽr, *n.* a changing over or being changed over, especially from one position, situation, method of operation, etc. to another; as, a *change-over* from war-time production to peace-time production.

chān′ġẽr, *n.* 1. one who alters anything.

2. a moneychanger. [Obs.]

3. one given to change or fickleness. [Rare.]

chānġe ring′ing, the ringing of a series of unrepeated changes on bells.

chānġe wheel, one of a series of interchangeable cogwheels used to transmit motion from the mandrel of a lathe-head to the guide screw for the cutting of screws of various pitches.

chañk, chañk shell, [Sans. *cankha*, a conch shell.] the common conch shell, *Turbinella pyrum*, found especially in the Indian Ocean: used for ornaments and bangles.

chan′nel, *n.* [ME. *chanel*; OFr. *chanel*, *canel*; L. *canalis*, a water pipe, canal.]

1. the bed of a stream, river, etc.; the hollow or course in which a stream flows.

2. the deeper part of a stream, estuary, harbor, etc.

3. a strait or narrow sea between two larger bodies of water; as, the English *Channel.*

4. a tubelike passage for liquids.

5. that by which something passes or is transmitted; means of passing, conveying, or transmitting; as, the news was conveyed to us by different *channels.*

6. the proper or official course of transmission of communications, as in the army; as, the soldier made his request through *channels.*

7. a long furrow or groove; as, the *channels* of a fluted column.

8. a long, grooved bar of rolled metal; channel bar, channel iron, etc.

9. a frequency band assigned to a single transmitting station, as in radio, television, telegraphy, etc.: the width and position of the band differ for each type of transmission.

10. in motion pictures, the complete set of equipment used for the recording or reproduction of sound.

chan′nel, *v.t.*; channeled *or* channelled, *pt., pp.*; channeling *or* channelling, *ppr.* 1. to form a channel in or cut channels in.

2. to groove; as, to *channel* a column.

3. to send through a channel.

chan′nel, *n.* [originally, *chain wale.*] formerly, any of several metal ledges projecting from the sides of a ship to secure the rigging and keep the ropes free of the gunwales.

chan′nel bär, same as *channel iron.*

chan′nel bȧss, the redfish or red bass of southern waters.

chan′nel·bill, *n.* an Australian cuckoo, *Scythrops novæ-hollandiæ*, of unusually large size.

chan′nel gọọse, the white gannet.

chan′nel·ing, *n.* 1. the act of making a channel or channels.

2. a channel; channels collectively.

chan′nel ī′ron (-ūrn), a rolled metal bar whose section is that of three sides of an oblong rectangle: called also *channel bar.*

ç̈hän·sōṅ′, *n.* [Fr.] a song.

ç̈hän·sōṅ′ de geste′ (ẓest′), [Fr., song of heroic acts.] an Old French epic tale in verse, especially of the type of the *Chanson de Roland* (*Song of Roland*), c. 1100: typically written in ten-syllable lines characterized by assonance and arranged in *laisses* (irregular stanzas), these poems fall into cycles organized around Charlemagne (*geste du roi*), William of Orange (*geste de Guillaume*), and the Northern traitors (*geste de Doon de Mayence*).

ç̈hän·sō·nette′, *n.* [Fr.] a short song.

chȧnt, *v.t.*; chanted, *pt., pp.*; chanting, *ppr.*

[ME. *chanten*; OFr. *chanter, canter*; L. *cantare*, freq. of *canere*, to sing.]

1. to sing; to utter with a melodious voice.
The cheerful birds do *chant* sweet music.
—Spenser.

2. to celebrate in song; as, to *chant* praises.
3. to sing or recite in the manner of a chant.
4. to say monotonously.

to chant (horses); to praise (horses) fraudulently in making a sale. [Slang.]

chȧnt, *v.i.* 1. to sing; to make melody with the voice. [Poetic.]
2. to sing a chant; to intone.
3. to say something monotonously or repetitiously.

chȧnt, *n.* [Fr. *chant*; L. *cantus*, a song, from *cantare*, to sing.]
1. a song or singing; melody.
2. a simple song in which a number of syllables or words are sung in a monotone.
3. words, as of a canticle or psalm, to be sung in this way.
4. a monotonous tone of voice; a singsong mode of speaking; intonation.

chant royal; in old French poetry, a composition consisting of five stanzas, each having eleven lines, and a concluding stanza, each of these parts in turn closing with a common refrain.

çhän·tȧge' (-tȧz'), *n.* [Fr.] blackmail.

çhȧn'tȧnt (*or Fr. pron.* shäṅ-täṅ'), *a.* [Fr. *chantant*, ppr. of *chanter*, to sing.] of an easy, smooth, and singing style.

chȧnt'ẽr, *n.* 1. one who chants; a singer.
2. the chief singer or priest of the chantry.
3. the pipe which sounds the tenor or treble in a bagpipe.
4. the hedge warbler.

çhȧn·te·relle', çhȧn·tȧ·relle', *n.* [Fr.] the *Cantharellus cibarius*, an edible, yellow mushroom that smells somewhat like a plum.

çhȧn·te·relle', *n.* [Fr.] the highest string of a musical instrument, as a guitar.

çhäṅ·tëuşe', *n.* [Fr.] a woman singer.

çhȧnt'ey (*or* chȧnt'), *n.* a song that sailors sing when working, to enliven the work by marking rhythm.

chan'ti·çleer, *n.* [name of the rooster in "Reynard the Fox."] a rooster: used as a proper name: so called from the clearness or loudness of his voice in crowing.

chȧnt'ing, *n.* the act of singing or uttering in the manner of a chant.

chȧnt'ŏr, *n.* one who chants; a chanter.

chȧnt'ress, *n.* a female singer or chanter.

chȧnt'ry, *n.*; *pl.* **chȧnt'rieş,** [OFr. *chanterie*, from *chanter*, to sing.]
1. an endowed chapel where one or more priests daily sing or say Mass for the souls of the specified persons.
2. an endowment for chanting Masses and offering prayers in such a chapel.

çhȧn'ty, *n.*; *pl.* **çhȧn'tieş,** a chantey.

chä'nụ·käh (khä'), *n.* same as *Hanukkah.*

çhā'ō·man·cy, *n.* [Gr. *chaos*, chaos, and *manteia*, divination.] divination by means of aerial visions.

çhā'os, *n.* [L. *chaos*; Gr. *chaos*, empty space, abyss, from *chainein*, to yawn, gape.]
1. confusion, or confused mass, of formless matter and infinite space, supposed to have existed before the ordered universe.
2. any mixed mass, without due form or order; confusion; as, a *chaos* of materials.
3. an empty, immeasurable space; an abyss. [Archaic.]

çhā·ot'iç, *a.* in a condition of chaos; in a completely confused or disordered condition.

çhā·ot'iç·ăl·ly, *adv.* in a chaotic way or state; in complete confusion.

chap, *v.t.*; chapped *or* chapt, *pt., pp.*; chapping, *ppr.* 1. to cause to crack or break open in cracks or slits; as, a cold wind *chaps* the skin.
2. to strike; to beat. [Scot.]

chap, *v.i.* to crack open; to break open in cracks or slits; as, the lips or hands *chap.*

chap, *n.* 1. a crack, chink, or cleft; specifically, a chapped place in the skin.
2. a stroke of any kind; a blow. [Scot.]

chäp, chop, *n.* [Scot. *chaft*; Ice. *kjaptr*; Dan. *kjæft*, a jaw, chap.]
1. the upper or lower part of the mouth; the jaw: commonly in the plural.
2. a cheek.
3. a jaw of a clamp or vise.

chap, *n.* [an abbrev. of *chapman*, a merchant.]
1. a buyer; a chapman. [Obs.]
2. a man or boy; a fellow; as, poor old *chap*; little *chap*. [Colloq.]

chap, *v.i.* and *v.t.* [AS. *ceápian*, from *ceáp*, a bargain, price.]
1. to buy or sell; to trade; to bargain. [Obs.]
2. to fix upon (any person or thing); to select and claim. [Scot.]

chä·pä·rä'jōs (-hōs), *n.pl.* [Mex. Sp.] leather trousers worn over ordinary trousers by cowboys to protect their legs: also called *chaps.*

chä·pä·re'jōs (-hōs), *n.pl.* same as *chaparajos.*

chȧ·par·ral', *n.* [Sp., from *chaparro*, an evergreen oak.]
1. a grove of low evergreen oaks.
2. a clump or thicket formed by thorny shrubs; sometimes a thick tangle of cacti.

chȧ·par·ral' çock, chȧ·par·ral' hen, a brownish, long-tailed bird, *Geococcyx californianus*, related to the cuckoo: also called *ground cuckoo* and *road runner.*

chȧ·par·ral' pēa, a thorny shrub of the pea family, growing in chaparrals along the western coast of the United States.

chȧ·pä'ti, *n.* same as *chupatty.*

chap'book, *n.* [*chap*, abbrev. of *chapman*, and *book*.] a small book or pamphlet containing a religious tract, verses, or the like, usually sold by peddlers, or chapmen.

chāpe, *n.* [Fr. *chape*, a cope, a cover, chape; LL. *cappa*, cape, hooded cloak.]
1. the catch of anything, as the hook of a scabbard, or the catch of a buckle, by which it is held to the strap.
2. a brass or silver tip, or case that strengthens the end of a scabbard and acts as a protection for the point.
3. in casting, the outer jacket or case holding together a mold.

çhȧ·peau' (-pō'), *n.*; *pl.* **çhȧ·peaux'** (-pō, -pōz') or **çhȧ·peauş'** (-pōz'), [Fr., from OFr. *chapel*, from LL. *capellus*, a hat, headdress.]
1. a hat.
2. in heraldry, a cap of maintenance.

chapeau bras; a three-cornered hat which may be folded flat and carried under the arm; worn chiefly by gentlemen in the latter half of the eighteenth century.

chāped (chāpt), *a.* furnished with a chape or chapes. [Obs.]

chap'el, *n.* [OFr. *chapele, capele*, from LL. *capella*, dim. of *cappa*, a cope, cape; originally a sanctuary in which the *cappa* or cope of St. Martin was preserved; then, any sanctuary.]
1. a secondary place of worship usually attached to a large church or cathedral, separately dedicated, and devoted to special services.
2. a building subsidiary to a parish church; as, a parochial *chapel*; a mission *chapel.*
3. in Great Britain, a place of worship used by those who are not members of an established church.
4. a private place of worship; as, a college *chapel*; hospital *chapel*; prison *chapel.*
5. a room or recess in a church, set apart for special services and having its own altar.
6. a service in a chapel, or any religious service, as at a school.
7. a choir or an orchestra connected with a nobleman's establishment or a prince's palace.
8. a printing office: said to be so called because Caxton, the pioneer English printer, first conducted an establishment of that kind in a chapel near Westminster Abbey. [Obs.]

chapel of ease; originally a chapel for the ease or accommodation of the parishioners that dwell too far away to be able to attend the parish church.

chapel royal; a chapel attached to a royal palace.

chap'el, *v.t.*; chapeled, *pt., pp.*; chapeling, *ppr.*
1. to place or bury in a chapel. [Rare.]
2. to turn (a ship) round in a light breeze, when closehauled, so that she will lie the same way as before.

chāpe'less, *a.* having no chape or scabbard tip: said of a sword.

chap'e·let, *n.* [Fr., a chaplet, a stirrup leather.]
1. a pair of stirrup straps, with stirrups, joined at the top in a sort of leather buckle, by which they are made fast to the framework of the saddle, after they have been adjusted to the length and bearing of the rider.
2. a dredging or water-raising machine, consisting of an endless chain provided with buckets or with pallets.

chap'el·lă·ny, *n.* [Fr. *chapellenie*; LL. *capellania*, a chaplaincy, from *capellanus*, a chaplain; *capella*, a chapel.] a chapel in the district of and, hence, under the jurisdiction of another. [Obs.]

chap'el·mȧs"tẽr, *n.* same as *kapellmeister.*

chap'el·ry, *n.* [OFr. *capelerie*; LL. *capellaria*, from *capella*, a chapel.] the bounds of jurisdiction of a chapel.

çhap'ẽr·ōn, çhap'ẽr·ōne, *n.* [Fr., a hood, shoulder knot, coping; from *chape*, a cope.]
1. a hood worn by the Knights of the Garter in their habits. It was worn by men and women in late medieval times.
2. a person, especially an older or married woman, who accompanies young unmarried people in public or is present at their parties, etc. for the sake of propriety or good form.

çhap'ẽr·ōn, çhap'ẽr·ōne, *v.t.*; chaperoned, *pt., pp.*; chaperoning, *ppr.* to attend (a person or persons) in the capacity of a chaperon; to act as a chaperon to.

çhap'ẽr·ōn·āġe, *n.* the duties or supervision of a chaperon.

chäp'fạll·en, *a.* having the lower chap depressed; hence, dejected; dispirited; silenced: also *chopfallen.*

chā'pin, *n.* same as *chopine.*

chap'i·tẽr, *n.* [a corruption of OFr. *chapitel*; LL. *capitellum*, a capital; L. *capitulum*, a chapter, a capital.]
1. in architecture, the capital of a column. [Archaic.]
2. a schedule of matters to be introduced at any session before the justice of the peace, assize, or eyre. [Obs.]

chap'lain (-lin), *n.* [OFr. *chapelain*; LL. *capellanus*, from *capella*, a chapel.]
1. a clergyman attached to a chapel, as of a royal court, prison, etc.
2. a clergyman or layman appointed to perform religious functions in a public institution, club, etc.
3. a minister, priest, or rabbi serving in a religious capacity with the armed forces.

chap'lain·cy, *n.*, *pl.* **chap'lain·cieş,** the position or term of office of a chaplain.

chap'lain·ship, *n.* a chaplaincy.

chap'less, *a.* without a lower jaw.

chap'let, *n.* [OFr. *chapelet*, a headdress, wreath, dim. of *chapel*, a headdress, cap.]
1. a garland or wreath to be worn on the head; a crown.
2. a string of prayer beads one-third the length of a rosary; also, the prayers told with such beads.
3. in architecture, a small convex molding somewhat resembling a string of beads.
4. in horsemanship, same as *chapelet.*
5. any string of beads; a necklace.
6. a device of bent sheet iron for keeping a core in position in a mold.

chap'let, *v.t.* to embellish with flowers, beads, or chaplets.

chap'let·ed, *a.* having a wreath or garland on the head.

chap'măn, *n.*; *pl.* **chap'men,** [ME. *chapman, chepman*; AS. *ceápman*, a buyer, seller, merchant; *ceáp*, a bargain, trade, and *man*.]
1. a peddler; a hawker. [Brit.]
2. a tradesman. [Archaic.]

chä·pō'tẹ, *n.* [Mex.] the black persimmon of Mexico.

çhȧ·pöur'net, *n.* [Fr. *chaperonnet*, dim. of *chaperon*, a hood, cope.] in heraldry, a chief divided by a curved line.

CHAPOURNET

chap'py, chap'pie, *n.* [dim. of *chap*.] a fellow; chap. [Colloq.]

chap'py, *a.* full of chaps; cleft.

chaps, *n.pl.* chaparajos. [Colloq.]

chaps (*or* chäps), *n.pl.* chops (jaws).

chapt, past tense and past participle of *chap.*

chap'tẽr, *n.* [Fr. *chapitre*; L. *capitulum*, a head, a chapter of a book, dim. of *caput*, a head.]
1. a division of a book or other writing; as, Genesis contains fifty *chapters.*
2. a thing like a chapter; a part; an episode; a section.
3. a society or community of clergymen, belonging to a cathedral or collegiate church; as, the dean and *chapter* of Westminster; also, a meeting of a religious body.
4. a local branch of some society, club, or fraternity.
5. a house where a chapter meets; a chapter house.

chapter and verse; (a) the exact Scriptural reference; hence, (b) authority (for a statement, belief, etc.).

chapter of accidents; a number of unforeseen happenings.

to the end of the chapter; throughout; to the end.

chap'tẽr, *v.t.* 1. to divide into chapters.
2. to correct. [Obs.]

chap'tẽr house, a house where a chapter, as of a cathedral, fraternity, etc., meets.

chap'trel, *n.* [dim. of *chapiter*, from OFr. *chapitel*, a chapter, capital.] the top of a pillar on which an arch rests; an impost.

chä·que′tä (-ke′), *n.* [Sp.] a heavy jacket worn by cowboys.

chär, *n.* and *v.i.*; charred, *pt.*, *pp.*; charring, *ppr.* chare (odd job).

chär, *n.*; *pl.* **chärs** or **chär,** [Gael. *ceara*; Ir. *cear*, blood-colored, blood.] a species of trout found in deep, mountainous lakes: so called from its red belly: also spelled *charr*.

chär, *n.* [Fr.] a chariot. [Obs.]

chär, *v.t.* [AS. *cerran, cyrran*, to turn.] to hew, as granite.

chär, *v.t.* and *v.i.*; charred, *pt.*, *pp.*; charring, *ppr.* [ME. *charren*, to turn, return. The meaning is influenced by *char* in *charcoal*.]

1. to turn into charcoal by burning.
2. to burn partially; to scorch.

chär, *n.* anything charred; cinders; charcoal.

Chā′rà, *n.* [Gr. *chara*, delight, from *chairein*, to rejoice.] a genus of plants growing in damp places, without flowers.

çhar′à·banc, char-à-banc′ (*Fr.* shȧr-ȧ-bäṅ′), *n.*; *pl.* **çhar′à·bancs, char-à-bancs′** (*Fr.* shȧr-ȧ-bäṅ′), [Fr.] a large excursion bus with transverse seats facing forward.

Çhā·rā′cē·ae, *n.pl.* [*chara* and *-aceæ*.] a family of chlorophyll-bearing plants allied to the algae.

çhā·rā′ceous, *a.* relating to or like the *Characeæ*.

çhar′a·cin, *n.* [from Mod. L. *characinidæ*, the name of the family, from Gr. *karax*, a kind of fish.] any of a large group of strong-jawed, fresh-water fish of Africa and South America.

çhar′açt, *n.* an inscription. [Obs.]

çhar′aç·tẽr, *n.* [L. *character*; Gr. *charaktēr*, from *charassein*, engrave.]

1. a distinctive mark.
2. any conventional mark, sign, or symbol used in writing and printing, as +, –, 7, 0, X, Y, Z, etc.
3. a style of printing or handwriting.
4. a mystic symbol; code; cipher.
5. a distinctive trait, quality, or attribute.
6. essential quality; nature; kind or sort.
7. an individual's pattern of behavior or personality; moral constitution.
8. moral strength; self-discipline, fortitude, etc.
9. reputation.
10. good reputation; as, left without a shred of *character*.
11. a description of the traits or qualities of a person or type; character sketch.
12. a statement about the behavior, qualities, etc. of a person; recommendation.
13. status; position; as, he spoke in the *character* of lawyer.
14. a personage; as, he was a great *character* in his day.
15. a person in a play, story, novel, etc.
16. a person conspicuously different from others; a queer or eccentric person. [Colloq.]

Syn.—symbol, letter, nature, type, disposition, temperament, cast, estimation, repute, office, species, mark, figure.

çhar′aç·tẽr, *v.t.* 1. to write; to print; to inscribe.

2. to represent; also, to distinguish by particular marks or traits. [Archaic.]

çhar′aç·tẽr aç′tŏr, an actor usually cast in the role of a person with pronounced or eccentric characteristics.

çhar′aç·tẽr·iṣm, *n.* (a) characterization; (b) a characteristic. [Obs.]

çhar″aç·tẽr·is′tiç, çhar″aç·tẽr·is′tiç·ăl, *a.* that constitutes the character; that marks the peculiar distinctive qualities of a person or thing; typical; distinctive; special; as, the *characteristic* odor of cabbage.

çhar″aç·tẽr·is′tiç, *n.* 1. that which constitutes a character; that which characterizes; a distinguishing trait, feature, or quality; a peculiarity.

> Invention is the *characteristic* of Homer.
> —Pope.

2. the whole number, or integral part, of a logarithm, as distinguished from the fractional remainder, or mantissa; as, 4 is the *characteristic* of the logarithm 4.7193.

Syn.—distinction, peculiarity, idiosyncrasy, specialty, individuality, personality, singularity.

çhar″aç·tẽr·is′tiç·ăl·ly, *adv.* in a manner that distinguishes character; typically.

çhar″aç·tẽr·is′tiç·ăl·ness, *n.* the state or quality of being characteristic.

çhar″aç·tẽr·i·zā′tion, *n.* 1. act of characterizing; description of characteristics.

2. the delineation of character or creation of characters in a play, story, etc., especially by imitating or describing actions, utterances, and gestures.

çhar′aç·tẽr·īze, *v.t.*; characterized, *pt.*, *pp.*; characterizing, *ppr.* [LL. *characterizare*; Gr. *charaktērizein*, to designate by a mark; from *charactēr*, a mark, character.]

1. to describe the particular qualities, features, or traits of.
2. to distinguish; to mark or tell the character of; to be the distinctive character of; as, a miser is *characterized* by greed.
3. to engrave or imprint. [Obs.]
4. to mark with a peculiar stamp or figure; to give character to.

çhar′aç·tẽr·less, *a.* without (a) character.

çhar′aç·tẽr sketch, 1. a short essay describing a person or type of person.

2. in the theater, a performance depicting a person of pronounced or unusual characteristics.

çhar′aç·tẽr·y, *n.*; *pl.* **çhar′aç·tẽr·ies,** 1. a system of symbols or characters used to express thoughts.

2. the expression of thought by such symbols.

çhà·rāde′, *n.* [Fr.] a game in which a chosen word or phrase to be guessed is acted out in pantomime, syllable by syllable or as a whole.

çhär′bŏn, *n.* [Fr.] anthrax.

çhär′broil, *v.t.*; charbroiled, *pt.*, *pp.*; charbroiling, *ppr.* [*char*coal and *broil*.] to broil over a charcoal fire: also written *char-broil*.

chär′çōal, *n.* [lit., turn coal; ME. *charren*, to turn, and *cole*, coal; i.e., wood turned to coal.]

1. a black form of carbon made by charring wood or other organic matter by a process of smothered combustion to exclude air: used as a fuel, filter, gas absorbent, etc.
2. a pencil or crayon made of this substance.
3. a drawing made with such a pencil or crayon.

animal charcoal; charcoal obtained by calcining bones, used for filtering and disinfecting.

mineral charcoal; a substance taking the form of layers of fine charcoal between beds of bituminous coal: also called *mother of coal*.

chär′çōal black, a pigment made from burnt ivory, burnt cork, etc.

chär′çōal bũrn′ẽr, 1. a device in which charcoal is burned.

2. a person whose work is producing charcoal.

chär′çōal ī′ron (-ũrn), iron smelted in furnaces heated with charcoal.

çhär·çût′ẽr·iē (*Fr.* shär-kü-trē′), *n.* [Fr., pork butcher's shop, from *chair*, meat, and *cuit*, pp. of *cuire*, to cook.]

1. sausage, ham, cold cuts of meat, pâtés, etc.
2. a delicatessen that specializes in charcuterie.

chärd, *n.* [Fr. *carde*; L. *carduus*, a thistle, artichoke.]

1. the leafstalks of artichokes, blanched for use as a vegetable.
2. a kind of beet whose large leaves and thick stalks are used as food: also *Swiss chard*.

chāre, *n.* [ME. *cher, cherre*; AS. *cerr, cierr, cyrr*, a turn, job, piece of work, from *cierran*, to turn.] an odd job; household task; chore: also spelled *char*.

chāre, *v.i.*; chared, *pt.*, *pp.*; charing, *ppr.* 1. to do odd jobs or chores.

2. to be a charwoman.

Also spelled *char*.

chärġe, *v.t.*; charged, *pt.*, *pp.*; charging, *ppr.* [ME. *chargen*; OFr. *charger*; LL. *carricare*, to load a wagon, from L. *carrus*, a car, wagon.]

1. to rush on; to bear down on; to attack; as, an army *charges* the enemy.
2. (a) to put a load on or in; to load or fill to usual capacity; (b) to load (a gun); (c) to fill (a substance) with another substance; as, the air was *charged* with steam; (d) to add carbon dioxide to (water, etc.); (e) to add an electrical charge to (a battery, etc.); to replenish.
3. to load or burden with that which oppresses. [Obs.]
4. to set or lay on; to impose, as a tax, or as a task; as, he *charged* the officer with the execution of the plan.

> The gospel *chargeth* us with piety toward God.
> —Tillotson.

5. to put or lay on, often implying superfluity; as, to *charge* a building with ornaments.
6. to entrust to; as, an officer is *charged* with dispatches.
7. to set to, as a debt; to place on the debit side of an account; as, to *charge* a man with the price of goods sold to him.
8. to put blame on; to censure; to accuse; as, to *charge* a man with theft.
9. (a) to put liability on (a person); (b) to make liable for (a purchase, error, etc.).
10. to lay on, give, or communicate, as an order, command, or earnest request; to enjoin or exhort; as, he *charged* his son not to act rashly.
11. to give directions to; to instruct authoritatively; as, the judge *charged* the grand jury to inquire respecting breaches of the peace.
12. to make or ask as a price; as, he *charged* ten dollars for it.
13. to put on, as a bearing in heraldry.
14. in military usage, to bring (a gun) to bear on; to level; to direct.

Syn.—accuse, arraign, impeach, indict.

chärġe, *v.i.* 1. to ask payment (*for*); as, we *charge for* this service.

2. to attack vigorously; to make a sudden rush; as, he *charged* on ahead.
3. to crouch or squat, as a trained dog when a command is given.

chärġe, *n.* [Fr. *charge*; LL. *carricare*, to load; *carrus*, a car, wagon.]

1. a load or burden.
2. the maximum or necessary quantity, as of electricity, explosive, fuel, etc., that a container or apparatus is built to accommodate.
3. an onset; an attack with maximum weight and speed.
4. an order; injunction; instruction; command; as, the officer gave *charge* concerning the prisoner.
5. responsibility or duty (*of*); as, to take *charge of* finances.
6. (a) care, safekeeping, or custody (*of*); hence, (b) the person or thing committed to another's custody, care, or management; a trust.

> The starry guardian drove his *charge* away
> To some fresh pasture. —Dryden.

7. in law, instructions given by a judge to a jury.
8. indictment; accusation; as, *charges* of cruelty.
9. a debt; an entry of money, or the price of goods, on the debit side of an account.
10. cost; price; expense; as, the *charges* of the war.
11. in military usage, a signal to attack; as, to sound the *charge*.
12. the position of a weapon fitted for an attack or combat.
13. in veterinary medicine, an ointment or plaster, used as a treatment for sprains and inflammations.
14. in heraldry, a bearing; that which is borne upon the color; the figures represented on the escutcheon.
15. anxiety; trouble; care; heed. [Obs.]
16. in physics and electricity, the accumulation of either positively or negatively charged electrons on the surface of a substance when it is electrified.

to sound the charge; to give the signal to make an attack.

char·gé′ (shär-zhā′), *n.* [Fr.] same as *chargé d'affaires*.

chärġe′à·ble, *a.* 1. capable of being charged; as, a duty of forty per cent is *chargeable* on this product.

2. subject to be charged; as, this product is *chargeable* with a duty of forty per cent.
3. expensive; costly; as, a *chargeable* family.
4. imputable; that may be laid or attributed as a crime, fault, or debt; as, a fault *chargeable* on a man.
5. subject to be charged or accused; as, a man *chargeable* with a fault or neglect.

chärġe′à·ble·ness, *n.* the state of being chargeable.

chärġe′à·bly, *adv.* in a chargeable manner.

chärġe aç·çount′, a business arrangement by which a customer may buy things and pay for them within a specified future period.

char·gé′ d'af·faires′ (shär-zhā′ dȧf-fãr′), *n.*; *pl.* **char·gés′ d'af·faires′** (-zhā′) [Fr., lit., entrusted with business.]

1. a government official who temporarily takes the place of a minister, ambassador, or other diplomat.
2. an official of lower rank than an ambassador or minister, sent as a diplomatic representative to a smaller or less important country than his own.

chärġe′fụl, *a.* expensive; costly. [Obs.]

chärġe′less, *a.* not expensive; free from expense.

chärġe plāte, a metal or plastic plate embossed with the owner's name and address, used as a stamp on bills in making purchases on credit. Also **chärġe′-ȧ-plāte.**

chär′ġẽr, *n.* 1. one who or that which charges.
2. an instrument used to measure or insert a charge, as in a gun.
3. a large dish. [Obs.]
4. a war horse.
5. in electricity, an apparatus used to charge storage batteries.

chärġe sheet, the daily record kept in a police station of all arrests made and charges preferred.

chãr′i·ly, *adv.* in a chary manner; carefully.

chãr′i·ness, *n.* the quality of being chary; caution; care; frugality.

char′i·ŏt, *n.* [OFr. *chariot*, dim. of *char, car*, a car, from L. *carrus*, a car, wagon.]
1. a light carriage with four wheels, used for pleasure or on some state occasions. [Archaic.]

GRECIAN CHARIOT

2. a two-wheeled cart, used formerly in war, racing, parades, etc., drawn by horses.

char′i·ŏt, *v.t.* and *v.i.*; charioted, *pt., pp.*; charioting, *ppr.* to drive or ride in a chariot.

char″i·ŏt·ee′, *n.* a light, four-wheeled pleasure carriage having two seats and a top.

char″i·ŏt·eer′, *n.* 1. the person who drives a chariot.
2. [C–] in astronomy, a constellation in the Northern Hemisphere: known also as *Auriga* and *Wagoner.*

ça·riş′mȧ, ça′riṣm, *n.*; *pl.* **ça·riş′mȧ·tȧ,** [Gr. *charisma*, a gift, from *charizesthai*, to favor, gratify; *charis*, favor, grace.]
1. in Christian theology, a divinely inspired gift, grace, or talent, as for prophesying, healing, etc.
2. a special quality of leadership that captures the popular imagination and inspires unswerving allegiance and devotion.

çar·iş·mat′iç, *a.* 1. pertaining to charisma.
2. designating or of any of various religious groups or movements that stress direct divine inspiration, manifested as in glossolalia, healing powers, etc.

çar·iş·mat′iç, *n.* 1. a member of a charismatic group or movement.
2. a person who supposedly has some divinely inspired power, as the ability to prophesy.

char′i·tȧ·ble, *a.* 1. showing charity, or love; benevolent and kind. [Archaic.]
2. liberal in gifts to the poor, and in relieving them in distress; as, a *charitable* man.
3. pertaining to charity; springing from charity, or intended for charity; benevolent; as, a *charitable* institution.
4. liberal in judgment of others; given neither to severe criticism nor to evil construction of motives.

Syn.—benevolent, generous, liberal, forgiving, benign, indulgent, lenient.

char′i·tȧ·ble·ness, *n.* the disposition to be charitable, or the exercise of charity.

char′i·ta·bly, *adv.* kindly; liberally; benevolently; with a disposition to help the poor.

char′i·ty, *n.* [OFr. *charite*, from L. *caritas* (*-atis*), dearness, affection, high regard, from *carus*, dear.]
1. love; benevolence; affection; good will; that disposition of heart which inclines men to think favorably of their fellow men, and to do them good. In a theological sense, it includes supreme love of God, and universal good will to men.
2. an act of good will or affection.
3. liberality to the poor, consisting in giving money or benefactions, or in free services to relieve them in distress.
4. alms; whatever is bestowed gratuitously on the poor for their relief.
5. an institution, organization, or fund for giving help to those in need.
6. liberality in judging of men and their actions; a disposition which inclines men to think and judge favorably, and to put the best construction on words and actions which the case will admit.
7. in law, grants or devises, which include relief of the poor and friendless, education, religious culture, and public institutions.

Syn.—alms, benevolence, good will, kindness.

char′i·ty sçhool, a school for poor children, maintained by voluntary contributions.

çhȧ·ri·vä′ri (*or* shȧ-riv″ȧ-rē′, *or* shiv′ȧ-ri), *n.* [Fr.] a mock serenade of discordant noises made on kettles, tin horns, etc.: often played as a practical joke on newly married couples: also *shivaree.*

chärk, *v.t.* [abbrev. from *charcoal.*] to burn to a charcoal; to char.

chärk, *n.* cinder; charcoal; coke.

chär′khȧ, chär′kȧ (*preferably* chũr′kȧ), *n.* [Hind.] in India, a spinning wheel, used especially for cotton.

chär′lā·dy, *n.*; *pl.* **chär′lā·dieṣ,** a charwoman. [Brit.]

çhär′lȧ·tăn, *n.* [Fr., from It. *ciarlatano*, a quack, from *ciarlare*, to prate.] one who makes untruthful pretensions; a quack; a mountebank; an impostor.

çhär·lȧ·tan′iç, çhär·lȧ·tan′iç·ăl, *a.* quackish; pertaining to a charlatan.

çhär·lȧ·tan′iç·ăl·ly, *adv.* in the manner of a charlatan.

çhär′lȧ·tăn·iṣm, *n.* [Fr. *charlatanisme.*] the methods of a charlatan; quackery.

çhär′lȧ·tăn·ry, *n.* same as *charlatanism.*

Chärleṣ″ṣ Wāin, [AS. *Carles wægn*, wagon of *Carl* (Charlemagne): so named because of confusion between Charlemagne and King Arthur (L. *Arcturus*), who were associated in popular legend; orig., the wain of *Arcturus* (star in the constellation Boötes).]
1. the Big Dipper.
2. occasionally, Ursa Major.

Chär′ley, Chär′lie (-li), *n.* 1. a night watchman. [Brit.]
2. a short pointed beard, as worn by Charles I.

chär′ley hŏrse, a cramp in the muscles of a leg or arm, resulting from strenuous activity. [Colloq.]

chär′lock, *n.* [ME. *carlok*; AS. *cerlic*, charlock.] the wild mustard, *Brassica sinapistrum*, a troublesome weed which does much damage in grain fields: also written *carlick.*
jointed or *white charlock*; the wild radish, *Raphanus raphanistrum.*

çhär′lŏtte, *n.* [Fr.] a light pudding or dessert made of fruit, gelatin, etc. in a mold of bread, cake, or graham-cracker crumbs.
charlotte russe, charlotte à la russe; a delicacy consisting mainly of whipped cream or custard enclosed in a cup of spongecake.

chärm, *n.* [Fr. *charme*; L. *carmen*, a song, poem, charm.]
1. a word, verse, action, gesture, object, etc. imagined to possess some occult or magic power; an enchantment, incantation, spell, or talisman.
2. power to gain affections; that which can please irresistibly; that which delights and attracts the heart; a fascinating or alluring quality; as, she influenced many by her *charm.*
3. a song or melody. [Obs.]
4. any object worn or carried in the hope of bringing good fortune, or averting evil.
5. an ornament worn on the person; as, a watch chain and its *charm.*
6. a hypothetical property of certain heavy elementary particles, described by a quantum number, observed only in matter excited to very high energies, and postulated to be a fourth quark.

Syn.—spell, incantation, enchantment, fascination, attraction, allurement.

chärm, *v.t.*; charmed, *pt., pp.*; charming, *ppr.*
1. to act on as though by magic.
2. to subdue, especially by that which pleases and delights the mind; to allay or appease; to soothe.

Music the fiercest grief can *charm.*
—Pope.

3. to give great pleasure to the mind or senses of; to fascinate; to enchant; to delight; as, we were *charmed* with the conversation.
4. to fortify with charms against evil.
5. to make powerful by charms.
6. to summon by incantation.
7. to tune or make music upon. [Obs.]

chärm, *v.i.* 1. to sound harmonically. [Obs.]
2. to use charms or practice magic.
3. to be charming; to please greatly.

Syn.—attract, bewitch, captivate; delight, enchant.

chärmed, *a.* subdued or protected by charms; delighted; enchanted.
charmed life; a life seemingly protected from harm as though by magic.

I bear a *charmed life*, which must not yield.
—Shak.

chärm′ẽr, *n.* 1. one that charms or has power to charm; one that uses or has the power of enchantment; a magician.
2. one who delights and attracts the affections: usually said of a woman.

çhär·mëuşe′, *n.* [Fr.] a soft, lightweight, satin-like cloth.

chärm′fųl, *a.* full of charms.

chärm′ing, *a.* 1. pleasing in a high degree; delighting; fascinating; of attractive character and personality; as, a *charming* maid; a *charming* song.
2. using a charm or charms.

Syn.—delightful, amiable, lovely, pleasing.

chärm′ing·ly, *adv.* delightfully; in a manner to charm, or to give delight.

She smiled very *charmingly.* —Addison.

chärm′ing·ness, *n.* the power to please.

chärm′less, *a.* without charms.

chär′nē·çō, *n.* [named from *Charneco*, Portugal] a sort of sweet wine. [Obs.]

chär′nel, *a.* [OFr. *charnel*, *carnel*; LL. *carnale*, neut. of *carnalis*, of flesh; L. *caro, carnis*, flesh.]
1. containing flesh or carcasses; containing dead bodies; as, *charnel* vaults.
2. like or fit for a charnel; deathlike.

chär′nel, *n.* a charnel house.

chär′nel house, 1. originally, a tomb or vault for the dead.
2. any place where there are corpses, bones of the dead, etc.

Çhā′ron, *n.* [Gr. *Charōn.*]
1. in Greek mythology, the son of Erebus and Nox, who ferried the souls of the deceased over the river Styx to Hades.

CHARON AND SPIRITS OF THE DECEASED

2. by humorous analogy, a ferryman.

chär′-ŏv″en, *n.* a furnace or kiln for burning turf to an ash.

chär′paī, *n.* a charpoy.

çhär′pie (-pi), *n.* [Fr., pp. of *charpir*, to pick to pieces, from L. *carpere*, to seize.] lint obtained from old linen, used for dressing wounds.

chär′poy, *n.* [Hindu *chārpāi*, a couch.] a cot or small bed used in India.

chär′qued (-kid), jerked: said of beef.

chär′qui (-ki), *n.* [Sp.] jerked beef; beef cut into strips and dried in the sun.

chärr, *n.* same as *char* (trout).

chär′ry, *a.* pertaining to charcoal; like charcoal.

chärt, *n.* [Fr. *charte*; L. *charta*, a leaf of paper, a writing, tablet; Gr. *chartē*, a leaf of paper, layer of papyrus bark.]
1. a hydrographic or marine map; a draft or projection on paper of some body of water with the coasts, islands, rocks, banks, channels, or entrances into harbors, rivers, and bays, the points of compass, soundings or depth of water, etc., to regulate the courses of ships and aid navigation.
2. a sheet giving information or facts, usually in tabular, diagrammatic, illustrative, or graphic form; as, a genealogical, historical, or statistical *chart.*
3. such a table, diagram, graph, etc.
4. a simple outline map on which information can be plotted or written; as, a weather *chart.*
5. a charter or written deed. [Obs.]
globular chart; a chart made on a globular projection.
heliographic chart; a chart showing the sun and its spots.
Mercator's chart; a chart made on the plan of projection adopted in the sixteenth century by the Flemish cartographer Mercator, in

which the meridians and parallels of latitude are projected in straight lines.

physical chart; a chart showing the physical geography of a section of the earth's surface.

plane chart; a chart of some part of the earth's surface in which its globular form is not considered and the meridians and parallels are projected as straight lines.

selenographic chart; a chart of the moon.

topographic chart; a chart showing in detail the topographic features of a particular place or a district of limited size.

chärt, *v.t.*; charted, *pt., pp.*; charting, *ppr.* 1. to map out in a chart; to delineate; as, to *chart* a part of the ocean; to *chart* a coast.

2. to plot (a course) on, or by reference to, a chart or charts.

3. to show by, on, or as by, a chart.

çhär'tȧ, *n.*; *pl.* **çhär'tae,** [L., leaf of paper.]

1. an instrument under which a grant is conveyed; a deed; a charter; a conveyance: see *Magna Charta.*

2. a parchment, paper, or letter. [Obs.]

3. in pharmacy, the paper used in wrapping up powders.

çhär·tā'ceous, *a.* [L. *chartaceus*, from *charta*, a leaf of paper.] resembling paper; having a paperlike texture.

Çharte, *n.* [Fr.] the constitution or fundamental law of the French monarchy, as established on the restoration of Louis XVIII, in 1814.

chär'tẽr, *n.* [ME. *chartre, chartere*; OFr. *chartre, cartre*; L. *chartula*, dim. of *charta*, a sheet of paper, a writing, tablet.]

1. an instrument, executed with due form, given as evidence of a grant, contract, etc.; a franchise or written grant conferring powers, rights, and privileges, as from a state or other sovereign power to a person, business corporation, etc.

2. permission from a society for the organization of a local chapter or lodge.

3. privilege; immunity; exemption.

My mother,
Who has a *charter* to extol her blood.
—Shak.

4. the hiring or leasing, as of a vessel, bus, airplane, etc., by contract; also, the contract itself; as, the ship was under *charter* to proceed to Europe.

5. [C–] the Charter of the United Nations.

charter member; an original member of an order, corporation, society, etc., particularly one involved in organizing it; one whose name appears in the charter of an organization.

Charter Oak; a historical oak tree at Hartford, Conn., first used as a place of safekeeping for the charter of the colony in 1687. The tree was destroyed by a gale in 1856.

Charter school; one of the free schools founded in Ireland in 1733, by the Protestants.

Great Charter; see *Magna Charta.*

chär'tẽr, *v.t.*; chartered, *pt., pp.*; chartering, *ppr.* 1. to establish by charter; to grant a charter to.

2. to hire or lease, as a ship, by charter.

3. to hire for exclusive use.

chär'tẽr·āġe, *n.* a chartering; grant of a charter.

chär'tẽred, *a.* 1. granted by charter; invested with privileges by charter; as, *chartered* rights; *chartered* power.

2. hired or let, as a ship.

chär'tẽred aç·çount'ănt, in Great Britain, a member of an Institute of Chartered Accountants.

chär'tẽr·ẽr, *n.* one who charters; especially, one who charters a ship.

Chär'tẽr·house, *n.* [altered (by folk etym.) from Anglo-Fr. *chartouse* (Fr. *chartreuse*), Carthusian monastery.]

1. a Carthusian monastery.

2. a London hospital founded (1611) on the site of a Carthusian monastery.

3. the school into which this hospital was later converted.

4. the modern boarding school (called *public school* in England) at Godalming, Surrey, which inherits the tradition of the former school.

Chär'tẽr·ist, *n.* same as *Chartist.*

chär'tẽr land, in old English law, land held by charter; freehold land.

Chär'tẽr of the Ū·nī'ted Nā'tions, the document establishing the United Nations and outlining its principles, functions, and organization, adopted at an international conference in San Francisco (1945).

chär'tẽr pär'ty, [Fr. *charte partie*, divided deed: so named because half was kept by each party to the transaction.]

1. an agreement between a shipowner and a carrier, merchant, etc. for the commercial lease of a ship or space on a ship, especially as recorded in a document.

2. the hiring or leasing of a vessel or space in a vessel by such agreement.

3. a party, as of amateur fishermen, etc., which hires or charters a vessel for sport fishing, cruising, etc. [Colloq.]

Chärt'iṣm, *n.* [Fr. *charte*, a charter, and *-ism.*]

1. in English history, the principles of a political movement which stood for universal suffrage, the vote by ballot, annual parliaments, and other reforms.

2. this movement (1836–1848).

Chärt'ist, *n.* one who upheld the principles of Chartism.

Chärt'ist, *a.* of Chartism or Chartists.

chärt'less, *a.* 1. without a chart; of which no chart has been made; vague; unknown; as, the *chartless* main.

2. unguided.

çhär·tog'rȧ·phẽr, *n.* a cartographer.

çhär·tō·graph'iç, *a.* cartographic.

çhär·tog'rȧ·phy, *n.* cartography.

çhär'tō·man·cy, *n.* same as *cartomancy.*

çhär·tom'e·tẽr, *n.* [L. *charta*, a map, and *metrum*, a measure.] an instrument for computing distances on charts and maps.

Çhär·trēuṣe', *n.* [Fr.]

1. a monastery of Carthusians, especially the original house, *La Grande Chartreuse*, near Grenoble, France.

2. [c–] a liqueur or cordial, yellow, pale-green, or white in color, made by the Carthusian monks.

3. [c–] pale, yellowish green.

çhär'trēuṣe', *a.* of a pale, yellowish-green color.

çhär'tū·lā·ry, çär'tū·lā·ry, *n.* [LL. *chartularium, cartularium*, from *chartula*, a charter, a record.] a list of charters; a book containing duplicates of all charters issued; also the official who keeps such a book.

chär'wom″ăn (-woom″), *n.*; *pl.* **chär'wom″en** (-wim″), [ME. *char*, a chore, and *woman.*] a woman who is hired to do cleaning or scrubbing, as in office buildings.

chār'y, *a.* [AS. *cearig*, careful, *cearu*, to care.]

1. careful; cautious; as, a burnt child is *chary* of fire.

2. shy; as, he was *chary* of strangers.

3. frugal; stingy; as, he was *chary* of his hospitality.

Çhȧ·ryb'dis, *n.* [L., from Gr. *Charybdis.*] a whirlpool off the coast of Sicily, opposite the rock Scylla, on the Italian coast.

between Scylla and Charybdis; figuratively, in a position of danger or difficulty; having the choice of two dangers.

chās'ȧ·ble, *a.* capable of being chased; fit for hunting: also spelled *chaseable.*

chāse, *v.t.*; chased (chāst), *pt., pp.*; chasing, *ppr.* [ME. *chasen, chacen*; OFr. *chacier, cacier*, from L. *captare*, to strive to seize, from *capere*, to take.]

1. to follow quickly or persistently in order to catch or harm.

2. to run after; follow; pursue.

3. to make run away; drive.

4. to hunt.

chāse, *v.i.* 1. to go in pursuit; follow along; as, *chase* after him.

2. to go hurriedly; rush; as, I *chased* around town looking for you. [Colloq.]

chāse, *n.* 1. a chasing or pursuit with a desire to obtain.

2. the hunting of game for sport.

3. that which is pursued or hunted.

4. in England, (a) an open ground or place of retreat for deer and other wild beasts: differing from a forest, which is not private property and is invested with privileges, and from a park, which is enclosed; (b) a license to hunt over a specified area or to keep animals there as game.

5. hunters collectively.

to give chase; to chase; pursue.

chāse, *v.t.* [a contr. of *enchase.*]

1. to ornament (metal) by such means as embossing, engraving, cutting, etc.

2. to cut like a screw thread.

chāse, *n.* [OFr. *chasse*, a frame, shrine, from *casse*, a box, chest, from L. *capsa*, a box, chest.]

1. a strong rectangular metal frame used by printers to lock up type when set in pages or columns and ready for electrotyping, stereotyping, or the press.

2. a wide groove or channel; a trench, as for the holding of a drainpipe.

3. the bore of a gun barrel.

4. a joint, as at the ends of a clinker-built boat, in which an overlapping joint merges into one that is flush.

5. a groove; furrow.

chāse, *v.t.* to make a groove or furrow in; to indent.

chāse'ȧ·ble, *a.* see *chasable.*

chāse gun, in an armed ship, a gun used in chasing an enemy or in defending a ship when pursued.

chāse port, the port of a chase gun.

chās'ẽr, *n.* 1. one who chases; a pursuer; a hunter.

2. a gun at the head or stern of a vessel for firing when in chase or being pursued: called also *chase gun.*

3. a mild drink taken after a strong one. [Colloq.]

4. in aeronautics, a light, fast airplane of small size used to ward off and pursue an enemy craft.

5. a small, speedy ship used in naval warfare for pursuing or attacking other vessels or submarines.

6. a steeplechaser.

chās'ẽr, *n.* 1. one skilled in the art of enchasing or engraving.

2. a finishing tool for threading screws, having several points that bear on work revolving on a lathe.

3. a tool for engraving.

chas'i·ble, *n.* see *chasuble.*

Çhas·i·dē'ăn, *n.* see *Assidean.*

chās'ing, *n.* the act or art of embossing on metals.

çhaṣm, *n.* [L. *chasma*; Gr. *chasma*, a yawning hollow, gulf, from *chainein*, to yawn, to gape.]

1. a deep cleft; a fissure; an abyss; an opening made by splitting, as a breach in the earth or a rock.

2. any break or gap; a hiatus.

3. a wide divergence of feelings, sentiments, interests, etc. between people or groups; a rift.

Syn.—abyss, gorge, depth, gulf, breach.

çhaṣ'mȧ, *n.* [Gr. *chasma*, from *chainein*, to yawn, gape.] in pathology, an abnormal spell of yawning. [Rare.]

çhaṣ'măl, *a.* of or like a chasm; abysmal.

çhaṣmed, *a.* having gaps or a chasm.

çhaṣ·mog'ȧ·my, *n.* [Gr. *chasma*, an opening, chasm, and *gamos*, marriage.] in botany, the opening of the perianth of a flower for the purpose of fertilization: opposed to *clistogamy.*

çhaṣ'my, *a.* filled with chasms.

chas·sé' (shȧ-sā'), *n.* [Fr., from *chasse*, pp. of *chasser*, to chase.]

1. originally, a dance step in which one foot rapidly followed the other during the execution of a glide.

2. a forward or sideways gliding step accompanied by one or two rapid linking steps.

chas·sé', *v.i.*; chasséd, *pt., pp.*; chasséing, *ppr.* 1. to make such a step or steps; to dance with such steps.

2. to walk as if in a series of such steps.

çhȧsse (shȧs), *n.* [Fr., from *chasser*, to chase.] a light liqueur served after the coffee: called also *chasse café.*

çhas'se·las, *n.* [named from the French village of *Chasselas*, where it is grown.] a fine, white variety of grape.

chasse″-ma″rée' (shȧs″mȧ″rā'), *n.* [Fr., from *chasser*, to chase, and *marée*, tide.] a small sailing vessel used in the French coasting trade; a lugger.

çhȧsse·pōt' (-pō'), *n.* [Fr., named after the inventor, A. A. *Chassepot.*] a breech-loading needle gun, or center-fire rifle, formerly used by the French, especially during the Franco-Prussian war of 1870–1871.

çhȧs·sēur', *n.* [Fr., a huntsman, from *chasser*, to hunt, chase.]

1. a soldier, especially one of certain French light infantry or cavalry troops, trained and equipped for rapid action.

2. a uniformed attendant.

3. a hunter; huntsman.

Çhas·sid'iç (*or* khä-sē'dik), *a.* of or characteristic of the Chassidim: also *Hasidic.*

Çhas'sid·im (*Heb.* khä-sē'dim), *n.pl.*; *sing.* **Çhas'sid** (*Heb.* khä'sid), the members of a sect of Jewish mystics that originated in Poland in the eighteenth century: also *Hasidim.*

chas'sis (*or* shas'i, *or* chas'i), *n.*; *pl.* **çhas'siṣ,** [Fr., from *chasse*, a frame.]

1. a frame on which the carriage of a gun moves back and forth.

2. the under framework of a motor vehicle, including the wheels and engine parts.

3. the frame supporting the body of an airplane.

4. in radio, (a) the framework to which the parts of a radio set, amplifier, etc. are attached; (b) the assembled frame and parts.
5. the body. [Slang.]

chāste, *v.t.* to chasten. [Obs.]

chāste, *a.* [OFr. *chaste, caste,* from L. *castus,* pure, chaste; Gr. *katharos,* pure.]
1. not indulging in unlawful sexual intercourse; virtuous: said especially of women.
2. free from obscenity; pure in thought and act; innocent; modest.
3. unmarried. [Obs.]
4. in literature, architecture, or the arts, indicative of simplicity and restraint; free from vulgarisms, affectations, or extravagancies; as, a *chaste* style; the building or the statue was *chaste* in design.
Syn.—immaculate, incorrupt, modest, pure, simple, unaffected, uncontaminated, undefiled, virtuous.

chāste′-eȳed (-id), *a.* having a modest look.

chāste′ly, *adv.* in a chaste manner; without obscenity; purely.

chās′ten (chās′n), *v.t.*; chastened, *pt., pp.*; chastening, *ppr.* [ME. *chastien;* OFr. *chastier,* from L. *castigare,* to punish, chastise; *castus,* pure, and *agere,* to lead, drive.]
1. to correct by punishment; to punish in order to make better; to discipline; as, to *chasten* a son with a rod.
2. to purify from errors or faults.
3. to restrain from excess; to subdue.
Syn.—chastise, discipline, correct, punish, purify.

chās′tened (chās′nd), *a.* corrected; punished; purified from faults.

chās′ten·ēr, *n.* one who chastens.

chāste′ness, *n.* 1. chastity; purity.
2. in literature and the arts, freedom from extravagances and mannerisms; the quality of being both simple and restrained.

chās′ten·ing, *n.* correction; punishment.

chāste tree, the agnus castus, or *Vitex,* a Mediterranean tree that grows to the height of eight or ten feet and whose aromatic properties were said to be productive of chastity.

chas·tiṡ′ȧ·ble, *a.* deserving of chastisement.

chas·tiṡe′, *v.t.*; chastised, *pt., pp.*; chastising, *ppr.* [ME. *chastisen,* an extended form of *chastien,* to chasten, punish.]
1. to punish; to inflict pain upon, by blows or otherwise, for the purpose of correction.
2. to restrain; to repress. [Obs.]
3. to purify by expunging faults. [Obs.]
Syn.—punish, chasten, afflict, correct, discipline.

chas′tiṡe·ment, *n.* correction; punishment; pain inflicted for punishment and correction, especially by beating.

chas·tiṡ′ēr, *n.* one who chastises; a punisher.

chas′ti·ty, *n.* [ME. *chastite, chastete;* OFr. *chastete, chasteit;* L. *castitas (-atis),* from *castus,* chaste, pure.]
1. abstinence from all unlawful sexual activity: said especially of women.
2. freedom from obscenity, as in language or conversation; decency; modesty.
3. simple refinement of design; lack of ornateness or excess.
4. purity; unadulterated state; as, the *chastity* of the gospel. [Rare.]
5. celibacy or virginity; sexual continence.

chas′ti·ty belt, a securely fastened, beltlike device of metal, leather, etc. worn by women in the Middle Ages to prevent sexual intercourse during the absence of their husbands.

chaṡ′ū·ble, *n.* [OFr. *chasuble;* LL. *casubula, casubla, casula,* a hooded garment; from L. *casa,* a hut, cottage.] a sleeveless outer vestment worn over the alb by the priest in saying Mass: also written *chasible* or *chesible.*

chat, *v.i.*; chatted, *pt., pp.*; chatting, *ppr.* [shortened from *chatter.*]
1. to talk in a familiar manner; to talk without form or ceremony.
2. to talk idly; to prate.

chat, *v.t.* to talk of. [Obs.]

chat, *n.* 1. free, familiar talk; informal conversation.
2. small talk; chit-chat; chatter.
3. a bird of the genus *Icteria,* related to the warblers, the best known varieties being the yellow-breasted chat (a fluent songster common in the United States) and the long-tailed chat. The name is also applied to several European birds of the family *Saxicolidæ,* including the stonechat, whinchat, and wheatear.

chat, *n.* 1. a twig or little stick. [Dial.]
2. [*pl.*] poor ore freely mixed with small stones. [Brit. Dial.]
3. a little potato. [Brit. Dial.]
4. an ament or catkin, as of a willow.
5. a samara, as of a maple.
6. a spike, as of plantain.

chȧ·teau′ (sha-tō′), *n.*; *pl.* **chȧ·teaux′** (sha-tōz′), [Fr., from OFr. *chastel, castel,* from L. *castellum,* a castle.]
1. in France, a feudal castle or a fortress.
2. any manor house, imposing country residence, or royal residence outside a city, especially in France.

Chȧ·teau′ wīne, any of certain wines made from grapes grown at some particular château in France, especially in the region of Bordeaux: each wine is designated by the name of its château; as, *Château Ausone.*

chat′e·lāin, *n.* the keeper of a castle; castellan.

chat′e·lāine, *n.* [Fr. *chatelaine,* a wife of a castellan, f. of *chatelain;* LL. *castellanus,* a keeper of a castle, from L. *castellum,* a castle.]
1. the lady of a castle; mistress of a château.
2. a woman's ornamental clasp worn at the waist, with keys, purses, watches, etc. fastened to it on a chain: so called from the keys carried by a medieval chatelaine.
3. a decorative chain suspended between two clasps or pins and worn as an ornament on women's clothing.

chat′e·let, *n.* a castellet. [Obs.]

chat′el·lā·ny, *n.* same as *castellany.*

chȧ·tī′, *n.* [S. Am.] a wildcat, *Felis mitis,* or tiger cat, of South America, small and spotted.

chȧ·toy′ăn·cy, *n.* the condition or quality of being chatoyant.

chȧ·toy′ănt, *a.* [Fr. *chatoyant,* ppr. of *chatoyer,* to change luster like the eye of a cat; *chat,* a cat.] having a changeable, undulating luster or color, like that of a cat's eye in the dark.

chȧ·toy′ănt, *n.* a hard stone, which, being cut smooth, has an undulating or wavy light.

chȧ·toy′ment, *n.* changeableness of color in a mineral; play of colors, as in the cat's-eye. [Rare.]

chat′täh, *n.* [Anglo-Ind.] in India, an umbrella.

chat′tel (chat′l), *n.* [ME. *chatel;* OFr. *chatel;* LL. *captale, capitale,* capital, property, goods; neut. of L. *capitalis,* chief, head, from *caput (-itis),* head.]
1. an article of personal or movable property as distinguished from real property: furniture, automobiles, livestock, farm equipment, etc. are chattels.
2. a slave. [Archaic.]
chattel mortgage; a mortgage on personal property, as distinguished from one on real estate.
chattel personal; any article of tangible personal property.
chattel real or *interest;* any right in land that is less than a freehold.

chat′tel·iṡm, *n.* the condition of holding chattels or of being a chattel.

chat′tēr, *v.i.*; chattered, *pt., pp.*; chattering, *ppr.* [imitative in origin.]
1. to utter sounds rapidly and indistinctly, as a magpie or a monkey.
2. to click together rapidly; as, the teeth *chatter* when one is chilly.
3. to talk idly, carelessly, or rapidly.
4. to rattle or vibrate, as a tool when not held with sufficient firmness, or when the tool itself is too flexible.

chat′tēr, *v.t.* to utter, as rapid indistinct sounds; as, to *chatter* nonsense.

chat′tēr, *n.* 1. short, indistinct sounds in rapid succession; also, rapid, idle talk.
2. noise made by clicking the teeth together.

chat·tēr·ā′tion, *n.* the act of habitual or excessive chattering. [Colloq.]

chat′tēr·box, *n.* one who talks incessantly.

chat′tēr·ēr, *n.* 1. a prater; an idle talker; a person who chatters.
2. any of various chattering birds, as the waxwing.

chat′tēr·ing, *n.* rapid, inarticulate sounds, as of birds; idle talk; rapid striking of the teeth, as from cold.

chat′tēr·märk, *n.* 1. one of the fine undulations formed on the surface of work by a cutting tool which chatters.
2. one of a series of small, curved abrasions of the surface of a glaciated rock, resulting from the vibrations of the glacier passing over.

chat thrush, same as *myna.*

chat′ti·ly, *adv.* in a chatty manner.

chat′ti·ness, *n.* the quality of being chatty.

chat′ty, *a.* 1. given to free conversation; talkative.
2. light, familiar, and informal: said of talk.

chat′ty, *n.* [Anglo-Ind.] a porous earthen pot or jar for cooling water by evaporation: used in the East Indies.

chat′wood, *n.* little sticks for fuel. [Dial.]

Chau·cē′ri·ăn, *a.* like or similar to Chaucer or his writings.

Chau·cē′ri·ăn, *n.* a scholar specializing in the life and works of Chaucer.

Chau′cēr text, a kind of text type.

chaud″froid′ (shō″frwȧ′), *n.* [Fr., *hot-cold.*] a cold dish consisting of choice bits of meat or game or poultry in aspic.

chaud′-mel′lé (shōd′-mel′ā), *n.* [Fr. *chaud-mêlée; chaud,* hot, and *mêler, medler,* to mingle.] unpremeditated homicide committed in passion but not in self-defense: sometimes confused with *chance-medley.*

chauf′fēr, *n.* [Fr. *chauffer,* to heat.] a small furnace, usually open at the top, with a grate near the bottom.

chauf′fēur (shō′fēr), *n.* [Fr. *chauffeur,* a stoker, from *chauffer,* to heat, get up steam.] a person whose work is to drive an automobile for someone else; driver.

chauf′fēur, *v.t.* to act as chauffeur to; drive (a person) in an automobile.

chaul·moo′grȧ, chaul·mū′grȧ, chaul·mau′grȧ, *n.* [E. Ind.] a tree of the East Indies belonging to the Indian plum family: it yields a large succulent fruit, the seeds of which yield a medicinal oil used in the treatment of leprosy and other diseases.

chau·mon·telle′ (shō-), *n.* [Fr.] a sort of pear.

chaun, *n.* a gap. [Obs.]

chaun, *v.i.* to open; to yawn. [Obs.]

chaunt, *n.* and *v.* chant. [Archaic.]

chaunt′ēr, *n.* chanter. [Archaic.]

chā′us, *n.* an animal of Asia and Africa like a lynx: called also the *jungle cat.*

chausses (shōs *or, formerly, Eng.* chou′siz), *n.pl.* [Fr.] trousers covering the hips, legs, and feet, worn in Europe in medieval times; also, flexible armor for the same parts.

chaus·sūre′ (shō-sēr′), *n.* [Fr., from *chausser,* to shoe; L. *calceare,* from *calceus,* shoe, from *calx,* the heel.] an article of footwear; shoe, boot, slipper, etc.

chau·tau′quȧ (shȧ-tô′kwȧ), *n.* [from the summer schools inaugurated at Chautauqua, New York, in 1874.] an assembly lasting several days, for educational and recreational purposes: the program includes lectures, concerts, etc.

chau′vin·iṡm (shō′), *n.* [Fr. *chauvinisme,* from Nicolas *Chauvin,* a soldier of Napoleon I, who, in 1815, acquired much notoriety by his bellicose attachment to the lost imperial cause.]
1. absurd, unreasoning, and belligerent patriotism; the quality of being wildly extravagant, demonstrative, or fanatical in regard to national glory and honor.
2. unreasoning devotion to one's race, sex, etc., with contempt for other races, the opposite sex, etc.; as, male *chauvinism.*

chau′vin·ist (shō′), *n.* 1. a person whose patriotism is unreasoning and fanatical; jingo.
2. a person unreasonably devoted to his own race, sex, etc. and contemptuous of other races, the opposite sex, etc.

chau′vin·ist, *a.* chauvinistic.

chau·vin·is′tic (shō-), *a.* pertaining to the qualities of chauvinism or chauvinists.

chau·vin·is′ti·căl·ly (shō-), *adv.* in the manner of a chauvinist.

chav′en·dēr, *n.* [Fr. *chevin;* OFr. *chevesne,* a chub.] see *chub.*

chav′i·chȧ, *n.* the Columbia salmon: the Alaskan Indian name.

chaw, *n.* and *v.* chew: now substandard or humorous. [Colloq.]

chaw′bā″cŏn, *n.* a country bumpkin; a lout; an uncouth rustic. [Colloq.]

chāy, chāy′root, *n.* [Tamil *chaya,* a root, and *root.*] the root of the *Oldenlandia umbellata,* from which a red dye is obtained: also called *shayaroot, chayaroot,* and *choyroot.*

chēap, *a.*; *comp.* cheaper; *superl.* cheapest, [shortened from *good cheap,* good bargain.]
1. low in price or cost; not expensive.
2. charging low prices; as, *cheap* jobbers.
3. worth more than the price.
4. costing little labor or trouble; easily got.
5. of little or no value; virtually worthless.
6. held in little esteem; common; as, don't make yourself *cheap.*
7. in economics, lowered in exchange value or buying power; as, *cheap* money is often a result of inflation.
to feel cheap; to feel embarrassed, ashamed, or somewhat contemptible. [Slang.]
Syn.—common, inexpensive, uncostly, mean, vile, worthless, low-priced.

chēap, *n.* [ME. *cheep, cheap*; AS. *ceáp*, trade, traffic, price, cattle.]
1. bargain; purchase; as in the phrases good *cheap*, better *cheap*. [Obs.]
2. a market: now only in place names, as *Cheapside*.

chēap, *adv.* in a cheap manner; cheaply.

chēap, *v.i.* to bargain. [Obs.]

chēap'en, *v.t.*; cheapened, *pt.*, *pp.*; cheapening, *ppr.* [ME. *cheapien, chepen*; AS. *ceápian*, to trade, buy.]
1. to attempt to buy; to ask the price of (a commodity); to chaffer; to bargain for. [Archaic.]
2. to make cheap or cheaper.
3. to depreciate, belittle, or bring into contempt.

chēap'en, *v.i.* to become cheap or cheaper.

chēap'en·ẽr, *n.* one who cheapens or bargains.

chēap'-jack, chēap'-john, *n.* one who hawks or sells cheap goods on the streets; also, one who ostensibly fixes a price and gradually reduces it to make a sale.

chēap'ly, *adv.* 1. at a small price; at a low rate.
2. in a cheap manner.

chēap'ness, *n.* the quality or condition of being cheap.

chēap skāte, a person unwilling to spend money; miserly, ungenerous person. [Slang.]

chēar, *n.* and *v.* cheer. [Obs.]

chēat, *v.t.*; cheated, *pt.*, *pp.*; cheating, *ppr.* [ME. *cheten*, to confiscate, seize; a contr. of *escheten*, escheat.]
1. to deceive and defraud in a bargain; to deceive for the purpose of gain in selling.
2. to impose on; to trick; to beguile: it may be followed by *of*, *out of*, or *into*; as, to *cheat* a child *into* a belief that a medicine is palatable.
3. to foil; elude; escape; as, to *cheat* death.
Syn.—defraud, trick, fleece, delude, cozen, overreach, swindle, dupe, beguile, deceive, hoodwink, prevaricate, gull, dissemble, inveigle.

chēat, *v.i.* to practice trickery or fraud; to act dishonestly; as, to *cheat* in business or at cards.
to cheat on; to be sexually unfaithful to. [Slang.]

chēat, *n.* 1. a fraud committed by deception; a trick; imposition; imposture.
2. a person who cheats; one guilty of fraud by deceitful practices.
3. a grass which grows among grain: also called *chess*.
4. in law, the obtaining of another's property by intentional and active misrepresentation.
Syn.—artifice, deception, imposture, chicanery, swindle, deceit, fraud, delusion, trick, imposition, guile, stratagem.

chēat'ȧ·ble, *a.* able to be defrauded.

chēat'ȧ·ble·ness, *n.* the quality of being cheatable.

chēat bread (bred), English wheaten bread second in grade to the finest, the latter being called *manchet*.

chēat'ẽr, *n.* 1. one who cheats.
2. an escheater. [Rare.]

chēat'ing, *a.* defrauding by deception; imposing on.

chēat'ing, *n.* the act of defrauding by deceitful means.

chēat'ing·ly, *adv.* in a cheating manner.

Çhē·baç'çō bōat, [from *Chebacco*, a river in Massachusetts, where such vessels were built.] a two-masted boat, with a broad bow and a narrow stern, formerly used in the Newfoundland cod and mackerel fisheries.

chē·beç', *n.* [echoic of the bird's note.] the least flycatcher, a small, eastern North American bird, *Empidonax minimus*.

check, *n.* [ME. *chek, chekke*; OFr. *eschek, eschec, eschac*, a check at chess, repulse, defeat; from Per. *shāh*, king, the principal piece in a game of chess.]
1. a sudden stop; abrupt halt.
2. a sudden restraint; curb; control.
3. a person or thing that controls or restrains.
4. a supervision of accuracy, efficiency, etc.; as, the foreman kept a *check* on his department.
5. a test of accuracy; comparison or standard of comparison; verification; examination.
6. a mark (✓) to show approval or verification of something, or to call attention to it.
7. a ticket or token given, (a) to show ownership or identify against loss; as, a baggage *check*; (b) to indicate one's bill at a restaurant or bar.
8. a gambling chip.
9. a written order to a bank for money payable as to a person named or to bearer: also spelled *cheque*.
10. a pattern of small squares like that of a chessboard.
11. one of the small squares of such a pattern.
12. a cloth with such a pattern.
13. a small split, crack, or chink.
14. in chess, the condition of a player's king that is in danger and must be put into a safe position.
in check; in restraint; under control.

check, *interj.* 1. agreed! correct! right! [Colloq.]
2. in chess, a call meaning that the opponent's king must be taken out of check.

check, *v.t.*; checked, *pt.*, *pp.*; checking, *ppr.*
1. to stop suddenly; to halt abruptly.
2. to restrain; to hinder or repress; to curb; to moderate.
3. to retard the growth of.
4. to rebuke; to chide or reprove.
5. to test, measure, verify, or control by investigation, comparison, or examination.
6. to mark with a check (✓).
7. to mark with a crisscross pattern.
8. to deposit temporarily; as, *check* your hat and coat.
9. to make cracks in; as, heat *checks* timber.
10. in agriculture, to plant in checkrows.
11. in chess, to place (an opponent's king) in check.
12. in seamanship, to ease off (a little of a rope, which is too taut); also, to stopper (the cable).
to check off; to mark as verified, examined, etc.
to check up on; to investigate the record, character, etc. of; to examine.
Syn.—control, curb, inhibit, govern, rebuke, repress, reprove, restrain, stop.

check, *v.i.* 1. to stop; to make a stop (with *at*). [Archaic.]
The mind *checks at* any vigorous undertaking. —Locke.
2. to clash or interfere. [Rare.]
3. to agree with one another item for item; as, the accounts *check*.
4. to write a check; draw a check on a bank account.
5. to crack in small checks, as wood subjected to heat, or varnish in drying.
6. to stop or pause to pick up the scent: said of hunting dogs.
7. in chess, to place an opponent's king in check.
8. in falconry, to turn or to abandon the chase of proper game in order to follow worse game (with *at*).
to check in; (a) to register at a hotel, convention, etc.; (b) [Slang.] to die.
to check out; (a) to settle one's bill and leave a hotel, etc.; (b) [Slang.] to die.

check, *a.* 1. used to check or verify; as, a *check* experiment.
2. having a crisscross pattern; checked.

check'āġe, *n.* the act of checking, as an item in a catalogue.

check'book, *n.* a book formed of a number of detachable blank checks, issued to a depositor by a bank.

checked, *a.* [pp. of *check*.] having a pattern of squares; as, a *checked* tablecloth.

check'ẽr, *n.* [ME. *cheker*, chessboard, from *escheker*; OFr. *eschequier*, from *eschec*, a check.]
1. a small square like those of a chessboard.
2. a pattern of such squares.
3. one of the flat, round pieces used in playing checkers or backgammon.
4. a chessboard. [Archaic.]
5. [*pl.*] in architecture, stones arranged like the squares of a chessboard.
6. in botany, (a) either of two European varieties of service tree resembling the mountain ash, but having a larger, spotted fruit: also *checker tree*; (b) [*pl.*] the fruit of either of these trees.

check'ẽr, *v.t.*; checkered, *pt.*, *pp.*; checkering, *ppr.* 1. to form into little squares, like a chessboard, by lines or stripes of different colors.
2. to diversify; to break the uniformity of.

check'ẽr, *n.* 1. one who examines or verifies.
2. a person who checks hats, luggage, etc.

check'ẽr·ber'ry, *n.*; *pl.* **check'ẽr·ber''rieṣ,**
1. the wintergreen plant, *Gaultheria procumbens*, or its edible, red, berrylike fruit.
2. the partridgeberry.

check'ẽr·bloom, *n.* a plant of the mallow family, with pinkish flowers.

check'ẽr·bōard, *n.* a board on which checkers or chess is played. It is laid out in sixty-four squares of two alternating colors.

check'ẽred, *a.* 1. diversified; varied; full of ups and downs; as, a *checkered* career.
2. patterned in alternate squares of color like a chessboard.
3. varied by the use of color and shading.

check'ẽrṣ, *n.pl.* [*construed as sing.*] draughts; a game played on a checkerboard by two persons, each having twelve pieces to move.

check'ẽr·wōrk, *n.* 1. any article exhibiting different colors, alternating and arranged in squares.
2. a condition or situation presenting diversified features, especially relating to misfortunes.

check'hook, *n.* 1. a hook on the saddle of a horse's harness through which the checkrein is fastened.
2. a device on a hoisting machine for checking excessive speed.

check'ing aç·çount', a bank account against which the depositor can draw checks at any time, without presenting a passbook.

check'lȧ·töun, *n.* same as *ciclaton*.

check'less, *a.* that cannot be checked or restrained.

check list, a list or catalogue used for verifying or checking.

check'māte, *n.* 1. a move in the game of chess, that checks the opponent's king so that it cannot be put into safety, thus ending the game.
2. the position of the king resulting from this.
3. figuratively, defeat; overthrow.

check'māte, *interj.* in chess, a call to indicate a checkmate.

check'māte, *v.t.*; checkmated, *pt.*, *pp.*; checkmating, *ppr.* in chess, to place in checkmate; hence, to arrest and defeat.

check nut, in mechanics, a nut which screws down upon the primary nut to secure it: called also *lock nut*.

check'ọff, *n.* an arrangement by which dues, assessments, etc. of trade-union members are withheld from wages and turned over to the union by the employer.

check'point, *n.* a place on a highway, a border between countries, etc. where traffic is stopped, as for inspection by authorities.

check'rein, *n.* 1. a strap looped around the checkhook to prevent a horse from lowering his head: also called *bearing rein*.
2. a rein or line which connects the driving rein of one horse of a double team with the bit of the other.
Also called *check line*.

check'rōll, *n.* a list of employees in a household.

check'rọom, *n.* a room in which hats, coats, baggage, etc. may be left until called for.

check'rōw, *n.* any of several rows planted in squares so that a cultivator can operate between them.

check'rōw, *v.t.* to plant (corn, grain, etc.) in checkrows.

check'string, *n.* a cord by which a person in a public conveyance may signal the driver to stop.

check'up, *n.* an examination; an investigation.

check valve, a valve that permits water, etc. to flow only in one direction and prevents a return flow.

check'y, *a.* arranged in checkerlike form, especially, in heraldry, applied to the checkerlike design of the border or field of an armorial bearing.

CHECKY FIELD

Ched'dar, *n.* see under *cheese*.

chedd'īte (*or* shed'), *n.* [from *Chedde*, France, where it was made.] an explosive for blasting, consisting of potassium chlorate or perchlorate mixed with a nitro compound and an oily substance, as castor oil.

cheek, *n.* [ME. *cheke, cheoke, choke*; AS. *ceace, ceoce*, the cheek; L.G. *koek*; D. *kaak*, jaw.]
1. the side of the face between the nose and the ear, below the eyes on each side.
2. a thing suggesting this in shape or position.
3. [*pl.*] in mechanics, those pieces of a machine which form corresponding sides, or which are double and alike; as, the *cheeks* of a printing press; the *cheeks* of a turner's lathe.
4. in founding, one of the side parts of a flask consisting of more than two parts.
5. a branch of a horse's bit.
6. impudence; sauciness; insolence; cool self-possession. [Colloq.]

cheek by jowl; (a) close together; (b) familiar; close; extremely intimate.
tongue in cheek; without sincerity; with the real meaning different from the ostensible one.
cheek, *v.t.* to speak saucily to; to confront in a bold or impudent manner. [Colloq.]
What does he come here *cheeking* us for?
—Dickens.
cheek'bōne, *n.* the bone of the upper cheek, just below the eye.
cheeked, *a.* with cheeks: used in hyphenated compounds.
cheek'i·ly, *adv.* saucily; impudently. [Colloq.]
cheek'i·ness, *n.* the quality or state of being cheeky; sauciness; impudence. [Colloq.]
cheek pouch, a pouchlike swelling in the cheek of certain rodents, monkeys, etc., used for holding food.
cheek strap, one of the side straps of a bridle, connecting the headband with the bit.
cheek tooth, a molar tooth or grinder.
cheek'y, *a.*; *comp.* cheekier; *superl.* cheekiest, saucy; impudent. [Colloq.]
cheep, *n.* a short, faint, shrill sound, as of a young bird; a chirp; a peep.
Come, screw the pegs in tunefu' *cheep*.
—Burns.
cheep, *v.i.*; cheeped, *pt.*, *pp.*; cheeping, *ppr.* to chirp as a bird.
cheep, *v.t.* to utter in a chirping tone; to pipe.
cheer, *n.* [ME. *chere*, the face, look, demeanor, welcome; OFr. *chere*, *chiere*, from LL. *cara*, the face; Gr. *kara*, the head; Sans. *ciras*, the head.]
1. a shout of joy used to urge on, welcome, approve, congratulate, etc.; as, they gave three *cheers*.
2. a state of gladness or joy; a state of animation; mirth; gaiety; jollity.
3. entertainment; that which makes cheerful; provisions for a feast.
The table was loaded with good *cheer*.
—Irving.
4. anything that makes one happy; encouragement.
5. a mood; disposition; state of mind or of feeling.
6. facial expression. [Archaic.]
His words their drooping *cheer*
Enlightened. —Milton.
to be of good cheer; (a) to have a cheerful countenance or manner; (b) to be cheerful.
with good cheer; in a cordial manner.
Syn.—hope, happiness, comfort, hospitality.
cheer, *v.i.*; cheered, *pt.*, *pp.*; cheering, *ppr.* 1. to grow cheerful; to become gladsome or joyous: often with *up*.
At sight of thee my gloomy soul *cheers up*.
—Phillips.
2. to utter a cheer or shout of acclamation or joy.
cheer, *v.t.* 1. to salute with cheers, or other expressions of approval.
2. to dispel gloom, sorrow, or apathy from; to fill with joy, good spirits, and hope; to gladden; as, to *cheer* the heart.
3. to urge, incite, or encourage by cheers; as, to *cheer* the hounds.
Syn.—inspire, encourage, comfort.
cheer'ẽr, *n.* one who or that which cheers or gladdens.
cheer'ful, *a.* 1. animated; having good spirits; full of life; gay; joyful.
2. filling with cheer; bright and attractive; as, a *cheerful* room.
3. willing; hearty; as, a *cheerful* helper.
Syn.—lively, gay, bright, happy, bonny, merry, joyful, pleasant, buoyant, sunny, sprightly, blithe, joyous.
cheer'ful·ly, *adv.* in a cheerful manner.
cheer'ful·ness, *n.* animation; good spirits; state or quality of being cheerful.
cheer'i·ly, *adv.* with cheerfulness; with spirit.
cheer'i·ness, *n.* cheerfulness.
cheer'ing·ly, *adv.* in a cheerful manner.
cheer'i·ō, *interj.* and *n.*; *pl.* **cheer'i·ōs**, 1. hello. [Brit. Colloq.]
2. good-by. [Brit Colloq.]
cheer'ish·ness, *n.* cheerfulness. [Rare.]
cheer'less, *a.* without joy, gladness, or comfort; gloomy; dreary.
cheer'less·ly, *adv.* in a cheerless manner.
cheer'less·ness, *n.* state of being cheerless.
cheer'ly, *a.* gay; cheerful; not gloomy. [Obs.]
cheer'ly, *adv.* 1. cheerily. [Archaic.]
2. in nautical usage, quickly; briskly.
cheer'y, *a.*; *comp.* cheerier; *superl.* cheeriest, gay; sprightly; pleasant; cheerful; bright.
cheeṣe, *n.* [ME. *chese*; AS. *cese*, *cysa*; LL. *casius*; L. *caseus*, cheese.]
1. a food made from the curd of milk, coagulated usually by rennet, separated from the whey, and pressed in a vat, hoop, or mold.
2. a shaped mass of this.
3. a thing like cheese in shape or consistency; as, damson *cheese*.
4. the wrinkled, flat, unripe fruit of dwarf mallow, somewhat resembling a cheese.
American cheese; a kind of fairly hard, mild Cheddar cheese, popular in the United States.
brick cheese; a semihard, elastic American cheese with a strong, sweetish taste, shaped like a brick and containing many small holes.
Brie cheese; (a) a soft, white cheese made in Brie, France; (b) an American cheese resembling this.
Camembert cheese; a soft, creamy cheese of a pale yellow color.
Cheddar cheese; a hard, smooth cheese, originally made in Cheddar, England.
cheese it! stop (whatever one is doing)! run! [Slang.]
cottage cheese; a soft, white cheese made by straining and seasoning the curds of sour milk: also called *Dutch cheese*, *pot cheese*, and *smeerkaas*.
cream cheese; a soft cheese made of cream or of milk with the addition of cream.
Dunlop cheese; a soft, white cheese, made in Ayrshire, Scotland.
Dutch cheese; (a) a hard cheese made from skim milk pressed into round molds, the outside being colored a reddish tint; (b) same as *cottage cheese*.
Edam cheese; a mild, yellow cheese made in a round mold and generally colored red on the outside.
filled cheese; a kind of cheese made from skim milk: so called because a fatty filling, as lard or oleomargarine, is used as a substitute for the cream.
Gloucester cheese; a rich English cheese of mild flavor.
Gruyère cheese; a light-yellow Swiss cheese, very rich in butterfat, or an American cheese resembling this.
Limburger cheese; a soft, white brick cheese with a strong odor, originally made near Limburg, Belgium, now also in the United States.
Neufchâtel cheese; a delicate cream cheese prepared from sweet milk with or without cream.
Parmesan cheese; a hard, dry, yellow Italian cheese of delicate flavor, made from skim milk and usually grated.
Roquefort cheese; a strong cheese with a bluish mold, made at Roquefort, in Guienne, France, from goats' and ewes' milk.
slipcoat cheese; a soft, rich cheese made from milk and resembling Camembert cheese.
Stilton cheese; a rich, waxy cheese having a blue-green mold, originally sold at Stilton, England.
cheeṣe, *n.* [prob. from Urdu *chīz*, thing.] the important thing; as, he's the big *cheese*. [Slang.]
cheeṣe'cāke, *n.* 1. a type of cake made of a mixture of sweetened curds, eggs, milk, etc.
2. display of the figure, especially the legs, of a pretty girl, as in some newspaper photographs. [Slang.]
cheeṣe'çloth, *n.* a thin, cotton cloth with a loose weave, used for wrapping cheese, and many other purposes, such as curtains, dustcloths, etc.
cheeṣe flȳ, a small, black dipterous insect bred in cheese, ham, etc., the *Piophila casei*, of the family *Muscidæ*, the same to which the housefly, blowfly, etc. belong. The maggot, called *cheese hopper*, is furnished with two horny, claw-shaped mandibles, which it uses both for digging and for moving itself, having no feet.
cheeṣe hop'pẽr, see *cheese fly*.
cheeṣe'lep, *n.* [AS. *cyslybb*, rennet.] rennet. [Dial.]
cheeṣe mīte, a mite, *Acarus siro*, which infests cheese, dried meat, etc.
cheeṣe'mŏñ''gẽr, *n.* one who deals in cheese.
cheeṣe'pär''ing, *a.* meanly economical; parsimonious; as, a *cheeseparing* policy.
cheeṣe'pär''ing, *n.* 1. a paring of the rind of cheese.
2. anything as worthless as such a paring.
3. stinginess.
cheeṣe press, a press or apparatus for pressing curd in the making of cheese.
cheeṣe ren'net, the yellow bedstraw, *Galium verum*, used for coagulating milk.
cheeṣe vat, the vat or case in which curds are kept for pressing.
cheeṣ'i·ness, *n.* the quality of being cheesy.
cheeṣ'y, *a.*; *comp.* cheesier; *superl.* cheesiest.
1. having the consistency, taste, odor, or form of cheese.
2. poor; inferior. [Slang.]
chee'tȧh, **chee'tȧ**, *n.* [Hind. *chītā*, leopard, from Sans. *citra*, variegated, spotted.] a leopardlike animal of Africa and southern Asia, with a small head, long legs, and a black-spotted, tawny coat: it can be trained to hunt: also spelled *chetah*.
chē'tăl, *n.* [Hind. *chītal*.] the chital.
çhef, *n.* [Fr.] 1. a head cook.
2. any cook.
çhef-d'oeuvre' (she-dūvr'), *n.*; *pl.* **çhefs-d'oeuvre'** (she-), [Fr.] a masterpiece, as in art, literature, etc.
cheg'ōe, *n.* same as *chigoe*.
Çhei·lan'thēṣ, *n.* [Gr. *cheilos*, a lip, and *anthos*, a flower, so called from the form of the indusium.] a genus of polypodiaceous ferns, distinguished by the small sori at the ends of the free veins, and covered by the bent-over margin of the frond.
çheir, *n.* [abbrev. of *Cheiranthus*.] the wallflower.
Çhei·ran'thus, *n.* [Gr. *cheir*, the hand, and *anthos*, a flower.] a genus of plants, of the family *Cruciferæ*, consisting of pubescent herbs or small shrubs with large yellow or purple, sweet-scented flowers. The wallflower, *Cheiranthus cheiri*, is the best-known species.
çhei'rō-, same as *chiro-*.
Chē'kȧ, *n.* [from Russ. names of initial letters of *Chrezvychainaya Kommissia*, the extraordinary commission.] a commission in the Soviet Union which acted as secret police against counterrevolutionists (1917–1921).
çhē'lȧ, *n.* [Hind. *celā*, a pupil, a disciple, a slave.] in India, a disciple or novice.
çhē'lȧ, *n.*; *pl.* **çhē'lae**, [Gr. *chēlē*, a claw.] one of the pincerlike claws with which some of the limbs are terminated in certain crustaceans, as the crab, lobster, etc.
çhē'lāte, *a.* having or resembling pincerlike claws.
çhē'lāte, *n.* a chemical compound in which the central atom (usually a metal ion) is attached to neighboring atoms by at least two bonds in such a way as to form a ring structure.
çhē'lāte, *v.t.*; chelated, *pt.*, *pp.*; chelating, *ppr.* to cause (a metal ion) to react with another molecule to form a chelate.
çhē·lā'tion, *n.* the act or process of chelating or the state of being chelated.
çhel·e·ryth'rine, **çhel·e·ryth'rin**, *n.* [Gr. *chelidonion*, celandine, and *erythros*, red, and *-in*.] a colorless, crystalline, acrid, poisonous narcotic obtained from the celandine plant.
çhē·lic'ẽr·ȧ, *n.*; *pl.* **çhē·lic'ẽr·ae**, [Gr. *chēlē*, a claw, and *keras*, a horn.] one of the prehensile claws of the scorpion and spider, which are the homologues of antennae.
çhel·i·don'iç, *a.* [Gr. *chelidonion*, the celandine.] pertaining to celandine.
chelidonic acid; an acid that crystallizes in silky needles, obtained from celandine.
çhel'i·fẽr, *n.* the book scorpion.
çhē·lif'ẽr·ous, *a.* [L. *chele*, a claw, and *ferre*, to bear.] furnished with chelae, as a lobster.
çhel'i·form, *a.* [L. *chele*, a claw, and *forma*, form.] having the form of a chela or pincerlike claw, like that of the lobster.
Çhel'lē·ăn, *a.* [Fr. *chelléen*, from *Chelles*, France, where the tools were found.] designating or of that division of the Paleolithic Age during which certain flint tools were used.
çhē'loid, *n.* same as *keloid*.
Çhē·lō'nē, *n.* [Gr. *chelōnē*, a tortoise.]
1. a genus of turtles, represented by the green turtle.
2. a genus of plants in which the corolla resembles the head of a tortoise.
Çhē·lō'ni·ȧ, *n.pl.* an order of reptiles, distinguished by the body being enclosed in a double shell, out of which the head, tail, and four extremities protrude: it includes the various species of tortoise and turtle.
çhē·lō'ni·ăn, *a.* pertaining to or designating tortoises or turtles.
çhē·lō'ni·ăn, *n.* a member of the order *Chelonia*.
Çhē·lū'rȧ, *n.* [Gr. *chēlē*, a claw, and *oura*, a tail.] a genus of marine shrimps that destroy timber by boring tunnels under the surface.
çhem'iç, *n.* [Fr. *chimique*; LL. *alchimicus*, from *alchimia*, alchemy.]
1. an alchemist; a chemist. [Obs.]
2. a solution of chloride of lime for bleaching purposes.
çhem'iç, *a.* 1. of alchemy. [Archaic.]
2. chemical. [Archaic.]

chem'ic·ăl, *a.* 1. pertaining to chemistry; as, a *chemical* laboratory.
2. made by or used in chemistry.
3. operated by the use of chemicals.
4. trained in the science of chemistry.
chemical attraction; see *attraction*.
chemical engineering; see *engineering*.
chemical warfare; warfare by means of chemicals and chemical devices other than explosives, as gases, flame throwers, incendiary bombs, smoke screens, etc.

chem'ic·ăl, *n.* any substance used in or obtained by a chemical process or processes.

chem'ic·ăl·ly, *adv.* according to chemical principles; also, by chemical process or operation.

che·min' de fer (she-maṅ' dẽ fãr), [Fr., road of iron.]
1. a railroad.
2. a kind of baccarat, a gambling game.

che·mise', *n.* [Fr. *chemise*; LL. *camisia*, a shirt, tunic.]
1. an undergarment, somewhat like a loose, short slip or long undershirt, worn by women.
2. a loose dress that hangs straight with no waistline.

chem·i·sette', *n.* [Fr., dim. of *chemise*.]
1. a short, sleeveless bodice formerly worn as an undergarment by women.
2. a detachable shirt front formerly worn by women to fill in the neckline of a dress.

chem'işm, *n.* chemical force, action, or affinity. [Rare.]

chem'i·sorb, *v.t.* [*chemical*, and ad*sorb*.] to bind (a substance) chemically onto the surface layer of an adsorbent.

chem"i·sorp'tion, *n.* [from *chemisorb*, after *adsorption*.] adsorption in which the substance adsorbed on a surface reacts chemically with the surface and becomes a fixed coating.

chem'ist, *n.* 1. a student of or specialist in chemistry.
2. a druggist. [Brit.]
3. an alchemist. [Obs.]

chem'is·try, *n.*; *pl.* **chem'is·trieş,** [from *chemist*, shortened form of *alchemist*, from *alchemy*.]
1. the science dealing with the composition and properties of substances, and with the reactions by which substances are produced from or converted into other substances.
2. the application of this to a specified subject or field of activity.
3. the chemical properties, composition, reactions, and uses of a substance.
4. any process of synthesis or analysis similar to that used in chemistry; as, the main trait of wit is its *chemistry* of incongruities.
5. alchemy. [Obs.]

chem'ō-, a combining form meaning, *having to do with chemicals, of chemical reactions*, as in *chemo*therapy; also, before a vowel, *chem-*.

chem"ō·rē·cep'tŏr, *n.* a nerve ending, or sense organ, that can respond to chemical stimuli, as the taste and smell receptors.

chē·mō'sis, *n.*; *pl.* **chē·mō'sēş,** [Gr. *chēmē*, a yawning, and *-osis*.] an infection of the conjunctiva of the eye.

chem·os·mō'sis, *n.* [*chemo-*, and *osmosis*.] chemical reactions occurring through an intervening semipermeable membrane.

chem·os·mot'iç, *a.* pertaining to chemosmosis.

chem'ō·sphēre, *n.* an atmospheric zone about 20 to 50 miles above the earth's surface, characterized by extensive photochemical activity.

chem"ō·ster'i·lănt, *n.* a chemical compound that can produce sterility, used especially in insect control.

chem"ō·sũr'gẽr·y, *n.* the removal of diseased tissue or abnormal growths by using chemical substances.

chem·ō·syn'thē·sis, *n.* the synthesis by plants of organic chemical compounds with energy derived from other chemical reactions, as from oxidation by bacteria.

chem·ō·tax'is, *n.* the property of certain living cells and organisms by which they are attracted to or repelled from chemical substances.

chem"ō·ther·ȧ·peū'tiç, *a.* pertaining to chemotherapy.

chem"ō·ther·ȧ·peū'tiçs, *n.pl.* [*construed as sing.*] chemotherapy.

chem·ō·ther'ȧ·py, *n.* [*chemo-*, and *therapy*.] the treatment of infection by the systemic administration of chemicals.

chē·mot'iç, *a.* pertaining to chemosis.

chem·ot'rō·pişm, *n.* the tendency of certain plants or other organisms to turn or bend under the influence of chemical substances.

chem·ũr'giç, *a.* of or produced by chemurgy.

chem'ũr·ġy, *n.* the application of a scientific knowledge of chemistry to the cultivation of the soil, so as to secure from it products not classed as food or clothing (e.g., soy beans as a base for plastics).

che·nille', *n.* [Fr., a caterpillar.]
1. a tufted, velvety cord used for making trimmings, fringes, laces, etc.
2. a fabric filled or woven with chenille, used for rugs, bedspreads, etc.

che·niṅ blänc' (she naṅ bläṅ' *or* shen'in bläṅk'), [*also* C- B-] [Fr.; OFr. (*reisin*) *chenin*, (grape) of the dog, and *blanc*, white] a light, dry or semisweet white wine.

chē'nō·pod, *n.* a chenopodiaceous plant.

Chē·nō·pō·di·ā'cē·ae, *n.pl.* [*Chenopodium*, and *-aceæ*.] a large family of widespread plants that bear inconspicuous flowers with no petals: a few genera, as beets and spinach, are grown for food, others for ornament, and many others include noxious weeds, as Russian thistle.

chē·nō·pō·di·ā'ceous, *a.* relating to the order *Chenopodiaceæ*.

Chē·nō·pō'di·um, *n.* [Gr. *chēn*, *chēnos*, a goose, and *pous*, *podos*, a foot.] a genus of variable herbs, the goosefoots or pigweeds, of the family *Chenopodiaceæ*.

che·ong'säm', che·ong'-säm', *n.* [Chin.] a high-necked, closefitting dress with the skirt slit part way up the sides, traditionally worn by Chinese women.

cheque, *n.* a (bank) check: British spelling.

cheq'uẽr, *n.* and *v.t.* checker: British spelling.

cheq'uẽrş, *n.pl.* [*construed as sing.*] checkers: British spelling.

chē·quin' (-kēn'), *n.* a sequin. [Obs.]

cher·chez' lȧ femme' (sher-shā' lȧ fȧm'), [Fr.] look for the woman: used, often facetiously, to imply that a woman is the cause of the trouble.

che·rif', *n.* [Fr.] same as *sherif*.

cher·i·moy'ẽr, *n.* [Fr. *chérimolier*, a corruption of *cherimoles*, the Peruvian name.]
1. the pulpy fruit of *Annona cherimola*, a tree of Peru: it is heart-shaped with a scaly exterior and numerous seeds.
2. the tree bearing this fruit.

cher'ish, *v.t.*; cherished, *pt.*, *pp.*; cherishing, *ppr.* [ME. *cherischen*, *cherisen*, from OFr. *cheris-*, the stem of *cherir*, to hold dear, cherish; *cher*, from L. *carus*, dear.]
1. to treat with tenderness and affection; to take care of; to foster; to nurture.
2. to hold dear; to value highly.
3. to indulge and encourage in the mind; to harbor; to cling to; as, to *cherish* the principles of virtue.

cher'ish·ẽr, *n.* one who cherishes; a supporter.

cher'ish·ment, *n.* encouragement. [Obs.]

Chẽr'mēş, *n.* 1. a genus of bark lice found chiefly on firs and larches.
2. [c-] same as *kermes* (the dye).

chẽr'nȧ, *n.* [Sp.] any of several fishes of the family *Serranidæ*, including the red grouper.

cher'nō·zem, *n.* [Russ., from *chernyi*, black, and *zemlya*, earth, soil.] rich, black topsoil, with a lower layer of lime, found characteristically in the grasslands of central European Russia.

Cher'ō·kee, *n.*; *pl.* **Cher'ō·kee, Cher'ō·keeş,** a member of a tribe of Iroquoian Indians formerly inhabiting the southeastern United States: now settled in the Southwest.

Cher'ō·kee rōşe, an evergreen climbing rose with fragrant, large, white flowers and glossy leaves.

che·root', *n.* [Fr. *cheroute*; Tamil *shuruttu*, a roll.] a kind of cigar having blunt ends, and thicker at one end than at the other.

cher'ry, *n.*; *pl.* **cher'rieş,** [ME. *chery*, *chere*; AS. *ciris*, *cyrs*; LL. *ceresia*; L. *cerasus*; Gr. *kerasos*, a cherry tree, from *keras*, a horn, from the hardness of the wood.]
1. a small, fleshy fruit containing a smooth, hard seed: cherries are bright red, reddish black, or yellowish.
2. any tree or shrub bearing such fruit; specifically, (a) the cultivated varieties of *Prunus cerasus* and *Prunus avium*; (b) *Prunus virginiana*, the wild chokecherry, and *Prunus serotina*, the wild black cherry; (c) a kind of evergreen tree, *Prunus laurocerasus*, having a small, tasteless fruit.
3. the wood of the various cherry trees, especially that of the black cherry.
4. any of several plants or fruits resembling the cherry; as, the dog *cherry*.
5. a bright red.
Barbados cherry; a tree growing in the West Indies, a species of *Malpighia*, producing a tart fruit.

cher'ry, *a.* 1. like a red cherry in color; bright-red; ruddy; blooming; as, *cherry* lips.
2. made of cherry wood.
3. made with or from cherries.
4. having a flavor like that of cherries.
cherry bounce; a drink consisting of burned brandy and sugar in which cherries have been steeped.
cherry brandy or *cordial*; a drink made by steeping cherries in alcohol or brandy.

cher'ry bird, a bird whose chief food is cherries, such as the Carolina cedar waxwing and the California house finch.

cher'ry bomb, a round, red, powerful firecracker.

cher'ry lau'rel, an evergreen shrub, *Prunus laurocerasus*, of the family *Rosaceæ*, a native of Asia Minor.

cher'ry pep'pẽr, a species of capsicum, having small, cherry-shaped fruit.

cher'ry pick'ẽr, an elevator tower mounted on a truck, with a platform from which spacecraft on launchers, raised electric power lines, etc. can be serviced. [Slang.]

cher'ry pit, 1. the seed of the cherry.
2. a child's game played with cherry stones.

cher'ry stōne, 1. the seed of the cherry.
2. a small quahog, a variety of clam.

chẽr'sō·nēşe, *n.* [Gr. *chersonēsos*; *chersos*, dry land, and *nēsos*, an island.] a peninsula; a tract of land nearly surrounded by water.

chẽrt, *n.* [Ir. *ceart*, a stone.]
1. a dull-colored, flintlike quartz often found in limestone.
2. any of certain similar rocks composed of hydrated silica and containing impurities.

chẽrt'y, *a.*; *comp.* chertier; *superl.* chertiest, like chert; full of chert; flinty.

cher'ub, *n.*; *pl.* **cher'ubs** or, for 1, 2, 3, **cher'ū·bim,** also, in the Vulgate, **cher'ū·bin,** [LL. *cherub*; Heb. *kerūb*, a cherub.]
1. a winged heavenly being described in Ezek. i. 5–11.
2. any of the second order of angels, usually ranked just below the seraphim and described as excelling in knowledge.
3. a representation of one of the cherubim as a winged angel clothed in red, as in early art, or a chubby, rosy-faced child with wings, as in later art.
4. a person, especially a child, with a sweet, innocent face.
5. an innocent or lovely child.

che·rū'biç, che·rū'biç·ăl, *a.* 1. pertaining to or resembling cherubs; angelic.
2. innocent and sweet.
3. chubby, rosy-faced, etc.

che·rū'biç·ăl·ly, *adv.* in a cherubic manner; angelically.

cher'ū·bim, *n.* alternative plural and, formerly, alternative singular of *cherub* (in senses 1, 2, 3).

cher·ū·bim'iç, *a.* pertaining to cherubim.

cher'ū·bin, *a.* cherubic; angelic. [Obs.]

cher'ū·bin, *n.* occasional plural and, formerly, singular of *cherub* (in senses 1, 2, 3).

cher'up, *v.t.* and *v.i.*; cheruped, *pt.*, *pp.*; cheruping, *ppr.* [echoic.] to chirrup; to chirp.

cher'up, *n.* a chirrup; a chirp.

chẽr'vil, *n.* [AS. *cerfille*; OFr. *cherfuel*; Sp. *cerafolio*; L. *cærafolium*, *cerafolium*; Gr. *chairephyllon*, chervil; *chairein*, to rejoice, and *phyllon*, a leaf.] any of various umbelliferous plants, as *Myrrhis odorata*, sweet chervil; *Anthriscus sylvestre*, cow chervil; but especially, *Anthriscus cerefolium*, garden chervil, used in salads.

cher·vō'nets, *n.*; *pl.* **cher·vŏnt'sï,** [Russ.]
1. the former monetary unit of the Soviet Union, equal to 10 gold rubles.
2. a gold coin of this value.
Also spelled *tchervonetz*.

chēşe, *v.t.* to choose. [Obs.]

Chesh'ire çat, a proverbial grinning cat from Cheshire, England: the one in Lewis Carroll's *Alice's Adventures in Wonderland* (1856) that disappeared gradually until only a fixed grin remained.

Chesh'văn (khesh'), *n.* [Heb.] the second month of the Jewish year.

ches'i·ble, *n.* see *chasuble*.

ches'key, *n.* [from Czech *český*, *a.*, Czech.]
1. a person of Czech extraction. [Slang.]
2. the Czech language. [Slang.]

chess, *n.* [ME. *ches*, *chesse*; OFr. *esches*, *eschas*; from Per. *shāh*, a king, the most important piece in the game.] a game of skill played by two persons, each having 16 pieces to move in different ways, on a board divided into 64 squares, alternately light and dark. Each player has eight principal pieces (a king, a queen, two bishops, two knights, and two rooks, or castles) and eight pawns. The game progresses by alternate moves until one player wins by checkmating his opponent's king or until neither can do so and a stalemate results.

chess, *n.* 1. a stalked plant, *Bromus secalinus,* resembling oats, often growing with wheat: also called *cheat.*
 2. the darnel.

chess ap′ple, a species of service tree, *Pyrus aria,* common in Europe.

chess′bōard, *n.* the checkered board upon which the games of chess and checkers are played.

ches′sel, *n.* [from *cheese,* and *well.*] a mold or vat in which cheese is formed.

chess′eṣ, *n.pl.*; *sing.* **chess,** [Fr. *chassis,* a frame, sash.] the boards used for the flooring of a temporary military bridge.

chess′măn, *n.*; *pl.* **chess′men,** any of the pieces used in the game of chess.

ches′sŏm, *n.* a kind of sandy, clayey earth. [Obs.]

chess′tree, *n.* in nautical usage, a piece of wood bolted perpendicularly on the side, to confine the clews of the mainsail.

ches′sy·līte, *n.* [from *Chessy,* a town near Lyons, in France, where the mineral occurs, and Gr. *lithos,* a stone.] azurite: also called *Chessy copper.*

chest, *n.* [ME. *chest, chist*; AS. *cist, cyst, cest,* a box, coffin; L. *cista*; Gr. *kiste,* a box, chest.]
 1. a box provided with a lid and, sometimes, a lock; as, tool *chest,* treasure *chest.*
 2. a box for the safe transportation of goods; as, a tea *chest.*
 3. the capacity of such a box; as, a *chest* of tea.
 4. the thorax: the part of the body enclosed by the ribs and breastbone.
 5. a tight box or closely fitted receptacle for gas, steam, etc.
 6. a piece of furniture with drawers; a bureau.
 7. the place where money, as of a club, is kept; a treasury.
 8. a fund; a public fund; as, the community *chest.*
 to get (something) off one's chest; to unburden oneself of (some trouble, annoyance, etc.) by talking about it. [Colloq.]

chest, *v.t.*; chested, *pt., pp.*; chesting, *ppr.* 1. to deposit in a chest; to hoard.
 2. to coffin. [Obs.]

chest, *n.* [ME. *chest*; AS. *ceast,* strife, contention.] debate; quarrel; strife; enmity. [Obs.]

chest′ed, *a.* having a (specified kind of) chest (thorax); as, broad-*chested,* narrow-*chested.*

ches′ten, *n.* the chestnut tree or its nut. [Obs.]

ches′tẽr·fiēld, *n.* [after a 19th-century Earl of *Chesterfield.*]
 1. a single-breasted topcoat, usually with a fly front and a velvet collar.
 2. a kind of sofa, heavily stuffed and with upright ends.

Ches·tẽr·fiēld′i·ȧn, *a.* resembling the fourth Earl of Chesterfield (1694–1773), who was distinguished for his courtliness; hence, extremely polite; polished; suave; urbane.

ches′tẽr·līte, *n.* [after *Chester* County, Pennsylvania, where it is found.] a variety of orthoclase.

Ches′tẽr White, [after *Chester* County, Pennsylvania, where the breed is said to have originated.] a variety of large, white hog.

chest found′ẽr, atrophy of the chest muscles, a disease of horses.

chest′nut (ches′), *n.* [from *chesten-nut*; ME. *chesten, chestein,* a chestnut; AS. *cisten* in *cistenbeam,* a chestnut; L. *castanea*; Gr. *kastanea,* a chestnut.]

CHESTNUT
(*Castanea vesca*)

 1. the smooth-shelled, sweet, edible nut of a tree belonging to the genus *Castanea.* It is enclosed in a prickly pericarp, which contains two or more seeds.
 2. *Castanea vesca,* the tree which produces this nut.
 3. the wood of this tree.
 4. the color of a chestnut, a reddish brown.
 5. any of certain trees or plants of other genera, or their fruit, as the horse chestnut, *Æsculus hippocastanum*; the wild chestnut, *Brabejum stellatum* of South Africa; the Tahiti, Otaheite, or Fiji chestnut, *Inocarpus edulis,* of the islands of the Pacific.
 6. a reddish-brown horse.
 7. a callous excrescence, composed of horny layers, on the inner side of a horse's foreleg.
 8. an old, worn-out joke or phrase; a cliché; also, a very familiar story, plot, or piece of music. [Colloq.]
 to pull someone's chestnuts out of the fire; to be persuaded or duped into doing a dangerous, painful, hard, or unpleasant thing for someone else.

chest′nut, *a.* of a reddish-brown color resembling that of the chestnut.

chest′nut bŭr, the prickly hull or bur of a chestnut.

chest′nut cōal, a size of hard coal which passes through screen meshes about an inch square.

chest of draw′ẽrṣ, an article of furniture, as for a bedroom, consisting of a frame containing a set of drawers for keeping clothing, etc.: usually distinguished from *dresser* or *bureau* by its lack of attached mirror.

chest′-on-chest′, *n.* a chest of drawers fitted onto another, somewhat larger one, generally resting on short feet.

chest′y, *a.*; *comp.* chestier; *superl.* chestiest, 1. having a large chest (thorax) or lung capacity.
 2. boastful, proud, or conceited.

chē′tȧh, *n.* same as *cheetah.*

cheth (kheth), *n.* same as *kheth.*

Chet′nik, *n.* [Serb.] a Serbian nationalist guerrilla fighter in World War II.

chet′vẽrt, *n.* [Russ.] a Russian measure of grain, equal to about six bushels.

çhev′ȧ·çhiē, *n.* an expedition with cavalry. [Obs.]

chē′vāġe, *n.* a head tax. [Obs.]

çhe·val′, *n.*; *pl.* **çhe·vaux′** (-vō′), [Fr.]
 1. a horse.
 2. a support or frame; as, a *cheval* glass.
 à cheval; on horseback; astraddle; hence, straddling (an issue).

çhe·val′-dē-friṣe′, *n.*; *pl.* **çhe·vaux′-dē-friṣe′** (-vō′), [Fr. *cheval,* a horse, and *de,* of, and *Frise,* Friesland: so called because first used by Netherlanders, who lacked cavalry, against Spaniards.]
 1. a piece of wood with projecting spikes, formerly used to hinder enemy horsemen.

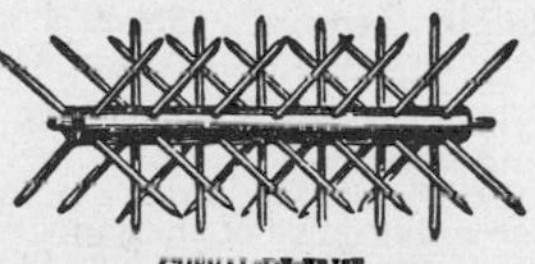

CHEVAL-DE-FRISE

 2. a row of spikes or jagged glass set into the masonry on top of a wall to prevent escape or trespassing.

çhe·val′ glȧss, a mirror mounted so as to swing in a frame, and large enough to reflect the whole figure.

çhev·ȧ·liẽr′, *n.* [Fr., from *cheval,* a horse.]
 1. a gallant; a cavalier.
 2. in heraldry, a horseman fully armed.
 3. a member of the lowest rank of the French Legion of Honor.
 4. in French history, a noble of the lowest rank.
 5. a knight. [Archaic.]
 chevalier of industry; one who gains a living by dishonest means; a sharper; a swindler.

çhev·ȧ·liẽr′ bīrd, a bird of the genus *Totanus,* commonly called *yellowlegs.*

çhev·ȧ·liẽr′ çrab, an ocypode, commonly called *horseman.*

çhev′ăl·ry, *n.* chivalry. [Obs.]

çhe·vaux′ (-vō′), *n.*, pl. of *cheval.*

chēve, *v.i.* and *v.t.* to bring to an end; to accomplish. [Obs.]

çhe·ve·lūre′, *n.* [Fr., head of hair.]
 1. in astronomy, the coma of a comet or other nebulous body.
 2. the hair of the head.

chev′en, *n.* [OFr. *chevesne,* a chub.] the chub. [Obs.]

chev′en·teīn, *n.* a chieftain. [Obs.]

chev′ẽr·el, chev′ẽr·il, *n.* [OFr. *chevrel,* a kid, dim. of *chevre*; L. *capra,* a goat.] soft leather made of kidskin; hence, a yielding disposition. [Obs.]

chev′ẽr·el, chev′ẽr·il, *a.* made of cheverel; hence, yielding; pliable. [Obs.]

çhe·vet′ (-vā′), *n.* [Fr., the head of a bed, dim. of *chef,* a head.] in architecture, the eastern end of the apse, especially in French Gothic churches.

Chev′i·ŏt (*for 2 and 3,* shev′), *n.* [from the *Cheviot* Hills in Scotland.]
 1. a breed of sheep with short, close-set wool.
 2. [c–] a kind of close-napped wool fabric in a twill weave, formerly made from the wool of the Cheviot sheep.
 3. [c–] a cotton cloth resembling this.

çhev′i·sänce, *n.* [Fr., from *chevir,* to come to an end, prevail; from *chef,* head, extremity.]
 1. achievement; deed; performance. [Obs.]
 2. formerly, in law, a making of contracts; a bargain; also, an unlawful agreement or contract.
 3. an agreement between a creditor and his debtor. [Obs.]

çhev·rette′, *n.* [Fr., from *chèvre,* L. *capra,* a goat.] a machine formerly used in handling heavy guns or mortars. [Obs.]

çhev′rŏn, *n.* [Fr., a rafter, chevron, from LL. *capro,* a rafter; L. *caper,* a goat.]
 1. in heraldry, a V-shaped device representing two rafters of a house meeting at the top.
 2. in architecture, an ornament in the form of zigzag work; zigzag molding.
 3. a V-shaped bar or bars worn on one or both of the sleeves of a military or police uniform, etc., to show rank or service.

CHEVRONS

çhev′rŏn bōne, one of the arched bones branching from the spinal column of many vertebrates.

çhev′rŏned, *a.* having or resembling a chevron.

çhev′rŏn·el, *n.* in heraldry, a half-chevron; a small chevron, half as wide as the ordinary chevron.

çhev′rŏn·wīṣe, *adv.* in heraldry, in the manner of a chevron.

çhev·rō·tāin′, *n.* [Fr., from OFr. *chevrot,* dim. of *chevre,* a goat.] the *Tragulus pygmæus,* a small, hornless animal resembling the musk deer, and classified with the genus *Tragulus,* family *Tragulidæ.*

chev′y, *n.*; *pl.* **chev′ieṣ,** [from hunting cry *chivy,* in the ballad of *Chevy Chase,* from *Cheviot.*]
 1. a hunting cry. [Brit.]
 2. a hunt; a chase. [Brit.]

chev′y, *v.t.* and *v.i.*; chevied, *pt., pp.*; chevying, *ppr.* 1. to chase; to hunt. [Brit.]
 2. to worry. [Brit.]

chew, *v.t.* and *v.i.*; chewed, *pt., pp.*; chewing, *ppr.* [ME. *chewen, cheowen*; AS. *ceowan,* to chew.]
 1. to bite and grind with the teeth; to masticate.
 2. to ruminate in the thoughts; to meditate; as, to *chew* revenge.
 Old politicians *chew* on wisdom past.
 —Pope.

chew, *n.* 1. the act of chewing.
 2. that which is chewed; that which is for chewing.

chew′ẽr, *n.* one who chews.

chew′et, *n.* 1. a kind of pie made of chopped substances.
 2. a chough, or red-legged crow; figuratively, a chatterer. [Obs.]

chew′ing gum, a flavored and sweetened preparation of chicle, used for chewing.

chē·wiṅk′, *n.* [echoic of its note.] an American finch with red eyes; the red-eyed towhee, *Pipilo erythrophthalmus.*

Çhey·enne′, *n.*; *pl.* **Çhey·enne′, Çhey·enneṣ′,** one of a tribe of Algonquian Indians who migrated from Minnesota to the headwaters of the Platte River.

çhe·yō′te, *n.* a Cuban fruit of a plant of the gourd family, *Sechium edule*: also called *choco.*

çhez (shā), *prep.* [Fr.] by; at; at the home of.

çhī, *n.* [Gr.] the 22nd letter of the Greek alphabet, transliterated into English by *ch.*

chi′ȧ, *n.* [Sp.] any of several species of *Salvia,* found in Mexico and the southwestern United States, especially *Salvia columbariæ,* which produces edible seeds.

Çhī′ăn, *a.* pertaining to Chios, a Greek island.
 Chian earth; a dense, compact kind of earth

from Chios, used in ancient times as an astringent and a cosmetic.

Chian or *Cyprus turpentine*; a turpentine obtained from the *Pistacia terebinthus*.

Chī'ăn, *n.* a native or inhabitant of Chios.

Chi·an'ti, *n.* [It.] a dry, red wine, originally made in Tuscany in the region of the Chianti mountains.

çhï·ä·rō·sçū'rist, *n.* an artist or photographer using or skilled in using chiaroscuro.

çhï·ä·rō·sçū'rō, çhï·ä"rō-os·çū'rō, *n.* [It., literally, clear dark; L. *clarus*, clear, and *obscurus*, dark.]

1. a style of painting, drawing, etc. using only light and shade, in order to achieve the effect of a third dimension.

2. the effect achieved by such a style.

3. the way that an artist uses light and shade.

4. a painting, etc. in which chiaroscuro is used.

çhī'aṣm, *n.* same as *chiasma*.

çhī·aṣ'mȧ, *n.*; *pl.* **çhī·aṣ'mȧ·tȧ,** [Gr. *chiasma*, two lines crossed, from *chiazein*, to mark with the Greek letter *chi*.]

1. in anatomy, a crossing or intersection of the optic nerves on the ventral surface of the brain.

2. any crosswise fusion.

çhī·aṣ'măl, *a.* pertaining to the chiasma.

çhī·aṣ'mȧ·tȳp·y, *n.* [from *chiasma*, *type*, and *-y*.] in genetics, a supposed twisting of homologous chromosomes about each other during one stage of meiosis, resulting in a possible interchange of genes by the chromosomes.

çhī·aṣ'mus, *n.*; *pl.* **çhī·aṣ'mī,** [Mod. L.; Gr. *chiasmos*, placing crosswise.] an inversion of the second of two parallel phrases, clauses, etc.; as, do not live to eat, but eat to live.

çhī·as'tō·līte, *n.* [Gr. *chiastos*, marked with a *chi* (X), and *lithos*, stone.] a variety of andalusite characterized by the diagonal arrangement of its crystals as seen when the stone is cut transversely: also called *macle*.

chiaus (chous), *n.* [Turk. *chāwush*.] in Turkey, a messenger, emissary, sergeant, etc.

Chib'chȧ, *n.* 1. a member of a tribe of Chibchan Indians who lived in eastern Colombia and had a highly developed civilization.

2. their language.

Chib'chăn, *a.* designating or of a linguistic group of South and Central American Indians.

chi·böuk', chi·böuque' (-bök'), *n.* [Turk. *chibuq*, a pipe.] a tobacco pipe used by the Turks, Persians, Arabs, etc., having a long, straight, wooden stem, and a clay bowl.

çhiç, *a.*; *comp.* chicquer; *superl.* chicquest; stylish and original; effective in style; elegant; clever and fashionable.

çhiç, *n.* [Fr., from M.H.G. *schic*, manner, or *schicken*, form, appearance, from *schicken*, to arrange, prepare.] elegance and originality in attire; cleverness of style: said especially of women or their clothes.

chï'çȧ, *n.* [Sp.] an orange-red coloring matter obtained from the *Bignonia chica*, a climbing plant of South America.

chi·çȧ·lō'tę, *n.* [Mex.] a prickly poppy of Mexico and the southwestern United States, *Argemone platyceras*.

çhi·çāne', *n.* [Fr., from Per. *chaugān*, the game of polo. The various senses are figurative of the methods of the game.]

1. the art of protracting a contest or discussion by the use of evasive stratagems or mean and unfair tricks and artifices; trickery.

2. in bridge, a hand without trumps.

çhi·çāne', *v.i.*; chicaned, *pt.*, *pp.*; chicaning, *ppr.* to use chicanery.

çhi·çāne, *v.t.* 1. to trick.

2. to get by chicanery.

çhi·çān'ēr, *n.* one who employs chicanery.

çhi·çān'ēr·y, *n.*; *pl.* **çhi·çān'ēr·ieş,** 1. trickery, especially legal trickery; mean or unfair artifices used in contest or discussion.

2. a trick or quibble.

Syn.—sophistry, caviling, quibble, trickery.

Chi·çä'nō, *n.*; *pl.* **Chi·çä'nōs,** [from Am. Sp. *(Me)chicano*, phonetic misspelling of *Mējicano*, a Mexican] [*also* c-] a U.S. citizen or inhabitant of Mexican descent.

chiç'çō·ry, *n.*; *pl.* **chiç'çō·rieş,** see *chicory*.

chich, *n.* [Fr. *chiche*, from L. *cicer*, chick-pea.] the dwarf pea or chick-pea. [Obs.]

chï'çhȧ, *n.* same as *chica*.

çhi'çhi, çhi'-çhi, *adj.* [Fr.] extremely chic; very smart, elegant, or sophisticated: usually used in a somewhat derogatory sense, suggesting affectation, showiness, effeteness, etc.

çhi'çhi, çhi'-çhi, *n.* a chichi quality, thing, or person.

chick, *v.i.* to sprout, as seed in the ground; to vegetate.

chick, *n.* 1. a young chicken.

2. a young bird.

3. a child: an endearing term.

chick'ȧ·bid·dy, *n.* 1. a fowl; a chick.

2. a child: an endearing term.

chick'ȧ·dee, *n.* [echoic of its note.] any of various small birds, genus *Penthestes*.

chick'ȧ·ree, *n.* [echoic of its cry.] the red squirrel, *Tamiasciurus hudsonicus*, one of the tree squirrels.

Chick'ȧ·şaw, *n.*; *pl.* **Chick'ȧ·şaw, Chick'ȧ·şawş,** one of a tribe of Muskhogean Indians who lived in the eastern portions of the lower Mississippi valley.

chick'en, *n.* [ME. *chiken*, *chekin*; AS. *cicen*, dim. of *coc*, a cock.]

1. the young of any breed of the common domestic fowl, particularly a fowl less than one year old; loosely, a fowl of any age; any hen or rooster; also, its meat.

2. a young bird of some other species.

3. a young or inexperienced person.

chicken cholera; see under *cholera*.

to count one's chickens before they are hatched; to count on something that may not materialize.

chick'en, *a.* 1. made of chicken; as, a *chicken* croquette.

2. small and tender; as, *chicken* lobster.

chick'en breast (brest), a chest condition in which the breast-bone is abnormally prominent, as in rickets: also called *pigeon breast*.

chick'en-breast"ed, *a.* having a chicken breast.

chick'en feed, 1. food for chickens.

2. small coins; negligible amount of money. [Slang.]

chick'en-frīed", *a.* coated with seasoned flour or batter and fried; as, *chicken-fried* steak.

chick'en hawk, any of various hawks that prey or are reputed to prey on chickens and other barnyard fowl; especially, the North American Cooper's hawk.

chick'en-heärt'ed, *a.* timid; fearful; cowardly.

chick'en-liv"ēred, *a.* cowardly; timid.

chick'en pox, an acute, infectious, eruptive virus disease, generally appearing in children: also called *varicella*.

chick'en·weed, *n.* same as *chickweed*.

chick'ling, *n.* a small chick or chicken.

chick'ling, *n.* a vetch or pea, *Lathyrus sativus*: also called *chichling*.

chick'-pēa, *n.* [for *chich pea*; OFr. *chiche*, from L. *cicer*, the chick, chick-pea.]

1. *Cicer arietinum*, a native plant of Spain, but also found all over southern Europe, and in many parts of Africa and Asia. It is smaller than the common pea.

2. the seed of this plant which is used for food.

chick'weed, *n.* any of several species of the pink family, especially *Stellaria media*, the common chickweed, much used as a food for birds.

chick'y, *n.* a chicken: a term especially used in calling fowls.

chiç'le (chik''l), *n.* [Sp. Am.] a gum obtained from the milky juice of the sapodilla, *Achras sapota*, and much used as a base in the manufacture of chewing gum.

chï'çō, *n.*; *pl.* **chï'çōş,** [from *chicalote*.] a spiny shrub with fleshy leaves, found in the western United States; greasewood.

chiç'ō·ry, *n.* [Fr. *chicorée*, *cichorée*; L. *cichorium*; Gr. *kichora*, *kichoreia*, chicory.] *Cichorium intybus*, a composite plant common in Europe, Asia, and America. The roots are used as a substitute for coffee, or to mix with coffee. The blanched leaves are sometimes used as a salad. Also called *succory*.

CHICORY
(*Cichorium intybus*)

chīde, *v.t.*; chid *or* chided, *pt.*; chid, chidden, *or* chided, *pp.*; chiding, *ppr.* [ME. *chiden*; AS. *cidan*, to chide, blame.]

1. to fret at or chafe against; as, the waves *chide* the shore.

2. to scold; to reprove; to rebuke; as, to *chide* one for his faults.

3. to blame; to reproach; as, to *chide* folly or negligence.

Syn.—reprimand, scold, rebuke, reprove, censure, blame.

chīde, *v.i.* 1. to scold; to clamor; to find fault: sometimes followed by *with*.

The people did *chide with* Moses.
—Ex. xvii. 2.

2. to quarrel.

3. to make a rough, clamorous, roaring noise; as, the flood *chides*.

chīde, *n.* a murmuring, chafing noise. [Rare.]

chīd'ēr, *n.* one who chides, clamors, reproves, or rebukes.

chīde'stēr, *n.* a scolding woman. [Obs.]

chīd'ing, *n.* a scolding or clamoring; rebuke; reproof.

chīd'ing·ly, *adv.* in a scolding or reproving manner.

chiēf, *a.* [ME. *cheef*, *chefe*, the head man; OFr. *chef*, leader, commander; L. *caput*, head.]

1. highest in office or rank; foremost; as, a *chief* priest; the *chief* butler.

2. principal or most eminent in any quality or action; most distinguished, valuable, important, etc.; as, agriculture is the *chief* employment of men.

3. first in affection; most dear and familiar; as, my *chief* friend. [Rare.]

chiēf, *adv.* chiefly. [Archaic.]

chiēf, *n.* 1. a commander; a leader; the person who heads any group or organization.

2. the head or leader of a tribe, family, or clan.

3. the principal officer of a department of administration or branch of military service, etc; as, a *chief* of police; *chief* of a fire department; *chief* of staff.

4. in heraldry, the upper third of an escutcheon.

CHIEF

5. [usually C-] in nautical usage, a chief engineer or chief officer.

6. the most valuable or main part of anything. [Archaic.]

in chief; (a) in or of the highest rank; as, commander *in chief*; (b) chiefly; (c) in feudal law, holding or held directly by contract with the chief or king; (d) in heraldry, borne in the upper third of the escutcheon.

Syn.—chieftain, commander, leader.

chiēf'āġe, *n.* [Fr. *chevage*.] a capitation tax. [Obs.]

chiēf'dǒm, *n.* sovereignty. [Rare.]

chiēf'est, *a.* archaic superlative of *chief*.

chiēf jus'tice, the presiding judge of a court made up of several judges.

chiēf'-jus'tice·ship, *n.* the office of chief justice.

chiēf'less, *a.* without a chief or leader.

chiēf'ly, *adv.* 1. principally; eminently; in the first place; as, it *chiefly* concerns you.

2. for the most part; mostly; mainly.

In the parts of the kingdom where the estates of the dissenters *chiefly* lay.
—Swift.

chiēf'ly, *a.* of or like a chief.

chiēf of stȧff, the head member of the staff officers of a division or higher unit in the armed forces.

chiēf pet'ty of'fi·cēr, a noncommissioned officer of the highest rank of petty officers in the navy.

chiēf'ry, chiēf'rie, *n.* 1. rent paid to a chief.

2. the domain or system of government of a lord or chief, especially of ancient Ireland.

chiēf'tain (-tin), *n.* [ME. *chefetain*; OFr. *chevetaine*; LL. *capitanus*, a commander, from L. caput, head.]

1. a chief of a clan or tribe.

2. any leader of a group.

chiēf'tain·cy, *n.*; *pl.* **chiēf'tain·cieş,** headship; captaincy; the rank or position of a chieftain.

chiēf'tain·ship, *n.* same as *chieftaincy*.

chiēld, *n.* a young man; a youth; a fellow. [Scot.]

chiēve, *v.i.* and *v.t.* to come or bring to an end; to prosper or accomplish. [Obs.]

chiff'chaff, *n.* [echoic of its cry.] a small European bird, *Phylloscopus collybita*, of the warbler family, feeding mainly on insects.

çhif'fŏn (*or* shi-fon'), *n.* [Fr.]

1. [*pl.*] any ornamental trifles worn by women; ribbons, laces, etc.

2. a sheer silk material used for women's dresses, blouses, etc.

çhif'fŏn, *a.* 1. made of chiffon.

2. light and fluffy from being whipped; as, a lemon *chiffon* pie filling.

chif·fō·niēr′, chif·fŏn·iēr′, *n.* [Fr. *chiffonnier*, orig., chest of drawers (now, ragpicker), from *chiffon*.] a narrow, high bureau or chest of drawers, sometimes with a mirror attached.

chif′fre (-fr), *n.* [Fr. *chiffre*, a cipher.] in music, a character indicating the harmony, as in figured bass.

chig′gēr, *n.* [from *chigoe*.]
1. the tiny, red larva of certain mites found especially in the southern United States and the tropics: its bite causes severe itching: also called *redbug*.
2. a kind of flea; chigoe.

chi′gnon (-nyon), *n.* [Fr. *chignon*; OFr. *chaignon*, the nape of the neck, from *chaine*, a chain.] a knot or coil of hair sometimes worn at the back part of the head and nape of the neck by women.

chig′ōe, cheg′ōe, chig′re (-ēr), *n.* [native name.]
1. a sand flea, *Tunga penetrans*, closely resembling the common flea, but smaller, found in tropical South America and Africa. The female burrows beneath the skin and causes painful sores. Also called *jigger*.
2. the larva of certain mites; chigger.

Chi·huä′huä (-wä′wä), *n.* [after *Chihuahua*, a state of Mexico.] any of a breed of very small dog with large pointed ears, originally from Mexico.

chi·kä′rȧ, *n.* [East Indian origin.] a goatlike antelope found in India, the male having four horns: also called *chousingha*.

chil′blāin, *n.* [*chill* and *blain*, from AS. *blegen*, a sore.] a sore caused by exposure to cold, affecting the hands and feet and accompanied with inflammation, itching, and sometimes ulceration.

chil′blāin, *v.t.* to produce chilblains in.

chil′blāined, *a.* having chilblains.

chīld, *n.*; *pl.* **chil′dren,** [ME. *child, childe*, pl. *childre*; AS. *cild*, pl. *cild, cildru*, child.]
1. an infant; a baby.
2. an unborn offspring.
3. a boy or girl in the period before puberty.
4. a son or a daughter; a male or female descendant, in the first degree; in law, a legitimate son or daughter.
5. a person like a child in knowledge, experience, judgment, or attainments; as, he is a mere *child*.
6. a person regarded as the product of a specified place, time, etc.; as, a *child* of the Renaissance.
7. a thing which is the product or effect of something else.
This noble passion, *child* of integrity.—Shak.
8. a descendant, however remote.
9. childe. [Archaic.]
with child; pregnant.

chīld′beār″ing, *a.* producing children.

chīld′beār″ing, *n.* the act of producing or bringing forth children; parturition.

chīld′bed, *n.* the state of a woman bringing forth a child or being in labor; parturition.

chīld′birth, *n.* 1. the act of bringing forth a child; labor; as, the pains of *childbirth*.
2 birth rate.

chīld′crōw″ing, *n.* an inflammatory affection of the trachea, false or spasmodic croup.

chīlde, *n.* a young man of noble birth: also spelled *child*. [Archaic.]

Chil′dēr·măs, *n.* [AS. *cildamæsse, cild*, child, and *mæsse*, mass.] December 28, a day commemorating the slaughter of the children of Bethlehem by Herod: called also *Holy Innocents' Day*. [Obs.]

chīld′hood, *n.* [ME. *childhod*; AS. *cildhād*, childhood; *cild*, a child, and *hād*, state.]
1. the state of a child.
2. the time in which persons are children, including the time from infancy to puberty.

chīld′ing, *a.* 1. bearing a child or children; pregnant. [Archaic.]
2. bearing a cluster of newer blossoms around an older blossom. [Archaic.]

chīld′ish, *a.* 1. belonging to a child or to childhood; trifling; puerile.
When I became a man, I put away *childish* things. —1 Cor. xiii. 11.
2. pertaining to a child; as, *childish* sports.
3. immature; silly; not fit for an adult; as, *childish* fear.
Syn.—childlike, foolish, imbecile, infantile, paltry, petty, puerile.

chīld′ish·ly, *adv.* in the manner of a child.

chīld′ish·ness, *n.* the state or quality of being childish.

chīld lā′bŏr, the regular, full-time employment of children under a legally defined age in factories, stores, offices, etc.: in the United States, the minimum legal age, as defined by the Fair Labor Standards Act of 1938, is 16 (in hazardous occupations, 18), but this standard is not observed by all States.

chīld′less, *a.* having no children or offspring.

chīld′less·ness, *n.* the state of having no children.

chīld′līke, *a.* resembling a child, or that which belongs to children; becoming a child; meek; submissive; dutiful; as, *childlike* obedience.

chīld′ly, *a.* childlike; childish. [Rare.]

chīld′ly, *adv.* in the manner of a child.

chīld′ness, *n.* the character or nature of a child. [Obs.]

chīld psȳ·chol′ō·gy (sy-), the branch of psychology that deals with the behavior and mental processes of children.

chil′dren, *n.*, plural of *child*.

chil′dren of Is′rā·el, the Jews; the Hebrews.

Chil′dren's Crū·sāde′, either of two ill-fated crusades for the recovery of Jerusalem from the Saracens, undertaken in 1212 by thousands of French and German children: in the first, those who reached the Mediterranean were sold into slavery; the survivors of the second turned back after crossing the Alps.

chīld′ship, *n.* the condition of being a child. [Rare.]

chīld's plāy, any very simple task.

chil′ē, *n.* same as *chili*.

Chil′ē·ăn, *a.* pertaining to Chile, its people, or culture: also spelled *Chilian*.

Chil′ē·ăn, *n.* 1. a native or inhabitant of Chile.
2. Spanish as spoken in Chile.

chil′ē con cär′nē, a pungent Mexican dish made usually of beans, red peppers, spices, and meat.

chil′i, *n.*; *pl.* **chil′ies,** [Sp., from native Mex. name.]
1. the dried pod of red pepper, a very hot seasoning.
2. the tropical American plant that bears this pod.
3. chile con carne.
Also spelled *chile, chilli*.

chil′i·ad, *n.* [Gr. *chilias*, the number 1,000, from *chilioi*, a thousand.]
1. a thousand; a collection or sum, containing a thousand individuals or particulars.
2. the period of a thousand years.

chil′i·ȧ·gon, *n.* [Gr. *chiliagōnos*, with a thousand angles; *chilioi*, a thousand, and *gōnia*, a corner.] a plane figure of a thousand angles and sides.

chil″i·ȧ·hē′drŏn, chil″i·ȧ·ē′drŏn, *n.* [Gr. *chilioi*, a thousand, and *hedra*, a base.] a solid figure of a thousand sides or faces. [Rare.]

Chil′i·ăn, *a.* see *Chilean*.

chil′i·ärch, *n.* [Gr. *chiliarchēs*, the commander of a thousand men, from *chilioi*, a thousand, and *archos*, a leader, from *archein*, to lead.] in ancient Greece, the commander or chief of a thousand men.

chil′i·ärch·y, *n.* a body consisting of a thousand men.

chil′i·asm, *n.* [Gr. *chiliasmos*, from *chiliazein*, to be a thousand years old; *chilioi*, a thousand.] the doctrine that Christ will personally reign on earth during the millennium.

chil′i·ast, *n.* one who believes in the doctrine of chiliasm; a millenarian.

chil·i·as′tic, *a.* millenarian.

chil′i con cär′ne, same as *chile con carne*.

chil′i pow′dēr, a powder made of dried chili pods, used as a condiment.

chil′i sauce, a tomato sauce spiced with chilies, used on meat, etc.

chill, *n.* [ME. *chil, chile*; AS. *ciele, cele*, chill, from *calan, celan*, to be cold.]
1. a bodily coldness with shivering; the cold fit that sometimes precedes a fever; chilliness.
2. a moderate coldness.
3. figuratively, a check to feelings of joy or sociability; as, a *chill* came over the assembly.
4. a sudden fear, apprehension, or discouragement.
5. coolness of manner; unfriendliness.
6. in metallurgy, a cooled iron mold designed to cool suddenly and harden the surface of a casting; also, the surface thus hardened.

chill, *a.* 1. uncomfortably cool; moderately cold; tending to cause shivering; as, the *chill* vapors of night.
2. shivering with cold.
3. cool; distant; formal; dull; not warm, enthusiastic, animated, or affectionate; as, a *chill* reception.
4. depressed; dispirited; dejected; discouraged.

chill, *v.t.*; chilled, *pt., pp.*; chilling, *ppr.* 1. to cause a shiver in; to affect with a chill.
2. to make cool; as, the evening air *chills* the earth.
3. to check (enthusiasm, etc.).
4. to depress; to deject; to discourage; as, to *chill* the gaiety of the spirits.
5. in metallurgy, to harden (metal) by rapid cooling.

chill, *v.i.* 1. to become cool.
2. to become cold; to feel cold.
3. in metallurgy, to become hardened on the surface by rapid cooling.

chilled, *a.* hardened on the surface by chilling; as, *chilled* iron.

chill fac′tŏr, the effect of low temperatures and high winds on exposed skin, expressed as a loss of body heat.

chil′li, *n.* see *chili*.

chill′i·ly, *adv.* in a chilly manner.

chill′i·ness, *n.* the state or quality of being chilly.

chill′ing, *a.* cooling; causing to shiver; discouraging; cold; as, a *chilling* wind, a *chilling* reply.

chill′ing·ly, *adv.* in a chilling manner.

chill′ness, *n.* coolness; coldness; a shivering.

chill′y, *a.*; *comp.* chillier; *superl.* chilliest.
1. uncomfortably cool; moderately cold, such as to cause shivering; as, a *chilly* day.
2. chilling; making cold.
3. cool in manner; unfriendly.
4. depressing; dispiriting.

chī′lō-, [from Gr. *cheilos*, lip.] a combining form meaning *lip*: also, before a vowel, *chil-*.

chī′log·nath, *n.* one of the *Chilognatha*.

Chī·log′nȧ·thȧ, *n.pl.* [L., from Gr. *cheilos*, lip, and *gnathos*, jaw.] a subclass of *Diplopoda*, represented by the millepedes, in which the two mandibles and the tongue are united to form a large lower lip.

chī·lō′mȧ, *n.*; *pl.* **chī·lō′mȧ·tȧ,** [Gr. *cheilōma*, lip.] in zoology, the upper lip or muzzle of a quadruped, when tumid and continued uninterruptedly from the nostril, as in the camel.

chī′lō·plas·ty, *n.* [Gr. *cheilos*, the lip, and *plassein*, to form, to mold.] the repair of some defect of the lip by plastic surgery.

chī′lō·pod, *n.* one of the *Chilopoda*.

Chī·lop′ō·dȧ, *n.pl.* [L., from Gr. *cheilos*, lip, and *pous, podos*, foot.] a class of terrestrial arthropods, represented by the centipedes, in which a pair of mandibles, or large jaws with small palpi, two pairs of maxillipeds, and a lower lip, are developed.

chi·los′chis·is, *n.* harelip.

Chī·lō·stom′ȧ·tȧ, *n.pl.* [Gr. *cheilos*, lip, and *stoma*, mouth.] an order of funnel-shaped marine *Bryozoa*, characterized by having the orifice of the cell filled with a thin membranous or calcareous plate, and a curved mouth furnished with a movable lip.

chī·lō·stom′ȧ·tous, *a.* pertaining to the *Chilostomata*.

Chil′tērn hun′dreds, [from tract of crown lands containing the Chiltern Hills.] in Great Britain, an ancient, now purely nominal, office of profit held from the crown: members of Parliament wishing to resign their seats are temporarily appointed to this office, thus automatically disqualifying themselves as members of Parliament.

chil′vēr, *n.* a ewe lamb or ewe mutton. [Brit. Dial.]

Chī·mae′rȧ, *n.* 1. a genus of cartilaginous fishes, of which the best known species is the *Chimæra monstrosa*, which inhabits the northern seas.

CHIMAERA

2. same as *chimera*.

chī·mae′roid, *a.* pertaining to or resembling the *Chimæra*.

Chī·maph′i·lȧ, *n.* [Gr. *cheima*, winter, and *philos*, loving.] a genus of perennial, North American, evergreen plants of the heath family, commonly called pipsissewa.

chim′ăr, *n.* same as *chimer* (robe).

chīmb (chīm), *n.* same as *chime* (rim).

chīme, *n.* [ME. *chimbe, chymbe*; AS. *cimbal, cimbala*; L. *cymbalum*; Gr. *kymbalon*, a cymbal, a bell.]

1. the consonant or harmonic sounds of musical instruments.

Instruments that made melodious *chime*. —Milton.

2. harmony; agreement.

3. [*usually pl.*] the musical sounds or harmony of a set of bells struck with hammers.

4. [*usually pl.*] a set of bells (generally five to twelve) which ring in harmony, and are usually placed in the belfry of a church or in a tower.

5. a contrivance for striking a bell or set of bells.

6. a single bell rung by a hammer, as in a clock or doorbell.

chīme, *v.i.*; chimed, *pt., pp.*; chiming, *ppr.* 1. to sound in consonance or harmony, as bells; to sound as a chime.

2. to correspond in relation or proportion; to agree; to harmonize.

Father and son, husband and wife, correlative terms, do readily *chime*. —Locke.

3. to recite in cadence or singsong.

chīme, *v.t.* 1. to ring, play, or strike (a bell, set of bells, etc.); to make musical sounds on.

2. to recite harmoniously; as, a child *chiming* verse.

3. to give (the hour of day) by striking bells.

chīme, *n.* [ME. *chymbe*, edge, brim; AS. *cim-*, in composition, *cim-stān*, the base of a column.] the edge or rim of a cask, barrel, etc., being the part formed by the projection of the stave ends: also spelled *chimb*.

chīme, *v.t.* to make the chime in (a cask, barrel, or tub); to chamfer the ends of (staves) in order to make a chime.

chīm′ēr, *n.* one who chimes.

chim′ēr (*or* ç**him′**), *n.* [ML. *chimera*, from MFr. *chamarre*, from Sp. *zamarra*, from Ar. *sammūr*, sable.] a loose, sleeveless robe to which lawn sleeves are attached, worn by Anglican bishops.

çhī·mē′rȧ, çhī·mac′rȧ, *n.* [L. *chimæra*; Gr. *chimaira*, a goat, a monstrous beast.]

1. [C–] in Greek mythology, a fire-breathing monster, represented with the head of a lion, the body of a goat, and the tail of a dragon: supposed to represent a volcanic mountain in Lycia, whose top was the resort of lions, the middle that of goats, and the foot that of serpents.

2. any similar fabulous monster.

3. an impossible or idle fancy.

çhī·mēre′, *n.* same as *chimer* (robe).

çhī·mer′iç, *a.* chimerical.

çhī·mer′iç·ȧl, *a.* 1. imaginary; fanciful; fantastic; wildly or vainly conceived; that has or can have no existence except in the imagination; as, *chimerical* plans.

2. absurd; impossible.

3. indulging in unrealistic fancies; visionary.

çhī·mer′iç·ȧl·ly, *adv.* so as to be chimerical.

chīmeṣ′mȧs″tēr, *n.* one in charge of playing the bell chimes.

çhim′i·nāge, *n.* [Fr. *chemin*; Sp. *camino*, a way.] in old law, a toll for passage through a forest. [Obs.]

chīm′ing bell, a plant of the genus *Mertensia*, of the United States.

chim′ley lug, the fireside or the side of a fireplace. [Scot.]

chim′ley neūck (nūk), the chimney corner. [Scot.]

chim′ney, *n.*; *pl.* **chim′neyṣ,** [ME. *chimny*, *chymney*; OFr. *cheminee*, chimney; LL. *caminata*, a fireplace; L. *caminus*, a furnace, a flue; Gr. *kaminos*, an oven, a furnace.]

1. (a) the passage through which smoke or fumes from a fire escape; flue; (b) a structure of brick, stone, etc. erected in a building, containing a flue or flues and extending above the roof, to convey smoke and other volatile matter from the stove, furnace, hearth, or fireplace where fuel is burned.

2. a fireplace; a hearth. [Now Dial.]

3. a tube of glass, etc. to surround the flame of a lamp or gas jet, and promote draft and protect the flame.

4. a deep, narrow fissure in a cliff, by which it can be climbed.

ELIZABETHAN CHIMNEY

5. something like a chimney, as the vent of a volcano.

6. a smokestack. [Chiefly Brit.]

7. in mining, any vertical mass of ore in a vein.

chim′ney bōard, a fireboard.

chim′ney breast (brest), the projection of a wall enclosing a chimney; especially, the projection inside a building.

chim′ney çap, a device, often ornamental, placed on the top of a chimney to improve the draft, or to keep out rain and snow.

chim′ney çor′nēr, 1. the corner of an open fireplace, or a space between the fire and the sides of the fireplace.

2. the fireside, or a place near the fire.

chim′ney hook, a hook in fireplaces on which to hang pots and kettles.

chim′ney mŏn′ey, a duty formerly paid in England for each chimney in a house: also called *hearth money*.

chim′ney piēce, *n.* 1. an ornamental structure of wood or stone set around a fireplace. [Archaic.]

2. a mantelpiece.

chim′ney pot, a pipe placed at the top of chimneys to increase the draft.

chim′ney shȧft, the part of a chimney above the roof.

chim′ney swăl′lōw, the chimney swift; also, the common English barn swallow, *Hirundo rustica*.

chim′ney sweep, chim′ney sweep′ēr, 1. one whose occupation is to sweep and scrape the soot from chimneys and flues.

2. a mechanical device for cleaning chimneys.

chim′ney swift, a sooty-brown North American bird resembling the swallow: so called from its habit of making a nest in an unused chimney.

chim·pan·zee′, *n.* [Fr. *chimpanzé*, from a native name.] an anthropoid ape of Africa, with black hair and large outstanding ears: it is smaller and less fierce than a gorilla, and is noted for its intelligence.

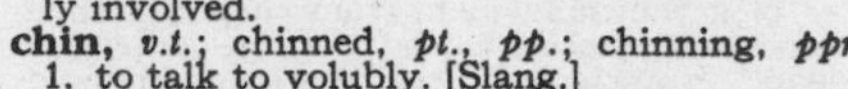

CHIMPANZEE (4 1/2 ft. standing)

chin, *n.* [ME. *chin*; AS. *cin*, chin.] the lower extremity of the face, below the mouth; the projecting part of the lower jaw in man, or a corresponding part in other animals.

up to the chin; deeply involved.

chin, *v.t.*; chinned, *pt., pp.*; chinning, *ppr.* 1. to talk to volubly. [Slang.]

2. in gymnastics, to pull (oneself) up, when hanging by the hands from a horizontal bar, until the chin is level with the bar.

chin, *v.i.* to chatter; to talk volubly. [Slang.]

chī′nȧ, *n.* 1. a fine porcelain made of clay specially baked, originally imported from China.

2. dishes, ornaments, etc. made of this porcelain.

3. any earthenware dishes or crockery. Also *chinaware*.

blue china; a kind of Chinese porcelain decorated in blue beneath the glazing.

Chī′nȧ as′tēr, a garden flower with large blooms of various colors, especially lavender and pink, originally native to China and Japan.

chī′nȧ bärk, [altered from Sp. *quina*, from Peruv. (Quechuan) native name.]

1. cinchona bark.

2. the bark of a cascarilla bush grown in Brazil.

chī′nȧ·ber·ry, *n.*; *pl.* **chī′nȧ·ber·rieṣ,** 1. the yellow, berrylike fruit of the China tree.

2. the orange-brown fruit of a tree that grows in dry areas of Mexico, the southwestern United States, and the West Indies; soapberry: it contains saponin and is used by natives as soap.

3. either of these trees.

Chī′nȧ çlāy, same as *kaolin*.

Chī′nȧ·măn, *n.*; *pl.* **Chī′nȧ·men,** 1. a Chinese: a contemptuous or patronizing term.

2. originally, a dealer in Chinese imports.

chi·när′, *n.* [Hind.] the plane tree of India, *Platanus orientalis*.

chī′nȧ·rọot, *n.* the rootstock of *Smilax china*, formerly used in medicine as a purgative. It is native to China and Japan.

chī′nȧ shop, a store in which chinaware, porcelain, or crockery is sold.

Chī′nȧ stōne, same as *kaolin*.

Chī′nȧ·town, *n.* the Chinese quarter of any city outside of China.

Chī′nȧ tree, a tall, graceful shade tree, *Melia azedarach*, native to Asia, widely cultivated in warm countries.

chī′nȧ·wāre, *n.* same as *china*.

chinch, *n.* [Sp. *chinche*; L. *cimex*, bug.]

1. a bedbug.

2. a chinch bug.

chinch bug, a kind of bug, with a disgusting odor, which does great injury to wheat and other grains in dry seasons; the *Blissus leucopterus*: called also *chinch*.

chin·chil′lȧ, *n.* [Sp.]

1. a small rodent *Chinchilla laniger* found in the Andes, South America.

2. the soft, pale-gray fur of the animal, very expensive commercially.

CHINCHILLA (15 in. long)

3. a heavy woolen cloth with a long nap, used for making overcoats.

4. a breed of domestic cat with long, soft, silver-gray hair.

chin·çhō′nȧ, chin·çō′nȧ, *n.* same as *cinchona*.

chin′çough (-kọf), *n.* same as *whooping cough*.

chīne, *n.* [ME. *chine*, *chyne*; OFr. *eschine*, the spine.]

1. the backbone or spine of an animal.

2. a piece of the backbone of an animal, with the adjoining parts, cut for cooking.

3. a ridge.

chīne, *n.* [ME. *chine*, *chyne*; AS. *cinu*, a crack, chink.] a cleft; a deep ravine. [Brit. Dial.]

chīne, *n.* a chime (the edge of a cask).

chīne, *v.t.*; chined, *pt., pp.*; chining, *ppr.* to cut through the backbone, or into chine pieces.

chi·né′ (shē-nā′), *a.* [Fr.] dyed or woven after the fashion of Chinese fabrics: applied to dress goods, etc.

chīned, *a.* 1. pertaining to or having a backbone.

2. back-broken. [Obs.]

Chī·nēṣe′ (*or* chī-nēs′), *a.* pertaining to China, its people, language, or culture.

Chinese wax; the secretion of certain Chinese insects, bleached white and resembling wax: it is used in China for candles.

Chī·nēṣe′, *n.* 1. *pl.* **Chī·nēṣe′,** a native of China or a descendant of the people of China.

2. the standard language of the Chinese, based on Peking speech.

3. any of the various languages of the Chinese.

4. a group of Sino-Tibetan languages comprising Mandarin and most of the other languages of China.

Chī·nēṣe′ çab′bāge, a vegetable with long, narrow, blanched leaves growing in loose, cylindrical heads and tasting somewhat like cabbage, to which it is related: also called *celery cabbage*.

Chī·nēṣe′ Em′pīre, China from the founding of its first dynasty, about 2200 B. C., to the revolution of 1911.

Chī·nēṣe′ lan′tērn, a lantern of brightly colored paper, used for outdoor parties, etc., and made so that it can be folded up.

Chī·nēṣe′-lan′tērn plant, a perennial herb, *Physalis alkekengi*, of the nightshade family, grown for winter bouquets because of the inflated, bladderlike, red calyx that surrounds the small, tomatolike fruit.

Chī·nēṣe′ puz′zle, 1. an intricate puzzle.

2. anything intricate and hard to solve.

Chī·nēṣe′ red, any of various shades of red, as chrome red or, especially, a brilliant orange-red.

Chī·nēṣe′ Rev·ō·lū′tion, a revolution (1911) in which forces led by Sun Yat-sen overthrew the Manchu dynasty and set up the Chinese republic.

Chī·nēṣe′ whīte, a dense white pigment made of zinc oxide or barium sulfate.

Chī·nēṣe′ wind′lȧss, a windlass with a barrel

consisting of two parts of different diameters; a differential windlass.
Chi·nēṣe' wood oil, tung oil.
chiñ'gle, *n.* gravel free from dirt; shingle.
Chiñk, *n.* a Chinese: vulgar term indicating a contemptuous or patronizing attitude. [Slang.]
chiñk, *n.* [ME. *chine*; AS. *cinu, cine*, a crack.] a small opening lengthwise; a cleft, rent, or fissure of greater length than breadth; a gap or crack; as, the *chinks* of a wall.
chiñk, *v.i.* to crack; to open.
chiñk, *v.t.* 1. to cause to part and form a fissure.
2. to fill up holes or chinks in; to fill (cracks).
chiñk, *n.* [imitative.] 1. a metallic sound; as, the *chink* of coins.
2. cash; money. [Slang.]
chiñk, *v.t.*; chinked, *pt., pp.*; chinking, *ppr.* to cause to sound, by shaking, as coins or small pieces of metal; as, to *chink* a purse of money.
chiñk, *v.i.* to make a sharp, clinking sound, as by coins striking together.
chiñ'kȧ·pin, chiñ'çȧ·pin, *n.* same as *chinquapin.*
chiñk'y, *a.* full of chinks or fissures; opening in narrow clefts.
chinned, *a.* having a chin: used in compounds; as, long-*chinned.*
chī'nō (*or* shē'-), *n.* [origin unknown.]
1. a strong, twilled cotton cloth used for work clothes, uniforms, etc.
2. [*pl.*] men's pants of chino for casual wear.
Chī'nō-, a combining form meaning *Chinese, Chinese and*, as in *Chino*-Soviet.
ċhi·noi″ṣe·riē' (shē-nwȧ″z-rē'), *n.* [Fr.] anything made by or peculiar to the Chinese.
ċhin'ō·līne, *n.* same as *quinoline.*
Chi·nọọk', *n.* [Am. Indian.]
1. any of various Penutian Indian tribes formerly inhabiting the Columbia River valley.
2. their language.
3. a dialect or pidgin language consisting of Indian, English, French, and other words and phrases, used in intercourse between Indians of various tribes, traders, and others, in the northwestern States. It contains many words from the language of the Chinook Indians, hence its name.
4. [c–] (a) on the eastern slope of the Rockies, a warm, dry wind from the west or north: probably so called because coming from the direction of the Chinook country; (b) a warm, moist southwest wind blowing from the sea onto the coast of Washington and Oregon in winter and spring.
Chi·nọọk'ăn, *a.* of the Chinooks, their culture, language, etc.
Chi·nọọk'ăn, *n.* a Chinook.
Chi·nọọk' jär'gŏn, same as *Chinook* (sense 3).
chi·nọọk salm'ŏn (sam'), a variety of Pacific salmon; quinnat salmon.
chiñ'quȧ·pin (-kȧ-), *n.* [of Am. Indian origin.]
1. the dwarf chestnut tree.
2. a related evergreen tree (called the *Giant Chinquapin*) growing in California and Oregon.
3. the edible nut of either of these trees.
Also spelled *chincapin, chinkapin.*
chinse, *v.t.*; chinsed, *pt., pp.*; chinsing, *ppr.* [perh. var. of *chink, v.*] in nautical usage, to put oakum into (the seams or chinks of a ship) with a chisel or point of a knife, as a temporary expedient for calking.
chintz, *n.* [Hind. *chhint*, chintz; Sans. *chitra*, spotted, bright.] a cotton cloth printed with flowers and other patterns in a number of different colors and usually glazed.
chintz'y, *a.*; *comp.* chintzier; *superl.* chintziest, [*chintz* and *-y*; from the sleazy quality of some chintz fabrics.]
1. like chintz.
2. cheap, stingy, petty, etc. [Colloq.]
chip, *n.* [ME. *chip, chippe*, a chip; AS. *cyp, cypp*; L. *cippus*, a stake, post.]
1. a small, thin piece of wood, stone, or other substance, cut or broken off.
2. a place where a fragment or piece has been broken off.
3. slips of wood, palm leaf, or straw, woven for the manufacture of hats and bonnets.
4. a worthless or useless thing.
5. a counter used in games to take the place of money, especially in the game of poker.
6. in nautical usage, the quadrant-shaped piece of wood fastened at the end of a log line: called also the *log.*
7. a fragment of dried dung used as fuel.
8. [*pl.*] (a) thin slices or shavings of food; as, potato *chips*; (b) French fried potatoes. [Brit.]
9. in electronics, (a) a semiconductor body in which an integrated circuit is formed or is to be formed; (b) an integrated circuit.
10. in golf, a chip shot.
a chip off the old block; a child who exhibits characteristics similar to those of his father.
Saratoga chips; very thin slices of potato fried to a chip, that is, fried crisp; potato chips.
chip, *v.t.*; chipped (chipt), *pt., pp.*; chipping, *ppr.* 1. to cut into small pieces or chips; to hew.
2. to shape by cutting or chopping.
3. in poker, to put up, as a stake.
4. to break off a small piece from; as, to *chip* crockery.
to chip in; to contribute; to add to a common fund; to share the expense of. [Colloq.]
chip, *v.i.* 1. to break off in small pieces, as earthenware.
2. in golf, to make a chip shot.
chip ax, a small ax for chipping wood.
chip bīrd, same as *chipping sparrow.*
chip'muck, chip'mŏñk, *n.* same as *chipmunk.*
chip'muñk, *n.* [Am. Indian origin.] a small animal, *Tamias striatus*, with striped markings on its back, resembling a squirrel, and common in the United States: called also *ground squirrel, striped squirrel, chipping squirrel*, etc.
chipped beef, dried or smoked beef sliced into shavings, usually served with a cream sauce.
Chip'pen·dāle, *a.* designating or of furniture made by, or in the style of, Thomas Chippendale (1718?–1779), an English cabinetmaker: it is characterized by graceful lines and, often, rococo ornamentation.
chip'pẽr, *n.* a person or thing that chips; especially, a tool for chipping.
chip'pẽr, *v.i.* 1. to chirp or twitter: said of birds.
2. to chatter or prattle; to babble. [Colloq.]
chip'pẽr, *a.* lively; cheerful; talkative. [Colloq.]
Chip'pe·wä, *n.* 1. *pl.* **Chip'pe·wä, Chip'pe·wäṣ,** [var. of *Ojibway.*] a member of a tribe of Algonquian Indians who lived in an area between western Lake Erie and North Dakota.
2. the Central Algonquian language of this tribe.
Also called *Ojibway.*
Chip'pe·wāyṣ, *n.* and *a.* Chippewa.
chip'ping, *n.* 1. a chip; a piece cut off or separated by cutting or breaking; a fragment.
2. the breaking off in small pieces of the edges of earthenware and porcelain.
3. the act of cutting or breaking off small pieces, as in dressing stone or timber.
chip'ping spar'rōw, [from *chip*, echoic word for its cry.] a small sparrow with a reddish-brown crown, native to eastern and central North America.
chip'ping squīr'rel, same as *chipmunk.*
chip'py, *a.* dry, like chips; abounding in chips.
chip'py, *n.*; *pl.* **chip'pieṣ,** 1. a chipping sparrow.
2. a chipmunk.
3. (a) a promiscuous young woman; (b) a prostitute. [Slang.]
chip shot, in golf, a short, lofting stroke, used when the ball is near the green.
ċhī·rag'rȧ, *n.* [Gr. *cheiragra*, gout in the hand; *cheir*, hand, and *agra*, seizure.] gout in the hand.
ċhī·rag'riç·ăl, *a.* having gout in the hand.
ċhī'răl, *a.* [*chiro-* and *-al.*] designating or of a three-dimensional form, as a molecule, that cannot be superimposed on its mirror image.
ċhī·ral'i·ty, *n.* the quality or condition of being chiral.
ċhī·ret'tȧ, *n.* [Hind. *chiraeta, chiraita*, a kind of gentian.] an herb of the gentian family found in northern India and used in medicine as a tonic, etc.
chīrk, *a.* lively; cheerful; in good spirits; in a comfortable state. [Colloq.]
chīrk, *v.t.* and *v.i.* to make or become cheerful; to cheer: with *up*; as, to *chirk* a man *up.* [Colloq.]
chīrk, *v.i.* [ME. *chirken*, to make a noise, as a bird; AS. *cearcian*, creak, crack.]
1. to chirp like a bird. [Obs.]
2. to screech; to shriek. [Obs.]
chīrm, *v.i.* [ME. *chirmen*; AS. *cirman*, to cry out, make a loud noise.] to twitter, warble, or hum, as birds, insects, etc. [Dial. or Rare.]
chīrm, *n.* a twittering, warbling, or humming sound. [Dial. or Rare.]
ċhī'rō-, a combining form from Greek *cheir*, the hand, meaning *hand.*
ċhī·rog'nō·my, *n.* [*chiro-*, and Gr. *gnōmē*, understanding.] the reading of character or fortune by the appearance or lines of the hand; palmistry.
ċhī'rō·ġraph, *n.* [*chiro-*, and Gr. *graphein*, to write.]
1. formerly, a writing which, requiring a duplicate, was engrossed twice on the same piece of parchment, with a space between, in which was written the word *chirographum*, or other word or words, through which the parchment was cut, and one part given to each party.
2. a written voucher of a debt signed by the debtor.
3. any written document.
ċhī·rog'rȧ·phẽr, *n.* 1. one who exercises or professes the art or business of writing; penman.
2. a palmist.
ċhī·rō·graph'iç, ċhī·rō·graph'iç·ăl, *a.* pertaining to chirography.
ċhī·rog'rȧ·phist, *n.* a chirographer.
ċhī·rog'rȧ·phy, *n.* [Gr. *cheirographos*, handwriting; *cheir*, the hand, and *graphein*, to write.]
1. the art of writing; handwriting.
2. palmistry.
ċhī·rō·ġym'nast, *n.* [*chiro-*, and Gr. *gymnastēs*, a trainer of athletes, from *gymnazein*, to train.] a device by means of which pianists may exercise their fingers.
ċhī·rol'ō·ġy, *n.* [*chiro-*, and Gr. *logos*, from *legein*, to speak.] dactylology. [Obs.]
ċhī'rō·man·cẽr, *n.* [*chiro-*, and Gr. *manteia*, divination.] one who professes to foretell future events, or to tell the fortunes and dispositions of persons, by inspecting the lines and marks of the palm of the hand; a palmist.
ċhī'rō·man·cy, *n.* palmistry; the art or practice of attempting to foretell events, or to discover the disposition of a person, by inspecting the lines and marks of his hand.
ċhī·rō·man'tiç, ċhī·rō·man'tiç·ăl, *a.* pertaining to chiromancy.
ċhī·rō·meg'ȧ·ly, *n.* abnormal size of one or both hands.
Ċhī'ron, *n.* [L.; Gr. *Cheirōn.*] in Greek mythology, the wisest of all Centaurs, famous for his knowledge of medicine: he taught Aesculapius, Achilles, and Hercules.
ċhī·rō·nom'iç, *a.* relating to chironomy.
ċhī·ron'ō·my, *n.* [*chiro-*, and Gr. *nemein*, to manage, wield.] the art of pantomimic gesticulation, especially in musical directing as practiced by the choirmasters of the early Western church.
ċhī'rō·plast, *n.* [*chiro-*, and Gr. *plastos*, formed, from *plassein*, to form.] an instrument to keep the hands in correct position when playing on the piano.
ċhī·rop'ō·dist, *n.* [*chiro-*, and Gr. *pous, podos*, foot.]
1. formerly, a person who treated diseases of the hands and feet.
2. one who treats foot ailments, removes corns, etc.
ċhī·rop'ō·dy, *n.* the occupation of a chiropodist.
ċhī″rō·praç'tiç, *n.* [Gr. *cheir*, hand, and *praktikos*, practical.]
1. a method of treating disease by manual manipulation of the joints of the body, especially the spinal column.
2. a chiropractor.
ċhī″rō·praç'tiç, *a.* having to do with the method of treatment used by a chiropractor.
ċhī'rō·praç″tŏr, *n.* one skilled in chiropractic.
ċhī·rop'tẽr, *n.* a mammal of the order *Chiroptera.*
Ċhī·rop'tē·rȧ, *n.pl.* [L., from Gr. *cheir*, hand, and *pteron*, wing.] an order of mammals, the bats. They are characterized by the elongation of all the fingers, save the thumbs, for the support of membranous wings which stretch along the sides of the body, and are attached to the posterior limbs.
ċhī·rop'tẽr·ăn, *a.* of or characteristic of the *Chiroptera.*
ċhī·rop'tẽr·ăn, *n.* a chiropter; a bat.
ċhī·rop'tē·rous, *a.* belonging to or having the characteristics of the *Chiroptera.*
ċhī·rop·tē·ryġ'i·um, *n.* [*chiro-*, and Gr. *pteryx*, wing.] the handlike forelimb of certain vertebrates.
ċhī·ros'ō·phy, *n.* same as *chiromancy.*
ċhī'rō·spaṣm, *n.* writer's cramp.
ċhī·rot'ō·ny, *n.* [Gr. *cheirotonia*, a stretching out of the hands; *cheir*, hand, and *teinein*, to stretch.]
1. a voting or electing by a show of hands.
2. a laying-on of hands, as in the ordination of a priest.

chirp, *v.i.*; chirped, *pt.*, *pp.*; chirping, *ppr.* [imitative.]
1. to make a short, shrill sound, as certain small birds or insects.
2. to speak in a lively, shrill fashion.

chirp, *v.t.* to utter in a high, cheerful tone.

chirp, *n.* the sharp, shrill note of certain birds or insects.

chirp'ẽr, *n.* one who chirps.

chirp'ing, *n.* the sharp, shrill noise of certain birds and insects.

chirp'ing·ly, *adv.* in a chirping manner.

chirp'y, *a.* inclined to chirp; lively; cheerful. [Colloq.]

chirr, chirre, *v.i.* and *v.t.* [AS. *ceorran*, to murmur.] to utter (a shrill, trilling sound), as a grasshopper or cricket.

chirr, chirre, *n.* a shrill, trilled sound, as of certain birds or insects.

chir'rup, *v.t.*; chirruped, *pt.*, *pp.*; chirruping, *ppr.* to urge on (a horse) by chirruping.

chir'rup, *v.i.* 1. to chirp repeatedly.
2. to make a series of sharp, short sounds, as in urging a horse on.

chir'rup, *n.* a chirruping sound.

chir'rup·y, *a.* joyful; cheerful; chirpy.

çhī·rūr'ġeŏn, *n.* [L. *chirurgus*; Gr. *cheirourgos*, a surgeon, one who operates with the hand; *cheir*, the hand, and *ergos*, work.] a surgeon. [Archaic.]

çhī·rūr'ġeŏn·ly, *adv.* in the manner of a chirurgeon; surgically. [Archaic.]

çhī·rūr'ġẽr·y, *n.* [Gr. *cheirourgia*.] surgery. [Archaic.]

çhī·rūr'ġiç, çhī·rūr'ġiç·ăl, *a.* surgical. [Archaic.]

chiș'el, *n.* [ME. *chisel*, *chysel*; OFr. *cisel*, chisel; LL. *cisellus*, forceps, from L. *cæsus*, pp. of *cædere*, to cut.] a tool used in carpentry, cabinetwork, masonry, sculpture, etc., for paring, hewing, or gouging. It consists of a metal blade with a cutting edge at one end, and a handle at the other to which the pressure is generally applied by a mallet or hammer, the hand, or a machine.

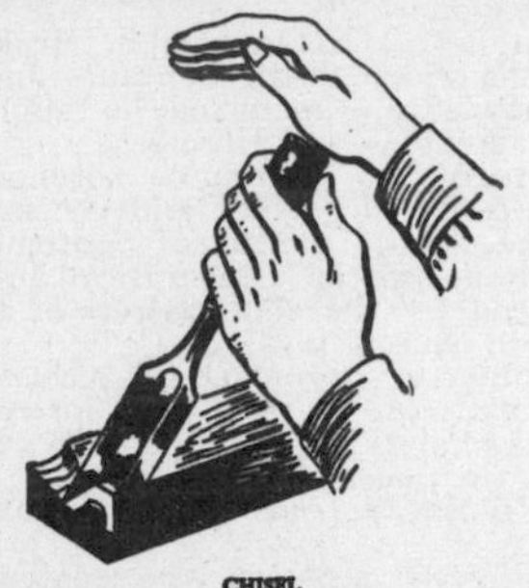
CHISEL

chiș'el, *v.i.* and *v.t.*; chiseled *or* chiselled, *pt.*, *pp.*; chiseling *or* chiselling, *ppr.* 1. to cut, pare, gouge, or engrave with a chisel.
2. to cheat; to swindle; also, to get (something) by cheating or swindling. [Colloq.]

chiș'el drȧft, in masonry, the dressed edge of a stone, serving as a guide in cutting the other edges and sides.

chiș'eled, chiș'elled, *a.* fashioned with a chisel; also, finely wrought, as if shaped by a chisel; clear-cut; statuesque.

chiș'el·ẽr, chiș'el·lẽr, *n.* 1. a person who uses a chisel.
2. a person who cheats; a swindler. [Colloq.]

chiș'el·ing, chiș'el·ling, *n.* obtaining of goods or money under false pretense or misrepresentation.

chiș'el tooth, one of the incisors of a rodent, having a chisel-shaped edge.

Çhis'leū (-lū), *n.* same as *Kislev*.

chiș'ley, *a.* [AS. *ceosel*, *ceosl*, gravel, sand.] containing chiefly gravel and sand; having a sandy and clayey character: applied to soils. [Dial.]

chit, *n.* [ME. *chitte*, variant of *kitte* for kitten; sense shows merging with *chit* (AS. *cith*) shoot, sprout.]
1. a child.
2. a pert, saucy girl.

chit, *n.* [AS. *cith*, a shoot or twig.] a shoot or sprout.

chit, *v.i.* to sprout; to shoot, as a seed or plant. [Dial.]

chit, *n.* [from *chitty*; Hind. *citthi*, letter, note.]
1. a note or short letter; any memorandum or brief writing. [Chiefly Brit.]
2. a voucher for a small sum owed for drink, food, etc.

chit'ăl, *n.* [Hind. *chītal*, spotted, a spotted snake; *chītāl*, a spotted deer.]
1. the axis, or Indian spotted deer, *Axis maculata*.
2. a venomous sea snake (genus *Hydrophis*) found off the coasts of India.

chit'chat, *n.* 1. prattle; familiar or trifling talk.
2. gossip.

çhī'tin, çhī'tine, *n.* [Gr. *chitōn*, a tunic.] a hard, amorphous compound, the chief constituent of the external covering or integument of crustaceans and insects.

çhī''ti·ni·zā'tion, *n.* the act or process of assuming a chitinous form.

çhī·ti·noġ'e·nous, *a.* [Gr. *chitōn*, a tunic, and *-genēs*, producing.] in biology, producing, or coated with chitin.

çhī'ti·nous, *a.* pertaining to, formed of, or containing chitin.

chit'lingș, chit'linș, *n.pl.* chitterlings. [Dial.]

çhī'tŏn, *n.* [Gr. *chitōn*, a woolen undergarment.]
1. an undergarment or shirt worn by the ancient Greeks; a kind of tunic.
2. [C–] in zoology, a genus of gastropods having an armored shell composed of eight pieces.

chit'rȧ, *n.* [native Indian name.] the Indian spotted hog deer: also spelled *chittra*.

chit'tăm·wood, *n.* in botany, *Rhus cotinoides*, the smoketree of southern United States; also, the orange-colored wood of the tree.

chit'tẽr, *v.i.* [ME. *chiteren*, to chirp, an imitative word.]
1. to twitter, as a bird. [Obs.]
2. to shiver with cold. [Scot.]

chit'tẽr·lingș, *n.pl.* [ME. *chitterlinge*, entrail; compare G. *kutteln*, entrails.]
1. the smaller intestines of swine, etc. used for food.
2. [*sing.*] a frill or ruff. [Obs.]

chit'trȧ, *n.* see *chitra*.

chit'ty, *a.* 1. full of chits or sprouts.
2. childish. [Obs.]
3. having warts or pimples. [Obs.]

chit'ty, *n.* [Hind. *chit hee*, a letter.] a short letter, memorandum, or certificate.

çhiv'ȧ·çhē, çhiv'ȧ·çhiē, *n.* chevachie. [Obs.]

çhiv'ăl·riç, *a.* partaking of the character of chivalry; knightly; gallant; chivalrous.

çhiv'ăl·rous, *a.* [ME. *chivalrous*; OFr. *chevalereus*, bold, gallant; *chevalier*, a knight.]
1. pertaining to chivalry or knight-errantry.
2. having the attributes of an ideal knight; gallant, courteous, honorable, etc.
Syn.—courageous, generous, knightly, gallant, heroic, valiant, high-minded.

çhiv'ăl·rous·ly, *adv.* in a chivalrous manner; boldly; gallantly.

çhiv'ăl·ry, *n.* [ME. *chivalrie*; OFr. *chevalerie*, knighthood, from *cheval*, a horse; L. *caballus*, horse, nag.]
1. the rank or position of a knight. [Obs.]
2. the qualifications of a knight, as valor, nobility, fairness, courtesy, respect for women, protection of the poor, etc.
3. the demonstration of any of the knightly qualities.
4. the medieval system of knighthood.
5. an adventure or exploit. [Obs.]
6. a group of knights or gallant gentlemen.
court of chivalry; a court, formerly held before the Lord High Constable and Earl Marshal of England, having cognizance of contracts and other matters relating to deeds of arms and war.

chive, *n.* in botany, a filament; a blade. [Obs.]

chive, *n.* [ME. and OFr. *cive*; L. *cepa*, onion.] a hardy plant, *Allium schoenoprasum*, of the onion family, with small, slender, hollow leaves used to flavor soups, stews, salads, etc.

chiv'y, chiv'vy, *n.*, *v.t.*, and *v.i.*, chevy.

çhlam'y·dāte, *a.* [L. *chlamydatus*, dressed in a cloak, from *chlamys*, Gr. *chlamys*, a cloak.] in zoology, having a mantle: said of certain mollusks.

çhlȧ·myd'ē·ous, *a.* [Gr. *chlamys*, cloak.] in botany, pertaining to the floral envelope of a plant.

çhlam'y·dēș, *n.* alternative plural of *chlamys*.

Çhlam·y·doph'ō·rus, *n.* [Gr. *chlamys*, a cloak, and *phoros*, bearing, from *pherein*, to bear.] a genus of small South American armadillos, covered with a shell or coat of leathery plates.

çhlam'y·dō·spōre, *n.* [Gr. *chlamys*, cloak, and *sporos*, a sowing.]
1. in biology, a spore furnished with protective envelopes.
2. one of certain protected spores generated in certain fungi.

çhlā'mys, *n.*; *pl.* **çhlā'mys·ēș, çhlam'y·dēș**, [L., from Gr. *chlamys*, a military cloak.] a short mantle clasped at the shoulder, worn by men in ancient Greece.

CHLAMYS

çhlō·aș'mȧ, *n.* [Gr. *chloazein*, to be or become green.] in medicine, a disease of the skin characterized by yellow patches.

çhlōr-, chloro-.

çhlōr·ȧ·cē'tiç (*or* -cet'ic), *a.* [*chlor-*, and L. *acetum*, vinegar.] in chemistry, pertaining to or obtained from chlorine and acetic acid.
chloracetic acid; an acid formed by the action of chlorine on acetic acid.

çhlō'răl, *n.* [*chlor-* and *al*cohol.]
1. a thin, oily, colorless liquid, CCl_3CHO, obtained by the action of chlorine on alcohol. It has a pungent odor and a dry, bitter taste.
2. chloral hydrate.

çhlō'răl hȳ'drāte, a colorless, crystalline compound, $CCl_3 \cdot CH(OH)_2$, produced by the reaction of water and chloral: used chiefly as a sedative.

çhlō'răl·ișm, *n.* an unhealthy condition of the system produced by excessive use of chloral.

çhlōr·al'um, *n.* a disinfectant and antiseptic containing chloride of aluminum, of which it is an aqueous solution.

çhlō·rȧ·mīne' (*or* klōr-ăm'in), *n.* [*chlor-*, and *amine*.] a colorless, pungent liquid, NH_2Cl, obtained by the action of ammonia on some hypochlorite.

çhlōr''am·phen'i·çol, *n.* [*chlor-*, and *am*id, and *phen-*, and *ni*tr-, and gly*col*.] an antibiotic drug, $C_{11}H_{12}Cl_2N_2O_5$, prepared synthetically or isolated from a bacillus (*Streptomyces venezuelae*): used against many bacterial and rickettsial diseases and some viruses.

çhlōr·an'il, *n.* [*chlor-* and *aniline*, from Ar. *an-nil*, the indigo plant.] a yellow crystalline compound, obtained by the action of chlorine on phenol and other benzene derivatives, as aniline.

Çhlō·ran·thā'cē·ae, *n.pl.* a family of tropical aromatic plants and small trees, of which *Chloranthus* is typical.

Çhlō·ran'thus, *n.* [*chlor-*, and Gr. *anthos*, flower.] a small genus of perennial plants of the family *Chloranthaceæ*, natives of Asia, and having spicy and tonic qualities.

çhlō·ran'thy, *n.* see *chlorosis*.

çhlō'rāte, *n.* a salt of chloric acid.

çhlōr·cȳ'cli·zīne, *n.* [*chlor-*, and *cyclo-*, and *-i-*, and pipera*zine*.] an antihistamine, $C_{18}H_{21}ClN_2$, for treating allergies and insect bites.

çhlōr'dāne, *n.* [*chlor-*, and in*dane*, a derivative of *indene*.] a chlorinated, highly poisonous, volatile oil, $C_{10}H_6Cl_8$, used as an insecticide, especially against soil grubs. Also **çhlōr'dan**.

çhlōr·hȳ'driç, *a.* same as *hydrochloric*.

çhlōr·hȳ'drin, *n.* [*chlor-*, and Gr. *hydōr*, water.] any one of a class of compounds formed by the substitution of chlorine for one to three hydroxyl groups in glycerin, etc.

çhlō'riç, *a.* [*chlor-*, and *-ic*.]
1. of, obtained from, or containing chlorine with a higher valence than that in corresponding chlorous compounds.
2. designating or of a colorless acid, $HClO_3$, whose salts are chlorates.
chloric ether; a compound made by subjecting alcohol to the action of hydrochloric acid; ethyl chloride. The name is also given to spirits of chloroform.

çhlō'ri·dāte, *v.t.* same as *chloridize*.

çhlō'rīde, çhlō'rid, *n.* [*chlor-*, and *-ide*.] a compound in which chlorine is combined with another element or radical (e.g., a salt of hydrochloric acid).

çhlō'rīde of līme, calcium chloride, $CaOCl_2$, a white powder obtained by treating slaked lime with chlorine, used for disinfecting and bleaching.

çhlō'rid·īze, *v.t.*; chloridized, *pt.*, *pp.*; chloridizing, *ppr.* to subject to or sensitize with a chloride; as, in photography, to *chloridize* a plate with chloride of silver.

çhlō·rim'e·try, *n.* see *chlorometry*.

çhlō'rin·āte, *v.t.*; chlorinated, *pt.*, *pp.*; chlorinating, *ppr.* to treat or combine (a substance) with chlorine; especially, to pass chlorine into (water or sewage) for purification.

çhlō·ri·nā′tion, *n.* the act or process of chlorinating, or subjecting anything to the action of chlorine. In mining, chlorination is used for the extraction of gold and silver from certain ores.

çhlō′rīne, çhlō′rin, *n.* [*chlor-*, and *-ine.*] a greenish-yellow, poisonous, gaseous chemical element with a disagreeable odor, used in the preparation of bleaching agents, in water purification, in various industrial processes, as a lung irritant in chemical warfare, etc.: symbol, Cl; atomic weight, 35.457; atomic number, 17.

çhlōr·i·od′iç, *a.* compounded of or containing chlorine and iodine.

çhlō′rīte, *n.* [L. *chloritis*; Gr. *chlōritis*, a light green stone, from *chlōros*, light green.] a bright-green, complex silicate mineral, similar in structure to the micas.

çhlō′rīte, *n.* [*chlor-*, and *-ite.*] a salt of chlorous acid.

çhlō·rit′iç, *a.* pertaining to or containing chlorite; as, *chloritic* sand.

çhlō′ri·toid, *n.* a chloritic mineral, shading from dark gray to greenish black in color and found in scales easily broken or split. It is a hydrous silicate of alumina, iron, and magnesia: also called *brittle mica.*

çhlō′rō-, [from Gr. *chlōros*, pale green.] a combining form meaning (a) *green*, as in *chloro*phyll, *chloro*sis; (b) *chlorine, having chlorine as an ingredient*, as in *chloro*form. Also, before a vowel, *chlor-*.

çhlō·rō·çrū′ō·rin, *n.* [*chloro-*, and L. *cruor*, blood.] a green coloring matter supposed to produce the green tinge of the blood in certain marine worms.

çhlō′rō·dȳne, *n.* a powerful anodyne remedy formerly much used, containing opium, chloroform, Indian hemp, etc.

çhlō′rō·fọrm, *n.* [*chloro-*, and *formyl*, from L. *formica*, an ant.] trichloromethane, or formyl trichloride, $CHCl_3$; a colorless, volatile liquid of a sweetish taste. It is used as an anesthetic in surgical operations, and as a solvent.

çhlō′rō·fọrm, *v.t.*; chloroformed, *pt.*, *pp.*; chloroforming, *ppr.* 1. to anesthetize with chloroform.
2. to kill with chloroform.

çhlō″rō·fọr′miç, *a.* containing or pertaining to chloroform or its use.

çhlō·rō·fọrm·işm, *n.* in medicine, the unhealthy condition resulting from the habitual use of chloroform.

çhlō′rō·fọrm″ist, *n.* the person giving chloroform as an anesthetic.

çhlō″rō·ġen′iç, *a.* in chemistry, pertaining to or designating a crystalline, colorless, tanninlike acid obtained from coffee berries or a similar source.

çhlō″rō·hy″drō·çär′bŏn, *n.* in chemistry, any chlorine derivative of a hydrocarbon.

çhlō″rō·ī′ō·dīde, *n.* in chemistry, an iodochloride.

çhlō·rō′mȧ, *n.* [Gr. *chlōros*, yellowish green.] a fleshy tumor of a greenish color, occurring usually in the membranes of the skull.

çhlō·rom′e·tẽr, *n.* [*chloro-*, and Gr. *metron*, a measure.] an instrument for testing the bleaching powers of chloride of lime.

çhlō·rom′e·try, *n.* the process for testing the bleaching power of any combination of chlorine.

çhlō″rō·mȳ·cē′tin, *n.* [*chloro-*, and *-mycete*, and *-in.*] a synthesized antibiotic drug used in the treatment of rickettsial and virus diseases.

çhlō·rō′păl, *n.* [*chloro-*, and L. *opalus*, opal; Gr. *opallios*, a rock, stone, precious stone.] a greenish, earthy mineral, consisting of silica and oxide of iron, with eighteen to twenty per cent of water.

çhlō′rō·phāne, *n.* [*chloro-*, and Gr. *-phanēs*, evident; from *phainein*, to show.]
1. a variety of fluor spar, from Siberia. When placed on a heated iron it gives a beautiful emerald-green light.
2. the pigment in the inner portion of the cones of the retina, yellowish-green in color.

Çhlō·rō·phyc′ē·ae (-fis′ē-ē), *n.pl.* [*chloro-*, and Gr. *phykos*, seaweed.] a large group of green algae or seaweeds.

çhlō·rō·phy′ceous (-fish′us), *a.* pertaining to the *Chlorophyceæ.*

çhlō′rō·phyll, çhlō′rō·phyl, *n.* [Fr. *chlorophylle*; Gr. *chlōros*, green, and *phyllon*, leaf.] the green coloring matter contained in plants: in the presence of sunlight it converts carbon dioxide and water into carbohydrates. It is used as a dye and in medicine, and certain derivatives, commercially added to various products, are claimed to eliminate offensive odors.

CHLOROPHYLL
a. spiral bands of chlorophyll in Spirogyra *b.* irregular mass in Zygnema *c.* granules in cells of the leaf

çhlō·rō·phyl′li·ăn, *a.* chlorophyllose.

çhlō″rō·phyl·lif′ẽr·ous, *a.* containing chlorophyll.

çhlō″rō·phyl·liġ′e·nous, *a.* [L., from Gr. *chlōro-*, green, and *phyllon*, a leaf, and *-genēs*, producing.] producing chlorophyll; produced by chlorophyll.

çhlō·rō·phyl′loid, *a.* [*chloro-*, and Gr. *phyllon*, leaf, and *eidos*, form.] resembling chlorophyll.

çhlō·rō·phyl′lōse, çhlō·rō·phyl′lous, *a.* 1. of or like chlorophyll.
2. having chlorophyll.

çhlō·rō·piç′rin, *n.* [from *chloro-*, and *picric*, and *-in.*] a colorless liquid, CCl_3NO_2, prepared by treating chloroform with concentrated nitric acid, and used in chemical warfare as a gas to cause vomiting: also called *nitrochloroform.*

çhlō′rō·plast, *n.* [*chloro-*, and *-plast.*] an oval, chlorophyll-bearing body found outside the nucleus in a cell.

çhlō·rō·plas′tid, *n.* same as *chloroplast.*

çhlō″rō·plȧ·tin′iç, *a.* designating an acid, composed of platinum chloride and hydrochloric acid, produced in the form of reddish-brown crystals, and largely used as a reagent.

çhlō′rō·prēne, *n.* [*chloro-*, and iso*prene.*] in chemistry, a colorless liquid obtained from acetylene and hydrochloric acid having the formula C_4H_5Cl: it can be polymerized to form a synthetic rubber.

çhlō·rō′sis, *n.* [Mod.L.; see *chloro-* and *-osis.*]
1. the green sickness, a kind of anemia sometimes affecting girls at puberty, characterized by a pale or greenish hue of the skin, weakness, palpitation, dyspepsia, etc.
2. in botany, (a) a disease of plants in which the green parts lose their color or turn yellow; (b) the transformation of the normally colored floral organs of a plant into green leaves; chloranthy.

çhlō·rot′iç, *a.* 1. pertaining to chlorosis.
2. affected by chlorosis.

çhlō′rous, *a.* [*chlor-*, and *-ous.*]
1. of, obtained from, or containing chlorine with a lower valence than that in corresponding chloric compounds.
2. designating or of an acid, $HClO_2$, whose salts are chlorites.

çhlōr·piç′rin, *n.* chloropicrin.

chōak, *v.* to choke. [Obs.]

çhō′ȧ·nȧ, *n.*; *pl.* **çhō′ȧ·nae,** [Gr. *choanē*, funnel.]
1. in anatomy, a funnellike opening; specifically, one of the funnellike nasal cavities.
2. the collarlike rim encircling the flagellum of some kinds of *Infusoria.*

çhō′ȧ·nāte, *a.* relating to or formed like a choana.

çhō′an·īte, *n.* a fossil zoophyte resembling a sponge.

çhō′ȧ·noid, *a.* [Gr. *choanē*, a funnel, and *eidos*, form.] having the shape of a funnel: specifically applied to a hollow muscle attached to the ball of the eye in a number of reptiles and mammals.

çhō′çärd, *n.* a kind of crow; the chough.

chock, *v.t.*; chocked (chokt), *pt.*, *pp.*; chocking, *ppr.* 1. to make fast or to stop, with a block or wedge; as, to *chock* a wheel or a barrel.
2. to place (a vessel) on chocks.

chock, *v.i.* [from *choke*; ME. *choken*; AS. *ceocian*, to choke, fill up.]
1. to fill up a cavity; as, the woodwork exactly *chocked* into the joints.
2. to encounter. [Obs.]

chock, *n.* 1. a wedge or block placed under a barrel, wheel, etc., to prevent motion.
2. an encounter. [Obs.]
3. in nautical usage, a metal casting, having two short, horn-shaped projections curving inward, between which ropes or hawsers are passed during the acts of hauling or warping.

chock, *adv.* completely, so as to be tight or full; thoroughly; as, a bin *chock* full of potatoes.

chock′ȧ·block, *a.* 1. lifted as far as the tackle will allow, the blocks being brought together, thus preventing further motion; jammed: said of a tackle, or a thing being hoisted.
2. crowded; squeezed together.

chock′ȧ·block, *adv.* tightly together.

chock′-fụll, *a.* as full as possible; filled to capacity: also written *choke-full, chuck-full.*

choç′ō·lāte, *n.* [Fr. *chocolat*; Sp. and Port. *chocolate*; Mex. *chocolatl*, chocolate; *choco*, cacao, and *latl*, water.]
1. a paste, powder, sirup, or bar made from cacao seeds that have been ground and roasted.
2. a drink made of chocolate, hot milk or water, and sugar.
3. a candy made of, containing, or coated with chocolate.
4. reddish brown.

choç′ō·lāte, *a.* 1. made of or containing chocolate; as, *chocolate* cake.
2. of the color of chocolate; reddish-brown.

Choç′tạw, *n.* 1. *pl.* **Choç′tạw, Choç′tạwṣ,** a member of a tribe of Muskhogean Indians who lived in southern Mississippi, Alabama, Georgia, and Louisiana.
2. the language of this tribe.

Choç′tạw, *a.* of the tribe or language of the Choctaws.

chog′set, *n.* see *cunner.*

choice, *n.* [ME. *chois, choise*; OFr. *chois, choix*, choice, from *choisir*, to choose.]
1. the act of choosing; the voluntary act of selecting or separating from two or more things that which is preferred; or the determination of the mind in preferring one thing to another; selection.
2. the right or power of choosing; option; as, he had the *choice* of two evils.
3. care in selecting; judgment or skill in distinguishing what is to be preferred, and in giving a preference.
I imagine Caesar's apophthegms were collected with judgment and *choice.*—Bacon.
4. the person or thing chosen; that which is approved and selected in preference to others; selection.
5. the best part of anything; that which is preferable, and properly the object of choice.
In the *choice* of our sepulchers bury thy dead.
—Gen. xxiii. 6.
6. a variety from which to choose.
7. a supply that is well chosen.
8. an alternative.
Syn.—election, option, preference, selection.

choice, *a.*; *comp.* choicer; *superl.* choicest. 1. worthy of being preferred; select; of special excellence.
My *choicest* hours of life are lost. —Swift.
2. holding dear; preserving or using with care, as valuable; frugal; as, to be *choice* of time, or of advantages. [Dial.]
3. selecting with care and due attention to preference; as, to be *choice* of one's company. [Dial.]
4. carefully chosen.

choice′-drạwn, *a.* selected with particular care. [Rare.]

choice′fụl, *a.* fickle.

choice′less, *a.* not having the power of choosing; not free. [Rare.]

choice′ly, *adv.* 1. with care in choosing; with exact choice; as, a band of men *choicely* collected.
2. valuably; excellently; preferably; curiously.
3. with great care; carefully; as, a thing *choicely* preserved.

choice′ness, *n.* valuableness; particular value or worth; as, the *choiceness* of a plant, or of wine.

choil, *n.* the part of a knife blade between the cutting edge and the tang.

çhoīr (kwīr), *n.* [ME. *queer, quere*; OFr. *cuer*, a choir; L. *chorus*; Gr. *choros*, a band of dancers and singers.]
1. a group of singers, especially in divine service, in a church.
2. any group of singers or dancers.
3. that part of a church reserved for the singers.
Also spelled *quire.*

çhoīr, *v.t.* and *v.i.* to sing in chorus: also spelled *quire.* [Poetic.]

çhoīr′boy *n.* a boy who sings in a choir.

çhoir loft, the gallery occupied by the choir in a church.
çhoir′mas·tẽr, *n.* the conductor of a choir.
çhoir or′găn, a part of the full church organ, complete in itself, and specially suited for choir accompaniments.
çhoir sçreen, a screen, in old churches, usually of carved woodwork, dividing the choir from the aisles.
çhoir sẽrv′ice, a religious observance in which the services of a choir are used.
chōke, *v.t.*; choked (chokt), *pt., pp.*; choking *ppr.* [ME. *choken, cheken*; AS. *ceocian*, to choke; probably imitative.]
1. to obstruct the breathing of, by blocking the windpipe or squeezing the neck; to suffocate; to strangle.
2. to stop by filling; to obstruct; to block up; as, to *choke* the entrance to a harbor.
3. to hinder by obstruction or impediments; to hinder or check the growth, expansion, or progress of.
4. to smother or extinguish, as fire.
5. to suppress or stifle: usually with *down*; as, he *choked down* his rising emotions.
6. to affect with a sense of choking, as in anger.
7. to narrow (a gun bore) at the muzzle.
8. to fill up.
9. to cut off the air from the carburetor of (a gasoline engine) in order to make a richer gasoline mixture.
to choke back; to hold back (feelings, sobs, etc.)
to choke off; to bring to an end; to end the growth of.
to choke up; (a) to bring up by choking; (b) to block up; clog; (c) to fill too full; (d) [Colloq.] to be speechless, as from strong emotion; (e) [Colloq.] to be unable to function efficiently in a critical situation because of tenseness.
chōke, *v.i.* 1. to be suffocated; to have difficulty in breathing.
2. to be blocked up; to be obstructed.
3. to stick, as if by choking; as, the words *choked* in his throat.
chōke, *n.* 1. the act of choking; the noise or stoppage in the windpipe, as in strangulation.
2. the constriction, or part of smallest caliber, in the bore of a chokebore.
3. the neck of a rocket, where the stick is attached.
4. the tie at the end of a nonmetallic cartridge.
5. the filamentous or capillary part of the artichoke.
6. the valve that shuts off air in the carburetor of a gasoline engine.
chōke′ber″ry, *n.*; *pl.* **chōke′ber″ries,** a North American shrub, *Aronia arbutifolia*, which belongs to the rose family and grows in damp thickets; also, its fruit, a small, red or purple, apple-shaped or pear-shaped, astringent berry.
chōke′bōre, *n.* a gun with the bore narrowing toward the muzzle to keep the charge of shot from spreading; also, the bore of a gun, so narrowed.
chōke′bōre, *v.t.*; chokebored, *pt., pp.*, chokeboring, *ppr.* to bore with a choke of gradually narrowing caliber.
chōke′cher″ry, *n.*; *pl.* **chōke′cher″ries,** either of two wild cherry trees of North America; also, the astringent fruit of either of these.
chōke çoil, a coil of wire with a core of iron or air, used for control of the alternating current in an electric circuit: it permits the passage of the direct-current component but has such a high reactance that little alternating current goes through: also *choking coil*.
chōke çol′lăr, a training collar for a dog, that tightens when the dog strains at the leash.
chōke′damp, *n.* a suffocating gas, chiefly carbon dioxide, found in wells, coal mines, and other pits: called also *blackdamp*.
chōke′-full, *a.* same as *chock-full*.
chōke peăr, 1. a kind of pear that has a rough, astringent taste and is therefore swallowed with difficulty.
2. hence, anything that stops the mouth; an unanswerable argument; an aspersion or sarcasm by which a person is put to silence. [Obs.]
chōk′ẽr, *n.* 1. one who or that which chokes; that which irritates with a sense of strangulation; something difficult to swallow.
2. that which puts another to silence; that which cannot be answered. [Colloq.]
3. a wide necktie or collar worn tight around the neck. [Colloq.]
4. a necklace that fits closely around the neck.
5. a narrow fur piece worn around the neck or on the shoulders.
6. in military engineering, a chain used to compress and measure fascines.
chōke′strap, *n.* in saddlery, a strap passing from the lower portion of the collar to the bellyband, to keep the collar in place when an animal is descending a hill or backing.
chōke′weed, chōke′wŏrt, *n.* any of several weeds of different genera that choke the growth of other plants.
chō′ki·där, chō′ke·där, *n.* [Hind. *chaukidar*, a watchman, policeman; *chauki*, watch, and *-dar*, holding.] in India, a watchman or policeman.
chōk′ing, *a.* 1. causing suffocation; tending to choke or suffocate; as, a *choking* cloud of dust.
2. strained or indistinct with emotion, as if about to choke; gasping; as, to speak with a *choking* voice.
chōk′y, chōk′ey, *a.*; *comp.* chokier; *superl.* chokiest. 1. that tends to suffocate, or has power to suffocate.
2. inclined to choke; affected as if being choked; as, he felt *choky*.
chō′ky, *n.* [Hind. *chauki*, a guard.]
1. in India, a customs station, a palanquin station, etc.
2. a prison or lockup.
chol-, cholo-.
chō·lae′mi·ȧ, *n.* same as cholemia.
çhol′ȧ·gogue (-gog), *n.* [Gr. *cholagōgos*, carrying off bile; *cholē*, bile, and *agōgos*, leading, from *agein*, to lead.] a medicine that has the specific quality of evacuating the bile.
çhō·lal′iç, *a.* same as *cholic*.
çhō′lāte, *n.* a salt of cholic acid.
çhol′ē-, cholo-.
çhol′ē·cyst, çhol·ē·cys′tis, *n.* [Mod. L. *cholecystis*, the gall bladder: Gr. *cholē*, bile, gall, and *kystis*, bladder.] the gall bladder.
çhol″ē·cys·teç′tō·my, *n.* in surgery, the operation of removing the gall bladder.
çhol″ē·cys·tot′ō·my, *n.* [Gr. *cholē*, bile, *kystis*, bladder, and *tomē*, a cutting, from *temnein*, to cut.] the surgical operation of opening the gall bladder by incision, as for the removal of gallstones.
çhol·ē·dol′ō·ġy, *n.* [Gr. *cholē*, bile, and *logos*, a description.] a medical treatise relating to bile or the secretion of bile.
çhō·lē′iç, *a.* [Gr. *cholē*, bile.] pertaining to or derived from bile.
çhō·lē′mi·ȧ, *n.* in medicine, a disease caused by the presence of bile in the blood, and producing extreme nervous symptoms: also spelled *cholaemia*.
çhol′ẽr, *n.* [ME. *coler, colere*; OFr. *colere*, anger, bile; L. *cholera*; Gr. *cholera*, a disease of the bile; *cholē*, bile.]
1. the bile: in medieval times it was considered one of the four humors of the body, and the source of anger and irritability. [Obs.]
2. anger; wrath; irritation of the passions.
çhol′ẽr·ȧ, *n.* [Gr. *cholera*, a disease of the bile from *cholē*, bile.]
1. bile; choler. [Obs.]
2. any of several intestinal diseases, (a) cholera morbus; (b) Asiatic cholera, an infectious disease, usually fatal, characterized by violent diarrhea and vomiting, muscular cramps, and collapse.
chicken cholera; an infectious, usually fatal, disease peculiar to fowls.
cholera bacillus; see *comma bacillus*.
cholera infantum; the "summer complaint" of infants and young children, an intestinal disease occurring in warm weather, and characterized by pain, vomiting, diarrhea, fever, and prostration.
cholera morbus; a noninfectious, rarely fatal cholera, with diarrhea and cramps: it is usually caused by contaminated foods: also called *sporadic cholera, bilious cholera*.
cholera nostras; same as *cholera morbus*.
hog cholera; a contagious disease affecting swine, characterized by a high fever, inflammation of the digestive and respiratory organs, diarrhea, cough, and the effusion of blood into the mucous membranes and skin: called also *swine plague*.
sporadic cholera; same as *cholera morbus*.
çhol·ẽr·ā′iç, *a.* pertaining to cholera; resulting from cholera.
çhol′ẽr·iç, *a.* [ME. *colerik*; OFr. *colerique*; L. *cholericus*, bilious, choleric; Gr. *cholerikos*, resembling the cholera, from *cholera*, cholera.]
1. bilious; causing biliousness. [Obs.]
2. easily irritated; irascible; inclined to anger; as, a *choleric* man.
3. angry; indicating anger; excited by anger; as, a *choleric* speech.
çhol′ẽr·iç·ly, *adv.* in a choleric manner; irascibly; angrily.
çhol′ẽr·iç·ness, *n.* irascibility; anger; peevishness.
çhol′ẽr·i·form, *a.* resembling cholera.
çhol·ẽr·iġ′e·nous, *a.* producing or generating cholera.
çhol′ẽr·ine, *n.* 1. a mild form of Asiatic cholera; also, the initial diarrheal stage of epidemic cholera.
2. the precursory symptoms of cholera.
çhol′ẽr·oid, *a.* resembling cholera.
çhō·les·ter′iç, *a.* pertaining to cholesterol, or obtained from it; as, *cholesteric* acid.
çhō·les′tẽr·in, çhō·les′tẽr·ine, *n.* same as *cholesterol*.
çhō·les′tẽr·ōl, *n.* [from *chole-*, and Gr. *stereos*, solid, stiff; and *-ol*.] a crystalline fatty alcohol, $C_{27}H_{45}OH$, found especially in animal fats, blood, nerve tissue, and bile: some gallstones are almost pure cholesterol.
çhō′li·amb, çhō·li·am′biç, *n.* [L. *choliambus*, choliambic; Gr. *chōliambos*, lame iambus, from *chōlos*, lame, and *iambos*, an iambus.] an iambic verse in poetry having a spondee in the sixth or last foot.
çhol′iç, *a.* [Gr. *cholē*, bile.] pertaining to or derived from the bile.
cholic acid; a compound found in the acids of the bile which may be chemically extracted as resinous crystals.
çhō′līne, *n.* [*chol-*, and *-ine*.] a viscous liquid ptomaine, $C_5H_{15}O_2N$, found in many animal and vegetable tissues: a vitamin of the B complex.
chōl′lä (-yä), *n.* [Sp. lit., skull, head.] a spiny cactus with cylindrical stems, growing in the southwestern United States.
çhol′ō-, [Gr. *cholē, cholos*, bile.] a combining form meaning *bile, gall*, as in *chololith*: also *chol-, chole-*.
çhol′ō·lith, *n.* [*cholo-*, and *-lith*.] a gallstone.
chōl′try, chōul′try, *n.* [Anglo-Ind. from Malayalam *chāwati*, an inn.] a Hindu caravansary for the use of travelers.
chomp, *v.t.* and *v.i.*; chomped, *pt., pp.*; chomping, *ppr.* [dial. var. of *champ*.]
1. to chew hard and noisily; champ.
2. to bite down (*on*), repeatedly and restlessly; as, a cigar-*chomping* general.
chomp, *n.* the act or sound of chomping.
çhon′drăl, *a.* [Gr. *chondros*, cartilage, grain.] pertaining to cartilage; cartilaginous.
çhon″dri·fi·çā′tion, *n.* [*chondr-*, and L. *facere*, to make.] the process of being converted into cartilage; the state of being chondrified.
çhon′dri·fȳ, *v.t.*; chondrified, *pt., pp.*; chondrifying, *ppr.* to convert into cartilage.
çhon′dri·fȳ, *v.i.* to be converted into cartilage.
çhon′dri·ġen, *n.* [*chondr-* and Gr. *-genēs*, producing.] the substance of hyaline cartilage from which chondrin is obtained after long boiling in water.
çhon·driġ′e·nous, *a.* [*chondr-*, and Gr. *-genēs*, producing.] yielding chondrin.
çhon′drin, çhon′drine, *n.* [Gr. *chondros*, cartilage.] a transparent substance similar to gelatin, without taste, odor, or color, obtained by long boiling of cartilaginous tissue with water. It is largely used as an ingredient of commercial gelatin.
çhon′dri·ō·sōme″, *n.* [from Gr. *chondrion*, little cartilage; and *-some*.] in biology, any of various very small structures found in different forms in the cytoplasm of cells.
çhon′drīte, *n.* a meteoric stone having chondrules in its composition.
çhon·drit′iç, *a.* granular in structure; having the peculiar granular structure characteristic of the meteorites called chondrites.
çhon·drī′tis, *n.* inflammation of cartilage or cartilaginous tissue.
çhon′drō-, [from Gr. *chondros*, a grain, cartilage.] a combining form meaning *of cartilage*: also, before a vowel, *chondr-*.
çhon′drō·blăst, *n.* [*chondro-*, and Gr. *blastos*, a bud, shoot.] a cell that produces cartilage.
Çhon·drō·den′drŏn, *n.* [*chondro-*, and Gr. *dendron*, a tree.] a small genus of woody vines or high-climbing shrubs, with large leaves, indigenous to Brazil and Peru. The root of *Chondrodendron tomentosum* yields pareira brava, a drug formerly taken for diseases of the bladder.
çhon′drō·dīte, *n.* [Gr. *chondros*, a grain of wheat, cartilage.] a light yellow, brittle min-

eral, occurring in granular form in primary limestone.

Çhon″drō·gȧ·noi′dē·ȧ, *n.pl.* [*chondro-*, and Gr. *ganoidea*, from *ganos*, brightness, and *eidos*, form.] same as *Chondrostei*.

çhon·drō·ġen′e·sis, *n.* [*chondro-*, and Gr. *genesis*, origin, source.] the formation or development of cartilage; the morbid conversion of parts into cartilage: also written *chondrogeny*.

çhon·droġ′e·ny, *n.* same as *chondrogenesis*.

çhon′droid, *a.* [Gr. *chondros*, cartilage, and *eidos*, appearance.] resembling cartilage.

çhon·drol′ō·ġy, *n.* [Gr. *chondros*, a cartilage, and *logos*, description.] the scientific study of cartilages.

çhon·drō′mȧ, *n.*; *pl.* **çhon·drō′mȧṣ, çhon·drō′mȧ·tȧ,** [*chondro-*, and Gr. *-ōma*, signifying a morbid condition.] a tumor which consists of cartilage.

çhon·drom′e·tẽr, *n.* [*chondro-*, and Gr. *metron*, a measure.] a device like a steelyard for weighing grain.

çhon·drop·tẽr·yġ′i·ăn, *n.* [*chondro-*, and Gr. *pterygion*, dim. of *pteryx*, a wing, fin.] one of the *Chondropterygii*.

çhon·drop·tẽr·yġ′i·ăn, *a.* pertaining to the *Chondropterygii*; having a cartilaginous skeleton.

Çhon·drop·tẽr·yġ′i·ī, *n.pl.* [L., from Gr. *chondros*, cartilage, and *pterygion*, a fin, dim. of *pteryx*, a wing.] a former group of fishes including the sturgeon, shark, ray, etc., distinguished from the fishes with true bone by the cartilaginous or gristly substance of which the skeleton is composed.

çhon·drō·skel′e·tŏn, *n.* a cartilaginous skeleton.

Çhon·dros′tē·ī, *n.pl.* [L., from Gr. *chondros*, cartilage, and *osteon*, bone.] an order of ganoid fishes, including the sturgeons, having the skeleton partly cartilaginous and partly bony.

çhon·drot′ō·my, *n.* [*chondro-*, and Gr. *tomē*, a cutting, from *temnein*, to cut.] in surgery and anatomy, the cutting and the dissection of cartilages.

çhon′drūle, *n.* [Mod. L. *chondrus*; Gr. *chondros*, grain.] a small rounded mass of various minerals, the size of a pea or smaller, contained in some stony meteorites.

çhon′drus, *n.*; *pl.* **çhon′drī,** [L.] same as *chondrule*.

chọọṣe, *v.t.*; chose, *pt.*; chosen, *pp.*; choosing, *ppr.* [ME. *cheosen*, *chesen*; AS. *ceosan*, to choose.]

1. to pick out by preference from all available; to select; as, to *choose* a wife.

2. to prefer; decide; think proper (with an infinitive object.).

3. to desire; want. [Colloq.]

chọọṣe, *v.i.* 1. to select; to make a choice; to decide; to exercise the power of choice; as, do as you *choose*.

2. to do as one pleases. [Obs.]

cannot choose but; cannot do otherwise than.

Syn.—select, pick out, prefer, cull, elect, adopt, follow.

chọọṣ′ẽr, *n.* one who chooses; specifically, formerly, an elector.

chọọṣ′ing, *n.* the act of making a choice.

chọọṣ′ing·ly, *adv.* by choosing or preference. [Rare.]

chọọṣ′ing stick, a divining stick. [Brit. Dial.]

chop, *v.t.*; chopped (chopt), *pt.*, *pp.*; chopping, *ppr.* [ME. *choppen*, *chappen*; G. and D. *kappen*, to chop; origin obscure.]

1. to cut into small pieces; to mince: often with *up*; as, to *chop up* meat; to *chop* straw.

2. to cut by blows with an ax or other sharp instrument: with *off*, *down*, etc.; as, to *chop off* a head; to *chop down* a tree.

3. to cause to cleave or open into chinks or fissures; to crack: in this sense usually *chap*.

4. to cut short.

chop, *v.i.* 1. to do something with sudden, unexpected motion; to make a hasty movement.

2. to make a cutting stroke or strokes with an ax, knife, or other sharp instrument.

3. to utter words abruptly; to interrupt by remarking: with *in* or *out*.

chop, *v.t.* [D. *koopen*, to buy.]

1. to barter; to truck. [Obs.]

2. to exchange; to put one thing in the place of another. [Obs.]

to chop logic; to dispute or argue in a sophistical manner, or with an affectation of logical terms or methods.

chop, *v.i.* 1. to bargain; to buy by way of truck.

2. to turn, vary, change, or shift suddenly; as, the wind *chops*, or *chops* about.

3. to bandy words; to dispute. [Obs.]

Let not the counsel at the bar *chop* with the judge. —Bacon.

chop, *n.* an exchange.

chop, *n.* 1. the act of chopping.

2. a short, sharp blow or stroke.

3. a piece chopped off.

4. a slice of lamb, pork, veal, etc.: chops are cut from the rib, loin, or shoulder.

5. a chapped place in the skin.

6. a short, broken movement of waves.

chop, *n.* [var. of *chap* (jaw).]

1. [*usually in pl.*] the chap; the jaw.

2. a movable jaw, as of a carpenter's vise.

3. [*pl.*] the mouth or entrance to a channel; as, the *chops* of the English Channel.

chop, *n.* [Hind. *chhāp*, a brand.]

1. an official seal, stamp, permit, or license in China and India.

2. in China, a brand on or of goods; as, silk or tea of the first *chop*.

3. quality; grade; brand: *first chop* means *first rate*. [Slang.]

chop′-chop′, *adv.* and *interj.* [Pidgin Eng.] quickly; at once.

chop dol′lăr, in certain Asiatic ports, a coin bearing the stamp of a trading company to attest its genuineness.

chop′fall·en (-fal′n), *a.* see *chapfallen*.

chop′house, *n.* a restaurant that specializes in chops and steaks.

chop′house, *n.* [see *chop* (a seal).] a Chinese customhouse.

chop′in, *n.* [ME. *chopyn*; OFr. *chopine*, a liquid measure.] a liquid measure formerly used in France and Great Britain, the capacity of which varied in different localities, ranging from half a pint to a quart.

chō·pïne′, *n.* [OFr. and Sp. *chapin*, a sock, pump.] an unusually high clog or patten, in some cases resembling a short stilt, worn by ladies in the seventeenth and eighteenth centuries: introduced into the West from Turkey.

CHOPINES

chop′log″iç, *n.* 1. an argumentative person.

2. pretentious and hair-splitting disputation. [Obs.]

chop′pẽr, *n.* 1. one who or that which chops.

2. a helicopter. [Colloq.]

3. a motorcycle. [Coloq.]

chop′ping, *a.* having tumbling broken waves which dash against each other with a short, quick motion; also, veering or shifting suddenly, as the wind.

chop′ping, *a.* vigorous; sturdy; bouncing. [Brit. Colloq.]

chop′ping, *n.* the act of cutting by a stroke or series of strokes.

chop′ping block, a solid block of wood on which anything may be chopped; specifically, a block of hardwood on which meat and vegetables are cut up in food preparation.

chop′ping knīfe (nīf), a knife with a curved blade or blades fixed to a handle, for mincing cooking materials.

chop′py, *a.*; *comp.* choppier; *superl.* choppiest, [from *chop* (to change).] changing constantly and abruptly, as the wind.

chop′py, *a.* 1. characterized by small, rough, tumultuous waves; as, a *choppy* sea.

2. with sharp, abrupt movements; jerky.

3. full of cracks; chapped.

chops, *n.pl.* [from *chap* (jaw).] 1. the jaws.

2. the mouth and lower cheeks.

3. technical skill, especially of a jazz or rock musician. [Slang.]

chop′sticks, *n.pl.* 1. small tapering sticks, usually of wood or ivory, held by the Chinese, Japanese, and some other Asian peoples, between the thumb and fingers, and used, in pairs, to convey food to the mouth.

2. a short, choppy melody played on the piano with one finger of each hand. [Colloq.]

chop strōke, in tennis, a stroke made with a cutting or slicing motion.

chop sū′ey, chop sọọ′y, [altered from Chin. *tsa-sui*, lit., various pieces.] a Chinese-American dish consisting of meat and various vegetables cooked together in a sauce and served with rice, etc.

çhō·rag′iç, *a.* pertaining to or connected with a choragus; as, a *choragic* monument.

choragic monument; in ancient Greece, a monument erected in honor of the choragus who gained the prize (a bronze tripod) by the exhibition of the best musical or theatrical entertainment at the festival of Bacchus: the prize itself was displayed on the monument.

çhō·rā′gus, *n.*; *pl.* **çhō·rā′ġī,** [L. *choragus*; Gr. *chorēgos*, the leader of a chorus, from *choros*, chorus, and *hēgeisthai*, to lead.]

1. in ancient Greece, the leader of a chorus or of a theatrical representation; especially, one who provided at his own expense the choruses for tragedies and comedies, and for the various religious festivals at Athens.

2. any leader of a chorus, choir, or band.

çhō′răl, *a.* [Fr.] pertaining to, for, sung by, or recited by a choir or chorus; as, *choral* service.

çhō·ral′, çhō·rale′, *n.* [from G. *choral* (*gesang*), choral (song), hymn.] a simple hymn tune sung by the choir and congregation, often in unison.

çhō″răl·cel′ō, *n.* in music, an instrument with a keyboard like the piano but having electromagnets to vibrate the strings, giving an organlike quality to the tone.

çhō′răl·ist, *n.* one who sings or composes chorals; also, a member of a choir.

çhō′răl·ly, *adv.* in the manner of a chorus.

çhō′răl sẽrv′ice, a song service, especially the full liturgy or a major part of it, in which the clergy, choir, and congregation join.

çhord, *n.* [L. *chorda*; Gr. *chordē*, the string of a musical instrument.]

1. the string of a musical instrument. [Poetic.]

2. a responsive emotional element; as, his speech struck a sympathetic *chord*.

3. in aeronautics, (a) a straight line extending directly across an airfoil from the leading to the trailing edge; (b) the length of such a line.

4. in anatomy, a structure, such as a tendon, resembling a cord.

5. in engineering, a principal horizontal member in a rigid framework, as of a bridge.

6. in geometry, a straight line joining any two points on an arc, curve, or circumference.

C A B

CHORDS (AC, AB)

çhord, *n.* [mistakenly altered (after L. *chorda*, string) from *cord*, contr. from *accord*.] in music, a combination of three or more tones sounded together in harmony.

çhord, *v.t.* and *v.i.* chorded, *pt.*, *pp.*; chording, *ppr.* to harmonize.

çhor′dȧ, *n.*; *pl.* **çhor′dae,** [L.]

1. in anatomy, a tendon.

2. [C–] in botany, a genus of algae. One species, *Chorda filum*, is known as sea lace.

chorda dorsalis; the notochord.

çhor′dăl, *a.* pertaining to a chord.

Çhor·dā′tȧ, *n.pl.* an extensive phylum of the animal kingdom, including those having a notochord.

çhor′dāte, *n.* [L. *chorda*, string, and *-ate*.] any animal having at some stage of its development a notochord, gill slits, and a dorsal tubular nerve cord: all the vertebrates, including man, are chordates.

çhor′dāte, *a.* 1. having a notochord.

2. of a chordate or chordates.

çhor·dō·tō′năl, *a.* [Gr. *chordē*, chord, and *tonos*, tone, measure.] affected by or responsive to sound vibrations, as certain organs in the legs of insects are believed to be.

chōre, *n.* [ME. *cheer*, *char*, a turning; AS. *cerr*, *cyrr*, turn, occasion, from *cerran*, *cyrran*, to turn.]

1. [*usually in pl.*] a small routine task, as of a housekeeper or farmer; odd job.

2. a hard or unpleasant task.

chōre, *v.i.*; chored, *pt.*, *pp.*; choring, *ppr.* to perform chores.

çhō·rē′ȧ, *n.* [L. *chorea*; Gr. *choreia*, a dance.] a nervous disease in which there are irregular, jerking movements caused by involuntary muscular contractions; St. Vitus's dance.

çhō·ree′, *n.* same as *choreus*.

çhō·rē′gus, *n.* same as *choragus*.

çhō·rē′iç, *a.* having the nature of, relating to, or having chorea.

çhō′rē·ō·graph″, *v.t.* and *v.i.*; choreographed, *pt.*, *pp.*; choreographing, *ppr.* [back-formation from *choreography*.] to design or plan the movements of (a dance, especially a ballet).

çhō·rē·og′rȧ·phẽr, *n.* a person who designs or arranges the movements of a ballet.

çhō·rē·og′rȧ·phy, *n.* [Gr. *choreia*, dance, and *graphein*, to describe.]

1. ballet dancing.

2. the arrangement, especially the written notation, of the movements of a ballet.

3. the art of devising ballets.

çhō·rē·pis′çō·păl, *a.* pertaining to the jurisdiction and power of a chorepiscopus.

çhō·rē·pis′çō·pus, *n.*; *pl.* **çhō·rē·pis′çō·pī,** [LL., from Gr. *chōra*, place, spot, and *episkopos*, an overseer; *epi*, over, and *skopein*, to examine.] a local or suffragan bishop; a bishop appointed in the early Christian church by the ordinary bishop of a diocese to assist him in taking charge of the outlying rural district of his diocese.

çhō·rē'us, çhō·ree', *n.* [L. *choreus*; Gr. *choreios*, in prosody, the trochee.] in prosody, (a) a foot of two syllables, the first long and the second short; a trochee; (b) with later prosodists, a tribrach: a foot consisting of three short syllables.

çhō'ri-, a combining form from Greek *choris*, apart.

çhō'ri·amb, *n.* [L. *choriambus*; Gr. *choriambos*, a choriambus, from *chorios*, a choreus, or trochee, and *iambos*, an iambus.] a metrical foot of four syllables, the first and last long, the middle two short, as in Greek and Latin verse, or the first and last stressed and the middle two unstressed, as in English verse; trochee and iamb combined.

çhō·ri·am'biç, *n.* a choriamb.

çhō·ri·am'biç, *a.* pertaining to a choriamb.

çhō·ri·am'bus, *n.*; *pl.* **çhō·ri·am'bī, çhō·ri·am'bus·eș,** same as *choriamb*.

çhō'riç, *a.* [Gr. *chorikos*, belonging to a choral dance.] pertaining to, for, or in the manner of, a chorus, especially in an ancient Greek play.

çhō'rīne, *n.* a chorus girl in a theater, cabaret, etc. [Colloq.]

çhō'ri·oid, *a.* and *n.* choroid.

çhō'ri·on, *n.* [Gr. *chorion*, leather, skin.]

1. in anatomy, the outer membrane which surrounds the fetus of a mammal, attaching it to the uterus.

2. a membrane or covering like a chorion, which invests various ova, as of insects or of seeds, at certain stages of development.

çhō·ri·pet'ăl·ous, *a.* [Gr. *chōris*, apart, and *petalon*, leaf.] polypetalous; having unconnected or separate petals.

çhō·ri·phyl'lous, *a.* [Gr. *chōris*, asunder, apart, and *phyllon*, leaf.] having the leaves distinct and separate, as a perianth.

çhō·ri·sep'ăl·ous, *a.* [Gr. *chōris*, apart, and L. *sepalum*, sepal.] polysepalous; having unconnected sepals.

çhō'ri·sis, *n.* [Gr. *chōrisis*, a separation, from *chōrizein*, to separate.] in botany, the congenital development of two or more parts from one: it may be either transverse or collateral.

çhō'rist, *n.* [Fr. *choriste*, a chorist, from L. *chorus*, choir.] one who sings in a choir. [Rare.]

çhō·ris'tāte, *a.* formed by chorisis.

çhor'is·tẽr, *n.* [from *chorus*, *choir*.]

1. a singer in a choir; especially, a boy who sings in a choir.

2. one who leads a choir in church music.

3. a songster; as, a feathered *chorister*.

çhō·ris'tiç, *a.* choral; choric. [Rare.]

çhō''ri·stō'mȧ, *n.* [Mod. L., from *chorist* and *-oma*.] in medicine, a malignant growth resulting from embryonic parts that are out of place.

çhor'is·try, *n.* the singing of choristers.

çhō''ri·zon'tēș, *n.pl.* [Mod. L., from Gr. *chorizontes*, separation.] in criticism of Homer, those who believe that the *Iliad* and *Odyssey* were written by different authors.

çhō'rō·grȧph, *n.* [Gr. *chōros*, place, and *graphein*, to describe.] an instrument for determining the location of a point from the angles made by lines to three points whose position is known.

çhō·rog'rȧ·phẽr, *n.* one who describes, or forms a map or maps of, particular regions or countries.

çhō·rō·graph'iç, çhō·rō·graph'iç·ăl, *a.* pertaining to chorography.

çhō·rō·graph'iç·ăl·ly, *adv.* in a chorographical manner.

çhō·rog'rȧ·phy, *n.* [Gr. *chōros*, place, and *graphein*, to describe.]

1. the art or practice of making a map or description of a particular region, country, or province.

2. such a map or description.

çhō'roid, çhō'ri·oid, *a.* [Gr. *choroeidēs*, contr. from *chorioeidēs*, from *chorion*, leather, skin, and *eidos*, form.] designating or of the chorion or certain other vascular membranes in the body.

choroid membrane; the dark, vascular membrane of the eye, situated between the sclera and the retina, and forming the middle coat of the eye.

choroid plexus; one of the membranous and vascular fringes of the pia mater where it covers the ventricles of the brain.

çhō'roid, çhō'ri·oid, *n.* the choroid membrane.

çhō·roid'ăl, *a.* same as *choroid*.

çhō·roid·ī'tis, *n.* inflammation of the choroid membrane.

çhō·rol'ō·ġy, *n.* [Gr. *chōros*, place, and *logos*, description.]

1. same as *chorography*.

2. the science which treats of the laws governing the geographical distribution of plants and animals.

çhō·rō·mā'ni·ȧ, *n.* [Gr. *choros*, a dance, and *mania*, madness.] epidemic chorea: written also *choreomania*.

çhō·rom'e·try, *n.* [Gr. *chōros*, place, and *metron*, measure.] the art of land surveying.

çhor'ten, *n. sing.* and *pl.* in Lamaism, a reliquary; a stupa.

Chor'ti (-tē), *n. sing.* and *pl.* a Mayan Indian.

çhor'tle, *v.i.* and *v.t.*; chortled, *pt.*, *pp.*; chortling, *ppr.* [coined by Lewis Carroll, in *Through the Looking Glass*; prob. from *chuckle* and *snort*.] to make or utter with a gleeful chuckling or snorting sound.

çhor'tle, *n.* a gleeful chuckling or snorting sound.

çhō'rus, *n.*; *pl.* **çhō'rus·eș,** [L. *chorus*; Gr. *choros*, a dance in a ring, a chorus.]

1. in Greek drama, a company of performers whose singing, dancing, and narration provided explanation and elaboration of the main action.

2. in Elizabethan drama, a person who recites the prologue and epilogue.

3. a group of dancers and singers performing together in a modern musical show, theatrical performance, opera, etc.

4. the part of a drama, song, etc. performed by a chorus.

5. a number of people singing or speaking something together simultaneously.

6. a simultaneous utterance by many; as, a *chorus* of protest.

7. that which is thus uttered.

8. music written for group singing.

9. that part of a musical composition in which the company joins the solo singer.

10. the refrain of a song, following the verse.

çhō'rus, *v.i.* and *v.t.*; chorused, *pt.*, *pp.*; chorusing, *ppr.* to sing or recite all together and simultaneously; to utter in unison.

çhō'rus girl (or **boy**), a woman (or man) singing or dancing in the chorus of a musical comedy, etc.

chōșe, *v.*, past tense and obsolete past participle of *choose*.

çhōșe, *n.* [Fr. *chose*, a thing; OFr. *cose*, *cosa*; LL. *causa*, a thing; L. *causa*, cause.] in law, a chattel; a piece of personal property.

chose in action; a right to a sum of money or a thing not actually in possession, but legally recoverable; also, a written obligation, as a note or bond, upon which suit may legally be brought.

chose in possession; a piece of personal property in actual and legal possession.

chose local; anything annexed to a place, as a mill or the like.

chose transitory; a piece of property which is portable or movable. [Rare.]

chō'șen, *v.*, past participle of *choose*.

chō'șen, *a.* 1. selected from a number; picked out by preference; choice.

2. in theology, elect; favored by God.

the chosen people; the Israelites.

Chōu (jō), *n.* a Chinese dynasty (1122?–249 B.C.).

Çhōu'ăn (*or Fr.* shö-oṅ'), *n.* [Fr. *chathuant*, a screech owl.] one of a band of insurgent royalists of Brittany who rose in 1793 against the French republic and carried on guerrilla warfare.

chough (chuf), *n.* [ME. *choughe*, *cheo*; AS. *ceō*, a chough or jackdaw.] a bird belonging to the genus *Pyrrhocorax*, of the crow family, with red legs and beak and glossy black feathers.

chöu'i·chȧ, *n.* same as *chavicha*.

choul'try, *n.* same as *choltry*.

chouse, *n.* [Turk. *cha'ush*, *chaush*, an interpreter; Ar. *khawas*; Hind. *khawas*, an attendant. The word is said to have been adopted because in 1609 a Turkish interpreter swindled several London merchants.]

1. one who is easily gulled. [Obs.]

2. an imposition; a trick. [Colloq.]

3. a rogue; a swindler. [Obs.]

chouse, *v.t.*; choused, *pt.*, *pp.*; chousing, *ppr.* to cheat; trick; defraud: followed by *of* or *out of*; as, to *chouse* one *out of* his money. [Colloq.]

chout, *n.* [Hind. *chauth*, a fourth of the revenue.] in the East Indies, a fourth part of the clear revenue, formerly exacted by the Mahrattas; hence, extortion of any kind.

chow, *n.* 1. a dog of a breed originally Chinese, having a thick, furry coat, a short tail curled over and close to the body, a leonine head and a characteristic blue-black tongue: its coloring is uniform, ranging from white or cream to black.

CHOW (20 in. high)

2. food; anything that may be eaten. [Slang.]

3. in China, a subordinate district or its principal city.

chow'chow, *a.* [Pidgin Eng.] mixed; assorted; as, *chowchow* sweetmeats.

chow'chow, *n.* 1. chopped pickles in a highly seasoned mustard sauce.

2. a chow (dog).

3. the yellow-billed cuckoo. [Dial.]

chow'dẽr, *n.* [prob. from Fr. *chaudière*, a caldron.]

1. a stewed dish of fish or clams containing salt pork, potatoes, onions, etc., usually in milk.

2. a picnic at which the making and serving of chowder is the chief feature.

chow'dẽr, *v.t.*; chowdered, *pt.*, *pp.*; chowdering, *ppr.* to make into a chowder.

chow'dẽr beer, a beverage made by boiling black spruce in water and mixing it with molasses.

chow·mein' (-mān'), *n.* [Chinese (Pekingese) *ch'ao*, to fry, and *mien*, flour.] a Chinese-American dish consisting of a stew made of shredded meat, onions, mushrooms, and celery, served with fried noodles.

chow'ry, *n.* [Hind.] in the East Indies, a whisk to keep off flies, often made of the tail of a yak.

choy'ro͞ot, *n.* same as *chay*.

çhrē·mȧ·tis'tiç, *a.* pertaining to chrematistics.

çhrē·mȧ·tis'tiçs, *n.* [Gr. *chrematistēs*, one who carries on business, from *chrēmatizein*, to transact business.] the science of wealth: that branch of political economy relating to the manipulation of property and wealth.

çhrē·ō·teçh'niçs, *n.* [Gr. *chreios*, useful, and *technē*, art.] the useful arts; specifically, agriculture, manufacturing, and commerce. [Rare.]

çhres·tō·math'iç, *a.* pertaining to the learning of useful things or to a chrestomathy.

çhres·tom'ȧ·thy, *n.*; *pl.* **çhres·tom'ȧ·thieș,** [Gr. *chrēstos*, useful, and *manthanein*, to learn.] a collection of passages from literature, used in studying a language or as literary specimens.

çhrișm, *n.* [ME. *chrisme*; AS. *crisma*; LL. *chrisma*, chrism oil; Gr. *chrisma*, an unguent, from *chriein*, to rub, anoint.]

1. olive oil or unguent, consecrated by a bishop and used in the administration of baptism, confirmation, ordination, and extreme unction in certain churches.

2. a sacramental anointing with such oil.

3. a chrisom. [Obs.]

çhriș'măl, *a.* pertaining to the chrism.

çhriș·mā'tion, *n.* the act of applying the chrism, or consecrated oil.

çhriș'mȧ·tō·ry, *n.*; *pl.* **çhriș'mȧ·tō·ries,** [ML. *chrismatorium*, from LL. *chrisma*, chrism oil.] a container or receptacle for the chrism.

CHRISMATORY

çhriș'mon, *n.* a monogram formed of the first two letters in the Greek name of Christ.

çhriș'ŏm, *n.* [var. of *chrism*; orig., cloth to keep chrism off the face.]

1. a white robe or cloth put on a baby at baptism as a symbol of innocence: it was used as a shroud if the baby died within a month of birth.

2. (a) a baby in its chrism; hence, (b) an innocent baby; an infant. [Archaic.]

Çhrist, *n.* [ME. *Crist*; AS. *Crist*; L. *Christus*, Christ; Gr. *Christos*, Christ, lit. the Anointed, from *chriein*, to anoint.]

1. the Messiah whose appearance is prophesied in the Old Testament.

2. Jesus of Nazareth, regarded by Christians as the realization of the Messianic prophecy: originally a title (*Jesus the Christ*), later used as part of the name (*Jesus Christ*).

Çhris·tȧ·del'phi·ăn, *n.* [Gr. *Christos*, Christ, and *adelphos*, brother.] a member of a small religious sect founded in the United States about 1833 by John Thomas, M. D., and later extending to England and other countries. They reject the Trinity, deny infant baptism, etc.: also called *Brothers of Christ* and *Thomasites*.

Çhrīst chīld, the representation of Jesus Christ as a child.

çhrist′çross (kris′), *n.* [from *Christ's cross.*]
1. the figure of a cross (✠) formerly placed before the alphabet in hornbooks, etc.; also, the mark of the cross (X) used as a signature by a person who cannot write. [Archaic.]
2. the alphabet. [Brit. Dial.]
See also *crisscross.*

çhrist′çross-rōw, *n.* the alphabet. [Archaic and Dial.]

çhris′ten (kris′n), *v.t.*; christened, *pt.*, *pp.*; christening, *ppr.* [ME. *christenen*; AS. *cristenian, cristnian,* to christen, from *Cristen,* a Christian, L. *Christianus*; Gr. *Christianos,* a Christian.]
1. to give a name to at baptism; as, the child was *christened* Edith.
2. to baptize; to take into a Christian church by baptism.
3. to name; to give a name to.
4. to use for the first time; as, to *christen* a house. [Colloq.]
5. to convert to Christianity. [Archaic.]

Çhris′ten·dŏm (kris′n-dum), *n.* [ME. *cristendom*; AS. *cristendom,* Christianity, from *Cristen,* Christian, and *dōm,* domain, jurisdiction, from *dōn,* to do.]
1. Christianity. [Obs.]
2. the territories, countries, or regions chiefly inhabited by those who profess to the Christian religion.
3. Christians collectively.
4. baptism; christening. [Obs.]

çhrist′en·ing, *n.* the act or ceremony of baptism, especially when accompanied by a naming of the baptized.

Çhrīst′hood, *n.* the state or fact of being the Christ.

Çhris′tiăn (kris′chăn), *n.* [ME. *Cristen*; AS. *Cristen, Cristena*; L. *Christianus*; Gr. *Christianos,* a Christian, from *Christos,* Christ.]
1. a person professing belief in Jesus as the Christ, or in the religion based on the teachings of Jesus.
2. the main character in Bunyan's *Pilgrim's Progress* (1678), a refugee fleeing the City of Destruction to seek Zion, the City of God.
3. a decent, respectable person. [Colloq.]
4. in a general sense, anyone born of Christian parents.
5. in church history, (a) a member of a sect which is the offshoot of three other churches, which rejects creeds, accepts the Bible literally, and believes in open communion and immersion; (b) one belonging to a similar sect founded by Thomas and Alexander Campbell: also called *Disciples of Christ* or *Campbellites.*

Çhris′tiăn, *a.* 1. of Jesus Christ.
2. of the teachings of Jesus Christ.
3. of or professing the religion based on these teachings.
4. having the qualities demonstrated and taught by Jesus Christ, as love, kindness, etc.
5. of or representing Christians or Christianity.
6. human, decent, etc. [Colloq.]

Çhris′tiăn Brŏth′ẽrs, a Roman Catholic lay order that undertakes the teaching of youth.

Çhris′tiăn Ē′rȧ, the era beginning with the year formerly thought to be that of the birth of Jesus Christ (born probably c. 4–6 B.C.): *A.D.* marks dates in this era, *B.C.* marks dates before it.

Çhris′tiăn·işm, *n.* the religious system or principles of Christians. [Rare.]

çhris′tiăn·ite, *n.* [after Prince *Christian* Frederick of Denmark.] a kind of anorthite from Mount Vesuvius.

Çhris·ti·an′i·ty (-chi-an′), *n.* [ME. *cristianite, cristiente*; OFr. *crestiente*; L. *christianitas,* from *Christianus,* a Christian.]
1. Christians collectively; Christendom.
2. the Christian religion; doctrines taught by Jesus Christ.
3. a particular Christian religious system; as, Eastern *Christianity.*
4. the state of being a Christian.
5. Christian character, practices, etc.

Çhris″tiăn·i·zā′tion, *n.* the act or process of converting to Christianity.

Çhris′tiăn·īze, *v.t.*; Christianized, *pt.*, *pp.*; Christianizing, *ppr.* 1. to make Christian; to convert to Christianity; as, to *Christianize* pagans.
2. to inspire with Christian principles.

Çhris′tiăn·īze, *v.i.* to adopt Christianity.

Çhris′tiăn·līke, *a.* having the qualities or habits of a Christian.

Çhris′tiăn·ly, *a.* and *adv.* like, characteristic of, or in the manner of a Christian.

Çhris′tiăn nāme, the baptismal name, as distinguished from the surname or family name; given name.

Çhris′tiăn·ness, *n.* the state or quality of being in accord with Christian doctrines. [Obs.]

Çhris′tiăn Scī′ence, a religion and system of healing founded by Mary Baker Eddy in 1866, based on an interpretation of the Scriptures as upholding the idea that disease, sin, etc. are caused by mental error and may be eliminated by spiritual treatment without medical aid: official name, *Church of Christ, Scientist.*

Çhris′tiăn Scī′en·tist, a person who believes in Christian Science.

Çhrīst′less, *a.* having no faith in Christ; unchristian.

Çhrīst′līke, *a.* like Jesus Christ in nature or character.

Çhrīst′like·ness, *n.* the state of being Christlike.

Çhrīst′li·ness, *n.* the state of being Christly.

Çhrīst′ly, *a.* like Jesus Christ.

Çhrist′măs (kris′), *n.* [ME. *Cristmas, Cristmes,* from *Christ,* and *mass,* from AS. *mæssa,* a church festival, from L. *missus,* pp. of *mittere,* to send.] the festival of the Christian church observed annually on the 25th day of December, in memory of the birth of Jesus Christ.
Christmas carol; a carol suitable for Christmas; a song or hymn in celebration of the nativity of Jesus Christ.
Christmas Day; December 25.
Christmas Eve; the evening before Christmas Day.
Christmas fern; a fern, *Aspidium acrostichoides,* used for decorative purposes in winter.
Christmas rose or *Christmas flower*; a plant, *Helleborus niger*: so called from its open roselike flower, which blossoms during the winter months.
Christmas tree; an evergreen tree hung with ornaments and lights, set up at Christmas time.

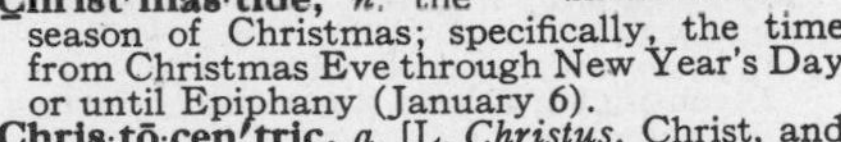
CHRISTMAS ROSE (*Helleborus niger*)

Çhrist′măs·tīde, *n.* the season of Christmas; specifically, the time from Christmas Eve through New Year's Day or until Epiphany (January 6).

Çhris·tō·cen′triç, *a.* [L. *Christus,* Christ, and *centrum,* center.] grouping all things about Christ as a center.

Çhrīst of the An′dēş, a bronze statue of Jesus Christ, unveiled in 1904 at Cambre Pass, a mountain frontier, 13,000 feet above sea level, between Chile and Argentina.

Çhris·tol′ō·ġy, *n.* [Gr. *Christos,* Christ, and *logos,* description.] a discourse or treatise concerning Christ.

Çhris·toph′ȧ·ny, *n.* [Gr. *Christos,* Christ, and *phainein,* to appear.] the appearance of Christ after his death, as recorded in the New Testament.

Çhrīst's thorn, one of several thorny shrubs, as *Paliurus aculeatus* of southern Europe and the Near East, supposed to have been used for Christ's crown of thorns.

çhrōm-, same as *chromo-.*

çhrō′mȧ, *n.* [Gr. *chrōma,* a color.] the purity of a color, determined by its degree of freedom from white or gray; color intensity.

çhrō′mȧ·sçōpe, *n.* [*chroma-,* and Gr. *skopein,* to view.] an instrument for showing the various optical effects of color and colored light.

çhrō′mat-, same as *chromato-.*

çhrō′māte, *n.* a salt formed by chromic acid, producing compounds used in dyeing and as pigments.

çhrō·mat′iç, *a.* [L. *chromaticus*; Gr. *chrōmatikos,* suited for color, from *chrōma,* color.]
1. of or containing color or colors.
2. in biology, readily stained.
3. in music, (a) using or progressing by half tones; as, a *chromatic* scale; (b) producing all the tones of such a scale; as, a *chromatic* instrument.
chromatic aberration; a property of lenses that causes the various colors in a beam of light to be focused at different points, thus causing a spectrum to appear.
chromatic printing; any method of color printing; specifically, the use of several plates printing different colors so as to blend and produce varying tints.
chromatic scale; in music, the scale embracing thirteen successive half tones to the octave.
chromatic semitone; the difference in pitch between a note and its sharp or flat.
chromatic sign; in music, an accidental.

çhrō·mat′iç, *n.* in music, a tone modified by an accidental.

çhrō·mat′iç·ăl, *a.* same as *chromatic.*

çhrō·mat′iç·ăl·ly, *adv.* 1. in a chromatic manner.
2. in a chromatic scale.

çhrō·mat′içs, *n.* [*construed as sing.*] the science of colors.

çhrō′mȧ·tin, *n.* [Gr. *chrōma,* color, and *-in.*] in biology, the protoplasmic substance in the nucleus of a cell, which is most subject to the action of dyes: chromatin contains the genes.

çhrō′mȧ·tişm, *n.* [Gr. *chrōmatismos,* coloring, from *chrōmatizein,* to color.]
1. chromatic aberration.
2. in botany, abnormal coloration in parts of a plant ordinarily green.

çhrō′mȧ·tō-, [from Gr. *chrōma, chrōmatos,* a color.] a combining form meaning (a) *color* or *pigmentation,* as in *chromato*logy; (b) *chromatin,* as in *chromato*lysis. Also, before a vowel, *chromat-.*

çhrō·mȧ·toġ′e·nous, *a.* [*chromato-,* and Gr. *-genēs,* producing.] yielding color.

çhrō′mȧ·tō·grȧph, *n.* [*chromato-,* and Gr. *graphein,* to write.] an instrument designed to show the synthetical production of color tones by the rotation of a circular disk bearing any combination of colors.

çhrō·mȧ·tog′rȧ·phy, *n.* [*chromato-,* and Gr. *graphē,* a representation, from *graphein,* to write.]
1. a treatise on colors.
2. chromatics.

çhrō·mȧ·tol′ō·ġy, *n.* [*chromato-,* and Gr. *logos,* a description.] chromatography.

çhrō·mȧ·tol′y·sis, *n.* [*chromato-,* and *-lysis.*] in medicine, the breakdown and dissolution of the chromatin in the cell nucleus.

çhrō·mȧ·tom′e·tẽr, *n.* [*chromato-,* and Gr. *metron,* a measure.] an arrangement of various colors which serve by comparison to classify other colors; a scale for colors.

çhrō′mȧ·tō·phōre, *n.* [*chromato-,* and Gr. *-phoros,* bearing, from *pherein,* to bear.]
1. in zoology, a pigment cell capable of contraction and expansion with consequent change of color, as in the chameleon.
2. in botany, a cell having coloring matter in its composition.

çhrō′mȧ·tō·sçōpe, *n.* [*chromato-,* and Gr. *skopein,* to view.]
1. in astronomy, a reflecting and revolving telescope by which the observer views a star as a ring of light instead of a point.
2. a chromatograph.

çhrō·mȧ·tos′çō·py, *n.* the study of color or of star scintillation by means of the chromatoscope.

çhrō′mȧ·trōpe, *n.* [*chroma-,* and Gr. *tropē,* a turn, from *trepein,* to turn.]
1. an instrument consisting of disks on which arcs of colors are so arranged that, when rotated rapidly, they present the appearance of streams of colors flowing to or from their center.
2. a kaleidoscopic attachment for a magic lantern.

çhrō′mȧ·tȳpe, *n.* same as *chromotype.*

çhrōme, *v.t.*; chromed, *pt.*, *pp.*; chroming, *ppr.*
1. to treat with a compound of chromium, as potassium dichromate, used in dyeing and oxidizing.
2. to plate with chromium.

çhrōme, *n.* [L. *chromium,* from Gr. *chrōma,* color.]
1. chromium.
2. chrome yellow.

-çhrōme, [from Gr. *chrōma,* a color.] a suffix meaning: (a) *color, coloring agent,* as in uro*chrome*; (b) *chromium,* as in ferro*chrome.*

çhrōme al′um, a crystallizable double salt formed from chromium and potassium.

çhrōme green, a dark green pigment prepared from, usually, chromic oxide and cobaltic oxide.

çhrōme ī′ron, chromite (the mineral): also *chrome iron ore.*

çhrōme leath′ẽr, leather tanned with chromium salts.

çhrōme red, any of various red pigments prepared from basic chromate of lead.

çhrōme steel, a very strong, hard alloy steel that contains chromium.

çhrōme yel′lōw, a neutral chromate of lead, used as a yellow pigment.

çhrō′miç, *a.* relating to or derived from chromium; especially, designating compounds of chromium in which the valence of chromium is higher than in the corresponding chromous compounds.

chromic acid; an acid, H_2CrO_4, whose salts are chromates.

chromic anhydrid; a crimson-red substance, CrO_3, readily forming chromic acid.

çhrō′mid, *n.* a fish of the family *Chromides.*

Çhrom′i·dēs, Çhrom′i·dae, *n.pl.* [Gr. *chromis,* a kind of sea fish, and *eidos,* resemblance.] a family of teleostean fishes, generally inhabiting tropical waters, allied to the *Labridæ,* or true wrasses.

çhrō·mid′i·um, *n.*; *pl.* **çhrō·mid′i·ȧ,** [dim., from Gr. *chrōma,* color.] in algae, one of the asexually produced reproductive cells.

çhrō·mi·drō′sis, *n.* [Gr. *chrōma,* color, and *hidrōs,* sweat.] a condition characterized by abnormally colored perspiration.

çhrō′mişm, *n.* same as *chromatism.*

çhrō′mīte, *n.* 1. a black mineral, the chief source of chromium, $FeCr_2O_4$, with a metallic luster and an uneven fracture.

2. a salt of chromous acid.

çhrō′mi·um, *n.* [L., from Gr. *chrōma,* color.] a white, crystalline, very hard, metallic chemical element with a high resistance to corrosion: used in chromium electroplating, in alloy steel, and in alloys containing nickel, copper, manganese, and other metals: symbol, Cr; atomic weight, 52.01; atomic number, 24.

çhrō′mi·um-plāt′ed, *a.* plated with chromium.

çhrō′mi·um steel, chrome steel.

çhrō′mō, *n.*; *pl.* **çhrō′mōş,** a chromolithograph.

çhrō′mō-, [from Gr. *chrōma,* a color.] a combining form meaning *color, colored, pigment, pigmentation,* as in *chromo*some, *chromo*lithograph: also, before a vowel, *chrom-.*

çhrō′mō·blȧst, *n.* [*chromo-,* and Gr. *blastos,* a bud, shoot.] a pigmented connective tissue cell, as in the skin of snakes.

çhrō′mō·ġen, *n.* [*chromo-,* and Gr. *-genēs,* producing.] any substance that can become a pigment or coloring matter, as a substance in organic fluids that forms colored compounds when oxidized, or a compound, not itself a dye, that can become a dye.

çhrō·mō·ġen′iç, *a.* 1. pertaining to chromogen or chromogens.

2. producing a color or pigment, as certain bacteria.

çhrō′mō·grȧph, *n.* [*chromo-,* and Gr. *graphein,* to write.] a hectograph.

çhrō·mō·leū′cīte, *n.* [*chromo-,* and Gr. *leukos,* white.] a chromoplast.

çhrō·mō·lip′oid, *n.* [*chromo-,* and Gr. *lipoid.*] same as *lipochrome.*

çhrō·mō·lith′ō·grȧph, *n.* a picture obtained by means of chromolithography.

çhrō″mō·li·thog′rȧ·phẽr, *n.* one who practices chromolithography.

çhrō″mō·lith·ō·graph′iç, *a.* relating to chromolithography or chromolithographs.

çhrō″mō·li·thog′rȧ·phy, *n.* [*chromo-,* and Gr. *lithos,* a stone, and *graphein,* to write.] a method of producing a colored lithographic picture, by using a series of stone or zinc plates having different portions of the picture drawn upon them with inks of various colors and so arranged as to blend into a complete picture.

çhrō′mō·mēre, *n.* [*chromo-,* and Gr. *meros,* part.] in physiology and pathology, one of the small particles of chromatin of which a chromosome is formed.

çhrō′mō·phāne, *n.* [*chromo-,* and Gr. *phainein,* to appear.] the coloring matter in the retinal cones of certain animals.

çhrō·moph′i·lous, *a.* [*chromo-,* and Gr. *philos,* friendly.] readily stained or colored.

çhrō′mō·phōre, *n.* any chemical group which, aside from its chemical action, imparts a color to a compound and unites with certain other groups to form dyes.

çhrō·mō·phō′tō·grȧph, *n.* [*chromo-* and *photograph,* from Gr. *phōs,* light, and *graphein,* to write, to represent.] any photograph reproducing the original colors.

çhrō″mō·phō·tog′rȧ·phy, *n.* the art or science of making chromophotographs.

çhrō′mō·phō″tō·lith′ō·grȧph, *n.* a photolithograph which is printed in colors.

çhrō′mō·plaşm, *n.* [*chromo-,* and *-plasm.*] chromatin.

çhrō′mō·plast, *n.* [*chromo-,* and *-plast.*]

1. in biology, any pigmented body found in the cell outside the nucleus.

2. in botany, a granule containing a pigment other than green.

çhrō·mō·plas′tid, *n.* same as *chromoplast.*

çhrō·mop·tom′e·tẽr, *n.* [*chromo-,* and Gr. *optikos,* of seeing, and *metron,* a measure.] a device for determining the keenness of the color sense.

çhrō′mō·sō·măl, *a.* of a chromosome or chromosomes.

çhrō′mō·sōme, *n.* [*chromo-,* and Gr. *sōma,* the body.] any of the microscopic rod-shaped bodies into which the chromatin separates during mitosis: they carry the genes that convey hereditary characteristics, and are constant in number for each species.

çhrō′mō·sphēre, *n.* [*chromo-,* and Gr. *sphaira,* a sphere.] the reddish gaseous envelope surrounding the body of the sun, through which the light of the photosphere passes; also, a similar envelope surrounding a star.

çhrō·mō·spher′iç, *a.* relating to or like a chromosphere.

çhrō·mō·ther′ȧ·py, *n.* the treatment of disease by colored lights.

çhrō′mō·tȳpe, *n.* [*chromo-,* and Gr. *typos,* an impression.]

1. a print made by any color process.

2. a chromophotograph.

çhrō′mous (-mus), *a.* relating to or denoting chromium, especially chromium compounds in which the valence of chromium is lower than in corresponding chromic compounds.

çhrō·mō·xȳ′lō·grȧph (-zī′), *n.* [*chromo-,* and Gr. *xylon,* wood, and *graphein,* to write, represent.] a color picture printed from a number of wooden blocks.

çhrō′mūle, *n.* [Gr. *chrōma,* color, and *hylē,* matter.] any coloring substance in plants other than chlorophyll. [Obs.]

çhrō′myl, *n.* [*chrom-,* and *-yl.*] in chemistry, the divalent radical CrO_2.

çhron-, same as *chrono-.*

çhrō·nax′i·ȧ, *n.* [*chron-,* and Gr. *axia,* value.] the minimum time necessary to excite a tissue, such as muscle or nerve tissue, with an electric current of twice the minimum potential for stimulation: used as an index of tissue excitability.

çhrō′nax·ie, çhrō′nax·y, *n.* same as *chronaxia.*

çhron′ic, *a.* [ME. *cronike, cronyke*; L. *chronicus*; Gr. *chronikos,* chronic, of or for the time, from *chronos,* time.]

1. perpetual; habitual; constant.

2. continuing a long time; also, recurring, as a disease.

3. having had an ailment or habit for a long time.

çhron′i·căl, *a.* chronic. [Rare.]

çhron′i·căl·ly, *a.* in a chronic manner; persistently; habitually; continually.

çhron′i·çle (-kl), *n.* [ME. *cronicle,* a chronicle, from Gr. *chronos,* time.] a historical account of facts or events recorded in the order in which they happened; also, a history.

> Irish *chronicles* which are most fabulous and forged. —Spenser.

Syn.—record, register, annals.

çhron′i·çle, *v.t.*; chronicled, *pt., pp.*; chronicling, *ppr.* to record in history or chronicle; to recount.

çhron′i·çle plāy, a historical play of or like a type that flourished in the Elizabethan period, characterized by free treatment of the facts of history.

çhron′i·çlẽr, *n.* a writer of a chronicle; a historian.

Çhron′i·çleş, *n.pl.* two books of the Old Testament, I and II Chronicles.

çhrō·nïque′ (-nēk′), *n.* a chronicle. [Obs.]

çhron′ō-, a combining form meaning *time.*

çhron′ō·gram, *n.* [*chrono-,* and Gr. *gramma,* a letter or writing, from *graphein,* to write.]

1. an inscription in which certain letters, more prominent than the others, express a date in Roman numerals when put together in order. Example: **M**er**C**y **M**i**X**ed with **L**o**V**e **I**n h**I**m—MCMXLVII = 1947.

2. the measured record of a chronograph.

çhron″ō·gram·mat′iç, çhron″ō·gram·mat′i·căl, *a.* of or containing a chronogram.

çhron·ō·gram′mȧ·tist, *n.* a writer of chronograms.

çhron′ō·grȧph, *n.* [*chrono-,* and Gr. *graphein,* to write, describe.]

1. a chronogram.

2. an instrument for measuring and registering very minute portions of time with extreme precision.

çhrō·nog′rȧ·phẽr, *n.* [*chrono-,* and Gr. *graphein,* to write, describe.] one who writes concerning time or the events of time; a chronologist.

çhron·ō·graph′iç, *a.* relating to chronography.

çhrō·nog′rȧ·phy, *n.* [*chrono-,* and Gr. *graphein,* to write]. the description or investigation of past events; chronology. [Obs.]

çhrō·nol′ō·ġẽr, *n.* one versed in chronology; a person who investigates and records in order the dates of past events.

çhron·ō·loġ′iç·ăl, çhron·ō·loġ′iç, *a.* 1. relating to or containing an account of events in the order of occurrence.

2. arranged in the order of occurrence.

çhron·ō·loġ′iç·ăl·ly, *adv.* in a chronological manner.

çhrō·nol′ō·ġist, *n.* an expert in chronology; a chronologer.

çhrō·nol′ō·ġy, *n.*; *pl.* **çhrō·nol′ō·ġieş,** [Gr. *chronos,* time, and *logos,* a description, from *legein,* to describe.]

1. the science of ascertaining the fixed periods when past events took place and of arranging them in the order of occurrence.

> If history without *chronology* is dark and confused, *chronology* without history is dry and insipid. —A. Holmes.

2. the arrangement of events, dates, etc. in the order of occurrence.

3. a list or table of dates in their proper sequence.

çhrō·nom′e·tẽr, *n.* [*chrono-,* and Gr. *metron,* a measure.]

1. any instrument that measures time precisely; specifically, a clock or watch of the highest possible accuracy, used on ships to determine longitude.

2. a metronome, or mechanism for measuring time in music.

çhron·ō·met′riç, çhron·ō·met′riç·ăl, *a.* pertaining to a chronometer; also, measured by a chronometer.

çhron·ō·met′ri·căl·ly, *adv.* as determined by a chronometer.

çhrō·nom′e·try, *n.* the science of measuring time; the measuring of time by periods or divisions.

çhron′ō·phẽr, *n.* [*chrono-,* and Gr. *pherein,* to carry.] an electrical instrument for signaling the time to distant points.

çhron′ō·sçōpe, *n.* [*chrono-,* and Gr. *skopein,* to view.] a chronograph; specifically, one used in measuring the velocity of projectiles or other rapidly moving bodies.

-çhrō·ous, [Gr. *-chroos,* from *chrōs, chroos,* color.] a terminal combining form meaning *colored,* as in xantho*chroous.*

çhrys-, same as *chryso-.*

çhrys′ăl, *n.* in archery, a small crack in the bow: written also *crysal.*

çhrys′ȧ·lid, *a.* pertaining to a chrysalis.

çhrys′ȧ·lid, *n.* same as *chrysalis.*

çhrys′ȧ·lis, *n.*; *pl.* **çhry·sal′i·sēş** or **çhry·sal′i·dēş,** [L. *chrysallis*; Gr. *chrysallis,* the chrysalis of a butterfly, from *chrysos,* gold.]

1. a form which butterflies, moths, and most other insects assume between the state of larva, or caterpillar, and the winged, or adult, state; pupa.

2. the case or cocoon enveloping the insect at this stage.

CHRYSALISES
1. 2. chrysalis of the white butterfly-moth. 3. chrysalis of the oak egger moth.

3. anything in a formative or undeveloped stage.

çhrys·an′i·line, *n.* [*chrys-* and *aniline.*] a derivative of rosaniline used as a golden-yellow dye.

Çhrys·an′thē·mum, *n.* [L. *chrysanthemum*; Gr. *chrysanthemon,* the marigold, lit., the gold flower; *chrysos,* gold, and *anthemon,* a flower.]

1. a large genus of composite plants, consisting of herbs or shrubs with single, showy, large-stalked flowers or with many small flowers, which bloom in the late summer and fall and have a characteristic odor and a variety of colors, mostly yellow, white, or red.

2. [c—] any plant or flower of this genus.

çhrys·ȧ·rō′bin, *n.* [L., from *chrys-,* and *araroba,*

a native name of Goa powder.] a yellow, crystalline substance, $C_{15}H_{12}O_3$, derived from Goa powder and used in the treatment of various skin disorders.

Chrȳ·sē'is, *n.* [L.; Gr. *Chryseïs.*] in Homer's *Iliad,* the beautiful daughter of Chryses, priest of Apollo: seized by the Greeks during the Trojan War and given to Agamemnon, she was returned to her father only after Apollo caused a plague to fall on the Greek camp.

chrys″el·e·phan'tine, *a.* [Gr. *chryselephantinos,* made of gold and ivory; *chrysos,* gold, and *elephas,* ivory.] composed or partly composed of gold and ivory: a term specially applied to statues overlaid with gold and ivory, as the statue of the Olympian Zeus by Phidias.

chrȳ'sēne, *n.* [Gr. *chrysos,* gold.] a hydrocarbon, which occurs in the least volatile portion of crude anthracene. It is crystalline, yellow, and without taste or smell.

chrys'ō-, [from Gr. *chrysos,* gold.] a combining form meaning *golden, yellow,* as in *chryso*beryl: also, before a vowel, *chrys-.*

Chrys·ō·bal'ȧ·nus, *n.* [*chryso-,* and Gr. *balanos,* an acorn.] a genus of trees or shrubs, natives of tropical America and Africa, natural order *Rosaceæ.*

chrys'ō·ber·yl, *n.* [*chryso-,* and Gr. *beryllos,* beryl.] a pale green or nearly yellow mineral, beryllium aluminate, crystallizing in the orthorhombic system. It is extremely hard, and the varieties, alexandrite and cat's-eye, are used as semiprecious stones.

chrys'ō·chlōre, *n.* [*chryso-,* and Gr. *chlōros,* a pale green.] a species of South African mole, the fur of which reflects metallic hues of green and gold.

chrys'ō·chrous (-krus), *a.* [*chryso-,* and Gr. *chrōa,* color.] of a golden-yellow color.

chrys·ō·col'lȧ, *n.* [Gr. *chrysokollos,* inlaid with gold; *chrysos,* gold, and *kolla,* glue, from *kollān,* to weld.] a silicate of copper of a fine emerald-green color.

chry·sog'rȧ·phy, *n.* [Gr. *chrysos,* gold, and *graphein,* to write.]
1. the art of writing in letters of gold.
2. the writing itself.

chry·soi'dine, *n.* [Gr. *chrysos,* gold, and *eidos,* form.] a crystalline dyestuff producing a bright yellow dye.

chrys·ō·lep'iç, *a.* [*chryso-,* and Gr. *lepis,* scale.] having or appearing to have golden scales or flakes.

chrys'ō·līte, *n.* [*chryso-,* and Gr. *lithos,* stone.] a mineral composed of silica, magnesium, and iron, generally of some shade of green. It is called *peridot* when used as a semiprecious stone.

chry·sol'ō·ġy, *n.* [*chryso-,* and Gr. *logos,* discourse.] that branch of political economy which relates to the production of wealth, especially of precious metals.

chrys'ō·phan, *n.* a glucoside of chrysophanic acid.

chrys·ō·phan'iç, *a.* [*chryso-,* and Gr. *phainein,* to show, appear.] relating to or derived from chrysophan.
chrysophanic acid; a crystalline compound found in Goa powder, cascara sagrada, in senna leaves, rhubarb root, etc.

chrys'ō·prāṣe, *n.* [*chryso-,* and Gr. *prason,* a leek.] a kind of quartz, a variety of chalcedony, apple-green in color and sometimes used as a semiprecious stone.

Chrȳ'sops, *n.* [L., from Gr. *chrysos,* gold, and *ōps,* eye.] a genus of dipterous insects of the family *Tabanidæ*; the clegs or gadflies.

CHRYSOPS (*Chrysops cæcutiens*)

chrys'ō·spērm, *n.* [*chryso-,* and Gr. *sperma,* seed.] in alchemy, a means of producing gold. [Obs.]

chrys'ō·tile, *n.* [Gr. *chrysōtos,* gilded, from *chrysoun,* to gild.] a fibrous variety of serpentine, resembling true asbestos and used as a substitute.

chrys'ō·tȳpe, *n.* [*chryso-,* and Gr. *typos,* impression.] a photographic process, the developing agent of which is chloride of gold; also, a picture so produced.

chthōn'i·ăn (thōn'), *a.* underground; subterranean; relating to the underworld; as, the *chthonian* deities: applied to such Greek gods as distinguished from those of Olympus.

chthon'iç (thon'), *a.* same as *chthonian.*

chthon·ō·phā'ġi·ȧ, chthon·oph'ȧ·ġy (thon-), *n.* [Gr. *chthōn,* earth, and *phagein,* to eat.] an abnormal impulse to eat clay or other soil.

chub, *n.* [Ice. *kubbr, kumbr,* a block, stump.]
1. a fresh-water fish of the family *Cyprinidæ,* the true minnows.

CHUB
Cyprinus (Leuciscus) cephalus

2. one of various other fishes found in the United States and elsewhere; as, the fallfish, *Semotilus corporalis*; the tautog; the chub sucker; the spot, *Leiostomus xanthurus*; the marine food fish, *Kyphosus sectatrix,* the Bermuda chub, found off Bermuda.

chub'bed, *a.* chubby. [Rare.]

chub'bed·ness, *n.* the state of being chubby.

chub'bi·ness, *n.* the state of being chubby.

chub'by, *a.* short and thick; plump; rounded; as, a *chubby* infant.

chub'-fāced (-fāst), *a.* having a plump, round face.

chub mack'ẽr·el, a kind of mackerel, *Scomber colias,* found on the Atlantic coast: called also *bull mackerel, big-eyed mackerel,* etc.

chub suck'ẽr, a common variety of sucker found in the United States, *Erimyzon sucetta.*

chuck, *v.i.*; chucked, *pt., pp.*; chucking, *ppr.* [ME. *chukken,* an imitative word.]
1. to make a clucking noise resembling that of a hen.
2. to laugh in a quiet manner; to chuckle. [Rare.]

chuck, *n.* 1. the cluck or call of a hen.
2. a term of endearment, perhaps corrupted from *chick.*

chuck, *v.t.* [from *shock,* to strike; AS. *scacan, sceacan,* to shake, strike.]
1. to strike or tap gently; as, to *chuck* one under the chin.
2. to throw, with quick motion, a short distance; to pitch. [Colloq.]

chuck, *n.* 1. a gentle tap under the chin.
2. a short throw or pitch.
3. any game of pitch and toss.
4. food. [Slang.]

chuck, *n.* 1. a small pebble: also called *chuck stone.* [Scot.]
2. [*pl.*] a child's game played with pebbles chucked or thrown in the air. [Scot.]

chuck, *n.* 1. that part of a side of dressed beef including the neck, shoulders, and first three ribs.
2. a clamplike device designed to hold a tool or a piece of wood, metal, or other material in place so that it may be rotated, as upon the mandrel of a lathe.
chuck wagon; a wagon, or other conveyance, equipped with a stove, cooking utensils, and food: used as a movable kitchen in lumber camps, on ranches, etc.
elliptic chuck; a chuck on which there is an eccentric circle and a slider, used in turning objects having an elliptic cross section.

CHUCK

chuck, *v.t.* to adjust in a chuck or hold in place by means of a chuck.

chuck'-a-luck, chuck'-luck, *n.* a gambling game in which bets are made that a certain number, numbers, or combination of numbers will appear on one, two, or all three of the dice used in playing, which are thrown by turning the handle of a cage containing them.

chuck and toss, pitch and toss.

chuck fär'thing, a game in which coins are pitched at a mark.

chuck'-full', *a.* chock-full.

chuck'hōle, a depression, hole, or rut in a road.

chuç'kle, *v.i.*; chuckled, *pt., pp.*; chuckling, *ppr.* [frequentative of *chuck,* to cluck.]
1. to laugh softly in a low tone, as in mild amusement or satisfaction.
2. to cluck, as a hen.

chuç'kle, *v.t.* to call together, as a hen her brood. [Obs.]

chuç'kle, *n.* a soft, low-toned laugh.

chuç'kle, *a.* [probably from *chuck, chock* (a block).] clumsy and stupid.

chuç'kle, *n.* a clumsy, stupid person.

chuç'kle·head (-hed), *n.* a stupid person; a blockhead; a numskull. [Colloq.]

chuç'kle·head·ed, *a.* thick-headed; stupid. [Colloq.]

chuç'klẽr, *n.* [Anglo-Ind.] in India, a tanner, cobbler, or shoemaker.

chuck'stōne, *n.* same as *chuck* (pebble).

chuck wag'ŏn, [*chuck* (a throw, food), and *wagon.*] a portable kitchen cart for serving food to lumbermen, ranch hands, etc. [Slang.]

chuck'wäl·lȧ, *n.* [Mex. Sp. *chacahuala,* from Am. Ind. (Cahuilla) *tcáxxwal.*] any of several large, edible lizards, genus *Sauromalus,* living in northwestern Mexico and southwestern United States.

chuck'-will's-wid'ōw, *n.* a bird (*Antrostomus carolinensis*) of the goatsucker family, found in southern United States and named from its note.

chud, *v.t.* to champ; to bite. [Obs.]

chud'dăr, chud'dẽr, chud'dȧ, chud'dȧh, *n.* [Anglo-Ind., from Hind. *chadar, chaddar,* sheet, tablecloth, cover; Per. *chadar,* a sheet, pavilion.] a large, square cloth worn by women in India as a shawl.

Chụ'diç, *a.* of or pertaining to the West Finnic subdivision of the Finno-Ugric languages.

chụ'et, *n.* chewet. [Obs.]

chụ'fȧ, *n.* [Sp.]
1. a species of sedge, *Cyperus esculentus,* bearing edible tubers, and widely cultivated.
2. the edible tuber of the plant: also called *earth almond.*

chuff, *n.* a coarse, heavy, dull fellow; a boor.

chuff, *a.* 1. chuffy; swollen. [Obs.]
2. surly; ill-tempered. [Brit. Dial.]

chuff'i·ly, *adv.* in a rough, surly manner.

chuff'i·ness, *n.* surliness.

chuff'y, *a.* [prob. from Sw. *kubbug,* fat, plump.]
1. originally, fat or swelled out, especially in the cheeks; as, a *chuffy* lad. [Dial.]
2. figuratively, surly; churlish. [Dial.]
chuffy brick; a brick swollen by air or steam in the process of burning.

chuff'y-cheeked (-chēkt), *a.* having plump or chubby cheeks.

chug, *n.* [echoic.] a loud, abrupt, explosive sound, as that made by the exhaust from an engine.

chug, *v.i.*; chugged, *pt., pp.*; chugging, *ppr.*
1. to make the sound of a chug or chugs.
2. to move while making such sounds; as, the train *chugged* along.

chuk'kẽr, chuk'kăr, *n.* [Hind. *cakkar, cakar,* from Sans. *cakra,* a wheel, circle.]
1. one of the periods into which a polo game is divided: a chukker lasts 7½ minutes.
2. a round or circular course; a wheel.

chụ'lăn, *n.* [Chin., from *chu,* pearl, and *lan,* a name given to plants of an orchideous character.] the flowers of a Chinese plant, the *Chloranthus inconspicuus,* used to scent tea.

chum, *n.* [prob. altered sp. of *cham,* clipped form of *chamber* in *chamber fellow, chamber mate.*]
1. originally, a roommate. [Colloq.]
2. a close friend. [Colloq.]

chum, *v.i.*; chummed, *pt., pp.*; chumming, *ppr.* 1. originally, to share the same room with another. [Colloq.]
2. to be intimate friends. [Colloq.]

chum, *v.t.* to put into the same room or rooms with another. [Colloq.]

chum, *n.* [origin obscure.] bits of fish, used as bait.

chum, *v.i.*; chummed, *pt., pp.*; chumming, *ppr.* to use chum for bait in fishing.

chum, *n.* [origin unknown, perhaps from Ice. *kumbr,* a log, block.] in the manufacture of pottery, the block on which an unburned piece of ware is placed for turning purposes.

chum'măġe, *n.* the act or system of placing people together as roommates; specifically, the proportionate share of expenses paid by each chum.

Your *chummage* ticket will be on twenty-seven, in the third. —Dickens.

chum'mi·ly, *adv.* in a chummy manner.

chum'my, *a.* intimate; companionable; friendly. [Colloq.]

chump, *n.* [origin uncertain, compare Ice. *kumbr,* a block.]
1. a short and heavy block of wood.
2. a thick, blunt end.
3. the head. [Slang.]
4. a stupid or silly person; a fool; one who lets his opportunities pass unimproved. [Colloq.]
off one's chump; insane; crazy. [Brit. Slang.]

chump end, the thick end: usually applied to a loin of veal or mutton.

chụ·nam', *n.* [Anglo-Ind.; Tamil. *chunnam*; Hind. *chūnā,* lime, from Sans. *chūrna,* meal.]
1. in the East Indies, a name given to lime,

or a mixture made of lime, as stucco, or the lime prepared from shells.

2. in northern India, a weight of gold equal to six grains troy.

chu·nam′, *v.t.*; chunammed, *pt.*, *pp.*; chunamming, *ppr.* to cover or plaster with chunam.

chuñk, *n.* [prob. a variant of *chump.*]

1. a short, thick piece. [Colloq.]

2. a fair portion. [Colloq.]

3. a stocky human being or animal. [Colloq.]

chuñk′i·ness, *n.* the state or quality of being chunky.

chuñk′y, *a.* short and thick; also, stocky; thickset; as, a *chunky* boy. [Colloq.]

chu·pat′ty, *n.* [Anglo-Ind., from Hind. *chapati*, *cha pata*, an unleavened cake.] in India, unleavened bread or cake, made of flour, water, and salt.

chŭrch, *v.t.*; churched, *pt.*, *pp.*; churching, *ppr.* to conduct a church service for; especially, to say prayers over (a woman) after childbirth.

chŭrch, *n.* [ME. *chirche*, *cherche*; AS. *circe*, *cyrce*; Late Gr. *kyriakon*, a church, from Gr. *kyriakē* (supply *dōma*, house), the Lord's house, from *kyriakos*, belonging to the Lord or Master; *kyrios*, lord, master; *kyros*, supreme power, authority.]

1. an edifice consecrated for public worship, especially one for Christian worship.

2. the collective body of Christians, composed of three great branches, the Roman Catholic, Protestant, and Orthodox Eastern.

> Probably we Christians are too familiarized with the presence of the *church* to do justice to her as a world-embracing institution. —Liddon.

3. [*usually* C–] a particular body of Christians united under one form of ecclesiastical government, in one creed, and using the same ritual and ceremonies; as, the Greek Church; the Anglican Church; the Roman Catholic Church.

4. ecclesiastical, as opposed to secular, government; ecclesiastical authority and influence; as, the union of *church* and state.

5. the organized body of Christians in any particular district, city, state, or country; as, the *church* at Ephesus.

> The American *church* at large did not do its whole duty in the conflict with slavery. —Jos. Cook.

6. the worshipers of God before the advent of Christ.

7. any group of worshipers.

8. any organized body of Christians occupying the same edifice for religious worship; a congregation; as, a pastor and his *church*.

9. the profession of the Christian ministry; as, he has gone into the *church*.

10. public worship; religious service.

church militant; the church on earth, distinguished from the *church triumphant*; the visible church in conflict with the powers of evil.

church triumphant; the church now glorified in heaven.

chŭrch, *a.* 1. pertaining to a church or to ecclesiastical matters; as, *church* music.

2. having to do with organized Christian worship.

church festival; a day or several days on which special religious services are held by the churches to pay honor to, and commemorate events in the life of Jesus, or in the lives of his apostles, or of various later saints.

church government; the polity and discipline of any church body in regard to its members; or the enforcement of its regulations by the heads or officers of a church.

church living; a benefice in an established church.

church service; the order of any religious observance held in a church.

church text; a rather thin pointed style of black letter, much used in engraved texts and ornamental lettering for ecclesiastical purposes; Old English type.

chŭrch′-āle, *n.* in England, ale formerly brewed for church festivals; also, the festival itself at which the ale was served. [Obs.]

chŭrch′dŏm, *n.* [AS. *circe*, church, and *dom*, jurisdiction.] the government or authority of the church.

chŭrch′-gärth, *n.* a churchyard.

chŭrch′gō″ẽr, *n.* one who attends church, especially one who does so regularly.

chŭrch′gō″ing, *a.* 1. regularly attending church.

2. calling to church.

> The sound of the *churchgoing* bell.—Cowper.

chŭrch′-hạwe, *n.* a churchyard. [Obs.]

chŭrch house, a building connected with a church and used for parish or diocesan purposes.

chŭrch′ịsm, *n.* adherence to ritual and forms.

chŭrch′less, *a.* without a church, or unattached to a church.

chŭrch′līke, *a.* like or fit for the church or a churchman.

chŭrch′li·ness, *n.* the quality or state of being churchly.

chŭrch′ly, *a.* ecclesiastical; appropriate for a church.

chŭrch′măn, *n.* 1. an ecclesiastic or clergyman; one who ministers in sacred things.

2. a member of a church, especially of an established church; in England, an Episcopalian, as distinguished from a Dissenter.

chŭrch′măn·ly, *a.* befitting a churchman.

chŭrch′măn·ship, *n.* the state of being a churchman, or of belonging to the established church [Chiefly Brit.]

chŭrch mem′bẽr, a person having membership in some church.

chŭrch mem′bẽr·ship, communicants of a church, considered collectively; also, membership in a church.

chŭrch mouse, a mouse that lives in a church.

poor as a church mouse; very poor.

Chŭrch of Çhrīst, Scī′en·tist, the official name of the Christian Science Church.

Chŭrch of Eng′lănd, the episcopal church of England; the Anglican Church: it was established during the Reformation when the authority of the king replaced that of the Pope, and is supported by the government.

Chŭrch of Jē′ṣus Çhrīst of Lat′tẽr-dāy Sāints, the official name of the Mormon Church.

Chŭrch of Rōme, the Roman Catholic Church.

chŭrch rāte, a rate formerly levied in England by the vestries on all parishioners.

chŭrch′reeve, *n.* [ME. *chirche-reve*; AS. *circe*, church, and *gerēfa*, steward.] a warden or steward of a church. [Obs.]

chŭrch′ship, *n.* condition of being a church. [Obs.]

chŭrch′wărd, *adv.* to or toward the church.

chŭrch′wạrd″en, *n.* [ME. *chirchewardein*, *kirkewardein*, a warden of the church; AS. *ciric*, church, and *weard*, a keeper.]

1. a lay officer of an Anglican or Episcopal church. Churchwardens are appointed by the minister, or elected by parishioners, to attend to the secular affairs of the church and (in England) to act as legal representatives of the parish.

2. a long-stemmed clay pipe. [Brit. Colloq.]

chŭrch′wạrd″en·ship, *n.* the office of a churchwarden.

chŭrch′wom″ăn (-woom″), *n.*; *pl.* **chŭrch′-wom″en** (-wim″), 1. a woman member of a church.

2. a woman active in church affairs.

chŭrch wŏrk, 1. work on a church building.

2. work to promote the religious interests of the church.

3. work that drags, or is slowly performed.

> This siege was *church work*, and therefore went on slowly. —Fuller.

chŭrch writ, a writ issued from an ecclesiastical court.

chŭrch′y, *a.* attaching extreme importance to church forms and rules. [Colloq.]

chŭrch′yärd, *n.* [ME. *chirchezeard*; AS. *cirice*, church, and *geard*, yard.] the ground adjoining a church, often used as a cemetery.

chụ′ri·ȧ, *n.* [native Mex. name.] the chaparral cock.

chŭrl, *n.* [ME. *churl*, *cherl*; AS. *ceorl*, a man, a countryman of the lowest rank.]

1. a rude, surly, ill-bred man.

2. a rustic; a countryman or peasant.

3. a miser; a niggard.

4. in early English history, a freeman of lowest rank.

chŭrl, *a.* churlish. [Rare.]

chŭrl′ish, *a.* 1. like a churl; rude; surly; sullen; rough in temper; unfeeling; uncivil.

2. selfish; miserly.

3. unpliant; unyielding; unmanageable: said of things; as, *churlish* metal.

4. of a churl or churls; rustic.

chŭrl′ish·ly, *adv.* in a churlish manner.

chŭrl′ish·ness, *n.* the state or quality of being churlish.

chŭrl′y, *a.* rude; boisterous.

chŭrm, *n.* chirm. [Obs.]

chŭrn, *n.* [ME. *cherne*, *chirne*; AS. *cyrin*, a churn.]

1. a vessel in which cream or milk is beaten, stirred, and shaken to form butter.

2. a violent stirring; agitation.

chŭrn, *v.t.*; churned, *pt.*, *pp.*; churning, *ppr.*

1. to stir or agitate (cream or milk) in a churn to make butter.

2. to make (butter) in a churn.

3. to shake or agitate with violence or continued motion; as, the steamer *churned* the sea into foam.

chŭrn, *v.i.* 1. to perform the act of churning cream or milk in making butter.

2. to be agitated or in a state of agitation; as, water *churning* over the shoals.

chŭrn′ing, *n.* 1. the act of a person who churns; a shaking or stirring.

2. the quantity of butter churned at one time.

chŭrr, *n.* [an imitative word.]

1. the whitethroat, *Sylvia cinerea*, and other trilling birds.

2. a whirring note of certain birds and insects; chirr.

chŭrr, *v.t.* and *v.i.* to chirr.

chur′rus, *n.* [Hind. *charas.*] a gum resin which oozes from the Indian hemp. It is a narcotic and intoxicant.

chŭrr′wŏrm, *n.* [AS. *cyrran*, to turn, and *wyrm*, worm.] the mole cricket.

chūṣe, *v.* choose. [Obs.]

çhụte, *n.* [Fr. *chute*; OFr. *cheute*, a fall, declivity.]

1. an inclined framework, trough, or conduit by means of which objects are made to slide from a higher to a lower level; a shoot; as, a water *chute*, a coal *chute*, etc.

2. an opening in a dam for the passage of timber, etc. with the current.

3. in the lower Mississippi region, a narrow channel between islands or between an island and the shore; a side channel.

4. the natural or artificial inclined plane of a toboggan slide.

5. a waterfall or rapids.

çhụte, ′çhụte, *n.* a parachute. [Colloq.]

chut′ney, chut′nee, *n.* [Hind. *chatni.*] a spicy relish composed of spices, herbs, and fruits: originally popular in India, its manufacture and sale are now widespread.

Chụ′väsh, *n.*; *pl.* **Chụ′väsh,** 1. a member of a Turkic-speaking Bulgarian people living chiefly in the Chuvash Autonomous Soviet Socialist Republic.

2. their language.

çhȳ·lā′ceous, *a.* having the properties of chyle; consisting of chyle.

çhȳ·lā′quē·ous, *a.* [L., from *chylus*, chyle, and *aqua*, water.] watery and chylaceous.

çhȳle, *n.* [L. *chylus*; Gr. *chylos*, juice, humor, chyle, from *chein*, to pour.] in physiology, a nutritive milky fluid containing lymph and the fatty matter of the food in a condition of emulsion, produced during digestion by the action of the pancreatic juices and the bile on the chyme. After absorption by the lacteals it is carried into the blood by the thoracic duct.

çhȳ′li-, same as *chylo-*.

çhȳl·i·faç′tion, *n.* [*chyli-*, and L. *factio*, a making, from *facere*, to make.] the act or process by which chyle is formed from food in animal bodies.

çhȳl·i·faç′tive, *a.* forming or changing into chyle; having the power to make chyle.

çhȳ·lif′ẽr·ous, *a.* [*chyli-*, and L. *ferre*, to bear.] transmitting chyle; as, *chyliferous* vessels.

çhȳ·lif′iç, *a.* chylifactive: applied especially to any portion of the digestive tract concerned in the production of chyle; as, in insects, the *chylific* ventricle, or last stomach.

çhȳl·i·fi·çā′tion, *n.* the formation of chyle; chylifaction.

çhȳ·lif′i·çȧ·tō″ry, *a.* producing chyle; chylifactive.

çhȳ′li·fȳ, *v.t.* and *v.i.* to convert, or to be converted, into chyle.

çhȳ′lō-, çhȳ′li-, çhȳl-, [L. *chylus*; Gr. *chylos*, juice, chyle, from *chein*, to pour.] combining forms denoting *relation to* or *connection with chyle*; as, *chylo*poietic, *chyli*fication, *chyl*uria, etc.

çhȳ′lō·cyst, *n.* [*chylo-*, and Gr. *kystis*, bladder.] in physiology, the reservoir at the lower end of the thoracic duct into which the lymphatic vessels convey the chyle.

çhȳ″lō·pō·et′iç, *a.* same as *chylopoietic*.

çhȳ″lō·poi·et′iç, *a.* [*chylo-*, and Gr. *poiētikos*, capable of making, from *poiein*, to make.] helping to make chyle; connected with chyle; as, the *chylopoietic* organs.

çhȳ·lō′sis, *n.* same as *chylifaction*.

ch̄y'lous, *a.* consisting of, relating to, or similar to chyle.

chȳ·lū'ri·ȧ, *n.* [*chyl-*, and Gr. *ouron*, urine.] an abnormal milky condition of the urine when it contains chyle or fatty matter.

chȳ·mā'quē·ous (-kwē-), *a.* [LL. *chymus*, chyle, juice, and L. *aqua*, water.] watery and chymous.

chȳme, *n.* [LL. *chymus*; Gr. *chymos*, juice, from *chein*, to pour.] the form which food assumes after it has undergone the action of the stomach, and is partly digested: it is a thick, semifluid mass which passes into the small intestine, where the process of digestion is completed by its conversion into chyle and by excretion.

chym'iç, chym'ist, chym'is·try, chemic, chemist, chemistry. [Obs.]

chȳ·mif'ẽr·ous, *a.* [LL. *chymus*, chyme, and L. *ferre*, to bear.] containing or conveying chyme.

chȳm"i·fi·çā'tion, *n.* [LL. *chymus*, chyme, and L. *facere*, to make.] the process of becoming or of forming chyme.

chȳm'i·fied, *a.* formed into chyme.

chȳm'i·fȳ, *v.t.* and *v.i.* to form, or to be formed into, chyme.

chȳ'mous, *a.* relating to chyme.

chȳ·om'e·tẽr, *n.* [Gr. *chy-*, the root of *chein*, to pour, and *metron*, a measure.] an instrument formerly used for measuring liquids. It was a device consisting mainly of a syringe with a graduated piston.

çhy'pre (shē'pr'), *n.* a type of perfume with a nonalcoholic oil base.

ci·bā'ri·ăn, *a.* [L. *cibarius*, pertaining to food, from *cibus*, food.] in zoology, pertaining to the organs of the mouth; as, the *cibarian* system of classifying insects and crustaceans.

ci·bā'ri·ous, *a.* pertaining to food; useful for food; edible.

ci·bā'tion, *n.* [L. *cibatio*, a feeding, from *cibare*, to feed.]
1. the act of taking nourishment. [Obs.]
2. in alchemy, the act of supplying the contents of a crucible with new material. [Obs.]

cib'ŏl, *n.* [ME. *chibolle*, *chebole*; Fr. *ciboule*, an onion, from L. *cæpa*, *cepa*, an onion.] a small onion used in cookery; the shallot; also, the Welsh onion, *Allium fistulosum*.

ci·bō'ri·um, *n.*; *pl.* **ci·bō'ri·ȧ,** [L. *ciborium*, a drinking vessel; Gr. *kibōrion*, a drinking cup made like the large pod of the Egyptian bean.]
1. a canopy of wood, stone, etc. that rests on four columns, especially one covering an altar.
2. a covered cup for holding the consecrated wafers of the Eucharist.

ci·çā'dȧ, *n.*; *pl.* **ci·çā'dȧş** or **ci·çā'dae,** [L. *cicada*, the cicada, or tree-cricket.]
1. any one of many species of insects, genus *Cicada*, living on trees, shrubs, etc. and having a characteristically sharp chirp produced by vibrating a tightly stretched membrane beneath the abdomen. The best known American species is *Cicada septendecim*, or seventeen-year locust.
2. [C–] the genus of insects of which the seventeen-year locust is a type.

ci·çä'lȧ, *n.* [It., from L. *cicada*.] a cicada.

ciç'ȧ·trice, *n.* [ME. *cicatrice*; Fr. *cicatrice*; L. *cicatrix*, a scar.] a cicatrix.

ciç·ȧ·tri'ciăl (-trish'ăl), *a.* pertaining to or characteristic of a cicatrix.

ciç'ȧ·tri·çle (-kl), *n.* [Fr. *cicatricule*; L. *cicatricula*, dim. of *cicatrix*, a scar.]
1. in botany, a cicatrix.
2. in embryology, the protoplasmic disc in the yolk of an egg from which the embryo develops.

ci·çat'ri·çōse, *a.* covered with scars or marked by cicatrices: said of plants.

ciç"ȧ·trī'sive, *a.* tending to promote the formation of a cicatrix; beneficial to the healing of a wound.

ciç'ȧ·trix, *n.*; *pl.* **ciç·ȧ·trī'çēş,** [L. *cicatrix*, a scar.]
1. in medicine, the contracted fibrous tissue at the place where a wound has healed; scar.
2. in botany, (a) the scar left on a stem where a branch, leaf, etc. was once attached; (b) the mark left where a wound has healed on a tree or plant; (c) the scarlike mark on a seed showing where it was attached to the pod; the hilum.
3. any scarlike marking, as the point of attachment of the adductor muscle of a bivalve to the shell.

ciç'ȧ·trī·zănt, *n.* a medicine or application that promotes the formation of a cicatrix, and the healing of the wounded part.

ciç"ȧ·tri·zā'tion, *n.* the process of healing or forming a cicatrix; the state of being healed or cicatrized.

ciç'ȧ·trīze, *v.t.* and *v.i.*; cicatrized, *pt.*, *pp.*; cicatrizing, *ppr.* [L. *cicatrix*, scar.] to heal or induce the formation of a cicatrix in, as wounded or ulcerated flesh; to heal by forming a cicatrix.

ciç'ȧ·trīzed, *a.* having a cicatrix formed.

ciç'ȧ·trōse, *a.* same as *cicatricose*.

cic'e·ly, *n.* [L. *seselis*; Gr. *seselis*, hartwort, seseli.] any of several plants of the parsley family, with fernlike leaves and umbrellalike clusters of white flowers. The sweet *cicely* of Europe is *Myrrhis odorata*; the sweet *cicely* of New England is *Osmorrhiza longistylis*.
wild cicely; an umbelliferous European herb, *Chærofilum sylvestre*.

cic·e·rō'nē (*or* chē-che-rō'ne), *n.*; *pl.* **cic·e·rō'nēş,** **ci·ce·rō'nï** (chē-che-), [It., from L. *Cicero*, the famous Roman orator: so called from the usual loquacity of guides.] a guide; one who shows sight-seers the features of a place.

Cic·e·rō'ni·ăn, *a.* [L. *Ciceronianus*, from the orator, *Cicero*.] resembling Cicero or his polished literary style; eloquent.

Cic·e·rō'ni·ăn·işm, *n.* imitation of or resemblance to the style or action of Cicero.

cich'lid, *n.* [from Mod. L. *Cichlidae*, name of the family, from Gr. *kichle*, thrush, also sea fish.] any of a family of spiny fresh-water fishes related to the American sunfishes.

cich'lid, *a.* of the family of cichlids.

Ci·chō·ri·ā'cē·ae, *n.pl.* [L., from *cichorium*, chicory.] a group of composite plants, including the chicory, dandelion, etc.

ci·chō·ri·ā'ceous, *a.* relating or akin to the *Cichoriaceæ*.

Ci·chō'ri·um, *n.* [L. *cichorium*; Gr. *kichōrion*, chicory, endive.] a genus of *Cichoriaceæ*, the species being found in Europe and the Mediterranean countries: it includes the chicory, endive, etc.

cich'-pēa, chick-pea. [Obs.]

ci·cis'bē·işm (*or* chē-chēz-be'izm), *n.* the state or condition of a cicisbeo.

ci·cis'bē·ō (*or* chē-chēz-be'ō), *n.* [It.] 1. the recognized lover of a married woman.
2. formerly, a piece of silk knotted to a fan, cane, etc.

ciç'lȧ·tōun, ciç'lȧ·tŏn, *n.* [ME. *ciclatoun*, *ciclatun*; OFr. *ciclaton*, *singlaton*, a kind of robe; L. *cyclas*; Gr. *kyklas*, a robe worn chiefly by women.] a costly medieval fabric, usually of silk: also written *checklatoun*. [Obs.]

ciç'ō·nīne, *a.* [L. *ciconia*, stork.] relating to or belonging to the stork family, *Ciconiidæ*.

ciç'ū·rāte, *v.t.* [L. *cicur*, tame, from *cicurare*, to tame.] to tame. [Obs.]

ciç·ū·rā'tion, *n.* the act of taming wild animals. [Obs.]

Ci·çū'tȧ, *n.* [L. *cicuta*, the hemlock. a genus of plants containing several poisonous species, one European and the others American. It includes the water hemlock or cowbane, *Cicuta maculata*, the root of which is a deadly poison.

ciç·ū·tox'in, *n.* [L. *cicuta*, hemlock, and *toxicum*, poison.] a poisonous substance extracted from the root of the water hemlock, *Cicuta maculata*.

Cid, *n.* [Sp., from Ar. *seid*, lord.]
1. leader, or commander-in-chief: the Spanish appellation for Ruy Diaz de Bivar (1040?–1099) a champion of Christianity against the Moors.
2. the title of a well known Spanish epic poem telling of the deeds of Ruy Diaz.

-cid'ăl, a suffix meaning: (a) *of a killer or killing*, as in homi*cidal*; (b) *that can kill*; as in fungi*cidal*.

cid'ȧ·ris, *n.*; *pl.* **cid'ȧ·rēş,** [L. *cidaris*; Gr. *kidaris*, a turban.] the royal headdress of ancient Persian kings.

-cīde, [from Fr. or L.; Fr. *-cide*; L. *-cida*, from *caedere*, to cut down, strike mortally, kill.] a suffix meaning *killer* or *killing*, as in regi*cide*, homi*cide*.

cī'dẽr, *n.* [ME. *cidre*, *cyder*; OFr. *sidre*, *cidere*, cider; L. *sicera*; Gr. *sikera*; Heb. *shekar*, a sweet fermented liquor, from *shakar*, to be intoxicated.] the juice pressed from apples, used as a beverage or for making vinegar: *sweet cider* is unfermented juice, *hard cider* is fermented juice. The word was formerly used to signify the juice of other fruits.

cī'dẽr bran'dy, a brandy distilled from cider: called also *apple jack*.

cī'dẽr·ist, *n.* a maker of cider.

cī'dẽr·kin, *n.* weak cider made by steeping the refuse from a cider press.

cī'dẽr mill, a mill in which cider is produced.

cī'dẽr press, a press for crushing apples to make cider.

cī'dẽr tree, an Australian tree, growing in the swamps, from the gum of which a cider is sometimes made.

cī'dẽr vin'e·gȧr, sour cider, or vinegar made from cider.

ci-de·vänt' (-väṅ'), *a.* [Fr., from *ci*, from *ici*, here, *de*, of, and *avant*, before.] former; recent; previous: used to designate men who have been in office and retired.

ci·é'nä·gȧ (thyā'), *n.* [Sp., a quagmire, from *cieno*, mud, from L. *cœnum*, mud.] a morass, swamp, or marsh.

ciẽrġe, *n.* a wax candle; cerge.

ci·gär', *n.* [Sp. *cigarro*, said to be from *cigarra*, cicada: from resemblance to the insect's body; originally the name of a variety of Cuban tobacco.] a compact roll of tobacco leaves, often tapered at the ends, used for smoking.

cig·ȧ·rette' (-ret'), **cig·ȧ·ret',** *n.* [Fr., dim. of *cigare*, cigar.]
1. a small quantity of fine tobacco rolled in paper (usually rice paper), cylindrical in shape, for smoking.
2. a similar cylinder filled with a drug or herb, as with cubeb, which is smoked to relieve asthma.

cig·ȧ·rette' hōld'ẽr, a slender tube with a mouthpiece at one end and a hole at the other for holding a cigarette to be smoked.

ci·gär'fish, *n.* a fish found in the Gulf of Mexico and the Caribbean Sea, resembling the mackerel.

ci·gär plant, a Mexican plant having a red and black corolla somewhat resembling a cigar in shape.

ci·lan'trō, *n.* [Sp., coriander.] coriander leaves used as an herb, especially in Latin American cooking.

cil'ẽr·y, *n.* the foliage, etc. carved on the heads of columns.

cil'i·ȧ, *n.pl.*; *sing.* **cil'i·um,** [L., pl. of *cilium*, eyelid.]
1. the eyelashes.
2. in biology, hairlike outgrowths of certain cells, capable of vibratory movement.
3. in botany, small hairlike processes extending from certain plant cells, often forming a fringe or hairy surface, as on the underside of some leaves.

cil'i·ăr·y, *a.* [L. *cilia*, the eyelashes.]
1. pertaining to the eyelashes, or related parts of the eye; as, the *ciliary* gland.
2. pertaining to the cilia in animals or plants.
ciliary muscle; the muscle attached to the eyeball which adjusts the crystalline lens to the required focus.

Cil·i·ā'tȧ, *n.pl.* [L. *ciliata*, neut. pl. of *ciliatus*, with cilia, from *cilium*, an eyelid.] an order of *Infusoria* distinguished by having cilia.

cil'i·āte, cil'i·ā·ted, *a.* [L. *ciliatus*, with cilia; from *cilia*, the eyelashes.] in botany and zoology, having cilia.

cil'i·āte, *n.* any of a class of microscopic protozoans characterized by cilia covering the body.

CILIATE LEAF

cil'ice, *n.* [L. *cilicium*; Gr. *kilikion*, a garment made of goat's hair, from *Kilikia*, Cilicia, a region in Asia Minor, noted for its goats.] a rough undergarment of haircloth, formerly worn by monks, etc. as an act of penance; also, the coarse cloth itself, sometimes made of goat's hair.

Ci·li'ciăn (-lish'ăn), *a.* relating to Cilicia, in Asia Minor.

Ci·li'ciăn, *n.* a native or inhabitant of Cilicia.

Cil'i·cişm, *n.* an idiom or expression of the Cilicians.

cil·i·el'lȧ, *n.*; *pl.* **cil·i·el'lae,** [L., dim. of *cilium*, eyelid.] in zoology, a fringe composed of fine hairs.

ci·lif'er·ous, *a.* having or bearing cilia; ciliate.

cil'i·i·form, *a.* [L. *cilium*, an eyelid, and *forma*, form.] extremely fine; slender like cilia; having the form of cilia.

cil'i·ō·grāde, *n.* [L. *cilium*, the eyelash, and *gradi*, to step, walk.] an animal that moves by means of cilia.

cil'i·ō·grāde, *a.* moving by the aid of cilia; as, the *ciliograde Medusæ*.

cil'i·ō·lāte, *a.* having very small cilia.

ci·li'ō·lum, *n.*; *pl.* **ci·li'ō·lȧ,** a very small cilium.

cil'i·um, *n.* sing. of *cilia*.

cil'lō, *n.* [L., from *cilium*, an eyelid.] a convulsive trembling or quivering of the upper eyelid.

cil·lō'sis, *n.* same as *cillo*.

cī'mȧ, *n.* same as *cyme*.

cī·mär·rōn′, *n.* [Sp.] 1. the Rocky Mountain sheep; the bighorn.
2. a runaway slave.

cim′bȧl, *n.* a kind of cake. [Obs.]

cim′bi·ȧ, cim′i·ȧ, *n.* [Sp. *cimbra*, an arched frame, a cincture.] in architecture, a strengthening band or cincture around a pillar.

Cim′brī, *n.pl.* [L. *Cimber*, pl. *Cimbri*.] a Germanic people, supposed to have originated in Jutland, who invaded Gaul and northern Italy at the end of the 2d century B.C. and were finally defeated by the Romans near Vercellae (101 B.C.): the first Germanic invaders of Italy.

Cim′bri·ăn, *a.* of or relating to the Cimbri.

Cim′bri·ăn, *n.* 1. one of the Cimbri.
2. the language of the Cimbri.

Cim′briç, *a.* and *n.* same as *Cimbrian*.

ci·mē′li·ärch, *n.* [Gr. *keimēliarchēs*, a treasurer; *keimēlion*, treasure, and *archein*, to rule.] a superintendent or keeper of valuable things belonging to a church. [Obs.]

cim′e·tẽr, *n.* same as *scimitar*.

Cī′mex, *n.* [L., a bug.]
1. a genus of hemipterous insects, the bedbugs.
2. [c–] *pl.* **cim′i·cēs̹,** a bedbug.

cim′i·ȧ, *n.* same as *cimbia*.

ci·mic′iç, *a.* pertaining to the genus *Cimex*.
cimicic acid; a yellow substance obtained from the oil of a species of *Cimex*.

cim′i·cid, *n.* a bug of the family *Cimicidæ*.

Ci·mic′i·dae, *n.pl.* [L., from *cimex*, a bug.] a family of insects which includes the typical genus *Cimex*.

cim′i·cine, *n.* the substance which is productive of the odor characteristic of the bedbug.

cī′miss, *n.* [L. *cimex*, a bug.] the bedbug. [Obs.]

Cim·mē′ri·ăn, *n.* any of a mythical people (*the Cimmerii*) whose land was described by Homer as a region of perpetual mist and darkness: written also *Kimmerian*.

Cim·mē′ri·ăn, *a.* 1. pertaining to the Cimmerians or their land.
2. dark; gloomy.

cim′ō·līte, *n.* [L. *cimolia* (supply *creta*, clay); Gr. *kimōlia* (supply *gē*, earth), the Cimolian earth: so named from *Kimolus* in the Cyclades.] a species of clay used by the ancients as a treatment for erysipelas and other inflammations. It is white, of a loose, soft texture, and is useful in taking spots from cloth.

cinch, *n.* [Sp. *cincha*; L. *cingula*, a girdle.]
1. a broad saddle girth, usually made of canvas or horsehair.
2. a hold; a tight grip. [Colloq.]
3. a thing easy to do; a sure thing. [Slang.]

cinch, *v.t.*; cinched, *pt.*, *pp.*; cinching, *ppr.*
1. to gird tightly; to fasten a cinch around.
2. to force into a tight place; to get a tight hold upon. [Slang.]
3. to make sure of. [Slang.]

cinch, *n.* [from Sp. *cinco*, five.] a game of cards in which the leading cards are the five of trumps, called *right pedro*, and the other five of the same color, called *left pedro*, each counting five in the score: also called *pedro* and *high-five*.

cinch′ẽr, *n.* a plaiter. [Brit.]

cin″çhō·loi′pon, *n.* [*cinchon*ine and Gr. *loipon*, remainder.] in chemistry, a yellow crystalline powder derived from cinchonine.

cin″çhō·mē·ron′iç ac′id, in chemistry, a colorless, crystalline acid, $C_7H_5O_4N$.

Cin·çhō′nȧ, *n.* [so named from the Countess del *Chinchon*, wife of a Peruvian viceroy of the seventeenth century, who was cured of a fever by the use of the bark.]
1. a genus of evergreen trees, family *Rubiaceæ*, native to South America. Several species furnish the valuable Peruvian bark, the cinchona of commerce, and quinine. These trees are now extensively cultivated in the East Indies. *Cinchona succirubra* furnishes red cinchona bark, *Cinchona calisaya* affords calisaya, or the yellow bark, and the ordinary Peruvian bark is obtained from *Cinchona officinalis*.
2. [c–] the bitter bark of any species of *Cinchona* which possesses medicinal properties; also, the tree itself.

CINCHONA
(*Cinchona succirubra*)

cin·çhō·nā′ceous, *a.* pertaining to or resembling cinchona or the trees producing it.

cin·çhō′ni·ȧ, *n.* same as *cinchonine*.

cin·çhon′iç, *a.* derived from or belonging to cinchona.

cin·çhon′i·cine, *n.* an alkaloid obtained from cinchonine.

cin·çhō·nid′i·ȧ, *n.* same as *cinchonidine*.

cin·çhon′i·dine, *n.* an alkaloid resembling quinine, obtained especially from red cinchona bark: used in the treatment of malaria and to reduce fever.

cin′çhō·nine, *n.* an alkaloid obtained from the bark of several species of *Cinchona*, and closely related to quinine.

cin′çhō·nis̹m, *n.* a pathological condition caused by excessive use of quinine: its symptoms are deafness, roaring in the ears, vertigo, and temporary loss of sight.

cin′çhō·nīze, *v.t.*; cinchonized, *pt.*, *pp.*; cinchonizing, *ppr.* to treat with cinchona, quinine, etc.

cin·cin′năl, *a.* of, pertaining to, or like a cincinnus.

Cin·cin·na′ti, Sō·cī′e·ty of the, a fraternal order or society founded in 1783 to perpetuate the friendship of officers in the Revolutionary Army, and relieve the widows and orphans of those killed: it still continues, the membership consisting of only the oldest living male lineal descendants of the original members.

cin·cin′nus, *n.* [L. *cincinnus*; Gr. *kikinnos*, a curl of hair.] in botany, a form of alternate branching in flower clusters.

ciñç′tūre, *n.* [L. *cinctura*, a girdle, from *cingere*, to surround, to gird.]
1. an encircling; an enclosing.
2. a belt, a girdle, or something worn around the body.
3. that which encompasses or encloses.
4. in architecture, a ring or molding at the top and bottom of a column, immediately above the base or below the capital.

ciñç′tūre, *v.t.*; cinctured, *pt.*, *pp.*; cincturing, *ppr.* to encircle with or as with a cincture.

ciñç′tūred, *a.* having a cincture or girdle.

cin′dẽr, *n.* [ME. *cinder*, *sinder*; AS. *sinder*, dross of iron, cinder; L. *cinis*, ashes.]
1. a small hot coal burning but not flaming; an ember; as, emptying a grate of *cinders*.
2. small particles of fuel or other matter, remaining after combustion, burned but not reduced to ashes; also, one such particle.
3. slag, as from the reduction of metallic ores.
4. volcanic slag.
5. [*pl.*] the ashes from coal or wood.

cin′dẽr, *v.t.* to burn to a cinder or cinders.

cin′dẽr çōne, a cone-shaped hill composed of successive deposits of volcanic cinders.

Cin·dẽr·el′lȧ, *n.* the heroine of a fairy tale, who is treated as a household drudge by a stepmother and stepsisters: a fairy godmother equips her to attend a grand ball given by a prince, where she loses a glass slipper. The prince finds the slipper and by means of it discovers Cinderella, whom he marries, to the great discomfiture of her taskmistresses; hence, a girl whose beauty or merit is for a time unrecognized.

cin′dẽr frāme, a wire device fixed in front of the tubes of a locomotive to prevent the escape of cinders.

cin′dẽr notch (noch), in a blast furnace, the opening for the removal of molten slag.

cin′dẽr pȧth, a path, walk, or track laid with cinders; specifically, a track for athletes.

cin′dẽr pig, pig iron composed of slagged ore.

cin′dẽr track, a racing track covered with fine cinders.

cin′dẽr wool, same as *mineral wool*.

cin′dẽr·y, *a.* of, resembling, or composed of cinders; full of cinders.

cin·ē·fac′tion, *n.* [L. *cinis*, ashes, and *factus*, pp. of *facere*, to make.] reduction to ashes. [Obs.]

cin′ē·mȧ, *n.* [from *cinematograph*.] a motion picture or motion-picture theater.
the cinema; (a) the art or business of motion pictures; (b) motion pictures collectively.

cin·ē·mat′iç, cin·ē·mat′iç·ăl, *a.* 1. same as *kinematic*.
2. of motion pictures.

cin·ē·mat′i·căl·ly, *adv.* 1. in a cinematic manner.
2. from the viewpoint of the cinema.

cin·ē·mat′içs, *n.pl.* 1. [*construed as sing.*] the art of motion pictures.
2. the artistic principles which can be observed in a motion picture or motion pictures.

cin′ē·mȧ·tīze, *v.t.* and *v.i.*; cinematized, *pt.*, *pp.*; cinematizing, *ppr.* to cinematograph.

cin·ē·mat′ō·grȧph, *n.* [Gr. *kinēma*, motion, and *graphein*, to write.]
1. a motion-picture projector. [Brit.]
2. a motion-picture camera.
3. a motion-picture theater. [Brit.]

cin·ē·mat′ō·grȧph, *v.t.* and *v.i.*; cinematographed, *pt.*, *pp.*; cinematographing, *ppr.*, to photograph with a cinematograph or a motion-picture camera; to take motion pictures (of).

cin·ē·mȧ·tog′rȧ·phẽr, *n.* one who operates a cinematograph or motion-picture camera; a cameraman; hence, one who films or produces motion pictures.

cin″ē·mat″ō·graph′iç, *a.* of a cinematograph.

cin·ē·mȧ·tog′rȧ·phy, *n.* the art of making motion pictures.

cin·é·ma vér·i·té (sē nā mä″ vā rē tā′), [Fr., lit., truth cinema.] a form of documentary film in which a small, hand-held camera and unobtrusive techniques are used to record scenes under the most natural conditions possible.

ci·neñ′çhy·mȧ, *n.* [Gr. *kinein*, to move, and *enchyma*, infusion.] in botany, tissue containing latex.

cin′ē·ōle, cin′ē·ōl, *n.* [from Mod. L. *ole*um *cinae* (oil of wormwood), with transposition of constituents.] a liquid substance, $C_{10}H_{18}O$, with a camphorlike odor, present in turpentine and many essential oils.

cin′e·phīle″, *n.* [Fr. *cinéphile*, from *cinéma*, cinema, and *-phile*, -phile.] a devotee of motion pictures.

cin·e·rā′ceous, *a.* [L. *cinereus*, ashy, from *cinis*, ashes.] like ashes; having the color of ashes.

Cin·e·rā′ri·ȧ, *n.* [L. *cinerarius*, pertaining to ashes, from *cinis*, ashes.] a genus of plants of the aster family, having velvety, heart-shaped leaves, and daisylike flowers in shades of purple, red, pink, blue, or white.

CINERARIA

cin·e·rā′ri·um, *n.*; *pl.* **cin·e·rā′ri·ȧ,** [L., from *cinis*, ashes.] a place to keep the ashes of cremated bodies.

cin′e·rā·ry, *a.* [L. *cinerarius*, from *cinis*, ashes.]
1. of or for ashes.
2. of or for the ashes of the cremated dead; as, a *cinerary* urn.

CINERARY URNS

cin·e·rā′tion, *n.* [L. *cinis*, ashes.] the reducing of anything to ashes.

cin′ẽr·ā·tŏr, *n.* [*cinerarium*, and *-ator*.] a furnace for cremation; a crematory.

ci·nē′rē·ȧ, *n.* [L., from *cinereus*, ashy.] in anatomy, the gray or cellular nerve tissue, as distinguished from the white or fibrous.

ci·nē′rē·ous, *a.* [L. *cinereus*, ashy; *cinis*, ashes.] having the color of ashes; ash-gray; ashen; like ashes.

Ciñ·gȧ·lēse′, *n.* and *a.* same as *Singhalese*.

ciñ′gle (-gl), *n.* [L. *cingula*, a girdle, from *cingere*, to gird.] a girth; a girdle; a belt.

ciñ′gū·lāte, *a.* [L. *cingula*, girdle.] having a cingulum.

ciñ′gū·lāt·ed, *a.* cingulate.

ciñ′gū·lum, *n.* 1. a band or girdle, as the raised spiral line seen on certain univalve shells, the zone of a tooth near the gum, or the clitellus of earth worms.
2. a bundle of nerve fibers in the brain.
3. a girdle; a belt.

cin′nȧ·bär, *n.* [Fr. *cinabre*; L. *cinnabaris*; Gr. *kinnabari*, cinnabar, vermilion.]
1. mercuric sulfide, HgS, a heavy, bright-red mineral, the principal ore of mercury.
2. artificial mercuric sulfide, used as a red pigment.
3. vermilion; brilliant red.

hepatic cinnabar; an impure cinnabar of a liver-brown color and submetallic luster.

cin·nȧ·bar′iç, *a.* pertaining to cinnabar; consisting of cinnabar, or containing it; as, *cinnabaric* sand.

cin·nȧ·bar′ine, *a.* same as *cinnabaric*.

cin′nȧ·mēne, *n.* a compound obtained from cinnamic acid: also called *styrolene* and *cinnamole*.

cin·nam′iç, *a.* [from L. *cinnamomum*, cinnamon.] obtained from or pertaining to cinnamon: also *cinnamomic*.

cinnamic acid; designating a white, crystalline, organic acid, $C_6H_5 \cdot CH:CH \cdot COOH$, produced from benzaldehyde: the corresponding aldehyde gives oil of cinnamon its characteristic flavor and odor.

cin·nȧ·mom′iç, *a.* same as *cinnamic*.

Cin·nȧ·mō′mum, *n.* [L., from Gr. *kinnamōmon*, cinnamon.] a genus of trees and shrubs of the laurel family, including the common cinnamon tree and the cassia tree.

cin′nȧ·mŏn, *n.* [ME. *cinamome*; L. *cinnamomum*; Gr. *kinnamōmon*; Heb. *qinnamon*, cinnamon.]

1. the inner bark of *Cinnamomum zeylanicum* of the East Indies, prepared by drying. It is made into an aromatic spice of a light yellowish-brown color, and has a sweetish taste; also, this spice.

2. any tree yielding cinnamon.

3. yellowish brown.

oil of cinnamon; an aromatic oil obtained from the bark of different trees of the genus *Cinnamomum*.

CINNAMON (*Cinnamomum zeylanicum*)

cin′nȧ·mŏn, *a.* 1. yellowish-brown.

2. made or flavored with cinnamon.

cin′nȧ·mŏn beãr, a brown variety of the American black bear.

cin′nȧ·mŏn stōne, a variety of garnet of a cinnamon color.

cin′nȧ·myl, *n.* in organic chemistry, the radical, C_8H_7CO, of cinnamic compounds.

ciñque (siñk), *n.* [Fr., OFr. *cinc*; L. *quinque*, five.]

1. a five on dice or playing cards.

2. a throw in dice in which a five turns up.

cin·que·cen′tist (chiñ-kwe-chen′tist), *n.* [It. *cinquecentista*, a writer of the sixteenth century, from *cinquecento*, lit. 500, used for the sixteenth century.] any Italian connected with the Italian revival in arts and letters in the sixteenth century.

cin·que·cen′tō (chiñ-kwe-chen′tō), *n.* 1. the sixteenth century in Italian art and literature.

2. the style of Italian art of this period.

ciñque′foil (siñk′foil), *n.* [Fr. *quintefeuille*; It. *cinquefoglie*; L. *quinte*, five, and *folium*, a leaf.]

1. in architecture, a circular design made up of five converging arcs. Circular windows frequently have this form.

CINQUEFOIL

2. any of several plants belonging to the genus *Potentilla*, of the rose family, with yellow flowers and leaves composed of five leaflets: also called *five finger*.

marsh cinquefoil; a purple-flowered plant, *Potentilla palustris*, growing in marshes inland.

ciñ′que·pāce (sing′ke-), *n.* [Fr., from *cinque*, five, and *pas*, pace.] a kind of dance, the steps of which were regulated by the number five. Obs.]

Ciñque Pōrts, originally, five ports on the southern shore of England, viz., Hastings, Romney, Hythe, Dover, and Sandwich, others being added afterward. These were deemed of so much importance that they received particular privileges, on condition of providing a certain number of ships in war.

Ci·nū′rȧ, *n.pl.* [L., from Gr. *kinein*, to move, and *oura*, tail.] a group of insects of the family *Thysanura*, whose tails end in bristles.

cī′ŏn, *n.* [OFr.] a shoot or bud of a plant, especially one for planting or grafting: also spelled *scion*.

cī′phẽr, *n.* [ME. *ciphre*; OFr. *cifre*; LL. *cifra*; Ar. *sifr*, *sefr*, a cipher, nothing, from *safara*, to be nothing.]

1. in arithmetic, a naught; a zero; 0, which, standing by itself, expresses the absence of any quantity, but increases or diminishes the value of other figures, according to its position. In whole numbers, when placed at the right of a figure it increases its value tenfold, but in decimal fractions, placed at the left of a figure, it diminishes the value of that figure tenfold.

2. a person or thing of no value or consequence; a nonentity.

Here he was a mere *cipher*, there he was lord of the ascendant. —Irving.

3. an intricate weaving together of letters, as the initials of a name, on a seal, plate, coach, tomb, picture, etc.; a monogram.

4. a secret or disguised manner of writing meant to be understood only by the persons who have the key to it; a code; also, the key to such a code.

5. any Arabic numeral.

cī′phẽr, *a.* useless; having no influence; without weight.

cī′phẽr, *v.i.*; ciphered, *pt.*, *pp.*; ciphering, *ppr.* 1. to solve arithmetical problems.

2. to use secret writing.

cī′phẽr, *v.t.* 1. to express in secret writing.

2. to find out by ciphering; to solve by arithmetic; as, to *cipher* the cost.

3. to make out; to interpret; to decipher. [Obs.]

cip′ō·lin, *n.* [It. *cipollino*, a granular limestone, from *cipolla*, an onion: so named on account of its being stratified or veined like an onion.] a variety of Italian marble containing streaks of color, especially of white and green.

cip′pus, *n.*; *pl.* **cip′pī,** [L., a stake, post, a gravestone.] in ancient times, a small pillar or column, usually having an inscription, used for various purposes, often as a funeral monument or landmark.

DIS MANIBVS SACRVM

SEPULCHRAL CIPPUS

cĩr′cȧ, *adv.* [L.] about; around: generally combined with dates or numerals to express approximation and lack of absolute certainty; as, *circa* 800 A.D.

cĩr·cȧ′dĭ·ăn, *adj.* [coined from L. *circa*, about, and *diem*, acc. sing. of *dies*, day.] in biology, designating or of behavioral or physiological rhythms associated with the 24-hour cycles of the earth's rotation, as, in man, the regular metabolic, glandular, and sleep rhythms which may persist through a dislocation of day and night caused by high-speed travel.

cĩr·cär′, *n.* same as *sircar*.

Cĩr·ças′siăn (-kash′ăn), *n.* [L., from Russ. *Zemlya Cherkesovŭ*, the land of the Circassians; *Zemlya*, land, and *Cherkesŭ*, a Circassian.]

1. a native or inhabitant of Circassia, a Russian district, situated on the Black Sea.

2. a member of a group of tribes of Circassia belonging to the Caucasian race.

3. the non-Indo-European, North Caucasian language of the Circassians.

Cĩr·ças′siăn, *a.* pertaining to Circassia, its people, or their language.

Cĩr′cē, *n.* in Homer's *Odyssey*, an enchantress who turned men into swine.

Cĩr·cē′ăn, Cĩr·caē′ăn, *a.* [L. *Circe*; Gr. *Kirkē*, Circe.] pertaining to or resembling Circe; hence, pleasing, but harmful; dangerously bewitching; as, the *Circean* spells of opium.

cĩr·cen′siăn (-shăn), **cĩr·cen′siăl** (-shăl), *a.* [L. *circensis*, pertaining to the circus, from *circus*, circus.] pertaining to the *circenses*, the athletic games held in the Circus Maximus, Rome.

cĩr′ci·năl, same as *circinate*.

cĩr′ci·nāte, *a.* [L. *circinus*; Gr. *kirkinos*, a pair of compasses, from *kirkos*, a circle.] rolled into a coil on its axis, the tip occupying the center: used of foliation or leafing, as in ferns.

cĩr′ci·nāte, *v.t.* to make a circle upon, or to encircle with a compass. [Obs.]

cĩr·ci·nā′tion, *n.* 1. a circling motion. [Obs.]

2. in botany, the quality of being circinate; as, the rings or *circinations* of onions.

CIRCINATE (fern)

cĩr′cle (-kl), *n.* [ME. *cercle*, *sercle*; OFr. *cercle*; AS. *circul*; L. *circulus*, a circle, dim. of *circus*; Gr. *kirkos*, a ring.]

1. a plane figure bounded by a single curved line, called its circumference, every point of which is equally distant from a point at the center of the figure: all lines drawn from the center to the circumference, or periphery, are equal to each other.

2. the line which bounds such a figure; circumference.

3. anything shaped like a circle, as the orb of a heavenly body, or a halo around it, a ring, a crown, etc.

4. the orbit of a planet.

5. compass; circuit; enclosure; as, the *circle* of the forest.

6. a group of people bound together by a common interest; a group; a coterie; as, a *circle* of friends.

7. a complete or recurring series, usually ending as it began; a going round; a cycle.

8. a semicircular tier of seats in a theater; as, the dress *circle*.

9. range; extent; scope, as of influence or interest.

10. an imaginary circle on the surface of the earth: the *great circle* is a circle with its plane passing through the center of the earth; the *Arctic Circle* is a parallel of latitude.

11. in logic, an inconclusive form of argument in which unproved statements are used to prove one another; e.g., heavy bodies descend by gravity, since gravity is a quality by which a heavy body descends: otherwise called *argument in a circle*.

12. a territorial division or district.

circle of altitude; same as *almucantar*.

circle of latitude; in astronomy, a great circle perpendicular to the plane of the ecliptic.

circle of longitude; in astronomy, a small circle parallel to the ecliptic.

circle of perpetual apparition; at any given place, the boundary of that space around the elevated celestial pole, within which the stars never set. Its distance from the pole is equal to the latitude of the place.

circle of perpetual occultation; at any given place, the boundary of that space around the depressed celestial pole, within which the stars never rise.

circle of Willis; in anatomy, a ring of arteries at the base of the brain: named after Thomas Willis (1621–1675), an English anatomist, who described it.

circles of the sphere; either great circles, which divide the sphere into equal parts, as the equator, etc., or small circles, which divide it into unequal parts, as the polar circles.

diurnal circle; the apparent circle described by a heavenly body on account of the rotation of the earth.

cĩr′cle, *v.t.*; circled, *pt.*, *pp.*; circling, *ppr.* 1. to move round, as in a circle; to revolve round.

And other planets *circle* other suns.—Pope.

2. to encircle; to encompass; to surround; to enclose.

cĩr′cle, *v.i.* to move circularly; to revolve; as, the *circling* years.

cĩr′cled, *a.* having the form of a circle; round; as, the moon's *circled* orb.

cĩr′clẽr, *n.* a person or thing that encircles or moves in a circle.

cĩr′clet, *n.* 1. a little circle.

2. a bracelet, ring, or other personal ornament in the form of a circle.

cĩr′çō·cēle, *n.* same as *cirsocele*.

cĩr′çuit (-kit), *n.* [ME. *circuit*; OFr. *circuit*; L. *circuitus*, a going round, a circuit; from *circum*, around, and *itus*, pp. of *ire*, to go.]

1. the act of moving or passing round; a revolving; a course or journey around; as, the periodical *circuit* of the earth round the sun, or of the moon round the earth.

2. the line or the length of the line forming the boundaries of an area.

3. the space or area enclosed in a circle, or within certain limits.
4. the regular journey of a person performing his duties, as of an itinerant preacher or a judge holding court at designated places.
5. the district periodically traveled through in the performance of duties, as the territory under the jurisdiction of certain judges.
6. a roundabout manner of speech; circumlocution. [Obs.]
7. a number of theaters or other places of amusement under the same management and successively engaging the same performers, plays, films, etc.
8. in electricity, the path of a current; as, to complete a *circuit*.
9. in radio, a hookup.

cĩr′cuit, *v.i.* to move in a circle; to go round.
cĩr′cuit, *v.t.* to make a circuit of.
cĩr′cuit bīnd′ing, a bookbinding with flexible edges projecting beyond the leaves to protect them.
cĩr′cuit breāk′ẽr, a device that automatically interrupts the flow of an electric current, as when the current becomes excessive.
cĩr′cuit çōurt, 1. formerly, a Federal court presided over by a judge or judges who held court regularly at designated places in a district: abolished in 1911.
2. a State court having original jurisdiction in several counties or a district.
cĩr′cuit edġ′eṣ (ej′), the projecting edges of a circuit binding.
cĩr·cuit·eer′, *n.* same as *circuiter*.
cĩr′cuit·ẽr, *n.* one who makes or travels a circuit, as a circuit preacher or circuit judge.
cĩr·çū·i′tion (-ish′un), *n.* [L. *circuitio*, a going round.] the act of going round; circumlocution. [Rare.]
cĩr·çū′i·tous, *a.* [L. *circuitus*, pp. of *circumire*, to go round.] going round in a circuit; not direct; roundabout; devious; as, a *circuitous* road; a *circuitous* way of doing things.
Syn.—winding, roundabout, sinuous, tortuous, devious, erratic, eccentric.
cĩr·çū′i·tous·ly, *adv.* in a circuitous way.
cĩr·çū′i·tous·ness, *n.* the act or manner of being circuitous.
cĩr′cuit rīd′ẽr, a Methodist minister who travels from station to station in his circuit to preach.
cĩr′cuit·ry, *n.* the scheme or system of an electric circuit, or the elements comprising such a circuit, as in a computer.
cĩr·çū′i·ty, *n.* [L. *circuitus*, a circuit.] the quality or state of being circuitous; indirection.
circuity of action; in law, an unnecessary length of procedure, or other means taken, with a view of delaying direct legal action.
cĩr′çū·là·ble, *a.* capable of being circulated.
cĩr′çū·lăr, *a.* [LL. *circularis*, in the form of a circle, from L. *circulus*, a circle.]
1. in the form of a circle; round; as, the sun appears to be *circular*.
2. relating to a circle.
3. moving in a circle.
4. roundabout; circuitous.
5. ending in itself: used of a paralogism, where the second proposition at once proves the first, and is proved by it; illogical; not conclusive.
6. intended for circulation among a number of people; addressed to persons having a common interest; as, a *circular* letter.
7. complete. [Obs.]
circular arc; part of the circumference of a circle.
circular insanity; manic-depressive psychosis.
circular instrument; a mathematical instrument having a complete circle of graduation from 1 to 360 degrees: used in measuring angles.
circular line; a straight line pertaining to the circle, as a sine, tangent, or secant.
circular measure; a system for measuring circles in which 1 circle equals 360 degrees, 1 degree equals 60 minutes, 1 minute equals 60 seconds.
circular mil; a unit of measurement for the thickness of wires, equal to the area of a circle with a diameter of one mil.
circular number; a number whose powers terminate in the same digit as the root itself, as 5, whose square is 25.
circular sailing; the method of sailing by the arc of a great circle.
circular saw; see under *saw*.
cĩr′çū·lăr, *n.* [LL. *circularis*, circular; L. *circulus*, a circle.]
1. a letter, advertisement, etc., usually printed in quantities, intended for circulation.
2. a loose round cloak, without sleeves, worn by women.
cĩr·çū·lar′i·ty, *n.*; *pl.* **cĩr·çū·lar′i·tieṣ,** the state of being circular; a circular form.
cĩr′çū·lăr·īze, *v.t.*; circularized, *pt.*, *pp.*; circularizing, *ppr.* 1. to give a round shape to.
2. to send circulars to; as, the advertisers *circularized* the entire city.
3. to canvass for opinions, support, etc.
cĩr′çū·lăr·īz·ẽr, *n.* one who or that which circularizes.
cĩr′çū·lăr·ly, *adv.* in a circular manner; in the form of a circle.
cĩr′çū·là·ry, *a.* roundabout; circular; as, *circulary* remarks. [Rare.]
cĩr′çū·lāte, *v.i.*; circulated, *pt.*, *pp.*; circulating, *ppr.* [L. *circulatus*, pp. of *circulari*, to form a circle.]
1. to move in a circle, circuit, or course and return to the same point; as, the blood *circulates* in the body.
2. to pass from place to place, from person to person, or from hand to hand; to move around; as, money *circulates* in the country.
3. to be distributed to a circle of readers.
4. in mathematics, to have an infinitely recurring series of digits: said of a decimal (e.g., .421421421 . . .).
cĩr′çū·lāte, *v.t.* to cause to pass from place to place, or from person to person; to place in circulation; as, to *circulate* a newspaper.
Syn.—diffuse, disseminate, spread, propagate, scatter.
cĩr′çū·lā·ting, *a.* moving or passing round; passing from one to another.
circulating library; see under *library*.
circulating medium; see under *medium*.
cĩr·çū·lā′tion, *n.* [L. *circulatio*, a circular course; *circulari*, to form a circle.]
1. the act of moving round, or in a circle, or in a course which brings or tends to bring the moving body to the point where its motion began; as, the *circulation* of steam through pipes.
2. a series in which the same order is preserved, and things return to the same state. [Obs.]
3. the passing of something, as money, news, etc., from place to place or from person to person.
4. currency; circulating coin, bills, etc.; the combined mediums of exchange, of a monetary system; as, the *circulation* of the country.
5. the movement of the blood in the veins and arteries throughout the body.
6. the flow of sap in a plant.
7. the distribution of newspapers, magazines, etc. among readers.
8. the extent to which something is circulated, as the average number of copies of a magazine sold in a given period.
collateral circulation; the passage of the blood from one part to another of the same system of vessels by collateral communicating channels when the main vessel is obstructed.
cĩr′çū·lā·tive, *a.* 1. promoting or causing circulation.
2. circulating or tending to circulate.
cĩr′çū·lā·tŏr, *n.* [L. *circulator*, a peddler; *circulari*, to form a circle.]
1. one who or that which circulates.
2. a circulating decimal: see *circulate* (sense 4).
cĩr′çū·là·tō·ry, *a.* 1. circular; as, a *circulatory* letter.
2. circulating; going in a circuit; as, *circulatory* travels.
3. relating to circulation, as of the blood.
circulatory system; the system in animals through which the blood circulates, made up of the heart and blood vessels.
cĩr′çū·là·tō·ry, *n.*; *pl.* **cĩr′çū·là·tō·rieṣ,** in old chemistry, a vessel consisting of two parts, unequally exposed to heat, in which fluids were distilled.
cĩr′çū·let, *n.* a ring; a circlet. [Obs.]
cĩr′çū·line, *a.* circular. [Obs.]
cĩr′çum-, a prefix from L. *circum*, meaning *around, about, on all sides, surrounding*, as in *circum*navigate, *circum*scribe.
cĩr·çum·aġ′i·tāte, *v.t.* to agitate on all sides.
cĩr″çum·am′bà·ġeṣ, *n.pl.* [*circum-* and *ambages*.] evasive speech. [Rare.]
cĩr·çum·am′bi·ence, *n.* a surrounding or encircling.
cĩr·çum·am′bi·en·cy, *n.* 1. the quality of being circumambient; the act of surrounding or encompassing.
2. surroundings; environment.
cĩr·çum·am′bi·ent, *a.* surrounding; encompassing; enclosing or being on all sides.
cĩr·çum·am′bū·lāte, *v.i.* and *v.t.*; circumambulated, *pt.*, *pp.*; circumambulating, *ppr.* [*circum-*, and L. *ambulare*, to walk.] to walk around.
cĩr·çum·am·bū·lā′tion, *n.* the act of walking around.
cĩr·çum·am′bū·là·tō·ry, *a.* circumambulating; roundabout.
cĩr·çum·ā′vi·āte, *v.i.* to pilot an airplane around an obstacle, such as a mountain.
cĩr·çum·bend′i·bus, *n.* a roundabout course or method; circumlocution. [Humorous.]
Cĩr·çum·cel′liŏn, *n.* [*circum-*, and L. *cella*, a cell.]
1. one of a set of fanatic Donatists in the fourth century, who roved through northern Africa seeking death by committing deeds of violence, so as to gain the glory of martyrdom.
2. [c–] a vagabond monk.
cĩr′çum·cen″tẽr, *n.* [*circum-*, and L. *centrum*, center.] in mathematics, the center of a circumscribed circle: the *circumcenter* of a triangle is the center of the circle circumscribed about it.
cĩr″çum·ciṅçt′, *a.* [L. *circumcinctus*.] girdled; cinctured. [Rare.]
cĩr″çum·ciṅç′tūre, *n.* [*circum-* and *cincture*.] a girdle or a belt.
cĩr′çum·cīṣe, *v.t.*; circumcised, *pt.*, *pp.*; circumcising, *ppr.* [ME. *circumcisen*; L. *circumcidere*, to cut around; *circum*, and *cædere*, to cut.]
1. to cut off the prepuce of (males); also, in certain primitive rituals, to cut off the labia minora of (females).
2. in the Bible, to put off the sins of (the flesh); to make spiritual or holy.
3. to cut round. [Obs.]
cĩr′çum·cīṣed, *a.* 1. having the prepuce cut off.
2. spiritually purified.
cĩr′çum·cī·ṣẽr, *n.* one who performs circumcision.
cĩr·çum·ci′ṣion, *n.* 1. the act or custom of cutting off the prepuce, or foreskin, of human males or (rarely) the labia minora of females: practiced either as a religious rite of Jews, Moslems, etc. or as a hygienic measure.
2. rejection of the sins of the flesh; spiritual purification, and acceptance of the Christian faith.
3. the Jews as a circumcised people.

> They that were of the *circumcision* contended with him. —Acts xi. 2.

4. a festival observed in the Anglican, Roman Catholic, and Orthodox Eastern Churches on January 1, the octave of Christmas Day, in commemoration of the circumcision of Jesus.
cĩr″çum·çlūde′ *v.t.* to confine; to shut in. [Rare.]
cĩr·çum·çlū′ṣion, *n.* [L. *circumcludere*, to enclose on every side.] the act of enclosing on all sides. [Rare.]
cĩr·çum·çōne, *n.* in mathematics, a cone surface all of whose parts are tangent to a given surface.
cĩr″çum·çon′iç, *a.* pertaining to circumcone.
cĩr″çum·çres′cence, *n.* in biology, an enveloping of some other object by a growth.
cĩr·çum·den·ū·dā′tion, *n.* [*circum-*, and L. *denudare*, to uncover.] in geology, denudation around an object so as to expose it or elevate it.
cĩr″çum·diç′tion, *n.* beating around the point; using words not directly applicable.
cĩr·çum·dūce′, *v.t.* same as *circumduct*, sense 3.
cĩr·çum·duçt′, *v.t.* [L. *circumducere*, to lead around; *circum*, and *ducere*, to lead.]
1. to contravene; to nullify: a term of civil law. [Rare.]
2. to lead about. [Rare.]
3. in Scots law, to deny the admission of (further evidence).
4. to revolve (as a line) round an axis, as in describing a cone.
cĩr·çum·duç′tion, *n.* 1. a leading about. [Rare.]
2. in old English law, an annulling or cancellation. [Rare.]
3. in physiology, the moving of a limb round an axis so as to describe an imaginary cone.
cĩr″çum·ē·sō·phaġ′ē·ăl, *a.* [*circum-*, and L. *œsophagus*, the esophagus.] in anatomy, surrounding the esophagus.
cĩr·çum·fẽr′, *v.t.* to bear or carry round. [Obs.]

cir·cum′fēr·ence, *n.* [ME. *circumference;* L. *circumferens,* ppr. of *circumferre,* to carry round.]

1. the line bounding a circle or other rounded surface; a periphery.

2. the space included in a circle. [Obs.]

3. an orb; a circle; anything circular or round, as a shield. [Obs.]

The broad *circumference*
Hung on his shoulders like the moon.
—Milton.

4. the external surface of any rounded body or sphere. [Obs.]

5. the distance around a circle, globe, etc.; circuit; compass; as, a chest *circumference* of thirty-six inches.

cir·cum′fēr·ence, *v.t.* to include in a circular space. [Obs.]

cir·cum·fēr·en′tiăl (-shăl), *a.* of, at, or close to the circumference.

cir·cum·fēr·en′tiăl·ly, *adv.* in the manner of a circumference.

cir·cum·fēr·en′tŏr, *n.* 1. an instrument used by surveyors for taking angles; a surveyor's compass. It consists of a compass with magnetic needle and dial graduated into 360 degrees, mounted on a horizontal brass bar at the ends of which are the sighting slits.

2. a small wheel formerly used for measuring tires.

CIRCUMFERENTOR

cir′cum·flect, *v.t.*; circumflected, *pt., pp.*; circumflecting, *ppr.* [L. *circumflectere; circum,* and *flectere,* to bend.]

1. to bend around.

2. to place a circumflex accent on (a word). [Rare.]

cir·cum·flec′tion, *n.* same as *circumflexion.*

cir′cum·flex, *n.* [L. *circumflexus,* pp. of *circumflectere; circum,* and *flectere,* to bend.]

1. a wave of the voice, embracing both a rise and fall on the same syllable.

2. a mark (^, ˆ, ˜) used over a vowel in certain languages, as French, or in phonetic keys to indicate some tone or quality of the pronunciation: also, *circumflex accent.*

cir′cum·flex, *v.t.*; circumflexed, *pt., pp.*; circumflexing, *ppr.* 1. to mark or pronounce with a circumflex.

2. to curve; to bend or twist around.

cir′cum·flex, *a.* 1. moving or bending around; circuitous.

2. curved in a circular manner: said of certain arteries and veins of the hip, thigh, or shoulder, and of a nerve of the shoulder.

3. of or marked by a circumflex.

cir·cum·flex′ion, *n.* a bending or winding around.

cir·cum′flu·ence, *n.* [L. *circumfluens,* ppr. of *circumfluere; circum,* and *fluere,* to flow.] a flowing round on all sides; an enclosure, as of water.

cir·cum′flu·ent, *a.* flowing round; surrounding as a fluid; as, *circumfluent* waves.

cir·cum′flu·ous, *a.* 1. flowing round; circumfluent.

2. surrounded by water.

cir″cum·fō·rā′nē·ous, cir″cum·fō·rā′nē·ăn, *a.* [L. *circumforaneus,* about the market place; *circum,* around, and *forum,* a market place.] going about; walking or wandering from house to house; as, a *circumforaneous* fiddler.

cir·cum·ful′gent, *a.* [*circum-,* and L. *fulgere,* to shine.] shining around.

cir·cum·fūse′, *v.t.* [L. *circumfusus,* pp. of *circumfundere; circum,* and *fundere,* to pour.]

1. to pour or spread (a fluid) around.

2. to spread round; to surround (*with* a fluid); to bathe or suffuse (*in*).

cir·cum·fū′sile, *a.* [*circum-,* and L. *fusilis,* fluid.] that may be poured or spread round; as, *circumfusile* gold.

cir·cum·fū′sion, *n.* the act of pouring or spreading round; also, the state of being poured round.

cir″cum·ges·tā′tion, *n.* a carrying about. [Obs.]

cir·cum·gȳ′rāte, *v.t.* to roll or turn round.

cir″cum·gȳ·rā′tion, *n.* [*circum-,* and L. *gyrus,* Gr. *gyros,* a circle.] the act of turning, rolling, or whirling round; as, the *circumgyration* of the planets.

cir·cum·gȳ′rȧ·tō·ry, *a.* moving in a circular manner.

cir·cum·gȳre′, *v.i.* to roll or turn round; to circumgyrate. [Obs.]

cir″cum·in·ces′sion, *n.* [*circum-,* and L. *incessus,* a going, walking, from *incedere,* to advance, to walk.] in theology, the existence of persons in one another.

cir·cum·in′sū·lăr, *a.* surrounding or around an island; in anatomy, around the insula of the cerebral cortex.

cir·cum·jā′cence, *n.* the state of bordering on every side, or of being circumjacent.

cir·cum·jā′cent, *a.* [L. *circumjacens,* ppr. of *circumjacere; circum,* and *jacere,* to lie.] lying round; bordering on every side.

cir·cum·jō′vi·ăl, *n.* one of Jupiter's satellites or moons.

cir·cum·jō′vi·ăl, *a.* moving or revolving around Jupiter.

cir″cum·li·gā′tion, *n.* [L. *circumligare; circum,* and *ligare,* to tie, bind.] the act of binding round; also, the bond with which anything is surrounded. [Obs.]

cir·cum·lit′tō·răl, *a.* [*circum-,* and L. *litus, litoris,* shore.] adjacent to the shore.

cir″cum·lō·cū′tion, *n.* [L. *circumlocutio,* circumlocution; *circum,* and *locutio,* a speaking, from *loqui,* to speak.] the use of a number of words to express an idea; an indirect or lengthy way of expressing something; also, an instance of this.

cir″cum·lō·cū′tion·ăl, *a.* pertaining to circumlocution.

cir·cum·loc′ū·tō·ry, *a.* pertaining to or characterized by circumlocution.

cir″cum·mē·rid′i·ăn, *a.* [*circum-,* and L. *meridies,* midday.] about, or in close proximity to, the meridian.

cir·cum·mūre′, *v.t.* [*circum-,* and L. *murus,* wall.] to surround with a wall.

cir·cum·nav′i·gȧ·ble, *a.* that may be sailed around.

cir·cum·nav′i·gāte, *v.t.*; circumnavigated, *pt., pp.*; circumnavigating, *ppr.* to sail around; to pass around by water; as, to *circumnavigate* the globe.

cir·cum·nav·i·gā′tion, *n.* the act of sailing around.

cir·cum·nav′i·gā·tŏr, *n.* one who circumnavigates.

cir·cum·nū′tāte, *v.i.* to exhibit circumnutation.

cir″cum·nū·tā′tion, *n.* [*circum-,* and L. *nutare,* to nod.] the act or inclination of the stems, roots, or shoots of plants to bend in various directions because of differences in the rate of growth of the opposite sides.

cir·cum·oc′ū·lăr, *a.* around or near the eye.

cir·cum·ō′răl, *a.* [*circum-,* and L. *os,* genit. *oris,* mouth.] being situated near, or encircling, the mouth.

cir″cum·pli·cā′tion, *n.* [L. *circumplicare; circum,* and *plicare,* to fold.] a folding, winding, or wrapping round.

cir·cum·pō′lăr, *a.* about the pole: said of stars which are so near either pole as to revolve around it without setting; as, *circumpolar* stars; *circumpolar* sea.

cir″cum·pō·si′tion, *n.* the act of placing in a circle, or the state of being so placed.

cir·cum·rō′tȧ·ry, *a.* turning, rolling, or whirling around.

cir·cum·rō′tāte, *v.t.* and *v.i.*; circumrotated, *pt., pp.*; circumrotating, *ppr.* to revolve; to rotate, as on an axis.

cir″cum·rō·tā′tion, *n.* the act of rolling or revolving around, as a wheel; circumvolution.

cir·cum·rō′tȧ·tō·ry, *a.* same as *circumrotary.*

cir·cum·scis′sile, *a.* [*circum-,* and L. *scissilis,* easily cut, from *scissus,* pp. of *scindere,* to cut.] in botany, opening or splitting by a transverse fissure around the circumference, leaving an upper and lower half: said of certain seed pods or capsules.

CIRCUMSCISSILE SEED PODS

cir·cum·scrīb′ȧ·ble, *a.* capable of being circumscribed.

cir·cum·scrībe′, *v.t.*; circumscribed, *pt., pp.*; circumscribing, *ppr.* [ME. *circumscrive;* L. *circumscribere,* to draw a line around.]

1. to draw a line around.

2. to enclose within a certain limit; to limit, bound, or confine.

3. to write around. [Rare.]

4. in geometry, (a) to draw a figure around (another figure) so as to touch it at as many points as possible; as, *circumscribe* a triangle with a circle; (b) to be thus drawn around; as, the hexagon *circumscribed* the square.

Syn.—bind, restrain, restrict, narrow.

cir·cum·scrībed′, *a.* 1. drawn around, as a line; limited; confined.

2. in geometry, designating or of a figure which is drawn around another figure, so as to touch it at as many points as possible.

cir·cum·scrīb′ēr, *n.* a person or object that circumscribes.

cir·cum·scrip′ti·ble, *a.* capable of being circumscribed or limited by bounds.

cir·cum·scrip′tion, *n.* [L. *circumscriptio,* an encircling, boundary, from *circumscribere,* to draw a line around; *circum,* and *scribere,* to draw, write.]

1. a line that limits; limitation; restriction; confinement.

2. the termination or limits of a body; the exterior line which determines the form or magnitude of a body; an outline.

3. an inscription around a coin, metal, etc.

4. a surrounding substance.

5. a circumscribed space.

cir·cum·scrip′tive, *a.* defining the external outline; marking or enclosing the limits in space.

cir·cum·scrip′tive·ly, *adv.* in a limited manner.

cir·cum·script′ly, *adv.* circumscriptively. [Rare.]

cir·cum·sō′lăr, *a.* revolving around the sun.

cir′cum·spect, *a.* [L. *circumspectus,* pp. of *circumspicere,* to look about; *circum,* and *specere,* to look.] cautious; prudent; watchful on all sides; examining carefully all the circumstances that may affect an action, judgment, conduct, etc.

Syn.—cautious, discreet, prudent, careful, scrupulous.

cir·cum·spec′tion, *n.* caution; attention to all the facts and circumstances of an action, judgment, etc., with a view to a correct course of conduct.

cir·cum·spec′tive, *a.* looking round in every direction; cautious; careful of consequences.

cir·cum·spec′tive·ly, *adv.* cautiously; vigilantly; heedfully.

cir′cum·spect·ly, *adv.* in a circumspect manner; cautiously.

cir′cum·spect·ness, *n.* caution; circumspection.

cir′cum·stance, *n.* [L. *circumstantia,* a standing around, condition, from *circumstare; circum,* and *stare,* to stand.]

1. something attending, appendant, or relative to a fact or event, either incidentally or as an essential condition or determining factor; as, the *circumstances* of time, place, and persons are to be considered.

2. one of the adjuncts of a fact, which makes it more or less criminal, or makes an accusation more or less probable.

3. [*pl.*] conditions surrounding and affecting a person; as, a man in easy *circumstances.*

4. ceremony; show; as, pomp and *circumstance.*

5. accompanying or surrounding detail, especially fullness of detail; as, the story was told with great *circumstance.*

under the circumstances; when everything is considered; conditions being what they are.

Syn.—fact, event, incident, position, situation.

cir′cum·stance, *v.t.*; circumstanced, *pt., pp.*; circumstancing, *ppr.* to place in certain circumstances.

cir′cum·stanced (-stanst), *a.* 1. placed in a particular circumstance or condition; as, *circumstanced* as we were, we could not escape.

2. governed or supported by circumstances or conditions.

cir′cum·stant, *a.* surrounding. [Obs.]

cir′cum·stant, *n.* a spectator. [Obs.]

cir·cum·stan′tiȧ·ble (-shȧ-bl), *a.* capable of being circumstantiated. [Obs.]

cir·cum·stan′tiăl (-shăl), *a.* 1. attending; relating to, but not essential; incidental.

2. pertaining to circumstances, or to particular incidents.

The usual character of human testimony is substantial truth under *circumstantial* variety. —Paley.

3. abounding with circumstances, or exhibiting all the circumstances; full of detail; complete; as, a *circumstantial* account or recital.

circumstantial evidence; in law, proof of certain attendant circumstances which is used as evidence to infer the proof of a fact; as, proof of possession of stolen property is *circumstantial evidence* in a case of theft.

cir·cum·stan′tiăl, *n.* something incidental to the main subject: usually in the plural; as, the *circumstantials* rather than the *essentials* of history.

cĩr·cum·stan·ti·al′i·ty (-shi-al′), *n.* the quality or state of being modified by circumstances; particularity; detail.

cĩr·cum·stan′tiăl·ly, *adv.* 1. according to circumstances; not essentially; accidentally.
2. minutely; exactly; in every detail or particular.

cĩr·cum·stan′ti·āte (-shi-āt), *v.t.*; circumstantiated, *pt., pp.*; circumstantiating, *ppr.* 1. to place in particular circumstances; to invest with particular accidents or adjuncts. [Obs.]
2. to prove or confirm by presenting circumstances; to verify in every particular.

cĩr·cum·stan·ti·ā′tion (-shi-ā′shun), *n.* a circumstantiating or being circumstantiated.

cĩr″cum·tẽr·rā′nē·ous, *a.* [*circum-*, and L. *terra*, earth.] around the earth. [Obs.]

cĩr·cum·un′dū·lāte, *v.t.* [*circum-*, and L. *undulatus*, waved, from *unda*, a wave.] to flow around, as waves. [Rare.]

cĩr·cum·val′lāte, *v.t.*; circumvallated, *pt., pp.*; circumvallating, *ppr.* to surround with a rampart or trench.

cĩr·cum·val′lāte, *a.* 1. enclosed or surrounded by a wall, trench, etc.
2. in anatomy, surrounded by a ridge.

cĩr″cum·val·lā′tion, *n.* [L. *circumvallare*, to surround with a rampart; *circum*, and *vallum*, a rampart.] in early warfare, a surrounding with a wall or rampart; also, a wall, rampart, or parapet with a trench, surrounding the camp of a besieging army.

cĩr·cum·vent′, *v.t.* [L. *circumventus*, pp. of *circumvenire*, to come round, encircle; *circum*, and *venire*, to come.]
1. to go around; surround.
2. to surround by trickery or craft.
3. to catch in a trap.
4. to gain superiority over; outwit.
5. to prevent from happening.

cĩr·cum·ven′tion, *n.* a circumventing or being circumvented.

cĩr·cum·vent′ive, *a.* circumventing.

cĩr·cum·vent′ŏr, *n.* a person who circumvents.

cĩr·cum·vest′, *v.t.* to cover around, as with a garment. [Obs.]

cĩr·cum′vō·lănt, *a.* flying about.

cĩr″cum·vō·lū′tion, *n.* [*circumvolutus*, pp. of *circumvolvere*, to roll round; *circum*, and *volvere*, to turn.]
1. a rolling, turning around, or coiling.
2. the state of being rolled around, folded, or coiled.
3. a fold or twist.
4. a circuitous course or form.

cĩr·cum·volve′, *v.t.*; circumvolved, *pt., pp.*; circumvolving, *ppr.* to cause to revolve; to put into a circular motion.

cĩr·cum·volve′, *v.i.* to revolve.

cĩr′cus, *n.*; *pl.* **cĩr′cus·es,** [L. *circus*, a circle, ring, racecourse; Gr. *kirkos*, a circle.]
1. in ancient Rome, an oval or oblong arena with tiers of seats around it, used for games, chariot races, etc.
2. a similar arena, usually enclosed in a tent, for a show of acrobats, wild animals, clowns, etc.
3. a traveling show of this sort.
4. the performance of such a show.
5. a circular open place where many streets come together; as, Piccadilly *Circus*. [Brit.]
6. any riotously entertaining person, thing, etc. [Colloq.]

cĩrl bun′ting, [It. *zirlo*, the whistling of a thrush; *zirlare*, to whistle like a thrush.] a species of bunting, *Emberiza cirlus*.

cĩrque (sẽrk), *n.* [Fr., from L. *circus*, a ring, circus.]
1. a circular arrangement or space.
2. a circle; ring. [Poetic.]
3. a circus. [Archaic.]
4. in geology, a natural amphitheater; steep, hollow excavation in a mountain, made by erosion, etc.

cĩr′rāte, *a.* [L. *cirratus*, having ringlets or tendrils, from *cirrus*, a ringlet.] in biology, having cirri.

cir·rhō′sis, *n.* [L., from Gr. *kirrhos*, tawny.] a degenerative disease in an organ of the body, especially the liver, marked by excess formation of connective tissue and the subsequent contraction of the organ.

cir·rhot′iç, *a.* caused by, having, or resembling cirrhosis.

cir′rī, *n.*, plural of *cirrus*.

cir′ri-, [from L. *cirrus*.] a combining form meaning *curl, ringlet*, as in *cirri*ped: also *cirro-, cirrhi-, cirrho-*.

Cir″ri·brañ″chi·ā′tȧ, *n.pl.* [*cirri-*, and Gr. *branchia*, gills.] an order of mollusks having slender cirriform gills.

cir·rif′ẽr·ous, *a.* [*cirri-*, and L. *ferre*, to bear.] producing tendrils or cirri, as a plant.

cir′ri·fọrm, *a.* [*cirri-*, and L. *forma*, form.] with a tendrillike form.

cir·rig′ẽr·ous, *a.* [*cirri-*, and L. *gerere*, to carry.] having curled locks of hair or hairlike appendages.

cir′ri·grāde, *a.* [*cirri-*, and L. *gradi*, to walk.] moving by means of cirri, or hairlike tendrils.

cir′ri·ped, cir′ri·pēde, *n.* [*cirri-*, and L. *pes, pedis*, foot.] any crustacean belonging to the order *Cirripedia*.

cir′ri·ped, cir′ri·pēde, *a.* of a cirriped or the cirripeds.

Cir·ri·pē′di·ȧ, *n.* an order of crustaceans, including barnacles, having curl-shaped appendages and attaching themselves parasitically, in the adult stage, to other organisms, rocks, the bottoms of ships, etc.

Cir″rō·brañ″chi·ā′tȧ, *n.* same as *Cirribranchiata*.

cir″rō·çū′mū·lus, *n.* [*cirro-*, and L. *cumulus*, a heap.] a formation of small, white, fleecy clouds in groups or rows: mean height, 27,000 ft.: also called *mackerel sky*.

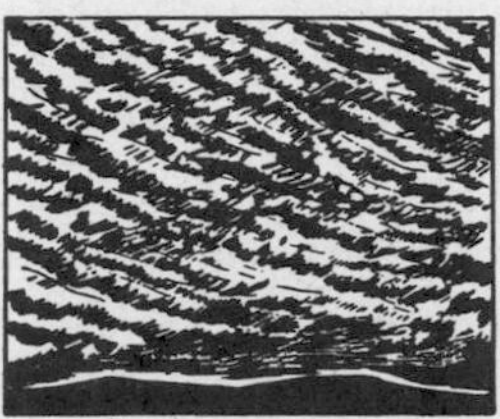

CIRRO-CUMULUS

cir′rōse, *a.* [from L. *cirrus*, a tendril; and *-ose*.] having or resembling a cirrus or cirri: applied to plants, birds, beetles, etc.

Cir·ros′tō·mī, *n.pl.* [*cirro-*, and Gr. *stoma*, mouth.] an order of vertebrates, having cirri around the mouth and forming the lowest group, the leptocardians.

cir″rō·strā′tus, *n.* [*cirro-*, and L. *stratus*, pp. of *sternere*, to spread out.] a high, thin, delicate formation of clouds, often resembling a tangled web: mean height, 32,000 ft.

cir′rous, *a.* same as *cirrose*.

cir′rus, *n.*; *pl.* **cir′rī,** [L. a lock, curl, tendril.]
1. in biology, (a) a plant tendril; (b) a flexible, threadlike appendage, as the feelers of certain organisms.
2. in meteorology, a formation of filmy, fleecy clouds, generally whitish: mean height, 33,000 ft.

CIRRUS

Cĩr′si·um, *n.* [L., from Gr. *kirsion*, a kind of thistle.] a large genus of prickly herbs belonging to the thistle family.

cĩr′sō-, [Gr. *kirso-*, *kirs*, from *kirsos*, enlargement of a vein.] a combining form meaning *an enlarged vein*: also, before a vowel, *cirs-*.

cĩr′sō·cēle, *n.* [Gr. *kirsos*, an enlarged vein, varicocele, and *kēlē*, a tumor.] a varix, or dilatation of the spermatic vein.

cĩr′soid, *a.* [Gr. *kirsos*, an enlarged vein, and *eidos*, form.] like a varix, or enlarged blood vessel; varicose.

cĩr·sot′ō·my, *n.* [Gr. *kirsos*, an enlarged vein, and *tomē*, from *temnein*, to cut.] a surgical operation for removing varicose veins.

cis-, [from L. *cis*, on this side.] a prefix meaning: (a) *on this side of*, as in *cis*alpine; (b) *subsequent to*.

cis·al′pīne, *a.* on this side of the Alps, from the viewpoint of Rome; that is, south of the alps: opposed to *transalpine*.

cis·at·lan′tiç, *a.* on this (the speaker's) side of the Atlantic Ocean.

cis′çō, *n.*; *pl.* **cis′çōes** or **cis′çōs,** [from Canadian Fr. *ciscovette* for *siskowet, siskowit*, from Algonquian.] any of a number of whitefishes of the genus *Leucichthys*, found in the Great Lakes of North America: called also the *lake herring*.

ci·se·lūre′, *n.* [Fr., from *ciseler*, to carve.] metal chased work; also, the art of metal chasing.

cis·leī′thăn, *a.* situated on the side of the river Leitha toward Vienna; Austrian as opposed to Hungarian.

cis·mon′tāne, *a.* situated on this side of the mountains, especially of the Alps.

cis′pȧ·dāne, *a.* [*cis-*, and L. *Padanus*, the river Po.] situated on this side of the Po, from the viewpoint of Rome; that is, south of the Po.

cis′soid, *n.* [Gr. *kissoeidēs*, like ivy; *kissos*, ivy, and *eidos*, form.] in geometry, a curve of the second order, invented by Diocles. In the diameter, A B, of a circle described about C, take B M = A N, and erect the ordinates M Q = N R, and join A Q; the locus of the point P, in which the line A Q cuts the ordinate N R, is the *cissoid*. To find its equation, let A N = x, P N = y, A C = a, then since

$$\frac{PN = y}{AN = x} = \frac{QM = \sqrt{2ax-x^2}}{AM = 2a-x}$$

the equation is $y^2\ (2a-x)=x^3$. The curve has an equal branch on the other side of A B; the two branches meet in a cusp at point A, and have the line H K as an asymptote. The area included between the curve and the asymptote is three times the area of the generating circle. In the cissoid of Diocles the generating curve is a circle, but this term has been applied in later times to all curves described in a similar manner, where the generating curve is not a circle.

cis′soid, *a.* designating the angle formed by the concave sides of two intersecting curves: opposed to *sistroid*.

cist, *n.* [L. *cista*; Gr. *kistē*, a chest.]
1. a primitive tomb made of stone slabs or hollowed out of rock: also *kist*.
2. in ancient Greece, a box or chest containing sacred utensils.

CIST

Cis·tā′cē·ae, *n.* [L., from Gr. *kistos*, *kisthos*, the rockrose.] the rockrose family of low shrubby plants or herbs, with entire leaves, and crumpled, showy flowers. Some species exude a balsamic resin.

cis·tā′ceous, *a.* resembling or belonging to the rockrose family, *Cistaceæ*.

cist′ed, *a.* containing a cist or cists.

Cis·tẽr′ciăn, *n.* [Fr. *Cistercien*, from LL. *Cistercium*, Fr. *Cîteaux*, the original convent.] a monk of the Cistercian Order.

Cis·tẽr′ciăn, *a.* belonging or pertaining to the Cistercians.

Cis·tẽr′ciăn Ọr′dẽr, a monastic order, a stricter branch of the Benedictine Order, established in 1098 at Cîteaux, France.

cis′tẽrn, *n.* [ME. *cisterne*; OFr. *cisterne*; L. *cisterna*, a reservoir for water, from *cista*, Gr. *kistē*, a chest, box.]
1. a large receptacle for storing water, beer, or other liquids, as in dwellings, distilleries, and breweries; especially, a tank in which rain water is collected for use.
2. a natural reservoir; a hollow place containing water, as a fountain or lake.
3. in anatomy, a sac or cavity containing a natural fluid of the body.

cis·tẽr′nȧ, *n.* [L.; see *cistern*.] in anatomy, a cistern; specifically, any of the enlarged spaces below the arachnoid.

cist′iç, *a.* same as *cystic*.

cis·tin′ē·ous, *a.* same as *cistaceous*.

Cis′tus, *n.* [L., from Gr. *kistos*, or *kisthos*, the rockrose.]
1. the rockrose, a genus of plants, family *Cistaceæ*, of many species, most of them native to southern Europe.
2. [c—] any plant of this genus.

cist′vaen, *n.* same as *cist* (a tomb).

cit, *n.* [contracted from *citizen*.] a citizen; an inhabitant of a city. [Colloq.]

cīt′ȧ·ble, *a.* capable of being cited or quoted: also spelled *citeable*.

cit′ȧ·del, *n.* [Fr. *citadelle*; LL. *civitatella*, a small city, from L. *civitas*, citizenship, a state or city.]
1. a fortress on a commanding height for defense of a city.
2. a fortified place; stronghold.

3. a refuge; place of retreat.
4. the heavily armored central structure of a warship, on which the guns are mounted.

cī·tā′tion, *n.* [ME. *citacion*, from L. *citare*, to arouse, summon.]
1. a summons; an official notice to appear in a court and answer to a demand.
2. a citing; quoting.
3. a passage cited; quotation.
4. honorable mention in an official report for bravery or meritorious service in the armed forces.
5. a reference to a legal statute, a previous law case, a written authority, etc.

cī·tā′tŏr, *n.* the person who cites. [Rare.]

cī′tȧ·tō·ry, *a.* of a citation; having the power or form of citation; as, letters *citatory*.

cīte, *v.t.*; cited, *pt.*, *pp.*; citing, *ppr.* [Fr. *citer*, to summon; L. *citare*, to arouse, summon.]
1. to call upon officially or authoritatively; to summon; to give legal or official notice, as to appear in court.
2. to enjoin; to direct; to order or urge.
3. to quote (a passage, book, speech, writer, etc.).
4. to name or refer to, in support, proof, or confirmation; as, to *cite* an authority in law.
5. to mention in an official report for bravery or meritorious service in the armed forces.
Syn.—summon, call, quote, mention, name.

cīt′ẽr, *n.* one who cites.

cith′ȧ·rȧ, *n.* [L. *cithara*; Gr. *kithara*, a kind of lyre, harp.] an ancient musical instrument somewhat resembling a lyre: precursor of the zither.

CITHARA

Cith·ȧ·rex′y·lum, *n.* [L., from Gr. *kithara*, a lyre, and *xylon*, wood.] a genus of shrubs and trees, native to tropical America and valuable for building material because of the hardness and durability of their wood: often called *fiddle wood*.

cith·ȧ·ris′tiç, *a.* [Gr. *kitharistikos*, pertaining to the lyre; *kithara*, a lyre.] pertaining to a cithara.

cith′ẽr, *n.* [Fr. *cithare*, from L. *cithara*.]
1. a cithara.
2. loosely, a cithern or zither.

cith′ẽrn, cit′tẽrn, *n.* [ME. *gitterne*; L. *cithara*; Gr. *kithara*, a kind of lyre, harp.] a stringed musical instrument of the sixteenth century: it bore some resemblance to the modern guitar.

cith′ẽrn head (hed), a stupid person: so called in reference to the carved head on the handle of a cithern. [Obs.]

CITHERN

cit′ied (-id), *a.* 1. belonging to a city. [Rare.]
2. resembling a city.
3. having a city or cities on it; as, the *citied* earth.

cit′i·fied, *a.* having the manners, dress, etc. attributed to city people; following city ways.

Cit·i·grā′dȧ, *n.pl.* [L., from *citus*, rapid, and *gradi*, to walk.] a family of spiders which catch their prey by swift running. It includes the European tarantula and the wolf spiders.

cit′i·grāde, *a.* relating to the *Citigrada*.

cit′i·nẽr, *n.* a city-born or city-bred person. [Obs.]

cit′i·zen (-zn), *n.* [ME. *citizen*; OFr. *citeein*, a citizen, from L. *civitas*, genit. *civitatis*, a state, city.]
1. formerly, a native or inhabitant, especially a freeman or burgess, of a town or city.
2. loosely, a native, inhabitant, or denizen of any place.
3. a member of a state or nation, especially one with a republican form of government, who owes allegiance to it by birth or naturalization and is entitled to full civil rights; as, this former British subject is now an American *citizen*.
4. a civilian, as distinguished from a person in military service, a policeman, etc.
citizen of the world; a person who feels at home in various countries; cosmopolitan person.

cit′i·zen, *a.* 1. having the qualities of a citizen; as, *citizen* soldiery.
2. town-bred; effeminate. [Obs.]

cit′i·zen·ess, *n.* a woman citizen.

cit′i·zen·ry, *n.* citizens collectively.

cit′i·zenṣ′ band, either of two bands of shortwave radio frequencies set aside by the Federal Communications Commission for local use at low power by private persons or businesses.

cit′i·zen·ship, *n.* [*citizen*, and *-ship*.]
1. the status or condition of a citizen.
2. the duties, rights, and privileges of this status.

cit′i·zen·ship pā′pẽrṣ, the document stating that a naturalized person has been formally declared a citizen.

cit′ōle, *n.* [OFr. *citole*, from L. *cithara*, a cithern.] a cithern.

cï·toy·eṅ′ (-twȧ-yaṅ′), *n.*; *pl.* **cï·toy·eṅs′** (-twȧ-yaṅ′), [Fr. (fem., *citoyenne*).] a citizen.

cit′rȧ-, [L. *citra*, on this side of, from *citer*, hither.] a combining form meaning *on this side of, cis-*, as in *citra*montane. [Rare.]

cit·rȧ·çon′iç, *a.* pertaining to or derived from citraconic acid.
citraconic acid; a white, odorless compound derived from citric acid.

cit′răl, *n.* [*cit*ron, and *al*dehyde.] a liquid aldehyde, $C_9H_{15}·CHO$, with a pleasant odor, found in oil of lemon, oil of lime, etc.

cit′rāte, *n.* [L. *citrus*, the citron tree.] in chemistry, a salt or ester of citric acid.

cit′rē·ăn, *a.* same as *citrine*.

cit′rēne, *n.* a crystalline compound obtained from the oil of lemon.

cit′rē·ous, *a.* [L. *citreus*; see *citrus*.] lemon-yellow.

cit′riç, *a.* [from *citrus*, and *-ic*.]
1. of or from citrons, lemons, oranges, or similar fruits.
2. designating or of an acid, $C_6H_8O_7$, obtained from such fruits, used in making flavoring extracts, dyes, citrates, etc.

cit′ril, *n.* [It. *citrinella*, dim. of *citrina*, the yellowhammer, citril, from LL. *citrinus*, yellow; L. *citrus*, the citron.] a small finch, *Fringilla citrinella*, of southern Europe.

cit′rin, *n.* [from *citrus*, and *-in*.] vitamin P, found in lemon juice and paprika.

cit·ri·nā′tion, *n.* the turning of a substance to a yellow-green color.

cit′rine, *a.* like a citron or lemon; of a lemon color; yellow or greenish-yellow.
citrine ointment; a yellow ointment containing mercuric nitrate.

cit′rine, *n.* [from *citrus*, and *-ine*.]
1. lemon yellow.
2. a yellow, semiprecious variety of quartz resembling topaz.

cit′rŏn, *n.* [Fr. *citron*; L. *citrus*; Gr. *kitron*, a citron.]
1. a yellow, thick-skinned fruit resembling a lime or lemon but larger and less acid.
2. the semitropical tree bearing this fruit.
3. the candied rind of this fruit, used as a confection, in fruitcake, etc.
4. the citron melon.

cit·rŏn·el′lȧ, *n.* [Mod.L., from *citron*.]
1. a volatile, sharp-smelling oil used in perfume, soap, etc. and to keep insects away: also *citronella oil*.
2. the southern Asiatic grass from which this oil is derived.

cit′rŏn mel′ŏn, a kind of watermelon with hard, white flesh.

cit′rŏn wood, 1. the wood of the Barbary pine or sandarac tree, *Callitris quadrivalvis*.
2. the wood of the citron tree.

cit′rous, *a.* 1. of fleshy fruits with a thick rind and acid flesh, as oranges, lemons, limes, grapefruit, and citrons.
2. of the trees that bear these fruits; citrus.

cit′rul, *n.* the watermelon, *Citrullus vulgaris*.

Cit′rus, *n.* [L., the citron tree.]
1. a genus of trees and shrubs, including the citron, orange, lemon, and lime trees.
2. [c–] any tree or shrub of the genus *Citrus*.
3. [c–] the fruit of any of these trees or shrubs.

cit′rus, *a.* relating to the genus *Citrus*.

cit′tẽrn, *n.* same as *cithern*.

cit′y, *n.*; *pl.* **cit′ieṣ,** [ME. *cite*, *citee*; OFr. *cite*, *citet*, city; L. *civitas*, citizenship, from *civis*, a citizen.]
1. a large, important town.
2. in the United States, an incorporated municipality whose boundaries and powers of self-government are defined by a charter from the State in which it is located.
3. in Canada, a municipality of the highest rank.
4. in Great Britain, a borough or town with a royal charter, usually a town that has been or is an episcopal see.
5. all the people of a city.
6. in ancient Greece, a city-state.
the City; the financial and commercial district of Greater London.

cit′y, *a.* pertaining to or in a city.
city editor; in the United States, the editor in charge of the local-news department of a newspaper; in England, a newspaper editor in charge of financial, or commercial, news.
city father; any of the important officials of a city; councilman, alderman, etc.
city hall; (a) a building which houses the offices of a municipal government; (b) the municipal government.
city manager; an administrator appointed by a city council or similar body to act as manager of the city.

cit′y-bo̤rn, *a.* born in a city.

cit′y-bred, *a.* raised in a city.

cit′y chick′en, strips of pork or veal wound on a skewer, breaded, and fried.

cit′y·fied, *a.* citified.

Cit′y of Brŏth′ẽr·ly Lŏve, Philadelphia, Pennsylvania: so called from the literal interpretation of its name.

Cit′y of Dā′vid, 1. Jerusalem: so called because David captured it and established his capital there: II Sam. v. 6.
2. Bethlehem: so called because David was born there: I Sam. xvi. 1.

Cit′y of God, heaven.

Cit′y of Sev′en Hillṣ, Rome.

cit′y-stāte, *n.* a state made up of an independent city and the territory directly controlled by it, as in ancient Greece.

cīve, *n.* same as *chive*.

civ′et, *n.* [Fr. *civette*; It. *cibetto*; Ar. *zabbad*, the civet.]
1. a substance of the consistency of butter or honey secreted by glands in the anal pouch of the civet cat. It is of a clear yellowish or brownish color, and is used in making some perfumes.
2. the civet cat.
3. its fur.

civ′et, *v.t.* to scent with civet.

civ′et çat, any of several varieties of a catlike, flesh-eating animal of Africa, India, Malaysia, and southern China, *Viverra civetta*, with a spotted, yellowish fur: valued for its civet.

civ′iç, *a.* [L. *civicus*, civil, from *civis*, a citizen.]
1. of a city.
2. of citizens.
3. of citizenship.
civic crown; in ancient Rome, a crown, wreath, or garland of oak leaves and acorns, given as a mark of public approbation to any Roman soldier who had saved the life of a citizen in battle.

civ′i·ciṣm, *n.* the principle of equal duties and rights among citizens.

civ′içṣ, *n.pl.* [*construed as sing.*] the branch of political science that deals with civic affairs and the duties and rights of citizenship.

civ′il, *a.* [Fr. *civil*; L. *civilis*, pertaining to a citizen, from *civis*, a citizen.]
1. of a citizen or citizens.
2. of a community of citizens, their government, or their interrelations; as, *civil* affairs; *civil* service, *civil* war.
3. suitable for a city dweller; not rustic.
4. polite; urbane.
5. civilized.
6. not military, naval, or ecclesiastical; as, *civil* law, *civil* marriage.
7. designating legally recognized divisions of time; as, a *civil* year.
8. [*sometimes* C–] of or according to Roman civil law or modern civil law.
9. in law, relating to the private rights of individuals and to legal actions involving these: distinguished from *criminal, political*.
civil action; any suit or action at law other than a criminal prosecution.
civil architecture; the architecture which is employed in constructing buildings for the purposes of civil life, in distinction from *military* and *naval architecture*.
civil death; in law, deprivation of all civil rights as a result of being convicted of treason or, sometimes, of being declared an outlaw.
civil defense; a system of warning devices, fallout shelters, volunteer workers, etc. organized as a defense of the population, especially against nuclear annihilation.
civil engineer; a specialist in civil engineering.
civil engineering; see under *engineering*.

civil law; see under *law*.

civil liberties; liberties guaranteed to the individual by law; rights of thinking, speaking, and acting as one likes without interference or restraint except in the interests of the public welfare.

civil list; in England, formerly, a list of the entire expenses of the civil government; now, the annual appropriation fixed by the legislature for the expenditures of the reigning monarch's household and the sovereign's allowances.

civil marriage; a marriage performed by a justice of the peace, judge, or similar official, not by a clergyman.

civil remedy; in law, remedy obtainable by a civil action.

civil rights; those rights guaranteed to the individual by the 13th and 14th Amendments to the Constitution of the United States and by certain other acts of Congress; especially, exemption from involuntary servitude and equal treatment of all people with respect to the enjoyment of life, liberty, and property and to the protection of law.

civil servant; a member of the civil service: in British usage, *Civil Servant*. [Chiefly Brit.]

civil service; [orig. applied to the civilian staff of the British East India Company.] (a) all those employed in government administration except in the army, navy, legislature, or judiciary; (b) any government service in which a position is secured through competitive public examination; (c) official regulations for such government service; as, he came under *civil service*. In British usage, *Civil Service*.

civil war; a war between geographical sections or political factions of the same nation.

civil year; a calendar year: distinguished from *astronomical year*.

the Civil War; the war between the North (the Union) and the South (the Confederacy) in the United States (1861–1865).

Syn.—courteous, obliging, well-bred, polite, affable, complaisant.

ci·vil'iăn (-yăn), *n.* [ME. *civilian*, a civilian; L. *civilis*, pertaining to a citizen.]
1. one who is skilled in civil or Roman law.
2. any person not in military or naval service.

ci·vil'iăn, *a.* relating to or characteristic of civilians; nonmilitary.

civ'il·ist, *n.* a civilian. [Obs.]

ci·vil'i·ty, *n.*; *pl.* **ci·vil'i·tieș**, [ME. *civylite*; OFr. *civilite*, civility; L. *civilitas*, the art of government, from *civilis*, civil.]
1. the state of being civilized. [Archaic.]
2. good breeding; politeness; consideration; courtesy.
3. a polite act or utterance.

civ·i·līz'à·ble, *a.* capable of becoming civilized.

civ″il·i·zā'tion, *n.* 1. the process of civilizing or becoming civilized.
2. the condition of being civilized; social organization of a high order, marked by advances in the arts, sciences, etc.
3. the total culture of a people, nation, period, etc.; as, the *civilization* of the Occident differs from that of the Orient.
4. the countries and peoples considered to have reached a high stage of social and cultural development.

civ'il·īze, *v.t.*; civilized, *pt.*, *pp.*; civilizing, *ppr.* [Fr. *civiliser*, to civilize; L. *civilis*, civil.]
1. to bring out of a condition of savagery or barbarism; instruct in the ways of an advanced society.
2. to better the habits or manners of; refine.

civ'il·īzed, *a.* [pp. of *civilize*.]
1. advanced in social organization and the arts and sciences.
2. of people or countries thus advanced.
3. cultured and courteous; refined.

civ'il·īz·ēr, *n.* one who or that which civilizes.

civ'il·ly, *adv.* 1. with civility; politely.
2. by civil law.

civ'ișm, *n.* [Fr. *civisme*, from L. *civis*, citizen.] the principles and ideals of good citizenship: term of the French Revolution.

civ'vieș, civ'ieș, *n.pl.* civilian clothes, as distinguished from military uniform; mufti. [Slang.]

ciz'ărș, *n.pl.* scissors. [Obs.]

Cl, in chemistry, chlorine.

çlab'bēr, *n.* [Ir. *clabar*.] thick, sour milk; curdled milk; bonnyclabber.

çlab'bēr, *v.i.* and *v.t.*; clabbered, *pt.*, *pp.*; clabbering, *ppr.* to curdle.

çlăch'ăn (klăkh'), *n.* [Scot. Gael.; prob. from *clach*, stone.] a hamlet, especially in the Highlands of Scotland. [Scot. or Irish.]

çlack, *v.i.*; clacked, *pt.*, *pp.*; clacking, *ppr.* [ME. *clacken*, to clack; an imitative word.]
1. to make a sudden, sharp noise, as by striking or cracking two hard substances together.
2. to chatter; prate; blab.
3. to make a clucking, cackling sound, as a hen.

çlack, *v.t.* 1. to cause to make an abrupt, sharp sound.
2. to blab.

çlack, *n.* 1. a sharp, abrupt sound, such as is made by striking two hard substances together.
2. something that makes this sound.
3. continual and heedless talk; prattle; chatter.

çlack box, the chamber in which a clack valve works.

çlack'dish, *n.* a dish or money box with a movable lid, formerly carried by beggars, who attracted attention by clacking the lid.

çlack'-dōor, *n.* an adjustable cover to an aperture in a clack box.

çlack'ēr, *n.* one who or that which clacks; especially, the clapper of a mill.

çlack goose, a barnacle goose.

çlack valve, a valve, often hinged at one edge, which closes with a clacking sound.

CLACK VALVE

çlad, *v.* occasional past tense and past participle of *clothe*.

çlad, *a.* clothed; dressed.

çlad, *v.t.* to clothe. [Obs.]

çlad'ine, *a.* same as *cladose*.

çlad'ō-, a combining form from Gr. *klados*, a shoot, branch, signifying *branched* or *having branches*, as in *clado*phyll.

Çlad·ō·çăr'pī, *n.pl.* in botany, a division of mosses having cladocarpous fruit.

çlad·ō·çăr'pous, *a.* [*clado-*, and Gr. *karpos*, fruit.] having the fruit at the end of a lateral shoot: said of mosses.

Çlà·doc'e·rà, *n.pl.* [*clado-*, and Gr. *keras*, horn.] an order of ostracoid entomostracans, having a bivalve shell covering the body but not the head, and branched antennae: it includes the water fleas.

çlad'ōde, çlà·dō'di·um, *n.* [*clado-*, and Gr. *eidos*, form.] same as *cladophyll*.

çlà·doġ'e·nous, *a.* same as *cladocarpous*.

çlad'ō·phyll, *n.* [from *clado-*, and *phyllon*, a leaf.] in botany, a branch with the shape and appearance of a leaf.

çlā'dōse, *a.* [L. *cladus*; Gr. *klados*, a branch.] in zoology, branched, as a sponge spicule; having many branches.

Çlad'ō·thrix, *n.* [*clado-*, and Gr. *thrix*, a hair.] a genus of threadlike bacteria, found on plants in a variety of forms.

çlag'gy, *a.* [Scot. *clag*, a clog, impediment.] sticky, adhesive. [Dial.]

çlāik (gōose), a barnacle goose.

çlāim, *v.t.*; claimed, *pt.*, *pp.*; claiming, *ppr.* [ME. *claimen*; OFr. *claimer*, to call, cry out, claim; L. *clamare*, to cry out; Gr. *kalein*, to call, cry out.]
1. to call for; to ask or seek to obtain by virtue of authority, right, or supposed right; to challenge as a right; to demand as due; as, to *claim* a debt; to *claim* obedience or respect.
2. to assert as a fact; to state; to maintain; as, he *claims* to speak good French: a frequent and valid use despite objections.
3. to call for; require; deserve; as, this problem *claims* our attention.
4. to proclaim. [Obs.]
5. to call, or name. [Obs.]

Syn.—ask, demand, insist, require, request, maintain.

çlāim, *v.i.* 1. to have a claim; to assert a right.
2. to cry out; to call. [Obs.]

çlāim, *n.* 1. a demand for something rightfully or allegedly due; assertion of one's right to something.
2. a right to demand; a title to any debt, privilege, or other thing in possession of another; as, the prince had a *claim* to the throne.
3. the thing claimed or demanded; as, a settler's *claim*; a miner's *claim*.
4. a statement of something as a fact; assertion.
5. a loud call. [Obs.]

to lay claim to; to assert one's right or title to.

Syn.—pretension, right, title, assertion, statement.

çlāim'à·ble, *a.* that can be claimed.

çlāim'ănt, *n.* a person who makes a claim.

çlāim'ēr, *n.* a claimant.

çlāim'ing rāce, a horse race in which each entering horse must be made available for purchase at a fixed price by anyone entering another horse in the meet.

çlāim'less, *a.* having no claim. [Rare.]

çlāir·ąu'di·ence, *n.* [Fr. *clair*, *clear*, and *audience*, hearing.] the supposed ability to hear or perceive sounds not normally audible: attributed especially to persons in a mesmeric trance.

çlāir·ąu'di·ent, *a.* relating to or having clairaudience.

çlāir·ąu'di·ent, *n.* one who is alleged to have clairaudience.

çlāir'çōle, çlēar'çōle, *n.* [Fr. *claire colle*, clear glue.] a kind of size used in house-painting and in applying gold leaf.

çlāir·voy'ănce, *n.* [Fr. *clair*, clear, and *voyant*, ppr. of *voir*, to see.]
1. a power, attributed to persons in a mesmeric trance, of discerning objects which are not present to the normal senses.
2. keen perception; great insight.

çlāir·voy'ănt, *a.* 1. apparently having clairvoyance.
2. pertaining to clairvoyance.

çlāir·voy'ănt, *n.* a clairvoyant person.

çlam, *n.*; *pl.* **clamș** or **clam**, [from *clamshell*, from *clam* (a clamp).]
1. any of a large variety of hard-shelled bivalve mollusks, some of which live in the shallows of the sea, others in fresh water. The name is variously applied to such bivalve mollusks of North America as the long, soft, or bait clam, *Mya arenaria*; the round or hard clam, or quahog, *Venus mercenaria*; the black clam, surf clam, or hen clam, *Spisula solidissima*, and numerous other species. The first two are highly esteemed as food.
2. the soft, edible part of such a mollusk.

çlam, *v.i.*; clammed, *pt.*, *pp.*; clamming, *ppr.* to dig, or go digging, for clams.

çlam, *n.* a wooden vise or clamp.

çlam, *n.* a cold dampness; clamminess.

çlam, *n.* [abbrev. of *clamor*.] the medley of sounds made by the simultaneous ringing of all the bells in a chime; a crash or clangor, as in a wedding peal.

çlam, *v.t.*; clammed, *pt.*, *pp.*; clamming, *ppr.* [from the same root as AS. *beclemman*, to fasten, stick, *clæman*, to clam, smear.] to clog with glutinous or viscous matter. [Dial.]

çlam, *v.t.* and *v.i.* in bell ringing, to produce a clam or clangor with (bells); to sound all the bells at once.

çlam, *v.i.* to be moist or sticky; to stick; to adhere. [Rare.]

çlā'mănt, *a.* [L. *clamans*, ppr. of *clamare*, to cry out.]
1. clamorous; noisy.
2. demanding attention; urgent.

çlà·mā'tion, *n.* [LL. *clamatio*, from L. *clamare*, to cry out.] the act of crying or calling out. [Obs.]

Çlam·à·tō'rēș, *n.pl.* [L. *clamator*, pl. *clamatores*, a bawler, from *clamare*, to cry out.] a suborder of passerine birds, including the nonoscine forms, which have poorly developed vocal muscles and so have little singing power.

çlam·à·tō'ri·ăl, *a.* pertaining to the *Clamatores*; belonging to the flycatcher family of birds.

çlam'bāke, *n.* 1. a picnic at which steamed or baked clams and other foods are served.
2. the steaming or baking of clams, usually on heated stones and with layers of other foods, as corn, fish, etc., under a covering of seaweed.

çlam'bēr, *v.i.* and *v.t.*; clambered, *pt.*, *pp.*; clambering, *ppr.* [ME. *clamberen*, *clameren*; akin to G. *klammern* in *sich klammern*, to hook oneself on; cling firmly.] to climb by using both hands and feet; climb with difficulty or in a clumsy manner.

çlam'bēr, *n.* the act of clambering; clumsy or hard climb.

çlam·jam'fe·ry, *n.* same as *clanjamfrie*.

çlam'mi·ly, *adv.* in a cold, sticky manner; in a clammy way.

çlam'mi·ness, *n.* the state of being clammy or viscous; stickiness.

çlam'my, *a.*; *comp.* clammier; *superl.* clammiest, [ME. *clam*, moist, clammy.] thick; viscous; adhesive; soft and sticky; glutinous; tenacious; uncomfortably moist and cool.

> Cold sweat, in *clammy* drops, his limbs o'erspread. —Dryden.

çlam'ŏr, *n.* [ME. *clamour*; OFr. *clamour*; L. *clamor*, a loud call, from *clamare*, to cry out.]
1. a great outcry; noise; exclamation; a continued, noisy complaint or demand.
2. figuratively, any loud and continued noise, as of a river or other inanimate thing.

3. a prolonged exhibition of discontent; violent agitation by a mob.

çlam′ŏr, *v.t.*; clamored, *pt.*, *pp.*; clamoring, *ppr.* 1. to stun with noise. [Rare.]
2. to salute loudly. [Rare.]
3. to express or effect with clamor.

çlam′ŏr, *v.i.* to utter loud sounds or outcries; to talk loudly; to complain or demand noisily; as, the crowd *clamored* for bread.

çlam′ŏr·ẽr, *n.* one who clamors.

çlam′ŏr·ous, *a.* 1. talking loudly and continuously; noisy; vociferous; loud; turbulent.
2. loudly demanding or complaining.

çlam′ŏr·ous·ly, *adv.* in a clamorous manner.

çlam′ŏr·ous·ness, *n.* the state or quality of being clamorous.

çlam′our, *n.*, *v.i.*, and *v.t.* clamor. [British spelling.]

çlamp, *n.* [AS. *clam*, *clom*, a band, bond, fetter.]
1. any of various devices for clasping or fastening things together, or for bracing or strengthening parts; especially, an appliance with two parts that can be brought together, usually by screws, to grip and hold something.
2. in nautical usage, (a) a thick plank on the inner part of a ship's side used to sustain the ends of the beams; (b) any plate of iron made to turn or open and shut so as to confine a spar or boom.

çlamp, *v.t.*; clamped, *pt.*, *pp.*; clamping, *ppr.* to fasten, strengthen, or brace with a clamp or clamps; to fix a clamp on.

çlamp, *n.* [var. of *clump*.] a heavy footstep or tread; a tramp.

çlamp, *v.i.* to tread heavily.

çlamp′ẽr, *n.* a metal plate having sharp prongs, designed to be fastened to the shoe or boot, so as to enable a person to walk safely on ice: also called *creeper* and *calk*.

çlamp ī′ron, an andiron.

çlam′shell, *n.* 1. the shell of a clam.
2. a dredging bucket, hinged like the shell of a clam.

çlan, *n.* [Gael. *clann*; Ir. *clann*, *cland*, offspring, children, a tribe, prob. from W. *plant*, offspring; L. *planta*, offshoot.]
1. an early form of social group, as in the Scottish Highlands, composed of several families claiming descent from a common ancestor, bearing the same family name, and following the same chieftain.
2. in certain primitive societies, a tribal division, usually exogamous, of matrilineal or patrilineal descent from a common ancestor.
3. a group of people with interests in common; clique; set.

çlañ′çū·lăr, *a.* clandestine; secret; private; concealed. [Obs.]

çlañ′çū·lăr·ly, *adv.* privately; secretly. [Obs.]

çlan·des′tine (-tin), *a.* [Fr. *clandestin*; L. *clandestinus*, secret, hidden.] secret; private; hidden; withdrawn from public view, generally implying craft, deception, or illicit purpose; furtive; underhand; as, *clandestine* meetings.
Syn.—concealed, secluded, unseen, unknown, private, covert.

çlan·des′tine·ly, *adv.* secretly; privately; in secret.

çlan·des′tine·ness, *n.* secrecy; a state of concealment.

çlan·des·tin′i·ty, *n.* privacy or secrecy.

çlang, *n.* [prob. echoic; compare O.H.G. *chlang*; L. *clangor*, clang, clangor.]
1. a loud, sharp, ringing sound, especially that produced by the collision of metallic bodies; a clank; clangor; as, the *clang* of arms.
2. the loud, harsh sound made by some birds, as cranes.
3. in music, klang.

çlang, *v.i.*; clanged, *pt.*, *pp.*; clanging, *ppr.* 1. to give out a clang; to clank; to resound.
The wood which grides and *clangs*.
—Tennyson.
2. to strike together with a clang.

çlang, *v.t.* 1. to cause to sound with a clang.
They *clanged* their sounding arms.—Prior.
2. to strike together with a clang.

çlañ′gŏr, *n.* [L.] 1. a sharp, shrill, harsh sound; a clang.
2. a persistent clanging.

çlañ′gŏr, *v.i.* to clang.

çlañ′gŏr·ous, *a.* clanging.

çlañ′gŏur, *n.* clangor. [British spelling.]

çlañ′gous, *a.* making a clang, or a shrill, harsh sound. [Obs.]

çlang tint, the quality of a complex tone: also called *clang color*.

çlan·jam′frie, çlan·jam′fry, *n.* rubbish or trumpery; persons who are collectively worthless; a rabble; a mob; canaille: also written *clamjamfery*. [Scot.]

çlañk, *n.* [of echoic origin.] the loud, shrill, sharp sound made by a collision of metallic or other sonorous bodies; a sound less resonant than a clang and shorter in duration.

çlañk, *v.t.*; clanked, *pt.*, *pp.*; clanking, *ppr.* to cause to sound with a clank; to strike with a sharp sound; as, the prisoners *clank* their chains.

çlañk, *v.i.* to sound with a clank.

çlañk′less, *a.* without a clank; not clanking.

çlan′nish, *a.* 1. of a clan.
2. closely united, like a clan; disposed to associate closely, to the exclusion of others, as the members of a clan; cliquish.

çlan′nish·ly, *adv.* in a clannish manner.

çlan′nish·ness, *n.* tendency to associate closely; cliquishness.

çlan′ship, *n.* a state of union, as in a family or clan; an association under a chieftain.

çlanş′măn, *n.*; *pl.* **çlanş′men,** a member of a clan.

çlap, *v.t.*; clapped *or archaic* clapt, *pt.*, *pp.*; clapping, *ppr.* [ME. *clappen*; AS. *clæppian*, to clap, knock; prob. echoic in origin.]
1. to strike together briskly and loudly; as, he *clapped* his hands.
2. to show pleasure at or approval of by clapping the hands.
3. to strike with an open hand, as in hearty greeting or encouragement.
4. to put, move, set, bring to, etc. swiftly and effectively; as, he was *clapped* into jail.
to clap eyes on; to look at; to catch sight of; to see. [Colloq.]
to clap up; (a) to make or complete hastily; as, *to clap up* a peace; (b) to imprison without formality or delay.

çlap, *v.i.* 1. to make a sudden, explosive sound, as of two flat surfaces being struck together.
2. to strike the hands together, usually as a sign of pleasure or approval.
3. to begin or set to work with alacrity and briskness. [Obs.]
4. to knock, as at a door. [Obs.]
5. to chatter; to prattle or prate continually or noisily. [Obs.]

çlap, *n.* 1. a sudden, explosive sound, as of two flat surfaces being struck together; as, a *clap* of thunder.
2. a sudden act or motion; generally in the phrase *at a clap*, that is, all at once.
What, fifty of my followers *at a clap*!
—Shak.
3. a sharp blow; a slap.
4. the act of striking the hands together, as in applauding.
5. in falconry, the lower part of the beak of a hawk.

çlap, *n.* [OFr. *clapoir*, brothel, orig., a rabbit hole.] gonorrhea (often with *the*): a vulgarism.

çlap′board (klab′ẽrd *or* klap′bōrd), *n.* [partial trans. of G. *klapholz*, or L.G. *klapholt*, from *klappen*, to fit, and *holz*, *holt*, wood, board.]
1. a thin, narrow board with one edge thicker than the other, used for covering the outer walls of frame houses.
2. in Great Britain, a small size of board for making wainscoting and barrel staves.

çlap′board (klab′ẽrd *or* klap′bōrd), *v.t.* to cover with clapboards.

çlap′bread, çlap′çāke, *n.* a kind of oatmeal cake rolled out thin and baked hard. [Brit. Dial.]

çlap′dish, *n.* a clackdish.

çlap′match (-mach), *n.* a hooded seal.

çlap′net, *n.* a net in hinged sections for capturing small birds.

çlap′pẽr, *n.* 1. a person who claps, or applauds by clapping.
2. that which makes a clapping sound, as the tongue of a bell, or the piece of wood that strikes a mill hopper.
3. a burrow or enclosure. [Obs.]

çlap′pẽr·çlaw, *v.t.* 1. to fight and scratch. [Archaic or Dial.]
2. to scold; to abuse with the tongue; to revile. [Archaic or Dial.]

çlap′pẽr rāil, a species of rail, *Rallus crepitans*, found in the eastern United States.

çlapse, *v.t.* clasp. [Obs.]

çlapt, *v.* archaic past tense and past participle of *clap*.

çlap′trap, *n.* 1. a contrivance for clapping in theaters. [Obs.]
2. showy, insincere, empty talk, expression, etc., intended only to get applause or notice.

çlap′trap, *a.* showy and cheap.

çlaque (klak), *n.* [Fr., from *claquer*, to clap the hands, to applaud.]
1. a group of people paid to go to a play, opera, etc. and applaud.
2. a group of admiring or fawning followers.

çlȧ·queūr′ (klȧ-kẽr′), *n.* [Fr.] a member of a claque.

çlar·ȧ·bel′lȧ, *n.* [L. *clarus*, clear, and *bellus*, beautiful.] an eight-foot stop in an organ, with open wood pipes, which produces a soft, melodious tone.

çlar′ence, *n.* [from the Duke of *Clarence*, later William IV.] a closed four-wheeled carriage with seats for four inside and a seat for the driver outside.

Çlar′en·cieūx, Çlar′en·ceūx (-sū), *n.* see *king-of-arms*.

çlar′en·dŏn, *n.* [from *Clarendon* Press, Oxford, England.] a style of type with narrow letters of thick, heavy lines.

çlar′et, *n.* [ME. *claret*; OFr. *claret*, clear, claret; L. *clarus*, clear.]
1. a dry red wine; especially, a dry, red Bordeaux wine.
2. purplish red: also *claret red*.

çlar′et, *a.* purplish-red.

çlar′et çup, an iced drink of claret, lemon juice, brandy, sugar, and soda.

çlar·i·bel′lȧ, *n.* same as *clarabella*.

çlar′i·çhord, *n.* [L. *clarus*, clear, and *chorda*, a string.] a clavichord. [Obs.]

çlar″i·fi·çā′tion, *n.* [LL. *clarificatio*, glorification, from L. *clarus*, clear, and *facere*, to make.] the act of clearing; the process of clarifying; as, the *clarification* of impure alcohol.

çlar′i·fi·ẽr, *n.* 1. a person or thing that clarifies; especially, a substance used to clarify wine.
2. a large metal pan in which sugar is clarified.

çlar′i·fȳ, *v.t.* and *v.i.*; clarified, *pt.*, *pp.*; clarifying, *ppr.* [ME. *clarifien*; OFr. *clarifier*; L. *clarificere*, from *clarus*, clear, bright, and *facere*, to make.]
1. to make or become clear and free from impurities: said of liquids, etc.
2. to make or become easier to understand; as, you must *clarify* your meaning.

çlar′i·gāte, *v.i.* to declare war formally. [Obs.]

çlar′i·net, *n.* [Fr. *clarinette*, dim. of *clarine*, little bell; LL. *clario*, a trumpet.] a single-reed, wood-wind instrument with a long wooden or metal tube and a flaring bell, played by means of holes and keys: it is made in various keys, and has a range of about $3\frac{1}{2}$ octaves.

CLARINET

çlar·i·net′ist, çlar·i·net′tist, *n.* a person who plays the clarinet.

çlȧ·rī′nō, *n.* [It., from L. *clarus*, clear.] a four-foot organ stop having reed pipes that sound like a trumpet: also written *clarion*.

çlar′i·ŏn, *n.* [ME. *clarioun*; OFr. *clarion*; LL. *clario*, a trumpet; L. *clarus*, clear.]
1. a kind of trumpet producing clear, sharp, shrill tones.
2. the sound of a clarion, or a sound like this. [Poetic.]

çlar′i·ŏn, *a.* clear, sharp, and shrill; as, a *clarion* call.

çlar′i·ŏn, *v.t.* to announce forcefully or loudly.

çlar″i·ō·net′, *n.* same as *clarinet*.

Çlȧ·risse′, *n.* [Fr.] a member of a Franciscan order of nuns, from the founder of the order, St. Clare, who died A.D. 1253.

çlȧ·ris′si·mō, *n.* a title given to a noble in Venice. [Obs.]

çlar′i·tūde, *n.* clearness; splendor. [Obs.]

çlar′i·ty, *n.* clearness (in various senses).

Çlär′ki·ȧ, *n.* [named after William *Clark* (1770–1838), American explorer.] a small herbaceous genus of annual plants characterized by showy purplish flowers.

çlä′rō, *a.* [Sp., from L. *clarus*, clear.] light-colored and mild: said of cigars.

çlä′rō, *n.* a light-colored and mild cigar.

çlä·rō·ob·sçū′rō, *n.* chiaroscuro. [Obs.]

çlar·rē′ (klar-rā′), *n.* [Fr.] wine mixed with honey and spices, and afterward strained until clear. [Obs.]

çlärt, *v.t.* to daub, smear, or spread with sticky dirt. [Scot. and Brit. Dial.]

çlärt′y, *a.*; *comp.* clartier; *superl.* clartiest, sticky and dirty. [Dial.]

çlăr′y, *v.i.*, to make a loud or shrill noise. [Obs.]

çlā′ry, *n.* [Fr. *sclarée*; LL. *sclarea*, clary.]

1. a plant of the genus *Salvia*, or sage, *Salvia sclarea*.
2. an ornamental variety of this plant.

çlash, *v.i.*; clashed (klasht), *pt., pp.*; clashing, *ppr.* [an imitative word.]
1. to collide or strike together with a loud, harsh, metallic noise.
2. to conflict; to disagree; to fail to harmonize; as, the opinions of men *clash*; *clashing* interests.
Independent jurisdictions could not fail to *clash*. —Dwight.

çlash, *v.t.* to strike together, bring together, shut, etc. with a loud, harsh, metallic noise.

çlash, *n.* 1. a loud, harsh noise, as of two metallic objects colliding.
2. opposition; conflict; disagreement; lack of harmony.

çlash'ing·ly, *adv.* with clashing.

çlȧsp, *n.* [ME. *claspe, clapse.*]
1. a fastening, as a hook, buckle, or catch, to hold two things or parts together.
2. a holding; grasping; embrace.
3. a grip of the hand.

çlȧsp, *v.t.*; clasped *or archaic* claspt, *pt., pp.*; clasping, *ppr.* [ME. *claspen*, from the *n.*]
1. to fasten with a clasp.
2. to hold tightly with the arms or hands; grasp firmly; embrace.
3. to grip with the hand.
4. to entwine about; cling to.

çlȧsp'ẽr, *n.* 1. one who or that which clasps.
2. in botany, a tendril.
3. in zoology, (a) a portion of the male reproductive organ used in a clasping manner, as by certain insects; (b) one of the organs on the ventral fins, used in sexual union, developed in some male fish, as the sharks and rays.

çlȧsp'ẽred, *a.* furnished with tendrils or claspers.

çlȧsp knīfe (nīf), a knife commonly used in hunting, having a folding blade which, when open, is generally held firmly by a catch.

çlȧsp lock, a lock in which the catch fastens itself automatically.

çlȧspt, *v.* archaic past tense and past participle of *clasp*.

çlȧss, *n.* [Fr. *classe*; L. *classis*, a class or division of the Roman people; Gr. *klēsis*, a calling, summons, from *kalein*, to call.]
1. a number of people or things grouped together because of certain likenesses or common traits; kind; sort; as, an inferior *class* of novels.
2. a group of people considered as a unit according to economic, occupational, or social status; especially, a social rank or caste; as, the working *class*, the middle *class*.
3. high social rank or caste.
4. the division of society into ranks or castes.
5. a group of students taught together according to standing, subject, etc.
6. a meeting of such a group.
7. a group of students graduating together; as, the *class* of 1960.
8. a division or grouping according to grade or quality.
9. grade or quality.
10. conscripted troops, or men liable to conscription, all of whom were born in the same year; as, they called up the *class* of 1931.
11. in biology, a group of animals or plants having a common basic structure and ranking below a *phylum* and above an *order*.
12. excellence, especially of style, appearance, etc. [Slang.]
13. in the Methodist Church, a section of the congregation under the leadership of one of their number.
class of a curve; in geometry, the numerical class to which a curve belongs as determined by the number of tangential lines which may be drawn to it from a given point. Thus, two lines may be drawn from a point tangent to a circle; consequently a circle is a curve of the second class.
class of a surface; in geometry, the numerical class to which a surface belongs as determined by the number of tangential planes which may be passed through a given line to a given surface.
Syn.—order, rank, degree, category, grade, division, genus, kind, group.

çlȧss, *v.t.*; classed, *pt., pp.*; classing, *ppr.* 1. to put in a class or classes; to rank together; to refer to a class or group; to classify.
2. to place in ranks or divisions, as students that are pursuing the same studies; to form into a class or classes.

çlȧss, *v.i.* to be grouped or arranged in classes.

çlȧss'ȧ·ble, *a.* adapted to arrangement in classes; capable of being classed.

çlȧss aç'tion sūit, a legal action brought by one or more persons on behalf of themselves and a much larger group, all of whom have the same grounds for action: also *class action*.

çlȧss book, 1. a book in which a teacher records grades, absences, etc.
2. a book published by members of a class in a school or college, containing pictures of students and teachers, an account of student activities, etc.

çlȧss'-çon'scious, *a.* having or showing class consciousness.

çlȧss çon'scious·ness, an awareness of belonging to or constituting a class in the social order, with definite economic interests; sense of class solidarity.

çlȧss dāy, a day set aside during the commencement period of American schools and colleges, for the presentation of a play, a class history, a class oration, etc. by the members of the senior class.

çlas'siç, *a.* [L. *classicus*, relating to the classes of the Roman people, especially to the highest class; hence, superior, from *classis*, a class.]
1. of the highest class; most representative of the excellence of its kind; having recognized worth.
2. in accordance with established principles of excellence in the arts and sciences.
3. of the art, literature, and culture of the ancient Greeks and Romans, or their writers, artists, etc.
4. like or characteristic of the literary and artistic standards, principles, and methods of the ancient Greeks and Romans.
5. balanced, formal, objective, austere, regular, simple, etc.: a term variously interpreted, generally opposed to *romantic*.
6. famous as traditional or typical. [Colloq.]

çlas'siç, *n.* 1. a writer, artist, etc. generally recognized as excellent.
2. a literary or artistic work generally recognized as of the highest excellence.
3. a classicist. [Rare.]
4. a famous traditional or typical event; as, this football game is a *classic*. [Colloq.]
5. a woman's suit, dress, etc. made in a traditional style. [Slang.]
the classics; the literature or language of the ancient Greeks and Romans.

çlas'siç·ăl, *a.* 1. classic (senses 1, 3, 4, 5).
2. learned in and devoted to Greek and Roman culture, literature, etc.
3. designating or of music that conforms to certain established standards of form, complexity, musical literacy, etc.; as, symphonies, concertos, sonatas, etc. are called *classical* music: variously distinguished from *popular, romantic, modern*.
4. designating or of a course of study that is standard and traditionally authoritative, not new and experimental; as, *classical* political science.

çlas'siç·ăl·iṣm, *n.* same as *classicism*.

çlas'siç·ăl·ist, *n.* same as *classicist*.

çlas·siç·al'i·ty, *n.* 1. the quality of being classical.
2. classical scholarship.
3. anything that has a classical quality.

çlas'siç·ăl·ly, *adv.* in a classical manner or style.

çlas'si·ciṣm, *n.* 1. the aesthetic principles and methods regarded as characteristic of ancient Greece and Rome; objectivity, formality, balance, simplicity, dignity, restraint, etc.: generally contrasted with *romanticism*.
2. adherence to these principles or to principles derived from them.
3. knowledge of the literature and art of ancient Greece and Rome; classical scholarship.
4. a Greek or Latin idiom or expression.

çlas'si·cist, *n.* 1. a person who advocates or follows the principles of classicism.
2. a student of or specialist in ancient Greek and Roman literature.
3. a person who advocates the teaching of Greek and Latin in the schools.

çlas'si·cize, *v.t.*; classicized, *pt., pp.*; classicizing, *ppr.* to make classic.

çlas'si·cize, *v.i.* to use or affect a classic style or form.

çlas'si·fī·ȧ·ble, *a.* capable of being classified.

çlas"si·fi·çā'tion, *n.* 1. a classifying or being classified; arrangement according to some systematic division into classes or groups.
2. in biology, a system of arranging all living organisms into groups based on some factor common to each, as structure or natural relationship: the categories now used are, from the broadest to the narrowest, *phylum* (in botany, *division*), *class, order, family, genus, species*, and *variety*.

çlas'si·fi·çā·tō·ry, *a.* relating to or using classification.

çlas'si·fied (-fīd), *a.* placed in or divided into groups or classes.
classified advertisement; an advertisement or other public notice listed categorically under its particular subject and printed in a part of a publication reserved for such material.
classified advertising; public notices or advertising, listed according to subject in a special section of a publication.
classified bonds or stocks; in finance, the bonds or stocks issued by a company and divided into different groups, each of which has some special characteristic such as a higher interest rate.
classified civil service; that type of service into which, according to acts of 1853 and 1949 U. S. government clerks are classified.

çlas'si·fī·ẽr, *n.* 1. a person who classifies.
2. a term used to designate a certain class of objects, as in Chinese grammar.
3. in ore dressing, a piece of machinery used to separate the ground-up ore into grades to expedite the refining process.

çlas'si·fȳ, *v.t.*; classified, *pt., pp.*; classifying, *ppr.* [L. *classis*, a class, and *facere*, to make.]
1. to arrange or group in classes according to some system or principle.
2. to place in a class or category.
3. to designate (governmental documents, reports, etc.) to be secret or confidential and available only to authorized persons.

çlas'sis, *n.*; *pl.* **çlas'sēṣ**, [L. *classis*, a class.]
1. a church court or governing group consisting of the pastors and elders from the churches in the district.
2. the jurisdiction of such a body.

çlass'less, *a.* having no distinct social or economic classes; as, a *classless* society.

çlȧss'măn, *n.*; *pl.* **çlȧss'men**, 1. a classmate.
2. in English universities, a candidate for graduation in arts who has passed an examination in one of the departments in which honors are conferred, and who is placed according to merit in one of several classes.

çlȧss'māte, *n.* a fellow member in a class at school or college.

çlȧss'room, *n.* a room for recitations, etc. of a class in a school or college.

çlȧss strug'gle, in Marxism, the constant economic and political struggle held to exist between social classes regarded as exploiting and those regarded as exploited; specifically, in capitalist countries, the struggle between the capitalists (bourgeoisie) and the industrial workers (proletariat).

çlȧss'y, *a.*; *comp.* classier; *superl.* classiest; first-class, especially in style or manner; elegant; fine. [Slang.]

çlas'tiç, *a.* [Gr. *klastos*, broken in pieces, from *klaein*, to break; and *-ic*.]
1. designating an anatomical model with removable sections to show internal structure.
2. in geology, consisting of fragments of older rocks.

çlatch (klach), *n.* 1. soft mud. [Scot.]
2. a slattern. [Scot.]

çlath'rāte, *a.* [L. *clathri*; Gr. *klēthra*, a trellis, grate.] in botany, latticed; divided like latticework; reticulated: also written *clathroid*.

çlath'rōse, *a.* in entomology, barred or latticed, sometimes at right angles.

çlat'tẽr, *v.i.*; clattered, *pt., pp.*; clattering, *ppr.* [ME. *clateren*, to clatter; AS. *clatrung*, a clattering; imitative in origin.]
1. to make rattling sounds; to make repeated sharp sounds, as by striking sonorous bodies; as, to *clatter* on a shield.
2. to talk fast and idly; to run on.

çlat'tẽr, *v.t.* to strike so as to produce a rattling noise from.

çlat'tẽr, *n.* 1. a rapid succession of abrupt, sharp sounds, made by the collision of metallic or other sonorous bodies; rattling sounds.
2. tumultuous and confused noise.
3. noisy chatter.

çlat'tẽr·ẽr, *n.* one who clatters; a babbler.

çlat'tẽr·ing·ly, *adv.* with a clattering noise.

çlău·di·çā'tion, *n.* [from L. *claudicare*, to limp.] a halting or limping.

çlauṣ'ăl, *a.* of or constituting a clause.

çlauṣe, *n.* [ME. *clause*; OFr. *clause*; I L. *clausa*, a clause; L. *clausula*, a clause, close of a period, from *clausus*, pp. of *claudere*, to close.]
1. a group of words containing a subject and verb, usually forming part of a compound

or complex sentence: a dependent (subordinate) clause functions as a noun, adjective, or adverb; an independent (principal) clause states the main predication. In English, the most obvious formal difference between a clause and a sentence is that the latter begins with silence and ends with an ending pitch, the former begins or ends with a suspension pitch: clauses may be joined by parataxis (The house is secluded; you will like it), by modified parataxis (The house is secluded, and you will like it), and by hypotaxis (Because the house is secluded, you will like it).

2. a particular article, stipulation, or provision in a formal or legal document.

çlause, *n.* close; conclusion. [Obs.]

çlaus'trăl, *a.* [L. *claustrum*, a fastening, an enclosed place, from *claudere*, to close.] relating to a cloister or religious house; cloistral.

çlaus·trō·phō'bi·à, *n.* abnormal fear of being confined, as in a room or small space.

çlaus'trum, *n.*; *pl.* **çlaus'trà**, [L. *claustra*, neut. pl., a bar, lock.] a thin layer of the cortical part of each cranial hemisphere in man.

çlau'sū·lăr, *a.* consisting of or having clauses.

çlau'şūre, *n.* [ME. *clausure*; L. *clausura*, an enclosure, from *claudere*, to close.] the act of shutting up or confining; confinement. [Obs.]

çlā'và, *n.*; *pl.* **çlā'vae**, [L. *clava*, a knotty branch or club.] the blunt, knobbed end of the antenna in some insects.

çlā'văl, *a.* pertaining to or resembling a clavus or clava.

çlā'vāte, çlā'vā·ted, *a.* [L. *clava*, a club.] club-shaped; having the form of a club; growing gradually thicker toward the top, as certain parts of a plant.

çlāve, archaic past tense of *cleave*.

çlav'e·cin, *n.* same as *harpsichord*.

çlav'el·lāte, *a.* diminutive of *clavate*.

çlav'el·lā·ted, *a.* designating potash made from the dried and calcined lees of wine.

çlav'ẽr, *n.* same as *clover*. [Brit. Dial.]

çlav'ẽr, *v.i.* to talk idly and foolishly; to talk much and at random. [Scot.]

çlav"i·à·tūre', *n.* [D. *claviatuur*, from L. *clavis*, a key.]

1. the part of a piano or organ occupied by the keys.

2. a system of fingering adapted to a musical keyboard.

çlav'i·çhord, *n.* [L. *clavis*, a key, and *chorda*, a string.] a stringed musical instrument with a keyboard, from which the piano developed: it somewhat resembles the harpsichord, except that when the keys are pressed, the strings are struck by little hammers rather than plucked.

çlav'i·çle (-kl), *n.* [L. *clavicula*, dim. of *clavis*, a key or lock.] the collarbone, forming one of the elements of the pectoral arch in vertebrate animals. In man and various quadrupeds there are two clavicles, each joined at one end to the scapula, or shoulder blade, and at the other to the sternum, or breastbone. In many quadrupeds the clavicles are absent or rudimentary, while in birds they are united in one piece, popularly called the *wishbone*.

çlav'i·çorn, *a.* [L. *clava*, a club, and *cornu*, a horn.] having the antennae club-shaped.

çlav'i·çorn, *n.* one of the family *Clavicornia*.

çlav·i·çor'nāte, *a.* in zoology, having club-shaped antennae.

Çlav·i·çor'ni·à, *n.pl.* [L., from *clava*, a club, and *cornu*, a horn.] a group of pentamerous beetles: so named from the antenna, which terminates in a club-shaped enlargement.

çlà·viç'ū·lăr, *a.* pertaining to the collarbone, or clavicle.

çlav'i·form, *a.* club-shaped.

çlav'i·ġẽr, *n.* [L. *clavis*, a key, and *gerere*, to carry.] one who keeps the keys of a place.

çlav'i·ġẽr, *n.* [L. *claviger*, a club bearer; *clava*, a club, and *gerere*, to bear.] a bearer of a club.

çlà·viġ'ẽr·ous, *a.* 1. bearing a club.

2. bearing a key or keys.

çlā'vis, *n.*; *pl.* **çlā'vēş**, [L.] a key, as to a book or cipher.

çlav'ō·là, *n.*; *pl.* **çlav'ō·lae**, [L., dim. of *clava*, a club.] the knobbed end of an antenna.

çlā'vus, *n.*; *pl.* **çlā'vī**, [L. *clavus*, a nail.]

1. a callous growth; a corn.

2. the thickened portion of the fore wings of certain insects.

çlaw, *n.* [ME. *claw*; AS. *clawu*, a claw, hoof.]

1. a sharp, hooked or curved nail on the foot of an animal or bird

2. a foot with such nails at its end.

3. the pincers (chela) of a lobster, crab, scorpion, etc.

4. anything resembling or regarded as a claw; as, the *claw* of a hammer.

çlaw, *v.t.* and *v.i.*; clawed, *pt.*, *pp.*; clawing, *ppr.* [ME. *clawen*; AS. *clawian*, to claw, scratch.]

1. to tear, scratch, pull, or seize with, or as with, claws or nails.

Like wild beasts shut up in a cage, to *claw* and bite each other to their mutual destruction. —Burke.

2. to scratch gently, as an itching part, with intent to gratify. [Brit. Dial.]

Look, whether the wither'd elder hath not his poll *claw'd* like a parrot. —Shak.

3. to fawn on; to flatter. [Brit. Dial.]

Rich men they *claw*, soothe up, and flatter; the poor they contemn and despise. —Holland.

4. in nautical usage, to beat to windward, to prevent falling on a lee shore or on another vessel.

to claw off, *to claw away*; to rail at; to scold. [Obs.]

çlaw'back, *n.* one who flatters; a sycophant; a wheedler. [Obs.]

çlaw'back, *a.* flattering. [Obs.]

çlaw'back, *v.t.* to flatter. [Obs.]

çlawed, *a.* furnished with claws.

çlaw ham'mẽr, a hammer with one end of the head forked and curved like a claw, for drawing nails out of wood.

claw-hammer coat; a full-dress or swallowtail coat: sometimes contracted to *claw hammer*. [Colloq.]

çlaw hatch'et, a hatchet with one end of the head forked.

çlaw'less, *a.* having no claws.

çlāy, *n.* [ME. *clay*, *cley*; AS. *clæg*, clay.]

1. a firm, plastic, fine-grained earth, chiefly aluminum silicate: it is produced by the deposit of fine rock particles in water, and used in the manufacture of bricks, pottery, and other ceramics.

2. (a) earth, especially as a symbol of the material of the human body; (b) the human body.

fatty clay; any clay having a greasy feeling.

firebrick clay; a clay having no fusible constituents.

porcelain clay; see *kaolin*.

potter's clay; any clay, including kaolin, suitable by reason of its composition for the making of earthenware, pottery, etc.

çlāy, *a.* formed or consisting of clay; as, a *clay* soil.

çlāy, *v.t.*; clayed, *pt.*, *pp.*, claying, *ppr.* 1. to cover with clay.

2. to purify and whiten by treating with clay, as sugar.

3. to mix with clay.

çlāy'bañk, *n.* a yellowish-brown color.

çlāy'-çōld, *a.* cold as clay or earth; lifeless.

çlāy'ey, *a.* 1. of, containing, or full of clay.

2. like clay.

3. soiled with clay.

çlāy'ish, *a.* partaking of the nature of clay, or containing particles of it.

çlāy märl, a whitish, smooth, chalky clay.

çlāy'mōre, *n.* [Gael. *claidheamhmor*, a great sword; *claidheamh*, a sword, and *mor*, great; comp. L. *gladius*, a sword, and *magnus*, great.] the large two-edged broadsword formerly used by the Scotch Highlanders.

çlāy piġ'eŏn, a disk of clay, etc. tossed into the air from the trap as a target in trap shooting.

çlāy pit, a pit from which clay is dug.

çlāy slāte, a rock consisting of clay which has been hardened and otherwise changed, for the most part extremely fissile and often producing good roofing slate.

çlāy stōne, 1. a rounded mass of limestone formed in a clay deposit.

2. a kind of rock containing clay.

Çlāy·tō'ni·à, *n.* [from John *Clayton*, a Virginia botanist.]

1. a genus of low, smooth herbs of the family *Portulacaceæ*, comprising the spring beauties.

2. [c—] any plant of this genus.

-cle, [from L. *-culus*, *-cula*, *-culum*.] a suffix added to nouns to form the diminutive, as in such words as arti*cle*, parti*cle*, mus*cle*, corpus*cle*, etc.

çlead'ing, *n.* [Brit. Dial. and Scot. form of *clothing*.]

1. in engines, the jacket or outer covering of the cylinder; also, a casing of a locomotive engine and firebox; also, the covering put on steam pipes to prevent the radiation of heat.

2. any kind of plank covering, such as the slating boards of a roof, the boards of a floor, the plank lining of a pit shaft, the planking of a cofferdam, etc.

çlēan, *a.* [ME. *clene*, *clæne*; AS. *clæne*, clean, bright.]

1. clear of dirt or filth; having all uncleanness removed; unmixed with matter foreign to the substance itself; unadulterated; pure; unsoiled; unstained.

2. free from flaws, imperfection, or defect; as, *clean* timber.

3. clean-limbed; well-proportioned; shapely; lithe.

Thy waist is straight and *clean*.—Waller.

4. free from awkwardness; not clumsy or bungling; dexterous; adroit; clever; deft; as, a *clean* boxer; a *clean* leap; a *clean* trick.

5. free from limitation or any modifying quality or circumstance; entire; complete; thorough.

6. in whale fishing, having no fish or oil aboard; as, the ship returned *clean*.

7. free from moral impurity, guilt, or blame; innocent; sinless; as, a *clean* man.

8. in the Bible, (a) free or freed from ceremonial defilement; (b) fit for food: said of certain animals.

9. free from vulgarism or indecency; as, *clean* literature.

10. recently laundered.

11. habitually avoiding filth.

12. free from writing: said of paper, etc.

13. legible; having few corrections; as, *clean* copy should be sent to the printer.

to come clean; to confess; to tell the truth. [Slang.]

with clean hands; without guilt.

Syn.—clear, spotless, pure, purified, cleansed, untarnished.

çlēan, *adv.* 1. quite; perfectly; wholly; entirely; fully.

The people passed *clean* over Jordan. —Josh. iii. 17.

2. in a clean manner.

çlēan, *v.t.*; cleaned; *pt.*, *pp.*; cleaning, *ppr.* 1. to make clean; to remove all foreign matter from; to purify; to cleanse; as, to *clean* a ship's bottom; to *clean* a house; to *clean* a field or garden.

2. to prepare (fish, fowl, etc.) for cooking.

3. in weight lifting, to lift (a barbell) from the floor to the shoulders in one continuous movement: cf. *clean and jerk*.

to clean out; (a) [Colloq.] to deprive of all available means; to exhaust the pecuniary resources of; (b) to empty so as to make clean; (c) to empty.

to clean up; (a) to make clean, neat, or orderly; (b) [Colloq.] to dispose of completely; to finish.

to clean up on; to defeat; to beat. [Slang.]

çlēan, *v.i.* 1. to be made clean.

2. to perform the act of cleaning.

to clean up; (a) to make oneself clean and neat; to get washed, combed, etc.; (b) [Slang.] to make much money or profit.

çlēan and jẽrk, in weight lifting, a lift in which the barbell is cleaned and then thrust quickly overhead so that the arms are completely extended.

çlēan'-bred, *a.* well-bred.

çlēan'-çut', *a.* 1. clearly and sharply outlined.

2. well-formed.

3. distinct; clear.

4. good-looking, trim, neat, etc.; as, a *clean-cut* young fellow.

çlēan'ẽr, *n.* 1. a person whose work is cleaning up rooms, buildings, etc.

2. a person who owns, operates, or works in a dry-cleaning establishment.

3. a tool or device for cleaning.

4. a preparation for removing stains, grease, or other dirt.

çlēan'-hand'ed, *a.* 1. having clean hands.

2. figuratively, free from moral taint or suspicion; as, he went out of court *clean-handed*.

çlēan"hand'ed·ness, *n.* the state or quality of being clean-handed.

çlēan'ing, *n.* 1. the act of making clean.

2. the afterbirth of cows, ewes, etc. [Brit. Dial.]

çlean'li·ly (klen'), *adv.* in a cleanly manner.

çlēan'-limbed' (-limd'), *a.* having well-proportioned, symmetrical limbs; lithe; lissome.

çlean'li·ness (klen'), *n.* the state or quality of being cleanly; freedom from dirt, filth, or any foul, extraneous matter; neatness of person or dress; purity.

çlean'ly (klen'), *a.*; *comp.* cleanlier; *superl.* cleanliest, 1. free from dirt, filth, or any foul matter; neat; carefully avoiding filth; having clean habits.

2. free from injurious or polluting influence; pure; innocent. [Obs.]
3. cleansing; making clean; as, *cleanly* powder. [Obs.]
4. nice; artful; dexterous; adroit; as, a *cleanly* play; a *cleanly* evasion. [Obs.]
5. always kept clean.

çlēan'ly, *adv.* 1. in a clean manner; neatly; as, he was *cleanly* dressed.
2. purely; innocently.
3. cleverly; adroitly; dexterously. [Obs.]

çlēan'ness, *n.* the state or quality of being clean; specifically, (a) freedom from dirt, filth, and foreign matter; neatness; (b) freedom from ceremonial pollution; (c) exactness, purity, justness, correctness: said of language or style; (d) purity; innocence.

çleanṣ'á·ble (klenz'), *a.* capable of being cleansed.

çleanṣe (klenz), *v.t.*; cleansed, *pt., pp.*; cleansing, *ppr.* 1. to make clean.
2. to purify; to free from impurity, guilt, infection, or whatever is unseemly, noxious, or offensive.
Cleanse thou me from secret faults.
—Ps. xix. 12.
3. to remove; to purge away.

çleanṣ'ẽr (klenz'), *n.* one who or that which cleanses; specifically, a preparation for cleaning.

çlēan'-shāv'en, *adj.* having all the hairs shaved off.

çleanṣ'ing (klenz'), *a.* adapted to cleanse.

çleanṣ'ing (klenz'), *n.* the act of cleaning, purifying, or purging.

çleanṣ'ing-dāyṣ, *n.pl.* Ash Wednesday and the three following days.

çleanṣ'ing week, the week beginning with Quinquagesima Sunday; also called *chaste week.*

çlēan'skin, çlēar'skin, *n.* in Australia, an unbranded bullock or calf: called a *maverick* in the United States.

çlēan'-tim"bẽred, *a.* well-proportioned; symmetrical in shape; clean-limbed. [Poet.]
I think Hector was not so *clean-timbered.*
—Shak.

çlēan'up, *n.* 1. a cleaning up.
2. in mining, the gathering together of gold after the process of washing or stamping; hence, the gold so gathered.
3. profit; gain. [Slang.]

çlēar, *a.* [ME. *clere, cler*; OFr. *cler, clair*; L. *clarus*, clear, bright.]
1. free from darkness or mist; brilliant; light; luminous; unclouded; not obscured; as, a *clear* day.
2. free from that which would dim the transparency or bright color of a thing; as, *clear* water; a *clear* complexion; *clear* sand.
The stream is so transparent, pure, and *clear*. —Denham.
3. not confused or dull; having the power of perceiving or comprehending quickly; orderly; acute; discriminating; as, a *clear* intellect.
4. easily seen or comprehended; free from obscurity; easily intelligible; perspicuous; distinct; lucid; as, a *clear* statement.
5. evident; manifest; indisputable; undeniable.
Remained to our Almighty foe *clear* victory.
—Milton.
6. free from that which perturbs; undisturbed by care or passion; unruffled; serene.
To whom the Son with calm aspect and *clear*. —Milton.
7. free from guilt or blame; morally unblemished; innocent.
Duncan hath been so *clear* in his great office.
—Shak.
8. free from a legal charge or suspicion of guilt.
9. free from debt.
To get *clear* of all the debts I owe.—Shak.
10. free from impediment or obstruction; unobstructed; as, a *clear* view.
11. sounding distinctly; distinctly audible; as, his voice was loud and *clear*; also, ringing; resonant; as, the bell has a *clear* tone.
12. without diminution or deduction; in full; net; as, *clear* profit or gain.
13. free from dimness or blur; easily seen; sharply defined; distinct; as, a *clear* outline.
14. certain; positive; as, I am *clear* on the matter.
15. free from qualification; absolute; complete.
16. free from contact or connection.
17. freed or emptied of freight or cargo.
clear breach; see under *breach*, n.
clear days; in law, days reckoned exclusively of the one at the beginning and the one at the end of the period under discussion; as, there are thirteen *clear days* between the first and fifteenth of a month.
clear stuff; lumber free from knots.
Syn.—lucid, bright, vivid, apparent, distinct, evident, free, guiltless, manifest, obvious, perspicuous, plain, pure.—A mere freedom from stain or dullness constitutes *clear*; *bright* supposes a certain strength of light; *vivid* a freshness combined with the strength, and even a degree of brilliancy.

çlēar, *n.* 1. a clear space.
2. clearance.
in the clear; (a) free from enclosing or limiting obstructions; (b) [Colloq.] free from suspicion, guilt, etc.

çlēar, *adv.* 1. in a clear manner; clearly; plainly; not obscurely; manifestly.
2. quite; entirely; wholly: used as an intensive; as, to go *clear* through; to cut a piece *clear* off; to go *clear* away. [Colloq.]

çlēar, *v.t.*; cleared, *pt., pp.*; clearing, *ppr.* 1. to make clear or bright; remove whatever diminishes the brightness, transparency, or purity of; as, to *clear* the sky.
2. to free from obscurity, perplexity, or ambiguity; to make intelligible, plain, or lucid; as, to *clear* a question or theory.
Let a god descend, and *clear* the business to the audience. —Dryden.
3. to free from obstructions; to free from any impediment or encumbrance; as, to *clear* land of trees.
4. to free; to liberate or disengage (a person or thing) *of* or *from* something; as, to *clear* a man *from* debt, obligation, or duty.
5. to free from a legal charge or suspicion of guilt; to justify or vindicate; to acquit.
That will by no means *clear* the guilty.
Ex. xxxiv. 7.
6. to gain or profit beyond all expenses and charges; to net.
He *clears* but two hundred thousand crowns a year. —Addison.
7. to leap over or pass by without touching; as, to *clear* a fence, hedge, or ditch; to *clear* a rock at sea.
8. in maritime affairs, to free (a ship or cargo) by satisfying harbor and customs requirements.
9. to remove; to get rid of; as, to *clear* the sea of pirates.
10. to unload; to empty; as, they *cleared* the freighter of cargo.
11. to pass without contact; as, the tug cleared the bridge.
12. to discharge (a debt) by paying it.
13. to rid (the throat) of phlegm by hawking or coughing.
14. to rid (the voice) of hoarseness in the same manner.
15. to make (the eyesight) clear or sharp.
16. in banking, to pass (a check, etc.) through a clearinghouse.
to clear away; (a) to take away so as to leave a cleared space; (b) to go away; to go out of sight.
to clear hawse; to disentangle twisted cables.
to clear off; (a) to clear away; (b) to remove something from in order to make clear.
to clear out; (a) to clear by emptying; (b) [Colloq.] to go away; depart.
to clear the air (or *atmosphere*); to get rid of emotional tensions, misunderstandings, etc.
to clear (*the decks*) *for action*; (a) to remove all encumbrances from the decks and prepare for a fight; hence, (b) to get ready for any action.
to clear the land; to gain such a distance from shore as to have open sea room and be out of danger from the land.
to clear up; (a) to make or become clear; (b) to make orderly; (c) to become unclouded, sunny, etc. after being cloudy or stormy; (d) to explain.
Syn.—exculpate, exonerate, absolve, acquit, relieve, justify, whitewash, release, set free, extricate, vindicate.

çlēar, *v.i.* 1. to become clear; to become free from clouds or fog; to become fair; also, to pass away or disappear from the sky; often followed by *up, off,* or *away*; as, the mist *clears off* or *away.*
So foul a sky *clears* not without a storm.
—Shak.
Advise him to stay till the weather *clears up.*
—Swift.
2. to be disengaged from encumbrances, distress, or entanglements; to become free or disengaged. [Obs.]
3. in banking, to exchange checks and bills and settle balances, as in clearinghouses.
4. to satisfy harbor and customs requirements in discharging a cargo or leaving a port (often with *in* or *out*): said of a ship.

çlēar'āġe, *n.* the act of removing anything; a clearing.

çlēar'ănce, *n.* 1. the act of clearing; as, the *clearance* of land from trees; the *clearance* of an estate from unprofitable tenantry.
2. clear or net profit; profit over all expenses. [Rare.]
3. (a) a certificate that a ship or vessel has been cleared at the customhouse and is authorized to enter or leave port: also called *clearance papers*; (b) the act or process of meeting the requirements for getting this certificate.
4. the clear space between a passing object and the sides or roof of its passageway, as on a bridge, in a tunnel, etc.
5. the distance separating moving objects or mechanical parts.
6. in banking, the adjustment of debits and credits, exchange of checks, etc. in a clearinghouse.

çlēar'ănce sāle, a sale to get rid of old merchandise and make room for new.

çlēar'çōle, *n.* see *clairecole.*

çlēar'-çut', *a.* 1. formed with clear, sharp, or delicately defined outlines, as if by cutting.
2. distinct; plain.

çlēar'ed·ness, *n.* the state or quality of being cleared. [Rare.]

çlēar'ẽr, *n.* 1. one who or that which clears.
2. a fine-toothed comb or tool on which hemp is finished for lines and twines used by sailmakers.

çlēar'eȳed (-īd), *a.* having bright, clear eyes; keen of sight or perception.

çlēar'head'ed (-hed'), *a.* clear in understanding; not confused or mentally clouded; quick to perceive and understand.

çlēar'head'ed·ness, *n.* the quality of being clearheaded; intelligence.

çlēar'ing, *n.* 1. the process of making clear or freeing from anything; as, the *clearing* of land; the *clearing* of a statement; the *clearing* of a suspect.
2. in banking, (a) the exchanging of checks, etc. and balancing of accounts between banks; (b) the procedure for doing this; (c) [*pl.*] the amount of the balances thus settled.
3. in English railway management, the act of distributing among the different companies the proceeds of the through traffic passing over several railways, the necessary calculations being made in the railway clearinghouse in London.
4. a place or tract of land cleared of wood and underbrush.

çlēar'ing·house, *n.* the place maintained by a group of banks as a center for exchanging checks and drafts drawn against one another, and adjusting balances.

çlēar'ing·house ā'ġent, in banking, a clearinghouse bank which puts through checks for banks which are not members.

çlēar'ing stōne, a whetstone used for sharpening curriers' knives after grinding.

çlēar'ly, *adv.* 1. in a clear manner; plainly; evidently; fully; as, the fact is *clearly* proved.
2. without obstruction; luminously; as, to shine *clearly.*
3. with clear discernment; as, to understand *clearly.*
4. without entanglement or confusion.
5. plainly; honestly; candidly.
Deal *clearly* and impartially with yourselves. —Tillotson.
6. without reserve, evasion, or subterfuge.
Syn.—plainly, distinctly, obviously, palpably, evidently, lucidly, perspicuously, explicitly.

çlēar'ness, *n.* 1. the state or quality of being clear; freedom from anything that diminishes brightness, transparency, or purity of color; as, the *clearness* of water or other liquid; *clearness* of skin.
2. freedom from obstruction or encumbrance; as, the *clearness* of the ground.
3. discernment; perceptiveness; as, *clearness* of understanding.
4. distinctness; perspicuity; lucidity; as, the *clearness* of views, of arguments, of explanations.

çlēar'-see"ing, *a.* having a clear sight or understanding.

çlēar'-shīn"ing, *a.* shining with brightness or unobstructed splendor.

çlēar'-sīght"ed (-sīt"ed), *a.* seeing with clearness; having acuteness of sight; also, discerning; perspicacious; as, *clear-sighted* reason; a *clear-sighted* judge.

çlēar″-sīght′ed·ness, *n.* the state or quality of being clear-sighted; acute discernment.

çlēar′skin, *n.* same as *cleanskin.*

çlēar′stärch, *v.t.* and *v.i.*; clearstarched, *pt., pp.*; clearstarching, *ppr.* to stiffen (laundry) with a colorless solution of starch.

çlēar′stärch″ēr, *n.* one who clearstarches.

çlēar′stärch″ing, *n.* the act of stiffening with starch.

çlēar′stō″ry, *n.* same as *clerestory.*

çlēar′weed, *n.* a variety of nettle, *Pilea pumila,* with a smooth pellucid stem, found in cool, moist soil.

çlēar′wing, *n.* a moth of the family *Ægeriidæ,* having wings transparent or partially transparent in the middle.

çlēat, *n.* [ME. *clete, clyte,* a wedge; from same root as D. *kloot,* a ball; G. *kloss,* lump, clod.]

1. CLEAT 2. DECK CLEAT 3. THUMB CLEAT

1. a piece of wood or metal used in a ship to fasten ropes to. It is formed with one arm or two, or with a hollow, to receive a rope, and is made fast to some part of a vessel. There are several kinds of cleats on board vessels, such as belaying cleats, deck cleats, and thumb cleats.

2. a piece of metal fastened to a shoe to give secure footing.

3. in joinery, a piece of wood nailed transversely or otherwise fastened, and used as a strengthener or support.

4. a strip of wood or metal fastened to something to prevent slipping, as on gangways, etc.

5. in coal mining, the principal set of planes or facings in the natural cleavage of coal.

çlēat, *v.t.*; cleated, *pt., pp.*; cleating, *ppr.* to fasten to or with a cleat.

çlēav′à·ble, *a.* capable of being cleft or divided.

çlēav′āġe, *n.* 1. the act of cleaving or splitting; the act of separating or dividing off.

2. the manner in which a thing splits.

3. a cleft; fissure; division.

4. the property observed in crystals of undergoing mechanical division in certain fixed directions. Cleavage is called basal, cubic, diagonal, lateral, or prismatic, according as it is parallel to the base of a crystal, to the faces of a cube, to a diagonal plane, to the lateral planes, or to a vertical prism.

5. in mineralogy and geology, the manner in which rocks regularly cleave or split. The term is used in relation to the fracture of minerals which possess a regular structure. Certain rocks, as slate rocks in the strictest sense, may be cleft into an indefinite number of thin laminae which are parallel to each other, but which are not necessarily parallel to the planes of the natural strata. Cleavage is the result of an operation which is subsequent to, and entirely independent of, the original stratification of the rocks.

6. in biology, (a) cell division, especially the series of mitotic cell divisions that transform the fertilized ovum into the blastula, the earliest embryonic stage; (b) any single division in this series.

çlēave, *v.i.*; cleaved *or archaic* clave, clove, *pt.*; cleaving, *ppr.*; cleaved, *pp.* [ME. *cleven, cleovien*; AS. *cleofian, clifian,* to stick, cleave.]

1. to stick; to adhere; to be attached; to cling: used both in a literal and figurative sense.

If any blot hath *cleaved* to mine hands.
—Job xxxi. 7.

2. to unite or be united closely in interest or affection; to adhere with strong attachment; to be faithful.

Who loved one only and *clave* to her.
—Tennyson.

çlēave, *v.t.*; cleft, cleaved, clove, *or archaic* clave, *pt.*; cleaving, *ppr.*; cleft, cloven, cleaved, *or poetic* clove, *pp.* [ME. *cleven, cleoven*; AS. *cleofan,* to split, divide.]

1. to part or divide by force; to split or rive; to hew apart; to cut; as, to *cleave* wood; to *cleave* a rock.

His heart was *cleft* with pain and rage,
His cheeks they quivered, his eyes were wild.
—Coleridge.

2. to pierce.

3. to sever; disunite.

çlēave, *v.i.* 1. to part; to open; to crack; to separate or fall apart, as parts of cohering bodies; as, the ground *cleaves* by frost.

2. to make one's way by cutting, as through underbrush.

çlēave′lănd·īte, *n.* [after Parker *Cleaveland,* American mineralogist.] a mineral, generally of a white or grayish-white color, sometimes blue, or bluish, or reddish: called also *silicious feldspar,* or *albite.*

çlēav′ēr, *n.* 1. one who or that which cleaves.

2. specifically, a butcher's heavy, sharp-edged cutting tool.

CLEAVER

çlēav′ērş, çlīv′ērş, *n. sing. and pl.* [from *cleave,* to stick.] a plant, *Galium aparine,* with a square, rough, jointed stem, the joints being hairy at the base, and each joint having eight or ten narrow leaves: its hooked prickles adhere to whatever they come in contact with: called also *goose grass.*

çlēav′ing, *n.* 1. the act of forcibly separating a body into parts.

2. in phonetics, the changing of single long vowels into two different sounds.

cle·ché′, cle·chée′ (kle-shā′), *a.* [Fr. *cléché, cléchée,* from L. *clāvis,* a key.] in heraldry, voided or hollowed throughout. Thus a cross *cleché* is a cross with the inside taken out, leaving only an edge.

CROSS CLECHÉ

çleck, *v.t.* and *v.i.* [ME. *cleken*; Ice. *klekja,* to hatch.] to hatch; to litter. [Scot.]

çledġe (klej), *n.* [AS. *clæg,* clay.] the upper stratum of fuller's earth. [Brit. Dial.]

çledġ′y, *a.* of the nature of sticky, tenacious soils, or those mixed with clay. [Brit. Dial.]

çlee, *n.* a claw. [Obs.]

çlee, *n.* the redshank.

çleek, *n.* [Scot., from obs. v. *cleek,* to clutch, snatch; ME. *clechen,* to seize, from *cleche,* a claw, fingernail.]

1. a large hook.

2. in golf, formerly, an iron-headed club with a narrow, slightly sloped face; now, a wooden-headed club with a small head, having slightly more loft than a spoon.

çleek, *v.t.* to hook; to snatch; to seize; to catch, as by a hook.

çleek, *v.i.* to take a person's arm; to link together.

çlef, *n.* [Fr. *clef*; OFr. *cle, clef*; L. *clavis,* a key.] a symbol in music, placed at the beginning of a staff to indicate the pitch of the notes on the staff. There are three clefs, G (treble), F (bass), and C (tenor or alto).

G CLEF F CLEF

C CLEFS

TYPES OF CLEF

çleft, alternative past tense and past participle of *cleave* (to split).

çleft, *a.* 1. divided or partly divided; split; parted asunder.

2. in botany, divided halfway down to the midrib or further; as, a *cleft* leaf.

çleft, *n.* [ME. *clift, clyft,* a cleft; AS. *cleofan,* to cut.]

1. a space or opening made by splitting; a crack; a crevice; as, the *cleft* of a rock.

2. a disease in horses characterized by a crack on the bend of the pastern.

3. a piece made by splitting; as, a *cleft* of wood.

Syn.—fissure, crack, crevice, chink, opening, chasm.

çleft′-foot″ed, *a.* having cleft or cloven feet.

çleft′gráft, *v.t.* to engraft a plant in (another) by cleaving the stock and inserting a scion.

çleft pal′ăte, a cleft from front to back along the middle of the palate or roof of the mouth, caused by the failure of the two parts of the palate to join in prenatal development.

çleg, *n.* [Scot. and Prov. Eng. *gleg*; Ice. *kleggi,* a horsefly.] any of various insects, the females of which are troublesome to horses, cattle, and man because of their blood-sucking habits; as the great horsefly or breeze, *Tabanus bovinus,* also called the gadfly; the *Chrysops cæcutiens,* and in Scotland the *Hæmatopota pluvialis,* a smaller grayish-colored fly. [Brit. Dial.]

çleī′dō-, same as *clido-.*

çleī′dō·man·cy, *n.* same as *clidomancy.*

çlēik, *n.* and *v.* same as *cleek.*

çleīs′tō-, [from Gr. *kleistos,* verbal adj. of *kleiein,* to close.] a combining form meaning *shut, closed,* as in *cleisto*carp.

çleīs′tō·cärp, *n.* [*cleisto-,* and Gr. *karpos,* fruit.] in botany, a form of ascocarp in which asci or spore cases develop, and from which they are liberated by bursting the walls of the cell.

Çleīs·tō·cär′pē·ae, *n.pl.* a group of mosses, the fruit of which usually opens by decay, thus discharging the spores.

çleīs·tō·çär′pous, *a.* of or pertaining to the *Cleistocarpeæ.*

çleīs·tō·gam′iç, *a.* same as *cleistogamous.*

çleīs·tog′à·mous, *a.* [*cleisto-,* and *-gamous.*] having small, closed, self-pollinating flowers.

çleīs·tog′à·my, *n.* [*cleisto-,* and *-gamy.*] self-pollination of certain closed flowers.

çleīs·toġ′e·nous, *a.* same as *cleistogamous.*

çleīth′răl, *a.* same as *clithral.*

çlem, *v.t.* to cause to perish of hunger; to starve. [Brit. Dial.]

çlem, *v.i.* to die of hunger; to starve. [Brit. Dial.]

Çlem′à·tis, *n.* [L., from Gr. *klēmatis,* brushwood, clematis, from *klēma,* a vine, twig.]

1. a genus of woody climbing plants of the crowfoot family, with bright-colored flowers. There are many species, natives of temperate climates. *Clematis vitalba* is the European traveler's joy, common on English hedgerows. Improved cultivated varieties are much in favor as garden vines.

2. [c-] any plant belonging to this genus.

çlem′ence, *n.* clemency. [Obs.]

çlem′en·cy, *n.* [L. *clementia,* mildness, from *clemens,* merciful.]

1. forbearance, leniency, or mercy, as toward an offender or enemy.

2. a merciful or lenient act.

3. mildness of the elements; as, the *clemency* of the weather.

Syn.—mercy, lenity, compassion, mildness, gentleness, tenderness.

çlem′ent, *a.* [Fr. *clement*; L. *clemens,* mild, calm.]

1. mild in temper and disposition; forbearing; lenient; merciful; kind; tender; compassionate.

2. of the weather, calm and mild.

Çlem′ent·ine (*or* -īn), *a.* pertaining to St. Clement, or to his reputed compilations; or to the constitutions of Pope Clement V.

Çlem′ent·ine, *n.* 1. one of a series of compilations ascribed to St. Clement.

2. a decretal of Pope Clement V.

çlem′ent·ly, *adv.* with mildness of temper; mercifully.

çlench, *v.t.*; clenched, *pt., pp.*; clenching, *ppr.* [ME. *clenchen,* to clench, from same root as AS. *beclencan,* to fasten, knit.]

1. to make fast by bending over; to clinch; as, to *clench* a nail.

2. to shut or bring together tightly; to close firmly, as the teeth or fist.

3. to grip tightly.

çlench, *n.* 1. the act of holding or grasping firmly; also, that which serves to hold fast; a clutch; a clasp; a grip; as, to have a *clench* of an opponent, or of a sword; to hold with convulsive *clenches*.

2. a method of securing a nail, a staple, etc., by turning over a portion of it and hammering it into the wood.

3. in nautical usage, a clinch.

4. a pun; a witty reply; a play on words. [Rare.]

Comick wit, degenerating into *clenches*. —Dryden.

clench'ėr, *n.* same as *clincher*.

Clē·ō'mē, *n.* [LL. *cleome*, an unidentified plant.] a large genus of herbaceous and shrubby plants with white, green, or purple flowers having feathery petals and long stamens, family *Capparidaceæ*, natives of tropical and warm regions of both hemispheres.

Clē·ō·pā'trà's Nee'dle, 1. an ancient Egyptian obelisk now in Central Park, New York City.

2. another such obelisk on the Thames Embankment, London.

clēpe, *v.t.* [ME. *clepen*; AS. *cleopian*, to call, cry out.]

1. to call or address (a person). [Obs.]

2. to call by name; to name: generally in the archaic past participle, *yclept, ycleped*. [Archaic.]

Clep'sī·nē, *n.* [L., from Gr. *klepsia*, theft, from *kleptein*, to steal.]

1. a genus of fresh-water leeches typical of *Clepsinidæ*, having an elongated proboscis and feeding mostly on worms and mollusks.

2. [c—] a leech of this genus.

Clep·sin'i·dae, *n.pl.* a family of leeches characterized by a protractile proboscis.

clep'sy·drà, *n.*; *pl.* **clep'sy·dràs** or **clep'sy·drae,** [L. *clepsydra*, Gr. *klepsydra*, a water clock; *kleptein*, to steal, and *hydōr*, water.] a device for measuring time by marking the gradual flow of liquid through a small opening; a water clock.

clep·tō·mā'ni·à, *n.* same as *kleptomania*.

clep·tō·mā'ni·ac, *n.* same as *kleptomaniac*.

clēre'stō"ry, *n.*; *pl.* **clēre'stō"ries,** [*clere* (for *clear*), and *story*, floor.]

1. the wall of a church rising above the roofs of the flanking aisles and containing windows for lighting the central part of the structure.

2. any similar windowed wall.

Also spelled *clearstory*.

clėr'gi·ăl, *a.* learned; clerkly. [Obs.]

Oure termes ben so *clergial*, and queynte. —Chaucer.

clėr'gi·căl, *a.* pertaining to the clergy. [Obs.]

clėr'gi·on, *n.* [Fr., dim. of *clerc*, a clergyman, scholar.] a young chorister or choir boy.

A litel *clergion*, sevene yere of age. —Chaucer.

clėr'gy, *n.*; *pl.* **clėr'gies,** [ME. *clergie*; OFr. *clergie*, the office or dignity of a clergyman; LL. *clericus*, a clergyman, from Gr. *klēros*, a lot; lit., that which is assigned by lot.]

1. men ordained for religious service, as ministers, priests, etc., collectively.

2. the benefit of clergy. [Obs.]

If convicted of a clergyable felony, he is entitled equally to his *clergy* after as before conviction. —Blackstone.

3. a learned profession; learning. [Obs.]

clėr'gy·à·ble, *a.* entitled to or admitting the benefit of clergy; as, a *clergyable* felony.

clėr'gy·măn, *n.*; *pl.* **clėr'gy·men,** a member of the clergy; a minister, priest, etc.; a man regularly authorized to preach the gospel, and administer its ordinances: in England, commonly restricted to a minister of the Established Church.

cler'ic, *n.* a clergyman.

cler'ic, *a.* same as *clerical* (sense 1).

cler'ic·ăl, *a.* 1. relating or pertaining to the clergy or a clergyman.

2. relating to a clerk or clerks; of office work, such as keeping records, copying, filing, etc.

3. favoring the influence of the clergy in political matters: often in a derogatory sense.

clerical error; an error inadvertently made by a person in writing or copying something.

cler'ic·ăl, *n.* 1. a clergyman.

2. a person who believes in advancing the political power of the clergy: often in a derogatory sense.

cler'ic·ăl·ism, *n.* political power or influence of the clergy; also, policies or principles favoring this. Generally a derogatory term.

cler'ic·ăl·ist, *n.* a person in favor of clericalism.

cler'ic·ăls, *n.pl.* clergymen's garments.

cler·ic'i·ty, *n.* the state or quality of being clerical. [Rare.]

clėr'i·sy, *n.* 1. learned people as a class; intellectuals collectively.

The *clerisy* of a nation, that is, its learned men, whether poets, philosophers, or scholars. —Coleridge.

2. the clergy, as opposed to the laity. [Rare.]

clėrk, *n.* [ME. *clerc, clærk*; AS. *clerc*; LL. *clericus*, a clergyman, priest, from Gr. *klēros*, the clergy, lit., a lot, or that which is chosen by lot.]

1. a clergyman, or ecclesiastic; a man in holy orders. [Archaic.]

2. a man who can read and write; a man of letters; a scholar. [Archaic.]

3. a layman who has certain minor duties in a church.

4. an office worker who keeps accounts and records, does filing and copying, etc.: in public service, other duties, responsibilities, etc. may be involved, as in the case of a city *clerk* or a *clerk* of courts.

5. a person in a shop or store who sells goods; a retail salesman or saleswoman; as, a grocery *clerk*.

clėrk, *v.i.* to work or be employed as a clerk.

clėrk āle, in England, a feast for the benefit of the parish clerk; also, the ale provided for it. [Obs.]

clėrk'less, *a.* ignorant; unlearned. [Obs.]

clėrk'līke, *a.* like a scholar; learned. [Obs.]

clėrk'li·ness, *n.* clerkly skill; scholarship. [Obs.]

clėrk'ly, *a.*; *comp.* clerklier; *superl.* clerkliest,

1. of or pertaining to a clerk.

2. of the clergy; clerical.

3. scholarly. [Archaic.]

clėrk'ly, *adv.* in a clerkly manner.

clėrk'ship, *n.* 1. the state of being in holy orders.

2. scholarship.

3. the office or business of a clerk or writer.

Clē·rō·den'drŏn, *n.* [L., from Gr. *klēros*, lot, chance, and *dendron*, tree.] a large genus of trees and shrubs found in the tropical and subtropical climates of both hemispheres. They are allied to the genus *Verbena*.

cler'ō·man·cy, *n.* [Gr. *klēros*, lot, and *manteia*, divination.] divination by throwing dice or beans, and observing the points or marks turned up.

clē·ron'ō·my, *n.* [Gr. *klēronomia*, an inheritance, from *klēros*, lot, and *nemesthai*, to possess.] inheritance; heritage or patrimony.

clē'rụ̈ch, *n.* [Gr. *klērouchia*, the allotment of land in a foreign country; *klēros*, lot, and *echein*, to hold.] in ancient Greece, a citizen who was given an allotment of land in a conquered country and moved to it without losing his citizenship.

clē·rụ̈'chi·ăl, *a.* of or pertaining to a cleruch, or the system of colonization by cleruchs.

Clē'thrà, *n.* [Gr. *klēthra*, alder, which these plants resemble in foliage.] a genus of plants, natural order *Ericaceæ*, natives of the Americas. They are shrubs or trees, with alternate serrate leaves. One species, *Clethra alnifolia*, a native of Virginia and the Carolinas, is widely cultivated as one of the most beautiful of flowering shrubs.

cleugh, cleuch (klụ̈k), *n.* a gorge; a ravine; also, a cliff or side of a ravine. [Scot.]

When in the *cleugh* the buck was ta'en. —Sir W. Scott.

clēve, *n.* cliff. [Now Dial.]

clēve'īte, *n.* a kind of uraninite found in Norway: named after P. T. Cleve (1840–1905), Swedish mineralogist.

clev'ėr, *a.* [East Anglican ME. and Early Mod. Eng. *cliver*, replacing earlier *deliver* in literary Eng.; perh. from AS. *clifian*, to cleave (hence, discern), either directly or via ME. *cliver*, claw, hand, in the sense, "adroit with the hand."]

1. (a) performing or acting with skill; having the art of doing or devising anything readily; possessing ability of any kind, especially such as involves quickness of intellect or mechanical dexterity; as, a *clever* workman or speaker; (b) intelligent; able to learn; (c) ingenious; quick-witted; bright.

2. indicative of or exhibiting cleverness; showing ingenuity or intelligence; as, a *clever* speech; a *clever* trick.

3. fit; suitable; convenient; proper; commodious. [Obs. or Brit. Dial.]

These *clever* apartments. —Cowper.

4. nice, handsome, etc. [Dial. or Slang.]

5. good-natured; obliging; possessing an agreeable mind or disposition. [Dial.]

Syn.—skillful, expert, dexterous, adroit, talented.

clev'ėr·ish, *a.* somewhat clever.

clev'ėr·ly, *adv.* in a clever or adroit manner.

clev'ėr·ness, *n.* the quality of being clever; dexterity; adroitness; skill.

clev'is, clev'y, *n.* [from ME. *cleven*; AS. *cleofan*, to split.] an iron bent to the form of a U, with the two ends perforated to receive a pin, as used on the end of a plow or wagon tongue to attach it to a whiffletree, etc.

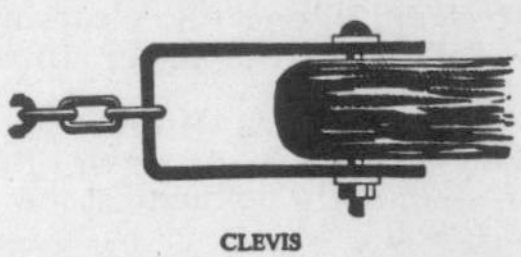

CLEVIS

clew, clūe, *n.* [ME. *clewe*; AS. *cleowen*.]

1. a ball of thread or yarn: in Greek legend, a thread was used by Theseus as a guide out of the labyrinth.

2. something that leads out of a maze, perplexity, etc., or helps to solve a problem: in this sense generally spelled *clue*.

3. in nautical usage, (a) either of the two lower corners of a square sail; (b) the lower corner aft of a fore-and-aft sail; (c) a metal loop fastened in the corner of a sail; (d) a combination of lines by which a hammock is hung.

clew, clūe, *v.t.* 1. to wind up into a ball (usually with *up*).

2. to indicate by or as by a clew (with *out*).

3. to trace, as by a clew.

clew gär'net, a rope and pulley fastened to the clews of the mainsail and foresail to truss them up to the yard.

clew līnes, the system of ropes and pulleys connecting the clew of a sail with the yard or mast, used in raising or lowering the sail.

Clī·an'thus, *n.* [L., from Gr. *kleos*, fame, glory, and *anthos*, a flower.] a genus of shrubs of the bean family, *Leguminosæ*, two species being in cultivation, *Clianthus dampieri*, or glory pea, of Australia, and *Clianthus puniceus*, or parrot's-bill, of New Zealand.

cli·ché' (klī-shā'), *n.* [Fr., pp. of *clicher*, to stereotype; OFr. *cliquer*, to clap.]

1. an electrotype or stereotype printing plate.

2. an expression or idea that has become trite.

click, *n.* [echoic.] 1. a slight, sharp sound like that of a door latch snapping into place.

2. a mechanical device, as a catch or pawl, that clicks into position.

3. in phonetics, any of a class of sounds, common in some African languages, made by drawing the breath into the mouth and clicking the tongue.

click, *v.i.* and *v.t.* 1. to make or cause to make a click.

2. to move with a clicking sound.

click bee'tle, a beetle of the family *Elateridæ*, so named because of the clicking noise which it makes when righting itself after being on its back.

click'ėr, *n.* 1. one who stands at a shop door to invite customers in. [Brit. Slang.]

2. in printing, a compositor who distributes copy and has general charge of the work in his group. [Brit.]

3. in shoemaking, one who cuts out the leather and distributes the work. [Brit. Slang.]

click'et, *n.* the latch of a door or gate. [Brit. Dial.]

click'ing, *n.* a small, sharp noise.

click'y, *a.* full of clicks.

Clī·das'tēs, *n.* [L. from Gr. *kleis*, a key.] a genus of marine reptiles now extinct. The specimens found in the North American cretaceous deposits vary from twelve to forty feet in length.

clī'dō-, clei'dō-, [from L. *clavis*, Gr. *kleis*, a key.] a combining form signifying *by means of* or *pertaining to a key*, as in *clidomancy*; or, in anatomy, *of* or *pertaining to the clavicle* (*and*), as in *clidomastoid*.

clī'dō·man·cy, *n.* [*clido-*, and Gr. *manteia*, divination.] divination by means of a key.

clī·dō·mas'toid, *a.* pertaining to the clavicle and the mastoid process; as, the *clidomastoid* muscle.

clī·dō·stėr'năl, *n.* pertaining to the clavicle and the sternum, or breastbone.

clī'en·cy, *n.* the state of being a client.

clī'ent, *n.* [OFr. *client*; L. *cliens*, a follower, retainer, one who hears (his patron), from *cluere*, to hear oneself called.]

1. among the ancient Romans, a citizen

who placed himself under the protection of a patrician, who was called his patron.
2. a dependent; one under the protection or patronage of another.
3. a person or company in its relationship to a lawyer, accountant, etc. engaged to act in its behalf.
4. loosely, a customer.
çlī'ent·āġe, *n.* same as *clientele.*
çlī·en'tăl, *a.* relating to a client or clients.
çlī'ent·ed, *a.* supplied with clients. [Rare.]
çlī·en'te·lāġe, *n.* clientele.
çlī·en·tele', *n.* [Fr.]
1. the condition or relation of a client. [Obs.]
2. clients collectively.
3. the clients of a lawyer, doctor, etc., or the habitual customers of a store, hotel, amusement place, etc.
4. the number of such clients or customers.
çlī'ent·ship, *n.* the relation or state of a client.
çliff, *n.* [ME. *clif, clef*; AS. *clif,* a cliff.]
1. a steep bank or rugged face of rock, especially one on a coast; as, the *cliffs* of Dover.
2. a high and steep rock; any precipice.
çliff, *n.* in music, a clef. [Obs.]
çliff brāke, a species of fern growing on cliffs and walls.
çliff dwell'ẽr, one of the race of Indians living in Mexico or the southwestern portion of the United States, who dwelt in hollows or caves of cliffs: they were ancestors of the Pueblo Indians.
çliff līme'stōne, a limestone found in the cliffs of the Ohio and Mississippi valleys, being of mixed Devonian and Silurian origin.
çliff swäl'lōw, *n.* a North American swallow that builds its gourdlike nest of mud, grass, and feathers against a cliff or under the eaves of a building.
çliff'y, *a.* having cliffs; broken; craggy.
çlift, *n.* a precipice; a cliff. [Obs.]
çlift, *n.* a cleft or fissure. [Obs.]
çlī·maç'tẽr, *n.* a climacteric. [Obs.]
çlī·maç'tẽr·iç, *n.* [L. *climactericus*; Gr. *klimakterikos* from *klimaktēr,* the step of a staircase, round of a ladder, from *klimax,* a ladder.]
1. a period in the life of a person when an important change in health or bodily function occurs, especially the period of the menopause in women. The critical periods were held by some to be the years produced by multiplying 7 by the odd numbers 3, 5, 7, and 9. The 63d year is called the *grand climacteric.* It has been supposed that these periods are attended with some radical change in respect to health, life, or fortune.
2. any crucial period or event.
çlī·maç'tẽr·iç, çlī·maç·ter'iç·ăl, *a.* pertaining to or resembling a climacteric.
çlī·maç'tiç, çlī·maç'tiç·ăl, *a.* tending or relating to a climax.
çlī'mȧ·tăl, *a.* climatic.
çlī·mȧ·tär'çhiç, *a.* [Gr. *klima,* a region, and *archein,* to rule.] presiding over climates. [Obs.]
çlī'māte, *n.* [ME. *climat,* OFr. *climat*; L. *clima*; Gr. *klima,* a region, zone.]
1. in old geography, one of thirty zones into which the surface of the earth was supposed to be divided from the equator to each pole. They were measured by lines parallel to the equator.
2. the prevailing or average weather conditions of a place, as determined by the temperature and meteorological changes over a period of years: distinguished from *weather.*
3. any prevailing conditions affecting life, activity, etc.
4. a region considered with reference to the kind of weather prevailing there; as, he went south to a warmer *climate.*
5. any distinct portion of the earth's surface; a region; a clime. [Obs.]
çlī'māte, *v.i.* to dwell; to reside in a particular region. [Poet.]
çlī·mat'iç, çlī·mat'iç·ăl, *a.* pertaining to a climate or climates; limited by a climate.
çlī·mat'iç·ăl·ly, *adv.* with regard to climate.
çlī·mȧ·tic'i·ty, *n.* the property of climatizing.
çlī'mȧ·tīze, *v.t.*; climatized, *pt., pp.*; climatizing, *ppr.* to accustom to a new climate, as a plant; to acclimatize.
çlī'mȧ·tīze, *v.i.* to become accustomed to a new climate; as, plants will *climatize* in foreign countries.
çlī·mȧ·tog'rȧ·phy, *n.* [Gr. *klima,* a region, zone, and *graphein,* to write.] an explanation or description of climates.
çlī″mȧ·tō·log'iç, çlī″mȧ·tō·log'iç·ăl, *a.* relating to climatology.
çlī·mȧ·tol'ō·ġist, *n.* a person who is expert in the science of climatology.
çlī·mȧ·tol'ō·ġy, *n.* [Gr. *klima,* climate, and *logos,* description.] the science dealing with climates and climatic phenomena.
çlī'mȧ·tūre, *n.* a climate or region. [Obs.]
çlī'max, *n.* [LL. *climax,* a climax, from Gr. *klimax,* a ladder, from *klinein,* to slope.]
1. a series of ideas or events arranged or occurring progressively so that the most forceful is last.
2. the final, culminating element in such a series: in dramatic structure, it is the decisive turning point of the action.
3. the highest point, as of interest, excitement, etc.; the culmination; the acme.
to cap the climax; to overtop the climax, as in absurdity.
çlī'max, *v.i.* and *v.t.* to reach, or bring to, a climax.
çlīmb (klīm), *v.i.* and *v.t.* climbed, *pt., pp.*; climbing, *ppr.* [ME. *climben*; AS. *climban,* to climb.]
1. to ascend step by step; to mount or ascend, by means of the hands and feet.
2. to ascend gradually or laboriously; as, he *climbed* to power in ten years.
3. in botany, to grow upward on (a wall, etc.) by means of tendrils or adhesive fibers.
Syn.—clamber, ascend, rise, mount.
çlīmb, *n.* 1. a climbing; rise; ascent; also, a distance which has been, or may be, climbed; as, it was a long *climb.*
2. a thing or place to be climbed.
çlīmb'ȧ·ble, *a.* capable of being climbed.
çlīmb'ẽr, *n.* 1. one who climbs, mounts, or rises, by the hands and feet.
2. a metal spike fastened to a shoe to aid in climbing telephone poles, etc.; a climbing iron.
3. a person who constantly tries to advance himself socially or in business. [Colloq.]
4. a plant that creeps and rises on some support.
5. one of an order of birds that climb, as the woodpecker.
çlīmb'ẽr, *v.i.* to climb; to mount with effort. [Obs.]
çlīmb in'di·çā·tŏr, an instrument for indicating the rate of ascent or descent of an aircraft: it is operated by changes in atmospheric pressure at different levels.
çlīmb'ing, *n.* the act of one who climbs.
çlīmb'ing fẽrn, a fern of the genus *Lygodium,* a climbing and decorative plant.
çlīmb'ing fish, a fresh-water fish of the East Indies, *Anabas scandens,* that can live out of water for some time, travel over the land, and is said to climb trees by means of the spiny coverings of its gills.
çlīmb'ing ī'ronș (-ũrnz), metal spikes fastened to a shoe to assist in climbing telegraph poles, etc.
çlīmb'ing pẽrch, same as *climbing fish.*
çlīme, *n.* [L. *clima.*] a climate; a tract or region. [Poet.]
Whatever *clime* the sun's bright circle warms. —Milton.
çlin-, same as *clino-.*
çlī·nā'men, *n.*; *pl.* **çlī·nā'mi·nȧ,** [L. *clinamen,* an inclination, from *inclinare,* to bend; Gr. *klinein,* to bend.] curve; turn; bend; bias.
çlī·nan'dri·um, *n.*; *pl.* **çlī·nan'dri·ȧ,** [L., from Gr. *klinē,* bed, and *aner,* genit. *andros,* man.] a cavity in the top of the column of some orchids in which the anthers rest: also called *androclinium.*
çlī·nan'thi·um, çlī·nan'thus, *n.* [L., from Gr. *klinē,* bed, and *anthos,* flower.] the flower receptacle of a composite plant.
çlinch, *v.t.* [ME. *clenchen*; var. of *clench* with vowel raised by nasalization.]
1. to fasten (a nail, bolt, etc. that has been driven through something) by bending or flattening the projecting end.
2. to fasten firmly together by this means.
3. to settle (an argument, bargain, etc.) definitely; to close conclusively.
çlinch, *v.i.* 1. to clinch a nail, bolt, etc.
2. in boxing, to grip the opponent's body with the arms so as to hinder his punching.
3. to embrace. [Slang.]
çlinch, *n.* 1. a fastening or fastening together.
2. a fastening in which the nail, bolt, etc. is clinched.
3. a clinched nail, bolt, etc.
4. the part clinched.
5. in boxing, an act of clinching.
6. an embrace. [Slang.]
7. in nautical usage, a kind of knot or noose in a rope; a clench.
çlinch'ẽr, *n.* 1. a person who clinches.
2. a tool for clinching nails.
3. a point that is conclusive or decisive, as in an argument. [Colloq.]
çlinch'ẽr-built (-bilt), *a.* same as *clinker-built.*
çling, *v.i.*; clung, *pt., pp.*; clinging, *ppr.* [ME. *clingen,* to adhere closely, to shrivel, shrink; AS. *clingan,* to shrink, shrivel.]
1. to adhere closely; to stick; to hold fast, especially by winding round or embracing; as, the tendril of a vine *clings* to its support.
2. to adhere or stick, as a viscous substance.
3. to adhere closely and firmly, in interest or affection; as, men of a party *cling* to their leader.
4. to be or stay near, as if by holding fast.
çling, *v.t.* 1. to dry up; to wither; to shrivel. [Obs.]
Till famine *cling* thee. —Shak.
2. to cause to fasten or adhere closely, as by embracing. [Rare.]
I *clung* my legs as close to his sides as I could. —Swift.
Syn.—adhere, clasp, cleave, hang, hold, stick.
çling, *n.* the act of holding fast; attachment; devotion; clasp; an embrace. [Rare.]
çling'fish, *n.*; *pl.* **çling'fish** or **çling'fish·eș,** any of a group of small, tropical marine fishes having a sucking disk on the ventral side of the body by which they adhere to rocks.
çling'ing vīne, a woman inclined to be helpless and dependent in her relationship with a man.
çling'stōne, *a.* having a stone that clings to the fleshy part: said of some peaches.
çling'stōne, *n.* a variety of peach, whose pulp adheres closely to the stone.
çling'y, *a.* apt to cling; adhesive; sticking; tenacious.
çlin'iç, *n.* [Fr. *clinique*; L. *clinicus,* a bedridden person, from Gr. *klinikos,* pertaining to the bed; *klinē,* a bed.]
1. the teaching of medicine by examining and treating patients in the presence of students.
2. a class getting such teaching.
3. a place where patients are studied or treated by physicians specializing in various ailments and practicing as a group; as, a cancer *clinic,* a tuberculosis *clinic.*
4. the dispensary or outpatient department of a hospital or medical school, where patients are treated free or for a small fee.
5. an organization or institution that offers some kind of advice or treatment: as, a domestic-relations *clinic.*
6. a brief, intensive session of group instruction in a specific skill, field of knowledge, etc.; as, a basketball *clinic.*
çlin'iç, *a.* same as *clinical.*
çlin'iç·ăl, *a.* 1. pertaining to a clinic.
2. pertaining to a sickbed.
3. having to do with medical study or practice based on actual treatment and observation of patients, as distinguished from experimental or laboratory study.
4. purely scientific; dispassionately curious; as, she regarded his death with *clinical* detachment.
5. in ecclesiastical usage, administered on a sickbed or deathbed.
clinical lecture; a discourse delivered by a medical instructor to students at the bedside of a patient.
clinical surgery or *medicine*; surgical or medical instruction which is imparted to the student at a clinic.
clinical thermometer; a thermometer with which the body temperature is measured.
çlin'iç·ăl·ly, *adv.* in a clinical manner or according to clinical procedure.
çli·ni'ciăn, *n.* one skilled in clinical medicine or surgery.
çli·nid'i·um, *n.*; *pl.* **çli·nid'i·ȧ,** [L., from Gr. *klinein,* to incline.] in botany, a filament that bears a spore, found in the follicle of some lichens.
çlī·nïque' (-nēk'), *n.* [Fr.] a clinic.
çlin'i·um, *n.* same as *clinanthium.*
çliñk, *v.t.* and *v.i.*; clinked, *pt., pp.*; clinking, *ppr.* [of echoic origin.] to make or cause to make a sharp sound or succession of such sounds; as, to *clink* glasses in drinking a toast.
çliñk, *n.* 1. a slight, sharp sound.
2. a jail; a prison. [Colloq.]
çliñk, *v.t.* to hold fast; to clinch. [Scot.]
çliñ'kănt, *a.* same as *clinquant.*
çliñk'ẽr, *n.* [D. *klinker,* a vitrified brick, which clinks when struck.]
1. a hard mass of fused stony matter formed

in a furnace from impurities in the coal or in the kiln.

2. a very hard kind of brick: sometimes called *Dutch clinker*.

3. a mass of fused bricks.

4. a scale of black oxide of iron formed when iron is heated to redness in the open air.

5. a brick with a surface made glassy by heat and fusion.

clink'ẽr-built (-bilt), *a.* [*clinker*, from *clink*, dial. var. of *clinch*.] built with overlapping boards or plates, as in shipbuilding.

clink'stōne, *n.* in mineralogy, any of various varieties of phonolite that make a clinking, metallic sound when struck.

clī'nō-, [from Gr. *klinein*, to bend or slope.] a combining form signifying *bent* or *inclined*, as in *clino*diagonal: also, before a vowel, *clin-*.

clī·nō·ax'is, *n.* same as *clinodiagonal*.

clī·nō·ceph'ȧ·ly, *n.* [*clino-*, and Gr. *kephalē*, head.] a flatness or slight depression in the skull.

clī'nō·chlōre, *n.* [*clino-*, and Gr. *chlōros*, yellowish green.] same as *ripidolite*.

clī"nō·di·ag'ō·năl, *n.* [*clino-*, and L. *diagonalis*; Gr. *diagōnios*, diagonal.] in crystallography, a diagonal or lateral axis in monoclinic crystals which forms an oblique angle with the vertical axis.

clī"nō·di·ag'ō·năl, *a.* pertaining to or in the direction of a clinodiagonal.

clī'nō·dōme, *n.* [*clino-*, and Gr. *dōma*, a house.] a plane in a monoclinic crystal that is parallel to the inclined lateral axis.

clī·nō·graph'iç, *a.* [*clino-*, and Gr. *graphein*, to write.] relating to the method of projection in drawing in which the rays of light are supposed to fall obliquely on the plane of projection.

clī'noid, *a.* [Fr. *clinoide*, from Gr. *klinē*, a bed, and *eidos*, form.] bedlike; in anatomy, designating the four processes which are arranged like posts of a bedstead on the inner side of the sphenoid bone.

clī·nom'e·tẽr, *n.* [*clino-*, and Gr. *metron*, a measure.] an instrument for measuring the dip of rock strata, the inclination of an embankment, or the degree of a slope.

clī·nō·met'riç, clī·nō·met'riç·ăl, *a.* 1. measured by or relating to a clinometer.

2. in mineralogy, relating to oblique crystalline forms, or to solids having oblique angles between the axes.

clī·nom'e·try, *n.* the science of measuring the inclination or dip of rock strata, the slope of an embankment, etc.

clī·nō·pin'ȧ·çoid, *n.* [*clino-*, and Gr. *pinax*, a tablet, and *eidos*, form.] in crystallography, either of the two planes that are parallel to the vertical and inclined lateral axes of a monoclinic crystal.

clī'nō·prişm, *n.* [*clino-*, and Gr. *prisma*, a prism.] a variety of prism in a monoclinic crystal.

clī·nō·rhom'biç (-rom'), *a.* [*clino-*, and Gr. *rhombos*, a rhombus.] in crystallography, monoclinic.

clī"nō·spō·ran'ġi·um, *n.*; *pl.* **clī"nō·spō·ran'ġi·ȧ**, [*clino-*, and Gr. *sporos*, a sowing, and *angeion*, a vessel.] a conceptacle in lichens which contains filaments bearing clinospores.

clī'nō·spōre, *n.* [*clino-*, and Gr. *sporos*, a sowing.] a spore produced at the summit of a spore-bearing filament in a clinosporangium.

clī'nō·stat, *n.* [*clino-*, and Gr. *statos*, verbal adj. from *istasthai*, to stand.] a device employed in the study of plant physiology consisting of a revolving disk controlled by clockwork: used to control the effects of such agents as light, gravity, etc. on growing plants.

clinquant (-kănt), *n.* [Fr., tinsel; D. *klinken*, tinsel.] tinsel; imitation gold leaf.

clin'quănt, *a.* glittering; dressed or adorned with or as with gold or silver.

Clin·tō'ni·ȧ, *n.* a genus of North American plants, named after the American statesman, DeWitt Clinton. They bear large, white or yellow lily-shaped flowers on a short peduncle, and blue berries.

Clī'ō, *n.* [L., from Gr. *Kleiō*, Clio, from *kleiein*, to celebrate; *kleos*, fame, glory.] in Greek mythology, the Muse of history.

Clī"ō·met'riçs, *n.pl.* [*construed as sing.*] [from *Clio*, and Gr. *metron*, measure.] the use of mathematical and statistical methods, and often of computers, in analyzing historical data.

Clī·ō'nē, *n.* [L., from Gr. *Kleiō*, Clio.] a genus of pteropods without gills, constituting a food for whales.

Clī·on'i·dae, *n.pl.* [L., from Gr. *Kleiō*, Clio.] the family of pteropods of which *Clione* is the type. They swim near the surface of the water by means of winglike appendages at the sides of the head.

clip, *v.t.*; clipped, *pt.*, *pp.*; clipping, *ppr.* [ME. *clippen*; Ice. *klippa*, to clip, shear.]

1. to cut or cut off with shears or scissors; to separate by a sudden stroke; as, to *clip* wool, to *clip* hair.

2. to cut off the edge of (coins, etc.).

3. to curtail; to cut short, as words; as, to *clip* one's speech.

To *clip* the divine prerogative. —South.

4. to cut the hair of.

5. to hit or punch with a quick, sharp blow. [Colloq.]

6. to cheat; to swindle; to rob. [Slang.]

to clip the wings; literally, to cut a bird's wings short, so as to deprive it of the power of flight; figuratively, to put a check on one's ambition; to render one less able to execute his schemes or realize his aspirations.

clip, *v.i.* 1. to move swiftly, as a horse, a falcon, etc. [Colloq.]

Clips it down the wind. —Dryden.

2. to cut something.

3. to cut out newspaper or magazine clippings.

clip, *n.* 1. a shearing; a clipping.

2. a thing clipped.

3. the amount of wool clipped from sheep at one time or in one season; as, there will be a large *clip* this year.

4. a blow or stroke with the hand; as, he hit him a *clip*. [Colloq.]

5. a rapid motion or pace. [Colloq.]

6. [*pl.*] shears. [Scot.]

clip, *v.i.* and *v.t.*; clipped *or archaic* clipt, *pt.*, *pp.*; clipping, *ppr.* [ME. *clippen*; AS. *clyppan*, to embrace.]

1. to grip tightly; fasten.

2. to hug; embrace closely. [Archaic and Dial.]

3. in football, to throw oneself from behind across the lower part of the leg or legs of (an opponent who is not carrying the ball), so as to cause him to fall: an illegal act.

clip, *n.* 1. anything that clips or fastens.

2. a cartridge clip.

3. an embrace. [Obs.]

4. in football, the act of clipping.

clip'bōard, *n.* a portable writing board with a hinged clip at the top to hold papers.

clip'-fed, *a.* automatically loaded from a cartridge clip: said of certain repeating firearms.

clipped fọrm (or **wōrd**), a shortened form of a word, as *pike* (for *turnpike*) or *fan* (for *fanatic*).

clip'pẽr, *n.* 1. one who clips, shears, etc.

2. a tool for clipping, as a shears for trimming hedges.

3. (a) a ship with a sharp, forward-raking bow and masts raking aft, built and rigged for fast sailing: called also *clipper ship*; (b) a modified form of this with less speed and greater cargo capacity.

CLIPPER

CLIPPER SHIP

4. (a) a horse, sled, automobile, airplane, etc. regarded as especially fast; (b) a person or thing especially admired.

5. the larva of a neuropter, used as bait by anglers.

clip'pẽr-built (-bilt), *a.* built with long, smooth lines for speed: said of ships.

clip'pẽrş, *n.pl.* a barber's tool for clipping hair.

clip'ping, *n.* 1. the act of cutting off, curtailing, or diminishing; as, the *clipping* of coins.

2. that which is clipped off or out of something.

3. an item cut out of a newspaper, magazine, etc.

clip'ping, *a.* 1. cutting.

2. swiftly moving.

clipt, *v.*, archaic past tense and past participle of *clip* (to embrace).

clique (klēk), *n.* [Fr.] a small, exclusive circle of persons; a snobbish or narrow coterie.

clique, *v.i.*; cliqued (klēkt), *pt.*, *pp.*; cliquing, *ppr.* to gather in, or act as, a clique. [Colloq.]

clī'quish (-kish), *a.* 1. like or pertaining to a clique.

2. inclined to form a clique or cliques.

clī'quish·ness, *n.* disposition to associate with a clique or in cliques.

clī'quişm (-kizm), *n.* cliquishness.

clī'quy, clī'quey (-ki), *a.* cliquish.

clish'-clash', *n.* [Scot.] chatter; gossip.

clīs'tō-, same as *cleisto-*.

clīs'tō·cärp, *n.* same as *cleistocarp*.

Clīs·tō·cär'pē·ae, *n.pl.* same as *Cleistocarpeæ*.

clīs·tō·cär'pous, *a.* same as *cleistocarpous*.

clīs·tō·gam'iç, *a.* same as *cleistogamic*.

clīs·tog'ȧ·mous, *a.* same as *cleistogamous*.

clīs·tog'ȧ·my, *n.* same as *cleistogamy*.

clīs·tog'e·nous, *a.* same as *cleistogenous*.

clīte, *n.* [ME. *clide*, *clete*; AS. *clite*, coltsfoot.]

1. the goose grass, *Galium aparine*.

2. the burdock, *Arctium lappa*.

clī·tel'lum, *n.*; *pl.* **clī·tel'lȧ**, [L. *clitellæ*, a pack saddle.] a part of the body of an earthworm, consisting of glands which have grown thick, various segments being joined together serving as a reproductive organ.

clī·tel'lus, *n.* same as *clitellum*.

clith'răl, *a.* [Gr. *kleithron*, a bar, from *kleiein*, to close.] in Greek architecture, having a roof that forms a complete covering: said of temples.

clith·rid'i·āte, *a.* [Gr. *kleithria*, a keyhole, from *kleiein*, to close.] in zoology, shaped like a keyhole.

clī'tō·ris, *n.* [L., from Gr. *kleitoris*, clitoris, from *kleiein*, to close, hide.] a small, sensitive, erectile organ at the upper end of the external female genital organ: it corresponds to the penis of the male.

cliv'ẽrş, *n.* same as *cleavers*.

cliv'es, *n.* [from ME. *cliven*; AS. *othclifan*, to adhere.] a clevis. [Dial.]

cliv'i·ty, *n.* inclination; ascent or descent. [Rare.]

clō·ā'çȧ, *n.*; *pl.* **clō·ā'cae**, [L. *cloaca*, a sewer, from *cluere*, to cleanse.]

1. a sewer.

2. in birds, reptiles, amphibians, and many fishes, the cavity of the body into which the intestinal and genito-urinary tracts empty.

clō·ā'çăl, *a.* pertaining to the cloaca.

clōak, *n.* [ME. *cloke*; OFr. *cloke*, a cloak; LL. *cloca*, a cloak.]

1. a loose, usually sleeveless outer garment worn over other clothes.

2. a cover; that which conceals; a disguise; as, a *cloak* for his faults.

clōak, *v.t.*; cloaked (klōkt), *pt.*, *pp.*; cloaking, *ppr.* 1. to cover with or as with a cloak.

2. to hide; to conceal.

Syn.—conceal, disguise, mask, veil, hide, cover, palliate, screen, mitigate, extenuate.

clōak, *v.i.* to put on a cloak; also, to intrigue.

clōak'-and-dag'gẽr, *a.* of or characteristic of the activities of spies and undercover agents, especially as extravagantly depicted in fiction.

clōak'ed·ly, *adv.* in a concealed manner.

clōak'ing, *n.* 1. the act of covering with a cloak, or of concealing anything.

2. material for cloaks.

clōak'rọọm, *n.* a room where wraps may be temporarily left.

clōam, *n.* [AS. *clām*, mud.] earthenware; crockery. [Brit. Dial.]

clob'bẽr, *v.t.* [origin uncertain.]

1. to beat or hit repeatedly; maul. [Slang.]

2. to defeat decisively. [Slang.]

clōche, *n.* [Fr.]

1. a bell-shaped glass jar used to cover delicate plants.

2. a closefitting, bell-shaped hat for women.

clō'chẽr, *n.* [Fr.] a bell tower or belfry. [Obs.]

clock, *n.* [ME. *clock*, clock; LL. *clocca*, bell.]

1. an instrument for the measurement of time by the motion of its parts, indicating the hours, minutes, and often seconds, by hands which move upon a dial plate. It usually consists of a frame containing a train of toothed wheels operated by springs or weights and regulated by a pendulum or balance wheel. It differs from a watch in that it is not worn or carried about in the pocket.

2. a time clock.

3. a measuring or recording device suggestive of a clock, as a taximeter.

around the clock; day and night, without stopping.

clock, *v.t.* to measure or record the time of (a race, runner, etc.) with a stop watch.

çlock, *n.* a woven or embroidered ornament on the side of a stocking, going up from the ankle.

çlock, *v.t.* to put a woven or embroidered ornament on.

çlock, *n.* the European dung beetle, *Scarabæus stercorarius*, or any related beetle.

çlocked, *a.* ornamented with clocks or embroidered figures; as, *clocked* stockings.

çlock'līke, *a.* with the precision or regularity of a clock.

çlock'māk″ẽr, *n.* one who makes or repairs clocks.

çlock rā'di·ō, a radio with a built-in clock that can be set to turn the radio on or off at any desired time.

çlock'wīse, *adv.* in the same direction in which the hands move around the dial of a clock.

çlock'wŏrk, *n.* 1. the machinery and movements of a clock.
2. any similar mechanism, consisting of springs and geared wheels, as in some mechanical toys.
like clockwork; very regularly, precisely, and evenly.

çlod, *n.* [ME. *clodde*; AS. *clott*, a round mass.]
1. a lump, especially a lump of earth or clay; a mass of earth and turf.
2. turf; soil; the ground. [Rare.]
3. that which is earthy, base, and vile, as the body of man compared with his soul. [Poet.]
4. a dull, gross, stupid fellow; a dolt.
5. the part of the neck of beef nearest the shoulder.
6. in coal mining, indurated clay; bind.
7. a clot; as, *clods* of blood. [Obs.]

çlod, *v.i.*; clodded, *pt., pp.*; clodding, *ppr.* to collect into concretions, or a thick mass; as, *clodded* in clayey lumps.

çlod, *v.t.* 1. to pelt with clods.
2. to throw in a violent manner; to hurl. [Scot.[

çlod'dish, *a.* having the characteristics of a clod; dull; awkward; stupid.

çlod'dish·ness, *n.* the state of being cloddish; boorishness.

çlod'dy, *a.* consisting of clods; full of clods.

çlod'hop″pẽr, *n.* 1. a plowman.
2. an awkward, clumsy fellow; a dolt; a boor.
3. a coarse, heavy shoe, such as is worn by a plowman.

çlod'hop″ping, *a.* rude; boorish; clumsy.

çlod'pāte, *n.* a stupid fellow; a dolt.

çlod'pāt″ed, *a.* stupid; dull; doltish.

çlod'pōll, çlod'pōle, *n.* a stupid fellow; a blockhead.

çloff, çlough (klof), *n.* [origin unknown.] formerly, in commerce, an allowance of two pounds made in every three hundredweight of certain goods.

çlog, *n.* [ME. *clogge*, a lump, block; Scot. *clag*, an impediment, clog; AS. *clæg*, clay.]
1. anything put upon an animal to hinder action, as a weight fastened to its leg.
2. an encumbrance; that which hinders motion, or renders it difficult; hindrance; impediment.

Slavery is the greatest *clog* to speculation.
—Swift.

3. a heavy shoe, usually with a wooden sole: light clogs are worn in clog dancing.
4. a clog dance.
5. a clog almanac.

çlog, *v.t.*; clogged, *pt., pp.*; clogging, *ppr.* 1. to load or fill with something that retards or hinders motion; as, to *clog* the channel of a river.
2. to hinder the action of; to shackle; as, to *clog* a steer.
3. to load with anything that encumbers; to burden; to embarrass; as, to *clog* commerce with impositions or restrictions.

çlog, *v.i.* 1. to become clogged or blocked up.
2. to unite and adhere in a cluster or mass, so as to clog.
3. to do a clog dance.

çlog al'mà·naç, a primitive calendar kept by cutting notches and figures on a clog, or block of wood, bone, etc.

çlog dȧnce, a dance in which clogs are worn to beat out the rhythm.

çlog'gi·ness, *n.* the state of being clogged.

çlog'gy, *a.* tending to clog; thick; gross.

çloi'sŏn, *n.* [Fr.] a dividing band or partition; especially, the wire band used in cloisonné work.

cloi·son·né' (kloi-zŏn-nā'), *a.* [Fr., partitioned; *cloison* a partition, from L. *claudere*, to close.] denoting a form of enamel work in which the surface decoration is set in hollows formed by thin strips of wire welded to a metal plate in a complex pattern.

cloi·son·né', *n.* cloisonné enamel.

çlois'tẽr, *n.* [ME. *cloister, cloyster*; OFr. *cloistre*, a cloister; L. *claustra*, that which closes, a bolt, a place shut in, from *claudere*, to close.]

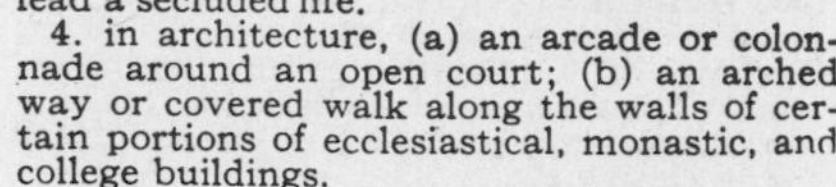
CLOISTER

1. a monastery or nunnery; a house inhabited by monks or nuns.
2. monastic life.
3. any place where one may lead a secluded life.
4. in architecture, (a) an arcade or colonnade around an open court; (b) an arched way or covered walk along the walls of certain portions of ecclesiastical, monastic, and college buildings.

Syn.—monastery, nunnery, convent, abbey, priory.—*Cloister* is generic, being a place of seclusion from the world; a *monastery* is usually for monks; a *convent* is always for women, formerly called a *nunnery*; an *abbey* and a *priory* are named from their heads, an abbot or prior.

çlois'tẽr, *v.t.*; cloistered, *pt., pp.*; cloistering, *ppr.* 1. to confine in a cloister or monastery.
2. to confine closely within walls; to shut up in retirement from the world.
3. to furnish or surround with a cloister.

çlois'tẽr·ăl, *a.* cloistral. [Obs.]

çlois'tẽred, *a.* 1. solitary; retired from the world.
2. furnished with cloisters.

çlois'tẽr·ẽr, *n.* one belonging to a cloister.

çlois'tẽr gärth, the garden or yard surrounded by a cloister.

çlois'trăl, *a.* 1. pertaining to or resembling a cloister.
2. confined in a cloister.
3. as if confined in a cloister; secluded; retired.

çlois'tress, *n.* a nun. [Rare.]

çlōke, *n.* cloak. [Archaic.]

çlōke, *v.t.*; cloked, *pt., pp.*; cloking, *ppr.* to cloak. [Archaic.]

çlōmb (klōm), archaic past tense and past participle of *climb*.

çlōne, çlon, *n.* [from Gr. *klōn*, a twig.]
1. a group of plants all of whose members are directly descended from a single individual, as by grafting or budding.
2. an individual produced by cloning.

çlōne, *v.t.*; cloned, *pt., pp.*; cloning, *ppr.* to produce by cloning.

çlon'iç, *a.* [L. *clonicus*, clonic, from Gr. *klonos*, any violent motion.] of clonus; shaking; convulsive; as, *clonic* spasm.
clonic spasm; clonus.

çlō·nic'i·ty, *n.* a clonic condition.

çlōn'ing, *n.* [from Gr. *klōn*, a twig.] the technique of producing a genetically identical duplicate of an organism by replacing the nucleus of an unfertilized ovum with the nucleus of a body cell from the organism.

çlō'nus, çlō'nŏs, *n.* [L., from Gr. *klonos*, any violent motion.] irregular, violent contractions and relaxations of a muscle or group of muscles.

çloop, *n.* [echoic.] the sound made when a cork is drawn from a bottle, or an imitation of it.

çloot, *n.* [Scot.] the whole or a part of a cloven hoof.

çloot'ie, *n.* [Scot.] 1. a small hoof.
2. [C–] the devil: with reference to the cloven hoofs.

çlōṣe, *v.t.*; closed, *pt., pp.*; closing, *ppr.* [ME. *closen*, to shut; AS. *clysung*, a closing; L. *clausus*, pp. of *claudere*, to close.]
1. to shut; to make fast by pressing together, or by stopping an open place, so as to intercept a passage; as, to *close* the eyes; to *close* a gate, door, or window.
2. to end; to finish; to conclude; to complete; as, to *close* a speech or contract.
3. to unite; to bind or bring together.
4. to fill up or stop (an opening).
to close down; to shut or stop entirely.
to close out; to dispose of (goods) by sale, as in ending a business.
to close round; to encircle; surround.
to close up; (a) to draw nearer together; (b) to shut or stop up entirely.

çlōṣe, *v.i.* 1. to unite; to coalesce; to come together: often followed by *on* or *upon*; as, the shades of night *close upon* us.
2. to come to an end; as, the debate *closed* at six o'clock.
3. to come close, in order to attack; to grapple.

If I can *close* with him, I care not for his thrust.
—Shak.

4. to become shut; to shut itself.
5. to agree; to come to an agreement.
to close in; to draw near from various directions, cutting off escape on all sides.
to close up; to heal, as a wound does.
to close with the land; in nautical usage, to approach the land.

çlōṣe, *n.* 1. conclusion; termination; final end; as, the *close* of life; the *close* of day or night.
2. the manner of shutting; junction. [Obs.]

The doors of plank were; their *close* exquisite.
—Chapman.

3. a grapple, as in wrestling.
4. in music, the conclusion of a strain.

çlōse, *n.* [ME. *clos, close*, a yard, bounds.]
1. an enclosed place; any place surrounded by a fence, wall, or hedge; specifically, the precinct of an abbey or cathedral.
2. in law, a piece of land held as private property, whether actually enclosed or not.
3. a narrow passage, leading from the street to a court and tenements. [Brit.]

çlōse, *a.* [ME. *close, clos*; OFr. *clos*, from *clore*, to shut.]
1. shut fast; tight; made fast, so as to have no opening; as, a *close* box.
2. having parts firmly united; compact; dense; as, the *close* texture of wood, *close* marching order.
3. having parts firmly adhering; viscous; tenacious, as oil or glue. [Rare.]
4. confined in circulation; stagnant; oppressive; humid: applied to the atmosphere, weather, etc.
5. in strict confinement; carefully guarded; as, a *close* secret.
6. shut away from observation; hidden; secluded.
7. confined or confining within narrow limits; narrow; as, a *close* alley.
8. near; within a short distance; as, a *close* fight or action.
9. enclosed or enclosing; shut in.
10. compressed, as thoughts or words; hence, brief; concise.

When the original is *close*, no version can reach it in the same compass.—Dryden.

11. confined to specific groups; not open to the public; restricted.
12. having the quality of keeping secrets, thoughts, or designs; cautious; reticent.
13. intimate; familiar; confidential; as, a *close* friend.
14. strict; thorough; attentive; careful; as, to give *close* attention.

Keep your mind *close* to the business.
—Locke.

15. nearly equal or alike; as, a *close* resemblance.
16. nearly equal; almost evenly balanced; as, a *close* vote.
17. near, proximate, or down to the surface on which something grows; as, a *close* shave.
18. not easily available; scarce; difficult to get; tight; as, credit is *close*.
19. niggardly; penurious; parsimonious; stingy; as, a *close* man.
20. in strict agreement with an original; literal; exact; strict; as, a *close* translation.
21. fitting tightly or snugly; as, a *close* cap.
22. in heraldry, (a) having the wings lying close to the body: said of birds; (b) having the vizor of a helmet down.
23. in phonetics, uttered with the tongue relatively near the palate: said of certain vowels, as (ē).
close communion; see under *communion*.
close corporation; a corporation in which a few persons hold all of the stock, which is rarely or never placed on the market: also *closed corporation*.
close harmony; in music, harmony consisting primarily of chords having all four tones within the compass of an octave.

Syn.—compact, compressed, dense, miserly, niggardly, firm, narrow.

çlōse, *adv.* at a little distance; very near; closely; pressingly.

Behind her Death
Close followed, pace for pace.—Milton.

close to the wind; (a) in nautical usage, heading as nearly as possible in the direction from which the wind blows; (b) barely avoiding what is unlawful.

çlōse'-bod'ied (-id), *a.* fitting the body exactly, as a garment.

close′-com·pact′ed, *a.* in compact order; compact.

close′-cur′tained (-tind), *a.* enclosed or surrounded with curtains.

closed chain, the structural form of the molecule of certain chemical compounds, represented in models and formulas as a ring of atoms.

closed gen′tian, a North American plant with dark-blue, closed, tubular flowers, blooming in the fall.

closed pri′mar·y, a direct primary election in which only the members of a given political party, as determined by enrollment, previous voting record, etc., may vote for candidates of that party.

closed sea′son, any of various annual periods during which it is illegal to kill or capture certain game or fish.

closed shop, 1. a factory, business, etc. operating under a contractual arrangement between a labor union and the employer by which only members of the union may be employed.
 2. this arrangement.
 Opposed to *open shop*.

closed syl′la·ble (-bl), a syllable that ends in a consonant.

close′-fights, *n.pl.* close quarters, or strong barriers of wood formerly used in a ship for defense when it was boarded.

close′fist′ed, *a.* extremely stingy or niggardly.

close′fit′ting, *a.* fitting tightly enough to show the contours of the body.

close′-grained, *a.* having a fine, compact grain or texture, as certain woods.

close′hand′ed, *a.* closefisted; covetous.

close′hand′ed·ness, *n.* covetousness.

close′-hauled, *a.* having the sails adjusted (hauled close) for heading as nearly as possible in the direction from which the wind is blowing.

close′-lipped, *a.* close-mouthed.

close′ly, *adv.* 1. in a close, compact manner.
 2. with little space or time intervening; as, to follow *closely* at one's heels; one event follows *closely* upon another.
 3. intently; attentively; with the mind or thoughts fixed; as, to look or attend *closely*.
 4. secretly; privately. [Rare.]
 5. with affection, attachment, or interest; intimately; as, men *closely* connected by friendship.
 6. strictly; within close limits; without communication abroad; as, a prisoner *closely* confined.
 7. with strict adherence to the original; as, to translate *closely*.

close′-mouthed′, *a.* reticent; not talking much; telling little; taciturn.

clos′en, *v.t.* to make close or closer. [Rare.]

close′ness, *n.* the condition or quality of being close.
 Syn.—nearness, narrowness, strictness, stinginess, intimacy, literalness.

close′-or″der drill, a series of military exercises in marching, maneuvering, the carrying and ceremonial handling of arms, etc., in which the troops are arranged in compact units at close intervals and distances.

close′-out″, *a.* of or designating a final sale of goods, as in ending a business, disposing of merchandise at the end of a season, etc.

close′-out″, *n.* an act or occasion of closing out, as by having a sale.

close′pent, *a.* shut close.

close quar′ters, 1. originally, an enclosed space on a ship, in which a last stand could be made against boarders; close-fights.
 2. (a) space that is narrow or crowded; (b) hand-to-hand encounter with an enemy.

clos′er, *n.* 1. one who or that which closes.
 2. in building, the last stone or brick in a horizontal row, of smaller size than the others and fitted to close the row.
 3. in shoemaking, one who or that which closes or sews the seams in boots or shoes.

close′-reef, *v.t.* to take in all the reefs of (a sail or ship).

close shave, a narrow escape from danger or misfortune. [Colloq.]

close′stool, *n.* a box with a tight cover containing a chamber pot.

clos′et, *n.* [ME. *closet*; OFr. *closet*, a small enclosure, dim. of *clos*, an enclosed place.]
 1. a small room for retirement; any room for privacy; as, a dressing *closet*.
 2. a small room or cupboard for depositing or storing articles; as, a china *closet*, a clothes *closet*.
 3. a privy; a water closet.
 4. a king's private room for prayer or consultation.
 5. in heraldry, a diminutive of the bar, having one half of its width.

clos′et, *v.t.*; closeted, *pt., pp.*; closeting, *ppr.*
 1. to shut up in or as in a closet; to conceal.
 2. to admit or take into a private room for consultation; to admit to a confidential conversation: usually reflexive; as, the treasurer *closeted* himself with the accountants for an hour.

clos′et, *a.* 1. private; concealed.
 2. designed or adapted only for private or secluded use; as, *closet* drama is written only to be read, not acted.

close time, a closed season. [Chiefly Brit.]

close′-tongued (-tungd), *a.* secretive; cautious in speaking; close-mouthed.

close′-up, *n.* 1. in motion pictures and television, a picture, as of a character, taken at very close range so as to give distinct detail.
 2. a close view.

closh, *n.* a bowling game, perhaps the game of ninepins. [Obs.]

clo′sure (-zhūr), *n.* [OFr. *closure*; L. *clausura*, a closing, from *claudere*, to close.]
 1. the act of shutting; a closing; as, the *closure* of a factory.
 2. that which closes, or shuts: that by which separate parts are fastened or made to adhere.
 3. enclosure; that which confines. [Obs.]
 4. a finish; end; conclusion.
 5. the parliamentary procedure for closing a debate so that a vote can be taken upon the measure under discussion without any delay.

clo′sure, *v.t.* and *v.i.*; closured, *pt., pp.*; closuring, *ppr.* to apply closure to (a debate, bill, etc.).

clot, *n.* [ME. *clot*, *clotte*; AS. *clott*, a round mass.] a coagulation, particularly of soft or fluid matter, which forms into a mass or lump; as, a *clot* of blood.

clot, *v.i.*; clotted, *pt., pp.*; clotting, *ppr.* to coagulate, as soft or fluid matter, into a thick mass; as, milk or blood *clots*.

clot, *v.t.* to cause to become a clot, or clots.

clot′bur, *n.* [G. *klette*.]
 1. burdock. [Brit. Dial.]
 2. the cocklebur. [Brit. Dial.]

clote, *n.* [ME. *clote*, *cloothe*; AS. *clate*, the burdock.] the burdock or clotbur. [Obs.]

cloth (*or* kloth), *n.*; *pl.* **cloths** (*or* kloths), [ME. *cloth*; AS. *clāth*, cloth.]
 1. a woven, knitted, or pressed fabric of fibrous material, as wool, hair, cotton, flax, hemp, synthetic fibers, etc., used for garments or other covering, and for various other purposes, as household furnishings.
 2. the covering of a table; a tablecloth.
 3. a texture or covering put to a specific use; as, a wash*cloth*, loin*cloth*.
 4. the usual or identifying dress of any profession.
 5. the profession itself, especially the profession of a clergyman.
 6. in nautical usage, canvas; sail.
 7. dress; raiment. [Obs.]
 cloth measure; the measure of length and width by which cloth was formerly sold. The standard yard was divided into quarters and nails, there being 4 nails of 2¼ inches each to a quarter yard.
 cloth paper; a coarse paper used in pressing woolen cloths.
 cloth shearer; one who shears cloth and removes the nap from its surface.

clothe, *v.t.*; clothed *or* clad, *pt., pp.*; clothing, *ppr.* [ME. *clothen*; AS. *clāthian*, to clothe.]
 1. to put garments on; to dress.
 The Lord God made coats of skin and *clothed* them. —Gen. iii. 21.
 2. to provide with clothes.
 3. to provide; to equip; to invest; to cover over, as if with a garment; as, to *clothe* thoughts with words.
 4. in nautical usage, to rig, as a mast.

clothe, *v.i.* to wear clothes. [Rare.]
 Care no more to *clothe* and eat. —Shak.

clothes (*or* klōz), *n.pl.* [ME. *clothes*; AS. *clāthas*, clothes, pl. of *clāth*, a garment.]
 1. covering for the human body; articles, usually of cloth, designed to cover, protect, or adorn the body; dress; vestments; vesture.
 2. the covering of a bed; bedclothes.
 Syn.—apparel, array, attire, dress, garments, raiment, vesture, habit, garb.

clothes′bas′ket, *n.* a large basket for holding or carrying clothes.

clothes′brush, *n.* a brush for removing dust, etc. from clothes.

clothes′horse, *n.* 1. a framework on which to hang clothes or household linen for airing or drying, usually so constructed that it may be either folded or expanded.
 2. a person regarded as paying too much attention to his clothes, or as having little talent except for dressing well. [Slang.]

clothes′line, *n.* a rope or wire on which clothes are hung to dry or to be aired.

clothes moth, a moth belonging to the genus *Tinea*, the larvae of which feed on furs, woolen goods, etc. They construct tubular cases from the material in which they live.

clothes′pin, *n.* a device for securing clothes on a line; made in the form of a small clip, as a forked piece of wood or plastic.

clothes pole, a pole for supporting a clothesline.

clothes′press, *n.* a case or closet in which clothes are kept; a wardrobe: also written *clothes press*.

clothes tree, an upright pole with branching hooks or pegs near the top to hold coats and hats.

cloth′ier, (-yēr), *n.* 1. a person who makes or sells clothes.
 2. a dealer in cloth.

cloth′ing, *n.* [ME. *clothing*, from AS. *clāth*, cloth.]
 1. garments in general; clothes; dress; raiment.
 2. a covering.
 3. the art or practice of manufacturing cloth. [Rare.]
 The king took measures to instruct the refugees from Flanders in the art of *clothing*. —Ray.
 4. a jacket of nonconducting material for a boiler, engine cylinder, or pipe to prevent radiation of heat.
 5. strips of wire-toothed card used on carding machines as a cover for the cylinders; card clothing.

cloth′ing wool, short strands of wool used in making woolen goods: called also *carding wool*.

Clo′tho, *n.* [L., from Gr. *Klōthō*, one of the three Fates, the spinster, from *klōthein*, to spin.] in Greek mythology, one of the three Fates, who holds the distaff and spins the thread of life.

cloth of ac′ca, a garment of cloth of gold shot with sky blue.

cloth of gold, cloth made from gold threads, either wholly or in part.

cloth of sil′ver, cloth made from silver threads, either wholly or in part.

cloth yard, 1. the yard used in measuring cloth, equal to 3 feet (36 inches).
 2. the arrow used with the long bow: so called from its length.

clot′poll, *n.* a clodpoll; a blockhead.

clot′ted, *a.* coagulated into a mass.
 clotted cream; cream processed by scalding and cooling.

clot′ty, *a.* full of clots; tending to clot.

clo′ture, *n.* closure: applied to parliamentary debate.

clo′ture, *v.t.*; clotured, *pt., pp.*; cloturing, *ppr.* to closure.

cloud, *n.* [ME. *cloud*, *cloude*, a cloud; AS. *clud*, a mass of rock.]
 1. a visible mass of vapor, especially one suspended in the sky.
 2. a mass of smoke, dust, steam, etc. rising or floating in the air.
 3. a vein or spot darker than the area surrounding it, as in stones, yarn, varnish, etc.
 4. a great number of things close together or in motion; as, a *cloud* of locusts.
 5. figuratively, a state of obscurity, darkness, or gloominess; as, amidst the *clouds* of war; a *cloud* hung over his character; there was a *cloud* thrown over their prospects.
 6. a soft, loosely knitted woolen scarf, worn by women as a wrap for the head and neck.
 7. an appearance of murkiness or dimness, as in a liquid or mirror.
 cloud on a (or *the*) *title*; a defect in a title to property which can often be cleared up by action in a court of chancery or by appeal to a legislative body.
 in the clouds; (a) high up in the sky; (b) fanciful; impractical; (c) in a reverie or daydream.
 under a cloud; (a) under suspicion of wrongdoing; (b) in a depressed or troubled state of mind.

cloud, *v.t.*; clouded, *pt., pp.*; clouding, *ppr.*

1. to overspread with a cloud or clouds; as, the sky is *clouded*.

2. to obscure; to darken; as, to *cloud* the rays of truth or reason.

3. to darken in veins or spots; to variegate with colors; as, to *cloud* yarn.

4. to make gloomy or troubled.

What sullen fury *clouds* his scornful brow. —Pope.

5. to sully; to tarnish (a reputation, etc.).

çloud, *v.i.* 1. to grow cloudy; to become obscure with clouds: sometimes followed by *over*; as, the sky *clouds over*.

2. to become gloomy or troubled.

çloud′āġe, *n.* prevalence of clouds. [Rare.]

çloud′ber″ry, *n.*; *pl.* **çloud′ber″ries,** a plant, *Rubus chamæmorus*, with yellowish-red fruit: also called *knotberry*.

CLOUDBERRY (*Rubus chamæmorus*)

çloud′-built (-bilt), *a.* located in or built of clouds; hence, imaginary.

çloud′bŭrst, *n.* a sudden, unusually heavy downpour of rain, accompanied sometimes by violent wind.

çloud′-capped, çloud′-çapt, *a.* capped with clouds; having clouds around the top; as, a *cloud-capped* mountain.

çloud chām′bẽr, an enclosed chamber supersaturated with water vapor for revealing the presence of moving charged particles by their ionization of the vapor.

çloud′-çŏm·pel″lẽr, *n.* he that drives clouds; Jove. [Poet.]

çloud′-çŏm·pel″ling, *a.* driving clouds; as, *cloud-compelling* Jove.

çloud′ed, *a.* (a) overcast; overspread with clouds; (b) obscured; darkened; (c) rendered gloomy or sullen; (d) variegated with colored spots or veins; as, the *clouded* sky, *clouded* marble.

çloud′i·ly, *adv.* in a cloudy manner; darkly; obscurely.

çloud′i·ness, *n.* 1. the state of being overcast with clouds; as, the *cloudiness* of the atmosphere.

2. darkness of appearance; variegation of colors.

çloud′ing, *n.* 1. a clouded appearance, especially like that given to ribbons and silks in the process of dyeing.

2. a variety of colors in yarn, appearing at regular intervals.

çloud′land, *n.* a visionary realm; the land of fancy and dreams.

çloud′less, *a.* without a cloud; unclouded; clear; bright; luminous; as, *cloudless* skies.

çloud′less·ly, *adv.* without clouds.

çloud′less·ness, *n.* the condition of being clear; the state of being without clouds.

çloud′let, *n.* a little cloud.

çloud rack, a drifting mass of clouds.

çloud′y, *a.*; *comp.* cloudier; *superl.* cloudiest. 1. overcast with clouds; obscured with clouds; as, a *cloudy* day.

2. of or like clouds.

The *cloudy* pillar descended. —Ex. xxxiii. 9.

3. obscure; dark; indistinct; not easily understood; as, *cloudy* notions.

4. having the appearance of gloom; indicating gloom, anxiety, sullenness, or ill nature; not open or cheerful; as, *cloudy* looks.

5. marked with veins or spots of dark or various hues, as marble.

6. lacking clearness or luster; opaque; not transparent; as, a *cloudy* diamond.

çlough (kluf), *n.* [ME. *clough*; Ice. *klofi*, a cleft or rift in a hill, from *kljufa*, to split.]

1. a narrow cleft, ravine, or gorge.

2. a kind of sluice for draining off water, employed in the operation of improving land by flooding it with muddy water; a clow.

çlough (kluf), *n.* same as *cloff*.

çlōur, *n.* [Scot.]

1. a blow.

2. an indentation produced by a blow, or a raised lump, as from a blow on the head.

çlout, *n.* [ME. *clout*, *clut*; AS. *clūt*; W. *clwt*, a patch.]

1. a patch; a piece of cloth or leather, etc. used to mend something. [Archaic or Dial.]

2. any piece of cloth, especially a worthless piece; sometimes, a swaddling band. [Archaic or Dial.]

3. in archery, (a) a target of white cloth on a frame; (b) a shot that strikes the target.

He'll ne'er hit the *clout*. —Shak.

4. an iron plate on an axletree to keep it from wearing.

5. a blow with or as with the hand; a rap. [Colloq.]

6. a long, powerful hit in baseball. [Slang.]

çlout, *v.t.* 1. to patch; to mend by sewing on a clout, or patch. [Archaic or Dial.]

2. to cover with a piece of cloth. [Archaic or Dial.]

3. to join clumsily.

4. to strike, as with the hand; to knock; to hit. [Colloq.]

5. to stud or fasten with clout nails.

çlout′ed, *a.* 1. patched; mended clumsily; covered with a clout. [Archaic or Dial.]

2. studded, strengthened, or fastened with clout nails.

3. clotted; as, *clouted* cream. [Brit. Dial.]

çlout nāil, a short, large-headed nail used as a stud or for securing clouts or small patches of iron.

çlōve, *n.* [D. *klove*, *kloof*, a cleft.] a cleft; a ravine; a gully.

çlōve, *n.* [ME. *clowe*; Sp. *clavo*, a clove, from L. *clavus*, a nail: so called from its shape.]

1. the dried flower bud of *Caryophyllus aromaticus*, a tree growing in the West Indies, British India, Ceylon, and Mauritius.

CLOVE (*Caryophyllus aromaticus*)

2. a pungent, fragrant spice obtained from these buds.

3. the tree.

çlōve, *n.* [ME. *clove*; AS. *clufu*, akin to *cleofan*, to cleave.] a segment of a bulb, as of garlic.

çlōve, *n.* [Anglo-Fr. *clou*, ult. from L. *clavus*, a nail.] a weight of about seven pounds, formerly used in weighing cheese or wool.

çlōve, *v.* 1. archaic past tense of *cleave* (to cling).

2. alternative past tense and poetic past participle of *cleave* (to split).

çlōve gil′ly·flow′ẽr, same as *clove pink*.

çlōve hitch, a kind of knot for fastening a rope around a spar, pole, or another rope.

çlōve hook, one of a pair of overlapping hooks: sometimes called *sister hook*.

çlō′ven, *a.* [ME. *cloven*; AS. *clofen*, pp. of *cleofan*, to cleave.] divided; parted.

çlō′ven, *v.* alternative past participle of *cleave* (to split).

çlō′ven foot, a cloven hoof.

çlō′ven-foot″ed, çlō′ven-hoo̤fed, *a.* 1. having cloven hoofs; bisulcate.

2. satanic; devilish.

çlō′ven hoo̤f, a hoof divided by a cleft, as in the ox, deer, and sheep: used as a symbol of the Devil, who is usually pictured with such hoofs.

çlōve piñk, a variety of pink, a plant with small flowers having a clovelike scent.

çlō′vẽr, *n.* [ME. *clover*; AS. *clafre*, clover.] a plant of the various species of the genus *Trifolium*, family *Leguminosæ*. The species are low-growing herbs, chiefly found in the temperate regions of the Northern Hemisphere. The *red clover*, *Trifolium pratense*, is generally cultivated for fodder and for enriching land. The *white clover*, *Trifolium repens*, is also used as fodder for cattle, either green or dry, and is also commonly used in lawn seed mixtures. The name *clover* is often applied to plants belonging to the same natural order, although not of the same genus, as *sweet clover*.

in clover; originally, in good pasture; hence, living in most enjoyable circumstances; living luxuriously, free from work and care.

çlō′vẽred, *a.* covered with clover.

çlō′vẽr·lēaf, *n.*; *pl.* **çlō′vẽr·lēaves,** a multiple highway intersection in the form of a four-leaf clover, which, by means of curving ramps from one level to another, permits traffic to move or turn in any of four directions without interference.

CLOVERLEAF

çlō′vẽr-lēaf, *a.* in the shape or pattern of a leaf of clover.

çlō′vẽr wee′vil, a kind of weevil, genus *Apion*, different species of which feed on the seeds of the clover and other leguminous plants.

çlō′vẽr wŏrm, a moth, *Asopia costalis*, the larvae of which are very destructive to clover hay.

çlow, *n.* same as *clough* (sluice).

çlowe′-gi·lof″re (-ẽr), *n.* the spice clove. [Obs.]

çlown, *n.* [ME. *cloune*; Ice. *klunni*, a clumsy, boorish fellow.]

1. originally, a peasant; a rustic.

2. one who has the manners of a rustic; a boor; a man of coarse manners; an ill-bred man.

3. a man whose work is entertaining in a circus or vaudeville by antics, jokes, tricks, etc.; a jester; a buffoon.

çlown, *v.i.* 1. to perform as a clown.

2. to play practical jokes, act silly, etc.

çlown′āġe, *n.* the manners of a clown. [Obs.]

çlown′ẽr·y, *n.*; *pl.* **çlown′ẽr·ies,** the actions or behavior of a clown; clowning.

çlown′hēal, *n.* a plant supposedly having healing properties: called also *clown's woundwort*.

çlown′ish, *a.* 1. pertaining to or resembling clowns.

2. having rough manners; ill-bred; awkward.

Syn.—boorish, bucolic, awkward, clumsy, rude.

çlown′ish·ly, *adv.* in a clownish manner.

çlown′ish·ness, *n.* the quality of being clownish.

çloy, *v.t.*; cloyed, *pt.*, *pp.*; cloying, *ppr.* [Fr. *clouer*, to nail; *clou*, a nail; L. *clavus*, a nail.]

1. to fill; to choke up; to obstruct. [Obs.]

2. to glut; to surfeit by too much of anything, especially anything too sweet, rich, etc.; to satiate.

Who can *cloy* the hungry edge of appetite
By bare imagination of a feast? —Shak.

3. to spike, as a gun; to drive a spike into, as a vent. [Obs.]

4. in farriery, to prick or lame (a horse) in shoeing. [Obs.]

5. to claw. [Obs.]

çloy′less, *a.* not cloying; not filling to satiety.

çloy′ment, *n.* surfeit; repletion beyond the demands of appetite. [Obs.]

çlub, *n.* [ME. *club*, *clubb*, a club; Ice. *klubba*, *klumba*, a club, a mass of anything.]

1. a stick or piece of wood, usually with one end thicker and heavier than the other, used as a weapon.

2. a variously shaped stick or bat used in certain games, as golf, hockey, polo, etc.

3. one of the suits of playing cards, characterized by a black trefoil or clover-leaf figure (♣).

4. [*pl.*] this suit of cards.

5. a group of people associated for a common purpose, usually in an organization that meets regularly.

6. the room, building, or facilities used by such an association.

çlub, *v.i.*; clubbed, *pt.*, *pp.*; clubbing, *ppr.*

1. to join, as a number of individuals, to the same end; to contribute separate powers to one end, purpose, or effect: usually with *together*.

Till grosser atoms, tumbling in the stream
Of fancy, madly met, and *clubbed* into a dream. —Dryden.

2. to pay an equal proportion of a common reckoning or charge.

3. in nautical usage, to be driven along by a current, with an anchor out.

çlub, *v.t.* 1. to strike with or as with a club.

2. to give or combine (something) for a common purpose; to pool (resources, etc.).

3. to use (a rifle) as a club by holding it so as to hit with the butt end.

4. to throw, or permit to fall, into disorder:

said in reference to a company of soldiers. [Brit.]

club′bȧ·ble, club′ȧ·ble, *a.* denoting possession of qualities that fit a person to be a member of a club; hence, sociable. [Colloq.]

clubbed, *a.* shaped like or used as a club.

club′bẽr, *n.* 1. a person or the thing that clubs.
2. a member of a party, club, or association. [Rare.]

club′bish, *a.* 1. rough; ill-mannered; rustic. [Obs.]
2. disposed to associate together; clubbable.

club′bist, *n.* one who belongs to or frequents clubs. [Rare.]

club cär, a railroad car with lounge chairs and, usually, a bar.

club′foot, *n.* 1. a congenital deformity of the foot, characterized by a misshapen or twisted, often clublike, appearance: also called *talipes.*
2. *pl.* **club′feet,** a foot so deformed.

club′-foot″ed, *a.* having clubfoot.

club gràss, cattail, a tall, reedy marsh plant.

club′hand, *n.* 1. a deformity of the hand analogous to clubfoot.
2. a hand so deformed.

club′haul, *v.t.*; clubhauled, *pt., pp.*; clubhauling, *ppr.* to tack (a ship in a precarious situation) by dropping the lee anchor as soon as the wind is out of the sails and maneuvering the ship's head to the wind: the cable is cut and the sails trimmed when the ship swings off from the wind onto the new tack.

club′house, *n.* the building occupied by a club.

club′măn, *n.*; *pl.* **club′men,** a man who is a member of a club or clubs, especially, one who spends much time at club social affairs, night clubs, etc.

club moss, any of a group of flowerless, evergreen plants of the order *Lycopodiaceæ*, genus *Lycopodium*: they reproduce by spores borne in club-shaped cases.

club′room, *n.* a room used by a club as a meeting place, for social affairs, etc.

club′root, *n.* a disease attacking cabbage, ruining the heads and twisting the roots in irregular growths.

club rush, any plant of the genus *Scirpus*; also, the cattail.

club sand′wich, a sandwich of two or more layers, often toasted, containing chicken, bacon, lettuce, mayonnaise, tomatoes, etc.

club′-shāped, *a.* having the shape of a club.

club steak (stāk), a small beefsteak cut from the loin tip.

club top′sāil (*or* -sl), an accessory sail; a kind of gaff topsail.

club′wom″ăn (-woom″), *n.*; *pl.* **club′wom″en** (-wim″), a woman member of a club or clubs.

cluck, *v.i.*; clucked (klukt), *pt., pp.*; clucking, *ppr.* [ME. *clokken*; AS. *cloccian*, to cluck; echoic.] to utter the call or cry of a hen calling her chickens or brooding.

cluck, *v.t.* 1. to call (chickens) by clucking.
2. to utter with such a sound; as, she *clucked* her disapproval.

cluck, *n.* 1. the sound made by a hen calling her chickens or when brooding.
2. a sound resembling or imitating this.

cluck′ing, *n.* the sound of a hen when she calls her chickens.

clūe, *n.* and *v.t.* clew: **usual spelling for** *n.*, sense 2.

clum, *interj.* be silent; hush! [Obs.]

clum′bẽr, *n.* [so named from *Clumber*, the estate of the Duke of Newcastle.] a kind of field spaniel having a stocky body with short legs and a thick coat of straight, white hair marked with yellow or orange: also *clumber spaniel.*

clump, *n.* [from AS. *clympre*, a lump of metal; compare Dan., Sw. *klump*, a clump, lump.]
1. a lump; a mass.
2. a cluster of trees or shrubs.
3. the compact layers of clay found in coal strata.
4. a mass of bacteria.
5. the sound of heavy footsteps.

clump, *v.t.*; clumped (klumpt), *pt., pp.*; clumping, *ppr.* 1. to plant in a clump; to group together in a cluster.
2. to cause to form clumps.

clump, *v.i.* 1. to walk clumsily or heavily.
2. to form clumps.

clump′ẽr, *v.t.* to form into clumps or masses. [Obs.]

clump′ish, *a.* heavy and clumsy.

clumps, *n.* a game of questions and answers: so named from the fact that the players divide into two clumps, or groups.

clump′y, *a.*; *comp.* clumpier; *superl.* clumpiest,
1. full of clumps.
2. like clumps.

clum′si·ly, *adv.* in a clumsy manner; awkwardly.

clum′si·ness, *n.* the state or quality of being clumsy.

clum′sy, *a.*; *comp.* clumsier; *superl.* clumsiest, [ME. *clumsid, clomsed*, pp. of *clumsen*, to benumb; Sw. dial. *klummsen*, to benumb with the cold; Norw. *klumsa*, speechless, palsied.]
1. stiffened with cold; benumbed. [Obs.]
2. moving heavily, slowly, or awkwardly; as, *clumsy* fingers.
3. awkward; ungainly; unhandy; lacking skill or grace; as, a *clumsy* fellow.
4. ill-made; badly constructed; as, a *clumsy* garment.
5. badly contrived; inelegant: said of style.

Syn.—awkward, bungling, inexpert, ungraceful, lubberly, troublesome.

clunch, *n.* [origin obscure, prob. from same root as AS. *clympre*, a lump of metal.]
1. indurated clay, found in coal pits.
2. a soft limestone.

clung, past tense and past participle of *cling.*

clung, *a.* shrunken. [Obs.]

Clū′ni·ac, *a.* relating to the monks of Cluny.

Clū′ni·ac, *n.* one of an order of Benedictine monks founded in the tenth century, taking their name from the town of *Cluny*, France.

clunk, *n.* [echoic.]
1. a dull metallic sound.
2. a heavy blow. [Colloq.]
3. a dull or stupid person. [Slang.]

clunk, *v.i.* and *v.t.*; clunked (klunkt), *pt., pp.*; clunking, *ppr.* to move or strike with a clunk or clunks.

clunk′ẽr, *n.* 1. an old machine in poor repair; especially, a noisy, dilapidated automobile. [Slang.]
2. a thing that is worthless, inferior, unsuccessful, etc. [Slang.]

Clū′ny lāce, [after *Cluny*, France.] a heavy bobbin lace with an open design, made of linen or cotton thread.

clū′pē·id, *n.* [from Mod.L. *Clupea*, name of the genus, from L. *clupea*, kind of small river fish.] any of a family of soft-finned fishes, as herring, sardines, etc.

clū′pē·id, *a.* of the clupeids.

clū′pē·i·form, *a.* [L. *clupea*, a small river fish, herring, and *forma*, form.] like a herring in form.

clū′pē·oid, *a.* [L. *clupea*, a small river fish, and Gr. *eidos*, shape.] of or like the fish of the herring family.

clū′pē·oid, *n.* any fish of the herring family.

clus′tẽr, *n.* [ME. *cluster*; AS. *cluster*, a cluster.]
1. a bunch; a number of things of the same kind growing together or gathered together; as, a *cluster* of grapes.
2. a number of persons, animals, or things grouped together; as, a *cluster* of bees, a *cluster* of people.

clus′tẽr, *v.i.* and *v.t.*; clustered, *pt., pp.*; clustering, *ppr.* to grow in clusters; to gather or unite in a bunch or bunches.

clus′tẽr cup, same as *aecium.*

clus′tẽr·ing·ly, *adv.* in clusters.

clus′tẽr·y, *a.* growing in clusters; full of clusters.

clutch (kluch), *n.* 1. a grip; seizure; grasp; as, to make a *clutch* at a thing.
2. a claw or hand in the act of seizing.

It was the hard fortune of a cock to fall into the *clutches* of a cat. —L'Estrange.

3. [*usually pl.*] power; control; as, to fall into the *clutches* of an enemy.
4. in an automobile, etc., the apparatus by means of which the gears on a motor crankshaft are temporarily connected to or disengaged from the gears on a drive shaft.
5. the lever or pedal by which this device is operated.
6. a device for gripping and holding, as in a crane.
7. a critical situation or emergency; as, he's dependable in the *clutch.* [Slang.]

clutch, *a.* 1. designating or done in a critical situation. [Colloq.]
2. likely to function well or be successful in such a situation. [Colloq.]

clutch, *v.t.*; clutched (klucht), *pt., pp.*; clutching, *ppr.* [ME. *clucchen*, to clutch; Scot., *cleuk*, a claw, talon; origin doubtful.]
1. to grasp or hold eagerly or tightly.
2. to seize, clasp, or grip with a hand or claw; as, to *clutch* a dagger.

clutch, *v.i.* to snatch or seize (with *at*).

clutch, *v.t.* [dial., from ME. *cleken*, to hatch, from ON. *klekja*, to hatch.] to hatch (chickens).

clutch, *n.* 1. a nest of eggs.
2. a brood of chicks.

clut′tẽr, *n.* [W. *cludair*, a heap, pile; *cludeirio*, to pile up; *cludo*, a heap.]
1. a heap or assemblage of things lying in confusion; confusion; litter.

He saw what a *clutter* there was with huge pots, pans, and spits. —L'Estrange.

2. confused noise; bustle; clamor.

Prithee, Tim, why all this *clutter?*
Why ever in these raging fits? —Swift.

clut′tẽr, *v.t.*; cluttered, *pt., pp.*; cluttering, *ppr.* to crowd together in disorder; to litter; to jumble (often with *up*); as, to *clutter up* a room.

The law of a history, which *clutters* not praises together upon the first mention of a name. —Bacon.

clut′tẽr, *v.i.* 1. to make a clatter.
2. to bustle; to fill with confusion.

Clȳdes′dāle, *n.* [after *Clydesdale*, the valley of the River Clyde, Scotland, where the breed originated.] any of a breed of heavy, strong draft horse.

Clȳdes′dāle ter′ri·ẽr, a small Scottish terrier of a breed developed from the Skye terrier.

clyp′ē-, [from L. *clipeus, clypeus*, a shield.] a combining form signifying *like a shield*, or *furnished with a shield*, as in *Clype*astridae.

Clyp·ē·as′tẽr, *n.* a genus of sea urchins typical of the *Clypeastridæ.*

Clyp·ē·as′tri·dae, *n.pl.* [L., from *clipeus*, a shield, and Gr. *astēr*, a star.] a subfamily of sea urchins, of a rounded form, having the mouth and vent on the underside.

clyp·ē·as′troid, *a.* [*clype-*, and Gr. *astēr*, a star, and *eidos*, form.] pertaining to the genus *Clypeaster.*

clyp·ē·as′troid, *n.* a sea urchin of the genus *Clypeaster.*

clyp′ē·āte, *a.* in biology, (a) shaped like a shield; (b) having a shieldlike process.

clyp′ē·āt·ed, *a.* clypeate.

clyp′ē·i·form, *a.* [*clype-*, and L. *forma*, form.] shield-shaped.

cly·pē′ō·lȧ, *n.*; *pl.* **cly·pē′ō·lae,** [L., dim. of *clipeus, clypeus*, a shield.] a modified leaf bearing spores; a sporophyll.

clyp′ē·us, *n.*; *pl.* **clyp′ē·ī,** [L. *clipeus, clypeus*, a shield.] a plate or shieldlike process on the head of certain insects.

clys′mic, *a.* [Gr. *klysma*, a liquid used for washing out, from *klyzein*, to wash.] washing; cleansing.

clys′tẽr, *n.* [OFr. *clistere*; L. *clyster*; Gr. *klystēr*, a clyster pipe, syringe, from *klyzein*, to wash.] in medicine, a rectal injection; an enema.

Clȳ·tem·nes′trȧ, Clȳ·taem·nes′trȧ, *n.* in Greek legend, the wife of Agamemnon: with the aid of her lover Aegisthus she murdered her husband when he came back from the Trojan War, and was consequently herself killed by their son Orestes.

Cm, in chemistry, curium.

cnē′mi·ăl (nē′), *a.* [Gr. *knēmē*, the tibia.] pertaining to the shinbone, or tibia.

Cnī′cus (nī′), *n.* [L. *cnicus*; Gr. *knēkos*, a plant of the thistle kind.] in botany, a genus of thistlelike composite plants, having a hard-spined involucre, including the genus *Cirsium.*

cnī′dȧ (nī′), *n.*; *pl.* **cnī′dae,** [L. *cnide*; Gr. *knidē*, a nettle, from *knizein*, to scrape.] a nematocyst, or stinging cell, of certain hydrozoans.

Cnī·dā′ri·ȧ (nī-), *n.pl.* [L., from Gr. *knidē*, a nettle.] the *Cœlenterata*, excluding the sponges.

cnī′dō·blast (nī′), *n.* [L. *cnide*; Gr. *knidē*, a nettle, and *blastos*, a germ.] a cell developing, or which has developed, a cnida.

cnī′dō·cil (nī′), *n.* [L. *cnide*, a nettle, and *cilium*, an eyelid.] the thread of a cnida.

cnī′dō·phōre (nī′), *n.* [L. *cnide*; Gr. *knidē*, a nettle, and *-phoros*, carrying, from *pherein*, to bear.] any part or organ developing cnidoblasts.

cō-, 1. a shortened form of *com-*, meaning: (a) *together, with*, as in *co*-operation; (b) *joint*, as in *co*-owner; (c) *equally*, as in *co*extensive.
2. a prefix formed from *complement*, meaning *complement of*, as in *co*sine.

-cō, [from *co.*, abbrev. of *company.*] a suffix used in forming the trade names of many business firms, commercial products, etc.

Co, in chemistry, cobalt.

cō·ȧ·cẽr′vāte, *v.t.* [L. *coacervatus*, pp. of *coacervare*, to heap together.] to heap up; to pile. [Rare.]

cō·ȧ·cẽr′vāte, *a.* heaped; raised into a pile;

collected into a crowd; accumulated. [Rare.]

çō·ac·ẽr·vā′tion, *n.* the act of heaping, or state of being heaped together. [Rare.]

çōach, *n.* [Fr. *coche*; Hung. *kocsi*, a coach, so called from *Kócs*, Hungary, where the coach was invented and first used.]

1. a large, covered, four-wheeled carriage with seats for passengers inside and an open, raised seat in front for the driver; stagecoach; four-in-hand.

2. a cabin in a large ship of war, near the stern and beneath the poop deck, usually occupied by the captain. [Obs.]

3. (a) a private tutor, generally employed to prepare a person for a specific examination; (b) a trainer or instructor in athletics, dramatics, etc.

4. a railroad passenger car furnishing the lowest-priced seating accommodations.

5. an enclosed automobile, usually a two-door sedan.

6. a bus.

7. in baseball, a member of the team at bat stationed near first or third base to advise the base runners.

çōach, *v.t.*; coached, *pt., pp.*; coaching, *ppr.*

1. to carry in a coach.

2. to instruct (a person) in a subject, or to prepare (a person) for an examination by private instruction.

3. to train and instruct (athletes, actors, etc.).

4. in baseball, to advise (base runners) in their movements.

çōach, *v.i.* 1. to ride or travel in a coach.

2. to act in the capacity of coach; as, he *coaches* at Harvard; also, to receive special instruction from a coach; as, he will *coach* in mathematics.

çōach′-and-fōur′, *n.* a coach drawn by four horses.

çōach box, the seat on which the driver of a coach sits.

çōach dog, a large, lean, short-haired dog, generally white, spotted with black; a Dalmatian: so called because formerly trained to run beside a carriage.

çōach′ee, *n.* a coach driver. [Old Slang.]

çōach′ẽr, *n.* 1. a person who coaches.

2. a horse used or trained to draw a coach.

çōach′fel″lōw, *n.* 1. a horse which draws a coach along with another.

2. one intimately connected with another; a close companion.

çōach′măn, *n.*; *pl.* **çōach′men,** 1. the driver of a coach or carriage.

2. a fish, *Dules auriga*, frequenting waters of the tropics: so named from its long, whiplike spine.

3. [said to be so named from a famous coachman-angler.] an artificial fly used in angling: it has a peacock-green body, brown hackles, and white wings.

çōach′măn·ship, *n.* skill in driving coaches.

çōach′whip (-hwip), *n.* a whip used in coach-driving.

coachwhip bird; an Australian passerine bird, *Psophodes crepitans*: also called *coachman* and *whipbird*.

coachwhip snake; a nonpoisonous snake of the genus *Masticophis*, having a tail resembling in its markings the strands of a braided whiplash. It is found in the southern United States.

çōach′wood, *n.* a large tree, *Ceratopetalum apetalum*, of the saxifrage family, found in Australasia, and valued for its compact, fine-grained wood.

çō·açt′, *v.t.* and *v.i.* to force together; to act together. [Rare.]

çō·aç′tion, *n.* [L. *coactio*, a collecting, from *coactus*, pp. of *cogere*, to drive together, collect.] force; compulsion, either in restraining or impelling.

çō·aç′tive, *a.* 1. forcing; compulsory; having the power to impel or restrain.

2. acting or occurring together.

çō·aç′tive·ly, *adv.* in a compulsory manner.

çō·aç·tiv′i·ty, *n.* the state of being coactive.

çō·ad·ap·tā′tion, *n.* [*co-*, and *adaptation*, from L. *adaptare*, to fit to; *ad*, to, and *aptare*, to fit.] reciprocal or mutual adaptation.

çō·ȧ·dapt′ed, *a.* mutually adapted.

çō·ad′jū·ment, *n.* mutual assistance.

çō·ad·just′ment, *n.* mutual adjustment.

çō·ad′jū·tănt, *a.* [*co-*, and L. *adjutans*, ppr. of *adjutare*, to help.] helping each other; co-operating.

çō·ad′jū·tănt, *n.* one who assists; an assistant.

çō·ad′jū·ting, *a.* mutually helping. [Rare.]

çō·ad′jū·tive, *a.* rendering mutual assistance; coadjutant. [Rare.]

çō·ad·jū′tŏr, *n.* 1. one who aids another; an assistant; a fellow helper.

2. a person, often another bishop, appointed to assist a bishop.

Syn.—assistant, helper, ally, associate, fellow worker, partner, colleague.

çō·ad·jū′tŏr·ship, *n.* the office of a coadjutor; joint assistance.

çō·ad·jū′tress, çō·ad·jū′trix, *n.* [*co-*, and L. *adjutrix*, a female assistant.] a woman coadjutor.

çō·ad′jū·văn·cy, *n.* joint help; assistance; concurrent aid; co-operation.

çō·ad′jū·vănt, *a.* co-operating with; assisting.

çō·ad′nāte, *a.* same as *adnate*.

çō·ad′ū·nāte, *a.* [LL. *coadunatus*, pp. of *coadunare*, to unite together; L. *co-*, together, *ad*, to, and *unus*, one.]

1. united; joined together.

2. in botany and zoology, grown together.

çō·ad·ū·nā′tion, *n.* union of constituent parts.

çō·ad·ū·ni′tion, *n.* coadunation. [Obs.]

çō·ad·ven′tūre, *n.* a joint adventure.

çō·ad·ven′tūre, *v.i.* to share with others in an adventure.

çō·ad·ven′tūr·ẽr, *n.* a fellow adventurer.

çō·af·for′est, *v.t.* to convert (land) into a forest.

çō·ā′gen·cy, *n.* joint agency.

çō·ā′gent, *n.* an assistant or associate agent.

çō·ag·ment′, *v.t.* to congregate or heap together. [Obs.]

çō·ag·men·tā′tion, *n.* collection into a mass or united body; union; conjunction. [Obs.]

çō·ag″ū·lȧ·bil′i·ty, *n.* the capacity of being coagulated.

çō·ag′ū·lȧ·ble, *a.* that can be coagulated.

çō·ag′ū·lănt, *n.* a substance which produces coagulation.

çō·ag′ū·lāte, *a.* coagulated. [Obs.]

çō·ag′ū·lāte, *v.t.*; coagulated, *pt., pp.*; coagulating, *ppr.* 1. to curdle; to congeal; to cause (a liquid) to become a soft, semisolid mass; as, to *coagulate* blood, rennet *coagulates* milk.

2. to form into a mass; to solidify. [Rare.]

çō·ag′ū·lāte, *v.i.* [L. *coagulatus*, pp. of *coagulare*, to curdle.] to become clotted or congealed.

çō·ag′ū·lā·ted, *a.* exhibiting coagulation.

çō·ag·ū·lā′tion, *n.* [L. *coagulatio*, coagulation, from *coagulare*, to coagulate.]

1. the act of changing from a fluid to a soft, semisolid state; also, the state of being coagulated.

2. the mass or result of such change.

çō·ag′ū·lā·tive, *a.* tending to cause coagulation or become coagulated.

çō·ag′ū·lā·tŏr, *n.* a substance which causes coagulation.

çō·ag′ū·lā·tō·ry, *a.* coagulative.

çō·ag′ū·lin, *n.* an antibody formed in animal tissue following the injection of a proteid serum, and capable of coagulating that serum.

çō·ag′ū·lum, *n.*; *pl.* **çō·ag′ū·lȧ,** [L. *coagulum*, a means of coagulation, rennet.] a coagulated mass, as curd, a clot of blood, etc.; the thick precipitate produced when albuminous matter coagulates.

çō·aī′tȧ, *n.* [native name.] a South American monkey, *Ateles paniscus*, about 18 inches in length; the black spider monkey.

çōak, *n.* see *coke* (coal).

çōak, *n.* [origin uncertain.]

1. in ship carpentry, a small hardwood pin let into the ends of pieces of wood intended to be joined, in order to strengthen the joining.

2. in nautical usage, the metal hole in a sheave through which the pin runs.

çōak, *v.t.* in ship carpentry, to unite together (two pieces of wood) by means of coaks, or hardwood pins.

çōal, *n.* [ME. *cole*, *col*; AS. *col*, coal.]

1. a piece of wood or other combustible substance ignited, burning, or charred; an ember; a cinder.

2. a black, combustible, mineral solid resulting from the partial decomposition of vegetable matter away from air and under varying degrees of high temperature and great pressure over a period of millions of years: used as a fuel and in the production of coke, coal gas, water gas, and many coal-tar compounds. It is generally divided into three chief kinds—*anthracite* or *glance* or *hard coal*, *bituminous* or *soft coal*, and *brown coal* or *lignite*.

3. a piece of this substance.

4. charcoal.

to haul (or *rake, drag, call*) *over the coals*; to criticize sharply; to censure; to scold.

çōal, *v.t.*; coaled, *pt., pp.*; coaling, *ppr.* 1. to reduce (a substance) to charcoal by burning.

2. to mark or delineate with charcoal.

3. to supply with coal; as, the captain *coaled* his ships at sea.

çōal, *v.i.* to take in a supply of coal; as, the ship *coaled* at Honolulu.

çōal bed, a geological formation in which there are strata of coal; the deposit of coal itself.

çōal′bin, *n.* a bin or locker for storing coal.

çōal′-black, *a.* black as a coal; very black.

çōal breāk′ẽr, 1. a machine or building used in the process of breaking coal.

2. one who breaks coal.

çōal çär, a railroad car designed for transporting coal, as from a mine.

çōal′ẽr, *n.* 1. a ship, railroad, freight car, etc. that transports or supplies coal.

2. a person who sells or supplies coal.

çōal′ẽr·y, *n.* a colliery. [Obs.]

çō·ȧ·lesce′ (-les′), *v.i.*; coalesced (-lest′), *pt., pp.*; coalescing, *ppr.* [L. *coalescere*, to grow together; *co-*, together, and *alescere*, to grow up, from *alere*, to nourish.]

1. to grow together, as the halves of a broken bone.

2. to unite or merge into one body or mass.

3. to unite, combine, or blend into a single body or group, as individuals, parties, or nations; as, the Populists *coalesced* with the Democrats.

çō·ȧ·les′cence, *n.* the act of growing together; the act of uniting; also, the state of being united; merger; combination.

çō·ȧ·les′cent, *a.* growing together; uniting.

çōal fiēld, a region where there are coal strata.

çōal′fish, *n.*; *pl.* **çōal′fish, çōal′fish·eṣ,** 1. a species of *Gadus* or cod, named from the dark color of its back: also called *black pollack*.

2. any of various other fishes, as the eulachon, the cobia, etc.

çōal gas, 1. a poisonous gas given off by burning coal.

2. a gas produced by the destructive distillation of bituminous coal and purified for lighting, cooking, and heating purposes.

çōal gọọse, the cormorant. [Brit. Dial.]

çōal hēav′ẽr, one who is employed in carrying and shoveling coal.

çōal hod, a kind of bucket for carrying coal; a scuttle.

çōal′ing stā′tion, a place, as a port or station, where ships or trains take on coal.

çō′ȧ·līte, *v.t.* to cause to coalesce. [Obs.]

çō′ȧ·līte, *v.i.* to coalesce. [Obs.]

çō′ȧ·līte, *a.* [L. *coalitus*, pp. of *coalescere*, to grow together.] coalesced; grown together. [Obs.]

çō·ȧ·li′tion (-lish′un), *n.* 1. the act of coalescing or the state of being joined by coalescence.

2. a combination; union.

3. a temporary alliance of factions, parties, etc., for some specific purpose, as of political parties in times of national emergency.

Syn.—alliance, combination, confederacy, league, union.

çō·ȧ·li′tion·ist, çō·ȧ·li′tion·ẽr, *n.* one who supports or promotes a political coalition.

çō-al·lȳ′, *n.*; *pl.* **çō-al·lieṣ′,** a joint ally; as, the army of a *co-ally*.

çōal meaṣ′ūreṣ (mezh′ūrz), 1. coal beds.

2. in geology, coal-bearing strata formed just after the Devonian strata and lying above them.

çōal′-mē′tẽr, *n.* formerly, in England, an official appointed to measure coal.

çōal mīne, a mine or pit from which coal is dug.

çōal′mouse, çōle′mouse, *n.* a small species of titmouse, with a black head: called also *coaltit*.

çōal oil, 1. kerosene or any other oil obtained by fractional distillation of petroleum.

2. crude petroleum.

çōal păss′ẽr, on board ships, one who carries coal from the bunkers to the furnaces.

çōal pīpe, the fossil of a tree in sandstone or other rock, sometimes found standing upright in coal mines.

çōal pit, 1. a pit or mine from which coal is dug.

2. a place where charcoal is made.

çōal plant, a fossil plant of the Carboniferous Era.

çōal′sack, *n.* 1. any dark space in the Milky Way.

2. [C—] such a space near the Southern Cross.

çōal sçut′tle, a bucketlike container for holding and carrying coal.

çōal tär, a thick, black, viscid, opaque liquid

obtained by the destructive distillation of bituminous coal: many synthetic compounds have been developed from it, including dyes, medicines, explosives, and perfumes.

çōal'tit, *n.* see *coalmouse.*

çōal'-whip"pẽr, *n.* in England, one who or that which raises coal out of the hold of a ship; a coal heaver.

çōal wŏrks, a coal mine; a colliery; a place where coal is dug.

çōal'y, *a.*; *comp.* coalier; *superl.* coaliest, like coal; containing coal; of the nature of coal; of the color of coal.

çōam'ing, *n.* [from ME. *comb*; AS. *camb*, a comb.]
1. a raised border around a roof opening, well, etc.
2. one of the raised borders or edges of the hatches of a ship, made to keep out water.

çō·an·nex', *v.t.* to annex with something else. [Rare.]

çō·apt', *v.t.* to fit together: also written *coaptate.*

çō·ap·tā'tion, *n.* [LL. *coaptatio*, from *coaptare*, to fit together.] the adaptation or adjustment of parts to each other, as of the ends of a broken bone.

çō·ärb', *n.* [Ir. *comharba*, a successor, abbot.] the abbot of a monastery: also called *comarb.*

çō·ärçt', *v.t.* to crowd; to restrain: also spelled *coarctate.* [Obs.]

çō·ärç'tāte, *a.* [L. *coarctatus*, pp. of *coarctare*, to compress; *co-*, together, and *arctare*, to press.] in biology, (a) closely connected; (b) having the thorax and abdomen separated only by a constriction.
coarctate pupa; a pupa enclosed by the stiffened larval skin.

çō·ärç·tā'tion, *n.* 1. confinement; restraint to a narrow space; restraint of liberty. [Obs.]
2. pressure; contraction; specifically, in medicine, the contraction or lessening of the diameter of a canal, as the intestinal canal or the urethra.

çōarse, *a.*; *comp.* coarser; *superl.* coarsest, [formerly written *course, cowrse*, and believed to be the same word as *course*. A thing *of course*, or *in course*, is what is natural, ordinary, common, and hence probably the development of the meaning.]
1. lacking in fineness of texture or structure, or in elegance of form; composed of large parts or particles; thick and rough in texture; as, *coarse* thread; *coarse* hair; *coarse* sand; *coarse* glass; *coarse* features.
2. rude; rough; unrefined; uncivil; unpolished; as, *coarse* manners.
3. gross; indelicate; as, he indulged in *coarse* language.
4. common; of inferior or poor quality.
Syn.—bluff, brutish, large, thick, blunt, uncouth, immodest, vulgar.

çōarse'-grāined', *a.* 1. consisting of large particles or constituent elements; having a coarse or rough texture; as, *coarse-grained* granite or wood.
2. lacking in refinement or delicacy; vulgar; as, a *coarse-grained* nature.

çōarse'ly, *adv.* in a coarse manner.

çōars'en, *v.t.* and *v.i.* to make or become coarse.

çōarse'ness, *n.* the state or quality of being coarse.

çō·är·tiç·ū·lā'tion, *n.* in anatomy, the fitting together of bones to form a joint. [Obs.]

çō"as·sess'ŏr, *n.* a joint assessor.

çōast, *n.* [ME. *coste, coost*, coast; OFr. *coste*, a rib, hill, shore, coast; L. *costa*, a rib, a side.]
1. the exterior line, limit, or border of a country. [Obs.]
2. the edge or margin of the land next to the sea; the seashore; also, the country near the seashore; as, populous towns along the *coast.*
3. the side of an object. [Obs.]
4. a slide downhill, as on a sled; a ride down an incline without using propelling power, as on a bicycle.
5. the incline down which a slide is taken.
the Coast; in the United States, the Pacific coast.
the coast is clear; there is no apparent danger or hindrance.

çōast, *v.i.*; coasted, *pt., pp.*; coasting, *ppr.*
1. to sail near a coast; to sail along or near the shore, or in sight of land.
The ancients *coasted* only in their navigation. —Arbuthnot.
2. to make short voyages from port to port.
3. to go down an incline on a sled.
4. to continue in motion on momentum or by the force of gravity after propelling power has stopped.
5. to behave aimlessly; not make any serious effort.
6. to approach. [Obs.]

çōast, *v.t.* 1. to sail along or near to; as, to *coast* the American shore.
2. to draw near; to approach; to follow. [Obs.]

çōast'ăl, *a.* of, at, near, or along a coast.

çōast'ăl plāin, level land extending along a coast.

çōast är·til'lẽr·y, that branch of the armed forces assigned to protect the harbors and coast lines of the nation, and generally armed with artillery and antiaircraft guns of the largest caliber: distinguished from *field artillery.*

çōast'ẽr, *n.* 1. a person or thing that coasts.
2. a vessel employed in sailing or in trading from port to port along a coast.
3. formerly, a small tray on wheels for passing a decanter around a table.
4. a small round tray placed under a glass or bottle to protect a table or other surface.
5. a sled, etc. suitable for coasting.
6. an amusement railway that runs on a specially constructed framework with sharp dips and curves; a roller coaster.

çōast'ẽr brāke, a brake in the hub of the rear wheel of a bicycle, operated by reversing the pressure on the pedals: it also releases the wheel from the driving mechanism to permit free coasting.

çōast guärd, 1. a group of men employed by a government to defend its coasts, prevent smuggling, aid vessels in distress, maintain lighthouses, etc.
2. [C– G–] such a group in the United States: normally under the control of the Treasury Department, in time of war it is placed under the control of the navy.
3. a member of a coast guard.

çōast'ing, *a.* sailing along or near a coast; as, a *coasting* schooner.
coasting trade; trade which is carried on along a coast from port to port, especially within one country.

çōast'ing, *n.* the act of one who or of that which coasts.

çōast land, *n.* land along a coast.

çōast līne, the contour or outline of a coast.

çōast rat, a small mammal, *Bathyergus maritimus*, of South Africa. It is about the size of a rabbit, and is also called *mole rat* or *sand mole.* Its burrows are exceedingly large.

çōast'wāit"ẽr, *n.* in England, a customs officer who oversees the loading and landing of goods in the coasting trade: also called *landwaiter.*

çōast'wărd, *a.* and *adv.* toward the coast.

çōast'wărdṣ, *adv.* coastward.

çōast'wāyṣ, *adv.* coastwise.

çōast'wīṣe, *adv.* and *a.* by way of or along the coast.

çōat, *n.* [ME. *cote, coote*; OFr. *cote*, a coat; LL. *cota, cotta*, a tunic.]
1. a sleeved outer garment opening down the front and extending usually just below the hips, worn as part of a suit or as a jacket.
2. a similar garment of varying length, worn out of doors over one's usual clothing.
3. a natural outer covering of an animal, as of skin, fur, wool, etc.
4. the outer covering of a plant or of an animal structure or tissue.
5. a layer of some substance, as paint, over a surface.
6. a petticoat or skirt. [Dial.]
7. customary garb showing one's position, class, etc. [Obs.]
coat of mail; a piece of armor, in the shape of a coat, made of joined metal links, or chain mail.

COATS OF MAIL—1. Roman 2. Greek

çōat, *v.t.*; coated, *pt., pp.*; coating, *ppr.* 1. to cover or spread over with a layer of any substance; as, to *coat* a ceiling with paint.
2. to provide or cover with a coat.

çōat är'mŏr, 1. an outer coat worn over the armor, bearing heraldic devices. [Obs.]
2. a coat of arms; an escutcheon with crest, motto, etc.

çōat çärd, the king, queen, or jack in a deck of playing cards; a face card: usually called *court card.*

çōat'ed pā'pẽr, a paper whose surface has been treated so that it will take half-tone impressions or color printing.

çōat·ee', *n.* a short, close-fitting coat, usually with a short skirt or tails.

çō·ä'ti, *n.* [native name.] a small, flesh-eating animal of Central and South America, resembling the raccoon, but with a longer body and a long flexible snout.

çō·ä'ti-mŏn'di, çō·ä'ti-mun'di, *n.* [Tupi; *coati*, and *mondi*, solitary.] a coati.

çōat'ing, *n.* 1. the act of covering; also, any substance spread over for cover or protection; as, a *coating* of enamel.
2. cloth for making coats; as, an assortment of *coatings.*

çōat liṅk, studs or buttons joined by a link, or a loop and button, for fastening a coat.

çōat of ärmṣ, [after Fr. *cotte d'armes*, light garment worn over armor, and generally blazoned with the heraldic arms of the wearer.]
1. a shield marked with the insignia or designs (heraldic bearings) of a person, family, institution, etc.
2. a representation of such a shield.

COAT OF ARMS

çōat'tāil, *n.* 1. the back part of a coat below the waist.
2. one half of the skirt of a coat that is divided in the back.
3. either of the two long, tapering skirts on the back of a man's dress coat.

çō·a̤u'thŏr, *n.* a joint author; collaborator.

çōax, *v.t.*; coaxed (kōxt), *pt., pp.*; coaxing, *ppr.* [from *coax*, a fool: origin obscure.]
1. to induce or try to induce to do something; to persuade by soothing words, flattery, etc.; to wheedle.
2. to get by coaxing.
Syn.—wheedle, cajole, flatter, entice.

çōax, *v.i.* to use persuasion, flattery, etc.

çō·ax'ăl, *a.* coaxial.

çōax'ẽr, *n.* a wheedler; someone who coaxes.

çō·ax'i·ăl, *a.* 1. having an axis, or axes, in common.
2. designating a compound loudspeaker consisting of a smaller unit mounted within and connected with a larger one on a common axis: the smaller unit reproduces the higher frequencies, beyond the range of the larger.

çō·ax'i·ăl çā'ble, a cable made up of an insulated conductor tube through which a number of conducting wires are passed, and by means of which many telephone, television, and telegraph impulses can be sent simultaneously.

çōax'ing, *n.* the act of wheedling or leading on by kind treatment.

çōax'ing·ly, *adv.* by coaxing; in a coaxing manner.

çob, *n.* [origin obscure; the primary idea doubtless being that of head; compare G. *kopf*; AS. *cop, copp*, head.]
1. the top or head. [Obs.]
2. the tough core on which the kernels of corn grow; a corncob; hence, a corncob pipe.
3. the black-backed sea gull; the sea cob: also spelled *cobb.*
4. a ball or pellet for feeding fowls.
5. a spider. [Rare.]
6. a short, thickset horse.
7. unburned clay mixed with straw, as in cobwalls, which are used in constructing cottages in some parts of England.
8. a large stone, lump of coal, or round mass of any material.

9. a leader, particularly if rich and grasping. [Obs.]
10. the early Spanish-American dollar. [Obs.]
11. a newly hatched herring. [Dial.]
12. a small fresh-water fish, the miller's-thumb.
13. a large hazelnut; the cobnut.
14. a beating or spanking, as with a piece of wood or a strap: also written *cobb*.
15. a swan of the male sex.
16. a wheat ear.

çob, çobb, *v.t.* 1. to punish by striking on the buttocks, as with a flat piece of wood.
2. to break with a hammer, as in mining ores.

Çō·bae′ȧ, *n.* [Latinized form from Barnabas *Cobo*, a Spanish naturalist.] a genus of Mexican and South American climbing vines.

çō′bạlt, *n.* [G. *kobalt*; the name is probably derived from *kobold*, a goblin, the demon of the mines, applied to cobalt by the miners, when they did not know its value, because it was troublesome.] a hard, lustrous, steel-gray, ductile metallic chemical element. It is found in various ores, usually as an oxide, or combined with arsenic or its acid, with sulfur, iron, etc. Cobalt is used in the preparation of alloys; its compounds are used in the production of inks and paints and to give a permanent blue color to glass and enamels upon metals, porcelain, and earthenware. Symbol, Co; atomic weight, 58.94; atomic number, 27.
cobalt blue; (a) a dark-blue pigment made from cobalt; (b) dark blue: also called *cobalt ultramarine*.
cobalt green; a pigment made from the oxides of zinc and cobalt.
cobalt yellow; the double nitrite of potassium and cobalt which yields a permanent yellow pigment much used by artists.

çō′bạlt blo͞om, an arsenate of cobalt occurring in needle-shaped crystals: also called *erythrite*.

çō′bạlt çrust, an earthy kind of erythrite.

çō′bạlt glance, same as *cobaltite*.

çō·bạlt′iç, *a.* 1. pertaining to cobalt, resembling cobalt, or containing it.
2. designating or of compounds in which cobalt has a valence of three.

çō·bạlt·if′ẽr·ous, *a.* containing or yielding cobalt.

çō′bạlt·ïne, *n.* cobaltite.

çō·bạlt′īte, *n.* cobalt sulfarsenide, CoAsS, a silver-white mineral: also called *cobalt glance*.

çō·bạlt′ous (-us), *a.* 1. containing or of the nature of cobalt.
2. designating or of compounds in which cobalt has a valence of two.
cobaltous chloride; a crystalline substance used in solution as an ink, the writing being almost colorless after drying, but becoming a bright blue upon the application of heat.

çō′bang, *n.* a Japanese gold coin: written also *kobang*.

çobb, *n.* a cob (gull).

çob′bing, *n.* a beating on the buttocks, as with a flat piece of wood.

çob′bing, *a.* acting like a cob (*n.*, sense 9). [Obs.]

çob′ble (-bl), *n.* [Scot.] a small fishing boat; coble.

çob′ble, *n.* [dim. of *cob*.]
1. a cobblestone.
2. [*pl.*] cob coal.

çob′ble, *v.t.*; cobbled, *pt.*, *pp.*; cobbling, *ppr.* [ME.: form suggests *cob* (a lump) plus *-le*, freq. suffix, in sense "to lump together."]
1. to make or mend, as shoes.
2. to make or do clumsily or unhandily.
3. to pave with cobblestones.

çob′blẽr, *n.* 1. a mender of shoes.
2. a clumsy workman.
3. a deep-dish fruit pie with no bottom crust and a thick top crust of biscuit dough.
4. an iced beverage containing wine, citrus fruit, and sugar.

çob′blẽr·fish, *n.* a fish found in the Atlantic: so called from its threadlike dorsal fin rays.

çob′ble·stōne, *n.* a roundish stone formerly much used for paving streets.

çob′by, *a.* 1. stout. [Obs.]
2. self-willed; obstinate. [Obs.]

çob çōal, coal in rounded lumps from about the size of a baseball to that of a basketball.

çō-bel·lig′ẽr·ent, *a.* carrying on war in conjunction with another power or powers, but without the status of an ally.

çō-bel·lig′ẽr·ent, *n.* a nation associated but not allied with another or other nations in waging war.

çob′head (-hed), *n.* the young of the goldeneye duck.

çō′bi·ȧ, *n.* [West Indian origin.] a large fish with a wide, flattened head: also called *sergeant fish*.

çob′ī″ron (-ũrn), *n.* an andiron with a knob at the top. [Obs.]

çō·bish′ŏp, *n.* a joint or coadjutor bishop. [Rare.]

çōb′le, *n.* [ME. *coble*; W. *ceubal*, a ferryboat, from *ceuo*, hollow.]
1. a small fishing boat having a flat bottom, deep stem, large rudder, and a lug sail, first used off the coast of Yorkshire, England: it was formerly much used in piloting.
2. in Scotland, a short, flat-bottomed rowboat.

çob′lōaf, *n.* a crusty loaf of bread with a round lump on the top.

çob mŏn′ey, gold and silver money, used during the eighteenth century in Spanish America.

çob′nut, *n.* 1. a kind of hazelnut.
2. the tree that it grows on.
3. a child's game using hazelnuts or other nuts.

çō·bō′lä, *n.* [Amer. Sp. (Costa Rica).] a tree of the genus *Podocarpus*, found in Central America.

çob′rȧ, *n.* same as *copra*.

çō′brȧ, *n.* [from Port. *cobra* (*de capello*), serpent (of the hood); L. *colubra*, a snake.]
1. a very poisonous snake of Asia and Africa, having around its neck loose skin which is expanded into a hood when the snake is excited.
2. leather made of the skin of this snake.

çō′brȧ dē çȧ·pel′lō, [Port., a hooded snake; *cobra*, a snake, *de*, of, *capello*, a hood.] a vari-colored cobra found especially in India.

COBRA DE CAPELLO (*Naia tripudians*)

çob′stōne, *n.* cobblestone. [Dial.]

çob′swän, *n.* a male swan.

çō′bũrg, *n.* [named from *Coburg*, in Germany.] a fabric for women's wear, made of worsted and silk or cotton.

çob′wạll, *n.* a wall made of unburned clay, mixed with straw.

çob′web, *n.* [ME. *copweb*; *cop*, abbrev. of AS. *attercoppe*, a spider, and *web*, from AS. *web*, from *wefan*, to weave.]
1. the line, thread, or filament which a spider spins from its abdomen.
2. the network spread by a spider to catch its prey.
3. anything flimsy, gauzy, or ensnaring like the web of a spider.
4. the spotted flycatcher of Europe: also called *cobweb bird*.
cobweb lawn; a linen of very fine texture made in the seventeenth century.

çob′web, *v.t.*; cobwebbed, *pt.*, *pp.*; cobwebbing, *ppr.* to cover with or as with cobwebs.

çob′webbed, *a.* 1. in botany, covered thickly with downy hairs.
2. covered with cobwebs.

çob′web·by, *a.* 1. covered with cobwebs.
2. pertaining to or resembling a cobweb or cobwebs.

çob′wŏrk, *n.* a structure of logs laid horizontally and securely held by dovetailing the ends where they meet.

çō′çȧ, *n.* [S. Am. name.] a highly stimulating narcotic, the dried leaf of the *Erythroxylon coca*, a plant found wild principally in the mountainous districts of Bolivia, and cultivated in various sections of South America and the West Indies; also, the plant itself.

Çōç·āgne′ (-āne′), *n.* see *Cockaigne*.

çō·çāine′, çō·çāin′ (*or* kō′kān), *n.* a white crystalline alkaloid extracted from coca leaves. It is a narcotic and local anesthetic.

çō·çāin′iṣm, *n.* a diseased condition resulting from excessive or habitual use of cocaine.

çō·çāin′īze, *v.t.*; cocainized, *pt.*, *pp.*; cocainizing, *ppr.* to anesthetize with cocaine.

çō·çärde′, *n.* [Fr.] one of the bright red lobed vesicles in the thorax of certain beetles.

-çoç′çăl, a combining form meaning *of* or *produced by a* (specified kind of) *coccus*, as in staphylo*coccal*.

Çoç·cē′iăn (-yăn), *n.* [Latinized form of *Koch*.] an adherent of the theology of the covenants founded by Johannes Koch or Cocceius (1603–1669), professor of theology at Leyden.

Çoç·cē′iăn·iṣm, *n.* the doctrine of the Cocceians.

çoç′ci-, see *cocco-*.

çoç′cī, *n.* plural of *coccus*.

-çoç′ciç, a combining form equivalent to *-coccal*, as in staphylo*coccic*.

çoç′cid, *a.* pertaining to the family *Coccidæ*.

çoç′cid, *n.* one of the *Coccidæ*.

Çoç′ci·dae, *n.pl.* [L., from *coccum*; Gr. *kokkos*, a kind of berry, now known to be the cochineal insect, found upon the scarlet dye oak.] a family of scale insects that live on plants.

çoç·cid·i·ō′sis, *n.* [Mod. L., from *coccidium*, little berry; and *-osis*.] any of various diseases of domestic animals, birds, and, rarely, man, caused by a class of protozoans living as parasites in the intestines.

çoç·cif′ẽr·ous, *a.* [*cocci-*, and L. *ferre*, to bear.] bearing or producing berries; as, *cocciferous* trees or plants. [Obs.]

Çoç·ci·nel′lȧ, *n.* [L., from *coccinus*; Gr. *kokkinos*, scarlet, from *kokkos*, a berry, especially the kermes insect, once thought to be a berry, used to dye scarlet.] a genus of beetles that feed on plant lice, including the ladybirds, or ladybugs.

çoç′çō-, çoç′ci-, combining forms from L. *coccum*, Gr. *kokkos*, a kernel, seed, berry.

çoç′çoid, *a.* like a coccus.

-çoç′çoid, a combining form meaning *like a* (specified kind of) *coccus*, as in staphylo*coccoid*.

çoç′çō·līte, *n.* [*cocco-*, and Gr. *lithos*, a stone.] a variety of pyroxene, usually green in color. It is composed of granular, distinct concretions, easily separable, some of which present the appearance of crystals whose angles and edges have been obliterated: called also *granuliform pyroxene*.

çoç′çō·lith, *n.* [*cocco-*, and Gr. *lithos*, a stone.] a minute organism abounding in the depths of the North Atlantic Ocean and probably one of the *Algæ*.

Çoç·çol′ō·bis, *n.* [*cocco-*, and Gr. *lobos*, a pod.] a genus of polygonaceous plants of the American tropics. It includes *Coccolobis ovifera*, the sea grape of the West Indies.

çoç′çō·sphēre, *n.* [*cocco-*, and Gr. *sphaira*, a sphere.] a spheroidal aggregation of coccoliths found in the ooze of the North Atlantic Ocean.

Çoç·ços′tē·us, *n.* [*cocco-*, and Gr. *osteon*, a bone.] a genus of fish of the Devonian Period having berrylike tubercles on the body and cranial plates.

Çoç′çū·lus, *n.* [L., dim. of *coccus*, a berry.] a genus of East Indian menispermaceous plants, consisting of climbers, whose leaves are usually more or less heart-shaped and the flowers small.
Cocculus indicus; the fruit of the *Anamirta cocculus*: it is a strong poison.

çoç′çus, *n.*; *pl.* **çoç′cī,** [L., from *coccum*, Gr. *kokkos*, a berry, kernel, seed.]
1. a bacterium having a spherical or oval shape.
2. in botany, a single-celled seed vessel; one of the parts of a compound carpel in fruit.
3. [C–] a genus of insects including the cochineal and scale insects.

-çoç′çus, *coccus*, used as a terminal combining form in names of various bacteria, as in gono*coccus*.

çoç·cyġ′ē·ăl, *a.* pertaining to the coccyx.
coccygeal gland; a gland located at the base of the tail of a bird and containing an oily fluid used in dressing the feathers: also called the *uropygial gland*. The term is also applied to a small vascular organ near the tip of the coccyx in man.

çoç·cyġ′ē·ous, *a.* same as *coccygeal*. [Rare.]

çoç′cyx, *n.*; *pl.* **çoç·cȳ′ġēṣ,** [L., from Gr. *kokkyx*, a cuckoo, so called from the cuckoo's beak, which it resembles.] a small, triangular bone at the lower end of the vertebral column, formed by the fusion of four rudimentary vertebrae and articulating with the sacrum.

Çō′chin, *n.* [from *Cochin-China*.] [also c–] a variety of domestic fowl of large size, full-breasted, with buff, black, white, or penciled gray plumage and heavily feathered legs.

Çō′chin-Chī′nȧ, [also c– c–] a variety of large domestic fowl originally brought from Cochin-China. From these have been bred the *brahma* and *cochin* varieties.

çoch·i·nēal′, *n.* [Sp. *cochinilla*, cochineal; L. *coccineus*, *coccinus*, scarlet, from *coccum*; Gr. *kokkos*, a berry.]
1. a scale insect, the *Coccus cacti*, a native of the warmer climates of America. It is found on several species of cactus, particularly on that called nopal or Indian fig tree.
2. a red dye made from the dried bodies of the females of this insect.

çoch·i·nēal′ fig, a plant of the cactus family, *Nopalea cochinillifera*, upon which the cochineal insect thrives. It is widely cultivated in the American tropics.

çoch′le·ȧ, *n.*; *pl.* **çoch′le·ae**, [L. *coclea*, or *cochlea*; Gr. *kochlias*, a snail, from *kochlos*, a shellfish.]
1. the spiral-shaped part of the internal ear, containing the auditory nerve endings.
2. in botany, any body or organ of a spiral form, especially a spiral legume.

çoch′le·ăn, *a.* same as *cochleate*.

çoch′le·ăr, *a.* 1. of or relating to the cochlea; as, the *cochlear* duct.
2. in botany, spoon-shaped.

çoch′le·ăr, *n.* [L. *coclear*, *cochlear*, a spoon, from *coclea*, *cochlea*, a snail.] in the Orthodox Eastern Church, the Eucharistic spoon in which the consecrated elements are administered to communicants: also called *labis*.

çoch·lē·ā′rē, *n.* [L. *coclear*, *cochlear*, spoon; from *coclea*, *cochlea*, a snail.] in medicine, a spoon; a spoonful.

Çoch·lē·ā′ri·ȧ, *n.* [L. *coclear*, *cochlear*, a spoon, from the shape of the leaves.] a genus of cruciferous plants, including the horseradish and common scurvy grass. The plants are perennial herbs with simple or pinnate leaves and small white flowers.

çoch·lē·ar′i·form, *a.* [L. *coclear*, *cochlear*, a spoon, and *forma*, shape.] having the form of a cochleare or spoon; spoon-shaped.

çoch′le·ā·ry, *a.* cochleate. [Obs.]

çoch′le·āte, **çoch′le·ā·ted**, *a.* [L. *cocleatus*, *cochleatus*, spiral, from *coclea*, *cochlea*, a snail.] shaped like the shell of a snail.

çoch·lē′i·form, *a.* [L. *coclea*, *cochlea*, a snail, and *forma*, form.] having the form of a snail's shell.

çoch′lē·ous, *a.* spiral in form; cochleate.

Çoch·lō·spēr′mum, *n.* [L., from Gr. *kochlos*, a shellfish, and *sperma*, seed.] a genus of small trees or shrubs found in the tropics of both hemispheres. They have palmately lobed leaves, large yellow flowers, and pear-shaped fruits.

çock, *n.* [ME. *cock*, *cok*; AS. *coc*, *cocc*, a cock; a word of imitative origin.]
1. (a) the male of the chicken; a rooster; (b) the male of other birds, particularly of gallinaceous fowls. The word is often used adjectively; as, a *cock* sparrow; and occasionally to signify the male of certain animals other than birds; as, a *cock* lobster. In composition it is sometimes applied to birds without regard to sex; as, pea*cock*, wood*cock*, etc.
2. the sound made by a rooster, especially at sunrise; crow.
3. a weathercock; a vane shaped like a rooster.
4. a faucet or valve for permitting or arresting the flow of fluids through a pipe; as, a feed *cock*, gauge *cock*, etc.
5. the style or gnomon of a sundial.
6. the needle or pointer of a balance. [Obs.]
7. the piece which covers the balance in a clock or watch.
8. the hammer of a firearm; also, its position when set for firing.
9. a leader; a chief among men or boys; as, the *cock* of the school.
10. a canard; a cock-and-bull story.
11. the act of turning or tilting upward, or the effect or form produced by such an act; as, a *cock* of the head, the *cock* of a hat.
at cock, at full cock; in firearms, having the hammer fully raised.
at half cock; having the hammer pulled halfway back.
cock-and-bull story; an absurd, improbable story.
cock of the plains; the largest kind of American grouse, *Centrocercus urophasianus*: also called *sage cock*, *sage grouse*.
cock of the rock; a beautiful bird of South America. It is about as large as a pigeon, orange colored, with black on the wings and tail. It forms the type of the genus *Rupicola*.
cock of the walk; the most important person in any group.
to go off at half cock; see under *half cock*.

çock, *v.t.*; cocked (kokt), *pt.*, *pp.*; cocking, *ppr.*
1. to tilt; to set (a hat, etc.) jauntily on one side.
2. to raise stiffly; as, a dog *cocks* his ears.
3. to turn (the eye or ear) toward something.
4. to set or draw back the hammer of (a gun) in order to fire.

çock, *v.i.* 1. to hold up the head; to strut; to look big, pert, or menacing.
2. to train or use fighting cocks. [Rare.]
3. to assume an erect or tilted position.

çock, *n.* [Dan. *kok*, a heap, a pile.] a small conical pile, as of hay.

çock, *v.t.*; cocked (kokt), *pt.*, *pp.*; cocking, *ppr* to pile (hay, etc.) in cocks.

çock, *v.t.* to calk or furnish (a horseshoe) with sharp points of iron to prevent slipping in frost.

> Cautious men when they went on the roads
> had their horses' shoes *cocked*.
> —Trollope.

çock, *n.* [ME. *cokboot*, cockboat; OFr. *coque*, a boat; L. *concha*, a shell.] a small boat; cockboat. [Obs.]

> Yond tall anchoring bark
> Diminished to her *cock*, her *cock* a buoy
> Almost too small for sight. —Shak.

çock·āde′, *n.* [Fr. *cocarde*, a cockade, from *coq*, a cock, on account of its resemblance to the crest of a cock.] a rosette, knot of ribbon, or the like, worn on the hat as a badge.

çock·ā′ded, *a.* wearing a cockade.

çock′-ȧ-dọọ·dle-dọọ′, *n.* [echoic.]
1. the shrill sound made by a rooster; crow.
2. a rooster; cock.

çock-ȧ-họọp′, *a.* [Fr. *coq à huppe*, cock with a crest.] strutting like a cock; triumphant; jubilant; elated; boastful; conceited.

çock-ȧ-họọp′, *adv.* in a triumphant or jubilant manner; boastingly.

Çock·āigne′, **Çọ·āgne′** (-ān′), *n.* [ME. *cokaygne*; OFr. (*pais de*) *cocaigne*, (land of) sugar cake.]
1. an imaginary country of idleness and luxury.
2. the land of cockneys; London and its suburbs: used in a humorous sense: also written *Cockayne*.

çock′ăl, *n.* [of doubtful origin.]
1. an old English game of chance, played with the anklebones of sheep instead of dice. [Obs.]
2. a bone used in playing the game. [Obs.]

çock·ȧ·lee′kie (-ki), *n.* [Scot.] in Scotland, a soup made of a capon boiled with leeks, etc.: also written *cockieleekie* and *cockyleeky*.

çock·ȧ·lō′rum, *n.* [pseudo L. extension of *cock* (male bird); perh. influenced by D. *kockeloeren*, to crow.]
1. a small rooster; a bantam.
2. a little man with an exaggerated idea of his own importance.

çock′ȧ·pērt, *a.* impudent; saucy. [Obs.]

çock·ȧ·teel′, **çock·ȧ·tiēl′**, *n.* a small Australian parrot.

çock·ȧ·tọọ′, *n.* [Hind. *kakatua*, a cockatoo.]
1. any of numerous bright-colored birds of the parrot kind, chiefly inhabiting Australia and the East Indies, distinguished by their high crests, which are composed of a tuft of elegant feathers. There are several species, as the broad-crested cockatoo, *Cacatua cristata*; the great sulfur-crested cockatoo, *Cacatua galerita*; the red-vented cockatoo, *Cacatua philippinarum*; the tricolor-crested or Leadbeaters' cockatoo, *Cacatua leadbeateri*.

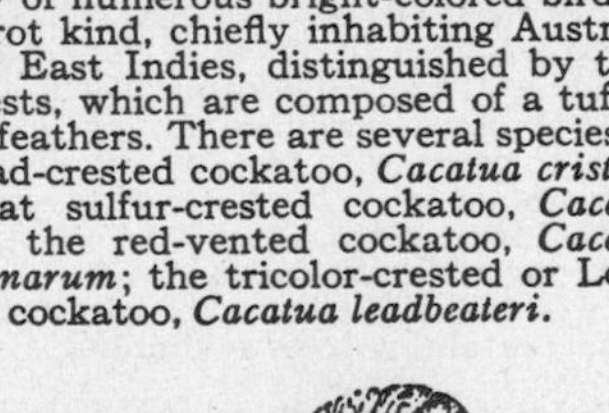

COCKATOO (*Cacatua leadbeateri*)

2. in Australia, a name for a small farmer: called also *cockatoo squatter*. [Colloq.]

çock′ȧ·trice (*or* -trīs), *n.* [ME. *cocatryse*, *kokatrice*; OFr. *cocatrice*, *cocatris*, a cockatrice, a corruption of L. *crocodilus*, a crocodile.]
1. a basilisk, a fabulous serpent, supposed to have been produced from a cock's egg hatched by a serpent. Its breath and glance were believed to be fatal to any who came within their influence.

COCKATRICE (sense 4)

2. in Scripture, an unidentified venomous serpent.
3. figuratively, anything venomous or deadly.
4. in heraldry, a basilisk combed, wattled, winged, and spurred, like the cock, and with a serpentine tail.

Çock·āyne′, *n.* same as *Cockaigne*.

çock′bill, *v.t.* to place acockbill, as a ship's yards or anchor. [see *acockbill*.]

çock′bōat, *n.* a small boat, especially one used as a ship's tender.

çock′-brāined, *a.* rash; giddy; flighty.

çock broth, broth made by boiling down a cock; cockaleekie.

çock′chāf″ẽr, *n.* [*cock*, for Scot. *clock*, a beetle, and *chafer*, from AS. *ceafor*, *ceafer*, the cockchafer.] the May bug, or dorbeetle, *Melolontha vulgaris*: it is a large European beetle whose grubs live in the soil for three years feeding on the roots of plants.

çock′çrōw, **çock′çrōw″ing**, *n.* the time at which cocks crow; early morning; dawn; as, I rose at *cockcrow*.

çocked hat, 1. a three-cornered hat with a turned-up brim.
2. a hat pointed in front and in back and with the crown rising to a point.
to knock into a cocked hat; to damage beyond recognition; to ruin. [Slang.]

çock·ee′, *n.* [Scot.] the mark aimed at in curling; the tee.

çock′ẽr, *v.t.* [ME. *cockeren*, to fondle; of uncertain origin.] to fondle; to indulge; to treat with tenderness; to pamper.

çock′ẽr, *n.* 1. one who follows cockfighting as a business, or as a sport.
2. a cocker spaniel.

COCKER SPANIEL (11 in. high)

çock′ẽr, *n.* [OE. *coker*, boot.] a half boot.

çock′ẽr·el, *n.* a young cock, less than a year old.

çock′ẽr·ing, *n.* indulgence.

çock′ẽr span′iel (-yel), *n.* [so called from its use in hunting woodcock.] any of a breed of small spaniels with a compact body, short legs, long, silky hair, and long, drooping ears. The coat may be black or liver-colored, sometimes combined with white.

çock′et, *a.* brisk; pert. [Obs.]

çock′et, *n.* [ME. *coket*, a seal; of uncertain origin.]
1. in England, formerly a seal of the customhouse; a royal seal; a scroll of parchment, sealed and delivered, by the officers of the customhouse, to merchants, as a warrant that their merchandise is entered. [Brit.]
2. a customhouse. [Brit.]
3. a bread measure. [Obs.]
4. cocket bread. [Obs.]

çock′et, *v.t.* in architecture, to fasten together. [Obs.]

çock′et bread (bred), in England, a former variety of wheat bread, second in quality to the finest.

çock′et cent′ẽr, in architecture, a bracing of the center of an arch to allow removal of the main tie beam, so as to permit more head room above the springers while the building is in progress.

çock′eȳe (-ī), *n.* 1. a squinting eye.
2. the socket in a millstone.

çock′eȳed (-īd), *a.* 1. having crossed or cocked eyes.
2. awry, twisted, crooked, or out of focus or line; as, a *cockeyed* picture. [Slang.]
3. fantastically absurd. [Slang.]
4. drunk, inebriated; as, he drank until he was *cockeyed*. [Slang.]

çock′fīght (-fīt), *n.* a match or contest of gamecocks, usually wearing metal spurs.

çock′fīght″ing, *n.* the pitting of gamecocks against each other in a fight: the sport is illegal in the United States.

çock'head (-hed), *n.* the point of the spindle of a millstone, on which it is balanced.
çock'hǫrse', *n.* 1. a child's toy horse, usually set on rockers; hobbyhorse.
2. any horse of unusual height. [Rare.]
çock'hǫrse', *a.* on horseback; exalted; exulting; as, a *cockhorse* general.
çock·ie·lee'kie, *n.* same as *cockaleekie.*
çock'i·ly, *adv.* in a cocky manner.
çock'i·ness, *n.* the quality of being cocky; jaunty conceit.
çock'ing, *n.* cockfighting.
çock'ing māin, a match of fighting cocks, consisting of several bouts.
çock'ish, *a.* like a cock in being self-assertive, arrogant, defiant, etc.; cocky.
çock'-lāird, *n.* in Scotland, a small landowner: a contemptuous term.
çoç'kle (kok'l), *n.* [ME. *cockle, cockel*; AS. *coccel*, tares.] a plant or weed that grows among grain, as the corn rose or corn *cockle*: also applied to *Lolium temulentum* or darnel.
çoç'kle, *n.* [ME. *cokel*, dim. of *cocke*, a shell; OFr. *coquille*, a shell, cockle; L. *conchylium*; Gr. *konchylion*, a shellfish, *konchē*, a mussel.]
1. any shellfish of the genus *Cardium*, especially the edible species *Cardium edule*, with two heart-shaped, radially ridged shells. The name is also applied to similar shells belonging to other genera.
2. a cockleshell.
3. a small, shallow boat.
4. a wrinkle; a pucker.
cockles of one's heart; [perh. for L. *cochlea*, winding cavity.] the deepest part of one's heart, or emotions.
çoç'kle, *n.* a mineral; a name given by the Cornish miners to black tourmalin: also called *shirl*, or *schorl*.
çoç'kle, *n.* [perh. from D. *kakel*; G. *kachel*, stove tile.]
1. the fire chamber of a furnace.
2. a kiln used for drying hops.
3. the rounded top of a hot-air furnace.
çoç'kle, *v.i.* and *v.t.*; cockled, *pt., pp.*; cockling, *ppr.* to contract into wrinkles; to shrink, pucker, or wrinkle, as cloth.
çoç'kle·bōat, *n.* a small, shallow, lightweight boat; a cockboat.
çoç'kle·bũr, *n.* 1. the clotbur, a coarse ragweed with prickly burs.
2. the common burdock.
çoç'kled (-klod), *a.* 1. enclosed in a shell.
2. contracted into wrinkles; shrunk and puckered, as cloth.
çoç'kle hat, a hat decorated with a cockleshell, formerly worn by pilgrims.
çoç'klẽr, *n.* one who deals in cockles.
çoç'kle·shell, *n.* 1. the shell of a cockle.
2. loosely, a scallop shell, etc.
3. a small skiff; a cockleboat.
çoç'kle stāirs, winding or spiral stairs. [Obs.]
çock'lǫft, *n.* the top loft; the upper room in a house or other building.
çock'mas″tẽr, *n.* one who breeds gamecocks.
çock'match (-mach), *n.* a match of cocks; a cockfight; a cocking main. [Rare.]
çock'ney, *n.* [ME. *cockeney, cocknaye*, a spoiled child; etym. uncertain.]
1. a native of the East End of London, England, traditionally one born within sound of the bells of St. Mary-le-Bow (Bow Bells) and speaking a characteristic dialect.
2. this dialect, characterized by extreme diphthongization of original vowels, loss of initial *h*, and use of an intrusive *r*.
3. loosely, any native or inhabitant of London: a humorous or disparaging usage.
4. an effeminate, cockered, or spoiled child or youth. [Obs.]
A young heir or *cockney*, that is his mother's darling. —Nash.
çock'ney, *a.* 1. pertaining to or resembling the cockneys of London; characteristic of cockneys; as, a *cockney* song; a *cockney* dialect.
2. loosely, of Londoners or of London.
çock'ney·dŏm, *n.* 1. the district where cockneys live.
2. cockneys as a class, or taken collectively.
çock·ney·ēse', *n.* the characteristic dialect of cockneys.
çock'ney·fȳ, *v.t.*; cockneyfied, *pt., pp.*; cockneyfying, *ppr.* to impart the qualities of a cockney to.
çock'ney·ish, *a.* like cockneys.
çock'ney·ism, *n.* an idiom, pronunciation, etc. characteristic of cockneys.
çock'pāi″dle, *n.* the lumpfish or lumpsucker.
çock'pit, *n.* 1. a pit or enclosed space for cockfighting.
2. a place where there have been many battles; as, Belgium is the *cockpit* of Europe.
3. any space throught to resemble a typical cockpit; specifically, (a) in small, decked vessels, a sunken space toward the stern used by the steersman, etc.; hence, (b) in some small airplanes, the space where the pilot and, sometimes, one or two passengers sit; (c) formerly, the quarters of junior officers on the after part of the lowest deck of a warship, used as a station for the wounded in battle; (d) [Obs.] the pit of a theater.
4. [C–] the English privy council room at Westminster: because built on the site of the cockpit of Whitehall palace.
çock'rōach, *n.* [Sp. *cucaracha*, a wood louse, a cockroach.] a straight-winged insect (family, *Blattidæ*) with a flat, yellowish-brown or black body, slender legs, and long feelers: it is a common kitchen pest, especially in warm, damp places.

COCKROACH (1 1/2 in. long)

çocks'çōmb (-kōm), *n.*
1. the caruncle or comb of a cock.
2. a jester's cap somewhat resembling this.
3. the points on such a cap.
4. a plant of the amaranth family, with red or yellow flower heads supposedly like a rooster's crest: some varieties have feathery heads.
5. a fop, or vain, silly fellow; coxcomb. [Obs.]
çocks'çōmbed (-kōmd), *a.* flattened and laterally widened; banded or compacted together; as, *cockscombed* strawberries.
çocks'fo͝ot, *n.* the orchard grass, *Dactylis glomerata*: also called *cocksfoot grass.*
çocks'head (-hed), *n.* a plant, *Onobrychis sativa*, or sainfoin, having small spiny-crested pods.
çock'shut, *n.* the close of the day, when fowls go to roost. [Obs. or Brit. Dial.]
çock'shȳ, *n.* 1. a game in which toys or trinkets are set up as targets at a carnival booth, to be shied or thrown at, and usually given as prizes to those who hit them: so named from the old sport of shying or throwing sticks at cocks.
2. any mark to be thrown at; also, a throw at a mark.
çock'spũr, *n.* 1. a kind of hawthorn having long, straight thorns: also called *cockspur thorn, Cratægus crus-galli.*
2. one of the sharp spines on the leg of a cock.
3. in ceramics, a small, flat piece of clay to separate pieces of pottery, especially while they are being glazed.
çock'sụre' (-shụr'), *a.* 1. absolutely certain.
2. sure or self-confident to an offensive degree.
çock'swāin (*or* kox'en), *n.* a coxswain.
çock'tāil, *n.* [c. 1806; prob. fanciful coinage; perh. influenced by Fr. *coquetel*, mixed drink popular around Bordeaux, France.]
1. a short mixed alcoholic drink made in various ways and usually iced.
2. an appetizer, as fruit juice, tomato juice, mixed diced fruits, or sea food seasoned with a sharp sauce, served usually at the beginning of a meal; as, a shrimp *cocktail.*
3. a horse with a docked tail.
4. an underbred horse, generally one having one-eighth or one-sixteenth outside blood in his veins; hence, a person of inferior breeding.
5. a kind of rove beetle with an elevated tail: also called the *devil's coach horse.*
çock'up, *n.* 1. a large predatory serranoid fish of India, highly esteemed for its food qualities.
2. a turning up of an end above the level of the rest.
3. a hat or cap turned up in front.
çock'weed, *n.* the peppergrass.
çock'y, *a.* pert or forward; jauntily conceited; self-confident in a swaggering way. [Colloq.]
çock·y·ol'y bīrd, the yellowhammer, a European bird; also, any small bird.
çō'çō, *n.*; *pl.* **çō'çōş**, [Sp.; Port., from L. *coccum*, a seed, kernel; Gr. *kokkos*, a berry.]
1. the coconut palm tree.
2. its fruit; coconut.
Also written, by confusion, *cocoa.*
çō'çō, *a.* made of the fiber from coconut husks.
çō'çōa (kō'kō), *n.* [Sp. and Port. *coco*, cocoa; Gr. *kouki*, the cocoa tree.]
1. powder made from cacao seeds that have been roasted and ground.
2. the beverage made from cocoa by adding sugar and hot water or milk.
3. reddish-yellow brown.
çō'çōa bēanş, the dried, partly fermented seeds of the cacao tree.
çō'çōa brown, a reddish-yellow brown.
çō'çōa-brown, *a.* of the color cocoa brown.
çō'çōa but'tẽr, a yellowish-white fat extracted from cocoa beans: used in pharmacy and in making cosmetics.
çō'çō·bō·lō, çō'çō·bō·lås, *n.* [Sp.] a hardwood tree that grows in the West Indies. It is used in cabinetwork and for ornamental and useful articles, as the handles of tools.
çō'çō·nut, çō'çōa·nut, *n.* the large nut or fruit of the coconut palm, the interior of which contains a milky liquid, called *coconut milk*, and is lined with a solid white meat used as a food and for making oil.
double coconut; the fruit of a palm, native only to the Seychelles in the Indian Ocean. It weighs 40 to 50 pounds.

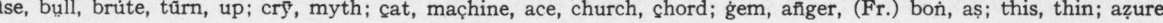

COCONUT AND FLOWER

çō'çō·nut çrab, any land crab of the genus *Birgus*, allied to the hermit crabs: they are very strong and able to crack coconuts with their large claws.
çō'çō·nut päłm (päm), a palm belonging to the genus *Cocos*, producing the coconut. The coconut palm, *Cocos nucifera*, is found in tropical regions. It has a cylindrical trunk, large featherlike leaves, and a subtriangular ovoid fruit which has a single seed enclosed in a very hard shell, and surrounded by a thick fibrous rind or husk.
ço·çoon', *n.* [Fr. *cocon*, dim. of *coque*, a shell, the shell of an egg, a cocoon; L. *concha*, a shellfish, shell.]
1. the silky case which the larvae of certain insects spin about themselves to shelter them during the pupa stage.
2. any protective cover like this.

COCONUT PALM (*Cocos nucifera*)

çō·çoon'ẽr·y, *n.* a place for silkworms when feeding and forming cocoons.
çō'çō päłm (päm), same as *coconut palm.*
çō'çō plum, a tree, *Chrysobalanus icaco*, which yields an edible fruit like a plum. It is native to tropical America, but grows as far north as southern Florida; also, its fruit.
çō·cotte', *n.* [Fr.; orig., hen, from *coq*, cock.] a woman who is sexually promiscuous.
çoç'ti·ble, *a.* capable of being boiled or baked.
çoç'tile, *a.* [L. *coctilis*, burned, baked, from *coctus*, pp. of *coquere*, to cook.] made by baking or exposing to heat, as a brick.
çoç'tion, *n.* [L. *coctio*, from *coquere*, to cook.]
1. the act of boiling or exposing to heat.
2. in medicine, digestion. [Obs.]
çō'çum, *n.* [prob. from native name.] a thick oil extracted from an East Indian tree, *Garcinia indica*: also called *cocum butter, cocum oil.*
çō'çus·wood, *n.* a close-grained wood of the West Indies, sometimes known as *American ebony*, which is used in the manufacture of musical instruments.
Çō·çȳ'tus, *n.* [L.; Gr. *Kōkytos*, lit., a shrieking, wailing, from *kōkyein*, to wail.] in Greek mythology, the river of wailing, a tributary of the Acheron in Hades.
çod, *n.* [ME. *cod, codde*; AS. *cod, codd*, a bag, pouch, cod.]
1. any husk, envelope, or case, containing the seeds of a plant; a pod. [Dial.]
2. a bag. [Archaic.]
3. a pillow. [Scot.]
4. the scrotum. [Obs.]
çod, çod'fish, *n.* [origin uncertain.]
1. an edible fish, of the genus *Gadus*, inhabiting northern seas, but particularly the banks

of Newfoundland and the shores of New England. It is usually salted and dried, and widely used for food. It is also the source of cod-liver oil.

COD (*Gadus morrhua*)

2. any one of several fishes inhabiting Australasian waters; as, (a) in Australia, the Murray cod, *Oligorus maquariensis*; (b) in New Zealand, the serranoid, *Polyprion prognathus*.

çō′dȧ, *n.* [It., from L. *coda, cauda*, tail.] in music, a final passage, which brings a composition to a definite, formal close.

çō′da·mīne, çō′da·min, *n.* [from *code*ine and *amine*.] a white crystalline alkaloid, found in the aqueous extract of opium.

çod′ded, *a.* enclosed in a pod.

çod′dẽr, *n.* a gatherer of cods or peas. [Dial.]

çod′ding, *a.* wanton; lustful. [Obs.]

çod′dle, *v.t.*; coddled, *pt., pp.*; coddling, *ppr.* [Ice. *kvotla*, to dabble.]

1. to cook gently, as an egg, by heating in water not quite at boiling temperature.

2. to treat with excessive care; to spoil; to pamper; to fondle.

çod′dy, *a.* husky. [Obs.]

çod′dy-mod″dy, *n.* a gull. [Brit. Dial.]

çōde, *n.* [Fr. *code*, a code; L. *codex*, the trunk of a tree, a wooden tablet covered with wax for writing.]

1. a body of laws of a nation, state, city, or organization, arranged systematically for easy reference.

In Roman law, *The Code* is the distinctive title which, by way of eminence, is applied to the collection of laws and constitutions of the Roman emperors, made by order of Justinian, containing twelve books.

2. any accepted system of rules and regulations pertaining to a given subject; as, the *medical code*, which governs the professional ethics of physicians; also, a system of rules and regulations governing the conduct in particular cases; as, the *social code*; the *code of honor*, etc.

3. a set of signals representing letters or numerals, used in sending messages, as by telegraph, flags, heliograph, etc.

4. a system of secret writing in which letters, figures, etc. are arbitrarily given certain meanings.

5. the symbols used in such a system.

Code Napoléon; a system of civil law established in France in 1804, compiled under the direction of Napoleon: it has served as the model for the civil codes of many nations.

çōde, *v.t.*; coded, *pt., pp.*; coding, *ppr.* to put in the form of a code; to translate into the symbols of a code.

çō·deç·li·nā′tion, *n.* in astronomy, the complement of the angle of declination: also called *polar distance*.

çō·dē·fend′ănt, *n.* a joint defendant.

çō·dē′lȧ, *n.* same as *codeine*.

çō·dē′ine, çō·dē′in, *n.* [Gr. *kōdeia*, a poppy head.] an alkaloid, $C_{18}H_{21}O_3N{\cdot}H_2O$, obtained from opium and similar to morphine, but milder in its action and less habit-forming: used for the relief of pain and as a sedative.

çō·det′tȧ, *n.* [It., dim. of *coda*, a tail; L. *coda, cauda*, a tail.] a short passage in music joining two sections, but not belonging to either; a short coda.

çō′dex, *n.*; *pl.* **çō′di·cēs,** [L.]

1. a digest or code of laws. [Archaic.]

2. an ancient manuscript of the Scriptures or of certain parts of them, especially of the New Testament; also, an old manuscript of a classic text; as, the *Codex Ambrosianus* of the *Iliad*.

3. a collection of canons or formulas, especially those relating to medicine.

Çō′dex Jū′ris Cȧ·no′ni·cī, [L., Code of Canon Law.] the laws governing the Roman Catholic Church since 1918: superseded the *Corpus Juris Canonici*.

çod′fish, *n.*; *pl.* **çod′fish, çod′fish·eṣ,** the cod.

codfish aristocracy; pretentious, newly-rich people: first said of certain rich New Englanders who made their money out of the codfish industry.

çodġ′ẽr (koj′), *n.* [prob. var. of *cadger*.]

1. a miserly man. [Brit. Dial.]

2. a peculiar person: usually preceded by *old*. [Colloq.]

Çō·di·ae′um, *n.* [L., origin uncertain, perhaps from Gr. *kōdeia*, head, because the leaves were used in making wreaths for the head.] a small genus of shrubs and trees, found in the islands of the Pacific, and valued for their beautiful foliage: also called *croton*.

çod′i·căl, *a.* pertaining to a code, or to a codex.

çō′di·cēṣ, *n.* pl. of *codex*.

çod′i·cil, *n.* [L. *codicillus*, a small tablet, a note, dim. of *codex*, a writing tablet.]

1. in law, an addition to a will, to change or explain some provisions or to add new ones.

2. an appendix or supplement.

çod·i·cil′lȧ·ry, *a.* of the nature of a codicil.

çō″di·fi·çā′tion, *n.* the act or process of arranging (laws) in a code or system.

çō′di·fī·ẽr, *n.* one who forms a code or reduces to codical form.

çō′di·fȳ (*or* cod′i-fȳ), *v.t.*; codified, *pt., pp.*; codifying, *ppr.* to arrange (laws, etc.) systematically; to reduce to a code or digest, as laws.

ço·dil′lȧ, *n.* [LL. *codicula*, dim. of L. *coda, cauda*, tail.] the coarse tow of hemp or flax.

çō·dille′ (-dil′), *n.* [Fr. *codille*; Sp. *codillo*, the knee, a joint, dim. of *codo*, the elbow; L. *cubitus*, the elbow, cubit.] a term in omber, used when the game is won.

çod′le, *v.t.* to coddle. [Obs.]

çod′lin, *n.* a codling (apple).

çod līne, an eighteen-thread line of hemp or cotton, used in cod fishing.

çod′ling, *n.* 1. a variety of elongated apple.

2. an unripe apple.

3. a small, inferior apple.

çod′ling, *n.*; *pl.* **çod′ling, çod′lingṣ,** 1. a young cod.

2. any of certain fishes related to the cod.

çod′ling (or **çod′lin**) **moth,** a small moth whose larva bores into and destroys apples, pears, and quinces: called also the *apple worm*.

çod liv′ẽr, the liver of the cod and allied species.

cod-liver oil; an oil obtained from the liver of the cod and allied fishes: it contains various vitamins and is used medicinally to increase the number of red blood corpuscles in the blood, thus increasing resistance to various diseases.

çod′pïēce, *n.* an ornamented bag or flap appended to the front of the tight breeches worn by men in the fifteenth and sixteenth centuries. [Archaic.]

çod′wŏrm, *n.* a caddis worm.

çoe·cil′i·ăn (sē-), *a.* same as *caecilian*.

çō′ed′, çō′-ed′, *n.* a girl attending a coeducational college. [Colloq.]

çō·ed·ū·çā′tion, *n.* [*co-*, and L. *educare*, to educate.] the education of students of both sexes together in the same classes: especially applied to collegiate or university education.

çō·ed·ū·çā′tion·ăl, *a.* relating to or having coeducation; as, a *coeducational* college.

çō·ef′fi·cȧ·cy, *n.* [*co-*, and L. *efficax*, powerful, from *efficere*, to do.] joint efficacy; the power of two or more things acting together to produce an effect.

çō·ef·fi′cien·cy (-fish′en-cy), *n.* co-operation; joint power of two or more things or causes acting to produce a result.

çō·ef·fi′cient (-fish′ent), *a.* co-operating; acting together to produce a result.

çō·ef·fi′cient, *n.* 1. that which unites in action with something else to produce a result.

2. in mathematics, a number or algebraic symbol prefixed as a multiplier to a variable or unknown quantity; as, in $3x$ and ax, 3 and a are the *coefficients* of x.

3. in physics, a number, constant for a given substance, used as a multiplier in measuring the change in some property of the substance under given conditions; as, the *coefficient* of expansion.

çō·ef·fi′cient·ly, *adv.* by co-operation.

çōe′horn, *n.* [from Baron *Coehorn*, the inventor.] a small military howitzer or mortar with two handles, by which it was carried short distances: also written *cohorn*. [Obs.]

coel- (sēl), same as *coelo-*.

coel′ȧ·çanth (sēl′-), *n.* [*coel-*, and Gr. *akantha*, spine.] any of several primitive ganoid fishes, possibly ancestors to land animals: so called because of their hollow spines: they were long believed to be extinct, but several living specimens have been found in recent times.

coe·lā′ri·um (sē-), *n.*; *pl.* **coe·lā′ri·ȧ,** [L., from Gr. *koilos*, hollow.] the surface layer of cells in the coelom.

-coele (-sēl), [from Gr. *koilia*, a cavity.] a combining form meaning *cavity, chamber of the body, chamber of an organ*, as in blasto*coele*: also *-cele*.

coel′el·minth (sēl′), *n.* a member of the *Cœlelmintha*.

Coel·el·min′thȧ (sēl-), *n.pl.* [*coel-*, and Gr. *helmins*, a worm.] a large group of parasitic worms infesting the cavities of the body: they are entozoons, having an intestinal canal, and include the threadworms.

Coe·len′te·rȧ, Coe·len·te·rā′tȧ (sē-), *n.pl.* [*coel-*, and Gr. *enteron*, intestine.] a phylum of invertebrates, mostly marine, having one large, central cavity: it includes the hydra, jellyfishes, sea anemones, etc.

coe·len′tẽr·āte (sē-), *a.* relating to the *Cœlentera*.

coe·len′tẽr·āte (sē-), *n.* a member of the *Cœlentera*.

coe·len′te·ron (sē-), *n.*; *pl.* **coe·len′te·rȧ,** [Mod.L., from Gr. *koilos*, hollow, and *enteron*, intestine.] the internal cavity of a coelenterate.

coe·les′tine (sē-), *n.* same as *celestite*.

coe′li·ȧ (sē′), *n.* [L., from Gr. *koilia*, a cavity, *koilos*, hollow.] a cavity, as a ventricle of the brain.

coe′li·aç, *a.* [L. *coeliacus*; Gr. *koiliakos*, from *koilia*, the belly, from *koilos*, hollow.] of or in the cavity of the abdomen: also spelled *celiac*.

coe′lō- (sē′-), [from Gr. *koilos*, hollow.] a combining form meaning *hollow, cavity*.

coel·ō·blas′tū·lȧ, *n.* [*coelo-*, and Gr. *blastos*, a shoot.] a blastula with a large center cavity.

coe′lō·dont, *a.* [*coelo-*, and Gr. *odous, odontos*, tooth.] having hollow teeth, as some lizards.

coe′lō·dont, *n.* one of a group of hollow-toothed lizards.

coel·ō·gas′trū·lȧ, *n.* [*coelo-*, and Gr. *gastēr*, belly.] a gastrula having an opening directly into the cavity by means of a blastopore.

Coe·loġ′y·nē (sē-), *n.* [*coelo-*, and Gr. *gyne*, a woman.] a large genus of orchids, native to the East Indies and the Malay Archipelago.

coe′lom, *n.* [Gr. *koiloma*, from *koilos*, hollow.] the embryonic cavity of nearly all multicellular animals, from which the main cavities of the body develop.

coe·lō′mȧ, *n.*; *pl.* **coe·lō′mȧ·tȧ,** same as *coelom*.

coe·lō′māte, *a.* having a coelom.

coe·lō′māte, *n.* an animal which has a coelom.

coe′lōme, *n.* same as *coelom*.

coe·lom′iç, *a.* relating to the coelom.

coel·ō·plan′ū·lȧ, *n.* [*coelo-*, and L. *planula*, dim. of *planum*, a plain.] a coelogastrula without a blastopore.

coel·ō·spẽr′mous, *a.* [*coelo-*, and Gr. *sperma*, a seed.] having hollow seeds.

çō·empt′, *v.t.* to gain control of by coemption.

çō·emp′tion, *n.* [L. *coemptio*; *co-*, together, and *emere*, to buy.] the act of purchasing the whole quantity of any commodity in order to gain a monopoly, control prices, etc.

coe·nan′thi·um, *n.*; *pl.* **coe·nan′thi·ȧ,** [*coen-*, and Gr. *anthos*, a flower.] same as *clinanthium*.

çō·en′dou (-dọọ), *n.* [native name.] the porcupine of Brazil, having a prehensile tail.

coe·neñ′çhym, *n.* same as *coenenchyma*.

coe·neñ′çhy·mȧ, *n.*; *pl.* **coe·neñ·çhy′mȧ·tȧ,** [*coen-*, and Gr. *enchyma*, an infusion, from *enchein*, to infuse; *en*, in, and *chein*, to pour.] the soft, or partly ossified, tissue which joins the polyps of a compound coral.

coen·es·thē′ṣi·ä, *n.* same as *coenesthesis*.

coen·es·thē′sis, *n.* [*coen-*, and Gr. *aisthēsis*, perception.] in psychology, the mass of undifferentiated sensations that make one aware of the body and its condition, as in the feeling of health, illness, discomfort, etc.

çō·en·joy′, *v.t.* to enjoy together. [Rare.]

coe′nō-, [from Gr. *koinos*, common.] a combining form signifying *in common*; *common*; as, *coeno*bium; also, before a vowel, *coen-*.

coe′nō·bīte, *n.* same as *cenobite*.

coe·nō′bi·um, *n.* [LL. from Gr. *koinos*, common, and *bios*, life.]

1. a monastery; a monastic community under one roof, governed by the same rules.

2. the conglomerate mass of a group of protozoa.

coe′nō·çȳte, *n.* [*coeno-*, and *-cyte*.] an organism consisting of several protoplasmic units contained within one cell wall.

coe·noe′ci·um, *n.* [*coeno-*, and Gr. *oikos*, a dwelling.] the tissue which covers a colony of hydroid hydrozoans.

coen′ō·särç, *n.* [*coeno-*, and Gr. *sarx*, flesh.] the soft tissues joining the polyps of a composite zoophyte into one living mass.

coen′ō·sīte, *n.* [*coeno-*, and Gr. *sitos*, food.] one who eats with another, or (as in zoology and botany) an animal or a plant living in, on, or with another but neither parasitic nor injured by it.

coe·nū′rus, *n.* [*coeno-*, and Gr. *oura*, tail.] a tapeworm which in the larval period infests the brains of sheep, causing any of various diseases, as staggers.

çō·en′zȳme, *n.* a substance that occurs with an enzyme and activates it.

çō·ē′quăl, *a.* [*co-*, and L. *æqualis*, equal.] equal with another person or thing; of the same rank, dignity, or power.

çō·ē′quăl, *n.* one who is equal to another.

çō·ē·quăl′i·ty, *n.* the state of being equal; equality.

çō·ē′quăl·ly, *adv.* with joint equality.

çō·ẽrce′, *v.t.*; coerced (-ẽrst′), *pt.*, *pp.*; coercing, *ppr.* [OFr. *coercer*, to coerce; L. *coercere*, to surround; *co-*, together, and *arcere*, to confine.]

1. to restrain by force; to keep from acting by force, especially by legal authority; to repress.
2. to compel; to constrain.
3. to effect by force; to enforce.

Syn.—compel, force, constrain.

çō·ẽr′ci·ble (-bl), *a.* capable of being restrained or compelled; also, condensible; as, a *coercible* gas.

çō·ẽr′ci·ble·ness, *n.* the state of being coercible.

çō·ẽr′cion (-shun), *n.* 1. restraint; hindrance, especially by legal authority; compulsion; force.

2. government by force.

çō·ẽr′ci·tive, *a.* same as *coercive*.

çō·ẽr′cive, *n.* that which has power to restrain by force, especially by legal authority.

çō·ẽr′cive, *a.* tending to coerce; constraining; forcing.

çō·ẽr′cive·ly, *adv.* by coercion.

çō·ẽr′cive·ness, *n.* the quality of being coercive.

coe·rụ′lē·in, *n.* same as *cerulein*.

coe·rụ·lig′nōne, *n.* same as *cerulignone*.

çō·es·sen′tiăl, *a.* [*co-*, and L. *essentia*, the being or essence of a thing.] having one and the same essence or nature.

> We bless and magnify that *coessential* Spirit, eternally proceeding from the Father and Son. —Hooker.

çō·es·sen·ti·al′i·ty (-shi-al′i-ty), *n.* the quality of being coessential.

çō·es·sen′tiăl·ly, *adv.* in a coessential manner.

çō·es·tab′lish·ment, *n.* joint establishment.

çō·es·tāte′, *n.* 1. an estate or state of equal rank to another.

2. a joint estate.

çō·ē·tā′nē·ăn, *n.* one who lives at the same time as another; a contemporary. [Rare.]

çō·ē·tā′nē·ous, *a.* [LL. *coætaneus*, of the same age; L. *co-*, together, and *ætas*, age.] of the same age as another; beginning to exist at the same time; contemporary.

çō·ē·tā′nē·ous·ly, *adv.* of or from the same age or beginning.

çō·ē·tẽr′năl, *a.* equally eternal; existing together eternally.

çō·ē·tẽr′năl·ly, *adv.* with joint eternity.

çō·ē·tẽr′ni·ty, *n.* [LL. *coæternus*, coexistent from eternity; L. *co-*, together, and *æternitas*, eternity.] in theology, existence together of eternal beings or things; joint eternity.

çoeūr (kẽr), *n.* [Fr.] in heraldry, the center or heart of a shield.

çō·ē′văl, *a.* [LL. *coævus*, of the same age; L. *co-*, together, and *ævum*, age.] of the same period; existing at the same time; of equal age; contemporary.

çō·ē′văl, *n.* one of the same age; one who begins to exist at the same time; a contemporary.

çō·ē′vous (-vus), *a.* coeval. [Obs.]

çō·ex·eç′ū·tŏr (-egz-ek′) *n.* a joint executor.

çō·ex·eç′ū·trix (-egz-ek′), *n.* a joint executrix.

çō·ex·ist′ (-eg-zist′), *v.i.*; coexisted, *pt.*, *pp.*; coexisting, *ppr.* to exist together at the same time or at the same place.

çō·ex·ist′ence, *n.* existence together at the same time or at the same place.

çō·ex·ist′ent, *a.* existing together at the same time or at the same place.

çō·ex·ist′ent, *n.* that which coexists.

çō·ex·ist′ing, *a.* existing together at the same time or at the same place.

çō·ex·tend′, *v.t.* and *v.i.*; coextended, *pt.*, *pp.*; coextending, *ppr.* to extend equally in space or time; as, one line *coextends* with another.

çō·ex·tend′ing, *a.* extending equally through the same space or time.

çō·ex·ten′sion, *n.* the act of extending equally, or the state of being equally extended.

çō·ex·ten′sive, *a.* equally extensive; having equal extent in time or space.

çō·ex·ten′sive·ly, *adv.* of equal extent.

çō·ex·ten′sive·ness, *n.* equal extension or extent.

çō·feof·fee′ (-fef-), *n.* [*co-*, and OFr. *feoffé*, a feoffee.] any of two or more individuals to whom a feoffment is granted jointly.

çof′fee (*or* kof′fē), *n.*; *pl.* **çof′fee, çof′fees** [It. *caffè*; Turk. *quahwe*; Ar. *qahwa*, *qahwe*, coffee.]

1. the seeds found in the red berries of a shrub belonging to the genus *Coffea*, growing in tropical climates. The stem of the shrub is upright, and covered with a light-brown bark; the branches are horizontal and opposite, crossing each other at every joint, and forming a sort of pyramid. The pure-white flowers grow in clusters at the root of the leaves, and close to the branches. The berry grows in clusters along the branches and under the axils of the leaves.

COFFEE PLANT (*Coffea Arabica*)

2. an aromatic drink made from the roasted and ground beanlike seeds of the coffee plant.
3. the coffee shrub, of which there are a number of species; as, *Coffea Arabica*, *Coffea occidentalis*, and *Coffea Liberica*.
4. the color of coffee containing milk or cream; brown.

California coffee; the buckthorn berry of California.

çof′fee bēan, the seed of the coffee plant.

çof′fee·ber″ry, *n.*; *pl.* **çof′fee·ber″ries**, 1. the fruit of the coffee plant.

2. the coffee bean.

çof′fee blīght (blīt), a rust blight of coffee leaves; specifically, the fungus *Hemileia vastatrix*.

çof′fee bug, a species of scale insect, *Lecanium coffeae*, which is destructive to the coffee tree.

çof′fee·çāke, *n.* a cake or other form of pastry, often containing nuts, raisins, etc. or coated with sugar or icing, to be eaten with coffee or the like.

çof′fee çrēam, sweet cream with a lower butter fat content than whipping cream.

çof′fee çup, a cup from which coffee is drunk.

çof′fee·house, *n.* a house of entertainment, where guests are supplied with coffee and other refreshments, and where men meet for conversation: popular in Great Britain and the United States in the seventeenth and eighteenth centuries.

çof′fee·man, *n.* one who keeps a coffeehouse.

çof′fee mill, a mill for grinding roasted coffee beans.

çof′fee·pot, *n.* a container, usually with a lid, in which coffee is made or served.

çof′fee·rọọm, *n.* a coffee shop.

çof′fee shop, a restaurant, as in a hotel, in which light refreshments, and now usually meals, may be obtained.

çof′fee tā′ble, a small, low table, usually in a living room, for serving refreshments.

çof′fee tree, 1. the tree that produces the coffee bean.

2. the Kentucky coffee tree.

çof′fẽr, *n.* [ME. *cofer*, *cofre*, a chest; OFr. *cofre*, a chest; L. *cophinus*; Gr. *kophinos*, a basket.]

1. a chest or trunk, especially one used for keeping money; as, the *coffers* of the king.
2. [*pl.*] money; a treasury.
3. in architecture, a decorative sunken panel in the ceiling of a vault or dome, or in the underside of a cornice.
4. a cofferdam.
5. a lock for a barge or ship in a canal, river, dock, etc.
6. in fortification, a trench dug across a dry moat, the upper part made of pieces of timber, raised above the level of the moat to serve as a parapet.

çof′fẽr, *v.t.*; coffered, *pt.*, *pp.*; coffering, *ppr.*

1. to enclose in a coffer.

COFFERED CEILING

2. in mining, to protect (a shaft) from leaking, with timbers or masonry, or by closing the spaces between timbers with clay or other material.
3. in architecture, to ornament with coffers, or to construct in the form of coffers, as a ceiling.

çof′fẽr·dam, *n.* 1. a watertight temporary structure fixed in the bottom of a river, lake, etc., to keep out water during the progress of work: used in laying foundations and abutments of bridges, dams, etc.

2. a watertight box or chamber attached to the side of a ship so that repairs can be made below the water line.

çof′fẽr·ẽr, *n.* 1. a treasurer. [Obs.]

2. formerly, in England, a principal officer of the king's household.

çof′fẽr·wŏrk, *n.* 1. in masonry, rubblework faced with stone.

2. in architecture, a paneled surface.

çof′fin (*or* kọf′), *n.* [ME. *cofin*, *coffin*, a basket, receptacle; OFr. *cofin*, basket, coffer; L. *cophinus*; Gr. *kophinos*, a basket.]

1. the case, chest, or box in which a dead person is placed for burial; a casket.
2. a mold of paste for a pie. [Obs.]
3. a paper bag, in the form of a cone, used by grocers. [Obs.]
4. in farriery, the hollow part of a horse's hoof.
5. in printing, a wooden frame enclosing the imposing stone.
6. a vessel that is not seaworthy. [Colloq.]

to put a nail in one's coffin; to do anything that may tend to shorten one's days.

çof′fin, *v.t.*; coffined, *pt.*, *pp.*; coffining, *ppr.*

1. to put in or enclose in a coffin.
2. to confine tightly; to seclude from sight.

çof′fin bōne, a small spongy bone enclosed in the hoof of a horse or other similar animal.

çof′fin çor′nẽr, [radio slang, prob. with reference to the grave of the defending team's hopes.] in football, any of the corners of the playing field formed by a goal line and side line: punts are often directed to a coffin corner so that the ball will roll out of bounds and be put back into play near the opponent's goal line.

çof′fin joint, the joint in a horse's foot above the coffin bone.

çof′fin nāil, a cigarette. [Slang.]

çof′fin plāte, an inscribed metal plate fastened to the lid of a coffin.

çof′fle, *n.* [Ar. *kāfila*, a caravan.] a number of persons or animals fastened together; especially a caravan or gang of slaves chained together or driven along together.

çof′fle, *v.t.*; coffled, *pt.*, *pp.*; coffling, *ppr.* to fasten together in or as in a coffle.

çof′fret, *n.* [Fr.] a small coffer; an ornamental casket.

çō·found′ẽr, *n.* a joint founder.

çog, *v.t.*; cogged, *pt.*, *pp.*; cogging, *ppr.* [prob. slang extension of *cog* (gear tooth).]

1. to flatter; to wheedle; to seduce or draw from, by adulation or artifice.

> I'll *cog* their hearts from them. —Shak.

2. to obtrude or thrust in, by falsehood or deception; as, to *cog* in a word to serve a purpose. [Rare.]
3. to load for cheating, as a die; to handle fraudulently; as, to play with *cogged* dice.
4. to cheat; to swindle.

to cog a die; to load a die so that it will fall in a desired position.

çog, *v.i.* 1. to deceive; to cheat; to lie.

2. to wheedle; to quibble. [Archaic.]
3. to cheat with dice which are loaded or cogged.

çog, *n.* 1. a cogging at dice. [Obs.]
2. a deception; a trick. [Obs.]

çog, *n.* [ME. *cog, cogge*; Gael., Ir. *cog*, a cog.]
1. one of a series of teeth on the rim of a wheel by which it is connected in motion with another wheel, or part of a machine; gear tooth.
2. a wheel with such teeth on its rim.
3. a person regarded as a minor part of the entire machinery of an activity, business, etc. [Colloq.]
to slip a cog; to make an error.

çog, *v.t.*; cogged, *pt., pp.*; cogging, *ppr.* to furnish with a cog or cogs.

çog, *n.* [altered (after *cog*, gear tooth) from earlier *cock*, to secure.]
1. a projection on a beam that fits into a corresponding groove or notch in another beam, making a joint.
2. in mining, one of the pillars supporting the roof of a mine; a chock.

çog, *v.t.* and *v.i.*; cogged, *pt., pp.*; cogging, *ppr.* to join by a cog (projection) or cogs.

çog, *n.* [ME. *cogge, coge*; OFr. *coque*, a small boat.]
1. formerly, a broadly built boat with a blunt bow and stern.
2. a small boat; cockboat.

çog, *n.* [Gael. *cogan*, a drinking vessel.] a cogue. [Scot.]

cō′gen·cy, *n.* 1. the quality or condition of being cogent; power to convince.
2. *pl.* **cō′gen·cieṣ**, a cogent statement.

cō·gē′ni·ăl, *a.* congenial. [Obs.]

cō′gent, *a.* [L. *cogens*, ppr. of *cogere*, to collect.]
1. forcible in a physical sense; as, the *cogent* force of nature.
2. urgent; compelling; convincing; having a powerful appeal to the mind; forcible; powerful; not easily resisted; as, a *cogent* reason or argument.

cō′gent·ly, *adv.* with urgent force; with powerful impulse; forcibly.

çogged, *a.* having cogs (gear teeth) or cogwheels.

çog′gẽr, *n.* a flatterer, or deceiver.

çog′gẽr·y, *n.* trickery; deception. [Obs.]

çog′gle, *n.* 1. a small round stone or cobble. [Brit. Dial.]
2. a small boat. [Obs.]

çog″i·tȧ·bil′i·ty, *n.* the quality of being conceivable or cogitable.

çog′i·tȧ·ble, *a.* [L. *cogitabilis*, conceivable, from *cogitare*, to think.] capable of being conceived or apprehended in thought; thinkable.

çog′i·tȧ·bund, *a.* [LL. *cogitabundus*, thoughtful, from L. *cogitare*, to think.] very thoughtful.

çog′i·tāte, *v.i.*; cogitated, *pt., pp.*; cogitating, *ppr.* to think seriously; to ponder; to meditate.

He that calleth a thing into his mind, *cogitateth* and considereth. —Bacon.

çog′i·tāte, *v.t.* to think earnestly about; to meditate or ponder upon; as, to *cogitate* plans for advancement.

çog·i·tā′tion, *n.* [ME. *cogitaciun*; OFr. *cogitaciun*; L. *cogitatio*, a thinking, from *cogitare*, to think.]
1. the act of thinking; thought; meditation; contemplation.
2. a thought; a reflection.

çog′i·tā·tive, *a.* 1. thinking; having the power of thinking, or meditating; as, a *cogitative* faculty.
2. tending to cogitate; thoughtful; meditative.

çog′i·tā·tŏr, *n.* a person who cogitates.

ço′gi·tō ẽr′gō sum, [L.] I think, therefore I exist: the basic tenet of the philosophy of Descartes.

cō′gnac (kō′nyak), *n.* [Fr.]
1. a French brandy distilled from wines produced near Cognac, in the department of Charente, France.
2. loosely, any French brandy or any brandy.

çog′nāte, *a.* [L. *cognatus*, related by birth; *co-*, together, and *natus*, pp. of *nasci*, to be born.]
1. related by family; having the same ancestor.
2. related through the same origin; derived from a common original form; as, English *apple* and German *apfel* are *cognate* words, English and Flemish are *cognate* languages.
3. having the same nature or quality.
cognate accusative or *objective*; an object of a verb that expresses or names the action of the verb; as, to fish *fish* from a river.

çog′nāte, *n.* 1. in Scottish law, any relation on the mother's side.
2. a person related to another by common ancestry.
3. a cognate word, language, or thing.

çog′nāte·ness, *n.* the state of being cognate.

çog·nā′tion, *n.* [ME. *cognacioun*; OFr. *cognacion*; L. *cognatio*, kindred, from *co-*, together, and *nasci*, to be born.]
1. relationship by descent from the same ancestor.
2. relationship by descent from the same source.

Pride and hard heartedness are of near *cognation* to ingratitude. —Wotton.

3. resemblance; likeness.

çog·ni′tion, *n.* [ME. *cognicion*; L. *cognitio*, knowledge, from *cognitus*, pp. of *cognoscere*, to know; *co-*, together, and *noscere*, to know.]
1. the process of knowing or perceiving; perception.
2. the faculty of knowing; the act of acquiring an idea.
3. that which is known or perceived.

çog′ni·tive, *a.* knowing; apprehending; as, *cognitive* power.

çog′ni·zȧ·ble (*or* kon′i-), *a.* [OFr. *cognoisable*, from *conoistre*; L. *cognoscere*, to know.]
1. in law, within the jurisdiction of a court; as, a cause is *cognizable* before the circuit court.
2. capable of being known, perceived, or recognized.

çog′ni·zȧ·bly, *adv.* in a cognizable manner.

çog′ni·zănce (*or* kon′i-), *n.* [ME. *cognisaunce*, *conoissance*; OFr. *cognoisance*, *connoissance*, knowledge, from *conoissant*, ppr. of *conoistre*, to know; L. *cognoscere*, to know.]
1. the fact of being aware; perception; knowledge.
2. notice; heed.
3. the range of knowledge possible through observation.
4. in heraldry, the distinguishing crest or other device by which the bearer is recognized.
5. in law, (a) the hearing of a case in court; (b) jurisdiction; the right or power of dealing with a matter judicially.
to take cognizance of; to notice; to recognize officially.

çog′ni·zănt (*or* kon′i-), *a.* having cognizance (*of* something); informed.

çog′nīze, *v.t.*; cognized, *pt., pp.*; cognizing, *ppr.* [L. *cognoscere*, to know.] to take cognizance of; to notice, perceive, or recognize.

çog·ni·zee′ (*or* kon-i-), *n.* in old law, the plaintiff in an action for the assurance of land by fine.

çog·ni·zor′ (*or* kon-i-), *n.* in old law, one who acknowledged the right of the cognizee, in a fine.

çog·nō′men, *n.*; *pl.* **çog·nō′menṣ, çog·nom′i·nȧ,** [L. *cognomen*, a Roman family name, a surname; *co-*, together, and *nomen*, name.]
1. the third or family name of an ancient Roman, as *Cicero* in *Marcus Tullius Cicero*.
2. a family name; surname; last name.
3. any name; especially, a nickname.

çog·nom′i·năl, *a.* 1. pertaining to a cognomen.
2. having the same cognomen.

çog·nom′i·năl, *n.* one having the same name; a namesake. [Obs.]

çog·nom·i·nā′tion, *n.* a surname; a cognomen; a name given by way of distinction; as, Alexander the *Great*.

çog′nosce, *v.t.*; cognosced, *pt., pp.*; cognoscing, *ppr.* to pronounce upon, mentally or morally; to investigate judicially. [Scot.]

çog·nos′cence, *n.* knowledge; the act or state of knowing. [Rare.]

çō·gno·scen′te (nyọ-shen′), *n.*; *pl.* **çō·gno·scen′ti,** [It., from L. *cognoscere*, to know.] a connoisseur.

çog·nos·ci·bil′i·ty, *n.* the quality of being cognoscible.

çog·nos′ci·ble, *a.* capable of being known or perceived.

çog·nos′ci·tive, *a.* having the power of knowing.

çog·nō′vit, *n.* [L., lit. he has acknowledged it; 3d pers. sing. perf. ind. of *cognoscere*, to know.] in law, a written acknowledgment of his liability made by a defendant in a civil suit to avoid the expense of contending.

çō·gōn′, *n.* [Sp. *cogón*, from native (Tagalog) name.] a tall, coarse grass growing in the Philippines and near-by lands, used as thatching.

çog′rāil, *n.* a rail of an inclined road, provided with cogs, or teeth, to engage the cogged driving gear of the locomotive.

çō·grē′di·ent, *a.* [*co-*, and L. *gradiens*, ppr. of *gradi*, to walk.] literally, coming together: a term used in mathematics to denote the relation of two sets of variables which are subject to similar linear transformation.

çō·guärd′i·ăn, *n.* a joint guardian.

çōgue (kōg), *n.* a small wooden vessel for holding liquids of various kinds; a cog. [Scot.]

çog′wāre, *n.* a kind of coarse cloth resembling frieze, worn by the poorer classes in England up to the sixteenth century. [Obs.]

çog′wheel (-hwēl), *n.* a wheel with a rim notched into teeth, which mesh with those of another wheel to transmit or receive motion.

COGWHEELS

çō·hab′it, *v.i.*; cohabited, *pt., pp.*; cohabiting, *ppr.* [LL. *cohabitare*, to dwell together; L. *co-*, together, and *habitare*, to dwell.]
1. to dwell together; to inhabit or reside in company or in the same place. [Archaic.]
2. to dwell or live together as husband and wife: the word usually implies sexual intercourse and is applied especially to those not legally married.

çō·hab′it·ănt, *n.* one who dwells with another or others.

çō·hab·i·tā′tion, *n.* 1. the act or state of dwelling together, or in the same place with another.
2. the state of living together as man and wife.

çō·hab′it·ẽr, *n.* a cohabitant; one who cohabits.

çō·heir′ (-âr′), *n.* [L. *coheres*, fellow heir; *co-*, together, and *heres*, an heir.] a joint heir; one who succeeds to a share of an inheritance.

çō·heir′ess, *n.* a girl or woman who inherits a share of an estate; a joint heiress.

çō·heir′ship, *n.* the condition of being a coheir.

çō·her′ăld, *n.* a joint herald.

çō·hēre′, *v.i.*; cohered, *pt., pp.*; cohering, *ppr.* [L. *cohærere*, to stick together.]
1. to stick together; to cleave; to be united; to hold fast, as parts of the same mass, or as two substances that attract each other; as, particles of clay *cohere*.
2. to be connected naturally or logically, as by a common principle; to be coherent, as the parts of a discourse, or arguments in a train of reasoning.
3. to suit; to be fitted; to agree.

çō·hēr′ence, çō·hēr′en·cy, *n.* 1. cohesion; the act or state of cohering.
2. connection; suitable connection or dependence, proceeding from the natural relation of parts or things to each other, as in the parts of a discourse, or of a system; consistency.

çō·hēr′ent, *a.* 1. sticking together; cleaving.
2. connected; united by some relation in form or order.
3. suitable or suited; regularly adapted.
4. consistent; clearly articulated and intelligible; as, a *coherent* discourse.
Syn.—connected, consistent, united, related.

çō·hēr′ent·ly, *adv.* in a coherent manner.

çō·hēr′ẽr, *n.* in radio, a kind of detector formerly used before the general adoption of the vacuum tube.

çō·hē′ṣi·bil′i·ty, *n.* the tendency to unite by cohesion.

çō·hē′ṣi·ble, *a.* capable of cohesion.

çō·hē′ṣion, *n.* [L. *cohæsus*, pp. of *cohærere*, to stick together.]
1. the act or condition of cohering; tendency to stick together.
2. in physics, the force by which the molecules of a substance are held together: distinguished from *adhesion*.

çō·hē′sive, *a.* having the power of cohering; causing or characterized by cohesion.

çō·hē′sive·ly, *adv.* in a cohesive manner.

çō·hē′sive·ness, *n.* the quality of being cohesive; the quality of adhering together.

çō·hib′it, *v.t.* to restrain.

çō·hi·bi′tion, *n.* hindrance.

çō′hō, *n.*; *pl.* **çō′hō, çō′hōs,** [origin unknown.] a comparatively small salmon, *Oncorhynchus kisutch*, native to the North Pacific Ocean and now widely introduced as a game fish into fresh waters of the northern United States: also *coho salmon*.

çō′hō·bāte, *v.t.* cohobated, *pt., pp.*; cohobating, *ppr.* [from ML. *cohobare*; said to be from Ar. *ka'aba*, to repeat (an action).] in chemistry, formerly, to redistill, often several times, by pouring the distillate back upon the residue in the retort or upon some matter like this, in an attempt to obtain greater purity.

cō·hō·bā′tion, *n.* the operation of repeatedly distilling the same liquid, or that from the same substance.

cō′horn, *n.* same as *coehorn.*

cō′hort, *n.* [L. *cohors,* a cohort.]
1. an ancient Roman military unit, of from three to six hundred soldiers: each cohort consisted of three maniples, and each maniple of two centuries: ten cohorts constituted a legion.
2. any band or body of soldiers.
3. a group; a band.

cō·hor·tā′tion, *n.* exhortation; encouragement. [Obs.]

cō·hor′tȧ·tive, *n.* [L. *cohortatus,* pp. of *cohortari,* to encourage.] in Hebrew grammar, the future paragogic.

cō·hosh′, *n.* [Am. Ind.] a perennial herb, *Caulophyllum thalictroides,* used in medicine; also, any of several species of the crowfoot family.

cō·hūne′, *n.* [from central Am. Ind. name, *cóhuṅ.*] a broad-leaved palm, *Attalea Cohune,* of Central America. It bears large nuts, which yield cohune oil, a substitute for coconut oil. Its wood is used in building.

çoif, *n.* [ME. *coif, coyfe;* OFr. *coife;* LL. *cofea,* a cap, hood.]
1. a cap that fits the head closely.
2. formerly, in England, a white cap worn by lawyers, particularly by sergeants-at-law.
3. the rank of sergeant-at-law.
4. a thick skullcap, as of leather, formerly worn under a hood of mail.

çoif, *v.t.* to cover or dress with or as with a coif.

çoifed (koift), *a.* wearing a coif.

çoiffe, *n.* same as *coif.*

çoif·feur′ (kwä-fũr′), *n.* [Fr.] a hairdresser.

çoif·fūre′ (kwä-), *n.* [Fr., from *coiffer,* to dress the head.] the arrangement of the hair; the style of dressing the hair; a headdress.

çoign, çoigne (koin), *n.* [var. of *coin,* quoin.] a projecting corner.
coign of vantage; a position of advantage for observation or action.

çoil, *v.t.;* coiled, *pt., pp.;* coiling, *ppr.* [OFr. *coillir,* to gather, pick; L. *colligere,* to gather together.]
1. to gather (a line, rope, etc.) into a circular form; to wind into a ring or spiral form.
2. to encircle and hold with or as with coils.
3. to gather up close. [Obs.]

çoil, *v.i.* 1. to wind or twine around something, as a vine around an oak tree.
2. to form rings or coils, or to move in a winding course.

çoil, *n.* 1. anything gathered into a series of rings or spirals; in nautical usage, a single turn or winding of a rope is called a *fake,* and a pile of fakes is calling a *tier.*
2. a series of rings or spirals.
3. a single turn of a coiled figure.
4. in plumbing, a series or group of connected pipes in spirals, rows, or layers, as in a steam-heating radiator.
5. in electricity, (a) a spiral of wire; (b) any device consisting essentially of such a spiral.
coil antenna; a radio antenna wound in the form of a coil.
Flemish coil; among sailors, a coil of rope laid flat and forming a sort of mat.

çoil, *n.* [Early Mod. Eng., from OFr. *acueil,* collision, etc.] commotion; turmoil. [Archaic.]

çoiled, *a.* gathered into a circular form, as a rope, etc.

çoil′lon, *n.* a cullion. [Obs.]

çoin, *n.* [ME. *coyn, coyne,* coin; OFr. *coin,* a wedge, stamp, die, also a corner; L. *cuneus,* a wedge.]
1. a cornerstone; wedge; quoin; coign.
2. a piece of metal with a distinctive stamp, and of a fixed value and weight, issued by a government and used as money.
3. such pieces collectively.
4. money. [Slang.]
5. a die used for stamping money.
to pay one back in his own coin; to retaliate in kind; to give tit for tat.

çoin, *v.t.;* coined, *pt., pp.;* coining, *ppr.* 1. (a) to make (coins) by stamping metal; (b) to make (metal) into coins.
2. to make up; devise; invent, as a new word or phrase.
to coin money; to make money rapidly; to be very successful or fortunate financially. [Colloq.]

çoin, *v.i.* to make coins.

çoin′āġe, *n.* 1. the act, art, or practice of coining.
2. a thing or things coined; coins; metal money.
3. a system of money or metal currency.
4. the right to coin money.
5. an invented word or expression; as, *radar* is a *coinage.*
6. invention; fabrication.

This is the very *coinage* of your brain.
—Shak.

çō·in·cīde′, *v.i.;* coincided, *pt., pp.;* coinciding, *ppr.* [Fr. *coincider;* ML. *coincidere;* L. *co-,* together, and *incidere,* to fall upon; *in,* upon, in, and *cadere,* to fall.]
1. to take up the same place in space; to be exactly alike in shape, position, and area.
2. to occur simultaneously; to take up the same period of time.
3. to concur; to be identical; to agree; as, the judges did not *coincide* in opinion.

çō·in′ci·dence, *n.* [Fr., from ML. *coincedens,* ppr.]
1. the fact or condition of coinciding.
2. an accidental and remarkable occurrence of events, ideas, etc. at the same time, in a way that sometimes suggests a causal relationship; as, their meeting on the train was pure *coincidence.*
Syn.—chance, fortuity, casualty, concurrence, harmony, agreement.

çō·in′ci·den·cy, *n.* coincidence. [Rare.]

çō·in′ci·dent, *a.* 1. taking up the same position in space at the same time.
2. concurrent; corresponding; consistent; agreeable to: followed by *with.*

Christianity teaches nothing but what is perfectly *coincident with* the ruling principles of a virtuous man. —South.

3. happening at the same time; coinciding.

çō·in′ci·dent, *n.* one of two or more coinciding events. [Rare.]

çō·in·ci·den′tăl, *a.* characterized by coincidence.

çō·in·ci·den′tăl·ly, *adv.* in a coincident manner.

çō·in′ci·dent·ly, *adv.* with coincidence.

çō·in·cīd′ẽr, *n.* one who or that which coincides or concurs.

çō·in·cīd′ing, *a.* meeting in the same point; agreeing; concurring.

çō·in·di·çā′tion, *n.* [*co-,* and L. *indicare,* to indicate, show.] a concurrent sign or indication.

çoin′ẽr, *n.* 1. one who stamps coin; a minter; a maker of money.
2. a counterfeiter of legal coin.
3. an inventor or maker, as of words.

çō·in·hab′it·ănt, *n.* one who dwells with another or others.

çō·in·hēre′, *v.i.;* coinhered, *pt., pp.;* coinhering, *ppr.* [*co-,* and L. *inhærere,* to adhere to, inhere.] to inhere or exist together; to be included in the same thing or substance.

çō·in·her′it·ȧnce, *n.* joint inheritance.

çō·in·her′it·ŏr, *n.* a person who inherits jointly with another or others.

çoin′ing, *n.* the act, art, or practice of making stamped metallic money.

çō·in·i′tiăl, *a.* [*co-,* and L. *initium,* a beginning.] having the same origin.

çō·in′qui·nāte, *v.t.* to pollute. [Obs.]

çō·in·qui·nā′tion, *n.* defilement. [Obs.]

çoin sil′vẽr, in metallurgy, silver of standard fineness for making coins.

çō·in·stan·tā′nē·ous, *a.* happening at the same instant.

çō·in·sūr′ănce (-shūr′), *n.* property insurance, especially fire insurance, in which the full value of the property is not covered by the policy: so called because insured and insurer carry the risk jointly.

çō·in·tense′, *a.* having the same intensity.

çō·in·ten′sion, *n.* the state or quality of being cointense.

çoir, *n.* [Port. *cairo;* Malayalam *kayar,* a rope, cord, from Tamil *kayaru,* to be twisted.] a material for cordage, consisting of the husks of the coconut; also, the cordage made of this material.

çois′trel, *n.* [OFr. *coustillier,* a soldier armed with a dagger, from *coustel,* a dagger.] a young lad or inferior groom, employed to take care of a knight's horses; hence, a mean, paltry fellow; knave; varlet. [Archaic.]

çoit, *n.* and *v.* quoit. [Obs.]

çō·i′tion, *n.* [L. *coitio,* a coming together, from *coitus,* pp. of *coire,* to come together; *co-,* together, and *ire,* to come.] a coming together; especially, sexual intercourse; copulation.

çō′i·tus, *n.* sexual intercourse; coition.

çō·join′, *v.t.* to conjoin. [Obs.]

çō·jū′rŏr, *n.* one who swears to another's credibility.

çōke, *n.* [North Eng. dial. *cokes, coaks,* cinders.] coal from which most of the gases have been removed by heating: it burns with intense heat and little smoke, and is used as an industrial fuel: sometimes spelled *coak.*

çōke, *v.t.;* coked (kokt), *pt., pp.;* coking, *ppr.* to convert (coal) into coke.

çōke, *v.i.* to become coke.

çōke, *n.* 1. cocaine. [Slang.]
2. a variety of soft drink containing no cocaine: a trade-mark (*Coke*). [Slang.]

çōke, *v.t.;* coked, *pt., pp.;* coking, *ppr.* to affect with cocaine: usually in the passive, with *up.* [Slang.]

çōke ŏv′en, an oven in which coke (coal) is made.

çō′kẽr·nut, *n.* same as *coconut.*

çōkes, *n.pl.* see *coaks.*

çōkes, *n.* a simpleton. [Obs.]

çōke′wōld, *n.* a cuckold. [Obs.]

çol, *n.* [Fr., neck, a pass; L. *collum,* the neck.] an elevated mountain pass between two higher summits; a mountain pass connecting two valleys, one on either side of a mountain; the most elevated part of a mountain pass.

çol-, com-: used before *l.*

Çō′lȧ, *n.* [Latinized form of a native name.]
1. a genus of trees found in Africa, whose nuts contain caffeine. It includes the kola nut species, *Cola acuminata.*
2. [c–] any tree of this genus.

çō′lȧ, *n.,* 1. alternative plural of *colon* (intestine).
2. plural of *colon* (in prosody).

çō·lā′bŏr·ẽr, *n.* one associated with another in some labor; a fellow worker.

çŏl′an·dẽr, *n.* [Sp. *colador,* a colander, from L. *colare,* to strain, filter, from *colum,* a strainer.] a vessel, having bottom and sides perforated, used in draining off liquids in cookery; a strainer: also spelled *cullender.*

çō′lȧ nut, same as *kola nut.*

çō·lā′tion, *n.* [from L. *colatus,* pp. of *colare,* to strain.] the act of straining or purifying. [Rare.]

çō·lat′i·tūde, *n.* [*co-,* abbrev. of L. *complementum,* the complement, and *latitudo,* breadth.] in astronomy, the complement of the latitude, or the difference in degrees between a given latitude and 90°.

çol′ȧ·tūre, *n.* [L. *colare,* to strain.] the act of straining; the matter strained; the vessel which strains. [Rare.]

çol′bẽr·tīne, çol′bẽr·teen, *n.* [so called after Jean Baptiste *Colbert,* a French minister in the seventeenth century, and a patron of the arts and crafts.] a kind of French lace. [Obs.]

çol·çan′nŏn, *n.* [Ir. *cāl ceannain,* from *cāl,* cabbage, and *ceannan,* white-headed.] an Irish dish made of potatoes, cabbage, and onions boiled together and mashed.

çŏl′chi·çīne, *n.* a poisonous, yellow crystalline alkaloid, $C_{22}H_{25}O_6N$, obtained from the seeds and bulbs of the common colchicum.

Çol′chi·çum, *n.* [L. *colchicum;* Gr. *kolchikon,* a plant having a poisonous root, prob. from *Kolchis,* Colchis, a country in Asia famous as the home of Medea, the sorceress and poisoner of ancient legend.]
1. a genus of plants of the lily family, with radical leaves generally produced in spring, and crocuslike flowers blooming in the autumn. About thirty species are known, the most familiar being *Colchicum autumnale* (the *meadow saffron* or *autumn crocus*), a plant with a solid bulblike rootstock, having purple flowers.
2. [c–] any plant belonging to this genus.
3. [c–] a medical preparation made from the seeds or bulbs of the meadow saffron, sometimes used in the treatment of rheumatism and gout.

COLCHICUM
meadow saffron (*Colchicum autumnale*)

çol′çō·thăr, *n.* [ML., prob. from Ar. *qulquṭār,* a rough metal.] a brownish-red oxide of iron, obtained by heating ferrous sulfate: it is used as a pigment, in polishing glass, and in cleaning metal: also called *crocus.*

çōld, *a.* [ME. *cold, cald;* AS. *ceald, cald,* from *calan,* to become cold.]

1. of a temperature much lower than that of the human body; very chilly; frigid.

2. lacking heat; having lost heat; of less heat than is required; as, this soup is *cold*.

3. having the sensation of cold; feeling chilled; shivering; as, I am *cold*.

4. bland; lacking pungency or acridity.

Cold plants have a quicker perception of the heat of the sun than the hot herbs. —Bacon.

5. dead; lifeless.

Ere the placid lips be *cold*. —Tennyson.

6. without warmth of feeling; without enthusiasm; indifferent; as, a *cold* personality.

7. not cordial; unfriendly; as, a *cold* reception.

8. chilling; gloomy; dispiriting; as, they had a *cold* realization of their plight.

9. calm; detached; objective; as, *cold* logic.

10. designating colors that suggest cold, as tones of blue, green, or gray.

11. still far from what is being sought: said of the seeker.

12. completely mastered; as, the actor had his lines down *cold*. [Slang.]

13. insensible; as, the boxer was knocked *cold*. [Slang.]

14. in hunting, faint; not strong: said of a scent.

cold comfort; little or no comfort at all.

in cold blood; without the excuse of passion; with deliberation.

to catch cold; to become ill with a cold: also *to take cold*.

to throw cold water on; to discourage where support was expected; to introduce unlooked-for objections.

Syn.—wintry, frosty, bleak, indifferent, unconcerned, passionless, apathetic, stoical, unfeeling, forbidding, distant, reserved, spiritless, lifeless.

cōld, *n.* [ME. *cold, cald*; AS. *ceald*, cold.]

1. the comparative absence of heat; lack of warmth: often thought of as an active force.

The parching air
Burns frore, and *cold* performs th' effect of fire. —Milton.

2. the sensation produced in animal bodies by the loss or absence of heat.

My teeth, which now are dropt away,
Would chatter with the *cold*. —Tennyson.

3. an acute inflammation of the mucous membranes of the respiratory passages, especially of the nose and throat, caused by a virus and characterized by sneezing, coughing, etc.; coryza.

to leave one out in the cold; to slight a person intentionally.

cōld, *v.i.* to grow cold. [Obs.]

cōld′-blood″ed (-blud″), *a.* 1. having blood that varies in temperature, approximating that of the surrounding air, land, or water; as, fishes and reptiles are *cold-blooded* animals.

2. without keen sensibility; unsympathetic; actuated by deliberate heartlessness or cruelty.

3. sensitive to the cold; as, sluggish circulation makes one *cold-blooded*.

4. not thoroughbred; of common or mongrel stock: said of livestock, especially horses.

cōld chis′el, a chisel whose cutting edge is formed of steel properly strengthened by tempering, for cutting or chipping cold metal.

cōld crēam, a creamy, soothing preparation for softening and cleansing the skin.

cōld′-drạw′, *v.t.* to draw or shape (unheated metal) through a die.

cōld duck, [transl. of G. *kalte ente*; origin unknown.] a drink made from equal parts of sparkling burgundy and champagne.

cōld frāme, an unheated, boxlike, glass structure for protecting young plants.

cōld front, in meteorology, the forward line of a cold air mass advancing into a warmer air mass.

cōld′-heart″ed, *a.* destitute of passion; without feeling; indifferent; unsympathetic.

cōld′-heart″ed·ness, *n.* lack of feeling or sympathy.

cōld light, light not accompanied by the heat of combustion or incandescence, as phosphorescent light.

cōld′ly, *adv.* in a cold manner; without warmth; without concern; without ardor or animation; without apparent emotion or feeling; with indifference or negligence; as, to answer one *coldly*; a proposition is *coldly* received.

cōld′ness, *n.* the condition, sensation, or quality of being cold; indifference; frigidity; lack of ardor, animation, or spirit.

cōld′-pack′, *v.t.* 1. to apply a cold pack to.

2. to can by cold pack.

cōld pack, 1. cold, wet blankets or sheets wrapped around a patient's body as a means of treatment.

2. a process of canning foodstuffs.

cōld rub′bẽr, a synthetic rubber formed by polymerizing and curing the starting materials, as butadiene-styrene, at a temperature of 41°F or lower: used in automobile tires because of its special resistance to abrasion.

cōld′-short, *a.* in metallurgy, brittle when not at a red heat.

cōld′-shōul′dẽr, *v.t.* to slight; to snub; to rebuff. [Colloq.]

cōld shōul′dẽr, deliberate neglect or indifference; slight; snub; unfriendly attitude.

cōld′-shut, *a.* brought together at too low a temperature to unite properly: said of a welding or casting.

cōld′-shut, *n.* a flaw in a casting, etc., caused by too rapid congealing in the mold.

cōld′slạw, *n.* same as *coleslaw*.

cōld snap, a sudden, brief spell of cold weather.

cōld sōre, a sore consisting of little blisters on or near the lips, coexistent with a cold or during a fever.

cōld steel, a weapon of steel, as a knife or bayonet.

cōld stōr′āge, storage of perishable foods, etc. in a very cold place, especially in a refrigerating chamber.

cōld sweat (swet), perspiration accompanied by a cold, clammy feeling, as during fear or shock.

cōld tũr′key, [*cold*, and *turkey*; reason for use obscure.]

1. the abrupt and total withdrawal of drugs from an addict, as during an attempted cure.

2. in a frank, blunt, or matter-of-fact way; as, to talk *cold turkey* about our chances. [Slang.]

3. without preparation or preliminaries; as, to approach a sales prospect *cold turkey*. [Slang.]

cōld wạr, sharp conflict in diplomacy, economics, etc. between states, regarded as potentially leading to actual war.

cōld wāve, 1. a period of weather colder than is normal.

2. a permanent wave in which the hair is set with a liquid preparation instead of heat.

cōle, *n.* [ME. *cold, cool*; AS. *cawel*; L. *caulis, colis*, a cabbage, cabbage stalk.] any of various plants of the genus *Brassica*, including all sorts of cabbage; especially, rape.

cō·lec′tō·my, *n.* the surgical removal of all or part of the colon.

cō″leg·ȧ·tee′, *n.* one who is a legatee jointly with another or others.

cōle′măn·īte, *n.* [after William T. *Coleman* (1824–1893), Am. manufacturer of borax.] a white or colorless crystalline substance, $Ca_2B_6O_{11}·5H_2O$, a hydrous borate of calcium.

cō·lē·op′tẽr, cō·lē·op′tẽr·ăn, *n.* an insect of the order *Coleoptera*.

Cō·lē·op′te·rȧ, *n.pl.* [L., from Gr. *koleos*, a sheath, and *pteron*, a wing.] an order of insects, including the beetles and weevils, the largest ordinal group in the animal kingdom. They are characterized by having four wings, of which the two anterior, called elytra, are not suited for flight, but form a covering and protection to the two posterior, and are of a hard or parchmentlike nature.

COLEOPTER
(*Cicindela campestris*)
a, head; *b*, thorax; *c*, abdomen; *d d*, elytra; *e e*, wings; *f f* antennae

cō·lē·op′tẽr·ăl, *a.* coleopterous.

cō·lē·op′tẽr·ist, *n.* one who makes a study of the *Coleoptera*.

cō·lē·op′tẽr·on, *n.*; *pl.* **cō·lē·op′tẽr·ȧ,** a coleopter.

cō·lē·op′tẽr·ous, *a.* pertaining or belonging to the *Coleoptera*.

cō″lē·ō·rhī′zȧ, *n.*; *pl.* **cō″lē·ō·rhī′zae,** [Mod. L., from Gr. *koleos*, a sheath, and *rhiza*, a root.] a sheath surrounding the early root of certain seedlings, through which the roots emerge.

cōle′seed, *n.* 1. the plant *Brassica napus*, the common winter rape.

2. the seed of the common rape.

cōle′slạw, *n.* [from D. *kool*, cabbage, and *sla*, for *salad*, salad.] a salad made of shredded raw cabbage, often mixed with salad dressing and seasoning: also written *cole slaw*.

cōle′tit, *n.* see *coalmouse*.

Cō′lē·us, *n.* [Mod.L., from Gr. *koleos*, a sheath.]

1. a genus of plants of the mint family, native to Africa and the East Indies, largely cultivated for their showy, bright-colored leaves.

2. [c—] any of various plants of this genus.

cōle′wŏrt, *n.* [ME. *colwort*, from AS. *cawl*, cabbage, and *wyrte*, a wort, root.]

1. cole.

2. any cabbage whose leaves do not form a compact head; also, a young cabbage cut before the head is formed.

col′iç, *n.* [ME. *colyke*; OFr. *colique*, colic; L. *colicus*, sick with the colic; Gr. *kōlikos*, colic, from *kolon*, the colon.] acute abdominal pain caused by various abnormal conditions in the bowels.

col′iç, *a.* 1. relating to colic; having action on the bowels.

2. relating to the colon (part of the large intestine).

col′iç·ăl, *a.* resembling colic. [Rare.]

col′ick·y, *a.* 1. afflicted with or subject to attacks of colic.

2. of or having a resemblance to colic.

3. liable to bring on colic; as, *colicky* fruits.

col′iç·rọọt, *n.* 1. a bitter herb of the lily family with white or yellow flowers.

2. any of a number of other plants supposedly beneficial in colic, as *Aletris farinosa*, *Aletris aurea*, and *Dioscorea villosa*.

col′ic·weed, *n.* any of several North American plants, as the Dutchman's-breeches.

col′in, *n.* [Sp. *colín*; Mex. *çolin*.]

1. the masked bobwhite.

2. any bird of the bobwhite family.

col·i·sē′um, *n.* [Mod.L., from L. *colosseum*, neut. of *colosseus*, colossal, huge.]

1. [C—] the Colosseum.

2. a large building or stadium for sports events and other public entertainments.

cō·lī′tis, *n.* [Mod.L., from Gr. *kolon*, the colon.] inflammation of the mucous membrane of the large intestine.

col′lȧ, *n.* plural of *collum*.

çol·lab′ō·rāte, *v.i.*; collaborated, *pt., pp.*; collaborating, *ppr.* [from L. *collaboratus*, pp. of *collaborare*, to work together, from *com-*, with, and *laborare*, to work.]

1. to labor, especially in literary or scientific pursuits, as the associate of another or others.

2. to co-operate with the enemy; to be a collaborationist.

çol·lab·ō·rā′tion, *n.* 1. the act of performing work or labor together; especially literary work or scientific research.

2. co-operation with the enemy.

çol·lab·ō·rā′tion·ist, *n.* a person who co-operates with an enemy invader of his country.

çol·lab′ō·rā·tive, *a.* 1. collaborating or tending to collaborate.

2. resulting from collaboration.

çol·lab′ō·rā·tŏr, *n.* [Fr. *collaborateur*, from L. *com-*, with, and *laborare*, to labor.] an associate in labor, as in scholarly pursuits.

çol·läge′ (-läzh′), *n.* [Fr., a pasting, paper hanging.]

1. a kind of surrealist art in which bits of flat objects, as newspaper, cloth, pressed flowers, etc., are pasted together in incongruous relationship for their symbolic or suggestive effect.

2. a picture so made.

col′lȧ·gen, *n.* [Gr. *kolla*, glue, and *-gen*.] a gelatinous substance found in connective tissue, bone, and cartilage: written also *collogen*.

col·laġ′e·nous, *a.* resembling or made up of collagen.

çol·lapse′, *v.i.*; collapsed, *pt., pp.*; collapsing, *ppr.* [L. *collapsus*, pp. of *collabi, conlabi*, to fall together or in; *com-*, together, and *lapsi*, to fall.]

1. to fall in or together, as the two sides of a vessel; to cave in, either from force exerted on the outside, or from the removal of support from within; as, a bladder when emptied of air *collapses*.

2. to come to nothing; to break down suddenly; to fail; to vanish; as, the project *collapsed*.

3. to break down or fail suddenly in health.

4. to fold or come together compactly.

5. to fall down, as from a blow or strain.

çol·lapse′, *v.t.* to cause to collapse.

çol·lapse′, *n.* 1. a falling in or together, as of the sides of a hollow vessel.

2. a sudden and entire failure of any kind; utter ruin; a breakdown.

3. a sudden breakdown in health; state of extreme physical depression and prostration with failure of circulation.

çŏl·laps·i·bil′i·ty, *n.* the quality or condition of being collapsible.

çŏl·laps′i·ble, *a.* made so that it can be folded up compactly.

çŏl·lap′sion, *n.* a state of falling together or collapsing. [Obs.]

çol′lăr, *n.* [ME. *coller*; OFr. *coler, colier*; L. *collare*, a band or chain for the neck, from *collum*, neck.]

1. the part of a dress, blouse, coat, shirt, etc. that encircles the neck.

2. the cloth band or folded-over piece attached to the neck of a shirt, blouse, dress, etc.

3. an ornamental band, chain, or circlet worn around the neck.

4. a band of leather or metal for a dog's neck.

5. a leather-covered roll for the neck of a horse or other draft animal; part of the harness against which the animal strains in pulling a weight.

6. a ring or flange, as on rods, shafts, or pipes, to prevent sideward motion, connect parts, etc.

7. a distinctive band, as of a different color, marking, or texture, around the neck of an animal, bird, etc.

8. the foam that forms on the top of a glass of beer.

9. in architecture, (a) a band or cincture; (b) a collar beam.

10. in botany, (a) the ring upon the stem of an agaric; (b) the point of divergence of the root and stem of a plant.

11. a steel ring which confines a planchet, in coining, and prevents spreading under the pressure of the coining press.

12. in nautical usage, (a) an eye in the end or bight of a shroud or stay, to slip over a masthead; (b) a rope formed into a wreath with a heart or deadeye in the bight, to which the stay is confined at the lower part.

13. in mining, the curb or lining of a shaft.

çol′lăr, *v.t.*; collared, *pt., pp.*; collaring, *ppr.*
1. to seize by or as by the collar; to capture.

2. to furnish with a collar.

3. to roll up and bind (meat, etc.).

4. to stop and talk to; as, she *collared* him in the hall. [Colloq.]

çol′lăr bēam, a beam or piece of timber extending between two opposite rafters, at some height above their base.

çol′lăr·bīrd, *n.* the bower bird of Australia, genus *Chlamydodera.*

çol′lăr·bōne, *n.* a flat, slender bone reaching from the breastbone to the shoulder; the clavicle.

çol′lăr but′tŏn, a small button, sometimes detachable, for fastening a shirt collar.

çŏl′lărd, *n.* [contr. from *colewort.*] a kind of kale whose coarse leaves are borne in tufts.

çol′lăr dāy, a day formerly observed in England, on which knights appeared at court wearing the jeweled collars of their orders.

çol′lăred, *a.* 1. having a collar about the neck: used especially in heraldry; as, a *collared* lion.

2. bound up in a roll, as a joint of meat.

çol·lăr·et′, çol·lăr·ette′, *n.* [Fr. *collarette*, from L. *collare*, collar.] a short cape, broad collar, or fichu, made of lace, fur, or other material, worn by women.

çŏl·lāt′ȧ·ble, *a.* capable of being collated.

çŏl·lāte′, *v.t.*; collated, *pt., pp.*; collating, *ppr.* [L. *collatus*, pp. of *conferre*, to bring together; *com-*, together, and *ferre*, to carry.]

1. to compare carefully, as texts, by examining point by point; as, to *collate* copies of the scriptures.

2. to present and institute (a clergyman) in a benefice, when the same person is both the ordinary and the patron: followed by *to*.

> If the patron neglects to present, the bishop may *collate* his clerk *to* the church.
> —Blackstone.

3. to bestow or confer. [Obs.]

4. to examine (the sheets of a book to be bound) to see that the pages, plates, etc. are in proper order.

5. in library usage, to examine (a book) page by page to see that none are missing.

çŏl·lāte′, *v.i.* to place a cleric in a benefice.

çŏl·lat′ẽr·ăl, *a.* [ME. *collateral*; L. *com-*, together, and *lateralis*, lateral, from *latus*, side.]

1. side by side; parallel.

2. accompanying; concomitant.

3. of a similar but subordinate nature; secondary.

4. of corresponding value or importance.

5. descended from the same ancestors but in a different line; as, Franklin D. Roosevelt and Theodore Roosevelt were *collateral* relatives.

6. designating or of security given as a pledge for the fulfillment of an obligation; hence, secured or guaranteed by property, as stock, bonds, etc.; as, a *collateral* loan.

collateral assurance; in law, assurance made in addition to the principal deed.

collateral issue; in law, an issue aside from the main question in the case.

collateral security; additional security, as property, a bill of sale, a stock certificate, or any other pledge deposited to secure the performance of a contract or the discharge of an obligation.

çŏl·lat′ẽr·ăl, *n.* 1. a collateral relative or kinsman.

2. anything of value pledged as additional security for the performance of the main obligation; collateral security: it is returned to the debtor when the obligation is fulfilled.

çŏl·lat′ẽr·ăl·ly, *adv.* 1. side by side.

2. indirectly; in the nature of a side issue.

3. in collateral relation; not in a direct line; not lineally.

çŏl·lat′ẽr·ăl·ness, *n.* the state of being collateral.

çŏl·lā′tion, *n.* [ME. *collacioun*; OFr. *collacion*, discourse; L. *collatio, conlatio*, a bringing together, collection, from *com-*, together, and *latus*, pp. of *ferre*, to bring.]

1. the act, process, or result of collating or comparing; a comparison of one copy, text, etc. with another.

2. the act of conferring or bestowing. [Obs.]

3. the appointment of a clergyman to a benefice.

4. in Scots law, the right which an heir has of throwing the whole heritable and movable estates of the deceased into one mass, and sharing it equally with others who are of the same degree of kindred.

5. a compilation; specifically, a collection of the lives of the fathers of the church; also, the act of reading and discussing this or some other religious book, a practice instituted in monasteries by St. Benedict.

6. a light repast: a term originally applied to the meal eaten by monks in monasteries after the reading of a religious book, as one containing the lives of the saints.

7. in bookbinding, the assembling of the printed sheets for a final inspection previous to binding.

8. a conference or consultation.

9. in library usage, the technical description of a book, including the number of pages, illustrations, etc.

collation of seals; the comparison of a seal with one whose authenticity is unquestioned to determine the reliability of the former.

çŏl·lā′tion, *v.i.* to partake of a light meal. [Obs.]

çol·lȧ·ti′tious (-tish′us), *a.* done by contributions. [Obs.]

çŏl·lā′tive, *a.* 1. having the power to confer or bestow.

2. bestowed or held by collation.

çŏl·lā′tŏr, *n.* 1. one who collates or compares manuscripts or editions of books.

2. one who collates to a benefice.

3. one who grants any benefit or bestows a gift of any kind.

çol′lēague (-lēg), *n.* [Fr. *collègue*; L. *collega, conlega*, a colleague; *com-*, together, and *legatus*, pp. of *legare*, to choose for an embassy.] a fellow worker in the same profession; a partner or associate in office.

Syn.—collaborator, associate, companion, coadjutor, ally, confederate.

çol·lēague′, *v.i.* to unite with one or more associates in the same office. [Rare.]

çol′lēague·ship, *n.* the state of being a colleague.

çŏl·leçt′, *v.t.*; collected, *pt., pp.*; collecting, *ppr.* [OFr. *collecter*, to collect, from L. *collectus*, pp. of *colligere*, to collect; *com-*, together, and *legere*, to gather.]

1. to gather together; to assemble or bring together; as, to *collect* men into an army; to *collect* ideas.

2. to gain by observation or information; as, to *collect* news.

3. to gather from premises; to infer. [Rare.]

> Which sequence, I conceive, is very ill *collected.* —Locke.

4. to receive or compel payment of, as debts; to demand and receive; as, to *collect* taxes; to *collect* accounts.

5. to obtain from contribution.

6. to gather (stamps, books, etc.) for a hobby.

7. to regain control of (oneself or one's wits); to summon up (one's faculties or powers).

Syn.—accumulate, assemble, amass, gather, congregate, convoke, garner, reap, convene, muster, aggregate, summon.

çŏl·leçt′, *v.i.* 1. to run together; to accumulate; as, pus *collects* in an abscess; snow *collects* in banks.

2. to gather; to assemble.

3. to collect payments, etc.; as, the landlord *collects* on the first of the month.

çŏl·leçt′, *a.* and *adv.* with payment to be made by the receiver; as, he telephoned *collect.*

çol′leçt, *n.* [ME. and OFr. *collecte*; LL. *collecta*, a gathering together of ideas from the day's reading; from L. *collectus, pp.* of *colligere*, from *com-*, together, and *legere*, to gather.]

1. a short prayer suitable to the time or occasion, used in certain church services.

2. a collection or gathering of money. [Obs.]

çŏl·leçt′ȧ·ble, *a.* and *n.* See *collectible.*

çol·lec·tā′nē·ȧ. *n.pl.* [LL., things collected, from L. *collectaneus*, gathered or collected.] a collection of passages from various authors, usually made for the purpose of instruction; an anthology.

çŏl·leçt′ed, *a.* 1. gathered together; assembled.

2. calm and self-possessed; undisturbed; not disconcerted; cool; composed.

Syn.—calm, composed, cool, placid, serene, unmoved.

çŏl·leçt′ed·ly, *adv.* 1. in a collected form or condition; in one body.

2. in a cool, self-possessed state of mind.

çŏl·leçt′ed·ness, *n.* a collected state of the mind; self-possession.

çŏl·leçt′i·ble, *a.* 1. that can be collected.

2. suitable for collecting, as for a hobby.

çŏl·leçt′i·ble, *n.* any of a class of old things, but not antiques, that people collect as a hobby, specifically a thing of no great intrinsic value.

çol·leç′tion, *n.* [L. *collectio*, a bringing together, from *collectus*, pp. of *colligere*, to collect.]

1. the act or process of collecting.

2. the body formed by gathering; an assemblage, or assembly; as, a *collection* of books or paintings; a *collection* of strangers.

3. a contribution; a sum collected for a charitable or religious purpose, especially during a meeting or religious service.

4. something that has gathered into a mass or pile; accumulation; as, a *collection* of dust.

5. [*pl.*] in English universities, an examination held at the end of a semester.

Syn.—assembly, assemblage, store, gathering, group, accumulation, aggregation, compilation, company, crowd, quantity, mass.

çŏl·leçt′ive, *a.* [L. *collectivus*, collective, from *collectus*, pp. of *colligere*, to collect.]

1. formed by gathering or assembling; gathered into a mass, sum, or body; congregated, or aggregated.

2. deducing consequences; reasoning; inferring. [Obs.]

3. of, as, or characteristic of a group; of or characteristic of individuals acting together; common to several or many; as, the *collective* effort of the students.

4. designating or of any enterprise in which people work collectively; as, there are *collective* farms in the Soviet Union.

5. in grammar, designating a noun which in the singular form denotes a collection of individuals (e.g., army, orchestra, crowd): it is treated as singular when the collection is thought of as a whole and as plural when the individual members are thought of as acting separately.

collective bargaining; bargaining carried on between an employer, or employers, and an organized group of workers in order to reach an agreement on wages, hours, working conditions, etc.

collective fruit; in botany, any fruit formed by a fused cluster of the ovaries of several flowers, as the pineapple, the mulberry, etc.: called also *multiple fruit.*

collective security; a system of international security in which the participating nations agree to take joint action against a nation that attacks any one of them.

çŏl·leçt′ive, *n.* 1. in grammar, a collective noun.

2. any collective enterprise.

3. the people who work together in such an enterprise.

çŏl·lect′ive·ly, *adv.* 1. in a collective manner; with all participating.
2. as a whole; as a group.

çŏl·lect′ive·ness, *n.* the state of being collective; union; mass.

çŏl·lect′iv·ism, *n.* the ownership and control of the means of production and distribution by the people as a whole; socialism.

çŏl·lect′iv·ist, *a.* pertaining to collectivism or collectivists.

çŏl·lect′iv·ist, *n.* one who advocates collectivism.

çŏl·lec·tiv·is′tiç, *a.* of collectivism or collectivists.

çŏl·lec·tiv′i·ty, *n.* 1. the quality or state of being collective.
2. a collective whole.
3. the people as a whole.
4. collectivism.

çŏl·lect′iv·īze, *v.t.*; collectivized, *pt., pp.*; collectivizing, *ppr.* 1. to establish collectivism in.
2. to transfer from private to public ownership.

çŏl·lect′ŏr, *n.* [LL. *collector*; L. *collectus*, pp. of *colligere*, to collect.]
1. a person or thing that collects; especially, one who collects objects of art, rare books, manuscripts, natural history specimens, and the like.
2. a compiler of books. [Obs.]
3. a person employed to collect commercial accounts, debts, rents, or the like.
4. a government official empowered to gather or receive public dues, as internal revenue taxes and customs duties.
5. in electricity, a disk or part of a machine used to collect currents and give to them a common direction.

çŏl·lect′ŏr·āte, *n.* a collectorship.

çŏl·lect′ŏr·ship, *n.* the office or district of a collector of customs or taxes; as, the *collectorship* of the port of New York.

çol′leen, *n.* [Ir. *cailin*, dim. of *caile*, girl.] a girl. [Irish.]

çŏl·leg′ȧ·tā·ry, *n.* in law, a person who has a legacy left to him, in common with one or more other persons; a colegatee.

çol′leġe, *n.* [L. *collegium*, a society, guild, or fraternity, from *collega*, a colleague; *com-*, together, and *legatus*, pp. of *legare*, to send on an embassy, choose for a mission.]
1. a collection, assemblage, body, or society of men, invested with special powers and rights, performing certain duties, or engaged in some common employment or pursuit; as, a *college* of physicians; a *college* of bishops; the electoral *college*.
2. a society of scholars and persons of learning formed into a corporation for the purposes of concerted study, scientific, literary, or historical research, and the instruction of students in the advanced branches of knowledge. A college generally has the right of conferring degrees upon individuals not members of the institution, as well as upon students who have completed courses of study; a university.
3. any of the schools of a university offering instruction and granting degrees in any of several specialized courses of study, as liberal arts, architecture, education, business administration, etc.
4. that division of a university which offers a general four-year course leading to the bachelor's degree: distinguished from the graduate and professional schools.
5. a school offering specialized instruction in some profession or occupation; as, business *college*, *college* of chiropody.
6. the building or group of buildings of a college.
7. figuratively, any assemblage; a community; as, a *college* of bees. [Rare.]
8. a prison, especially a debtors' prison. [Brit. Slang.]
9. an assembly for the study of special subjects; as, the *college* of war.
apostolic college; (a) the apostles of Christ, considered collectively as being invested with corporate authority; (b) the whole body of bishops of the historical church, regarded as continuing the authority possessed by the original apostles.
college church; (a) a church connected with a college; (b) a collegiate church: see under *collegiate*.
College of Cardinals; the cardinals of the Roman Catholic Church, serving as a privy council to the Pope: it administers the Holy See in the absence of the Pope and elects his successor.
College of Justice; in Scotland, the whole system of supreme civil courts, together with their judges and officers.
Heralds' College; see under *Herald*.
Sacred College; the College of Cardinals.

çol′leġ·ẽr, *n.* 1. a member of, or student at, a college.
2. at Eton College, England, a student supported by endowment of the college.

çol′leġe wid′ōw, a young, unmarried woman in a college town who has had social engagements with male students at the college over a number of years.

çŏl·lē′ġi·ȧ, *n.*, plural of *collegium*.

çŏl·lē′ġi·ăl, *a.* relating to a college; belonging to a college; having the nature of a college.

çŏl·lē′ġi·ăl·ism, *n.* the ecclesiastical theory that the church is an organization (the collegium) independent of and equal to the state, with its highest authority resting in its entire membership.

çŏl·lē′ġi·ăn, *n.* 1. a member of a college; a college student.
2. one in prison for debt. [Brit. Slang.]

Çŏl·lē′ġi·ănt, *n.* a member of a Dutch sect with no formulated creed or organized ministry. The sect was founded in 1619, and its members are also known as *Holland* or *Dutch Quakers*.

çŏl·lē′ġi·āte, *a.* [L. *collegium*, a society, fraternity.]
1. pertaining to or like a college; as, *collegiate* studies; a *collegiate* society.
2. containing a college; as, a *collegiate* town.
3. collected; united. [Rare.]
4. of, like, or characteristic of college students.
collegiate church; (a) a church with a chapter (college) of canons although it is not a bishop's see; (b) in Scotland, a church with two or more ministers serving together jointly; (c) in the United States, a church associated with others under a joint body of pastors; (d) such an association of churches.

çŏl·lē′ġi·āte, *n.* a student at a college; a collegian.

çŏl·lē′ġi·um, *n.*; *pl.* **çŏl·lē′ġi·ȧ,** [L. *collegium*, a society, college.] an ecclesiastical body of independent powers, and free of governmental control.

Çŏl·le′mȧ, *n.* [L., from Gr. *kollan*, to glue together, from *kolla*, glue.] in botany, a large genus of gelatinous lichens.

çŏl·lē·mā′ceous, *a.* belonging to or characteristic of the genus *Collema*.

Çŏl·lem′bō·lȧ, *n.pl.* [L., from Gr. *kolla*, glue, and *embolē*, a throwing or putting in, from *emballein*, to throw, or put in.] an order of insects containing the most primitive types, including the podurids and related species.

çŏl·lē′moid, *a.* same as *collemaceous*.

çŏl·len′chy·mȧ, *n.* [L., from Gr. *kolla*, glue, and *enchyma*, an infusion.] in botany, a layer of elastic plant tissue composed of elongated cells, having walls which are thickened at the angles by a gluelike mass.

çol′let, *n.* [Fr. *collet*, a collar, from L. *collum*, neck.]
1. among jewelers, the horizontal face or plane at the base of brilliants; the culet; also, the ring of metal in which a jewel is set.
2. a narrow collar or neckband. [Obs.]
3. a metal band or ring, such as is used in a watch to hold the end of the spring.
4. in glassmaking, that part of glass vessels which sticks to the pontil or iron instrument used in taking the substance from the melting pot. [Obs.]

çol′let, *v.t.* to set in or furnish with a collet.

çol·lē·tē′ri·ăl, *a.* relating to or deposited by the colleterium of insects.

çol·lē·tē′ri·um, *n.* [L., from Gr. *kollan*, to glue, from *kolla*, glue.] an abdominal organ in insects, containing a cement for gluing together the ova after they have been deposited.

çŏl·let′iç, *a.* having the property of gluing; agglutinant.

çŏl·let′iç, *n.* an agglutinant substance.

çol′ley, *n.* same as *collie*.

çŏl·līde′, *v.i.*; collided, *pt., pp.*; colliding, *ppr.* [L. *collidere*, to strike or dash together; *com-* together, and *lædere*, to strike, injure.] to strike or dash against each other; to encounter violently; to meet in shock; to crash; hence, to meet in opposition or antagonism; to conflict; to clash; as, their interests *collided*.

çŏl·līde′, *v.t.* to strike against; to dash against. [Obs.]

çol′li·dine, *n.* [from Gr. *kolla*, glue.] an oily, poisonous liquid, derived from coal tar and belonging to the pyridine series. It may be formed by the distillation of various alkaloids or made synthetically.

çol′lie, *n.* [origin uncertain; probably from *coaly*, coal-black, from the color of some of the breed.] any of a breed of large, long-haired Scottish sheep dog with a long, narrow head and pointed nose: written also *colly*, *colley*.

çol′lied, *a.* begrimed or darkened; made black, as with soot.

çol′liẽr (-yẽr), *n.* [ME. *colyer*, *colier*, from *col*, coal, and *-yer*.]
1. a coal miner; one who works in a coal mine.
2. a ship for carrying coal.
3. any of its crew.
collier's lung; an occupational disease of miners; miner's lung, or anthracosis.

çol′liẽr·y, *n.*; *pl.* **çol′liẽr·ieș,** 1. a coal mine and its buildings, equipment, etc.
2. the coal trade. [Obs.]

çol′li·fọrm, *a.* [L. *collum*, neck, and *forma*, shape.] shaped like a neck, or collar.

çol′li·gāte, *v.t.*; colligated, *pt., pp.*; colligating, *ppr.* [L. *colligatus*, pp. of *colligare*, to bind together; *co-*, together, and *ligare*, to bind.]
1. to tie or bind together.
The pieces of insinglass are *colligated* in rows. —Nicholson.
2. in logic, to relate (isolated facts) by some reasonable explanation, especially so as to evolve a general principle.

çol·li·gā′tion, *n.* [L. *colligatio*, a binding together, from *colligare*, to bind together.] a colligating or being colligated.

çol′li·māte, *v.t.*; collimated, *pt., pp.*; collimating, *ppr.* [from *collimare*, false reading of L. *collineare*, to direct in a straight line, from *com-*, with, and *lineare*, to make straight, from *linea*, a line.]
1. to make parallel, as light rays.
2. to adjust the line of sight of (a telescope, etc.).

çol·li·mā′tion, *n.* [*col-*, and L. *limes*, a boundary, limit.] a collimating or being collimated.

çol′li·mā·tŏr, *n.* 1. a small telescope with cross hairs at its focus, fixed to another telescope, surveying instrument, etc. for adjusting the line of sight.
2. the tube of a spectroscope that receives the light and casts it upon the prism in parallel rays; also, the lens used in this.

çol′lin, *n.* [Gr. *kolla*, glue.] the purest form of gelatin, taken as the type of all similar substances.

çol′line, *n.* [Fr. *colline*, from L. *collis*, a hill.] a little hill; a mount. [Obs.]

çŏl·lin′ē·ăr, *a.* [*col-*, and L. *linea*, a line.] in the same straight line; as, a series of points *collinear* with another series.

çŏl·lin·ē·ā′tion, *n.* [L. *collineare*, to direct in a straight line; *com-*, together, and *lineare*, to make straight, from *linea*, a straight line.] the act of aiming at, or directing in a line to, a fixed object.

çoll′ing·ly, *adv.* with an embrace.

çŏl·lin′guăl (-gwăl), *a.* [*col-*, and L. *lingua*, the tongue.] having or pertaining to the same language.

Çol′linș, *n.* [supposedly after its inventor, a bartender named Tom *Collins*.] any of several mixed drinks made with lemon or lime juice, sugar, carbonated water, ice, and either gin (*Tom Collins*), rum (*Rum Collins*), or whisky (*John Collins*).

çŏl·lin′si·ȧ, *n.* [Mod.L., after Amer. botanist Zaccheus *Collins* (1764–1831).] any of a group of hardy, low-growing plants of the figwort family, with flowers arranged in whorls.

çŏl·liq′uȧ·ble (-wȧ-bl), *a.* capable of being liquefied, or melted; liable to melt, grow soft, or become fluid. [Obs.]

çŏl·liq′uȧ·ment, *n.* 1. that which is melted. [Obs.]
2. the first rudiments of an embryo. [Obs.]

çol′li·quāte, *v.t.* and *v.i.*; colliquated, *pt., pp.*; colliquating, *ppr.* to melt; to dissolve; to change from solid to fluid; to become liquid. [Obs.]

çol·li·quā′tion, *n.* [*col-*, and L. *liquare*, to become a liquid.]
1. the act of melting; a melting or fusing together. [Obs.]
2. formerly, in medicine, a wasting away of solid parts, accompanied by an excessive excretion of fluids.

çŏl·liq′uȧ·tive (-wȧ-), *a.* in medicine, profuse or excessive, so as to cause exhaustion: said of discharges; as, a *colliquative* sweat.

çŏl·liq·uē·fac′tion (-wē-), *n.* [L. *colliquefacere*, to become liquid; *com-*, together, and *liquefacere*, to make liquid.] a melting together;

the reduction of different bodies to one mass, by fusion. [Obs.]

çol·li′sion, *n.* [LL. *collisio*, pp. of *collidere*, to strike together; *col-*, *com-*, together, and *lædere*, to strike, injure.]

1. the act of striking or dashing together; a striking together of two bodies, as motor vehicles, trains, or ships; the meeting and mutual striking of two or more moving bodies, or of a moving body with a stationary one.

2. a clash of opinions, interests, etc.; opposition; antagonism; interference.

Syn.—clash, concussion, conflict, contact, encounter, impact, shock.

çŏl·lī′sive, *a.* causing collision; clashing. [Rare.]

çol′lō·çāte, *v.t.*; collocated, *pt.*, *pp.*; collocating, *ppr.* [L. *collocatus*, pp. of *collocare*, *conlocare*, to place together; *com-*, together, and *locare*, to place.]

1. to arrange.

2. to place side by side.

çol′lō·çāte, *a.* set; placed. [Obs.]

çol·lō·çā′tion, *n.* [L. *collocatio*, an arrangement, from *collocare*, to place together.]

1. a setting; the act of placing; disposition in place.

2. the state of being placed or arranged with something else.

çol·lō·çū′tion, *n.* [L. *collocutio*, a conversation, from *collocutus*, pp. of *colloqui*, to speak together.] a speaking or conversing together; conference; mutual discourse.

çol′lō·çū·tŏr, *n.* one of the speakers in a dialogue.

çŏl·lō′di·ŏn, *n.* [Gr. *kolla*, glue, and *eidos*, resemblance.] a highly inflammable, colorless or pale-yellow, viscous solution of nitrated cellulose in a mixture of alcohol and ether: it dries quickly, forming a tough, elastic film, and is used as a protective coating for wounds, photographic plates, etc.

collodion process; the wet process of photography, in which the plate used is sensitized with collodion and a salt of silver: now superseded by the common dry plate and film processes.

çŏl·lō′di·ŏn·īze, *v.t.*; collodionized, *pt.*, *pp.*; collodionizing, *ppr.* to treat with collodion.

çŏl·lō′di·ō·tȳpe, *n.* [*collodion*, and Gr. *typos*, a mark, stamp.] a picture produced by the collodion process, or the method by which such pictures are produced.

çŏl·lō′di·um, *n.* same as *collodion*.

çol′lō·ġen, *n.* same as *collagen*.

çŏl·lōgue′ (-lōg′), *v.i.*; collogued, *pt.*, *pp.*; colloguing, *ppr.* [L. *colloqui*, to speak together.] to confer or converse confidentially and secretly; to converse with deceitful intentions; to lay schemes in concert with another: often used in a humorous sense. [Colloq.]

He had been *colloguing* with my wife.
—Thackeray.

çol′loid, *n.* [Gr. *kolla*, glue, and *-oid*.]

1. a gelatinous substance made up of very small, insoluble, nondiffusible particles larger than molecules but small enough so that they remain suspended in a fluid medium without settling to the bottom: a colloid does not affect the freezing point, boiling point, or vapor tension of the medium in which it is suspended.

2. the hormonal material secreted by the thyroid gland: it is a protein containing iodine.

3. a clear, structureless material appearing in various body tissues under abnormal conditions: also called *hyalin*.

çol′loid, *a.* same as *colloidal*.

çŏl·loid′ăl, *a.* 1. of, like, or containing a colloid.

2. of the nature, or in the form, of a colloid.

çŏl·loi·dal′i·ty, *n.* the state or quality of being colloidal.

çol′lŏp, *n.* [ME. *collop*, *colop*, a slice of meat; G. *klops*, a dish of meat made tender by beating, from L.G. *kloppen*, to beat; OFr. *colp*, a blow.]

1. a fold of flesh on the body. [Archaic.]

2. a slice or piece of anything, especially of meat.

This, indeed, with the former, cut two good *collops* out of the crown land. —Fuller.

çol′lŏped, *a.* having collop like folds of flesh.

çol′lō·phōre, *n.* [Gr. *kolla*, glue, and *-phoros*, bearing, from *pherein*, to bear.] a suckerlike, subabdominal organ of certain insects of the genus *Collembola*.

çŏl·lō′qui·ăl (-kwi-), *a.* [L. *colloquium*, conversation.]

1. pertaining to conversation; conversational.

His (Johnson's) *colloquial* talents were, indeed, of the highest order. —Macaulay.

2. belonging to the words, phrases, and idioms characteristic of conversation and informal writing; informal: the label [Colloq.] is used throughout this dictionary in this sense, and does not indicate substandard or illiterate usage.

çŏl·lō′qui·ăl·işm, *n.* 1. colloquial quality, style, or usage.

2. a colloquial word or expression.

çŏl·lō′qui·ăl·īze, *v.t.* to make colloquial.

çŏl·lō′qui·ăl·ly, *adv.* in a colloquial manner.

çol′lō·quist, *n.* a participant in a colloquy.

çŏl·lō′qui·um, *n.*; *pl.* **çŏl·lō′qui·ȧ,** [L., conversation.] in law, the portion of a complaint in a suit for slander, which alleges the speaking of the words which constitute the offense, and connects them with the plaintiff.

çol′lō·quy, *n.*; *pl.* **çol′lō·quieş,** [L. *colloquium*, a conversation; *com-*, together, and *loqui*, to speak.]

1. the mutual discourse of two or more; a conference; a dialogue; a conversation.

In retirement make frequent *colloquies* or short discoursings between God and your own soul. —Jer. Taylor.

2. a literary work written in dialogue or conversation form; as, the *Colloquies* of Erasmus.

çol′lō·tȳpe, *n.* [Gr. *kolla*, glue; and *-type*.]

1. a photographic plate made from gelatin film in such a way that inked reproductions can be printed from it.

2. the process by which such a plate is made.

3. the printed reproduction.

çol′lōw, *n.* see first *colly*, n.

çŏl·luç′tăn·cy, *n.* colluctation. [Obs.]

çol·luç·tā′tion, *n.* [*col-*, and L. *luctari*, to struggle.] a struggling to resist; contest; resistance; opposition; contrariety. [Rare.]

çŏl·lūde′, *v.i.*; colluded, *pt.*, *pp.*; colluding, *ppr.* [L. *colludere*, *conludere*, to play together; *col-*, *com-*, together, and *ludere*, to play.] to have a secret share in a scheme; to conspire in a fraud; to act in collusion.

çŏl·lūd′ẽr, *n.* one who colludes.

çol′lum, *n.*; *pl.* **çol′lȧ,** [L., the neck.]

1. in anatomy, the neck, or a necklike part.

2. in botany, same as *collar*.

çol·lū·nār′i·um, *n.* [L.] in medicine, any solution to be applied to the nasal passages, as nose drops or a nasal douche.

çŏl·lū′şion, *n.* [L. *collusio*, a secret understanding, from *collusus*, pp. of *colludere*, to play together.]

1. secret agreement for a fraudulent or illegal purpose; conspiracy.

2. specifically, in law, a secret understanding between two parties, who plead, testify, or proceed fraudulently against each other in order to defraud a third person.

Syn.—connivance.—In *connivance*, one overlooks and thus sanctions what he was bound to prevent; in *collusion*, he unites with others for fraudulent purposes.

çŏl·lū′sive, *a.* [L. *collusus*, pp. of *colludere*, to play together, to act fraudulently.] characterized by or involving collusion; fraudulent.

çŏl·lū′sive·ly, *adv.* in a collusive manner.

çŏl·lū′sive·ness, *n.* the quality of being collusive.

çŏl·lū′sō·ry, *a.* collusive.

çol·lū·tō′ri·um, *n.* [L., from *collutus*, pp. of *colluere*, to wash, rinse.] in medicine, a mouth wash; a gargle.

çol′lū·tō·ry, *n.* a collutorium.

çŏl·lū′vi·ăl, *a.* pertaining to or composed of colluvies.

çŏl·lū′vi·ēş, *n.* [L., from *colluvio*, *colluvies*, washings, filth, from *colluere*, to wash thoroughly.]

1. filth; excrement; impure matter.

2. figuratively, offscourings of humanity; a rabble. [Rare.]

çol′ly, *v.t.*; collied, *pt.*, *pp.*; collying, *ppr.* to make foul; to blacken as with soot or grime. [Dial.]

çol′ly, çol′lōw, *n.* [supposed to be from *coal*.] the black grime or soot of coal or burnt wood. [Dial.]

çol′ly, *n.* see *collie*.

çol′ly·bist, *n.* [Gr. *kollybos*, a small coin.] a moneychanger. [Obs.]

çol′ly·rīte, *n.* [Gr. *kollyrion*, collyrium.] a hydrous silicate of aluminium resembling ordinary clay.

çŏl·lyr′i·um, *n.*; *pl.* **çŏl·lyr′i·ȧ** or **çŏl·lyr′i·umş,** [L., from Gr. *kollyrion*, an eye salve, dim. of *kollyra*, a long roll of coarse bread.]

1. any medicated preparation for the eyes; eyewash.

2. formerly, a suppository.

çol′ly·wob·bleş, *n.pl.* [prob. from *colic*, and *wobble*.] a pain in the bowels, usually with diarrhea. [Colloq.]

çō′lō-, [from Gr. *kolon*, the colon.] a combining form meaning *the colon*, as in *colo*stomy: also, before a vowel, *col-*.

çol′ō·bin, *n.* [Gr. *kolobos*, curtailed, mutilated.] an African monkey of the genus *Colobus*, having no thumbs, or only rudimentary ones.

çō·lō′bi·um, *n.*; *pl.* **çō·lō′bi·ȧ,** [L., from Gr. *kolobos*, docked, curtailed.]

1. the sleeveless dress of a monk; also, an episcopal vestment, similar in kind to the tunic, with or without sleeves.

2. a dress worn by a king at his coronation, corresponding to the clerical dalmatic.

çol·ō·bō′mȧ, *n.*; *pl.* **çol·ō·bō′mȧ·tȧ,** [L., from Gr. *koloboun*, to mutilate; *kolobos*, mutilated.] in anatomy, a mutilated organ; specifically, a congenital fissure of the iris, choroid, or eyelids.

Çol′ō·bus, *n.* [Gr. *kolobos*, docked.] a genus of African monkeys possessing only rudimentary thumbs.

çol·ō·çō′lȧ, *n.* [native name.] a small, ferocious South American wildcat, *Felis colocolo*: also written *colocolo*.

çol′ō·cynth, *n.* [L. *colocynthis*; Gr. *kolokynthis*, the colocynth and its fruit; *kolokynthē*, the round gourd or pumpkin.]

1. the coloquintida, a kind of cucumber, the bitter fruit of *Citrullus colocynthis*, family *Cucurbitaceæ*, a vine of the gourd family which grows in Mediterranean regions.

2. the vine on which this fruit grows.

3. a cathartic prepared from this bitter fruit.

Also called *bitter apple*.

COLOCYNTH
(*Citrullus colocynthis*)

çol·ō·cyn′thē·in, *n.* a resinous, soluble, extremely bitter substance obtained from colocynthin.

çol·ō·cyn′thin, *n.* a soft, yellow, semitransparent glucoside obtained from colocynth and many species of gourds.

çō·lōgne′ (-lōn′), *n.* [so named because first made in *Cologne*, Germany.] a fragrant liquid made of alcohol and various aromatic oils, used like perfume: called also *Cologne water* and *eau de Cologne*.

cologne earth; see under *earth*.

çol′ō·līte, *n.* [Gr. *kolon*, the colon, and *lithos*, a stone.] an oölite resembling the fossil intestines of fishes.

Çō·lŏm′bi·ăn, *a.* of Colombia, its people, etc.

Çō·lŏm′bi·ăn, *n.* a native or inhabitant of Colombia.

çol′ŏm·biẽr, *n.* [Fr.] same as *columbier*.

çō·lom′e·try, *n.* [Gr. *kōlon*, a clause, and *metron*, a measure.] the system or practice of measuring with the colon as a unit, as verses or ancient manuscripts.

çō′lŏn, *n.*; *pl.* **çō′lŏnş** or **çō′lȧ,** [L. *colon*; Gr. *kolon*, the large intestine, colon.] that part of the large intestine extending from the caecum to the rectum.

çō′lŏn, *n.* [L. *colon*, a clause, member of a verse or poem; Gr. *kōlon*, a member, limb, part of a verse.]

1. a mark of punctuation (:) used before an extended quotation, explanation, example, series, etc., and after the salutation of a formal letter.

2. *pl.* **çō′lȧ,** in classical prosody, a section of a period, consisting of a group of two to six feet forming a rhythmic unit with a principal accent.

çō·lōn′, *n.*; *pl.* **çō·lōnş′,** Sp. **çō·lō′nes,** [Am. Sp. *colón*, from Sp. *Colón*, Columbus.]

1. the monetary unit of Costa Rica.

2. the monetary unit of El Salvador.

çolo′nel (kẽr′nl), *n.* [earlier *coronel*; Fr. *colonel*, *coronel*; It. *colonello*, from *colonna*, (military) column; L. *columna*, a column; Fr. and Eng. sp. modified after L. and It., but older pronun. kept in Eng.] an army officer ranking just above a lieutenant colonel and below a brigadier general, and corresponding to a captain in the navy: the usual commanding officer of a regiment in the army or of a group in the air force.

çolo′nel·cy (kẽr′nl-), *n.*; *pl.* **çolo′nel·cieş,** the office, rank, or commission of a colonel.

çolo'nel·ship (kẽr'nl-), *n.* a colonelcy.
çō·lō'ni·ăl, *a.* [Fr. *colonial*, from L. *colonia*, a colony.]
 1. of or relating to a colony or colonies; as, *colonial* government; *colonial* rights; *colonial* trade.
 2. pertaining to or characteristic of the thirteen British colonies which became the thirteen original states of the United States, or of their period; as, the *colonial* troops; *colonial* furniture.
 3. in zoology, forming or living in colonies.
çō·lō'ni·ăl, *n.* an inhabitant of a colony.
çō·lō'ni·ăl·iṣm, *n.* 1. a phrase, idiom, practice, etc. peculiar to a colony.
 2. the colonial policy or system of extending territory.
çō·lon'iç, *a.* of the colon (intestine).
çō·lon'i·çăl, *a.* [L. *colonus*, a husbandman.] pertaining to farmers. [Obs.]
çol'ō·nist, *n.* 1. one of the original settlers or founders of a colony.
 2. an inhabitant of a colony.
çol·ō·nī'tis, *n.* same as *colitis*.
çol″ō·ni·zā'tion, *n.* the act of colonizing, or state of being colonized; the establishment of a colony or colonies; also, in politics, the fraudulent temporary settlement of a voting district.
 Colonization Society; formerly, a society in the United States designed to aid free Negroes in emigrating to Africa.
çol″ō·ni·zā'tion·ist, *n.* a friend to colonization, particularly to the colonization of Africa by emigrants from the Negro population of the United States.
çol'ō·nīze, *v.t.*; colonized, *pt.*, *pp.*; colonizing, *ppr.* 1. to found or establish a colony or colonies in; to send a colony to; as, England *colonized* Australia.
 2. to place or settle (persons) in a colony.
çol'ō·nīze, *v.i.* 1. to found or establish a colony or colonies.
 2. to settle in a colony.
çol'ō·nīz·ẽr, *n.* one who establishes colonies; a colonist.
çol·ŏn·nāde', *n.* [Fr. *colonnade*; It *colonnato*, a series of columns; L. *columna*, a column.] in architecture, any series or range of columns placed at certain intervals, called intercolumniations, from each other.
çol·ŏn·nād'ed, *a.* furnished with a colonnade.
çol'ō·ny, *n.*; *pl.* **çol'ō·nieṣ,** [Fr. *colonie*; L. *colonia*, a colony, from *colonus*, a husbandman; *colere*, to cultivate.]
 1. a group of people who settle in a distant land but remain under the political jurisdiction of their native land.
 2. the region thus settled.
 3. a territory distant from the state having jurisdiction or nominal control over it.
 4. [C-] [*pl.*] the thirteen British colonies in North America that won their independence in the Revolutionary War and became the United States: they were Virginia, New York, Massachusetts, Connecticut, Rhode Island, New Hampshire, Maryland, New Jersey, North Carolina, South Carolina, Pennsylvania, Delaware, and Georgia.
 5. a community of people of the same nationality or pursuits concentrated in a particular district or place; as, the Hungarian *colony* of Cleveland; an artist's *colony*.
 6. such a district or place.
 7. in bacteriology, a group of similar bacteria growing in or on a culture medium.
 8. in biology, a group of similar plants or animals living or growing together.
çol'ō·phā·ny, *n.* same as *colophony*.
çō'lō·phēne, *n.* a colorless, oily liquid obtained by the distillation of oil of turpentine with sulfuric acid: also called *diterebene*.
çol'ō·phon, *n.* [Gr. *kolophōn*, a summit, top, finishing.]
 1. an inscription at the end of a book, giving facts about its production: much of this information is now usually on the title page.
 2. an emblematic or ornamental device, the publisher's trade-mark, put on the last page or title page of a book.
çol·ō·phon'iç, *a.* derived from colophony, as various acids.
çol'ō·phō·nīte, *n.* a variety of garnet, of a reddish-yellow or brown color.
çol'ō·phō·ny, *n.* [L. *colophonia*; Gr. *kolophōnia* (supply *rētinē*, resin), Colophonian resin, so called from *Colophon*, a city of Ionia.] rosin.
çol·ō·quin'ti·dȧ, *n.* same as *colocynth*.
çŏl'ŏr, çŏl'ŏur, *n.* [ME. *colour*; OFr. *colur*; L. *color*; Old L. *colos*, color; original sense, a covering, from *celare*, to cover, hide.]
 1. the sensation resulting from stimulation of the retina of the eye by light waves of certain lengths.
 2. the property of reflecting light waves of a particular length: the *primary colors* of the spectrum are red, orange, yellow, green, blue, indigo, and violet.
 3. any coloring matter; dye; pigment; paint: in painting, etc., red, yellow, and blue are the *primary colors*, which, when mixed in various ways, produce the *secondary colors* (green, orange, purple, etc.); black, white, and gray are often called colors (*achromatic colors*), although black is caused by the complete absorption of light rays, white by the reflection of all the rays that produce color, and gray by an imperfect absorption of all these rays (i.e., a mixture of black and white pigments).
 4. any color other than black, white, and gray; chromatic color; as, she likes *colors* better than black or white.
 5. color of the face, especially healthy rosiness.
 6. the color of a person's skin.
 7. the color of the skin of a Negro or other person not classified as Caucasian.
 8. [*pl.*] a colored badge, ribbon, costume, etc. that identifies the wearer or shows his connection with something or someone.
 9. [*pl.*] a flag or banner of a country, regiment, etc.
 10. [*pl.*] the side that a person is on; one's position or opinion; as, stick to your *colors*.
 11. outward appearance; semblance; aspect.
 12. appearance of truth, likelihood, validity, or right; justification; as, the circumstances gave *color* to his contention.
 13. kind; sort.
 14. vivid and picturesque quality or character; as, there is *color* in his writing.
 15. in art, the way of using color.
 16. in mining, a bit of gold.
 17. in music, timbre, as of a voice or instrument: also *tone color*.
 18. in phonetics, the degree of openness of a vowel: the dark vowels are more open.
 19. in law, an apparent or prima-facie right; a sufficient warrant for action; as, *color* of title.
 20. in phrenology, aptitude for perceiving colors or of distinguishing their shades.
 local colors; those which are natural to a particular object in a picture, and by which it is distinguished from other objects.
 to lose color; to become pale.
 to serve with the colors; to serve in the armed forces of one's country.
 to show one's colors; (a) to reveal one's true self; (b) to make one's opinions, position, etc. known.
 under color of; under the pretext or guise of.
 with flying colors; with great success.
çŏl'ŏr, *v.t.*; colored, *pt.*, *pp.*; coloring, *ppr.* 1. to give color to; to impregnate or cover with color; paint; stain; dye.
 2. to change the color of.
 3. to give fair or reasonable appearance to; to make plausible.
 4. to alter or influence to some degree, especially by distortion or exaggeration; as, his experience *colored* his views.
çŏl'ŏr, *v.i.* 1. to become colored.
 2. to change color, as ripening fruit.
 3. to turn red; to have color come into the cheeks from embarrassment, anger, or other cause; to blush; to flush.
çŏl'ŏr·ȧ·ble, *a.* 1. capable of being colored.
 2. designed to cover or conceal; apparently valid or plausible, but actually specious; as, a *colorable* pretense; a *colorable* excuse.
çŏl'ŏr·ȧ·bly, *adv.* in a colorable manner.
Çol·ō·ra'dăn (*or* -rä'dăn), *a.* of Colorado.
Çol·ō·ra'dăn, *n.* a native or inhabitant of Colorado.
çol·ō·ra'dō (*or* -rä'dō), *a.* [Sp., red, lit., colored, pp. of *colorar*, from L. *colarare*, from *color*.] of medium strength and color: said of cigars.
Çol·ō·ra'dō bee'tle, see under *beetle*.
çol·ō·ra'dō·īte, *n.* a rare iron-black metallic mineral, found in Colorado; mercury telluride.
çol·ŏr·ā'tion, *n.* [L. *coloratus*, pp. of *colorare*, to color.]
 1. the art or practice of coloring, or the state of being colored.
 2. coloring; as, some animals have protective *coloration*.
çŏl″ō·rȧ·tū'rȧ, *n.* in music, a variety of trills, runs, and scales, used to display a singer's skill; also the music so ornamented.
çŏl″ō·rȧ·tū'rȧ, *a.* characterized by coloratura.
çŏl″ō·rȧ·tū'rȧ sō·prȧ'nō, a high soprano voice adapted in range and flexibility to the singing of coloratura; also, a person with such a voice.
çŏl'ŏr·ȧ·tūre', *n.* coloratura.
çŏl'ŏr bär, same as *color line*.
çŏl'ŏr-beãr″ẽr, *n.* a person who carries the colors (flag); a standard-bearer.
çŏl'ŏr-blīnd″, *a.* 1. incapable of distinguishing or perceiving certain colors or any color.
 2. not influenced by considerations of race.
çŏl'ŏr·blīnd″ness, *n.* the condition of being colorblind.
çŏl'ŏr çam'ẽr·ȧ, a camera designed for photographing scenes and people in color.
çŏl'ŏr·çȧst″, *n.* [*color*, and tele*cast*.] a television broadcast in color.
çŏl'ŏr·çȧst″, *v.t.* and *v.i.*; colorcast or colorcasted, *pt.*, *pp.*; colorcasting, *ppr.* to televise in color.
çŏl'ŏr çin·ē·mȧ·tog'rȧ·phy, the art or practice of making motion pictures in color.
çŏl'ŏred, *a.* [pp. of *color*.]
 1. having color.
 2. of a (specified) color.
 3. of a race other than the Caucasian; specifically, Negro.
 4. altered, influenced, distorted, or exaggerated to some degree; as, his remarks were *colored* by prejudice.
 5. in botany, having any color except green; as, *colored* foliage.
çŏl'ŏr·fast″, *a.* that will keep its original color without fading or running.
çŏl'ŏr fil'tẽr, a colored and transparent screen of glass, etc., designed to halt all light waves except those of certain lengths, and used in photography to control the color or light effects: also called a *color screen*.
çŏl'ŏr·fụl, *a.* 1. full of color; vividly colored; as, a *colorful* costume.
 2. vivid; stimulating; full of startling contrasts; as, a *colorful* story.
çŏl'ŏr guärd, the persons carrying and escorting the colors (flag).
çŏl″ŏr·if'iç, *a.* [L. *color*, color, and *-ficus*, making, from *facere*, to make.]
 1. producing or imparting color.
 2. pertaining to color.
çŏl″ŏr·im'e·tẽr, *n.* [L. *color*, color, and *metrum*, a measure.] a device for measuring the depth or strength of color; also, in chemistry, an apparatus for the analysis of liquids by comparing the color of the liquid being tested with standard colors.
çŏl″ŏr·i·met'riç, *a.* of colorimetry.
çŏl″ŏr·i·met'ri·çal·ly, *adv.* as measured or analyzed by a colorimeter.
çŏl″ŏr·im'e·try, *n.* the use of the colorimeter in the analysis or measurement of color.
çŏl'ŏr·ing, *n.* 1. the act or art of applying colors; the state of being colored; color.
 2. anything applied to impart color; pigment, dye, stain, etc.: often called *coloring matter*.
 3. appearance with reference to color.
 4. a specious appearance; pretense; show; artificial representation; as, the story has a *coloring* of truth.
çŏl'ŏr·ist, *n.* 1. one who uses colors.
 2. a painter who excels in the use of color.
çŏl'ŏr·less, *a.* 1. without color; transparent; as, *colorless* water.
 2. lacking expression or feeling; without distinction; not vivid; dull; as, she is a *colorless* person; his speech was *colorless*.
çŏl'ŏr līne, 1. the barrier of social, political, and economic restrictions imposed on Negroes or other colored races.
 2. [*pl.*] in heraldry, a number of parallel lines engraved upon the field for the conventional expression of heraldic colors.
 to draw the color line; to accept and keep the color line (sense 1).
çŏl'ŏr·măn, *n.*; *pl.* **çŏl'ŏr·men,** 1. one who sells paints and colors.
 2. in leather making, one who mixes dyes.
çŏl'ŏr phō·tog'rȧ·phy, the art or practice of producing photographs in color.
çŏl'ŏr print, a print executed in two or more colors.
çŏl'ŏr proc'ess, any one of several methods of printing or lithographing by which work in different colors is produced: called two-color, three-color, etc.
çŏl'ŏr sçhēme, a pattern, combination, or arrangement of colors designed to produce a harmonious or other desired effect.
çŏl'ŏr sçreen, same as *color filter*.
çŏl'ŏr sep·ȧ·rā'tion (-shun), in photography and photoengraving, the recording on different negatives, by the use of color filters, of the parts of a picture to be printed in each of the

desired colors; also, the blocking out, by means of an acid-resisting agent, of parts of a plate, in order that only those portions of a picture or design to be printed in the same color may be produced.

çŏl′ŏr sėr′ġeant (sär′jent), a sergeant whose special duty is to carry or attend to the colors (flag) of his regiment or battalion in the field.

çō·los′săl, *a.* 1. like a colossus in size; huge; gigantic: used loosely, as in the motion-picture industry, to denote approval.
 2. in sculpture and painting, larger than heroic size.

çol·os·sē′ăn, *a.* colossal. [Rare.]

Çol·os·sē′um, *n.* [L. *Colosseum,* from *colosseus,* large, gigantic.]
 1. an amphitheater in Rome, an immense building enclosing an arena anciently used for gladiatorial combats, fights of wild beasts, and other sports. It was begun by Vespasian in 75 A.D. and finished by Titus about five years later. A large portion of the structure still stands. The outline of the Colosseum is elliptic, the exterior length of the building being about 620 and its breadth about 513 feet. It is pierced with eighty openings, or vomitories, in the ground story, over which are superimposed three other stories, the whole rising perpendicularly to a height of 160 feet. It is estimated that it provided seats for 87,000 spectators.
 2. [c–] a coliseum.

Çō·los′siăn (-losh′ăn), *n.* a native or inhabitant of Colossae, a city in ancient Phrygia.

Çō·los′siăns (-losh′ănz), *n.pl.* [*construed as sing.*] the Epistle to the Colossians, a book of the New Testament which was a message from the Apostle Paul to the Christians of Colossae.

çō·los′sus, *n.*; *pl.* **çō·los′sī** or **çō·los′sus·eṣ,** [L. *colossus*; Gr. *kolossos,* a gigantic statue.]
 1. a statue of gigantic size; especially, [C–], that of Apollo set at the entrance to the harbor of Rhodes c. 280 B.C. and considered among the seven wonders of the ancient world.
 2. any person or thing of extraordinary size or importance.

çō·los′sus·wīṣe, *adv.* in the manner of a colossus; astride: from the erroneous belief that the Colossus at Rhodes stood astride the entrance to the harbor.

çō·los′tō·my, *n.* [Gr. *kolon,* the colon, and *tomē,* a cutting, from *temnein,* to cut.] the surgical operation of forming an artificial anal opening in the colon.

çō·los′trum, *n.* [L.] the fluid secreted by the mammary glands for several days just before and after childbirth.

çō·lot′ō·my, *n.* [Gr. *kolon,* the colon, and *tomē,* a cutting, from *temnein,* to cut.] a surgical incision of the colon.

çŏl′ŏur, *n.* and *v.* color: British spelling.

-ço·lous, [from base of L. *colere,* to cultivate, inhabit; and *-ous.*] a combining form meaning *growing* (or *living*) *in* or *among,* as in *arenicolous.*

çolp, *n.* same as *collop.*

çol·pī′tis, *n.* [L., from Gr. *kolpos,* bosom, womb.] inflammation of the vagina; vaginitis.

çol′pō-, çolp-, combining forms from Gr. *kolpos,* the bosom, womb, signifying *pertaining to the vagina,* as in *colpocele.*

çol′pō·cēle, *n.* hernia of the vagina.

çol·por·rhā′ġi·ȧ (-rā′), *n.* [*colpo-,* and Gr. *rhagē,* a rent, from *rhēgnynai,* to break.] hemorrhage from the vagina.

çol·por′rhȧ·phy, *n.* [*colpo-,* and Gr. *rhaphē,* a sewing, from *rhaptein,* to sew.] in surgery, suture of the vagina.

çol′pōr·tāġe, *n.* [Fr.] the system of distributing Bibles, tracts, etc. by colporteurs.

çol′pōr·tėur, çol′pōr·tēr, *n.* [Fr. *colporteur,* a hawker, peddler; *col,* neck, and *porter,* to carry; L. *collum,* neck, and *portare,* to carry.] literally, a peddler; in modern usage, one who travels from place to place distributing Bibles, religious tracts, etc.

çol′stȧff, *n.* same as *cowlstaff.*

çōlt, *n.* [ME. *colt,* a young horse or ass; AS. *colt,* a young ass, or camel.]
 1. a young horse, donkey, zebra, etc.: commonly applied to the male, the young female being termed a *filly.*
 2. a young person without experience or stability; hence, a novice.
 3. in nautical usage, a rope knotted at the end, formerly used for flogging.
 colt's tooth; any tooth of a horse's first set of teeth.

çōlt, *v.i.* to frisk, riot, or frolic, like a colt; to be licentious. [Obs.]

çōlt, *v.t.* to befool. [Obs.]

çōl′tēr, çoul′tēr, *n.* [ME. *colter, culter*; AS. *culter,* a knife, from L. *culter,* a knife.] a knife, in the form of an iron blade or sharp-edged wheel, attached to the beam of a plow to make vertical cuts in the soil and facilitate the work of the plowshare.

çōlt′ish, *a.* of or like a colt; wanton; frisky; gay.

çōlt′ish·ly, *adv.* in a coltish manner.

çōlt′ish·ness, *n.* the condition of being coltish.

çōlts′foot, *n.*; *pl.* **çōlts′foots,** [so called from shape of the leaves.] a plant of the composite family, with small, yellow flowers and large, heart-shaped leaves, used medicinally.

çōlt′s′-tāil, *n.* in botany, the horseweed or fleabane, *Erigeron canadensis.*

Çol′ū·bēr, *n.* [L., a serpent or adder.] in zoology, a large genus of nonvenomous snakes.

çol′ū·brine, *a.* [L. *colubrinus,* like a serpent, from *coluber,* a serpent.]
 1. relating to the genus *Coluber.*
 2. of, characteristic of, or like a snake.

çol′ū·broid, *a.* same as *colubrine.*

çō·lū′gō, *n.* an East Indian tree-dwelling mammal having a fold of skin on each side that enables it to make long, sailing leaps; flying lemur.

Çō·lum′bȧ, *n.* a genus of pigeons typical of the family *Columbidæ,* and including the domestic pigeon, *Columba livia.*

çō·lum′bȧ, *n.* see *columbo.*

çol·um·bā′ceous, *a.* [L. *columba,* a dove.] relating to pigeons or doves.

Çō·lum′bae, *n.pl.* [L.] an order of birds of the pigeon kind.

çol·um·bā′ri·um, *n.*; *pl.* **çol·um·bā′ri·ȧ,** [L.]
 1. a vault with niches for urns that contain the ashes of cremated bodies.
 2. any of these niches.
 3. a columbary.

çol′um·bȧ·ry, *n.*; *pl.* **çol′um·bā·rieṣ,** a house for pigeons or doves; a dovecote.

çō·lum′bāte, *n.* a salt of columbic acid.

Çol·um·bel′lȧ, *n.* [L., from *columba,* a dove; so called from the dovelike color of the shell.] a genus of tropical mollusks bearing a fancied resemblance to a dove, both in color and form.

Çō·lum′bi·ȧ, *n.* [from Christopher *Columbus.*] the United States: feminine symbol. [Poetic.]

çō·lum′bi·ad, *n.* [from *Columbia.*]
 1. an epic of America.
 2. a long, heavy cannon formerly used for coast defense.

Çō·lum′bi·ăn, *a.* 1. of Columbia.
 2. of Christopher Columbus.

çō·lum′bi·ăn, *n.* a size of type, 16 point.

çō·lum′biç, *a.* designating or of compounds containing columbium with a valence of five; as, *columbic* acid, more commonly called *niobic* acid.

çō·lum′biç, *a.* derived from columbo root.
 columbic acid; a yellow and bitter compound obtained from columbo root.

Çō·lum′bi·dae, *n.pl.* the leading family of the order *Columbæ,* including the true doves or pigeons.

çō·lum′bi·ēr, *n.* a size of drawing paper, 23 x 33¹/₄ inches: also spelled *colombier.*

çol·um·bif′ēr·ous, *a.* [L. *columbium,* columbium, and *ferre,* to carry.] producing or containing columbium.

Çol′um·bīne, *n.* [It. *Colombina,* from L. *columbina,* fem. of *columbinus,* dovelike.] daughter of Pantaloon and sweetheart of Harlequin, a stock character in early Italian comedy and in pantomime.

çol′um·bīne, *n.* [Fr.; ML. *columbina,* from *columbinus,* dovelike: so named because the flower is thought to resemble a group of pigeons.] any of a genus, *Aquilegia,* of plants of the crowfoot family, with showy, spurred flowers of various colors.

çol′um·bīne, *a.* like or pertaining to a pigeon or dove; of a dove color, or like the neck of a dove.

çō·lum′bīte, *n.* a black mineral, $Fe(CbO_3)_2$, a compound of columbium and iron: called also *niobite.*

çō·lum′bi·um, *n.* niobium: the former name.

çō·lum′bō, çȧ·lum′bȧ, *n.* [from *Colombo,* in Ceylon, where the plant is supposed to have originated.] a shrub, *Jateorhiza calumba,* and its root, which is bitter and aromatic to the taste and much used in mild tonics. It is native to Mozambique and is cultivated in some islands of Africa and the East Indies. Written also *columba.*
 American columbo; an herb, *Frasera carolinensis,* the root of which is bitter and used as a tonic: also called *American gentian.*

çō·lum′boid, *a.* pertaining to pigeons.

çō·lum′bous, *a.* designating or of compounds containing columbium with a valence of three.

Çō·lum′bus Dāy, October 12, a legal holiday in most States, commemorating the discovery of America by Columbus in 1492: also called *Discovery Day.*

çol·ū·mel′lȧ, *n.*; *pl.* **çol·ū·mel′lae,** [L., dim. of *columen,* or *columna,* a column.]
 1. in botany, the central column in a capsule, having the seeds fixed around it; the axis of the fruit.
 2. in conchology, the upright pillar in the center of most of the univalve shells.
 3. in anatomy, any of several columnlike parts, as in the ears and skulls of certain birds and reptiles.

çol·ū·mel′li·form, *a.* [L. *columella,* a small column, and *forma,* form.] formed like a little column.

çol′umn (-um), *n.* [ME. *columne,* a column in a page; L. *columna,* a column, pillar.]
 1. a slender upright structure, generally consisting of a cylindrical shaft, a base, and a capital; pillar: it is usually a supporting or ornamental member in a building.

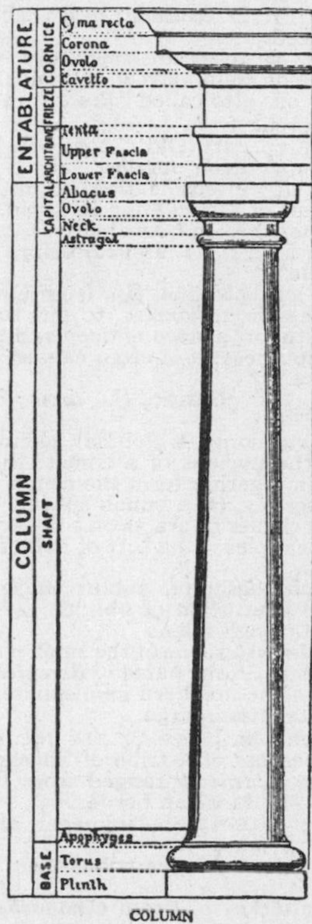

COLUMN

 2. anything resembling a column in shape or function; as, a *column* of water or mercury; the spinal *column.*
 3. in botany, the united stamens and styles of plants when they form a solid central body, as in the genus *Orchis.*
 4. in military and naval usage, a formation in which the elements, as troops or ships, are placed one behind another.
 5. one of two or more vertical sections of printed matter lying side by side on a page and separated by a rule or blank space.
 6. a feature article appearing daily or at intervals in a newspaper or magazine and written by a special writer or devoted to a certain subject.
 clustered column; a column presenting the appearance of several pillars clustered together.

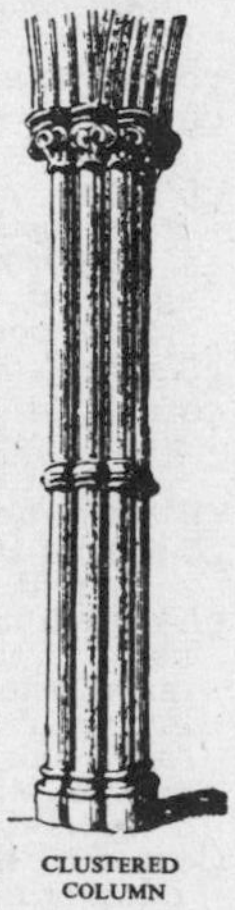

çō·lum′năr, *a.* 1. like a column.
 2. formed in or composed of columns.
 3. written or printed in columns.
 columnar structure; a geological structure that has a columnar form, illustrated in rocks of basaltic character, as in the Giant's Causeway.

CLUSTERED COLUMN

çol·um·nar′i·ty, *n.* the condition of being formed in columns.

çō·lum′nā·ted, *a.* columned.

çol′umned, *a.* 1. having columns.
2. columnar.

çō·lum″ni·ā′tion (-shun), *n.* the architectural use or arrangement of columns.

çol′um·nist, *n.* one who writes or conducts a special column for a newspaper or periodical: the contents may treat of a special subject or of a variety of subjects, and are often highly personalized.

çol′umn rūle, a strip of brass, type-high, used by printers to separate columns, and making an impression of a vertical line.

çō·lūre′, *n.* [LL. *colurus*, with tail docked; Gr. *kolos*, shortened, docked, and *oura*, tail.] in astronomy, either of two imaginary circles of the celestial sphere intersecting each other at right angles at the poles: one passes through the ecliptic at the solstice, the other at the equinox.

çō′ly, *n.*; *pl.* **çō′lies,** [LL. *colius*; Gr. *kolios*, green woodpecker.] any of a group of small African birds, constituting the genus *Colius*, with long tails and crested heads.

çol′zà, *n.* [Fr.; D. *koolzaad*; *kool*, a cabbage, and *zaad*, a seed.]
1. cole or coleseed: especially, rapeseed, which yields an oil burned in lamps.
2. this oil: also called *colza oil, rape oil*.

çom-, a prefix from L. *com-*, with, together, from L. prep. *cum* (Old L. *com*, with), and signifying: (a) *with, together*, as in *com*bine, *com*pact; (b) intensification, as in *com*mand. As a result of assimilation in Latin, *com-* appears as *col-* before *l*, *cor-* before *r*, *con-* before *c, d, g, j, n, q, s, t, v*, and *co-* before *h, w*, and all vowels.

çō′mà, *n.*; *pl.* **çō′màs,** [L., from Gr. *kōma*, a deep sleep, from *koiman*, to put to sleep.] a kind of stupor; a state of deep and prolonged unconsciousness: it is often caused by injury or disease.

çō′mà, *n.*; *pl.* **çō′mae,** [L. *coma*; Gr. *komē*, hair.]
1. in astronomy, a globular, cloudlike mass around the nucleus of a comet: the nucleus and coma together form the comet's head.
2. in botany, (a) a bunch of branches; (b) a terminal cluster of bracts on a flowering stem, as in pineapples; (c) a tuft of hairs at the end of a seed.
3. in photography, a blur caused by the spherical aberration of oblique rays of light passing through a lens.
Coma Berenices; one of the smaller constellations, sometimes named *Berenice's Hair*, located in the northern hemisphere, north of the constellation Virgo.

Çō·man′chē, *n.* [Mex. Sp., of unc. meaning.]
1. a member of a tribe of Shoshonean Indians who formerly ranged from the Platte River to the Mexican border.
2. their Uto-Aztec language: also called *Shoshone-Comanche*.

Çō·man′chē, *a.* of this tribe, their language, or culture.

Çō·man′chē·ăn, *a.* [from *Comanche* County, Texas.] designating or of a geologic epoch between the Jurassic and Cretaceous Periods or its series of rocks, as typified by those found in the region of the Gulf of Mexico.
the Comanchean; the Comanchean Epoch or its series of rocks.

çō′märb, *n.* same as *coarb*.

çō′märt, *n.* a treaty; article; agreement. [Obs.]

çō′māte, *a.* [L. *comatus*, covered with hair, from *coma*, hair.]
1. in astronomy, surrounded by a coma (globular, cloudlike mass).
2. in botany, hairy; tufted.

çō·māte′ (*or* kō′māt), *n.* a companion; mate.

çom′à·tōse (*or* kō′mà-tōs), *a.* 1. of, like, or in a coma (stupor).
2. as if in a coma; lethargic; torpid.

çō′mà·tous, *a.* same as *comatose*.

çō·mat′ū·là, *n.*; *pl.* **çō·mat′ū·lae,** same as *comatulid*.

çō·mat′ū·lid, *n.* [from Mod.L. *Comatulidæ*, name of the family, from L. *comatulus*, having hair neatly curled, dim. of *comatus*, having long hair, pp. of *comare*, to have hair, from *coma*, hair, from Gr. *kōme*.] a free-swimming animal related to the starfish; one of the *Comatulidæ*.

Çom·à·tū′li·dae, *n.pl.* a family of free-swimming crinoids: also called *feather stars*.

çōmb (kōm), *n.* [ME. *comb*; AS. *camb*, a comb.]
1. a thin strip of bone, plastic, metal, etc. with teeth, which is passed through the hair to arrange or clean it, or is set in the hair to hold it in place or as an ornament.
2. the crest, caruncle, or red, fleshy tuft, growing on the head of certain fowls, as on that of a rooster: so called from its indentures, which resemble the teeth of a comb.
3. the substance in which bees lodge their honey, in small, hexagonal cells; honeycomb.
4. an instrument for currying or cleaning the coats of animals: more commonly called *currycomb*.
5. anything that resembles a comb; as, (a) a hat manufacturer's tool, used for stiffening the soft fibers of a felt hat; (b) a chasing tool with teeth used on a lathe in screw work; (c) an instrument with teeth for separating and cleansing wool or flax; (d) the toothed knife in a carding machine; (e) the collector of an electrical machine; (f) the notched measuring scale of a wire micrometer.
6. the top or crest of a wave.
7. the thumb piece of a gun hammer.

çōmb, *v.t.*; combed, *pt., pp.*; combing, *ppr.*
1. to separate, disentangle, straighten, clean, or adjust, with a comb; as, to *comb* hair; to *comb* wool.
2. to search thoroughly; to look everywhere in; as, we've *combed* the house for that book.

çōmb, *v.i.* to roll over, as the top of a wave; to break with a white foam.

çōmb, *n.* same as *coomb*.

çom′bat (*or* kum′), *v.i.*; combated, or combatted, *pt., pp.*; combating or combatting, *ppr.* [Fr. *combattre*, to combat; L. *com-*, together, and LL. *battere*, to beat, fight.] to fight; to battle; to struggle or contend with an opposing force.

> After the fall of the republic, the Romans *combated* only for the choice of masters.
> —Gibbon.

çom′bat (*or* cŏm-bat′), *v.t.* to fight against; to oppose by force; as, to *combat* an antagonist.

çom′bat, *n.* 1. a fight; a struggle to resist, overthrow, or conquer; a contest by force; an engagement; an armed battle; as, the *combat* of armies.
2. struggle; strife.
3. a duel; a formal contest at arms between two persons.

çom′bat, *a.* in military use, of or for combat.

çom·bat′à·ble, *a.* capable of being disputed or opposed.

çom′bat·ănt, *a.* 1. contending; fighting.
2. ready or eager to fight.
3. in heraldry, ready to fight, or in a fighting position, as two leopards rampant face to face on opposite sides of the shield.

çom′bat·ănt, *n.* [Fr. *combattant*, ppr. of *combattre*, to fight.]
1. one who combats; any person who fights with another or others.
2. in military usage, a member of the armed forces who takes part in actual fighting.
3. a duelist; one who fights or contends in battle, for the decision of a private quarrel or difference.

çom′bat·ẽr, *n.* one who fights or contends. [Rare.]

çom′bat fà·tïgue′ (-tēg′), a psychoneurotic condition characterized by anxiety, irritability, depression, etc., often occurring after extreme exertion and lack of sleep in armed combat: also called *battle fatigue*.

çom′bat in′făn·try·măn's badge, a badge awarded to United States infantrymen of World War II for exemplary conduct in a combat action of a major operation.

çom′bat·ive, *a.* disposed to combat; fond of fighting or opposing; pugnacious.

çom·bat′ive·ness, *n.* disposition to fight; pugnacity.

çōmb′brōach (kōm′brōch), *n.* a tooth of a comb for dressing wool.

çōmbe, *n.* same as *coomb*.

çōmbed, *a.* 1. separated, cleaned, or dressed with a comb.
2. having a comb.

çōmb′ẽr (kōm′), *n.* 1. one who combs; especially, a person or machine that combs wool, etc.
2. a long, rolling wave that breaks on a beach, reef, etc.

çŏm′bẽr, *v.t.* to cumber. [Obs.]

çom′bẽr, *n.* a fish, *Serranus cabrilla*, common on the south coast of England. [Brit. Dial.]

çŏm·bīn′à·ble, *a.* capable of combining or being combined.

çŏm·bīn′à·ble·ness, *n.* the state of being combinable.

çom′bi·nănt (*or* kŏm-bī′), *n.* [from LL. *combinans*, ppr. of *combinare*, to combine; L. *com-*, together, and *bini*, two by two.] in certain mathematical quantics, the invariant which remains unaltered, except by a change in the factor, when a linear function of the quantics replaces any quantic, as well as when the variables are linearly unchanged.

çom′bi·nāte, *a.* espoused; betrothed. [Rare.]

çom·bi·nā′tion, *n.* [LL. *combinatus*, pp. of *combinare*, to combine; L. *com-*, together, and *bini*, two by two.]
1. a combining or being combined.
2. a thing made by combining.
3. union or association of two or more persons or things, by set purpose or agreement, in order to effect some object by joint operation; as, a *combination* of capital, or of labor.
4. in chemistry, the uniting of substances to form a compound.
5. in mathematics, the union of a number of individuals in different groups, each containing a certain number of the individuals. Thus, the number of combinations of 1, 2, 3, and 4, taking two together, is six (12, 13, 14, 23, 24, 34).
6. the series of numbers or letters used in opening a combination lock.
7. the mechanism operating such a lock.
8. a one-piece undergarment combining an undershirt and drawers.
combination car; a railway car containing compartments for different purposes; as, for example, part for passengers and part for baggage.
combination last; a style of shoe last in which an unusually narrow heel is combined with a forepart of standard dimensions.
combination lock; a lock operated by a dial that is turned to a specified series of numbers or letters to work the mechanism that opens it.

Syn.—union, association, alliance, party, faction, league, conspiracy, cabal.

çom′bi·nā·tive, *a.* 1. of or characterized by combination.
2. having the ability to combine.
3. resulting from combination.

çŏm·bīne′, *v.t.* and *v.i.*; combined, *pt., pp.*; combining, *ppr.* [ME. *combinen*; LL. *combinare*, to unite; L. *com-*, together, and *bini*, two by two.]
1. to come or bring into union; to unite or join.
2. to unite to form a chemical compound.
combining weight; the exact proportional weight with which one element combines with another in making a definite compound.

çom′bīne, *n.* 1. a union or combination of individuals, firms, etc. for commercial or political purposes; as, a *combine* of manufacturers to advance prices above their natural level by means of unlawful restraint of trade; a *combine* of aldermen, etc. [Colloq.]
2. a type of threshing machine having a harvesting apparatus attached to it: the machine acts as a cleanser and header, leaving the straw behind as it moves across the field.

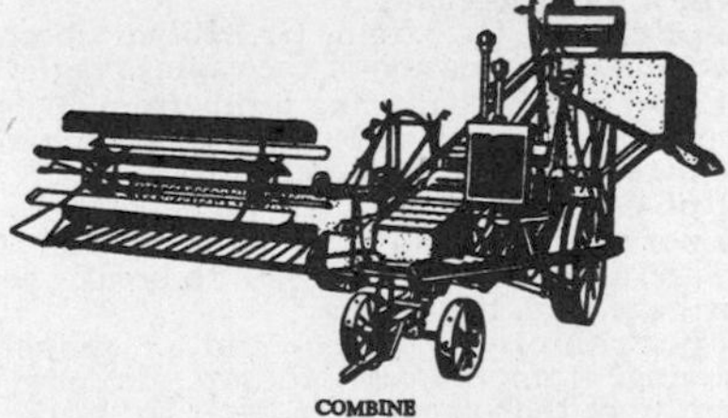
COMBINE

çŏm·bīned′, *a.* united closely; associated; confederated; leagued; chemically united.

çŏm·bīn′ed·ly, *adv.* jointly; in combination.

çŏm·bīn′ẽr, *n.* one who or that which combines.

çōmb′ing (kōm′), *n.* 1. the act of using a comb; the process of carding wool.
2. [*pl.*] that which is collected in or removed by a comb, as loose hair, wool, etc.

çōmb′ing mà·chïne′, a machine for carding wool.

çŏm·bīn′ing fọrm, a word or word base used as an element in word formation, as *jack-* in *jackknife*, *tele-* in *telephone*: the word bases used in English word formation are often from Greek and Latin, which used a special form of the word (the *stem*) for combining purposes.

çōmb jel′ly, a ctenophore.

çōmb′less, *a.* without a comb or crest; as, a *combless* cock.

çom′bō, *n.*; *pl.* **çom′bōṣ,** a combination; specifically, a small jazz ensemble. [Colloq.]

çom·bō·lō′iō (-yō), *n.* a rosary of ninety-nine beads, used by Mohammedans.

çŏm′boy, *n.* [Singhalese *kambāya.*] in Ceylon, a sarong.

çomb pot′tēr·y, in archaeology, a kind of neolithic pottery found in the Baltic countries.

Çom·brē·tā′cē·ae, *n.pl.* [L. *combretum,* a kind of rush.] an order of tropical shrubs containing about 250 species, characterized by their bright-colored flowers: some species are astringent and used in tanning.

çom·brē·tā′ceous, *a.* pertaining to the order *Combretaceæ.*

Çom·brē′tum, *n.* [L., a kind of rush.] an extensive genus of tropical shrubs, typical of the *Combretaceæ.*

çŏm·bust′, *a.* [ME. *combust,* L. *combustus,* pp. of *comburere,* to burn up.]

1. in astrology, designating or of a star or planet when in conjunction with the sun, or apparently very near it.

2. consumed as by fire. [Obs.]

çŏm·bust′, *v.t.* and *v.i.*; to undergo or cause to undergo combustion; burn.

çŏm·bus·ti·bil′i·ty, *n.* same as *combustibleness.*

çŏm·bus′ti·ble, *a.* [Fr. *combustible*; L. *combustus,* pp. of *comburere,* to burn up.]

1. capable of taking fire; that can be easily burned up; inflammable; as, wood and coal are *combustible.*

2. fiery; readily aroused; easily excited.

çŏm·bus′ti·ble, *n.* a substance that will take fire and burn; as, the building was full of *combustibles.*

çŏm·bus′ti·ble·ness, *n.* the quality or state of being combustible.

çŏm·bus′tion (-bus′chun), *n.* [Fr. *combustion*; LL. *combustio,* combustion, from L. *combustus,* pp. of *comburere,* to burn up.]

1. the act or process of burning.

2. rapid oxidation generating heat, or both light and heat; also, slow oxidation accompanied by relatively little heat and no light.

3. any sudden outbreak of inflammatory excitement; violent agitation; tumult; uproar.

4. in astrology, the state of being in a position near the sun.

spontaneous combustion; the process of catching fire and burning as a result of heat generated by internal chemical action.

çŏm·bus′tion tūbe, a tube of heat-resistant glass in which a substance can be reduced by combustion, as in a furnace.

çŏm·bus′tious (-chus), *a.* inflammable. [Obs.]

çŏm·bus′tive, *a.* disposed to take fire.

çŏme (kum), *v.i.*; came, *pt.*; coming, *ppr.*; come, *pp.* [ME. *cumen*; AS. *cuman,* to come.]

1. to move from a place thought of as "there" to or into a place thought of as "here": (a) in the second person, with relation to the speaker; as, *come* to me, will you *come* to the dance tonight? (b) in the first person, with relation to the person addressed; as, I will *come* to see you; (c) in the third person, with relation to the person or thing approached; as, he *came* to her and wept, he *came* into the room.

2. to arrive; to complete a movement toward some place, as the result of motion or progress; to attain to an end; to achieve completion; as, they *came* to land.

3. to enter into a certain state or condition; as, the ships *came* into action; the players *came* to blows; also, to be manifest or to appear; to develop, evolve, sprout, take form, or be formed; as, the butter *comes* (from churning); peace will *come* in time.

4. to become perceptible; to appear; to begin to be; as, the shadows *come* and go in the firelight.

5. to draw near or arrive in time; to be present; as, the hour has *come*; when Easter *comes.*

6. to approach or arrive as a result of circumstances, or of the acts of another; as, both riches and honor *come.*

7. to exist in a certain place or order; as, after 9 *comes* 10.

8. to happen; to take place; to occur; as, misfortune in some form *comes* alike to all.

9. to become; to get to be; as, my shoe *came* loose.

10. to emanate from a source; to be derived or descended; as, this word *comes* from the Latin; light *comes* from the sun.

11. to extend; to reach; as, the bus line *comes* near the hotel.

12. to be caused; to result; as, illness may *come* from a poor diet.

13. to be obtainable or available; as, this dress *comes* in four sizes.

14. to amount; as, the bill *comes* to $5.68.

15. to have a sexual orgasm. [Colloq.]

to come about; (a) to happen; to occur; to come to pass; (b) to turn about; (c) in nautical usage, to change from one tack to another.

to come across; (a) to meet or find suddenly or by chance; (b) [Colloq.] to be effective, readily understood, etc.; (c) [Slang.] to give, do, or say what is wanted.

to come along; (a) to appear or arrive; (b) to proceed or succeed.

to come around (or *round*); (a) to revive; recover; (b) to make a turn or change in direction; (c) to influence, outwit, or gain favor with by cajoling, flattering, etc.; (d) [Colloq.] to concede or yield, as to a demand; (e) [Colloq.] to come to visit.

to come at; (a) to reach; to arrive within reach of; to gain; as, *to come at* a true idea of the situation; (b) to approach angrily or swiftly, as in a violent attack.

to come between; to cause estrangement between; to part.

to come by; (a) to gain or obtain; (b) to pay a visit.

to come down; (a) to be handed down, as from generation to generation; (b) to be humbled or to suffer loss in dignity, wealth, etc.

to come down upon; to rebuke. [Colloq.]

to come home; (a) to come close; to touch the feelings, interest, or reason; (b) in nautical usage, to become loosened from the ground: said of an anchor.

to come in; (a) to enter, as a town, a house, an enclosure; (b) to arrive; as, the fleet has *come in*; (c) to comply; to yield; to submit; (d) to assume official duties; as, when the new president *came in*; (e) to become fashionable; to be brought into use; (f) to enter into as an ingredient or part of a composition; (g) to mature and yield a harvest; as, crops *come in* well; (h) to accrue, as profit from investment; (i) to bring forth young: said of livestock; as, the cow will *come in* next spring.

to come in for; to get; to receive, as a share. [Colloq.]

to come into; (a) to join with; to enter into; (b) to agree to; to comply with; to unite with others in adopting; as, *to come into* a plan; (c) to get; acquire; (d) to inherit.

to come it over; to fool; to deceive. [Colloq.]

to come of; (a) to issue from; to proceed from, as a descendant; (b) to result from, as an effect from a cause.

to come off; (a) to become unfastened or detached; (b) to escape; to get free; (c) [Colloq.] to end; to arrive at the final issue; as, *to come off* with honor; (d) to take place; as, the meeting *came off* at such a time.

to come on; (a) to go forward; to proceed; as, night is *coming on*; (b) to improve; to thrive; as, the sweet peas are *coming on* nicely; (c) to meet by accident; to find; (d) to invade; to attack; (e) in the theater, to make an entrance.

to come out; (a) to be disclosed; become evident; (b) to become public or to be published; (c) to end; to result; (d) to be formally introduced into society; (e) to appear; as, the sun *came out.*

to come out with; (a) to say; to utter; (b) to make a public disclosure; to disclose.

to come over; (a) to pass from one place or party to another; (b) to happen to; to occur to; to seize; as, these feelings often *come over* me.

to come short; to be lacking or to fall short of attaining.

to come to; (a) to yield; (b) to bring the ship's head nearer the wind; (c) to anchor; (d) to regain consciousness; (e) to amount to.

to come to a head; (a) to arrive at the stage of suppuration, as a boil; (b) to culminate or come to an issue.

to come to oneself; to recover one's senses.

to come to pass; to happen; to occur.

to come to the scratch; to toe the mark in a prize fight or a race: said of combatants or contestants at the starting point; hence, [Colloq.] to fulfill one's agreements promptly or to meet difficulties bravely.

to come to time; to be ready when time is called, after an interval of rest: said of prize fighters and contestants in various athletic sports; hence, [Colloq.] to keep engagements or discharge obligations promptly.

to come true; to happen according to prediction or expectation; to be verified.

to come under; (a) to belong to, as an animal to a species or an individual to a class; (b) to pass under the control of; to be under the authority of.

to come up; (a) to ascend; to rise; (b) to spring; to rise above a surface, as a plant; (c) to come into use, as a fashion; (d) to arise, as in discussion.

to come upon; (a) to fall on; to attack or invade; (b) to become dependent upon; as, *to come upon* the county; (c) to meet by accident; to find.

to come up to; (a) to reach or extend to; (b) to equal; (c) to amount to; (d) to advance to; to rise to.

to come up with; (a) to overtake; (b) to propose; to suggest.

Syn.—arrive, approach, attain, bechance, befall, betide, ensue, enter, follow, happen, invade, occur, penetrate, reach, result, succeed.

çŏme, *v.t.* to carry through; to act; to practice. [Colloq.]

çŏme, *n.* coming; arrival. [Obs.]

çŏme, *interj.* look! see here! stop!: used to express irritation, impatience, remonstrance, etc.

çŏme, *n.* 1. a sprout. [Obs.]

2. the rootlet that appears on barley during the malting process, subsequently dropping off and drying up to form malt dust: also written *coom.*

çŏme-at″-ȧ·bil′i·ty, *n.* accessibility; approachableness. [Colloq.]

çŏme-at′-ȧ·ble, *a.* easily approached; readily obtained; accessible or attainable. [Colloq.]

çŏme′back, *n.* 1. a return to a previous state or position, as of power, success, etc. [Colloq.]

2. a witty answer; retort. [Slang.]

3. ground for action or complaint; recourse. [Slang.]

çō·mē′di·ăn, *n.* [Fr. *comédien,* a comedian, from *comédie,* comedy.]

1. an actor or player in comedy; occasionally, an actor in general.

2. a writer of comedy.

3. an entertainer who tells jokes, sings comic songs, etc.

4. a person who amuses or tries to amuse others by clowning, telling jokes, etc.

çō·mē′diç, *a.* of or having to do with comedy.

çō·mē·di·enne′, *n.* [Fr., f. of *comédien,* comedian.]

1. an actress who plays in comedy.

2. a woman entertainer who tells jokes, sings comic songs, etc.

çō·mē·di·et′tȧ, *n.* [It., dim. of *commedia,* a comedy.] a short comedy or farce.

çom′ē·dō, *n.*; *pl.* **çom·ē·dō′nēṣ,** [L., a glutton, from *comedere,* to eat up, devour; *com-,* intens., and *edere,* to eat.] in medicine, a small nodule, due to a plug of dirt or fatty matter in a skin gland: also called *blackhead.*

çŏme′down, *n.* a loss of status, wealth, etc.; a downfall; a humiliation.

çom′e·dy, *n.*; *pl.* **çom′e·dieṣ,** [ME. *commedy*; OFr. *comedie*; L. *comœdia*; Gr. *kōmōdia,* a comedy, from *kōmos,* a festival, and *ōdos,* a singer; *ōdē,* a song.]

1. originally, any play or other literary composition with a nontragic ending.

2. any of various types of play or motion picture with more or less humorous treatment of characters and situation, and a nontragic ending.

3. the art, technique, or theory of writing, producing, or acting such plays or motion pictures.

4. comedies collectively.

5. the branch of the drama having to do with comedies.

6. a work of literature having a theme suitable for comedy or certain characteristics of comedy.

7. any amusing incident or event; as, the whole affair became a regular *comedy.*

çom′e·dy of man′nērṣ, a type of comedy depicting and satirizing the manners and customs of fashionable society.

çŏme′-hith′ēr, *a.* flirtatious or inviting; as, a *come-hither* look. [Colloq.]

çŏme′li·ly, *adv.* in a suitable or decent manner. [Rare.]

çŏme′li·ness, *n.* the state or quality of being comely.

His face, as I grant, in spite of spite
Has a broad-blown *comeliness,* red and white. —Tennyson.

çŏme′ly, *a.* [ME. *comly, cumly*; AS. *cymlic,* fit, comely, from *cyme,* fit, suitable, from *cuman,* to come.]

1. handsome; attractive; good-looking.

I have seen a son of Jesse—a *comely* person. —I Sam. xvi. 18.

2. decent; suitable; proper; becoming;

suited to time, place, circumstances, or persons.

Is it *comely* that a woman pray to God uncovered? —1 Cor. xi. 13.

Syn.—graceful, seemly, pleasing, pretty, handsome.

çŏme′-off, *n.* means of escape; excuse. [Rare.]

çŏme′-ŏn, *n.* 1. a confidence man. [Slang.]

2. an inviting look or gesture. [Slang.]

3. something offered as an inducement. [Slang.]

çŏme-out′ẽr, *n.* one who leaves an association, a party, or a religious body on account of differences of opinion. [Slang.]

çŏm′ẽr, *n.* 1. one who comes; one who approaches; one who has lately arrived and is present.

2. a person or thing that shows promise of being a success. [Slang.]

çō′mēş, *n.*; *pl.* **çom′i·tēş,** [L., a companion.]

1. in music, the answer to the theme of a fugue.

2. in anatomy, a vessel accompanying another vessel or other structure.

çom·es·sā′tion, *n.* [L. *comessatio*, a bacchanalian procession, a reveling, from *comissari*; Gr. *komazein*, to revel.] feasting or reveling. [Obs.]

çō·mes′ti·ble, *a.* [Fr. *comestible*, eatable, from L. *comestus*, *comesus*, pp. of *comedere*, to eat; *com-*, intens., and *edere*, to eat.] eatable; fit to be eaten.

çō·mes′ti·ble, *n.* [*usually in pl.*] food.

çom′et, *n.* [ME. *comete*; AS. *cometa*; L. *cometa*: so named from the appearance of its tail, from *komē*, hair.]

1. a heavenly body having a starlike nucleus with a luminous mass around it, and, usually, a long, luminous tail; comets follow an elliptical or parabolic orbit around the sun.

COMET

2. an old game of cards. [Obs.]

3. one of a group of brilliant hummingbirds found in tropical South America; as, the Sappho *comet*.

çom·e·tā′ri·um, *n.* [L., from *cometes*, a comet.] an astronomical instrument, intended to represent the revolution of a comet around the sun.

çom′et·ā·ry, *a.* pertaining to a comet or comets.

çom′et fīnd′ẽr (or **seek′ẽr**), a telescope made expressly for the purpose of discovering comets, being of low power and exceptionally wide range.

çō·meth′ẽr, *n.* [dial. contr., from *come hither*.]

1. an affair; circumstance. [Anglo-Irish Dial.]

2. friendship; friendly relationship. [Anglo-Irish Dial.]

çō·met′iç, *a.* relating to a comet or comets.

çom·et·og′rȧ·phẽr, *n.* one who writes about comets.

çom·et·og′rȧ·phy, *n.* [Gr. *komētēs*, a comet, and *graphein*, to write.] a description of or treatise on comets.

çom·et·ol′ō·ġy, *n.* the science of comets, a branch of astronomy.

çŏme·up′pănce, *n.* [from *come*, and *up*, and *-ance*.] deserved punishment; retribution. [Slang.]

çŏm′fit, *n.* [ME. *confit*; OFr. *confit*, a confect; L. *confectus*, pp. of *conficere*, to put together.] a sweetmeat; any kind of fruit or root preserved with sugar and dried; a bonbon.

çŏm′fit, *v.t.* to preserve with sugar; to make into candy. [Obs.]

çŏm′fi·tūre, *n.* comfit. [Rare.]

çŏm′fŏrt, *v.t.*; comforted, *pt.*, *pp.*; comforting, *ppr.* [ME. *comforten*, *cumforten*; OFr. *conforter*, to comfort; L. *com-*, together, and *fortis*, strong.]

1. to strengthen; to invigorate; to cheer or enliven. [Obs.]

2. to soothe in distress or sorrow; to ease the misery or grief of; to bring consolation or hope to.

3. in law, to relieve, assist, or help, as the accessory to a crime after the fact.

Syn.—console, encourage, cheer, enliven, gladden, support, refresh, inspirit.

çŏm′fŏrt, *n.* 1. relief from pain, grief, distress, etc.

2. a state of ease and quiet enjoyment, free from worry, pain, etc.

3. a person or thing that comforts.

4. anything that makes life easy and comfortable.

5. in law, support; assistance; countenance; encouragement: now only in *aid and comfort*.

6. a quilted covering for a bed; a comforter.

Syn.—consolation, solace, relief, support.

çŏm′fŏrt·ȧ·ble, *a.* [ME. *comfortable*; OFr. *confortable*, comfortable, from *conforter*, to strengthen.]

1. providing comfort; as, *comfortable* shoes.

2. in a state of comfort; at ease in body or mind; contented; as, he felt *comfortable* after his bath and dinner.

3. sufficient to satisfy; adequate; as, a *comfortable* salary. [Colloq.]

Syn.—snug, satisfied, pleasant, agreeable, cozy, convenient, consoled.

çŏm′fŏrt·ȧ·ble, *n.* a quilted bed covering; a comforter.

çŏm′fŏrt·ȧ·ble·ness, *n.* the state of being comfortable.

çŏm′fŏrt·ȧ·bly, *adv.* in a comfortable manner.

çŏm′fŏrt·ẽr, *n.* 1. a person or thing that comforts.

2. [C—] in theology, the Holy Spirit.

But the *Comforter*, the Holy Ghost, whom the Father will send in my name, he shall teach you all things. —John xiv. 26.

3. a knitted woolen scarf, long and narrow.

4. a quilted bed cover.

çŏm′fŏrt·ful, *a.* full of comfort.

çŏm′fŏrt·ing, *a.* encouraging; heartening; consoling.

çŏm′fŏrt·less, *a.* 1. without comfort; without anything to alleviate misfortune or distress; as, in his old age he was left *comfortless*.

2. providing no comfort.

Syn.—desolate, disconsolate, lonely, forsaken, miserable.

çŏm′fŏrt·less·ly, *adv.* in a comfortless manner.

çŏm′fŏrt·less·ness, *n.* the state of being comfortless.

çŏm′fŏrt·ment, *n.* the act of giving comfort. [Obs.]

çŏm′fŏrt·ress, *n.* a woman who comforts. [Rare.]

çŏm′fŏrt stā′tion, a public toilet or restroom.

çŏm′frey, *n.*; *pl.* **çŏm′freyş,** [ME. *cumfirie*, *comfory*; OFr. *cumfirie*, comfrey, perh. from L. *confirmare*, to strengthen.] a genus of plants, *Symphytum*. A preparation of the root of the common comfrey, *Symphytum officinale*, is used in treating coughs, intestinal disorders, etc.

çom′iç, *a.* [L. *comicus*; Gr. *kōmikos*, comic, relating to comedy, from *kōmos*, a revel, carousal; *kōmōdia*, comedy.]

1. relating to comedy.

2. amusing or intended to be amusing; comical.

3. of comic strips or cartoons.

çom′iç, *n.* 1. a comic actor or singer; a comedian.

2. the humorous part of art or life.

3. [*usually in pl.*] a comic cartoon or strip of cartoons. [Colloq.]

çom′iç·ăl, *a.* 1. relating to comedy; comic. [Obs.]

2. causing amusement; humorous; funny; droll; as, a *comical* fellow.

Syn.—droll, absurd, laughable, ludicrous, preposterous.

çom·i·căl′i·ty, *n.* the quality of being comical.

çom′iç·ăl·ly, *adv.* in a comical manner.

çom′iç·ăl·ness, *n.* the quality of being comical.

çom′iç op′ẽr·ȧ, opera with humorous situations, a story that ends happily, and, usually, some spoken dialogue.

çom′iç·ry, *n.* comicality. [Rare.]

çom′iç strip, a series of cartoons, usually telling a humorous or adventurous story and appearing in newspapers or other publications.

Çom′in·fŏrm, *n.* [from *Com*munist *Informa*tion.] the Communist Information Bureau, established in October, 1947, by the Communist Parties of Bulgaria, Czechoslovakia, France, Hungary, Italy, Poland, Romania, the Soviet Union, and, originally, Yugoslavia to exchange information and coordinate activities.

çŏm′ing, *a.* 1. drawing nearer or nigh, approaching; advancing.

2. future; immediately following; as, in *coming* ages.

3. forward; ready to come.

4. showing promise of being successful or famous; as, a *coming* young actor. [Colloq.]

çŏm′ing, *n.* approach; arrival; advent.

Çom′in·tẽrn, *n.* the Third International.

çō·mi′ti·ȧ (-mish′i-ȧ), *n.pl.* [L. *comitia*, nom. pl. of *comitium*, the place where the assembly was held; *com-*, together, and *itus*, pp. of *ire*, to come.] in ancient Rome, an assembly of the people, for electing officers, passing laws, etc.

çō·mi′tiăl (-mish′ăl), *a.* relating to the comitia, or popular assemblies, of the Romans; also, pertaining to an order of Presbyterian assemblies.

çom′i·ty, *n.* [L. *comitas*, courteousness, from *comis*, courteous, kind.] politeness; courtesy; civility; as, well-bred people are characterized by their *comity*.

comity of nations; the friendly relation existing between nations by which the laws and institutions of each country are recognized and respected; also, loosely, the nations practicing this.

çom′mȧ, *n.* [L. *comma*; Gr. *komma*, a short clause in a sentence; that which is struck or cut off, from *koptein*, to cut off.]

1. a mark of punctuation (,) used to indicate a slight separation of sentence elements: commas are used to set off nonrestrictive or parenthetical elements, quotations, items in a series, etc.

2. a slight pause.

3. in music, any of various minute intervals, as that between the major and the minor tone.

4. in ancient prosody, a phrase or short clause.

5. a butterfly, *Grapta comma-album*, bearing a white, comma-shaped mark on the lower wings.

comma bacillus; a comma-shaped bacillus, also known as the *cholera bacillus*, because it causes Asiatic cholera.

çŏm·mȧnd′, *v.t.*; commanded, *pt.*, *pp.*; commanding, *ppr.* [ME. *commanden*; OFr. *commander*, to command; L. *com-*, intens., and *mandare*, to commit, entrust.]

1. to order; to direct with authority.

2. to govern, lead, or control; to have or to exercise authority over; as, Grant *commanded* the Army of the Potomac.

3. to be able to have and use; as, he *commands* a large vocabulary.

4. to overlook; to control (a position).

One side *commands* a view of the finest garden in the world. —Addison.

5. to direct; to send; to bestow. [Obs.]

The Lord shall *command* the blessing on thee. —Deut. xxviii. 8.

6. to require and get; to have or to exercise a controlling influence over; as, a good magistrate *commands* the respect of the community.

çŏm·mȧnd′, *v.i.* 1. to have or to exercise authority or power; to govern; to be in control.

2. to be in a position of superiority or advantage.

Not music so *commands*, nor so the muse. —Crabbe.

çŏm·mȧnd′, *n.* 1. the right or power of governing with authority; as, to take *command*.

2. the act of commanding; exercise of authority or influence.

Command and force may often create, but can never cure an aversion. —Locke.

3. the thing commanded; a direction; mandate; order.

The captain gives *command*. —Dryden.

4. power to control or dominate by position; as, the troops were so posted as to have *command* of the road.

5. any naval or military force under the direction of a particular officer; as, the captain was entrusted with an independent *command*; also, the post where the person in command is stationed.

6. ability to have and use; mastery.

Syn.—behest, injunction, mandate, order, control, sway, power, authority, charge, bidding, requisition.

çŏm·mȧnd′ȧ·ble, *a.* capable of being commanded.

çom·măn·dănt′, *n.* [Fr., lit. ppr. of *commander*, to command.] a commander; a commanding officer of a district, fort, etc.

çŏm·mȧnd′ȧ·tō·ry, *a.* having the force of a command. [Obs.]

çŏm·măn·deer′, *v.t.* [D. *kommandeeren*, to command; Fr. *commander*, to command.]

1. to force into military service.

2. to seize (property) for military or governmental use.

3. to take forcibly. [Colloq.]

çŏm·măn·deer′, *v.i.* to commandeer men or property.

çŏm·mȧnd′ẽr, *n.* [ME. *commaundour*; OFr.

 fāte, fär, fȧst, fạll, finăl, cãre, at; mēte, prey, hẽr, met; pīne, marïne, bīrd, pin; nōte, mōve, fọr, atŏm, not; moon, book;

commandeor, a commander, from L. *commendatus*, pp. of *commendare*, to commit to one's charge.]

1. one who commands; one who has authority; a leader.

2. in the United States Navy, an officer who ranks above a lieutenant commander and below a captain.

3. a high ranking member in certain secret orders, medieval and modern, as in the Knights Templars and Hospitalers.

4. the officer in charge of a military unit: a functional title, not a rank.

5. a heavy beetle or wooden mallet, used in paving, etc.

çŏm·månd′ẽr in chiēf, 1. an officer exercising supreme military or naval authority; as, the President is the *commander in chief* of the armed forces of the United States.

2. an officer in command of all armed forces in a certain theater of war.

çŏm·månd′ẽr·ship, *n.* the rank or position of a commander.

çŏm·månd′ẽr·y, *n.*; *pl.* **çŏm·månd′ẽr·ieṣ,** [Fr. *commanderie*, from *commander*, to command.]

1. the office or station of a commander.

2. among several orders of knights, such as the medieval Templars and Hospitalers, a district under the control of a member of the order.

3. the rank of a commander in an order of knights.

4. a branch in certain fraternal orders.

5. a district under the authority and control of a military commander. [Rare.]

çŏm·månd′ing, *a.* 1. controlling or dominating by position; having a free view over a wide region; as, a *commanding* position.

2. controlling by influence, authority, or dignity; dominating; as, a man of *commanding* manners; a *commanding* eloquence.

3. in command.

Syn.—imperious, imperative, authoritative, lordly.

çŏm·månd′ing·ly, *adv.* in a commanding manner.

çŏm·månd′ment, *n.* [ME. *commandement*; OFr. *commandement*, a commandment, from L. *commendatus*, pp. of *commendare*, to commit to one's charge, command.]

1. a command; a mandate; an order or injunction given by authority; a charge; a precept.

A new *commandment* I give unto you, that ye love one another. —John xiii. 34.

2. any of the Ten Commandments, laws described in the Bible as given by God to Moses on Mount Sinai: Ex. xx. 2–17, Deut. v. 6–21.

3. authority; command; power of commanding.

4. in old English law, the offense of inducing another to commit a violation of the law. [Obs.]

çŏm·man′dō (*or* -män′), *n.*; *pl.* **çŏm·man′dōṣ, çŏm·man′dōeṣ,** [D.; Port., lit., party commanded, from *commandar*, to govern, command; LL. *commandare*.]

1. originally, in South Africa, a force of Boer troops.

2. a raid made by such troops.

3. in World War II, a small raiding force trained to operate inside territory held by the enemy.

4. a member of such a group.

çŏm·månd′ pẽr·fôrm′ănce, a performance, as of a play, put on for royalty, etc. by command or request.

çŏm·månd′ pōst, the field headquarters of an army unit, from which the commander directs operations.

çŏm·månd′ry, *n.* same as *commandery*.

çom′märk, *n.* [Fr. *comarque*.] the frontier of a country. [Obs.]

çom·mȧ·tē′ri·ăl, *a.* consisting of the same material. [Obs.]

çŏm·mat′iç, *a.* [LL. *commaticus*; Gr. *kommatikos*, framed in short clauses.] having short clauses or sentences; brief; concise.

çom′mȧ·tiṣm, *n.* briefness; conciseness in writing.

çom·meaṣ′ūr·ȧ·ble (-mezh′), *a.* having an equal measure or size; commensurate.

çom·meaṣ′ure (-mezh′), *v.t.*; commeasured, *pt.*, *pp.*; commeasuring, *ppr.* to equal in measure; to coincide with.

çomme il faut′ (-fō′), [Fr.] as it should be; proper; fitting.

Çom·me·lī′nȧ, *n.* the type genus of the family of plants, *Commelinaceæ*, having branching foliage and, for the most part, blue flowers: generally known as *day flowers*.

Çom·mel·i·nā′cē·ae, *n.pl.* [Latinized from the names of J. and K. *Commelin*, Dutch botanists.] a family of herbaceous endogens, natives of warm climates. The spiderwort, *Tradescantia virginiana*, belongs to this family.

çom·mel·i·nā′ceous, *a.* belonging or relating to the family *Commelinaceæ*.

çŏm·mem′ō·rȧ·ble, *a.* memorable; worthy to be remembered or noticed with honor.

çŏm·mem′ō·rāte, *v.t.*; commemorated, *pt.*, *pp.*; commemorating, *ppr.* [L. *commemoratus*, pp. of *commemorare*, to call to mind; *com-*, intens., and *memorare*, to mention, remind.]

1. to call to remembrance by a ceremony, etc.; to honor by some act of respect or affection intended to preserve the memory of a person or event.

2. to preserve the memory of; to serve as a memorial to.

çŏm·mem·ō·rā′tion, *n.* [L. *commemoratio*, a reminding, from *commemorare*, to commemorate, call to mind.]

1. the act of commemorating.

2. a celebration in memory of someone or something.

commemoration day; at Oxford University, the annual ceremony in honor of the founders and benefactors of that institution, when orations are delivered and honorary degrees conferred.

çŏm·mem′ō·rā·tive, *a.* tending to preserve the remembrance of something; serving to commemorate.

çŏm·mem′ō·rā·tive, *n.* anything that commemorates.

çŏm·mem′ō·rā·tŏr, *n.* [L.] one who commemorates.

çŏm·mem′ō·rȧ·tō·ry, *a.* serving to commemorate.

çŏm·mence′, *v.i.*; commenced, *pt.*, *pp.*; commencing, *ppr.* [OFr. *comencer*, to begin; L. *com-*, together, and *initiare*, to begin.]

1. to begin; to take rise or origin; to start; as, this republic *commenced* at a late period.

2. to begin to be, or act as. [Rare.]

Let not learning, too, *commence* its foe. —Pope.

3. to take a degree in a university or college. [Brit.]

çŏm·mence′, *v.t.* to begin; to enter upon; to perform the first act of; as, to *commence* operations.

Syn.—begin, start, set about, originate.

çŏm·mence′ment, *n.* [ME. *commencement*; OFr. *commencement*, from *commencer*, to commence.]

1. beginning; rise; origin; start; as, the *commencement* of hostilities.

2. the time of commencing or beginning.

3. the day upon which degrees are conferred in schools and colleges; also, the ceremonies in connection with this.

çŏm·mend′, *v.t.*; commended, *pt.*, *pp.*; commending, *ppr.* [ME. *commenden*, to commend; L. *commendare*, to entrust to, commend; *com-*, intens., and *mandare*, to put in one's hands, commit to one's charge.]

1. to commit; to deliver; to entrust or put in the care of another.

Father, into thy hands I *commend* my spirit. —Luke xxiii. 46.

2. to represent as worthy of confidence, notice, regard, or kindness; to recommend; as, this subject *commends* itself to our careful attention.

3. to praise; to mention with approbation.

The Lord *commended* the unjust steward. —Luke xvi. 8.

4. to mention by way of keeping in memory; to send greeting or compliments from. [Archaic.]

Signior Antonio
Commends him to you. —Shak.

Syn.—praise, approve, eulogize, applaud, entrust, recommend.

çŏm·mend′, *n.* 1. commendation. [Obs.]

2. greeting; compliment. [Obs.]

çŏm·mend′ȧ·ble, *a.* [L. *commendabilis*, commendable, from *commendare*, to entrust to one, commend.] worthy of approbation, praise, or commendation; laudable.

çŏm·mend′ȧ·ble·ness, *n.* the state of being commendable.

çŏm·mend′ȧ·bly, *adv.* laudably; in a commendable manner.

çŏm·men′dam, *n.* [LL., acc. of *commenda*, a trust, used in the phrase *dare in commendam*, to give in trust, from L. *commendare*, to commit, entrust.] formerly, in ecclesiastical law, the entrusting of a benefice by the king or head of the church to the care of a layman, to retain till a proper pastor is provided; also, a benefice held in this way.

çŏm·mend′ȧ·tā·ry, *n.* one who holds a benefice in commendam.

çom·men·dā′tion, *n.* [ME. *commendacion*; L. *commendatio*, a recommendation, from *commendare*, to commend.]

1. the act of commending; praise; approval; declaration of esteem.

Good nature is the most godlike *commendation* of a man. —Dryden.

2. a putting in the care of another; entrusting.

3. recommendation.

4. [*usually in pl.*] a greeting or remembrance, as to a friend. [Archaic.]

Mistress Page hath her hearty *commendations* to you too. —Shak.

çŏm·mend′ȧ·tŏr, *n.* one who holds a benefice in commendam; a commendatary.

çŏm·mend′ȧ·tō·ry, *a.* 1. serving to commend; expressing approval or praise; as, a *commendatory* letter.

2. recommending.

3. holding a benefice in commendam; as, a *commendatory* bishop.

çŏm·mend′ȧ·tō·ry, *n.* a commendation; eulogy.

çŏm·mend′ẽr, *n.* one who commends or praises.

çŏm·men′săl, *n.* [ME. *commensal*; L. *com-*, with, and *mensa*, table.]

1. one who eats at the same table.

2. an animal or plant living with another for support or sometimes for mutual advantage, but not as a parasite.

çŏm·men′săl, *a.* designating, of, characteristic of, or like a commensal.

çŏm·men′săl·iṣm, *n.* the state of being commensal.

çom·men·sal′i·ty, *n.* same as *commensalism*.

çom·men·sā′tion, *n.* commensalism. [Obs.]

çŏm·men″sū·rȧ·bil′i·ty, *n.* the quality or state of being commensurable.

çŏm·men′sū·rȧ·ble, *a.* [LL. *commensurabilis*, having a common measure, L. *com-*, together, and *mensura*, a measurement.]

1. having a common measure, or reducible to one; as, a yard and a foot are *commensurable*, since both may be measured by inches.

2. proportionable; fitly proportioned.

commensurable numbers; numbers which may be measured or divided by another number without a remainder, as 12 and 18 may be divided by 6 and 3.

çŏm·men′sū·rȧ·ble·ness, *n.* commensurability.

çŏm·men′sū·rȧ·bly, *adv.* in a commensurable manner.

çŏm·men′sū·rāte, *a.* 1. proportionate; corresponding in measure.

2. equal; proportional; having equal measure or size.

3. measurable by the same standard or measure; commensurable.

Syn.—adequate, proportionate, sufficient, suitable, competent.

çŏm·men′sū·rāte, *v.t.* and *v.i.*; commensurated, *pt.*, *pp.*; commensurating, *ppr.* [*com-*, and LL. *mensuratus*, pp. of *mensurare*, to measure; L. *mensura*, a measurement.] to make or be commensurate.

çŏm·men′sū·rāte·ly, *adv.* in a commensurate manner; correspondingly.

çŏm·men′sū·rāte·ness, *n.* the quality of being commensurate.

çŏm·men·sū·rā′tion, *n.* the state of being commensurate.

çom′ment, *v.i.*; commented, *pt.*, *pp.*; commenting, *ppr.* [Fr. *commenter*, to comment; L. *commentari*, to meditate, freq. of *comminisci*, to think, devise; *com-*, intens., and *meminisse*, to remember.]

1. to make notes with a view to illustrating, criticizing, or explaining something written or said; to annotate; as, to *comment* on the writings of an author.

2. to make remarks, or criticisms, as on publications, actions, events, or opinions.

3. to talk; to chatter; to gossip.

çom′ment, *v.t.* to explain; to annotate. [Archaic.]

çom′ment, *n.* 1. a note, intended to illustrate, explain, or criticize a writing, passage, etc.; annotation; explanation; exposition; as, the *comments* of Scott on the Scriptures.

2. that which explains or illustrates; as, a man's conduct is the best *comment* on his declarations.

3. remark; observation.

In such a time as this, it is not meet
That every nice offense should bear its *comment.* —Shak.

4. talk; chatter; gossip.

Syn.—annotation, elucidation, explanation, exposition, note, observation, remark.

com·men·tăr'i·ăl, *a.* of, or having the nature of, a commentary.

com'men·tā·ry, *n.* 1. a comment.

2. a series of explanatory notes or annotations.

3. a series of remarks or observations.

4. a historical narrative; a memoir of particular transactions; as, the *Commentaries* of Caesar.

com'men·tāte, *v.i.* to make comments. [Rare.]

com·men·tā'tion, *n.* [L. *commentatio,* diligent meditation, from *commentari,* to meditate.]

1. the practice or process of making comments.

2. a criticism, explanation, or illustration. [Obs.]

com'men·tā·tŏr, *n.* 1. one who comments; one who writes a series of explanatory notes or annotations; an expositor; an annotator.

2. a person whose profession is reporting, analyzing, and evaluating events, trends, etc.; as, a news *commentator.*

com"men·tȧ·tō'ri·ăl, *a.* relating to commentators or commentaries.

com'men·tā·tŏr·ship, *n.* the office of a commentator.

com'ment·ẽr, *n.* 1. one who comments; an annotator.

2. one who makes remarks.

com·men·ti'tious (-tish'us), *a.* [L. *commenticius,* thought out, feigned, from *commentus,* pp. of *comminisci,* to devise, invent.] invented; feigned; imaginary; fictitious.

com'mẽrce, *n.* [L. *commercium,* commerce; *com-,* together, and *merx,* genit. *mercis,* merchandise.]

1. an interchange of goods, wares, productions, or property of any kind, between nations or individuals, either by barter, or by purchase and sale; trade; traffic.

2. intercourse between individuals; mutual dealings in social life.

3. sexual intercourse. [Rare.]

4. interchange; reciprocal communications; as, there is a vast *commerce* of ideas.

5. a card game played by exchanging or bartering cards.

Syn.—barter, business, communication, dealing, exchange, intercourse, trade, traffic.

cŏm·mẽrce', *v.i.*; commerced, *pt., pp.*; commercing, *ppr.* 1. to traffic; to carry on trade. [Obs.]

2. to hold social intercourse (*with*).

cŏm·mẽr'ciăl (-shăl), *a.* 1. of or pertaining to commerce; as, *commercial* affairs.

2. designating unrefined products bought and sold in large quantities for industrial uses; as, *commercial* sulfuric acid.

3. made or done primarily for sale or profit.

commercial art; paintings, drawings, or other art work used to illustrate advertisements or for other commercial purposes.

commercial artist; one who makes illustrations for advertisements or for other commercial uses.

commercial college; a college or school offering instruction in business or commerce; business college.

commercial note; a writing paper, $5^1/_2$ x $8^1/_2$ inches.

commercial paper; paper used in business having a monetary or exchangeable value, such as bank checks, promissory notes, etc.

commercial traveler; a traveling salesman. [Brit.]

cŏm·mẽr'ciăl, *n.* in radio and television, the part of a broadcast devoted to advertising of the sponsor's product; a paid advertisement.

cŏm·mẽr'ciăl·ism, *n.* 1. the methods and spirit of commerce and business; the spirit or principles of trade.

2. a business practice, custom, or idiom.

cŏm·mẽr"ciăl·i·zā'tion, *n.* a commercializing or being commercialized.

cŏm·mẽr'ciăl·īze, *v.t.*; commercialized, *pt., pp.*; commercializing, *ppr.* 1. to put on a business basis; apply commercial methods to.

2. to make the profit motive dominant in; make or do mainly for profit.

3. to put on the market; make a commodity of.

cŏm·mẽr'ciăl·ly, *adv.* 1. in a commercial manner.

2. from the viewpoint of business.

com'mi·grāte, *v.i.* [L. *commigrare,* to move in a body.] to migrate together in a body. [Obs.]

com·mi·grā'tion, *n.* the migration of a group of people. [Obs.]

com'mi·nāte, *v.t.* and *v.i.*; comminated, *pt., pp.*; comminating, *ppr.* 1. to threaten, especially with anathema.

2. to curse or ban solemnly; to anathematize.

com·mi·nā'tion, *n.* [L. *comminatio,* a threatening, from *comminari,* to threaten; *com-,* intens., and *minari,* to threaten.]

1. a threat or threatening, especially of punishment or vengeance.

2. a recital of divine threats against sinners: read in the Church of England on Ash Wednesday.

com·min'ȧ·tō·ry, *a.* threatening; denunciatory.

cŏm·miñ'gle, *v.t.* and *v.i.*; commingled, *pt., pp.*; commingling, *ppr.* to mix together; to mingle; to blend.

com·min'ū·i·ble, *a.* reducible to powder. [Obs.]

com'mi·nūte, *v.t.*; comminuted, *pt., pp.*; comminuting, *ppr.* [L. *comminutus,* pp. of *comminuere,* to make small; *com-,* intens., and *minuere,* to make small.] to make small or fine; to reduce to minute particles, or to a fine powder, by breaking, pounding, rasping, or grinding; to pulverize.

com'mi·nūt·ed frac'tūre, a fracture in which the bone is splintered or broken into many small pieces.

com·mi·nū'tion, *n.* 1. the act of reducing to a fine powder or to small particles; pulverization.

2. in surgery, fracture, as of a bone, into numerous pieces.

3. a lessening; a gradual wearing away by the gradual breaking off of small pieces.

Com·miph'ō·rȧ, *n.* [L., from Gr. *kommi,* gum, and *-phoros,* bearing.] a genus of shrubs and trees which yield valuable balsams. They are natives of Africa, Arabia, and the East Indies.

cŏm·mis' (kō-mē'), *n.* [Fr., from L. *commissus,* pp. of *committere,* to commit.] in French law, a person appointed by another to act as his representative in any kind of transaction; also, a clerk; a deputy.

cŏm·miṣ'ẽr·ȧ·ble, *a.* deserving of commiseration or pity; pitiable; capable of exciting sympathy or sorrow.

cŏm·miṣ'ẽr·āte, *v.t.*; commiserated, *pt., pp.*; commiserating, *ppr.* [L. *commiseratus,* pp. of *commiserari,* to pity; *com-,* intens., and *miserari,* to pity.] to feel or show sorrow or pity for; to sympathize with in distress.

We should *commiserate* those who groan beneath the weight of age, disease, or want. —Denham.

cŏm·miṣ'ẽr·āte, *v.i.* to condole (*with*).

cŏm·miṣ·ẽr·ā'tion, *n.* pity; compassion; a sympathetic sorrow for the wants, afflictions, or distresses of another; as, they thought of the poor man with *commiseration.*

Syn.—pity, sympathy, compassion, fellow feeling.

cŏm·miṣ'ẽr·ȧ·tive, *a.* feeling or expressing pity; compassionate.

cŏm·miṣ'ẽr·ȧ·tive·ly, *adv.* in a compassionate manner; with compassion.

cŏm·miṣ'ẽr·ā·tŏr, *n.* one who commiserates.

com'mis·săr, *n.* a commissioner; specifically, formerly, a chief or head of any of the commissariats in any of the separate states that make up the Union of Soviet Socialist Republics: now officially called *minister.*

com·mis·sā'ri·ăl, *a.* pertaining to a commissary.

com·mis·sā'ri·at, *n.* [Fr.]

1. the office or employment of a commissar.

2. the department of an army whose duties consist in providing food and supplies for the troops; also, the body of officers in that department.

3. food supply.

4. a department headed by a commissar.

5. formerly, any of the government departments in the republics of the Soviet Union: now officially called *ministry.*

6. a group of commissars.

com'mis·sȧ·ry, *n.* [from L. *commissus,* pp. of *committere,* to commit; *com-,* with, and *mittere,* to send.]

1. a person to whom some duty is given by authority; a representative; a deputy; specifically, (a) in France, a police official; (b) a person representing a bishop in a part of his diocese; (c) in the Soviet Union, a commissar.

2. formerly, (a) an army officer in charge of providing soldiers with food and other supplies; (b) the buildings and personnel in his charge.

3. a store in a lumber camp, army camp, etc. where food and supplies can be obtained.

com'mis·sȧ·ry ġen'ẽr·ăl, the head of the commissary department.

com'mis·sȧ·ry·ship, *n.* the office of commissary.

cŏm·mis'sion (-mish'un), *n.* [ME. *commission*; OFr. *commission*; LL. *commissio,* a delegation of business to any one; L. *commissus,* pp. of *committere,* to commit, give in charge; *com-,* with, and *mittere,* to send.]

1. an authorization to perform certain duties or tasks, or to take on certain powers.

2. a document giving such authorization.

3. authority to act for another.

4. a thing that a person is authorized to do for another.

5. the state of being authorized to perform certain duties or tasks.

6. a group of people chosen to perform specified duties.

7. a committing; a doing.

8. the thing done.

9. a percentage of the money taken in on sales, given as pay to a salesclerk or agent, usually in addition to salary or wages.

10. in military usage, (a) an official certificate conferring rank; specifically, a document issued by the President, making one a commissioned officer in the United States armed forces; (b) the rank thus granted.

commission of the peace; in England, a commission issuing under the great seal for the appointment of justices of the peace.

in commission; (a) in use; (b) in fit condition for use.

military commission; in United States military law, a tribunal composed of military officers to try offenders during a time when civil law is suspended.

out of commission; (a) not in use; (b) not in fit condition for use.

to put a ship into commission; to send a vessel out on public service after it has been laid up; to equip and man a government vessel for service; to take command, as a captain, hoist the flag, etc., in readiness for service.

to put a ship out of commission; to detach or transfer the officers and crew and withdraw a vessel from active service, either temporarily or permanently.

United States Christian Commission; during the Civil War, a society of Christians of the Northern States, formed to look after the spiritual and physical needs of the Union soldiers in the camps and hospitals.

United States Sanitary Commission; an organization in the North during the Civil War, formed to co-operate with and supplement the medical departments of the Union armies in furnishing medical and surgical aid to soldiers, especially in camps and field hospitals.

cŏm·mis'sion, *v.t.*; commissioned, *pt., pp.*; commissioning, *ppr.* 1. to give a commission to; to empower or authorize by commission; as, the President *commissions* an officer.

2. to send with a mandate or authority; to empower; to delegate.

3. in nautical usage, to put (a vessel) into service.

Syn.—delegate, authorize, appoint, depute, ordain, constitute, empower.

cŏm·mis·sion·āire', *n.* [Fr. *commissionnaire.*]

1. a messenger or light porter; especially, one of the *Corps of Commissionaires,* of London, England, organized in 1859, a body of pensioned and partly disabled soldiers.

2. any person commissioned to perform miscellaneous small services, as a porter, doorkeeper, messenger, etc.

cŏm·mis'sion·ăl, *a.* pertaining to a commission; conferring a commission or conferred by a commission.

cŏm·mis'sion·ȧ·ry, *a.* same as *commissioned.* [Rare.]

cŏm·mis'sion·āte, *v.t.* to commission. [Obs.]

cŏm·mis'sioned, *a.* furnished with a commission; holding rank in the armed forces by a commission from the proper authority: the lowest rank of commissioned officer in the United States Army is second lieutenant, in the Navy, ensign.

cŏm·mis'sion·ẽr, *n.* [LL. *commissionarius,* one to whom a commission is entrusted, from *commissio,* a commission; L. *commissus,* pp. of *committere,* to entrust, commit.]

1. one who is included in a warrant of au-

thority; one who has a commission or warrant from proper authority to perform some office or execute some business for the person or government which employs him and gives him authority; as, *commissioners* for adjusting claims; *commissioners* for settling a boundary dispute; *commissioners* to an international exposition.

2. specifically, an officer who has charge of some branch of the public service; as, the *commissioner* of highways.

3. a commissionaire. [Rare.]

4. in Scotland, one of the persons elected to manage the affairs of a police burgh or noncorporate town, corresponding to a bailie or town councilor in a corporate town.

5. a member of a commission.

6. one of a group chosen to govern a local political unit.

commissioner of deeds; in the United States, an officer authorized to take acknowledgments and depositions, to probate accounts, etc., especially in one State for use in another.

county commissioner; one of a board of officers elected in the several counties of many of the States to administer county affairs. They usually have control of the public highways, the county buildings, finances, etc.

police commissioner; in many cities of the United States, one of a municipal board, appointive or elective, having control of police matters.

çŏm·mis′sion·ẽr·ship″, *n.* the office or position of a commissioner.

çŏm·mis′sion house, a stockbroker's office that buys and sells stock for customers on a commission basis.

çŏm·mis′sion mẽr′chănt, one who buys or sells goods or commodities on commission as the representative of others, receiving for his compensation a percentage of the value involved.

çŏm·mis′sion plan, a form of city government in which all legislative and administrative powers are in the hands of an elected commission (usually five or six members) instead of a mayor and council.

çŏm·mis′sive, *a.* [L. *commissus*, pp. of *committere*, to commit.]

1. of or pertaining to a commission; of the nature of, or involving, a commission. [Rare.]

2. committing. [Rare.]

çŏm·mis·sū′răl (*or* çŏ-mish′ū-răl), *a.* of or pertaining to a commissure.

çom′mis·sūre, *n.* [L. *commissura*, a joining together, from *commissus*, pp. of *committere*, to put together.]

1. a joint, seam, or closure; the place where two bodies, or parts of a body, meet and unite; an interstice or cleft between particles or parts, as between plates or lamellae.

2. in architecture, the joint between two stones.

3. in anatomy, a band of fibers joining symmetrical parts, as of the right and left sides of the brain and spinal cord.

4. in botany, the line of junction of two carpels, as in the *Umbelliferæ*.

çŏm·mit′, *v.t.*; committed, *pt.*, *pp.*; committing, *ppr.* [ME. *committen*, to commit; L. *committere*, to bring together, commit; *com-*, together, and *mittere*, to send.]

1. to do; to effect or perpetrate; as, to *commit* murder.

2. to give in trust; to put into custody or charge; to entrust; to consign or surrender for safekeeping; as, to *commit* an inheritance to the care of trustees; to *commit* a prisoner to jail.

> *Commit* him to the grave. —Shak.

3. to join or put together, for a contest; to match; followed by *with*: a Latinism. [Obs.]

> How does Philopolis *commit* the opponent *with* the respondent? —More.

4. to engage; to pledge, or to pledge by implication; to bind: often with reflexive pronouns; as, to *commit oneself*.

5. to refer (a bill, etc.) to a committee for their consideration and report.

6. to confound. [Obs.]

7. to memorize, as a speech or a passage in a book.

to commit oneself; to speak or act in such a manner as to bind oneself to a certain line of conduct.

to commit to memory; to learn by heart; to learn so as to be able to repeat from memory.

to commit to paper (or *writing*); to write down; to record.

Syn.—entrust, consign.—*Entrust* signifies to put into the care of another, implying a degree of confidence in the person to whom the trust is given; *commit*, to give into the care of another, implying some sort of formality in the act; *consign*, to give over to another in the most positive manner and with formality, implying that the thing given over passes entirely into another's charge.

çŏm·mit′, *v.i.* 1. to be guilty of incontinency. [Obs.]

> *Commit* not with man's sworn spouse. —Shak.

2. to consign a person or persons to prison.

çŏm·mit′ment, *n.* 1. a committing or being committed; the act or process of consigning, delivering, or entrusting, as for safekeeping; committal.

2. specifically, the act of delivering in charge to the authorities of an institution; as, the *commitment* of a prisoner to jail.

3. the act of pledging or engaging oneself; also, the state of being pledged or engaged.

4. a court order for confining in prison: also called a *mittimus*.

5. the act of referring or entrusting to a committee for consideration and report: said of a legislative bill, petition, etc.

6. a financial liability undertaken; an agreement to buy or sell securities, etc.

çŏm·mit′tȧ·ble, *a.* 1. capable of being committed.

2. liable to be committed to prison, to an institution for the mentally ill, etc.

3. making a person liable to such commitment: said of offenses.

çŏm·mit′tăl, *n.* the act of committing in all its senses; commitment; commission; as, the *committal* of a trust to a person, of a body to the grave, of a criminal to prison, etc.

çŏm·mit′tee, *n.* [from L. *committere*, to commit.]

1. a group of people elected or appointed to attend to any matter or business referred to them, as by a legislative body, court, corporation, society, club, etc.

2. in law, a person to whom someone or something is given in charge.

committee of the whole; the committee of a legislative body consisting of all the members present sitting for purposes of deliberation, permitting operation under rules of order different from those used in a regular session.

in committee; under consideration by a committee, as a resolution or bill.

standing committee; any of various committees in a legislative body or other organization, appointed at the opening of a session and continuing during the existence of such body; as, the *standing committee* on elections.

çŏm·mit′tee·măn, *n.*; *pl.* **çŏm·mit′tee·men,** a member of a committee.

çŏm·mit′tee·ship, *n.* the office or function of a committee.

çŏm·mit′tee·wom″ăn (-woom″ăn), *n.*; *pl.* **çŏm·mit′tee·wom″en** (-wim″en), a woman member of a committee.

çŏm·mit′tẽr, *n.* 1. one who commits (a crime, etc.); one who perpetrates.

2. a fornicator; an adulterer. [Obs.]

çŏm·mit′ti·ble, *a.* committable.

çŏm·mit′tŏr, *n.* in law, a magistrate who commits persons of unsound mind to the charge of a committee.

çŏm·mix′, *v.t.* and *v.i.*; commixed, *pt.*, *pp.*; commixing, *ppr.* [ME. *commixen*; L. *commixtus*, pp. of *commiscere*, to mix together; *com-*, together, and *miscere*, to mix.] to mix or mingle; to blend, as different substances. [Archaic or Poet.]

çŏm·mix′iŏn (-shun), *n.* same as *commixtion*.

çŏm·mix′tiŏn (-chun), *n.* mixture; a blending of different ingredients in one mass or compound. [Obs.]

çŏm·mix′tūre, *n.* 1. the act or process of mixing; also, the state or being mixed.

2. the mass formed by mixing different things; composition; compound.

3. in Scots law, the blending of different substances belonging to different proprietors, as two kinds of corn, giving rise to certain questions regarding rights of property.

çŏm′mō·dāte, *n.* [L. *commodatus*, pp. of *commodare*, to make fit, from *commodus*, adapted, suitable.] in Scots law, a loan, with no payment to the lender, by which the borrower is obliged to restore the object lent, in the same condition in which he received it.

çŏm·mōde′, *n.* [Fr. *commode*, n., a chest of drawers; adj., fit, suitable; L. *commodus*, fit, suitable.]

1. a kind of headdress worn by women at the beginning of the eighteenth century, raising the front hair and cap to a great height.

2. any of several articles of furniture; (a) a chiffonier, or set of drawers; (b) an enclosed, movable washstand, with basin, waste pipe, etc.; (c) a piece of furniture containing a chamber pot; (d) a toilet: euphemistic term.

3. a procuress; a bawd. [Obs.]

çŏm·mō′di·ous, *a.* [ME. *commodious*; L. *commodus*, adapted to, suitable; *com-*, with, and *modus*, a measure.]

1. suitable; fit; proper; useful; serviceable; beneficial. [Obs.]

> If they think we ought to prove the ceremonies *commodious*, they do greatly deceive themselves. —Hooker.

2. roomy; spacious; as, a *commodious* dwelling.

> The haven was not *commodious* to winter in. —Acts xxvii. 12.

Syn.—convenient, suitable, comfortable, spacious, useful, fit, advantageous.

çŏm·mō′di·ous·ly, *adv.* in a commodious manner; conveniently.

çŏm·mō′di·ous·ness, *n.* 1. convenience; fitness; suitableness for its purpose. [Obs.]

2. the state or quality of being commodious.

çŏm·mod′i·ty, *n.*; *pl.* **çŏm·mod′i·tieṣ,** [Fr. *commodité*, comfort, convenience; L. *commoditas*, fitness, adaptation, from *commodus*, fit.]

1. convenience; profit; advantage; interest; as, men seek their own *commodity*. [Obs.]

2. that which affords ease, convenience, profit, or advantage; anything that is useful.

3. in commerce, any article that is bought and sold.

> *Commodities* are movables, valuable by money, the common measure.—Locke.

4. quantity of wares; parcel; supply. [Obs.]

> Now Jove, in his next *commodity* of hair, send thee a beard! —Shak.

Syn.—merchandise, goods, wares, stock.

çŏm·mod′i·ty mŏn′ey, a proposed system of currency whose unit (*commodity dollar*) would have a fluctuating gold value determined at regular intervals on the basis of an official index of commodity prices.

çom′mŏ·dōre, *n.* [Sp. *comendador*, a knight, superior of a monastery, from *comendar*, to charge with; L. *commendare*, to entrust with.]

1. a naval officer ranking above a captain and below a rear admiral. This rank was abolished in the United States Navy in 1899, but has been temporarily restored in times of war.

2. in the British Navy, the captain who temporarily commands a squadron or detachment of a fleet: the title is unofficial and carries no rating.

3. a courtesy title given to the senior captain of a line of merchant vessels, the chief officer of a yachting club, etc.

4. the leading ship in a fleet of merchantmen, which carries a light in her top by night, as a guide to the other ships.

çom·moigne′ (-moin′), *n.* [Fr.] a monk of the same convent. [Obs.]

çom′mŏn, *a.* [ME. *comon*, *comun*; OFr. *comun*; L. *communis*, common, general.]

1. belonging or pertaining equally to more than one, or to many indefinitely.

2. belonging to all, that is, either to the human race generally, or to all the people of a certain country, region, or locality; general; universal; public; as, the *common* schools.

3. of frequent or usual occurrence; not extraordinary; general; frequent; usual; ordinary; habitual.

> It is no act of *common* passage, but
> A strain of rareness. —Shak.

4. not distinguished; not of superior excellence; ordinary.

5. of no rank; as, a *common* soldier.

6. below ordinary.

7. not refined; vulgar; low; coarse.

8. in mathematics, belonging equally to two or more quantities; as, a *common* denominator.

9. polluted; profane; not clean.

10. in botany, designating a part or organ having functions of a dual or general nature: thus, a *common* bud is one that contains both leaves and flowers; a *common* peduncle, one that bears several flowers.

11. in grammar, (a) designating a verb that has both active and passive meanings, as Latin *aspernor*, I despise or am despised; (b) designating gender that is either masculine or feminine; as, parent, horse, ant, trout, etc. are of *common* gender; (c) designating a noun that is the name of all the objects possessing the attributes denoted by the noun: in this

sense opposed to *proper*; as, river is a *common* noun, but Mississippi is a *proper* noun.

common barrator; in law, one who willfully stirs up or instigates litigation, especially one who makes it a business to do so.

Common Bench; in England, the Court of Common Pleas.

common carrier, council, divisor, multiple, law, etc.; see under the nouns.

common-law marriage; see under *marriage*.

common pleas; in law, civil suits between private parties.

in common; equally with another, or with others; to be equally shared by two or more.

out of the common; extraordinary; unusual.

to make common cause with; see under *cause*.

Syn.—frequent, customary, ordinary, usual, habitual, vulgar, mean.

çom′mŏn, *n.* [ME. *comon, comun*; OFr. *commune*; L. *commune*, that which is common, the community, from *communis*, common.]

1. [*sometimes pl.*] a tract of ground, the use of which is not appropriated to an individual, but belongs to or is used by the public.

2. in law, a right which a person has to pasture his cattle on land of another, or to dig turf, or catch fish, or cut wood, or the like: called *common* of pasture, of turbary, of piscary, of estovers, etc.

3. the public; the people. [Obs. in sing.]

4. [*sometimes* C–] in ecclesiastical usage, a service suitable for any class of festivals.

common appendant; in English law, a right belonging to the owners or occupiers of arable land to put commonable beasts upon waste land, within the same manor.

common appurtenant; a right similar to the above applying to lands in other manors, or extending to other beasts besides those which are generally commonable.

çom′mŏn, *v.i.* [ME. *comonen*; OFr. *comunier*; L. *communicare*, to have in common, from *communis*, common.]

1. to have a joint right with others in common ground.

2. to board together; to eat at a table in common.

3. to discourse together; to confer. [Obs.]

4. to participate or share. [Obs.]

çom′mŏn·ȧ·ble, *a.* 1. held in common.

2. qualified to be pastured on common land.

Commonable beasts are either beasts of the plow, or such as manure the ground. —Blackstone.

çom′mŏn·āġe, *n.* [OFr. *communage*, the use of anything in common.]

1. the right of pasturing on a common; also, the joint right of using anything in common with others.

2. the state of land owned in common.

3. the land so owned.

4. the common people; commonalty.

çom′mŏn·ăl·ty, *n.*; *pl.* **çom′mŏn·ăl·tieș,** 1. the common people. In Great Britain, all classes and conditions of people who are below the rank of nobility.

The *commonalty*, like the nobility, are divided into several degrees. —Blackstone.

2. people in general.

3. a body corporate or its membership.

çom′mŏn dē·nom′i·nā·tŏr, 1. a common multiple of the denominators of two or more fractions; as, 10 is a *common denominator* of $^1/_2$ and $^1/_5$.

2. a characteristic, element, etc. held in common.

çom′mŏn·ẽr, *n.* 1. one of the common people; one not of the nobility.

2. a member of the British House of Commons. [Rare.]

3. one who has a joint right in common ground.

4. a student at the University of Oxford who is not dependent on the foundation for support, but pays for his board, or commons.

5. a prostitute. [Obs.]

Çom′mŏn E′rȧ, same as *Christian Era*.

çom′mŏn frac′tion, a fraction with the numerator separated from the denominator by a diagonal or horizontal line, as 5/11 or $\frac{3}{4}$.

çom·mō·ni′tion, *n.* [L. *commonitio*, admonition, from *commonere*, to advise.] advice; warning; caution. [Obs.]

çom·mon′i·tō·ry, *a.* calling to mind.

çom′mŏn log′ȧ·rithm, in mathematics, a logarithm having 10 for its base.

çom′mŏn·ly, *adv.* 1. usually; generally; ordinarily; frequently; for the most part; as, confirmed habits *commonly* continue through life.

2. in a common or mean manner; as, they live *commonly*.

3. in common. [Obs.]

çom′mŏn man, one of the common people.

Çom′mŏn Mär′ket, an association formed in 1958 by Belgium, France, West Germany, Italy, Luxemburg, and the Netherlands, and joined, in 1973, by Denmark, Ireland, and the United Kingdom, to effect a closer economic union, especially by means of mutual tariff concessions: official name, *European Economic Community*.

çom′mŏn meaș′ūre (mezh′), in music, common time.

çom′mŏn·ness, *n.* 1. frequent occurrence; a state of being common or usual.

2. equal participation by two or more.

3. meanness; poorness.

çom′mŏn pēo′ple, the people of the world, of a country, etc. who are not of the upper classes; masses.

çom′mŏn·plāce, *a.* common; trite; not new or extraordinary.

çom′mŏn·plāce, *n.* 1. memorandum; a note made for future reference.

2. an expression or idea having no originality; a trite saying.

3. anything of ordinary or usual character.

çom′mŏn·plāce, *v.i.* to speak commonplaces. [Obs.]

çom′mŏn·plāce, *v.t.* to enter in a commonplace book, or to reduce to general heads.

çom′mŏn·plāce book, a book in which things to be remembered are recorded.

çom′mŏn·plāce·ness, *n.* the state or quality of being commonplace, trite, or platitudinous; commonness.

Çom′mŏn Prāyer (prār), the prayer book of the Anglican Communion; Book of Common Prayer.

çom′mŏnș, *n.pl.* 1. the common people; people who inherit or possess no honors or titles.

Come in your war array gentles and *commons*. —Scott.

2. [C–] in Great Britain or Canada, the lower house of Parliament: in full, the *House of Commons*.

3. [*construed as sing.*] provisions or food provided for meals in common for all members of a group; especially, such food provided by a college at a fixed charge.

4. a room, building, table, or tables where such food is served.

5. any dining room at a college or similar institution.

Doctors' Commons; in London, formerly, the buildings in which the doctors of the civil law were accommodated, and where business connected with ecclesiastical and certain other courts, wills, divorce, etc. was carried on.

çom′mŏn sçhool (sköl), a public elementary school: also called *grade school*.

çom′mŏn-sense, *a.* having or showing common sense; sound and practical; sensible.

çom′mŏn sense, 1. originally, the faculty which supposedly united and interpreted impressions of the five senses.

2. practical judgment or intelligence; ordinary good sense.

çom′mŏn stock, ordinary capital stock in a company, without a definite dividend rate or the privileges of preferred stock, but usually giving its owner a vote at shareholders' meetings in proportion to his holdings.

çom′mŏn time, in music, a rhythm of two beats to the measure or any multiple of this; especially, 4/4 time: also called *common measure*.

çom′mŏn·ty, *n.* in Scots law, a piece of land belonging to two or more common proprietors.

çom′mŏn·wēal, *n.* 1. the common or public good.

2. a commonwealth. [Archaic.]

çom′mŏn·wealth (-welth), *n.* 1. the whole body of people in a state: the body politic; the public.

You are a good member of the *commonwealth*. —Shak.

2. a republic or democracy; a nation or state in which there is self-government.

3. [C–] any of the dominions in the British Commonwealth of Nations: especially, Australia (official title, *Commonwealth of Australia*).

4. loosely, any State of the United States: strictly, Kentucky, Massachusetts, Pennsylvania, or Virginia, which are so termed by charter.

5. the general welfare; commonweal. [Obs.]

the Commonwealth; the government in England under the Cromwells and, later, parliament from 1649–1660.

çom′mō·răn·cy, çom′mō·rănce, *n.* [L. *commorans*, ppr. of *commorari*, to abide; *com-*, intens., and *morari*, to delay.] in law, a dwelling, abiding, or ordinary residence in a place; abode; habitation.

Commorancy consists in usually lying there. —Blackstone.

çom′mō·rănt, *a.* [L. *commorans*, ppr. of *commorari*, to abide, stay.] dwelling; ordinarily residing; inhabiting.

çom·mo′ri·ent, *a.* [L. *commoriens*, ppr. of *commori*, to die together; *com-*, with, and *mori*, to die.] dying at the same time. [Rare.]

çŏm′mŏt, çŏm′mŏte, *n.* [W. *cwmmwd*.] in Wales, formerly one of the minor political divisions, usually a subdivision of a cantred.

çŏm·mōte′, *v.t.* to stir into commotion; to agitate; to disturb. [Rare.]

çŏm·mō′tion, *n.* [L. *commotio*, a violent motion, from *commotus*, pp. of *commovere*, to *move*, disturb; *com-*, together, and *movere*, to move.]

1. a violent movement; agitation; as, the *commotion* of the sea.

2. tumult of people; disturbance; disorder; as, the *commotion* in the schoolyard.

3. perturbation; disorder of mind; heat; excitement. [Obs.]

Syn.—agitation, tumult, turmoil, disturbance, perturbation.

çŏm·mōve′, *v.t.*; commoved, *pt., pp.*; commoving, *ppr.* 1. to put in motion; to disturb; to agitate; to unsettle.

Like wild waves all our designs *commove*. —Drummond.

2. to incite; to stir the emotions of. [Obs.]

çom′mū·năl, *a.* 1. pertaining to a commune or communalism.

2. of a community; belonging to the community; public.

çom′mū·năl·ișm, *n.* [Fr. *communalisme*, from L. *communis*, common.] the theory of government by communes or corporations of towns and districts. The doctrine is that every commune, or at least every important city commune, should be a kind of independent state in itself, and the nation merely a federation of such states.

çom′mū·năl·ist, *n.* one who advocates communalism or lives under it.

çom″mū·năl·is′tiç, *a.* pertaining to communalism.

çom′mū·năl·īze, *v.t.*; communalized, *pt., pp.*; communalizing, *ppr.* to make communal; make (something) the property of the entire community.

Çom′mū·närd, *n.* [Fr.] a person who supported or took part in the Commune of Paris (1871).

çŏm·mūne′, *v.i.*; communed, *pt., pp.*; communing, *ppr.* [Fr. *communier*, to administer the sacrament; L. *communicare*, to share, have in common, from *communis*, common.]

1. to converse; to talk together familiarly; to impart sentiments mutually; to interchange ideas or feelings.

And there will I meet and *commune* with thee. —Ex. xxv. 22.

2. to partake of the sacrament or Lord's Supper; to receive Holy Communion.

to commune with oneself; to think; to consider; to deliberate.

çom′mūne, *n.* familiar interchange of ideas or sentiments; communion; intercourse; friendly conversation.

çom′mūne, *n.* [Fr.]

1. the smallest territorial district in France, Belgium, and some other European countries: a subordinate political division, corresponding to a township in the United States.

2. the inhabitants of a commune; a community.

3. the common people.

4. a strictly organized collective farm, as in China.

5. a small group of people living communally and sharing in work, earnings, etc.

the Commune (*of Paris*); (a) the revolutionary government of Paris from 1792 until suppressed in 1794; (b) the revolutionary government established in Paris on March 18, 1871, after the Franco-Prussian War. It was suppressed by the Versailles government on May 28, 1871.

çŏm·mū″ni·cȧ·bil′i·ty, *n.* the quality of being communicable; capability of being imparted from one to another.

cŏm·mū'ni·că·ble, *a.* 1. capable of being communicated; capable of impartation from one to another; as, knowledge is *communicable* by words.

2. communicative; ready to impart. [Archaic.]

Perhaps Sir Hugo would have been *communicable* enough without that kind motive. —George Eliot.

3. capable of being transmitted: said of a disease, etc.

cŏm·mū'ni·că·ble·ness, *n.* the quality of being communicable.

cŏm·mū'ni·că·bly, *adv.* in a communicable manner.

cŏm·mū'ni·cănt, *n.* 1. one who receives Holy Communion or belongs to a church that celebrates this sacrament; as, a *communicant* of the Catholic Church.

2. one who communicates information.

cŏm·mū'ni·cāte, *v.t.*; communicated, *pt., pp.*; communicating, *ppr.* [L. *communicatus*, pp. of *communicare*, to impart, share, from *communis*, common.]

1. to impart to another or others; to give to another, as a partaker; to make known, generally something intangible; as, to *communicate* intelligence, news, opinions, or facts.

They read all they would *communicate* to their hearers. —Watts.

2. to share in or participate. [Obs.]

3. to admit to the sacraments of the church; to administer the Eucharist or Communion to. [Rare.]

Syn.—reveal, disclose, divulge, impart, announce, publish, promulgate.

cŏm·mū'ni·cāte, *v.i.* 1. to share; to participate. [Obs.]

2. to have a connection or passage from one to another: said of things, and generally followed by *with*.

The whole body is nothing but a system of such canals which all *communicate with* one another. —Arbuthnot.

3. to have or hold intercourse or interchange of thoughts; to give, or give and receive, information, signals, or messages in any way, as by talk, gestures, writing, etc.

But in dear words of human speech
We two *communicate* no more.
—Tennyson.

4. to partake of the Lord's Supper; to receive Holy Communion.

cŏm·mū·ni·cā'tion, *n.* [Fr. *communication*; L. *communicatio*, communication, from *communicare*, to communicate, share.]

1. the act of imparting, conferring, or delivering, from one to another; as, the *communication* of knowledge, opinions, or facts.

2. intercourse by words, letters, or messages; interchange of thoughts or opinions, by conference or other means.

3. the science and art of communicating as a branch of study.

4. means of communicating; specifically, (a) connecting passage; means of passing from place to place; (b) [*pl.*] a system for sending and receiving messages, as by telephone, telegraph, radio, etc.; (c) [*pl.*] a system for moving troops and matériel.

5. that which is communicated or imparted; information or intelligence imparted by word or writing; as, the general received an important *communication*.

6. participation in the sacrament of the Lord's Supper. [Obs.]

privileged communications; see under *privileged*.

Syn.—discourse, intercourse, correspondence.

cŏm·mū·ni·cā'tions zōne, in military usage, the area between the zone of the interior and the combat zone, serving as a center for communications, supply, evacuation of wounded, troop replacements, etc.

cŏm·mū'ni·că·tive, *a.* 1. inclined to communicate; ready to impart to others.

We have paid for our want of prudence, and determine for the future to be less *communicative*. —Swift.

2. of communication.

cŏm·mū'ni·că·tive·ness, *n.* the quality of being communicative.

cŏm·mū'ni·cā·tŏr, *n.* one who communicates.

cŏm·mū'ni·că·tō"ry, *a.* of communication or tending to communicate. [Rare.]

cŏm·mūn'iŏn (-yun), *n.* [ME. (late) *communyone*; L. *communio*, a fellowship, communion.]

1. fellowship; intercourse between two or more persons; interchange of thoughts or interests; a state of giving and receiving; agreement; concord.

We are naturally led to seek *communion* and fellowship with others. —Hooker.

2. mutual intercourse or union in religious worship, or in doctrine and discipline.

3. a group of people professing the same religious faith and practicing the same rites.

4. [C–] the act of communicating the sacrament of the Eucharist (*Holy Communion*); the celebration of the Lord's Supper.

5. a sharing; possession in common; participation.

close communion; in the Baptist Church, restriction of the sacrament of the Lord's Supper to those who have been baptized by immersion.

Communion elements; the bread and wine used in a Communion service.

Communion in both kinds; Communion in which both the bread and the wine are partaken of by all the communicants.

Communion in one kind; Communion in which one element only of the Eucharist is partaken of by the laity, as in the Roman Catholic Church at most services.

Communion service; the religious ceremony attending the celebration of the Lord's Supper.

Communion table; the table on which the bread and wine of a Communion service are placed.

Syn.—converse, fellowship, intercourse, unity, concord, agreement.

cŏm·mūn'iŏn·ist, *n.* 1. one of the same communion.

2. a person who believes in a definite theory about Holy Communion.

3. one who receives Holy Communion.

com·mu·ni·qué' (cŏm-mū-ni-kā'), *n.* [Fr.] any communication or item of information spoken, written, or printed, as an official utterance.

com'mū·nism, *n.* [Fr. *communisme*, from L. *communis*, common.]

1. (a) an economic theory or system of the ownership of all property by the community as a whole; (b) a theory or system of the ownership of all means of production (and distribution) by the community or society, with all members of the community or society sharing in the work and the products; specifically, such a system as practiced in the Soviet Union since 1917, and later in China, Poland, Czechoslovakia, and other communist countries, theoretically based on the doctrines of Marx, Engels, Lenin, and, latterly, Stalin, characterized by state planning and control of the economy, ruthless suppression of all opposition political parties and all deviation within the Party, and the suppression of individual liberties under a dictatorship; since 1940 expansionist by military action and subversion in Estonia, Latvia, Lithuania, Czechoslovakia, etc.

2. [*often* C–] (a) a political movement for establishing such a system; (b) the doctrines, methods, etc. of the Communist parties.

3. loosely, communalism.

com'mū·nist, *n.* 1. one who holds the doctrines of, or practices, communism.

2. one who advocates government by communes.

3. [C–] one who supported the Paris Commune in 1871.

4. [C–] a member of a Communist party.

Bible communist; see *Perfectionist*.

com'mū·nist, *a.* 1. of, characteristic of, or like communism or communists.

2. advocating or supporting communism.

Communist Party; a political party favoring the beliefs of communism as developed by Marx, Engels, Lenin, and Stalin: dedicated to the establishment of international communism.

com·mū·nis'tic, *a.* 1. communist.

2. in zoology, living in or sharing nests in common: said of certain birds.

com·mū·nis'tic·ăl·ly, *adv.* 1. in a communistic manner.

2. toward communism; as, *communistically* inclined.

Com'mū·nist In·tẽr·na'tion·ăl, the Comintern.

Com'mū·nist Man·i·fes'tō, a document written in 1848 by Karl Marx and Friedrich Engels, summarizing their theory and program of communism.

cŏm·mū·ni·tā'ri·ăn, *n.* one who believes in or is a member of a communistic community.

cŏm·mū'ni·ty, *n.* [L. *communitas*, a community, fellowship, from *communis*, common.]

1. common possession or enjoyment; as, a *community* of goods.

The original *community* of all things. —Locke.

2. a society of people having common rights and privileges, or common interests, civil, political, etc. or living under the same laws and regulations; as, a *community* of farmers.

3. society at large; the public, or people in general: in this sense used with the definite article; as, burdens laid upon the poorer classes of *the community*.

4. common character; similarity; likeness; as, *community* of spirit.

The essential *community* of nature between organic growth and inorganic growth. —Spencer.

5. commonness; frequency. [Obs.]

Sick and blunted with *community*. —Shak.

6. the people living in the same district, city, etc. under the same laws.

7. the district, city, etc. where they live.

8. a group of animals or plants living together in the same environment.

Syn.—aggregation, association, commonwealth, society, order, class, brotherhood, fraternity, polity, unity, nationality, similarity.

cŏm·mū'ni·ty an·ten'nȧ tel'ē·vi·ṣiŏn, a television system by which a single, high antenna receives signals from distant stations and transmits those signals by direct cable to the receivers of persons subscribing to the system.

cŏm·mū'ni·ty cen'tẽr, a building or club in which recreational and cultural activities may be pursued by the residents of the neighborhood in which it is situated or located.

cŏm·mū'ni·ty chest (or **fund**), a fund raised annually by popular subscription for the relief of indigent members of a community and for contributing to the support of charitable organizations, hospitals, etc.

cŏm·mū'ni·ty col'leġe, a junior college established to serve a certain community and supported in part by it.

cŏm·mū'ni·ty sing'ing, singing by all those present at a gathering.

com"mū·ni·zā'tion (*or* -nī-), *n.* a communizing or being communized.

com'mū·nīze, *v.t.*; communized, *pt., pp.*; communizing, *ppr.* 1. to subject to communal ownership and control.

2. to cause to become communistic.

cŏm·mū·tȧ·bil'i·ty, *n.* the quality or capability of being commutable.

cŏm·mūt'ȧ·ble, *a.* [L. *commutabilis*, changeable, from *commutare*, to change; *com-*, intens., and *mutare*, to change.] capable of being commuted; that may be exchanged or interchanged.

com'mū·tāte, *v.t.*; commutated, *pt., pp.*; commutating, *ppr.* [L. *commutatus*, pp. of *commutare*, to change.] in electricity, to change the direction of (an electric current); as, to *commutate* alternating current to direct current.

com·mū·tā'tion, *n.* [L. *commutatio*, a changing, from *commutatus*, pp. of *commutare*, to change.]

1. a passing from one state to another; change; alteration. [Rare.]

So great is the *commutation*, that the soul then hated only that which now only it loves. —South.

2. the act of giving one thing for another; exchange; barter. [Obs.]

The use of money in the commerce and traffick of mankind, is that of saving the *commutation* of more bulky commodities. —Arbuthnot.

3. the act of substituting; substitution.

4. in law, the change of a penalty or punishment to a less severe one.

5. the act of substituting one sort of payment for another.

6. the payment made in such substitution.

7. daily or regular travel by train, etc. between an outlying district and one's place of work in the city; use of a commutation ticket.

8. in electricity, change of the direction of a current by a commutator.

commutation ticket; a ticket issued at a reduced rate by a railroad company or other public carrier, which entitles the holder to repeated passage for a limited number of times, or for an unlimited number of times within a stated period.

cŏm·mūt'ȧ·tive, *a.* relating to exchange; mutually passing from one to another; as, the *commutative* justice of society.

cŏm·mūt'ȧ·tive lạw, in logic, a law stating

that the order in which the elements of certain operations are given is immaterial, as in arithmetic, 6 times 9 is the same as 9 times 6.

çŏm·mūt′ȧ·tive·ly, *adv.* by way of reciprocal exchange.

çom′mū·tā·tŏr, *n.* [from L. *commutatus*, pp. of *commutare*, to change.]

1. a device used in electricity, by means of which alternating currents are changed into direct currents and vice versa, or by means of which the direction of electromotive currents in one part of a circuit is changed in another part.

2. in a dynamo or motor, a revolving part that collects the current from, or distributes it to, the brushes.

çŏm·mūte′, *v.t.*; commuted, *pt., pp.*; commuting, *ppr.* [L. *commutare*, to change; *com-*, intens., and *mutare*, to change.]

1. to exchange; to put (one thing) in the place of another; to give or receive (one thing) for another; as, to *commute* pain for pleasure.

2. to change (one penalty or punishment) to another of less severity; as, to *commute* a sentence of death to life imprisonment.

3. to substitute (one sort of burden) for another, especially to substitute (money payment) for the performance of a payment in kind or a compulsory duty; as, to *commute* tithes.

4. in electricity, to commutate.

5. to pay in one sum, instead of in installments; as, to *commute* a pension.

Syn.—exchange, barter, alter, mitigate.

çŏm·mūte′, *v.i.* 1. to be a substitute; to stand in the place (of); as, one penalty *commutes* for another.

2. to pay in an aggregate sum, often reduced, instead of in installments; as, to *commute* for annual railroad fare or freight charges.

3. to pay in money instead of in kind or in service.

4. to travel daily or regularly by train, etc. between an outlying district and one's place of work in the city; use a commutation ticket.

çŏm·mūt′ẽr, *n.* one who commutes; particularly, one who uses a commutation ticket.

çŏm·mū′tū·ăl (-chọọ-), *a.* [*com-*, and L. *mutuus*, mutual.] mutual; reciprocal.

There, with *commutual* zeal, we both had strove
In acts of dear benevolence and love.
—Pope.

çō·mol′e·çūle, *n.* in physical chemistry, a molecule whose atoms are joined together by pairs of electrons.

çō′mōse, *a.* [L. *comosus*, hairy, from *coma*, hair.] in botany, having a tuft of hairs.

Çō′mox, *n.* a native of the British Columbian coast belonging to the Salishan tribes of Indians.

çŏm·paçt′ (*or* çom′paçt), *a.* [Fr. *compacte*, a compact, from L. *compactus*, pp. of *compingere*, to join; *com-*, together, and *pangere*, to fasten.]

1. closely and firmly united, as the particles of solid bodies; solid; dense; as, a *compact* mass of people; a *compact* body or substance.

2. composed; consisting: with *of*.

A wandering fire,
Compact of unctuous vapor. —Milton.

3. joined; held together. [Obs.]

A pipe of seven reeds *compact* with wax together. —Peacham.

4. brief; terse; pithy; not diffuse; not verbose; as, a *compact* discourse.

5. taking little space; arranged neatly in a small space.

6. designating or of a relatively small, light, economical model of automobile.

Syn.—close, condensed, hard, solid.

çom′paçt, *n.* [L. *compactum*, an agreement, from *compactus, compectus*, pp. of *compacisci*, or *compecisci*, to make an agreement; *com-*, with, and *pacisci*, to fix, settle.] an agreement; a contract between parties: applied, in a general sense, to any covenant or contract between individuals, but more generally applied to agreements between nations and states, as treaties and conventions.

çom′paçt, *n.* a small case, fitted with a mirror and containing face powder, a powder puff, and, sometimes, rouge and lipstick: usually designed to be carried in a purse.

çŏm·paçt′, *v.t.*; compacted, *pt., pp.*; compacting, *ppr.* 1. to press closely together; to join firmly; to consolidate; to make close, as the parts which compose a body.

Now the bright sun *compacts* the precious stone. —Blackmore.

2. to unite or connect firmly, as in a system; to make by joining together.

The whole body fitly joined together and *compacted*. —Eph. iv. 16.

3. to condense.

çŏm·paçt′ed, *a.* pressed close; firmly united or connected.

çŏm·paçt′ed·ly, *adv.* in a compact manner.

çŏm·paçt′ed·ness, *n.* a state of being compact; firmness; closeness of parts; density.

çŏm·paçt′ẽr, *n.* one who makes a compact.

çŏm·paçt′i·ble, *a.* capable of being closely joined or united.

çŏm·paç′tion, *n.* the act of making compact; also, the state of being compact. [Obs.]

çŏm·paçt′ly, *adv.* closely; densely; with close union of parts.

çŏm·paçt′ness, *n.* firmness; close union of parts; density.

çŏm·paç′tŏr, *n.* **a device that compresses trash into small bundles for easy disposal.**

çŏm·paç′tūre, *n.* close union or connection of parts; manner of compacting. [Obs.]

çŏm·pā′ġēş, *n.* [L. *compages*, a joining together, from *compingere*, to fix, fasten together; *com-*, together, and *pangere*, to fasten.] a system or structure of many parts united.

çŏm·paġ′i·nāte, *v.t.* **to unite or join. [Obs.]**

çŏm·paġ·i·nā′tion, *n.* [LL. *compaginatio*, a joining, from *compaginare*; L. *compingere*, to join together.] union of parts; connection; contexture. [Obs.]

çŏm·pȧ·gnie′ (kōṅ-pȧ-nyē′), *n.* [Fr.] company.

com·pa·ñi′a (kọm-pä-nyē′ä), *n.* [Sp.] company.

çŏm·pan′i·ȧ·ble, *a.* companionable. [Obs.]

çŏm·pan′i·ȧ·ble·ness, *n.* sociableness. [Obs.]

çŏm·pan′iŏn (-yun), *n.* [ME. *compainoun*; OFr. *compainon*, companion; L. *com-*, with, and *panis*, bread.]

1. one who keeps company with another; one with whom a person associates. The word often connotes friendship or comradeship.

2. one who accompanies another; specifically, a person employed to live or travel with another.

3. a partner; an associate. [Obs.]

4. a mate; a thing that matches another in sort, color, etc.; one of a set of things.

5. [C—] one of the lowest rank in an English order of knighthood; as, a *Companion* of the Bath.

companion hatch; a wooden covering placed over the staircase to the cabin in a merchant ship: the cabin stairs are called the *companionway*.

companion ladder; (a) the ladder by which officers ascend to and descend from the quarter-deck; (b) the ladder or stairs in a companionway.

Syn.—associate, comrade, consort, friend.

çŏm·pan′iŏn, *v.t.* to attend on; to act as a companion to; to accompany.

çŏm·pan′iŏn, *n.* [D. *kampagne*, quarter-deck, from OFr. *compagne*, steward's room in a galley; It. (*camera della*) *compagna* (room of the) company, crew.]

1. a companion hatch.

2. a companionway.

çŏm·pan″iŏn·ȧ·bil′i·ty, *n.* **the quality of being companionable.**

çŏm·pan′iŏn·ȧ·ble, *a.* fit for good fellowship; sociable; agreeable as a companion.

çŏm·pan′iŏn·ȧ·ble·ness, *n.* agreeableness; good fellowship.

çŏm·pan′iŏn·ȧ·bly, *adv.* in a companionable manner; sociably.

çŏm·pan′iŏn·ăte, *n.* of or characteristic of companions.

çŏm·pan′iŏn·ăte mar′riaġe (-rij), marriage in which the couple would not have children until they are sure that they wish to stay married: divorce by mutual consent would be permitted before children are born.

çŏm·pan′iŏn·less, *a.* having no companion.

çŏm·pan′iŏn·ship, *n.* 1. good fellowship; association; the state of being a companion.

2. a group of companions.

3. [C—] the lowest rank in an order of knighthood.

çŏm·pan′iŏn·wāy, *n.* 1. on shipboard, the stairway leading from the deck to the cabins or space below.

2. the space taken up by this stairway.

çŏm′pȧ·ny, *n.* [ME. *companye*; OFr. *compainie*, company; L. *com-*, with, and *panis*, bread.]

1. in military affairs, the body of soldiers united under the command of a captain: it is the lowest administrative unit, usually a subdivision of a regiment, and is equivalent to *battery* (artillery), *flight* (air forces), *troop* (cavalry).

2. an assemblage of persons; a collection of men, or, rarely, of animals, in an indefinite sense.

3. an assemblage of persons for social purposes.

4. persons that associate with others habitually; as, let your children keep good *company*.

5. the state of being a companion; the act of accompanying; fellowship; society; as, we should not frequent the *company* of licentious men.

6. a number of persons united for the same purpose, either in private partnership or as a business concern; as, an insurance *company*; a theatrical *company*.

7. (a) the crew of a ship, including the officers; (b) [Obs.] a fleet.

8. the members of a firm whose names do not appear in the firm name: generally shortened to *Co.*

9. a guest or guests; a visitor or visitors. [Colloq.]

Company of Jesus; see *Jesuit*.

to bear company; to accompany; to attend.

to keep company; to accompany; to attend; also, to associate (*with*) frequently or habitually; to associate (*with*), as a lover or suitor.

to part company; (a) to stop associating (*with*); (b) to separate and go in different directions.

Syn.—assembly, association, congregation, corporation, syndicate, trust, collection, group, gathering, crowd, band, horde, crew, gang, troop.

çŏm′pȧ·ny, *v.t.*; companied, *pt., pp.*; companying, *ppr.* to accompany; to go with; to be a companion to. [Archaic.]

çŏm′pȧ·ny, *v.i.* 1. to associate; to keep company. [Archaic.]

2. to be a gay companion. [Obs.]

3. to have sexual intercourse. [Obs.]

çŏm′pȧ·ny of′fi·cẽr, in military usage, any commissioned officer below the rank of major.

çŏm′pȧ·ny ūn′iŏn (-yun), an organization of workers in one company, factory, or business establishment, not affiliated with any group of labor unions: the term generally implies control by the employers.

çom″pȧ·rȧ·bil′i·ty, *n.* the quality or state of being comparable.

çom′pȧ·rȧ·ble, *a.* [L. *comparabilis*, comparable, from *comparare*, to compare.] capable of being compared or equaled; worthy of comparison; being of equal regard.

There is no blessing of life *comparable* to the enjoyment of a discreet and virtuous friend. —Addison.

çom′pȧ·rȧ·ble·ness, *n.* the quality of being comparable.

çom′pȧ·rȧ·bly, *adv.* 1. in a comparable manner.

2. to a comparable degree.

çom′pȧ·rāte, *n.* [from L. *comparatus*, pp. of *comparare*, to compare.] in logic, one of two things which are compared. [Obs.]

çom·pȧ·rā′tion, *n.* comparison. [Obs.]

çŏm·par′ȧ·tive, *a.* [L. *comparativus*, comparative, from *comparatus*, pp. of *comparare*, to compare.]

1. pertaining to or making use of comparison; involving comparison as a method, especially in a branch of study; as, the *comparative* sciences.

2. estimated by comparison; not positive or absolute; relative; as, *comparative* good or evil; the *comparative* weight of a body.

3. having the power of comparing different things; as, a *comparative* faculty.

4. in grammar, designating the second degree of comparison of adjectives and adverbs; expressing a greater degree of a quality than the positive degree.

comparative anatomy, psychology, etc.; see under the nouns.

comparative sciences; those sciences which endeavor to deduce scientific conclusions from various groups of related phenomena, as comparative anatomy, comparative psychology, etc.

çŏm·par′ȧ·tive, *n.* 1. a rival; one who is equal or aspires to be an equal. [Obs.]

2. one who makes comparisons. [Obs.]

3. in grammar, (a) the comparative degree; as, *prettier* and *more beautiful* are the *comparatives* of *pretty* and *beautiful*; (b) an adjective or adverb in the comparative degree.

çom·par′ȧ·tive liñ·guis′tiçs, the branch of linguistics which discovers and describes genetic relationships between languages.

çŏm·par′ȧ·tive·ly, *adv.* in comparison; by comparison; according to estimate made by comparison; not positively or absolutely.

çom′pȧ·rā·tŏr, *n.* any of various instruments for making comparisons of some measurement or other aspect of something, as for comparing the lengths of nearly equal bars.

çŏm·pāre′, *v.t.*; compared, *pt., pp.*; comparing, *ppr.* [L. *comparare,* to compare; *com-,* with, and *par,* equal.]

1. to set or bring (things) together in fact or in contemplation, and to examine the relations they bear to each other, especially with a view to ascertain their agreement or disagreement, points of resemblance or difference (often followed by *with*); as, to *compare* pieces of cloth, tables, or two coins; to *compare* reasons and arguments.

2. to liken; to represent as similar, for the purpose of illustration (followed by *to*).

Solon *compared* the people *to* the sea, and orators and counselors *to* the winds. —Bacon.

3. in grammar, to form in the positive, comparative, and superlative degrees of comparison, as an adjective or adverb; as, *black, blacker, blackest.*

to compare notes; to exchange opinions or views; to compare the results of inquiry or investigation.

çŏm·pāre′, *v.i.* 1. to be worthy or admit of comparison (*with* anything else); to be regarded as similar or equal.

2. to vie; to emulate.

çŏm·pāre′, *n.* 1. comparison. [Poet.]

Their small galleys may not hold *compare* With our tall ships. —Waller.

2. simile; similitude; illustration by comparison. [Obs.]

Protest, and oath, and big *compare.* —Shak.

beyond (or *past* or *without*) *compare*; without equal; incomparably good, bad, great, etc.

çŏm·pāre′, *v.t.* to get; to procure. [Obs.]

çŏm·pâr′ẽr, *n.* one who compares or makes a comparison.

çŏm·par′i·sŏn, *n.* [ME. *comparison*; OFr. *comparaisun*; L. *comparatio,* a comparison, from *comparare,* to compare.]

1. the act of comparing; the act of considering the relation between persons or things, in order to estimate their similarities or differences.

2. the state of being compared; a comparative estimate.

3. in grammar, the modification of an adjective or adverb to show its three degrees of quality; as, *strong, stronger, strongest; glorious, more glorious, most glorious; slowly, more slowly, most slowly.*

4. a simile; similitude, or illustration by similitude; a parallel.

Whereunto shall we liken the kingdom of God? Or with what *comparison* shall we compare it? —Mark iv. 30.

5. in rhetoric, a figure of speech by which two things are compared.

6. in phrenology, the faculty of reasoning, analyzing, or making contrasts.

7. the quality of being capable or worthy of comparison; similarity; likeness.

beyond comparison; so surpassing in quality as not to admit comparison with anything else.

in comparison with; as contrasted with, or with reference to.

no comparison between; no basis for comparison between: implying great superiority of one person or thing to another.

Syn.—likeness, analogy, similitude.

çŏm·par′i·sŏn, *v.t.* and *v.i.* to compare. [Obs.]

çŏm·pärt′, *v.t.*; comparted, *pt., pp.*; comparting, *ppr.* [OFr. *compartir,* to divide; L. *compartiri,* to share; *com-,* with, and *partiri,* to divide.] to subdivide; to divide into parts or subdivisions.

çōm·pär·tï·men′tō, *n.*; *pl.* **çōm·pär·tï·men′tï,** [It.] one of the conventional divisions into which the provinces of Italy are grouped.

çom·pär·ti′tion, *n.* the act of dividing into parts or compartments.

çŏm·pärt′ment, *n.* [Fr. *compartiment,* compartment; L. *com-,* with, and *partiri,* to divide, from *pars,* part.]

1. any of the divisions into which a space is partitioned off.

2. a small, private section of a railroad car with sleeping accommodations.

3. in art and architecture, a division of a work or design, as a painting, a wall, or a ceiling; a panel.

çŏm′pȧss, *n.* [ME. *compas, cumpas,* a circle, compass; OFr. *compas,* a circle; L. *com-,* with, and *passus,* a pace.]

1. stretch; reach; extent; the limit or boundary of a space, and the space included: applied to time, space, sound, etc.; as, our knowledge lies within a very narrow *compass*; the universe extends beyond the *compass* of our thoughts.

DRAWING COMPASS

2. moderate bounds; limits of truth; moderation.

In two hundred years (I speak within *compass*) no such commission had been executed. —Davies.

3. a passing around; a course; a circuit. [Archaic.]

My life has run its *compass.* —Shak.

4. in music, the range of notes that can be covered by any voice or instrument.

5. [*often pl.*] an instrument consisting of two pointed legs connected at one end by a pivot, used for drawing arcs or circles and taking measurements.

6. a boundary; circumference.

7. an enclosed area.

8. any of various instruments for showing direction, especially one consisting of a magnetic needle swinging freely on a pivot and pointing to the magnetic north.

9. intent; purpose; design. [Rare.]

10. in zoology, a forked structure in the dental system of an echinoderm.

11. a circle; the circle of the earth. [Obs.]

12. in archery, the curve described by an arrow in its flight.

azimuth compass; see under *azimuth.*

dumb compass; a compass card without a needle, but sometimes furnished with sight vanes: used in taking bearings.

gyrostatic compass; same as *gyrocompass.*

mariner's compass; a compass used for directing or ascertaining the course of ships at sea. It consists of a circular box or bowl, containing a card marked with the thirty-two points of the compass, with a magnetic needle attached, that always points to the magnetic north. The needle, with the card attached to it, turns on a pivot in the center of the box. The box is covered with glass, and is so suspended as to remain always in a horizontal position, notwithstanding the motion of the ship. On many ships the compass used is a *liquid compass,* the card floating on a fluid consisting of a mixture of alcohol and water, the box or bowl being hermetically sealed.

plain compass; an instrument used by surveyors, including a compass, level, and horizontal circle, attached to a staff.

points of the compass; the thirty-two points of direction into which the card of the mariner's compass is divided.

pole or *masthead compass*; a compass elevated above the deck of a ship to diminish the effect of the ship's magnetic attraction.

surveyor's compass; an instrument used by surveyors for measuring horizontal angles.

to fetch a compass; to make a circuit or go in a roundabout way.

variation compass; a compass of especially fine construction used in making observations and calculations of the variation of the magnetic needle from true north.

çŏm′pȧss, *v.t.*; compassed, *pt., pp.*; compassing, *ppr.* [ME. *compassen, cumpassen*; OFr. *compasser,* to go around, from *compas,* a circle.]

1. to grasp mentally; understand; comprehend.

2. to surround; to environ; to enclose on all sides: sometimes followed by *around, round,* or *about.*

Now, all the blessings
Of a glad father *compass* thee *about.* —Shak.

3. to go or walk round.

Ye shall *compass* the city . . . and the seventh day ye shall *compass* the city seven times. —Josh. vi. 3, 4.

4. to besiege; to beleaguer; to block up.

5. to obtain; to attain; to bring within one's power; to accomplish.

How can you hope to *compass* your designs? —Denham.

6. to purpose; to intend; to imagine; to plot; to contrive (something harmful); as, to *compass* the death of the king.

7. to bend into a curve or circle: a term used in ship carpentry. [Obs.]

Syn.—acquire, master, attain, realize, obtain, gain, accomplish, achieve, effect, secure.

çŏm′pȧss, *a.* round; circular or semicircular.

çŏm′pȧss·ȧ·ble, *a.* capable of being compassed; attainable.

çŏm′pȧss bōwl, çŏm′pȧss box, the glass-covered, metal box or receptacle of a mariner's compass.

çŏm′pȧss brick, a kind of curved brick.

çŏm′pȧss çärd, the circular card over which the magnetic needle of a compass swings, marked with the thirty-two points of the compass and, often, the degrees of the circle.

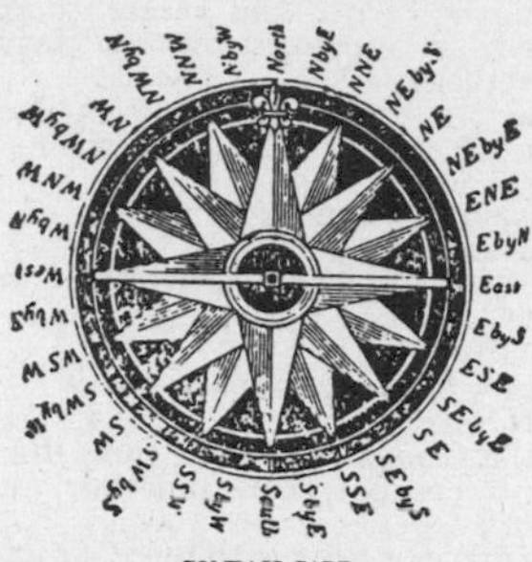

COMPASS CARD

çŏm′pȧss dī′ăl, a compass card; also, a compass combined with a small sundial.

çŏm′pȧssed (-pȧst), *a.* arched; rounded; as, a *compassed* window. [Obs.]

çŏm′pȧss·eș, *n.pl.* a compass (sense 5).

çŏm′pȧss-head″ed (-hed″), *a.* in architecture, semicircular at the top.

çŏm′pȧss·ing, *a.* arched; curved.

çŏm·pas′sion, *n.* [ME. *compassion*; OFr. *compassion*; LL. *compassio,* sympathy; L. *com-,* with, and *passus,* pp. of *pati,* to suffer.] a suffering with another; hence, sympathy; sorrow for the distress or misfortunes of another, with the desire to help; pity; commiseration.

Syn.—pity, commiseration, fellow feeling, sympathy, kindness, tenderness, clemency.

çŏm·pas′sion, *v.t.* to pity. [Obs.]

çŏm·pas′sion·ȧ·ble, *a.* deserving of pity. [Rare.]

çŏm·pas′sion·āte, *a.* 1. having a disposition to pity; full of compassion; inclined to show mercy or pity; sympathetic.

There never was a heart truly great and generous, that was not also tender and *compassionate.* —South.

2. inviting compassion; pitiable; piteous. [Obs.]

Syn.—merciful, tender, soft, indulgent, kind, clement, gracious.

çŏm·pas′sion·āte, *v.t.*; compassionated, *pt., pp.*; compassionating, *ppr.* to pity; to commiserate; to have compassion for.

Compassionates my pains, and pities me. —Addison.

çŏm·pas′sion·āte·ly, *adv.* with compassion; in a compassionate manner.

çŏm·pas′sion·āte·ness, *n.* the quality of being compassionate.

çŏm′pȧss·less, *a.* having no compass.

çŏm′pȧss plāne, a plane used by carpenters for smoothing concave surfaces. Its under surface is convex.

çŏm′pȧss plant, an American prairie plant, *Silphium laciniatum,* whose lower leaves have their vertical edges in a north-and-south direction: called also *rosinweed* and *polar plant.*

çŏm′pȧss sąw, a saw with a narrow, tapering blade that can cut in a circular manner, as a keyhole saw.

çŏm′pȧss sig′năl, a signal showing a particular point of the compass.

çŏm′pȧss tim′bẽr, any timber that is not straight: a ship carpenter's term.

çŏm′pȧss win′dōw, a window shaped like the arc of a circle; a bow window.

çom·pȧ·tẽr′ni·ty, *n.* the relationship of a godparent to the real parent of a child.

çŏm·pat·i·bil′i·ty, *n.* the quality of being compatible.

çŏm·pat′i·ble, *a.* [Fr. *compatible,* compatible; L. *com-,* with, and *pati,* to suffer.] capable of living together harmoniously or getting along well together; in agreement; congruous: often followed by *with*.

The poets have joined qualities which by nature are the most *compatible*. —Broome.

cŏm·pat′i·ble·ness, *n.* compatibility.

cŏm·pat′i·bly, *adv.* in a compatible manner; fitly; suitably; consistently.

çom·pā′tient (-shent), *a.* suffering together. [Obs.]

çom·pā′tri·ŏt, *n.* [Fr. *compatriote*; L. *com-*, with, and LL. *patriota*; Gr. *patriōtēs*, a fellow countryman.] a fellow countryman.

çom·pā′tri·ŏt, *a.* of the same country.

çom·pā′tri·ŏt·ism, *n.* the state of being a compatriot.

çom·pēar′, çom·peer′, *v.i.* [L. *comparere*, to appear; *com-*, with, and *parere*, to appear.] in Scots law, to appear in court either in person or by attorney.

çom·peer′, *n.* [ME. *compeer*, *compere*; L. *compar*, equal, an equal; *com-*, with, and *par*, equal.]

1. an equal; a peer; a person of the same rank or status.

2. a companion; an associate; a mate.

çom·peer′, *v.t.* to equal; to match; to be equal with. [Obs.]

çom·peer′, *v.i.* to compear.

cŏm·pel′, *v.t.*; compelled, *pt.*, *pp.*; compelling, *ppr.* [ME. *compellen*; OFr. *compellir*; L. *compellere*, to compel; *com-*, together, and *pellere*, to drive.]

1. to drive or urge with force, or irresistibly; to constrain; to oblige; to necessitate, either by physical or moral force; as, circumstances *compel* us to practice economy.

2. to take by force or violence; to bring about by force.

The subjects' grief
Comes through commissions, which *compel* from each
A sixth part of his substance. —Shak.

3. to drive together; to gather; to unite in a crowd or company: a Latinism.

4. to overpower; to cause to yield.

And easy sleep their weary limbs *compelled*. —Dryden.

5. to call forth. [Poet.]

Syn.—constrain, coerce, oblige, drive, force.

cŏm·pel′, *v.i.* to use irresistible force; as, if necessity *compels*, I will submit.

cŏm·pel′lȧ·ble, *a.* capable of being driven, forced, or constrained.

cŏm·pel′lȧ·bly, *adv.* by compulsion.

çom·pel·lā′tion, *n.* [L. *compellatio*, an accosting, from *compellare*, to address, rebuke.]

1. a ceremonious appellation; a name or title used in direct address; as, the *compellation* of the kings of France was *Sire*.

2. an addressing or calling upon by such a name or title.

cŏm·pel′lȧ·tive, *n.* a descriptive name; a proper name; an appellative.

cŏm·pel′lȧ·tive, *a.* denoting address: applied to grammatical forms.

cŏm·pel′lȧ·tō·ry, *a.* capable of compelling; tending to compel or constrain; compulsory. [Rare.]

cŏm·pel′lẽr, *n.* one who compels or constrains

çom′pend, *n.* same as *compendium*.

cŏm·pen·di·ā′ri·ous, *a.* short; contracted; compendious. [Obs.]

cŏm·pen′di·āte, *v.t.* to sum up in a concise manner. [Obs.]

cŏm·pen′di·ous, *a.* [L. *compendiosus*, short, from *compendium*, a weighing together; abridgment.] short; succinct; abridged; comprehensive; containing the substance or general principles of a subject or work in a brief form.

cŏm·pen′di·ous·ly, *adv.* in a short or brief manner; summarily; in brief; in epitome; as, *compendiously* written.

cŏm·pen′di·ous·ness, *n.* shortness; brevity; comprehension within a narrow compass.

cŏm·pen′di·um, *n.* [L. *compendium*, a weighing together, an abridgment, from *compendere*, to weigh together; *com-*, together, and *pendere*, to weigh.] a composition containing, in a brief form, the substance of a larger work or the leading features of a subject; a summary; an abstract.

cŏm·pen′sȧ·ble, *a.* [Fr.] entitling to compensation, as an injury.

çom′pen·sāte, *v.t.*; compensated, *pt.*, *pp.*; compensating, *ppr.* [L. *compensatus*, pp. of *compensare*, to weigh together, or weigh one thing against another; *com-*, with, and *pensare*, to weigh.]

1. to give equal value to; to recompense; to pay; as, to *compensate* a laborer for his work.

2. to be equivalent in value or effect to; to counterbalance; to make up for.

The length of the night and the dews do *compensate* the heat of the day. —Bacon.

3. in mechanics, to counteract or make allowance for (a variation).

4. in psychology, to disguise (an undesired trait) by exaggerating a desired or socially approved one.

çom′pen·sāte, *v.i.* to make compensation; to make amends; to supply an equivalent: often followed by *for*; as, nothing can *compensate for* the loss of a good reputation.

Syn.—recompense, remunerate, reward, indemnify, requite, countervail, counterbalance.

çom·pen·sā′tion, *n.* [L. *compensatio*, a weighing together, a compensation, from *compensare*, to weigh together, compensate.]

1. that which is given or received as an equivalent for services, debt, want, loss, suffering, etc.; amends; remuneration; recompense.

All other debts may *compensation* find. —Dryden.

2. the act of compensating or state of being compensated.

3. in law, a setoff; the settlement of debt by the debtor's establishment of a counterclaim against his creditor.

4. an instance or means of compensating.

5. in biology, the counterbalancing of a defect in the structure or function of a part by a greater activity or development of another or other parts.

6. in psychology, an attempt to disguise an undesired trait by exaggerating a desired or socially approved trait.

7. in mechanics, any means employed to counteract the effect upon the precision of a piece of mechanism of such exterior forces as temperature.

compensation balance; a balance wheel or pendulum in a timepiece, having several varieties of metal varying in degrees of expansibility, thereby providing for uniformity of movement in all temperatures.

compensation bars; bars formed of two or more metals of different expansibilities, used to produce perfect equality of motion in the balances of watches and chronometers and the pendulums of clocks.

Syn.—remuneration, amends, recompense, indemnity, requital, satisfaction.

çom·pen·sā′tion·ăl, *a.* of or as compensation.

cŏm·pen′sȧ·tive, *a.* making amends or affording compensation.

cŏm·pen′sȧ·tive, *n.* compensation. [Rare.]

çom′pen·sā·tŏr, *n.* 1. one who or that which compensates.

2. any of a number of mechanical or electrical devices for equalizing, counteracting, or correcting deviations in speed, direction, flow, etc.

3. a magnet or sheet of iron placed in proximity to a compass in order to counteract the ship's attraction on the magnetic needle.

4. an automatic appliance to regulate the pressure of gas in the cylinders of gasworks or in the mains.

cŏm·pen′sȧ·tō·ry, *a.* serving to compensate.

cŏm·pense′, *v.t.* and *v.i.* to compensate. [Obs.]

çom·pe·ren′di·nāte, *v.t.* to delay. [Obs.]

çom·pesce′, *v.t.* [L. *compescere*, to restrain; *com-*, with, and *pes*, foot.] to restrain. [Rare.]

cŏm·pēte′, *v.i.*; competed, *pt.*, *pp.*; competing, *ppr.* [L. *competere*, to strive together, compete; *com-*, together, and *petere*, to seek.]

1. to seek or strive for the same thing as another; to carry on competition or rivalry; to strive in opposition.

The sages of antiquity will not dare to *compete* with the inspired authors. —Milner.

2. to enter or participate (*in* a contest, athletic meet, etc.).

çom′pe·tence, çom′pe·ten·cy, *n.* [L. *competens*, ppr. of *competere*, to strive together, be fit, suitable.]

1. capacity equal to requirement; adequate fitness or ability; the state of being competent.

2. property or means of subsistence sufficient to furnish the necessaries and conveniences of life, without superfluity.

Happy years of health and *competence*. —Tennyson.

3. in law, legal capacity, qualification, power, jurisdiction, or fitness; as, the *competence* of a witness to testify; the *competence* of a judge to try a case.

çom′pe·tent, *a.* [OFr. *competent*, competent; L. *competens*, ppr. of *competere*, to be sufficient, strive for.]

1. answering all requirements; suitable; fit; convenient; hence, sufficient; fit for the purpose; adequate; as, a *competent* force.

2. having ability or capacity; duly qualified; as, a *competent* workman.

3. permissible or properly belonging: followed by *to*.

4. in law, legally qualified, authorized, or fit; as, a *competent* judge or court; a *competent* witness.

A *competent* judge is one who has jurisdiction in the case. —Johnson.

çom·pe·ten′tēs, *n.pl.* [LL., from L. *competens*, ppr. of *competere*, to be competent, to compete.] in the early church, such neophytes as, after having received a course of instruction, had applied to be baptized.

çom′pe·tent·ly, *adv.* sufficiently; adequately; suitably; as, the fact has been *competently* proved; a church is *competently* endowed.

çom·pe·ti′tion (-tish′un), *n.* [L. *competitio*, an agreement, rivalry, from L. *competitus*, pp. of *competere*, to compete.]

1. the act of seeking or endeavoring to gain that for which another is also striving; rivalry; strife for superiority; as, the *competition* of two candidates for an office.

2. a contest; a match.

3. official participation in organized sport.

4. opposition, or effective opposition, in a contest or match.

5. business rivalry; competing for customers or markets.

Syn.—emulation, rivalry, contention.

cŏm·pet′i·tive, *a.* relating to or involving competition; inducing competition; based on or determined by competition; as, a *competitive* examination.

cŏm·pet′i·tŏr, *n.* [L. *competitor*, a rival, from *competitus*, pp. of *competere*, to compete.]

1. one who endeavors to obtain what another seeks; one who claims what another claims; a rival; one who competes.

2. a friendly associate in the same cause. [Obs.]

cŏm·pet′i·tō·ry, *a.* rivaling; acting or done in competition; competitive.

cŏm·pet′i·tress, cŏm·pet′i·trix, *n.* a woman competitor.

çom·pi·lā′tion, *n.* [Fr. *compilation*, compilation; L. *compilatio*, a pillaging, plundering; hence, contemptuously of a collection of documents, a compilation, from *compilatus*, pp. of *compilare*, to plunder, pilfer.]

1. the act of compiling or collecting from different sources.

2. that which is compiled or collected from different sources, as a collection of material from various publications, to form a separate work.

çom′pi·lā·tŏr, *n.* a compiler.

cŏm·pīle′, *v.t.*; compiled, *pt.*, *pp.*; compiling, *ppr.* 1. to collect (material) from different sources and put in a new form; especially, to prepare, as a written or printed work, by collecting and collating literary material; as, to *compile* a gazetteer; to *compile* a history of the world.

2. to write; to compose. [Obs.]

3. to put together; to build. [Obs.]

4. to contain; to comprise. [Obs.]

cŏm·pīle′ment, *n.* compilation. [Rare.]

cŏm·pī′lẽr, *n.* [ME. *compilour*; OFr. *compileor*; L. *compilator*, a compiler, from *compilare*, to snatch together.] one who compiles; especially, one who gathers literary material from different sources for publication in a new form.

cŏm·pinġe′, *v.t.* to confine; to compress; to close up. [Obs.]

cŏm·plā′cen·cy, cŏm·plā′cence, *n.* [L. *complacens*, ppr. of *complacere*, to be very pleasing; *com-*, with, and *placere*, to please.]

1. quiet satisfaction; contentment.

2. self-satisfaction; smugness.

3. complaisance; civility; disposition to please.

Every moment of her life brings me fresh instances of her *complacency* to my inclinations. —Steele.

cŏm·plā′cent, *a.* 1. displaying complacence;

self-satisfied; smug; as, a *complacent* look or smile.
2. kindly; complaisant.

çom·plā·cen'tiăl (-shăl), *a.* marked by complacence.

çŏm·plā'cent·ly, *adv.* in a complacent manner.

çŏm·plāin', *v.i.*; complained, *pt., pp.*; complaining, *ppr.* [ME. *complaynen*; OFr. *complaindre*, to complain; L. *com-*, with, and *plangere*, to strike.]
1. to utter expressions of grief, pain, dissatisfaction, etc.; to lament; as, he *complained* tearfully of his condition.
2. to utter expressions of annoyance or resentment; to find fault; as, he *complained* bitterly of his treatment.
3. to accuse formally of an offense; to present an accusation.
Syn.—bewail, bemoan, deplore, murmur, grumble, grieve, repine.

çŏm·plāin'ȧ·ble, *a.* that may be complained of.

çŏm·plāin'ănt, *n.* 1. one who makes a complaint; a complainer.
2. in law, a person who files a charge or makes the complaint in court; a plaintiff.

çŏm·plāin'ẽr, *n.* one who complains.

çŏm·plāin'fụl, *a.* full of complaint. [Rare.]

çŏm·plāin'ing, *n.* complaint.

çŏm·plāint', *n.* 1. expression of grief, regret, discomfort, dissatisfaction, pain, censure, or resentment; a finding fault.
2. the cause or subject of complaint; a grievance.
The poverty of the clergy hath been the *complaint* of all who wish well to the church. —Swift.
3. an illness; an ailment; a disease; as, his physical *complaints* were aggravated by his mental troubles.
4. in law, a formal charge or accusation.

çŏm·plāint'fụl, *a.* prone to complain; complainful. [Rare.]

çom'plāi·ṣănce, *n.* [Fr. *complaisance*, complaisance, from *complaire*; L. *complacere*, to please.]
1. willingness to please; disposition to be obliging and agreeable; courtesy; politeness; as, the gentleman received us with *complaisance*.
2. an act or instance of this.

çom'plāi·ṣănt, *a.* [Fr. *complaisant*, pleasing, ppr. of *complaire*; L. *complacere*, to please.] pleasing in manners; courteous; obliging; desirous to please; as, a *complaisant* gentleman.
Syn.—affable, gracious, benign, condescending, benignant, urbane, courteous.

çom'plāi·ṣănt·ly, *adv.* in a complaisant manner.

çom'plāi·ṣănt·ness, *n.* civility; complaisance. [Rare.]

çom'plā·nāte, *a.* 1. leveled; reduced to an even surface.
2. in botany, lying in the same plane, as the leaves of certain mosses.

çom'plā·nāte, *v.t.* [L. *complanatus*, pp. of *complanare*, to make level; *com-*, together, and *planum*, a plain.] to make level; to reduce to an even surface. [Obs.]

çŏm·plect', *v.t.* 1. to place the arms around; to embrace. [Obs.]
2. to twine together; to interweave.

çŏm·plect'ed, *a.* pertaining to the complexion; of a specified complexion; as, a light-*complected* man. [Dial. or Colloq.]

çom'plē·ment, *n.* [L. *complementum*, that which fills up or completes, from *complere*, to complete; *com-*, intens., and *plere*, to fill.]
1. full quantity or number; full amount; an entirety; a complete set; as, a company has its *complement* of men; a ship has its *complement* of stores.
2. perfect state; fullness; completeness. [Obs.]
3. (a) what is needed to complete or fill up something; (b) that which completes or brings to perfection; (c) something added to complete a whole; either of two parts that complete each other.
4. in grammar, a word or group of words completing a predication. Examples: *president* in *elect him president* (*objective complement*), *pretty* in *she was pretty* (*predicate complement*).
5. in immunology, a protein in the blood or lymph acting with immune bodies to destroy bacteria.
6. in mathematics, the number of degrees that must be added to a given angle or arc to make it equal 90 degrees.
7. in nautical usage, the full crew of officers and men assigned to a ship.
8. in music, the interval needed to complete an octave; as, the *complement* of a third is a sixth; that of a fourth, a fifth; of a fifth, a fourth.
9. in optics, either of two complementary colors with reference to the other.

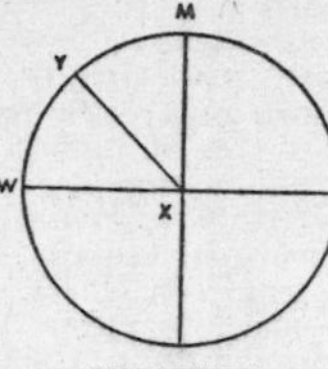

COMPLEMENT
arc YM, complement of arc WY; angle YXM, complement of angle WXY

10. that which is added, not as necessary, but as ornamental; outward show; an accessory. [Obs.]
11. compliment. [Obs.]
arithmetical complement of a number; the difference between a number and the power of ten next in series; as, 2 is the complement of 8, and 24 of 76.

çom'plē·ment, *v.t.* 1. to make complete; to be a complement to.
2. to compliment. [Obs.]

çom·plē·men'tăl, *a.* 1. filling; supplying a deficiency; completing; forming a complement.
2. flattering; courteous. [Obs.]
complemental air; the amount of air which the lungs will hold in addition to an ordinary inhalation.
complemental males; imperfect organisms, such as are found in cirripeds, which are in reality rudimentary males parasitic on hermaphrodites: a term coined by Darwin.

çom·plē·men'tȧ·ry, *n.* anything which complements.

çom·plē·men'tȧ·ry, *a.* 1. helping to fill out; acting as a complement; completing.
2. mutually making up what is lacking.
complementary angle; the angle that is the complement of another, specified angle.
complementary colors; any two colors of the spectrum that combine to form white or whitish light: if a disk colored half yellow and half blue is rotated rapidly, it looks white or gray.

çŏm·plēte', *a.* [ME. *compleet*; OFr. *complet*, complete, full, from L. *completus*, pp. of *complere*, to fill up, complete; *com-*, intens., and *plere*, to fill.]
1. lacking none of the parts; full; whole; entire.
2. finished; ended; concluded; as, the edifice is *complete*.
3. in botany, furnished with all the normal parts; as, a *complete* flower is one having calyx, corolla, stamens, and pistils.
4. perfect; thorough.
5. accomplished; skilled; consummate. [Archaic.]

çŏm·plēte', *v.t.*; completed, *pt., pp.*; completing, *ppr.* 1. to finish; to end; to conclude; as, to *complete* an edifice; to *complete* an education.
2. to make entire, thorough, or perfect.
3. to fulfill; as, to *complete* one's desires.
Syn.—perform, execute, terminate, conclude, finish, end, achieve, realize, effect, consummate, accomplish.

çŏm·plēte'ly, *adv.* fully; perfectly; entirely.

çŏm·plēte'ment, *n.* the act of completing; a finishing. [Obs.]

çŏm·plēte'ness, *n.* the state of being complete.

çŏm·plē'tion, *n.* [LL. *completio*, a filling up, from L. *complere*, to fill up.]
1. fulfillment; accomplishment.
2. the act of completing; the state of being completed; utmost extent; perfect state; as, the *completion* of an education.

çŏm·plē'tive, *a.* filling; making complete. [Rare.]

çom·plē·tō'ri·um, *n.*; *pl.* **çom·plē·tō'ri·ȧ,** [LL., from L. *completus*, pp. of *complere*, to fill up, complete.]
1. the last canonical or daily public prayer of the Roman Catholic breviary; the complin.
2. in the Ambrosian ritual, an evening song of praise.

çŏm·plē'tō·ry, *a.* tending or serving to complete. [Obs.]

çŏm·plē'tō·ry, *n.* same as *complin*.

çom'plex, *a.* [L. *complexus*, pp. of *complecti*, to encircle, embrace; *com-*, with, and *plectere*, to weave, braid.]
1. composed of two or more related parts; composite; not simple; as, a *complex* being.
2. involved; perplexing; difficult; complicated; intricate; as, a *complex* subject.
Syn.—abstruse, complicated, composite, confused, conglomerate, entangled, heterogeneous, intricate, involved.

çom'plex, *n.* 1. a more or less complicated collection or system of related things or parts.
2. in psychoanalysis, (a) a group of emotional attitudes associated with a particular object, activity, etc. and remaining partly unconscious but strongly influencing the individual's behavior; (b) popularly, an exaggerated dislike or fear; an obsession.

çom'plexed, *a.* complex; intricate. [Obs.]

çŏm·plex'ed·ness, *n.* complexity; the state or quality of being complex; as, the *complexedness* of moral ideas.

çom'plex frac'tion, a fraction with a fraction in its numerator or denominator, or in both, as, $\frac{1\,^3/_8}{6\,^1/_4}$: also called *compound fraction*.

çŏm·plex'iŏn (-plek'shun), *n.* [ME. *complexion*; OFr. *complexion*, complexion, constitution; L. *complexio*, a combination, connection, from *complexus*, pp. of *complecti*, to entwine.]
1. originally, the combination of the four humors, or the qualities of cold, heat, dryness, and moisture, in certain proportions believed to determine the temperament and constitution of the body.
2. the temperament or constitution.
3. the color, texture, and general appearance of the skin, particularly of the face.
4. the general appearance of anything; aspect; character; nature.
Men judge by the *complexion* of the sky
The state and inclination of the day. —Shak.
5. the state of being complex; complexity. [Obs.]

çŏm·plex'iŏn·ăl, *a.* depending on or pertaining to complexion; constitutional; as, *complexional* prejudices.

çŏm·plex'iŏn·ăl·ly, *adv.* by complexion; constitutionally. [Rare.]

çŏm·plex'iŏn·ā·ry, *a.* pertaining to the complexion, or to the care of it. [Rare.]

çŏm·plex'iŏned (-shund), *a.* 1. having a certain temperament or state. [Rare.]
2. having a (specified) complexion of the skin: used in hyphenated compounds; as, a dark-*complexioned* man.

çŏm·plex'i·ty, *n.* 1. the state or quality of being complex; complexness.
2. *pl.* **çŏm·plex'i·ties,** that which is fashioned complexly; as, the palace was a network of *complexities*.

çom'plex·ly, *adv.* in a complex manner; not simply.

çom'plex·ness, *n.* the state of being complex.

çom'plex sen'tence, a sentence consisting of a main clause and one or more subordinate clauses (e.g., I would go home if I didn't have to work).

çŏm·plex'us, *n.* [L. *complexus*, an encircling, surrounding, from *complexus*, pp. of *complecti*, to encircle.]
1. a complex or complication.
2. in anatomy, the large muscle connecting the upper vertebrae with the head and chiefly governing its motions.

çŏm·plī'ȧ·ble, *a.* capable of bending or yielding; compliant.

çŏm·plī'ȧ·bly, *adv.* in a compliable manner; in compliance.

çŏm·plī'ănce, *n.* [from L. *complere*, to fill up.]
1. the act of complying; a yielding, as to a request, wish, desire, demand, or proposal; concession; submission.
Let the king meet *compliance* in your looks,
A free and ready yielding to his wishes. —Rowe.
2. a disposition to yield to others; complaisance.
He was a man of few words and great *compliance*. —Clarendon.
Syn.—acquiescence, assent, concession, consent, execution, obedience, performance, submission.

çŏm·plī'ăn·cy, *n.* same as *compliance*.

çŏm·plī'ănt, *a.* complying or tending to comply; yielding; pliant; bending; as, the *compliant* boughs.

çŏm·plī'ănt·ly, *adv.* in a yielding manner.

çom'pli·cȧ·cy, *n.* 1. a state of being complex or complicated.
2. *pl.* **çom'pli·cȧ·cieș,** anything complicated; a complication.

çom′pli·çănt, *a.* folding over: applied to the anterior wings of beetles.

çom′pli·çāte, *v.t.* and *v.i.*; complicated, *pt.*, *pp.*; complicating, *ppr.* [L. *complicatus*, pp. of *complicare*, to fold together; *com-*, together, and *plicare*, to fold, weave.]

1. to fold or twist together; to entangle; to intertwine; to interweave.

2. to make or become intricate, difficult, or involved; as, to *complicate* matters, he was suddenly taken ill.

çom′pli·çāte, *a.* 1. complex; complicated. [Archaic.]

2. in biology, folded lengthwise, as some leaves or insects' wings.

çom′pli·çāt·ed, *a.* [pp. of *complicate.*] made up of parts intricately involved or combined; hard to untangle, solve, understand, analyze, etc.

çom′pli·çāte·ly, *adv.* in a complicated manner. [Obs.]

çom′pli·çāte·ness, *n.* the state of being complicated. [Obs.]

çom·pli·çā′tion, *n.* 1. a complicating.

2. a complicated condition or structure; a complex, involved, or confused relationship of parts.

3. a complicating factor, as in the plot of a story or play.

4. in medicine, a disease or abnormal condition that occurs during another disease.

çom′plice, *n.* an accomplice; an associate. [Archaic.]

çŏm·plic′i·ty, *n.*; *pl.* **çŏm·plic′i·ties,** [LL. *complex*, genit. *complicis*, a participant, from L. *complicare*, to fold together, involve.]

1. the state or fact of being an accomplice; partnership in wrongdoing.

2. complexity.

çŏm·plī′ẽr, *n.* one who complies.

çom′pli·ment, *n.* [Fr. *compliment*; It. *complimento*, a compliment, an expression of civility; L. *complementum*, that which fills up or completes, from *completus*, pp. of *complere*, to fill up; *com-*, intens., and *plere*, to fill.]

1. a formal act or expression of civility, respect, or regard.

Compliments of congratulation are always kindly taken, and cost one nothing but pen, ink, and paper. —Chesterfield.

2. something said in admiration or praise.

3. [*pl.*] courteous greetings; respects: as, please accept this free offer with our *compliments.*

4. a gift given for services. [Archaic and Dial.]

left-handed compliment; an insincere or dubious complimentary expression.

çom′pli·ment, *v.t.*; complimented, *pt.*, *pp.*; complimenting, *ppr.* 1. to praise; to flatter by expressions of approbation, esteem, or respect; to congratulate or pay a compliment to.

She *compliments* Menelaus very handsomely. —Pope.

2. to present something to (a person) as an act of politeness or respect.

Syn.—congratulate, flatter, felicitate, praise.

çom′pli·ment, *v.i.* to pass compliments; to use ceremony or ceremonious language. [Rare.]

çom·pli·men′tăl, *a.* expressive of civility or respect; implying compliments. [Obs.]

çom·pli·men′tăl·ly, *adv.* in the nature of a compliment; by way of civility or ceremony. [Obs.]

çom·pli·men′tăl·ness, *n.* the tendency to be complimentary. [Obs.]

çom·pli·men′tȧ·ry, *a.* 1. expressing civility, regard, or praise; conveying a compliment; as, *complimentary* remarks.

2. given free as a courtesy or in return for a favor; as, a *complimentary* ticket.

çom·pli·men′tȧ·tive, *a.* complimentary.

çom′pli·ment·ẽr, *n.* one who compliments; a flatterer.

çom′plin, çom′pline, *n.* [ME. *complyn*; OFr. *complie*; LL. *completa*, the complin, from f. of L. *completus*, pp. of *complere*, to fill up.] the last of the seven canonical hours; also, the last prayer at night, to be recited after sunset: so called because it closes the service of the day.

çom′plot, *n.* [Fr. *complot*, a plot, conspiracy; OFr. *complot*, a crowd, a battle, a plot, from L. *complicatus*, pp. of *complicare*, to confuse, fold together.] a plotting together; a joint plot; a conspiracy.

I know their *complot* is to have my life. —Shak.

çŏm·plot′, *v.t.* and *v.i.*; complotted, *pt.*, *pp.*; complotting, *ppr.* to plot together; to conspire.

çŏm·plot′ment, *n.* a plotting together; conspiracy. [Rare.]

çŏm·plot′tẽr, *n.* one joined in a plot; a conspirator.

çŏm·plot′ting·ly, *adv.* by complotting.

Çom·plū·ten′siăn, *a.* designating the copy of the Bible first published in 1522 by Cardinal Ximenes, and printed at Complutum, or Alcala de Henares, a city near Madrid.

çom·plu′vi·um, *n.*; *pl.* **çom·plu′vi·ȧ,** [L., from *compluere*, to flow together, in raining; *com-*, together, and *pluere*, to rain.] a large opening in the roof of an ancient Roman house for the admittance of light and air, and through which rain fell into the cistern, or impluvium.

çŏm·plȳ′, *v.i.*; complied, *pt.*, *pp.*; complying, *ppr.* [L. *complere*, to fill up, supply, satiate.]

1. to yield; to yield in compliance; to accord; to act in accordance with a request, demand, order, rule, etc.

2. to be formally polite. [Obs.]

Syn.—accede, assent, concur.

çŏm·plȳ′, *v.t.* to fulfill; also, to bring into conformity. [Obs.]

çŏm·pōne′, *v.t.* to compose; to settle. [Obs.]

com·po′né (çom-pō′nā), *a.* [Fr. *componé*, composed, from L. *componere*, to place together.] in heraldry, composed of small squares of two tinctures alternately in one row: said of a bordure, bend, or other ordinary.

BORDURE COMPONÉ

çŏm·pō′nent, *a.* [L. *componens*, ppr. of *componere*, to place together, compose; *com-*, together, and *ponere*, to place.] serving as one of the parts of a whole; constituent; as, the *component* parts of a vegetable substance; the *component* parts of society.

çŏm·pō′nent, *n.* 1. a part; a constituent; an ingredient.

2. in mechanics, one of the elements into which a vector quantity, as force, velocity, etc., may be resolved on analysis.

çŏm·pō′ny, same as *componé.*

çŏm·pōrt′, *v.i.*; comported, *pt.*, *pp.*; comporting, *ppr.* [Fr. *comporter*, allow, admit of; L. *comportare*, bring together; *com-*, together, and *portare*, to bring.]

1. to bear. [Archaic.]

2. to agree or suit; to accord: followed by *with*; as, charity should *comport with* prudence; his behavior does not *comport with* his station.

çŏm·pōrt′, *v.t.* 1. to behave or conduct (oneself) in a specified manner.

2. to bear; to endure. [Obs.]

çom′pōrt, *n.* behavior; conduct; manner of acting; comportment. [Obs.]

I knew them well, and marked their rude *comport.* —Dryden.

çŏm·pōrt′ȧ·ble, *a.* suitable; consistent. [Obs.]

çŏm·pōrt′ănce, *n.* behavior; deportment. [Obs.]

çom·pōr·tā′tion, *n.* an assemblage. [Obs.]

çŏm·pōrt′ment, *n.* behavior; demeanor; manner of acting; deportment.

çom′pō·sănt, *n.* same as *corposant.*

çŏm·pōṣe′, *v.t.*; composed, *pt.*, *pp.*; composing, *ppr.* [OFr. *composer*, to compose, adjust, settle; L. *componere*, to put together, arrange; *com-*, together, and *ponere*, to put, place.]

1. to form by uniting two or more things; to put together; to form, frame, or fashion.

A casque *composed* by Vulcan's skill. —Shak.

2. to form by being combined or united; to form the substance or constituents of; to constitute; to make up; as, mortar is *composed* of lime, sand, and water.

3. to create (an original musical or literary work); as, to *compose* a sermon; to *compose* a sonata for the piano.

4. to calm; to quiet; to appease.

Compose thy mind;
Nor frauds are here contrived, nor force design'd. —Dryden.

5. to settle; to adjust; as, to *compose* differences.

6. to place in proper form or in a quiet state.

In a peaceful grave my corpse *compose.* —Dryden.

7. to dispose; to put in a proper state or temper for any purpose.

Compose yourself to the situation. —Dickens.

8. in printing, to set (type or matter to be printed).

Syn.—construct, form, frame, fashion, make, constitute, arrange, write, draw up, soothe, calm, pacify, allay, quiet.

çŏm·pōṣe′, *v.i.* 1. to come to terms; to arrange. [Obs.]

2. to create literary or musical works; as, she *composes* well.

3. to set type.

çŏm·pōṣed′, *a.* calm; sedate; quiet; tranquil; free from agitation.

çŏm·pōṣ′ed·ly, *adv.* in a composed manner; calmly; sedately.

çŏm·pōṣ′ed·ness, *n.* the state of being composed; calmness; sedateness; tranquillity.

çŏm·pōṣ′ẽr, *n.* 1. one who composes; especially one who composes music; as, Mozart, the great *composer.*

2. one who or that which quiets or calms.

çŏm·pōṣ′ing, *a.* 1. pertaining to composition.

2. quieting; soothing.

çŏm·pōṣ′ing frāme, in printing, a working stand of wood or metal for holding cases of type when in use by a compositor.

çŏm·pōṣ′ing rọom, a room in which typesetting is done.

çŏm·pōṣ′ing rule, in printing, a thin strip of steel or brass against which type is set in a composing stick.

çŏm·pōṣ′ing stick, in printing, a metal tray in which type is set from the cases. It has one side open and one end adjustable to various lengths of line. It is held in one hand by the compositor.

COMPOSING STICK

Çom·poṣ′i·tae, *n.pl.* [L., from *compositus*, composite, pp. of *componere*, to put together, compose.] a large group of plants, containing over 12,000 described species of herbs or shrubs distributed all over the world. The flowers are generally numerous and sessile, forming a head consisting of a large number of small flowers in clusters surrounded by small leaves. Many varieties are common weeds, as the daisy, dandelion, and thistle, while many are cultivated in gardens, such as the aster, marigold, etc.

çom·poṣ′ite, *a.* [L. *compositus*, compound, composite, pp. of *componere*, to put together; *com-*, together, and *ponere*, to put.]

1. made up of distinct parts, elements, or substances; compounded; as, a *composite* language.

Happiness, like air and water, is *composite.* —Landor.

2. [C–] in architecture, designating one of the classic orders: so called because the capital belonging to it is composed of the features of the other orders, borrowing a quarter-round from the Tuscan and Doric, leaves from the Corinthian, and volutes from the Ionic.

COMPOSITE ORDER

3. in shipbuilding, having a wooden covering over a metal framework; as, a vessel built on the *composite* principle.

4. in botany, belonging to the group *Compositæ*; having the characters of this group; as, a *composite* plant; *composite* flowers.

composite carriage; in England, a railway carriage made up of compartments of different classes, as first, second, and third.

composite number; a number that can be divided without a remainder by some number other than itself or 1: distinguished from *prime number.*

composite photograph; a photograph made by superimposing one or more photographs on another, either on a single negative or on one print from several negatives.

çom·poṣ′ite, *n.* 1. anything made up of separate parts; a compound.

2. in botany, a composite plant.

çom·pō·si′tion, *n.* [ME. *composicion*; OFr. *composition*; L. *compositio*, a putting together, (in rhetoric) a proper arrangement of words, from *compositus*, pp. of *componere*, to put together, arrange; *com-*, together, and *ponere*, to put.]

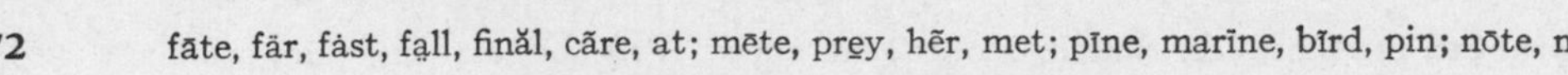

1. the act of composing or compounding, or the state of being composed or compounded.

2. the act of writing prose or poetry; the putting together of words; as, to learn Latin and Greek *composition*.

3. adjustment; orderly disposition; regulation. [Obs.]

4. (a) an agreement; a settlement, often by compromise; (b) in law, a settlement by which a potential bankrupt agrees to pay his creditors part of their claim.

5. that combination of the several parts whereby a subject or object is agreeably presented as a unified harmonious whole, as the arrangement of figures, trees, and vessels in a painting or piece of sculpture, or of doors, windows, piers, columns, pilasters, and cornices in a building, with the view of setting off the whole to the best advantage.

6. in linguistics, the act of forming compounds from separate words.

7. in printing, the act of setting type.

8. the result of an act of composing; that which is composed.

9. relation in a group; the state of being placed together. [Obs.]

10. the creation of musical works.

11. the make-up of a thing; aggregate of ingredients and manner of their combination; constitution.

12. a mixture of various ingredients.

13. a work of music, literature, or art.

14. an exercise in writing done as schoolwork.

composition cloth; a material made from long flax, and dressed with a solution which renders it waterproof.

composition deed; the agreement between an insolvent debtor and those having claims against him.

composition face or *plane*; the common plane in a twin crystal.

composition metal; a kind of brass made of copper, zinc, etc., used as sheathing for vessels.

composition of forces; in mechanics, the process of finding a force (called the *resultant*) whose effect will equal that of two or more given forces (called the *components*).

composition of proportion; in mathematics, the substitution, in a series of four proportionals, of the sum of the first and second terms for the first term, and the sum of the third and fourth for the third, the same equality of proportion subsisting in the second series as in the first.

Syn.—compound, conformation, structure, mixture, combination, compromise, adjustment, settlement.

çŏm·poṣ'i·tive, *a.* compounded; synthetic.

çŏm·poṣ'i·tŏr, *n.* [L. *compositor*, an arranger, or disposer, from *compositus*, pp. of *componere*, to arrange, put together.]

1. in printing, one who sets type; a typesetter.

2. one who composes or settles.

çŏm·poṣ''i·tō'ri·ăl, *a.* having to do with compositors or composers.

çŏm·poṣ'i·tous, *a.* composite; denoting one of the *Compositæ*. [Rare.]

çom'pos men'tis, [L. *compos mentis*, lit., having control of one's mind; *compos*, having control of, and *mens*, genit., *mentis*, mind.] in law, of sound mind; sane: used commonly to denote a sane and responsible person as distinguished from one who is insane and irresponsible.

çom·pos'si·ble, *a.* consistent. [Rare.]

çom'pōst, *n.* [ME. *compost*; OFr. *composte*, a condiment, pickle; It. *composta*, a mixture, conserve, from L. *compositus*, pp. of *componere*, to bring together.]

1. a mixture or composition of decomposing vegetable refuse, manure, etc., used for fertilizing the soil.

2. a composition; a compound; a mixture.

çom'pōst, *v.t.*; composted, *pt.*, *pp.*; composting, *ppr.* to treat with compost.

çom·pos'tūre, *n.* manure. [Obs.]

çŏm·pō'ṣūre, *n.* [from L. *compositus*, pp. of *componere*, to compose, put together.]

1. the act of composing, or that which is composed; as, a form of prayer of public *composure*; a hasty *composure*. [Obs.]

2. composition; arrangement; order. [Obs.]

From the various *composures* of these corpuscles, happen all the varieties of bodies formed out of them. —Woodward.

3. the form, adjustment or disposition of the various parts; as, the *composure* of the body.

4. frame; make; temperament. [Obs.]

His *composure* must be rare indeed,
Whom these things cannot blemish. —Shak.

5. a settled state of the mind; sedateness; calmness; tranquillity; self-possession.

When the passions are silent, the mind enjoys its most perfect *composure*. —Watts.

6. combination; bond. [Obs.]

It was a strong *composure* a fool could disunite. —Shak.

çom·pō·tā'tion, *n.* [L. *compotatio*, a drinking together; *com-*, together, and *potatio*, a drinking, from *potare*, to drink.] the act of drinking or tippling together.

çom'pō·tā·tŏr, *n.* one who drinks with another.

çom'pōte, *n.* [Fr.] 1. a preparation of fruit stewed in sirup so as to retain the form.

2. a long-stemmed dish for candy, fruit, etc.

çom·pō·tier' (-tyā'), *n.* [Fr.] a compote (sense 2).

çŏm·pound' (*or* çom'pound), *v.t.*; compounded, *pt.*, *pp.*; compounding, *ppr.* [ME. *compounen*; OFr. *compondre*, to arrange, direct; L. *componere*, to arrange, put together; *com-*, together, and *ponere*, to put.]

1. to mix; to combine.

We have the power of altering and *compounding* images into all the varieties of picture. —Addison

2. to make by combining parts or elements.

3. to compose; to constitute. [Obs.]

4. in grammar, to unite (two or more words); to form (one word) of two or more.

5. to settle amicably; to adjust by agreement, as a difference or controversy.

I pray, my lords, let me *compound* this strife. —Shak.

6. to settle (a debt) by a compromise payment of less than the total claim.

7. in pharmacy, to mix (substances) according to prescription.

to compound a felony or *crime*; to agree, for a consideration, not to inform about or prosecute for a felony or crime committed: it is an illegal act.

çŏm·pound', *v.i.* 1. to agree; to come to terms of agreement.

They were glad to *compound* for his bare commitment to the Tower. —Clarendon.

2. to come to terms, by granting something on each side.

Cornwall *compounded* to furnish ten oxen for thirty pounds. —Carew.

3. to settle with a creditor by agreement.

çom'pound, *a.* [ME. *compouned*, compound, from *compounen*, to put together, compound.] composed of two or more elements, parts, or ingredients.

compound addition, subtraction, etc.; the addition, subtraction, etc. of compound numbers.

compound engine; an engine in which the steam is expanded under progressively lower pressures from cylinder to cylinder, to avoid excessive loss of steam by condensation.

compound eye; an eye made up of numerous simple eyes (*ocelli*), as in insects and crustaceans.

compound flower; the flower head of a plant of the order *Compositæ*.

compound fraction; a complex fraction.

compound fracture; a fracture in which the broken bone has pierced the skin.

compound householder; in England, one who makes an agreement with his landlord to include his rates in the rent.

compound interest; interest paid on both the principal and the accumulated unpaid interest: distinguished from *simple interest*.

compound interval; in music, any interval greater than an octave.

compound leaf; a leaf composed of several leaflets on one petiole called a common petiole.

compound numbers; quantities consisting of two or more sorts of related units, as 16 days, 8 hours, 7 minutes, 6 seconds.

compound pier; see *clustered column* under *column*.

compound quantities; in algebra, expressions consisting of two or more terms; as, $a + b - c$ and $b^2 - b$ are *compound quantities*.

compound ratio; the ratio which the product of the antecedents of two or more ratios has to the product of their consequents.

compound screw; two or more screws on the same axis. They may vary in size, or run in different directions.

compound sentence; a sentence consisting of two or more independent, co-ordinate clauses (e.g., I came, I saw, I conquered).

compound time; in music, time in which the bar is divided into two or more groups of simple measures, as $\frac{6}{8}$ or $\frac{9}{8}$.

çom'pound, *n.* 1. something produced by combining or mixing two or more ingredients, parts, or elements.

Man is a *compound* of flesh and spirit. —South.

2. a substance containing two or more elements combined in fixed proportions: distinguished from *mixture* in that the constituents of a compound lose their individual characteristics and the compound has new characteristics.

3. a word composed of two or more other words (*free morphemes*), whether hyphenated or not: English compounds are distinguished from phrases by reduced stress on one of the elements (e.g., *black'-bird''*, *black' bird'*) and by reduced pause between the elements (*internal open juncture*); many words conventionally written as phrases are actually compounds and may be treated as such (e.g., *ice' cream'*, *ice'cream''*, *push' but'ton*, *push'-but''ton*).

Syn.—amalgamation, combination, mixture, medley.

çom'pound, *n.* [Malay *campong*, an enclosure.]

1. in the Orient, an enclosed space with a building or group of buildings in it, especially if occupied by foreigners.

2. any similar enclosed space, as for the temporary confinement of prisoners of war.

çŏm·pound'ȧ·ble, *a.* capable of being compounded.

çŏm·pound'ẽr, *n.* 1. one who compounds or mixes.

2. one who attempts to bring parties to terms of agreement. [Rare.]

3. one who compounds with a debtor or felon.

4. one at an English university who pays extraordinary fees, according to his means, for the degree he is to take. [Obs.]

5. in English history, a member of one of the two divisions of the Jacobite party soon after the Revolution, wishing a restoration of James II, accompanied by amnesty and constitutional guarantees.

çom·prä·dōr', çom·prä·dōre', *n.* [Port. and Sp. *comprador*; LL. *comparator*, a buyer; L. *comparatus*, pp. of *comparare*, to prepare, provide.] in China and other Eastern countries, a native agent for a foreign business, who has charge over the native workers, etc.

çom·prē·çā'tion, *n.* a praying together. [Obs.]

çom·prē·hend', *v.t.*; comprehended, *pt.*, *pp.*; comprehending, *ppr.* [ME. *comprehenden*; OFr. *comprendre*; L. *comprehendere*, to seize, lay hold of, comprehend; *com-*, with, and *prehendere*, or *prendere*, to catch hold of, seize.]

1. to include by implication or signification; to imply.

2. to include; to take in; to comprise.

3. to take into the mind; to grasp by the understanding; to possess or have in idea; to understand.

Fantasies that apprehend more than cool reason ever *comprehends*. —Shak.

Syn.—include, comprise, embody, embrace, encompass, contain, involve, understand, apprehend, conceive, discern, perceive, grasp.

çom·prē·hen·si·bil'i·ty, *n.* the quality or fact of being comprehensible; comprehensibleness.

çom·prē·hen'si·ble, *a.* [L. *comprehensibilis*, comprehensible, from *comprehensus*, pp. of *comprehendere*, to lay hold of, comprehend.]

1. capable of being comprehended or included.

2. capable of being understood; intelligible; conceivable.

çom·prē·hen'si·ble·ness, *n.* capability of being comprehensible.

çom·prē·hen'si·bly, *adv.* in a comprehensive manner.

çom·prē·hen'sion, *n.* [L. *comprehensio*, a seizing, laying hold of, comprehension, from *comprehensus*, pp. of *comprehendere*, to lay hold of.]

1. the act of comprehending, including, or comprising.

2. that which comprehends or contains within itself; a summary; an epitome. [Obs.]

3. the act of or capacity for understanding.

4. in rhetoric, a trope or figure, by which

the name of a whole is put for a part, or that of a part for a whole. [Rare.]

5. in logic, all those attributes which make up the notion signified by a general term; all those attributes which are essential to the existence of an object as such.

Body, in its *comprehension*, takes in solidity, figure, quantity, mobility. —Watts.

Syn.—understanding, knowledge, capacity, conception, perception, summary, epitome.

çom·prē·hen′sive, *a.* [LL. *comprehensivus*, comprehensive, from L. *comprehensus*, pp. of *comprehendere*, to comprehend.]

1. having the quality of comprehending well; understanding much.

2. including much; inclusive; as, a *comprehensive* survey.

çom·prē·hen′sive·ly, *adv.* in a comprehensive manner.

çom·prē·hen′sive·ness, *n.* the quality of being comprehensive; as, the *comprehensiveness* of a view.

Compare the beauty and *comprehensiveness* of legends on ancient coins. —Addison.

çom·prē·hen′sŏr, *n.* one who has obtained knowledge. [Obs.]

çŏm·press′, *v.t.*; compressed, *pt., pp.*; compressing, *ppr.* [L. *compressus*, pp. of *comprimere*, to press together, squeeze; *com-*, together, and *premere*, to press.]

1. to press together; to force, urge, or drive into a smaller compass; to condense; as, the air was *compressed.*

2. to embrace sexually. [Obs.]

Syn.—crowd, press, squeeze, condense.

çom′press, *n.* 1. a pad of folded cloth applied to a part of the body to exert pressure.

2. such a pad medicated or dipped in hot or cold water, and used to lessen soreness or inflammation.

3. an apparatus for compressing cotton into bales.

çŏm·pressed′ (-prest′), *a.* 1. pressed together; condensed.

2. flattened laterally or lengthwise; having the two opposite sides flat; as, a *compressed* stem; the *compressed* bill of a bird: chiefly used in botany and zoology.

çŏm·pressed′ âir, air reduced in volume by pressure, held in a container: the force with which it expands when released is used to operate various mechanisms.

çŏm·press·i·bil′i·ty, *n.* the quality or state of being compressible; as, the *compressibility* of elastic fluids.

çŏm·press′i·ble, *a.* capable of being compressed; as, elastic fluids are *compressible.*

çŏm·press′i·ble·ness, *n.* compressibility; the quality of being compressible.

çŏm·pres′sion, *n.* [L. *compressio*, a pressing together, from *compressus*, pp. of *comprimere*, to press or squeeze together.]

1. the act of compressing, or the state of being compressed.

2. in mechanics, the compressing, or the degree of compressing, of a working fluid in an engine, as of steam in the cylinder of a steam engine after the exhaust valve is closed, or of gas in an internal-combustion engine just before ignition.

çŏm·press′ive, *a.* compressing or tending to compress.

çŏm·press′ŏr, *n.* [L., from *compressus*, pp. of *comprimere*, to squeeze, compress.] one who or that which compresses; specifically, (a) in anatomy, a muscle which presses together the parts on which it acts; as, the *compressor naris*, a muscle of the nose; (b) in surgery, an instrument used for compressing different parts of the body, as arteries; (c) an attachment to a microscope, used for compressing objects with the view of rendering the examination of them more complete; (d) in gunnery, a mechanism for compressing a gun carriage to its slide or platform during recoil; (e) a machine for compressing air, gas, etc.

çŏm·pres′sūre (-presh′ūr), *n.* compression.

çom·print′, *v.t.* and *v.i.* to print concurrently. [Obs.]

çŏm·priș′ȧ·ble, çŏm·prīz′ȧ·ble, *a.* that can be comprised.

çŏm·priș′ăl, çŏm·prīz′ăl, *n.* 1. the act of comprising.

2. a summary; an abstract.

çŏm·prīșe′, çŏm·prīze′, *v.t.*; comprised, *pt., pp.*; comprising, *ppr.* [Fr. *compris*, pp. of *comprendre*, to comprehend, include; L. *comprehensus*, or *comprensus*, pp. of *comprehendere*, to comprehend, comprise.]

1. to contain; to include; as, the German empire *comprised* a number of separate states.

Friendship does two souls in one *comprise.* —Roscommon.

2. to consist of; to be composed of.

Syn.—embrace, include, comprehend, contain, encircle, enclose, involve.

çom′prō·bāte, *v.t.* to approve. [Obs.]

çom·prō·bā′tion, *n.* 1. proof; joint attestation. [Obs.]

2. joint approval or approbation. [Obs.]

çom′prō·mīșe, *n.* [Fr. *compromis*; LL. *compromissum*, a compromise, originally a mutual promise, from L. *compromissus*, pp. of *compromittere*, to make a mutual promise, to abide by the decision of an arbiter; *com-*, together, and *promittere*, to promise.]

1. a settlement in which each side gives up some demands or makes concessions.

2. an adjustment of opposing principles, etc. in which part of each is given up.

3. the result of such an adjustment.

4. something midway between different things.

5. a laying open to danger, suspicion, or disrepute; as, a *compromise* of one's good name.

Missouri Compromise; a compromise between the advocates and opponents of slavery, incorporated in the Congressional act by which Missouri was admitted into the Union as a Slave State (1820), and by which in all the other territory of the United States north of 36° 30′ slavery was prohibited: repealed in 1854.

çom′prō·mīșe, *v.t.*; compromised, *pt., pp.*; compromising, *ppr.* 1. to adjust and settle (a difference) by mutual agreement, with concessions on both sides.

2. to agree; to accord. [Obs.]

3. to lay open to danger, suspicion, or disrepute; to endanger the interests of.

4. to surrender or give up (one's interests, principles, etc.).

çom′prō·mīșe, *v.i.* 1. to make a compromise or compromises.

2. to agree. [Obs.]

çom′prō·mī·șẽr, *n.* one who compromises or believes in compromises.

çom″prō·mis·sō′ri·ăl, *a.* relating to a compromise. [Rare.]

çom·prō·mit′, *v.t.*; compromitted, *pt., pp.*; compromitting, *ppr.* [ME. *compromytte*; L. *compromittere*, to make a mutual promise.]

1. to pledge or engage mutually, by some act or declaration. [Obs.]

2. to put to hazard, by some previous act or measure, which cannot be recalled; to compromise; as, to *compromit* the honor or the safety of a nation. [Obs.]

çom·prō·vin′ciăl (-shăl), *n.* one belonging to the same province or archiepiscopal jurisdiction. [Obs.]

çom·prō·vin′ciăl, *a.* relating to or emanating from the same province.

Çomp·sog′nā·thus, *n.* [Gr. *kompsos*, elegant, and *gnathos*, jaw.] a genus of extinct reptiles, of the order *Dinosauria*, having some characteristics of birds.

çompt (kount), *n.* [Fr. *compte*, from L. *computo.*] count. [Obs.]

çompt, *v.t.* to count. [Obs.]

çompt, *a.* neat; spruce. [Obs.]

çompt′ẽr, *n.* counter. [Obs.]

çōmpte ren·dū′ (kōnt räṅ-dü′), **[Fr.]** an account rendered; report; statement.

çompt′i·ble (kount′), *a.* countable. [Obs.]

çompt′ō·grȧph (kount′), *n.* [Fr. *compter*; L. *computare*, to compute, count, and Gr. *graphein*, to write.] an adding machine that automatically makes a record of the results.

çomp·tom′e·tẽr (kom-), *n.* [Fr. *compter*; L. *computare*, to compute, and *metrum*, a measure.] a machine for doing addition, subtraction, multiplication, and division mechanically: a trade-mark (*Comptometer*).

çŏmp·trōl′ (kŏn-), *n.* and *v.* same as *control.*

çŏmp·trōl′lẽr (kŏn-), *n.* an official in charge of expenditures; a controller.

çŏmp·trōl′lẽr·ship (kŏn-), *n.* the position or tenure of office of a comptroller.

çŏm·pul′sȧ·tive, *a.* compulsory. [Rare.]

çŏm·pul′sȧ·tive·ly, *adv.* by constraint or compulsion. [Rare.]

çŏm·pul′sȧ·tō·ry, *a.* compulsory. [Rare.]

çŏm·pul′sion, *n.* [LL. *compulsio*, compulsion, from L. *compulsus*, pp. of *compellere*, to force, drive together, compel; *com-*, together, and *pellere*, to strike.]

1. the act of compelling.

2. the state or fact of being compelled; force; coercion; constraint.

3. in psychopathology, an irresistible impulse to perform some irrational act.

Syn.—coercion, constraint, force, restraint, urgency, necessity, violence, obligation.

çŏm·pul′sive, *a.* having power to compel; driving; forcing; constraining; applying force; as, uniformity of opinions cannot be effected by *compulsive* measures.

çŏm·pul′sive·ly, *adv.* by compulsion; by force.

çŏm·pul′sive·ness, *n.* force; compulsion.

çŏm·pul′sō·ri·ly, *adv.* in a compulsory manner; by force or constraint.

çŏm·pul′sō·ri·ness, *n.* the quality of being compulsory.

çŏm·pul′sō·ry, *a.* 1. having compelling power; coercive; constraining.

2. prescribed by proper authority; obligatory; required; as, *compulsory* studies.

çŏm·puṅçt′, *a.* having compunction. [Obs.]

çŏm·puṅç′tion, *n.* [LL. *compunctio*, a sticking or pricking; L. *compunctus*, pp. of *compungere*, to prick, sting; *com-*, intens., and *pungere*, to prick.]

1. literally, a pricking; stimulation. [Obs.]

2. a sharp feeling of uneasiness brought on by a sense of guilt; twinge of conscience; remorse; scruple.

3. a feeling of slight regret for some wrong done and of pity for the one wronged.

Syn.—contrition, penitence, regret, remorse, repentance, sorrow.

çom·puṅç′tion·less, *a.* having no compunction.

çŏm·puṅç′tious, *a.* 1. causing or actuated by compunction.

2. having compunction.

çŏm·puṅç′tious·ly, *adv.* with a feeling of compunction.

çŏm·puṅç′tive, *a.* 1. causing remorse. [Obs.]

2. sensitive to remorse. [Rare.]

çom·pũr·gā′tion, *n.* [LL. *compurgatio*, a purifying, from L. *compurgatus*, pp. of *compurgare*, to purge, purify; *com-*, intens., and *purgare*, to purge, purify.]

1. in law, the act or practice of clearing an accused person by the oath of others, who swear to their belief in his innocence; specifically, in early English law, the privilege by which the accused could call upon twelve witnesses to swear to such belief.

2. testimony of a vindicatory nature; exculpation.

çom′pũr·gā·tŏr, *n.* one who bears testimony or swears to the veracity or innocence of another.

çŏm·pũr·gȧ·tō′ri·ăl, *a.* pertaining to compurgation or compurgators.

çom·pũr′sion, *n.* drawing up or wrinkling of the features; as, *compursion* of the mouth. [Rare].

çŏm·pūt·ȧ·bil′i·ty, *n.* the quality of being computable.

çŏm·pūt′ȧ·ble, *a.* capable of being computed.

çom·pū·tā′tion, *n.* [L. *computatio*, a reckoning, from *computare*, to compute, reckon.]

1. the act of computing, numbering, reckoning, or estimating; the process by which different sums or items are numbered, estimated, or compared; as, a *computation* of the time required to do a certain thing.

2. the sum, quantity, or amount ascertained by computing or reckoning.

We pass for women of fifty: many additional years are thrown into female *computations* of this nature. —Addison.

3. a method of computing.

çŏm·pūte′, *v.t.* and *v.i.*; computed, *pt., pp.*; computing, *ppr.* to number; to count; to reckon; to determine (a number, amount, etc.) by reckoning; to ascertain the amount, aggregate, or other result of; as, to *compute* the quantity of water that will fill a vessel.

Syn.—calculate, appraise, estimate, number, cast up, reckon, count, value, rate.

çŏm·pūte′, *n.* computation: chiefly in *beyond compute.*

çŏm·pūt′ẽr, *n.* a person who computes or a device used for computing; specifically, an electronic machine which, by means of stored instructions and information, performs rapid, often complex calculations or compiles, correlates, and selects data.

çŏm·pūt′ẽr·īze″, *v.t.*; computerized, *pt., pp.*; computerizing, *ppr.* 1. to equip with electronic computers so as to facilitate or automate procedures.

2. to operate, produce, control, etc. by or as if by means of electronic computers.

çom′pū·tist, *n.* a computer.

çom′rade, *n.* [ME. *comered*; Fr. *camerade*, a company, society, comrade; Sp. *camarada*, a chamber mate; L. *camera*, a chamber.]

1. a friend; a close companion.

2. a person who has interests and concerns

in common with others and shares in their activities; partner; associate; fellow: used as a form of address, as in the Communist party; hence, [C-] [Colloq.] a member of the Communist party.

com'rade in ärms, a fellow soldier.

com'rade·ry, *n.* comradeship. [Rare.]

com'rade·ship, *n.* 1. the state of being comrades.

2. the relation of comrades; friendship; companionship.

com'rōgue (-rōg), *n.* a fellow rogue. [Obs.]

com'sat, *n.* [*com*munications, and *sat*ellite.] any of various communications satellites for relaying microwave transmissions, as of telephone, television, etc.

Com'stock·ẽr·y, *n.* [after Anthony *Comstock* (1844–1915), head of the N.Y. Society for Suppression of Vice; prob. coined by G. B. Shaw.] zealous suppression of plays, books, etc. considered offensive or dangerous to public morals.

comte (kont), *n.* [Fr.] in France, a count: a hereditary title of nobility.

Com'ti·ăn (kon'), *a.* pertaining to Auguste Comte, a French philosopher (1798–1857), or to his positivist philosophy.

Com'tism (kon'), *n.* the philosophy taught by Comte; positivism.

Com'tist (kon'), *n.* a student or adherent of Comte's philosophy; a positivist.

Cō'mus, *n.* [L.; Gr. *komos*, festival.]

1. in Greek and Roman mythology, a young god of festivity and revelry.

2. a masque (1634) by John Milton, praising chastity and showing Comus as a sorcerer.

con-, com-: used before all consonants except the cluster *gn*, the lip sounds *p*, *b*, *m*, and the glides *l*, *r*, *h*.

con, *adv.* [an abbrev. of L. *contra*, against.] in opposition; against; as, they argued the matter pro and *con*.

con, *n.* an argument, reason, vote, person, etc. in opposition.

con, *v.t.*; conned, *pt.*, *pp.*; conning, *ppr* [ME. *cunnen*; AS. *cunnian*, to try, test.]

1. to know. [Obs.]

2. to peruse or study carefully; to memorize; to learn; as, to *con* a speech.

con, *v.t.* [earlier *cond*, from ME. *conduen*, to conduct; OFr. *conduire*; L. *conducere*, to lead or bring together.] to direct the course or steering of (a ship); as, he *conned* the ship from the main rigging.

con, *n.* 1. the station of a person who cons.

2. the act of conning.

con, *a.* confidence; as, a *con* man. [Slang.]

con, *v.t.* 1. to swindle (a victim) by first gaining his confidence. [Slang.]

2. to trick or fool, esp. by glib persuasion.

con·ā'cre (-kẽr), *v.t.* to let on the conacre system.

con·ā'cre, *n.* in Ireland, formerly, the custom of letting land in small portions for a single crop, the rent being paid in money or in labor.

con·ā'cre, *a.* relating to the custom of conacre, or of letting land in this way; as, the *conacre* system.

cŏn ä·mō're, [It.]

1. with love or tenderness; as, in music, to play or sing *con amore*.

2. with enthusiasm.

cō·nā'ri·um, *n.* [L., from Gr. *kōnarion*, the pineal gland, dim. of *kōnos*, a cone.] in anatomy, the pineal gland, or pineal body of the brain.

cō·nā'tion, *n.* [L. *conatio*, an attempt, from *conari*, to undertake, attempt.] in psychology, the act or faculty of impelling or directing muscular or mental effort.

cō'nȧ·tive, *a.* 1. relating to conation.

The exertive or *conative* powers.
—Hamilton.

2. in linguistics, expressing endeavor or effort, especially as an aspect of the action of verbs. Example: Ar. *qātala*, he has tried to kill (as contrasted with *qatala*, he has killed).

cō·nā'tus, *n.*; *pl.* **cō·nā'tus**, 1. a natural, active force, as of plants or animals, analogous to human effort.

2. an effort or attempt; an endeavor.

cŏn brï'ō, [It.] with spirit; spiritedly: a direction to the performer in music.

con·cam'ẽr·āte, *v.t.*; concamerated, *pt.*, *pp.*; concamerating, *ppr.* [L. *concameratus*, pp. of *concamerare*, to arch over.] to arch over; to vault; to lay a concave over. [Rare.]

con·cam·ẽr·ā'tion, *n.* an arching; an arch or vault; an arched chamber. [Rare.]

con·cat'e·nāte, *v.t.*; concatenated, *pt.*, *pp.*; concatenating, *ppr.* [LL. *concatenatus*, pp. of *concatenare*, to link together.] to link together, to unite in a successive series or chain, as things depending on each other; as, all the affairs of human life are *concatenated*.

con·cat'e·nāte, *a.* linked together; connected.

con·cat·e·nā'tion, *n.* 1. a series of links united; a successive series or order of things or events regarded as causally or dependently related; as, a *concatenation* of causes.

2. the condition of being concatenated.

con·cau·les'cence, *n.* [L. *con-*, with, and *caulis*, a stalk.] in botany, the gradual approach and union of axes, or of an organ and an axis.

con·cause', *n.* joint cause. [Rare.]

con·cā·vā'tion, *n.* the act of making concave.

con'cāve, *a.* [Fr. *concave*; L. *concavus*, hollow; *con-*, intens., and *cavus*, hollow.] hollow and curved like a section of the inner surface of a spherical body: opposed to *convex*; as, a *concave* lens; a *concave* mirror.

concave lens; a lens which has either one or both sides arched in toward the center; if both, the lens is said to be *double concave*, or *concavo-concave*.

CONCAVE OR PLANO-CONCAVE LENS

con'cāve, *n.* a concave surface, line, object, etc.

con'cāve, *v.t.*; concaved, *pt.*, *pp.*; concaving, *ppr.* to make concave.

con'cāved, *a.* arched; shaped like an arch.

con'cāve·ness, *n.* hollowness.

con·cav'i·ty, *n.* [LL. *concavitas*, concavity; L. *concavus*, hollow.]

1. the quality or condition of being concave.

2. *pl.* **con·cav'i·ties**, a concave surface or object.

CONCAVO-CONCAVE LENS

con·cā'vō-con'cāve, *a.* concave or hollow on both surfaces: usually applied to lenses.

con·cā'vō-con'vex, *a.* concave on one side, and convex on the other.

concavo-convex lens; in optics, a lens in which the convex face has a slighter curvature than the concave.

CONCAVO-CONVEX LENS

con·cā'vous, *a.* concave. [Obs.]

con·cā'vous·ly, *adv.* in a concave manner; so as to show a concave surface; concavely.

cŏn·cēal', *v.t.*; concealed, *pt.*, *pp.*; concealing, *ppr.* [ME. *concelen*; L. *concelare*, to hide; *con-*, together, and *celare*, to hide.]

1. to keep close or secret; to forbear to disclose; to withhold from utterance or declaration; as, to *conceal* one's thoughts or opinions.

2. to hide; to withdraw from observation; to cover or keep from sight; as, a party of men *concealed* themselves behind a wall; a mask *conceals* the face.

Syn.—cover, disguise, dissemble, withhold, secrete, hide, mask, screen, veil, cloak, bury.

cŏn·cēal'ȧ·ble, *a.* capable of being concealed, hidden, withheld, or kept close.

cŏn·cēaled', *a.* kept close or secret; hidden; withdrawn from sight; covered.

concealed weapons; weapons, such as firearms or knives, hidden upon the person, but ready for use, to carry such being, generally, a violation of law.

cŏn·cēal'ed·ly, *adv.* so as not to be detected; secretly.

cŏn·cēal'ed·ness, *n.* the state of being concealed.

cŏn·cēal'ẽr, *n.* one who conceals something; as, the *concealer* of a crime.

cŏn·cēal'ment, *n.* 1. forbearance of disclosure; a keeping close or secret; as, the *concealment* of opinions or passions.

2. the act of hiding, covering, or withdrawing from sight; as, the *concealment* of the face by a mask; the *concealment* of a person in a house.

3. the state of being hidden or concealed; privacy; as, a project formed in *concealment*.

4. a place or means of hiding; a secret place; as, his *concealment* was a deep forest.

5. secret knowledge; a secret. [Obs.]

6. in law, the suppression of truth to the injury or prejudice of another; the withholding of knowledge which one is bound in justice to reveal.

cŏn·cēde', *v.t.*; conceded, *pt.*, *pp.*; conceding, *ppr.* [L. *concedere*, to yield, grant; *con-*, with, and *cedere*, to go, cede, grant.]

1. to yield, as in argument; to admit as true, just, or proper; to grant; to let pass undisputed; as, the advocate *concedes* the point in question.

We *concede* that their citizens were those who lived under different forms.
—Burke.

2. to grant as a right; to admit the justice of; as, he *conceded* the victory.

cŏn·cēde', *v.i.* to assent, yield, permit, or make concession.

Syn.—yield, admit, grant, suffer, permit, allow, acquiesce, assent, surrender.

cŏn·cēit', *n.* [ME. *conceit*, *conseit*; OFr. *concept*, conceit, from L. *conceptus*, a collecting, taking, from *concipere*, to take, lay hold of, perceive.]

1. (a) a concept; that which is conceived, imagined, or formed in the mind; idea; thought; image; as, his *conceit* of happiness was vague indeed; (b) personal opinion. [Rare.]

2. understanding; power or faculty of conceiving; apprehension; as, a man of quick *conceit*. [Obs.]

3. fancy; imagination.

4. [from It. *concetto*, of same ult. origin.] (a) an affectation in style or in expression of ideas; a fanciful or witty expression or notion; a startling or strained figure of speech; (b) the use of such figures in writing or speaking.

5. favorable or self-flattering opinion of oneself; a lofty or vain conception of one's own person or accomplishments.

By a little study and a great *conceit* of himself, he has lost his religion. —Bentley.

6. a trifling article, ingeniously contrived; a fanciful device; a pretty or attractive trifle. [Obs.]

out of conceit with; not having a favorable opinion of; no longer pleased with; as, a man *out of conceit with* his neighbor.

Syn.—conception, thought, image, apprehension, fancy, device, whim, idea, vagary, vanity, egotism, pride.

cŏn·cēit', *v.t.* 1. to conceive; to imagine; to think; to fancy. [Obs.]

The strong, by *conceiting* themselves weak, are thereby rendered inactive. —South.

2. to think well of; to take a fancy to. [Dial.]

cŏn·cēit', *v.i.* to conceive an idea; to think. [Obs.]

cŏn·cēit'ed, *a.* 1. endowed with fancy or imagination. [Obs.]

2. entertaining a flattering opinion of oneself; having a vain conception of one's own person or accomplishments; vain.

3. ingeniously contrived; curiously designed. [Obs.]

4. full of whims and fanciful notions. [Dial.]

Syn.—egotistical, opinionated, proud, self-important, vain.

cŏn·cēit'ed·ly, *adv.* in a conceited manner.

cŏn·cēit'ed·ness, *n.* the state of being conceited; conceit; vanity; an overweening sense of one's own importance.

cŏn·cēit'less, *a.* of dull conception; stupid; dull of apprehension. [Obs.]

cŏn·cēiv·ȧ·bil'i·ty, *n.* the quality of being conceivable.

cŏn·cēiv'ȧ·ble, *a.* [Fr. *concevable*.]

1. capable of being imagined or thought.

2. capable of being understood or believed.

cŏn·cēiv'ȧ·ble·ness, *n.* the quality of being conceivable.

cŏn·cēiv'ȧ·bly, *adv.* in a conceivable or intelligible manner.

cŏn·cēive', *v.t.*; conceived, *pt.*, *pp.*; conceiving, *ppr.* [ME. *conceiven*, *conceyven*; OFr. *concever*, *conciver*; L. *concipere*, to take in, receive; *con-*, together, and *capere*, to take.]

1. to become pregnant with; to begin the formation of the embryo or fetus of.

2. to form in the mind; to imagine; to devise; as, to *conceive* a plan of escape.

3. to understand; to comprehend; to apprehend; as, we cannot *conceive* the manner in which spirit operates upon matter.

4. to think; to believe or suppose.

You can hardly *conceive* this man to have been bred in the same climate. —Swift.

5. to express; to represent in words.

cŏn·cēive', *v.i.* 1. to have a fetus formed in the womb; to become pregnant.

2. to think; to have a conception or idea: used with *of*.

Syn.—engender, originate, formulate, comprehend, apprehend, perceive, suppose, understand, think.

cŏn·cēiv'ẽr, *n.* a person who conceives or comprehends.

con·cel'ē·brāte, *v.t.* to celebrate together. [Obs.]

con·cent', *n.* [L. *concentus*, harmony, from *con-*

cinere, to sing, play, or sound together; *con-*, together, and *canere*, to sing.]

1. concert of voices; concord of sounds; harmony; as, a *concent* of notes. [Rare.]

2. consistency; accordance; as, in *concent* to a man's own principles. [Rare.]

cŏn·cen′tẽr, *v.i.*; concentered, *pt., pp.*; concentering, *ppr.* [Fr. *concentrer*, to center; L. *con-*, together, and *centrum*, center.] to come to a point, or to meet in a common center; to converge.

All these are like so many lines drawn from several objects, that in some way relate to him, and *concenter* in him. —Hale.

cŏn·cen′tẽr, *v.t.* to bring to a common center; to focus; to concentrate.

All is *concentered* in a life intense.—Byron

çon′cen·trāte, *v.t.*; concentrated, *pt., pp.*; concentrating, *ppr.* 1. to bring to, or direct toward, a common center.

2. to collect or focus (one's thoughts, efforts, etc.).

3. to increase the strength or density of.

çon′cen·trāte, *v.i.* 1. to come to or toward a common center.

2. to direct one's thoughts or efforts; to fix one's attention (*on* or *upon*).

3. to increase in strength or density.

çon′cen·trāte, *a.* concentrated.

çon′cen·trāte, *n.* a substance that has been concentrated.

çon′cen·trā·ted, *a.* 1. brought to or directed toward a common center; focused.

2. intensified in strength or density by a process of concentration.

çon·cen·trā′tion, *n.* [from L. *con-*, together, and *centrum*, a center.]

1. a concentrating or being concentrated.

2. fixed or close attention.

3. in chemistry, the volatilization of part of a liquid, in order to increase the strength of the remainder.

4. the strength or density, as of a solution.

5. in mining, the act or process of separating waste matter, as earth and rock from ore, as by washing or by chemical action in a reduction mill.

6. the result of concentrating.

çon·cen·trā′tion çamp, 1. a place where troops are massed, as before distribution.

2. a place in which enemy aliens or prisoners of war are kept under guard.

3. a place of confinement for those considered dangerous to the regime: used especially in Nazi Germany for antifascists, Jews, etc.

çon′cen·trā·tive, *a.* concentrating or tending to concentrate.

çon′cen·trā·tive·ness, *n.* the quality or faculty of concentrating; specifically, in phrenology, the power by which mental concentration (or the centering of the mentality upon one object) is assured.

çon′cen·trā·tŏr, *n.* 1. one who concentrates.

2. any of various devices for concentrating solutions, ores, etc.

çon·cen′tre (-tẽr), *v.t.* and *v.i.* concenter: British spelling.

çon·cen′triç, çon·cen′triç·ăl, *a.* 1. having a common center; as, the *concentric* layers of an onion; the *concentric* orbits of the planets.

2. in military usage, concentrated upon a given point; as, *concentric* fire.

CONCENTRIC CIRCLES

çon·cen′triç, *n.* anything which has a common center with another thing. [Rare.]

Its peculiar relations to its *concentrics*. —Coleridge.

çon·cen′triç·ăl·ly, *adv.* in a concentric manner; with a center in common.

çon·cen·tric′i·ty, *n.* the state of being concentric; the state of having a center in common with another body or figure.

çon·cen′tū·ăl, *a.* [L. *concentus*, harmony, from *concinere*, to play or sing together.] harmonious; accordant. [Rare.]

çon′cept, *n.* [L. *conceptus*, a collecting, gathering, a thought, from *concipere*, to take in, conceive; *con-*, and *capere*, to take.] an idea, especially a generalized idea of a class of objects; a thought; general notion.

çŏn·cep′tȧ·çle, *n.* 1. that in which anything is contained; receptacle. [Obs.]

2. in botany, a sac opening outward and containing reproductive cells, found in certain primitive plants.

çŏn·cep·ti·bil′i·ty, *n.* conceivability. [Obs.]

çŏn·cep′ti·ble, *a.* conceivable. [Obs.]

çŏn·cep′tion, *n.* [ME. *conceptioun*; L. *conceptio*, a comprehending, a conception, from *conceptus*, pp. of *concipere*, to conceive.]

1. a conceiving or being conceived in the womb.

2. that which is so conceived; embryo; fetus.

3. the beginning of some process, chain of events, etc.

4. the act, process, or power of conceiving mentally; formulation of ideas.

5. a mental impression or image; general notion; concept.

6. a conceit; a fanciful thought; a fantastic thought or figure of speech. [Obs.]

7. an original idea, design, plan, etc.; as, an architect's *conception* of a building.

false conception; an apparent conception in which an abnormal, fleshy mass, as a tumor or mole, is produced, instead of a normally developed fetus.

Syn.—apprehension, comprehension, concept, image, imagination, thought, notion, idea, sentiment, view.

çŏn·cep′tion·ăl, *a.* relating to a conception or image.

çŏn·cep′tion·ăl·ist, *n.* same as *conceptualist*.

çŏn·cep′tious (-shus), *a.* apt to conceive; fruitful; pregnant. [Obs.]

çŏn·cep′tive, *a.* having the power of conception: generally said of the mind.

çŏn·cep′tū·ăl, *a.* of conception or concepts.

çŏn·cep′tū·ăl·iṣm, *n.* [*conceptual*, and *-ism*.] in philosophy, the doctrine that universals exist as realities in the mind only and that the mind can form an image corresponding to the general term for a particular concept: distinguished from *realism* and *nominalism*.

çŏn·cep′tū·ăl·ist, *n.* one who holds the doctrine of conceptualism.

çŏn·cep′tū·ăl·ist, *a.* of conceptualism or conceptualists.

çŏn·cẽrn′, *v.t.*; concerned, *pt., pp.*; concerning, *ppr.* [Fr. *concerner*, to concern; LL. *concernere*, to mix, mingle, as in a sieve; L. *con-*, and *cernere*, to separate, sift.]

1. to have a relation to or bearing on; to be of interest or importance to; as, this *concerns* all of us.

2. to involve or interest (used in the passive).

3. to cause to feel uneasy or anxious.

to concern oneself; (a) to busy oneself (*with, about, over, in* something); to take an interest; (b) to be worried, anxious, or uneasy.

çŏn·cẽrn′, *n.* 1. that which busies or occupies one's thoughts; that which relates or pertains to one; business; matter; interest; affair; as, each one has his own *concerns* to attend to.

2. that which pertains to or affects in any way one's interests, welfare, or happiness; a matter of importance.

'Tis all mankind's *concern* that he should live. —Dryden.

3. (a) interest in or regard for a person or thing; (b) solicitude; anxiety; agitation or uneasiness of mind; disturbed state of feeling.

Why all this *concern* for the poor? We want them not. —Swift.

4. an establishment or firm for the transaction of business; a manufacturing or commercial establishment; as, two banking *concerns* closed their doors at noon.

5. an object generally, especially one that is large and somewhat clumsily constructed; a contrivance. [Colloq.]

The hackney coach, a great, lumbering, square *concern*. —Dickens.

6. relation; reference.

Syn.—matter, affair, business, interest, regard, moment, importance, care, solicitude, anxiety.

çŏn·cẽrned′, *a.* 1. interested or involved (*in* some matter).

2. uneasy; solicitous; anxious; as, we are *concerned* for the fate of our fleet.

çŏn·cẽrn′ed·ly, *adv.* with affection or interest.

çŏn·cẽrn′ing, *prep.* pertaining to; regarding; about; having relation to; with reference to; as, he spoke only good *concerning* the man.

çŏn·cẽrn′ing, *a.* affecting the interests; important. [Obs.]

çŏn·cẽrn′ing, *n.* a matter of concern, interest, or importance. [Obs.]

çŏn·cẽrn′ment, *n.* 1. the thing in which one is concerned or interested; concern; affair; business; interest.

The great *concernment* of men is with men. —Locke.

2. importance; moment; interest; consequence.

Experimental truths are matters of great *concernment* to mankind. —Boyle.

3. concern; participation; involvement; as, the father's *concernment* in the marriage of his daughter was slight.

4. worry; anxiety; solicitude; as, their ambition is manifest in their *concernment*.

5. relation; reference.

çŏn·cẽrt′, *v.t.* and *v.i.*; concerted, *pt., pp.*; concerting, *ppr.* [Fr. *concerter*; It. *concertare*; L. *concertare*, to contend, contest; *con-*, and *certare*, to strive.] to arrange or settle by mutual understanding; to contrive or plan together; to devise.

çon′cẽrt, *n.* [Fr. *concert*; It. *concerto*, an agreement, union, from *concertare*, to contest together; L. *concertare*, to strive.]

1. agreement of two or more in a design or plan; union formed by mutual communication of opinions and views; harmony of action; concord; as, the allies acted in *concert*.

2. a performance of vocal or instrumental music, usually one in which a number of musicians participate.

3. musical consonance.

in concert; in unison; in agreement; together.

çon′cẽrt, *a.* of or for concerts.

çon·cẽr·tan′tē (*or It. pron.*, kōn-chār-tän′te), *n.* and *a.* [It., ppr. of *concertare*, to form a concert.] a composition for the orchestra in which there are special parts for solo instruments: now generally used as an adjective, indicating certain prominent solo parts in an orchestral composition, which are spoken of as *concertante* parts.

çon·cẽr·tā′tion, *n.* strife; contention. [Obs.]

çŏn·cẽrt′ed, *a.* 1. mutually planned, arranged, or agreed on; combined; as, a *concerted* scheme.

2. in music, arranged in parts for several voices or instruments, as a trio, a quartet, etc.

çon′cẽrt grand (pi·an′ō), the largest size of grand piano, for concert performance.

çon·cẽr·tī′nȧ, *n.* [*concert*, and *-ina*: coined by Sir Charles Wheatstone (1802–1875), Eng. physicist who invented it.] a small musical instrument of the accordion type, with bellows and keys.

CONCERTINA

çon·cẽr·tī′nō, *n.* [It., dim. of *concerto*.] a brief concerto.

çŏn·cẽr′tion, *n.* concert; contrivance; adjustment. [Rare.]

çon′cẽrt·mȧs″tẽr, *n.* [after G. *konzertmeister*.] the leader of the first violin section of a symphony orchestra, who plays the solo passages and often serves as assistant to the conductor.

çon′cẽrt·meis·tẽr, *n.* [G., older form of *konzertmeister*.] a concertmaster.

çon·cer′tō (-chār′), *n.*; *pl.* **çon·cer′tōṣ,** It. **çon·cer′ti,** [It.]

1. formerly, a musical composition with the several distinct movements of an orchestral suite, but played by a small group of solo instruments with a larger orchestral ensemble.

2. a composition for one, or two or three, solo instruments and an orchestra: it is based on the sonata form and has, usually, three movements.

çon·cer′tō grōs′sō, [It., lit., big concerto.] a concerto for a small group of solo instruments and a full orchestra.

çon′cẽrt pitch, in music, a pitch, slightly higher than the usual pitch, to which concert instruments are tuned in order to compensate acoustically for the relatively high room temperature of crowded concert halls.

çŏn·ces′sion, *n.* [Fr. *concession*; L. *concessio*, a concession, from *concessus*, pp. of *concedere*, to concede, grant.]

1. a conceding; granting; giving in; yielding.

2. a thing conceded or granted; acknowledgment, as of an argument or claim.

3. a privilege granted by a government, company, etc.; especially, (a) the right to use land; (b) the right to sell food, check hats and coats, etc., as at a park, theater, etc.

4. the land, trading rights, etc. so granted.

çŏn·ces·sion·āire′, *n.* [Fr. *concessionnaire*.] the holder of a concession granted by a government, company, etc.

çŏn·ces′sion·ā·ry, *a.* of a concession.

çŏn·ces′sion·ā·ry, *n.*; *pl.* **çŏn·ces′sion·ā·rieș,** a concessionaire.

çŏn·ces′sion·ẽr, *n.* [Fr. *concessionnaire.*] a concessionaire.

çŏn·ces′sion·ist, *n.* one who is in favor of making concessions.

çŏn·ces′sive, *a.* 1. having the character of concession; conceding or tending to concede.
2. in grammar, expressing concession; as, *though* is a *concessive* conjunction.

çŏn·ces′sive·ly, *adv.* by way of concession or yielding.

çŏn·ces′sō·ry, *a.* conceding; yielding; permissive. [Rare.]

çon·cet′ti, *n.*, pl. of *concetto.*

çon·cet′tism, *n.* [It. *concetto,* conceit.] the use of concetti.

çon·cet′tō, *n.*; *pl.* **çon·cet′ti,** [It.] a conceit; a witty expression or notion.

coñch (*or* çonch), *n.*; *pl.* **coñchs** or **çon′cheș,** [L. *concha*; Gr. *konchē,* a mussel, shell.]
1. the spiral, one-piece shell of certain sea mollusks.
2. in Roman mythology, such a shell used as a trumpet by the Tritons.
3. a concha.
4. an inhabitant of the Bahamas and other neighboring islands. [Colloq.]
5. any large shell used as a horn or instrument for calling.

CONCH

coñ′chȧ, *n.*; *pl.* **coñ′chae,** [L. *concha*; Gr. *konchē,* a shell.]
1. in anatomy, any of several structures resembling a shell in form, as a thin, bony projection inside the nasal cavity, the largest hollow of the external ear, or the whole external ear.
2. in architecture, (a) the half dome covering an apse; (b) the apse.

coñ′chăl, *a.* pertaining to a concha.

coñ′chi·fẽr, *n.* [L. *concha,* a shell, and *ferre,* to bear.] one of the *Conchifera*; any of the bivalve mollusks.

Coñ·chif′ẽ·rȧ, *n.pl.* [L., from *concha,* a shell, and *ferre,* to bear.] the large class of acephalous molluscous animals commonly called bivalves, and including the *Lamellibranchiata* and the *Brachiopoda.*

coñ·chif′ẽr·ous, *a.* 1. pertaining to the *Conchifera.*
2. having or bearing a shell.

coñ′chi·form, *a.* [L. *concha,* a shell, and *forma,* shape.] having the shape of a shell.

coñ·chī′ō·lin, *n.* the organic base of mollusk shells.

coñ′chīte, *n.* a fossil or petrified conch or shell. [Obs.]

coñ·chit′iç, *a.* [Gr. *konchitēs,* a shelly marble, from *konchē,* a shell.] composed of or containing shells: applied to limestones and marbles in which the remains of shells are a characteristic feature.

Coñ′chō·bar (-wẽr, *or* kon′oor), *n.* in Irish legend, a king of Ulster, the guardian and intended husband of Deirdre.

coñ′chō gràss, the millet of Texas, *Panicum texanum.*

coñ′choid, *n.* [Gr. *konchē,* a shell, and *eidos,* form.] a plane curve of the fourth degree: so called by its inventor Nicomedes.

coñ·choid′ăl, *a.* in mineralogy, having curved elevations or depressions like those of a bivalve shell in cross section.

coñ·chō·log′iç·ăl, *a.* [*conch,* and Gr. *logos,* a discourse.] pertaining to conchology.

coñ·chol′ō·ġist, *n.* a student of or a specialist in conchology; one who collects shells.

coñ·chol′ō·ġy, *n.* [Gr. *konchē,* a shell, and *logos,* a description.] that branch of zoology which treats of the nature, formation, and classification of mollusks and shells: also called *malacology.*

coñ·chom′e·tẽr, *n.* [Gr. *konchē,* a shell, and *metron,* a measure.] an instrument for measuring shells or the angle of their spire.

coñ·chom′e·try, *n.* the practice or art of measuring shells; the use of the conchometer.

coñ·chō·spī′răl, *n.* a variety of spiral curve existing in many univalve shells.

çon′chy (*or* -shi), *n.*; *pl.* **çon′chieș** (*or* -shēz), a conscientious objector. [Slang.]

coñ·chy·lā′ceous, coñ·chyl·i·ā′ceous, *a.* [L. *conchylium*; Gr. *konchylion,* dim. of *konchē,* a shell.] pertaining to shells; resembling a shell; as, *conchylaceous* impressions.

coñ·chy·lif′ẽr·ous, *a.* same as *conchiferous.*

coñ·chyl·i·ol′ō·ġy, *n.* conchology. [Obs.]

coñ·chyl·i·om′e·try, *n.* same as *conchometry.*

coñ·chyl′i·ous, *a.* pertaining to *Conchifera* or their shells; conchylaceous.

coñ·chyl′i·um, *n.*; *pl.* **coñ·chyl′i·ȧ,** [L. *conchylium*; Gr. *konchylion,* dim. of *konchē,* a shell.] any shell of a mollusk; a conch.

çon′ci·ā·tōr, *n.* [It. *conciatore,* from *conciare,* to fit, adorn, from L. *comptus,* adorned, elegant, pp. of *comere,* to dress, adorn.] in glassmaking, one who weighs, proportions, works, and tempers the materials used.

çọn·ci·erge′ (-ārzh′), *n.* [Fr.]
1. a doorkeeper.
2. a caretaker, as of an apartment house; a janitor; a custodian.

çŏn·cil′i·ȧ·ble, *n.* a small or secret assembly. [Obs.]

çŏn·cil′i·ȧ·ble, *a.* [from L. *conciliare,* to conciliate.] capable of being conciliated.

çŏn·cil′i·ȧ·būle, *n.* [L. *conciliabulum,* a place of assembly, from *conciliare,* to call together, conciliate.] a private ecclesiastical assembly; an obscure council. [Rare.]

çŏn·cil′i·ăr, çŏn·cil′i·ā·ry, *a.* [L. *concilium,* a council.] pertaining to a council.

çŏn·cil′i·āte, *v.t.*; conciliated, *pt., pp.*; conciliating, *ppr.* [L. *conciliatus,* pp. of *conciliare,* to call or bring together, to win over, from *concilium,* a meeting, assembly.]
1. to win over; soothe the anger of; make friendly; placate.
2. to gain (regard, favor, good will, esteem, etc.) by friendly acts.
3. to reconcile; make consistent. [Archaic.]
Syn.—win, gain, engage, propitiate, reconcile, appease, pacify.

çŏn·cil·i·ā′tion, *n.* the act of conciliating or state of being conciliated.

çŏn·cil′i·ȧ·tive, *a.* conciliatory; reconciling; pacific.

çŏn·cil′i·ā·tōr, *n.* one who conciliates or reconciles.

çŏn·cil′i·ȧ·tō·ry, *a.* tending to conciliate or reconcile; tending to make peace between persons at variance; pacific; as, the general made *conciliatory* propositions to the insurgents.
Syn.—pacific, winning, engaging.

çŏn·cin′nāte, *v.t.* to unite becomingly; to adapt; to adjust. [Obs.]

çŏn·cin′ni·ty, *n.*; *pl.* **çŏn·cin′ni·tieș,** [L. *concinnitas,* fitness, elegance.] a skillful arrangement of parts; harmony; elegance, especially of literary style.
An exact *concinnity* and evenness of fancy.
—Howell.

çŏn·cin′nous, *a.* fit; suitable; agreeable; harmonious; pleasant; as, a *concinnous* interval in music; a *concinnous* system. [Rare.]

çon′ciŏn·āte (-shun-), *v.i.* to preach. [Obs.]

çon′ciŏn·ā·tive, *a.* pertaining to preaching or public speaking. [Rare.]

çon′ciŏn·ā·tōr, *n.* [L. *contionator,* a haranguer, from *contio,* an assembly.]
1. a preacher.
2. in old English law, a common councilman; a freeman. [Obs.]

çon′ciŏn·ā·tō·ry, *a.* concionative. [Obs.]

çŏn·cīse′, *a.* [L. *concisus,* cut off, brief, from *concidere,* to cut off; *con-,* and *cædere,* to cut.] brief and to the point; containing few words; comprehensive; employing as few words as possible; as, a *concise* summary.
Syn.—succinct, brief, condensed, terse.

çŏn·cīse′ly, *adv.* briefly; in a few words.

çŏn·cīse′ness, *n.* brevity in speaking or writing; as, the *conciseness* of Demosthenes.

çŏn·ci′siŏn (-sizh′un), *n.* 1. originally, a cutting off; a schism; a faction; a division; a sect.
2. conciseness.
His wonted vigor and *concision.*
—Brougham.

çon·ci·tā′tion, *n.* the act of stirring up, exciting, or putting in motion. [Obs.]

çon·cīte′, *v.t.* to excite. [Obs.]

çon·clȧ·mā′tion, *n.* [L. *conclamatio,* from *conclamare*; *con-,* and *clamare,* to cry out.] an outcry or shout of many together. [Rare.]

çon′clāve, *n.* [ME. *conclave*; OFr. *conclave*; L. *conclave,* a room or closet; *con-,* with, and *clavis,* a key.]
1. an apartment in which the cardinals of the Roman Catholic Church meet in privacy for the election of a pope.
2. the secret assembly or meeting of the cardinals for the election of a pope; hence, the cardinals collectively.
3. any private meeting; a close assembly.
In close recess and secret *conclave* sat.
—Milton.

çon′clā·vist, *n.* [It. *conclavista.*] either of two persons, a secretary and a servant, who attend a cardinal in conclave.

çŏn·clūde′, *v.t.*; concluded, *pt., pp.*; concluding, *ppr.* [ME. *concluden,* to conclude; L. *concludere,* to shut up closely, enclose; *con-,* together, and *claudere,* to shut.]
1. to shut up; to enclose. [Obs.]
2. to include; to comprehend. [Obs.]
The Scripture hath *concluded* all under sin.
—Gal. iii. 22.
3. to arrive at by reasoning; to infer; to deduce.
Therefore we *conclude,* that a man is justified by faith without the deeds of the law.
—Rom. iii. 28.
4. to decide; to determine; to make a final determination concerning; as, we have *concluded* not to go.
5. to bring to a close; to end; to finish.
I will *conclude* this part with the speech of a counselor of state.
—Bacon.
6. to stop or restrain, or, as in law, to estop from further argument or proceedings; to oblige or bind, as by authority, or by one's own argument or concession: generally in the passive; as, the defendant is *concluded* by his own plea.
7. to settle or arrange finally; to come to an agreement about; as, to *conclude* a bargain, to *conclude* a peace.
Syn.—infer, decide, determine, close, finish, terminate, end, arrange, settle.

çŏn·clūde′, *v.i.* 1. to settle an opinion; to come to an agreement; to form a final judgment.
Can we *conclude* upon Luther's instability?
—Atterbury.
2. to come to a close; to end; to terminate.
A train of lies,
That, made in lust, *conclude* in perjuries.
—Dryden.

çŏn·clūd′en·cy, *n.* inference; logical deduction from premises. [Obs.]

çŏn·clūd′ent, *a.* bringing to a close; decisive. [Obs.]

çŏn·clūd′ẽr, *n.* one who concludes.

çŏn·clūd′ing, *a.* final; ending; closing; as, the *concluding* sentence of an essay.

çŏn·clūd′ing·ly, *adv.* conclusively; with incontrovertible evidence. [Obs.]

çŏn·clū′si·ble, *a.* capable of being concluded or inferred; determinable. [Obs.]

çŏn·clū′sion, *n.* 1. the end; the close; the last part; as, the *conclusion* of an address.
2. the close of an argument, debate, or reasoning; judgment, decision, or opinion formed after investigation or thought.
Let us hear the *conclusion* of the whole matter: Fear God, and keep his commandments; for this is the whole duty of man.
—Eccles. xii. 13.
3. in logic, inference; the third and last part of a syllogism; deduction from propositions, facts, experience, or reasoning.
4. the result of experiments; experiment. [Obs.]
We practice all *conclusions* of grafting and inoculating.
—Bacon.
5. in law, (a) the formal end of a plea; (b) an estoppel; (c) a binding act.
6. a concluding; final arrangement (*of* a peace treaty, etc.)
7. the last part of a chain of events; outcome.
conclusion of fact; a conclusion from testimony as to the verity of an alleged fact.
conclusion of law; the decision or decree of a court as to the law applying to a given state of facts.
conclusion to the country; in law, the formal end of a plea, demanding a trial by jury.
foregone conclusion; something decided upon in advance that cannot be changed by argument or influence.
in conclusion; finally; lastly; in closing.
to try conclusions with; to engage in an argument, a contest, etc. with.
Syn.—decision, determination, inference, deduction, result, consequence, end.

çŏn·clū′sion·ăl, *a.* concluding; final. [Obs.]

çŏn·clū′sive, *a.* 1. final; forming the end.
2. decisive; settling the question; putting an end to debate; convincing; leaving no room for doubt; as, a *conclusive* argument.
Syn.—convincing, decisive, final, ultimate, unanswerable.

çŏn·clū′sive·ly, *adv.* in a conclusive manner; decisively; with final determination; as, the point of law is *conclusively* settled.

çŏn·clū′sive·ness, *n.* the quality of being conclusive, or decisive; as, the *conclusiveness* of evidence, or of an argument.

çŏn·clū′sō·ry, *a.* conclusive. [Rare.]

çŏn·coct′, *v.t.*; concocted, *pt.*, *pp.*; concocting, *ppr.* [L. *concoctus*, pp. of *concoquere*, to boil together, prepare; from *com-*, together, and *coquere*, to cook.]

1. to digest. [Obs.]

The vital functions are performed by general and constant laws; the food is *concocted.* —Cheyne.

2. to purify chemically; to refine by separation. [Obs.]

3. to ripen. [Obs.]

Fruits and grains are half a year in *concocting* their products. —Bacon.

4. to form and prepare in the mind; to plan; as, to *concoct* a scheme.

5. to prepare from raw materials, or by mixing various ingredients; to compound; as, to *concoct* a new dish.

çŏn·coct′ẽr, *n.* a person who concocts.

çŏn·coc′tion, *n.* 1. digestion of food. [Obs.]

2. maturation; the process by which morbid matter was supposed to be separated from the bodily fluids, preparatory to being thrown off. [Obs.]

3. a ripening. [Obs.]

4. the act of concocting, or preparing from raw materials, or by mixing a variety of ingredients.

5. the result of concocting; anything produced by concocting; as, a medical *concoction.*

çŏn·coct′ive, *a.* digestive; having the power of digesting or ripening.

çŏn·çŏl′ŏr, *a.* of one color; having the same coloration. [Rare.]

çŏn·çŏl′ŏr·ous, *a.* in zoology, having a uniform color throughout; concolor.

çŏn·com′i·tănce, çŏn·com′i·tăn·cy, *n.* [Fr. *concomitance*, from L. *con-*, together, and *comitari*, to accompany; *comes*, a companion.]

1. the fact of being concomitant; accompaniment; existence in association.

2. in the Roman Catholic Church, the doctrine that both the body and blood of Jesus exist in each element of the Eucharist, so that both are partaken of or received by communicating in one element only.

çŏn·com′i·tănt, *a.* accompanying; conjoined; concurrent; attendant; as, a *concomitant* cause.

çŏn·com′i·tănt, *n.* 1. an accompanying or attendant condition, circumstance, or thing.

Reproach is a *concomitant* to greatness. —Addison.

2. any algebraic function the relations of which to a given quantic are unchanged by linear transformation of the variables which the function represents.

çŏn·com′i·tănt·ly, *adv.* in company with; concurrently.

çon′çord, *n.* [L. *concordia*, agreement, union, from *concors*, genit. *concordis*, of the same mind; from *com-*, together, and *cor*, heart.]

1. agreement between persons or things; union in opinions, sentiments, views, or interests; accordance; harmony.

What *concord* hath Christ with Belial? —2 Cor. vi. 15.

2. in music, a combination of simultaneous and harmonious tones.

The true *concord* of well-tuned sounds. —Shak.

3. a compact; an agreement by stipulation; a treaty.

4. in old English law, an agreement between the parties in a fine, made by leave of the court.

5. in grammar, agreement of words in construction, as adjectives with nouns in gender, number, and case, or verbs with nouns or pronouns in number and person.

6. friendly and peaceful relations, as between nations.

Syn.—agreement, harmony, accordance, concurrence, conformity, consonance, uniformity, unison.

çŏn·çord′, *v.i.* [L. *concordare*, to agree.] to cooperate; to agree; to accord. [Obs.]

çŏn·çord′, *v.t.* to reconcile; to bring into harmony. [Obs.]

çŏn·çord′á·ble, *a.* capable of according; agreeing; harmonizing. [Obs.]

çŏn·çord′á·bly, *adv.* with agreement. [Obs.]

çŏn·çord′ănce, *n.* [ME. *concordaunce*; OFr. *concordance*, agreement, a concordance, from L. *concordans*, ppr. of *concordare*, to agree.]

1. agreement; accordance; the state of being concordant.

2. in grammar, concord. [Obs.]

3. an index in which the principal words used in any work, as the Bible, Shakespeare, Milton, Tennyson, etc., are arranged alphabetically, with references to the passages in which they occur.

His knowledge of the Bible was such that he might be called a living *concordance.* —Macaulay.

çŏn·çord′ăn·cy, *n.* agreement. [Obs.]

çŏn·çord′ănt, *a.* [L. *concordans*, ppr. of *concordare*, to agree.] agreeing; agreeable; correspondent; harmonious.

çŏn·çord′ănt·ly, *adv.* in a concordant manner.

çon·çor′dat, *n.* [L. *concordatus*, pp. of *concordare*, to agree.]

1. a compact; formal agreement; covenant.

2. an agreement between the Pope and a government on church matters.

Çon′çord çōach, a type of stagecoach used by early settlers of the western United States.

Çon′çord grāpe, a large, dark-blue grape native to North America.

çŏn·çord′ist, *n.* the compiler of a concordance.

çon·çor′pō·rāte, *v.t.* and *v.i.* to unite in one mass or body; to incorporate. [Obs.]

çon·çor′pō·rāte, *a.* united in the same body; incorporated. [Obs.]

çon·çor·pō·rā′tion, *n.* union of things in one mass or body. [Rare.]

çon′çōurse, *n.* [Fr. *concours*, from L. *concursus*, a running together, from *concurrere*, to run together.]

1. a moving, flowing, or running together; confluence.

2. a crowd; a throng; a gathering.

3. a place where crowds gather.

4. a place or point of meeting; the point of junction of two or more bodies. [Rare.]

5. an open space, as in a park or railroad station.

6. a broad thoroughfare or boulevard.

7. a working together; concurrence. [Obs.]

8. in Scots law, concurrence by a person having legal qualification to grant it; as, the lord advocate's *concourse* to a libel.

çon·çrē·āte′, *v.t.* to create with, or at the same time. [Rare.]

çon·çrē·mā′tion, *n.* the act of burning different things together. [Obs.]

çon′çrē·ment, *n.* a growing together; the collection or mass formed by concretion, or natural union. [Obs.]

çŏn·çres′cence, *n.* [L. *concrescentia*, a growing together, from *concrescere*, to grow together; from *com-*, together, and *crescere*, to grow.]

1. growth or increase; the act of growing or increasing by spontaneous union, or the coalescence of separate particles; increment.

2. in biology, a joining or growing together of two or more individual cells or parts.

çŏn·çres′ci·ble, *a.* 1. capable of growing together.

2. that can change or be changed from a liquid to a solid state.

çŏn·çres′cive, *a.* growing together. [Rare.]

çŏn·çrēte′ (*or* kon′krēt), *a.* [L. *concretus*, pp. of *concrescere*, to grow together, to be solid; from *com-*, together, and *crescere*, to grow.]

1. united in growth; hence, formed by coalition of separate particles into one body; formed into a solid mass.

The first *concrete* state or consistent surface of the chaos. —Burnet.

2. having a material, perceptible existence; of, belonging to, or characterized by things or events that can be perceived by the senses; real; actual.

3. referring to a particular; specific, not general or abstract.

4. made of concrete; as, a *concrete* floor.

5. in grammar, designating a thing or class of things that can be perceived by the senses: opposed to *abstract.*

concrete number; a number telling how many or how much of a specific thing (e.g., *seven* apples, *four* miles).

concrete sound; a gliding sound or movement of the voice, as distinguished from a *discrete sound*, in which the transition from one pitch to another is abrupt.

çon′çrēte (*or* kon-krēt′), *n.* 1. anything concrete.

2. a hard, compact substance made of sand, gravel, cement, and water, used in the construction of bridges, dams, buildings, etc.

çŏn·çrēte′ (*or* kon′krēt), *v.i.*; concreted, *pt.*, *pp.*; concreting, *ppr.* to unite or coalesce into a mass or solid body by cohesion, growing together, or other natural process; as, saline particles *concrete* into crystals.

çŏn·çrēte′ (*or* kon′krēt), *v.t.* 1. to form into a mass by the cohesion or coalescence of separate particles; to solidify.

2. to construct of, or cover with, concrete (cement); as, to *concrete* a roadway.

çŏn·çrēte′ly, *adv.* in a concrete manner; not abstractly.

çŏn·çrēte′ness, *n.* the state of being concrete; coagulation.

çŏn·çrē′tion, *n.* [L. *concretio*, a uniting, condensing, from *concretus*, pp. of *concrescere*, to grow together; from *com-*, together, and *crescere*, to grow.]

1. a solidifying or being solidified.

2. a solidified mass.

3. in geology, an inclusion in sedimentary rock, usually rounded, resulting from the formation of succeeding layers of mineral matter about some nucleus, as a fossil or grain of sand.

4. in medicine, a solidified mass, usually inorganic, deposited in a tissue or cavity of the body; a calculus.

çŏn·çrē′tion·ăl, *a.* concretionary.

çŏn·çrē′tion·ā·ry, *a.* 1. pertaining to or formed by concretions.

2. containing concretion.

çŏn·çrē′tive, *a.* producing or tending to produce concretion; as, *concretive* juices.

çŏn·çrē′tive·ly, *adv.* in a concretive manner.

çon′çrēt·īze, *v.t.*; concretized, *pt.*, *pp.*; concretizing, *ppr.* to make (something) concrete; to make specific; to give definite form to.

çon·çrew′, *v.i.* to grow together. [Obs.]

çon·çrim·i·nā′tion, *n.* a joint accusation.

çŏn·çū′bi·nā·çy, *n.* concubinage. [Obs.]

çŏn·çū′bi·nāġe, *n.* [Fr. *concubinage*, from *concubine*, a concubine.]

1. the cohabitation of a man and concubine.

2. the state of being a concubine.

çŏn·çū′bi·năl, *a.* pertaining to concubinage.

çŏn·çū·bi·nā′ri·ăn, *a.* and *n.* concubinary.

çŏn·çū′bi·nā·ry, *a.* relating to, living in, or born from concubinage.

çŏn·çū′bi·nā·ry, *n.*; *pl.* **çŏn·çū′bi·nā·rieș,** one living in concubinage.

çŏn·çū′bi·nāte, *n.* concubinage. [Obs.]

çoñ′çū·bīne, *n.* [ME. *concubine*; OFr. masc. *concubin*; f. *concubine*; L. masc. *concubinus*, f. *concubina*, one who lives in concubinage, from *concumbere*, to lie together or with; from *com-*, with, and *cubare*, to lie down.]

1. a male paramour. [Obs.]

2. a woman who cohabits with a man without being legally married to him.

I know I am too mean to be your queen,
And yet too good to be your *concubine.* —Shak.

3. in certain polygamous societies, a secondary wife; a wife of inferior social and legal status: the children of such a union are generally regarded as legitimate.

çŏn·çul′çāte, *v.t.* to tread on; to trample under foot. [Obs.]

çon·çul·çā′tion, *n.* a trampling under foot. [Obs.]

çŏn·çū′pis·cence, *n.* [ME. *concupiscence*; Fr. *concupiscence*; LL. *concupiscentia*, an eager desire; L. *concupiscens*, ppr. of *concupiscere*, to desire eagerly; *com-*, together, and *cupere*, to desire.] strong or abnormal desire or appetite; especially, sexual desire; lust.

çŏn·çū′pis·cent, *a.* strongly desirous; especially, sexually desirous; lustful.

çŏn·çū·pis·cen′tiăl (-shăl), *a.* relating to concupiscence. [Obs.]

çŏn·çū·pis·cen′tious, *a.* concupiscent. [Obs.]

çŏn·çū′pis·ci·ble, *a.* concupiscent; lustful.

çŏn·çū′pis·ci·ble·ness, *n.* the state or quality of being concupiscible; concupiscence. [Rare.]

çŏn·çũr′, *v.i.*; concurred, *pt.*, *pp.*; concurring, *ppr.* [L. *concurrere*, to run together; from *com-*, together, and *currere*, to run.]

1. to run together; to meet in the same point. [Obs.]

2. to agree; to be in accord; to have the same opinion.

3. to assent: with *to.* [Rare.]

4. to unite or be conjoined; to meet together; to be combined.

In whom all these qualities do *concur.* —Whitgift.

5. to combine in having an effect; to act together; as, various causes may *concur* in the changes of temperature.

6. to coincide; to happen together; to occur at the same time.

Syn.—agree, join, unite, combine, meet, conjoin, coincide, approve.

çŏn·çũr′rence, *n.* [L. *concurrens*, ppr. of *concurrere*, to run together; from *com-*, together, and *currere*, to run.]

1. agreement in opinion; accord.

2. a happening together in time or place;

combination of agents, circumstances, or events; as, the *concurrence* of great historical events.

3. a combining to produce or bring about something.

4. in law, a joint right or claim; as, a *con-concurrence* of jurisdiction in two different courts.

5. in ecclesiastical usage, the falling together wholly or in part of two or more festivals.

6. in geometry, (a) the point where three or more lines meet; (b) the junction of lines or surfaces.

Syn.—agreement, bargain, compact, stipulation, covenant.

çŏn·çûr′ren·cy, *n.*; *pl.* **çŏn·çûr′ren·cieṣ,** concurrence.

çŏn·çûr′rent, *a.* 1. acting in conjunction; coöperating.

A *concurrent* cause of this reformation. —Davies.

2. occurring at the same time; existing together.

3. in geometry, meeting in or going toward the same point; converging.

4. in agreement; harmonious.

5. in law, having equal jurisdiction or authority.

çŏn·çûr′rent, *n.* 1. that which concurs; joint or contributory cause.

2. one who concurs or agrees with another in opinion, etc.

3. one who is aiming at the same object as another; hence, a rival. [Rare.]

4. the day or days in excess of 52 weeks in any one year: so called because they concur with the solar cycle.

çŏn·çûr′rent·ly, *adv.* with concurrence; unitedly; at the same time.

çŏn·çûr′rent·ness, *n.* concurrence.

çŏn·çûr′rent reṣ·ō·lū′tion, a resolution passed by one branch of a bicameral legislature and concurred in by the other, indicating the opinion of the legislature on some matter: it does not have the force of law and, hence, does not require the signature of the chief executive: distinguished from *joint resolution*.

çŏn·çûr′ring, *a.* agreeing; acting together; contributing to the same event or effect; consenting.

concurring figure; in geometry, a figure which, being laid on another, corresponds with it in every part; a congruent figure.

çon·çûr′sō, *n.* [Sp., Port., from L. *concursus*, a running together, from *com-*, together, and *currere*, to run.] a civil law process by which each creditor may maintain his right to payment out of the assets of a debtor without regard to the claims of the other creditors.

çŏn·çuss′, *v.t.* [L. *concussus*, pp. of *concutere*, to shake together; from *com-*, together, and *quatere*, to shake.]

1. to shake, jar, or agitate violently; to shock. [Rare.]

2. in law, to compel the surrender of (something) or the performance of (an act) by force or threats. [Rare.]

çon·çus·sā′tion, *n.* a violent shock or agitation. [Obs.]

çŏn·çus′sion, *n.* [L. *concussio*, a violent shock, from *concutere*, to shake violently, shake together; from *com-*, together, and *quatere*, to shake.]

1. the act of violently shaking or agitating; a shock, as from impact.

2. in medicine, a condition of impaired functioning of some organ, especially the brain, as a result of a violent blow or impact.

3. in civil law, extortion by intimidation. [Rare.]

çŏn·çus′sion fūṣe, a shell fuse which ignites upon the impact of the shell with some solid.

çŏn·çus′sive, *a.* 1. of concussion.

2. tending to cause concussion.

çŏn·çȳ′liç, *a.* [*con-*, and Gr. *kyklos*, a circle.] located in the same circumference, or possessing parallel cyclic planes.

çond, *v.t.* to con (a ship). [Obs.]

çŏn·demn′ (-dem′), *v.t.*; condemned, *pt.*, *pp.*; condemning, *ppr.* [L. *condemnare*, to condemn, doom, blame; from *com-*, intens., and *damnare*, to harm, condemn.]

1. to pass an adverse judgment on; to utter a sentence of disapprobation against; to censure; to blame.

2. to convict; to show or prove (a person) to be wrong, or guilty.

3. to sentence to a fine or other punishment; to utter sentence against judicially; to doom; as, the judge *condemned* him to death.

4. to declare unfit for use or service; as, the ship was *condemned* as unseaworthy.

5. to declare (property) forfeited or legally appropriated for public use.

6. to declare (a sick person) incurable.

Syn.—blame, censure, upbraid, convict, sentence, adjudge, reprove, doom, reprobate, reproach.

çŏn·dem′nȧ·ble, *a.* deserving to be condemned; blamable; culpable.

çon·dem·nā′tion, *n.* [LL. *condemnatio*, condemnation, from L. *condemnare*, to condemn.]

1. the act of condemning; the judicial act of declaring one guilty, and sentencing him to punishment.

2. the state of being condemned; as, the *condemnation* of the wicked.

3. a cause for condemning.

çŏn·dem′nȧ·tō·ry, *a.* condemning; expressing condemnation, explicitly or implicitly; as, a *condemnatory* sentence or decree.

çŏn·demned′, *a.* 1. censured; declared to be wrong, guilty, worthless, or forfeited; adjudged or sentenced to punishment; as, the *condemned* criminal.

2. intended for persons under sentence of death; as, the *condemned* cell.

çŏn·dem′nẽr, *n.* one who condemns.

çŏn·den·sȧ·bil′i·ty, *n.* the quality of being condensable.

çŏn·den′sȧ·ble, *a.* that can be condensed.

çŏn·den′sāte, *v.t.* and *v.i.*; condensated, *pt.*, *pp.*; condensating, *ppr.* to condense. [Rare.]

çŏn·den′sāte, *a.* condensed. [Archaic.]

çŏn·den′sāte, *n.* a product of condensation.

çon·den·sā′tion, *n.* [LL. *condensatio*, condensation, from L. *condensare*, to condense.]

1. the act of making dense or compact; the process of condensing or the state of being condensed.

2. the result or product of condensing.

çŏn·den′sȧ·tive, *a.* having the power or tendency to condense.

çŏn·dense′, *v.t.*; condensed, *pt.*, *pp.*; condensing, *ppr.* [Fr. *condenser*; L. *condensare*, from *condensus*, very dense, from *com-*, intens., and *densus*, dense.]

1. to make more close, dense, or compact; to reduce the volume of; to compress.

2. to express in fewer words; to make concise.

3. to concentrate; to intensify: said of light rays.

4. to change (a substance) to a denser form, as from a gas to a liquid.

Syn.—compress, squeeze, abridge, contract, epitomize, reduce.

çŏn·dense′, *v.i.* 1. to become more dense or compact.

2. to become reduced to a denser form, as a vapor into a liquid.

3. in chemistry, to join with other atoms in the same or different molecules, so as to form a new, more complex compound: said of an atom or atoms.

çŏn·dense′, *a.* close in texture or composition; compact; firm; dense. [Obs.]

çŏn·densed′ (-denst), *a.* made more dense; contracted.

çŏn·densed′ milk, a thick, sweetened milk made by evaporating part of the water from cow's milk and adding sugar: distinguished from *evaporated milk*.

çŏn·densed′ tȳpe, in printing, a type face of narrower width than the standard type for the series.

çŏn·dens′ẽr, *n.* 1. one who or that which condenses.

2. an apparatus for converting gases or vapors to a liquid state.

3. a lens or series of lenses for concentrating light rays on an object or area.

4. in electricity, a device consisting of two or more conductor plates separated from one another by a dielectric and used for receiving and storing an electric charge.

5. in cloth manufacturing, (a) an apparatus (part of a cotton gin) for compressing lint; (b) a device for forming carded wool into rolls.

injection condenser; a condenser in which steam comes in contact with a jet of cold water: called also *jet condenser* and *siphon condenser*.

surface condenser; in steam engines, an apparatus for condensing steam by bringing it into contact with cold metallic surfaces.

çŏn·dens′ẽr an·ten′nȧ, an antenna system consisting of an overhead conductor or aerial and a lower conductor which is grounded.

çŏn·den·si·bil′i·ty, *n.* condensability.

çŏn·den′si·ble, *a.* condensable.

çŏn·den′si·ty, *n.* the state of being condensed; denseness; density. [Obs.]

çond′ẽr, *n.* a conner, or lookout on a ship. [Obs.]

çon·dē·scend′, *v.i.*; condescended, *pt.*, *pp.*; condescending, *ppr.* [ME. *condescenden*; OFr. *condescendre*; LL. *condescendere*, let oneself down, condescend; from *com-*, together, and *descendere*, to come down; *de-*, from, and *scandere*, to climb.]

1. to descend voluntarily to the level, regarded as lower, of the person or persons that one is dealing with; to be gracious or affable to inferiors; to deign.

2. to deal with others in a patronizing manner.

3. to lower or degrade oneself; as, he *condescended* to accept a bribe.

4. to make concessions; agree; assent. [Obs.]

çon·dē·scend′ence, *n.* 1. the act of condescending; condescension.

2. a listing of particulars. [Scot.]

çon·dē·scend′en·cy, *n.* condescension. [Obs.]

çon·dē·scend′ing, *a.* showing condescension; especially, patronizing.

çon·dē·scend′ing·ly, *adv.* in a condescending manner.

çon·dē·scen′sion, *n.* act or instance of condescending; patronizing manner or behavior.

çŏn·dīgn′ (-dīn′), *a.* [L. *condignus*, very worthy; from *com-*, intens., and *dignus*, worthy.]

1. deserved; suitable; adequate: used especially with reference to punishment for wrongdoing; as, the prisoner has suffered *condign* punishment.

2. worthy; merited; as, *condign* praise. [Obs.]

çŏn·dig′ni·ty, *n.* 1. worthiness; merit. [Obs.]

2. the merit of human actions, which claims reward on the score of justice.

çŏn·dīgn′ly, *adv.* according to merit.

çŏn·dīgn′ness, *n.* accordance with merits.

çon′di·ment, *n.* [Fr. *condiment*; L. *condimentum*, a spice, seasoning, from *condire*, to pickle.] seasoning; that which is used to give relish to meat or other food, as pepper, mustard, sauces, etc.

çon·dis·ci′ple, *n.* 1. a fellow disciple.

2. a fellow student.

çŏn·dīte′, *v.t.* to preserve with sugar, salt, spices, or the like; to pickle. [Obs.]

çon′dīte, *a.* pickled; preserved. [Obs.]

çŏn·di′tion, *n.* [ME. *condicion*; OFr. *condicion*; L. *condicio*, an agreement, stipulation, condition, situation, from *condicere*, to speak with, agree; from *com-*, together, and *dicere*, to speak.]

1. anything called for as a requirement before the performance, completion, or effectiveness of something else; provision; stipulation; as, this contract imposes several *conditions*.

2. anything essential to the existence or occurrence of something else; prerequisite; as, health is a *condition* of happiness.

3. anything that modifies or restricts the nature, existence, or occurrence of something else; external circumstance or factor; as, *conditions* were favorable for business.

4. manner or state of being.

5. proper or healthy state; as, athletes must train to be in *condition*.

6. rank; station; social position.

7. in education, (a) the requirement imposed on a student that he make up deficiencies in a certain subject in order to pass it; (b) the grade or mark stating this requirement.

8. in grammar, a clause expressing a condition, as one beginning with *if*.

9. in logic, a proposition on which the truth of another proposition depends.

10. in law, a clause in a contract, will, or other document which provides that one or more of its stipulations may be qualified, suspended, or nullified, under stated circumstances.

on or *upon condition that*; provided that; if.

çŏn·di′tion, *v.i.*; conditioned, *pt.*, *pp.*; conditioning, *ppr.* to make terms; to negotiate about conditions.

çŏn·di′tion, *v.t.* 1. to contract; to stipulate; to make terms concerning.

2. to place conditions upon; to subject to a condition or conditions.

3. in education, to require (a student) to make up deficiencies in a course in order to pass it.

4. in psychology, to cause to respond in a certain way to a certain stimulus; to develop

a conditioned reflex or behavior pattern in (a person or animal).

5. loosely, to accustom (a person) to.

6. to be a condition of.

7. to bring into proper or fit condition.

çŏn·dĭ'tion·ăl, *a.* 1. containing, implying, or depending on a condition or conditions; made with limitations; not absolute; as, a *conditional* promise, a *conditional* fee.

2. in grammar and logic, expressing a condition or supposition; as, a *conditional* clause.

çon·dĭ'tion·ăl, *n.* a word, clause, or proposition expressing a condition.

çŏn·dĭ·tion·al'i·ty, *n.* the quality or state of being conditional.

çŏn·dĭ'tion·ăl·ly, *adv.* with or under certain conditions; subject to particular terms or stipulations; not absolutely or positively.

çŏn·dĭ'tion·āte, *v.t.* and *v.i.* 1. to qualify. [Obs.]

2. to make subject to conditions.

çŏn·dĭ'tioned (-shund), *a.* 1. stipulated; depending on certain conditions.

2. in a (specified) condition; as, well-*conditioned*; ill-*conditioned*.

3. in a fit or proper condition.

4. having developed a conditioned reflex or behavior pattern.

5. loosely, accustomed (*to*).

conditioned reflex or *response*; a reflex in which the response (e.g., secretion of saliva in a dog) is occasioned by a secondary stimulus (e.g., the ringing of a bell) repeatedly associated with the primary stimulus (e.g., the sight of meat).

çŏn·dĭ'tioned, *n.* in philosophy or metaphysics, that which depends upon or is determined by something else (with *the*): opposed to *the absolute*.

çon'dĭ·tō·ry, *n.* [L. *conditorium*, a place where anything is put away, from *condire*, to preserve, put aside.] a repository. [Obs.]

çon'dō, *n.*; *pl.* **çon'dōş** or **çon'dōeş** same as *condominium* (sense 3). [Colloq.]

çŏn·dō'lȧ·tō·ry, *a.* expressing condolence.

çŏn·dōle', *v.i.*; condoled, *pt.*, *pp.*; condoling *ppr.* [LL. *condolere*, to condole; from *com-*, with, and *dolere*, to grieve.] to express sympathy; to mourn in sympathy; commiserate.

çŏn·dōle', *v.t.* to grieve over. [Rare.]

çŏn·dōle'ment, *n.* same as *condolence*.

çŏn·dō'lence, *n.* the expression of sympathy with another in grief.

çŏn·dōl'ẽr, *n.* one who condoles.

con dō·lō're, [It.] with grief; sadly: a direction to the performer in music.

çon'dŏm, *n.* [perh. altered from *Conton*, name of 18th-c. Eng. doctor, the reputed inventor.] a thin protective sheath, generally of rubber, used to prevent venereal infection or as a contraceptive.

çon·dō·min'i·um, *n.* 1. joint or concurrent dominion or jurisdiction of a country or region by two or more states.

2. the territory so governed.

3. (a) an arrangement under which a tenant in an apartment building or in a complex of multiple-unit dwellings holds full title to his unit and joint ownership in the common grounds; (b) *pl.* **çon·dō·min'i·umş, çon·dō·min'i·ȧ,** such a building or complex.

çon·dō·nā'tion, *n.* [L. *condonatio*, a giving away, pardoning, from *condonare*, to give as a present, to pardon.]

1. the act of condoning.

2. in law, an expressed or implied forgiving by a husband or wife of the other's adultery.

çŏn·dōne', *v.t.*; condoned, *pt.*, *pp.*; condoning, *ppr.* [L. *condonare*, to give up, pardon; from *com-*, intens., and *donare*, to give.] to pardon, forgive, or overlook (an offense).

çon'dŏr, *n.* [Sp., from Peruv. *cuntur*, condor.]

1. a large vulture, *Sarcorhamphus gryphus*, found in the most elevated parts of the South American Andes, with black plumage, bare head and neck, and a ruff of downy white feathers at the base of the neck.

2. a similar vulture found in California.

3. *pl.* **çon·dōr'eş,** any of various gold coins, stamped with a condor's figure, and used in several South American countries.

CONDOR (4 ft. long; 9 ft. wingspread)

çon·dot·tiẹ're (-tyā'), *n.*; *pl.* **çon·dot·tiẹ'ri,** [It., from L. *conducti*, mercenary soldiers, from *conductus*, pp. of *conducere*, to hire.] in Europe from the fourteenth to the sixteenth centuries, a captain of a band of adventurers, hired to lead his mercenaries in battle.

çŏn·dūce', *v.i.*; conduced (-dūst), *pt.*, *pp.*; conducing, *ppr.* [OFr. *conduire*; L. *conducere*, to lead, draw or bring together, hire, conduce; from *com-*, together, and *ducere*, to lead.] to lead or tend; to contribute to a result: followed by *to* or *toward*; as, insecurity often *conduces to* fear.

They may *conduce to* further discoveries for completing the theory of light.—Newton.

çŏn·dūce', *v.t.* to conduct; to bring about. [Obs.]

çŏn·dūce'ment, *n.* a leading or tending to; tendency. [Obs.]

çŏn·dū'cent, *a.* tending or contributing to.

çŏn·dū·ci·bil'i·ty, *n.* the state of contributing to an end.

çŏn·dū'ci·ble, *a.* leading or tending to; conducive.

çŏn·dū'ci·ble·ness, *n.* the quality of leading or contributing to any end.

çŏn·dū'ci·bly, *adv.* in a conducive manner.

çŏn·dū'cive, *a.* conducing; contributing; tending; helpful (*to*).

An action, however *conducive to* the good of our country, will be represented as prejudicial to it. —Addison.

çŏn·dū'cive·ness, *n.* the quality of being conducive.

çon'duçt, *n.* [L. *conductus*, pp. of *conducere*, to bring together, collect.]

1. the act of leading; guidance; as, the *conduct* of a campaign.

2. management; handling.

3. a convoy; escort. [Obs.]

4. personal behavior; deportment; way that one acts.

5. in ethics, the voluntary control and direction of one's actions toward moral or spiritual development.

6. a conveyor; conduit; a carrier; an instrument; that which conducts. [Obs.]

7. construction; action; plot; literary or dramatic development; as, the *conduct* of a novel.

Syn.—deportment, behavior, demeanor, management, guidance.

çŏn·duçt', *v.t.*; conducted, *pt.*, *pp.*; conducting, *ppr.* [L. *conductus*, pp. of *conducere*, to bring or lead together; from *com-*, together, and *ducere*, to lead.]

1. to introduce; to escort; to attend; to usher; to guide; to lead; as, to *conduct* a lady to a seat.

2. to direct; to manage; to command; as, to *conduct* one's affairs.

3. to direct (an orchestra, etc.).

4. to behave (oneself).

5. to serve as a channel for; to convey; to transmit.

çŏn·duçt', *v.i.* 1. to act as a conveyor, transmitter, or conductor, as of electricity, heat, etc.

2. to behave. [Rare.]

3. to lead.

çŏn·duçt'ănce, *n.* the ability of a substance to conduct electricity, measured by the ratio of the current to the applied electromotive force: also called *reciprocal of resistance*.

çŏn·duçt·i·bil'i·ty, *n.* capacity for conducting (electricity, heat, etc.).

çŏn·duçt'i·ble, *a.* 1. that can conduct (electricity, heat, etc.).

2. that can be conducted.

çŏn·duç'tion, *n.* 1. a conveying, as of liquid through a channel.

2. in physics, (a) transmission (of electricity, heat, etc.) by the passage of energy from particle to particle; (b) conductivity.

çŏn·duçt'ive, *a.* 1. having the power of conducting.

2. having to do with conduction.

çon·duç·tiv'i·ty, *n.* 1. the power of conducting heat, electricity, etc.; the property of being conductive.

2. in electricity, the quantity of electricity that will flow through a unit cube of a given substance in a unit of time; the reciprocal of resistivity.

çŏn·duçt'ŏr, *n.* [L. *conductor*, a lessee, a contractor, from *conducere*, to lead, bring together.]

1. a leader; a guide; one who conducts.

2. a chief; a commander; one who leads an army or a people. [Obs.]

3. a director; a manager; a superintendent; as, the *conductor* of an enterprise.

4. in surgery, a grooved staff which serves to direct the knife.

5. a thing or substance which conducts heat, electricity, etc.

6. the official in charge of the passengers and collection of fares on a railroad train, streetcar, bus, etc.

7. the director of an orchestra or other musical group.

prime conductor; the largest of the conductors in a static electrical apparatus, which collects and retains the electricity.

çŏn·duçt'ō·ry, *a.* having the property of conducting. [Rare.]

çŏn·duçt'ress, *n.* a woman conductor.

çon'duit (-dit *or* -doo-it), *n.* [ME. *conduit*; OFr. *conduit*, conduct, guidance, from L. *conductus*, pp. of *conducere*, to bring or lead together, conduct.]

1. in architecture, a narrow passage, usually underground, for the purpose of secret communication between apartments. [Archaic.]

2. a canal, pipe, or passageway for the conveyance of fluids.

The *conduits* of my blood. —Shak.

3. a tube or protected trough for electric wires.

4. a fountain. [Archaic.]

çon·dū'pli·çāte, *a.* [L. *conduplicatus*, pp. of *conduplicare*, to double, fold together; from *com-*, together, and *duplicare*, to double.] folded lengthwise through the middle, as certain leaves or petals in the bud.

çon·dū'pli·çā·ted, *a.* doubled; folded together.

çon·dū·pli·çā'tion, *n.* a doubling; a duplication.

çon·dū·rañ'gō, *n.* see *cundurango*.

çon·dur'rīte, *n.* a form of domeykite, an arsenide of copper, taken from the Condurrow mine in Cornwall, England.

çon'dy·lăr, *a.* pertaining to or resembling a condyle.

Çon·dy·lär'thrȧ, *n.pl.* [L., from Gr. *kondylos*, a knuckle, and *arthron*, a joint.] an extinct order of Eocene mammals, characterized by having a third femoral trochanter.

çon''dy·lär·thrō'sis, *n.* in anatomy, a form of movable joint of which the articular surfaces are spheroidal, permitting angular motion in any direction; condylar articulation.

çon'dyle (*or* -dil), *n.* [L. *condylus*; Gr. *kondylos*, a knob, knuckle, joint.]

1. a rounded process at the end of a bone, forming a ball-and-socket joint with the hollow part of another bone.

2. a rounded part of the hard integument covering the joints of the limbs in arthropods.

çon'dy·loid, *a.* pertaining to or resembling a condyle.

condyloid process; in anatomy, an oblong rounded process on the lower jawbone which is received into the fossa of the temporal bone, forming a movable articulation.

çon·dy·lō'mȧ, *n.*; *pl.* **çon·dy·lō'mȧ·tȧ,** [L., from Gr. *kondylos*, a knob, knuckle, and *-ōma*, from *ōmos*, raw, like a tumor.] a wartlike, inflammatory growth on the epidermis or adjacent mucous membrane of the anus or genitals, occurring especially in the secondary stage of syphilis.

çon'dy·lōpe, *n.* a condylopod. [Obs.]

çon·dyl'ō·pod, *n.* [L. *condylopus*, from Gr. *kondylos*, a knuckle, and *pous*, *podos*, a foot.] an arthropod: so called by Cuvier because of its jointed feet.

çōne, *n.* [Fr. *cone*; L. *conus*; Gr. *kōnos*, a wedge, peak, cone.]

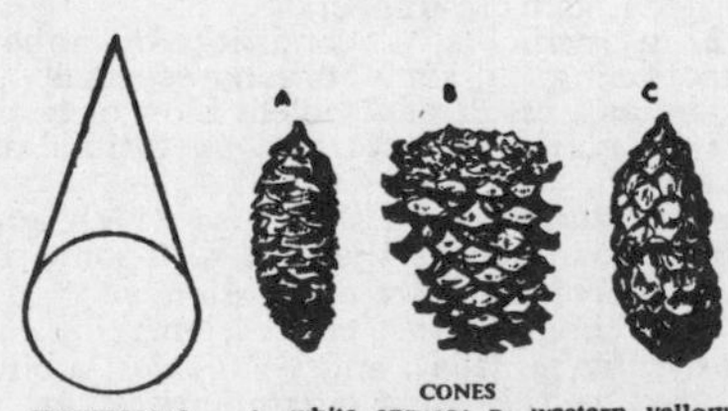

GEOMETRICAL CONE

CONES A. white spruce; B. western yellow pine; C. airplane spruce

1. in geometry, (a) a solid with a circle for its base and a curved surface tapering evenly to an apex so that any point on this surface is in a straight line between the circumference of the base and the apex; (b) a solid described by the hypotenuse of a right triangle rotated about either of its legs as an axis; (c) a surface described by a moving straight line passing through a fixed point (called the *vertex*) and tracing any fixed curve, as a circle, ellipse, etc., at another point.

2. in botany, the fruit of several evergreen trees, as of the pine, fir, and spruce. It

is composed of a woody axis on which are arranged stiff, leaflike scales containing ovules or pollen.

3. any object or mass having the shape of a cone, as the peak of a volcano, a crisp shell of pastry for holding a scoop of ice cream, any of various machine parts, etc.

4. a shell belonging to the genus *Conus*; a cone shell.

cone of rays; in optics, all the rays of light which proceed from a radiant point and fall upon a given flat surface.

cones of the retina; the crystalline cones of the eye.

oblique or *scalene cone*; a cone the axis of which is inclined to the plane of its base, the sides being unequal.

right cone; a cone of which the axis is perpendicular to the plane of its base, the sides being equal.

çōne, *v.t.*; coned, *pt.*, *pp.*; coning, *ppr.* to shape like a cone or conical segment.

çōne bēar′ing, a bearing in which a conelike end supports the revolving part.

çōne′flow″ẽr, *n.* any of the composite plants belonging to the genus *Rudbeckia*, with flowers, mostly yellow, having petals radiating from a cone-shaped axis, as the black-eyed Susan.

çōne′-in-çōne′, *a.* in geology, having a concentric series of cones with parallel bases and axes, as seen in the texture of some shales.

çō·nē′ine, *n.* see *conine*.

çō·neñ′çhy·mȧ, *n.* [L., from Gr. *kōnos*, a cone, and *enchyma*, an infusion.] plant tissue found in the form of conical cells.

çōne′nōṣe, *n.* any of various blood-sucking insects belonging to the genus *Conorhinus*, having conelike sucking organs, found in the southern and southwestern United States.

çō′ne·pä·te, çō′ne·patl, *n.* a skunk of Latin America, with a solid white back.

çōne pụl′ley, a pulley made in sections of graduating diameters, giving it the shape of a cone.

Çon·es·tō′gȧ wag′ŏn, [after *Conestoga*, Lancaster County, Pennsylvania, where the wagons were manufactured.] a broad-wheeled covered wagon used by American pioneers crossing the prairies.

çō′ney, *n.*; *pl.* **çō′neyṣ,** see *cony*.

çon′fab, *n.* familiar and easy conversation; confabulation. [Colloq.]

çŏn·fab′ū·lāte, *v.i.*; confabulated, *pt.*, *pp.*; confabulating, *ppr.* [L. *confabulatus*, pp. of *confabulari*, to talk together.] to talk familiarly together; to chat; to prattle.

çŏn·fab·ū·lā′tion, *n.* familiar talk; easy, unrestrained, unceremonious conversation; chat.

çŏn·fab′ū·lā·tō·ry, *a.* pertaining to familiar talk or confabulation; colloquial. [Rare.]

çon·far·rē·ā′tion, *n.* [L. *confarreatio*, from *confarreare*, to connect in marriage by an offering of bread; from *com-*, together, and *farreus*, of grain, from *far*, grain, spelt.] in ancient Rome, the most solemn form of marriage among the patricians, marked by the offering of a cake of spelt as a sacrifice to Jupiter.

çŏn·fāt′ed, *a.* fated together with something else. [Rare.]

çŏn·feçt′, *v.t.*; confected, *pt.*, *pp.*; confecting, *ppr.* 1. to make into sweetmeats. [Obs.]

Saffron *confected* in Cilicia. —Browne.

2. to put together; to prepare or make, especially by mixing or combining.

çon′feçt, *n.* something prepared with sugar or honey, as fruit, herbs, roots, and the like; a confection; a comfit; a sweetmeat. [Obs.]

çŏn·feç′tion, *n.* [ME. *confection*, *confeccioun*; OFr. *confection*, *confession*, a confection, preparation, from L. *confectus*, pp. of *conficere*, to prepare, put together; from *com-*, with, and *facere*, to make.]

1. anything prepared or preserved with sugar, as a bonbon, candy, ice cream, etc.

2. a confecting.

3. a sweetened compound of drugs; electuary.

4. a fancy, stylish article of women's clothing.

çŏn·feç′tion, *v.t.* to prepare as a confection.

çŏn·feç′tion·ā·ry, *n.*; *pl.* **çon·feç′tion·ā·rieṣ,** 1. a confectioner. [Archaic.]

2. a confection; a sweetmeat.

3. a confectionery; a confectioner's shop.

çŏn·feç′tion·ā·ry, *a.* 1. relating to or consisting of confections; as, *confectionary* wares.

The biscuit, or *confectionary* plum. —Cowper.

2. of a confectioner or his work.

çŏn·feç′tion·ẽr, *n.* 1. one who manufactures or deals in confections, such as candies, bonbons, cakes, ice cream, etc.

2. one who compounds drugs, such as conserves, electuaries, etc. [Obs.]

çŏn·feç′tion·ẽr′ṣ sụg′ăr (shụg′), see under *sugar*.

çŏn·feç′tion·ẽr·y, *n.* 1. a place where candy and other confections are made or sold; a confectioner's store or shop: sometimes spelled *confectionary*.

2. candies, ice cream, and other confections; things prepared or sold by a confectioner.

3. the business or work of a confectioner.

çŏn·feç′tō·ry, *a.* pertaining to the art of making confections. [Obs.]

çŏn·fec′tūre, *n.* a confection. [Obs.]

çŏn·fed′ẽr, *v.t.* and *v.i.* to confederate. [Obs.]

çŏn·fed′ẽr·ȧ·cy, *n.*; *pl.* **çŏn·fed′ẽr·ȧ·cieṣ,** [ME. *confederacie*; OFr. *confederacie*, a league, from LL. *confœderatus*, pp. of *confœderare*, to league together; from L. *com-*, together, and *fœdus*, a league.]

1. a league or alliance between two or more people, groups, nations, or states, in support of some common act or enterprise; a federation.

The friendships of the world are oft
Confederacies in vice. —Addison.

2. the persons, states, or nations united by such a league.

3. people united to commit an unlawful act; a conspiracy.

the Confederacy; the group of Southern States that seceded from the United States in 1860 and 1861; Alabama, Arkansas, Florida, Georgia, Louisiana, Mississippi, North Carolina, South Carolina, Tennessee, Texas, and Virginia: also called *Confederate States of America*, *Southern Confederacy*.

Syn.—alliance, league, association, combination, union, covenant, confederation.

çŏn·fed′ẽr·āte, *a.* 1. united in a league; engaged in a confederacy; pertaining to a confederacy.

All the swords
In Italy, and her *confederate* arms,
Could not have made this peace. —Shak.

2. [C-] of or pertaining to the Confederacy; as, the *Confederate* Congress.

Confederate States of America; the Confederacy.

çŏn·fed′ẽr·āte, *n.* 1. a person, group, nation, or state united with another or others for some common purpose; an ally; an accomplice.

2. [C-] any Southerner who sided with the Confederacy in the Civil War (1861–1865), especially, a soldier or sailor of the Southern forces, as distinguished from a *Federal* or *Union* soldier or sailor.

3. an associate in an unlawful act or plot; an accomplice; a co-conspirator.

Syn.—friend, companion, associate, accomplice, accessory, abetter, ally.

çŏn·fed′ẽr·āte, *v.t.* and *v.i.*; confederated, *pt.*, *pp.*; confederating, *ppr.* to unite in a league; to join together; to ally.

çŏn·fed′ẽr·ā·tẽr, çŏn·fed′ẽr·ā·tŏr, *n.* a confederate. [Obs.]

çŏn·fed·ẽr·ā′tion, *n.* 1. a uniting or being united in a league or alliance.

2. the states or nations joined in a league or union for a special purpose that is not merely temporary.

Articles of Confederation; see under *article*, *n.*

the Confederation; the union of the American States (1781–1789) under the Articles of Confederation.

çŏn·fed′ẽr·ā·tive, *a.* of confederates or a confederation.

çŏn·fẽr′, *v.t.*; conferred, *pt.*, *pp.*; conferring, *ppr.* [OFr. *conferer*; L. *conferre*, to bring together, compare, confer; from *com-*, together, and *ferre*, to bring.]

1. to compare; to examine by comparison; to collate: now obsolete except in the imperative, usually abbreviated *cf.*

2. to give or bestow.

Coronation *confers* on the king no royal authority. —South.

3. to bring or carry to; hence, to contribute; to conduce. [Obs.]

çŏn·fẽr′, *v.i.* to consult together; to compare opinions; to carry on a discussion or deliberation; to converse.

When they had commanded them to go aside out of the council they *conferred* among themselves. —Acts iv. 15.

Syn.—consult, discuss, converse, advise, discourse.

çon·fẽr·ee′, *n.* 1. one who participates in a conference; one who is conferred with.

2. one upon whom something, as an honor, a title, a gift, or the like, is conferred.

Also written *conferree*.

çon′fẽr·ence, *n.* [Fr. *conférence*, conference, from L. *conferens*, ppr. of *conferre*, to compare, bring together.]

1. comparison; examination of things by comparison. [Obs.]

The mutual *conference* of all men's collections and observations. —Hooker.

2. the act of conferring or consulting together.

3. a formal meeting of a number of people for consultation or discussion.

4. a meeting at which committees from the two branches of a legislature adjust differences respecting bills passed by both houses.

5. [C-] an assembly of ministers of either the Methodist Church or the Mennonite Church for legislating on church matters.

6. an association of religious bodies, schools, athletic teams, etc., for some common purpose.

çon·fẽr·en′tiăl (-shăl), *a.* of or relating to conference.

çŏn·fẽr′ment, *n.* the act of conferring; as, the *conferment* of a title or a degree.

çŏn·fẽr′rȧ·ble, *a.* capable of being conferred.

çon·fẽr·ree′, *n.* same as *conferee*.

çŏn·fẽr′rẽr, *n.* one who confers something; one who bestows.

çon·fer·rū′mi·nāte, çon·fer·rū′mi·nā·ted, *a.* [L. *conferruminatus*, pp. of *conferruminare*, to solder together; from *com-*, together, and *ferruminare*, to solder, from *ferrumen*, solder, cement; *ferrum*, iron.] in botany, firmly united together.

Çon·fẽr′vȧ, *n.* [L. *conferva*, an aquatic plant.] a genus of green algae, consisting of fresh-water species.

çŏn·fẽr′vȧ, *n.*; *pl.* **çŏn·fẽr′vae, çŏn·fẽr′vȧṣ,** an alga of the genus *Conferva*.

Çon·fẽr·vā′cē·ae, *n.pl.* a family of fresh-water algae having green fronds which are composed of articulated filaments, simple or branched. *Conferva* is the type genus.

çon·fẽr·vā′ceous, *a.* of or belonging to the *Confervaceæ*.

çŏn·fẽr′văl, *a.* of or like the genus *Conferva*.

çŏn·fẽr′văl, *n.* a plant of the family *Confervaceæ*.

çŏn·fẽr′vīte, *n.* a fossil plant, occurring chiefly in chalk, apparently allied to the aquatic confervae.

çŏn·fẽr′void, *a.* [L. *conferva*, and Gr. *eidos*, form.] like a conferva.

çŏn·fẽr′void, *n.* a conferva.

Çon·fẽr·voi′dē·ae, *n.pl.* the green-spored algae, or *Chlorospermeæ*, the lowest order of water plants.

çŏn·fẽr′vous, *a.* conferval.

çŏn·fess′, *v.t.*; confessed (-fest), *pt.*, *pp.*; confessing, *ppr.* [ME. *confessen*; OFr. *confesser*, to confess; L. *confessus*, pp. of *confiteri*, to confess, own; from *com-*, together, and *fateri*, to acknowledge.]

1. to own, acknowledge, or avow; to make avowal or admission of (a crime, fault, opinion, etc.).

And there *confess*
Humbly our faults, and pardon beg. —Milton.

2. in ecclesiastical usage, (a) to tell (one's sins) to a priest in private in order to receive absolution; (b) to hear or receive the confession of (a penitent): said of a priest.

I have *confessed* her and I know her virtue. —Shak.

3. to acknowledge as having a certain character or certain claims; to declare belief or faith in.

Whosoever therefore shall *confess* me before men, him will I *confess* also before my Father which is in heaven.—Matt. x. 32.

4. to grant; to admit; not to dispute.

5. to show by the effect; to manifest; to attest; to reveal. [Poet.]

The lovely stranger stands *confessed*
A maid in all her charms. —Goldsmith.

Syn.—acknowledge, own, reveal, concede, avow, admit, attest, accept, grant, assent, recognize, prove, exhibit.

çŏn·fess′, *v.i.* 1. to admit or acknowledge one's faults or crimes; own up to one's guilt.

2. in ecclesiastical usage, (a) to tell one's sins in order to receive absolution; (b) to hear a person tell his sins; serve as a confessor.

çŏn·fess′ănt, *n.* one who confesses to a priest.

çŏn·fess′ȧ·ry, *n.* one who makes a confession. [Obs.]

çŏn·fess′ed·ly, *adv.* by one's own confession or acknowledgment; avowedly; admittedly; without denial.

çŏn·fess′ẽr, *n.* one who confesses.

çŏn·fes′sion, *n.* [ME. *confession,* OFr. *confession;* L. *confessio,* confession.]

1. the act of confessing; especially, the acknowledgment of anything adverse to one's interest or reputation.

2. something confessed.

3. a disclosing of sins or faults to a priest in order to receive absolution; in the Roman Catholic Church, part of the sacrament of penance: often called *auricular confession.*

4. a formulary which comprises the articles of faith; a creed to be assented to or signed as a preliminary to admission into a church: usually called a *confession of faith.*

5. in law, an acknowledgment of guilt by a person charged with a crime. A *judicial confession* is one made before a magistrate or in court; an *extrajudicial confession* is one made out of court, whether to an official or a nonofficial.

6. a form used in public worship, expressing a general acknowledgment of sin.

7. a group of people adhering to a certain creed; church; sect; denomination.

8. the tomb or shrine of a martyr or confessor.

confession and avoidance; in law, a form of pleading, as when a party confesses the facts in the declaration to be true, but presents some new matter by way of avoiding the legal effect.

general confession; the joint confession of sins by a number of persons, as in public worship.

çŏn·fes′sion·ăl, *n.* 1. a small, enclosed place in a church, where a priest hears confessions.

2. the confession of sins to a priest.

çŏn·fes′sion·ăl, *a.* 1. of, like, or for confession.

2. of creeds.

çŏn·fes′sion·ăl·ism, *n.* extreme adherence to the letter of a particular creed or confession of faith. [Rare.]

çŏn·fes′sion·ăl·ist, *n.* a priest who sits in the confessional; a confessor.

çŏn·fes′sion·ā·ry, *a.* and *n.*; *pl.* **çŏn·fes′sion·ā·ries,** confessional. [Rare.]

çŏn·fes′sion·ist, *n.* 1. one who makes a profession of faith.

2. [C-] a Lutheran; one who held to the Augsburg formulary.

çŏn·fes′sion of fāith, 1. a declaration of belief.

2. a declaration of the beliefs or doctrines of a religion; creed.

çŏn·fess′ŏr, *n.* 1. one who confesses; one who acknowledges a crime, fault, or sin.

2. one who makes a profession of his faith in the Christian religion; specifically, one who avows his religion in the face of danger, or adheres to it in defiance of persecution and torture; as, Edward the *Confessor:* distinguished from *martyr.*

3. one who hears confessions, specifically, a priest who is authorized to hear confessions and grant absolution.

çŏn·fess′ŏr·ship, *n.* the state of being persecuted on account of religious faith.

çŏn·fest′ly, *adv.* see *confessedly.*

çŏn·fet′ti, *n.pl.*; *sing.* **çŏn·fet′tō,** [It., pl. of *confetto,* sweetmeat.]

1. candies, or plaster imitations of candies, formerly scattered about at carnivals or other celebrations.

2. [*construed as sing.*] bits of colored paper now used in this way.

çon·fi·dant′, *n.* [Fr.] a person entrusted with the confidence of another; one to whom secrets are confided; a confidential friend.

çon·fi·dante′, *n.* a confidant who is a woman.

çŏn·fīde′, *v.i.*; confided, *pt., pp.*; confiding, *ppr.* [L. *confidere,* to trust; *com-,* together, and *fidere,* to trust.] to trust (*in* someone); share secrets or discuss private affairs; as, the prince *confides in* his ministers.

çŏn·fīde′, *v.t.* 1. to tell or talk about as a secret; as, she *confided* her difficulties to her friend.

2. to entrust (a duty, object, person, etc., *to* someone); give into the keeping of a trusted person.

Syn.—trust to, rely on, depend on.

çon′fi·dence, *n.* [L. *confidentia,* confidence, trust, from *confidens,* ppr. of *confidere,* to trust.]

1. an assurance of mind or firm belief in the trustworthiness of another, or in the truth and reality of a fact; trust; reliance: usually followed by *in.*

A cheerful *confidence in* the mercy of God. —Macaulay.

2. reliance on one's own abilities, fortune, or circumstances; belief in one's own competency; self-reliance; assurance.

3. someone or something in which trust is placed.

The Lord shall be thy *confidence.* —Prov. iii. 26.

4. boldness; courage; defiance of danger.

But *confidence* then bore thee on.—Milton.

5. something told as a secret; a private or confidential communication.

6. a relationship as confidant; as, take me into your *confidence.*

7. the belief that another will keep a secret; assurance of secrecy; as, told in strict *confidence.*

confidence game; a swindling operation, in which the swindlers first gain the confidence of the victim.

confidence man; a swindler who tries to gain the confidence of his victim in order to defraud him.

Syn.—trust, faith, reliance, belief, assurance, self-reliance.

çon′fi·dent, *a.* 1. having full belief; fully assured; certain; as, we are *confident* of victory.

2. confiding; not entertaining suspicion or distrust. [Archaic.]

3. relying on oneself; full of assurance; bold; sometimes overbold, impudent, or presumptuous.

The fool rageth and is *confident.* —Prov. xiv. 16.

4. trustworthy; as, a *confident* servant. [Obs.]

5. in Scots law, confidential.

Syn.—positive, assured, sure, certain, sanguine, bold, impudent.

çon′fi·dent, *n.* same as *confidant.*

çon·fi·den′tiăl, *a.* [Fr. *confidentiel,* from L. *confidentia,* confidence.]

1. entrusted with private or secret matters; as, a *confidential* friend.

2. imparted in secret; told in confidence; private; as, a *confidential* matter.

3. of or showing confidence.

çon·fi·den′tiăl çŏm·mū·ni·çā′tion, a statement made in confidence to one's attorney, physician, clergyman, husband, or wife, who cannot then be compelled to divulge this in a court of law.

çon·fi·den′tiăl·ly, *adv.* in confidence; in reliance on secrecy.

çon′fi·dent·ly, *adv.* with firm trust; with strong assurance; without doubt or wavering of opinion; positively; as, to believe *confidently,* to assert *confidently.*

çon′fi·dent·ness, *n.* confidence; the quality or state of having full reliance.

çŏn·fīd′ẽr, *n.* one who confides; one who trusts in or entrusts to another.

çŏn·fīd′ing, *a.* trusting; reposing confidence; trustful or inclined to trust; credulous.

çŏn·fīd′ing·ly, *adv.* in a confiding manner; trustfully.

çŏn·fīd′ing·ness, *n.* the quality of being trustful; confidence; confiding disposition; trustfulness.

çŏn·fig′ūr·āte, *v.i.*; configurated, *pt., pp.*; configurating, *ppr.* [L. *configuratus,* pp. of *configurare,* to form after something; *com-,* together, and *figurare,* to form, from *figura,* a form, figure.] to exhibit uniformity of plan or balance of parts. [Rare.]

The whole structure doth *configurate.* —Jordan.

çŏn·fig·ū·rā′tion, *n.* 1. external form, figure, or shape of a thing as resulting from the disposition and shape of its parts; external aspect or appearance; contour; outline.

2. in astrology, relative position or aspect of the planets; the face of the horoscope, according to the relative positions of the planets at any time.

3. in astronomy, the position of the stars in regard to each other.

4. [after G. *gestalt.*] in Gestalt psychology, an integrated whole with independent properties and functions over and above the sum of the properties and functions of its parts.

çŏn·fig·ū·rā′tion·ism, *n.* Gestalt psychology.

çŏn·fig′ūre, *v.t.*; configured, *pt., pp.*; configuring, *ppr.* to form; to dispose in a certain form, figure, or shape.

çŏn·fīn′ȧ·ble, çŏn·fīne′ȧ·ble, *a.* capable of being confined or limited.

çon′fīne, *n.* [Fr. *confin;* OFr. *confin,* a border, boundary; L. *confinis,* bordering on, from *confinium,* a boundary, border; *com-,* with, and *finis,* an end, limit.]

1. [*usually in pl.*] a boundary or bounded region; border; limit.

2. confinement. [Poet.]

3. a place of confinement. [Obs.]

çon′fīne, *v.i.*; confined, *pt., pp.*; confining, *ppr.* to border (*on*); to be adjacent or contiguous (*with* or *to* another region); as, England *confines on* Scotland. [Rare.]

çŏn·fīne′, *v.t.* 1. to bound or limit; to restrain within limits; to imprison; to shut up; to restrain from forcible escape; as, to *confine* horses or cattle to an enclosure; to *confine* water in a pond; to *confine* a garrison in a town; to *confine* a criminal in prison.

2. to keep shut up, as in prison, in bed because of illness, indoors, etc.

3. to restrain by a moral force; as, to *confine* men by laws; the Constitution of the United States *confines* the States to the exercise of powers of a local nature.

to be confined; to be undergoing childbirth.

Syn.—imprison, incarcerate, immure, restrict, bound, limit, circumscribe, enclose.

çŏn·fīned′, *a.* restrained within limits; imprisoned; limited; secluded; close.

çŏn·fīne′less, *a.* boundless; without end.

çŏn·fīne′ment, *n.* a confining or being confined; specifically, (a) imprisonment; (b) limitation; restriction; restraint; (c) childbirth; lying-in.

çon′fī·nẽr, *n.* a borderer; one who lives on confines, or near the border of a country. [Obs.]

çŏn·fīn′ẽr, *n.* one who or that which limits or restrains.

çŏn·fin′i·ty, *n.* [L. *confinis,* bordering upon.] contiguity; nearness; neighborhood. [Rare.]

çŏn·fĩrm′, *v.t.*; confirmed, *pt., pp.*; confirming, *ppr.* [ME. *confermen;* OFr. *confermer;* L. *confirmare,* to make firm, strengthen; *com-,* intens., and *firmare,* to strengthen, from *firmus,* firm, strong.]

1. to make firm, or more firm; to strengthen; to establish; to encourage; as, health is *confirmed* by exercise.

2. to make certain; to give new assurance of truth or certainty; to assure; to verify; as, my suspicions are now fully *confirmed.*

3. to sanction; to ratify; as, to *confirm* an agreement, promise, covenant, or title; the Senate *confirms* or rejects the appointments brought before it by the President of the United States.

4. in ecclesiastical usage, to admit (a person of a certain age) to full membership in a church by a ceremony in which he reaffirms the vows made for him when he was a child.

Syn.—corroborate, establish, substantiate, settle, strengthen, fix, ratify.

çŏn·fĩrm′ȧ·ble, *a.* capable of being confirmed.

çŏn·fĩrm′ănce, *n.* confirmation. [Obs.]

çon·fĩr·mand′, *n.* in ecclesiastical usage, a person who is to be confirmed.

çon·fĩr·mā′tion, *n.* 1. a confirming or being confirmed; corroboration; ratification; verification.

2. something that confirms or proves.

3. a religious ceremony in which a person of a certain age is admitted to full membership in a church.

4. in law, an assurance of title, by the conveyance of an estate or right *in esse* from one man to another, by which a voidable estate is made sure or valid, or a specific estate is increased.

çŏn·fĩrm′ȧ·tive, *a.* confirming or tending to confirm.

çŏn·fĩrm′ȧ·tive·ly, *adv.* in a confirmative manner; so as to confirm.

çon′fĩr·mā·tŏr, *n.* a confirmer. [Obs.]

çŏn·fĩrm′ȧ·tō·ry, *a.* 1. confirming or serving to confirm.

2. pertaining to the rite of confirmation.

çŏn·fĩrmed′, *a.* 1. firmly established, as in a habit or condition; habitual; as, a *confirmed* bachelor.

2. chronic, as a disease.

3. corroborated; proved.

4. having gone through the religious ceremony of confirmation.

çŏn·fĩrm′ed·ly, *adv.* in a confirmed manner; with confirmation.

çŏn·fĩrm′ed·ness, *n.* the state or quality of being confirmed.

çon·fĩr·mee′, *n.* in law, one to whom anything is confirmed.

çŏn·fĩrm′ẽr, *n.* one who or that which confirms, establishes, or ratifies.

çŏn·firm′ing·ly, *adv.* in such a manner as to strengthen or corroborate.

çon·firm·ọr′ (*or* kŏn-fir′mẽr), *n.* a person who ratifies another's legal title.

çŏn·fis′çȧ·ble, *a.* capable of being confiscated; liable to forfeiture.

çon′fis·çāte, *v.t.*; confiscated, *pt., pp.*, confiscating, *ppr.* [L. *confiscatus*, pp. of *confiscare*, to lay up in a chest, to seize for the public treasury, confiscate; *com-*, together, and *fiscus*, a wicker basket, a money basket or chest, the public treasury.]

1. to seize (private property) for the public treasury, usually as a penalty.

2. to seize by or as by authority; appropriate.

çon′fis·çāte, *a.* 1. confiscated.

2. having property confiscated.

çon·fis·çā′tion, *n.* 1. a confiscating or being confiscated.

2. something confiscated.

çon′fis·çȧ·tŏr, *n.* one who confiscates.

çŏn·fis′çȧ·tō·ry, *a.* 1. of, constituting, or effecting confiscation; as, a *confiscatory* tax.

2. confiscating.

çon′fit, *n.* a sweetmeat; confection; comfit. [Obs.]

çon′fi·tent, *n.* [L. *confitens*, pp. of *confiteri*, to confess.] one who confesses his sins and faults.

çŏn·fit′ē·ọr, *n.* [L., I confess, 1st pers. sing. pres. ind. of *confiteri*, to confess.] a formal prayer in which sins are confessed.

çon′fi·tūre, *n.* 1. a sweetmeat; confection; comfit.

2. a composition, as of various drugs. [Obs.]

çŏn·fix′, *v.t.*; confixed (-fixt), *pt., pp.*, confixing, *ppr.* to fasten or fix firmly.

çŏn·fix′ūre, *n.* the act of fastening. [Obs.]

çŏn·flā′grȧnt, *a.* burning; ablaze.

çon′flȧ·grāte, *v.t.*; conflagrated, *pt., pp.*; conflagrating, *ppr.* [L. *conflagratus*, pp. of *conflagrare*, to burn together; *com-*, intens., and *flagrare*, to burn.] to burn up utterly; to consume.

çon′flȧ·grāte, *v.i.* to burn or blaze with flame.

çon·flȧ·grā′tion, *n.* a great, destructive fire.

çon′flȧ·grā·tive, *a.* tending to produce or causing a conflagration.

çŏn·flāte′, *v.t.*; conflated, *pt., pp.*; conflating, *ppr.* [L. *conflatus*, pp. of *conflare*, to blow together, kindle, *com-*, together, and *flare*, to blow.]

1. to blow together; to bring together; to collect.

2. to combine into a composite text or reading from various sources, as extracts from old manuscripts: used in the passive.

3. to melt together; to fuse; to join. [Obs.]

çŏn·flāte′, *a.* 1. blown together; brought together from several sources.

2. formed by combining different readings, as a composite text.

çŏn·flā′tion, *n.* [LL. *conflatio*, a blowing together, from *conflare*, to blow together.] the act of fusing or combining, as of variant readings into a text.

çŏn·fliçt′, *v.i.*; conflicted, *pt., pp.*; conflicting, *ppr.* [L. *conflictus*, a striking together, a contest, from *confligere*, to strike together; *com-*, together, and *fligere*, to strike.]

1. originally, to fight; battle; contend.

2. to clash; be antagonistic, incompatible, or contradictory; be in opposition; as, his interests *conflict* with mine.

çon′fliçt, *n.* 1. a fight; battle; struggle.

2. sharp disagreement or opposition, as of interests, ideas, etc.; clash.

3. emotional disturbance resulting from a clash of impulses in a person.

conflict of laws; the opposition between the laws of different countries, in the case of an individual who may have acquired rights or become subject to duties within the limits of more than one nation or state.

irrepressible conflict; in the United States, the unavoidable conflict over the slavery question: first used by William H. Seward.

Syn.—contention, contest, fight, struggle, combat, encounter.

çŏn·fliçt′ing, *a.* being in opposition; contrary; contradictory; incompatible; as, *conflicting* jurisdiction, *conflicting* evidence.

çŏn·fliç′tion, *n.* the act of conflicting or clashing; the state of being in a conflict.

çŏn·fliçt′ive, *a.* tending to conflict; clashing; conflicting; as, *conflictive* systems of theology.

çon′flū·ence, *n.* [LL. *confluentia*, a flowing together.]

1. a flowing together; the meeting or junction of two or more streams; also, the place of, or a stream formed by, this; as, the *confluence* of the Ohio and Mississippi.

2. a flocking together of people; the act of meeting and crowding in a place; a crowd; a concourse.

3. in philology, the tendency by which words become similar in form, or figuratively run together.

çon′flū·ent, *a.* 1. flowing together so as to form one; as, *confluent* streams.

2. in anatomy, united, blended, or grown together, as two bones which originally were separate; connate.

3. in medicine, running together so as to form a merged mass, as sores, pimples, etc.

çon′flū·ent, *n.* 1. a stream uniting with another.

2. loosely, a tributary.

çon′flū·ent·ly, *adv.* in a flowing or blending manner.

çon′flux, *n.* same as *confluence*.

çŏn·flux·i·bil′i·ty, *n.* the tendency to flow or run together. [Rare.]

çŏn·flux′i·ble, *a.* having a tendency to flow or run together.

çŏn·flux′i·ble·ness, *n.* same as *confluxibility*.

çŏn·fō′çȧl, *a.* [*con-*, and L. *focus*, a hearth, in modern sense, a center.] in mathematics, having the same focus or foci; as, *confocal* quadrics, *confocal* conics, *confocal* surfaces.

çŏn·fọrm′, *v.t.*; conformed, *pt., pp.*; conforming, *ppr.* [ME. *conformen*; OFr. *conformer*; L. *conformare*, to fashion, form.]

1. to give the same form or character to; to make like; as, to *conform* anything to a model.

2. to bring into harmony or agreement; to make agreeable; to adapt; to submit: often used reflexively.

> Demand of them why they *conform* not themselves unto the order of the church.
> —Hooker.

çŏn·fọrm′, *v.i.* 1. to have the same form; be or become similar.

2. to be in accord or agreement; as, the novel *conformed* to my notion of a good story.

3. to act in accordance with rules, customs, etc.

4. in English history, to accept and adhere to the usages of the Established Church.

çŏn·fọrm′, *a.* conformable. [Rare.]

çŏn·fọrm·ȧ·bil′i·ty, *n.* the state or quality of being conformable.

çŏn·fọrm′ȧ·ble, *a.* [from L. *conformare*, to conform.]

1. that conforms; specifically, (a) similar; (b) in harmony or agreement; (c) adapted; suited; corresponding.

2. quick to conform; obedient; submissive; compliant.

3. in geology, uninterruptedly parallel: said of contiguous strata.

çŏn·fọrm′ȧ·ble·ness, *n.* conformability.

çŏn·fọrm′ȧ·bly, *adv.* in a conformable manner; in conformity with; suitably; agreeably.

çŏn·fọrm′ănce, *n.* conformity.

çŏn·fọrm′āte, *a.* having the same form. [Rare.]

çon·fọr·mā′tion, *n.* [L. *conformatio*, a forming, fashioning, conforming, from *conformare*, to conform.]

1. a conforming or being conformed; adaptation. [Rare.]

2. a completed or symmetrical formation and arrangement of the parts of a thing.

3. the structure or form of a thing as determined by the arrangement of its parts.

çŏn·fọrm′ẽr, *n.* one who conforms; one who complies with established forms or doctrines.

çŏn·fọrm′ist, *n.* one who conforms or complies; specifically, in English history, one who complies with the usages of the Church of England, or the Established Church, as distinguished from a dissenter or nonconformist.

çŏn·fọrm′i·ty, *n.*; *pl.* **çŏn·fọrm′i·tieṣ,** 1. correspondence in form or manner; resemblance; agreement; congruity; likeness; harmony.

2. correspondence with the decrees, rules, or customs; accordance.

> We cannot be otherwise happy but by our *conformity* to God. —Tillotson.

3. in English history, compliance with the usages or principles of the Established Church.

> A proclamation requiring all ecclesiastical and civil officers to do their duty by enforcing *conformity*. —Hallam.

Syn.—consistency, harmony, similitude, resemblance, accordance, agreement.

çŏn·found′ (*or* kon-found′), *v.t.*; confounded, *pt., pp.*; confounding, *ppr.* [ME. *confounden*; OFr. *confondre*; L. *confundere*, to pour or mingle together, confuse, confound; *com-*, together, and *fundere*, to pour.]

1. to mingle and blend so that forms or natures cannot be distinguished; to throw into disorder; to confuse.

> Let us go down, and there *confound* their language. —Gen. xi. 7.

2. to mistake one for another; to cause to become confused; to bewilder.

3. to throw into consternation; to perplex with terror, surprise, or astonishment; to stupefy with amazement; to abash. [Archaic.]

4. to destroy; to overthrow; to ruin; to defeat. [Archaic.]

> Which infinite calamity shall cause
> To human life, and household peace *confound*. —Milton.

5. to waste or spend uselessly, as time. [Obs.]

6. to damn: used as a mild oath.

Syn.—abash, astonish, baffle, confuse, defeat, dismay, intermingle, mix, terrify.

çŏn·found′ed, *a.* 1. confused; bewildered.

2. damned: a mild oath.

3. detestable; abominable.

çŏn·found′ed·ly, *adv.* in a confounded manner.

çŏn·found′ed·ness, *n.* the state of being confounded.

çŏn·found′ẽr, *n.* one who or that which confounds.

çon′fraçt, *a.* broken. [Obs.]

çon·frȧ·gōse′, *a.* broken; uneven. [Obs.]

çon·frȧ·tẽr′ni·ty, *n.*; *pl.* **çon·frȧ·tẽr′ni·tieṣ,** [LL. *confraternitas*, brotherhood.]

1. a brotherhood.

2. a group of men united for some purpose or in some profession; as, a *confraternity* of artists.

çon·frere′ (-frâr′), *n.* [Fr.] a colleague; a fellow member; an associate.

çon·frī′ăr, çon·frī′ẽr, *n.* a confrere. [Obs.]

çon·fri·çā′tion, *n.* [LL. *confricatio*, from L. *confricare*, to rub together.] a rubbing against; friction. [Obs.]

çŏn·frŏnt′, *v.t.*; confronted, *pt., pp.*; confronting, *ppr.* [Fr. *confronter*, to confront; L. *com-*, together, and *frons*, forehead.]

1. to stand facing; to face; to stand in front of.

> He spoke and then *confronts* the bull. —Dryden.

2. to face boldly, defiantly, or antagonistically; to meet in hostility; to oppose.

> Strength match'd with strength, and power *confronted* power. —Shak.

3. to set face to face; to bring into the presence of, as an accused person and a witness, in court: followed by *with*; as, the witness was *confronted with* the accused.

4. to set together for comparison; to compare.

> When I *confront* a medal with a verse I only show you the same design executed by different hands. —Addison.

çon·frŏn·tā′tion, *n.* the act of confronting.

çon·fron·té′ (çoṅ-frọṅ-tā′), *a.* same as *affronté*.

çŏn·frŏnt′ẽr, *n.* one who or that which confronts.

çŏn·frŏnt′ment, *n.* the act of confronting. [Rare.]

Çŏn·fū′ciăn, *a.* relating to Confucius, his teachings, or his followers.

Çŏn·fū′ciăn, *n.* a Confucianist.

Çŏn·fū′ciăn·iṣm, *n.* the ethical teachings formulated by Confucius and introduced into the Chinese religion, emphasizing devotion to parents, family, and friends, ancestor worship, and the maintenance of justice and peace.

Çŏn·fū′ciăn·ist, *a.* of Confucianism or Confucianists.

Çŏn·fū′ciăn·ist, *n.* an adherent of Confucianism.

çŏn·fūṣ·ȧ·bil′i·ty, *n.* liability to be confused.

çŏn·fūṣ′ȧ·ble, *a.* liable to be confused.

çŏn·fūṣe′, *v.t.*; confused, *pt., pp.*; confusing, *ppr.* [L. *confusus*, pp. of *confundere*, to pour together, confuse; *com-*, together, and *fundere*, to pour.]

1. to mix up; to bring disorder among; to throw together indiscriminately; to disorder; to jumble; as, the accounts were *confused*.

2. to perplex or mix up the mind or ideas of; specifically, (a) to embarrass; to disconcert; to cause to lose self-possession; (b) to bewilder; to perplex; (c) to fail to distinguish between; to mistake the identity of.

> The want of arrangement and connexion *confuses* the reader. —Whately.

Syn.—derange, disorder, jumble, involve, abash, disconcert, confound, embarrass, distract.

çŏn·fūṣe′, *a.* mixed; confounded. [Obs.]

çŏn·fūş′ed·ly, *adv.* in a confused manner.
çŏn·fūş′ed·ness, *n.* the state of being in confusion.
çŏn·fūse′ly, *adv.* confusedly. [Obs.]
çŏn·fū′şion, *n.* 1. a confusing or being confused; disorder; as, the *confusion* of the crowd; a *confusion* of ideas.
2. embarrassment.
We lie down in our shame, and our *confusion* covereth us. —Jer. iii. 25.
3. bewilderment.
4. failure to distinguish between things.
5. overthrow; defeat; ruin. [Obs.]
Ruin seize thee, ruthless king!
Confusion on thy banners wait. —Gray.
6. one who confuses; a confounder. [Obs.]
çŏn·fū′şion·ăl, *a.* characterized by confusion.
çŏn·fū′sive, *a.* having a tendency to confuse.
çŏn·fūt′ȧ·ble, *a.* capable of being confuted.
çŏn·fūt′ănt, *n.* a confuter.
çon·fū·tā′tion, *n.* [L. *confutatio*, from *confutare*, to confute.]
1. the act of confuting or proving to be false.
2. an argument, evidence, etc. that confutes.
çŏn·fūt′ȧ·tive, *a.* confuting or tending to confute.
çŏn·fūte′, *v.t.*; confuted, *pt.*, *pp.*; confuting, *ppr.* [L. *confutare*, to confute, from *com-*, intens., and hyp. *futare*.]
1. to disprove; to prove to be false or invalid; as, to *confute* arguments.
2. to prove (a person) to be wrong; to overcome by argument or proof; as, to *confute* an advocate at the bar; to *confute* a writer.
3. to make useless; to defeat; to confound.
çŏn·fūte′ment, *n.* confutation. [Obs.]
çŏn·fūt′ẽr, *n.* one who confutes.
çoṅ′gȧ, *n.* [Am. Sp.]
1. a modern ballroom dance of Latin-American origin, in which the dancers form a winding line.
2. the music for this dance, in 4/4 syncopated time, with a heavy accent on the fourth beat of every measure.
çoṅ′gȧ, *v.i.* to dance the conga.
çon·ġé′ (çoṅ-zhā′), *n.* [Fr., leave, departure; OFr. *congie, congiet*, leave, permission to depart; L. *commeatus*, a leave of absence, furlough.]
1. a curt dismissal; as, to give one his *congé*.
2. a formal leave-taking or farewell.
3. a bow or curtsy, especially when leaving. [Archaic.]
The captain salutes you with *congé* profound. —Swift.
4. in architecture, a kind of molding.
congé d'élire; in ecclesiastical usage, the sovereign's license or permission to a dean and chapter to choose a bishop.
çon′ġé (çoṅ′zhā), *v.i.*; congéed, *pt.*, *pp.*; congéing, *ppr.* to take leave with the customary civilities; to bow or curtsy.
çon′ġé·ȧ·ble, *a.* in old English law, allowable; permissible. [Obs.]
çŏn·ġēal′, *v.t.* and *v.i.*; congealed, *pt.*, *pp.*; congealing, *ppr.* [L. *congelare*, to cause to freeze together, to thicken; *com-*, together, and *gelare*, to freeze.]
1. to change from a fluid to a solid state, as water in freezing, liquid metal or wax in cooling, etc.; to harden.
(The island of Sal) hath its name from the abundance of salt that is naturally *congealed* there. —Dampier.
2. to thicken; to coagulate; to jell.
çŏn·ġēal′ȧ·ble, *a.* capable of being congealed.
çŏn·ġēal′ȧ·ble·ness, *n.* capability of congealing.
çŏn·ġēal′ed·ness, *n.* the state of being congealed.
çŏn·ġēal′ment, *n.* 1. a clot, concretion, etc. formed by congelation.
2. congelation.
çon′ġee, *n.* [ME. *conge*; OFr. *congie*, from L. *commeare*, to come and go, leave.] congé. [Now Rare.]
çon′ġee, *v.i.* to take formal leave; especially, to bow in leaving. [Now Rare.]
çon·ġee′, *n.* [Hind. *kanji*; Pali *kanjikam*, rice water.]
1. in the East Indies, boiled rice.
2. an East Indian jail: also called *congee house*.
çon·ġee′wa′tẽr, in India, rice water.
çon·ġē·lā′tion, *n.* [L. *congelatio*, a congealing, from *congelatus*, pp. of *congelare*, to congeal.]
1. the act or process of congealing; the state of being congealed.
The capillary tubes are obstructed either by outward compression or *congelation* of the fluid. —Arbuthnot.
2. what is congealed or solidified; a concretion; as, a *congelation* of blood.
çon′ġē·nẽr, *n.* [L., of the same race; *com-*, together, and *genus*, genit. *generis*, race, kind.] a person or thing of the same kind, class, race, or genus.
çon·ġē·ner′iç, çon·ġē·ner′iç·ăl, *a.* [L. *com-*, together, and *genus*, kind, race.] being of the same kind, class, race, or genus.
çon·ġen′ẽr·ous, *a.* congeneric.
çon·ġen′ẽr·ous·ness, *n.* the quality of being congenerous.
çŏn·ġēn′iăl (-yăl), *a.* [L. *com-*, together, and *genialis*, of the same nature or birth, from *genus*, kind.]
1. partaking of the same nature or natural characteristics; kindred; compatible; as, *congenial* tastes.
Smit with the love of sister arts we came
And met *congenial*. —Pope.
2. having the same tastes and temperament; friendly; sympathetic; as, *congenial* friends.
3. suited to one's needs or disposition; agreeable; as, *congenial* work.
çŏn·ġē·ni·al′i·ty, *n.* the quality or condition of being congenial.
çŏn·ġēn′iăl·ize, *v.t.* and *v.i.* to make congenial. [Rare.]
çŏn·ġēn′iăl·ly, *adv.* in a congenial manner.
çŏn·ġēn′iăl·ness, *n.* congeniality.
çŏn·ġēn′ious (-yus), *a.* congeneric. [Obs.]
çŏn·ġen′i·tăl, *a.* [L. *congenitus*, born together with; *com-*, together, and *genitus*, pp. of *gignere*, to bear.] belonging or pertaining to an individual from birth; resulting from one's heredity or prenatal development; as, a *congenital* disease, a *congenital* deformity.
çŏn·ġen′i·tăl·ly, *adv.* from birth; as a result of congenital factors.
çŏn·ġen′ite, *a.* congenital. [Obs.]
çoṅ′gẽr, *n.* [L. *conger*; Gr. *gongros*, the sea-eel.]
1. the *Conger vulgaris*, a large, edible, saltwater eel, pale brown above and grayish-white below, sometimes ten feet in length.
2. the eelpout or the *Sidera mordax* of the coast of California.
Also *conger eel*.
çon·ġē′ri·ēş, *n.*; *pl.* **çon·ġē′ri·ēş,** [L. *congeries*, that which is brought together, a pile, from *congerere*, to bring together.] a collection of things or parts in one mass or aggregate; a heap; a pile.
çŏn·ġest′, *v.t.*; congested, *pt.*, *pp.*; congesting, *ppr.* [L. *congestus*, pp. of *congerere*, to bring together.]
1. to collect or gather into a mass; to overcrowd; to fill to excess.
2. in medicine, to cause too much blood to accumulate in (a part of the body).
çŏn·ġest′, *v.i.* to become congested.
çŏn·ġest′ed, *a.* 1. crowded very closely; overcrowded; obstructed by crowding or massing together.
2. in medicine, affected with congestion, as blood.
çŏn·ġes′tion (-chun), *n.* 1. the act of gathering or heaping together; aggregation. [Obs.]
2. crowded condition; condition of overcrowding; as, *congestion* of risks in fire insurance.
3. in medicine, an excessive accumulation of blood in a part of the body.
çŏn·ġest′ive, *a.* pertaining to congestion; causing or resulting from congestion.
çon′ġi·ā·ry, *n.*; *pl.* **çon′ġi·ā·rieş,** [L. *congiarium (donum)*, a gift to the people consisting of a congius for each one.] a largess or distribution of corn, oil, or wine, afterward of money, to the people or soldiers of ancient Rome.
çon′ġi·us, *n.*; *pl.* **çon′ġi·ī,** [L.]
1. a liquid measure among the ancient Romans, equal to a little less than seven pints.
2. in pharmacy, a gallon.
çŏn·glā′ci·āte (-shi-), *v.i.* to turn to ice; to freeze. [Obs.]
çŏn·glā·ci·ā′tion, *n.* [L. *conglaciatus*, pp. of *conglaciare*, to turn to ice, freeze; *com-*, together, and *glaciare*, to freeze.] the act of changing into ice, or the state of being converted to ice; a freezing; congelation. [Obs.]
çŏn·glō′bāte, *a.* [L. *conglobatus*, from *conglobare*; *com-*, with, and *globare*, to collect, or to make round; *globus*, a ball.] formed or gathered into a ball or rounded mass.
çŏn·glō′bāte, *v.t.*; conglobated, *pt.*, *pp.*; conglobating, *ppr.* to collect or form into a ball or rounded mass.
çŏn·glō′bāte·ly, *adv.* in a round or rounded form.
çon·glō·bā′tion, *n.* the act of forming into a ball or the ball so formed.
çŏn·glōbe′, *v.t.* and *v.i.* conglobed, *pt.*, *pp.*; conglobing, *ppr.* to conglobate.
çŏn·glob′ū·lāte, *v.i.* to conglobate. [Rare.]
çŏn·glom′ẽr·āte, *v.t.* and *v.i.*; conglomerated, *pt.*, *pp.*; conglomerating, *ppr.* [L. *conglomeratus*, pp. of *conglomerare*, to roll together, wind up; *com-*, together, and *glomerare*, to gather into a ball, from *glomus*, a ball.] to form or gather into a ball or round body; to collect into a round mass.
çŏn·glom′ẽr·āte, *a.* 1. gathered into a ball or round body; crowded together; clustered.
The beams of light when they are multiplied and *conglomerate* generate heat.—Bacon.
2. made up of separate parts or substances collected together into a single mass.
3. in geology, denoting rocks composed of smaller rock particles cemented together in a mass of hardened clay and sand.
çŏn·glom′ẽr·āte, *n.* 1. a conglomerate mass; a cluster.
2. in geology, a rock composed of rounded fragments of various rocks cemented together in a mass of hardened clay and sand.
çŏn·glom·ẽr·at′iç, *a.* in geology, conglomerate.
çŏn·glom·ẽr·ā′tion, *n.* 1. a conglomerating or being conglomerated.
2. a collection, mixture, or mass of miscellaneous things.
çŏn·glom·ẽr·it′iç, *a.* in geology, conglomerate.
çŏn·glū′tin, *n.* one of the proteins found in peas, beans, almonds, wheat, etc.
çŏn·glū′ti·nănt, *a.* gluing; uniting; healing. [Obs.]
çŏn·glū′ti·nāte, *v.t.* and *v.i.*; conglutinated, *pt.*, *pp.*; conglutinating, *ppr.* [L. *conglutinatus*, pp. of *conglutinare*, to glue together; *com-*, together, and *glutinare*, to glue, from *gluten*, glue.] to glue together; to unite by or as by adhesion.
çŏn·glū′ti·nāte, *a.* glued together; united by adhesion.
çŏn·glū·ti·nā′tion, *n.* the act of gluing together; a joining by means of adhesion.
çŏn·glū′ti·nȧ·tive, *a.* causing conglutination.
çŏn·glū′ti·nā·tŏr, *n.* a medicine having the power of uniting by adhesion.
çoṅ′gō, *n.* same as *congou*.
Çoṅ′gō dȳe (or **çŏl′ŏr**), any of certain azo dyes, derived mainly from benzidine.
çoṅ′gō eel, same as *congo snake*.
Çoṅ′gō pā′pẽr, a paper colored with Congo red, used to test for the presence of acids.
Çoṅ′gō red, a sodium salt of a complex organic acid, used for dyeing wool and cotton and as an acid-base indicator: it becomes blue in an acid solution and remains red in an alkaline or neutral solution.
çoṅ′gō snāke, an eellike amphibious animal with two pairs of small, weak legs, found in the swamps of the southeastern United States.
çoṅ′gou, *n.* [Chin. *kung-fu*, labor.] a variety of black Chinese tea.
çŏn·grat′ū·lănt, *a.* congratulating; expressing congratulations.
çŏn·grat′ū·lănt, *n.* a congratulator.
çŏn·grat′ū·lāte, *v.t.*; congratulated, *pt.*, *pp.*; congratulating, *ppr.* [L. *congratulatus*, pp. of *congratulari*, to wish joy; *com-*, together, and *gratulari*, to manifest joy, wish joy.]
1. to address with expressions of pleasure to (a person who has been fortunate, successful, etc.); to compliment upon a happy event; to wish joy to; as, to *congratulate* the nation on the restoration of peace.
2. to welcome; to hail; to greet. [Obs.]
3. to rejoice at; to celebrate. [Obs.]
çŏn·grat′ū·lāte, *v.i.* to express or feel sympathetic joy: followed by *with*. [Rare.]
I cannot but *congratulate with* my country, which hath outdone all Europe in advancing conversation. —Swift.
çŏn·grat·ū·lā′tion, *n.* 1. the act of congratulating.
2. [*pl.*] expressions of pleasure and good wishes on the occasion of another's fortune or success.
çŏn·grat′ū·lā·tŏr, *n.* one who offers congratulation.
çŏn·grat′ū·lȧ·tō·ry, *a.* expressing congratulations.
çŏn·gree′, *v.i.* to agree. [Obs.]
çŏn·greet′, *v.i.* to salute mutually. [Obs.]
çoṅ′grē·gāte, *v.t.* and *v.i.*; congregated, *pt.*,

pp.; congregating, *ppr.* [L. *congregatus*, pp. of *congregare*, to collect into a flock, congregate; *com-*, together, and *gregare*, to collect into a flock, to gather, from *grex*, a flock.] to gather into a mass or crowd; to collect; to assemble.
Equals with equals often *congregate*.
—Denham.

çon'grē·gāte, *a.* 1. collected; assembled.
2. collective.

çon·grē·gā'tion, *n.* 1. the act of congregating or being congregated; the act of bringing together or assembling; as, by *congregation* of the separate particles.
2. a collection or assemblage of people or things.
3. an assembly of persons, especially one meeting at a stated time and place for the holding of religious services.
4. the members of a particular place of worship.
5. a settlement, town, or parish in the colonies of early New England where Congregationalism was established.
6. in the Old Testament, the Jews.
7. in the Roman Catholic Church, (a) an assembly of cardinals appointed by the Pope, to which is entrusted the management of some important branch of the affairs of the church; (b) a fraternity of religious persons forming a subdivision of a monastic order; (c) a religious community or order not necessarily under solemn vows but bound by a common rule.
8. at Oxford and Cambridge, the assembly of masters and doctors which confers degrees.

çon·grē·gā'tion·ăl, *a.* 1. of, relating to, or pertaining to a congregation; as, *congregational* music.
2. of, relating to, or pertaining to congregationalism; as, *congregational* methods.
3. [C–] of Congregationalism or Congregationalists; as, a *Congregational* church.

çon·grē·gā'tion·ăl·iṣm, *n.* 1. that system of church government which vests all ecclesiastical power in the assembled brotherhood of each local church, as an independent body.
2. [C–] the doctrinal belief and mode of government of the Congregational church.

Çon·grē·gā'tion·ăl·ist, *n.* one who believes in Congregationalism, or belongs to a Congregational church.

Çon·grē·gā'tion·ăl·ist, *a.* of Congregationalism or Congregationalists.

çon'grē·gā·tive, *a.* congregating or tending to congregate.

çoṅ'gress, *n.* [L. *congressus*, a meeting, an interview, a hostile encounter, from *congredi*, to come together; *com-*, together, and *gradi*, to step, walk, from *gradus*, a step.]
1. a meeting; a coming together.
2. a meeting of two or more persons in a contest; an encounter; a conflict. [Obs.]
3. social intercourse.
4. sexual intercourse.
5. an assembly or conference.
6. a formal assembly of envoys, commissioners, deputies, etc. to discuss problems.
7. [C–] (a) the legislature of the United States, comprising the Senate and the House of Representatives. Members of the Senate are elected for a period of six years, one-third of whom are elected every two years. Members of the House of Representatives are elected for a term of two years, the terms of all Representatives beginning and ending at the same time, being coincident with a single Congress; (b) a session of this legislature; (c) the body of Senators and Representatives serving together for any two-year term.
8. the lower house of various legislative bodies, especially the national legislature of a republic.
congress boot; a shoe having an elastic material inserted at the side so as to hold the shoe snugly on the foot.
Congress water; a mineral water from the Congress Spring at Saratoga, New York.

çŏn·gres'sion, *n.* 1. a coming together; as, sexual *congression*. [Obs.]
2. a bringing together for comparison. [Obs.]

çŏn·gres'sion·ăl, *a.* 1. of or pertaining to a congress.
2. [C–] of or designating the Congress of the United States.
Congressional district; a division of a State entitled, by reason of its population, to one representative in Congress.
Congressional Medal of Honor; the highest United States military decoration, awarded by Congress for gallantry at the risk of life above and beyond the call of duty: instituted 1862: also called *Medal of Honor*.
Congressional Record; a daily publication of the proceedings of Congress, including a complete stenographic report of all remarks and debate.

çŏn·gres'sion·ăl·ist, *n.* a supporter of a congress.

çŏn·gres'sive, *a.* coming together, as in sexual intercourse. [Obs.]

çoṅ'gress·măn, *n.*; *pl.* **çoṅ'gress·men,** a member of either house of Congress, especially the House of Representatives.

Çoṅ'gress of In·dus'tri·ăl Or·găn·i·zā'tionṣ, a federation of labor unions in the United States and Canada, originally composed of a dissenting faction of the American Federation of Labor and organized as the *Committee for Industrial Organization*: it was reorganized in 1938 under its present name: its chief aims are organization of workers in mass-production industries instead of by crafts, and the establishment of collective bargaining.

Çoṅ'gress of Vi·en'nȧ, a conference of the major European powers held at Vienna in 1814–1815, at the end of the Napoleonic Wars: its purpose was to restore monarchical governments and readjust territories throughout Europe; its leading figure was Metternich.

çoṅ'gress·wom″ăn (-woom″), *n.*; *pl.* **çoṅ'gress·wom″en** (-wim″), a woman member of either the House of Representatives or the Senate, but usually the former.

Çon'grēve match, [after Sir William *Congreve* (1772-1828), the inventor.] an early kind of friction match.

Çon'grēve rock'et, a kind of rocket formerly used as a weapon of war.

çoṅ'grid, *n.* an eel of the family *Congridæ*.

Çoṅ'gri·dae, *n.pl.* [L. from *conger*, Gr. *gongros*, the conger.] a family of eellike fishes, especially the conger eel.

çoṅ'groid, *a.* [L. *conger*; Gr. *gongros*, the conger, and *eidos*, form, resemblance.] belonging or pertaining to the *Congridæ*.

çoṅ'groid, *n.* one of the *Congridæ*.

çon·grūe', *v.i.* to agree. [Obs.]

çoṅ'grū·ence, *n.* [L. *congruentia*, agreement, from *congruens*, ppr. of *congruere*, to run together, agree.]
1. agreement; correspondence; harmony.
2. correspondence to what is right, proper, or reasonable; suitability; appropriateness.
3. in English grammar, concord.
4. in mathematics, the relation between two numbers each of which, when divided by a third (called the *modulus*), leaves the same remainder.

çoṅ'grū·en·cy, *n.* congruence.

çoṅ'grū·ent, *a.* [L. *congruens*, ppr. of *congruere*, to run together, agree.]
1. agreeing; corresponding; harmonious.
2. in English grammar, showing concord.
3. in geometry, of the same shape and size: congruent figures, if placed one upon another, coincide exactly in all their parts.
4. in mathematics, in congruence; as, *congruent* numbers.

çŏn·grū'i·ty, *n.*; *pl.* **çŏn·grū'i·tieṣ,** [ME. *congruite*; OFr. *congruite*, congruity, agreement, from L. *congruus*, suitable, agreeing, from *congruere*, to agree.]
1. the condition, quality, or fact of being congruous; specifically, (a) agreement; harmony; (b) fitness; appropriateness.
2. in geometry, exact coincidence: said of two or more figures.

çoṅ'grū·ous, *a.* 1. corresponding to what is right, proper, and reasonable; fitting; suitable; appropriate.
2. congruent.

çoṅ'grū·ous·ly, *adv.* in a congruous manner.

çon·hȳ'drine, *n.* [from *con*ium and *hydro*gen.] a narcotic alkaloid contained in the flowers and seeds of hemlock.

çō'ni·ȧ, *n.* same as *Conine*.

çon'iç, *a.* [Gr. *konikos*, conic, from *kōnos*, a peak or cone.] same as *conical*.

çon'iç, *n.* a conic section.

çon'i·căl, *a.* 1. of a cone.
2. resembling or shaped like a cone.

çon·i·çal'i·ty, *n.* conicalness.

çon'iç·ăl·ly, *adv.* in the form of a cone.

çon'iç·ăl·ness, *n.* the state or quality of being conic.

çon'i·çoid, *n.* a quadric surface.

çon'iç prō·jeç'tion, a type of map projection formed by projecting the surface of the earth on the surface of a cone and unrolling this to a plane surface on which the parallels of latitude are then concentric circles and the meridians equally spaced radii.

çon'içs, *n. pl.* [*construed as sing.*] the branch of geometry dealing with conic sections.

çon'iç seç'tion, in geometry, a curve, as an ellipse, parabola, or hyperbola, produced by the intersection of a plane with a right circular cone.

çon'iç seç'tionṣ, the branch of geometry dealing with ellipses, parabolas, and hyperbolas.

çō·nid'i·ȧ, *n.*, plural of *conidium*.

çō·nid'i·ăl, çō·nid'i·ăn, *a.* 1. of or like conidia.
2. producing conidia.

çō·nid'i·oid, *a.* same as *conidial*.

çō·nid'i·ō·phōre, *n.* [L. *conidium*, the conidium, from Gr. *konis*, dust, and *-phoros*, bearing, from *pherein*, to bear.] a specialized, threadlike part that bears conidia, found in certain fungi.

çō·nid'i·ō·spōre, *n.* same as *conidium*.

çō·nid'i·um, *n.*, *pl.* **çō·nid'i·ȧ,** [Mod. L., from Gr. *konis*, dust.] in botany, a small asexual spore occurring in certain fungi.

çō'ni·fēr, (*or* kon'i-), *n.* [from L. *conus*, a cone, and *ferre*, to bear.] any of a large group of cone-bearing trees and shrubs, mostly evergreens, as the pine, spruce, fir, cedar, yew, etc.; one of the *Coniferæ*.

Çō·nif'e·rae, *n.pl.* [L. *conifer*, cone-bearing; *conus*, a cone, and *ferre*, to bear.] a natural order of gymnospermous exogens, consisting of trees or shrubs, found throughout the world, especially in cold regions.

çō·nif'ẽr·in, *n.* a glucoside crystallizing in needle-shaped crystals, a constituent of the sap of coniferous trees.

çō·nif'ẽr·ous, *a.* 1. cone-bearing.
2. relating to the order *Coniferæ*.

çō'ni·form, *a.* cone-shaped; conical.

çō'ni·ïne, *n.* same as *conine*.

çon'i·mȧ, *n.* [native name.] a medicinal resin obtained from a tropical American tree, the incense tree.

çō'nine, *n.* [see *conium*.] a very poisonous, oily alkaloid, $C_8H_{17}N$, extracted from the poison hemlock.

çō·ni·ros'tẽr, *n.* a bird of the suborder *Conirostres*.

çō·ni·ros'trăl, *a.* 1. having a thick, conical beak, as crows and finches.
2. of or pertaining to the *Conirostres*.

Çō·ni·ros'trēṣ, *n.pl.* [L., from *conus*, a cone, and *rostrum*, beak.] a group of perching, walking birds, having a conical bill, including the crows, finches, etc.

çō'nīte, *n.* [from Gr. *konis*, dust.] a variety of dolomite.

Çō'ni·um (*or* kō-nī'), *n.* [L., from Gr. *kōneion*, hemlock.]
1. in botany, a genus of poisonous plants belonging to the carrot family, *Umbelliferæ*. The most widely known species is the white hemlock, *Conium maculatum*, which is cultivated in this country for medicinal purposes.
2. [c–] any plant of this genus.

çŏn·jeçt', *v.t.* to throw together, or to throw. [Obs.]

çŏn·jeçt', *v.i.* to guess. [Obs.]

çŏn·jeçt'ŏr, *n.* one who guesses or conjectures. [Obs.]

çŏn·jeç'tūr·ȧ·ble, *a.* capable of being guessed or conjectured.

çŏn·jeç'tūr·ăl, *a.* 1. based on or involving conjecture.
2. inclined to make conjectures.

çŏn·jeç'tūr·ăl·ist, *n.* one who conjectures; a conjecturer. [Rare.]

çŏn·jeç·tūr·ăl'i·ty, *n.* the quality of being conjectural. [Rare.]

çŏn·jeç'tūr·ăl·ly, *adv.* by conjecture; by guess; as, this opinion was given *conjecturally*.

çŏn·jeç'tūre, *n.* [L. *conjectura*, a putting together, a guess, an inference, from *conjectus*, pp. of *conjicere*, to throw or bring together, to guess.]
1. guesswork; inferring, theorizing, or predicting from incomplete or uncertain evidence; as, this critic is too fond of *conjecture*.
2. a guess; inference, theory, or prediction based on guesswork.

çŏn·jeç'tūre, *v.t.*; conjectured, *pt.*, *pp.*; conjecturing, *ppr.* to guess; to arrive at, propose, or predict by conjecture; as, he *conjectured* that some misfortune had happened.

çŏn·jeç'tūre, *v.i.* to make a conjecture.
Syn.—surmise, guess, suppose, imagine.

çŏn·jeç'tūr·ẽr, *n.* one who conjectures, or guesses.

çŏn·join', *v.t.*; conjoined, *pt.*, *pp.*; conjoining, *ppr.* [ME. *conjoignen*; OFr. *conjoindre*; L. *conjungere*, to join together.]
1. to join together; to unite, as two or more persons or things in close connection; as, to *conjoin* friends.
2. to associate or connect.
Let that which he learns next be nearly *con-*

joined with what he knows already.
—Locke.

çŏn·join′, *v.i.* to unite; to join; to combine.

çŏn·joined′, *a.* joined to or with; united; associated; in heraldry, touching or joined together.

çŏn·joint′, *a.* 1. joined together; united; connected; associated.
2. of or involving two or more in association; joint.

çŏn·joint′, *n.* in law, one associated with another in interest or obligation; specifically, [*pl.*] married persons.

çŏn·joint′ly, *adv.* jointly; in union; together.

çŏn·joint′ness, *n.* state of being joined or united.

çŏn·jū′bi·lănt, *a.* jubilant together. [Rare.]

çon′jū·găl, *a.* [L. *conjugalis*, relating to marriage, conjugal, from *conjunx*, husband or wife, from *conjungere*, to unite, to join together; *com-*, together, and *jungere*, to unite.] belonging to marriage or the relation between husband and wife; matrimonial; connubial; as, the *conjugal* relation; *conjugal* ties.

çon·jū·gal′i·ty, *n.* the married state.

çon′jū·găl·ly, *adv.* matrimonially; connubially.

Çon·jū·gā′tae, *n.pl.* [L., f. pl. of *conjugatus*, pp. of *conjugare*, to join, unite.] in botany, a class of algae, the *Chlorophyceæ*, embracing several families of fresh-water plants which reproduce by conjugation.

CONJUGATAE

çon′jū·gāte, *a.* [L. *conjugatus*, pp. of *conjugare*, to join together, from *com-*, together, and *jugare*, to join, from *jugum*, a yoke.]
1. joined together, especially in a pair; coupled.
2. in botany, growing in pairs, as leaflets on the axis of some leaves.
3. in grammar, derived from the same base and, usually, related in meaning: said of words.
4. in mathematics, reciprocally related, and interchangeable as to properties, as two points, lines, quantities, etc.
conjugate axis; see under *axis*.
conjugate diameter; one of the two diameters of an ellipse or hyperbola, so related that the tangents at the ends of either diameter parallel the other.
conjugate hyperbola; a hyperbola whose transverse axis is the minor axis of the given hyperbola.
conjugate lines on a surface; in geometry, lines whose directions at any point are those of conjugate diameters of the indicatrix at the same point.
conjugate mirrors; in optics, two mirrors so arranged that rays reflected from the focus of one meet at the focus of the other.
conjugate point; in geometry, an acnode.

çon′jū·gāte, *v.t.*; conjugated, *pt.*, *pp.*; conjugating, *ppr.* 1. to join together; to couple; to unite.
2. in grammar, to inflect (a verb) systematically, giving its different forms according to voice, mood, tense, number, and person.

çon′jū·gāte, *v.i.* 1. to unite sexually. [Rare.]
2. in biology, to unite in conjugation.
3. in grammar, (a) to conjugate a verb; (b) to be conjugated.

çon′jū·gāte, *n.* 1. in grammar, a conjugate word.
2. a conjugate point, line, quantity, etc.

çon·jū·gā′tion, *n.* 1. a conjugating or being conjugated; union.
2. in biology, the fusion of two gametes or one-celled organisms for reproduction.
3. in grammar, (a) a methodical presentation or arrangement of the inflectional forms of a verb; paradigm; (b) a class of verbs with similar inflectional forms.

çon·jū·gā′tion·ăl, *a.* pertaining to conjugation.

çon′jū·gā·tive, *a.* 1. of conjugation.
2. conjugating or tending to conjugate.

çon′jū·gā·tŏr, *n.* a person or thing that conjugates.

çŏn·jū′gi·ăl, *a.* conjugal. [Rare.]

çon·jū′gi·um, *n.* [L., a connection, union, the married state.] in Roman law, the matrimonial bond.

çŏn·juñçt′, *a.* [L. *conjunctus*, pp. of *conjungere*, to join together.] conjoined; united; joint; associated. [Archaic.]
conjunct degrees; in music, adjacent degrees on the staff, representing notes which follow each other immediately in the scale.
conjunct tetrachords; in music, two tetrachords, or fourths, where the same note is the highest of one and the lowest of the other.

çŏn·juñç′tion, *n.* [ME. *conjunccion*; OFr. *conjunction*; L. *conjunctio*, from pp. of *conjungere*; see *conjoin*.]
1. a joining together or being joined together; union; association; combination; as, carelessness, in *conjunction* with laziness, made her a poor worker.
2. coincidence; as, the *conjunction* of events.
3. in astronomy and astrology, the meeting of two or more stars or planets in the same degree of the zodiac; as, the *conjunction* of the moon with the sun, or of Jupiter and Saturn. Heavenly bodies are said to be in *conjunction* when they are seen in the same part of the heavens, or have the same longitude. The *inferior conjunction* of a planet is its position when in conjunction on the same side of the sun with the earth; the *superior conjunction* is its position when on the side of the sun most distant from the earth.
4. in grammar, an uninflected word used to connect words, phrases, clauses, or sentences; connective: conjunctions may be co-ordinating (e.g., *and, but, or*), subordinating (e.g., *if, when, as, because, though*, etc.), or correlative (e.g., *either . . . or, both . . . and*, etc.).
5. sexual copulation. [Obs.]

çŏn·juñç′tion·ăl, *a.* pertaining to a conjunction.

çon·juñç·tī′vȧ, *n.*; *pl.* **çon·juñç·tī′vȧs**, **çon·juñç·tī′vae**, the mucous membrane lining the inner surface of the eyelids and covering the front part of the eyeball.

çon·juñç·tī′văl, *a.* of the conjunctiva.

çŏn·juñç′tive, *a.* [LL. *conjunctivus*, from pp. of L. *conjungere*; see *conjoin*.]
1. serving to join together; connective.
2. united; combined; joint.
3. in grammar, (a) used as a conjunction; as, a *conjunctive* adverb; (b) connecting both the meaning and the construction of sentence elements; as, *and* and *moreover* are *conjunctive*; (c) always used in conjunction with the verb: said of unstressed forms of personal, reflexive, or reciprocal pronouns in some Romance languages (e.g., *il*, in French *il me faut*).

çŏn·juñç′tive, *n.* in grammar, a conjunctive word, especially a conjunction.

çŏn·juñç′tive·ly, *adv.* 1. jointly; in conjunction or union; together.
2. by a conjunction.

çŏn·juñç′tive·ness, *n.* the quality of conjoining or uniting.

çŏn·juñç·ti·vī′tis, *n.* [Mod. L., from *conjunctiva*, and *-itis*.] inflammation of the conjunctiva.

çŏn·juñçt′ly, *adv.* in union; jointly; together.

çŏn·juñç′tūre, *n.* 1. a joining; a combination or union, as of causes, events, or circumstances; as, an unhappy *conjuncture* of affairs.
2. an occasion; a critical time, proceeding from a union of circumstances; as, at that *conjuncture* peace was very desirable.

çon·jụ̇·rā′tion, *n.* [ME. *conjuracioun*; OFr. *conjuration*; L. *conjuratio*, a swearing together, conspiracy, in LL. enchantment, adjuration, from *conjuratus*, pp. of *conjurare*, to swear together, combine; from *com-*, together, and *jurare*, to swear.]
1. a conjuring; invocation.
2. a magic spell; incantation.
3. magic; sorcery.
4. a solemn entreaty to a deity. [Archaic.]

çon′jụ̇·rā·tŏr, *n.* [LL.] a fellow conspirator; one who enters by an oath into an agreement with others.

çŏn·jụ̇re′, *v.t.*; conjured, *pt.*, *pp.*; conjuring, *ppr.* [ME. *conjuren*; OFr. *conjurer*; L. *conjurare*, to conspire.]
1. to call upon, appeal to, or entreat solemnly, especially by some oath; as, I *conjure* you in the name of God to help me.
2. (kun′jẽr *or* kon′) to summon (a devil, etc.) by an oath or magic spell.
3. (kun′jẽr *or* kon′) to cause to be, appear, come (*up*), or go (*away*, etc.) by or as by magic; as, the music *conjured* my troubles away; the story *conjured up* visions of faraway lands.

çŏn·jụ̇re′, *v.i.* 1. originally, to be sworn in a conspiracy.
2. (kun′jẽr *or* kon′) to summon a demon, spirit, etc. by an oath or magic spell.
3. (kun′jẽr *or* kon′) to practice magic or legerdemain.

çŏn·jụ̇re′ment, *n.* serious injunction; solemn demand.

çon′jụ̇r·ẽr, **çon′jur·ŏr**, *n.* [OFr. *conjureur*; LL. *conjurator*, one bound with an oath, a conjurer, from *conjurare*, to swear together.]
1. (kŏn-jụ̇r′) a person who solemnly entreats or appeals to someone.
2. a person who practices magic; magician; sorcerer.
3. a person skilled in legerdemain.

çon·jụ̇r′ŏr, *n.* [L. *conjuratus*, pp. of *conjurare*, to swear together; *com-*, together, and *jurare*, to swear.] in law, one who is bound by an oath taken with others.

çon′jụ̇·ry, *n.* the art or practice of conjuring, or magic; enchantment. [Rare.]

çoñk, *n.* [from *conch*.]
1. the nose. [British Slang.]
2. the head. [Slang.]
3. a blow on the head. [Slang.]

çoñk, *v.t.* to strike or hit, especially on the head. [Slang.]
to conk out; to fail suddenly in operation, as a motor. [Slang.]

çon man, a confidence man; a swindler. [Slang.]

çonn, *v.t.* and *n.* con (nautical term).

çon·nas′cence, *n.* [LL. *connascens*, pp. of *connasci*, to be born at the same time; L. *com-*, together, and *nasci*, to be born.]
1. the common birth of two or more at the same time; production of two or more together. [Rare.]
2. the act of growing together, or at the same time. [Obs.]

çon·nas′cent, *a.* growing together; born or produced at the same time. [Rare.]

çon′nāte, *a.* [LL. *connatus*, pp. of *connasci*, to be born at the same time; L. *com-*, together, and *nasci*, to be born.]
1. inborn; innate; congenital.
2. coexisting since birth or the beginning.
3. having the same origin or agreeing in nature; cognate.
4. in biology, congenitally or firmly united.

CONNATE-PERFOLIATE LEAVES

çon′nāte-pẽr·fō′li·āte, *a.* connate at the base and about the stem, so as to produce a broad body through which the stem passes, as opposite sessile leaves.

çon·nā′tion, *n.* the condition of being connate; union from birth.

çon·nat′ū·răl, *a.* [L. *com-*, together, and *naturalis*, natural, from *natura*, nature.]
1. innate; natural.
2. related in nature; cognate.

çon·nat·ū·ral′i·ty, *n.* connatural quality.

çon·nat′ū·răl·īze, *v.t.*; connaturalized, *pt.*, *pp.*; connaturalizing, *ppr.* to make connatural, or cognate.

çon·nat′ū·răl·ly, *adv.* by the act of nature; originally.

çon·nat′ū·răl·ness, *n.* connatural condition.

çon·nā′tūre, *n.* likeness or identity in nature or character.

çŏn·neçt′, *v.t.*; connected, *pt.*, *pp.*; connecting, *ppr.* [L. *connectere*, to bind together.]
1. to join or fasten (two things together, or one thing, *with* or *to* another); link; couple.
2. to show or think of as related; associate; as, we *connect* orange blossoms with weddings.
3. to provide with a circuit for communicating by telephone; as, the operator will *connect* you with Cleveland.
4. in electricity, to plug into a circuit; hook up.

çŏn·neçt′, *v.i.* 1. to join or be joined.
2. to meet so that passengers can transfer promptly: said of trains, buses, etc.
3. to be properly related; fit in; as, your second paragraph doesn't *connect* with the others.
4. to reach the thing aimed at; have or get a desired effect; as, that right to the jaw didn't quite *connect*. [Slang.]

çŏn·neçt′ed, *a.* 1. joined together; fastened.
2. joined in proper order; coherent, as ideas, parts of a story, etc.
3. related; affiliated; associated; having something to do (*with*).

çŏn·neçt′ed·ly, *adv.* by connection; in a connected manner; logically; coherently.

çŏn·neç′tẽr, *n.* same as *connector*.

çŏn·neçt′ing liñk, 1. a movable link used to connect one chain with another.
2. figuratively, any circumstance, fact, or

thought which may be used to complete a logical chain.

çŏn·nect'ing rod, a rod or bar connecting two or more moving parts of a machine; especially, a rod connecting the crank shaft and pistons of an automobile.

çŏn·neç'tion, *n.* 1. the act of joining, or state of being joined; a state of being knit or fastened together; union.

2. that which connects or unites; a tie; a bond; means of joining.

3. a relation; association; specifically, (a) the relation between things that depend on, involve, or follow each other; (b) the logical linking together of words or ideas; coherence; (c) the relation of a word, sentence, etc. to the surrounding text as it affects and influences the meaning; context; (d) relation by family ties, business, etc.

4. [*usually in pl.*] (a) a relative, especially by marriage; (b) a business associate, acquaintance, etc., especially an influential one; as, he has powerful *connections.*

5. [*usually in pl.*] the act, fact, or means of meeting buses, trains, etc., or transferring from one to another, at points along a route.

6. a group of people associated together in politics, business, worship, etc.

7. a religious sect or denomination: usually *connexion.*

8. in electricity, a circuit.

9. in telephony and telegraphy, a line of communication from one point to another.

in connection with; (a) together with; in conjunction with; (b) with reference to.

çŏn·neçt'ive, *a.* connecting or serving to connect.

çŏn·neçt'ive, *n.* something that connects; especially, a word that connects phrases, clauses, or other words, as a conjunction or relative pronoun.

çŏn·neçt'ive·ly, *adv.* in union or conjunction; jointly.

çŏn·neçt'ive tis'sūe (tish'ū), tissue found throughout the body, serving to bind together and support other tissues and organs: it is made up of various kinds of fibrils contained in a matrix of intercellular material.

çon·neç·tiv'i·ty, *n.* the quality or condition of being connective.

çŏn·neçt'ŏr, *n.* a person or thing that connects: also spelled *connecter.*

çŏn'nēr, *n.* same as *cunner.*

çon'nēr, *n.* [from ME. *cunnen*; AS. *cunnian*, to try, test, examine.] an examiner; one who inspects or tests. [Archaic.]

çon'nēr, *n.* a lookout on shore or on shipboard.

çon'nex, *v.t.* to link together; to join. [Obs.]

çŏn·nex'ion, *n.* connection: chiefly British spelling.

çŏn·nex'ive, *a.* connective. [Obs.]

çon'ning tow'ēr, [ppr. of *con, conn* (to direct).]

1. an armored pilothouse on the deck of a warship, used as an observation and control station.

2. in submarines, a low observation tower serving also as an entrance to the interior.

CONNING TOWER OF SUBMARINE

çŏn·nip'tion, *n.* [arbitrary pseudo-Latin coinage.] a fit of anger, hysteria, etc.; tantrum: also *conniption fit.* [Colloq.]

çŏn·nīv'ănce, *n.* [Fr. *connivence*; L. *conniventia*, connivance, from *connivere*, to wink, connive.] a conniving; passive co-operation, as by consent or pretended ignorance, especially in wrongdoing.

çŏn·nīv'ăn·cy, *n.* connivance. [Rare.]

çŏn·nīve', *v.t.*; connived, *pt., pp.*; conniving, *ppr.* to feign ignorance of. [Obs.]

çŏn·nīve', *v.i.* [L. *connivere*, to wink, wink at, overlook.]

1. to wink; to close and open the eyelids rapidly. [Obs.]

2. to pretend not to look (*at* crime, deceit, etc.), thus giving tacit consent or co-operation; pretend ignorance of another's wrongdoing.

3. to co-operate secretly (*with* someone), especially in wrongdoing; conspire.

çŏn·nīv'en·cy, *n.* connivance. [Obs.]

çŏn·nīv'ent, *a.* 1. conniving. [Obs.]

2. in biology, with the ends inclined toward each other, as wings, anthers, etc.

çŏn·nīv'ēr, *n.* one who connives.

çon·nois·seūr' (-nis-sẽr' *or* -nis-sūr'), *n.* [Fr. *connaisseur*, formerly *connoisseur*; OFr. *conoisseor*, a judge, one well versed in anything, from *conoistre*; L. *cognoscere*, to know.] a person who has expert knowledge and keen discrimination in some field, especially in the fine arts or in matters of taste.

çon·nois·seūr'ship, *n.* the skill of a connoisseur.

çon'nō·tāte, *v.t.* to connote. [Obs.]

çon·nō·tā'tion, *n.* [L. *com-*, together, and *notare*, to mark, note.]

1. the act or process of connoting.

2. something connoted; idea suggested by or associated with a word, phrase, etc. in addition to its explicit meaning, or denotation; as, *politician* has different *connotations* from *statesman.*

3. in logic, the sum of all the attributes thought of as essential to the meaning of a term.

çon·nō'tȧ·tive, *a.* connoting, or involving connotation.

connotative term; a term which denotes a subject and gives its attributes by implication.

çon·nō'tȧ·tive·ly, *adv.* in the manner of connotation.

çŏn·nōte', *v.t.*; connoted, *pt., pp.*; connoting, *ppr.* 1. to suggest or convey (associations, overtones, etc.) in addition to the explicit, or denoted, meaning; as, the word *mother* means "female parent," but it generally *connotes* love, care, tenderness, etc.

2. to imply or involve.

çŏn·nū'bi·ăl, *a.* [L. *connubialis*, pertaining to marriage, from *connubium*, marriage; from *com-*, together, and *nubere*, to veil, marry.]

1. of marriage or the state of being married; conjugal.

2. married.

çŏn·nū·bi·al'i·ty, *n.*; *pl.* **çŏn·nū·bi·al'i·tieş,** 1. marriage.

2. a thing characteristic of marriage.

çon·nū·mēr·ā'tion, *n.* a reckoning together. [Rare.]

çon'nu·sănce, *n.* cognizance. [Obs.]

çon'nu·sănt, *a.* cognizant. [Obs.]

çon·nu·sor', *n.* cognizor. [Obs.]

çon·nū·tri'tious (-trish'us), *a.* fed or nourished together. [Obs.]

çon'ny, *n.* canny. [Brit. Dial.]

çō'nō·dont, *n.* [Gr. *kōnos*, a cone, and *odous*, a tooth.] any of various toothlike fossils, occurring especially in carboniferous rocks, believed to be the remains of annelids.

çō'noid, *n.* [Gr. *kōnoeidēs*, cone-shaped.]

1. in geometry, a solid formed by the revolution of a conic section about its axis. If the conic section is a parabola, the resulting solid is a parabolic conoid, or paraboloid; if a hyperbola, the solid is a hyperbolic conoid, or hyperboloid; if an ellipse, an elliptic conoid, a spheroid, or an ellipsoid.

2. in anatomy, the pineal gland. [Obs.]

3. anything having the form of a cone.

çō'noid, *a.* same as *conoidal.*

çō·noid'ăl, *a.* of or shaped like a cone or conoid.

conoidal ligament; a ligament, conical in form, which serves to protect the collarbone and to hold it in place at its distal end.

çō·noid'iç, çō·noid'iç·ăl, *a.* pertaining to a conoid; having the form of a conoid.

çō·nom·i·nee', *n.* one nominated in conjunction with another; a joint nominee.

çō'nō·sçōpe, *n.* [Gr. *kōnos*, a cone, and *skopein*, to view.] a kind of polariscope for the examination of crystals in converging rays of light.

çon·quăd'rāte, *v.t.* [L. *conquadratus*, pp. of *conquadrare*, to make square; *con-*, and *quadrare*, to make square.] to bring into a square.

çon·quas'sāte, *v.t.* to shake. [Obs.]

çon·quas·sā'tion, *n.* a shaking; an agitation. [Obs.]

çoñ'quēr (-kẽr), *v.t.*; conquered, *pt., pp.*; conquering, *ppr.* [ME. *conqueren*; OFr. *conquerre*, to conquer, seek after; L. *conquirere*, to seek after, procure.]

1. to subdue; to gain by force; to take possession or control of by or as by winning a war.

2. to overcome by physical, mental, or moral force; defeat; get the better of.

3. to gain or obtain by effort; as, to *conquer* freedom; to *conquer* peace. [Obs.]

çoñ'quēr (-kẽr), *v.i.* to win; to gain the victory.

> The champions resolved to *conquer* or to die.
> —Waller.

Syn.—beat, crush, defeat, discomfit, down, humble, master, overcome, overpower, overthrow, prevail over, reduce, rout, subdue, subject, subjugate, surmount, vanquish, win, worst.

çoñ'quēr·ȧ·ble, *a.* capable of being conquered, overcome, or subdued.

çoñ'quēr·ȧ·ble·ness, *n.* a state of being conquerable.

çoñ'quēr·ess, *n.* a woman who conquers.

çoñ'quēr·ing·ly, *adv.* in a conquering manner.

çoñ'quēr·ŏr, *n.* one who conquers.

çoñ'quest (-kwest), *n.* [ME. *conquest*; OFr. *conquest*; L. *conquisitus*, pp. of *conquirere*, to seek for; from *con-*, and *quærere*, to seek.]

1. the act or process of conquering; the act of overcoming or vanquishing opposition by force, physical, mental, or moral; victory; subjugation.

> In joys of *conquest* he resigns his breath.
> —Addison.

2. that which is conquered; as, Jamaica was a valuable *conquest* for England.

3. in a feudal sense, acquisition; the acquiring of property by other means than inheritance.

4. the act of gaining or regaining by effort; as, the *conquest* of liberty or peace. [Obs.]

5. (a) a winning of someone's affection or favor; (b) a person whose affection or favor has been won.

Syn.—victory, triumph, mastery, reduction, subjugation, subjection, achievement.

çoñ'qui·ȧn (-ki-ȧn), *n.* a card game like rummy, for two players.

çoñ·quis'tȧ·dōr, *n.* [Sp.] any one of the Spanish conquerors of South or Central America in the sixteenth century.

çon·sañ'guine (-gwin), *a.* consanguineous.

çon·sañ·guin'ē·ăl (-gwin'), *a.* consanguineous.

çon·sañ'guined, *a.* related by blood. [Rare.]

çon·sañ·guin'ē·ous, *a.* [L. *consanguineus*; *con-*, and *sanguis*, blood.]

1. of the same blood; related by birth; descended from the same ancestor.

2. of blood relationship.

çon·sañ·guin'i·ty, *n.* 1. the relation or connection of persons descended from the same ancestor; blood relationship.

2. close relationship; affinity.

çon·sär·ci·nā'tion, *n.* [L. *consarcinatus*, pp. of *consarcinare*, to patch together.] the act of patching together. [Obs.]

çon'science (-shens), *n.* [Fr. *conscience*, from L. *conscientia*, a joint knowledge, feeling, from *conscire*; from *com-*, together with, and *scire*, to know.]

1. knowledge or feeling of right and wrong; the faculty, power, or principle of a person which decides on the lawfulness or unlawfulness of his actions, with a compulsion to do right; moral judgment that prohibits or opposes the violation of a previously recognized ethical principle.

> *Conscience* is first occupied in ascertaining our duty, before we proceed to action; then in judging of our actions when performed.
> —J. M. Mason.

2. consciousness; knowledge of our own actions or thoughts. [Obs.]

> The sweetest cordial we receive, at last,
> Is *conscience* of our virtuous actions past.
> —Denham.

3. the estimate or determination of justice, honesty, etc.

> What you require cannot, in *conscience*, be deferred.
> —Milton.

a matter of conscience; a matter in which one is bound to act according to the dictates of conscience.

conscience clause; a clause in a law exempting certain persons from doing certain things prescribed for others, when they have religious or conscientious scruples against performing such acts, as taking oaths, rendering military service, etc.

conscience money; money paid to relieve one's conscience, as if to compensate for some previous fraud, or in atonement for theft, etc.

in all conscience; in all reason or reasonableness.

çon'scienced (-shenst), *a.* having a conscience.

çon′science·less, *a.* having no conscience; unscrupulous.

çon′science-strick″en, *a.* feeling guilty or bad because of having done something wrong.

çon′scient, *a.* conscious. [Rare.]

çon·sci·en′tious (-shi-en′shus), *a.* influenced or governed by conscience; governed by the known or accepted rules of right and wrong; scrupulous; honest; as, a *conscientious* judge.

çon·sci·en′tious·ly, *adv.* according to the dictates of conscience; faithfully; scrupulously; as, a man may err *conscientiously.*

çon·sci·en′tious·ness, *n.* the state or quality of being conscientious.

çon·sci·en′tious ob·jeçt′ŏr, a person who objects to warfare because he believes that it is wrong to kill; especially, a member of any of various religious sects whose tenets prohibit military service.

çon′sciŏn·à·ble (-shun-), *a.* according to conscience; reasonable; just. [Rare.]

Let my debtors have *conscionable* satisfaction. —Wotton.

çon′scious (-shus), *a.* [L. *conscius,* knowing, aware, from *conscire,* to know with, be cognizant of; from *com-,* with, and *scire,* to know.]

1. having a feeling or knowledge (*of* one's sensations, feelings, etc., or external things); knowing or feeling (*that* something is or was happening or existing); aware; cognizant.

2. able to feel and think; awake.

3. aware of oneself as a thinking being; knowing what one is doing and why.

4. painfully aware of oneself; self-conscious; embarrassed.

5. accompanied by an awareness of what one is thinking, feeling, and doing; intentional; as, *conscious* humor.

6. known to or felt by oneself; as, *conscious* guilt.

Syn.—aware, sensible, felt, known, cognizant, apprised.

çon′scious·ly, *adv.* with knowledge of one's own mental operations or actions.

çon′scious·ness, *n.* 1. the knowledge of what is happening around one; the state of being conscious.

2. the totality of one's thoughts, feelings, and impressions; mind.

Syn.—feeling, attention, sensation.

çon′scious·ness-rāiṣ″ing, *n.* the process of seeking, especially through group sessions, to increase awareness of one's own role, attitudes, needs, etc. in connection with the personal, social, economic, sexual, etc. problems of modern life.

cŏn·sçrībe′, *v.t.* to force to do military service; to draft; to conscript. [Obs.]

cŏn·sçript′, *v.t.*; conscripted, *pt., pp.*; conscripting, *ppr.* [L. *conscriptus,* pp. of *conscribere,* to enroll; from *com-,* together with, and *scribere,* to write.]

1. to draft for military service; to enroll in a compulsory manner in the armed forces.

2. to force (labor, capital, etc.) into service for the government.

çon′sçript, *a.* conscripted; drafted.

çon′sçript, *n.* a conscripted person; a draftee.

çon′sçript fä′thẽrṣ, 1. the senators of ancient Rome.

2. legislators of any nation, state, etc.

cŏn·sçrip′tion, *n.* 1. an enrolling or registering. [Obs.]

2. a compulsory enrollment of men, or sometimes women, in the armed forces.

3. a forcing of labor, capital, etc. into government service.

çon′sē·crāte, *v.t.*; consecrated, *pt., pp.*; consecrating, *ppr.* [L. *consecratus,* pp. of *consecrare,* to dedicate; from *com-,* together, and *sacrare,* to consecrate, devote to a divinity, from *sacer,* sacred.]

1. to make or declare to be sacred, by certain ceremonies or rites; to appropriate to sacred uses; to set apart or dedicate as holy; as, to *consecrate* a church, to *consecrate* a bishop.

2. to make (someone) a bishop, ruler, etc. by a religious ceremony.

3. to make respected; to cause to be revered or honored; as, customs or principles *consecrated* by time.

4. to devote to a sacred or high purpose; to dedicate; as, he *consecrated* his life to the glory of his country.

çon′sē·crāte, *a.* sacred; consecrated; devoted; dedicated.

They were assembled in that *consecrate* place. —Bacon.

çon′sē·crā·ted·ness, *n.* the state of being consecrated.

çon·sē·crā′tion, *n.* the act of consecrating or the state of being consecrated; also, a ceremony for this.

çon′sē·crā·tŏr, *n.* a person or thing that consecrates.

çon′sē·crā·tō·ry, *a.* of or for consecration.

çon·seç·tā′nē·ous, *a.* following or deducible as a matter of course.

çon′seç·tā·ry, *a.* [L. *consectarius,* from *consectari,* to follow after; from *com-,* with, and *sectari,* to follow.] following; consequent; consequential; deducible. [Rare.]

çon′seç·tā·ry, *n.* that which follows; consequence. [Rare.]

çon′sē·cūte, *v.t.* to follow closely after. [Obs.]

çon·sē·cū′tion, *n.* [L. *consecutio,* from *consequi,* to follow; from *com-,* with, and *sequi,* to follow.]

1. a following or sequel; a train of reasoning; logical sequence.

2. succession; a series of things that follow each other; as, a *consecution* of colors.

consecution month; in astronomy, the lunar month.

cŏn·seç′ū·tive, *a.* 1. following in order; succeeding one another in a regular course; successive; uninterrupted in succession; as, fifty *consecutive* years.

2. proceeding from one part or idea to the next in logical order, as a story, reasoning, etc.

3. in grammar, stating a result, as a clause.

consecutive chords; a succession or repetition of musical chords having the same intervals.

consecutive symptoms; in medicine, symptoms appearing on the cessation of a disease or during convalescence, but having neither direct nor certain connection with the disease.

cŏn·seç′ū·tive·ly, *adv.* in a consecutive manner; in regular succession; successively.

cŏn·seç′ū·tive·ness, *n.* the state of being consecutive.

cŏn·sen′sion, *n.* [Fr. *consension*; L. *consensio,* from *consentire,* to be of one opinion, to agree.] agreement; accord. [Rare.]

cŏn·sen′sū·ăl, *a.* in law, formed or existing by mere mutual consent; as, a *consensual* marriage; a *consensual* contract, etc.

consensual motions; in physiology, involuntary motions following or accompanying voluntary motions. Thus the iris contracts when the eye is open to admit the light.

cŏn·sen′sus, *n.* unanimity; agreement, especially in opinion; hence, general opinion.

cŏn·sent′, *n.* [L. *consensus,* from *consentio,* to be of one mind, to agree; from *com-,* with, and *sentire,* to think, feel, or perceive.]

1. agreement in sentiment, opinion, etc.; accord of minds; concord.

They all with one *consent* began to make excuse. —Luke xiv. 18.

2. voluntary allowance or acceptance of something done or proposed; permission; approval; compliance; acquiescence; as, he gave his *consent* to the marriage of his daughter.

3. agreement; coherence; correspondence in parts, qualities, or operation. [Rare.]

Such is the world's great harmony that springs
From union, order, full *consent* of things. —Pope.

4. in physiology, sympathy.

5. in law, deliberate concurrence in the terms of a contract or agreement, of such a nature as to bind the party consenting.

Syn.—concord, assent, compliance, concurrence, agreement, approval, permission.

cŏn·sent′, *v.i.*; consented, *pt., pp.*; consenting, *ppr.* 1. to acquiesce; to approve or give permission (*to* something proposed or requested); as, I cannot *consent* to the request.

2. to be of the same opinion; to agree or accord. [Archaic.]

Syn.—accede, agree, assent, comply, yield, allow, permit, approve.

cŏn·sent′, *v.t.* to give assent to; to acknowledge; to grant. [Obs.]

cŏn·sent′à·ble, *a.* established by common consent; agreed upon: applied in Pennsylvania law to a property boundary line.

çon·sen·tà·nē′i·ty, *n.* mutual agreement. [Rare.]

çon·sen·tā′nē·ous, *a.* 1. agreeable; accordant; consistent; suitable.

A good law and *consentaneous* to reason. —Howell.

2. unanimous.

çon·sen·tā′nē·ous·ly, *adv.* agreeably; consistently; suitably.

cŏn·sent′ẽr, *n.* a person who consents.

cŏn·sen′tient (-shent), *a.* agreeing in mind; united in opinion; unanimous.

The *consentient* judgment of the church. —Pearson.

cŏn·sent′ing·ly, *adv.* in a consenting manner.

cŏn·sen′tū·ăl, *a.* [from *consent,* and *-al.*] involving consent, especially mutual consent; as, *consentual* divorce.

çon′sē·quence, *n.* [Fr. *consequence*; L. *consequentia,* from *consequens* (*-entis*), ppr. of *consequi,* to follow after; from *com-,* with, and *sequi,* to follow.]

1. that which follows from any act, cause, principle, or series of actions; an event or effect produced by some preceding act or cause; a result.

Shun the bitter *consequence.* —Milton.

2. a logical result or conclusion; inference; deduction.

3. connection of cause and effect.

4. logical sequence.

5. importance as a cause or influence; significance; as, a matter of little *consequence.*

6. importance in rank; influence; distinction; as, a man of great *consequence* in society.

in consequence; as a result; for this reason; hence; therefore.

in consequence of; as a result or effect of; because of; through.

Syn.—effect, result, outgrowth, end, consequent, issue.

çon′sē·quence, *v.i.* to draw inferences; to form deductions. [Obs.]

Moses condescends to such a methodical and school-like way of defining and *consequencing.* —Milton.

çon′sē·quent, *a.* 1. following as a result; resulting; as, favorable weather and *consequent* abundant crops; distress *consequent* on the war.

The right was *consequent* to, and built on, an act perfectly personal. —Locke.

2. following as a logical inference or deduction; as, a proposition *consequent* to other propositions.

3. proceeding in logical sequence.

çon′sē·quent, *n.* 1. that which follows something else.

2. that which follows as a result or effect.

3. in logic, that which follows from propositions by rational deduction; especially, (a) the second term of a conditional proposition; (b) an inference.

4. in mathematics, the second of the two terms of a ratio, or that with which the antecedent is compared.

çon·sē·quen′tiăl (-shăl), *a.* 1. following as the natural effect; resulting; consequent; as, a *consequential* failure.

2. having the consequence justly connected with the premises; conclusive. [Obs.]

3. assuming the air of a person of importance; pompous; as, a very *consequential* delegation.

4. important; as, a *consequential* event. [Rare.]

consequential losses or *damages*; in law, such losses or damages as arise not from the primary cause, but as an incidental result of it.

çon·sē·quen′tiăl·ly, *adv.* same as *consequently.*

çon·sē·quen′tiăl·ness, *n.* 1. the state or quality of being consequential.

2. conceit; pompousness; the assumption of importance.

çon′sē·quent·ly, *adv.* by necessary connection of effects with their causes; as a result; by logical inference; therefore; accordingly.

çon′sē·quent·ness, *n.* the quality or condition of being consequential. [Obs.]

cŏn·sẽrv′à·ble, *a.* capable of being kept or preserved.

cŏn·sẽrv′ăn·cy, *n.* 1. the act of preserving; conservation; preservation from injury or improper use; as, the *conservancy* of fisheries or forests.

2. a commission authorized to supervise a forest, river, or port. [Brit.]

cŏn·sẽrv′ănt, *a.* conserving; having the power or quality of preserving.

çon·sẽr·vā′tion, *n.* [L. *conservatio,* from *conservare,* to keep; from *com-,* together, and *servare,* to keep, save.]

1. the act of preserving, guarding, or protecting; preservation from loss, decay, injury, or violation; as, the *conservation* of the peace of society.

2. the official care and protection of natural resources, as forests.

3. a forest, fishery, etc., or a part of one, under official supervision.

conservation of areas; the theory that a planetary radius vector traverses equal areas in equal times.

conservation of energy or *of force*; the principle that the aggregate of energy in any physical system is a constant quantity, transformable in countless ways, but never increased or diminished.

çon·sẽr·vā′tion·ăl, *a.* tending toward conservation; preservative.

çon·sẽr·vā′tion·ist, *n.* a person who advocates conservation of the natural resources of a country or region.

çŏn·sẽrv′ȧ·tiṣm, *n.* 1. the practice of preserving what is established; disposition to oppose change in established institutions and methods.

2. [C–] the political principles and opinions maintained by the Conservative party of either Great Britain or Canada.

çŏn·sẽrv′ȧ·tive, *a.* 1. conserving or tending to conserve; preservative.

2. tending to preserve old institutions, methods, customs, and the like; adhering to what is old or established; opposing or resisting change; as, a *conservative* political party, *conservative* art.

3. of or characteristic of a conservative; as, *conservative* views.

The slow progress which Sweden has made in introducing needful reforms, is owing to the *conservative* spirit of the nobility and the priesthood. —Bayard Taylor.

4. moderate; prudent; safe; as, a *conservative* estimate.

5. [C–] pertaining to the English or Canadian Conservatives or their principles.

conservative system; any physical system exemplifying the principle of the conservation of energy; any system the total energy of which is constant, whatever form or forms that energy may take.

çŏn·sẽrv′ȧ·tive, *n.* 1. a person or thing tending to preserve; a preservative.

2. one who wishes to preserve traditions or institutions and resists innovation or change; a conservative person.

3. [C–] a member of the major right-wing political party of Great Britain or of the similar one in Canada.

çŏn·sẽrv′ȧ·tive·ness, *n.* the state or quality of being conservative.

çŏn·sẽr·vȧ·toire′ (-twär′), *n.* [Fr.] a school for special instruction, especially in art, music, etc.; a conservatory.

çon′sẽr·vā·tŏr, *n.* [L.] 1. a protector; a guardian; a custodian; one who or that which preserves from injury or violation; as, a *conservator* of the public peace.

2. a person appointed by a court to manage the affairs of mental incompetents, minors, etc.

çŏn·sẽrv′ȧ·tō·ry, *a.* having the quality of preserving.

çŏn·sẽrv′ȧ·tō·ry, *n.*; *pl.* **çŏn·sẽrv′ȧ·tō·ries,** 1. a preservative; as, a *conservatory* of life. [Obs.]

2. a room enclosed in glass, for growing and showing flowers and other plants; greenhouse, especially of a private home, museum, etc.

3. a school for giving instruction and training in some special branch of study, especially in the arts or music.

çon·sẽr·vā′trix, *n.* [L.] a woman conservator.

çŏn·sẽrve′, *v.t.*; conserved, *pt., pp.*; conserving, *ppr.* [L. *conservare*, to keep, preserve.]

1. to keep in a safe or sound state; to save; to preserve from loss, decay, waste, or injury; to defend from violation; as, to *conserve* the peace of society.

2. to preserve with sugar, in order to prevent decay; to make into preserves, as fruits.

çon′sẽrve, *n.* 1. [*usually in pl.*] a kind of jam made of fruits, etc. and sugar.

2. a pharmaceutical preparation of vegetable substances and sugar.

3. a conservatory. [Obs.]

çŏn·sẽrv′ẽr, *n.* one who conserves.

çŏn·ses′sion, *n.* a sitting together. [Obs.]

çŏn·ses′sŏr, *n.* one who sits with others. [Obs.]

çŏn·sid′ẽr, *v.t.*; considered, *pt., pp.*; considering, *ppr.* [ME. *consideren*; OFr. *considerer*; L. *considerare*, to look at closely, observe; from *com-*, with, and *sidus, sideris*, a star.]

1. to fix the mind on in order to understand; to think on with care; to ponder; to study; to meditate on; as, the commissioners met to *consider* the matter.

2. to view attentively; to observe carefully; to examine. [Archaic.]

3. to believe after thought; as, we *consider* the plaintiff not guilty.

4. to respect; to show consideration for (others, their feelings, etc.).

5. to take into account; to have or keep in mind; to make allowance for; as, *consider* hereditary tendencies when judging character.

6. to think of as acceptable or possible; as, would you *consider* going with us?

7. to regard in a particular light; to judge to be; to esteem; to think; as, I *consider* him a rascal.

Syn.—deliberate, ponder, reflect, contemplate, examine, regard.

çŏn·sid′ẽr, *v.i.* to think seriously, maturely, or carefully; to reflect; as, take time to *consider* well.

çŏn·sid′ẽr·ȧ·ble, *a.* [Fr. *considérable*; L. *considerabilis*, from *considerare*, to observe closely, consider.]

1. that should receive consideration. [Obs.]

2. worth considering; important; noteworthy.

Men *considerable* in all worthy professions, eminent in many ways of life. —Spratt.

3. more than a little; moderately large; as, a *considerable* estate; a body of a *considerable* thickness.

çŏn·sid′ẽr·ȧ·ble·ness, *n.* a degree of value or importance that deserves notice. [Rare.]

çŏn·sid′ẽr·ȧ·bly, *adv.* to a considerable degree; a great deal; much.

çŏn·sid′ẽr·ănce, *n.* consideration; reflection; sober thought. [Obs.]

çŏn·sid′ẽr·āte, *a.* 1. given to consideration or to sober reflection; serious; discreet.

Aeneas is patient, *considerate*, and careful of his people. —Dryden.

2. having respect for; regardful; as, *considerate* of praise. [Rare.]

3. characterized by consideration or regard for another's circumstances and feelings; thoughtful; as, a *considerate* master, *considerate* treatment.

Syn.—careful, cautious, prudent, thoughtful, serious, kind, unselfish, charitable.

çŏn·sid′ẽr·āte·ly, *adv.* 1. with deliberation; with due consideration; prudently.

2. kindly; with regard for others.

çŏn·sid′ẽr·āte·ness, *n.* the state or quality of being considerate.

çŏn·sid·ẽr·ā′tion, *n.* 1. the act of considering; careful thought or attention; deliberation or meditation; as, let us take into *consideration* the consequences of a hasty decision.

2. thoughtful or sympathetic regard or respect, as for others.

3. something that is, or should be, considered, as in making a decision.

4. a thought or opinion produced by considering; reflection.

5. importance; claim to notice or regard.

Lucan is an author of *consideration* among the Latin poets. —Addison.

6. fee for trouble or for services; compensation; as, he will do it for a *consideration*.

7. in law, the reason which moves a contracting party to enter into an agreement; the material cause of a contract; the price or motive of a stipulation. In all contracts, each party gives or does something in exchange for what he receives.

8. respect or regard; esteem; as, *consideration* for the feelings of others.

Syn.—attention, friendliness, motive, prudence, reflection.

çŏn·sid′ẽr·ȧ·tive, *a.* taking into consideration; careful; thoughtful. [Rare.]

çŏn·sid′ẽr·ā·tŏr, *n.* one who considers. [Obs.]

çŏn·sid′ẽred, *a.* 1. arrived at after careful thought; thought out.

2. respected; esteemed.

çŏn·sid′ẽr·ẽr, *n.* one who considers.

çŏn·sid′ẽr·ing, *prep.* in view of; taking into account; making allowance for.

çŏn·sid′ẽr·ing, *adv.* taking all the circumstances into account; all things considered. [Colloq.]

çŏn·sid′ẽr·ing·ly, *adv.* with consideration or deliberation.

çŏn·sīgn′ (-sīn′), *v.t.*; consigned, *pt., pp.*; consigning, *ppr.* [Fr. *consigner*, present, deliver; L. *consignare*, to seal, attest, register; from *com-*, together, and *signare*, to sign, mark; *signum*, a mark, sign.]

1. to give, send, or set over; to transfer or deliver; as, at death the body is *consigned* to the grave.

At the day of general account, good men are to be *consigned* over to another state. —Atterbury.

2. to put in the charge of; entrust; as, *consign* the orphan to her uncle's care.

3. to assign; give over or set apart (*to* a purpose, a person's use, etc.).

4. to send or deliver, as goods to be sold.

5. to impress or stamp, as with a seal. [Obs.]

Syn.—commit, entrust, make over, transfer, deliver, resign.

çŏn·sīgn′, *v.i.* to submit to the same terms as another; also, to sign; to agree or consent. [Obs.]

çŏn·sig′nȧ·tā·ry, *n.* a person to whom anything is consigned; a consignee. [Obs.]

çon·sig·nā′tion, *n.* 1. the act of consigning; the act of delivering or committing to another person, place, or state.

Despair is a certain *consignation* to eternal ruin. —Taylor.

2. ratification; attestation; the act of confirming or establishing. [Obs.]

3. in Scots law, the depositing in the hands of a third party of a sum of money about which there is either a dispute or a competition.

4. in the Greek and other churches, the act of consecrating by marking with the sign of the cross.

çŏn·sig′nȧ·tō·ry, *n.* same as *cosignatory*.

çŏn·sig′nȧ·tūre, *n.* full signature; joint signing. [Rare.]

çon′sīgne (-sīn), *n.* [Fr. *consigne*, from *consigner*, to confine, put under orders.] in military usage, a countersign; a password.

con·si·gné′ (kọṅ-sē-nyā′), *n.* [Fr.] a person who is commanded to keep within certain limits, as an army officer under arrest.

con·sign·ee′ (-sīn-), *n.* the person to whom goods or other things are consigned.

çŏn·sīgn′ẽr (-sīn′), *n.* same as *consignor*.

çon·sig·nif′i·çănt, *a.* expressing the same meaning or significance; synonymous.

çon·sig″ni·fi·çā′tion, *n.* joint signification. [Rare.]

çon·sig·nif′i·çā·tive, *a.* having a like signification, or jointly significative. [Rare.]

çŏn·sig′ni·fȳ, *v.t.*; consignified, *pt., pp.*; consignifying, *ppr.* to signify in conjunction with something else. [Rare.]

çŏn·sīgn′ment (-sīn′), *n.* 1. the act of consigning or the state of being consigned, as of goods to an agent.

2. the thing consigned or shipped; the goods sent or delivered to an agent for sale or safekeeping.

3. the writing by which anything is consigned.

çŏn·sīgn′ŏr (-sīn′), *n.* a person or business firm that consigns or delivers goods to an agent.

çŏn·sil′i·ā·ry, *a.* [L. *consiliarius*, from *consilium*, counsel.] of or pertaining to counsel or advice; of the nature of advice.

çŏn·sil′i·ence, *n.* [L. *com-*, together, and *salire*, to leap.] a coincidence; the act of concurring.

çon·sim′i·lăr, *a.* having common resemblance. [Obs.]

çon·si·mil′i·tūde, *n.* resemblance. [Obs.]

çon·si·mil′i·ty, *n.* resemblance. [Obs.]

çŏn·sist′, *v.i.*; consisted, *pt., pp.*; consisting, *ppr.* [L. *consistere*, to stand together, stand still; from *com-*, together, and *sistere*, to stand, cause to stand; caus. of *stare*, to stand.]

1. to hold together or be held together; to exist. [Archaic.]

He is before all things, and by him all things *consist*. —Col. i. 17.

2. to be contained, comprised, or inherent: followed by *in*; as, the beauty of letter writing *consists in* ease and freedom.

3. to be composed, made up, or formed: followed by *of*; as, a landscape should *consist of* a variety of scenery.

4. to agree; to be in accordance (*with*); to be compatible; to harmonize.

5. to insist: followed by *on*. [Obs.]

çŏn·sist′en·cy, çŏn·sist′ence, *n.* 1. the condition of holding together; that state of a body in which its component parts remain fixed; firmness; solidity; as, the *consistency* of wood or iron.

The *consistency* of bodies is divers; dense, rare, tangible, pneumatic, volatile, etc. —Bacon.

2. the degree of density, firmness, or thickness.

Let the juices or liquor be boiled into the *consistence* of a syrup. —Arbuthnot.

3. agreement; harmony; logical connection; as, these accounts show no *consistency*.

4. agreement or harmony with what has already been done, agreed on, or expressed;

congruity; uniformity; as, the *consistency* of laws, regulations, or judicial decisions.

There is harmony and *consistency* in all God's works. —J. Lathrop.

çŏn·sist′ent, *a.* 1. fixed; firm; solid; holding together; as, the *consistent* parts of a body.

2. in agreement; compatible; congruous; uniform; not contradictory or opposed; as, overeating is not *consistent* with good health.

3. conducting oneself in harmony with one's belief or profession; as, a *consistent* Methodist.

Syn.—accordant, consonant, changeless.

çon·sis·tent′ēs, *n.pl.* the fourth or highest order of penitents in the early church. They were permitted to be present at the celebration of the Eucharist, but were not allowed to participate.

çŏn·sist′ent·ly, *adv.* in a consistent manner; as, to command confidence a man must act *consistently.*

çon·sis·tō′ri·ăl, *a.* pertaining to a consistory, or ecclesiastical court; as, *consistorial* laws.

çon·sis·tō′ri·ăn, *a.* consistorial.

çŏn·sis′tō·ry, *n.* [L. *consistorium,* a place of assembly, a council, from *consistere,* to stand together.]

1. originally, a place of meeting; a council house, or place of justice; hence, any assembly or council.

2. a church council or court, as the court of every diocesan bishop; also, the session of such a body.

3. in the Roman Catholic Church, an assembly of prelates; the college of cardinals at Rome.

Pius was then hearing causes in *consistory.* —Bacon.

4. in some religious bodies, as the Dutch Reformed Church, the lowest tribunal, corresponding to a church session, or one composed of ministers and elders, corresponding to a presbytery.

5. a civil court or seat of justice. [Obs.]

çŏn·sō′ci·āte (-shi-āt), *n.* an associate; a partner.

çŏn·sō′ci·āte, *v.t.* and *v.i.*; consociated, *pt., pp.*; consociating, *ppr.* [L. *consociatus,* pp. of *consociare,* to unite, associate; from *com-,* together, and *sociare,* from *socius,* joined with.] to join together; to unite in association.

çŏn·sō′ci·āte, *a.* associated; united.

çŏn·sō·ci·ā′tion, *n.* 1. intimate union of persons; fellowship; alliance; companionship; association.

2. an assembly of the pastors and delegates of the Congregational churches within a certain district.

çŏn·sō·ci·ā′tion·ăl, *a.* pertaining to a consociation.

çon′sol (*or* kŏn-sol′), *n.* singular of *consols.*

çŏn·sōl′ȧ·ble, *a.* that can be consoled; capable of receiving consolation.

çon′sō·lāte, *v.t.* to console. [Obs.]

çon·sō·lā′tion, *n.* [L. *consolatio,* from *consolari,* to console.]

1. a consoling or being consoled; comfort; alleviation of misery or distress of mind.

Against such cruelties,
With inward *consolations* recompensed.
—Milton.

2. a person or thing that consoles.

Syn.—alleviation, comfort, condolence, relief, solace, support.

çon·sō·lā′tion prīze, a prize given to a person who does well but does not win, or who wins in a match for those previously defeated.

çon′sō·lā·tŏr, *n.* one who consoles.

çŏn·sol′ȧ·tō·ry, *a.* [L. *consolatorius.*] consoling or tending to console.

çŏn·sol′ȧ·tō·ry, *n.* a consoling speech or writing.

çŏn·sōle′, *v.t.*; consoled, *pt., pp.*; consoling, *ppr.* to comfort; to cheer, especially by making up for loss or disappointment; to give (someone) contentment or moderate happiness, by relieving from distress.

Syn.—comfort, solace, soothe, cheer, sustain.

çon′sōle, *n.* [Fr., origin unknown.]

1. in architecture, an ornamental bracket used to support a cornice, bust, vase, or the like.

2. in a breech-loading cannon, a platform for supporting a withdrawn breech pin.

3. a console table.

4. the desklike frame containing the keys, stops, pedals, and other controls of an organ: it is often situated at a distance from the pipes, which are connected to it by an electric cable.

5. a radio or phonograph cabinet meant to stand on the floor.

çŏn·sōl′ẽr, *n.* one who consoles.

çon′sōle tā′ble, 1. a table supported by consoles.

2. a small table with legs curved or carved to resemble consoles, placed against a wall.

çŏn·sol′i·dȧ, *n.* a consound. [Obs.]

çŏn·sol′i·dănt, *a.* tending to consolidate or make firm; specifically, in medicine, having the quality of healing wounds, or forming new flesh.

çŏn·sol′i·dănt, *n.* a medicine used to heal wounds.

çŏn·sol′i·dāte, *v.t.*; consolidated, *pt., pp.*; consolidating, *ppr.* [L. *consolidatus,* pp. of *consolidare*; from *com-,* together, and *solidare,* to make solid, from *solidus,* solid.]

1. to make solid; to unite or press together (loose or separate parts), and form a compact mass; to harden or make dense and firm.

He fixed and *consolidated* the earth.
—Burnet.

2. to unite (the parts of a broken bone, etc.) by means of applications.

3. to unite (various units) into one mass or body; as, to *consolidate* the forces of an army; to *consolidate* various funds.

çŏn·sol′i·dāte, *v.i.* to grow firm and hard; to unite and become solid; as, moist clay *consolidates* by drying.

In hurts and ulcers of the head, dryness maketh them more apt to *consolidate.*
—Bacon.

Syn.—unite, combine, harden, compact, condense, compress.

çŏn·sol′i·dāte, *a.* formed into a solid mass; consolidated.

Consolidate in mind and frame.
—Tennyson.

çon·sol′i·dā·ted, *a.* made solid, hard, or compact; united.

consolidated annuities; same as *consols.*

Consolidated Fund; a British national fund, created by consolidating certain revenues and used for the payment of the interest on the national debt, the civil list, grants to the royal family, and other specified expenses.

consolidated school; a school attended by pupils from several adjoining districts.

çŏn·sol·i·dā′tion, *n.* 1. the act of making, or process of becoming, solid; the act of forming into a firm, compact mass, body, or system, or the uniting of several particulars into one body; as, a *consolidation* of the funds.

2. the annexing of one bill to another in parliament or legislation.

3. in law, the combining of two benefices in one.

4. in botany, adnation.

çŏn·sol′i·dā·tive, *a.* tending to consolidate; healing.

çŏn·sol′i·dā·tŏr, *n.* a person or thing that consolidates.

çŏn·sōl′ing, *a.* that consoles or comforts; as, *consoling* news.

çon′solṣ (*or* -solz′), *n.pl.* [contr. of *consolidated annuities.*] the government securities of Great Britain, including a large part of the national debt, consisting originally of public securities in great variety, these being consolidated in 1751 into a single 3 per cent stock. Reductions in interest have since been made; in 1889 to $2^3/_4$ per cent and in **1903** to the current rate of $2^1/_2$ per cent.

con·som·mé′ (çon-sŏm-mā′), *n.* [Fr. pp. of *consommer*; L. *consummare,* to finish, make perfect.] a clear soup made by boiling meat and, sometimes, grains or vegetables, in water.

çon′sō·nănce, çon′sō·năn·cy, *n.* [Fr. *consonance*; L. *consonantia,* from *consonans* (*-antis*), ppr. of *consonare,* to sound together with; from *com-,* with, and *sonare,* to sound; *sonus,* a sound.]

1. in music, accord or agreement of sounds; a pleasing combination of sounds simultaneously produced.

2. agreement; accord; congruity; consistency.

Syn.—agreement, accord; consistency, unison, harmony, congruity, suitableness, agreeableness.

çon′sō·nănt, *a.* 1. agreeing; according; congruous; consistent: followed generally by *with* or *to.*

2. in music, composed of consonances; harmonious; as, *consonant* intervals.

3. having rhyme or assonance.

4. of or pertaining to consonants.

çon′sō·nănt, *n.* 1. any speech sound produced by stopping and releasing the air stream (p, t, k, b, d, g), or stopping it at one point while it escapes at another (m, n, n, l, r), or forcing it through a loosely closed or very narrow passage (f, v, s, zh, sh, z, th, th, h, w, y), or by a combination of these means (ch, j).

2. loosely, a letter representing such a sound (k, s, etc.) or combination of such sounds (x = ks or gz): distinguished from *vowel.*

3. in linguistics, (a) any phoneme, especially one produced as described above, that functions in a word or syllable as a less audible sound, introducing, connecting, or following the more audible sounds (called *sonants*); (b) any sound, in any language, that does not function as a syllabic.

çon·sō·nan′tăl, *a.* 1. having the characteristics or function of a consonant or consonants.

2. of or having a consonant or consonants.

çon′sō·nănt·īze, *v.t.*; consonantized, *pt., pp.*; consonantizing, *ppr.* to use as a consonant or to make (a vowel) into a consonant.

çon′sō·nănt·ly, *adv.* consistently; in agreement.

çon′sō·nănt·ness, *n.* agreeableness; consistency. [Rare.]

çon′sō·nous, *a.* [L. *consonus,* sounding together.] agreeing in sound; harmonious.

çon′sō·pīte, *v.t.* [L. *consopitus,* pp. of *consopire,* to lull to sleep.] to quiet or compose; to lull to sleep. [Obs.]

çon′sō·pīte, *a.* calm; composed. [Obs.]

çon·sō·pi′tion, *n.* a lulling to sleep. [Obs.]

çon′sọrt, *n.* [OFr. *consort*; L. *consors* (*consortis*), a partner, neighbor; from *com-,* with, and *sors* (*sortis*), a lot.]

1. originally, a companion; a partner; hence, a wife or husband, especially of a reigning king or queen.

2. an assembly or association of persons. [Obs.]

3. agreement; accord. [Obs.]

4. [altered from *concert.*] harmony of sounds. [Obs.]

5. in navigation, any ship traveling along with another.

çŏn·sọrt′, *v.i.*; consorted, *pt., pp.*; consorting, *ppr.* 1. to associate; to keep company: followed by *with.*

Which of the Grecian chiefs *consorts with* thee? —Dryden.

2. to be in harmony or agreement; to be in accord.

çŏn·sọrt′, *v.t.* 1. to join; to marry. [Obs.]

With his *consorted* Eve. —Milton.

2. to associate; to join.

He begins to *consort* himself with men.
—Locke.

3. to accompany. [Obs.]

4. to sound in harmony. [Obs.]

çŏn·sọrt′ȧ·ble, *a.* that can be consorted. [Obs.]

çŏn·sọr′tion, *n.* a consorting. [Obs.]

çon′sọrt·iṣm, *n.* symbiosis.

çŏn·sọr′ti·um (-shi-), *n.*; *pl.* **çŏn·sọr′ti·ȧ,** [L., community of goods.]

1. a partnership.

2. an agreement or association of the banking interests of two or more nations, as for giving joint financial aid to another nation.

çon′sọrt·ship, *n.* fellowship; partnership.

çon′sound, *n.* [a corruption of Fr. *consoude,* from L. *consolida,* a comfrey; *consolidare,* to make solid.] any of a large number of plants supposed to have healing qualities.

çon·spē·cif′iç, *a.* of or pertaining to the same species.

çon·speç·tū′i·ty, *n.* sight; view. [Obs.]

çŏn·speç′tus, *n.* [L.]

1. a general view; a survey.

2. a summary; an outline; a synopsis.

çŏn·spẽrse′, *a.* [L. *conspersus,* pp. of *conspergere,* to sprinkle; from *com-,* with, and *spargere,* to scatter, sprinkle.] having irregular blotches or dots: said of the eggs of certain birds.

çŏn·spẽr′sion, *n.* a sprinkling. [Rare.]

çon·spi·çū′i·ty, *n.* conspicuousness. [Rare.]

çŏn·spiç′ū·ous, *a.* [L. *conspicuus,* open to view, from *conspicere,* to look at, observe.]

1. easy to see or perceive; obvious; manifest; as, to stand in a *conspicuous* place.

Or come I less *conspicuous.* —Milton.

2. attracting attention by being unexpected, unusual, or outstanding; remarkable; striking; as, she was *conspicuous* for her beauty.

Syn.—eminent, famous, distinguished, illustrious, prominent, celebrated, noted.

çŏn·spiç′ū·ous·ly, *adv.* in a conspicuous manner.

çŏn·spiç′ū·ous·ness, *n.* the state or quality of being conspicuous.

çŏn·spir′ȧ·cy, *n.*; *pl.* **çŏn·spir′ȧ·cieṣ,** [ME. *conspiracie*; OFr. *conspiracie*, from L. *conspirare*, to breathe together, conspire, agree; from *com-*, together, and *spirare*, to breathe.]

1. a planning and acting together secretly, especially for an unlawful or harmful purpose, such as murder or treason.

2. the plan agreed on; plot.

3. the group taking part in such a plan.

4. a combining or working together; as, the *conspiracy* of events.

Syn.—combination, plot, cabal, collusion, connivance.

çŏn·spīr′ănt, *a.* conspiring; plotting. [Obs.]

çon·spi·rā′tion, *n.* conspiracy. [Rare.]

çŏn·spir′ȧ·tŏr, *n.* one who conspires; one who engages in a plot to commit a crime, particularly treason.

çŏn·spir·ȧ·tō′ri·ăl, *a.* 1. of or characteristic of a conspirator or conspiracy.

2. conspiring or fond of conspiracy.

çŏn·spīre′, *v.i.*; conspired, *pt., pp.*; conspiring, *ppr.* 1. to plan and act together secretly, especially to commit a crime; to plot.

The servants of Amon *conspired* against him,
and slew the king in his own house.
—2 Kings xxi. 23.

2. to agree; to concur to one end; as, events *conspired* to ruin him.

Syn.—unite, concur, combine, confederate, league.

çŏn·spīre′, *v.t.* to plan for, usually in secret. [Rare.]

çŏn·spīr′ẽr, *n.* one who conspires or plots; a conspirator.

çŏn·spīr′ing·ly, *adv.* in the manner of a conspiracy; by conspiracy.

çon·spis·sā′tion, *n.* [L. *conspissatio*, from *conspissare*, to thicken.] the act of making thick or viscous; thickness. [Rare.]

çon·spūr′çāte, *v.t.* [L. *conspurcatus*, pp. of *conspurcare*, to defile.] to make impure. [Obs.]

çon·spūr·çā′tion, *n.* the act of defiling; defilement; pollution. [Obs.]

çon′stȧ·ble, *n.* [ME. *constable*, *conestable*; OFr. *conestable*; L. *conestabulus*, *comistabuli*, a constable, from *comes stabuli*, a count of the stable; *comes*, a count, and *stabulum*, a stable.]

1. in the Middle Ages, the highest ranking official of a royal household, court, etc.

2. the warden or keeper of a royal fortress or castle.

3. a policeman.

çon′stȧ·blẽr·y, *n.* constableship. [Obs.]

çon′stȧ·ble·ship, *n.* the position or term of office of a constable.

çon′stȧ·bless, *n.* a constable's wife. [Obs.]

çon′stȧ·ble·wick, *n.* the district to which a constable's power is limited. [Obs.]

çŏn·stab′ū·lā·ry, çŏn·stab′ū·lȧr, *a.* pertaining to constables or a constabulary.

çŏn·stab′ū·lā·ry, *n.*; *pl.* **çŏn·stab′ū·lȧr·ieṣ,** 1. the body of constables of a district, city, or country, collectively.

2. a district under a constable.

3. a police force characterized by a military organization but distinct from the regular army; state police.

4. the police: humorous usage.

çŏn·stab′ū·lȧ·tō·ry, *n.* and *a.* same as *constabulary*.

çon′stăn·cy, *n.* [ME. *constance*; OFr. *constance*; L. *constantia*, firmness, unchangeableness, from *constans*, ppr. of *constare*; from *com-*, together, and *stare*, to stand.]

1. the state or condition of being constant.

2. firmness of mind or purpose; resoluteness.

3. steadiness in affections or loyalties; faithfulness.

4. uniformity in nature, value, extent, etc.; regularity; stability.

5. certainty. [Obs.]

Syn.—fixedness, stability, firmness, steadiness, permanence, steadfastness, resolution.

çon′stănt, *a.* 1. fixed; firm: opposed to *fluid*. [Obs.]

To turn two fluid liquors into a *constant*
body. —Boyle.

2. not changing; remaining the same; specifically, (a) remaining firm in purpose; resolute; (b) remaining steady in affections or loyalties; faithful; (c) remaining uniform in nature, value, extent, etc.; regular; stable.

3. going on all the time; continual; persistent; as, *constant* interruptions.

Syn.—fixed, steadfast, unchanging, permanent, unalterable, immutable, invariable, perpetual, continual, resolute, firm, unshaken, determined.

çon′stănt, *n.* 1. anything that does not change or vary.

2. in mathematics and physics, a quantity or factor that does not vary throughout a discussion or investigation: opposed to *variable*.

absolute constant; in mathematics, a constant that never varies, as a cardinal number.

çon′stănt·an, *n.* [coined from *constant*.] an alloy of copper (60 per cent) and nickel (40 per cent), used for electrical resistance heating and thermocouples.

çon′stănt·in, *n.* same as *constantan*.

Çon·stan″ti·nō·pol′i·tăn, *a.* relating to Constantinople, the capital of the Ottoman empire.

Constantinopolitan creed; the creed adopted by a council at Constantinople in 381 A.D., which was a revision of the Nicene creed: called also *Niceno-Constantinopolitan creed*.

çon′stănt·ly, *adv.* in a constant manner.

çon′stat, *n.* [L., it appears.] a certificate given by the auditors of the exchequer to a person who intends to plead or move for a discharge of anything in that court, showing what appears upon the record respecting the matter in question. [Obs.]

çŏn·stāte′, *v.t.* [Fr. *constater*, to verify, take down; L. *constatus*, pp. of *constare*; from *com-*, together, and *stare*, to stand.] to find out; to determine; to verify.

çon′stel·lāte, *v.i.* and *v.t.*; constellated, *pt., pp.*; constellating, *ppr.* [LL. *constellatus*.] to unite in or as in a constellation; cluster.

çon·stel·lā′tion, *n.* [ME. and OFr. *constellacion*; L. *constellatio*, a collection of stars, from *constellatus*, set with stars; from *com-*, together, and *stellare*, to shine; *stella*, a star.]

1. a number of fixed stars arbitrarily considered as a group, usually named after some mythological being that they supposedly resemble in outline.

2. the part of the heavens occupied by such a group.

3. any brilliant cluster or gathering; as, a *constellation* of beautiful women.

4. in astrology, (a) the grouping of the planets at any particular time, especially at a person's birth; (b) one's disposition or fate as supposedly influenced by such grouping.

5. in psychology, a group of related thoughts regarded as clustered about one central idea.

çon′stẽr, *v.t.* and *v.i.* to construe. [Obs. or Dial.]

çon′stẽr·nāte, *v.t.*; consternated, *pt., pp.*; consternating, *ppr.* [L. *consternatus*, pp. of *consternare*; see *consternation*.] to paralyze with fright or horror; dismay.

çon·stẽr·nā′tion, *n.* [L. *consternatio*, from *consternare*, intens. form of *consternere*, to throw down, bestrew; from *com-*, together, and *sternere*, to strew.] paralyzing amazement or horror; great terror, wonder, or surprise.

Syn.—dismay, alarm, terror, panic, horror.

çon′sti·pāte, *v.t.*; constipated, *pt., pp.*; constipating, *ppr.* [L. *constipatus*, pp. of *constipare*, to press or crowd together; from *com-*, together, and *stipare*, to cram, pack.]

1. to crowd into a narrow compass; to condense. [Obs.]

2. to stop or close (pores, vessels, etc.); as, to *constipate* capillary vessels.

3. to cause constipation in.

çon′sti·pāt·ed, *a.* having constipation; costive.

çon·sti·pā′tion, *n.* 1. the act of crowding anything; condensation; as, a close *constipation* of particles. [Obs.]

2. a condition of the bowels in which the emptying of waste matter from the bowels is infrequent and difficult; costiveness.

çŏn·stit′ū·en·cy, *n.*; *pl.* **çŏn·stit′ū·en·cieṣ,** 1. the voters, or, loosely, the residents in a district, regarded as a group.

2. the district of such a group of voters, etc.

3. a group of clients, supporters, etc.

çŏn·stit′ū·ent, *a.* 1. necessary in the formation of the whole; forming, composing, or making as an essential part; component; elementary; as, oxygen and hydrogen are the *constituent* parts of water.

Body, soul, and reason are the three *constituent* parts of a man. —Dryden.

2. that can or does appoint or vote for a representative.

3. authorized to make or revise a political constitution; as, a *constituent* assembly.

çŏn·stit′ū·ent, *n.* 1. a necessary part or element; a component.

2. one who elects or assists in electing another as his representative in a deliberative or administrative assembly; as, the representative took up the claims of his *constituents*.

3. one who empowers another to transact business for him; one who appoints another as his agent; a principal; as, the agent said he could do nothing till he consulted his *constituent*.

çon′sti·tūte, *v.t.*; constituted, *pt., pp.*; constituting, *ppr.* [L. *constitutus*, pp. of *constituere*, to set up, establish; from *com-*, together, and *statuere*, to set.]

1. to set up (a law, government, institution, etc.); establish.

2. to set up (an assembly, proceeding, etc.) in a legal or official form.

3. to set up as; appoint; ordain; as, the students *constituted* him their spokesman.

4. to make up; form; compose; be the components or elements of; as, twelve people *constitute* a jury.

5. to make up or form of elements, material, etc.

constituted authorities; the magistrates or officers of a nation, people, municipality, etc.

çon′sti·tūte, *n.* an established law. [Obs.]

çon′sti·tū·tẽr, *n.* one who constitutes or appoints.

çon·sti·tū′tion, *n.* [ME. *constitucion*; OFr. *constitution*; L. *constitutio*, from *constituere*, to establish; from *com-*, together, and *statuere*, to set.]

1. a setting up; establishment.

2. an appointing.

3. a making up; composition.

4. the way in which a thing is made up; structure; organization; make-up.

5. the way in which a person is made up; physical or mental make-up; as, a man of strong *constitution*.

6. the way in which a government, state, society, etc. is organized.

7. the system of fundamental laws and principles of a government, state, society, corporation, etc., written or unwritten.

8. a document or set of documents in which these laws and principles are written down.

9. [C—] the Constitution of the United States: it consists of seven articles and twenty-two amendments, and has been the supreme law of the Federal government since its adoption in 1789.

çon·sti·tū′tion·ăl, *a.* 1. of, pertaining to, or inherent in, the constitution of a person or thing; basic; essential; as, a *constitutional* infirmity.

2. of, in, authorized by, subject to, dependent on, or in accordance with the constitution of a government, state, society, etc.; as, *constitutional* rights, *constitutional* rule.

3. upholding the constitution.

4. beneficial to or having a tendency to benefit the constitution; good for one's health; as, a *constitutional* walk.

Constitutional Democrat; a member of the Constitutional Democratic party formed in Russia in 1905, which advocated a federal constitution for the Russian Empire.

constitutional law; the branch of law relating to the fundamental rules and principles of a political government, or dealing with matters involved under the constitution, as distinguished from the common or the statutory law.

çon·sti·tū′tion·ăl, *n.* some form of exercise, particularly a walk, taken for one's health. [Colloq.]

Çon·sti·tū′tion·ăl Çŏn·ven′tion, the convention held in May, 1787, at Philadelphia, to draw up the Constitution of the United States: it was attended by representatives of all States except Rhode Island.

çon·sti·tū′tion·ăl·iṣm, *n.* 1. government according to a constitution.

2. adherence to constitutional principles or government.

çon·sti·tū′tion·ăl·ist, *n.* 1. a person who believes in government by constitution.

2. an advocate of a particular constitution.

3. a specialist in the study of constitutions and constitutionalism.

çon·sti·tū·tion·al′i·ty, *n.* 1. the quality or condition of being constitutional; the state of being inherent in the natural frame; as, the *constitutionality* of disease.

2. the state of being consistent with the con-

stitution of a government or state, or of being authorized by its provisions.

çon·sti·tū′tion·ăl·ly, *adv.* 1. in composition, physique, or temperament; by nature; as, he is *constitutionally* frail.

2. in accordance with the (or a) constitution; as, social change can often be brought about *constitutionally*.

çon·sti·tū′tion·ăl mon′ärch·y, a monarchy in which the powers of a sovereign are limited by a constitution.

çon·sti·tū′tion·ist, *n.* one who adheres to the constitution of the country. [Rare.]

çon′sti·tū·tive, *a.* 1. making a thing what it is; basic; elemental; essential.

2. having power to enact, establish, or appoint; instituting.

3. forming a part (*of*); constituent; component.

çon′sti·tū·tive·ly, *adv.* in a constitutive manner.

çon′sti·tū·tŏr, *n.* [L. *constitutor*, from *constituere* to establish; from *com-*, together, and *statuere*, to place.] a person or thing that constitutes.

çŏn·strāin′, *v.t.*; constrained, *pt.*, *pp.*; constraining, *ppr.* [ME. *constrainen*; OFr. *constraindre*; L. *constringere*, to bind together, to draw together; from *com-*, together, and *stringere*, to draw tight.]

1. to compel or force; to urge with irresistible power.

I was *constrained* to appeal to Caesar.
—Acts xxviii. 19.

2. to confine by force; to restrain from escape or action; to repress; to bind or confine.

My sire in caves *constrains* the winds.
—Dryden.

3. to get or produce by force or strain, as a person's consent, an unnatural laugh, etc.

4. to force; to ravish. [Obs.]

5. in mechanics, to control or limit the motion of (a body or mass) to some particular direction or manner.

Syn.—necessitate, compel, force, oblige, urge, drive, restrain, repress.

çŏn·strāin′ȧ·ble, *a.* able to be constrained, forced, or repressed.

çŏn·strāined′, *a.* 1. urged irresistibly or powerfully; compelled; produced by force.

2. resulting from or exhibiting unusual constraint; repressed; unnatural; embarrassed; as, a *constrained* voice.

çŏn·strāin′ed·ly, *adv.* in a constrained manner; with embarrassment.

çŏn·strāin′ẽr, *n.* one who or that which constrains.

çŏn·strāint′, *n.* [OFr. *constrainte*, pp. of *constraindre*, to constrain.]

1. confinement; restriction.

2. force; compulsion; coercion.

3. repression of natural feelings or behavior; forced, unnatural, awkward quality of manner.

4. a constraining or being constrained.

5. something that constrains.

Syn.—necessity, coercion, compulsion, violence, reserve, restraint.

çŏn·strāint′ive, *a.* having power to compel. [Rare.]

çŏn·strict′, *v.t.*; constricted, *pt.*, *pp.*; constricting, *ppr.* [L. *constrictus*, pp. of *constringere*, to draw together, draw tight; from *com-*, together, and *stringere*, to draw tight, bind together.] to draw together; to bind; to cramp; to make smaller or narrower, especially at one place, by binding, squeezing, or shrinking; to contract; to compress.

çŏn·strict′ed, *a.* 1. drawn together; bound; contracted.

2. in botany, contracted or irregularly small at some places; as, a *constricted* pod.

çŏn·stric′tion, *n.* 1. a constricting or being constricted; compression; contraction.

2. a feeling of tightness or pressure, as in the chest.

3. something that constricts.

4. a constricted part.

çŏn·strict′ive, *a.* 1. constricting; tending to contract or compress.

2. of or characterized by constriction.

çŏn·strict′ŏr, *n.* 1. that which draws together or contracts.

2. in anatomy, a muscle which compresses an organ, draws parts together, or closes an orifice of the body; as, the *constrictor labiorum*, a muscle of the lips.

3. a snake that kills by coiling around its prey and squeezing.

çŏn·stringe′, *v.t.*; constringed, *pt.*, *pp.*; constringing, *ppr.* [L. *constringere*, to draw together; from *com-*, together, and *stringere*, to draw together, to bind.] to draw together; to contract; to compress.

çŏn·strin′ġen·cy, *n.* 1. the quality of being constringent.

2. a constringing.

çŏn·strin′ġent, *a.* having the quality of contracting, binding, or compressing; causing constriction; astringent.

çŏn·strụ′ȧ·ble, *a.* that can be construed.

çŏn·struct′, *v.t.*; constructed, *pt.*, *pp.*; constructing, *ppr.* [L. *constructus*, pp. of *construere*, to heap together, build; from *com-*, together, and *struere*, to heap or pile up.]

1. to put together the parts of in their proper place and order; to build; to form; as, to *construct* an edifice; to *construct* a telescope.

2. to devise and put into orderly arrangement; to form by the mind; to originate or invent; as, to *construct* a plausible story.

3. to interpret or construe. [Obs.]

4. to draw (a figure, plan, sketch, etc.) to meet certain requirements; as, to *construct* a regular hexagon.

Syn.—make, erect, build, form, compose, fabricate, invent.

çon′struct, *a.* relating to construction; expressing the genitive relation.

construct state or *form*; in Hebrew and other Semitic languages, that form of a noun used when it is followed by a second noun which bears the genitive relation to it; annexion.

çon′struct, *n.* 1. something built or put together systematically.

2. an idea or perception resulting from the orderly arrangement of facts, impressions, etc.

3. in linguistics, any larger unit of discourse built up of phrases; syntactical construction.

çŏn·struct′ẽr, *n.* same as *constructor*.

çŏn·struc′tion, *n.* [L. *constructio*, from *construere*, to heap together, build; from *com-*, together, and *struere*, to heap, pile up.]

1. the act or process of building, or of devising and forming; fabrication; erection.

2. the manner or method of building; the way in which a thing is made or put together; structure; organization; as, a machine of intricate *construction*.

3. in grammar, the arrangement and connection of words in a clause, sentence, etc.; syntax; as, involved *constructions* are seldom necessary in ordinary writing.

4. sense; meaning; interpretation; explanation; the manner of understanding the arrangement of words, or of explaining facts; as, what *construction* shall we put upon his conduct?

5. in geometry, the manner of drawing a figure to fulfill certain conditions; also, the figure so constructed; as, the *construction* of an equilateral triangle is simple.

6. something constructed; structure; building.

çŏn·struc′tion·ăl, *a.* pertaining to or in construction; deduced from construction or interpretation.

çŏn·struc′tion·ist, *n.* one who puts a specific construction upon a law, a document, etc.; as, a broad *constructionist* of license laws.

çŏn·struc′tion trāin, in railroad building and operation, a train for the transportation of men and materials needed in construction or repair work.

çŏn·struct′ive, *a.* 1. by construction; created or deduced by construction or interpretation; not directly expressed, but inferred; as, *constructive* treason.

2. able or helping to construct; leading to improvements or advances; formative; positive; as, a *constructive* thinker, *constructive* criticism.

3. pertaining to or involving construction or structure; as, *constructive* architecture.

çŏn·struct′ive·ly, *adv.* in a constructive manner; by construction or interpretation; by fair inference.

çŏn·struct′ive·ness, *n.* 1. the ability or proclivity to make, devise, or construct; especially, mechanical ability.

2. in phrenology, the faculty that leads a person to construct.

çŏn·struc′tiv·ism, *n.* a movement in painting, sculpture, architecture, etc., especially in Russia during the 1920's, characterized by abstract and geometric design and massive structural form.

çŏn·struct′ŏr, çon·struct′ẽr, *n.* [L. *constructor*, from *construere*, to heap together, build; from *com-*, together, and *struere*, to heap, pile up.]

1. one who constructs; a maker of things; a builder; as, a naval *constructor*.

2. one who construes.

çŏn·struc′tūre, *n.* an edifice; a structure; a construction. [Obs.]

çŏn·strụe′, *v.t.*; construed, *pt.*, *pp.*; construing, *ppr.* [ME. *construen*, to interpret, construe; L. *construere*, to heap up, bring together; from *com-*, together, and *struere*, to heap, or pile up.]

1. to analyze (a clause, etc.) so as to show its grammatical construction and meaning.

2. to translate.

3. to explain or deduce the meaning of; interpret; as, her sudden departure was *construed* as an insult.

4. to infer or deduce.

5. in grammar, to combine in syntax; as, the verb *let*, unlike *permit*, is *construed* with an infinitive omitting the *to*.

çŏn·strụe′, *v.i.* 1. to analyze sentence structure.

2. to be construable, as a sentence.

3. to translate something.

4. to make deductions; judge by inference.

çon′stū·prāte, *v.t.* [L. *constupratus*, pp. of *constuprare*; from *com-*, with, and *stuprare*, to ravish; *stuprum*, dishonor.] to violate; to debauch. [Obs.]

çon·stū·prā′tion, *n.* the act of ravishing; violation; defilement. [Obs.]

çon·sub·stan′tiăl (-shăl), *a.* [L. *consubstantialis*; from *com-*, together, and *substantialis*, from *substantia*, material, substance.]

1. having the same substance or essential nature; coessential: term used especially in Christian theology in reference to the Trinity.

2. of the same kind or nature.

çon·sub·stan′tiăl·işm, *n.* the doctrine of consubstantiation.

çon·sub·stan′tiăl·ist, *n.* one who believes in consubstantiation.

çon·sub·stan·ti·al′i·ty (-shi-al′), *n.* the state or fact of being consubstantial.

çon·sub·stan′tiăl·ly, *adv.* in a consubstantial manner.

çon·sub·stan′ti·āte (-shi-āt), *v.t.*; consubstantiated, *pt.*, *pp.*; consubstantiating, *ppr.* [from ML. *consubstantiatus*, pp. of *consubstantiare*, from L. *com-*, together, and *substantia*, substance.]

1. to unite in one common substance or nature.

2. to regard as thus united.

çon·sub·stan′ti·āte, *v.i.* 1. to profess consubstantiation.

2. to become united in one common substance.

çon·sub·stan′ti·āte, *a.* consubstantial.

çon·sub·stan·ti·ā′tion, *n.* 1. in theology, the doctrine that the substance of the bread and wine of the Eucharist exists, after consecration, side by side with the substance of the body and blood of Christ but is not changed into it: distinguished from *transubstantiation*.

2. a consubstantiating. [Obs.]

çon′sue·tūde (-swi-), *n.* [OFr. *consuetude*; L. *consuetudo* (*-tudinis*), custom, habit; from *consuescere*, to accustom; from *consuere*; from *com-*, with, and *suere*, to be accustomed; from *suus*, one's own.] custom; usage; habit.

çon·sue·tū′di·năl, *a.* customary.

çon·sue·tū′di·nā·ry, *a.* customary; habitual.

çon·sue·tū′di·nā·ry, *n.*; *pl.* **çon·sue·tū′di·nā·rieş,** a ritual of devotions common to any particular diocese or religious order.

çon′sul, *n.* [L. *consul*, from *consulere*, to deliberate, take counsel.]

1. either of the two chief magistrates of the ancient Roman republic, invested with regal authority for one year.

2. one of the three highest officials of the French republic from 1799 to 1804; Napoleon Bonaparte was First Consul.

3. a person appointed by his government to live in a certain city in some foreign country and look after his country's citizens and business interests.

4. a senator. [Obs.]

çon′sul·āġe, *n.* same as *consulate*.

çon′sū·lăr, *a.* 1. pertaining to a consul or consulate; as, *consular* power; *consular* dignity or privileges.

2. functioning as a consul.

çon′sū·lăr ā′ġent, an official who does the work of a consul at a place that is commercially unimportant.

çon′sū·lȧ·ry, *a.* consular. [Rare.]

çon′sū·lāte, *n.* [L. *consulatus*, from *consul*, a consul.]

1. the position, powers, and functions of a consul.

2. the office or residence of a consul.
3. the term of office of a consul; consulship.
4. government by consuls.
the Consulate; the consular government of France from 1799 to 1804.

çon'sul ġen'ẽr·ăl, *pl.* **çon'suls ġen'ẽr·ăl, çon'sul ġen'ẽr·ăls,** a consul stationed in a principal commercial city, who supervises other consuls within his district.

çon'sul·ship, *n.* 1. the position, powers, and functions of a consul.
2. the term of office of a consul.

çŏn·sult', *v.i.*; consulted, *pt., pp.*; consulting, *ppr.* [L. *consultare*, freq. of *consulere*, to deliberate, consider, ask advice.]
1. to seek the opinion or advice of another; to confer or converse in order to decide or plan something.
2. to take counsel together; as, they *consulted* some time.

çŏn·sult', *v.t.* 1. to ask advice of; to seek the opinion of as a guide to one's own judgment; as, to *consult* a friend or parent.
2. to seek information or facts from, as by examining books or papers; as, to *consult* official documents.
3. to consider; to show regard for; to have reference or respect to in judging or acting.
Ere fancy you *consult*, *consult* your purse.
—Franklin.
4. (a) to confer about; (b) to plan for. [Obs.]
Syn.—interrogate, canvass, question, deliberate, confer, advise with, regard, consider.

çŏn·sult', *n.* 1. a consultation. [Obs.]
2. a deliberating assembly; a council. [Obs.]

çŏn·sult'ȧ·ry, *a.* consultatory.
consultary response; the opinion on a special case by a court.

çon·sul·tā'tion, *n.* 1. a consulting.
2. a meeting of persons to discuss, decide, or plan something.

çŏn·sult'ȧ·tive, *a.* having the privilege of consulting; of or pertaining to consultation; advisory; as, his function was *consultative*.

çŏn·sult'ȧ·tō·ry, *a.* consultative.

çŏn·sult'ẽr, *n.* one who consults, or asks counsel or information.

çŏn·sult'ing, *a.* consulted for professional or technical advice in special cases; acting in an advisory capacity; as, a *consulting* engineer.

çŏn·sult'ive, *a.* consultative.

çŏn·sūm'ȧ·ble, *a.* that can be consumed.

çŏn·sūm'ȧ·ble, *n.* a consumable commodity.

çŏn·sūme', *v.t.*; consumed, *pt., pp.*; consuming, *ppr.* [ME. *consumen*; OFr. *consumer*; L. *consumere*, to eat, use up, destroy; from *com-*, together, and *sumere*, to take; *sub*, under, and *emere*, to buy, take.]
1. to destroy, as by fire; to do away with.
2. to use up; spend wastefully; squander (time, energy, money, etc.).
3. to drink or eat up; devour.
Syn.—destroy, swallow up, waste, exhaust, spend, expend, squander, lavish, dissipate, burn.

çŏn·sūme', *v.i.* to waste away; to perish.

çŏn·sūm'ed·ly, *adv.* extremely; to an excessive degree.

çŏn·sūm'ẽr, *n.* 1. one who consumes, spends, wastes, or destroys; that which consumes.
2. in economics, a person who uses goods or services to satisfy his needs rather than to resell them or produce other goods with them: opposed to *producer*.

çon·sūm'ẽr·iṣm, *n.* 1. the practice and policies of protecting the consumer by making him aware of defective and unsafe products, misleading business practices, etc.
2. the consumption of goods and services.

çŏn·sūm'ẽrṣ' goodṣ, in economics, goods, such as food, clothing, etc., for satisfying people's needs rather than for producing other goods or services: opposed to *producers' goods*.

çŏn·sūm'ing·ly, *adv.* in a destructive manner.

çon'sum·māte, *v.t.*; consummated, *pt.*, pp.; consummating, *ppr.* [L. *consummatus*, pp. of *consummare*, to sum up, finish; *com-*, together, and *summa*, a sum.]
1. to end; to finish by completing or fulfilling; to perfect; to bring or carry to the utmost point or degree.
2. to make (marriage) actual by sexual intercourse.

çon'sum·māte, *v.i.*, to arrive at completion, fulfillment, or perfection.

çŏn·sum'māte, *a.* complete; perfect; carried to the utmost extent or degree; as, *consummate* greatness or felicity.

çŏn·sum'māte·ly, *adv.* completely; perfectly.

çon·sum·mā'tion, *n.* 1. a consummating or being consummated; completion; fulfillment.
2. an end; conclusion; outcome.

çon'sum·mā·tive, *a.* consummating or helping to consummate; completing.

çon'sum·mā·tŏr, *n.* a person or thing that consummates.

çŏn·sump'tion, *n.* [L. *consumptio*, a consuming, wasting, from *consumere*, to consume, destroy.]
1. a consuming or being consumed; waste; destruction; as, the *consumption* of fuel, of food, of time, etc.
2. a disease that causes the body or part of the body to waste away; especially, tuberculosis of the lungs.
3. in economics, (a) the using up of goods or services: opposed to *production*; (b) the amount used up.
Syn.—decay, decline, waste, destruction.

çŏn·sump'tive, *a.* 1. destructive; wasting; exhausting; having the quality of consuming, or dissipating; as, a long, *consumptive* war.
2. in economics, of or for consumers' goods.
3. in medicine, (a) of tuberculosis of the lungs; (b) having or inclined to have tuberculosis of the lungs; tuberculous.

çŏn·sump'tive, *n.* a person who has tuberculosis of the lungs.

çŏn·sump'tive·ly, *adv.* in a way tending to consumption.

çŏn·sump'tive·ness, *n.* a state of being consumptive, or a tendency to consumption.

çŏn·sūte', *a.* [L. *consutus*, pp. of *consuere*, to stitch together; *com-*, together, and *suere*, to sew.] in entomology, having stitchlike markings, as the elytra of some beetles.

çon·tȧ·bes'cence, *n.* 1. in medicine, disease marked by a wasting away, as atrophy, consumption, etc.
2. in botany, a contabescent condition.

çon·tȧ·bes'cent, *a.* [L. *contabescens* (*-entis*), pp. of *contabescere*, to waste away.]
1. wasting away; atrophied.
2. in botany, having abortive stamens and pollen.

çon·tab·ū·lā'tion, *n.* the act of laying with boards, or of flooring. [Obs.]

çon'taçt, *n.* [L. *contactus*, from *contingere*, to touch, seize; *com-*, together, and *tangere*, to touch.]
1. the act of touching or meeting; as, some shells explode only by *contact* with other objects.
2. the state of being in touch or association (*with*); as, you will come into *contact with* many new ideas.
3. connection; as, he made some valuable *contacts* at the convention; the pilot of the airplane tried to make *contact* with his base.
4. in electricity, (a) a connection or point of connection between two conductors in a circuit; (b) a device for making such a connection.
5. in mathematics, tangency; coincidence.
6. in mining, the plane marking the limit of an ore-producing vein.
7. in medicine, close juxtaposition or touching of the bodies or persons; also, one who has been near enough to a person with a contagious disease to have been exposed.

çon'taçt, *v.t.*; contacted, *pt., pp.*; contacting, *ppr.* 1. to place in contact.
2. to come into contact with.

çon'taçt, *v.i.* to be in touch or juxtaposition; to come into contact.

çon'taçt, *a.* that keeps or forms contact; as, a *contact* officer.

çon'taçt, *interj.* ready!: a signal in aviation that everything is set for the engine to be started.

çon'taçt bed, a bed of coke or similar material through which water cannot seep; utilized in purifying sewage.

çon'taçt breāk'ẽr, any device for interrupting a circuit, as in an induction coil.

çon'taçt flȳ'ing, flying an airplane at a low altitude, so that the course can be determined by observing objects on the ground, as streams, buildings, etc.

çon'taçt lenṣ'eṣ, small, thin lenses of glass or plastic worn next to the eyeballs, with the edges under the eyelids, sometimes used instead of ordinary eyeglasses.

çon'taçt lev'el, an apparatus used in determining minute differences in length by means of a transversely pivoted spirit level.

çon'taçt pō·ten'tiăl, an electromotive force resulting from the contact of two plates of dissimilar metals and equal to the difference in their potentials.

çon·tȧ·dī'nȧ, *n.*; *pl.* **çon·tȧ·dī'ne,** [It.] a peasant woman of Italy.

çon·tȧ·dī'nō, *n.*; *pl.* **çon·tȧ·dī'nī,** [It.] a peasant of Italy.

çŏn·tā'ġiŏn, *n.* [L. *contagio* (*-onis*), a touching, from *contingere*; *com-*, together, and *tangere*, to touch.]
1. the spreading of disease from one individual to another by direct or indirect contact.
2. any disease thus spread; contagious disease.
3. a means or medium by which disease is spread.
4. a poison.
5. the spreading of an emotion, idea, custom, etc. from person to person until many are affected; as, the *contagion* of gaiety.
6. a bad influence that tends to spread; corruption; as, racial hatred is a *contagion*.

çŏn·tā'ġiŏned, *a.* affected by contagion.

çŏn·tā'ġiŏn·ist, *n.* one who believes in the contagious character of certain diseases.

çŏn·tā'ġious, *a.* 1. spread by direct or indirect contact; communicable: said of diseases.
2. carrying, or liable to transmit, the causative agent of a contagious disease.
3. spreading or tending to spread from person to person; as, *contagious* laughter.
Syn.—epidemic, pestilential, infectious.

çŏn·tā'ġious·ly, *adv.* by contagion.

çŏn·tā'ġious·ness, *n.* the quality or state of being contagious.

çŏn·tā'ġi·um, *n.*; *pl.* **çŏn·tā'ġi·ȧ,** [L.]
1. a contagious substance.
2. contagion.

çŏn·tāin', *v.t.*; contained, *pt., pp.*; containing, *ppr.* [ME. *conteinen*; OFr. *contenir*; L. *continere*, to hold, keep together; *com-*, together, and *tenere*, to hold.]
1. to have in it; hold; enclose or include.
2. to have the capacity for holding.
3. to be equal or equivalent to; as, a gallon *contains* four quarts.
4. to hold back or within fixed limits.
5. to control or restrain (one's feelings, oneself, etc.).
6. to be divisible by, especially without a remainder; as, 10 *contains* 5 and 2.
Syn.—comprise, embrace, enclose, include.

çŏn·tāin', *v.i.* to live in continence. [Obs.]

çŏn·tāin'ȧ·ble, *a.* that can be contained.

çŏn·tāin'ẽr, *n.* a thing that contains or can contain something; a box, crate, can, jar, etc.

çŏn·tāin'ẽr·īze, *v.t.*; containerized, *pt., pp.*; containerizing, *ppr.* to pack (general cargo) into huge, standardized, usually metal, containers for more efficient shipment, as in transferring from one mode of transportation to another.

çŏn·tāin'ment, *n.* the fact or act of containing.

çŏn·tam'i·nȧ·ble, *a.* capable of contamination.

çŏn·tam'i·nănt, *n.* a substance that contaminates another substance, the air, water, etc.

çŏn·tam'i·nāte, *v.t.*; contaminated, *pt., pp.*; contaminating, *ppr.* [L. *contaminatus*, pp. of *contaminare*, to defile; *contamen*, contact, contagion, from *contingere*; *com-*, together, and *tangere*, to touch.] to make impure, unclean, or corrupt by contact; to corrupt; to pollute; to sully; to tarnish; to taint; as, cowardice *contaminates* honor.
Shall we now
Contaminate our fingers with base bribes?
—Shak.

çŏn·tam'i·nāte, *a.* contaminated. [Archaic.]

çŏn·tam·i·nā'tion, *n.* 1. a contaminating or being contaminated.
2. something that contaminates.

çŏn·tam'i·nā·tive, *a.* contaminating or tending to contaminate.

çŏn·tam'i·nā·tŏr, *n.* a person or thing that contaminates.

çŏn·tañ'gō, *n.*; *pl.* **çŏn·tañ'gōeṣ,** [of doubtful origin.] in English stock transactions, interest paid to a seller for accommodating a buyer, by carrying over the engagement to pay the price of shares until the next settling day.

çōnte, *n.*; *pl.* **çōntes** (kōnts), [Fr., from *conter*, to tell.]
1. formerly, any short fictional tale of adventure.
2. a short story; tale.

çon'teck, çon'tek, *n.* [OFr. *contek*, contention.] quarrel; contention. [Obs.]

çŏn·teç'tion, *n.* [L. *contectio*, from *contegere*, to cover.] a covering. [Obs.]

çŏn·temn' (-tem'), *v.t.*; contemned, *pt., pp.*; contemning, *ppr.* [L. *contemnere*, to despise; *com-*, intens., and *temnere*, to scorn, despise.]

to despise; to consider and treat as mean and despicable; to scorn; to slight; to neglect as unworthy of regard; to reject with disdain.

In whose eyes a vile person is *contemned*.
—Ps. xv. 4.

Syn.—scorn, despise, disdain, spurn, slight, neglect, underrate, overlook.

çŏn·temn′ẽr (-tem′), *n.* one who contemns; a despiser; a scorner.

çŏn·temn′ing·ly, *adv.* in a contemptuous manner; slightingly.

çŏn·tem′nŏr, *n.* a person who contemns.

çŏn·tem′pẽr, *v.t.* [L. *contemperare*, to temper, mix; *com-*, together, and *temperare*, to mix, temper.] to moderate; to temper. [Obs.]

çŏn·tem′pẽr·ȧ·ment, *n.* contemperation. [Obs.]

çŏn·tem′pẽr·āte, *v.t.* to contemper. [Obs.]

çŏn·tem·pẽr·ā′tion, *n.* the act of moderating or tempering. [Obs.]

çŏn·tem′pẽr·ȧ·tūre, *n.* proportionate mixture. [Obs.]

çŏn·tem′plȧ·ble, *a.* that can be contemplated.

çŏn·tem′plănce, *n.* [OFr.] contemplation; meditation. [Obs.]

çŏn·tem′plănt, *a.* meditative; contemplative.

çon′tem·plāte, *v.t.*; contemplated, *pt.*, *pp.*; contemplating, *ppr.* [L. *contemplatus*, pp. of *contemplari*, to gaze attentively, observe; lit., to mark out an augural temple; *com-*, with, and *templum*, temple.]

1. to look at with continued attention; to gaze at; to behold.

2. to think about intently; to consider; to meditate on; to study; to ponder on.

3. to look forward to; to consider or have in view in reference to a future act or event; to intend or expect.

Syn.—study, ponder, meditate on, dwell on, consider, intend, design, plan, purpose.

çon′tem·plāte, *v.i.* to think studiously; to study; to muse; to meditate; to ponder.

çon·tem·plā′tion, 1. the act of looking at something intently.

2. the act of the mind in considering with attention; meditation; study; consideration; the act of thinking about something intently.

3. meditation on spiritual things.

4. the act of looking forward to; intention or expectation.

çŏn·tem′plȧ·tist, *n.* one who contemplates. [Rare.]

çon′tem·plā·tive (*or* kŏn-tem′plȧ-), *a.* 1. given to contemplation, or continued application of the mind to a subject; studious; thoughtful; as, a *contemplative* philosopher or mind.

2. having the power of thought or meditation; as, the *contemplative* faculty of man.

çon′tem·plā·tive(*or* kŏn-tem′plȧ-), *n.* a religious person devoted to contemplation and prayer.

çŏn·tem′plȧ·tive·ly, *adv.* in a contemplative manner; attentively; thoughtfully.

çŏn·tem′plȧ·tive·ness, *n.* the condition of being contemplative or thoughtful; meditativeness.

çon′tem·plā·tŏr, *n.* one who contemplates; one employed in study or meditation.

çŏn·tem″pō·rȧ·nē′i·ty, *n.* the condition or quality of being contemporaneous, or existing at the same time.

çŏn·tem·pō·rā′nē·ous, *a.* existing or happening in the same period of time.

contemporaneous with; existing or happening at the same time as.

çŏn·tem·pō·rā′nē·ous·ly, *adv.* at the same time; in or during the same period of time.

çŏn·tem·pō·rā′nē·ous·ness, *n.* the condition or quality of being contemporaneous.

çŏn·tem′pō·rā·ri·ness, *n.* the condition or quality of being contemporary.

çŏn·tem′pō·rā·ry, *a.* [L. *com-*, with, and *temporarius*, pertaining to time, from *tempus*, time.]

1. living or happening in the same period of time.

2. of about the same age.

3. coeval. [Rare.]

contemporary with; living or happening at the same time as.

çŏn·tem′pō·rā·ry, *n.*; *pl.* **çŏn·tem′pō·rā·ries,**

1. a person living in the same period of history as another or others.

2. a person or thing of about the same age or date of origin, publication, etc.

çŏn·tem′pō·rize, *v.t.* and *v.i.*; contemporized, *pt.*, *pp.*; contemporizing, *ppr.* to make or be contemporary; synchronize.

çŏn·tempt′, *n.* [L. *contemptus*, scorn, from *contemnere*, to despise, scorn; *com-*, intens., and *temnere*, to despise.]

1. the feeling or actions of a person toward something he considers low, worthless, or beneath notice; disrespect; scorn.

2. the condition of being despised.

3. in law, the punishable act of showing disrespect for the authority or dignity of a court (or legislature), as by disobedience, disorderly conduct, etc.: in full, *contempt of court* (or *congress*, etc.).

Syn.—disdain, scorn, derision, mockery, contumely, neglect, disregard, slight.

çŏn·tempt·i·bil′i·ty, *n.* the quality of being contemptible.

çŏn·tempt′i·ble, *a.* 1. worthy of contempt; that deserves scorn or disdain; despicable; mean; vile; despised; neglected.

2. apt to despise; contemptuous. [Obs.]

Syn.—despicable, abject, vile, mean, base, paltry, worthless, sorry.

çŏn·tempt′i·ble·ness, *n.* the state of being contemptible, or of being despised; despicableness; meanness; vileness.

çŏn·tempt′i·bly, *adv.* in a contemptible manner; meanly.

çŏn·temp′tū·ous, *a.* manifesting or expressing contempt or disdain; scornful; as, *contemptuous* language, a *contemptuous* opinion.

Syn.—haughty, insolent, insulting, scornful, supercilious, contumelious.

çŏn·temp′tū·ous·ly, *adv.* in a contemptuous manner; with scorn or disdain.

çŏn·temp′tū·ous·ness, *n.* disposition to contempt; act of contempt; insolence; scornfulness; haughtiness.

çŏn·tend′, *v.i.*; contended, *pt.*, *pp.*; contending, *ppr.* [L. *contendere*, to stretch out, strive after; *com-*, together, and *tendere*, to stretch, extend.]

1. to strive in opposition or combat; to fight; to struggle.

2. to strive in debate or controversy; argue; dispute.

3. to strive in competition; compete; vie; as, he will *contend* for the prize.

çŏn·tend′, *v.t.* 1. to dispute; to contest. [Rare.]

Carthage shall *contend* the world with Rome. —Dryden.

2. to hold to be a fact; assert; argue; as, we *contend* that he is guilty.

çŏn·tend′ent, *n.* an antagonist or opposer.

çŏn·tend′ẽr, *n.* one who contends.

çŏn·tend′ress, *n.* a woman who contends. [Rare.]

çŏn·tent′, *a.* [ME. *content*; OFr. *content*; L. *contentus*, pp. of *continere*, to hold in, contain; *com-*, together, and *tenere*, to hold.]

1. happy enough with what one has or is; not desiring something more or different; satisfied.

2. willing: used in the British House of Lords as an affirmative vote.

çŏn·tent′, *v.t.*; contented, *pt.*, *pp.*; contenting, *ppr.* 1. to satisfy the mind of; to make quiet, so as to stop complaint or opposition; to appease; to make easy in any situation: often used reflexively.

Do not *content yourselves* with obscure and confused ideas. —Watts.

2. to pay or reward. [Obs.]

Syn.—satisfy, appease, favor, gratify, humor, please.

çŏn·tent′, *n.* 1. contentment; satisfaction.

A wise *content* his even soul secured.—Smith.

2. satisfaction without examination. [Obs.]

The style is excellent;
The sense they humbly take upon *content*.
—Pope.

3. a vote of *aye*; an assenting or affirmative vote. [Brit.]

çon′tent, *n.* [L. *contentum*, neut. pl. of *continere*, to hold.]

1. [*usually pl.*] (a) all that is contained in something; everything inside; as, the *contents* of a jar, trunk, etc.; (b) all that is contained or expressed in a writing or speech; as, a table of *contents* is a list of chapters, topics, etc. in a book.

2. the main substance or meaning; as, the *content* of a poem is distinguished from its form.

3. holding power; capacity.

4. volume or area.

5. the amount (of a specified substance) contained; as, cast iron has a high carbon *content*.

çon·ten·tā′tion, *n.* content. [Obs.]

çŏn·tent′ed, *a.* not desiring something more or different; satisfied; quiet; easy in mind; not complaining.

Syn.—satisfied, comfortable, satiated, willing, ready, resigned, passive.

çŏn·tent′ed·ly, *adv.* in a contented manner.

çŏn·tent′ed·ness, *n.* the state or quality of being content.

çŏn·ten′tion, *n.* [L. *contentio*, from *contendere*; *com-*, together, and *tendere*, to stretch.]

1. verbal strife; argument; controversy; dispute; quarrel; altercation.

2. a statement or point that one argues for as true or valid.

3. strife; struggle; contest; competition.

Syn.—struggle, contest, litigation, controversy, quarrel, conflict, feud, dissension, variance, disagreement, debate, competition, emulation, discord.

çŏn·ten′tious (-shus), *a.* 1. apt to contend; argumentative; quarrelsome; perverse.

A continual dropping in a rainy day, and a *contentious* woman, are alike.
—Prov. xxvii. 15.

2. relating to or characterized by contention, or strife; involving contention; controversial.

3. in law, having power to decide causes between contending parties; as, a court of *contentious* jurisdiction.

çŏn·ten′tious·ly, *adv.* in a contentious manner; perversely.

çŏn·ten′tious·ness, *n.* the state or condition of being contentious.

çŏn·tent′less, *a.* discontented.

çŏn·tent′ly, *adv.* in a contented way.

çŏn·tent′ment, *n.* 1. the state, quality, or fact of being contented.

2. a satisfying or being satisfied. [Archaic.]

Syn.—comfort, satisfaction, repose, acquiescence, gratification.

çŏn·tẽr′min·ȧ·ble, *a.* limited or terminated by the same bounds; terminating at the same point, whether of space or time. [Rare.]

çŏn·tẽr′mi·năl, *a.* same as *conterminous*.

çŏn·tẽr′mi·nănt, *a.* conterminous. [Obs.]

çŏn·tẽr′mi·nāte, *a.* conterminous.

çŏn·tẽr′mi·nous, *a.* [L. *conterminus*, bordering upon.]

1. having a common boundary at some point; contiguous.

2. having the same boundaries or limits.

çon·tẽr·rā′nē·ăn, çon·tẽr·rā′nē·ous, *a.* [L. *conterraneus*; *com-*, together, and *terra*, land.] being of the same country. [Obs.]

çŏn·tes·sẽr·ā′tion, *n.* contraction of friendship. [Obs.]

çŏn·test′, *v.t.*; contested, *pt.*, *pp.*; contesting, *ppr.* [Fr. *contester*, to contest; L. *contestari*, to call to witness, to bring action; *com-*, together, and *testari*, to bear witness, from *testis*, a witness.]

1. to dispute; to strive earnestly to hold or maintain; to struggle to win or keep; as, the troops *contested* every inch of ground.

2. to dispute; to argue in opposition to; to controvert; to oppose; to litigate; to call in question; as, to *contest* a will.

çŏn·test′, *v.i.* to strive; to contend; to vie; followed by *with* or *against*.

The difficulty of an argument adds to the pleasure of *contesting with* it. —Burnet.

çon′test, *n.* 1. strife; struggle; conflict; fight.

2. dispute; debate; controversy; verbal strife.

Leave all noisy *contests*, all immodest clamors, and brawling language. —Watts.

3. any race, game, debate, etc. in which there is a struggle to be the winner.

Syn.—conflict, combat, battle, feud, dispute, altercation, debate, controversy, difference, fray.

çŏn·test′ȧ·ble, *a.* that may be disputed or debated; disputable; controvertible.

çŏn·test′ȧ·ble·ness, *n.* the state or quality of being contestable.

çŏn·test′ănt, *n.* one who contests or competes in a contest.

çon·tes·tā′tion, *n.* 1. the act of contesting; strife; dispute.

2. testimony; proof by witnesses. [Obs.]

3. in ecclesiastical usage, the preface to the Eucharistic service in the Gallican liturgy.

çŏn·test′ing·ly, *adv.* in a contending manner.

çŏn·tex′, *v.t.* to weave together. [Obs.]

çon′text, *n.* [L. *contextus*, from *contexere*, to weave together.]

1. the parts of a sentence, paragraph, discourse, etc. that occur just before and after a specified word or passage, and determine its exact meaning; as, it is unfair to quote this remark out of its *context*.

2. the whole situation, background, or environment relevant to some happening or personality.

çŏn·text′, *a.* knit or woven together; close; firm. [Obs.]

çŏn·text′, *v.t.* to knit together. [Obs.]

çŏn·tex′tū·ăl, *a.* of, connected with, or depending on the context.

çŏn·tex′tū·ăl·ly, *adv.* according to, or by referring to, the context.

çŏn·tex′tūr·ăl, *a.* pertaining to contexture.

çŏn·tex′tūre, *n.* [Fr. *contexture*, from L. *contextus*, pp. of *contexere*; *com-*, together, and *texere*, to weave.]
 1. a weaving together; fabrication.
 2. an interwoven mass; fabric.
 3. the way in which a thing is put together; structure; composition.

çŏn·tex′tūred, *a.* woven; formed into texture. [Rare.]

çon′ti·cent, *a.* [L. *conticens*, pp. of *conticere*, to be silent.] hushed; quiet; silent. [Rare.]

çon·tig·nā′tion, *n.* [L. *contignatio*, from *contignari*, to join with beams.]
 1. a frame of beams; a story. [Archaic.]
 2. the act of framing together, or uniting beams. [Archaic.]

çŏn·tig′ū·āte, *a.* contiguous. [Obs.]

çon·ti·gū′i·ty, *n.*; *pl.* **çon·ti·gū′i·tieș,** [Fr. *contiguïté*; ML. *contiguitas*.]
 1. nearness or contact.
 2. continuous mass or unbroken series. [Rare.]

çŏn·tig′ū·ous, *a.* [L. *contiguus*, touching, from *contingere*; *com-*, together, and *tangere*, to touch.] touching; meeting or joining at the surface or border; close together; neighboring; bordering or adjoining; as, two *contiguous* bodies, houses, or countries.
 contiguous angles; in geometry, adjacent angles.
 Syn.—adjoining, adjacent, touching.

çŏn·tig′u·ous·ly, *adv.* in such a way as to be contiguous.

çŏn·tig′ū·ous·ness, *n.* a state of contact; close union of surfaces or borders; close proximity.

çon′ti·nence, çon′ti·nen·cy, *n.* [OFr. *continence*; L. *continentia*, ppr. of *continere*, to hold back or together.]
 1. the restraint which a person imposes upon his desires and passions; moderation.
 2. self-restraint in sexual activity; especially, complete abstinence.
 3. continuity; uninterrupted course. [Obs.]

çon′ti·nent, *a.* [from L. *continens*, ppr. of *continere*; see *contain*.]
 1. self-restrained; temperate.
 2. characterized by self-restraint, especially by complete abstinence, in sexual activity.
 3. opposing; restraining. [Obs.]
 4. continuous; connected; not interrupted; as, a *continent* fever. [Obs.]

çon′ti·nent, *n.* 1. that which contains or retains something. [Rare.]
 2. a large and extensive land mass; mainland, as distinguished from outlying islands: now rare except in *the Continent*.
 3. any of the six largest land masses of the earth, conventionally regarded (with or without outlying islands) as units; Africa, Asia, Australia, Europe, North America, and South America: Antarctica is sometimes regarded as the seventh continent.
 4. land in general; earth. [Obs.]
 the Continent; the mainland of Europe; all of Europe except the British Isles.

çon·ti·nen′tăl, *a.* 1. of a continent.
 2. [*sometimes* C–] of or characteristic of the Continent; European.
 3. [C–] of the American colonies at the time of the American Revolution, or of the States just after this.
 Continental Congress; either of two assemblies of representatives from the American colonies during the Revolutionary period: the first was held in 1774 to express grievances against British colonial policy; the second convened in 1775, created the Continental army, issued the Declaration of Independence (1776) and the Articles of Confederation (1778), and operated as the legislative body of the United States for several years.
 Continental Divide; the ridge of the Rocky Mountains that separates rivers flowing toward the Atlantic from those flowing toward the Pacific.
 continental shelf; the submerged shelf of land that slopes gradually from the exposed edge of a continent for a variable distance to the point where the steep descent to the ocean bottom begins.
 Continental system; the plan of Napoleon I for excluding the merchandise of England from all parts of the Continent.

çon·ti·nen′tăl, *n.* 1. [*usually* C–] a person living on the Continent; a European.
 2. [C–] a soldier of the American army during the Revolutionary period.
 3. a piece of paper money issued by the Continental Congress: it became almost worthless before the end of the war, hence the phrase *not worth a continental*, worthless.

Çon·ti·nen′tăl·ẽr, *n.* a Continental (a soldier).

çon·ti·nen′tăl·ist, *n.* 1. a Continental; a European.
 2. [C–] in United States history, a believer in a close political union of the separate States at the close of the Revolution.

çon′ti·nent·ly, *adv.* in a continent manner; chastely; moderately; temperately.

çŏn·tin′ġence, *n.* contingency.

çŏn·tin′ġen·cy, *n.*; *pl.* **çŏn·tin′ġen·cieș,** 1. the quality or condition of being contingent.
 2. dependence on chance or uncertain conditions; uncertainty of occurrence.
 3. something whose occurrence depends on chance or uncertain conditions; a possible, accidental, or chance event; as, be prepared for any *contingency*.
 4. something incidental to another thing.
 5. contact. [Obs.]
 Syn.—casualty, accident, chance.

çŏn·tin′ġent, *a.* [L. *contingens* (*-entis*), ppr. of *contingere*, to touch, meet, happen; *com-*, together, and *tangere*, to touch.]
 1. that may or may not happen; possible.
 2. happening by chance; accidental; fortuitous.
 3. dependent (*on* or *upon* something uncertain); conditional.
 4. touching; tangential. [Archaic.]
 5. in logic, true only with certain conditions or contexts; not always or necessarily true.
 Syn.—incidental, accidental, casual, fortuitous.

çŏn·tin′ġent, *n.* 1. an accidental or chance happening.
 2. a share, proportion, or quota, as of troops, ships, laborers, delegates, etc.
 3. a group or body forming part of a larger one.

çŏn·tin′ġent fee, a fee of a lawyer or agent the amount or payment of which depends upon the outcome of a particular litigation or transaction.

çŏn·tin′ġent·ly, *adv.* accidentally; without design or foresight.

çŏn·tin′ġent·ness, *n.* the state of being contingent; fortuitousness.

çŏn·tin′ū·ȧ·ble, *a.* that can be continued.

çŏn·tin′ū·ăl, *a.* [OFr. *continuel*, from L. *continuus*, continuous.]
 1. proceeding without interruption or cessation; unceasing; continuous.
 2. very frequent; often repeated; happening over and over again; going on in rapid succession.
 continual proportional; see *continued proportion* under *continued*.
 Syn.—constant, continuous, perpetual, incessant, uninterrupted, unceasing, invariable, regular, unbroken, unvarying.

çŏn·tin′u·ăl·ly, *adv.* 1. all the time; without pause or cessation; unceasingly; as, the ocean is *continually* in motion.
 2. very often; in repeated succession; again and again.

çŏn·tin′ū·ăl·ness, *n.* permanence.

çŏn·tin′ū·ȧnce, *n.* 1. a keeping up, going on, going on with, or lasting (*of* an action, process, or state).
 2. the time during which an action, process, or state lasts; duration.
 3. a remaining (*in* a place, position, or state); stay.
 4. an unbroken succession.
 5. a continuation; sequel.
 6. in law, adjournment or putting off, as of a case, from day to day or from term to term; also, the complete record of such adjournment.

çŏn·tin′ū·ȧnt, *a.* characterized by continuance.

çŏn·tin′ū·ȧnt, *n.* [from L. *continuans*, ppr.; see *continue*.] a speech sound that can be prolonged as long as the breath lasts, with no change in the quality of the sound: continuants are called *fricatives* (s, f, th, etc.), *nasals* (m, n, ñ), *liquids* (l, r), or *vowels*: distinguished from *stop*.

çŏn·tin′ū·āte, *v.t.* to make continuous. [Obs.]

çŏn·tin′ū·āte, *a.* 1. immediately united; holding together. [Obs.]
 2. uninterrupted; unbroken.

çŏn·tin′ū·āte·ly, *adv.* with continuity; without interruption.

çŏn·tin·ū·ā′tion, *n.* 1. a keeping up or going on without interruption; prolonged and unbroken existence or maintenance.
 2. a taking up or beginning again after an interruption; resumption.
 3. a part or thing added to make something reach further or last longer; extension; supplement; sequel.

çŏn·tin·ū·ā′tion sçhool, a school offering instruction in elementary and vocational subjects to adults who wish to continue their education: classes are held mainly in the evening.

çŏn·tin′ū·ȧ·tive, *a.* 1. continuing something.
 2. in grammar, expressing continuation, or sequel, as the subordinate clause in the sentence "I gave the check to the teller, who cashed it for me."

çŏn·tin′ū·ȧ·tive, *n.* 1. in logic, an expression denoting continuance, permanence, or duration.

> To these may be added *continuatives*; as, Rome remains to this day; which includes at least two propositions, viz., Rome was, and Rome is. —Watts.

 2 in grammar, a continuative word or clause.

çŏn·tin′ū·ā·tŏr, *n.* a person who continues something, as a literary work started by another.

çŏn·tin′ūe, *v.i.*; continued, *pt.*, *pp.*; continuing, *ppr.* [ME. *continuen*; OFr. *continuer*; L. *continuare*, to join, unite, make continuous, from *continuus*, continuous, from *continere*; *com-*, together, and *tenere*, to hold.]
 1. to remain in existence or effect; last; endure; as, the war *continued* for five years.
 2. to go on in a specified condition or course of action; as, we *continued* to let him have his way; she *continued* ailing.
 3. to remain in the same place or position; stay; as, the chairman *continued* in office for another year.
 4. to keep on; persist; persevere; as, we *continued* to demand our rights.
 5. to go on again after an interruption; resume; as, after a sip of water, the speaker *continued*.

çŏn·tin′ūe, *v.t.* 1. to go on with; carry on; keep up; persist in.
 2. to carry further; extend.
 3. to go on with (an activity, story, etc.) again after an interruption; resume.
 4. to cause to remain; keep; retain; as, the people *continued* Roosevelt in office for four terms.
 5. in law, to postpone or adjourn to a later date.

çŏn·tin′ūed, *a.* 1. continual; going on in rapid succession or in a series.
 2. continuous; extending without interruption or break.
 continued fever; a fever which runs its course without interruption.
 continued fraction; a fraction whose denominator contains a fraction whose denominator contains a fraction, and so forth (e. g., $\frac{5}{6 + \frac{3}{8 + \frac{4}{5 + \ldots}}}$).
 continued proportion; a series of three or more quantities with the same ratio between each two adjacent terms (e.g., 3,6,12,24).
 continued story; a story, usually a novel, published in installments in a magazine or newspaper; serial.
 continued or *continuous voyage*; a voyage considered as a single voyage in regard to its objective, no account being made of intermediate stoppages.

çŏn·tin′ūed·ly, *adv.* continuously; without interruption; without ceasing.

çŏn·tin′ū·ẽr, *n.* one who or that which continues.

çon·ti·nū′i·ty, *n.*; *pl.* **çon·ti·nū′i·tieș,** 1. the state or quality of being continuous.
 2. a continuous series or succession; unbroken, coherent whole.
 3. a written plan detailing the succession and connection of scenes in a motion picture.
 4. in radio and television, (a) a series of comments or announcements connecting the parts of a program; (b) the script of a program.
 law of continuity; the principle that nothing passes from one state to another without passing through all the intermediate states.

çon·ti·nū′i·ty wrīt′ẽr, one who writes continuity for radio, television, or motion pictures.

çon·ti′nū·ō, *n.* [It.] continued bass; thorough bass.

çŏn·tin′ū·ous, *a.* [L. *continuus,* from *continere,* to hold together; *com-,* together, and *tenere,* to hold.]

1. joined without intervening space; without cessation or interruption; unbroken; constant; connected; as, *continuous* depth.

2. in botany, being uniform throughout; lacking joints or articulations.

continuous brake; a series of railway car brakes, as the air brake, capable of operation at any point of its extent.

continuous current; see *direct current,* under *current.*

continuous impost; in architecture, the moldings of an arch continued along the pillar that supports it down to the ground without a break.

continuous wave; a form of electromagnetic wave having a constant amplitude and no damping effect.

Syn.—incessant, continual, perpetual.

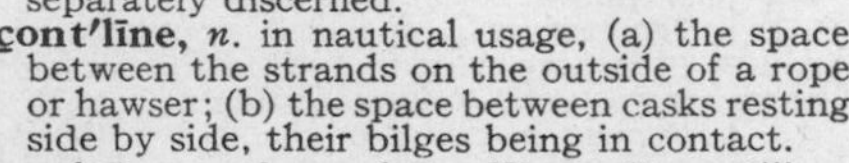
CONTINUOUS IMPOST

çŏn·tin′ū·ous·ly, *adv.* in a continuous manner.

çŏn·tin′ū·ous·ness, *n.* the state or quality of being continuous.

çŏn·tin′ū·um, *n.*; *pl.* **çŏn·tin′ū·à,** [L., neut. of *continuus.*] a continuous whole, quantity, or series; thing whose parts cannot be separated or separately discerned.

çont′līne, *n.* in nautical usage, (a) the space between the strands on the outside of a rope or hawser; (b) the space between casks resting side by side, their bilges being in contact.

çon′tō, *n.*; *pl.* **çon′tōṣ,** [Port., lit., million, from L. *computus.*] a money of account in Brazil and Portugal, formerly equal to 1,000,000 reis, now equal to 1,000 cruzeiros in Brazil and 1,000 escudos in Portugal.

çŏn·tọr′ni·āte, *a.* having edges that have been furrowed: applied to medals.

çŏn·tọr′ni·āte, çŏn·tọr·ni·ā′tō, *n.* [Fr. *contorniate*; It. *contorniato,* from *contorno,* a circuit, circumference, from LL. *contornare*; *com-,* intens., and *tornare,* to turn.] a species of medal or medallion in bronze, having a curved furrow on each side, supposedly made in the days of Constantine the Great and his successors.

çŏn·tọr′sion, *n.* contortion. [Obs.]

çŏn·tọrt′, *v.t.*; contorted, *pt., pp.*; contorting, *ppr.* [L. *contortus,* pp. of *contorquere,* to whirl, to twist; *com-,* together, and *torquere,* to twist.] to twist together or out of shape by or as by twisting, wrenching, etc.; to distort; as, disease *contorted* his limbs.

çŏn·tọrt′ed, *a.* 1. twisted; distorted.

2. in botany, convolute.

çŏn·tọr′tion, *n.* 1. a contorting or being contorted; distortion, especially of the face or body.

2. a contorted condition, position, or shape.

çŏn·tọr′tion·ist, *n.* a person who can contort his body into unnatural positions.

çŏn·tọr′tive, *a.* causing or exhibiting contortion.

çon·tọr·tū′pli·çāte, *a.* [L. *contortuplicatus*; *contortus,* twisted, and *plicatus,* pp. of *plicare,* to fold, double up.] in botany, turned back on itself.

çon′tōur, *n.* [Fr. *contour,* a circuit, circumference, from LL. *contornare,* to go around; from *com-,* intens., and *tornare,* to turn; *tornus,* a lathe; Gr. *torsios,* a tool to make a circle with.]

1. the outline of a figure, mass, land, etc.

2. the representation of such an outline.

3. in fortification, the horizontal outline of works of defense.

çon′tōur, *a.* characterized by furrows along the natural contour lines so as to avoid erosion; as, *contour* farming.

çon′tōur, *v.t.*; contoured, *pt., pp.*; contouring, *ppr.* 1. to make an outline of; to represent in contour.

2. to construct (a road, etc.) in accordance with natural contours.

çon′tōur feath′ẽrṣ (feth′-), feathers that form the surface plumage of a bird and determine the outer contour, apart from wings, tail, etc.

çon′tōur in′tẽr·văl, the difference in elevation represented by each of the contour lines on a map.

çon′tōur līne, 1. an imaginary line connecting all points of the same elevation on a part of the earth's surface.

2. a line on a map, representing this line.

çon′tōur map, a map showing the physical features of an area of land by means of contour lines.

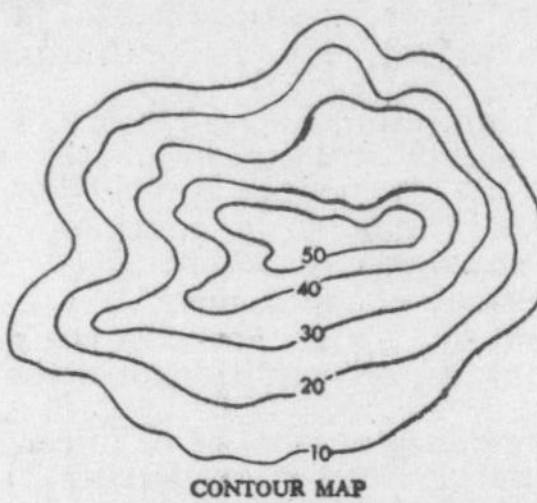

CONTOUR MAP

con·tour·né′ (çon-tör-nā′), *a.* [Fr.] in heraldry, twisted about: used when a beast is represented standing, passant, courant, etc., with its face to the sinister side of the escutcheon.

çon′trȧ, *adv.* [L.] to the contrary; contrariwise.

çon′trȧ, *n.* something contrary or opposite.

çon′trȧ-, a prefix, from Latin *contra,* a preposition and adverb, signifying *against, contrary, opposite,* as in *contra*diction, *contra*bass.

çon′trȧ·band, *a.* [It. *contrabbando,* from L. *contra,* against, and LL. *bandum,* bannum, a proclamation.] prohibited or excluded by proclamation, law, or treaty; forbidden by law to be exported or imported.

çon′trȧ·band, *n.* 1. illegal or prohibited trade.

2. articles prohibited by law to be imported or exported; smuggled merchandise.

3. contraband of war.

4. during the Civil War, a Negro slave who fled to or was smuggled behind the Union lines or remained in territory captured by the Union Army.

çon′trȧ·band, *v.t.* and *v.i.* to declare prohibited; also, to smuggle. [Rare.]

çon′trȧ·band·iṣm, *n.* illegal trade.

çon′trȧ·band·ist, *n.* a person who trades in contraband goods; a smuggler.

çon′trȧ·band of wạr, goods essential to warfare, as ammunition, weapons, etc., which, according to international law, may rightfully be intercepted and seized by either belligerent when shipped to the other one by a neutral country.

çon·trȧ·bȧss′, *a.* of deep tone; specifically, having its pitch an octave lower than normal bass; double-bass.

çon·trȧ·bȧss′, *n.* an instrument or voice having the lowest bass tone; specifically, the largest, and deepest-toned, instrument of the viol class; double bass.

çon·trȧ·bȧss′ist, *n.* a person who plays the contrabass.

çon·trȧ·bȧs′sō, *n.* [It., from L. *contra,* opposite, and *basso,* L. *bassus,* low.] a contrabass.

çon·trȧ·bas·sọon′, *n.* the double bassoon, which is larger than the regular bassoon and an octave lower in pitch.

CONTRABASS

çon·trȧ·cep′tion, *n.* artificial prevention of the fertilization of the human ovum: often called *birth control.*

çon·trȧ·cep′tive, *a.* of or used for contraception.

çon·trȧ·cep′tive, *n.* any contraceptive device.

çon·trȧ·çlock′wīṣe, *a.* and *adv.* counterclockwise.

çŏn·traçt′, *v.t.*; contracted, *pt., pp.*; contracting, *ppr.* [L. *contractus,* pp. of *contrahere,* to draw together, make a bargain; *com-,* together, and *trahere,* to draw.]

1. (*often* kon′trakt), to enter upon, or undertake, by contract.

2. to betroth. [Rare.]

3. to get; acquire; incur; as, he *contracted* the disease.

4. to reduce in size; draw together; narrow; shrink; as, cold *contracts* metals, the brows are *contracted* when the forehead is wrinkled.

5. in grammar, to shorten (a word or phrase) by the omission of a letter or part, as in *I'm, e'er, can't.*

6. to epitomize; to abridge; as, to *contract* an essay. [Obs.]

çŏn·traçt′, *v.i.* 1. to shrink; to become less in size or bulk; to draw together; to narrow; as, iron *contracts* on cooling.

2. to bargain; to agree formally; to make a mutual agreement, as between two or more persons; as, we have *contracted* for a load of flour.

3. to betroth in marriage. [Rare.]

Syn.—abbreviate, shorten, narrow, lessen, condense, reduce, assume.

çŏn·traçt′, *a.* contracted.

çon′traçt, *n.* 1. an agreement or covenant between two or more persons, in which each party binds himself to do or forbear some act, and each acquires a right to what the other promises; a mutual promise upon lawful consideration or cause which binds the parties to a performance; a bargain; a compact.

2. an agreement, usually written, enforceable by law.

3. a formal agreement of marriage or betrothal.

4. a document containing the terms of an agreement.

5. in bridge, (a) the verbal agreement made by the highest bidder to make a number of tricks; (b) the number of tricks that he bids; (c) contract bridge.

Syn.—covenant, agreement, compact, stipulation, bargain, arrangement, obligation, promise, engagement.

çŏn·traçt′ănt, *n.* a person who contracts.

çon′traçt bridġe (brij), a form of auction bridge in which only the number of tricks named in the contract may be counted toward a game, additional tricks being counted as honors.

çŏn·traçt′ed, *a.* 1. drawn together, or into a shorter or narrower compass; shrunken; shortened; reduced in size or bulk.

2. bargained for; betrothed.

3. incurred; as, a debt improperly *contracted.*

4. narrowed in mental scope; narrow-minded; mean; selfish; as, a man of a *contracted* soul or mind.

çŏn·traçt′ed·ly, *adv.* in a contracted manner.

çŏn·traçt′ed·ness, *n.* the state of being contracted; narrowness; meanness; excessive selfishness.

çŏn·traçt·i·bil′i·ty, *n.* the quality of being contractible.

çŏn·traçt′i·ble, *a.* capable of contraction.

çŏn·traçt′i·ble·ness, *n.* contractibility.

çŏn·traçt′ile, *a.* 1. tending to contract; having the power of contracting.

2. producing contraction.

çon·traç·til′i·ty, *n.* 1. the ability to contract, or shrink.

2. the contracting or shortening power possessed by fibers of living muscles.

çŏn·traç′tion, *n.* 1. a contracting or being contracted.

2. the drawing up and thickening of a muscle fiber or a muscle in action.

3. in grammar, (a) the shortening of a word or phrase by the omission of one or more letters or sounds (e.g., *aren't* for *are not, dep't* for *department*); (b) a word form resulting from this.

4. a contract; marriage contract. [Obs.]

çŏn·traçt′ive, *a.* 1. having the power of contracting.

2. producing or tending to produce contraction.

3. of contraction.

çon′traçt·ŏr (*or* kŏn-trak′tŏr), *n.* 1. one of the parties to a contract.

2. a person who contracts to supply certain materials or do certain work for a stipulated sum; especially, one whose business is contracting to erect buildings.

3. (*usually* kŏn-trak′tŏr), a thing that contracts, narrows, or shortens; especially, a muscle that contracts.

çŏn·traç′tū·ăl, *a.* of or pertaining to a contract; of the nature of a contract; implying a contract.

çŏn·traç′tūre, *n.* permanent muscle shortening.

çon′trȧ·dȧnce, *n.* [Fr. *contredanse*; *contre,* opposite, and *danse,* dance.] a contredanse.

çon·trȧ·diçt′, *v.t.*; contradicted, *pt., pp.*; contradicting, *ppr.* [L. *contradictus,* pp. of *contradicere*; *contra,* against, and *dicere,* to speak.]

1. (a) to assert the opposite of (what someone else has said); (b) to deny the statement of (a person).

2. to declare (a statement, report, etc.) to be false or incorrect; to deny.
3. to be contrary to; to go against.

çon·trȧ·diçt′, *v.i.* to utter a contradiction; to speak in denial; to oppose verbally.
Syn.—oppose, gainsay, deny, resist, impugn, correct, rectify, retract, recall.

çon·trȧ·diçt′ȧ·ble, *a.* that is capable of contradiction.

çon·trȧ·diçt′ẽr, *n.* same as *contradictor*.

çon·trȧ·diç′tion, *n.* 1. a contradicting or being contradicted.
2. a statement in opposition to another; denial.
3. a condition in which things tend to be contrary to each other; inconsistency; discrepancy.
4. a statement that contradicts itself.
5. a person or thing containing or composed of contradictory elements.
principle of contradiction; the axiom that truth and falsity are never inherent in the same thing simultaneously in the same sense.

çon·trȧ·diç′tion·ăl, *a.* contradictory. [Rare.]

çon·trȧ·diç′tious (-shus), *a.* 1. (a) contradictory [Archaic.]; (b) self-contradictory [Archaic.].
2. inclined to contradict; contentious.

çon·trȧ·diç′tious·ness, *n.* the quality of being contradictious. [Rare.]

çon·trȧ·diçt′ive, *a.* contradictory.

çon·trȧ·diçt′ive·ly, *adv.* by contradiction.

çon·trȧ·diçt′ŏr, *n.* a person or thing that contradicts: also spelled *contradicter*.

çon·trȧ·diçt′ō·ri·ly, *adv.* in a contradictory manner.

çon·trȧ·diçt′ō·ri·ness, *n.* the quality of being contradictory.

çon·trȧ·diçt′ō·ry, *a.* 1. affirming the contrary; inclined to contradict or deny; as, *contradictory* assertions.
2. inconsistent or mutually inconsistent; opposite; contrary; as, *contradictory* schemes.
Syn.—adverse, alien, incompatible, inconsistent, opposite, repugnant, contrary.

çon·trȧ·diçt′ō·ry, *n.*; *pl.* **çon·trȧ·diçt′ō·rieṣ**, a proposition which denies or opposes another in all its terms; contrariety; inconsistency.
It is common with princes to will *contradictories*. —Bacon.

çon″trȧ·dis·tinçt′, *a.* [*contra-*, and L. *distinctus*, pp. of *distinguere*, to distinguish.] distinguished by opposite qualities.

çon″trȧ·dis·tinç′tion, *n.* distinction by opposite qualities or by contrast.
We speak of sins of infirmity, in *contradistinction* to those of presumption.—South.

çon″trȧ·dis·tinç′tive, *a.* characterized by contradistinction.

çon″trȧ·dis·tinç′tive, *n.* that which contradistinguishes.

çon″trȧ·dis·tiṅ′guish (-gwish), *v.t.*; contradistinguished, *pt.*, *pp.*; contradistinguishing, *ppr.* to distinguish (one thing from another) by contrasting.

çon″trȧ·fȧ·got′tō, *n.* [It.] the double bassoon.

çon·trȧ·fis′sūre (-fish′ūr), *n.* [*contra-*, and L. *fissura*, from *findere*, to cleave.] in surgery, a fissure or fracture in the cranium, on the side opposite to that which received the blow, or at some distance from it.

çon·trȧ·grē′di·ent, *a.* in mathematics, denoting the relation of one system of variables to another when one is subject to undergo linear substitution simultaneously with the other, but of a contrary kind.

çon′trȧ·hent, *a.* contracting; agreeing.

çon′trāil, *n.* [*con*densation *trail*.] a white trail of condensed water vapor that sometimes forms in the wake of an aircraft.

çon·trȧ·in′di·çant, *n.* a contraindication.

çon·trȧ·in′di·çāte, *v.t.*; contraindicated, *pt.*, *pp.*; contraindicating, *ppr.* [*contra-*, and L. *indicatus*, pp. of *indicare*, to point out; *in*, in, and *dicare*, to proclaim.] in medicine, to make (the indicated, or expected, treatment) inadvisable: said of a symptom or condition.

çon·trȧ·in·di·çā′tion, *n.* in medicine, any condition of disease which makes the indicated medication or treatment inadvisable.

çŏn·tral′tō, *n.*; *pl.* **çŏn·tral′tōṣ**, **cŏntral′ti**, [It.] 1. the part sung by the lowest female voice or, formerly, the highest male voice.
2. a female voice of the lowest range.
3. a woman or girl who sings in this range.

çŏn·tral′tō, *a.* of or for a contralto.

çon′trȧ·mūre, *n.* countermure. [Obs.]

çon·trȧ·nat′ū·răl, *a.* contrary to nature.

çon′trȧ·oç′tāve, *n.* [*contra-*, and L. *octava*, an eighth, from *octo*, eight.] that octave on the piano which begins with lowest C; also, the corresponding octave on other instruments.

çon′trȧ·plex, *a.* same as *duplex*.

çon·trȧ·pōṣe′, *v.t.*; contraposed, *pt.*, *pp.*; contraposing, *ppr.* [*contra-*, and L. *positus*, pp. of *ponere*, to place.]
1. to set in opposition.
2. in logic, to transpose (the terms of a proposition) by contraposition.

çon″trȧ·pō·ṣi′tion (-zish′un), *n.* 1. a placing opposite or over against.
2. a position directly opposite; antithesis.
3. in logic, conversion, in particular negative propositions, effected by separating the word *not* from the copula and attaching it to the predicate.

çŏn·trap′tion, *n.* [perh. formed on *contrive* and words ending in *-ption* (e.g., *deception*).] a contrivance; gadget; makeshift: often used humorously or contemptuously. [Colloq.]

çon·trȧ·pun′tăl, *a.* [It. *contrappunto*, counterpoint.] pertaining to counterpoint, or conforming to its rules.

çon·trȧ·pun′tăl·ly, *adv.* in a manner conformable to the rules of counterpoint.

çon·trȧ·pun′tist, *n.* one skilled in counterpoint.

çon·trȧ·pun′tō, *n.* same as *counterpoint*.

çon″trȧ·rē·mon′strănt, *n.* one who remonstrates against a remonstrance.

çŏn·trā′ri·ănt, *a.* [Fr., from L. *contrarians*, ppr. of *contrariare*, to contradict, from *contrarius*, opposite; *contra*, against.] contradictory; opposite; inconsistent; opposing. [Rare.]

çŏn·trā′ri·ănt, *n.* a contrariant person, applied particularly, in English history, to Thomas, Earl of Lancaster, and the barons who took part with him against King Edward II.

çŏn·trā′ri·ănt·ly, *adv.* in a contrary manner. [Obs.]

çon·trȧ·rī′e·ty, *n.* [L. *contrarietas*, from *contrarius*, opposite, opposed; *contra*, against.]
1. the condition of being opposed in fact, essence, quality, or principle; the quality of being contrary; lack of agreement.
There is nothing more common than *contrariety* of opinions. —Locke.
2. *pl.* **çŏn·trȧ·rī′e·tieṣ**, an inconsistency; any quality or thing contrary or opposed to another; as, political *contrarieties*.
Syn.—disagreement, discrepancy, dissimilarity, inconsistency, antagonism.

çon′trȧ·ri·ly, *adv.* in a contrary manner.

çon′trā·ri·ness, *n.* the state or quality of being contrary.

çŏn·trā′ri·ous, *a.* contrary; opposing, especially (a) perverse; (b) adverse. [Rare or Obs.]

çŏn·trā′ri·ous·ly, *adv.* contrarily; oppositely. [Rare.]

çon′trā·ri·wīṣe, *adv.* 1. on the contrary; oppositely; on the other hand.
Not rendering evil for evil, or railing for railing; but *contrariwise* blessing.
—1 Pet. iii. 9.
2. conversely; in reverse order; in the opposite way.

çon″trȧ·rō·tā′tion, *n.* rotation in a direction opposite to another motion.

çon′trā·ry, *a.* [L. *contrarius*, opposite, opposed, from *contra*, against.]
1. opposite; adverse; in an opposite direction or position; as, *contrary* winds.
2. opposed; altogether different; as, an idea *contrary* to accepted theories.
3. disposed to contrariness; characterized by opposition; perverse; as, an exasperatingly *contrary* person.
4. unfavorable; as, *contrary* weather.
contrary motion; in music, a simultaneous progression of voice parts, in which one ascends while another descends.
Syn.—dissimilar, unlike, opposite, opposed, conflicting, antagonistic.

çon′trā·ry, *n.*; *pl.* **çon′trā·rieṣ**, 1. a thing that is the opposite of another; the opposite.
No *contraries* hold more antipathy
Than I and such a knave. —Shak.
2. an antagonist. [Obs.]
on the contrary; in opposition; on the other side.
to the contrary; to an opposite effect.

çon′trā·ry, *adv.* in opposition; counter.

çon′trā·ry, *v.t.* to contradict or oppose. [Obs.]

çŏn·trȧst′, *v.t.*; contrasted, *pt.*, *pp.*; contrasting, *ppr.* [Fr. *contraster*; LL. *contrastare*, to stand opposed to, withstand; *contra*, against, and *stare*, to stand.]
1. to set in opposition (different things or qualities) to show the comparative excellences of, or the differences between; to compare so as to point out differences; as, to *contrast* night and day.
2. in painting and sculpture, to place in such relation of opposition, as color, form, etc., that the effect of the whole is heightened.
The figures of the groups must *contrast* each other. —Dryden.

çŏn·trȧst′, *v.i.* to stand in contrast or opposition; to show differences or dissimilarity when compared; to form a contrast.
The joints which divide the sandstone *contrast* finely with the divisional planes which separate the basalt into pillars.—Lyell.

çon′trȧst, *n.* 1. the act or process of contrasting, or the state of being contrasted.
2. a difference, especially a striking difference, between things being compared; as, the *contrast* between a well-bred man and a boor.
3. a person or thing showing differences when compared with another.
4. in painting, sculpture, and other arts, the opposition or dissimilarity of figures, colors, etc., by which one heightens the effect of the other.

çon·trȧ·stim′ū·lănt, *a.* having the properties of or acting as a contrastimulant.

çon·trȧ·stim′ū·lănt, *n.* a remedy or treatment tending to counteract the effects of a stimulant or an excessive use of stimulants.

çŏn·trȧst′y, *a.* in photography, characterized by sharp contrasts or gradations of tone, as between light and dark areas, resulting from overdevelopment or underexposure of the negative.

çon′trāte, *a.* [from L. *contra*, opposite, against.] bearing teeth on the rim cogs parallel to the axis: applied to clockwork wheels.

çon′trȧ·ten″ŏr, *n.* [It.] in music, a countertenor.

çon′trāte wheel, same as *crown wheel*.

çon″trȧ·val·lā′tion, *n.* [Fr. *contrevallation*, from L. *contra*, against, and *vallum*, a rampart.] in fortification, a trench guarded with a parapet, formed by the besiegers between their camp and the place besieged, to protect themselves and check sallies of the besieged garrison.

çon·trȧ·vā′ri·ănt, *n.* a function which stands in the same relation to the primitive function from which it is derived as any of its linear transforms to an inversely derived transform of its primitive.

çon·trȧ·vēne′, *v.t.*; contravened, *pt.*, *pp.*; contravening, *ppr.* [LL. *contravenire*; *contra*, against, and *venire*, to come.]
1. to go against; to oppose; to conflict with; to infringe; to violate; as, such a ruling will *contravene* all precedent.
2. to disagree with in argument; to contradict.
Syn.—oppose, run counter to, contradict, nullify, thwart, defeat.

çon·trȧ·vēn′ẽr, *n.* one who contravenes.

çon·trȧ·ven′tion, *n.* 1. the act of contravening or opposing; violation; opposition; as, the proceedings of the allies were in *contravention* of the treaty.
2. contradiction.

çon·trȧ·vẽr′sion, *n.* [L. *contraversus*; *contra*, against, and *versus*, pp. of *vertere*, to turn.] a turning to the opposite side. [Rare.]

çon·trȧ·yẽr′vȧ, *n.* [from Sp. *contrayerba*, a counter herb, antidote; L. *contra*, against, and *herba*, an herb.] in botany, a South American plant of the mulberry family, *Dorstenia contrayerva*, which possesses an aromatic root having medicinal qualities.

çon′tre·çoup [kon′tr-kö), *n.* [Fr. *contre*, L. *contra*, against, and *coup*, a blow.] an injury, as to the brain, resulting from a blow but produced in a part opposite to or distant from the part that received the blow: also *counterstroke*.

çon·treç·tā′tion, *n.* [L. *contrectatio*, from *con-*, and *trectare*, to handle, touch.] a touching or handling. [Rare.]

çŏṅ·tre·däṅse′ (-tr-däṅs′), *n.* [Fr., altered from Eng. *country-dance* through confusion of *country* with Fr. *contre*, against, opposite.]
1. a dance in which the partners form two facing lines; country-dance.
2. music for this dance.
Also *contradance*.

çŏṅ·tre·temps′ (-tr-täṅ′), *n.*; *pl.* **çŏṅ·tre·temps′** (-täṅ′), [Fr., from L. *contra*, against, and *tempus*, time.] an inopportune happening which causes confusion; an embarrassing occurrence.

çŏn·trib′ū·tȧ·ble, *a.* able to contribute or be contributed.

çŏn·trib'ū·tā·ry, *a.* tributary. [Obs.]

It was situated on the Ganges, at the place where this river received a *contributary* stream. —D'Anville.

çŏn·trib'ūte, *v.t.*; contributed, *pt., pp.*; contributing, *ppr.* [L. *contributus*, pp. of *contribuere*, to throw together, unite; *com-*, together, and *tribuere*, to grant, assign.]

1. to give or grant in common with others; to give to a common fund or for a common purpose; to pay a share of or make a gift toward; as, to *contribute* money to a famine fund.

2. to write and give or sell (an article, story, poem, etc.) to a magazine, newspaper, etc.

3. to give or furnish (knowledge, etc.).

çŏn·trib'ūte, *v.i.* to give a part; to lend a portion of power, aid, or influence; to have a share in any act or effect; to make a contribution; as, he *contributed* to the success of the evening.

There is not a single beauty in the piece, to which the invention must not *contribute*. —Pope.

Syn.—add, subscribe, give, co-operate, assist, supply, tend, conduce.

çon·tri·bū'tion, *n.* 1. a contributing.

2. money, aid, etc. contributed.

3. a levy or tax for a special purpose, as for supporting an army in the field.

4. something written for, and given or sold to, a magazine, newspaper, etc.

5. in law, the share of a common loss, obligation, or benefit, paid or to be paid by each of the persons concerned.

çon·tri·bū'tion·ăl, *a.* of or pertaining to a contribution; making contributions.

çŏn·trib'ū·tive, *a.* tending to contribute; contributing.

çŏn·trib'ū·tŏr, *n.* 1. one who contributes money, aid, etc.

2. a person who gives or sells his writings to a magazine, newspaper, etc.

çŏn·trib'ū·tō·ry, *a.* 1. contributing; having a share in bringing about a result.

2. involving, or having the nature of, a contribution.

contributory negligence; in law, negligence on the part of an injured person, which helped to bring about the cause of the injury and therefore usually precludes him from winning in an action for damages.

çŏn·trib'ū·tō·ry, *n.*; *pl.* **çŏn·trib'ū·tō·rieș,** 1. a person or thing that contributes; a contributor.

2. in law, a member liable to help make up a deficiency in the assets of a company being dissolved.

çŏn·trist', *v.t.* to make sorrowful; to sadden. [Obs.]

çŏn·tris'tāte, *v.t.* [L. *contristatus*, pp. of *contristare*, to make sad.] to make sorrowful. [Obs.]

çon·tris·tā'tion, *n.* the act of making sad; sadness; dejection; sorrowfulness. [Obs.]

çŏn·trīte', *a.* [L. *contritus*, pp. of *conterere*, to bruise, rub; *com-*, together, and *terere*, to rub.]

1. worn or bruised. [Obs.]

2. deeply affected with grief and sorrow for having done wrong; humbled; penitent; as, a *contrite* sinner.

A broken and a *contrite* heart, O God, thou wilt not despise. —Ps. li. 17.

3. showing or resulting from remorse or guilt.

çon'trīte, *n.* one who is penitent.

çon'trīte·ly, *adv.* in a contrite manner; with penitence.

çon'trīte·ness, *n.* contrition; deep sorrow and penitence for sin.

çŏn·tri'tion, *n.* 1. attrition; the act of grinding or rubbing to powder. [Obs.]

2. penitence; deep sorrow for sin; remorse for having done wrong.

Syn.—penitence, sorrow, repentance, compunction, remorse.

çŏn·trit'ū·rāte, *v.t.*; contriturated, *pt., pp.*; contriturating, *ppr.* to pulverize or reduce to small particles; to triturate.

çŏn·trīv'ȧ·ble, *a.* able to be contrived; capable of being planned, invented, or devised.

çŏn·trīv'ănce, *n.* 1. the act, way, or power of contriving.

2. the thing contrived; arrangement; plan; scheme; artifice; mechanical device; invention.

Syn.—appliance, mechanism, project, device, design, ruse, trick.

çŏn·trīve', *v.t.*; contrived, *pt., pp.*; contriving, *ppr.* [ME. *contriven, controven*; OFr. *controver*, to find out, contrive; *con-*, and *trover*, to find.]

1. to devise; to plan; to scheme.

2. to invent; to design; to fabricate; as, they have *contrived* an automatic dishwasher.

3. to carry to completion or success by scheming or using ingenuity; to manage; as, he *contrived* to pull through.

Syn.—invent, form, arrange, frame, design, devise, scheme, plot.

çŏn·trīve', *v.i.* to form a plan; to scheme.

çŏn·trīve'ment, *n.* contrivance; invention; scheme. [Obs.]

çŏn·trīv'ẽr, *n.* one who contrives; an inventor; one who plans or devises; a schemer.

çŏn·trōl', *n.* [Fr. *controle*; OFr. *contrerole*; LL. *contrarotulum*, a counterroll or register; L. *contra*, against, and *rotula*, a roll.]

1. the act of controlling; the power to control, regulate, or guide; as, out of one's *control*.

2. a holding back; a restraint, a curb.

3. a means of restraint; a check.

4. a standard of comparison for verifying or checking the findings of an experiment.

5. [*often in pl.*] an instrument or apparatus to regulate a mechanism; as, the *controls* of an airplane.

6. in spiritualism, a spirit supposed to direct the actions and speech of the medium.

board of control; a governing body which has authority over another body.

Syn.—regulation, check, restraint, ascendancy, dominion, influence.

çŏn·trōl', *v.t.*; controlled, *pt., pp.*; controlling, *ppr.* 1. to check or verify (payments, etc.) by a counter-register or double account. [Obs.]

2. to regulate (financial affairs).

3. to verify, as an experiment, by comparison with a standard, or by other experiments.

4. to exercise authority over; direct; command.

5. to curb; restrain; hold back.

I feel my virtue struggling in my soul;
But stronger passion does its power *control*. —Dryden.

Syn.—restrain, rule, govern, direct, check, curb, overpower, counteract.

çŏn·trōl' ex·per'i·ment, an experiment in which the variable factors are controlled so as to make it possible to observe the results of varying one factor at a time.

çŏn·trōl·lȧ·bil'i·ty, *n.* the quality of being controllable; controllableness.

çŏn·trōl'lȧ·ble, *a.* that may be controlled, checked, or restrained.

Passion is the drunkenness of the mind, and not always *controllable* by reason. —South.

çŏn·trōl'lȧ·ble·ness, *n.* controllability.

çŏn·trōl'lẽr, *n.* 1. a keeper of counterrolls. [Obs.]

2. one who controls or restrains; one that has the power or authority to govern or control.

The great *Controller* of our fate
Deigned to be man, and lived in low estate. —Dryden.

3. an officer having specified duties in connection with the management of financial affairs; especially, a government official so employed: in this sense also spelled *comptroller*.

4. any device for controlling the speed, power, etc. of a machine.

çŏn·trōl'lẽr·ship, *n.* the position or term of office of a controller.

çŏn·trōl'ment, *n.* the power or act of controlling; the state of being restrained; control; restraint.

çŏn·trōl' stick, the lever by which the pilot moves the ailerons and the elevators of an airplane to control its flight.

çon·trō·vẽr'săl, *a.* inclined or faced in opposite directions. [Obs.]

çon·trō·vẽr'sȧ·ry, *a.* controversial. [Obs.]

çon'trō·vẽrse, *n.* controversy. [Obs.]

çon'trō·vẽrse, *v.t.* to dispute; to debate. [Obs.]

çon'trō·vẽr·sẽr, *n.* one who disputes. [Obs.]

çon·trō·vẽr'siăl (-shăl), *a.* 1. subject to controversy; debatable.

2. of controversy.

3. liking to take part in controversy; disputatious.

çon·trō·vẽr'siăl·ist, *n.* one who carries on a controversy; a disputant.

çon·trō·vẽr'siăl·ly, *adv.* in a controversial manner.

çon·trō·vẽr'sion, *n.* controversy. [Obs.]

çon'trō·vẽr·sŏr, *n.* a disputant. [Obs.]

çon'trō·vẽr·sy, *n.*; *pl.* **çon'trō·vẽr·sieș,** [L. *controversia*, from *controversus*, turned in an opposite direction; *contra*, against, and *versus*, pp. of *vertere*, to turn.]

1. a suit in law.

2. a discussion of a question in which opposing opinions clash; debate; disputation.

3. a quarrel; a dispute.

Syn.—dispute.—A *dispute* is commonly oral, and is generally of short continuance. It may be defined as a temporary debate, and involves the idea of heat. A *controversy* may be oral, but is commonly in writing, and is frequently continued for a long period of time, many persons taking part in it.

çon'trō·vẽrt, *v.t.*; controverted, *pt., pp.*; controverting, *ppr.* [L. *contravertere*, to turn in an opposite direction; *contra*, against, and *vertere*, to turn.]

1. to dispute; to deny and attempt to disprove or confute; to argue against; as, to *controvert* opinions or principles.

2. to argue about; to debate; to discuss.

çon'trō·vẽr·tẽr, *n.* one who controverts.

çon·trō·vẽr'ti·ble, *a.* capable of being disputed; disputable; not too evident to exclude difference of opinion; as, this is a *controvertible* point of law.

çon·trō·vẽr'ti·bly, *adv.* in a controvertible manner.

çon'trō·vẽr·tist, *n.* one who controverts; a disputant; one versed in or given to disputation.

How unfriendly is the spirit of the *controvertist* to the discernment of the critic! —Campbell.

çon·tū'bẽr·năl, çon·tū·bẽr'ni·ăl, *a.* [L. *contubernalis*, from *contubernium*, companionship in a tent; from *com-*, together, and *taberna*, a tent.] living together familiarly.

çon·tū·mā'cious, *a.* [L. *contumax*, from *com-*, intens., and *tumere*, to swell.]

1. insubordinate; rebellious; disobedient; as, a *contumacious* child.

2. in law, willfully resisting authority.

Syn.—obstinate, obdurate, stubborn, disobedient, perverse, unyielding, headstrong.

çon·tū·mā'cious·ly, *adv.* obstinately; stubbornly; perversely; in disobedience of orders.

çon'tū·mȧ·cy, *n.*; *pl.* **çon'tū·mȧ·cieș,** [L. *contumacia*, from *contumax*, haughty, stubborn; from *com-*, intens., and *tumere*, to swell up.]

1. insubordination; disobedience.

2. in law, a willful contempt of, and disobedience to, any lawful summons or order of court.

Syn.—stubbornness, obstinacy, perverseness, obduracy.

çon·tū·mē'li·ous, *a.* [L. *contumeliosus*, from *contumelia*, abuse, reproach.]

1. haughty and contemptuous; insulting; insolent; rude; as, a *contumelious* person.

2. reproachful; shameful; ignominious. [Obs.]

çon·tū·mē'li·ous·ly, *adv.* in a contumelious manner.

çon·tū·mē'li·ous·ness, *n.* reproach; rudeness.

çon'tū·mē·ly, *n.* [L. *contumelia*, reproach, abuse.] haughtiness and contempt; contemptuousness; insolence; contemptuous language or conduct; also, an instance of this; a scornful insult.

The oppressor's wrong, the proud man's *contumely*. —Shak.

çŏn·tūșe', *v.t.*; contused, *pt., pp.*; contusing, *ppr.* [L. *contusus*, pp. of *contundere*, to bruise, beat together.]

1. to beat together; to bray. [Obs.]

2. to injure or bruise without breaking the skin.

çŏn·tū'șion, *n.* 1. the act of bruising or the state of being bruised.

2. a bruise; an injury in which the skin is not broken.

cō·nun'drum, *n.* [16th-c. university Latin slang for pedant, pedantic whim, word play, etc.; early sp. *quonundrum*.]

1. a riddle whose answer involves a pun.

2. any question or thing of a perplexing nature; as, life is full of *conundrums*.

çon"ũr·bā'tion, *n.* [*con-*, and L. *urbs*, city; and *-ation*.] an extremely large, densely populated urban area, usually a complex of suburbs and smaller towns together with the large city at their center.

çō·nūre', *n.* [L. *conurus*, from Gr. *kōnos*, a cone, and *oura*, a tail.] one of several species of American parrots, genus *Conurus*, so named from their tapering tails, as the Carolina parakeet.

çō'nus, *n.*; *pl.* **çō'nī,** [L.]

1. a cone or cone-shaped organ.

2. [C–] a genus of mollusks of the family *Conidæ*, having cone-shaped shells.

çon'ū·sȧ·ble, *a.* liable to be tried or judged. [Obs.]

çon'ū·sănt, *a.* in law, knowing; having knowledge of; cognizant. [Obs.]

çon·ū·sor', *n.* cognizor. [Archaic.]

çon·vȧ·lesce', *v.i.*; convalesced, *pt.*, *pp.*; convalescing, *ppr.* [L. *convalescere*, to begin to grow strong; from *com-*, intens., and *valescere*, incept. of *valere*, to be strong.] to get better after illness; to recover strength and health.

çon·vȧ·les'cence, çon·vȧ·les'cen·cy, *n.* the gradual recovery of health and strength after an illness; also, the period of such recovery.

çon·vȧ·les'cent, *a.* 1. recovering health and strength after illness.
 2. relating to convalescence; as, a *convalescent* diet.

çon·vȧ·les'cent, *n.* one recovering from illness or regaining strength.

çon·vȧ·les'cent·ly, *adv.* in the manner of one convalescing; with gradually increasing strength.

çon·val·lȧ·mā'rin, *n.* [*convall-*, from *Convallaria*, and L. *amarus*, bitter.] in chemistry, a bitter, poisonous compound extracted from the lily of the valley.

Çon·văl·lā'ri·ȧ, *n.* [Mod. L., from *convallis*, a valley enclosed on all sides; from *com-*, intens., and *vallis*, a valley.]
 1. in botany, a genus of herbs of the lily family, *Liliaceæ*, having only one species, the lily of the valley, *Convallaria majalis*.
 2. [c–] the lily of the valley.

çon·văl·lăr·i·ā'ceous, *a.* [Mod. L. *Convallaria*; and *-aceous*.] of a group of bulbless plants with pulpy fruits, as the asparagus.

çon·văl·lā'rin, *n.* in chemistry, an acrid, crystalline glucoside extracted from the *Convallaria*.

çŏn·veç'tion, *n.* [L. *convectio*, from *convehere*, to bring together.]
 1. a transmitting or conveying.
 2. in physics, the transmission of heat or electricity by the mass movement of the heated or electrified particles, as in air, gas, or liquid currents.

çŏn·veç'tion·ăl, *a.* of convection.

çŏn·veç'tive, *a.* 1. resulting from or caused by convection; as, a *convective* discharge of electricity.
 2. conveying.

çŏn·veç'tive·ly, *adv.* in a convective manner.

çŏn·veç'tŏr, *n.* a medium of convection.

çŏn·vēn'ȧ·ble, *a.* that may be convened or assembled.

çon'vē·nänce, *n.*; *pl.* **çon'vē·nän·ceş,** [Fr.]
 1. that which is proper, suitable, or in accordance with established customs.
 2. [*pl.*] the conventionalities.

çŏn·vēne', *v.i.*; convened, *pt.*, *pp.*; convening, *ppr.* [L. *convenire*, to come together, fit, join.]
 1. to come together; to meet; to unite, as things. [Rare.]
 The rays of light converge and *convene* in the eyes. —Newton.
 2. to come together; to meet together; to assemble, implying a common purpose; as, the meeting *convened* in the schoolhouse.
 Syn.—meet, assemble, congregate.

çŏn·vēne', *v.t.* 1. to cause to assemble; to call together; to convoke; as, to *convene* Congress.
 2. to summon before a court of law.

çŏn·vēn'ẽr, *n.* 1. one who convenes or meets with others.
 2. one who convenes or calls a meeting together; specifically, in Scotland, one appointed to call an organized body together, as a committee, of which he is generally chairman.

çŏn·vēn'ience (-yens), **çŏn·vēn'ien·cy,** *n.* [L. *convenientia*, from *convenire*, to come together, join, suit.]
 1. the state or quality of being convenient; fitness; serviceableness.
 2. absence of that which annoys; personal well being; comfort.
 3. that which gives ease or comfort or makes work less difficult and complicated; a handy device, article, etc.; as, an apartment with modern *conveniences*.
 A man alters his mind as the work proceeds, and will have this or that *convenience* more. —Dryden.
 4. a condition personally favorable or suitable; advantage.
 at one's convenience; at a time, or in a place or manner, suitable to one; as one wishes.

çŏn·vēn'ient, *a.* 1. fit; suitable; appropriate. [Obs.]
 Some arts are peculiarly *convenient* to particular nations. —Tillotson.
 2. favorable to one's comfort; easy to do, use, or get to; causing little trouble, work, etc.; handy.
 Obstinate heretics used to be brought thither *convenient* for burning hard by. —Thackeray.
 convenient to; easily accessible to; near. [Colloq.]

çŏn·vēn'ient·ly, *adv.* in a convenient manner; without trouble or difficulty.

çon'vent, *n.* [Fr. *convent*; L. *conventus*, from *convenire*, to come together, assemble.]
 1. a gathering; a meeting. [Obs.]
 2. a community of nuns or, sometimes, monks, living under strict religious vows.
 3. the building or buildings occupied by such a group; a nunnery or, sometimes, a monastery.

çŏn·vent'iç·ăl, *a.* of, relating to, or pertaining to a convent.

çŏn·ven'ti·çle, *n.* [L. *conventiculum*, dim. of *conventus*, an assembly.]
 1. a religious assembly; especially, a secret or illegal one.
 2. the meeting place of such a body.
 3. in English history, a prohibited meeting of any religious sect that disputed the authority of the Church of England, as of certain Protestants in the sixteenth and seventeenth centuries.

çŏn·ven'ti·çle, *v.i.* to belong to a conventicle. [Rare.]

çŏn·ven'ti·çlẽr, *n.* one who supports or attends conventicles.

çŏn·ven'tion, *n.* [L. *conventio*, from *convenire*, to come together.]
 1. the act of coming together; a convening or being convened.
 2. an assembly, often periodical, of delegates or representatives, as of a political or religious group, commercial organization, professional association, fraternal society, etc.
 3. the members or delegates at such an assembly.
 4. originally, an agreement as reached by such an assembly; hence, (a) an agreement between persons, nations, etc.; (b) general agreement on the usages and practices of social life; (c) custom; usage.

çŏn·ven'tion·ăl, *a.* [LL. *conventionalis*, pertaining to an agreement, from *conventio*, an assembly, agreement.]
 1. stipulated; formed by agreement.
 Conventional services reserved by tenures on grants, made out of the crown or knights service. —Hale.
 2. arising out of custom or usage; customary; as, a *conventional* use of language.
 3. depending on or conforming to accepted models or traditions rather than nature; not natural, original, or spontaneous; as, *conventional* behavior.
 4. stylized; conventionalized.
 5. having to do with a convention.
 Syn.—customary, usual, ordinary, stipulated, prevalent, social.

çŏn·ven'tion·ăl·işm, *n.* 1. adherence to conventional customs and rules; formalism.
 2. a conventional idea, usage, or verbal expression; formality.

çŏn·ven'tion·ăl·ist, *n.* 1. one who is faithful to a treaty or agreement.
 2. an adherent to conventional forms or usages.

çŏn·ven·tion·al'i·ty, *n.*; *pl.* **çŏn·ven·tion·al'i·tieş,** 1. the fact, condition, or quality of being conventional.
 2. conventional behavior or act.
 3. a conventional form, usage, or rule.
 It is strong and sturdy writing; and breaks up a whole legion of *conventionalities*. —Lamb.

çŏn·ven″tion·ăl·i·zā'tion, *n.* the practice or result of conventionalizing.

çŏn·ven'tion·ăl·īze, *v.t.*; conventionalized, *pt.*, *pp.*; conventionalizing, *ppr.* 1. to render conventional; to bring under the influence of conventional rules; to render observant of the conventional rules of society.
 2. in the fine arts, to render or represent in accordance with usual patterns; to treat in a conventional or standardized manner.

çŏn·ven'tion·ăl·ly, *adv.* in a conventional manner.

çŏn·ven'tion·ăl wiş'dŏm, the generally accepted belief with regard to some matter, or the set of beliefs held by most people.

çŏn·ven'tion·ā·ry, *a.* acting under contract; as, *conventionary* tenants. [Obs.]

çŏn·ven'tion·ẽr, *n.* one who belongs to a convention.

çŏn·ven'tion·ist, *n.* one who makes a contract.

çŏn·ven'tū·ăl, *a.* of, like, or characteristic of a convent; as, *conventual* priors.

çŏn·ven'tū·ăl, *n.* 1. a member of a convent.
 2. [C–] one of a branch of the Franciscan order which believes in accumulating and holding property in common.

çŏn·vẽrġe', *v.i.*; converged, *pt.*, *pp.*; converging, *ppr.* [LL. *convergere*, to incline together; from *com-*, together, and *vergere*, to turn, bend.]
 1. to tend to come together at one point.
 2. to move, turn, or be directed toward each other or toward the same place: opposed to *diverge*.

çŏn·vẽrġe', *v.t.* to cause to converge.

çŏn·vẽr'ġence, *n.* 1. the act, fact, or condition of converging.
 2. (a) the degree of converging; (b) the point at which things converge.
 3. in biology, the formation of similarities in unrelated organisms living in the same environment.

çŏn·vẽr'ġen·cy, *n.*; *pl.* **çŏn·vẽr'ġen·cieş,** convergence.

çŏn·vẽr'ġent, *a.* converging or tending to converge.

çŏn·vẽr'ġi·nẽrved, *a.* in botany, designating the venation of leaves in which the ribs form a curve and meet at the point, as in *Plantago lanceolata*.

CONVERGI-NERVED LEAF

çŏn·vẽr'ġing, *a.* tending to one point; approaching each other, as lines extended.
 converging lens; a lens that increases the convergence or decreases the divergence of a beam of light passing through it.
 converging rays; in optics, those rays of light, which, proceeding from different points of an object, tend toward a single point.

çŏn·vẽrs'ȧ·ble, *a.* 1. of or fit for conversation.
 2. disposed to converse; liking to talk; sociable.
 3. easy to talk to; free in discourse; affable.

çon'vẽr·sănce, *n.* familiarity or acquaintance (*with*).

çon'vẽr·săn·cy, *n.* conversance.

çon'vẽr·sănt, *a.* [L. *conversans* (*-antis*), ppr. of *conversari*, to live with, converse, freq. of *convertere*; from *com-*, together, and *vertere*, to turn.]
 1. familiar or acquainted: followed by *with*; as, a student *conversant with* his instructors.
 Never to be infected with delight,
 Nor *conversant with* ease and idleness. —Shak.
 2. acquainted by familiar use or study; having a thorough understanding; proficient: followed by *with*; as, one *conversant with* politics.
 3. concerning; having concern or relation to; having for its object: followed by *about* or *with*. [Obs.]
 Education is *conversant about* children. —Wotton.

çŏn·vẽrs'ănt, *n.* a converser.

çon'vẽr·sănt·ly, *adv.* in a conversant or familiar manner.

çon·vẽr·sā'tion, *n.* [Fr. *conversation*; L. *conversatio*, intercourse, conversation.]
 1. general behavior; deportment. [Archaic.]
 2. social intercourse.
 3. sexual intercourse: now only in the legal phrase *criminal conversation*, i.e., adultery as grounds for divorce.
 4. knowledge or familiarity based on study or use.
 5. a talking together; informal or familiar talk; verbal exchange of ideas, information, etc.
 What I mentioned in *conversation* was not a new thought. —Swift.
 Syn.—talk, intercourse, communion, communication, discourse, conference, colloquy.

çon·vẽr·sā'tion·ăl, *a.* 1. pertaining to conversation; done in mutual discourse or talk.
 2. fond of or adept at conversation.

çon·vẽr·sā'tion·ăl·ist, *n.* one who excels in conversation.

çon·vẽr·sā'tion·ăl·ly, *adv.* 1. in a manner appropriate to conversation.
 2. in conversation.

çon·vẽr·sā'tioned, *a.* having a certain behavior or deportment. [Obs.]

çon·vẽr·sā'tion·işm, *n.* a conversational term; a colloquialism.

çon·vẽr·sā'tion·ist, *n.* one who excels in or is given to conversation; a conversationalist.
 I must not quite omit the talking sage,
 Kit Cat, the famous *conversationist*. —Byron.

çon·vẽr·sā′tion piēce (pēs), a type of genre painting in which a group of people, usually of the upper classes, are shown in an appropriate setting: it was popular in the eighteenth century.

çon·vẽr′sȧ·tive, *a.* conversable; sociable.

çon·ver·sȧ·zi·ō′ne (-sȧt-si-ō′), *n.*; *pl.* **çon·ver·sȧ·zi·ō′nï,** [It.] a social meeting for conversation about literature, the arts, etc.

cŏn·vẽrse′, *v.i.*; conversed, *pt.*, *pp.*; conversing, *ppr.* [ME. *conversen*; OFr. *converser*; L. *conversari*, to dwell, keep company with, freq. of *convertere*; from *com-*, together, and *vertere*, to turn.]

1. to associate; to be intimately acquainted (*with*); as, to *converse with* nature. [Archaic.]

2. to have sexual intercourse. [Archaic.]

3. to have free intercourse in mutual communication of thoughts and opinions; to hold a conversation; to talk.

So she goes by him attended,
Hears him lovingly *converse*. —Tennyson.

Syn.—talk, commune, communicate, confer, discourse, chat, speak.

çon′vẽrse, *n.* 1. conversation; familiar discourse or talk; free interchange of thoughts or opinions.

Formed by thy *converse* happily to steer
From grave to gay, from lively to severe.
—Pope.

2. friendly intercourse; association; communion.

3. sexual intercourse. [Obs.]

çon′vẽrse (*or* cŏn-vẽrs′), *a.* reversed; opposite; contrary; turned about.

çon′vẽrse, *n.* [L. *conversus*, pp. of *convertere*, to turn around; from *com-*, together, and *vertere*, to turn.]

1. a thing reversed in position, order, action, etc.; the opposite.

2. in logic and mathematics, an opposite proposition; thus, after drawing a conclusion from something supposed, we invert the order, making the conclusion the supposition or premises, and draw from it what was first supposed; as, "truth is the best guide," would be the *converse* of "the best guide is truth"; and, "the area of a circle equals πR^2," would be the *converse* of "πR^2 equals the area of a circle."

çon′vẽrse·ly, *adv.* contrarily; on the contrary; if or when reversed; as, some are well but unhappy; *conversely*, others are happy but ill.

cŏn·vẽrs′ẽr, *n.* one who converses.

cŏn·vẽr′si·ble, *a.* capable of conversion; reversible.

cŏn·vẽr′sion (*or* -zhun), *n.* 1. a turning or change from one state to another; a converting or being converted; transmutation; as, a *conversion* of water into ice.

2. in military usage, (a) a change of front, as of a body of troops attacked on the flank; (b) an alteration, as of firearms from one bore or style of bore to another.

3. a change from lack of faith to religious belief; adoption of a religion, especially Christianity.

4. a change in which one believes or advocates views at variance with those held in the past.

That *conversion* will be suspected that apparently concurs with interest.—Johnson.

5. in finance, a change of a security, currency, etc. from one form to another.

6. in law, (a) unlawful appropriation and use of another's property; (b) the exchange of property from real property to personal, or the reverse.

7. in logic, the producing of a new proposition by transposing the subject and predicate of the original proposition.

8. in mathematics, a change in the form of a quantity or an expression without a change in the value.

cŏn·vẽr′sion·ăl, *a.* of conversion.

cŏn·vẽr′sion·ăr·y, *a.* of conversion.

cŏn·vẽr′sive, *a.* capable of being converted or changed; convertible. [Rare.]

cŏn·vẽr′sive, *a.* conversable; social. [Rare.]

cŏn·vẽrt′, *v.t.*; converted, *pt.*, *pp.*; converting, *ppr.* [L. *convertere*, to turn round, turn toward; from *com-*, together, and *vertere*, to turn.]

1. to turn; to move. [Obs.]

2. to change or turn into another substance or form; to transform; to transmute; as, to *convert* steam into water, or water into ice.

3. to change from one religion, doctrine, opinion, course, or action to another.

4. to exchange for something equal in value.

5. in finance, to change (a security, currency, etc.) from one form into an equivalent of another form.

6. in football, to score (an extra point) after a touchdown, as by kicking a field goal with a place kick.

7. in law, (a) to appropriate and use (another's property) unlawfully; (b) to change (property) from real to personal, or the reverse.

8. in logic, to change (a proposition) by transposing the subject and predicate.

9. to turn into another language. [Obs.]

cŏn·vẽrt′, *v.i.* to turn or be changed; to undergo a change.

The love of wicked friends *converts* to fear;
That fear, to hate. —Shak.

çon′vẽrt, *n.* 1. a person who is converted, as to a religion.

2. a lay friar or brother. [Obs.]

çon·vẽr·tend′, *n.* something to be converted; specifically, in logic, a proposition to undergo, or that has undergone, conversion.

cŏn·vẽrt′ẽr, *n.* 1. one who or that which converts.

2. a furnace for converting pig iron into steel in the Bessemer process.

3. a device for transforming electrical energy, as from direct to alternating current.

4. a wholesale textile dealer who buys gray goods and has them dyed and finished at his own risk and expense.

Also spelled *convertor*.

cŏn·vẽrt·i·bil′i·ty, *n.* the quality or condition of being convertible.

cŏn·vẽrt′i·ble, *a.* 1. that may be converted; transmutable; transformable.

Minerals are not *convertible* into another species, though of the same genus.
—Harvey.

2. so much alike that one may be used for another; interchangeable.

cŏn·vẽrt′i·ble, *n.* 1. a thing that can be converted.

2. an automobile with a top of canvas, etc. that can be folded back.

cŏn·vẽrt′i·ble·ness, *n.* convertibility.

cŏn·vẽrt′i·bly, *adv.* in a convertible manner.

çon′vẽrt·ite, *n.* 1. a convert. [Archaic.]

2. a reformed prostitute; a magdalen. [Archaic.]

çon′vex, *a.* [L. *convexus*, vaulted, arched; pp. of *convehere*, to bring together; from *com-*, together, and *vehere*, to bring.] having a surface that curves outward, like the surface of a sphere: opposed to *concave*; as, a *convex* mirror or lens.

PLANO-CONVEX LENS

çon′vex, *n.* a convex body, surface, lens, etc.

çon′vexed (-vext) *a.* made convex.

çon·vex′ed·ly, *adv.* in a convex form.

çon·vex′ed·ness, *n.* convexity.

çon·vex′i·ty, *n.*; *pl.* **çon·vex′i·ties,** 1. a convex body, surface, lens, etc.

2. the state or quality of being convex.

çon′vex·ly, *adv.* in a convex form; as, a body *convexly* conical.

çon′vex·ness, *n.* convexity.

çon·vex′ō-cŏn·çāve′, *a.* 1. convex on one side and concave on the other; having the hollow on the inside corresponding to the convex surface.

2. in optics, designating a lens whose convex face has a greater degree of curvature than its concave face, so that the lens is thickest in the middle.

CONVEXO-CONCAVE LENS

çon·vex′ō-cŏn·vex′, *a.* convex on both sides, as some lenses: also called *double-convex*.

CONVEXO-CONVEX LENS

çon·vex′ō-plāne′, *a.* plano-convex.

cŏn·vey′, *v.t.*; conveyed (-vād′), *pt.*, *pp.*; conveying, *ppr.* [ME. *conveyen*, *conveien*; OFr. *conveier*, to escort, convoy; LL. *conviare*, to accompany on the way; from L. *com-*, together, and *via*, way.]

1. to carry, bear, or transport; to take from one place to another.

There was one *conveyed* out of my house yesterday in this basket. —Shak.

2. to transfer, as property or title to property, from one person to another.

3. to serve as a medium or channel for; to transmit; as, air *conveys* sound; words *convey* ideas.

Full well the busy whisper, circling round,
Convey'd the dismal tidings when he frown'd.
—Goldsmith.

4. to manage; to carry on. [Obs.]

I will *convey* the business as I shall find means. —Shak.

5. to impart; to communicate; to represent in words.

To *convey* our thoughts in ardent and intense phrases. —Addison.

6. to steal. [Obs.]

Convey, the wise it call. Steal!—foh, a fico for the phrase. —Shak.

cŏn·vey′, *v.i.* to play the thief. [Old Slang.]

cŏn·vey′ȧ·ble, *a.* that can be conveyed or transferred.

cŏn·vey′ănce, *n.* 1. the act of conveying; transportation; carriage; transference.

2. the means by which anything is conveyed or transported from one place to another, especially a vehicle.

Bethink you of some *conveyance*.—Shak.

3. (a) the transfer of the ownership of real property from one person to another; (b) the document of such transfer; a deed.

4. the act of removing; removal; conduct; convoy. [Obs.]

Mad'st quick *conveyance* with her good aunt Anne. —Shak.

5. management; artifice; secret practices. [Obs.]

Since Henry's death, I fear there is *conveyance*. —Shak.

cŏn·vey′ăn·cẽr, *n.* a lawyer who draws up deeds, etc. transferring the ownership of real property from one person to another.

cŏn·vey′ăn·cing, *n.* the business of a conveyancer.

cŏn·vey′ẽr, *n.* 1. one who or that which conveys; especially, a mechanical contrivance, as a continuous chain or belt (*conveyer belt*), used to move something from one place to another: also spelled *conveyor*.

2. a tricky fellow; a thief. [Obs.]

cŏn·vi′ci·āte (-vish′i-), *v.t.* to reproach. [Obs.]

çon·vi·cin′i·ty, *n.*; *pl.* **çon·vi·cin′i·ties,** neighborhood; vicinity. [Obs.]

cŏn·vi′cious (-vish′us), *a.* railing; reproaching. [Obs.]

cŏn·viçt′, *v.t.*; convicted, *pt.*, *pp.*; convicting, *ppr.* [L. *convictus*, pp. of *convincere*, to overcome, conquer; from *com-*, intens., and *vincere*, to conquer.]

1. to prove (a person) guilty; as, the evidence *convicts* him of theft.

2. to find or declare (a person) guilty of an offense charged; as, the jury *convicted* him of theft.

3. to bring to the realization of one's guilt, as by the conscience.

4. to confute. [Archaic.]

5. to show by proof or evidence. [Obs.]

cŏn·viçt′, *a.* proved or found guilty. [Obs.]

çon′viçt, *n.* 1. a person proved or found guilty of a crime and sentenced by a law court.

2. a person serving a sentence of confinement, as in a penitentiary.

Syn.—malefactor, culprit, felon, criminal.

cŏn·viçt′i·ble, *a.* capable of being found guilty or convicted.

cŏn·viç′tion, *n.* 1. the act of proving, finding, or determining to be guilty of an offense; specifically, in law, the act of finding or the state of being found guilty of crime by a law court.

2. strong belief.

3. a convincing or being convinced.

çon′viçt·iṣm, *n.* any system of disposition of convicts.

cŏn·viçt′ive, *a.* having power to convince or convict.

cŏn·viçt′ive·ly, *adv.* in a convincing manner.

cŏn·viçt′ive·ness, *n.* power of convicting.

cŏn·viç′tŏr, *n.* [L. *convictor*, from *convivere*, to live together.] a messmate; a table associate. [Archaic.]

cŏn·vince′, *v.t.*; convinced, *pt.*, *pp.*; convincing, *ppr.* [L. *convincere*, to overcome, convict of error; from *com-*, intens., and *vincere*, to conquer.]

1. originally, to overcome or convict.

2. to persuade or satisfy by evidence or argument; to overcome the doubts of; to cause to feel certain; as, to *convince* a man of his errors; to *convince* him of the truth.

Proofs as might enable them to *convince* others. —Atterbury.

Syn.—persuade.—To *convince* a person is to satisfy his understanding as to the truth of a certain statement; to *persuade* him is to influence his feelings or will.

cŏn·vin′cẽr, *n.* one who or that which convinces.

cŏn·vin′ci·ble, *a.* 1. that can be convinced.

2. capable of being disproved or refuted. [Obs.]

cŏn·vin′cing, *a.* [ppr. of *convince*.] persuading by argument or evidence; causing to feel certain.

çŏn·vin′çing·ly, *adv.* in a convincing manner.

çŏn·vin′çing·ness, *n.* the power of convincing.

çŏn·viv′i·ăl, *a.* [L. *convivialis*, from *convivium*, a feast, from *convivere*; from *com-*, together, and *vivere*, to live.]

1. relating to a feast or entertainment; festive.

2. fond of eating, drinking, and good company; social; jovial.

cŏn·viv′i·ăl·ist, *n.* one of convivial habits.

çŏn·viv·i·al′i·ty, *n.*; *pl.* **çŏn·viv·i·al′i·ties,** 1. the quality or condition of being convivial; festivity; sociability.

2. a convivial act or remark.

çŏn·viv′i·ăl·ly, *adv.* in a convivial manner.

çon·vō·çā′tion, *n.* 1. a convoking; a calling together; an assembling by summons.

2. a group of people called together by summons; especially, an ecclesiastical or academic assembly.

3. [C—] in the Church of England, an assembly of the clergy, by their representatives, to consult on ecclesiastical affairs.

Syn.—meeting, assembly, congregation, congress, diet, convention, synod, council.

çon·vō·çā′tion·ăl, *a.* pertaining to a convocation.

çon·vō·çā′tion·ist, *n.* in the Church of England, one who supports Convocation.

çon·vō·çā′tŏr, *n.* 1. a person who orders a convocation.

2. a participant in a convocation.

çŏn·vōke′, *v.t.*; convoked, *pt.*, *pp.*; convoking, *ppr.* [L. *convocare*, to call together; from *com-*, together, and *vocare*, to call.] to call together; to summon to meet.

Syn.—summon, assemble, convene, call, collect, muster.

çon′vō·lūte, çon′vō·lū·ted, *a.* [L. *convolutus*, pp. of *convolvere*, to roll together.] rolled up in the form of a spiral with the coils falling one upon the other; coiled.

çon′vō·lūte, *v.t.* and *v.i.*; convoluted, *pt. pp.*; convoluting, *ppr.* to wind around; to coil.

çon·vō·lū′tion, *n.* 1. a twisting, rolling, or winding together.

O'er the calm sky in *convolution* swift
The feathered eddy floats. —Thomson.

2. a convoluted condition.

3. a fold, twist, or coil of something convoluted.

The *convolutions* of a smooth-lipped shell.
—Wordsworth.

4. any of the irregular folds or ridges on the surface of the brain.

çŏn·volve′, *v.t.*; convolved, *pt.*, *pp.*; convolving, *ppr.* [L. *convolvere*, to roll together.] to roll, coil, or wind together.

çŏn·volve′, *v.i.* to revolve together; to intertwine.

Çon·vol·vū·lā′cē·ae, *n.pl.* [L. *convolvulus*, from *convolvere*, to roll together, and *-aceæ*.] the morning-glory family of twining, trailing, or erect plants with funnel-shaped flowers.

çon·vol·vū·lā′ceous, *a.* of or pertaining to the *Convolvulaceæ*.

çŏn·vol′vū·lin, *n.* a colorless, transparent resin contained in jalap root.

Çŏn·vol′vū·lus, *n.* [L., from **convolvere**, to roll together.]

1. bindweed, a genus of plants, family *Convolvulaceæ*, consisting of slender, twining herbs, with milky juice.

2. [c—] any plant of this or a related genus.

JALAP CONVOLVULUS
(*Exogonium purga*)

çŏn·voy′, *v.t.*; convoyed, *pt.*, *pp.*; convoying, *ppr.* [Fr. *convoyer*; OFr. *convoier*, to escort, convoy; LL. *conviare*, to accompany on the way; from *com-*, with, and *via*, way.]

1. to accompany for protection, by either sea or land; to escort.

2. to convey. [Obs.]

çon′voy, *n.* 1. a protecting force accompanying ships or property on their way from place to place, by either sea or land.

2. the ship, fleet, troops, etc. conducted and protected; that which is convoyed.

3. a convoying or being convoyed.

çŏn·vul′sănt, *a.* causing convulsions.

çŏn·vul′sănt, *n.* anything that produces convulsions.

çŏn·vulse′, *v.t.*; convulsed (-vulst), *pt.*, *pp.*; convulsing, *ppr.* [L. *convulsus*, pp. of *convellere*, to tear up, wrench away; from *com-*, together, and *vellere*, to pluck, pull.]

1. to draw or contract, as the muscular parts of an animal body; to affect by irregular spasms.

2. to shake or disturb violently; to agitate.

Convulsing heaven and earth. —Thomson.

3. to cause to shake with laughter, rage, grief, etc.

Syn.—agitate, disturb, shake.

çŏn·vul′sion, *n.* 1. [*usually in pl.*] a violent and involuntary contraction of the muscles.

2. any violent and irregular motion; a great agitation; tumult; commotion; as, political *convulsions*.

3. a violent fit of laughter.

Syn.—agitation, commotion, tumult, disturbance, turmoil, tremor, perturbation.

çŏn·vul′sion·ăl, *a.* convulsionary. [Rare.]

çŏn·vul′sion·ā·ry, *a.* 1. pertaining to or having convulsions; convulsive.

2. having to do with a convulsionary.

çŏn·vul′sion·ā·ry, *n.*; *pl.* **çŏn·vul′sion·ā·ries,** a person who has convulsions in a religious frenzy.

çŏn·vul′sion·ist, *n.* a convulsionary.

çŏn·vul′sive, *a.* 1. having the nature of a convulsion.

2. having or characterized by convulsions.

3. producing convulsions.

çŏn·vul′sive·ly, *adv.* with violent shaking or agitation; in a convulsive manner.

çō′ny, *n.*; *pl.* **çō′nies,** [ME. *cony, conyng, conig*; OFr. *conin, counin*, from L. *cuniculus*, a rabbit.]

1. a rabbit; especially, the *lepus cuniculus* of Europe.

2. a small animal mentioned in the Bible, probably the hydrax or daman.

The high hills are a refuge for the wild goats;
and the rocks for the *conies*.—Ps. civ. 18.

3. the pika, *lagomys princeps*, a small rodent of Asia and western North America.

4. rabbit fur.

5. a gullible person; a dupe. [Archaic.]

6. in heraldry, the representation of a rabbit used as a bearing.

7. any of various fishes, as the *Epinephelus apua*, or hind, of the West Indies, and, in England, the burbot.

Also spelled *coney*.

çō′ny-çatch, *v.i.* to cheat; to trick. [Obs.]

çō′ny·çatch″ẽr, *n.* a cheat; a swindler. [Obs.]

çoo, *v.i.*; cooed, *pt.*, *pp.*; cooing, *ppr.* [echoic.]

1. to make the soft, murmuring sound of pigeons or doves or a sound like this.

2. to speak gently and lovingly: now only in the phrase *bill and coo*.

çoo, *v.t.* to speak or express gently and lovingly; utter with a coo or coos.

çoo, *n.* 1. the sound made by pigeons or doves.

2. any sound like this.

çoo, *interj.* an expression of surprise, disappointment, irritation, etc. [Brit.]

çō″-ob·li·gor′, *n.* in law, one jointly obligated with another.

çoo′ee, çoo′ey, *n.* [of native echoic origin.] a long, penetrating cry or call of the Australian aborigines and bushmen, used as a means of attracting attention or signaling.

çoo′ee, çoo′ey, *v.i.*; cooeed *or* cooeyed, *pt.*, *pp.*; cooeeing *or* cooeying, *ppr.* to call *cooee*, as a signal or to attract attention.

çoo′ing, *a.* uttering a low sound, as a dove.

çook, *n.* one whose occupation is to prepare food for eating.

çook, *v.t.*; cooked (kookt), *pt.*, *pp.*; cooking, *ppr.* [ME. *coken*, from L. *coquere*, to cook.]

1. to prepare (food) for eating, by boiling, roasting, baking, broiling, frying, etc.

2. to subject to heat or to some treatment suggestive of a heating process.

3. to tamper with; to falsify. [Brit. Colloq.]

4. to spoil; to ruin. [Slang.]

to cook up; (a) to concoct; to devise; (b) to devise fraudulently. [Colloq.]

çook, *v.i.* 1. to act as cook; to do the work of a cook; as, to *cook* for a living.

2. to undergo cooking; to be cooked.

3. to spoil; to ruin. [Slang.]

what's cooking? what's happening? [Slang.]

çook, *v.t.* to pitch; to throw. [Brit. Dial.]

çook, *v.i.* to make the noise of the cuckoo. [Rare.]

çook′book, *n.* a book containing directions for cooking, recipes for various dishes, and other information for the preparation of food.

çook′ee, *n.* an assistant to the cook in a lumber camp. [Dial.]

çook′ẽr, *n.* 1. a stove for cooking.

2. a container in which food is cooked.

çook′ẽr·y, *n.*; *pl.* **çook′ẽr·ies,** 1. the art or practice of preparing food for eating.

2. cooked dishes; cooking. [Rare.]

3. a place for cooking.

çook′ey, çook′ie, *n.* same as *cooky*.

çook′house, *n.* a place for cooking, as a ship's galley.

çook′ing, *a.* of or pertaining to cookery; as, a *cooking* utensil.

çook′ing, *n.* the art or process of preparing food for eating; cookery.

çook′māid, *n.* a maid who helps a cook.

çook′room, *n.* a room for cooking; a kitchen; a ship's galley or caboose.

çook′shop, *n.* an eating house; a place where cooked food is sold.

çook′stōve, *n.* a stove for cooking.

çook′y, *n.*; *pl.* **çook′ies,** [D. *koekje*, dim. of *koek*, a cake.]

1. a thin, crisp cake, usually sugared or spiced and cut in fancy or circular shapes before baking.

2. a bun. [Scot.]

çool, *a.*; *comp.* cooler; *superl.* coolest, [ME. *cool, cole*; AS. *col*, cool, from *calan*, to be cold.]

1. moderately cold; neither warm nor very cold; as, *cool* winds, *cool* water.

2. (a) not excited; calm; composed; as, *cool* in an emergency; (b) marked by control of the emotions; restrained; as, *cool* jazz; (c) [Slang.] emotionally uninvolved; uncommitted; dispassionate.

3. impudent in a deliberate or bold way.

4. tending to reduce discomfort in warm or hot weather; as, a *cool* dress.

5. showing indifference or dislike; as, a *cool* manner.

6. without exaggeration; as, he lost a *cool* million. [Colloq.]

7. not suggesting warmth: said of colors in the blue-green end of the spectrum.

8. very good, pleasing, etc.; excellent. [Slang.]

Syn.—calm, dispassionate, self-possessed, composed, frigid, impudent, cold, fresh.

çool, *adv.* in a cool manner.

to play it cool; to exercise strict control over one's emotions; stay aloof, unenthusiastic, or uncommitted. [Slang.]

çool, *v.t.*; cooled, *pt.*, *pp.*; cooling, *ppr.* 1. to allay heat in; to make cool or cold; to reduce the temperature of; as, ice *cools* water.

Send Lazarus, that he may dip the tip of his
finger in water, and *cool* my tongue.
—Luke xvi. 24.

2. to moderate the excitement or intensity of; to allay, as passion of any kind; to calm or abate; to moderate; as, to *cool* his ire.

to cool one's heels; to wait long and tediously. [Colloq.]

çool, *v.i.* to become cool.

to cool off; (a) to calm down; (b) to lose enthusiasm, interest, etc.

çool, *n.* a cool place, time, thing, part, etc.; as, the *cool* of the morning or evening.

çool′ănt, *n.* a substance, usually a fluid, used to remove heat, as from a nuclear reactor, an internal-combustion engine, molten metal, etc.

çool′ẽr, *n.* 1. anything which cools, as a refreshing drink.

2. any vessel, receptacle, or apparatus in which liquids or other things are cooled; as, a water *cooler*.

3. a prison; a jail. [Slang.]

çoo′ley, çoo′lie, *n.* same as *coulee*.

çool′-head″ed, *a.* mentally calm; having a temper not easily excited; free from passion.

çool″head′ed·ness, *n.* the state or quality of being cool-headed.

Çool′idge (-ij) **tūbe,** [after W. D. *Coolidge*, American physicist who invented it.] a vacuum tube for the generation of X rays: a spiral, incandescent tungsten filament and a massive tungsten anode generate the rays, the hardness of which depends on the speed with which the cathode electrons strike the anode or target.

çoo′lie, *n.* [Hind. *qūlī*, hired servant.]

1. in the Orient, an unskilled native laborer.

2. a person doing heavy labor for little pay, especially one transported from the Orient.

çool′ing, *a.* that which cools and refreshes; as, a *cooling* drink.

cooling card; a setback; hence, figuratively, something to dampen one's hopes. [Obs.]

çool·ing-off′ pē′ri·ŏd, a period of time required to pass before strike action may begin.

çool′ish, *a.* somewhat cool.

çool′ly, *adv.* 1. without heat or extreme cold; moderately.

2. in a cool or indifferent manner; not cordially; without passion or ardor.

3. without haste; calmly; deliberately.
4. nonchalantly; audaciously; impudently. [Colloq.]

çool'ness, *n.* 1. a moderate degree of cold; a temperature between cold and heat; as, the *coolness* of the summer evening; also, a lack of passion, ardor, or zeal; indifference; lack of affection or cordiality; as, they parted with *coolness*.
2. calmness; deliberateness; self-possession.
3. quiet and unabashed impudence. [Colloq.]

çool tank'ärd, an old English spiced beverage made with ale, wine, etc.

çool'weed, *n.* clearweed.

çool'wŏrt, *n.* false miterwort, a perennial herb of the United States.

çoo'ly, *n.*; *pl.* **çoo'lieș,** same as *coolie*.

çoom, *n.* dust; refuse; soot. [Scot. and Brit. Dial.]

çoomb (kөөm), *n.* [ME. *coomb*; AS. *cumb.*] a deep, narrow valley; a ravine: also spelled *combe, comb.* [Dial.]

çoon, *n.* 1. racoon. [Colloq.]
2. a Negro: vulgar term of prejudice and contempt. [Slang.]

çoon'çan, *n.* [var. of *conquian.*] a card game like rummy, for two players.

çoon's āġe, an indefinitely long time. [Colloq.]

çoon'tie, çoon'ty, *n.* [Am. Ind.] any of several tropical American plants of the cycad family, somewhat resembling ferns or palms, with large, dark-green, feathery leaves and underground trunks and roots that yield a starch.

co-op', co·öp' (kō-op' *or* kō'op), *n.* a co-operative society, store, rooming house, etc. [Colloq.]

çoop, *n.* [ME. *coop, coppe,* a cup; D. *kuip,* a tub; M.H.G. *kuofe*; G. *kufe,* a coop, tub; L. *copa, cupa,* a tub, vat, cask; Gr. *kypē*; Sans. *kūpa,* a pit, well, vat.]
1. a small cage or pen for poultry, small animals, etc.
2. a place of confinement.

çoop, *v.t.*; cooped, *pt., pp.*; cooping, *ppr.* 1. to put in a coop; to confine in or as in a coop: usually followed by *up* or *in*.

They are *cooped in* close by the laws of the country. —Locke.

2. to repair, as a cooper. [Obs.]
Syn.—cage, enclose, imprison, confine.

çoop, *v.i.* to sleep while on duty: said of a policeman. [Slang.]

çoo·pee', *n.* coupee. [Obs.]

çoop'ēr, *n.* 1. one whose occupation is to make and repair barrels and casks of various kinds.
2. an English beverage, consisting of one half stout and one half porter.

çoop'ēr, *v.t.*; coopered, *pt., pp.*; coopering, *ppr.* to do the work of a cooper upon; to make or repair (casks, barrels, etc.).

çoop'ēr·āġe, *n.* 1. the work or business of a cooper.
2. the price paid for such work.
3. the workshop of a cooper.

çō-op'ēr·ānt, *a.* acting together; co-operating: also written *coöperant, cooperant.*

çō-op'ēr·āte, *v.i.*; co-operated, *pt., pp.*; co-operating, *ppr.* [LL. *cooperatus,* pp. of *cooperari* to work together, *co-,* with, and *operari,* to work, from *opus, operis,* work.]
1. to act or operate jointly with another or others, to the same end; to work or labor with mutual efforts to promote the same object.
2. to act together; to unite in producing an effect: said of things.
3. to practice economic co-operation.
Also written *coöperate, cooperate.*

çō-op·ēr·ā'tion, *n.* 1. the act of working or operating together to one end; joint operation; concurrent effort or labor.
2. the association of a number of people in an enterprise, as an industry, credit union, consumers' organization, etc., the benefits or profits of which are shared by all the members.
Also written *coöperation, cooperation.*

çō-op'ēr·ȧ·tive, *a.* 1. operating jointly to the same end; inclined to co-operate.
2. designating or of an organization, as for the production or marketing of goods, owned collectively by members who share in its benefits.
Also written *coöperative, cooperative.*

çō-op'ēr·ȧ·tive, *n.* 1. a co-operator.
2. a co-operative society or enterprise; also, a member of such a society or enterprise.

çō-op'ēr·ȧ·tive plan, in education, a system of instruction in which the student's time is divided between classroom work and outside occupation.

çō-op'ēr·ā·tŏr, *a.* 1. one who works jointly with others to promote the same end.
2. a member of a co-operative society.
Also written *coöperator, cooperator.*

çoop'ēr·ing, *n.* the making or repairing of casks, barrels, etc.; cooperage.

çoop'ēr·y, *n.*; *pl.* **çoop'ēr·ieș,** the work, shop, or product of a cooper.

çō-opt', *v.t.*; co-opted, *pt., pp.*; co-opting, *ppr.* [L. *cooptare,* to choose, elect; *co-, cum,* with, and *optare,* to choose.]
1. to add (a person or persons) to a group by vote of those already members.
2. to appoint as an associate.
3. to persuade or lure (an opponent) to join one's own system, party, etc.
Also written *coöpt.*

ço-op'tāte, *v.t.* to co-opt; to select by common choice: also written *coöptate.* [Rare.]

çō-op·tā'tion, *n.* 1. adoption; assumption. [Obs.]
2. a co-opting or being co-opted; the election of a person to some body by those who are already members.
Also written *coöptation.*

çō-op'tȧ·tive, *a.* co-opting: also written *coöptative.*

çō-ọr·dāin', *v.t.*; co-ordained, *pt., pp.*; co-ordaining, *ppr.* to appoint together with another: also written *coördain.*

çō-ọr'di·nāte, *a.* [ML. *coordinatus,* pp. of *coordinare,* to arrange together; *co-,* with, and *ordinare,* from *ordo* (*ordinis*), order.]
1. being of equal order, or of the same rank or degree; not subordinate; as, a compound sentence has two or more *co-ordinate* clauses.
2. pertaining to or involving co-ordination or co-ordinates.

çō-ọr'di·nāte, *v.t.*; co-ordinated, *pt., pp.*; co-ordinating, *ppr.* 1. to place in the same rank; to make of equal value.
2. to bring into proper and relative order; to harmonize; to adjust.

The founders of universities held the theory that . . . the business of philosophy was to interpret and *co-ordinate* these two. —Huxley.

3. to design as co-ordinates; as, color-*co-ordinated* luggage.

çō-ọr'di·nāte, *v.i.* to become co-ordinate; to function harmoniously.

çō-ọr'di·nāte, *n.* 1. a person or thing of the same rank with another, and working or employed to the same end.
2. [*pl.*] articles of clothing, luggage, etc. designed to form a pleasing ensemble when worn or used together.
3. in mathematics, any magnitude of a system of two or more magnitudes used to define the position of a point, line, curve, or plane.
geographical co-ordinates; latitude and longitude; also, height above sea level, regarded as a third co-ordinate.
spherical co-ordinates; the distances from two great circles of a sphere which locate a point on its surface; quantities corresponding to latitude and longitude.
trilinear co-ordinates; the distances of a point from the sides of a triangle, called the fixed triangle of reference.

çō-ọr'di·nāte·ly, *adv.* in a co-ordinate manner: also written *coördinately, coordinately.*

çō-ọr'di·nāte·ness, *n.* the state of being co-ordinate; equality of rank and authority: also written *coördinateness, coordinateness.*

çō-ọr'di·nāt·ing çŏn·junç'tion, a conjunction that connects co-ordinate words, phrases, or clauses (e.g., *and, but, for, or, nor, yet*).

çō-ọr·di·nā'tion, *n.* 1. a co-ordinating or being co-ordinated.
2. the state or relation of being co-ordinate; harmonious adjustment or functioning, as of muscles in producing complex movements.
Also written *coördination, coordination.*

çō-ọr'di·nā·tive, *a.* indicating co-ordination.

çō-ọr'di·nā·tŏr, *n.* a person or thing that co-ordinates: also written *coördinator, coordinator.*

çoo'rong, *n.* a tree of the pine family found in Australia, the *Frenela robusta.* Its wood is used in cabinetmaking.

Çoos, *n.* [from native name.] any of several Penutian languages.

çō-os'si·fȳ, *v.i.*; co-ossified, *pt., pp.*; co-ossifying, *ppr.* [*co-,* and Fr. *ossifier,* from L. *os* (*ossis*), a bone.] to become united by ossification; to form one bone; as, several bony elements *co-ossify* in man to form the sphenoid bone.

çoot, *n.*; *pl.* **çoots** or **çoot,** [ME. *coote*; M. D. *koet.*]
1. a water fowl of the genus *Fulica,* found in most parts of the world. The common coot has an extension of the culmen of the bill, a black body, and webbed toes. The common European and Asiatic species is the bald coot, the *Fulica atra.* The North American coot is recognized as a distinct species, the *Fulica americana.*

COMMON COOT (*Fulica atra*)

2. a northern sea duck of the genus *Œdemia,* the scoter.
3. a foolish person; a dolt. [Colloq.]

çoot'ēr, *n.* any of various tortoises, especially the common box tortoise, the snapping turtle, and a fresh-water terrapin of Florida, the *Preudemus concinna.*

çoot'foot, *n.* the phalarope.

çoo·thāy', *n.* [Ind. name.] a striped satin cloth manufactured in India.

çoo'tie, *n.* [Brit. World War I army slang; said to be seaman's term from Polynesian *kutu,* parasitic insect.] a louse. [Slang.]

çop, *n.* [ME. *cop,* top, head; AS. *cop,* top, summit.]
1. the top, as of a hill, or the crest, as of a bird's head.
2. the conical ball of thread or yarn coiled round a spindle of a wheel or spinning frame: sometimes called *coppin.*
3. the tube used in a spinning machine, on which silk thread or yarn is wound.
4. a merlon or portion of a battlement.

çop, *v.t.*; copped, *pt., pp.*; copping, *ppr.* [from north Brit. dial. form of obs. *cap,* to seize; prob. from OFr. *caper,* from L. *capere,* to take.] to seize; to steal. [Slang.]

çop, *n.* a policeman. [Slang.]

çō'pȧ, *n.* 1. a tropical American tree, *Protium panamense,* yielding a gum.
2. the horizontal parts of the crown of a Panama hat.
3. in the southwestern U. S., a landmark.

çō·pāi'bȧ, çō·pāi'vȧ, *n.* [Sp. and Port. from the Braz. name.] a resin obtained from certain South American plants, having a whitish or pale yellowish color, an agreeable smell, and a somewhat bitter, pungent taste. It is used in medicine as a stimulant, diuretic, etc. Written also *copayva* and *capivi.*

çō·pāi'viç, *a.* derived from copaiba.

çō·pāi'yẹ wood (-yā), [*copaiye,* native name.] the wood obtained from a tree native to British Guiana, the *Vochysia guianensis.*

çō'păl, *n.* [Sp. from Mex. *copalli,* a generic name of resins.] a hard resin obtained from several different tropical trees, used in varnishes.

çō·pal'chē, çō·pal'chi, *n.* [native name.]
1. a Brazilian tree, the bark of which has medicinal properties, the *Strychnos pseudoquina.*
2. a shrub native to Mexico, the *Croton niveus*: its bark is used medicinally.

çō·păl·if'ēr·ous, *a.* [*copal,* and L. *ferre,* to bear.] productive of copal.

çō'păl·in, çō'păl·ine, *n.* a fossil resin found in roundish lumps in the blue clay of Highgate Hill, London, resembling copal resin in appearance and some of its characteristics: called also *copalite.*

çō'pälm (-päm), *n.* [perh. from *copal,* and *palm* (because of the palmate leaves of the sweet gum tree).]
1. a yellowish, aromatic resin obtained from the sweet gum tree.
2. the tree.

çō·pär'ce·nā·ry, *n.*; *pl.* **çō·pär'ce·nā·rieș,**
1. in law, partnership in inheritance; joint heirship; joint right of succession or joint succession to an estate of inheritance.
2. joint partnership or ownership.

çō·pär'ce·nā·ry, *a.* of coparcenary or coparceners.

çō·pär'ce·nēr, *n.* [*co-,* and Fr. *parcener, parcenier,* from L. *partitio,* a sharing, distribution; *pars,* a part.] in law, a coheir; one who has an equal portion with another or others in the inheritance of an estate.

çō·pär'ce·ny, *n.* coparcenary.

çō·pärt', *v.t.* to share. [Obs.]

çō·pärt'ment, *n.* a compartment. [Obs.]

çō·pärt′nẽr, *n.* [*co-*, and *partner*, for *parcener*, influenced by *part.*] one who has a share with one or more persons in any enterprise; a partner; an associate.

çō·pärt′nẽr·ship, *n.* the state of having a joint share or concern in some common undertaking or interest; partnership.

çō·pärt′nẽr·y, *n.* the state of being copartners in any undertaking. [Rare.]

çō·pā′tri·ŏt, *n.* a joint patriot; a compatriot.

çōpe, *n.* [ME. *cope*; OFr. *cape*; from L. *cappa*, *capa*, a cape, cope.]
1. anything used as a covering for the head. [Obs.]
2. an ecclesiastical vestment resembling a cape, worn by priests at certain ceremonies.
3. anything spread or extended over the head, as the arch of the sky, the roof of a house, the arch over a door, etc.
4. in founding, the top part of a mold.

çōpe, *v.t.*; coped, *pt., pp.*; coping, *ppr.* to cover with or as with a cope; to furnish with a coping.

çōpe, *v.i.* in architecture, to form a cope; to bend, as an arch or vault.

çōpe, *v.t.* and *v.i.* [ME. *copen*, to buy, pay for, from D. *koopen*, to buy.] to barter; to reward. [Obs.]

çōpe, *v.t.* [ME. *copen*, from OFr. *coup*, *colp*; LL. *colpus*, a blow, stroke, from *colaphus*, Gr. *kolaphos*, from *kolaptein*, to peck, strike.]
1. to meet; to engage against; to match against. [Archaic.]
I love to *cope* him in these sullen fits. —Shak.
2. to requite. [Obs.]
3. to cope with. [Brit. Colloq.]

çōpe, *v.i.* 1. to strive or contend (*with*) successfully or on equal terms; to be a match for.
Their generals have not been able to *cope with* the troops of Athens. —Addison.
2. to meet, encounter, or have to do (*with*). [Archaic.]
Host *coped with* host, dire was the din of war. —Philips.

çōpe, *v.t.* to pare (the beak or talons of a hawk).

çōpe chiṣ′el, a chisel with a narrow blade, used to cut grooves.

çō′peck, *n.* [Russ. *kopieika*, from *kopati*, to cut, dig.] a kopeck, a small Russian coin.

çōped (kōpt), *a.* covered with a cope.

Çōp·ē·lā′tae, Çōp·ē·lā′tȧ, *n.pl.* [L., from Gr. *kōpēlatēs*, a rower.] in zoology, an order of tunicates: usually called *Larvalia*.

çōpe′măn, *n.* a merchant; a peddler; a hawker. [Obs.]

çō·pen·hā′gen blūe, [after *Copenhagen*, Denmark.] a dull, light blue.

çō′pē·pod, *a.* pertaining or belonging to the order *Copepoda*.

çō′pē·pod, *n.* a crustacean of the *Copepoda*.

Çō·pep′ō·dȧ, *n.pl.* [L., from Gr. *kōpē*, an oar, and *pous*, *podos*, a foot.] an order of very small fresh-water and marine crustaceans.

çōp′ẽr, *n.* [from D. *koopen*, to buy, bargain.] a peddler; a seller. [Brit.]

Çō·pẽr′ni·căn, *a.* pertaining to Copernicus, or his astronomical system.

Çō·pẽr′ni·çăn sys′tem, the theory of Copernicus that the planets revolve around the sun and that the turning of the earth on its axis accounts for the apparent rising and setting of the stars: basis of modern astronomy.

çōpes′māte, *n.* a friend; an associate or partner. [Obs.]

çōpe′stōne, *n.* [AS. *cop*, top, summit, and Eng. *stone*.]
1. the top stone of a wall or building; the stone in or for a coping.
2. a culmination; a finishing stroke.

çō·phō′sis, *n.* [L., from Gr. *kōphōsis*, deafness, from *kōphos*, deaf.] deafness; inability to hear.

çop′i·ȧ·ble, *a.* capable of being copied.

çō′pi·ȧ·pīte, *n.* [from *Copiapo*, Chile, where it is found, and *-ite.*] a hydrated iron sulfate, found massive or in crystalline scales. Also called *yellow copperas* and *misy*.

çop′i·ẽr, *n.* one who copies; one who writes or transcribes from an original or form; a transcriber; also, an imitator.

çō′pī·lŏt, *n.* the assistant pilot of an aircraft.

çōp′ing, *n.* [from fig. use of *cope* (a cloak).] the top course or cover of a wall, usually made sloping to carry off the water.

çōp′ing saw, a saw with a narrow blade in a U-shaped frame, for cutting curved outlines.

çō′pi·ous, *a.* [ME. *copious*, from L. *copiosus*, plentiful, from *copia*, abundance.]
1. abundant; plentiful; in great quantities; full; ample; furnishing full supplies.
The tender heart is peace,
And kindly pours its *copious* treasures forth.
—Thomson.
2. showing or employing an abundance of words, ideas, etc.; wordy; profuse or diffuse; as, a *copious* argument.
Syn.—abundant, plenteous, rich, fruitful, ample, overflowing, full.

çō′pi·ous·ly, *adv.* 1. abundantly; plentifully; in large quantities.
2. largely; fully; amply; diffusely.
The remains of antiquity have been *copiously* described by travelers. —Addison.

çō′pi·ous·ness, *n.* 1. abundance; plenty; great quantity; full supply.
2. diffusiveness of style or manner of treating a subject; as, the *copiousness* of Tolstoy.

çop′ist, *n.* a copier. [Obs.]

çō·plăn′ăr, *a.* in mathematics, lying or situated in the same plane: said of figures.

çop′land, *n.* a piece of ground terminating in a cop or acute angle.

çō·pol′y·mẽr, *n.* in chemistry, a compound produced by copolymerization.

çō·pol″y·mẽr·i·zā′tion, *n.* a process resembling polymerization but in which unlike molecules are arranged in alternate sequence in a chain.

çō·pol′y·mẽr·īze, *v.t.* and *v.i.* to subject to or undergo copolymerization.

çō·pōr′tion, *n.* equal share. [Obs.]

çopped (kopt), *a.* [ME. *cop*; AS. *cop*, a summit, head.] rising to a point or head; peaked; conical.

çop′pel, *n.* and *v.* same as *cupel*.

çop′pẽr, *n.* [ME. *coper*; LL. *cuper*, *cuprum*, contr. of *cyprium*, in *Cyprium æs*, Cyprian brass, from Gr. *Kyprios*, the island where the best copper was produced.]
1. a reddish-brown, malleable, ductile, metallic element that is an excellent conductor of electricity and heat; symbol, Cu; atomic weight, 63.54; atomic number, 29.
2. a thing made of copper.
3. a large boiler or container, now often made of iron.
4. a small coin of copper or bronze, as a penny.
My friends filled my pockets with *coppers*. —Franklin.
5. the color of copper; reddish brown.
6. in faro, a coin or object resembling a coin, used to copper a card.
7. a butterfly, the copperwing.

çop′pẽr, *a.* 1. made of copper; as, a *copper* wire.
2. copper-colored; reddish-brown.

çop′pẽr, *v.t.*; coppered, *pt., pp.*; coppering, *ppr.*
1. to cover with copper.
2. in faro, to denote (the card a player wishes to bet against) by placing a chip or other token upon such a card; to bet against.

çop′pẽr, *n.* [prob. from *cop* (to seize).] a policeman. [Slang.]

çop′pẽr·ȧh, *n.* copra.

çop′pẽr·ȧs, *n.* [ME. *coperose*; OFr. *couperose*; from L. *cupri*, genit. of *cuprum*, copper, and *rosa*, rose.] ferrous sulfate, $FeSO_4 \cdot 7H_2O$, a green, crystalline compound used in dyeing, the making of ink, etc.

çop′pẽr bȧ·ril′lȧ, a native concentrate of copper.

çop′pẽr-bel″ly, *n.* the common water snake of America.

çop′pẽr-bot″tŏmed, *a.* having a bottom covered with or made of copper.

çop′pẽr-fāced, *a.* faced or covered with copper, as some type.

çop′pẽr-fȧs″tened (-nd), *a.* fastened with copper bolts: said of ship planking.

çop′pẽr·finch, *n.* same as *chaffinch*.

çop′pẽr·head (-hed), *n.* 1. a poisonous snake, *Ancistrodon contortrix*, with a copper-colored head, found in North America: it is related to the rattlesnake but has no rattles.
2. [C-] a Northerner who sympathized with the South at the time of the Civil War: contemptuous and hostile term used in the North.

COPPERHEAD
(24 in. long)

çop′pẽr·ing, *n.* a copper covering; the act of facing or covering with copper.

çop′pẽr·ish, *a.* containing or like copper. [Rare.]

çop′pẽr nick′el, niccolite.

çop′pẽr·plāte, *n.* 1. a flat piece of copper on which lettering or a design is engraved, the sunken lines being filled with prepared ink.
2. a print or engraving made from a copperplate.
3. copperplate printing or engraving.

çop′pẽr pȳ′rītes, copper-iron sulfide, $CuFeS_2$; chalcopyrite.

çop′pẽr rōse, the scarlet field poppy: also written *coprose*, *cuprose*. [Brit. Dial.]

çop′pẽr·smith, *n.* one whose occupation is making copper utensils.

çop′pẽr sul′fāte, a blue, crystalline substance, $CuSO_4 \cdot 5H_2O$, which effloresces and turns white when heated; cupric sulfate; blue vitriol: used in making pigments, germicides, electric batteries, etc.

çop′pẽr·wing, *n.* a butterfly of the family *Lycænidæ*.

çop′pẽr·wŏrks, *n.*; *pl.* **çop′pẽr·wŏrks,** a place where copper is wrought or manufactured.

çop′pẽr·wŏrm, *n.* any of various insects, as (a) the teredo; (b) the clothes moth; (c) the itch mite.

çop′pẽr·y, *a.* 1. mixed with copper; containing copper, or made of copper.
2. like copper, as in color.

çop′pice, çopse, *n.* [OFr. *copeiz*, wood newly cut, from *coper*, *copper*, to cut, from *cop*, *colp*; LL. *colpus*, from *colaphos*, Gr. *kolaphos*, a blow, from *kolaptein*, to peck, strike.]
1. a thicket of small trees or shrubbery.
2. wood cut at certain times for fuel or other purposes.

çop′pice, *v.t.*; coppiced, *pt., pp.*; coppicing, *ppr.* to cut back, so as to form a coppice.

çop′pin, *n.* a cone of thread; a cop.

çop′ple, *n.* an elevation; a conical hill.

çop′ple·çrown, *n.* 1. a tuft of feathers on the head of a fowl.
2. a hen having such a crest.

çop′pled, *a.* [from *copple*, dim. of *cop*, a hill, summit.] rising to a point; conical. [Obs.]

çop′ple·stōne, *n.* a cobblestone. [Obs.]

çopps, *n.* a coppice. [Obs.]

çō′prȧ, *n.* [Malay *koppara.*] the dried kernel of the coconut, from which coconut oil is extracted: also *cobra*, *coprah*, *copperah*.

çō·prē′mi·ȧ, çō·prae′mi·ȧ, *n.* [L., from Gr. *kopros*, dung, and *haima*, blood.] blood poisoning caused by the absorption of fecal matter.

çop′rō-, [from Gr. *kopros*, dung.] a combining form meaning *dung*, *excrement*, *feces*, as in *copro*lite: also, before a vowel, *copr-*.

çop′rō·līte, *n.* [*copro-*, and *-lite.*] fossilized excrement of animals.

çop·rō·lit′iç, *a.* containing or resembling coprolites.

çop·rol′ō·ġy, *n.* [*copro-*, and -logy.] the study or treatment of pornography in art and literature.

çō·proph′ȧ·găn, *n.* a dung-eating beetle of the *Coprophagi*.

Çō·proph′ȧ·ġī, *n.pl.* [L., from Gr. *koprophagos*; *kopros*, dung, and *phagein*, to eat.] a family of lamellicorn beetles, which live in and upon the dung of animals.

çō·proph′ȧ·gous, *a.* feeding on excrement.

çop·rō·phil′i·ȧ, *n.* [*copro-*, and *-philia.*]
1. in psychology, attraction to feces.
2. preoccupation with obscenity; fondness for pornography.

çō·proph′i·lous, *a.* growing from or upon dung, as certain fungi.

çop′rōṣe, *n.* [Fr.] for the copper rose.

çops, *n.* the hook for connecting parts of a harrow. [Brit. Dial.]

çopse, *n.* a coppice.

çopse, *v.t.*; copsed, *pt., pp.*; copsing, *ppr.* to coppice.

çopse′wood, *n.* coppice.

çops′y, *a.* having a copse or copses.

Çopt, *n.* [LL. *Cophti*; Ar. *Qobt*, *Kibti*, probably from *-gypt* in Gr. *Aigyptos*, Egypt.]
1. a native of Egypt descended from the ancient inhabitants of that country.
2. a member of the Coptic Church.

Çop′tiç, *a.* [L. *Copticus*, from *Cophti*, Copts.]
1. pertaining to the Copts, their language, culture, etc.
2. of the Coptic Church.

Çop′tiç, *n.* the ancient Hamitic language of the Copts, now used only in the ritual of the Coptic Church; New Egyptian.

Çop′tiç Church, the native Christian church of Egypt and, at one time, of Ethiopia.

çop′ū·lȧ, *n.*; *pl.* **çop′ū·lȧṣ,** [L. *copula*, a band, link, for *coapula*; *co-*, together, and *apere*, to join.]
1. something that connects or links together.
2. a bone, cartilage, ligament, etc. connecting parts of the body.

3. in grammar, a weakened verbal form, especially a form of *be* or any similar verb, as *seem, appear*, etc., which links a subject with a predicate complement.

4. in logic, the connecting link between the subject and predicate of a proposition.

5. in law, sexual intercourse.

çop′ū·lãr, *a.* of, or having the nature of, a copula.

çop′ū·lāte, *a.* joined. [Obs.]

çop′ū·lāte, *v.t.* [L. *copulatus*, pp. of *copulare*, to unite, couple, from *copula*, a band, bond.] to unite. [Obs.]

çop′ū·lāte, *v.i.*; copulated, *pt., pp.*; copulating, *ppr.* to unite in sexual intercourse.

çop·ū·lā′tion, *n.* 1. a joining together; coupling.

2. the state of being coupled.

3. the act of copulating.

çop′ū·lā·tive, *a.* 1. joining together; coupling.

2. involving or comprising connected words or clauses.

3. having the nature of a copula; as, a *copulative* verb.

4. of or for copulating.

çop′ū·lā·tive, *n.* a copulative word.

çop′ū·lā·tive·ly, *adv.* in a copulative manner.

çop′ū·lȧ·tō·ry, *a.* copulative.

çop′y, *n.*; *pl.* **çop′ieș,** [OFr. *copie*, abundance, transcript, copy; ML. *copia*, copious transcript; L. *copia*, plenty; *co-*, together, and *opes*, riches.]

1. abundance. [Obs.]

2. copyhold; also, copyright. [Obs.]

3. a full reproduction or transcription; an imitation of a prototype; one thing like another; a duplicate; as, a *copy* of a letter or work of art.

4. a pattern to be followed in producing a duplicate, or for instruction; a model; as, a penmanship *copy*.

5. any of a number of books, magazines, engravings, etc. having the same composition or printed matter; as, he has two *copies* of *Tom Jones*.

6. a manuscript to be reproduced in printing; as, *copy* for the compositor or lithographer.

7. a size of writing paper measuring 16 x 20 inches.

8. anything that can provide subject matter for a novelist, journalist, etc.

certified or *office copy*; in law, a transcript attested by the officer having legal care of the original.

çop′y, *v.t.* and *v.i.*; copied, *pt., pp.*; copying, *ppr.* [ME. *copien*; OFr. *copier*, from ML. *copiare*, to copy, from *copia*, a copy; L., abundance.]

1. to make a copy or copies of (a piece of writing, etc.); to make a reproduction or imitation of; to reproduce; to transcribe: sometimes with *out*; as, to *copy* a pattern of a machine; to *copy out* a page of a book.

2. to make or do something in imitation of (some thing or person); to imitate; to ape; as, to *copy* the habits of the rich.

çop′y·book, *n.* 1. a book containing examples of penmanship to be imitated by students.

2. a book containing copies, as of accounts.

çop′y·book, *a.* ordinary; trite; commonplace; as, *copybook* maxims.

çop′y boy, a boy who runs errands and carries copy from the writers to the editor in a newspaper office.

çop′y·çat, *n.* a person who habitually imitates or mimics: a child's term.

çop′y desk, the desk in a newspaper office where copy is edited and headlines are written.

çop′y ed′i·tŏr, one who reads and prepares manuscripts for publication.

çop′y·grȧph, *n.* [ML. *copia*, copy, and Gr. *graphein*, to write.] a hectograph.

çop′y·hōld, *n.* in English law, (a) tenure of property proved by a written transcript or record in the rolls of a manorial court; (b) land so held.

çop′y·hōld″ẽr, *n.* 1. in English law, one who is possessed of land in copyhold.

2. a person who reads the manuscript to a proofreader.

3. any device for holding copy on the printer's frame, typesetting machine, or typewriter.

çop′y·ing ink, an ink used in printing or writing which may be reproduced in the copying press.

çop′y·ing pā′pẽr, thin paper for use in a copying press.

çop′y·ing press, a machine used in the duplication of matter produced in copying ink. The paper to receive the duplicate is dampened and pressure applied.

çop′y·ing rib′bŏn, a typewriter ribbon inked with copying ink, to make impressions suitable for reproducing by means of a copying press.

çop′y·ist, *n.* 1. a person who makes written copies; transcriber.

2. a person who imitates; copier.

çop′y·man, *n.* a copy editor.

çop′y·rēad·ẽr, *n.* in journalism, one who reads and edits material presented for publication in a newspaper and sometimes writes the headlines; also, in printing, a copyholder.

çop′y·rīght (-rīt), *n.* the exclusive right to the publication, production, or sale of the rights to a literary, dramatic, musical, or artistic work, or to the use of a manufacturing or merchandising label, granted by law for a definite period of years to an author, composer, artist, distributor, etc. In the United States copyright may be secured for a term of twenty-eight years, renewable only once for another twenty-eight years.

international copyright; an arrangement between different countries giving reciprocal copyright privileges to citizens of such countries as are in the copyright union.

çop′y·rīght, *v.t.*; copyrighted, *pt., pp.*; copyrighting, *ppr.* to protect by copyright; as, a *copyrighted* book.

çop′y·rīght, *a.* protected by copyright.

çop′y·rīght·ẽr, *n.* one who obtains a copyright; a holder of copyright privileges.

çop′y·wrīt·ẽr, *n.* one who writes copy, especially, advertising copy.

coque (kok), *n.* [Fr.] a small loop or bow of ribbon used in trimming.

çōque′lï·çōt (kōk′lē-kō), *n.* [Fr.]

1. the corn poppy.

2. the color of this flower, a mixture of orange and scarlet.

çō·quet′ (-ket′), *v.t.*; coquetted, *pt., pp.*; coquetting, *ppr.* [Fr. *coqueter*, to coquet, flirt, to strut like a cock, from *coquet*, a little cock.] to attempt to attract the notice, admiration, or love of, from vanity; to flirt with. [Rare.]

You are *coquetting* a maid of honor.—Swift.

çō·quet′, *v.i.* 1. to trifle in love; to treat a person with an appearance of favor, but with a design to deceive and disappoint; to flirt: usually said of a woman.

2. to trifle (*with* an idea, etc.); dally.

çō′quet·ry, *n.*; *pl.* **çō′quet·rieș,** attempts to attract admiration, notice, or love, merely from vanity; a trifling in love.

çō·quette′ (-ket′), *n.* [Fr. *coquette*, f. of *coquet*, a beau, flirt, lit., a little cock.]

1. a vain girl or woman who endeavors to attract amorous advances and rejects them when offered; a jilt; a flirt.

A *coquette* and a tinder box are spark-led.
—Pope.

2. one of a group of crested hummingbirds.

çō·quette′, *v.i.* to coquet.

çō·quet′tish, *a.* practicing or displaying coquetry; of, like, or characteristic of a coquette.

çō·quet′tish·ly (kō-ket′ish-ly), *adv.* in a coquettish manner.

çō·quïl′lȧ nut (-kēl′yȧ), [Port. *coquilho*; Sp. *coquillo*, dim. of *coco*, a coconut.] the seed of the palm *Attalea funifera*, one of the coconut group, native to Brazil. The nuts are three or four inches long, oval, of a rich brown color and very hard. The ivorylike shell is used by turners and carvers.

çō·quïl′lō (-kēl′yō), *n.* [Sp., dim. of *coco*, a coconut.] the physic nut.

çō·quim′bīte (-kim′), *n.* an astringent, hydrous iron sulfate, first found in the province of Coquimbo, Chile.

çō·quï′nȧ (-kē′), *n.* [Sp., shellfish, cockle.] a soft, whitish limestone made up of shell fragments and corals. It is used as a building stone, particularly in Florida.

çō·quï′tō (-kē′), *n.* [Sp.] the *Jubæa spectabilis*, a very beautiful palm of Chile, allied to the coconut, growing to the height of forty or fifty feet: its sweet sap and seeds are used for food.

çọr-, com-: used before *r*, as in *cor*rupt.

çọr, *n.* [Heb. *kor*.] an ancient Hebrew measure of capacity containing about 11½ bushels; a homer.

çō′rȧ, *n.* the Arabian gazel.

çọr·ȧ·çī′i·fọrm, *a.* [from Mod. L. *Coracii*, name of the suborder, from Gr. *korax*, raven; and *-form*.] of a kind of tree-dwelling birds that neither perch nor sing, as kingfishers, hornbills, etc.; of nonpasserine birds.

çor′ȧ·cine, *n.* [L. *coracinus*; Gr. *korakinos*, from *korax*, a raven, so named from its black color.] a perchlike fish of the river Nile.

çor′ȧ·cle, *n.* [from W. *corwgl*, a coracle, from *corwg*, a frame, boat.] a boat used in Wales by fishermen, made by covering a wicker frame with leather or oilcloth, being so light as to be easily carried on the back.

FISHERMAN WITH CORACLE

çor′ȧ·çō-, a combining form used in anatomy and medicine to mean *connection with*, or *relation to, the coracoid bone* or *process*; as, *coraco*-acromial, pertaining to the coracoid and acromion.

çor′ȧ·çoid, *n.* [L. *coracoides*, from Gr. *korakœidēs*, like a raven; *korax*, a raven, and *eidos*, form.]

1. a small, sharp process, shaped like a crow's beak, extending from the shoulder blade toward the breastbone in mammals.

2. a bone in birds and reptiles that extends from the shoulder blade to the breastbone.

çor′ȧ·çoid, *a.* 1. shaped like a crow's beak.

2. of or pertaining to a coracoid.

çō·rad′i·çāte, *a.* in linguistics, derived from the same root.

çō′rȧh, *a.* [Hind. *korā*, new, plain.] of the natural color, as silk.

çō′rȧh, *n.* undyed silk; also, a silk handkerchief.

çor′ăl, *n.* [OFr. *coral*; LL. *corallum*; Gr. *korallion*, coral.]

1. the hard, calcareous substance made up of the skeletons of marine coelenterate polyps: reefs, shelves, and atolls of coral are found in tropical seas.

2. any of a number of such animals living in colonies: their skeletons form a stony mass.

3. a piece of coral, especially the red kind used in jewelry.

4. the ovaries of the lobster, resembling coral when boiled.

5. a teething toy for babies, made of coral.

6. coral red.

coral reef; a reef built up by the action of ocean waves which deposit the limestone skeletons of certain types of coral living in warm tropical waters.

CORAL

çor′ăl, *a.* 1. made of coral.

2. resembling coral; coral-red.

çor′ăl-ber″ry, *n.* the shrub *Symphoricarpus vulgaris*, the Indian currant.

çor′ăled, çor′ălled, *a.* having corals.

çor′ăl fish, a fish of the family *Chætodontidæ* or *Pomacentridæ*, frequenting coral reefs.

çor′ăl in′seçt, one of the polyps by which coral is produced: a popular but erroneous name.

çor·ăl·lā′ceous, *a.* resembling coral. [Rare.]

çŏ·ral′li·ăn, *n.* coral rag.

çor·ăl·lif′ẽr·ous, *a.* containing or consisting of coral; producing coral.

çor·al′li·fọrm, *a.* resembling coral.

Çor·ăl·lig′e·nȧ, *n.pl.* same as *Anthozoa*.

çor·ăl·lig′e·nous, *a.* [L. *coralligenus*; *corallum*, coral, and *-genus*, producing.] producing coral.

çor·ăl·lig′ẽr·ous, *a.* same as *coralliferous*.

çor′ăl·lin, *n.* [named from its resemblance to *coral* red; L. *corallinus*, from *corallum*, coral.] a red dye prepared by the action of sulfuric and oxalic acids on phenol: also spelled *coralline*.

Çor·ăl·lī′nȧ, *n.* a genus of rose-spored algae with calcareous jointed fronds.

çor′ăl·līne, *a.* [LL. *corallinus*, coral-red, from *corallum*, coral.] consisting of coral or corallines; containing coral; also, resembling coral in color.

çor'ăl·līne, *n.* 1. any of various algae or seaweeds with rigid, calcareous fronds: so named from their resemblance to coral.

2. any animal related to or resembling the corals, as the zoophytes or *Polyzoa.*

3. same as *corallin.*

çor'ăl·lin·īte, *n.* fossil coral.

çor'ăl·līte, *n.* 1. corallinite.

2. a skeleton of a single polyp of a coral.

çor'ăl·loid, *n.* any organism resembling or related to coral, as several of the *Polyzoa.*

çor'ăl·loid, çor·ăl·loid'ăl, *a.* [LL. *corallum,* coral, and Gr. *eidos,* form.] having the form of coral; branching like coral.

çō·ral'lum, *n.* [LL.] a compound coral.

çor'ăl plant, an East Indian plant, *Jatropha multifida,* having deeply cut foliage and beautiful scarlet flowers.

çor'ăl rag, a limestone formation containing an abundance of petrified corals, found in a division of the Jurassic Period.

çor'ăl-red, *a.* yellowish-red.

çor'ăl red, yellowish red.

çor'ăl·root, *n.* any of a group of brownish orchids with branched, corallike rootstocks and no leaves.

çor'ăl snāke, a small, poisonous snake with coral-red, yellow, and black bands around its body, found in the southeastern United States and subtropical America.

çor'ăl stitch, a stitch in embroidery so worked as to give the appearance of finely branched coral.

çor'ăl sū'maç, poisonwood.

çor'ăl tree, a genus of plants, *Erythrina,* of several species, native to Asia and America. They are all shrubby, flowering plants, adorned chiefly with three-lobed leaves and scarlet spikes of papilionaceous flowers.

çor'ăl wood, a fine-grained cabinet wood, yellow when first cut, but afterward becoming a coral red.

çor'ăl·wŏrt, *n.* coralroot.

çor'ȧ·nach, *n.* see *coronach.*

çō·ran'tō, çō·rant', *n.* a dance, the courante.

çorb, *n.* [O.H.G. *corb,* from L. *corbis,* a basket.] a basket used in coal mines; corf.

çor'băn, *n.* [Heb. *korbān,* an offering, sacrifice, from *karab,* to approach, offer.]

1. in Jewish antiquity, an offering to God, usually to fulfill a vow.

2. a corbana. [Obs.]

3. the host of the Coptic liturgy.

çor·bā'nȧ, *n.* in the early church, the treasury, where money offerings were deposited. [Obs.]

çorbe, *a.* curved. [Obs.]

çor'beil (-bel), *n.* [Fr. *corbeille,* from LL. *corbicula,* dim. of L. *corbis,* a basket.]

1. in fortification, a basket filled with earth and set upon a parapet, to shelter men from the fire of besiegers. [Obs.]

2. in architecture, a carved basket with sculptured flowers and fruits.

çor'bel, *n.* [OFr., dim. of *corb,* raven; L. *corvus,* raven: so called from its beaked shape.]

1. in architecture, a form of bracket used in the Gothic style for the purpose of supporting the ends of timbers, arches, parapets, floors, cornices, etc.

2. a short timber placed lengthwise under a beam or girder.

CORBEL

çor'bel, *v.t.*; corbeled, *pt., pp.*; corbeling, *ppr.* to furnish with a corbel; to form like a corbel.

çor'bel·ing, çor'bel·ling, *n.* 1. the fashioning of corbels; corbel work.

2. a series of corbels.

çor'bel step, a corbiestep.

çor'bel tā'ble, any architectural arrangement requiring the support of a number of corbels.

çor'bet, *n.* a corbel. [Obs.]

Çor·biç'ū·lȧ, *n.* [LL. *corbicula,* a little basket, dim. of *corbis,* a basket.]

1. a genus of bivalve mollusks similar to the clam.

2. [c–] a corbiculum.

çor·biç'ū·lum, *n.*; *pl.* **çor·biç'ū·lȧ,** the pollen basket of a bee.

çor'bie, çor'by, *n.* a crow; a raven. [Scot.]

çor'bie crōw, a corby, especially the carrion crow.

çor'bie gā'ble, a gable with corbiesteps.

çor'bie·step, *n.* [*corbie,* and *step.*] one of a series of steps forming the roofs of certain gabled houses.

Çor'chō·rus, *n.* [L., from Gr. *korchoros,* a wild plant of bitter taste.]

1. a genus of tropical plants of the linden family. The species *capsularis* and *olitorius* of this genus furnish jute.

2. [c–] a Japanese shrub, *Kerria japonica,* cultivated for its roselike flower.

çor'cle, çor'cūle, *n.* [L. *corculum,* dim. of *cor,* heart.] the heart or embryo of a seed. [Obs.]

çord, *n.* [OFr. *corde;* L. *chorda,* from Gr. *chorde,* catgut, chord, cord.]

1. a thick string, or thin rope, composed of several strands twisted together.

2. anything resembling a cord, as the string of an instrument.

3. a measure of wood cut for fuel (128 cubic feet, as arranged in a pile 4x4x8 feet).

4. in fabrics, (a) corduroy; (b) a rib on the surface of a fabric.

5. any influence that binds and holds; as, the *cords* of love.

6. [*pl.*] corduroy trousers.

7. in anatomy, any part resembling a cord; as, the spinal *cord,* vocal *cords,* umbilical *cord.*

8. in electricity, a small, flexible insulated cable fitted with a plug or plugs.

çord, *v.t.*; corded, *pt., pp.*; cording, *ppr.* 1. to bind with a cord or rope; to fasten with cords; to connect with a cord or cords.

2. to pile (wood or other material) in cords.

çord'āġe, *n.* [Fr. *cordage,* from *cord* and *-age.*]

1. ropes or cords collectively.

2. the ropes or rigging of a ship.

3. the amount of wood, measured in cords, in a given area.

Çor·dȧ·ī'tēş, *n.* [named after *Corda,* an Austrian botanist.] a genus of immense, arborescent trees of the Carboniferous epoch, belonging to the cycad family.

çord'ăl, *n.* [OFr. *cordal, cordail,* from *corde,* a cord.] in heraldry, a string of the mantle or robe of estate, made of silk and gold threads interwoven like a cord, with tassels at the ends. [Obs.]

çor'dāte, *a.* [from L. *cor, cordis,* a heart.] having the form of a heart; heart-shaped; as, a *cordate* leaf. Hence, *cordate*-oblong, heart-shaped, lengthened; *cordate*-lanceolate, heart-shaped, gradually tapering toward the extremity, like the head of a lance; *cordate*-sagittate, heart-shaped, but resembling the head of an arrow.

CORDATE LEAF

çor'dāte·ly, *adv.* in a cordate form or manner.

çord'ed, *a.* 1. bound or fastened with cords.

2. piled in a form for measurement by the cord.

3. made of cords; furnished with cords.

4. striped or furrowed, as by cords.

5. having a ribbed or twilled surface, as corduroy.

Çor·dēl'iȧ (-yȧ), *n.* in Shakespeare's *King Lear,* the youngest of Lear's three daughters, and the only one faithful to him.

Çor·de·liēr', *n.* [Fr. *cordelière,* a cord or girdle worn by the order, from *corde,* a cord.]

1. a member of the Franciscan friars: so named from their wearing a girdle of knotted cord.

2. a member of a Parisian political club in the time of the Revolution, which numbered Danton and Marat among its chief members: named from an old convent of the *Cordeliers,* where their meetings were held.

çor'del·ing, çor'del·ling, *a.* [Fr. *cordeler,* to twist.] twisting.

çor·delle', *n.* [Fr. *cordelle,* dim. of *corde,* a cord.]

1. a twisted cord; a tassel. [Obs.]

2. a towline, especially as formerly used on Mississippi flatboats and keelboats.

çor·delle', *v.t.*; cordelled, *pt., pp.*; cordelling, *ppr.* to tow with or as with a cordelle.

Çor'di·ȧ, *n.* [named after *Cordus,* a German botanist.] a large genus of plants of the borage family, consisting of some 200 species scattered over the warm regions of the world, especially in America. It consists of trees or shrubs with alternate simple leaves. The fruit is drupaceous, and that of some species, as sebesten, is eaten.

çor'diăl (-jăl *or* -dyăl), *a.* [Fr. *cordial;* LL. *cordialis,* from *cor, cordis,* heart.]

1. relating to the heart. [Obs.]

2. proceeding as from the heart; hearty; sincere; not hypocritical; warm; affectionate; as, we give our friends a *cordial* reception.

With looks of *cordial* love. —Milton.

3. reviving the spirits; cheering; invigorating; giving strength or spirits; stimulating the heart; as, *cordial* waters.

çor'diăl, *n.* 1. that which revives the spirits; an exhilarant; specifically, an exhilarating draught; a refreshing medicine that stimulates the heart.

2. a liqueur; an aromatic, sirupy, alcoholic drink.

çor·dial'i·ty (-ji-al' *or* -jal'), *n.* 1. relation to the heart. [Obs.]

2. sincerity; freedom from hypocrisy; sincere affection and kindness; as, our friends were received with *cordiality.*

3. *pl.* **çor·dial'i·tieş,** a cordial act or remark.

çor'diăl·īze (-jăl-īz), *v.t.*; cordialized, *pt., pp.*; cordializing, *ppr.* 1. to make into a cordial.

2. to make cordial or warm in feeling or manner; to render genial or hearty.

çor'diăl·īze, *v.i.* to feel or show cordiality.

çor'diăl·ly, *adv.* in a cordial manner.

çor'diăl·ness, *n.* cordiality; hearty good will. [Rare.]

çor'di·ẽr·īte, *n.* [named after *Cordier,* a French geologist.] iolite.

çor'di·form, *a.* [L. *cor, cordis,* the heart, and *forma,* form.] heart-shaped.

çor·dil'lẽr·ȧ, *n.* [Sp., from O.Sp. *cordilla, cordiella,* dim. of *cuerda,* a rope, string, from L. *chorda,* a cord, string.] a ridge or chain of mountains: first applied (*the Cordilleras*) to the ranges of the Andes in South America, and then also to their continuation into Mexico and further north. Now the term is used generally for the principal mountain range of a continent.

çor·dil'lẽr·ăn, *a.* 1. of a cordillera or cordilleras.

2. [C–] of the Cordilleras.

çor'di·nẽr, *n.* a cordwainer. [Obs.]

çord'ing, *n.* 1. the ribbed surface of corded cloth.

2. cordage.

çor'dīte, *n.* a smokeless high explosive made in the form of a cord. It is of a brown color and composed principally of nitroglycerine, guncotton, petroleum jelly, and acetone.

çord'lēaf, *n.* a plant of the family *Restionaceæ.*

çor'dō·bȧ, *n.* [Sp. *córdoba:* so named in honor of the explorer Francisco F. de *Córdoba.*]

1. the monetary unit of Nicaragua.

2. a silver coin of this value.

çor'dŏn, *n.* [Fr. and Sp. *cordon;* It. *cordone,* from LL. *corda,* L. *chorda,* a cord, string.]

1. in fortification, a row of stones jutting out between the rampart and the basis of the parapet; also, a row of stones between the wall of a fortress which lies aslope, and the parapet, which is perpendicular.

2. a line or circle of people, forts, ships, etc. enclosing or guarding any particular place; as, a *cordon* of troops.

3. a ribbon or cord worn as the badge of an order or as a decoration.

4. in architecture, a projecting band of stone on the exterior of a building or the surface of a wall.

5. in heraldry, a baldric or ribbon worn across the breast by knights of the first class or order.

6. in horticulture, a tree pruned of most of its branches to obtain fruit of fine quality.

cordon bleu; (a) the blue ribbon worn as a scarf or badge of the Order of the Holy Ghost, the highest order of the old French chivalry under the Bourbon monarchy; hence, any very high distinction; (b) one entitled to wear the cordon bleu; hence, any person of great eminence in his profession or calling.

cordon sanitaire; (a) a line of troops or military posts on the borders of a district infected with disease, to cut off communication, and thus prevent the disease from spreading; hence, (b) a belt of countries serving to isolate another country and lessen its influence.

çor·don·net' (-nā'), *n.* 1. a raised edge or border of a point-lace pattern.

2. an edging of small cord or piping.

çọr'dō·văn, *n.* [Sp. *cordoban*, from *Córdoba*, in Spain.]
 1. a soft, colored leather, usually of sheepskin or split horsehide, originally made at Córdoba, Spain.
 2. [*pl.*] shoes made of this leather.
 3. [C–] a native or inhabitant of Córdoba.

çọr'dō·văn, *a.* 1. made of cordovan.
 2. [C–] of Córdoba.

çọr'du·roy, *n.* [of doubtful origin.]
 1. a stout, ribbed cotton fabric, made with a pile, so cut as to leave a velvety surface ridged in the direction of the warp.
 2. a corduroy road.
 3. [*pl.*] trousers or, sometimes, a suit made of corduroy.
 corduroy road; a road constructed with logs laid together crosswise. It is used in swampy places, and derives its name from its ribbed appearance, resembling corduroy.

çọr'du·roy, *v.t.*; corduroyed, *pt., pp.*; corduroying, *ppr.* to construct of logs, in the manner of a corduroy road.

çọr'du·roy, *a.* 1. made of corduroy.
 2. ribbed like corduroy.

çọrd'wāin, *n.* [ME. *cordwane*; OFr. *cordowan*; Sp. *cordoban*, from *Córdoba*, in Spain.] cordovan leather. [Archaic.]

çọrd'wāin·ẽr, *n.* a worker in cordwain; also, a shoemaker. [Archaic.]

çọrd'wood, *n.* 1. wood cut and stacked in cords or sold by the cord.
 2. wood cut in lengths of 4 feet.

Çọr'dy·ceps, *n.* [L., from Gr. *kordylē*, a club, and L. *-ceps*, from *caput*, head.] a genus of ascomycetous fungi. Some species grow upon decaying leaves and branches on plants affected by ergot, others on living insects.

çōre, *n.* [ME. *core*; OFr. *cor, coer*; L. *cor*, heart.]
 1. the central or inner part of anything; particularly, the central part of fruit, containing the kernels or seeds; as, the *core* of an apple.
 2. the inner part of an ulcer or boil.
 3. in architecture, the interior part of a column or wall.
 4. a disorder of sheep, caused by worms in the liver.
 5. figuratively, the essence or most important part of a matter; as, the *core* of a question.
 This obscure belief lies at the very *core* of our spiritual nature. —J. A. Froude.
 6. in molding, the internal part of a mold, which forms a hollow in the casting.
 7. the bony center of a ruminant's horn.
 8. in electrodynamics, a mass of ferromagnetic material around which a helix or coil is wound, serving to increase the external magnetic field.
 9. in ethnological archaeology, a piece of flint or other similar material from which stone implements have been chipped.
 10. in telegraphy, the cord of insulated conducting wires in the heart of a cable.

çōre, *v.t.*; cored, *pt., pp.*; coring, *ppr.* 1. to remove the core of (an apple or other fruit, etc.).
 2. to mold or cast by means of a core.
 3. to roll in salt and prepare for drying, as herrings.

çōre, *n.* [phonetic spelling of Fr. *corps*, a body.] a body; party; company. [Scot.]

çōre, *n.* [an alteration of *chore*.] in mining, the shift worked by each group of miners. [Brit.]

çōre bar'rel, a vertical iron tube or pipe, wrapped with straw and covered with sand and clay, used in casting guns.

çōre box, a box in which clay is rammed to form cores for molding.

çō·reç'tōme, *n.* [Gr. *korē*, the pupil, and *ektomos*, from *ektemnein*, to cut out; *ek*, out, and *temnein*, to cut.] an instrument for cutting through the iris to form an artificial pupil.

çōre disk, a disk cut or stamped out of sheet iron and used for the laminated core of any dynamo-electric apparatus.

çō·rē'ġent, *n.* a joint regent or ruler.

Çor·ē·gō'nus, *n.* a genus of fishes, distinguished from the salmons in having the first dorsal fin further forward than the ventrals, the scales large, and the teeth either minute or lacking.

Çō·rē'i·dae, *n.pl.* [L., from Gr. *koris*, a bug, and *-idæ*.] a family of insects of the order *Hemiptera*, remarkable for their size and grotesque shapes.

çō·rē·lā'tion, *n.* correlation.

çōre'less, *a.* 1. having no core.
 2. figuratively, without pith or stamina; weak.

çō·rē·liġ'iŏn·ist, *n.* one of the same religion or sect as another.

çō·rel'lȧ, *n.* [L., dim. of *cora*; Gr. *korē*, a girl, doll.] a yellow-crested parakeet, *Nymphicus novæ-hollandiæ*, of Australia.

Çō·rē·op'sis, *n.* [L., from Gr. *koris*, a bug, and *opsis*, appearance, in allusion to the form of the seed which has two little horns at the end.]
 1. a genus of plants, natural order *Compositæ*. Most of the species are herbaceous perennials, with opposite leaves and yellow or parti-colored rays. The fruit is an achene, flat on one side and convex on the other, slightly winged, and with two awns. The species are native to North America and South Africa.
 2. [c–] a plant of this genus, or its flower.

çōre print, a projecting piece on a pattern for molding, forming a hole in the mold to receive the end of the core, by which it is held in the mold in proper position relative to the object cast.

çōr'ẽr, *n.* an instrument for removing the core from fruit; as, an apple *corer*.

çor'e·sēs̤, *n.pl.* [L., from Gr. *koris*, a bug, pl. *koreis*; named from the resemblance to a bug.] dark red, broad, discoid bodies found beneath the epicarp of grapes.

çō·rē·spond'en·cy, *n.* the state of being a corespondent.

çō·rē·spond'ent, *n.* in law, one who is made a joint respondent with another in a suit; especially one who is charged with adultery with the wife or husband of the plaintiff, and made a party to a suit for divorce.

çō'ret, *n.* a pond snail of the genus *Planorbis*.

Çō'rē·us, *n.* [L., from Gr. *koris*, a bug.] the typical genus of *Coreidæ*.

çōre wheel, a wheel having a rim furnished with cavities to receive cogs.

çọrf, *n.*; *pl.* **çọrveṣ,** [M.D.; L. *corbis*, a basket.] formerly, a basket, now a low wheeled vehicle for carrying coal, ore, etc. in a mine. [Brit.]

çọrf house, in Scotland, a shed where the nets and other material used in salmon fishing are stored, and where the fish are cured.

Çọr'fi·ōte, Çọr'fūte, *n.* a native or inhabitant of Corfu, one of the Ionian islands.

çō·ri·ā'ceous, *a.* [L. *coriaceus*, from *corium*, leather.] consisting of leather, or resembling leather; tough; as, *coriaceous* concretions.

çō·ri·an'dẽr, *n.* [Fr. *coriandre*; L. *coriandrum*, from Gr. *koriannon, korion*, the coriander; perhaps from *koris*, a bug, because of the smell of its leaves.] an umbelliferous plant, *Coriandrum sativum*; also, its seedlike, strong-smelling fruit (commonly called *coriander seeds*), used in cooking for flavoring, and in medicine as a stomachic and carminative.

CORIANDER (*Coriandrum sativum*)

Çō·ri·an'drum, *n.* a genus of plants, family *Umbelliferæ*, containing two species. They are slender annual herbs with white flowers, natives of the Mediterranean region. *Coriandrum sativum*, the medicinal coriander, is cultivated on account of its seeds, or rather fruit.

Çō·ri·ā·ri·ā'cē·ae, *n.pl.* [L. *coriarius*, from *corium*, leather.] a small family of polypetalous exogens, consisting of six known species of shrubs included in a single genus, *Coriaria*. The best known species is the *myrtifolia*, of southern Europe, used as a black dye.

çō'ri·dine, *n.* [from L. *corium*, leather.] a compound, $C_{10}H_{15}N$, obtained from coal tar, Dippel's oil, etc., having an odor like new leather.

çō·rin'dŏn, *n.* corundum. [Obs.]

çō·rinne' (-rin'), *n.* [from Fr. *corinnes*, the gazel.]
 1. the common gazel.
 2. a hummingbird having a long, lancelike bill and very brilliant coloration.

çor'inth, *n.* [from *Corinth*, an ancient city in Greece near which the fruit grows.] a small dried grape; a currant.

Çō·rin'thi·aç, *a.* Corinthian; of or pertaining to Corinth.

Çō·rin'thi·ăn, *a.* 1. pertaining to Corinth, Greece, its people, or culture.
 2. licentious; dissipated and given to luxury, as the people of Corinth were reputed to be.
 3. in the style of the art of Corinth; elaborately graceful.
 4. designating or relating to the most elaborate of the three orders (Doric, Ionic, Corinthian) of Greek architecture, distinguished by a slender, fluted column and a bell-shaped capital decorated with a design of acanthus leaves.
 5. amateur: applied especially to a yacht race for amateurs.

CORINTHIAN ORDER

Çō·rin'thi·ăn, *n.* 1. an inhabitant or native of Corinth: often with reference to dissoluteness.
 2. a wealthy man about town.
 3. an amateur yachtsman.
 4. a gentleman amateur in sports, especially boxing, horse racing, and cricket.

Çō·rin'thi·ănṣ, *n.pl.* [*construed as sing.*] either of the Epistles to the Corinthians, two books of the New Testament which were messages from the Apostle Paul to the Christians of Corinth.

Çọr·i·ō'lis force, [after G. *Coriolis*, 19th-c. Fr. scientist who first discussed it.] the force created by the earth's rotation, acting upon anything moving above the earth's surface by causing it to curve to the right in the Northern Hemisphere and to the left in the Southern Hemisphere.

çō'ri·um, *n.* [L.] 1. a kind of body armor, composed of scales or small plates of leather, worn by ancient Roman soldiers: in England, used until the reign of Edward I.
 2. the innermost layer of the skin in mammals, lying beneath the epidermis and containing its blood and nerve supply; dermis; the true skin.
 3. in entomology, the main portion of the hemelytron of a hemipterous insect.

ROMAN CORIUM

çō·rī'văl, *n., v.i.* and *v.t.* same as *corrival*.

çō·rī'văl·ry, çō·rī'văl·ship, *n.* joint rivalry.

çọrk, *n.* [ME. *cork*, from Sp. *al·corque*, corkwood slippers; Ar. *alcorque*, perh. from L. *quercus*, oak.]
 1. a glandiferous tree, the cork oak, *Quercus suber*, growing in Spain and Portugal, having a thick, rough, fungous, cleft bark.
 2. the outer bark of this tree; it is stripped off in large plates every 12 to 15 years and is used for various purposes.
 3. anything made of cork; as, (a) a fishing float; (b) a bottle stopper; (c) a shoe sole.
 4. a bottle stopper, similar to a cork stopper, made of glass, rubber, metal, etc.
 5. the suberous bark of any tree.

çọrk, *a.* made of cork.

çọrk, *v.t.*; corked (kọrkt), *pt., pp.*; corking, *ppr.* 1. to stop with a cork, as bottles or casks.
 2. to confine, hold back, or check.
 3. to blacken with burnt cork.

çọrk, *n.* and *v.* same as *calk*. [U. S.]

çọrk'āġe, *n.* a charge made at a tavern, restaurant, hotel, etc. for every bottle of wine or liquor uncorked and served, especially for bottles bought elsewhere and brought in by guests.

çọrk çam'bi·um, in botany, the tissue between the bark and the wood, from which the protective outer bark is formed; phellogen.

çọrked (kọrkt), *a.* 1. stopped with a cork.
 2. fitted with or raised on cork. [Obs.]
 A *corked* shoe or slipper. —Huloet.
 3. having acquired the taste and smell of cork: said of wine, etc. which has been bottled with unsound cork.
 4. blackened with burnt cork.

çọrk'ẽr, *n.* 1. one who or that which corks.
 2. a conclusive argument, statement, or circumstance. [Slang.]

3. a remarkable person or thing. [Slang.]
4. a preposterous lie. [Slang.]

çork fos'sil, a kind of hornblende: so named from its lightness.

çork'ing, *a.* and *interj.* [from *cork.*] very good; excellent. [Slang.]

çork'ing pin, a pin of a large size. [Obs.]

çork jack'et, a jacket lined with cork for use as a life preserver.

çork'sçrew (-skrü), *n.* a device to draw corks from bottles, usually a spiral-shaped piece of steel with a point at one end and a handle at the other.

çork'sçrew, *v.t.* and *v.i.* to move in a twisting or winding way; to zigzag.

çork'sçrew, *a.* formed like a corkscrew; spiral; as, *corkscrew* stairs, a *corkscrew* curl.

çork tree, same as *cork, n.* (sense 1).

çork'wing, *n.* a fish, *Crenilabrus melops*: commonly called *goldfinny.*

çork'wood, *n.* any of several trees having light and porous wood, as the *Anona palustris* or the *Ochroma lagopus*; also, the wood.

çork'wood çot'tŏn, the cottony or silky covering of the seeds of the bombacaceous tropical tree, *Ochroma lagopus.*

çork'y, *a.*; *comp.* corkier; *superl.* corkiest, consisting of cork; resembling cork; dry and tough like cork.
Bind fast his *corky* arms. —Shak.

çorm, *n.* [L. *cormus*; Gr. *kormos*, the trunk of a tree with the boughs lopped off, from *keirein*, to cut, shear.]
1. in botany, the short, fleshy, underground stem of certain plants, as the crocus or gladiolus: it resembles a bulb and is covered with several scalelike leaves.

CORM OF CROCUS

2. in zoology, same as *cormus.*

çorm'el, *n.* [dim. of *corm.*] a small, secondary corm.

çor'mī, *n.* plural of *cormus.*

çor·mid'i·um, *n.*; *pl.* **çor·mid'i·ȧ,** [L., dim. from Gr. *kormos*, the trunk of a tree.] a group of zooids budding from a medusa, the individuals of which are heteromorphic.

Çor·moph'y·tȧ, *n.pl.* [L., from Gr. *kormos*, a trunk, and *phyton*, plant.] formerly, a division comprising all plants having a stem and root.

çor'mō·phȳte, *n.* [*cormo-* (from Gr. *kormos*, the trunk of a tree), and *-phyte.*] any plant with a stem and root.

çor·mō·phyt'iç, *a.* of, or having the nature of, a cormophyte.

çor'mō·rȧnt, *n.* [ME. *cormerawnt*; OFr. *cormoran*; L. *corvus marinus*, sea crow.]
1. a large, voracious, web-footed sea bird of the pelican family. The common species, *Phalacrocorax carbo*, has a black head and neck; the coverts of the wings, the scapulars, and the back are a deep green, edged with black, and glossed with blue. Called also *sea raven, coal goose.*
2. a greedy fellow; a glutton.
Light vanity, insatiate *cormorant*, soon preys upon itself. —Shak.

çor'mō·rȧnt, *a.* having the qualities of a cormorant; greedy; rapacious.
If thou be still human and not *cormorant.* —Carlyle.

çor'mus, *n.*; *pl.* **çor'mī,** [L. from Gr. *kormos*, the trunk of a tree with the branches lopped off.]
1. in botany, a corm.
2. in zoology, a colony of individuals of a compound animal.

çorn, *n.* [AS. *corn*, a grain, seed, corn; D. *koren*; O.H.G. *koren*; Ice. and Sw. *korn*; Goth. *kaurn*, grain.]
1. a single, small, hard seed or seedlike fruit, especially the seed of cereal plants, as wheat, rye, barley, and maize; a grain; a kernel.
2. (a) a kind of grain, *Zea mays*, that grows in kernels on large ears; maize; (b) its ears. Also, and originally, called *Indian corn.*
3. in England, wheat.
4. in Scotland and Ireland, oats.
5. the seeds of the small grains, wheat, oats, rye or barley, or the plants producing them. [Brit.]
6. a small, hard particle. [Dial.]
7. corn whisky. [Colloq.]
8. ideas, humor, music, etc. regarded as old-fashioned, trite, banal, or sentimental. [Slang.]

çorn, *v.t.*; corned, *pt., pp.*; corning, *ppr.* 1. to preserve and season or pickle in brine, or with salt in grains, or corns; as, to *corn* beef.
2. to granulate; to form into small grains.
3. to feed with grain, as a horse.
4. to intoxicate. [Colloq.]

çorn, *n.* a horny thickening of the skin, usually painful when subjected to pressure, most common on the toes, being caused by friction or compression.

-çorn, [from L. *cornu*, a horn.] a terminal combining form meaning *horn*, as in Capri*corn*, uni*corn*.

Çor·nā'cē·ae, *n.pl.* [Mod. L. *cornus*, the dogwood, and *-aceæ.*] a family of epigynous exogens, the dogwood family, mostly trees, herbs, or shrubs, found in Europe, Asia, and America.

çor·nā'ceous, *a.* of or pertaining to the *Cornaceæ.*

çor'nāġe, *n.* [OFr. *cornage*, a hornblowing, from *corne*, L. *cornus*, a horn.] a feudal tax or rent paid by a tenant on his horned cattle.

çor'nȧ·mūte, *n.* a cornemuse. [Obs.]

çorn ball, popped corn formed into a ball held together by a sticky sirup; a popcorn ball.

çorn bee'tle, a minute beetle, *Cucujus testaceus*, having a larva that destroys wheat in the bin; the wheat beetle.

çorn'bell, *n.* a fungoid growth, *Cyathus vernicosus*, attacking growing grain.

Çorn Belt, the Upper Mississippi Valley, or that portion of the Middle West which extends from central Ohio to central Kansas and Nebraska, where large harvests of corn are reaped.

çorn'bīnd, *n.* any of several twining weeds; as, (a) bindweed; (b) the climbing buckwheat.

çorn bŏr'ẽr, a moth larva that feeds on corn, etc.

çorn bread (bred), bread made of corn meal.

çorn'cāke, *n.* johnnycake.

çorn'çob, *n.* 1. the woody core of an ear of corn bearing the kernels in rows.
2. a corncob pipe.

çorn'çob pīpe, a tobacco pipe with a bowl made of a hollowed piece of dried corncob.

çorn çoç'kle, a weed, *Lychnis githago*, growing in grainfields and having purple, bell-shaped flowers and hard black seeds: often called *cockle.*

çorn çŏl'ŏr, light yellow.

çorn'çrack''ẽr, *n.* 1. a native Kentuckian. [Colloq.]
2. a corn crake.

çorn çrāke, [*corn* and *crake*, Ice. *kraka*, a crow.] a short-billed bird of the rail family, common in Europe, frequenting grainfields and meadows: also called *land rail.*

çorn'çrib, *n.* a small, ventilated structure for holding corn before shelling, usually made of slats and somewhat elevated from the ground.

çorn'çut''tẽr, *n.* 1. a corn shredder.
2. a hooked or machetelike knife for cutting standing corn by hand; also, a corn harvester.

çorn'dodġ''ẽr (-doj''), *n.* a hard-baked bread of corn meal made in small pones; also, such a pone: also written *corn-dodger, corn dodger.*

çor'nē·ȧ, [L. f. sing. of *corneus*, horny, from *cornu*, a horn.]
1. the transparent tissue forming the outer coat of the eyeball and covering the iris and pupil.
2. in entomology, the exterior of a compound eye.

çor'nē·ăl, *a.* of or pertaining to a cornea.

çorn'ēar wŏrm, a certain moth larva that feeds on corn, cotton, etc.; bollworm.

çorned, *a.* preserved with salt or brine; as, *corned* beef.

çor'nel, *n.* [OFr. *cornille*; LL. *cornolium*, the cornel tree; from L. *cornus*, a cornel tree.]
1. the cornelian cherry or dogwood, the popular name of *Cornus mascula*, of the dogwood family, a European and Asiatic shrub having very hard wood, small yellowish-green flowers and cherrylike fruit.
2. any tree or shrub of the genus *Cornus*: also called *cornel tree, cornelian tree.*

çor·nēl'i·ăn, *n.* the carnelian.

çorne'mūşe, *n.* an early type of bagpipe.

çor''nē·ō·çal·çā'rē·ous, *a.* [L. *corneus*, horny, and *calcareus*, pertaining to lime.] made up of horny and calcareous matter.

çor'nē·ous, *a.* [L. *corneus*, from *cornu*, a horn.] horny; hard; consisting of some substance resembling horn.

çor'nẽr, *n.* [ME. *corner, cornier*; OFr. *corniere*; LL. *cornerium*, from *corne*, a corner, angle; from *cornu*, a horn, projecting point.]
1. the point of meeting of two lines; the line or point of meeting of two or more planes or surfaces forming an angle.
2. the space between two converging lines or walls which meet in a point; angle; as, a piano in the *corner* of the room.
3. a secluded, secret, or remote place.
This thing was not done in a *corner.* —Acts xxvi. 26.
4. the place where two streets meet.
5. a piece used to form, mark, guard, or ornament a corner.
6. an awkward position, from which escape is difficult; as, he was driven into a *corner.*
7. a part; region; quarter; as, all *corners* of the country.
8. in surveying, a mark placed at the corner of a surveyed tract.
9. a bookbinder's tool for corner ornamentation.
10. a device for protecting the corner of anything, as of the cover of a book.
11. a speculative monopoly of a certain product or commodity, so as to be able to regulate the supply or raise the price at will; as, a *corner* in corn.
the (four) corners of the earth; (a) the farthest parts of the earth; (b) everywhere.
to cut corners; (a) to take a direct route by going across corners; (b) to cut down expenses, time or labor required, etc.
to turn the corner; to get safely past the critical point.

çor'nẽr, *v.t.*; cornered, *pt., pp.*; cornering, *ppr.*
1. to furnish with corners.
2. to put into a corner.
3. to force or drive into a difficult or embarrassing position; as, to *corner* a witness.
4. to obtain control of (any commodity) for the purpose of fixing the price; as, to *corner* wheat.

çor'nẽr, *v.i.* 1. to form a corner or angle.
2. to be situated on or at a corner.

çor'nẽr, *a.* 1. at or on a corner; as, a *corner* store.
2. used in a corner.

çor'nẽr·çap, *n.* a cap with three or four corners worn in the sixteenth and seventeenth centuries by ecclesiastics and members of universities. [Obs.]

çor'nẽred, *a.* 1. having corners.
2. driven into a corner, or into a difficult or embarrassing position.

çor'nẽr·ẽr, *n.* one who corners, especially one who controls a commodity so as to fix the price.

çor'nẽr·stōne, *n.* 1. the stone which lies at the corner of a building.
2. such a stone, often inscribed, laid at a ceremony formally beginning the erection of a building.
3. something fundamental or of primary importance; foundation.

çor'nẽr tooth, one of the four teeth of a horse between the middle teeth and the tushes, two above and two below, on each side of the jaw.

çor'nẽr·wāyş, *adv.* same as *cornerwise.*

çor'nẽr·wīse, *adv.* 1. diagonally; from one corner to an opposite corner.
2. with the corner in front; so as to form a corner.

çor'net (*or* kor-net'), *n.* [OFr. *cornet*; LL. *cornetum*, a horn, bugle, a kind of hood, from *corneta*, a kind of hood; L. *cornu*, a horn.]
1. in music, (a) the smallest of the brass-wind instruments of the trumpet class, consisting of a variously curved metal tube with a cup-shaped, removal mouthpiece, three valves controlled by pistons: also called *cornet-à-pistons*; (b) [Rare.] a loud organ stop; (c) an instrument resembling the oboe, now no longer used.

CORNET

2. a woman's headdress worn about the sixteenth century; also, the spreading white headdress that a Sister of Charity wears.
3. in military affairs, (a) a flag; (b) a company of cavalry; (c) a British cavalry officer of the lowest rank, who carried his troops' flag. [Obs.]
4. a piece of paper twisted like a cone, for holding sugar, candy, etc.

cor'net-à-pis'tons (kor'net à-pis'tŏnş), *n.*; *pl.* **cor'nets-à-pis'tons** (kor'net-à-pis'tŏnş), [Fr., a cornet with pistons.] a musical instrument, the cornet.

çor′net·cy, *n.*; *pl.* **çor′net·cieș,** the commission or rank of a cornet (cavalry officer). [Obs.]

çor′net·ẽr, *n.* one who plays a cornet.

çor·net′tist, çor·net′ist, *n.* a cornet player.

çor′nē·ūle, *n.* [Fr., dim. of *cornée*, the cornea.] the cornea of an ocellus.

çorn′fed, *a.* 1. fed on corn.
 2. countrified; healthy and strong but unsophisticated. [Slang.]

çorn′fiēld, *n.* a field where corn is grown.

çorn flag, any of a genus of plants, the *Gladiolus*, bearing red or white flowers.

çorn′flōor, *n.* a floor for threshing corn.

çorn′flour, *n.* 1. flour made from corn (maize).
 2. flour made from some other grain. [Brit.]

çorn′flow″ẽr, *n.* 1. the bachelor's-button.
 2. the corn cockle.

çorn här′vest·ẽr, a machine, similar to a self-binder, for cutting and binding corn.

çorn′husk, *n.* any of the tough, fibrous leaves acting as an envelope for an ear of corn.

çorn′husk″ing, *n.* 1. the husking of corn.
 2. a gathering of friends and neighbors for husking corn; husking bee: it is generally a festive event, followed by dancing, etc.

çor′niç, *a.* pertaining to cornin.

çor′nice, *n.* [OFr. *cornice*; It. *cornice*; L. *cornix, coronix*, from *coronis*, a curved line, a flourish with a pen at the end of a book; Gr. *korōnis*, a wreath, garland.]
 1. the highest part of an entablature resting on the frieze.
 2. a horizontal molding projecting along the top of a wall, building, etc.
 3. an ornamental band for covering a curtain rod.

çor′nice, *v.t.*; corniced, *pt., pp.*; cornicing, *ppr.* to top with a cornice or something like a cornice.

çor′niced (-nist), *a.* provided with a cornice.

çor′nice ring, the ring on a cannon behind the muzzle ring. [Obs.]

çor′ni·çle, *n.* [L. *corniculum*, dim. of *cornu*, a horn.] a little horn. [Obs.]

çor·niç′ū·lāte, *a.* [LL. *corniculatus*, from *corniculum*, dim. of *cornu*, a horn.] horned; having horns or hornlike projections.

çor·niç′ū·lẽr, *n.* a secretary; a clerk. [Obs.]

çor·niç′ū·lum, *n.*; *pl.* **çor·niç′ū·lȧ,** [L. *corniculum*, dim. of *cornu*, a horn.] a hornlike process, as one of the cartilaginous bodies of the larynx.

çor·nif′iç, *a.* [L. *cornu*, a horn, and *-ficus*, from *facere*, to make.] producing a horn or horns.

çor″ni·fi·çā′tion, *n.* the transformation into a hornlike substance.

çor′ni·fied, *a.* transformed into horn.

çor′ni·form, *a.* [L. *cornu*, a horn, and *forma*, form.] having the form of a horn.

çor·nig′ẽr·ous, *a.* [L. *corniger*; *cornu*, a horn, and *gerere*, to bear.] horned; having horns.

çor′nin, *n.* a bitter, crystalline substance extracted from the root of the flowering dogwood, *Cornus florida*; cornic acid.

çorn′ing house, a house or place where powder is granulated.

çor′ni·plūme, *n.* [L. *cornu*, a horn, and *pluma*, a feather.] in ornithology, a horny tuft of feathers.

Çor′nish, *a.* pertaining to Cornwall, its people, or culture.
 Cornish engine; an old form of single-acting engine, first used for pumping up water in the Cornwall mines.

Çor′nish, *n.* the Brythonic Celtic language spoken by the people of Cornwall until c. 1800, closely related to Breton and Welsh.

Çor′nish·măn, *n.*; *pl.* **Çor′nish·men,** a native or inhabitant of Cornwall.

çorn′land, *n.* land suitable for the production of corn.

Çorn Lạwș, in England, certain laws imposing heavy duties on the importation of wheat, repealed in 1846.

çorn lil′y, any of a number of related bulb plants native to South Africa, with slender, grasslike leaves and spikes of showy, funnel-shaped flowers.

çorn′loft, *n.* a granary.

çorn mar′i·gōld, a variety of marigold growing in cornfields.

çorn mēal, 1. meal of corn; maize ground up.
 2. meal made from some other grain, as in Scotland, oats.

çorn mil′dew, a rust that attacks wheat.

çorn mill, a gristmill; specifically, one grinding corn on the cob.

çorn moth, a small moth, *Tinea granella*, destructive to wheat in the shock or bin.

çorn′mūșe, *n.* a cornemuse. [Obs.]

çor·nō′pē·ăn, *n.* the cornet-à-pistons.

çorn pick′ẽr, a machine for picking ears of corn from standing stalks and removing the husks.

çorn pit, that part of a produce exchange where trading in corn futures goes on.

çorn plant′ẽr, a device for planting corn.

çorn pōne, a kind of corn bread usually made without milk or eggs.

çorn pop′py, a red, black-spotted poppy, *Papaver rhœas*, often growing in cornfields of Europe and Asia.

çorn rōșe, 1. the corn cockle.
 2. the corn poppy.

çorn sal′ăd, *Fedia* or *Valerianella olitoria*, a European plant whose leaves are used in salads.

çorn shel′lẽr, an implement for shelling corn from the cob.

çorn shock, a stack of cut cornstalks set up in a field to dry.

çorn shred′dẽr, a machine for preparing corn for fodder or the silo.

çorn shuck, a cornhusk. [Colloq.]

çorn silk, a tassel of silky fibers growing at the end of an ear of corn, serving to receive pollen.

çorn sir′up, a sweet sirup made from cornstarch.

çorn smut, 1. a fungus disease of corn marked by large, black swellings on the ear and tassel.
 2. the fungus causing this disease.

çorn snāke, a nonpoisonous North American snake, *Scotophis guttatus*.

çorn′stạlk (-stọk), *n.* a stalk of corn.
 cornstalk disease; a generally fatal disease, attacking cattle and, sometimes, horses and sheep after pasturing in cornfields. Its cause is undetermined but thought to come from corn smut.

çorn′stärch, *n.* a fine, starchy flour made from Indian corn and used in making puddings, etc.

çorn sụg′ăr (shụg′), a dextrose made from cornstarch.

çor′nū, *n.*; *pl.* **çor′nū·ȧ,** [L.] 1. a horn.
 2. that which resembles a horn; in anatomy, a hornlike part; in conchology, an ammonite.

çor·nū·çō′pi·ȧ, *n.* [L. *cornu copiæ*, horn of plenty.]
 1. in Greek mythology, the horn of the goat that suckled Zeus.
 2. a horn of plenty; a representation, in painting, sculpture, etc., of a horn overflowing with fruits, flowers, and grain.
 3. an overflowing fullness; abundance.
 4. a cone-shaped paper container for nuts, candy, etc.

CORNUCOPIA

Çor′nus, *n.* a genus of plants of the cornel or dogwood family, consisting of shrubs, trees, or, rarely, herbs, with small, white or yellowish flowers and ovoid drupes.

çor′nus, *n.* [L.] a cornel.

çor·nūte′, çor·nūt′ed, *a.* 1. grafted with horns; horned; also, horn-shaped.
 2. cuckolded. [Archaic.]

çorn vī′ō·let, a species of *Campanula*.

çorn wee′vil, an insect, as *Sphenophorus zeæ*, attacking roots of growing corn, or *Calandra granaria*, which destroys grain in the bin.

çorn whis′ky, whisky made from corn (maize).

çorn′y, *a.*; *comp.* cornier; *superl.* corniest, [L. *corneus*, horny, from *cornu*, a horn.] having or relating to corns on the feet.

çorn′y, *a.*; *comp.* cornier; *superl.* corniest,
 1. producing corn; containing corn.
 2. intoxicated. [Slang.]
 3. countrified; unsophisticated. [Slang.]
 4. old-fashioned, trite, banal, sentimental, etc. [Slang.]

çor′ō·çōre, *n.* [native name.] an East Indian boat, sometimes masted.

çor′ō·dy, *n.*; *pl.* **çor′ō·dieș,** [LL. *corrodium, corredium*, furniture, provision, equipment.] in old law, (a) originally, an allowance of meat, drink, or clothing, due to the king from an abbey or other religious house, for the sustenance of his servants; (b) later, an allowance of food, etc. for one's maintenance; also, the right to this.

çor′ŏl, *n.* a corolla.

çō·rol′lȧ, *n.* [L. *corolla*, a little crown, dim. of *corona*, a crown, wreath.] in botany, the petals or inner leaves of a flower. It is distinguished from the perianth by its fine texture and bright colors.

COROLLAS
a a, many-petaled or many-leaved corollas; *b b*, single-petaled or single-leaved corollas

çor·ŏl·lā′ceous, *a.* pertaining to a corolla; also, having a corolla.

çor′ŏl·lā·ry, *n.*; *pl.* **çor′ŏl·lā·rieș,** [LL. *corollarium*, additional inference, corollary, from L. *corolla*, dim. of *corona*, a crown.]
 1. a proposition which follows from another that has been proved.
 2. an inference or deduction.
 3. anything that follows as a normal result; as, improved health is a *corollary* of slum clearance.
 4. anything in excess; a surplus. [Obs.]

çor′ŏl·lāte, çor′ŏl·lā·ted, *a.* having or like a corolla.

çor′ŏl·let, *n.* [dim. of *corolla*.] one of the small flowers which make up a compound one.

çor·ŏl·lif′ẽr·ous, *a.* corolla-bearing.

Çō·rol·li·flō′rae, *n.pl.* one of the subdivisions of exogenous plants, distinguished by a gamopetalous corolla, attached below the ovary, and having the stamens attached to the corolla. The primrose, heath, gentian, verbena, etc. are included in this division.

çō·rol·li·flō′răl, çō·rol·li·flō′rous, *a.* [L. *corolla*, a little wreath, and *flos, floris*, a flower.] of or pertaining to the *Corollifloræ*.

çor′ŏl·line, *a.* relating to a corolla.

Çor·ō·man′del wood, calamander wood.

çō·rō′nȧ, *n.*; *pl.* **çō·rō′nȧș, çō·rō′nae,** [L., a crown.]
 1. a crown; especially, one bestowed by the Romans as a reward for distinguished military service.
 2. in architecture, the top of a cornice, situated between the bed molding and the cymatium.
 3. in anatomy and zoology, (a) any crown or crownlike part; (b) the upper part of a tooth, a skull, etc.
 4. in botany, (a) the circle of florets of a composite flower; (b) a cuplike appendage of the corolla or petals attached to the stem, as the daffodil, milkweed, etc.; (c) the appendage at the top of seeds enabling them to disperse.
 5. in astronomy, (a) a luminous circle around the sun or moon; (b) the halo around the sun, seen only during a total eclipse.
 6. in ecclesiastical usage, the stripe passing horizontally about the lower edge of a miter.
 7. a chandelier hung in the roof of a church, having the lights arranged in one or more circles and illuminated on ceremonial occasions: called also *corona lucis*.

CORONA OF SUN

 8. in music, a pause. [Rare.]
 9. a type of cigar characterized by a long, nontapering body, rounded off bluntly at the ends.
 10. in electricity, a sometimes visible electric discharge resulting from a partial electric breakdown in a gas, as in the air surrounding a wire at high potential.

Çō·rō′nȧ Ạus·trā′lis, [L., Southern Crown.] a southern constellation near Sagittarius: also called the *Southern Crown*.

Çō·rō′nȧ Bọ·rē·a′lis, [L., Northern Crown.] a northern constellation between Hercules and Boötes, consisting of a semicircular group of stars: also called the *Northern Crown*.

çor′ō·nach, çor′ȧ·nach, *n.* [Ir. *coranach* and Scot. Gael. *corranach* from *comh-*, together, and *ranach*, outcry.]
 1. a dirge, sung or played on bagpipes. [Scot.]
 2. a wailing lament for the dead; a keening. [Ir.]

çor′ō·năl, *n.* [LL. *coronalis,* from L. *corona,* a crown.]
1. a wreath; a garland; anything resembling a crown.
2. the coronal suture; also, occasionally, the frontal bone.
3. a circlet for the head; a diadem; a crown; a coronet.
4. the head of a jousting lance, constructed to unhorse but not to wound a knight; sometimes, the lance itself.

çor′ō·năl, *a.* 1. pertaining or belonging to a crown, coronet, or halo.
2. of or pertaining to a corona.
3. in anatomy, (a) of the corona of the skull; (b) designating, of, or lying in the direction of, the suture between the frontal and parietal bones of the skull.
coronal suture; that suture of the skull between the frontal and the parietal bones; the frontoparietal suture.

çor·ō·nā′men, *n.* in farriery, a coronet.

çor′ō·nā·ry, *a.* [L. *coronarius,* from *corona,* a crown.]
1. pertaining to, or in the form of, a crown.
2. in anatomy, (a) like a crown; encircling; (b) designating or relating to either of two arteries branching from the aorta and supplying blood directly to the heart tissues.
coronary thrombosis; the formation of a clot in one of the coronary arteries, resulting in obstruction of that artery.

çor′ō·nā·ry, *n.*; *pl.* **çor′ō·nā·rieș,** the small pastern bone of a horse.

çor′ō·nāte, çor′ō·nā·ted, *a.* [L. *coronatus,* pp. of *coronare,* to crown, from *corona,* a crown.] wearing a crown; having some appendage or process resembling a crown; crowned; specifically, (a) in botany, having a corona; (b) in ornithology, crested, with conspicuous coronal feathers; (c) in zoology, surmounted with rows of spines, tubercles, etc., as certain spiral shells.

çor·ō·nā′tion, *n.* the act or ceremony of crowning a sovereign.

çor′ō·nel (*or* kũr′nel), a colonel. [Obs.]

çor′ō·nel, *n.* a coronal (head of a lance). [Obs.]

çor′ō·nẽr, *n.* [ME. *coroner*; Anglo-Fr. *corouner,* from *coroune, corone,* a crown; L. *corona,* a crown.]
1. a public officer whose chief duty is to determine by inquest before a jury the causes of any deaths not obviously due to natural causes. In some places the office of coroner has been superseded by that of medical examiner.
2. in England, formerly, an officer having charge of the private property of the crown.

çor′ō·nẽr′ș jụ̈′ry, a group of people summoned to witness a coroner's inquest and submit a verdict as to the cause of the death investigated.

çor′ō·net, *n.* [OFr. *coronette, coronete,* a little crown, dim. of *corone*; L. *corona,* a crown.]
1. a small crown worn by princes and others of high rank.

CORONETS

2. an ornamental headdress; a coronal.
3. the margin around the upper part of the hoof of a horse, where the skin joins the horn: called also *coronamen.*
4. in zoology, a row of spines or hairlike processes encircling some part.

çor′ō·net brāid, braided hair worn in the manner of a coronet.

çor′ō·net·ed, çor′ō·net·ted, *a.* wearing or entitled to wear a coronet.

çō·rō′ni·fọrm, *a.* [L. *corona,* a crown, and *forma,* form.] having the form of a crown.

Çor·ō·nil′lȧ, *n.* [Mod. L., from L. *corona,* a crown.] a genus of annual or perennial plants of the pea family, having stalked umbels of yellow flowers.

çō·rō′nis, *n.* [Gr. *korōnis,* a curved line or stroke.]
1. in Greek grammar, the sign (') of the contraction of two vowels into a long vowel or a diphthong, the first vowel ending a word and the second beginning the succeeding word.
2. a double flourish used in ancient manuscripts to indicate the end of a section or chapter; hence, the end. [Rare or Obs.]

çō·rō′ni·um, *n.* a hypothetical element, known only through its spectrum, supposed to exist in a gaseous state in the sun's corona.

çor′ō·noid, *a.* [Gr. *korōnē,* a crow, and *eidos,* form.] in anatomy, (a) like the beak of a crow: applied to certain processes of the bones; as, the *coronoid* process of the lower jaw; (b) pertaining to a coronoid process.

çor′ō·nūle, *n.* [L. *coronula,* dim. of *corona,* a crown.] a coronet, or little crown, of a seed.

çō·roune′, çō·roun′, *n.* and *v.* crown. [Obs.]

çō·rō′zō, çō·rō′sō, *n.* [Sp.] 1. the seed of a tropical American palm, the *Phytelephas macrocarpa,* whose hardened albumen (called vegetable ivory) is used for the manufacture of small ornamental articles: called also *ivory nut.*
2. the *Attalea cohune,* a palm of Central America, the nuts of which are oil-producing.

çọr′pō·rȧ, *n.* plural of *corpus.*

çọr′pō·rāce, *n.* corporal (linen cloth). [Obs.]

çọr′pō·răl, *n.* [corrupted from Fr. *caporal*; It. *caporale,* a corporal, from *capo,* the head; L. *caput,* the head.]
1. in the United States armed forces, the lowest-ranking noncommissioned officer, just below a sergeant: in the Army, it is the fourth grade of enlisted man (formerly *sergeant*); in the Marine Corps and Air Force, it is the fifth grade.
2. in the British armed forces, (a) the lowest-ranking noncommissioned officer in the Army; (b) a naval petty officer who assists the master-at-arms.
3. the fish *Semotilus bullaris* or *corporalis*: also called *fallfish, silver chub,* etc.
corporal's guard; a small detachment of soldiers under command of a corporal, as assigned to guard duty, etc.

çọr′pō·răl, *a.* [L. *corporalis,* from *corpus,* body.]
1. belonging or relating to the body; physical; as, *corporal* punishment.
2. corporeal; material; not spiritual. [Archaic.]
3. personal.
4. in zoology, pertaining to the body or trunk, as distinguished from the head, limbs, etc.

çọr′pō·răl, *n.* [OFr. *corporal*; LL. *corporale* (*pallium,* pall, understood), neut. of *corporalis,* from *corpus, corporis,* body.] a fine linen cloth, used in the celebration of the Eucharist to cover the altar, on which the bread and wine are placed; Communion cloth: called also *corporal cloth, corporale,* and, formerly, *corporace, corporas.*
corporal oath; a solemn oath: so called from the ancient usage of touching the *corporal,* or cloth that covered the consecrated elements, while taking an oath.

çọr′pō·răl·cy, *n.*; *pl.* **çọr′pō·răl·cieș,** the rank of a corporal.

çọr·pō·rā′lē, *n.* same as *corporal* (linen cloth).

çọr·pō·ral′i·ty, *n.*; *pl.* **çọr·pō·ral′i·tieș,** 1. the state or quality of having a body; bodily existence or substance.
2. a guild or corporation. [Obs.]

çọr′pō·răl·ly, *adv.* bodily; in or with the body; as, to be *corporally* present.

çọr′pō·răl pun′ish·ment, punishment inflicted directly on the body, as flogging: now distinguished from capital punishment, imprisonment, etc.

çọr′pō·răl·ship, *n.* a corporal's rank or command.

çọr′pō·răs, *n.* a cloth, the corporal. [Obs.]

çọr′pō·rāte, *a.* [L. *corporatus,* pp. of *corporare,* to make into a body, from *corpus, corporis,* a body.]
1. united; combined.
2. united in a legal body, as a number of individuals who are empowered to transact business as an individual; formed into a corporation; incorporated; as, a *corporate* town.
3. belonging or pertaining to a corporation; as, *corporate* interests.
4. shared by all members of a unified group; common; joint; as, *corporate* responsibility.
corporate member; a voting member of a corporation; an active member as distinguished from an honorary member.

çọr′pō·rāte, *v.t.* and *v.i.* to incorporate. [Obs.]

çọr′pō·rāte·ly, *adv.* 1. in a corporate manner or capacity.
2. bodily. [Obs.]

çọr′pō·rāte·ness, *n.* the state of being a corporate body.

çọr·pō·rā′tion, *n.* [LL. *corporatio,* the assumption of a body, from L. *corporare,* to form into a body, from *corpus,* a body.]
1. a group of people who get a charter granting them as a body certain of the legal powers, rights, privileges, and liabilities of an individual, distinct from those of the individuals making up the group: a corporation can buy, sell, and inherit property.
2. a group of people, as the mayor and aldermen of an incorporated town, legally authorized to act as an individual.
3. any of the political and economic bodies forming a corporative state, each being composed of the employers and employees in a certain sphere, as agriculture, industry, finance, etc.
4. a large and prominent abdomen. [Colloq.]
corporation aggregate; a corporation consisting of two or more persons, as the mayor and aldermen of cities, the head and fellows of a college, the dean and chapter of a cathedral church, the stockholders of a bank or insurance company, etc.
corporation sole; especially in England, a corporation consisting of one person at a time, as a king or bishop, who among other legal rights has that of official succession.
private corporation; a corporation which is not public.
public or *municipal corporation*; a corporation formed for purposes of government, such as a town, county, etc.

çọr′pōr·ȧ·tist, of or characteristic of a corporative state or its corporations.

çọr′pō·rā·tive, *a.* of or connected with a corporation.

çọr′pō·rā·tive (or **çọr′pō·răte**) **stāte,** a government, as theoretically in Italy under Fascism (1924–1943), centering absolute authority in one corporate body consisting of representatives of major industries, as employer-employee groups, each of which controls all phases of its own field of endeavor.

çọr′pō·rā·tŏr, *n.* a member of a corporation.

çọr·pō′rē·ăl, *a.* [L. *corporeus,* from *corpus, corporis,* a body.]
1. consisting of material substance; material; physical; tangible.
2. of, for, or having the nature of, the body; bodily.

çọr·pō′rē·ăl·ișm, *n.* the principles of a corporealist; materialism. [Rare.]

çọr·pō′rē·ăl·ist, *n.* one who believes in materialism. [Rare.]

çọr·pō·rē·al′i·ty, *n.* the state of being corporeal.

çọr·pō′rē·ăl·ly, *adv.* bodily; in a corporeal form or manner.

çọr·pō′rē·ăl·ness, *n.* corporeality.

çọr·pō·rē′i·ty, *n.* 1. the state or quality of being corporeal; bodily existence.
2. material or bodily substance.

çọr·pō′rē·ous, *a.* same as *corporeal.*

çọr·por″i·fi·çā′tion, *n.* the act of giving body to. [Obs.]

çọr·por′i·fy, *v.t.* to embody; to form into a body. [Obs.]

çọr′pō·șănt, *n.* [Port. *corpo santo,* from L. *corpus sanctum,* holy body.] a glowing ball of electrical discharge sometimes seen on church steeples or at the ends of a ship's masts, etc. during a storm: also called *St. Elmo's fire.*

çōrps (kōr), *n.*; *pl.* **çōrpș** (kōrz), [Fr. *corps,* from OFr. *corps,* the body; L. *corpus,* the body.]
1. any body of persons associated in some common work or interest; as, a *corps* of teachers.
2. in military usage, (a) a separate branch of the armed forces having some specialized function; as, the Signal *Corps,* the Marine *Corps*; (b) a tactical subdivision of an army, normally headed by a lieutenant general and composed of two or more divisions, plus auxiliary service troops.
3. a society formed by the students of a German university.
4. a body of laws. [Obs.]
5. a dead body; a corpse. [Obs.]

çōrps ā′rē·ȧ, formerly, any of the nine geographical divisions of the United States, formed on the basis of population, for purposes of military administration and training: now called *service command.*

çōrps de bal′let (ba′lā), [Fr.] a troupe or company of ballet dancers.

çọrpse, *n.* [earlier sp. *corps* (kōrs); ME. and OFr. *cors, corps*; see *corps.*]

1. a dead body, usually of a person.
2. a body, living or dead. [Obs.]
3. the endowment of an ecclesiastical office.

çorpse çan'dle, 1. a candle used at ceremonial vigils of a corpse before interment. [Obs.]
2. in England, an ignis fatuus, or phosphorescent light, sometimes seen in graveyards.

çorpse gāte, a covered gateway at the entrance to churchyards, intended to shelter the burial procession from rain: called also *lich gate.*

çorpse līght, 1. St. Elmo's fire.
2. a corpse candle, sense 2.

çorpse plant, the Indian pipe.

çorps'măn (kōr'), *n.*; *pl.* **çorps'men** (kōr'),
1. an enlisted man of the United States Army Medical Corps assigned to a combat area to give first aid and remove the wounded.
2. an enlisted pharmacist in the United States Navy.

çor'pū·lence, çor'pū·len·cy, *n.* fleshiness; excessive fatness; bulkiness of figure.

çor'pū·lent, *a.* [Fr. *corpulent,* from L. *corpulentus,* fleshy, fat, from *corpus,* a body.]
1. fleshy; having a great or excessive quantity of fat or flesh; obese; stout; bulky.
2. solid; dense; opaque. [Obs.]
Syn.—fat, portly, fleshy, stout.

çor'pū·lent·ly, *adv.* in a corpulent manner.

çor'pus, *n.*; *pl.* **çor'pō·rȧ,** [L.] 1. a human or animal body, especially a dead one: now used humorously.
2. a complete or comprehensive collection, as of laws or writings of a specified type; as, the *corpus* of a civil law.
3. the main body or substance of anything.
4. the principal, as distinguished from the interest or income, of an estate, investment, etc.
5. in anatomy, the main part of an organ; the solid and relatively homogeneous part.

çor'pus çal·lō'sum, *pl.* **çor'pō·rȧ çal·lō'sȧ,** [Mod. L., lit., callous body.] a mass of white, transverse fibers connecting the cerebral hemispheres in the higher mammals.

Çor'pus Çhris'tī, [L., Body of Christ.] in the Roman Catholic Church, a festival celebrated on the Thursday after Trinity Sunday, in honor of the Eucharist.

Çor'pus Çhris'tī cloth, the cloth used to cover the pyx: usually called *pyx cloth.*

çor'pus·cle (-sl), *n.* [L. *corpusculum,* dim. of *corpus,* body.]
1. a very small particle.
2. in anatomy, a protoplasmic particle with a special function; especially, any of the red cells (*erythrocytes*) or white cells (*leucocytes*) that float in the blood, lymph, etc. of vertebrates: red corpuscles contain hemoglobin, which carries oxygen to the body tissues, and certain white corpuscles sometimes kill harmful microorganisms.

çor·pus'çū·lăr, *a.* [Fr. *corpusculaire,* from L. *corpusculum,* dim. of *corpus,* a body.] pertaining to corpuscles; consisting of corpuscles or small particles; characteristic of corpuscles.
corpuscular philosophy; that system of philosophy that attempts to account for the phenomena of nature, by the motion, figure, rest, position, etc. of the minute particles of matter.
corpuscular theory; a theory for explaining the nature of light, adopted and advocated by Newton, but now rejected. According to this theory, the sun and all other luminous bodies have the property of emitting exceedingly minute particles of their substance with prodigious velocity, and these particles entering the eye produce the sensation of vision. It has also been termed the *Newtonian theory.*

çor·pus·çū·lā'ri·ăn, *a.* corpuscular.

çor·pus·çū·lā'ri·ăn, *n.* an advocate of or believer in corpuscular philosophy.

çor·pus'çūle, *n.* same as *corpuscle.*

çor·pus'çū·lous, *a.* same as *corpuscular.*

çor'pus dē·liç'tī, [L., lit., body of the crime.]
1. the facts constituting or proving a crime: the corpus delicti in a murder case is not the body of the victim, but the fact that death has occurred and that it is the result of murder.
2. loosely, the body of the victim in a murder case.

çor'pus jụ'ris, [L., a body of law.] a collection of all the laws of a nation or district.

Çor'pus Jụ'ris Çȧ·nō'ni·çī, [L., lit., body of canon law.] the decrees and canons of the Roman Catholic Church up to 1918.

Çor'pus Jụ'ris Ci·vī'lis, [L., lit., body of civil law.] the body of Civil, or Roman, law, compiled and issued during the reign of Justinian (528–534 A.D.): it has been the basis of most European law.

çor'pus lū'tē·um, *pl.* **çor'pō·rȧ lū'tē·ȧ,** [Mod. L., lit., luteous body.]
1. in anatomy, a mass of yellow tissue formed in the ovary by a ruptured Graafian follicle that has discharged its ovum: if the ovum is fertilized, this tissue secretes a necessary hormone.
2. a preparation containing this hormone, used in ovarian therapy.

çor'pus strī·ā'tum, *pl.* **çor'pō·rȧ strī·ā'tȧ,** [Mod. L., lit., striated body.] in anatomy, either of two striated ganglia in front of the thalamus in each half of the brain.

çŏr·rāde', *v.t.*; corraded, *pt., pp.*; corrading, *ppr.* [L. *corradere,* to scrape together; *com-,* together, and *radere,* to scrape, rub.]
1. to rub off; to scrape. [Obs.]
2. in geology, to wear away, erode, or disintegrate by the action of running water.

çŏr·rā'di·ăl, *a.* radiating from one center; converging to one point. [Rare.]

çŏr·rā'di·āte, *v.t.*; corradiated, *pt., pp.*; corradiating, *ppr.* [L. *com-,* together, and *radiatus,* pp. of *radiare,* to beam; *radius,* a staff, spoke.] to converge or focus to a single point. [Rare.]

çŏr·rȧ·di·ā'tion, *n.* a conjunction of rays in one point. [Rare.]

çŏr·ral', *n.* [Sp. *corral,* a pen or enclosure, for cattle, from *corro,* a circle or ring; L. *currere,* to run.]
1. a pen or enclosure for horses, cattle, and other animals.
2. an enclosure formed of wagons, used as a means of defense against attack and for confining the horses and other grazing animals.
3. a strong stockade or enclosure for capturing wild animals.

çŏr·ral', *v.t.*; corralled, *pt., pp.*; corralling, *ppr.*
1. to drive into or confine in a corral.
2. to surround or capture; round up.
3. to arrange (wagons) in the form of a corral.
4. to take possession of; lay hold of. [Slang.]

çŏr·rā'şion, *n.* [L. *corrasus,* pp. of *corradere*; *com-,* together, and *radere,* to scrape, rub off.] erosion by the abrasive action of running water containing sand, pebbles, and other debris.

çŏr·rā'sive, *a.* same as *corrosive.*

çor'rē·ăl, *a.* [LL. *correus,* an accomplice; *com-,* together, and *reus,* one accused; *res,* a thing, case.] relating to or having joint obligation.

çŏr·reçt', *v.t.*; corrected, *pt., pp.*; correcting, *ppr.* [from L. *correctus,* pp. of *corrigere*; *com-,* together, and *regere,* to lead straight, direct.]
1. to make right; to rectify; to bring to the standard of truth, justice, or propriety; as, to *correct* manners or principles.
2. to amend; to point out or remove faults or errors in; to set right; as, to *correct* a manuscript, to *correct* a student's work.
3. to bring back or attempt to bring back to propriety in morals; to punish for faults or deviations from moral rectitude; to chastise; to discipline; to reprove or rebuke; as, a child should be *corrected* for lying.

Correct thy son, and he shall give thee rest.
—Prov. xxix. 17.

4. to obviate or remove (something wrong or inconvenient); to reduce or change the qualities of; to counteract; to remedy; to rectify or destroy; as, to *correct* the acidity of the stomach by alkaline preparations; to *correct* errors and abuses.
Syn.—amend, improve, reform, rectify, reprove, punish.

çŏr·reçt', *a.* 1. conforming with or adhering to a conventional standard; proper; as, *correct* behavior.
2. conforming with fact or logic; true; accurate; right; free from errors.
Syn.—right, proper, faultless, exact, precise, accurate.

çŏr·reçt'ȧ·ble, çŏr·reçt'i·ble, *a.* that can be corrected or made right.

çŏr·reçt'i·fȳ, *v.t.* to set right. [Obs.]

çŏr·reçt'ing plāte, a thin lens for correcting incoming light rays in certain reflecting telescopes.

çŏr·reç'tion, *n.* 1. the act of correcting; the act of pointing out errors, mistakes, etc., or of setting right according to a just standard, as to truth, rectitude, justice, or propriety; as, the *correction* of opinions or manners.
2. that which is substituted or suggested in the place of what is wrong; a change or amendment; emendation; rectification; improvement; as, the *corrections* in his manuscripts were few.
3. that which is intended to rectify or to cure faults; the act of punishing or reproving; a reprimand or rebuke; discipline; chastisement.
4. the act or process of counteracting or removing what is inconvenient or painful in its effects; as, the *correction* of acidity in the stomach.
5. an amount added or taken away in correcting; as, a compass *correction*; a *correction* for temperature.
house of correction; a place of short-term confinement for persons convicted of minor offenses and regarded as capable of being reformed.
under correction; open to correction.

çŏr·reç'tion·ăl, *a.* 1. of correction.
2. tending to or intended for correction.

çŏr·reç'tion·ẽr, *n.* one who corrects or punishes. [Obs.]

çŏr·reç'tion līne, in the United States survey, one of the parallels of latitude taken as a new base line, thus partially correcting the convergence of north and south lines.

çŏr·reçt'i·tūde, *n.* [from *correct,* after *rectitude.*] the quality of being correct, especially in conduct; propriety.

çŏr·reçt'ive, *a.* tending or intending to correct or improve; remedial.

çŏr·reçt'ive, *n.* that which has the power of correcting; that which has the quality of altering or removing what is wrong or injurious; counteractive; something corrective; remedy; as, alkalis are *correctives* of acids; penalties are *correctives* of immoral conduct.

çŏr·reçt'ly, *adv.* in a correct manner; accurately; without fault or error.

çŏr·reçt'ness, *n.* the state or quality of exactness or precision.
Syn.—accuracy, exactness, precision, propriety.

çŏr·reçt'ŏr, *n.* 1. one who corrects.
2. that which corrects; as, a *corrector* of wrongs; an alkali is a *corrector* of acids.

çŏr·reçt'ō·ry, *a.* and *n.* corrective. [Obs.]

çŏr·reçt'ress, *n.* a woman who corrects.

çŏr·reg'i·dor (*or* Sp. -rā'hē-dōr), *n.* [Sp., a corrector, from *corregir,* to correct.] in Spain, a chief magistrate.

çor'rei (kor'i), *n.* same as *corrie.*

çor·rē·lāt'ȧ·ble, *a.* that can be correlated; as, *correlatable* divisions.

çor'rē·lāte, *n.* [L. *com-,* together, and *relatus,* related, pp. of *referre,* to bear back.] one who or that which stands in a reciprocal relation to something else, as father and son.

çor'rē·lāte, *a.* closely and naturally related.

çor'rē·lāte, *v.i.*; correlated, *pt., pp.*; correlating, *ppr.* to have a reciprocal relation; to be reciprocally related (*to* or *with*), as father and son.

çor'rē·lāte, *v.t.* to bring (a thing) into mutual relation (*with* another thing); to calculate or show the reciprocal relation between (two things); as, *correlate* the findings of psychology with those of sociology.

çor·rē·lā'tion, *n.* 1. a close or mutual relation; as, the *correlation* between illiteracy and prejudice.
2. the degree of relative correspondence, as between two sets of data; as, a *correlation* of 75 per cent.
3. a correlating or being correlated.
4. in geometry, the reciprocal relation between propositions, figures, etc. derivable from each other by interchanging the words *point* and *plane,* or *point* and *line.*

çŏr·rel'ȧ·tive, *a.* 1. having a reciprocal relation; reciprocally dependent.
2. in grammar, expressing mutual relation and used in pairs; as, *both . . . and* and *neither . . . nor* are *correlative* conjunctions.

çŏr·rel'ȧ·tive, *n.* 1. that which is correlative; correlate.
2. a correlative word: also called *correlator.*

çŏr·rel'ȧ·tive·ly, *adv.* in a correlative relation.

çŏr·rel'ȧ·tive·ness, *n.* the state of being correlative.

çŏr·rel·ȧ·tiv'i·ty, *n.* 1. the state of being correlative.
2. the degree of correlation.

çor·rē·lig'ion·ist, *n.* a coreligionist.

çŏr·rep'tion, *n.* [L. *correptio,* from *corripere,* to seize upon, reproach.] chiding; reproof; reprimand. [Obs.]

çor·re·spond', *v.i.*; corresponded, *pt., pp.*; corresponding, *ppr.* [Fr. *correspondre,* from L. *com-,* together, and *respondere,* to answer.]
1. to be in agreement (*with* something); be congruent (*to* something); suit; match.
2. to be similar, analogous, or equal (*to* something).

3. to communicate (*with* someone) by exchanging letters, usually habitually.
Syn.—suit, agree, fit, answer.

çor·re·spond′ence, *n.* 1. relation; fitness; congruity; mutual adaptation of one thing to another; as, *correspondence* of two theories.
2. similarity; analogy.
3. communication by exchange of letters; letter writing.
4. the letters or the quantity of letters which pass between correspondents; as, the *correspondence* of Washington and Jefferson.
5. friendly intercourse; reciprocal exchange of offices or civilities; connection. [Rare.]

çor·re·spond′ence çourse, a series of lessons and examinations in a course given by a correspondence school.

çor·re·spond′ence school, a school that gives instruction by mail, sending lessons and examinations to a student periodically, and correcting and grading the answers returned by him.

çor·re·spond′en·cy, *n.*; *pl.* **çor·re·spond′en·cies,** same as *correspondence.*

çor·re·spond′ent, *a.* suitable; fit; congruous; agreeable; answerable; adapted.

çor·re·spond′ent, *n.* 1. a thing that corresponds; correlate.
2. a person who exchanges letters with another, or who writes to a magazine, newspaper, etc.
3. a person hired by a magazine or newspaper to furnish news, articles, etc. of a certain type or from a certain place.
4. a person or firm acting for, or having regular commerce with, another at a distance.

çor·re·spond′ent·ly, *adv.* in a corresponding manner.

çor·re·spond′ing, *a.* 1. agreeing; equivalent.
2. similar; analogous.
3. exchanging, or communicating by, letters; handling correspondence; as, a *corresponding* secretary.
corresponding member; a member of a society residing at a distance, who is invited to aid in carrying out its designs.

çor·re·spond′ing·ly, *adv.* in a corresponding manner.

çor·re·spon′sion, *n.* correspondence. [Rare.]

çor·re·spon′sive, *a.* answering mutually; corresponding. [Archaic.]

çor·re·spon′sive·ly, *adv.* in a corresponsive manner.

çor′ri·dọr, *n.* [Fr., from It. *corridore,* a gallery, corridor, runner, from L. *currere,* to run.]
1. in architecture, a gallery or open communication around a building, leading to several chambers at a distance from each other.
2. in fortification, the covered way surrounding the fortifications of a place. [Obs.]
3. a long passageway or hall, especially one on which several rooms open.
4. a strip of land forming a passageway between two otherwise separated parts of a country, or between an inland country and a seaport.

çor′rie, çor′ri (kor′i), *n.* [Scot.] a round hollow in a hillside, often sheltering game: spelled also *correi.*

Çor′rie·dāle, *n.* [from *Corriedale,* New Zealand.] a breed of rather large, white-faced sheep, originally developed in New Zealand: they produce good wool and mutton lambs.

çor·ri·gen′dum, *n.*; *pl.* **çor·ri·ġen′dȧ,** [L., gerund of *corrigere,* to correct.]
1. an error to be corrected, especially one in a manuscript or book.
2. [*pl.*] a list of such errors with their corrections.

çor′ri·ġent, *n.* [L. *corrigens* (*-entis*), ppr. of *corrigere,* to correct.] in medicine, a substance used to modify the taste or effect of another ingredient.

çor′ri·ġent, *a.* corrective; modifying.

çor″ri·ġi·bil′i·ty, *n.* the quality of being corrigible.

çor′ri·ġi·ble, *a.* [Fr., from L. *corrigere,* to correct.]
1. that can be corrected, set right, or amended; as, a *corrigible* defect.
2. submitting to correction or punishment; willing to be reformed.
3. punishable; that can be chastised for correction. [Obs.]
4. corrective. [Obs.]

çor′ri·ġi·ble·ness, *n.* corrigibility.

çor′ri·ġi·bly, *adv.* in a corrigible manner.

çŏr·rī′văl, *n.* 1. a fellow rival; a competitor.
2. a companion. [Obs.]

çŏr·rī′văl, *a.* competitive; rivaling.

çŏr·rī′văl, *v.i.* and *v.t.* to rival.

çŏr·rī′văl·ry, *n.* competition. [Rare.]

çŏr·rī′văl·ship, *n.* competition. [Rare.]

çor′ri·vāte, *v.t.* [L. *corrivatus,* pp. of *corrivare,* to corrivate.] to cause to flow together. [Rare.]

çor·ri·vā′tion, *n.* the flowing together of different streams into one. [Rare.]

çŏr·rob′ō·rănt, *a.* 1. corroborating.
2. invigorating; strengthening; having the power or quality of giving strength; as, a *corroborant* medicine.

çŏr·rob′ō·rănt, *n.* 1. a medicine that strengthens; a tonic.
2. a fact that corroborates.

çŏr·rob′ō·rāte, *v.t.*; corroborated, *pt., pp.*; corroborating, *ppr.* [L. *corroboratus,* pp. of *corroborare,* to strengthen; *com-,* intens., and *roborare,* from *robur, roboris,* strength.]
1. to strengthen.
2. to confirm; to make more certain; as, to *corroborate* a suspicion.

çŏr·rob′ō·rāte, *a.* confirmed. [Archaic.]

çŏr·rob·ō·rā′tion, *n.* 1. a corroborating or being corroborated; addition of strength, assurance, or security; confirmation; as, the *corroboration* of an argument, or of intelligence.
2. anything that corroborates.

çŏr·rob′ō·rȧ·tive, *a.* corrobating or tending to corroborate; tending to confirm.

çŏr·rob′ō·rȧ·tive, *n.* a medicine that strengthens; a corroborant.

çŏr·rob′ō·rā·tŏr, *n.* a person or thing that corroborates.

çŏr·rob′ō·rȧ·tō·ry, *a.* corroborative.

çor·rob′ō·ree, çor·rob′ō·ri, *n.* [from native *korobra,* dance.]
1. a dance festival held at night by Australian aborigines to celebrate tribal victories and similar events.
2. in Australia, (a) a large or noisy festivity; (b) an uproar; tumult.

çor·rob′ō·ree, çor·rob′ō·ri, *v.i.* to participate in a corroboree.

çŏr·rōde′, *v.t.*; corroded, *pt., pp.*; corroding, *ppr.* [L. *corrodere,* to gnaw to pieces; *com-,* intens., and *rodere,* to gnaw.] to eat away by degrees; to wear away or diminish gradually, as if by gnawing; rust; consume; destroy: said of the action of chemicals, and often used figuratively; as, nitric acid *corrodes* copper.

çŏr·rōde′, *v.i.* to act, or be acted on, corrosively, used literally and figuratively.
Syn.—canker, gnaw, rust, waste, attack.

çŏr·rōd′ent, *a.* corroding.

çŏr·rōd′ent, *n.* a corrosive.

çŏr·rō·di·bil′i·ty, *n.* the quality of being corrodible.

çŏr·rōd′i·ble, *a.* that can be corroded.

çor′rō·dy, *n.* same as *corody.*

çŏr·rō·si·bil′i·ty, *n.* same as *corrodibility.*

çŏr·rō′si·ble, *a.* same as *corrodible.*

çŏr·rō′si·ble·ness, *n.* the quality of being corrosible.

çŏr·rō′ṣion, *n.* [Fr.; LL. *corrosio* (*-onis*), from L. *corrodere,* to corrode, gnaw to pieces.]
1. a corroding or being corroded.
2. a substance, as rust, formed by corroding.

çŏr·rō′sive, *a.* corroding or causing corrosion: often used figuratively; as, *corrosive* care, a *corrosive* ulcer.

çŏr·rō′sive, *n.* something causing corrosion.

çŏr·rō′sive·ly, *adv.* in a corrosive manner.

çŏr·rō′sive·ness, *n.* the quality of corroding, eating away, or fretting.

çŏr·rō′sive sub′li·māte, mercuric chloride, a poisonous, white, crystalline salt, $HgCl_2$.

çor′rụ·gănt, *a.* having the power of contracting into wrinkles.

çor′rụ·gāte, *v.t.* and *v.i.*; corrugated, *pt., pp.*; corrugating, *ppr.* [L. *corrugatus,* pp. of *corrugare*; *com-,* intens., and *rugare,* to wrinkle; from *ruga,* a wrinkle, fold.] to wrinkle; to draw or contract into folds, or into parallel grooves and ridges; furrow; as, to *corrugate* the brow.

çor′rụ·gāte, *a.* corrugated.

çor′rụ·gā·ted, *a.* folded or shaped into parallel ridges and furrows so as to form a wavy surface.

çor′rụ·gā·ted ī′ron (ī′ŭrn), sheet iron or steel, usually galvanized, corrugated to give it added strength in construction.

çor′rụ·gā·ted pā′pẽr, paper or pasteboard corrugated so as to be resilient, used for wrapping or packing.

çor·rụ·gā′tion, *n.* 1. a corrugating or being corrugated.
2. any of a series of parallel folds, ridges, wrinkles, or furrows.

çor′rụ·gā·tŏr, *n.* [L., from *corrugare,* to wrinkle.] a muscle which contracts the skin into wrinkles.

çor·rụ′ġent, *a.* in anatomy, contracting; drawing together. [Obs.]

çor·rump′, *v.t.* to corrupt. [Obs.]

çor·rump′ȧ·ble, *a.* corruptible. [Obs.]

çŏr·rupt′, *a.* [L. *corruptus,* pp. of *corrumpere,* to destroy, spoil, bribe, from *com-,* together, and *rumpere,* to break in pieces.]
1. originally, changed from a sound condition to an unsound one; spoiled; contaminated; rotten.
2. deteriorated from the normal or standard; specifically, (a) morally unsound or debased; perverted; evil; depraved; (b) taking bribes; (c) containing alterations, foreign admixtures, or errors: said of languages, texts, etc.

çŏr·rupt′, *v.t.* and *v.i.* to make or become corrupt (in various senses).

çŏr·rupt′ẽr, *n.* one who or that which corrupts.

çŏr·rupt′fụl, *a.* inclined to corrupt. [Rare.]

çŏr·rupt·i·bil′i·ty, *n.* the quality or state of being corruptible.

çŏr·rupt′i·ble, *a.* that can be corrupted; specifically, (a) that can be bribed; (b) liable to decay or destruction.

çŏr·rupt′i·ble, *n.* that which can become corrupted or decayed.

çŏr·rupt′i·ble·ness, *n.* corruptibility.

çŏr·rupt′i·bly, *adv.* in a corruptible manner.

çŏr·rup′tion, *n.* 1. decay; rottenness.
2. putrid matter; pus. [Dial.]
3. a changing or being changed for the worse; a making, becoming, or being corrupt.
4. depravity; wickedness; perversion or deterioration of moral principles; loss of purity or integrity.

Having escaped the *corruption* that is in the world through lust. —2 Pet. i. 4.

5. an instance of becoming or causing to be corrupt; as, a *corruption* of language.
6. bribery.
7. a thing or influence that corrupts.

Corruption in elections is the great enemy of freedom. —J. Adams.

corruption of blood; in old English law, the effect of an act of attainder of treason or felony, by which a person was disqualified from inheriting lands from an ancestor, and could neither retain those in his possession nor transmit them by descent to his heirs.
Syn.—putrescence, putrefaction, pollution, defilement, contamination, depravation, debasement, adulteration, depravity, taint, bribery.

çŏr·rup′tion·ist, *n.* a person who engages in or upholds corrupt practices, such as bribery, especially in public life.

çŏr·rupt′ive, *a.* tending to corrupt or produce corruption.

çŏr·rupt′less, *a.* not susceptible to corruption or decay.

çŏr·rupt′ly, *adv.* in a corrupt manner; by means of bribery.

çŏr·rupt′ness, *n.* the state of being corrupt.

çŏr·rupt′ress, *n.* a woman who corrupts others.

çor′saç, *n.* same as *corsak.*

çọr·säge′ (-säzh′), *n.* [Fr. *corsage,* a bust, trunk; OFr. *cors,* a body.]
1. a bodice; the waist of a woman's dress; as, an openwork *corsage.*
2. a small bouquet for a woman to wear, usually at the waist or shoulder.

çor′sāir, *n.* [Fr. *corsaire*; Pr. *corsari*; Sp. *corsario,* a corsair; Pr. *corsa,* a cruise, course; from L. *cursus,* a running; *currere,* to run.]
1. a pirate.
2. a pirate ship.
3. a privateer, especially of Barbary.
4. a fish, *Sebastichthys rosaceus,* of the Pacific coast.

çor′sak, *n.* [native name.] a species of yellowish fox found in India, the *Vulpes corsak.*

çorse, *n.* [OFr. *cors, corps,* from L. *corpus,* a body.]
1. a corpse; a dead body. [Archaic and Poet.]
2. the living body; bodily frame. [Obs.]

çorse′let, *n.* [Fr. *corselet,* dim. of OFr. *cors,* a body.]
1. armor to cover and protect the body, worn in medieval times.
2. (kọr-se-let′), a woman's lightweight corset, usually without stays.
3. that part of a winged insect to which the wings and legs are attached; the thorax.

çorse′let, *v.t.* to encircle with a corselet. [Rare.]

çorse′preș″ent, *n.* formerly, a present paid at the interment of a dead body.

çor′set, *n.* [Fr. *corset*, dim. of OFr. *cors*, a body.]
1. [*sometimes pl.*] a woman's close-fitting undergarment, often tightened with laces and reinforced with stays, worn to give support or a desired figure to the body from the hips to the breast.
2. a bodice. [Archaic.]
3. a quilted garment of defensive armor; a gambeson of metal. [Obs.]

çor′set, *v.t.*; corseted, *pt., pp.*; corseting, *ppr.* to dress in a corset; to fit a corset on.

Çor′si·căn, *a.* of or pertaining to Corsica, its people, or their dialect.

Çor′si·căn, *n.* 1. a native or inhabitant of Corsica.
2. the Italian dialect spoken by Corsicans.

çors′let, *n.* a corselet (armor).

çors′ned, *n.* [AS. *corsnæd*; *cor-*, from *coren*, *ceósan*, to choose, and *snæd*, a piece cut off; from *snidan*, to cut.] consecrated bread used by the Anglo-Saxons as an ordeal, supposed to choke the guilty. [Obs.]

çor·tège′, cor·tège′ (kọr-tezh′), *n.* [Fr., from It. *corteggio*, a retinue, from *corte*, a court.]
1. a train of attendants.
2. a ceremonial procession.

Çor′tes, *n.pl.* [Sp. and Port., pl. of *corte*, a court.] the national legislative body of Portugal; also, the legislature of Spain before the seizure of power by Franco. Both have two houses.

çor′tex, *n.*; *pl.* **çor′ti·cēș,** [L.]
1. bark, as of a tree.
2. in medicine, cinchona bark.
3. in anatomy, the outer part or external layers of an internal organ, as of the kidney; especially, the layer of gray matter over most of the brain.

çor′ti·căl, *a.* [from L. *cortex*, *corticis*, bark of a tree.]
1. of or pertaining to a cortex.
2. consisting of cortex.
3. involving, or in some way caused by, the brain cortex.

Çor·ti·cā′tȧ, *n.pl.* [L., neut. pl. of *corticatus*, from *cortex*, *corticis*, bark.] the barked corals; the *Alcyonaria*.

çor′ti·çāte, çor′ti·çā·ted, *a.* 1. having a bark, rind, or other barklike covering.
2. having a cortex.
3. of or relating to the *Corticata*.

çor′ti·cēș, *n.* plural of *cortex*.

çor·ti·cif′ẽr·ous, *a.* [L. *cortex*, *corticis*, bark, and *ferre*, to bear.] producing bark, or that which resembles it.

çor·tic′i·form, *a.* [L. *cortex*, *corticis*, bark, and *forma*, form.] resembling bark.

çor′ti·cine, *n.* 1. an alkaloid derived from the bark of the *Populus tremula*.
2. a floor covering resembling linoleum.

çor′ti·çōle, çor·tiç′ō·lous, *a.* growing on bark, as certain fungi.

çor′ti·çōse, çor′ti·çous, *a.* barky; covered with bark; corticate.

çor′tile, *n.* [It., from *corte*, a court.] in architecture, a small court enclosed by the walls of a building.

çor′tin, *n.* [*cort*ex, and *-in*.] the hormone secreted by the adrenal cortex.

çor·tī′nȧ, *n.* [LL. *cortina*, a curtain, small court, from *cortis*, court.] that portion of the veil of fungi which adheres to the margin of the pileus in fragments.

çor′ti·sōne (*or* -zōn), *n.* an adrenal-gland hormone extracted from ox bile or prepared synthetically from certain tropical plants, used experimentally in the treatment of rheumatoid arthritis and certain other diseases.

çō·run′dum, *n.* [L., from Hind. *kurand*, corundum.] a common mineral, aluminum oxide, Al_2O_3, second only to the diamond in hardness: a dark, granular variety is used for grinding and polishing; pure, transparent varieties are the ruby, sapphire, Oriental amethyst, and Oriental topaz.

çō·rus′cănt, *a.* flashing; glittering by flashes.

çor′us·çāte, *v.i.*; coruscated, *pt., pp.*; coruscating, *ppr.* [L. *coruscatus*, pp. of *coruscare*, to move quickly, glitter.] to flash; to sparkle; to glitter.
Syn.—glisten, gleam, sparkle, radiate, shine.

çor·us·çā′tion, *n.* 1. any sudden flash of light.
2. a coruscating; a sparkling; a flashing.
3. a sudden brilliant display, as of wit.
Syn.—flash, glitter, radiation, gleam, sparkle.

cor·vée′ (çor-vā′), *n.* [Fr., from LL. *corvata*, from *corrogare*, to bring together by entreaty; *com-*, together, and *rogare*, to ask.]
1. in feudal law, an obligation on the inhabitants of a district to perform certain services, as the repair of roads, etc., for the sovereign or the feudal lord.
2. forced labor exacted by a government, as for the construction of public works.

çorveș, *n.* plural of *corf*.

çor·vette′, çor·vet′, *n.* [Fr., from Sp. *corveta*, *corbeta*; L. *corbita*, a slow-sailing ship of burden, from *corbis*, a wicker basket.]
1. formerly, a sailing warship larger than a sloop and smaller than a frigate: it had only one tier of guns.
2. a small warship of about 1,000 tons, used for antisubmarine and convoy duty.

çor·vet′tō, *n.* a curvet.

çor′vi·form, *a.* resembling a crow; crowlike.

çor·vī′nȧ, *n.* [L. *corvinus*, from *corvus*, a raven.] a California bluefish, *Cynoscion parvipinnis*, related to the weakfish.

çor′vine, *a.* [L. *corvinus*, from *corvus*, a raven.] pertaining to the crow family.

Çor′vus, *n.* [L., a raven.]
1. in astronomy, a small southern constellation near Virgo; the Crow or Raven.
2. [c–] a name given to several ancient military weapons because of a fancied resemblance to a crow's beak.
3. in zoology, a genus of birds, including the crow, jackdaw, raven, and rook.

Çor′y·bant, *n.*; *pl.* **Çor′y·bants** or **Çor·y·ban′tēș,** [L. *Corybas* (*-antis*); Gr. *Korybas*.]
1. in Greek mythology, (a) one of the attendants who followed the Phrygian goddess Cybele with dancing and revelry in her nightly wanderings; (b) a priest in the worship of Cybele.
2. [c–] a reveler.

Çor·y·ban′ti·ăn, *a.* of or pertaining to the Corybants.

Çor·y·ban′tiç, *a.* 1. [c–] wild and frenzied, as the Corybants.
2. of the Corybants.

çō·ryd′ȧ·līne, çō·ryd′ȧ·lin, *n.* a vegetable base found in the roots of the plants *Corydalis bulbosa* and *Corydalis fabacea*.

Çō·ryd′ȧ·lis, *n.* [L., from Gr. *korydallis*, a lark; the spur of the flower resembling the crest of the lark; *korys*, a helmet.] a genus of dicotyledonous plants with yellow, rose, blue, or purple flowers resembling those of the bleeding heart; also, [c–] any plant of this genus.

Çor′y·don, *n.* [L.; Gr. *Korydōn*.]
1. a shepherd: traditional name used in pastoral poems.
2. a young country fellow.

Çor′y·lus, *n.* [L., from Gr. *korylos*, a hazel or filbert tree, from *korys*, a helmet, in allusion to the shape of the involucre.] a genus of shrubs or small trees, the hazels, which bear hazelnuts, or filberts.

çor′ymb, *n.* [L. *corymbus*; Gr. *korymbos*, the uppermost point, a cluster of fruit or flowers, from *korys*, a helmet.] in botany, a cluster of flowers in which the stems are of different lengths, so arranged along a common axis as to form a flat, broad mass of flowers with a convex or level top, as in the hawthorn and candytuft.

CORYMB

çor′ymbed, *a.* corymbose.

çō·rym′bi·āte, çō·rym′bi·ā·ted, *a.* [LL. *corymbiatus*, from *corymbus*, a cluster, corymb.] of or like a corymb; also, in the form of corymbs.

çor·ym·bif′ẽr·ous, *a.* producing corymbs; bearing fruit, berries, or flowers in clusters.

çō·rym′bōse, çō·rym′bous, çō·rym′bū·lous, *a.* 1. consisting of or resembling corymbs.
2. growing in corymbs.

çō·rym′bōse·ly, *adv.* in a corymbose manner.

çor·y·phae′noid, *a.* of or pertaining to the genus *Coryphæna*, a family of fishes including the dolphins.

çor·y·phae′us, *n.*; *pl.* **çor·y·phae′ī,** [L. *coryphæus*; Gr. *koryphaios*, the leader of a chorus, from *koryphē*, the head.]
1. the leader of the ancient Greek dramatic chorus; hence, a leader of any chorus.
2. any leader or chief.

> . . . *corypheus* of the Independent faction.
> —South.

çō·ry·phee′ (-rē-fā′), *n.* [Fr.] a ballet dancer, especially one who leads a ballet.

çor′y·phēne, *n.* any coryphaenoid fish.

Çō-ryph′ō·don, *n.* [L., from Gr. *koryphē*, head, summit, and *adōn*, tooth.] a genus of extinct animals, forming a link between the elephants and tapirs: so named because the ridges of the molars are developed into points: found in the Eocene of England and the United States.

çō·ryph′ō·dont, *a.* of or pertaining to the genus *Coryphodon*.

çō·rȳ′zȧ, *n.* [L., from Gr. *koryza*, catarrh.] catarrh of the nose; a cold in the head.

ços, *n.* [from *Cos* (Gr. *Kōs*), island in the Aegean from which the variety was introduced.] a kind of lettuce with a cylindrical or conical head.

ços·cin′ō·man·cy, *n.* [Gr. *koskinon*, a sieve, and *manteia*, divination.] divination by the turning of a sieve suspended on a pair of shears: a practice of voodooism.

ços·çō·rō′bȧ, *n.* a white South American duck resembling a swan.

çōșe, *v.i.*; cosed, *pt., pp.*; cosing, *ppr.* same as *coze*.

çōșe, *n.* same as *coze*.

çō·sē′çant, *n.* [abbrev. of L. *complementi secans*, secant of the complement.] in trigonometry, the secant of the complement of an angle or arc.

COSECANT
$\frac{R}{Y}$, cosecant of angle BAC

çō·seīs′măl, *a.* [*co-*, and Gr. *seismos*, earthquake, from *seiein*, to shake.] denoting the points, or lines connecting such points, simultaneously affected by an earthquake shock.

çō·seīs′măl, *n.* a coseismal line.

çō·seīs′miç, *a.* coseismal.

çō·sen′tient (-shent), *a.* [*co-*, and L. *sentiens* (*-entis*), ppr. of *sentire*, to know, perceive.] perceiving together.

çō′șey, *a.*; *comp.* cosier; *superl.* cosiest; cozy.

çō′șey, *n.*; *pl.* **çō′șeyș,** cozy.

çosh′ẽr, *v.t.* [Ir. *cosair*, a feast.] to levy (exactions), as formerly Irish landlords did on their tenants.

çosh′ẽr, *v.t.* to feed with delicacies; to treat kindly and fondly; to fondle; to pet (sometimes with *up*). [Colloq.]

> Thus she *coshered up* Eleanor with cold fowl and port wine. —Trollope.

çosh′ẽr·ẽr, *n.* one who coshers.

çosh′ẽr·ing, *n.* in Ireland, an old feudal custom whereby the lord of the soil was entitled to quarter and feast himself and his followers at a tenant's house.

çō′șie, *a.* cozy.

çō′șiẽr (-zhẽr), *n.* a cobbler. [Obs.]

çō·sig′nȧ·tō·ry, *a.* [*co-*, and L. *signatorius*, from *signare*, to sign.] signing a document, as a treaty, along with others.

çō·sig′nȧ·tō·ry, *n.*; *pl.* **çō·sig′nȧ·tō·rieș,** one who signs a document, as a treaty, along with others.

çō-sīgn′ẽr, *n.* a person who signs a promissory note in addition to the maker, thus becoming responsible for the obligation if the maker should default: also called *co-maker*.

çō·sig′ni·tā·ry, *a.* and *n.* cosignatory.

çō′și·ly, *adv.* cozily.

çōș′in·āġe, *n.* [OFr. *cosinage*, *cousinage*, from *cosin*, *cousin*, a cousin, kinsman.] in law, (a) anciently, a writ to recover possession of an estate in lands, when a stranger has entered and abated, after the death of the grandfather's grandfather, or of certain collateral relations; (b) now, blood relation.

çō′sīne, *n.* [for *co-sinus*, abbrev. of *complementi sinus*, sine of the complement.] in trigonometry, the sine of the complement of an angle or arc.

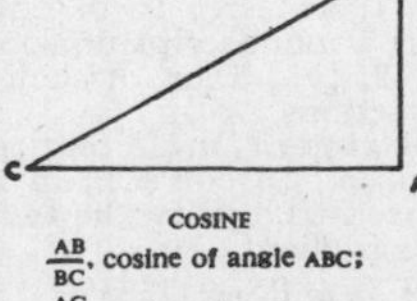

COSINE
$\frac{AB}{BC}$, cosine of angle ABC;
$\frac{AC}{BC}$, cosine of angle ACB

çoș·met′iç, çoș·met′iç·ăl, *a.* [Gr. *kosmētikos*, from *kosmein*, to decorate, adorn; *kosmos*, order, adornment.] beautifying or designed to beautify the skin, hair, etc.

çoș·met′iç, *n.* any preparation that helps to beautify the skin, hair, etc., as rouge and powder.

çoș·met′i·căl·ly, *adv.* 1. by means of cosmetics.
2. as regards cosmetics.

çoș·me·ti′ciăn (-tish′ăn), *n.* same as *cosmetologist*.

çoș·me·tol′ō·ġist, *n.* one who makes or sells cosmetics or who practices cosmetology; one skilled in giving cosmetic treatments.

çoș·me·tol′ō·ġy, *n.* the study of cosmetics and their use.

çoș′miç, çoș′miç·ăl, *a.* [Gr. *kosmikos*, from *kosmos*, order, universe.]

1. relating to the universe as a whole.
2. harmonious; orderly. [Rare.]
The dark chaotic dullard, who knows the meaning of nothing *cosmic* or noble. —Carlyle.
3. of the universe exclusive of the earth.
4. vast; grandiose.
A result of the play between organism and environment through *cosmic* ranges of time. —Tyndall.

çoṣ'miç·ăl·ly, *adv.* 1. in relation to, or according to the principles of, the cosmos.
2. on a grandiose scale.

çoṣ'miç dust, small particles, probably meteoric fragments, falling from interstellar space to the earth.

çoṣ'miç rāyṣ, rays of extremely short wave length and great penetrating power, which bombard the earth from beyond its atmosphere: also called *ultragamma rays.*

çoṣ'miṣm, *n.* the philosophy of the evolution of the universe; the theory that the cosmos can be scientifically explained as a self-existent system.

çoṣ'mō-, [from Gr. *kosmos,* universe, world, order.] a combining form meaning *world, universe,* as in *cosmology:* also, before a vowel, *cosm-.*

çoṣ·mō·gon'iç, çoṣ·mog'ō·năl, çoṣ·mō·gon'iç·ăl, *a.* of or pertaining to cosmogony.

çoṣ·mog'ō·nist, *n.* one versed in cosmogony.

çoṣ·mog'ō·ny, *n.*; *pl.* **çoṣ·mog'ō·nieṣ,** [Gr. *kosmogonia,* the creation or origin of the world; from *kosmogonos; kosmos,* order, universe, and *-gonos,* from the root of *gignesthai,* to produce.] the generation or origin of the universe; also, a theory or account of this.

çoṣ·mog'rȧ·phẽr, *n.* [Gr. *kosmographos; kosmos,* universe, and *graphos,* from *graphein,* to write.] one who is an expert in cosmography.

çoṣ·mō·graph'iç, çoṣ·mō·graph'iç·ăl, *a.* relating or pertaining to cosmography.

çoṣ·mō·graph'iç·ăl·ly, *adv.* in a manner corresponding to cosmography.

çoṣ·mog'rȧ·phy, *n.*; *pl.* **çoṣ·mog'rȧ·phieṣ,**
1. a general description of the world.
2. the science dealing with the structure of the universe as a whole and of its related parts: geology, geography, and astronomy are branches of cosmography.

çoṣ'mō·lābe, *n.* [Gr. *kosmos,* universe, and *lambanein,* to take.] an ancient instrument resembling the astrolabe, formerly used in astronomical observations.

çoṣ·mol'ȧ·try, *n.* [Gr. *kosmos,* universe, and *latreia,* worship.] the worship of the world.

çoṣ'mō·līne, *n.* [*cos*metic, and L. *oleum,* oil.] a heavy grease used in cosmetics and especially as a protective coating for firearms, etc.

çoṣ'mō·līne, *v.t.*; cosmolined, *pt., pp.*; cosmolining, *ppr.* to coat with cosmoline.

çoṣ·mō·log'iç·ăl, *a.* relating or pertaining to cosmology.

çoṣ·mol'ō·ġist, *n.* one versed in cosmology.

çoṣ·mol'ō·ġy, *n.* [Fr. *cosmologie,* from Gr. *kosmos,* universe, and *-logia,* from *legein,* to speak.] theory or philosophy of the nature and principles of the universe.

çoṣ·mom'e·try, *n.* [Gr. *kosmos,* the world, and *-metria,* from *metron,* a measure.] the art of measuring the universe.

çoṣ'mō·naut, *n.* [Russ. *kosmonaut,* from Gr. *kosmos,* universe, and *nautēs,* sailor.] a person trained to make rocket flights in outer space; astronaut.

çoṣ·mō·plas'tiç, *a.* [Gr. *kosmoplastēs,* the framer of the world; *kosmos,* universe, and *plassein,* to form.] pertaining to the formation of the universe.

çoṣ·mō·pol'i·tăn, *a.* [Gr. *kosmopolitēs,* a citizen of the world; *kosmos,* world, and *politēs,* a citizen.]
1. belonging to the whole world; not national or local.
2. not bound by local or national habits or prejudices; at home in all countries or places.

çoṣ·mō·pol'i·tăn, *n.* a cosmopolitan person or thing; a cosmopolite.

çoṣ·mō·pol'i·tăn·iṣm, *n.* the quality or condition of being cosmopolitan.

çoṣ·mop'ō·līte, *n.* 1. a cosmopolitan person; a citizen of the world.
2. a plant or animal common to all or most parts of the world.

çoṣ·mop'ō·līte, *a.* cosmopolitan.

çoṣ·mop'ō·lī·tiṣm, *n.* same as *cosmopolitanism.*

çoṣ·mō·rä'mȧ, *n.* [Gr. *kosmos,* the world, and *horama,* from *horan,* to see.] an exhibition of scenes of various parts of the world.

çoṣ·mō·ram'iç, *a.* pertaining to a cosmorama.

çoṣ'mos, *n.* [Gr. *kosmos,* order, harmony, ornament, hence the world as an orderly system.]
1. order; harmony.
2. the universe as an embodiment of order and harmony; the system of order and harmony combined in the universe.
. . . first received the title of "*cosmos,*" or "beautiful order." —Trench.
3. any complete and orderly system.
4. [C–] a small genus of American composite plants with feathery leaves and white, pink, or purple flowers.

çoṣ'mō·sphēre, *n.* [Gr. *kosmos,* the world, and *sphaira,* a sphere.] an apparatus for showing the position of the earth, at any given time, with respect to the fixed stars. It consists of a hollow glass globe, on which are depicted the stars, and within which is a terrestrial globe.

çoṣ'mō·thē·iṣm, *n.* [Gr. *kosmos,* world, and *theos,* god.] pantheism. [Rare.]

çoṣ·mō·thet'iç, *a.* [Gr. *kosmos,* world, and *thetikos,* from *tithenai,* to fix, set up.] believing in the real and substantial existence of an external world.

çoṣ'mō·tron, *n.* [*cos*mic rays, and cyclo*tron.*] a high-energy proton accelerator.

cō·sov'ẽr·eign (-in), *n.* a joint sovereign; a king or queen consort.

cō·spon'sŏr, *n.* a joint sponsor, as of a proposed piece of legislation.

cō·spon'sŏr, *v.t.* to be a cosponsor of.

Ços'sack, *n.* [Russ. *Kozakŭ.*] one of a people, very expert on horseback, inhabiting the steppes in the southern Soviet Union.

Ços'sack, *a.* of or characteristic of the Cossacks.

ços'săṣ, *n.pl.* [E. Ind.] plain India muslins of various qualities and breadths.

ços'set, *n.* [Domesday Bk. form *cozez* [for *cotsets*] suggests AS. *cot-sæta,* cot dweller.] a lamb brought up without the aid of the dam; a pet lamb; also, any pet.

ços'set, *v.t.*; cosseted, *pt., pp.*; cosseting, *ppr.* to pet; to fondle.

ços'siç, ços'siç·ăl, *a.* relating to algebra. [Obs.]

Ços'sus, *n.* [L., a kind of larvae.] a genus of moths of the family *Epialidæ,* including the species, *Cossus ligniperda,* the goat moth.

çost, *n.* [L. *costa,* rib, side.] in heraldry, a cottise.

çost, *v.t.*; cost, *pt., pp.*; costing, *ppr.* [ME. *costen;* OFr. *coster;* LL. *costare,* contr. of L. *constare,* to stand together, stand at, cost; *com-,* together, and *stare,* to stand.]
1. (a) to be obtained or obtainable for (a set price); be priced at; (b) to cause or require the expenditure, loss, or experience of; as, victory *cost* him his health. Originally construed as a *v.i.* with the apparent object an adverbial adjunct, and still felt as a *v.i.* when used with an adverb; as, it *cost* him dearly.
2. in business, to estimate the cost of making, producing, carrying out, etc., as a product or program (often with *out*).

çost, *n.* 1. (a) the amount of money or the like asked or paid for a thing; price; (b) the amount spent in producing or manufacturing a commodity; (c) the amount paid for something by a dealer, contractor, etc.: a markup is usually added to this amount to arrive at a selling price; as, stoves sold at *cost* in a sale.
2. (a) the amount of money, time, effort, etc. required to achieve an end; (b) loss; sacrifice; detriment.
3. *pl.* in law, the expenses of a lawsuit, especially those assessed by the court against the losing party.
at all costs; regardless of the cost or difficulty involved; by any means required: also *at any cost.*

çost-, same as *costo-.*

ços'tȧ, *n.*; *pl.* **ços'tae,** [L., a rib.] in biology, a rib, or part resembling a rib; specifically, (a) the midrib of a leaf; (b) the anterior marginal rib of an insect's wing; (c) the ridge of a shell.

çost aç·çount'ănt, an accountant who specializes in cost accounting.

çost aç·çount'ing, in accounting, any system whereby the costs of production, manufacture, sales, overhead, etc. are shown; also, the maintenance of such a system.

ços'tăl, *a.* [Fr. *costal,* from L. *costa,* a rib.] pertaining to or near a rib or the ribs.

ços'tăl-nẽrved, *a.* branching from the costa, as the nerves of a leaf.

ços'tărd, *n.* [ME. *costard,* a ribbed apple, from L. *costa,* a rib.] an apple; also, a head. [Obs.]

ços'tărd·mŏn″gẽr, *n.* a costermonger. [Obs.]

ços'tāte, ços'tā·ted, *a.* [L. *costatus,* from *costa,* rib.] ribbed; having ribs or the appearance of ribs.

ços'tēan, *v.i.* [Corn. *cothas,* dropped, and *stean,* tin.] to prospect for a lode by sinking pits to the bedrock. [Brit.]

ços'tēan·ing, *n.* the process of prospecting by sinking pits. [Brit.]

çost'-ef·fect'ive, *a.* producing good results for the amount of money spent; efficient or economical.

çost'-ef·fect'ive·ness, *n.* the quality of being cost-effective.

ços·tel'lāte, *a.* [L. *costellatus,* from *costellum,* dim. of *costa,* a rib.] having fine ribs; costate.

ços'tẽr, *n.* a costermonger.

ços'tẽr·mŏn″gẽr, *n.* a person who sells fruit, vegetables, etc. from a cart or street stand. [Brit.]

ços'ti-, same as *costo-.*

ços'tive, *a.* [OFr. *costevé,* from L. *constipatus,* pp. of *constipare,* to cram, stuff; *com-,* together, and *stipare,* to crowd, press together.]
1. dry and hard; also, cold; formal. [Obs.]
2. constipated.

ços'tive·ly, *adv.* with costiveness.

ços'tive·ness, *n.* constipation.

çost'less, *a.* costing nothing.

çost'li·ness, *n.* the quality or state of being costly; expensiveness.

çost'ly, *a.*; *comp.* costlier; *superl.* costliest,
1. of a high price; expensive, purchased at a great expense; as, a *costly* habit; *costly* furniture.
2. very valuable; magnificent; sumptuous.
3. lavish; extravagant. [Archaic.]
Syn.—choice, gorgeous, precious, expensive.

çost'mā·ry, *n.* [L. *costus;* Gr. *kostos,* an Oriental aromatic plant, and *Maria,* Mary.]
1. *Tanacetum balsamita,* a perennial plant of the family *Compositæ,* a native of the south of Europe.
2. a kind of chrysanthemum with many small flowers and sweet-smelling leaves.

ços'tō-, a combining form from L. *costa,* a rib, used to express relation between a rib and the thing designated, as in *costotome.*

ços'tō·tōme, *n.* a dissecting instrument used to sever the ribs.

ços'trel, *n.* [W. *costrel,* a cup, flagon.] a large bottle or flask with a loop or loops by which it can be hung from the shoulders or waist. [Archaic or Dial.]

çost sys'tem, same as *cost accounting.*

ços'tūme, *n.* [Fr., *costume;* LL., *costuma;* L. *consuetudo,* custom.]
1. a style of dress; dress in general, including accessories, style of the hair, etc.
2. the style of dress typical of a certain country, period, people, etc., often worn at a masquerade or in a play.
3. a complete set of outer clothes considered as a unit and worn for a particular purpose; as, a riding *costume.*

ços·tūme', *v.t.*; costumed, *pt., pp.*; costuming, *ppr.* to provide with a costume; to put a costume on; to dress.

ços'tūme jew'el·ry, jewelry made of or with relatively inexpensive materials.

ços'tūm·ẽr, *n.* a costume maker or dealer.

ços'tus-root, *n.* the root of a Kashmirian plant, *Saussurea lappa,* the oil of which is used in perfumery, etc. for the East Indian market.

cō·sū·prēme', *n.* a partaker of supremacy. [Obs.]

cō·sụre'ty (-shụr'), *n.*; *pl.* **cō·sụre'tieṣ,** one who is surety with another.

cō'ṣy, *a.*; *comp.* cosier; *superl.* cosiest, and *n.*; *pl.* **cō'ṣieṣ,** cozy.

çot, *n.* [ME. *cot;* AS. *cot,* a cot, cottage, hut.]
1. a cottage; a hut; a small house. [Poetic.]
2. a protective covering or sheath, as for a sore finger.
3. a small shelter; a cote.

çot, *n.* [Ir.] a little boat. [Irish.]

çot, *n.* a cotquean (sense 1). [Obs.]

çot, *n.* [orig. military term, from Hind. *khāt,* from Sans. *khatvā.*] a narrow bed, especially one made of canvas on a frame that can be folded up.

cō·tan'ġent, *n.* [Mod. L. *cotangens,* from *co. tangens,* short for *complementi tangens,* lit., tangent of the complement.] in trigonometry, the tangent of the complement of an angle or arc.

cō·tan·ġen'tiăl (-shăl), *a.* of, or having the nature of, a cotangent.

cō·tär'nine, *n.* [by transposition of *narcotine.*] an organic base, $C_{12}H_{15}NO_4$, obtained by the oxidation of narcotine.

çōte, *n.* [ME. *cote*; AS. *cote*, a cot, cottage, chamber.]
1. a small shelter or shed for birds, chickens, sheep, etc.
2. a cottage. [Dial.]

çōte, *v.t.*; coted, *pt.*, *pp.*; coting, *ppr.* [Fr. *côtoyer*, to go by the side of; OFr. *costoier*, from L. *costa*, a rib, side.] to pass by; surpass. [Obs.]

çō·teau′ (-tō′), *n.*; *pl.* **çō·teaux′** (-tōz′), [Fr., a little hill.] a divide of land; also, a small plateau.

çō·tem·pō·rā′nē·ous, *a.* same as *contemporaneous.*

çō·tem′pō·rā·ry, *a.* and *n.* same as *contemporary.*

çō·ten′ăn·cy, *n.* combined tenancy.

çō·ten′ănt, *n.* one of two or more tenants who share a place; a joint tenant.

çō′te·riē, *n.* [Fr., orig., organization of peasants holding land from a feudal lord, from *cote*, hut, from M.D. *kote.*] a group of people who often gather for social purposes; social circle or set; clique.

çō·tẽr′mi·nous, *a.* conterminous.

çō′thũrn, *n.* same as *cothurnus.*

çō·thũr′nus, *n.*; *pl.* **çō·thũr′nī,** [L.]
1. a high, thick-soled boot or buskin worn by actors in ancient Greek and Roman tragedies.
2. tragedy or a lofty, tragic style in drama.

COTHURNUS

çō·tiç′ū·lăr, *a.* [L., *coticula*, dim. of *cos*, a whetstone.] pertaining to whetstones; like or suitable for whetstones. [Obs.]

çō·tīd′ăl, *a.* indicating the coincidence in time or extent of tides; as, *cotidal* lines on a map.

çō·til′liŏn, çō·til′lon (-yun), *n.* [Fr. *cotillon*, a dance, a petticoat, dim. of OFr. *cote*, a coat.]
1. a brisk, lively dance of the nineteenth century, characterized by many intricate figures and variations and the continual changing of partners.
2. the music for such a dance.
3. black and white woolen skirting.

Çō·tin′gȧ, *n.* [L., from S. Am. native name.]
1. a genus of birds, the chatterers.
2. [c—] any bird of this genus.

çot′ise, *n.* cottise.

çot′ised (-ist), *a.* cottised.

çot′land, *n.* land belonging to a cottage.

Çō·tō·nē·as′tẽr, *n.* [Mod. L., from L. *cotonea*, a quince, and *-aster.*] a genus of shrubby trees of the apple family.

çot′quēan (-kwēn), *n.* [ME. *cot*, a cottage, and *quean*, a woman.]
1. a man who busies himself with housework and other work regarded as women's. [Archaic.]
2. a vulgar, scolding woman; a shrew. [Archaic.]

çō·trus·tee′, *n.* a joint trustee.

Çots′wōld, *n.* any of a breed of sheep with long wool, originally from the Cotswolds, a range of hills in Gloucestershire, England.

çot′tȧ, *n.* [ML.] a short surplice worn in some churches.

çot′tȧ·bus, *n.* [L., from Gr. *kottabos.*] an ancient Greek game, which consisted in throwing wine from cups, without spilling, into metal basins.

çot′tāġe, *n.* [ME. *cotage*; Anglo-Fr. *cotage*, from OFr. *cote*; see *cot* (cottage).]
1. a small house, usually of one story.
2. a house at a resort or in the country, used for vacations or as a summer home.
cottage allotment; in Great Britain, a laborer's allowance of land for his use, gratis.
cottage cheese; a soft white cheese made by straining and seasoning the curds of sour milk.
cottage pudding; cake without icing, covered with a sweet sauce.

çot′tāġed, *a.* set or covered with cottages.

çot′tāġe in′dus·try, 1. a manufacturing activity carried on, as in the early part of the Industrial Revolution, by farming out work to be done in the workers' homes.
2. any relatively small-scale business operation carried on as from the home.

çot′tā·ġẽr, *n.* 1. one who lives in a cottage.
2. a farm laborer. [Brit.]

çot′tẽr, çot′tăr, *n.* [ME. *cottier*, from LL. *cota*, a cot.]
1. a cottager.
2. a tenant farmer. [Scot.]
3. a cottier. [Irish.]

çot′tẽr, *n.* [Early Mod. Eng. (also *cotterel*); apparently from L.G.]
1. a bolt or wedge put through a slot to hold together parts of machinery.
2. a cotter pin.

çot′tẽr, *v.t.*; cottered, *pt.*, *pp.*; cottering, *ppr.* to fasten by use of a cotter.

çot′tẽr·el, *n.* 1. a key; a cotter. [Brit. Dial.]
2. a pot support in a fireplace. [Brit. Dial.]

çot′tẽr pin, a split pin used as a cotter, fastened in place by spreading apart its ends after it is inserted.

COTTER PIN

çot′ti·ẽr, *n.* [ME. and OFr. *cotier*, from *cote*; see *cot* (cottage).]
1. in Great Britain and Ireland, a farmer who lives in a cottage: also *cotter, cottar.*
2. in Ireland, a peasant renting a small piece of land under a system (called *cottier tenure*) of renting land to the highest bidder. [Archaic.]

çot′tise, çot′ise, *n.* [Fr. *côte*; L. *costa*, a rib.] in heraldry, a diminutive of the bend, containing in breadth one half of the bendlet.

çot′tised (-tist), *a.* in heraldry, having cottises.

COTTISED BEND

çot′toid, *a.* [L. *cottus*, a kind of fish, and Gr. *eidos*, form.] belonging to the family of fishes of which the typical genus is *Cottus.*

çot′toid, *n.* a fish of the genus *Cottus.*

çot′tŏn, *a.* pertaining to cotton; made of cotton; consisting of cotton; as, *cotton* cloth.

çot′tŏn, *n.* [ME. *cotoun*; OFr. *coton*; Sp. *coton*, from Ar. *qūtun, qūtn*, cotton.]
1. the soft, white, fibrous matter around the seeds of various shrubs or woody herbs of the mallow family.
2. a plant or plants, especially of the genus *Gossypium*, producing this material.
3. the crop of such plants.
4. thread or cloth made of cotton.
5. a downy, cottonlike substance growing on other plants.
mineral cotton; see *mineral wool*, under *wool.*

COTTON PLANT
(3-4 ft. high)

çot′tŏn, *v.i.*; cottoned, *pt.*, *pp.*; cottoning, *ppr.* 1. to rise with a nap. [Obs.]
2. to agree with; to be in harmony with: used with *to.* [Colloq.]
3. to become friends with; to associate with: used with *to.* [Colloq.]
4. to begin to like; to become attached to by liking: used with *to.* [Colloq.]

çot′tŏn·āde, *n.* a thick, stout cotton fabric.

çot′tŏn bat′ting, thin, pressed layers of fluffy, absorbent cotton, used for surgical dressing, etc.

Çot′tŏn Belt, the region in the southern part of the United States where much cotton is grown: it extends from the eastern coast through Texas.

çot′tŏn çāke, a mass of compressed cottonseed from which the oil has been extracted, used as feed.

çot′tŏn çan′dy, a cottony candy consisting of threadlike fibers of melted sugar spun into a fluffy mass around a paper cone.

çot′tŏn flan′nel, a strong cotton cloth with a long, fleecy nap: also called *Canton flannel.*

çot′tŏn ġin, [see *gin* (snare).] a machine for separating cotton fibers from the seeds.

çot′tŏn grȧss, any of a genus (*Eriphorum*) of grasslike plants of the sedge family, with flower heads resembling cotton.

Çot·tō′ni·ăn, *a.* pertaining to Sir Robert Cotton (1571–1631), known mostly through his valuable library, now in the British Museum.

çot′tŏn mill, a factory for making cotton thread or cloth.

çot′tŏn mouse, the *Hesperomys gossypinus*, a field mouse injuring cotton plants.

çot′tŏn·mouth, *n.* a large, poisonous snake, *Agkistrodon piscivorus*, with a thick body and a whitish mouth, found in the southern United States; water moccasin: also called *cottonmouth moccasin.*

çot′tŏn·ous (-us), *a.* cottony. [Obs.]

çot′tŏn pick′ẽr, 1. a person or machine that picks cotton.
2. a machine for cleaning raw cotton.

çot′tŏn press, a machine for pressing cotton into bales.

çot′tŏn rat, a rodent native to the cotton plantations of the United States.

çot′tŏn rōṣe, a plant of the composite genus *Filago.*

çot′tŏn sçāle, *Pulvinaria innumerabilis*, a louse infesting the bark of the cotton plant.

çot′tŏn·seed, *n.* the seed of the cotton plant: also *cotton-seed, cotton seed.*

çot′tŏn·seed mēal, hulled cottonseed ground up after the oil has been removed, used as fertilizer and fodder.

çot′tŏn·seed oil, an oil pressed from cottonseed, used to make shortening, soap, etc.

çot′tŏn shrub, the cotton plant.

çot′tŏn stāin′ẽr, *Dysdercus suturellus*, a small, red bug that harms cotton fibers by giving them an indelible red or yellow stain.

çot′tŏn·tāil, *n.* *Lepus sylvaticus*, the common rabbit of the United States, with a short, fluffy tail that is white underneath.

çot′tŏn this′tle (-sl), *Onopordon acanthium*, a Scotch thistle.

çot′tŏn tree, the American cottonwood; also, a tree of the genus *Bombax.*

çot′tŏn vel′vet, same as *velveteen.*

çot′tŏn wāste, refuse cotton fiber or yarn, used as box packing and in wiping oily machinery.

çot′tŏn·weed, *n.* any of various plants with white, cottony hairs, as the cudweed.

çot′tŏn·wood, *n.* 1. one of several trees of the genus *Populus*, as *Populus heterophylla*, of eastern United States: so named from their cottony catkins.
2. the wood of any of these trees.

çot′tŏn wool, natural or raw cotton; cotton batting.

çot′tŏn wŏrm, *Aletia xylina*, a moth having a larva destructive to growing cotton.

çot′tŏn·y, *a.* 1. of or consisting of cotton.
2. like cotton; downy; fluffy.

çot′trel, *n.* a cotterel (sense 2).

çot′y·le, *n.* [Gr. *kotylē*, a hollow, a cup.]
1. in anatomy, an acetabulum: also spelled *cotyla.*
2. in ancient Greece, (a) a drinking cup; (b) a unit of liquid measure, varying in different localities.

çot·y·lē′dŏn, *n.* [L., from Gr. *kotylēdōn*, from *kotylē*, a hollow or cavity.]
1. in the embryo of a plant, a seed leaf; the earliest leaf or one of the earliest leaves growing out of a seed and usually having the function of nourishing the elementary plant. Plants may have one, two, or more cotyledons, being mono-, di-, or polycotyledonous.
2. [C—] a genus of polypetalous herbs of the houseleek family; the navelworts.
3. in anatomy, a villous, placental area.

çot·y·led′ŏn·ăl, *a.* of, relating to, or pertaining to a cotyledon.

çot·y·led′ŏn·ā·ry, *a.* having a cotyledon or cotyledons.

çot·y·led′ŏn·ous, *a.* of, like, or having cotyledons.

çō·tyl′i·fọrm, *a.* [L. *cotyla*; Gr. *kotylē*, a hollow, and *forma*, form.] cup-shaped.

çot·y·liġ′ẽr·ous, *a.* [L. *cotyla*, a cotyle, and *gerere*, to carry.] possessing cotyledons.

çot′y·loid, *a.* [Gr. *kotylē*, a cup, and *eidos*, form.]
1. cup-shaped; cupped; as, a *cotyloid* socket.
2. pertaining to a cotyle.

çöu′çăl, *n.* [prob. native name.] a tropical cuckoo of the genus *Centropus.*

couch, *v.t.*; couched, *pt.*, *pp.*; couching, *ppr.* [ME. *couchen*; OFr. *coucher*; Pr. *colcar*; It. *colcare*; L. *collocari*, to place together; from *com-*, together, and *locare*, to place; *locus*, a place.]
1. to lay upon a bed or place of rest.

Where unbruised youth, with unstuffed brain,
Doth *couch* his limbs. —Shak.

2. in brewing, to spread (grain) in a thin layer to germinate.
3. to lay close, or in a stratum; to make to stoop and lie close.

The water *couch* themselves, as close as may be, to the center of the globe. —Burnet.

4. to hide; also, to inlay. [Obs.]
5. in papermaking, to pass (a pulp sheet) to a drier, from the mold.
6. to express; to put into words; to state; as, to *couch* a proposition skillfully.

7. to lower or bring down; especially, to lower (a spear, lance, etc.) to an attacking position.
8. to embroider with thread laid flat.
9. to put in a layer. [Archaic.]
10. in surgery, formerly, to treat (a cataract) by forcing down the lens until it no longer intercepts the line of vision.

çouch, *v.i.* 1. to lie down on a bed; to recline.
2. to lie in hiding; to crouch; to hide.
Fierce tigers *couched* around. —Dryden.
3. to bend or stoop, as in pain.
4. to be in a pile, as leaves.

çouch, *n.* [ME. *couche*, a lair; OFr. *couche*, *colche*; a bed, from *coucher*, to lie down.]
1. an article of furniture on which one may sit or lie down; sofa; divan.
2. any resting place.
3. a bed; a place for sleeping. [Chiefly Poetic.]
4. an animal's lair or den. [Obs.]
5. in brewing, a layer of grain spread to germinate.
6. a preliminary layer, coating, or stratum; specifically, (a) in painting, a ground or coat of color, varnish, or size, covering the canvas, wall, or other surface; (b) a coat of gold or silver leaf laid on any substance to be gilded or silvered; (c) in bookbinding, a layer or single thickness of leather.

çouch'ăn·cy, *n.* the act of lying; repose. [Rare.]

çouch'ănt, *a.* [Fr. *couchant*, ppr. of *coucher*, to lie down.]
1. lying down: said especially of animals.
2. in heraldry, lying down with the head raised, which distinguishes the posture of *couchant* from that of *dormant*, or sleeping: applied to a lion or other beast.
levant and couchant; in law, rising up and lying down: applied to beasts, and indicating that they have been long enough on land not their owner's to lie down and rise up to feed, or for one night at least.

cou·ché' (kö-shā'), *a.* [Fr., pp. of *coucher*, to lie down.] in heraldry, (a) inclined; reclining partly; (b) lying on the side or sides; as, chevrons *couché*.

çouched (koucht), *a.* in heraldry, couché.

çöu·çhee', *n.* [Fr., f. of *couché*, pp. of *coucher*, to lie down.] bedtime, or visits received about bedtime. [Obs.]

çouch'ẽr, *n.* 1. formerly, one who couched cataracts.
2. in papermaking, one who couches the pulp on the felt as it comes from the mold in sheets.

çouch'ẽr, *n.* in old English law, a factor; a resident in a country for trade. [Obs.]

çouch'ẽr, *n.* [from LL. *collectarius*, a factor, moneychanger.]
1. a book in which a corporation or religious house registers its acts. [Obs.]
2. a book of services or collects. [Obs.]

çouch grȧss, *Triticum* (or *Agropyrum*) *repens*, a species of grass, a great pest from the rapidity with which it spreads and the difficulty with which it is eradicated: also called *quitch grass*, *cutch grass*, etc.

çouch'ing, *n.* 1. the act of bending.
2. formerly, the act or process of treating a cataract by depressing the crystalline lens.
3. a kind of embroidery done by laying threads flat on the surface to be embroidered and fastening them with fine stitches so as to form a design.

çouch'less, *a.* having no couch or bed.

çöu'dee, *n.* [Fr. *coudée*, from *coude*, elbow.] a linear measure, the cubit.

çöu'gär, *n.*; *pl.* **çöu'gärș, çöu'gär,** [Fr., earlier *cuguacuarana*, apparently for Tupi *suçuarana*, lit., false deer, from *susuú*, deer, and *rana*, false: so named from its color.] a tawny-brown animal (*Felis concolor*) of the cat family, with a long, slender body and a long tail, found from Canada to Patagonia. It is known by various other names, as puma, panther, catamount, and mountain lion. Spelled also *couguar*, *cougouar*, *cuguar*.

çough (kof), *v.i.*; coughed, *pt.*, *pp.*; coughing, *ppr.* [ME. coughen: from echoic base.] to expel air suddenly and noisily from the lungs through the glottis, either as the result of an involuntary muscular spasm in the throat or to clear the air passages.

çough, *v.t.* 1. to expel by coughing.
2. to cause (some result) or to bring about (a condition) by coughing; as, to *cough* oneself weak.
3. to express or utter by coughing.
to cough down; to silence, as an unpopular or too lengthy speaker, by pretended coughing.
to cough up; (a) to bring up or eject (phlegm, etc.) by coughing; (b) [Slang.] to hand over (money, etc.).

çough, *n.* 1. a coughing.
2. a diseased state of the lungs or throat, causing frequent coughing.

çough drop, a small medicated tablet, often sweetened and flavored, for the relief of coughs, hoarseness, etc.

çough'ẽr, *n.* one who coughs.

çough'wŏrt, *n.* an herb, coltsfoot.

çöug'när, *n.* [Malay.] a three-masted Malay vessel, rigged with square sails.

COUGNAR

çou'hāġe (-āj), *n.* same as *cowhage*.

could (kud), *v.* 1. past tense of *can*.
2. an auxiliary with present or future sense, generally equivalent to *can* in meaning and use, expressing especially a shade of doubt or a smaller degree of ability or possibility (e.g., it *could* be so) or permission (e.g., *could* I go?).

could'n't, could not.

couldst, second person singular, past indicative, of *can*: used with *thou*. [Archaic or Poetic.]

çöu'lee, *n.* [Fr., f. of pp. of *couler*, to flow.]
1. in geology, a stream of lava, whether flowing or solidified.
2. a ravine or deep gully, usually dry in summer.

cou·lée' (kö-lā'), *n.* [Fr.] a coulee.

çöu·leūr', *n.* [Fr., color, from L. *color*, color.] in certain French card games, suit.
couleur de rose; rose color; adverbially, full of promise.

çöu·lisse', *n.* [Fr., a groove, slide, from *couler*, to slide, glide.]
1. a timber with a channel or groove in it in which a sluice gate, etc. slides.
2. in a theater, one of the side scenes; also, the space between two side scenes on either side of the stage.

çöu·loir' (-lwär'), *n.* [Fr., from *couler*, to slide.]
1. a deep mountain ravine or gorge.
2. a dredging machine employing buckets.

çöu·lomb' (-lom'), *n.* [after Charles Augustin de *Coulomb* (1736–1806), Fr. physicist.] a unit for measuring the quantity of an electric current; the amount of electricity provided by a current of one ampere flowing for one second: symbol, C (no period).
Coulomb's law; the law that the attraction or repulsion between two electric charges or two magnetic poles is directly proportional to the product of the charges and inversely proportional to the square of the distance between them.

çōul'tẽr, *n.* same as *colter*.

çöu·mar'iç, *a.* pertaining to or derived from coumarin.
coumaric acid; an acid, $C_9H_8O_3$, found in coumarin.

çöu'mȧ·rin, çöu'mȧ·rine, *n.* [Fr. *coumarine*, from *coumaron*, tonka bean; Sp. *cumarú* or Port. *cumaru*, both from Tupi *cumarú*.] a white, vanilla-flavored, crystalline substance obtained from the tonka bean and certain plants or made synthetically: used as a flavoring in baking, in perfumes, etc.

çöu'mȧ·röu, *n.* the tree, *Dipteryx odorata*, which yields the sweet-scented tonka bean. It is a native of French Guiana.

çoun'cil, *n.* [ME. *counceil*; OFr. *concile*; L. *concilium*, an assembly; *com-*, together, and *calare*, to call, convoke.]
1. an assembly of people summoned or convened for consultation, deliberation, advice, etc.; as, a *council* of physicians.
2. a group of people chosen as an administrative, advisory, or legislative assembly.
3. the legislative body of a city or town.
4. an assembly of church officials to discuss points of doctrine, etc.
5. a body of delegates from labor unions in a city, town, etc.
6. the discussion or deliberation in a council.
7. counsel. [Obs.]
common council; the legislative body of a municipal corporation; a city council. It is generally the representative body, composed of one or more aldermen elected from each of the city wards, but is sometimes the designation of a co-ordinate or lower branch of a municipal legislature. In the latter case the two bodies taken together are called the *city council*.
council of war; (a) a conference of leading military or naval officers to discuss important military affairs in connection with a campaign; (b) any conference to discuss plans for action.
ecumenical council; in church history, a general council or assembly of prelates and divines, representing the whole church, as the council of Nice.
executive council; the persons designated to act as advisers to a chief executive officer.
legislative council; the senate of a territorial legislature.
privy council; a select council for advising a sovereign in the administration of the government.
Syn.—meeting, conference, assembly, convention, convocation, congress, parliament.

çoun'cil bōard, the table around which a council holds consultation; hence, the council itself in deliberation or session.

çoun'cil fīre, a camp fire kept burning during the councils of North American Indians.

çoun'cil·ist, *n.* a councilor. [Obs.]

çoun'cil·măn, *n.*; *pl.* **çoun'cil·men,** one who belongs to a council, particularly a city council.

çoun'cil-man'ȧ·ġẽr plan, a system of municipal government in which the chief administrative official is a manager chosen by the city council.

çoun'cil·ŏr, çoun'cil·lŏr, *n.* a member of a council.

çoun'cil tā'ble, a council board.

çō·ūne', *v.t.* [L. *com-*, together, and *unus*, one.] to unite. [Obs.]

çō·ū·nīte', *a.* combined; united. [Obs.]

çō·ū·nīte', *v.t.* [L. *com-*, together, and *unitus*, pp. of *unire*, to unite.] to unite.

çoun'sel, *n.* [ME. *counseil*; OFr. *conseil*; L. *consilium*, deliberation, counsel, from *consulere*, to consult.]
1. consultation; mutual interchange of opinions, ideas, etc.; discussion and deliberation.
We took sweet *counsel* together. —Ps. lv. 14.
2. wisdom; prudence; examination of consequences; deliberate opinion or judgment, or the faculty or habit of judging with caution. [Archaic.]
They all confess that, in the working of that first cause, *counsel* is used, reason followed, and a way observed.—Hooker.
3. advice; opinion or instruction given for directing the judgment or conduct of another; opinion or direction given upon request or upon deliberation or consultation.
Ill *counsel* had misled the girl. —Tennyson.
4. purpose; design; will; plan.
To show . . . the immutability of his *counsel*. —Heb. vi. 17.
5. a confidential idea, plan, etc.; a secret. [Obs.]
6. one who gives legal advice; a lawyer retained to conduct or manage a case in court; also used collectively for any number of attorneys, counselors, or barristers, engaged on the same case; as, the plaintiff's *counsel*, or the defendant's *counsel*.
to keep one's own counsel; to keep one's opinions, purposes, etc. to oneself.
to take counsel; to invite consultation; to ask advice; to consult.
Syn.—advice, suggestion, recommendation, warning, admonition, instruction.

çoun'sel, *v.t.*; counseled *or* counselled, *pt.*, *pp.*; counseling *or* counselling, *ppr.* 1. to give advice to; to advise; to exhort, warn, admonish, or instruct; as, we should *counsel* our children.
They that will not be *counseled* cannot be helped. —Franklin.
2. to advise or recommend; as, to *counsel* submission.

çoun'sel, *v.i.* to deliberate; to give or take advice.

çoun'sel·ȧ·ble, çoun'sel·lȧ·ble, *a.* 1. willing to receive counsel; disposed to follow advice. [Rare.]
2. wise; expedient. [Obs.]

çoun'sel·ŏr, çoun'sel·lŏr, *n.* [ME. *counselour, counseiller*; OFr. *consellier*; L. *consiliarius*, a counselor, adviser, from *consilium*, counsel.]
1. one who gives counsel or advice.
2. a legal adviser, as of an embassy or legation.
3. a lawyer, especially one who conducts cases in court: in full, *counselor-at-law*.
4. a person in charge of a group of children at a camp.

çoun'sel·ŏr·ship, *n.* the office of a counselor.

çount, *v.t.*; counted, *pt., pp.*; counting, *ppr.* [ME. *counten*; OFr. *conter*; It. *contare*, from L. *computare*, to count, compute; *com-*, together, and *putare*, to cleanse, prune, adjust.]
1. to name numbers in regular order to (a certain number); as, he *counted* five.
2. to name, one by one, by units or groups, to reach a total; to add; as, *count* the money.
3. to check by numbering off; to inventory.
4. to take account of; include.
5. to consider; believe to be; as, he *counts* himself fortunate.
6. to ascribe; attribute. [Archaic.]
to count in; to include.
to count on or *upon*; to rely or depend on.
to count out; (a) to disregard; omit; (b) [Brit.] to end a sitting of (Parliament) when the members present are not enough for a quorum; (c) [Colloq.] to keep (a candidate) from office by counting the ballots incorrectly; (d) in boxing, to declare (a boxer) defeated when he has remained down for a count of ten.
Syn.—calculate, number, reckon, compute, enumerate.

çount, *v.i.* 1. to take account: with *of*. [Obs.]
2. to name numbers or things in order.
3. to be included in counting; be taken into account.
4. to have importance, weight, etc.; be worth consideration; as, his foolish opinions don't *count*.
5. in music, to keep time by counting.
6. in law, to plead or argue a case in court. [Obs.]
to count for; to be worth.
to count off; to separate into equal divisions by counting.

çount, *n.* 1. a counting; an adding or numbering.
2. the number reached by counting; total number or quantity.
3. a reckoning; accounting.
4. regard; notice; account. [Archaic.]
5. in boxing, ten seconds counted to give a boxer who has been knocked down time to rise before he loses the match.
6. in law, any of the charges in an indictment, each of which gives a reason and is alone sufficient for prosecution.

çount, *n.* [OFr. *conte, comte*, from L. *comes, comitis*, a companion.] a nobleman in some European countries, having a rank equivalent to that of an earl in England.

çount'ȧ·ble, *n.* 1. any object or term, etc. which can be counted.
2. [*pl.*] in grammar, those things which occur in distinct units and can be referred to numerically, or by such words as *many, numerous*.

çoun'te·nănce, *n.* [ME. and OFr. *contenance*; L. *continentia*, countenance, demeanor, from *continere*; from *com-*, together, and *tenere*, to hold.]
1. the expression of the face.
2. the face; facial features; visage.
3. a look of approval on the face.
4. approval; support.
5. composure; calm control.
6. show; resemblance; appearance. [Obs.]
in countenance; with assurance; calm; composed.
to put out of countenance; to cause to lose composure; to make feel embarrassed and uneasy; disconcert.

çoun'te·nănce, *v.t.*; countenanced (-nanst), *pt., pp.*; countenancing, *ppr.* 1. to favor; to approve; to give support to; to abet; as to *countenance* vice.
2. to make a show of. [Obs.]

çoun'te·năn·cẽr, *n.* one who countenances, favors, or supports.

çoun'tẽr-, [Fr. *contre-*; L. *contra-*, against, opposite.] a combining form meaning: (a) *opposite, contrary to*, as in *counter*clockwise; (b) *in retaliation*, as in *counter*plot; (c) *opposed to but like, complementary*, as in *counter*part.

çoun'tẽr, *adv.* [Fr. *contre*; L. *contra*, against, opposite.]
1. contrary; in opposition; in a contrary direction, manner, etc.; as, he went *counter* to his own interest.
2. in the wrong way; contrary to the right course; contrariwise.
3. in the face, or at the face. [Obs.]

çoun'tẽr, *a.* adverse; opposite; contrary; opposed.

çoun'tẽr, *n.* 1. the opposite; contrary.
2. the part of a horse's breast between the shoulders and under the neck.
3. a stiff leather piece around the heel of a shoe.
4. the part of a ship's stern between the water line and the arched or curved part.
5. a depression between the raised parts of a type face.
6. in boxing, (a) a blow given while parrying an opponent's blow; (b) the act of giving such a blow.
7. in fencing, a circular parry of the foil.
8. same as *countertenor*.

çoun'tẽr, *v.t.* and *v.i.* 1. to act, do, move, etc. counter to (a person or thing); oppose.
2. in boxing, to attack or strike one's opponent while parrying (his blow).

çoun'tẽr, *n.* [ME. *countour*; in senses 1 and 2 from OFr. *conteor*; L. *computator*, from *computare*; in senses 3, 4, 5 from OFr. *contouer*, counting room, table of a bank; ML. *computatorium*, from L. *computare*, to compute.]
1. a person or thing that counts; computer.
2. an indicator on a machine, for keeping count of turns, strokes, etc. of the machine or its parts.
3. a small device of metal, wood, etc. used for keeping count, especially for keeping score in some games.
4. an imitation coin.
5. a long board or table in a store, behind which the seller stands and on which goods are displayed, wrapped, etc.; also, a similar table in a restaurant, etc.
over the counter; in an office instead of through the stock exchange: said of sales of stock.
under the counter; in a surreptitious manner: said of merchandise sold illegally, especially at prices higher than those established by governmental regulation.

çoun'tẽr, *n.* and *v.t.* encounter. [Archaic.]

çoun·tẽr·act', *v.t.*; counteracted, *pt., pp.*; counteracting, *ppr.* [*counter-*, and L. *actus*, pp. of *agere*, to lead, drive, do.] to act directly against; to check, neutralize, or mitigate the effect of with opposing action.

çoun·tẽr·ac'tion, *n.* 1. action in opposition.
2. an action that opposes, checks, etc. another action.

çoun·tẽr·act'ive, *n.* one who or that which counteracts.

çoun·tẽr·act'ive, *a.* counteracting or tending to counteract.

çoun·tẽr·act'ive·ly, *adv.* by counteraction.

çoun·tẽr·ap·prōach, *n.* in fortification, a work constructed to aid in resisting besiegers.

çoun'tẽr·at·tack, *n.* an attack made in opposition to, or in reprisal for, another attack.

çoun·tẽr·at·tack', *v.t.* and *v.i.* to attack in reprisal, or so as to offset the enemy's attack.

çoun'tẽr·at·trac''tion, *n.* an attraction opposed to or rivaling another attraction.

çoun'tẽr·at·tract''ive, *a.* attracting in an opposite way.

çoun'tẽr·bal·ănce, *n.* 1. a weight used to balance another weight; a counterpoise.
2. any force or influence that balances or offsets another force or influence.

çoun·tẽr·bal'ănce, *v.t.*; counterbalanced, *pt., pp.*; counterbalancing, *ppr.* to be a counterbalance to; to offset.

çoun'tẽr·blȧst, *n.* 1. an opposing or answering blast.
2. an expression of strong opposition to someone or something.

çoun'tẽr·blōw, *n.* a blow given in return.

çoun'tẽr·bond, *n.* a bond to secure one who has given bond for another.

çoun'tẽr·bōre, *n.* 1. in any bore or cylindrical cavity, an enlargement of an orifice, as for the insertion of a head.
2. a drill for making such an enlargement.

çoun·tẽr·bōre', *v.t.*; counterbored, *pt., pp.*; counterboring, *ppr.* to furnish, as a cylinder, with a counterbore.

çoun'tẽr·brāce, *n.* 1. in nautical usage, the lee brace of the foretopsail yard.
2. in engineering, diagonal bracing, as in a girder, giving additional support and relieving the main brace of stress.

çoun·tẽr·brāce', *v.t.*; counterbraced, *pt., pp.*; counterbracing, *ppr.* 1. in nautical usage, to brace (the yards) in opposite directions.
2. in engineering, to furnish with a counterbrace.

çoun·tẽr·buff', *v.t.*; counterbuffed (-buft), *pt., pp.*; counterbuffing, *ppr.* to strike back or in an opposite direction; to drive back; to stop by a blow or impulse in front.

çoun'tẽr·buff, *n.* a blow in an opposite direction; a stroke that stops motion or causes a recoil.

çoun'tẽr·çȧst, *n.* delusive contrivance; contrary cast. [Obs.]

çoun'tẽr·çȧst''ẽr, *n.* a caster of accounts; a reckoner; a bookkeeper: used in contempt. [Obs.]

çoun'tẽr·chānġe, *n.* exchange; reciprocation. [Obs.]

çoun·tẽr·chānġe', *v.t.*; counterchanged, *pt., pp.*; counterchanging, *ppr.* 1. to transpose; interchange.
2. to checker; variegate.
3. to exchange. [Obs.]

çoun·tẽr·chānġed', *a.* [Fr. *contre-changé*; *contre*, opposite, and *changé*, from *changer*, LL. *cambiare*, to exchange; barter.]
1. exchanged.
2. in heraldry, having a field of two tinctures, metal and color, and a charge upon it partaking of both, the charge or part of the charge which lies in the metal being of color, and vice versa.

A BOAR PASSANT COUNTERCHANGED

çoun'tẽr·chärġe, *n.* 1. a charge in answer to another charge or against the accuser.
2. an attack in return.

çoun·tẽr·chärġe', *v.t.* 1. to attack in return.
2. to charge or accuse in return.

çoun'tẽr·chärm, *n.* that which has the power of dissolving or opposing the effect of a charm.

çoun·tẽr·chärm', *v.t.*; countercharmed, *pt., pp.*; countercharming, *ppr.* to destroy the effect of (enchantment).

çoun·tẽr·check', *v.t.*; counterchecked, *pt., pp.*; counterchecking, *ppr.* 1. to check or restrain by a counteraction.
2. to check again; confirm by a second check.

çoun'tẽr·check, *n.* 1. anything that checks, restrains, etc.
2. a check upon a check; a double check to make certain.

çoun'tẽr check, a bank check kept on the counter for the use of depositors in making a withdrawal.

çoun'tẽr·çlāim, *n.* an opposing claim, as by a defendant against a plaintiff, made to offset another claim.

çoun·tẽr·çlāim', *v.t.* and *v.i.*; counterclaimed, *pt., pp.*; counterclaiming, *ppr.* to present as, or make, a counterclaim.

çoun·tẽr·çlāim'ănt, *n.* a person who makes a counterclaim.

çoun·tẽr·çlock'wīse, *a.* and *adv.* in a direction opposite to that in which the hands of a clock move.

çoun''tẽr·çom·pō'ny, *a.* [Fr. *contre-componé*; *contre-*, opposite, and *componé*, from L. *componere*, to place together.] in heraldry, denoting a border, bend, or other ordinary, which is compounded of two ranks of panes, or rows of checkers, of alternate metals and colors.

A BEND COUNTER-COMPONY

çoun''tẽr·çouch'ănt, *a.* in heraldry, denoting animals borne couchant, and having their heads in contrary directions.

çoun''tẽr·çou·ränt', *a.* in heraldry, denoting animals borne running in opposite directions.

COUNTERCOURANT

çoun'tẽr·çul''tūre, *n.* the culture of many young people of the 1960's and 1970's manifested by a life style that is opposed to the prevailing culture.

çoun'tẽr·çũr·rent, *a.* running in an opposite direction.

çoun'tẽr·çũr·rent, *n.* a current in an opposite direction to another current; an opposing current.

çoun''tẽr·dem''ŏn·strā'tion, *n.* a demonstration to oppose or counter the effect of another demonstration.

çoun'tẽr·dis·tinc''tion, *n.* contradistinction.

çoun·tẽr·drąw', *v.t.*; counterdrew, *pt.*; counterdrawing, *ppr.*; counterdrawn, *pp.* in painting, to trace; to copy by means of a transparent substance.

çoun″tẽr·em·bat′tled (-tld), *a.* in heraldry, denoting an ordinary, embattled on both sides.

COUNTEREMBATTLED

çoun·tẽr·es′pi·ŏn·äge, *n.* actions to prevent or thwart enemy espionage.

çoun′tẽr·ev″i·dence, *n.* opposite evidence; evidence or testimony which opposes other evidence.

çoun′tẽr·ex·ten″sion, *n.* in surgery, a means of reducing a fracture by making extension in the opposite direction.

çoun′tẽr·fąll″ẽr, *n.* in a spinning mule, a counterweighted wire which is depressed when the faller wire lowers the row of yarns to wind them on the spindle.

çoun·tẽr·fēi′ṣănce, *n.* [Fr. *contrefaisance*, from *contrefaire*, counterfeit, imitate.] the act of forging; forgery: also written *counterfaisance*. [Obs.]

çoun′tẽr·feit (-fit), *a.* [OFr. *contrefait*; LL. *contrafactus*, counterfeit, pp. of *contrafacere*; *contra*, against, opposite, and *facere*, to make.]
1. forged; false; fabricated without right; made in imitation of something else with a view to defraud by passing the false copy for genuine or original; as, a *counterfeit* coin, a *counterfeit* deed or bond.
2. pretended; sham; feigned; dissembled; as, *counterfeit* sorrow.
Syn.—bogus, deceptive, false, fictitious, forged, fraudulent, mock, sham, spurious.

çoun′tẽr·feit, *n.* 1. a cheat; an impostor. [Archaic.]
2. one thing made like or resembling another; specifically, an imitation without lawful authority, made with intent to defraud by passing the false for the true; as, the note is a poor *counterfeit*.
3. a copy or likeness, as in painting, sculpture, etc. [Archaic.]

çoun′tẽr·feit, *v.t.* and *v.i.* 1. to make an imitation of (money, pictures, etc.), usually with intention to deceive or defraud.
2. to pretend.
3. to resemble or make resemble.

çoun′tẽr·feit·ẽr, *n.* one who counterfeits; specifically, a maker or circulator of counterfeit money.

çoun′tẽr·feit·ly, *adv.* by forgery; falsely.

çoun″tẽr·flō′ry, çoun″tẽr·fleū′ry, *a.* [*counter-*, and Fr. *fleuré*, from *fleur*, a flower.] in heraldry, denoting that the flowers with which an ordinary is adorned stand opposite to each other alternately.

çoun′tẽr·foil, *n.* [*counter-*, and *foil* (a leaf).]
1. same as *counterstock*.
2. the part of a check, postal money order, receipt, etc. kept by the issuer as a record of the transaction.

çoun′tẽr·fōrce, *n.* an opposing or counteracting force.

çoun′tẽr·fōrt, *n.* 1. in architecture, a buttress or other support.
2. a projecting crag of a mountain.

çoun′tẽr·gauġe, çoun′tẽr·gāġe, *n.* in carpentry, a double-pointed gauge used to measure the joints, by transferring the breadth of a mortise to the place where the tenon is to be, in order to make them fit each other.

çoun′tẽr·guärd, *n.* in fortification, a redan-shaped work having its faces parallel to the faces of the bastion.

çoun·tẽr·in′flu·ence, *v.t.* to hinder by opposing influence.

çoun″tẽr·in·sũr′ġen·cy, *n.* military and political action carried on to defeat an insurgency.

çoun″tẽr·in·tel′li·ġence, *n.* counterespionage, censorship, etc. to keep the enemy from getting information that may be of value to him.

çoun·tẽr·ir′ri·tănt, *n.* anything used to produce a slight irritation, as of an area of the skin, to relieve more serious irritation elsewhere.

çoun·tẽr·ir′ri·tāte, *v.t.*; counterirritated, *pt., pp.*; counterirritating, *ppr.* to use a counterirritant on.

çoun′tẽr·ir·ri·tā″tion, *n.* the effect brought about by a counterirritant.

çoun′tẽr·jum″pẽr, *n.* a person who works behind the counter of a shop; a salesman or saleswoman in a store: contemptuous term.

çoun′tẽr·măn, *n.*; *pl.* **çoun′tẽr·men,** a man whose work is serving customers at the counter of a lunchroom or cafeteria.

çoun·tẽr·mȧnd′, *v.t.*; countermanded, *pt., pp.*; countermanding, *ppr.* [Fr. *contremander*; L. *contramandare*; *contra*, opposite, and *mandare*, to command.]
1. to cancel or revoke (a command or order).
2. to call back or order back by a contrary order.
3. to prohibit. [Obs.]

çoun′tẽr·mȧnd, *n.* a contrary order; revocation of a former order or command.

çoun·tẽr·mȧnd′ȧ·ble, *a.* subject to countermand.

çoun′tẽr·märch, *n.* 1. a march back or in the opposite direction.
2. a marching movement in which a file or column reverses its direction, the individuals remaining in the same order and position: used especially by marching bands.

çoun·tẽr·märch′, *v.t.* and *v.i.*; countermarched, *pt., pp.*; countermarching, *ppr.* to march back; to perform, or cause to perform, a countermarch.

çoun′tẽr·märk, *n.* 1. a supplementary mark put on a bale of goods belonging to several merchants, that it may be opened only in the presence of all the owners.
2. the mark of the Goldsmiths' Company (London), added to that of the artificer, to show the metal to be standard.
3. an artificial cavity made in the teeth of horses that have outgrown their natural mark, to disguise their age.

çoun·tẽr·märk′, *v.t.*; countermarked, *pt., pp.*; countermarking, *ppr.* to affix a countermark on.

çoun′tẽr·meaṣ·ūre (-mezh-ūr), *n.* a measure, or action, taken in opposition or retaliation.

çoun′tẽr·mīne, *n.* [from *counter*, and *mine* after Fr. *contremine* and It. *contramina*.]
1. a tunnel dug underground and filled with a charge of explosive to destroy an enemy tunnel.
2. a charge of explosive sunk under water to destroy enemy submarine mines.
3. a plot to defeat another plot.

çoun·tẽr·mīne′, *v.t.* and *v.i.*; countermined, *pt., pp.*; countermining, *ppr.* 1. to intercept (an enemy mine) with a countermine.
2. to defeat (a plot) with another plot.

çoun·tẽr·möve′, *v.t.* and *v.i.*; countermoved, *pt., pp.*; countermoving, *ppr.* to move in opposition or retaliation.

çoun′tẽr·möve, çoun′tẽr·möve·ment, *n.* a movement made in opposition or retaliation.

çoun′tẽr·mūre, *n.* [Fr. *contremur*; L. *contra*, against, and *murus*, a wall.] a wall raised behind another, to supply its place when a breach is made.

çoun·tẽr·mūre′, *v.t.* to fortify with a wall behind another.

çoun″tẽr·of·fen′sive, *n.* an attack in force by troops who have been defending a position.

çoun′tẽr·of″fẽr, *n.* an offer proposed in response to one that is unsatisfactory.

çoun′tẽr·ō″pen·ing, *n.* an aperture or vent on the opposite side or in a different place.

çoun′tẽr·pāce, *n.* a step or measure in opposition to another; contrary measure or attempt.

çoun′tẽr·pāled, çoun′tẽr·pā″ly, *a.* in heraldry, denoting an escutcheon divided into an equal number of pieces palewise by a line fesswise, the two tinctures above and below the fess line being counterchanged.

çoun′tẽr·pāne, *n.* [a corruption of *counterpoint*; OFr. *contrepointe*, a quilt, from LL. *culcita puncta*; *culcita*, a quilt, and *puncta*, f. of pp. of *pungere*, to prick.] a bedspread; a coverlet.

çoun′tẽr·pāne, *n.* [OFr. *contrepan*, a pledge, pawn; *contre*, opposite, and *pan*, a pledge, pawn.] one part of an indenture; a counterpart or duplicate.

çoun′tẽr·pȧ·rōle″, *n.* in military usage, a word in addition to the password, which is given in any time of alarm as a signal.

çoun′tẽr·pärt, *n.* 1. a copy; a duplicate. [Obs.]
2. a person or thing resembling or corresponding to another.
3. a thing which, when added to another, completes or complements it; hence, a person having qualities wanting in another, and such as make him or her complete.
4. in music, a part serving as accompaniment to another; as, the bass is the *counterpart* to the treble.

çoun·tẽr·pas′sănt, *a.* [OFr. *contrepassant*; *contre*, opposite, and *passer*, to pass, go over.] in heraldry, going opposite directions, as animals.

çoun′tẽr·plēa, *n.* in law, a replication to a plea or request.

çoun·tẽr·plēad′, *v.t.* to plead in opposition to; to contradict; to deny.

çoun·tẽr·plot′, *v.t.* and *v.i.*; counterplotted, *pt., pp.*; counterplotting, *ppr.* to plot against (a plot); to defeat (a plot) with another plot.

çoun′tẽr·plot, *n.* a plot or artifice to defeat another plot.

çoun·tẽr·plot′ting, *n.* a plotting in opposition to a stratagem.

çoun′tẽr·point, *n.* [Fr. *contrepoint*; It. *contrappunto*, from L. *contra*, against, and *punctum*, a prick, small hole.]
1. an opposite point or course.
2. a melody accompanying another melody note for note.
3. the art of adding a related but independent melody or melodies to a basic melody, in accordance with the fixed rules of harmony, to make a harmonic whole.
4. this kind of composition.

çoun′tẽr·point, *n.* [OFr. *contrepointe*, *contrepoinct*, a quilt, from LL. *culcita puncta*, a stitched quilt, counterpane.] a coverlet; a counterpane. [Obs.]

coun″ter·poin·té′ (koun″tẽr-poin-tā′), *a.* in heraldry, a term denoting two chevrons meeting with their points in the center of an escutcheon.

TWO CHEVRONS COUNTER-POINTÉ

çoun·tẽr·poiṣe′, *v.t.*; counterpoised, *pt., pp.*; counterpoising, *ppr.* [ME. *counterpeisen*; OFr. *contrepeser*, to counterpoise.]
1. to counterbalance; to act against with equal weight; to equal in weight.
2. to act against with equal power or effect; to balance.

çoun′tẽr·poiṣe, *n.* [OFr. *contrepois*; L. *contra*, against, and *pensum*, a weight, pound, from *pendere*, to weigh.]
1. a weight that balances another.
2. a force, influence, etc. that balances or neutralizes another.
3. a state of balance or equilibrium.

çoun′tẽr·poi·ṣŏn, *n.* 1. a substance that counteracts a poison; an antidote. [Obs.]
2. a poison that counteracts another poison.

çoun′tẽr·prō·duç″tive, *a.* bringing about effects or results that are contrary to those intended.

çoun′tẽr·proj·eçt, *n.* a project, scheme, or undertaking proposed in opposition to another.

çoun′tẽr·proọf, *n.* in engraving, a print taken off from another fresh printed, which, by being passed through the press, gives the figure of the former, but inverted.

çoun″tẽr·prop·ȧ·gan′dȧ, *n.* propaganda to counteract enemy propaganda.

çoun′tẽr·prō·pō″ṣăl, *n.* a proposal in response to one that is unsatisfactory.

çoun·tẽr·prövė′, *v.t.*; counterproved, *pt., pp.*; counterproving, *ppr.* to take a counterproof of.

çoun′tẽr·punch″, *n.* in boxing, a punch delivered in countering an opponent's lead.

çoun″tẽr·ref·ọr·mā′tion, *n.* a reform movement to oppose a previous one.

Çoun′tẽr Ref·ọr·mā′tion, the reform movement in the Roman Catholic Church in the sixteenth century, following the Protestant Reformation and in answer to it.

çoun′tẽr·rev·ō·lū′tion, *n.* 1. a political movement or revolution against a government or social system set up by a previous revolution.
2. a movement to combat revolutionary tendencies.

çoun″tẽr·rev·ō·lū′tion·ãr·y, *a.* of, advocating, or promoting a counterrevolution.

çoun″tẽr·rev·ō·lū′tion·ãr·y, *n.* a person who advocates or takes part in a counterrevolution.

çoun′tẽr·rev·ō·lū′tion·ist, *n.* one taking part in a counterrevolution.

çoun′tẽr·round, *n.* a body of officers going to visit and inspect the sentinels.

çoun″tẽr·sā′li·ent, *a.* [from Fr. *contre*, opposite, and *saillir*, to leap.] in heraldry, denoting two beasts, borne on a coat of arms, leaping from each other.

çoun′tẽr·sçāle, *n.* counterbalance. [Obs.]

çoun′tẽr·sçärp, çoun′tẽr·sçärf, *n.* [Fr. *contrescarpe*; *contre*, against, opposite, and *escarpe*, from *escarper*, to cut slopewise, scarp.] the outer slope or wall of a ditch, moat, etc. in a fortification.

çoun′tẽr·sēa, *n.* a sea running against the ship's course or against another sea. [Rare.]

çoun·tẽr·sēal′, *v.t.*; countersealed, *pt., pp.*; countersealing, *ppr.* to seal with another or others.

çoun″tẽr·sē·çūre′, *v.t.* to render more secure by additional guarantee.

çoun′tẽr·sē·çū″ri·ty, *n.* security given to one who has become surety for another.

çoun′tẽr·sense, *n.* opposite meaning.

çoun′tẽr·shąft, *n.* an intermediate shaft that

transmits motion from the main shaft of a machine to a working part.

çoun·tẽr·sign′ (-sīn′), *v.t.*; countersigned, *pt.*, *pp.*; countersigning, *ppr.* [OFr. *contresigner*; *contre*, against, opposite, and *signer*, to sign.]
 1. to authenticate or confirm (a previously signed piece of writing) by signing.
 2. to corroborate.

çoun′tẽr·sign, *n.* 1. a signature added to a previously signed piece of writing in order to authenticate or confirm it.
 2. a secret sign or signal in answer to another, as in a secret society.
 3. in military usage, a secret word or signal, usually changed daily, which must be given to a guard or sentry by someone wishing to pass; password.

çoun′tẽr·sig·năl, *n.* a signal to answer or correspond to another.

çoun′tẽr·sig″nȧ·tūre, *n.* a signature made in countersigning.

çoun·tẽr·sink′, *v.t.*; countersunk, *pt.*, *pp.*; countersinking, *ppr.* 1. to enlarge the top part of (a hole in metal, wood, etc.) so that the head of a bolt, screw, etc. will fit flush with or below the surface.
 2. to sink (the head of a bolt, screw, etc.) into such a hole.

çoun′tẽr·sink, *n.* 1. a drill or brace bit for countersinking holes.
 2. a countersunk hole.

çoun′tẽr·slōpe, *n.* any slope that overhangs.

çoun′tẽr·stand, *n.* ground for opposition.

çoun′tẽr·stāte·ment, *n.* a statement made in denial or refutation of another statement.

çoun′tẽr·stat·ūte, *n.* a contrary statute or ordinance.

çoun′tẽr·step, *n.* an opposite step or procedure; an opposite course of action.

çoun′tẽr·stock, *n.* that part of a tally kept by the payee.

çoun′tẽr·strōke, *n.* 1. a contrary stroke; a stroke given in return.
 2. a contrecoup.

çoun′tẽr·sūre·ty (-shůr-), *n.* a counterbond, or a surety to secure one that has given security.

çoun′tẽr·swāy, *n.* contrary sway; opposite influence. [Obs.]

çoun′tẽr·tal·ly, *n.* a tally corresponding to another.

çoun·tẽr·tend′en·cy, *n.*; *pl.* **çoun·tẽr·tend′en·cies,** an opposing tendency.

çoun·tẽr·ten′ŏr, *n.* [OFr. *contreteneur*; see *counter-* and *tenor*.]
 1. a part for a male voice higher in pitch than the tenor.
 2. a male voice of this kind.
 3. a singer who has such a voice.

çoun′tẽr·tẽrm, *n.* an antithetical term; an antonym.

çoun′tẽr·thrust, *n.* a thrust to counter another thrust.

çoun′tẽr·tīde, *n.* contrary tide.

çoun′tẽr·tīme, *n.* in horsemanship, the defense or resistance of a horse, that interrupts his cadence and the measure of his manège.

çoun″tẽr·trip′pănt, *a.* in heraldry, a term applied to two animals in an escutcheon, tripping in opposite directions: also *counter-tripping.*

çoun′tẽr·tũrn, *n.* an unexpected climax in the plot of a play.

çoun′tẽr·tȳpe, *n.* 1. an opposite type.
 2. a parallel type.

çoun·tẽr·vāil′, *v.t.*; countervailed, *pt.*, *pp.*; countervailing, *ppr.* [OFr. *contrevaleir*; *contre-*, L. *contra*, against, and *valeir*, L. *valere*, to be strong.]
 1. to have or use equal force against.
 2. to make up for; compensate.
 3. to counteract; be successful, useful, etc. against; avail against.

çoun·tẽr·vāil′, *v.i.* to avail (*against*).

çoun′tẽr·vāil, *n.* equal weight or strength; compensation; requital.

çoun·tẽr·vāir′y, çoun′tẽr·vāir, *a.* in heraldry, charged with vair (one of the furs), differing from it in having the bells or cups arranged base against base and point against point.

COUNTERVAIRY

çoun′tẽr·view (-vū), *n.* 1. an opposite or opposing view; opposition; a posture in which two persons front each other.
 2. contrast; a position in which two dissimilar things illustrate each other by opposition.

çoun·tẽr·vōte′, *v.t.* to vote in opposition; to outvote.

çoun·tẽr·wāit′, *v.t.* to watch for. [Obs.]

çoun·tẽr·weigh′ (-wā′), *v.t.* to weigh against; to counterbalance.

çoun′tẽr·weight (-wāt), *n.* a weight equal to another; a counterbalance.

çoun′tẽr·weight, *v.t.* to counterweigh.

çoun·tẽr·wheel′, *v.t.* to cause to wheel in an opposite direction.

çoun·tẽr·wŏrk′, *v.t.* and *v.i.*; counterworked, *pt.*, *pp.*; counterworking, *ppr.* to work in opposition to (someone or something); to counteract; to hinder any effect by contrary operations.

 That *counterworks* each folly and caprice.
 —Pope.

çoun′tẽr·wŏrk, *n.* 1. anything done or made to oppose something else.
 2. a fortification to oppose an enemy fortification.

çount′ess, *n.*; *pl.* **çount′ess·eş,** [Fr. *comtesse*; It. *contessa*; Sp. *condesa*, a female associate or companion; from L. *comes*, *comitis*, a companion.]
 1. the wife or widow of an earl or count.
 2. a noblewoman whose rank is equal to that of a count or earl.

çount′ing·house, *n.* a building or office in which a business firm keeps records, handles correspondence, etc.

çount′ing room, same as *countinghouse.*

çount′less, *a.* too many to count; innumerable.

çount′ŏr, *n.* an accountant. [Obs.]

çoun′tōur, *n.* an accountant. [Obs.]

çount pal′ȧ·tīne, 1. in German history, formerly, a count granted certain powers from the emperor in his own territory.
 2. in English history, formerly, a count or earl with supreme power in his county.

çoun′tre-, contra-. [Obs.]

çŏun′tri·fīed (kun′), *a.* rustic; rural; also, having the appearance and manners generally attributed to country people.

çŏun′tri·fȳ, *v.t.*; countrified, *pt.*, *pp.*; countrifying, *ppr.* to make rustic or rural.

çŏun′try (kun′), *n.*; *pl.* **çŏun′trieş,** [ME. *countre*; OFr. *contree*, *contrie*; Port. and It. *contrada*; LL. *contrata*, a region, country, that which is before, or over against one; from *contra*, opposite, over against.]
 1. a land; the whole territory of a nation or state.
 2. a tract of land; area; region; as, the train passed through an arid *country.*
 3. the land of one's birth or citizenship.
 4. the inhabitants of a nation or state; as, the whole *country* distrusted him.
 5. a rural part or agricultural region, as distinguished from a city or town; as, a vacation in the *country.*
 6. in law, a jury: in reference to the fact that the jury was originally a group of men from the vicinity; jury trial was called *trial by the country.*
 7. any field of activity or sphere of knowledge; as, this subject is strange *country* to me.
 8. in mining, the rock or stratum in which a mineral deposit is found; country rock.
 to put oneself upon the country; to demand a jury trial.

çŏun′try, *a.* 1. pertaining to the country or territory at a distance from a city; rural; as, a *country* town.
 2. like or characteristic of the country; rustic.
 3. of one's own country; native. [Dial.]

çŏun′try bāse, a game, prisoner's base.

çŏun′try çlub, a club, situated in a suburb or rural community, equipped with a clubhouse, golf course, etc.

çŏun′try çŏuş′in, a person not used to city life and confused by it.

çŏun′try-dȧnce, *n.* a folk dance in which the partners are arranged in two lines facing each other.

çŏun′try·fīed, *a.* same as *countrified.*

çŏun′try·fōlk (-fōk), *n.* people living in the country; rural people.

çŏun′try ġen′tle·măn, 1. a man of some wealth who lives on a country estate.
 2. [C– G–] a variety of sweet corn.

çŏun′try house, a house on a country estate; home of a country gentleman.

çŏun′try·măn, *n.*; *pl.* **çŏun′try·men,** 1. a man of one's own country; a compatriot.
 2. one who dwells in the country, as opposed to one living in a town or city; a rustic; a farmer.

çŏun′try rock, same as *country*, n. 8.

çŏun′try·sēat, *n.* a mansion in the country; a dwelling used as a place of retirement from the city.

çŏun′try·sīde, *n.* 1. a rural region; country or district of the country.
 2. the people of such a district.

çŏun′try stōre, a retail store in a rural community, where many sorts of merchandise are sold.

çŏun′try-wīde, *a.* throughout the country.

çŏun′try·wom″ăn (-woom″), *n.*; *pl.* **çŏun′-try·wom″en** (-wim″), 1. a woman living in the country.
 2. a woman of one's own country; a woman compatriot.

çount wheel, the wheel of a clock which causes it to strike the correct number of hours.

çoun′ty, *n.*; *pl.* **çoun′tieş,** [ME. *countee*; OFr. *counte*, *contee*; It. *contado*, from LL. *comitatus*, the office or jurisdiction of a count or earl, from L. *comes*, *comitis*, a companion.]
 1. a small administrative district of a country; especially, (a) a local administrative subdivision of a State, which in turn is divided into townships; (b) [Brit.] a shire considered as an administrative, judicial, and political district.
 2. the inhabitants of a county, taken collectively.
 3. the district of an earl or count; also, a count or earl. [Obs.]
 county corporate; in Great Britain, a city or town having privilege of being a county by itself, as London.
 county palatine; the land held by a count palatine.

çoun′ty, *a.* of a county.
 county commissioner; see under *commissioner.*
 county court; a court having jurisdiction only in a county.
 county fair; a fair, usually held annually, to exhibit the products of a county.
 county farm; a farm maintained by a county as a home for people without means of support.
 county seat; a town or city that is the center of a county government.
 county sessions; the general quarter sessions of the peace for each county. [Brit.]
 county town; a county seat.

çŏup (kö), *n.*; *pl.* **çŏupş** (köz), [Fr., a stroke, blow.]
 1. literally, a stroke or blow.
 2. a sudden, successful move or action; a brilliant stroke; a clever stratagem.
 3. in certain tribes of Indians of North America, a stroke or maneuver against an enemy so done as to constitute a deed of bravery.
 coup de grâce; the blow, shot, etc. that brings death to a sufferer; a death blow; hence, the finishing stroke.
 coup de main; a surprise attack, as in war.
 coup de soleil; a sunstroke.
 coup d'état; a sudden, forceful stroke in politics; especially, the sudden, forcible overthrow of a government.
 coup de théâtre; (a) a surprising or startling turn in a drama; (b) an action for sensational effect; theatrical action.
 coup d'oeil; a rapid glance; a quick view or survey.

çŏu′pȧ·ble, *a.* culpable. [Obs.]

çŏupe (köp), *n.* a closed, two-door automobile that seats two to six people.

çou·pé′ (kö-pā′), *n.* [Fr., pp. of *couper*, to cut.]
 1. the front seats of a continental diligence; also, in European railway cars, a half-compartment at the end, with seats on only one side.
 2. a four-wheeled closed carriage carrying two passengers inside, with a seat for the driver on the outside.
 3. a coupe: now the less common form of the word.

çŏuped (köpt), *a.* in heraldry, denoting that the head or any limb of an animal is cut off smoothly from the trunk: distinguished from *erased*, which indicates that the head or limb is torn off.

COUPED

çŏu·pee′, *n.* [Fr., from *couper*, to cut.] a motion in dancing made when one leg is resting while with the other a motion is made forward.

çŏupe gọrge (gọrzh), [Fr. *coupé*, from *couper*, to cut, and *gorge*, a throat.] in military usage, a position in which troops are unable to resist and must surrender or be annihilated.

çŏu′ple (kup′pl), *n.* [ME. *couple*; OFr. *cuple*, *cople*; L. *copula*, a band, bond.]
 1. two of the same species or kind, and near in place, or considered together; a pair; as, a *couple* of men.

2. a man and woman who are engaged, married, or joined as partners in dances, games, etc.
3. that which links or connects two things together.
4. in mechanics, two equal and parallel forces producing rotation by acting in opposite directions.
5. in electricity, two metals in contact with each other to form a galvanic or thermoelectric current; voltaic couple.
6. one of a pair of opposite rafters in a roof nailed at the top where they meet, and connected by a tie at or near their lower ends.
7. a few; several; as, I've a *couple* of things to do. [Colloq.]
Syn.—brace, pair, two.

çŏu′ple, *v.t.*; coupled, *pt.*, *pp.*; coupling, *ppr.* [Fr. *coupler*; L. *copulare*, to couple, from *copula*, band, bond.]
1. to link, join, or connect (one thing) with another.
2. to marry; to wed; to unite as husband and wife.
3. in electricity, to join (two electric currents) magnetically or by direct connection.

çŏu′ple, *v.i.* 1. to copulate.
2. to unite in a pair or pairs; to pair.

çŏu′ple-beg″găr, *n.* one who made it his business to marry beggars to each other. [Obs.]

çŏu′ple-çlōṣe, *n.* 1. in heraldry, the fourth of a chevron, always appearing in pairs, usually with a chevron between them.
2. in architecture, couples, collectively.

çŏu′ple·ment (kup′pl-), *n.* union. [Obs.]

çŏup′lẽr, *n.* one who or that which couples; as, (a) any device in an organ for depressing another key or keys when one is played; (b) a pneumatic device for coupling two railroad cars.

çŏup′let, *n.* [Fr., dim. of *couple*, a couple.]
1. two lines of verse in immediate succession, especially two of the same length that rhyme.
2. a pair; as, a *couplet* of doves. [Rare.]

çŏup′ling, *n.* 1. a joining together; pairing.
2. any mechanical device or appliance serving to unite two or more parts or things.
3. a device for joining two railroad cars together.
4. the part of the body of a dog, horse, etc. between the forequarters and hindquarters.
5. a method or device for joining two electric circuits for the transference of energy from one to the other.

COUPLING OF SHAFT

çŏup′ling box, a box-shaped fixture for joining the ends of two shafts.

çŏup′ling pin, a pin used for coupling together railroad cars or machinery.

çōu′pon (*or* kū′), *n.* [Fr., a remnant, from *couper*, to cut, cut off.]
1. an interest certificate, printed at the bottom of transferable bonds (state, railroad, etc.), given for a term of years. There are as many of these certificates as there are payments of interest to be made. At each time of payment one is cut off and presented for payment.
2. a portion, generally detachable, of a ticket given with package goods entitling the buyer to a specified privilege, as the right to certain transportation, a certain seat in a theater, etc.
3. a part of a printed advertisement that can be used to order goods, samples, etc.

çōup′stick, *n.* a stick carried by certain North American Indians, with which to execute a coup.

çōu′pūre, *n.* [Fr., from *couper*, to cut.]
1. in fortification, (a) an entrenchment made behind a breach by the besieged, with a view to defense; (b) a passage cut through the glacis to facilitate sallies by the besieged.
2. in the theory of functions, a cutting of a Riemann's surface.

çŏur′āġe (kūr′), *n.* [OFr. *courage*, *corage*, mind, heart, spirit, from L. *cor*, heart.]
1. the attitude or response of facing and dealing with anything recognized as dangerous, difficult, or painful, instead of withdrawing from it; the quality of being fearless or brave; valor; pluck.
2. spirit; desire; temper. [Obs.]
Syn.—bravery, intrepidity, valor, boldness, resolution, fortitude, firmness, fearlessness, daring, enterprise, hardihood, heroism, gallantry, dauntlessness, mettle, pluck.

çŏur·ā′ġeous (-jus), *a.* [OFr. *corageus*, from *corage*, mind, heart, spirit.] having or exhibiting courage; brave; daring; as, a *courageous* deed.

çŏur·ā′ġeous·ly, *adv.* in a courageous manner; bravely.

çŏur·ā′ġeous·ness, *n.* the state or quality of being courageous.

çōu′rant, *a.* running: applied, in heraldry, to animals.

çōu′rant (*or* cōu-rant′), *n.* a newspaper: obsolete except in newspaper titles.

çōu·ränt′, çōu·ränte′, *n.* [Fr. *courant*, running, pp. of *courir*, to run.] a piece of music in triple time; also, an old, lively French dance with gliding or running steps.

çōu·rap′, *n.* [E. Ind.] an eruptive disease or itch, especially on the groin, face, breast, and armpits: common in India.

çōurb, *v.i.* [Fr. *courber*.] to bend. [Obs.]

çōur′bȧ·ril, *n.* [from S. Am. name.] a resin; animé.

çōurbed, *a.* crooked. [Obs.]

çōurçhe, *n.* [Scot.] a kerchief. [Obs.]

çōu′ri·ẽr, *n.* [OFr. *courier*, from *courir*, to run; L. *currere*, to run.]
1. a messenger, usually one sent in haste with important letters or messages.
2. a person hired to accompany travelers and take care of hotel accommodations, luggage, etc.

çōur′lăn, *n.* [Fr., from S. Am. name.] any tropical American raillike bird of the genus *Aramus*.

çōurse, *n.* [Fr. *course*; OFr. *curs*; L. *cursus*, a running, from *currere*, to run.]
1. a moving or motion forward in any direction; a continuous progression or advance; progress.
When his fair *course* is not hindered.
—Shak.
2. the direction of motion; the line in which a body moves; as, what *course* shall the pilot steer?
3. the progress or duration of time; as, in the *course* of a week.
4. the charge of one mounted knight or champion against another in a tournament.
5. the continual or gradual advance or progress of anything; as, the *course* of an argument.
Time rolls his ceaseless *course*. —Scott.
6. a number of like things in some regular order; a series.
7. a regular mode or pattern of action or behavior; customary or established sequence of events; recurrence of events according to certain laws.
Seed time and harvest, heat and hoary frost,
Shall hold their *course*. —Milton.
8. a way, path, or channel of movement; as, a race *course*, golf *course*.
9. in education, (a) a complete, progressive series of studies necessary for graduation, for a degree, etc.; (b) any of the studies; a unit of instruction in a subject, made up of recitations, lectures, etc.; as, the psychology *course* was interesting.
10. the part of a meal served at one time; as, the dinner consisted of four *courses*.
11. in architecture, a continuous range of stones or bricks on the face or roof of a building.
12. in nautical usage, (a) one of the sails that hangs from a ship's lower yards; as, the mainsail, foresail, and mizzen; (b) the point of the compass toward which a ship sails.
13. [*pl.*] the menses.
in course; regularly; in sequence.
matter of course; something to be expected in the natural order of things.
of course; (a) as a matter of course; (b) certainly.
Syn.—way, road, route, passage, race, procedure, series, succession, rotation, manner, method, mode.

çōurse, *v.t.*; coursed, *pt.*, *pp.*; coursing, *ppr.*
1. to hunt; to pursue; to chase.
We *coursed* him at the heels. —Shak.
2. to cause to chase, as hounds in a hunt.
3. to run through or over; as, the blood *courses* the arteries.

çōurse, *v.i.* 1. to run; to move with speed; to run or move about; as, the blood *courses*.
2. to hunt with dogs.

çōursed (kōrst), *a.* hunted; also, arranged in courses.

çōurs′ẽr, *n.* [ME. *courser*; OFr. *corsier*; LL. *cursarius*, from L. *cursus*, a running; *currere*, to run.] a swift horse; a runner; a war horse. [Poetic.]

çōurs′ẽr, *n.* [from L. *cursorius*, pertaining to running.] any of various Asian and African birds related to the plover, known for their swift running.

çōurṣ′ẽr, *n.* 1. a person or thing that courses.
2. a dog for coursing.

çōur′sey, *n.* a narrow aisle in a galley separating slaves from each other.

çōurs′ing, *n.* 1. pursuit of game by dogs using the sense of sight rather than smell to follow the quarry.
2. the action of a person or thing that courses.

çōurs′ing joint, a joint between two courses of masonry.

çōurt, *n.* [ME. *court*, *cort*; OFr. *curt*, *cort*; LL. *cortis*, a courtyard, yard, villa, palace; L. *cors*, contr. of *cohors*, a place enclosed.]
1. an uncovered area wholly or partly surrounded by buildings or walls; a courtyard; also, a special section or area of a museum, somewhat like such a space but roofed, as with a skylight.
2. a palace; the place of residence of a king or sovereign prince.
This our *court*,
Shows like a riotous inn. —Shak.
3. all the people surrounding a sovereign in his regal state; specifically, the collective body of persons who compose the retinue or council of a sovereign.
Love rules the *court*, the camp, the grove.
—Scott.
4. a sovereign and his councilors, ministers, etc. as a governing body.
5. any formal gathering, reception, etc. held by a sovereign.
6. the hall, chamber, or place where justice is administered, trials are held, investigations made, etc.
7. the persons or judges assembled for hearing and deciding cases, civil, criminal, military, naval, or ecclesiastical, as distinguished from the counsel or jury; as, a *court* of law, a *court* of chancery.
8. a judicial assembly.
The archbishop . . .
Held a late *court* at Dunstable. —Shak.
9. the sitting of a judicial assembly.
10. the meeting of a corporation or the principal members of a corporation; as, the *court* of directors; the *court* of aldermen.
11. attention directed to a person in order to get something; flattery; address to gain favor; as, to pay *court* to wealth.
12. courtship; wooing.
13. a short street, often closed at one end.
14. a specially prepared area for playing any of several ball games, as basketball, handball, tennis, etc.
15. a part of such an area.
16. formerly, a mansion or manor with a large, uncovered entrance area: now used occasionally in proper names, as Hampton *Court*.
Court Circular; news of the court and sovereign of Great Britain, as furnished by authority to the press.
court day; the day of a court's sitting.
court dress; a dress suitable for an appearance at the court of a sovereign.
court guide; a directory or book containing the addresses of the nobility and gentry. [Brit.]
court of claims; the United States court that investigates claims against the government.
Court of Common Pleas; in some States of the United States, a court having jurisdiction over civil suits between private parties.
court of error; a court having jurisdiction in cases of alleged error.
court of inquiry; a court convened to investigate and report on questions of military law or precedent, generally as a preliminary to a court martial.
Court of St. James; the British royal court.
district court; (a) the federal trial court sitting in each district of the United States; (b) in some States, the court of general jurisdiction.
General Court; (a) originally, a Colonial legislative assembly with judicial powers; (b) now, the legislature of New Hampshire or Massachusetts: the official title.
Permanent Court of International Justice; same as *World Court*.
Superior Court; (a) in the United States, a court having jurisdiction between the inferior courts and the supreme court; (b) in England, one of the main courts sitting at Westminster.

Supreme Court; see under *supreme*.
the courts of the Lord; the temple at Jerusalem; hence, any house of public worship.
World Court; see under *world*.

çōurt, *v.t.*; courted, *pt., pp.*; courting, *ppr.*
1. to endeavor to gain the favor of or win over by attention and address; to flatter in order to get something.
2. to seek the affections or love of; to woo; to solicit for marriage.

A thousand *court* you, though they court in vain. —Pope.

3. to try to get; to solicit; to seek, as, to *court* commendation or applause.
4. to hold out inducements to; to invite.

A well-worn pathway *courted* us. —Tennyson.

çōurt, *v.i.* to carry on a courtship; to woo.

çōurt′-bar′ŏn, *n.* a baron's court. [Obs.]

çōurt′bred, *a.* used to the ways of a court; easy; polished.

çōurt breed′ing, the etiquette of a court.

çōurt çärd, [altered from *coat card*.] same as *face card*.

çōurt′çrȧft, *n.* intrigue, as at court.

çōurt çup′bōard (kub′ẽrd), a sideboard. [Obs.]

çoūr′tē·ous, *a.* [ME. *curteous, curteis, corteis*; OFr. *curteis, corteis*, from LL. *cortis*, a court.] having courtlike manners; using or characterized by courtesy; well-bred; polite and gracious; considerate of others; as, a *courteous* gentleman, *courteous* words.

Syn.—civil, polite, obliging, urbane, affable, conciliating, attentive, respectful.

çoūr′tē·ous·ly, *adv.* in a courteous manner.

çoūr′tē·ous·ness, *n.* the state or quality of being courteous.

çoūr′tē·py, *n.* [D. *kort*, short, and *pije*, a coarse cloth.] a coarse, short coat. [Obs.]

çōurt′ẽr, *n.* one who courts.

çoūr′tē·săn, çoūr′tē·zăn, *n.* [ME. *courtezane*; Fr. *courtesan*, a court lady; from *corte*, a court.]
1. a courtier. [Obs.]
2. a prostitute.

çoūr′tē·săn·ship, çoūr′tē·zăn·ship, *n.* prostitution.

çoūr′te·sy, *n.* [ME. *curtesie*; OFr. *curteisie*, from *curteis*, courteous; LL. *cortis*, a court.]
1. politeness of manners; especially, politeness connected with kindness; civility; considerateness; as, a *courtesy* done a stranger.
2. a polite or considerate act or remark.
3. favor; approval: opposed to legal right; as, a title of *courtesy*.
4. (kũrt′si), a curtsy.

courtesy card; a card entitling the bearer to special privileges, as at a hotel, bank, etc.

Courtesy (or *Curtesy*) *of England*; the status of one who marries a woman having an estate by inheritance, and has by her issue capable of inheriting her estate; in this case, on the death of his wife, he holds the lands for his life, as tenant by courtesy.

courtesy title; a title of address not legally valid but given by custom, as to the children of British dukes.

Syn.—urbanity, civility, complaisance, condescension, affability, courteousness.

çoūrte′sy (kũrt′), *v.i.*; courtesied, *pt., pp.*; courtesying, *ppr.* to make a courtesy (sense 4).

çoūrte′sy, *v.t.* to treat courteously. [Obs.]

çōurt hand, the old Gothic or Saxon handwriting formerly used in English records and judicial proceedings.

çōurt′house, *n.* a building used for the regular holding of a court; also, a building that houses the offices of a county government.

çōurt′iẽr (-yẽr), *n.* [OFr. *courtier*, a judge, courtier, from LL. *cortis*, a court, palace.]
1. one who attends or frequents the royal court.
2. a person who uses flattery to get something or to win favor.

çōurt′iẽr·y, *n.* manners of a courtier. [Obs.]

çōurt landṣ, in English law, lands of domain retained as a homestead.

çōurt leet, in English law, formerly, a court of record held once a year, in a particular hundred, lordship, or manor, before the steward of the court.

çōurt′like, *a.* polite; elegant.

çōurt′li·ness, *n.* the quality of being courtly.

çōurt′ling, *n.* a courtier.

çōurt′ly, *a.*; *comp.* courtlier; *superl.* courtliest,
1. suitable for a king's court; dignified, polite, elegant, etc.; as, *courtly* manners.
2. flattering, especially in a servile way.

çōurt′ly, *adv.* in a courtly manner; politely.

çōurt mär′shăl, one acting as marshal of a law court.

çōurt′-mär′tiăl (-shăl), *n.*; *pl.* **çōurts′-mär′tiăl,** 1. a court made up of military or naval personnel convened for trial of military offenses, or of army or navy personnel: in the United States, the three kinds, employed according to the seriousness of the offense, are *summary, special*, and *general*.
2. *pl. now often* **çōurt′-mär′tiălṣ,** a trial by a court-martial.

çōurt′-mär′tiăl, *v.t.*; court-martialed *or* court-martialled, *pt., pp.*; court-martialing *or* court-martialling, *ppr.* to try by court-martial.

çōurt plȧs′tẽr, fine cloth treated with an adhesive substance, often medicated, to protect minor cuts and scratches in the skin.

çōurt rōllṣ, records of a court.

çōurt′ro͝om, *n.* a room in which a law court is held.

çōurt′ship, *n.* 1. the act of soliciting favor.
2. the act, process, or period of courting a woman.
3. civility; elegance of manners. [Obs.]

çōurt ten′nis, see *tennis*.

çōurt′yärd, *n.* a space enclosed by walls, adjoining or in a castle or other large building.

çōus′çōus, *n.* [W. Afr.] in Africa, a food made of baobab leaves, millet flour, and meat.

çōuṣ′in (kuz′n), *n.* [OFr. *cousin, cosin*; LL. *cosinus*, contr. of *consobrinus*, the child of a mother's sister, a cousin, relation; from *soror*, a sister.]
1. originally, one collaterally related more remotely than a brother or sister, descended from a common ancestor.
2. the son or daughter of one's uncle or aunt: also called *cousin-german, first* (or *full* or *own*) *cousin*: you are a *first cousin* to the child of your uncle or aunt; you are a *second cousin* to the children of your parents' first cousins; you are a *first cousin once removed* (sometimes called *second cousin*) to the children of your first cousins.
3. loosely, any relative by blood or marriage.
4. a person of a nation thought of as related to another nation; as, the English and Australians are sometimes called *cousins*.
5. a title of address used by a sovereign to another sovereign or to a nobleman.
6. a rival or competitor who unwittingly or unintentionally advances one's interests. [Slang.]

çōuṣ′in·ăġe, *n.* cousinhood. [Obs.]

çōuṣ′in-ġẽr′măn, *n.*; *pl.* **çōuṣ′inṣ-ġẽr′măn,** a first cousin; a child of one's uncle or aunt.

çōuṣ′in·hood, *n.* 1. the state of being cousins.
2. the individuals connected with a family; cousins collectively.

çōuṣ′in·ly, *a.* of, like, characteristic of, or fit for a cousin.

çōuṣ′in·ly, *adv.* in a cousinly manner.

çōuṣ′in·ry, *n.*; *pl.* **çōuṣ′in·rieṣ,** cousins or other relatives, collectively.

çōuṣ′in·ship, *n.* the relationship of cousins.

çōus′si·net, *n.* [Fr., a little cushion.] in architecture, (a) a stone placed on the impost of a pier for receiving the first stone of an arch; (b) that part of the Ionic capital between the abacus and quarter round, which serves to form the volute.

çōu·teau′ (-tō′), *n.*; *pl.* **çōu·teaux′** (-tō′), [Fr., a knife.]
1. a two-edged dagger.
2. a large knife carried as a weapon.

çōuth, obs. pt. and pp. of *can* (to be able).

çōuth, *a.* known. [Archaic.]

çōu′til, *n.* [Fr.] a linen or cotton cloth of a specially heavy close texture, used in making corsets, etc.

çōu·tūre′, *n.* [Fr., sewing, seam, from Vulgar L. *consutura*, seam, from L. *consutus*, pp. of *consuere*, to sew, stitch, join, from *con-*, together, and *suere*, to sew.] the work or business of designing new fashions in women's clothes; also, women's clothes in new or specially designed fashions.

çōu·tū·rier′ (-ryā′), *n.* [Fr.] a man dressmaker.

cou·tu·rière′ (kö-tụ̈-ryâr′), *n.* a woman dressmaker.

çōu·văde′, *n.* [Fr., from *couver*, to brood, hatch, sit.] a custom among some of the primitive tribes, in which the father goes to bed as if for childbearing when his wife is having a baby.

çōu′xi·ȧ (-shi-), *n.* [S. Am. name.] the black saki of South America; also, the couxio.

çōu′xi·ō (-shi-), *n.* *Pithecia chiropotes*, the red-backed saki.

çō·vā′lence, *n.* 1. the number of pairs of electrons that an atom can share with its neighboring atoms.
2. the bond formed by shared pairs of electrons between two atoms.

çō·vā′ri·ănce, *n.* in statistics, a measure of the relationship between two variables whose values are observed at the same time; specifically, the average value of the product of the two variables diminished by the product of their average values.

çōve, *n.* [AS. *cofa*, a room, chamber; Norw. *kove*, a closet.]
1. a small inlet, creek, or bay.

At length I spied a little *cove* on the right shore of the creek. —Defoe.

2. a sheltered recess, as in a mountain; a secluded hollow or dell.
3. a strip of open land extending into a forest.
4. in architecture, (a) a concave molding, especially one next to a ceiling; (b) a trough for concealed light fixtures on a wall near a ceiling; (c) a concave arch or vault.

çōve, *v.t.* and *v.i.*; coved, *pt., pp.*; coving, *ppr.* in architecture, to arch over or slope inward.

çōve, *n.* [Gypsy *cova*, a thing, *covo*, that man, *covi*, that woman.] a man or boy; a chap; a fellow; as, a queer *cove*. [Brit. Slang.]

çōved, *a.* forming an arch; arched; curving.

coved ceiling; a ceiling formed in a coved or arched manner at its junction with the side walls. Such ceilings are frequently highly ornamented with panels enriched with moldings or carvings.

COVED CEILING

coved vault; a vault formed by the meeting in a central point of four sections curving concavely from wall to ceiling.

çō·vel′lin, çō·vel′line, *n.* [named after *Covelli*, the discoverer.] a native form of copper sulfide, massive, and of an indigo-blue color: called also *indigo copper* and *covellite*.

çŏv′en (*or* kōv′-), *n.* [ME. *covin*, a group of confederates; OFr. *covine*, a band; ultimately from L. *convenire*, to come together, be of one mind, agree; from *com-*, together, and *venire*, to come.] a gathering or meeting, especially of witches.

çŏv′e·nȧ·ble, *a.* [OFr.] fit; suitable. [Obs.]

çŏv′e·nănt, *n.* [OFr. *covenant*, an agreement, from *covenir*; L. *convenire*, to agree, be of one mind, come together; from *com-*, together, and *venire*, to come.]
1. a binding and solemn agreement by two or more persons, parties, etc. to do or keep from doing some specified thing; a compact.
2. in theology, the promises of God to man, usually carrying with them conditions to be fulfilled by man, as recorded in the Bible.
3. a solemn agreement between the members of a church, that they will hold to points of doctrine, faith, etc.
4. in law, (a) a writing, under seal, containing the terms of agreement or contract between parties; also, a clause containing a subordinate agreement or stipulation in a deed or other sealed instrument; (b) a suit claiming damages for breach of contract under seal.
5. [C-] an agreement of Presbyterians in Scotland in 1638 to oppose episcopacy: also called *National Covenant*.
6. [C-] an agreement between the parliaments of Scotland and England in 1643 to extend and preserve Presbyterianism in England: also called *Solemn League and Covenant*.
7. [C-] the Covenant of the League of Nations.

Syn.—contract, bargain, stipulation, agreement, promise, engagement.

çŏv′e·nănt, *v.t.* and *v.i.*; covenanted, *pt., pp.*; covenanting, *ppr.* to promise by or in a covenant.

çŏv″e·năn·tee′, *n.* the person to whom the promises of a covenant are made.

çŏv′e·nănt·ẽr, *n.* 1. a person who makes a covenant.
2. [C-] in Scottish history, a subscriber to the National Covenant (1638), or to the Solemn League and Covenant (1643); also, in a later and more general sense, anyone uphold-

ing the principles of the Reformed Presbyterian Church.

çŏv′e·nănt·ing, *a.* 1. of, entering into, or pertaining to a covenant.

2. relating or belonging to the Scottish Covenanters, or, later, to the Reformed Presbyterian Church.

Çŏv′e·nănt of the Lēague of Nā′tions, the first section of the Treaty of Versailles (1919): it was the constitution of the League of Nations.

çŏv′e·nănt·ŏr, *n.* the person responsible for the performance of the stipulations of a covenant.

çŏv′e·nous, *a.* see *covinous.*

çŏv′ent, *n.* [OFr. *covent,* convent, from L. *conventus,* an assembly, agreement.]

1. a convent or monastery. [Obs.]

2. a gathering or assembly; also, an agreement or promise. [Obs.]

Çov′en·try, *n.* [prob. 17th-c. Cavalier phrase: the town of Coventry, England, was strongly Roundhead.] a state of banishment or exclusion from society; ostracism.

send to Coventry; to ostracize; to refuse to speak to or deal with socially.

Çov′en·try bell, any of several bellflowers more commonly called *canterbury bell.*

Çov′en·try blüe, blue thread of a superior dye, made at Coventry, England, and used for embroidery.

Çov′en·try rāpe, a European bellflower, the rampion.

çŏv′ẽr, *v.t.*; covered, *pt., pp.*; covering, *ppr.* [ME. *coveren*; OFr. *covrir, couvrir,* from L. *cooperire*; *co-,* intens., and *operire,* to hide.]

1. to place something on, over, or in front of, so as to hide or protect; overlay with or as with a covering.

2. to extend over; lie upon; as, snow *covered* the highway.

3. to clothe; as, to *cover* with a robe or mantle.

4. to conceal; hide; screen.

5. to pardon or remit.

Blessed is he whose sin is *covered.*
—Ps. xxxii. 1.

6. to shelter; to protect; to defend; to keep from harm or injury by shielding.

7. to attract to or bring upon (oneself) by one's actions; to invest (oneself) with; as, she *covered* herself with fame and renown.

8. to sit on (eggs); incubate; brood; as, a hen *covers* her eggs faithfully.

9. to copulate with (female).

10. to put the usual headdress on.

Nay, pray be *covered.* —Shak.

11. to place within range; to have direct aim at; to point a firearm at; as, to *cover* an enemy with a rifle; also, to have a superior strategic position in relation to; to occupy a vantage point which gives command of; as, the battery *covered* the bridge.

12. in commerce, to equal, or be of equal extent to; to be equivalent to or adequate for; to include, comprehend, or comprise; to compensate for or counterbalance; as, the receipts do not *cover* the expenses; this principle will *cover* the majority of cases.

13. in journalism, to report, by assignment or otherwise, the news of, or items of interest concerning; as, to *cover* city hall; to *cover* a convention.

14. to coat, sprinkle, etc. thickly; as, he was *covered* with mud.

15. to accept (a bet); stake the equivalent of (an opponent's stake) in a wager.

16. to travel over; go through; as, he *covered* the distance in ten minutes.

17. to include; deal with; as, the book *covers* the subject thoroughly.

18. in card games, to put a higher card on (a previously played card).

19 in military usage, to stand or move behind (a man or men) in order to observe and protect from enemy action.

20. in sports, to watch, guard, or defend (an opponent or area); be responsible for.

to cover shorts; on the stock exchange, to buy property of any kind to fill contracts previously made.

to cover up; (a) to cover entirely; envelop; wrap; (b) to conceal; be secretive.

Syn.—overspread, cloak, shield, protect, shelter, hide, disguise.

çŏv′ẽr, *v.i.* 1. to prepare a table for a banquet. [Obs.]

2. to spread or distribute in such a way as to hide something; to overspread; as, this paint *covers* better than the other.

3. to put one's hat on.

çŏv′ẽr, *n.* 1. anything which is laid, set, or spread over another thing; anything that covers.

2. anything which veils or conceals; a screen; disguise; pretense; as, gravity may serve as a *cover* for a deceitful heart.

3. shelter; defense; protection; as, the troops fought under *cover* of the batteries.

4. the tablecloth and setting for a meal, especially for one person, such as plate, spoons, knives, forks, napkin, glasses, etc.; as, *covers* were laid for ten.

5. in hunting, the woods or shrubbery which hide game.

6. the part of a shingle, slate, etc. placed in a roof or other portion of a building, that is covered by the row or course above.

7. the amount of lap of a slide valve of a steam engine.

8. a cover charge.

9. an envelope with a newly issued stamp, which has passed through a post office on the date of issue: valued by stamp collectors because of its dated postal markings.

to break cover; to come out from a hiding place or den.

to take cover; to seek protective shelter or concealment.

under cover; (a) enclosed in a wrapper or contained in a letter; (b) under protection from gunfire; (c) in secret; (d) by pretense; (e) hidden.

çŏv′ẽr·ăġe, *n.* [*cover* and *-age.*]

1. the amount, extent, etc. covered by something.

2. in insurance, all the risks covered by an insurance policy.

3. in journalism, the extent to which a news story is covered.

çŏv′ẽr·all, *n.* [*usually pl.*] a one-piece, loose-fitting garment with sleeves, worn by mechanics, etc.

çŏv′ẽr chärġe, [see *cover, n.* sense 4.] a charge added to the cost of food and drink at a night club or restaurant.

çŏv′ẽr·chief (-chif), *n.* a covering for the head. [Obs.]

çŏv′ẽr-çloth, *n.* a piece of cloth forming the outside of a lace maker's pillow.

çŏv′ẽr çrop, a crop, as rye, vetch, or red clover, grown to protect soil from erosion and loss by bleaching.

Çŏv′ẽr·dāle Bī′ble (-bl), a translation of the Bible by Miles Coverdale, afterwards Bishop of Exeter, issued in 1535, and dedicated to Henry VIII: it was the first Bible sanctioned by royal authority.

çŏv′ẽred (-ẽrd), *a.* [pp. of *cover.*] 1. having a cover or covering.

2. having a cover on.

3. having a hat, cap, etc. on the head.

çŏv′ẽred wag′ŏn, a large wagon with an arched cover of canvas, used by American pioneers: also called *schooner, prairie schooner.*

çŏv′ẽr·ẽr, *n.* a person or the thing that covers.

çŏv′ẽr girl, a pretty girl whose picture is often put on magazine covers, etc. [Colloq.]

çŏv′ẽr glȧss, a thin glass slide used to cover specimens prepared for the microscope.

çŏv′ẽr·ing, *n.* 1. that which covers; anything spread or laid over something else.

2. the act of providing a cover for.

çŏv′ẽr·ing let′tẽr, a letter sent with a package, another letter, etc. as an explanation or introduction.

çŏv′ẽr·let, *n.* [Fr. *couvre-lit,* a bed cover; *couvrir,* to cover, and *lit,* from L. *lectus,* a bed.]

1. the cover of a bed; a quilt, usually ornamental, designed to be spread over all the other coverings of a bed.

2. any covering.

çŏv′ẽr·lid, *n.* a coverlet.

çŏv′ẽr-point, *n.* 1. in cricket, a fielder backing point; also, the position he occupies.

2. in lacrosse, a player in front of point; also, the position he occupies.

çō′vẽrsed (-vẽrst) **sīne,** in trigonometry, the versed sine of the complement of an arc or angle.

çŏv′ẽr-shāme, *n.* something used to conceal infamy. [Obs.]

çŏv′ẽr slip, see *cover glass.*

çŏv′ẽr stō′ry, the special article or story in a magazine that deals with the subject depicted on the cover.

çŏv′ẽrt, *a.* [OFr. *covert, couvert,* pp. of *couvrir,* to cover.]

1. covered; hid; private; secret; concealed; disguised; insidious.

Whether of open war, or *covert* guile.
—Milton.

2. sheltered; not open or exposed; as, a *covert* corner or place.

3. in law, under cover, authority, or protection; as, a *feme covert,* a married woman, regarded as being under the influence and protection of her husband.

Syn.—close, concealed, hidden, secret, disguised, veiled, obscure.

çŏv′ẽrt, *n.* 1. a covering, or covering place; a place which covers and shelters; a shelter.

2. a thicket; a shady place; a hiding place for game.

3. that which hides or disguises; a pretext.

4. in fowling, a flock; a covey. [Obs.]

5. in ornithology, one of the small feathers on the under part of the wing or on the tail, which lie over and cover the bases of the quills.

çŏv′ẽrt-bar″ŏn, *n.* [Fr. *covert,* pp. of *couvrir,* to cover, and *baron,* a baron.] the status of a woman who is married, or a feme covert.

çŏv′ẽrt çlŏth, a smooth, twilled cloth of wool with cotton, rayon, or silk: used for suits, topcoats, etc.

çŏv′ẽrt·ly, *adv.* secretly; closely; in private; insidiously.

Among the poets, Persius *covertly* strikes at Nero. —Dryden.

çŏv′ẽrt·ness, *n.* secrecy; privacy.

çŏv′ẽr·tūre, *n.* [OFr. *coverture,* from LL. *coopertura,* from L. *cooperire,* to cover; *co-,* intens., and *operire,* to cover.]

1. covering; shelter; defense.

2. a concealment; disguise.

3. in law, the status of a married woman.

çov′ẽr-up, *n.* something used for hiding one's real activities, intentions, etc.; front.

çŏv′et, *v.t.*; coveted, *pt., pp.*; coveting, *ppr.* [ME. *coveten*; OFr. *coveitier,* from L. *cupidus,* eager, desirous of.]

1. to desire, or wish for, with eagerness; to desire earnestly.

Covet earnestly the best gifts.
—1 Cor. xii. 31.

2. to desire inordinately; to long for (that which another person has).

Thou shalt not *covet* thy neighbour's house.
—Ex. xx. 17.

çŏv′et, *v.i.* to have or to satisfy an extreme desire.

çŏv′et·ȧ·ble, *a.* that may be coveted.

çŏv′et·ẽr, *n.* one who covets.

çŏv′et·ing·ly, *adv.* with eager desire to possess.

çŏv′et·ise (-is), *n.* avarice. [Obs.]

çŏv′e·tive·ness, *n.* in phrenology, acquisitiveness.

çŏv′et·ous (-us), *a.* [ME. *coveitous*; OFr. *covoitous,* from L. *cupidus,* eager, desirous of.]

1. very desirous; eager to obtain; as, *covetous* of wisdom, virtue, or learning. [Archaic.]

2. inordinately desirous; excessively eager to obtain and possess; avaricious; grasping; greedy; miserly.

çŏv′et·ous·ly, *adv.* in a covetous manner.

çŏv′et·ous·ness, *n.* 1. a strong or inordinate desire of obtaining and possessing that which belongs to another.

2. strong desire; eagerness. [Rare.]

çŏv′ey, *n.* [OFr. *coveye, covee,* a brood, flock of birds, from *cover,* to brood, sit on; L. *cubare,* to lie down.]

1. a brood or hatch of birds; a small flock or number of birds together, especially partridges or quail.

2. a company; a set; a party; a small group of people.

çŏv′ey, *v.i.* to brood; hatch. [Obs.]

çŏv′ey, *n.* a closet or pantry. [Brit. Dial.]

çō′vey, *n.* same as *cove* (a fellow). [Slang.]

çŏv′in, çŏv′ine, çŏv′en, *n.* [OFr. *covine,* a secret agreement, plot, from *covenir,* to come together, agree.]

1. in law, a collusive or deceitful agreement between two or more persons to defraud or swindle another or others.

2. a secret agreement. [Obs.]

3. deceit; fraud. [Archaic.]

çō′ving, *n.* the projection of the upper stories of buildings over the lower ones: formerly a prevalent style of building.

çŏv′in·ous, çŏv′en·ous, *a.* deceitful; collusive; fraudulent.

çow, *n.*; *pl.* **çowṣ** *or archaic or poet.* **kīne,** [ME. *cow, cou, cu*; AS. *cu*; D. *koe*; G. *kuh*; Sw. *ko*; L. *bos*; Gr. *bous*; Per. *koh*; Sans. *go,* a cow, ox.]

1. the mature female of domestic cattle, genus *Bos*; especially, a familiar farm animal domesticated for its milk.

2. the female of various other mammals, as the elephant, the whale, the walrus, etc.

çow, *v.t.*; cowed, *pt., pp.*; cowing, *ppr.* to depress with fear; to lower the spirits or courage of; to oppress with habitual timidity; to intimidate.

çow, *n.* in mining, a wedge-shaped brake.
çow′āġe, *n.* a plant, cowhage.
çow′ăn, *n.* a mason who has picked up the trade without serving an apprenticeship. [Scot.]
çow′ărd, *a.* relating to a coward; pertaining to cowardice; timid; cowardly.
çow′ărd, *n.* [ME. *coward, couard,* from OFr. *coue, coe,* from L. *coda, cauda,* a tail, and the depreciatory suffix *-ard;* originally an epithet of the hare, "short-tailed."]
1. a person who lacks courage to meet danger, difficulty, or pain; a poltroon; a timid or pusillanimous man.

Where's the *coward* that would not dare
To fight for such a land. —Scott.

2. in heraldry, an animal borne in the escutcheon with its tail between its legs.
Syn.—poltroon, craven, dastard.—A *coward* is, in a general sense, one who is afraid to meet danger, real or imaginary; a *poltroon* is a mean-spirited and contemptible coward; a *craven* is one who shrinks back at the approach of danger; a *dastard* is a sneaking, malicious coward.
çow′ărd, *v.t.* to frighten. [Obs.]
çow′ărd·ice, *n.* lack of courage to face danger; timidity; pusillanimity; fear of exposing one's person to difficulty or pain.

Cowardice alone is loss of fame.—Dryden.

çow′ărd·ie, *n.* cowardice. [Obs.]
çow′ărd·ish, *a.* cowardly. [Obs.]
çow′ărd·īze, *v.t.* to make cowardly. [Obs.]
çow′ărd·li·ness, *n.* lack of courage; cowardice.
çow′ărd·ly, *a.* 1. lacking courage to face danger; timid; timorous; fearful; pusillanimous; of, or characteristic of, a coward.
2. mean; base; befitting a coward; as, a *cowardly* action.
çow′ărd·ly, *adv.* in the manner of a coward; meanly; basely.
çow′ărd·ous, *a.* cowardly. [Obs.]
çow′ărd·ship, *n.* cowardice. [Obs.]
çow′bāne, *n.* *Cicuta virosa,* the English water hemlock, or *Cicuta maculata,* an American plant resembling it, or any of several other plants of the carrot family. They have poisonous roots and clusters of small, white flowers.
çow′bell, *n.* a bell hung from a cow's neck to tinkle when she moves and thus indicate where she is.
çow′ber″ry, *n.;* *pl.* **çow′ber″ries,** 1. a shrub with white or pink flowers and dark-red berries, *Vaccinium Vitis-Idæa,* the red huckleberry.
2. a plant of the rose family, with purple flowers.
3. the fruit of either of these plants.
çow′bīnd, *n.* a vine with large, fleshy roots, clusters of greenish-white flowers, and red berries; white bryony.
çow′bīrd, *n.* an American blackbird frequenting the grounds around grazing cattle. *Molothrus ater* is the common species. Cowbirds lay their eggs in other bird's nests, and leave the care of their young to other birds, as does the European cuckoo.
çow′boy, *n.* 1. a boy cattle herder.
2. an employee of a ranchman having care of the ranging cattle, usually herding them on horseback.
3. in the Revolutionary War, one of a plundering band that marauded near New York City.
çow′catch″ẽr (kou′kach″ẽr), *n.* a strong, metal frame in front of a locomotive or streetcar, for removing obstructions, such as strayed cattle and the like, from the tracks; the pilot.
çow chẽr′vil, cow parsley.
çow çress, *Lepidium campestre,* the field cress.
çow′die, *n.* a tree, the kauri.
çow′ẽr, *v.i.;* cowered, *pt., pp.;* cowering, *ppr.* [ME. *couren;* Ice. *kura;* Sw. *kura,* to lie quiet, rest.]
1. to sink by bending the knees; to crouch; to bend down, as from cold or fear.
2. to shrink and tremble, as from someone's anger, threats, or blows; cringe.
çow′ẽr, *v.t.* to cherish with care. [Obs.]
çow′fish, *n.* one of various cetaceans and fishes; as, (a) the sea cow; (b) the California porpoise; (c) the grampus; (d) the tropical, horned *Ostracion quadricorne;* trunkfish.
çow′girl, *n.* a girl who helps to herd cattle, etc. on a ranch.
çow grȧss, *Trifolium medium,* a red clover.
çow′hāġe (-āj), *n.* [Hind. *kawānch, koānch,* cowhage.]
1. the hairs of the pods of a leguminous plant, *Mucuna pruriens,* which easily penetrate animal or human skin, causing intense itching.
2. a single pod; also, the entire plant bearing these hairs.
çow′hand, *n.* a cowboy: also written *cow hand.*
çow′heärt″ed, *a.* cowardly.
çow′hẽrb (-ẽrb), *n.* *Vaccaria vulgaris,* a soapwort.
çow′hẽrd, *n.* one whose work is tending cows at pasture.
çow′hīde, *n.* 1. the hide of a cow made, or to be made, into leather.
2. a heavy whip, often braided.
çow′hīde, *v.t.;* cowhided, *pt., pp.;* cowhiding, *ppr.* to beat or whip with a cowhide; flog.
çow′ish, *a.* cowardly. [Rare.]
çow kil′lẽr, a wasp of the southern United States that looks like a large ant: so called from the notion that its sting can kill cattle.
çowl, *n.* [ME. *cowle, cuvel;* AS. *cule;* OFr. *coule;* Pr. *cogula,* from L. *cucullus,* a cap, hood.]
1. a hood, especially one worn by a monk; by extension, the hood and cloak of a monk.
2. a vanelike, hood-shaped ventilator, placed over the top of a chimney or shaft to increase the draft.
3. the spark arrester of a locomotive or other steam engine.

MONK'S COWL

4. at the front of an automobile, the part behind the hood to which the windshield and dashboard are fastened.
5. a cowling.
çowl, *n.* a large two-handled water vessel carried on a pole. [Archaic.]
çowle, *n.* [Anglo-Ind.] a grant, particularly one giving protection.
çowled, *a.* wearing a cowl; hooded; also, shaped like a cowl; as, a *cowled* leaf.
çow′lick, *n.* a reversed tuft of hair on the human head that cannot easily be made to lie flat: so called from the notion that it looks as if it had been licked by a cow.
çowl′ing, *n.* a detachable metal covering for an airplane engine.

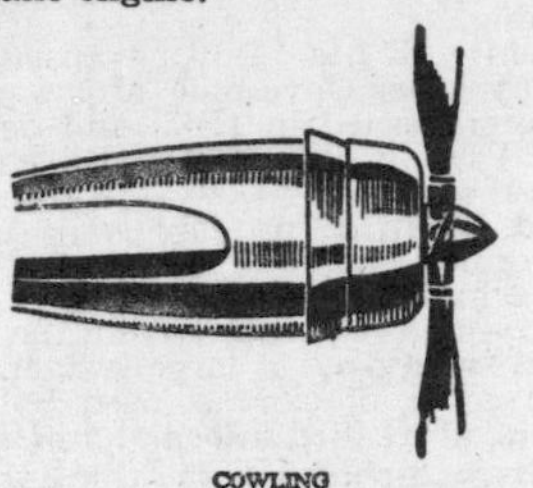

COWLING

çowl′stȧff, *n.* [OFr. *cuvel,* dim. of *cuve,* a tub, from L. *cupa,* a tub, vat, and *staff,* from AS. *stæf,* stick, staff.] a staff or pole run through the handles of a large tub, as a cowl, and supported between two persons. [Archaic.]
çow′măn, *n.;* *pl.* **çow′men,** a man who owns or operates a cattle ranch.
çō-wŏrk′ẽr, *n.* one who works with another or others; a fellow worker; a co-operator.
çow pärs′ley, a plant with many lobed leaves and large, flattened clusters of white or purple flowers: also called *cow chervil.*
çow pärs′nip, any weed of the genus *Heracleum* having some of the characteristics of the parsnip and flattened clusters of white or purple flowers.
çow′pēa, *n.* *Vigna sinensis,* cultivated in the southern United States, Asia, and Africa; also, its edible seed.
Çow′pẽr's (koo′) **glandş,** [after William *Cowper* (1666–1709), Eng. anatomist.] a pair of small glands with ducts opening into the urethra, found in various male mammals: during sexual excitement they secrete a mucous substance.
çow pī′lŏt, *Pomacentrus saxatilis,* a fish frequenting the coasts of Florida and the West Indies, having bands of bright green and black around its body.
çow poi′ṣŏn, *Delphinium trollifolium,* a larkspur of California.
çow pō′ny, a pony used in herding cattle.
çow′pox, *n.* a contagious disease of cows, characterized by vesicles containing the virus used in vaccinating people and thus making them temporarily immune to smallpox; vaccinia: called also *cowpock, kinepox.*
çow′punch″ẽr, *a.* [so named from prodding animals in herding.] a cowboy. [Colloq.]
çow′quākes (-kwāks), *n.* *Briza media,* quaking grass.
çow′rie, *n.* a tree, kauri.
çow′ry, çow′rie, *n.;* *pl.* **çow′rieş,** [Hind. *kaurī,* a cowry.] a small gastropodous shell, the *Cypræa moneta,* used for coin on the coast of Guinea in Africa, and in many parts of southern Asia; also, any shell of the genus *Cypræa.*
çow shärk, a large shark of European and West Indian waters.
çow′shed, *n.* a shelter for cows.
çow′slip, *n.* 1. in the United States, *Caltha palustris,* the marsh marigold, a swamp plant with yellow flowers.
2. the English primrose, *Primula veris,* a wildflower found in pastures and hedgebanks of England. It has umbels of small, buff-yellow, scented flowers on short pedicels.
çow′slipped (-slipt), *a.* bearing or covered with cowslips.
çow tree, any of various trees having an abundance of milky juice; especially, *Brosimum galactodendron,* a South American tree common in Venezuela.

TWIG AND FRUIT OF COW TREE (*Brosimum galactodendron*)

çow′weed, *n.* a plant, cow parsley.
çow′whēat, *n.* any of the plants of the genus *Melampyrum.*
çox, *n.* a coxswain. [Colloq.]
çox, *v.t.* and *v.i.* to act as coxswain to (a boat). [Colloq.]
çox′ȧ, *n.;* *pl.* **çox′ae,** [L.]
1. in anatomy, the hip or hip joint; also, the coccyx.
2. in entomology, the first joint of the leg of an insect or other arthropod, next to the body.
çox′ăl, *a.* of or relating to the coxa or coxae.
çox·al′ġi·ȧ, *n.* [L., from *coxa,* hip, and Gr. *algos,* pain.] a pain in, or disease of, the hip or hip joint.
çox′al·ġy, *n.* coxalgia.
çox′cōmb (-kōm), *n.* [corruption of *cockscomb,* cock's comb.]
1. the top of the head; by extension, the head. [Rare.]
2. a strip of red cloth notched like the comb of a cock, which jesters formerly wore in their caps; also, the cap itself.
3. a fop; a vain, showy fellow; a superficial pretender to knowledge or accomplishments.
4. a flower, the cockscomb.
çox·çomb′iç·ăl (-kom′ik-), *a.* resembling or of a coxcomb; foppish.
çox·çomb′iç·ăl·ly, *adv.* after the manner of a coxcomb; conceitedly.
çox′çōmb·ly, *a.* like a coxcomb. [Obs.]
çox′çōmb·ry, *n.* the manners of a coxcomb; silly conceit or vanity.
çox·çom′iç·ăl, *a.* foppish. [Rare.]
çox·çom′iç·ăl·ly, *adv.* foppishly. [Rare.]
çox·oc′ẽr·īte, *n.* [L. *coxa,* the hip, and Gr. *keras,* a horn.] the first or basal joint of an antenna of a crustacean.
çox·op′ō·dīte, *n.* [L. *coxa,* the hip, and Gr. *pous, podos,* a foot.] the first leg joint of a crustacean.
çox′swain (kok′sn *or* kok′swān), *n.* [*cock* (cockboat) and *swain.*] the person who steers a boat or racing shell: also spelled *cockswain.*
çoy, *a.* [ME. *coy;* OFr. *coi, quoi,* quiet, still, secret; Sp. *quieto,* from L. *quietus,* quiet, calm, still.]
1. (a) disdainful; (b) quiet; still. [Obs.]
2. avoiding familiarity; modest; bashful; shy: applied mostly to women.

The *coy* maid, half willing to be pressed.
—Goldsmith.

3. pretending shyness to attract; coquettish.
Syn.—shrinking, shy, distant, reserved, modest, bashful, backward.

çoy, *v.t.*; coyed, *pt., pp.*; coying, *ppr.* 1. to decoy; to allure. [Obs.]
 2. to pet; to stroke. [Obs.]
 Pleasure, being *coyed*, follows us.—**Hall.**
 3. to quiet; to soothe. [Obs.]

çoy, *v.i.* to act coyly. [Archaic.]

çoy′ish, *a.* somewhat coy or reserved.

çoy′ly, *adv.* in a coy manner.

çoy′ness, *n.* the quality or state of being coy.
 When the kind nymph would *coyness* feign,
 And hides but to be found again.
 —Dryden.

 Syn.—reserve, shyness, backwardness, modesty, bashfulness.

çoy′ō·te (kī′ōt *or* kī-ō′tē), *n.* [Sp. Am., from Mex. *coyotl.*] the prairie wolf, *Canis latrans*, a carnivorous animal related to the wolf, found in the western part of North America.

COYOTE (4 ft. long)

çō·yō·til′lō (-tēl′yō), *n.* [Am. Sp. dim. from Nahuatl *coyotl*, coyote.] a thorny, poisonous plant found in Mexico and the southwestern United States.

çoy′pu̇, çoy′pöu, *n.* same as *nutria.*

çoys′trel, çoys′tril, *n.* same as *coistrel.*

çŏz, *n.* cousin. [Colloq.]

çōze, *v.i.*; cozed, *pt.*; *pp.*; cozing, *ppr.* [prob. from Fr. *causer*, to chat, from LL. *causare*, to complain; L. *causari*, to plead, debate, from *causa*.] to have a friendly talk; chat.

çōze, *n.* a friendly talk.

çŏz′en, *v.t.*; cozened, *pt., pp.*; cozening, *ppr.* [OFr. *cousiner*, to claim kindred for advantage, to sponge.] to cheat; to defraud; to deceive; to beguile.

çŏz′en, *v.i.* to be a deceiver.

çŏz′en·āġe, *n.* cheating; fraud; deceit.

çŏz′en·ẽr, *n.* one who cheats or defrauds.

çō′zey, *a.* cozy.

çō′zieṙ (-zhẽr), *n.* same as *cosier.*

çō′zi·ly, *adv.* snugly; comfortably.

çō′zi·ness, *n.* a cozy condition.

çō′zy, *a.*; *comp.* cozier; *superl.* coziest, [Scot. *cosie*, *cozie*; Gael. *cosach*, abounding in hollows, snug, sheltered; from *cos*, a hollow.] snug, implying warmth and comfort; sociable; as, a *cozy* room: also written *cosy*.
 to cozy up to; to try to ingratiate oneself, or make friends, with. [Colloq.]
 to play it cozy; to act cautiously so as to avoid risk. [Slang.]

çō′zy, *n.*; *pl.* **çō′zieṣ,** a padded covering for a teapot to keep the contents hot.

çrab, *n.* [ME. *crabbe*; AS. *crabba*, a crab; D. *krab*; Sw. *krabba*; Dan. *krabbe*; perhaps from O.H.G. *chrapfo*, a hook, claw.]
 1. any of the short-tailed crustaceans constituting the suborder *Brachyura*, order *Decapoda*, comprising many genera, distinguished from the lobster and other macrurous decapods by the shortness of the tail, which is folded under the thorax. The front pair of feet are modified into pincers. The common large edible crab belongs to the genus *Cancer*; the small edible crab to the genus *Carcinus*; the long-armed crab to the genus *Corystes*; the hermit crab to the genus *Pagurus*, and the land crab to the genus *Gecarcinus*.
 2. [C–] Cancer, the constellation and fourth sign of the Zodiac.
 3. the crab louse.
 4. [*pl.*] the lowest throw of a pair of dice, two aces.
 5. in mechanics, (a) an engine with claws for launching ships and moving them in the dock; (b) a pillar used sometimes for the same purpose as a capstan; (c) a kind of windlass or machine for raising weights, etc.; (d) a yarn stretcher used in rope manufacturing.
 6. any of several animals similar to the crab.
 7. in aviation, the apparent sidewise motion of an airplane with respect to the ground when headed into a cross wind.
 to catch a crab; in rowing, to miss a stroke by missing the water, or to fail to clear the water on the recovery stroke.

çrab, *v.i.*; crabbed, *pt., pp.*; crabbing, *ppr.* 1. to fish for or catch crabs.
 2. to recede from a position; to back out: usually with *out*; as, to *crab out* of an agreement. [Colloq. U.S.]
 3. in nautical usage, to drift sidewise.
 4. to fight by seizing, scratching, clawing, etc., as hawks.

crab, *v.t.* in aviation, to head (an airplane) into a cross wind in order to counteract drift, thus causing apparent sidewise motion with respect to the ground.

çrab, *n.* [ME. *crabbe*; Sw. in composition, *krabb-äple*, a crab apple; prob. from *krabba*, a crab: so called because of its sharp taste.]
 1. a person who has a sour temper or is always complaining.
 2. a crab apple.
 3. a stick from a crab tree; a crabstick.

çrab, *v.t.* 1. to beat. [Obs.]
 2. to make crabbed.
 3. to complain about or find fault with (a person or thing).
 to crab one's act (*the deal*, etc.); to ruin or frustrate one's scheme (the deal, etc.). [Colloq.]

çrab, *v.i.* 1. to be crabbed or cross.
 2. to complain about or find fault with a person or thing.

çrab, *a.* 1. austere; sour; severe.
 2. of a crab apple or the tree that it grows on.

çrab ap′ple, 1. any of several varieties of small, very sour apple, growing wild or cultivated, used for making jellies and preserves.
 2. a tree bearing crab apples.

çrab′bed, *a.* 1. cross; morose; peevish.
 2. rough; harsh: applied to things. [Archaic.]
 3. hard to understand because intricate or complicated; difficult; perplexing; as, a *crabbed* author or subject.
 4. very intricate or irregular; hard to read because cramped; as, *crabbed* writing.

çrab′bed·ly, *adv.* in a crabbed manner.

çrab′bed·ness, *n.* the state or quality of being crabbed.

çrab′bẽr, *n.* 1. one who fishes for crabs.
 2. the boat used in fishing for crabs.
 3. [from *crab* (apple).] a person who constantly complains or finds fault. [Colloq.]

çrab′bing, *n.* crab fishing.

çrab′bing, *n.* a process by which cloth is given a finish that prevents its wrinkling.

çrab′bish, *a.* inclined to be cross or surly. [Obs.]

çrab′by, *a.* difficult; peevish; ill-tempered.

çrab′ēat″ẽr, *n.* 1. a fish, the cobia.
 2. the least bittern; also, certain other herons.

çrab′ẽr, *n.* the water rat.

çrab′fāced (-fāst), *a.* of a surly countenance.

çrab grass, a coarse grass that spreads quickly because of its freely rooting stems, especially (a) *Panicum sanguinale*, common finger grass; (b) *Eleusine indica*, wire grass.

çrab louse, *Phthirius pubis*, a body louse sometimes found in the pubic hair of the body: it somewhat resembles a crab in shape.

çrab plŏv′ẽr, *Dromas ardeola*, an East Indian bird resembling the plover.

çrab′sī″dle, *v.i.* to have a sidewise movement. [Humorous.]

çrab spī′dẽr, 1. a spider of the division *Laterigradæ*, moving laterally.
 2. a scorpion.

çrab′stick, *n.* 1. a walking stick made of the wood of the crab tree; hence, a stick of any kind.
 2. a crabbed, ill-tempered person.

çrab tree, a tree bearing crab apples.

çrab wood, the wood of *Carapa guianensis*, a South American tree.

çrab′-yawṣ, *n.* a West Indian disease, characterized by ulcers on the soles of the feet, with hard callous edges.

çracche (krach), *v.t.* and *v.i.* to scratch. [Obs.]

çrack, *v.t.*; cracked (krakt), *pt., pp.*; cracking, *ppr.* [ME. *crakken*, *craken*; AS. *cracian*, to crack; Gael. *crac*, a crack, break: an imitative word.]
 1. to break, or cause a narrow split in, by a sharp, sudden blow, or by pressure, heat, etc.; to break without an entire severance of the parts; as, to *crack* glass.
 2. to break in pieces.
 3. to break with grief; to affect deeply.
 O madam, my old heart is *cracked*.—Shak.
 4. to open and drink; as, to *crack* a bottle of wine.
 5. to utter with smartness; as, to *crack* a joke. [Slang.]
 6. to snap; to cause to make a sharp sudden noise; as, to *crack* a whip.
 7. to break, damage, or destroy.
 8. to disorder; to make mentally unbalanced.
 9. to cause (the voice) to crack.
 10. to subject (petroleum) to the process of cracking.
 11. to hit with a sudden, sharp noise; strike with the fist, open hand, etc. [Colloq.]
 12. to find the solution of; as, the police have finally *cracked* that murder case. [Colloq.]
 13. to break open or into; as, the thief *cracked* the safe. [Slang.]
 to crack a book; to open and study or read a book, especially a textbook. [Slang.]
 to crack a crib; to commit burglary. [Slang.]
 to crack a smile; to smile. [Slang.]

çrack, *v.i.* 1. to break with a sharp, sudden sound.
 2. to burst; to open in chinks; to be fractured, usually without quite separating into different parts.
 3. to fall to ruin, or to be impaired. [Colloq.]
 Credit . . . *cracks* when little comes in and
 much goes out. —Dryden.
 4. to utter a loud or sharp sudden sound; as, the whip *cracked*.
 5. to boast; to brag; to utter vain, pompous, blustering words. [Dial.]
 The Ethiops of their sweet complexion
 crack. —Shak.
 6. to chat. [Scot.]
 7. to become harsh or rasping, as the voice when hoarse.
 8. to change suddenly from one register to another, as the voice of a boy in adolescence.
 9. to move with speed: now chiefly in the phrase *get cracking*. [Colloq.]
 10. to break down; as, will he *crack* under the strain? [Slang.]
 11. to joke, gibe, or make sharp remarks. [Slang.]
 to crack down (*on*); to become strict or stricter (with). [Colloq.]
 to crack up; (a) to crash, as in an airplane; (b) to break down physically or mentally. [Colloq.]; (c) to break into a fit of laughter or tears. [Colloq.]
 to crack wise; to wisecrack. [Slang.]

çrack, *n.* 1. a chink or fissure; a narrow breach; a crevice; a separation; a slight opening; as, a *crack* between boards.
 2. a break, usually without complete separation of parts; partial fracture; flaw.
 3. a burst of sound; a sudden, sharp noise; a violent report; as, a loud *crack* of thunder; the *crack* of a whip.
 4. the cracking of the voice when changed at puberty or in hoarseness.
 5. lunacy; insanity.
 6. an insane person. [Obs.]
 7. a boast; also, a boaster. [Archaic.]
 8. a fault, flaw, or blemish; a breach.
 9. a prostitute. [Obs.]
 10. a pert, lively boy. [Obs.]
 When he was a *crack* not this high.
 —Shak.
 11. an instant; as, I'll be with you in a *crack*. [Colloq.]
 12. free familiar conversation; chat. [Scot.]
 13. a sharp, resonant blow. [Colloq.]
 14. a burglar or burglary. [Thieves' slang.]
 15. an attempt; try. [Slang.]
 16. a joke, gibe, or sharp remark. [Slang.]

çrack, *a.* excellent; first-rate; having qualities to be proud of. [Colloq.]

çrack′á·jack, *a.* and *n.* crackerjack. [Slang.]

çrack′brāin, *n.* a crackbrained person.

çrack′brāined, *a.* foolhardy; crazy; so senseless or unreasonable as to seem insane.

çrack′down, *n.* a resorting to strict or stricter measures of discipline or punishment.

çracked (krakt), *a.* 1. split; rent; broken or fractured without complete separation into parts; partially severed; having a crack or cracks; hence, blemished in reputation.
 2. mentally impaired; crazy. [Colloq.]
 3. harsh or strident: said of a voice.
 cracked up to be; alleged or believed to be. [Colloq.]

çrack′ẽr, *n.* 1. one who or that which cracks; specifically, (a) a firecracker; (b) a grinding machine for raw rubber; (c) a person who breaks flints; (d) [Obs.] a braggart; (e) a little paper roll containing candy, etc., which explodes when the ends are pulled; cracker bonbon: used as a favor at parties.
 2. a hard-baked biscuit; thin, crisp wafer of unleavened dough.
 3. an impoverished white person in the rural sections of the southern United States, especially in Georgia and Florida: contemptuous term.

çrack′ẽr-bar·rel, *a.* [from the large barrel of soda crackers formerly found in general stores.] designating, like, or characteristic of the informal discussions on all subjects by persons gathered at a country store; as, a *cracker-barrel* philosopher. [Colloq.]

çrack′ẽr·jack, *a.* [late 19th-c. slang; extension of *crack, a.*, and *Jack* (nickname).] excellent; first-rate, as in skill or ability. [Slang.]

çrack′ẽr·jack, *n.* 1. anything excellent. [Slang.]

2. a person of recognized excellence or skill. [Slang.]

çrack′ing, *n.* [from *crack, v.*] the process of breaking down hydrocarbons by heat and pressure into lighter hydrocarbons of lower molecular weight: by this method the complex hydrocarbons of the heavier fractions of petroleum can be broken down into the simpler hydrocarbons of gasoline.

çraç′kle (krak′l), *v.i.*; crackled, *pt., pp.*; crackling, *ppr.* [ME. *crackelen*, to crackle, quaver in singing; dim. of *crack.*] to make small, abrupt noises, rapidly or frequently repeated; to decrepitate; as, burning thorns *crackle.*

çraç′kle, *v.t.* to crush or break with the sounds of crackling.

çraç′kle, *n.* 1. a crackling; a succession of slight, sharp, sudden sounds.

2. a minute crack.

3. the network of intersecting cracks which cover the glaze of various ceramic wares, glassware, etc.

4. ware having such a surface; crackleware.

5. in medicine, abnormal breathing marked by a crackling sound.

çraç′kled (-kld), *a.* marked by numerous intersecting cracks, as some china.

çraç′kle·wâre, *n.* pottery or porcelain with a finely crackled surface.

çraç′kling, *a.* making slight cracks or abrupt noises.

çraç′kling, *n.* 1. the making of small, abrupt cracks or reports, frequently repeated.

2. the browned, crisp rind of roasted pork.

3. [*pl.*] lard or tallow scraps made into food for dogs.

4. [*pl.*] the crisp part remaining after the lard has been removed from hog fat by frying.

çrack′ly, *a.* crackling or inclined to crackle.

çrack′nel, *n.* [ME. *crakenelle*; D. *krakeling*, a cake, crackling, from *kraken*, to crack.]

1. a hard, brittle biscuit.

2. [*pl.*] pork, in small pieces, fried till crisp.

3. [*pl.*] cracklings.

çrack of doom, [phrase in *Macbeth*, IV, i.] the signal for the beginning of the Day of Judgment.

çrack′pot, *n.* a person so senseless or unreasonable as to seem insane; crazy person. [Colloq.]

çrack′pot, *a.* characteristic of a lunatic; foolish and impractical; as, a *crackpot* scheme. [Colloq.]

çracks′măn, *n.*; *pl.* **çracks′men,** a burglar. [Slang.]

çrack′-up, *n.* a cracking up; specifically, (a) a crash, as of an airplane; (b) a mental or physical breakdown.

çrack′y, *interj.* an exclamation used, usually in the phrase *by cracky*, to lend emphasis to a remark.

çrā′çoweș, *n.pl.*, long-toed boots or shoes introduced into England in 1384: named from the city of Cracow, where the fashion is supposed to have originated. [Obs.]

CRACOWES

-çrȧ·cy, [Fr. or ML.; Fr. *-cratie*; ML. *-cratia*; Gr. *-kratia*, rule, from *kratos*, rule, power.] a terminal combining form meaning *a* (specified) *type of government, rule by*, as in auto*cracy*, theo*cracy*.

çrā′dle, *n.* [ME. *cradel*; AS. *cradel*, *cradol*; Gael. *creathall*, a cradle, grade.]

1. a crib for an infant, usually free to rock or swing.

2. infancy; also, the place of a thing's beginning or early development; as, Boston was the *cradle* of the Revolution.

MINER'S CRADLE

3. a place of rest; as, rocked in the *cradle* of the deep. [Poet.]

4. a framework of bars, cords, rods, etc., for support or protection.

5. a flat, wheeled frame for a mechanic to lie on when working under an automobile.

6. a wooden or metal framework to support a boat, ship, aircraft, etc. while it is being built, repaired, or lifted.

7. the supporting part of a cradle telephone.

8. in agriculture, a frame of wood, with long, bending teeth, to which is fastened a scythe, for cutting and laying grain evenly in a swath; also, the frame itself.

9. in surgery, (a) a supporting case for a broken or dislocated limb; (b) a frame protecting an injured part of the body from contact with the bedclothes.

10. in mezzotint engraving, a grooved instrument which, when rocked back and forth, makes a zigzag series of raised burs upon a printing plate.

11. in mining, (a) a suspended scaffold; (b) a rocking box for washing out earth holding gold.

12. in carpentry, the ribbing for vaulted ceilings to be covered with plaster.

13. in life-saving apparatus, the basketlike structure running on a line from ship to shore.

14. in hat making, a circular support having inwardly jutting pegs, supporting hats to be dipped in the dye.

15. a standing bedstead for wounded seamen to sleep in, instead of a hammock. [Obs.]

16. a child's game, cat's cradle.

çrā′dle, *v.t.*; cradled, *pt., pp.*; cradling, *ppr.* 1. to lay, rock, or hold in or as in a cradle; to compose or quiet.

It *cradles* their fears to sleep.
—D. A. Clark.

2. to nurse or take care of in infancy.

3. to use a cradle for, in various ways; as, to *cradle* grain; to *cradle* pay dirt; to *cradle* a boat or a limb.

çrā′dle, *v.i.* 1. to lie or lodge in or as in a cradle.

2. to cut grain with a cradle scythe.

to rob the cradle; to take as one's wife, husband, sweetheart, etc. a person much younger than oneself.

çrā′dle-hōle, *n.* a rut in a vehicle track, as in snow or softening frozen ground. [U. S.]

Çrā′dle of Lib′ẽr·ty, Faneuil Hall, Boston, the place where the Revolutionary leaders often met and spoke.

çrā′dle sçythe (sīth), a broad-bladed scythe with a frame fastened to it for laying the cut grain evenly.

çrā′dle·sọng, *n.* a lullaby.

çrā′dle tel′e·phōne, a telephone in which the mouthpiece and receiver form a unit, which lies on the connecting switch between U-shaped supports when the telephone is not in use.

çrā′dling, *n.* 1. the act of using a cradle.

2. in carpentry, same as *cradle* (sense 12).

CRADLE SCYTHE

çrȧft, *n.* [AS. *cræft*, art, cunning, power, a craft, bark.]

1. power; also, any artifice or device. [Obs.]

2. cunning, art, or skill, as applied to a bad purpose; artifice; guile; skill or dexterity employed in deceiving.

3. some special art or skill; dexterity in a particular manual occupation; hence, the occupation or employment itself; manual art; trade.

Ye know that by this *craft* we have our wealth. —Acts xix. 25.

4. the members of a skilled trade, collectively.

5. a boat, ship, or aircraft; as, she is a tidy *craft*; also used in a collective sense for vessels or aircraft of any kind.

small craft; small vessels of all kinds, as sloops, cutters, etc.

çrȧft, *v.i.* to play tricks. [Obs.]

-çrȧft, [from *craft.*] a terminal combining form meaning *the work, skill*, or *practice of*, as in handi*craft*, witch*craft*.

çrȧft′i·ly, *adv.* with craft; cunningly.

çrȧft′i·ness, *n.* artfulness; cunning; artifice; stratagem.

çrȧft′less, *a.* without craft.

çrȧfts′măn, *n.*; *pl.* **çrȧfts′men,** 1. an artisan; an artificer; a mechanic; one skilled in a manual occupation or trade.

2. an artist: sometimes said of one skilled in the mechanics of his art, but lacking higher excellence.

çrȧfts′măn·ship, *n.* mastery of a craft; the skill, art, or work of a craftsman.

çrȧfts′mȧs″tẽr, *n.* one skilled in his craft or trade. [Archaic.]

çrȧft ūn′iŏn (-yun), a labor union to which only workers in a certain trade, craft, or occupation can belong: distinguished from *industrial* (or *vertical*) *union*: also called *horizontal union.*

çrȧft′y, *a.* 1. dexterous; handy. [Obs.]

2. versed in deceit; skillful at fraud; artful; sly; cunning; fraudulent.

Syn.—skillful, wily, sly, astute, insidious, politic, deceitful, subtle, shrewd, cunning.

çrag, *n.* [ME. *crag*; W. *craig*; Gael. *creag*, a rock, crag.]

1. a steep, rugged rock that rises above others or projects from a rock mass; a rough, broken rock, or point of a rock.

2. in geology, shelly deposits in Norfolk and Suffolk, England, usually of gravel and sand, of the older Pliocene period.

crag and tail; a form of secondary hills, common in Britain, in which a steep front faces to the west or northwest, while the opposite side is formed of a sloping declivity.

çrag, *n.* [M.D. *krage*, neck, throat; M.L.G. *krage*, neck, throat.] the neck, throat, or craw. [Scot. and Brit. Dial.]

çrag′ged, *a.* full of crags or broken rocks; rough; rugged; steep.

çrag′ged·ness, *n.* cragginess.

çrag′gi·ness, *n.* the state of being craggy.

çrag′gy, *a.* cragged.

çragș′măn, *n.*; *pl.* **çragș′men,** one who scales crags; specifically, one who gathers eggs on cliffs adjoining the sea.

çrāie (krā), *n.* crare. [Obs.]

çrāig floun′dẽr, çrāig flu̇ke, [Scot. *craig*, a rock.] the pole flounder.

çrāil, *n.* a creel. [Obs.]

çrāi′șey, *n.* the buttercup. [Brit. Dial.]

çrāke, *v.i.* to crack; to boast. [Obs.]

çrāke, *n.* a boast. [Obs.]

çrāke, *v.i.*; craked, *pt., pp.*; craking, *ppr.* to utter a sound like that of a corncrake.

çrāke, *n.* [ME. *crake*; Ice. *kraka*, a crow; imitative, from the noise.]

1. a crow; also, the raven. [Brit. Dial.]

2. the corncrake, *Crex pratensis*, of the British Isles; also, any raillike short-billed bird of the same or an allied genus, as *Porzana carolina*, the sora.

çrāke′ber″ry, *n.*; *pl.* **çrāke′ber″rieș,** the crowberry, an evergreen shrub.

çrāke′-nee′dleș (-dlz), *n.* crow needles, a plant.

çrāk′ẽr, *n.* a boaster. [Obs.]

çram, *v.t.*; crammed, *pt., pp.*; cramming, *ppr.* [ME. *crammen*; AS. *crammian*, to cram, from *crimman*, to press, bruise.]

1. to fill (a space, etc.) beyond normal capacity by pressing or squeezing; to stuff; to crowd; to fill to superfluity; as, to *cram* papers into a drawer; to *cram* a room with people.

2. to fill with food to satiety; to stuff.

3. to prepare (a person) or review (a subject) for examination, usually in a hurried way or comparatively short time, by stuffing the mind with information. [Colloq.]

4. to tell lies to; to fill up with false stories. [Slang.]

çram, *v.i.* 1. to stuff oneself with food; to eat too much or too quickly.

2. to stuff the mind full of a subject, as in preparation for an examination, usually in a hurried or intensive way. [Colloq.]

çram, *n.* 1. a crammed condition; a crush. [Colloq.]

2. (a) the act of cramming information; (b) the information so obtained. [Colloq.]

3. a lie. [Slang.]

çram′bō, *n.* 1. a game in which one person gives a word, to which another finds a rhyme.

2. a rhyme or rhyming: contemptuous term for inferior poetry.

dumb crambo; a game in which the rhyming word is acted out in pantomime by the guesser.

çram'mẽr, *n.* 1. one who or that which crams.
2. a lie. [Slang.]

çram'oi·ṣy, çram'oi·ṣie, *a.* crimson. [Archaic.]

çram'oi·ṣy, çram'oi·ṣie, *n.* crimson cloth. [Archaic.]

çramp, *n.* [OFr. *crampe*; D. *krampe*; Dan. *krampe*; Ice. *krappr*, strait, narrow.]
1. a metal bar with both ends bent, for holding together blocks of stone, timbers, etc.
2. a clamp.
3. anything that confines or hampers.
4. a cramped condition or part.
5. a piece of wood shaped like the upper part of the instep, over which leather is formed in making the upper part of a boot or shoe.

çramp, *a.* 1. confined; restricted; narrowed.
2. hard to read or understand; crabbed, as some handwriting.

çramp, *v.t.*; cramped (krampt), *pt.*, *pp.*; cramping, *ppr.* 1. to confine; to restrain; to hinder from action or expansion; as, to *cramp* the exertions.
2. to fasten, confine, or hold with or as with a cramp.
3. to form (the upper part of a boot or shoe) by the use of a cramp.
4. to turn (the front wheels of a vehicle) so as to be at an angle with the rear wheels.
to cramp one's style; to hamper one's usual skill, confidence, etc. in doing something. [Slang.]

çramp, *n.* [ME. *crampe, craumpe*; OFr. *crampe*; D. *krampe*; Sw. *kramp*, a cramp, spasm.]
1. a sudden, painful, involuntary contraction of a muscle or muscles from chill, strain, etc.
2. paralysis of a muscle or set of muscles by reason of excessive use; as, writers' *cramp*.
3. [*usually in pl.*] intestinal griping and pain.

çramp, *v.t.* 1. to affect with cramp; as, to be *cramped* with rheumatism.
2. to cause to be affected with a cramp.

çramp bōne, a sheep's kneepan: formerly thought a charm against cramps.

çram'pet, *n.* see *crampit.*

çramp'fish, *n.*; *pl.* **çramp'fish** *or* **çramp'-fish·eṣ,** a kind of fish that can produce an electric current: also called *electric ray, torpedo fish.*

çramp ī'ron (-ũrn), a piece of metal, usually iron, bent at each end, for holding stones, etc. securely together, as in a building.

çram'pit, *n.* 1. a piece of metal at the end of the scabbard of a sword.
2. (a) a cramp iron; (b) a calk to prevent slipping on ice. [Scot.]

çram'pŏn, çram·pọọn', *n.* [Fr. *crampon*, a cramp iron.]
1. either of a pair of iron hooks for raising heavy weights; grappling iron.
2. [*usually in pl.*] a spiked iron plate used on shoes to prevent slipping; climbing iron.
3. in botany, an aerial root which serves as a fulcrum or support, as in the ivy.

çram·pŏn·nee', *a.* [Fr. *cramponné*, pp. of *cramponner*, to fasten with a clamp; *crampon*, a cramp iron.] in heraldry, denoting a cross having a cramp, or square hook, at each end.

çramp'y, *a.* having or producing cramps.

çran, çrāne, *n.* [Scot.] a British measure of fresh herring, equal to 45 gallons.

çrān'āġe, *n.* the use of a crane at a wharf for raising wares from a vessel; also, the price paid for the use of a crane.

çran'ber"ry, *n.*; *pl.* **çran'ber"rieṣ,** [for D. *kranebere*, G. *kranbeere*, lit., crane berry; name used by early D. and G. settlers in U. S., replacing earlier Brit. *fen berry*, etc.]
1. a firm, sour, edible, red berry, the fruit of certain species of the genus *Vaccinium*, that grow in bogs or marshes. *Vaccinium macrocarpon* is the American species, being larger than *Vaccinium oxycoccus*, the mossberry of Europe.
2. the trailing, evergreen shrub producing this fruit.

çran'ber"ry tree, a shrub or small tree of the honeysuckle family, bearing clusters of white flowers followed by red fruit resembling the cranberry: also called *bush cranberry.*

çran'dȧll, *n.* [from proper name *Crandall.*] a tool with which to dress stone, resembling a hammer in form, the head of which is made up of a number of sharp steel bars.

çran'dȧll, *v.t.* to dress, as stone, with a crandall.

çrāne, *n.*; *pl.* **çrāneṣ** *or* **çrāne,** [ME. *crane*; AS. *cran*; akin to D. *kraan*, a crane.]
1. a migratory grallatorial or wading bird of the genus *Grus*, family *Gruidæ*, with very long legs and neck and a long, straight bill. The European crane is *Grus cinerea*; the Siberian crane, *Grus gigantea*; the sandhill crane of America is *Grus canadensis*. The crowned crane is classed by some in a separate genus (*Balearica*).
2. popularly, any of certain herons, as *Ardea herodias*, and storks.

CRANE (4 ft. tall)

3. any of various machines for lifting or moving heavy weights by means of a movable projecting arm or a horizontal beam that travels over a factory yard, etc.
4. any device with a swinging arm fixed on a vertical axis; as, a fireplace *crane* is used for holding a kettle.
5. in nautical usage, a bracket on a ship's side, for supporting spars, etc.
6. a siphon or crooked pipe for drawing liquor out of a cask.

çrāne, *v.t.* and *v.i.*; craned, *pt.*, *pp.*; craning, *ppr.* 1. to raise or move by or as by a crane.
2. to stretch (the neck) as a crane does, as in straining to see something beyond an obstacle or in the distance.

çrāne flȳ, any of various two-winged, slender flies of the genus *Tipula.*

çrāne'ṣ'-bill, çrāneṣ'bill, *n.* 1. the geranium, especially the wild geranium.
2. a pair of pincers used by surgeons.

çrang, *n.* same as *krang.*

Çrā'ni·ȧ, *n.* [LL. *cranium*, a skull.] a genus of mollusks typical of the family *Craniidæ.*

çrā'ni·ȧ, *n.* alternative plural of *cranium.*

çrā"ni·ȧ·çrō'mi·ăl, *a.* [*cranium*, and Gr. *akrōmion*; *akros*, extreme, and *ōmos*, shoulder.] in anatomy, of or denoting the cranium and shoulder.

çrā'ni·ăl, *a.* [L. *cranialis*, from *cranium*, a skull.] of or denoting the cranium or skull.

çrā'ni·ăl in'dex, in craniometry, the ratio of the greatest breadth of the skull to its greatest length from front to back, multiplied by 100.

çrā'ni·ăl nẽrve, a peripheral nerve connected directly with the brain: there are twelve pairs of such nerves in man, including the olfactory, optic, trigeminal, facial, and auditory nerves.

Çrā·ni·ā'tȧ, *n.pl.* same as *Craniota.*

çrā'ni·āte, *a.* having a skull or cranium, as fishes, reptiles, birds, and mammals.

çrā'ni·āte, *n.* a craniate animal.

Çrā·nī'i·dae, *n.pl.* a family of brachiopods, characterized by the absence of a hinge and peduncle, the shells being attached by the lower valve.

çrā'ni·ō-, a combining form from L. *cranium*, Gr. *kranion*, a skull, meaning *of the head, cranial*, as in *cranio*clast, *cranio*facial.

çrā'ni·ō·çlaṣm, *n.* same as *craniotomy.*

çrā'ni·ō·çlȧst, *n.* [*cranio-*, and Gr. *klastos*, from *klān*, to break.] delivery forceps used in craniotomy.

çrā"ni·ō·fā'ciăl (-shăl), *a.* [*cranio-*, and L. *facies*, the face, appearance.] of or denoting the cranium and face; as, the *craniofacial* angle.

çrā'ni·ō·gràph, *n.* [*cranio-*, and Gr. *graphein*, to write.] an instrument with which to make topographical outlines of the skull.

çrā"ni·ō·loġ'iç·ăl, *a.* pertaining to craniology.

çrā·ni·ol'ō·ġist, *n.* a specialist in craniology.

çrā·ni·ol'ō·ġy, *n.* [*cranio-*, and Gr. *-logia*, from *legein*, to speak.] the scientific study of skulls, especially human skulls, and their characteristics, including differences in size, shape, etc.

çrā·ni·om'e·tẽr, *n.* [*cranio-*, and Gr. *metron*, a measure.] an instrument for measuring skulls.

çrā"ni·ō·met'riç, çrā"ni·ō·met'riç·al, *a.* pertaining to craniometry.

çrā·ni·om'e·try, *n.* the science of measuring skulls; cranial measurement.

Çrā·ni·ō'tȧ, *n.pl.* [L., from *cranium*; Gr. *kranion*, a skull.] a class of vertebrates composed of animals having a cranium.

çrā·ni·ot'ō·my, *n.*; *pl.* **çrā·ni·ot'ō·mieṣ,** [*cranio-*, and Gr. *temnē*, from *temnein*, to cut.] the surgical operation of opening the skull.

çrā'ni·um, *n.*; *pl.* **çrā'ni·umṣ, çrā'ni·ȧ,** [L., from Gr. *kranion*, a skull.]
1. the skull.
2. the bones which form the enclosure of the brain, excluding the lower jaw.

çrañk, *a.* [AS. *cranc*, weak; D. *krank*; Ice. *krankr*, sick, weak.]
1. in nautical usage, liable to lurch or capsize.
2. shaky; unsteady.
3. ill; infirm; feeble. [Obs.]

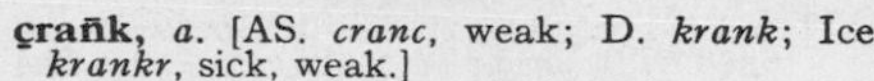
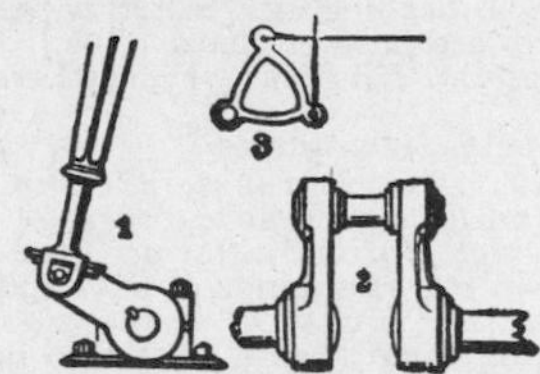

TYPES OF CRANK
1. single crank 2. double crank 3. bell crank

çrañk, *n.* [ME. *crank*, yarn reel; AS. *cranc* in *crancstæf*, yarn comb, but later influenced by L. G.; closely akin to *cringe, crinkle.*]
1. a part, as a handle, connected at right angles to a shaft of a machine in order to transmit motion.
2. any bend, turn, or winding.
3. a metal brace or bracket used for various purposes.
4. a former instrument of prison discipline, consisting of a small wheel which, when the prisoner turned a handle outside, revolved in a box partially filled with gravel.
5. a twisting or turning in speech; a whim; a caprice.

Quips, and *cranks*, and wanton wiles.
—Milton.

6. a queer action or idea.
7. a person given to queer actions, ideas, manners, etc.; an eccentric. [Colloq.]
8. an irritable, complaining person; cranky person. [Colloq.]

çrañk, *v.t.*; cranked, *pt.*, *pp.*; cranking, *ppr.*
1. to form into the shape of a crank.
2. to provide with a crank.
3. to start or operate by a crank.

çrañk, *v.i.* 1. to turn a crank, as in starting an engine or operating a device.
2. to run in a winding course; to bend, wind, and turn. [Obs.]

See how this river comes me *cranking* in.
—Shak.

çrañk'bĩrd, *n.* the spotted woodpecker of Europe, *Picus minor.*

çrañk'çāse, *n.* the metal casing that encloses the crankshaft of an internal-combustion engine.

çrañked (krañkt), *a.* having a bend; formed with a crank; as, a *cranked* shaft.

çrañk'i·ly, *adv.* in a cranky manner.

çrañk'i·ness, *n.* the quality or state of being cranky.

çrañ'kle (krañ'kl), *v.t.*; crankled, *pt.*, *pp.*; crankling, *ppr.* to break into bends, turns, or angles; to crinkle.

Old Vaga's stream . . .
Crankling her banks. —Philips.

çrañ'kle, *v.i.* to bend, wind, or twist; to move in a zigzag course.

çrañ'kle, *n.* a bend or turn; a crinkle.

çrañk'ness, *n.* 1. liability to be capsized, as a ship.
2. shakiness; unsteadiness.

çrañk'ous, *a.* cranky; irritable. [Scot.]

çrañk'pin, *n.* a cylindrical bar attaching a connecting rod to a crank: also written *crank pin.*

çrañk'shȧft, *n.* a shaft turning a crank or turned by a crank: in a gasoline engine the movement of the pistons is transmitted to the crankshaft by cranks.

çrañk'y, *a.*; *comp.* crankier; *superl.* crankiest,
1. out of order; out of gear; shaky, loose.
2. ill-tempered; irritable; cross.
3. queer; eccentric.
4. in nautical usage, liable to be upset, as a vessel; unsteady.
5. in feeble health; sickly. [Brit. Dial.]

çran'nied (-nid), *a.* having rents, chinks, or fissures; as, a *crannied* wall.

çran'nog, *n.* [Ir. *crannog*; Gael. *crannag*, a pulpit, top of a mast.] a lake dwelling built on an artificial island or shallows, such as remain as ruins from prehistoric times in Scotland and Ireland.

çran'nōġe, *n.* a crannog: erroneous form.

çran'ny, *n.*; *pl.* **çran'nieṣ,** [ME. *crany*; OFr. *cran*, from LL. *crena*, a notch.]
1. a rent; a small, narrow opening, fissure, crevice, or chink, as in a wall.

In a firm building, the cavities ought to be filled with brick or stone, fitted to the *crannies*. —Dryden.

2. in glassmaking, an iron instrument for forming the necks of bottles.

çran'ny, *v.i.*; crannied, *pt.*, *pp.*; crannying, *ppr.* 1. to become intersected with or penetrated by crannies or clefts. [Obs.]

The ground did *cranny* everywhere. —Golding.

2. to enter by crannies.

çran·tä'rȧ, *n.* [Gael. *cranntara*; *crann*, a beam, shaft, and *tair*, reproach, disgrace.] the fiery cross which formerly formed the rallying symbol in the Highlands of Scotland.

çrants, *n.* [Ice. *krants*; G. *kranz*, a garland.] a garland or wreath, as that carried before the bier of a maiden, and hung over her grave. [Obs.]

çrap, *n.* [ME. *crappe*, chaff; OFr. *crape*; LL. *crappa*, siftings.] buckwheat; also, darnel. [Brit. Dial.]

çrap, *n.* 1. craps.

2. any throw that causes the thrower to lose at craps.

to crap out; to lose at craps by throwing a two, three, or twelve on the first throw or a seven after the point has been established.

çrap'ạu·dine, *n.* [Fr. *crapaudine*, a socket, sole, step, a toadstone, from *crapaud*, a toad.] ulceration of the coronet of a horse.

çrāpe, *v.t.*; craped, *pt.*, *pp.*; craping, *ppr.* [Fr. *creper*, to crisp, curl, from L. *crispus*, crisped, curled.] to curl, to form into ringlets; as, to *crape* the hair.

çrāpe, *n.* [Fr. *crêpe*, *crespe*, crepe, a silk tissue curled into minute wrinkles, from *creper*; L. *crispare*, to crisp, curl; *crispus*, curled, crisped.]

1. a thin, crinkled cloth of silk, rayon, cotton, or wool; crepe.

2. a piece of black crepe as a sign of mourning, often in the form of a band worn around the arm.

çrāpe'fish, *n.* salted and pressed codfish.

çrāpe'hang·ẽr, *n.* a person with a gloomy outlook on things; a pessimist. [Slang.]

çrāpe myr'tle (mẽr'tl), a shrub, *Lagerstrœmia indica*, native to China and the East Indies, and cultivated in the United States. It bears large, rose-colored flowers.

çrap'nel, *n.* a hook or drag. [Obs.]

çrap'pie, *n.*; *pl.* **çrap'pieṣ** *or* **çrap'pie,** [origin unknown.] a small food fish, *Pomoxys annularis*: it is found in sluggish streams and ponds of the eastern and central United States: also called *croppie*.

çraps, *n.pl.* [Fr. *crabs*, *craps*, from Eng. *crabs*, lowest throw at hazard, two aces.] [*construed as sing.*] a gambling game played with two dice: a first throw of seven or eleven wins, and a first throw of two, three, or twelve loses; any other first throw, to win, must be repeated before a seven appears.

çrap'shọọt″ẽr, *n.* a person playing a game of craps, or one who habitually plays craps.

çrap'ū·lä, çrap'ūle, *n.* same as *crapulence*.

çrap'ū·lence, *n.* [LL. *crapulentus*, from L. *crapula*; Gr. *kraipalē*, a drunken sickness, intoxication.]

1. sickness caused by overindulgence in food or drink.

2. gross intemperance, especially in drinking; debauchery.

çrap'ū·lent, *a.* of, suffering from, or characterized by excess or gross intemperance in drinking or eating.

çrap'ū·lous, *a.* 1. characterized by intemperance, especially in drinking; debauched.

2. sick as a result of such intemperance.

çrāp'y, *a.* like crape; crimped.

çrāre, *n.* [OFr. *craier*; LL. *craiera*, a kind of ship used by the Scandinavians.] an unwieldy trading vessel: also spelled *crayer*. [Obs.]

çrash, *v.i.*; crashed (krasht), *pt.*, *pp.*; crashing, *ppr.* [ME. *craschen*, *crasshen*, to crash, break, shatter; prob. echoic.]

1. to fall, collide, or break with violence, accompanied by a loud, relatively prolonged noise; to smash; as, the shell *crashed* through the roof.

2. to make a sudden, loud noise, as of something brittle falling and breaking.

3. to move or go with such a noise.

4. to fall or land violently out of control so as to damage or destroy the craft: said of aircraft.

5. to collapse; to come to sudden ruin; fail; as, their business *crashed*.

6. (a) to sleep; (b) to get a place to sleep temporarily. [Slang.]

çrash, *v.t.* 1. to cause (a car, airplane, etc.) to crash.

2. to force or impel with a crashing noise (with *in*, *out*, *through*, etc.).

3. to get into (a party, theater, etc.) without an invitation, ticket, etc. [Colloq.]

çrash, *n.* 1. a loud, sudden noise, as of something brittle falling and breaking.

2. the collapse of a commercial undertaking; bankruptcy; by extension, commercial depression or panic.

3. a forced landing or a fall of an airplane, causing damage to the craft; also, a traffic accident.

çrash, *n.* [earlier *crasko*, *crasho*, "Russian linen," prob. a trade contraction of Russ. *krashenina*, colored linen.] a coarse cotton or linen cloth used for furniture covers, towels, etc.

çrash dīve, a sudden submergence of a submarine to escape from a threatened attack.

çrā'sis, *n.* [L., from Gr. *krasis*, a mingling, mixing, from *kerannynai*, to mix.]

1. formerly, the mixture of the constituents of a fluid, as of the blood. [Obs.]

2. in grammar, the contraction of two different letters into one long letter or into a diphthong; syneresis.

çras·ped'ō·drōme, *a.* [Gr. *kraspedon*, a border, and *dromos*, running.] in botany, denoting a system of nervation in which the nerves of a leaf run to and meet the margin.

Çras·pe·dō'tȧ, *n.pl.* [L., pl. of *craspedotus*, from Gr. *kraspedoun*, to surround with a border; *kraspedon*, a border.] a division of jellyfishes, the *Hydromedusæ*.

çras'pe·dōte, *a.* relating or pertaining to *Craspedota*.

çrass, *a.* [L. *crassus*, thick, dense.]

1. gross; thick; coarse. [Rare.]

2. grossly stupid, dull, or obtuse; as, *crass* ignorance.

3. tasteless, insensitive, materialistic, uncultured, etc.

çras'sȧ·ment, *n.* [L. *crassamentum*, thickness, thick sediment, from *crassus*, thick, dense.] crassamentum. [Obs.]

çras·sȧ·men'tum, *n.* [L. *thickness*, thick sediment, from *crassus*, thick, dense.] the thick, red part of the blood, as distinct from the serum or aqueous part; the clot.

çras'si·tūde, *n.* [L. *crassitudo*, from *crassus*, thick, dense.]

1. gross stupidity or ignorance.

2. grossness; coarseness; thickness.

çrass'ness, *n.* grossness.

Çras'sū·lȧ, *n.* [from L. *crassus*, thick, coarse.] a genus of plants of the natural order *Crassulaceæ*, consisting of herbs and shrubs found chiefly in South Africa.

Çras·sū·lā'cē·ae, *n.pl.* [L., from *crassula*, dim. of *crassus*, thick, dense.] the houseleek family, a natural order of juicy plants, with herbaceous or shrubby stems, and annual or perennial roots, growing in hot, dry, exposed places in the more temperate parts of the world, but chiefly in South Africa.

çras·sū·lā'ceous, *a.* of or pertaining to the *Crassulaceæ*.

çras·ti·nā'tion, *n.* [LL. *crastinatio*, from *crastinus*, of tomorrow; *cras*, tomorrow.] procrastination. [Obs.]

-çrat, [Fr. *-crate*; Gr. *-kratēs*, from *kratos*, rule, power.] a terminal combining form meaning *participant in* or *supporter of* (a specified kind of) *government* or *ruling body*, as in demo*crat*, aristo*crat*.

Çrȧ·tae'gus, *n.* [L., from Gr. *krataigos*, a flowering thorn.] an extensive genus of hardy, flowering trees and bushes, including the hawthorns.

çratch, *n.* [ME. *cratche*, *crecche*; OFr. *creche*, a crib, manger; O.H.G. *crippa*, a crib.] a rack or crib. [Dial.]

çratch çrā'dle, cat's cradle.

çratch'eṣ, *n.pl.* [G. *krätze*, the itch, cratches; *kratzen*, to scratch.] scratches, a disease of horses.

çrāte, *n.* [L. *cratis*, wickerwork.]

1. a wickerwork hamper for preventing the breakage of fragile ware, or any case made up of slats to protect goods in transit; also, the amount held by such a case; as, a *crate* of tomatoes.

2. an old or decrepit automobile or airplane. [Slang.]

çrāte, *v.t.*; crated, *pt.*, *pp.*; crating, *ppr.* to pack or enclose in a crate; as, to *crate* china.

çrā'tẽr, *n.* [L. *crater*, mixing bowl, mouth of a volcano, from Gr. *kratēr*, from *kerannynai*, to mix.]

1. in ancient Greece, a kind of bowl or jar.

2. the bowl-shaped cavity at the mouth of a volcano.

3. a pit resembling this, especially one made by an explosion, as of a bomb.

4. [C-] in astronomy, a southern constellation.

5. in electric lighting, the depression at the point of a positive carbon in the voltaic arc.

CRATER (of a volcano)

çrā·ter'i·fọrm, *a.* [L. *crater*, from Gr. *kratēr*, a crater, and *forma*, form.] in botany, having the form of a crater; shaped like a bowl.

çrā'tẽr·ous, *a.* pertaining to or like a crater.

çräunch, *v.t.* and *v.i.*; craunched, *pt.*, *pp.*; craunching, *ppr.* [earlier form of *crunch*.] to crush with the teeth; to chew; to crunch.

çräunch, *n.* a crunching.

çrȧ·vat', *n.* [Fr. *cravate*, from *Cravate*, a Croat.]

1. a neckcloth or scarf.

2. a necktie.

çrāve, *v.t.*; craved, *pt.*, *pp.*; craving, *ppr.* [ME. *craven*; AS. *crafian*, to crave, ask, demand.]

1. to ask for with earnestness or importunity; to beseech; to implore; to beg; to entreat.

As for my nobler friends, I *crave* their pardons. —Shak.

2. to long for eagerly; to desire intensely.

3. to be in great need of.

Syn.—desire, entreat, beseech, implore, adjure, request, supplicate, solicit, ask.

çrāve, *v.i.* to have an eager longing or intense desire (*for*).

çrā'ven, *a.* [ME. *cravant*, conquered, cowardly; OFr. *cravanté*, pp. of *craventer*, to break, overcome, conquer.]

1. vanquished. [Obs.]

2. cowardly; base.

to cry craven; to surrender; to give up.

çrā'ven, *n.* a coward; a poltroon.

çrav·en·ette', *n.* [after *Craven* Street, London.]

1. a finish for making certain fabrics waterproof.

2. a fabric with this finish.

A trade-mark (*Cravanette*).

çrāv'ẽr, *n.* one who craves or begs.

çrāv'ing, *n.* vehement and prolonged desire; a longing, as for food, drink, etc.

çrāv'ing·ly, *adv.* in a craving manner.

çrāv'ing·ness, *n.* the state of craving.

çrạw, *n.* [Dan. *kro*, the craw; Sw. *kräfva*; D. *kraag*, the neck.] the crop of a bird or insect; by extension, the stomach of any animal.

to stick in the (or *one's*) *craw*; to be unacceptable or displeasing to one.

çrạw'fish, *n.*; *pl.* **çrạw'fish** *or* **çrạw'fish·eṣ,** a crayfish: the form preferred in the U. S., except among zoologists.

çrạw'fish, *v.i.* to try to avoid the keeping of a promise; to fail to stick to a statement made; to back down. [Colloq.]

çrạw'foot, *n.* [var. of *crowfoot*.]

1. a kind of orchis.

2. the creeping crowfoot.

3. a buttercup, *Ranunculus acris*.

Çrạw'ford (-fẽrd), *n.* either of two varieties of peach, one ripening late, the other early.

çrạwl, *v.i.*; crawled, *pt.*, *pp.*; crawling, *ppr.* [Ice. *krafla*, to paw, scrabble; Dan. *kravle*, to crawl, creep.]

1. to move slowly by dragging the body along the ground, as a worm.

2. to move slowly on the hands and knees; to creep.

3. to move weakly, slowly, or timorously.

4. to swarm or teem with crawling things.

5. to have a sensation as of insects creeping upon the skin.

6. to move or act in an abjectly servile manner.

çrạwl, *n.* 1. the act of crawling; slow, creeping motion.

2. a swimming stroke in which one lies face downward, with the mouth and nose under

water except when turned briefly sideward for breathing, and uses alternate overarm movements and a continuous up-and-down kick.

çrawl, *n.* [W. Ind. D. *kraal*, an enclosure, a cattle pen.] a pen or enclosure made in shallow water by setting stakes vertically, in which to confine fish or other aquatic animals.

çrawl'ẽr, *n.* one who or that which crawls.

çraw'ley-root, *n.* same as *coralroot.*

çrawl'ing·ly, *adv.* in a crawling manner.

çrawl space, a shallow or narrow space, as under a roof or floor, allowing access to wiring, plumbing, etc.

çrawl'y, *a.*; *comp.* crawlier; *superl.* crawliest, creepy. [Colloq.]

Çrax, *n.* [L., from Gr. *krazein, kraxein*, to croak like a raven.] the curassows, a genus of gallinaceous birds of the family *Cracidæ.*

çrāyer, *n.* see *crare.*

çrāy'fish, *n.*; *pl.* **çrāy'fish** *or* **çrāy'fish·eṣ,** [altered, after *fish*, from ME. *crevis, crevice*; OFr. *crevice*; O.H.G. *krebiz.*]

1. a small, fresh-water crustacean somewhat resembling a little lobster.

2. a sea shellfish resembling a lobster but without the large pincers: also called *spiny lobster.*

çrāy'ŏn, *n.* [Fr., from *craie*, chalk, from L. *creta*, chalk, said to be from *creta*, Cretan earth; *Creta*, Crete.]

1. a small stick of chalk, waxy material, charcoal, etc., used for drawing, coloring, or writing: it may be white or colored.

2. a drawing made with crayons.

3. the carbon pencil of an arc lamp.

çrāy'ŏn, *v.t.*; crayoned, *pt., pp.*; crayoning, *ppr.* to sketch or design with a crayon or crayons.

çrāy'ŏn bōard, prepared cardboard for drawing on with crayons.

çrāze, *v.t.*; crazed, *pt., pp.*; crazing, *ppr.* [ME. *crasen*, to break, break in pieces; Sw. *krasa*; Dan. *krase*, to break, crackle.]

1. to break. [Obs.]

2. to cause to become mentally ill; make insane.

3. to produce a crackled surface or small cracks in the glaze of (pottery, porcelain, etc.)

çrāze, *v.i.* 1. to burst apart. [Obs.]

2. to become mentally ill.

3. to become finely cracked, as the glaze of pottery.

çrāze, *n.* 1. an exaggerated enthusiasm; mania.

2. something that is temporarily the fashion; fad.

3. a little crack in the glaze or enamel, as of pottery.

çrāz'ed·ness, *n.* a broken state; decrepitude.

çrāze'mill, çrāz'ing-mill, *n.* a mill resembling a gristmill, used for grinding tin ore. [Brit. Dial.]

çrā'zi·ly, *adv.* in a crazy manner.

çrā'zi·ness, *n.* the quality or state of being crazy.

çrāz'ing, *n.* a cracking of the glaze on pottery, etc.

çrā'zy, *a.*; *comp.* crazier; *superl.* craziest, [from *craze.*]

1. unsound; cracked; shaky; rickety.

2. unsound of mind; mentally unbalanced or deranged; psychopathic; insane.

3. of or fit for an insane person.

4. temporarily unbalanced, as with great excitement, rage, etc.

5. very enthusiastic; very eager; as, she's *crazy* about the movies. [Colloq.]

çrā'zy bōne, the funny bone.

çrā'zy quilt (kwilt), a quilt made up of pieces of cloth arranged without pattern or order.

çrā'zy·weed, *n.* same as *locoweed.*

çrā'zy-wŏrk, *n.* patchwork making up a crazy quilt.

çrē'ȧ·ble, *a.* creatable. [Obs.]

çreaght (krāt), *n.* [Ir. *graigh*, a herd, flock.] a herd of cattle. [Obs.]

çreaght, *v.i.* to graze. [Obs.]

çrēak, *v.t.* and *v.i.*; creaked (krēkt), *pt., pp.*; creaking, *ppr.* [ME. *creken*, to make a harsh, grating sound; echoic of the sound.] to make, cause to make, or move with a sharp, harsh, grating sound, as rusted hinges.

çrēak, *n.* a sharp, harsh, grating sound, as that produced by rusted hinges.

çrēak'i·ly, *adv.* in a creaky manner.

çrēak'i·ness, *n.* the quality or state of being creaky.

çrēak'y, *a.*; *comp.* creakier; *superl.* creakiest, making or likely to make a creak; as, a *creaky* old bed.

çrēam, *n.* [ME. *creme*; OFr. *cresme, creme*; LL. *chrisma*, an anointing, unction.]

1. the oily, yellowish part of milk, which rises to the top.

2. any of various foods made of cream or having a creamy consistency.

3. a cosmetic or emulsion with a creamy consistency.

4. a thick liqueur.

5. the best part of a thing, the choicest part.

Welcome, O flower and *cream* of knights-
errant. —Shelton.

6. the color of cream; yellowish white.

cream of; creamed puree of; as, *cream of* tomato soup.

cream of lime; a mixture of slaked lime and water, having a creamy consistency.

çrēam, *a.* 1. containing cream; made of cream.

2. having the consistency of cream; creamy.

3. cream-colored.

çrēam, *v.i.*; creamed, *pt., pp.*; creaming, *ppr.*

1. to form into cream or a foamy substance.

2. to form a foam or scum on top.

çrēam, *v.t.* 1. to skim; to take the cream from, by skimming.

2. to remove the best part of.

3. to add cream to.

4. to cook with cream or a cream sauce.

5. to beat into a creamy consistency; make into a creamy mixture.

6. to let (milk) form cream.

7. to separate as cream.

8. to beat or defeat soundly. [Slang.]

çrēam'çāke, *n.* a cake having a custardlike filling made of cream, eggs, sugar, etc.

çrēam cheeṣe, see under *cheese.*

çrēam-çŏl'ŏred, *a.* yellowish-white.

çrēam'çups, *n.*; *pl.* **çrēam'çups,** *Platystemon californicus*, a California plant of the poppy family, with small, creamy flowers.

çrēam'ẽr, *n.* 1. a cream separator.

2. a pitcher or jug for cream.

3. a refrigerator in which milk is put to form cream.

4. a person or thing that creams.

çrēam'ẽr·y, *n.*; *pl.* **çrēam'ẽr·ieṣ,** 1. a place where milk and cream are pasteurized, separated, and bottled, and butter and cheese are made.

2. a shop where dairy products are sold.

3. a place where milk is put for creaming.

çrēam'-fāced (-fāst), *a.* white or pale, as from fear.

çrēam'fruit, *n.* a plant of the dogbane family growing in western Africa, having a creamy, edible fruit.

çrēam gāuġe, same as *creamometer.*

çrēam'i·ness, *n.* the state or quality of being creamy.

çrēam nut, the fruit of the *Bertholletia excelsa* of South America; the Brazil nut.

çrēam of tär'tãr, a white, acid, crystalline substance, $KHC_4H_4O_6$, used in medicine and cooking: also called *potassium acid tartrate* or *potassium bitartrate.*

çrēam-of-tär'tãr tree, a North Australian tree, *Adansonia gregorii.*

çrēam·om'e·tẽr, *n.* an instrument for determining the percentage of cream in milk.

çrēam puff, a round shell of pastry filled with whipped cream or having a cream filling.

çrēam sauce, a sauce made of butter and flour cooked together with milk or cream.

çrēam sep'ȧ·rā·tŏr, a machine which has a rapidly revolving drum, separating cream from skim milk by centrifugal action.

çrēam slīce, 1. a wooden knife used in skimming milk or cutting ice cream.

2. a kind of pastry made with a layer of cream.

çrēam sō'dȧ, soda pop, usually colorless, that is flavored with vanilla.

çrēam soup, soup made with cream or milk, or, sometimes, with a cream sauce.

cream-soup cup; a large, shallow cup for soup, often having two handles.

cream-soup spoon; a spoon having a round bowl, used with a cream-soup cup.

çrēam'y, *a.*; *comp.* creamier; *superl.* creamiest, containing cream; like cream in consistency or color.

çrē'ănce, *n.* [OFr. *creance*, faith, confidence, from LL. *credentia*; from *credere*, to trust.]

1. belief; faith; also, credit. [Obs.]

2. in falconry, a small line fastened to a hawk's leash when it is first lured.

çrē'ănt, *a.* [L. *creans* (*-antis*), ppr. of *creare*, to create.] constructive; creative. [Rare.]

çrēase, *n.* same as *creese.*

çrēase, *n.* [Breton *kriz*, a crease, wrinkle; *kriza*, to crease, wrinkle.]

1. a line or mark made by folding and pressing cloth, paper, etc.; a ridge, as that pressed into men's trousers.

2. any mark resembling that of a wrinkle or fold; as, her dress was full of *creases.*

3. in cricket, any of certain lines that mark off an area on the ground showing the station of the batsman or the bowler.

4. in hockey, a rectangular area marked off by lines in front of the goal cage, which cannot be entered by attacking players except under certain special conditions.

çrēase, *v.t.*; creased (krēst), *pt., pp.*; creasing, *ppr.* 1. to make a crease or mark in, by folding, pressing, etc.

2. to wrinkle; muss.

3. (a) originally, to put a shot through the ridge of a horse's neck; (b) to graze and injure slightly with a bullet.

çrēase, *v.i.* to become creased.

çrēas'ẽr, *n.* any of various tools used for making creases; as, (a) a tool used in bookbinding to trace depressed lines in the covers; (b) an attachment to a sewing machine that marks a guide line for stitching.

çrē'ȧ·sol, *n.* see *creosol.*

çrē'ȧ·sōte, *n.* and *v.t.* see *creosote.*

çrēas'y, *a.* full of creases; creased; wrinkled.

çrē·āt'ȧ·ble, *a.* that can be created.

çre·āte', *v.t.*; created, *pt., pp.*; creating, *ppr.* [L. *creatus*, pp. of *creare*, to make, create; Gr. *krainein*, to accomplish; Sans. *kar*, to make.]

1. to originate; to bring into being from nothing; to cause to exist.

In the beginning, God *created* the heaven
and the earth. —Gen. i. 1.

2. to produce; to cause; to bring about; to give rise to; as, hurry *creates* confusion.

Your eye, in Scotland,
Would *create* soldiers, and make women
fight. —Shak.

3. to invest with a new rank, function, etc.; as, to *create* one a peer or baron.

4. to portray (a character) effectively for the first time: said of an actor.

Syn.—constitute, form, make, occasion, originate, produce, generate.

çrē·āte', *a.* created. [Archaic.]

çrē·at'iç, *a.* [Gr. *kreas* (*-atos*), flesh.] occasioned by or pertaining to animal food; as, *creatic* nausea: also spelled *kreatic.*

çrē'ȧ·tine, çrē'ȧ·tin, *n.* [from Gr. *kreas*, flesh, and *-ine.*] a white, crystalline substance, an alkaloid or amino acid, $C_4H_9N_3O_2$, present chiefly in the muscle tissue of vertebrates: written also *kreatine, kreatin.*

çrē·at'i·nine, çrē·at'i·nin, *n.* [G. *kreatinin*, from *kreatin*, creatine, and *-in*, -ine.] a nitrogen compound, $C_4H_7N_3O$, an anhydride of creatine, found in blood, muscle, and especially urine, where measurement of its excretion is used to evaluate kidney function.

çrē·ā'tion, *n.* 1. a creating or being created; the act of bringing into existence.

2. the act of investing with a new rank, function, etc.; as, the *creation* of peers in England.

3. the thing or things created; all the world; the universe and everything in it.

As subjects then the whole *creation* came.
—Denham.

4. anything produced or created in mechanics, science, or art; especially, something created by the imagination; an invention.

A false *creation*,
Proceeding from the heat-oppressed brain.
—Shak.

the Creation; in theology, God's creating of the world.

çrē·ā'tion·ăl, *a.* pertaining to creation.

çrē·ā'tion·iṣm, *n.* in theology, (a) the doctrine that God creates a new soul for every human being born; (b) the doctrine that ascribes the origin of matter and of distinct species of animals and plants to acts of creation by God.

çrē·ā'tion·ist, *n.* a person who believes in creationism.

çrē·ā'tive, *a.* having the power to create; pertaining to creation; inventive; productive (*of*); as, a *creative* mind, *creative* power.

çrē·ā'tive·ness, *n.* the state or quality of being creative.

çrē·ā·tiv'i·ty, *n.* creative ability; artistic or intellectual inventiveness.

çrē·ā'tŏr, *n.* [L.] 1. a person or, sometimes, thing that creates.

2. [C–] God; the Supreme Being.

Remember now thy *Creator* in the days of
thy youth. —Eccles. xii. 1.

çrē·ā'tŏr·ship, *n.* the state or condition of being a creator.

çrē·ā'tress, *n.* a woman who creates anything.

çrē·ā'trix, *n.* [L.] same as *creatress.*

çrēa'tūr·ăl, *a.* same as *creaturely.*

çrēa'tūre, *n.* [OFr. *creature*; LL. *creatura,* a creature, creation, from L. *creare,* to create.]

1. that which is created; anything created, animate or inanimate.

2. a living being of any kind; usually, a beast or domestic animal.

3. a human being: used in a contemptuous, commiserating, or endearing sense; as, an idle *creature,* a poor *creature.*

4. a person who owes his rise and fortune to another; one who is completely dominated by or dependent on another.

Great princes thus, when favorites they raise,
To justify their grace, their *creatures* praise.
—Dryden.

5. a strange or imaginary being.

çrēa'tūre çŏm'fŏrt, anything providing bodily comfort, as food, clothing, or shelter.

çrēa'tūre·ly, *a.* having the nature of or pertaining to a creature; creatural.

çrēaze, *n.* in tin mining, the ore that gathers in the middle of the washing pit. [Brit. Dial.]

çrē·bri·ços'tāte, *a.* [L. *creber,* close, frequent, and *costa,* a rib.] in conchology, having ridges or marks like ribs set closely together.

çrē·bri·sul'çāte, *a.* [L. *creber,* frequent, close, and *sulcus,* a furrow.] in conchology, marked with closely set furrows or grooves, running transversely.

çrē'brous, *a.* [L. *creber,* close, frequent.] frequent. [Rare.]

crèche (krāsh), *n.* [Fr., from OFr. *creche,* a crib.]

1. a miniature representation of the stable in which Jesus was born, with figures of the infant Jesus, Mary, Joseph, the Magi, etc.

2. a home for foundlings.

3. a public nursery where mothers who work can leave their children during the day.

çrē'dence, *n.* [OFr. *credence*; ML. *credentia,* faith, from L. *credens (-entis),* ppr. of *credere,* to believe, put faith in.]

1. belief, especially in the reports or testimony of another; as, give no *credence* to rumors.

2. credential; as, a letter of *credence.*

3. in ecclesiastical usage, a small table near the altar, on which the bread and wine to be used in the Eucharist are placed before consecration.

CREDENCE (sense 4)

4. in the Middle Ages, a kind of buffet or sideboard where the meats were tasted before they were served to the guests, as a precaution against poisoning.

Syn.—belief, credit, confidence, trust, faith.

çrē'dence, *v.t.* to believe. [Obs.]

çrē·den'dȧ, *n.pl.*; *sing.* **çrē·den'dum,** [L., pl. of gerundive of *credere,* to believe, put faith in.] in theology, doctrines to be believed; articles of faith.

çrē'dent, *a.* [L. *credens (-entis),* ppr. of *credere,* to believe.]

1. believing; giving credence.

2. having credit; credible. [Obs.]

çrē·den'tiăl, *a.* [from ML. *credentia,* belief, faith, from L. *credere,* to believe, put trust in.] entitled to credit, confidence, etc.; establishing reliability. [Rare.]

çrē·den'tiăl, *n.* 1. that which gives credit; that which entitles to credit, confidence, etc.

2. [*usually in pl.*] a letter or certificate given to a person to show that he has a right to confidence or to the exercise of a certain position or authority.

çrē·den'zȧ, *n.*; *pl.* **çrē·den'zȧṣ** *or It.* **çrē·den'zē,** [It.] a type of buffet, or sideboard.

çred·i·bil'i·ty, *n.* [Fr. *crédibilité*; L. *credibilitas,* from *credibilis,* worthy of belief, from *credere,* to believe, put faith in.] the state or quality of being credible.

credibility gap; (a) an apparent disparity between what is said and the actual facts; (b) the inability to have one's statements accepted as factual or one's professed motives accepted as the true ones.

çred'i·ble, *a.* [L. *credibilis,* from *credere,* to believe, put trust in.]

1. worthy of credence; believable, as a book.

2. entitled to belief or trust; trustworthy; reliable, as a person.

çred'i·ble·ness, *n.* credibility.

çred'i·bly, *adv.* in a credible manner.

çred'it, *n.* [Fr. *crédit*; L. *creditum,* a loan, neut. of *creditus,* pp. of *credere,* to trust, believe.]

1. belief; faith; confidence; trust.

What though no *credit* doubting wits may give? —Pope.

2. the quality of being credible or trustworthy.

3. the favorable reputation derived from the confidence of others; esteem; honor; good opinion founded on the belief of a man's veracity, integrity, abilities, and virtue.

4. praise or approval to which a person or thing is entitled; commendation; as, he deserves *credit* for telling the truth.

5. one who or that which augments reputation, honor, or fame; as, a *credit* to his family.

6. [*usually pl.*] acknowledgment of work done, as in the preparation of a motion picture.

7. the amount of money remaining in a person's account in a bank, etc.

8. in business, (a) trust in one's integrity in money matters and confidence of future payment; (b) the time allowed for payment.

9. in accounting, (a) the acknowledgment of payment on a debt by entry of the amount in an account; (b) the right-hand side of an account in which such amounts are entered; (c) an entry on this side; (d) the sum of such entries.

10. in education, (a) the certification of a student's successful completion of a unit or course of study; (b) a unit of work so certified.

on credit; with the agreement that payment will be made at a future date.

to do credit to; to bring approval or honor to.

to give credit to; (a) to believe; to have confidence or trust in; (b) to commend.

to give one credit for; (a) to commend one for; (b) to believe that one has.

to one's credit; bringing approval or honor to one.

Syn.—belief, faith, trust, confidence, favor, influence, name, character, reputation, honor.

çred'it, *v.t.*; credited, *pt., pp.*; crediting, *ppr.* [from L. *creditus,* pp. of *credere,* to trust.]

1. to believe; to trust; to have confidence or faith in.

2. to bring approval or honor to; to do credit to; to give reputation or honor to.

May here her monument stand so,
To *credit* this rude age. —Waller.

3. to give deserved commendation for.

4. to give credit in a bank account, etc.

5. to enter on the credit side of an account; to give credit for; as, to *credit* the amount paid.

6. in education, to enter a credit or credits on the record of (a student).

to credit one with; to ascribe to one.

to credit to one; to believe that one has.

çred'it·ȧ·ble, *a.* 1. believable. [Obs.]

2. reputable; that may be enjoyed or exercised with reputation or esteem; praiseworthy; as, a *creditable* way of living.

çred'it·ȧ·ble·ness, *n.* the state or quality of being creditable; reputableness.

çred'it·ȧ·bly, *adv.* in a creditable manner.

çred'it bū'reau, an agency that collects and disseminates information on the credit rating of individuals or firms.

çred'it çärd, a card establishing the privilege of the person to whom it is issued to charge bills at certain restaurants, hotels, airlines, gas stations, etc.

çred'it līne, an acknowledgment of work done or a contribution made, as in a newspaper or motion picture.

çred'it·ŏr, *n.* [L. *creditor,* a truster, lender, from *credere,* to trust, put faith in.]

1. one who believes. [Obs.]

2. one to whom a sum of money or other thing is due by obligation, promise, or in law; one who gives credit or has a just claim for money.

Creditors have better memories than debtors. —Franklin.

3. in bookkeeping, (a) the credit side of an account; (b) any entry on this side.

çred'it rāt'ing, the rating of an individual or firm as a credit risk, based on past records of debt repayment, financial status, etc.

çred'it ūn'iŏn (-yun), a co-operative association for pooling savings of members and making loans to them at a low rate of interest.

çrē'dō, *n.*; *pl.* **çrē'dōṣ,** [L., I believe; see *creed.*]

1. a creed.

2. [*usually* C–] (a) the Apostles' Creed or the Nicene Creed, both of which begin with *credo*; (b) the music for either of these.

çrē·dū'li·ty, *n.*; *pl.* **çrē·dū'li·tieṣ,** lack of doubt or skepticism; easiness of belief; readiness to believe without sufficient evidence.

çred'ū·lous, *a.* [L. *credulus,* from *credere,* to trust, put faith in.] tending to believe too readily; easily convinced.

çred'ū·lous·ly, *adv.* with credulity.

çred'ū·lous·ness, *n.* credulity.

Çree, *n.*; *pl.* **Çree, Çreeṣ,** [from Am. Ind. (Algonquian) name.]

1. a member of a tribe of Algonquian Indians who lived in an area extending from the southern end of Hudson Bay to northern Alberta, Canada.

2. the language of this tribe.

çreed, *n.* [ME. *crede*; AS. *creda*; from L. *credo,* I believe, the first word of the Latin version of the Apostles' Creed; 1st pers. sing. pres. ind. act. of *credere,* to trust, put faith in.]

1. a brief statement of religious belief; a confession of faith.

2. a specific statement of this kind, accepted as authoritative by a church; especially, the Apostles' Creed, the Nicene Creed, or the Athanasian Creed.

3. a statement of belief, principles, or opinions on any subject.

Apostles' Creed; see under *Apostle.*

Athanasian Creed; see under *Athanasian.*

Nicene Creed; see under *Nicene.*

the Creed; the Apostles' Creed.

çreed'less, *a.* without a creed.

çreek (*or* krik), *n.* [ME. *creke, crike,* an inlet, cove; Ice. *kriki,* a nook; Sw. *krik,* a bend, cove, creek; D. *kreek,* a bay, creek.]

1. a small stream, somewhat larger than a brook.

2. a small inlet, bay, or cove; a recess in the shore of the sea or of a river.

3. any turn or winding.

up the creek; in trouble. [Slang.]

Çreek, *n.* [perh. from *creek* (with reference to the many creeks in the tribal territory).]

1. an American Indian of any of several tribes, mainly Muskhogean, now living in Oklahoma.

2. an Indian of the Creek Confederacy or the Creek Nation.

3. the Muskhogean language of the Creeks.

Çreek Çŏn·fed'ẽr·ȧ·cy, a former tribal league of Muskhogean Indians in Georgia and Alabama.

çreek'fish, *n.*; *pl.* **çreek'fish** *or* **çreek'fish·eṣ,** a fish, the chub sucker.

Çreek Nā'tion, a former semiautonomous league of Indian tribes set up by the Creeks in the Indian Territory.

çreek'y, *a.* full of creeks.

çreel, *n.* [ME. *crelle*; MFr. *crille,* dial., var. of *grille,* a grill.]

1. a wicker basket for holding fish: creels are often worn on the back by fishermen.

2. a basketlike cage for trapping fish, shellfish, etc.

3. in spinning, the bar which holds the bobbins.

çreel, *v.t.*; creeled, *pt., pp.*; creeling, *ppr.* to place in a creel.

çreep, *v.i.*; crept, *pt., pp.*; creeping, *ppr.* [ME. *crepen*; AS. *creopan,* to creep, crawl; D. *criupen*; L.G. *krupen,* to creep, crawl.]

1. to move along with the body close to the ground, as on hands and knees.

2. to move slowly.

We took a little boat to *creep* along the seashore as far as Genoa. —Addison.

3. to move stealthily, timidly, or furtively.

4. to move secretly; to move so as to escape detection or prevent suspicion; to enter unobserved (often with *up*).

The sophistry which *creeps* into most of the books of argument. —Locke.

5. to move or behave with extreme servility or humility; to move as if affected with a sense of humiliation or fear.

Like a guilty thing I *creep.* —Tennyson.

6. to grow along the ground or a wall, as a vine.

Oh, a dainty plant is the ivy green,
That *creepeth* o'er ruins old. —Dickens.

7. to feel as if insects were creeping on the skin of the body; as, the sight made my flesh *creep.*

8. to slip slightly out of position.

to make one's flesh creep; to cause one to feel fear, repugnance, etc. as if insects were creeping on one's skin.

çreep, *n.* 1. the act of creeping.

2. a creeping movement.

3. in mining, a sinking down of the strata overlying a working, the floor being at the same time pushed up.

the creeps; a feeling of fear, repugnance, etc. as if insects were creeping on one's skin. [Colloq.]

çreep'ẽr, *n.* 1. one who or that which creeps.
2. any plant whose stem puts out tendrils or rootlets by which it can creep along a surface as it grows.
3. any of various small birds that creep on trees and bushes looking for insects, larvae, etc. to eat, as the American brown creeper, certain warblers, etc.
4. [*usually pl.*] a metal plate with spikes fixed on a shoe to prevent slipping.
5. an instrument of iron with hooks or claws for dragging the bottom of a river, harbor, etc.
6. [*pl.*] climbing irons, as those used by telephone linemen.
7. [*pl.*] a baby's one-piece garment, combining pants and waist.

çreep'hōle, *n.* a hole into which an animal may creep to escape notice or danger; also, a subterfuge; an excuse.

çreep'ie, *n.* a kind of low stool. [Brit. Dial.]

çreep'i·ness, *n.* the quality or state of being creepy.

çreep'ing bent grȧss, any of a large group of low-growing grasses, including some lawn and pasture varieties, that root along the stem.

çreep'ing·ly, *adv.* by creeping movement; slowly.

çreep'y, *a.*; *comp.* creepier; *superl.* creepiest. 1. creeping; moving slowly.
2. having a feeling of fear, horror, or repugnance, as if insects were creeping on one's skin.
3. fearful; producing a chilled and scared sensation.

çreese, *n.* [from Malay *kris*, a dagger.] a dagger with a wavy blade, used by Malays: also spelled *crease, cris, kris.*

çreesh, *n.* and *v.t.* [from OFr. *cresse, craisse, n.*, from L. *crassa*, fem. of *crassus*, thick, gross, fat.] grease. [Scot.]

cré·mail·lère' (krā-mā-yãr'), *n.* [Fr.] in fortification, a defensive line in the form of a saw, making possible both oblique and cross fires.

çrē·mas'tẽr, *n.* [L., from Gr. *kremastēr*, a suspender, from *kremannynai*, to hang.]
1. in anatomy, a muscle suspending the testicle.
2. in entomology, the abdominal point of the pupa of a lepidopter.

çrem·as·ter'iç, *a.* pertaining to the cremaster.

çrē'māte, *v.t.*; cremated, *pt., pp.*; cremating, *ppr.* [L. *crematus*, pp. of *cremare*, to burn.]
1. to burn up; to consume by fire.
2. to burn (a dead body) to ashes.

çrē·mā'tion, *n.* [L. *crematio*, from *cremare*, to burn.] the act or process of cremating; a burning of a dead body to ashes.

çrē·mā'tion·ist, *n.* an advocate of cremation in preference to burial.

çrē·mā'tŏr, *n.* 1. one who cremates.
2. a furnace for cremating dead bodies.
3. an incinerator for garbage, trash, etc.

çrem·ȧ·tō'ri·um, *n.*; *pl.* **çrem·ȧ·tō'ri·ȧ,** a crematory. [Chiefly Brit.]

çrem'ȧ·tō·ry, *n.*; *pl.* **çrem'ȧ·tō·rieṣ,** [Mod. L. *crematorium*, from *cremare*, to burn.] a building at which dead bodies are cremated; also, the furnace so employed.

çrem'ȧ·tō·ry, *a.* connected with or relating to cremation.

crème (krem), *n.* [Fr., cream.]
1. cream.
2. a thick liqueur.
crème de cacao; liqueur flavored with chocolate.
crème de menthe; liqueur flavored with mint.
crème de moka; liqueur flavored with coffee.

crème de la crème (krem dẽ lȧ krem), [Fr., lit., cream of the cream.] the very best (of something).

çrem'ō·çȧrp, *n.* [Gr. *kremannynai*, to hang, and *karpos*, fruit.] a fruit, as that of umbellifers, consisting of two or more indehiscent, one-seeded carpels, adhering around a distinct and separable axis.

Çrē·mō'nȧ, *n.* any of the famous violins made at Cremona, Italy by Nicola Amati (1596–1684) or a member of his family, his pupil Antonio Stradivari (1644–1737), or Guiseppe Guarneri (1683–1745).

çrē'mọr, *n.* [L.] cream; any substance resembling cream.

çrem'ō·sin, *n.* crimson. [Obs.]

çremṣ, *n.* same as *krems.*

çrē'nȧ, *n.*; *pl.* **çrē'nae,** [L., a notch.] in zoology, a notch.

çrē'nāte, çrē'nāt·ed, *a.* [Mod. L. *crenatus*, from *crena*, a notch.] in botany, having a notched, indented, or scalloped edge, as certain leaves.

CRENATE LEAF

çrē·nā'tion, *n.* 1. the condition of being crenate.
2. a crenate formation.

çren'ȧ·tūre, *n.* 1. a rounded projection on the margin of a crenate leaf, or any other part that is crenate.
2. a notch between such projections.

çren'el, çrē·nelle', *n.* [OFr., dim., from LL. *crena*, a notch, groove.] an indentation or loophole in the top of a battlement or wall; embrasure.

çren'el, *v.t.*; creneled *or* crenelled, *pt., pp.*; creneling *or* crenelling, *ppr.* to crenelate.

çren'el·āte, *v.t.*; crenelated, *pt., pp.*; crenelating, *ppr.* [OFr. *creneler*, to indent, from LL. *crenellus*, an embrasure, battlement.] to furnish, as a parapet or breastwork, with battlements or crenels: written also *crenellate.*

çren'el·ā·ted, *a.* furnished with crenels, as a parapet or breastwork; embattled: written also *crenellated.*

CRENELATED MOLDING

çren·el·ā'tion, *n.* 1. the act of forming crenels.
2. the state or condition of being crenelated.
3. a battlement; a notch or indentation. Written also *crenellation.*

çrē·nelle', *n.* same as *crenel.*

çrē·nelled', *a.* same as *crenelated.*

çreñ'gle (-gl), **çreñ'kle,** *n.* in nautical usage, a cringle.

çrē·nit'iç, *a.* [Gr. *krēnē*, a spring.] in geology, pertaining to the upward shifting of matter through the agency of springs.

çren'ū·lȧ, *n.*; *pl.* **çren'ū·lae,** [L., dim. of *crena*, a notch.] a small notch or crena.

çren'ū·lāte, çren'ū·lā·ted, *a.* [dim. of *crenate.*] having very small notches or scallops, as some leaves or shells.

çren·ū·lā'tion, *n.* that which has very small notches; also, a notched state or condition.

çrē'ō·dont, *n.* [from Mod. L. *Creodonta, pl.*, from Gr. *kreas*, flesh, and *odons*, tooth.] any of a group of primitive, flesh-eating mammals with small brains.

Çrē'ōle, *n.* [Fr. *créole*; Sp. *criollo*, a native (of a tropic dependency); assumed to be for *criadillo*, nurseling, dim. of *criado*, lit., created, from *criar*; L. *creare*, to create, produce.]
1. originally, a native, especially of the West Indies, Central America, tropical South America, the Gulf States, or Mauritius, of nonnative descent.
2. a person of French or Spanish descent born in the Americas.
3. [c–] a person of Negro descent born in the Americas: usually *creole Negro.*
4. a person descended from or culturally related to the original French settlers of Louisiana and New Orleans; hence, French as spoken by such people.
5. loosely, anyone from Louisiana.
6. a person descended from or culturally related to original Spanish settlers in the Gulf States, especially Texas.
7. [c–] loosely, a person of mixed Creole and Negro stock.
8. [from Sp. *criollo.*] in parts of tropical South America, the child of a white father and a mestiza mother.

Çrē'ōle, *a.* 1. of, characteristic of, or relating to a Creole or Creoles.
2. [c–] designating, of, or characteristic of, a creole, or creoles.
3. of Creole.

Çrē·ō'lē·ăn, çrē·ō'lē·ăn, *a.* creole. [Rare.]

Çrē·ō'li·ăn, çrē·ō'li·ăn, *a.* and *n.* Creole. [Obs.]

çrē'ō·lin, *n.* [Gr. *kreas*, flesh, and L. *oleum*, oil.] a liquid preparation made from coal tar, used as an antiseptic.

çrē'ōl·īzed lañ'guȧġe (-gwăj), [from *Creole.*] the form of mixed language (e.g., Gullah) that develops when speakers of mutually unintelligible languages remain in persistent, long-lasting, and thorough contact with each other.

Çrē'on, *n.* [Gr. *Kreōn.*] in Greek legend, the King of Thebes who had his niece Antigone buried alive because she disobeyed him by performing funeral rites over the body of her brother Polynices.

çrē·oph'ȧ·gous, *a.* [Gr. *kreophagos*, flesh-eating; *kreas*, flesh, and *phagein*, to eat.] carnivorous.

çrē'ō·sol, çrē'ȧ·sol, *n.* [*creosote* and phen*ol.*] a colorless, pungent, oily liquid, $C_8H_{10}O_2$, obtained from beechwood tar and the resin guaiacum: it is used as an antiseptic.

çrē'ō·sōte, çrē'ȧ·sōte, *n.* [L. *creosota*, from Gr. *kreas*, flesh, and *sōtēr*, from *sōzein*, to save.] a transparent, oily liquid with a pungent odor, resulting from wood-tar or coal-tar distillation: it is used as an antiseptic and as a preservative for wood.

çrē'ō·sōte, *v.t.*; creosoted, *pt., pp.*; creosoting, *ppr.* to treat (wood, etc.) with creosote.

çrē'ō·sōte bụsh, *Laurea mexicana*, a desert shrub of northern Mexico and the southwestern United States.

çrē'pănce, *n.* [L. *crepare*, to crack, burst.] a wound in a horse's leg, caused by interfering.

çrepe, crêpe (krāp), *n.* [Fr. *crêpe*, from L. *crispa*, curled, crisp.]
1. a thin, crinkled cloth of silk, rayon, cotton, wool, etc.; crape.
2. a piece of black crepe as a sign of mourning, often in the form of a band worn around the arm: usually spelled *crape.*
3. thin paper crinkled like crepe: also *crepe paper.*

çrepe de Chïne, [Fr., lit., crepe of China.] a soft, rather thin silk crepe, used for women's blouses, etc.

crêpes sụ·zette' (krep), [Fr.; *crêpe*, pancake, crepe, and *Suzette*, dim. of *Suzanne.*] very thin pancakes rolled up and sprinkled with sugar, sometimes served with a flaming brandy sauce.

çrep·i·taç'ū·lum, *n.*; *pl.* **çrep·i·taç'ū·lȧ,** [L., a rattle, from *crepitare*, freq. of *crepare*, to creak.] in zoology, (a) a rattlelike organ, as of the rattlesnake; (b) a stridulating organ at the base of a wing of certain insects, as the katydid.

çrep'i·tănt, *a.* [L. *crepitans* (-*antis*), ppr. of *crepitare*, to rattle.] rattling; crackling.

çrep'i·tāte, *v.i.*; crepitated, *pt., pp.*; crepitating, *ppr.* [L. *crepitatus*, pp. of *crepitare*, to rattle, freq. of *crepare*, to creak, burst.] to crackle; to make small, sharp, and repeated crackling sounds.

çrep·i·tā'tion, *n.* 1. a crackling.
2. in medicine, (a) the grating of fractured bones when moved; (b) an abnormal rattling sound detected in the lungs by auscultation and usually indicating a diseased condition.

çrep'i·tus, *n.* [L., a rattling, from *crepitare*, freq. of *crepare*, to creak, burst.] in medicine, crepitation.

çrē'pon, *n.* [Fr.] a fabric made of wool or of wool and silk, cotton, etc., resembling crepe.

çrept, past tense and past participle of *creep.*

çrē·pus'cle (-sl), **çrē·pus'çūle,** *n.* [L. *crepusculum*, twilight, from *creper*, dusky, dark.] twilight.

çrē·pus'çū·lăr, *a.* 1. pertaining to twilight; glimmering.
2. becoming active, flying, or appearing in the twilight; as, *crepuscular* insects.

çrē·pus'çū·line, *a.* crepuscular. [Obs.]

çrē·pus'çū·lous, *a.* glimmering.

çreṣ'cence, *n.* growth. [Obs.]

çres·cen'dō (kre-shen'dō), *a.* and *adv.* [It., from *crescere*, to increase.] in music, gradually increasing loudness and fullness of tone.

çres·cen'dō, *n.*; *pl.* **çres·cen'dōṣ,** 1. a gradually swelling tone in a musical passage.
2. a passage thus rendered.

çres'cent, *n.* [Latinized sp. (cf. L. *crescens*) of ME. *cressant*; OFr. *creissant*, ppr. of *creistre*, to increase; L. *crescere*, to come forth, grow.]
1. the moon in its first or last quarter, when it appears to have one concave edge and one convex edge.
2. the figure or likeness of the moon in either of these phases, as that borne in the Turkish flag or national standard; hence, the standard itself, and, figuratively, the Turkish power or Moslem power.
3. in heraldry, a bearing in the form of a young or new moon.
4. any of three orders of knighthood having a crescent-shaped symbol or badge: the first instituted by Charles I of Naples and Sicily in 1268; the second instituted at Angiers in 1464 by René of Anjou, being a revival of the former; and the third instituted by Selim, sultan of Turkey, in 1801.
5. a Turkish military musical instrument with bells or jingles.
6. in architecture, a range of buildings in the form of a crescent or half-moon.

CRESCENT

çres'cent, *a.* 1. increasing; growing. [Poet.]

2. shaped like the moon in its first or last quarter.

çres'cent, *v.t.* 1. to form into a crescent.
2. to embellish with a crescent or crescents.

çres·cen'tiç, *a.* shaped like a crescent.

çres'cent·wiṣe, *adv.* in the form of a crescent.

çres'cive, *a.* [from L. *crescere*, to grow, increase.] increasing; growing. [Rare.]

çrē'sōl, *n.* [Gr. *kreas*, flesh, and L. *oleum*, oil.] any of three isomeric, colorless, oily liquids or solids with the formula C_7H_8O, prepared by the fractional distillation of coal tar and used in the preparation of disinfectants, fumigating compounds, and dyestuffs: also called *cresylic acid*.

çrē·sor'cin, *n.* same as *isorcin*.

çrē·sot'iç, *a.* of or designating any of a group of isomeric acids obtained from the cresols.

çress, *n.* [ME. *cresse*; AS. *cresse*; OFr. *kerson, creson*; LL. *cresso, cresco*, the cress.] any of various plants of the mustard family, as water cress, the pungent leaves of which are used in salads and as garnishes.
not worth a cress; not worth a curse: the original form of the phrase: see under *curse*.

çres·selle', *n.* a wooden rattle used in some Roman Catholic countries during Passion week instead of bells, to give notice of divine worship.

çres'set, *n.* [OFr. *cresset, crasset*, a kind of lamp or torch; D. *kruysel*, a hanging lamp.]
1. a metal container for burning oil, wood, etc., fastened to a pole, wall, etc., and used as a torch or lantern.
2. an iron frame used by coopers in heating barrels.
3. a chafing dish.

CRESSETS

Çres'si·dȧ, *n.* in medieval legend, a Trojan woman who was unfaithful to her lover, Troilus: the legend is the source of Shakespeare's *Troilus and Cressida*: also spelled *Criseyde* (in Chaucer).

çress rock'et, *Vella pseudocytisus*, a plant of the mustard family with yellow flowers.

çress'y, *a.* abounding in or covered with cresses.

çrest, *n.* [ME. *crest, creste*; OFr. *creste*; L. *crista*, a comb or tuft on the head of a bird, a crest.]
1. a tuft or other growth on the top of an animal's head, as the comb of a cock.
2. in ancient armor, the plume of feathers, or an emblem or decoration, affixed to the top of a helmet; hence, a helmet.
3. a heraldic device placed above the shield in a coat of arms, and used separately on seals, silverware, note paper, etc.
4. the top of anything, or the line or surface along the top; summit; ridge; as, the *crest* of a wave, a mountain *crest*.
5. a projecting ridge along a bone.
6. the rising part of the neck of a horse, lion, etc.; also, the mane growing on this.
7. pride; courage; spirit. [Archaic.]

CREST ON A HELMET

çrest, *v.t.*; crested, *pt., pp.*; cresting, *ppr.* 1. to furnish with a crest; to serve as a crest for.
2. to lie at the top of; to crown.
3. to reach the crest of.

çrest, *v.i.* to form a crest or crests, as waves.

çrest'ed, *a.* wearing a crest; adorned with a crest; as, a *crested* helmet.

çrest'ed flȳ'çatch"ẽr, any of various crested birds that catch insects in flight.

çrest'fạll"en, *a.* 1. with drooping crest or bowed head; hence, dejected; dispirited.
2. having the upper part of the neck hanging on one side, as a horse.

çrest'ing, *n.* in architecture, carving or ornamental work, as on the peak of a roof.

çrest'less, *a.* without a crest; of low birth.

çrest tīle, a tile shaped like an inverted V, covering the ridge of a roof.

çrē'syl, *n.* [from *cre(o)sote* and *-yl*.] an unsaturated hydrocarbon, C_7H_7, of the aromatic series.

çrē·syl'iç, *a.* pertaining to or derived from cresol or creosote.
cresylic acid; cresol.

çrē·tā'ceous, *a.* [L. *cretaceus*, from *creta*, chalk.]
1. chalky; like chalk; abounding with chalk.
2. [C–] designating or of the third geological period, following the Jurassic, in the Mesozoic Era: it is marked by the dying out of toothed birds and dinosaurs, the development of early mammals and flowering plants, and the deposit of chalk beds.
the Cretaceous; the Cretaceous Period or its rocks.

çrē·tā'ceous·ly, *adv.* in a chalky manner.

Çrē·tac'iç, *a.* cretaceous.

Çrē'tăn, *a.* relating or pertaining to Crete, its people, or culture.

Çrē'tăn, *n.* a native or inhabitant of Crete.

çrē'tā·ted, *a.* rubbed with chalk. [Rare.]

Çrēte, *n.* a Cretan.

çrē·tē·fac'tion, *n.* chalk formation.

Çrē'tiăn, *a.* and *n.* same as *Cretan*.

çrē'tiç, *n.* [L. *Creticus*; Gr. *krētikos* (supply *pous*, foot), a Cretan foot.] in prosody, a poetic foot of three syllables, one short between two long syllables.

Çrē'ti·ciṣm, *n.* deceit; lying; Cretism.

çrē'tin, *n.* [Fr. *crétin*; origin uncertain.] one afflicted with cretinism.

çrē'tin·iṣm, *n.* in medicine, a congenital deficiency of thyroid secretion, characterized by a stunted and malformed body and arrested mental development.

çrē'tin·ous, *a.* characteristic of a cretin; also, having cretinism.

Çrē'tiṣm, *n.* [Gr. *krētismos*, lying, from *Krētizein*, to speak like a Cretan, to lie; *Krēs, Krētos*, a Cretan.] deceit; lying; falsehood.

çrē·tonne' (-ton'), [Fr., from *Creton*, village in Normandy.] a heavy, unglazed cotton or linen cloth having patterns printed in colors on one or both sides: used for curtains, draperies, etc.

Cre·ü'sa (krē-ọọ'sȧ), *n.* in Greek legend, (a) the bride of Jason, killed by the sorcery of the jealous Medea; (b) the wife of Aeneas and daughter of Priam, lost in the flight from captured Troy.

çreut'zẽr (kroit'sẽr), *n.* same as *kreutzer*.

cre·val·lé' (krẹ-vȧl-lā'), *n.* [Port. *cavalla*, a fish.] a fish, the cavalla.

çre·vàsse', *n.* [Fr. *crevasse*, a chink, cleft, from *crever*, to break; L. *crepare*, to break, burst, crack.]
1. a deep crack; a fissure, as in a glacier.
2. a break in a river embankment, usually occasioned by pressure or high water.

çre·vàsse', *v.t.*; crevassed, *pt., pp.*; crevassing, *ppr.* to make a crevasse or crevasses in.

çrev'et, *n.* [a variant of *cruet*.] a melting pot used by goldsmiths.

çrev'ice, *n.* [ME. *crevace, crevasse*; OFr. *crevace*, a chink, cleft, from *crever*, to break; L. *crepare*, to crack, burst, break.] a cleft; a fissure; a narrow opening caused by a crack or split; as, a *crevice* in a wall.

çrev'iced (-ist), *a.* having a crevice or crevices.

çrev'is, *n.* the crawfish. [Rare.]

çrew, *n.* [ME. *crewe*, a form of *accrue*, an accession, addition, company; OFr. *acreue*, pp. of *accroître*, to increase, from L. *adcrescere*; *ad*, to, and *crescere*, to grow.]
1. a reinforcement. [Obs.]
2. a company of persons associating together.
3. any body of workers assigned to a definite undertaking, usually under the direction of a foreman or leader; as, a threshing *crew*.
4. all the men working on a ship, aircraft, etc.
5. all of a ship's personnel except the officers.
6. a group; set; crowd; gang; mob; as, the arrested men were a dangerous *crew*.
7. a rowing team, usually of eight men.
8. the sport of rowing in races (at colleges, etc.).
Syn.—band, company, complement, force, gang, set.

çrew, *n.* the shearwater of the Isle of Man. [Brit. Dial.]

çrew, *v.*, alternative past tense of *crow* (sense 1).

çrew'el, *n.* [dim. of *clew*, a ball of thread.] a worsted yarn loosely twisted and used in embroidery and fancywork.

çrew'elṣ, *n.pl.* [Scot., from Fr. *écrouelles*, scrofula.] scrofulous swellings of the glands of the neck: written also *cruels*.

çrew'el stitch, an embroidery stitch in crewelwork.

çrew'el·wŏrk, *n.* work done with crewels; embroidery with a design worked in worsted on a cloth background.

çrew'et, *n.* same as *cruet*.

çrew neck, a round, closefitting neckline, as on a T-shirt.

çrib, *n.* [AS. *crib, cryb*; D. *krib*; L.G. *kribbe*; Ice. *krubba*; Dan. *krybbe*, a crib, manger.]
1. a small, crude house or room.
2. an open wooden rack at which livestock feed; a manger; also, a stall for cattle, oxen, etc.
3. a bin for grain, etc.; as, a corn*crib*.
4. a small bed for a child, with high sides and ends to keep him from falling out.
5. a house, shop, etc. [Slang.]
6. a framework of wooden or metal bars for support or strengthening, as in a mine.
7. the act of passing off another's ideas or writings as one's own; plagiarism. [Colloq.]
8. (a) a literal translation of a literary work in a foreign language, used in doing schoolwork, often dishonestly; (b) notes or similar aids dishonestly used in doing schoolwork. [Colloq.]
9. in cribbage, a set of cards made up of two thrown from the hand of each player, used by the dealer in scoring his points.
10. a raft.

çrib, *v.t.*; cribbed, *pt., pp.*; cribbing, *ppr.* 1. to enclose, as in a crib; to confine; as, *cribbed* in a narrow space.
2. to put away (produce) in a crib; as, to *crib* fifty bushels of corn.
3. to steal. [Colloq.]
4. to pass off (another's ideas or writings) as one's own; to plagiarize. [Colloq.]
5. to furnish with a crib or cribs.

çrib, *v.i.* 1. to be confined.
2. to do schoolwork dishonestly by using a crib. [Colloq.]
3. to do crib biting, as a horse.

çrib'bāġe, *n.* a game of cards in which the dealer counts the cards of his hand, those of the crib, and a turned card, toward his score. It is played by two, three, or four players: the object is to form various combinations that count for points: the score is kept on a small board with rows of holes into which pegs are inserted.

çrib'bāġe bōard, a board having holes supporting pegs with which to score at cribbage.

çrib'bẽr, *n.* 1. one who cribs.
2. a horse characterized by crib biting.

çrib'bing, *n.* 1. crib biting.
2. a plank lining, as of a well or shaft, keeping the dirt from caving, etc.
3. something cribbed.
4. the action of one that cribs.

çrib'-bīte, *v.t.*; crib-bit, *pt.* crib-bitten *or* crib-bit, *pp.*; crib-biting, *ppr.* to practice crib biting, as some horses.

çrib bīt'ing, a habit of horses in which they bite on the feeding trough or some other object, simultaneously swallowing air.

çrib'ble, *n.* [ME. *cribil*; Fr. *crible*, a sieve; LL. *cribellum*, dim. of L. *cribrum*, a sieve.]
1. a sieve or screen.
2. coarse flour or meal.

çrib'ble, *v.t.*; cribbled, *pt., pp.*; cribbling, *ppr.* to sift; to cause to pass through a sieve.

çrib death, same as *sudden infant death syndrome*.

çri·bel'lum, *n.*; *pl.* **çri·bel'lȧ**, [LL. *cribellum*, dim. of *cribrum*, a sieve.] a sievelike spinning organ accessory to the spinneret of certain spiders of the family *Ciniflonidæ*.

çri·brā'tion, *n.* [from L. *cribrare*, to sift; *cribrum*, a sieve.] in pharmacy, separation by sifting. [Obs.]

çrib'ri·fọrm, *a.* having holes like those of a sieve; perforated like a sieve.

çrib'rōse, *a.* cribriform.

çrib'wŏrk, *n.* the framework of a crib, consisting of layers of beams, logs, etc. built up one above another, each layer having its beams or logs at right angles to those of the layer immediately below.

çriç, *n.* [Fr. *cric*, a jackscrew.] a device for regulating the flame of a lamp having a circular wick.

çrick, *n.* a creek. [Obs.]

çrick, *n.* [ME. *cricke, crykke*, a crick in the neck, a twist or bend.] a painful muscular cramp or spasm of some part of the body, as of the neck or back, making it difficult to move the part affected.

çrick, *v.t.* to cause a crick, or muscle spasm, in.

çrick'et, *n.* [ME. *creket, crykette*; OFr. *crequet*; Pr. *cricot*, a cricket; M.D. *krieck-er*, a cricket, a creaker. Imitative of the sharp sound.] any of a large group of leaping insects of the genus *Gryllus*, belonging to the order *Orthoptera*: they are related to the locusts and grasshoppers but usually having long antennae: the males produce a characteristic chirping noise by rubbing parts of the forewings together.

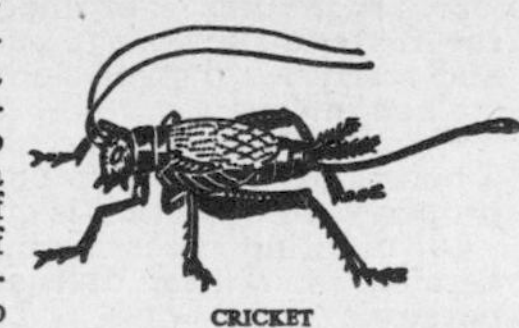
CRICKET

çrick'et, *n.* [prob. from OFr. *criquet*, a stick used in a game.]
1. an outdoor game played by two teams of eleven men each, in which a ball, bats, and wickets are used: it is one of the most popular sports in England.
2. fair play; sportsmanship. [Colloq.]

çrick'et, *v.i.* to play cricket.

çrick'et, *n.* [AS. *cricc, crycc*, a crooked staff, crutch, used in the sense of a stool or wicket.] a wooden footstool.

çrick'et bĩrd, the grasshopper warbler, *Sylvia locustella*: so called from its note resembling that of a cricket.

çrick'et·ẽr, *n.* one who plays cricket.

çrick'et frog, *Acris gryllus*, or any similar chirping tree frog.

çrī'çō-, a combining form, from Greek *krikos*, a ring, circle, and used in anatomy and medicine to indicate relation to the cricoid cartilage; as, *crico*thyroid.

çrī'çoid, *a.* [Gr. *krikos*, a ring, and *eidos*, form.] designating or of the round ringlike cartilage forming the lower part of the larynx.

çrī·çō·thy'roid, *a.* [*crico-*, and Gr. *thyreoeidēs*, shield-shaped; *thyreos*, a large shield, and *eidos*, form.] relating to or connected with both the cricoid and thyroid cartilages.

çrīed, *v.* past tense and past participle of *cry*.

çrī'ẽr, *n.* [ME. *cryour, cryar*; OFr. *crieor*, a crier, from *crier*, to cry.]
1. one who cries.
2. a person who shouts out announcements of news, court orders, etc.; as, town *criers* were formerly common in New England.
3. a person who shouts out announcements about his wares.
town crier; formerly, one who cried public announcements through the streets of a city or town.

çrīme, *n.* [OFr. *crime*; L. *crimen*, an accusation, fault, crime, from *cernere*; Gr. *krinein*, to decide, judge.]
1. an act committed in violation of a law prohibiting it, or omitted in violation of a law ordering it: crimes are variously punishable by death, imprisonment, or the imposition of certain fines or restrictions.
2. extreme violation of the law; wrongdoing of a criminal nature, as felony or treason, which affects the whole public and not just the rights of an individual: distinguished from *misdemeanor*.
3. an offense against morality; sin.
4. the acts of criminals; habitual violation of the law.

Çrī·mē'ăn, *a.* of the Crimea.

Çrī·mē'ăn Wär, a war (1854–1856) over the domination of southeastern Europe, in which England, France, Turkey, and Sardinia defeated Russia.

çrīme'fụl, *a.* criminal. [Obs.]

çrīme'less, *a.* free from crime; innocent.

çrim'i·năl, *a.* [LL. *criminalis*, from *crimen*, a crime, fault.]
1. guilty of a crime.
2. having the nature of a crime; that violates a law of morality or well-doing; as, theft is a *criminal* act.
Ornaments only indications of vice, not *criminal* in themselves. —Addison.
3. involving or relating to crime; as, a *criminal* code, *criminal* law.
criminal conversation; adultery.

çrim'i·năl, *n.* 1. one who has committed a crime.
2. one who has been legally convicted of crime.
Syn.—culprit, malefactor, evildoer, transgressor, felon, convict.

çrim'i·năl·ist, *n.* an authority in criminal law.

çrim·i·nal'i·ty, *n.* [LL. *criminalitas*, from *criminalis*, pertaining to crime; *crimen*, a crime.]
1. the quality, state, or fact of being criminal, or of being guilty of crime.
This is by no means the only criterion of *criminality*. —Blackstone.
2. *pl.* **çrim·i·nal'i·tieş,** a criminal action.

çrim'i·năl·ly, *adv.* 1. in a criminal manner.
2. according to criminal law.

çrim'i·năl·ness, *n.* criminality. [Rare.]

çrim'i·năl·oid, *a.* [L. *criminalis*, pertaining to crime, and Gr. *eidos*, form.] having a tendency to crime.

çrim'i·năl·oid, *n.* one having a tendency to criminality.

çrim'i·nāte, *v.t.*; criminated, *pt., pp.*; criminating, *ppr.* [L. *criminatus*, pp. of *criminari*, to accuse of a crime; *crimen*, a crime.]
1. to accuse of or charge with a crime or crimes.
2. to incriminate; to give proof of the guilt of.
Our municipal laws do not require the offender to plead guilty or *criminate* himself. —Scott.
3. to condemn; to censure.

çrim·i·nā'tion, *n.* [L. *criminatio*, from *criminari*, to accuse of a crime; *crimen*, a crime.] the act of accusing; accusation.

çrim'i·nȧ·tive, *a.* accusing of crime; criminatory.

çrim'i·nȧ·tō·ry, *a.* of or concerned with crimination or accusation; criminative.

çrim·i·nō·loġ'i·căl, *a.* of criminology.

çrim·i·nō·loġ'i·căl·ly, *adv.* by or according to criminology.

çrim·i·nol'ō·ġist, *n.* an expert in criminology.

çrim·i·nol'ō·ġy, *n.* [L. *crimen*, a crime, and Gr. *-logia*, from *legein*, to speak.] the scientific study and investigation of crime and criminals.

çrim'i·nous, *a.* criminal.

çrim'i·nous·ly, *adv.* criminally.

çrim'i·nous·ness, *n.* criminality.

çrim'mẽr, *n.* krimmer, a kind of fur.

çrim'o·şin, *a.* and *n.* crimson. [Obs.]

çrimp, *v.t.*; crimped, *pt., pp.*; crimping, *ppr.* [D. *krimpen*; Dan. *krympe*, to shrink; W. *crimpiaw*, to pinch, crimp, from *crimp*, a sharp edge.]
1. to form into waves or curls; as, to *crimp* the hair.
2. to press into narrow, regular folds; to pleat.
3. to close or indent (a cartridge case); to crease.
4. to shape, as leather for shoe uppers.
5. in cookery, to gash, as the flesh of a fish, so as to make the muscles contract and stay firm in cooking.

çrimp, *n.* 1. a crimping.
2. that which is crimped; as, a dress all ruffles and *crimps*.
3. [*usually pl.*] crimped hair.
4. a game at cards. [Obs.]
to put a crimp in; to obstruct; hinder. [Slang.]

çrimp, *a.* 1. easily crumbled; friable; brittle.
2. not consistent. [Rare.]

çrimp, *n.* [from *crimp* (to pleat); prob. via 17th-c. game of cards.] a person who gets men to serve as sailors or soldiers by force or trickery.

çrimp, *v.t.* to get (men) to serve as sailors or soldiers by force or trickery.

çrimp'ẽr, *n.* one who or that which crimps; also, a crimping machine.

çrimp'ing house, a house where men are crimped into service as sailors or soldiers.

çrimp'ing ī'ron (-ŭrn), a curling iron for the hair; also, an appliance for fluting or waving cloth.

çrimp'ing mȧ·çhïne, one of various machines used in corrugating, fluting, crimping, etc.

çrimp'ing pin, a kind of hairpin used to wave the hair.

çrim'ple, *v.t.* and *v.i.*; crimpled, *pt., pp.*; crimpling, *ppr.* [dim. of *crimp*.] to wrinkle; to crinkle; to crumple.

çrimp'y, *a.*; *comp.* crimpier; *superl.* crimpiest, having a frizzled or crimped appearance; curly; wavy.

çrim'şŏn, *n.* [ME. *crimosin, cramosin*; OFr. *cramoisyne*; LL. *carmesinus*; from Ar. *qermez*, crimson; from Sans. *krmija*, produced by a worm; *krmi*, a worm, insect, and *jan*, to produce.] deep red; also, deep-red coloring matter.

çrim'şŏn, *a.* 1. deep-red; as, the *crimson* blush of modesty.
2. bloody.

çrim'şŏn, *v.t.* and *v.i.*; crimsoned, *pt., pp.*; crimsoning, *ppr.* to make or become crimson.

çrim'şŏn çlō'vẽr, a plant of the pea family, with dark-red flower heads: used in scientific farming to enrich the soil for crop rotation.

çrim'şŏn ram'blẽr, a small, climbing, bright-red rose.

çrī'năl, *a.* [L. *crinalis*, from *crinis*, hair.] of or pertaining to hair.

çrī'nȧ·ted, *a.* hairy.

çrī'nȧ·tō·ry, *a.* same as *crinitory*.

çriñ'çum, *n.* a turn or bend; a whimsy. [Colloq.]

çrīned, *a.* [Fr. *crin*; L. *crinis*, a hair.] in heraldry, having hair.

çrī'nel, *n.* same as *crinet*.

çrī'net, *n.* [dim. of Fr. *crin*; L. *crinis*, a hair.] a small, thin feather.

çrinġe, *v.t.* [AS. *cringan, crincan*, to yield, fall.] to contract; to draw together. [Obs.]

çrinġe, *v.i.* 1. to draw back, bend, crouch, etc., as when afraid; to shrink from something dangerous or painful; to cower.
2. to act in a timid, servile manner; to fawn.
Flatterers are always bowing and *cringing*. —Arbuthnot.
Syn.—crouch, fawn, flatter, grovel, truckle.

çrinġe, *n.* a cringing.

çrinġe'ling, *n.* one who cringes.

çrin'ġẽr, *n.* one who cringes.

çrin'ġing·ly, *adv.* in a cringing manner.

çriñ'gle, *n.* [L.G. *kringel*; Ice. *kringla*, a disk, orb, circle.]
1. a withe for fastening a gate. [Brit.]
2. a small ring or loop of rope or metal on the edge of a sail, through which a rope may be run for fastening the sail.

CRINGLE

çrin·i·çul'tūr·ăl, *a.* [L. *crinis*, hair, and *cultura*, culture.] relating to the growth of hair.

çri·niġ'ẽr·ous, *a.* [L. *criniger*, from *crinis*, hair, and *gerere*, to bear.] covered with hair; hairy.

çrī'nīte, *a.* [L. *crinitus*, haired, pp. of *crinire*, to cover with hair; *crinis*, hair.]
1. hairy.
2. having a hairy or hairlike tail.
3. in biology, bearded with long hairs, or having tufts of long hairs on the surface.

çrī'nīte, *n.* [crinoid, and *-ite*.] a fossil crinoid.

çrī'ni·tō·ry, *a.* made of or pertaining to hair.

çriñ'kle, *v.t.* and *v.i.*; crinkled, *pt., pp.*; crinkling, *ppr.* [ME. *crenklen*, to bend, turn; D. *krinkelen*, to turn, wind.]
1. to be or cause to be undulated; to wrinkle; to ripple.
2. to rustle, as paper when crushed.

çriñ'kle, *n.* a wrinkle; a ripple; an undulation.

çriñ'kle·rọot, *n.* *Dentaria diphylla*, an American variety of toothwort, with small, white or lilac-colored flowers and a white, tuberous, strong-smelling rootstock.

çriñ'kly, *a.*; *comp.* crinklier; *superl.* crinkliest, full of crinkles; wrinkled; ripply; wavy.

çriñ'kum-çrañ'kum, *n.* 1. anything full of twists and turns, as an elaborate ornamentation. [Colloq.]
2. a whimsy. [Colloq.]

çrī'noid, *n.* a member of the *Crinoidea*: also called *sea lily*.

çrī'noid, *a.* 1. lily-shaped.
2. designating or of the *Crinoidea*.

çrī·noi'dăl, *a.* of or pertaining to the *Crinoidea*.

Çri·noid'ē·ȧ, *n.pl.* [L., from Gr. *krinoeidēs*; *krinon*, a lily, and *eidos*, form.] a large group of small marine animals of the phylum *Echinodermata*: they are somewhat flowerlike in form and generally anchored by a stalk opposite the mouth.

çri·noid'ē·ăn, *n.* a crinoid.

çrin'ō·line, *n.* [Fr. *crinoline*, haircloth, crinoline; L. *crinis*, hair, and *linum*, flax.]
1. a stiff cloth of cotton or silk, originally of horsehair and linen, used as a lining for stiffening garments.
2. a petticoat of crinoline worn under a skirt to make it bulge out widely from the waist; also, a hoop skirt.

çrī'nōse, *a.* hairy.

çrī·nos'i·ty, *n.* hairiness.

Çrī'num, *n.* [L., from Gr. *krinon*, a lily.] a genus of bulbous tropical plants, of the amaryllis family, with thick, straplike leaves and large, tubular flowers of white, pink, or red; also, [c—] any plant of this genus.

çrī'ō·sphiñx, *n.* [Gr. *krios*, a ram, and *sphinx*, a sphinx.] one of the three varieties of the Egyptian sphinx, having the head of a ram, as distinguished from the *androsphinx*, with the head of a human being, and *hieracosphinx* or hawk-headed sphinx.

CRIOSPHINX

çrip′ple, *n.* [ME. *cripel*, *crypel*; L.G. *kropel*; D. *kroppel*; O.H.G. *kruppel*; Ice. *kryppill*, from AS. *creopan*, to creep.]
1. a person or animal that is lame or otherwise disabled as a result of injury, disease, or a condition existing from birth.
2. a bog; also, a shallow. [Dial.]

çrip′ple, *a.* lame. [Rare.]

çrip′ple, *v.t.*; crippled, *pt.*, *pp.*; crippling, *ppr.* 1. to lame; to make a cripple of.
2. to disable, damage, or impair.
Embarrassments *crippling* the energy of the settlement in the Bay. —Palfrey.

çrip′ple·ness, *n.* lameness.

çrip′plẽr, *n.* same as *graining board*.

çrip′pling, *n.* one of a number of spars or timbers set up as supports against the side of a building.

çrip′ply, *a.* crippled.

çris, *n.* same as *creese*.

Çri·sey′de, *n.* Cressida: so spelled by Chaucer.

çrī′sis, *n.*; *pl.* **çrī′sēs,** [L. *crisis*; Gr. *krisis*, a separating, decision, from *krinein*, to decide, separate.]
1. a serious or decisive state of things, or the turning point when an affair must soon terminate or suffer a material change; a decisive or crucial time, stage, or event.
This hour's the very *crisis* of your fate. —Dryden.
2. in medicine, the turning point in the course of a disease, which indicates recovery or death.
3. a crucial situation; a situation whose outcome decides whether possible bad consequences will follow; as, an economic *crisis*.

çrisp, *a.*; *comp.* crisper; *superl.* crispest, [AS. *crisp*, *cirps*, from L. *crispus*, curled, crisp.]
1. curled; wavy; wrinkled; formed into stiff curls or ringlets.
2. brittle; easily broken or crumbled; as, *crisp* crackers.
3. lively; brisk; sharp or stimulating; as, *crisp* wine or *crisp* air.
4. fresh; not wilted; as, *crisp* vegetables.
5. sharp; pointed; witty; short or terse; as, a *crisp* literary style, a *crisp* answer.
6. in botany, curled: applied to a leaf when the border is so much more dilated than the disk that it necessarily becomes crinkled and twisted.

çrisp, *v.t.*; crisped, *pt.*, *pp.*; crisping, *ppr.* [ME. *crispen*; L. *crispare*, to curl, from *crispus*, curled, crisp.]
1. to curl; to twist; to contract or form into ringlets, as the hair; to wreathe or interweave, as the branches of trees.
2. to wrinkle or curl into little undulations; to ripple; to cause to be crinkled or wavy.
3. to make crisp; as, to *crisp* potatoes.

çrisp, *v.i.* 1. to form little curls or undulations; to curl.
The bubbling runnel *crispeth*. —Tennyson.
2. to snap lightly; to crackle.
3. to become crisp.

çris′pāte, çris′pā·ted, *a.* [L. *crispatus*, pp. of *crispare*, to curl, crisp; *crispus*, curled, crisp.] curled or wavy; crisped.

çris·pā′tion, *n.* 1. the act of curling, or state of being curled.
2. a slight involuntary contraction of the muscles or skin.
3. a minute undulation or quiver on the surface of a liquid caused by vibrations of the containing vessel.

çris′pȧ·tūre, *n.* a curling; also, the state of being curled.

çrisp′ẽr, *n.* one who or that which crisps; specifically, a crisping iron.

Çris′pin, *n.* a shoemaker: so called from Crispin, the patron saint of shoemakers.

çrisp′ing ī′ron (-ũrn), an instrument for curling hair or crimping cloth.

çrisp′ly, *adv.* in a crisp manner.

çrisp′ness, *n.* a state of being crisp, curled, or brittle.

çrisp′y, *a.*; *comp.* crispier; *superl.* crispiest,
1. curled; formed into ringlets; as, *crispy* locks.
2. brittle; easy to break; as, a *crispy* cake.
3. brisk; fresh; sharp; exhilarating; as, *crispy* air.

çris′sȧ, *n.*, pl. of *crissum*.

çris′săl, *a.* in ornithology, (a) of or pertaining to the crissum; (b) having a crissum that is bright-colored.

çriss′çross, *n.* [earlier *Christ-cross.*]
1. a mark made of two crossed lines (×), often used as a signature by people who cannot write their names.
2. a pattern made of crossed lines.
3. tick-tack-toe.

çriss′çross, *v.t.*; crisscrossed, *pt.*, *pp.*; crisscrossing, *ppr.* to mark or cover with intersecting or crisscross lines.

çriss′çross, *v.i.* to move crosswise.

çriss′çross, *adv.* 1. crosswise; in different or contrary directions.
2. inharmoniously; unpleasingly; contrarily; awry; as, things are going *crisscross.*

çriss′çross, *a.* crossing; crossed; marked by crossings.

çriss′çross rōw, same as *christcross row*.

çris′sum, *n.*; *pl.* **çris′sȧ,** [L., from *crissare*, to move the thighs.]
1. the area under the tail of a bird, around the cloacal opening.
2. the feathers covering this area.

çris′tȧ, *n.*; *pl.* **çris′tae,** [L., a crest, tuft on the head of animals.] in anatomy, a crest or ridge.
crista acustica; a ridge in the semicircular canals of the ear, on which the branches of the auditory nerve terminate.
crista galli; a projection of the mesethmoid to which the outer fibrous covering of the brain is attached.

çris′tāte, çris′tā·ted, *a.* [L. *cristatus*, from *crista*, a crest.]
1. in botany, crested; tufted; having an appendage like a crest or tuft, as some anthers and flowers.
2. in zoology, having a crest or crestlike process on some part, generally the head, as some birds.

çrī·tē′ri·ŏn, *n.*; *pl.* **çrī·tē′ri·ȧ,** [Gr. *kritērion*, a test, means of judging, from *kritēs*, a judge, from *krinein*, to judge.] a standard of judging; any established law, rule, principle, or fact by which a correct judgment may be formed: spelled also, rarely, *criterium*.
Syn.—rule, measure, test, standard.

çrī·tē′ri·ŏn·ăl, *a.* relating to or serving as a criterion.

çrith, *n.* [Gr. *krithē*, a barleycorn, a weight.] a name given to the weight of one liter of hydrogen at 0° C. and 760 millimeters' pressure, which is 0.0896 of a gram. This was formerly proposed as the unit of weight of gaseous chemical substances. [Rare.]

çrith′ō·man·cy, *n.* [Gr. *krithē*, barley, and *manteia*, divination.] a kind of divination by means of the dough of cakes, and the meal strewn over the victims, in ancient sacrifices.

çrit′iç, *n.* [L. *criticus*; Gr. *kritikos*, from *krites*, a judge, discerner, from *krinein*, to judge, to separate, to distinguish.]
1. one who compares, judges, or estimates any person or thing.
2. a person who forms and expresses judgments of the qualities and comparative worth of books, music, paintings, sculpture, plays, motion pictures, etc., especially one who writes such judgments professionally.
3. one who censures or finds fault; a caviler or carper.
4. the art of criticism. [Obs.]
5. a critical examination or review. [Obs.]
Syn.—judge, censor, connoisseur.

çrit′iç, *a.* critical; relating to criticism, or to a critic or critics. [Obs.]
Critic learning flourished most in France. —Pope.

çrit′iç, *v.i.* and *v.t.* to criticize. [Obs.]

çrit′i·căl, *a.* 1. relating to critics or criticism; based on or in accordance with the principles of criticism; as, a *critical* dissertation on Homer.
2. characterized by careful analysis; as, a sound *critical* estimate of the problem.
3. inclined to find fault; carping; criticizing harshly.
4. pertaining to a crisis; decisive; denoting a time or state on which the issue of things depends; as, a *critical* time or moment.
5. in medicine, of a crisis or change in a disease.
6. formed or situated to determine or decide; important or essential for determining; as, a *critical* post.
7. dangerous or risky; perilous; hazardous; as, a *critical* undertaking.
8. designating or of important products or raw materials subject to increased production and restricted distribution under strict control, as in wartime.
9. in mathematics and physics, designating a point, etc. at which a change in character, property, or condition is effected.
10. differing in or distinguished by slight details; as, *critical* divisions of a group in botany.
critical angle; (a) in optics, the smallest angle of incidence giving rise to total reflection of a ray of light; (b) in aeronautics, that angle of attack at which the flow of air around an airfoil suddenly changes, with similar changes in lift and drag.
critical constants; the critical temperature, pressure, density, and volume of a substance.
critical philosophy; the philosophy of Immanuel Kant.
critical point; (a) in mathematics, that point at which some two or more values of a function of a complex variable are equal; (b) the stage in temperature and pressure at which the liquid and vapor phases of a substance are indistinguishable from each other.
critical pressure; the vapor tension of a liquid at the critical temperature.
critical state; that condition of a substance in which the liquid state and the vapor state have equal density.
critical temperature; that temperature of a gas above which it cannot be liquefied by pressure alone, regardless of the amount applied.
Syn.—nice, discriminating, captious, faultfinding, decisive, important, momentous.

çrit′iç·ăl·ly, *adv.* in a critical manner.

çrit′iç·ăl·ness, *n.* the state of being critical.

çrit′iç·as·tẽr, *n.* [L. *criticus*, a critic, and dim. *-aster.*] an incompetent, inferior critic.

çrit′i·çīṣe, *v.t.* and *v.i.*; criticised, *pt.*, *pp.*; criticising, *ppr.* to criticize: British spelling.

çrit′i·çiṣm, *n.* 1. the act of making judgments; analysis of qualities and evaluation of comparative worth; especially, the definition and judgment of literary or artistic work.
2. a review, article, etc. expressing such analysis and judgment.
3. a finding fault; censuring; disapproval.
4. the art, principles, or methods of a critic or critics.
5. the scientific investigation of literary documents to discover their origin, history, or original form: usually called *textual criticism.*

çrit′i·cīz·ȧ·ble, *a.* subject to criticism.

çrit′i·cīze, *v.t.*; criticized, *pt.*, *pp.*; criticizing, *ppr.* 1. to make a critical estimate of; to utter or write a critical opinion on the merit of; as, to *criticize* the writings of Milton.
2. to point out the faults in; to judge adversely; to express disapproval of; to censure.

çrit′i·cīze, *v.i.* 1. to judge critically; to express criticisms.
2. to find fault; to express harsh and severe judgments.

çrit′i·cī·zẽr, *n.* a person who criticizes; a critic.

çri·tique′ (-tēk′), *n.* [Fr. *critique*, from Gr. *kritikos* (supply *technē*, art), critical, from *krinein*, to separate, judge.]
1. a critical analysis or examination of the merits of a work of art or literature; as, Addison's *critique* on "Paradise Lost."
2. the art of criticism; the judging of the merit of any work.
3. a critic. [Obs.]

çri·tique′, *v.t.* to criticize.

çrit′tẽr, çrit′tũr, *n.* a creature; specifically, (a) a domestic animal, especially a cow, steer, etc.; (b) a bear, wolf, etc.; (c) a human being: usually depreciatory or humorous. [Dial.]

çriz′zle, çriz′zel, *n.* a kind of roughness, as on the surface of glass or on the skin. [Brit. Dial.]

çriz′zle, *v.i.*; crizzled, *pt.*, *pp.*; crizzling, *ppr.* to become rough; to have the surface, as of glass or skin, wrinkled or drawn. [Brit. Dial.]

çrōak, *v.i.*; croaked, *pt.*, *pp.*; croaking, *ppr.* [ME. *crouken*; AS. *cracettan*, to croak; O.H.G. *chrockezan*, to croak; an imitative word.]
1. to make a low, hoarse noise in the throat, as a frog, crow, or the like.
2. to speak with a low, hollow voice; to cry dismally; to forebode evil; to complain; to grumble.
3. to die. [Slang.]

çrōak, *v.t.* 1. to utter hoarsely.
2. to kill. [Slang.]

çrōak, *n.* the low, harsh sound uttered by a frog or a raven, or a like sound.

çrōak'ẽr, *n.* 1. one who croaks, murmurs, or grumbles; one who complains unreasonably.
 2. any bird or animal that makes a croaking sound.
 3. any of several fishes of the family *Sciænidæ*, as the drum, the queenfish, etc.: from the croaking or grunting sound they make.

çrōak'y, *a.*; *comp.* croakier; *superl.* croakiest; croaking or inclined to croak.

Çrō'at, *n.* 1. a native or inhabitant of Croatia.
 2. the Slavic language of the Croats.
 3. formerly, a member of a somewhat irregular cavalry force made up in large part of Croats and serving in the Austrian army.

Çrō·ā'tiăn (-shăn), *a.* relating to Croatia, its people, language, or culture.

Çrō·ā'tiăn, *n.* 1. a Croat.
 2. the South Slavic language of the Croats.

çrō'cē·in, *n.* [from L. *croceus*, saffron-colored, and *-in*.] a red azo dye.

çrō'cē·ine, *n.* same as *crocein.*

çrō'ce·tin, *n.* [L. *crocus*, saffron.] a brilliant yellow dye made from crocin.

çrōçhe, *n.* crotch. [Obs.]

çrō·çhet' (-shā'), *n.* [Fr., dim. of *croc*, a hook.] a kind of knitting in which thread is looped and interwoven by means of one hooked needle, the stitches used being generally more elaborate than the regular knitting stitch.

çrō·çhet' (-shā'), *v.t.* and *v.i.*; crocheted, *pt.*, *pp.*; crocheting, *ppr.* to knit with one hooked needle.

çrō·çhet' nee'dle (-shā'), a hooked needle used in crocheting.

çrō·cid'ō·līte, *n.* [Gr. *krokis*, *krokidos*, the nap on cloth, and *lithos*, stone.] a bluish-green silicate of iron and sodium, occurring in asbestoslike fibers: also called *blue asbestos.*

çrō'cin, *n.* [Gr. *krokos*, saffron.] a red or reddish-yellow coloring matter obtained from the pods of the *Gardenia grandiflora* of China, and from saffron, *Crocus sativus.*

çrock, *n.* an old sheep. [Scot.]

çrock, *n.* [ME. *crocke*, *crokk*; AS. *crocca*; Ice. *krukka*; Sw. *kruka*; Dan. *krukke*, a crock.]
 1. an earthenware pot or jar.
 2. a broken piece of crockery.
 3. something said or done that is absurd, insincere, exaggerated, etc.; nonsense.

çrock, *n.* [ON. *kraki*, a weak, crippled person, originally, a bent object.]
 1. an old broken-down horse.
 2. anyone or anything worthless, useless, or worn-out, as from old age. [Slang.]
 3. a medical patient who complains chronically of his minor or imaginary illnesses. [Slang.]

çrock, *n.* soot, the black matter collected from combustion, as on pots and kettles, or in a chimney; also, stain or discoloration, as from the coloring in dyed fabrics. [Dial.]

çrock, *v.t.*; crocked (krokt), *pt.*, *pp.*; crocking, *ppr.* to soil with soot or smut; to soil or stain with the coloring matter of cloth. [Dial.]

çrock, *v.i.* to give off crock, stain, or smut.

çrock'ẽr, *n.* a maker of crockery. [Obs.]

çrock'ẽr·y, *n.* earthenware; pots, jars, dishes, etc. made of baked clay.

çrock'et, *n.* [ME. *croket*, a roll, or lock of hair; OFr. *croquet*, *crochet*, dim. of *croc*, a hook.]
 1. in architecture, an ornament placed at the angles of pediments, canopies, pinnacles, etc., resembling buds of trees or bunches of foliage.
 2. one of the terminal snags on a stag's horn.
 3. a woman's coiffure. [Obs.]

çrock'et·ed, *a.* in architecture, furnished or ornamented with crockets.

PINNACLE DECORATED WITH CROCKETS

çrock'et·ing, *n.* embellishment with crockets.

çrock'y, *a.* smutty; sooty.

çroç'ō·dīle, *n.* [L. *crocodilus*; Gr. *krokodeilos*, a kind of lizard, a crocodile.]
 1. a genus of large, lizardlike amphibious reptiles, the type of the family *Crocodilidæ*, comprising the largest living forms of reptiles. Crocodiles have a thick, horny skin composed of scales and plates, a long tail, and a long, narrow, triangular head with massive jaws and cone-shaped teeth. They are oviparous, depositing eggs in the sand. *Crocodilus niloticus* or *vulgaris* is the species frequenting the Nile; *Crocodilus acutus* is found in Florida, the gavial is termed the Ganges *crocodile.*

CROCODILE (*Crocodilus niloticus* or *vulgaris*)

 2. loosely, any crocodilian.
 3. in logic, a captious and sophistical argument contrived to draw one into a snare.

çroç'ō·dīle bīrd, *Pluvianus ægyptius*, a small African bird like the plover, which feeds on the insect parasites of the crocodile.

çroç'ō·dīle tēarṣ, insincere tears or a hypocritical show of grief: from an old belief that crocodiles shed tears while eating their prey.

Çroç·ō·dil'i·ȧ, *n.pl.* [L., from *crocodilus*; Gr. *krokodeilos*, a lizard, crocodile.] an order of saurian reptiles, found in the Old and New Worlds, including the crocodiles, gavials, alligators, and like animals now extinct.

çroç·ō·dil'i·ăn, *a.* 1. of or like a crocodile.
 2. of a group of reptiles including the crocodile, alligator, cayman, and gavial.

çroç·ō·dil'i·ăn, *n.* any reptile of the crocodilian group.

Çroç·ō·dil'i·dae, *n.pl.* the family typical of *Crocodilia.*

çroç·ō·dil'i·ty, *n.* in logic, a false or captious mode of arguing.

çrō·çō'i·sīte, *n.* same as *crocoite.*

çrō'çō·īte, *n.* [Gr. *krokoeis*, of a saffron color, from *krokos*, saffron.] native chromate of lead, $PbCrO_4$, a red or orange mineral.

çrō'çōn·āte, *n.* a salt of croconic acid.

çrō·çon'iç, *a.* [L. *crocus*; Gr. *krokos*, saffron.] of, pertaining to, or designating croconic acid.
 croconic acid; a yellow crystalline substance, $C_6H_2O_6$, strongly acid and of a yellow color.

çrō'çus, *n.*; *pl.* **çrō'çus·eṣ, çrō'cī,** [L. *crocus*; Gr. *krokos*, saffron, also the crocus, from its color.]
 1. [C-] a genus of iridaceous herbaceous plants with a bulblike stem, grasslike leaves, and a yellow, purple, or white flower: it is among the earliest flowers to bloom in the spring. *Crocus sativus* is common saffron.
 2. any plant of this genus.
 3. an orange-yellow color; saffron.
 4. powdered iron oxide used for polishing.

Çroē'sus, *n.* a very rich man: so called after *Croesus*, a fabulously rich Lydian king of the sixth century B. C.

çroft, *v.t.*; crofted, *pt.*, *pp.*; crofting, *ppr.* to subject (linen) to the sun's rays after treatment with an alkaline dye.

çroft, *n.* [AS. *croft*, a small enclosed field; D. *kroft*, a hillock; Gael. *croit*, a hump, hillock.]
 1. a small enclosed field. [Brit.]
 2. a small farm, especially one worked by a renter. [Brit.]

çroft'ẽr, *n.* one who rents a croft and works it; a peasant farmer. [Brit.]

çrois, *n.* a cross. [Obs.]

çroiṣe, *v.t.* [Fr. *croisé*, a crusader.] to make the sign of the cross over. [Obs.]

çrois·sänt' (krŏ-sänt'), *n.* [Fr. *croissant*, a crescent.] a rich, flaky bread roll made in the shape of a crescent.

çroix de guerre (krwä″ dē gār'), [Fr., cross of war.] a French military decoration awarded for bravery in action.

çrō'ki·nōle, *n.* a parlor game played with small wooden disks on a table; squails.

Çrō-Ma'gnon (-mag'non; Fr. krō″mȧ″nyōn'), *a.* [after the *Cro-Magnon* cave near Dordogne, France, where remains were discovered.] belonging to a prehistoric race of men who lived on the European continent, distinguished by their height and erect stature, and their use of stone and bone implements.

Çrō-Ma'gnon, *n.* a member of the Cro-Magnon race.

çrom'leçh, *n.* [W. *cromlec*; *crom*, bent, bowed, and *llec*, a flat stone.]
 1. a prehistoric tomb or monument consisting of a large, flat stone laid across upright stones; dolmen.
 2. an ancient monument of monoliths, arranged in a circle and surrounding a mound.

CROMLECH

çrō·mor'nȧ, *n.* [Fr. *cromorne*; G. *krummhorn*, a crooked horn, cornet; *krumm*, crooked, and *horn*, horn.] a reed stop of an organ, similar in tone to a clarinet: sometimes written *cremona.*

çrōne, *n.* [Ir. *criona*, old; *crion*, dry, withered; *crionaim*, to wither, fade, decay; W. *crina*, to wither.]
 1. an old ewe.
 2. a withered old woman.

çrō'nel, *n.* coronal. [Obs.]

Çrō'ni·ăn, *a.* [L. *Cronius*, neut. *Cronium* (supply *mare*, sea); Gr. *Kronios ōkeanos*, northern or Saturnian sea.] denoting the Arctic Ocean. [Rare.]

çron'stedt·īte (-stet-), *n.* [named after A. F. *Cronstedt*, a Swedish mineralogist.] a brilliantly vitreous mineral, found crystalline in hexagonal prisms: it is a hydrous silicate of iron.

çrō'ny, *n.*; *pl.* **çrō'nieṣ,** 1. a crone. [Obs.]
 2. an intimate companion; a familiar friend.

çrō'ny·iṣm, *n.* favoritism shown to close friends, especially in political appointments to office.

çroo'dle, *v.i.* to coo. [Scot.]

çrook, *n.* [ME. *crok*; Ice. *krokr*, a hook, bend; D. *kroke*, a hook; Sw. *kroka*; Gael. *crocan*, a crook, hook.]
 1. any bend, turn, or curve; as, a *crook* in a stick of timber, or in a river.
 2. a curving or crooked part; a turn; as, a cane with a large *crook.*
 3. something having a turn or curve; as, (a) a shepherd's staff, curving at the end; (b) the pastoral staff of a bishop or abbot; (c) in Scotland, a pothook; (d) an accessory tube inserted in a wind instrument, as a cornet, to change its key.
 4. a genuflection.
 5. a gibbet or gibbetlike object. [Obs.]
 6. an artifice; a trick.
 7. a thief; a swindler; a rogue. [Colloq.]
 by hook or crook; by some means; if not one way, then by another.

çrook, *v.t.*; crooked (krookt), *pt.*, *pp.*; crooking, *ppr.* 1. to bend; to turn from a straight line; to make a curve or hook in.
 2. to turn from rectitude; to pervert.

çrook, *v.i.* to bend or be bent; to be turned from a right line; to curve; to wind.

çrook'back, *n.* a hunchback. [Rare.]

çrook'backed (-bakt), *a.* hunchbacked.

çrook'bill, *n.* *Anarhynchus frontalis*, a plover of New Zealand, having a bent bill.

çrook'ed, *a.* 1. having a crook; not straight; bent; curving; winding.
 2. tricky as regards conduct; not to be trusted; dishonest; swindling.
 3. made illegally; illicit; as, *crooked* liquor. [Colloq.]
 Syn.—curved, curving, winding, bowed, awry, oblique, wry, deformed, perverse, deceitful.

çrook'ed·ly, *adv.* in a crooked manner.

çrook'ed·ness, *n.* the state or quality of being crooked.

çrook'en, *v.t.* to make crooked. [Obs.]

Çrookes lay'ẽr, [after Sir William *Crookes* (1832–1919), Eng. chemist and physicist.] a layer or stratum in the residual atmosphere of a vacuous space, in which the molecules recoiling from a heated or electrified surface do not meet other molecules, but impinge on the enclosing walls.

Çrookes spāce, the dark space that appears around the cathode of a vacuum tube when the pressure is low.

Çrookes tūbe, a vacuum tube in which gases are rarefied to a high degree: used by Sir William Crookes in the study of electrical discharge in a gas at low pressure.

çrook'neck, *n.* either of two varieties of squash with a long, tapering, curved neck.

çroon, *v.i.* and *v.t.* crooned, *pt.*, *pp.*; crooning, *ppr.* [ME. (northern dial.), from M.L.G.]
 1. to sing or hum in a low, gentle tone.
 2. to sing (popular songs) in a soft, sentimental manner.

çroon, *n.* a low, gentle singing, humming, or murmuring.

çroon'ẽr, *n.* one who croons; especially, a man

who sings popular songs in a soft, sentimental manner.

çrop, *n.* [AS. *crop, croppe,* craw, top, or head of a plant; D. *krop,* an excrescence, the gullet, craw.]

1. a saclike enlargement of a bird's gullet, with thick muscular walls in which food is softened for digestion; craw.

2. any agricultural product, growing or harvested, as wheat, cotton, fruit, etc.

3. the yield of any product in one season or place.

4. a group or collection appearing together; as, a new *crop* of students, a *crop* of suggestions.

5. the entire tanned hide of an animal.

6. the handle or butt of a whip.

7. a whip with a looped lash and a short stock, used in horseback riding.

8. the act or result of cropping; especially, (a) hair cut close to the head; (b) this style of haircut; (c) an earmark made by clipping.

9. the top or end of a thing. [Obs.]

10. in mining, an outcropping lode.

11. in architecture, an apex ornament. [Obs.]

çrop, *v.t.*; cropped (kropt) *or occas.* cropt, *pt., pp.*; cropping, *ppr.* 1. to cut off the ends of (anything); to eat off; to pull off; to pluck; to mow; to reap; as, to *crop* flowers, trees, or grass.

2. to cut off prematurely.

3. to cause to bear a crop; as, to *crop* a field.

4. to cut (hair, etc.) short.

çrop, *v.i.* 1. to bear a crop or crops.

2. to plant or grow a crop.

to crop out (or *up*); (a) to appear unexpectedly; (b) to appear at the surface.

çrop'-ēar, *n.* one having cropped ears.

çrop'-ēared, *a.* 1. having the ears cropped.

2. having the hair cut short, so that the ears show.

çrop'ful, *a.* having a full crop or belly; satiated.

çrop'pēr, *n.* a pigeon, the pouter.

çrop'pēr, *n.* 1. a person or thing that crops.

2. a machine for cutting or shearing.

3. a person whose work is shearing the nap from cloth.

4. a farmer who works another's land and receives a share of the crop as wages; a sharecropper.

5. a heavy or headlong fall. [Colloq.]

6. a failure; a disastrous occurrence. [Colloq.]

to come a cropper; (a) to fall heavily or headlong; (b) to come to ruin; fail. [Colloq.]

çrop'pie, *n.*; *pl.* **çrop'pieṣ** *or* **çrop'pie,** a fish, the crappie.

çrop'ple-çrown, *n.* a copple crown.

çrop rō·tā'tion, a system of growing successive crops that have different food requirements, to prevent soil depletion, break up a disease cycle, etc.

çrop'sick, *a.* sick from repletion. [Obs.]

çrop'sick″ness, *n.* sickness from repletion. [Obs.]

çropt, occasional past tense and past participle of *crop*.

çrop'weed, *n.* a plant, the knapweed.

çrō·quet' (-kā'), *n.* [Fr., from *croquer,* to crack; Walloon, *croque,* a blow, fillip.]

1. an outdoor game played with mallets, balls, posts, and a series of hoops on a prepared lawn, the object of the game being the driving of a ball through the hoops subject to certain rules.

2. the act of croqueting.

çrō·quet', *v.t.*; croqueted (-kād'), *pt., pp.*; croqueting, *ppr.* in croquet, to drive away (an opponent's ball) by hitting one's own which has been placed in contact with it.

çrō·quette' (-ket'), *n.* [Fr., from *croquet,* a crisp cake, from *croquer,* to crunch.] a small, rounded or cone-shaped mass of chopped meat, fish, or vegetables, fried in deep fat until browned.

çrō'qui·gnōle (-ki-nōl *or* -kin-yōl), *n.* [Fr., fillip, from *croquer,* Norm. form of *crocher,* to hook up, crook, from *croc,* a hook.] a method of imparting a wave to the hair by winding strands of the hair around metal rods and applying heat by chemical or electrical means.

çrōre, *n.* [Hind. *kror, koti*; Sans. *koti,* ten millions.] in India, one hundred lacs, or ten millions (of rupees).

çrosh'ȧ·bell, *n.* a courtezan. [Obs.]

çrō'ṣiēr (-zhēr), *n.* [ME. *crocer, croyser*; OFr. *crocier, crossier,* bearer of a staff, from *croce, crosse,* bishop's staff.] the staff carried by or before a bishop or abbot as a symbol of his function as a pastor: also spelled *crozier.*

çrō'ṣiēred, *a.* having a crosier.

çrǫs'let, *n.* see *crosslet.*

çrǫss, *n.* [ME. *cros, crosse, crois*; OFr. *crois, croiz*; Pr. *cros, croitz*; L. *crux,* a cross.]

GREEK PRE-CHRISTIAN MALTESE

CROSS PATÉE LATIN CROSS FITCHEE

TYPES OF CROSS

1. a gibbet or ancient instrument of torture, generally made of two pieces of timber placed across each other, usually with an upright set in the ground and a horizontal crosspiece below the top of the upright. Upon this, criminals were in ancient times nailed or bound and left to die.

2. the emblem of the Christian religion; a symbol representing the cross on which Jesus died.

3. a mark of a cross instead of a signature, used by those unable to write.

4. a monument in the form of a cross, or surmounted by a cross, set up as a shrine, memorial, or landmark or to designate a market place.

5. formerly, in England, a coin stamped with the figure of a cross.

6. [C–] in theology, the sufferings of Christ by crucifixion; the atonement.

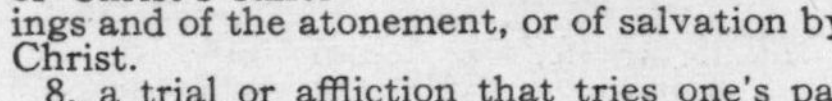
MONUMENTAL CROSS

7. the doctrine of Christ's sufferings and of the atonement, or of salvation by Christ.

8. a trial or affliction that tries one's patience or virtue.

9. anything that thwarts, obstructs, or perplexes; hindrance; vexation.

10. a crossing, or mixing, of varieties, breeds, or races; hybridization.

11. the result of such mixing; a hybrid.

12. [C–] in astronomy, (a) the Northern Cross; (b) the Southern Cross.

13. a casual electrical contact of two wires by which electricity passes from one to the other.

14. a representation or figure of a cross, given as a distinction, or worn as a token of membership in some order or society; as, the *cross* of the Legion of Honor; the Victoria *cross.*

15. any of various charges used in heraldry.

HERALDIC CROSS

16. a crucifix such as may be attached to a rosary or worn about the neck.

17. a contest decided dishonestly, as through one of the parties allowing himself to be beaten for the sake of gaining money by bribery. [Slang.]

18. anything in the form of a cross.

19. a crozier, or pastoral staff.

20. a pipe fitting having two arms at right angles to each other; a four-way joint.

cross and pile; the ancient English game of heads and tails.

surveyor's cross; an apparatus for determining perpendiculars to a given line.

the Cross; (a) the cross on which Jesus was put to death; (b) the suffering and death of Jesus; (c) Christianity or Christendom.

to take the cross; to become a crusader.

çrǫss, *v.t.* 1. to make the sign of the cross over or upon.

2. to place across or crosswise; as, *cross* your fingers.

3. to lie or cut across; intersect; as, Broadway *crosses* Seventh Avenue at Times Square.

4. to draw or put a line or lines across.

5. to pass over; go from one side to the other of; go across; as, he *crossed* the ocean.

6. to carry (troops, etc.) across.

7. to extend or reach across; as, the bridge *crosses* a river.

8. to meet (each other) in passing.

9. to thwart; oppose; go counter to; as, no one likes to be *crossed.*

10. to interbreed (animals or plants); hybridize; cross-fertilize.

to cross off (or *out*); to cancel by or as by drawing crosses over or lines across.

to cross oneself; to outline the form of a cross by moving the hand from the forehead to the breast and then from one shoulder to another: a religious gesture.

to cross one's fingers; to cross one finger over another of the same hand: superstitiously believed to bring good luck or mitigate the wrong of telling a half-truth.

to cross one's heart; to make the sign of the cross over one's heart as a token that one is telling the truth.

to cross one's mind; to suggest itself to one.

to cross one's palm; (a) to make a cross on one's hand with a coin, specifically in paying a fortune teller; (b) to pay one money, especially as a bribe.

to cross one's path; to meet one.

çrǫss, *v.i.* 1. to lie across; intersect.

2. to go or extend from one side to the other.

3. to meet in passing.

4. to interbreed; hybridize; cross-fertilize.

to cross over; to pass over from one chromosome to another that is homologous: said of chromatin material in a gene or factor.

çrǫss, *prep.* athwart; transversely; over; from side to side; across. [Dial. or Poet.]

And *cross* their limits cut a sloping way. —Dryden.

çrǫss, *a.* 1. transverse; oblique; intersecting; passing from side to side; crossing or crossed; lying or passing across.

2. adverse; thwarting; obstructing: sometimes with *to*; as, an event *cross to* our inclinations.

3. peevish; fretful; ill-humored; quick-tempered; as, a *cross* person; a *cross* answer.

4. contrary; opposed; counter.

5. involving reciprocation.

6. of mixed variety, breed, or race; hybrid; crossbred.

Syn.—counter, contrary, opposite, morose, sullen, peevish, petulant, perverse, ill-tempered, fractious, crusty, fretful, irritable.

çrǫss-, *cross* used as a combining form in forming words containing any of the various senses of the word, as *cross*bow, *cross*bred, *cross*breed.

çrǫss aç'tion, in law, an action brought against a plaintiff by a defendant, arising out of the same transaction as occasioned the first suit.

çrǫss aīsle (-īl), a transept. [Obs.]

çrǫss'-ärmed, *a.* 1. with arms across.

2. in botany, brachiate; decussate.

çrǫss ax'le (ak'sl), 1. a device like a windlass, operated by two levers, one at either end.

2. a driving axle in a steam engine turned by cranks placed at right angles to one another.

çrǫss'-band″ed, *a.* in architecture, having the grain of the wood in a veneer crossing that of the rail: applied to hand rails.

çrǫss'bär, *n.* a bar, line, or stripe placed crosswise, as a bar placed between goal posts on a football field.

çrǫss'bär, *v.t.* to furnish or mark with crossbars.

çrǫss'bär shot, a shot so constructed that when it left the gun it expanded into the form of a cross with the four quarters of the ball at its radial points. It was formerly used in naval battles because it was so highly destructive to a ship's rigging.

çrǫss'bēak, *n.* a bird, the crossbill.

çrǫss'bēam, *n.* a beam placed across another or from one wall to another; a transverse beam.

çrǫss'-beār″ēr, *n.* 1. a person who bears or wears a cross.

2. in a furnace, a support for grate bars.

çrǫss'bed·ded, *a.* in geology, having irregular laminations oblique to the main beds of stratified rock.

çrǫss bill, a bill in an equity suit in which the defendant alleges certain charges against the plaintiff as regards the subject matter of that suit.

çrǫss'bill, *n.* any passerine bird of the genus *Loxia* and family *Fringillidæ,* having the mandibles of the bill curving oppositely and crossing; the crossbeak. *Loxia curvirostra* is the common species.

çrǫss'bīrth, *n.* in obstetrics, any abnormal presentation of the fetus requiring manual turning in the uterus.

çrọss′bīte, *n.* a deception; a cheat. [Obs.]
çrọss′bīte, *v.t.* to deceive. [Obs.]
çrọss bitt, in nautical usage, a piece of timber bolted across two bitts.
çrọss bond, a bond in bricklaying consisting of headers and stretchers arranged as in the English bond, but having alternate stretcher courses breaking joints with each other.
çrọss′bōneṣ, *n.* a representation of two thighbones placed across each other, usually under that of a skull, used as a symbol of death or danger, as on a pirate flag or a bottle of poison.
çrọss′bōw, *n.* a medieval weapon consisting of a bow set transversely on a wooden stock: the stock is grooved to direct an arrow or stone and notched to hold the bowstring, which is drawn up by a small windlass and released by a trigger.

CROSSBOW

çrọss′bōw″ẽr, *n.* a crossbowman. [Obs.]
çrọss′bōw″măn, *n.*; *pl.* **çrọss′bōw″men,** a man armed with a crossbow.
çrọss′bred′, *a.* produced by the union of different varieties, breeds, or races.
çrọss′bred′, *n.* a crossbred plant or animal; hybrid; mongrel.
çrọss′breed′, *v.t.* and *v.i.* crossbred, *pt.*, *pp.*; crossbreeding, *ppr.* to hybridize; interbreed; cross.
çrọss′breed, *n.* an individual or breed produced by the crossing of different varieties or, more rarely, species; a hybrid.
çrọss bun, a hot cross bun.
çrọss′-but′tŏck, *n.* in wrestling, a method of throwing one's opponent over one's hip; hence, any unlooked-for discouragement or defeat.
çrọss′-çoun″try, *a.* not following the traveled roads, but pursuing a course across fields and over fences; as, a *cross-country* run.
çrọss′çut, *a.* 1. made or used for cutting across.
2. cut across.
çrọss′çut, *n.* 1. a cut across.
2. a crosscut saw.
3. a direct path oblique to the main path; a short cut.
4. in mining, a cutting made across a vein.
çrọss′çut, *v.t.* and *v.i.*; crosscut, *pt.*, *pp.*; crosscutting, *ppr.* to cut across.
çrọss′çut sąw, a saw for cutting wood across the grain.
çrọss′-dāyṣ, *n.pl.* Rogation days. [Obs.]
çrọsse, *n.* [Fr. *crosier*, a hockey stick.] the long-handled, pouched racket used in playing lacrosse: also called *lacrosse stick*.
çrọ·sette′, *n.* [Fr.] in architecture, any of the small, projecting pieces in arch stones, which hang upon the adjacent stones; also, the return on the corners of door cases or window frames: called also an *ear*, *elbow*, *ancon*.
çrọss′-ex·am·i·nā′tion, *n.* a cross-examining or being cross-examined.
çrọss′-ex·am′ine, *v.t.* and *v.i.*; cross-examined, *pt.*, *pp.*; cross-examining, *ppr.* 1. to question closely.
2. in law, to question (a witness already questioned by the opposing side) in order to determine the validity of previous statements.
çrọss′-ex·am′in·ẽr, *n.* one who cross-examines.
çrọss′-eȳe (-ī), *n.* an abnormal condition in which the eyes are turned toward each other; convergent strabismus.
çrọss′-eȳed (-īd), *a.* having cross-eye.
çrọss′-fẽr·ti·li·zā′tion, *n.* a cross-fertilizing or being cross-fertilized.
çrọss′-fẽr′ti·līze, *v.t.* and *v.i*; cross-fertilized, *pt.*, *pp.*; cross-fertilizing, *ppr.* 1. to fertilize or be fertilized by pollen from another flower.
2. to fertilize or be fertilized by a sperm (or male gamete) from another individual.
çrọss fīle, a file having two surfaces unequally convex.
çrọss fīre, in military usage, fire directed at a single objective from two or more positions so that the lines of fire cross at or near the objective.
çrọss′fish, *n.* a starfish.
çrọss fox, 1. a fox marked with a dark cross along the spine and shoulders.
2. the yellowish, black-marked fur of this fox.
çrọss frog, in railroading, a frog permitting the crossing of tracks.

çrọss′-gär″net, *n.* a T-shaped hinge.
çrọss′-grāined′, *a.* 1. having an irregular or transverse grain: said of wood.
2. untractable; perverse; cantankerous; contrary.
çrọss guärd, a defensive guard on a weapon, as at the hilt of a sword or head of a spear.
çrọss hāirs, crossed lines, as of fine hair or cobweb, mounted on the front lens of a telescopic gunsight, surveyor's level, etc. to assist in precise aiming or centering of the instrument.
çrọss′hatch, *v.t.* and *v.i.*; crosshatched (-hacht), *pt.*, *pp.*; crosshatching, *ppr.* to shade, as a drawing, by the use of crosshatching.
çrọss′hatch″ing, *n.* representation of light and shade, as in drawing, by means of parallel intersecting lines.
çrọss′head (-hed), *n.* 1. a bar across the end of a piston rod.
2. one of the headings inserted at intervals in a newspaper article, describing the part of the article that follows.
çrọss′ing, *n.* 1. the act of passing across, thwarting, interbreeding, etc.
2. an intersection, as of lines, streets, etc.
3. a place where a street, river, etc. may be crossed.
4. the place in a cruciform church where the transept crosses the nave.
çrọss′-in″tẽr·rog′ȧ·tō·ry, *n.*; *pl.* **çrọss′-in″tẽr·rog′ȧ·tō·rieṣ,** a question asked a witness by the party whose interest is opposed to the party taking the deposition.
çrọss′jack, *n.* a large square sail extended on the lower yard on the mizzenmast or crossjack yard.
çrọss lam·i·nā′tion, [*cross*, and *lamination*, from L. *lamina*, a plate, layer.] a deposit of strata out of parallel to the general dip, caused by the action of water during stratification: called also *cross bedding* and *false bedding*.
çrọss′-leg′ged, *a.* having one leg crossed over another, as in sitting, or having the ankles crossed and the knees apart.
çrọss′let, çrọs′let, *a.* [Anglo-Fr. *croiselette*, dim. of OFr. *crois*, a cross.] in heraldry, a small cross.
çrọss′let, çrọs′let, *n.* an alchemists' crucible. [Obs.]
çrọss′-liñk, *n.* a crosswise connecting part; specifically, an atom or group connecting parallel chains in a complex molecule.
çrọss′link, *v.t.* to join crosswise.
çrọss lōde, in mining, a less productive lode intersecting the true lode.
çrọs·sop·te·ryġ′i·ăn, *a.* pertaining to or having the characteristics of the *Crossopterygii*.
çrọs·sop·te·ryġ′i·ăn, *n.* an individual of the *Crossopterygii*: crossopterygians are extinct except for one species and are regarded as the ancestors of amphibians and land vertebrates in general.
Çrọs·sop·te·ryġ′i·ī, *n.pl.* [L., from Gr. *krossoi*, tassels, fringe, and *pterygion*, dim. of *pteryx*, a wing, fin.] a group of fishes, almost extinct, with the fin rays of the paired fins being arranged so as to form a fringe round a central lobe. They are represented among living forms by the genus *Polypterus*.
çrọss′ō·ver, *n.* 1. a connecting track by which a railroad train can be switched from one line to another.
2. in biology, (a) a crossing over: see phrase under *cross*, *v.i.*; (b) a character resulting from this.
çrọss′patch, *n.* an ill-natured person. [Colloq.]
çrọss′-pawl, *n.* see *cross-spale*.
çrọss′pīece, *n.* 1. a piece of anything placed crosswise on something else.
2. in nautical usage, a cross bitt.
3. the corpus callosum of the brain. [Rare.]
çrọss′-pol′li·nāte, *v.t.* and *v.i.* to subject or be subjected to cross-pollination.
çrọss′-pol·li·nā′tion, *n.* the transfer of pollen from the anther of one flower to the stigma of another, as by action of the wind or insects.
çrọss′-pũr′pŏse, *n.* 1. a purpose or aim at variance with another; an inconsistency.
2. [*pl.*] a game in which questions and answers having no connection are joined to make ridiculous combinations.
to be at cross-purposes; to misunderstand one another, and so to act in a contradictory manner without intending it.
çrọss′-ques′tiŏn (-kwes′chun), *v.t.*; cross-questioned, *pt.*, *pp.*; cross-questioning, *ppr.* to cross-examine.
çrọss′-ques′tiŏn, *n.* a question asked in cross-examination.

çrọss rēad′ing, the reading of the lines of a newspaper directly across the page, through the adjoining columns, thus producing a ludicrous combination of ideas.
çrọss-rē·fẽr′, *v.t.* to refer from one part to another.
çrọss-rē·fẽr′, *v.i.* to make a cross reference.
çrọss ref′ẽr·ence, a reference from one part of a book, catalogue, index, etc. to another part, for additional information.
çrọss re·lā′tion, in music, a relationship between two successive tones in different voices that ordinarily occurs in one voice: also called *false relation*.
çrọss riv′et·ing, riveting in which the rivets of one row are opposite spaces in succeeding rows.
çrọss′rōad, *n.* 1. a road that crosses another road.
2. a road that connects two or more main roads.
3. [*usually pl.*] the place where two or more roads intersect: often regarded metaphorically as the gathering point of the near-by rural inhabitants.
at the crossroads; at the point where one must choose between different courses of action.
çrọss′rōw (-rō), *n.* 1. the alphabet; christcross row. [Obs.]
2. a row that crosses others.
çrọss′ruff, *n.* in card games, a play in which each of two partners in turn leads a suit that the other will be able to trump: also called *seesaw*.
çrọss sēa, a condition at sea when the waves run contrary to the winds; a choppy sea.
çrọss seç′tion, 1. a cutting through something, especially at right angles to its axis.
2. a piece so cut off.
3. a representative part or selection serving to demonstrate the qualities of the whole.
4. in surveying, a vertical section of the ground surface taken at right angles to a survey line.
çrọss′-spāle, çrọss′-spąll, *n.* a horizontal timber used as a temporary brace to support the frame of a ship during its construction: called also *cross-pawl*.
çrọss spring′ẽr, in groined vaulting, the rib which extends diagonally from the one pier to the other.
çrọss′-stäff, *n.* 1. a surveyor's instrument used for sighting at right angles.
2. an early form of the quadrant.
çrọss′-stitch (-stich), *n.* 1. a stitch made by crossing two stitches diagonally in the form of an X.
2. needlework made with this stitch.
çrọss′-stitch, *v.t.* and *v.i.* to sew or embroider with cross-stitch; to do cross-stitch.
çrọss′-stōne, *n.* any one of the minerals andalusite, staurolite, or harmotome.
çrọss street, 1. a street that crosses another street.
2. a street that connects two or more main streets.
çrọss′tāil, *n.* in a marine steam engine, a strong iron bar connecting the side lever with the piston rod.
çrọss tąlk (tąk), in radio and telephony, interference in one channel from another or others.
çrọss′-tīe, *n.* a beam, post, rod, etc. placed crosswise to give support or strength; specifically, any of the transverse timbers supporting the rails of a railroad track.
çrọss′-tīn″ing, *n.* in agriculture, a mode of harrowing crosswise, or in a direction across the ridges.
çrọss′-town, *a.* going across the main avenues or transportation lines of a city or town; as, a *cross-town* bus route is needed.
çrọss′treeṣ, *n.pl.* two short, horizontal bars across a ship's masthead, which spread the rigging that supports the mast.

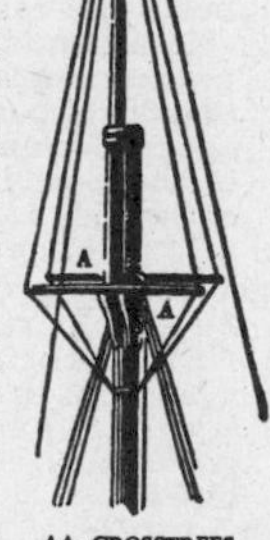

AA. CROSSTREES

çrọss′-vault″ing, *n.* vaulting formed by the intersection of two or more simple vaults.
çrọss′wąlk (-wąk), *n.* a lane marked off for pedestrians to use in crossing a street.
çrọss′wāy, *n.* same as *crossroad*.
çrọss′wāyṣ, *adv.* crosswise.
çrọss week, Rogation week.
çrọss wind, a wind blowing at right angles to the line of flight of an aircraft, the course of a ship, or any given course or direction.
çrọss wīre, a cross hair.
çrọss′wīṣe, *adv.* 1. across.

2. in the form of a cross.
3. in a contrary manner.

cross′wŏrd puz′zle, an arrangement or numbered squares to be filled in with words, a letter to each square, so that a letter appearing in a word placed horizontally is usually also part of a word placed vertically: numbered definitions, etc. are given as clues for the words to be entered in the corresponding squares.

crōt′ȧ·lȧ, *n.*, pl. of *crotalum*.

Crōt·ȧ·lā′ri·ȧ, *n.* [L., from Gr. *krotalon*, a rattle.] rattlewort; a very extensive genus of plants of the family *Fabaceæ*, containing several hundred known species, all natives of warm climates.

crōt′ȧ·lid, *n.* one of the *Crotalidæ*.

Crōt·al′i·dae, *n.pl.* [L., from Gr. *krotalon*, a rattle.] a family of venomous serpents, order *Ophidia*, having a large pit on each side of the face, between the eye and nostril; the pit vipers.

crōt′ȧ·line, *a.* of or relating to the rattlesnakes.

crōt′ȧ·lō, *n.* [Gr. *krotalon*, a rattle, castanet.] a Turkish musical instrument, corresponding to the ancient cymbalum.

crōt′ȧ·loid, *n.* [Gr. *krotalon*, a rattle, and *eidos*, form.] any serpent of the family *Crotalidæ*.

crōt′ȧ·lum, *n.*; *pl.* **crōt′ȧ·lȧ,** [L., from Gr. *krotalon*, a rattle, castanet.]
1. a kind of castanet used by the ancient Egyptians and Greeks.
2. a bell, particularly a small one.

Crōt′ȧ·lus, *n.* [L., from Gr. *krotalon*, a rattle.] the genus of the *Crotalidæ* comprising the rattlesnakes.

crōt′ȧ·phīte, *a.* [Gr. *krotaphos*, the side of the forehead.] in anatomy, temporal: sometimes used as a noun. [Rare.]

crōt·ȧ·phit′ic, *a.* same as *crotaphite*.

crotch, *n.*; *pl.* **crotch′es,** [Fr. *croche*, a hook, from *croc*; see *crosier*.]
1. a pole forked on top.
2. a place where two branches or limbs fork from a tree.
3. the place where the legs fork from the human body.
4. in nautical usage, a crutch.
5. in billiards, a small square at the corner of the table.

crotched (krocht), *a.* 1. having a crotch; forked.
2. cross; peevish. [Dial.]

crotch′et, *n.* [OFr. *crochet*, a little hook, dim. of *croc*, a hook.]
1. a small hook.
2. a hooklike part or process.
3. in printing, a bracket. [Obs.]
4. in music, a quarter note.
5. in fortification, an indentation in a covered way, opposite to a traverse.
6. in military usage, disposal of troops in a line forming right angles to the general line of battle.
7. in anatomy, a hook at the anterior extremity of the uncinate convolution of the brain.
8. a hooklike device or hooked instrument; specifically, in surgery, a curved instrument with a sharp hook, used to extract the fetus in the operation of embryotomy.
9. a peculiar turn of the mind; a whim, or fancy; a stubborn notion.

crotch′et, *v.i.* to perform music or to sing in quick time. [Obs.]

crotch′et·ed, *a.* marked with crotchets.

crotch′et·i·ness, *n.* the state or quality of being crotchety; eccentricity.

crotch′et·y, *a.* 1. full of peculiar whims or stubborn notions; cantankerous; eccentric.
2. having the nature of a crotchet.

Crō′tŏn, *n.* [Gr. *krotōn*, a tick, the plant which bears the castor-oil berry.]
1. a genus of euphorbiaceous plants, comprehending a large number of species, many of which possess important medicinal properties. *Croton tiglium*, a native of several parts of the East Indies, yields croton oil, a strong cathartic.
2. [c–] any foliage plant of this genus.

crō′tŏn bug, Crō′tŏn bug, [from *Croton* aqueduct (a part of the water-supply system of New York City): so named from becoming numerous in the city after the opening of the aqueduct.] a small, winged cockroach, *Blatta germanica*, common in houses having water pipes.

crō·ton′ic, *a.* of or pertaining to plants of the genus *Croton*.

crotonic acid; a colorless, crystalline compound, $C_4H_6O_2$, used in organic synthesis.

crō′tŏn·in, crō′tŏn·ine, *n.* an alkaloid found in the seeds of *Croton tiglium*.

crō′tŏn oil, a thick, bitter oil obtained from croton seeds: it is used externally as a counterirritant and internally as a strong cathartic.

crō·ton′y·len, crō·ton′y·lēne, *n.* the unsaturated hydrocarbon, C_4H_6.

crot′tles (-tlz), *n.pl.* [Gael. *crotal*, a name for lichens.] certain lichens used as dyestuffs. [Scot.]

crouch, *v.i.*; crouched (kroucht), *pt.*, *pp.*; crouching, *ppr.* [ME. *crouchen*, *crouken*, to crouch, bend; *croken*, to crook.]
1. to bend down; to stoop low with the limbs drawn close to the body; to lie close to the ground, as an animal ready to pounce or cowering in fear.
2. to bend servilely; to stoop meanly; to fawn; to cringe.

crouch, *v.t.* to bow or bend (the knee, etc.) low.

crouch, *n.* 1. a crouching.
2. the posture assumed when crouching.

crouch, *v.t.* to sign with the cross; to bless. [Obs.]

croud, *n.* same as *crowd* (a large number of people).

crouke, *n.* a jar of earthenware; a crock. [Obs.]

cröup, *n.* [OFr. *croupe*, the rump; Ice. *kryppa*, a hump.] the rump or buttocks; also, the part of a horse behind the saddle.

cröup, *n.* [Scot. *croup*, *crope*, *crupe*, *crowp*, to croak, to cry or speak with a hoarse voice; Goth. *hropyan*; AS. *hreopan*, to call out.] an inflammation of the respiratory passages, with labored breathing, hoarse coughing, and laryngeal spasm.
false croup; a catarrhal affection of the larynx.

cröu·pāde′, *n.* [Fr., from *croupe*, the hind quarters.] in horsemanship, a leap in which the horse pulls his hind legs up under his belly.

cröup′ăl, *a.* croupy.

cröup′ẽr, *n.* same as *crupper*.

cröu′pi·ẽr, *n.* [Fr.] 1. one who collects and pays the money at a gaming table.
2. one who acts as assistant chairman at a public dinner party.

crou·pi·ère′ (crö-pi-ār′), *n.* [Fr., from *croup*, the hind quarters.] armor for the buttocks of a horse.

cröup′ous, *a.* croupy.

cröup′y, *a.* 1. having the disease of croup.
2. having the characteristic harsh breathing and hoarseness of croup.
3. of or like croup.

cröuse, *a.* [Scot.] brisk; full of heart; courageous; self-satisfied; self-complacent. [Dial.]

cröu·stāde′, *n.* [Fr., from OFr. *crouste*, a crust.] a dish prepared with crusts of bread.

crout, *n.* same as *sauerkraut*.

cröu·ton′, *n.* [Fr. *croûton*, from *croûte*, a crust; L. *crusta*, crust.] one of the small, crisp pieces of toasted or fried bread often served in soup.

crōw, *n.* [ME. *crowe*, *craw*; AS. *crawe*; D. *kraai*; O.H.G. *chraja*, *chrawa*, a crow.]
1. a large, nonmigrating bird with glossy, black plumage, of the genus *Corvus*: the beak is convex and pointed, the nostrils are covered with bristly feathers, the tongue is forked and cartilaginous. It utters a harsh call, imitatively called a *caw*. The common or carrion crow is the *Corvus americanus*; the raven is the *Corvus corax*; the hooded crow, *Corvus cornix*; the rook, *Corvus frugilegus*; the jackdaw, *Corvus monedula*.

HOODED CROW CARRION CROW

2. a crowbar.
3. [C–] the southern constellation Corvus.
4. one who watches while another steals; a confederate in a robbery. [Thieves' Slang.]
as the crow flies; in the most direct line between two points.
red-legged or *Cornish crow*; the chough.

crōw, *v.i.*; crowed *or*, *for sense 1*, crew, *pt.*, crowed, *pp.*; crowing, *ppr.* [ME. *crowen*, *crawen*; AS. *crawan*, to crow; D. *kraaijen*; G. *krahen*, to crow.]
1. to make the shrill cry of a rooster.
2. to boast in triumph; to vaunt; to exult.
3. to utter a cry of pleasure or victory.
4. to express pleasure by a cooing sound, as an infant.
to crow over one; to express elation at a triumph over one; to be exultant at another's expense.

Crōw, *n.* [trans., via Fr. *gens de corbeaux*, of their native name, *Absaroke*, crow people.]
1. *pl.* **Crōws, Crōw,** a member of a tribe of Siouan Indians who lived in the upper basins of the Yellowstone and Big Horn Rivers.
2. their Siouan language.

crōw′bär, *n.* a bar of iron sharpened at one end, used as a lever for prying: often fitted with a claw on the other end.

crōw′bells, *n.* the bluebell; also, the daffodil. [Obs.]

crōw′ber″ry, *n.*; *pl.* **crōw′ber″ries,** 1. a black, edible berry of *Empetrum nigrum*; also, the plant itself, a heathlike evergreen shrub common in Scotland and northern North America: also called *black crowberry*, *crakeberry*, and *heathberry*.
2. a variety of large cranberry.

crōw black′bird, *Quiscalus quiscula*, the American purple grackle; also, any of a number of North American birds resembling the crow.

crowd, *n.* [ME. *crowde*, *croude*; W. *crwth*, a bulge, crowd, violin; Gael. *cruit*, a violin, harp.] an ancient Celtic six-stringed violin, four of the strings being bowed and two struck by the thumb in playing: also written *croud*, *crowth*, and (Welsh) *crwth*.

CROWD

crowd, *v.i.* to play the crowd. [Obs.]

crowd, *v.t.*; crowded, *pt.*, *pp.*; crowding, *ppr.* [ME. *crowden*, *cruden*; AS. *creodan*, to crowd, push.]
1. to press; push; shove.
2. to press or force closely together; cram.
3. to fill too full; occupy to excess, as by pressing or thronging.
4. to put (a person) under pressure or stress. [Colloq.]
5. to press urgently for payment; dun. [Colloq.]
6. in basketball, to guard (an opponent) closely to prevent his getting the ball.
to crowd sail; in nautical usage, to make all possible speed by spreading all the sails.

crowd, *v.i.* 1. to press; push; shove.
2. to press forward; push one's way (*forward*, *into*, *through*, etc.).
3. to gather closely together, pressing upon one another; throng.

crowd, *n.* 1. a collection; a number of things collected, or closely pressed together.
2. a large number of people congregated closely together; a throng.
3. any company of persons having something in common; a clique; a set; as, to frequent the fast *crowd*. [Colloq.]
4. the common people; the populace.
Syn.—concourse, confluence, gathering, assembly, throng, group, swarm.

crowd′ed, *a.* 1. filled with people or things; packed.
2. packed too full.
3. close together; inconveniently lacking room.

crowd′ẽr, *n.* a crowd player; a fiddler. [Obs.]

crowd′ẽr, *n.* one who crowds; a pusher.

crowd′ie, crowd′y, *n.* a gruel of meal stirred into cold water or milk. [Scot.]

crōw′flow″ẽr, *n.* 1. a buttercup.
2. a ragged robin. [Obs.]

crōw′foot, *n.*; *pl.* **crōw′foots** for senses 1 and 2, **crōw′feet** for senses 3, 4, and 5, 1. any of a number of plants of the buttercup family, characterized by simple or variously lobed leaves somewhat resembling a crow's foot.
2. any of several other plants with leaves or other parts somewhat resembling a crow's foot, as the plantain.
3. in electricity, a zinc electrode shaped somewhat like a crow's foot.
4. in military usage, a device with several sharp metal points, placed on the ground to hinder enemy cavalry; caltrop.
5. in nautical usage, an arrangement of small cords run through a block pulley to suspend an awning, etc.

crow′foot fam·i·ly, the *Ranunculaceæ*.

crōw′foot gram′ȧ, the blue grama.

çrōw′foot gråss, crab grass, *Digitaria sauguinalis,* or Egyptian grass.

çrōw′foot vī′ō·let, bird's-foot violet.

çrōw′keep″ẽr, *n.* one who scares crows from a field; also, a scarecrow. [Obs.]

çrown, *n.* [ME. *croun, corone, coroun;* OFr. *corone, coroune;* L. *corona,* a crown, wreath; Gr. *koronē,* the tip of a bow, anything curved.]

1. an ornamented circlet or head covering worn by kings and those having sovereign power, as an emblem of their office.

CROWN OF ENGLAND

2. regal power in a monarchy; sovereignty; kingly government or imperial dominion.

3. a wreath or garland worn on the head as an ornament, sign of honor, victory, etc.

4. honorary distinction; reward; honor.

5. a reigning monarch; a sovereign; as, the debts of the *crown* were by this time enormous.

6. anything serving to adorn or honor like a crown.

7. a thing like a crown in shape, position, etc.

8. the highest or most perfect state of anything; acme.

A sorrow's *crown* of sorrow is remembering happier things. —Tennyson.

9. the top of anything; the highest part, as the summit of a mountain, the dome of a furnace, the face of an anvil, etc.

10. the upper part of a rounding or convex surface, as in a bridge, a road, the deck of a ship, etc.

11. the top part of the skull or head.

12. the top part of a hat.

13. clerical tonsure in a circular form. [Obs.]

14. in nautical usage, (a) the end of an anchor, or the point from which the arms proceed; (b) a kind of knot made at the end of a rope to prevent the strands from raveling.

15. the enamel-covered part of a tooth which appears beyond the gum; also, an artificial cap for a tooth.

16. the top portion of a cut gem; the uppermost circle of facets.

17. in architecture, the uppermost member of a cornice; also, the top part of an arch or of a lantern made by the meeting of several flying buttresses.

18. in botany, (a) a corona; (b) the part of the root which joins with the stem; (c) the leafy head of a tree.

19. (a) formerly, any coin stamped with the figure of a crown or a crowned head; (b) a silver coin of Great Britain equal to five shillings; (c) any of various coins whose name means *crown,* as the *krona, krone,* etc.

20. in zoology, (a) the crest of an animal; (b) the flowerlike part of certain sea animals.

21. a size of paper, in the United States, 15 x 19 inches

çrown, *v.t.*; crowned, *pt., pp.*; crowning, *ppr.* [ME. *crownen, corownen,* OFr. *coroner;* L. *coronare,* to crown; *corona,* a crown.]

1. to cover with a crown; to put a crown on.

And peaceful olives *crowned* his hoary head. —Dryden.

2. to invest with regal power; to enthrone.

3. to honor; to dignify; to adorn; to recompense or reward; to bestow an honorary reward or distinction upon; as, to *crown* the victor with laurel.

Thou . . . hast *crowned* him with glory and honor. —Ps. viii. 5.

4. to complete; to perfect; to put the finishing touch on.

5. to top; to surmount (often followed by *with*); as, an observatory *crowned* the height.

6. to be the crown, highest part, or chief ornament of.

7. to hit (a person) on the head. [Slang.]

8. in checkers, to make a king of.

9. in military usage, to secure a foothold in; to gain and hold a position upon.

10. in nautical usage, to make a finishing knot on the end of (a rope) by interweaving the strands.

çrown ant′lẽr, the topmost prong of an antler.

çrown ärch, a solid arched plate above the firebox of a boiler.

çrown bär, one of the bars by which the crown sheet of the firebox of a steam boiler is supported.

çrown′bēard, *n.* any plant of the aster family belonging to the genus *Verbesina.*

çrown çap, a cork-lined metal stopper whose edges are crimped over the mouth of the bottle.

çrown çol′ō·ny, a British colony directly under the control of the home government.

çrown çrāne, a bird, the demoiselle.

çrowned, *a.* 1. invested with a crown, or with regal power and dignity; also, honored; dignified; rewarded with a crown, wreath, or garland.

2. in zoology, having the head marked in some distinguishing manner, as by a crest or by coloring; crested; coronate.

3. in botany, having a corona.

4. finished off with a crown knot: said of a rope.

çrown′ẽr, *n.* one who or that which crowns.

çrown′ẽr, *n.* a coroner. [Brit. Dial.]

çrown′et, *n.* a coronet. [Archaic.]

çrown gāte, the head gate of a lock of a canal.

çrown glåss, 1. window glass made in flat, circular plates by blowing and whirling, with a small knot in the center left by the blower's rod.

2. a very clear optical glass.

çrown gråft, a plant graft in which the shoot or twig is inserted at the crown of the main stem or trunk.

çrown head (hed), on a checkerboard, the king row.

çrown im·pē′ri·ăl, a liliaceous plant, *Fritillaria imperialis,* cultivated for its flowers.

çrown′ing, *a.* 1. bulging at the top.

2. completing; perfecting; putting the finishing touch on.

The *crowning* act of a long career. —Buckle.

çrown′ing, *n.* 1. the act of investing with a crown; the state of being crowned; coronation.

2. in architecture, the upper part, as of an arch.

3. in nautical usage, a finishing knot; a crown.

çrown jew′els, the jewels belonging to a sovereign which pass on to his successor.

çrown land, land owned by the crown, the income from which goes to the reigning monarch.

çrown lạw, in England, that part of the common law governing criminal matters.

çrown lens, a lens made of crown glass; specifically, the convex member of an achromatic lens.

çrown′less, *a.* without a crown.

çrown′let, *n.* [dim. of *crown.*] a small crown.

çrown of′fice, in English law, a department of the King's (or Queen's) Bench division of the High Court of Justice which handles certain procedure in all criminal cases.

çrown′piēce, *n.* 1. the strap of a bridle passing over the top of the horse's head back of the ears.

2. a piece forming the crown or top.

çrown pōst, same as *king post.*

çrown prince, the heir apparent to a throne; a monarch's oldest living son.

çrown prin′cess, the wife of a crown prince.

çrown sạw, a kind of circular saw, a cylinder with cutting teeth round the bottom edge.

çrown sçab, a painful sore of an ulcerous nature that forms on a horse's hoof.

çrown sheet, the sheet or plate forming the top of the firebox of a steam boiler.

çrown spar′rōw, any bird of the genus *Zonotrichia;* particularly, the Peabody bird.

çrown tīle, a common roof tile.

çrown valve, a crown-shaped valve.

çrown wheel, a wheel with teeth set at right angles to its plane: in certain watches, the wheel that drives the balance. It is also called a *contrate wheel* or *face wheel.*

CROWN WHEEL

çrown′wŏrk, *n.* 1. in fortification, an outwork running into the field, consisting of two demibastions (*a a*) at the extremes, and an entire bastion (*b*) in the middle, with curtains (*c c*). It is designed to protect some hill or advantageous post, and cover the other works.

CROWNWORK

2. in dentistry, (a) the making or insertion of an artificial crown; (b) an artificial crown or crowns collectively.

çrōw pheaṣ′ănt (fez′), the coucal.

çrōw′-quill (kwil), *n.* 1. a quill of a crow; also, a pen made from a crow's quill.

2. a steel pen having a fine point and a cylindrical shank, much used in very fine work.

çrōw′ṣ′-foot, *n.*; *pl.* **çrōw′ṣ′-feet,** 1. one of the wrinkles which form under the eye of adults and extend from the outer corner radially: most commonly used in the plural.

2. a three-pointed, stitched design put on a garment, as at the end of a seam.

3. in military usage, a device with several sharp metal points, placed on the ground to hinder enemy cavalry; a caltrop.

çrōw′shrīke, *n.* the piping crow.

çrōw′-silk, *n.* any of the various algae of the order *Confervaceæ.*

çrōw′ṣ′-nest, *n.* 1. a small, sheltered platform close to the top of a ship's mast, used by the lookout.

2. any platform like this.

CROW'S-NEST

çrōw′step, *n.* same as *corbiestep.*

çrōw′stōne, *n.* the topmost stone in a gable.

çrōw′tōe, *n.* [*also pl.*] *Lotus corniculatus,* bird's-foot trefoil.

çroyl′stōne, *n.* crystallized cauk, in which the crystals are small.

çrōze, *n.* [origin unknown.] a plane used to cut grooves in barrel staves for insertion of the head; also, the groove so cut.

çrō′ziẽr (-zhẽr), *n.* same as *crosier.*

çrō′ziẽred, *a.* same as *crosiered.*

çrū′çēs, *n.* alternative pl. of *crux.*

çrū′ciăl (-shul), *a.* [Fr. *cruciale,* from L. *crux, crucis,* a cross.]

1. of supreme importance; decisive; critical; as, a *crucial* decision.

2. extremely trying; severe; difficult.

3. in anatomy, cross-shaped; intersecting; cruciform; as, the *crucial* ligaments of the knee joint.

çrū′ciăn, çrū′siăn, *n.* [Fr. *carassin;* LL. *coracinus;* Gr. *korakinos,* a fish like a perch.] a short, thick, broad fish, of a deep-yellow color, the German carp, *Carassius carassius,* or *vulgaris,* family *Cyprinidæ.* It inhabits the lakes and ponds of northern Europe and Asia, and differs from the common carp in having no barbels at its mouth: called also *Prussian carp* or *crucian carp.*

çrū′ci·āte (-shi-āt), *v.t.* [L. *cruciatus,* pp. of *cruciare,* to torture; *crux,* a cross, torture.] to torture. [Archaic.]

çrū′ci·āte, *a.* 1. tormented. [Obs.]

2. cross-shaped; marked as by a cross; cruciform.

3. in botany, having petals or leaves in the form of a cross.

4. in zoology, crossing: said of wings.

çrū·ci·ā′tion, *n.* 1. torment. [Obs.]

2. a crossing or being crossed.

çrū′ci·ble, *n.* [LL. *crucibulum,* a lamp, a pot for melting metals; OFr. *croche,* an earthen pot; D. *kroes;* Sw. *krus,* a cup, crucible.]

CRUCIBLES

1. a vessel or pot made of graphite, porcelain, platinum, or other material, so baked or tempered as to resist extreme heat. It is used for melting ores, metals, etc.

2. in metallurgy, a hollow place at the bottom of a furnace to receive the molten metal.

3. a severe test; a hard trial; as, his probity was tried in the *crucible* of temptation and poverty.

Hessian crucible; a crucible made of coarse sand and infusible clay, used in melting metals.

çrū′ci·ble steel, a high-grade steel made by melting blister steel or by fusing flux, wrought iron, and carbon in crucibles: used for making knives, tools, etc.

çrū′ci·fẽr, *n.* [LL. *crucifer; crux, crucis,* a cross, and *ferre,* to bear.]

1. a cross bearer in religious processions.

2. in botany, any plant of the mustard family, including the mustards, cabbages,

cresses, etc., with flowers having four parts that form a cross.

Çru·cif′e·rae, *n.pl.* a very extensive family of dicotyledonous plants, the mustard family, consisting of annual or perennial herbs with a pungent or acrid watery juice, all having flowers with six stamens, two of which are short, and four sepals and petals, the spreading limbs of which form a cross. The fruit is a pod divided into two cells. The mustard, watercress, turnip, cabbage, radish, horseradish, etc. belong to this family.

çru·cif′ẽr·ous, *a.* [LL. *crucifer*, bearing a cross; *crux, crucis*, a cross, and *ferre*, to bear.]
1. bearing a cross.
2. in botany, pertaining to or like the *Cruciferæ*.

çru′ci·fi·ẽr, *n.* one who crucifies.

çru′ci·fix, *n.* [LL. *crucifixum*, a crucifix, neut. of *crucifus*, pp. of *crucifigere*, to crucify; *crux, crucis*, a cross, and *figere*, to fix, fasten.]
1. a religious symbol consisting of a cross, or a representation of a cross, with the figure of Jesus crucified upon it.
2. the cross as a religious symbol.

çru·ci·fix′ion (-fik′shun), *n.* 1. the act of nailing or fastening a person to a cross, for the purpose of putting him to death.
2. the state of being nailed or fastened to a cross; death upon a cross.
3. [C–] the crucifying of Jesus, or a representation of this in painting, statuary, etc.
4. intense suffering or affliction; great mental trial.

çru′ci·form, *a.* [L. *crux, crucis*, a cross, and *forma*, form.] cross-shaped.

çru′ci·fȳ, *v.t.*; crucified, *pt., pp.*; crucifying, *ppr.* [OFr. *crucifier*; LL. *crucifigere, cruci figere*, to fasten to a cross; *crux, crucis*, a cross, and *figere*, to fasten.]
1. to put to death by suspending from a cross, with the hands and feet nailed or bound to it.
2. to subdue; to mortify; to destroy the power or ruling influence of.

They that are Christ's have *crucified* the flesh with the affections and lusts.
—Gal. v. 24.

3. to torment; to torture.

çrud, *n.* [said to be from W. *cryd*, fever, plague.] an imaginary disease: used as a general term for any vague disorder or ailment. [Military Slang.]

çrud, *v.t.* and *v.i.* to coagulate; to curd. [Dial.]

çrud′dle, *v.i.* to curdle. [Obs.]

çrude, *a.*; *comp.* cruder; *superl.* crudest, [L. *crudus*, bloody, raw, unripe, from *cruor*, blood.]
1. in a raw or natural condition; not refined; not prepared, as by heating or other processes.
2. immature; unripe; not mellowed; as, the harsh flavor of *crude* fruit.
3. unadorned; bare; as, *crude* reality.
4. not well formed, arranged, or prepared; rough; imperfect; as, a *crude* plan or theory; *crude* work.
5. lacking finish, grace, tact, taste, etc.; uncultured; as, a *crude* fellow.

çrude′ly, *adv.* in a crude manner.

crude′ness, *n.* the state of being crude.

çru″di·tés′ (-tā′), *n.pl.* [Fr., lit., something raw.] raw vegetables cut up and served as hors d'oeuvres, usually with a dip.

çru′di·ty, *n.* [L. *cruditas* (*-atis*), from *crudus*, raw, rough, undigested.]
1. the condition or quality of being crude.
2. *pl.* **çru′di·ties,** a crude action, remark, etc.

çru′dle, *v.i.* same as *cruddle*.

çrud′y, *a.* coagulated, thickened, or curdled. [Obs.]

çru′el, *a.* [Fr. *cruel*; L. *crudelis*, raw, unfeeling, rough.]
1. disposed to inflict pain or suffering; willing or pleased to torment, vex, or afflict; without pity, compassion, or kindness; fierce; savage; hard-hearted.

They are *cruel*, and have no mercy.
—Jer. vi. 23.

2. causing, or of a kind to cause, pain, grief, or distress; tormenting, vexing, or afflicting; harsh; painful; as, *cruel* words or acts.

Syn.—barbarous, brutal, ferocious, inhuman, inexorable, merciless, pitiless.

çru′el, *adv.* extremely. [Dial.]

çru′el, *n.* same as *crewel*. [Obs.]

çru′el·ly, *adv.* 1. in a cruel or harsh manner; with cruelty; inhumanly; barbarously; without pity.
2. with great suffering; painfully.
3. exceedingly; in a high degree; very; as, he is *cruelly* strong in body. [Colloq.]

çru′el·ness, *n.* inhumanity; cruelty. [Rare.]

çru′els, *n.pl.* same as *crewels*.

çru′el·ty, *n.*; *pl.* **çru′el·ties,** [OFr. *cruelte*; It. *crudelita*; L. *crudelitas*, cruelty, barbarity, from *crudelis*, raw, rough, unfeeling.]
1. the quality or condition of being cruel; inhumanity; a savage or barbarous disposition or temper, which is gratified in giving unnecessary pain or distress to others; barbarity.
2. a cruel action, remark, etc.

çru·en′tous, *a.* bloody; cruentate. [Obs.]

çru′et, *n.* [ME. *cruet, crewet*, dim. of OFr. *cruye, cruie*, a pitcher.]
1. a vial or small glass bottle, particularly one used on the table for holding vinegar, oil, etc.
2. ecclesiastically, one of the vessels used for wine or water in the celebration of the Eucharist.

çruise, *n.* same as *cruse*.

çruise, *v.i.*; cruised, *pt., pp.*; cruising, *ppr.* [D. *kruisen*, to move crosswise or in a zigzag course; *kruis*, a cross; OFr. *crois*; L. *crux*, a cross.]
1. to sail from place to place, as for pleasure, without a set destination.
2. to wander about on land in a similar manner; as, a taxi *cruises* in search of passengers.
3. to move at a speed fit for sustained travel; as, the airplane *cruised* at 270 miles an hour.
4. in forestry, to explore or examine forests to estimate the quantity and quality of timber to be cut therefrom.

çruise, *v.t.* 1. to sail or journey over, about, or through; as, yachts that *cruise* the small lakes.
2. in forestry, to explore, in order to estimate the actual or possible timber yield; as, to *cruise* a river valley.

çruise, *n.* a sailing from place to place; a cruising voyage, especially a sea voyage.

çruise mis′sile (-sil), a long-range, jet-propelled winged bomb that can be launched from an airplane, submarine, or ship and guided to a target by remote control.

çruis′ẽr, *n.* 1. a person, ship, plane, auto, etc. that cruises; particularly, an armed ship that sails to and fro, capturing an enemy's ships or protecting the commerce of its own country: generally applied to vessels of less size and military power than battleships, but of high speed and adapted to long voyages.
2. an explorer or estimator of standing timber.
3. a police squad car.
4. a powerboat with a cabin and the necessary equipment for living on board.

çruis′ing, *a.* designating or at the most efficient, though not the highest, speed of an airplane.

cruising radius, the greatest distance that an aircraft or ship can cruise, usually from and back to a base, without refueling.

çruis′ken, çruis′keen, *n.* a small cruse; especially, one containing a dram of whisky.

çruive, *n.* 1. a sty or hovel. [Scot.]
2. a tidal fish trap of wattles. [Brit.]

çrul′lẽr, krul′lẽr, *n.* [D. *krullen*, to curl.] a small cake cut from a soft, sweet dough, and fried in deep fat until crisp; a kind of doughnut.

çrum, *n.* and *v.* crumb: former spelling.

çrumb (krum), *n.* [AS. *cruma*, a crumb, from *crummen*, pp. of *crimman*, to break into pieces.]
1. a small fragment or piece; a small particle or bit, especially of bread, cake, etc.
2. the soft inner part of bread: distinguished from *crust*.
3. any bit or scrap; as, *crumbs* of knowledge.
4. a louse, the grayback. [Dial.]
to a crumb; exactly; with great precision in every detail.

çrumb, *v.t.*; crumbed *or* crummed, *pt., pp.*; crumbing *or* crumming, *ppr.* 1. to break into small pieces with the fingers; to crumble; as, to *crumb* bread into milk.
2. to remove the crumbs from; as, to *crumb* the table. [Colloq.]
3. in cooking, to cover or thicken with bread or cracker crumbs; as, to *crumb* cutlets.

çrumb, *v.i.* to come apart in crumbs.

çrumb′cloth, *n.* a cloth protecting a floor or carpet from food crumbs.

çrum′ble, *v.t.*; crumbled, *pt., pp.*; crumbling, *ppr.* [dim. of *crumb*.] to break into crumbs or small pieces; to divide into minute parts.

çrum′ble, *v.i.* 1. to fall into small pieces; to break or part into small fragments.

If a stone is brittle, it will *crumble* into gravel.
—Arbuthnot.

2. to fall to decay; to perish; to disintegrate; to dwindle away; to become wasted or scattered; as, the political alliance will soon *crumble*.

çrum′ble, *n.* a substance that is crumbling. [Rare.]

çrum′bli·ness, *n.* the quality of being crumbly.

çrum′bly, *a.*; *comp.* crumblier; *superl.* crumbliest, brittle; easy to crumble; apt to break.

çrum′by (krum′i), *a.*; *comp.* crumbier; *superl.* crumbiest, 1. full of crumbs.
2. soft.

çru′men, *n.* [L. *crumena*, a purse.] a larmier or tearpit.

çru′me·năl, *n.* [L. *crumena*.] a purse. [Obs.]

çrum′ma·ble, *a.* capable of being crumbed.

çrum′mie, çrum′my, *n.*; *pl.* **çrum′mies** [via dial. from AS. *crump, crumb*, crooked; and *-y*.] a cow with crooked horns: sometimes used as an epithet for any cow. [Scot. and Brit. Dial.]

çrum′my, *a.*; *comp.* crummier; *superl.* crummiest, [understood as *crumb*, and *-y*, with basic notion "brittle, friable, hence worthless."] of poor quality, character, or appearance; inferior, shabby, contemptible, etc. [Slang.]

çrump, *v.t.* and *v.i.* [echoic.] to explode with a crunching sound: said of shells, etc.

çrump, *n.* a crumping.

çrump, *a.* [AS. *crumb*, stooping, bent down; G. *krumm*, crooked.]
1. crooked. [Obs.]
2. brittle; crusty; dry-baked; crisp. [Scot. and Brit. Dial.]

çrump′et, *n.* [W. *crempog*, a pancake, fritter.] an unsweetened batter cake, very light and spongy: it is baked on a griddle and usually toasted and buttered before serving.

çrum′ple, *v.t.*; crumpled, *pt., pp.*; crumpling, *ppr.* [ME. *crumplen, cromplen*, to make crooked; dim. of *crump*.]
1. to deform. [Obs.]
2. to crush together so as to make wrinkled; to rumple.

çrum′ple, *v.i.* 1. to become corrugated or crumpled; to shrink; to shrivel.
2. to collapse; to break down.

çrum′ple, *n.* a crease or wrinkle.

çrump′y, *a.* easily broken; brittle; crump. [Dial.]

çrunch, *v.t.* and *v.i.*; crunched (kruncht), *pt., pp.*; crunching, *ppr.* [imitative of the sound.]
1. to bite or chew with a noisy crackling sound.
2. to press through or against something so as to produce a grinding or crushing noise; as, to *crunch* through a crust of snow.

çrunch, *n.* 1. a crunching.
2. a crunching sound.

çrunch′y, *a.* making a crunching sound.

çruñk, çruñ′kle, *v.i.* [imitative word.] to cry like a crane. [Obs.]

çru′node, *n.* [L. *crux, crucis*, a cross, and *nodus*, a knot.] the point where a curve crosses itself.

çru′or, *n.* [L.] coagulated blood; gore.

çru′ŏ·rin, çru′ŏ·rine, *n.* [L. *cruor*, blood.] hemoglobin: the former name. [Brit. Dial.]

çrup, *a.* 1. short; crisp.
2. snappish; crabbed; testy. [Brit. Dial.]

çrup, *n.* [Fr. *croupe*, crupper, rump.] croup (a horse's rump). [Obs.]

çrup′pẽr, *n.* [Fr. *croupière*, from *croupe*, the buttocks of a horse.]
1. the rump of a horse.
2. the loop in a harness passing under the tail; also, a similar strap attached to a saddle.

çrup′pẽr, *v.t.* to put a crupper on; as, to *crupper* a horse.

çru′rȧ, *n.*, pl. of *crus*.

çru′răl, *a.* [L. *cruralis*, from *crus, cruris*, the leg.]
1. of or pertaining to a crus or crura; as, the *crural* arteries.
2. shaped like a leg.

çrus, *n.*; *pl.* **çru′rȧ,** [L., the leg.]
1. the part of a leg or hind limb between the knee and the ankle: the shank.
2. in anatomy, any leglike part or (in the plural) any structure resembling a pair of legs, as the cerebral peduncles.

çru·sāde′, *n.* [Fr. *croisade*; Pr. *crozada*; Sp. *cruzada*, a crusade; It. *crociata*; LL. *cruciata*, a crusade, from L. *crux, crucis*, a cross.]

1. [*sometimes* C–] any of the military expeditions which were undertaken by the Christians from 1096 to 1271 to recover the Holy Land from the Mohammedans.
2. any war or expedition having a religious object and sanctioned by the church.
3. an enterprise projected in a spirit of enthusiasm and conducted with earnestness for some cause or idea, or against some social or economic wrong; as, a *crusade* against the slave trade, a *crusade* against impure milk.

çru·sāde′, *v.i.* crusaded, *pt.*, *pp.*; crusading, *ppr.* to participate in a crusade; to support or oppose any cause with zeal.

çru·sāde′, *n.* same as *crusado.*

çru·sād′ẽr, *n.* a person engaged in a crusade; specifically, a participant in the medieval crusades.

çru·sād′ing, *a.* engaged in or relating to the crusades.
Some gray *crusading* knight. —M. Arnold.

çru·ṣā′dō, çru·zā′dō, *n.* [Port. *cruzado*, marked with a cross, from *cruz*; L. *crux*, a cross.] an obsolete Portuguese silver coin with the figure of a cross on it.

çruse, *n.* [ME. *cruse*; Ice. *krus*, a pot, tankard; D. *kroes*, a cup, cruse.] a small cup; a bottle or cruet for water, oil, honey, etc. [Archaic.]

çru′set, *n.* [Fr. *creuset*, *cruset*, a melting pot, crucible.] a goldsmith's crucible or melting pot. [Obs.]

çrush, *v.t.*; crushed (krusht), *pt.*, *pp.*; crushing, *ppr.* [ME. *cruschen*, *crousshen*; OFr. *cruissor*, *croissir*; LL. *cruscire*, to crush, break.]
1. to press between two opposing forces so as to break or injure; to squeeze so as to force a thing out of its natural shape; to bruise by pressure; as, to *crush* a finger in a door.
The ass *crushed* Balaam's foot against the wall. —Num. xxii. 25.
2. to overwhelm by power; to subdue; to suppress; to conquer beyond resistance; as, to *crush* one's enemies, to *crush* a rebellion.
3. to oppress grievously.
Thou shalt be only oppressed and *crushed* alway. —Deut. xxviii. 33.
4. to bruise and break into fine particles or powder by beating or grinding; to comminute.
5. to extract by pressing or squeezing.
to crush a cup of wine; to drink in company; to open a bottle together.

çrush, *v.i.* to be or become crushed; to be pressed into a smaller space by external pressure.

çrush, *n.* 1. a crushing; severe pressure; destruction.
The wreck of matter and the *crush* of worlds. —Addison.
2. the pressure caused by a crowd of persons or animals; the mass of separate bodies crowded together; as, a person fainted in the *crush.*
3. an infatuation. [Colloq.]

çrush′ẽr, *n.* 1. one who or the thing which exerts a crushing force.
2. a power machine in which hard substances such as ore and boulders are crushed.
3. anything which bears down with compelling force, as a blow or a reproof. [Colloq.]

çrush′ẽr gauġe, any appliance for determining the projectile force of a charge in a gun.

çrush hat, a soft hat; also, an opera hat.

çrush rọọm, a lobby or foyer.

Çru′sōe, Rob′in·sŏn, the hero of Daniel Defoe's novel *Robinson Crusoe* (1719), who is stranded on an island, as the result of a shipwreck.

çrust, *n.* [L. *crusta*, the hard surface of a body, shell, rind.]
1. an external coat or covering of a thing, which is hard or harder than the internal substance; as, the *crust* of bread, the *crust* of snow.
2. a collection of matter into a hard body; an incrustation; specifically, a hard deposit formed by wine on the inside surface of a bottle.
3. a piece of bread that is mostly crust; also, any dry, hard piece of bread.
Give me again a hollow tree,
A *crust* of bread and liberty. —Pope.
4. a shell, as the hard covering of a crab and some other animals.
5. in cookery, (a) the hard outside part of a loaf of bread, opposed to the *crumb*; (b) the enclosing shell of pastry, as of a pie or dumpling.
6. in anatomy, a crusta.
7. in geology, the outer part of the earth.
8. that part of a horse's hoof serving to hold the nails of a shoe.
9. audacity; insolence; forwardness.[Slang.]
10. in medicine, a dry, hard outer layer of blood, pus, or other bodily secretion; scab.

çrust, *v.t.* and *v.i.* 1. to cover or become covered with a crust.
2. to form or harden into a crust.

çrus′tȧ, *n.*; *pl.* **çrus′tae,** [L., a shell, crust.]
1. a hardened coating; a crust.
2. a medallion or gem to be set in an incrusted surface.
3. in zoology, the bony covering of a crustacean; a crust.
4. in botany, the brittle crustaceous thallus of lichens.
5. in anatomy, formerly, the layer of true bone, *crusta petrosa*, which covers the root of a tooth, as the enamel covers the exposed crown.

Çrus·tā′ce·ȧ (-shi-ȧ), *n.pl.* [L., from *crusta*, the hard shell of a body, rind, and *-acea.*] in zoology, a class of invertebrates, characterized by a hard outer shell and jointed appendages and bodies, that usually live in the water and breathe through gills. The higher forms of this class include lobsters, shrimps, crawfish, etc.; the lower animals are of varied forms, as barnacles, wood lice, fish lice, etc.

çrus·tā′ceăn (-shăn), *a.* belonging to or characteristic of the *Crustacea*; crustaceous.

çrus·tā′ceăn, *n.* an individual of the *Crustacea.*

çrus·tā″cē·ō·loġ′iç·ăl, *a.* pertaining to crustaceology.

çrus·tā·cē·ol′ō·ġist, *n.* one versed in crustaceology.

çrus·tā·cē·ol′ō·ġy, *n.* [L. *crusta*, crust, rind, and *-acea*, and Gr. *-logia*, from *legein*, to speak.] that division of zoology which has to do with crustaceans.

çrus·tā′ceous, *a.* [L. *crustaceus*, from *crusta*, crust, rind.]
1. pertaining to or of the nature of a crust.
2. having a hard crust or shell.
3. in zoology, belonging to the *Crustacea.*
4. in botany, (a) brittle; (b) having a brittle thallus, as certain lichens.

çrus·tā′ceous·ness, *n.* the quality of being crustaceous.

çrus′tae, *n.*, pl. of *crusta.*

çrust′ăl, *a.* of the nature of a crust, especially the earth's crust; relating to a crust; crustaceous.

çrus·tȧ·loġ′iç·ăl, *a.* same as *crustaceological.*

çrus·tal′ō·ġist, *n.* same as *crustaceologist.*

çrus·tal′ō·ġy, *n.* same as *crustaceology.*

çrus′tāte, çrus′tā·ted, *a.* [L. *crustatus.*] covered with a crust; as, *crustate* basalt.

çrus·tā′tion, *n.* an incrustation.

çrust′ed, *a.* 1. having a crust.
2. designating wine that has deposited a crust.
3. antiquated.

çrus·tif′iç, *a.* forming or depositing a crust. [Rare.]

çrust′i·ly, *adv.* in a crusty manner; harshly; morosely.

çrust′i·ness, *n.* 1. incrustation; hardness.
2. peevishness; moroseness; surliness.

çrust′y, *a.* 1. having a crust.
2. like crust; of the nature of crust; hard.
3. irritable or cross in manner or speech; peevish; testy; petulant; surly.
Thou *crusty* batch of nature, what's the news? —Shak.

çrut, *n.* [Fr. *croûte*; L. *crusta*, crust.] the rough, shaggy part of oak bark.

çrutch, *n.* [ME. *crutche*, *crucche*; AS. *crycc*; D. *kruk*; Dan. *krykke*; Sw. *krycka*, a crutch.]
1. any of various devices held in the hand to support the lame in walking; especially, a staff with a curving crosspiece at the top to be placed under the arm or shoulder.
2. a forked leg rest on a sidesaddle.
3. in nautical usage, (a) a piece of knee timber placed inside of a ship, for the security of the heels of the cant timbers abaft; (b) a forked stanchion of wood or iron; any fixture or adjustment with a head or top like that of a crutch.
4. figuratively, any prop or support.
5. the crotch of the human body.

çrutch, *v.t.*; crutched (krutcht), *pt.*, *pp.*; crutching, *ppr.* to support on crutches; to prop or sustain, as that which is feeble, with or as with a crutch.
Fools that *crutch* their feeble sense on verse. —Dryden.

çrutched, *a.* 1. supported with crutches.
2. bearing the sign of the cross.
crutched Friars; an early order of English friars, who wore crosses on their robes.

çrux, *n.*; *pl.* **çrux′eṣ** or **çru′cēṣ,** [L. *crux*, a cross.]
1. anything that puzzles, vexes, or tries, in the highest degree.
2. a crucial point; critical moment.
3. the essential or most important point.
4. a cross.
5. [C–] the Southern Cross, a constellation.
crux ansata; a tau cross surmounted by a circle; an ankh, ancient Egyptian cross.

çruy′shāġe, *n.* [origin unknown.] the porbeagle.

çru·zā′dō, *n.* see *crusado.*

çru·zei′rō, *n.* [Port., from *cruz*, a cross, from L. *crux.*] the gold monetary unit of Brazil.

çrwth (kröth), *n.* [W.] the crowd (stringed instrument).

çrȳ, *v.i.*; cried, *pt.*, *pp.*; crying, *ppr.* [ME. *crien*; OFr. *crier*; Pr. *cridar*; LL. *cridare*, to clamor, cry; L. *quiritare*, freq. of *queri*, to lament, complain.]
1. to shout in a loud voice, as in pain, anger, fright, sorrow, pleading, warning, etc.; to speak, call, or exclaim with vehemence; to call importunately.
The people *cried* to Pharaoh for bread. —Gen. xli. 55.
2. to express sorrow, pain, fear, etc. by sobbing or shedding tears; to lament.
3. to utter its characteristic call, as a dog or a bird.
In a cowslip's bell I lie;
There I couch when owls do *cry*. —Shak.
to cry off; to withdraw from an agreement or undertaking; refuse to do something undertaken.
to cry out; to shout; to vociferate; to complain loudly; to expostulate.
And lo, a spirit taketh him, and he suddenly *crieth out.* —Luke ix. 39.
to cry out against; to complain loudly, with a view to censure; to blame; to utter censure.
to cry quits; to declare that an affair is settled and that one is willing to let the matter rest.

çrȳ, *v.t.* 1. to proclaim; to name loudly and publicly for giving notice; as, to *cry* goods; to *cry* a lost child.
2. to beg; plead for; implore; beseech; as, the beaten knight *cried* quarter.
3. to utter loudly; shout; exclaim.
4. to bring to some specified condition as a result of crying or weeping; as, to *cry* oneself hoarse; to *cry* oneself sick.
5. to publish the banns of. [Dial.]
to cry down; (a) to cheapen or belittle anything in the eyes of others; as, *to cry down* goods offered for sale; (b) to condemn.
to cry for; (a) to plead for; (b) to need greatly.
to cry up; to praise so as to enhance the value of a thing.
Syn.—call, shout, exclaim, pray, implore, appeal, clamor, shed tears, sob, weep, proclaim, hawk, advertise.

çrȳ, *n.*; *pl.* **çrīeṣ,** 1. a loud vocal sound uttered by either a man or an animal, expressing pain, anger, fright, etc.
2. any loud utterance; shout.
3. an exclamation of triumph, wonder, etc.
4. a proclamation; public notice.
5. a public outcry; clamor.
6. a call by a hawker or peddler announcing the goods he has for sale.
7. an entreaty; urgent appeal.
8. a popular report; rumor.
9. a sobbing and shedding of tears; a fit of weeping.
10. the characteristic vocal sound of an animal.
11. the baying of hounds in the chase.
12. a pack of hunting dogs.
13. an object for which a political party professes great earnestness for electioneering purposes; a political catchword; a battle cry; a slogan; as, the party *cry* of the Democrats.
14. the peculiar sound produced by the bending and breaking of tin.
a far cry; (a) a long distance; a wide separation; as, from anticipation to realization is *a far cry*; (b) a thing much different.
in full cry; in eager pursuit: originally a term in hunting signifying that all the hounds have caught the scent and bark in chorus.
Syn.—call, shout, sound, utterance, outcry, tumult, clamor, proclamation, demand, requisition, vociferation, watchword.

çrȳ′ăl, *n.* [W. *cregyr*, a heron, a screamer.] the heron. [Obs.]

çrȳ·al·ġē′si·ȧ, *n.* pain due to cold.

çrȳ′bā·by, *n.* 1. a person, especially a child, who cries often or with little cause.

2. a person who complains constantly or accepts defeat unwillingly.
çrȳ'ẽr, *n.* 1. a falcon-gentle.
2. same as *crier.*
çry·es·thē'si·ȧ, *n.* sensitiveness to cold.
çrȳ'ing, *a.* 1. calling for immediate notice or remedy; notorious; great.
Heinous offences are called *crying* sins.
—Lowth.
2. that cries.
çrȳ'ing bîrd, same as *courlan.*
çrȳ"mō·ther'ȧ·py, *n.* same as *cryotherapy.*
çrȳ'ō-, [from Gr. *kryos,* cold, frost.] a combining form meaning *cold, freezing,* as in *cryo*gen.
çrȳ"ō·bi·ol'ō·ġy, *n.* [*cryo-,* and *biology.*] the science that deals with the study of organisms, especially warm-blooded animals, at low temperatures.
çrȳ'ō·ġen, *n.* [Gr. *kryos,* cold, frost, and *-genēs,* producing.] a refrigerant.
çrȳ"ō·ġen'içs, *n.pl.* [*construed as sing.*], [*cryogen,* and *-ics.*] the science that deals with the production of very low temperatures and their effect on the properties of matter.
çry·ō·hȳ'drāte, *n.* [Gr. *kryos,* cold, frost, and *hydōr,* water.] a crystalline solid formed by the combination of some substance, as salt, with ice at a temperature below the normal freezing point of water.
çrȳ'ō·līte, *n.* [Gr. *kryos,* cold, frost, and *lithos,* stone.] a fluoride of sodium and aluminum found in Greenland. It occurs in masses of a foliated structure, and has a glistening, vitreous luster. It is used in the manufacture of aluminum, soda, and certain grades of glass.
çrȳ·om'e·tẽr, *n.* [*cryo-* and *-meter.*] a thermometer, usually filled with alcohol, for measuring lower temperatures than a mercury thermometer will register.
çry·on'içs, *n.pl.* [*construed as sing.*], [*cryo-* and *-n-* and *-ics.*] the practice of freezing the body of a person who has just died in order to preserve it for possible resuscitation in the future, as when a cure for the disease that caused death has been found.
çry·oph'o·rus, *n.* [L., from Gr. *kryos,* cold, frost, and *-phoros,* from *phērein,* to bear.] an instrument for showing the lowering of the temperature of water by evaporation.

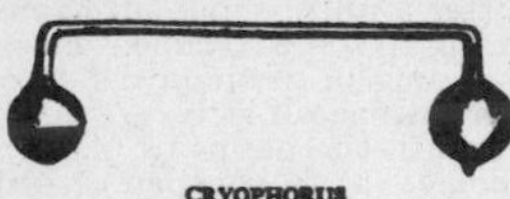

CRYOPHORUS

çrȳ·os'çō·py, *n.* [*cryo-,* and *-scopy.*] the science dealing with the determination of the freezing points of liquids.
çrȳ'ō·stat, *n.* [*cryo-* and *-stat.*] a regulator for maintaining a constant, low temperature.
çrȳ"ō·sûr'ġẽr·y, *n.* [*cryo-,* and *surgery.*] surgery involving the selective destruction of tissues by freezing them, as with liquid nitrogen: also *cryogenic surgery.*
çrȳ"ō·ther'ȧ·py, *n.* the use of low temperatures in the treatment of disease, as by the application of ice packs.
çrypt, *n.* [L. *crypta;* Gr. *kryptē,* a vault, crypt; from *kryptein,* to hide.]
1. a subterranean cell or cave, especially one constructed for the interment of bodies.
2. that part of a basilica or cathedral below the floor, set apart for burial purposes.
3. in anatomy, a recess, glandular cavity, or follicle, in the body.
çrypt'ăl, *a.* of or connected with a crypt.
çrypt"ȧ·nal'y·sis, *n.* [*crypto*gram, and *analysis.*] the art or science of deciphering a code or coded message without a prior knowledge of the key.
çryp'tiç, çryp'tiç·ăl, *a.* [LL. *crypticus;* Gr. *kryptikos,* from *kryptein,* to hide.]
1. hidden; secret; occult.
2. having a hidden or ambiguous meaning.
3. in zoology, serving to conceal, as the form or coloring of certain animals.
çryp'tiç·ăl·ly, *adv.* covertly; in secret; occultly.
çryp'ti·dine, *n.* [Gr. *kryptos,* hidden.] a derivative of coal tar, $C_{11}H_{11}N$, one of the quinoline bases.
çryp'tō-, çrypt-, [from Gr. *kryptos,* hidden, secret.] a combining form meaning *hidden, covered, secret,* as in *crypto*gram, *crypto*dont.
çryp'tō·branch, *a.* [*crypto-,* and Gr. *branchia,* gills.] same as *cryptobranchiate.*
çryp'tō·branch, *n.* an animal having concealed or internal branchiae.
Çryp·tō·bran·chi·ā'tȧ, *n.pl.* a division of animals comprising those with concealed gills.
çryp·tō·bran'chi·āte, *a.* in zoology, having concealed gills.
çryp"tō-Çal'vin·ism, *n.* [*crypto-,* and *Calvinism.*] the doctrine held by the adherents of Melanchthon, following Luther's death, who accepted Calvin's doctrine of the real presence rather than Luther's: an opprobrious term used by Lutherans.
çryp"tō-Çal'vin·ist, *n.* one who accepted the doctrine of crypto-Calvinism.
çryp'tō·çärp, *n.* see *cystocarp.*
çryp·tō·ceph'ȧ·lous, *a.* [*crypto-,* and Gr. *kephalē,* head.] having the head deeply inserted in the thorax.
çryp·toc'ẽr·ous, *a.* [*crypto-,* and Gr. *keras,* a horn.] having the antennae hidden underneath the head.
çryp·tō·clas'tiç, *a.* [*crypto-* and *-clastic.*] in mineralogy, consisting of fragmental grains too small to be seen with the unaided eye.
çryp·tō·crys'tăl·line, *a.* [*crypto-,* and Gr. *krystallinos,* from *krystallos,* crystal, ice; *kryos,* cold, frost.] made up of crystalline particles too small to be distinguished even under the microscope: applied to minerals.
çryp·tō·dī'rous, *a.* [*crypto-,* and Gr. *deirē,* neck, throat.] having a retractile neck which, with the head, may be entirely withdrawn beneath the exoskeleton, as in turtles.
çryp'tō·dont, *a.* [*crypto-,* and Gr. *odous, odontos,* tooth.] having rudimentary tooth-like processes, as certain bivalve mollusks.
çryp'tō·gam, *n.* a plant of *Cryptogamia.*
Çryp·tō·gā'mi·ȧ, *n.pl.* [L., from Gr. *kryptos,* hidden, and *gamos,* marriage.] the large division of plants, such as the algae, mosses, and ferns, which do not bear true flowers, but grow from spores.
çryp·tō·gā'mi·ăn, çryp·tō·gam'iç, çryp·tog'ȧ·mous, *a.* pertaining to plants of the division *Cryptogamia.*
çryp·tō·gen'iç, *a.* [*crypto-,* and *-genic.*] of unknown or obscure origin: said of a disease.
çryp'tō·gram, *n.* [*crypto-,* and Gr. *gramma,* a writing, from *graphein,* to write.] a writing in cipher or code; a cryptograph.
çryp·tō·gram'miç, *a.* of or like a cryptogram.
çryp'tō·gràph, *n.* [*crypto-,* and Gr. *graphein,* to write.] something written in code or cipher, as a message.
çryp·tog'rȧ·phẽr, çryp·tog'rȧ·phist, *n.* one who writes in or deciphers code.
çryp·tō·graph'iç, çryp·tō·graph'iç·ăl, *a.* having to do with cryptography; written in secret characters or in cipher.
çryp·tog'rȧ·phy, *n.* 1. the act or art of writing in or deciphering secret characters.
2. secret characters or cipher, or a system of writing with them.
çryp·tol'ō·ġy, *n.* 1. secret or enigmatical language.
2. cryptography.
Çryp·tō·mē'ri·ȧ, *n.* a genus of cypresslike conifers native to China but now grown as ornamental trees in the United States. *Cryptomeria japonica,* the Japanese cedar, is the only species.
çryp·tō·neū'rous, *a.* [*crypto-,* and Gr. *neuron,* a nerve.] without nerves or a nervous system.
çryp'tō·nym, *n.* [*crypto-,* and Gr. *onyma,* name.] a secret name, as of an initiate.
çryp·ton'y·mous, *a.* [*cryptonym* and *-ous.*] having a secret or concealed name.
çryp'tō·phȳte, *n.* a cryptogram.
çryp'tō·pine, *n.* [*crypto-,* and Gr. *opion,* poppy juice.] a colorless opium alkaloid, $C_{21}H_{23}NO_5$.
çryp·tor'chis, çryp·tor'chid, *n.* one whose testicles have failed to descend into the scrotum.
Çryp·tō·zō'iç, *a.* [*crypto-,* and *-zoic.*] Proterozoic.
çrys'tăl, *n.* [L. *crystallum;* Gr. *krystallos,* ice, crystal, from *kryos,* cold, frost.]
1. a clear, transparent quartz; rock crystal.
2. a piece of this cut in the form of an ornament.

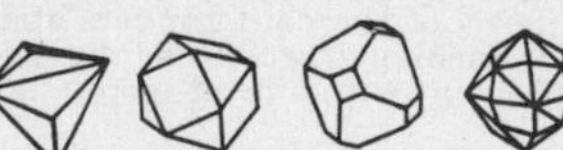

TYPES OF CRYSTAL

3. a kind of heavy, clear glass; hence, an article or articles, as decanters, cruets, etc., made of this material.
4. the thin, transparent, protective shield which covers the dial of a watch.
5. anything resembling crystal in its qualities, as in clearness, transparency, or purity.
Down the liquid *crystal* dropt.
—Tennyson.
6. a solidified form of a substance in which the atoms or molecules are arranged in a definite repeating pattern so that the external shape of a particle or mass of the substance is made up of plane faces in a symmetrical arrangement.
7. in radio, a crystal detector.
compound crystal; a crystal composed of two united crystals.
Iceland crystal; Iceland spar.
cry'stăl, *a.* 1. like crystal; clear; transparent.
By *crystal* streams that murmur through the meads.
—Dryden.
2. of or composed of crystal.
3. in radio, of or using a crystal.
çrys'tăl ball, a large ball of rock crystal or, more commonly, of glass, used in crystal gazing.
çrys'tăl dē·teçt'ŏr, in radio, a rectifier consisting of a semiconductor (e.g., silica) in contact with the sharp edge of a conductor (e.g., tungsten).
çrys'tăl gāz'ing, the practice of gazing into a crystal ball and pretending to see certain images, especially of future events.
çrys'tăll-, crystallo-.
çrys·tăl·lif'ẽr·ous, *a.* producing or composed of crystals.
çrys·tăl·liġ'ẽr·ous, *a.* [L. *crystallum,* a crystal, ice, and L. *gerere,* to bear.] bearing or producing crystals; crystalliferous.
çrys'tăl·lin, çrys'tăl·line, *n.* a globulin found in the crystalline lens.
çrys'tăl·line (*or* -lĭn), *a.* 1. consisting or made of crystal; as, a *crystalline* palace.
2. relating or pertaining to crystals or crystallography.
3. formed by crystallization; having the character or structure of a crystal.
4. resembling crystal; pure; clear; transparent; pellucid; as, a *crystalline* sky.
5. consisting of crystals.
crystalline heavens; in ancient astronomy, two spheres imagined between the *primum mobile* and the firmament, in the Ptolemaic system, which supposed the heavens to be solid and susceptible of only a single motion.
crystalline lens; the double convex, transparent part of the eye lying behind the iris and in front of the vitreous body of the eye. It serves to refract the various rays of light so as to form an image on the retina.
crystalline style; a semitransparent caecal organ of certain bivalves.
crystalline system; any of the six groups (isometric, hexagonal, tetragonal, orthorhombic, monoclinic, and triclinic) into which crystalline species are classified on the basis of the relationships of their crystallographic axes (imaginary lines drawn from each face or edge through the center of the crystal).
çrys'tăl·line, *n.* a crystallized rock, or one only partially crystallized, as granite.
çrys'tăl·līte, *n.* [Gr. *krystallos,* crystal, ice, and *-ite.*] a hairlike formation found in igneous and volcanic rocks that are beginning to crystallize.
çrys·tăl·lit'iç, *a.* 1. of or containing crystallite.
2. of the nature of crystallite.
çrys'tăl·lī·zȧ·ble, *a.* that may be crystallized; that may form or be formed into crystals.
çrys"tăl·li·zā'tion, *n.* 1. the act or process of crystallizing or being crystallized.
2. the mass or body formed by the process of crystallizing.
çrys'tăl·līze, *v.t.;* crystallized, *pt., pp.;* crystallizing, *ppr.* 1. to cause to form crystals or take on a crystalline structure.
2. to give a definite form to; as, to *crystallize* public opinion.
3. to coat with sugar.
çrys'tăl·līze, *v.i.* 1. to become a crystal or crystalline in form.
2. to take on a definite form; as, our unfavorable impressions *crystallized* into a strong dislike.
çrys'tăl·lō-, [Gr. *krystallos.*] a combining form meaning *crystal.*
çrys'tăl·lod, *n.* [Gr. *krystallos,* crystal, and Gr. *od,* from *hodos,* way.] the imagined odic force of crystallization.
çrys"tăl·lō·ġen'iç, çrys"tăl·lō·ġen'iç·ăl, *a.* relating to crystallogeny; pertaining to crystal formation.
çrys·tăl·loġ'e·ny, *n.* [*crystallo-,* and Gr. *-geneia,* from *genēs,* producing.] the science which has to do with the formation of crystals.
çrys·tăl·log'rȧ·phẽr, *n.* one who has made a study of crystallography.
çrys"tăl·lō·graph'iç, çrys"tăl·lō·graph'iç·ăl,

a. relating to crystallography; as, a *crystallographic* axis.

çrys″tăl·lō·graph′iç·ăl·ly, *adv.* according to the manner of crystallography; by crystallization.

çrys·tăl·log′rȧ·phy, *n.* [*crystallo-*, and Gr. *-graphia*, from *graphein*, to write.]
1. the science of the form, structure, properties, and classification of crystals.
2. a discourse or treatise on crystallization.

çrys′tăl·loid, *a.* [Gr. *krystallos*, crystal, and *eidos*, form.]
1. like a crystal.
2. having the nature of a crystalloid.

çrys′tăl·loid, *n.* 1. a substance, usually crystallizable, which, when in solution, readily passes through vegetable and animal membranes: opposed to *colloid*.
2. a protein crystal present in some vegetable cells.

çrys·tăl·loi′dăl, *a.* of a crystalloid.

çrys·tăl·lol′ō·ġy, *n.* [*crystallo-*, and Gr. *-logia*, from *legein*, to speak.] same as *crystallography*.

çrys′tăl·lō·man·cy, *n.* [*crystallo-*, and Gr. *manteia*, divination.] crystal gazing.

çrys·tăl·lom′e·try, *n.* [*crystallo-*, and Gr. *-metria*, from *metron*, a measure.] the art or process of measuring crystals.

çrys′tăl·lōse, *a.* [*crystall-* and *-ose*.] the sodium salt of saccharin, used for the same purposes as saccharin: also called *soluble saccharin*.

çrys′tăl·lūr·ġy, *n.* [*crystallo-*, and Gr. *ergon*, work.] formation of crystals; the process of producing crystals. [Obs.]

çrys′tăl pick′up, a pickup with a quartz crystal, often used on electric phonographs: distinguished from *magnetic pickup*.

çrys′tăl set, a simple type of radio receiver with a crystal detector instead of an electron tube detector.

çrys′tăl vī′ō·let, a rosaniline dye used in medicine as an antiseptic, an indicator, and a Gram stain for bacteria.

çrys′tăl vi′şion (-zhun), 1. the alleged faculty of divination by crystal gazing.
2. the images supposed to be seen in crystal gazing.

çrys′tăl·wŏrt, *n.* a plant of the *Hepaticæ* or liverwort family.

cte·nid′i·um (te-), *n.*; *pl.* **cte·nid′i·ȧ,** [L., from Gr. *ktenidion*, dim. of *kteis*, a comb.] the filamentous respiratory organ of a mollusk; a branchia.

cten′ō- (ten′ō-), [Gr. *kteis*, *ktenos*.] a combining form meaning a *comb*.

cten′ō·brañçh, cten·ō·brañ′çhi·āte (ten-), *a.* having comblike gills, as the *Ctenobranchiata*.

cten′ō·brañçh, cten·ō·brañ′çhi·āte, *n.* one of the *Ctenobranchiata*.

Cten·ō·brañ·çhi·ā′tȧ, Cten·ō·brañ′çhi·ȧ, *n. pl.* a family of mollusks, the *Pectinibranchiata*.

ctē′nō·cyst (tē′), *n.* [*cteno-*, and Gr. *kystis*, a bladder.] a sensory organ found in the *Ctenophora*.

cten′ō·dont, *a.* [*cteno-*, and Gr. *odous*, *odontos*, a tooth.] having the teeth ctenoid.

ctē′noid (tē′), *a.* [*cteno-*, and Gr. *eidos*, form.]
1. relating to fish of the *Ctenoidei*.
2. having an edge with projections like the teeth of a comb, as the scales and teeth of certain fishes.

ctē′noid, *n.* a ctenoidean. [Obs.]

ctē·noid′ē·ăn, ctē·noid′i·ăn, *a.* of or relating to the *Ctenoidei*.

ctē·noid′ē·ăn, ctē·noid′i·ăn, *n.* a ctenoid fish.

Ctē·noid′ē·ī, *n.pl.* [L., from Gr. *kteis*, *ktenos*, a comb, and *eidos*, form.] a group of fishes having scales jagged or pectinate like the teeth of a comb.

Cte·noph′ō·rȧ, *n.pl.* [L., from Gr. *kteis*, *ktenos*, a comb, and *-phoros*, from *pherein*, to bear.] a large group of sea animals with an oval, transparent, gelatinous body. Eight rows of comblike plates covered with cilia run from pole to pole, and are used in swimming.

cte·noph′ō·răn, *a.* of a ctenophore.

cte·noph′ō·răn, *n.* a member of the *Ctenophora*.

cten′ō·phōre, *n.* 1. an individual of the *Ctenophora*.
2. one of the comblike plates of the *Ctenophora*.

cte·noph′ō·rous, cten·ō·phor′iç, *a.* pertaining to or resembling the *Ctenophora*.

Cten·ō·stom′ȧ·tȧ, *n.pl.* [*cteno-*, and Gr. *stoma*, *stomatos*, a mouth.] a suborder of marine *Polyzoa*, having the terminal mouths closed by means of a fringe of hair.

çuär·tïl′lä (kwär-tēl′yä), *n.* [Sp., dim. of *cuarta*, fourth.] a Spanish measure; (a) eight liquid pints or one-fourth of an arroba; (b) one-fourth of a fanega.

çub, *n.* [Ir. *cuib*, a young dog, whelp; *cu*, a dog.]
1. the young of certain mammals, as of the bear and the fox; a whelp.
2. an inexperienced youth; an awkward young person.
3. a novice or beginner, especially in newspaper reporting.
4. a member of a division of the Boy Scouts for boys between the ages of eight and eleven.

çub, *v.t.* and *v.i.*; cubbed, *pt.*, *pp.*; cubbing, *ppr.* to bring forth, as a cub or cubs; also, to bring forth young: a contemptuous usage.

çub, *v.t.* to restrain; to confine. [Obs.]

çub, *n.* 1. a stall for cattle. [Obs.]
2. a cubby; a cupboard; a chest. [Obs.]

çūb′āġe, *n.* [*cube* and *-age*.] cubic content; cubature.

Çū′bȧ lïb′re, [Sp., lit., free Cuba.] an alcoholic drink made by mixing a cola beverage with rum and fresh lime or lemon juice.

Çū′băn, *a.* of or relating to the island of Cuba, its people, or culture.

Çū′băn, *n.* a native or inhabitant of Cuba.

Çū′băn heel, a heel of medium height, used on some types of women's shoes.

çū′băn·īte, *n.* [so named because first found in *Cuba*.] a sulfide of iron and copper, resembling chalcopyrite.

çū·bā′tion, *n.* [L. *cubatio*, from *cubare*, to lie down.] a reclining. [Obs.]

çū′bȧ·tō·ry, *a.* [LL. *cubator*, one who lies down, from *cubare*, to lie down.] recumbent. [Rare.]

çū′bȧ·tūre, *n.* [from L. *cubus*, a cube.] the determination of the cubic content of a body; also, the contents so found.

çub′bridġe·head (-brij-hed), *n.* [*cubbord*, cupboard, and *-age* and *head*.] a partition made of boards, etc. across the forecastle and half-deck of a ship.

çub′by, *n.* [LG. *kubje*, a shed.] a secluded nook indoors; a close, snug corner.

çub′by·hōle, *n.* a small, enclosed space; a pigeonhole; a recess.

çub′by·yew, *n.* [a corruption of *cobia*, of W. Ind. origin.] a fish, the cobia.

çub′-drạwn, *a.* sucked by its cubs: applied to the bear.

çūbe, *n.* [Fr. *cube*; L. *cubus*; Gr. *kybos*, a cube, die.]
1. in geometry, a regular solid with six equal square sides.
2. in arithmetic, the third power; the product obtained by multiplying a given number or quantity by its square; as, 4 × 4 = 16, and 16 × 4 = 64, the *cube* of 4, (4 × 4 × 4).

CUBE

cube root; the number or quantity of which a given number or quantity is the cube: as, the *cube root* of 8 is 2.

çūbe, *v.t.*; cubed, *pt.*, *pp.*; cubing, *ppr.* 1. to raise to the third power by multiplying (a number) by itself twice.
2. to form or cut into the shape of a cube or cubes; as, *cube* the vegetables.
3. to measure the cubic content of.

çū′beb, *n.* [Sp. *cubeba*; Ar. *kababa*; Hind. *kababa*.].
1. the small, spicy berry of the *Piper cubeba*, from Java and other East Indian islands, used in diseases of the urinary system, and sometimes made into cigarettes, smoked for catarrh or bronchial disease.
2. such a cigarette.

çū·beb′iç, *a.* relating to or obtained from cubebs.

çūbe ọre, a mineral, pharmacosiderite.

çūbe spär, a mineral, anhydrite.

çub′hood, *n.* the condition of being a cub.

çū′biç, *a.* [L. *cubicus*; Gr. *kybikos*, from *kybos*, a cube.]
1. having the form of a cube.
2. having three dimensions; measured by, or capable of being measured by, a unit of volume (e.g., a cubic foot) which is the volume of a cube whose length, width, and breadth each measure that linear unit (a foot).
3. in mathematics, denoting the third power or degree; relating to the cubes of numbers or quantities.

cubic equation; an equation in which the highest exponent of the unknown quantity or quantities is three.

cubic number; in arithmetic, a cube.

cubic parabola; a curve equationally expressed by $y^m = ax^n$, in which one exponent is 3, and greater than the other.

çū′biç, *n.* in mathematics, (a) a cubic expression or equation; (b) a cubic curve.

çū′biç·ăl, *a.* 1. cubic.
2. of or pertaining to a cube.

çū′biç·ăl·ly, *adv.* by a cubical method.

çū′biç·ăl·ness, *n.* the state or quality of being cubical.

çū′bi·çle, *n.* [L. *cubiculum*, a bedroom, from *cubare*, to lie down.] a small sleeping compartment, as in a dormitory; also, any small compartment.

çū′biç meaṣ′ūre (mezh′), a system of measuring volume in cubic units, as the system in which 1,728 cubic inches = 1 cubic foot and 27 cubic feet = 1 cubic yard.

çū·biç′ū·lăr, *a.* pertaining to a private chamber; as, *cubicular* devotions. [Obs.]

çū·biç′ū·lum, *n.*; *pl.* **çū·biç′ū·lȧ,** [L., lit., a sleeping chamber.] a burial chamber, as in the Roman catacombs.

çū′bi·fọrm, *a.* having the form of a cube.

çū·bi′lē, *n.* [L., a bed, resting place, from *cubare*, to lie down.] the groundwork or lowest course of stones in a building.

çūb′işm, *n.* a school of modern art characterized by the use of cubes and other abstract geometric forms rather than by a realistic representation of nature.

çūb′ist, *n.* an adherent of cubism.

çūb′ist, *a.* of cubism or cubists.

çū′bit, *n.* [L. *cubitum*, the elbow, a cubit.]
1. in anatomy, the forearm; the ulna, a bone of the arm from the elbow to the wrist. [Obs.]
2. a measure of length, originally the distance from the elbow to the end of the middle finger. The ancient Egyptian cubit measured 20.64 inches; the Roman cubit was equal to 17.4 inches; and the English cubit is a measure of 18 inches.
3. a cubitus.

çū′bit·ăl, *a.* 1. of the length or measure of a cubit.
2. pertaining to the cubit or ulna; as, the *cubital* nerve.
3. in zoology, relating to the cubitus.

çū′bit·ăl, *n.* [L. *cubital*, an elbow cushion, from *cubitum*, an elbow.]
1. an oversleeve covering the forearm from the wrist to the elbow. [Obs.]
2. a pillow upon which to lean the elbow when in a half-reclining position.
3. in entomology, a cubitus.

çū′bit·ed, *a.* having the measure of a cubit.

çū′bi·tus, *n.*; *pl.* **çū′bi·tī,** [L. *cubitus*, the elbow.]
1. in entomology, the primary nervure of an insect's wing, lying between the media and the first anal vein.
2. in anatomy, same as *cubit*.

çū·bō-, [L. *cubus*, Gr. *kybos*.] a combining form meaning *a cube*, used to signify, (a) in mathematics, *relating to a cube*, and (b) in anatomy, *of or pertaining to the cuboid bone in the foot*.

çū″bō·dō″deç·ȧ·hē′drăl, *a.* [*cubo-*, and Gr. *dōdekaedron*; *dōdeka*, twelve, and *hedra*, a seat, base.] presenting the two forms, a cube and a dodecahedron.

çū′boid, *a.* [Gr. *kyboidēs*.]
1. shaped like a cube.
2. designating a cubelike bone between the instep and the heel bone.

çū′boid, *n.* 1. a six-sided figure each face of which is a rectangle.
2. the cuboid bone.

çū·boid′ăl, *a.* 1. cuboid.
2. of the cuboid bone.

çū″bō-oç·tȧ·hē′drăl, *a.* presenting the two forms, a cube and an octahedron.

çū″bō-oç·tȧ·hē′drŏn, *n.* [*cubo-*, and Gr. *oktaedron*, from *oktaedros*, eight-sided; *oktō*, eight, and *hedra*, a seat, base.] a fourteen-sided figure having twelve vertices, being a combination of the cube and octahedron.

çub rē·pōrt′ēr, an inexperienced newspaper reporter.

çū′çȧ, *n.* see *coca*.

çuck′ing stọọl, [ME. *cokinge-stole*, lit., toilet seat, from ME. *coken*, from ON. *kūka*, to defecate: the instrument was orig. made to resemble a toilet seat to heighten the victim's indignity.] a kind of chair in which disorderly women, scolds, dishonest tradespeople, etc. were fastened and exposed to public ridicule, or sometimes ducked.

çuck′ōld, *n.* [ME. *cokewold*, *cukeweld*; OFr. *cucuault*, from *cucu* (see *cuckoo*).]
1. a man whose wife has committed adultery.
2. the horned cowfish, *Ostracion quadricorne*.
3. the cowbird, *Molothrus ater*: so called

from its habit of laying its eggs in nests not of its own building.

cuckold's knot or *neck*; in nautical usage, a knot securing a rope to a spar, the two parts being crossed and seized together.

çuck'ōld, *v.t.*; cuckolded, *pt., pp.*; cuckolding, *ppr.* to make a cuckold of.

çuck'ōld·īze, *v.t.* to cuckold. [Obs.]

çuck'ōld·ly, *a.* having the qualities of a cuckold; mean; sneaking. [Obs.]

çuck'ōl·dŏm, *n.* the condition of being a cuckold.

çuck'ōld·ry, *n.* the act of making a cuckold of a husband; adultery.

çuck'o͝o, *n.* [ME. *cuckoo*, from OFr. *coucou*, *cucu*, echoic of the bird's cry.]

1. a bird of the family *Cuculidæ*, named in imitation of the call of the male during the mating season. It is of many genera, and is found in most temperate and tropical regions. The typical genus, *Cuculus*, comprises the

CUCKOO (*Cuculus canorus*)

common European cuckoo, *Cuculus canorus*, a zygodactylous bird about the size of a small pigeon, having an abundance of ashy plumage streaked with white and black. It deposits its eggs in the nests of other birds. The principal American species are *Coccyzus americanus*, the yellow-billed cuckoo, and *Coccyzus erythrophthalmus*, the black-billed cuckoo: both species hatch and rear their own young.

2. the call of a cuckoo, which sounds somewhat like its name.

3. an imitation of this call.

4. an idiot; a fool: used in jest or contempt.

çuck'o͝o, *v.i.* to utter or imitate the call of the cuckoo.

çuck'o͝o, *v.t.* to repeat continually: from the cuckoo's habit of sounding its call again and again.

çuck'o͝o, *a.* crazy; foolish; silly. [Slang.]

çuck'o͝o bee, a bee of any of several genera, as the *Nomada, Epeolus, Cælioxys*, etc. It lays its eggs in the nests of other bees.

çuck'o͝o-bread, çuck'o͝o's-bread (-bred), *n.* a plant, wood sorrel.

çuck'o͝o-bud, *n.* the buttercup. [Obs.]

çuck'o͝o çlock, a clock with a small toy figure of a cuckoo in it, which appears at regular intervals, usually on the hour, to the accompaniment of a sound imitating the bird's call.

çuck'o͝o dŏve, a pigeon of the genus *Macropygia*.

çuck'o͝o fạl'cŏn (fa'k'n), one of a group of East Indian falconine birds.

çuck'o͝o fish, in England, (a) *Trigla cuculus*, the red gurnard; (b) the boarfish; (c) the striped wrasse.

çuck'o͝o-flow"ẽr, *n.* any of several plants; especially, (a) lady's-smock; (b) ragged robin.

çuck'o͝o flȳ, any of various parasitic insects, as the ichneumon fly or one of the *Chrysididæ*.

çuck'o͝o-pīnt, *n. Arum maculatum*, the wake robin.

çuck'o͝o-shrīke, *n.* a bird, the caterpillar catcher.

çuck'o͝o spit, çuck'o͝o spit'tle, 1. a frothy substance produced on plants by the nymphs of certain insects to envelop their larvae.

2. such an insect.

çuck'quēan, *n.* [*cuck*old, and *quean*, a woman.] a woman whose husband has committed adultery. [Obs.]

çu·çū'jō, *n.* see *fire beetle*, sense 1.

çū·çū'li·fọrm, *a.* [L. *cuculus*, a cuckoo, and *forma*, form.] of or like the cuckoos or the order of birds to which they belong.

çū'çū·līne, *a.* [from L. *cuculus*, a cuckoo.] pertaining or related to the cuckoos; having the characteristics of a cuckoo.

çū'çul·lāte, çū'çul·lā·ted, *a.* [LL. *cucullatus*, from *cucullus*, a hood, cowl.]

1. hooded; cowled; covered as with a hood.

2. in botany, having the shape or resemblance of a hood; wide at the top and drawn to a point below, in the shape of a conical roll of paper; as, a *cucullate* leaf.

3. in zoology, bearing some process or marking resembling a hood; especially, having the first segment of the thorax raised to cover the head like a hood, as some insects.

çū·çul'lī, *n.*, pl. of *cucullus*.

çū·çul'li·fọrm, *a.* [L. *cucullus*, a hood, and *forma*, form.] formed like or resembling a hood.

çū·çul'lus, *n.*; *pl.* **çū·çul'lī,** [L.]

1. a cowl or hood worn by the ancient Romans.

2. in biology, a marking or a part or process, like a hood.

çū'çū·loid, *a.* [L. *cuculus*, a cuckoo, and Gr. *eidos*, form.] of or pertaining to the typical genus of cuckoos, *Cuculus*; also, resembling the cuckoos.

çū'çum·bẽr, *n.* [ME. *cucumber, cocumber*; OFr. *cocombre*; LL. *cucumer*; L. *cucumis, cucumeris*, a cucumber.]

1. any of various plants of the genus *Cucumis* or of related genera; also, the fruit of such plants.

2. *Cucumis sativus*, a common garden vegetable. The plant has long rough stalks, creeping or climbing, and yellow flowers. The fruit is fleshy, cylindrical in shape, and edible when unripe. It is also much used for pickling.

bitter cucumber; the colocynth.

cool as a cucumber; exceedingly cool; also, composed and self-possessed.

creeping cucumber; a climbing vine of the southeastern United States, the *Melothria pendula*.

Jamaica (or *Jerusalem*) *cucumber*; *Cucumis anguria*, the prickly cucumber, the fruit of which is used for pickles.

squirting (or *wild*) *cucumber*; a cucurbitaceous plant, *Ecballium elaterium*: the fruit, when ripe, separates from the stem and, by sudden contraction of the rind, forces out the seeds and juice through the opening left at the point of attachment.

çū'çum·bẽr bee'tle, a beetle that feeds upon the leaves of cucumber, melon, squash, and similar vines; especially, a flea beetle, *Crepidodera cucumeris*, and the squash beetle, *Diabrotica vittata*.

çū'çum·bẽr ro͞ot, the Indian cucumber.

çū'çum·bẽr tree, 1. any of several varieties of magnolia trees cultivated for shade and ornament; especially, the *Magnolia acuminata*, which bears a fruit somewhat resembling a small cucumber in shape.

2. the bilimbi of the East Indies.

çū·çū'mi·fọrm, *a.* [L. *cucumis*, a cucumber, and *forma*, form.] cucumber-shaped.

Çū'çū·mis, *n.* [L., a cucumber.] a genus of plants, family *Cucurbitaceæ*, containing about thirty species. They are annual herbs, with hairy stems and leaves, spreading over the ground or climbing. They have yellow flowers, and a roundish, cylindrical, or angular fleshy fruit. The best known species are *Cucumis sativus*, the cucumber, and *Cucumis melo*, the muskmelon.

çū·çũr'bit, çū·çũr'bite, *n.* [Fr. *cucurbite*; L. *cucurbita*, a gourd.]

1. a chemical vessel originally in the shape of a gourd, but sometimes shallow, with a wide mouth, formerly used in distillation.

2. any vessel that is gourd-shaped, as a cupping glass.

3. a plant belonging to the order *Cucurbitaceæ*.

Çū·çũr'bi·tȧ, *n.* a genus of plants typical of the family *Cucurbitaceæ*. There are about a dozen species inhabiting the warmer regions of the world. They are creeping annuals, with lobed, cordate leaves, large yellow flowers, and fleshy, generally very large fruits. The pumpkin and the longneck squashes belong to *Cucurbita pepo*, and the winter squash to *Cucurbita maxima*.

Çū·çũr·bi·tā'çē·ae, *n.pl.* a family of polypetalous dicotyledonous plants, with the petals more or less united into a monopetalous corolla, consisting of climbing or trailing species with unisexual flowers, scabrous stems and leaves, and a more or less pulpy fruit. The order includes the melon, gourd, cucumber, pumpkin, squash, colocynth, bryony, and other plants, ranged into more than eighty genera and six hundred species.

çū·çũr·bi·tā'ceous, *a.* pertaining or belonging to the *Cucurbitaceæ*; having the characteristics of the gourd family.

çū·çũr'bi·tăl, *a.* of or pertaining to the order *Cucurbitaceæ* or the type genus *Cucurbita*.

çū·çũr'bi·tive, *a.* shaped like the seed of a gourd: a term applied to certain kinds of small worms.

çud, *n.* [ME. *cudde, cude*; AS. *cudu*; *cwidu*, cud, from *ceowan*, to chew.]

1. a mouthful of previously swallowed food regurgitated from the first stomach of cattle and other ruminants back to the mouth, where it is chewed slowly a second time.

2. a portion of tobacco held in the mouth and chewed. [Slang.]

3. the first stomach of ruminants; the rumen.

to chew the cud; to ponder; to reflect; to ruminate.

çud'beãr, *n.* [coined from *Cuthbert*, after Dr. *Cuthbert* Gordon, who first brought it into notice.]

1. a purple or violet-colored powder, used in dyeing violet, purple, and crimson, prepared from various species of lichens, especially from *Lecanora tartarea*.

2. the lichen yielding such dye.

çud'den, *n.* a clown; a low rustic; a dolt. [Obs.]

çud'den, çud'die, *n.* the coalfish. [Brit. Dial.]

çud'dle, *v.i.*; cuddled (-dld), *pt., pp.*; cuddling, *ppr.* [an alteration of ME. *cuthen*, to cuddle, make known; AS. *cuth*, pp. of *cunnan*, to know.] to snuggle; to lie close or snug.

çud'dle, *v.t.* to hug; to embrace and fondle.

çud'dle, *n.* 1. a cuddling.

2. a hug; an embrace.

çud'dle·sŏme, *a.* [*cuddle*, and *-some*.] inviting cuddling; embraceable.

çud'dly, *a.*; *comp.* cuddlier; *superl.* cuddliest; fond of cuddling; cuddlesome.

çud'dy, *n.*; *pl.* **çud'dieș,** [perhaps a contr. of D. *kajuit*, a cabin.]

1. (a) a small room or cabin on a ship; (b) on a small ship, the cook's galley or a shelter cabin.

2. a small room, cupboard, or closet.

çud'dy, *n.*; *pl.* **çud'dieș,** an ass; a donkey; also, a stupid fellow; a simpleton or clown. [Scot.]

çud'dy, *n.*; *pl.* **çud'dieș,** a fish of the cod family, the coalfish: written also *cudden*, *cuddie*. [Scot.]

çudġ'el (kuj'el), *n.* [ME. *cuggel*; W. *cogyl*, a club, cudgel.] a short, thick stick of wood, such as may be used as a weapon.

to take up the cudgels for; to come to the defense of.

çudġ'el, *v.t.*; cudgeled, cudgelled, *pt., pp.*; cudgeling, cudgelling, *ppr.* to beat with a cudgel.

to cudgel one's brains; to think hard.

çudġ'el·ẽr, çudġ'el·lẽr, *n.* one who beats with a cudgel.

çudġ'el plāy, a fight with cudgels, especially as a contest.

çud'weed, *n.* any of several plants, as *Gnaphalium, Filago*, and *Antennaria*, with cottony or woolly leaves.

çūe, *n.* [from *q*, used on plays in 16th and 17th c. to indicate actors' entrances; prob. abbrev. of some L. word, as *quando*, when.]

1. a signal in dialogue, action, or music for an actor's entrance or speech, or for the working of curtains, lights, sound effects, etc.

2. the few notes or bars of music directly preceding an instrumentalist's or vocalist's part and serving as a signal for him to begin.

3. any signal or motion to begin or enter.

4. a hint; intimation; suggestion.

5. the part that an actor is assigned to play.

6. a course of action.

7. frame of mind; mood; temperament.

8. in psychology, a secondary stimulus that guides behavior, often without entering consciousness.

çūe, *v.t.*; cued, *pt., pp.*; cuing, *ppr.* to give a cue to. [Colloq.]

çūe, *n.* [Fr. *queue*, pigtail; OFr. *coue*; It. *coda*; L. *coda, cauda*, a tail.]

1. the tail end of a thing, as the long curl of a wig, or a long roll or braid of hair: written also *queue*.

2. a line of waiting persons, as that formed in front of a ticket window: written also *queue*.

3. a long, tapering, tipped rod used in billiards and similar games to strike the cue ball.

çūe, *v.t.*; cued, *pt., pp.*; cuing, *ppr.* to braid, twist, or curl; to tie in a cue.

çūe, *n.* [for *q.*, an abbrev. of L. *quadrans*, a farthing.] a half farthing or a half farthing's worth.

çūe bạll, the ball that a player strikes with his cue in billiards or pool: it is usually white or yellowish.

çuer'pō (kwer'), *n.* [Sp., from L. *corpus*, a body.] the body; the form of the body.

in cuerpo; without a cloak or upper garment,

or without the formalities of full dress; by extension, undressed; unprotected; naked.

çues'tȧ (kwes'), *n.* [Sp.] a ridge or hill characterized by a steep escarpment on one side and a long gentle slope on the other.

çuff, *v.t.*; cuffed, *pt., pp.*; cuffing, *ppr.* [perhaps from ON.; cf. Sw. *kuffa*, to thrust, push; *kufva*, to subdue, oppress.] to strike with the hand, especially with the open hand; to box or slap; also, to beat or buffet.

çuff, *v.i.* to fight; to scuffle.

çuff, *n.* a blow with the fist, or, more generally, with the open hand; a slap; a box.

çuff, *n.* [ME. *cuffe, coffe*, a glove or mitten; AS. *cuffie*, cap, hood.]
1. a band at the wrist end of the sleeve of a garment, either fastened to the sleeve or separate.
2. the wrist end of a sleeve.
3. a turned-up fold at the bottom of a trouser leg.
4. a handcuff.
5. that portion of a gauntlet glove which is stiffened and covers the wrist and forearm.
on the cuff; with payment deferred. [Slang.]

çuff, *v.t.* to put a cuff or cuffs on.

çuff but'tŏn, a button for the cuff of a shirt.

çuff liñk, a pair of linked buttons or similar small device for keeping a shirt cuff closed.

Çū'fiç, *a.* same as *Kufic.*

çui bō'nō (kwē *or* kī), [L., lit., to whom for a good.]
1. for whose benefit?
2. to what purpose?

çuin'ȧġe (kwin'), *n.* corrupted from *coinage.*] the stamping of pigs of tin, by the proper officer. [Brit.]

çui·rȧss' (kwi-), *n.* [Fr. *cuirasse*; L. *coratia, coratium*, a breastplate of leather; L. *corium*, skin, leather.]
1. a piece of close-fitting armor for protecting the breast and back: it was originally made of leather.
2. the breastplate of such armor.
3. in zoology, a protective structure of bony plates.

çui·rȧss' (kwi-), *v.t.* to cover with or as with a cuirass.

çui·rȧssed' (kwi-), *a.* provided with a cuirass; as, a *cuirassed* fish; a *cuirassed* sentry.

çui·rȧs·siēr' (kwi-), *n.* [Fr.] a cavalryman wearing a cuirass.

çuir-bōuil·li' (kwēr-bö-yē'), *n.* [Fr. *cuir bouilli*, boiled leather.] leather that is soaked in hot water or boiled, and pressed into some shape or stamped with a pattern, which is permanently retained when the leather dries and hardens. Formerly used for armor, helmets, etc., now used in decorative art.

çuish (kwish), *n.* same as *cuisse.*

çui·ṣine' (kwē-zēn'), *n.* [Fr., from L. *coquina*, a kitchen; *coquere*, to cook.]
1. the kitchen.
2. the manner of preparing food for eating; the style of cooking; cookery.
3. the food prepared, as at a restaurant.

çuisse (kwis), *n.* [ME. *cuissues*; OFr. *cuisseaux*, pl. of *cuissel*, from *cuisse*, thigh, from L. *coxa*, hip.] [*usually in pl.*] a piece of armor for protection of the thigh; thigh piece: also *cuish.*

çu·lasse', *n.* [Fr., from *cul*, back.] the lower portion of a gem cut as a brilliant.

çulch, *n.* same as *cultch.*

Çul·dee', *n.* [Gael. *ceile*, servant, and *De*, of God.] one of an ancient order of monks who lived in Scotland, Ireland, and Wales.

çul'-de-föur', *n.*; *pl.* **çuls'-de-föur',** [Fr., bottom of an oven.] in architecture, a vault that is a quarter sphere in form; a semidome.

çul'-de-saç' (*Fr.* kü'), *n.*; *pl.* **çul'-de-saçs',** Fr. **çuls'-de-saç'** (kü'), [Fr., the bottom of a bag.]
1. a passage or position with only one outlet; a blind alley.
2. a situation from which there is no escape.
3. militarily, the situation of an army when it is hemmed in and has no exit except behind.
4. in anatomy, any natural cavity or bag, or tubular vessel, having but one end open.

-çūle, [from Fr. or L.; Fr. *-cule*; L. *-culus, -cula, -culum.*] a suffix added to nouns to indicate the diminutive, as in animal*cule.*

çul'ēr·ȧġe, *n.* culrage. [Obs.]

çū'let, *n.* [OFr., from *cul*, bottom; L. *culus*, anus.]
1. the flat face on the lower side of a gem cut as a brilliant: spelled also *cullet, collet.*
2. [*pl.*] in ancient armor, the overlapping plates from the waist to the hip which protected the back of the knight.

Çū'lex, *n.* [L., a gnat.]
1. the genus of insects regarded as the type of the family *Culicidæ.*
2. any of a large group of mosquitoes including the most common species found in North America and Europe.

çū'li·cid, *a.* of or pertaining to the family *Culicidæ*; having characteristics like those of the mosquito family.

çū'li·cid, *n.* an insect of the family *Culicidæ.*

Çū·lic'i·dae, *n.pl.* [L., from *culex, culicis*, a gnat, and *-idæ.*] a family of insects including mosquitoes, gnats, etc.

çū·lic'i·fọrm, *a.* [L. *culex, culicis*, a gnat, and *forma*, form.] of the form or shape of a gnat; resembling a gnat.

çū'li·nā·ri·ly, *adv.* in the manner of cookery, with reference to the process or place of cooking; in relation to a kitchen.

çū'li·nā·ry, *a.* [L. *culinarius*, from *culina*, a kitchen.] relating to the kitchen, or to the art of cookery; used in kitchens or in the process of cooking, as, *culinary* knowledge; a *culinary* vessel.

çull, *v.t.*; culled, *pt., pp.*; culling, *ppr.* [ME. *cullen*, to gather, pick, OFr. *cuillir, coillir*; L. *colligere*, to collect.]
1. to pick out; to separate (one or more things) from others; to select and gather together from many; to collect; as, to *cull* flowers.
2. to sort over; to measure and to examine for quality; as, to *cull* lumber.

çull, *n.* anything selected from others; especially, something inferior picked out and set aside.

çull, *n.* a cully. [Slang.]

çull bōard, a table or stand for holding articles to be sorted.

çul'len·dẽr, *n.* see *colander.*

çull'ẽr, *n.* one who culls.

çul'let, *n.* [from Fr. *collet*, dim. of *col*, neck, with reference to glass debris at the neck of a bottle in blowing.] scraps of waste glass that can be remelted.

çul'let, *n.* see *culet.*

çul·li·bil'i·ty, *n.* credulity; easiness in being gulled. [Obs.]

çul'li·ble, *a.* gullible. [Obs.]

çull'ing, *n.* 1. the act or process of sorting out or selecting.
2. anything separated or selected from a mass as inferior; refuse: generally used in the plural.

çul'liŏn (-yun), *n.* [OFr. *couillon, coillon*, a vile fellow, coward, testicle; L. *coleus*, scrotum.]
1. a low, contemptible fellow. [Obs.]
2. a round or bulbous root, an orchis.

çul'liŏn·ly, *a.* mean, base. [Obs.]

çul'lis, *n.* [Fr. *couler*, to strain, to run.]
1. a broth of boiled meat strained. [Obs.]
2. a kind of jelly. [Obs.]

çul'lis, *n.* 1. a trough or gutter in a roof.
2. a groove in which some piece is fitted to run, as a side scene on the stage of a theater.

çull'-mē-to'-you, *n.* the pansy. [Brit. Dial.]

çul'ly, *n.*; *pl.* **çul'lieṣ,** [17th-c. thieves' slang; perhaps contr. of *cullion.*]
1. a person easily deceived; dupe. [Rare.]
2. fellow; pal; buddy. [Brit. Slang.]

çul'ly, *v.t.*; cullied, *pt., pp.*; cullying, *ppr.* to deceive; to trick, cheat, or impose on; to jilt. [Obs.]

çul'ly·iṣm, *n.* the state of being a cully. [Slang.]

çulm, *n.* [L. *culmus*, a stock, stem.] in botany, the stalk or stem of grasses, usually jointed and hollow.

çulm, *v.i.* to grow or develop into a culm.

çulm, *n.* [ME. *culme, colm*, soot, smoke.]
1. coal dust or slack; small pieces of anthracite.
2. in geology, a Lower Carboniferous formation of shale or sandstone containing beds of impure anthracite: also *culm measures.*

çul'men, *n.* [L., the top, summit.]
1. top; summit.
2. in ornithology, the ridge running lengthwise down the middle of the upper mandible.
3. in anatomy, a small protuberance on the upper surface of the median lobe of the cerebellum.

çul·miç'ō·lous, *a.* [L. *culmus*, a stock, stem, and *colere*, to inhabit.] growing on grass stems: applied to certain fungi.

çul·mif'ẽr·ous, *a.* [L. *culmus*, a stalk, and *ferre*, to bear.] bearing culms, or grass stems.

çul·mif'ẽr·ous, *a.* [ME. *culm*, soot, smoke, and *ferre*, to bear.] in geology, producing or containing culm.

çul'mi·năl, *a.* [from L. *culmen, culminis*, the top, summit.] of or pertaining to the summit or culmen; at or belonging to the apex; topmost.

çul'mi·nănt, *a.* approaching or situated at the highest point or altitude; culminating.

çul'mi·nāte, *v.i.*; culminated, *pt., pp.*; culminating, *ppr.* [LL. *culminatus*, pp. of *culminare*, from *culmen*, top, summit.]
1. to reach its highest altitude: said of a celestial body.
2. to reach its highest point or climax; result (*in*).

çul'mi·nāte, *a.* growing upward, as distinguished from a lateral growth: applied specifically to the growth of corals.

çul·mi·nā'tion, *n.* 1. the transit of a heavenly body over the meridian; the attainment by a heavenly body of its greatest altitude.
2. the act of attaining the highest point; the state of being at the apex; also, the highest point of any ascending progress; the top; summit; acme.

çū·lottes', *n.pl.* [Fr.] knee-length trousers made full in the legs to resemble a skirt, worn by women and girls for sports, etc.

çul'pȧ, *n.* [L.]
1. fault; guilt.
2. in law, negligence; carelessness.

çul·pȧ·bil'i·ty, *n.* blamableness; liability to blame.

çul'pȧ·ble, *a.* [L. *culpabilis*, blameworthy, from *culpare*, to find fault with, condemn; *culpa*, a fault, crime.]
1. blameworthy; deserving censure, as the person who has done wrong, or the act, conduct, or negligence of the person; as, the man is *culpable*; voluntary ignorance is *culpable.*
2. guilty, as, *culpable* of a crime. [Obs.]

çul'pȧ·ble·ness, *n.* the quality of deserving blame; the state of being censurable; blamableness.

çul'pȧ·bly, *adv.* in a culpable manner.

çul'pȧ·tō·ry, *a.* [L. *culpatus*, pp. of *culpare*, to blame, condemn; *culpa*, a fault, crime.] censuring or accusing; expressing blame or charging with guilt. [Rare.]

çulpe, *n.* [Fr. *coulpe*; L. *culpa*, fault, crime.] an offense or fault; also, guilt, blameworthiness. [Obs.]

çul'pon, *n.* [ME. *culpe*, a fragment, chip; OFr. *coupon*, from *couper*, to cut.] a piece of something cut, torn, or split off; a slice, shred, or splinter. [Obs.]

çul'prit, *n.* [from Anglo-Fr. *cul. prit*, contr. for phr. *culpable, prit* (*à averer nostre bille*), lit., guilty, ready (to prove our case): words used by prosecutor in opening case.]
1. a person accused of a crime or offense, as in court; prisoner at the bar.
2. a person guilty of a crime or offense; offender.

çul'rȧġe, *n.* [ME. *culrage*; OFr. *culrage, curage*, from *cul* (L. *culus*), the posteriors, and *rage*, L. *rabies*, madness.] *Polygonum hydropiper*, smartweed. [Obs.]

çult, *n.* [Fr. *culte*, L. *cultus*, from *colere*, to cultivate, worship.]
1. worship; reverential honor; religious devotion. [Obs.]
2. the system of outward forms and ceremonies used in worship; religious rites and formalities.
3. devoted attachment to, or extravagant admiration for, a person, principle, etc., especially when regarded as a fad; as, the *cult* of nudism.
4. a group of followers; sect.

çultch, çulch, *n.* [origin uncertain.]
1. rubbish.
2. the various materials, such as shells, gravel, etc., out of which a spawning bed for oysters is made.
3. the spawn of oysters.

çul'tẽr, *n.* [L.] a colter.

çul·ti·ros'trăl, *a.* [L. *culter*, a colter, and *rostrum*, a beak.] same as *cultrirostral.*

Çul·ti·ros'trēṣ, *n.pl.* same as *Cultrirostres.*

çul'ti·vȧ·ble, *a.* capable of being tilled or cultivated.

çul'ti·vā·tȧ·ble, *a.* cultivable.

çul'ti·vāte, *v.t.*; cultivated, *pt., pp.*; cultivating, *ppr.* [L. *cultus*, cultivation, from *colere*, to cultivate.]
1. to prepare and use (soil, land, etc.) for growing crops; to till.
2. to break up the surface soil around (plants) in order to destroy weeds, prevent crusting, and preserve moisture.
3. to grow (plants or crops) from seeds, bulbs, shoots, etc.
4. to improve or develop (plants) by various horticultural techniques.

5. to improve by care, training, or study; refine; as, *cultivate* your mind.
6. to promote the development or growth of; acquire and develop; as, he *cultivated* a social conscience.
7. to seek to develop a familiarity with; give one's attention to; pursue.

çul'ti·vāt·ed, *a.* 1. prepared and used for growing crops; tilled; as, *cultivated* land.
2. grown by cultivation: opposed to *wild*.
3. trained and developed; refined; cultured; as, a *cultivated* person.

çul·ti·vā'tion, *n.* 1. the art or practice of cultivating land, plants, etc.; husbandry; the management of land for agriculture.
2. study, care, and practice directed to improving or advancing something; as, men may grow wiser by the *cultivation* of talents.
3. the state of being cultivated or refined; refinement; culture.
Syn.—civilization, culture, improvement, husbandry, refinement, melioration.

çul'ti·vā·tŏr, *n.* 1. one who cultivates; as, a *cultivator* of land; a *cultivator* of friendship.
2. a machine or implement, as a harrow, hoe, etc., used in loosening the soil or ridding it of weeds.

çul'trāte, *a.* [L. *cultratus*, knife-shaped, from *culter*, a knife.] sharp-edged and pointed; shaped like a pruning knife; as, the beak of a bird is convex and *cultrate*.

çul'trā·ted, *a.* cultrate.

çul'tri·fọrm, *a.* cultrate; having the shape of a pruning knife.

çul·tri·ros'trăl, *a.* [L. *culter*, a knife, and *rostrum*, a beak.] having a cultrate beak.

Çul·tri·ros'trēs, *n.pl.* an obsolete group of birds distinguished by a bill which is large, long, and strong, as cranes, herons, storks, etc.

çul'tūr·ȧ·ble, *a.* capable of being cultivated or cultured; suitable for cultivation.

çul'tūr·ăl, *a.* 1. of culture.
2. obtained by breeding.

çul'tūr·ăl fēa'tūreș, man-made landmarks, as cities, highways, dams, etc., especially as seen from the air.

çul'tūre, *n.* [Fr. *culture*, from L. *cultura*, cultivation, care, from *cultus*, pp. of *colere*, to till.]
1. the act or process of tilling and preparing the earth for crops; cultivation of soil.
2. the raising, improvement, or development of some plant, animal, or product.
3. the growth of bacteria or other microorganisms in a specially prepared nourishing substance, as agar.
4. a colony of microorganisms thus grown.
5. improvement, refinement, or development by study, training, etc.
6. the training and refining of the mind, emotions, manners, taste, etc.
7. the result of this; refinement of thought, emotion, manners, taste, etc.
8. the concepts, habits, skills, art, instruments, institutions, etc. of a given people in a given period; civilization.

çul'tūre, *v.t.*; cultured, *pt., pp.*; culturing, *ppr.*
1. to cultivate; to refine; to educate.
2. to grow (microorganisms) in a specially prepared medium.

çul'tūred, *a.* 1. cultivated; under cultivation or culture; as, *cultured* fields.
2. possessing culture and refinement; as, *cultured* people.
Syn.—refined, accomplished, cultivated, learned, erudite, polished.

çul'tūre (*or* **çul'tūr·ăl**) **dif·fū'sion,** in sociology, the spread of a culture trait or pattern from its point of origin to other areas.

çul'tūred pēarl, a pearl grown within a mollusk by controlled stimulation, as by insertion of a bead of mother-of-pearl.

çul'tūre (or **çul'tūr·ăl**) **lag,** in sociology, the failure of one aspect of a cultural complex to keep pace with the changes in some other related aspect, as the failure of social institutions to keep pace with the rapid advances in science.

çul'tūre·less, *a.* having no culture.

çul'tūre mē'di·um, a nutrient substance sterilized and suitably prepared for the controlled growth of microorganisms.

çul'tūr·ist, *n.* 1. a person engaged in the culture of plants or animals.
2. one who advocates, or is devoted to, general cultural advancement.

çul'tus, *n.* [L., care, cultivation, from *cultus*, pp. of *colere*, to till, care for.] a cult, especially a religious cult.

çul'tus çod, [probably from Chinook *cultus*, worthless.] an edible fish of large size, *Ophiodon elongatus*, found along the northern Pacific coast.

çul'vẽr, *n.* same as *culverin*.

çul'vẽr, *n.* [ME. *culver*; AS. *culfre*, *culufre*, a dove.] a pigeon or wood pigeon; a dove.

çul'vẽr·house, *n.* a dovecote.

çul'vẽr·in, *n.* [OFr. *couleuvrine*, *colouvrine*, a serpent; L. *colubra*, f. of *coluber*, a serpent.]
1. a kind of musket used in the Middle Ages.
2. a long, heavy cannon of the sixteenth and seventeenth centuries.

çul·vẽr·in·eer', *n.* one whose duty it was to load and fire a culverin.

çul'vẽr·kēy, *n.* [*culver*, from AS. *culfre*, a dove, and *key*, from AS. *cæg*, key.]
1. an English meadow plant or flower. [Obs.]
2. a bunch of the keys or pods of the ash tree.

Çul'vẽr's phyș'iç, the root of *Veronica* (*Leptandra*) *virginica*, a tall herb having a medicinal use; also, the plant itself. It was used by a Dr. *Culver*, and named after him.

çul'vẽrt, *n.* [Fr. *coulvir*, a channel or gutter, from *couler*, to drop or trickle; OFr. *coulouere*, a channel.] a passage under a road, railroad or canal, covered with an arch or bridge; an arched drain for the passage of water.

CULVERT

çul'vẽrt·āġe, *n.* [OFr. *culvertage*, serfage, from *culvert*, low, mean, a serf, wretch, rascal.] in feudal law, forfeiture of a vassal's holding to the lord of the manor, and his consequent reduction to serfdom.

çul'vẽr·tāil, *n.* in carpentry, a dovetail. [Obs.]

çum, *prep.* [L.] with: used, chiefly in hyphenated compounds, with the general meaning "combined with" or "plus;" as, vaudeville-*cum*-burlesque.

Çū·mā'cē·ȧ, *n.pl.* [from Gr. *kyma*, a wave.] an order of small crustaceans, resembling the *Schizopoda*.

Çū·maē'ăn, *a.* of a famous sibyl of Cumae, an ancient city in Italy.

çū'mȧ·rin, *n.* same as *coumarin*.

çum'bent, *a.* [L. *cubere*, to lie down.] lying down. [Rare.]

çum'bẽr, *v.t.*; cumbered, *pt., pp.*; cumbering, *ppr.* [ME. *cumbren*, *combren*; OFr. *combrer*, to hinder, obstruct; from L. *cumulus*, a heap.]
1. to overload; to overburden.
2. to check, stop, or retard, as by a load or weight; to make motion difficult; to obstruct.
3. to perplex or trouble. [Obs.]

çum'bẽr, *n.* hindrance; obstruction; embarrassment; distress.

çum'bẽr·sŏme, *a.* 1. troublesome; burdensome; embarrassing; vexatious; as, *cumbersome* obedience.
2. unwieldy; unmanageable; not easily borne or managed; as, a *cumbersome* load.

çum'bẽr·sŏme·ly, *adv.* in a cumbersome way.

çum'bẽr·sŏme·ness, *n.* burdensomeness; the quality of being cumbersome.

çum'brănce, *n.* that which obstructs; burden.

Çum'bri·ăn, *a.* [L. *Cumbria*, Cumberland.] pertaining to Cumbria, an early British kingdom, or to Cumberland, a county in the north of England, formerly part of Cumbria.

çum'brŏus, *a.* cumbersome.

çum'brŏus·ly, *adv.* in a cumbrous manner.

çum'brŏus·ness, *n.* the state of being cumbrous.

çū'mēne, *n.* one of the hydrocarbons, C_6H_5-C_3H_7, prepared from coal tar.

çum'frey, *n.* see *comfrey*.

çum grā'nō sā'lis, [L., lit., with a grain of salt.] with due skepticism.

çū'miç, *a.* same as *cuminic*.

çū'mi·din, çū'mi·dine, *n.* in chemistry, an organic compound obtained from cumene.

çum'in, çum'min, *n.* [ME. *cummin*; AS. *cumin*, *cymen*; L. *cuminum*; Gr. *kyminon*, the cumin plant.]
1. a small plant, *Cuminum cyminum*, of the carrot family, bearing clusters of small, white or rose flowers.
2. its aromatic seeds used for flavoring pickles and soups, and as an ingredient of curry powder.
black cumin; the plant *Nigella sativa*; also, its pungent seeds.
sweet cumin; the anise, *Pimpinella anisum*.
wild cumin; *Lagæcia cuminoides*, a European plant of the parsley family.

çū·min'iç, *a.* pertaining to or derived from cumin; as, *cuminic* acid.

çū'mi·nil, *n.* a yellow crystalline compound, $C_{20}H_{22}O_2$.

çū'mi·nōl, *n.* a colorless oil, $C_{10}H_{12}O$.

çum lau'dē, [L.] with praise: phrase used to signify graduation with honors from a college.

çum'mẽr, *n.* [Fr. *commère*; LL. *commater*, from L. *com-*, with, and *mater*, mother.]
1. a godmother. [Scot.]
2. a woman companion. [Scot.]
3. a woman or girl. [Scot.]

çum'mẽr·bund, *n.* [Hind. *kamarband*; *kamar*, the loins, and *band*, *bandh*, a band.] a sash for the waist, worn originally by men in India: also written *kummerbund*, *kamarband*.

çū'mōl, *n.* same as *cumene*.

çum'quăt (-kwăt), *n.* a small Chinese orange, the fruit of the *Citrus aurantium*: also written *kumquat*.

çum'shaw, *n.* [from dial. form of Chin. *kan hsieh*, grateful thanks; *kan*, to be thankful, and *hsieh*, thanks.] a tip; gratuity.

çum'shaw, *v.t.* to give a present to; to tip.

çū'mū·lāte, *v.t.*; cumulated, *pt., pp.*; cumulating, *ppr.* [L. *cumulatus*, pp. of *cumulare*, to heap or pile up.]
1. to gather or throw into a heap; to form into a heap; to heap together.
2. in law, to unite in one action; as, to *cumulate* actions or causes of actions.

çū'mū·lāte, *a.* gathered into a heap.

çū·mū·lā'tion, *n.* 1. a cumulating.
2. an accumulation; a heap.

çū'mū·lā·tist, *n.* one who accumulates, gathers, or collects. [Rare.]

çū'mū·lā·tive, *a.* 1. composed of parts in a heap; forming a mass. [Obs.]
2. increasing in effect, size, quantity, etc. by successive additions; accumulated; as, *cumulative* interest is interest that is added to the principal and draws additional interest.
3. in law, (a) augmenting or tending to establish a point already proved by other evidence; (b) designating a legacy where the legatee is more than once provided for in the same testament.
cumulative action; in medicine, the sudden action of certain drugs after several doses which have produced no apparent effect.
cumulative voting; a system of voting for members of a legislature whereby each voter can record as many votes as there are candidates for election, either giving them all to one candidate or dividing them among the several candidates.

çū'mū·lā·tive·ly, *adv.* in a cumulative manner.

çū'mū·lī, *n.*, pl. of *cumulus*.

çū'mū·li·fọrm, *a.* designating, or having the form of, a cumulus (cloud).

çū"mū·lō-cir"rō-strā'tus, *n.* [L. *cumulus*, a heap, *cirrus*, a curl or spiral, *stratus*, pp. of *sternere*, to spread out.] a form of cloud which expands into a crown of cirrus and breaks into a shower; a rain cloud.

çū"mū·lō-cir'rus, *n.* a small cumulus that is white and filmy like a cirrus.

çū"mū·lō-nim'bus, *n.* [L. *cumulus*, a heap, and *nimbus*, a cloud.] a thick, towering cloud formation, usually producing rain.

çū'mū·lōse, *a.* full of heaps.

çū"mū·lō-strā'tus, *n.* [L. *cumulus*, a heap, and *stratus*, pp. of *sternere*, to strew.] a cumulus (cloud) with a horizontal base like a stratus.

çū'mū·lous, *a.* of, or having the form of, a cumulus (cloud), or consisting of cumuli.

çū'mū·lus, *n.*; *pl.* **çū'mū·lī,** [L., a heap.]
1. a heap; mass; pile.
2. a thick cloud formation with a horizontal base and rounded masses piled up on each other.

çum'yl, *n.* [from L. *cuminum*; Gr. *kyminon*, the cumin plant, and *hylē*, matter.] in chemistry, a monovalent radical, C_3H_7·C_6H_4, derived from cumene.

çun, *v.t.* to know. [Obs.]

çun, *v.t.* to con or direct the course of (a ship). [Obs.]

çū·nab'ū·lȧ, *n.pl.* [L. *cunabula*, neut. pl., early abode, cradle; dim. of *cunæ*, cradle.]
1. the early abode or birthplace; the beginnings; as, the *cunabula* of anarchism.
2. same as *incunabula*.

çunç·tā'tion, *n.* [L. *cunctatio*, a delay, from *cunctari*, to delay.] a delaying or delay. [Rare.]

çunç'tȧ·tive, *a.* slow-moving; sluggish; dilatory. [Rare.]

çunç·tā'tŏr, *n.* [L. *cunctator*, a loiterer, from *cunctari*, to delay.] one who waits or delays. [Rare.]

çunç·tip'ō·tent, *a.* [L. *cunctus*, all, entire, and *potens*, ppr. of *posse*, to be able, to be powerful.] all-powerful; omnipotent. [Rare.]

çund, *v.t.* to direct, as a ship. [Obs.]

çun·dū·rañ'gō, *n.* [native name.] a vine, *Marsdenia cundurango*, of South America.

çū'nē·ăl, *a.* [L. *cuneus*, a wedge.] pertaining to, or having the form of, a wedge.

çū'nē·āte, *a.* [L. *cuneatus*, wedge-shaped, from *cuneus*, a wedge.] in botany, wedge-shaped: said of a leaf which terminates abruptly with a blunted point and tapers gradually downward.

CUNEATE LEAF

çū'nē·ā·ted, *a.* cuneate.

çū'nē·āte·ly, *adv.* in the form of a wedge.

çū·nē·at'iç, *a.* cuneal.

çū'nē·ā·tŏr, *n.* [from LL. *cuneare*, to shape like a wedge; from L. *cuneus*, a wedge.] formerly, an officer having charge of the dies used in the mints in England.

çū·nē'i·fọrm, *a.* [from L. *cuneus*, genit. *cunei*, a wedge, and *forma*, form.] shaped like a wedge: especially applied to (a) any of the wedge-shaped bones of the ankle or of the wrist; (b) the wedge-shaped characters in the inscriptions of the ancient Akkadians, Persians, Babylonians, and Assyrians, or the inscriptions themselves.

THE SUN
GOD
MOUNTAIN
MAN
OX
CUNEIFORM CHARACTERS

çū·nē'i·fọrm, *n.* 1. cuneiform characters or inscriptions.

2. in anatomy, a cuneiform bone.

çū·nette', *n.* [Fr., possibly dim. formed from L. *cuneus*, a wedge.] in fortification, (a) a small trench in the middle of a larger one, for drainage purposes; (b) a deep trench dug along the middle of a dry moat, to increase the difficulty of passing over it.

çū'nē·us, *n.*; *pl.* **çū'nē·ī**, [L. *cuneus*, a wedge.]

1. in zoology, a triangular or wedge-shaped portion of the forewings of certain heteropterous insects.

2. in anatomy, a cuneate or wedge-shaped convolution on the mesial aspect of the occipital lobe of the brain.

çū·niç'ū·lăr, *a.* [from L. *cuniculus*, a rabbit; by metonymy, a passage underground.] relating to or resembling rabbitlike burrows underground.

çū·niç'ū·lāte, *a.* in botany, traversed by a long passage open at one end, as the peduncle of the nasturtium.

çū·niç'ū·lous, *a.* relating to rabbits. [Rare.]

çū·niç'ū·lus, *n.*; *pl.* **çū·niç'ū·lī**, [L., a rabbit; by metonymy, a passage underground.]

1. a small, subterranean passage; specifically, one of the ancient subterranean drains about Rome and other districts of Italy.

2. the burrow of the itch insect.

çū'ni·fọrm, *a.* and *n.* same as *cuneiform.*

Çū·nī'là, *n.* [L. *cunila*, a plant.] a genus of shrubby plants belonging to the family *Labiatæ*: the fragrant herb, *Cunila origanoides*, of the eastern United States, commonly called dittany, is the best known species.

çun'nẽr, çŏn'nẽr, *n.* [a local Eng. word; origin obscure.] a small, salt-water food fish, *Tautogolabrus adspersus*, found along the coast of eastern North America.

çun·ni·liñ'gus, *n.* [L., lit., vulva-licker, from *cunnus*, vulva, and *lingere*, to lick.] a sexual activity involving oral contact with the female genitals.

çun'ning, *a.* [ME. *cunning*, *connyng*, skillful; AS. *cunnian*, to try, test.]

1. skillful; clever; shrewd.

2. skillful in deception; sly; crafty.

3. created with skill; ingenious.

All the more do I admire
Joints of *cunning* workmanship.
—Tennyson.

4. pleasing; attractive; pretty in a delicate way; as, a *cunning* child.

Syn.—artful, crafty, designing, sly, astute, subtle, wily, insidious.

çun'ning, *n.* 1. knowledge; art; skill; dexterity; as, a workman of great *cunning*. [Archaic.]

Let my right hand forget her *cunning*.
—Ps. cxxxvii. 5.

2. artfulness; craft; shrewdness; slyness; skill in deception.

Discourage *cunning* in a child; *cunning* is the ape of wisdom. —Locke.

çun'ning·ly, *adv.* in a cunning manner.

çun'ning man, a man who tells fortunes. [Obs.]

çun'ning·ness, *n.* the quality of being cunning.

çun'ning wom'ăn (woom'), a woman fortuneteller. [Obs.]

çup, *n.* [ME. *cup*, *cuppe*; AS. *cuppe*, a cup; LL. *copa*, *coppa*, a cup; L. *cupa*, a tub, cask.]

1. a small, open container for beverages, usually bowl-shaped and with a handle.

2. the bowl of a drinking container.

3. a cup and its contents.

4. as much as a cup will hold; cupful: usually half a pint.

5. one's portion, share, or allotment (*of* a given experience); as, his *cup of* happiness was full.

6. the chalice containing the sacramental wine at Communion; also, the wine itself.

7. anything shaped like a cup; as, an acorn *cup*.

8. a vessel shaped like a cup, usually made of silver, offered as a prize to be contended for in horseracing, yachting, and other sports.

9. [C—] in astronomy, the constellation Crater.

10. a mixed drink of wine, etc., usually iced, flavored, and sweetened; as, claret *cup*.

11. in medicine, a small glass vessel used in cupping.

12. in biology, any cuplike organ or structure.

13. in golf, (a) the metal container in a hole; (b) a hole.

cup and ball; a toy consisting of a cup or hole at the end of a stick to which a ball is attached by a cord. The ball is tossed up and the player tries to catch it in the cup.

to be in one's cups; to be intoxicated.

çup, *v.t.*; cupped (kupt), *pt.*, *pp.*; cupping, *ppr.*

1. to give cups of liquor to; to make drunk. [Obs.]

2. to treat with or subject to cupping.

3. to take in or put into a cup.

4. to shape like a cup; to make concave.

çup, *v.i.* 1. to drink. [Obs.]

2. in surgery, to operate by cupping.

3. in golf, to make a hole or depression in the ground when striking the ball.

çup'beãr"ẽr, *n.* a person who fills and serves the wine cups, as in a king's palace.

çup'bŏard (kub'ẽrd), *n.* 1. a table or shelf for holding cups. [Obs.]

2. a cabinet or closet fitted with shelves for cups, plates, dishes, etc.

3. any small closet, cabinet, etc. [Brit.]

cupboard love; insincere professions of love, motivated by self-interest and a desire for gain.

çup'bŏard, *v.t.* to collect into a cupboard. [Obs.]

çup'çāke, *n.* a small cake, sometimes baked in a paper cup.

çup çor'ăl, a coral shaped like a cup.

çū'pel, *n.* [Fr. *coupelle*, a cupel; ML. *cupella*, a cup; dim. of L. *cupa*, a tub, cask.]

1. a small cup, shallow and porous, used in assaying gold, silver, etc.

2. a receptacle or furnace bottom for refining silver.

çū·pel', *v.t.*; cupeled *or* cupelled, *pt.*, *pp.*; cupeling *or* cupelling, *ppr.* to assay or refine in a cupel, as gold or silver.

çū'pel dust, powder used in refining metals.

çū·pel·lā'tion, *n.* the process of assaying or refining gold, silver, or other metals in a cupel.

çup'fụl, *n.*; *pl.* **çup'fụls**, 1. the contents of a cup; the quantity that a cup will hold.

2. in cookery, half a pint.

Çū'phē·à, *n.* [Gr. *kyphos*, a hump, with reference to the protuberant base of the calyx.] a genus of plants, order *Lythraceæ*, found in tropical America. *Cuphea platycentra*, the cigar plant, is widely cultivated.

Çū'phiç, *a.* same as *Kufic.*

Çū'pid, *n.* [L. *Cupido*, the god of love, from *cupido*, passion, desire of love, from *cupere*, to desire.]

1. in Roman mythology, the god of love, son of Venus: usually represented as a naked boy with wings, and carrying a bow and quiver of arrows, and identified with the Greek god Eros.

2. [c—] a representation of Cupid as a naked, winged boy, as on a valentine.

çū·pid'i·ty, *n.* [Fr. *cupidité*; L. *cupiditas*, desire, wish, from *cupere*, to desire.]

1. inordinate greed for wealth or power; avarice; covetousness.

2. passionate carnal desire; sexual love. [Obs.]

çū'pi·dōne, *n.* [Fr. *Cupidon*, the name of a flower; L. *Cupido*, Cupid.] in botany, a composite plant bearing blue flowers, *Catananche cærulea.*

çū'pid's-bōw', *a.* in the shape of the bow that Cupid is usually pictured as carrying; as, a *cupid's-bow* mouth.

çup lī'çhen, same as *cup moss.*

çup mọss, in botany, a lichen of the genus *Cladonia*, having a cup-shaped podetium.

çup of tēa, a favorite thing, activity, etc.; as, golf isn't his *cup of tea*. [Brit. Colloq.]

çū'pō·là, *n.* [It. *cupola*, a dome; LL. *cupula*, a cup, dim. of L. *cupa*, a tub, cask.]

1. in architecture, a small dome or similar structure on a roof.

2. a rounded roof or ceiling.

3. a furnace used in foundries for melting metals: usually of firebrick cased with iron.

CUPOLA

4. a dome-shaped, armor-plated, revolving gun turret on a battleship.

5. in anatomy, a dome-shaped process or organ.

çū'pō·là, *v.t.*; cupolaed (-lȧd), *pt.*, *pp.*; cupolaing, *ppr.* 1. to provide with a cupola.

2. to make in the shape of a cupola.

çupped, *a.* shaped like a cup.

çup'ping, *n.* in medicine, the act of drawing blood to the surface of the skin of a body by means of the vacuum created in a cupping glass.

dry cupping; cupping without cutting the skin.

wet cupping; the application of a cupping glass to a cut surface.

çup'ping glȧss, a small bell-shaped glass used in cupping to produce a vacuum.

çup plant, a tall, composite American plant, *Silphium perfoliatum*, bearing large, yellow flowers and opposite leaves, the upper pairs curving into the shape of a cup.

çup'py, *a.* having hollows resembling a cup; cuplike.

çū'prē·ous, *a.* [L. *cupreus*, coppery, from *cuprum*, copper, from Gr. *Kypros*, Cyprus island, abounding in copper.]

1. of, like, or consisting of copper.

2. copper-colored.

çū·pres'site, *n.* [from L. *cupressus*, the cypress tree.] a coniferous fossil plant occurring in the Trias and other formations, and supposedly allied to the cypress.

Çū·pres'sus, *n.* [L. *cupressus*; Gr. *kyparissos*, the cypress tree.] a genus of coniferous evergreen trees having appressed leaves and scaly cones; the cypress: native to Asia and western America.

çū'pri-, a combining form meaning copper, as in *cupri*ferous.

çū'priç, *a.* [L. *cuprum*, copper; from Gr. *Kypros*, the island of Cyprus, famous for its copper.] in chemistry, containing, derived from, or pertaining to copper with a valence of two.

çū·prif'ẽr·ous, *a.* [from L. *cuprum*, copper, and *ferre*, to bear.] containing copper; as, *cupriferous* silver.

çū'prīte, *n.* [L. *cuprum*, copper.] in mineralogy, a dark-red copper ore, Cu_2O, found massive and in isomeric crystals.

çū'prō-, [from L. *cuprum*, copper.] a combining form meaning *copper and*, as in *cupro*magnesite: also, before a vowel, *cupr-*.

çū'proid, *n.* [from L. *cuprum*, copper, and Gr. *eidos*, form.] in crystallography, a solid related to a tetrahedron, and having twelve equal triangular faces.

çū·prō·mag'nē·site, *n.* a mineral containing copper and magnesium.

çū'prō·nick·el, *n.* an alloy of copper and nickel, used in the manufacture of hardware and in some coins.

çū'prous, *a.* [from L. *cuprum*, copper, and *-ous*.] in chemistry, of or containing copper with a valence of one.

çū'prum, *n.* [L.] copper.

çup'seed, *n.* a climbing vine, *Calycocarpum lyoni*, native to the southeastern United States.

çup spọṅge, a variety of sponge resembling a cup in form.

çū'pū·là, *n.* same as *cupule.*

çū′pū·lăr, *a.* bearing cupules; cup-shaped.
çū′pū·lāte, *a.* cupular.
çū′pūle, *n.* [L. *cupula*, dim. of *cupa*, a tub or cask; Gr. *kypē*, anything hollow.]
1. in botany, a cup-shaped part, as the involucre of the acorn.
2. any small cup-shaped depression in a level surface, as in rock.
3. in zoology, a sucking disk.
çū·pū·lif′ẽr·ous, *a.* [from L. *cupula*, a cup, and *ferre*, to bear.] having the form of a cupule; bearing cupules.
çup valve, a valve with a seat made to fit a cover in the form of a cup or section of a sphere.

CUP VALVE

çŭr, *n.* [ME. *curre*, *kur*; prob. from Sw. dial. *kurre*, a dog; Ice. *kurra*, to mumble.]
1. a dog of mixed breed; a mongrel.
2. a person who is mean, contemptible, cowardly, etc.
çūr·ȧ·bil′i·ty, *n.* the state or quality of being cured.
çūr′ȧ·ble, *a.* capable of being cured.
çūr′ȧ·ble·ness, *n.* curability.
cu·ra·çao′ (çū-rȧ-sō′), *n.* a sweet liqueur flavored with orange peel, cinnamon, and mace, and deriving its name from the island of Curaçao, north of Venezuela, its place of origin: also written *curaçoa.*
çū′rȧ·cy, *n.*; *pl.* **çū′rȧ·cieṣ,** the office, duties, or tenure of a curate.
çù·rä′rē, *n.* [native S. Am. name.]
1. a black, resinous extract obtained from *Strychnos toxifera* and other trees and used by South American Indians to poison arrow-points, especially those of the arrows used with the blowgun: it causes motor paralysis when introduced into the blood stream and is now used in medicine to reduce spasm in various conditions of muscular rigidity, as in tetanus and spastic paralysis.
2. any of certain plants from which this substance is prepared.
Also *curari*, *curara*, *ourali*, *wourali*, *urari*, etc.
çù′rȧ·rine, *n.* an extremely poisonous alkaloid obtained from curare.
çù′rȧ·rīze, *v.t.*; curarized, *pt.*, *pp.*; curarizing, *ppr.* to treat or poison with curare.
çū·ras′sōw, *n.* [named from the island of *Curaçao.*] any bird of South and Central America belonging to the genera *Crax* and *Pauxi*, family *Cracidæ*. There are a dozen or more species. The crested curassow, *Crax alector*, is native to Guiana, Mexico, and Brazil: called also *curaçao bird*. Several species are domesticated in South America, being similar to the turkey.
çū′rat, *n.* a breastplate; a cuirass. [Obs.]
çū′rāte, *n.* [ME. *curat*; ML. *curatus*, a priest, from L. *curare*, to care for.]
1. originally, a clergyman.
2. a clergyman who assists a rector or vicar.
3. a guardian or protector. [Obs.]
çū′rāte·ship, *n.* a curacy.
çū·rā′tion, *n.* the act of healing. [Obs.]
çūr′ȧ·tive, *a.* 1. of or relating to the cure of diseases.
2. curing, tending to cure, or having the power to cure.
çūr′ȧ·tive, *n.* that which cures; a remedy.
çū·rā′tŏr, *n.* [L. *curator*, a manager, overseer, from *curare*, to care for.]
1. one who has the care and superintendence of anything, as a museum, library, etc.
2. in law, a guardian of a minor or of an incompetent.
çū·rā′tŏr·ship, *n.* the office or position of a curator.
çū·rā′trix, *n.* [LL., f., from L. *curator*, a manager.]
1. a woman curator or custodian.
2. a woman who cures. [Rare.]
çũrb, *n.* [Fr. *courbe*, a curve, the knee; L. *curvus*, crooked, from *curvare*, to bend.]
1. a chain or strap passed around a horse's lower jaw and attached to the bit: the curb checks the horse when the reins are pulled.
2. anything that checks, restrains, or subdues.
3. an enclosing framework.
4. a raised margin around or along an edge, to strengthen or confine.
5. a stone or concrete edging of a sidewalk or pavement: British spelling *kerb*.
6. a market dealing in stocks and bonds not listed on the stock exchange: so called from the fact that early markets conducted their business on the street.
7. a hard callous swelling on a horse's leg, attended with stiffness, and sometimes pain and lameness.
curb market; same as *curb* (sense 6).
çũrb, *v.t.* 1. to restrain; check; control.
2. to provide with a curb.
çũrb bit, a horse's bit having a curb.
çũrb chāin, a chain that curbs or checks the motion of machinery.
çũrb′ing, *n.* 1. curbstones collectively.
2. the material for making a curb.
3. a curb or part of a curb (sense 5): British spelling *kerbing.*
çũrb′less, *a.* having no curb; unrestrained.
çũrb pin, a pin that controls the balance-wheel of a watch and regulates the vibrations.
çũrb plāte, in architecture, any plate that serves as a curb.
çũrb roof, in architecture, a gambrel roof; a roof having a double slant on each side, the lower one being the steeper.

RAFTERS
BEAMS
WALL
WALL
CURB ROOF

çũrb send′ẽr, in telegraphy, an automatic signaling device that sends alternate opposing electric currents, the second curbing the indication produced by the first and making it sharp and distinct.
çũrb′stōne, *n.* a stone or concrete edge at the margin of a sidewalk or pavement; also, a series of such stones forming the curb: British spelling *kerbstone.*
çũrch, *n.* a woman's head covering; a kerchief. [Scot.]
çũr·çū′li·ō, *n.*; *pl.* **çũr·çū′li·ōṣ,** [L. *curculio*, a corn worm.] an insect of the family *Curculionidæ.*
çũr·çū·li·on′id, *a.* pertaining to the *Curculionidæ.*
Çũr·çū·li·on′i·dae, *n.pl.* a large family of coleopterous insects, the weevils or snout beetles: the head is prolonged into a beak or snout, furnished with sharp jaws: some are harmful to fruit.
Çũr′çū·mȧ, *n.* [Ar. *kurkum*, saffron.] a genus of plants of the family *Scitamineæ*, having perennial roots and annual stems. *Curcuma longa* yields turmeric.
çũr′çū·mȧ pā′pẽr, same as *turmeric paper.*
çũr′çū·min, *n.* [Ar. *kurkum*, saffron.] in chemistry, the yellowish coloring matter of turmeric.
çũrd, *n.* [15th-c. form, metathesized from ME. *crudde*, from AS. *crudan*, to press.]
1. the coagulated or thickened part of milk, which is made into various kinds of cheese: it is formed when milk sours and is distinguished from whey, the watery part.
2. any chemical coagulation.
çũrd, *v.t.* and *v.i.*; curded, *pt.*, *pp.*; curding, *ppr.* to form into a curd; to curdle.
çũrd′i·ness, *n.* the quality or state of being curdy.
çũr′dle, *v.t.* and *v.i.*; curdled, *pt.*, *pp.*; curdling, *ppr.* to coagulate; to thicken or change into curd; to congeal; as, milk *curdles* by a mixture of rennet.
to curdle one's blood; to horrify or terrify one.
çũrd′less, *a.* without curd.
çũrd′y, *a.* 1. full of curd.
2. like curd; coagulated.
çūre, *n.* [ME. *cure*; OFr. *cure*, cure; L. *cura*, care.]
1. a healing; the act of healing; restoration to health.
2. a remedy; that which makes one well.
Cold, hunger, prisons, ills without a *cure.*
—Dryden.
3. a system or method of medical treatment.
4. the care of souls; spiritual charge; curacy.
5. the office or work of a curate.
6. attention; care. [Obs.]
7. the preserving of fish, meat, etc., as by salting or smoking.
çūre, *v.t.*; cured, *pt.*, *pp.*; curing, *ppr.* 1. to heal; to restore to health; to make well.
2. to get rid of or provide a remedy for (an ailment, evil, etc.).
3. to prepare by salting or smoking, so as to preserve; as, to *cure* fish or beef.
Syn.—heal, make well, remedy, restore.
çūre, *v.i.* 1. to be or become preserved.
2. to bring about a cure.
3. to heed; to take care. [Obs.]
cu·ré′ (çū-rā′), *n.* [Fr., from L. *curare*, to care for.] in France, a parish priest.
çūre′-ąll, *n.* a remedy for all diseases or evils; a panacea.
çūre′less, *a.* incurable.
çūr′ẽr, *n.* 1. a healer; one who heals.
2. one who prepares meats to be preserved.
çū·ret′tāġe, *n.* in surgery, the process of curetting.
çū·rette′, *n.* [Fr., a scoop, scraper, from *curer*, to cleanse.] a spoon-shaped surgical instrument for removing tissue from the walls of body cavities.
çū·rette′, *v.t.*; curetted, *pt.*, *pp.*; curetting, *ppr.* to scrape and cleanse with a curette.
çũr′few, *n.* [ME. *curfewe*; OFr. *courfeu*, curfew, contr. of *couvre-feu*, lit., cover fire; *couvrir* (L. *cooperire*), to hide, and *feu*, fire; L. *focus*, hearth.]
1. in the Middle Ages, a regulation causing a bell to be rung every evening at a certain time as a signal to the inhabitants to rake up their fires, put out lights, and retire.
2. the ringing of such a bell.
3. the hour for ringing it.
4. the bell.
5. a time, generally in the evening, set as a deadline beyond which children, inhabitants of cities occupied by the enemy in wartime, etc. may not appear on the streets or in public places.
6. the regulation establishing this time.
7. a cover for a fire. [Obs.]
çū′ri·ȧ, *n.*; *pl.* **çū′ri·ae,** [L.]
1. in ancient Rome, any of the ten political subdivisions into which the Latin, Sabine, and Etruscan tribes were each divided.
2. the meeting place of one of these divisions.
3. the Roman senate house.
4. in the Middle Ages, a judicial council or court held in the king's name.
5. [C–] the collective body of officials of the papal government: also called *Curia Romana.*
çū′ri·ăl, *a.* [L. *cuiralis*, pertaining to the curia.]
1. pertaining to a curia.
2. courtly. [Obs.]
çū′ri·ȧ·liṣm, *n.* the political doctrines or policy of the Italian party in the Roman Catholic Church; ultramontanism.
çū′ri·ȧ·list, *n.* in the Roman Catholic Church, an ultramontanist.
çū″ri·ȧ·lis′tiç, *a.* pertaining to a court.
çū·ri·al′i·ty, *n.* the privileges, prerogatives, or retinue of a court. [Obs.]
Çū′ri·ȧ Rō·mā′nȧ, [L.] the papal court, including all the officials and authorities that help the Pope in the government of the Roman Catholic Church.
çū′riē, *n.* [named for Marie Sklodowska *Curie*, 1867–1934, Polish scientist.] the unit used in measuring radioactivity: the quantity of any radioactive atom of a specific nuclear constitution in which the number of disintegrations per second is 3.700×10^{10}.
Çū′riē's ląw, [after Pierre *Curie* (1859–1906), Fr. physicist.] the law that the ratio of the magnetization of a paramagnetic substance to the magnetizing force is in inverse proportion to the absolute temperature.
çū′ri·et, *n.* a cuirass. [Obs.]
çūr′ing house, 1. any building in which the curing, or preserving, process is done.
2. a building in which sugar is drained and dried.
çū′ri·ō, *n.*; *pl.* **çū′ri·ōṣ,** [contr. of *curiosity.*] an art object regarded as rare or curious.
çū″ri·ō·loġ′iç, *a.* [Gr. *kyriologikos*, one who speaks literally, from *kyros*, authority or power, and *legein*, to speak.] designating a kind of heiroglyphics, in which a thing is represented by its picture rather than by a symbol.
çū·ri·ō′sȧ, *n.pl.* [L., lit., curious objects.] curiosities; novelties; specifically, books, etc. dealing with strange or unusual, especially pornographic, subjects.
çū·ri·os′i·ty, *n.*; *pl.* **çū·ri·os′i·tieṣ,** [ME. *curiosite*; OFr. *curiosetē*; L. *curiositas*, curiosity; *curiosus*, curious.]
1. a desire to gratify the senses with a sight of what is new or unusual, or to gratify the mind with new discoveries.
2. a desire to learn about things that do not necessarily concern one; inquisitiveness.
3. anything novel, extraordinary, rare, or strange.
4. accuracy; exactness; nicety; delicacy. [Obs.]
çū·ri·ō′sō, *n.*; *pl.* **çū·ri·ō′si** or **çū·ri·ō′sōṣ,** [It.] an admirer or collector of curios.
çū′ri·ous, *a.* [ME. *curious*, *corious*; OFr. *curious*; L. *curiousus*, careful, diligent, akin to *cura*, care.]
1. strongly desirous to learn or know.
2. unnecessarily inquisitive; prying.

3. accurate; careful; detailed.
4. rare; singular; strange; arousing curiosity; as, a *curious* fact.
5. very careful; scrupulous; fastidious. [Obs.]
Syn.—inquisitive, prying, rare.

çū'ri·ous·ly, *adv.* attentively; with care and accuracy; also, strangely; inquisitively.

çū'ri·ous·ness, *n.* the state or quality of being curious.

çū'ri·um, *n.* [after Pierre and Marie *Curie.*] a chemical element of the transuranium group, produced by atomic fission: symbol, Cm; atomic weight, 242 (?); atomic number, 96.

çũrl, *v.t.*; curled, *pt., pp.*; curling, *ppr.* [ME. *curlen,* metathesized from *crulled, crolled,* curled, from *crull, a.,* curly.]
1. to wind or twist (hair, etc.) into ringlets or coils.
2. to dress with curls; to adorn.
3. to raise in waves or undulations; to ripple.

Seas would be pools, without the brushing air
To *curl* the waves. —Dryden.

4. to cause to roll over or bend around.

çũrl, *v.i.* 1. to bend in curves; to take the form of ringlets; to assume a curved or spiral form; to appear curly.

It'll make your hair *curl.* —Thackeray.

2. to move in waves or undulations; to ripple; to rise in a winding outline; as, *curling* smoke; *curling* waves.
3. to writhe; to twist.

Then round her slender waist he *curled.* —Dryden.

4. to play the game of curling.
to curl up; (a) to gather into spirals or curls; to roll up; (b) to sit or lie with the legs drawn up; (c) [Colloq.] to collapse; to break down.

çũrl, *n.* [ME. *crull, crulle,* curly, from M.D. *krul, krol,* a curl.]
1. a ringlet of hair, or anything of a like form.
2. undulation; a waving; sinuosity; a winding.
3. any of various diseases of plants in which the leaves curl up.
in curl; curled.

çũrled, *a.* having curls; wavy.

çũrl'ed·ness, *n.* the state of being curled; curliness. [Rare.]

çũrl'ẽr, *n.* 1. one who or that which curls.
2. one who plays the game of curling.

çũr'lew, *n.*; *pl.* **çũr'lews, çũr'lew,** [ME. *curlewe*; OFr. *corlieu,* the curlew bird; name prob. echoic of the bird's cry.]
1. a large, brownish wading bird, of the genus *Numenius.* It has a long bill that curves downward. It is of the same family as the woodcock and sandpiper, and is widely scattered in Europe and America.

EUROPEAN CURLEW (*Numenius arquatus*)

2. any of certain wading birds, not of the genus *Numenius*; as, the pygmy *curlew,* the stone *curlew.*

çũr'lew·ber''ry, *n.* the black crowberry, *Empetrum nigrum.*

çũr'lew jack, the European whimbrel, *Numenius phæopus.*

çũr'lew knot (not), the curlew jack.

çũr'lew sand'pī''pẽr, a European sandpiper, *Tringa ferruginea,* having a bill like that of a curlew.

çũrl'i·çūe, *n.* a fancy curve, flourish, etc., as in handwriting: also written *curlycue.*

çũrl'i·ness, *n.* the quality or state of being curly.

çũrl'ing, *n.* 1. the act of making curls.
2. a game played by sliding a large, smooth stone of a circular form along the ice at a mark (called the *tee*) 38 yards away.

çũrl'ing ī'ron (-ũrn) or **ī'rons,** an instrument for curling the hair, generally consisting of a kind of metal tongs: a lock of hair is lifted with the heated tongs and rolled into a ringlet.

çũrl'ing stōne, a smooth, round stone used in the game of curling, having a handle attached to the upper side.

çũrl'ing tongs, a curling iron.

çũrl'pā''pẽr, *n.* a piece of paper around which a lock of hair may be wrapped to make a curl.

çũrl'y, *a.*; *comp.* curlier; *superl.* curliest. 1. having curls.
2. tending to curl.
3. having curled or undulating grain, as certain woods.

çũrl'y·çūe, *n.* same as *curlicue.*

çũrl'y-head''ed, *a.* having curly hair; as, a *curly-headed* boy.

çũrl'y-pā''ted, *a.* curly-headed.

çũr·mudġ'eŏn (-muj'un), *n.* [perh. from medieval name *Curmegan,* perh. equivalent to Fr. *coeur méchant,* evil heart.] an avaricious, churlish fellow; a miser; a cantankerous fellow.

çũr·mudġ'eŏn·ly, *a.* avaricious; cantankerous; churlish.

çũr·mũr'ring, *n.* [Scot.; echoic.] a murmuring or rumbling sound. [Scot. and Brit. Dial.]

çũrn, *n.* [var. of *corn,* grain.]
1. a grain. [Scot.]
2. a small number or quantity; a few. [Scot.]

çũrr, *v.i.* [echoic or ON. *kurra,* to growl, coo, rumble.] to coo or purr as a dove or cat.

çur'rach, çur'ragh (-rakh), *n.* [Gael.]
1. a coracle or light skiff for one person. [Ir. and Scot.]
2. a small cart made of wickerwork. [Scot.]

çũr'rȧ·jong, çũr're·jong, çũr'ri·jong, *n.* the kurrajong, an Australian tree, *Plagianthus sidoides.*

çur'rănt, *n.* [ME. *raisins of corans*; Fr. *raisins de Corinth,* raisins of Corinth: so named from being imported from Corinth.]
1. the dried fruit of a small, seedless grape grown in the Mediterranean region, used in cookery.
2. the fruit of several species of *Ribes,* so named because the berries resemble in size the small grapes from the Mediterranean region. The red currant is *Ribes rubrum,* of which the white currant is a variety; the black currant is *Ribes nigrum.*
3. the shrub bearing this fruit.
4. in Australia, any of several species of trees and shrubs bearing fruit resembling the true currant.

çur'rănt bŏr'ẽr, in zoology, the larva of a clearwing moth, *Ægeria tipuliformis,* which infests the stems of currant bushes.

çur'rănt gall, a small, round gall resembling an unripe currant, formed upon the flowers and leaves of the oak tree by an insect, *Spathegaster baccarum.*

çur'rănt wŏrm, in zoology, the larva of any insect that devours the currant; especially, *Nematus ventricosus,* a European species of sawfly, *Pristiphora grossulariæ,* an American sawfly, and *Eufitchia ribearia,* the spanworm.

çur'ren·cy, *n.*; *pl.* **çur'ren·cieş,** [hyp. ML. *currentia,* a current, from L. *currens,* ppr. of *currere,* to run.]
1. literally, a flowing, running, or passing; a continued or uninterrupted course like that of a stream; as, the *currency* of time. [Obs.]
2. a continual passing from hand to hand, as of coins or bills of credit; circulation.
3. that which is current or in circulation as a medium of trade or exchange; as, paper *currency.*
4. general estimation; common acceptance; the rate at which anything is generally valued.

He takes greatness of kingdoms according to their bulk and *currency,* and not after intrinsic value. —Bacon.

5. the time during which anything is current.
fractional currency; coins or paper money in circulation, worth less than the monetary unit; as, the dime is *fractional currency,* being worth less than the standard unit, the dollar.
paper currency; paper issued as a substitute for money; the certificates issued by a government, or by a bank on the authority of a government.

çur'rent, *a.* [ME. *currant, coraunt*; OFr. *curant*; L. *currens,* ppr. of *currere,* to run, hasten.]
1. running; flowing; passing. [Rare.]
2. now in progress; of this day, week, month, or year; as, the *current* issue of a magazine.
3. passing from person to person, or from hand to hand; common; general; circulating; as, *current* opinions.
4. established by common estimation; generally received; as, the *current* value of coin.
5. passable; that may be accepted or admitted; authentic; genuine. [Obs.]

çur'rent, *n.* 1. a body of water or air flowing in a definite direction; as, a *current* of air; the *current* of the Gulf Stream.
2. a running or flowing.
3. general or main course; progressive motion or movement; continuation; successive course; as, the *current* of time; the *current* of events.
4. in electricity, the flow or rate of flow of electric force in a conductor, from a point of higher potential to one of lower potential.
alternating current; in electricity, a current which changes its direction at regular intervals: abbreviated *A. C.*
commuted current; in electricity, a current which alternates when generated, but is made to flow continuously in one direction by a commutator.
direct current; in electricity, a current which flows in one direction only: also called *continuous current* when the flow is steady and free of pulsations: abbreviated *D. C.*
eddy current or *Foucault current*; in electricity, a current created in a mass of metal by movement through magnetic induction, which is converted into heat and causes waste.
galvanic current; a voltaic current.
rotating current; in electricity, a current inducing a rotating magnetic field; a polyphase current.
undulatory current; in electricity, a current whose direction is constant, but whose strength is continuously varying.
voltaic current; in electricity, a current produced chemically, as in a battery.
Syn.—flow, stream, course, tide, flux.

çur'rent den'si·ty, the amount of electric current passing through a cross-sectional area of the conductor in a given unit of time: commonly expressed in amperes per square centimeter.

çur'rent ex·pens'eş, the regular and continuing expenses of maintaining a going business.

çur'rent·ly, *adv.* 1. now.
2. generally; commonly; popularly.

çur'rent mē'tẽr, an instrument for measuring the strength and velocity of a current in a river, etc.

çur'rent mill, a mill having for its motor a current wheel.

çur'rent·ness, *n.* 1. the state or quality of being current; currency; circulation; general reception.
2. fluency; easiness of pronunciation. [Obs.]

çur'rent wheel, a wheel driven by a current of water or by a tide.

çur'ri·çle, *n.* [L. *curriculum,* a race, a racecourse, from *currere,* to run.]
1. a light carriage with two wheels, drawn by two horses abreast.
2. a short course. [Obs.]

çur·riç'ū·lăr, *a.* [L. *curriculum,* a chariot.] pertaining to carriages, to driving, or to a racecourse. [Rare.]

çur·riç'ū·lăr, *a.* pertaining to a curriculum.

çur·riç'ū·lum, *n.*; *pl.* **çur·riç'ū·lumş** or **çur·riç'ū·lȧ,** [L., a race, course, career, from *currere,* to run; figurative use.] a specific course of study or, collectively, all the courses of study in a university, college, or school.

çur'rie, *n.* see *curry.*

çur'ried (-rid), *a.* dressed by currying; dressed as leather; cleaned; prepared.

çur'ried, *a.* made with curry powder; as, *curried* chicken.

çũr'ri·ẽr, *n.* [ME. *coriour*; OFr. *corier, corrier,* a worker in leather; L. *coriarius,* a tanner, from *corium,* leather.]
1. one who dresses and colors leather after it is tanned.
2. one who curries horses, etc.

çũr'ri·ẽr, *n.* a firearm of the sixteenth century similar to the harquebus. [Obs.]

Çur'ri·ẽr and Iveş, [after the founders, Nathaniel *Currier* (1813–1888) and James M. Ives (1824–1895).]
1. a nineteenth-century lithographing firm in the United States that published a series of prints showing the manners, people, and events of the times.
2. any of these prints.

çur'ri·ẽr·y *n.*; *pl.* **çur'ri·ẽr·ieş,** the work or shop of a leather currier.

çũr'rish, *a.* like a cur; having the qualities of a cur; brutal; mean; snarling; churlish; quarrelsome.

çũr'rish·ly, *adv.* in a currish manner.

çũr'rish·ness, *n.* the state or quality of being currish.

çur'ry, *v.t.*; curried, *pt., pp.*; currying, *ppr.* [ME. *curreyen, currayan,* to curry a horse, to prepare leather; OFr. *correier, coreer,* to put in order, prepare, from *conroy, corroi*, preparation, order.]

1. to dress (leather) after it is tanned; to soak, scrape, cleanse, beat, and color (tanned hides), and prepare for use.

2. to rub down and clean the coat of (a horse or other animal) with a currycomb; to groom.

3. to beat; to thrash.

By setting brother against brother,
To claw and *curry* one another.—Butler.

to curry favor; to seek to gain favor by flattery, fawning, etc.

çur'ry, çur'rie, *n.*; *pl.* **çur'rieș,** [Tamil *kari*, sauce.]

1. curry powder or a sauce made with this, used especially in the East Indies.

2. a stew of fowl, fish, etc. cooked with curry.

çur'ry, *v.t.*; curried, *pt., pp.*; currying, *ppr.* to prepare or flavor with curry; as, to *curry* rice.

çur'ry·cōmb (-kōm), *n.* a comb with metal teeth, for grooming and cleaning a horse's coat.

çur'ry·cōmb, *v.t.*; currycombed, *pt., pp.*; currycombing, *ppr.* to comb with a currycomb; to curry.

çur'ry lēaf, the aromatic leaf of an East Indian rutaceous tree, *Murraya kœnigii*, sometimes used as a flavoring for curries.

çur'ry pow'dẽr, a powder prepared from turmeric and various spices and herbs, used as a seasoning in cooking.

çũrse, *n.* [ME. *curs*; Late AS. *curs*, from Anglo-Fr. *curuz*, wrath, and *curcier*, to call down wrath upon, from LL. *corruptiare*, to corrupt.]

1. a calling on God or the gods to send evil or injury down on some person or thing.

2. a blasphemous oath; imprecation.

3. a thing cursed.

4. evil or injury that seems to come in answer to a curse.

5. any cause of evil or injury.

not worth a curse; no good; useless.

Syn.—malediction, anathema, execration, imprecation, oath.

çũrse, *v.t.*; cursed *or* curst, *pt., pp.*; cursing, *ppr.* [ME. *cursien, cursen*, Late AS. *cursian*, to curse.]

1. to utter a wish of evil against; to imprecate evil upon; to call injury down on; to execrate.

Thou shalt not *curse* the ruler of thy people.
—Ex. xxii. 28.

2. to swear at; to use blasphemous language against.

3. to afflict; to subject to evil; to blight with a curse; to bring evil or injury on.

On impious realms and barbarous kings impose
Thy plagues, and *curse* 'em with such sons as those. —Pope.

çũrse, *v.i.* to utter a curse or curses; to swear; to blaspheme.

Then began he to *curse* and to swear.
—Matt. xxvi. 74.

çũrs'ed, *a.* 1. under a curse.

2. execrable; hateful; odious; abhorred; detestable; deserving a curse.

3. malevolent; quarrelsome: usually *curst*. [Archaic.]

çũrs'ed·ly, *adv.* in a cursed manner; miserably; in a manner to be cursed or detested.

çũrs'ed·ness, *n.* 1. the state of being under a curse, or of being doomed to execration or to evil.

2. blasphemy; cursing. [Obs.]

3. shrewishness; contrariness. [Archaic.]

çũrs'ẽr, *n.* one who curses.

çũr'si·tŏr, *n.* [L. *cursor*, a runner, from *currere*, to run.]

1. formerly, in England, a clerk in the court of chancery who made out original writs.

2. a courier. [Obs.]

çũr'sive, *a.* [ML. *cursivus*, running, from *cursus*, a running, course.] running; flowing; designating writing in which the strokes of the letters are joined in each word.

çũr'sive, *n.* 1. a character or letter used in cursive writing.

2. a manuscript written in cursive characters.

3. in printing, a type face that looks like writing.

çũr'sive·ly, *adv.* in a cursive manner.

çũr'sŏr, *n.* [L., a runner, from *currere*, to run.] any part of a mathematical instrument that slides backward and forward upon another part, as the point that slides along a beam compass.

çũr'sō·rā·ry, *a.* cursory; hasty. [Obs.]

Çũr·sō'rēș, *n.pl.* [L. *cursores*, runners, pl. of *cursor*, a runner.]

1. an order of birds, the *Ratitæ*, or *Brevipennes*, which have long legs and undeveloped wings. The order comprises the ostrich, cassowary, emu, rhea, and apteryx.

2. any of a group of spiders which make no webs, but catch their prey by swift pursuit, such as the wolf spiders, *Lycosidæ*.

Çũr·sō'ri·ȧ, *n.pl.* [LL., neut. pl. of *cursorius*, running, L. *currere*, to run.] a suborder of insects of the order *Orthoptera*, including the cockroaches.

çũr·sō'ri·ăl, *a.* 1. adapted, or having legs adapted, for running.

2. pertaining to the *Cursores*.

çũr'sō·ri·ly, *adv.* in a cursory manner; hastily; without close attention.

çũr'sō·ri·ness, *n.* the quality of being cursory; superficiality.

Çũr·sō'ri·us, *n.* [LL., running; L. *cursor*, a runner.] a genus of grallatorial birds of the plover family, including the black-bellied courier, the brazen-winged courser, and the swiftfoot. These birds chiefly inhabit Africa.

çũr'sō·ry, *a.* [L. *cursor*, a runner.]

1. hasty; slight; superficial; careless; without close attention; as, a *cursory* reading, a *cursory* view.

2. running about; not stationary. [Obs.]

Syn.—careless, desultory, hasty, slight, superficial, rapid.

çũrst, alternative past tense and past participle of *curse*.

çũrst, *a.* cursed.

çũrst'fụl·ly, *adv.* cursedly. [Obs.]

çũrst'ness, *n.* cursedness. [Obs.]

çũr'sus, *n.* [L.] a regular order of service in a church; the office of daily prayer.

çũrt, *a.* [L. *curtus*, shortened, mutilated.]

1. short; shortened.

2. rudely short or concise; terse and abrupt; as, a *curt* reply.

Syn.—short, brief, sharp, concise, acute, abrupt.

çũr·tāil', *v.t.*; curtailed, *pt., pp.*; curtailing, *ppr.* [altered (by association with *tail*) from *curtal*.] to shorten; to cut off the end or a part of; to lessen; as, to *curtail* expenses, to *curtail* an allowance.

Syn.—reduce, lessen, diminish, abridge, abbreviate, shorten, dock, retrench, decrease.

çũr'tāil, *n.* in architecture, the scroll-shaped end of any part.

çũr·tāil'ẽr, *n.* one who curtails; one who cuts off or shortens anything.

çũr·tāil'ment, *n.* the act of curtailing; also, the result of curtailing; a diminution.

çũr'tāil step, the lowest step in a flight of stairs, shaped at the end like a scroll.

çũr'tain (-tin), *n.* [ME. *curteyn*; OFr. *curtine*, a curtain; LL. *cortina*, a small court, a screen of cloth; dim. of *cortis*, a court; L. *cohors*, a court, an enclosed space; Gr. *chortos*, a yard, court.]

1. a piece of cloth, etc., sometimes arranged so that it can be drawn up or sideways, hung for decoration, as at a window, or to cover, conceal, or shut off something.

2. anything that conceals, covers, or shuts off as a curtain.

3. in fortification, that part of the rampart which is between the flanks of two bastions, bordered with a parapet, behind which the soldiers stand to fire.

4. in architecture, an enclosing wall that does not support a roof.

5. in the theater, (a) the large drape or hanging screen at the front of the stage, which may be drawn up or aside to reveal the stage; (b) an effect, line, or situation in a play immediately before the fall of the curtain.

6. [*pl.*] death; the end. [Slang.]

7. the cortina of a fungus.

to draw the curtain on; (a) to end; (b) to conceal.

to lift the curtain on; (a) to begin; (b) to reveal.

çũr'tain, *v.t.*; curtained, *pt., pp.*; curtaining, *ppr.* 1. to furnish or decorate with a curtain.

2. to conceal, cover, or shut off as with a curtain.

çũr'tain an'gle, in fortification, the angle between the curtain and a bastion flank.

çũr'tain çạll, a call, usually by continued applause, for a performer to return to the stage at the end of a play, act, etc. and acknowledge the applause.

çũr'tain leç'tūre, a private reproof or scolding given to a husband by his wife: so called from the curtained beds in which such reproofs were conventionally given.

çũr'tain rāiș'ẽr, a short play or skit, presented before a longer or more elaborate production.

çũr'tain speech, a speech delivered from in front of the curtain at the end of a theatrical performance.

çũr'tăl, *a.* [OFr. *cortald, curtald*; prob. from *court*, short; L. *curtus*, shortened.] shortened; curtailed. [Obs.]

çũr'tăl, *n.* 1. a horse with a docked tail. [Obs.]

2. anything cut short or shortened. [Obs.]

çũr'tăl ax, [altered from *cutlass*.] a cutlass. [Archaic.]

Çũr·tā'nȧ, *n.* the blunt sword displayed before English monarchs at their coronation, symbolizing mercy: also called *the sword of Edward the Confessor*.

çũr'tāte, *a.* [L. *curtatus*, pp. of *curtare*, to shorten.] reduced; shortened.

curtate cycloid; see *cycloid*.

curtate distance; in astronomy, the distance from the earth or sun to that point where a perpendicular from the planet meets the plane of the ecliptic.

çũr·tā'tion, *n.* [L. *curtatus*, pp. of *curtare*, to shorten.] the interval between a planet's true distance from the sun and the curtate distance.

çũr'tē·sy, *n.*; *pl.* **çũr'tē·sieș,** [var. of *courtesy*.] in law, the right that a husband has in the lands of his dead wife, when they have had children capable of inheriting.

çũr'ti·lāġe, *n.* [OFr. *cortillage*, from *courtil*, a court; L. *cohors*, a yard.] in law, a yard, garden, enclosure, or field, near and belonging to a dwelling.

çũr'tle ax, a cutlass. [Archaic.]

çũrt'ly, *adv.* briefly; in a curt manner.

çũrt'ness, *n.* shortness; the quality of being curt.

çũrt'sy, *n.*; *pl.* **çũrt'sieș,** [var. of *courtesy*.] a salutation made by bending the knees and dipping the body slightly, as a mark of respect or a step in dancing: now only of women and girls: also spelled *curtsey*.

çũrt'sy, *v.i.*; curtsied, *pt., pp.*; curtsying, *ppr.* to make a curtsy: also spelled *curtsey*.

çụ'rụ·bȧ, *n.* [from native name.] the sweet calabash of the West Indies; the fruit of *Passiflora multiformis*.

çụ·rụ·çụ'çụ, *n.* see *bushmaster*.

çụ'rụ·çui (-kwi), *n.* [native Brazilian name.] a Brazilian bird, the trogon.

çū'rūle, *a.* [L. *curulis*, pertaining to a chariot, from *currus*, a chariot, car; *currere*, to run.] privileged to sit in a *curule* chair; as, a *curule* magistrate.

curule chair; in ancient Rome, a chair or stool without a back, so made as to be folded up and opened in the manner of a campstool, but with heavy curved legs and upholstered seat: used by dictators, consuls, pretors, censors, and ediles.

CURULE CHAIR

çụ·rụ'rō, *n.*; *pl.* **çụ·rụ'rōș,** [native name.] a burrowing rodent of Chile, genus *Spalacopus*.

çũr·vā'ceous, *a.* [from *curve*, and *-aceous*.] having a full, shapely figure: said of a woman. [Colloq.]

çũr'văl, *a.* same as *curvant*.

çũr'vănt, *a.* in heraldry, bowed or curved.

çũr'vāte, çũr'vā·ted, *a.* [L. *curvatus*, pp. of *curvare*, to bend.] curved; bent in a regular form.

çũr·vā'tion, *n.* the act of bending or curving.

çũr'vȧ·tive, *a.* in botany, slightly curved, as the margins of leaves. [Rare.]

çũr'vȧ·tūre, *n.* [L. *curvatura*, a bending, from *curvare*, to bend.]

1. the flexure or bending of a line from a rectilinear direction; a curve.

2. in geometry, the rate of deviation of a curve or curved surface from a straight line or plane surface tangent to it.

3. the act of curving; the state of being bent.

curvature of the spine; in medicine, an abnormal curving of the spinal column, either angular or lateral.

çũrve, *a.* [L. *curvus*, bent, crooked; Gr. *kyrtos*, curved, bent.] bending; crooked; inflected in a regular form and forming part of a circle; as, a *curve* line.

çũrve, *n.* [L. *curvum*, from *curvus*, bent.]

1. (a) a bend without angles; that which is bent; a curving; (b) the amount of this.
2. a line which changes its direction at every point; a line of which no three consecutive points are in the same direction or straight line.
3. an instrument for making curved figures, used by draftsmen.
4. a thing or part having the shape of a curve.
5. in baseball, a pitched ball thrown with spin so that it curves to one side or the other before crossing the plate.
6. in mathematics, a line whose path is traced by an equation that can be applied to every point on it.

çũrve, *v.t.* and *v.i.*; curved, *pt.*, *pp.*; curving, *ppr.* [L. *curvare*, to bend, curve.]
1. to form a curve by bending.
2. to move in a curved path.

çũr'ved·ness, *n.* the state of being curved. [Rare.]

çũr'vet, *n.* [It. *corvetta*, a leap, curvet, from *corvare*, to bend, stoop; L. *curvare*, to bend.]
1. an upward leap made by a horse in which the hind legs are raised from the ground just before the forelegs come down again.
2. a prank; a frolic.

çũr'vet, *v.i.*; curvetted *or* curveted, *pt.*, *pp.*; curvetting *or* curveting, *ppr.* [It. *corvettare*; Fr. *courbetter*; Sp. *corvetear*.]
1. to leap; to bound; to make a curvet.
2. to leap and frisk.

çũr'vet, *v.t.* to cause to curvet; to cause to leap or prance.

çũr'vi-, [from L. *curvus*, curved.] a combining form meaning *curved, bent*, as in *curvi*linear.

çũr·vi·çau'dāte, *a.* [*curvi-*, and L. *cauda*, tail.] in zoology, having a bent or curved tail.

çũr·vi·ços'tāte, *a.* [*curvi-*, and L. *costa*, rib.] having crooked or curved ribs.

çũr·vi·den'tāte, *a.* [*curvi-*, and L. *dens*, tooth.] having curved teeth.

çũr·vi·fō'li·āte, *a.* [*curvi-*, and L. *folium*, leaf.] having curved leaves.

çũr'vi·form, *a.* having the form of a curve; curved.

çũr·vi·lin'ē·ad, *n.* [*curvi-*, and L. *linea*, a line.] an instrument for making curved lines.

çũr·vi·lin'ē·ăr, çũr·vi·lin'ē·ăl, *a.* [*curvi-*, and L. *linea*, line.] consisting of a curved line or lines; bounded by a curved line or lines; as, a *curvilinear* figure.

çũr·vi·lin·ē·ar'i·ty, *n.* the state of being curvilinear, or of consisting of curved lines.

çũr·vi·lin'ē·ăr·ly, *adv.* in a curvilinear manner.

çũr·vi·nẽr'vāte, *a.* [*curvi-*, and L. *nervus*, nerve.] having the veins or nerves curved: said of the leaves of plants and the wings of insects.

çũr'vi·nẽrved, *a.* same as *curvinervate*.

çũr·vi·ros'trăl, *a.* [*curvi-*, and L. *rostrum*, a beak.] in ornithology, (a) having a downward curving beak, as the curlew; (b) having the mandibles curved and crossed, as the crossbill.

Çũr·vi·ros'trēṣ, *n.pl.* in ornithology, a group of passerine birds, including the creepers and nuthatches.

çũr·vi·sē'ri·ăl, *a.* [*curvi-*, and L. *series*, series.] arranged in a series describing a curve or spiral, as leaves about a stem.

çũr'vi·tăl, *a.* pertaining to curves.

çũr'vi·ty, *n.* a bending in a regular form; crookedness; curvature; the state of being curved.

çũr'vō·grȧph, *n.* [L. *curvus*; Gr. *kyrtos*, curved, and *graphein*, to write.] in geometry, an arcograph or cyclograph.

çũr'vū·lāte, *a.* slightly curved.

çus'çus, *n.* [Fr. *couscous*; Ar. *kuskus*.] the rootstock of an Indian grass, *Andropogon muricatus*.

çū'seç, *n.* [*cu*bic, and *sec*ond.] one cubic foot per second.

Çush, *n.* in the Bible, the oldest of Ham's sons: also spelled *Kush*.

çush, *n.* [Anglo-Ind.] sorghum.

çush'at, *n.* [ME. *cowscot, couscot*; AS. *cuscoet, cusceote*, the ringdove; *cwicu*, quick, and *sceotan*, to shoot.] the European ringdove or wood pigeon.

çu·shaw', *n.* [prob. from Chin. *k'u kua*, lit., bitter melon.] a winter squash, usually oblong, with a large, smooth crookneck: also called *winter crookneck pumpkin, China squash*.

çush'ew·bĩrd, *n.* the cashew bird.

çush'iŏn (-un), *n.* [ME. *cushone*; OFr. *cuissin*; LL. *cussinus*, cushion; L. *culcita*, a cushion, pillow.]
1. a pillow or soft pad for sitting or kneeling on, or reclining against.
2. anything having the appearance or use of a cushion; specifically, (a) a small pillow used in lacemaking; (b) anything serving to absorb shocks or jolts, as air or steam in machinery, or the elastic inner rim of a billiard table.

çush'iŏn, *v.t.*; cushioned, *pt.*, *pp.*; cushioning, *ppr.* 1. to seat or set on a cushion; to prop up with cushions.
2. to cover or furnish with a cushion or cushions.
3. to hide, as if under a cushion.
4. to protect (a part) from shock by means of a cushion, as of air or steam.
5. to absorb (shock).

çush'iŏn çap'i·tăl, in architecture, a capital of such form as to appear like a cushion flattened by the weight of the superstructure; also, the Norman capital, which consists of a cube rounded off at its base.

NORMAN CUSHION CAPITAL

çush'iŏn çar'ŏm, in billiards, a carom in which the cue ball touches the cushion before contact with the second object ball.

çush'iŏn dȧnce, a rustic dance, formerly popular in England and Scotland, in which each dancer, at recurring intervals, dropped before another of the opposite sex a cushion, on which they knelt and exchanged kisses.

çush'iŏned (-und), *a.* supported by cushions; furnished with cushions.

çush'iŏn·et, *n.* a little cushion.

çush'iŏn rȧft'ẽr, in architecture, an auxiliary rafter, used to relieve the strain on a principal rafter.

çush'iŏn sçāle, an insect harmful to certain fruit trees, *Icerya purchasi*: the females have a cushion-shaped ovisac.

çush'iŏn stär, any of several species of pentagonal starfish, as the *Goniaster equestris* of Great Britain.

çush'iŏn stitch, a straight, short embroidery stitch used in the groundwork of designs intended to imitate painting.

çush'iŏn·y, *a.* like a cushion; elastic; soft.

Çush·it'iç, *a.* [from *Cush*.] designating or of a group of Hamitic languages spoken in Ethiopia and Eastern Africa: also spelled *Kushitic*.

Çush·it'iç, *n.* the Cushitic group of languages: also spelled *Kushitic*.

çush'y, *adj.*; *comp.* cushier; *superl.* cushiest; [orig. Brit. army slang, from Hind. *khush*, pleasant; Per. *khūsh*.] comfortable; easy. [Slang.]

çusk, *n.*; *pl.* **çusk** or **çusks,** 1. a large, edible sea fish, *Brosmius brosme*, related to the cod.
2. the burbot, *Lota maculosa*.

çusp, *n.* [L. *cuspis*, a point.]
1. in astronomy, either horn of a crescent moon.
2. in architecture, a projecting point where two arcs meet, as in the internal curve of an arch.
3. in astrology, the initial entrance of a house in the calculation of nativities.
4. in botany, a rigid, sharp point, especially on a leaf.
5. in anatomy, (a) any prominence on the chewing surface of a tooth; (b) one of the triangular parts of a heart valve.
6. in geometry, a point or pointed end formed where two curves meet.

çus'pāte, *a.* 1. having a cusp or cusps.
2. shaped like a cusp.

çus'pā·ted, *a.* cuspate.

çusped (kuspt), *a.* cuspate.

çus'pid, *n.* [L. *cuspis*, a point.] a canine tooth; a tooth with one cusp.

çus'pid, *a.* cuspidate.

çus'pi·dăl, *a.* 1. of or like a cusp.
2. having a cusp; ending in a point.

çus'pi·dāte, çus'pi·dā·ted, *a.* [L. *cuspidatus*, pp. of *cuspidare*, to make pointed; *cuspis*, a point.] having a sharp end, like the point of a spear; terminating in a point, as some leaves.

çus'pi·dāte, *v.t.*; cuspidated, *pt.*, *pp.*; cuspidating, *ppr.* to make pointed; to form like a cusp.

çus·pi·dā'tion, *n.* the use of cusps for decoration, as in architecture.

çus'pi·dīne, *n.* [L. *cuspis*, a point, spear.] in mineralogy, a silicate containing fluorine, lime, and carbon dioxide, occurring in pale red, spear-shaped crystals.

çus'pi·dọr, *n.* [Port. *cuspideira*, a spittoon, from *cuspir*, to spit; L. *conspuere*, to spit upon.] a spittoon.

çus'pis, *n.*; *pl.* **çus'pi·dēṣ,** [L. *cuspis*, a point.] a point; a cusp.

çuss, *n.* [from *curse*; in sense **2**, perh. from *customer*.]
1. a curse. [Colloq.]
2. a person or animal, especially when regarded as queer or annoying: used humorously or contemptuously. [Colloq.]

çuss, *v.t.* and *v.i.* to curse. [Colloq.]

çuss'ed, *a.* 1. cursed. [Colloq.]
2. perverse; stubborn. [Colloq.]

çuss'ed·ness, *n.* cantankerousness; meanness. [Colloq.]

çus'sō, *n.* [Eth.] 1. a rosaceous tree of Ethiopia, *Brayera anthelmintica*.
2. a vermifuge made of the dried flowers of *Brayera anthelmintica*: also written *kousso*.

çus'tărd, *n.* [OFr. *croustade*, pie, pastry; from L. *crustatus*, pp. of *crustare*, to crust, *crusta*, a crust, shell.] a mixture of milk, eggs, sugar, flavoring, etc., either baked or boiled.
custard cup; a small cup having no handles, made of a heat-resistant material, in which an individual portion of custard is boiled or baked and then served.

çus'tărd ap'ple, [from *custard*: with reference to the flavor.]
1. a species of small tree grown, especially in the West Indies, for its edible, heart-shaped fruit.
2. any of various related trees and shrubs, as the sweetsop, sugar apple, and soursop.
3. the fruit of any of these plants.

çus·tō'dēṣ, *n.* plural of *custos*.

çus·tō'di·ȧ, *n.*; *pl.* **çus·tō'di·ae,** [L., guard, a prison.] a custodial.

çus·tō'di·ăl, *a.* relating to custody or custodians.

çus·tō'di·ăl, *n.* a container for relics.

çus·tō'di·ăn, *n.* [L. *custodia*, a watch, guard; *custodire*, to guard.]
1. one who has the care of something, as of the exhibits in a museum; a caretaker; a keeper.
2. one who is responsible for the care and maintenance of a building; a janitor.

çus·tō'di·ăn·ship, *n.* the position or work of a custodian.

çus·tō'di·ẽr, *n.* a custodian. [Obs.]

çus'tō·dy, *n. pl.* **çus'tō·dieṣ,** [L. *custodia*, a watch, guard, from *custos*, a watchman; Gr. *keuthein*, to hide, conceal.]
1. a keeping safe or guarding; care; protection; guardianship.
2. imprisonment; confinement; restraint of liberty.

çus'tŏm, *n.* [ME. *custom, custome*; OFr. *costume*, custom; from L. *consuetudo*, custom, habit, from *consuescere*, to accustom, habituate, from *com-*, intens., and *suescere*, to become accustomed, from *suere*, to be accustomed.]
1. frequent or common use or practice; a frequent repetition of the same act; usage; habit.
2. established usage; social conventions carried on by tradition and enforced by social disapproval of any violation.
3. a service, rent, etc. regularly paid to a feudal lord.
4. [*pl.*] (a) duties or taxes imposed by a government on imported and, occasionally, exported goods; (b) the government agency in charge of collecting these duties.
5. the regular support or patronage of a business establishment.
6. in law, such usage as by long-established, uniform practice and common consent has taken on the force of law.
custom of merchants; the code or unwritten law in commerce which governs contracts, exchange, insurance, etc.
customs union; a union of two or more nations that agree to eliminate customs restrictions among them and to follow a common tariff policy toward all other nations.

Syn.—habit, practice, habitude, usage, wont.

çus'tŏm, *a.* 1. made to order: sometimes loosely said of a ready-made article regarded as resembling one made to order, extra fine, etc.
2. making things to order, or dealing in things made to order.

çus'tŏm·à·ble, *a.* liable to payment of duties; taxable as imported. [Rare.]

çus'tŏm·ā·ri·ly, *adv.* according to custom; ordinarily.

çus'tŏm·ā·ri·ness, *n.* the quality or state of being customary; frequency; commonness; habitual use or practice.

çus'tŏm·ā·ry, *a.* [ME. *customere*; OFr. *costumier*; LL. *custumarius*, subject to tax; *custuma*, custom.]

1. according to custom, or to established or common usage; conventional; habitual; usual.

2. in law, (a) subject to customs; (b) holding or held by custom; as, *customary* tenants.

çus'tŏm·ā·ry, *n.*; *pl.* **çus'tŏm·ā·rieş,** a collection of laws established by custom.

çus'tŏm-built', *a.* built to order; not ready-made; as, *custom-built* furniture.

çus'tŏm·ẽr, *n.* [OFr. *costumier*, customer; LL. *custumarius*, toll gatherer, from *custuma*, tax, custom.]

1. a person who buys, especially one who buys regularly; as, she is one of our *customers*.

2. a person with whom one has to deal; as, he's a rough *customer*. [Colloq.]

3. a toll gatherer. [Obs.]

çus'tŏm·house, *n.* the office or building where ships are cleared for entering or leaving, and where customs duties are paid on imported and, sometimes, exported goods.

customhouse broker; an agent or broker who attends to the clearing of ships and cargoes, payment of customs duties, etc.

çus'tŏm-māde', *a.* made to order; as, *custom-made* hats.

çus'tos, *n.*; *pl.* **çus·tō'dēş,** [L. *custos*, a keeper, guardian, from *custodire*, to guard.] a custodian; a keeper.

Custos Rotulorum; in English law, the principal justice of the peace in a county, who is keeper of the rolls and records of the sessions of the peace.

çus'trel, *n.* 1. an armorbearer.

2. a vessel for holding wine. [Obs.]

çus'tū·măl, *a.* of the customs of a manor, district, etc.

çus'tū·măl, *n.* a collection of the customs of a manor, district, etc.; a customary.

çus'tum·ā·ry, *n.* a customary. [Obs.]

çut, *v.t.*; cut, *pt., pp.*; cutting, *ppr.* [ME. *cutten, kutten, kytten*, to cut; hyp. Late AS. *cyttan*, from Anglo-N.]

1. to make an opening in with a sharp-edged instrument; to gash; to incise.

2. to penetrate; to pierce or hit sharply so as to hurt.

3. to affect deeply; to hurt the feelings of.

4. to get (a new tooth cutting its way through the gum).

5. to remove or divide into parts by means of a sharp-edged instrument; to sever.

6. to carve (meat).

7. to cause to fall by severing; to fell; to hew.

8. to mow or reap with a scythe, sickle, etc.; as, to *cut* grass or corn.

9. to divide; to pass through or across; to intersect; as, a ship *cuts* the waves.

10. to divide (a pack of cards) at random after shuffling and before dealing.

11. to castrate; to geld.

12. to remain away from (a school class, etc.) without being excused. [Colloq.]

13. to pass with intentional lack of recognition; to ignore; as, to *cut* an acquaintance on the street. [Colloq.]

14. to stop; to discontinue; as, *cut* the noise. [Slang.]

15. to curtail; to reduce in quantity or extent by or as by severing a part or parts; to shorten; as, to *cut* expenses.

16. to make shorter by severing the ends of (the fingernails, hair, branches, etc.); to trim; to shear; to pare.

17. to dilute (alcohol, etc.).

18. to dissolve or break up the fat globules of; as, lye *cuts* grease.

19. to make (an opening, clearing, channel, etc.) by incising, drilling, hacking, or excavating.

20. to make ready or form by cutting; as, to *cut* a dress.

21. to carve or engrave; as, to *cut* a jewel or an inscription.

22. to perform; as, he *cut* a caper.

23. in motion pictures, to edit (film) by deleting some scenes and assembling others into their proper sequence.

24. in sports, to hit, drive, or throw (a ball) so that it spins or is deflected.

to cut across; to take a shorter course by going straight across in a diagonal direction.

to cut a figure; (a) to attract attention; (b) to make a (specified kind of) display or impression. [Colloq.]

to cut back; (a) to make shorter by cutting off the end; (b) to reduce or discontinue (a contract, etc.) before the completion of what was originally called for.

to cut down; (a) to fell; to cause to fall by severing; (b) to reduce; to curtail; as, *to cut down* expenditure; (c) to kill, as by striking with a sword.

to cut off; (a) to separate from other parts; to sever; (b) to put an end to suddenly; (c) to interrupt; to stop; (d) to intercept; (e) to omit from the benefits of a will or testament; to disinherit.

to cut one's teeth on; to learn or use at an early age.

to cut out; (a) to remove by cutting or carving; (b) to remove and take the place of (a rival); (c) to make or shape by or as by cutting; (d) to remove; (e) to leave out; to omit; to eliminate; to quit; to cease. [Colloq.]

to cut short; to terminate abruptly or suddenly before the end.

to cut through; (a) to penetrate or go through by cutting; (b) to go straight through.

to cut up; (a) to cut into pieces; (b) to inflict cuts or lacerations on; (c) [Colloq.] to cause to be dejected or distressed.

Syn.—hew, chop, cleave, sever, gash, incise, dissect, carve.

çut, *v.i.* 1. to do the work of a sharp-edged instrument; to pierce, sever, gash, etc.

2. to take cutting, incision, or division; as, the wood *cuts* easily.

3. to do cutting, severing, dissecting, or incising; to work as a cutter.

4. to use a knife or instrument that cuts.

5. to interfere, as a horse.

6. to hurt by or as by sharp, piercing strokes; as, the wind *cut* through his thin clothes.

7. in motion pictures, (a) to stop the camera or cameras; (b) to edit film.

8. in sports, (a) to hit, drive, or throw a ball so that it spins or is deflected; (b) to change direction suddenly while running.

to cut and run; (a) to cut the cable and set sail immediately, leaving the anchor behind; (b) to get away quickly.

to cut back; (a) to go back, as in telling a story; (b) to change direction suddenly, as a football player running with the ball.

to cut in; (a) to move in suddenly; (b) to join, or take part, in anything suddenly; (c) to interrupt two people dancing together in order to dance with one of them.

to cut loose; (a) to cut a ship's moorings; (b) [Colloq.] to act or speak without restraint.

to cut up; to play pranks, clown, etc. to attract attention. [Slang.]

çut, *n.* 1. a cutting or being cut.

2. a stroke or blow, with a sharp-edged instrument, whip, etc.

3. a cleft; a gash; a notch; a wound; the opening made by a sharp-edged instrument.

4. the omission of a part.

5. a part omitted.

6. a piece cut; specifically, (a) any of the divisions or segments of a meat animal; (b) a slice from such a segment.

7. a reduction; lessening; decrease.

8. a route that is the shortest distance across: usually *short cut*.

9. a channel made by cutting or digging; a ditch; a groove; a furrow; a canal.

10. the act of dividing a pack of cards.

11. the style in which a thing is cut; form; shape; fashion; as, the *cut* of a garment.

12. an act, remark, etc. that hurts one's feelings.

13. a block or plate engraved for printing.

14. the impression from such a block or plate.

15. an intentional failure to recognize the greeting of an acquaintance; a snub. [Colloq.]

16. an unauthorized absence from a school class, etc. [Colloq.]

17. a share, as of profits or loot. [Slang.]

18. in sports, a stroke that causes a ball to spin or be deflected from its course.

a cut above; somewhat better than. [Colloq.]

çut, *a.* 1. that has been cut.

2. shaped by cutting; hewn or chiseled; carved; polished; dressed; as, *cut* stone, *cut* glass.

3. castrated.

4. reduced; lessened.

5. in botany, having an indented edge; incised, as some leaves or petals.

cut and dried; (a) prepared for the occasion; (b) lacking spontaneity; lifeless; boring.

cut out for; fitted for; suited for.

cut terrace; a terrace formed by the erosive action of waves upon a cliff.

çut, *n.* [perh. from W. *cwt*, lot, or OFr. *courte*, short; modified by ME. *cutten*.] one of the bits of straw, stick, paper, etc. used in drawing lots to decide something.

çū·tā'nē·ous, *a.* [L. *cutis*, skin.] belonging to the skin; existing on, or affecting the skin; as, a *cutaneous* disease, *cutaneous* eruption.

çū·tā'nē·ous·ly, *adv.* in a manner affecting the skin.

çut'à·wāy, *n.* a coat, worn by men for formal daytime occasions, with the skirt cut so as to curve back to the tails: also called *cutaway coat*.

çut'back, *n.* 1. the act or result of shortening by cutting off the end.

2. reduction or discontinuance, as of a contract, before the completion of what was originally called for.

3. a sequence of earlier narrative events introduced at a later point in a novel, motion picture, etc.

4. in football, a play in which the player carrying the ball suddenly changes the direction of his run, as in avoiding opposing players.

çutch, *n.* same as *cultch*.

çutch, *n.* catechu.

çutch, *n.* couch grass.

çutch, *n.* the package of vellum leaves between which gold is placed to be beaten into gold leaf.

çutch'ẽr, *n.* a cylinder in a paper-making machine around which an endless felt apron is carried.

çut·cher'ry, *n.*; *pl.* **çut·cher'rieş,** [Hind. *kachahrī*, a court, courthouse.] in India, a court of justice or an administrative office.

çutch'ẽr·y, *n.* a cutcherry.

çūte, *a.* [from *acute*; L. *acutus*, sharp.]

1. clever; sharp; cunning; as, a *cute* swindle. [Colloq.]

2. pretty or attractive, especially in a delicate or dainty way. [Colloq.]

çūte'ly, *adv.* in a cute manner. [Colloq.]

çūte'ness, *n.* the state or quality of being cute. [Colloq.]

çut glȧss, glass, especially flint glass, shaped or ornamented by grinding and polishing.

çut'-grȧss, *n.* a species of swamp grass, the blades of which have many tiny hooks along the edges that cut the flesh readily; spear grass.

çū'ti·çle, *n.* [L. *cuticula*, dim. of *cutis*, skin.]

1. the outermost thin layer of the skin; the epidermis or scarfskin.

2. hardened skin, such as accumulates at the base and sides of a fingernail.

3. in botany, the thin external covering over the outer surface of the epidermis of plants: it contains cutin and protects against water and gases.

4. a thin skin formed on the surface of a liquid.

çū·tiç'ū·lȧ, *n.*; *pl.* **çū·tiç'ū·lae,** [L.] a cuticle; especially, the tough outer layer of skin of certain lower organisms.

çū·tiç'ū·lăr, *a.* pertaining to the cuticle.

çū·tiç''ū·lăr·i·zā'tion, *n.* same as *cutinization*.

çū·tiç'ū·lăr·īze, *v.t.* and *v.i.*; cuticularized, *pt., pp.*; cuticularizing, *ppr.* to make cuticular; to give the character, nature, or composition of the cuticle to.

çū'ti·fȳ, *v.i.*; cutified, *pt., pp.*; cutifying, *ppr.* to form skin.

çū'tin, *n.* [L. *cutis*, the skin.] a waxy substance which, together with cellulose, forms the outer layer of the skin of many plants.

çut'-in, *n.* in motion pictures, the close-up of a pertinent object, as a newspaper headline, a book, etc., inserted into the sequence of a scene: also called *insert*.

çū''tin·i·zā'tion, *n.* in botany, a process in which the outermost plant cells become thickened and covered with cutin, making them waterproof.

çū'tin·īze, *v.t.* and *v.i.*; cutinized, *pt., pp.*; cutinizing, *ppr.* to undergo or cause to undergo cutinization.

çū'tis, *n.* the layer of skin beneath the epidermis; derma; dermis; corium.

çū'tis vē'rȧ, [L., true skin.] the cutis.

çut'lăss, çut'lăs, *n.* [Fr. *coutelas*, a cutlass; OFr. *coutel*, a knife, dagger; L. *cultellus*, dim. of *culter*, a knife.] a short, broad, curving sword with a single cutting edge, formerly used especially by seamen.

çut'lăss fish, a long, thin fish, *Trichiurus lepturus*, found in the West Indies: also called *scabbard fish, saber fish*, and *silver eel*.

çut'lẽr, *n.* [ME. *coteler*; OFr. *coutelier*; LL. *cultellarius*, a maker of knives; from L. *cultellus*, dim. of *culter*, a knife.] one who manufactures, repairs, or sells cutlery.

çut'lẽr·y, *n.* 1. the occupation of a cutler.
2. knives or other cutting instruments, collectively.
3. implements used in eating; knives, forks, and spoons.

çut'let, *n.* [Fr. *côtelette*, a chop, dim. of *côte*, rib, side; OFr. *coste*; L. *costa*, a rib.]
1. a small piece of meat from the ribs or leg, for broiling or frying, often served breaded.
2. a small, flat croquette of chopped meat or fish.

çut'ling, *n.* the art of cutlery. [Obs.]

çut'lips, *n.* 1. the stone toter, *Exoglossum maxillingua*, a cyprinoid fish.
2. the harelipped sucker of the Mississippi Valley.

çut'off, *n.* 1. that which cuts off or shortens, as a short road or path; a short cut.
2. the act of cutting off steam, etc. from the cylinder of an engine.
3. a device for doing this, or the point at which this is done.
4. the shorter channel formed when a river or stream cuts through a bend in its course.
5. the water thus cut off.
6. an arm on a reaping machine which supports the grain as it is about to fall, while that which has fallen on the platform is being removed.

çut'out, *n.* 1. a switch or other device for breaking or closing an electric circuit.
2. a device for letting the exhaust gases of an internal-combustion engine pass directly into the air instead of through a muffler.
3. a design cut out of something, or to be cut out.

çut'ō·vẽr, *a.* cleared of trees.

çut'ō·vẽr, *n.* land cleared of trees.

çut'pũrse, *n.* originally, one who cut purses from the belts or girdles to which they were attached, in order to steal them or their contents; hence, a pickpocket.

çut'-rāte, *a.* 1. on sale at a lower price.
2. having articles for sale at a lower price.

çut'tāġe, *n.* the method of propagating plants by means of cuttings.

çut'tẽr, *v.i.* [Eng. dial. for *quitter*, to speak low.] to speak in a whisper; to murmur, as a dove. [Rare.]

çut'tẽr, *n.* 1. one who cuts or hews; one who shapes or forms by cutting; specifically, one who cuts out cloth for garments according to measurements.
2. that which cuts; an instrument that cuts; as, a paper *cutter*.
3. a front tooth that cuts, as distinguished from a grinder; an incisor.
4. a boat, motor-powered or rowed, carried aboard large ships as a communications tender: also called *ship's cutter*.
5. an armed, single-masted, gaff-rigged sailing vessel, formerly used by revenue authorities to pursue smugglers, etc.: also called *revenue cutter*.
6. a small steamer or motor ship, armed and often designed for speed, now employed by the coast guard for coastal or ocean patrol, etc.: also called *coast-guard cutter*.
7. a gaff-rigged racing yacht with one mast, a straight running-in bowsprit, a deep keel, and narrow beam: also called *British cutter*.
8. a modern single-masted yacht or sailboat carrying two headsails under normal wind conditions: distinguished from *sloop*.
9. a small one-horse sleigh.
10. a ruffian; a bravo. [Obs.]
11. a soft, yellow brick, easily cut and used for face work.
12. a colter.
13. [*usually in pl.*] in mining, a crack or fissure cutting across the strata.

çut'tẽr bär, 1. the bar of a reaping machine which carries the triangular knives or cutters.
2. the bar of a boring machine, in which the cutters or cutting tools are fixed.

çut'tẽr-head (-hed), *n.* a rotating cutter or a stock to carry cutters, as in a planing machine.

çut'thrōat, *n.* 1. a murderer; an assassin; a ruffian.
2. the mustang grape of Texas, *Vitis candicans*: so called from its acrid taste.

çut'thrōat, *a.* 1. murderous; cruel; barbarous.
2. merciless; ruthless, relentless.
3. played by three people: said of some card games, as *cutthroat* bridge.

çut'ting, *n.* 1. the act of a person or thing that cuts.
2. something cut off or made by cutting, as a slip or shoot cut away from a plant for the purpose of grafting or rooting, or a passage through a hill in constructing a railroad, canal, etc.
3. a clipping from a newspaper, etc. [Brit.]
4. the editing of a motion-picture film by deleting certain scenes and assembling others into their proper sequence.

çut'ting, *a.* 1. adapted for cutting; serving to sever or divide; as, a *cutting* instrument.
2. wounding the feelings; sarcastic; as, a *cutting* remark.
3. piercing; keen; chilling; as, a *cutting* blast of wind.

çut'ting·ly, *adv.* in a cutting manner.

çut'tle, *n.* a knife. [Obs.]

çut'tle, *n.* [ME. *cotul, cotull*; AS. *cudele*, the cuttlefish.]
1. a cuttlefish.
2. cuttlebone.

çut'tle·bōne, *n.* the internal shell or bone of a cuttlefish, used as a food for birds and, when powdered, as a polishing agent.

çut'tle·fish, *n.*; *pl.* **çut'tle·fish** or **çut'tle·fish·eṣ,** any of the *Cephalopoda*, especially any of the genus *Sepia*, dibranchiate cephalopodous mollusks, with a depressed body, enclosed in a sac. It has ten sucker-bearing arms and a hard internal shell. It has the power of ejecting a black, inklike fluid from a bag or sac, so as to darken the water and conceal itself when in danger.

CUTTLEFISH

çut'too plāte, a hood attached to the end of a wagon axle to protect it from mud.

çut'ty, *a.* short; as, a *cutty* spoon. [Scot. and Dial.]

Her *cutty* sark o' Paisley harn. —Burns.

çut'ty, *n.*; *pl.* **çut'tieṣ,** 1. a short pipe or spoon.
2. a slatternly woman or girl; a wanton.

çut'ty stool, 1. a low stool. [Scot.]
2. formerly, a seat in a church where offenders against chastity were seated and publicly rebuked by the minister. [Scot.]

çut'up, *n.* a person who clowns, plays practical jokes, etc. to attract attention. [Slang.]

çut'wạl, *n.* [Per. *kotwal*, chief officer of police.] in the East Indies, the chief police officer in a city.

çut'wạ''tẽr, *n.* 1. the fore part of a ship's prow, which cuts the water.
2. the angular edge of the pier of a bridge.
3. a sea bird, the skimmer, *Rhynchops nigra*.

çut'weed, *n.* any of several varieties of coarse marine algae, as *Fucus vesiculosus, Fucus serratus*, and *Laminaria digitata*.

çut'wŏrk, *n.* openwork embroidery in which part of the cloth is cut away from the design.

çut'wŏrm, *n.* any of a number of caterpillars, especially the larvae of various night-flying moths, which attack the young plants of cabbage, corn, beans, etc., cutting them off at ground level.

çū·vette', *n.* [Fr., dim. of *cuve*, a tub; L. *cupa*, a tub.]
1. a vessel used to carry molten glass from the melting pot to the rolling table.
2. in fortification, a cunette.

Çū·vi·ē'ri·ăn, *a.* in zoology, pertaining to Georges Cuvier, a French naturalist (1769–1832), or to his system of classification.

-cy, [ME. *-cie*; OFr. *-cie*; L. *-cia, -tia*; Gr. *-kia, -keia, -tia, -teia*.] a suffix denoting: (a) *quality, condition, state*, or *fact of being*, as in innocen*cy*, democra*cy*, aristocra*cy*; (b) *position, rank*, or *office of*, as in captain*cy*, cura*cy*.

cȳ·am'e·līde (*or* -lid), *n.* in chemistry, a white, amorphous compound $(CNOH)_3$.

cȳ'an-, same as *cyano-*.

cȳ·an·am'id, *n.* same as *cyanamide*.

cȳ·an·am'īde (*or* -id), *n.* [*cyan-*, and *amide*.] a white, crystalline compound, $CN{\cdot}NH_2$, prepared by the reaction of carbon dioxide and hot sodium amide, and by other reactions.

cȳ'ȧ·nāte, *n.* a salt or ester of cyanic acid.
ammonium cyanate; a white, crystalline compound, NH_4CNO, easily passing into urea.

cȳ·ā'nē·ăn, *a.* [Gr. *kyaneos*, dark blue.] azure-blue; cerulean.

cȳ·ā'nē·ous, *a.* cyanean.

cȳ·an·hȳ'driç, *a.* [Gr. *kyanos*, dark blue, and *hydōr*, water.] in chemistry, hydrocyanic.

cȳ·an'iç, *a.* [*cyan-*, and *-ic*.]
1. relating to or containing cyanogen.
2. blue.
cyanic acid; a colorless, poisonous, unstable acid, HOCN, prepared by heating cyanuric acid.
cyanic colors; in botany, a series of colors in flowers, having a blue tinge: opposed to *xanthic colors*, which have a yellow tinge.

cȳ'ȧ·nid, *n.* same as *cyanide*.

cȳ'ȧ·nīde (*or* -nid), *n.* a substance composed of cyanogen in combination with some element or radical; especially, potassium cyanide, KCN, or sodium cyanide, NaCN, extremely poisonous, white, crystalline compounds with an odor of bitter almonds: used in extracting gold from low-grade ores, electroplating, case-hardening of steel, and as a fluxing material.

cȳ'ȧ·nīde proc'ess, a process of extracting gold or silver from low-grade ores by treating them with a solution of sodium cyanide or potassium cyanide and then recovering the gold or silver by electrolysis.

cȳ'ȧ·nin, *n.* same as *cyanine*.

cȳ'ȧ·nīne, *n.* [*cyan-*, and *-ine*.] a soluble, crystalline, blue dye, $C_{29}H_{35}N_2I$, derived from quiniline and used as a sensitizer in photography.

cȳ'ȧ·nīte, *n.* [*cyan-*, and *-ite*.] a silicate of aluminum, Al_2SiO_5, occurring usually in long, thin, bladelike crystals, of a clear blue or bluish-white color: also called *kyanite*.

cȳ'an·ō-, [from Gr. *kyanos*, dark blue.] a combining form meaning: (a) *dark-blue*, as in *cyanosis*; (b) in chemistry, *of* or *containing cyanogen*. Also, before a vowel, *cyan-*.

cȳ·an'ō·ġen, *n.* [L. *cyano-*, and Gr. *genos*, kind.]
1. a colorless, poisonous, inflammable gas, C_2N_2, with a strong odor, resembling that of peach blossoms.
2. the univalent radical CN, occurring in cyanides.

cȳ''ȧ·nō·hȳ'drin, *n.* [*cyano-*, *hydro-*, and *-in*.] any of a class of organic chemical compounds containing both the CN and OH radicals.

cȳ·ȧ·nom'e·tẽr, *n.* [*cyano-*, and Gr. *metron*, a measure.] an instrument for measuring degrees of blueness, as of the ocean or sky.

cȳ·ȧ·nom'e·try, *n.* the science of measuring the intensity of blue light, especially that of the sky.

cȳ·ȧ·nop'ȧ·thy, *n.* [*cyano-*, and Gr. *pathos*, suffering.] cyanosis.

Cȳ''ȧ·nō·phyc'ē·ae, *n.pl.* [*cyano-*, and Gr. *phykos*, seaweed.] a class of algae of a blue-green color.

cȳ''ȧ·nō·phy'ceous (-fish'us), *a.* pertaining to the *Cyanophyceæ*.

cȳ'ȧ·nōsed, *a.* cyanotic.

cȳ·ȧ·nō'sis, *n.* [Mod. L. *cyanosis*; Gr. *kyanōsis*, dark-blue color, from *kyanos*, dark blue.] a bluish coloration of the skin, caused by lack of oxygen in the blood.

cȳ·an'ō·sīte, *n.* [Gr. *kyanos*, dark blue.] blue vitriol; chalcanthite.

cȳ·ȧ·not'iç, *a.* pertaining to or characterized by cyanosis.

cȳ·ȧ·not'ri·ċhīte, *n.* [*cyano-*, and Gr. *thrix*, hair.] a hydrous sulfate of copper and aluminum: also called *lettsomite*.

cȳ·an'ō·tȳpe, *n.* [*cyano-*, and Gr. *typos*, stamp, impression.] a photographic picture produced on paper sensitized by a cyanide; a blueprint.

cȳ·an·ū·ram'īde (*or* -id), *n.* see *melamine*.

cȳ·an'ū·rāte, *n.* a salt of cyanuric acid.

cȳ·an'ū·ret, *n.* cyanide. [Obs.]

cȳ·ȧ·nū'riç, *a.* [Gr. *kyanos*, dark blue, and *ouron*, urine.] in chemistry, relating to or designating cyanuric acid.
cyanuric acid; a white, crystalline acid, $C_3N_3(OH)_3$, made by heating urea, yielding cyanic acid when subjected to a heating process.

Cȳ·ath'ē·ȧ, *n.* [Gr. *kyathos*, a cup.] a genus of tropical tree ferns, of the order *Polypodiaceæ*, having the spores enclosed in a cup-shaped indusium.

cy̆·ath·ē·ā′ceous, *a.* pertaining to or characteristic of the genus *Cyathea.*

cy̆·ath′i·form, *a.* [L. *cyathus*; Gr. *kyathos*, a cup, and *forma*, shape.] in the form of a cup.

CYATHIFORM FLOWER

cy̆′ath·oid, *a.* same as *cyathiform.*

cy̆·ath′ō·lith, *n.* [Gr. *kyathos*, cup, and *lithos*, stone.] a coccolith shaped like a cup.

Cy̆″ȧ·thō·phyl′li·dae, *n.pl.* [Gr. *kyathos*, a cup, *phyllon*, a leaf, and *eidos*, form.] a family of fossil stone corals of the group *Rugosa*, the species of which are called cup corals.

cy̆″ȧ·thō·phyl′loid, *a.* pertaining to the family *Cyathophyllidæ.*

cy̆″ȧ·thō·zō′oid, *n.* [Gr. *kyathos*, a cup, *zōos*, alive, and *eidos*, form.] an imperfect rudimentary zooid of certain ascidians, as of those belonging to the genus *Pyrosoma.*

cy̆′ȧ·thus, *n.*; *pl.* **cy̆′ȧ·thī,** [L. *cyathus*; Gr. *kyathos*, a cup.]

1. in ancient Greece, a small, long-handled ladle or cup used especially for filling wine glasses.

2. an Attic liquid measure, equivalent to about 1/24 of a quart.

3. in botany, a small, conical organ or cavity in some cryptogams.

4. [C–] a genus of nidulariaceous fungi.

Cyb′e·lē, *n.* [L. *Cybele*; Gr. *Kybelē*, the goddess Cybele.] in ancient Phyrgian mythology, the goddess of nature: identified with the Greek goddess Rhea.

cy̆·bẽr·net′iç, *a.* of cybernetics.

cy̆·bẽr·net′iç̧s, *n. pl.* [*construed as sing.*] [from Gr. *kybernetes*, helmsman, and *-ics.*] the comparative study of the human nervous system and of complex electronic calculating machines, aimed at increasing the understanding of how the human brain functions.

cy̆′bọrg, *n.* [*cyb*ernetic *org*anism.] a hypothetical human being modified for life in a nonearth environment by the substitution of artificial organs and other body parts.

cy̆′çad, *n.* any plant of the family *Cycadaceæ.*

Cyç·ȧ·dā′cē·ae, *n.pl.* [Gr. *kykas*, the African cocoa palm.] a family of primitive tropical plants, resembling palms in appearance and having fernlike leaves growing in a top cluster.

cyç·ȧ·dā′ceous, *a.* in botany, belonging to or characteristic of the order *Cycadaceæ.*

cy·çā′dē·ăn, *a.* cycadaceous.

Cy̆′ças, *n.* [Gr. *kykas*, the African cocoa palm.] a genus of cycadaceous trees resembling the palms. They are native to Asia, Australia, and Polynesia. From the pith of the trunk of certain species a coarse sago is obtained: the tree is sometimes called *sago palm.*

Cyç′lȧ·men, *n.* [Gr. *kyklaminos*, the cyclamen; *kyklos*, a circle.]

1. a genus of bulbous plants of the family *Primulaceæ*, having heart-shaped leaves

CYCLAMEN

spotted with white along the veins, and white, pink, or red flowers with reflexed petals.

2. [c–] *pl.* **cyç′lȧ·menş,** a plant of this genus.

cyç′lȧ·min, *n.* the bitter principle of the root of *Cyclamen europæum.*

Cyç·lan·thā′cē·ae, *n.pl.* [Gr. *kyklos*, circle, and *anthos*, a flower.] a small family of tropical plants intermediate between the palms and the screw pines. The typical genus is *Cyclanthus*, and its species are found in tropical America.

cyç·lan·thā′ceous, *a.* belonging to or characteristic of the family *Cyclanthaceæ.*

cy̆′çlas, *n.* 1. in ancient Rome, an upper garment worn by both men and women, usually made of silk: it was somewhat similar to the surcoat and embroidered with gold.

2. an outer gown of the fourteenth century, worn by women and also by knights over their armor.

cy̆·çlȧ·zō′cīne, *n.* [from *cyclo-*, and *azo-*, and *-ocin*, suffix for an 8-membered ring, and *-e.*] a pain-killing, nonaddictive, synthetic drug that blocks the effects of heroin or morphine.

cy̆′çle, *n.* [Fr. *cycle*; LL. *cyclus*; Gr. *kyklos*, a circle.]

1. a recurring period of a definite number of years, used as a measure of time.

2. a period of time within which a round of regularly recurring events or phenomena is completed; as, the business *cycle.*

3. a complete set of events or phenomena recurring in the same sequence.

4. any long period; an age.

Better fifty years of Europe than a *cycle* of Cathay. —Tennyson.

5. in literature, the aggregate of legendary or traditional matter accumulated round some mythical or heroic event or character embodied in poetry, songs, etc.; as, the ballads of the Arthurian *cycle.*

6. a series of poems or songs on the same theme.

7. a bicycle, tricycle, or motorcycle.

8. a set of equal septa in corals.

9. in astronomy, the orbit of a heavenly body.

10. in biology, a recurring series of functional changes or events.

11. in botany, (a) in the theory of spiral leaf arrangement, a complete turn of the spire; (b) an entire circle of leaves.

12. in electricity, (a) a complete alternation of a current that changes from positive to negative and back again; (b) the time necessary for such an alternation.

Callippic cycle; a period of seventy-six years, or four Metonic cycles.

cycle of eclipses; a period required for the revolution of the moon's node, about eighteen years eleven days, after which eclipses usually return in a similar order.

cycle of indiction; a period of fifteen years in Roman chronology.

cycle of the sun, or *solar cycle*; a period of twenty-eight years, which having elapsed, the days of the month again fall upon the same days of the week.

Metonic cycle; a period of nineteen years at the end of which the new moon reappears on the same day as at the beginning of the cycle.

cy̆′çle, *v.i.*; cycled, *pt., pp.*; cycling, *ppr.* 1. to recur in cycles; to pass through a cycle.

2. to ride a bicycle, tricycle, or motorcycle.

cy̆′çlẽr, *n.* a cyclist.

cy̆′ç̧liç (*or* sik′), a. 1. pertaining to or moving in a cycle.

All the *cyclic* heavens around me spun. —E. B. Browning.

2. connected with a cycle of legends, etc.

3. in ancient prosody, having a certain shortened measure in which the time of three syllables is occupied instead of four; designating certain dactyls and anapests.

4. in botany, having the parts arranged in the form of a whorl.

5. in chemistry, arranged in a ring or closed-chain structure: said of atoms.

cyclic chorus; in ancient Greece, the chorus which performed the songs and dances of the dithyrambic odes at Athens, dancing round the altar of Dionysus in a circle.

cyclic poets; the epic poets who followed Homer, and wrote on the Trojan war.

cy̆ç′liç (*or* sik′), *n.* a poem in cyclic meter.

cy̆ç′liç·ăl, *a.* cyclic.

cy̆′çling, *n.* the act or sport of riding a cycle, especially a bicycle.

cy̆′çlist, *n.* 1. one who rides a cycle, especially a bicycle.

2. one who believes in the cyclic recurrence of events or phenomena.

cyç·lī′tis, *n.* inflammation of the ciliary body.

cy̆′çlō-, [Gr. *kyklos*, circle, wheel.] a combining form meaning *of a wheel* or *circle, circular*, as in *cyclo*graph: also, before a vowel, *cycl-.*

cy̆·çlō·bran′çhi·āte, *a.* [*cyclo-*, and Gr. *branchia*, gills.] in zoology, having the gills arranged in a circle about the body, as a limpet.

cy̆·çlō·coe′liç (-sē′lik), *a.* [*cyclo-*, and Gr. *koilia*, the belly, intestines.] arranged in coils, as the intestines of certain birds.

cy̆′çlō·ġen, *n.* [*cyclo-*, and Gr. *genos*, kind.] an exogen.

cy̆′çlō·gràph, *n.* [*cyclo-*, and Gr. *graphein*, to describe.]

1. an instrument for describing the arcs of circles; an arcograph.

2. a camera that can take a panoramic view of half the surface of a spherical object.

3. an electronic tool for determining the hardness of metals.

cy̆′çloid, *n.* [Gr. *kyklos*, a circle, and *eidos*, form.]

1. in geometry, a curve traced by a point on the circumference, or on a radius, of a circle that makes one complete revolution along a straight line and kept always in the same plane. The *common cycloid* is described

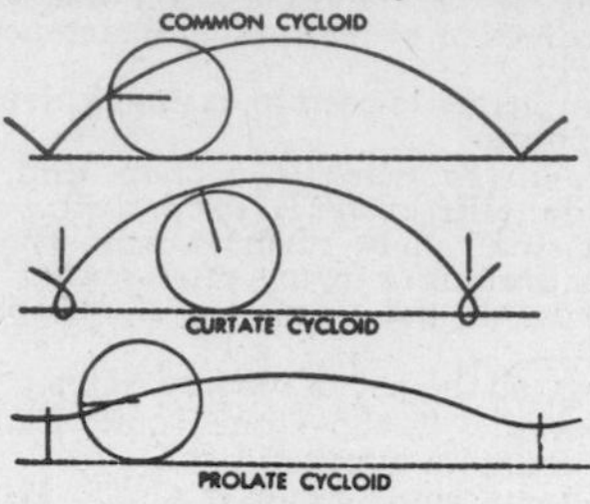

CYCLOIDS

by a point on the circumference; the *curtate cycloid* is the cycloid described when the generating point lies outside the circumference of the circle; the *prolate* or *inflected cycloid* is the cycloid described when the point lies within the circumference.

2. any of the *Cycloidei.*

cy̆′çloid, *a.* 1. circular.

2. designating or of a person who has cyclothymia.

3. relating to the *Cycloidei.*

cy̆·çloid′ăl, *a.* pertaining to, or having the shape of, a cycloid.

cy̆·çloi′dē·ăn, *a.* pertaining to the *Cycloidei.*

cy̆·çloi′dē·ăn, *n.* any of the *Cycloidei.*

Cy̆·çloi′dē·ī, *n.pl.* [L., from Gr. *kyklos*, circle, and *eidos*, form.] in former classifications, a group of fishes having cycloid scales.

cy̆·çlom′e·tẽr, *n.* [*cyclo-*, and Gr. *metron*, a measure.] 1. an instrument for recording a wheel's revolutions or the number of miles traveled by a wheeled vehicle: used with automobiles, bicycles, etc.

2. an instrument for measuring the arcs of circles.

cy̆·çlom′e·try, *n.* [*cyclo-*, and Gr. *metron*, a measure.] in geometry, the measuring of circles.

cy̆′çlōne, *n.* [Gr. *kyklōn*, ppr. of *kykloun*, to whirl around, twist.]

1. in meteorology, a violent, circular storm with heavy rainfall and winds rotating about a calm center of low atmospheric pressure, that moves forward at a rate of from 2 to 40 miles per hour.

2. any violent windstorm having a rotary motion; a tornado or hurricane.

cy̆′çlōne cel′lăr, a deep cellar beneath a building, for shelter during heavy windstorms.

cy̆·çlon′iç, *a.* pertaining to or resembling a cyclone.

cy̆·çlon′i·çăl, *a.* same as *cyclonic.*

cy̆·çlō′nō·sçōpe, *n.* [from *cyclone*, and *-scope.*] in meteorology, a device for locating the center of a cyclone.

cy̆·çlō·pē′ăn, *a.* [L. *Cyclopeus*; Gr. *Kyklōpeios*, Cyclopean, from *Kyklōps*, Cyclops.]

1. [C–] pertaining to the Cyclopes.

2. gigantic; enormous; massive; vast; as, a *cyclopean* work.

3. in zoology, having a single eye in the center of the forehead.

cy̆·çlō·pē′di·ȧ, cy̆·çlō·pae′di·ȧ, *n.* [Gr. *kyklos*, a circle, and *paideia*, education.]

1. a book dealing comprehensively with one branch of learning; as, a *cyclopedia* of electricity.

2. a book with subjects alphabetically arranged, containing an extensive account of many branches of knowledge; an encyclopedia.

cy̆·çlō·pē′diç, cy̆·çlō·pae′diç, *a.* 1. pertaining to a cyclopedia.

2. of the nature of a cyclopedia; exhaustive; thorough.

cy̆·çlō·pē′dist, cy̆·çlō·pae′dist, *n.* one who compiles or writes for a cyclopedia.

cy̆·çlō·pen′tāne, *n.* [*cyclo-*, and *pentane.*] a saturated, colorless liquid hydrocarbon, C_5H_{10}, derived from certain petroleums.

cy̆·çlop′iç, *a.* pertaining to, or resembling, the Cyclopes; cyclopean.

cy̆′çlō·pid, *n.* in zoology, one of the *Cyclopidæ.*

Cȳ·çlop′i·dae, *n.pl.* [Gr. *Kyklōps*, Cyclops, and *eidos*, form, shape.] a family of minute crustaceans having but one eye.

cȳ·çlō·plē′ġi·ȧ, *n.* paralysis of those muscles of the eye responsible for visual accommodation.

cȳ′çlō·poid, *a.* pertaining to the *Cyclopidæ.*

cȳ·çlō·prō′pāne, *n.* [*cyclo-*, and *-propane.*] a colorless, inflammable gas, C_3H_6, used as a general anesthetic.

Cȳ′çlops, *n.*; *pl.* **Cȳ′çlō·pēṣ,** [L. *Cyclops*, pl. *Cyclopes*; Gr. *Kyklōps*, pl. *Kyklōpes*, Cyclops; *kyklos*, a circle, and *ōps*, eye.]
1. in Greek mythology, one of a race of giants supposedly living in Sicily, having but one circular eye in the middle of the forehead.
2. a typical genus of the *Cyclopidæ.*

cȳ·çlō·rä′mȧ, *n.* [*cyclo-*, and Gr. *horama*, a view.]
1. a pictorial representation, usually of a battle or landscape, displayed on a circular wall in imitation of natural perspective, and viewed from a central point; a circular panorama.
2. a large, curved curtain or screen used as a background for stage settings.

cȳ·çlō·ram′iç, *a.* pertaining to or resembling a cyclorama.

cȳ′çlō·sçōpe, *n.* [*cyclo-*, and Gr. *skopein*, to look at, view.] an automatic apparatus for measuring velocity of revolution.

cȳ·çlō′sis, *n.* [Gr. *kyklōsis*, a surrounding, from *kykloun*, to enclose.] in biology, circulation of the life-giving fluids.

Cȳ·çlos′tō·mȧ, *n.* [*cyclo-*, and Gr. *stoma*, mouth.] a genus of gastropods whose shells have circular apertures; type of the family *Cyclostomidæ.*

Cȳ·çlō·stō′mȧ·tȧ, *n.pl.* [*cyclo-*, and Gr. *stoma*, mouth.] in zoology, (a) a genus of gymnolaematous polyzoans having circular apertures; (b) the order *Marsipobranchii.*

cȳ·çlos′tō·māte, *a.* 1. having a round mouth.
2. of a cyclostome or the cyclostomes.

cȳ·çlō·stom′ȧ·tous, *a.* same as *cyclostomate.*

cȳ′çlō·stōme, *n.* any of a group of primitive fishes, including the lamprey and hagfish, which are vertebrates with an eellike body and a circular, sucking mouth; any of the *Cyclostomi.*

cȳ′çlō·stōme, *a.* same as *cyclostomous.*

Cȳ·çlos′tō·mī, *n.pl.* an order of eellike fishes with sucking mouths; the *Marsipobranchii.*

cȳ·çlos′tō·mous, *a.* 1. having a circular mouth.
2. of or relating to the *Cyclostomi.*

cȳ·çlō·stȳ′lăr, *a.* 1. made by, or pertaining to, a cyclostyle.
2. in architecture, resembling or pertaining to a cyclostyle.

cȳ′çlō·stȳle, *n.* [*cyclo-*, and Gr. *stylos*, a pillar.]
1. in architecture, a circular arrangement of columns supporting a roof, without a core or building within.
2. an apparatus for producing a number of copies of a writing or drawing by means of a stencil in which very small holes are cut with a small, toothed wheel on a stylus.

cȳ·çlō·thȳ′mi·ȧ, *n.* [Mod. L., from *cyclo-*, and Gr. *thymos*, spirit.] an abnormal condition characterized by alternate periods of elation and depression; manic-depressive psychosis.

cȳ·çlō·thȳ′miç, *a.* of, characteristic of, or having cyclothymia.

cȳ·çlō·thȳ′miç, *n.* a cyclothymic person.

cȳ·çlō·tom′iç, *a.* pertaining to cyclotomy.

cȳ·çlot′ō·my, *n.* [*cyclo-*, and Gr. *tomē*, a cutting, from *temnein*, to cut.]
1. in geometry, the theory of the division of a circle into equal parts.
2. in surgery, an operation consisting of an incision into the ciliary body.

cȳ′çlō·tron, *n.* [*cyclo-*, and elec*tron.*] an apparatus for giving high energy to particles, usually protons and deuterons: through the combined action of a homogeneous magnetic field and an oscillating electrostatic field it causes a particle to move in a spiral path with increasing kinetic energy until the particle attains a velocity sufficiently high for the purpose intended, usually to initiate nuclear transformations upon collision with a suitable target. By modulating the oscillations of the electric field it is also possible to accelerate electrons in a cyclotron.

CYCLOTRON

cȳ′dẽr, *n.* same as *cider.*

cȳ·dō′nin, *n.* [L. *cydonia*, a quince, a Cydonian apple, from Cydonia, a town in Crete.] in chemistry, an amyloid extract of quince seeds resembling mucilage.

cȳ·dō′ni·um, *n.* in pharmacy, quince seed.

cȳ·ē·si·ol′ō·ġy, *n.* [Gr. *kyēsis*, pregnancy, and *legein*, to describe.] that branch of physiology that deals with pregnancy.

cȳ·ē′sis, *n.* [Gr. *kyēsis*, pregnancy.] pregnancy.

cyg′nē·ous, *a.* [L. *cygneus*, pertaining to a swan, from *cygnus*, a swan.] in botany, curved to resemble a swan's neck.

cyg′net, *n.* [Fr., dim. of *cygne*, a swan; L. *cygnus*; Gr. *kyknos*, a swan.] a young swan.

Cyg′nus, *n.* [L. *Cygnus*; Gr. *kyknos*, a swan.]
1. in astronomy, a northern constellation, the Swan, in the Milky Way.
2. a genus of birds typical of *Cygninæ*, the swans.

cyl′in·dẽr, *n.* [Fr. *cylindre*; L. *cylindrus*; Gr. *kylindros*, a cylinder, roller, from *kylindein*, to roll.]
1. in geometry, a solid body described by the rotation of a parallelogram round one of its sides: the ends of a cylinder are equal and parallel circles. When the axis is at right angles to the planes, it is called a *right cylinder*; otherwise, it is an *oblique cylinder.*

RIGHT CYLINDER

2. anything having the shape of a cylinder, whether hollow or solid; specifically, (a) the turning part of a revolver, containing chambers for cartridges; (b) a chamber in which force is exerted on the piston of a reciprocating engine; (c) the barrel of a pump; (d) on a printing press, a roller carrying the printing plates or the part receiving the impression; (e) a roller-shaped stone with cuneiform inscriptions.

cyl′in·dẽr bōre, a gun having a bore of uniform diameter throughout.

cyl′in·dẽr çock, a cock at the end of a steam cylinder through which water may be blown out or steam blown in.

cyl′in·dẽr head (hed), the closed end, usually detachable, of a cylinder in an internal-combustion engine, often containing the seatings for the valves and the inlet and exhaust passages.

cyl′in·dẽr wrench, a pipe wrench.

cyl·in·drā′ceous, *a.* approximately cylindrical.

cyl·in·dren′chy·mȧ, *n.* [Gr. *kylindros*, a cylinder, and *enchyma*, an infusion; *en*, in, and *chein*, to pour.] in botany, plant tissue composed of cylindrical cells, as in the genus *Conferva.*

cy·lin′driç·ăl, cy·lin′driç, *a.* having the shape of a cylinder; like a cylinder; also, of a cylinder.
cylindrical lens; a lens having cylindrical surfaces, as in spectacles.
cylindrical surface; in geometry, a surface described by a straight line moving parallel to a fixed straight line.

cy·lin·dri·cal′i·ty, *n.* the quality or state of being cylindrical.

cyl·in·dric′i·ty, *n.* same as *cylindricality.*

cy·lin′dri·çūle, *n.* a small cylinder.

cy·lin′dri·form, *a.* [L. *cylindrus*, a cylinder, and *forma*, shape.] having the form of a cylinder.

cyl′in·droid, *a.* [Gr. *kylindros*, a cylinder, and *eidos*, form.] of cylindrical form.

cyl′in·droid, *n.* a solid body resembling a cylinder but having the bases or ends elliptical.

cy·lin·drō·met′riç, *a.* [Gr. *kylindros*, a cylinder, and *metron*, a measure.] belonging to a scale used in measuring cylinders.

cȳ′lix, *n.*; *pl.* **cyl′i·çēṣ,** [Gr. *kylix.*] a two-handled drinking cup with a stem and a wide, shallow bowl, used in ancient Greece: also *kylix.*

Cyl·lē′ni·ăn, *a.* 1. of Mount Cyllene, in Greece.
2. of Hermes, who was regarded as having been born there, or of the arts and practices of which he was the patron god.

cȳ′mȧ, *n.*; *pl.* **cȳ′mae,** [Mod. L. *cyma*; Gr. *kyma*, wave, from *kyein*, to swell.]
1. in architecture, a molding of a cornice, the profile of which is partly concave and partly convex. *Cyma recta* is concave at the top and convex at the bottom, and *cyma reversa*, convex at the top and concave at the bottom.
2. in botany, a cyme.

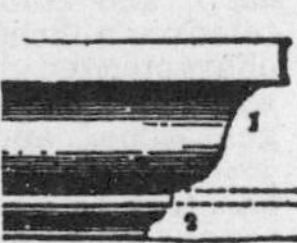

CYMA
1. cyma recta; 2. cyma reversa

cȳ′mȧ·gràph, *n.* same as *cymograph.*

cy·mär′, *n.* [Fr. *simarre.*] a chemise or other loose, lightweight garment for women.

cȳ·mā′ti·um (-shi-um), *n.* [L. *cymatium*, a waved molding, from Gr. *kyma*, a wave.] in architecture, a molding topping an entablature; also, a cyma.

cym′băl, *n.* [ME. *cimbale, cymbale*; OFr. *cimbale*; L. *cymbalum*; Gr. *kymbalon*, a cymbal, from *kymbē*, a hollow vessel.]
1. either of a pair of circular, concave brass or bronze plates which have handles at the back and make a ringing sound when clashed together: used as percussion instruments in orchestras or bands.
2. a single brass plate, struck with a drumstick.
3. a musical instrument consisting of a triangular wire strung with movable rings.
4. a stop of high pitch in an organ.

CYMBALS

cym′băl·ist, *n.* [L. *cymba*; Gr. *kymbē*, a boat, skiff.] one who plays the cymbals.

cym′bāte, *a.* shaped like a boat; cymbiform.

cym′bi·form, *a.* [L. *cymba*, a boat, and *forma*, shape.] having the form of a boat.

cym·bō·ceph′ȧ·ly, *n.* [Gr. *kymbē*, a boat, and *kephalē*, head.] in craniology, a bilobate skull.

cȳme, *n.* [L., from Gr. *kyma*, a wave, from *kyein*, to swell.]
1. a cluster of flowers in which each main and secondary stem bears a single flower, the bud on the main stem blooming first, as in phlox and sweet William.
2. in architecture, the cyma.

cȳme′let, *n.* same as *cymule.*

cȳ′mēne, *n.* [L. *cuminum*; Gr. *kyminon*, cumin.] a hydrocarbon, $C_{10}H_{14}$, occurring in three isomeric forms (*orthocymene, metacymene*, and *paracymene*), derived from benzene: the most common form, paracymene, is found in the oil of certain plants, as cumin and wild thyme.

cȳ·mif′ẽr·ous, *a.* [L. *cyma*, cyme, and *ferre*, to bear.] in botany, bearing cymes.

cȳ′mō-, [Gr. *kymo-*, from *kyma*, cyme.] a combining form meaning *wave*, as in *cymo*scope.

cȳ′mō·ġēne, *n.* [L. *cuminum*; Gr. *kyminon*, cumin, and *-genēs*, producing.] in chemistry, a volatile liquid mixture of hydrocarbons obtained from petroleum which, when condensed, is used as a refrigerant.

cȳ′mō·gràph, *n.* [*cymo-*, and *-graph.*] an instrument for making tracings, as of profiles, contours, etc.; kymograph.

cȳ′moid, *a.* having the form of a cyme or cyma.

cȳ′mōl, *n.* same as *cymene.*

cȳ·mom′e·tẽr, *n.* [*cymo-*, and *-meter.*] an instrument for measuring the frequency of electrical oscillations or radio waves.

cȳ′mō·phāne, *n.* [*cymo-*, and *-phane.*] an opalescent variety of chrysoberyl.

cȳ·moph′ȧ·nous, *a.* [Gr. *kyma*, a wave, and *phanein*, to appear.] having a wavy, floating light; opalescent; chatoyant.

cȳ′mō·sçōpe, *n.* [*cymo-*, and *-scope.*] an instrument for detecting the presence of electric waves.

cȳ′mōse, cȳ′mous, *a.* 1. bearing a cyme or cymes.
2. in the form of a cyme.

Çym′riç, *a.* 1. of the Celtic people of Wales.
2. of their language.

Çym′riç, *n.* the group of Brythonic Celtic languages that includes Welsh, Breton, and extinct Cornish.

Çym′ry, *n.pl.* [W. *Cymro*, a Welshman, pl. *Cymry*, the Welsh.] the Welsh; also, the division of the Celtic race including the Cornishmen and Bretons: also *Kymry.*

cȳ′mūle, *n.* in botany, a simple or small cyme; a cymelet.

cȳ·nan′çhē, *n.* [L., from Gr. *kynanche*, a dog collar, a bad kind of sore throat; *kyōn*, a dog, and *anchein*, to press, choke.] in medicine, any disease of the throat or windpipe attended with inflammation, swelling, and difficulty in breathing and swallowing.

cȳ·nan′thrō·py, *n.* [Gr. *kyōn*, a dog, and *anthrōpos*, man.] a kind of insanity in which the patient believes himself to be a dog, and behaves like a dog.

Cyn′ȧ·rȧ, *n.* [L., from Gr. *kynara*, a plant, either the dog thorn or artichoke.] in botany, a genus of composite herbs allied to the thistle, found in the Mediterranean regions, and including the cultivated artichoke and cardoon.

cyn·à·rā′ceous, *a.* pertaining to or resembling the genus *Cynara*; cynareous.

cyn·ärç·tom′à·çhy, *n.* [Gr. *kyōn*, a dog, *arktos*, a bear, and *machē*, a fight.] bearbaiting with a dog.

cy·nā′rē·ous, *a.* cynaraceous.

cyn·à·roid′, *a.* cynaraceous.

cyn·ar·rhō′di·um, *n.*; *pl.* **cyn·ar·rhō′di·à,** [L., from Gr. *kynorodon*, the dogrose; *kyōn*, dog, and *rhodon*, rose.] in botany, a fruit in which the receptacle is deeply concave or urn-shaped, enclosed by the calyx, and bearing numerous bony achenia on its inner surface, as in the rose.

cyn·ar′rhō·don, *n.* same as *cynarrhodium*.

cyn·ē·ġet′içs, *n.* [Gr. *kynēgetēs*, a hunter; *kyōn*, a dog, and *ēgeisthai*, to lead.] hunting with dogs.

cyn′iç, *n.* [L. *cynicus*, cynical; Gr. *kynikos*, doglike, from *kyōn*, a dog.]
1. [C–] a member of a sect of ancient Greek philosophers who held virtue to be the only good, and stressed independence from worldly needs and pleasures: they became critical of the rest of society and its material interests.
2. a cynical person.
3. a person who believes that people are motivated in all their actions entirely by selfishness.

cyn′iç, *a.* 1. [C–] of or like the Cynics or their doctrines.
2. cynical.
3. pertaining to the Dog Star.
4. doglike.
cynic spasm; in medicine, a contraction of the muscles on one side of the face, suggesting the movements of a dog's upper lip.

cyn′iç·ăl, *a.* [from L. *cynicus*, of the Cynics; Gr. *kynikos*, lit., canine, like a dog, from *kyōn*, *kynos*, dog.]
1. inclined to question the sincerity and goodness of people's motives and actions, or the value of living.
2. morose, sarcastic, sneering, etc.

cyn′iç·ăl·ly, *adv.* in a cynical manner.

cyn′iç·ăl·ness, *n.* the state or quality of being cynical.

cyn′i·çişm, *n.* [LL. *cynismus*; Gr. *kynismos*, cynicism, from *kynizein*, to be a cynic.]
1. [C–] the philosophy of the Cynics.
2. the attitude or beliefs of a cynic.
3. a cynical expression or view.

cyn′i·pid, *a.* pertaining to the *Cynipidæ*.

cyn′i·pid, *n.* an insect of the family *Cynipidæ*.

Cy·nip′i·dae, *n.pl.* [LL. *cyniphes*, a kind of gallfly; Gr. *knips*, a kind of emmet, from *knizein*, to tease.] a family of hymenopterous insects, the gallflies.

cyn·i·pid′ē·ous, *a.* cynipidous.

cy·nip′i·dous, *a.* characteristic of or pertaining to the gallflies, or *Cynipidæ*.

cyn′i·poid, *a.* pertaining to or resembling the *Cynipidæ*; cynipid.

Cȳ′nips, *n.* 1. a genus of gallflies, type of the family *Cynipidæ*.
2. [c–] an insect of this genus; a gallfly.

cyn·ō·cē·phal′iç, *a.* pertaining to a cynocephalus; dog-headed.

cyn·ō·ceph′à·lous, *a.* cynocephalic.

Cyn·ō·ceph′à·lus, *n.* [L. *cynocephalus*; Gr. *kynokephalos*, the African dog-headed ape; *kyōn*, a dog, and *kephalē*, head.]
1. a genus of baboons of the family *Cynopithecidæ*.
2. [c–] a dog-faced baboon.

Cyn·ō·glos′sum, *n.* [L. *cynoglossus*, a plant named the dog-tongued by Pliny.] a genus of plants of the borage family, having about sixty species, of which six are found in North America. *Cynoglossum officinale* is the hound's-tongue.

cȳ′noid, *a.* [Gr. *kynōdes*, doglike.]
1. pertaining to the *Cynoidea*.
2. canine; doglike.

Cȳ·noi′dē·à, *n.pl.* a group of the *Carnivora*, including the dog, fox, and wolf, or family *Canidæ*.

cȳ·nop′ō·dous, *a.* [L., from Gr. *kyōn*, a dog, and *pous*, genit. *podos*, foot.] having feet resembling those of a dog, with blunt, nonretractile claws.

cyn·ō·rex′i·à, *n.* [Gr. *kyōn*, a dog, and *orexis*, appetite; *orexein*, to reach out, desire.] a voracious, doglike appetite; insatiable hunger.

cȳ·nō·sū′răl (*or* sin′ō-), *a.* pertaining to a cynosure; strongly attractive.

cȳ′nō·sūre (*or* sin′ō-), *n.* [L. *cynosura*; Gr. *kynosoura*, the constellation Ursa Minor; *kyōn*, dog, and *oura*, tail; the *cynosure* forms the tip of the tail.]
1. [C–] the constellation Ursa Minor.
2. [C–] the North Star, which is in this constellation.
3. anything that guides or directs.
4. anything which strongly attracts attention; a center of attraction.

Where perhaps some beauty lies,
The *Cynosure* of neighb'ring eyes.
—Milton.

Cyn′thi·à, *n.* [L., f. adj. from *Cynthus*; Gr. *Kynthos*, a mountain in Delos.]
1. Artemis (Diana), goddess of the moon.
2. the moon personified.

cȳ′on, *n.* scion. [Obs.]

Cyp·e·rā′cē·ae, *n.pl.* [L. *cyperos*; Gr. *kypeiron*, a marsh plant.] a large family of rushlike monocotyledonous plants of the sedge family: they resemble the grasses but have solid stems and seeds in closed sheaths.

cyp·ē̃r·ā′ceous, *a.* of or pertaining to the *Cyperaceæ*.

Cyp′e·rus, *n.* a genus of herbs of the sedge family embracing seven hundred species, of which more than fifty are found in the United States as annuals or perennials. *Cyperus papyrus* is the papyrus of Egypt.

cȳ·phel′là, *n.*; *pl.* **cȳ·phel′lae,** [L., from Gr. *kyphella*, the hollow of the ear; *kypelion*, a drinking cup.] a small, cuplike pit on the under surface of the thallus of some lichens.

cȳ·phel′lāte, *a.* in botany, showing cuplike pits; having cyphellae.

cȳ′phē̃r, *n.* and *v.* same as *cipher*.

cyph·ō·nau′tēş, *n.* [L., from Gr. *kyphos*, bent, and *nautes*, a sailor.] in zoology, the larva of a bryozoan of the genus *Membranipora*.

cyph′ŏn·işm, *n.* [Gr. *kyphōn*, a kind of pillory.] an ancient form of punishment consisting of smearing the victim with honey, and exposing him to insects; also, punishment by a pillory.

Cy·prae′à, *n.* [L., from *Cypria*; Gr. *Kypris*, a name for Venus, from the isle of Cyprus, where she was most worshiped.] a genus of gastropods; the cowries.

cy·prae′id, *n.* any of the *Cypræa*; a cowry.

cy pres (sē prā), [OFr. *cyprès*, near to, so near; *cy*, here, *pres*, near; L. *pressus*, pressed, close.] in law, as nearly as possible: applied to the interpretation of wills, as in cases of trust funds when the terms cannot be carried out literally and an effort is made to adhere to the general intent.

cȳ′press, *n.* [ME. *cipres*; OFr. *cypres*; L. *cypressus*, *cupressus*; Gr. *kyparissos*, the cypress tree.]
1. any of a large group of evergreen, cone-bearing trees of the pine family, native to North America, Europe, and Asia: they have dark foliage and a distinctive symmetrical form.
2. the hard wood of one of these trees.
3. the branches or sprigs of the cypress used as an emblem of mourning for the dead.
4. any of a number of related coniferous trees allied to or resembling the true cypresses.

cȳ′press, *a.* made of or resembling cypress.

cȳ′press, *n.* [ME. *cipres*; OFr. *Cipre*, *Cypre*, *Cypres*, Cyprus.] any of various textile fabrics, originally made in Cyprus; specifically, (a) a cloth of gold; (b) a heavy satin; (c) a fine, gauzelike lawn or silk. Also spelled *cyprus*.

cȳ′press knee (nē), a large, hollow tumor or coneshaped outgrowth on the roots of the swamp cypress.

cȳ′press vine, a tropical American climbing plant with showy, trumpet-shaped flowers of scarlet or white, related to the morning-glory.

Cyp′ri·ăn, *n.* [L. *Cyprius*; Gr. *Kyprios*, a Cyprian, from *Kypros*, Cyprus, noted for its temple to Venus.]
1. a native or inhabitant of Cyprus.
2. the Greek dialect of Cyprus.
3. (a) a licentious person; (b) a prostitute. [Obs.]

Cyp′ri·ăn, *a.* 1. of Cyprus, its people, or its language.
2. wanton; licentious: in reference to the worship of Aphrodite there in ancient times.

cyp′rine, *a.* pertaining to the cypress.

cy·prī′nid, *n.* and *a.* same as *cyprinoid*.

Cy·prin′i·dae, *n.pl.* [L., from Gr. *kyprinos*, a carp, and *eidos*, resemblance.] a family of teleostean fishes, the species of which are characterized by a small mouth generally without teeth, strong teeth on the pharyngeal bones, and large scales. The genus *Cyprinus* is the type of the family, which, in addition to the carp, includes the goldfish, tench, roach, loach, bleak, barbel, etc.

cy·prin′ō·dont, *a.* pertaining to the *Cyprinodontidæ*.

cy·prin′ō·dont, *n.* a fish of the family *Cyprinodontidæ*.

Cy·prin·ō·don′ti·dae, *n. pl.* [L., from Gr. *kyprinos*, a carp, and *odous*, a tooth.] a family of very small fishes with soft fins, allied to *Cyprinidæ*, but having toothed, more protractile jaws: it includes the killifishes, minnows, etc.

CYPRINOID
(*Barbus vulgaris*)

cy·prin·ō·don′toid, *a.* and *n.* same as *cyprinodont*.

cyp′ri·noid, *a.* of or like the fishes of the carp family.

cyp′ri·noid, *n.* any of the carp family or a related family.

Cy·prī′nus, *n.* [L. *cyprinus*; Gr. *kyprinos*, a carp.] a genus of fishes typical of the family *Cyprinidæ*; the true carps.

Cyp′ri·ōte, Cyp′ri·ŏt, *a.* and *n.* same as *Cyprian*.

Cyp·ri·pē′di·um, *n.* [Mod. L., from Gr. *Kypris*, Aphrodite, and *pedion*, an open plain, dim. of *pedon*, the ground.]
1. a genus of orchids with showy, drooping flowers, including the lady's slipper, moccasin flower, etc.
2. [c–] *pl.* **cyp·ri·pē′di·à,** a plant of this genus.

cȳ′prus, *n.* same as *cypress* (cloth).

cyp′se·là, *n.*; *pl.* **cyp′se·lae,** [Mod. L., from Gr. *kypselē*, a hollow vessel.] a kind of seed pod (*achene*) with two spore-bearing organs (*carpels*) and a calyx directly attached to it, as in the sunflower.

Cyp·sel′i·dae, *n.pl.* a family of insessorial birds, including the swifts.

cyp·sel′i·fọrm, *a.* [L. *cypsellus*, a swift, and *forma*, form.] in ornithology, pertaining to or resembling the swifts; cypseline.

cyp′se·line, *a.* [L. *cypsellus*, a swift.] pertaining to the *Cypselidæ* or swifts.

cyp′se·loid, *a.* same as *cypseline*.

Cȳ·rē·nā′iç, *a.* [L. *Cyreniacus*; Gr. *Kyrenaikos*, a Cyrenaic, from *Kyrene*, Cyrene.]
1. pertaining to Cyrene or Cyrenaica.
2. pertaining to the Greek school of philosophy founded by Aristippus of Cyrene, who believed pleasure to be the greatest good.

Cȳ·rē·nā′iç, *n.* 1. a philosopher of the Cyrenaic school.
2. a native of Cyrene or Cyrenaica.

Cȳ·rē′ni·ăn, *n.* and *a.* same as *Cyrenaic*.

Cyr·il·lā′cē·ae, *n.pl.* [LL. *cyrillus*; Gr. *kyrillos*, Cyril.] a family of tropical American evergreen trees or shrubs, closely allied to the *Ericaceæ*.

cyr·il·lā′ceous, *a.* pertaining to the *Cyrillaceæ*.

Cy·ril′liç, *a.* pertaining to St. Cyril, ninth-century apostle to the Slavs, or to the alphabet invented by him.
Cyrillic alphabet; an old Slavic alphabet based on the Greek, invented by St. Cyril: in modified form, it is still used in Russia, Bulgaria, and other Slavic countries.

cyr·tom′e·tē̃r (sē̃r-), *n.* [Gr. *kyrtos*, curved, bent, and *metron*, a measure.] in medicine, an instrument for measuring the circumference of the chest.

cyr′tō·style (sē̃r-), *n.* [Gr. *kyrtos*, curved, and *stylos*, a pillar.] in architecture, a circular portico projecting from the front of a building.

cyst, *n.* [L., from Gr. *kystis*, a bladder, a pouch, from *kyein*, to be pregnant.]
1. any of certain saclike structures in plants or animals.
2. any saclike structure or pocket in the body, especially if filled with fluid or diseased matter.
3. in botany, (a) the envelope surrounding the spores in certain seaweeds; (b) a minute cavity containing oil in the rind of certain fruits; (c) the seed cells of some cryptogamous plants.

cyst-, same as *cysto-*.

-cyst, [from Gr. *kystis*, sac, bladder.] a suffix meaning *sac*, *pouch*, *bladder*, as in en*cyst*.

cys·tal′ġi·à, *n.* pain in the bladder.

cys·teç′tō·my, *n.*; *pl.* **cys·teç′tō·mieş,** 1. excision of the gall bladder or a part of the urinary bladder.
2. the excision of a cyst.

cyst'ed, *a.* surrounded by a cyst.
cys'te·ine, *n.* an amino acid, $C_3H_7O_2NS$, derived from cystine and produced by the acid hydrolysis of proteins in digestion.
cys'tel·minth, *n.* [Gr. *kystis*, a bladder, and *elmins*, a worm.] in zoology, any worm enclosing itself in a cyst.
cys'ti-, same as *cysto-*.
cyst'ic, *a.* 1. of or like a cyst.
2. having or containing a cyst or cysts.
3. enclosed in a cyst.
4. in anatomy, of the gall bladder or the urinary bladder.
cystic duct; in anatomy, the membranous canal that conveys the bile from the hepatic duct into the gall bladder.
cystic worm; in zoology, a hydatid, or immature entozoan.
cys·ti·cėr'çoid, *a.* of or like a cysticercus.
cys·ti·cėr'çoid, *n.* the larva of certain tapeworms, similar to a cysticercus but having a much smaller bladder.
cys·ti·cėr'çus, *n.*; *pl.* **cys·ti·cėr'cī,** [Mod. L., from Gr. *kystis*, a bladder, and *kerkos*, tail.] a tapeworm in larval form in which the head and neck are partly enclosed in a bladderlike cyst.
cyst'iç fī·brō'sis, a congenital disease of children, characterized by fibrosis and malfunctioning of the pancreas, and frequent respiratory infections.
cys'ti·çle, *n.* [dim. from L. *cystis*; Gr. *kystis*, a bladder.] a small cyst.
cys'tid, *n.* [Gr. *kystis*, a sac, bladder.] any of the *Cystidea*.
Cys·tid'ē·ȧ, *n.pl.* same as *Cystoidea*.
cys·tid'ē·ăn, *a.* pertaining to the *Cystidea*.
cys·tid'ē·ăn, *n.* same as *cystid*.
cys·ti·diç'ō·lous, *a.* [L. *cystis*; Gr. *kystis*, a bladder, and L. *colere*, to inhabit.] in zoology, living in a cyst.
cys·tid'i·um, *n.*; *pl.* **cys·tid'i·ȧ,** [L., dim. of Gr. *kystis*, bladder.] in hymenomycetous fungi, a spherical cell, supposedly sterile, emerging from the basidia and paraphyses, and projecting beyond them.
cys'tin, *n.* same as *cystine*.
cys'tine, *n.* [from Gr. *kystis*, sac, bladder, and *-ine*: so named from having been found first in urinary calculi.] a crystalline amino acid, $C_4H_4(NH_2)_2S_2(COOH)_2$, produced in the digestion of proteins.
cys'tis, *n.*; *pl.* **cys'ti·dēş,** same as *cyst*.
cys·tī'tis, *n.* in medicine, inflammation of the urinary bladder.
cys'tō-, [from L. *cystis*; Gr. *kystis*, bladder, sac.] a combining form meaning *of* or *like a bladder* or *sac*, as in *cysto*cele: also *cyst-*, *cysti-*.
cys'tō·çärp, *n.* [*cysto-*, and Gr. *karpos*, fruit.] in botany, a small sac or pericarp containing the spores of reproduction of red algae: called also *sporocarp*.
cys'tō·cēle, *n.* [*cysto-*, and Gr. *kēlē*, a rupture.] in medicine, a hernia or rupture of the urinary bladder.
cys'toid, *a.* resembling a cyst or bladder; cystiform.
cys'toid, *n.* a cystlike formation.
Cys·toi'dē·ȧ, *n.pl.* [Gr. *kystis*, bladder, and *eidos*, form.] a class of crinoid Paleozoic fossils, having a roundish body enclosed in sutured plates and a lateral orifice closed by jointed plates: called also *Cystidea*.
cys·toi'dē·ăn, *a.* pertaining to the *Cystoidea*.
cys·toi'dē·ăn, *n.* any of the *Cystoidea*.
cys'tō·lith, *n.* [*cysto-*, and Gr. *lithos*, stone.]
1. in botany, a crystalline concretion of calcium carbonate found in the cell of a plant.
2. in medicine, a urinary calculus.
cys·tō·lith'iç, *a.* pertaining to a cystolith.
cys'tō·plȧst, *n.* [*cysto-*, and Gr. *plastos*, anything formed or molded, from *plassein*, to form.] in anatomy, a cell consisting of an enveloped nucleus.
cys″tō·plē'ġi·ȧ, *n.* paralysis of the bladder.
Cys'to·pus, *n.* [*cysto-*, and Gr. *ōps*, face, appearance.] in botany, a genus of parasitic fungi affecting flowering plants.
cys'tō·sçōpe, *n.* [*cysto-*, and *-scope*.] an instrument for examining the interior of the urinary bladder.
cys'tō·sçōpe, *v.t.*; cystoscoped, *pt.*, *pp.*; cystoscoping, *ppr.* to examine with a cystoscope.
cys·tos'çō·py, *n.* examination of the urinary bladder with the aid of a cystoscope.
cys'tōse, *a.* containing cysts.
cys'tō·tōme, *n.* [*cysto-*, and Gr. *tomos*, a cutting, from *temnein*, to cut.] in surgery, an instrument for making incisions in the bladder.
cys·tot'ō·my, *n.* in surgery, cutting into the urinary bladder, as for removing calcium formations.
cȳt-, same as *cyto-*.
cy·tas'tēr, *n.* [Gr. *kytos*, a cavity, and *astēr*, star.] in biology, a radiate shape occurring in a cell undergoing mitosis.
-cȳte, [from Gr. *kytos*, a hollow.] a terminal combining form meaning *a cell*, as in lympho*cyte*.
Cyth·e·rē'ȧ, *n.* [L.; Gr. *Kythereia*, from *Kythera*, name of a Greek island near which the goddess is fabled to have risen from the sea.] Aphrodite; Venus.
Cyth·e·rē'ăn, *a.* 1. in astronomy, pertaining to the planet Venus.
2. in mythology, pertaining to the goddess Cytherea (Venus).
Cyt'i·sus, *n.* [L. *cytisus*, shrubby lucerne, a kind of clover.] a genus of hardy, leguminous shrubs. The leaves are usually composed of three leaflets, though some species are leafless. The large flowers are purple, white, or yellow. *Cytisus scoparius* is the broom.
cȳ'tō-, [from Gr. *kytos*, a hollow.] a combining form, meaning *of a cell* or *cells*, as in *cyto*logy.
cȳ'tō·blȧst, *n.* [*cyto-*, and Gr. *blastos*, a bud, shoot.] the nucleus of a cell.
cȳ″tō·çhem'is·try, *n.* the study of the chemical constituents of tissues and cells, as with a microscope.
cȳ'tō·çhrōme, *n.* [*cyto-*, and *-chrome*.] any of several iron-containing enzymes found in almost all animal and plant cells, very important in cell respiration.
cȳ″tō·çhy·lē'mȧ, *n.* same as *cytolymph*.
cȳ'tōde, *n.* [Gr. *kytos*, a hollow, and *eidos*, form.] in biology, a cell without a nucleus.
cȳ'tō·dėrm, *n.* [*cyto-*, and Gr. *derma*, skin.] in biology, the wall of a cell.
cȳ·tō·ġen'e·sis, *n.* [*cyto-*, and Gr. *genesis*, birth, origin.] in biology, the formation or development of cells.
cȳ″tō·ġe·net'iç, *a.* 1. pertaining to cytogenesis.
2. of or having to do with cytogenetics.
cȳ″tō·ġe·net'içs, *n.pl.* [*construed as sing.*] the science correlating cytology and genetics as they relate to the behavior of chromosomes and genes in cells with regard to heredity and variation.
cȳ·toġ'e·nous, *a.* [*cyto-*, and Gr. *-genēs*, producing.] in anatomy, producing cells; cytogenetic.
cȳ·toġ'e·ny, *n.* same as *cytogenesis*.
cȳ'toid, *a.* [Gr. *kytos*, a hollow, and *eidos*, form.] cell-like.
cȳ·tō·ki·nē'sis, *n.* [Mod. L.; *cyto-*, and *kinesis*.] the changes that take place in the cytoplasm of a cell during the stages of its development.
cy·tō·ki'nin, *n.* [from *cyto-*, and *kinetic*, and *-in*.] any of a group of organic compounds which behave like hormones in plants, promoting cell division and cell differentiation into roots and shoots, inhibiting aging, etc.
cȳ·tol'ō·ġy, *n.* [*cyto-*, and Gr. *logos*, description, from *legein*, to speak.] the branch of biology dealing with the structure, function, pathology, and life history of cells.
cȳ'tō·lymph, *n.* [*cyto-*, and L. *lympha*, water.] in biology, the more fluid portion of cytoplasm; cytochylema.
cȳ·tol'y·sin, *n.* a substance or antibody that produces cytolysis.
cȳ·tol'y·sis, *n.* [*cyto-*, and *-lysis*.] in biology, the degeneration of cells.
cȳ'tō·plaşm, *n.* [*cyto-*, and Gr. *plasma*, anything formed, image; from *plassein*, to form.] in biology, the protoplasm of a cell, exclusive of the nucleus.
cȳ·tō·plaş'miç, *a.* pertaining to or contained in cytoplasm.
cȳ'tō·plȧst, *n.* same as *cytoplasm*.
cȳ'tō·pȳġe, *n.* the excretory aperture of a unicellular animal.
cȳ'tō·sine, *n.* [G. *zytosin*, from *zyt-*, cyto-, and *-os*, -ose, and *-in*, -ine.] a nitrogenous base, $C_4H_5N_3O$, a constituent of various nucleic acids, and one of the substances constituting the genetic code in DNA molecules.
cȳ'tō·stōme, *n.* [*cyto-*, and Gr. *stoma*, mouth.] in biology, the mouth of a unicellular organism.
cȳ″tō·tax·on'ō·my, *n.* the branch of taxonomy that uses cytological structures, especially the chromosomes, as an aid in classifying organisms.
cyt'ū·lȧ, *n.* [L., from Gr. *kytos*, a hollow.] in biology, the fertilized ovum or parent cell from which any organism is developed.
czär (zär), *n.* [Russ. *tsare*; O.H.G. *keisar*; L. *Cæsar*, emperor, from the cognomen of Caius Julius *Cæsar*.]
1. an emperor: title of any of the former emperors of Russia and, at various times, the sovereigns of other Slavic nations.
2. an autocrat; despot; absolute ruler.
Also *tsar*, *tzar*.
czär'däs (chär'däsh), *n.* [Hung. *csárdás*.]
1. a Hungarian dance consisting of a fast movement and a slow movement.
2. the music for this dance.
czär'dŏm, *n.* 1. the position or power of a czar.
2. the territory ruled over by a czar.
Also *tsardom*, *tzardom*.
czär'e·vitch, *n.* [Russ. *tsarevichu*, prince.]
1. the eldest son of a czar of Russia.
2. formerly, any son of a czar of Russia: in later times the title *grand duke* was borne by all sons but the eldest.
Also *tsarevitch*, *tzarevitch*.
czä·rev'nȧ, *n.* [Russ. *tsarevna*, *tsesarevna*, princess.] the wife of a czarevitch; also, a Russian czar's daughter: also *tsarevna*, *tzarevna*.
czä·rï'nȧ, *n.* [Russ. f. of *czar*.] the wife of a czar of Russia, or a reigning empress of Russia; also *tsarina*, *tzarina*.
czär'işm, *n.* czarist system of government; absolute rule; autocracy: also *tsarism*, *tzarism*.
czär'ist, *a.* 1. of, characteristic of, or like the czars; autocratic.
2. of the time of the czars in Russia; pre-Soviet.
3. supporting a czar or czarism.
Also *tsarist*, *tzarist*.
czär'ist, *n.* a follower or supporter of a czar or czarism: also *tsarist*, *tzarist*.
czä·rit'zȧ (-sȧ), *n.* [Russ.] czarina: also *tsaritza*, *tzaritza*.
Czeçh (chek), *n.* [Bohem. *Chekh*; named from their chieftain *Czech*.]
1. a member of the Slavic people inhabiting Bohemia, Moravia, and Silesia.
2. the West Slavic language of the Czechs: also called *Bohemian*.
Czeçh (chek), *a.* of Czechoslovakia, its people, or their language.
Czeçh'iç (chek'), *a.* same as *Czech*.
Czeçh'ish (chek'), *a.* same as *Czech*.
Czeçh″ō·slō'vak, Czeçh″ō-Slō'vak, *a.* pertaining to the people of Czechoslovakia, to the country, or to the language.
Czeçh″ō·slō'vak, Czeçh″ō-Slō·vak, *n.* 1. a Czech or a Slovak living in Czechoslovakia.
2. the West Slavic language spoken there, including the Czech, Slovak, and Moravian dialects.
Czeçh″ō·slō·vak'i·ăn, Czeçh″ō-Slō·vak'i·ăn, *n.* and *a.* same as *Czechoslovak*.

D

D, d (dē), *n.*; *pl.* **D's, d's, Ds, ds** (dēz). 1. the fourth letter of the English alphabet: from the Greek *delta*, a borrowing from the Phoenician.
2. the sound of D or d.
3. a type or impression for D or d.
4. *a symbol for* the fourth in a sequence or group.

D, d (dē), *a.* 1. of D or d.
2. fourth in a sequence or group.

D (dē), *n.* 1. an object shaped like D.
2. a Roman numeral for 500; with a superior bar ($\overline{D}$), 500,000, or, less often, 5,000.
3. in chemistry, *the symbol for*, (a) deuterium; (b) formerly, didymium.
4. in education, a grade fourth in quality, or merely passing; as, a *D* in history.
5. in music, (a) the second tone or note in the scale of C major, or the fourth in the scale of A minor; (b) a key, string, etc. producing this tone; (c) the scale having D as the keynote.
6. in physics, *the symbol for* density.

D (dē), *a.* shaped like D.

'd, 1. abbreviated spelling of ***had*** or ***would*** in contracted auxiliary forms, as ***I'd, they'd***, etc.
2. -ed, as in foster'*d*.

dab, *v.t.* and *v.i.*; dabbed, *pt.*, *pp.*; dabbing, *ppr.* [ME. *dabben*, to strike; akin to M.D. *dabben* and Norw. *dabba*.]
1. to strike or touch quickly and gently.
2. to pat gently with some soft or moist substance; as, to *dab* a sore with lint.
3. to strike or stab with a pointed weapon; as, he was *dabbed* in the side. [Obs.]
4. to peck.
5. to put on (paint, etc.) with light, quick strokes.

dab, *n.* 1. a gentle, quick blow; a tap; a pat.
2. a small bit of anything soft or moist; as, a *dab* of rouge.

dab, *n.* an expert. [Colloq.]

dab, *n.* 1. a small fish belonging to any of several species allied to the flounder, especially *Pleuronectes limanda*. It averages about

DAB (*Pleuronectes limanda*)

a foot in length and is a common food fish on the British coasts.
2. any small, edible flatfish.

dȧbb, *n.* in zoology, *Uromastix spinipes*, a large lizard with a spiny tail found in the northern part of Africa.

dab'bẽr, *n.* one who or that which dabs; specifically, a kind of pad used by engravers, etchers, printers, etc., for applying ink, color, etc. to plates and type.

dab'ble, *v.t*; dabbled, *pt.*, *pp.*; dabbling, *ppr.*
1. to dip lightly in and out of a liquid.
2. to wet; to moisten; to spatter; to wet by little dips; to sprinkle.

dab'ble, *v.i.* 1. to play in water, as with the hands.
2. to do anything in a slight or superficial manner (with *in* or *at*); as, he *dabbles in* art.
3. to tamper. [Obs.]

You have, I think, been *dabbling* with the text. —Atterbury.

dab'blẽr, *n.* one who dabbles; specifically, one who enters slightly into anything; a superficial worker or thinker; as, a *dabbler* in politics.

dab'bling·ly, *adv.* in a dabbling manner.

dab'chick, *n.* 1. the European little grebe, remarkable for the rapidity with which it dives.
2. the American pied-billed grebe.

dȧ·boy'ȧ, *n.* [E. Ind. name.] *Daboia xanthica*, a large venomous snake of Asia.

dab'stẽr, *n.* 1. one who is skilled; one who is expert; a master of his business. [Brit. Dial.]
2. a clumsy, amateurish worker; a dabbler. [Colloq.]

dä çä'pō, [It., from the beginning; *de*, L. *de*, from, and *capo*, L. *caput*, head] in music, from the commencement; a direction to return to the beginning of a section and repeat it: abbreviated *D. C.*

d'ȧç·çord' (dȧ-kọr'), [Fr.] in accord; agreed.

dāce, *n.* [ME. *darce, darse*; OFr. *dars*, a dart, a dace: so named from its swiftness.]
1. a small cyprinoid fish of Europe, genus *Leuciscus*, gregarious and frequenting fresh waters.

DACE (*Leuciscus vulgaris*)

2. any of a number of small North American fishes like or related to the carp, found in fresh-water streams or ponds.

däçhs'hụnd, *n.* [G. *dachs*, badger, and *hund*, dog.] a small dog of German breed, with a long body, drooping ears, and short legs: known also as the *badger dog*.

DACHSHUND (8-10 in. high)

Dā'ciăn, *a.* [L. *Dacus*, or *Dacicus*, Dacian, from *Dacia*, Dacia.] relating to the old Roman province of Dacia or to its people.

Dā'ciăn, *n.* a native or inhabitant of Dacia.

dā'cīte, *n.* [from *Dacia*, where the mineral is found.] in mineralogy, a volcanic rock consisting essentially of plagioclase and quartz, together with either hornblende, biotite, or pyroxene.

dack'ẽr, *v.i.* 1. to be unsettled; to waver; to be undetermined. [Brit. Dial. and Scot.]
2. to loiter; to walk about carelessly; to saunter. [Brit. Dial. and Scot.]
3. to potter; to work with little purpose. [Brit. Dial. and Scot.]
4. to search, as for smuggled goods. [Brit. Dial. and Scot.]

dack'ẽr, *v.t.* to examine; search for; as, to *dacker* a house. [Brit. Dial. and Scot.]

dȧ·çoit', *n.* [Hind. *dakait*, robber, from *dākā*, attack by robbers.] a member of a gang of robbers in India or Burma.

dȧ·çoit'y, dȧ·çoit'āġe, *n.* robbery by dacoits.

Dȧ·çō'tȧh, *n.* same as *Dakota*.

dā'çron, *n.* a washable synthetic fabric that is mothproof and resistant to wrinkling: a trademark (*Dacron*).

daç'ry·ō-, daç'ry-, [from Gr. *dakryon*, a tear.] combining forms meaning *tear*.

daç''ry·ō·cys·tī'tis, *n.* [*dacryo-*, and Gr. *kystis*, a vessel.] inflammation of the lachrymal sac.

daç'ry·ō·līte, daç'ry·ō·lith, *n.* [*dacryo-*, and Gr. *lithos*, a stone.] a calculous concretion in the lachrymal passage.

daç'tyl, *n.* [L. *dactylus*; Gr. *daktylos*, a finger, a measure of length, a dactyl.]
1. a metrical foot consisting of three syllables, the first long or accented, and the others short or unaccented: so called because like the joints of a finger. Example: "Thĭs ĭs thĕ/fórĕst prĭ/mévăl. Thĕ/múrmŭrĭng / pínes ănd thĕ / hémlŏcks." /
2. a finger or toe; a digit.
3. same as *dactylus*.
4. a unit of measure used by the ancients equal to a fingerbreadth.

daç'tyl·ăr, *a.* 1. pertaining to a dactyl; dactylic. [Rare.]
2. in zoology, relating to a finger, toe, or claw.

daç'tyl·et, *n.* a small dactyl. [Obs.]

-daç·tyl'i·ȧ, -dactyly.

daç·tyl'iç, *a.* pertaining to or consisting chiefly or wholly of dactyls; as, *dactylic* verses.

daç·tyl'iç, *n.* 1. a line or verse consisting chiefly or wholly of dactyls.

daç·tyl'i·ō·glyph, *n.* [Gr. *daktylioglyphos*, an engraver of gems; *daktylios*, a finger ring, from *daktylos*, a finger, and *glyphein*, to cut, engrave.]
1. the inscription of the name of the artist on a finger ring or gem.
2. one who engraves precious stones for rings and other adornments.

daç·tyl''i·ō·glyph'iç, *a.* relating to or characteristic of dactylioglyphy.

daç·tyl·i·og'ly·phist, *n.* same as *dactylioglyph*, sense 2.

daç·tyl·i·og'ly·phy, *n.* the art of engraving precious stones.

daç·tyl·i·og'rȧ·phy, *n.* [Gr. *daktylios*, a finger ring, and *graphein*, to write.] the study or science of gem engraving.

daç·tyl·i·ol'ō·ġy, *n.* study of finger rings.

daç·tyl'i·ō·man''cy, *n.* [Gr. *daktylios*, a finger ring, and *manteia*, divination.] the supposed art of divining by finger rings.

daç·tyl'i·ŏn, *n.* [Gr. *daktylos*, a finger.]
1. a condition of the fingers or toes in which they are joined together from birth, or by accident or disease; syndactylism.
2. a device invented by Henri Herz in 1835 for developing the fingers of piano players: now obsolete.

Daç'ty·lis, *n.* [Mod.L., from Gr. *daktylos*, finger.] in botany, a genus of Eurasian grasses, the most important being *Dactylis glomerata*.

daç'tyl·ist, *n.* one who writes dactylic verse.

daç·tyl·ī'tis, *n.* [Gr. *daktylos*, finger or toe.] in medicine, inflammation of a digit.

daç'tyl·ō-, [from Gr. *daktylos*, a finger or toe.] a combining form meaning *a finger* or *toe*.

daç·tyl'ō·gram, *n.* [*dactylo-*, and Gr. *gramma*, writing.] a dactylograph; a fingerprint.

daç·tyl'ō·grȧph, *n.* [*dactylo-*, and Gr. *graphein*, to write.] a fingerprint impression or record.

daç''tyl·ō·grȧph'iç, *a.* pertaining to a dactylograph or dactylography.

daç·tyl·og'rȧ·phy, *n.* 1. the art of recording and studying fingerprints as a means of identification.
2. dactylology.

daç'tyl·oid, *a.* [*dactylo-*, and Gr. *eidos*, form.] shaped like a finger.

daç·tyl·ol'ō·ġy, *n.* [*dactylo-*, and Gr. *logos*, description.] the act, study, or art of communicating ideas or thoughts by the fingers; the finger-alphabet language of the deaf-mutes.

daç·tyl·on'ō·my, *n.* [*dactylo-*, and Gr. *nemein*, to deal out, distribute.] the art of counting or numbering on the fingers.

daç·tyl·op'ō·dīte, *n.* [*dactylo-*, and Gr. *pous*, genit. *podos*, a foot.] in crustaceans, the terminal segment of a limb.

daç·tyl·op'tẽr·ous, *a.* [*dactylo-*, and Gr. *pteron*, a wing.] having the inferior rays of the pectoral fins free, either wholly or in part, as in certain fishes.

daç·tyl·os'çō·py, *n.* [*dactylo-*, and Gr. *skopein*, to view.] the scientific study and utilization of fingerprints.

daç''tyl·ō·thē'çȧ, *n.* [L., from Gr. *daktylos*, finger. and *thēkē*, a case, covering.] the scaly integument of the toes of a bird.

daç″tyl·o·zō′oid, *n.* [*dactylo-*, and Gr. *zōon*, an animal.] in zoology, an elongated, mouthless appendage of hydrozoans, resembling a worm and having one tentacle.

daç′ty·lus, *n.*; *pl.* **daç′ty·lī,** [L., from Gr. *daktylos*, a finger, toe.]
1. in anatomy, a digit.
2. in zoology, (a) the last segment of a crustacean's limb; (b) the second tarsal joint or those following the first joint of an insect's leg.
3. *Pholas dactylus*, a European piddock.

-daç′ty·ly, [from Gr. *daktylos*, a finger.] a combining form meaning *a* (specified) *condition of the fingers, toes*, etc.: also *-dactylia*.

dad, *n.* [ME. *dadd, dadde*; Ir. *daid*, imitative of a child's cry.] father. [Colloq.]

dad, daud, *n.* 1. a severe blow. [Brit. Dial. and Scot.]
2. a lump or fragment of anything broken off by a blow. [Brit. Dial. and Scot.]

Dä′dä, *n.* [Fr.; prob. from child's cry; term chosen by Tristan Tsara, leader of cult, because of its meaninglessness.] a cult (1916–1922) in painting, sculpture, and literature characterized by fantastic, symbolic, often formless expression of supposedly subconscious matter, and by nihilistic satire: also *Dadaism*.

Dä′dä·işm, *n.* Dada.

dad′dle, *v.i.* to do anything slowly; to walk slowly or feebly, like a child or an old man. [Rare.]

dad′dŏck, *n.* [etym. unknown.] the rotten heart or body of a tree. [Brit. Dial.]

dad′dy, *n.* dad, father. [Colloq.]

dad·dy-lọng′legş, *n.* 1. a species of the crane fly, *Tipula oleracea*, having two wings and very long legs: called also *father longlegs*. [Brit.]
2. an arachnid belonging to the genus *Phalangium*, having a small body and eight very long legs, known also as *carter, harvestman*, and *grandfather longlegs*.

dāde, *v.t.* to hold up or support by leading strings, as a child learning to walk. [Dial.]

dāde, *v.i.* to toddle; to move slowly and unsteadily, as a child learning to walk. [Dial.]

dā′dō, *n.*; *pl.* **dā′dōeş,** [It.] 1. part of a pedestal between the cap and the base.
2. the lower part of the wall of a room if decorated differently from the upper part, as with panels or an ornamental border.

CAP
DADO
BASE
DADO

dā′dō, *v.t.*; dadoed, *pt., pp.*; dadoing, *ppr.*
1. to furnish with a dado.
2. to groove.
3. to insert or fit into a groove.

dae′dăl, *a.* [L. *daedalus*; Gr. *daidalos*, from *daidallein*, to work artfully; akin to L. *dolare*, to hew.]
1. skillful in workmanship; ingenious.
2. highly wrought; intricate; varied.
Also spelled *dedal*.

Dae·dā′li·ăn, Dae·dā′lē·ăn, *a.* 1. of Daedalus.
2. [d–] daedal; ingenious or intricate.
Also spelled *Dedalian, Dedalean*.

daed′à·lous (ded′), *a.* in botany, having a margin that turns and winds, as some leaves: also spelled *dedalous*. [Obs.]

Daed′à·lus (*or* ded′), *n.* [L.; Gr. *Daidalos*, lit., the artful craftsman, from *daidalos*.] in Greek legend, the skillful artist and inventor who built the labyrinth in Crete for King Minos and was then imprisoned in it with his son Icarus: they escaped by means of wings that he had made.

dae′mŏn, *n.* [L.; Gr. *daimōn*.]
1. in Greek mythology, any of the secondary divinities ranking between the gods and men.
2. a guardian spirit; inspiring or inner spirit.
3. a demon; a devil.

dae·mon′iç, *a.* 1. of or possessed by a daemon.
2. demonic.

dàff, *v.t.* 1. to toss aside. [Archaic.]
2. to doff; to take off (an article of clothing). [Obs.]

dàff, *n.* a stupid, simple fellow; fool; idiot. [Obs.]

dàff, *v.i.* to be foolish; to toy; to make sport. [Scot.]

dàff, *v.t.* to intimidate; to daunt. [Brit. Dial.]

daf′fà·down·dil′ly, daf′fy·down·dil′ly, *n.*; *pl.* **daf′fà·down·dil′lieş, daf′fy·down·dil′lieş,** a daffodil. [Poet. or Dial.]

daf′fō·dil, *n.* [ME. *affodylle*; LL. *affodillus*; L. *asphodilus*; Gr. *asphodelos*, the asphodel.]
1. a plant of the genus *Narcissus*, having a bulbous root, long, narrow leaves, and flowers with a trumpetlike corona of a deep yellow hue. The genus includes many species. Known also as *daffadilly, daffodilly, daffodowndilly*, etc.
2. the flower of this plant.
3. yellow.

daf′fō·dil gär′liç, a European onion, *Allium neapolitanum*, bearing white flowers.

daf′fō·dil lil′y, the atamasco lily.

daf′fō·dil·ly, *n.*; *pl.* **daf′fō·dil·lieş,** a daffodil: also spelled *daffadilly*. [Poet. or Dial.]

daf′fy, *a.*; *comp.* daffier; *superl.* daffiest, [prob. from obs. *daff*, a fool, idiot.] crazy, idiotic, silly. [Colloq.]

dàft, *a.* 1. insane.
2. foolish; silly.
3. weak-minded.
4. frolicsome; playful; wanton. [Scot.]

dàft′ly, *adv.* in a daft manner.

dàft′ness, *n.* the state or quality of being daft.

dag, *n.* [OFr. *dague*, a dagger, from *daguer*, to thrust.] an unbranched antler.

dag, *n.* [origin uncertain.] a handgun; pistol. [Obs.]

dag, *n.* dew; thick mist. [Dial.]

dag, *v.i.* to drizzle. [Brit. Dial.]

dag, *n.* [ME. *dagge*, an ornamental point on the edge of garments, from OFr. *dague*, a dagger.]
1. a loose end, as of locks of wool. [Obs.]
2. a deep, ornamental cut in the edge of a garment. [Obs.]

Dä′găn, *n.* [Assyr.-Bab. *Dagān*.] in Babylonian mythology, the god of the earth.

dag′gẽr, *n.* [ME. *dagger*; W. *dagr*, a dagger; of Celtic origin.]
1. a short weapon with a sharp point, used for stabbing; a poniard.

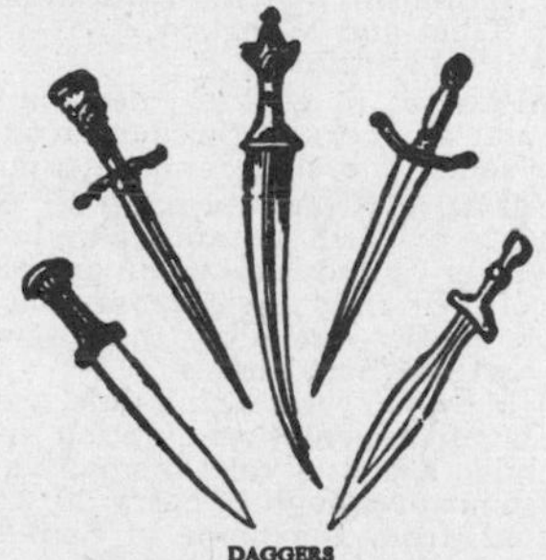

DAGGERS

2. in printing, an obelisk, a mark of reference (†) in the form of a dagger.
at daggers drawn; ready for attack, violence, hostility, etc.
double dagger; in printing, a mark of reference (‡).
to look daggers at; to look at with anger or hatred.

dag′gẽr, *v.t.* 1. to pierce with a dagger; to stab.
2. to mark with a dagger.

dag′gẽr, *n.* [prob. a corruption of *diagonal*.] in shipbuilding, any timber resting diagonally in the frame.

dag′gẽr mọth, a moth of the genus *Apatela*, the larvae of which infest fruit trees and their foliage: so named from a daggerlike mark on its forewing.

dag′gẽr plant, a plant having leaves with sharp points, belonging to the genus *Yucca*.

dag′gle, *v.t.* and *v.i.*; daggled, *pt., pp.*; daggling, *ppr.* [Sw. *dagga*, to bedew.] to trail; to make or become dirty by trailing through mud, as the lower end of a garment; to draggle.

dag′gle-tāil, *n.* a slatternly woman; a draggle tail. [Dial.]

dag′gle-tāiled, *a.* having the lower ends of a garment dirtied with mud. [Dial.]

dä·ghes·tän′ (-ges-), *n.* a type of heavy carpet: after Daghestan, a division of the U. S. S. R. in the Caucasus.

dag′lock, *n.* a lock of wool, hair, or fur that is dirty or matted or that hangs and drags in the wet; a taglock.

dā′gō, *n.*; *pl.* **dā′gōş, dā′gōeş,** [Sp. *Diego*, a name equivalent to James, very common in Spanish.] [also D–] a dark-skinned person of Italian, Spanish, Portuguese, or other Latin descent: vulgar term of prejudice and contempt. [Slang.]

dä·gō′bà, *n.* [Singhalese.] in Buddhist countries, a monumental structure containing relics of Buddha or of some Buddhist saint.

dag′ŏn, *n.* an end; a piece or slip. [Obs.]

Dā′gon, *n.* [L. *Dagon*; Gr. *Dagōn*; Heb. *dag*, a fish.] the main god of the Philistines and later of the Phoenicians, represented with the upper part of a man and the tail of a fish.

DAGON OF THE PHILISTINES

dag′swāin, *n.* [ME. *daggysweyne*, origin obscure.] a rough or coarse cover for a bed. [Obs.]

dà·guer′rē·ăn, dà·guer′ri·ăn (dà-ger′rē-ăn), *a.* 1. pertaining to a daguerreotype.
2. [D–] pertaining to Daguerre, the inventor of the daguerreotype.

dà·guerre′ō·tȳpe, *n.* [Fr.] 1. an early photographic process, invented by L. J. M. Daguerre (1789–1851), French painter, by which pictures were produced on plates of chemically treated metal or glass.
2. a picture produced by such a process.

dà·guerre′ō·tȳpe, *v.t.*; daguerreotyped, *pt., pp.*; daguerreotyping, *ppr.* 1. to photograph by the daguerreotypic process.
2. to imitate exactly; to impress with great distinctness. [Rare.]

dà·guerre′ō·tȳ·pẽr, dà·guerre′ō·tȳ·pist, *n.* one who takes pictures by the daguerreotypic process.

dà·guerre·ō·typ′iç, *a.* pertaining to or characteristic of a daguerreotype.

dà·guerre·ō·typ′iç·ăl, *a.* daguerreotypic.

dà·guerre′ō·tȳ·py, *n.* the art of producing daguerreotypes.

dä·hä·bē′áh, dä·hä·bee′yáh, dä·hä·bī′áh, *n.* [Ar. *dhahabīya*.] a large boat, originally having one or two masts with a long yard supporting a triangular sail, now generally equipped with steam or gasoline engines: used on the Nile for the conveyance of passengers.

DAHABEAH

Däh′lià (däl′yà *or* dāl′yà), *n.* [from *Dahl*, 18th-c. Swedish botanist.]
1. a genus of composite plants of which several species are known, native to Mexico and Central America. *Dahlia variabilis*, one of the species, is extensively cultivated.
2. [d–] any plant of the genus *Dahlia* having tuberous roots, or its large, showy, bright-colored flower.
3. [d–] in dyeing, a violet coal-tar pigment obtained from rosaniline: also called *Hofmann's violet* and *primula*.

däh′lin, *n.* same as *inulin*.

Dä·hō′măn, *a.* of Dahomey, a French colony of French West Africa, or its people.

Dä·hō′măn, *n.* a native or inhabitant of Dahomey.

dà·họọn′, *n.* a small evergreen tree, *Ilex dahoon*, growing in the southern United States and having white, soft, close-grained wood: called also *dahoon holly*.

dāik′ẽr, *v.i.* and *v.t.* same as *dacker*.

Dāil Eir′eann (däl âr′in), the Chamber of Deputies or Lower House of the Irish Legislature in Dublin.

dāi′li·ness, *n.* daily occurrence. [Rare.]

dāi′ly, *a.* [ME. *dayly*; AS. *dæglic*, daily, from *dæg*, day.] relating to, done, happening, or published every day or every weekday; diurnal; as, *daily* labor.

dāi′ly, *adv.* every day; day after day.

dāi'ly, *n.*; *pl.* **dāi'lieṣ**, a newspaper or other publication issued each day or each weekday.

dāi'ly dŏu'ble (dub'l), in horse racing, a bet the success of which depends on choosing both winners in two specified races during the day.

dāi'ly dŏz'en (duz'n), gymnastic setting-up exercises (originally twelve) done daily. [Colloq.]

dai'miō (dī'myō), *n.*; *pl.* **dai'miō, dai'miōṣ**, [Japan. from Chin. *dai*, great, and *mio*, name.] a hereditary feudal nobleman of Japan under a former regime: also spelled *daimyo*.

dai'mōn, *n.* same as *daemon*.

dāint, *a.* dainty. [Obs.]

dāin'ti·fȳ, *v.t.* to make dainty or delicate; to render fastidious.

dāin'ti·ly, *adv.* in a dainty manner; elegantly; delicately; fastidiously.

dāin'ti·ness, *n.* the quality of being dainty.

dāin'trel, *n.* a dainty. [Obs.]

dāin'ty, *n.*; *pl.* **dāin'tieṣ**, [ME. *daynte*; OFr. *daintie*, worth, value, a delicacy, from L. *dignitas*, worth, dignity.]

1. something nice and delicate to the taste; that which is exquisitely delicious; a delicacy.
2. darling: a term of fondness. [Obs.]
3. estimation or value; the pleasure taken in anything. [Obs.]

dāin'ty, *a.* 1. nice; pleasing to the palate; of exquisite taste; delicious; as, *dainty* food.

2. of delicate and refined taste.
3. elegant; tender; delicately lovely or pretty.
4. fastidious; squeamish; overnice; affectedly fine; as, *dainty* standards.

Syn.—choice, delicate, elegant, exquisite, fine, neat, nice, rare, refined.

Dai'qui·ri (dī'kēr-i), *n.* [after *Daiquirí*, Cuba, source of the rum first used in this drink.] a cocktail made of rum, sugar, and lime or lemon juice.

dai'rï, *n.* 1. the court or palace of the emperor of Japan.

2. a term of respect applied to the mikado.

dāi'ry, *n.* [ME. *deyery*, dairy, from *deye*, *deie*, a dairymaid, from Ice. *deija*, a dairymaid, originally a dough kneader, from *deig*, dough.]

1. the place where milk and cream are kept and converted into butter or cheese.
2. a dairy farm.
3. a store where milk and milk products are sold.
4. dairying.

dairy lunch; a public lunchroom where simple dishes are served, especially those containing dairy products.

dāi'ry çat'tle, cows raised mainly for their milk.

dāi'ry färm, a farm devoted to the production of dairy products.

dāi'ry·ing, *n.* the business of producing, making, or selling dairy products.

dāi'ry·māid, *n.* a girl or woman who works in a dairy.

dāi'ry·măn, *n.*; *pl.* **dāi'ry·men**, 1. a man who owns a dairy.

2. a man who works in or for a dairy.

dā'is, *n.* [ME. *deis*, *deys*; OFr. *deis*, *dois*, a high table in a hall; LL. *discus*, a table; L. *discus*, a platter, quoit, discus.]

1. a platform or raised floor at the end or side of a room or hall, as one on which are placed tables and chairs for specially honored guests.
2. a long board, seat, or settle erected against a wall, and sometimes so constructed as to serve both for a settee and a table. [Scot.]

dāi'ṣied (-zid), *a.* full of daisies; decorated with daisies.

dāi'ṣy, *n.*; *pl.* **dāi'ṣieṣ**, [ME. *daysie*, *daysy*; AS. *dæges*, the daisy, lit. day's eye, from *dæg*, day, and *eage*, eye.]

1. a common plant of the genus *Bellis*, family *Compositæ*, having a yellow disk, with white, pinkish, or rose-colored rays: often called *English daisy*.
2. its flower.
3. a related tall chrysanthemum, *Chrysanthemum leucanthemum*, with large flowers that have long, white rays around a yellow disk: also called *oxeye*.
4. any elegant or excellent person or thing. [Slang.]

to push up (the) daisies; to be dead and buried. [Slang.]

dāi'ṣy çut'tēr, 1. in baseball and cricket, a batted ball which skims along the ground. [Slang.]

2. a horse that trots with only slightly raised feet.

dąk, dąwk, *n.* [Hind. *dak*, the post, post office, a relay of men.] in India, a method of transporting passengers or news by relays of men and horses; hence, the mail.

dąk buṅ'gȧ·lōw, in India, a hotel at the end of a relay or dak stage.

dā'kēr, *n.* same as *dicker* (a quantity of ten).

dā'kēr hen, in ornithology, the corn crake or land rail.

Dā'kin's sō·lū'tion, [after Henry Drysdale *Dakin* (1880–1952), Eng. chemist in America.] a mildly alkaline solution of sodium hypochlorite, used as an antiseptic in the treatment of wounds.

dȧ·koit', *n.* [Hind. *dakait*, a robber, from *daka*, an attack by robbers.] one of a gang of robbers in India and Burma; a dacoit.

dȧ·koit'y, *n.* the system of robbery conducted by dakoits.

Dȧ·kō'tȧ, *n.* 1. a member of a group of Siouan tribes that lived in North and South Dakota.

2. the Siouan language of the Dakotas.
3. a Sioux: Indian name.

Dȧ·kō'tȧ, *a.* Dakotan.

Dȧ·kō'tȧ mil'let, a variety of millet used as hay.

Dȧ·kō'tăn, *a.* of or relating to (a) the Dakota Indians; (b) the former territory of Dakota; (c) the present states of North and South Dakota.

Dȧ·kō'tăn, *n.* an inhabitant or native of North Dakota or South Dakota.

Da·kō'tȧ pō·tā'tō, the groundnut, *Apios tuberosa*.

Dȧ·kō'tȧ tũr'nip, the breadroot.

Dȧ·kō'tȧ vetch, a kind of grass, *Hosackia americana*, used in the western U. S. as fodder.

Dăk'shȧ, *n.* in Hindu mythology, a son of Brahma, who sacrificed himself to save Rudra, or Siva, and thus incurred the wrath of Vishnu.

dal, *n.* [Hind. *dal*, a kind of pulse.] in botany, split pulse. an East Indian food; also, a vetch cultivated in East India as a fodder plant.

Dä·lai' Lä'mȧ, the Grand Lama or spiritual head of Lamaism, a form of Buddhism practiced in Tibet and Mongolia.

dä'lär, *n.* [Pol.] a thaler.

Dȧ·lär'ni·ăn, *a.* in geology, designating the pre-Cambrian rocks of Sweden, a 6,000-foot layer of sandstone, shale, and other materials.

Dal·bẽr'gi·ȧ, *n.* [from the name of Nicholas *Dalberg*, a Swedish botanist.] in botany, a large genus of tropical trees and climbing shrubs of the family *Leguminosæ* that furnish valuable timber, including the rosewoods of Brazil and the East Indies.

dāle, *n.* [ME. *dale*; AS. *dæl*, a dale, valley.]

1. a level or gently undulating space between hills; a dell; a vale; a small valley.
2. a spout or trough to carry off water.

Dā'lē·ȧ, *n.* [from the name of Samuel *Dale*, an English physician.] in botany, a genus of American herbs or shrubs of the family *Leguminosæ*, having gaudy flowers and pointed leaves: it is native to the western U. S. and Mexico.

dāle'-land, *n.* low-lying land.

dāleṣ'măn, *n.* one dwelling in a dale; particularly, one living in the dale-lands of England and Scotland.

dä'leth, dä'ledh (-led *or* -leth), *n.* [Heb., door.] the fourth letter of the Hebrew alphabet, corresponding to English *D*, *d*.

dä'li, *n.* [native name.] in botany, a large tree, allied to the nutmeg tree, growing in tropical America: the wood is used in cooperage and the seeds yield an illuminant.

Dal·i·bär'dȧ, *n.* [Mod. L., named after T. F. *Dalibard* (1703–1799), French botanist.] in botany, an herb of the *Rosaceæ* family, the only known species being the dewdrop, *Dalibarda repens*.

dalle, *n.* [Fr. *dalle*, gutter, tube, trough.]

1. in decorative art, a slab of marble, stone, etc. bearing ornamentations, such as those used in medieval church pavements and walls; any slab or tile.
2. [*pl.*] the rapids of a river flowing swiftly over a narrow, troughlike, rock-covered bed, as those of the Columbia River.

Dal'li·ȧ, *n.* [from W. H. *Dall*, an American naturalist.] a genus of mud minnows of the family *Umbridæ*. The edible blackfish of Alaska is a well-known species.

dal'li·ȧnce, *n.* [ME. *daliance*, from *dalien*, to delay.]

1. the act of dallying; delay; a lingering or loitering.
2. a fondling; a toying; interchange of caresses

dal'li·ẽr, *n.* one who fondles; a trifler; as, a *dallier* with pleasant words.

Dal'lis gräss, [origin unknown.] a tall, succulent, forage grass, *Paspalum dilatatum*, much grown in the southern United States.

dal'ly, *v.i.*; dallied, *pt.*, *pp.*; dallying, *ppr.* [ME. *dalien*, from OFr. *dalier*, to converse, trifle.]

1. to delay; to linger; to wait; to lose time in idleness and trifles; to amuse oneself with idle play.
2. to flirt or toy; as, she *dallied* with the idea.
3. to play, especially in making love; to toy; to interchange caresses; to fondle.

dal'ly, *v.t.* 1. to delay; to put off. [Obs.]

2. to spend (time) in trifling (with *away*).

Dal·mā'tiăn, *n.* 1. a native or inhabitant of Dalmatia, especially a Slavic-speaking native.

DALMATIAN (23 in. high)

2. a large, lean, short-haired dog with a black-and-white coat, of a breed supposed to have originated in Dalmatia: also called *coach dog*.

Dal·mā'tiăn, *a.* pertaining to Dalmatia or the Dalmatians.

dal·mat'iç, dal·mat'i·çȧ, *n.* [LL. *dalmatica*, from *Dalmatia*.]

1. in the Roman Catholic Church, a long, wide-sleeved, loose-fitting vestment with open sides, worn by deacons over the alb and cassock at communion or mass, or by bishops, cardinals, and abbots under the chasuble and over the tunicle at pontifical Mass.
2. in medieval history, a senatorial or coronation robe of Dalmatian origin.

dāl se'gnō (se'nyō), [It., lit. from the sign.] a direction used in music to signify that the performer is to go back to S and repeat to the end: abbreviated *D. S.*

dąl'tŏn, *n.* [after John *Dalton*, the chemist.] in biochemistry, a unit of mass, 1/16 of an oxygen atom: approximately 1.65 x 10^{-24} gram.

Dąl·tō'ni·ăn, *n.* a person who cannot distinguish colors; one who is color-blind.

Dąl·tō'ni·ăn, *a.* 1. pertaining to John Dalton, the chemist, or to his atomic theory of chemical combination.

2. of Daltonism.

Dąl'tŏn·işm, *n.* [named from John *Dalton*, the chemist, who had color blindness.] incapacity to distinguish colors; especially, red-green blindness.

Dąl'tŏn plan, [after *Dalton*, Mass.] a system of education in which pupils are given individual instruction and are advanced as fast as their ability allows, without regard to the rate of the group.

dam, *n.* [ME. *damme*, a woman, dame; OFr. *dame*; L. *domina*, a lady, f. of *dominus*, lord, master.]

1. a female parent: used of beasts, particularly of quadrupeds.
2. a mother. [Archaic.]

dam, *n.* a king in the game of checkers. [Obs.]

DAM

dam, *n.* [ME. *dam*, *damme*, a dam, from AS. *fordemman*, to stop up.]

1. a bank or mound of earth, or any wall or framework, raised to obstruct a current of water.

2. the body of water thus held back.
3. in mining, any contrivance for the exclusion of air, gas, or water.
4. in metallurgy, a wall of firebrick or stone that forms the hearth front of a blast furnace.
5. in dentistry, a thin rubber guard stretched tightly around a tooth to exclude moisture during treatment.
floating dam; a caisson used to close the entrance to a dry dock.
movable dam; in engineering, a barrage.

dam, *v.t.*; dammed, *pt., pp.*; damming, *ppr.* 1. to put a dam in.
2. to keep back by means of a dam; to obstruct or stop the current of, as a stream of water.
3. to close up; to stop up; confine; restrain (usually with *in* or *up*).

dam'ăġe, *n.* [ME. *damage*; OFr. *damage*; L. *damnum*, loss, injury.]
1. any hurt, injury, or harm to one's person or estate causing any loss of property, etc.
2. the loss so caused.
3. [*pl.*] in law, money claimed or ordered paid as a recompense for injury or loss that is the fault of someone else.
4. [*usually pl.*] cost or expense. [Colloq.]
damage feasant; in law, doing injury; trespassing, as cattle.
nominal damages; in law, in a case where no appreciable loss has been inflicted, damages assessed to sustain right of action.
Syn.—detriment, harm, injury, loss.

dam'ăġe, *v.t.*; damaged; *pt., pp.*; damaging, *ppr.* to hurt or harm; to injure; to impair; to lessen the soundness, goodness, or value of.

dam'ăġe, *v.i.* to receive harm; to be injured or impaired in soundness or value.

dam'ăġe·ȧ·ble, *a.* 1. able to be injured or impaired; susceptible of damage.
2. hurtful; pernicious. [Obs.]

dam'ăn, dam'ŏn, *n.* [Syrian.] in zoology, a small, herbivorous, rodentlike, hoofed mammal of the Syrian genus *Hyrax*: in the Bible called *cony*.

dam'ăr, *n.* same as *dammar*.

Dam'ăs·cēne, *n.* [ME. *Damascene*; L. *Damascenus*; Gr. *Damaskēnos*, of Damascus, from *Damaskos*, Damascus.]
1. an inhabitant or native of Damascus.
2. [d–] in botany, a small plum, the damson.
3. [d–] damascened work.

Dam'ăs·cēne, *a.* 1. pertaining to Damascus, in Syria, its people, etc.
2. [d–] relating to the art of damascening, or to damask.
damascene work; metal that has been damascened.

dam·ăs·cēne', *v.t.* to decorate (metal) with wavy markings: also *damaskeen*.

dam·ăs·cēn'ing, *n.* 1. the act or art of decorating a metal with wavy lines by engraving it or inlaying it with another or other metals: this may be effected in many different ways.
2. the decorative markings thus produced.

Dȧ·mȧs'çus blāde, a noted kind of sword or blade, formerly made in Damascus, of fine steel, and artistically finished by damascening.

Dȧ·mȧs'çus steel, damask steel.

dam'ăsk, *n.* [ME. *damaske*, named from the city of *Damascus*.]
1. a silk fabric, having some parts raised in the form of flowers and other figures, originally made in Damascus: now also applied to other, similar fabrics, as linen.
2. a fine, twilled table linen, in imitation of damask silks.
3. red or pink color: from the damask rose.
4. damascened steel.
5. the wavy markings of such steel.
6. a mixed modern fabric of cotton, silk wool, etc., used in upholstery, hangings, etc

dam'ăsk, *a.* 1. having a pinkish color, as the damask rose.
2. of, originating at, or pertaining to Damascus.
3. like damask.
4. made of damask (metal or cloth); as, a *damask* tablecloth.
damask plum; a small, purple plum; the damson. [Obs.]
damask rose; a fragrant, pink rose used in the Orient for making attar of roses.
damask steel; (a) steel decorated with wavy lines or inlaid gold and silver, originally made in Damascus and used for sword blades; (b) any steel like this.
damask violet; see *dame's violet*.

dam'ăsk, *v.t.*; damasked (-ăskt), *pt., pp.*; damasking, *ppr.* 1. to decorate with flowered designs or wavy lines, as in the cloth or metal.
2. to variegate; to diversify.
3. to make deep-pink or rose.

dam'ăsked (-ăskt), *a.* 1. in heraldry, having an ornamented pattern, as the field. [Rare.]
2. having a surface with wavy markings, as damascened metal.

dam·ăs·keen', *v.t.* to damascene.

dam·ăs·keen'ing, *n.* damascening.

dam'ăs·kin, *n.* a sword made of damask steel; a damascened blade. [Obs.]

dam'ăsk·ing, *n.* same as *damascening*.

da·mas·sé' (dȧ-mȧs-sā'), *n.* [Fr., pp. of *damasser*, to damask.] a kind of linen, so woven that the surface resembles damask.

da·mas·sé', *a.* 1. in dress fabrics, woven with a figured or flowered surface, as certain silks.
2. in ceramics, having white ornamentation on a white ground.

dam'ăs·sin, *n.* [from Fr. *damasser*, to damask.] a damask fabric or brocade having threads of gold or silver.

dam'bō·nīte, *n.* [from *n'dambo*, the native African name for the tree.] in chemistry, a white crystalline substance found in small percentage in the caoutchouc obtained along the Gabon River, in West Africa.

dam'bōse, *n.* in chemistry, a kind of sugar obtained from dambonite.

dāme, *n.* [ME. *dame*; OFr. *dame*; L. *domina*, a lady, f. of *dominus*, lord.]
1. in Great Britain, (a) the title borne by the wife or widow of a baronet or knight; (b) a title awarded to a woman as the equivalent of a knight's title, *Sir*: used always with the given name; as, *Dame* Sybil Thorndike.
2. a title formerly given to a woman in authority or head of a household: now only in *Dame Care, Dame Fortune*, etc.
3. a woman of rank or high social position; a lady.
4. a mature or elderly woman, married or single.
5. the mistress of a school for children.
6. at Eton college, England, the person with whom the pupils board, whether man or woman.
7. a dam; a mother: used in reference to animals.
8. a girl or woman. [Slang.]

dāmeș vī'ō·let, in botany, a fragrant plant bearing large purple or white flowers, the *Hesperis matronalis*: called also *damask violet, damewort*, and *rocket*.

dam·i·an'ȧ, *n.* [L., origin uncertain.] in medicine, a drug composed of the leaves of Mexican plants of the genus *Turnera*: used as an aphrodisiac, or tonic.

Dā'mi·ăn·īte, Dā'mi·ăn·ist, *n.* in ecclesiastical history, one of the followers of Damianus, patriarch of Alexandria in the sixth century, who concentered all the personal attributes of the Father, Son, and Holy Ghost in the one God, and therefore was accused of teaching Sabellianism.

dam'măr, dam'mŏr, *n.* [Malay *damar*.] the resin from various pine trees of Australia, New Zealand, and the East Indies, used in making varnish.

Dam'mȧ·rȧ, *n.* [L., from Hind. *damar*, resin, pitch.] in botany, a genus of large, coniferous trees of the East Indies and Australasia, having several species which yield dammar: called also *Agathis*.

damn (dam), *v.t.*; damned, *pt., pp.*; damning, *ppr.* [ME. *damnen*; OFr. *damner*; L. *damnare*, to condemn, fine, from *damnum*, loss, injury.]
1. originally, to condemn as guilty.
2. to condemn as bad, inferior, etc.: often used in the imperative as a curse.
3. to criticize adversely.
4. to ruin the chances of for success; to make fail.
5. to swear at by saying "damn"; as, he *damned* the weather.
6. in theology, to condemn to eternal punishment, as in hell.

damn, *v.i.* to swear profanely; to curse; to say "damn," etc.; as, to *damn* right and left.

damn, *n.* the saying of "damn" as a curse.
not care (or *give*) *a damn*; not care at all. [Colloq.]

damn, *a.* and *adv.* damned: **a clipped form**, used as a curse or strong intensive. [Colloq.]

damn, *interj.* an expression of anger, annoyance, disappointment, etc. Often euphemized as *darn, dog-gone*, etc.

dam'nȧ·ble, *a.* 1. capable of being damned or condemned; deserving damnation; worthy of punishment.
2. deserving to be sworn at; execrable.

dam'nȧ·ble·ness, *n.* the state or quality of deserving damnation.

dam'nȧ·bly, *adv.* 1. in a damnable manner.
2. very; extremely. [Colloq.]

dam·nā'tion, *n.* 1. in theology, condemnation to endless punishment, as in hell.
2. endless punishment.
3. a damning or being damned.
4. ruination by adverse criticism.

dam·nā'tion, *interj.* an expression of anger, annoyance, etc.

dam'nȧ·tō·ry, *a.* [L. *damnatorius*.]
1. threatening with damnation; damning.
2. condemning; as, *damnatory* evidence.

damned (damd), *a.* 1. condemned or deserving condemnation.
2. cursed or deserving cursing; outrageous; as, a *damn(ed)* shame. [Colloq.]
3. in theology, doomed to endless punishment, as in hell.

damned, *adv.* very; as, you know *damn(ed)* well. [Colloq.]

dam'ni·fȳ, *v.t.*; damnified, *pt., pp.*; damnifying, *ppr.* [Early Mod. Eng.; OFr. *damnifier*; L. *damnificare*, to harm, from *damnum*.] in law, to cause injury, damage, or loss to.

damn'ing, *a.* exposing to damnation or condemnation; as, a *damning* sin, *damning* evidence.

damn'ing·ness, *n.* tendency to bring damnation.

dam'num, *n.*; *pl.* **dam'nȧ,** [L. *damnum*, loss, injury.] in law, damage; harm; loss.
damnum absque injuria; loss without any injury of which the law can take cognizance.

Dam'ō·clēș, *n.* in Greek legend, a courtier of ancient Syracuse who talked so much about the happiness of being a king that his own king, Dionysius, demonstrated the dangers of a ruler's life by seating him at a banquet just below a sword hanging by a hair.
sword of Damocles; any imminent danger.

dam'ōi·șelle, dam'ō·șel, dam'ō·zel, *n.* a damsel. [Archaic.]

Dā'mŏn and Pyth'i·ăs, in Roman legend, friends so devoted to each other that when Pythias, condemned to death for plotting against King Dionysius of Syracuse, wanted time to arrange his affairs, Damon pledged his life that his friend would return: Pythias returned and was pardoned.

dam·ōur'īte, *n.* [named from *Damour*, a French chemist.] in mineralogy, a yellowish muscovite or potash mica, holding water in combination.

damp, *n.* [M.D., vapor, steam.]
1. wetness; humidity; moisture; fog.
2. a dampened condition; dejection; depression of spirits.
3. a harmful gas sometimes found in coal mines and other excavations; firedamp; chokedamp.
damp sheet; in mining, a curtain so arranged in a gallery as to direct air currents and rid the mine of foul air and gas.

damp, *a.* [ME. *dampen*, to extinguish.]
1. moist; humid; moderately wet; as, a *damp* cloth; *damp* air.
2. dejected; depressed. [Archaic.]

damp, *v.t.*; damped (dampt), *pt., pp.*; damping, *ppr.* 1. to moisten; to make humid, or moderately wet.
2. to stifle; to make choke.
3. to check or reduce (energy, action, etc.).
4. in acoustics, to check or deaden the vibration of (a string, etc.).
5. in electricity, to reduce the amplitude of (oscillations, waves, etc.).
to damp off; to wither and die because of mildew, as seedlings, plant shoots, etc.

damp'en, *v.t.* 1. to make damp; moisten.
2. to depress; dishearten.
3. to deaden, reduce, or lessen.

damp'en, *v.i.* to become damp.

damp'ẽr, *n.* 1. a person or thing that depresses or disheartens.
2. a movable plate or valve in the flue of a stove or furnace, for controlling the draft.
3. a device to check vibration in the strings of a stringed keyboard instrument.
4. a copper part in or near the poles of certain electric motors, generators, etc., to lessen variation from the proper rate of speed.
5. a device for lessening the oscillation of a magnetic needle, a moving coil, etc.
6. in Australia, an unfermented bread made of flour and water and baked on a stone or in ashes.

damp'ẽr ped'ăl, in pianofortes, the pedal that

raises all the dampers from the strings, prolonging vibration: called also *loud pedal.*

damp'ing, *n.* in physics, a progressive reduction in amplitude of oscillations.

damp'ish, *a.* moderately damp, or moist.

damp'ish·ly, *adv.* in a dampish manner.

damp'ish·ness, *n.* a moderate degree of dampness, or moistness; slight humidity.

dam plāte, an iron plate attached to the front of the dam in a blast furnace to reinforce it.

damp'ness, *n.* moisture; fogginess; moistness; humidity.

damp'y, *a.* 1. dejected; gloomy. [Obs.]

2. in coal mining, affected by chokedamp, as the underground air.

dam'sel, *n.* [ME. *damesele*; OFr. *dameisele*; LL. *domicella*, a young lady, girl, from L. *domina*, a lady.]

1. a young woman of noble or genteel extraction. [Obs.]

2. a young unmarried woman; a maiden. [Archaic.]

3. in milling, the hopper shaker, attached to the millstone spindle.

dam'sel fly̆, any of a species of slow-flying dragonfly with a slender body and long wings that fold over its back when at rest.

dam'ṣŏn, *n.* [ME. *damasyn*; L. *Damascenus*, of Damascus.]

1. the fruit of a variety of the *Prunus domestica*, a small blue or purple plum: called also *damask plum.*

2. the tree that it grows on.

bitter or *mountain damson*; in botany, the *Simaruba amara* of Guiana and the West Indies, whose bitter bark has medicinal qualities.

damson cheese; conserved damsons pressed into the shape of a cheese.

dam stōne, the stone closing the front of the hearth in a blast furnace, to which the dam plate is attached.

Dan, *n.* 1. in the Bible, the fifth son of Jacob.

2. the tribe of Israel descended from him, which settled in northern Palestine.

Dan, *n.* [ME.; OFr. *dan, danz*, from L. *dominus*, a master, lord.] master; sir: a title; as, *Dan* Cupid. [Archaic.]

dan, *n.* [etym. unknown.] in mining, a small coal-carrying truck or sled.

Dan'ā·ē, *n.* in Greek mythology, the mother of Perseus: she was visited by Zeus in the form of a shower of gold. Also written *Danaë.*

dan'ā·īde, *n.* [named for the *Danaides* of mythology, condemned to dip water with sieves.] a water wheel, consisting of two tapering shells, one within the other.

Dȧ·nā'i·dēṣ, *n. pl.*; *sing.* **Dan'ā·id,** [Gr.] in Greek legend, the fifty daughters of Danaus, a king of Argos, who were married to their fifty cousins: forty-nine murdered their husbands at their father's command, and were condemned in Hades to pour water forever into a broken cistern or draw it with a sieve. Also written *Danaïdes* (*sing. Danaïd*).

dā'nȧ·īte, *n.* [named from J. F. *Dana*, an American chemist.] in mineralogy, a variety of cobaltiferous arsenopyrite.

dā'nȧ·līte, *n.* [named from J. D. *Dana*, an American mineralogist.] in mineralogy, a silicate of iron, zinc, manganese, and beryllium, containing a small percentage of sulfur, and occurring in crystals.

Dan'ā·us, *n.* in Greek legend, a king of Argos: see *Danaides.* Also written *Danaüs.*

dan'bũr·īte, *n.* [named from *Danbury*, Conn., where first found.] in mineralogy, a white or pale yellow borosilicate of calcium, occurring in crystals.

dȧnce, *v.i.*; danced (dȧnst), *pt., pp.*; dancing, *ppr.* [ME. *dauncen*; OFr. *dancer*, to dance; probably from O.H.G. *danson*, to draw or drag along, *dinsan*, to trail, drag.]

1. to move the body, especially the feet, in rhythm, ordinarily to music.

2. to move lightly and gaily about; to caper.

3. to bob up and down.

4. to be stirred into rapid movement, as leaves in a wind.

to dance on nothing; to dangle from a gibbet; to be hanged.

dȧnce, *v.t.* 1. to take part in (a dance); perform (a dance).

2. to cause to dance.

3. to bring into a specified condition by dancing; as, he *danced* her weary.

4. to dandle.

to dance attendance; to wait with obsequiousness; to strive to please and gain favor by assiduous attentions and civilities; as, *to dance attendance* at court.

dȧnce, *n.* 1. rhythmic movement of the feet or body, ordinarily to music.

2. a particular kind of dance, as the waltz, tango, etc.

3. the art of dancing.

4. one round of a dance.

5. a party to which people come to dance.

6. a piece of music for dancing.

7. rapid, lively movement.

dance of death; in painting and sculpture, an allegorical illustration of the power of death, in which a skeleton leads a group of live persons or skeletons to the grave; danse macabre.

pyrrhic dance; in ancient Greece, a war dance symbolizing attack and defense.

St. Vitus's dance; chorea.

dȧn'cẽr, *n.* one who practices dancing, or is skillful in the performance; particularly, one whose profession is dancing.

merry dancers; the aurora borealis. [Scot. and Brit. Dial.]

dȧn'cẽr·ess, *n.* a woman dancer. [Obs.]

dȧnce sçript, written directions and diagrams to show the movements in a ballet or other dance.

dan·cet·té' (-tā'), *a.* [Fr., from OFr. *dent*, L. *dens*, tooth.] in heraldry, having large indentations.

DANCETTÉ

dan·cette', *n.* in architecture, a chevron or zigzag molding.

dȧn'cing, *n.* the act or art of moving in measured step corresponding to the time of the music.

dȧn'cing diṣ·ēase', same as *tarantism.*

dȧn'cing gi̇rl, 1. a professional female dancer; in India, a nautch girl.

2. in botany, an East Indian plant, *Mantisia saltatoria*, whose purple and yellow flowers bear a fancied resemblance to a dancing girl.

DANCETTE

dȧn'cing mȧs'tẽr, one who teaches the art of dancing.

dȧn'cing pär'ty, a social gathering at which dancing is the principal form of entertainment.

dȧn'cing sçhọọl, a school in which the art of dancing is taught.

dan'cy, *a.* same as *dancetté.*

dan'dē·lī·ŏn, *n.* [Fr. *dent de lion*, lit. tooth of the lion; from L. *dens* (*dentis*), tooth, *de*, of, and *leo*, lion.] in botany, a common plant, *Taraxacum officinale*, having a milky, perennial root, naked stalk, deeply notched leaves, and a single large, yellow flower.

dan'dẽr, *v.i.* to wander about; to talk incoherently. [Brit. Dial.]

dan'dẽr, *n.* same as *dandruff.*

dan'dẽr, *n.* [perhaps var. of Scot. *dunder*, resounding.] anger; temper. [Colloq.]

to get one's dander up; to become enraged; to lose one's temper. [Colloq.]

dan'dẽr, *n.* [etym. obscure.] a cinder; refuse from a furnace. [Scot.]

dan'di·ȧ·căl, *a.* pertaining to or like a dandy; dandified.

Dan'die Din'mŏnt ter'ri·ẽr, [after *Dandie* (Andrew) *Dinmont*, character in Scott's *Guy Mannering.*] a small active dog with drooping ears, short legs, and a rough coat, usually gray or tan, of a breed originated in Scotland.

dan'di·fīed, *a.* having the characteristic dress or manners of a dandy; foppish; as, *dandified* ways.

dan'di·fȳ, *v.t.*; dandified, *pt., pp.*; dandifying, *ppr.* to cause to resemble a dandy; to make foppish.

dan'di·prat, *n.* [etym. obscure.]

1. a little fellow; an urchin; a dapperling: used as a word both of affection and contempt. [Archaic.]

2. an English silver coin of the value of three halfpence, coined by Henry VII.

dan'dle, *v.t.*; dandled, *pt., pp.*; dandling, *ppr.* [cf. Scot. *dandill*, to go about idly; G. *tandeln*, to trifle, dandle.]

1. to dance (a child, etc.) up and down on the knee or in the arms.

2. to fondle; to pet; to treat as a child; to toy with.

3. to delay; to protract by trifles. [Obs.]

dan'dlẽr, *n.* one who dandles or fondles.

dan'driff, *n.* same as *dandruff.*

dan'druff, *n.* [folk etym. of earlier *dandro, dander*; prob. of Fr. origin; second element is Eng. dial. *hurf*, scab, from ON. *hrufa.*] little scales of dead skin formed on the scalp.

dan'dy, *n.*; *pl.* **dan'dieṣ,** [playful Scot. form of *Andy*, from *Andrew.*]

1. a fastidious dresser; a fop; a coxcomb.

2. in technical usage, (a) a preliminary heating chamber in a puddling furnace; (b) in tin-plate making, a portable furnace that permits of access from all sides; (c) an accessory or attachment to a machine; (d) in papermaking, the dandy roller.

3. something very good; a first-class thing. [Slang.]

4. in England, a kind of light cart with two wheels.

5. in Ireland, a small drinking glass.

6. in navigation, (a) a sloop-rigged vessel carrying a jigger mast; (b) a small jiggermast sail.

dan'dy, *n.* same as *dandy fever.*

dan'dy, dan'dee, *n.* [Hind. *dandi*, a boatman, a rower, from *dand*, an oar, a staff.]

1. a boatman on the Ganges river.

2. a cloth hammock or litter attached to a bamboo staff and carried by bearers.

dan'dy, *a.* 1. dressed like a coxcomb or fop.

2. very good; first-class. [Slang.]

dan'dy-cock, *n.* a bantam cock. [Brit. Dial.]

dan'dy fē'vẽr, same as *dengue.*

dan'dy·hen, *n.* a bantam hen. [Brit. Dial.]

dan'dy·ish, *a.* of or like a dandy; foppish.

dan'dy·iṣm, *n.* the characteristics or dress of a dandy; foppishness.

dan'dy·īze, *v.t.* to dandify.

dan'dy·īze, *v.i.* to become or be a dandy.

dan'dy·ling, *n.* a little dandy: an absurd or contemptible fop.

dan'dy nōte, in Great Britain, a permit from the customs authorities to remove goods.

dan'dy-rōll, *n.* in papermaking, a cylinder that puts on the watermark: also *dandy roll, dandy roller.*

Dāne, *n.* a native or inhabitant of Denmark.

Dan'e·brog, Dan'ne·brog, *n.* 1. a Danish order of knighthood, founded in 1219.

2. the national standard of Denmark, a white cross on a red field.

Dāne'flow·ẽr, *n.* in botany, the pasqueflower, *Anemone pulsatilla.*

Dāne'geld, Dāne'gelt, *n.* [ME. *Danegeld*, from AS. *Dene*, the Danes, and *geld, gild*, a payment, from *gildan*, to pay, yield.] in English history, an annual tax levied, from the tenth into the twelfth century, on the English nation, originally (it is thought) for maintaining forces to oppose the Danes, or to furnish tribute to procure peace, and later as a land tax.

Dāne'lạw, Dāne'lạgh (dān'lạ), *n.* [ME. *Danelagh* from Anglo-N.; AS. *Dena lagu*, Danes' law.]

1. the code of Scandinavian laws established in eastern and northern England by Norse invaders and settlers in the ninth and tenth centuries A.D.

2. the eastern and northern section of England that was ruled under these laws.

Dānes'-blood (-blud), *n.* in botany, the clustered bellflower, the pasqueflower, or the dwarf elder, fancied to have sprung up from the blood of Danes killed in battle. [Brit. Dial.]

Dāne'weed, *n.* in botany, Danewort; also, the plant, *Eryngium campestre*, of the parsley family.

Dāne'wŏrt, *n.* in botany, the dwarf elder, *Sambucus ebulus*, of Europe; Danes-blood.

dān'ġẽr, *n.* [ME. *daunger*; OFr. *danger*, absolute power, from L. *dominium*, right of ownership, power, from *dominus*, a ruler.]

1. liability to injury, pain, damage, or loss; hazard; insecurity; peril; risk.

2. jurisdiction; power to inflict harm. [Obs.]

3. hesitation; difficulty. [Obs.]

4. disdain; coyness. [Obs.]

5. a thing that may cause injury, pain, etc.

Syn.—peril, hazard, risk, jeopardy, venture, exposure.—*Danger* is the general term for this concept. *Peril* is instant or impending danger. *Hazard* arises from something fortuitous or beyond our control; as, the *hazard* of the seas. *Risk* is doubtful or uncertain danger, often incurred voluntarily. *Jeopardy* is extreme danger.

dān'ġẽr, *v.t.* to place in danger; to hazard. [Obs.]

dān'ġẽr·fụl, *a.* dangerous. [Obs.]

dān'ġẽr·fụl·ly, *adv.* in a dangerous manner. [Obs.]

dān'ġẽr·less, *a.* devoid of danger. [Rare.]

dān'ġẽr list, in a hospital, the official list of names of patients who are dangerously ill.

dān'ġẽr·ous, *a.* 1. beset with danger; hazardous; perilous; risky; unsafe; as, a *dangerous* experiment.

2. creating danger; causing menace; as, a *dangerous* man.

3. in danger or peril, as from illness. [Dial.]

4. hard to please; critical; haughty; reserved; unaffable. [Obs.]

dān′ġẽr·ous·ly, *adv.* with danger; with risk of injury, pain, etc.; hazardously.

dān′ġẽr·ous·ness, *n.* the quality or condition of being dangerous.

dān′ġẽr point, a time, place, or situation at or in which imminent danger threatens.

dān′ġẽr sig′năl, a sign so placed as to forewarn of danger.

dañ′gle, *v.i.*; dangled, *pt., pp.*; dangling, *ppr.* [Dan. *dangle,* to dangle, bob.]

1. to hang swinging loosely.

2. to follow; to be a hanger-on (usually with *after*).

3. in grammar, to lack clear connection with the proper substantive: in "Having broken his legs, the bystanders took the old man into the house," the participle *having broken* is *dangling.*

dañ′gle, *v.t.* to cause to dangle; to hold (something) so that it hangs and swings loosely or with a swaying motion; as, he *dangled* the necklace before her eyes.

dañ′gle·ber″ry, *n.* the blue huckleberry of the United States; also, the shrub that bears it: also called *blue tangle, tangleberry.*

dañ′gle·ment, *n.* the act of dangling; the condition of being dangled.

dañ′glẽr, *n.* one who dangles about or after others; particularly, one who dangles about women; a trifler.

Dān′i·cişm, *n.* any idiom of the Danish language: also written *Danism.*

Dan′i·el (*or* -yel), *n.* [Heb., a divine judge.]

1. in the Bible, a Hebrew prophet whose faith saved him in the lion's den. Dan. vi. 16–27.

2. the book of the Old Testament with his stories and prophecies.

Dān′ish, *a.* pertaining to Denmark, to the Danes, or to their language.

Danish ax; a battle-ax of peculiar form, with elongated blade.

Danish dog; same as *great Dane.*

Dān′ish, *n.* the North Germanic language of the Danes.

Dān′işm, *n.* same as *Danicism.*

Dan′īte, *a.* of the Hebrew tribe of Dan.

Dan′īte, *n.* 1. a descendant of Dan, the son of Jacob; a member of the Hebrew tribe of Dan.

2. in the United States, one of an alleged secret society supposed to have been formed among the Mormons about 1837.

dañk, *a.* [ME. *dank*; prob. from ON.] disagreeably damp; humid; moist; wet.

dañk, *n.* humidity; moisture; water. [Obs.]

dan′ke schön (dän′ke shān), [G.] thank you.

dañk′ish, *a.* slightly dank; moist.

dañk′ness, *n.* the state of being dank.

dän·sänt′ (-säñ′), *n.* [Fr.] a small, informal dancing party; a tea dance.

dänse ma·cä′bre (-brȧ), [Fr.] dance of death.

dän·sēuse′ (-sēz′), *n.*; *pl.* **dän·sēuş′eş** (Fr. -sēz′), [Fr., f. of *danseur,* a dancer, from *danser,* to dance.] a girl or woman dancer, especially a ballet dancer.

première danseuse; a danseuse who leads in a ballet.

Dansk′ẽr, *n.* a Dane. [Obs.]

dant, *v.t.* to daunt. [Obs.]

Dan′tē·ăn (*or* dan·tē′an), *a.* 1. of Dante or his writings.

2. Dantesque.

Dan′tē·ăn, *n.* a person who makes a special study of Dante and his writings.

Dan·tesque′ (-tesk′), *a.* like Dante or his writings.

Dan′tist, *n.* an admirer of Dante, or one versed in his writings.

Dan′tŏn·ist, *n.* a political adherent of Georges Jacques Danton, a leader in the French Revolution.

Dȧ·nū′bi·ăn, *a.* of the Danube, a river in southern Europe, or the regions and peoples near it.

dap, *v.i.*; dapped, *pt., pp.*; dapping, *ppr.* [prob. var. of *dab,* influenced by *dip.*]

1. to fish by dropping the bait gently on the water.

2. to dip lightly and suddenly into water, as a bird.

3. to bounce or skip, as a stone thrown along the surface of water.

dap, *n.* a bounce or hop, as of a ball or stone. [Obs. or Brit. Dial.]

daph′nad, *n.* in botany, any plant or shrub of the spurge-laurel family, *Thymeleaceæ,* of which *Daphne* is the typical genus.

Daph′nē, *n.* [L. *daphne*; Gr. *daphnē,* the laurel or bay tree.]

1. in botany, a genus of shrubs of the family *Thymeleaceæ,* including about forty species, mainly evergreens, and bearing fragrant blooms of different colors.

2. [d–] a shrub of the genus *Daphne.*

3. [d–] the laurel tree.

4. in Greek mythology, a nymph said to have been changed into a laurel tree while fleeing from Apollo.

daph′ne·tin, *n.* in chemistry, a crystalline substance found in daphnin.

Daph′ni·ȧ, *n.* [Mod. L., from Gr. *daphnē,* the laurel tree.] in zoology, a genus of minute entomostracans typical of the *Daphniidæ*: called also *water flea.*

daph′nid, *a.* pertaining to or resembling the *Daphnia.*

daph′nid, *n.* one of the *Daphnia.*

Daph·nī′i·dae, *n.pl.* a family of minute entomostracans.

daph′nin, *n.* in chemistry, a bitter, transparent, crystalline glucoside found in the bark and flowers of various species of *Daphne.*

daph′ni·oid, daph′noid, *a.* [from Mod. L. *Daphnia,* and Gr. *eidos,* form.] pertaining to the *Daphniidæ.*

Daph′nis and Çhlō′ē, two lovers in an old Greek pastoral romance attributed to Longus (fourth or fifth century A.D.).

dap′i·fẽr, *n.* [L. *daps,* a feast, and *ferre,* to bear.] the steward of a royal or noble household.

dap′pẽr, *a.* [ME. *daper,* pretty, neat; D. *dapper,* brave, valiant.]

1. small and active.

2. neat in dress; spruce; trim.

dap′pẽr·ling, *n.* a dapper little person.

dap′ple, *a.* [ME. in comp. *dappul-gray,* dapple-gray; Ice. *depill,* a spot, dot, a splash of water, from *dapi,* a pool.] spotted; mottled; variegated.

dap′ple, *n.* 1. a spotted condition.

2. an animal whose skin is spotted.

dap′ple, *v.t.*; dappled, *pt., pp.*; dappling, *ppr.* to bespot; to variegate with spots.

dap′ple bāy, a dappled bay horse.

dap′pled (-pld), *a.* marked with variegated spots; mottled.

dap′ple-grāy, *a.* gray spotted with darker gray.

dap′ple-grāy, *n.* a dapple-gray horse.

där′by, *n.*; *pl.* **där′bieş,** [prob. from the personal name *Darby* or *Derby.*]

1. a mason's or plasterer's float.

2. [*pl.*] handcuffs. [Slang.]

Där′by and Jōan, [from an old song (1753).] an old married couple who are devoted to each other and live in perfect harmony.

Där′by·ītes, *n.pl.* one of the Plymouth Brethren or of a sect of these called the Exclusive Brethren, founded in England by John N. Darby (1800–1882).

Där′dăn, *a.* and *n.* [L. *Dardanus*; Gr. *Dardanos,* from *Dardanoi,* a people allied with the Trojans in the Trojan War; later identified with them.] Trojan.

Där·dā′ni·ăn, *a.* and *n.* Trojan.

dāre, *n.* the dace. [Obs.]

dāre, *v. i.*; dared *or archaic* durst, *pt.*; dared, *pp.*; daring, *ppr.*; dare *or* dares, *third pers. sing. pres. ind.* [ME. *dar, der*; AS. *dear, dearr,* first pers. sing. pres. ind. of *durran,* to dare.] to have enough courage or boldness for some act; to be fearless; venture.

dāre, *v.t.* 1. to have courage for; venture upon.

2. to face; oppose and defy.

3. to challenge (someone) to do something hard or dangerous as a test of courage.

to dare say; to think very likely; consider probable; as, I *dare say* you're right.

dāre, *n.* 1. a challenge.

2. boldness. [Obs.]

dāre′dev″il, *a.* reckless; bold; foolhardy.

dāre′dev″il, *n.* a bold, foolhardy fellow; a reckless person.

dāre′dev″il·işm, *n.* daredeviltry.

dāre′dev″il·try, *n.* the conduct of a daredevil; recklessness.

dāre′fụl, *a.* full of daring.

dār′ẽr, *n.* one who dares or defies.

därg, därgue, *n.* a day's work; also, a certain quantity of work, whether more or less than that supposed to be done in a day. [Scot.]

därg, *v.i.* to be employed by the day. [Scot.]

dar′iç, *n.* [Gr. *dareikos,* a Per. gold coin, from *Dareios,* Darius, by whom it was supposedly first coined, from Per. *dara,* a ruler.] an ancient Persian gold coin.

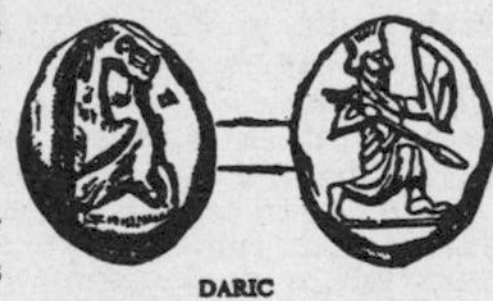
DARIC

dā′ri·ī, *n.* one of the valid modes in logic.

dâr′ing, *n.* a bold act; a hazardous attempt; boldness; adventurousness; intrepid courage.

dâr′ing, *a.* bold; courageous; intrepid; fearless; adventurous; brave; stout.

dâr′ing·ly, *adv.* in a daring manner.

dâr′ing·ness, *n.* the quality of being daring.

dȧ′ri·ōle, *n.* a little French sweet cake filled with cream, macaroons, fruit, etc.

därk, *a.* [ME. *dark, derk*; AS. *deorc,* dark.]

1. entirely or partly without light; neither illuminated nor illuminating; obscure.

2. wholly or partially black; having the quality opposite to white; as, a *dark* color or substance.

3. gloomy; disheartening; having unfavorable prospects; as, a *dark* time in political affairs.

4. concealed; mysterious; secret; not easily explained or understood.

The words of the wise, and their *dark* sayings. —Prov. i. 6.

5. not enlightened with knowledge; without learning and science; rude; ignorant; as, a *dark* age.

6. wanting sight; blind. [Obs.]

7. evil; wicked; sinister; as, *dark* designs.

8. not fair; not light in color or complexion; brunet; as, a *dark* skin.

Dark Ages, dark ages; (a) the period from the fall of the Western Roman Empire (476 A.D.) to the beginning of the modern era (c. 1450); the Middle Ages; (b) the earlier part of the Middle Ages, to about the end of the tenth century. The term arose from the idea that this period in Europe was characterized by widespread ignorance, lack of progress, etc.

Dark Continent; Africa: so called because it was little known until the late nineteenth century.

dark heat; in physics, the heat produced by the infrared rays of the spectrum.

dark horse; (a) an unexpected, almost unknown winner in a horse race, previously supposed to have little chance; (b) an almost unknown contestant regarded by only a few as having a chance to win; (c) in politics, a person who gets or may get the nomination unexpectedly, often as the result of a compromise. [Colloq.]

dark lantern; a lantern with a shutter that can hide the light.

dark space; in physics, a space in an exhausted tube near the cathode or negative pole, which remains obscure while an electric discharge is passing; particularly, that space within the glow of both electrodes: called also *first dark space* or *Crookes' space.*

the dark and bloody ground; Kentucky: a nickname given to the state by reason of the many bloody conflicts carried on there by Indians.

to keep dark; to keep secret and hidden.

Syn.—obscure, opaque, dismal, dim, gloomy, mysterious, dusky, shady, somber, black, shadowy, murky.

därk, *v.t.* to darken; to obscure. [Obs.]

därk, *n.* 1. darkness; obscurity; absence of light; also, a place deprived of light.

2. night; nightfall.

3. obscurity; a state of ignorance; as, we are all in the *dark* concerning his plans.

4. secrecy; as, plans hatched in the *dark.*

5. in art, a shade or shadow in a picture; as, *darks* and lights are both necessary.

in the dark; uninformed; ignorant.

därk′en, *v.t.*; darkened, *pt., pp.*; darkening, *ppr.* 1. to make dark or darker; to deprive of light; as, to *darken* a room.

2. to make dim; to deprive of vision; as, deep sorrow *darkened* his mind.

3. to render gloomy; as, sorrow *darkened* the home.

4. to obscure; to perplex; to render less clear or intelligible; as, her foolish words *darkened* the solution of the question.

5. to sully; to make foul; to render less bright.

to darken one's door; to call upon; to visit: usually implying unwelcomeness.

därk'en, *v.i.* to grow dark or darker; also, to grow less white or clear.
därk'en·ẽr, *n.* one who or that which darkens.
därk'en·ing, *n.* twilight; gloaming. [Scot. and Brit. Dial.]
därk'ey, därk'ie, *n.* see *darky*.
därk'-fīred, *a.* dark in color: used especially in reference to certain fire-cured tobaccos.
därk'ful, *a.* full of darkness. [Rare.]
därk'ish, *a.* dusky; somewhat dark.
där'kle, *v.i.*; darkled, *pt., pp.*; darkling, *ppr.*
1. to appear dark; to show indistinctly.
2. to grow dark, gloomy, obscure, etc.
därk'ling, *adv.* in the dark; at night. [Poetic.]
därk'ling, *a.* 1. dark or growing dark; dusky; dim.
2. happening in darkness.
därk'ly, *adv.* 1. in a dark manner; obscurely; mysteriously; dimly; blindly; uncertainly; with imperfect light, clearness, or knowledge; as, *darkly* seen against the cloudy sky, *darkly* perceived by the clouded mind.
2. in a gloomy or sinister manner.
därk'ness, *n.* 1. absence of light; obscurity; gloom.
2. obscurity; lack of clearness or perspicuity; that quality or state which renders anything difficult to be understood.
3. a state of being intellectually clouded; ignorance; hence, sin; wickedness.
4. secrecy; privacy.
What I tell you in *darkness*, that speak ye in light. —Matt. x. 27.
5. great trouble and distress.
6. blindness.
Prince of Darkness; the Devil; Satan.
Syn.—dimness, obscurity, gloom.—*Darkness* implies a total, and *dimness* a partial, absence of light. A thing is *obscure* when so overclouded or covered as not to be easily perceived. As the obscurity increases, it deepens into *gloom*. When taken figuratively, these words have a like use; as, the *darkness* of ignorance, *dimness* of discernment, *obscurity* of reasoning, and *gloom* of superstition.
därk'rọọm, *n.* a room from which all actinic rays are excluded, so that photographs can be developed in it.
därk'sōme, *a.* dark; gloomy; obscure; as, a *darksome* house. [Poetic.]
därk'y, *n.*; *pl.* **därk'ieṣ,** a Negro: patronizing or contemptuous term: also spelled *darkey, darkie*. [Colloq.]
där'ling, *n.* [ME. *derling, durling*; AS. *deorling*, a favorite, dim. of *deor*, dear.]
1. a person much loved by another: often a term of affectionate address.
2. a favorite.
där'ling, *a.* 1. very dear; beloved.
2. cherished; yearned for.
Där·ling·tō'ni·ȧ, *n.* [named after Dr. William *Darlington*, an American botanist.] a genus of pitcher plants with only one species, *Darlingtonia californica*, found in the northern part of California.
därn, *v.t.* and *v.i.*; darned, *pt., pp.*; darning, *ppr.* [prob. from MFr. dial. *darner*, to mend, from Bret. *darn*, a piece (torn out of something).] to mend (cloth, etc.) or repair (a hole or tear in cloth) by sewing a network of stitches across the gap.
därn, *n.* 1. a darning.
2. a darned place in fabric.
därn, *v.t., n., adj., adv., interj.* [from *damn*.] damn: a euphemism for the curse. [Colloq.]
där'nel, *n.* [ME. *darnel*; Fr. dial. *darnelle*, the darnel, from OFr. *darne*, stupefied: so called from its supposed stupefying or intoxicating qualities.] any grass of the genus *Lolium*, particularly *Lolium temulentum*, often found in grain fields: also called *rye grass*. The name was formerly given to any weed in grain.
därn'ẽr, *n.* 1. a person who darns.
2. a darning needle.
3. a wooden ball or similar device placed under a hole to be darned.
där'nex, där'niç, *n.* same as *dornick*.
därn'ing, *n.* the act of mending, as a hole in a garment; also, things darned or to be darned; as, a bundle of *darning*.
därn'ing nee'dle, 1. a large needle for darning.
2. a dragonfly.
dȧ·rō'gȧ, dȧ·rō'ghȧ, *n.* [Hind. *daroga*, from Per. *daroga*, a manager, superintendent.] in India, a native chief of any of the various departments; a superintendent; a manager; a chief of police.
dȧ·rọọ', *n.* [Egypt.] *Ficus sycomorus*, the sycamore of Egypt.
därr, *n.* the black tern of Europe.

dar'rāign, dar'rāin (or dar-rān'), *v.t.* to deraign. [Obs.]
dar'rein (-rin), *a.* [OFr. *darrain*, last, from L. *de*, from, and *retro*, back.] in old law, last; as, *darrein* continuance, the last continuance.
där'shăn, *n.* [Hindi *darśan* from Sans. *darśana*, a seeing.] the virtue, uplift, blessing, etc. which many Hindus believe one gets in the presence of a great man.
därt, *n.* [ME. *dart*; OFr. *dart*, a dart.]
1. a small, pointed weapon, to be thrown or shot; a short lance; any missile.
Time shall throw a *dart* at thee. —B. Jonson.
2. that which pierces or wounds; anything resembling a *dart*; a piercing look or word.
If there be such a *dart* in princes' frowns. —Shak.
3. the dace. [Obs.]
4. a sudden, quick movement; as, to make a *dart* at anything.
5. in entomology, the sting of an insect.
6. a short, tapered seam to make the garment fit the figure.
7. [*pl., construed as sing.*] a game in which a number of small, pointed missiles are hurled at a target.
därt, *v.t.* and *v.i.*; darted, *pt., pp.*; darting, *ppr.*
1. to throw, shoot, etc. suddenly and fast.
2. to move suddenly and fast.
där'tărṣ, *n.* [Fr. *dartre*, tetter, ringworm.] a scab or ulcer under the skin of lambs.
därt'ẽr, *n.* 1. one who throws a dart.
2. one who or that which springs or darts forward.
3. *Anhinga anhinga*, the snakebird or water turkey, so named from the way it darts upon its prey.
4. *Toxotes jaculator*, the archerfish.
5. a small American fresh-water fish of the family *Percidæ*, somewhat resembling the common yellow perch: so named from the rapidity with which it darts.
därt'ẽr fish, same as *archerfish*.
därt'ing·ly, *adv.* rapidly; like a dart.
där'tle, *v.t.* and *v.i*; dartled, *pt., pp.*; dartling, *ppr.* to dart again and again; to dart about.
där'toid, där·tō'iç, *a.* [Gr. *dartos*, skinned, and *eidos*, form.] relating to the dartos; as, *dartoid* tissue.
där'tos, *n.* [Gr. *dartos*, skinned, from *derein*, to skin, flay.] a contractile, fibrous layer of tissue immediately beneath the skin of the scrotum.
därt snāke, a serpentlike lizard of the genus *Acontias*, so called from its dartlike motions.
där'von, *n.* 1. a pain-killing drug that contains an analgesic, $C_{22}H_{29}NO_2 \cdot HCl$, related to methadone: a trade-mark (*Darvon*).
2. this drug combined with phenacetin, aspirin, etc.: a trade-mark (*Darvon Compound*).
Där·win'i·ăn, *a.* of or pertaining to Charles Darwin (1809–1882), English naturalist, or his theory of evolution.
Darwinian theory; Darwin's theory of evolution, which holds that all species of plants and animals developed from earlier forms by hereditary transmission of slight variations in successive generations, those forms surviving which are best adapted to the environment (*natural selection* and *survival of the fittest*).
Darwinian tubercle; a nodule on the edge of the external ear of man, said to correspond to the pointed portion of the ear of quadrupeds.
Där·win'i·ăn, *n.* a believer in the Darwinian theory.
Där·win'i·ăn·iṣm, *n.* Darwinism.
Där'win·iṣm, *n.* the Darwinian theory; also, belief in or support of the Darwinian theory.
Där'win tū'lip, [after C. *Darwin*, the naturalist.] a tulip with globular flowers.
dāṣe, *v.t.* to daze. [Obs.]
dash, *v.t.*; dashed (dasht), *pt., pp.*; dashing, *ppr.* [ME. *daschen*, to rush with violence, strike with violence; prob. from ON.]
1. to smash.
2. to strike violently against.
3. to throw, knock, or thrust (with *away, down*, etc.).
4. to splash.
5. to mix with a little of another substance.
6. to destroy.
7. to frustrate; discourage.
8. to abash.
9. to do, write, etc. hastily (with *off*).
10. [from the dash in *d—d*, a euphemistic form of *damned*.] to damn: usually in the imperative as a mild curse. [Colloq.]
dash, *v.i.* to move rapidly; to rush violently and furiously; as, the waves *dashed* against the shore; he *dashed* here and there.

dash, *n.* 1. collision; a violent striking of two bodies; a smash.
2. infusion; admixture, especially in small proportion.
Innocence with a *dash* of folly.—Addison.
3. a rush; a short, quick movement; as, to make a *dash* upon the enemy.
4. a sudden check; frustration; abashment; as, his hopes met with a *dash*.
5. capacity for prompt action; boldness; hence, spirit; liveliness; vivacity; showy appearance or action.
6. a splash.
7. the mark (—), used in printing and writing to indicate a break in a sentence, a parenthetical element, or an omission.
8. in music, (a) a small mark (ꞌ) denoting that the note over which it is placed is to be given the staccato effect; (b) a line drawn through a figure in thorough bass, denoting that the note is to be raised a semitone.
9. a short, swift run or running race; as, a hundred-yard *dash*.
10. in telegraphy, a long sound or signal, as in the Morse code: opposed to *dot*.
11. a dashboard.
to cut a dash; to have a showy appearance. [Colloq.]
dash, *n.* a gift, tip, present, or gratuity.
dash'bōard, *n.* 1. a board or screen at the front or side of a carriage, boat, etc. for protection against splashing; splashboard.
2. a panel with instruments and gauges on it, as in an automobile.
dȧ·sheen', *n.* [perhaps from Fr. *de*, of, and *Chine*, China.] the edible sprouts of the taro, a tropical plant.
dash'ẽr, *n.* 1. one who or that which dashes.
2. a rotating device for whipping cream in a churn or ice-cream freezer.
3. a dashboard.
4. one who makes an ostentatious parade; a bold, showy person. [Colloq.]
dash'ẽr block, a small block fastened to the end of the spanker gaff for reeving the ensign halyards.
dȧ·shi'kï, *n.* [coined in 1967 by J. Benning, its U.S. manufacturer.] a loose-fitting, usually brightly colored, robe or tunic modeled after an African tribal garment.
dash'ing, *a.* 1. spirited; impetuous; bold and lively; as, a *dashing* attack.
2. showy; ostentatious; as, a *dashing* girl.
dash'ing·ly, *adv.* ostentatiously; showily.
dash lamp, a small lamp usually provided with a reflector, hung upon the dashboard of a vehicle.
dash light (līt), a light which illuminates the dashboard of a motor vehicle.
dash'pot, *n.* in machinery, an apparatus for deadening the blow of any falling weight, and preventing any jar in the machinery, as in the valve gear of an engine.
dash'y, *a.*; *comp.* dashier; *superl.* dashiest,
1. having dash; showy.
2. full of dashes.
das'sie, *n.* [native name.] *Procavia capensis*, a small, harelike mammal of Africa.
das'tărd, *n.* [ME. *dastard*, a dullard, from Ice. *dæstr*, exhausted.] a coward; a poltroon; one who meanly shrinks from danger; a craven.
das'tărd, *a.* cowardly; meanly shrinking from danger.
das'tărd, *v.t.* to make cowardly; intimidate; dispirit. [Obs.]
das'tărd·īze, *v.t.* to make cowardly.
das'tărd·li·ness, *n.* the state or quality of being dastardly.
das'tărd·ly, *a.* cowardly and brutal; mean and skulking; base; sneaking.
das'tărd·ness, *n.* dastardliness. [Obs.]
das'tărd·y, *n.* dastardliness. [Archaic.]
däs·tụr', *n.* [Anglo-Ind.]
1. one of the priests, especially a chief priest, of the Parsees: written also *destour*.
2. the commission or bribe paid to servants by native tradesmen in India, in order to secure the trade of employers or masters: also written *dustoor*.
daṣ'wen, *v.i.* to be or become dim. [Obs.]
das'y-, [from Greek *dasys*.] a combining form meaning *hairy, dense, thick*.
dȧ·sym'e·tẽr, *n.* [*dasy-*, and Gr. *metron*, a measure.] formerly, an instrument used in testing the density of gases.
Das·y·pod'i·dae, *n.pl.* a South American family of armadillos, typical of this variety of edentate quadrupeds.
das'y·ūre, *n.* [*dasy-*, and Gr. *oura*, tail.] an Australian and Tasmanian animal, family *Dasyuridæ*, of which there are several species;

species; especially, *Dasyurus maculatus*, a small, spotted marsupial.

das·y·ū'rine, *a.* pertaining to the dasyures.

dā'tȧ, *n.pl.* [*construed as sing.*] [see *datum.*] things known or assumed; facts or figures from which conclusions can be inferred; information.

dā'tȧ bāse, dā'tȧ bank, a large collection of data in a computer, organized so that it can be expanded, updated, and retrieved rapidly for various uses: also written *database, databank.*

dāt'ȧ·ble, *a.* capable of being dated.

dā·tȧ·mā'tion, *n.* [*data,* and auto*mation.*] electronic data processing.

dā'tȧ proc'ess·ing, the recording and handling of information by means of mechanical or electronic equipment.

dā'tȧ·ry, *n.*; *pl.* **dā'tȧ·ries,** [ML. *dataria,* from L. *datarius,* for giving away, from *datus,* pp. of *dare,* to give.] in the Roman Catholic Church, a curial official in charge of examining candidates for papal benefices and handling the claims of those with rights to pensions.

dāte, *n.* [ME. *date*; OFr. *date,* the fruit of the date palm; L. *dactylus*; Gr. *daktylos,* a date, lit., a finger, so named from its shape.]
 1. the sweet, fleshy fruit of the date palm, *Phœnix dactylifera.*
 2. the date palm.

dāte, *n.* [ME. *date*; OFr. *date,* date; L. *data,* neut. pl. of *datus,* pp. of *dare,* to give; the first word in Roman letters or documents, giving the place and time of writing, as *data Romæ,* lit., given at Rome.]
 1. a statement on a writing, coin, etc. of when it was made.
 2. the time at which a thing happens.
 3. the time that anything lasts or goes on.
 4. a season or period of time. [Rare.]
 5. the day of the month.
 6. an appointment for a set time; specifically, a social appointment with a person of the opposite sex.
 7. a person of the opposite sex with whom one has such an appointment.
 out of date; old-fashioned; no longer in use.
 to date; until now; as yet.
 up to date; modern; now fashionable.

dāte, *v.t.*; dated, *pt., pp.*; dating, *ppr.* 1. to mark (a letter, etc.) with a date.
 2. to find out, determine, set, or give the date of.
 3. to give a date to.
 4. to reckon by dates.
 5. to have a social appointment with.

dāte, *v.i.* 1. to be dated (usually with *from*).
 2. to belong to, or have origin in, a definite period in the past (usually with *from*).
 3. to be old-fashioned.
 4. to have social appointments with persons of the opposite sex. [Colloq.]

dāt'ed, *a.* [pp. of *date.*]
 1. marked with or showing a date.
 2. out of date; old-fashioned.

dāte'less, *a.* 1. without a date.
 2. without limit or end.
 3. too old for its date to be fixed.
 4. still good or interesting though old.

dāte line, 1. a line on which the date of writing or issue is given, as in a letter, a newspaper, etc.

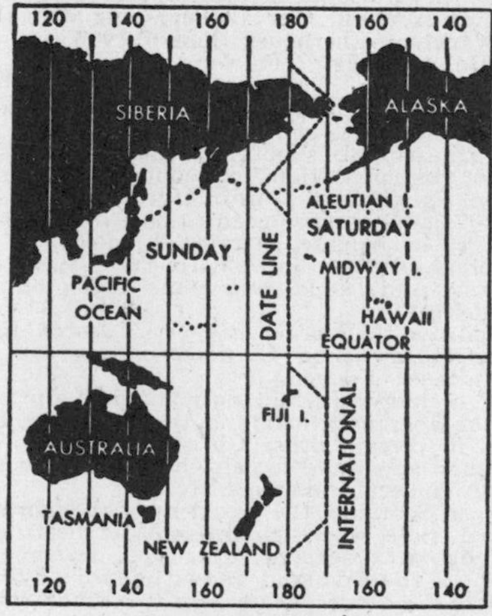

INTERNATIONAL DATE LINE

 2. an imaginary line drawn north and south through the Pacific Ocean, largely along the 180th meridian: it is the line at which, by international agreement, each calendar day begins at midnight, so that when it is Sunday just west of the line, it is Saturday just east of it.

dāte palm, a palm tree that bears dates: some date palms have a tall, slender trunk with foliage at the top, others have a bushy appearance.

dāte plum, the edible fruit of various species of the genus *Diospyros*; also, any of the trees themselves.

dāt'ēr, *n.* one who or that which dates.

Dȧ·tis'çȧ, *n.* [L.] a genus of tall exogenous herbs of the family *Datiscaceæ.*

dȧ·tis'cin, *n.* [from *Datisca.*] in chemistry, a crystalline compound extracted from the leaves and roots of *Datisca cannabina.* It has been used as a yellow dye.

dȧ·tī'sī, *n.* in logic, one of the valid moods.

dā·tī'vȧl, *a.* in the dative case.

dā'tive, *a.* [L. *dativus,* relating to giving; in LL. *casus dativus,* or *dativus* alone, the dative case, from *datus,* pp. of *dare,* to give.]
 1. in grammar, denoting or belonging to that case of a noun, pronoun, or adjective which expresses the indirect object of a verb and, in many languages, approach toward something.
 2. in law, (a) capable of being given or disposed of at pleasure; being in one's gift; (b) removable, in distinction from *perpetual*: said of an officer; (c) given or appointed by a magistrate or court of justice, in distinction from what is given by law or by a testator; as, in Scottish law, an executor *dative,* whose office is equivalent to that of an administrator.

dā'tive, *n.* 1. the dative case: in English, the dative notion is expressed by *to, for,* or word order (e.g., I gave the book *to Jack,* I did the task *for Jack,* I gave *Jack* the book).
 2. a word or phrase in the dative case.

dā'tive·ly, *adv.* as a dative; in the dative case.

dä'tō, *n.*; *pl.* **dä'tōs,** [from Malay *datōq.*]
 1. the chief of a Moslem Moro tribe in the Philippine Islands.
 2. the chief of a barrio in Malay countries.

dat'ō·līte, dath'ō·līte, *n.* [Gr. *dateisthai,* to divide, and *lithos,* stone.] a borosilicate of calcium, occurring usually in glassy crystals.

dat'tock, *n.* [W. African name.] *Detarium senegalense,* a tropical African tree of the pea family, having hard wood that resembles mahogany in color.

dā'tum, *n.*; *pl.* **dā'tȧ,** [L. *datum,* a gift, present, from neut. of *datus,* pp. of *dare,* to give.]
 1. [*usually in pl.*] something given, granted, or admitted; a premise upon which something can be argued or inferred; as, the problem could not be solved, owing to insufficient *data.*
 2. a real or assumed thing, used as a basis for calculations; as, *datum* point, line, etc.
 3. [*pl.*] in mathematics, certain relations or quantities, given or known, from which unknown quantities are determined.

dā'tum līne, the horizontal or base line of a section, from which the heights and depths are reckoned or measured.

dā'tum plāne, an assumed plane of reference forming a basis for measuring heights and depths: sea level is often so used.

Dā·tū'rȧ, *n.* [L., from Hind. *dhatūrā,* a plant.]
 1. a genus of poisonous plants of several species, belonging to the potato family, and having large, funnel-shaped, bad-smelling flowers. *Datura stramonium,* the thorn apple, is a common species.
 2. [d–] any plant of this genus.
 3. [d–] the flower of the datura.

dā·tū'rine, *n.* a poisonous alkaloid found in the thorn apple: called also *atropine.*

daub, *v.t.* and *v.i.*; daubed, *pt., pp.*; daubing, *ppr.* [ME. *dauben,* to daub; OFr. *dauber,* to whiten, whitewash; L. *dealbare,* to whiten, whitewash; *de-,* intens., and *albus,* white.]
 1. to smear with soft, adhesive matter, such as plaster, grease, etc.; to cover with mud, slime, or other soft substance; to smear.
 2. to paint badly and coarsely.
 If a picture is *daubed* with many bright colors, the vulgar admire it. —Watts.
 3. to cover with something gross or specious; to disguise with an artificial covering.
 So smooth he *daubed* his vice with show of virtue. —Shak.
 4. to lay or put on without taste; to deck awkwardly or ostentatiously. [Rare.]
 Let him be *daubed* with lace. —Dryden.

daub, *n.* 1. anything daubed on, as plaster grease, etc.
 2. a daubing stroke or splash.
 3. a poorly painted picture.
 4. a kind of mortar; plaster made of mud.

daub'ēr, *n.* 1. one who or that which daubs; especially, an unskillful painter.
 2. a flatterer.
 3. a thing to daub with.
 4. a mud wasp: so named from the manner in which it daubs mud in building its nest.

daub'ēr·y, daub'ry, *n.* a daubing; painting or work done in an inartistic or unskillful manner.

daub'ing, *n.* 1. the act of one who daubs.
 2. a material used in daubing.

dau·bree'līte, *n.* [from G. A. *Daubrée,* a Fr. mineralogist, and Gr. *lithos,* stone.] a metallic sulfide of chromium, a rare mineral of a black color occurring in certain meteoric irons.

dau·brē'īte, *n.* [named from G. A. *Daubrée,* a Fr. mineralogist.] bismuth oxychloride of a yellowish color.

daub'y, *a.* of the nature of a daub; viscous; adhesive.

Dau'çus, *n.* [L., from *daucus, daucum*; Gr. *daukos, daukon,* a carrotlike plant growing in Crete.] a genus of umbelliferous plants of several species, with spinous fruit of a somewhat compressed ovate or oblong form. *Daucus carota* is the cultivated carrot.

daud, *n.* same as *dad* (a blow).

daugh'tēr (da'), *n.* [ME. *doughter*; AS. *dohtor,* daughter, prob. from Sans. *duhitár,* daughter, lit., milker, from *duh,* milk.]
 1. a girl or woman in her relationship to either or both parents.
 2. a female descendant.
 3. a female thought of as if in the relation of child to parent; as, a *daughter* of France.
 4. anything thought of as like a daughter in relation to its source or origin; as, the colonies are the *daughters* of the mother country.

daugh'tēr, *a.* having the natural characteristics of a daughter; also, in biology, related in the first degree or generation, without reference to sex.

daugh'tēr cell, in biology, one of the cells formed by the division of another cell.

daugh'tēr-in-law, *n.*; *pl.* **daugh'tērs-in-law,** the wife of one's son.

daugh'tēr·li·ness, *n.* the state or quality of being daughterly.

daugh'tēr·ly, *a.* 1. of a daughter.
 2. like, characteristic of, or becoming a daughter; dutiful; as, *daughterly* affection.

daugh'tēr of Eve, any woman or girl.

Daun, *n.* Dan: a title of respect. [Obs.]

daun'dēr, *v.i.* same as *dander.*

däunt, *v.t.*; daunted, *pt., pp.*; daunting, *ppr.* [ME. *daunten*; OFr. *danter, donter,* to daunt, subdue, tame, from L. *domitare,* to tame, break in, freq. of *domare,* to tame, subdue.]
 1. to make afraid; to intimidate.
 2. to dishearten.
 3. to conquer; to subdue. [Obs.]
 Syn.—intimidate, dismay, frighten, dishearten, cow, appal, terrify.

däunt'ēr, *n.* one who daunts.

däunt'less, *a.* that cannot be daunted; bold; fearless; not timid; not discouraged; as, a *dauntless* spirit.

däunt'less·ly, *adv.* in a dauntless manner.

däunt'less·ness, *n.* the state or quality of being dauntless.

dau'phin, *n.* [Fr., from OFr. *dauphin, daulphin,* the dauphin, from L. *delphinus,* a dolphin: a name assumed about the middle of the ninth century by the lord of the French province of Dauphiny, which was bequeathed by Humbert III to the king of France, in 1349, on condition that the heir of the throne should bear the title of *Dauphin* of Viennois.] the eldest son of the king of France: a title used from 1349 to 1830.

dau'phin·ess, dau'phīne, *n.* the wife of a dauphin.

daut, *v.t.* [Scot. Gael.] to fondle; to pet; to caress: also spelled *dawt.* [Scot.]

dauw (da), *n.* [S. Afr. D. form of native name.] *Equus burchelli,* a South African zebra: it somewhat resembles the quagga.

dä'ven, *v.i.*; davened, *pt., pp.*; davening, *ppr.* [Yid. *davnen,* to pray.] in Judaism, to recite the prayers of the daily or of a holiday liturgy.

dav'en·port, *n.* [from the name of the original manufacturer (19th c.).]
 1. a small desk with a hinged lid that opens out for writing.
 2. a large couch or sofa, sometimes convertible into a bed.

Dā'vid, *n.* in the Bible, the second king of Israel and Judah, succeeding Saul and followed by his son Solomon: the reputed writer of the Psalms.

Dā·vid′iç, Dā·vid′iç·ăl, *a.* of or pertaining to David, king of Israel.

Dā′vid·ist, *n.* 1. a follower of David of Dinant, Belgium, who held extreme pantheistic views. His book *Quaternuli* was burned in 1209, and his followers scattered.
2. a follower of David Joris, of Delft, Holland, who founded an Anabaptist sect in the sixteenth century.

Dā′vid's root, the Brazilian cahinca root, used for snake bites.

dav′it, *n.* 1. either of two curved uprights of timber or iron projecting over the side or stern of a vessel, used for suspending, hoisting, or lowering a small boat by means of sheave and pulley.
2. a crane in a ship's bow, used to hoist the flukes of the anchor to the top of the bow, without injuring the sides of the ship: called also *fish davit.*

DAVITS

dā′vy, *n.* an affidavit. [Slang.]

Dā′vy Jōnes, the spirit of the sea: a humorous name among seamen.
Davy Jones's locker; the bottom of the ocean; specifically, the ocean regarded as the grave of those drowned at sea or buried there.

Dā′vy lamp, [from Sir Humphry *Davy,* 1778–1829, Eng. chemist who invented it.] formerly, a miner's safety lamp in which the flame was enclosed by a screen of wire gauze as a protection against firedamp.

daw, *n.* [ME. *dawe.*]
1. a jackdaw, a bird allied to the crows.
2. a sluggard. [Brit. Dial. and Scot.]
3. a simpleton. [Brit. Dial.]

daw, *v.i.* to dawn. [Obs.]

daw, *v.t.* to daunt; to frighten. [Obs.]

daw′dle, *v.i.* and *v.t.*; dawdled, *pt., pp.*; dawdling, *ppr.* [from Scot. *daidle,* to walk with tottering steps, to daddle.] to waste (time) by trifling; to loiter: often with *away*; as, to *dawdle away* an afternoon.

daw′dle, *n.* a trifler; a dawdler.

daw′dlẽr, *n.* one who dawdles; a trifler; an idler.

daw′dy, *n.* same as *dowdy.*

dawe, *n.* day. [Obs.]

daw′ish, *a.* like a daw; slatternly. [Obs.]

dawk, *n.* same as *dak.*

dawk, *n.* [a variant of *dalk,* from ME. *dale, dal,* a hollow; AS. *dæl,* a pit, hole, hollow.] a hollow or incision.

dawk, *v.t.* to cut or mark with an incision.

dawn, *v.i.*; dawned, *pt., pp.*; dawning, *ppr.* [ME. *dawnen, dawen,* to become day; AS. *dagian,* to become day, from *dæg,* day.]
1. to begin to grow light in the morning; to grow light; as, the day *dawns.*
2. to begin to appear, develop, etc.; as, the genius of the youth begins to *dawn.*
3. to begin to be clear to the mind; to begin to become visible in consequence of more light shining upon (usually with *on* or *upon*); as, the truth *dawns upon* me.

dawn, *n.* 1. the break of day; the first appearance of light in the morning.
2. first appearance (*of* something); beginning; rise; as, the *dawn of* a new era.

dawn′ing, *n.* dawn.

dawn red′wood, a coniferous Chinese tree, *Metasequoia glyptostroboides,* resembling the coastal redwood of California but having deciduous twigs and needles: now in the U.S.

daw′pāte, *n.* a simpleton; a fool. [Obs.]

daw′sŏn·ite, *n.* [named after J. W. *Dawson* (1820–1899), Canadian geologist.] a hydrous carbonate of aluminum and sodium.

dawt, *v.t.* same as *daut.*

dāy, *n.* [ME. *day*; AS. *dæg,* day.]
1. the period of time between the rising and setting of the sun.
2. the whole time or period of one revolution of the earth on its axis, twenty-four hours: called the *astronomical day.* In this sense, the day begins and ends at noon. The *civil* or *legal day* begins and ends at midnight.
3. daylight.
4. sunshine.
5. [often D-] a particular or special day; as, Decoration *Day,* D-*Day.*
6. a period of time; number of years; as, the best writer of his *day.*
7. a period of flourishing, power, glory, etc.; as, he has had his *day.*
8. the struggle or contest occurring on a certain day; as, we lost the *day.*
9. hours of work; shift; as, an eight-hour *day.*
10. an unspecified past or future; as, one of these *days.*
11. opportunity; as, my *day* has come.
12. [*pl.*] time; era; as, in *days* of old.
13. [*pl.*] life; as, he spent his *days* in study.
14. in astronomy, the time that it takes a celestial body to revolve once on its axis.
calendar day; the twenty-four hours from one midnight to the next midnight.
day after day; every day.
day by day; daily; every day; each day in succession; continually; without intermission of a day.
day in, day out; every day.
days in bank; in English law, set days for return of writs and appearance of parties to suits.
days of grace; (a) in some States, the three days after the date of maturity specified in a note which the law allows for its payment; (b) any extension of time.
from day to day; from one day to the next; without thought of or provision for the future.

Day′ak, *n.* same as *Dyak.*

dāy bed, a couch or sofa that can also be used as a bed.

dāy′ber″ry, *n.* the wild gooseberry.

dāy blīnd′ness, a defect of the eye by which vision is obscured by daylight.

dāy′book, *n.* 1. in bookkeeping, a journal of accounts; a book in which are recorded the debits and credits or accounts of the day as they occur.
2. a diary.

dāy′breăk, *n.* the dawn or first appearance of light in the morning.

dāy çōach, a regular passenger car of a railroad train, as distinguished from a sleeping car, chair car, etc.

dāy′drēam, *n.* 1. a pleasant, dreamy thought; reverie.
2. a pleasing but visionary notion or scheme.

dāy′drēam, *v.i.* to have a daydream or daydreams.

dāy′drēam″y, *a.* indulging in daydreams.

dāy′flow″ẽr, *n.* 1. any of a number of related plants of the spiderwort family, with jointed stems, grasslike leaves, and short-lived, usually blue flowers.
2. the flower.

dāy′flȳ, *n.* any of a group of neuropterous insects which belong to the genus *Ephemera*: so called because, though they may exist in the nymph stage for several years, in the adult stage they exist only from a few hours to a few days, taking no food, but only propagating their species and then dying: also called *May fly.*

DAYFLY (*Ephemera vulgata*)

dāy′-glō, *n.* a coloring agent added to pigments, dyes, etc. to produce any of a variety of brilliant fluorescent colors: a trade-mark (*Day-Glo*).

dāy′-house, *n.* in astrology, the house that is ruled by a planet by day; as, Libra is the *day-house* of Venus.

dāy in çourt, 1. a day on which one may present his case or claim in court.
2. any opportunity to present one's arguments; hearing.

dāy lā′bŏr, labor hired or performed by the day.

dāy lā′bŏr·ẽr, an unskilled worker who is paid by the day.

dāy let′tẽr, a telegram with a minimum charge for fifty words or fewer, sent in the daytime: it is cheaper but slower than a regular telegram.

dāy′light, *n.* 1. the light of day; the light of the sun.
2. the beginning of the day; dawn; as, the fire lasted until *daylight.*
3. daytime.
4. understanding; solution (of a problem).
5. publicity; as, let *daylight* into the affair.
6. the approaching end of a task or an ordeal; as, we can now see *daylight* ahead.
7. the empty space left at the top of a drinking glass, as usually filled. [Slang.]
8. [*pl.*] the eyes. [Slang.]
daylight saving; a method of saving or making use of daylight by setting the clock ahead, usually one hour, of standard time: this gives an hour more of daylight at the end of the usual working day.
daylight-saving time; time according to daylight saving; as, 6:00 A. M. *daylight-saving time* is the same as 5:00 A. M. standard.

dāy′light lamp, a lamp with an incandescent electric bulb and color screens which gives a light similar to daylight: used as a protection against eyestrain.

dāy lil′y, a garden plant of the genus *Hemerocallis,* whose tawny or yellow flowers last but one day.

dāy′lŏng, *a.* and *adv.* lasting throughout the day.

dāy′man, *n.*; *pl.* **dāy′men,** one who is hired by the day; a day laborer.

dāy′măre, *n.* in medicine, a nightmare occurring during waking hours.

dāy nŭrs′ẽr·y, a place where small children are cared for during the day.

Dāy of A·tōne′ment, Yom Kippur, a Jewish holiday.

Dāy of Judġ′ment, same as *judgment day.*

dāy owl, a hawk owl, *Surnia ulula.*

dāy′-peep, *n.* the dawn.

dāy room, in military usage, a recreation room for a company, troop, or battery.

dāy sçhol′ăr, a boarding-school pupil who lives at home and attends classes daily.

dāy sçhool, 1. a school that has classes only in the daytime: opposed to *night school.*
2. a private school whose students live at home and attend classes daily: opposed to *boarding school.*

dāyṣ′man, *n.*; *pl.* **dāyṣ′men,** an umpire or arbiter; a mediator. [Archaic.]

dāy′spring, *n.* the dawn. [Poetic.]

dāy′stăr, *n.* 1. the morning star; the star which precedes the sunrise.
2. the sun. [Poetic.]

dāy′tăle, *n.* the work of a day. [Brit. Dial.]

dāy′tīme, *n.* the interval during which the sun is above the horizon; the time of daylight.

dāy′-tō-dāy′, *a.* everyday; daily; routine.

dāy′wŏrk, *n.* work by the day; day labor.

dāze, *v.t.*; dazed, *pt., pp.*; dazing, *ppr.* [ME. *dasen,* to stupefy; Ice. *dasask,* to become weary.]
1. to confuse, stun, or stupefy, as by a blow.
2. to dazzle.

dāze, *n.* 1. the condition of being dazed.
2. in mining, a glittering or shining stone.

dāz′ed·ly, *adv.* in a dazed manner.

daz′zle, *v.t.*; dazzled, *pt., pp.*; dazzling, *ppr.*
1. to overpower with light; to hinder distinct vision of by intense light.
2. to surprise, confuse, or overpower with brilliant qualities, display, etc.

daz′zle, *v.i.* 1. to be overpowered by glare.
2. to arouse profound admiration by brilliant display.

daz′zle, *n.* 1. a dazzling.
2. something that dazzles.

daz′zle·ment, *n.* the act, power, or effect of dazzling.

daz′zle păint′ing, a style or system of painting ships developed during World War I by which the lines of the vessels were distorted in a way that gave observers a false idea of their course so as to avoid submarine attacks.

daz′zling·ly, *adv.* in a dazzling manner.

D′-dāy, *n.* 1. the unspecified day on which a military operation is to take place.
2. the day of the invasion of Europe by the Allies in World War II, beginning with the advance on Cherbourg; June 6, 1944.

de, De, *prep.* [Fr.; OFr. *des*; L. *dis-,* dis-.]
1. of.
2. from: in French family names, it indicates place of origin.

de-, [L., a prefix signifying separation, cessation, intensification, or contraction; also, from Fr. *dé,* from L. *de* or OFr. *des-,* from L. *dis-,* dis-.] a prefix meaning: (a) *away from, off,* as in *de*pilate, *de*train; (b) *down,* as in *de*press, *de*cline; (c) *wholly, entirely,* as in *de*funct; (d) *undo, reverse the action of,* as in *de*frost.

dēa′çŏn, *n.* [ME. *deken, dekyn*; AS. *deacon*; LL. *diaconus,* a deacon; Gr. *diakonos,* a servant, a messenger, a deacon.]
1. a clergyman ranking just below a priest in the Roman Catholic and Anglican churches.
2. in certain other Christian churches, a layman appointed to help the minister, especially in secular matters, etc.
3. in Scotland, the president of an incorporated trade, who is chairman of its meetings.

dēa′çŏn, *v.t.*; deaconed, *pt., pp.*; deaconing, *ppr.* 1. to read aloud, as two lines of a hymn before the congregation sings it (usually with *off*).

2. to deceive by placing the best uppermost, as fruit in a measure.
3. to adulterate or do (something) dishonestly.
4. to kill for food while very young; as, to *deacon* veal. [Slang.]

dēa′cŏn·ess, *n.* [LL. *diaconissa*, f. of *diaconus*, a deacon.]
1. a member of the Institution of Deaconesses, an order devoted to charitable work.
2. a woman appointed as a helper or assistant in a church.
3. in the Anglican and Protestant Episcopal churches, a woman church worker appointed by a bishop.

dēa′cŏn·hood, *n.* the condition of being a deacon; the office and duties of a deacon.

dēa′cŏn·ry, *n.* the office or position of a deacon; also, deacons collectively.

dēa′cŏn·ship, *n.* same as *deaconry*.

dē·aç′ti·vāte, *v.t.*; deactivated, *pt., pp.*; deactivating, *ppr.* in military usage, to place (a division, regiment, etc.) on a nonactive status; to demobilize.

dead (ded), *a.* [ME. *ded, deed*; AS. *dead*, dead.]
1. no longer living; having died.
2. without life; inanimate; lifeless; as, a *dead* tree.
3. imitating death; deathlike; as, a *dead* sleep.
4. perfectly still; inert; motionless; as, a *dead* calm, a *dead* weight.
5. (a) conducting sound imperfectly; as, a *dead* floor; (b) nonresonant; as, a *dead* sound.
6. barren; useless; unprofitable; unproductive; as, *dead* soil.
7. assured; unerring; unfailing; as, a *dead* shot.
8. lacking feeling, energy, sensitivity, warmth, etc.
9. inelastic; as, a *dead* tennis ball.
10. no longer used or significant; obsolete; as, *dead* languages, *dead* laws.
11. lacking interest, taste, zest, color, etc.; dull; flat; as, a *dead* picture.
12. complete; absolute; as, a *dead* loss.
13. unvarying; as, a *dead* level.
14. unclaimed; as, *dead* letters.
15. very tired; exhausted. [Colloq.]
16. in electricity, with no current going through it; uncharged; as, a *dead* wire.
17. in law, deprived of civil rights.
18. in printing, (a) set up but not to be used; (b) already used; as, *dead* type.
19. in radio, not operating; as, a *dead* microphone.
20. in sports, not in actual play; as, a *dead* ball.
dead cotton; in dyeing, the unripe cotton fibers that cannot be dyed.
dead freight; in maritime law, the sum paid for unoccupied space in a chartered vessel.
dead horse; work done in payment of debt, as for wages advanced.
dead men; the empty bottles at a banquet's end. [Slang.]
Syn.—deceased, extinct, defunct, inanimate, lifeless.

dead (ded), *n.* 1. the time of most cold, most darkness, etc.; a time of profound gloom or stillness; as, the *dead* of winter; the *dead* of night.
2. among students, failure in recitation. [Slang.]
3. [*pl.*] in mining, unproductive rock.
the dead; those who have died.

dead, *v.t.* to deprive of life; to make dead. [Obs.]

dead, *v.i.* to lose life; to die. [Obs.]

dead, *adv.* in a deathlike degree; absolutely; completely; also, directly.

dead an′gle, in fortification, any space that is not visible from the parapet or that cannot be defended from behind it.

dead′bēat, *a.* in mechanics, beating without recoil.

dead′bēat, *n.* a beat without a recoil.

dead′-bēat′, *a.* tired out; exhausted. [Colloq.]

dead beat, 1. a person who tries to evade paying for things; sponge. [Slang.]
2. a lazy, idle person. [Slang.]

dead block, either of two iron or wooden blocks that serve as buffers at the end of a freight car.

dead′bọrn, *a.* stillborn.

dead cen′tẽr, in mechanics, the position of a steam engine's connecting rod and crank axle in which both are in a straight line, so that no force is exerted; also, a nonrevolving center.

dead çlōtheṣ, clothes used to dress a corpse.

dead-çŏl′ŏr·ing, *n.* in oil painting, the first layer of color, usually gray, on which are superimposed the finishing colors of the picture.

dead dip′ping, the process of giving to brass a dead, or dull, color, by dipping in acid.

dead′en, *v.t.*; deadened, *pt., pp.*; deadening, *ppr.* [ME. *deden*; AS. *dydan*, to kill, deprive of life.]
1. to lessen the vigor or force of; to dull; to muffle; to abate (vigor or action); as, to *deaden* the force of a ball.
2. to make numb; to take away the sensitivity of.
3. to girdle with incisions, as a tree.
4. to make soundproof.
5. to retard; to lessen velocity or motion of; as, to *deaden* a ship's way.
6. to make vapid or spiritless; as, to *deaden* wine or beer.
7. to deprive of gloss or brilliancy; as, to *deaden* gilding by a coat of size.

dead′en, *v.i.* to become as if dead; lose vigor, intensity, etc.

dead′-end, *a.* 1. having one end closed; as, a *dead-end* street.
2. [from *Dead End*, a play (1935) by Sidney Kingsley about New York slum life.] of or characteristic of slums or slum life. [Colloq.]

dead end, 1. a street, alley, etc. closed at one end.
2. an impasse.
3. in radio, any part of a coil not connected with the circuit.

dead′en·ẽr, *n.* one who or that which deadens.

dead′en·ing, *n.* 1. material used to make rooms soundproof.
2. material used to take off gloss.

dead′eȳe (ded′ī), *n.* a round, flat wooden block, pierced with three holes, to receive the lanyard: used on a ship to extend the shrouds and stays, and for other purposes.

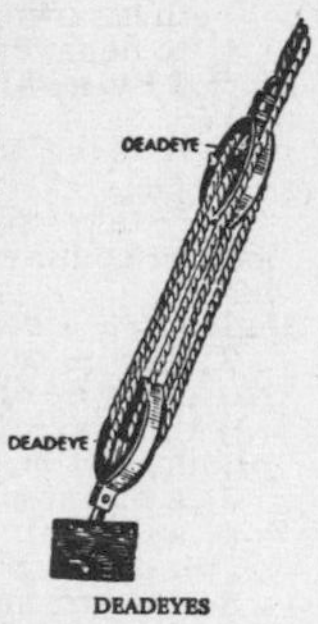

DEADEYE
DEADEYE
DEADEYES

dead′fall, *n.* 1. a trap for animals, arranged so that a heavy weight will fall upon and crush the game sought.
2. fallen trees and undergrowth that make a matted mass.
3. a drinking or gambling house of bad repute. [Slang.]

dead flat, in shipbuilding, a ship's widest cross section; the midship frame.

dead ground, in mining, unproductive ground which must be worked through to reach ore-bearing rock.

dead hand, in law, inalienable tenure; mortmain.

dead′head (ded′hed), *n.* 1. in founding, the extra length given to a casting, as a gun; sprue.
2. the tailstock of a lathe.
3. a rough block of wood used as an anchor buoy.

dead′head, *n.* [from *dead head* of cattle.]
1. a person who receives transportation, admission, goods, services, etc. without paying for them.
2. a truck, train, etc. that travels without a pay load. [Slang.]

dead′head, *v.t.*; deadheaded, *pt., pp.*; deadheading, *ppr.* to furnish free admission, use, or transportation to.

dead′head, *v.i.* 1. to receive transportation, admission, goods, services, etc. without paying for them; to sponge; to behave as a parasite or deadhead.
2. to travel without carrying a pay load, as trucks, trains, etc., or their operators. [Slang.]

dead′head, *adv.* 1. without paying.
2. without a pay load. [Slang.]

dead′head, *a.* 1. costing nothing; free.
2. traveling without a pay load; unprofitable; unremunerative; noncompensating. [Slang.]

dead′heärt″ed, *a.* listless; unfeeling; insensible; callous.

dead hēat, a race in which two or more contestants reach the finish line at exactly the same time; a tie.

dead′house, *n.* in hospitals, etc., a house or room in which the dead are placed temporarily; a morgue.

dead′latch, *n.* a latch which may be made immovable by a detent, or catch.

dead let′tẽr, 1. a law or ordinance no longer enforced but not repealed.
2. an unclaimed letter, or one that cannot be delivered because of an incorrect address, etc.

dead′-let′tẽr of′fice, the postal department to which dead letters are sent to be opened and, if possible, returned to the writer, or destroyed.

dead lift, 1. a direct lifting without any mechanical assistance, as of a dead weight.
2. a difficult task requiring all one's powers.

dead′līght, *n.* 1. a strong shutter fitted to a cabin window or ship's porthole, to shut out water in stormy weather.
2. a window of heavy glass in the deck or side of a ship.
3. a skylight made so as not to be opened.

dead′līne, *n.* 1. originally, in a military prison, a line beyond which a prisoner could go only at the risk of being shot by a guard.
2. any line the crossing of which entails penalty or is forbidden.
3. a time limit, as for a payment, news story, etc.

dead′li·ness, *n.* the quality or state of being deadly.

dead lōad, in engineering, a uniform pressure or weight, as of a structure: opposed to *moving load*.

dead′lock, *n.* 1. a lock so constructed that it must be worked on one side by a handle and on the other by a key.
2. a complete blocking or stoppage resulting from the action of equal and opposed forces; as, the *deadlock* of a jury or legislature.

dead′lock, *v.t.* to bring to a deadlock.

dead′lock, *v.i.* to come to a deadlock.

dead′ly, *a.*; *comp.* deadlier; *superl.* deadliest.
1. capable of causing death; mortal; fatal; destructive; as, a *deadly* blow or wound.
2. implacable; aiming to kill or destroy; as, a *deadly* enemy.
3. liable to death; mortal. [Obs.]
4. bearing a resemblance to death; deathly.
5. very great; excessive.
A *deadly* number of pardons. —Pepys.
6. until death; as, *deadly* combat.
7. unbearable; as, a *deadly* party. [Colloq.]
8. in theology, causing spiritual death; as, the seven *deadly* sins.
Syn.—destructive, fatal, mortal.

dead′ly, *adv.* 1. in a manner resembling death; as, *deadly* pale or wan.
2. mortally. [Archaic.]
3. implacably. [Obs.]
4. extremely; excessively.
5. as if dead.

dead′ly nīght′shāde, the belladonna, a poisonous plant whose leaves and roots are used in medicine.

dead′ly sinṣ, in theology, the seven capital sins (pride, covetousness, lust, anger, gluttony, envy, and sloth): so called because regarded as causing spiritual death.

dead′măn, *n.*; *pl.* **dead′men,** 1. a log or beam sunk in the ground and used as an anchor for guy ropes, or the like.
2. [*pl.*] in nautical usage, the gasket ends or reef ends not tucked in when furling the sail.

dead′-man′ṣ-hand′, *n.* 1. *Nephrodium filixmas*, the male fern.
2. *Laminaria digitata*, the devil's-apron.

dead märch, a piece of solemn funeral music in slow march tempo; especially, a military funeral march.

dead′-men′ṣ-fiñ′gẽrṣ, *n.* 1. *Orchis maculata*, a species of the genus *Orchis*, having pale, handlike tubers; also, any of the other species of the same genus.
2. *Alcyonium digitatum*, a polyp having a resemblance to the human hand.

dead′-men′ṣ-līneṣ′, *n. Chorda filum*, a species of seaweed having long, cordlike fronds.

dead nēap, the lowest point reached by a neap tide.

dead′ness, *n.* the state of being dead, in any sense.

dead net′tle, any of the species of plants of the genus *Lamium*, from the resemblance of their leaves to those of the nettle: they are stingless, however; hence the name.

dead oil, an oil, heavier than water, containing naphthalin, carbolic acid, etc., obtained in the distillation of coal-tar.

dead′-pan, *a.* and *adv.* with an expressionless face. [Slang.]

dead pan, an expressionless face; also, one whose facial expression never varies or reflects any emotion: usually said of a comedian or actor. [Slang.]

dead plāte, a flat, iron plate sometimes attached to the bars of a furnace and used to coke bituminous coal before it is finally consumed as fuel.

dead pledġe (plej), a mortgage or pawning of lands or goods, or the thing pawned.

dead point, same as *dead center*.

dead reck′ŏn·ing, the calculation of a ship's position at sea by using compass readings and data recorded in the log (speed, course, and distance traveled) rather than astronomical observations: used in fog, etc.

dead rīṣe, in shipbuilding, the distance between the top of the keel and a horizontal line joining the top of the floor timbers amidships.

dead rīṣ′ing, same as *dead rise*.

dead set, 1. the unmoving position of a hunting dog in pointing game.
 2. a resolute attack or effort.
 3. stubbornly determined; as, he was *dead set* on having his own way. [Colloq.]

dead shēave, a scored opening in the heel of the topmast of a ship, through which a second top tackle can be rove.

dead shọre, a piece of wood built up vertically in a wall which has been broken through.

dead′-strōke, *a.* without recoil, as certain power hammers.

dead′-strōke, *n.* a stroke, as by certain power hammers, in which the recoil is resisted by a spring.

dead′tongue (-tung), *n.* *Œnanthe crocata*, the water hemlock, an umbelliferous plant of Europe.

dead wạll, a blank wall in which there is no opening.

dead wạ′tẽr, 1. still water.
 2. the water which eddies about the stern of a ship as it passes through the water: also called *eddy water*.

dead wẹight (wāt), 1. the weight of an inert person or thing.
 2. a heavy or oppressive burden.
 3. formerly, an advance by the Bank of England to the government for the payment of pensions to retired officers of the army or navy.
 4. the lading of a vessel when it consists of heavy goods; that portion of the cargo, as coal, iron, etc., which pays freight according to its weight and not its bulk.
 5. the weight of a vehicle without a load, as distinguished from the live weight or load.

dead wind, a wind blowing in the direction opposite to a ship's course; head wind.

dead′wood, *n.* 1. dead wood on trees.
 2. anything useless; burdensome person or thing.
 3. blocks of timber laid upon the keel of a ship, especially at the stern.
 4. a buffer block.
 5. in bowling, the pins that have been knocked down.
 to get the deadwood on one; to obtain the advantage over one. [Slang.]

dead wool, wool taken from the skin of sheep which have been slaughtered or have died.

dead wŏrk, work from which no direct profit is derived, but which is preliminary to that which is profitable; specifically, the work of opening a mine.

dead′wŏrks, *n.pl.* the parts of a ship which are above the surface of the water when the ballast or the cargo is on board: called also *upper works*. [Obs.]

deaf (def), *a.* [ME. *def, deef*; AS. *deaf*, deaf.]
 1. not perceiving sounds; totally or partially unable to hear; as, a *deaf* ear, a *deaf* man.
 2. not listening, or refusing to listen; not moved, persuaded, or convinced; as, *deaf* to all entreaties; *deaf* to argument.
 3. stifled; imperfect; obscurely heard. [Rare.]

 A *deaf* noise of sounds that never cease.
 —Dryden.

 4. barren; unproductive; empty; as, a *deaf* field. [Obs. or Brit. Dial.]

deaf, *v.t.* to deafen. [Archaic or Dial.]

deaf′-and-dumb′ (-dum′), *a.* 1. deaf-mute.
 2. of or for deaf-mutes.
 Now regarded as opprobrious.

deaf′en, *v.t.*; deafened, *pt., pp.*; deafening, *ppr.*
 1. to make deaf.
 2. to overwhelm with noise.
 3. to drown out (a sound) with a louder sound.
 4. in architecture, to make soundproof, as a floor or partition.

deaf′en·ing, *a.* [ppr. of *deafen*.] 1. making deaf.
 2. very noisy.
 3. making soundproof.

deaf′en·ing, *n.* material used in floors or walls to make them soundproof.

deaf′ly, *adv.* without sense of sounds; obscurely heard.

deaf′ly, *a.* lonely. [Brit. Dial.]

deaf′-mūte, *n.* a person who is deaf, especially from birth, and therefore unable to speak: most deaf-mutes, having the necessary vocal organs, can be taught to speak.

deaf′-mūte, *a.* unable to hear and speak, especially because deaf from birth.

deaf′-mūt′iṣm, *n.* 1. the condition of being a deaf-mute.
 2. any incorrect language usage of a deaf-mute: sometimes because of a transposition of letters; as, the writing of *stale* for *slate*; *kinfe* for *knife*.

deaf′ness, *n.* 1. incapacity of perceiving sounds; the state of the organs which prevents the reception of auditory impressions.
 2. unwillingness to hear and regard; complete rejection of what is said to one.
 nervous deafness; deafness resulting from injury to the auditory nerve.

dēal, *v.t.*; dealt (delt), *pt., pp.*; dealing, *ppr.* [ME. *delen*; AS. *dælan*, to divide, share.]
 1. to portion out.
 2. to distribute.
 3. to give; administer; as, he *dealt* his opponent a blow.
 4. to distribute (playing cards) to the players.

dēal, *v.i.* 1. to distribute in portions, as in card playing.
 2. to traffic; to trade; to do business (*with* or *in*); as, to *deal in* coffee; to *deal with* a merchant.
 3. to act between man and man; to transact or negotiate between men. [Archaic.]

 He that *deals* between man and man, raiseth his own credit with both. —Bacon.

 4. to behave; to act or conduct oneself (followed by *with*); as, he *dealt* dishonestly *with* others.
 5. to have to do (*with*); as, science *deals with* facts.
 6. to take up or consider (followed by *with*); as, the committee will *deal with* these problems.

dēal, *n.* 1. a dealing.
 2. (a) the act of distributing playing cards; (b) cards dealt; (c) a player's turn to deal; (d) the playing of one deal of cards; (e) the privilege of dealing.
 3. a business transaction. [Colloq.]
 4. a bargain or agreement, especially a secret one in politics. [Colloq.]
 5. an arrangement, treatment, or plan, usually involving some sort of distribution; as, a fair *deal*. [Colloq.]

dēal, *n.* [ME. *dele, deel*; AS. *dæl*, a part, share.] a division, part, or portion; hence, an indefinite quantity, degree, or extent; as, a *deal* of time and trouble.
 a good (or *great*) *deal*; (a) a large quantity or amount; as, you've wasted *a good deal* of time; (b) very much; as, I can't walk *a great deal* faster.

dēal, *n.* [from D. *deel*, a board, plank.]
 1. the division of a piece of fir or pine timber made by sawing it into any of several sizes; a board or plank.
 2. fir or pine wood.

dēal, *a.* made of deal.

dē·al′bāte, *v.t.* to whiten. [Obs.]

dē·al·bā′tion, *n.* the act of bleaching; a whitening.

dēal endṣ, boards or planks less than six feet in length. [Brit.]

dēal′ẽr, *n.* one who deals; specifically, (a) a trader; a trafficker; a shopkeeper; a broker; a merchant; as, a *dealer* in dry goods; (b) the person who shuffles and distributes the cards in a card game.

dēal′fish, *n.*; *pl.* **dēal′fish** or **dēal′fish·eṣ,** any of a number of related deep-sea fishes of the genus *Trachypterus*, with a long, thin body; ribbonfish.

dēal frāme, a sawing machine for cutting deals, or logs.

dēal′ing, *n.* 1. the act of one who deals; distribution.
 2. behavior; way of acting.
 3. [*usually pl.*] transactions or relations, usually of business.
 4. doing business.
 5. way of doing business.

dealt (delt), past tense and past participle of *deal*.

dēal tree, the fir tree: so called because deals are commonly made of it. [Brit. Dial.]

dē·am′bū·lāte, *v.i.* to walk abroad. [Obs.]

dē·am·bū·lā′tion, *n.* the act of walking abroad; a promenading. [Obs.]

dē·am′bū·lȧ·tọ·ry, *a.* relating to walks; strolling.

dē·am′bū·lȧ·tọ·ry, *n.* a covered place in which to promenade, as a gallery.

dēan, *n.* [ME. *deen, dene*; OFr. *deien*, a dean; LL. *decanus*, one who is head of ten soldiers, from L. *decem*, ten.]
 1. a dignitary, in the Roman Catholic and Anglican churches, subordinate to the bishop.
 2. the presiding official of a cathedral or collegiate church.
 3. in some English universities, an officer who attends to matters of conduct and discipline of the students in addition to his other regular duties.
 4. a member of a college or university administration in charge of a school, faculty, or class, or of the men or women students.
 5. the member of an association or group who has belonged to it longer than anyone else; as, he is the *dean* of American novelists.
 Dean of Arches; in England, the chief judicial officer of the ecclesiastical court of appeal, known as the Court of Arches.
 Dean of Faculty; in Scotland, the president of the Faculty of Advocates.
 dean of guild; a Scottish magistrate who supervises all matters relative to the erection of new structures.
 dean of peculiars; a dean not subject to direct diocesan rule.
 rural dean; originally, a beneficed clergyman appointed by a bishop to exercise a certain jurisdiction in districts of his diocese remote from his personal superintendence. The duties of *rural deans* are now usually performed by archdeacons.

dēan, *n.* a small, narrow valley. [Obs.]

dēan′ẽr·y, *n.*; *pl.* **dēan′ẽr·ieṣ,** 1. the office, authority, or jurisdiction of a dean.
 2. the official residence of a dean.

dē·an′i·măl·īze, *v.t.* [*de-* priv., and L. *animal*, a living being, animal.] to free from animal qualities. [Rare.]

dēan′ship, *n.* the position, rank, or term of office of a dean.

dēar, *a.*; *comp.* dearer; *superl.* dearest, [ME. *deere, dere*; AS. *deore*, beloved, precious, very valuable.]
 1. (a) charging high prices; (b) high in price; more costly than usual; expensive.

 The cheapest of us is ten groats too *dear*.
 —Shak.

 2. marked or characterized by scarcity; as, a *dear* season. [Obs.]
 3. of a high value in estimation; greatly valued; highly thought of: used as a polite form of address in speaking or letter writing; as, *Dear* Sir.
 4. much loved; beloved; precious; as, a *dear* mother.
 5. earnest; as, our *dearest* hope.
 6. high in degree; intense; dangerous; as, *dear* peril. [Obs.]

dēar, *adv.* 1. with deep affection.
 2. at a high cost.

 If thou attempt it, it will cost thee *dear*.
 —Shak.

dēar, *n.* a darling; a sweetheart; a loved person; a word denoting tender affection or endearment; as, my *dear*.

dēar, *interj.* an expression of distress, annoyance, surprise, pity, etc.

dēar, *v.t.* to make dear. [Obs.]

dēar′bọrn, *n.* a light four-wheeled carriage: probably named after General Henry Dearborn.

dēar′-bọught (-bọt), *a.* dearly bought; as, *dear-bought* experience.

dēare, *v., n.,* and *a.* dere. [Obs.]

dēar′ie, *n.* same as *deary*.

dēar′ling, *n.* a darling. [Obs.]

dēar′-lŏved (-luvd), *a.* greatly beloved. [Rare.]

dēar′ly, *adv.* 1. at a high price; as, he pays *dearly* for his rashness.
 2. with great fondness; as, we love our children *dearly*.
 3. earnestly; as, I *dearly* wish to go.
 4. richly; exquisitely. [Obs.]

dēar′ness, *n.* 1. costliness; high price, or a higher price than the customary one; as, the *dearness* of corn.
 2. fondness; nearness to the heart or affections; great value in estimation; preciousness; tender love; as, the *dearness* of friendship.

dēarth, *n.* [ME. *derth, derthe*, scarcity, from *deere, dere*; AS. *deore*, dear, of great value.]

1. originally, costliness; dearness.
2. scarcity of food supply; famine; privation; want; as, a *dearth* of corn.
3. scarcity; lack.

dē·är·tiç′ū·lāte, *v.t.* [*de-* priv., and L. *articulare,* to divide into joints, from *articulus,* a joint.] to disjoint.

dēar′y, *n.*; *pl.* **dēar′ieṣ,** [dim. of *dear.*] one who is a dear; a darling: now often ironic or humorous.

dē′as, *n.* dais. [Scot.]

death, (deth), *n.* [ME. *deth, deeth*; AS. *death,* death.]
1. the act or fact of dying; permanent cessation of life in a person, animal, or plant, in which all vital functions cease permanently.
2. any ending resembling death; total extinction; destruction; as, the *death* of love.
3. the state of being dead.
4. in theology, separation or alienation of the soul from God; a being under the dominion of sin, and destitute of grace or divine life: called *spiritual death.*
5. the cause or agent of death; as, he will be the *death* of his father.
6. murder; slaughter; as, a man of *death.*
7. a disease generally fatal; pestilence; as, the Black *Death.* [Obs.]
8. something deemed as dreadful as death; any condition or experience thought of as like dying or being dead; as, friendlessness is *death* itself.
9. [D-] the personification of death, usually pictured as a skeleton in a black robe, holding a scythe.
at death's door; nearly dead.
Black Death; see under *black, adj.*
civil death; the deprivation of all civil rights, as by banishment, life imprisonment, etc.
in at the death; (a) present at the death (of the quarry): hunter's term; (b) present at the end or culmination.
second death; in theology, the death of the soul after the death of the body.
to be death on; to be superior in doing anything; to have a particular fondness for. [Slang.]
to death, or *to the death*; to the utmost extremity; very much; to the end.
to do to death; to kill.
to put to death; to slay or cause to be slain; to execute.
Syn.—decease, demise, departure, dissolution, release.

death ad′dẽr, *Acanthophis antarctica,* a venomous Australian snake.

death′bed, *n.* 1. the bed on which one dies.
2. the last hours of a person's life.

death′bed, *a.* done or made in the last hours of life; as, a *deathbed* will.

death bell, 1. a bell whose ringing announces death; the passing bell.
2. a monotonous ringing sound in either ear, thought by the superstitious to foretell death.

death′bīrd, *n.* 1. a small North American owl, *Nyctala richardsoni.*
2. the death's-head moth.

death′blōw, *n.* 1. a mortal blow or shock.
2. figuratively, a thing destructive or fatal (*to* something).

death′-bōd″ing, *a.* foretokening death.

death çam′ăss, a lilylike plant with a poisonous bulb, grasslike leaves, and clusters of small, greenish-white flowers.

death chām′bẽr, 1. a room in which someone has died.
2. a room in which condemned prisoners are put to death.

death çord, the hangman's halter; gallows rope.

death çup, a poisonous mushroom with a swollen, cuplike base.

death dȧnce, see *dance of death* under *dance.*

death′dāy, *n.* the day on which death comes, or its anniversary.

death dū′ty, an inheritance tax. [Brit.]

death fīre, the ignis fatuus, thought by the superstitious to foretell death.

death′fụl, *a.* 1. murderous; deadly; destructive.
2. deathlike; deathly.
3. liable to death; mortal. [Archaic.]

death′fụl·ness, *n.* an appearance as of death; the quality of suggesting death.

death grap′ple, a desperate struggle or grapple upon which life depends.

death house, a place, as a cell block, where prisoners condemned to die are kept until the time of execution.

death′less, *a.* 1. not subject to death; immortal; as, *deathless* beings.
2. imperishable; unending; as, *deathless* fame.

death′less·ness, *n.* the condition of being deathless; immortality.

death′līke, *a.* 1. having the appearance of death; as in death; deathly.
2. fatal; deadly. [Obs.]

death′li·ness, *n.* likeness to death.

death′ly, *a.* 1. having the appearance or nature of death; as, *deathly* pallor.
2. causing or threatening death; deadly.
3. of death. [Poet.]

death′ly, *adv.* 1. in such manner as to resemble death; as, *deathly* sick.
2. extremely; deadly; as, *deathly* serious.

death mȧsk, a cast of a person's face, taken soon after his death.

death point, that degree of cold or heat at which life ceases.

death rāte, the ratio of deaths to population for a specified period; usually, the number of deaths per year per thousand of population in a given community, area, or group.

death rat′tle, a rattling or gurgling sound caused by air passing through mucus which sometimes accompanies the breathing of a dying person.

death rāy, a ray that can supposedly kill at a distance.

death's′-head (deths′hed), *n.* 1. the skull of a human skeleton or a figure representing it, symbolizing death.
2. in zoology, one of the saimiri; the squirrel monkey of South America.
death's-head moth; a large European moth, *Acherontia atropos,* having on the back of its thorax markings like a human skull.

death′s′hẽrb, *n.* in botany, the deadly nightshade, *Atropa belladonna.*

deaths′măn, *n.* a public executioner; a hangman. [Archaic.]

death tick, in entomology, the deathwatch.

death trȧnce, in medicine, a deathlike condition, resulting from reduced action of the vital organs.

death′trap, *n.* 1. any place or structure that especially endangers life, as a railway crossing or an insecure building.
2. a very dangerous set of circumstances.

death′wȧrd, *adv.* toward death.

death wär′rănt, 1. in law, an official order directing the execution of a criminal.
2. figuratively, anything that ends hope, joy, etc.

death′wätch, *n.* 1. in entomology, any of various insects, especially a small beetle, *Anobium tessellatum,* whose ticking is superstitiously thought by some persons to prognosticate death, but in fact is only the call of the sexes to each other. The beetle produces this ticking sound by raising itself upon its hind legs and rapidly beating its head against woodwork. Called also *death tick.*
2. a guard set over a condemned criminal during his last hours.
3. the vigil kept beside a dying person or a corpse before burial.

death wöund, a wound that is mortal.

death′y, *a.* and *adv.* deathly. [Rare.]

dē·au′rāte, *a.* [*de-,* and L. *auratus,* ornamented with gold; *aurum,* gold.]
1. in entomology, having a golden color.
2. gilded. [Obs.]

dē·au′rāte, *v.t.* to gild. [Obs.]

dēave, *v.t.*; deaved, *pt., pp.*; deaving, *ppr.* to confuse or stun with noise; to deafen. [Scot. and Brit. Dial.]

dēave, *v.i.* to become deaf. [Obs.]

deb, *n.* short for *debutante.* [Colloq.]

dē·baç′chāte, *v.i.* to rave and bluster as a bacchanal. [Obs.]

dē·baç·chā′tion, *n.* a raving. [Obs.]

dē·baç′le (*or* dā-bä′kl), *n.* [Fr. *debacle,* a breakup, overthrow, from *debacler,* to break up.]
1. a breaking up of ice in a river, etc.
2. a rush of debris-filled waters.
3. an overthrow; a rout.
4. a sudden great disaster.

dē·bär′, *v.t.*; debarred, *pt., pp.*; debarring, *ppr.* 1. to cut off from entrance; to preclude; to hinder from approach, entry, or enjoyment; to shut out or exclude: used with *from* or *of.*
2. to prevent, hinder, or prohibit.

dē·bärb′, *v.t.* to deprive of the beard. [Obs.]

dē·bärk′, *v.t.* [Fr. *débarquer; de,* from, and *barque,* a ship, bark, from LL. *barca,* a bark.] to land (passengers or goods) from a ship or boat; to remove from on board any watercraft and place on land; to disembark; to unload; as, to *debark* artillery.

dē·bärk′, *v.i.* to go ashore from a boat or ship; to disembark.

dē·bär·kā′tion, *n.* a going ashore or being taken ashore from a vessel; disembarkation.

dē·bär′ment, *n.* the act of debarring or prohibiting; the state of being debarred; hindrance from approach; exclusion.

dē·bar′răss, *v.t.* to relieve from embarrassment; to disembarrass. [Rare.]

dē·bāse′, *v.t.*; debased, *pt., pp.*; debasing, *ppr.* [*de-,* and Fr. *bas*; LL. *bassus,* low.]
1. to reduce from a higher to a lower state in character or dignity.
2. to reduce or lower in quality, purity, or value; to adulterate; as, to *debase* gold or silver by alloy.
3. to lower or degrade; to make mean or despicable; as, vicious habits *debase* the mind as well as the body.
4. to impair in purity or elegance; to vitiate by meanness; as, to *debase* literary style by vulgar expressions.
Syn.—abase, corrupt, degrade, impair, lower, taint.

dē·bāsed′ (dē-bāst′), *a.* 1. in heraldry, turned over or downward from its proper position or use; inverted; reversed.
2. lowered in quality, value, purity, dignity, etc.
3. corrupted; degraded.

ESCUTCHEON DEBASED

dē·bāse′ment, *n.* the act of debasing; also, the fact or condition of being debased.

dē·bās′ẽr, *n.* one who debases or lowers in estimation or in value; one who degrades or renders mean; that which debases.

dē·bās′ing·ly, *adv.* in such manner as to debase or degrade.

dē·bāt′ȧ·ble, *a.* 1. capable of being debated; disputable; subject to controversy or contention; as, a *debatable* question.
2. being disputed; undecided.
debatable ground; figuratively, any question or subject open to discussion.
Debatable Land; formerly, a tract of land, situated between the rivers Esk and Sark, claimed by both England and Scotland.

dē·bāte′, *n.* [ME. *debate*; OFr. *debat,* a debate, from *debatre,* to fight, contend, debate.]
1. contention in words or arguments; discussion of opposing reasons; argument or reasoning, especially between those of diametrical views; dispute; controversy; as, the *debates* in Parliament or in Congress.
2. a formal contest of skill in reasoned argument, with two teams taking opposite sides of a specified question (the resolution).
3. the art or study of formal debate.
4. strife; contention. [Archaic.]
5. subject of discussion. [Rare.]

Statutes and edicts concerning this *debate.*
—Milton.

dē·bāte′, *v.t.*; debated, *pt., pp.*; debating, *ppr.* 1. to contend; to dispute; to discuss; to argue, especially in a meeting or legislature; as, they *debated* the question with vigor.
2. to argue (a question) formally.
3. to consider reasons for and against (*with* oneself, or *in* one's own mind).
Syn.—argue, contest, controvert, dispute.

dē·bāte′, *v.i.* 1. to consider.
2. to discuss opposing reasons; to argue.
3. to take part in a formal argument; to be a debater.
4. to fight or quarrel. [Obs.]

dē·bāte′fụl, *a.* contentious; quarrelsome.

dē·bāte′fụl·ly, *adv.* with contention.

dē·bāte′ment, *n.* the act of debating; controversy; debate. [Rare.]

dē·bāt′ẽr, *n.* one who debates; a disputant; a controvertist; one who takes part in a formal debate, usually as one of a team.

dē·bāt′ing, *n.* the act of a person or persons who debate.
debating society; a society for the purpose of formal debate and improvement in extemporaneous speaking.

dē·bāt′ing·ly, *adv.* in the manner of a debate.

dē·bạuch′, *v.t.*; debauched (dē-bạcht′), *pt., pp.*; debauching, *ppr.* [OFr. *desbaucher,* to corrupt, seduce, lit. to hew away; *des-* priv., away from, and *baucher,* to hew, chip.]
1. to corrupt or vitiate; as, to *debauch* a youth, to *debauch* good principles.
2. to corrupt with lewdness; to seduce; as, to *debauch* a woman.
3. to seduce from duty or allegiance; as, to *debauch* an army.

dē·bạuch′, *v.i.* to take part in debauchery; to dissipate.

dē·bạuch′, *n.* 1. excess in eating or drinking; intemperance; drunkenness; gluttony; lewdness; debauchery.
 2. a time or period of debauchery; an orgy.

dē·bạuched′ (-bạcht′), *a.* corrupted; vitiated in habits and character; profligate.

dē·bạuch′ed·ly, *adv.* in a debauched manner.

dē·bạuch′ed·ness, *n.* the condition of being debauched; intemperance.

deb·au·chee′, *n.* one given to debauchery; one habitually lewd or profligate; a dissipated or depraved person.

dē·bạuch′ẽr, *n.* one who debauches or corrupts others.

dē·bạuch′ẽr·y, *n.*; *pl.* **dē·bạuch′ẽr·ies**, 1. extreme indulgence of one's appetites, especially for sensual pleasure; gross intemperance; lustfulness; gluttony.
 2. seduction from duty or allegiance; a leading astray morally.
 3. [*pl.*] orgies.

dē·bạuch′ment, *n.* the act of debauching or corrupting; the act of seducing from virtue or duty.

dē·bạuch′ness, *n.* debauchedness. [Obs.]

dē·bel′, *v.t.* to subdue. [Obs.]

dē·bel′lāte, *v.t.* to debel. [Obs.]

deb·el·lā′tion, *n.* the act of conquering or subduing. [Obs.]

dē bē′ne es′sē, [L. *de*, of, for, *bene*, well, *esse*, to be.] well-being, or conditional allowance. In law, to take an order or testimony *de bene esse* is to take or allow it for the present, but subject to be suppressed or disallowed on a further or full examination.

dē·ben′tūre, *n.* [Fr., from L. *debentur*, 3d pers. pl. ind. pres. of *debere*, to owe; so called because these receipts began with the Latin words *debentur mihi*, there are owing to me.]
 1. a voucher or certificate acknowledging that a debt is owed by the signer.
 2. a customhouse order for payment of a drawback, as to an importer.
 3. a government voucher of indebtedness.
 4. an interest-bearing bond issued, often without security, by a corporation.

dē·ben′tūred, *a.* entitled to a drawback; as, *debentured* goods.

deb′ile, *a.* [OFr. *debile*; L. *debilis*, weak; *de-* priv., and *habilis*, able.] weak; feeble.

dē·bil′i·tāte, *v.t.*; debilitated, *pt.*, *pp.*; debilitating, *ppr.* [L. *debilitatus*, pp. of *debilitare*, to weaken, from *debilis*, weak.] to weaken; to impair the strength of; to enfeeble; to make faint or languid; as, excessive indulgence *debilitates* the system.
 Syn.—enervate, enfeeble, impair.

dē·bil·i·tā′tion, *n.* the act of debilitating or the state of being debilitated.

dē·bil′i·ty, *n.*; *pl.* **dē·bil′i·ties**, [Fr. *débilité*; L. *debilitas*, weakness, from *debilis*, weak.] weakness; feebleness; languor of body; faintness: usually applied to the body; as, his *debility* was extreme.

deb′it, *n.* [L. *debitum*, what is owing, a debt; neut. pp. of *debere*, to owe.]
 1. a debt. [Obs.]
 2. an entry on the left-hand side of an account, as of money owed; also, the total of such entries.
 3. the left-hand side or column of an account, where such entries are made.

deb′it, *v.t.*; debited, *pt.*, *pp.*; debiting, *ppr.*
 1. to charge with a debt; as, to *debit* a purchaser.
 2. to enter as a debit or debits; to enter on the left-hand side of an account; as, to *debit* the amount of goods sold.

deb′it·ŏr, *n.* a debtor. [Obs.]

dē·bi·tū″mi·ni·zā′tion, *n.* the act of debituminizing.

dē·bi·tū′mi·nīze, *v.t.* to remove bitumen from.

dé·blai′ (dā-blā′), *n.* [Fr.] in fortification, the place from which earth is removed in building a parapet.

deb·ō·nāir′, **deb·ō·nāire′**, *a.* [ME. *debonaire*; OFr. *de bon aire*, lit. of good mien.]
 1. having an affable manner; genial; courteous.
 2. gay; jaunty.

deb·ō·nāir′i·ty, *n.* the state of being debonair. [Obs.]

deb·ō·nāir′ly, *adv.* in a debonair manner.

deb·ō·nāir′ness, *n.* the quality of being debonair.

de bọnne″ grȧce′, [Fr.] with good grace; graciously.

Deb′ō·rȧh, *n.* [Heb. *debōrāh*, lit., a bee.] in the Bible, a prophetess and one of the judges of Israel, who helped the Israelites free themselves from the Canaanites. Jud. iv. v.

dē·bosh′, **dē·bosh′ment**, *etc.* obsolete or archaic forms of *debauch*, *debauchment*, etc.

dē·bouçh′, *v.i.* [Fr. *deboucher*, to emerge from; *de*, from, and *boucher*, to stop up, from *bouche*, mouth; L. *bucca*, cheek.]
 1. in military usage, to march out of a confined place, as a defile, into open country.
 2. to issue; to come forth; to emerge.

dé·bou·ché′ (dā-bö-shā′), *n.* [Fr., from *deboucher*, to open up.]
 1. an opening for troops to debouch through.
 2. a commercial outlet for goods.

de·bouçh′ment, *n.* [Fr. *débouchement*.]
 1. a debouching.
 2. a mouth (of a river); an outlet.

dé·bou·chure′ (dā-bö-shụr′), *n.* [Fr.] the outlet of a valley or an extended body of water.

dé·bride′ment (dā-brēd′mäṅ), *n.* [Fr., from *debrider*, to unbridle; *de-* priv., and *bride*, bridle, from AS. *bridel*, bridle.] in surgery, the cutting away of dead or contaminated tissue from a wound to prevent infection.

dē·brïef′, *v.t.* [*de-*, and *brief*.] to receive information from (a pilot, emissary, etc.) concerning a flight or mission just completed and, often, to instruct as to restrictions in making this information public.

de·bris′, **dé·bris′** (de-brē′ *or* dā-brē′), *n.* [Fr. *débris*, fragments, from *desbriser*, to break apart.]
 1. scattered fragments; remains; rubbish, especially that caused by destruction; ruins.
 2. in geology, any heap of rock fragments, as at the bases of cliffs, or in drift.

dē·brụiṣe′, *v.t.* and *v.i.* to bruise or be bruised. [Obs.]

dē·brụiṣed′, *a.* [ME. *debrusen*, *debrisen*, to break apart; OFr. *debruiser*, to break, break open; *de*, apart, and *brusier*, to break.] in heraldry, surmounted or partly covered by an ordinary; as, a lion *debruised*.

A LION DEBRUISED

debt (det), *n.* [ME. *det*, *dette*; OFr. *dette*, *debte*, debt, from L. *debitum*, neut. pp. of *debere*, to owe; *de*, from, and *habere*, to have.]
 1. that which is due from one person to another or others, whether goods, money, or services; something owed.
 2. an obligation or liability to pay or return something.
 3. the condition of being under obligation to pay money to, or perform services for, another; as, I am in his *debt*.
 4. neglected moral duty; sin; trespass.
 Forgive us our *debts*. — Matt. vi. 12.
 action of debt; in law, an action for the recovery of a specified sum of money alleged to be due.
 bonded debt; see under *bonded*.
 debt of honor; a debt, such as a gambling debt, which cannot be collected by law.
 debt of nature; death.
 floating debt; the unfunded debt of a corporation or government.
 funded debt; see under *funded*.
 national debt; indebtedness of government to creditors: it is funded and based upon public securities.
 preferred debt; a debt of such a character as to have priority of payment.

debt′ed (det′ed), *a.* indebted; bounden. [Obs.]

debt·ee′, *n.* in law, a creditor.

debt′less, *a.* free from debt.

debt′ŏr, *n.* [ME. *dettur*; OFr. *detor*; L. *debitor*, a debtor, from *debitus*, pp. of *debere*, to owe.] one who owes goods, money, or services to another; one who is in debt: opposed to *creditor*.

dē·bug′, *v.t.*; debugged, *pt.*, *pp.*; debugging, *ppr.* [*de-*, and *bug*.]
 1. to remove insects from.
 2. to find and correct the defects, errors, malfunctioning parts, etc. in. [Slang.]
 3. to find and remove hidden electronic listening devices from (a room, building, etc.). [Slang.]

dē·bul′li·āte, *v.i.* to boil over. [Obs.]

deb·ul·li′tion, *n.* a boiling over. [Obs.]

dē·buṅk′, *v.t.*; debunked, *pt.*, *pp.*; debunking, *ppr.* [*de-*, and *bunk* (nonsense).] to expose the false or exaggerated claims, pretensions, glamour, etc. of. [Colloq.]

dē·bũrse′, *v.t.* and *v.i.* to disburse. [Obs.]

dẹ·būt′, **dé·but′** (dā-bū′ *or* dā′bū), *n.* [Fr. *début*, from *débuter*, to lead off (at bowls, etc.), from (*jouer*) *de but*, (to play) for the mark.]
 1. a first appearance before the public, as of an actor.
 2. the formal introduction of a girl to society.
 3. the beginning of a career, course, etc.

de·būt′, **dé·but′**, *v.i.* to make a debut.

deb·ū·tänt′, **dé·bu·tant′** (dā-bū-tänt′), *n.* [Fr. *débutant*, ppr. of *débuter*; see *debut*.] a person making a debut.

deb·ū·tänte′, **dé·bu·tante′** (dā-bū-tänt′), *n.* [Fr., fem. of *débutant*.] a girl or woman making a debut, especially into high society.

deç·a-, [from L. *decem*, Gr. *deka*, ten.] a combining form meaning *ten*, as in *decagon*, *decameter*: also, before a vowel, *dec-*.

De·çac′e·rȧ, *n.pl.* [*deca-*, and Gr. *keras*, horn.] in zoology, an order of cephalopods having five pairs of arms or tentacles: also called *Decapoda*.

dē·çac′ẽr·ous, *a.* pertaining to the *Decacera*.

deç′ȧ·çhord, *n.* [*deca-*, and Gr. *chordē*, a chord.] a harplike musical instrument having ten strings.

deç·ȧ·çhor′dŏn, *n.* decachord. [Obs.]

deç′ad, *n.* [L. *decas*; Gr. *dekas*, the number ten; *deka*, ten.]
 1. in ancient philosophy, the number ten, considered to be the perfect number by the Pythagoreans.
 2. a decade.

deç′ȧ·dăl, *a.* pertaining to or consisting of tens.

deç′ȧ·dā·ry, *a.* pertaining to a period of ten days.

deç·ȧ·dā′tion, *n.* in music, the process of modulation by decades.

deç′āde, *n.* [L. *decas*; Gr. *dekas*, the number ten; *deka*, ten.]
 1. a period of time covering ten years.
 2. any group or set of ten.
 3. one of ten parts or divisions of a literary work; as, the third *decade* of Livy.

dē·çā′dence, **dē·çā′den·cy** (*or* dek′ȧ-), *n.* [Fr. *décadence*, a falling away, from L. *de*, from, and *cadens*, ppr. of *cadere*, to fall.] a decline in force or quality; a falling away; process, condition, or period of decline, as in morals, art, literature, etc.; decay; deterioration.

dē·çā′dent (*or* dek′ȧ-), *a.* [Fr. *décadent*: term applied to themselves by young Fr. writers of late 19th c. who openly admired Roman decadence.] in a state of decline; characterized by decadence.

dē·çā′dent (*or* dek′ȧ-), *n.* a decadent person, especially a decadent writer or artist.

deç′ȧ·dist, *n.* [from Gr. *deka*, ten.] an author whose writings comprise ten parts or volumes. [Rare.]

deç′ȧ·drachm (-dram), *n.* same as *dekadrachm*.

dē·caf′fē·in·āte, *v.t.*; decaffeinated, *pt.*, *pp.*; decaffeinating, *ppr.* to remove the caffein from.

dē·caf′fē·in·īze, *v.t.*; decaffeinized, *pt.*, *pp.*; decaffeinizing, *ppr.* to decaffeinate.

deç′ȧ·gon, *n.* [*deca*, and Gr. *gonia*, an angle.] in geometry, a plane figure having ten sides and ten angles.
 regular decagon; in geometry, a decagon whose sides and angles are equal.

de·cag′ō·năl, *a.* pertaining to or resembling a decagon; ten-sided.

deç′ȧ·gram, **deç′ȧ·gramme**, *n.* [*deca-*, and Gr. *gramma*, a thing drawn or written.] in the metric system, a weight equal to ten grams, 154.32349 troy grains, or 0.353 ounce avoirdupois.

deç′ȧ·gyn, *n.* [*deca-*, and Gr. *gynē*, a woman.] in botany, a plant of the order *Decagynia*, having ten pistils.

Deç·ȧ·gyn′i·ȧ, *n.pl.* [L., from Gr. *deka*, ten, and *gynē*, a woman.] in the Linnaean botanic system, the tenth order in the first thirteen classes, including plants with ten pistils.

deç·ȧ·gyn′i·ăn, *a.* in botany, belonging to the order *Decagynia*.

de·çag′y·nous, *a.* same as *decagynian*.

deç·ȧ·hē′drăl, *a.* resembling a decahedron.

deç·ȧ·hē′drŏn, *n.*; *pl.* **deç·ȧ·hē′drŏnṣ**, **deç·ȧ·hē′drȧ**, [*deca-*, and Gr. *hedra*, a seat, base.] in geometry, a solid having ten plane surfaces.

dē·cal″ci·fi·çā′tion, *n.* a decalcifying or being decalcified.

dē·cal′ci·fī·ẽr, *n.* a thing that decalcifies.

dē·cal′ci·fȳ, *v.t.*; decalcified, *pt.*, *pp.*; decalcifying, *ppr.* to remove calcareous matter from (bones, teeth, etc.).

dē·cal·cō·mā′ni·ȧ, *n.* [Fr. *décalcomanie*, from *décalquer*, to counterdraw, and Gr. *mania*, madness.]
 1. the art of transferring pictures and ornamental designs from specially prepared paper to china, glass, wood, etc., and fixing them permanently.
 2. a picture or design of this kind.

dē·çȧ·les′cence, *n.* [*de*, from, and L. *calescere*,

to become warm.] a sudden decrease in the rate of temperature rise of heated metal after a certain degree of temperature has been reached (795° C. for iron), due to greater absorption of heat.

dē·ca·les′cent, *a.* of or subject to decalescence.

deç′ȧ·lī·tẽr, deç′ȧ·lī·tre(-tẽr), *n.* [*deca-*, and Fr. *litre*, a liter; Gr. *litra*, a pound.] in the metric system, a measure of capacity equal to ten liters (2.64 gallons liquid measure or 9.08 quarts dry measure).

Dē·çal′ō·ġist, *n.* a commentator or expounder of the decalogue.

Deç′ȧ·logue (-log), **Deç′ȧ·log,** *n.* [ME. *decaloge*; LL. *decalogus*; Gr. *dekalogos*, the decalogue; *deka*, ten, and *logos*, word or speech, from *legein*, to speak.] [*sometimes* d–] the Ten Commandments; the precepts received by Moses on Mount Sinai, originally written on two tables of stone.

dē·çal′vănt, *a.* hair-removing; denoting that which destroys hair roots.

Dē·çam′e·ron, *n.* [It. *Decamerone*, from Gr. *deka*, ten, and *meros*, part, share.]

1. a collection of a hundred tales written by Boccaccio in the fourteenth century.

2. [d–] any book or literary work divided into ten parts; a decade.

Dē·çam·e·ron′iç, *a.* pertaining to or in the style of the Decameron.

dē·çam′ẽr·ous, *a.* [*deca-*, and Gr. *meros*, part.] in botany, having the parts in tens: said of flowers: also written *10-merous.*

deç′ȧ·mē·tẽr, deç′ȧ·mē·tre, *n.* [Fr. *décamètre*, a length of ten meters; Gr. *deka*, ten, and *metron*, a measure.] in the metric system, a measure of length containing ten meters, equal to 393.70 inches or 32.81 feet.

dē·çamp′, *v.i.*; decamped, *pt.*, *pp.*; decamping, *ppr.* [Fr. *décamper*, to break camp; L. *de*, from, and *campus*, a camp.]

1. to depart from a camping ground; to break camp and resume the march, as troops.

2. to run away; to go away suddenly and secretly.

3. to camp. [Rare.]

dē·çamp′ment, *n.* a decamping.

deç′ȧ·năl, *a.* 1. pertaining to a dean or to a deanery.

2. same as *decani*.

deç′ȧ·nāte, *n.* [from LL. *decanatus*, the office of a *decanus*, or dean, from L. *decem*, ten.] in astrology, one of the zodiacal divisions of ten degrees.

dē·çan′dẽr, *n.* in botany, a plant with ten stamens.

Dē·çan′dri·ȧ, *n.pl.* [L., from Gr. *deka*, ten, and *anēr* (*andros*), a man.] in botany, the tenth class of plants in the Linnaean system. These plants have ten stamens.

DECANDER

dē·çan′drous, dē·çan′dri·ăn, *a.* in botany, pertaining to the class *Decandria.*

deç′āne, *n.* [from *deca-*, and *-ane.*] any of the isomeric hydrocarbons having the formula $C_{10}H_{22}$ and belonging to the methane series, present in petroleum or in certain petroleum products, such as kerosene.

deç·an′gū·lăr, *a.* [*deca-*, and L. *angulus*, an angle.] having ten angles.

dē·çā′nī, *a.* [L., genit. of *decanus*, a dean.] pertaining to a dean; as, the *decani* side of a church, the side on which the dean's stall is located.

dē·çant′, *v.t.*; decanted, *pt.*, *pp.*; decanting, *ppr.* [Fr. *décanter*, to pour off from the edge of a vessel; *de*, from, and OFr. *cant*, edge; L. *canthus*, the iron ring round a carriage wheel.] to pour off gently, as liquor from its sediment; also, to pour from one vessel into another; as, to *decant* wine.

dē·çan′tāte, *v.t.* and *v.i.* to sing or say repeatedly. [Obs.]

dē·çan·tā′tion, *n.* the act of pouring off a clear fluid gently from its lees or sediment, or from one vessel into another.

dē·çant′ẽr, *n.* 1. a vessel used to decant liquors, or for receiving decanted liquors; a glass bottle for table service used for holding wine or other liquors.

2. one who decants liquors.

deç·ȧ·pet′ăl·ous, *a.* [*deca-*, and Gr. *petalon*, a leaf.] in botany, having ten petals.

deç·ȧ·phyl′lous, *a.* [*deca-*, and Gr. *phyllon*, a leaf.] in botany, having ten leaves.

dē·çap′i·tāte, *v.t.*; decapitated, *pt.*, *pp.*; decapitating, *ppr.* [L. *de*, off, and *caput*, head.]

1. to behead; to cut off the head of.

2. to remove from office. [Colloq.]

dē·çap·i·tā′tion, *n.* a beheading or being beheaded; execution by beheading.

2. dismissal from office. [Colloq.]

dē·çap′i·tā·tŏr, *n.* a person or thing that decapitates.

deç′ȧ·pod, dē·çap′ō·dăl, dē·çap′ō·dous, *a.* pertaining to the *Decapoda*; having ten arms or legs.

deç′ȧ·pod, *n.* [*deca-*, and *-pod.*] one of the *Decapoda.*

Dē·çap′ō·dȧ, *n.pl.* [L., from Gr. *deka*, ten, and *pous* (*podos*), foot.]

1. an order of crustaceans having five pairs of legs, including crabs, lobsters, shrimps, etc.

2. the ten-armed cephalopods, including the cuttlefishes, squids, etc.: also called *Decacera.*

dē·çap′ō·dăl, *a.* same as *decapod.*

deç·ȧ·pod′i·form, *a.* [L. *decapus*, the decapod, and *forma*, shape.] in entomology, having the form of a crawfish or lobster.

dē·çap′ō·dous, *a.* same as *decapod.*

dē·çär′bŏn·āte, *v.t.* to remove carbon dioxide or carbonic acid from.

dē·çär″bŏn·i·zā′tion, *n.* the act or process of decarbonizing.

dē·çär′bŏn·īze, *v.t.* to remove carbon from.

dē·çär·box·y·lā′tion, *n.* [*de-*, and *carboxyl*, and *-ation.*] the removal of a molecule of carbon dioxide from amino acids and proteins by bacterial action, with the resultant formation of amines.

dē·çär″bū·ri·zā′tion, *n.* the act or process of decarbonizing.

dē·çär′bū·rīze, *v.t.*; decarburized, *pt.*, *pp.*; decarburizing, *ppr.* to decarbonize.

dē·çärd′, *v.t.* to discard. [Obs.]

dē·çär′di·năl·īze, *v.t.* to remove from the rank of a cardinal.

deç′āre, *n.* [Fr.] in the metric system, a unit of surface measure equal to ten ares (0.2471 acre).

deç·ȧ·sep′ăl·ous, *a.* [*deca-*, and L. *sepalum*, a leaf.] in botany, having ten sepals.

deç′ȧ·stēre, *n.* [Fr. *decastere*; Gr. *deka*, ten, and *stereos*, solid.] in the metric system, a measure of volume equal to ten steres, or ten cubic meters (13.08 cubic yards).

deç′ȧ·stiçh, *n.* [*deca-*, and Gr. *stichos*, a verse.] a poem containing ten lines.

deç′ȧ·style, *a.* [*deca-*, and Gr. *stylos*, a column.] having or consisting of ten columns; as, a *decastyle* portico, a *decastyle* temple.

deç″ȧ·syl·lab′iç, *a.* [*deca-*, and Gr. *syllabē*, a syllable.]

1. having ten syllables.

2. of a decasyllable.

deç″ȧ·syl·lab′iç, *n.* a decasyllable.

deç′ȧ·syl·lȧ·ble, *n.* a line of verse having ten syllables.

deç·ath′lŏn, *n.* [from *deca-*, and Gr. *athlon*, a contest.] an athletic contest in which each contestant takes part in ten events (100-meter dash, broad jump, 16-pound shot-put, high jump, 400-meter dash, 110-meter hurdles, discus throw, pole vault, javelin throw, and 1500-meter run): the winner is the contestant receiving the highest total of points.

deç·ȧ·tō′iç, *a.* in chemistry, relating to or derived from decane.

dē·çau′dāte, *v.t.* [*de-* priv., and L. *cauda*, tail.] to deprive of the tail.

dē·çāy′, *v.i.*; decayed, *pt.*, *pp.*; decaying, *ppr.* [OFr. dial. *decair*, decay, decline, from L. *decidere*, to fall down, to fall away; *de*, down, and *cadere*, to fall.]

1. to pass gradually from a sound or prosperous state to one of less perfection; to fail; to be gradually impaired; to deteriorate.

2. to become rotten.

dē·çāy′, *v.t.* to cause to fail, deteriorate, rot, etc.; to impair.

dē·çāy′, *n.* 1. gradual decline of health, strength, soundness, prosperity, etc.; tendency toward dissolution or extinction.

2. a wasting away.

3. a rotting or chemical decomposition, as of vegetable matter.

4. rottenness.

5. the gradual disintegration of radioactive substances.

6. destruction; death. [Obs.]

7. cause of decay. [Rare.]

Syn.—decline, decadence, degeneracy, collapse, downfall.

dē·çāyed′, *a.* having deteriorated; impaired; weakened.

dē·çāy′ed·ness, *n.* a state of being impaired; a decayed state.

dē·çāy′ẽr, *n.* that which causes decay. [Rare.]

dē·cēase′, *n.* [ME. *deces*, *deses*; OFr. *deces*, death, departure, from L. *decessus*, pp. of *decedere*, to depart, go away; *de*, from, and *cedere*, to go, move.] departure from this life; death.

Syn.—death, demise, departure, dissolution, release.

dē·cēase′, *v.i.* deceased (-sēst), *pt.*, *pp.*; deceasing, *ppr.* to depart from this life; to die.

dē·cēased′ (-sēst′), *a.* departed from life; dead. *the deceased*; (a) the dead person; (b) dead persons; the dead.

dē·cēde′, *v.i.* to depart. [Obs.]

dē·cē′dent, *n.* [L. *decedens*, ppr. of *decedere*, to depart.] in law, the deceased; dead person.

dē·cēit′, *n.* [ME. *deceite*; OFr. *deceite*, deceit; L. *deceptus*, pp. of *decipere*, to deceive; *de*, from, and *capere*, to take.]

1. the act of representing as true what is known to be false; deceiving; lying; the misleading of a person.

2. the quality of being deceitful.

3. in law, any trick, device, collusion, shift, or underhand practice, used to defraud another.

Syn.—deception, double-dealing, cunning, duplicity, fraud, guile, trickery, hypocrisy.

dē·cēit′fụl, *a.* 1. tending to mislead, deceive, or ensnare; apt to lie or cheat; as, a *deceitful* man.

2. intended to deceive; deceptive; false; tricky; fraudulent; cheating; as, *deceitful* practices.

dē·cēit′fụl·ly, *adv.* in a deceitful manner; fraudulently.

dē·cēit′fụl·ness, *n.* 1. tendency to mislead or deceive; as, the *deceitfulness* of sin.

2. the quality of being fraudulent; as, the *deceitfulness* of a man's practices.

3. the disposition to deceive; as, a man's *deceitfulness* may be habitual.

dē·cēit′less, *a.* free from deceit. [Rare.]

dē·cēiv′ȧ·ble, *a.* 1. subject to deceit or imposition; capable of being misled or entrapped; as, young persons are very *deceivable.* [Rare.]

2. apt to produce error or deception; deceitful. [Archaic.]

dē·cēiv′ȧ·ble·ness, *n.* liability to deceive or be deceived. [Rare.]

dē·cēiv′ȧ·bly, *adv.* in a deceivable manner. [Rare.]

dē·cēive′, *v.t.*; deceived, *pt.*, *pp.*; deceiving, *ppr.* [ME. *deceyven*; OFr. *decever*; L. *decipere*, to take down or from, to beguile, deceive; *de*, from, and *capere*, to take.]

1. to make (a person) believe what is not true; to mislead; to cause to err; to impose on; to delude; to cheat.

2. to beguile; to divert; to while away (time). [Archaic.]

dē·cēive′, *v.i.* to use deceit; to lie, etc.

dē·cēiv′ẽr, *n.* one who deceives; one who leads into error; a cheat; an impostor.

dē·cel′ẽr·āte, *v.t.* and *v.i.*; decelerated, *pt.*, *pp.*; decelerating, *ppr.* [*de-*, and *accelerate.*] to slow down: opposed to *accelerate.*

dē·cel″ẽr·ā′tion, *n.* a decelerating or being decelerated.

dē·cel′ẽr·ā·tŏr (-tẽr), *n.* a person or thing that decelerates.

dē·cel″ẽr·om′e·tẽr, *n.* [*deceleration*, and *-meter.*] an instrument used to measure the rate of deceleration of a moving vehicle.

dē′cem-, [from L. *decem*, ten.] a combining form meaning *ten.*

Dē·cem′bẽr, *n.* [OFr. *decembre*; L. *December*, from *decem*, ten, this being the tenth month among the early Romans, who reckoned from March.]

1. the twelfth and last month of the year, in which the sun enters the Tropic of Capricorn, and makes the winter solstice. It has thirty-one days.

2. figuratively, the period of old age; as, he had reached the *December* of life.

Dē·cem′brist, *n.* in Russian history, one of the conspirators against Czar Nicholas I on his accession to the Russian throne in December, 1825.

dē·cem·den′tāte, *a.* [*decem-*, and L. *dentatus*, having teeth.] having ten points or teeth.

dē·cem′fid, *a.* [*decem-*, and L. *findere*, to divide.]

1. cleft or divided into ten parts.

2. in botany, separated into ten lobes or segments.

dē·cem·loç′ū·lăr, *a.* [*decem-*, and L. *loculus*, a

small receptacle, dim. of *locus*, a place.] in botany, having ten cells for seeds.

dē·cem·pär′tīte, *a.* same as *decamerous.*

dē·cem′pe·dăl, *a.* [LL. *decempedalis*, ten feet in length; L. *decem*, ten, and *pes* (*pedis*), a foot.]

1. ten feet in length. [Obs.]

2. same as *decapod.*

dē·cem·pen′nāte, *a.* [*decem-*, and L. *penna*, a wing.] in ornithology, having ten developed flight feathers.

dē·cem′vĭr, *n.*; *pl.* **dē·cem′vĭrș, dē·cem′vi·rī,** [L. *decem*, ten, and *vir*, a man.]

1. one of ten magistrates who had absolute authority in ancient Rome: in 450 B. C. this body drew up the first Roman code of laws.

2. a member of any official body consisting of ten men.

dē·cem′vi·răl, *a.* pertaining to the Roman decemvirs.

dē·cem′vi·rāte, *n.* [L. *decemviratus*, the rank or office of the decemvirs.]

1. the office or term of office of the Roman decemvirs.

2. any body of ten men in authority.

dē·cem′vĭr·ship, *n.* the office, rank, or dignity of a decemvir.

dē·cen′ȧ·ry, dē·cen′nȧ·ry, *a.* [ML. *decenarius*, from *decena*, a tithing, from L. *decem*, ten.] of a tithing.

dē·cen′ȧ·ry, dē·cen′nȧ·ry, *n.*; *pl.* **dē·cen′ȧ·rieș, dē·cen′nȧ·rieș,** a tithing.

dē′cence, *n.* decency. [Obs.]

dē′cen·cy, *n.*; *pl.* **dē′cen·cieș,** [OFr. *decence*; L. *decentia*, comeliness.]

1. the quality or condition of being decent; propriety of conduct and speech; proper observance of the requirements of modesty, good taste, etc.

2. [*pl.*] socially proper actions; as, observe the *decencies.*

3. [*pl.*] things needed for a proper or comfortable standard of living.

Syn.—decorum, propriety, modesty, suitableness, becomingness.

dē·cen′nȧ·ry, *n.*; *pl.* **dē·cen′nȧ·rieș,** [L. *decennis*, lasting ten years; *decem*, ten, and *annus*, a year.] a period of ten years.

dē·cen′nȧ·ry, *a.* ten-year; decennial.

dē·cen′ni·ăl, *a.* [L. *decem*, ten, and *annus*, a year.]

1. of or continuing for ten years.

2. happening every ten years; as, *decennial* games.

dē·cen′ni·ăl, *n.* a tenth anniversary or its celebration.

dē·cen′ni·um, *n.*; *pl.* **dē·cen′ni·umș, dē·cen′ni·ȧ,** [L., from *decem*, ten, and *annus*, a year.] a period covering ten years; a decade.

dē·cen′nō·văl, *a.* [LL. *decennovalis*, of nineteen years; L. *decem*, ten, and *novem*, nine.] pertaining to the number nineteen; designating a period or cycle of nineteen years. [Obs.]

dē·cen′nō·vā·ry, *a.* decennoval. [Obs.]

dē′cent, *a.* [Fr. *decent*; L. *decens* (*decentis*), *comely*, fitting, ppr. of *decere*, to become, be fitting.]

1. proper and fitting.

2. not immodest; not obscene; chaste.

3. conforming to approved social standards; respectable.

4. satisfactory; fairly good; adequate; as, *decent* wages.

5. fair; kind; generous; as, he is very *decent* to me.

6. adequately clothed for propriety. [Colloq.]

7. comely; shapely. [Obs.]

A sable stole of Cyprus lawn,
O'er the *decent* shoulders drawn.
—Milton.

Syn.—suitable, modest, respectable, befitting, decorous, proper, seemly, becoming.

dē·cen′tẽr, dē·cen′tre (-tẽr), *v.t.* 1. to put out of center; to make (a thing) eccentric.

2. to cut (a lens) so that the optical and geometrical centers are not the same.

dē′cent·ly, *adv.* in a decent manner.

dē′cent·ness, *n.* decency; the quality of being decent.

dē·cen″trăl·i·zā′tion, *n.* the act of decentralizing or the state of being decentralized.

dē·cen′trăl·īze, *v.t.* to break up the centralization of authority, as in a government or industry, and distribute among more places, local authorities, etc.

dē·ceph″ȧ·li·zā′tion, *n.* [*de-* priv., and Gr. *kephalē*, head.] in zoology, degeneration or degradation of cephalic parts: opposed to *cephalization.*

dē·ceph′ȧ·līze, *v.t.*; decephalized, *pt.*, *pp.*; decephalizing, *ppr.* to effect decephalization of; to degrade or simplify the cephalic parts of.

dē·cep·ti·bil′i·ty, *n.* the liability or capability of being deceived. [Rare.]

dē·cep′ti·ble, *a.* [from L. *deceptus*, pp. of *decipere*, to deceive.] capable of being deceived; deceivable. [Rare.]

dē·cep′tion, *n.* 1. the act or practice of deceiving or misleading.

2. the fact or condition of being deceived or misled.

3. something deceiving, as an illusion, or meant to deceive, as a fraud, imposture, etc.

Syn.—deceit, fraud, imposition, artifice, cheat, ruse, stratagem, trick.—*Deception* usually refers to the act, and *deceit*, to the habit of the mind; hence, a person is spoken of as skilled in *deception* and addicted to *deceit*. An *imposition* is an act of deception practiced upon someone to his annoyance or injury; a *fraud* implies the use of stratagem with a view to some unlawful gain or advantage.

dē·cep′tious, *a.* tending to deceive; deceitful. [Rare.]

dē·cep′tive, *a.* deceiving or intended to deceive.

deceptive cadence; in music, the close of a phrase on any other chord than that of the tonic preceded by that of the dominant.

dē·cep′tive·ly, *adv.* in a deceptive manner.

dē·cep′tive·ness, *n.* the power of deceiving; the tendency or aptness to deceive.

dē·cep·tiv′i·ty, *n.* 1. that which deceives; a sham. [Rare.]

2. the power or tendency to deceive.

dē·cep′tō·ry, *a.* deceptive. [Obs.]

dē·cer′ē·brize, *v.t.* to remove the cerebrum from. [Rare.]

dē·cẽrn′, *v.t.* [OFr. *decerner*; L. *decernere*, to decide, judge; *de*, from, and *cernere*, to separate, distinguish.]

1. to discern. [Obs.]

2. in Scots law, to decree by judicial sentence.

dē·cẽrn′i·tūre, *n.* in Scots law, a decree or sentence of a court; as, he resolved to appeal against the *decerniture* of the judge.

dē·cẽrp′, *v.t.* to pluck off; to crop. [Obs.]

dē·cẽrp′tion, *n.* [L. *decerpere*, to pluck off; *de*, from, and *carpere*, to pluck.]

1. a pulling or plucking off; a cropping. [Obs.]

2. that which is pulled off or separated; a fragment. [Obs.]

dē·cẽr·tā′tion, *n.* [L. *decertare*, to fight, contend; *de*, and *certare*, to fight, contend.] strife; contest for mastery. [Obs.]

dē·ces′sion (-sesh′un), *n.* departure; decrease; diminution. [Rare.]

dē·chärm′, *v.t.* to remove the spell or enchantment of; to disenchant. [Obs.]

deçh′en·īte, *n.* [named after Von *Dechen*, a German geologist.] in mineralogy, a vanadate of lead found free in nature and occurring in massive form.

dē·çhris′tiăn·īze, *v.t.*; dechristianized, *pt.*, *pp.*; dechristianizing, *ppr.* to turn from Christianity; to banish Christian belief and principles from.

dec′i-, [from L. *decimus*, tenth, from *decem*, ten.] a combining form meaning *one tenth of* (a specified unit), as in *deci*gram, *deci*meter: used in the metric system.

dec′i·āre, *n.* in the metric system, a measure of surface, one tenth of an are (10 square meters or 11.96 square yards).

dec′i·bel, *n.* [*deci-*, and *bel.*] a unit for measuring the volume of a sound, equal to the logarithm of the ratio of the intensity of the sound to the intensity of an arbitrarily chosen standard sound.

dē·cīd′ȧ·ble, *a.* capable of being decided.

dē·cīde′, *v.t.*; decided, *pt.*, *pp.*; deciding, *ppr.* [Fr. *décider*; L. *decidere*, to cut off, to decide; *de*, off, from, and *cædere*, to cut.]

1. to cut off; to separate. [Obs.]

2. to bring to an end; to determine, as a question, contest, controversy, or struggle, by some recognized authority; to settle in favor of one side or the other; to determine the issue or result of; as, the court *decided* the case for the plaintiff.

3. to cause to reach a decision.

Syn.—determine, resolve, settle, fix, adjust, regulate, arrange.

dē·cīde′, *v.i.* 1. to pass judgment.

2. to make up one's mind; to form a definite opinion; to come to a conclusion.

dē·cīd′ed, *a.* 1. undoubted; definite; clear-cut; unmistakable; unquestionable.

2. resolute; determined; as, a *decided* character.

dē·cīd′ed·ly, *adv.* 1. definitely; unmistakably; certainly.

2. without hesitation; determinedly.

dē·cīd′ed·ness, *n.* the state of being decided.

dē·cīde′ment, *n.* the act of deciding; decision. [Obs.]

dec′i·dence, *n.* a falling off. [Rare.]

dē·cīd′ẽr, *n.* one who determines a cause or contest.

dē·cīd′ing·ly, *adv.* in a deciding manner.

dē·cid′ū·ȧ, *n.* [Mod. L., f. of *deciduus*, that which falls down, from *decidere*, to fall down.] in physiology, a membrane arising from alteration of the upper layer of the mucous membrane of the uterus, after the reception into the latter of the impregnated ovum, the name being given to it because it is discharged at parturition.

dē·cid′ū·ăl, *a.* of the decidua.

Dē·cid·ū·ā′tȧ, *n.pl.* in zoology, the division of mammals throwing off a decidua during parturition.

dē·cid′ū·āte, *a.* having a decidua; characteristic of the *Deciduata.*

dec·i·dū′i·ty, *n.* deciduousness. [Rare.]

dē·cid′ū·ous, *a.* [L. *deciduus*, that which falls down, from *decidere*, to fall down; *de*, down, and *cadere*, to fall.]

1. falling off at a certain season or stage of growth, as some leaves, antlers, the wings of certain insects, etc.

2. shedding leaves annually: opposed to *evergreen.*

3. short-lived; temporary.

dē·cid′ū·ous·ness, *n.* the quality of being deciduous.

dec′i·gram, dec′i·gramme, *n.* [Fr. *décigramme*, from L. *decimus*, tenth, and *gramma*, a gram.] a metric weight, equal to 1/10 gram (1.5432 grains or .003527 ounce).

dec′ile, dec′il, *n.* [Fr., from L. *decimus*, tenth, from *decem*, ten.]

1. an aspect or position of two planets, when they are distant from each other a tenth part of the zodiac.

2. in statistics, any of the values in a series dividing the distribution of the individuals in the series into ten groups of equal frequency; also, any of these groups.

dec′i·lī·tẽr, dec′i·lī·tre (-tẽr), *n.* [Fr. *décilitre*; L. *decimus*, tenth, and *litra*, a liter, from Gr. *litra*, a pound.] a metric measure of volume, equal to 1/10 liter (3.38 fluid ounces or 6.1025 cubic inches).

dē·cil′liŏn, *n.* [*decem-*, and *million.*]

1. in the United States and France, 1 followed by 33 zeros.

2. in England and Germany, 1 followed by 60 zeros.

dē·cil′liŏn, *a.* amounting to one decillion in number.

dē·cil′liŏnth, *a.* pertaining to a decillion; having the magnitude or position of one of a decillion equal parts.

dē·cil′liŏnth, *n.* one of a decillion equal parts.

dec′i·mȧ, *n.* 1. in music, an interval of ten diatonic degrees.

2. a Spanish coin.

dec′i·măl, *a.* [OFr. *decimal*; L. *decimus*, tenth, from *decem*, ten.]

1. relating to decimals; numbered by tens; increasing or diminishing by tens; as, *decimal* fractions, *decimal* coinage.

2. relating to tithes.

decimal arithmetic; the common system of arithmetic in which the decimal scale of numbers is used.

decimal fraction; a fraction whose denominator is ten or some power of ten, as $^7/_{10}$, $^{40}/_{100}$, $^{50}/_{1000}$. In the notation of decimals the denominator is usually omitted, and to indicate its value a point is placed to the left of the numerator, as .5 = $^5/_{10}$, .07 = $^7/_{100}$.

decimal measure; a measure the unit of which is divided into ten equal parts.

decimal notation or *numeration*; a system of numeral notation based on powers of ten.

decimal place; the position of a figure after the decimal point.

decimal point; a period placed just to the left of a decimal fraction.

decimal system; any system of measuring or reckoning by tenths, tens, or powers of ten.

dec′i·măl, *n.* a decimal fraction.

circulating decimal; a recurring decimal which repeats one figure or a set of figures indefinitely: also called *circulatory decimal.*

recurring decimal; same as *circulating decimal.*

repeating decimal; a recurring decimal fraction which repeats one figure indefinitely.

dec′i·măl·ism, *n.* the theory or system of

reckoning by decimals, as in systems of weights, measures, etc.

dec′i·măl·ist, *n.* one who employs or is an advocate of the decimal system.

dec″i·măl·i·zā′tion, *n.* the act of reducing or causing to conform to the decimal system.

dec′i·măl·īze, *v.t.* 1. to adopt the decimal system for; as, to *decimalize* currency, weights, measures, etc.
 2. to change into a decimal or decimals.

dec′i·măl·ly, *adv.* by tens; also, by means of decimals.

dec′i·māte, *v.t.*; decimated, *pt., pp.*; decimating, *ppr.* [L. *decimare*, from *decem*, ten.]
 1. to take or destroy a tenth part of.
 2. to select by lot and kill every tenth one of; as, to *decimate* an army or a collection of prisoners.
 3. to destroy or kill a great but indefinite number of; as, the inhabitants were *decimated* by fever.

dec·i·mā′tion, *n.* [L. *decimatio*, from *decimare*, to select the tenth by lot, to pay tithes; from *decimus*, tenth; *decem*, ten.] a decimating or being decimated.

dec′i·mā·tŏr, *n.* one who or that which decimates.

de·cime′, *n.* [Fr., from L. *decimus*, tenth.] a French coin, the tenth part of a franc.

dec′i·mē·tēr, dec′i·mē·tre (-tēr), *n.* [Fr., from *deci-*, and Gr. *metron*, a measure.] a measure of length in the metric system, equal to 1/10 meter (3.937 inches).

dec″i·mō·sex′tō, *a.* and *n.* same as *sextodecimo.*

dē·cī′phēr, *v.t.*; deciphered, *pt., pp.*; deciphering, *ppr.* [OFr. *de chiffrer*; *de*, from, and *cifre*, a cipher.]
 1. to translate from secret writing or code into comprehensible terms; to decode.
 2. to read, as that written in obscure, partially obliterated, or badly formed characters; to unfold.
 3. to discover or explain the meaning of, as of something that is obscure or difficult to be understood; as, to *decipher* an ambiguous speech.
 Syn.—interpret, translate, reveal, unravel, unfold, solve.

dē·cī′phēr·ȧ·ble, *a.* capable of being deciphered or interpreted.

dē·cī′phēr·ēr, *n.* a person who deciphers.

dē·cī′phēr·ess, *n.* a woman who deciphers.

dē·cī′phēr·ment, *n.* the act of deciphering.

dē·cip′i·um, *n.* [L., from *decipere*, to deceive.] formerly, a hypothetical metallic substance intermediate between cerium and yttrium.

dē·ci′ṣion (-sizh′un), *n.* [L. *decisio*, a cutting short, a decision, from *decisus*, pp. of *decidere*, to cut short, to decide.]
 1. the act of separating or cutting off; detachment of a part. [Obs.]
 2. the act of deciding or settling a dispute or question by giving a judgment.
 3. the act of making up one's mind.
 4. a judgment or conclusion reached or given.
 5. the quality of being decided; prompt determination; as, a man of *decision.*
 6. in boxing, a victory on points instead of by a knockout.
 Syn.—conclusion, disposal, resolution, determination, opinion.

dē·cī′sive, *a.* 1. having the power or quality of settling a dispute, question, doubt, contest, event, etc.; final; conclusive; as, the judgment of the court is *decisive*, a *decisive* victory.
 2. marked by decision or prompt determination; as, a *decisive* character.
 Syn.—decided, final, conclusive, unquestionable, unmistakable, positive.

dē·cī′sive·ly, *adv.* in a decisive manner.

dē·cī′sive·ness, *n.* the quality of being decisive.

dē·cī′sō·ry, *a.* same as *decisive.*

dec′i·stēre, *n.* [Fr., from *deci-*, tenth, and Gr. *stereos*, solid.] in the metric system, a measure of volume equal to 1/10 cubic meter (3.53 cubic feet).

dē·cit′i·zen·īze, *v.t.* to deprive of citizenship. [Rare.]

dē·civ′i·līze, *v.t.*; decivilized, *pt., pp.*; decivilizing, *ppr.* to reduce from a civilized to a wild or savage state.

deck, *v.t.*; decked (dekt), *pt., pp.*; decking, *ppr.* [ME. *decken*, to cover; M.D. *decken*, to hide.]
 1. to cover; to clothe, especially with elegance; to array; to embellish; as, she *decked* herself in all her finery.

 The dew with spangles *decked* the ground.
 —Dryden.

 2. to furnish with a deck, as a vessel.
 3. to cover. [Archaic.]
 Syn.—adorn embellish, array, decorate, ornament, beautify, bedeck, garnish.

deck, *n.* [M.D. *decke*, a cover.]
 1. a platform or roof over a section of a ship's hold, serving as a floor.
 2. any platform or floor like a ship's deck.
 3. in card playing, (a) the pack required to play any specified game; as, a euchre *deck*; (b) that part of the pack remaining after the players have received their hands.
 4. a pile; a heap. [Obs.]
 5. in mining, the platform of a cage.
 6. the roof of a railroad passenger car.
 cold deck; a pack of playing cards arranged before being dealt; a stacked deck. [Slang.]
 flush deck; a continued deck from stem to stern.
 on deck; ready for duty or action; hence, in baseball, next in turn to bat. [Colloq.]
 protective deck; a curved steel deck below the water, about three inches thick, serving to protect the machinery.
 to clear the decks; to prepare for action.
 to sweep the deck; (a) to carry away everything movable from the deck, as by a wave; (b) to command all parts of the deck; (c) in card playing, to take all the stakes on the table.

deck bēam, a strong, transverse piece of timber stretching across a ship from side to side, serving to support a deck.

deck bridge (brij), in railroad engineering, a bridge carrying the track upon the top, and not between the girders.

deck chāir, a lightweight, portable folding chair, generally with arms and a leg rest, used by passengers on ships, etc.

deck′el, *n.* same as *deckle.*

deck′ēr, *n.* one who or that which decks or adorns; a coverer; as, a table *decker.*

-deck′ēr, a combining form meaning *having* (a specified number of) *decks, layers*, etc., as in two-*decker*, triple-*decker.*

deck feath′ēr (feth′ēr), one of the pair of middle tail feathers of a bird, which cover those below and form a sort of deck.

deck hand, a sailor, especially one whose duty it is to work about the deck.

deck hook, the compass timber bolted horizontally athwart a ship's bow, connecting the stem, timbers, and deck planks of the fore part of a ship.

deç′kle (dek′l), *n.* [L.G. *dekkel*, a cover, lid.] in papermaking, a thin frame of wood fitting on the shallow mold in which the paper pulp is placed, serving to regulate the size or width of the sheet.

deç′kle edġe, the untrimmed edge of paper made in a deckle.

deç′kle-edġed (-ejd), *a.* having a deckle edge.

deck light, a thick piece of glass fitted into the deck to light the quarters below.

deck load, cargo carried above the upper deck of a ship.

deck quoits (kwoits), the game of quoits, when played on the deck of a ship.

deck ten′nis, a game resembling tennis, in which a small ring of rope, etc. is tossed back and forth over a net, often played on the deck of a ship.

dē·çlāim′, *v.i.*; declaimed, *pt., pp.*; declaiming, *ppr.* [ME. *declamen*; L. *declamare*, to cry aloud, declaim; *de-*, intens., and *clamare*, to cry, shout.]
 1. to make a formal speech or oration; to give a recitation; as, the students *declaim* twice a week.
 2. to speak or write for rhetorical display; to speak or write pompously or elaborately.
 3. to attack in an emotional speech: with *against.*

dē·çlāim′, *v.t.* 1. to recite or say in a rhetorical manner.
 2. to decry. [Obs.]
 3. to speak in favor of; to advocate. [Obs.]

dē·çlāim′ănt, *n.* a declaimer. [Rare.]

dē·çlāim′ēr, *n.* one who declaims.

deç·lȧ·mā′tion, *n.* [Fr. *declamation*; L. *declamatio*, declamation, from *declamare*, to speak aloud, declaim.]
 1. a declaiming or being declaimed.
 2. the act or art of speaking in public or of giving formal recitations.
 3. a speech or a selection of prose or poetry recited, or for recitation, in public.
 4. a harangue; bombastic oratory.
 5. in singing, clear and correct enunciation, especially in rendering dramatic compositions.

deç′lȧ·mā·tŏr, *n.* a declaimer. [Rare.]

dē·çlam′ȧ·tō·ry, *a.* [L. *declamatorius*, belonging to the exercise of speaking aloud, from *declamare*, to speak aloud.]
 1. pertaining to or fit for declamation; as, a *declamatory* theme.
 2. noisily rhetorical; oratorical; as, a *declamatory* style.

dē·çlār′ȧ·ble, *a.* capable of being declared or proved.

dē·çlar′ănt, *n.* in law, one who declares.

deç·lȧ·rā′tion, *n.* [ME. *declaracion*; L. *declaratio*, a declaration, from *declarare*, to make clear, declare; *de-*, intens., and *clarus*, clear.]
 1. a declaring or being declared; announcement.
 2. a thing declared.
 3. an affirmation; a formal statement of facts or opinions; proclamation; as, he declared his sentiments, and I rely on his *declaration.*
 4. a statement of taxable goods; as, a *declaration* at the customs office.
 5. in bezique, an indication of the combination that a player holds, given by laying the cards face up on the table.
 6. in bridge, a bid; especially, the winning bid.
 7. in law, (a) a statement of the plaintiff's cause for complaint in a court action; (b) a witness's statement, subject to penalty in case of perjury: distinguished from *oath.*
 Declaration of Independence; see under *Independence.*
 declaration of intention; the statement of an alien, when applying for naturalization under the United States laws, declaratory of his intention to become a citizen.
 declaration of trust; in law, the creation of a trust in writing, or the declaration thereof.

dē·çlar′ȧ·tive, *a.* [LL. *declarativus*, from L. *declarare*, to declare.]
 1. making a declaration or proclamation; explanatory; as, the name of a thing may be *declarative* of its form or nature.
 2. in grammar, making a statement or assertion; as, a *declarative* sentence.

dē·çlar′ȧ·tive·ly, *adv.* by distinct statement; specifically.

deç′lȧ·rā″tŏr, *n.* in Scots law, an action praying for the judicial declaration of some right or interest.

dē·çlar′ȧ·tō·ri·ly, *adv.* in a clear, explanatory manner.

dē·çlar′ȧ·tō·ry, *a.* same as *declarative.*

dē·çlāre′, *v.t.*; declared, *pt., pp.*; declaring, *ppr.* [ME. *declaren*; OFr. *declarer*; L. *declarare*, to make clear, to declare; *de-*, intens., and *clarus*, clear.]
 1. to clear; to free from obscurity; to make plain. [Obs.]
 2. to make known; to tell explicitly; to state or announce openly, formally, or in definite terms.
 3. to show; to reveal.
 4. to assert positively; to avow; to state in an unmistakable manner.
 5. to announce the existence of, in an official manner; as, to *declare* war.
 6. to make a statement concerning (goods liable to duty, taxes, etc.).
 7. in law, to state in a formal manner before witnesses.
 8. in bridge, to bid to play the hand in (a specific suit or no trump).
 to declare off; to recede from a position taken; to announce discontinuance; as, to *declare* a strike *off*, to *declare* the contest *off.*
 to declare oneself; (a) to throw off reserve and avow one's opinion; to state openly what one thinks, or which side one espouses; (b) to reveal one's true character, identity, etc.

dē·çlāre′, *v.i.* 1. to make a declaration.
 2. to proclaim or avow some opinion or resolution; to make known explicitly some determination: with *for* or *against.*
 3. in law, to recite the cause of complaint against the defendant; as, the plaintiff *declares* in debt or trespass.

dē·çlāred′, *a.* avowed; exhibited; manifested; published; proclaimed; recited.

dē·çlār′ed·ly, *adv.* avowedly; explicitly.

dē·çlār′ed·ness, *n.* the state of being declared.

dē·çlāre′ment, *n.* declaration. [Obs.]

dē·çlār′ēr, *n.* one who declares; one who makes known or publishes.

dé·clas·sé′ (dā-klȧ-sā′), *a.* having fallen or been forced from one's proper or former place in society; having lost class.

dē·çlȧssed′, *a.* same as *déclassé.*

dē·çlen′sion, *n.* [L. *declinatio*, a bending aside, from *declinare*, to bend or turn aside.]

1. in grammar, (a) the inflection of nouns, adjectives, and pronouns; the change of endings undergone by them to express their different relations of gender, person, number, and case; (b) the act of so inflecting words; (c) a class of nouns, pronouns, or adjectives showing the same or a similar system of inflections; as, the third *declension*.
2. a bending or moving downward; descent; slope.
3. act of declining; a refusal. [Rare.]
4. the process of falling or sinking lower; deterioration; decay; as, the *declension* of learning.
5. a deviation, as from a faith or standard.

dē·çlen'sion·ăl, *a.* in grammar, belonging or pertaining to declension.

dē·çlīn'ȧ·ble, *a.* in grammar, capable of being declined; having case inflections; as, a *declinable* noun.

dē·çlīn'ăl, *a.* declining; refusing. [Rare.]

deç'li·nănt, *a.* in heraldry, having the tail vertically downward; as, a serpent *declinant.*

deç'li·nāte, *a.* in botany, bent downward or aside, as the stamens of flowers.

deç·li·nā'tion, *n.* [ME. *declinacion*; L. *declinatio*, a bending aside, deflection, from *declinare*, to turn or bend aside.]
1. a bending or sloping downward; deviation from the horizontal or vertical.
2. the angle that a freely turning magnetic needle makes with the imaginary line pointing to true north.
3. a declining; decay; deterioration; gradual diminution of strength, soundness, vigor, or excellence. [Archaic.]
4. an oblique deviation from a definite direction; oblique motion; as, the *declination* of a descending body.
5. the act or state of declining; refusal.
6. in astronomy, the angular distance of any object from the celestial equator, either northward or southward.
7. in grammar, declension. [Obs.]
8. in dialing, an arc of the horizon contained between the vertical plane and the prime vertical circle if reckoned from the east or west, or between the meridian and the plane if reckoned from the north or south.
angle of declination; the angle described by a descending line or plane with one which is horizontal.
circle of declination; a great circle passing through the poles and cutting the equator at right angles.
declination compass; a compass designed to ascertain the variations of the magnetic needle.

deç'li·nā·tŏr, *n.* [L., from *declinare*, to decline.]
1. an instrument for taking the declination or inclination of a plane; an instrument in dialing: also written *declinatory*.
2. a dissentient. [Rare.]

dē·çlīn'ȧ·tō·ry, *a.* pertaining to, conveying, or involving a declination, or refusal.
declinatory plea; in old English law, a plea before trial or conviction, intended to show that the party was not liable to the penalty of the law, or was specially exempt from the jurisdiction of the court.

dē·çlīn'ȧ·tō·ry, *n.* same as *declinator*.

dē·çlīn'ȧ·tūre, *n.* a declining; declension; refusal.

dē·çlīne', *v.t.*; declined, *pt., pp.*; declining, *ppr.* [ME. *declinen*; OFr. *decliner*; L. *declinare*, to bend, turn aside.]
1. to cause to bend or slope downward or aside.
2. to refuse, especially politely; as, he *declined* the offer.
3. in grammar, to inflect; to change the endings of (a noun, pronoun, or adjective), in order to express the different relations of gender, person, number, and case.
4. to cause to decrease. [Obs.]

dē·çlīne', *v.i.* 1. to bend or slope downward or aside.
2. to sink, as the setting sun.
3. to lessen in force, health, value, etc.; deteriorate; decay.
4. to refuse something, especially in a polite manner.
5. to deviate from the prevailing intellectual or moral standard.

dē·çlīne', *n.* 1. a falling off; diminution; deterioration, decay; as, the *decline* of life, the *decline* of agriculture, the *decline* of learning.
2. a failing of health.
3. a period of decline.
4. the last part; as, the *decline* of life.
5. a wasting disease, especially tuberculosis of the lungs.
6. a downward slope.
Syn.—decay, consumption.

dē·çlīned', *a.* in botany, declinate.

dē·çlīn'ẽr, *n.* one who rejects or refuses.

deç·li·nom'e·tẽr, *n.* [from L. *declinare*, to decline, and Gr. *metron*, a measure.] an instrument for measuring the declination of the magnetic needle.

dē·çlīn'ous, *a.* bent downward.

deç'li·vănt, *a.* same as *declinant.*

dē·çliv'i·tous, *a.* same as *declivous.*

dē·çliv'i·ty, *n.* [L. *declivitas*, a sloping place, declivity, from *declivis*, sloping downward; *de*, down, from, and *clivus*, a slope, a hill.] declination from a horizontal line; descent; a slope downward, as of a hill: opposed to *acclivity.*

dē·çlī'vous, *a.* gradually descending; not precipitous; sloping.

dē·çoct', *v.t.* [ME. *decocten*; L. *decoctus*, pp. of *decoquere*, to boil down; *de*, down, and *coquere*, to cook.]
1. to prepare by boiling; to extract the essence, flavor, etc. of by boiling.
2. to digest in the stomach. [Obs.]

dē·çoct'i·ble, *a.* capable of being boiled or digested.

dē·çoç'tion, *n.* 1. the act of boiling a substance in water, for the purpose of extracting its flavor, essence, etc.
2. an extract produced by decocting or boiling.

dē·çōde, *v.i.* and *v.t.* to translate from code into language easily understood.

dē·çōd'ẽr, *n.* 1. a person who deciphers messages written in code.
2. a device that automatically decodes scrambled messages sent by telephone.

dē·çō·hēre', *v.t.* and *v.i.* in electricity, to change back to the normal condition of sensitivity: said of a coherer.

dē·çō·hēr'ẽr, *n.* in electricity, a vibrating device for changing a coherer back to its normal condition of sensitivity after a current has gone through it.

dē·çō·hē'ṣion, *n.* a decohering or being decohered.

dē·çol'lāte, *v.t.*; decollated, *pt., pp.*; decollating, *ppr.* [L. *decollatus*, pp. of *decollare*, to behead; *de*, from, and *collum*, neck.] to behead.

dē·çol'lā·ted, *a.* 1. beheaded.
2. in conchology, having the head or apex worn off, as certain univalve shells.

dē·çol·lā'tion, *n.* 1. the act of beheading or being beheaded; decapitation.
2. in surgery, removal of the head of the fetus in difficult parturition.

dē'çol·lā·tŏr, *n.* a person or thing that decollates.

dé·col·le·tage' (dā-koll-täzh'), *n.* [Fr., from *décolleter*, to bare one's neck and shoulders.]
1. the neckline of a dress cut low so as to bare the neck and shoulders.
2. a décolleté dress, etc.

dé·colle·té' (dā-kol-tā'), *a.* [Fr., pp. of *décolleter*, to bare one's neck and shoulders; *de*, from, and *cou*, neck; L. *de*, from, down, and *collum*, neck.]
1. cut low so as to bare the neck and shoulders, as some dresses.
2. wearing a décolleté dress, etc.

dē·çŏl'ŏr, *v.t.*; decolored, *pt., pp.*; decoloring, *ppr.* to deprive of color; to bleach; decolorize.

dē·çŏl'ŏr·ănt, *a.* tending to remove color; bleaching.

dē·çŏl'ŏr·ănt, *n.* a substance which decolorizes.

dē·çŏl'ŏr·āte, *a.* deprived of color; bleached.

dē·çŏl'ŏr·āte, *v.t.* to remove the color from; to decolor.

dē·çŏl·ŏr·ā'tion, *n.* the removal or absence of color.

dē·çŏl''ŏr·i·zā'tion, *n.* the act or art of removing color.

dē·çŏl'ŏr·īze, *v.t.*; decolorized, *pt., pp.*; decolorizing, *ppr.* to take the color out of; to bleach.

dē·çom·pen·sā'tion, *n.* failure of the heart muscle to compensate for a valvular or myocardial defect; heart failure.

dē·çŏm·plex', *a.* made up of complex constituents.

dē·çŏm·pōṣ'ȧ·ble, *a.* capable of being decomposed or resolved into constituent elements.

dē·çŏm·pōṣe', *v.t.* and *v.i.*; decomposed, *pt., pp.*; decomposing, *ppr.* [L. *de-* priv., and *componere*, to put together, to compose; *com-*, together, and *ponere*, to put, place.]
1. to break up or separate into basic components or parts.
2. to rot.

dē·çŏm·pōṣed', *a.* 1. in a state of decomposition; rotten.
2. in ornithology, standing apart; divergent; as, a *decomposed* crest.

dē·çŏm·pō'ṣẽr, *n.* anything that causes decomposition.

dē·çŏm·poṣ'ite, *a.* 1. compounded a second time, or with things already composite.
2. in botany, much divided, as a leaf or stem; decompound.

dē·çŏm·poṣ'ite, *n.* anything compounded with things already composite.

dē·çŏm·pō·ṣi'tion (zish'un), *n.* 1. a decomposing; the act of separating the constituent parts of a compound body or substance.
2. the fact or state of being decomposed.
3. a combination of things already compounded. [Obs.]
decomposition of forces; the process by which a given force or forces is resolved into several minor forces or motions.
decomposition of light; separation of a beam of light into the prismatic colors.

dē·çŏm·pound', *v.t.*; decompounded, *pt., pp.*; decompounding, *ppr.* [L. *de-* priv., and *componere*, to put together.]
1. to compound (things already compounded); to form by a second composition.
2. to decompose.

dē·çŏm·pound', *a.* 1. compounded of things already compounded.
2. in botany, made up of a number of compound divisions, as, a *decompound* leaf.

dē·çŏm·pound', *n.* a decomposite.

dē·çŏm·pound'ȧ·ble, *a.* capable of being decompounded.

dē·çŏm·pound'ly, *adv.* in a decompound manner.

DECOMPOUND LEAF

dē·çŏm·press', *v.t.* 1. to free from pressure.
2. to free (a worker in compressed air) from compression or air pressure by means of an air lock.

dē·çŏm·pres'sion, *n.* 1. release from pressure.
2. the lowering of air pressure on deep-sea divers, tunnel workers, etc.
3. a surgical operation to relieve excessive pressure, as in the cranium, a body cavity, etc.

dē·çŏm·pres'sion sick'ness, a condition caused by the formation of air bubbles in the blood or body tissues as the result of a sudden lowering of pressure, as in deep-sea divers returning to the surface too quickly: it is characterized by tightness in the chest, pains in the joints, and convulsions and collapse in severe cases: commonly called *caisson disease, bends, diver's disease, tunnel disease.*

dē·çŏn·cen'trāte, *v.t.* to scatter from a center; to distribute; to decentralize.

dē·çon·cen·trā'tion, *n.* the act of deconcentrating; the state of being deconcentrated.

dē·çŏn·çoct', *v.t.* to decompose. [Obs.]

dē·çon·ġest'ănt, *n.* a medication or treatment that relieves congestion, as in the nasal passages.

dē·çon'sē·crāte, *v.t.* to deprive of sacred character or of consecration; to secularize.

dē·çŏn·tam'i·nāte, *v.t.* to rid of a polluting or harmful substance, as poison gas.

dē·çŏn·trōl', *v.t.*; decontrolled, *pt., pp.*; decontrolling, *ppr.* to free from controls.

dē·çŏn·trōl', *n.* a decontrolling or being decontrolled.

dē·çop''pẽr·i·zā'tion, *n.* the process of freeing from copper.

dē·çop'pẽr·īze, *v.t.* to free from copper.

dé·cor' (dā-çor'), *n.* [Fr. *décor*, decoration.]
1. decoration.
2. the decorative scheme of a room, stage set, etc.

deç'ō·rȧ·ment, *n.* ornament. [Obs.]

deç'ō·rāte, *v.t.*; decorated, *pt., pp.*; decorating

ppr. [L. *decoratus*, pp. of *decorare*, to decorate, adorn, from *decus*, ornament, pride, from *decere*, to befit, become.]

1. to deck with something becoming or ornamental; to adorn; to beautify; to embellish; as, to *decorate* a hall with bunting.

2. to plan and furnish a color scheme, drapes, etc. for.

3. to paint or wallpaper; as, to *decorate* a room.

4. to give a medal or similar sign of honor to; as, he was *decorated* for heroism.

deç'ō·rāte, *v.i.* to put decorations on something; to decorate a room, house, etc.

Deç'ō·rāt·ed style, the second style of English Pointed architecture, flourishing from the end of the thirteenth to the commencement of the fifteenth century, when it was superseded by the Perpendicular.

WINDOW, DECORATED STYLE

deç·ō·rā'tion, *n.* 1. the act of decorating.

2. the fact or state of being decorated.

3. that which decorates or adorns; an ornament.

4. any badge, as a medal, cross of honor, etc., bestowed for distinguished services; the conferring of such a mark of honor.

5. in pyrotechny, the compositions placed in rockets, etc. which make the display when the explosion takes place.

Decoration Day; Memorial Day.

deç'ō·rā·tive, *a.* decorating; used for decorating; ornamental.

deç'ō·rā·tive·ness, *n.* the quality of being decorative.

deç'ō·rā·tŏr, *n.* one who decorates; specifically, one whose business is interior decoration; an interior decorator.

dē·çōre', *v.t.* to decorate; to honor. [Obs.]

dē·çōre'ment, *n.* decoration; ornament. [Obs.]

deç'ō·rous (*or* dē-kō'), *a.* [L. *decorus*, becoming, from *decor*, comeliness, grace.] characterized by or showing decorum, propriety, good taste, etc.; proper; becoming; befitting; as, *decorous* behavior, a *decorous* speech.

deç'ō·rous·ly, *adv.* in a decorous manner.

deç'ō·rous·ness, *n.* the quality of being decorous.

dē·çor'ti·çāte, *v.t.*; decorticated, *pt.*, *pp.*; decorticating, *ppr.* [L. *decorticatus*, pp. of *decorticare*, to strip the bark off; *de*, from, and *cortex*, bark.] to strip the bark from; to husk; to remove the cortex or outer covering from; as, to *decorticate* barley, or a tree.

dē·çor·ti·çā'tion, *n.* the act of stripping off the cortex, or outer covering of anything.

dē·çor'ti·çā·tŏr, *n.* a tool or machine for decorticating.

dē·çō'rum, *n.*; *pl.* **dē·çō'rums, dē·çō'rȧ,** [L., neut. of *decorus*, fit, proper, from *decor*, beauty, from *decere*, to become.]

1. whatever is suitable or proper; propriety; congruity.

2. propriety and good taste in behavior, speech, dress, etc.

3. [*often in pl.*] an act or requirement of polite behavior.

de·cou·page', dé·cou·page' (dā-ko̤o̤-päzh'), *n.* [Fr., the act of cutting up or carving.]

1. the art of cutting out designs or illustrations from paper, foil, etc. and mounting them on a surface in a decorative arrangement.

2. work done by decoupage.

dē·çoy' (*or* dē'koy), *n.* [earlier *coy*, from D. *kooi*, a cage.]

1. a place into which wild ducks, etc. are lured for capture.

2. an artificial or trained bird or animal used to lure game to a place where it can be shot.

3. a thing or person used to lure or tempt into danger or a trap; as, a police *decoy*.

dē·çoy', *v.t.* and *v.i.*; decoyed, *pt.*, *pp.*; decoying, *ppr.* to lure or be lured into a trap, danger, etc.

dē·çoy' duck, a duck, or an imitation of a duck, used as a decoy; hence, a person who decoys.

dē·çoy'ēr, *n.* a person employed to decoy others.

dē·çras'si·fȳ, *v.t.* to make less crass; to free from grossness.

dē·çrēase', *v.i.*; decreased (dē-krēst'), *pt.*, *pp.*; decreasing, *ppr.* [ME. *decresen*; OFr. *decresser*; L. *decrescere*, to decrease, become less; *de*, from, away, and *crescere*, to grow, increase.] to become less, smaller, etc.; to be diminished gradually; as, his capital *decreased*; the days are *decreasing* in length.

dē·çrēase', *v.t.* to lessen or make smaller; to diminish gradually or by small deductions; as, dissipation *decreases* one's vitality.

Syn.—diminish, lessen, abate, minimize, lower, reduce.—Things usually *decrease* by degrees, and from within, or through some cause which is imperceptible. They commonly *diminish* or are *diminished* by an action from without, or one which is apparent.

dē·çrēase', *n.* 1. a decreasing; a lessening; a diminution.

2. amount of decreasing.

3. the wane of the moon.

dē·çrēase'less, *a.* without decrease. [Rare.]

dē·çrēas'ing·ly, *adv.* in a decreasing manner.

dē·çree', *n.* [ME. *decre*; OFr. *decret*; L. *decretum*, a decree, neut. of *decretus*, pp. of *decernere*, to decree; *de*, from, and *cernere*, to see, to judge.]

1. an ordinance or order issued by a person or body of persons in authority deciding what is to be done in a certain matter, or what is to take place; an edict; a decision; a command; as, the *decree* of the emperor; an ecclesiastical *decree*.

2. in Roman law, a determination or judgment of the emperor on a suit between parties.

3. a judicial decision, or determination of a litigated case; as, a *decree* of a court of chancery.

4. the judgment or award of an umpire in a case submitted to him.

5. in theology, the purpose of God concerning future events.

6. anything settled and unchangeable; as, a *decree* of fate.

Syn.—edict, judgment, law, order, ordinance, proclamation.

dē·çree', *v.t.*; decreed, *pt.*, *pp.*; decreeing, *ppr.* to order, decide, or appoint by decree or officially.

dē·çree', *v.i.* to issue a decree.

dē·çree'ȧ·ble, *a.* capable of being decreed.

dē·çrē'ēr, *n.* one who decrees.

dē·çreet', *n.* in Scots law, a decree; a final judgment.

deç'rē·ment, *n.* [LL. *decrementum*, a decrease, from L. *decrescere*, to decrease.]

1. a decreasing or decrease; waste; loss.

2. the quantity lost by gradual diminution or waste: opposed to *increment*.

3. in mathematics, the quantity by which a variable decreases or is decreased.

4. in crystallography, a successive diminution of the layers of molecules, applied to the faces of the primitive form, by which the secondary forms are supposed to be produced.

5. in heraldry, the wane of the moon.

6. in radio and electricity, a measure of the rate of decrease of vibrations or oscillations: said of damped waves.

equal decrement of life; in the doctrine of annuities, the theory that of a given number of persons there should be an equal annual decrease by death within a given period.

dē·çrem'ē·tēr (*or* dek're-mē''tēr), *n.* [*decrement*, and *-meter*.] an instrument used in radiotelegraphy and electricity to measure the damping of electric waves or alternating currents: it also measures the logarithmic decrement of a circuit.

dē·çrep'it, *a.* [Fr. *décrépit*; L. *decrepitus*, broken down, worn out, very old, from *de-* priv., and *crepare*, to make a noise.] broken down or worn out by old age, illness, or long use.

dē·çrep'i·tāte, *v.t.*; decrepitated, *pt.*, *pp.*; decrepitating, *ppr.* [*de-*, intens., and L. *crepitatus*, pp. of *crepitare*, to crackle, rattle, break with a noise.] to roast or calcine (salts, minerals, etc.) in a strong heat, with a continual bursting or crackling of the substance.

dē·çrep'i·tāte, *v.i.* to crackle, as salts when roasting.

dē·çrep·i·tā'tion, *n.* the act of decrepitating; also, the noise made by minerals, salts, etc. when roasting.

dē·çrep'it·ly, *adv.* in a decrepit manner.

dē·çrep'it·ness, *n.* decrepitude.

dē·çrep'i·tūde, *n.* [Fr. *décrépitude*, from L. *decrepitus*, decrepit.] the condition of being decrepit; feebleness; infirmity, as from age.

dē·çre·scen'dō (-shen'), *a.* and *adv.* [It.] in music, with a gradual decrease in loudness or intensity; diminuendo: indicated by the sign >.

dē·çre·scen'dō, *n.*; *pl.* **dē·çre·scen'dōs,** in music, (a) a gradual decrease in loudness or intensity; (b) a passage played decrescendo.

dē·çres'cent, *a.* [L. *decrescens*, ppr. of *decrescere*, to decrease.] decreasing; becoming less by gradual diminution; waning; as, a *decrescent* moon.

dē·çres'cent, *n.* in heraldry, the moon when declining from the full to the last quarter: used as a bearing.

dē·çrē'tăl, *a.* pertaining to a decree; containing a decree; as, a *decretal* epistle.

dē·çrē'tăl, *n.* 1. a decree.

2. in the Roman Catholic Church, (a) a decree by the Pope on a question of doctrine or ecclesiastical law; (b) [*usually pl.*] a collection of such decrees forming a part of canon law.

dē·çrē'tist, *n.* [from L. *decretum*, a decree.] an expert in canon law.

dē·çrē'tive, *a.* 1. of a decree.

2. having the force of a decree.

deç·rē·tō'ri·ăl, *a.* decretory. [Obs.]

deç'rē·tō·ri·ly, *adv.* in a definitive manner.

deç'rē·tō·ry, *a.* 1. judicial; definitive; of, involving, or established by a decree.

2. of the nature of a decree.

3. critical; determining. [Obs.]

dē·çrī'ăl, *n.* a crying down; a clamorous censure; condemnation by censure.

dē·çrī'ēr, *n.* one who decries.

dē·çrim'i·năl·īze, *v.t.*; decriminalized, *pt.*, *pp.*; decriminalizing, *ppr.* to eliminate or reduce the legal penalties for (a specified crime); as, to *decriminalize* the use of marijuana.

dē·çrus·tā'tion, *n.* the removal of a crust from.

dē·çrȳ', *v.t.*; decried, *pt.*, *pp.*; decrying, *ppr.* [Fr. *decrier*; OFr. *descrier*, to decry, to cry down; *des*, down, and *crier*, to cry; L. *de*, down, and *queri*, to complain, lament.]

1. to denounce or condemn openly; to cry down; to censure as faulty or worthless; to clamor against; as, to *decry* religious intolerance.

2. to depreciate (money, etc.) officially.

Syn.—depreciate, detract, disparage.—One *decries* his rivals and *depreciates* their accomplishments. The envious *detract* from the merit of a good action, and *disparage* the motives of him who performs it.

dē·crypt, *v.t.*; decrypted, *pt.*, *pp.*; decrypting, *ppr.* [*de-*, and *crypto*gram.] to decode or decipher.

dē·çū'bi·tăl, *a.* in medicine, relating to or caused by (a) decubitus.

dē·çū'bi·tus, *n.* [L., from *decumbere*, to lie down.] in medicine, (a) the manner or posture of lying in bed; (b) a bedsore.

deç'ū·măn, *a.* [L. *decimanus*, or *decumanus*, belonging to the tenth part; *decumus*, tenth; *decem*, ten.]

1. in ancient Roman military usage, pertaining to the tenth cohort: applied to a gate of a Roman camp near which the tenth cohorts of the legions were encamped. The decuman gate was the principal entrance to the camp, and was that farthest from the enemy.

2. of great size; huge: said especially of waves, from the notion that every tenth wave was the largest.

dē·çum'bence, *n.* same as *decumbency*.

dē·çum'ben·cy, *n.* a decumbent condition or position.

dē·çum'bent, *a.* [L. *decumbens*, ppr. of *decumbere*, to lie down, from *de-*, down, and *cumbere* (in combination only), *cubare*, to recline, lie down.]

1. lying down; reclining.

2. in botany, trailing on the ground and rising at the tip, as some stems.

dē·çum'bent·ly, *adv.* in a decumbent posture.

dē·çum'bi·tūre, *n.* [from L. *decumbere*, to lie down.]

1. the time at which a sick person takes to bed, or during which he is confined to bed.

2. in astrology, the scheme or aspect of the heavens at this time, by which the prognostics of recovery or death were made.

deç'ū·ple (-pl), *a.* [L. *decuplus*, tenfold, from *decem*, ten, and *plus*, more.]

1. tenfold; containing ten times as many.

2. in tens.

deç'ū·ple, *n.* a number or quantity ten times as large as another one, or repeated ten times.

deç'ū·ple, *v.t.*; decupled, *pt.*, *pp.*; decupling, *ppr.* to increase tenfold; to multiply by ten.

dē·çū'ri·ŏn, *n.* [L. *decurio*, from *decuria*, a company of ten men; *decem*, ten.]

1. in Roman history, (a) an officer having

charge of ten men; (b) a member of a municipal or colonial senate.

2. formerly, in England, any commander or overseer of ten; a tithingman.

dē·çū′ri·ŏn·āte, *n.* the state or office of a decurion.

dē·çūr′rence, *n.* a running down; a lapse. [Rare.]

dē·çūr′rent, *a.* [L. *decurrens,* ppr. of *decurrere,* to run down; *de,* down, and *currere,* to run.] in botany, extending downward beyond the place of insertion; as, a *decurrent* leaf, having its base extending downward along the stem.

DECURRENT LEAVES

dē·çūr′rent·ly, *adv.* in a decurrent manner.

dē·çūr′ṣion, *n.* 1. the act of running down. [Obs.]

2. in Roman antiquity, a military maneuver or march; a parade.

dē·çūr′sive, *a.* running down; decurrent.

dē·çūr′sive·ly, *adv.* in a decursive manner.

dē·çūrt′, *v.t.* to shorten by cutting off; to abridge. [Obs.]

dē·çūr·tā′tion, *n.* abridgment. [Obs.]

dē·çūr·vā′tion, *n.* the act of decurving; the state of being curved downward.

dē·çūr′vȧ·tūre, *n.* decurvation.

dē·çūrve′ *v.t.*; decurved, *pt., pp.*; decurving, *ppr.* to curve downward.

deç′ū·ry, *n.*; *pl.* **deç′ū·rieṣ,** [L. *decuria,* from *decem,* ten.] in Roman history, (a) the group commanded by a decurion; (b) any of various divisions or classes, as of the judges, the curiae etc.

dē·çus′sāte, *v.t.* and *v.i.*; decussated, *pt., pp.*; decussating, *ppr.* [L. *decussatus,* pp. of *decussare,* to divide crosswise in the form of an X, from *decussis,* the figure ten (X), from *decem,* ten.] to cross or cut so as to form an X; to intersect.

dē·çus′sāte, *a.* 1. decussated.

2. in botany, arranged in pairs growing at right angles to those above and below; as, *decussate* leaves and branches.

dē·çus′sāte·ly, *adv.* in a decussate manner.

dē·çus·sā′tion, *n.* [L. *decussatio,* from *decussare,* to cross.]

1. a decussating or being decussated.

DECUSSATE LEAVES

2. an intersection in the form of X.

dē·çus′sȧ·tive, *a.* crossing; intersecting.

dē·çus′sȧ·tive·ly, *adv.* crosswise; in the form of an X.

dē′cyl, *n.* [Gr. *deka,* ten, and *hylē,* wood, material.] a univalent, organic, hydrocarbon radical, $C_{10}H_{21}$.

dē·cyl′iç, *a.* pertaining to decyl.

dē′dăl, *a.* same as *daedal.*

Dē·dā′li·ăn, Dē·dā′lē·ăn, *a.* same as *Daedalian.*

ded′ȧ·lous, *a.* same as *daedalous.*

de·däṅs′ (-däṅ′), *n.* [Fr. *dedans,* the inside.] in court tennis, the space reserved at one end of the tennis court for those looking on.

dede, *a.* dead. [Obs.]

dē·deç′ō·rāte, *v.t.* to disgrace. [Obs.]

dē·deç·ō·rā′tion, *n.* disgrace. [Obs.]

dē·deç′ō·rous, *a.* disgraceful; unbecoming. [Rare.]

dē·den·ti′tion (-tish′un), *n.* the shedding of teeth. [Rare.]

ded′i·çȧnt, *n.* one who dedicates.

ded′i·çāte, *v.t.*; dedicated, *pt., pp.*; dedicating, *ppr.* [L. *dedicatus,* pp. of *dedicare,* to consecrate, declare.]

1. to set apart and consecrate to a deity or to a sacred purpose; to devote to a sacred use, by a solemn act or by religious ceremonies; as, to *dedicate* a temple or a church.

2. to set apart for a special purpose; to devote to some work, duty, etc.

3. to address or inscribe (a book, artistic performance, etc.) to someone as a sign of honor, affection, etc.

4. to open formally (a public building, fair, etc.).

5. in law, to devote (land, etc.) to public use.

Syn.—devote, consecrate, hallow, set apart.

ded′i·çāte, *a.* dedicated. [Archaic and Poetic.]

ded″i·çȧ·tee′, *n.* one to whom a thing is dedicated.

ded·i·çā′tion, *n.* 1. a dedicating or being dedicated.

2. an inscription in a book, etc., in which the author dedicates the work to a patron, friend, or cause.

ded′i·çā·tive, *a.* dedicatory.

ded′i·çā·tŏr, *n.* one who dedicates.

ded″i·çȧ·tō′ri·ăl, *a.* of the nature of a dedication; dedicatory.

ded′i·çȧ·tō·ry, *a.* of or as a dedication; as, an epistle *dedicatory.*

ded′i·çȧ·tō·ry, *n.* a dedication. [Rare.]

ded′i·mus, *n.* [L., we have given, 1st pers. pl. perf. ind. act. of *dare,* to give.] in law, a writ to commission private persons to do some act in place of a judge, as to examine a witness, etc.

dē·dit′ (dā-dē′), *n.* [Fr.] in French and Canadian law, the sum named in the penalty clause of a contract; a forfeit.

dē·di′tion (-dish′un), *n.* [L. *deditio,* a surrender, giving up, from *dedere,* to give up, surrender; *de,* from, and *dare,* to give.] the act of yielding anything; surrender. [Rare.]

ded·i·ti′tiăn·cy (-tish′ăn-cy), *n.* in old Roman law, the state of a freedman denied full citizenship because of gross misbehavior while a slave.

ded′ō·lent, *a.* [L. *dedolens,* ppr. of *dedolere,* to cease to grieve; *de-* priv., and *dolere,* to grieve.] feeling no compunction or regret. [Obs.]

dē·dūce′, *v.t.*; deduced, *pt., pp.*; deducing, *ppr.* [L. *deducere,* to lead or draw down, to bring away; *de,* down, away, and *ducere,* to lead.]

1. to draw; to bring; to lead forth. [Archaic.]

2. to draw from, in reasoning; to attain or arrive at, as a truth, opinion, or proposition, from premises; to infer from what precedes; to conclude.

Reasoning is nothing but the faculty of *deducing* unknown truths from principles already known. —Locke.

3. to trace the course or derivation of.

dē·dūce′ment, *n.* the conclusion of a deduction; inference. [Obs.]

dē·dū·ci·bil′i·ty, *n.* deducibleness.

dē·dū′ci·ble, *a.* 1. that can be deduced.

2. capable of being brought down. [Obs.]

dē·dū′ci·ble·ness, *n.* capability of being deduced; deducibility.

dē·dū′çi·bly, *adv.* by means of deduction.

dē·dū′cive, *a.* performing the act of deduction; inferential. [Rare.]

dē·duçt′, *v.t.*; deducted, *pt., pp.*; deducting, *ppr.* [L. *deductus,* pp. of *deducere,* to lead away; *de,* from, and *ducere,* to lead.]

1. to take away, separate, or remove, in numbering, estimating, or calculating; to subtract; as, from the sum of two numbers *deduct* the lesser number.

2. to reduce; to bring down. [Obs.]

Do not *deduct* it to days. —Massinger.

3. to lead forth, as a colony; to deduce. [Obs.]

dē·duçt′i·ble, *a.* 1. capable of being deducted or subtracted.

2. capable of being deduced; consequential. [Rare.]

dē·duç′tion, *n.* 1. the act of deducting; subtraction.

2. that which is deducted; the sum or amount taken from another; abatement; as, this sum is a *deduction* from the yearly rent.

3. in logic, (a) the act or process of deducing; reasoning from a known principle to an unknown, from the general to the specific, or from a premise to a logical conclusion; (b) a conclusion so deduced. Opposed to *induction.*

Syn.—abatement, discount, diminution, inference, consequence, conclusion.

dē·duçt′ive, *a.* 1. of or based on deduction.

2. reasoning by deduction.

dē·duçt′ive·ly, *adv.* by deduction; by way of inference; by consequence.

dē·duit′ (-dwit′), *n.* delight; sport. [Obs.]

dē·dū·pli·çā′tion, *n.* [*de-,* and L. *duplicare,* to double.] in botany, chorisis.

deed, *a.* dead. [Obs.]

deed, *n.* [ME. *deed, dede*; AS. *dæd,* a deed, a thing done, from *don,* to do.]

1. that which is done, acted, or effected; an act; a fact.

2. a feat of courage, skill, etc.; exploit; achievement; illustrious act.

3. action; doing.

4. in law, a document under seal that states a contract, agreement, transfer of property, etc.

deed of trust; a conveyance of property to one person to be held in trust for another.

deed poll; a deed not indented, that is, polled or even, made by one party only.

in deed; in fact; actually.

Syn.—action, achievement, accomplishment, exploit, feat.

deed, *v.t.*; deeded, *pt., pp.*; deeding, *ppr.* to convey or transfer by deed; as, to *deed* realty to a wife.

deed′fu̇l, *a.* filled with deeds; active; stirring. [Rare.]

deed′less, *a.* inactive; not performing or having performed deeds or exploits.

deed′y, *a.* industrious; active. [Rare.]

deem, *v.t.*; deemed, *pt., pp.*; deeming, *ppr.* [ME. *demen*; AS. *deman,* to judge, deem, from *dom,* judgment, doom.]

1. to think; to judge; to hold in opinion; to conclude on consideration; as, he *deems* it prudent to be silent.

2. to doom; to judge; to decide. [Obs.]

deem, *v.i.* 1. to be of opinion; to judge; to think.

deem, *n.* opinion; judgment; surmise. [Obs.]

deem′stẽr, demp′stẽr, *n.* one of the two judges in the Isle of Man acting as the chief justices of the island.

deep, *a.* [ME. *deep, depe*; AS. *deop,* deep.]

1. extending far downward from the top or top edges, inward from the surface, backward from the front, or far to the sides or edge.

2. extending thus for a specified length or distance; as, eight feet *deep.*

3. placed far down or back.

4. coming from far down or back.

5. hard to understand; abstruse.

6. serious; extreme; as, *deep* disgrace.

7. strongly felt: as, *deep* love.

8. wise; sagacious.

9. tricky and sly.

10. dark and rich: said of colors.

11. sunk in or absorbed by (with *in*); as, he was *deep in* thought.

12. great in degree; intense; profound; as, a *deep* sleep.

13. much involved; as, *deep* in debt.

14. of low pitch: said of sound.

deep, *adv.* deeply; far down, far in, far back, far on, etc.

Drink *deep,* or taste not the Pierian spring. —Pope.

deep, *n.* [ME. *deepe*; AS. *dype,* the deep sea, from *deop,* deep.]

1. a deep place, as in water or earth.

2. the extent of space, time, the unknown, etc.

3. the middle part; the part that is darkest, most silent, etc.; as, in the *deep* of night.

4. in nautical usage, any unmarked point between two consecutive fathom marks on a sounding line.

deep′-chest·ed, *a.* having or from a thick chest; as, a *deep-chested* roar.

deep′-dish pie, a fruit pie baked in a deep dish and having only a top crust.

deep′-dȳed, *a.* 1. stained throughout.

2. thoroughgoing; unmitigated; as, a *deep-dyed* villain.

deep′en, *v.t.*; deepened, *pt., pp.*; deepening, *ppr.* 1. to make deep or deeper; to sink lower; as, to *deepen* the channel of a river or harbor; to *deepen* a well.

2. to make dark or darker; to make thicker or more gloomy; as, to *deepen* the shades of night; to *deepen* gloom.

3. to make more poignant or absorbing; as, to *deepen* grief or sorrow.

4. to make graver; as, to *deepen* the tones of an organ.

deep′en, *v.i.* to become deeper; as, the water *deepens* at every cast of the lead.

deep′-fet, *a.* fetched or brought from a deep place. [Obs.]

deep′freeze′, *n.* a refrigerator for keeping perishable foods at a very low temperature for long periods of time: a trade-mark (*Deepfreeze*).

deep′freeze′, *v.t.* to put or keep (foods) in a deepfreeze refrigerator.

deep′-frȳ′, *v.t.*; deep-fried, *pt., pp.*; deep-frying, *ppr.* to fry by immersing in a deep pan of boiling fat.

deep′-lāid, *a.* carefully worked out and kept secret; as, *deep-laid* plans.

deep′ly, *adv.* 1. at or to a great depth; far below the surface; as, a passion *deeply* rooted in our nature.

2. profoundly; thoroughly; as, *deeply* skilled in ethics or anatomy.

3. with a deep or low tone; as, a *deeply* toned instrument.

4. with profound skill; with art or intricacy; as, a *deeply* laid plot or intrigue.

deep′mouthed, *a.* having a hoarse, loud, hollow voice; as, a *deepmouthed* dog.

deep′ness, *n.* the state of being deep, in all its senses; depth.
deep′-read (-red), *a.* having fully read; profoundly versed.
deep′-root·ed, *a.* 1. having deep roots.
2. firmly established; hard to remove; as, *deep-rooted* prejudice.
deep′-sēa, *a.* pertaining to or used in the deeper parts of the sea; as, *deep-sea* fishing.
deep′-sēat′ed, *a.* 1. placed or originating far beneath the surface.
2. firmly established; hard to remove.
deep′-set, *a.* 1. deeply set.
2. firmly established.
deep′-six′, *n.* [from the custom of burial at sea in at least six fathoms.]
1. originally, burial at sea. [Slang.]
2. a discarding or disposal of something. [Slang.]
deep′-six′, *v.t.*; deep-sixed, *pt., pp.*; deep-sixing, *ppr.* to get rid of, as by throwing into the water. [Slang.]
deep space, same as *outer space.*
deep struc′tūre, in transformational grammar, the underlying relationship of the parts of a sentence that gives that sentence meaning.
deep′-wāist″ed, *a.* having a deep waist, as a ship when the quarter-deck and forecastle are raised from four to six feet above the level of the main deck.
deer, *n.*; *pl.* **deer,** *occas.* **deers,** [ME. *der*; AS. *deor*, a wild animal.]
1. any quadruped, particularly if wild. [Obs.]

RED DEER (*Cervus elaphus*)

2. one of a large group of hoofed, cud-chewing mammals in the family *Cervidae*, including the mule deer, elk, reindeer, moose, etc., the males of which usually bear antlers that are shed annually: popularly used only of the smaller species of this family.
deer′flȳ, *n.*; *pl.* **deer′flīes,** any of a group of blood-sucking flies related to the horsefly, but smaller and with mottled wings.
deer′grȧss, *n.* any plant of the genus *Rhexia*, the meadow beauty.
deer′hâir, *n.* *Scirpus cæspitosus*, heath club rush.
deer′hound, *n.* any of a Scottish breed of large, shaggy-haired dog, used in hunting deer; a staghound.
deer′let, *n.* any small deer, as the chevrotain.
deer lick, any damp, salty place where deer come to lick the salty earth.
deer mouse, 1. a small, white-footed mouse, *Peromyscus leucopus.*
2. a light-brown jumping mouse.
Both are American varieties.
deer′skin, *n.* 1. the raw skin of a deer.
2. the dressed leather made of the raw skin; buckskin.
deer′skin, *a.* made of deerskin.
deer′stalk″ẽr (-stạk″), *n.* 1. a hunter who stalks deer.
2. a tight-fitting cap with a low crown, used by hunters.
deer′stalk″ing, *n.* the hunting of deer by stalking instead of pursuit or in the open.
deer′s-tŏngue (-tung), *n.* *Trilisa odoratissima*, a plant having leaves of a vanillalike odor.
dees, *n.* dice. [Obs.]
dees, *n.* a dais. [Obs.]
dē·ē′sis, *n.* [Gr. *deēsis*, a supplication.] in rhetoric, an invocation to a deity.
dē′ess, *n.* a goddess. [Obs.]
dē-eth′i·cīze, *v.t.*; de-ethicized, *pt., pp.*; de-ethicizing, *ppr.* to rid of ethical qualities; to cause to be separated from ethics.
deev, *n.* same as *deva.*
dē·fāce′, *v.t.*; defaced (dē-fāst′), *pt., pp.*; defacing, *ppr.* [ME. *defacen*; OFr. *defacier*; L. *de-* priv., and *facies*, face.]
1. to destroy or mar the face or surface of; to injure the beauty of; to disfigure; as, to *deface* a monument, to *deface* an edifice.
2. to make illegible by injuring the surface of; to erase or obliterate; as, to *deface* letters or writing, to *deface* a record.
Syn.—disfigure, deform.—A thing is *defaced* usually by design; it is *disfigured* either by design or accident; it is *deformed* either by an error or by the nature of the thing. Inanimate objects are mostly *defaced* or *disfigured*, but seldom *deformed*; animate objects are either *disfigured* or *deformed*, but seldom *defaced.*
dē·fāce′ment, *n.* 1. a defacing or being defaced.
2. that which defaces.
dē·fā′cẽr, *n.* one who or that which defaces.
dē fac′tō, [L. *de*, of, from; *facto*, ablative of *factum*, a fact, from *facere*, to do.] actual; in fact; in reality; existing (regardless of legal or moral considerations); as, a *de facto* government, distinguished from a *de jure* government.
dē·fāil′, *v.t.* and *v.i.* to fail. [Obs.]
dē·fāil′ănce, *n.* failure. [Obs.]
dē·fāil′ūre, *n.* failure. [Obs.]
dē·fal′cāte, *v.t.*; defalcated, *pt., pp.*; defalcating, *ppr.* [LL. *defalcatus*, pp. of *defalcare*, to cut off; L. *de*, from, and *falx*, a sickle.] to cut off; to take away or deduct a part of: used chiefly of money, accounts, rents, income, etc. [Rare.]
dē·fal′cāte, *v.i.* to steal or misuse funds entrusted to one's care; to be guilty of defalcation; to embezzle.
dē·fal·cā′tion, *n.* 1. misappropriation of money; embezzlement; also, the sum embezzled.
2. in law, the reduction of a claim by the allowance of a setoff; abatement; also, the amount so abated. [Rare.]
dē·fal′cā·tŏr, *n.* a person who defalcates; an embezzler.
dē·falk′, *v.t.* to defalcate; to cut off. [Obs.]
def·ȧ·mā′tion, *n.* [ME. *diffamacioun*; LL. *diffamatio*, libel, defamation, from L. *diffamare*, to defame.] the uttering of slanderous words or writings; the malicious uttering of falsehood respecting another, which tends to destroy or impair his good name, character, or occupation; aspersion; calumny. Defamation, in law, embraces libel and slander.
dē·fam′ȧ·tō·ry, *a.* calumnious; slanderous; containing defamation; false and injurious to reputation; as, *defamatory* words.
dē·fāme′, *v.t.*; defamed, *pt., pp.*; defaming, *ppr.* [ME. *defamen*, *diffamen*; L. *diffamare*, to spread an evil report, defame.]
1. to slander or libel; to attack the reputation of; to speak evil of; to dishonor by false reports; to calumniate.
2. to accuse, especially if the charge is false. [Rare.]
3. to lower the fame of; to bring into disrepute; to make infamous. [Archaic.]
Syn.—asperse, calumniate, libel, slander, traduce, vilify.
dē·fāme′, *n.* disrepute. [Obs.]
dē·fām′ẽr, *n.* a slanderer; a detractor; a calumniator.
dē·fām′ing·ly, *adv.* in a calumnious manner.
def′ȧ·mous, *a.* defamatory; slanderous. [Obs.]
dē·fat′i·gȧ·ble, *a.* [L. *defatigare*, to weary, tire out.] liable to be wearied. [Obs.]
dē·fat′i·gāte, *v.t.* to weary or tire. [Obs.]
dē·fat·i·gā′tion, *n.* weariness. [Obs.]
dē·fault′, *n.* [ME. *defaulte*; OFr. *defaute*, a failure, from L. *de*, away, and *fallere*, to fall, to deceive.]
1. failure to do something or be somewhere when required; as, he lost the tennis match by *default.*
2. failure to pay money due.
3. failure to appear in court to defend or prosecute a case.
4. an offense; fault; wrong act. [Rare.]
in default of; through lack or neglect of; in the absence of.
judgment by default; a judgment rendered against a litigant who fails to plead.
to suffer default; to fail to answer when a case is called for trial.
Syn.—delinquency, failure, omission, neglect.
dē·fault′, *v.i.* [ME. *defauten*; OFr. *defauter*; see the *n.*]
1. to fail to do something or be somewhere when required.
2. to fail to make payment when due.
3. to fail to appear in court.
4. to fail to take part in or finish a contest.
5. to lose by default.
6. to offend. [Rare.]
dē·fault′, *v.t.* 1. to fail to do or pay (something) when required.
2. to fail to take part in or finish (a contest).
3. to lose (a contest, etc.) by default; to forfeit.
dē·fault′ẽr, *n.* 1. one who makes default; one who fails to appear in court when called.
2. one who fails to account for money entrusted to his care; an embezzler.
3. a soldier guilty of a military offense. [Brit.]
dē·fēa′ṣănce, *n.* [OFr. *defeisance*, a rendering void, from *defeisant*, ppr. of *defaire*, to render void, undo.]
1. defeat. [Obs.]
2. the annulment of a contract or deed.
3. a clause stating a condition the fulfillment of which makes the deed, contract, etc. void in whole or in part.
dē·fēa′ṣănced, *a.* liable to be forfeited; subject to defeasance.
dē·fēa′ṣi·ble, *a.* that can be undone or made void.
dē·fēa′ṣi·ble·ness, *n.* the quality of being defeasible.
dē·fēat′, *v.t.*; defeated, *pt., pp.*; defeating, *ppr.* [ME. *defeten*, *deffeten*, from OFr. *defait*, pp. of *defaire*, to undo, defeat; L. *de-* or *dis-* priv., and *facere*, to do.]
1. to overcome or vanquish, as an army; to win victory over; to beat.
2. to frustrate; to bring to nothing; to prevent the success of; to disappoint; as, our dearest hopes are often *defeated.*
3. to render null and void; as, to *defeat* a title to an estate.
4. to undo; to destroy. [Obs.]
Syn.—overpower, overthrow, beat, rout, discomfit, vanquish, subdue, conquer, frustrate, foil, disconcert, baffle.
dē·fēat′, *n.* [from the *v.*; prob. after Fr. *défaite.*]
1. overthrow; loss of battle; check, rout, or destruction, as of an army by the victory of an enemy.
2. frustration by rendering null and void, or by prevention of success; as, the *defeat* of one's hopes.
3. an undoing; destruction. [Obs.]
dē·fēat′iṣm, *n.* the actions or state of mind of a defeatist.
dē·fēat′ist, *a.* relating to, or characteristic of, a defeatist.
dē·fēat′ist, *n.* [Fr. *défaitiste.*] a person who too readily accepts defeat for himself or his side, and acts accordingly.
dē·fēa′tūre, *n.* 1. defeat. [Obs.]
2. disfigurement. [Archaic.]
dē·fēa′tūre, *v.t.*; defeatured, *pt., pp.*; defeaturing, *ppr.* to disfigure.
def′ē·cāte, *a.* having every impurity removed; cleared; refined.
def′ē·cāte, *v.t.*; defecated, *pt., pp.*; defecating, *ppr.* [L. *defæcatus*, pp. of *defæcare*, to cleanse from dregs, to strain; *de*, from, and *fæx*, grounds, dregs.]
1. to purify; to refine; to clear from dregs or impurities; to clarify; as, to *defecate* liquor.
2. figuratively, to purify from admixture; to clear; to purge of extraneous matter.
def′ē·cāte, *v.i.* 1. to become free from impurities.
2. to excrete waste matter from the bowels.
def·ē·cā′tion, *n.* the act or process of defecating.
def′ē·cā·tŏr, *n.* one who or that which defecates; specifically, an apparatus for removing impure matter, as in sugar refining.
dē·fect′, *n.* [ME. *defaicte*; OFr. *defait*, from L. *defectus*, a failure, lack, from *defectus*, pp. of *deficere*, to fail, to lack.]
1. lack or absence of something necessary for completeness; shortcoming.
2. an imperfection; fault; flaw; blemish; deformity; as, a *defect* in timber, a *defect* of memory.
dē·fect′, *v.i.* to be deficient. [Obs.]
dē·fect′, *v.t.* to harm; to injure. [Rare.]
dē·fect·i·bil′i·ty, *n.* deficiency; imperfection. [Rare.]
dē·fect′i·ble, *a.* imperfect; deficient. [Rare.]
dē·fec′tion, *n.* [L. *defectio*, a failure, defection, from *defectus*, pp. of *deficere*, to fail.]
1. a failing; failure.
2. the act of abandoning a person or cause to which one is bound by allegiance or duty, or to which one has attached himself; desertion.
dē·fec′tion·ist, *n.* one who encourages or incites defection.
dē·fec′tious, *a.* full of imperfections. [Obs.]
dē·fec′tive, *a.* 1. having a defect or defects; incomplete; faulty.

2. in grammar, lacking some of the usual grammatical forms, as a noun or verb.
3. subnormal in intelligence, memory, etc.
Syn.—imperfect, deficient, incomplete, inadequate, insufficient, faulty, blamable.

dē·fect'ive, *n.* 1. one having some mental or physical defect.
2. in grammar, a defective word.

dē·fect'ive·ly, *adv.* in a defective manner.

dē·fect'ive·ness, *n.* the state of being defective; faultiness.

dē·fect·ū·os'i·ty, *n.* defectiveness. [Obs.]

dē·fect'ū·ous, *a.* full of defects. [Obs.]

def·ē·dā'tion, *n.* pollution. [Obs.]

dē·fence', *n.* and *v.t.* defense: British spelling.

dē·fend', *v.t.*; defended, *pt., pp.*; defending, *ppr.* [ME. *defenden*; OFr. *defendre*; L. *defendere,* to ward off, repel; *de-*, away, from, and *fendere,* to strike.]
1. to fend or ward off. [Scot.]
2. to forbid; to prohibit. [Obs.]
3. to support or maintain by speech or act.
4. to guard from attack; to protect by opposition or resistance; to prevent from being injured or destroyed.
There arose to *defend* Israel, Tola, the son of Puah. —Jud. x. 1.
5. to try to justify; as, to *defend* one's conduct.
6. in law, (a) to oppose (an action, etc.); (b) to plead (one's cause) in defense; (c) to act for (an accused).
Syn.—protect. —To *defend* is literally to ward off; to *protect* is to cover over. We *defend* those who are attacked; we *protect* those who are liable to injury or invasion. A fortress is *defended* by its guns, and *protected* by its walls.

dē·fend', *v.i.* to make a defense.

dē·fend'ȧ·ble, *a.* that can be defended.

dē·fend'ănt, *a.* 1. defensive. [Obs.]
2. making defense; defending.

dē·fend'ănt, *n.* 1. one who defends. [Obs.]
2. in law, the defending party; one who is sued or accused: opposed to *plaintiff*.

dē·fend'ēr, *n.* one who defends by opposition; one who maintains, supports, protects, or vindicates; a protector.
Syn.—advocate, pleader, vindicator, champion.

Dē·fend'ēr of the Fāith, a hereditary title of English sovereigns, first conferred upon Henry VIII by Pope Leo X (1521).

dē·fend'ress, *n.* a woman defender. [Rare.]

dē·fen·es·trā'tion, *n.* [*de-*, and *fenestration.*] a throwing or being thrown out of a window.

dē·fen'sȧ·tive, *n.* that which defends or protects; a defense; a guard. [Rare.]

dē·fense', *n.* [ME. *defense,* L. *defensus,* pp. of *defendere,* to defend.]
1. the act of defending; a guarding against attack; a keeping from harm or danger.
2. the fact or state of being defended.
3. something that defends; a means of defense.
4. justification or support by speech or writing.
5. an argument to justify or vindicate.
6. self-protection, as by boxing.
7. the side that is defending in any contest.
8. (a) the arguments of the defendant or his lawyer in contesting a case; (b) the defendant and his lawyer or lawyers, collectively.
9. prohibition. [Obs.]
angle of defense; in fortification, the angle formed by the meeting of the line of defense with a diverging flank.

dē·fense', *v.t.* to defend by fortification. [Obs.]

dē·fense'less, *a.* being without defense; unable to defend oneself; open to attack; helpless; unprotected.

dē·fense'less·ness, *n.* the state of being defenseless.

dē·fense' mech'ȧ·nism, 1. any self-protective physiological reaction of an organism.
2. in psychology, any behavior pattern in which there is an unconscious tendency to keep from oneself or others unpleasant or uncomfortable feelings, memories, etc.
Also called *defense reaction*.

dē·fen·si·bil'i·ty, *n.* capability of being defended; defensibleness.

dē·fen'si·ble, *a.* 1. that can be defended.
2. that can be vindicated, maintained, or justified; as, a *defensible* cause.

dē·fen'si·ble·ness, *n.* defensibility.

dē·fen'sive, *a.* 1. that serves to defend; for defense; as, *defensive* armor.
2. carried on in resisting attack or aggression; defending; as, *defensive* war.

dē·fen'sive, *n.* 1. that which defends. [Obs.]
2. attitude, position, or operation of defense (often with *the*).

dē·fen'sive·ly, *adv.* in a defensive manner; on the defensive.

dē·fen'sŏr, *n.* 1. one who defends; a defender. [Obs.]
2. in law, a defender in court; an advocate.

dē·fen'sō·ry, *a.* defensive.

dē·fēr', *v.t.* and *v.i.*; deferred, *pt., pp.*; deferring, *ppr.* [ME. *differren*; OFr. *differer*; L. *differre,* to carry asunder or different ways, to defer, put off; *dis-*, apart, and *ferre,* to carry.] to delay; to put off; to postpone to a future time.
Syn.—delay, postpone, procrastinate, prolong, protract, retard, adjourn.

dē·fēr', *v.i.* [Fr. *déférer,* from L. *deferre,* to bring down, give, grant; *de-*, down, and *ferre,* to bring.] to yield with courtesy; to submit in opinion or judgment; as, he *defers* to the opinion of his father.

dē·fēr', *v.t.* 1. to offer; to render; to give. [Obs.]
2. to refer; to leave to another's judgment and determination: with *to*.

def'ēr·ence, *n.* [Fr. *déférence,* from L. *deferens,* ppr. of *deferre,* to bring down, to grant; *de-*, down, and *ferre,* to bring.]
1. a yielding in opinion; submission of judgment to the opinion or judgment of another.
2. courteous regard or respect.
in deference to; because of regard or respect for (a person, his wishes, position, etc.).

def'ēr·ent, *a.* deferential.

def'ēr·ent, *a.* [Fr. *déférent*; L. *deferens,* ppr. of *deferre.*]
1. carrying down or out.
2. in anatomy, carrying fluids, impulses, etc. away from an organ or part.

def'ēr·ent, *n.* [L. *deferens,* ppr. of *deferre,* to carry down.]
1. that which carries or conveys.
2. in Ptolemaic astronomy, a circle surrounding the earth, in whose periphery the center of the epicycle was supposed to move around.

def·ēr·en'tiăl (-shăl), *a.* expressing deference.

def·ēr·en'tiăl·ly, *adv.* with deference.

dē·fēr'ment, *n.* the act of putting off or delaying; postponement.

dē·fērred', *a.* 1. postponed.
2. with rights, interest, etc. withheld until a certain date; as, a *deferred* annuity.
3. classified as not subject to immediate induction into the armed forces.

dē·fēr'rēr, *n.* one who delays or puts off.

dē·fēr·ves'cence, *n.* [L. *defervescens,* ppr. of *defervescere,* to cease boiling; *de-*, from, and *fervescere,* to begin to boil, from *fervere,* to boil.]
1. abatement of heat; the state of growing cool; coolness.
2. in medicine, abatement or decrease of fever or feverish symptoms.

dē·fēr·ves'cen·cy, *n.* defervescence.

dē·feū'dăl·ize, *v.t.* to remove the feudal attributes of.

dē·fī'ănce, *n.* [ME. *defyaunce*; OFr. *defiance,* distrust, defiance, lack of faith, from *defier,* to distrust, defy, from L. *dis-*, from, and *fidus,* faithful.]
1. a defying; open, bold resistance to authority or opposition.
2. a challenge.
3. rejection; refusal. [Obs.]
in defiance of; (a) defying; (b) in spite of.
to bid defiance to; to defy.
to set at defiance; to defy.

dē·fī'ănt, *a.* full of defiance, boldness, or insolence; challenging.

dē·fī'ănt·ly, *adv.* in a defiant manner.

dē·fī'ănt·ness, *n.* the quality of being defiant.

dē·fī'ȧ·tō·ry, *a.* bidding or bearing defiance. [Obs.]

dē·fī'bri·nāte, *v.t.*; defibrinated, *pt., pp.*; defibrinating, *ppr.* to deprive of fibrin; specifically, to remove fibrin from lymph or fresh blood by stirring.

dē·fī·bri·nā'tion, *n.* the act or process of defibrinating.

dē·fī'bri·nīze, *v.t.*; defibrinized, *pt., pp.*; defibrinizing, *ppr.* to defibrinate.

dē·fi'cience (-fish'ens), *n.* deficiency. [Obs.]

dē·fi'cien·cy (-fish'en-cy), *n.*; *pl.* **dē·fi'cien·cieṣ,** [LL. *deficientia,* from L. *deficiens,* ppr. of *deficere,* to lack, fail; *de-*, from, and *facere,* to do.]
1. the state or quality of being deficient; absence of something essential; incompleteness.
2. (a) a shortage; (b) the amount of shortage; deficit.
deficiency of a curve; in geometry, the number by which its double points fall short of the highest number possible in a curve of the same order.

dē·fi'cien·cy diṣ·ēaṣe', a disease, as rickets, scurvy, or pellagra, caused by a lack of vitamins, etc. in the diet.

dē·fi'cien·cy judġ'ment, in law, a judgment in favor of a mortgagee for the remainder of a debt not completely cleared by foreclosure of the mortgage.

dē·fi'cient (-fish'ent), *a.* 1. lacking in some essential; defective; imperfect.
2. not sufficient; inadequate in amount, quality, degree, etc.
deficient number; see *abundant number* under *abundant*.
Syn.—defective, inadequate, imperfect, incomplete.

dē·fi'cient, *n.* a deficient person or thing.

dē·fi'cient·ly, *adv.* in a deficient manner.

def'i·cit, *n.* [L., 3d pers. sing. pres. ind. of *deficere,* to be wanting, to fail.] the amount by which a sum of money is less than what is expected, due, needed, etc.; shortage.

dē fi'dē, [L.] of the faith: used in the Roman Catholic Church to designate a truth regarded as revealed.

dē·fī'ēr, *n.* one who defies; as, a *defier* of the laws.

dē·fig·ū·rā'tion, *n.* a disfiguring. [Obs.]

dē·fig'ūre, *v.t.* to delineate. [Obs.]

def·i·lāde', *v.t.* and *v.i.*; defiladed, *pt., pp.*; defilading, *ppr.* [Fr.] to arrange (troops and fortifications) so that the terrain will protect them, especially from enfilading fire.

def·i·lāde' (*or* def'i-lād), *n.* 1. the act of defilading.
2. the protection or concealment afforded by defilading.

dē·fīle', *v.t.*; defiled, *pt., pp.*; defiling, *ppr.* [ME. *defoulen*; OFr. *defouler,* to tread underfoot; insult; influenced by ME. *filen,* to foul, from AS. *fylan,* to make foul, from *ful,* foul.]
1. to make filthy; to dirty; to make impure; to pollute.
2. to soil or sully; to tarnish, as reputation.
He is among the greatest prelates of the age, however his character may be *defiled* by dirty hands. —Swift.
3. to make ceremonially unclean.
That which dieth of itself, he shall not eat, to *defile* himself therewith. —Lev. xxii. 8.
4. to violate the chastity of; to debauch; to deflower. [Archaic.]
Shechem lay with her, and *defiled* her. —Gen. xxxiv. 2.
5. to corrupt; to vitiate.
Defile not yourselves with the idols of Egypt. —Ezek. xx. 7.
Syn.—contaminate, corrupt, pollute, tarnish, taint, vitiate, sully, soil, stain, befoul, debauch.

dē·fīle', *v.i.* [Fr. *défiler,* to file off, unravel; *dé-*, from, and *filer,* to spin threads, from *fil,* L. *filium,* a thread.]
1. to march in a line, in single file.
2. to march by files.

dē·fīle' (*or* dē'fīl), *n.* [Fr. *défilé,* from *défiler,* to file off.]
1. a narrow passage or way through which troops can march only in single file or in files.
2. any long, narrow valley or mountain pass.
3. a march in single file or in files.

dē·fīle', *v.t.* to defilade.

dē·fīle'ment, *n.* 1. the act of defiling, or the state of being defiled; foulness; dirtiness; uncleanness.
2. corruption of morals, principles, or character; impurity; pollution.
The chaste can not rake into such filth without danger of *defilement*. —Addison.
3. a thing that defiles.

dē·fīle'ment, *n.* same as *defilade*.

dē·fīl'ēr, *n.* one who defiles something.

dē·fil·i·ā'tion, *n.* [*de-* priv., and L. *filius,* a son, *filia,* a daughter.] the act of making childless by abduction. [Rare.]

dē·fīn'ȧ·ble, *a.* that can be defined; ascertainable; determinable; as, *definable* limits.

dē·fīn'ȧ·bly, *adv.* in a definable manner.

dē·fīne', *v.t.*; defined, *pt., pp.*; defining, *ppr.* [ME. *definen*; OFr. *definer*; L. *definire,* to limit, define; *de-*, from, and *finire,* to set a limit to, to bound, from *finis,* a boundary.]
1. to determine or describe the limits of; to determine or set down the precise outlines of.
2. to determine and state the limits and nature of; to describe exactly.
3. to state or explain the meaning or meanings of (a word, etc.).

4. to give the distinctive properties or characteristics of a thing; as, to *define* a line or an angle.
5. to constitute the definition of; as, the characteristics that *define* man.
6. to settle; to decide. [Obs.]
dē·fīne′, *v.i.* to determine; to decide. [Obs.]
dē·fīne′ment, *n.* the act of defining or describing; definition.
dē·fīn′ēr, *n.* one who defines.
def′i·nite, *a.* [L. *definitus*, pp. of *definire*, to define, bound.]
1. having certain limits; bounded with precision; fixed; determinate; as, a *definite* extent of land, *definite* dimensions, *definite* measure.
2. having certain limits in meaning; determinate; explicit; precise; as, a *definite* word, term, or expression.
3. certain; positive; as, it's *definite* that he'll go.
4. in botany, having a constant number of stamens, etc., less than 20 but always a multiple of the number of petals.
5. in grammar, limiting or pointing out; as, *the* is the *definite* article.
Syn.—bounded, certain, determinate, limited, fixed, precise, positive.
def′i·nite, *n.* a thing defined. [Obs.]
def′i·nite·ly, *adv.* in a definite manner.
def′i·nite·ness, *n.* the quality of being definite; precision; certainty of extent.
def·i·ni′tion (-nish′un), *n.* [L. *definitio*, a boundary, a definition, from pp. of *definire*, to define.]
1. the act of defining, determining, distinguishing, or explaining.
2. a brief description of what a thing is.
3. an explanation or statement of what a word or phrase means or has meant.
4. a putting or being in clear, sharp outline.
5. the power of a lens to give a distinct image of an object in all its details.
6. the degree of distinctness of a photograph, etc.
7. in radio and television, the degree of accuracy with which sounds or images are reproduced.
def·i·ni′tion·ăl, *a.* pertaining to definition; used in defining; abounding in definitions.
dē·fin′i·tive, *a.* 1. decisive; conclusive; final.
2. most nearly complete and accurate; as, a *definitive* edition of Shakespeare.
3. serving to define; limiting; distinguishing.
4. in biology, complete in development or formation; as, a *definitive* organ.
dē·fin′i·tive, *n.* in grammar, a word that defines or limits a noun, as *this, that, some*, etc.
dē·fin′i·tive hōst, the organism on or in which a parasite lives in the adult stage.
dē·fin′i·tive·ly, *adv.* in a definitive manner.
dē·fin′i·tive·ness, *n.* the state or quality of being definitive.
dē·fin′i·tūde, *n.* definiteness; precision.
dē·fix′, *v.t.* to fix; to fasten. [Obs.]
def″lȧ·grȧ·bil′i·ty, *n.* combustibility.
dē·flā′grȧ·ble, *a.* having the quality of burning rapidly.
def′lȧ·grāte, *v.t.* and *v.i.*; deflagrated, *pt., pp.*; deflagrating, *ppr.* [L. *deflagratus*, pp. of *deflagrare*, to burn, consume; *de-*, intens., and *flagrare*, to burn.] to burn rapidly, with intense heat and dazzling light.
def·lȧ·grā′tion, *n.* combustion.
dē·flāte′, *v.t.*; deflated, *pt., pp.*; deflating, *ppr.* [L. *de-*, from, and *flatus*, pp. of *flare*, to blow.]
1. to collapse by letting out air or gas; as, to *deflate* a balloon or pneumatic tire.
2. to lessen in amount, importance, etc., as currency.
Opposed to *inflate*.
dē·flā′tion, *n.* 1. a deflating or being deflated.
2. a lessening of the amount of money in circulation, resulting in a relatively sharp and sudden rise in its value and fall in prices.
3. in geology, a wearing away of land by the action of the wind.
dē·flā′tion·ăr·y, *a.* of, causing, or characterized by deflation.
dē·flā′tŏr, *n.* a person or thing that deflates.
dē·flect′, *v.t.* and *v.i.*; deflected, *pt., pp.*; deflecting, *ppr.* [L. *deflectere*, to bend aside; *de-*, from, and *flectere*, to bend.] to turn or bend to one side; to swerve.
dē·flect′ȧ·ble, *a.* capable of being deflected.
dē·flect′ed, *a.* 1. turned aside, or from a direct line or course.
2. in biology, bending downward; deflexed.
dē·flec′tion, *n.* [LL. *deflexio*, a bending aside, from L. *deflexus*, pp. of *deflectere*, to bend aside.]
1. deviation; the act of turning aside; a deflecting or being deflected.

King David found out the *deflection* and indirectness of our minds. —Montague.

2. the amount of deviation.
3. the deviation from the zero mark of the needle or pointer of a measuring instrument.
4. in optics, diffraction. [Obs.]
5. in mathematics, the distance by which a curve departs from another curve, or from a straight line.
6. in mechanics, the bending of any material exposed to a transverse strain.
dē·flec″tion·i·zā′tion, *n.* removal of inflections.
dē·flec′tion·īze, *v.t.* to free from inflections.
dē·flect′ive, *a.* causing deflection or tending to deflect.
dē·flec·tom′e·tēr, *n.* [L. *deflectere*, to bend aside, deflect, and *metrum*, a measure.] an instrument for measuring deflection, as that of a bridge under a certain stress.
dē·flect′ŏr, *n.* a thing that deflects; especially, a device for deflecting a current of air, gas, sound, etc.
dē·flex′, *v.t.*; deflexed (-flext), *pt., pp.*; deflexing, *ppr.* [L. *deflexus*, pp. of *deflectere*, to turn aside.] to turn aside or down.
dē·flexed′ (-flext′), *a.* bent down; deflected.
dē·flex′iŏn (-flek′shun), *n.* deflection: British spelling.
dē·flex′ūre, *n.* a bending down; a turning aside; deviation.
dē·flō′rāte, *a.* in botany, (a) having cast its pollen, as a flower; (b) having shed its flowers, as a plant.
def·lō·rā′tion, *n.* the act of deflowering.
dē·flour′, *v.t.* same as *deflower*.
dē·flour′ēr, *n.* same as *deflowerer*.
dē·flōw′, *v.i.* to flow down. [Obs.]
dē·flow′ēr, *v.t.*; deflowered, *pt., pp.*; deflowering, *ppr.* [ME. *deflouren*; OFr. *desflorir*; LL. *deflorare*, to deprive of flowers.]
1. to take away the virginity of (a woman).
2. to ravish; to ravage; to spoil.
3. to remove flowers from (a plant).
dē·flow′ēr·ēr, *n.* one who deflowers.
def′lū·ous, *a.* flowing down; falling off. [Obs.]
dē·flux′, *n.* a flowing down; a running downward. [Obs.]
dē·flux′iŏn (-fluk′shun), *n.* [LL. *defluxio*, a flowing down, from L. *defluere*, to flow down.] in medicine, a flow or discharge, as from the nose. [Rare.]
dē·fō′li·ănt, *n.* a chemical spray that strips growing plants of their leaves.
dē·fō′li·āte, *v.t.*; defoliated, *pt., pp.*; defoliating, *ppr.* [ML. *defoliatus*, pp. of *defoliare*, from L. *de-*, from, and *folium*, a leaf.]
1. to strip (trees, plants, etc.) of leaves.
2. to use a defoliant on.
dē·fō′li·āte, *v.i.* to be stripped of leaves.
dē·fō′li·āte, *a.* in botany, devoid of leaves; having shed the leaves.
dē·fō·li·ā′tion, *n.* a defoliating or being defoliated.
dē·fō′li·ā·tŏr, *n.* that which defoliates, as a leaf-destroying insect.
dē·fōrce′, *v.t.*; deforced, *pt., pp.*; deforcing, *ppr.* [OFr. *deforcer*, to take away by violence, LL. *de-*, from, and *fortia*, violence, from L. *fortis*, strong.]
1. in law, (a) to withhold the possession of (property, etc.) from the rightful owner by force; (b) to keep (a person) from rightful possession by force.
2. in Scottish law, to resist (an officer) in the execution of his official duty.
dē·fōrce′ment, *n.* 1. in law, the unjust holding of property, etc. to which another person has a right.
2. in Scottish law, a resisting of an officer in the execution of law.
dē·fōr′ciănt, *n.* in law, a person who deforces another or another's property.
dē·for′est, *v.t.*; deforested, *pt., pp.*; deforesting, *ppr.* to remove forests or trees from.
dē·for·es·tā′tion, *n.* a deforesting or being deforested.
dē·fọrm′, *v.t.*; deformed, *pt., pp.*; deforming, *ppr.* [ME. *deformen*; OFr. *deformer*; L. *deformare*, to put out of shape; *de-*, from, and *forma*, shape.]
1. to mar or injure the form or shape of.
2. to make ugly; to disfigure.
3. in physics, to change the shape of by pressure or stress.
Syn.—deface, disfigure, mar, mutilate.
dē·fọrm′, *v.i.* to become deformed.
dē·fọrm′, *a.* deformed. [Archaic.]
dē·fọrm′ȧ·ble, *a.* capable of being deformed, or changed in shape, as by pressure, etc.
dē·fọr·mā′tion, *n.* [L. *deformatio*, a deforming, disfiguring, from *deformare*, to deform.]
1. the act of deforming.
2. the fact or state of being deformed.
3. the result of deforming; disfigurement.
4. a change in form for the worse.
5. in physics, etc., (a) change of form or shape; (b) a changed form (of something).
dē·fọrmed′, *a.* 1. changed, especially marred, in form; disfigured; distorted; misshapen.

Deformed, unfinished, sent before my time
Into this breathing world. —Shak.

2. ugly, offensive, hateful, etc.
Syn.—ugly, disfigured, distorted.
dē·fọrm′ed·ly, *adv.* in a deformed manner.
dē·fọrm′ed·ness, *n.* the state of being deformed.
dē·fọrm′ēr, *n.* one who or that which deforms.
dē·fọrm′i·ty, *n.*; *pl.* **dē·fọrm′i·tieș**, [OFr. *deformeté*; L. *deformitas*, unshapeliness, from *deformis*, misshapen, deformed.]
1. the condition of being deformed.
2. abnormal bodily formation.
3. a deformed part, as of the body.
4. ugliness; depravity.
5. a deformed person or thing.
dē·fraud′, *v.t.*; defrauded, *pt., pp.*; defrauding, *ppr.* [ME. *defrauden*; OFr. *defrauder*; L. *defraudare*, to cheat, defraud; *de-*, intens., and *fraudare*, to cheat, from *fraus* (*-dis*), deceit, fraud.] to deprive of rights, property, etc. by deception or fraud; to cheat; to cozen.
Syn.—cheat, deceive, rob, cozen, dupe.
dē·frau·dā′tion, *n.* the act of defrauding.
dē·fraud′ēr, *n.* one who defrauds; a cheat; an embezzler; a peculator.
dē·fraud′ment, *n.* defraudation.
dē·frāy′, *v.t.*; defrayed, *pt., pp.*; defraying, *ppr.* [OFr. *defrayer, defraier*, to pay the expense, *de-*, from, off, and *frait*, expense, cost.]
1. to satisfy; as, to *defray* anger. [Obs.]
2. to bear, pay, or settle (the cost or expenses).
dē·frāy′ăl, *n.* the act of paying or defraying.
dē·frāy′ēr, *n.* one who defrays expenses.
dē·frāy′ment, *n.* payment; defrayal.
dē·frock′, *v.t.* to take priestly dress or church position from; to unfrock.
dē·frost′, *v.t.*; defrosted, *pt., pp.*; defrosting, *ppr.* to remove frost or ice from, as refrigerating coils.
dē·frost′, *v.i.* to become rid of ice or frost.
dē·frost′ēr, *n.* any device for melting ice and frost or preventing their formation, as on an airplane wing, automobile windshield, etc.
deft, *a.* [ME. *defte*, simple, meek, from AS. *ge-dæfte*, meek, gentle, from *dæftan*, to prepare, to put in order.]
1. showing skill and aptness; subtly apt; handy; dexterous; as, *deft* workmanship.
2. modest; also, neat. [Obs.]
def′tēr·där, *n.* [Turk.] in Turkey, a minister of finance; a treasurer.
deft′ly, *adv.* in a deft manner; skillfully.
deft′ness, *n.* the quality of being deft.
dē·funct′, *a.* [L. *defunctus*, pp. of *defungi*, to do, perform, finish anything, finish life, die; *de-*, from, off, and *fungi*, to perform.] no longer living or existing; dead; extinct.
dē·funct′, *n.* a dead person. [Rare.]
dē·func′tion, *n.* death. [Obs.]
dē·func′tive, *a.* funereal. [Obs.]
dē·fūșe′, *v.t.* to diffuse. [Obs.]
dē·fūșe′, dē-fūșe′, *v.t.*; defused, de-fused, *pt., pp.*; defusing, de-fusing, *ppr.* 1. to remove the fuse from (a bomb or the like).
2. to render harmless.
dē·fȳ′, *v.t.*; defied, *pt., pp.*; defying, *ppr.* [ME. *defien, diffyen*; OFr. *defier*, to distrust, repudiate, defy, from hyp. LL. *disfidare*, from L. *dis-*, from, and *fidus*, faithful.]
1. to repudiate; to recoil from. [Obs.]
2. to challenge (someone) to fight; to provoke by daring to a combat. [Archaic.]

I once again
Defy thee to the trial of mortal fight.
—Milton.

3. to dare (someone) to do or prove something.
4. to brave; to offer to hazard a conflict by resisting or opposing boldly or openly; as, to *defy* the arguments of an opponent.
5. to resist completely; to baffle; to foil.
dē·fȳ′, *n.*; *pl.* **dē·fieș′**, a defiance; a challenge. [Slang.]
deg, *v.t.* and *v.i.*; degged, *pt., pp.*; degging, *ppr.* to sprinkle. [Brit. Dial.]
dé·gȧ·gé′ (dā-gȧ-zhā′), *a.* [Fr., pp. of *dégager*, to release, redeem.]
1. unconstrained; unconventional; easy and free in manner.
2. uncommitted, uninvolved, detached, etc.

dē·gär′nish, *v.t.*; degarnished, *pt., pp.*; degarnishing, *ppr.* to strip, as a house of furnishings; to dismantle, as a fort.

dē·gär′nish·ment, *n.* the act of degarnishing.

dē·gas′, *v.t.*; degassed, *pt., pp.*; degassing, *ppr.* to remove gas from; specifically, (a) to evacuate the gases from (a vacuum tube, etc.); (b) to decontaminate (an area or person affected with a poison gas).

dē·gauss′, *v.t.* [*de-*, and *gauss.*] to neutralize the magnetic field surrounding (a ship) as a protection against magnetic mines.

dē·ġen′dēr, dē·ġen′ēr, *v.i.* to degenerate. [Obs.]

dē·ġen′ēr·ȧ·cy, *n.* 1. a degenerating; a growing worse or inferior; as, the *degeneracy* of a plant.

2. the quality or condition of being degenerate; lowness; meanness.

dē·ġen′ēr·āte, *a.* [L. *degeneratus*, pp. of *degenerare*, to become unlike one's race, fall off, degenerate, from *degener*, not genuine, base, from *de-*, from, and *genus*, race, kind.] having sunk below a former or normal condition, character, etc.; deteriorated; degraded; as, a *degenerate* plant, a *degenerate* empire.

dē·ġen′ēr·āte, *n.* a person who has deteriorated from the normal condition or standard, especially one who is subnormal mentally or morally.

dē·ġen′ēr·āte, *v.i.*; degenerated, *pt., pp.*; degenerating, *ppr.* 1. to pass from a good to a bad or worse state; to lose former, normal, or higher qualities.

2. in biology, to become gradually of a lower type; to deteriorate: said of species, etc.

dē·ġen′ēr·āte′ly, *adv.* in a degenerate or base manner.

dē·ġen′ēr·āte·ness, *n.* degeneracy.

dē·ġen·ēr·ā′tion, *n.* 1. degeneracy.

2. in biology, a gradual falling off or deterioration to a lower form of development.

3. in medicine, biochemical change in tissues or organs, caused by injury or disease and leading to loss of vitality, of function, etc.

4. the thing degenerated. [Rare.]

amyloid degeneration; see under *amyloid.*

caseous degeneration; see under *caseous.*

dē·ġen·ēr·ā′tion·ist, *n.* one believing that the tendency of all life is toward degeneration.

dē·ġen′ēr·ȧ·tive, *a.* 1. of, showing, or causing degeneration.

2. tending to degenerate; making worse.

dē·ġen′ēr·ous, *a.* degenerated. [Obs.]

dē·ġen′ēr·ous·ly, *adv.* meanly. [Obs.]

dē·ġērm′, *v.t.*; degermed, *pt., pp.*; degerming, *ppr.* to remove the germs from; as, to *degerm* wheat.

dē·ġēr·mi·nā′tŏr, *n.* a machine which crushes grain and removes the germ.

dē·glāze′, *v.t.*; deglazed, *pt., pp.*; deglazing, *ppr.* to remove the glaze from (pottery, etc.).

dē·glō′ry, *v.t.* to dishonor. [Obs.]

dē·glū′ti·nāte, *v.t.*; deglutinated, *pt., pp.*; deglutinating, *ppr.* [L. *deglutinatus*, pp. of *deglutinare*, to unglue; *de-*, from, and *glutinare*, to glue, from *gluten*, glue.]

1. to unglue; to loosen or separate (substances glued together).

2. to extract gluten from.

dē·glū·ti·nā′tion, *n.* the act or process of deglutinating.

dē·glū·ti′tion, *n.* [LL. *deglutire*, to swallow down; L. *de-*, from, down, and *glutire*, to swallow.] the act, process, or power of swallowing.

dē·glū·ti′tious, *a.* relating to deglutition. [Rare.]

dē·glū′ti·tō·ry, *a.* acting as an aid to deglutition.

deg·rȧ·dā′tion, *n.* [ML. *degradatio*, a reducing in rank, from L. *de-*, down, and *gradus*, a step.]

1. a reducing in rank; the act of depriving one of a degree of honor, dignity, or rank; also, deposition, removal, or dismissal from office; as, the *degradation* of a public official, *degradation* of a priest.

2. the state of being reduced from a higher or more honorable station to a lower one.

The descent of Spain, once the first among monarchies, to the lower depths of *degradation.* —Macaulay.

3. diminution or reduction of strength, efficacy, value, altitude, or magnitude.

4. in painting, a lessening and obscuring of distant objects in a landscape so that they appear in perspective.

5. in geology, the lowering or wearing down of higher lands, rocks, strata, etc. by erosion.

6. in biology, the condition of a type which exhibits degraded forms; degeneration.

The *degradation* of the species man is observed in some of its varieties. —Dana.

degradation of energy; in physics, any process by which available energy becomes unavailable, as by conversion into heat.

Syn.—debasement, abasement, dishonor, depression, disgrace, degeneracy, baseness, deposition.

dē·grāde′, *v.t.*; degraded, *pt., pp.*; degrading, *ppr.* [ME. *degraden*; OFr. *degrader*; LL. *degradare*, to reduce in rank.]

1. to reduce from a higher to a lower rank or status; to deprive of a position of honor.

Prynne was sentenced to be *degraded* from the bar. —Palfrey.

2. to lower or corrupt in quality, moral character, etc.

3. to bring into dishonor or contempt.

4. to lower in value, price, quality, etc.

5. in geology, to lower (a surface) by erosion; to wear down.

6. in biology, to place in a lower classification.

Syn.—depress, humble, debase, lower, sink, bring down, depose, dishonor, disgrace.

dē·grāde′, *v.i.* to degenerate; to sink to a lower position or type.

dē·grād′ed, *a.* 1. reduced in rank; deprived of an office or dignity; lowered; sunk; reduced in estimation or value; debased; low.

2. in biology, reduced to a lower classification.

dē·grāde′ment, *n.* degradation. [Rare.]

dē·grād′ing, *a.* that degrades; debasing.

dē·grād′ing·ly, *adv.* in a degrading manner.

dē grā′ti·ȧ (-shi-ȧ), [L.] in law, by grace or favor.

deg·rȧ·vā′tion, *n.* the act of making heavy. [Obs.]

dē·gree′, *n.* [ME. *degre, degree*; OFr. *degre*, a degree, step, rank; hyp. LL. *degradus*, from *degradare*, from L. *de-*, down, and *gradus*, a step, from *gradi*, to walk.]

1. a step; a stair, or set of steps.

2. a step or single movement, upward or downward, toward any end; any of the successive steps or stages in a process or series.

We have feet to scale and climb
By slow *degrees.* —Longfellow.

3. a step in the direct line of descent; as, a cousin in the third *degree.*

4. social or official rank, position, or class; as, a man of low *degree.*

5. the relative condition, way, or respect; as, each contributing to victory in his *degree.*

6. intensity, amount, or extent; as, the light is intense to a *degree* that is intolerable; we suffer an extreme *degree* of heat or cold.

7. in algebra, rank as determined by the sum of a term's exponents; as, a^3c^2 and x^5 are each of the fifth *degree.*

8. in arithmetic, three figures taken together in numeration; thus, the number 270,360 consists of two *degrees.*

9. in education, a rank given by a college or university to a student who has completed a required course of study, or to a distinguished person as an honor; as, an M.A. *degree*, a Litt.D. *degree.*

10. in grammar, a grade of comparison of adjectives and adverbs; as, the positive *degree* of *good* is *good*, the comparative *degree* is *better*, and the superlative *degree* is *best.*

11. in law, the seriousness of a crime; as, murder in the first *degree.*

12. in mathematics, astronomy, geography, etc., a unit of measure for angles or arcs, one 360th part of the circumference of a circle: the measure of an angle is the number of degrees between its sides considered as radii of a circle; as, a right angle has 90 *degrees.*

13. in music, (a) a line or space on the staff; (b) the interval between any two notes on an adjacent line and space, as between E and F, E♭ and F♯, or G♯ and A♭.

14. in physics, (a) a unit of measure for temperature; as, the boiling point of water is 212 *degrees* Fahrenheit (212° F.); (b) a line marking a degree on a thermometer.

by degrees; by moderate advances; step by step.

to a degree; (a) exceedingly; extremely; as, rash *to a degree*; (b) somewhat.

dē·gree′-dāy′, *n.* a unit of heat measurement equal to one degree of variation from a standard temperature in the average temperature of one day.

dē·gres′sion, *n.* [LL. *degressio*, from L. *degressus*, pp. of *degredi*, to go down; *de-*, down, and *gredi*, to go.] a going down; descent or decrease; specifically, a decrease in the rate of taxation on sums below a specified amount.

dē·gres′sive, *a.* designating or of a system of taxation in which the rate of taxation becomes progressively lower on sums below a specified amount.

dẹ′gŭ, *n.* [native S. Am. name.] any South American rodent of the genus *Octodon.*

dē·gum′, *v.t.*; degummed, *pt., pp.*; degumming, *ppr.* to rid of gum; to deglutinate; as, to *degum* raw silk.

dē·gust′, *v.t.* and *v.i.*; degusted, *pt., pp.*; degusting, *ppr.* [L. *degustare*, to taste of; *de-*, and *gustare*, to taste.] to taste; especially, to taste attentively so as to perceive the flavor. [Rare.]

dē·gus′tāte, *v.t.* to degust. [Rare.]

dē·gus·tā′tion, *n.* [LL. *degustatio*, tasting, from L. *degustare*, to taste.] a tasting. [Rare.]

dē gus′ti·bus non dis·pū·tan′dum (est), [L.] there is no disputing about tastes.

dē·hisce′, *v.i.*; dehisced, *pt., pp.*; dehiscing, *ppr.* [L. *dehiscere*, to gape open; *de-*, off, from, and *hiscere*, to gape, yawn.] to gape; specifically, in botany, to burst or split open, as the seed capsules of plants.

dē·his′cence, *n.* 1. a gaping.

2. in botany, a bursting or splitting open of a seed capsule, the cells of anthers, etc.

dē·his′cent, *a.* bursting or splitting open, as a seed capsule; exhibiting dehiscence.

DEHISCENT SEED CAPSULE

dē·hō·nes′tāte, *v.t.* to dishonor. [Obs.]

dē·hon·es·tā′tion, *n.* a dishonoring. [Obs.]

dē·hǫrn′, *v.t.*; dehorned, *pt., pp.*; dehorning, *ppr.* to prevent the growth of the horns of (a calf) by cauterization; to remove the horns from (cattle).

dē·hǫrṣ′, *prep.* [Fr. *dehors*; OFr. *defors*, out of doors, outside.] in law, outside of; foreign to; irrelevant to.

dē·hǫrṣ′, *n.* in fortification, collectively, accessory works outside of the main fort.

dē·hort′, *v.t.* to dissuade. [Rare.]

dē·hor·tā′tion, *n.* [L. *dehortari*, to dissuade; *de-*, from, and *hortari*, to persuade.] dissuasion; advice or counsel against something.

dē·hort′ȧ·tive, *a.* dehortatory. [Rare.]

dē·hort′ȧ·tō·ry, *a.* dissuading; belonging or tending to dissuasion.

dē·hort′ēr, *n.* a dissuader.

dē·hū′măn·īze, *v.t.*; dehumanized, *pt., pp.*; dehumanizing, *ppr.* to divest of those qualities characteristically human, as pity, kindness, etc.

dē″hū·mid′i·fī·ēr, *n.* an apparatus that removes part of the water vapor from air that is forced through it.

dē″hū·mid′i·fȳ, *v.t.*; dehumidified, *pt., pp.*; dehumidifying, *ppr.* [*de-*, and *humidify.*] to remove moisture from (the air, etc.).

dē·hȳ′drāte, *v.t.*; dehydrated, *pt., pp.*; dehydrating, *ppr.* [*de-*, and Gr. *hydōr*, water, and *-ate.*] to remove water from; to dry; as, alcohol *dehydrates* animal tissue.

dē·hȳ′drāte, *v.i.* to lose water; to become dry.

dē·hȳ·drā′tion, *n.* the act of dehydrating or the state of being dehydrated.

dē·hȳ′drā·tŏr, *n.* that which dehydrates.

dē·hȳ′drō·ġen·āte, *v.t.* to dehydrogenize.

dē·hȳ″drō·ġen·i·zā′tion, *n.* the removal of hydrogen from a compound.

dē·hȳ′drō·ġen·īze, *v.t.*; dehydrogenized, *pt., pp.*; dehydrogenizing, *ppr.* to remove hydrogen from.

dē·hyp′nō·tīze, *v.t.* to arouse from a hypnotic trance.

Dē·iȧ·nī′rȧ, Dē·iȧ·neī′rȧ, *n.* [L. *Deianira*; Gr. *Dēianeira.*] in Greek mythology, the second wife of Hercules, who unknowingly killed him by sending him a garment steeped in the poisoned blood of the centaur Nessus, thinking that it was a love charm.

dē·īc′ēr, *n.* an apparatus or heating device used to prevent or remove ice formations, as on the wings of an airplane while in flight.

dē′i·cīde, *n.* [L. *deus*, a god, and *cædere*, to kill, slay.]

1. the killing of a god.

2. the killer of a god.

deīç′tiç, *a.* [Gr. *deiktikos*, capable of proving, from *deiknynai*, to show, prove.]

1. in grammar, pointing out; demonstrative; as, *that* is a *deictic* pronoun.

2. in logic, proving directly: opposed to *elenctic.*

Also written *dictic.*

deīç′tiç·ăl·ly, *adv.* with directness and definiteness; pointedly.

dē·if′iç, dē·if′iç·ăl, *a.* [L. *deificus*, from *deus*, god, and *facere*, to make.]
1. tending to make divine; deifying; as, a *deific* impulse.
2. loosely, godlike.

dē″i·fi·çā′tion, *n.* 1. the act of deifying or the condition of being deified; apotheosis.
2. a deified person or embodiment.

dē′i·fī·ẽr, *n.* one who deifies.

dē′i·form, *a.* [L. *deus*, a god, and *forma*, form.]
1. like a god; of a godlike form.
2. divine.

dē·i·for′mi·ty, *n.* resemblance to a god. [Obs.]

dē′i·fȳ, *v.t.*; deified, *pt., pp.*; deifying, *ppr.* [ME. *deifien*; OFr. *deifier*; LL. *deificare*, to make divine; L. *deus*, a god, and *facere*, to make.]
1. to make a god of; to exalt to the rank of a deity; to rank among the deities.
2. to exalt into an object of worship; to treat as a god; as, to *deify* riches.
3. to idealize; to adore.

deign (dān), *v.t.*; deigned, *pt., pp.*; deigning, *ppr.* [ME. *deignen*; OFr. *deigner*; L. *dignari*, to deem worthy, from *dignus*, worthy.]
1. to accept with condescension. [Obs.]
2. to grant or allow with condescension; to vouchsafe; as, will you *deign* no answer?

deign, *v.i.* to think befitting one's dignity (*to do* something); to condescend; to lower oneself.

deign′ous (dān′us), *a.* arrogant; haughty. [Obs.]

Dē′ī grā′ti·ȧ (-shi-ȧ), [L.] by the grace of God.

dēil, *n.* [Scot.] 1. the devil.
2. a mischievous fellow.

Deī′mos, *n.* [Gr. *deimos*, fear, terror, personified by Homer in the *Iliad* and regarded later by the Greeks as the son of Ares.] a satellite of the planet Mars making a revolution in thirty hours and eighteen minutes: discovered by Asaph Hall, American astronomer, in 1877.

Deī·noc′e·ras, *n.* same as *Dinoceras*.

Deī·nor′nis, *n.* same as *Dinornis*.

deī′nō·saur, *n.* same as *dinosaur*.

Deī·nō·thē′ri·um, *n.* same as *Dinotherium*.

dē·ī′ŏn·īze, *v.t.* 1. to remove ions from.
2. to restore (gas that has become ionized) to its former condition.

Dē·ip′ȧ·rȧ, *n.* [LL., from L. *deus*, god, and *parere*, to bring forth.] a title of the Virgin Mary, meaning Mother of God.

dē·ip′ȧ·rous, *a.* bearing or bringing forth a god: applied to the Virgin Mary.

Dē·iph′ō·bus, *n.* [L.; Gr. *Dēiphobos*.] in Greek legend, a Trojan hero, son of Priam and Hecuba: he married Helen after the death of Paris, and was eventually killed by Menelaus.

deīp·nos′ō·phist, *n.* [Gr. *deipnon*, a dinner, and *sophistēs*, a learned man.] one who discourses learnedly at meals; a table philosopher.

Dēir′drē, *n.* [O.Ir. *Derdriu*, lit., the raging one.] in Irish legend, a princess of Ulster who eloped to Scotland with her lover: when he was treacherously killed by her guardian, she committed suicide.

dē′işm, *n.* [Fr. *déisme*, from L. *deus*, god.]
1. the belief that God exists and created the world but thereafter assumed no control over it or the lives of people.
2. in philosophy, the belief that reason is sufficient to prove the existence of God, with the consequent rejection of revelation and authority.

dē′ist, *n.* [Fr. *déiste*, from L. *deus*, god.] one who believes in deism.

dē·is′tiç, dē·is′tiç·ăl, *a.* pertaining to deism or to deists; embracing deism; as, a *deistic* writer.

dē·is′tiç·ăl·ly, *adv.* in a deistic manner.

dē·is′tiç·ăl·ness, *n.* the state or quality of being deistic.

dē′i·tāte, *a.* deified. [Obs.]

dē′i·ty, *n.*; *pl.* **dē′i·tieş,** [ME. *deite*; OFr. *deite*; LL. *deitas* (*-atis*), the divinity, from L. *divinitas* (*-atis*), divinity, from *deus*, god.]
1. the state of being a god; divine nature; godhood.
2. a god.
3. a goddess.
the Deity; God.

dé·jà vu (dā″zhȧ″vü′), [Fr., lit., already seen.] in psychology, the illusion that one has previously had a given experience.

dē·jeçt′, *v.t.*; dejected, *pt., pp.*; dejecting, *ppr.* [L. *dejectus*, pp. of *dejicere*, to throw or cast down.]
1. to throw down; also, to abate. [Obs.]
2. to depress the spirits of; to dispirit; to discourage; to dishearten.

Nor think, to die *dejects* my lofty mind.
—Pope.

dē·jeçt′, *a.* dejected; low-spirited. [Archaic.]

dē·jeç′tȧ, *n.pl.* [L., neut. pl. of *dejectus*, pp. of *dejicere*, to throw or cast down.] excrements.

dē·jeçt′ed, *a.* downcast; depressed; grieved; discouraged; as, a *dejected* look.

dē·jeçt′ed·ly, *adv.* in a dejected manner.

dē·jeçt′ed·ness, *n.* the state or quality of being dejected.

dē·jeçt′ẽr, *n.* one who or that which dejects.

dē·jeç′tion, *n.* 1. the state of being downcast; depression; melancholy; lowness of spirits, occasioned by grief or misfortune.

Of sorrow, *dejection*, and despair.
—Milton.

2. weakness; as, *dejection* of appetite. [Rare.]
3. in medicine, (a) an evacuation of the bowels; (b) the matter evacuated; excrement.
4. a casting or bowing down. [Rare.]

Syn.—depression, despondency, gloom, melancholy, sadness.

dē·jeçt′ly, *adv.* dejectedly. [Obs.]

dē·jeç′tō·ry, *a.* having the power or tending to cast down; specifically, in medicine, purgative.

dē·jeç′tūre, *n.* that which is ejected; excrement.

dej′ẽr·āte, *v.i.* [L. *dejerare*, *dejurare*, to take an oath.] to swear, as in taking an oath. [Obs.]

dej·ẽr·ā′tion, *n.* an oath. [Obs.]

dé·jeu·né′ (dā-zhē̃-nā′), *n.* a breakfast. [Obs.]

dé·jeu·ner′ (dā-zhē̃-nā′), *n.* [Fr.] a breakfast, especially a late one; hence, a luncheon.
déjeuner à la fourchette; literally, breakfast with the fork; a meal in the middle of the day, with meat and wine.

dē jū′rē, [L.] by right; in accordance with law; as, *de jure* government: distinguished from *de facto*.

dek′ȧ-, same as *deca-*.

Dek′ȧ·brist, *n.* [Russ. *Dekabr*, December, and *-ist*.] same as *Decembrist*.

dek′ȧ·drachm (-dram), *n.* [Gr. *deka*, ten, and *drachmē*, drachma.] a silver coin of ancient Greece, equal to ten drachms.

dek′ȧ·gram, *n.* same as *decagram*.

dek′ȧ·lī·tẽr, *n.* same as *decaliter*.

dek′ȧ·mē·tẽr, *n.* same as *decameter*.

dek′ȧ·stēre, *n.* same as *decastere*.

dek′le, *n.* same as *deckle*.

del, *n.* a part or portion. [Obs.]

dē·lac·ẽr·ā′tion, *n.* a tearing in pieces.

dē·laç·ri·mā′tion, dē·laç·ry·mā′tion, *n.* wateriness of the eyes. [Obs.]

del·aç·tā′tion, *n.* the act of weaning. [Obs.]

dē·lāine′, *n.* [Fr. *de laine*, of wool; L. *de-*, of, from, and *lana*, wool.] a lightweight fabric made originally of wool, now usually of cotton and wool.

dē·lam′i·nāte, *v.t.* and *v.i.* [*de-*, and *laminate*.] to separate into layers.

dē·lam·i·nā′tion, *n.* the process of splitting into separate layers; specifically, in embryology, a splitting of the blastoderm into two layers of cells.

dē·lapse′, *v.i.* to fall or slide down. [Obs.]

dē·lap′sion, *n.* [L. *delapsus*, pp. of *delabi*, to fall or sink down; *de-*, down, and *labi*, to fall.] a falling down, as of the uterus. [Obs.]

dē·las·sā′tion, *n.* [from L. *delassatus*, pp. of *delassare*, to weary, tire out; *de-*, and *lassare*, to tire, weary.] fatigue; weariness. [Obs.]

dē·lāte′, *v.t.*; delated, *pt., pp.*; delating, *ppr.* [L. *delatus*, pp. of *deferre*, to bring or carry down, report, announce, accuse.]
1. to carry; to convey; to transmit. [Obs.]
2. to relate; to announce; to make public.
3. to bring a charge against; to accuse; to inform against; to denounce. [Chiefly Scot.]

As men were *delated*, they were marked down for such a fine. —Burnet.

dē·lā′tion, *n.* 1. carriage; conveyance. [Obs.]
2. in law, accusation; act of charging with a crime or informing against.

The accusers were not to be liable to the charge of *delation*. —Milman.

dē·lā′tŏr, *n.* an accuser; an informer.

del·ȧ·tō′ri·ăn, *a.* characteristic of or pertaining to a delator.

Del′ȧ·wāre, *n.* an American hybrid grape, reddish in color, having a sweet flavor.

Del·ȧ·wār′ē·ăn, *a.* of the State of Delaware.

Del·ȧ·wār′ē·ăn, *n.* a native or inhabitant of the State of Delaware.

Del′ȧ·wāreş, *n.pl.* a tribe of Algonquian Indians who lived in the Delaware River valley.

dē·lāy′, *v.t.*; delayed, *pt., pp.*; delaying, *ppr.* [ME. *delayen*, *delaien*; OFr. *delaier*, from *de-*, from, and *laier*, to leave, let.]
1. to put off to a future time; to defer; to postpone.
2. to retard; to stop, detain, or hinder for a time; to restrain or retard the motion of; as, the mail is *delayed*.
3. to allay. [Obs.]

Syn.—defer, postpone, procrastinate, prolong, protract, retard.

dē·lāy′, *v.i.* to linger; to move slowly; to loiter; to stop for a time.

dē·lāy′, *n.* [ME. *delay*; OFr. *delai*, from *delaier*, *delayer*, to delay.] a delaying or being delayed; procrastination; hindrance; lingering; stay.

dē·lāy′ẽr, *n.* one who or that which delays.

dē·lāy′ing aç′tion, maneuvers to cover a retreat, gain time, etc.

dē·lāy′ing·ly, *adv.* in a manner to cause delay.

dē·lāy′ment, *n.* hindrance; loitering. [Obs.]

del çred′ẽr·e, [It., of belief, or trust; *del*, for *de il*, of the, and *credere*, trust; L. *de*, of, and *credere*, to believe.] a guaranty given by a factor, broker, or mercantile agent, binding him to warrant the solvency of the purchasers of goods which he sells on credit.

dē′lē, *v.t.*; deled, *pt., pp.*; deleing, *ppr.* [L., imper. sing. of *delere*, to blot out, erase.] in printing, to take out (a letter, etc.); delete: usually in the imperative as a direction to the printer.

dē′lē, *n.* a mark (₰) showing that a letter, word, etc. is to be taken out.

del′e·ble, *a.* same as *delible*.

dē·leç·tȧ·bil′i·ty, *n.* the quality of being delectable.

dē·leç′tȧ·ble, *a.* [L. *delectabilis*, delightful, from *delectare*, to delight.] delightful; highly pleasing; that gives joy or pleasure.

dē·leç′tȧ·ble·ness, *n.* delectability.

dē·leç′tȧ·bly, *adv.* delightfully; charmingly.

dē·leç′tāte, *v.t.* to please; to charm; to delight.

dē·leç·tā′tion, *n.* great pleasure; enjoyment; delight.

dē·leç′tus, *n.* [L., from *delectus*, pp. of *deligere*, to select, choose.] a book containing selected passages, used in the study of Greek or Latin.

del′ē·gȧ·cy, *n.*; *pl.* **del′ē·gȧ·cieş,** 1. the act of delegating or state of being delegated.
2. authority to act as a delegate.
3. a delegation.

dē·lē′găl·īze, *v.t.* to make no longer legal.

del′ē·gāte, *n.* [L. *delegatus*, pp. of *delegare*, to appoint.]
1. a person authorized or sent to act for others; a deputy; a representative.
2. a representative of a United States Territory in the House of Representatives, who has the right to speak but not to vote.
3. in England, (a) one of the commissioners formerly appointed by the crown to hear and determine appeals from the ecclesiastical courts; (b) an acting committeeman in the University of Oxford.

Syn.—deputy, representative, commissioner, vicar, attorney, substitute.

del′ē·gāte, *a.* deputed; sent to act for or represent another; as, a *delegate* judge.

del′ē·gāte, *v.t.*; delegated, *pt., pp.*; delegating, *ppr.* [L. *delegatus*, pp. of *delegare*, to send or remove from one place to another, to appoint, assign; *de-*, from, and *legare*, to send, appoint.]
1. to authorize, send, or appoint as a delegate.
2. to entrust (authority, power, etc.) to a person acting as one's agent or representative.
3. in law, to assign (one's debtor) as debtor to one's creditor in place of oneself.

del·ē·gā′tion, *n.* 1. a delegating or being delegated.
2. the commission given to a delegate.
3. a delegate or group of delegates.

del′ē·gȧ·tō·ry, *a.* having a delegated position. [Obs.]

dē·len′dȧ, *n.pl.* [L., neut. pl. of *delendus*, gerundive of *delere*, to erase.] things to be blotted out or erased.

dē·len′dȧ est Çär·thā′gō, [L.] Carthage must be destroyed: Roman view of the proper fate for a traditional enemy.

dē·lēte′, *v.t.*; deleted, *pt., pp.*; deleting, *ppr.* [L. *deletus*, pp. of *delere*, to blot out, destroy.] to remove (a printed or written letter, word, etc.); to cross out; to cancel; to dele.

del·ē·tē′ri·ous, *a.* [Gr. *dēlētērios*, baneful, destructive, from *dēlētēr*, a destroyer, from *dēleisthai*, to injure, to destroy.] harmful to health, well-being, etc.; destructive; injurious; pernicious; unwholesome.

del·ē·tē′ri·ous·ly, *adv.* in a deleterious manner.

del·ē·tē′ri·ous·ness, *n.* the quality of being deleterious.

del′ē·ter·y, *a.* destructive; poisonous. [Obs.]

del′ē·ter·y, *n.* any destructive agent. [Obs.]

dē·lē′tion, *n.* 1. the act of deleting or erasing.

2. an erasure; a passage deleted.
3. destruction, as by blotting out; extinction. [Rare.]

dē·lē′tive, *a.* pertaining to deletion; tending to delete or erase. [Rare.]

del′ē·tō·ry, *n.* that which deletes.

delf, *n.* [ME. *delf,* a quarry, a grave; AS. *dælf,* a ditch, from *delfan,* to dig.]
1. the result of digging, as a pit, ditch, mine, etc. [Obs.]
2. a drain, as one on the landward side of a sea wall.
3. in heraldry, an abatement in the form of a square sod.

delf, delft, *n.* delftware.

delft′wāre, *n.* 1. glazed pottery, usually blue, which originated at Delft, Holland.
2. any similar ware.
3. brown earthenware covered with a white glaze and decorated.

del′ī, *n.* a delicatessen. [Colloq.]

Dē′li·ȧ, *n.* in Greek mythology, Artemis.

Dē′li·ăn, *a.* of or pertaining to Delos, a small island in the Aegean Sea, or its people.
Delian problem; the problem of finding the length of the side of a cube when the volume is doubled: so termed from the advice of the oracle of Apollo at Delos, that the plague then raging would cease were the cubical altar doubled.

Dē′li·ăn, *n.* a native or inhabitant of Delos.

del′i·bāte, *v.t.* to taste; to take a sip of. [Obs.]

del·i·bā′tion, *n.* a taste; a sip. [Obs.]

del′i·bẽr, *v.t.* and *v.i.* to deliberate. [Obs.]

dē·lib′ẽr·āte, *a.* [L. *deliberatus,* pp. of *deliberare,* to consider, weigh well, from *de-,* intens., and *librare,* to weigh, from *libra,* a scales.]
1. carefully thought out or formed; premeditated; done on purpose.
2. formed with deliberation; careful in considering; not sudden or rash; as, a *deliberate* opinion; a *deliberate* measure or result.
3. lacking rapidity; slow; unhurried; as, a *deliberate* move.
Syn.—careful, cautious, intentional, purposed, thoughtful.

dē·lib′ẽr·āte, *v.i.;* deliberated, *pt., pp.;* deliberating, *ppr.* to estimate the weight or force of arguments, or the probable consequences of a measure, in order to make a choice or decision; to consider carefully and fully.

The woman that *deliberates* is lost.
—Addison.

dē·lib′ẽr·āte, *v.t.* to weigh in the mind; to consider and examine the reasons for and against; to consider carefully; to ponder on; as, to *deliberate* questions of state.

dē·lib′ẽr·āte·ly, *adv.* with careful consideration or deliberation; circumspectly; not hastily or rashly; slowly; as, a resolution *deliberately* formed.

dē·lib′ẽr·āte·ness, *n.* calm consideration; circumspection; due attention to the arguments for and against a measure; caution.

dē·lib′ẽr·ā·tẽr, *n.* same as *deliberator.*

dē·lib·ẽr·ā′tion, *n.* 1. the act of deliberating; a considering carefully.
2. [*often pl.*] discussion and consideration of the reasons for and against a measure; as, the *deliberations* of a legislative body or council.
3. the quality or condition of being deliberate; carefulness; slowness.
Syn.—thoughtfulness, circumspection, reflection, consideration, wariness, caution, coolness, prudence.

dē·lib′ẽr·ā·tive, *a.* 1. of or for deliberating; considering and debating; as, a *deliberative* assembly.
2. characterized by or resulting from deliberation.

dē·lib′ẽr·ā·tive, *n.* a discourse in which a question is discussed and examined. [Obs.]

dē·lib′ẽr·ā·tive·ly, *adv.* by deliberation; in a deliberative manner.

dē·lib′ẽr·ā·tōr, *n.* one who deliberates.

del′i·ble, del′e·ble, *a.* [L. *delebilis,* from *delere,* to blot out.] that can be deleted.

del′i·cȧ·cy, *n.; pl.* **del′i·cȧ·cies,** 1. the quality of being delicate.
2. fineness; frailty; graceful slightness, softness, etc.; as, the *delicacy* of a petal, of Venetian glass, of a child's face.
3. weakness of constitution or health; as, the *delicacy* of an invalid.
4. the condition or quality of requiring careful and deft handling; as, the *delicacy* of a point or question.
5. fineness of feeling, observing, or appreciating; as, *delicacy* of musical taste.
6. sensitiveness of response; as, the *delicacy* of a compass.
7. fineness of touch, skill, etc.
8. a fine regard for the feelings of others.
9. a sensitive distaste for what is considered improper or offensive.
10. a choice food; as, caviar and other *delicacies.*
11. the quality of being addicted to pleasure; luxuriousness. [Obs.]
12. pleasure; self-gratification. [Obs.]

del′i·cāte, *a.* [ME. *delicat;* L. *delicatus,* giving pleasure, delightful, from *delicere,* to allure; *de-,* intens., and *lacere,* to draw gently, to charm.]
1. pleasing to the senses; as, a *delicate* odor.
2. beautifully fine in texture, quality, workmanship, etc.; as, a *delicate* fabric, *delicate* skin.
3. deliciously mild, light, or soft; as, a *delicate* color, air, etc.
4. slight and subtle; as, a *delicate* difference.
5. easily damaged, spoiled, disordered, etc.; as, a *delicate* vase, a *delicate* stomach.
6. frail in health; as, a *delicate* child.
7. needing careful handling; as, a *delicate* diplomatic question.
8. finely sensitive in feeling, understanding, or responding; as, a *delicate* ear for music, a *delicate* gauge.
9. finely skilled.
10. considerate and tactful.
11. having or showing a sensitive distaste for anything offensive or improper.

del′i·cāte, *n.* a delicacy; a dainty. [Archaic and Poet.]

del′i·cāte·ly, *adv.* in a delicate manner.

del′i·cāte·ness, *n.* the state of being delicate.

del″i·cȧ·tes′sen, *n.pl.* [G. *delikatessen,* from Fr. *délicatesse,* a delicacy.]
1. delicacies for the table; prepared cooked foods, especially meats; also, pickles, preserves, relishes, etc.
2. a store where such foods are sold.

dē·li′cious, *a.* [ME. *delicious;* L. *deliciosus,* delicious, from *deliciae,* an allurement, charm, from *delicere,* to allure.]
1. highly pleasing, especially to taste or smell; as, *delicious* fruit or wine.
2. very pleasing to the mind; delightful; as, a *delicious* entertainment.
3. pleasure-seeking; effeminate. [Obs.]
Syn.—delightful.—*Delicious* refers to the pleasure derived from certain of the senses; as, *delicious* food, a *delicious* fragrance; *delightful* may also refer to most of the senses, but has a higher application to matters of taste, feeling, and sentiment; as, a *delightful* abode, conversation, etc.

Dē·li′cious, *n.* a variety of sweet, red winter apple.

dē·li′cious·ly, *adv.* in a delicious manner; sweetly; pleasantly; delightfully.

dē·li′cious·ness, *n.* 1. the quality of being delicious.
2. great pleasure; luxury. [Obs.]

dē·lict′, *n.* [L. *delictum,* a fault, from *delinquere,* to fail, commit a fault; *de-,* from, and *linquere,* to leave.] in law, an offense; a misdemeanor.

del·i·gā′tion, *n.* [from L. *deligatus,* pp. of *deligare,* to bind down.] in surgery, a binding up; a bandaging.

dē·light′ (-līt′), *v.t.;* delighted, *pt., pp.;* delighting, *ppr.* [ME. *deliten;* L. *delectare,* to delight.] to please highly; to give great pleasure or joy to; as, a beautiful landscape *delights* the eye.

dē·light′, *v.i.* 1. to give great pleasure or joy.
2. to be greatly pleased; to rejoice: often followed by *in* or an infinitive; as, to *delight in* doing good.

I *delight to do* thy will, O my God.
—Ps. xl. 8.

dē·light′, *n.* 1. a high degree of pleasure or satisfaction of mind; joy.

His *delight* is in the law of the Lord.
—Ps. i. 2.

2. that which gives great pleasure; that which affords rapture.

Angels listen when she speaks,
She's my *delight* and mankind's wonder.
—Rochester.

3. the power of pleasing greatly. [Poet.]
Syn.—rapture, joy, charm, gratification, satisfaction.

dē·light′ȧ·ble, *a.* capable of giving delight. [Rare.]

dē·light′ed, *a.* greatly pleased; full of joy; as, a *delighted* child.
Syn.—pleased, glad, happy, joyous, joyful, gratified.

dē·light′ed·ly, *adv.* in a delighted manner; with delight.

dē·light′ẽr, *n.* one who takes delight. [Rare.]

dē·light′ful, *a.* highly pleasing; giving great pleasure and satisfaction; charming.
Syn.—beautiful, charming, gladsome, lovely, delicious, agreeable, captivating, enjoyable.

dē·light′ful·ly, *adv.* in a delightful manner.

dē·light′ful·ness, *n.* the quality of being delightful.

dē·light′ing, *a.* giving great pleasure; making glad.

dē·light′ing·ly, *adv.* in a delighting manner.

dē·light′sōme, *a.* very pleasing; delightful. [Archaic and Poet.]

dē·light′sōme·ly, *adv.* very pleasingly; in a delightful manner. [Archaic and Poet.]

dē·light′sōme·ness, *n.* delightfulness. [Archaic and Poet.]

dē·lig′nāte, *v.t.* to deprive of wood by felling trees. [Rare.]

Dē·lī′lȧh, *n.* [Heb. *delīlāh,* lit., delicate.]
1. in the Bible, the mistress of Samson, who betrayed him to the Philistines by having his hair cut off while he was asleep, thus depriving him of his strength: Jud. xvi.
2. a false woman; temptress; harlot.

dē·lim′it, *v.t.* [Fr. *délimiter,* to limit; L. *delimitare,* to mark out the limits.] to set the limits of; to bound; to mark the boundaries of.

dē·lim′i·tāte, *v.t.;* delimitated, *pt., pp.;* delimitating, *ppr.* [from L. *delimitatus,* pp. of *delimitare.*] to delimit.

dē·lim·i·tā′tion, *n.* 1. the act of delimiting or being delimited.
2. a thing that serves as a limit.

dē·line′, *v.t.* to delineate. [Obs.]

dē·lin′ē·ȧ·ble, *a.* that may be delineated.

dē·lin′ē·ȧ·ment, *n.* representation by delineation; sketch; picture.

dē·lin′ē·āte, *v.t.;* delineated, *pt., pp.;* delineating, *ppr.* [L. *delineatus,* pp. of *delineare,* to mark out, sketch.]
1. to trace the form or outline of; to sketch out; as, to *delineate* the form of the earth.
2. to draw; to depict.
3. to describe; to depict in words; as, to *delineate* the character of Whitman.

Customs or habits *delineated* with great accuracy. —Walpole.

Syn.—depict, represent, describe, design, draw, outline, sketch, portray.

dē·lin·ē·ā′tion, *n.* 1. the act or process of delineating; the act of representing, portraying, or describing; as, the *delineation* of a person's features.
2. a drawing; sketch; portrait.
3. representation in words; description; as, the *delineation* of a character.
Syn.—sketch, picture, description, outline, figure, design.

dē·lin′ē·ā·tive, *a.* of delineation or tending to delineate.

dē·lin′ē·ā·tōr, *n.* 1. one who or that which delineates.
2. an adjustable pattern used by tailors.
3. a surveying instrument on wheels which makes a record of the distance traversed by it and delineates profiles, as of roads; a perambulator.

dē·lin′ē·ȧ·tō·ry, *a.* of, or having the nature of, delineation.

dē·lin′ē·ȧ·tūre, *n.* delineation. [Obs.]

dē·lin·ē·ā′vit, [L.] he (or she) drew (this): used with the artist's name on a painting, etc.

del·i·ni′tion (-nish′un), *n.* the act of smearing. [Obs.]

dē·lin′quen·cy, *n.; pl.* **dē·lin′quen·cies,** [LL. *delinquentia,* a fault, delinquency, from L. *delinquens,* ppr. of *delinquere,* to be wanting, to commit a fault.]
1. failure or neglect to do what duty or law requires; guilt.
2. a fault; misdeed.
3. in law, the act or acts of a juvenile delinquent.
4. an overdue debt, tax, etc.

dē·lin′quent, *a.* 1. failing or neglecting to do what duty or law requires; guilty of a fault or misdeed.
2. overdue; as, *delinquent* taxes.

dē·lin′quent, *n.* a delinquent person; especially, a delinquent juvenile.

A *delinquent* ought to be cited in the place or jurisdiction where the delinquency was committed. —Ayliffe.

Syn.—offender, transgressor, misdoer, culprit, defaulter.

dē·lin′quent·ly, *adv.* in a delinquent manner.

del′i·quāte, *v.i.* [L. *deliquatus,* pp. of *deliquare,* to clarify, to strain, to pour off.] to melt or be dissolved. [Obs.]

fāte, fär, fȧst, fạll, finăl, cāre, at; mēte, prey, hẽr, met; pīne, marine, bïrd, pin; nōte, mōve, fọr, atŏm, not; mọọn, book;

del′i·quāte, *v.t.* to cause to melt; to dissolve away. [Obs.]

del·i·quā′tion, *n.* a melting. [Obs.]

del·i·quesce′ (-kwes′), *v.i.*; deliquesced (-kwest′), *pt., pp.*; deliquescing, *ppr.* [L. *deliquescere,* to melt away, to dissolve.]
 1. to melt away.
 2. in chemistry, to become liquid by attracting and absorbing moisture from the air, as certain salts, acids, and alkalis.
 3. in biology, (a) to melt away in the course of growth or decay, as parts of certain fungi; (b) to branch into many fine divisions, as leaf veins.

del·i·ques′cence, *n.* the act, process, result, or quality of deliquescing.

del·i·ques′cent, *a.* 1. in chemistry, liquefying in the air; capable of absorbing moisture from the atmosphere and becoming liquid; as, *deliquescent* salts.
 2. in botany, dividing into many branches.

dē·liq′ui·āte (-lik′wē-āt), *v.i.* deliquesce. [Obs.]

dē·liq·ui·ā′tion, *n.* deliquescence. [Obs.]

dē·liq′ui·um, *n.* [LL. *deliquium,* a flowing down, from L. *de-,* down, and *liquere,* to melt.] deliquescence. [Obs.]

dē·liq′ui·um, *n.* 1. cessation of the sun's light, as by an eclipse. [Obs.]
 2. a fainting; a swoon. [Archaic.]

dē·lir′ȧ·cy, *n.* delirium. [Obs.]

dē·lir′ȧ·ment, *n.* a wandering of the mind; foolish fancy. [Obs.]

dē·lir′ăn·cy, *n.* delirium. [Obs.]

dē·lī′rănt, *a.* delirious. [Obs.]

dē·lī′rāte, *v.t.* and *v.i.* to rave, as a madman. [Obs.]

del·i·rā′tion, *n.* a demented state of mind; delirium; madness.

dē·lir′i·ănt, *n.* a substance inducing mental aberration.

dē·lir·i·fā′cient (-fā′shent), *a.* [L. *delirium,* madness, and *faciens* (-*entis*), ppr. of *facere,* to make.] causing delirium.

dē·lir′i·ous, *a.* 1. in a state of delirium; mentally wandering; incoherently raving.
 2. of, characteristic of, or caused by delirium.
 3. in a state of wild excitement; as, *delirious* with joy.

dē·lir′i·ous·ly, *adv.* in a delirious manner.

dē·lir′i·ous·ness, *n.* the state of being delirious; delirium.

dē·lir′i·um, *n.*; *pl.* **dē·lir′i·umṣ, dē·lir′i·ȧ,** [L. *delirium,* madness, from *delirare,* to rave, to be crazy, lit. to make the furrow awry in plowing, to deviate from the straight line; *de-,* from, and *lira,* a line, furrow.]
 1. a temporary state of extreme mental excitement, marked by restlessness, confused speech, and hallucinations: it sometimes occurs during fever, as in certain diseases, in some forms of insanity, etc.
 2. an uncontrollably wild excitement or emotion; as, a *delirium* of joy.
 3. wildly irrational, confused, or frenzied thought or speech.
 delirium tremens; an affection of the brain induced by the excessive and prolonged use of intoxicating liquors, and characterized by sweating, trembling, anxiety, and hallucinations.
 Syn.—madness, mania, aberration, frenzy, lunacy, insanity.

dē·list′, *v.t.* to remove (a name, item, etc.) from a list, directory, catalog, etc.

dē·līt′, *n.* delight. [Obs.]

dé·lit′ (dā-lē′), *n.* [Fr.] in law, a mild offense or misdemeanor against penal law.

dē·līt′ȧ·ble, *a.* delightful, delectable. [Obs.]

del·i·tes′cence, *n.* [L. *delitescens* (-*entis*), ppr. of *delitescere,* to lie hid, to lurk.]
 1. retirement; obscurity; the state of being concealed.
 2. in surgery, the sudden disappearance of inflammatory symptoms.

del·i·tes′cen·cy, *n.* delitescence.

del·i·tes′cent, *a.* concealed; lying hidden; latent or inactive.

dē·lit′i·gāte, *v.i.* to chide or contend in words. [Obs.]

dē·lit·i·gā′tion, *n.* a chiding; a brawl. [Obs.]

dē·liv′ēr, *v.t.*; delivered, *pt., pp.*; delivering, *ppr.* [ME. *deliveren*; LL. *deliberare,* to deliver; L. *de-,* from, and *liberare,* to set free; *liber,* free.]
 1. to free; to release; to set at liberty; to rescue or save from evil, danger, etc.; as, to *deliver* one from captivity.
 Deliver me, O my God, out of the hand of the wicked. —Ps. lxxi. 4.
 2. to give or transfer; to put into another's possession or power; to commit; to pass from one to another: with *to.*
 3. to utter; to speak; as, to *deliver* a sermon, an address, or an oration.
 4. to assist at the birth of (an offspring); as, the doctor *delivered* the child.
 5. to give out; distribute; as, *deliver* the mail.
 6. to give forth; as, the well *delivers* much water.
 7. to strike (a blow).
 8. to throw or toss; as, the pitcher *delivered* a curve.
 9. to cause (votes, etc.) to be directed toward the support of a particular candidate or cause. [Colloq.]
 to be delivered of; to give birth to.
 Syn.—free, save, rescue, emancipate, release, discharge, liberate, surrender, utter, pronounce.

dē·liv′ēr, *v.i.* 1. to give birth to a child.
 2. to make deliveries, as of merchandise.
 3. in molding, to disunite from the mold.

dē·liv′ēr, *a.* free; nimble; active. [Archaic.]

dē·liv′ēr·ȧ·ble, *a.* that can be or is to be delivered.

dē·liv′ēr·ănce, *n.* 1. the act of delivering or the state of being delivered; rescue or release, as from captivity, slavery, oppression, etc.
 2. an opinion, judgment, etc. formally or publicly expressed.
 3. the act of bringing forth children; parturition; delivery. [Obs.]
 4. in Scots law, the expressed decision of a judge or arbitrator, interlocutory or final.

dē·liv′ēr·ēr, *n.* 1. one who delivers; one who releases or rescues; a preserver.
 The Lord raised up a *deliverer* to Israel. —Jud. iii. 9.
 2. one who relates or communicates. [Rare].

dē·liv′ēr·ess, *n.* a woman deliverer. [Rare.]

dē·liv′ēr·ly, *adv.* nimbly; actively. [Archaic.]

dē·liv′ēr·ness, *n.* nimbleness; agility. [Obs.]

dē·liv′ēr·y, *n.*; *pl.* **dē·liv′ēr·ieṣ,** 1. a giving or handing over; transfer.
 2. a giving out or distributing, as of goods or mail.
 3. a giving birth; childbirth.
 4. a giving forth in words; utterance.
 5. any giving forth.
 6. a striking (of a blow).
 7. a throwing (of a ball).
 8. the manner or style of speaking, singing, striking, throwing, etc.; as, an actor's poor *delivery.*
 9. something delivered or to be delivered, as mail, parcels, a pitched ball, etc.
 10. a setting free. [Archaic.]
 11. in law, (a) the irrevocable transfer of a deed; (b) the transfer of goods from a consignor to a consignee.

dē·liv′ēr·y·man, *n.*; *pl.* **dē·liv′ēr·y·men,** a man whose work is delivering goods.

dell, *n.* [ME. *dell*; D. *del,* a dale, valley.] a small, narrow valley or ravine, usually a wooded one.

dell, *n.* a girl; a wench. [Obs.]

Del′lȧ Çrus′çȧ, [It., a shortened form of *Accademia della Crusca,* lit. the Academy of Chaff; *della,* of the, and *crusca,* bran, chaff.] an academy founded at Florence, Italy, in 1582, mainly for promoting the purity of the Italian language.

Del·lȧ-Çrus′căn, *a.* 1. relating to or characteristic of the Academy Della Crusca.
 2. designating or of a school of English poetry started by some Englishmen at Florence toward the close of the eighteenth century.

dellṣ, *n.pl.* same as *dalles* (sense 2).

dē·lō′căl·īze, *v.t.* 1. to free from associations or limitations of locality; to widen the scope of.
 2. to remove (a thing) from its locality.

dē′loo, *n.* [native North African name.] an antelope, the duykerbok.

dē·louse′ (*or* -louz′), *v.t.*; deloused, *pt., pp.*; delousing, *ppr.* to rid of lice.

delph, *n.* same as *delf.*

Del′phi·ăn, *a.* same as *Delphic.*

Del′phi·ăn, *n.* an inhabitant of Delphi.

Del′phiç, *a.* 1. of Delphi, in ancient Greece, or the oracle of Apollo there.
 2. oracular; obscure in meaning; ambiguous.

Del′phin, Del′phine, *a.* pertaining to the dauphin of France: applied particularly to an edition of the Latin classics prepared under Louis XIV for the dauphin's use.

del′phi·nāte, *n.* a salt of delphinic acid.

del′phine, *a.* [L. *delphinus*; Gr. *delphin,* a dolphin.] pertaining to the dolphins, or to the *Delphinidæ.*

del·phin′iç, *a.* [from L. *delphinus,* a dolphin.] pertaining to an acid discovered by Chevreul, first in dolphin oil and afterward in the ripe berries of the guelder rose. It is now known to be identical with valeric acid.

del·phin′iç, *a.* pertaining to or derived from the larkspur.

Del·phin′i·dae, *n.pl.* a family of cetaceous animals, including the dolphins, porpoises, etc., characterized by the moderate size of the head, by the presence of teeth in both jaws, and by a dorsal fin.

del′phi·nine, *n.* [*delphin*ium, and *-ine.*] a poisonous, white crystalline substance prepared from the seeds of certain larkspurs.

Del·phin′i·um, *n.* [L., from Gr. *delphinion,* the larkspur, so called on account of the resemblance of the nectary to a dolphin; Gr. *delphis, delphin,* a dolphin.]
 1. an extensive genus of plants (the larkspurs) of the crowfoot family, with spikes of spurred, irregular flowers of a blue, purple, or white color on tall stalks. The genus embraces fifty species found in the North Temperate Zone.
 2. [d–] a plant of this genus.

del′phi·noid, *a.* [Gr. *delphis, delphin,* a dolphin, and *eidos,* form.] pertaining to or characteristic of the dolphin.

del′phi·noid, *n.* any species of dolphin of the family *Delphinoidea.*

Del·phi·noi′dē·ȧ, *n.pl.* [L., from Gr. *delphin,* a dolphin, and *eidos,* form.] a superfamily of cetaceans, comprising the suborder *Denticete,* excepting only the sperm whales.

del·phi·noi′dine, *n.* an alkaloid derived from the seeds of *Delphinium staphisagria.*

Del·phī′nus, *n.* [L., from Gr. *delphis, delphin,* a dolphin.]
 1. a cetacean genus containing the dolphin and kindred species.
 2. in astronomy, a small northern constellation between Pegasus and Aquila.

Del·särte′ sys′tem, [after François *Delsarte* (1811–1871), Fr. teacher of music and dramatics.] a system of calisthenics combined with singing, declamation, and dancing to develop bodily grace and poise.

Del·sär′ti·ăn, *a.* pertaining to François Delsarte or his system of calisthenics.

del′tȧ, *n.* [L. *delta*; Gr. *delta*; Heb. *daleth,* the fourth letter of the alphabet; lit., a door.]
 1. the fourth letter of the Greek alphabet, corresponding to the English *D.*
 2. a triangular-shaped tract of alluvial land at the mouth of a river; as, the *delta* of the Nile or of the Mississippi.

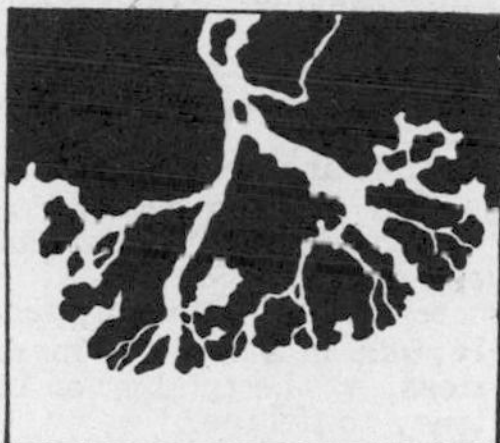

DELTA OF RIVER

del″tȧ·fi·cā′tion, *n.* [L. *delta,* and *facere,* to make.] the act or process of forming a delta at the mouth of a river.

del·tā′iç, *a.* pertaining to, resembling, or forming a delta.

del′tȧ met′ăl, a nonoxidizing alloy of zinc, copper, and iron: so named because composed of three metals, in allusion to the fact that the Greek letter *delta* is formed by three lines.

del′tȧ rāy, a particle, especially an electron, ejected by primary ionizing particles passing through matter.

del′tȧ wing, the triangular structure of certain jet aircraft.

del′tic, *a.* same as *deltaic.*

del·tid′i·um, *n.* [L., from Gr. *delta,* the letter delta, Δ.] in zoology, the triangular space between the beak and the hinge of brachiopod shells, usually covered by a shelly plate.

del·tō·hē′drŏn, *n.* [Gr. *delta,* delta, and *hedra,* a seat, base.] in crystallography, a hemihedral isometric solid included under twelve quadrilateral faces.

del'toid, *a.* [Gr. *delta,* and *eidos,* form.] shaped like the Greek letter *delta;* triangular; specifically, (a) in anatomy, denoting the large, triangular muscle of the shoulder which raises the arm away from the side; (b) in botany, triangular or trowel-shaped; as, a *deltoid* leaf.

DELTOID LEAF

del'toid, *n.* in anatomy, the deltoid muscle.

del·toi'dăl, *a.* triangular; deltoid.

dē·lū'brum, *n.*; *pl.* **dē·lū'brȧ,** [L. *delubrum,* a shrine, temple, a place of religious purification, from *de,* off, from, and *luere,* to wash.]
  1. in Roman antiquity, a temple or shrine.
  2. in ecclesiastical architecture, a church furnished with a font.
  3. a font or baptismal basin.

dē·lūd'ȧ·ble, *a.* that can be deluded or deceived.

dē·lūde', *v.t.*; deluded, *pt., pp.*; deluding, *ppr.* [ME. *deluden*; L. *deludere,* to play false with, to delude, deceive.]
  1. to deceive; to lead from truth or into error; to mislead; to beguile.
   To *delude* the nation by an airy phantom. —Burke.
  2. to frustrate or disappoint. [Obs.]
  Syn.—deceive, mislead, cheat, beguile, misguide.

dē·lūd'ẽr, *n.* one who deceives; a deceiver.

del'ūġe, *n.* [ME. *deluge*; L. *diluvium,* a flood, deluge, from *diluere,* to wash away; *dis-,* off, from, and *luere,* to wash.]
  1. a great overflowing of water; an inundation; a flood; also, a heavy rainfall.
  2. anything resembling an inundation, either in destructiveness or volume; as, a *deluge* of molten lava, a *deluge* of letters.

del'ūġe, *v.t.*; deluged, *pt., pp.*; deluging, *ppr.*
  1. to overflow with water; to inundate; to flood; as, too abundant rains have *deluged* the lowlands.
  2. to overwhelm by or as by a deluge; as, the armies *deluged* the country; *deluged* by requests.

dē·lụl', *n.* [Ar.] a female dromedary.

dē·lun'dung, *n.* [native name.] *Prionodon gracilis,* a catlike animal inhabiting Java and Malacca, allied to the civets.

dē·lū'ṣion, *n.* [L. *delusio,* delusion, from *delusus,* pp. of *deludere,* to cheat, delude.]
  1. the act of deluding; deception; a misleading of the mind.
   Under the influence of love's *delusion.* —Thackeray.
  2. the state of being deluded.
  3. a false belief or opinion.
  4. in psychiatry, a false, persistent belief not substantiated by sensory evidence.
  Syn.—illusion, fallacy, deception, error, hallucination.

dē·lū'ṣion·ăl, *a.* characterized by delusions; afflicted with delusions; as, a *delusional* patient.

dē·lū'ṣion·ist, *n.* one deluded or deluding.

dē·lū'sive, *a.* 1. apt to deceive; tending to mislead; deceptive; beguiling; as, *delusive* arts, *delusive* appearances.
  2. characterized by delusion; deceptive.

dē·lū'sive·ly, *adv.* in a delusive manner.

dē·lū'sive·ness, *n.* the quality of being delusive; tendency to delude.

dē·lū'sō·ry, *a.* apt to deceive; deceptive; delusive.

dē lụxe (*or* luks), [Fr. *de luxe,* of luxury.] elaborate; elegant; of especially good quality.

delve, *v.i.*; delved, *pt., pp.*; delving, *ppr.* [ME. *delven*; AS. *delfan,* to dig.]
  1. to dig. [Archaic or Brit. Dial.]
  2. to make an investigation; to search for facts; as, to *delve* into books, into the past, etc.

delve, *v.t.* 1. to dig or turn up (ground) with a spade. [Archaic or Brit. Dial.]
  2. to bury. [Obs.]

delve, *n.* a place dug; a pit; a pitfall; a ditch; a den; a cave. [Rare.]

delv'ẽr, *n.* one who delves.

dē·mag''net·i·zā'tion, *n.* the act or process of depriving of magnetic properties.

dē·mag'net·īze, *v.t.*; demagnetized, *pt., pp.*; demagnetizing, *ppr.* 1. to deprive of magnetism or magnetic properties.
  2. to deprive of mesmeric influence; to bring from a hypnotic state. [Obs.]

dē·mag'net·ī·zẽr, *n.* one who or that which demagnetizes.

dem'ȧ·gog, *n.* same as *demagogue.*

dem·ȧ·goġ'iç, dem·ȧ·goġ'iç·ăl (*or* -gog'), *a.* relating to or like a demagogue or demagogy.

dem·ȧ·goġ'iç·ăl·ly (*or* -gog'), *adv.* 1. in the manner of a demagogue.
  2. by means of demagogy.

dem'ȧ·gog·iṣm, *n.* the methods, actions, or principles of a demagogue: also spelled *demagoguism.*

dem'ȧ·gogue (-gog), *n.* [Fr. *demagogue*; Gr. *dēmagōgos,* a leader of the people; *dēmos,* the people, and *agōgos,* a leader, from *agein,* to lead.]
  1. anciently, a leader of the common people.
  2. a person who tries to stir up the people by appeals to emotion, prejudice, etc. in order to become a leader and achieve selfish ends.
   A plausible insignificant word, in the mouth of an expert *demagogue,* is a dangerous and deceitful weapon. —South.

dem'ȧ·gog·uẽr·y, *n.* demagogy.

dem'ȧ·goġ·y (*or* -gog-), *n.* the methods, actions, or principles of a demagogue.

dē·māin', *n.* [ME. *demayn*; OFr. *demaine*; L. *dominium,* right of ownership, dominion.]
  1. domain. [Obs.]
  2. in law, demesne. [Obs.]

dē·mȧnd', *v.t.*; demanded, *pt., pp.*; demanding, *ppr.* [OFr. *demander,* to demand; L. *demandare,* to give in charge, hand over, entrust; *de,* away, from, and *mandare,* to entrust, lit., to put in one's hands, from *manus,* hand, and *dare,* to give.]
  1. to ask or call for as a right or with authority; to claim or seek as due by right; as, the creditor *demands* principal and interest of his debt.
  2. to ask for boldly or urgently.
  3. to ask to know or be informed.
  4. to require; to need; as, the execution of this work *demands* great industry and care.
  5. in law, to summon to court.
  Syn.—ask, request, solicit, seek, inquire.

dē·mȧnd', *v.i.* to make a demand.

dē·mȧnd', *n.* 1. a demanding; an asking with authority; a request made with authority; as, the *demand* of the creditor for payment.
   Confidence to turn his wishes into *demands.* —Locke.
  2. that which is demanded; as, unexpected *demands* on one's resources.
  3. a requirement or claim.
  4. an emphatic inquiry.
  5. in economics, (a) the desire for a commodity together with ability to pay for it; (b) the amount people are ready and able to buy at a certain price. Opposed to *supply.*
  6. in law, (a) a valid claim against a person, whether coming from contract, damage, or otherwise; (b) the asking or seeking for what is due or claimed as due.
  in demand; called for; demanded or sought.
  on demand; when presented for payment; as, a certificate payable *on demand.*

dē·mȧnd'ȧ·ble, *a.* that can be demanded or required.

dē·mȧnd'ȧnt, *n.* 1. one who demands.
  2. the plaintiff in a real action; also, any plaintiff.

dē·mȧnd' bill, a bill payable on demand.

dē·mȧnd' dē·poṣ'it, in banking a deposit that may be withdrawn on demand, without advance notice.

dē·mȧnd'ẽr, *n.* one who demands.

dē·mȧnd' lōan, a loan payable on demand; a call loan.

dē·mȧnd' nōte, a promissory note payable on demand.

dē·mȧnd'ress, *n.* a woman demandant.

dē·man'toid, *n.* [G. *demant,* a diamond, from L. *adamas,* Gr. *adamas,* the diamond, and *eidos,* form.] a kind of garnet, emerald-green in color.

dē·mär'çāte, *v.t.*; demarcated, *pt., pp.*; demarcating, *ppr.* [Fr. *demarquer,* to mark off, from L. *de,* off, and O.H.G. *marca,* a boundary.]
  1. to mark the limits or boundaries of; to bound.
  2. to distinguish; to discriminate; to separate.

dē·mär·çā'tion, *n.* [Fr. *demarcation,* from *demarquer,* to mark off.]
  1. the act of marking the limits of.
  2. a limit or boundary line.
  3. a separating.

dē'märçh, *n.* [L. *demarchus,* in Rome a tribune of the people; Gr. *dēmarchos,* the head of a deme, or tribe; *dēmos,* a deme, and *archein,* to rule.] the ruler or magistrate of a deme in ancient Attica; also, the mayor of a modern Greek town.

dé·marche' (dā-märsh'), *n.* [Fr.]
  1. a line of action.
  2. in diplomacy, a new line of action; a change of policy.

dē·märk', *v.t.* same as *demarcate.*

dē·mär·kā'tion, *n.* same as *demarcation.*

dē·mȧ·tē'ri·ăl·īze, *v.t.* to rid of material elements or attributes; to cause to lose material form.

dē·mȧ·tē'ri·ăl·īze, *v.i.* to lose, or be deprived of, material form.

dēme, *n.* [Gr. *dēmos,* a country district, town, the people.]
  1. (a) a township of ancient Attica; (b) a commune in modern Greece.
  2. in biology, any homogeneous mass of elementary organisms. [Rare.]

dē·mēan', *v.t.*; demeaned, *pt., pp.*; demeaning, *ppr.* [ME. *demenen*; OFr. *demener,* to drive, lead, conduct, do, from *de,* down, and LL. *minare,* to drive, to drive animals by threatening cries, from L. *minari,* to threaten.]
  1. to do; to manage; to guide. [Obs.]
  2. to behave; to comport; to conduct: used reflexively; as, they promised to *demean themselves* properly.
   How with so high a nymph he might
   Demean himself the marriage night. —Swift.

dē·mēan', *n.* mien; demeanor; behavior; conduct. [Obs.]

dē·mēan', *v.t.* [*de-,* and *mean* (low): on analogy with *debase.*] to lower in status or character; to degrade; to humble; as, he would not *demean* himself by taking the bribe.

dē·mēan'ănce, *n.* behavior; demeanor. [Obs].

dē·mēan'ŏr, *n.* outward behavior; manner; conduct; deportment; as, decent *demeanor,* sad *demeanor.*
  Syn.—air, bearing, behavior, manner.

dē·mēan'ŏur, *n.* demeanor: British spelling.

dē·mem·brā'tion, *n.* in Scots law, dismemberment.

dē'men·cy, *n.* dementia. [Rare.]

dē·ment', *v.t.* to make insane.

dē·ment', *a.* [L. *demens* (*-entis*), out of one's mind, mad; *de-* priv., and *mens* (*-entis*), mind.] devoid of reason; insane. [Rare.]

dē·ment', *n.* a demented person.

dē·men'tāte, *a.* mad; demented.

dē·men'tāte, *v.t.* to dement. [Rare.]

dē·men·tā'tion, *n.* the act of making mad; also, the state of being demented. [Rare.]

dē·ment'ed, *a.* devoid of reason; affected with dementia; insane.

dē·ment'ed·ness, *n.* the condition of being demented; mental unsoundness.

dé·men·ti' (dā-mäṅ-tē'), *n.* [Fr. from *dêmentir,* to give the lie to, contradict; *dē-,* from, and *mentir,* from L. *mentire,* to lie.] in diplomacy, an official denial, as of a rumor.

dē·men'tiȧ (-shiȧ), *n.* [L. *dementia,* madness, insanity, from *demens* (*-entis*), mad, out of one's mind.] impairment or loss of mental powers.
  dementia praecox (prē'); in psychiatry, a psychosis or form of dementia, usually beginning in late adolescence, characterized by melancholia, withdrawal, hallucinations, delusions, etc.

dē·meph''i·ti·zā'tion, *n.* the act of purifying from mephitic or foul air.

dē·meph'i·tīze, *v.t.*; demephitized, *pt., pp.*; demephitizing, *ppr.* [*de-* priv., and L. *mephitis,* foul air, ill smell.] to purify from foul, unwholesome air.

dē·mẽrġe', *v.t.* to immerse. [Obs.]

dē·mer'it, *n.* [Fr. *dêmérit*; LL. *demeritum,* a transgression, from *demerere,* to deserve ill.]
  1. a quality deserving blame; fault; defect.
  2. a mark recorded against a student, etc. for unsatisfactory work or conduct.
  3. merit. [Obs.]

dē·mer'it, *v.t.* 1. to deserve. [Obs.]
  2. to depreciate. [Obs.]

dē·mer'it, *v.i.* to be deserving of blame.

dem'e·rōl, *n.* a synthetic drug used in medicine as a sedative and analgesic: a trade-mark (*Demerol*).

dē·mẽrse', *v.t.* to immerse. [Obs.]

dē·mẽrsed' (-mẽrst'), *a.* in botany, submersed.

dē·mẽr'sion, *n.* [LL. *demersio,* immersion, from L. *demersus,* pp. of *demergere,* to dip under, plunge into.] submergence.

dē·meṣ'mẽr·īze, *v.t.* to relieve from mesmeric influence.

dē·mesne' (-mēn' *or* -mēn'), *n.* [ME. *demaine*; OFr. *demaine* (Fr. *domaine*), a right of ownership, from L. *dominium,* property, right of ownership.]
  1. possession; dominion. [Obs.]

2. in law, possession (of real estate) as one's own.
3. formerly, the land or estate belonging to a lord and not rented or let but kept in his hands.
4. a lord's mansion and the land around it.
5. a region; domain.
6. a realm (of activity); as, the *demesne* of science.

dē·mēsn'i·ăl (-mē'ni-ăl), *a.* pertaining to a demesne.

Dē·mē'tēr, *n.* [Gr. *Dēmētēr*; Doric *Damatēr*, prob. from Gr. *gē*, Doric *da*, earth, and *mētēr*, mother.] in Greek mythology, a goddess, corresponding in some respects to the Latin Ceres, the goddess of agriculture and fruitfulness, and protectress of marriage. She was mother of Bacchus.

dē'mī, *n.* plural of *demos*.

dem'i-, [OFr. *demi-*, half, from L. *dimidius*, half; *dis*, *di*, apart, and *medius*, middle.] a prefix meaning: (a) *half*, as in *demi*semiquaver, *demi*volt; (b) *less than usual in size, power*, etc., as in *demi*god, *demi*tasse.

dem'i·bas·tiŏn (-chun), *n.* [Fr., from *demi*, half, and *bastion*, a bastion.] in fortification, a bastion that has only one face and one flank.

dem'i·bȧth, *n.* a bath in which only the lower part of the body is immersed.

dem'i·bri·gāde', *n.* a half brigade.

dem'i·cā·dence, *n.* [*demi-*, and L. *cadens*, ppr. of *cadere*, to fall.] in music, a half cadence.

dem'i·çan·nŏn, *n.* an obsolete piece of ordnance carrying a ball of from 30 to 36 pounds in weight.

dem'i·çap·ō·nière', *n.* in fortification, a single caponiere.

dem'i·cīr·çle, *n.* a simple instrument for measuring and indicating angles, having much the same use as the theodolite.

dem·i·dē'i·fȳ, *v.t.* to deify in part. [Rare.]

dem'i·dis·tȧnce, *n.* in fortification, the distance between the outward polygons and the flank.

dem'i·dī·tōne, *n.* in music, a minor third.

dem'i·god, *n.* 1. in mythology, (a) a lesser god; minor deity; (b) the offspring of a human being and a god or goddess.
2. a person regarded as partly divine.
3. a hero declared to be a god.

dem'i·god·dess, *n.* a woman demigod.

dem'i·gorġe, *n.* in fortification, that part of the polygon which remains after the flank is raised, extending from the curtain to the angle of the polygon.

dem'i·grōat, *n.* a half groat.

dem'i-īs''lănd (-ī''lănd), *n.* a peninsula. [Obs.]

dem'i·john (-jon), *n.* [Fr. *damejeanne*, a demijohn, lit., Dame Jeanne; prob. orig. a fanciful name for the bottle.] a large bottle of glass or earthenware, with a narrow neck and a wicker casing and handle.

dem'i·lȧnce, *n.* a light lance; a short spear; also, one using such a weapon.

dē·mil''i·tȧ·ri·zā'tion, *n.* a demilitarizing or being demilitarized.

dē·mil'i·tȧ·rīze, *v.t.* 1. to free from organized military control.
2. to abolish the military character or militarism of.

dem'i·lūne, *n.* [Fr., from *demi*, half, and *lune*, moon.]
1. a crescent.
2. in fortification, a crescent-shaped outwork of two faces and two small flanks, constructed to cover the curtain and shoulders of the bastion.
demilunes of Heidenhain; in physiology, crescentic, protoplasmic bodies present in the salivary glands.

dem'i·man, *n.* a half man.

dem'i·men·ton·nière' (-nyăr'), *n.* in medieval armor, a half mentonnière attached to the breastplate for the protection of the throat and chin on the left side.

dem''i·mon·dāine', *n.* [Fr.] a woman of the demimonde.

dem'i·monde, *n.* [Fr., from *demi*, half, and *monde*, the world, society, from L. *mundus*, the world.] the class of women who have lost social standing because of sexual promiscuity.

dem'i·par·ăl·lel, *n.* in military usage, a shorter entrenchment thrown up between the main parallels of attack.

dem'i·pīke, *n.* a half pike.

dem'i·pïque (-pēk), *a.* [from *demi-*, and *peak*; sp. influenced by association with Fr. *pique*, a pike.] having a low pommel: said formerly of certain military saddles.

dem'i·pïque, *n.* a demipique saddle.

dem'i·quā·vēr, *n.* in music, a sixteenth note; a semiquaver.

dem'i·rē·liēf'', *n.* same as *mezzo-relievo*.

dem'i·rep, *n.* [*demi-* and *rep*utation.] a woman, or sometimes a man, of poor reputation, suspected of loose sexual behavior.

dē·mīṣ·ȧ·bil'i·ty, *n.* the state of being demisable.

dē·mīṣ'ȧ·ble, *a.* capable of being demised or leased; as, a *demisable* estate.

dē·mīṣe', *n.* [Fr. *démis*, pp. of *démettre*, to resign, from L. *demittere*, to send away, release, resign; *de-*, down, and *mittere*, to send.]
1. the transfer of an estate by will or lease.
2. the transfer of sovereignty by death or abdication.
3. death; decease.
demise and redemise; in law, a conveyance in which there are mutual leases made from one to another of the same land, or something out of it.

dē·mīṣe', *v.t.*; demised, *pt.*, *pp.*; demising, *ppr.* 1. to give, grant, or transfer (an estate) by will or lease.
2. to transfer (sovereignty) by death or abdication.

dē·mīṣe', *v.i.* to be passed on by bequest or inheritance, as property.

dem''i·sem'i·quā''vēr, *n.* [*demi-*, *semi-*, and *quaver*.] in music, a thirty-second note. (𝅘𝅥𝅰)

dē·miss', *a.* [L. *demissus*, pp. of *demittere*, to let down, cast down.]
1. downcast; humble. [Rare.]
2. in botany, depressed.

dē·mis'sion, *n.* [Fr. *démission*; L. *demissio*, a letting down, from *demissus*, pp. of *demittere*.] a demitting; resignation or abdication (of an office).

dē·mis'sion·ȧ·ry, *a.* 1. tending to degrade or lower.
2. relating to the transfer or demise of an estate.

dē·miss'ive, *a.* humble. [Obs.]

dē·miss'ly, *adv.* in a humble manner. [Obs.]

dē·mit', *v.t.*; demitted, *pt.*, *pp.*; demitting, *ppr.* [L. *demittere*, to send or cast down; *de-*, down, and *mittere*, to send.]
1. to let fall; to depress. [Obs.]
2. to submit; to humble. [Obs.]
3. to resign (a position or office) voluntarily.
4. to dismiss. [Archaic.]

dē·mit', *v.i.* to resign.

dē·mit', *n.* in Freemasonry, a dimit.

dem'i·tasse, *n.* [Fr.; *demi-*, demi-, and *tasse*, a cup.] a small cup of or for after-dinner black coffee.

dem'i·tint, *n.* in painting, a gradation of color between positive light and positive shade: also called *half tint*.

dem'i·tōne, *n.* in music, a semitone.

dem'i·ūrġe, *n.* [L. *demiurgus*; Gr. *dēmiourgos*, skilled workman, creator.]
1. [D–] in Plato's philosophy, a secondary deity, the creative spirit who made the world.
2. [D–] in Gnostic philosophy, a god subordinate to the supreme god, sometimes considered the originator of evil, or identified with the Jehovah of the Bible.
3. in Greek history, a magistrate in certain states.

dem·i·ūr'ġiç, dem·i·ūr'ġiç·ăl, *a.* pertaining to a demiurge or to creative power.

dem'i·vōlt, *n.* [Fr. *demi-volte*, from *demi*, half, and *volte*, a leap.] in horseback riding, a half turn with the forelegs of the horse raised.

dem'i·wolf (-wụlf), *n.* a half wolf; a hybrid between a dog and a wolf.

dem'ō, *n.* 1. a phonograph or tape recording made to demonstrate the talent of a performer, quality of a song, etc. [Colloq.]
2. a demonstration (senses 2 and 4). [Colloq.]
3. a product used as a demonstrator. [Colloq.]

dē·mob', *v.t.*; demobbed, *pt.*, *pp.*; demobbing, *ppr.* to demobilize. [Brit. Colloq.]

dē·mō''bi·li·zā'tion, *n.* a demobilizing or being demobilized.

dē·mō'bi·līze, *v.t.* and *v.i.*; demobilized, *pt.*, *pp.*; demobilizing, *ppr.* 1. to disband or dismiss (troops that have been mobilized).
2. to change over from a war footing to a peace footing.

dē·moç'rȧ·cy, *n.*; *pl.* **dē·moç'rȧ·cieṣ,** [Fr. *démocratie*; Gr. *dēmokratia*, democracy, popular government, from *dēmos*, the people, and *kratein*, to rule.]
1. government by the people, either directly or through elected representatives; rule by the ruled.
2. a country, state, community, etc. with such government.
3. majority rule.
4. the acceptance and practice of the principle of equality of rights, opportunity, and treatment; lack of snobbery; as, there is real *democracy* in this school.
5. the common people.
6. [D–] the Democratic Party of the United States, or the principles of this party.

dem'ō·çrat, *n.* 1. a person who believes in and upholds government by the people; advocate of rule by the majority.
2. a person who believes in and practices the principle of equality of rights, opportunity, and treatment.
3. [D–] a member or adherent of the Democratic Party.
4. a light wagon having several seats and no top.

dem·ō·çrat'iç, *a.* [Gr. *dēmokratikos*, suited to a democracy, from *dēmokratia*, a democracy; *dēmos*, the people, and *kratein*, to rule.]
1. of, belonging to, or upholding democracy or a democracy.
2. of or for all the people; as, *democratic* entertainment.
3. considering and treating others as one's equals; not snobbish.
4. [D–] of, belonging to, or characteristic of the Democratic Party.
Democratic Party; one of the two major political parties in the United States: it descended from the Democratic-Republican Party (c. 1830), developed from the Republican Party led by Thomas Jefferson.

dem·ō·çrat'iç·ăl, *a.* democratic.

dem·ō·çrat'iç·ăl·ly, *adv.* in a democratical manner.

dē·moç''rȧ·ti·zā'tion, *n.* a democratizing or being democratized.

dē·moç'rȧ·tīze, *v.t.* and *v.i.*; democratized, *pt.*, *pp.*; democratizing, *ppr.* to make or become democratic.

De·moç·ri·tē'ăn, *a.* of or like Democritus or his philosophy.

dé·mo·dé' (dā-mō-dā'), *a.* [Fr.] out-of-date; old-fashioned.

dē·mod'ū·lāte, *v.t.*; demodulated, *pt.*, *pp.*; demodulating, *ppr.* to cause demodulation.

dē·mod·ū·lā'tion, *n.* in radio, the process of recovering at the receiver a signal that has been modulated on a carrier wave; detection.

dē·mod'ū·lā·tŏr, *n.* same as *detector* (sense 3).

Dē·mō·gor'gŏn, *n.* [LL. *Demogorgo*, from Gr. *daimōn*, a demon, and *gorgos*, grim, dreadful.] a terrifying and mysterious god or demon of the underworld, to whom sinister powers were attributed: he is sometimes described in medieval writings as a primeval creator.

dē·mog'rȧ·phēr, *n.* a student of demography.

dē·mō·graph'iç, *a.* pertaining to demography.

dē·mog'rȧ·phy, *n.* [Gr. *dēmos*, people, and *graphein*, to write.] the science of vital statistics, as of births, deaths, marriages, etc. of populations.

dem·oi·ṣelle' (-wä-), *n.* [Fr.] 1. a damsel; a maid.
2. *Anthropoides virgo*, the Numidian crane, a small crane of Africa, Asia, and Europe.
3. any of various dragonflies with a small head, slender body, and wings held vertically when at rest.

dē·mol'ish, *v.t.*; demolished, *pt.*, *pp.*; demolishing, *ppr.* [L. *demoliri*, to pull down, destroy; *de*, down, and *moliri*, to build, construct, exert oneself, from *moles*, a mass.]
1. to pull or tear down (a building, etc.).
2. to destroy; ruin.
Syn.—overturn, overthrow, destroy, dismantle, raze.—That is *overturned* or *overthrown* which had stood upright; that is *destroyed* whose component parts are scattered; that is *demolished* which had formed a mass or structure; that is *dismantled* which is stripped of its covering; that is *razed* which is brought down smooth and level to the ground.

dē·mol'ish·ēr, *n.* one who or that which demolishes.

dē·mol'ish·ment, *n.* demolition.

dem·ō·li'tion, *n.* a demolishing or being demolished; destruction.

dem·ō·li'tion dēr'by, a public show in which old automobiles are driven into one another repeatedly until only one is still moving.

dem·ō·li'tion·ist, *n.* one who advocates demolition.

dē'mŏn, *n.* [L. *dæmon*; Gr. *daimon*, a deity, spirit, one's genius, an evil spirit.]
1. a daemon.
2. a devil; evil spirit.
3. a person or thing regarded as evil, cruel, etc.; as, the *demon* of jealousy.
4. a person who has great energy or skill; as, a *demon* at golf.

dē'mŏn-, same as *demono-*.

dē·mŏn″e·ti·zā′tion, *n.* the act of demonetizing or the condition of being demonetized.

dē·mŏn′e·tīze, *v.t.*; demonetized, *pt.*, *pp.*; demonetizing, *ppr.* [*de-* priv., and L. *moneta*, money.]
1. to deprive (currency) of its standard value.
2. to stop using as money; as, silver was *demonetized*.

dē·mō′ni·ac, *a.* 1. pertaining to, produced, or influenced by a demon or demons.
2. resembling a demon in nature; hence, frenzied; frantic; cruel; as, *demoniac* crimes.

dē·mō′ni·ac, *n.* 1. a human being supposedly possessed by a demon.
2. [D–] in church history, one of a sect of the Anabaptists who maintain that the devils will ultimately be saved.

dē·mō·nī′ȧ·căl, *a.* demoniac.

dē·mō·nī′ȧ·căl·ly, *adv.* in a demoniacal manner.

dē·mō·nī′ȧ·cism, *n.* the state of being demoniac; the practices of demoniacs.

dē·mō′ni·ăl, *a.* demoniac. [Rare.]

dē·mō′ni·ăn, *a.* pertaining to or characteristic of a demon.

dē·mō′ni·ăn·ism, *n.* the state of being possessed, supposedly, by a demon. [Rare.]

dē·mon′ic, *a.* [Gr. *daimonikos*, demoniac, from *daimōn*, a demon.]
1. of or like a demon or demons.
2. having a guiding spirit; daemonic.
3. inspired.

dē′mŏn·ism, *n.* 1. the belief in the existence and powers of demons.
2. demonolatry.

dē′mŏn·ist, *n.* one who believes in or worships demons.

dē′mŏn·īze, *v.t.*; demonized, *pt.*, *pp.*; demonizing, *ppr.* [LL. *demonizare*, to make demoniac.]
1. to make into, or like, a demon.
2. to bring under the influence of demons.

dē′mŏn·ō-, [Gr. *daimono*, from *daimōn*, a demon.] a combining form meaning *demon*, as in *demon*ology: also, before a vowel, *demon-*.

dē·mŏn·oc′rȧ·cy, *n.* [Gr. *daimōn*, a demon, and *kratein*, to rule.] the power or government of demons.

dē·mŏn·og′rȧ·phẽr, *n.* a demonologist.

dē·mŏn·og′rȧ·phy, *n.* [Gr. *daimōn*, a demon, and *graphein*, to write.] demonology.

dē·mŏn·ol′ȧ·tẽr, *n.* one who worships demons.

dē·mŏn·ol′ȧ·try, *n.* [Gr. *daimōn*, a demon, and *latreia*, worship, from *latreuein*, to worship, serve.] the worship of demons or of evil spirits.

dē·mŏn·ol′ō·gẽr, *n.* a demonologist. [Obs.]

dē″mŏn·ō·log′ic, dē″mŏn·ō·log′ic·ăl, *a.* pertaining to demonology.

dē·mŏn·ol′ō·gist, *n.* one versed in demonology.

dē·mŏn·ol′ō·gy, *n.* [Gr. *daimōn*, a demon, and *logos*, discourse.]
1. the study or science of demons; also, the investigation of legends and superstitions concerning demons.
2. a treatise on demons.

dē·mŏn·om′ȧ·gy, *n.* [Gr. *daimōn*, a demon, and *magos*, magic.] magic invoking or requiring the aid of demons. [Obs.]

dē′mŏn·ō·man·cy, *n.* [Gr. *daimōn*, a demon, and *manteia*, divination.] divination with the aid of the devil or demons. [Obs.]

dē″mŏn·ō·mā′ni·ȧ, *n.* [Gr. *daimōn*, a demon, and *mania*, madness.] a form of insanity in which the patient shows morbid fear of evil spirits and believes himself possessed of devils; demonopathy.

dē·mon′ō·mist, *n.* [Gr. *daimōn*, a demon, and *nōmos*, law, from *nemein*, to regulate.] one that lives in subjection to the devil, or to evil spirits. [Obs.]

dē·mon′ō·my, *n.* the dominion of demons. [Obs.]

dē·mŏn·op′ȧ·thy, *n.* [Gr. *daimōn*, a demon, and *pathos*, suffering.] demonomania.

dē′mŏn·ry, *n.* demoniacal influence.

dē′mŏn·ship, *n.* the state of a demon. [Rare.]

dē·mŏn·strȧ·bil′i·ty, *n.* the quality or state of being demonstrable.

dē·mon′strȧ·ble, *a.* capable of being demonstrated; provable.

dē·mon′strȧ·ble·ness, *n.* demonstrability.

dē·mon′strȧ·bly, *adv.* 1. in a demonstrable manner; plainly.
2. by means of demonstration.

dē·mon′strănce, *n.* demonstration. [Obs.]

dē·mon′strănt, *n.* a person who takes part in a public demonstration.

dem′ŏn·strāte, *v.t.*; demonstrated, *pt.*, *pp.*; demonstrating, *ppr.* [L. *demonstratus*, pp. of *demonstrare*, to point out, to show; *de*, out, from, and *monstrare*, to show.]
1. to show by reasoning; prove.
2. to explain or make clear by using examples, experiments, etc.
3. to show the operation or working of.
4. to advertise by showing the working or use of (a commodity).
5. to show (feelings) plainly.

dem′ŏn·strāte, *v.i.* 1. to show feelings or ideas by public meetings, parades, etc.
2. to show military power or preparedness.

dem′ŏn·strā·tẽr, *n.* same as *demonstrator*.

dem·ŏn·strā′tion, *n.* 1. the act, process, or means of making evident or proving.
2. an explanation by example, experiment, etc.; practical showing of how something works or is used.
3. a display or outward show; as, a *demonstration* of grief.
4. a public show of feeling or opinion, as by a mass meeting or parade.
5. a show of military force or preparedness.
6. in mathematics and logic, the act or process of proving that certain results follow from certain premises.
direct (or *positive*) *demonstration*; a method of proceeding by positive or affirmative propositions to the correct conclusion.
indirect (or *negative*) *demonstration*; that by which a thing is shown to be true by proving the absurdity of a contrary supposition: called also *reductio ad absurdum*.

dē·mon′strȧ·tive, *a.* 1. having the power of showing with clearness and certainty; as, a *demonstrative* figure in painting.
2. giving evidence or conclusive proof (usually with *of*).
3. having to do with demonstration; as, a *demonstrative* science.
4. characterized by or given to the strong exhibition of any feeling or quality; energetically expressive; as, a *demonstrative* manner, a *demonstrative* person.
5. in grammar, pointing out; as, *that* is a *demonstrative* pronoun.

dē·mon′strȧ·tive, *n.* a demonstrative pronoun or adjective.

dē·mon′strȧ·tive·ly, *adv.* 1. so as to demonstrate; certainly; clearly; convincingly.
2. in a demonstrative manner, or with the energetic exhibition of any feeling or quality; as, he spoke very *demonstratively*.

dē·mon′strȧ·tive·ness, *n.* the state or quality of being demonstrative.

dem′ŏn·strȧ·tŏr, *n.* a person or thing that demonstrates, as a person engaged to exhibit and explain the method, process, application, advantages, or merits of an article offered for sale; also, a sample article or product used to demonstrate.

dē·mon′strȧ·tō·ry, *a.* demonstrative. [Rare.]

dē·mor′āge, *n.* demurrage. [Obs.]

dē·mor″ăl·i·zā′tion, *n.* the act of demoralizing or the state of being demoralized.

dē·mor′ăl·īze, *v.t.*; demoralized, *pt.*, *pp.*; demoralizing, *ppr.* [coined by Noah Webster, from *de-*, and moralize.]
1. to corrupt or undermine the morals of; to render corrupt in morals.
2. to lower the morale of; to weaken the spirit, courage, discipline, or staying power of; as, hunger and cold *demoralized* the army.
3. to confuse or disorder mentally; as, the examiner's questions *demoralized* the applicant.

dē′mos, *n.*; *pl.* **dē′mī,** [Gr. *dēmos*, a deme, the common people.]
1. a deme.
2. the people or commonalty of an ancient Greek state.
3. the common people; the people; the masses.

Dem·os·then′ic, *a.* pertaining to or characteristic of Demosthenes, the Greek orator.

dē·mōte′, *v.t.*; demoted, *pt.*, *pp.*; demoting, *ppr.* [*de-*, and *-mote* as in *promote*.] to reduce to a lower grade; to lower in rank: opposed to *promote*.

dē·mot′ic, *a.* [Gr. *dēmotikos*, suiting the people, popular, public, from *dēmos*, the people.]
1. of the people; popular. [Rare.]
2. in ancient Egyptian history, designating or of a simplified system of writing; distinguished from *hieratic*.

dē·mot′ics, *n.pl.* [*construed as sing.*] sociology in its widest sense.

dē·mō′tion, *n.* a demoting or being demoted.

dē·mount′, *v.t.* to remove from a mounting or mounted position; as, *demount* the motor.

dē·mount′, *v.i.* to dismount. [Rare.]

dē·mount′ȧ·ble, *a.* capable of being demounted; as, a *demountable* motor.

demp′ne, *v.t.* to condemn. [Obs.]

demp′stẽr, *n.* see *deemster*.

dē·mulce′, *v.t.* [L. *demulcere*, to stroke down, soften.] to soothe; to soften or pacify. [Rare.]

dē·mul′cent, *a.* soothing; emollient.

dē·mul′cent, *n.* a medicine or ointment having a soothing or emollient effect on inflamed surfaces.

dē·mul′sion, *n.* [from L. *demulctus*, pp. of *demulcere*, to stroke, soften.]
1. the act of soothing or pacifying.
2. that which soothes or comforts; flattery.

dē·mũr′, *v.i.*; demurred, *pt.*, *pp.*; demurring, *ppr.* [OFr. *demorer*; L. *demorari*, to delay; *de-*, from, and *morari*, to delay, from *mora*, delay.]
1. to stay; to linger. [Obs.]
2. to have or to state scruples or difficulties; to take exceptions; to hesitate; to object (with *at*).
3. in law, to enter a demurrer.

dē·mũr′, *v.t.*; demurred, *pt.*, *pp.*; demurring, *ppr.* 1. to delay; to postpone. [Obs.]
2. to hesitate about; as, to *demur* proceedings.

dē·mũr′, *n.* 1. a stop; pause; scruple; suspense of proceeding or decision.
2. an exception taken; objection made.

dē·mūre′, *a.* [ME. *demure*, from OFr. *de murs*, of manners, for *de bounes mures*, of good manners.]
1. sober; grave; modest; sedate; as, a *demure* countenance.
2. affecting modesty or decorum; making a pretense of gravity.

dē·mūre′, *v.i.* to look demurely. [Obs.]

dē·mūre′ly, *adv.* with a grave, solemn countenance; with a show of solemn gravity.

dē·mūre′ness, *n.* the state or quality of being demure; gravity of countenance real or affected; a show of modesty.

dē·mũr′i·ty, *n.* demureness; also, one who acts demurely.

dē·mũr′rȧ·ble, *a.* that may be demurred to; that exception may be taken to.

dē·mũr′rāge, *n.* [OFr. *demorage*, delay, from *demorer*, to delay.]
1. the detention of a ship, freight car, etc. by the freighter beyond the time originally stipulated, in loading or unloading.
2. the compensation which the freighter has to pay for such delay or detention.

dē·mũr′răl, *n.* a demurring; a demur; a delay.

dē·mũr′rẽr, *n.* 1. one who demurs.
2. a plea for the dismissal of a lawsuit on the grounds that even if the statements of the opposition are true, they do not sustain the claim because they are insufficient or otherwise legally defective.
3. an objection; a demur.
demurrer to evidence; an acknowledgment at trial that the evidence presented by the opposing party is true but inadequate, with a consequent submission of the issue to the court.

dē·mȳ′, *n.*; *pl.* **dē·mīeṣ′,** [Fr. *demi*, half.]
1. any of several sizes of writing and printing paper, averaging from 15½ by 20 to 18 by 23 inches.
2. a foundation scholar at Magdalen College, Oxford: also written *demi*.
3. a gold coin of Scotland of the fifteenth century.

dē·mȳ′, *a.* denoting a certain size of paper called demy.

dē·mȳ′ship, *n.* a foundation scholarship in Magdalen College, Oxford.

den, *n.* [ME. *den*, *denne*, a den, lair; AS. *denn*, a den, a lair of wild animals.]
1. the lair or hiding place of a wild animal.
2. a cage for a wild animal, as in a zoo.
3. a cave as a place to hide.
4. a retreat or headquarters, as of thieves or vagrants; haunt.
5. a small, squalid room.
6. a small, cozy room where one can be alone to read, work, etc.
7. a narrow glen; a gully; a dell. [Brit.]

den, *v.i.*; denned, *pt.*, *pp.*; denning, *ppr.* to live or hide in or as in a den.

dē·när″cō·ti·zā′tion, *n.* the state of being denarcotized.

dē·när′cō·tīze, *v.t.*; denarcotized, *pt.*, *pp.*; denarcotizing, *ppr.* [*de-*, and *narcotic*.] to deprive of narcotine; as, to *denarcotize* opium.

dē·nā′ri·us, *n.*; *pl.* **dē·nā′ri·ī,** [L. *denarius*, containing ten, from *deni*, ten by ten, from *decem*, ten.]
1. an ancient Roman silver coin, the penny

of the New Testament: the initial letter is now the symbol (d) for British pence.
2. an ancient Roman gold coin, worth 25 silver denarii.

DENARIUS

den′à·ry, *a.* [L. *denarius*, containing ten.] having to do with the number ten; tenfold; decimal.

den′à·ry, *n.*; *pl.* **den′à·ries,** 1. the number ten.
2. a tithing; a division into tens.
3. a denarius. [Obs.]

dē·na″tion·ăl·i·zā′tion, *n.* the act of denationalizing or the state of being denationalized.

dē·na′tion·ăl·īze, *v.t.*; denationalized, *pt.*, *pp.*; denationalizing, *ppr.* to deprive of national rights, status, scope, etc.

dē·nat′ū·răl·īze, *v.t.*; denaturalized, *pt.*, *pp.*; denaturalizing, *ppr.* 1. to render unnatural; to alienate from nature.
2. to deprive of citizenship.

dē·nā′tūr·ȧnt, *n.* a denaturing agent.

dē·nā·tūr·ā′tion, *n.* a denaturing or being denatured.

dē·nā′tūre, *v.t.*; denatured, *pt.*, *pp.*; denaturing, *ppr.* [L. *de*, away, and *nature*.]
1. to change the nature of; take natural qualities away from.
2. to render unfit for usual use: applied mainly to alcohol, rendering it unfit as beverage or medicine, but valuable as a fuel for various engines, cooking, etc.

dē·nā′tūred al′cō·hol, ethyl alcohol mixed with a small amount of pyridine, methyl alcohol, or certain other compounds to make it unfit to drink: used as an antifreeze for automobile radiators, etc.

dē·nā′tūr·īze, *v.t.*; denaturized, *pt.*, *pp.*; denaturizing, *ppr.* to denature.

dē·nāy′, *n.* denial; refusal. [Obs.]

dē·nāy′, *v.t.* to deny. [Obs.]

dē·nä′zi·fȳ (-nä′tsē-), *v.t.* to rid of all Nazi elements, as by removal of Nazis from positions of importance, by education, etc.

dendr-, den′dri-, den′drō-, [from Gr. *dendron*, tree.] combining forms meaning *tree*.

den′drȧ·chāte, *n.* [*dendr-*, and Gr. *achdtēs*, agate.] arborescent agate; agate containing the figures of shrubs or parts of plants.

den′drăl, *a.* [from Gr. *dendron*, a tree.] pertaining to a tree or trees; of the nature of a tree; arboreal. [Rare.]

den′dri·form, *a.* [*dendri-*, and L. *forma*, form.] having the form or appearance of a tree; arborescent.

den′drīte, *n.* [Gr. *dendritēs*, of or belonging to a tree, from *dendron*, a tree.]
1. a stone or mineral on or in which are the figures of shrubs or trees, produced usually by the presence of hydrous oxide of manganese.
2. a branching, treelike mark made by one mineral crystallizing in another.
3. the branched part of a nerve cell that carries impulses toward the cell body: also called *dendron*, *neurodendron*.
4. [*pl.*] the protoplasmic filaments of a nerve cell body.

den·drit′iç, den·drit′iç·ăl, *a.* 1. resembling a tree; treelike; dendriform.
2. marked by figures resembling shrubs, moss, etc.; like a dendrite: said of minerals.

den·drit′iç·ăl·ly, *adv.* in a dendritic manner.

den′drōbe, *n.* an orchid of the genus *Dendrobium*.

Den·drō′bi·um, *n.* [Mod.L., from Gr. *dendron*, a tree, and *bios*, life.] an extensive genus of epiphytic orchids, distributed over the whole of the damp tropical parts of Asia and cultivated in hothouses.

Den·drō·çal′ȧ·mus, *n.* [*dendro-*, and Gr. *kalamos*, a reed.] a small genus of arborescent grasses growing in the East Indies, resembling the bamboo, but bearing a berrylike fruit.

Den·drō·coe′lȧ, *n.pl.* [*dendro-*, and Gr. *koilos*, hollow.] a division of turbellarian worms characterized by a broad, thin, flat body; the planarians.

den·drō·coe′lăn, *n.* a turbellarian worm of the division *Dendrocœla*; a planarian.

den·drō·den′tine, *n.* [*dendro-*, and L. *dens* (*-entis*), a tooth.] that modification of the fundamental dentine of the teeth produced by the aggregation of many simple teeth into a mass.

den′drō·dont, *a.* [Gr. *dendron*, a tree, and *odous* (*odontos*), tooth.] having teeth presenting a dendriform appearance in section, as certain fossil vertebrates.

den′drō·dont, *n.* one of a dendrodont fossil family of vertebrates.

den·drog′rȧ·phy, *n.* [*dendro-*, and Gr. *graphein*, to write.] same as *dendrology*.

den′droid, *a.* [Gr. *dendron*, a tree, and *eidos*, form.] resembling a shrub or small tree; dendriform.

den·droid′ăl, *a.* dendroid.

den′drō·līte, *n.* [*dendro-*, and Gr. *lithos*, a stone.] a petrified or fossil shrub, plant, or part of a plant.

den·drō·log′iç·ăl, *a.* pertaining to dendrology.

den·drol′ō·ġist, *n.* one who specializes in dendrology.

den·drol′ō·gous, *a.* pertaining to dendrology.

den·drol′ō·ġy, *n.* [Gr. *dendron*, a tree, and *logos*, description, from *legein*, to speak.] a discourse or treatise on trees; the scientific study of trees.

den·drom′e·tẽr, *n.* [*dendro-*, and Gr. *metron*, a measure.] an instrument to measure the height and diameter of trees.

-den′drŏn, [from Gr. *dendron*, a tree.] a combining form meaning *tree* or *treelike structure*, as in rhodo*dendron*.

dēne, *n.* [var. of *dune*.] a low mound of loose sand near a seashore; dune. [Brit. Dial.]

dēne, *n.* a valley; a dean or den. [Obs.]

Den′eb, *n.* [Ar. *dhanab*, short for *dhanab aldajājah*, tail of the hen.] a first-magnitude star in the constellation Cygnus (Swan).

den′ē·gāte, *v.t.* to deny. [Obs.]

den·ē·gā′tion, *n.* denial.

dēne′hōle, *n.* [ME. *dene*; AS. *denu*, a valley, and *hol*, a hole.] any of a large number of ancient artificial pits or excavations, often found in the chalk formation in the southeastern part of England.

deñ′guē, *n.* [W. Ind. Sp. *dengue*, from Swahili *dinga*, *dyenga*, cramplike attack; confused with Sp. *dengue*, affected contortion, prudery (with reference to the position of the neck and shoulders).] an infectious tropical disease transmitted by mosquitoes and characterized by severe pains in the joints and back, fever, and rash: also called *dandy fever*, *breakbone fever*.

dē·nī′ȧ·ble, *a.* that can be denied or contradicted.

dē·nī′ăl, *n.* [from L. *denegare*, to deny; *de-*, intens., and *negare*, to deny.]
1. the act of denying or contradicting; an assertion that a declaration or fact stated is not true; negation; contradiction: opposed to *affirmation*.
2. refusal to grant; the negation of a request or petition; as, his request met with a direct *denial*: opposed to *compliance*.
3. a rejection or refusing to acknowledge; a disowning; as, the *denial* of one's family.
4. a refusing to receive, believe, accept, or embrace; as, a *denial* of the faith or the truth.
5. a refusal to give.
6. abstinence from desired things: called also *denial of oneself*, *self-denial*.
7. in law, a defense; a formal contradiction of a statement made by the opposing party.
Syn.—disavowal, renunciation, contradiction, dissent, rejection, abnegation.

dē·nī′ănce, *n.* denial. [Obs.]

dē·nic′ō·tin·īze, *v.t.*; denicotinized, *pt.*, *pp.*; denicotinizing, *ppr.* [*de-*, *nicotine*, and *-ize*.] to remove nicotine from (tobacco).

dē·nī′ẽr, *n.* one who denies.

dē·nier′, *n.* [OFr. *denier*, from L. *denarius*, lit. containing ten, a denarius.]
1. a small French coin, originally made of silver, later of copper, no longer current; the twelfth part of a sou.
2. a unit of weight for threads of silk, rayon, etc., equal to .05 gram per 450 meters.

den′i·grāte, *v.t.* [L. *denigratus*, pp. of *denigrare*, to blacken; *de-*, intens., and *nigrare*, to blacken.]
1. to blacken; to make black.
2. to blacken the name of; defame.

den·i·grā′tion, *n.* 1. the act of making black; a blackening.
2. a blackening of character; defamation.

den′i·grā·tŏr, *n.* 1. one who or that which blackens something.
2. a person who blackens another's character; defamer.

den′im, *n.* a coarse, twilled cotton drilling largely used for overalls, uniforms, etc.

dē·nī′trāte, *v.t.*; denitrated, *pt.*, *pp.*; denitrating, *ppr.* to remove nitric acid, the nitrate ion or radical, the nitro group, or the oxides of nitrogen from.

dē·nī·trā′tion, *n.* the process of denitrating.

dē·nī″tri·fi·çā′tion, *n.* the act or process of denitrifying.

dē·nī′tri·fȳ, *v.t.*; denitrified, *pt.*, *pp.*; denitrifying, *ppr.* to free from nitrogen or nitrogen compounds.

den·i·zā′tion, *n.* the act of making one a denizen, subject, or citizen.

dē·nīze′, *v.t.* to make a denizen, subject, or citizen of. [Obs.]

den′i·zen, *n.* [ME. *denesyn*; OFr. *denzein*, one living within a city, from LL. *de intus*, from within.]
1. a foreigner granted specified rights of citizenship.
2. a dweller; as, the *denizens* of the jungle.
3. an animal, plant, foreign word, etc. that has become naturalized.

den′i·zen, *v.t.*; denizened, *pt.*, *pp.*; denizening, *ppr.* 1. to make a denizen of; to admit to residence with certain rights and privileges; to enfranchise.
2. to furnish with denizens. [Rare.]

den″i·zen·ā′tion, *n.* denization.

den′i·zen·īze, *v.t.* to denizen, or naturalize.

den′i·zen·ship, *n.* the state of being a denizen.

den′net, *n.* [origin uncertain.] a light, open, two-wheeled carriage, resembling a gig.

dē·nom′i·nȧ·ble, *a.* capable of being denominated or named.

dē·nom′i·nănt, *n.* [L. *denominans* (*-antis*), ppr. of *denominare*, to name.] that which names or denotes a quality; as, boldness is the *denominant* of bold. [Rare.]

dē·nom′i·nāte, *v.t.*; denominated, *pt.*, *pp.*; denominating, *ppr.* [L. *denominatus*, pp. of *denominare*, to name; *de-*, intens., and *nominare*, to name, from *nomen*, a name.] to name; to give a name or epithet to; to call; to designate.
Syn.—name, designate, call, style, entitle.

dē·nom′i·nāte, *a.* in arithmetic, denoting a number which expresses a specific kind of unit; qualifying: opposed to *abstract*; thus, seven pounds is a *denominate* number, while seven, without reference to concrete units, is *abstract*.

dē·nom·i·nā′tion, *n.* 1. the act of naming.
2. a name or appellation.
3. the name of a class of things.
4. a class or kind (especially of units) having a specific name or value; as, coins of different *denominations*.
5. a religious sect; as, a Protestant *denomination*.
Syn.—name, designation, appellation, title, epithet.

dē·nom·i·nā′tion·ăl, *a.* of, sponsored by, or under the control of, some religious sect or sects; sectarian; as, *denominational* education.

dē·nom·i·nā′tion·ăl·iṣm, *n.* 1. denominational principles.
2. a denominational system.
3. acceptance or support of such principles or system.
4. division into denominations.

dē·nom·i·nā′tion·ăl·ist, *n.* an advocate or believer in denominationalism; a sectarian.

dē·nom·i·nā′tion·ăl·ly, *adv.* in a denominational manner; by denomination or sect.

dē·nom′i·nā·tive, *a.* 1. that may be denominated; namable.
2. that may constitute a distinct designation; appelative; naming.
3. in grammar, formed from a noun or adjective root; as, *to eye* is a *denominative* verb.
4. in logic, connotative; as, a *denominative* name.

dē·nom′i·nā·tive, *n.* that which has the character of a denomination; specifically, in grammar, a word, especially a verb, formed from either a substantive or adjective.

dē·nom′i·nā·tive·ly, *adv.* by denomination.

dē·nom′i·nā·tŏr, *n.* 1. one who or that which denominates; one from whom or that from which a name is derived.
2. in arithmetic and algebra, that number placed below or to the right of the line in fractions, which shows into how many equal parts the whole is divided. Thus, in 3/5, 5 is the *denominator*, showing that the whole is divided into five parts; and the numerator, 3, shows how many parts are taken.
3. a denominant. [Obs.]

dē·nōt′ȧ·ble, *a.* that can be denoted or marked.

dē·nō′tāte, *v.t.* to denote. [Obs.]

dē·nō·tā′tion, *n.* [LL. *denotatio*, a marking or

pointing out, from L. *denotare*, to mark out, denote.]
1. a denoting.
2. a marking out or off.
3. the direct, explicit meaning or reference of a word or term: distinguished from *connotation*.
4. an indication or sign.

dē·nōt′ȧ·tive, *a.* having power to denote; designative.

dē·nōt′ȧ·tive·ly, *adv.* in a denotative manner.

dē·nōte′, *v.t.*; denoted, *pt., pp.*; denoting, *ppr.* [L. *denotare*, to mark out, denote; *de-*, down, and *notare*, to mark, from *nota*, a mark.]
1. to mark; to signify by a visible sign; to indicate; to express; to designate; to refer to: said of words, signs, or symbols, and distinguished from *connote*.
2. to be the sign or symptom of; to show; to betoken; to indicate; as, a quick pulse *denotes* fever.
Syn.—mean, indicate, imply, signify, express, show, betoken, mark.

dē·nōte′ment, *n.* sign; indication.

dē·nō′tive, *a.* denoting; indicative.

de·nöue′ment, dé·noue′ment (dā-nö′moṅ), *n.* [Fr., from *dénouer*, to untie; *dé-* priv., and *nouer*, to tie.]
1. the outcome, solution, unraveling, or clarification of a plot in a drama, story, etc.
2. the point in the plot where this occurs.
3. any final revelation or outcome.

dē·nounce′, *v.t.*; denounced, *pt., pp.*; denouncing, *ppr.* [ME. *denouncen*; L. *denuntiare*, to give notice to, threaten, denounce.]
1. to declare solemnly; to announce. [Obs.]
I *denounce* unto you this day, that ye shall surely perish. —Deut. xxx. 18.
2. to threaten by some outward sign or expression.
His look *denounced* revenge. —Milton.
3. to inform against; to accuse; as, he was *denounced* to the authorities.
4. to condemn strongly as evil.
5. to give formal notice of the ending of (a treaty, armistice, etc.).
6. in Mexican and Spanish mining law, (a) to formally lay claim to (a mine abandoned or inadequately worked); (b) to establish a claim to (a new mine).

dē·nounce′ment, *n.* 1. the declaration of a menace, or of evil; denunciation.
2. in Mexican and Spanish mining law, the act of denouncing. [see *denounce*, sense 6.]

dē·noun′cẽr, *n.* one who denounces.

dē nō′vō, [L.] anew; once more; again.

dense, *a.* [L. *densus*, thick, close.]
1. close; compact; having the constituent parts closely packed; as, a *dense* body.
2. thick; impenetrable; as, a *dense* fog.
3. stupid; dull; thick-headed; as, a *dense* student.
4. in photography, opaque, with good contrast in light and shade: said of a negative.

dense′ly, *adv.* in a dense manner; compactly.

dense′ness, *n.* density.

den′shīre, den′shẽr, *v.t.* [from *Denshire*, contr. of the proper name *Devonshire*.] to fertilize (land) with burnt refuse. [Brit. Dial.]

den·sim′e·tẽr, *n.* [L. *densus*, dense, and *metrum*, a measure.] an instrument for determining the specific gravity or density of a solid or liquid.

den·si·tom′ē·tẽr, *n.* [from *density*, and *-meter*.] an optical device for measuring the density of a photographic negative.

den′si·ty, *n.*; *pl.* **den′si·ties,** [L. *densitas*, thickness, from *densus*, thick.]
1. the quality of being dense, close, or compact; closeness of constituent parts; compactness.
2. quantity or number per unit, as of area; as, the *density* of population.
3. stupidity.
4. in electricity, (a) the amount of a charge of electricity flowing through a unit of area in a unit of time; (b) current density.
5. in photography, opaque quality; amount of light-stopping material on an exposed negative.
6. in physics, the ratio of the mass of an object to its volume.

dent, *n.* [ME. *dent*, from AS. *dynt*, a stroke or blow.]
1. a stroke; a blow. [Obs.]
2. a mark made by a blow or pressure, as a gap or notch; especially, a hollow or depression made on the surface of a solid body; an indentation.

dent, *v.t.*; dented, *pt., pp.*; denting, *ppr.* to make a dent or small hollow in; to indent.

dent, *v.i.* to become dented.

dent, *n.* [Fr. *dent*; L. *dens* (*dentis*), a tooth.] a toothlike projection, as of a comb, gearwheel, lock, etc.; also, a cane or wire of the reed frame of a weaver's loom.

den·tag′rȧ, *n.* [L. *dens* (*dentis*), a tooth, and Gr. *agra*, a catching, hunting.]
1. toothache.
2. a forceps used in pulling teeth.

den′tăl, *a.* 1. pertaining to the teeth; as, *dental* surgery.
2. relating to dentistry; as, a *dental* saw.
3. in phonetics, formed or pronounced by placing the tip of the tongue against or near the upper front teeth; as, *d* and *t* are *dental* letters.
dental floss; thin, strong thread for removing food particles from between the teeth.
dental formula; an arrangement of symbols and numbers used to signify the number and kinds of teeth of a mammal. The *dental formula* of man is: I. $\frac{2-2}{2-2}$, C. $\frac{1-1}{1-1}$, P. M. $\frac{2-2}{2-2}$, M. $\frac{3-3}{3-3}$ = 32. The numerators designate the upper, and the denominators the lower incisors, canines, premolars, and molars, respectively.

den′tăl, *n.* 1. in phonetics, a dental consonant, as *t*, *d*, or *th*.
2. in zoology, a shell of the genus *Dentalium*, resembling a tooth; a tooth shell. [Obs.]

den·tal′i·ty, *n.* the state or quality of being dental (pronunciation).

Den·tā′li·um, *n.* [L., from *dens* (*dentis*), a tooth.] a genus of gasteropodous mollusks, the shell of which consists of a tubular arcuate cone, open at both ends. There are many species commonly called *tooth shells*.

den″tăl·i·zā′tion, *n.* change to a dental letter, as the change of *f* in the German *f*ein to *th* in the English *th*in.

Den·tā′ri·ȧ, *n.* [from LL. *dentarius*, pertaining to the teeth, from L. *dens* (*dentis*), tooth.] a genus of cruciferous, ornamental herbs, with creeping, scaly rootstocks, large, purple flowers, and stem leaves which are opposite or in whorls of three: also called *coralroot*, *toothwort*.

den′tȧ·ry, *n.* the bone in the lower jaw of fishes and reptiles that supports the teeth, if any.

den′tȧ·ry, *a.* relating to the teeth; bearing teeth; as, the *dentary* bone in fishes.

den·tā′tȧ, *n.* in anatomy, the axis of the vertebral column.

den′tāte, *a.* having teeth or toothlike projections; toothed or notched; specifically, (a) in botany, toothed; having sharp teeth which project outward; as, a *dentate* leaf; (b) in zoology, having toothlike processes or points; denticulate.

DENTATE LEAF

den′tāte-cil′i·āte, *a.* [L. *dentatus*, toothed, from *dens*, a tooth, and *cilium*, an eyelid.] in botany, having the margin dentate, and fringed or tipped with cilia, or hairs.

den′tā·ted, *a.* dentate.

den′tāte·ly, *adv.* in a dentate manner.

den′tāte-ser′rāte, *a.* serrated, and having each projection toothed.

den′tāte-sin′ū·āte, *a.* having angular teeth separated from each other by incurved spaces.

den·tā′tion, *n.* 1. the quality or condition of being dentate.
2. a toothlike projection, as on a leaf.

dent ċorn, a variety of corn having the kernel furrowed or depressed at the large end.

dent′ed, *a.* 1. indented.
2. impressed with little hollows.

dent′ed, *a.* having teeth; toothed.

den′tel, *n.* see *dentil*.

den′te·lā·ted, *a.* toothed or notched.

den·telle′, *n.* [Fr., lace, edging, from L. *dens*, a tooth.]
1. lace.
2. in bookbinding, a toothed or lacy decoration.

den′tex, *n.* [L. *dentix*, a seafish, from *dens* (*dentis*), tooth.] a sparoid marine food fish of the genus *Dentex*.

den′ti-, [from L. *dens*, *dentis*, a tooth.] a combining form meaning: (a) *tooth* or *teeth*, as in *denti*form; (b) in phonetics, *dental and*, as in *denti*labial.

Den·ti·cē′tē, *n.pl.* [*denti-*, and L. *cetus*, any large sea animal, a whale.] a suborder of *Cetacea* including the dolphins, in which the teeth are more or less permanent.

den′ti·ċle, *n.* 1. a small tooth or toothlike projecting point.
2. a dentil.

den·tiċ′ū·lāte, *a.* 1. having small teeth; finely dentate; as, a *denticulate* leaf.
2. in architecture, formed into dentils.

den·tiċ′ū·lā·ted, *a.* denticulate.

den·tiċ′ū·lāte·ly, *adv.* in a denticulate manner.

den·tiċ·ū·lā′tion, *n.* 1. the quality or condition of being denticulate.
2. a denticle; a set of small teeth or notches.

den′ti·ċūle, *n.* a dentil.

den′ti·faċ·tŏr, *n.* [*denti-*, and L. *factus*, pp. of *facere*, to make.] a machine for the manufacture of the artificial teeth, gums, and palate used in dental surgery.

den′ti·fọrm, *a.* having the form of a tooth; of the shape of a tooth or teeth.

den′ti·frice, *n.* [L. *dentifricium*, a tooth powder, from *dens*, a tooth, and *fricare*, to rub.] a powder, paste, liquid, etc., used in cleaning the teeth.

den·tiġ′ẽr·ous, *a.* [*denti-*, and L. *gerere*, to carry.] bearing or supporting teeth; supplied with teeth.

den′til, den′tel, *n.* [LL. *dentillus*; L. *denticulus*, dim. of *dens*, a tooth.]
1. in architecture, any of the small cubes into which the square member in the bed molding of an Ionic, Corinthian, Composite, and, occasionally, a Doric cornice is divided.
2. in heraldry, a tooth or notch.

den·ti·lā′bi·ăl, *a.* and *n.* [*denti-*, and L. *labium*, lip.] labiodental.

den′ti·lā·ted, *a.* toothed or notched. [Rare.]

den·ti·lā′tion, *n.* dentition.

den′tile, *n.* [LL. *dentillus*; L. *denticulus*, dim. of *dens* (*dentis*), a tooth.] a small tooth; a denticle.

den·ti·liṅ′guăl (-gwăl), *a.* [*denti-*, and L. *lingua*, the tongue.] formed by inserting the tongue between the teeth, as *th* in *th*ose and *th*ick: now usually *interdental*.

den·ti·liṅ′guăl, *n.* a dentilingual consonant.

den·ti·liṅ′guăl·ly, *adv.* in a dentilingual manner.

den·til′ō·quist, *n.* one who practices dentiloquy; one who speaks with the teeth closed.

den·til′ō·quy, *n.* [*denti-*, and L. *loqui*, to speak.] the act or habit of speaking with the teeth closed.

den′ti·năl, *a.* of or pertaining to dentine.
dentinal tubules; the minute tubules of the dentine.

den′tine, den′tin, *n.* [L. *dens* (*dentis*), tooth.] the hard, dense, calcareous tissue lying below the enamel and constituting the body of the tooth.

den′ti·phōne, *n.* [*denti-*, and Gr. *phōnē*, voice, sound.] an instrument by which sound waves are collected and conveyed to the auditory nerve through the teeth.

den·ti·ros′tẽr, *n.* a bird of the family *Dentirostres*.

den·ti·ros′trăl, *a.* [L. *dens* (*dentis*), a tooth, and *rostrum*, a beak.] pertaining to or characteristic of the *Dentirostres*.

den·ti·ros′trāte, *a.* dentirostral.

Den·ti·ros′trēṣ, *n.pl.* a suborder of insessorial birds, characterized by having a notch and toothlike process on each side of the margin of the upper mandible. The butcherbirds, shrikes, etc. belong to this suborder.

den′ti·sċalp, *n.* [*denti-*, and L. *scalpere*, to scrape.] an instrument for scraping or cleaning the teeth.

den′tist, *n.* [from L. *dens* (*dentis*), a tooth.] a person whose profession is the care of teeth, including the filling of cavities, the extraction of teeth beyond repair, and the replacement of missing teeth with artificial ones; doctor of dental surgery.

den·tis′tiċ, den·tis′ti·ċăl, *a.* dental. [Rare.]

den′tist·ry, *n.* the art or profession of a dentist; the branch of medical science that deals with the teeth and their care.

den·ti′tion, *n.* [L. *dentitio*, teething, from *dentire*, to cut teeth.]
1. the cutting or protrusion of the teeth; teething.
2. the period of development and cutting of the teeth.
3. the nature, number, and system of the teeth; as, the *dentition* of man differs from that of the dog.

den′tō-, 1. denti-.
2. a combining form meaning *dental*, *dental and*, as in *dento*surgical.

den′toid, *a.* resembling a tooth; shaped like a tooth.

den·tō·liṅ′guăl (-gwăl), *a.* and *n.* dentilingual.

den·tō·sũr′ġi·ċăl, *a.* relating to or used in both dentistry and surgery.

den′tūre, *n.* [L. *dens* (*dentis*), a tooth.] in dentistry, a set of teeth; especially, a partial or complete set of artificial teeth.

dē·nū′çlē·ā·ted, *a.* divested of a nucleus.

den′ū·dāte (*or* dē·nū′), *v.t.*; denudated, *pt.*, *pp.*; denudating, *ppr.* [L. *denudatus*, pp. of *denudare*, to strip off; *de-*, off, from, and *nudare*, to strip.] to strip; to denude.

dē·nūd′āte, dē·nūd′ā·ted (*or* den′ū-), *a.* nude; naked; denuded.

den·ū·dā′tion, *n.* 1. the act of stripping off covering; a making bare.

2. the fact or condition of being denuded.

dē·nūde′, *v.t.*; denuded, *pt.*, *pp.*; denuding, *ppr.* [L. *denudare*, to make bare, strip off.]

1. to strip; to divest of all covering; to make bare or naked.

2. in geology, to lay bare by erosion.

dē·nū′mẽr·ănt, *n.* [L. *denumerans*, ppr. of *denumerare*, to number; *de*, down, from, and *numerare*, to count.] in mathematics, the number denoting how many solutions are possible in a given system of equations.

dē·nū·mẽr·ā′tion, *n.* in law, a down payment.

dē·nún′ci·ä (-thi-ä), *n.* [Sp., from *denunciar*, to denounce.] in Mexico and Spanish America, (a) the judicial proceedings necessary to denounce a mine; (b) a similar method essential to land pre-emption.

dē·nun′ci·ā·ble (*or* -shi-), *a.* fit or liable to be denounced.

dē·nun′ci·ănt (*or* -shi-), *a.* denunciatory.

dē·nun′ci·āte (*or* -shi-āt), *v.t.*; denunciated, *pt.*, *pp.*; denunciating, *ppr.* to denounce.

dē·nun·ci·ā′tion, *n.* [L. *denuntiatio*, an announcement, forewarning, from *denuntiatus*, pp. of *denuntiare*, to announce, to denounce; *de-*, intens., and *nuntiare*, to announce.]

1. announcement; proclamation. [Obs.]

2. a denouncing.

3. a threat or warning of evil, punishment, etc.

4. an informing against (someone) to the authorities; accusation.

5. a notice by a nation of its intention to end a treaty, armistice, etc.

6. in Scottish law, the act by which a person is proclaimed outlawed or a rebel.

dē·nun′ci·ā·tive (*or* -shi-), *a.* denunciatory.

dē·nun′ci·ā·tŏr, *n.* [LL. *denuntiator*, a police office, from L. *denuntiare*, to announce.]

1. one who denounces or threatens.

2. in civil law, one who accuses another.

dē·nun′ci·ā·tō·ry, *a.* relating to or implying denunciation; containing a public threat; comminatory.

dē·nū·tri′tion, *n.* lack of nutrition.

dē·nȳ′, *v.t.*; denied, *pt.*, *pp.*; denying, *ppr.* [ME. *denyen*; L. *denegare*, to deny, from *de-*, intens., and *negare*, to deny.]

1. to contradict; to gainsay; to declare (a statement or position) not to be true; as, to *deny* a proposition.

2. to refuse to grant; to withhold; as, to *deny* aid.

3. to refuse to accept as true or right; to reject as unfounded, unreal, etc.

4. to repudiate; to disown; to refuse to receive or embrace; as, to *deny* one's friends.

5. to refuse access to.

6. to refuse (a person who makes a request).

7. to forbid. [Obs.]

to deny oneself; to decline the gratification of appetites or desires; also, to refrain from; to abstain.

to deny oneself to; to refuse access to (visitors).

Syn.—contradict, disavow, disclaim, disown, oppose, refuse.

dē·nȳ′, *v.i.* to give a negative answer; to maintain a negative attitude.

dē·nȳ′ing·ly, *adv.* in a manner indicating denial.

dē·ob·struçt′, *v.t.*; deobstructed, *pt.*, *pp.*; deobstructing, *ppr.* to remove obstructions or impediments from; as, to *deobstruct* the pores or lacteals.

dē·ob′strū·ent, *a.* removing obstructions; having power to clear or open the natural ducts of the fluids and secretions of the body, dissolving viscidities; aperient.

dē·ob′strū·ent, *n.* a medicine having the power of removing obstructions.

dē′ō·dand, *n.* [from L. *deodandum*, a thing to be given to God; *Deo*, dat. of *Deus*, God, and *dandum*, neut. of *dandus*, gerundive of *dare*, to give.] in early English law, a personal chattel which was instrumental in the death of a person and, for that reason, forfeited to the king, to be used for some pious purpose.

dē·ō·där′, *n.* [L. *deodara*, from Sans. *devadāru*, divine tree; *deva*, divine, and *dāru*, wood.]

1. a kind of cedar tree with durable, light-red wood, native to the Himalayas.

2. its wood.

dē′ō·dāte, *n.* an offering to or gift from God. [Obs.]

dē·ō′dŏr·ănt, *a.* [*de-* priv., and *odorans*, ppr. of *odorare*, to smell, from *odor*, a smell.] having the power of destroying or counteracting undesired odors.

dē·ō′dŏr·ănt, *n.* any deodorant substance or preparation.

dē·ō″dŏr·i·zā′tion, *n.* the act of removing odor; the condition of being deodorized.

dē·ō′dŏr·īze, *v.t.*; deodorized, *pt.*, *pp.*; deodorizing, *ppr.* to remove or counteract the odor of.

dē·ō′dŏr·ī·zẽr, *n.* a deodorizing agent.

Dē′ō grā′ti·as (-shi-as), [L.] thanks to God.

dē·on′ẽr·āte, *v.t.* to unload. [Obs.]

dē·on·tō·loġ′iç·ăl, *a.* relating to deontology.

dē·on·tol′ō·ġist, *n.* one versed in deontology.

dē·on·tol′ō·ġy, *n.* [Gr. *deon*, that which is binding, proper, from *dein*, to bind, and *logos*, description.] the theory of duty or moral obligation; ethics.

dē·ō·pẽr′çū·lāte, *a.* [*de-* priv., and L. *operculum*, a lid, covering.] in botany, pertaining to mosses having an operculum that does not separate spontaneously from the spore cases.

dē·op′pi·lāte, *v.t.* to free from obstruction. [Obs.]

dē·op·pi·lā′tion, *n.* the removal of obstruction. [Obs.]

dē·op′pi·lā·tive, *a.* deobstruent; removing obstruction. [Obs.]

dē·ọr·di·nā′tion, *n.* disorder. [Obs.]

dē·ọr′găn·īze, *v.t.*; deorganized, *pt.*, *pp.*; deorganizing, *ppr.* to destroy the organic character of.

dē·os′çū·lāte, *v.t.* to kiss. [Obs.]

dē·os·çū·lā′tion, *n.* a kissing [Obs.]

dē·os′si·fȳ, *v.t.*; deossified, *pt.*, *pp.*; deossifying, *ppr.* to deprive of bones or bony structure; to make weak.

Dē′ō vō·len′tē, [L.] (if) God is willing.

dē·ox′i·dāte, *v.t.*; deoxidated, *pt.*, *pp.*; deoxidating, *ppr.* to deoxidize.

dē·ox·i·dā′tion, *n.* the act or process of deoxidizing.

dē·ox″i·di·zā′tion, *n.* deoxidation.

dē·ox′i·dīze, *v.t.*; deoxidized, *pt.*, *pp.*; deoxidizing, *ppr.* to remove oxygen, especially chemically combined oxygen, from.

dē·ox′i·dī·zẽr, *n.* any agent that removes oxygen.

dē·ox′y·ġen·āte, *v.t.* to remove oxygen, especially free oxygen, from (water, air, etc.).

dē·ox″y·ġen·ā′tion, *n.* the act or operation of removing oxygen.

dē·ox′y·ġen·īze, *v.t.* to deoxygenate.

dē·pāint′, *v.t.* [ME. *depeynten*; OFr. *depeint*, from L. *depingere*, to paint; *de*, and *pingere*, to paint.] to depict or portray, either by painting or by words. [Rare or Obs.]

dē·pāint′ẽr, *n.* a painter. [Obs.]

de·pär′dieu″ (-dyö″), *interj.* [OFr.] in God's name.

dē·pärt′, *v.i.*; departed, *pt.*, *pp.*; departing, *ppr.* [ME. *departen*; L. *dispertire* or *dispartire*, to divide, separate; *dis-*, apart, and *partire*, to divide, from *pars* (*partis*), a part, share.]

1. to share. [Obs.]

2. to separate; to part; to withdraw; to go away (*from*).

He which hath no stomach to this fight
Let him *depart*. —Shak.

Depart from me, ye cursed, into everlasting fire. —Matt. xxv. 41.

3. to start; to set out.

4. to turn aside (*from* something); as, we cannot *depart from* our rules.

I have not *departed from* thy judgments. —Ps. cxix. 102.

5. in law, to forsake or abandon the ground assumed in a former pleading and assume a new one.

6. to die.

Lord, now lettest thou thy servant *depart* in peace, according to thy word. —Luke ii. 29.

to depart with; to yield. [Obs.]

Syn.—leave, retire, go, desert, apostatize, deviate, vary, decease, die.

dē·pärt′, *v.t.* 1. to divide. [Obs.]

2. to separate; as, till death us *depart*. [Obs.]

3. to retire from; to leave; to quit: now only in *depart this life*. [Archaic.]

dē·pärt′, *n.* 1. division, as of a compound into its elements. [Obs.]

2. a departure. [Obs.]

dē·pärt′ȧ·ble, *a.* divisible; separable. [Obs.]

dē·pärt′ed, *a.* 1. gone away; past; bygone.

2. dead.

the departed; (a) the dead person; (b) dead persons; the dead.

dē·pärt′ẽr, *n.* one who departs.

dē·pärt′ment, *n.* [OFr. *departement*, a division, department, from L. *dispartire, dispertire*, to divide, depart.]

1. the act of departing; departure. [Obs.]

2. a separate part, division, or branch, as of a government or business; a section; a subdivision; as, the accounting *department*, the police *department*.

3. a field of knowledge or activity; as, rewriting is his *department*.

4. a government administrative district in France.

5. in education, a subdivision of a college or school, for the teaching and studying of a branch of knowledge; as, the *department* of sociology.

department store; a large retail store not confined to one kind of goods but handling various kinds arranged in departments.

dē·pärt·men′tăl, *a.* 1. pertaining to a department or departments.

2. arranged into or according to departments; as, *departmental* instruction in grammar schools.

dē·pärt·men′tăl·iṣm, *n.* 1. strict following of departmental rules, practices, etc.

2. bureaucracy.

dē·pär′tūre, *n.* [OFr. *departeure*, from *despartir*, to depart.]

1. a separating or parting. [Obs.]

2. the act of going away; a moving from or leaving a place; as, a *departure* from San Francisco.

3. death. [Archaic.]

4. a starting out, as on a trip or new course of action; as, political action is a new *departure* for labor.

5. a deviation or turning aside (*from* something).

6. in nautical usage, (a) the distance of a ship due east or west from the meridian of its starting point; (b) a ship's position in latitude and longitude at the start of a voyage, from which the dead reckoning is begun.

7. in law, the abandonment of the ground taken in a former pleading, and the adoption of another.

dē·pas′cent, *a.* [L. *depascens*, ppr. of *depascere*, to feed upon; *de*, and *pasci*, to feed.] feeding. [Rare.]

dē·pȧs′tūre, *v.t.* 1. to eat up; to consume the herbage of (a piece of land): said of cattle, etc.

2. to pasture (cattle, etc.); to graze.

dē·pȧs′tūre, *v.i.* to feed; to graze.

dē·pā′tri·āte, *v.i.* to leave one's country. [Obs.]

dē·pau′pẽr·āte, *v.t.*; depauperated, *pt.*, *pp.*; depauperating, *ppr.* [*de-*, and L. *pauperare*, to make poor, from *pauper*, poor.] to make poor; to impoverish; to deprive of fertility or richness.

dē·pau′pẽr·āte, *a.* impoverished; made poor; specifically, in botany, imperfectly developed.

dē·pau′pẽr·īze, *v.t.*; depauperized, *pt.*, *pp.*; depauperizing, *ppr.* to raise from a condition of poverty or pauperism; to free from pauperism.

dē·pēach′, *v.t.* to dispatch. [Obs.]

dē·peç·ū·lā′tion, *n.* a robbing or embezzlement. [Obs.]

dē·peinct′ (-pānt′), *v.t.* to paint. [Obs.]

dē·pend′, *v.i.*; depended, *pt.*, *pp.*; depending, *ppr.* [ME. *dependen*; OFr. *dependre*; L. *dependere*, to hang down from, to depend; *de-*, down, and *pendere*, to hang.]

1. to be influenced or determined by something else; be contingent (*on*).

2. to rely; to rest with confidence; to trust; to confide; to have full confidence or belief; as, we *depend* on the word or assurance of our friends; we *depend* on the arrival of the mail.

3. to rely on for support or aid.

4. to be in suspense; to be undetermined; as, the suit is still *depending* in court.

5. to hang down; to be sustained by being fastened or attached to something above. [Archaic.]

6. to impend. [Obs.]

dē·pend·ȧ·bil′i·ty, *n.* the quality of being dependable.

dē·pend′ȧ·ble, *a.* that can be depended on; reliable; trustworthy.

dē·pend′ȧ·ble·ness, *n.* the quality of being dependable.

dē·pend′ȧ·bly, *adv.* in a dependable manner.

dē·pend′ănce, *n.* same as *dependence*.

dē·pend′ăn·cy, *n.* same as *dependency*.

dē·pend′ănt, *a.* and *n.* same as *dependent*.

dē·pend′ence, *n.* [L. *dependens*, ppr. of *dependere*, to hang from.]
1. the condition or fact of being dependent.
2. the state of being dependent on, or of being influenced, controlled, or determined by something else.
3. subordination.
4. reliance (*on* someone else) for support or aid.
5. reliance; confidence; trust; as, to place great *dependence* on a person.
6. that on which one depends or relies; as, the son was his mother's chief *dependence*. [Rare.]
7. that which hangs or is suspended. [Archaic.]
And make a large *dependence* from the bough. —Dryden.
8. a subject of quarrel or controversy. [Obs.]
Syn.—reliance.

dē·pend′en·cy, *n.*; *pl.* **dē·pend′en·cies,** 1. dependence; the state of being dependent; reliance; confidence.
Their *dependency* upon the crown of England. —Bacon.
2. that which is dependent or subordinate.
3. a land or territory geographically distinct from the country governing it, but belonging to it and subject to its laws; as, Alaska is a *dependency* of the United States.

dē·pend′ent, *a.* 1. hanging down; as, a *dependent* leaf.
2. influenced, controlled, or determined by something else; contingent.
3. relying (*on* someone or something) for support or aid.
4. subordinate.
dependent clause; in grammar, a subordinate clause.
dependent contract; in law, a contract, invalid until some stipulation has been performed.
dependent variable; in mathematics and science, a variable depending for its value on another variable, which is called the *independent variable*.

dē·pend′ent, *n.* 1. one who relies on another for support, existence, aid, etc.
2. that which depends on something else.

dē·pend′ent·ly, *adv.* in a dependent manner.

dē·pend′ẽr, *n.* one who depends; a dependent.

dē·pend′ing·ly, *adv.* in a dependent or subordinate manner.

dē·pēo′ple (-pē′pl), *v.t.* to depopulate.

dē·pẽr′dit, *n.* that which is lost or abandoned. [Obs.]

dē·pẽr′dite·ly, *adv.* in the manner of a deperdit. [Obs.]

dep·ẽr·di′tion, *n.* loss; destruction. [Obs.]

dē·pẽr′sŏn·ăl·īze, *v.t.*; depersonalized, *pt.*, *pp.*; depersonalizing, *ppr.* to destroy the personality of.

dē·pẽr′ti·ble, *a.* divisible. [Obs.]

dep′hal, *n.* [Bengalese.] *Artocarpus lakoocha*, an Indian tree of the same genus as the breadfruit and jack, and cultivated for its fruit.

dē·phlegm′ (-flem′), *v.t.* to dephlegmate. [Obs.]

dē·phleg′māte, *v.t.*; dephlegmated, *pt.*, *pp.*; dephlegmating, *ppr.* [*de-* priv., and L. *phlegma*, phlegm.] to free from excess water, as by evaporation or distillation; to rectify: said of spirits or acids.

dē·phleg·mā′tion, *n.* the process of separating water from spirits or acids, by evaporation or repeated distillation.

dē·phleg′mā·tŏr, *n.* a condensing apparatus for purifying liquids.

dē·phleg′mȧ·tō·ry, *a* pertaining to or producing dephlegmation.

dē·phlegm′ed·ness (-flem′), *n.* a state of being freed from excess water. [Obs.]

dē·phlō·ġis′ti·ċāte, *v.t.*; dephlogisticated, *pt.*, *pp.*; dephlogisticating, *ppr.* [*de-*, and Gr. *phlogistos*, burnt, from *phlogizein*, to burn.] to deprive of phlogiston, formerly the supposed principle of inflammability; as, *dephlogisticated* air was the former term for oxygen.

dē·phlō·ġis·ti·ċā′tion, *n.* a process by which phlogiston was supposedly separated from bodies.

dē·phos″phŏr·i·zā′tion, *n.* the act or process of depriving of phosphorus.

dē·phos′phŏr·īze, *v.t.*; dephosphorized, *pt.*, *pp.*; dephosphorizing, *ppr.* to deprive of or free from phosphorus.

dē·piçt′, *v.t.*; depicted, *pt.*, *pp.*; depicting, *ppr.* [OFr. *depicter*, to depict, from L. *depictus*, pp. of *depingere*, to paint, depict.]
1. to paint; to portray; to form a likeness of by drawing, painting, sculpturing, etc.; as, to *depict* a lion on a shield.
2. to describe; to represent in words; as, the poet *depicts* the virtues of his hero.
Syn.—delineate, portray, describe, picture, represent, sketch.

dē·piçt′, *a.* depicted.

dē·piçt′ẽr, *n.* one who depicts.

dē·piç′tion, *n.* 1. a depicting or being depicted.
2. a picture, sculpture, etc. depicting something.
3. description.

dē·piç′tūre, *v.t.*; depictured, *pt.*, *pp.*; depicturing, *ppr.* to represent in a picture or words; to depict.

dē·pig·men·tā′tion, *n.* the act or process of depigmentizing, or, the state of being depigmentized.

dē·pig′ment·īze, *v.t.*; depigmentized, *pt.*, *pp.*; depigmentizing, *ppr.* to take away the pigment from; to make white; to bleach.

dep′i·lāte, *v.t.*; depilated, *pt.*, *pp.*; depilating, *ppr.* [L. *depilatus*, pp. of *depilare*, to deprive of hair.] to remove hair from (a part of the body).

dep·i·lā′tion, *n.* the act or process of removing hair from the body.

dep′i·lā·tŏr, *n.* a person or instrument for removing hair.

dē·pil′ȧ·tō·ry, *a.* having the quality or power to remove hair, especially unwanted hair.

dē·pil′ȧ·tō·ry, *n.*; *pl.* **dē·pil′ȧ·tō·ries,** any substance or device which is used to remove hair.

dep′i·lous, *a.* without hair.

dē·plā′nāte (*or* dep′lȧ-nāt), *a.* [LL. *deplanatus*, pp. of *deplanare*, to make level; L. *de*, down, from, and *planus*, flat, level.] in botany, flattened; made level.

dē·plane′, *v.t.* and *v.i.*; deplaned, *pt.*, *pp.*; deplaning, *ppr.* to take (anything) out of an aircraft, especially out of an airplane after a flight.

dē·plant′, *v.t.*; deplanted, *pt.*, *pp.*; deplanting, *ppr.* to remove (plants) from beds; to transplant. [Rare.]

dē·plen′ish, *v.t.*; deplenished, *pt.*, *pp.*; deplenishing, *ppr.* to reduce, exhaust, or deplete.

dē·plēte′, *v.t.*; depleted, *pt.*, *pp.*; depleting, *ppr.* [L. *depletus*, pp. of *deplere*, to empty, from *de-*, from, and *plere*, to fill.]
1. to empty wholly or partly.
2. to reduce, or exhaust by draining away, as the strength, vital powers, resources, etc.; as, to *deplete* the treasury.
3. in medicine, to relieve of fluid, as congested blood, by draining.

dē·pleth′ō·riç, *a.* lacking plethora.

dē·plē′tion, *n.* 1. the act of depleting or the state of being depleted.
2. in medicine, a state of exhaustion resulting from excessive loss of blood.

dē·plē′tive, *a.* capable of depleting; causing depletion.

dē·plē′tive, *n.* that which depletes; specifically, any medical agent of depletion.

dē·plē′tō·ry, *a.* depletive.

dē·ploi·tā′tion, *n.* same as *exploitation*.

dē·plōr·ȧ·bil′i·ty, *n.* deplorableness. [Rare.]

dē·plōr′ȧ·ble, *a.* [from L. *deplorare*, to deplore, to weep bitterly.] that may be deplored; lamentable; that demands or causes lamentation; hence, sad; calamitous; grievous; miserable; wretched; pitiable.
Syn.—lamentable, sad, dismal, wretched, pitiable, calamitous, grievous, miserable.

dē·plōr′ȧ·ble·ness, *n.* the state of being deplorable; misery; wretchedness.

dē·plōr′ȧ·bly, *adv.* 1. in a deplorable manner.
2. to a deplorable extent.

dē·plō′rāte, *a.* deplorable. [Obs.]

dēp·lō·rā′tion (*or* dē-plō-), *n.* the act of lamenting. [Obs.]

dē·plōre′, *v.t.*; deplored, *pt.*, *pp.*; deploring, *ppr.* [L. *deplorare*, to weep bitterly, lament; *de-*, intens., and *plorare*, to weep.]
1. to lament; to bewail; to mourn; to be regretful or sorry about.
Thou art gone to the grave! but we will not *deplore* thee. —Heber.
2. to despair of. [Obs.]
Syn.—mourn, lament, bewail, bemoan.

dē·plōre′, *v.i.* to lament; to moan. [Rare.]

dē·plōr′ed·ly, *adv.* lamentably. [Rare.]

dē·plōr′ed·ness, *n.* the state of being deplored. [Rare.]

dē·plōre′ment, *n.* the act of deploring. [Obs.]

dē·plōr′ẽr, *n.* one who deplores.

dē·plōr′ing·ly, *adv.* in a deploring manner.

dē·ploy′, *v.t.* and *v.i.*; deployed, *pt.*, *pp.*; deploying, *ppr.* [Fr. *deployer*, to unfold, to display; OFr. *desployer*, to unfold, unroll, from L. *dis-*, from, and *plicare*, to fold.] in military science, to spread out so as to form a wider front of narrow depth.

dē·ploy′, *n.* a deploying. [Rare.]

dē·ploy′ment, *n.* the act of deploying.

dē·plū′māte, *a.* denuded of feathers; deplumed.

dep·lū·mā′tion, *n.* 1. a depluming or being deplumed.
2. the falling off of feathers, as in molting.
3. in medicine, a disease of the eyelids in which the eyelashes fall off.

dē·plūme′, *v.t.*; deplumed, *pt.*, *pp.*; depluming, *ppr.* [ME. *deplumen*, from L. *de*, off, from, and *plumare*, to cover with feathers, from *pluma*, a feather.]
1. to strip or pluck feathers from; to deprive of plumage; to pluck.
2. to strip of honor, riches, possessions, etc.

dē·pō″lăr·i·zā′tion, *n.* a depolarizing or being depolarized.

dē·pō′lăr·īze, *v.t.*; depolarized, *pt.*, *pp.*; depolarizing, *ppr.* to destroy or counteract the polarity or polarization of.

dē·pō′lăr·ī·zẽr, *n.* one who or that which depolarizes.

dē·pol′ish, *v.t.* to destroy the polish or glaze of.

dē·pol′ish·ing, *n.* the act or process of removing polish or glaze; specifically, in ceramics, the process of removing the glaze from porcelain, which in its deglazed state is called *ivory porcelain*.

dē·pōne′, *v.t.*; deponed, *pt.*, *pp.*; deponing, *ppr.* [L. *deponere*, to lay aside, put down; *de*, from, and *ponere*, to put.]
1. to lay down; to deposit. [Obs.]
2. to wager. [Obs.]
3. in law, to depose; to testify.

dē·pōne′, *v.i.* to declare in writing under oath; to testify.

dē·pō′nent, *a.* [from L. *deponens*, ppr. of *deponere*, to lay aside; *de*, from, and *ponere*, to place, put.] in Latin and Greek grammar, denoting a verb with a passive or middle voice form and an active meaning: so called because thought of as laying aside the original passive quality.

dē·pō′nent, *n.* 1. in law, (a) one who deposes or makes a deposition under oath; one who gives written testimony under oath; (b) one who makes an affidavit.
2. in Latin and Greek grammar, a deponent verb.

dē·pop′ū·lȧ·cy, *n.* depopulation. [Obs.]

dē·pop′ū·lăr·īze, *v.t.* to make unpopular.

dē·pop′ū·lāte, *v.t.*; depopulated, *pt.*, *pp.*; depopulating, *ppr.* [L. *depopulatus*, pp. of *depopulari*, to lay waste, devastate; *de-*, from, and *populari*, to lay waste, ravage, ruin, from *populus*, people.] to deprive of inhabitants; to reduce the population of, especially by violence, pestilence, etc.

dē·pop′ū·lāte, *v.i.* to become depopulated. [Rare.]

dē·pop′ū·lāte, *a.* depopulated. [Archaic.]

dē·pop·ū·lā′tion, *n.* the act of depopulating or the state of being depopulated.

dē·pop′ū·lā·tŏr, *n.* one who depopulates; that which depopulates.

dē·pōrt′, *v.t.*; deported, *pt.*, *pp.*; deporting, *ppr.* [OFr. *deporter*, to bear, to suffer, to desist from; L. *deportare*, to carry or bring away; *de*, from, and *portare*, to bring.]
1. to behave or conduct (oneself) in a specified manner.
Let an ambassador *deport* himself in the most graceful manner before a prince. —Pope.
2. to banish or send out of the country, as an undesirable alien.
Syn.—carry, behave, conduct, demean.

dē·pōrt′, *n.* behavior; carriage; demeanor; deportment. [Obs.]

dē·pōr·tā′tion, *n.* [Fr. *déportation*; L. *deportatio*, a carrying away, a removal, from *deportare*, to carry or bring away.] a deporting or being deported; expulsion, as of an undesirable alien, from a country.

dē·pōr·tee′, *n.* 1. a deported person.
2. a person sentenced to deportation.

dē·pōrt′ment, *n.* [OFr. *deportement*, from L. *deportare*, to carry away, to deport; *de*, from, and *portare*, to bring.] the manner of conducting or bearing oneself; behavior; demeanor; conduct; management.
The utmost propriety and dignity of *deportment* prevailed. —Irving.

dē·pōș′ȧ·ble, *a.* capable of being deposed, or deprived of office.

dē·pōș′ăl, *n.* the act of deposing, or divesting of office.

dē·pōṣe′, *v.t.*; deposed, *pt., pp.*; deposing, *ppr.* [ME. *deposen*, to lay aside, deprive of office, degrade, from OFr. *deposer*, to lay down, deposit; *de-* (L. *de*), from, away, and *poser*, to cease, lie down; confused in sense and form with L. *deponere* (pp. *depositus*), to lay down, lay aside.]
1. to remove from a throne or other high office; to dethrone; to degrade; to divest of office.
2. in law, to state on oath; to bear witness to; to testify.
3. to lay down; to let fall; to deposit. [Obs.]
4. to put under oath; to examine on oath. [Rare.]

dē·pōṣe′, *v.i.* to bear witness.

dē·pōṣ′ẽr, *n.* 1. one who deposes, or removes from office.
2. a witness; a deponent.

dē·poṣ′it, *v.t.*; deposited, *pt., pp.*; depositing, *ppr.* [L. *depositus*, pp. of *deponere*, to lay aside; *de*, from, and *ponere*, to place.]
1. to lay down; to put; to place; as, a bird *deposits* her eggs in a nest.
2. to put or lay in a place for safekeeping or preservation; to store; as, to *deposit* goods in a warehouse.
3. to put (money) in the bank, as for safekeeping or to earn interest.
4. to put down as a pledge or partial payment; as, they *deposited* $500 on a new house.
5. to leave lying, as sediment.
6. to lay aside; to get rid of. [Obs.]

dē·poṣ′it, *v.i.* to be formed by deposition.

dē·poṣ′it, *n.* 1. anything entrusted to the care of another; a thing given as security or for preservation.
2. a place where things are deposited; a depository.
3. the state of being deposited for safekeeping or convenience, as in a bank; as, to place a hundred dollars on *deposit*.
4. money put in a bank.
5. a pledge or part payment.
6. a depositing.
7. something deposited or left lying.
8. in geology and mining, sand, clay, mineral masses, etc. deposited by the action of wind, water, volcanic eruption, or ice.

dē·poṣ′i·tā·ry, *n.*; *pl.* **dē·poṣ′i·tā·rieṣ**, [LL. *depositarius*, from L. *depositum*, a deposit.]
1. a person, firm, etc. entrusted with something for safekeeping; trustee.
2. a depository; storehouse.
3. in law, one to whom goods are bailed, to be kept for the bailor without a recompense.

dē·poṣ′i·tā·ry, *a.* receiving deposits: said of banks.

dē·poṣ·i·tā′tion, *n.* in Scottish law, a contract by which a subject belonging to one person is entrusted to the gratuitous custody of another (the depositary), to be redelivered on demand.

dep·ō·si′tion (*or* dē-pō-), *n.* [OFr. *deposition*; LL. *depositio*, a laying or putting down, from L. *depositus*, pp. of *deponere*, to lay or put down.]
1. a deposing or being deposed; removal from office or position of power.
2. a testifying.
3. testimony.
4. a depositing or being deposited.
5. something deposited; deposit.
6. in law, a written statement by a witness, made under oath, to be used as testimony in court.
7. burial; the disposal of a saint's body in a new resting place; also, a celebration of such an event.

dē·poṣ′i·tŏr, *n.* [LL. *depositor*, from L. *depositus*, pp. of *deponere*, to deposit.] one who deposits something, especially money in a bank.

dē·poṣ′i·tō·ry, *n.*; *pl.* **dē·poṣ′i·tō·rieṣ**, 1. a place where anything is lodged for safekeeping; as, a warehouse is a *depository* for goods.
2. a depositary; a trustee.

dē·poṣ′i·tum, *n.* [L.] in law, a deposit.

dē·poṣ′i·tūre, *n.* the act of depositing. [Rare.]

dē′pōt (dē′pō; *Brit. or military* dep′ō), *n.* [Fr. *dépôt*, a deposit, storehouse; OFr. *depost*, a deposit, pledge, from L. *depositum*, a deposit, from *depositus*, pp. of *deponere*, to lay aside.]
1. a place for storage; a warehouse; as, a flour *depot*.
2. a railroad station: used originally of a freight station.
3. in military usage, (a) a storage place for supplies; (b) a station for assembling either recruits for training or combat replacements for assignment to a unit.

dep·rȧ·vā′tion, *n.* [L. *depravatio*, a making crooked; a perverting, from *depravare*, to make crooked.]
1. censure; defamation. [Obs.]
2. the act of making bad or worse; the act of corrupting, impairing, or degenerating.
3. the state of being made bad or worse; degeneracy.
Syn.—deterioration, degeneracy, corruption, contamination, vitiation.

dē·prāve′, *v.t.*; depraved, *pt., pp.*; depraving, *ppr.* 1. to make morally bad; to lead into bad habits; to corrupt; to pervert.
2. to defame; to vilify. [Obs.]
Syn.—contaminate, corrupt, pollute, vitiate.

dē·prāved′, *a.* morally bad; corrupt; perverted.

dē·prāv′ed·ly, *adv.* in a depraved manner.

dē·prāv′ed·ness, *n.* depravity.

dē·prāve′ment, *n.* depravity. [Obs.]

dē·prāv′ẽr, *n.* one who depraves; a corrupter.

dē·prāv′ing·ly, *adv.* in a depraving manner.

dē·prav′i·ty, *n.* 1. corruption; a depraved condition.
2. in theology, wickedness; the innate corruption of unregenerate man.
3. *pl.* **dē·prav′i·tieṣ**, a depraved act or practice.
total depravity; in theology, the doctrine that man's nature is innately bad and perverse because of original sin.
Syn.—depravation, corruption.—*Depravity* is a disposition or settled tendency to evil; *depravation* is the act or process of making depraved; as, the *depravation* of morals. *Corruption* applies to anything which is greatly vitiated; as, a *corruption* of morals, taste, language, etc.

dep′rē·çȧ·ble, *a.* liable to or deserving deprecation.

dep′rē·çāte, *v.t.*; deprecated, *pt., pp.*; deprecating, *ppr.* [L. *deprecatus*, pp. of *deprecari*, to pray against, to avert by prayer, to pray for; *de-*, off, from, and *precari*, to pray.]
1. to pray against; to pray deliverance from; as, to *deprecate* the return of war. [Archaic.]
2. to plead or argue earnestly against; to urge reasons against; to feel and express strong disapproval of.
3. to implore mercy of. [Obs.]

dep·rē·çā′ting·ly, *adv.* in a deprecating manner.

dep·rē·çā′tion, *n.* 1. a praying against; a praying that an evil may be removed or prevented. [Archaic.]
2. disapproval or protest; disapprobation.
3. a malediction; a curse. [Obs.]

dep′rē·çȧ·tive, *a.* deprecatory.

dep′rē·çȧ·tive·ly, *adv.* in a deprecative manner.

dep′rē·çȧ·tŏr, *n.* one who deprecates.

dep′rē·çȧ·tō·ry, *a.* 1. deprecating.
2. apologetic.

dē·prē′ci·ȧ·ble (-shi-), *a.* that can be depreciated; that may be lessened in value.

dē·prē′ci·āte, *v.t.* and *v.i.*; depreciated, *pt., pp.*; depreciating, *ppr.* [LL. *depreciatus*, pp. of *depretiare*, to lower the price, to undervalue, from L. *de-*, from, and *pretiare*, to value, from *pretium*, price.]
1. to lessen in value or price.
2. to undervalue; to belittle; to disparage.
Syn.—disparage, traduce, decry, lower, detract, undervalue, underrate.

dē·prē·ci·ā′tion, *n.* 1. a decrease in value of property through wear, deterioration, or obsolescence.
2. the allowance made for this in bookkeeping, accounting, etc.
3. a decrease in the purchasing power of money.
4. a belittling; disparagement.

dē·prē′ci·ȧ·tive, *a.* depreciatory.

dē·prē′ci·ȧ·tive·ly, *adv.* in a depreciative manner.

dē·prē′ci·ā·tŏr, *n.* one who or that which depreciates.

dē·prē′ci·ȧ·tō·ry, *a.* 1. tending to depreciate; lessening in value.
2. disparaging.

dep′rē·dȧ·ble, *a.* liable to depredation. [Obs.]

dep′rē·dāte, *v.t.* and *v.i.*; depredated, *pt., pp.*; depredating, *ppr.* [LL. *depraedatus*, pp. of *depraedare*, to plunder, from L. *de-*, intens., and *praedari*, to rob, plunder, from *praeda*, booty, prey.] to plunder. [Archaic.]

dep·rē·dā′tion, *n.* 1. a plundering or laying waste; robbery.
2. in Scottish law, the offense of forcibly driving away numbers of cattle, etc.: also called *hership*.

dep′rē·dā·tŏr, *n.* one who or that which depredates.

dep′rē·dȧ·tō·ry, *a.* depredating.

dē·pred′i·çāte, *v.t.* to publish; to proclaim. [Rare.]

dep·rē·hend′, *v.t.*; deprehended, *pt., pp.*; deprehending, *ppr.* [L. *deprehendere* or *deprendere*, to lay hold of, seize; *de*, and *prehendere*, to seize, take.] to catch; to take unawares or by surprise; to seize; to discover. [Obs.]

dep·rē·hen′si·ble, *a.* that may be caught or discovered. [Obs.]

dep·rē·hen′si·ble·ness, *n.* capability of being caught or discovered. [Obs.]

dep·rē·hen′sion, *n.* a catching or seizing; a discovery. [Obs.]

dē·press′, *v.t.*; depressed, *pt., pp.*; depressing, *ppr.* [ME. *depressen*; L. *depressus*, pp. of *deprimere*, to press down.]
1. to press down; to push or pull down; to lower.
2. to render dull or languid; to decrease the force or activity of; to weaken; as, to *depress* commerce.
3. to deject; to make sad or gloomy; to discourage; as, to *depress* the spirits.
4. to humble; to abase; as, to *depress* pride. [Archaic.]
5. to lower in value, price, or amount.
6. in algebra, to reduce to a lower degree, as an equation.
7. in music, to lower the pitch of.
8. to suppress. [Obs.]
to depress the pole; in nautical usage, to cause the pole to appear lower or nearer the horizon, as by sailing toward the equator.
Syn.—sink, lower, abase, cast down, deject, humble, degrade, dispirit.

dē·press′ănt, *a.* lowering the rate of muscular or nervous activity.

dē·press′ănt, *n.* a depressant medicine, drug, etc.; a sedative.

dē·pressed′ (-prest′), *a.* 1. pressed down.
2. lowered in position, intensity, amount, or degree.
3. flattened or hollowed, as if pressed down.
4. gloomy; dejected; sad.
5. in botany, flattened vertically, as if from downward pressure.
6. in zoology, having the horizontal diameter longer than the vertical; broader than high.
7. in heraldry, same as *debruised*.

dē·pres′si·ble, *a.* that can be depressed.

dē·press′ing·ly, *adv.* in a depressing manner.

dē·pres′sion, *n.* [ME. *depressioun*; L. *depressio*, a pressing down.]
1. a depressing or being depressed.
2. a depressed part or place; a hollow or low place on a surface.
3. low spirits; gloominess; dejection; sadness.
4. a decrease in force, activity, amount, etc.
5. in astronomy, the angular distance of a heavenly body below the horizon.
6. in economics, a period marked by slackening of business activity, much unemployment, falling prices and wages, etc.
7. in medicine, a decrease in functional activity.
8. in meteorology, (a) a lowering of the atmospheric pressure; (b) the fall of mercury indicating this in a barometer.
9 in psychology, an emotional condition, either normal or pathological, characterized by discouragement, a feeling of inadequacy, etc.
10. the act of humbling; abasement; as, the *depression* of pride. [Rare.]
11. in music, the lowering of a tone by flatting.
depression of the dew point; the difference in degrees at a given time between atmospheric temperature and the dew point.
Syn.—abasement, reduction, sinking, fall, humiliation, dejection, melancholy.

dē·press′ive, *a.* able or tending to depress; characterized by depression.

dē·press′ive·ness, *n.* the quality of being depressive.

dē·pres′sō·mō·tŏr, *a.* slowing down or decreasing motor activity.

dē·pres·sō·mō′tŏr, *n.* any depressomotor drug or other agent.

dē·press′ŏr, *n.* 1. one who or that which depresses.
2. any of various muscles that draw down a part of the body.
3. a nerve the stimulation of which decreases the activity of a part of the body.
4. an instrument that presses a protruding

part out of the way during a medical examination or operation; as, a tongue *depressor*.

dep′ri·ment, *a.* [L. *deprimens*, ppr. of *deprimere*, to press down.] same as *depressive*.

dē·prī′ṣūre, *n.* disesteem. [Obs.]

dē·prīv′ȧ·ble, *a.* that can be deprived.

dē·prīv′ăl, *n.* same as *deprivation*.

dep·ri·vā′tion, *n.* 1. the act of depriving; a taking away.

2. a state of being deprived; loss; want; bereavement.

3. dismissal from office; specifically, in ecclesiastical law, the act of divesting a bishop or other clergyman of his spiritual promotion or dignity.

dē·prīve′, *v.t.*; deprived, *pt.*, *pp.*; depriving, *ppr.* [ME. *depriven*; OFr. *depriver*, to deprive, take away, depose; L. *de-*, intens., and *privare*, to deprive, separate.]

1. to take away from forcibly; dispossess; as, he was *deprived* of his property.

2. to keep from having, using, or enjoying; as, no citizen should be *deprived* of his rights.

3. to remove from office, especially ecclesiastical office.

4. to end; to remove. [Obs.]

dē·prīved′, *a.* that has undergone deprivation; specifically, of or from a poor or depressed area; underprivileged.

dē·prīve′ment, *n.* deprivation. [Obs.]

dē·prīv′ẽr, *n.* one who or that which deprives.

dē prō·fun′dis, [L., out of the depths.]

1. from the deepest distress.

2. [D– P–] Psalm 130: from the first words of the Latin version.

dep′sīde, dep′sid, *n.* [from Gr. *depsein*, to tan; and *-ide*.] any of a class of anhydrides of phenol carboxylic acids, similar to esters.

depth, *n.* [ME. *depthe*, depth, from *dep*; AS. *deop*, deep.]

1. the distance from the top straight downward, from the surface or edge inward, or from front to back.

2. the quality or condition of being deep; deepness.

3. intensity (of colors, silence, etc.).

4. deepness of thought; profundity.

5. strength (of emotion).

6. lowness (of tone).

7. the middle (of night or winter).

8. [*usually pl.*] the far inner or inmost part; as, the *depths* of a wood.

9. [*usually pl.*] the deep or deepest place or part (of the sea, earth, sky, etc.).

10. [*usually pl.*] emotional depression; as, in the *depths* of despair.

11. reserve strength, as of suitable substitute players for a team.

12. in nautical usage, the extent of the square sails from the headrope to the foot rope.

in depth; in a thorough, comprehensive way.

out of (or *beyond*) *one's depth*; (a) in water too deep for one; (b) past one's ability or understanding.

depth chärġe, a powerful explosive charge timed to explode at a certain depth, and used against submarines or other underwater targets: also called *depth bomb*.

depth′en, *v.t.* to make deep. [Rare.]

depth′less, *a.* having no depth.

depth pẽr·cep′tion, the ability to perceive objects in perspective.

depth psȳ·chol′ō·ġy, any system of psychology, as psychoanalysis, dealing with the processes of the unconscious.

dep′ū·rănt, *a.* and *n.* [from *de-*, intens., and L. *purus*, pure.] depurative; purgative.

dep′ū·rāte, *v.t.*; depurated, *pt.*, *pp.*; depurating, *ppr.* [ML. *depuratus*, pp. of *depurare*, to purify, from L. *de-*, intens., and *purare*, to purify, from *purus*, pure.] to purify; to free from impurities; to cleanse.

dep′ū·rate, *v.i.* to become purified.

dep′ū·rāte, *a.* cleansed; pure. [Obs.]

dep·ū·rā′tion, *n.* the act of purifying.

dep′ū·rā·tive, *a.* purifying; tending to cleanse; depurating.

dep′ū·rā·tive, *n.* a purifying substance.

dep′ū·rā·tŏr, *n.* one who or that which cleanses.

dep′ū·rā·tō·ry, *a.* and *n.* depurative. [Obs.]

dep′ū·tȧ·ble, *a.* capable of being deputed; fit to be deputed.

dep·ū·tā′tion, *n.* [ME. *deputation*, from L. *deputatus*, pp. of *deputare*, to cut off, prune down, select; *de-*, off, from, and *putare*, to prune, cleanse, think, estimate.]

1. the act of deputing; the state of being deputed; the act of appointing a representative or representatives to act for another or others.

2. the person or persons appointed to represent another or others; delegation; as, the general sent a *deputation* to the enemy to offer terms of peace.

3. in English forestry law, a license giving to a gamekeeper certain privileges and rights.

dep′ū·tā·tŏr, *n.* a deputy. [Rare.]

dē·pūte′, *v.t.*; deputed, *pt.*, *pp.*; deputing, *ppr.* [L. *deputare*, to cut off, prune down, select, depute.]

1. to give (authority, functions, etc.) to someone else as deputy.

2. to appoint as a substitute or agent to act for another; to appoint and send with a special commission or authority to transact business in another's name; to delegate; as, the sheriff *deputes* a man to serve a writ.

3. to set aside or apart; to assign. [Obs.]

dē·pūte′, *n.* a deputy; as, a sheriff *depute*. [Scot.]

dep′ū·tīze, *v.t.*; deputized, *pt.*, *pp.*; deputizing, *ppr.* to appoint as a deputy; to empower to act for another; to depute.

dep′ū·tīze, *v.i.* to act as deputy.

dep′ū·ty, *n.*; *pl.* **dep′ū·tieṣ,** [Fr. *député*, pp. of *députer*, to depute.]

1. a person appointed to act for, or in the place of, another or others; one who exercises an office in another's right; a delegate; a representative; an agent.

2. a member of a legislature such as the Chamber of Deputies of the Third French Republic.

dep′ū·ty, *a.* acting as deputy.

dē·rac′i·nāte, *v.t.*; deracinated, *pt.*, *pp.*; deracinating, *ppr.* [Fr. *déraciner*; OFr. *desraciner*, to root out, uproot; *des-* priv., and *racine*, a root; L. *de-* priv., and *radix* (*-icis*), a root.]

1. to pluck up by the roots; to uproot.

2. to extirpate.

dē·rac·i·nā′tion, *n.* the act of pulling up by the roots. [Rare.]

dē·rāign′ (-rān′), *v.t.* [ME. *dereinen*; OFr. *derainier*, *deraisnier*, to plead, vindicate; *de-* (L. *de*), from, and *raisnier*, from L. *ratio*, reason.] formerly, in law, to determine (an issue), especially by personal combat between the litigants. [Rare.]

dē·rāign′ment, *n.* 1. the act of deraigning; proof; justification. [Obs.]

2. a renunciation, as of religious or monastic vows. [Obs.]

dē·rāil′, *v.t.*; derailed, *pt.*, *pp.*; derailing, *ppr.* to cause (a train, etc.) to run off the rails.

dē·rāil′, *v.i.* to run off the rails or track.

de·rai′lleur (di-rā′lẽr), *n.* [Fr.] a mechanism on a bicycle for controlling its speed by shifting the sprocket chain from one to another of a set of different-sized sprocket wheels.

dē·rāil′ment, *n.* the act of derailing or the condition of being derailed.

dē·rānġe′, *v.t.*; deranged, *pt.*, *pp.*; deranging, *ppr.* [Fr. *déranger*; OFr. *desrengier*, to put out of order; *des-*, apart, and *rengier*, to put in order, to arrange.]

1. to put out of order; to disturb the arrangement or order of; to throw into confusion; to disarrange; to disorder.

2. to disturb the normal condition or working of; to unsettle; as, to *derange* a machine.

3. to make insane; to unsettle the reason of; as, he is *deranged* by anxiety.

Syn.—disarrange, confuse, disturb, unbalance, disconcert, disorder, displace.

dē·rānġe′ȧ·ble, *a.* that can be deranged; liable to derangement.

dē·rānġed′, *a.* 1. disordered.

2. disordered in mind; insane.

dē·rānġe′ment, *n.* 1. an upsetting of order or arrangement; disorder.

2. disorder of the mind or reason; insanity.

de·ray′, *n.* [ME. *dereie*, *deraie*; OFr. *desrei*.] tumult; disorder; merriment. [Obs.]

dē·rāy′, *v.t.* and *v.i.* to derange; to rage. [Obs.]

Dẽr′by (*Brit.* där′bi), *n.*; *pl.* **Dẽr′bieṣ,** 1. a race for three-year-old horses, founded in 1780 by the twelfth Earl of Derby, and run annually at Epsom Downs, in Surrey, England.

2. any similar horse race, especially the Kentucky Derby.

3. [d–] a stiff felt hat having a rounded crown and a curved brim: also called *bowler*.

dēre, *v.t.* to hurt. [Obs.]

dēre, *n.* harm. [Obs.]

dēre, *a.* dear. [Obs.]

dē·rē″ăl·i·zā′tion, *n.* a loss or lessening of one's sense of the reality of things, as in the reaction to certain drugs.

dḙ·rḙ′chō, *n.* [Sp.] in Mexican and Spanish law, (a) right; just claim; (b) [*pl.*] imposts; taxes.

de rè′gle (re′gl), [Fr.] according to the rule or correct form.

dē·reg′ū·lāte, *v.t.*; deregulated, *pt.*, *pp.*; deregulating, *ppr.* to remove regulations governing; as, to *deregulate* the price of natural gas.

dē·reg″ū·lā′tion, *n.* 1. the act of deregulating.

2. the state of being deregulated.

dē·rē′iṣm, *n.* [L. *de re* unreal, literally, away from fact, and *-ism*.] a mental condition in which there is a loss of interest in external reality and deviation from normal logic.

der′e·liçt, *a.* [L. *derelictus*, pp. of *derelinquere*, to forsake utterly, to abandon; *de-*, intens., and *relinquere*, to leave, forsake.]

1. left; forsaken; abandoned by the guardian or owner; as, *derelict* property, *derelict* children.

2. remiss; negligent; neglectful of duty.

der′e·liçt, *n.* 1. a property thrown away, relinquished, or abandoned by the owner; especially, a ship abandoned at sea.

2. a person or thing abandoned as worthless; as, the streets were full of shabby *derelicts*.

3. a person neglectful of duty or trust.

4. a tract of land exposed by the receding of the sea.

der·e·liç′tion, *n.* 1. the act of leaving with an intention not to reclaim or resume; an utter forsaking; abandonment.

2. the state of being left or abandoned.

3. a neglect of, or failure in, duty.

4. in law, the gaining of land from the water by the gradual retreat of the sea below the usual watermark; also, this land.

dẽrf, *a.* brave; bold; powerful. [Obs.]

der′iç, *a.* [from Gr. *deros*, skin.] of or pertaining to the skin.

dē·rīde′, *v.t.*; derided, *pt.*, *pp.*; deriding, *ppr.* [L. *deridere*, to mock, laugh at, deride; *de-*, intens., and *ridere*, to laugh.] to laugh at in contempt; to ridicule or make fun of; to mock.

Syn.—ridicule, mock, taunt.—A person may *ridicule* without unkindness of feeling; his object may be to correct. He who *derides* is motivated by scorn or malicious contempt. To *mock* is stronger, denoting open and scoffing derision; to *taunt* is to reproach with bitter insult.

dē·rīd′ing·ly, *adv.* by means of derision or mockery.

de ri·gueur′ (-gẽr′), [Fr.] required by etiquette; according to good form.

dē·ris′i·ble, *a.* deserving to be derided.

dē·ri′sion, *n.* [LL. *derisio*, derision, from L. *derisus*, pp. of *deridere*, to deride.]

1. the act of deriding or the state of being derided; contempt manifested by laughter; scorn; ridicule.

2. an object of derision or contempt; a laughingstock; a person or thing derided. [Rare.]

Syn.—contempt, scorn, disregard, ridicule, mockery, insult, disdain.

dē·rī′sive, *a.* characterized by or expressing derision; as, *derisive* taunts.

dē·rī′sive·ly, *adv.* with mockery or contempt.

dē·rī′sive·ness, *n.* the state of being derisive.

dē·rī′sō·ry, *a.* derisive.

dē·rīv·ȧ·bil′i·ty, *n.* the quality of being derivable.

dē·rīv′ȧ·ble, *a.* that can be derived; as, income *derivable* from land.

dē·rīv′ȧ·bly, *adv.* by derivation.

der′i·vāte, *a.* derived. [Rare.]

der′i·vāte, *n.* a thing derived from another; a derivative. [Rare.]

der·i·vā′tion, *n.* [L. *derivatio*, a turning aside into another channel, a derivation, from *derivare*, to divert, derive; *de-*, from, and *rivus*, a stream.]

1. a deriving or being derived.

2. descent.

3. something derived; a derivative.

4. the source or origin of something.

5. the origin and development of a word; etymology.

6. the process of tracing this.

7. the process of forming words from bases by the addition of affixes, by internal phonetic change, etc. (e.g., *warmth*, from *warm*, *deem*, from *doom*).

8. in mathematics, the deriving of a solution expressed in terms of an equation; deducing of one function from another according to some definite principle.

9. a drawing from or turning aside from a natural course or channel; as, the *derivation*

of water from its channel by lateral drains. [Obs.]

10. in medicine, a drawing of fluids from one part of the body to another, to diminish or remedy inflammation or congestion.

11. in biology, descent of organisms from former organisms, the process being accompanied by certain structural changes; the theory of evolution.

der·i·vā'tion·ăl, *a.* relating to derivation.

der·i·vā'tion·ist, dē·riv'ȧ·tist, *n.* and *a.* evolutionist. [Archaic.]

dē·riv'ȧ·tive, *a.* [LL. *derivativus*, derivative, from L. *derivatus*, pp. of *derivare*, to derive, to turn aside.]

1. derived; taken or having proceeded from another or something preceding; hence, not original; secondary.

2. of or relating to derivation.

3. in medicine, producing derivation.

derivative circulation; a circulation existing in certain parts of the body, in which the veins receive the blood directly from the arteries.

derivative conveyance; in law, a secondary deed, as a release, confirmation, surrender, consignment, and defeasance.

dē·riv'ȧ·tive, *n.* 1. something derived.

2. in chemistry, a substance derived from, or of such composition and properties that it may be considered as derived from, another substance by chemical change, especially by the substitution of one or more elements or radicals for one or more constituents of the original substance.

3. in linguistics, a word derived from another or others.

4. in mathematics, a differential coefficient.

5. in music, a chord not fundamental, but derived from another by inversion.

6. in medicine, an agent or method for producing derivation.

dē·riv'ȧ·tive·ly, *adv.* in a derivative manner; by derivation.

dē·riv'ȧ·tive·ness, *n.* the state of being derivative.

dē·rīve', *v.t.*; derived, *pt.*, *pp.*; deriving, *ppr.* [ME. *deriven*; L. *derivare*, to turn a stream from its channel, to derive.]

1. to draw from, as in a regular course or channel; to receive or get (*from* a source); as, the heir *derives* an estate from his ancestors; we *derive* instruction from books.

2. to turn from its natural course; to divert; as, to *derive* water from the main channel or current into smaller ones. [Obs.]

3. to trace to or from a source; to show the derivation of, as a word.

4. to deduce or infer; to get by reasoning.

5. to originate (used reflexively).

6. in chemistry, to obtain or produce (a compound) from another compound by replacing one element with another.

Syn.—deduce, trace.

dē·rīve', *v.i.* to proceed (*from* a source); to be derived; to originate.

dē·rīve'ment, *n.* that which is derived. [Obs.]

dē·rīv'ēr, *n.* one who derives.

dẽrk, *a.* dark. [Obs.]

dẽrm, *n.* same as *dermis*.

dẽrm-, same as *dermo-*.

-dẽrm, [from Greek *derma*, skin.] a suffix used in forming biological terms, and meaning *skin* or *covering*, as in blasto*derm*, endo*derm*.

dẽr'mȧ, *n.* [Mod.L., from Gr. *derma*, skin.] same as *dermis*.

dẽr'mȧ, *n.* [Yid. *derme*, pl. of *darm*, gut.] beef casing stuffed with a filling of bread crumbs, seasoning, etc. and roasted.

dẽr·mȧ·brā'ṣion, *n.* [*derma* (dermis), and *abrasion*.] the surgical procedure of scraping off upper layers of the epidermis with an abrasive device, as in repairing acne scars, blemishes, etc.

dẽrm'ad, *adv.* toward the skin.

dẽrm'ăl, *a.* of the skin or the dermis.

Dẽr·map'te·rȧ, *n.pl.* [L., from Gr. *derma*, skin, and *pteron*, wing.] an order of insects including the earwigs: also called *Dermatoptera*.

dẽr·map'tẽr·ăn, *a.* pertaining to the *Dermaptera*.

dẽr·map'tẽr·ăn, *n.* an insect of the *Dermaptera*.

dẽr·map'tẽr·ous, *a.* pertaining to the *Dermaptera*.

dẽr'mat-, same as *dermato-*.

dẽr·mȧ·tal'ġi·ȧ, *n.* neuralgia of the skin.

dẽr·mat'iç, *a.* same as *dermal*.

dẽr'mȧ·tine, *a.* same as *dermal*.

dẽr·mȧ·tī'tis, *n.* [L., from Gr. *derma*, skin.] inflammation of the skin.

dẽr·mȧ·tō-, dẽr·mat-, dẽr·mō-, dẽrm-, [from Gr. *derma*, skin.] combining forms meaning *skin* or *hide* or *covering*.

Dẽr''mȧ·tō·brañ'ḉhi·ȧ, Dẽr''mȧ·tō·brañ·ḉhi·ā'tȧ, *n.pl.* same as *Dermobranchia*.

dẽr·mat'ō·ġen, *n.* [*dermato-*, and Gr. *-genēs*, producing.] in botany, a layer of dividing cells which develops into the epidermis.

dẽr·mȧ·tog'rȧ·phy, *n.* [*dermato-*, and Gr. *graphein*, to write.] the anatomical description of the skin.

dẽr'mȧ·toid, *a.* [Gr. *derma* (*-matos*), skin, and *eidos*, form.] resembling skin; skinlike.

dẽr''mȧ·tō·loġ'iç·ăl, *a.* relating to dermatology.

dẽr·mȧ·tol'ō·ġist, *n.* a skin specialist; an expert in dermatology.

dẽr·mȧ·tol'ō·ġy, *n.* [*dermato-*, and Gr. *logos*, discourse.] the branch of medicine dealing with the skin and its diseases.

dẽr·mȧ·tol'y·sis, *n.* [*dermato-*, skin, and Gr. *lysis*, a loosing, from *lyein*, to loose.] in medicine, an abnormal condition of the skin in which it becomes relaxed and pendulous.

dẽr'mȧ·tōme, *n.* [*derma*, skin, and *-tome*, division.] any of the segmentally arranged mesodermal masses in a vertebrate embryo, destined to form dermis.

dẽr''mȧ·tō·mȳ·cō'sis, *n.* [*dermato-*, and Gr. *mykēs*, fungus.] in medicine, any skin disease caused by a vegetable parasite.

dẽr''mȧ·tō·nō'sis (*or* -ton'ō-sis), *n.* [*dermato-*, and Gr. *nosos*, disease.] any skin disease.

dẽr''mȧ·tō·path'iç, *a.* [*dermato-*, and Gr. *pathos*, suffering.] pertaining to skin diseases or the methods of curing them.

dẽr·mȧ·top'ȧ·thy, dẽr''mȧ·tō·path'i·ȧ, *n.* any disease of the skin.

dẽr'mȧ·tō·phȳte'', *n.* [*dermato-*, and Gr. *phyton*, a growth, plant.] any plant parasitic on the skin, as the fungus that causes ringworm.

dẽr''mȧ·tō·phyt'iç, *a.* pertaining to or produced by dermatophytes; as, *dermatophytic* diseases.

dẽr'mȧ·tō·plas''ty, *n.* [*dermato-*, and Gr. *plassein*, to mold, form.] plastic surgery of the skin, as by skin grafts.

Dẽr·mȧ·top'te·rȧ, *n.pl.* [L., from Gr. *derma*, skin, and *pteron*, a wing.]

1. in entomology, same as *Dermaptera*.

2. in mammalogy, same as *Dermoptera*.

dẽr''mȧ·tō·sçlē·rō'sis, *n.* [*dermato-*, and Gr. *sklērōsis*, a hardening.] same as *scleroderma*.

dẽr·mȧ·tō'sis, *n.* [L., from Gr. *derma*, skin.] in pathology, any skin disease.

Dẽr·mes'tēṣ, *n.* [L., from Gr. *derma*, skin, and *esthiein*, to eat.] a genus of coleopterous insects, the type of the family *Dermestidæ*. The larvae of this genus devour dead bodies, skins, leather, and other animal substances. One species, *Dermestes lardarius*, is known by the name of bacon beetle.

dẽr·mes'tid, *n.* one of the *Dermestidæ*.

dẽr·mes'tid, *a.* relating to the *Dermestidæ*.

Dẽr·mes'ti·dae, *n.pl.* [L., from Gr. *derma*, skin, and *esthiein*, to eat.] a family of coleopterous insects, the species of which are for the most part of small size. Their larvae feed upon animal substances.

dẽr·mes'toid, *a.* characteristic of the genus *Dermestes*; relating to the *Dermestidæ*.

dẽr'miç, *a.* [Gr. *derma*, the skin.] of the skin; dermal.

dẽr'mis, *n.* [Mod. L., from Gr. *epidermis*, epidermis.]

1. the layer of skin just below the epidermis; the derma.

2. the skin in general.

dẽr·mō-, [from Gr. *derma*, skin.] same as *dermato-*.

Dẽr·mō·brañ'ḉhi·ȧ, *n.pl.* [*dermo-*, and Gr. *branchia*, gills.] a group of mollusks with external branchiae, or gills, occurring in the form of thin membranous plates, tufts, or filaments. They are more commonly called *Nudibranchiata*. Called also *Dermobranchiata*, *Dermatobranchia*, *Dermatobranchiata*.

Dẽr''mō·brañ·ḉhi·ā'tȧ, *n.pl.* same as *Dermobranchia*.

dẽr·mō·brañ'ḉhi·āte, *a.* relating to the *Dermobranchia*.

dẽr·mō·gas'triç, *a.* [*dermo-*, and Gr. *gastēr*, stomach.] relating to the skin and the alimentary canal; connecting the alimentary canal and the skin; as, a *dermogastric* pore.

dẽr·mog'rȧ·phy, *n.* same as *dermatography*.

dẽr·mō·hē'măl, dẽr·mȧ·hē'măl, *a.* [*dermo-*, and Gr. *haima*, blood.] pertaining to the skin on the ventral side of the body: written also *dermohaemal*, *dermahaemal*.

dẽr·mō·hē'mi·ȧ, dẽr·mō·hae'mi·ȧ, *n.* [L., from Gr. *derma*, skin, and *haima*, blood.] in pathology, hyperemia, or congestion, of the skin.

dẽr·mō·hū'mẽr·ăl, *a.* [*dermo-*, and L. *humerus*, the upper bone of the arm, the humerus.] relating to or connecting the humerus and skin; specifically, relating to a muscle in certain animals.

dẽr'moid, *a.* same as *dermatoid*.

dẽr·mol'ō·ġy, *n.* same as *dermatology*.

dẽr·mō·mus'çū·lăr, *a.* relating to the skin and muscles.

dẽr·mō·neū'răl, *a.* [*dermo-*, and Gr. *neuron*, nerve.] in zoology, designating or of the upper row of spines in the back of a fish, from their connection with the skin and their relation to that surface of the body on which the nervous system is placed.

dẽr·mō·path'iç, *a.* same as *dermatopathic*.

dẽr·mop'ȧ·thy, *n.* same as *dermatopathy*.

dẽr'mō·phȳte, *n.* same as *dermatophyte*.

Dẽr·mop'te·rȧ, *n.pl.* [L., from Gr. *dermopteros*, having membranous wings like a bat; *derma*, skin, and *pteron*, wing.] an order of *Mammalia*, with a membrane connecting the fore and hind limbs: it is typified by the colugo, *Galeopithecus volans*, or flying lemur.

dẽr·mop'tẽr·ous, *a.* having membranous wings (or fins).

dẽr·mō·sclē'rīte, *n.* [*dermo-*, and Gr. *sklēros*, hard.] a mass of spicules which occurs in the tissues of some of the *Actinozoa*.

dẽr·mō·skel'e·tăl, *a.* pertaining to the dermoskeleton.

dẽr·mō·skel'e·tŏn, *n.* [L., from Gr. *derma*, skin, and *skeleton*.] the coriaceous, crustaceous, testaceous, or osseous integument, such as covers many invertebrate and some vertebrate animals; exoskeleton.

dẽr·mos·tō'sis, *n.* [L., from Gr. *derma*, skin, and *osteon*, a bone.] in physiology, formation of bone in the skin.

dẽr·mot'ō·my, *n.* [*dermo-*, and Gr. *tomē*, a cutting, from *temnein*, to cut.] the anatomy or dissection of the skin.

dẽrn, *a.* hidden; secret; private. [Obs.]

dẽrn, *n.* in architecture, same as *durn*.

dẽrn, *v.t.* and *v.i.* to hide; to conceal; to skulk. [Obs.]

dẽrn, *v.t.*, *n.*, *adj.*, *adv.*, *interj.* darn (damn). [Dial.]

dẽrn'ful, *a.* solitary; hence, sad; mournful. [Obs.]

dẽr'ni·ẽr (*or Fr.* där-nyā'), *a.* [Fr.] last; final; ultimate; as, in the French phrases, *dernier cri*, the latest fashion, *dernier ressort*, last resort.

dẽrn'ly, *adv.* secretly; hence, sadly. [Obs.]

der'ō·gāte, *v.t.*; derogated, *pt. pp.*; derogating, *ppr.* [L. *derogatus*, pp. of *derogare*, to repeal part of a law, to take away, detract from; *de-*, from, and *rogare*, to ask.]

1. to invalidate some part of, as a law or established rule; to annul in part. [Obs.]

2. to lessen the worth of; to disparage. [Obs.]

3. to take away (*from*) so as to lessen or impair; detract. [Archaic.]

der'ō·gāte, *v.i.* 1. to detract; to lessen by taking away a part: with *from*; as, to *derogate from* reputation.

2. to do something derogatory to oneself or one's position; degenerate.

der'ō·gāte, *a.* diminished in force; degraded. [Rare.]

der'ō·gāte·ly, *adv.* derogatorily. [Rare.]

der·ō·gā'tion, *n.* 1. a lessening or weakening (*of* power, authority, position, etc.).

2. disparagement; detraction.

3. a decline; deterioration.

dē·rog'ȧ·tive, *a.* derogatory.

dē·rog'ȧ·tive·ly, *adv.* in a derogative manner.

der'ō·gā·tŏr, *n.* one who derogates; a detractor.

dē·rog'ȧ·tō·ri·ly, *adv.* in a derogatory manner.

dē·rog'ȧ·tō·ri·ness, *n.* the quality of being derogatory.

dē·rog'ȧ·tō·ry, *a.* [LL. *derogatorius*, derogatory, from L. *derogare*, to detract from.]

1. detracting or tending to lessen or impair.

2. disparaging; belittling.

derogatory clause; in law, a clause inserted by the testator, of which he reserves the knowledge to himself, with a condition that no will he may make hereafter shall be valid, unless this clause is inserted word for word: a precaution to guard against later wills extorted by violence, or obtained by suggestion.

der'rick, *n.* originally applied to a gallows; named after *Derrick*, a London hangman, who lived in the 17th century.]

1. an apparatus for hoisting and moving heavy weights, variously constructed, but

usually consisting of a long, moving beam pivoted at the base of a vertical, stationary beam and guided by ropes running on pulleys: this type is also called a *derrick crane*.

2. a tall, tapering framework, as over an oil well, to support drilling machinery, etc.

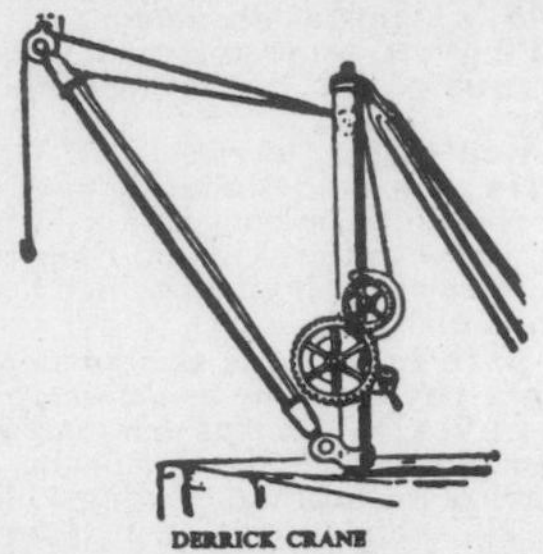
DERRICK CRANE

der·ri·ère′ (-i-er′ *or Fr.* -ryâr′), *n.* [Fr.] back part; rear; hence, the buttocks.

der′ring·do, *n.* [ME. *derryinge do, durring don,* lit., daring to do; misunderstood as abstract n. by Spenser and thence popularized as n. by Scott (*Ivanhoe*).] daring action; reckless courage.

der′rin·ġẽr, *n.* [from *Derringer,* Am. gunsmith who invented it.] a short-barreled pistol having a large caliber.

der′ris, *n.* [from Gr. *derris,* a covering.] any of a group of woody, leguminous plants of the East Indies, from whose roots is extracted rotenone, used as an insecticide.

der′ry, *n.*; *pl.* **der′ries,** a meaningless word in the refrains of old ballads; hence, a ballad.

der′ry-down, *n.* a derry.

dẽrth, *n.* dearth. [Obs.]

dẽr·trō·thē′çȧ, *n.* [Gr. *dertron,* a vulture's beak, and *thēkē,* a case, sheath.] the outer covering of the dertrum of a bird.

dẽr′trum, *n.*; *pl.* **dẽr′trȧ,** [Gr. *dertron,* the caul, a vulture's beak, from *derein,* to skin, flay.] the point of the upper mandible of a bird, when characterized by some difference from the remainder of the bill.

dẽr′vish, *n.* [Turk. *dervish*; Ar. *darwish*; Per. *derwesch,* a dervish, from Old Per. *derew,* to beg.]

1. a member of any of various Moslem orders, dedicated to a life of poverty and chastity: some dervishes practice whirling, howling, etc. as religious acts.

2. a Sudanese follower of the Mahdi.

dē·sal·i·nā′tion, *n.* [*de-,* and *salination.*] the removal of salt, especially from sea water to make it drinkable: also **dē·sal·i·ni·zā′tion.**

dē·sạlt′, *v.t.* to remove salt from (especially sea water).

deş′ărt, *a.* and *n.* desert. [Obs.]

des′çant, *n.* [OFr. *descanter,* to descant, from L. *dis-,* apart, and *cantare,* to sing.]

1. in medieval music, (a) a counterpoint or melody sung above the main melody; (b) the art of composing part music; (c) a piece of part music; (d) the highest voice in part singing; (e) a variation on the chief melody.

2. a song or tune with various modulations.

3. a discourse; criticism; comment.

des·çant′, *v.i.*; descanted, *pt., pp.*; descanting, *ppr.* 1. to comment (*on* or *upon*).

2. to talk at length; discourse.

3. to sing or play a counterpoint to the main melody.

4. to sing.

des·çant′ẽr, *n.* one who descants.

dē·scend′, *v.i.*; descended, *pt., pp.*; descending, *ppr.* [ME. *descenden*; OFr. *descendre*; L. *descendere,* to climb down, to fall, descend.]

1. to move or pass from a higher to a lower place; to move, come or go downward.

The rain *descended,* and the floods came.
—Matt. vii. 25.

2. to pass from an earlier to a later time, from greater to less, from general to particular, etc.

3. to slope or extend downward.

4. to come down (*from* a source): of ancestry, usually with auxiliary *be*; as, he *is descended from* pioneers.

5. to pass by inheritance or heredity; as, the estate *descended* to the nephew.

6. to lower oneself or stoop (*to* some act).

7. to make a sudden attack, raid, or visit (with *on* or *upon*).

8. in music, to move down the scale.

9. in astronomy, to move southward or toward the horizon.

dē·scend′, *v.t.* to come from a higher part of to a lower; to move down, along, or through.

dē·scend′ȧ·ble, *a.* same as *descendible.*

dē·scend′ănt, *a.* [OFr. *descendant,* from L. *descendens,* ppr. of *descendere,* to descend; *de,* down, and *scandere,* to climb.] descending; descendent. [Rare.]

dē·scend′ănt, *n.* an individual proceeding from an ancestor in any degree; offspring of a certain ancestor, family, group, etc.; as, the *descendants* of Adam and Eve.

dē·scend′ent, *a.* 1. descending.

2. proceeding from an original or ancestor.

dē·scend′ẽr, *n.* 1. one who or that which descends.

2. in typography, (a) a letter, such as *g* or *y,* that extends below the line; (b) the part below the line.

dē·scend·i·bil′i·ty, *n.* the quality of being descendible, or capable of being transmitted from ancestors; as, the *descendibility* of an estate or of a crown.

dē·scend′i·ble, *a.* 1. that can be descended; as, the hill is *descendible.* [Rare.]

2. that may or does descend from an ancestor to an heir; as, a *descendible* estate.

dē·scend′ing, *a.* 1. moving downward; pertaining to descent; marked by downward motion.

2. in heraldry, a term used for a bird, lion, etc., the head of which is turned toward the base of the shield.

descending constellations or signs; constellations or signs through which the planets pass in moving southward.

descending series; in mathematics, a series in which each term is numerically less than that preceding it.

dē·scend′ing·ly, *adv.* in a descending manner.

dē·scen′sion, *n.* [L. *descensio,* a going downward, descent, from *descendere,* to go down, descend.] the act of going downward; descent. [Rare.]

oblique descension; the arc of the equator which descends, with the sign or star, below the horizon in an oblique sphere. [Obs.]

right descension; the arc of the equator which descends, with the sign or star, below the horizon in a right sphere. [Obs.]

dē·scen′sion·ăl, *a.* pertaining to descension.

dē·scen′sive, *a.* descending; tending downward; having power to descend.

dē·scen′sō·ry, *n.* [from L. *descendere,* to descend.] a distillation vessel used in alchemy. [Obs.]

dē·scent′, *n.* [ME. *descent*; L. *descendere,* to descend.]

1. the act of descending; the act of passing from a higher to a lower place; a coming or going down; downward motion.

2. inclination downward; a downward slope.

3. a sinking or decline, as in station, virtue, quality, or the like; fall from a higher to a lower state or station.

O foul *descent* . . . into a beast. —Milton.

4. a way down or downward.

5. a stooping (*to* an act).

6. an invasion, sudden attack, or raid (with *on* or *upon*).

A *descent upon* their coasts. —Jortin.

7. in law, a passing from an ancestor to an heir; transmission (of property) by succession or inheritance.

8. a proceeding from an original or progenitor; hence, lineage; ancestry.

Smile at the claims of long *descent.*
—Tennyson.

9. a generation (of a specified lineage).

10. offspring; descendants. [Obs.]

11. a step or degree downward. [Obs.]

12. lowest place. [Obs.]

Syn.—declivity, slope, gradient, fall, degradation, debasement, extraction, pedigree, generation, lineage, assault, invasion, incursion, attack.

dē·sçrīb′ȧ·ble, *a.* that can be described; capable of description.

dē·sçrībe′, *v.t.*; described, *pt., pp.*; describing, *ppr.* [ME. *descriven*; L. *describere,* to write down or from, to copy, to transcribe, to describe; *de,* from, and *scribere,* to write.]

1. to delineate; to portray in art. [Archaic.]

2. to trace the form or outline of; as, to *describe* a circle with the compasses.

3. to tell or write about; to give a detailed account of; as, to *describe* the working of a mechanism.

4. to picture in words; as, she *described* the garden.

5. to descry: so used through confusion.

6. to distribute into classes or divisions. [Obs.]

Syn.—represent, delineate, relate, recount, narrate, express, explain, depict, portray.

dē·sçrībe′, *v.i.* to give a description; as, Milton *describes* with uncommon force and beauty.

dē·sçrīb′ẽr, *n.* one who describes.

dē·sçrī′ẽr, *n.* one who descries.

dē·sçrip′tion, *n.* [L. *descriptio,* a marking out, delineation.]

1. the act of delineating or outlining.

2. the act, process, art, or technique of describing; a picturing verbally; a giving an account of in words.

3. a statement or passage that describes.

4. sort, kind, or variety; as, books of every *description.*

Syn.—account, statement, delineation, representation, sketch.

dē·sçrip′tive, *a.* containing description; tending to describe; of or characterized by description; as, a *descriptive* figure, a *descriptive* narration.

descriptive anatomy; the study of the separate parts of the body aside from their relation to other parts.

descriptive geometry; geometry in which the situation of points in space is represented by their orthographical projections, on two planes at right angles to each other.

descriptive linguistics; the branch of linguistics which describes the structures of languages as they exist, without reference to their histories or to comparison with other languages.

dē·sçrip′tive·ly, *adv.* by description.

dē·sçrip′tive·ness, *n.* the state or quality of being descriptive.

dē·sçrīve′, *v.t.* to describe. [Obs.]

dē·sçrȳ′, *v.t.*; descried, *pt., pp.*; descrying, *ppr.* [ME. *descryen, descrien*; OFr. *descrier,* to proclaim; L. *de,* from, down, and *quiritare,* to cry, freq. of *queri,* to complain.]

1. to explore; to examine by observation. [Obs.]

The house of Joseph sent to *descry* Bethel.
—Jud. i. 23.

2. to detect; to look for and discover; as, to *descry* a distant foe.

3. to discern (distant or obscure objects); to have a sight of from a distance; as, the seamen *descried* land.

dē·sçrȳ′, *n.* perception from a distance. [Obs.]

Deş·de·mō′nȧ, *n.* in Shakespeare's *Othello,* the innocent wife of Othello, whom he smothers to death as a result of jealousy incited by Iago.

des′ē·çāte, *v.t.* to cut off; to mow. [Obs.]

des′ē·çrāte, *v.t.*; desecrated, *pt., pp.*; desecrating, *ppr.* [from L. *de-* priv., and *sacrare,* to make sacred, to consecrate, from *sacer,* sacred.] to divest of sacredness; to profane; to treat as not sacred; as, to *desecrate* a holy temple.

des′ē·çrā·tẽr, *n.* one who desecrates.

des·ē·çrā′tion, *n.* the act of desecrating or state of being desecrated; profanation; as, the *desecration* of the Sabbath.

des′ē·çrā·tŏr, *n.* one who desecrates.

dē·seg·men·tā′tion, *n.* in zoology, the coalescence of separate segments.

dē·seg′rē·gāte″, *vt.* and *vi.*; desegregated, *pt. pp.*; desegregating, *ppr.* to abolish the segregation of races in (public schools, etc.).

dē·seg″rē·gā′tion, *n.* a desegregating or being desegregated.

dē·sen′si·tīze, *v.t.* 1. to take away the sensitivity of; to make less sensitive.

2. in photography, to make (a plate or film) less sensitive to light, so that it may be developed in a brighter light than ordinarily.

3. in physiology, to make (a person, animal, or tissue) nonreactive or nonallergic to a substance by removing the antibodies from sensitized cells.

deş′ẽrt, *n.* [ME. *desert*; OFr. *desert,* a desert, from L. *desertum,* a desert, neut. of *desertus,* deserted, solitary, waste, pp. of *deserere,* to desert, abandon; *de-* priv., and *serere,* to join, unite.]

1. an uninhabited tract of land; a region in its natural state; a wilderness.

2. a dry, barren region, largely treeless and sandy.

deş′ẽrt, *a.* 1. of a desert or deserts.

2. wild and uninhabited; as, a *desert* island.

dē·şẽrt′, *n.* [ME. *deserte*; OFr. *deserte,* merit, recompense, from *deservir,* to deserve; L. *de-,* intens., and *servire,* to serve.]

1. the fact of deserving reward or punishment.

2. [*often pl.*] deserved reward or punishment; as, he got his just *deserts.*

Render to them their *desert.*—Ps. xxviii. 4.

3. the quality of deserving reward; merit.

Syn.—merit, worth, excellence, due.

dē·ṣẽrt′, *v.t.*; deserted, *pt.*, *pp.*; deserting, *ppr.* [L. *deserere*, to desert, abandon.]
1. to forsake; to leave in the lurch; to abandon; to quit with a view not to return to; as, to *desert* a friend, to *desert* a cause.
2. to leave, without permission; to forsake (the service in which one is engaged), in violation of duty; as, to *desert* the army, to *desert* one's colors, to *desert* a ship.
3. to fail (one) when most needed.
Syn.—abandon, abdicate, forsake, leave.

dē·ṣẽrt′, *v.i.* to run away; to leave one's post, military position, etc. without permission; as, to *desert* from the army.

dē·ṣẽrt′ẽr, *n.* [Fr. *deserteur*; L. *desertor*, a deserter, from *desertus*, pp. of *deserere*, to desert.]
1. a person who forsakes his cause, post, party, family, etc.
2. a member of the armed forces who leaves his post without permission and with no intent to return or, in time of war, who leaves his post to avoid hazardous duty.

dē·ṣẽrt′fụl, *a.* deserving; meritorious. [Rare.]

dē·ṣẽr′tion, *n.* [LL. *desertio*, desertion, from L. *desertus*, pp. of *deserere*, to desert.]
1. a deserting; action of a deserter.
2. the fact or state of being deserted.
3. the state of being forsaken by God; spiritual despondency. [Obs.]
4. desolation; abandonment. [Rare.]

dē·ṣẽrt′less, *a.* without merit or claim to favor or reward. [Rare.]

dē·ṣẽrt′less·ly, *adv.* undeservedly.

deṣ′ẽrt lynx, the caracal.

deṣ′ẽrt mouse, a variety of American field mouse.

deṣ′ẽrt vär′nish, a dark, glistening coating of iron or manganese oxide, formed on rock surfaces in deserts.

dē·ṣẽrve′, *v.t.*; deserved, *pt.*, *pp.*; deserving, *ppr.* [ME. *deserven*; OFr. *deservir*, to deserve; from L. *deservire*, to serve diligently; *de-*, intens., and *servire*, to serve.]
1. to be worthy of (either good or ill); to merit; to earn; as, such conduct *deserves* reward; to *deserve* punishment.
2. to benefit by service. [Obs.]

dē·ṣẽrve′, *v.i.* to merit; to be worthy or deserving: chiefly in *to deserve well* (or *ill*) *of*.

dē·ṣẽrved′, *a.* well earned; merited.

dē·ṣẽrv′ed·ly, *adv.* justly; according to desert.

dē·ṣẽrv′ed·ness, *n.* the quality of being deserving; meritoriousness.

dē·ṣẽrv′ẽr, *n.* one who deserves.

dē·ṣẽrv′ing, *a.* worthy of reward or praise; meritorious.

dē·ṣẽrv′ing, *n.* desert; merit or demerit.

dē·ṣẽrv′ing·ly, *adv.* meritoriously; with just desert.

dē·sex′, *v.t.*; desexed, *pt.*, *pp.*; desexing, *ppr.*
1. to remove the sex organs of.
2. to suppress or lessen the sexual characteristics of.

dē·sex″ū·ăl·i·zā′tion (*or* -ī-zā′shun), *n.* the act or process of desexualizing.

dē·sex′ū·ăl·īze, *v.t.*; desexualized, *pt.*, *pp.*; desexualizing, *ppr.* [*de-*, and *sexualize*.] 1. in medicine, to unsex; to cause to be without sexual power or sex qualities.
2. in psychoanalysis, to unsex by causing the libido or sex desire to be diverted to other interests and desires, especially by sublimating the libido; also, in cases of perversion, to cause (the sex desire or libido) to be focused in any part of the body other than the genital.

des·hȧ·bille′ (dez-ȧ-bēl′), *n.* same as *dishabille*.

des′iç·cănt, *a.* tending to dry or desiccate.

des′iç·cănt, *n.* a substance, drug, etc. for drying something.

des′iç·cāte, *v.t.*; desiccated, *pt.*, *pp.*; desiccating, *ppr.* [L. *desiccatus*, pp. of *desiccare*, to dry up completely, to drain; *de-*, intens., and *siccare*, to dry, from *siccus*, dry.]
1. to dry completely.
2. to preserve (food) by drying.

des′iç·cāte, *v.i.* to become dry.

des·iç·cā′tion, *n.* the act or process of desiccating, or the condition of being desiccated.

des′iç·cā·tive, *a.* drying; tending to dry.

des′iç·cā·tive, *n.* a desiccant.

des′iç·cā·tŏr, *n.* 1. one who or that which desiccates or dries.
2. an apparatus for drying foods, etc.
3. in chemistry, a vessel of glass or earthenware provided with an airtight cover, in which are contained some chemical absorbent and the substance to be desiccated.

dē·siç′cȧ·tō·ry, *a.* desiccative.

dē·sid′ẽr·ȧ·ble, *a.* desirable. [Obs.]

dē·sid·e·rā′tȧ, *n.*, pl. of *desideratum*.

dē·sid′ẽr·āte, *v.t.*; desiderated, *pt.*, *pp.*; desiderating, *ppr.* [L. *desideratus*, pp. of *desiderare*, to desire.] to want; to feel the need for; to miss; to desire.

dē·sid·ẽr·ā′tion, *n.* 1. the act of desiderating.
2. the thing desiderated. [Rare.]

dē·sid′ẽr·ȧ·tive, *a.* denoting desire; as, *desiderative* verbs.

dē·sid′ẽr·ȧ·tive, *n.* 1. that which is desired.
2. in Latin grammar, a verb formed from another verb, and expressing a desire of doing the action implied in the original verb.

dē·sid·e·rā′tum, *n.*; *pl.* **dē·sid·e·rā′tȧ**, [L., from neut. of *desideratus*, pp. of *desiderare*, to desire.] that which is desired; that which is needed and wanted.

dē·sid′i·ōse, dē·sid′i·ous, *a.* idle; lazy. [Obs.]

dē·sid′i·ous·ness, *n.* laziness; indolence. [Obs.]

dē·sīght′ (-sīt′), *n.* an unsightly object. [Obs.]

dē·sīght′ment, *n.* the act of making unsightly; disfigurement. [Rare.]

dē·ṣign′ (-zīn′), *v.t.*; designed, *pt.*, *pp.*; designing, *ppr.* [OFr. *designer*; L. *designare*, to mark out, to define; *de*, out, from, and *signare*, to mark, from *signum*, a mark, sign.]
1. to plan and delineate by drawing the outline or figure of; to sketch, as in painting and other works of art, as for a pattern or model.
2. to contrive; to project with an end in view; to form in idea, as a scheme.

Ask of politicians the end for which laws were originally *designed*. —Burke.

3. to intend or set apart for some purpose.

One of those places was *designed* by the old man to his son. —Clarendon.

4. to purpose; to intend; as, a man *designs* to write an essay, or to study law.
5. to decide upon and outline the main features of; to plan.
6. to indicate. [Rare.]
Syn.—intend, plan, propose, purpose, sketch.

dē·ṣign′, *v.i.* 1. to make designs.
2. to make original plans, sketches, patterns, etc.; as, she *designs* for a coat manufacturer.

dē·ṣign′, *n.* 1. a plan; scheme; project.
2. purpose; intention; aim.
3. a thing planned for or outcome aimed at.
4. a working out by plan; as, do we find a *design* in history?
5. [*pl.*] a secret or sinister scheme (often with *on* or *upon*); as, he has *designs* on her property.
6. a plan or sketch to work from; a pattern; as, a *design* for a house.
7. the art of making designs or patterns.
8. the arrangement of parts, details, form, color, etc., especially so as to produce a complete and artistic unit; artistic invention; as, the *design* of a rug.
9. a finished artistic work.

dē·ṣign′ȧ·ble, *a.* capable of being designed or marked out; distinguishable.

deṣ′ig·nāte, *a.* appointed; named for office, etc.

deṣ′ig·nāte, *v.t.*; designated, *pt.*, *pp.*; designating, *ppr.* [L. *designatus*, pp. of *designare*, to mark out, define.]
1. to mark out or show, so as to make known; to indicate; to specify; as, to *designate* the place where the troops are to land.
2. to name; to entitle.
3. to appoint; to select or distinguish for a particular purpose; to assign: often with *for* or *to*; as, to *designate* an officer *for* the command of a station.
Syn.—name, appoint, indicate, specify, characterize, denominate.

deṣ′ig·nāt·ed hit′tẽr, in baseball, a player in the regular lineup who does not play a defensive position: he bats in place of the pitcher whose position is otherwise unaffected.

deṣ·ig·nā′tion, *n.* 1. the act of pointing or marking out; specific indication; as, the *designation* of an estate by boundaries.
2. appointment; a selecting; assignment; as, the *designation* of an officer to a particular command.
3. that which designates; a distinguishing name, title, etc.

deṣ′ig·nā·tive, *a.* serving to designate or indicate.

deṣ′ig·nā·tŏr, *n.* 1. one who or that which designates.
2. in Roman antiquity, an officer who assigned to each person his rank and place in public shows and ceremonies.

deṣ′ig·nȧ·tō·ry, *a.* designative. [Rare.]

dē·ṣigned′ (-zīnd′), *a.* formed or done according to design; planned; purposed; intended.

dē·ṣign′ed·ly, *adv.* by design; purposely; intentionally.

deṣ·ig·nee′, *n.* a person designated.

dē·ṣign′ẽr, *n.* 1. one who designs.
2. one who conceives or forms original designs; one who designs figures and patterns for ornamental or artistic purposes.
3. a schemer; a plotter.

dē·ṣign′fụl, *a.* full of design; designing.

dē·ṣign′fụl·ness, *n.* the state or quality of being designful.

dē·ṣign′ing, *n.* the art of making sketches or original patterns.

dē·ṣign′ing, *a.* 1. that designs; of or for making designs, original patterns, etc.
2. planning.
3. scheming; crafty; artful.

dē·ṣign′less, *a.* without design.

dē·ṣign′less·ly, *adv.* without design.

dē·ṣign′ment, *n.* 1. design; sketch; delineation. [Obs.]
2. design; purpose; aim. [Obs.]

dē·sil′i·çā·ted, *a.* freed of silica.

dē·si·lic″i·fi·çā′tion, *n.* the act or process of removing silicon or siliceous matter from a substance.

dē·si·lic′i·fȳ, *v.t.* to subject to desilicification.

dē·sil′i·çŏn·īze, *v.t.* to deprive of silicon.

dē·sil′vẽr, *v.t.* to free from silver, as lead.

dē·sil″vẽr·i·zā′tion, *n.* the act or process of depriving lead, etc. of the silver present in its ore.

dē·sil′vẽr·īze, *v.t.* to free from silver, as lead.

des′i·nence, *n.* [L. *desinens*, ppr. of *desinere*, to leave off, cease; *de*, off, from, and *sinere*, to leave.] ending; close; specifically, in grammar, a formative suffix.

des′i·nent, *a.* ending.

des·i·nen′tiăl (-shăl), *a.* desinent.

dē·sip′i·ence, *n.* trifling; foolishness. [Rare.]

dē·sip′i·ent, *a.* [L. *desipiens* (*-entis*), ppr. of *desipere*, to lack sense; *de-* priv., and *sapere*, to be wise.] trifling; foolish. [Rare.]

dē·ṣīr·ȧ·bil′i·ty, *n.* the state or quality of being desirable; desirableness.

dē·ṣīr′ȧ·ble, *a.* [ME. *desirable*; L. *desiderabilis*, worthy of desire, from *desiderare*, to desire.] worthy of desire; that is to be wished for; calculated or fitted to excite a wish to possess; pleasing, beautiful, excellent, etc.

de·ṣīr′ȧ·ble, *n.* a desirable person or thing.

dē·ṣīr′ȧ·ble·ness, *n.* the state or quality of being desirable.

dē·ṣīr′ȧ·bly, *adv.* in a desirable manner; in accordance with what is desirable.

dē·ṣīre′, *v.t.*; desired, *pt.*, *pp.*; desiring, *ppr.* [L. *desiderare*, to long for, to desire.]
1. to wish for the possession and enjoyment of, with earnestness; to long for; to covet; as, to *desire* wealth.

Ye *desire* your child to live.—Tennyson.

2. to express a wish to obtain; to ask for.
3. to want sexually.
4. to require; to claim. [Obs.]
5. to regret; to miss. [Archaic.]
Syn.—request, wish, covet, solicit, want, long for.

dē·ṣīre′, *n.* [ME. *desire*; L. *desiderium*, desire, longing, appetite, from *desiderare*, to desire.]
1. an emotion directed to the attainment or possession of an object; a wish or craving.

By this time the Pilgrims had a *desire* to go forward. —Bunyan.

2. a request; a petition; as, a *desire* for aid.
3. that which is desired; an object of longing.

The *desire* of all nations shall come. —Hag. ii. 7.

4. sexual appetite; lust.

Fulfilling the *desires* of the flesh. —Eph. ii. 3.

Syn.—wish, longing, appetency, hankering, inclination, craving, eagerness.

dē·ṣīre′fụl, *a.* full of desire. [Archaic.]

dē·ṣīre′fụl·ness, *n.* the state of being desireful. [Archaic.]

dē·ṣīre′less, *a.* free from desire.

dē·ṣīr′ẽr, *n.* one who desires or asks; one who wishes.

dē·ṣīr′ous, *a.* wishing for; desiring; covetous; solicitous.

dē·ṣīr′ous·ly, *adv.* with earnest desire; longingly.

dē·ṣīr′ous·ness, *n.* the state of being desirous.

dē·ṣist′, *v.i.*; desisted, *pt.*, *pp.*; desisting, *ppr.* [L. *desistere*, to leave off, to cease; *de*, from, and *sistere*, to set, put, stand.] to stop; to cease to act or proceed; to forbear: frequently with *from*; as, he *desisted from* his purpose.
Syn.—cease, stop, discontinue, forbear, abstain.

dē·ṣist′ănce, dē·ṣist′ence, *n.* a ceasing to act or proceed; a stopping.

dē·ṣist′ive, *a.* final; conclusive. [Rare.]

dē·si′tion (-sish′un), *n.* end; conclusion.

des′i·tive, *a.* final; conclusive. [Obs.]

des′i·tive, *n.* in logic, a proposition which relates to a conclusion. [Obs.]

desk, *n.* [ME. *deske*, a desk; L. *discus*; Gr. *diskos*, a round plate, a quoit, anything round like a quoit; hence, a table.]

1. a frame or table equipped with drawers, compartments, etc., and a flat or sloping top for writing, drawing, or reading.

2. a pulpit.

3. the post of a clerk, official, etc. in a department or office.

4. a musician's stand in an orchestra.

5. a (specified) position in an orchestra.

cylinder or *roll-top desk*; one with a rounded, flexible cover, which can be rolled up and down.

desk, *v.t.*; desked, *pt., pp.*; desking, *ppr.* to enclose, as in a desk. [Obs.]

desk′wŏrk, *n.* work done at a desk, as by a bookkeeper, etc.

des′mȧ, *n.*; *pl.* **des′mȧ·tȧ,** [L., from Gr. *desma*, a band, from *dein*, to bind.] in sponges, a spicale with irregular branches.

des′mȧ·chȳme, *n.* [Gr. *desma*, a band, and *chymos*, juice.] the connective tissue of sponges.

des′mȧ·cȳte, *n.* [Gr. *desma*, a band, and *kytos*, a hollow.] a cell of the connective tissue of sponges.

des′măn, *n.* [Sw. *desman*, musk.] in zoology, an aquatic, insectivorous, molelike mammal, with webbed feet and a long, flexible snout, found in Russia. Another species is found in the Pyrenees.

des′mid, des·mid′i·ăn, *n.* in botany, any one of the plants of the family *Desmidiaceæ*.

Des·mid·i·ā′cē·ae, Des·mid·ī′ē·ae, *n.pl.* [L., from Gr. *desmos*, a band, fetter, from *dein*, to bind.] a family of microscopic, unicellular, fresh-water algae of the class *Conjugatæ*, sometimes found joined in chainlike groups.

des·mid·i·ā′ceous, *a.* of or pertaining to the order *Desmidiaceæ*.

des′mine, *n.* [Gr. *desmos*, a band, *desmē*, a bundle.] stilbite, a zeolitic mineral crystallizing in the monoclinic system.

des·mī′tis, *n.* [L., from Gr. *desmos*, a band.] in pathology, inflammation of a ligament.

des·mō-, [Gr. *desmos*, a band, fetter, bond, from *dein*, to bind.] a combining form signifying *a bond, band, ligament*.

Des·mob′ry·ȧ, *n.pl.* [L., from Gr. *desmos*, a band, and *bryon*, moss, lichen.] in botany, ferns in which the fronds are produced from the apex of the caudex, and are adherent to it.

Des·mō′di·um, *n.* [L., from Gr. *desmos*, a band, and *eidos*, form.] a genus of herbs of the bean family, with leaves of three or five leaflets, or sometimes reduced to a single leaflet. The small flowers are in terminal or lateral racemes, and the pods are flat and jointed. The species *Desmodium gyrans* is remarkable for the peculiar rotatory movements of its leaflets.

des′mọ·dont, *a.* 1. pertaining to the *Desmodonta*.

2. pertaining to the *Desmodontes*.

des′mō·dont, *n.* 1. one of the *Desmodonta*.

2. one of the *Desmodontes*.

Des·mō·don′tȧ, *n.pl.* [L., from Gr. *desmos*, a band, and *odous* (*-ontos*), a tooth.] an order of bivalve mollusks having irregular hinge teeth connected by a ligament.

Des·mō·don′tēs, *n.pl.* in zoology, a group of bloodsucking bats found in Central and South America, typified by the genera *Desmodus* and *Diphylla*.

Des′mō·dus, *n.* a genus of bloodsucking bats native to South America: also called *vampire bat*.

des′mo·ġen, *n.* in botany, vascular tissue which may be of two types, primary (or embryonic) tissue from which vascular tissue is later formed, and secondary, which is formed from the nascent layer of tissue between the bast and the wood, later becoming permanent vascular strands.

Des·mog′nȧ·thae (-thē), *n. pl.* in zoology, a primary division of birds having ridged palatal bones: storks, parrots, ducks, herons, geese, and the like are included in this classification.

des·mog′nă·thism, *n.* [L., from Gr. *desmos*, a band, and *gnathos*, a jaw.] in ornithology, the union of the maxillopalatine bones, as exhibited by the *Desmognathæ*.

des·mog′nȧ·thous, *a.* pertaining to or exhibiting desmognathism.

des·mog′rȧ·phy, *n.* [*desmo-*, and Gr. *-graphia*, from *graphein*, to write.] in anatomy, a description of the ligaments.

des·mō·hem′ō·blăst, *n.* same as *mesenchyme*.

des′moid, *a.* [Gr. *desmos*, a band, ligament, and *eidos*, form, appearance.] in anatomy, having the appearance or characteristics of a ligament; ligamentous; tendinous; also, of fibrous texture, as certain tumors.

Des Moines sē′riēs (de moin), [from Des Moines, capital city of Iowa.] in geology, the lower coal beds of Iowa and surrounding territory.

des·mol′ō·ġy, *n.* [*desmo-*, and Gr. *logos*, a description.] that branch of anatomy which treats of the ligaments.

Des″mō·mȳ·ā′ri·ȧ, *n.pl.* [*desmo-*, and Gr. *mys*, *myos*, muscle, and *-aria*.] a group of tunicates, including the salps.

des′mon, *n.* 1. in immunology, a hypothetical substance supposedly in the blood serum and functioning as one of the active agents in the destruction or dissolution of cells.

2. in pathology, a hypothetical substance believed to exist and circulate in protoplasm, going from one cell to another and controlling the reproduction and growth of tissues.

Des·mon′çus, *n.* a genus of palm trees, family *Arecaceæ*, found from Mexico to Brazil.

des·mop′ȧ·thy, *n.* [*desmo-*, and Gr. *pathos*, suffering.] in pathology, any disease of the ligaments.

des·mō·pel′mous, *a.* [*desmo-*, and Gr. *pelma*, the sole of the foot.] in ornithology, having the plantar tendons connected by a band, rendering the hind toe incapable of being bent independently.

des′ō·lāte, *a.* [ME. *desolat*; L. *desolatus*, pp. of *desolare*, to leave alone, to forsake, to strip of inhabitants; *de-*, intens., and *solare*, to make lonely, or desolate, from *solus*, alone.]

1. destitute or deprived of inhabitants; deserted; uninhabited; as, a *desolate* wilderness.

2. laid waste; in a ruinous condition; made uninhabitable; neglected; destroyed; as, *desolate* altars, *desolate* towers.

3. solitary; forsaken; lonely.

Have mercy upon me, for I am *desolate*.
—Ps. xxv. 16.

4. forlorn, wretched.

5. shameless; dissolute. [Obs.]

6. destitute. [Obs.]

Syn.—deserted, lonely, dreary, waste, abandoned, uninhabited.

des′ō·lāte, *v.t.*; desolated, *pt., pp.*; desolating, *ppr.* 1. to rid of inhabitants; to make desolate; as, the town was nearly *desolated* by the flood.

2. to lay waste; to ruin; to ravage; to make uninhabitable.

3. to forsake; to abandon.

4. to make forlorn, wretched, etc.

des′ō·lāte·ly, *adv.* in a desolate manner.

des′ō·lāte·ness, *n.* the state of being desolate.

des′ō·lā·tẽr, *n.* same as *desolator*.

des·ō·lā′tion, *n.* 1. the act of desolating; destruction or expulsion of inhabitants: devastation.

2. a place deprived of inhabitants, or otherwise wasted, ravaged, and forsaken.

3. a desolate state; destitution; ruin.

4. lonely grief; misery.

5. loneliness.

Syn.—devastation, havoc, ruin, destitution, gloom, waste.

des′ō·lā·tŏr, *n.* one who or that which desolates.

des′ō·lȧ·tō·ry, *a.* causing desolation. [Rare.]

dē·sō·phis′ti·cāte, *v.t.* to clear from sophism or error.

des·ox′ȧ·lāte, *n.* in chemistry, a salt of desoxalic acid.

des·ox·al′iç, *a.* pertaining to or obtained from oxalic acid.

de·spāir′, *v.i.*; despaired, *pt., pp.*; despairing, *ppr.* [L. *desperare*, to be without hope; *de-* priv., and *sperare*, to hope, from *spes*, hope.] to be without hope; to give up all hope or expectation: often followed by *of*; as, to *despair of* life.

de·spāir′, *v.t.* 1. to give up hope of; to lose confidence in. [Archaic.]

2. to cause to despair; to deprive of hope. [Archaic.]

de·spair′, *n.* 1. hopelessness; a hopeless state; a lack of hope or expectation.

2. a person or thing despaired of or causing despair.

The mere *despair* of surgery he cures.
—Shak.

Syn.—desperation, despondency, hopelessness, discouragement.

de·spāir′ẽr, *n.* one without hope.

de·spāir′fụl, *a.* hopeless. [Obs.]

de·spāir′ing, *a.* given to despair; indicating despair; hopeless.

de·spāir′ing·ly, *adv.* in a despairing manner.

de·spāir′ing·ness, *n.* the state of being despairing; hopelessness.

de·spär′ple, *v.t.* and *v.i.* to scatter. [Obs.]

des·patch′, *n.* and *v.* [OFr. *despeche*, haste, riddance, despatch, from *despechier*, to rid, discharge, hasten, despatch.] dispatch.

des·patch′ẽr, *n.* same as *dispatcher*.

des·patch′fụl, *a.* same as *dispatchful*.

dē·spē·cif′i·cāte, *v.t.* [*de-*, intens., and L. *species*, kind, and *facere*, to make.] to deprive of specific meaning. [Rare.]

dē·spec″i·fi·cā′tion, *n.* a despecificating. [Rare.]

dē·speçt′, *n.* [L. *despectus*, a looking down upon, properly, pp. of *despicere*, to look down upon.] despection; contempt. [Rare.]

dē·speç′tion, *n.* a looking down; a despising. [Rare.]

dē·speed′, *v.t.* to send in haste. [Obs.]

dē·spend′, *v.t.* same as *dispend*.

des·pẽr·ā′dō (*or* -ä′dō), *n.*; *pl.* **des·pẽr·ā′dōeş, des·pẽr·ā′dōş,** [OSp. *desperado*, from L. *desperatus*, given up, despaired of, desperate.] a desperate, lawless fellow; a bold outlaw.

des′pẽr·āte, *a.* [L. *desperatus*, pp. of *desperare*, to be without hope, to despair of.]

1. without hope; hopeless; despairing. [Archaic.]

2. having no regard for danger or safety; extremely reckless; as, a *desperate* man.

3. done or applied without regard to consequences, or in the last extreme; resulting from desperation; proceeding from despair; rash; reckless; as, a *desperate* effort.

4. despaired of; beyond hope of recovery; irretrievable; hopeless; extremely dangerous or serious; as, *desperate* fortunes, *desperate* conditions.

5. great in the extreme; hopelessly bad; as, a *desperate* reprobate.

Syn.—despairing, rash, reckless, furious, hopeless, irretrievable.

des′pẽr·āte, *n.* one who is desperate. [Obs.]

des′pẽr·āte·ly, *adv.* in a desperate manner; furiously; without regard to danger or safety; as, the troops fought *desperately*.

des′pẽr·āte·ness, *n.* desperation; fury; rash precipitance.

des·pẽr·ā′tion, *n.* [L. *desperatio*, hopelessness, despair, from *desperare*, to give up hope, to despair.]

1. a despairing; a giving up of hope. [Rare.]

2. the state of being desperate.

3. recklessness resulting from despair; as, the men fought with *desperation*.

des″pi·çȧ·bil′i·ty, *n.* despicableness.

des′pi·çȧ·ble, *a.* [LL. *despicabilis*, contemptible, from L. *despicere*, to despise.] that is or deserves to be despised; contemptible; mean; vile; worthless; as, a *despicable* man, *despicable* manners.

Syn.—mean, contemptible, pitiful, worthless, base.

des′pi·çȧ·ble·ness, *n.* the quality or state of being despicable; meanness; vileness; worthlessness.

des′pi·çȧ·bly, *adv.* meanly; vilely; contemptibly.

des·pi′cience, des·pi′cien·cy (-pish′ence, -ency), *n.* [L. *despicio.*] a looking down; a despising. [Obs.]

dē·spīş′ȧ·ble, *a.* despicable; contemptible.

dē·spīş′ăl, *n.* contempt.

dē·spīşe′, *v.t.*; despised, *pt., pp.*; despising, *ppr.* [ME. *despisen*; OFr. *despiser*, to despise, from L. *despicere*, to look down upon, to despise; *de*, down, from, and *specere*, to look at, behold.] to look down on; to scorn; to disdain; to have a low opinion of; to regard as contemptible.

Syn.—scorn, disdain, contemn, spurn.

dē·spīş′ed·ness, *n.* the state of being despised.

dē·spīş·ẽr, *n.* one who despises; a scorner.

dē·spīş′ing·ly, *adv.* with contempt.

dē·spīte′, *n.* [ME. *despite*; OFr. *despit*; L. *despectus*, a looking down upon, a despising, contempt, from *despicere*, to look down upon, to despise; *de*, down, from, and *specere*, to look.]

1. extreme malice; violent hatred; malignity; spite.

2. a contemptuous act; insult; injury.

3. contempt; scorn. [Archaic.]

in despite of; (a) in defiance of; (b) in spite of.

dē·spīte′, *v.t.* 1. to vex; to offend. [Obs.]

2. to scorn. [Archaic.]

dē·spīte′, *prep.* against; notwithstanding; in spite of; as, *despite* his intentions.

dē·spīte′ful, *a.* full of spite; malicious; malignant; as, a *despiteful* enemy. [Archaic.]

dē·spīte′ful·ly, *adv.* with despite; maliciously. [Archaic.]

dē·spīte′ful·ness, *n.* malice; hatred; malignity. [Archaic.]

des·pit′ē·ous, dis·pit′ē·ous, *a.* malicious; despiteful.

des·pit′ē·ous·ly, *adv.* despitefully.

dē·spīt′ous, di·spīt′ous, *a.* despiteous. [Obs.]

dē·spīt′ous·ly, di·spīt′ous·ly, *adv.* despiteously. [Obs.]

dē·spoil′, *v.t.*; despoiled, *pt.*, *pp.*; despoiling, *ppr.* [ME. *despoilen*; OFr. *despoiller*; L. *despoliare*, to plunder, rob; *de-*, intens., and *spoliare*, to strip, rob, plunder.]

1. to strip; to rob; to plunder; to pillage: often followed by *of*.

Despoiled of innocence, *of* faith, *of* bliss. —Milton.

2. to divest, as of clothing; to strip. [Obs.]

Syn.—deprive, plunder, pillage, rifle, strip, rob.

dē·spoil′, *n.* spoil. [Obs.]

dē·spoil′ēr, *n.* one who despoils; a plunderer.

dē·spoil′ment, *n.* the act of despoiling; despoliation.

dē·spō·li·ā′tion, *n.* the act of despoiling; a stripping; robbery; pillage.

dē·spond′, *v.i.*; desponded, *pt.*, *pp.*; desponding, *ppr.* [L. *despondere*, to promise, to pledge, (with or without *animum*, mind, courage), to lose courage, to despair; *de-* priv., and *spondere*, to promise.] to be cast down; to be depressed or dejected in mind; to lose courage, confidence, or hope.

Others depress their own minds, and *despond* at the first difficulty. —Locke.

dē·spond′, *n.* despondency: now only in *slough of despond*.

dē·spond′ence, *n.* despondency.

dē·spond′en·cy, *n.* dejection or depression of spirits; loss of courage, confidence, or hope.

Let not disappointment cause *despondency*. —Sir T. Browne.

dē·spond′ent, *a.* losing courage; depressed; disheartened; low-spirited.

dē·spond′ent·ly, *adv.* in a despondent manner.

dē·spond′ēr, *n.* one who desponds.

dē·spond′ing, *a.* despondent.

dē·spond′ing·ly, *adv.* in a desponding manner; with dejection of spirits.

dē·spon′sāte, *a.* betrothed. [Obs.]

des·pon·sā′tion, *n.* a betrothing. [Obs.]

dē·spon′sō·ries, *n. sing.* and *pl.* a betrothal or a formal written announcement of betrothal. [Obs.]

des′pōt, *n.* [OFr. *despot*; LL. *despotus*; Gr. *despotēs*, a master, lord.]

1. originally, a title meaning "master," applied to certain classes of rulers, as Byzantine emperors, bishops of the Greek church, etc.

2. an absolute ruler; king with unlimited powers; autocrat.

3. a tyrant.

Syn.—tyrant, autocrat, master, oppressor, dictator.

des′pō·tat, *n.* government by a despot; the territory governed by a despot. [Rare.]

des·pot′iç, des·pot′iç·ăl, *a.* [from Gr. *despotikos*, of a master, despotic, from *despotēs*, a lord or master.] absolute in power; unrestrained; arbitrary; tyrannical; characteristic of despotism or a despot; as, a *despotic* sovereign, *despotic* power.

des·pot′iç·ăl·ly, *adv.* with unlimited power; arbitrarily; in a despotic manner.

des·pot′iç·ăl·ness, *n.* absolute or arbitrary authority.

des·pot′i·çon, *n.* [Gr. *despoticon*, supply *sōma*, body, the body of the Lord.] in the ritual of the Coptic church, the most important of the nine parts into which the host is separated.

des′pō·tişm, *n.* 1. rule or government by a despot; autocracy.

2. the methods or acts of a despot; tyranny.

3. a government, political system, or state dominated by a despot.

4. figuratively, absolute power or influence of any kind.

Such is the *despotism* of the imagination over uncultivated minds. —Macaulay.

des′pō·tist, *n.* one who upholds or advocates despotism.

des′pō·tīze, *v.i.* to be a despot; to act despotically.

des′pū·māte (*or* **dē·spū′**), *v.t.*; despumated, *pt.*, *pp.*; despumating, *ppr.* [L. *despumatus*, pp. of *despumare*, to skim off; *de*, off, from, and *spumare*, to foam, from *spuma*, foam.]

1. to throw off in foam or as froth.

2. to take the scum off; to skim.

des′pū·māte, *v.i.* to become rid of scum.

des·pū·mā′tion, *n.* the act of despumating; clarification; scumming.

des′quȧ·māte, *v.i.*; desquamated, *pt.*, *pp.*; desquamating, *ppr.* [L. *desquamatus*, pp. of *desquamare*, to scale off; *de*, off, *squama*, a scale.] to scale off; to peel off; to exfoliate.

des·quȧ·mā′tion, *n.* the removal or peeling off of scales; especially, in medicine, the shedding of the superficial epithelium, as of the skin, mucous membranes, and renal tubules.

dē·squam′ȧ·tive, *a.* characterized by desquamation.

dē·squam′ȧ·tō·ry, *a.* desquamative.

dess, *v.t.* [Ice. *des*, a heap, mound.]

1. to place together closely; to pile. [Scot. and Brit. Dial.]

2. to cut out, as a portion of hay or straw from a stack. [Scot. and Brit. Dial.]

dess, *n.* 1. that part of a pile of hay or of a stack of sheaf grain remaining after a portion has been removed. [Scot. and Brit. Dial.]

2. a portion of hay cut from a stack for use. [Scot. and Brit. Dial.]

desse, *n.* a dais. [Obs.]

deș·ṣērt′, *n.* [Fr., from OFr. *dessert*, dessert, from *desservir*, to clear the table; *des*, *de*, away, from, and *servir*, to serve; L. *de*, from, and *servire*, to serve.]

1. a course as of fruits, pudding, pie, ice cream, etc., served at the end of a meal.

2. uncooked fruit and nuts served after the sweet course of cake, pudding, etc. [Brit.]

deș·ṣērt′spoon, *n.* a spoon intermediate in size between a tablespoon and a teaspoon, used for eating dessert.

des′siȧ·tīne, des′yȧ·tīne, *n.* [Russ. *desiatina*, a tenth.] a land measure in Russia, equal to about 2.7 English acres.

dē·stāin′, *v.t.* to remove stain from (a specimen or part of a specimen) to facilitate microscopic study.

dē-Stäl″i·ni·zā′tion, *n.* the progressive elimination by the Soviet government of political methods or influences derived from Stalinism.

des·tem′pēr, *n.* distemper. [Obs.]

dē·ster′i·līze, *v.t.* to bring back from a state of sterilization; especially, to return (sterilized gold) to a productive capacity as the basis for the further issuance of currency.

de Stijl (dē stil), *n.* [D., literally, the Style, name of a journal founded in 1917 in Holland.] an abstract art movement marked by the use of rectangular forms and by emphasis on primary colors or grays and blacks.

des′tin, *n.* destiny. [Obs.]

des′ti·nȧ·ble, *a.* capable of being destined or determined; fated. [Obs.]

des′ti·năl, *a.* pertaining to destiny; determined by destiny; fated. [Obs.]

des′ti·nāte, *v.t.* to design or appoint.

des′ti·nāte, *a.* appointed; destined. [Obs.]

des·ti·nā′tion, *n.* [L. *destinatio*, a settlement, appointment, from *destinare*, to fasten down, to secure, to determine, destine; from *de-*, intens., and *stare*, to stand.]

1. the act of destining or appointing. [Rare.]

2. the purpose for which something or someone is intended or appointed; end or ultimate design.

3. the place to which a person or thing is going or sent; the predetermined end of a journey or voyage; as, the ship reached her *destination*.

4. in Scots law, (a) the series of heirs called to the succession of heritable or movable property, by the provision of the law or title or by the will of the proprietor; (b) a nomination of successors in a certain order, regulated by the will of the proprietor.

Syn.—goal, end, appointment, destiny, fate, design, intention, purpose, lot.

des′tine, *v.t.*; destined, *pt.*, *pp.*; destining, *ppr.* [ME. *destenen*; L. *destinare*, to fasten down, to secure, determine.]

1. to set, ordain, or appoint to a use, purpose, state, or place.

2. to fix unalterably, as by a divine decree; to appoint unalterably; to predetermine, as by fate: usually in the passive.

destined for; (a) headed for; bound for; as, *destined for* Asia; (b) intended for; as, *destined for* leadership.

des′ti·ny, *n.*; *pl.* **des′ti·nieș**, [ME. *destynie*; OFr. *destinee*, destiny, from L. *destinare*, to make firm, to destine.]

1. state or condition appointed or predetermined; ultimate fate; doom; lot; fortune; destination; as, men are solicitous to know their future *destiny*.

2. invincible necessity; fate; a necessity or fixed order of things established, as by a divine decree, or by an indissoluble connection of causes and effects.

But who can turn the stream of *destiny*? —Spenser.

3. that which determines events: said of either a supernatural agency or necessity.

4. [D-] in Greek and Roman mythology, (a) the goddess of destiny; (b) [pl.] the three Fates.

Syn.—fate, doom, lot, fortune.

dē·stit′ū·ent, *a.* wanting; deficient. [Obs.]

des′ti·tūte, *a.* [ME. *destitute*, from L. *destitutus*, pp. of *destituere*, to forsake, abandon; *de*, down, away, and *statuere*, to set, put, place.]

1. not having or possessing; wanting; devoid; lacking: followed by *of*; as, *destitute of* virtue, *destitute of* food and clothing.

Totally *destitute of* all shadow of influence. —Burke.

2. not possessing the necessities of life; needy; as, the family is completely *destitute*.

3. abandoned. [Obs.]

des′ti·tūte, *v.t.* 1. to forsake; to desert; to abandon; to leave destitute. [Rare.]

2. to deprive; to divest. [Rare.]

3. to disappoint. [Obs.]

des′ti·tūte·ly, *adv.* in a destitute condition.

des′ti·tūte·ness, *n.* the state of being destitute; destitution. [Rare.]

des·ti·tū′tion, *n.* [L. *destitutio*, a forsaking, deserting, from *destituere*, to forsake.]

1. the state of being destitute; want; lack.

2. complete poverty; indigence; as, the fire caused much *destitution*.

Syn.—indigence, poverty, want, privation, distress, need, deficiency, pauperism.

des′tō, *adv.* [It.] in music, in a sprightly manner; briskly.

des·tōur′, *n.* see *dastur*.

des′trēr, *n.* a war horse: written also *destrier*, *dextrer*. [Obs.]

des′tri·ēr, *n.* a war horse; charger. [Archaic.]

dē·stroy′, *v.t.*; destroyed, *pt.*, *pp.*; destroying, *ppr.* [ME. *destroyen*; OFr. *destruire*; L. *destruere*, to pull down, to tear to pieces, to destroy; *de-* priv., and *struere*, to build.]

1. to demolish; to tear down; as, to *destroy* a house, to *destroy* a city.

2. to ruin; to bring to naught; to spoil completely; as, to *destroy* a scheme, to *destroy* a government, to *destroy* one's happiness.

3. to take away the utility of; to make useless.

4. to put an end to; to do away with.

5. to kill.

6. to neutralize the effect of.

7. to confute; to disprove.

Syn.—annihilate, demolish, extirpate, ruin, exterminate, overthrow, devastate, kill, consume, extinguish, dismantle.

dē·stroy′ȧ·ble, *a.* destructible. [Rare.]

dē·stroy′ēr, *n.* 1. one who or that which destroys; one who or that which kills, ruins, etc.

2. a small, fast, powerful, heavily armed warship with high maneuverability: originally called *torpedo-boat destroyer*.

dē·stroy′ing ăn′ġel, same as *death cup*.

dē·struçt′, *n.* [back-formation from *destruction*.] the deliberate destruction of a malfunctioning missile, rocket, etc. after its launch.

dē·struçt′, *v.i.* to be automatically destroyed.

dē·struçt′, *v.t.* to destroy. [Obs.]

dē·struç·ti·bil′i·ty, *n.* the quality of being destructible.

dē·struç′ti·ble, *a.* liable to destruction; capable of being destroyed.

dē·struç′ti·ble·ness, *n.* the quality of being destructible.

dē·struç′tion, *n.* [ME. *destruction*; OFr. *destruction*; L. *destructio*, a pulling down, destruction, from *destructus*, pp. of *destruere*, to pull down, to destroy.]

1. the act of destroying; demolition; a pulling down; ruin; as, the *destruction* of buildings or of towns.

2. the fact or state of being destroyed; ruin.

So near *destruction* brought. —Waller.

3. the cause or means of destruction.

Syn.—devastation, ruin, demolition, extermination, extinction, subversion, downfall, extirpation, eradication.

dē·struç′tion·ist, *n.* 1. one who favors destruction, as of the existing social order.

2. in theology, one who believes in the final complete destruction or annihilation of the wicked; an annihilationist.

dē·struç′tive, *a.* 1. tending or likely to cause destruction.
2. destroying; causing or producing destruction.
3. tearing down; as, *destructive* criticism.
4. in logic, tending to disprove; refuting; as, a *destructive* dilemma.
Syn.—ruinous, fatal, mischievous, pernicious, detrimental, deadly.
dē·struç′tive, *n.* one who or that which destroys; a destructionist.
dē·struç′tive dis·til·lā′tion, the decomposition of a material, as coal, wood, etc., by heat in the absence of air, followed by the recovery of volatile products of the decomposition by condensation or other means.
dē·struç′tive·ly, *adv.* in a destructive manner.
dē·struç′tive·ness, *n.* 1. the quality of being destructive.
2. in phrenology, a propensity whose function is to produce the impulse to destroy.
dē·struç·tiv′i·ty, *n.* power or tendency to destroy; destructiveness.
dē·struç′tŏr, *n.* 1. a destroyer; a consumer. [Obs.]
2. an oven or incinerator for burning refuse. [Brit.]
dē·struiē, *v.t.* to destroy. [Obs.]
des·ū·dā′tion, *n.* [LL. *desudatio*, a very profuse sweating, from L. *desudare*, to sweat violently.] in medicine, a sweating; a profuse or morbid sweating, often succeeded by an eruption of pustules called heat pimples.
de·suēte′ (-swēt′), *a.* out of use; fallen into desuetude. [Rare.]
des′uē·tūde (des′wē-), *n.* [L. *desuetudo*, disuse, from *desuetus*, pp. of *desuescere*, to disuse.] the cessation of use; disuse; as, laws fallen into *desuetude*.
dē·sul′fūr, *v.t.*; desulfured, *pt.*, *pp.*; desulfuring, *ppr.* to desulferize.
dē·sul′fū·rāte, *v.t.*; desulfurated, *pt.*, *pp.*; desulfurating, *ppr.* to desulfurize.
dē·sul·fū·rā′tion, *n.* same as *desulfurization*.
dē·sul″fūr·i·zā′tion, *n.* the act or process of depriving of sulfur.
dē·sul′fūr·īze, *v.t.*; desulfurized, *pt.*, *pp.*; desulfurizing, *ppr.* to deprive of sulfur, as an ore, mineral, etc.
des′ul·tō·ri·ly, *adv.* in a desultory manner; without method; loosely.
des′ul·tō·ri·ness, *n.* the character of being desultory; disconnectedness; discursiveness; as, the *desultoriness* of a speaker's remarks.
des·ul·tō′ri·ous, *a.* desultory.
des′ul·tō·ry, *a.* [L. *desultorius*, pertaining to a vaulter or rider in a circus, from *desultor*, a leaper, vaulter, one who vaulted from one horse to another in the games of the circus, from *desultus*, pp. of *desilire*, to leap down; *de*, down, from, and *salire*, to leap.]
1. passing from one thing or subject to another without order or natural connection; disconnected; not methodical; as, a *desultory* conversation.
2. random; as, a *desultory* thought.
Syn.—cursory, rambling, discursive, loose, immethodical, irregular.
dē·sūme′, *v.t.* to take from; to borrow. [Obs.]
dē·syn·on″y·mi·zā′tion, *n.* the act of desynonymizing, or depriving of synonymous character.
dē·syn·on′y·mīze, *v.t.*; desynonymized, *pt.*, *pp.*; desynonymizing, *ppr.* to deprive of synonymous character; to give a turn of meaning to (words), so as to prevent from being absolutely synonymous.
dē·tach′, *v.t.*; detached (-tacht′), *pt.*, *pp.*; detaching, *ppr.* [Fr. *détacher*; OFr. *destacher*, to detach, loosen, unfasten.]
1. to separate or disunite; to disengage; to part from; as, to *detach* the coats of a bulbous root from each other; to *detach* a man from a party.
2. to separate for a special purpose or service: used chiefly in a military sense; as, to *detach* a ship from a fleet or a regiment from an army.
Syn.—separate, withdraw, disengage, disconnect, detail, disunite.
dē·tach′, *v.i.* to become detached or separated; to separate or disunite itself or oneself.
dē·tach·ȧ·bil′i·ty, *n.* the condition of being detachable.
dē·tach′ȧ·ble, *a.* capable of being detached.
dē·tached′ (-tacht′), *a.* 1. separated; disunited; disjoined; as, *detached* portions, *detached* territories.
2. drawn and sent on a separate service: used chiefly in a military sense; as, a *detached* body of infantry.
3. not involved by emotion, interests, etc.; aloof; impartial.
detached work; in fortification, a work situated so far from the body of a fort that it is not protected by it, although forming part of the defense.
dē·tach′ment, *n.* [Fr. *détachement*, from *détacher*, to detach.]
1. the act of detaching or separating.
2. the sending of troops or ships on special service.
3. (a) a body of troops, selected or taken from the main army, and employed on some special service or expedition; (b) a number of ships taken from a fleet and sent on a separate service.
4. an order detaching an officer from duty at a certain military station.
5. the state of being on special service.
6. the state of being disinterested or impartial.
dē·tāil′, *v.t.*; detailed, *pt.*, *pp.*; detailing, *ppr.* [OFr. *detailler*, to cut up, divide, narrate in particulars; *de*, apart, and *tailler*, to cut; L. *dis-*, apart, and *talea*, a cutting.]
1. to relate, report, or narrate in particulars; to recite the particulars of; to particularize; as, he *detailed* all the facts in due order.
2. to choose for or send on a special task; as, to *detail* a man for sentry duty.
dē·tāil′, *v.i.* to give details about something; to particularize.
dē·tāil′ (*or* dē′tāl), *n.* 1. the act of dealing with things item by item.
2. an individual part; an item; a particular; as, the account is accurate in all its *details*.
3. a minute account; a narrative or report of particulars; as, he gave a *detail* of the entire transaction.
4. small secondary or accessory part or parts of a picture, statue, building, etc.
5. in military usage, (a) one or more soldiers, sailors, etc. chosen for or sent on a special task; (b) the special task.
detail drawing; a drawing showing plainly all parts or details of some portion of a house, machine, etc.
detail man; a salesman for a pharmaceutical firm who visits doctors, dentists, etc. in a certain district to describe and promote the sales of new drugs.
in detail; circumstantially; item by item; individually; part by part.
dē·tāil′ẽr, *n.* one who details.
dē·tāin′, *v.t.*; detained, *pt.*, *pp.*; detaining, *ppr.* [L. *detinere*, to hold down or off, to keep back, to detain; *de*, off, from, and *tenere*, to hold.]
1. to keep back or from; to withhold.

Detain not the wages of the hireling.
—Taylor.

2. to keep or restrain from proceeding; to delay; as, we were *detained* by the rain.
3. in law, to hold in custody; to confine.
dē·tāin′, *n.* detention. [Obs.]
dē·tāin′dẽr, *n.* a detainer. [Obs.]
dē·tāin′ẽr, *n.* 1. one who or that which detains.
2. in law, (a) a holding or keeping possession of what belongs to another; unlawful detention of what is another's, though the original taking may be lawful; (b) detention of a person without his consent; (c) a writ for continuing to hold a person already in custody.
dē·tāin′ment, *n.* same as *detention*.
dē·teçt′, *v.t.*; detected, *pt.*, *pp.*; detecting, *ppr.* [L. *detectus*, pp. of *detegere*, to uncover; *de-*, priv., and *tegere*, to cover.]
1. to discover; to find out.
2. to discover the presence or existence of (anything hidden, not clear, etc.).
3. in radio, to rectify.
4. to uncover; to reveal. [Obs.]
Syn.—discover, expose, discern, find out, ascertain, determine.
dē·teçt′ȧ·ble, dē·teçt′i·ble, *a.* that can be detected.

These errors are *detectible* at a glance.
—Latham.

dē·teçt′ȧ·phōne, *n.* a type of telephonic contrivance, having a microphone transmitter attached, by which conversations can be overheard by a listener.
dē·teçt′ẽr, *n.* same as *detector*.
dē·teç′tion, *n.* [LL. *detectio*, a revealing, from L. *detectus*, pp. of *detegere*, to uncover, reveal.]
1. the act of detecting or the state of being detected; the finding out of what was concealed, hidden, or formerly unknown; discovery; as, the *detection* of an error, the *detection* of a thief, the *detection* of fraud or forgery.
2. in radio, the process of receiving a radio wave and separating the signal wave from its carrier wave in order to reproduce it as sound; rectification.
dē·teçt′ive, *a.* 1. fitted for detecting; employed in detecting; of or for detection.
2. pertaining to detectives and their work; as, a *detective* story, a *detective* bureau.
dē·teçt′ive, *n.* a person, often a policeman, whose work is investigating and trying to solve crimes, watching suspected persons, getting information, etc.
dē·teçt′ŏr, *n.* [LL. *detector*, a revealer, one who detects, from L. *detectus*, pp. of *detegere*, to uncover, reveal.]
1. one who or that which detects or brings to light; one who finds out what another attempts to conceal; a revealer; a discoverer.
2. an apparatus or device for indicating the presence of something, as electric waves.
3. in radio, a device, usually a vacuum tube, for separating a signal wave from its carrier wave in order to reproduce it as sound; a rectifier.
dē·teçt′ŏr lock, a lock fitted with a contrivance for indicating any attempt to tamper with it.
dē·ten′ē·brāte, *v.t.* to remove darkness from. [Obs.]
dē·tent′, *n.* [Fr. *détente*, from *détendre*, to relax, unbend; *dé-*, from, and *tendre*, to stretch, from L. *tendere*, to stretch out.] in mechanics, a part that stops or releases a movement, as a lever, pin, or stud forming a check in a clock, watch, tumblerlock, or other machine. The detent in a clock falls into the striking wheel, and stops it when the right number of strokes has been given. The detent of a rachet wheel prevents reverse motion.
dé·tente′, de·tente′ (dā-tänt′), *n.* [Fr., see *detent*.] a lessening of tension or hostility, especially between nations, as through treaties, trade agreements, etc.
dē·ten′tion, *n.* [L. *detentus*, pp. of *detinere*, to hold back, detain.]
1. a detaining or being detained.
2. a withholding; retention.
3. a keeping in custody; confinement.
4. an enforced delay.
detention home; a place where juvenile offenders or delinquents are held in custody, especially temporarily, pending disposition of their cases by the juvenile court.
dē·ten′tive, *a.* able to detain.
dē·tẽr′, *v.t.*; deterred, *pt.*, *pp.*; deterring, *ppr.* [L. *deterrere*, to frighten from, to deter; *de*, from, and *terrere*, to frighten.] to discourage or keep (a person) from doing something through fear, anxiety, doubt, etc.

A million of frustrated hopes will not *deter* us from new experiments. —Mason.

Syn.—discourage, hinder, prevent, restrain.
dē·tẽrġe′, *v.t.*; deterged, *pt.*, *pp.*; deterging, *ppr.* [L. *detergere*, to wipe off, wipe away; *de*, off, from, and *tergere*, to wipe, cleanse.] to cleanse, as a wound.
dē·tẽr′ġence, *n.* same as *detergency*.
dē·tẽr′ġen·cy, *n.* a detergent quality or power.
dē·tẽr′ġent, *a.* cleansing; purging.
dē·tẽr′ġent, *n.* [L. *detergens* (*-entis*), ppr. of *detergere*, to wipe off.] a cleansing substance.
dē·tē′ri·ō·rāte, *v.t.*; deteriorated, *pt.*, *pp.*; deteriorating, *ppr.* [LL. *deterioratus*, pp. of *deteriorare*, to make worse, from L. *deterior*, worse, inferior.] to make worse; to lower the value of; to reduce in quality; to depreciate.
Syn.—degrade, depreciate, degenerate, impair, corrupt, debase.
dē·tē′ri·ō·rāte, *v.i.* to grow worse; to be impaired in quality; to degenerate.
dē·tē″ri·ō·rā′tion, *n.* 1. a deteriorating.
2. a deteriorated condition.
dē·tē′ri·ō·rā·tive, *a.* deteriorating or tending to deteriorate.
dē·tē·ri·or′i·ty, *n.* worse state or quality. [Rare.]
dē·tẽr′ment, *n.* 1. the act of deterring or the state of being deterred.
2. that which deters.
dē·tẽr″mi·nȧ·bil′i·ty, *n.* the quality of being determinable.
dē·tẽr′mi·nȧ·ble, *a.* [LL. *determinabilis*, determinable, from L. *determinare*, to determine.]
1. that can be determined, decided, or ascertained with positiveness; as, a *determinable* function.
2. in law, liable to termination; as, a *determinable* lease.
dē·tẽr′mi·nȧ·ble·ness, *n.* the quality of being determinable; determinability. [Rare.]

dē·tẽr′mi·nȧ·cy, *n.* determinateness. [Rare.]

dē·tẽr′mi·nănt, *a.* serving to determine; determinative.

dē·tẽr′mi·nănt, *n.* 1. a thing or factor that determines.

2. in mathematics, the sum of the products formed, in accordance with certain laws, from a series of quantities arranged in an equal number of rows and columns.

3. in some old universities, one who, having graduated as a bachelor of arts, proceeded to take the degree of master of arts.

4. in biology, one of the hypothetical minute subdivisions of chromatin, beyond the power of the microscope to reveal. It is made up of other theoretical divisions, the biophores. According to Weismann, biophores are united to form determinants, determinants to form ids (chromatin granules), and ids to form idants (chromosomes). It is believed that these units differ qualitatively and the manner of their combination determines the ultimate development of any cell or group of cells.

dē·tẽr′mi·nănt·ăl, *a.* in mathematics, relating to determinants.

dē·tẽr′mi·nāte, *v.t.* to bring to an end; to terminate. [Obs.]

dē·tẽr′mi·nāte, *a.* [L. *determinatus,* pp. of *determinare,* to determine.]

1. having defined limits; limited; fixed; definite; specific; as, a *determinate* quantity of matter.

2. established; settled; conclusive; as, a *determinate* rule or order.

3. resolved on.

4. fixed; resolute.

5. in botany, having a flower at the end of the primary axis and of each secondary axis: said of the inflorescence of certain plants.

6. in mathematics, (a) having a fixed value; (b) of problems, having a fixed solution or solutions.

dē·tẽr′mi·nāte·ly, *adv.* 1. with certainty; precisely; with exact specification.

2. resolutely; with fixed resolve.

dē·tẽr′mi·nāte·ness, *n.* the state of being determinate, certain, or precise.

dē·tẽr·mi·nā′tion, *n.* [ME. *determynation;* L. *determinatio,* a boundary, conclusion, from *determinare,* to bound, limit, determine; *de,* and *terminare,* to bound, limit, from *terminus,* a boundary, limit.]

1. the act of determining or the state of being determined.

2. an ending; a putting an end to; termination. [Archaic.]

3. direction to a certain end.

With a constant *determination* of the will to the greatest apparent good. —Locke.

4. the mental habit of settling upon some line of action with a fixed purpose to adhere to it; adherence to aims or purposes; resoluteness; as, a man of *determination.*

5. judicial decision; the ending, as of a controversy or suit; as, justice is promoted by a speedy *determination* of cases, civil and criminal.

6. fixed purpose; resolution; intention.

A *determination* to obtain convictions. —Hallam.

7. in medicine, tendency to flow to, more copiously than is normal; as, *determination* of blood to the head.

8. in physical science, the act, process, or result of determining the nature, quantity, intensity, etc. of anything; as, the *determination* of nitrogen in the atmosphere.

9. in logic, the act of defining a notion by adding differentia, and thus rendering it more definite.

10. in natural history, the referring of minerals, plants, etc. to the species to which they belong; classification; as, I am indebted to a friend for the *determination* of the greater part of these shells.

11. in some old universities, a solemn disputation enjoined upon one who has taken the degree of bachelor of arts, preparatory to working for the degree of master of arts.

12. in law, the ending of an estate or of an interest in property.

Syn.—decision, resolution.

dē·tẽr′mi·nȧ·tive, *a.* 1. having power to determine or direct to a certain end; conclusive.

2. serving to determine the species; having the power of ascertaining precisely; as, *determinative* tables in the natural sciences, that is, tables arranged for determining the specific character of minerals, plants, etc., and to assist in assigning them to their species.

dē·tẽr′mi·nȧ·tive, *n.* that which determines the nature or quality of something else; specifically, (a) in grammar, a demonstrative word; (b) in hieroglyphics, an ideographic sign annexed to a word expressed by a phonetic sign for the purpose of defining its signification.

dē·tẽr′mi·nā·tŏr, *n.* one who or that which determines; a determiner.

dē·tẽr′mine, *v.t.;* determined, *pt., pp.;* determining, *ppr.* [L. *determinare,* to bound, limit, prescribe.]

1. to set limits to; bound; define.

2. to settle conclusively or beforehand; decide; resolve.

3. to reach a decision about after thought and investigation; decide upon.

4. to be the cause of; be the deciding or regulating factor in.

5. to find out exactly; ascertain; calculate; fix precisely.

6. to give a definite aim or direction to; direct.

7. to end; terminate.

8. in logic, to define or limit by adding differences.

Syn.—decide, define, limit, fix, resolve, settle, conclude.

dē·tẽr′mine, *v.i.* 1. to resolve; to conclude; to come to a decision, frequently followed by *on;* as, to *determine on* a course.

2. in law, to come to an end; to terminate.

dē·tẽr′mined, *a.* 1. having one's mind made up; decided; resolved.

2. resolute; unwavering.

Syn.—decided, firm, fixed, immovable, obstinate, resolute, steady.

dē·tẽr′min·ed·ly (*or* -mind-ly), *adv.* in a determined manner.

dē·tẽr′min·ẽr, *n.* one who decides or determines; that which determines.

dē·tẽr′min·iṣm, *n.* 1. the doctrine that everything is entirely determined by a sequence of causes.

2. the doctrine that one's choice of action is not free, but is determined by a sequence of causes independent of his will.

dē·tẽr′min·ist, *n.* one who believes in determinism.

dē·tẽr′min·ist, *a.* of determinism or determinists.

dē·tẽr·min·is′tiç, *a.* same as *determinist.*

dē·tẽr·rā′tion, *n.* [from L. *de,* from, and *terra,* earth.] the carrying down of topsoil, etc. from hills into valleys by rain, etc. [Obs.]

dē·tẽr′rence, *n.* 1. a deterring.

2. a hindrance; a deterrent.

dē·tẽr′rent, *a.* having the power or tendency to deter; as, a *deterrent* principle.

dē·tẽr′rent, *n.* a thing or factor which deters or tends to deter.

dē·tẽr′ṣion, *n.* [from L. *detersus,* pp. of *detergere,* to wipe off, cleanse.] the act of cleansing, as a sore.

dē·tẽr′sive, *a.* cleansing; detergent.

dē·tẽr′sive, *n.* a detergent.

dē·tẽr′sive·ly, *adv.* in a detersive manner.

dē·tẽr′sive·ness, *n.* the quality of being detersive.

dē·test′, *v.t.;* detested, *pt., pp.;* detesting, *ppr.* [Fr. *detester,* to detest; L. *detestari,* to curse by calling on the gods to witness, to execrate, to detest; *de,* and *testari,* to witness; *testis,* a witness.]

1. to abhor; to abominate; to dislike intensely; as, to *detest* crimes or meanness.

And love the offender, yet *detest* th' offense. —Pope.

2. to denounce; to testify against. [Obs.]

Syn.—hate, abhor, abominate, loathe.

dē·test·ȧ·bil′i·ty, *n.* the quality of being detestable.

dē·test′ȧ·ble, *a.* [OFr. *detestable;* L. *detestabilis,* execrable, abominable, detestable.] extremely hateful; abominable; very odious; deserving abhorrence.

Syn.—execrable, abhorred, odious, abominable.

dē·test′ȧ·ble·ness, *n.* the quality of being detestable.

dē·test′ȧ·bly, *adv.* in a detestable manner; abominably.

dē·tes′tāte, *v.t.* to detest. [Obs.]

det·es·tā′tion, *n.* 1. extreme hatred; abhorrence; loathing.

2. a detested person or thing.

dē·test′ẽr, *n.* one who detests.

dē·thrōne′, *v.t.;* dethroned, *pt., pp.;* dethroning, *ppr.* [from L. *de-* priv., and *thronus,* a seat, throne.] to remove or drive from a throne; to depose; hence, to oust from any high position; to divest of authority and dignity.

dē·thrōne′ment, *n.* a dethroning or being dethroned.

dē·thrōn′ẽr, *n.* one who dethrones.

dē·thrōn·i·zā′tion, *n.* the act of dethroning. [Rare.]

dē·thrōn′īze, *v.t.* to dethrone. [Obs.]

det′i·nūe, *n.* [OFr. *detinu,* pp. of *detenir,* to detain; L. *detinere,* to detain.]

1. the unlawful detention of personal property.

2. an action or writ for the recovery of property unlawfully detained, as in a pawnshop.

det′ō·nȧ·ble, *a.* capable of detonating.

det′ō·nāte, *v.i.;* detonated, *pt., pp.;* detonating, *ppr.* [L. *detonatus,* pp. of *detonare,* to thunder, to make a loud noise; *de-,* intens., and *tonare,* to make a sound.] to explode violently and noisily.

det′ō·nāte, *v.t.* to cause to explode by setting off with a fuse, percussion cap, etc.

det′ō·nā·ting, *a.* exploding violently.

det′ō·nā·ting bulb, a small glass bulb, shaped like a pear, rendered brittle by cooling in the making. It flies into bits when scratched: called also *Prince Rupert's drop.*

det′ō·nā·ting pow′dẽr, any of certain chemical compounds which, when struck or exposed to heat, explode violently.

det′o·nā·ting prīm′ẽr, a primer for exploding guncotton or other explosive used in blasting. The primer itself is exploded by a fuse.

det′ō·nā·ting tūbe, a kind of eudiometer, a stout glass tube used in chemical analysis for detonating gases. It is generally graduated into centesimal parts, and perforated by two opposed wires for the purpose of passing an electric spark through the gases which are introduced into it.

DETONATING TUBE

det·ō·nā′tion, *n.* [from L. *detonare,* to thunder, to make a loud noise.]

1. a detonating or being detonated.

2. a loud, violent explosion.

3. a loud noise.

det′ō·nā·tive, *a.* detonable.

det′ō·nā·tŏr, *n.* that which sets off explosives, as a percussion cap; also, an explosive.

det″ō·ni·zā′tion, *n.* detonation. [Obs.]

det′ō·nīze, *v.t.* and *v.i.;* detonized, *pt., pp.;* detonizing, *ppr.* to detonate. [Obs.]

dē·tọr′sion, *n.* same as *detortion.*

dē·tọrt′, *v.t.;* detorted, *pt., pp.;* detorting, *ppr.* [L. *detortus,* pp. of *detorquere,* to turn aside, to turn off; *de,* off, from, and *torquere,* to turn.] to twist; to wrest; to pervert; to turn from the original meaning. [Obs.]

dē·tọr′tion, *n.* the act of detorting; the state of being detorted. [Obs.]

dē′tö̤ur, *n.* [Fr. *detour,* a turning, an evasion, excuse, from *detourner,* to turn aside, divert, evade.]

1. a turning; a circuitous or roundabout way; a deviation from the direct or shortest path, road, or route; as, the *detours* of a river.

2. a route used when the direct or regular route is closed to traffic.

dē′tö̤ur, *v.i.* to go by way of a detour.

dē′tö̤ur, *v.t.* to cause to go by way of a detour.

dē·traçt′, *v.t.;* detracted, *pt., pp.;* detracting, *ppr.* [L. *detractare,* to draw away from, decline, detract; *de,* from, and *trahere,* to draw.]

1. to take away.

2. to belittle; to disparage. [Rare.]

Syn.—defame, vilify, derogate, slander, decry, depreciate, calumniate.

dē·traçt′, *v.i.* to take something desirable away (*from*); as, anger *detracts from* her beauty.

dē·traçt′ẽr, *n.* same as *detractor.*

dē·traçt′ing·ly, *adv.* in a detracting manner.

dē·traç′tion, *n.* [ME. *detraction;* L. *detractio,* a taking away, drawing off, detraction, from *detractare, detrectare,* to draw away, detract.]

1. a detracting; a taking away.

2. the act of taking away from the reputation or worth of another; the act of depreciating another from envy or malice; a belittling.

Syn.—slander, defamation, calumny, depreciation, aspersion, derogation, disparagement.

dē·traç′tious, *a.* containing detraction; lessening reputation. [Obs.]

dē·traçt′ive, *a.* 1. having the quality of detraction.
2. tending to take away.
3. disparaging.

dē·traçt′ive·ness, *n.* the quality of being detractive.

dē·traçt′ŏr, *n.* one who detracts; one who takes away or impairs the reputation of another; one who attempts to lessen the worth or honor of another; a defamer; a calumniator.
Syn.—defamer, calumniator, slanderer, vilifier, derogator.

dē·traçt′ō·ry, *a.* same as *detractive.*

dē·traçt′ress, *n.* a woman detractor.

dē·trāin′, *v.t.* and *v.i.* to remove from or get off a railway train.

dē·trāin′ment, *n.* a detraining or being detrained.

dē·treçt′, *v.t.* and *v.i.* to refuse. [Obs.]

det′ri·ment, *n.* [OFr. *detriment*; L. *detrimentum*, a rubbing off, loss, damage, from *detritus*, pp. of *deterere*, to rub off, wear away, weaken; *de*, off, from, and *terere*, to rub, wear.]
1. damage; injury; harm.
2. that which causes damage, harm, or injury.
3. in England, a charge made upon barristers and students for repair of damages to the rooms they occupy.
4. in heraldry, same as *decrement.*
5. in astrology, a sign of mishap, distress, weakness, etc.
Syn.—injury, harm, evil, loss, hurt, damage, disadvantage.

det′ri·ment, *v.t.* to injure; to harm. [Obs.]

det·ri·men′tăl, *a.* injurious; harmful; causing loss or damage.
Syn.—injurious, damaging, mischievous, disadvantageous, harmful, prejudicial.

det·ri·men′tăl·ly, *adv.* in a detrimental manner.

det·ri·men′tăl·ness, *n.* the quality of being detrimental.

dē·trī′tăl, *a.* in geology, pertaining to or consisting of detritus.

dē·trīt′ed, *a.* [L. *detritus*, pp. of *deterere*, to rub down, to wear away; *de*, down, from, and *terere*, to rub.] worn down.

dē·tri′tion (-trish′un), *n.* [from L. *deterere*, to wear or rub away.] a wearing away or down by friction.

dē·trī′tus, *n.* [L. *detritus*, a rubbing away, from *deterere*, to rub or wear away.]
1. in geology, fragments of rock, etc. produced by disintegration or wearing away; debris.
2. any fragmentary material; waste; disintegrated matter.

de trōp (trō′), [Fr.] 1. literally, too much; too many.
2. unwanted; superfluous.

dē·trụde′, *v.t.*; detruded, *pt., pp.*; detruding, *ppr.* [L. *detrudere*, to thrust or push down.]
1. to thrust or force down.
2. to thrust away or out.

dē·truñ′çāte, *v.t.*; detruncated, *pt., pp.*; detruncating, *ppr.* [L. *detruncatus*, pp. of *detruncare*, to cut or lop off.] to cut off; to lop; to shorten by cutting.

dē·truñ·çā′tion, *n.* [L. *detruncatio*, from *detruncare*, to cut or lop off.]
1. the act of detruncating.
2. in obstetrics, separation of the trunk and head of the fetus.

dē·trụ′sion, *n.* [LL. *detrusio*, a thrusting away, from L. *detrudere*, to drive or thrust away.] the act of thrusting; the act of driving down or out.

dē·trụ′sive, *a.* tending to detrude.

dē·trụ′sŏr, *n.* in anatomy, a muscle which expels or ejects.

dette, *n.* debt. [Obs.]

dē·tū·mes′cence, *n.* [L. *detumescens*, (*-entis*), ppr. of *detumescere*, to cease swelling; *de*, from, and *tumescere*, incept. of *tumere*, to swell.] diminution of swelling.

dē′tũr, *n.* [L. *detur*, lit., let it be given; third pers. sing. pres. subj. pass. of *dare*, to give.] a prize of books annually awarded to meritorious undergraduate students at Harvard University.

dē·tũrb′, *v.t.* to throw into confusion; to throw down with violence. [Obs.]

dē·tũr′bāte, *v.t.* to evict. [Obs.]

det·ũr·bā′tion, *n.* eviction. [Obs.]

dē·tũrn′, *v.t.* to turn away. [Obs.]

dē·tũr′pāte, *v.t.* to defile. [Obs.]

det·ũr·pā′tion, *n.* the act of defiling. [Obs.]

Deū·çā′li·ŏn, *n.* [L.; Gr. *Deukaliōn.*] in Greek mythology, a son of Prometheus: Deucalion and his wife, Pyrrha, were the only survivors of a great flood sent by Zeus to punish mankind for wickedness, and their son, Hellen, was the fabled ancestor of the Hellenic race.

deūce, *n.* [Fr. *deux*; OFr. *deus*; L. *duo*, two.]
1. the side of a die bearing two spots, or a throw of the dice totaling two.
2. a playing card with two spots; as, the *deuce* of clubs.
3. in tennis, a score of 40 each (or five games each) after which one player or side must get two successive points (or games) to win the game (or set).

deūce, *n.* and *interj.* [ME. *dewes*; OFr. *Deus*; L. *Deus*, God.] the devil, bad luck, etc.: used in exclamatory or interjectional phrases; expressive of impatience or annoyance; as, go to the *deuce! deuce* take you!
to play the *deuce with*; to injure; to damage; to perplex; to annoy: used of persons or things. [Slang.]

deūce′-āce, *n.* a throw of two dice, one of which turns up one and the other two.

deū′ced, *a.* devilish; excessive; confounded: used in mild cursing.

deū′ced·ly, deū′sed·ly, *adv.* devilishly; confoundedly.

Dē′us, *n.* [L.] God.

deūse, *n.* deuce. [Obs.]

dē·us ex ma′çhi·nȧ, [L., god from a machine.]
1. in ancient Greek and Roman plays, a deity brought in by stage machinery to intervene in the action.
2. any character or happening artificially, suddenly, or improbably introduced to resolve a situation, as in some fiction.
3. anyone who unexpectedly intervenes to change the course of events.

Dē′us vō·bis′çum, [L.] (may) God (be) with you.

deūt-, same as *deuto-.*

deū″ten·ceph·al′iç, *a.* [from Gr. *deuteros*, second, and *enkephalos*, brain.] same as *diencephalic.*

deū·ten·ceph′ȧ·lon, *n.* same as *diencephalon.*

deū′tẽr-, same as *deutero-.*

deū·tẽr·ag′ō·nist, *n.* [from *deutero-*, and Gr. *agōnizesthai*, to contend for a prize.] in ancient Greek drama, the character second in importance to the protagonist.

deū·ter′i·um, *n.* [Mod.L., *deuter-*, and *-ium.*] the hydrogen isotope having an atomic weight of approximately 2; heavy hydrogen: it has the symbol D, and is a constituent of heavy water, D_2O.
deuterium oxide; heavy water.

deū′tẽr·ō-, [from Gr. *deuteros*, second.] a combining form meaning *second* or *secondary*, as in *deutero*plasm: also *deuto-, deuter-, deut-.*

deū″tẽr·ō·çȧ·non′iç·ăl, *a.* [*deutero-*, and L. *canon*; Gr. *kanōn*, a rule.] belonging to a second or subsequent canon: in the Roman Catholic Church, applied to those books of the Bible which were admitted into the canon after the rest.

deū·tẽr·og′ȧ·mist, *n.* one who marries the second time after the death of the first spouse.

deū·tẽr·og′ȧ·my, *n.* [Gr. *deuterogamia*, a second marriage; *deuteros*, second, and *gamos*, marriage.] a second marriage after the death of the first husband or wife.

deū″tẽr·ō·gen′iç, *a.* [*deutero-*, and Gr. *genos*, race.] of secondary origin.

deū′tẽr·on, *n.* the nucleus of an atom of deuterium: also *deutron, deuton.*

Deū″tẽr·ō·nom′iç, Deū″tẽr·ō·nom′iç·ăl, *a.* pertaining to the book of Deuteronomy.

Deū·tẽr·on′ō·mist, *n.* the assumed writer or one of the assumed writers of the book of Deuteronomy.

Deū·tẽr·on·ō·mis′tiç, *a.* relating to the Deuteronomist(s).

Deū·tẽr·on′ō·my, *n.* [L. *deuteronomium*, lit. the second law, Deuteronomy, from Gr. *deuteros*, second, and *nomos*, law.] the fifth book of the Pentateuch in the Old Testament, in which the law of Moses is set down in full for the second time.

deū″tẽr·ō·path′iç, *a.* of or pertaining to deuteropathy.

deū·tẽr·op′ȧ·thy, *n.* [*deutero-*, and Gr. *pathos*, suffering.] a secondary affection of any part of the body, resulting from another affection.

deū′tẽr·ō·plaṣm, *n.* same as *deutoplasm.*

deū·tẽr·os′çō·py, *n.* [*deutero-*, and Gr. *skopein*, to see.]
1. the second view; the hidden meaning. [Obs.]
2. prophetic or second sight. [Rare.]

deū·tẽr·os′tō·mȧ, *n.*; *pl.* **deū″tẽr·os·tō′mȧ·tȧ,** [L., from Gr. *deuteros*, second, and *stoma*, mouth.] a blastopore derived from an archaeostoma; a secondary blastopore.

deū″tẽr·ō·zō′oid, *n.* [*deutero-*, and Gr. *zōon*, an animal, and *eidos*, form.] a zooid produced by gemmation from a zooid.

deū·tō-, deutero-: also, before a vowel, *deut-.*

deū′ton, *n.* same as *deuteron.*

deū′tō·plaṣm, *n.* [*deuto-*, and Gr. *plasma*, anything formed, from *plassein*, to form.] in biology, that portion of the yolk of ova which furnishes materials for the nourishment of the embryo.

deū·tō·plaṣ′miç, *a.* deutoplastic.

deū·tō·plas′tiç, *a.* of or pertaining to deutoplasm.

deū·tō·sçō′lex, *n.* a secondary scolex.

deū′tron, *n.* same as *deuteron.*

Deut′sche·märk (doi′che-), *n.*; *pl.* **Deut′sche·märk,** Eng. **Deut′sche·märks,** the monetary unit of West Germany.

Deut′zi·ȧ (doit′), *n.* [named after *Deutz*, a Dutch botanist.] in botany, a genus of saxifragaceous shrubs, often cultivated, having ovate leaves and white flowers.

dẹ′vȧ, dẹv, *n.* [Sans. *deva*, a god, deity.]
1. in Hindu mythology, a deity or good spirit.
2. in Zoroastrian mythology, a demon or evil spirit.

dē·val′ū·āte, *v.t.*; devaluated, *pt., pp.*; devaluating, *ppr.* to decrease the value of; specifically, to set the value of, as a currency, lower than par on account of emergency circumstances.

dē·val″ū·ā′tion (-shun), *n.* 1. a devaluating or being devaluated.
2. the amount of this.

Dẹ·vȧ·nä′gȧ·rï, *n.* [from Sans. *deva*, god, and *nagari*, one of the alphabets of India, the one in which Sanskrit is usually written, from *nagara*, a city.] the alphabet used in Sanskrit.

dē·vap·ō·rā′tion, *n.* the change of vapor into water, as in rain.

dē·vȧst′, *v.t.* to lay waste. [Obs.]

dev′ȧs·tāte, *v.t.*; devastated, *pt., pp.*; devastating, *ppr.* [L. *devastatus*, pp. of *devastare*, to lay waste.] to lay waste; to ravage; to make desolate; to destroy.
Syn.—despoil, desolate, ravage, sack, strip.

dev·ȧs·tā′tion, *n.* 1. the act of devastating or the state of being devastated; a laying waste; desolation; as, the *devastation* of war.
2. in law, the waste of the property of a deceased person by an executor or administrator.
Syn.—desolation, ravage, waste, havoc, destruction, ruin, overthrow.

dev′ȧs·tā·tŏr, *n.* one who or that which devastates.

dev·ȧs·tā′vit, *n.* [L., lit. he has laid waste; third pers. sing. perf. ind. act. of *devastare*, to lay waste.] in law, a writ against an executor or administrator for waste of the property of a deceased person.

dēve, *a.* deaf. [Obs.]

dev′el, *v.t.* to strike with force. [Scot.]

dev′el, *n.* a heavy blow. [Scot.]

dev′el·in, *n.* the swift, *Cypselus apus.* [Brit. Dial.]

dē·vel′ŏp, *v.t.*; developed, *pt., pp.*; developing, *ppr.* [Fr. *développer*; OFr. *desvelopper*, to unfold, unwrap; perhaps from L. *de*, from, and *volutus*, pp. of *volvere*, to roll.]
1. to cause to grow gradually in some way; to cause to become gradually fuller, larger, better, etc.
2. to expand, as a business.
3. to strengthen, as muscles.
4. to bring into activity, as an idea.
5. to unfold gradually, as a bud.
6. to make more available or extensive, as electric power.
7. in music, to elaborate (a theme).
8. in photography, (a) to put (an exposed film, plate, or printing paper) in various chemical solutions in order to make the picture visible; (b) to make (a picture) visible by doing this.
9. to show or work out by degrees; reveal; disclose.
10. to make known gradually, as a plot.
11. to explain more clearly; to enlarge upon.
12. in mathematics, to work out in detail or expand (a function or expression).
Syn.—uncover, unfold, disclose, exhibit, unravel, disentangle.

dē·vel′ŏp, *v.i.* 1. to come into being or activity.
2. to become larger, fuller, better, etc.; grow; evolve.
3. to become known or apparent; to be disclosed.

dē·vel′ŏp·ȧ·ble, *a.* that can be developed.

dē·vel′ŏp·ȧ·ble, *n.* in mathematics, a developable surface; a torse.

dē·vel′ŏpe, *v.t.* and *v.i.*; developed, *pt., pp.*; developing, *ppr.* to develop.

dē·vel′ŏp·ẽr, *n.* one who or that which develops; specifically, in photography, a chemical or mixture used in the process of developing.

dē·vel′ŏp·ment, *n.* [Fr. *développement*, from *développer*, to develop.]
1. a developing or being developed (in all senses of the verb).
2. a step or stage in growth, advancement, etc.
3. an event or happening.
4. a thing that is developed; result of developing.
5. in music, (a) the elaboration of a theme by rhythmic, harmonic, or melodic changes; (b) the middle part of the sonata form.
Also spelled *developement*.
Syn.—unfolding, unraveling, disentanglement, growth, increase, evolution, progress.

dē·vel·ŏp·men′tăl, *a.* relating to development; evolutionary.

dev·ē·nus′tāte, *v.t.* to deprive of beauty or grace. [Obs.]

dē·vest′, *v.t.*; devested, *pt., pp.*; devesting, *ppr.* [L. *devestire*, to undress; *de-* priv., and *vestire*, to dress, from *vestis*, a dress, garment.]
1. to undress; to strip. [Obs.]
2. in law, (a) to take away (a right, etc.); (b) [Archaic.] to strip (*of* a title, etc.).

dē·vest′, *v.i.* in law, to be lost or taken away, as a title or an estate.

dē·vex′, *a.* bending down. [Obs.]

dē·vex′, *n.* devexity; slope. [Obs.]

dē·vex′i·ty, *n.* [L. *devexitas*, a bending downward, a sloping, from *devehere*, to go down.] a bending or sloping downward. [Obs.]

Dē′vĭ, *n.* [Sans., fem. of *deva*, god.] a Hindu goddess, Sakti, the consort of Siva.

dē′vi·ănt, *a.* deviating, especially from what is considered normal in a group or for a society.

dē′vi·ănt, *n.* a person whose behavior is deviant.

dē′vi·āte, *v.i.*; deviated, *pt., pp.*; deviating, *ppr.* [LL. *deviatus*, pp. of *deviare*, to turn aside, from L. *devius*, out of the way; *de*, from, and *via*, way, path.] to turn aside or wander from the common or right way, course, or line; to diverge; to differ; as, to *deviate* from the truth.

dē′vi·āte, *v.t.* to cause to deviate.
Syn.—deflect; digress; swerve; wander.

dē′vi·ăte, *a.* deviant.

dē′vi·ăte, *n.* a deviant; especially, one whose sexual behavior is deviant.

dē·vi·ā′tion, *n.* [LL. *deviatio*, from *deviare*, to deviate.]
1. a turning aside from a course, standard, etc.; also, the amount of this.
2. in commerce, the voluntary departure of a ship, without necessity, from the regular and usual course of the specific voyage insured. This discharges the underwriters from their responsibility.
deviation of a falling body; that deviation from the perpendicular line of descent which falling bodies exhibit in their descent, in consequence of the rotation of the earth on its axis.
deviation of the compass; the deviation of a ship's compass from the true magnetic meridian, caused by the magnetism of the iron in the ship.
deviation of the line of the vertical; deviation of a plumb line caused by side attraction, as that of an adjacent mountain.

dē′vi·ā·tŏr, *n.* one who or that which deviates.

dē′vi·ȧ·tō·ry, *a.* deviating.

dē·vīce′, *n.* [ME. *devise*; OFr. *devise, divise*, will, intention, opinion, division, from L. *divisus*, pp. of *dividere*, to divide.]
1. that which is formed by design; a thing devised; a plan; a scheme.
His *device* is against Babylon, to destroy it. —Jer. li. 11.
2. an underhanded scheme; a trick.
3. a mechanical contrivance for some purpose; an invention.
4. invention; faculty of devising. [Archaic.]
Full of noble *device*. —Shak.
5. anything fancifully conceived, as a picture, pattern, piece of embroidery, etc.
6. an emblem intended to represent a family, person, action, or quality, with a suitable motto: used in painting, sculpture, and heraldry.
7. the motto attached to or suited for such an emblem.
A youth, who bore, 'mid snow and ice,
A banner with the strange *device*,
Excelsior! —Longfellow.

DEVICES
1. device of Henry VII. 2. device of Anne Boleyn

8. the act or power of inventing or contriving. [Archaic.]
Syn.—contrivance, invention, design, scheme, project, stratagem, emblem, motto.

dē·vīce′fu̇l, *a.* full of devices; inventive. [Rare.]

dē·vīce′fu̇l·ly, *adv.* inventively. [Rare.]

dev′il, *n.* [ME. *devil*; AS. *deoful*; LL. *diabolus*, the devil; Gr. *diabolos*, the devil, lit. a slanderer, from *dia-*, through, across, and *ballein*, to throw.]
1. [sometimes D–] in theology, (a) the chief evil spirit, a supernatural being subordinate to, and the foe of, God and the tempter of man; Satan (with *the*): he is typically depicted as a man with horns, a tail, and cloven feet; (b) any of such subordinate beings who reside in hell; a demon.
2. a very wicked person.
Have I not chosen you twelve, and one of you is a *devil?* —John vi. 70.
3. any great evil.
To be tax'd, and beaten, is the *devil*. —Granville.
4. a person who is sprightly, mischievous, energetic, etc.
5. an unlucky, unhappy person; as, that poor *devil* has had a hard time.
6. anything difficult; a thing hard to operate or control, etc.
7. a marsupial animal, *Dasyurus ursinus*, of great ferocity: native to Tasmania.
8. a printer's errand boy or apprentice; formerly, the boy who took the printed sheets from the tympan of the press.
9. a machine with teeth for cutting up rags.
between the devil and the deep; between equally unpleasant alternatives.
devil's advocate; in the Roman Catholic Church, the Promotor of the Faith, the official critic of names proposed for canonization; hence, a person who upholds the wrong side, perversely or for argument's sake.
devil's-coach horse; (a) the wheel bug; (b) in England, *Ocypus olens*, the rove beetle.
printer's devil; see *devil*, n. 8.
Tasmanian devil; see *devil*, n. 7.
the devil's tattoo; a monotonous, rapid, drumming, as with the hands or feet.
the devil take the hindmost; leave the last, slowest, or least able to his fate without bothering about him.
the devil to pay; trouble ahead.
to give the devil his due; to acknowledge the ability or success of even a wicked or unpleasant person.
to play the devil with; to upset; to mismanage; to render inefficient or valueless.

dev′il, *v.t.*; deviled *or* devilled, *pt., pp.*; deviling *or* devilling, *ppr.* 1. [from the notion of heat.] to prepare (food) with seasoning, condiments, etc.
2. to tear up (rags, etc.) with a special machine.
3. to annoy; torment; tease.

dev′il·bĭrd, *n.* a bird of the genus *Dicrurus*, native to India; the drongo shrike.

dev′il dog, [English of *Teufel Hund*.] a U. S. marine: a name applied by the Germans in in World War I.

dev′iled, *a.* [pp. of *devil*: with reference to heat.] prepared with strong seasoning; as, *deviled* ham: also spelled *devilled*.

dev′il·ess, *n.* a she-devil. [Rare.]

dev′il·et, *n.* a devilkin; a little devil. [Rare.]

dev′il·fish, *n.*; *pl.* **dev′il·fish, dev′il·fish·eṣ,**
1. the largest kind of ray: so called because its pectoral fins are hornlike when rolled up.
2. any large cephalopod, especially the octopus.
3. the angler (a fish).
4. the gray whale.

DEVILFISH (20 ft. across)

dev′il·ing, *n.* a young devil.

dev′il·ish, *a.* [ME. *deoflich*; AS. *deoflic*, devilish, from *deoful*, devil.]
1. having the qualities of a devil or devils; diabolical; very evil and mischievous; malicious; as, a *devilish* scheme.
2. mischievous; energetic; reckless.
3. extremely bad. [Colloq.]
4. excessive; enormous; as, a *devilish* cheat. [Colloq.]
Syn.—atrocious, diabolical, impious, malicious, satanic, wicked.

dev′il·ish, *adv.* extremely; excessively; very. [Colloq.]

dev′il·ish·ly, *adv.* in a manner suiting the devil; diabolically; wickedly.

dev′il·ish·ness, *n.* the quality of being devilish.

dev′il·iṣm, *n.* same as *devilishness*.

dev′il·īze, *v.t.*; devilized, *pt., pp.*; devilizing, *ppr.* to make devilish.

dev′il·kin, *n.* a little devil.

dev′illed, *a.* same as *deviled*.

dev′il-māy-ċāre′, *a.* careless; heedless; reckless.

dev′il·ment, *n.* 1. evil behavior or action.
2. roguish mischief or trickery without ill intent.

dev′il·ry, *n.*; *pl.* **dev′il·rieṣ,** 1. evil conduct; malice.
2. reckless mischief, fun, etc.; deviltry.
3. devils or evil spirits collectively.

dev′il′ṣ-ā″prŏn, *n.* an alga of the genus *Laminaria*.

dev′il′ṣ-bit, *n.* the blazing star, a plant; also, any plant of the genus *Scabiosa*.

dev′il′ṣ-ċot″tŏn, *n.* *Abroma augusta*, an East Indian fiber plant.

dev′il′ṣ dāi′ṣy, the whiteweed, or oxeye daisy.

dev′il′ṣ-därn′ing-nee′dle, *n.* a dragonfly.

dev′il′ṣ-fo͞od ċāke, reddish-brown chocolate cake made with sour milk.

dev′il′ṣ-guts, *n.* *Cuscuta epithymum*, dodder, a plant parasitic on furze, heath, thyme, and other plants.

dev′il·ship, *n.* the person or character of a devil.

dev′il′ṣ-tree, *n.* *Alstonia scholaris*, an evergreen tropical tree of the eastern hemisphere producing dita bark: also called *devil tree*.

dev′il·try, *n.*; *pl.* **dev′il·trieṣ,** reckless mischief; fun, etc.; devilry.

dev′il·wood, *n.* *Osmanthus americanus*, the American olive, growing in the southern United States. It has whitish bark, glossy leaves, greenish flowers, and hard wood.

dev′il wŏr′ship, worship paid to the devil or an evil spirit.

dē′vi·ous, *a.* [L. *devius*, out of the way, off the road; *de*, off, from, and *via*, road.]
1. roundabout; winding; rambling.
2. deviating from the proper course; going astray; crooked.
Thoughts of love on a darkened and *devious* spirit. —Longfellow.
Syn.—circuitous, roundabout, erratic, roving, rambling, erring, straying.

dē′vi·ous·ly, *adv.* in a devious manner.

dē′vi·ous·ness, *n.* departure from a regular course; wandering.

dē·vĩr′ġin·āte, *a.* deflowered. [Obs.]

dē·vĩr′ġin·āte, *v.t.* to deflower. [Obs.]

dē·vĩr·ġi·nā′tion, *n.* a deflowering. [Obs.]

dē·viṣ′ȧ·ble, *a.* that can be devised.

dē·viṣ′ăl, *n.* a devising.

dē·vīṣe′, *v.t.* and *v.i.*; devised, *pt., pp.*; devising, *ppr.* [ME. *devisen, devysen*; OFr. *deviser*, to distribute, direct, regulate, talk, from L. *divisus*, pp. of *dividere*, to divide.]

1. to invent; to contrive; to form in the mind by new combinations of ideas, new applications of principles, or new arrangements of parts; to plan; to scheme; to project.

2. in law, to give or bequeath (real property) by will.

3. to divide. [Obs.]

4. to guess; to divine. [Obs.]

dē·vīse′, *n.* 1. a gift of real property by will. The term was formerly sometimes applied, though improperly, to bequest of personal estate.

2. a will, or clause in a will, granting such a gift.

dev·i·see′, *n.* the person to whom a devise is made; one to whom real property is bequeathed.

dē·vīs′ẽr, *n.* one who contrives or invents.

dē·vīs′ŏr, *n.* in law, a person who devises property; a testator.

dē·vī″tăl·i·zā′tion, *n.* 1. a devitalizing.

2. a divitalized condition.

dē·vī′tăl·īze, *v.t.* 1. to kill; to make lifeless.

2. to weaken; to deprive of vitality or the power to sustain vitality.

dev·i·tā′tion, *n.* an escaping; a warning off. [Obs.]

dē·vit″ri·fi·çā′tion, *n.* a devitrifying or being devitrified.

dē·vit′ri·fȳ, *v.t.*; devitrified, *pt., pp.*; devitrifying, *ppr.* 1. to take away or destroy the glassy qualities of.

2. to make (glass, etc.) opaque, hard, and crystalline, as by prolonged heating.

dē·vō″căl·i·zā′tion, *n.* the act of devocalizing or state of being devocalized.

dē·vō′căl·īze, *v.t.*; devocalized, *pt., pp.*; devocalizing, *ppr.* in phonetics, to make (a voiced sound) voiceless.

dē·voice′, *v.t.*; devoiced, *pt., pp.*; devoicing, *ppr.* same as *unvoice.*

dē·void′, *v.t.* [ME. *devoiden*, to make empty, to leave; OFr. *desvoidier*, to empty out; *des-*, from, and *voidier*, to make empty; *void*, empty.] to avoid; also, to destroy. [Obs.]

dē·void′, *a.* 1. void; empty; vacant. [Obs.]

2. destitute; not possessing: with *of*; as, *devoid of* understanding.

de·voir′ (de-vwär′), *n.*; *pl.* **de·voirs′,** [Fr., duty, from *devoir*, to owe; L. *debere*, to owe, to be indebted to.]

1. duty.

2. an act of due respect or courtesy: now used in the plural; as, pay your *devoirs* to her.

dev·ō·lū′tion, *n.* [L. *devolutus*, pp. of *devolvere*, to roll down.]

1. originally, a rolling down or falling.

2. a passing down from stage to stage.

3. the passing (of property, qualities, rights, authority, etc.) from one person to another.

4. a delegating (of duties) to a substitute or subordinate.

5. in biology, degeneration: opposed to *evolution*.

dē·volve′, *v.t.* and *v.i.*; devolved, *pt., pp.*; devolving, *ppr.* [L. *devolvere*, to roll down.]

1. originally, to roll down or onward.

2. to pass (*on*) to another or others: said of duties, responsibilities, etc.; as, the work *devolves on* the foreman when the superintendent is ill.

dē·volve′ment, *n.* the act of devolving; devolution.

Dev′ŏn, *n.* one of a breed of red, hardy, small-sized cattle, originally raised in Devonshire, England.

Dē·vō′ni·ăn, *a.* 1. of or pertaining to Devonshire, England.

2. in geology, designating or of the period after the Silurian and before the Carboniferous in the Paleozoic Era, marked by the dominance of the fish and the appearance of the first amphibians: so called because its rocks were first studied in Devonshire.

Dē·vō′ni·ăn, *n.* 1. a native or inhabitant of Devon or Devonshire.

2. in geology, the Devonian period.

dev·ō·rā′tion, *n.* the act of devouring. [Obs.]

dē·vō′tȧ·ry, *n.* a votary. [Obs.]

dē·vōte′, *v.t.*; devoted, *pt., pp.*; devoting, *ppr.* [L. *devotus*, pp. of *devovere*, to vow; *de-*, from, and *vovere*, to vow.]

1. to appropriate by vow; to set apart or dedicate by a solemn act; to consecrate.

2. to give up or apply (oneself or one's time, energy, etc.) to some purpose, activity, or person.

3. to doom; to consign to destruction; to curse. [Rare.]

Syn.—dedicate, hallow, destine, consign, doom.

dē·vōte′, *a.* devoted; devout [Archaic.]

dē·vōte′, *n.* a devotee. [Obs.]

dē·vōt′ed, *a.* 1. vowed; dedicated; consecrated.

2. very loyal; faithful.

3. doomed. [Rare.]

dē·vōt′ed·ly, *adv.* in a devoted manner.

dē·vōt′ed·ness, *n.* the state of being devoted.

dev·ō·tee′, *n.* 1. one who is wholly devoted to something or someone.

2. one given wholly to religion; one who is superstitiously given to religious duties and ceremonies; a bigot.

dev·ō·tee′ism, *n.* the state of a devotee; the tendency to become a devotee.

dē·vōte′ment, *n.* the act of devoting; the state of being devoted.

dē·vōt′ẽr, *n.* one who devotes; a worshiper.

dē·vō′tion, *n.* [ME. *devotioun*; OFr. *devotion*; L. *devotio*, a devoting, consecrating, from *devovere*, to vow, devote.]

1. the fact, quality, or state of being devoted.

2. piety; devoutness.

3. religious worship.

4. [*pl.*] prayers.

5. loyalty; faithfulness; deep affection.

6. the act of devoting.

7. something consecrated; an object of devotion. [Rare.]

8. disposal; power of disposing. [Obs.]

Syn.—consecration, devotedness, piety, zeal, ardor, earnestness, devoutness.

dē·vō′tion·ăl, *a.* pertaining to devotion; used in devotion; having to do with worship.

dē·vō′tion·ăl·ist, *n.* a devotionist. [Rare.]

dē·vō·tion·al′i·ty, *n.* devotion as practiced by a devotionist. [Rare.]

dē·vō′tion·ăl·ly, *adv.* in a devotional manner; toward devotion; as, *devotionally* inclined.

dē·vō′tion·ist, *n.* a person given to devotion; one superstitiously or formally devout. [Rare.]

dē·vō′tō, *n.*; *pl.* **dē·vō′tōes,** [It.] a devotee. [Obs.]

dē·vour′, *v.t.*; devoured, *pt., pp.*; devouring, *ppr.* [ME. *devouren*; OFr. *devorer*; L. *devorare*, to devour, to eat greedily; *de-*, intens., and *vorare*, to swallow whole.]

1. to eat up; to eat with greediness; to eat ravenously, as a beast of prey.

2. to destroy; to consume wantonly and with violence; to annihilate; to waste.

I waste my life and do my days *devour*.
—Spenser.

3. to enjoy with avidity; to gaze upon or listen to eagerly.

4. to absorb completely; engross; as, he is *devoured* by curiosity.

5. to swallow up; engulf.

Syn.—consume, annihilate, waste, destroy.

dē·vour′ẽr, *n.* one who or that which devours.

dē·vour′ing·ly, *adv.* in a devouring manner.

dē·vour′ment, *n.* the act or process of devouring.

dē·vout′, *a.* [ME. *devout*; OFr. *devot*, devout; L. *devotus*, pp. of *devovere*, to vow, devote.]

1. pious; very religious.

We must be constant and *devout* in the worship of God. —Rogers.

2. expressing devotion or piety; as, eyes *devout*.

3. sincere; earnest; as, you have my *devout* wishes for your safety.

Syn.—holy, pious, religious, reverent, sincere, earnest.

dē·vout′, *n.* 1. a devotee. [Obs.]

2. the whole or a part of a devotional composition. [Obs.]

dē·vout′fụl, *a.* full of or characterized by devoutness; devout. [Rare.]

dē·vout′less, *a.* without devoutness.

dē·vout′less·ly, *adv.* without devotion.

dē·vout′less·ness, *n.* lack of devotion.

dē·vout′ly, *adv.* 1. in a devout manner; with ardent devotion; piously; religiously.

2. sincerely; solemnly; earnestly.

dē·vout′ness, *n.* the quality or state of being devout.

dē·vōve′, *v.t.* to devote. [Obs.]

dē·vow′, *v.t.* 1. to give up. [Obs.]

2. to disavow; to disclaim. [Obs.]

dē·vul′găr·īze, *v.t.* to deprive of what is vulgar, commonplace, or narrow.

dew, *n.* [ME. *dew*; AS. *deaw*, dew.]

1. the atmospheric moisture that condenses after a warm day and appears during the night in little drops on cool surfaces.

2. anything regarded as refreshing, gently falling, pure, etc., like dew.

3. any moisture in small drops; as, the *dew* of his brow.

4. something emblematic of dawn, youth, freshness, and vigor.

Having the *dew* of his youth, and the beauty thereof. —Longfellow.

dew, *v.t.* to wet with or as with dew; to moisten.

dē·wan′, *n.* [Hind. *diwan*, a council, minister, a head officer in charge of finance and revenue, from Per. *divan*, an account book.] in India, any of various governmental officials.

dē·wa′ni, dē·wan′ny, *n.* [Hind.] the office held by a dewan.

Dew′ăr (flask), [after Sir James *Dewar* (1842–1923), Scot. physicist who invented it.] a double-walled flask with a vacuum between the walls that are silvered on the inside, used especially for storage of liquefied gases.

dē·wa′tẽr, *v.t.* to remove water from.

dew′ber″ry, *n.*; *pl.* **dew′ber″ries,** 1. any of various trailing blackberry plants belonging to the genus *Rubus*; especially in England, *Rubus cæsius*.

2. the fruit of any of these plants.

dew′cląw, *n.* 1. a functionless digit on the foot of some animals, as on the inner side of a dog's hind leg or above the true hoof in cattle, deer, etc.

2. the claw or hoof at the end of such a digit.

dew′çup, *n.* *Alchemilla vulgaris*, the lady's-mantle.

dew′drop, *n.* a drop of dew.

dew′fąll, *n.* 1. the falling of dew.

2. the early evening when dew begins to fall.

dew′i·ly, *adv.* in the manner of dew.

dew′i·ness, *n.* the condition or quality of being dewy; moisture; freshness.

dew′lap, *n.* 1. a loose fold of skin that hangs from the throat of cattle and certain other animals.

2. the flesh on the human throat when flaccid with age.

And on the withered *dewlap* pour the ale.
—Shak.

dew′lapped (-lapt), *a.* provided with a dewlap.

dew′less, *a.* having no dew.

DEW līne (dọọ), [*D*istant *E*arly *W*arning.] a line of radar stations near the 70th parallel in North America.

dē·worm′, *v.t.* same as *worm* (*v.t.* 4).

dew point, the temperature at which dew begins to form or vapor to condense into a liquid.

dew′ret, *v.t.* to rot, as hemp or flax, by subjecting to the process of dewretting.

dew′ret″ting, *n.* the spreading of hemp or flax on grass to expose it to the action of dew, rain, and sunshine, so as to hasten the separation of the fiber from the feculent matter.

dew′rot, *v.t.* to dewret.

dew′wŏrm, *n.* same as *earthworm*.

dew′y, *a.*; *comp.* dewier; *superl.* dewiest, 1. pertaining to, resembling, or characterized by dew; moist with dew; abounding in dew.

A *dewey* mist
Went up, and watered all the ground.
—Milton.

2. falling gently, or refreshing, like dew. [Poet.]

Dewey sleep ambrosial. —Cowper

dew′y-eyed (-īd), *a.* trustful, innocent, optimistic, etc.; not cynical or suspicious.

dex′e·drīne, *n.* a derivative of amphetamine, $(C_9H_{13}N)_2 \cdot H_2SO_4$, used as a central nervous system stimulant and appetite depressant: a trade-mark (*Dexedrine*).

dex·i·ō-, [from Gr. *dexios*.] a combining form meaning *on the right side*.

dex″i·ō·trop′iç, *a.* [*dexio-*, and Gr. *tropos*, a turning, from *trepein*, to turn.] turning or turned to the right; dextral, as a shell: opposed to *laeotropic*.

dex′tẽr, *a.* [L. *dexter*, on the right side, right.]

1. pertaining to or situated on the right hand; right, as opposed to left.

2. in heraldry, placed on that side of a shield which is toward the right of the wearer, or toward the left of the spectator in front: opposed to *sinister*.

3. favorable; auspicious. [Obs.]

dex·ter′i·ty, *n.* [L. *dexteritas*, skillfulness, handiness, from *dexter*, right, fit, prompt.]

1. ability to use the right hand more readily than the left; right-handedness. [Rare.]

2. suppleness; adroitness; expertness; skill in using one's hands or body.

Dexterity of hand, even in common trades, cannot be acquired without much practice and experience. —A. Smith.

3. readiness of mind in managing or controlling a scheme of operations; cleverness; mental adroitness.

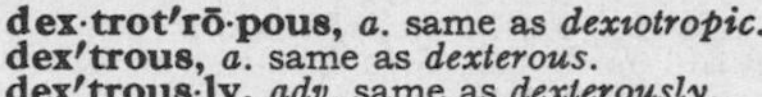

By his incomparable *dexterity*, he raised himself to the first throne of Italy. —Macaulay.

Syn.—art, ability, expertness, aptness, facility, aptitude, adroitness, skill, cleverness.

dex'tẽr·ous, dex'trous, *a.* [L. *dexter*, right.]
1. ready and expert in the use of the body or hands; skillful and active in manual employment; adroit; as, a *dexterous* workman.
2. having or showing mental skill; expert; quick at inventing expedients; as, a *dexterous* manager.
Dexterous the craving, fawning crowd to quit. —Pope.
3. right-handed. [Rare.]
Syn.—artful, skillful, clever, adroit, expert, apt, active.

dex'tẽr·ous·ly, dex'trous·ly, *adv.* with dexterity; expertly; skillfully; artfully; adroitly; promptly.

dex'tẽr·ous·ness, dex'trous·ness, *n.* dexterity; adroitness.

dextr-, same as *dextro-*.

dex'trad, *adv.* toward the right hand; to the right side; dextrally.

dex'trăl, *a.* 1. on the right-hand side; right.
2. right-handed.
3. having whorls that rise to the apex in counterclockwise spirals: said of the shells of certain mollusks.
Opposed to *sinistral*.

dex·tral'i·ty, *n.* 1. the state of having the right side differing from the left.
2. right-handedness.

dex'trăl·ly, *adv.* in a dextral way or direction.

dex'trăn, dex'trāne, *n.* [from L. *dexter*, right.] a white, amorphous gum, $C_6H_{10}O_5$, formed in milk by fermentation. It also occurs in unripe beet root.

dex·trẽr', *n.* a destrer. [Obs.]

dex'trin, dex'trine, *n.* [from L. *dexter*, right, and *-ine*: so called from its property of rotating the plane of polarization to the right.] a soluble, gummy substance obtained from starch and used as an adhesive, for sizing, etc. Its composition is the same as that of starch. By the action of hot diluted acids, or of an infusion of malt, dextrin is finally converted into grape sugar. It is used as a substitute for gum arabic in medicine. Called also *gommelin*, *British gum*, *starch gum*.

dex'trō, *a.* in chemistry, dextrorotatory.

dex·trō-, [from Latin *dexter*, right.] a combining form meaning: (a) *toward* (or *on*) *the right-hand side*, as in *dextro*rotatory; (b) in chemistry, *dextrorotatory*. Also, before a vowel, *dextr-*.

dex·trō·cär'di·a, *n.* [*dextro-*, and Gr. *kardia*, the heart.] same as *dexiocardia*.

dex'trō·com"pound, *n.* a chemical compound which causes the plane of a ray of polarized light to rotate to the right, as dextrin, dextroglucose, malic acid, etc.

dex·trō·glū'cōse, *n.* same as *dextrose*.

dex·trō·gȳ'rāte, *a.* [*dextro-*, and L. *gyratus*, circular, pp. of *gyrare*, to turn, from *gyrus*, a circle.] same as *dextrorotatory*.

dex·trō·gȳ'rous, *a.* [*dextro-*, and L. *gyrus*, a circle.] same as *dextrorotatory*.

dex·tron'iç, *a.* pertaining to dextrose; obtained from dextrose.
dextronic acid; a compound obtained as a sirupy liquid from glucose, starch, dextrine, etc.: called also *gluconic acid*, *maltonic acid*.

dex·trō·rō'tȧ·ry, *a.* same as *dextrorotatory*.

dex"trō·rō·tā'tion, *n.* dextrorotatory direction or movement.

dex·trō·rō'tȧ·tō·ry, *a.* 1. turning or circling to the right, in a clockwise direction.
2. that turns the plane of polarized light clockwise: said of certain crystals, etc.
Opposed to *levorotatory*.

dex·tror'săl, *a.* same as *dextrorse*.

dex'trorse, *a.* [L. *dextrorsum*, or *dextrovorsum*, toward the right; *dexter*, right, and *versus* or *vorsus*, pp. of *vertere* or *vortere*, to turn.] in botany, twining upward to the right, as the stem of the hop: opposed to *sinistrorse*.

dex'trōse, *n.* a crystalline, dextrorotatory sugar, $C_6H_{12}O_6$, found in plants and animals and in the human body, and made commercially by the reaction of starch and sulfuric acid; glucose: called also *dextroglucose*, *grape sugar*, and *starch sugar*.

DEXTRORSE VINE (of morning-glory)

dex·trō·trop'iç, *a.* same as *dexiotropic*.

dex·trot'rō·pous, *a.* same as *dexiotropic*.

dex'trous, *a.* same as *dexterous*.

dex'trous·ly, *adv.* same as *dexterously*.

dex'trous·ness, *n.* same as *dexterousness*.

dey, *n.* [Fr. *dey*; Turk. *day*, a maternal uncle, a friendly title formerly given to middle-aged or old people.
1. a Turkish title of the governor of Algiers before the French conquest in 1830.
2. formerly, a pasha or ruler of Tunis or Tripoli.

dey, *n.* [ME. *dey*, *deye*; Ice. *deigja*, a maidservant.] a dairy servant, usually a woman; any woman servant. [Dial.]

deye (dā), *v.i.* to die. [Obs.]

dē·ziñç"i·fi·çā'tion, *n.* the act or process of dezincifying.

dē·ziñç'i·fȳ, *v.t.*; dezincified, *pt.*, *pp.*; dezincifying, *ppr.* to free from zinc.

dhak (dak), *n.* [Hind.] an East Indian tree, *Butea frondosa*.

dhäl (dol), *n.* same as *dal*.

dham'noo (dam'), *n.* an East Indian tree which yields a very tough, pliable wood.

dhär'mȧ (där'), *n.* [Sans., law.] in Buddhism and Hinduism, religious observances; conformity to the law; duty; virtue.

dhär'nȧ (där'), *n.* [Hind. *dharnā*.] in India, a method of trying to get justice by sitting at the door of one's debtor or wrongdoer and fasting to death or until satisfaction is given: also *dhurna*.

dhō'bie, dhō'by (dō'bi), *n.* [Hind. *dhobī*, a washerman, from *dhob*, a washing.] an East Indian term for a manservant who does washing.

dhōle (dōl), *n.*; *pl.* **dhōleş, dhōle,** [E. Ind. name.] a wild mountain dog, *Canis dukhunensis*, found in the southeastern part of Asia. It seldom hunts alone, but pursues its prey in packs.

dhōll (dōl), *n.* an East Indian name for the pigeon pea.

dhō'ney, dhō'ny (dō'), *n.* same as *doni*.

dhō'ti, dhōo'ti (dō'), *n.* [Hind. *dhotī*.] 1. the loincloth worn by Hindus.
2. the cloth used for it.

dhöur'rȧ, dhụr'rȧ (dür'), *n.* same as *durra*.

dhow (dou), *n.* [Ar.] a single-masted ship with a lateen sail, sharp prow, deep forefoot, and raised deck at the stern, used in the Red Sea and Indian Ocean.

dhun'chee (dun'chē), *n.* [E. Ind.] a tropical shrub, *Sesbania aculeata*, having a hemplike fiber.

dhūr'nȧ, *n.* same as *dharna*.

dī, *n.* [arbitrary modification of *do*.] in music, a syllable representing the tone intermediate between do and re of the diatonic scale.

di-, [from L. *di-*, Gr. *di-*, two, double, from Gr. *dyo*, two.] a prefix meaning: (a) *twice*, *double*, *twofold*, as in *di*chroism, *di*cotyledon; (b) in chemistry, *having two* (atoms, molecules, radicals, etc.), as in *di*acid.

di-, same as *dis-* (separation, deprivation, etc.).

Di, in chemistry, *the symbol for* didymium.

di'a-, di-, [from L. *dia-*, Gr. *dia-*, through, from *dia*, through.] prefixes meaning: (a) *through*, *throughout*, *across*, as in *dia*phragm, *dia*gonal; (b) *apart*, *between*, as in *dia*gnose, *dia*critical.

dī'ȧ·bāse, *n.* [Fr., from Gr. *diabasis*, a crossing over; *dia-*, through, and *bainein*, to go.]
1. formerly, diorite.
2. a dark-colored igneous rock, made up largely of augite and feldspar.

dī·ab·ȧ·tē'ri·ăl, *a.* [Gr. *diabatēria* (supply *hiera*), sacrifices, offerings for a happy passage, from *diabainein*, to go across.] crossing the limits. [Rare.]

dī·ȧ·bē'tēş, *n.* [L., from Gr. *diabētēs*, a siphon, from *diabainein*, to pass through.] a diseased condition of the system, characterized by an excessive discharge of urine: there are various types of diabetes.
diabetes insipidus; diabetes in which the urine is normal, of low specific gravity, and excessive.
diabetes mellitus; a chronic form of diabetes characterized by excess of sugar in the blood and urine, hunger, thirst, and gradual loss of weight: also called *sugar diabetes*.

dī·ȧ·bet'iç, dī·ȧ·bet'iç·ăl, *a.* pertaining to diabetes; affected with diabetes.

dī·ȧ·bet'iç, *n.* a person who has diabetes.

di·äb'le·rie, di·äb'le·ry, *n.* [Fr. *diablerie*; OFr. *diablerie*, from *diable*, devil.]
1. sorcery; devil's work; witchcraft.
2. devil lore.
3. deviltry; diabolic acts or practices.

dī·ȧ·bol'iç, dī·ȧ·bol'iç·ăl, *a.* [LL. *diabolicus*, devilish, from *diabolus*; Gr. *diabolos*, the devil.]
1. of the Devil or devils.
2. very wicked or cruel; fiendish; devilish; demoniacal.

dī·ȧ·bol'iç·ăl·ly, *adv.* in a diabolical manner; very wickedly; nefariously.

dī·ȧ·bol'iç·ăl·ness, *n.* the state of being diabolic.

dī·ȧ·bol'i·fȳ, *v.t.*; diabolified, *pt.*, *pp.*; diabolifying, *ppr.* to ascribe diabolical qualities to.

dī·ab'ō·lişm, *n.* 1. dealing or dealings with the Devil or devils; sorcery; witchcraft.
2. belief in or worship of the Devil or devils.
3. diabolical action or behavior.
4. the character or condition of the Devil or a devil.

dī·ab'ō·list, *n.* 1. an authority on diabolism.
2. a devil worshiper.

dī·ab'ō·lō, *n.* [c. 1907; prob. from Gr. *dia-*, across, and *bolē*, a throw, from *ballein*, to throw, but associated with It. *diavolo*, a devil.] a game played with a wooden spool which is whirled and tossed on a string tied to two sticks held one in each hand.

dī"ȧ·bō·lol'ō·ġy, *n.* [Gr. *diabolos*, the devil, and *logos*, a description, from *legein*, to speak.] the literature, legends, and traditions about the devil; devil lore.

Dī·ȧ·brot'i·çȧ, *n.* [L., from Gr. *diabrotikos*, able to eat through; *dia*, through, and *bibrōskein*, to devour.] a large genus of beetles, including the common striped cucumber beetle. They are very destructive to fruit trees, vegetables, etc.

dī"ȧ·çȧ·thol'i·çon, *n.* [L., from Gr. *dia*, through, and *katholikos*, universal.] a purgative having a number of constituents, supposed to be of general efficacy. [Obs.]

dī·ȧ·çaus'tiç, *a.* in mathematics, belonging to a species of caustic curves or surfaces formed by refraction.

dī·ȧ·çaus'tiç, *n.* 1. a diacaustic curve or surface.
2. in medicine, a double-convex lens sometimes used for cauterization.

dī·ȧ·chē'ni·um, *n.*; *pl.* **dī·ȧ·chē'ni·ȧ,** same as *cremocarp*.

dī·ach'y·lon, dī·ach'y·lum, *n.* [ML., from Gr. *diachylos*, very juicy; *dia-*, through, and *chylos*, juice.] a plaster, originally composed of the juices of several plants, whence its name, now made of lead oxide, olive oil, and water.

dī·ac'id, *a.* 1. containing in each molecule two atoms of hydrogen replaceable by basic atoms or radicals: usually said of acids and acid salts.
2. capable of forming a salt or ester by reacting with one molecule of a diacid, or two of a monoacid: usually said of bases and alcohols.

dī·ac'id, *n.* an acid having in each molecule two hydrogen atoms which can be replaced by a metal or react with basic substances.

dī·aç'lȧ·sis, *n.* [L., from Gr. *diaklan*, to break in two; *dia*, through, apart, and *klan*, to break.] refraction.

dī·ȧ·clī'năl, *a.* [*dia-*, and Gr. *klinein*, to lean.] in geology, crossing a fold; as, a *diaclinal* fissure.

dī·ȧ·cō'di·um, *n.* [L. *diacodion*, a medicine made from poppy juice, from Gr. *dia*, through, from, and *kōdeia*, a poppy head.] a sirup of poppies.

dī·aç'ō·năl, *a.* [L. *diaconus*, a deacon.] pertaining to a deacon or deacons.

dī·aç'ō·nāte, *n.* 1. the rank, tenure, or office of a deacon.
2. a board of deacons; deacons collectively.

dī·ȧ·çon'i·çon, dī·ȧ·çon'i·çum, *n.*; *pl.* **dī·ȧ·çon'i·çȧ,** [L. *diaconicum*; Gr. *diakonikon*, a place for storing the vessels, vestments, etc., from *diakonos*, a servant, a deacon.] in the Orthodox Eastern Church, (a) the sacristy; (b) [*pl.*] a deacon's manual.

dī·aç'ō·pē, *n.* [Gr. *diakopē*, a gash, from *diakoptein*, to cut through.]
1. in surgery, a deep cut; a longitudinal fracture. [Rare.]
2. in grammar, same as *tmesis*.

dī·ȧ·çöus'tiç (*or* -kows'), *a.* [Gr. *diakouein*, to hear through; *dia*, through, and *akouein*, to hear.] pertaining to the science or doctrine of refracted sounds.

dī·ȧ·çöus'tiçs, *n.* the science which treats of the properties of sound refracted by passing through different mediums: called also *diaphonics*.

dī"ȧ·çran·tē'ri·ăn, dī"ȧ·çran·ter'iç, *a.* [*dia-*, and Gr. *krantēres*, the wisdom teeth, lit. the performers or completers, from *krainein*, to accomplish, complete.] having the posterior and anterior teeth in rows somewhat apart, as certain snakes.

dī·ȧ·çrit′iç, *a.* [Gr. *diakritikos,* able to distinguish, from *diakrinein,* to separate, distinguish; *dia-,* across, and *krinein,* to divide, distinguish.]
1. diacritical.
2. in medicine, diagnostic.

dī·ȧ·çrit′iç, *n.* a diacritical mark.

dī·ȧ·çrit′iç·ăl, *a.* used to distinguish; distinguishing.
diacritical mark, sign, or *point;* any mark used with a letter or character to distinguish it from another or to indicate how it is pronounced. Examples: ä, ā, å, é.

dī·aç′ti·năl, dī·aç′tine, *a.* [*di-,* two, and Gr. *aktis* (*-inos*), a ray.] tapering at both ends; having two axes.

dī·aç·tin′iç, *a.* capable of transmitting actinic rays of light.

Dī·ȧ·del′phi·ȧ, *n.pl.* [Gr. *di-,* twice, and *adelphos,* brother.] a class of plants in the Linnaean system whose stamens are united into two bodies or bundles by their filaments.

dī·ȧ·del′phi·ăn, *a.* same as *diadelphous.*

dī·ȧ·del′phous, *a.* [from *di-,* twice, and Gr. *adelphos,* brother; and *-ous.*]
1. arranged in two bundles or sets by the fusion of the filaments: said of stamens.
2. having the stamens so arranged.

DIADELPHOUS STAMENS (of pea)

dī′ȧ·dem, *n.* [ME. *diademe;* OFr. *diademe;* L. *diadema;* Gr. *diadēma,* a band or fillet, from *diadein,* to bind round, encircle; *dia-,* through, and *dein,* to bind.]
1. a crown.
2. an ornamental cloth headband worn as a crown by Eastern kings, especially in ancient Persia.
3. a thing like a crown.
4. kingly power, authority, or dignity.
5. in heraldry, the arch supporting the globe at the top of a crown.

dī′ȧ·dem, *v.t.* to crown; to put a diadem on.

dī′ȧ·dem lē′mŭr, a Madagascan ruffed lemur, *Propithecus diadema,* about the size of a cat.

dī′ȧ·dem spī′dēr, the common spider, *Epeira diadema.*

Dī·ad′ō·chī, *n.pl.* [L., from Gr. *diadochoi,* pl. of *diadochos,* a successor, from *diadechesthai,* to receive from another, to succeed to; *dia,* through, and *dechesthai,* to take, receive.] the Macedonian generals who divided the empire of Alexander the Great among themselves, after his death.

Dī·ȧ·dō′chi·ăn, *a.* of or pertaining to the Diadochi.

Dī·ȧ·dō′chi·ăn, *n.* a member of the Diadochi.

dī′ȧ·drom, *n.* a course or passing; a vibration; the time in which the vibration of a pendulum is performed. [Obs.]

dī·aer′e·sis (-er′), *n.;* *pl.* **dī·aer′e·sēs,** same as *dieresis.*

dī·ae·ret′iç, *a.* same as *dieretic.*

dī·ȧ·ġē·ō·trop′iç, *a.* [*dia-,* and Gr. *gē,* earth, and *tropos,* a turning, from *trepein,* to turn.] of the nature of, relating to, or characterized by diageotropism.

dī″ȧ·ġē·ot′rō·piṣm, *n.* the inclination of the parts of a plant to form a right angle to the direction of gravitation.

dī′ȧ·glyph, *n.* [Gr. *diaglyphein,* to carve through; *dia,* through, and *glyphein,* to carve, hollow out.] an intaglio.

dī·ȧ·glyph′iç, dī·ȧ·glyp′tiç, *a.* depressed; pertaining to or having the characteristics of a diaglyph.

dī·ag·nōse′ (*or* -nōz′), *v.t.;* diagnosed, *pt., pp.;* diagnosing, *ppr.* to make a diagnosis of; recognize and identify (a disease, etc.) by examination and observation.

dī·ag·nōse′, *v.i.* to make diagnoses.

dī·ag·nō′sis, *n.;* *pl.* **dī·ag·nō′sēṣ,** [L., from Gr. *diagnōsis,* a distinguishing, discrimination, from *diagignōskein,* to distinguish, discern between; *dia-,* through, between, and *gignōskein,* to know.]
1. the act or process of deciding the nature of a diseased condition by examination.
2. a careful investigation of the facts to determine the nature of a thing.
3. the decision or opinion resulting from such examination or investigation.

dī·ag·nos′tiç, *a.* 1. of or constituting a diagnosis.
2. of value for a diagnosis; specifically characteristic.

dī·ag·nos′tiç, *n.* [Gr. *diagnōstikos,* able to distinguish.] in medicine, (a) the sign or symptom by which a disease is known or distinguished from others; (b) diagnosis.

dī·ag·nos′ti·căl·ly, *adv.* 1. by diagnosis.
2. with regard to diagnosis.

dī·ag·nos′ti·çāte, *v.t.* and *v.i.;* diagnosticated, *pt., pp.;* diagnosticating, *ppr.* to diagnose.

dī″ag·nos·ti′ciăn, *n.* a person who makes diagnoses; specifically, a specialist in diagnostics.

dī·ag·nos′tiçs, *n.pl.* [*construed as sing.*] that branch of medical science which treats of diagnosis.

dī·ȧ·gom′e·tẽr, *n.* [from Gr. *diagein,* to conduct; *dia,* through, and *agein,* to lead, and *metron,* a measure.] an instrument used to determine the relative conductivity of different substances, as of coffee and chicory. It is used to detect adulterants.

dī·ag′ō·năl, *a.* [L. *diagonalis;* Gr. *diagōnios,* from angle to angle, diagonal; *dia-,* through, and *gōnia,* an angle, corner.]
1. extending between the vertices of any two nonadjacent angles in a polygonal or polyhedral figure; extending slantingly between opposite corners.
2. having the general direction of a diagonal; slanting; oblique.
3. having slanting markings, lines, etc.
diagonal bond; masonry in which the stones are laid obliquely, instead of being bedded flat; herringbone work.
diagonal scale; a scale upon a flat ruler, in which equidistant parallels are laid down, with oblique lines crossing them: used for measuring small fractions of the unit of measure.

dī·ag′ō·năl, *n.* 1. a diagonal line or plane.
2. any diagonal course, row, order, or part.
3. cloth woven with diagonal lines.

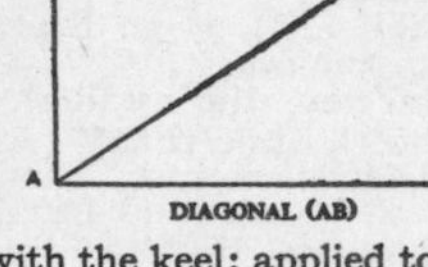

DIAGONAL (AB)

dī·ag′ō·năl-built (-bilt), *a.* sheathed in two transverse layers running oppositely, making an angle of 45 degrees with the keel: applied to a ship.

dī·ag′ō·năl·ly, *adv.* in a diagonal direction or manner; obliquely.

dī·ȧ·gō′ni·ăl, *a.* diagonal; opposite. [Obs.]

dī′ȧ·gram, *n.* [Fr. *diagramme;* L. *diagramma;* Gr. *diagramma,* that which is marked out by lines, a diagram, a scale, from *diagraphein,* to mark out by lines, to draw; *dia-,* through, across, and *graphein,* to write.]
1. a geometrical figure, often used to illustrate a theorem.
2. a sketch, drawing, or plan that explains a thing by outlining its parts, workings, etc.
3. a chart or graph explaining or illustrating ideas, statistics, etc.
4. formerly, in music, a scale.

dī′ȧ·gram, *v.t.;* diagramed *or* diagrammed, *pt., pp.;* diagraming *or* diagramming, *ppr.* to show or represent by a diagram; to make a diagram of; as, to *diagram* a sentence.

dī″ȧ·gram·mat′iç, *a.* 1. of, or having the form of, a diagram or diagrams.
2. merely outlined; sketchy.

dī″ȧ·gram·mat′i·çăl, *a.* same as *diagrammatic.*

dī″ȧ·gram·mat′iç·ăl·ly, *adv.* 1. in the form of a diagram.
2. by the use of a diagram; according to a diagram.

dī′ȧ·grȧph, *n.* [Fr. *diagraphe,* from Gr. *diagraphein,* to mark out by lines.] an instrument for drawing figures or projections of objects, used in drafting, consisting of a protractor and a scale.

dī·ȧ·graph′iç, dī·ȧ·graph′iç·ăl, *a.* of or pertaining to graphic representation. [Rare.]

dī·ȧ·graph′içs, *n.* the art or science of descriptive or mathematical drawing.

dī·ȧ·hē″li·ō·trop′iç, *a.* pertaining to diaheliotropism; showing a tendency to turn away from the sun.

dī·ȧ·hē·li·ot′rō·piṣm, *n.* the tendency of plants or their organs to assume a position transverse to the light.

dī″ȧ·ki·nē′sis, *n.* [from *dia-,* and Gr. *kinēsis,* motion.] in the meiosis of germ cells, a stage in which the maternal and paternal chromosomes have paired and lie near or on the nuclear membrane.

dī′ăl, *n.* [ME. *dial, dyal,* from ML. *dialis,* daily, from L. *dies,* day.]
1. an instrument for showing the hour of the day from the shadow thrown by a style or gnomon upon a graduated surface. When the shadow is cast by the sun it is called a sundial.
2. the face of a watch, clock, or other timekeeper, on which the time of the day is indicated.
3. a clock; a watch. [Obs.]
He drew a *dial* from his poke. —Shak.
4. a miner's compass.
5. any plate or face on which a pointer or index revolves, moves backward and forward, or oscillates, marking revolutions, pressure, etc., according to the nature of the machinery of which it forms part; as, the *dial* of a steam gauge, gas meter, or telegraphic instrument.
6. a vise to hold the stone in jewel cutting.
7. a graduated disk on a radio, especially one for tuning in stations.
8. a rotating disk on a telephone, used in making connections automatically: it consists of a circular plate marked around the rim with numbers and letters, combined with a perforated movable disk, by means of which the numbers and letters may be designated.
dial telephone; a telephone provided with and operated by a dial.

dī′ăl, *v.t.* and *v.i.;* dialed *or* dialled, *pt., pp.,* dialing *or* dialling, *ppr.* 1. to measure, survey, etc. with or as with a dial.
2. to show on a dial.
3. to tune in (a radio station, program, etc.).
4. to call by using a telephone dial.

dī′ăl bĭrd, a robinlike bird of the genus *Copsichus,* of India.

dī′ȧ·leçt, *n.* [Fr. *dialecte;* L. *dialectus;* Gr. *dialektos,* discourse, discussion, dialect, from *dialegesthai,* to discourse, talk; *dia-,* between, and *legein,* to choose, talk.]
1. the sum total of local characteristics of speech.
2. the sum total of an individual's characteristics of speech.
3. any form of speech considered as deviating from a real or imaginary standard speech.
4. English speech as employed by a foreign-born or minority group; as, the Milwaukee Polish *dialect.*
5. loosely, any jargon, cant, or patois.
6. in linguistics, the form or variety of a spoken language peculiar to a region, community, social group, or occupational group: in this sense, *dialects* are regarded as being, to some degree, mutually intelligible while *languages* are mutually unintelligible.
7. any language as part of a larger group or family of languages; as, English is a West Germanic *dialect.*

dī′ȧ·leçt, *a.* of or in dialect; as, *dialect* ballads.

dī·ȧ·leç′tăl, *a.* having the character of dialect.

dī·ȧ·leç′tăl·ly, *adv.* in the manner or form of dialect.

dī′ȧ·leçt at′lȧs, a collection of maps illustrating the regional distribution of dialect characteristics.

dī·ȧ·leç′tiç, *n.* [ME. *dialatik;* OFr. *dialetique;* L. *dialectica* (*ars*); Gr. *dialetikē* (*technē*), the dialectic (*art*), from *dialektikos,* dialect.]
1. the art or practice of examining opinions or ideas logically, often by the method of question and answer, so as to determine their validity; dialectics.
2. logical argumentation.
3. the method of logic used by Hegel and adapted by Marx to his materialist philosophy: it is based on the concept of the contradiction of opposites (*thesis* and *antithesis*) and their continual resolution (*synthesis*).

dī·ȧ·leç′tiç, dī·ȧ·leç′tiç·ăl, *a.* 1. dialectal.
2. of or using dialectic.

dī·ȧ·leç′tiç·ăl·ly, *adv.* 1. in a dialectical manner.
2. by means of dialectic.

dī·ȧ·leç′tiç·ăl mȧ·tē′ri·ăl·iṣm, the philosophy originated by Karl Marx and Friedrich Engels, an application of Hegel's logical method (dialectic) to philosophical materialism: the official doctrine of Communism.

dī″ȧ·leç·ti′ciăn (-tish′un), *n.* a logician; an expert in dialectic.

dī·ȧ·leç′ti·ciṣm, *n.* 1. the nature or effect of dialect.
2. a dialectical locution.
3. the use of dialectic.

dī·ȧ·leç′tiçs, *n.pl.* [*construed as sing.*] dialectic (sense 1).

dī″ȧ·leç·tol′ō·ġy, *n.* [Gr. *dialektos,* speech, dialect, and *logos,* description.] the branch of the science of language which has to do with dialects.

dī·ȧ·leç′tŏr, *n.* a dialectician.

dī′ăl·ing, dī′ăl·ling, *n.* 1. the act of one who dials.
 2. the art of making dials.
 3. measurement of time by dials.
 4. a method of surveying using a miner's compass.

dī′ăl·ist, *n.* a constructor of dials.

dī·al′lȧ·ġē, *n.* [Gr. *diallagē*, a change, from *diallassein*, to change, interchange; *dia-*, through, and *allassein*, to make a thing other than it is, to change, from *allos*, other, another.] a rhetorical figure by which arguments are considered from various points of view, and then turned to one point.

dī′ăl·lāġe, *n.* [Gr. *diallagē*, a change: so named from having unlike fracture planes.] a dark-green or bronze laminated mineral, a variety of pyroxene.

dī′ăl·lel, *a.* intersecting; not parallel. [Obs.]

dī·al′lyl, *n.* see *allyl*.

dī′ȧ·log, *n.*, *v.i.*, and *v.t.* same as *dialogue*.

dī·ȧ·log′iç, dī·ȧ·log′iç·ăl, *a.* of the form of, or pertaining to, a dialogue.

dī·ȧ·log′iç·ăl·ly, *adv.* in the manner of a dialogue.

dī·al′ō·ġiṣm, *n.* [from *dialogue*, and *-ism*.] a discussion of some subject in the form of an imaginary dialogue.

dī·al′ō·ġist, *n.* a speaker in a dialogue; also, a writer of dialogues.

dī″ăl·ō·ġis′tiç, dī″ăl·ō·ġis′tiç·ăl, *a.* having the form of a dialogue.

dī″ăl·ō·ġis′tiç·ăl·ly, *adv.* in the manner of a dialogue.

dī·al′ō·ġīte, *n.* [Gr. *dialogē*, an argument, doubt.] a rose-red mineral carbonate of manganese; rhodochrosite.

dī·al′ō·ġīze, *v.i.*; dialogized, *pt.*, *pp.*; dialogizing, *ppr.* to carry on a dialogue.

dī′ȧ·logue (-log), **dī′ȧ·log,** *n.* [Fr. *dialogue*; L. *dialogus*; Gr. *dialogos*, dialogue, conversation, from *dialegesthai*, to talk, converse; *dia-*, between, and *legein*, to talk.]
 1. a talking together; conversation.
 2. interchange and discussion of ideas, especially when open and frank, as in seeking mutual understanding or harmony.
 3. a written work in the form of a conversation.
 4. the passages of talk in a play, story, radio act, etc.

dī′ȧ·logue, *v.i.*; dialogued, *pt.*, *pp.*; dialoguing, *ppr.* to hold a conversation: also spelled *dialog*.

dī′ȧ·logue, dī′ȧ·log, *v.t.* to express in dialogue.

dī′ăl plāte, 1. the plate of a dial on which the lines are drawn to show the time of the day.
 2. the face of a clock or watch, on which the time of the day is shown.
 3. any kind of index plate.

dī′ăl tōne, a low buzzing sound indicating to the user of a dial telephone that the line is open and a number may be dialed.

dī·ȧ·lū′riç, *a.* [*di-*, and *alloxan*, and *uric*.] of or relating to an acid obtained from the action of uric acid on alloxan.

dī·al·y-, [from Gr. *dialyein*, to separate; *dia*, through, and *lyein*, to loose.] a combining form signifying *separate*, *distinct*.

dī″al·y·cär′pous, *a.* see *apocarpous*.

Dī″al·y·pet′ȧ·lae, *n.pl.* same as *polypetalæ*.

dī″al·y·pet′ăl·ous, *a.* same as *polypetalous*.

dī·ȧ·lyph′yl·lous, *a.* [*dialy-*, and Gr. *phyllon*, a leaf.] having distinct leaves, as a calyx.

dī″al·y·sep′ăl·ous, *a.* [*dialy-*, and L. *sephalum*, a sepal.] having separate sepals making up a calyx; polysepalous.

dī·al′y·sis, *n.*; *pl.* **dī·al′y·sēṣ,** [L.; Gr. *dialysis*, a separation, dissolution, from *dialyein*, to separate, dissolve; *dia-*, apart, and *lyein*, to loose.]
 1. in grammar, dieresis; specifically, in Latin grammar, the change of *j* into *i*, and *v* into *u*.
 2. in rhetoric, parenthesis or asyndeton.
 3. separation; dissolution.
 4. in chemistry, the act or process of separating mixed substances in solution, as crystalloids and colloids, by means of a moist membrane through which the crystalloids will pass easily, and the colloids very slowly, if at all.

dī·ȧ·lyt′iç, *a.* of or resembling dialysis.

dī·ȧ·lyt′iç·ăl·ly, *adv.* by means of dialysis.

dī·al′y·zāte, *n.* either of the parts of a mixture separated by dialysis; generally, the part that is diffused.

dī″ȧ·ly·zā′tion, *n.* dialysis.

dī′ȧ·lȳze, *v.t.*; dialyzed, *pt.*, *pp.*; dialyzing, *ppr.* to subject to or to separate by dialysis.

dī′ȧ·lȳ·zẽr, *n.* the apparatus by which chemical dialysis is accomplished.

dī·ȧ·mag′net, *n.* [*dia-*, and Gr. *magnēs*, a magnet.] any diamagnetic body.

dī″ȧ·mag·net′iç, *a.* pertaining to or characterized by diamagnetism.

dī″ȧ·mag·net′iç, *n.* any substance, as glass, bismuth, zinc, etc., which is diamagnetic in a magnetic field of force.

dī″ȧ·mag·net′iç·ăl·ly, *adv.* in a diamagnetic manner.

dī·ȧ·mag′net·iṣm, *n.* [*dia-*, and Gr. *magnēs*, a magnet.]
 1. the property that certain substances have of being repelled by both poles of a magnet and hence taking a position at right angles to the magnet's line of influence.
 2. diamagnetic force.
 3. diamagnetic phenomena.
 4. the science that deals with such phenomena and substances.

dī·ȧ·mag·net·om′e·tẽr, *n.* [*dia-*, and Gr. *magnēs*, a magnet, and *metron*, a measure.] an instrument for measuring the relative diamagnetism of substances.

dī″ȧ·man·tif′ẽr·ous, *a.* [Fr. *diamantifère*, from *diamant*, diamond, and L. *ferre*, to bear, carry.] yielding or producing diamonds.

dī·ȧ·man′tine, *a.* adamantine. [Obs.]

dī·am′e·tẽr, *n.* [ME. *diametre*; OFr. *diametre*; L. *diametros*; Gr. *diametros*, a diameter; *dia-*, through, and *metron*, a measure.]
 1. a straight line passing through the center of a circle, sphere, etc. from one side to the other.

DIAMETER

 2. the length of such a line; measurement across; width or thickness of a thing; as, the *diameter* of the tube is one inch.
 3. in optics, the unit of measure of the magnifying power of a lens.
 4. in architecture, the measure across the lower part of the shaft of a column, which, being divided into 60 parts, forms a scale by which all the parts of the order are measured.

dī·am′e·trăl, *a.* diametrical; relating or pertaining to a diameter.
 diametral curve; a bisector of parallel chords drawn in a curve.
 diametral plane; a plane which bisects a system of parallel chords drawn in a surface.

dī·am′e·trăl, *n.* the diameter. [Obs.]

dī·am′e·trăl·ly, *adv.* diametrically.

dī·ȧ·met′riç·ăl, dī·ȧ·met′riç, *a.* 1. of or pertaining to a diameter.
 2. directly opposed; contrary.
 3. direct; exact: said of opposites.

dī·ȧ·met′riç·ăl·ly, *adv.* 1. in a diametrical way; as a diameter; straight through.
 2. directly or exactly (with *opposed*, *opposite*, etc.).

dī·am′ide, *n.* [*di-*, two, *ammonia*, and *-ide*.] any of a class of compounds formed from a double molecule of ammonia $(NH_3)_2$, by replacement of hydrogen with a bivalent acid radical.

dī·am′īne, dī·am′in (*or* dī′ȧ-min), *n.* any of a group of chemical compounds containing two NH_2 radicals; double amine.

dī′ȧ·mŏnd (*or* dī′mŏnd), *n.* [ME. *diamaunde*; OFr. *diamant*, diamond; L. *adamas* (*-antis*); Gr. *adamas*, adamant, the diamond.]
 1. nearly pure carbon in crystalline form: it is noted for its power of refracting light, its great brilliance, and it is one of the hardest of known substances. Its specific gravity is 3.5 to 3.6. The greater part of the supply of diamonds is from South Africa, but some are found in Brazil, India, Borneo, and, rarely, in the United States.
 2. a piece of this substance, used as a gem and in cutting tools, wiredrawing dies, etc.
 3. a plane figure made up of four straight lines, the opposite sides equal and parallel, two of the interior angles acute and two obtuse; a lozenge; a rhombus.
 4. a red, lozenge-shaped mark on some playing cards.
 5. [*pl.*] the suit of cards with this mark.
 6. a card of this suit.
 7. in baseball, (a) the infield; (b) the whole playing field.
 8. in printing, a small size of type, 4 1/2 point.
 diamond in the rough; (a) a diamond in its natural state; (b) a person or thing having fine qualities but lacking in polish.

dī′ȧ·mŏnd, *a.* containing or consisting of diamonds; of the nature of or like a diamond.

dī′ȧ·mŏnd, *v.t.* to adorn with or as with diamonds.

dī′ȧ·mŏnd an·ni·vẽr′sȧ·ry, the sixtieth, or sometimes seventy-fifth, anniversary of an event.

dī′ȧ·mŏnd·back, *a.* having diamond-shaped markings on the back; as, a *diamondback* rattlesnake.

dī′ȧ·mŏnd·back, *n.* 1. a kind of moth.
 2. a diamondback terrapin.

dī′ȧ·mŏnd·back ter′rȧ·pin, an edible North American turtle, *Malaclemmys palustris*, with diamond-shaped ridges on its shell, found in salt marshes along the Atlantic and Gulf coasts.

dī′ȧ·mŏnd bee′tle, a weevil, *Entimus imperialis*, native to South America and characterized by its ornamental, sparkling scales.

dī′ȧ·mŏnd bīrd, an Australian shrike of the genus *Pardalotus*, having brilliant, spangled plumage.

dī′ȧ·mŏnd çut′tẽr, a lapidary.

dī′ȧ·mŏnd drill, a drill used for boring, the tip of which is set with bort diamonds.

dī′ȧ·mŏnd dust, same as *diamond powder*.

dī′ȧ·mŏnd·ed, *a.* 1. furnished, ornamented, or covered with diamonds.
 2. having the form of or marked with the form of a diamond.

dī′ȧ·mŏnd·īze, *v.t.*; diamondized, *pt.*, *pp.*; diamondizing, *ppr.* to stud with diamonds; to ornament with or as with diamonds.

dī′ȧ·mŏnd jū′bi·lee, a diamond anniversary.

dī′ȧ·mŏnd mor′tăr, a hardened steel mortar with a close-fitting pestle for pulverizing hard substances.

dī′ȧ·mŏnd point, a stylus, having a diamond tip, used by etchers or glaziers.

dī′ȧ·mŏnd pow′dẽr, the fine powder resulting in diamond cutting from cutting one diamond with another; diamond dust. It is used in cutting and polishing gems, making cameos, etc.

dī′ȧ·mŏnd-shāped (-shāpt), *a.* having the figure of an oblique-angled parallelogram or rhombus.

dī′ȧ·mŏnd snāke, 1. a large boa or python of Australia, *Morelia spilotes*: so called because its skin is marked with diamond-shaped figures.
 2. any snake having diamond-shaped markings.

dī′ȧ·mŏnd wed′ding, a sixtieth, or sometimes seventy-fifth, wedding anniversary.

dī′ȧ·mŏnd wee′vil, same as *diamond beetle*.

Dī′ăn, *n.* Diana. [Poet.]

Dī·an′ȧ, *n.* [L.] 1. in Roman mythology, the goddess of the chase, of chastity, and of the moon: identified with the Greek Artemus.
 2. the moon. [Poet.]

DIANA

Dī·an′ȧ mŏn′key, a large monkey, *Cercopithecus diana*, of Africa, having a white beard and a white cross on its forehead.

Dī·an′dri·ȧ, *n.pl.* [L., from Gr. *di-*, two, and *anēr* (*andros*), a man.] a Linnaean class of plants having perfect flowers and two distinct stamens.

DIANDRIA

dī·an′drous, dī·an′dri·an, *a.* having two stamens; of or relating to the class *Diandria*.

dī″ȧ·nō·et′iç, *a.* [Gr. *dianoētikos*, intellectual, capable of thought, from *dianoeisthai*, to think over, intend; *dia-*, through, and *noein*, to think, from *noos*, mind.] relating to the thought process, particularly as proceeding from logical, rather than intuitive, reasoning.

dī″ȧ·noi·al′ō·ġy, *n.* that branch of philosophy which treats of the dianoetic propositions.

Dī·an′thus, *n.* [L., from Gr. *dios*, divine, and *anthos*, flower.]
 1. a large genus of ornamental plants of the

pink family, native to the Mediterranean region and the temperate parts of Asia. It includes the various pinks, as the carnation and sweet William.

2. [d–] any of the plants of this genus.

dī·ȧ·pāṣe′, *n.* diapason. [Rare.]

dī′ȧ·paṣm, *n.* a powder or perfume. [Obs.]

dī·ȧ·pā′ṣŏn, *n.* [Gr. *diapasōn*, the concord of the first and last notes; *dia*, through, and *pasōn*, genit. pl. of *pas*, all.]

1. the entire range of a musical instrument or voice.

2. either of two principal stops of an organ (*open diapason* and *stopped diapason*), covering the entire range: when either is used, any note played is sounded in two or more octaves.

3. a swelling burst of harmony.

4. a standard of musical pitch; as, normal *diapason*.

5. a tuning fork or pitch pipe.

6. the interval of an octave. [Obs.]

7. complete harmony. [Obs.]

dī″ȧ·pē·dē′sis, *n.* [Gr. *diapēdēsis*, a leaping through, from *diapēdan*, to leap through or across.] the oozing of the blood corpuscles into the surrounding tissues through the natural pores of the blood vessels.

dī″ȧ·pē·det′iç, *a.* of the nature of, or pertaining to, diapedesis.

Dī·ȧ·pen·si·ȧ′cē·ae, *n.pl.* [L., from Gr. *dia pente*, by fives.] a small order of shrubby plants, allied to the heaths, growing in Europe and America, with pentamerous gamopetalous flowers, and three-celled erect capsules.

dī·ȧ·pen′te, *n.* [L., from Gr. *dia pente*, by fives.]

1. formerly, in music, the interval or consonance of a fifth.

2. in medicine, a composition of five ingredients.

dī′ȧ·pẽr, *n.* [ME. *dyaper*, *diapery*; OFr. *diapre*, a kind of ornamented cloth; ML. *diasprus*, a kind of precious cloth.]

1. a white cotton or linen cloth woven in a pattern formed by a repeated, small, diamond-shaped figure.

2. such a pattern.

3. a towel or napkin of such cloth.

4. (*or* dī′pẽr) a small cloth usually of cotton, folded to form a baby's breechcloth.

DIAPER (sense 2)

dī′ȧ·pẽr, *a.* 1. of diaper.

2. diapered.

3. for diapers.

dī′ȧ·pẽr, *v.t.*; diapered, *pt.*, *pp.*; diapering, *ppr.* 1. to pattern with diamond-shaped figures.

2. to put a diaper on (a baby).

dī′ȧ·pẽr, *v.i.* to draw diamond-shaped figures, as on cloth.

dī′ȧ·pẽr·ing, *n.* a diaper pattern or the thing which it ornaments.

dī′ȧ·phāne, *n.* [Gr. *diaphanēs*, transparent, from *diaphainein*, to show through, see through.] a woven silk cloth with transparent figures.

dī′ȧ·phāned, *a.* transparent. [Rare.]

dī″ȧ·phā·nē′i·ty, *n.* [Gr. *diaphaneia*, transparency, from *diaphanēs*, transparent; *dia-*, through, and *phainein*, to show.] the quality of being transparent.

dī·ȧ·phan′iç, *a.* same as *diaphanous*.

dī·aph′ȧ·niē, *n.* the art or process of ornamenting plain glass with transparent pictures, in imitation of stained glass.

dī″ȧ·phā·nom′e·tẽr, *n.* [Gr. *diaphanēs*, transparent, and *metron*, a measure.]

1. an instrument to determine the transparency of the atmosphere.

2. a testing instrument, to determine the purity of liquids by their relative transparency.

dī·ȧ·phan′ō·sçōpe, *n.* [Gr. *diaphanēs*, transparent, and *skopein*, to view.] a box for viewing transparent photographic positives.

dī·ȧ·phan′ō·tȳpe, *n.* [Gr. *diaphanēs*, transparent, and *typos*, an impression.] a picture made by the superposition of a positive having a tinted back upon an uncolored, heavily printed duplicate.

dī·aph′ȧ·nous, *a.* [Gr. *diaphanēs*, transparent, from *diaphainein*, to show through; *dia-*, through, and *phainein*, to show.] transparent or translucent, as gauzy cloth.

dī·aph′ȧ·nous·ly, *adv.* transparently.

dī′ȧ·phōne, *n.* a group of sounds popularly recognized as being the same although pronounced with slight differences by various speakers.

dī·ȧ·phon′iç, dī·ȧ·phon′iç·ăl, *a.* [*dia-*, and Gr. *phōnē*, sound.] same as *diacoustic*.

dī·ȧ·phon′içṣ, *n.* same as *diacoustics*.

dī″ȧ·phō·rē′sis, *n.* [LL. *diaphoresis*, perspiration; Gr. *diaphorēsis*, a carrying away, perspiration, from *diaphorein*, to carry off, throw off by perspiration.] perspiration, especially when profuse and caused by artificial means.

dī″ȧ·phō·ret′iç, dī″ȧ·phō·ret′iç·ăl, *a.* [Gr. *diaphorētikos*, causing perspiration.] having the power of producing or increasing perspiration.

dī″ȧ·phō·ret′iç, *n.* a medicine, treatment, etc. which increases perspiration; a sudorific.

dī′ȧ·phōte, *n.* same as *telephote*.

dī′ȧ·phragm (-fram), *n.* [LL. *diaphragma*, *diaphragmatis*; Gr. *diaphragma*, from *dia-*, through, and *phragma*, a fence, from *phrassein*, to enclose.]

1. the midriff; a muscular, membranous partition separating the chest cavity from the abdominal cavity in mammals.

2. any membrane or partition that separates one thing from another.

3. a device to regulate the amount of light entering the lens of a camera, microscope, etc.

4. a kind of contraceptive pessary.

5. a vibrating disk or cone that produces sound waves, as in an earphone, telephone receiver, or loudspeaker.

6. the divisional structure or septum found in certain shells.

dī″ȧ·phrag·mat′iç, *a.* of, pertaining to, or resembling a diaphragm.

dī″ȧ·phrag·mat′i·căl·ly, *adv.* by means of a diaphragm.

dī′ȧ·phragm pump, a pump which has a pliable diaphragm instead of a piston.

dī·ȧ·phyṣ′i·ăl, *a.* pertaining to the diaphysis.

dī·aph′y·sis, *n.*; *pl.* **dī·aph′y·sēṣ**, [Gr. *diaphysis*, a growing through; *dia-*, through, and *phyein*, to bring forth.]

1. in anatomy, the shaft of a long bone between its two growing ends; the part of a bone which ossifies first.

2. in botany, an abnormal extension of the center of a flower, or of an inflorescence.

dī·ap·nō′iç, *a.* [Gr. *diapnoē*, an outlet, from *dia*, through, and *pnein*, to blow.] diaphoretic in a mild degree.

dī·ap·nō′iç, *n.* a mild diaphoretic.

dī″ap·ō·phyṣ′i·ăl, *a.* of or relating to a diapophysis.

dī·ȧ·poph′y·sis, *n.*; *pl.* **dī·ȧ·poph′y·sēṣ**, [L., from Gr. *dia*, through, and *apophysis*, outgrowth.] in anatomy, the transverse process of a vertebra.

dī′ärçh·y, *n.*; *pl.* **dī′ärçh·ieṣ**, [*di-*, and Gr. *archos*, a ruler, from *archein*, to rule.] government shared by two rulers, powers, etc.: sometimes written *dyarchy*.

dī·ā′ri·ăn, dī·ā′ri·ăl, *a.* of, pertaining to, or resembling a diary.

dī′ȧ·rist, *n.* one who keeps a diary.

dī·ăr·rhē′ȧ, dī·ăr·rhoe′ȧ (-rē′ȧ), *n.* [LL. *diarrhœa*; Gr. *diarrhoia*, a flowing through, diarrhea, from *dia-*, through, and *rheein*, to flow.] a profuse, frequent, and loose discharge from the bowels.

dī·ăr·rhē′ăl, dī·ăr·rhoe′ăl, *a.* pertaining to or having the characteristics of diarrhea.

dī·ăr·rhē′iç, dī·ăr·rhoe′iç, *a.* same as *diarrheal*.

dī·är·thrō′di·ăl, *a.* of or pertaining to diarthrosis.

dī·är·thrō′sis, *n.* [Gr. *diarthrōsis*, a division by joints, from *diarthroun*, to divide by joints.] in anatomy, a joint, as the hip, so articulated as to move freely in any direction; also, the motion of such a joint.

dī′ȧ·ry, *n.*; *pl.* **dī′ȧ·rieṣ**, [L. *diarium*, a daily allowance (of food or pay), from *dies*, day.]

1. a daily written record, especially of the writer's own experiences, thoughts, etc.

2. a book in which such a record is kept.

3. a daily calendar or memorandum pad.

dī′ȧ·ry, *a.* lasting but one day; as, a *diary* fever. [Obs.]

dī·ȧ·skeū′ȧ·sis, *n.* [L., from Gr. *diaskeuazein*, to put in order; *dia*, through, and *skeuazein*, to prepare, make ready, from *skeuos*, an implement.] revision; editing.

dī·ȧ·skeū′ast, *n.* one who revises; an editor.

Dī·as′pō·rȧ, *n.* [Gr. *diaspora*, a dispersion, from *dia-*, through, and *speirein*, to scatter or sow.]

1. the dispersion of the Jews after the Babylonian exile.

2. the Jews thus dispersed.

3. in the time of the apostles, Jewish Christians who lived outside of Palestine.

dī′ȧ·spōre, *n.* [Gr. *diaspora*, a dispersion; *dia-*, through, and *speirein*, to scatter.] a variously colored native hydrate of aluminum, $HAlO_2$, occurring in lamellar masses and orthorhombic crystals. It is infusible, and receives its name from the fact that when exposed to heat it crackles and disperses.

dī·ȧ·stal′tiç, *a.* [Gr. *diastaltikos*, able to distinguish, dilating, from *diastellein*, to separate, to distinguish; *dia-*, apart, and *stellein*, to send.] dilated; extended: in Greek music, applied to certain intervals.

dī′ȧ·stāse, *n.* [Gr. *diastasis*, a standing apart, separation, from *dia-*, apart, and *histanai*, to stand.] an enzyme that changes starches into maltose and later into dextrose; amylase.

dī·ȧ·stā′siç, *a.* pertaining to or having the quality of diastase.

dī·as′tȧ·sis, *n.* in surgery, a dislocation; a separation of the bones without breaking.

dī·ȧ·stat′iç, *a.* of, pertaining to, or having the properties of diastase; changing starch into sugar.

dī′ȧ·stem, *n.* in Greek music, an interval.

dī·ȧ·stē′mȧ, *n.*; *pl.* **dī·ȧ·stē′mȧ·tȧ**, [Gr. *diastēma*, an interval, difference, from *dihistanai*, aor. *diastēnai*, to stand apart, divide; *dia*, apart, and *histanai*, to stand.]

1. in anatomy and zoology, a space between any two adjacent teeth or kinds of teeth.

2. a diastem.

dī·as′tẽr, *n.* [*di-*, two, and Gr. *astēr*, a star.] the stage of mitosis in which there is a set of chromosomes near each pole of the spindle.

dī·as′tō·lē, *n.* [Gr. *diastolē*, distinction, difference, from *diastellein*, to separate, dilate; *dia*, apart, and *stellein*, to put, arrange.]

1. the usual rhythmic dilatation of the heart, especially of the ventricles, following each contraction (*systole*), during which the heart muscle relaxes and the chambers fill with blood.

2. in Greek and Latin prosody, the lengthening of a short syllable.

dī·as·tol′iç, *a.* of, pertaining to, or caused by diastole.

dī·as′trăl, *a.* in biology, of or in the stage of diaster.

dī·as·troph′iç, *a.* of or pertaining to diastrophism.

dī·as′trō·phiṣm, *n.* [Gr. *diastrophē*, distortion, from *diastrephein*, to turn aside, distort; *dia-*, aside, and *strephein*, to turn.]

1. the process by which the internal structure and external configuration of the earth's crust are reshaped by internal forces, producing continents, ocean beds, mountains, strata, etc.

2. formation so made.

dī′ȧ·stȳle, *n.* [L. *diastylos*; Gr. *diastylos*, with columns wide apart; *dia*, apart, and *stylos*, column.] see *intercolumniation*.

dī·ȧ·tes′sȧ·ron, *n.* [L., from Gr. *dia tessarōn*, lit., through four, the interval of a fourth; *dia*, through, and *tessarōn*, genit. pl. of *tessares*, four.]

1. formerly, in music, the interval of a fourth.

2. formerly, in pharmacy, a mixture of four medicines in sirup or honey.

3. in theology, a continuous narrative of the four Gospels, to prove their agreement or harmony; Gospel harmony.

dī·ȧ·thẽr′măl, *a.* same as *diathermic*.

dī·ȧ·thẽr′măn·cy, dī·ȧ·thẽr′mănce, *n.* [Fr. *diathermansie*, from Gr. *dia-*, through, and *thermansis*, a heating.] the property of transmitting infrared or heat rays.

dī·ȧ·thẽr·mȧ·nē′i·ty, *n.* diathermancy. [Rare.]

dī·ȧ·thẽr′mȧ·niṣm, *n.* same as *diathermancy*.

dī·ȧ·thẽr′mȧ·nous, *a.* same as *diathermic*.

dī·ȧ·thẽr′mi·ȧ, *n.* [Mod. L.] diathermy.

dī·ȧ·thẽr′miç, *a.* 1. relating to diathermy.

2. letting heat rays pass through freely.

dī″ȧ·thẽr′mīze, *v.t.*; diathermized, *pt.*, *pp.*; diathermizing, *ppr.* to treat by diathermy.

dī″ȧ·thẽr·mom′e·tẽr, *n.* [*dia-*, and Gr. *thermos*, heat, and *metron*, a measure.] an instrument to measure the comparative power of heat transmission of various substances.

dī′ȧ·thẽr″my, *n.* [Gr. *dia-*, through, and *thermē*, heat.]

1. medical treatment in which heat is produced in the tissues beneath the skin by a high-frequency electric current.

2. the apparatus used in diathermy; also, the current so used.

dī·ath′e·sis, *n.* [Gr. *diathesis*, an arrangement, from *diatithenai*, to arrange; *dia-*, apart, and *tithenai*, to place, put.] in medicine, a congenital susceptibility or liability to certain diseases.

dī·à·thet′iç, *a.* of the nature of or dependent on diathesis.

dī′à·tom, *n.* any plant of the *Diatomaceæ*.

Dī·at′ō·mà, *n.* [L., from Gr. *dia*, through, and *tomē*, a cutting, from *temnein*, to cut.] in botany, a genus of *Diatomaceæ*.

Dī″à·tō·mā′cē·ae, *n.pl.* in botany, a family of algae, consisting of microscopic plants found in fresh and salt water. The frond secretes a very large quantity of silica, which is formed in each cell into two generally symmetrical valves. The species consist of single free cells, cells in colonies, or in some cases the cells or frustules are enclosed in a transparent gelatinous sheath or frond.

dī″à·tō·mā′cē·àn, *n.* a diatom.

dī″à·tō·mā′ceous, *a.* of, containing, or consisting of diatoms or their fossils.

dī·à·tom′iç, *a.* [*di-*, two, and Gr. *atomos*, an atom.]
1. consisting of two atoms in the molecule.
2. having two replaceable atoms or radicals in the molecule; bivalent.

dī·à·tom·if′ẽr·ous, *a.* [L. *Diatoma*, and *ferre*, to bear.] bearing or yielding diatoms.

dī·at′ō·min, dī·at′ō·mine, *n.* the buff or brownish pigment of some diatoms.

dī·at′ōm·īte, *n.* diatomaceous earth, forming, when dry, a fine powder used as an abrasive, as a pottery glaze, etc.

dī·at′ō·mous, *a.* [*dia-*, and Gr. *tomos*, a cut, from *temnein*, to cut.] in mineralogy, having crystals with one distinct, diagonal cleavage.

dī·à·ton′iç, *a.* [LL. *diatonicus*; Gr. *diatonikon*, or *diatonon* (supply *genos*, kind), the diatonic scale, from *diatonos*, extending through; *dia-*, through, and *teinein*, to stretch, from *tonos*, a chord, tone.] in music, designating, of, or using any standard major or minor scale of eight tones without the chromatic intervals.
diatonic scale; a major or minor scale of diatonic notes.

dī·à·ton′iç·ăl·ly, *adv.* in a diatonic manner; with reference to a diatonic scale.

dī·at′ō·nous, *a.* [Gr. *diatonos*, extending through; *dia*, through, and *teinein*, to stretch.] showing on two surfaces: said of a stone extending through a wall.

dī′à·trībe, *n.* [Gr. *diatribē*, a wearing away, waste of time, pastime, from *diatribein*, to rub away, waste.] a discourse or dispute; specifically, one of bitter, malicious criticism and abuse.

dī′à·tri·bist, *n.* one who makes a diatribe.

dī·à·trop′iç, *a.* of or showing diatropism.

dī·at′rō·piṣm, *n.* in botany, the tendency of some plant parts to place themselves crosswise to the line of force of a stimulus.

Dī·à·trȳ′mà, *n.* [L., from Gr. *dia*, through, and *trymē*, a hole, from *tryein*, to wear out, bore, pierce.] a genus of large fossil birds of the earliest epoch of the Tertiary.

dī·au′los, *n.*; *pl.* **dī·au′lī,** [Gr. *diaulos*, a double race track, a double pipe or channel; *di-*, two, and *aulos*, a pipe, flute.]
1. in ancient Greece, a double track for foot racing.
2. in Greek music, two flutes controlled by a single mouthpiece.

dī·à·zeūç′tiç, *a.* [Gr. *diazeutikos*, disjunctive, from *diazeugnynai*, to unyoke, disjoin; *dia*, apart, and *zeugnynai*, to join, yoke.] disjoining.
diazeuctic tone; in ancient music, a tone between two tetrachords.

dī′à·zīne, dī′à·zin, *n.* any chemical compound with a molecular structure consisting of four atoms of carbon and two of nitrogen, arranged in a ring.

dī·az′ō, *a.* [*di-*, and *azo*.] having a group of two nitrogen atoms combined directly with one hydrocarbon radical.

dī·az′ō-, a combining form meaning *diazo*: also *diaz-*.

dī·a′zō·à·mī′nō, *a.* denoting or of a diazo compound in which the N_2 group is attached to the nitrogen atom of an amino radical, replacing one of the atoms normally present in that radical.

dī′à·zōle (*or* dī-az′ōl), *n.* 1. any chemical compound with a molecular structure consisting of three atoms of carbon and two of nitrogen, arranged in a ring.
2. a derivative of such a compound.

dī·à·zō′mà, *n.*; *pl.* **dī·à·zō′mà·tà,** [L., from Gr. *diazōma*, a girdle, partition, from *diazōnnynai*, to gird around; *dia*, through, and *zōnnynai*, to gird, from *zōma*, a girdle.] in the theaters of ancient Greece, a horizontal passageway through the auditorium about halfway up and crossing the staircases.

dī·à·zō′ni·um, *a.* [*diaz-*, and ammo*nium*.] designating or containing the bivalent organic radical =N:N in which one nitrogen atom has a valence of three and the other a valence of five: it occurs in a series of aromatic compounds (*diazonium compounds*).

dī·az′ō rē·aç′tion, a chemical reaction in which a diazo compound is used.

dī·az′ō·tīze, *v.t.*; diazotized, *pt.*, *pp.*; diazotizing, *ppr.* to convert chemically into a diazo compound.

dib, *v.i.* [ME. *dibben*; AS. *dyppan*, to dip, plunge.] to dip; especially, to dip bait into the water.

dī·bā′siç, *a.* [*di-*, and Gr. *basis*, base.]
1. denoting or of an acid with two hydrogen atoms either or both of which may be replaced by basic radicals or atoms to form a salt.
2. having two atoms of a univalent metal.

dib′bẽr, *n.* a dibble.

dib′ble, *n.* [Eng. dial. var. of *dabble*.] a pointed instrument used to make holes for planting seeds, bulbs, or young plants.

dib′ble, *v.t.*; dibbled, *pt.*, *pp.*; dibbling, *ppr.* 1. to plant with a dibble.
2. to make holes in with a dibble.

dib′ble, *v.i.* 1. to use a dibble.
2. to dabble.
3. to dip bait gently into the water.

DIBBLE

dib′blẽr, *n.* one who or that which dibbles.

Dī·brañ·chi·ā′tà, *n.pl.* [Mod. L., from Gr. *di-*, two, and *branchia*, gills.] an order of cephalopods having two gills, many armlike appendages, and a sac for ejecting an inky liquid.

dī·brañ′chi·āte, *a.* having two gills; of or belonging to the *Dibranchiata*.

dī·brañ′chi·āte, *n.* any of the *Dibranchiata*, as an octopus, squid, etc.

dibs̹, *n.* [Ar.] a Syrian sirup made from the concentrated juice of grapes, dates, or figs.

dib′stōne, *n.* a bone or stone used in the child's game of jackstones.

di·çā′cious, *a.* saucy; impudent. [Obs.]

di·çac′i·ty, *n.* [L. *dicacitas*, biting wit, from *dicax* (*-cacis*), witty, sharp in speech, from *dicere*, to speak.] pertness. [Rare.]

dī·çal′ciç, *a.* having two atoms of calcium to the molecule.

dī·çär·bon′iç, *a.* having two carboxyl radicals $(CO\cdot OH)_2$ as a constituent.

dī′çast, *n.* [Gr. *dikastēs*, from *dikazein*, to judge, from *dikē*, right, justice.] in ancient Athens, an officer in a high court of justice, who combined the duties of a present-day juror and judge, chosen annually from 6,000 citizens.

dī·ças′tẽr·y, *n.* in ancient Athens, a court of justice; dicasts collectively.

dīce, *n.pl.*; *sing.* **dīe, dīce,** 1. small cubes of bone, plastic, etc. marked on each side with a different number of spots (from one to six) and used in games of chance.
2. [*construed as sing.*] a gambling game played with dice.
3. any small cubes.

dīce, *v.i.*; diced (dīst), *pt.*, *pp.*; dicing, *ppr.* to play or gamble with dice, by throwing them to see what the spots on the upturned faces total.

dīce, *v.t.* 1. to lose by gambling with dice.
2. to cut (vegetables, etc.) into small cubes.
3. to mark with a pattern of cubes or squares; checker.

dīce′box, *n.* a box from which dice are thrown in games of chance.

dīce çōal, coal which breaks easily into dice-shaped pieces.

dī·cel′lāte, *a.* [Gr. *dikella*, a mattock or pickax with two teeth.] in zoology, having two prongs, as a spicule of a sponge.

Dī·cen′trà, *n.pl.* [Mod. L., from Gr. *dikentros*, with two stings or points.] a genus of herbaceous plants of the order *Fumariaceæ*, widely distributed. They are ornamental and have finely cut leaves and heart-shaped flowers. Well-known species are the bleeding heart, squirrel corn, and Dutchman's-breeches.

dī·ceph′à·lous, *a.* [Gr. *dikephalos*, two-headed.] two-headed, as certain fetal monsters.

dī′çẽr, *n.* a player at dice.

dī·cer′i·on, *n.*; *pl.* **dī·cer′i·à,** [Gr. *dikerōs*, two-horned; *di-*, two, and *keras*, a horn.] a symbolic, two-branched candlestick used in ceremonials of the Orthodox Eastern Church.

dich-, same as *dicho-*.

dī·çhā′si·um, *n.*; *pl.* **dī·çhā′si·à,** [Mod. L., from Gr. *dichasis*, a division, from *dichazein*, to divide, from *dicha*, in two.] in botany, a cyme having two branches.

dī·çhas′tà·sis, *n.* [Gr. *dichasis*, a division.] spontaneous subdivision.

dī·çhas′tiç, *a.* capable of subdividing spontaneously.

dī·çhlā·myd′ē·ous, *a.* [*di-*, and Gr. *chlamys* (*-ydos*), a cloak, mantle.] in botany, having two coverings, a calyx and a corolla.

dī·çhlō′ride, dī·çhlō′rid, *n.* any chemical compound in which two atoms of chlorine are combined with an element or radical.

dī·çhlō″rō·phē·nox·y·à·cē′tiç ac′id, a chlorine derivative of phenol and acetic acid, $C_7H_6Cl_2O\cdot COOH$, used as a weed killer: also called *2,4–D*.

dī·çhō-, [from Gr. *dicha*, in two, from *dis*, twice, from *dyo*, two.] a combining form signifying *in two* or *into two, asunder*, as in *dicho*tomy, *dicho*gamy.

dī·çhog′à·mous, *a.* characterized by dichogamy.

dī·çhog′à·my, *n.* [*dicho-*, and Gr. *gamos*, marriage.] in botany, a condition in hermaphrodite flowers to prevent self-fertilization, as the maturing of stamens and pistils within the same flower at different times.

dī·çhō′ree, *n.* same as *dichoreus*.

dī·çhō·rē′us, *n.*; *pl.* **dī·çhō·rē′ī,** [L., from Gr. *dichoreios*, a double choreus; *di-*, two, and *choreios*, choreus, from *choros*, dance.] in prosody, two trochees considered as a single foot: also called *dichoree* and *ditrochee*.

dī·çhot′ō·măl, *a.* pertaining to or situated in a dichotomy.

dī·çhot′ō·mist, *n.* one who classifies by division into pairs.

dī·çhot′ō·mīze, *v.t.*; dichotomized, *pt.*, *pp.*; dichotomizing, *ppr.* [Gr. *dichotomein*, to cut in two.]
1. to cut into two parts; to divide into pairs.
2. in astronomy, to show (a planet) as if bisected.

dī·çhot′ō·mīze, *v.i.* to divide into two repeatedly, as a stem or root.

dī·çhot′ō·mous, *a.* [LL. *dichotomos*; Gr. *dichotomos*, a cutting in two, from *dichotomein*, to cut in two; *dicha*, in two parts, and *temnein*, to cut.]
1. having or consisting of a pair or pairs; paired.
2. of or characterized by dichotomy.

dī·çhot′ō·mous·ly, *adv.* in a dichotomous manner.

dī·çhot′ō·my, *n.* [Gr. *dichotomia*, a division into two parts; *dicha*, in two, and *temnein*, to cut.]
1. division of things by pairs.
2. a division.
3. in astronomy, that phase of the moon or of a planet in which only half of its apparently flat surface seems to be illuminated.
4. in biology, a dividing or forking into parts; bifurcation.
5. in botany, a system of branching by repeated divisions into two.
6. in logic, division of a class into two opposed subclasses, as *real* and *unreal*.

dī·çhrō′iç, *a.* of, pertaining to, or characterized by dichroism or dichromatism.

dī′çhrō·iṣm, *n.* [*di-*, and Gr. *chroia*, color.]
1. the property possessed by some crystals of reflecting two different colors when viewed in two different directions.
2. in physics, that property of a substance which results in its showing different colors of transmitted light, depending on the length of the light path in the substance: also called *dichromatism*.

dī′çhrō·īte, *n.* same as *iolite*.

dī·çhrō·it′iç, *a.* same as *dichroic*.

dī·çhrō′māte, *n.* any salt of dichromic acid: also called *bichromate*.

dī·çhrō·mat′iç, *a.* [*di-*, and Gr. *chrōma*, color.]
1. having two colors.
2. of or characterized by dichromatism.
3. in biology, having two different colors, not characteristics of sex or age, as certain species of insects, owls, parrots, etc.

dī·çhrō′mà·tiṣm, *n.* 1. the condition or quality of being dichromatic.
2. color blindness characterized by inability to see more than two of the three primary colors, with their variants.
3. dichroism.

dī·çhrō′miç, *a.* 1. able to distinguish only two of the three primary colors.
2. in chemistry, (a) having two atoms of chromium per molecule; (b) designating an acid, $H_2Cr_2O_7$, which forms dichromates.

dī′çhrō·ō·sçōpe, *n.* [Gr. *dichroos*, two-colored, and *skopein*, to view.] an instrument for studying dichroism, especially of crystals.

dī′çhrō·ous, *a.* same as *dichroic*.

dī′çhrō·sçōpe, *n.* same as *dichrooscope*.

dī·chrō·scop'iç, *a.* relating to the dichrooscope or to observations made by its use.

dī'cing, *n.* 1. the act or pastime of gambling with dice.
2. decoration of leather with stamped squares or diamonds.
3. leather so decorated.
4. a cutting into small cubes.

dī'cing house, a gambling house. [Rare.]

dick, *n.* a detective. [Slang.]

dick·cis'sel, *n.* [echoic of its cry.] the black-throated American bunting.

dick'enș, *n.* and *interj.* devil; deuce: a mild substitute for *devil*, as in *what the dickens!* [Colloq.]

Dick·en'și·ăn, *a.* of or characteristic of Charles Dickens or his writings.

dick'ẽr, *n.* [ME. *dycer*, from L. *decuria*, a military division of ten, from *decem*, ten.] a number or quantity of ten, especially ten hides or skins: also applied to other things; as, a *dicker* of gloves, etc. [Obs.]

dick'ẽr, *v.t.* and *v.i.* [from *dicker*, ten, ten hides, from ME. *dycer*.] to trade by bargaining, especially on a small scale; to barter.

dick'ẽr, *n.* the act of dickering.

dick'ey, *n.*; *pl.* **dick'eyș,** [from the nickname *Dick*.]
1. a man's detachable shirt front.
2. a woman's detachable collar or blouse front.
3. a child's bib or pinafore.
4. a donkey.
5. a small bird.
6. the driver's seat in a carriage: also *dickey box*.
7. a back seat or rumble seat for servants in a carriage.
Also spelled *dicky*.

Dick·sō'ni·ȧ, *n.* [named after James *Dickson*, Scot. botanist.] a genus of tree ferns with large fronds, having spores enclosed in a coriaceous two-valved indusium.

Dick test, [after G. F. *Dick*, b. 1881, Am. physician who devised it.] a skin test for determining susceptibility or immunity to scarlet fever.

dick'y, *n.*; *pl.* **dick'ieș,** same as *dickey*.

dick'y·bĩrd, *n.* any small bird.

dī·çlin'iç, diç'li·nāte, *a.* [*di-*, and Gr. *klinein*, to incline.] in crystallography, having two of the axes obliquely inclined, as in an oblique rectangular prism.

dī'çli·nișm, *n.* the quality or state of being diclinous.

dī'çli·nous, *a.* [*di-*, and Gr. *klinē*, a bed, from *klinein*, to incline, lean.]
1. having the pistils in one flower and the stamens in another, as in the oak.
2. having only stamens or only pistils, as some flowers.

dī·çoç'çous, *a.* [*di-*, and L. *coccum*; Gr. *kokkos*, a berry.] consisting of two cocci.

dī·coe'lous (-sē'), *a.* [*di-*, and Gr. *koilos*, hollow.] in anatomy, having both ends concave; also, possessing two cavities.

dī·çō'lȧ, *n.* plural of *dicolon*.

dī·çō'liç, *a.* [L., from Gr. *di-*, two, and *kōlon*, a member, a clause.] in prosody, having two cola.

dī·çō'lon, *n.*; *pl.* **dī·çō'lȧ,** a verse having two cola.

dī·çon·dyl'i·ăn, *a.* [Gr. *dikondylos*, double-knuckled; *di-*, two, and *kondylos*, a knuckle.] having two cavities in the lower back part of the skull.

dī·çot·y·lē'dŏn, *n.* [*di-*, and Gr. *kotylēdōn*, a cavity.] a plant with two seed leaves (cotyledons); specifically, any plant belonging to that one of the two subclasses of seed plants which is characterized by embryos with two cotyledons, as most shrubs and deciduous trees.

dī·çot·y·lē'dŏn·ous, *a.* of or relating to a dicotyledon or dicotyledons.

Dī·çot'y·lēș, *n.* the type genus of the *Dicotylidæ*.

Dī·çō·tyl'i·dae, *n.pl.* [L., from Gr. *dikotylos*, with two hollows.] a family of pachydermatous mammalia, the peccaries, found in tropical America. They have a glandular organ on the back, which secretes a strongly scented fluid.

dī·çou'mȧ·rin, *n.* a chemical compound extracted from spoiled sweet clover or prepared synthetically, used to retard blood clotting.

dī·çrā'noid, *a.* of or resembling plants of the genus *Dicranum*.

dī·çran·tē'ri·ăn, *a.* same as *diacranterian*.

Dī·çrā'num, *n.* [L., from Gr. *dikranos*, two-headed; *di-*, two, and *kranion*, the skull.] a genus of apocarpous operculate mosses, having the teeth of the peristome deeply bifid.

dī·çrō'tăl, *a.* same as *dicrotic*.

dī·çrot'iç, *a.* [from Gr. *dikrotos*, double-beating (*di-*, two, and *krotos*, rattling noise, clapping), and *-ic*.] of or having a double pulse beat with each heart beat; as, a *dicrotic* artery.

dī'çrō·tișm, *n.* the quality or state of being dicrotic.

dī'çrō·tous, *a.* same as *dicrotic*.

Dī·çrụ'ri·dae, *n.pl.* [L., from Gr. *dikros*, forked, and *oura*, tail.] the drongo shrikes, a subfamily of dentirostral birds, order *Passeres* and family *Ampelidæ*. They resemble crows and are found in India, China, Madagascar, and South Africa.

dic'tȧ, *n.* alternative plural of *dictum*.

diç'tȧ·grȧph, *n.* same as *dictograph*.

diç'tȧ·ment, *n.* a command; a dictate. [Obs.]

Diç·tam'nus, *n.* [L., from Gr. *diktamnos*, the dittany plant, from *Diktē*, a mountain in Crete, where the plant grows.]
1. a genus of plants of the order *Rutaceæ* found in southern Europe and Asia Minor, of which there is but one species, *Dictamnus fraxinella*, the fraxinella or dittany.
2. [d–] a plant of this genus.

diç'tȧ·phōne, *n.* a machine which records and reproduces words spoken into its mouthpiece, as for transcription by a stenographer: a trade-mark (*Dictaphone*).

diç'tāte, *v.t.* and *v.i.*; dictated, *pt.*, *pp.*; dictating, *ppr.* [L. *dictatus*, pp. of *dictare*, freq. of *dicere*, to speak.]
1. to deliver orally for another to write down.
2. to command expressly.
3. to impose or give (orders) with or as with authority.
4. to give (orders or instructions) arbitrarily.

Syn.—direct, instruct, order, prescribe.

diç'tāte, *n.* [L. *dictatum*, generally in pl. *dictata*, things dictated, lessons, commands, from *dictatus*, pp. of *dictare*, to dictate.] an authoritative order; a command.

diç·tā'tion, *n.* 1. the act of speaking or reading (something) aloud for someone else to write down.
2. the words so spoken, written down, or transcribed from shorthand.
3. the act of giving authoritative orders.

diç·tā'tŏr, *n.* [L. *dictator*, a commander.]
1. in ancient Rome, a magistrate appointed by the Senate in times of emergency and invested with absolute authority.
2. a ruler who has absolute power and unlimited authority; as, the *dictator* of a fascist state.
3. one who prescribes rules for others to follow; one who dictates; as, a *dictator* of fashions.
4. a person who reads aloud or speaks words for another person to write down.

diç·tȧ·tō'ri·ăl, *a.* 1. pertaining to a dictator; absolute.
2. like or characteristic of a dictator; imperious; dogmatic; overbearing; as, the officer assumed a *dictatorial* tone.

diç·tȧ·tō'ri·ăl·ly, *adv.* in a dictatorial manner.

diç·tȧ·tō'ri·ăl·ness, *n.* the quality of being dictatorial.

diç·tȧ·tō'ri·ăn, *a.* dictatorial. [Obs.]

diç·tā'tŏr·ship, *n.* 1. the position or office of a dictator.
2. the term of a dictator's office.
3. a dictatorial government; a state ruled by a dictator.
4. absolute power or authority.

diç·tā'tŏr·ship of the prō·lē·tār'i·ăt, absolute control of economic and political power in a country by a government of the working class (proletariat): regarded in Communist theory as a means of effecting the transition from capitalism to socialism.

diç'tȧ·tō·ry, *a.* dictatorial. [Obs.]

diç·tā'tress, diç·tā'trix, *n.* a woman who dictates or exercises authority.

diç·tā'tūre, *n.* the office of a dictator; dictatorship.

diç'tiç, *a.* same as *deictic*.

diç'tion, *n.* [L. *dictio*, a saying, delivery, diction, from *dicere*, to speak.]
1. choice of words; style or manner of expression in words; wording.
2. manner of speaking or singing; enunciation.

Syn.—style, phraseology.—*Style* relates both to language and thought; *diction* to language only; *phraseology* to the mechanical structure of sentences or the mode in which they are phrased.

diç·tion·ā'ri·ăn, *n.* a lexicographer. [Rare.]

diç'tion·ȧ·ry, *n.*; *pl.* **diç'tion·ȧ·rieș,** [ML. *dictionarium*, from L. *dictio*, a saying, from *dicere*, to speak.]
1. a book containing the words of a language, arranged in alphabetical order, with definitions, etymologies, pronunciations, and other information; a lexicon.
2. a book of alphabetically listed words in a language with their equivalents in another language; as, a Spanish-English *dictionary*.
3. a book of alphabetically arranged terms used in any science, art, or other branch of knowledge or work, or by any class of people; as, a geological *dictionary*, a *dictionary* of slang.

diç'tō·grȧph, *n.* [from L. *dictus*, pp. of *dicere*, to speak, and *-graph*.] a telephonic instrument with a small, very sensitive, easily concealed transmitter, used for secretly listening to or recording conversations carried on in another room: a trade-mark (*Dictograph*).

diç'tum, *n.*; *pl.* **diç'tumș, diç'tȧ,** [L. *dictum*, something said, a saying, a word, a witty remark, neut. of *dictus*, pp. of *dicere*, to speak.]
1. an authoritative assertion.
2. a saying.
3. in law, a statement of opinion expressed by the judge on some point not vital to the principal issue of the case.

diç·ty·ō-, [from Gr. *diktyon*, a net.] a combining form meaning *of* or *like a net*.

diç'ty·ō·ġen, *n.* [*dictyo-*, and Gr. *-genēs*, producing.] in botany, any of a group of monocotyledonous plants, with net-veined leaves, intermediate between the monocotyledons and dicotyledons.

diç·ty·oġ'en·ous, *a.* of, pertaining to, or resembling the dictyogens.

dī·çy'ȧ·nide, *n.* [*di-*, and *cyan*ogen.] a salt having two cyanide radicals.

dī·çȳ·ē'mid, *a.* of or pertaining to the *Dicyemida*.

dī·çȳ·ē'mid, *n.* one of the *Dicyemida*.

Dic·y·em'i·dȧ, Dī·çȳ·ē'mȧ·tȧ, *n.pl.* [L., from Gr. *di-*, two, and *kyēma*, an embryo, fetus, from *kyein*, to be pregnant.] a genus of parasitic worms, found in the renal organs of cephalopods. Their organism is very simple and the embryos are of two kinds, vermiform and infusoriform.

dī·cyn'ō·dont, *a.* [*di-*, and Gr. *kyōn*, dog, and *odous* (*odontos*), tooth.] of or pertaining to the *Dicynodontia*.

dī·cyn'ō·dont, *n.* one of the *Dicynodontia*.

Dī·cyn·ō·don'ti·ȧ (-shi·ȧ), *n.pl.* see *Anomodontia*.

dī·cyn·ō·don'ti·ăn, *a.* and *n.* dicynodont.

did, past tense of *do*.

Did'ȧ·çhē, *n.* [Gr. *didachē*, a teaching.] an anonymous Christian treatise of the early second century.

dī·daç'tiç, dī·daç'tic·ăl, *a.* [Gr. *didaktikos*, apt at teaching, from *didaskein*, to teach.]
1. used for teaching; preceptive; containing doctrines, precepts, principles, or rules; intended to instruct; as, a *didactic* poem or essay.
2. morally instructive, or intended to be so.
3. too much inclined to teach others; pedantic: used generally in an unfavorable sense.

dī·daç'tiç, *n.* a treatise on the theory and practice of teaching. [Obs.]

dī·daç'tiç·ăl·ly, *adv.* in a didactic manner; so as to teach.

dī·daç·ti'ciăn (-tish'un), *n.* a teacher; a student, advocate, or promulgator of didactic principles.

dī·daç'ti·cișm, *n.* 1. the quality of being didactic.
2. a didactic manner.

dī·daç·tic'i·ty, *n.* the characteristic or quality of being didactic.

dī·daç'tiçș, *n.* the art or science of teaching; pedagogy.

dī·daç'tyl, dī·daç'tyle, *a.* [Gr. *didaktylos*, two-fingered, from *di-*, two, and *daktylos*, a finger.] having only two digits; two-toed or two-fingered.

dī·daç'tyl, dī·daç'tyle, *n.* an animal with only two toes on each foot.

dī·daç'tyl·ous, *a.* same as *didactyl*.

dī'dăl, *n.* a triangular spade. [Obs.]

dī'dap·pẽr, *n.* [ME. *dydoppar*; AS. *dufedoppa*, the diving bird; *dufan*, to dive, and *doppettan*, to dip.] a small diving bird, the little grebe or dabchick.

dī·das·căl'iç, dī·das'çȧ·lăr, *a.* [Gr. *didaskalikos*, of or for teaching, from *didaskalos*, a teacher, from *didaskein*, to teach.] didactic; preceptive; giving precepts. [Rare.]

did'dẽr, *v.i.* to shake; to tremble. [Brit. Dial.]

did'dle, *v.t.* and *v.i.*; diddled, *pt.*, *pp.*; diddling, *ppr.* 1. to overreach; to cheat; to swindle.
2. to ruin (a person).
3. to waste (time) in trifling.
[Colloq. in all senses.]

did'dle, *v.t.* and *v.i.*; diddled, *pt.*, *pp.*; diddling, *ppr.* 1. to totter, as a child in walking; to toddle. [Brit. Dial. and Scot.]
2. to move back and forth jerkily; to shake; to jiggle. [Colloq.]

did'dlẽr, *n.* a cheat; a swindler. [Colloq.]

dī·deç·ȧ·hē'drăl, *a.* [*di-*, and Gr. *deka*, ten, and *hedra*, a seat.] in crystallography, having the form of a decahedral, or ten-sided, prism with pentahedral summits.

dī'delph, *n.* a marsupial; one of the *Didelphia*.

Dī·del'phi·ȧ, *n.pl.* [L., from Gr. *di-*, two, and *delphys*, womb.] the *Marsupialia*, one of the three subclasses of *Mammalia* (the other two being *Ornithodelphia* and *Monodelphia*): so called because of the double uterus.

dī·del'phi·ăn, dī·del'phiç, *a.* of or pertaining to the *Didelphia*.

dī·del'phid, *n.* a marsupial; an animal belonging to the *Didelphia*.

dī·del'phid, *a.* didelphian.

dī·del'phoid, *a.* same as *didelphian*.

dī·del'phous, *a.* same as *didelphian*.

Dī·del'phys, *n.* [*di-*, and Gr. *delphys*, womb.] a genus of marsupial animals, which is comprised of only the opossums.

dī'dine, *a.* pertaining to or resembling the dodo.

did'n't, did not.

Dī'dō, *n.* [L.; Gr. *Didō*.] in Roman legend, a Tyrian princess who founded Carthage and ruled there as queen: in Virgil's *Aeneid*, she greets Aeneas when he comes to Carthage after the fall of Troy, falls in love with him, and kills herself when he leaves.

dī'dō, *n.*; *pl.* **dī'dōs, dī'dōeş,** [perh. from *Dido*: because of the story that Dido, in buying as much land as could be covered by the hide of a bull, had the hide cut into long, thin strips and thus enclosed a large tract.] a clever trick; a caper; a prank. [Colloq.]

dī·dō''deç·ȧ·hē'drăl, *a.* [*di-*, and Gr. *dōdeka*, twelve, and *hedra*, a seat.] in crystallography, having the form of a dodecahedral, or twelve-sided, prism with hexahedral summits.

dī·dō''deç·ȧ·hē'dron, *n.* in crystallography, a diploid.

dī·draçh'mȧ, dī'drachm (-dram), *n.* [Gr. *didrachmon*, a double drachma; *di-*, two, and *drachmē*, a drachma.] a silver coin of ancient Greece, worth two drachmas.

didst, archaic second person singular, past indicative, of *do*: used with *thou*.

dī·duç'tion, *n.* [L. *diductio*, a leading away, from *diductus*, pp. of *diducere*, to lead or draw away; *di-*, from, and *ducere*, to lead or draw.] separation or the act of separating into distinct parts. [Obs.]

dī'dy, *n.*; *pl.* **dī'dieş,** a diaper (sense 4).

dī'dym, *n.* same as *didymium*.

dī·dym'i·um, *n.* [Mod. L., from Gr. *didymos*, twin (with lanthanum).] a rare metal, formerly considered an element but later found to be a mixture of neodymium and praseodymium, usually found associated with cerium and lanthanum: symbol, D or Di (no period).

did'y·mous, *a.* [Gr. *didymos*, double.] in botany and zoology, growing in pairs or twins.

Did·y·nā'mi·ȧ, *n.* [L., from Gr. *di-*, two, and *dynamis*, power.] the fourteenth class in the Linean system of plants, which have two pairs of stamens, of which one pair is longer than the other.

did·y·nā'mi·ăn, did·y·nam'iç, *a.* same as *didynamous*.

dī·dyn'ȧ·mous, *a.* containing two pairs of stamens, one pair shorter than the other; of or pertaining to the *Didynamia*.

dīe, *v.i.*; died, *pt.*, *pp.*; dying, *ppr.* [ME. *dien*, *deyen*; Ice. *deyja*, to die.]
1. to cease to live; to become dead; to expire; to decease; to perish.
2. to suffer the agony of death, or an agony regarded as similar.
3. to come to an end; to cease; as, let the secret *die* in your own breast.
4. to vanish or recede gradually, as if by death; to grow fainter, weaker, etc.; to lose force or activity.
5. to lose vital power; to become extinct; to wither: said of plants or parts of plants; as, the branch *died* slowly.
6. to become vapid or spiritless, as liquors.
7. to become indifferent (*to*), as if dead.
8. in theology, to suffer spiritual death.
9. in architecture, to disappear gradually or be merged into another part.

The curious zigzag with which its triangles *die* away is one of the most curious features of the structure. —Ruskin.

10. to pine away, as with desire.
11. to wish very much, as if suffering or pining away; as, he was *dying* to go. [Colloq.]
to die away; to become weaker and cease gradually.
to die back; to wither to the roots or woody part.
to die down; (a) to die away; (b) to wither to the ground.
to die hard; to cling to life, a cause, etc.; to resist to the last.
to die in harness; to die in the midst of the usual work; to attend to duties up to the time of death.
to die in the last ditch; to fight to the bitter end; to resist desperately and beyond hope of success; to choose death rather than surrender.
to die off; to die one by one until all are gone.
to die out; (a) to die away; (b) to go out of existence.
Syn.—decease, expire, perish.

dīe, *n.*; *pl.* **dīce, dīeş** in senses 4 and 5, [ME. *dee*, a die; OFr. *de*, pl. *dez*, a die, dice, from hyp. LL. *datum*, from L. *datus*, pp. of *dare*, to give or throw.]
1. either of a pair of dice; a small cube, marked on each side with a different number of spots (from one to six), used in games of chance.
2. any small cube resembling this; as, vegetables cut into *dice*.
3. hazard; chance.

Such is the *die* of war. —Spenser.

4. in architecture, the cubical part of a plinth or pedestal, between the base and the cap.
5. in mechanics, any of various tools or devices, originally cubical in form, for molding, stamping, cutting, or shaping; specifically, (a) a piece of engraved metal used for stamping money, medals, etc.; (b) the stationary part of a machine for shaping or punching holes in sheet metal, etc.; matrix: distinguished from *punch*; (c) the punch and matrix as a unit; (d) a tool used for cutting threads, as of screws or bolts; (e) a piece of metal with a hole through it, used in drawing wire, extruding rods, etc.
the die is cast; the decision is made; the step has been taken and to turn back is impossible.

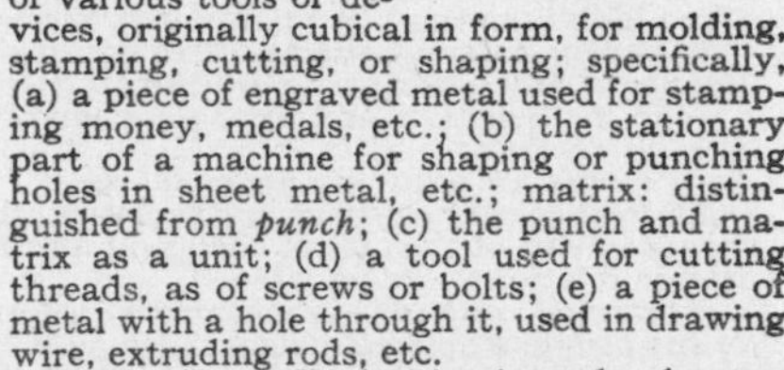

TYPES OF DIE
A, bolt die; B, rethreading die; C, adjustable dies

dīe, *v.t.*; died, *pt.*, *pp.*; dieing, *ppr.* to mold, stamp, cut, or shape with a die.

dīe cȧst'ing, 1. the process of making a casting by forcing molten metal into a metallic mold, or die, under great pressure.
2. a casting made in this way.

dī·ē'cious, dī·ē'ciăn, *a.* same as *dioecious*.

dī·ē'drăl, *a.* same as *dihedral*.

Dieƒ·fen·baçh'i·a, *n.* [L., from *Dieffenbach*, a German botanist.] a small genus of South American and West Indian plants of the order *Araceæ*, cultivated for their foliage.

dī·ē·ġē'sis, *n.* [L., from Gr. *diēgēsis*, a narration, from *diēgeisthai*, to narrate; *dia*, through, and *ēgeisthai*, to lead.] a narration; a recital of facts.

dīe'-härd, dīe'härd, *a.* stubborn in resistance; unwilling to give in.

dīe'-härd, dīe'härd, *n.* a stubborn or resistant person; especially, an extreme conservative.

dī·ē·leç'triç, *n.* [from *dia-*, through, across, and *electric*: so called because it permits the passage of the lines of force of an electrostatic field, but does not conduct the current.] a material, as rubber or glass, that does not conduct electricity; an insulator.

dī·ē·leç'triç, *a.* nonconducting; insulating.

Dī·el'y·trȧ, *n.* [L., from Gr. *di-*, two, and *elytron*, a covering, sheath.] same as *Dicentra*.

dī·en·ceph'ȧ·liç, *a.* of or pertaining to the diencephalon.

dī·en·ceph'ȧ·lon, *n.* [*di-*, and *encephalon*.] the posterior end of the prosencephalon, or forebrain.

dī·er'e·sis, *n.*; *pl.* **dī·er'e·sēş,** [LL. *diæresis*; Gr. *diairesis*, a division, from *diairein*, to divide, separate; *dia*, apart, and *hairein*, to take.]
1. the separation of two consecutive vowels, especially of a diphthong, into two syllables.
2. the mark (¨), placed over the second of two consecutive vowels to show that it is pronounced in a separate syllable: sometimes the dieresis is replaced by a hyphen (*coöperate*, *co-operate*). In this and some other dictionaries, the mark is also used to show a certain pronunciation of a vowel (ä, ï, ö).
3. in prosody, a slight break or pause, made in a line of verse, when the end of a metrical foot is also the end of a word.
Also spelled *diaeresis*.

dī·ē·ret'iç, dī·ae·ret'iç, *a.* [Gr. *diairetikos*, from *diairein*, to divide.] of dieresis.

Dī·ẽr·vil'lȧ, *n.* [from *Dierville*, Fr. surgeon.] a genus of caprifoliaceous shrubs, growing in North America, China, and Japan. They belong to the honeysuckle family, and are characterized by a funnel-shaped, three-cleft corolla and a two-celled capsule.

dī'ēş, *n.* [L.] a day.

Dīe'şel, *n.* [after Rudolf *Diesel* (1858–1913), G. inventor.] a type of internal-combustion engine that burns crude oil: the ignition is brought about by heat resulting from air compression, instead of by an electric spark as in a gasoline engine: also *diesel*, *Diesel engine* (or *motor*).
Diesel cycle; the four-stroke cycle of the piston upon which the Diesel engine operates: this cycle consists of a downward stroke, in which the air is injected into the cylinder; an upward stroke, in which the air is compressed and heated, after which the fuel is injected at the top of the stroke; a second downward stroke caused by the combustion and expansion of the fuel, and a final upward stroke in which the exhaust gases are forced from the cylinder.

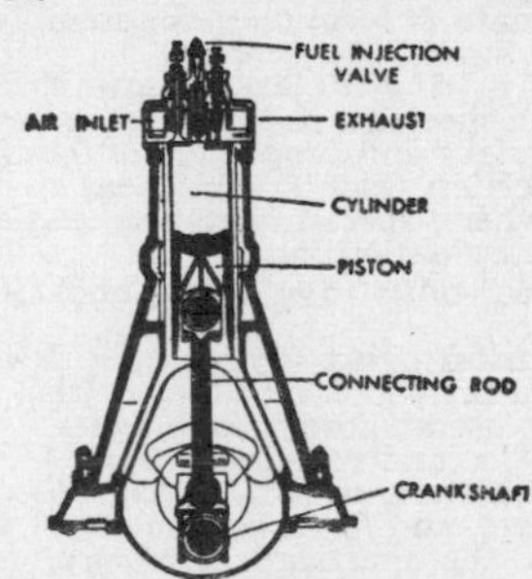

DIESEL ENGINE

Dīe'şel-ē·leç'triç, *a.* pertaining to a combination of a Diesel engine driving an electric generator.

dīe'sink''ẽr, *n.* one who cuts dies for stamping or shaping.

dīe'sink''ing, *n.* the process of cutting dies for stamping or shaping.

Dī'ēş Ī'rae, [L., Day of Wrath.]
1. Judgment Day.
2. a medieval Latin hymn about Judgment Day, beginning *Dies Irae*, now often included in the Requiem Mass.

dī'e·sis, *n.*; *pl.* **dī'e·sēş,** [L., *diesis*; Gr. *diesis*, a sending through, in music a semitone; later a quarter tone; *dia*, through, and *hienai*, to send.]
1. in music, the division of a tone, less than a semitone; also, an interval of less than a half step.
2. in printing, a reference mark (‡): also called *double dagger*.

dī'ēş non, [L. *dies non* (*juridicus*), not a (court) day.] in law, a day on which the business of courts cannot be transacted; a legal holiday.

dīe'stock, *n.* the frame for holding the dies used for cutting threads, as on water pipes, screws, bolts, etc.

dī'et, *n.* [ME. *diete*; OFr. *diete*, diet; LL. *dieta*; L. *diæta*; Gr. *diaita*, a manner of living, a place for living, a summerhouse.]
1. what a person or animal usually eats and drinks; daily fare.
2. special, limited food and drink, chosen or prescribed for health or to gain or lose weight.
3. a regulated manner of living, with special reference to eating habits.
4. allowance of provision. [Obs.]

For his *diet* there was a continual *diet* given
him by the king. —Jer. lii. 34.

5. allowance for food or expenses, as of one in the service of the government. [Obs.]

dī′et, *v.t.*; dieted, *pt., pp.*; dieting, *ppr.* 1. to feed; to board; to furnish provisions for; as, the master *diets* his apprentice. [Rare.]

2. to cause to eat a special selection of food and drink, especially for losing weight.

dī′et, *v.i.* 1. to eat a special selection of food and drink, especially for losing weight.

2. to eat; to feed; as, the students *diet* in common. [Rare.]

dī′et, *n.* [OFr. *diete*, ML. *dieta*, an assembly, a day's journey, from L. *dies*, day.]

1. a day's session of an assembly. [Scot.]

2. a formal assembly.

3. in some countries, a national or, sometimes, local legislative assembly.

dī-ē-tā′ri-ăn, *n.* one who follows or advocates prescribed rules for diet; one who diets.

dī′et-ā-ry, *n.*; *pl.* **dī′et-ā-ries,** 1. a system of diet.

2. a daily allowance of food, especially in prisons, hospitals, charitable institutions, etc.

dī′et-ā-ry, *a.* 1. pertaining to diet.

2. pertaining to a dietary.

dī′et-ẽr, *n.* one who diets.

dī-ē-tet′iç, dī-ē-tet′iç-ăl, *a.* pertaining to diet, or to the rules for regulating the kind and quantity of food to be eaten.

dī-ē-tet′iç-ăl-ly, *adv.* with reference to dietetics.

dī-ē-tet′içs, *n.pl.* [*construed as sing.*] the study of the kinds and quantities of food needed for health.

dī-eth-yl-am′ine, *n.* [*di-*, and *ethylamine*.] a liquid hydrocarbon, $NH(C_2H_5)_2$, having a fishlike smell.

dī-eth″yl-bär″bi-tū′riç ac′id, a compound, $C_8H_{12}O_3N_2$, derived from barbituric acid and used as a soporific: also called *veronal, barbital.*

dī-et′ic, dī-et′iç-ăl, *a.* same as *dietetic.*

dī′et-ine, *n.* [Fr. *diètine*, dim. of *diète*, diet.] a subordinate or local diet, or assembly.

dī′et-ist, *n.* same as *dietitian.*

dī-e-ti′tiăn, dī-e-ti′ciăn, *n.* an expert in dietetics; a specialist in planning meals with the right variety and proportion of foods.

dī′et kitch′en (kich′), a kitchen, as in a hospital, where special diets for patients are planned by a dietitian.

Dieu ä-veç′ nous (dyṳ ä-vek′ nọọ), [Fr.] God with us.

Dieu et mŏṅ droit (dyṳ ā mŏṅ drwä), [Fr.] God and my right: motto of British royalty.

dif-, dis-: used before *f*, as in *differ.*

dif-fāme′, *v.* and *n.* defame. [Rare.]

dif-far-rē-ā′tion, *n.* [LL. *diffarreatio*, from L. *dis-*, apart, and *farreatio*, the use of the spelt cake in the marriage ceremony, from *far* (*farris*), grain, spelt.] the parting of a cake, a ceremony among the ancient Romans at the divorce of man and wife.

dif′fẽr, *v.i.*; differed, *pt., pp.*; differing, *ppr.* [ME. *differen*; L. *differre*, to carry apart, differ, protract; *dis-*, apart, and *ferre*, to bring, carry.]

1. to be unlike, dissimilar, distinct, or various in nature, condition, form, or qualities: often with from; as, wisdom *differs from* folly.

One star *differeth from* another star in glory.
—1 Cor. xv. 41.

2. to disagree; to be of opposite or contrary opinions.

3. to contend; to be at variance; to strive or debate in words; to dispute; to quarrel (*with*).

We'll never *differ with* a crowded pit.
—Rowe.

Syn.—disagree; dissent, vary, dispute, oppose, contend, quarrel, wrangle.

dif′fẽr, *v.t.* to cause to be different; as, his early life *differed* his manners. [Rare.]

dif′fẽr-ence, *n.* [ME. *difference*; OFr. *difference*; L. *differentia*, difference, from *differens*, ppr. of *differre*, to carry apart, to differ.]

1. condition, quality, fact, or instance of being different.

2. the quality which distinguishes one thing or person from another; a distinguishing characteristic.

3. the state of holding an opinion unlike that of others; disagreement.

4. dispute; debate; contention; quarrel; controversy.

What was the *difference?* It was a contention in public. —Shak.

5. an evidence or mark of distinction. [Obs.]

The marks and *differences* of sovereignty.
—Davies.

6. distinction; discrimination; as, a mother makes no *difference* between her children.

There is no *difference* between the Jew and the Greek. —Rom. x. 12.

7. in mathematics, the remainder of a sum or quantity left after a lesser sum or quantity is subtracted; the amount by which one quantity is greater or less than another.

8. in logic, the differentia.

9. in heraldry, a certain figure added to a coat of arms, serving to distinguish one family from another, or to show how distant a younger branch is from the elder or principal branch.

to make a difference; (a) to have an effect; to matter; (b) to change the outlook or situation; (c) to give different treatment; to discriminate; to differentiate.

to split the difference; (a) to share equally what is left over; (b) to make a compromise.

what's the difference?; what does it matter? [Colloq.]

Syn.—distinction, dissimilarity, contrariety, dissimilitude, variation, divergence, contention, dispute.

dif′fẽr-ence, *v.t.*; differenced, *pt., pp.*; differencing, *ppr.* 1. to differentiate.

2. in heraldry, to add a difference or distinguishing mark to.

dif′fẽr-ent, *a.* 1. not alike; dissimilar (with *from*, or, more colloquially, *than*, and, in British usage, *to*).

2. not the same; distinct; separate; as, we belong to *different* churches.

3. various.

4. unlike most others; unusual.

Syn.—distinct, diverse, unlike, various.

dif-fẽr-en′ti-ȧ (-shi-), *n.*; *pl.* **dif-fẽr-en′ti-ae,** [L. *differentia*, difference.]

1. in logic, a distinguishing characteristic, especially one that distinguishes one species from another of the same genus.

The material part, which is called the *genus*, or the formal and distinguishing part, which is called *differentia*. —Whately.

2. a concise cadence characteristic of Gregorian chants.

dif-fẽr-en′ti-ȧ-ble (-shi-), *a.* capable of being differentiated.

dif-fẽr-en′tiăl (-shăl), *a.* 1. of, showing, or depending on a difference or differences; as, *differential* rates on a railroad.

2. making a specific difference or distinction; discriminating; distinguishing; special.

3. having different effects or results; making use of differences; as, a *differential* gear.

4. in mathematics and mechanics, involving differentials.

differential calculus; see under *calculus.*

differential coefficient; in mathematics, the measurement of the rate of change of a function in relation to its variable.

differential coupling; in machinery, a form of slip coupling applied in light machinery for the purpose of regulating the velocity of the connected shaft. In the figure, A is the power shaft having the wheel *a a* fixed to the shaft,

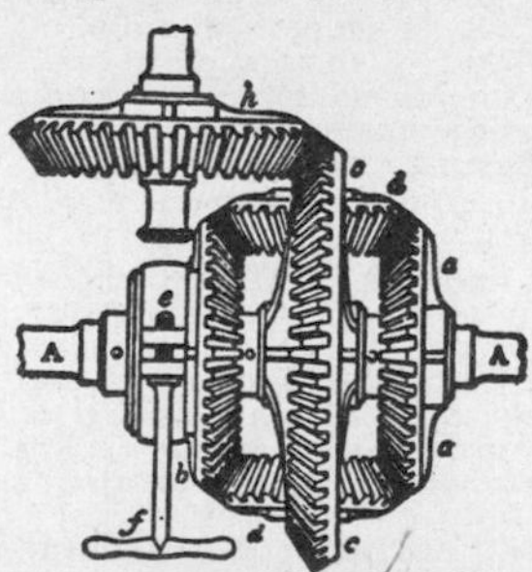

DIFFERENTIAL COUPLING

and *b* and *c c* loose. The pinions *d d* have their bearings in *c c* and gear in *a a* and *b*. A communicates opposite motion to *b*, *c c* remaining at rest until the friction clutch *e f* is engaged, making the teeth of *b* fulcra to *d d*, carrying *c c*, which, gearing with the wheel *h* on the second shaft, communicates motion to it of any degree of velocity not greater than half that of the driving shaft.

differential diagnosis; in medicine, the way and method of determining which of several related diseases or disorders is causing a particular illness, done by observing and comparing symptoms and test data.

differential duties; in political economy, duties which are not levied equally upon the products of different countries.

differential equation; in mathematics, an equation involving or containing differentials or differential coefficients.

differential gear; a certain arrangement of gears (epicyclic train) connecting two axles in the same line and dividing the driving force between them, but allowing one axle to turn faster than the other: it is used in automobile transmissions to permit a difference in axle speeds while turning curves.

differential pulley; (a) a portable differential windlass; (b) differential gearing applied to a pulley.

differential quotient; same as *differential coefficient.*

differential screw; a screw having two threads, one of which unwinds as the other winds; as, in the figure, the pitch of the

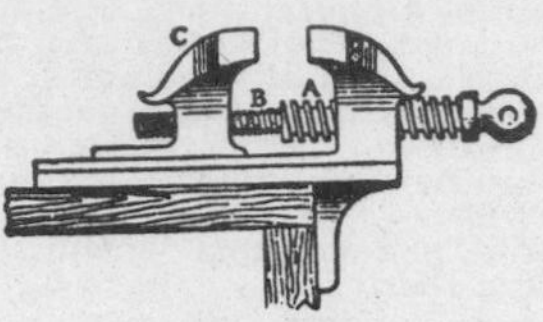

DIFFERENTIAL SCREW

threads at A and B being different, the jaw C moves a distance equal to the difference in the pitch of A and B at each revolution of A B.

differential thermometer; a U-shaped tube, each end of which terminates in an air bulb, the bend being filled with a colored liquid. A graduated scale measures differing temperatures of the two bulbs.

DIFFERENTIAL THERMOMETER

differential winding; in electricity, the winding of two insulated parallel wires of an instrument so that there is no third current induced when equal currents are passed in opposite directions through them: used in duplex telegraphy, galvanometers, etc.

differential or *Chinese windlass*; a windlass with two drums of different diameters to increase the lifting power. The cylinders A and B having a common axis, in the forward motion of B, A unwinds, communicating a motion to C equal to half the difference of the surface velocities of the two cylinders.

DIFFERENTIAL WINDLASS

dif-fẽr-en′tiăl, *n.* 1. a thing that is differential.

2. in electricity, one of two wire coils so arranged as to produce opposite polarities at some desired point of a circuit.

3. in mathematics, an infinitesimal difference between two consecutive values of a variable quantity.

4. in mechanics, a differential gear.

5. in railroading, a difference in rates, as between different routes.

partial differential; in mathematics, an increment, infinitesimally small, of a function of two or more variables resulting from a similar increment in only one of the variables.

total differential; in mathematics, the resultant of simultaneous infinitesimal increments of all of the variables.

dif-fẽr-en′tiăl-ly (-shăl-), *adv.* 1. in a differential manner.

2. distinctively.

dif-fẽr-en′ti-āte (-shi-), *v.t.*; differentiated, *pt., pp.*; differentiating, *ppr.* [ML. *differentiare*, from L. *differentia*, difference.]

1. to constitute a difference in or between.

2. to make unlike; to develop specialized differences in.

3. to perceive or express the difference in; to distinguish between.

4. in mathematics, to work out the differential or differential coefficient of.

dif-fẽr-en′ti-āte (-shi-), *v.i.* 1. to become different or differentiated; to develop new, distinguishing characteristics.

2. to perceive or express a difference.

dif-fẽr-en-ti-ā′tion (-shi-), *n.* 1. a differentiating or being differentiated.

2. in biology, the modification of tissues,

organs, etc. in structure or function during the course of development.
3. in mathematics, the working out of the differential or differential coefficient.
dif·fẽr·en′ti·ā·tŏr (-shi-), *n.* one who or that which differentiates.
dif′fẽr·ent·ly, *adv.* in a different manner; variously.
dif′fẽr·ing·ly, *adv.* same as *differently.*
dif·fi·cile′, *a.* [Fr., from L. *difficilis,* difficult; now used purely as a French expression.] hard, or difficult; especially, hard to deal with, please, or satisfy: said of persons.
dif·fi·cile′ness, *n.* the quality of being difficile. [Rare.]
dif′fi·cult, *a.* [from *difficulty.*]
1. hard to be made, done, or performed; not easy; attended with labor and pains; as, our task is *difficult*; it is *difficult* to ascend a steep hill or travel a bad road.
2. hard to be pleased or satisfied; not readily yielding; not compliant; unaccommodating; rigid; austere; not easily managed or persuaded; as, a *difficult* man; a person of a *difficult* temper.
3. hard to understand or expound; perplexing; as, a *difficult* problem.
Syn.—hard, arduous, laborious, toilsome, troublesome, unaccommodating.
dif′fi·cult, *v.t.* to make difficult; to hinder; to impede. [Obs.]
dif′fi·cult·āte, *v.t.* to make difficult. [Obs.]
dif′fi·cult·ly, *adv.* with difficulty. [Rare.]
dif′fi·cult·ness, *n.* difficulty. [Rare.]
dif′fi·cul·ty, *n.*; *pl.* **dif′fi·cul·tieṣ,** [ME. *difficultee*; OFr. *difficulte*; L. *difficultas,* difficulty; *dis-* priv., and *facilis,* easy.]
1. the condition or fact of being difficult.
2. that which is hard to be performed or surmounted; as, we often mistake *difficulties* for impossibilities.
3. perplexity; trouble; whatever renders progress or execution of designs laborious.
4. objection; obstacle to belief; that which cannot be easily understood, explained, or believed; as, science often raises *difficulties* concerning miracles.
5. a disagreement; a quarrel; a contention.
Syn.—obstacle, obstruction, impediment, perplexity, trouble, embarrassment.
to be in difficulties; to have financial troubles.
to make a difficulty; (a) to cause a difficulty; (b) to offer objections; be reluctant; demur.
dif′fi·dence, *n.* [L. *diffidentia,* distrust, from *diffidens* (*-entis*), ppr. of *diffidere,* to distrust; *dis-* priv., and *fidere,* to trust.]
1. lack of self-confidence; want of confidence in one's own power, ability, correctness, or wisdom; hesitancy to assert oneself; shyness; as, fearing the critics he wrote with *diffidence.*
2. distrust; doubt of the power, ability, or disposition of others. [Archaic.]
Syn.—bashfulness, modesty, humility, reserve, shyness.
dif′fi·den·cy, *n.* diffidence. [Obs.]
dif′fi·dent, *a.* having or showing diffidence.
Syn.—modest, reserved, retiring, humble, bashful, shy.
dif′fi·dent·ly, *adv.* in a diffident manner.
dif·fin′i·tive, *a.* determinate; definitive. [Obs.]
dif·flā′tion, *n.* the act of scattering by a gust of wind. [Obs.]
dif′flū·ence, dif′flū·en·cy, *n.* [L. *diffluo.*] a flowing or falling away on all sides. [Obs.]
dif′flū·ent, *a.* flowing away on all sides; not fixed.
dif′form, *a.* [L. *deformis,* deformed; *de-, dis-* priv., and *forma,* form, shape.] not uniform; dissimilar.
dif·form′i·ty, *n.* irregularity of form; lack of uniformity.
dif·fraçt′, *v.t.*; diffracted, *pt., pp.*; diffracting, *ppr.* [L. *diffractus,* pp. of *diffringere,* to break in pieces.]
1. to break or separate into parts.
2. to cause to undergo diffraction.
dif·fraçt′, *a.* broken; having distinct areolae: applied to the thalli of lichens.
dif·fraç′tion, *n.* [L. *diffractus,* pp. of *diffringere,* to break in pieces.]
1. the breaking up of a ray of light into dark and light bands or into the colors of the spectrum, caused by the interference of one part of a beam with another when the ray is deflected at the edge of an opaque object or passes through a narrow slit.
2. a similar breaking up of other kinds of wave motion, as of sound or electricity.
diffraction grating; in optics, a plate of glass or polished metal ruled with a series of very close, equidistant, parallel lines, used to produce a spectrum by the diffraction of reflected or transmitted light.
diffraction spectra; spectra produced by diffraction instead of other means, as by a prism.
dif·fraç′tive, *a.* pertaining to or causing diffraction.
dif·fran′chīṣe, *v.t.* to disfranchise. [Obs.]
dif·fran′chiṣe·ment, *n.* disfranchisement. [Obs.]
dif·fran·ġi·bil′i·ty, *n.* the state or quality of being diffrangible.
dif·fran′ġi·ble, *a.* [L. *diffringere,* to break in pieces.] capable of diffraction or causing diffraction.
dif·fūṣ′āte, *n.* in dialysis, the diffusible resultant.
dif·fūse′, *a.* [L. *diffusus,* pp. of *diffundere,* to pour in different directions; *dis-,* apart, and *fundere,* to pour.]
1. spread out; not concentrated.
2. using more words than are needed; long-winded; wordy.
dif·fūṣe′, *v.t.* and *v.i.*; diffused, *pt., pp.*; diffusing, *ppr.* 1. to pour in every direction; spread out; spread widely; scatter.
2. in physics, to mix by diffusion, as gases, liquids, etc.
dif·fūṣed′, *a.* spread out; scattered; flowing.
dif·fūṣ′ed·ly, *adv.* in a diffused manner.
dif·fūṣ′ed·ness, *n.* the state or condition of being diffused.
dif·fūse′ly, *adv.* in a diffuse manner.
dif·fūse′ness, *n.* the state or quality of being diffuse; copiousness; prolixity.
dif·fūṣ′ẽr, *n.* one who or that which diffuses: also spelled *diffusor.*
dif·fū·ṣi·bil′i·ty, *n.* the quality of being diffusible; as, the *diffusibility* of clay in water.
dif·fū′ṣi·ble, *a.* that can be diffused.
dif·fū′ṣi·ble·ness, *n.* diffusibility.
dif·fū·ṣi·om′e·tẽr, dif·fū·sim′e·tẽr, *n.* [L. *diffusio,* diffusion, and *metrum,* a measure.] an apparatus used to measure the rate of diffusion of gases.
dif·fū′ṣion, *n.* [L. *diffusio* (*-onis*), diffusion, from *diffusus,* pp. of *diffundere,* to pour in different directions, to diffuse.]
1. a diffusing or being diffused; a spreading; dissemination; as, the *diffusion* of cultural patterns.
2. wordiness.
3. the intermingling of the molecules of two or more substances.
4. a reflection, as of light, from an irregular surface.
dif·fū′sive, *a.* [L. *diffusus,* pp. of *diffundere,* to diffuse.]
1. tending to diffuse.
2. characterized by diffusion.
3. diffuse.
dif·fū′sive·ly, *adv.* in a diffusive manner.
dif·fū′sive·ness, *n.* the quality or state of being diffuse.
dif·fūṣ′ŏr, *n.* same as *diffuser.*
dig, *v.t.*; dug *or archaic and poetic* digged, *pt., pp.*; digging, *ppr.* [ME. *diggen, dyggen,* to dig; AS. *dician,* to make a ditch, from *dic,* a ditch.]
1. to excavate; to open and break, or turn up (the earth), with a spade or other sharp instrument, or with the hand, claws, etc.
2. to make (a hole, cellar, one's way, etc.) by digging.
3. to obtain or draw forth from the earth, by digging; as, to *dig* gold or potatoes.
4. to break up the earth or force a passage through: usually with *up*; as, the mole *dug up* the garden.
5. to find out, as by careful study or investigation; to unearth (usually with *up* or *out*); as, we *dug out* the truth.
6. to thrust; to nudge; to prod; to poke.
7. to understand; to comprehend. [Slang.]
to dig down; to undermine and cause to fall by digging; as, *to dig down* a wall.
to dig in; to mix in by covering with a layer of earth; as, *to dig in* fertilizers.
to dig into; (a) to penetrate by or as by digging; (b) [Colloq.] to work hard at.
to dig up; to obtain something from the earth by opening it, or uncovering the thing with a spade or other instrument, or by forcing out from the earth by a bar; as, *to dig up* a stone.
dig, *v.i.* 1. to dig the ground or any surface; to excavate.
2. to make a way by digging (*through, into, under*).
3. to work or study hard. [Colloq.]
to dig in; (a) to dig trenches or foxholes for cover; (b) to entrench oneself; (c) [Colloq.] to begin to work intensively.
dig, *n.* 1. the act of digging.
2. a nudge; a thrust; a prod; a poke. [Colloq.]
3. a sarcastic comment; a taunt; a jeer. [Colloq.]
4. in mining, same as *gouge.*
dī·gal′liç, *a.* [*di-* and *gallic,* from L. *galla,* the gallnut.] of or pertaining to an acid, *digallic acid,* the same as tannic acid.
dig′ȧ·mist, *n.* one who has married a second time.
dī·gam′mȧ, *n.* [Gr. *digamma, digammos,* the letter digamma, so called because it resembles two gammas in form; *di-,* two, and *gamma,* gamma.] the sixth letter of the early Greek alphabet, derived from the Semitic *vav* and having the sound of English *w*: it was replaced in the Latin alphabet by *F.*
dī·gam′mā·ted, dī·gam′māte, *a.* resembling or using a digamma or its representative sound.
dig′ȧ·mous, *a.* 1. married a second time.
2. pertaining to digamy.
dig′ȧ·my, *n.* [*di-,* and Gr. *gamos,* marriage.] a second legal marriage; marriage to a second husband or wife after the death or divorce of the first.
dī·gas′triç, *a.* [*di-,* and Gr. *gastēr,* belly.]
1. having two fleshy parts with a connecting tendon between them: the *digastric muscle* depresses the lower jaw and indirectly moves the tongue.
2. of or pertaining to a digastric muscle.
Dī·ġe′nē·ȧ, *n.pl.* [L., from Gr. *digenēs,* of two kinds or sexes; *di-,* two, and *genos,* kind.] a division of worms or flukes, parasitic in nature, having alternate characteristics in successive generations.
dī·ġen′e·sis, *n.* [L., from Gr. *di-,* two, and *genesis,* origin, generation.] in biology, successive reproduction by two processes, sexual in one generation and asexual in the next.
dī·ġē·net′iç, *a.* in biology, of or characterized by digenesis.
diġ′e·nous, *a.* [L., from Gr. *di-,* two, and *genos,* kind.] bisexual.
diġ′ẽr·ent, *a.* digesting. [Obs.]
dī′ġest, *n.* [ME. *digest*; LL. *digestum,* a collection of writings arranged under different heads, a code of laws, as that of Justinian, from L. *digestus,* pp. of *digerere,* to distribute, arrange.]
1. [D–] [*often pl.*] a collection or body of Roman laws, digested or arranged under proper titles by order of the emperor Justinian; the Pandects.
2. any collection, compilation, abridgment, or summary of laws, arranged under proper heads or titles; as, the *digest* of Comyn.
3. any compilation, abridgment, or summary of literary, historical, or other writings, arranged systematically.
Syn.—code, abridgment, abstract, compendium, epitome, summary, synopsis, system.
di·ġest′, *v.t.*; digested, *pt., pp.*; digesting, *ppr.* [L. *digestus,* pp. of *digerere,* to carry apart, distribute, set in order, arrange; *dis-,* apart, and *gerere,* to carry.]
1. to distribute into suitable classes, or under proper heads or titles; to arrange systematically, usually in condensed form; to summarize; as, to *digest* the Roman laws or the common law.
2. [after L. *digerere cibum,* to cut up (dissolve) food.] to change (food) in the mouth, stomach, and intestines by the action of gastric and intestinal juices, enzymes, and bacteria so that it can be absorbed by the body.
3. to aid the digestion of (food).
4. to think over; to absorb mentally.
5 to tolerate or accept.
6. in chemistry, to soften or make soluble with heat and moisture.
7. to cause (an ulcer or wound) to suppurate. [Obs.]
di·ġest′, *v.i.* 1. to be digested.
2. to digest food.
di·ġest′ănt, *a.* and *n.* same as *digestive.*
di·ġest′ed·ly, *adv.* in a well-arranged manner.
di·ġest′ẽr, di·ġest′ŏr, *n.* 1. one who digests or makes a digest.
2. one who digests his food.
3. a medicine or article of food that aids digestion.
4. a heavy metal container in which substances are heated or cooked to soften them or extract soluble elements from them.
di·ġest·i·bil′i·ty, *n.* the quality of being digestible.
di·ġest′i·ble, *a.* capable of being digested.
di·ġes′tion, *n.* [ME. *digestioun*; OFr. *digestion*; L. *digestio,* digestion, an orderly distribution.]

1. a digesting or being digested: said of food.
2. the ability to digest food.
3. the absorption of ideas; understanding.

di·ġest′ive, *a.* [LL. *digestivus*, from L. *digestus*, pp. of *digerere*, to digest.] of, for, or aiding digestion.

di·ġest′ive, *n.* any substance, etc. that aids digestion.

di·ġest′ŏr, *n.* see *digester*.

di·ġes′tūre, *n.* concoction; digestion. [Obs.]

digged (digd), original past tense and past participle of *dig*, now archaic or poetic.

dig′ġẽr, *n.* 1. one who or that which digs.
2. a tool or machine for digging.
3. the digging part of such a machine.
4. [D–] a member of any of several tribes of Indians in the western United States who dug up roots for food.
5. a digger wasp.

dig′ġẽr wăsp, any of various wasps that dig a nest in the ground or in wood.

dig′gings, *n.pl.* 1. materials dug out.
2. [*often construed as sing.*] a place where digging or mining, especially gold mining, is carried on.
3. originally, a gold miner's camp; hence, the place where one lives; quarters. [Slang.]

dīght (dīt), *v.t.*; dight *or* dighted, *pt., pp.*; dighting, *ppr.* [ME. *dighten*; AS. *dihtan*, to set in order, arrange, from L. *dictare*, to say.]
1. to prepare; to put in order; hence, to dress or put on; to array; to adorn.
2. to equip.
3. to have sexual intercourse with. [Obs.] [Archaic and Poet. in senses 1, 2.]

diġ′it, *n.* [L. *digitus*, a finger.]
1. a finger or toe.
2. any one of the ten Arabic numerals or symbols, 0, 1, 2, 3, 4, 5, 6, 7, 8, 9, by combinations of which all numbers are expressed: so called from counting on the fingers.
3. the measure of a finger's breadth, or three-fourths of an inch.
4. in astronomy, the twelfth part of the diameter of the sun or moon: a term used to express the quantity of an eclipse; as, an eclipse of six *digits* is one which hides one-half of the disk.

diġ′it, *v.t.* to point at with the finger. [Obs.]

diġ′i·tăl, *a.* 1. of, pertaining to, or resembling a digit or digits.
2. digitate.
3. performed with the finger.
4. using numbers that are digits to represent all the variables involved in calculation.
5. showing the time, temperature, etc. by a row of digits rather than by numbers on a dial, etc.; as, a *digital* watch.

diġ′i·tăl, *n.* 1. a finger.
2. a key played with a finger, as on a piano or similar musical instrument.
3. the final articulation of a spider's pedipalpus.

diġ′i·tăl çŏm·pūt′ẽr, a computer that uses numbers to perform logical and numerical calculations, usually in a binary system.

diġ·i·tal′in, *n.* [from *digitalis*, and *-in.*] a poisonous crystalline glucoside, $C_{36}H_{56}O_{14}$, obtained from the seed of the digitalis.

diġ·i·tal′is (*or* -tā′lis), *n.* [ML. *digitalis*, foxglove: so named by Fuchs (1542) from its thimblelike flowers, after the G. name *fingerhut*, lit., finger hat, i.e., thimble.]
1. [D-] a genus of plants of the figwort family, with long spikes of thimblelike flowers; foxglove.
2. the dried leaves of the purple foxglove.
3. a medicine made from these leaves, used as a heart stimulant.

diġ′i·tăl·iṣm, *n.* a condition of the body caused by excessive use of digitalis.

diġ′it·ăl·ly, *adv.* with the finger or fingers.

diġ′i·tāte, *v.t.* to point out, as with the finger. [Rare.]

diġ′i·tāte, *a.* 1. having separate fingers or toes.
2. like a digit; fingerlike.
3. in botany, having fingerlike divisions, as some leaves.

diġ′i·tā·ted, *a.* same as *digitate*.

diġ′i·tāte·ly, *adv.* in a digitate manner.

diġ·i·tā′tion, *n.* in botany, (a) a digitate condition; (b) a fingerlike part.

diġ·i·ti-, [from Latin *digitus*, finger.] a combining form meaning *finger* or *toe*.

diġ′i·ti·fọrm, *a.* [*digiti-*, and L. *forma*, form.] in the shape of a finger or arranged like fingers; digitate.

Diġ·i·tig′rȧ·dȧ, *n.pl.* [*digiti-*, and L. *gradi*, to walk.] the second tribe, in Cuvier's arrangement, of *Carnivora*, including those animals which walk on the toes only, as the lion, tiger, cat, weasel, civet, hyena, etc.: distinguished from the *Plantigrada*, which walk on the broad sole of the foot.

diġ′i·ti·grāde, *a.* 1. walking on the toes with the heels not touching the ground, as cats, dogs, horses, etc.
2. of, or relating to the *Digitigrada*.

diġ′i·ti·grāde, *n.* any animal that is digitigrade.

diġ′i·ti·nẽrved, *a.* [*digiti-*, and L. *nervus*, nerve.] in botany, having radiate nervation from the apex of the leaf.

diġ″i·ti·pär′tīte, *a.* in botany, parted like the extended fingers.

diġ′i·tīze, *v.t.* to finger; to handle. [Rare.]

diġ·i·tox′in, *n.* [*digitalis*, and *toxin*.] a glucoside, $C_{41}H_{64}O_{13}$, extracted from digitalis leaves, like digitalis in physiological action, but more potent.

diġ′i·tūle, *n.* [L. *digitulus*, dim. of *digitus*, a finger.] in zoology, a small finger or toe.

diġ′i·tus, *n.*; *pl.* **diġ′i·tī,** [L.] in entomology, the final articulation of the tarsus.

dī·glad′i·āte, *v.t.* [L. *digladiari*, to fight for life or death.] to fence; to quarrel. [Rare.]

dī·glad′i·ā′tion, *n.* a combat with swords; a quarrel. [Obs.]

dī′glot, *a.* [Gr. *diglōssos*, speaking two languages; *di-*, two, and *glōssa*, tongue.] in or using two languages; bilingual.

dī′glot, *n.* a diglot edition of a book.

dī·glot′tiṣm, *n.* the use of two languages; bilingualism. [Rare.]

dī′glyph, *n.* [Gr. *diglyphos*, doubly indented; *di-*, two, and *glyphein*, to hollow out, carve, cut.] in architecture, an imperfect triglyph having two channels instead of three.

diġ·nā′tion, *n.* the act of believing worthy or of conferring honor. [Obs.]

dīgne (dīn *or* dēn), *a.* worthy; proud. [Obs.]

diġ″ni·fi·çā′tion, *n.* the act of dignifying; exaltation; promotion.

diġ′ni·fīed, *a.* having or showing dignity; as, a *dignified* bearing.

diġ′ni·fȳ, *v.t.*; dignified, *pt., pp.*; dignifying, *ppr.* [OFr. *dignifier*, to dignify, from L. *dignus*, worthy, and *facere*, to make.]
1. to invest with honor or dignity; to exalt in rank; to promote; to make worthy.
2. to give a high-sounding name to; as, he *dignified* cowardice with the name of prudence.

Syn.—exalt, elevate, prefer, advance, honor, adorn, ennoble.

diġ′ni·tā·ry, *n.*; *pl.* **diġ′ni·tā·rieṣ,** [L. *dignitas*, dignity.] a person holding a high, dignified position or office, as in a church.

diġ′ni·ty, *n.*; *pl.* **diġ′ni·tieṣ,** [ME. *dignitee*; OFr. *dignite*; L. *dignitas*, worth, merit, from *dignus*, worthy.]
1. worthiness; nobility.
2. high repute; honor.
3. the degree of worth, repute, or honor.
4. a high position, rank, or title.
5. a dignitary. [Rare.]
6. loftiness of appearance or manner; stateliness.
7. calm self-possession and self-respect.
8. a general maxim or principle. [Obs.]
9. in astrology, an advantage which a planet has on account of its being in some particular place of the zodiac, or in a particular station in respect to other planets.

to stand upon one's dignity; to have or assume an exalted idea of one's own importance, especially if offended.

diġ·nō′tion, *n.* distinguishing mark; distinction. [Obs.]

dī·gō·neū′tiç, *a.* having broods twice a year: said of insects.

diġ′ō·nous, *a.* [*di-*, and Gr. *gōnia*, an angle.] in botany, having two angles, as a stem.

dī′gram, *n.* a digraph.

dī′grȧph, *n.* [*di-*, and Gr. *graphein*, to write.] a combination of two letters to represent one simple sound, as *read*, *show*, *graphic*, etc.

dī·graph′iç, *a.* of or pertaining to a digraph.

di·gress′, *v.i.*; digressed (-grest), *pt., pp.*; digressing, *ppr.* [L. *digressus*, pp. of *digredi*, to go apart, separate; *dis-*, apart, and *gradi*, to go, step.]
1. literally, to step or go from the way or road; hence, to depart temporarily from the main subject in talking or writing; to ramble.
2. to stray from the right way or common track; to deviate. [Obs.]

di·gress′, *n.* a digression. [Obs.]

di·gres′sion (-gresh′un), *n.* [ME. *digression*; L. *digressio*, a parting, separating, from *digressus*, pp. of *digredi*, to go apart, separate.]
1. a digressing; a temporary departure from the main subject in talking or writing.
2. deviation from a regular course; as, the *digression* of a ship.
3. departure from virtue; transgression. [Rare.]
4. in astronony, the apparent distance of the inferior planets, Mercury and Venus, from the sun; elongation.

di·gres′sion·ăl, *a.* same as *digressive*.

di·gress′ive, *a.* departing from the main subject; given to digression; digressing.

di·gress′ive·ly, *adv.* by way of digression.

digue (dig), *n.* a dike.

Dī·ġyn′i·ȧ, *n.pl.* [L., from Gr. *di-*, two, and *gynē*, a woman, a female.] in the Linnaean system, an order of plants having two pistils.

dī·ġyn′i·ăn, diġ′yn·ous, *a.* in botany, having two pistils.

dī·hē′drăl, *a.* [from *di-*, and Gr. *hedra*, a seat, base.]
1. having two plane faces or sides; as, a *dihedral* angle.
2. having wings that form a dihedral angle with each other, as some airplanes.
3. in solid geometry, formed by two intersecting planes.

dī·hē′drăl, *n.* 1. a dihedral angle.
2. the angle between either wing of an airplane and the horizontal plane of its transverse axis.

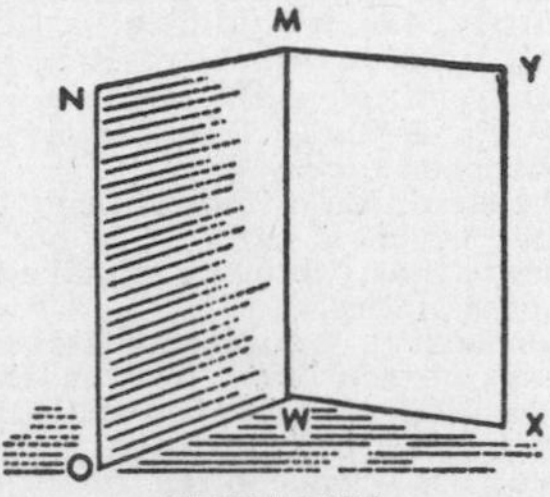

DIHEDRAL ANGLE
angle formed by planes MWON and MWXY

dī·hex·ag′ō·năl, *a.* [*di-*, and Gr. *hexagōnos*, six-cornered; *hex*, six, and *gōnia*, corner.] twelve-sided; doubly hexagonal.

dī·hex·ȧ·hē′drăl, *a.* in crystallography, having the form of a hexahedral prism with trihedral summits.

dī·hex·ȧ·hē′drŏn, *n.* [*di*, and Gr. *hex*, six, and *hedra*, a seat, base.] in crystallography, a dihexahedral prism.

dī·i·amb′, *n.* [Gr. *diiambos*, a diiamb; *di-*, two, and *iambos*, an iambus.] in prosody, a double iamb; a foot consisting of two iambs.

dī·i·am′bus, *n.*; *pl.* **dī·i·am′bī,** same as *diiamb*.

dī·i·sat′ō·ġen, *n.* [*di-*, and *isatine*, and *-gen.*] a red crystalline compound easily transformed into indigo.

Dī·jŏn′ mus′tȧrd (-zhōn̄), [after *Dijon*, city in France where orig. made.] a seasoning of mild mustard paste, usually blended with wine.

dī·jū′di·çănt, *n.* one who dijudicates. [Obs.]

dī·jū′di·çāte, *v.t.* and *v.i.* [L. *dijudicatus*, pp. of *dijudicare*, to judge between, decide; *dis-*, apart, and *judicare*, to judge.] to judge or determine.

dī·jū·di·çā′tion, *n.* a judging between; judicial distinction.

dī′kȧ, *n.* [native West African name.] dika bread.

dī′kȧ bread (bred), an oily chocolatelike substance, prepared by the West Africans from the nuts of the tree *Irvingia gabonensis*, and used as food.

dik·ȧ·mä′li, *n.* [E. Ind. name.] a fragrant resinous gum used as a lotion, exuding from the ends of young shoots of *Gardenia lucida*, an East Indian tree.

dik′-dik, *n.* [from the Ethiopian native name.] a very small African antelope.

dīke, dȳke, *n.* [ME. *dike*, *dyke*; AS. *dic*, a ditch, channel, dike.]
1. a ditch or watercourse.
2. the bank of earth thrown up in digging a ditch.
3. a causeway, embankment, or low dividing wall of earth or stone.
4. an embankment or dam made to prevent flooding by the sea or by a stream.
5. a protective barrier or obstacle.

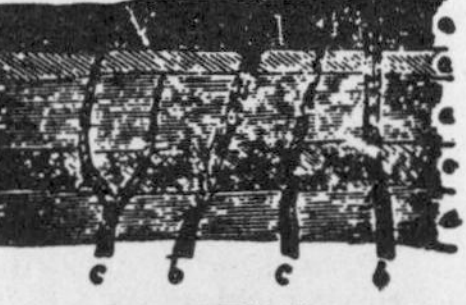
DIKE (Fig. 1)

6. a stone or turf fence. [Scot. and Brit. Dial.]

7. in geology, a vein of basalt, greenstone, or other igneous rock which has been intruded in a melted state into rents or fissures of rocks. When a mass of the unstratified or igneous rocks, such as granite, trap, and lava, appears as if injected into a great rent in the stratified rocks, cutting across the strata, it forms a *dike*. In fig. 1, *a a* are horizontal strata, *b c* dikes of lava forced through the strata; *b b* are of equal breadth throughout their entire length, and *c c* decrease upward. In fig. 2, the horizontal strata are shown worn away by the action of the weather, and the vertical veins of lava *d d* (marked *c b* in fig. 1), being harder, have resisted its effects, and consequently remain projecting in the form of walls or dikes.

DIKE (Fig. 2)

dīke, dȳke, *v.t.*; diked (dīkt), *pt., pp.*; diking, *ppr.* 1. to surround or protect with a dike.
2. to drain by a ditch.

dīke, *v.i.* to dig.

dīke′grāve, *n.* [D. *dijkgraaf.*] in Holland, a dike superintendent.

dīk′ẽr, *n.* one who builds dikes or ditches.

dīke′reeve, *n.* [AS. *dic,* a ditch, and *gerefa,* a superintendent.] a superintendent of dikes and ditches. [Brit.]

dī·lac′ẽr·āte, *v.t.*; dilacerated, *pt., pp.*; dilacerating, *ppr.* [L. *dilaceratus,* pp. of *dilacerare,* to tear to pieces.] to tear to pieces; to rip; to rend asunder.

di·lā′ni·āte, *v.t.* [L. *dilaniatus,* pp. of *dilaniare,* to tear in pieces.] to tear; to rend in pieces; to mangle. [Obs.]

di·lā·ni·ā′tion, *n.* a tearing in pieces. [Obs.]

di·lan′tin, *n.* [from *di*phenyl*hydantoin* sodium.] a drug used in the treatment of epileptic attacks: in full, *dilantin sodium*: a trademark (*Dilantin*).

di·lap′i·dāte, *v.t.*; dilapidated, *pt., pp.*; dilapidating, *ppr.* [L. *dilapidatus,* pp. of *dilapidare,* to squander, consume, demolish, scatter like stones; *dis-,* apart, and *lapidare,* to throw stones at, from *lapis* (*-idis*), a stone.]
1. to pull down; to waste or destroy partially; to allow to go to ruin.
2. to waste; to squander.

di·lap′i·dāte, *v.i.* to go to ruin; to become partially ruined and in need of repairs.

di·lap′i·dā·ted, *a.* 1. falling to pieces or into disrepair; broken down; ruined.
2. shabby and neglected.

di·lap·i·dā′tion, *n.* 1. a dilapidating or becoming dilapidated.
2. a dilapidated condition.

di·lap′i·dā·tŏr, *n.* one who causes dilapidation.

dī·lā·tȧ·bil′i·ty, *n.* the quality of being dilatable.

dī·lāt′ȧ·ble, *a.* [L. *dilatare,* to expand.] that can be dilated.

dī·lāt′ăn·cy, *n.* that characteristic of matter in granular form, which makes a change of shape result in an increase of volume.

dī·lāt′ănt, *a.* 1. dilating or tending to dilate.
2. expanding in bulk when the shape changes: said of certain granular substances.

dī·lāt′ănt, *n.* 1. a thing that can dilate.
2. a surgical instrument for dilating; dilator.

dil·ȧ·tā′tion, *n.* [ME. *dilatacioun*; LL. *dilatatio,* an extension, expansion, from L. *dilatatus,* pp. of *dilatare,* to expand.]
1. dilation.
2. in medicine, enlargement of an organ, cavity, duct, or opening of the body, beyond normal size.
3. verbosity; wordiness; as, *dilatation* of speech.

dil·ȧ·tā′tŏr, *n.* anything that dilates; specifically, in anatomy, a muscle which dilates any part or organ.

dī·lāte′, *v.t.*; dilated, *pt., pp.*; dilating, *ppr.* [L. *dilatare,* to spread out, extend, make wider; *dis-,* apart, and *latus,* pp. of *ferre,* to bring.]
1. to make wider or larger; to cause to expand or swell: opposed to *contract*; as, air *dilates* the lungs.
2. to enlarge upon; to relate at large; to tell copiously or diffusely. [Rare.]
Syn.—expand, swell, distend, enlarge, amplify, expatiate.

dī·lāte′, *v.i.* 1. to become wider or larger; to swell.
2. to speak or write in detail (*on* or *upon* a subject): as, an advocate may weaken his argument by *dilating on* trivial circumstances.

dī·lāte′, *a.* expanded; expansive. [Obs.]

dī·lāt′ed, *a.* 1. expanded; distended; enlarged so as to occupy a greater space.
2. in biology, unusually widened or broad as a part or organ.

dī·lāt′ed·ly, *adv.* in a dilated manner.

dī·lāt′ẽr, *n.* same as *dilator.*

dī·lā′tion, *n.* delay. [Obs.]

dī·lā′tion, *n.* 1. a dilating or being dilated.
2. a dilated part.

dī·lāt′ive, *a.* causing dilation; having a tendency to dilate or distend.

dil·ȧ·tom′e·tẽr, *n.* [LL. *dilatatio,* an extension, and L. *metrum,* a measure.] an apparatus for measuring the dilatation, or expansion, of a substance.

dī·lāt′ŏr, *n.* 1. one who or that which widens or expands.
2. a muscle that dilates a part of the body.
3. a surgical instrument for dilating an opening, wound, etc.

dil′ȧ·tō·ri·ly, *adv.* in a dilatory manner.

dil′ȧ·tō·ri·ness, *n.* the quality of being dilatory or late; lateness; slowness in motion; delay in proceeding; tardiness.

dil′ȧ·tō·ry, *a.* [LL. *dilatorius,* tending to delay, from L. *dilator,* a dilatory person, from *dilatus,* pp. of *differre,* to put off, delay.]
1. causing or tending to cause delay; meant to gain time, defer action, etc.
2. inclined to delay; slow or late in doing things; procrastinating.

dil′dō, *n.* a refrain or nonsense word in old songs, often implying obscenity. [Obs.]

dil′dō, *n.* a cactus, *Lemaireocereus hystrix,* found in the West Indies.

dil′dō, *n.*; *pl.* **dil′dōs, dil′dōes,** [perh. from It. *diletto,* delight.] a device of rubber, etc., shaped like an erect penis and used as a sexual stimulator: also spelled *dildoe.*

di·leç′tion, *n.* a loving; a preference. [Obs.]

di·lem′mȧ, *n.* [LL. *dilemma*; Gr. *dilēmma,* an argument which presents two or more alternatives; *di-,* two, and *lēmma,* a proposition or assumption, from *lambanein,* to take.]
1. in logic, an argument which presents an antagonist with a choice between equally unfavorable or disagreeable alternatives.
2. any situation necessitating a choice between unpleasant alternatives; a perplexing or awkward situation.

A strong *dilemma* in a desperate case!
To act with infamy, or quit the place.
—Swift.

on the horns of a dilemma; faced with a choice between alternatives which are equally undesirable or dangerous.

dil·et·tȧnt′, *a.* and *n.* same as dilettante.

dil·et·tȧn′te, *n.*; *pl.* **dil·et·tȧn′tes, dil·et·tȧn′ti,** [It., from ppr. of *dilettare,* to delight; L. *delectare,* to charm, delight.]
1. an admirer or lover of the fine arts.
2. a dabbler; a trifler; one who pursues an art desultorily and for amusement: sometimes applied contemptuously to one who affects a taste for, or a degree of acquaintance with, or skill in, art which he does not possess.

dil·et·tȧn′te, *a.* of or having the characteristics of a dilettante.

dil·et·tȧn′te·ish, *a.* same as *dilettantish.*

dil·et·tȧn′te·ism, *n.* same as *dilettantism.*

dil·et·tȧnt′ish, *a.* of the nature of or inclined toward dilettantism.

dil·et·tȧnt′ism, *n.* the pursuits and characteristics of a dilettante; specifically, an aimless, trifling, or affected pursuit of art, literature, or science.

dil′i·gence, *n.* [ME. *diligence*; OFr., *diligence*; L. *diligentia,* carefulness, diligence, from *diligens,* careful, diligent, ppr. of *diligere,* to choose apart, esteem highly, select; *dis-,* apart, and *legere,* to choose.]
1. the quality of being diligent.
2. steady application to business of any kind; constant effort to accomplish what is undertaken: perseverance; industry; assiduity.
3. care; caution. [Obs.]
4. in Scots law, (a) the warrant issued by a court for enforcing the attendance of witnesses or the production of writings; (b) the process of law by which persons, lands, or effects are attached on execution, or in security for debt.

dil′i·gence (*or Fr.* dēl-ē-zhoṅs′), *n.* a kind of stagecoach formerly much used in France and other European countries.

dil′i·gen·cy, *n.* diligence.

dil′i·gent, *a.* 1. steady in application to business; constant in effort or exertion to accomplish what is undertaken; assiduous; attentive; industrious; not idle or negligent: applied to persons.

Seest thou a man *diligent* in his business?
He shall stand before kings.—Prov. xxii. 29.

2. steadily applied; done with care and constant effort; careful; painstaking; as, make *diligent* search.

The judges shall make *diligent* inquisition.
—Deut. xix. 18.

Syn.—active, assiduous, sedulous, laborious, persevering, attentive, industrious, indefatigable, unremitting, untiring, careful.

dil′i·gent·ly, *adv.* in a diligent manner.

dill, *n.* [ME. *dille, dylle*: AS. *dile,* the dill plant.]
1. an annual plant, *Anethum graveolens,* of the parsley family, the aromatic seeds of which are used to flavor pickles, etc. The plant is native to the Mediterranean region, but is cultivated extensively in gardens. It is the anise of the Bible.
2. the seeds of this plant.

dill, *v.t.* to soothe; to allay, as pain. [Scot. and Brit. Dial.]

Dil·lē′ni·ȧ, *n.* [from *Dillen,* a professor of botany at Oxford (1728–1747).] the type genus of the family *Dilleniaceæ,* consisting of lofty forest trees, natives of tropical Asia. They have large leaves and showy white or yellow flowers.

Dil·lē·ni·ā′cē·ae, *n.pl.* a family of plants belonging to the polypetalous, albuminous exogens and having a persistent calyx and arillate seeds. Seventeen genera and about two hundred species are included in the order. They are trees or shrubs, with alternate leaves, found in warmer regions.

dil·lē·ni·ā′ceous, *a.* of or pertaining to the *Dilleniaceæ.*

dil′ling, *n.* a last child born in a family. [Now Dial.]

dill pick′le, a large cucumber pickle flavored with dill.

dil′lūe, *v.t.* to sift (tin ore) through a sieve. [Brit. Dial.]

dil′ly, *n.* 1. a diligence (stagecoach). [Obs.]
2. a cart, truck, wagon, or similar vehicle. [Now Dial.]

dil′ly, *n.* same as *daffodil.* [Colloq.]

dil′ly, *n.* a small tree, *Mimusops sieberi,* of the star apple family, native to Florida and the West Indies.

dil′ly·dal′ly, *v.i.*; dillydallied, *pt., pp.*; dillydallying, *ppr.* to consume time by hesitating, vacillating, loitering, trifling, etc.

di·log′iç·ăl, *a.* conveying a double meaning; ambiguous.

dil′ō·ġy, *n.* [L. *dilogia*; Gr. *dilogia,* repetition; *di-,* twice, and *legein,* to speak.] in rhetoric, (a) repetition, particularly to give emphasis; (b) an expression having (intentionally) more than one meaning.

di·lū′ci·dāte, *v.t.* to make clear; to elucidate. [Obs.]

di·lū·ci·dā′tion, *n.* the act of making clear. [Obs.]

di·lū·en′dō, *a.* and *adv.* same as *diminuendo.*

dil′ū·ent, *a.* [L. *diluens* (*-entis*), ppr. of *diluere,* to dilute.]
1. diluting; tending to weaken or dilute.
2. dissolving.

dil′ū·ent, *n.* 1. that which dilutes or dissolves; that which makes more liquid.
2. in medicine, any substance which thins the blood.

di·lūte′, *v.t.*; diluted, *pt., pp.*; diluting, *ppr.* [L. *dilutus,* pp. of *diluere,* to wash away; *dis-,* off, from, and *luere,* to wash.]
1. to thin down or weaken by mixing with water or other liquid.
2. to change or weaken (in brilliancy, force, etc.) by mixing with something else.

di·lūte′, *v.i.* to become weak or thin.

di·lūte′, *a.* thin; attenuated; reduced in strength, as spirit or color.

di·lūt′ed, *a.* weakened; made thin, as liquids.

di·lūt′ed·ly, *adv.* in a diluted form.

di·lūte′ness, *n.* the quality or state of being dilute.

di·lūt′ẽr, *n.* one who or that which dilutes.

di·lū'tion, *n.* [L. *dilutus*, pp. of *diluere*, to wash away.]
1. the act of diluting or the state of being diluted.
2. a substance which has been diluted.

di·lū'vi·ăl, *a.* [LL. *diluvialis*, pertaining to a flood, from L. *diluvium*, a flood, deluge, from *diluere*, to wash away.]
1. pertaining to a flood or deluge, especially to the Deluge in Noah's days.
2. of, pertaining to, or consisting of diluvium.

di·lū'vi·ăl·ist, *n.* one who explains geological phenomena by reference to a general deluge, especially the one in the days of Noah.

di·lū'vi·ăn, *a.* diluvial.

di·lū'vi·ăn·ism, *n.* the theory that a former universal deluge explains all geological phenomena.

di·lū'vi·āte, *v.i.* to flow as a flood. [Obs.]

di·lū'vi·um, *n.* [L. *diluvium*, a deluge, from *diluere*, to wash away.] in geology, a deposit of superficial loam, sand, gravel, pebbles, etc. left by a flood or glacier.

dim, *a.*; *comp.* dimmer; *superl.* dimmest, [ME. *dim*, *dym*; AS. *dim*, *dimm*, dim, dark.]
1. not seeing or hearing clearly; having the vision or hearing obscured and indistinct.
My heart is breaking and my eyes are *dim*. —Tennyson.
2. not clearly seen, heard, perceived, or understood; faint; vague; as, a *dim* recollection.
Dim with the mist of the years, gray flits the shade of power. —Byron.
3. somewhat dark; dusky; not luminous or bright; as, a *dim* shade.
And storied windows richly dight
Casting a *dim* religious light. —Milton.
4. dull of apprehension; slow to perceive.
The understanding is *dim*. —Rogers.
5. having its luster obscured; sullied; tarnished.
How is the gold become *dim*!—Lam. iv. 1.
6. not clear; indistinct.
to take a dim view of; to view skeptically, pessimistically, without enthusiasm, etc.
Syn.—obscure, dusky, dark, mysterious, indistinct, ill-defined, indefinite, imperfect, dull, sullied, tarnished.

dim, *v.t.* and *v.i.*; dimmed, *pt.*, *pp.*; dimming, *ppr.* [ME. *dimmen*; AS. *dimmian*, to make dim.]
1. to make or grow dim.
2. to make seem dim, as by comparison.

Dī·mas'ti·gȧ, *n.pl.* [L., from Gr. *di-*, two, and *mastix* (*-igos*), a whip.] a division of *Infusoria* having two whiplike flagella.

dī·mas'ti·gāte, *a.* of or pertaining to the *Dimastiga*; having two flagella.

dim'ble, *n.* a dingle; a dell. [Obs.]

dīme, *n.* [ME. *dyme*, *disme*; OFr. *disme*, a tithe, tenth; L. *decimus*, a tenth, from *decem*, ten.] a silver coin of the United States and Canada equal to ten cents or one-tenth of a dollar.
a dime a dozen; existing in great quantity and easily obtained; cheap. [Colloq.]

dīme, *a.* costing a dime; sold for a dime.
dime novel; a paper-covered book very melodramatic as to style and without literary worth, originally costing a dime.

di·men'sion, *n.* [OFr. *dimension*; L. *dimensio*, a measuring, from *dimensus*, pp. of *dimetiri*, to measure off; *dis-*, off, from, and *metiri*, to measure.]
1. extension in a single line or direction, as length, breadth, and thickness or depth; as, a line has one *dimension*, length; a plane has two *dimensions*, length and breadth; and a solid has three *dimensions*, length, breadth, and thickness or depth.
2. [*pl.*] measurement in length, breadth, and, often, height; as, the *dimensions* of a room, of a ship, of a farm, of a kingdom, etc.
3. extent; size; degree.
4. [*often pl.*] outline; shape; form; proportions: especially applied to the human body. [Obs.]
In *dimension*, and the shape of nature, a gracious person. —Shak.
5. figuratively, consequence; importance; scope; as, the question is assuming great *dimensions*.
6. in algebra, the sum of the exponents in a term; as, xy^2z and a^2b^2cd are terms of five and six *dimensions*, respectively.
7. in physics, a fundamental quantity, as mass, length, or time, in terms of which all other physical quantities, as those of area, velocity, power, etc. are measured; as, the *dimensions* of density are mass divided by the cube of length.

di·men'sion·ăl, *a.* 1. having (a specified number of) dimensions; measurable; as, a cube is a three-*dimensional* object.
2. pertaining to dimension or dimensions.

di·men'sioned, *a.* having dimensions.

di·men'sion·less, *a.* without definite measure or extent; boundless.

di·men'sion lum'bẽr, lumber cut to definite and precise sizes.

di·men'sion stōne, rough stone which will dress to a specified size; sometimes, the dressed stone.

di·men'sion wŏrk, masonry in which dimension stones are used.

di·men'si·ty, *n.* dimension. [Rare.]

di·men'sive, *a.* pertaining to boundaries or outlines. [Rare.]

Dim'e·rȧ, *n.pl.* [LL., from Gr. *dimerēs*, divided into two parts, *di-*, two, and *meros*, a part.] a group of homopterous insects having two-jointed tarsi, including the aphids.

dim'ẽr·ăn, *a.* pertaining to or of the nature of the *Dimera*.

dim'ẽr·ăn, *n.* one of the *Dimera*.

dim'ẽr·ous, *a.* 1. composed of two parts; bipartite.
2. in botany, having two members in each whorl or verticil.
3. in entomology, having two-jointed tarsi.

dīme stōre, a store where a wide variety of low-priced articles is sold, many for five or ten cents.

dim'e·tẽr, *a.* [Gr. *dimetros*, consisting of two feet or measures; *di-*, two, and *metron*, a measure.] having two measures.

dim'e·tẽr, *n.* in prosody, a line consisting of two measures (two or four feet).

dī·meth'yl, *n.* ethane.

dī·meth·yl·an'i·line, *n.* [*di-*, and *methyl*, and *aniline*.] an oily liquid $C_8H_{11}N$, the base of many coal tar colors.

dī·met'riç, *a.* [*di-*, two, and Gr. *metron*, a measure.] in crystallography, tetragonal.

dim·i·çā'tion, *n.* a battle or fight; contest. [Rare.]

di·mid'i·āte, *v.t.* [L. *dimidiatus*, pp. of *dimidiare*, to divide into halves, from *dimidium*, a half; *dis-*, apart, from, and *medius*, middle.]
1. to divide into two equal parts or reduce to half.
2. in heraldry, to divide into two parts, showing but one.

di·mid'i·āte, *a.* [L. *dimidiatus*, pp. of *dimidiare*, to halve.]
1. halved.
2. in zoology and anatomy, one-sided, as in hermaphroditism when the organs on one side are male and on the other, female.
3. in biology, having only one half developed.
4. in botany, split on one side, as some capsules.
5. in heraldry, reduced by half.

di·mid·i·ā'tion, *n.* the act of halving; the condition of being dimidiated.

di·min'ish, *v.t.*; diminished (-isht), *pt.*, *pp.*; diminishing, *ppr.* [Fr. *diminuer*; L. *deminuere*, to make smaller; diminish; *de*, from, and *minuere*, to make smaller, from *minus*, small.]
1. to lessen; to make less or smaller; to reduce in size or degree: opposed to *increase* and *augment*; as, to *diminish* the size of a thing by contraction or by cutting off a part; to *diminish* a number by subtraction; to *diminish* the revenue by limiting commerce or reducing the customs; to *diminish* strength or safety; to *diminish* the heat of a room.
2. to impair; to degrade; to reduce in importance.
I will *diminish* them, that they shall no more rule over the nations. —Ezek. xxix. 15.
3. in music, to reduce (a minor interval) by a semitone.
Syn.—decrease, reduce, abate, curtail.

di·min'ish, *v.i.* to lessen; to become smaller.

di·min'ish·ȧ·ble, *a.* capable of being reduced or diminished.

di·min'ished, *a.* [pp. of *diminish*.]
1. made smaller; lessened; reduced.
2. in music, lessened by a semitone: said of intervals or of chords formed with such an interval.
diminished arch; an arch less than a semicircle.
diminished bar; in joinery, the bar of a sash which is thinnest on its inner edge.
diminished column; a column tapering from bottom to top.

di·min'ish·ẽr, *n.* one who or that which diminishes.

di·min'ish·ing·ly, *adv.* in a diminishing manner.

di·min'ish·ing rē·tŭrn', in economics, the proportionately smaller increase in productivity observed after a certain point in the increase of capital or labor.

di·min'ish·ing rûle, a concave rule to measure the swell of a column.

di·min'ish·ing sçāle, a scale used in plotting the spiral of the scroll of an Ionic column.

di·min'ish·ment, *n.* diminution. [Rare.]

di·min·ū·en'dō, *a.* and *adv.* [It., from *diminuere*, to diminish.] in music, gradually diminishing in volume of sound; decrescendo.

di·min·ū·en'dō, *n.*; *pl.* **di·min·ū·en'dōṣ**, 1. a gradual decrease in loudness.
2. a passage played diminuendo.

di·min'ū·ent, *a.* lessening. [Obs.]

dim·i·nū'tăl, *a.* pertaining to diminution. [Obs.]

dim'i·nūte, *a.* small. [Obs.]

dim'i·nūte·ly, *adv.* minutely. [Obs.]

dim·i·nū'tion, *n.* [ME. *diminution*; L. *deminutio*, a lessening, diminishing, from *deminuere*, to diminish.]
1. the act of lessening; a making smaller: opposed to *augmentation*; as, the *diminution* of size, of wealth, of power, of safety.
2. the state of becoming or appearing less: opposed to *increase*; as, the *diminution* of the apparent diameter of a receding body.
3. deprivation of dignity; a lessening of estimation; degradation.
4. in architecture, the contraction of the upper part of a column, by which its diameter is made less than that of the lower part.
5. in music, the imitation of or reply to a subject in notes of one-half or one-quarter the length of those of the subject itself.
6. in law, an omission in the record, or in some point of the proceedings, which is certified in a writ of error on the part of either plaintiff or defendant.
7. in heraldry, the defacing of some particular point in the escutcheon.

di·min·ū·tī'văl, *a.* and *n.* same as *diminutive*.

di·min'ū·tive, *a.* [LL. *diminutivus*, from L. *deminutus*, pp. of *deminuere*, to make small.]
1. smaller than ordinary or average; very small; tiny; as, a *diminutive* race of men.
2. having the power or tendency to lessen, decrease, or abridge. [Archaic.]
3. in grammar, expressing smallness or diminution; as, a *diminutive* suffix.

di·min'ū·tive, *n.* 1. in grammar, a word formed from another word, usually an appellative or generic term, to express smallness in size and, sometimes, endearment, as *ringlet*, *sonny*, or *lambkin*.
2. anything very small in size, importance, etc.

di·min'ū·tive·ly, *adv.* in a diminutive manner.

di·min'ū·tive·ness, *n.* smallness; littleness.

dim'ish, *a.* same as *dimmish*.

di·mis'sion (-mish'un), *n.* leave to depart. [Obs.]

dim'is·sō·ry, *a.* [LL. *dimissorius*, from L. *dimissus*, pp. of *dimittere*, to send away.]
1. sending away; dismissing to another jurisdiction.
2. granting leave to depart.
a letter dimissory; one given by a bishop dismissing a person who is removing into another diocese, and recommending him for reception there.

di·mit', *v.t.* [L. *dimittere*, to send away.]
1. to permit to go; specifically, in Freemasonry, to give a dimit.
2. to grant; to let.

di·mit', *n.* in Freemasonry, a letter from a lodge, permitting a member in good standing to affiliate with another Masonic lodge.

dim'i·ty, *n.* [Gr. *dimitos*, two-threaded, dimity; *dis-*, two, and *mitos*, thread.]
1. a stout cotton fabric with raised stripes or patterns, sometimes printed in colors, used for hangings and upholstering.
2. a lightweight cotton fabric, with fine twills, much used for dresses.

dim'ly, *adv.* [ME. *dimly*, *dimliche*, from AS. *dimlic*, dim.] in a dim or obscure manner; with a faint light; not brightly or clearly; with imperfect sight.

dim'mẽr, *n.* 1. a person that dims.
2. a device for dimming an electric light, as in automobile headlights or theater stage lights.

dim'mẽr, *a.* comp. of *dim*.

dim'mest, *a.* superl. of *dim*.

dim'mish, dim'my, *a.* slightly dim: also written *dimish*.

dim′ness, *n.* [ME. *dimnes*; AS. *dimnes*, from *dim*, dim.] the state or quality of being dim.

dī′morph, *n.* [L. *dimorphus*; Gr. *dimorphos*, having two forms; *di-*, two, and *morphē*, form.] either form taken by a dimorphous substance.

dī·mor′phiç, *a.* characterized by dimorphism; dimorphous.

dī·mor′phism, *n.* [Gr. *di-*, two, and *morphē*, form.]

1. in crystallography, the property of crystallizing in two distinct forms not derivable from one another.

2. in botany, the state of having two different kinds of leaves, flowers, stamens, etc. on the same plant or in the same species.

3. in zoology, the existence of two types, exclusive of sex, in the same species, distinct in coloring, size, etc.

dī·mor′phous, *a.* [Gr. *dimorphos*, having two forms; *di-*, two, and *morphē*, form.] characterized by dimorphism; dimorphic.

dim′ple (-pl), *n.* [Late ME. *dimpul*, from base of Eng. dial. *dump*, deep pit filled with water, and *-le*, dim. suffix.]

1. a slight depression or dent occurring in some soft part of the body, as on the cheek or chin.

2. a slight dent or cavity on any surface.

dim′ple, *v.i.*; dimpled, *pt.*, *pp.*; dimpling, *ppr.* to form dimples; to sink into depressions or little inequalities.

And smiling eddies *dimpled* on the main.
—Dryden.

dim′ple, *v.t.* to make dimples in; to mark with a dimple or dimples.

dim′ple·ment, *n.* the state of being dimpled. [Rare.]

dim′ply, *a.* full of dimples or small depressions.

dim sum (tsoom), [Chin.]

1. a small casing of dough filled variously with minced meat, vegetables, etc. and steamed.

2. a variety of these and similar delicacies served as a light meal.

dim′wit, *n.* a stupid person; a simpleton. [Slang.]

dim′wit″ted, *a.* like or characteristic of a dimwit. [Slang.]

din, *n.* [ME. *dyn*; AS. *dyne*, a loud noise, a rumbling.] noise; a loud sound; particularly, a rattling, clattering, or rumbling sound, long continued; as, the *din* of arms, the *din* of war.

The guests are met, the feast is set:
May'st hear the merry *din*. —Coleridge.

din, *v.t.*; dinned, *pt.*, *pp.*; dinning, *ppr.* 1. to strike with continued or confused sound; to stun with noise; to harass with clamor; as, to *din* the ear with cries.

2. to tell repeatedly or persistently; as, he *dinned* his story into my ears.

din, *v.i.* to make a din or noisy clamor.

dī·nän·de·riē′, *n.* [Fr., from *Dinant*, a city in Belgium, noted for its copperware.]

1. utensils of copper, originally intended for use in the kitchen, and oftentimes ornamented with coats of arms and other devices.

2. ornamental brasswork of the Orient.

dī·naph′thyl, *n.* [*di-* and *naphthylene*.] a crystalline substance, $C_{20}H_{14}$, formed from naphthylene.

dī·när′, *n.* [Ar., from L. *denarius*, a silver coin containing originally ten asses, from *decem*, ten.]

1. a medieval gold coin of some Moslem countries; specifically, one issued by the Damascene caliphs.

2. an Iranian coin equal to 1/100 rial.

3. the monetary unit of Algeria, Iraq, Jordan, Kuwait, Libya, Tunisia, People's Democratic Republic of Yemen, and Yugoslavia.

din′är·çhy, *n.* [*di-*, and Gr. *archein*, to rule.] a form of government in which the supreme power is vested in two persons.

din′-din″, *n.* dinner: orig., a child's word. [Colloq.]

din′dle, *n.* the common or corn sow thistle; also, the hawkweed.

din′dle, *v.t.* and *v.i.*; dindled, *pt.*, *pp.*; dindling, *ppr.* [prob. from *din*, and *-le*, freq. suffix, with intrusive *-d-*.] to tingle or vibrate, as with or from a loud sound, shock, etc. [Scot. and Brit. Dial.]

din′dle, *n.* a tingling; thrill. [Scot. and Brit. Dial.]

dīne, *v.i.*; dined, *pt.*, *pp.*; dining, *ppr.* [ME. *dinen*, *dynen*; OFr. *disner*, *disgner*, to dine; origin uncertain, thought to be from L. *de-*, intens., and *cenare*, to dine, from *cena*, dinner.] to take dinner; to eat the principal meal of the day.

to dine out; to eat dinner away from home.

to dine with Duke Humphrey; to be dinnerless.

dīne, *v.t.* 1. to give a dinner to; to furnish with the principal meal; to feed; to entertain at a dinner: used especially in the sense of festivities for an honored guest; as, society wined and *dined* the poet.

2. to dine upon; as, what will you *dine*? [Obs.]

dīn′ẽr, *n.* 1. one who dines.

2. a railroad car equipped to serve meals to passengers.

3. a small restaurant built to look like such a car.

dī·ner′iç, *a.* [from *di-* and Gr. *nēron*, *nēros*, water; and *-ic*.] in physics, constituting, or having to do with, the surface of contact between two liquids in the same container.

dīn′ẽr-out, *n.* one who is often entertained at dinner away from home.

di·net′iç·ăl, *a.* whirling around; turning on an axis; rotatory. [Obs.]

dī·nette′, *n.* 1. a dining alcove; the wing of a room in a small-sized apartment used in place of a dining room.

2. in England, a hot luncheon.

ding, *v.t.*; dinged, *pt.*, *pp.*; dinging, *ppr.* [ME. *dingen*, to strike, beat.]

1. to thrust violently; to pound; to punch, [Dial.]

2. to throw away with violence. [Dial.]

3. to sound or urge repeatedly. [Colloq.]

to ding in one's ears; to make an impression by frequent repetition.

ding, *v.i.* 1. to strike; to pound. [Dial.]

2. to resound, as a bell; to toll; to ring; to clang.

3. to repeat vehemently and monotonously; to scold; to bluster. [Colloq.]

ding, *n.* the sound of a bell, or a similar sound.

ding′-ă-ling′, *n.* [from the ringing in the head of a punch-drunk boxer.] a crazy or unbalanced person. [Slang.]

ding′bat, *n.* 1. a stone, stick, or other object suitable for throwing. [Colloq.]

2. a doohickey. [Colloq.]

ding′-dong, *n.* [imitative origin.]

1. the sound of bells, or any similar sound of continuous strokes.

2. a device in a clock by which the quarter-hours are struck upon bells of variant pitch.

ding′-dong, *a.* carried out, as a contest, fight, etc., with continual, successive changes in the lead or advantage; vigorously contested. [Colloq.]

ding′-dong, *adv.* with a will; vigorously.

dinge, *v.t.*; dinged, *pt.*, *pp.*; dingeing, *ppr.* to make hollows or indentations in; to dint; to dent. [Brit.]

dinge, *v.t.* to make dingy. [Brit. Dial.]

diñ′ghy, diñ′gey, diñ′gy, dhiñ′gy, *n.* [Bengalese, *dingi*, a boat.]

1. an East Indian boat varying in size in different localities; as, the *dinghies* of Bombay and Calcutta.

2. a ship's small boat, used as a tender; also, the smallest boat of a ship of war.

3. in some parts of the United States, a flat-bottomed boat; a dory.

4. a small, undecked, single-masted racing boat.

5. an inflatable, pneumatic life raft.

din′ġi·ly, *adv.* in a dingy manner or condition.

din′ġi·ness, *n.* the quality or condition of being dingy.

diñ′gle, *n.* a narrow, wooded dale or valley between hills; a small, secluded valley.

diñ′gle-dañ′gle, *adv.* in a loose or dangling manner.

diñ′gō, *n.* [native Australian name.] a wild dog of Australia, of a wolflike appearance. The ears are short and erect, the tail rather bushy, and the hair of a reddish-dun color. It is very destructive to the flocks and is systematically hunted and killed.

ding′us, *n.* [S.Afr.D. from *ding*, thing.] any device; contrivance; gadget: humorous substitute for a name not known or temporarily forgotten. [Slang.]

din′ġy, *a.*; *comp.* dingier; *superl.* dingiest, [AS. *dung*, a heap.]

1. soiled; sullied; of a dark color; not bright or clean.

2. dismal; shabby.

diñ′gy, *n.*; *pl.* **diñ′gieṣ,** a dinghy.

Dī·nich′thys, *n.* [Gr. *deinos*, terrible, and *ichthys*, fish.] a genus of large extinct fishes of the Devonian period: their fossil remains, found in Ohio, indicate that they attained a length of twenty feet.

dīn′ing, *n.* the act of eating dinner.

dīn′ing çär, a railroad car equipped to serve meals to passengers.

dīn′ing rōōm, a room in which people eat their meals, especially dinner.

dī·nī′trō-, a combining form meaning ***having two nitro groups per molecule***, as in ***dinitro*benzene**.

dī·nī·trō·ben′zēne, *n.* a chemical compound, $C_6H_4(NO_2)_2$, formed by the reaction of nitric acid and benzene or nitrobenzene: it crystallizes as flexible needles.

dī·nī·trō·cel′lū·lōse, *n.* [*di-*, and *nitric*, and *cellulose*.] a substance resembling guncotton, produced by the action of a mixture of sulfuric and nitric acids on cotton: also called *soluble pyroxylin*.

diñk, *a.* dressed in fine array; tidy; trim. [Scot.]

diñk, *v.t.*; dinked, *pt.*, *pp.*; dinking, *ppr.* to dress (oneself) in fine array; to adorn; to deck. [Scot.]

Diñ′kä, *n.* 1. a member of a group of Sudanic Negroid tribes living in the southern Anglo-Egyptian Sudan.

2. the East Sudanic language of the Dinkas.

diñ′key, *n.*; *pl.* **diñ′keyṣ,** 1. a small locomotive for hauling cars, shunting, etc. in a railroad yard. [Colloq.]

2. a small trolley car. [Colloq.]

diñk′ly, *adv.* in a neat, trim fashion. [Scot.]

diñ′ky, *a.*; *comp.* dinkier; *superl.* dinkiest, [Scot. and N. Eng. dial. *dink*, trim, neat; and *-y*.] small; of no consequence. [Slang.]

diñ′ky, *n.* a dinkey.

din′mŏnt, *n.* a wether which has been sheared once. [Scot.]

din′nȧ, contraction of *do not*. [Scot. and Brit. Dial.]

din′nẽr, *n.* [ME. *diner*, *dyner*; OFr. *disner*, dinner.]

1. the principal meal of the day, often eaten at noon or in the late afternoon or early evening.

2. a banquet or formal meal in honor of some person or event.

din′nẽr dress, a woman's long, semiformal dress, usually with sleeves or worn with a jacket.

din′nẽr jack′et, a tuxedo jacket.

din′nẽr·less, *a.* without dinner.

din′nẽr·ly, *a.* pertaining to dinner. [Rare.]

din′nẽr ring, a ring with a large setting, worn on formal occasions.

din′nẽr·wāre, *n.* 1. plates, cups, saucers, etc., collectively.

2. a set of such dishes.

dī·nō-, [Gr. *deinos*, terrible, mighty, from *deos*, fear.] a combining form signifying ***terrible, fearful, mighty, huge***.

Dī·noc′e·ras, *n.* [L., from Gr. *deinos*, huge, and *keras*, horn.] a genus of huge extinct mammals, so called from the three pairs of horny projections on its head. Their remains are found in the early Tertiary deposits of North America.

Dī·nor′nis, *n.* [L., from Gr. *deinos*, huge, terrible, and *ornis*, a bird.] a genus of enormous extinct birds, resembling but much larger than the ostrich, and found in New Zealand.

Dī·nor·nith′i·dae, *n.pl.* a family of enormous extinct birds of which *Dinornis* is the type genus; a general name for the moas.

dī′nō·saur, *n.* one of the *Dinosauria*.

Dī·nō·sau′ri·ȧ, *n.pl.* [L., from Gr. *deinos*, terrible, and *sauros*, a lizard.] a group of extinct Mesozoic reptiles with four limbs and a long, tapering tail: *Dinosauria* ranged in size from a few feet to almost 100 feet long.

DINOSAUR
(*Tyrannosaurus*; 18 ft. high)

dī·nō·sau′ri·ăn, *a.* pertaining to the *Dinosauria*.

dī·nō·sau′ri·ăn, *n.* same as *dinosaur*.

dī′nō·thēre, *n.* a dinotherium.

Dī·nō·thē′ri·um, *n.* [L., from Gr. *deinos*, terrible, and *thērion*, a wild beast.]

1. a genus of enormous extinct elephantlike mammals, noted for a pair of immense lower incisors, turned down or away from the lower jaw. There are several species from the Miocene of Europe and Asia.

2. [d–] an animal of this genus.

din·ox′īde, *n.* dioxide: incorrect form.

din′sŏme, *a.* full of din; noisy; loud. [Scot.]

dint, *n.* [ME. *dint, dynt*; AS. *dynt*, a blow, stroke.]

1. a blow; a stroke. [Archaic.]

2. force; violence; power exerted; as, to win by *dint* of arms, by *dint* of war, by *dint* of argument.

3. the mark made by a blow; a dent.

His hands had made a *dint*. —Dryden.

dint, *v.t.*; dinted, *pt., pp.*; dinting, *ppr.* to dent.

dī·nū·mĕr·ā′tion, *n.* enumeration; a counting. [Obs.]

dī·oc′ē·săn (*or* dī-ō-cē′săn), *a.* pertaining to a diocese.

dī·oc′ē·săn, *n.* [ME. *dyocesan*; OFr. *diocesain*, pertaining to a diocese, from LL. *diœcesis*, a diocese.]

1. a bishop who has authority over a diocese.

2. one of the people or clergy belonging to a diocese. [Rare.]

dī′ō·cēse, *n.* [ME. *diocise*; OFr. *diocise*; LL. *diœcesis*, a bishop's jurisdiction; L. *diœcesis*, a district, government.] the circuit or extent of a bishop's jurisdiction; an ecclesiastical division subject to the authority of a bishop; a bishopric.

dī·ō·cē′se·nĕr, *n.* a person belonging to a diocese. [Obs.]

dī·oç·tȧ·hē′drăl, *a.* [*di-*, and Gr. *oktō*, eight, and *hedra*, a seat, base.] in crystallography, having the form of an octahedral prism with tetrahedral summits.

dī′ōde, *n.* [*di-*, and *-ode*.] a vacuum tube with a cold anode and a heated cathode, used as a rectifier of alternating current.

Dī′ō·don, *n.* [L. *diodon*, from Gr. *di-*, two, and *odous* (*odontos*), tooth.] a genus of teleostean fishes belonging to the family *Diodontidæ* of the order *Plectognathi*: so called because their jaws are not divided, but exhibit one piece of bony substance above and another below, so that they appear to have only two teeth. Also called ***porcupine fish, sea porcupine, sea hedgehog,*** and ***prickly globe fish.***

DIODONT
(*Diodon hystrix*)

dī′ō·dont, *a.* having two teeth; of or pertaining to the *Diodontidæ*.

dī′ō·dont, *n.* one of the *Diodontidæ*, a porcupine fish.

Dī·ō·don′ti·dae, *n.pl.* a family of fishes named from its type genus, the *Diodon*.

Dī·oe′ci·ȧ (-ē′shi-ȧ), *n.* [L., from Gr. *di-*, two, and *oikos*, house.] a class of plants having the stamens on one plant and the pistils on another.

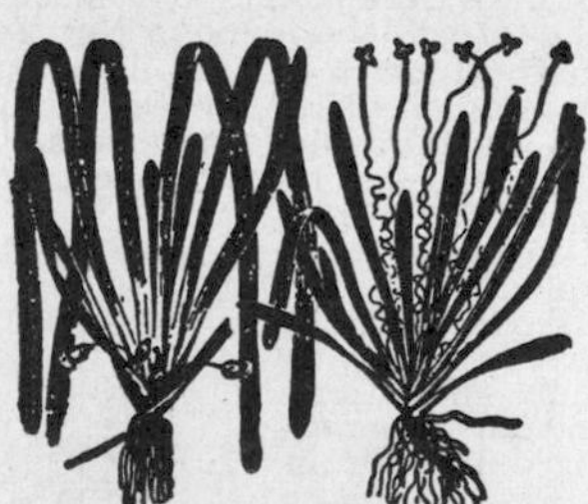

DIOECIA
(male and female plants of *Vallisneria spiralis*)

dī·oe′cious, dī·oe′ciăn, *a.* [L., from Gr. *di-*, two, and *oikos*, house.]

1. in botany, unisexual, the stamens being on one plant and the pistils on another: opposed to *monoecious*.

2. in zoology, sexually distinct; having the germ cell or ovum produced by one individual, the female, and the sperm cell or spermatozoid, by another, the male: opposed to *monoecious*.

dī·oe′cious·ly, *adv.* in a dioecious manner.

dī·oe′cious·ness, *n.* in biology, the state or quality of being dioecious.

dī·oe′ciṣm, *n.* dioeciousness.

dī·oes′trum (*or* -ēs′), *n.* [Mod. L.; *di-*, and *oestrum*.] the interval between successive periods of sexual heat, especially in female animals.

Dī·oḡ′e·nēs çrab, a hermit crab, *Cenobita diogenes*, of the West Indies.

Dī·ō·ḡen′iç, *a.* of, pertaining to, or resembling Diogenes, a Greek Cynic philosopher of the fourth century B.C.; cynical.

dī·oi′çous, dī′oiç, *a.* same as *dioecious*.

Dī′ō·med, Dī′ō·mēde, *n.* same as *Diomedes*.

Dī″ō·mē·dē′ȧ, *n.* [Mod. L., from *Diomedes*.] the type genus of the albatross family.

Dī·ō·mē′dēṣ, *n.* [Gr. *Diomēdēs*, lit., Zeus-counseled, from *Dios* (genit. of *Zeus*), and *medos*, council.] in Greek legend, a Greek warrior at the siege of Troy, who helped Odysseus steal the statue of Athena.

Dī′on, *n.* same as *Dioön*.

Dī·ō·nae′ȧ (-nē′ȧ), *n.* [L., from Gr. *Diōnē*, the mother of Aphrodite, also a name for Aphrodite.]

1. a genus of plants of the order *Droseraceæ*. Only one species is known, *Dionæa muscipula*, or Venus's-flytrap, a native of the Carolinas and Florida. It has a rosette of root leaves, from which rises a naked scape bearing a corymb of large white flowers. The bristles on the leaves are extremely sensitive, and when touched by a fly or other insect the lobes of the leaf suddenly close upon and capture the insect.

DIONAEA
(*Dionæa muscipula*)

2. [d–] a plant of this genus: also called *Venus's-flytrap*.

dī′ō·nym, *n.* a two-termed name, particularly in zoology.

Dī·ō·nys′i·ȧ, *n.pl.* [L., from Gr. *Dionysia* (supply *hiera*, offerings), the Dionysia, from *Dionysos*.] any set of the various Greek festivals in honor of Dionysus, especially those at Athens from which the Greek drama originated.

Dī·ō·nys′i·aç, *a.* of or pertaining to the Dionysia or Dionysus.

Dī·ō·nys′i·ăn, *a.* [Gr. *Dionysios*, pertaining to Dionysus, from *Dionysos*.]

1. same as *Dionysiac*.

2. of or pertaining to any of several historical figures named Dionysius.

Dionysian period; a period of 532 Julian years.

Dī·ō·nȳ′sus, Dī·ō·nȳ′sos, *n.* [L.; Gr. *Dionysos*.] in Greek mythology, the god of vegetation and wine: identified with the Roman god Bacchus.

Dī·o′ŏn (dī-ō′on), *n.* [L., from Gr. *di-*, two, and *ōon*, an egg.] a genus of plants of the *Cycadaceæ* family, palmlike in appearance, with short, stout trunks and large pinnate leaves with spiny tips. There are only two species, both of them native to tropical Mexico.

Dī·ō·phan′tine, *a.* pertaining to Diophantus, the ancient Greek authority on algebra.

Diophantine analysis; in algebra, a method of solution for indeterminate equations by determining a rational number which may be substituted for one of the unknown quantities.

dī·op′side (*or* -sīd), *n.* [Gr. *diopsis*, a view through; *dia*, through, and *opsis*, a view.] a variety of pyroxene, (Mg, Ca)SiO_3, usually transparent.

Dī·op′sis, *n.* [L., from Gr. *di-*, two, and *opsis*, a view.] a genus of dipterous insects, family *Muscidæ*, the members of which are characterized by prolongation of the sides of the head, the head appearing as if it were furnished with two long horns, each having a knob at its apex. All the known species are from the tropical parts of the Old World.

DIOPSIS

dī·op′tāse, *n.* a hydrous silicate of copper: it occurs in rich, emerald-green crystals, having the form of six-sided prisms.

dī·op′tēr, *n.* [L. *dioptra*; Gr. *dioptra*, a leveling instrument invented by Hipparchus.]

1. in optics, a unit of measure of the refractive power of a lens, equal to the power of a lens with a focal distance of one meter.

2. the theodolite as anciently made.

3. the indicator of a graduated circle.

4. an appliance for measuring skull projections.

dī·op·tom′e·tēr, *n.* an instrument for testing the refraction of the eye.

dī·op′trāte, *a.* [*dia-*, and Gr. *opt-*, from root of *opsesthai*, to see.] in entomology, having transverse divisions or partitions: applied to the eyes, as of certain beetles.

dī·op′tre, *n.* a diopter (unit of measure). [Obs.]

dī·op′triç, dī·op′triç·ăl, *a.* [Gr. *dioptrikos*, pertaining to the use of the diopter.]

1. of optical lenses or the method of numbering them according to their refractive powers; dioptral.

2. pertaining to dioptrics; refractive.

dī·op′triç, *n.* same as *diopter* (unit of measure).

dī·op′triçs, *n.* that part of optics which treats of the refraction of light passing through lenses.

dī·op′try, *n.* same as *diopter* (unit of measure).

dī·ō·rä′mȧ (*or* -ram′ȧ), *n.* [from Gr. *diorân*, to see through; *dia*, through, and *horân*, to see.]

1. a miniature scene, wholly or partially three-dimensional, depicting figures in a naturalistic setting.

2. a contrivance for giving a high degree of optical illusion to paintings exhibited in a building prepared for the purpose. A great diversity of scenic effect is produced by means of transparent paintings, through which the light is admitted, varying in intensity and color at different times.

3. a building used for this purpose.

dī·ō·ram′iç, *a.* pertaining to a diorama.

dī′ō·riṣm, *n.* [Gr. *diorismos*, division, distinction, from *diorizein*, to divide.] definition. [Rare.]

dī·ō·ris′tic, *a.* distinguishing; defining. [Rare.]

dī·ō·ris′tiç·ăl·ly, *adv.* in a distinguishing manner. [Rare.]

dī′ō·rīte, *n.* [from Gr. *diorizein*, to divide.] a dark-gray or greenish igneous rock composed of hornblende and triclinic feldspar.

dī·ō·rit′iç, *a.* relating to or containing diorite.

dī·ọr·thō′sis, *n.* [L., from Gr. *diorthōsis*, a making straight, correcting, from *diorthoun*, to make straight; *dia*, through, and *orthoun*, to make straight, from *orthos*, straight.]

1. a surgical operation, by which crooked or distorted limbs are restored to their proper shape.

2. a recension of a literary work.

dī·ọr·thot′iç, *a.* of the nature of or pertaining to diorthosis.

Dī·os·çō′rē·ȧ, *n.* [L., from *Dioscorides*, a Greek physician.] the genus of plants, family *Dioscoreaceæ*, which comprise the yams. They are perennial fleshy-rooted or tuberous dioecious plants, with annual twining stems and loose clusters of small green flowers.

Dī·os·çō·rē·ā′cē·ae, *n.pl.* a family of tropical plants including eight genera and about 160 species; the yam family.

dī·os·çō·rē·ā′ceous, *a.* of, pertaining to, or resembling the *Dioscoreaceæ*.

Dī·os·cū′ri, *n.pl.* [Gr. *Dioskouroi*, from *Dios* (genit. of *Zeus*), and *kouroi*, pl. of *kouros*, boy, son.] in Greek mythology, Castor and Pollux, twin sons of Zeus: after their death they became the constellation Gemini (the twins).

dī·oṣ′mōse, *n.* and *v.t.* same as *osmose*.

dī·oṣ·mō′sis, *n.* same as *osmosis*.

dī·oṣ·mot′iç, *a.* of or pertaining to diosmosis; osmotic.

Dī·os′py·ros, *n.* [Gr. *diospyros*, lit. Zeus's wheat, a certain plant; *Dios*, genit. of *Zeus*, Zeus, and *pyros*, wheat.] a large genus of trees and shrubs of the ebony family, found in tropical regions. They are noted for their valuable hard wood and delicious fruit. The persimmon or date plum, *Diospyros virginiana*, is the best known species in the United States.

dī·ox′īde, dī·ox′id, *n.* [*di-*, and *oxide*.] an oxide containing two atoms of oxygen per molecule.

dip, *v.t.*; dipped *or* dipt, *pt., pp.*; dipping, *ppr.* [ME. *dippen*; AS. *dyppan, dippan*, to dip, plunge, from *deop*, deep.]

1. to plunge or immerse, for a short time, in water or other liquid substance; to put into a fluid and withdraw.

The priest shall *dip* his finger in the blood. —Lev. iv. 6.

2. to dye in this way.
3. to clean (sheep) by bathing in disinfectant.
4. to make (a candle) by putting a wick in melted tallow or wax.
5. to plate or galvanize by immersion.
6. to get or take out by, or as if by, scooping up with a container, the hand, etc.
7. to put (snuff) on the gums.
8. to engage as a pledge; to mortgage. [Obs.]
9. to baptize by immersion.
10. to lower and raise again; as, to *dip* a flag in salute.

dip, *v.i.* 1. to plunge into water, etc. and quickly come out.
2. to sink or drop down suddenly.
3. to seem to sink; as, the sun *dips* into the ocean.
4. to slope down.
5. to lower a container, the hand, etc. into water, etc., especially in order to take something out.
6. to read here and there in a book, etc., or inquire into a subject superficially (with *into*).
7. in aeronautics, to drop suddenly before climbing.

dip, *n.* 1. a dipping or being dipped.
2. a plunge into water or other liquid.
3. a liquid into which something is dipped.
4. whatever is removed by or used in dipping.
5. a candle made by dipping.
6. a downward slope or inclination.
7. the amount of this.
8. a slight hollow.
9. a short downward plunge, as of an airplane.
10. liquid sauce. [Colloq.]
11. in geology and mining, the downward inclination of a stratum or vein, with reference to a horizontal plane.

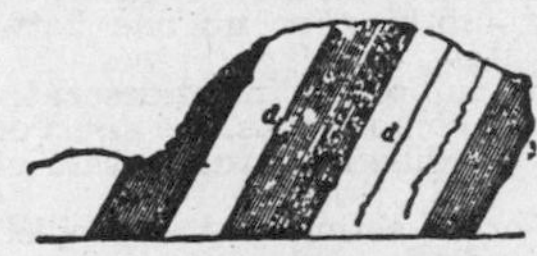

GEOLOGICAL DIP
d d, direction or angle of dip

12. in gymnastics, the act of lowering oneself by the arms between parallel bars until the chin reaches the bar level, and then raising oneself by straightening the arms.
13. in physics, the deviation of a dip needle from the horizontal; also, the amount of such deviation: also called *inclination*.
14. in surveying, the angular amount by which the horizon is below eye level.
dip of the horizon; the angle contained by two straight lines drawn from the observer's eye, the one to a point in the visible horizon, and the other parallel to the horizon, the eye of the observer being supposed to be elevated above the level of the sea. Hence, the greater the elevation of the observer's eye, the greater the dip of the horizon.
dip of the needle; the angle which a magnetic needle, freely suspended, makes, at a given place, with the horizon: also called *inclination of the needle*.

dī·pas′chăl, *a.* [*di-*, and Gr. *pascha*, a passover.] including two passovers.

dip′chick, *n.* same as *dabchick*.

dip cĩr′çle, a dipping compass.

dī·pet′ăl·ous, *a.* [*di-*, and Gr. *petalon*, a leaf.] having two petals; two-petaled.

dī′phāṣe, *a.* [*di-*, and Gr. *phasis*, an appearance, from *phainein*, to appear.] of or denoting an electrical circuit made up of two alternating currents, one of which has a maximum value when the other is zero, the phase difference between them being 90°.

dī·phāṣ′iç, *a.* same as *diphase*.

dī·phē′nyl, *n.* a chemical compound, $(C_6H_5)_2$, the molecule of which consists of two chemically combined phenyl groups; biphenyl.

dī·phē″nyl·ȧ·mīne′, *n.* a colorless, crystalline chemical compound, $(C_6H_5)_2NH$, used as a stabilizer of explosives, as a test for nitric acid, and in making dyes.

dī·phē″nyl·çhlō″rō·är′sīne, *n.* in chemistry, an arsenical compound: it is colorless but produces a noxious smoke which causes vomiting and sneezing: also called *adamsite*.

dī·phos′ġēne, *n.* a poisonous liquid compound, $ClCO_2CCl_3$, related to phosgene and used as a lung-irritant gas in warfare.

diph·thē′ri·ȧ (*or* dip-), *n.* [Gr. *diphthera*, a prepared skin, leather, from *dephein*, to soften hides, to tan.] an acute, infectious disease of the air passages, and especially of the throat, characterized by weakness, high fever, and the formation of a membrane which interferes with breathing: it is caused by a bacillus.

diph·thē′ri·ăl, *a.* of or characteristic of diphtheria; diphtheritic.

diph·ther′iç, *a.* same as *diphtheritic*.

diph·thē·rit′iç, *a.* of the nature of, pertaining to, caused by, or affected by diphtheria.

diph′thē·roid, *a.* having the nature of or similar to diphtheria.

diph′thong, *n.* [LL. *diphthongus*; Gr. *diphthongos*, a diphthong; *di-*, two, and *phongos*, voice, sound, from *phthengesthai*, to utter.] in phonetics, a complex sound made by gliding continuously from the position for one vowel to that for another within the same syllable; e.g., *ou* in *house*, *oi* in *coil*. In many languages, diphthongs can be interpreted and phonetically written as a vowel followed by a semivowel (glide).

diph′thong, *v.t.* same as *diphthongize*.

diph·thoṅ′găl, *a.* of, like, or constituting a diphthong.

diph·thoṅ′găl·īze, *v.t.* same as *diphthongize*.

diph·thoṅ′găl·ly, *adv.* in a diphthongal manner.

diph·thoṅ·gā′tion, *n.* same as *diphthongization*.

diph·thong′iç, *a.* of or pertaining to a diphthong.

diph·thong·i·zā′tion, *n.* a diphthongizing or being diphthongized.

diph′thong·īze, *v.t.*; diphthongized, *pt.*, *pp.*; diphthongizing, *ppr.* to change into a diphthong; to pronounce as a diphthong.

diph′thong·īze, *v.i.* to become a diphthong.

diph·y·cẽr′căl, diph′y·cẽrç, *a.* [Gr. *diphyēs*, of a double nature or form, and *kerkos*, a tail.] in ichthyology, having the tail divided symmetrically, as by the spinal column.

diph′y·cẽr·cy, *n.* the state of having the tail diphycercal: applied to fishes.

diph·y·ġen′ic, *a.* [Gr. *diphyēs*, of a double nature or form, and *genesis*, origin, birth.] in zoology, having two forms of embryo.

diph′yl·lous, *a.* [*di-*, and Gr. *phyllon*, a leaf.] in botany, having two leaves or sepals.

diph′y·ō·dont, *a.* growing in two sets: applied to teeth.

diph′y·ō·dont, *n.* [L. *diphyodons* (*-ontis*); Gr. *diphyēs*, of a double form, and *odous* (*-ontos*), a tooth.] one of that group of mammals which possess two successive sets of teeth, a deciduous set, and a permanent set: distinguished from the *monophyodonts*, which develop only one set.

diph′y·sīte, *n.* one who believes in diphysitism.

diph′y·sī·tism, *n.* [*di-*, and Gr. *physis*, nature.] in theology, the belief that Christ possessed two distinct natures, one human, one divine: opposed to *monophysitism*.

diph·y·zō′oid, *n.* [Gr. *diphyēs*, of a double nature, *zōon*, an animal, and *eidos*, form.] one of the detached reproductive zooids of adult members of an order of oceanic *Hydrozoa*.

dī·plā′năr, *a.* having or pertaining to two planes.

dī·plā·net′iç, *a.* [*di-*, and Gr. *planētikos*, disposed to wander, from *planan*, to wander.] in botany, having a period of rest alternating with two active periods.

dī·plā·si·as′mus, *n.* [Gr. *diplasiasmos*, a doubling, from *diplasiazein*, to double, from *diplasios*, double; *di-*, two, and *plasios*, fold.]
1. in orthography, the doubling of a letter; as, *petalled* for *petaled*.
2. in rhetoric, the repetition of a word for the purpose of emphasis; as, "Break! break! break! on thy cold, gray stones, O sea!"

dī·plas′iç, *a.* [Gr. *diplasios*, double.] in the ratio of two to one: applied specifically in ancient prosody to a class of feet in which the (accented) arsis has twice the length of the (unaccented) thesis.

dī·plē′ġi·ȧ, *n.* [L., from Gr. *di-*, two, and *plēgē*, a stroke.] paralysis in which similar parts on the two sides of the body are affected.

dī·pleī′dō·sçōpe, *n.* [Gr. *diploos*, double, *eidos*, appearance, and *skopein*, to see.] an instrument for indicating the passage of the sun or a star over the meridian, by the coincidence of two images of the object, the one formed by single and the other by double reflection.

dī′plex, *a.* see *duplex*.

dip′lō-, [from Greek *diploos*, double.] a combining form signifying *two*, *double*, *twin*, etc.: also, before a vowel, *dipl-*.

dip″lō·baç·tē′ri·ȧ, *n.pl.* [*diplo-*, and L. *bacteria*, bacteria, from Gr. *baktron*, a staff.] bacteria which are two-celled or exist in pairs.

dip·lō·blas′tiç, *a.* [*diplo-*, and Gr. *blastos*, a germ.] in embryology, having a two-layered germinal membrane.

dip·lō·cär′di·aç, *a.* [*diplo-*, and Gr. *kardia*, heart.] having the heart doubled, with the right and left sides distinctly separate, as in birds and mammals.

dip·lō·çoç′çus, *n.*; *pl.* **dip·lō·çoç′cī,** [L., from Gr. *diploos*, double, and *coccus*, a berry.] any of a group of parasitic bacteria occurring in pairs, as the pneumococcus that causes lobar pneumonia.

dī·plod′ō·çus, *n.* [Mod. L., from *diplo-*, and Gr. *dokos*, a beam, shaft.] a huge, herbivorous dinosaur of the Upper Jurassic of western North America.

dip′lō·ē, *n.* [L., from Gr. *diploē*, f. of *diploos*, double.] the soft, medullary substance or porous part between the plates of the skull.

dip·lō·et′iç, *a.* same as *diploic*.

dip·lō·ġen′e·sis, *n.* [L., from Gr. *diploos*, double, and *genesis*, origin, generation.] in biology, the abnormal doubling of parts or organs.

dip″lō·ġē·net′iç, *a.* of or pertaining to diplogenesis.

dip·lō·ġen′iç, *a.* diplogenetic.

di·plō′iç, *a.* of or pertaining to the diploe.

dip′loid, *a.* [*dipl-*, and *-oid*.]
1. twofold.
2. in biology, having twice the number of chromosōmes normally occurring in a germ cell: most somatic cells are diploid.

dip′loid, *n.* 1. in crystallography, a solid included under twenty-four equal, trapezoidal planes.
2. in biology, a diploid cell.

di·plō′mȧ, *n.* [L. *diploma*; Gr. *diploma*, a letter folded double.]
1. an official state document or historical document; a charter.
2. a certificate conferring honors, privileges, etc.
3. a certificate issued to a student by a school, college, or university, indicating the completion of a prescribed course of study, or conferring a degree.

di·plō′mȧ·cy, *n.*; *pl.* **di·plō′mȧ·cieṣ,** [Fr. *diplomatie*, from L. *diploma*, a diploma.]
1. the conducting of relations between nations, by their heads directly, or through accredited representatives; the art of managing international negotiations.
2. skill in conducting such negotiations.
3. a diplomatic body. [Obs.]
4. skill in dealing with people; tact.

dip′lō·mat, *n.* [Fr. *diplomate*, from L. *diploma*, a diploma.]
1. a representative of a government who conducts relations with another government in the interests of his own country; a person whose career or profession is diplomacy.
2. a person skilled in dealing with other people; a tactful person.

dip′lō·māte, *v.t.* to confer a diploma upon; to invest with authority or privilege by a diploma. [Rare.]

dip·lō·mā′tiăl (-shăl), *a.* diplomatic. [Rare.]

dip·lō·mat′iç, dip·lō·mat′iç·ăl, *a.* 1. of or pertaining to diplomas or diplomatics.
2. of, pertaining to, or concerned with diplomacy.
3. characterized by tact and cleverness in dealing with people; politic in conduct.
diplomatic corps; the entire body of ministers or official agents accredited to and resident at the capital of a nation.

dip·lō·mat′iç·ăl·ly, *adv.* according to the rules of diplomacy; artfully; tactfully.

dip·lō·mat′içs, *n.pl.* [*construed as sing.*] 1. diplomacy.
2. the science of deciphering old official and historical documents, determining their authenticity and age, etc.

di·plō′mȧ·tist, *n.* a diplomat.

dip·lō·neū′răl, *a.* [*diplo-*, and Gr. *neuron*, nerve.] in anatomy, supplied by two nerves different in origin.

di·plō′pi·ȧ, dip′lō·py, *n.* [L., from Gr. *di-*

ploos, double, and *ōps* (*ōpis*), eye.] an eye defect in which an object appears double; double vision.

dī·plop′iç, *a.* pertaining to, caused by, or suffering with diplopia.

dip·lō·plaç′ū·lȧ, *n.*; *pl.* **dip·lō·plaç′ū·lae,** [L., from Gr. *diploos*, double, and *plax*, a plate.] a placula having two layers of cells.

dip′lō·pod, *a.* of or pertaining to the *Diplopoda*.

dip′lō·pod, *n.* one of the *Diplopoda*.

Di·plop′ō·dȧ, *n.pl.* [L., from Gr. *diploos*, double, and *pous* (*podos*), foot.] one of the two divisions of the *Myriapoda*: synonymous with *Chilognatha*.

di·plop′ō·dous, *a.* diplopod.

Di·plop′tēr·ȧ, *n.pl.* [L., from Gr. *diploos*, double, and *pteron*, a wing.] a group of hymenopterous insects, having the upper wings folded longitudinally when at rest, as in the hornet.

di·plop′tēr·ous, *a.* of or pertaining to the *Diploptera*.

di·plō′sis, *n.* [Gr. *diplōsis*, a doubling.] in biology, doubling of the number of chromosomes through the fusion of two haploid sets in the union of gametes.

dip·lō·stem′ō·nous, *a.* [*diplo-*, and Gr. *stēmōn*, the warp, from *histanai*, to stand.] having two stamens to every petal.

dip·lō·stem′ō·ny, *n.* diplostemonous growth or condition.

dip nee′dle, a magnetic needle vertically suspended and freely moving, used to indicate the direction of the earth's magnetism: it is horizontal at the magnetic equator (*aclinic line*) but vertical at the magnetic poles.

Dip·neū′mō·nȧ, *n.pl.* [L., from Gr. *di-*, two, and *pneumōn*, lung.]
1. a division of *Dipnoi*, having paired lungs.
2. a division of holothurian enchinoderms, having two branching gills.

dip·neū′mō·nous, *a.* having two lungs or respiratory organs; of or pertaining to the *Dipneumona*.

dip·neūs′tăl, *a.* same as *dipnoan*.

dip′nō·ăn, *a.* pertaining to or resembling the *Dipnoi*.

dip′nō·ăn, *n.* one of the *Dipnoi*.

Dip′nō·ī, *n.pl.* [L., from Gr. *di-*, two, double, and *pnein*, to breathe.] an order of fishes with lungs as well as gills.

dip′noid, *a.* and *n.* same as *dipnoan*.

dī·pod′iç, *a.* of or in a dipody or dipodies.

dip′ō·dy, *n.*; *pl.* **dip′ō·dieș,** [Gr. *dipodia*, a dipody, from *dipous* (*-podos*), two-footed.] in prosody, a double foot; a pair of like feet composing a verse.

dī·pō′lăr, *a.* of, pertaining to, or having two poles.

dī′pōle, *n.* in physics and physical chemistry, anything having two equal but opposite electric charges or magnetic poles, as a hydrogen atom with its positive nucleus and negative electron.

dip′pēr, *n.* [ME. *dippere*, from *dippen*, *dyppen*; AS. *dyppan*, *dippan*, to dip.]

DIPPER
(*Cinclus aquaticus*)

1. one whose work is dipping something in liquid.
2. a vessel used to dip water or other liquid; a ladle.
3. one of certain swimming and diving birds; as, (a) any bird of the family *Cinclidæ*, of which *Cinclus* is the type genus, the water ouzel being *Cinclus aquaticus*; (b) any aquatic bird which is an active diver, particularly the buffle duck; also the grebe or the dabchick.
4. [D–] either of two groups of stars in the shape of a dipper, one (*Big Dipper*) in Ursa Major, the other (*Little Dipper*) in Ursa Minor.
5. [D–] a Dunker.

dip′ping, *n.* the act or process of one who dips.

dip′ping çŏm′păss, a combination of a dipping needle and a vertical graduated indicator in the form of a circle, to measure the angular inclination of the magnetic needle.

dip′ping nee′dle, a magnetized needle suspended by its center of gravity for determining the earth's magnetic direction.

dī·priș·mat′iç, *a.* [*di-*, and Gr. *prisma*, a prism.] doubly prismatic.

dī·prō·pär′ġyl, *n.* [*di-*, and *propargyl*.] an isomer of benzene, being a volatile, pungent liquid distilled from certain diallyl compounds.

Dī·prō′tō·don, *n.* [L., from Gr. *di-*, two, *prōtos*, first, and *odous* (*odontos*), tooth.] a genus of extinct gigantic marsupial mammals, characterized by two large upper incisor teeth: it is found in the Pleistocene deposits of Australia.

dī·prō′tō·dont, *a.* having two front teeth on the lower jaw; of or pertaining to the *Diprotodon*.

Dip·sȧ·çā′cē·ae, *n.pl.* [L., from Gr. *dipsakos*, the teazel, from *dipsa*, thirst, from *dipsan*, to thirst.] a family of herbs of the Old World, having two cotyledons and flowers with both calyx and corolla. They are nearly allied to the *Compositæ*, but have distinct anthers.

dip·sȧ·çā′ceous, dip·sā′ceous, *a.* of, pertaining to, or having the characteristics of the *Dipsacaceæ*.

Dip′sȧ·çus, *n.* the type genus of the order *Dipsacaceæ*, consisting of coarse, prickly, biennial herbs. The principal species is *Dipsacus fullonum*, or fuller's-teazel, the prickly flower heads of which are used to raise a nap on woolen cloth.

dip′sas, *n.* [L., from Gr. *dipsas*, a serpent whose bite was thought to produce thirst, from *dipsios*, thirsty, from *dipsa*, thirst.]
1. a serpent whose bite was believed to produce a great thirst.
2. [D–] a genus of tropical American and Asiatic nonvenomous serpents.

dip·set′iç, *a.* producing thirst.

dip′sey, dip′sy, *n.* [local U. S.; probably a nautical corruption of *deep-sea*.] a deep-sea fishing tackle; also, a sinker attached to such a line.

dip·sō·mā′ni·ȧ, *n.* [L., from Gr. *dipsa*, thirst, and *mania*, madness.] an abnormal and insatiable craving for alcoholic drink.

dip·sō·mā′ni·aç, *n.* a person who has dipsomania.

dip″sō·mȧ·nī′ȧ·çăl, *a.* of, like, or having dipsomania.

dip·sō′sis, *n.* [L., from Gr. *dipsa*, thirst.] in medicine, morbid thirst.

dipt, occasional past tense and past participle of *dip*.

dip′tēr, *n.* same as *dipteron*.

Dip′te·rȧ, *n.pl.* [L., from Gr. *di-*, two, and *pteron*, wing.] an order of insects, including the housefly, mosquito, gnat, etc., having only two wings with two halteres, or poisers, instead of the posterior pair of wings. They have six legs, furnished with five-jointed tarsi, two maxillary palpi, two antennae, three ocelli, or simple eyes, and a suctorial proboscis.

dip′tēr·ăl, *a.* [Gr. *dipteros*, having two wings; *di-*, two, and *pteron*, a wing.]
1. dipterous.
2. in architecture, surrounded by a double row of columns.

dip′tēr·ăn, *n.* same as *dipteron*.

dip·tēr·o-, [from Gr. *dipteros*, two-winged; *di-*, two, and *pteron*, a wing.] a combining form meaning *having two wings*.

dip″te·rō·çär·pā′ceous, *a.* of or pertaining to the order *Dipterocarpeæ*.

Dip″te·rō·çär′pē·ae, *n.pl.* [L., from Gr. *dipteros*, two-winged, and *karpos*, fruit.] an order of East Indian trees, bearing fruit with two long wings. Some species produce wood oil and some a fragrant resin.

Dip″te·rō·çär′pus, *n.* a genus of East Indian trees, the type of the order *Dipterocarpeæ*.

dip·tēr·ol′ō·ġy, *n.* [*diptero-*, and Gr. *logos*, description.] that branch of entomology treating of dipterous insects.

dip′tēr·on, *n.* any dipterous insect.

dip′te·ros, *n.* in architecture, a dipteral temple or portico.

dip′tēr·ous, *a.* 1. having two wings, as some insects, or two winglike appendages, as some seeds.
2. of the *Diptera*.

Dip′te·ryx, *n.* [L., from Gr. *di-*, two, and *pteryx*, a wing.] a genus of trees of the bean family, found in tropical South America. One species yields the tonka bean. The wood is hard and durable and is called *camara wood*.

dip′tōte, *n.* [LL. *diptota*; Gr. *diptōtos*, with a double case ending; *di-*, two, and *ptōsis*, a falling, a case, from *piptein*, to fall.] in grammar, a noun having only two cases.

dip′tyçh, *n.* [Gr. *diptycha*, a pair of writing tablets, neut. pl. of *diptychos*, folded together, double-folded; *di-*, two, and *ptychē*, a fold, from *ptyssein*, to fold.]
1. anything folded so as to have two leaves.
2. an ancient writing tablet made up of a hinged pair of wooden or ivory pieces folding to protect the inner waxed writing surfaces.
3. a picture painted or carved on two hinged tablets.

dī·pȳre′, *n.* [Gr. *dipyros*, with double lights, twice put in the fire; *di-*, twice, and *pyr* (*pyros*), fire.] a silicate of alumina, a mineral occurring in minute prisms, either single or adhering to each other in fascicular groups.

dī·pȳ·rē′nous, *a.* in botany, having two pyrenes or stones: said of fruit.

dī·rā·di·ā′tion, *n.* [L. *dis-*, apart, and *radiatio*, radiation.] radiation.

dir′dum, *n.* a loud outcry of blame or rebuke. [Scot. and Brit. Dial.]

dīre, *a.*; *comp.* direr; *superl.* direst, [L. *dirus*, fearful, awful.] dreadful; dismal; horrible; terrible; disastrous.

Dire was the tossing, deep the groans.
—Milton.

di·reçt′, *a.* [ME. and OFr. *directe*; L. *directus*, straight, upright, pp. of *dirigere*, to lay straight, put in a straight line, direct; *di-* for *dis-*, apart, from, and *regere*, to keep straight, to rule, control.]
1. straight; not deviating; not roundabout; not turned aside; not interrupted.
2. straightforward; not vague; frank; as, a *direct* answer.
3. immediate; as, a *direct* result.
4. with nothing or no one between; as, *direct* contact.
5. in an unbroken line of descent; lineal.
6. exact; complete; as, the *direct* opposite.
7. not needing a mordant: said of certain dyes.
8. by or of action of the people through popular vote instead of through representatives or delegates.
9. in astronomy, from west to east: opposed to *retrograde*.

di·reçt′, *v.t.*; directed, *pt.*, *pp.*; directing, *ppr.* [ME. *directen*, from L. *directus*, pp. of *dirigere*, to direct.]
1. to manage the affairs of; guide; conduct; regulate; control.
2. to give authoritative instructions to (a person); ordain (*that* a thing be done); order; command.
3. to move, turn, or point (a person or thing) toward a place, object, or goal; aim; head.
4. to tell (a person) the way to a place.
5. to say (words, etc.) to a specific person or persons, or in a specific direction; address (remarks).
6. to write the address on (a letter, etc.)
7. to plan the action and effects of (a play, motion picture, etc.) and to supervise and instruct (the actors and technicians) in the carrying out of such a plan.

Syn.—conduct, guide, dispose, order, contrive, manage, regulate, sway.

di·reçt′, *v.i.* 1. to give directions; make a practice of directing.
2. to be a director, as of a group of musicians.

di·reçt′, *n.* in music, a character formerly placed at the end of a staff to direct the performer to the first note of the next staff.

di·reçt′, *adv.* in a direct manner; directly.

di·reçt′-aç″tion, *a.* acting directly: applied specifically, in mechanics, to those steam engines and steam pumps in which connection is made from the piston rod of the engine directly to the crank or plunger, without intervening gears or other working parts: also *direct-acting*.

di·reçt′ aç′tion, action aimed directly at achieving an objective; especially, the use of strikes, demonstrations, etc. in disputes between labor and management.

di·reçt′ çur′rent, see *direct current*, under *current*.

di·reçt′ dis′çourse, quotation of a person's exact words.

di·reçt′ēr, *n.* same as *director*.

di·reçt ev′i·dence, in law, evidence which directly establishes the fact which it is intended to prove: distinguished from *circumstantial evidence*.

di·reç′tion, *n.* [L. *directio*, a making straight, the act of directing.]
1. a directing; management; control.
2. the address on a letter or parcel.
3. [*usually in pl.*] instruction for doing, operating, using, preparing, etc.
4. an order; command.
5. the line in which or point toward which a moving person or thing goes.
6. the way a person or thing faces or points.
7. the line leading to a place; as, in the *direction* of Berlin.
8. an aspect, line of development, way, etc.; as, work in that *direction*.
9. in the theater, (a) the director's plan for achieving certain effects, as of acting, lighting, etc.; (b) his instructions to the actors, etc.
10. in music, a word, phrase, or sign showing how a note, chord, passage, etc. is to be played.
line of direction; (a) in gunnery, the direct line in which a piece is pointed; (b) in mechanics, the line in which a body moves.
Syn.—administration, guidance, management, superintendence, oversight, government, control, order, command, instruction.

di·reç′tion·ăl, *a.* 1. of direction in space.
2. in radio, (a) for telling the direction from which signals are coming; (b) for sending radio waves on one directed beam; as, a *directional* antenna.

di·reç′tion fīnd′ẽr, a device for finding out the direction from which radio waves or signals are coming, as a loop antenna that can be rotated freely in any direction on a vertical axis.

di·reçt′ive, *a.* 1. directing; tending or intended to direct.
2. indicating direction; instructing; showing the way.
3. capable of being directed.
directive corpuscle; in biology, one of the bodies or corpuscles which detach from the ovum at maturation.

di·reç′tive, *n.* a general instruction or order issued by a central office, military unit, etc.

di·reçt′ly, *adv.* 1. in a direct way, line, or course; straight; not in a winding course; as, aim *directly* at the object.
2. immediately; without a person or thing coming between.
3. right away; instantly; soon; without delay; as, he will be with us *directly*.
4. exactly; completely; as, *directly* opposite.
5. openly; expressly; without circumlocution or ambiguity; without a train of inferences.
Syn.—immediately, instantly, instantaneously, forthwith, at once, promptly.

di·reçt′ly, *conj.* as soon as. [Chiefly Brit.]

di·reçt′ness, *n.* the state or quality of being direct; a straight course; straightforwardness.

di·reçt′ ob′jeçt, the word or words denoting the thing or person that receives the action of a transitive verb; goal of a verbal action, as *ball* in *he hit the ball*.

Dī·reç·toire′ (-twär′), *n.* [Fr., from ML. *directorium*: see *directory*.] an executive body of five men in the First Republic in France, given office October 27, 1795, and ousted November 9, 1799.

Dī·reç·toire′, *a.* of or characteristic of the Directoire period: said of furniture, dress, etc.

di·reçt′ŏr, *n.* [L. *directus*, pp. of *dirigere*, to direct.]
1. a person who directs or controls; supervisor; manager.
2. a member of a board chosen to direct the affairs of a corporation or institution.
3. a person who directs the production of a play or film, or the lighting, dancing, etc.
4. in music, a conductor.
5. that which directs; specifically, in surgery, a grooved probe, intended to direct the edge of the knife or scissors.

di·reçt′ō·rāte, *n.* 1. a board of directors, considered collectively.
2. the office or authority of a director.

di·reç·tō′ri·ăl, *a.* 1. of directing or management; also, capable of directing or commanding; directive.
2. of or pertaining to a director, a directorate, or a directory, specifically the Directory of France.

di·reçt′ŏr·ship, *n.* the position or term of office of a director.

di·reçt′ō·ry, *a.* containing directions; directing; guiding; advising; instructing.

di·reçt′ō·ry, *n.*; *pl.* **di·reçt′ō·rieș,** [LL. *directorius*, serving to direct, from L. *directus*, pp. of *dirigere*, to direct.]
1. a thing that directs.
2. a book of directions.
3. a book listing the names and addresses (and, often, occupations) of a specific group of persons; as, a telephone *directory*.
4. a directorate.
5. in the Anglican and Roman Catholic Churches, directions for worship.
6. [D–] in French history, the Directoire.

di·reçt′ prī′măr·y ē·leç′tion, a preliminary election at which candidates for public office are chosen by direct vote of the people instead of by delegates at a convention: also *primary* (*election*): *closed primary elections* are those in which voters must declare party affiliation and are prohibited from voting for candidates of another party.

di·reçt′ proc′ess, in mining, a process whereby metal in a working condition is obtained from the ore, in a single stage.

di·reçt′ress, *n.* a woman who directs or manages; a directrix.

di·reçt′rix, *n.*; *pl.* **di·reçt′rix·eș** or **di·reçt·rī′cēș,** 1. a directress.
2. in geometry, a fixed line that serves as a guide in drawing a curve or surface.

di·reçt′ tax, a tax levied directly on the person by whom it is to be paid, as an income tax or property tax.

dīre′fụl, *a.* dire; dreadful; terrible; calamitous; as, *direful* fiend; a *direful* misfortune.

dīre′fụl·ly, *adv.* in a dire or dreadful manner.

dīre′fụl·ness, *n.* the state of being direful; calamitousness.

dīre′ly, *adv.* in a dire manner.

di·rempt′, *a.* separated; parted. [Obs.]

di·rempt′, *v.t.* to separate; to tear apart forcibly. [Obs.]

di·remp′tion, *n.* [L. *diremptio*.] a forcible separation. [Obs.]

dīre′ness, *n.* terribleness; horror; dismalness.

di·rep′tion, *n.* the act of plundering. [Obs.]

di·rep·ti′tious (-tish′us), *a.* of the nature of or pertaining to direption. [Obs.]

di·rep·ti′tious·ly, *adv.* in a direptitious manner. [Obs.]

dirġe, *n.* [ME. *dirge*, *dorge*, from L. *dirige*, imper. of *dirigere*, to direct: so called from the first word of a funeral hymn, taken from Vulgate, Psalm v. 8: "*Dirige*, Domine, Deus meus, in conspectu tuo, viam meam," Direct, O Lord, my God, my way in thy sight.]
1. a funeral hymn or requiem mass.
2. a song, poem, or musical composition of grief or mourning; a lament.

dirġe′fụl, *a.* moaning; funereal; like a dirge.

dir′i·ġē, *n.* a service for the dead; a dirge. [Obs.]

dir′i·ġent, *a.* [L. *dirigens* (*-gentis*), ppr. of *dirigere*, to direct.] directing.

dir′i·ġent, *n.* in geometry, the line or plane along which another line or plane is supposed to move in the generation of a surface or solid; a directrix.

dir′i·ġi·ble, *a.* capable of being guided, steered, or controlled; as, a *dirigible* balloon.

dir′i·ġi·ble, *n.* a balloon that can be steered, especially such a long, cigar-shaped, motor-driven balloon with a cabin underneath.

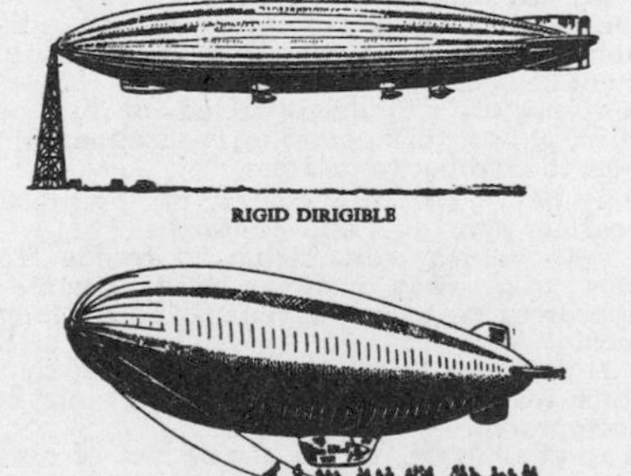

RIGID DIRIGIBLE

NONRIGID DIRIGIBLE

dir′i·ment, *a.* [L. *dirimens* (*-mentis*), ppr. of *dirimere*, to separate; *dis-*, from, and *emere*, to take.] in law, nullifying; making absolutely void.
diriment impediment of marriage; in the Roman Catholic Church, any obstacle that automatically annuls a marriage.

dĩrk, *n.* [so spelled by Dr. Johnson; earlier *dork*, *durk*; perhaps akin to G. *dolch*.] a short, straight dagger.

dĩrk, *v.t.* dirked, *pt.*, *pp.*; dirking, *ppr.* to stab with a dirk.

dĩrl, *v.t.* and *v.i.* [var. of Scot. *thirl*, to pierce, from ME. *thirlen*, *thrillen*.] to vibrate or tingle.

dĩrl, *n.* a tingling; a vibration.

dĩrn′dl, *n.* 1. a kind of dress with a gathered waist, full skirt, and close-fitting bodice.
2. such a skirt without a bodice.

dĩrt, *n.* [ME. *dirt*, from *drit*.]
1. any unclean or soiling matter, as mud, dust, trash, etc.; filth.
2. earth or garden soil.
3. anything common or filthy; as, he treats me like *dirt*.
4. dirtiness; uncleanness; meanness.
5. obscene writing or speaking; pornography.
6. malicious talk or gossip.
7. in gold mining, the gravel, soil, etc. from which gold is separated by washing or panning.
to do one dirt; to do harm to one, as by deception or malicious gossip. [Slang.]
to eat dirt; to submit humbly to an insult or degradation; to retract one's own words.

DIRK (front and profile)

dĩrt, *v.t.* to make foul or filthy; to soil; to bedaub; to pollute; to defile. [Rare.]

dĩrt′ bed, a bed or layer of mold with the remains of trees and plants, found especially in working the freestone in the oölite formation of Portland, England.

dĩrt′-chēap′, *a.* and *adv.* as cheap as dirt; very cheap. [Colloq.]

dĩrt fãrm′ẽr, a farmer who does his own farming: distinguished from *gentleman farmer*. [Colloq.]

dĩrt′i·ly, *adv.* in a dirty manner.

dĩrt′i·ness, *n.* the quality or state of being dirty.

dĩrt′y, *a.*; *comp.* dirtier; *superl.* dirtiest, 1. soiled or soiling with dirt; unclean.
2. obscene; pornographic; as, *dirty* jokes.
3. contemptible; mean.
4. grayish, muddy, or clouded; as, a *dirty* green.
5. in nautical usage, squally; rough; as, *dirty* weather.

dĩrt′y, *v.t.* and *v.i.*; dirtied, *pt.*, *pp.*; dirtying, *ppr.* to make or become dirty; to soil; to tarnish; to stain.

di·rup′tion, *n.* disruption. [Obs.]

dis-, [from OFr. or (usually) L.; OFr. *des-*, from L. *dis-* (*di-* before *b*, *d*, *g*, *v*, *m*, *n*, *l*, *r*; *dif-* before *f*).]
1. a prefix denoting, in general, *separation*, *negation*, or *reversal*, used to form verbs: (a) from word bases not actually found as individual English words: meaning *away*, *apart*, as in *dis*miss, *dis*perse; (b) from nouns: meaning *deprive of*, *expel from*, as in *dis*frock, *dis*bar; (c) from adjectives: meaning *cause to be the opposite of*, as in *dis*able; (d) from other verbs: meaning *fail*, *cease*, *refuse to*, as in *dis*satisfy, *dis*appear, *dis*allow; *do the opposite of*, as in *dis*join, *dis*integrate; intensifying the action, as in *dis*annul.
2. a prefix used to form adjectives from other simple or verbal adjectives: meaning *not*, *un-*, *the opposite of*, as in *dis*honest, *dis*satisfied, *dis*pleasing.
3. a prefix used to form nouns from other simple or verbal nouns: meaning *opposite of*, *lack of*, as in *dis*ease, *dis*union.

dis-, di- (twice, double).

Dis, *n.* [L.] in Roman mythology, (a) the god of the lower world: identified with the Greek god Pluto; (b) his realm; the lower world; Hades.

dis·ȧ·bil′i·ty, *n.*; *pl.* **dis·ȧ·bil′i·tieș,** [*dis-* priv., and L. *habilitas*, ability.]
1. a disabled condition.
2. that which disables, as illness, insanity, etc.
3. a legal disqualification or incapacity.

dis·ȧ·bil′i·ty çlauṣe, in life insurance, a clause entitling a policyholder who becomes totally and permanently disabled to cease premium payments and, often, to receive a specified monthly income, without losing any part of the life insurance given by the policy.

dis·ā′ble, *a.* unable; incompetent. [Obs.]

dis·ā′ble, *v.t.*; disabled, *pt.*, *pp.*; disabling, *ppr.* 1. to make unable or unfit; to deprive of normal strength or power; as, a broken leg *disables* a man.

2. to deprive of mental power, as by destroying or weakening the understanding.

3. to deprive of adequate means, instruments, or resources; as, lack of funds *disables* a nation to carry on war.

4. to deprive of legal qualifications; to disqualify legally.

dis·ā′ble·ment, *n.* weakness; disability; legal impediment.

dis·ȧ·būṣe′, *v.t.*; disabused, *pt., pp.*; disabusing, *ppr.* to free from mistake; to undeceive; to rid of false ideas; to set right.

> Now sufficiently enlightened to *disabuse* themselves of artifice, hypocrisy, and superstition. —J. Adams.

dī·saç′ċhȧ·rīde (*or* -rid), *n.* any of a group of sugars with a common formula, $C_{12}H_{22}O_{11}$, as sucrose, maltose, and lactose, which on hydrolysis yield two monosaccharides.

dis·aç·com′mō·dāte, *v.t.* to inconvenience; to discommode. [Rare.]

dis·aç·com·mō·dā′tion, *n.* the state of being inconvenienced. [Rare.]

dis·aç·ċord′, *v.i.* to refuse assent; to disagree.

dis·aç·ċord′, *n.* disagreement; incongruity.

dis·aç·ċord′ănt, *a.* not accordant.

dis·aç·ċred′it, *v.t.* to cause to be no longer accredited, or authorized.

dis·aç·ċus′tŏm, *v.t.*; disaccustomed, *pt., pp.*; disaccustoming, *ppr.* to cause to be unaccustomed (*to* something); to rid of a habit.

dis·ȧ·cid′i·fȳ, *v.t.* to deprive of acid.

dis·aç·knowl′edġe (-nol′ej), *v.t.* to deny; to disown.

dis·aç·quāint′ (-kwānt′), *v.t.* to dissolve acquaintance with. [Obs.]

dis·aç·quāint′ănce, *n.* lack or loss of familiarity (*with*) or familiar knowledge of.

dis·ȧ·dorn′, *v.t.* to deprive of ornaments. [Obs.]

dis·ad·vȧnce′, *v.t.* and *v.i.* to check; to halt; to stop. [Obs.]

dis·ad·vȧn′tȧġe, *n.* [ME. *disadvauntage*; OFr. *desavantage*; *des-* priv., and *avantage*, advantage.]

1. that which prevents success, or makes it difficult; an unfavorable situation or circumstance; a drawback; a handicap; as, the *disadvantage* of ill health.

2. loss; injury; hindrance; prejudice to interest, fame, credit, profit, etc.; as, to sell goods at a *disadvantage*.

Syn.—hurt, injury, detriment, loss, damage.

dis·ad·vȧn′tȧġe, *v.t.*; disadvantaged, *pt., pp.*; disadvantaging, *ppr.* to act to the disadvantage of.

dis·ad·vȧn′tȧġed, *adj.* deprived of a decent standard of living, education, etc., by poverty and lack of opportunity; underprivileged.

dis·ad·văn·tā′ġeous, *a.* causing or characterized by disadvantage; unfavorable to success or prosperity; inconvenient; adverse.

dis·ad·văn·tā′ġeous·ly, *adv.* in a manner not favorable to success.

dis·ad·văn·tā′ġeous·ness, *n.* unfavorableness to success; inconvenience.

dis·ad·ven′tūre, *n.* misfortune. [Obs.]

dis·ad·ven′tūr·ous, *a.* unprosperous. [Obs.]

dis·af·feçt′, *v.t.*; disaffected, *pt., pp.*; disaffecting, *ppr.* 1. to alienate the affection of; to make less friendly or less faithful, as to a person, party, or cause; to make discontented or unfriendly; as, an attempt was made to *disaffect* the army.

2. to disdain or dislike. [Rare.]

3. to throw into disorder. [Obs.]

dis·af·feçt′ed, *a.* having the affections alienated; unfriendly, discontented, or disloyal, especially toward the government.

dis·af·feçt′ed·ly, *adv.* in a disaffected manner.

dis·af·feçt′ed·ness, *n.* the state or quality of being disaffected.

dis·af·feç′tion, *n.* [Fr. *désaffection*; *des-* priv., and *affection*.]

1. the absence or alienation of affection, attachment, or good will; discontent or disloyalty, especially toward the government.

2. disorder; bad constitution. [Rare.]

dis·af·feç′tion·āte, *a.* disaffected; not friendly. [Rare.]

dis·af·firm′, *v.t.*; disaffirmed, *pt., pp.*; disaffirming, *ppr.* 1. to deny or contradict (a former statement).

2. in law, (a) to refuse to abide by (a contract, agreement, etc.); repudiate; (b) to reverse or set aside (a former decision).

dis·af·firm′ănce, dis″af·fir·mā′tion, *n.* a disaffirming; a denial; a refutation.

dis·af·for′est, *v.t.* 1. in English law, to reduce from the legal status of a forest to that of ordinary land.

2. to deforest.

dis·ag′grē·gāte, *v.t.*; disaggregated, *pt., pp.*; disaggregating, *ppr.* to separate into component parts, as an aggregate mass.

dis·ag·grē·gā′tion, *n.* the act or operation of separating an aggregate body into its component parts.

dis·ag′i·ō, *n.* [see *agio*.] the discount on any currency not standard.

dis·ȧ·gree′, *v.i.*; disagreed, *pt., pp.*; disagreeing, *ppr.* 1. to differ; to be different; to fail to agree; to be not the same; as, histories often *disagree*.

2. to differ in opinion; as, the best judges sometimes *disagree*.

3. to be unsuitable or harmful (followed by *with*); as, medicine sometimes *disagrees with* the patient.

4. to quarrel; to contend.

Syn.—differ, dissent, quarrel, vary.

dis·ȧ·gree′ȧ·ble, *a.* 1. not to one's taste; unpleasant; repugnant; offensive.

2. hard to get along with; quarrelsome.

dis·ȧ·gree′ȧ·ble·ness, dis·ȧ·gree·ȧ·bil′i·ty, *n.* unpleasantness; the quality of being disagreeable.

dis·ȧ·gree′ȧ·bly, *adv.* 1. in a disagreeable manner.

2. to a disagreeable extent.

dis·ȧ·gree′ănce, *n.* disagreement. [Obs.]

dis·ȧ·gree′ment, *n.* 1. difference; incongruity; discrepancy; as, the *disagreement* between two versions.

2. difference of opinion or sentiments.

3. a disagreeing; a refusal to agree.

4. a controversy; a contention; a quarrel; a difference.

Syn.—difference, diversity, unlikeness, discrepancy, variance, dissent, misunderstanding, dissension, division, dispute, discord.

dis·ȧ·grē′ēr, *n.* one who disagrees.

dis·al·liēġe′, *v.t.* to alienate from allegiance. [Obs.]

dis·al·low′, *v.t.*; disallowed, *pt., pp.*; disallowing, *ppr.* to refuse to allow; to reject as untrue, invalid, or illegal.

dis·al·low′ȧ·ble, *a.* not allowable; not to be suffered.

dis·al·low′ȧ·ble·ness, *n.* the state of being disallowable.

dis·al·low′ănce, *n.* disapprobation; refusal to admit or permit; rejection.

dis·al·lȳ′, *v.t.*; disallied, *pt., pp.*; disallying, *ppr.* to free from an alliance.

dis′ȧ·mis, *n.* in logic, one of the valid moods.

dis·an′ċhŏr, *v.t* and *v.i.*; disanchored, *pt., pp.*; disanchoring, *ppr.* 1. to loosen from its anchorage, as a ship. [Obs.]

2. to weigh anchor. [Obs.]

dis·an·ġel′iç·ăl, *a.* not angelical. [Obs.]

dis·an′i·māte, *v.t.*; disanimated, *pt., pp.*; disanimating, *ppr.* 1. to deprive of life. [Rare.]

2. to deprive of spirit or courage; to discourage; to dishearten; to deject.

dis·an·i·mā′tion, *n.* 1. the act of discouraging; depression of spirits.

2. privation of life. [Rare.]

dis·an·nex′, *v.t.* to disunite.

dis·an·nul′, *v.t.*; disannulled, *pt., pp.*; disannulling, *ppr.* 1. to annul completely; to render absolutely void.

2. to divest of. [Obs.]

dis·an·nul′lēr, *n.* one who disannuls.

dis·an·nul′ment, *n.* annulment.

dis·ȧ·noint′, *v.t.*; disanointed, *pt., pp.*; disanointing, *ppr.* to render invalid the anointment or consecration of.

dis·ap·par′el, *v.t.*; disappareled *or* disapparelled, *pt., pp.*; disappareling *or* disapparelling, *ppr.* to disrobe; to undress.

dis·ap·pēar′, *v.i.*; disappeared, *pt., pp.*; disappearing, *ppr.* [*dis-*, and *appear*.]

1. to vanish from sight; to recede from view; to go away or out of sight; to cease to appear or to be perceived; to be no longer seen.

2. to cease; to go out of existence; to become lost or extinct; as, the epidemic had *disappeared*.

dis·ap·pēar′ănce, *n.* the act or fact of disappearing.

dis·ap·pend′en·cy, *n.* a detachment or separation from a connection or union. [Rare.]

dis·ap·pend′ent, *a.* detached; disconnected. [Rare.]

dis·ap·point′, *v.t.*; disappointed, *pt., pp.*; disappointing, *ppr.* [OFr. *desapointer*, to disappoint; *des-* priv., and *apointer*, to appoint; L. *dis-* priv., *ad*, to, and *punctum*, point.]

1. to fail to satisfy the hopes or expectations of.

2. to break one's promise to.

3. to prevent or undo the intended result of; balk; thwart; as, the weather *disappointed* their plans.

Syn.—frustrate, balk, baffle, delude, foil, defeat.

dis·ap·point′ed, *a.* 1. thwarted; frustrated; brought to nothing; as, a *disappointed* lover or a *disappointed* hope.

2. unprepared or poorly prepared. [Obs.]

disappointed of; prevented from fulfilling, achieving, or obtaining.

dis·ap·point′ment, *n.* 1. a disappointing.

2. the condition or feeling of being disappointed.

3. a person or thing that causes this.

dis·ap·prē′ci·āte (-shi-), *v.t.*; disappreciated, *pt., pp.*; disappreciating, *ppr.* to undervalue; to fail to appreciate.

dis·ap·prē·ci·ā′tion, *n.* the act of undervaluing.

dis″ap·prō·bā′tion, *n.* disapproval; dislike.

dis·ap′prō·bȧ·tō·ry, *a.* containing disapprobation; tending to disapprove.

dis·ap·prō′pri·āte, *a.* in English law, disappropriated; severed from connection with a church.

dis·ap·prō′pri·āte, *v.t.*; disappropriated, *pt., pp.*; disappropriating, *ppr.* 1. to sever or separate, as an appropriation; to withdraw from an appropriate use.

2. to deprive of appropriated property, as a church.

dis·ap·prō·pri·ā′tion, *n.* the act of disappropriating.

dis·ap·pröv′ăl, *n.* 1. a disapproving; failure to approve.

2. unfavorable opinion; dislike.

dis·ap·pröve′, *v.t.*; disapproved, *pt., pp.*; disapproving, *ppr.* 1. to have or express an unfavorable opinion of; to consider (something) wrong.

2. to refuse to approve; to reject; as, the sentence of the court-martial was *disapproved* by the President.

dis·ap·pröve′, *v.i.* to have or express disapproval (*of*).

dis·ap·pröv′ēr, *n.* a person who disapproves.

dis·ap·pröv′ing·ly, *adv.* in a manner that shows disapproval.

dis′ärd, *n.* a prattler; a boasting talker. [Obs.]

dis·ärm′, *v.t.*; disarmed, *pt., pp.*; disarming, *ppr.* [ME. *desarmen*; OFr. *desarmer*, to disarm; L. *dis-* priv., and *armare*, to arm.]

1. to deprive of arms; to take the arms or weapons from, usually by force or authority; as, he *disarmed* his foes: with *of* before the thing taken away; as, to *disarm* one *of* his weapons.

2. to deprive of means of attack or defense; to make harmless; as, to *disarm* a venomous serpent.

3. to overcome the hostility of; to make friendly.

dis·ärm′, *v.i.* 1. to lay down arms; to divest oneself of arms.

2. to reduce or do away with armed forces and armaments.

dis·ärm′ȧ·ment, *n.* 1. a disarming.

2. the reduction of armed forces and armaments, as to a limitation set by treaty.

3. a disarmed condition.

dis·är′mȧ·tūre, *n.* disarmament. [Rare.]

dis·ärmed′, *a.* 1. deprived of arms; stripped of the means of defense or attack; rendered harmless; subdued.

2. in heraldry, having no claws, teeth, or beak: applied to animals or birds of prey.

dis·ärm′ēr, *n.* one who disarms.

dis·ärm′ing, *a.* [ppr. of *disarm*.] removing suspicions, fears, or hostility.

dis·ar·rānġe′, *v.t.*; disarranged, *pt., pp.*; disarranging, *ppr.* to put out of order; to unsettle or disturb the order or proper arrangement of, as the parts of anything.

dis·ar·rānġe′ment, *n.* a disarranging or being disarranged.

dis·ar·rāy′, *v.t.*; disarrayed, *pt., pp.*; disarraying, *ppr.* [OFr. *desareer*; *des-* priv., and *areer*, to array.]

1. to undress; to take the clothes off.

2. to throw into disorder; to rout, as troops.

dis·ar·rāy′, *n.* 1. disorder; confusion.

2. undress; incomplete or disorderly attire.

dis·ar·rāy′ment, *n.* disorder; disturbance. [Rare.]

dis·är·tiç′ū·lāte, *v.t.*; disarticulated, *pt., pp.*; disarticulating, *ppr.* to separate or amputate at the joint or joints; to disjoint.

dis·är·tic·ū·lā′tion, *n.* a disarticulating or being disarticulated.
dis·är·tic′ū·lā·tŏr, *n.* one who disarticulates or sunders.
dis·as·sem′ble, *v.t.* [*dis-*, and *assemble.*] to take apart.
dis·as·sem′bly, *n.* a disassembling or being disassembled.
dis·as·sent′, *v.i.* to dissent. [Obs.]
dis·as·sent′, *n.* dissent; refusal. [Obs.]
dis·as·sent′ẽr, *n.* a dissenter. [Obs.]
dis·as·si·dū′i·ty, *n.* lack of assiduity or care. [Obs.]
dis·as·sim′i·lāte, *v.t.* in physiology, to subject to the process of disassimilation.
dis·as·sim·i·lā′tion, *n.* destructive metabolism; catabolism.
dis·as·sim′i·lā·tive, *a.* of the nature of disassimilation; capable of disassimilation.
dis·as·sō′ci·āte (-shi-āt), *v.t.*; disassociated, *pt., pp.*; disassociating, *ppr.* same as *dissociate.*
dis·as·sō·ci·ā′tion, *n.* same as *dissociation.*
dis̤·ȧs′tẽr, *n.* [OFr. *desastre*, disaster, misfortune; L. *dis-*, from, and *astrum*, from Gr. *astron*, a star: from astrological notions.]
1. an unfavorable aspect of a star or planet. [Obs.]
2. misfortune; mishap; calamity; any unfortunate event, especially a sudden, serious misfortune.
Syn.—calamity, mischance, misfortune, mishap.
dis̤·ȧs′tẽr, *v.t.* to bring disaster upon; to injure; to afflict. [Obs.]
dis̤·ȧs′tẽr·ly, *adv.* disastrously. [Obs.]
dis̤·ȧs′trous, *a.* 1. unlucky; unfortunate; calamitous; causing loss or injury.
2. gloomy; dismal; threatening disaster. [Archaic.]
The moon,
In dim eclipse, *disastrous* twilight sheds.
—Milton.
dis̤·ȧs′trous·ly, *adv.* unfortunately; in a disastrous manner.
dis̤·ȧs′trous·ness, *n.* unfortunateness; calamitousness.
dis·at·tīre′, *v.t.* to disrobe; to undress. [Obs.]
dis·at·tūne′, *v.t.* to put out of tune or harmony.
dis·aug·ment′, *v.t.* to decrease; to diminish. [Rare.]
dis·au′thŏr·īze, *v.t.* to deprive of authority or credit.
dis·ȧ·vaunce′, *v.t.* to drive back; to repel. [Obs.]
dis·ȧ·ven′tūre, *n.* a misadventure; a misfortune. [Obs.]
dis·ȧ·vouch′, *v.t.* to disavow. [Obs.]
dis·ȧ·vow′, *v.t.* [ME. *disavouen*; OFr. *desavouer*, to disavow; *des-* priv., and *avouer*, to avow.]
1. to deny; to disown; to deny to be true, as a fact or charge respecting oneself; to disclaim responsibility for or connection with.
2. to refuse; to decline. [Obs.]
dis·ȧ·vow′ăl, *n.* a disavowing; refusal to acknowledge, approve, etc.; repudiation.
dis·ȧ·vow′ănce, *n.* disavowal. [Obs.]
dis·ȧ·vow′ẽr, *n.* one who disavows.
dis·ȧ·vow′ment, *n.* same as *disavowal.*
dis·band′, *v.t.*; disbanded, *pt., pp.*; disbanding, *ppr.* 1. to dismiss from military service.
2. to break up (an association or organization).
dis·band′, *v.i.* [OFr. *desbander*, to loosen, scatter; *des-* priv., and *bander*, to tie.]
1. to cease to exist or function as an organization; as, the army, at the close of the war, *disbanded.*
2. to scatter; to disperse.
dis·band′ment, *n.* a disbanding or being disbanded.
dis·bär′, *v.t.*; disbarred, *pt., pp.*; disbarring, *ppr.* in law, to deprive of the right to practice law; to expel (a lawyer) from the bar.
dis·bärk′, *v.t.* and *v.i.* [OFr. *desbarquer*; *des-* priv., and *barque*, a bark.] to land from a ship; to disembark. [Obs.]
dis·bärk′, *v.t.* to peel the bark from.
dis·bär′ment, *n.* a disbarring or being disbarred.
dis·bāse′, *v.t.* to debase. [Obs.]
dis·bē·c̤ome′, *v.t.* to misbecome. [Obs.]
dis·bē·lief′, *n.* refusal to believe; denial of belief; the act of disbelieving.
Our belief or *disbelief* of a thing does not alter the nature of the thing.—Tillotson.
Syn.—unbelief.—*Unbelief* is a mere failure to admit; *disbelief* is a positive rejection.
dis·bē·liēve′, *v.t.*; disbelieved, *pt., pp.*; disbelieving, *ppr.* to fail to believe; to hold not to be true.
dis·bē·liēve′, *v.i.* to fail to believe (*in*).
dis·bē·liēv′ẽr, *n.* one who refuses belief; one who denies a thing to be true; an unbeliever.
dis·bench′, *v.t.* [*dis-*, and *bench.*]
1. to drive from a bench or seat. [Rare.]
2. in English law, to deprive (a bencher) of status and privileges.
dis·bend′, *v.t.* to unbend. [Obs.]
dis·bīnd′, *v.t.* to loosen. [Obs.]
dis·blāme′, *v.t.* to clear from blame. [Obs.]
dis·bōard′, *v.i.* to disembark. [Obs.]
dis·bod′ied (-bod′id), *a.* disembodied.
dis·bos·çā′tion, *n.* [*dis-*, and ME. *boskage*; OFr. *boscage*, a grove.] the clearing of forest land; the act of deforesting.
dis·bow′el, *v.t.* to take out the intestines of; to disembowel.
dis·brȧnch′, *v.t.* 1. to break or cut off (a branch).
2. to cut the branches from; prune.
dis·bud′, *v.t.*; disbudded, *pt., pp.*; disbudding, *ppr.* to deprive of buds or shoots.
dis·bũr′den, *v.t.* [*dis-*, and *burden.*]
1. to remove a burden from; to get rid of (a burden).
2. to cast a burden from; to clear of anything weighty, troublesome, or cumbersome; as, to *disburden* oneself of grief.
dis·bũr′den, *v.i.* to rid oneself of a burden.
dis·bũr′ġeŏn, *v.t.* to deprive of sprouts or buds. [Rare.]
dis·bũrs′ȧ·ble, *a.* that can be disbursed; to be disbursed.
dis·bũrse′, *v.t.*; disbursed, *pt., pp.*; disbursing, *ppr.* [OFr. *disbourser*; *des-*, from, and *bourse*, a purse.] to pay out, as money; to spend or lay out; to expend.
dis·bũrse′ment, *n.* 1. the act of paying out; a disbursing.
2. the money or sum paid out; as, the annual *disbursements* exceed the income.
dis·bũrs′ẽr, *n.* one who pays out or disburses money.
disç, *n.* same as *disk.*
dis·çāġe′, *v.t.* to free from a cage. [Rare.]
dis′çăl, *a.* of, pertaining to, or resembling a disk.
dis·çal′cē·āte, *v.t.* and *v.i.* [L. *discalceatus*, unshod; *dis-*, not, and *calceatus*, pp. of *calceare*, to shoe, from *calceus*, a shoe.] to pull off the shoes or sandals from. [Obs.]
dis·çal·cē·ā′tion, *n.* the act of pulling off the shoes or sandals. [Obs.]
dis·çalced′ (-kalst′), *a.* [L. *discalceatus*, unshod; *dis-*, not, and *calceatus*, pp. of *calceare*, to shoe, from *calceus*, a shoe, from *calx* (*calcis*), heel.] without covering for the feet; barefooted: applied especially to members of certain religious orders.
dis·çamp′, *v.t.* to break up, or drive from, a camp. [Obs.]
dis·çan′dy, *v.i.* to melt; to dissolve. [Obs.]
dis′çant, *n.* and *v.i.* same as *descant.*
dis·ça·pac′i·tāte, *v.t.* to incapacitate. [Rare.]
dis·çärd′, *v.t.*; discarded, *pt., pp.*; discarding, *ppr.* 1. in card playing, (a) to throw out of the hand (a card which is undesired); (b) in some games, as whist, to throw away on a trick (a card that is not trump or of a suit other than the one led).
2. to throw away, abandon, or get rid of as no longer valuable or useful.
Syn.—discharge, dismiss, reject, displace, abjure.
dis·çärd′, *v.i.* in card playing, to throw a card or cards out of one's hand; to make a discard.
dis′çärd, *n.* 1. the act of discarding or the state of being discarded.
2. one who or that which is discarded.
3. in card games, the card or cards discarded.
dis·çär′dūre, *n.* rejection. [Rare.]
dis·çär′nāte, *a.* stripped of flesh. [Obs.]
dis·çāse′, *v.t.* to take off a covering from; to strip; to undress. [Obs.]
dis·cēde′, *v.i.* to depart. [Obs.]
dis·cept′, *v.i.* to discuss; to debate; to dispute. [Obs.]
dis·cep·tā′tion, *n.* controversy. [Obs.]
dis·cep·tā′tŏr, *n.* one who discepts. [Obs.]
dis̤·cẽrn′ (di-zẽrn′), *v.t.*; discerned, *pt., pp.*; discerning, *ppr.* [ME. *discernen*; OFr. *discerner*; L. *discernere*, to separate, divide, distinguish between; *dis-*, apart, and *cernere*, to separate.]
1. to see distinctly; to separate from surrounding objects; to perceive by the eye; as, he *discerned* the sail at a distance.
2. to distinguish mentally; to see the difference between (two or more things); to discriminate.
So is my lord the king to *discern* good and bad. —2 Sam. xiv. 17.
Syn.—descry, discriminate, distinguish, penetrate, perceive.
dis̤·cẽrn′, *v.i.* 1. to see or understand the difference; to make distinction; as, to *discern* between good and evil.
2. to have judicial cognizance. [Obs.]
dis̤·cẽrn′ănce, *n.* discernment. [Obs.]
dis̤·cẽrn′ẽr, *n.* one who discerns, discovers, or distinguishes.
He was a great observer and *discerner* of men's natures and humors.—Clarendon.
dis̤·cẽrn′i·ble, *a.* that can be discerned; perceptible.
Syn.—apparent, evident, manifest, palpable, perceptible.
dis̤·cẽrn′i·ble·ness, *n.* the state or quality of being discernible.
dis̤·cẽrn′i·bly, *adv.* in a manner to be discerned, seen, or discovered; visibly; perceptibly.
dis̤·cẽrn′ing, *a.* having power to discern; capable of seeing, discriminating, knowing, and judging; sharp-sighted; shrewd; astute; as, a *discerning* man or mind.
dis̤·cẽrn′ing·ly, *adv.* with discernment; shrewdly.
dis̤·cẽrn′ment, *n.* 1. the act of discerning.
2. the power or faculty of the mind by which it distinguishes one thing from another; acuteness of judgment; power of perceiving differences of things or ideas; insight; acumen; as, the errors of youth often proceed from the want of *discernment.*
Syn.—penetration, discrimination.
dis·cẽrp′, *v.t.*; discerped (-sẽrpt), *pt., pp.*; discerping, *ppr.* [L. *discerpere*, to pluck or tear to pieces; *dis-*, apart, and *carpere*, to pluck.] to separate; to pluck apart. [Rare.]
dis·cẽrp·ti·bil′i·ty, dis·cẽrp·i·bil′i·ty, *n.* capability or liability to be torn apart or disunited. [Obs.]
dis·cẽrp′ti·ble, dis·cẽrp′i·ble, *a.* capable of being torn apart or divided; separable; capable of being disunited by violence.
dis·cẽrp′tion, *n.* the act of pulling to pieces or of separating the parts.
dis·cẽrp′tive, *a.* having a tendency to separate or divide.
dis·ces′sion (-sesh′un), *n.* a leaving. [Obs.]
dis·chärġe′, *v.t.*; discharged, *pt., pp.*; discharging, *ppr.* [ME. *dischargen*; OFr. *descharger*, to unload, disburden, discharge; LL. *discargare*, *discarricare*, to unload; L. *dis-*, from, and *carrus*, a wagon, car.]
1. to relieve of or release from something; as, *discharged* of suspicion, *discharged* from the army.
2. to relieve of or release from a burden; specifically, (a) to remove the cargo of (a ship); unload; (b) to release the charge of (a gun); fire; (c) to relieve (a servant, jury, etc.) of office; dismiss from service; (d) to release (a prisoner) from jail, (a defendant) from suspicion, (a patient) as cured, (a bankrupt) from obligations.
3. to release or remove (that with which a person or thing is burdened, etc.); specifically, (a) to unload (a cargo); (b) to shoot (a projectile); (c) to remove (dye) from cloth.
4. to relieve oneself or itself of (a burden, load, etc.); specifically, (a) to throw off; send forth; emit; as, the sore *discharges* pus; (b) to get rid of; acquit oneself of; pay (a debt) or perform (a duty).
5. in architecture, (a) to relieve (a wall, etc.) of excess pressure by distribution of weight; (b) to distribute (weight) evenly over a supporting part.
6. in electricity, to remove stored energy from (a battery or condenser).
7. in law, to release (a person) from debt, duty, etc.
dis·chärġe′, *v.i.* 1. to be released or thrown off.
2. to get rid of a burden, load, etc.
3. to fire; go off: said of a gun, etc.
4. to emit waste matter: said of a wound, etc.
5. to smear; to blur, as the lines of a drawing not waterproof.
dis·chärġe′, *n.* [OFr. *descharge*, an unloading.]
1. a discharging or being discharged (in all senses).
2. that which discharges, as a legal order for release, a certificate of dismissal from military service, etc.
3. a seaman's record of service.

4. that which is discharged, as matter from a sore.
5. a flow of electricity across a gap, as in a spark.
6. a substance, such as chloride of lime or nitric acid, used by printers to remove a color from the parts on which the pattern is printed.
discharge style; a method of printing in which a piece of cloth is colored, and from parts of it, forming a pattern, the color is afterward removed by bleaching.

dis·chär′ġẽr, *n.* one who or that which discharges; specifically, in electricity, an instrument for discharging a Leyden jar by making a connection between the two surfaces.

dis′chärġe tūbe, a device in which a gas or metal vapor conducting an electric discharge is the source of light, as in a mercury-vapor lamp.

dis·chär′ġing ärch, in architecture, an arch formed in the substance of a wall to distribute

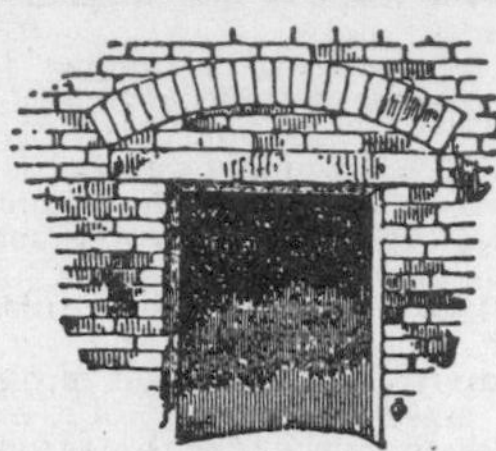

DISCHARGING ARCH

weight more evenly. Such arches are commonly used over lintels.

dis·chär′ġing rod, in electricity, a discharger.

dis·chũrch′, *v.t.*; dischurched, *pt.*, *pp.*; dischurching, *ppr.* 1. to deprive of the rank of a church. [Obs.]
2. to expel (a person) from church membership. [Obs.]

dis·cif′ẽr·ous, *a.* [L. *discus*, disk, and *ferre*, to bear.] having disks.

dis·ci·flō′răl, dis·ci·flō′rous, *a.* [L. *discus*, a disk, and *flos* (*floris*), flower.] of or relating to a number of polypetalous orders of flowers characterized by a conspicuous, expanded disk about the ovary.

dis′ci·fọrm, *a.* [L. *discus*, a disk, and *forma*, shape.] having the form of a disk or circular plate.

dis·cinçt′, *a.* ungirded. [Obs.]

dis·cī′ple, *n.* [ME. *disciple, desciple*; OFr. *disciple*; L. *discipulus*, a learner, from hyp. *discipere*, to learn.]
1. a pupil, follower, or adherent of any teacher or school of religion, learning, art, etc.
2. an early follower of Jesus, especially one of the twelve apostles.
3. [D–] a member of the Disciples of Christ.
Disciples of Christ; a Christian denomination which makes the Bible the only basis for faith and practice, holds Communion every Sunday, and baptizes by immersion: organized in 1809 by Alexander Campbell.
the disciples; the twelve disciples of Jesus.
Syn.—learner, scholar, pupil, follower, adherent.

dis·cī′ple, *v.t.*; discipled, *pt.*, *pp.*; discipling, *ppr.* 1. to teach; to train or bring up. [Obs.]
2. to punish; to discipline. [Obs.]
3. to make disciples of; to convert.
This authority he employed in sending missionaries to *disciple* all nations.—Griffin.

dis·cī′ple·ship, *n.* the position of a disciple; also, the duration of this.

dis·cī′pless, *n.* a woman disciple. [Obs.]

dis′ci·plin·ȧ·ble, *a.* 1. capable of instruction and improvement in learning.
2. capable of subjection to discipline.
3. subject or liable to discipline.

dis′ci·plin·ȧ·ble·ness, *n.* the state or quality of being disciplinable.

dis′ci·plin·ăl, *a.* pertaining to, or having the nature of, discipline.

dis′ci·plin·ănt, *n.* a person who disciplines himself; specifically, [D–] any member of a former Christian sect in Spain who flagellated and otherwise tortured themselves publicly as a means of discipline.

dis″ci·plin·ā′ri·ăn, *a.* pertaining to discipline; disciplinary.

dis″ci·plin·ā′ri·ăn, *n.* 1. one who enforces discipline.
2. a believer in strict discipline.
3. [D–] a Puritan or Presbyterian: so called from his rigid adherence to religious discipline. [Obs.]

dis′ci·plin·ȧ·ry, *a.* pertaining to discipline; intended for discipline; promoting discipline; as, *disciplinary* measures.

dis′ci·pline, *n.* [ME. *discipline*; L. *disciplina*, instruction, training, discipline, from *discipulus*, a learner.]
1. training that develops self-control, character, or orderliness and efficiency.
2. the result of such training; self-control; orderly conduct.
3. a system of rules or methods, as for the conduct of members of a monastic order.
4. subjection to rule; submissiveness to control.
The most perfect, who have their passions in the best *discipline*. —Rogers.
5. correction; chastisement; punishment inflicted by way of correction and training.
A sharp *discipline* of half a century had sufficed to educate us. —Macaulay.
6. anything taught; branch of knowledge or learning.

dis′ci·pline, *v.t.*; disciplined, *pt.*, *pp.*; disciplining, *ppr.* 1. to subject to discipline; to instruct or educate; to prepare by instruction; to train; as, to *discipline* youth for a profession.
They were with care prepared and *disciplined* for confirmation. —Addison.
2. to chastise; to punish.
3. to execute the laws of a church on.
4. to keep in subjection; to regulate; to govern.
Syn.—train, form, educate, instruct, drill, regulate, correct, chastise, punish.

dis′ci·plin·ẽr, *n.* one who or that which disciplines.

dis·cip′ū·lăr, *a.* of or becoming to a disciple.

dis·cis′sion, *n.* [LL. *discissio*, a separation, from *discissus*, pp. of *discindere*, to cut apart; *dis-*, apart, and *scindere*, to cut.] in surgery, a cutting apart.

disç jock′ey, same as *disk jockey*.

dis·çlāim′, *v.t.*; disclaimed, *pt.*, *pp.*; disclaiming, *ppr.* [OFr. *desclamer*; LL. *disclamare*, to renounce; L. *dis-* priv., and *clamare*, to cry out.]
1. to deny or relinquish all claim to; to reject as not belonging to oneself; to disown.
Here I *disclaim* all my paternal care. —Shak.
2. to refuse to acknowledge; to renounce; to deny.
He *disclaims* the authority of Jesus. —Farmer.
3. in law, (a) to deny or disavow (another's claim); (b) to decline accepting, as an estate, interest, office, etc.
Syn.—disown, disavow, deny, reject, renounce.

dis·çlāim′, *v.i.* to disavow all part or share. [Obs.]
Nature *disclaims* in thee. —Shak.

dis·çlāim′ẽr, *n.* 1. a person who disclaims, disowns, or renounces.
2. in law, an express or implied denial or renunciation of certain things in question.
3. a public disavowal, as of pretensions, etc.

dis·çlȧ·mā′tion, *n.* the act of disclaiming; specifically, in Scots law, the act of a tenant disclaiming a person as his superior, whether the person so disclaimed be the superior or not.

dis·clan′dẽr, *v.t.* to slander or abuse. [Obs.]

dis·clōṣe′, *v.t.*; disclosed, *pt.*, *pp.*; disclosing, *ppr.* [ME. *disclosen*; L. *discludere*, to shut up separately, to keep apart; *dis-*, apart, and *claudere*, to close.]
1. to uncover; to lay open to view.
The shells being broken, the stone included in them is *disclosed*. —Woodward.
2. to reveal; to make known; as, to *disclose* the secret thoughts of the heart.
3. to open; to hatch. [Obs.]
The ostrich layeth her eggs under sand, where the heat of the sun *discloseth* them. —Bacon.
Syn.—uncover, unveil, discover, reveal, divulge, tell, utter.

dis·clōṣe′, *n.* an uncovering; disclosure. [Obs.]

dis·clōṣed′, *a.* 1. uncovered; exposed to view; made known; revealed; told; uttered.
2. in heraldry, with the wings spread open or expanded on each side, but with the points downward: applied to tame fowls.

DOVE DISCLOSED

dis·clōṣ′ẽr, *n.* one who or that which discloses.

dis·clō′ṣūre (-zhūr), *n.* the act of disclosing or being disclosed; also, that which is disclosed.

dis·çloud′, *v.t.* to free from clouds or obscurity. [Obs.]

dis′çō, *n.* [shortened form of *discothèque*.]
1. *pl.* **dis′çōṣ,** a nightclub or other public place for dancing to recorded music.
2. a kind of popular dance music with a strong beat, elements of the blues and Latin American rhythms, and simple and repetitious lyrics, usually accompanied by pulsating lights, etc.

dis′çō-, [from L. *discus*, Gr. *diskos*, a quoit, disk.] a combining form meaning *disk-shaped*, *connected with disk.*

dis·çō·blas′tiç, *a.* [*disco-*, and Gr. *blastos*, a germ.] having discoidal segmentation of the formative yolk.

dis·çō·blas′tū·lȧ, *n.* the blastula which a discoblastic ovum yields.

dis·çob′ō·lus, *n.*; *pl.* **dis·çob′ō·lī,** [L., from Gr. *diskobolos*, a discus thrower; *diskos*, a discus, and *ballein*, to throw.]
1. a discus thrower.
2. [D–] a famous Greek statue said to have been sculptured by Myron about 450 B.C., being the representation of an athlete throwing the discus.

DISCOBOLUS

dis′çō·çärp, *n.* [*disco-*, and Gr. *karpos*, fruit.] in botany, (a) a collection of fruit in a hollow receptacle, as in many roseworts; (b) an apothecium.

Dis·çō·ceph′ȧ·lī, *n.pl.* [*disco-*, and Gr. *kephalē*, head.] a suborder of fishes; the sucking fishes, of which the remora is the best known example.

dis·çō·ceph′ȧ·lous, *a.* having a sucking disk attached to the head; of or pertaining to the *Discocephali*.

dis·çō·daç′tyl, *a.* of or pertaining to the *Discodactylia*.

dis·çō·daç′tyl, *n.* any of the *Discodactylia*.

Dis″çō·daç·tyl′i·ȧ, *n.pl.* [*disco-*, and Gr. *daktylos*, finger, toe.] a division of amphibians having terminally dilated toes by which they adhere to plane surfaces; the tree toads and tree frogs.

dis·çō·daç′tyl·ous, *a.* having terminally dilated toes; discodactyl.

dis·çō·gas′trụ·lȧ, *n.* [*disco-*, and L. *gastrula*, dim. of *gaster*; Gr. *gastēr*, belly.] the gastrula which develops from a discoblastic ovum.

dis′çoid, dis·çoid′ăl, *a.* [LL. *discoides*; Gr. *diskoeidēs*, disk-shaped; *diskos*, a disk, and *eidos*, form.] having the form of a disk.
discoid flower; a compound flower not radiated, but with tubular florets, as the tansy.

dis′çoid, *n.* 1. something in the form of a discus or disk.
2. a dental instrument with a circular or disklike blade.
3. a univalve shell whose whorls are arranged vertically in the same plane, so as to form a disk.

dis′çō·lith, *n.* [*disco-*, and Gr. *lithos*, a stone.] a disklike calcareous body with an organic structure found embedded in the ocean floor.

dis·çŏl′ŏr, *v.t.* and *v.i.*; discolored, *pt.*, *pp.*; discoloring, *ppr.* [LL., *discolorare*, to deprive of color.] to change in color or shade; to stain; to tinge.

dis·çŏl·ŏr·ā′tion, *n.* 1. a discoloring or being discolored.
2. a discolored spot or mark.

dis·çŏl′ŏr·ment, *n.* same as *discoloration*.

dis·çŏl′ŏur, *v.t.* and *v.i.* to discolor: British spelling.

dis·çŏm·bob′ū·lāte, *v.t.* to upset. [Slang.]

Dis″çō·mē·dū′sae, *n.pl.* [*disco-*, and L. *Medusæ*, a genus of jelly fishes.] an order of hydrozoans including *Discophora*.

dis″çō·mē·dū′săn, *a.* of or pertaining to the *Discomedusæ*.

dis″çō·mē·dū′săn, *n.* any of the *Discomedusæ*.

dis·çŏm′fit, *v.t.*; discomfited, *pt.*, *pp.*; discomfiting, *ppr.* [ME. *discomfiten*; OFr. *desconfire*; LL. *disconficere*, to defeat, discomfit; L. *dis-* priv., and *conficere*, to do, achieve; from *com-* intens., and *facere*, to do.]
1. originally, to rout; to defeat; to cause to flee; to vanquish.

2. to overthrow the plans or expectations of; thwart; frustrate.
3. to make uneasy; confuse; embarrass; disconcert.

dis·cŏm′fit, *a.* discomfited. [Obs.]

dis·cŏm′fit, *n.* discomfiture. [Obs.]

dis·cŏm′fi·tūre, *n.* 1. a discomfiting or being discomfited.
2. confusion; embarrassment.

After five days' exertion, this man resigns the task in *discomfiture* and despair. —Disraeli.

dis·cŏm′fŏrt, *n.* [ME.; OFr. *desconfort*, from *desconforter*, to discourage; L. *dis-* priv., and LL. *confortare*, to comfort.]
1. absence of comfort; uneasiness; inconvenience; hardship; distress.
2. anything causing this.

dis·cŏm′fŏrt, *v.t.* to cause discomfort to.

dis·cŏm′fŏrt·ȧ·ble, *a.* uncomfortable. [Rare.]

dis·cŏm′fŏrt·ȧ·ble·ness, *n.* discomfort. [Obs.]

dis·cŏm·mend′, *v.t.*; discommended, *pt.*, *pp.*; discommending, *ppr.* 1. to express disapproval of: opposed to *commend.*
2. to speak of dissuasively: opposed to *recommend.*
3. to cause to be viewed or received with disfavor. [Obs.]

dis·cŏm·mend′ȧ·ble, *a.* blamable; censurable; deserving disapprobation.

dis·cŏm·mend′ȧ·ble·ness, *n.* blamableness; the quality of being worthy of disapprobation.

dis·cŏm·men·dā′tion, *n.* blame; censure; reproach.

dis·cŏm·mend′ẽr, *n.* one who discommends.

dis·cŏm·mis′sion, *v.t.* to dispossess of a commission.

dis·com′mō·dāte, *v.t.* to inconvenience. [Obs.]

dis·cŏm·mōde′, *v.t.*; discommoded, *pt.*, *pp.*; discommoding, *ppr.* [OFr. *descommoder*; L. *dis-* priv., and *commodare*, to make fit or suitable, from *commodus*, fit, suitable.] to put to inconvenience; to incommode; to trouble.

dis·cŏm·mō′di·ous, *a.* inconvenient; troublesome.

dis·cŏm·mō′di·ous·ly, *adv.* in a discommodious manner.

dis·cŏm·mō′di·ous·ness, *n.* discommodity.

dis·cŏm·mod′i·ty, *n.*; *pl.* **dis·cŏm·mod′i·tieṣ,** 1. inconvenience; trouble; disadvantage.
2. in economics, anything that lacks utility.

dis·com′mŏn, *v.t.* 1. at Oxford and Cambridge universities, to prohibit (a tradesman) from dealing with the undergraduates, as for some infraction of the rules.
2. in law, (a) to deprive of the right of using a common, as for pasturage; (b) to cause (a common) to become private property.

dis·cŏm·mū′ni·ty, *n.* a state in which there is an absence of community, as in relationship or characteristics. [Rare.]

dis·cŏm·plex′ion (-plek′shun), *v.t.* to change the complexion or color of. [Obs.]

dis·cŏm·plī′ănce, *n.* noncompliance.

dis·cŏm·pōṣe′, *v.t.*; discomposed, *pt.*, *pp.*; discomposing, *ppr.* [L. *dis-* priv., and *componere*, to put in order, compose.]
1. to unsettle; to disarrange; to disorder.
2. to disturb peace and quietness in; to agitate, to ruffle.

Ill in death it shows,
Your peace of mind by rage to *discompose.* —Dryden.

3. to displace; to discharge. [Obs.]

He never put down or *discomposed* counsellor, save only Stanley. —Bacon.

Syn.—disorder, derange, unsettle, disturb, disconcert, agitate, ruffle, fret, vex.

dis·cŏm·pōṣed′, *a.* unsettled; disordered; ruffled; agitated; disturbed.

dis·cŏm·pōṣ′ed·ly, *adv.* in a discomposed manner.

dis·cŏm·pōṣ′ed·ness, *n.* the state or quality of being discomposed.

dis·com·pō·ṣi′tion, *n.* discomposure. [Obs.]

dis·cŏm·pō′ṣūre, *n.* 1. lack of composure; disorder; agitation; disturbance; perturbation; as, *discomposure* of mind.
2. inconsistency; disagreement. [Obs.]

dis·compt′, *v.t.* to discount. [Obs.]

Dis″ҫō·mȳ·cē′tēṣ, *n.pl.* [L., from Gr. *diskos*, a disk, and *mykes* (pl. *mykētes*), fungus.] an order of small fungi having the openings of the fruit above, and waxlike or fleshy tissue, including *Peziza* and the common morel.

dis″ҫō·mȳ·cē′tous, *a.* of or pertaining to the order *Discomycetes.*

dis·cŏn·cẽrt′, *v.t.*; disconcerted, *pt.*, *pp.*; disconcerting, *ppr.* [L. *dis-* priv., and *concertare*, to contend.]
1. to throw into disorder; to undo (plans, etc.); to defeat; to frustrate.
2. to unsettle the mind of; to discompose; to disturb the self-possession of; to confuse.

dis·con′cẽrt, *n.* lack of concert or harmony. [Rare.]

dis·cŏn·cẽr′tion, *n.* the act of disconcerting; the state of being disconcerted or confused.

dis·cŏn·dū′cive, *a.* not conducive; tending to hinder or prevent. [Rare.]

dis·cŏn·fọrm′ȧ·ble, *a.* lacking conformity.

dis·cŏn·fọrm′i·ty, *n.* lack of agreement or conformity; inconsistency.

dis·cŏn·grụ′i·ty, *n.* lack of congruity; incongruity; disagreement; inconsistency.

dis·cŏn·neçt′, *v.t.*; disconnected, *pt.*, *pp.*; disconnecting, *ppr.* 1. to separate; to disunite; to dissolve connection between; to detach.
2. to turn off the current in (an electrical appliance) by breaking the connection with the main circuit.

dis·cŏn·neçt′ed, *a.* 1. separated; detached; unrelated.
2. broken up into unrelated parts; incoherent.

dis·cŏn·neçt′ed·ly, *adv.* in a disconnected manner.

dis·cŏn·neç′tion, *n.* the act of disconnecting; also, the condition of being disconnected.

dis·cŏn·sent′, *v.i.* to refuse consent. [Obs.]

dis·con′sō·lȧ·cy, *n.* the state or quality of being disconsolate. [Obs.]

dis·con′sō·lāte, *a.* [ME. *disconsolat*; ML. *disconsolatus*, comfortless; L. *dis-* priv., and *consolatus*, pp. of *consolari*, to console.]
1. without comfort or consolation; sorrowful; hopeless; sad; dejected; melancholy; as, a *disconsolate* widow.
2. causing or suggesting discomfort or dejection; cheerless; as, the *disconsolate* darkness of a winter's night.

dis·con′sō·lā·ted, *a.* disconsolate. [Obs.]

dis·con′sō·lāte·ly, *adv.* in a disconsolate manner; without comfort.

dis·con′sō·lāte·ness, *n.* the state of being disconsolate or comfortless.

dis·con·sō·lā′tion, *n.* lack of comfort; disconsolateness.

dis·cŏn·tent′, *a.* discontented.

dis·cŏn·tent′, *n.* 1. lack of contentment; uneasiness; dissatisfaction at any present state of things; restless desire for something more or different; as, discomforts produce *discontent.*
2. one dissatisfied or rebellious. [Rare.]

Changelings and poor *discontents.*—Shak.

dis·cŏn·tent′, *v.t.*; discontented, *pt.*, *pp.*; discontenting, *ppr.* to make discontented.

dis·con·ten·tā′tion, *n.* discontent. [Obs.]

dis·cŏn·tent′ed, *a.* not contented; uneasy in mind; dissatisfied.

dis·cŏn·tent′ed·ly, *adv.* in a discontented manner or mood.

dis·cŏn·tent′ed·ness, *n.* uneasiness of mind; dissatisfaction.

dis·cŏn·tent′fụl, *a.* full of discontent.

dis·cŏn·tent′ing, *a.* 1. discontented. [Obs.]
2 giving discontent; disappointing.

dis·cŏn·tent′ive, *a.* pertaining to or causing discontent. [Rare.]

dis·cŏn·tent′ment, *n.* the state of being uneasy in mind; uneasiness; discontent.

dis·cŏn·tin′ū·ȧ·ble, *a.* capable of being discontinued. [Rare.]

dis·cŏn·tin′ū·ănce, *n.* 1. a stopping or being stopped; cessation; interruption.
2. in law, the interruption or termination of a suit by reason of the plaintiff's failure to prosecute it properly, or as the result of a dismissal.
3. in old English law, an interruption or break of a right of entry, consequent upon a wrongful alienation by the tenant in possession, for an estate larger than that to which he was entitled.

dis·cŏn·tin·ū·ā′tion, *n.* same as *discontinuance.*

dis·cŏn·tin′ūe, *v.t.*; discontinued, *pt.*, *pp.*; discontinuing, *ppr.* [L. *dis-* priv., and *continuare*, to continue.]
1. to cease; to stop; to put an end to; as, to *discontinue* the use of steam as a motive power.
2. in law, to effect a discontinuance of (a suit).

dis·cŏn·tin′ūe, *v.i.* 1. to stop; to end.

Thyself shalt *discontinue* from thine heritage. —Jer. xvii. 4.

2. to lose the cohesion of parts. [Obs.]

dis·cŏn·tin·ū·ee′, *n.* in law, one of whom an estate is discontinued.

dis·cŏn·tin′ū·ẽr, *n.* one who discontinues.

dis·con·ti·nū′i·ty, *n.* 1. lack of continuity; lack of logical sequence.
2. a gap or break.

dis·cŏn·tin′ū·ŏr, *n.* in law, a discontinuer.

dis·cŏn·tin′ū·ous, *a.* not continuous; broken off; interrupted; intermittent; gaping.
discontinuous function; in mathematics, a function that varies discontinuously, and whose differential coefficient may therefore become infinite.

dis·cŏn·tin′ū·ous·ly, *adv.* in a discontinuous manner.

dis·cŏn·vēn′ience (-yens), *n.* incongruity; disagreement. [Obs.]

dis·cŏn·vēn′ient, *a.* incongruous. [Obs.]

Dis·coph′ō·rȧ, *n.pl.* [Gr. *diskophoros*, bringing the discus; *diskos*, a disk, and *pherein*, to carry, bring.]
1. a group of the *Hydrozoa*, comprising the jelly fishes.
2. an order of annelids, *Hirudinea*, to which the leech belongs.

dis·coph′ō·rous, *a.* resembling or pertaining to the *Discophora.*

dis″ҫō·plȧ·cen′tȧ, *n.* [*disco-*, and L. *placenta*, a round, flat cake, the placenta.] a placenta having a disklike form.

dis″ҫō·plȧ·cen′tăl, *a.* pertaining to a discoplacenta.

dis′ҫọrd, *n.* [ME. *discord*; OFr. *descorde*; L. *discordare*, to be at variance, differ, from *discors*, unlike, discordant, from *dis-*, apart, and *cor* (*cordis*), the heart.]
1. disagreement; lack of concord or harmony; dissension; incompatibility; conflict.
2. a harsh or confused noise, as the sound of battle; clash; din.
3. in music, a lack of harmony in tones simultaneously sounded; inharmonious combination of tones; dissonance.

Syn.—disagreement, discordance, variance, difference, opposition, dissension, contention, strife, rupture, clashing, dissonance.

dis·ҫọrd′, *v.i.* to disagree; to jar; to clash; to be inharmonious.

dis·ҫọrd′ȧ·ble, *a.* discordant. [Obs.]

dis·ҫọrd′ănce, *n.* [L. *discordans.*] disagreement; inconsistency; lack of harmony; as, a *discordance* of opinions, sounds, etc.

dis·ҫọrd′ăn·cy, *n.*, *pl.* **dis·ҫọrd′ăn·cieṣ,** same as *discordance.*

dis·ҫọrd′ănt, *a.* [ME. *descordaunt*; L. *discordans* (*-antis*), ppr. of *discordare*, to disagree.]
1. disagreeing; incongruous; contradictory; being at variance; as, *discordant* rules or principles.
2. dissonant; not in unison; not harmonious; harsh; jarring; as, *discordant* notes.
3. in geology, lacking parallelism: applied to strata.

dis·ҫọrd′ănt·ly, *adv.* dissonantly; in a discordant manner.

dis·ҫọrd′ănt·ness, *n.* the state of being discordant.

dis·ҫor·re·spond′ent, *a.* lacking in correspondence. [Rare.]

dis·ҫos′tāte, *a.* [L. *dis-*, apart, and *costa*, rib.] having leaves with ribs radiating like the spokes of a wheel.

dis′ҫō·thèque (-tek), *n.* [Fr., from *disque*, disk, record (from L. *discus*, a disk), and *bibliothèque*, from L. *bibliotheca*, library.] a café or other public place for dancing to recorded popular music.

dis·ҫoun′sel, *v.t.* to dissuade. [Obs.]

dis′ҫount, *n.* [from OFr. *desconter*, to reckon off; LL. hyp. *discomputare*, to reckon off, discount; *dis-*, off, from, and *computare*, to reckon, count.]
1. a deduction from an original price or debt, allowed for paying promptly or in cash.
2. the interest deducted in advance by one who buys, or lends money on, a bill of exchange, promissory note, etc.
3. the rate of interest charged for discounting a bill, note, etc.: also called *discount rate.*
4. the act of discounting; as, a note may be deposited at a bank subject to *discount.*
5. in billiards, a handicap by which the player giving odds has deducted from his string an agreed number of counts for every count made by his opponent.
at a discount; (a) below the regular price; below face value; (b) not worth much; unwanted and easily obtained; (c) with allowance for exaggeration, bias, etc.

dis′ҫount (*or* dis-kount′), *v.t.*; discounted, *pt.*, *pp.*; discounting, *ppr.* 1. to deduct; to subtract.
2. to pay or receive the present value of (a

bill of exchange, promissory note, etc.), minus a deduction to cover interest for the purchaser.

3. to deduct from; reduce the quantity, cost, or value of.

4. to take (a story, statement, opinion, etc.) at less than face value, allowing for exaggeration, bias, etc.

5. to disbelieve or disregard entirely; to set aside as inaccurate or irrelevant.

His application is to be *discounted*, as here irrelevant. —Hamilton.

6. to estimate beforehand; to lessen the effect of by anticipating; to discuss and form conclusions before an event occurs; as, he *discounted* all the pleasure of the journey before setting out.

7. in billiards, to give (an opponent) a discount.

dis′çount, *v.i.* to lend or make a practice of lending money, deducting the interest at the time of the loan; as, the banks *discount* for sixty or ninety days.

dis·çount′ȧ·ble, *a.* capable of being discounted; as, a *discountable* note.

dis·coun′tē·nănce, *v.t.*; discountenanced, *pt., pp.*; discountenancing, *ppr.* [*dis-*, and *countenance.*]

1. to abash; to ruffle the countenance of; to put to shame.

2. to discourage; to refuse approval or support of; to frown on; as, to *discountenance* drunkenness.

dis·coun′tē·nănce, *n.* disapprobation; whatever tends to check or discourage. [Obs.]

dis·coun′tē·năn·cẽr, *n.* one who discountenances.

dis·çount′ẽr, *n.* one who discounts.

dis·çŏur′ȧġe, *v.t.*; discouraged, *pt., pp.*; discouraging, *ppr.* [ME. *discouragen*; OFr. *descoragier*, to discourage; *des-* priv., and *coragier*, to encourage.]

1. to deprive of courage; to dishearten; to depress the spirits of; to deject; to deprive of confidence.

Fathers, provoke not your children, lest they be *discouraged.* —Col. iii. 21.

2. to advise or persuade (a person) to refrain; as, she *discouraged* him from the rash attempt.

3. to attempt to repress or prevent by disapproving or raising objections or obstacles; to dissuade from; as, to *discourage* an effort.

Syn.—dishearten, depress, dissuade, dispirit, deter.

dis·çŏur′ȧġe, *n.* discouragement. [Obs.]

dis·çŏur′ȧġe·ȧ·ble, *a.* capable of discouragement.

dis·çŏur′ȧġe·ment, *n.* 1. the act of disheartening or depriving of courage; the act of deterring or dissuading from an undertaking.

2. the state, fact, or feeling of being discouraged.

3. that which destroys or abates courage; that which lessens confidence or hope; that which deters, or tends to deter, from an undertaking or from the prosecution of anything.

dis·çŏur′ȧ·ġẽr, *n.* one who or that which discourages.

dis·çŏur′ȧ·ġing, *a.* that discourages; disheartening; depressing; as, *discouraging* prospects.

dis·çŏur′ȧ·ġing·ly, *adv.* in a discouraging manner.

dis′çōurse (*or* dis-kōrs′), *n.* [ME. *discourse*; OFr. *discours*; LL. *discursus*, discourse, conversation; L. *discursus*, a running to and fro, from *discursus*, pp. of *discurrere*, to run to and fro; *dis-*, from, in different directions, and *currere*, to run.]

1. a communication of thoughts by words; expression of ideas; conversation.

The vanquished party with the victors joined,
Nor wanted sweet *discourse*, the banquet of the mind. —Dryden.

2. communication in general, especially as a subject of study.

3. a written treatise; a formal dissertation; a lecture; a sermon; as, the *discourse* of Plutarch on garrulity.

4. ability to reason; rationality. [Archaic.]

dis·çōurse′, *v.i.*; discoursed, *pt., pp.*; discoursing, *ppr.* 1. to converse; to speak; to talk.

2. to speak or write (*on* or *upon* a subject) formally and at some length.

3. to reason. [Obs.]

dis·çōurse′, *v.t.* 1. to treat of; to talk over; to tell. [Archaic.]

Let us *discourse* our fortunes. —Shak.

2. to utter; as, to *discourse* excellent music.

3. to talk, reason, or confer with. [Obs.]

dis·çōurs′ẽr, *n.* 1. one who discourses; a speaker.

2. the writer of a treatise or dissertation.

dis·çōurs′ive, *a.* 1. reasoning. [Obs.]

2. containing dialogue or conversation; interlocutory. [Obs.]

3. talkative; as, a *discoursive* woman. [Obs.]

dis·çōurs′ive·ness, *n.* the state of being discoursive. [Obs.]

dis·çoŭr′tē·ous, *a.* not courteous; impolite; uncivil; rude; lacking in good manners.

dis·çoŭr′tē·ous·ly, *adv.* in a discourteous manner.

dis·çoŭr′tē·ous·ness, *n.* discourtesy.

dis·çoŭr′tē·sy, *n.* 1. lack of courtesy; rudeness; bad manners.

2. *pl.* **dis·çoŭr′tē·sieṣ,** a rude or impolite act or remark.

dis·çōurt′ship, *n.* discourtesy. [Obs.]

disç′ous, *a.* discoid.

dis·çŏv′e·nănt, *v.t.* to dissolve covenant with. [Obs.]

dis·çŏv′ẽr, *v.t.*; discovered, *pt., pp.*; discovering, *ppr.* [ME. *discoveren*; OFr. *descovrir*; LL. *discooperire*, to discover, reveal; L. *dis-* priv., and *cooperire*, to cover.]

1. to be the first to find out, see, or know about.

2. to find out; learn of the existence of; realize.

3. (a) to reveal; disclose; expose; (b) to uncover. [Archaic.]

Syn.—invent, manifest, declare, disclose, reveal, divulge, uncover.

dis·çŏv′ẽr, *v.i.* to uncover. [Obs.]

dis·çŏv″ẽr·ȧ·bil′i·ty, *n.* the state or quality of being discoverable.

dis·çŏv′ẽr·ȧ·ble, *a.* capable of being discovered.

dis·çŏv′ẽr·ẽr, *n.* 1. one who discovers; one who first sees or finds out something.

2. a scout; an explorer. [Obs.]

dis·çŏv′ẽr·ment, *n.* discovery. [Obs.]

dis·çŏv′ẽrt, *a.* [ME. *discovert*; OFr. *descovert*, lit., not covered, hence not protected, from LL. *discoopertus*, pp. of *discooperire*, to uncover; L. *dis-* priv., and *cooperire*, to cover.] in law, having no husband: said of a spinster, widow, or divorcée.

dis·çŏv′ẽrt·ūre, *n.* in law, the state or condition of being discovert.

dis·çŏv′ẽr·y, *n.*; *pl.* **dis·çŏv′ẽr·ieṣ,** 1. a discovering.

2. that which is discovered.

3. the unraveling of a plot in a poem, play, etc.

4. exploration. [Obs.]

Dis·çŏv′ẽr·y Dāy, same as *Columbus Day.*

dis·crā′dle, *v.i.* to come forth from or as if from a cradle; to emerge. [Obs.]

dis·cred′it, *v.t.*; discredited, *pt., pp.*; discrediting, *ppr.* [LL. *discredere*, to disbelieve; L. *dis-* priv., and *credere*, to believe.]

1. to disbelieve; to give no credit to; not to credit or believe; as, the report is *discredited.*

2. to show reason for disbelieving or distrusting; to cast doubt on.

3. to damage the credit or reputation of; disgrace.

dis·cred′it, *n.* 1. lack of belief, trust, or confidence; disbelief; as, later accounts have brought the story into discredit.

2. damage to one's reputation; loss of respect or status; disgrace; dishonor.

3. something that causes disgrace or loss of status.

Syn.—disgrace, dishonor, disrepute, ignominy, reproach, scandal.

dis·cred′it·ȧ·ble, *a.* that discredits; injurious to reputation or status; disgraceful; disreputable.

dis·cred′it·ȧ·bly, *adv.* in a discreditable manner; also, to a discreditable extent.

dis·cred′it·ŏr, *n.* one who discredits. [Obs.]

dis·creet′, *a.* [ME. *discret*; OFr. *discret*, prudent, discreet, from L. *discretus*, pp. of *discernere*, to distinguish, discern; *dis-*, apart, from, and *cernere*, to separate, to see.]

1. prudent; cautious; wary; careful about what one says or does.

2. polite; courteous; civil. [Scot.]

dis·creet′ly, *adv.* in a discreet manner.

dis·creet′ness, *n.* the quality of being discreet; discretion.

dis·crep′ănce, *n.* discrepancy. [Rare.]

dis·crep′ăn·cy, *n.*; *pl.* **dis·crep′ăn·cieṣ,** [OFr. *discrepance*; L. *discrepantia*, discordance, disagreement, from *discrepare*, to sound differently.]

1. difference; disagreement; contrariety.

2. an instance of this.

dis·crep′ănt, *a.* different; disagreeing; contrary; characterized by discrepancy.

dis·crep′ănt, *n.* a dissenter. [Obs.]

dis·crēte′, *a.* [L. *discretus*, pp. of *discernere*, to distinguish, separate.]

1. separate; distinct; disjunct.

The parts are not *discrete* or dissentany. —Milton.

2. made up of distinct parts.

3. in logic, disjunctive.

discrete proportion; proportion where the ratio of two or more pairs of numbers or quantities is the same, but there is not the same proportion between all the numbers; as, 3:6::8:16, 3 bearing the same proportion to 6 as 8 does to 16. But 3 is not to 6 as 6 is to 8. Opposed to a *continued* or *continual proportion*; as, 3:6::12:24.

dis·crēte′, *v.t.* to separate; to divide. [Obs.]

dis·crēte′ly, *adv.* in a discrete manner.

dis·cre′tion, *n.* [ME. *discrecion*; OFr. *discrecion*; L. *discretio* (*-onis*), a separation, distinction, from *discretus*, pp. of *discernere*, to discern.]

1. the quality of being discrete; distinction; disjunction; separation.

2. the quality of being discreet; prudence; a being careful about what one does or says.

Discretion is the victor of the war,
Valour the pupil. —Massinger.

3. liberty or power of deciding or acting without other control than one's own judgment; as, the management of affairs was left to the *discretion* of the president.

4. the action or power of discerning; judgment. [Rare.]

at one's discretion; in accordance with one's judgment.

Syn.—circumspection, wariness, prudence, caution.

dis·cre′tion·ăl, *a.* discretionary.

dis·cre′tion·ăl·ly, *adv.* discretionarily.

dis·cre′tion·ā·ri·ly, *adv.* at discretion; according to discretion.

dis·cre′tion·ā·ry, *a.* left to discretion; regulated by one's own discretion or judgment; as, *discretionary* powers of an appointing officer.

dis·crē′tive, *a.* [LL. *discretivus*, serving to distinguish, from L. *discretus*, pp. of *discernere*, to distinguish, discern.] disjunctive; noting separation or opposition.

discretive proposition; in logic, a proposition which expresses some distinction, opposition, or variety, by means of *but, though, yet*, etc.; as, travelers change their climate, *but* not their temper.

dis·crē′tive·ly, *adv.* in a discretive manner.

dis·crim′i·nȧ·ble, *a.* that can be discriminated.

dis·crim′i·năl, *a.* making division; separating; specifically, in palmistry, denoting the dividing line between the hand and the arm.

dis·crim′i·nănt, *n.* in mathematics, the eliminant of the *n* first derived functions of a homogeneous function of *n* variables.

dis·crim′i·nāte, *v.t.*; discriminated, *pt., pp.*; discriminating, *ppr.* [L. *discriminatus*, pp. of *discriminare*, to divide, distinguish, from *discrimen*, a division, distinction, interval, from *dis-*, apart, and *crimen*, verdict, judgment.]

1. to distinguish; to observe the difference between; to select from others.

When a prisoner first leaves his cell he is unable to *discriminate* colors or recognize faces. —Macaulay.

2. to constitute a difference between; to differentiate.

In outward fashion . . . *discriminated* from all the nations of the earth.—Hammond.

dis·crim′i·nāte, *v.i.* 1. to see the difference (*between* things); distinguish.

2. to make distinctions in treatment; show partiality (*in favor of*) or prejudice (*against*).

dis·crim′i·nāte, *a.* 1. distinguished; distinct.

2. involving discrimination; distinguishing carefully.

dis·crim′i·nāte·ly, *adv.* distinctly; with careful distinction.

dis·crim′i·nāte·ness, *n.* distinctness; marked difference.

dis·crim′i·nā·ting, *a.* 1. that discriminates; differentiating.

2. able to make or see fine distinctions; discerning.

3. treating differently; differential, as a tariff.

dis·crim′i·nā·ting·ly, *adv.* in a discriminating manner.

dis·crim·i·nā′tion, *n.* 1. the act of distinguishing; the act of making or observing a difference; distinction; as, the *discrimination* between right and wrong.

2. the ability to make or perceive distinc-

tions; penetration; judgment; perception; discernment.

Their own desire of glory would . . . baffle their *discrimination.* —Milman.

3. the state of being discriminated, distinguished, or set apart; a showing of difference or favoritism in treatment.

There is a reverence to be showed them on the account of their *discrimination* from other places. —Stillingfleet.

4. that which discriminates; mark of distinction.

Take heed of abetting any factions, or applying any public *discriminations* in matters of religion. —Gauden.

Syn.—discernment, penetration, clearness, acuteness, acumen, judgment, distinction.

dis·çrim′i·nā·tive, *a.* marked by or observing discrimination; discriminating; as, a *discriminative* decision, *discriminative* tariffs.

dis·çrim′i·nā·tive·ly, *adv.* with discrimination or distinction.

dis·çrim′i·nā·tŏr, *n.* one who discriminates.

dis·çrim′i·nā·tō·ry, *a.* discriminative; characterized by discrimination.

dis·çrim′i·nous, *a.* hazardous. [Obs.]

dis·crīve′, *v.t.* to describe. [Obs.]

dis·crown′, *v.t.*; discrowned, *pt., pp.*; discrowning, *ppr.* to deprive of a crown; dethrone; depose.

dis·crū′ci·āte (-shi-āt), *v.t.* to torment; to torture. [Obs.]

dis·cū′bi·tō·ry, *a.* leaning; inclining. [Obs.]

dis·cul′pāte, *v.t.* [L. *dis-* priv., and *culpare,* to blame, from *culpa,* a fault.] to free from blame or fault; to exculpate; to excuse.

dis·cul·pā′tion, *n.* exculpation.

dis·cul′pa·tō·ry, *a.* tending to exculpate.

dis·çum′ben·cy, *n.* [L. *discumbens* (*-entis*), ppr. of *discumbere,* to lie down; *dis-,* intens., and *cubare,* to lie down, recline.] the act of leaning or reclining at meals. [Obs.]

dis·çum′bĕr, *v.t.* to unburden; to disencumber.

dis·çūre′, *v.t.* to discover; to reveal. [Obs.]

dis·cur′rent, *a.* not current. [Obs.]

dis·çûr′sion, *n.* [LL. *discursio,* a running different ways, from L. *discursus,* pp. of *discurrere,* to run different ways.]

1. a running or rambling about.

2. the act of discoursing or reasoning.

dis·çûr′sive, *a.* 1. moving or roving about from one topic to another; skimming over many apparently unconnected subjects; digressive; desultory.

2. in philosophy, going from premises to conclusions in a series of logical steps: distinguished from *intuitive.*

dis·çûr′sive·ly, *adv.* in a discursive manner; argumentatively.

dis·çûr′sive·ness, *n.* the state or quality of being discursive.

dis·çûr′sō·ry, *a.* argumental; rational; discursive. [Rare.]

dis·çûr′sus, *n.* [L.] ratiocination; discursive reasoning.

dis′çus, *n.*; *pl.* **dis′çus·eș, dis′cī,** [L. *discus*; Gr. *diskos,* a discus, quoit.]

1. a disk of metal or stone, thrown for distance as a test of strength and skill.

DISCUS THROWER

2. the throwing of the discus as a contest of strength and skill: often *discus throw.*

3. a disk: used especially in biology.

dis·cuss′, *v.t.*; discussed, *pt., pp.*; discussing, *ppr.* [ME. *discussen,* to examine, scatter, from L. *discussus,* pp. of *discutire,* to strike asunder, shake apart, scatter; *dis-,* apart, and *quatere,* to shake.]

1. to shake or strike asunder; to dissolve; to repel. [Obs.]

2. to shake off; to put away. [Obs.]

3. to talk or write about; take up in conversation or in a discourse; consider and argue the pros and cons of.

We might *discuss* the Northern sin,
Which made a selfish war begin.
—Tennyson.

4. to speak; to declare; to explain. [Obs.]

Discuss the same in French to him. —Shak.

5. to eat or drink with enjoyment. [Colloq.]

6. in law, to proceed against (a principal debtor) before calling upon his surety or sureties.

Syn.—debate, argue, dispute, controvert.

dis·çuss′ĕr, *n.* one who discusses.

dis·çuss′i·ble, *a.* that can be discussed.

dis·çus′sion, *n.* 1. the act or process of breaking up or dissolving; dispersion, as of a tumor, coagulated matter, and the like. [Obs.]

2. a discussing; talk or writing in which the pros and cons of a subject are considered.

Compatible with a liberty of *discussion* and of individual action never before known. —Macaulay.

3. in civil law, the act of thorough procedure against a debtor before calling upon his surety or sureties.

under discussion; being discussed.

dis·çus′sion·ăl, *a.* of or relating to discussion.

dis·çuss′ive, *a.* having the power to dissolve or disperse, as tumors or coagulated matter. [Obs.]

dis·çuss′ive, *n.* a medicine that dissolves or disperses tumors, etc.; a discutient. [Obs.]

dis·çū′tient (-kū′shent), *a.* and *n.* [L. *discutiens.*] same as *resolvent.*

dis·dāin′, *v.t.*; disdained, *pt., pp.*; disdaining, *ppr.* [ME. *disdainen*; OFr. *desdaignier,* to disdain; L. *dis-,* not, and *dignari,* to deign, deem worthy, from *dignus,* worthy.] to think unworthy; to deem worthless; to consider or treat as unworthy of notice, care, regard, or esteem; to scorn; to contemn; to reject as unworthy of oneself; as, the man of elevated mind *disdains* a mean action.

Whose fathers I would have *disdained* to set with the dogs of my flock.—Job xxx. 1.

dis·dāin′, *v.i.* to be filled with scorn or anger; to take offense; to be indignant.

Ajax, deprived of Achilles's armor, *disdains,* rageth and runs mad. —Jonson.

dis·dāin′, *n.* 1. the feeling, attitude, or expression of disdaining; aloof contempt or scorn.

2. state of being despised; the state of feeling oneself disgraced; ignominy; disgrace. [Obs.]

The *disdain* and shame whereof hath ever since kept Hector fasting and waking. —Shak.

3. that which is worthy of disdain. [Obs.]

Most loathsome, filthy, foul, and full of vile *disdain.* —Spenser.

Syn.—scorn, scornfulness, contempt, arrogance, haughtiness, pride, superciliousness.

dis·dāined′, *a.* disdainful. [Obs.]

dis·dāin′fụl, *a.* full of disdain; expressing disdain; scornful and aloof; as, a *disdainful* look.

Syn.—contemptuous, scornful, haughty, indignant.

dis·dāin′fụl·ly, *adv.* contemptuously; with scorn; in a haughty manner.

dis·dāin′fụl·ness, *n.* contempt; contemptuousness; haughty scorn.

dis·dāin′ous, *a.* disdainful. [Obs.]

dis·dāin′ous·ly, *adv.* disdainfully. [Obs.]

dis·dē′i·fȳ, *v.t.* to reduce from or deprive of deity or of the rank of deity. [Obs.]

dis·deign′ (-dān′), *v.t.* to disdain. [Obs.]

dis·dī′ȧ·clȧst, *n.* [from Gr. *dis-,* twice, and *diaklan,* to break apart; *dia-,* through, and *klan,* to break.] any of the dark particles forming, by their apposition on the same plane, the doubly refracting disk, band, or layer of striated muscular tissue.

dis·dī·ȧ·clas′tiç, *a.* doubly refractive. [Rare.]

dis·dī·ȧ·pā′sŏn, *n.* [LL., from Gr. *dis dia pasōn,* lit. twice through all.] in music, the interval of two octaves; a fifteenth.

diș·ēașe′, *n.* [ME. *disese*; OFr. *desaise,* disease; *des-* priv., and *aise,* ease; L. *dis-* priv., and *esse,* to be.]

1. uneasiness; distress. [Obs.]

2. any departure from health; illness in general.

3. a particular destructive process in the body, with a specific cause and characteristic symptoms; specific illness; ailment; malady.

4. an evil or destructive tendency or state of affairs; as, bigotry is a *disease* of society.

Basedow's disease; an exophthalmic goiter: named after the German physician who first described it.

Syn.—distemper, ailment, malady, disorder, sickness, illness, indisposition, complaint, infirmity.

diș·ēașe′, *v.t.*; diseased, *pt., pp.*; diseasing, *ppr.* 1. to cause disease in; to interrupt or impair any or all the natural and regular functions of (an organ of a living body); to afflict with pain or sickness; to derange; to corrupt.

2. to distress; to make uneasy. [Obs.]

diș·ēașed′, *a.* 1. affected by disease; sick.

2. abnormal; unhealthy; disordered; deranged.

diș·ēaș′ed·ness, *n.* the state of being diseased; sickness.

diș·ēașe′fụl, *a.* 1. abounding with or producing disease; unhealthy; as, a *diseaseful* climate. [Obs.]

2. causing uneasiness.

diș·ēașe′fụl·ness, *n.* the state of being diseaseful; sickness. [Rare.]

diș·ēașe′ment, *n.* lack of ease. [Obs.]

dis·edġe′ (-ej′), *v.t.* to destroy or dull the edge of.

dis·ed′i·fȳ, *v.t.* to shock or weaken the moral or religious feelings of.

dis·eld′ĕr, *v.t.* to dispossess of an elder or elders.

dī·sel′e·nīde, *n.* [*di-* and *selenide.*] in chemistry, a compound in which the molecule has two atoms of selenium.

dis·em·bärk′, *v.t.*; disembarked, *pt., pp.*; disembarking, *ppr.* [OFr. *desembarquer,* to disembark.] to land; to unload; to remove from a ship to the land; to put on shore.

dis·em·bärk′, *v.i.* to land; to debark; to go ashore from a ship.

dis·em·bär·kā′tion, dis·em·bär·çā′tion, *n.* the act of disembarking or the state of being disembarked.

dis·em·bärk′ment, *n.* disembarkation. [Rare.]

dis·em·bar′răss, *v.t.*; disembarrassed, *pt., pp.*; disembarrassing, *ppr.* [*dis-,* and *embarrass.*] to free from embarrassment, annoyance, entanglement, or perplexity; to clear; to extricate.

dis·em·bar′răss·ment, *n.* the act of extricating from perplexity.

dis·em·bāy′, *v.t.* to clear from a bay. [Obs.]

dis·em·bel′lish, *v.t.* to deprive of embellishment.

dis·em·bit′tĕr, *v.t.*; disembittered, *pt., pp.*; disembittering, *ppr.* to free from bitterness; to clear from acrimony; to make sweet or pleasant.

dis·em·bod′ied (-bod′id), *a.* freed from the body; incorporeal.

dis·em·bod′i·ment, *n.* the act of disembodying or the state of being disembodied.

dis·em·bod′y, *v.t.*; disembodied, *pt., pp.*; disembodying, *ppr.* 1. to free (a spirit, etc.) from bodily existence; to make incorporeal.

2. to discharge from military incorporation; as, the militia was *disembodied.*

dis·em·bōgue′ (-bōg′), *v.t.* and *v.i.*; disembogued, *pt., pp.*; disemboguing, *ppr.* [Sp. *desembocar*; *des-* priv., and *embocar,* to enter by the mouth; L. *dis-* priv., and *in,* in, and *bucca,* cheek.]

1. to pour out or discharge (its waters) at the mouth; to vent; to discharge (itself): said of a stream, etc.

Rolling down, the steep Timavus raves,
And through nine channels *disembogues* his waves. —Addison.

2. to sail out of an estuary or harbor. [Archaic.]

dis·em·bōgue′ment, *n.* discharge of waters into an ocean, lake, etc.

dis·em·boș′ŏm (-booz′), *v.t.* and *v.i.* to separate from the bosom; to reveal (a secret, etc.); to unbosom (oneself).

dis·em·bow′el, *v.t.*; disemboweled *or* disembowelled, *pt., pp.*; disemboweling *or* disembowelling, *ppr.* 1. to take out the bowels of; to eviscerate.

2. to take or draw from the body, as the web of a spider. [Rare.]

dis·em·bow′el·ment, *n.* the act of disemboweling or the state of being disemboweled.

dis·em·bow′ĕred, *a.* removed from, or deprived of, a bower.

dis·em·brañ′gle, *v.t.* to free from confusion or complication. [Obs.]

dis·em·broil′, *v.t.*; disembroiled, *pt., pp.*; disembroiling, *ppr.* to disentangle; to free from perplexity; to extricate from confusion.

dī·sē′miç, *a.* [Gr. *disēmos,* having two morae; *di-,* two, and *sēma,* a mark, mora.] containing two units of time or morae: applied in ancient prosody to meter.

dis·em·ploy′, *v.t.* to dismiss from employment; to discharge.

dis·em·ploy′ment, *n.* the state of being dismissed from employment.

dis·em·pow′ĕr, *v.t.* to deprive of authority.

dis·en·ā′ble, *v.t.*; disenabled, *pt., pp.*; disenabling, *ppr.* to disable; to prevent; to cause to become unable or incapable.

dis·en·am′ŏr, *v.t.* to free from love and desire.
Don Quixote *disenamored* of Dulcinea del Toboso. —Shelton.

dis·en·chāin′, *v.t.* to release from chains. [Rare.]

dis·en·chȧnt′, *v.t.*; disenchanted, *pt., pp.*; disenchanting, *ppr.* [OFr. *desenchanter*; L. *dis-* priv., and *incantare*, to enchant.] to free from enchantment; to deliver from the power of charms or spells; to disillusion.

dis·en·chȧnt′ẽr, *n.* one who or that which disenchants.

dis·en·chȧnt′ment, *n.* 1. the act of disenchanting.
2. the fact or state of being disenchanted.

dis·en·chärm′, *v.t.* to deliver from the power of a charm. [Rare.]

dis·en·çlōșe′, *v.t.*; disenclosed, *pt., pp.*; disenclosing, *ppr.* to open (an enclosure); to throw open (that which has been enclosed).

dis·en·çŏur′ȧġe, *v.t.* to discourage. [Obs.]

dis·en·çŏur′ȧġe·ment, *n.* discouragement. [Obs.]

dis·en·çrēase′, *v.i.* and *n.* decrease. [Obs.]

dis·en·çum′bẽr, *v.t.*; disencumbered, *pt., pp.*; disencumbering, *ppr.* to free from encumbrance; to deliver from a hindrance or annoyance; to disburden; as, to *disencumber* troops of their baggage.
Ere dim night had *disencumbered* Heaven. —Milton.

dis·en·çum′brănce, *n.* freedom or release from encumbrance, or anything burdensome or troublesome.

dis·en·dow′, *v.t.* to take away an endowment from.

dis·en·dow′ment, *n.* the act of disendowing.

dis·en·frȧn′chīșe, *v.t.* to disfranchise.

dis·en·frȧn′chīșe·ment, *n.* disfranchisement.

dis·en·gāġe′, *v.t.*; disengaged, *pt., pp.*; disengaging, *ppr.* [OFr. *desengager*; *des-* priv., and *engager*, to promise, engage.] to release or liberate from something that holds, complicates, entangles, or binds; to set free by dissolving an engagement; to unfasten, extricate, or disentangle; to detach; as, the men who were enlisted are now *disengaged*.
Syn.—separate, liberate, free, loose, extricate, clear, disentangle, detach, withdraw, wean.

dis·en·gāġe′, *v.i.* 1. to get loose; to withdraw; to free oneself; as, we *disengage* reluctantly from old associations.
2. in fencing, to transpose the position of the sword, so as to bring the advantage in favor of the one making the movement.

dis·en·gāġed′, *a.* [pp. of *disengage*.]
1. having no engagements; at leisure; at liberty.
2. detached; set loose.

dis·en·gā′ġed·ness, *n.* the quality or state of being disengaged.

dis·en·gāġe′ment, *n.* 1. the state of being disengaged or the act of disengaging.
2. freedom from attention, obligation, occupation, etc.; ease; leisure.
3. the move in fencing by which one disengages his weapon.

dis·en·gāġ′ing aç′tion, a voluntary tactical withdrawal of troops in a critical situation: sometimes a euphemism for *retreat*.

dis·en·nō′ble, *v.t.*; disennobled, *pt., pp.*; disennobling, *ppr.* to deprive of a title or that which ennobles.

dis·en·rōll′, *v.t.*; disenrolled, *pt., pp.*; disenrolling, *ppr.* to erase from a roll or list: also spelled *disenrol*. [Obs.]

dis·en·san′i·ty, *n.* insanity. [Obs.]

dis·en·shroud′, *v.t.* to remove from a shroud; to unveil. [Rare.]

dis·en·slāve′, *v.t.* to free, as from slavery.

dis·en·tāil′, *v.t.*; disentailed, *pt., pp.*; disentailing, *ppr.* to break the entail of (an estate).

dis·en·tan′gle, *v.t.*; disentangled, *pt., pp.*; disentangling, *ppr.* 1. to free from something that entangles, confuses, etc.; extricate; disengage.
2. to straighten out (anything tangled, confused, etc.); unravel; untangle.
Syn.—unravel, untwist, loosen, extricate, disembroil, clear, disengage, separate.

dis·en·tan′gle, *v.i.* to get free from a tangle.

dis·en·tan′gle·ment, *n.* a disentangling or being disentangled.

dis·en·tẽr′, *v.t.* to disinter. [Obs.]

dis·en·thrąll′, *v.t.* to liberate from slavery, bondage, or servitude; to free from oppression: also spelled *disenthral*.
In straits and in distress
Thou didst me *disenthrall*. —Milton.

dis·en·thrąll′ment, *n.* the state of being disenthralled.

dis·en·thrōne′, *v.t.*; disenthroned, *pt., pp.*; disenthroning, *ppr.* to dethrone; to depose.

dis·en·tī′tle, *v.t.*; disentitled, *pt., pp.*; disentitling, *ppr.* to deprive of a title, right, or claim.

dis·en·tömb′ (-töm′), *v.t.* to remove from a tomb; to disinter.

dis·en·trāil′, *v.t.* to deprive of the entrails or bowels; to disembowel; to draw forth from the body. [Obs.]

dis·en·trȧnce′, *v.t.*; disentranced, *pt., pp.*; disentrancing, *ppr.* to awaken from a trance or deep sleep; to arouse from a trance, sleep, or reverie.

dis·en·twīne′, *v.t.* and *v.i.* to release from a twisted state; to untwine; to unwind.

dī·sep′ăl·ous, *a.* in botany, having two sepals.

dis·ẽrt′, *a.* eloquent. [Obs.]

dis·es·pouse′, *v.t.* to separate after espousal or betrothal; to divorce. [Obs.]

dis·es·tab′lish, *v.t.*; disestablished, *pt., pp.*; disestablishing, *ppr.* 1. to remove from establishment; to deprive of the status of being established.
2. to withdraw (a state church) from its official connection with the government.

dis·es·tab′lish·ment, *n.* a disestablishing or being disestablished.

dis·es·teem′, *v.t.*; disesteemed, *pt., pp.*; disesteeming, *ppr.* [OFr. *desestimer*; *des-* priv., and *estimer*, to esteem.]
1. to dislike; to consider with disregard, disapprobation, dislike, or slight contempt; to slight.
2. to withdraw esteem from; to cause to be brought into disrepute. [Obs.]

dis·es·teem′, *n.* lack of esteem; dislike; disregard.

dis·es·teem′ẽr, *n.* one who disesteems.

dis·es·ti·mā′tion, *n.* disesteem; bad repute. [Rare.]

dī·sēuse′, *n.* [Fr.; lit., feminine speaker, from base *dis-* of *dire* (L. *dicere*), to say, speak.] a woman entertainer who performs monologues, dramatic impersonations, etc.

dis·ex′ẽr·çīse, *v.t.* to deprive of exercise. [Obs.]

dis·fāme′, *n.* defamation. [Rare.]

dis·fash′iŏn, *v.t.* to injure or mar. [Obs.]

dis·fā′vŏr, *n.* [L. *dis-* priv., and *favor*, favor.]
1. dislike; displeasure; unfavorable regard; disesteem.
2. the state of being disliked or disapproved of; a state in which one is not esteemed or favored, or not patronized, promoted, or befriended; as, to be in *disfavor* at court.

dis·fā′vŏr, *v.t.*; disfavored, *pt., pp.*; disfavoring, *ppr.* 1. to discountenance; to regard or treat unfavorably; to withdraw or withhold kindness, friendship, or support from; to slight.
2. to mar; to deface. [Obs.]

dis·fā′vŏr·ȧ·ble, *a.* not favorable. [Obs.]

dis·fā′vŏr·ȧ·bly, *adv.* not favorably. [Obs.]

dis·fā′vŏr·ẽr, *n.* one who disfavors.

dis·fēa′tūre, *v.t.* to impair the features of; to disfigure.

dis·fel′lōw·ship, *v.t.*; disfellowshiped *or* disfellowshipped, *pt., pp.*; disfellowshiping *or* disfellowshipping, *ppr.* to refuse to associate with: used especially in reference to church fellowship or communion.

dis·fig·ū·rā′tion, *n.* same as *disfigurement*.

dis·fig′ūre, *v.t.*; disfigured, *pt., pp.*; disfiguring, *ppr.* [ME. *disfiguren*; OFr. *desfigurer*; L. *dis-* priv., and *figurare*, to fashion, form, from *figura*, figure.] to deform; to impair, as shape or form; to mar; to deface; to injure the appearance or attractiveness of.
Syn.—deface, botch, injure, mar.

dis·fig′ūre, *n.* a deformity. [Obs.]

dis·fig′ūre·ment, *n.* 1. a disfiguring.
2. anything that disfigures or defaces; blemish; defect; deformity.
3. the fact or state of being disfigured.

dis·fig′ūr·ẽr, *n.* one who or that which disfigures.

dis·flesh′, *v.t.* to take off flesh from. [Obs.]

dis·for′est, *v.t.*; disforested, *pt., pp.*; disforesting, *ppr.* 1. same as *disafforest*.
2. to clear (land) of timber or forest; to deforest.

dis·for·es·tā′tion, *n.* the act of deforesting a piece of land.

dis·form′i·ty, *n.* deformity; difformity. [Obs.]

dis·fran′chīșe, *v.t.*; disfranchised, *pt., pp.*; disfranchising, *ppr.* 1. to deprive of the rights and privileges of a free citizen, as of the right to vote and hold office.
2. to deprive of any right, privilege, or power.

dis·fran′chīșe·ment, *n.* a disfranchising or being disfranchised.

dis·frī′ăr, *v.t.* to unfrock; to depose from a friarship. [Obs.]

dis·frock′, *v.t.* to unfrock.

dis·fũr′nish, *v.t.*; disfurnished, *pt., pp.*; disfurnishing, *ppr.* to deprive of furniture; to strip of equipment.

dis·fũr′nish·ment, *n.* the state of being disfurnished.

dis·fũr′ni·tūre, *n.* disfurnishment. [Obs.]

dis·gāġe′, *v.t.* to redeem from pawn; to disengage. [Obs.]

dis·gal′lănt, *v.t.* to deprive of gallantry. [Obs.]

dis·gär′lănd, *v.t.* to divest of a garland or garlands. [Rare.]

dis·gär′nish, *v.t.* to divest of garniture or ornaments. [Rare.]

dis·gar′ri·sŏn, *v.t.* to deprive of a garrison. [Rare.]

dis·gav′el, *v.t.*; disgaveled *or* disgavelled, *pt., pp.*; disgaveling *or* disgavelling, *ppr.* in English law, to take away the tenure of gavelkind from.

dis·ġē·ner′iç, *a.* of different genera: opposed to *congeneric*.

dis·glō′ri·fȳ, *v.t.* to dishonor; to treat with disrespect. [Rare.]

dis·glō′ry, *n.* disrespect; dishonor. [Obs.]

dis·gorġe′, *v.t.* and *v.i.*; disgorged, *pt., pp.*; disgorging, *ppr.* [OFr. *desgorger*; *des-*, from, and *gorge*, throat.]
1. to eject or discharge from the stomach, throat, or mouth; to vomit.
2. to throw out with violence; to discharge violently or in great quantities from a confined place; as, volcanoes *disgorge* streams of burning lava, ashes, and stones.
3. to yield or give up (something wrongfully obtained); as, to *disgorge* his ill-gotten gains.

dis·gorġe′ment, *n.* the act of disgorging.

dis·gos′pel, *v.i.* to deprive of the gospel. [Obs.]

dis·grāce′, *n.* [Fr. *disgrâce*; It. *disgrazia*, from *dis-*, (L. *dis-*), not, and *grazia*, favor, from L. *gratia*, favor.]
1. a state of being out of favor because of bad conduct; as, he is in *disgrace*.
2. ignominy; disrepute; loss of favor or respect; public dishonor; shame.
3. a person or thing that brings shame, dishonor, or reproach (*to* one, etc.); a cause of shame.
4. an act of unkindness. [Obs.]
Syn.—ignominy, dishonor, shame, infamy, odium, scandal.

dis·grāce′, *v.t.*; disgraced, *pt., pp.*; disgracing, *ppr.* 1. to put out of favor; to dismiss in dishonor; to punish by degrading; as, the officer was *disgraced* for his treachery.
2. to bring shame or dishonor upon; to be unworthy of; to be a discredit to; as, his theft *disgraced* his family.
3. to revile; to reproach. [Obs.]
Syn.—abase, degrade, humiliate, defame, humble, dishonor.

dis·grāce′fųl, *a.* shameful; reproachful; dishonorable; causing or characterized by disgrace.

dis·grāce′fųl·ly, *adv.* with disgrace; shamefully; reproachfully; ignominiously; in a disgraceful manner; as, the troops fled *disgracefully*.

dis·grāce′fųl·ness, *n.* ignominy; shamefulness.

dis·grā′cẽr, *n.* one who disgraces; one who exposes to disgrace; one who brings into disgrace, shame, or contempt.

dis·grā′cious, *a.* ungracious; disliked. [Obs.]

dis·grā′cive, *a.* disgracing. [Obs.]

dis·grā·dā′tion, *n.* degradation. [Obs.]

dis·grāde′, dis·grad′ū·āte, *v.t.* to degrade. [Obs.]

dis′grē·gāte, *v.t.* and *v.i.* to separate; to disperse.

dis·grē·gā′tion, *n.* separation; dissociation; specifically, in chemistry, decomposition.

dis·grun′tle, *v.t.*; disgruntled, *pt., pp.*; disgruntling, *ppr.* [*dis-*, and obs. *gruntle*, freq. of *grunt*.] to make peevishly discontented or disappointed; displease and make sulky.

dis·guīșe′ (-gīz′), *v.t.*; disguised, *pt., pp.*; disguising, *ppr.* [ME. *disguisen*; OFr. *desguiser*, to counterfeit, disguise; *des-* priv., and *guise*, manner, fashion.]
1. to make appear, sound, etc. different from usual so as to be unrecognizable; as, he *disguised* himself as a beggar, *disguise* your voice.
2. to hide or conceal the real nature of; to cloak by a false show, language, or manner; as, to *disguise* anger, sentiments, or intentions.

3. to disfigure or deform by liquor; to intoxicate. [Rare.]

Syn.—mask, dissemble, hide, change, conceal, feign, pretend.

dis·guīṣe′, *n.* 1. that which disguises or makes recognition difficult; any deceptive dress, action, manner, or speech; as, treachery is often concealed under the *disguise* of great candor.

2. the act or practice of disguising.

3. the state of being disguised.

4. a masquerade. [Obs.]

5. change of manner by drink; intoxication.

dis·guīṣ′ed·ly, *adv.* 1. in a manner that disguises.

2. in disguise; incognito.

dis·guīṣ′ed·ness, *n.* the state of being disguised.

dis·guīṣe′ment, *n.* the act of disguising; a disguise.

dis·guīṣ′ẽr, *n.* 1. one who or that which disguises.

Death's a great *disguiser*. —Shak.

2. a masker. [Obs.]

dis·guīṣ′ing, *n.* 1. the act of giving a false appearance.

2. theatrical mummery or masking. [Obs.]

dis·gust′, *n.* [MFr. *desgoust*, distaste, from *des-* priv., and L. *gustus*, a taste, relish.] a sickening distaste or dislike; deep aversion; repugnance.

Syn.—abhorrence, loathing, nausea, aversion, antipathy, dislike, distaste.

dis·gust′, *v.t.*; disgusted, *pt., pp.*; disgusting, *ppr.* [MFr. *desgouster*; L. *dis-* priv., and *gustare*, to taste, from *gustus*, a tasting.] to cause to feel disgust; to be sickening, repulsive, or very disagreeable to.

dis·gust′fụl, *a.* disgusting.

dis·gust′fụl·ness, *n.* the condition of being disgustful.

dis·gust′ing, *a.* causing disgust; offensive; sickening; repulsive; very disagreeable.

dis·gust′ing·ly, *adv.* in a disgusting manner.

dish, *n.* [ME. *dissh, disch*; AS. *disc*, a dish, plate, from L. *discus*, Gr. *diskos*, a discus, disk, a round plate, a trencher.]

1. any container, generally shallow and concave, for serving or holding food: dishes are usually made of porcelain, earthenware, glass, metal, or plastic, and comprise plates, bowls, saucers, cups, etc.

2. the food in a dish; a particular kind of food; as, my favorite *dish* is baked beans.

3. a dishful.

4. a dish-shaped object.

5. a dishlike concavity.

6. the amount of such concavity.

7. in English mining, a trough for measuring ore.

dish, *v.t.*; dished (disht), *pt., pp.*; dishing, *ppr.* 1. to serve (food) in a dish or dishes: usually with *up* or *out*; as, to *dish up* the dessert.

2. to shape (an object, surface, or hole) like a dish; make concave (usually with *out*).

3. to baffle; cheat; frustrate; ruin. [Slang, chiefly Brit.]

to dish it out; to administer punishment, reprimands, etc. [Slang.]

to dish out; in architecture, to make a gutter in.

dish, *v.i.* to be or become concave like a dish; to cave in; as, the ground *dished*.

dis·ha·bil′i·tāte, *v.t.* to disqualify. [Rare.]

dis·hȧ·bille′ (dis-ȧ-bēl′), *n.* [Fr. *déshabillé*, undress, a morning wrapper, from pp. of *déshabiller*, to undress.]

1. the state of being dressed only partially or in night clothes.

2. clothing or a garment worn in this state. Also *deshabille*.

dis·hab′it, *v.t.* to dislodge. [Obs.]

dis·ha·bit′ū·āte, *v.t.* to make strange or unaccustomed.

dis·hā′ble, *v.t.* to disable. [Obs.]

dis·hal′lōw, *v.t.* to desecrate; to profane.

dis·här·mō′ni·ous, *a.* not harmonious; discordant.

dis·här′mō·nīze, *v.t.* and *v.i.* to put or be out of harmony; make or be discordant.

dis·här′mō·ny, *n.* absence of harmony; discord.

dis·hạunt′, *v.t.* to cease to haunt or frequent. [Obs.]

dish′çloth, *n.* a cloth used for washing dishes; a dishrag.

dish′clout, *n.* a dishrag.

dis·heärt′, *v.t.* to dishearten. [Obs.]

dis·heärt′en, *v.t.*; disheartened, *pt., pp.*; disheartening, *ppr.* to discourage; to deprive of courage; to depress the spirits of; to deject.

dis·heärt′en·ment, *n.* a disheartening or being disheartened.

dished, *a.* 1. dish-shaped; concave.

2. farther apart at the top than at the bottom: said of parallel wheels.

dis·heir′ (-âr′), *v.t.* to disinherit. [Obs.]

dis·helm′, *v.t.* and *v.i.* to take the helmet off.

dis·her′i·ṣŏn, *n.* [OFr. *desheriteisun*, disinheritance; L. *dis-* priv., and *heres* (*heredis*), an heir.] a disinheriting or being disinherited. [Archaic.]

dis·her′it, *v.t.* to disinherit.

dis·her′it·ȧnce, *n.* disinheritance.

dis·her′it·ŏr, *n.* one who disinherits or deprives another of an inheritance.

di·shev′el, *v.t.*; disheveled *or* dishevelled, *pt., pp.*; disheveling *or* dishevelling, *ppr.* [ME. *dischevelen*; OFr. *descheveler*, to tear, pull, or disorder the hair, dishevel; L. *dis-*, apart, and *capillus*, hair.]

1. to cause (hair, clothing, etc.) to become disarranged and untidy, as by pulling or loosening, etc.; tousle; rumple.

2. to cause the hair or clothes of (a person) to become thus disarranged.

di·shev′el, *v.i.* to be in disorder; to be spread out carelessly, as the hair. [Rare.]

di·shev′eled, di·shev′elled, *a.* 1. disarranged and untidy; tousled; rumpled: said of hair or clothing.

2. having disheveled hair or clothing.

di·shev′el·ment, *n.* a disheveled condition.

di·shev′el·y, *a.* disheveled. [Obs.]

dish′-fāced (-fāst), *a.* having a somewhat concave face: said of dogs, cattle, and certain other animals.

dish′fụl, *n.* the amount which a dish can hold.

dis·hon′est (-on′est), *a.* [ME. *dishonest*; OFr. *deshoneste*, dishonest; L. *dis-* priv., and *honestus*, honest.]

1. not honest; faithless; fraudulent; knavish; deceiving, cheating, defrauding, etc.; as, a *dishonest* man.

2. resulting from or characterized by fraud; fraudulent; knavish; as, a *dishonest* transaction.

3. disgraced; dishonored. [Obs.]

4. disgraceful; ignominious. [Obs.]

Inglorious triumphs and *dishonest* scars. —Pope.

5. unchaste; lewd. [Obs.]

Syn.—unfaithful, faithless, fraudulent, knavish, perfidious.

dis·hon′est, *v.t.* to bring dishonor or disgrace to. [Obs.]

dis·hon′est·ly, *adv.* in a dishonest manner.

dis·hon′es·ty (-on′es-ty), *n.* 1. the quality of being dishonest; dishonest behavior; deceiving, stealing, etc.

2. *pl.* **dis·hon′es·tieṣ**, a dishonest act or statement; fraud, lie, etc.

3. unchastity; incontinence; lewdness. [Obs.]

dis·hon′ŏr, *n.* [ME. *deshonour*; OFr. *deshonor*, dishonor, disgrace, from L. *dis-* priv., and *honor*, honor.]

1. loss of honor; loss of status, respect, or reputation; disgrace; ignominy; shame.

2. a person, thing, or action that brings dishonor; discredit; insult.

3. the act of refusing or failing to pay a check, draft, bill of exchange, etc.

Syn.—ignominy, blemish, opprobrium, disgrace, shame, censure, disrespect.

dis·hon′ŏr, *v.t.*; dishonored, *pt., pp.*; dishonoring, *ppr.* 1. to disgrace; to bring reproach or shame on; to stain the character of; to lessen the reputation of.

2. to treat disrespectfully; to insult.

3. to violate the chastity or virginity of.

4. to refuse or fail to pay (a check, draft, bill of exchange, etc.).

Syn.—disgrace, shame, abase, disparage, degrade, seduce, ravish.

dis·hon′ŏr·ȧ·ble, *a.* 1. causing or deserving dishonor; shameful; reproachful; base; vile.

2. destitute of honor; as, a *dishonorable* man.

3. in a state of neglect or disesteem. [Rare.]

He that is *dishonorable* in riches, how much more in poverty! —Eccles. x. 31.

dis·hon′ŏr·ȧ·ble·ness, *n.* the quality of being dishonorable.

dis·hon′ŏr·ȧ·bly, *adv.* 1. in a dishonorable manner.

2. with dishonor; as, *dishonorably* discharged.

dis·hon′ŏr·ā·ry, *a.* bringing dishonor on; tending to disgrace; lessening reputation. [Rare.]

dis·hon′ŏr·ẽr, *n.* one who dishonors.

dis·hŏrn′, *v.t.* to deprive of horns.

dis·hŏrṣe′, *v.t.*; dishorsed, *pt., pp.*; dishorsing, *ppr.* to unhorse.

dis·hŏrṣe′, *v.i.* to dismount.

dis·houṣe′, *v.t.* to dislodge; to take away the house or home of. [Rare.]

dish′pan, *n.* a pan in which dishes and cooking utensils are washed.

dish′rag, *n.* a dishcloth.

dis·hū′mŏr, *n.* peevishness; ill humor. [Obs.]

dis·hū′mŏr, *v.t.* to put out of humor; to disgruntle. [Obs.]

dish′wäsh″ẽr, *n.* 1. a person or machine that washes dishes and cooking utensils.

2. a bird, the pied wagtail. [Brit. Dial.]

dish′wạ·tẽr, *n.* the water in which dishes and cooking utensils have been or are to be washed.

dis·il·lū′ṣion, *n.* same as *disillusionment*.

dis·il·lū′ṣion, *v.t.* to free from that which deludes or is illusory; to disenchant.

dis·il·lū′ṣion·īze, *v.t.* to disillusion.

dis·il·lū′ṣion·ment, *n.* 1. a disillusioning.

2. the fact or the state of being disillusioned.

dis·im·bit′tẽr, *v.t.* to disembitter.

dis·im·pärk′, *v.t.* to free from the barriers of a park; to free from restraints or seclusion. [Rare.]

dis·im·pas′sioned, *a.* unimpassioned; calm; tranquil.

dis·im·priṣ′ŏn, *v.t.* to free from imprisonment.

dis·im·pröve′, *v.t.* to make poorer in quality. [Rare.]

dis·im·pröve′, *v.i.* to deteriorate. [Rare.]

dis·im·pröve′ment, *n.* reduction from a better to a worse state; as, the *disimprovement* of the earth. [Rare.]

dis·in·çär′cẽr·āte, *v.t.* to liberate from prison; to set free from confinement. [Rare.]

dis·in·cli·nā′tion, *n.* a dislike or lack of desire (*for*); aversion (*to*); reluctance.

Disappointment gave him a *disinclination to* the fair sex. —Arbuthnot.

Syn.—unwillingness, dislike, aversion, repugnance.

dis·in·çlīne′, *v.t.*; disinclined, *pt., pp.*; disinclining, *ppr.* to excite dislike or aversion in; to make unwilling; to alienate from; as, his timidity *disinclined* him from such an arduous enterprise.

dis·in·çlīne′, *v.i.* to be unwilling.

dis·in·çlīned′, *a.* unwilling; reluctant.

dis·in·clōṣe′, *v.t.* same as *disenclose*.

dis·in·çor′pō·rāte, *v.t.*; disincorporated, *pt., pp.*; disincorporating, *ppr.* 1. to deprive of corporate powers; to disunite (a corporate body or an established society).

2. to detach or separate from a corporation or society.

dis·in·çor′pō·rāte, *a.* disincorporated; separated from or not included in a body or society. [Obs.]

dis·in·çor·pō·rā′tion, *n.* deprivation of the rights and privileges of a corporation.

dis·in·çrust′ănt, *n.* that which prevents the formation of crust or scale in boilers, etc.

dis·in·feçt′, *v.t.*; disinfected, *pt., pp.*; disinfecting, *ppr.* to destroy or make inactive the harmful bacteria, viruses, etc. in; to sterilize.

dis·in·feçt′ănt, *a.* disinfecting.

dis·in·feçt′ănt, *n.* anything that disinfects; means for destroying harmful bacteria, viruses, etc. or for making them inactive.

dis·in·feç′tion, *n.* a disinfecting or being disinfected.

dis·in·feçt′ŏr, *n.* one who or that which disinfects; a disinfecting apparatus.

dis·in·flāme′, *v.t.* to deprive of flame. [Obs.]

dis·in·ġe·nū′i·ty, *n.*; *pl.* **dis·in·ġe·nū′i·tieṣ**, disingenuousness.

dis·in·ġen′ū·ous, *a.* not ingenuous; not candid; not straightforward; insincere.

Persons entirely *disingenuous* who really do not believe the opinions they defend. —Hume.

Syn.—unfair, uncandid, insincere, crafty, sly, cunning.

dis·in·ġen′ū·ous·ly, *adv.* in a disingenuous manner.

dis·in·ġen′ū·ous·ness, *n.* the quality of being disingenuous; insincerity.

dis·in·hab′it·ed, *a.* deprived of inhabitants. [Obs.]

dis·in·her′i·ṣŏn, *n.* same as *disherison*.

dis·in·her′it, *v.t.*; disinherited, *pt., pp.*; disinheriting, *ppr.* to cut off from hereditary right; to deprive of an inheritance; to prevent, as an heir, from coming into possession of any property or right which by law or custom would devolve on him in the course of descent; as, a father sometimes *disinherits* his children by will.

dis·in·her'it·ănce, *n.* the act of disinheriting or the state of being disinherited; disherison.
dis·in·hūme', *v.t.* to disinter. [Rare.]
dis·in·sūre', *v.t.* to render unsafe; to place in danger.
dis·in'tē·grȧ·ble, *a.* capable of disintegration.
dis·in'tē·grāte, *v.t.* and *v.i.*; disintegrated, *pt., pp.*; disintegrating, *ppr.* [*dis-* priv., and L. *integratus,* pp. of *integrare,* to renew, repair, from *integer,* whole.] to separate into parts or fragments; to lose or cause to lose wholeness; to disunite.
dis·in·tē·grā'tion, *n.* a disintegrating or being disintegrated; specifically, in geology, the breaking up of rocks by natural causes, as by the action of water, wind, or frost.
dis·in'tē·grāt·ŏr, *n.* one who or that which causes something to disintegrate; specifically, in mechanics, a crusher or stamper used for breaking up ore.
dis·in·tẽr', *v.t.*; disinterred, *pt., pp.*; disinterring, *ppr.* [Fr. *désenterrer*; see *dis-* and *inter.*]
1. to take out of a grave, tomb, etc.; to dig up (what is buried); to exhume.
2. to take out as from a grave; to bring (something hidden) to light.
The philosopher may be concealed in a plebeian, which a proper education might have *disinterred.* —Addison.
dis·in'tẽr·ess, *v.t.* to disinterest. [Obs.]
dis·in'tẽr·ess·ment, *n.* disinterestedness. [Obs.]
dis·in'tẽr·est, *n.* 1. what is contrary to interest or advantage; disadvantage; injury.
2. disinterestedness.
dis·in'tẽr·est, *v.t.* to disengage from private interest or personal advantage.
dis·in'tẽr·est·ed, *a.* 1. not influenced by personal interest or selfish motives; impartial; unbiased.
2. uninterested; indifferent. [Colloq.]
Every true patriot is *disinterested.* —Whately.
Syn.—unbiased, impartial.
dis·in'tẽr·est·ed·ly, *adv.* in a disinterested manner.
dis·in'tẽr·est·ed·ness, *n.* the state or quality of being disinterested.
dis·in'tẽr·est·ing, *a.* uninteresting.
dis·in·tẽr'ment, *n.* 1. a disinterring or being disinterred.
2. anything disinterred.
dis·in·thrall', dis·in·thrąl', *v.t.* to disenthrall.
dis·in·thrąll'ment, *n.* disenthrallment.
dis·in·ūre', *v.t.* to deprive of familiarity or custom. [Obs.]
dis·in·ves'ti·tūre, *n.* the act of depriving of investiture or the state of being deprived of investiture.
dis·in·vig'ŏr·āte, *v.t.* to weaken; to deprive of force or strength. [Rare.]
dis·in·vīte', *v.t.* to cancel or recall an invitation to. [Obs.]
dis·in·volve', *v.t.* to uncover; to unfold or unroll; to disentangle. [Rare.]
dis·jeçt', *v.t.* [from L. *disjectum,* pp. of *disjicere,* to throw apart, from *dis-,* apart, and *jacere,* to throw.] to throw or break apart; to disperse.
dis·jeç'tȧ mem'brȧ, [L.] scattered parts or fragments.
dis·jeç'tion, *n.* the act of throwing apart or dissipating; dispersion.
dis·join', *v.t.*; disjoined, *pt., pp.*; disjoining, *ppr.* [OFr. *desjoindre*; L. *disjungere,* to separate; *dis-,* apart, and *jungere,* to join.] to prevent the joining of; to detach; to disunite; to separate; to sunder.
dis·join', *v.i.* to become separated; to part.
dis·joint', *a.* [ME.; OFr. *disjoint,* pp. of *disjoindre*; see *disjoin.*] disjointed. [Obs.]
dis·joint', *v.t.* [from the *a.*] 1. to put out of joint; dislocate.
2. to take apart joint by joint; dismember.
3. to destroy the unity, connections, or orderliness of.
dis·joint', *v.i.* to come apart at the joints; to go out of joint.
dis·joint'ed, *a.* 1. out of joint.
2. dismembered.
3. disconnected; without unity or coherence.
dis·joint'ed·ly, *adv.* in a disjointed manner.
dis·joint'ed·ness, *n.* the state of being disjointed.
dis·joint'ly, *adv.* 1. separately.
2. disconnectedly.
dis·junçt', *a.* [L. *disjunctus,* pp. of *disjungere,* to disjoin, separate.] disjoined; separated.
disjunct tetrachords; in music, tetrachords having such a relation to each other that the lowest interval of the upper is one note above the highest interval of the other.
dis·junç'tion, *n.* [from OFr. or L.; OFr. *disjunction*; L. *disjunctio,* from pp. of *disjungere*; see *disjoin.*]
1. a disjoining or being disjoined; separation.
2. in logic, the relation between two or more alternatives of a disjunctive proposition.
dis·junç'tive, *a.* [LL. *disjunctivus,* from L. *disjunctus,* pp. of *disjungere,* to disjoin, separate; *dis-,* apart, and *jungere,* to join.]
1. separating or causing to separate; disjoining.
2. having to do with disjunction.
3. in grammar, indicating a contrast or an alternative between ideas, clauses, etc.; as, *either . . . or, but,* and *although* are *disjunctive* conjunctions.
4. in logic, presenting alternatives.
5. in music, pertaining to disjunct tetrachords; as, a *disjunctive* interval.
dis·junç'tive, *n.* 1. in grammar, a disjunctive conjunction.
2. in logic, a disjunctive proposition. Example: Either all men are free, or no man is free.
dis·junç'tive·ly, *adv.* in a disjunctive manner; separately.
dis·junç'tūre, *n.* same as *disjunction.*
disk, disç, *n.* [L. *discus*; Gr. *diskos,* a discus, dish, trencher, disk.]
1. a discus. [Obs.]
2. a thin, flat, circular thing of any material; specifically, in mechanics, a thin circular plate: also used attributively; as, a *disk* pulverizer, a *disk* crank.
3. anything resembling this in shape; as, the moon's *disk.*
4. (a) a phonograph record; (b) a thin, flat circular plate coated with ferromagnetic particles, on which computer data can be stored.
5. any of the sharp, circular blades on a disc harrow.
6. in botany, (a) one of the rings of the woody fiber of certain trees, as conifers, visible in a longitudinal section of the wood; (b) the surface of an organ, as a leaf or petal: opposed to *margin*; (c) the convex center (sometimes the whole head) of composite flowers exclusive of the rays; (d) an expanded receptacle, commonly a nectary, taking a variety of forms.
7. in zoology, any discoid part; a discus; as, (a) a surface used for locomotion or for attachment, such as creeping or sucking discs; (b) the area about the mouth of certain of the *Cœlentera*; (c) the set of feathers extending radially around the eye of an owl; (d) the space in a bivalve shell included between the margin and the umbo.
Senses 4, 5, 6 and 7 are usually spelled *disc.*
disk är'mȧ·tūre, an armature consisting of thin, flat coils mounted on the periphery of a thin disk.
disk flow'ẽr, disç flow'ẽr, any of the little flowers that make up the central disc of a composite flower.
disk har'rōw, disç har'rōw, a harrow with sharp discs that can revolve, used to break up the soil for sowing.
dis·kīnd'ness, *n.* unkindness. [Rare.]
disk jock'ey, disç jock'ey, a person who conducts a radio program of recorded music, interspersed with chatter, jokes, commercials, etc.
disk'less, *a.* without a disk or disks.
disk wheel, a wheel made solid from rim to hub instead of with spokes.
dis·lēal', *a.* disloyal. [Obs.]
dis·lēave', *v.t.* to rid of leaves.
dis·līke', *n.* 1. a feeling of not liking; distaste; displeasure; aversion.
Our likings and *dislikes* are founded rather upon fancy than upon reason. —L'Estrange.
2. discord; disagreement. [Obs.]
A murmur rose
That showed *dislike* among the Christian peers. —Fairfax.
Syn.—disapprobation, disinclination, displeasure, disrelish, distaste, aversion, antipathy, repugnance, disgust.
dis·līke', *v.t.*; disliked (-līkt), *pt., pp.*; disliking, *ppr.* 1. to have a feeling of not liking; to disapprove of; to regard with some aversion or displeasure; as, we *dislike* proceedings which we deem wrong; we *dislike* persons of evil habits.
2. to displease. [Obs.]
I'll do't; but it *dislikes* me. —Shak.
3. to express disapprobation of. [Obs.]
dis·līke'fųl, *a.* disaffected. [Obs.]
dis·līke'li·hood, *n.* the state of being improbable. [Rare.]
dis·līk'en, *v.t.* to make unlike. [Obs.]
dis·līke'ness, *n.* unlikeness; want of resemblance; dissimilitude. [Obs.]
dis·līk'ẽr, *n.* one who dislikes.
dis·limb' (-lim'), *v.t.* to tear the limbs from.
dis·limn' (-lim'), *v.t.* to destroy the outlines of; to obliterate; to efface; to blot out. [Obs. or Poet.]
dis·liñk', *v.t.* to separate. [Rare.]
dis·līve', *v.t.* to kill. [Obs.]
dis'lō·çāte, *v.t.*; dislocated, *pt., pp.*; dislocating, *ppr.* [LL. *dislocatus,* pp. of *dislocare,* to dislocate; L. *dis-* priv., and *locare,* to place, from *locus,* place.]
1. to displace; to put out of its proper place; particularly, to put out of joint; to disjoint.
2. to upset the order of; to disarrange.
dis·lō·çā'tion, *n.* 1. the act of moving from its proper place; a dislocating.
2. the state of being dislocated.
3. in geology, the displacement of parts of rocks, or portions of strata, from the positions which they originally occupied.
dis·lodġe' (-loj'), *v.t.*; dislodged, *pt., pp.*; dislodging, *ppr.* [OFr. *desloger*; *des-* priv., and *loger,* to lodge; L. *dis-* priv., and LL. *lobia,* a gallery, lobby.]
1. to remove or drive from a place of lodgment or rest; to force out.
The shellfish resident in the depths are never *dislodged* by storms. —Woodward.
2. to drive from any place of hiding or defense, or from any station; as, to *dislodge* the enemy from a hill.
dis·lodġe', *v.i.* to go from a place of lodgment.
dis·lodġe', *n.* a dislodgment. [Obs.]
dis·lodġ'ment (-loj'), *n.* a dislodging or being dislodged.
dis·loign' (-loin'), *v.t.* to remove. [Obs.]
dis·loy'ăl, *a.* not loyal or faithful, as to a government, movement, principle, or obligation; exhibiting neglect or treachery where support is due; as, a *disloyal* citizen, a *disloyal* disciple, a *disloyal* wife.
Syn.—faithless, false, treacherous, perfidious, dishonest, inconstant.
dis·loy'ăl·ly, *adv.* in a disloyal manner.
dis·loy'ăl·ty, *n.* 1. the quality of being disloyal.
2. *pl.* **dis·loy'ăl·tieș,** a disloyal act.
dis·māil', *v.t.* to remove a coat of mail from. [Archaic.]
diș'măl, *a.*; *comp.* dismaller; *superl.* dismallest, [from ME. *dysmal,* pl. *dismale,* evil days (of the medieval calendar), from OFr. *dis mal,* from L. *dies mali,* evil days.]
1. causing gloom or misery; depressing.
The very *dismallest* of all the entertainments which Amelia had in her honeymoon. —Thackeray.
2. dark and gloomy; bleak; dreary.
3. depressed; miserable.
Syn.—dreary, gloomy, dark, doleful, horrid, dire, direful, frightful, horrible, lamentable, dolorous, calamitous, sorrowful, sad, melancholy, unfortunate, unhappy.
diș'măl, *n.* 1. Satan. [Obs.]
2. [*pl.*] mourning garb; weeds. [Obs.]
3. [*pl.*] mental depression; the blues; low spirits; as, in the *dismals.*
4. a swamp or bog: a term used in southern United States.
diș'măl·ly, *adv.* in a dismal manner.
diș'măl·ness, *n.* the state or quality of being dismal.
dis·man', *v.t.* 1. to unman. [Obs.]
2. to remove the men of; as, to *disman* a province.
dis·man'tle, *v.t.*; dismantled, *pt., pp.*; dismantling, *ppr.* [OFr. *desmanteller,* to take off one's cloak, to raze or beat down the wall of a fortress; L. *dis-* priv., and *mantellum,* a cloak.]
1. to deprive of dress; to strip of covering.
2. to strip or deprive of accessory or essential parts; to remove the furniture, equipment, or rigging of; as, to *dismantle* a house, ship, cannon, etc.
3. to take apart; to raze; to make unusable for its original purpose.
dis·märch', *v.i.* to march back; to retreat. [Obs.]
dis·mär'shăl, *v.t.* to derange or throw into disorder. [Rare.]
dis·mȧsk', *v.t.* to strip off, as a mask; to uncover; to remove, as that which conceals. [Obs.]

dis·mȧst′, *v.t.*; dismȧsted, *pt., pp.*; dismasting, *ppr.* to deprive of a mast or masts; to break and carry away the masts from; as, a storm *dismasted* the ship.

dis·mȧst′ment, *n.* the act of dismasting; the state of being dismasted. [Rare.]

dis·ma̤w′, *v.t.* to disgorge. [Rare.]

dis·māy′, *v.t.*; dismayed, *pt., pp.*; dismaying, *ppr.* [ME. *dismayen*, from *dis-* priv., and O.H.G. *magan*, to have power, be strong.]

1. to make afraid or discouraged at the prospect of trouble or danger; to fill with apprehension or alarm; to daunt.

Be strong, and of a good courage; be not afraid, neither be thou *dismayed*. —Josh. i. 9.

2. to subdue; to defeat. [Obs.]

Syn.—terrify, fright, affright, frighten, appall, daunt, dishearten, dispirit, discourage, deject, depress.

dis·māy′, *v.i.* to have or exhibit dismay; to fear.

Dismay not, princes, at this accident. —Shak.

dis·māy′, *n.* 1. a loss of courage or confidence at the prospect of trouble or danger; consternation.

And each
In other's countenance read his own *dismay*. —Milton.

2. ruin; defeat; destruction. [Obs.]

Like as a ship, whom cruell tempest drives
Upon a rocke with horrible *dismay*. —Spenser.

Syn.—dejection, discouragement, depression, fear, fright, terror.

dis·māy′ed·ness, *n.* a state of being dismayed; dispiritedness.

dis·māy′fụl, *a.* dreadful.

dīsme (dĭm), *n.* a dime. [Obs.]

dis·mem′bẽr, *v.t.*; dismembered, *pt., pp.*; dismembering, *ppr.* 1. to tear limb from limb; to separate a member or members from.

2. to cut or pull to pieces; to separate into parts.

3. to take away the membership of; as, to *dismember* one from a church. [Rare.]

Syn.—disjoint, dislocate, dilacerate, mutilate, divide, sever.

dis·mem′bẽr·ment, *n.* the act of dismembering or state of being dismembered.

dis·met′tled, *a.* without spirit. [Rare.]

dis·miss′, *v.t.*; dismissed (-mist), *pt., pp.*; dismissing, *ppr.* [L. *dismissus* or *dimissus*, pp. of *dimittere*, to send away; *di-*, from, and *mittere*, to send.]

1. to send away; to give leave of departure; to permit to depart.

With thanks, and pardon to you all,
I do *dismiss* you to your several countries. —Shak.

2. to remove or discharge from an office, service, employment, etc.

3. to put out of one's mind; as, he *dismissed* his fears.

4. in law, to discontinue or reject (a claim or action) as unworthy of notice or of being granted; as, to *dismiss* a petition or a motion in a court.

Syn.—discharge, banish, abandon, remove, reject.

dis·miss′, *n.* discharge; dismissal. [Obs.]

dis·miss′ăl, *n.* 1. a dismissing or being dismissed.

2. a notice or order for the dismissing of someone.

dis·miss′i·ble, *a.* that can be dismissed.

dis·mis′sion (-mish′un), *n.* dismissal. [Rare.]

dis·miss′ive, *a.* giving dismissal.

dis·mọrt′gāġe (-mọr′găj), *v.t.* to redeem from mortgage. [Obs.]

dis·mount′, *v.i.*; dismounted, *pt., pp.*; dismounting, *ppr.* 1. to alight from a horse, bicycle, etc.; to descend or get off, as a rider from a beast; as, the officer ordered his troops to *dismount*.

2. to descend from an elevation.

dis·mount′, *v.t.* 1. to throw or remove from a horse; to unhorse; as, the soldier *dismounted* his adversary.

2. to remove (a thing) from its mounting or setting.

3. to cause to get off or down; also, to get off or come down from.

4. to take (a machine) apart.

5. to throw or remove, as cannon or other artillery from their carriages; to break the carriages or wheels of and render useless.

dis·nat′ū·răl·īze, *v.t.* to denaturalize.

dis·nā′tūre, *v.t.*; disnatured, *pt., pp.*; disnaturing, *ppr.* to cause to lose its natural quality, appearance, etc.; to make unnatural.

dis·nā′tūred, *a.* deprived or destitute of natural qualities, etc.; unnatural.

dis·ō·bē′di·ence, *n.* neglect or refusal to obey; failure to do that which is commanded to be done, or the doing of that which is forbidden; breach of duty prescribed by authority; insubordination.

dis·ō·bē′di·en·cy, *n.* disobedience. [Obs.]

dis·ō·bē′di·ent, *a.* 1. not obedient; neglecting or refusing to obey; omitting to do what is commanded, or doing what is prohibited; refractory; insubordinate; not observant of duty or rules prescribed by authority; as, children *disobedient* to parents, citizens *disobedient* to the laws.

I was not *disobedient* unto the heavenly vision. —Acts xxvi. 19.

2. not yielding; as, nerves *disobedient* to the brain.

dis·ō·bē′di·ent·ly, *adv.* in a disobedient manner.

dis·ō·bēi′sănce, *n.* disobedience. [Obs.]

dis·ō·bēi′sănt, *a.* disobedient. [Obs.]

dis·ō·bẹy′, *v.t.*; disobeyed, *pt., pp.*; disobeying, *ppr.* to neglect or refuse to obey; to fail to obey; as, refractory children *disobey* their parents; men *disobey* the laws.

dis·ō·bẹy′, *v.i.* to refuse obedience; to be neglectful of commands.

dis·ō·bẹy′ẽr, *n.* one who disobeys.

dis·ob·li·gā′tion, *n.* the state or condition of being without obligation; also, a disobliging act. [Obs.]

dis·ob′li·gā·tō·ry, *a.* releasing from obligation. [Obs.]

dis·ō·blīġe′, *v.t.*; disobliged, *pt., pp.*; disobliging, *ppr.* 1. to refuse to oblige; not do for (another) what he wants done.

2. to slight; to offend.

My plan has given offense to some gentlemen whom it would not be very safe to *disoblige*. —Addison.

3. to inconvenience.

dis·ō·blīġe′ment, *n.* the act of disobliging.

dis·ō·blī′ġẽr, *n.* one who disobliges.

dis·ō·blī′ġing, *a.* not obliging; not disposed to gratify the wishes of another; not disposed to please; unaccommodating.

dis·ō·blī′ġing·ly, *adv.* in a disobliging manner; offensively.

dis·ō·blī′ġing·ness, *n.* offensiveness; disposition to displease, or want of readiness to please.

dis·oc′ci·dent, *v.t.* 1. to veer from a westerly line. [Obs.]

2. to impair the sense of direction of. [Obs.]

dis·oc·cū·pā′tion, *n.* the state of being without occupation.

dī·som′ȧ·tous, *a.* [Gr. *disōmatos*, double-bodied; *di-*, two, and *sōma*, body.] double-bodied.

dis·ō·pin′iŏn (-yun), *n.* dissent. [Obs.]

dis·op′pi·lāte, *v.t.* to open. [Obs.]

dis·ọrb′, *v.t.* to displace from an orbit, as a star.

dis·ọr′dẽr, *n.* [OFr. *désordre*, disorder; L. *dis-* priv., and *ordo*, order, arrangement.]

1. a lack of order; confusion; as, the troops were thrown into *disorder*; the papers are in *disorder*.

2. neglect or disregard of system; irregularity.

From vulgar bounds with brave *disorder* part,
And snatch a grace beyond the reach of art. —Pope.

3. breach of public peace; a riot.

4. irregularity, disturbance, or interruption of the normal functions; disease; as, a mental disorder.

Syn.—irregularity, disarrangement, confusion, tumult, bustle, disturbance, illness, indisposition, sickness, malady, distemper, disease.

dis·ọr′dẽr, *v.t.*; disordered, *pt., pp.*; disordering, *ppr.* [OFr. *desordrer*; L. *dis-* priv., and *ordinare*, to order, regulate.]

1. to break the order of; to derange; to disturb the regular order of; to throw into confusion; to confuse.

The incursions of the Goths and other barbarous nations *disordered* the affairs of the Roman Empire. —Arbuthnot.

2. to disturb or interrupt the normal functions or health of; as, the man's mentality is *disordered*.

3. to discompose; to ruffle. [Obs.]

Disordered into a wanton frame.—Barrow.

4. to depose from holy orders. [Obs.]

Let him be stripped and *disordered*, that the world may behold the inside of a friar. —Dryden.

Syn.—disarrange, derange, confuse, discompose, disturb, ruffle.

dis·ọr′dẽred, *a.* 1. put out of order; jumbled.

2. ill; deranged; as, a *disordered* stomach, a *disordered* mind.

Syn.—confused, deranged, disturbed, diseased.

dis·ọr′dẽred·ly, *adv.* in a disordered manner.

dis·ọr′dẽred·ness, *n.* a state of disorder or irregularity; confusion.

dis·ọr′dẽr·li·ness, *n.* the state of being disorderly.

dis·ọr′dẽr·ly, *a.* 1. being without proper order or disposition; confused; not methodical; irregular; as, the books and papers are in a *disorderly* state.

2. causing a disturbance; unruly; turbulent; rebellious.

3. in law, violating public peace, safety, or order.

4. not functioning in an orderly or regular way. [Obs.]

Syn.—irregular, immethodical, confused, tumultuous, inordinate, intemperate, unruly, lawless, vicious, loose.

dis·ọr′dẽr·ly, *adv.* in a disorderly manner.

dis·ọr′dẽr·ly cọn′duct, in law, any petty offense against public peace, safety, or order.

dis·ọr′dẽr·ly house, in law, any establishment where offenses against public peace, safety, or order habitually occur, as a house of prostitution or a gambling house.

dis·ọr′di·nănce, *n.* disarrangement. [Obs.]

dis·ọr′di·nāte, *a.* disorderly. [Obs.]

dis·ọr′di·nāte·ly, *adv.* inordinately; irregularly. [Obs.]

dis·ọr·di·nā′tion, *n.* disorder. [Obs.]

dis·ọr″găn·i·zā′tion, *n.* 1. the act of disorganizing.

2. the state of being disorganized; as, the *disorganization* of the body, or of government, or of society, or of an army.

dis·ọr′găn·īze, *v.t.*; disorganized, *pt., pp.*; disorganizing, *ppr.* to break up the order, arrangement, or system of; to throw into confusion or disorder.

dis·ọr′găn·īz·ẽr, *n.* one who or that which disorganizes.

dis·ō′ri·ent, **dis·ō·ri·en′tāte**, *v.t.* to change from an easterly line; to turn from the east, as the altar of a church; hence, to cause to lose one's bearings; to confuse.

dis·ō″ri·en·tā′tion, *n.* a loss of orientation; specifically, in psychiatry, a condition of mental confusion with respect to time, place, and the identity of persons and objects.

dis·ōwn′, *v.t.*; disowned, *pt., pp.*; disowning, *ppr.* 1. to repudiate, to cast off; to refuse to acknowledge as belonging to oneself; as, he *disowned* his profligate son.

2. to deny; not to allow.

dis·ōwn′ment, *n.* act of disowning.

dis·ox′i·dāte, *v.t.* to deoxidate. [Rare.]

dis·ox·i·dā′tion, *n.* deoxidation. [Rare.]

dis·ox′y·ġen·āte, *v.t.* to deprive of oxygen. [Rare.]

dis·ox·y·ġen·ā′tion, *n.* the act or process of separating oxygen from any substance containing it. [Rare.]

dis·pāce′, *v.i.* to move about. [Obs.]

dis·pāir′, *v.t.* to separate (a pair or couple). [Rare.]

dis·pand′, *v.t.* to expand. [Obs.]

dis·pan′sion, *n.* the act of expanding. [Obs.]

dis·par′ȧ·dīsed (-dĭst), *a.* removed from paradise. [Rare.]

dis·par′ăġe, *v.t.*; disparaged, *pt., pp.*; disparaging, *ppr.* [ME. *disparagen*; OFr. *desparager*, to marry one of inferior rank; *des-* priv., and *parage*, rank, condition; L. *dis-* priv., and *par*, equal.]

1. to marry unequally, as to one of inferior position in life. [Obs.]

2. to match unequally; to injure or dishonor by union with something inferior or by a comparison with something of less value or worth. [Rare.]

3. to lower in esteem; to discredit.

4. to speak slightingly of; to show disrespect for; to belittle.

Syn.—depreciate, undervalue, vilify, reproach, detract from, derogate from, decry, degrade.

dis′pȧ·rāġe, *n.* a misalliance. [Obs.]

dis·par′ăġe·ment, *n.* 1. misalliance. [Obs.]

2. a disparaging; detraction.

It ought to be no *disparagement* to a star that it is not the sun. —South.

3. anything that detracts or discredits.

Syn.—derogation, detraction, reproach, dishonor, debasement, degradation, disgrace.

dis·par′ăg·ẽr, *n.* one who disparages or dishonors.

dis·par′ăg·ing, *a.* that disparages; slighting; belittling.

dis·par′ăg·ing·ly, *adv.* in a manner to disparage or dishonor.

dis′pȧ·rāte, *a.* [L. *disparatus*, pp. of *disparare*, to separate; *dis-* priv., and *parare*, to make equal, from *par*, equal.] essentially not alike; distinct or different in kind; dissimilar; unequal.

dis′pȧ·rātes, *n.pl.* things so unequal or unlike that they cannot be compared with each other.

dis·pȧ·ri′tion, *n.* a disappearing. [Obs.]

dis·par′i·ty, *n.* [Fr. *disparite*; LL. *disparitas*, difference, disparity; L. *dispar*, unequal.]
 1. inequality or difference, as in degree, rank, amount, condition, or excellence; as, a *disparity* of years or of age.
 2. unlikeness; incongruity; as, the *disparity* in their accounts of the incident.

dis·pärk′, *v.t.*; disparked, *pt., pp.*; disparking, *ppr.* 1. to throw open, as a park.
 2. to set at large; to release from enclosure or confinement.

dis·pär′kle, *v.t.* and *v.i.* to disperse; to scatter. [Obs.]

dis·pärt′, *v.t.* [OFr. *despartir*; L. *dispartire*, to divide, distribute; *dis-*, apart, from, and *partire*, to part, divide, from *pars*, part.]
 1. to part asunder; to divide; to separate; to sever; to burst; to rend.
 2. in gunnery, (a) in taking aim, to make allowance for the dispart of; (b) to fix, as a piece of ordnance, with a dispart sight.

dis·pärt′, *v.i.* to separate; to open; to cleave.

dis·pärt′, *n.* in gunnery, (a) the difference in radius of the bore between the muzzle end and the breech end of a firearm; (b) a dispart sight.

dis·pärt′ sīght (sīt), in gunnery, a piece of metal cast on the muzzle of a firearm to make the line of sight parallel to the axis of the bore.

dis·pas′sion (-pash′un), *n.* freedom from passion, from emotion, or from bias.

dis·pas′sion·āte, *a.* free from passion, emotion, or bias; calm; composed; impartial; temperate; unmoved by feelings; as, *dispassionate* men or judges.

dis·pas′sion·āte·ly, *adv.* in a dispassionate manner.

dis·pas′sion·āte·ness, *n.* the state or quality of being dispassionate.

dis·patch′, *v.t.* [Sp. *despachar* and It. *dispacciare*, to send off, hasten.]
 1. to send off or out, usually on a specific errand or official business.
 2. to put an end to; to kill.
 3. to finish quickly or promptly.
 4. to eat up. [Colloq.]

dis·patch′, *v.i.* to make haste; to dispose of a matter; to finish. [Obs.]

dis·patch′, *n.* 1. a dispatching; a sending out or off.
 2. a putting to death; killing.
 3. speed; haste; promptness.
 4. a message, especially an official message.
 5. a news story sent to a paper, as by a syndicate or special reporter.
 6. a dispatching agency.

dis·patch′ bōat, a swift vessel for carrying official dispatches.

dis·patch′ box, a box in which official messages are sent.

dis·patch′ẽr, *n.* 1. a person who dispatches.
 2. a transportation worker who sends out trains, buses, trucks, etc. according to a schedule.

dis·patch′fụl, *a.* indicating haste; intent on speedy execution of business.

dis′pȧ·thy, *n.* same as *dyspathy*.

dis·pạu′pẽr, *v.t.* to deprive of the claim of a pauper to public support, or of the capacity of suing *in forma pauperis*.

dis·pạu′pẽr·īze, *v.t.* to liberate from a state of pauperism.

dis·peed′, *v.t.* to despatch. [Obs.]

dis·pel′, *v.t.*; dispelled, *pt., pp.*; dispelling, *ppr.* [L. *dispellere*, to drive away, disperse; *dis-*, apart, away, and *pellere*, to drive.] to scatter and drive away; to cause to vanish; to disperse; to dissipate; as, to *dispel* vapors, to *dispel* darkness or gloom, to *dispel* fears.
 Syn.—disperse, scatter, dissipate, drive away, dismiss.

dis·pend′, *v.t.* to spend; especially, to spend lavishly; to squander. [Obs.]

dis·pend′ẽr, *n.* one who dispends. [Obs.]

dis·pen′sȧ·ble, *a.* 1. that can be dispensed; that can be dealt out or administered.
 2. that can be dispensed with; not important; not needed.
 3. admitting of dispensation, as a sin, etc.; condonable.
 4. that can be considered not binding.

dis·pen′sȧ·ble·ness, *n.* the state or quality of being dispensable.

dis·pen′sȧ·ry, *n.*; *pl.* **dis·pen′sȧ·ries,** 1. that part of a building or institution where medicines are made up and dispensed; as, the *dispensary* adjoined the operating room.
 2. a place where medicines and medical treatment are given free or for a small fee.
 3. in South Carolina, formerly, a store or other place where intoxicating liquors were sold, not to be drunk on the premises. According to the Dispensary Law of this state, the sale of intoxicating liquors was otherwise forbidden (1892–1907).

dis·pen·sā′tion, *n.* [OFr. *despensation*; L. *dispensatio*, management, charge, from *dispensare*, to weigh out, pay; *dis-*, apart, and *pensare*, freq. of *pendere*, to weigh.]
 1. a dispensing; giving out; distribution.
 2. anything dispensed or distributed.
 3. the system by which anything is administered; management.
 4. any release from an obligation; special exemption or remission.
 5. in law, the suspension of a statute in a specific case for extenuating reasons.
 6. in the Roman Catholic Church, an official exemption or release from the provisions of a specific church law; as, a papal *dispensation* for divorce.
 7. in theology, (a) the ordering of events under divine authority; (b) any religious system; as, the Moslem *dispensation* differs from the Christian.

dis·pen′sȧ·tive, *a.* granting dispensation.

dis·pen′sȧ·tive·ly, *adv.* by dispensation.

dis′pen·sā·tŏr, *n.* [L.] a dispenser.

dis·pen′sȧ·tō·ry, *a.* granting privilege by dispensation.

dis·pen′sȧ·tō·ry, *n.*; *pl.* **dis·pen′sȧ·tō·ries,** [L. *dispensator*, a steward, treasurer, from *dispensare*, to weigh out, dispense.]
 1. a book containing the method of preparing the various kinds of medicines used in pharmacy, or containing directions for the composition of medicines, with the proportions of the ingredients, and the methods of preparing them.
 2. a dispensary. [Archaic.]

dis·pense′, *v.t.*; dispensed (-penst), *pt., pp.*; dispensing, *ppr.* [L. *dispensare*, to weigh out, pay out; *dis-*, out, from, and *pensare*, freq. of *pendere*, to weigh.]
 1. to deal out; to give out; to distribute; as, the steward *dispenses* provisions, the society *dispenses* medicines.
 2. to administer; to apply, as laws to particular cases.

> While you *dispense* the laws and guide the state. —Dryden.

 3. to prepare and give out (medicines, prescriptions, etc.).
 4. to grant dispensation to; to relieve; to excuse; to set free from an obligation; to exempt; as, good management *dispenses* one from many troubles.
 to dispense with; (a) to get rid of; do away with; (b) to do without; manage without.

dis·pense′, *v.i.* 1. to make amends; to counterbalance. [Obs.]
 2. to issue dispensation.

dis·pense′, *n.* 1. dispensation. [Obs.]
 2. expense; profusion. [Obs.]

dis·pens′ẽr, *n.* one who or that which dispenses.

dis·pēo′ple, *v.t.*; dispeopled, *pt., pp.*; dispeopling, *ppr.* to depopulate; to strip of all or many inhabitants, as by destruction, expulsion, or other means.

dis·pēo′plẽr, *n.* one who depopulates; a depopulator; that which deprives of inhabitants.

dis·pẽrġe′, *v.t.* to disperse. [Obs.]

dī·spẽr′mous, *a.* [*di-*, and Gr. *sperma*, a seed.] in botany, having two seeds.

dis·pẽr′ple, *v.t.* to disparkle. [Obs.]

dis·pẽr′săl, *n.* a dispersing or being dispersed; distribution.

dis·pẽrse′, *v.t.*; dispersed, *pt., pp.*; dispersing, *ppr.* [L. *dispersus*, pp. of *dispergere*, to scatter abroad.]
 1. to break up and scatter in all directions; to spread about or out; to distribute widely.
 2. to dispel (mist, etc.).
 3. to break up (light) into its component colored rays.
 Syn.—spread, scatter, dissipate, dispel, disseminate, distribute.

dis·pẽrse′, *v.i.* to become scattered; to separate; to go or move in different directions; as, the company *dispersed* at ten o'clock.

dis·pẽrsed′ (-pẽrst′), *a.* scattered.
 dispersed harmony; see under *harmony*.

dis·pẽrs′ed·ly, *adv.* in a dispersed manner; separately.

dis·pẽrs′ed·ness, *n.* the state of being dispersed or scattered.

dis·pẽrs′ẽr, *n.* one who or that which disperses.

dis·pẽrs′i·ble, *a.* that can be dispersed.

dis·pẽr′sion, *n.* [Fr.; L. *dispersio*, a scattering, dispersion, from *dispersus*, pp. of *dispergere*, to scatter.]
 1. a dispersing or being dispersed.
 2. the breaking up of light into its component color rays, as by means of a prism.
 3. the similar breaking up of electric waves, etc.
 dispersion of the optic axes; in crystallography, the phenomenon presented by a crystal in having two axes along which a ray of light can proceed without bifurcation.
 the Dispersion; the Diaspora.

dis·pẽrs′ive, *a.* dispersing or tending to disperse.
 dispersive power; in optics, the ratio of the angle of dispersion to the mean deviation of the two rays from which it is measured.

dis·pẽrs′ive·ly, *adv.* in a dispersive manner; due to dispersion.

dis·pẽrs′ive·ness, *n.* the state or quality of being dispersive.

dis·pẽr′sŏn·ăl·īze, dis·pẽr′sŏn·āte, *v.t.* to disguise, destroy, or change the individuality of. [Rare.]

dis·pir′it, *v.t.*; dispirited, *pt., pp.*; dispiriting, *ppr.* 1. to lower the spirits of; to deprive of courage; to discourage; to dishearten; to deject; to cast down.
 2. to transfuse the spirit of (a book). [Obs.]

dis·pir′it·ed·ly, *adv.* dejectedly.

dis·pir′it·ed·ness, *n.* lack of courage; depression of spirits.

dis·pir′it·ment, *n.* the state of being in a dispirited condition; the act of dispiriting.

dis·pit′ē·ous, *a.* having no pity or mercy; ruthless.

dis·pit′ē·ous·ly, *adv.* cruelly.

dis·plāce′, *v.t.*; displaced, *pt., pp.*; displacing, *ppr.* [OFr. *desplacer*, to displace; *des-* priv., and *placer*, to place.]
 1. to put out of the usual or proper place; to remove from its place; as, the books in the library are all *displaced*.
 2. to remove from any state, condition, office, or dignity; as, to *displace* an officer.
 3. to take the place of; to replace; as, a ship *displaces* a certain amount of water.

dis·plāced′ pẽr′sŏn (-plāst′), a person left homeless in a foreign country as a result of war.

dis·plāce′ment, *n.* 1. a displacing or being displaced.
 2. the weight or volume of air, water, or other fluid displaced by a floating object, as a balloon or a ship.
 3. the difference between a later position of a thing and its original position.
 4. in geology, a fault.
 5. in psychiatry, the transference of an emotion to a logically inappropriate object.
 6. in pharmacy, the method by which the active principles of a powder are extracted by filtering a liquid through it; percolation.
 7. in a machine having a piston, as a steam pump, the measure of space acted through or the amount of fluid displaced during each piston stroke.

dis·plā′cen·cy, *n.* [L. *displicentia*, from *displicere*, to displease; *dis-*, and *placere*, to please.] dissatisfaction; dislike; displeasure. [Now Rare.]

dis·plā′cẽr, *n.* one who or that which displaces.

dis·plant′, *v.t.*; displanted, *pt., pp.*; displanting; *ppr.* to move from the normal or settled place; specifically, (a) to transplant; (b) to dislodge or displace. [Obs.]

dis·plan·tā′tion, *n.* the act of displanting. [Obs.]

dis·plat′, *v.t.* to untwist; to uncurl. [Obs.]

dis·plāy′, *v.t.*; displayed, *pt., pp.*; displaying, *ppr.* [ME. *displayen*; L. *dis-*, apart, and *plicare*, to fold.]
 1. to unfold; to open; to spread wide; to expand.

> The northern wind his wings did broad *display*. —Spenser.

2. to spread before the view; to show; to exhibit to advantage.
3. to unfold to the mind; to disclose; to reveal.
4. to print conspicuously, as in large or fancy type.
5. to discover; to spy out. [Obs.]

dis·plāy′, *v.i.* 1. to make a show or display.
2. to lay anything open, as in carving or dissection.
He carves, *displays*, and cuts up to a wonder. —*Spectator*.

dis·plāy′, *n.* 1. a displaying; exhibition.
2. anything displayed; exhibit.
3. ostentation; show.
4. a manifestation; as, a *display* of courage.
5. in printing, the variation of type faces to attract attention.
display advertising; (a) advertising, as in a newspaper, magazine, etc., that is set apart from the classified-advertising section; (b) advertising intended to attract by the illustrations used, or on account of the copy, the prominence, the space, the lettering, etc.
display card; a placard on which something is advertised, the card being prominently displayed.

dis·plāyed′, *a.* 1. unfolded; opened; spread; expanded; manifested.
2. in heraldry, with wings expanded: said of any bird of prey presented as a bearing in this position.

dis·plāy′ẽr, *n.* one who or that which displays.

dis′ple (-pl), *v.t.* to discipline. [Obs.]

dis·pleas′ănce (-plez′), *n.* anger; discontent. [Obs.]

dis·pleas′ănt, *a.* 1. displeased. [Obs.]
2. displeasing. [Obs.]

dis·pleas′ănt·ly, *adv.* unpleasantly. [Obs.]

dis·pleas′ănt·ness, *n.* unpleasantness. [Obs.]

dis·plēase′, *v.t.*; displeased, *pt.*, *pp.*; displeasing, *ppr.* [ME. *displesen*; L. *displicere*, to displease; *dis-* priv., and *placere*, to please.]
1. to offend; to make angry in a slight degree; to fail to please; to be disagreeable to; as, his coarseness *displeased* his friends; stale food *displeases* the taste; a deformity *displeases* the eye.
2. to fail to accomplish; to fall short of satisfying. [Obs.]
Syn.—offend, anger, vex, disgust, provoke, dissatisfy, pique.

dis·plēase′, *v.i.* to cause displeasure, annoyance, etc.

dis·plēas′ed·ly, *adv.* in a displeased manner. [Rare.]

dis·plēas′ed·ness, *n.* displeasure; uneasiness. [Rare.]

dis·plēas′ẽr, *n.* one who or that which displeases.

dis·plēas′ing, *a.* offensive to the eye, to the mind, or to any of the senses; annoying; disagreeable.

dis·plēas′ing·ly, *adv.* in a displeasing manner.

dis·plēas′ing·ness, *n.* offensiveness; the quality of being displeasing.

dis·pleas′ūre (-plezh′), *n.* 1. the fact or feeling of being displeased; vexation; dissatisfaction; disapproval; annoyance.
2. an offense; an injury. [Archaic.]
Now shall I be more blameless than the Philistines, though I do them a *displeasure*. —Judges xv. 3.
3. discomfort; trouble. [Archaic.]
Syn.—dissatisfaction, anger, pique, vexation, dislike, indignation, resentment, annoyance.

dis·pleas′ūre, *v.t.* to displease. [Archaic.]

dis·plen′ish, *v.t.* to disfurnish; to strip. [Scot.]

dis′pli·cence, dis′pli·cen·cy, *n.* dissatisfaction; dislike. [Rare.]

dis·plōde′, *v.t.* and *v.i.*; disploded, *pt.*, *pp.*; disploding, *ppr.* [L. *displodere*, from *dis-*, apart, and *plaudere*, to strike, beat.] to explode. [Obs.]

dis·plō′sion, *n.* an explosion. [Obs.]

dis·plō′sive, *a.* explosive. [Obs.]

dis·plūme′, *v.t.*; displumed, *pt.*, *pp.*; displuming, *ppr.* [L. *dis-* priv., and *plumare*, to cover with feathers, from *pluma*, a feather.] to deplume. [Rare.]

dis·pond′, *n.* same as *despond*.

dī·spon′dee, *n.* [L. *dispondeus*; Gr. *dispondeios*, a double spondee; *di-*, two, and *spondeios*, a spondee.] in Greek and Latin prosody, a double spondee, consisting of four long syllables.

dis·pōne′, *v.t.*; disponed, *pt.*, *pp.*; disponing, *ppr.* [ME. *disponen*; OFr. *disponer*, to dispose, from L. *disponere*, to set in different places, distribute, dispose.]
1. to set in order; to arrange. [Obs.]
2. in Scots law, to make over or give to another, as property.

dis·pōne′, *v.i.* to dispose; to decide; to settle. [Obs.]

dis·pō·nee′, *n.* in Scots law, the one to whom anything is made over or deeded.

dis·pō′nent, *a.* disposing or preparing for what is sought.

dis·pōn′ẽr, *n.* in Scots law, the one who makes over or deeds property to another.

dis·pŏnge′, *v.t.* same as *dispunge*.

dis·pōpe′, *v.t.*; dispoped, *pt.*, *pp.*; dispoping, *ppr.* to deprive of the power or dignity of a pope.

dī·spōr′ous, *a.* in biology, two-spored.

dis·pōrt′, *n.* play; sport; pastime; diversion; amusement; merriment. [Archaic.]

dis·pōrt′, *v.i.*; disported, *pt.*, *pp.*; disporting, *ppr.* [ME. *disporten*, to bear, support, manage, from L. *deportare*, to carry away, transport; *de*, away, and *portare*, to carry.] to play; to indulge in amusement; to frolic; as, lambs *disporting* on the mead.
Where light *disports* in ever-mingling dyes. —Pope.

dis·pōrt′, *v.t.* 1. to divert or amuse (oneself).
2. to remove from a port; to transport; to deport. [Obs.]

dis·pōrt′ment, *n.* the act of disporting; play. [Obs.]

dis·pōs′ȧ·ble, *a.* 1. that can be disposed of; easy to get rid of.
2. that can be disposed; not put to any particular use; subject to disposal.

dis·pōs′ăl, *n.* 1. a disposing; arrangement in a particular order; as, the *disposal* of the troops in two lines.
2. regulation, order, or arrangement of things, by right of acknowledged authority or possession; dispensation.
Tax not divine *disposal*. —Milton.
3. a dealing with matters; settling affairs.
4. a giving away; transfer; bestowal.
5. a disposing of; getting rid of.
6. the power to dispose of.
7. management; control.
at one's disposal; available to be used as one wishes; at one's service.

dis·pōse′, *v.t.*; disposed, *pt.*, *pp.*; disposing, *ppr.* [ME. *disposen*; OFr. *disposer*, to dispose, put in order, arrange; L. *disponere*, to arrange, dispose; *dis-*, apart, and *ponere*, to place.]
1. to put in a certain order or arrangement; to place or distribute; to arrange; as, the general *disposed* his troops in three lines.
2. to regulate or settle (affairs); to arrange (matters).
3. to apply to a particular purpose; to give; to place; to bestow; as, you have *disposed* much in works of public piety.
4. to set, place, or turn to a particular end or consequence; to make some use of; to employ.
Endure and conquer; Jove will soon *dispose*
To future good our past and present woes. —Dryden.
5. to make willing; to incline; as, I am *disposed* to agree with you.
6. to make susceptible or liable; as, the climate *disposes* the people to laziness.
to dispose of; to come to a determination concerning; to make a disposal of; specifically, (a) to part with; to alienate; to sell; as, the man has *disposed of* his house; (b) to part with to another; to put into another's hand or power; to bestow; as, the father has *disposed of* his daughter to a man of worth; (c) to give away or transfer by authority; as, to *dispose of* a prize; (d) to use or employ; as, they know not how to *dispose of* their time; (e) to put away; to get rid of; as, the stream supplies more water than can be *disposed of*.
Syn.—arrange, settle, adjust, regulate, bestow, give.

dis·pōse′, *v.i.* 1. to bargain; to make terms. [Obs.]
2. to have the power or privilege of disposing.
Man proposes, God *disposes*. —Old Proverb.

dis·pōse′, *n.* 1. disposal; power of disposing; management. [Obs.]
2. disposition; cast of mind; inclination. [Obs.]

dis·pōsed′, *a.* inclined; having a certain tendency (usually preceded by an adverb); as, he feels well-*disposed* toward you.

dis·pōs′ed·ness, *n.* inclination; disposition; tendency. [Rare.]

dis·pōse′ment, *n.* disposal. [Obs.]

dis·pōs′ẽr, *n.* one who or that which disposes.

dis·pōs′ing·ly, *adv.* in a manner to dispose, settle, or govern.

dis·pō·si′tion (-zish′un), *n.* [ME. *disposition*; L. *dispositio*, arrangement, from *disponere*, to put in different places, to dispose.]
1. the act of disposing or state of being disposed.
2. the manner in which things, or the parts of a complex body, are placed or arranged; order; method; distribution; arrangement; as, the *disposition* of the trees in an orchard; the *disposition* of the several parts of an edifice, of the parts of a discourse, or of the figures in painting.
3. arrangement or management of affairs.
4. natural fitness or tendency; as, a *disposition* in plants to grow in a direction upward; a *disposition* in bodies to putrefaction.
5. one's customary frame of mind; one's nature or temperament; as, an amiable or an irritable *disposition*.
6. inclination; propensity; the temper or frame of mind as directed to particular objects; as, the *disposition* of a person to undertake a particular work; the *dispositions* of men toward each other; a *disposition* friendly to any design.
7. disposal; the giving away or giving up (*of* something); as, he has made *disposition of* his effects; he has satisfied his friends by the judicious *disposition of* his property.
8. the power or authority to arrange, settle, or manage; control.
9. in Scots law, a unilateral deed of alienation, by which a right to property, especially heritable, is conveyed.

dis·pō·si′tion·ăl, *a.* pertaining to disposition.

dis·pō·si′tioned, *a.* having a particular disposition, or bent of mind: used in compounds; as, mean-*dispositioned*.

dis·pos′i·tive, *a.* 1. of or relating to disposal or control; disposing.
2. of or relating to natural disposition. [Obs.]

dis·pos′i·tive·ly, *adv.* in a dispositive manner.

dis·pos′i·tŏr, *n.* in astrology, the planet which is lord of the sign where another planet is. [Obs.]

dis·pŏs·sess′, *v.t.*; dispossessed (-zest′), *pt.*, *pp.*; dispossessing, *ppr.* [OFr. *despossesser*, from L. *dis-* priv., and *possessus*, pp. of *possidere*, to possess.] to deprive of the possession of a thing, particularly of land or real estate; to disseize.

dis·pŏs·ses′sion (-zesh′un), *n.* 1. a dispossessing or being dispossessed.
2. in law, an ousting by legal process.

dis·pŏs·sess′ŏr, *n.* one who or that which dispossesses.

dis·pōst′, *v.t.* to deprive of a post.

dis·pōs′ūre (-pōzh′), *n.* disposition or disposal (in various senses). [Rare.]

dis·prāis′ȧ·ble, *a.* blameworthy. [Rare.]

dis·prāise′, *v.t.*; dispraised, *pt.*, *pp.*; dispraising, *ppr.* [ME. *dispreisen*; OFr. *despreiser*, to dispraise, blame; L. *dis-* priv., and LL. *pretiare*, to prize, praise, from L. *pretium*, price, prize.] to blame; to censure; to mention with disapprobation, or some degree of reproach.
I *dispraised* him before the wicked. —Shak.

dis·prāise′, *n.* the state of being dispraised; censure; reproach.

dis·prāis′ẽr, *n.* one who or that which dispraises.

dis·prāis′ing·ly, *adv.* by way of dispraise; with blame or some degree of reproach.

dis·pread′ (-pred′), *v.t.* to spread in different ways; to extend or flow in different directions.

dis·pread′, *v.i.* to expand or be extended. [Rare.]

dis·pread′ẽr, *n.* one who spreads abroad; a divulger. [Rare.]

dis·prej′ū·dice, *v.t.* to remove prejudice from.

dis·prē·pāre′, *v.t.* to make unprepared. [Obs.]

dis·prince′, *v.t.* to rid of princely characteristics. [Rare.]

dis·pris′ŏn, *v.t.* to let loose from prison; to set at liberty.

dis·priv′i·lege, *v.t.* to deprive of a privilege. [Rare.]

dis·prize′, *v.t.* to regard as of low value; not prize. [Archaic.]

dis·prō·fess′, *v.t.* to give up the profession of. [Rare.]

dis·prof′it, *n.* loss; detriment; damage. [Rare.]

dis·prof′it·ȧ·ble, *a.* unprofitable. [Obs.]

dis·proof′, *n.* 1. confutation; refutation; a proving to be false or erroneous; as, to offer

evidence in *disproof* of a fact, argument, principle, or allegation.
 2. evidence that disproves.
dis·prop′ẽr·ty, *v.t.* to deprive of property; to dispossess. [Obs.]
dis·prō·pōr′tion, *n.* 1. lack of proportion of one thing to another, or between the parts of a thing; lack of symmetry; as, the *disproportion* of a man's arms to his body; the *disproportion* of the length of an edifice to its height.
 2. lack of suitableness or adequacy; disparity; inequality; unsuitableness; as, the *disproportion* of his wrath to the provocation.
dis·prō·pōr′tion, *v.t.*; disproportioned, *pt., pp.*; disproportioning, *ppr.* to cause to be disproportionate.

To shape my legs of an unequal size,
To *disproportion* me in every part.—Shak.

dis·prō·pōr′tion·ȧ·ble, *a.* disproportional; not in proportion; unsuitable in form, size, or quantity, to something else; inadequate.
dis·prō·pōr′tion·ȧ·ble·ness, *n.* lack of proportion or symmetry; unsuitableness to something else.
dis·prō·pōr′tion·ȧ·bly, *adv.* with lack of proportion or symmetry; unsuitably to something else.
dis·prō·pōr′tion·ăl, *a.* disproportionate.
dis·prō·pōr·tion·al′i·ty, *n.* the state of being disproportional.
dis·prō·pōr′tion·ăl·ly, *adv.* not proportionally; not equally.
dis·prō·pōr′tion·āte, *a.* not proportionate; not in proportion; unsymmetrical; unsuitable to something else in size, amount, form, or value.
dis·prō·pōr′tion·āte·ly, *adv.* 1. in a manner characterized by disproportion.
 2. to a disproportionate extent.
dis·prō·pōr′tion·āte·ness, *n.* the condition, quality, or state of being disproportionate.
dis·prō′pri·āte, *v.t.* to dispossess; to withdraw from an appropriate use. [Obs.]
dis·prōv′ȧ·ble, *a.* capable of being disproved or refuted.
dis·prōv′ăl, *n.* a disproving or disproof.
dis·prōve′, *v.t.*; disproved, *pt., pp.*; disproving, *ppr.* [ME. *disproven*; OFr. *desprover*, to refute; *des-* priv., and *prover*, to prove; L. *dis-* priv., and *probare*, to test, prove.]
 1. to prove (something or someone) to be false or in error; to refute.
 2. to disallow or disapprove. [Obs.]
dis·prōv′ẽr, *n.* one who disproves or confutes.
dis·prō·vīde′, *v.t.* to fail to provide for. [Obs.]
dis·punct′, *v.t.* to strike off; to take out. [Obs.]
dis·punct′, *a.* ill-mannered; rude; discourteous. [Obs.]
dis·punge′, *v.t.* to expunge; to erase; also, to discharge, as from a sponge. [Archaic.]
dis·pun′ish·ȧ·ble, *a.* not punishable.
dis·pūr′pōse, *v.t.* to turn or divert from a purpose or aim. [Obs.]
dis·pūrse′, *v.t.* to disburse; to expend. [Obs.]
dis·pūr·vey′, *v.t.* to rob of provisions. [Obs.]
dis·pūr·vey′ănce, *n.* lack of provisions. [Obs.]
dis′pū·tȧ·ble (*or* dis-pū′), *a.* [L. *disputabilis*, disputable, from *disputare*, to dispute.]
 1. that can be disputed; liable to be called in question, controverted, or contested; controvertible; of doubtful certainty; as, *disputable* opinions, statements, propositions, arguments, points, cases, questions, etc.
 2. given to controversy; disputatious. [Obs.]
dis′pū·tȧ·ble·ness, *n.* the quality or state of being disputable.
dis′pū·tȧ·bly, *adv.* in a disputable manner.
dis·pū·tac′i·ty, *n.* proneness to dispute. [Obs.]
dis′pū·tănt, *a.* [L. *disputans*, ppr. of *disputare*.] disputing.
dis′pū·tănt, *n.* a person who disputes, or debates.
dis·pū·tā′tion, *n.* [L. *disputatio*.]
 1. a disputing; dispute.
 2. controversial discussion; debate.
 3. discussion or conversation. [Obs.]
dis·pū·tā′tious (-shus), *a.* inclined to dispute; fond of arguing; contentious; as, a *disputatious* person or temper.
dis·pū·tā′tious·ly, *adv.* in a disputatious manner.
dis·pū·tā′tious·ness, *n.* inclination to dispute.
dis·pū′tȧ·tive, *a.* 1. disputatious.
 2. having to do with disputation.
dis·pūte′, *v.i.*; disputed, *pt., pp.*; disputing, *ppr.* [ME. *disputen*; OFr. *desputer*, from L. *disputare*, to dispute, discuss.]
 1. to argue; to reason or argue in opposition; to debate; as, to *dispute* in a certain case.
 2. to quarrel; to wrangle; as, to *dispute* about trifles.
 3. to debate or contest against a rival; as, to *dispute* for a medal. [Archaic.]
 Syn.—argue, discuss, debate, question.
dis·pūte′, *v.t.* 1. to argue or debate (a question); to discuss pro and con.
 2. to question the truth of; to doubt.
 3. to oppose in any way; to resist.
 4. to try to win (a game, prize, etc.).
dis·pūte′, *n.* 1. strife or contest in words, or by arguments; an attempt to prove and maintain one's own opinions or claims in opposition to the opinions, arguments, or claims of another; controversy in words; debate; as, a *dispute* on the situation in Turkey.
 2. a quarrel; an ill-natured wrangle; a clash; as, family *disputes*.
 3. a fight. [Obs.]
 beyond, past, or *without dispute*; (a) not open to dispute or question; (b) indisputably.
 to be in dispute; to be unsettled; to be the subject of disputation or controversy.
 Syn.—controversy, quarrel, argument, disagreement, contention.
dis·pūt′ẽr, *n.* one who disputes or who is given to disputes; a controversialist.
dis·pū′ti·sŏun, *n.* disputation. [Obs.]
dis·qual″i·fi·cā′tion, *n.* 1. a disqualifying or being disqualified.
 2. anything that disqualifies; that which renders unfit, unsuitable, or inadequate; as, a grade under seventy is a *disqualification* for the advanced course.
dis·qual′i·fȳ, *v.t.*; disqualified, *pt., pp.*; disqualifying, *ppr.* 1. to make unfit or unqualified; disable; incapacitate.
 2. to make or declare ineligible; to take a right or privilege away from, as of further participation in a sport, for breaking rules; as, the boxer was *disqualified* because he struck a foul blow.
dis·quan′ti·ty (-kwän′), *v.t.* to diminish. [Obs.]
dis·quī′et, *v.t.*; disquieted, *pt., pp.*; disquieting, *ppr.* [*dis-* and *quiet*.] to disturb; to deprive of peace, rest, or tranquillity; to make anxious, uneasy, or restless; to vex the mind of.

That he may *disquiet* the inhabitants of Babylon. —Jer. i. 34.

 Syn.—excite, disturb, annoy, irritate.
dis·quī′et, *n.* uneasiness; restlessness; lack of tranquillity; disturbance; anxiety.
dis·quī′et (-kwī′), *a.* unquiet; restless; uneasy. [Rare.]
dis·quī′et·ăl, *n.* the act of disquieting. [Obs.]
dis·quī′et·ẽr, *n.* one who disquiets; he or that which makes uneasy.
dis·quī′et·ful, *a.* producing disquietude or restlessness. [Rare.]
dis·quī′et·ive, *a.* tending to disquiet. [Rare.]
dis·quī′et·ly, *adv.* in a disquiet manner; as, he rested *disquietly* that night. [Rare.]
dis·quī′et·ment, *n.* act of disquieting. [Obs.]
dis·quī′et·ness, *n.* uneasiness; restlessness; disturbance of peace in body or mind.
dis·quī′et·ous, *a.* causing uneasiness. [Rare.]
dis·quī′e·tūde, *n.* restlessness; uneasiness; disturbance; agitation; anxiety.
dis·quip′ȧ·răn·cy, dis·quip′ȧ·rănce, *n.* [LL. *disquiparantia*, from L. *dis-* priv., and *æquiparans*, ppr. of *æquiparare*, to put on a level, compare; *æquus*, equal, level, and *parare*, to make equal, from *par*, equal.] in logic, that relation which exists between two objects mutually implying each other yet not having sameness of relationship, as in the phrase mother and daughter: opposed to *equiparancy*, a state of equality, as in the phrase sister and sister.
dis·qui·si′tion, *n.* [L. *disquisitio* (-*onis*), an inquiry, investigation, from *disquisitus*, pp. of *disquirere*, to investigate, inquire; *dis-*, apart, and *quærere*, to seek.] a formal discussion of some subject, often in writing; a discourse or treatise.
dis·qui·si′tion·ăl, *a.* of or relating to a disquisition.
dis·qui·si′tion·ā·ry, *a.* disquisitional.
dis·quis′i·tive, *a.* disquisitorial.
dis·quis·i·tō′ri·ăl, dis·quis′i·tō·ry, *a.* of the nature of a disquisition; critical.
dis·rānge′, *v.t.* to disarrange. [Obs.]
dis·rank′, *v.t.* 1. to degrade from rank.
 2. to throw out of rank or into confusion. [Obs.]
dis·rāte′, *v.t.* to lower in rank; to abase.
dis·rāy′, *v.t.* to disarray. [Obs.]
dis·rē′ăl·īze, *v.t.* to make unreal. [Obs.]
dis·rē·gärd′, *v.t.*; disregarded, *pt., pp.*; disregarding, *ppr.* [*dis-* and *regard*.]
 1. to pay little or no attention to.
 2. to treat without due respect; to slight.
dis·rē·gärd′, *n.* 1. lack of attention.
 2. lack of due regard or respect; disdain.
dis·rē·gärd′ẽr, *n.* one who neglects.
dis·rē·gärd′ful, *a.* neglectful; negligent; heedless.
dis·rē·gärd′ful·ly, *adv.* negligently; heedlessly.
dis·rel′ish, *n.* and *v.t.* dislike.
dis·rē·mem′bẽr, *v.t.* to forget; to be unable to remember. [Dial. and Colloq.]

Not to *disremember* the old saying, but let every man skin his own skunks. —Crockett.

dis·rē·pāir′, *n.* the condition of needing repairs; state of neglect.
dis·rep″ū·tȧ·bil′i·ty, *n.* the state of being disreputable.
dis·rep′ū·tȧ·ble, *a.* 1. not reputable; discreditable.
 2. not respectable.
dis·rep′ū·tȧ·bly, *adv.* in a disreputable manner.
dis·rep·ū·tā′tion, *n.* same as *disrepute*.
dis·rē·pūte′, *n.* loss or lack of repute; bad reputation; disfavor; discredit; dishonor.
dis·rē·pūte′, *v.t.* to bring into disrepute. [Obs.]
dis·rē·spect′, *n.* lack of respect or reverence; incivility; rudeness.
dis·rē·spect′, *v.t.* to have or show lack of respect for.
dis·rē·spect·ȧ·bil′i·ty, *n.* lack of respectability.
dis·rē·spect′ȧ·ble, *a.* lacking respectability; in disrepute; unworthy of respect.
dis·rē·spect′ẽr, *n.* one who exhibits disrespect.
dis·rē·spect′ful, *a.* having or showing lack of respect; discourteous; impolite; rude.
dis·rē·spect′ful·ly, *adv.* in a disrespectful manner.
dis·rē·spect′ful·ness, *n.* the state or quality of being disrespectful.
dis·rē·spect′ive, *a.* disrespectful. [Obs.]
dis·rev′ẽr·ence, *v.t.* to treat with irreverence. [Obs.]
dis·rōbe′, *v.t.* and *v.i.*; disrobed, *pt., pp.*; disrobing, *ppr.* 1. to divest of a robe; to divest of garments; to undress.
 2. to strip of covering: used figuratively.

These two peers were *disrobed* of their glory. —Wotton.

dis·rōb′ẽr, *n.* one who disrobes.
dis·rōof′, *v.t.* to unroof.
dis·rōot′, *v.t.*; disrooted, *pt., pp.*; disrooting, *ppr.* 1. to tear up the roots of, or by the roots.
 2. to tear from a foundation; to loosen or undermine.

A piece of ground *disrooted* from its situation by subterraneous inundations. —Goldsmith.

dis·rout′, *v.t.* to put to rout. [Obs.]
dis·rud′dẽr, *v.t.* to make rudderless.
dis·rụ′li·ly, *adv.* in a disruly manner. [Obs.]
dis·rụ′ly, *a.* unruly. [Obs.]
dis·rupt′, *v.t.* and *v.i.*; disrupted, *pt., pp.*; disrupting, *ppr.* [from L. *disruptus*, pp. of *disrumpere*, to break or burst apart.] to break apart; to split up; to rend asunder.
dis·rupt′, *a.* rent or torn asunder; disrupted.
dis·rup′tion, *n.* [L. *disruptio*, a tearing to pieces.]
 1. a disrupting; breaking up; splitting.
 2. the fact or state of being disrupted.
 3. the rupture which took place in the Established Church of Scotland in 1843.
dis·rupt′ive, *a.* 1. causing disruption.
 2. produced by disruption.
dis·rup′tŏr, *n.* a person who disrupts something: also spelled *disrupter*.
dis·rup′tūre, *n.* disruption. [Rare.]
diss, *n.* [Ar. *dīs*.] a reedy, Mediterranean grass, *Ampelodesma tenax*, the fiber of which is used for twine, rope, baskets, etc.
dis·sat·is·fac′tion, *n.* 1. the condition of being dissatisfied or displeased; discontent.
 2. anything that dissatisfies.

The ambitious man is subject to uneasiness and *dissatisfaction*. —Addison.

 Syn.—discontent, discontentment, mortification, disappointment, displeasure, disapprobation, distaste, dislike.
dis·sat·is·fac′tō·ri·ness, *n.* state, quality, or condition of being dissatisfactory.
dis·sat·is·fac′tō·ry, *a.* causing dissatisfaction; giving discontent; not satisfying; unsatisfactory.

One uniform rule would probably have been as *dissatisfactory* to some of the states, as difficult for the convention.—Hamilton.

dis·sat′is·fīed, *a.* 1. not satisfied; displeased; discontented.
2. showing displeasure or dissatisfaction.

dis·sat′is·fȳ, *v.t.*; dissatisfied, *pt., pp.*; dissatisfying, *ppr.* to fail to satisfy; to discontent; to displease.

dis·sēat′, *v.t.* to unseat.

dis·sect′, *v.t.*; dissected, *pt., pp.*; dissecting, *ppr.* [L. *dissectus*, pp. of *dissecare*, to cut apart, cut up; *dis-*, apart, and *secare*, to cut.]
1. to cut apart piece by piece; to separate into parts, as a body for purposes of study; to anatomize.
2. to examine or analyze closely.

dis·sect′ed, *a.* 1. cut up into parts.
2. in botany, consisting of many lobes or segments, as some leaves.
3. in physical geography, cut up by valleys and ravines.

dis·sect′i·ble, *a.* capable of dissection.

dis·sect′ing, *a.* 1. of or relating to dissection; as, a *dissecting* scalpel.
2. causing the disconnection of integral parts; as, a *dissecting* medium.

dis·sec′tion, *n.* [from L. *dissectus*, pp. of *dissecare*, to cut up.]
1. a dissecting or being dissected.
2. anything dissected, as a plant or animal for study.
3. analysis part by part; detailed examination.

dis·sect′ŏr, *n.* 1. a person who dissects.
2. an instrument used in dissecting.

dis·sēize′, dis·sēiṣe′, *v.t.*; disseized *or* disseised, *pt., pp.*; disseizing *or* disseising, *ppr.* [OFr. *desseisir*, to dispossess; *des-* priv., and *seisir*, to take possession of.] in law, to dispossess wrongfully; to deprive of actual seizin or possession: followed by *of*; as, to *disseize* a tenant *of* his freehold.

dis·sēi·zee′, dis·sēi·ṣee′, *n.* in law, a disseized person.

dis·sēi′zin, dis·sēi′ṣin, *n.* [OFr. *disseisin*, from *disseisir*, to disseize.] in law, the act of disseizing; an unlawful dispossessing of a person of his lands, tenements, etc.; a deprivation of actual seizin.

dis·sēi′zŏr, dis·sēi′ṣŏr, *n.* in law, a person who disseizes.

dis·sēi′zŏr·ess, dis·sēi′ṣŏr·ess, *n.* a woman who disseizes.

dis·sēi′zūre, dis·sēi′ṣūre, *n.* disseizin. [Obs.]

dis′sel·bo͝om, *n.* [D. *disselboom*, a wagon pole; *dissel*, an axletree; and *boom*, pole.] a wagon tongue.

dis·sem′blănce, *n.* [from *dissemble*, and *-ance*.]
1. a dissembling; dissimulating.
2. [OFr. *dessemblance*; see *dis-*, and *semblance*.] lack of resemblance. [Archaic.]

dis·sem′ble, *v.t.*; dissembled, *pt., pp.*; dissembling, *ppr.* [OFr. *dessembler*, to be unlike; L. *dissimulare*, to feign to be different, dissemble; *dis-* priv., and *similis*, like.]
1. to hide under a false appearance; to conceal; to disguise; to pretend (that) not to be which really is; as, I will not *dissemble* the truth; I cannot *dissemble* my real sentiments.
2. to resemble falsely; to simulate; to feign; as, vice sometimes *dissembles* virtue.
3. to pretend not to observe; to feign ignorance of.
4. to disguise. [Obs.]
Syn.—hide, screen, disguise, cloak, cover, veil, conceal.

dis·sem′ble, *v.i.* to be hypocritical; to assume a false appearance; to conceal the real fact, motives, intention, or sentiments under some pretense.

dis·sem′blẽr, *n.* one who dissembles; a hypocrite; one who conceals his opinions or dispositions under a false appearance.
Syn.—hypocrite, pretender, deceiver.

dis·sem′bling, *a.* hiding under a false appearance; acting the hypocrite.

dis·sem′bling·ly, *adv.* in a dissembling manner.

dis·sem′i·nāte, *v.t.* and *v.i.*; disseminated, *pt., pp.*; disseminating, *ppr.* [L. *disseminatus*, pp. of *disseminare*, to scatter seed, spread abroad, disseminate; *dis-*, apart, and *seminare*, to sow, from *semen*, seed.]
1. to scatter far and wide; to spread abroad, as if sowing; to promulgate widely.
2. to spread by diffusion or dispersion.

> A uniform heat *disseminated* through the body of the earth. —Woodward.

Syn.—spread, diffuse, propagate, publish, promulgate, circulate, disperse.

dis·sem′i·nā·ted, *a.* in mineralogy, occurring in small, scattered portions; scattered; diffused: said of one mineral embedded in another.

dis·sem·i·nā′tion, *n.* the act of scattering and propagating, like seed; the act of spreading or promulgating; as, the *dissemination* of altruistic doctrines; also, the state of being disseminated.

dis·sem′i·nā·tive, *a.* conducive to dissemination.

dis·sem′i·nā·tŏr, *n.* one who disseminates; one who spreads or propagates.

dis·sen′sion, *n.* [ME. *dissencion*; OFr. *dissension*; L. *dissensio*, difference of opinion, disagreement, from *dissensus*, pp. of *dissentire*, to disagree; *dis-*, apart, and *sentire*, to think.]
1. disagreement in opinion; difference; discord.
2. contention in words; strife; quarrel.

> Debates, *dissensions*, uproars are thy joy. —Dryden.

Syn.—contention, discord, dispute, disagreement, strife, quarrel.

dis·sen′sious (-shus), *a.* dissentious. [Rare.]

dis·sen′sious·ly, *adv.* dissentiously. [Rare.]

dis·sent′, *v.i.*; dissented, *pt., pp.*; dissenting, *ppr.* [ME. *dissenten*; L. *dissentire*, to differ in opinion, disagree.]
1. to disagree in opinion; to differ; to think in a contrary manner: often with *from*; as, they *dissent from* each other.
2. to differ from an established church in regard to doctrines, rites, or government.
3. to differ; to be of a contrary nature. [Obs.]

dis·sent′, *n.* 1. difference of opinion; disagreement.
2. declaration of disagreement in opinion; the rendering of a minority opinion in the decision of a law case.
3. separation from an established church, especially that of England.
4. contrariety of nature; opposite quality. [Obs.]

dis·sen·tā′nē·ous, *a.* disagreeable; contrary. [Rare.]

dis·sen′tă·ny, *a.* dissentaneous. [Obs.]

dis·sen·tā′tion, *n.* act of dissenting. [Obs.]

dis·sent′ẽr, *n.* 1. one who dissents; one who differs in opinion; one who declares his disagreement.
2. one who separates from an established church; especially [D-], in England and Scotland, a Protestant who separates from or who does not unite with the Church of England.

dis·sent′ẽr·iṣm, *n.* the beliefs or doctrine of dissenters.

dis·sen′ti·āte (-shi-), *v.t.* to disturb; to make dissent in. [Obs.]

dis·sen′tient (-shent), *a.* disagreeing; declaring dissent, especially from the majority opinion.

dis·sen′tient, *n.* one who disagrees and declares his dissent.

dis·sen′tious (-shus), *a.* disposed to disagreement or discord. [Rare.]

> In religion they have a *dissentious* head; in the commonwealth a factious head. —Ascham.

dis·sen′tious·ly, *adv.* in a dissentious manner. [Rare.]

dis·sent′ive, *a.* dissenting. [Obs.]

dis·sep′i·ment, *n.* [LL. *dissæpimentum*, a partition, from L. *dissæpire*, to hedge in, separate; *dis-*, apart, and *sæpire*, to hedge in, from *sæpes*, or *sepes*, a hedge.]
1. a partition; a septum.
2. in botany, a partition formed in an ovary by the united sides of cohering carpels, separating the inside into cells.
3. in zoology, the imperfect horizontal plates which connect the vertical septa in corals, and divide the loculi enclosed between the septa into a series of cells communicating with each other.

dis·sẽrt′, *v.i.* to discourse or dissertate. [Rare.]

dis′sẽr·tāte, *v.i.* to discuss formally; to discourse; to write dissertations. [Rare.]

dis·sẽr·tā′tion, *n.* [LL. *dissertatio*, a treatise, discourse, from L. *dissertatus*, pp. of *dissertare*, to discuss; *dis-*, apart, and *serere*, to join.]
1. an elaborate, lengthy, and formal discourse in speech or writing, intended to illustrate a subject.
2. a written essay, treatise, or disquisition, especially one required by colleges and universities as partial fulfillment of requirements for a degree; thesis.
Syn.—disquisition, essay, discourse, treatise.

dis·sẽr·tā′tion·ăl, *a.* pertaining to a dissertation.

dis·sẽr·tā′tion·ist, *n.* one who writes dissertations.

dis′sẽr·tā·tŏr, *n.* one who writes a dissertation; one who dissertates.

dis·sẽrt′ly, *adv.* disertly; eloquently. [Obs.]

dis·sẽrve′, *v.t.*; disserved, *pt., pp.*; disserving, *ppr.* [OFr. *desservir*, to disserve, injure, from L. *dis-* priv., and *servire*, to serve.] to injure; to hurt; to harm; to do injury or a disservice to; as, too much zeal may *disserve* a good cause. [Rare.]

dis·sẽrv′ice, *n.* injury; harm; mischief, as, violent remedies often do a *disservice*.

dis·sẽrv′ice·ȧ·ble, *a.* injurious; hurtful.

dis·sẽrv′ice·ȧ·ble·ness, *n.* the quality of being injurious; tendency to harm.

dis·sẽrv′ice·ȧ·bly, *adv.* in a disserviceable manner.

dis·set′tle, *v.t.* to unsettle. [Obs.]

dis·set′tle·ment, *n.* the act of unsettling.

dis·sev′ẽr, *v.t.*; dissevered, *pt., pp.*; dissevering, *ppr.* [ME. *disseveren*; OFr. *dessevrer*, to sever, from L. *dis-*, apart, and *separare*, to sever, separate.]
1. to cut apart; to separate; to disunite; as, jealousy *dissevers* the bonds of friendship.
2. to divide into parts.

dis·sev′ẽr, *v.i.* to part company; to separate.

dis·sev′ẽr·ănce, *n.* the act of dissevering; separation.

dis·sev·ẽr·ā′tion, *n.* disseverance. [Obs.]

dis·sev′ẽr·ment, *n.* disseverance.

dis·shad′ōw, *v.t.* to bring forth from shadow, shade, or obscurity. [Obs.]

dis·shēathe′, *v.t.* and *v.i.* to draw from, as a sheath; to unsheathe. [Obs.]

dis·ship′, *v.t.* to remove from a ship. [Obs.]

dis·shiv′ẽr, *v.t.* and *v.i.* to shiver; to break into pieces; to shatter. [Obs.]

dis′si·dence, *n.* [L. *dissidentia*, disagreement, from *dissidens* (*-entis*), ppr. of *dissidere*, to disagree.] disagreement; dissent; nonconformity.

dis′si·dent, *n.* one who dissents from others; specifically, (a) one who separates from an established religion; (b) a Protestant or adherent of the Greek church in Poland, who, under the old elective monarchy, was allowed the free exercise of his faith.

dis′si·dent, *a.* not agreeing; dissenting.

dis′si·dent·ly, *adv.* with dissidence.

dis·sil′i·ence, dis·sil′i·en·cy, *n.* the act or quality of springing apart. [Rare.]

dis·sil′i·ent, *a.* [L. *dissiliens*, ppr. of *dissilire*, to leap or burst apart; *dis-*, apart, and *salire*, to leap.]
1. springing apart; bursting apart.
2. in botany, bursting and opening with an elastic force, as the dry pod or capsule of a plant; as, a *dissilient* pericarp.

dis·si·li′tion, *n.* the act of bursting open; the act of springing apart. [Obs.]

dis·sim′i·lăr, *a.* [L. *dissimilis*, unlike; *dis-* priv., and *similis*, like.] unlike in nature, properties, or form; not similar; as, the tempers of men are as *dissimilar* as their features.

dis·sim·i·lar′i·ty, *n.* 1. unlikeness; want of resemblance; dissimilitude; as, the *dissimilarity* of human faces and forms.
2. *pl.* **dis·sim·i·lar′i·ties,** an instance or point of difference, or unlikeness.

dis·sim′i·lăr·ly, *adv.* in a dissimilar manner.

dis·sim′i·lāte, *v.t.* 1. to make dissimilar.
2. to cause to undergo dissimilation.

dis·sim·i·lā′tion, *n.* [from L. *dissimilis*, unlike.]
1. the act of changing similarity to dissimilarity; the process of making unlike.
2. in biology, disassimilation.
3. in linguistics, (a) the mutual repulsion of sounds (phonemes) which are identical, similar, or formed with neighboring tongue positions; especially, (b) the replacement or disappearance of a sound (usually *l*, *r*, or *n*) when it recurs within the same word or form; as, It. *pellegrino* from L. *peregrinus*; Eng. *marble* from OFr. *marbre*.

dis·sim′i·lā·tive, *a.* of or tending toward dissimilation; specifically, in biology, catabolic.

dis·sim′i·lē, *n.* same as *dissimilitude*, sense 2.

dis·si·mil′i·tūde, *n.* [L. *dissimilitudo*, unlikeness, from *dissimilis*, unlike.]
1. unlikeness; difference; lack of resemblance; as, a *dissimilitude* of form or character.
2. in rhetoric, comparison or illustration by contrasts.

dis·sim′ū·lāte, *v.t.*; dissimulated, *pt.*, *pp.*; dissimulating, *ppr.* to hide (one's feelings, motives, etc.) by pretense; to simulate the opposite of.

dis·sim′ū·lāte, *v.i.* to feign; to pretend; to dissemble.

dis·sim′ū·lāte, *a.* feigning; dissembling. [Obs.]

dis·sim·ū·lā′tion, *n.* [ME. *dissimulation*; L. *dissimulatio*, a dissembling, from *dissimulare*, to dissemble; *dis-* priv., and *similis*, like.] the act of dissembling; a hiding under a false appearance; a feigning.

dis·sim′ū·lā·tive, *a.* characterized by dissimulation.

dis·sim′ū·lā·tŏr, *n.* one who dissimulates.

dis·sim′ūle, *v.t.* to dissemble. [Obs.]

dis·sim′ū·lẽr, *n.* one who dissembles. [Obs.]

dis′si·pȧ·ble, *a.* liable to be dissipated; that may be scattered or dispersed. [Rare.]

The heat of those plants is very *dissipable.* —Bacon.

dis′si·pāte, *v.t.*; dissipated, *pt.*, *pp.*; dissipating, *ppr.* [L. *dissipatus*, pp. of *dissipare*, to scatter, disperse; *dis-*, apart, and *supare*, to throw.]

1. to scatter; to disperse; to dispel; as, wind *dissipates* fog.

2. to drive completely away; to make disappear; as, mirth *dissipates* care and anxiety.

3. to expend; to squander, as property or physical or mental powers in wasteful extravagance; to waste; to consume; as, to *dissipate* a fortune in the pursuit of pleasure.

dis′si·pāte, *v.i.* 1. to scatter; to disperse; to separate into parts and disappear; to vanish; as, a fog gradually *dissipates* before the rays of the sun.

2. to be extravagant or reckless in the gratification of one's senses; to waste one's time and energy on frivolities; to indulge in drinking, gambling, etc. to the point of harming oneself.

dis′si·pā·ted, *a.* 1. scattered.

2. squandered; wasted.

3. wasting time and energy on frivolities; indulging in pleasure to excess; dissolute.

4. showing the harmful effects of dissipation.

dis·si·pā′tion, *n.* 1. the act of scattering; dispersion; also, the state of being dispersed; as, the *dissipation* of vapor or heat.

2. any wasteful use of time or energy; frivolous diversion.

3. a wasting or squandering.

4. a dissolute, irregular course of life; excessive indulgence in pleasure; dissoluteness.

What! is it proposed, then, to reclaim the spendthrift from his *dissipation* and extravagance, by filling his pockets with money? —P. Henry.

dis′si·pȧ·tive, *a.* having or exhibiting a tendency toward dissipation.

dissipative system; in physics, a system in which energy is dissipated.

dis″si·pȧ·tiv′i·ty, *n.* in physics, the rate of dissipation of energy divided by two.

dis′si·pā·tŏr, *n.* a person who dissipates: also spelled *dissipater.*

dis′sīte, *a.* separate; found apart. [Obs.]

dis·slan′dẽr, *v.t.* to slander. [Obs.]

dis·slan′dẽr, *n.* defamation; slander. [Obs.]

dis·slan′dẽr·ous, *a.* slanderous. [Obs.]

dis·sō·ciȧ·bil′i·ty (-shi-ȧ- *or* -shȧ-), *n.* 1. lack of sociability; unfriendliness.

2. capability of dissociation.

dis·sō′ciȧ·ble (-shi-ȧ- *or* -shȧ-), *a.* [Fr. *dissociable*, unsociable; L. *dissociabilis*, incompatible, from *dissociare*, to separate; *dis-* priv., and *sociare*, to associate, from *socius*, a companion.]

1. not well associated, assorted, or united; incongruous; ill-matched.

2. capable of being dissociated; separable; distinguishable.

dis·sō′ciă·ble (-shȧ-), *a.* [*dis-*, not, and *sociable*]. unsociable.

dis·sō′ciăl (-shăl), *a.* 1. not social; having a tendency to avoid society.

2. lacking in sympathy and friendship.

dis·sō′ciăl·īze, *v.t.*; dissocialized, *pt.*, *pp.*; dissocializing, *ppr.* to make unsocial; to separate; to disunite.

dis·sō′ci·āte (-shi-āt), *v.t.*; dissociated, *pt.*, *pp.*; dissociating, *ppr.* [L. *dissociatus*, pp. of *dissociare*, to separate from fellowship.]

1. to separate; disconnect; to sever the association of.

2. to think of as separate or distinct.

3. in chemistry, to cause to undergo dissociation.

dis·sō′ci·āte, *v.i.* 1. to part company; to stop associating.

2. in chemistry, to undergo dissociation.

dis·sō·ci·ā′tion, *n.* [L. *dissociatio* (*-onis*), a separation, from *dissociare*, to separate.]

1. the act of taking apart or dissociating; a state of disunion; separation.

2. in chemistry, the breaking up of a compound into simpler components.

3. in psychology, the process in which a group of mental activities breaks away from the main stream of consciousness and functions as a separate unit: an intensified dissociation can lead to multiple personality.

dis·sō′ci·ā·tive (-shi-ā-), *a.* 1. relating to dissociation.

2. causing or tending to cause dissociation.

dis·sol·ū·bil′i·ty, *n.* the quality or state of being dissoluble; solubility.

dis·sol′ū·ble, *a.* [L. *dissolubilis*, from *dissolvere*, to dissolve.]

1. that can be dissolved.

2. capable of being disunited or divided into parts.

dis·sol′ū·ble·ness, *n.* the quality of being dissoluble.

dis′sō·lūte, *a.* [L. *dissolutus*, loose, careless, licentious, pp. of *dissolvere*, to loosen; *dis-*, apart, and *solvere*, to loosen.] loose in behavior and morals; given to vice and dissipation; wanton; lewd; debauched.

Syn.—abandoned, profligate, loose, licentious, wanton, vicious.

dis′sō·lūte·ly, *adv.* in a dissolute manner.

dis′sō·lūte·ness, *n.* looseness of manners and morals; excessive indulgence in pleasure; dissipation.

dis·sō·lū′tion, *n.* [L. *dissolutio*, a breaking up, dissolution, from *dissolutus*, pp. of *dissolvere*, to dissolve.]

1. a dissolving or being dissolved.

2. a breaking up into parts; disintegration.

3. an ending; termination.

4. in finance, the surrender of a charter; liquidation.

5. in law, the annulment of a contract.

6. in chemistry, the reduction of a substance into its components.

7. the substance formed by dissolving a body in a menstruum; solution. [Obs.]

8. death.

9. the adjournment of a formal meeting; the breaking up of an assembly, or the putting an end to its existence.

Dissolution is the civil death of Parliament. —Blackstone.

10. looseness of morals; dissipation. [Obs.]

11. retrogression, as opposed to *evolution.* [Rare.]

diș·șolv·ȧ·bil′i·ty, *n.* solubility.

diș·șolv′ȧ·ble, *a.* capable of being dissolved; capable of being melted or converted into a fluid; as, sugar and ice are *dissolvable*: also spelled *dissolvible.*

diș·șolv′ȧ·ble·ness, *n.* the state of being dissolvable.

diș·șolv′ȧ·tive, *a.* solvent. [Obs.]

diș·șolve′, *v.t.*; dissolved, *pt.*, *pp.*; dissolving, *ppr.* [ME. *dissolven*, from L. *dissolvere*, to loosen; *dis-*, apart, and *solvere*, to loosen.]

1. to convert from a solid to a liquid state by merging with a liquid; to make a solution of; as, to *dissolve* sugar in water.

2. to melt; to liquefy; as, the sun *dissolves* the snow.

3. to disunite; to break up; to decompose; to disintegrate; to cause to separate into parts.

4. to destroy; to end; to terminate; as, to *dissolve* a friendship.

5. to make languid; to relax; as, *dissolved* in pleasure. [Obs.]

6. in law, to annul; to rescind; as, to *dissolve* an injunction.

7. to clear; to solve; to remove; to make disappear; to dissipate or to explain; as, to *dissolve* doubts.

8. in motion pictures, to make fade into or out of view.

diș·șolve′, *v.i.* 1. to be melted; to be converted from a solid to a liquid state; also, to pass into solution.

2. to fade slowly; to vanish by degrees; to disappear; as, the hills *dissolved* in the darkness.

3. to melt away in weakness; to relax; to lose force; to become soft or languid. [Obs.]

4. to fall asunder; to crumble; to be broken; to disunite; to decompose; to disintegrate; as, a government may *dissolve* by its own weight.

5. to waste away; to perish; to end; to terminate.

6. in motion pictures, to fade into or out of view.

dissolved in tears; weeping.

diș·șolve′, *n.* in motion pictures, (a) a fade-in; (b) a fade-out.

diș·șolv′ent, *a.* having power to melt or dissolve other substances; as, the *dissolvent* juices of the stomach.

diș·șolv′ent, *n.* 1. anything which has the power to dissolve; a solvent.

2. in early medicine, a remedy supposed to be capable of dissolving concretions in the body, such as calculi, tubercles, etc. [Obs.]

diș·șolv′ẽr, *n.* one who or that which dissolves or has the power of dissolving.

diș·șolv′ing, *a.* melting; fading.

dissolving view; an effect produced with a magic lantern or motion-picture projector, in which as one view fades from sight another takes its place so gradually that there is neither a pause nor an abrupt change.

diș·șolv′ing·ly, *adv.* in a dissolving manner.

dis′sō·nănce, *n.* [Fr. *dissonance*; LL. *dissonantia*, dissonance, from L. *dissonans*, disagreeing in sound; *dis-*, from, and *sonus*, a sound.]

1. discord; an inharmonious sound or combination of sounds.

2. any lack of harmony or agreement; incongruity; disagreement.

3. in music, a chord that sounds harsh and incomplete until resolved to a harmonious chord.

dis′sō·năn·cy, *n.* same as *dissonance.*

dis′sō·nănt, *a.* 1. discordant; harsh; jarring; inharmonious; unpleasant to the ear; as, *dissonant* notes or intervals.

2. disagreeing; incongruous; opposing in opinion, temperament, etc.: usually with *from* or *to*; as, he advanced propositions very *dissonant from* truth.

dis·spir′it, *v.t.* to dispirit. [Obs.]

dis·suāde′ (-swād′), *v.t.*; dissuaded, *pt.*, *pp.*, dissuading, *ppr.* [L. *dissuadere*, to dissuade; *dis-*, away, from, and *suadere*, to persuade, from *suavis*, sweet.]

1. to advise or exhort against (an action). [Archaic.]

War therefore, open or concealed, alike
My voice *dissuades.* —Milton.

2. to turn (a person) aside (*from* a course, etc.) by giving reasons or motives; as, the minister *dissuaded* the prince *from* adopting the measure.

dis·suād′ẽr, *n.* a person or thing that dissuades.

dis·suā′șion (-swā′), *n.* [L. *dissuasio*, an advising to the contrary, dissuasion, from *dissuadere*, to dissuade.]

1. the act of dissuading; also, the state of being dissuaded; as, the *dissuasion* of friends.

2. a dissuasive motive. [Rare.]

dis·suā′sive, *a.* trying, meant, or tending to dissuade from a measure or purpose.

dis·suā′sive, *n.* reason, argument, or counsel intended to dissuade one from a measure or purpose.

dis·suā′sive·ly, *adv.* in a dissuasive manner.

dis·suā′sō·ry, *a.* and *n.* dissuasive. [Rare.]

dis·sun′dẽr, *v.t.* to separate; to rend. [Obs.]

dis·sweet′en, *v.t.* to deprive of sweetness. [Obs.]

dis·syl·lab′iç, *a.* consisting of two syllables only; as, a *dissyllabic* foot in poetry.

dis·syl·lab″i·fi·çā′tion, *n.* a division into two syllables.

dis·syl·lab′i·fȳ, *v.t.* to divide into two syllables.

dis·syl′lȧ·bīze, *v.t.* same as *dissyllabify.*

dis·syl′lȧ·ble (*or* dis′syl-), *n.* [L. *disyllabus*; Gr. *disyllabos*, of two syllables.] a word consisting of two syllables only, as *paper.*

dis·sym·met′ri·căl, dis·sym·met′riç, *a.* [*dis-* priv., and Gr. *symmetros*, symmetric.]

1. not symmetrical.

2. symmetrical in opposite directions, as are a person's hands.

dis·sym′me·try, *n.*; *pl.* **dis·sym′me·trieș,** 1. a lack or deficiency of symmetry.

2. symmetry in opposite directions, as of a person's hands.

dis·sym′pȧ·thy, *n.* disinterest. [Rare.]

dis′tad, *adv.* in anatomy, away from the center; toward the far extremity; toward the distal aspect of the body.

dis′tȧff, *n.*; *pl.* **dis′tȧffs** or rarely **dis′tȧveṣ,** [ME. *distaf, dystaf*; AS. *distæf*, a distaff.]
1. the staff to which a bunch of flax, wool, or tow is tied, from which the thread is drawn in spinning.

DISTAFF AND SPINDLE

She layeth her hands to the spindle, and her hands hold the *distaff*.—Prov. xxxi. 19.
2. woman's work or concerns.
3. a woman or the female sex.
His crown usurped, a *distaff* on the throne. —Dryden.
Distaff Day or *St. Distaff's Day*; January 7th, the day which marked the resumption of spinning after the festivities of Christmas.
distaff side; the female or maternal line of a family.

dis·tāin′, *v.t.* [ME. *disteinen*; OFr. *desteindre*, to distain, discolor; *dis-* priv., and *tingere*, to tinge, color.]
1. to stain; to tinge; to discolor: mainly used poetically. [Archaic.]
That crown *distained* with gore.—Pope.
2. to blot, sully, defile, tarnish, or disgrace the honor of. [Archaic.]
She *distained* her honorable blood. —Spenser.

dis′tăl, *a.* in biology, farthest removed from the center or the point of attachment or origin; terminal: opposed to *proximal*; as, the *distal* aspect of a bone.

dis′tăl·ly, *adv.* in a distal direction.

dis′tănce, *n.* [ME. *distance*; L. *distantia*, distance, remoteness, from *distans* (*-antis*), ppr. of *distare*, to stand apart, to be separate; *dis-*, off, from, and *stare*, to stand.]
1. an interval or space between two points.
2. an interval between two points in time.
3. the measure of a space or interval; as, a great *distance*.
4. a remoteness in relationship; as, the *distance* between health and illness.
5. remoteness of place; a faraway location.
He waits at *distance* till he hears from Cato. —Addison.
6. a faraway point of time; as, at this *distance* we cannot know Neanderthal man.
7. space or separation; the fact or condition of being separated or removed in space or time; remoteness.
8. contrariety; opposition; discord. [Obs.]
Banquo was your enemy,
So he is mine, and in such bloody *distance*. —Shak.
9. a remoteness in behavior; coolness of manner; reserve; as, I will keep my *distance* from that fellow.
On the part of heaven,
Now alienated, *distance* and distaste. —Milton.
10. remoteness in succession or relation; as, the *distance* between a descendant and his ancestor.
11. in music, the interval between two notes; as, the *distance* of a fourth or seventh.
12. in horse racing, a specified length back from the winning post. If any horse has not reached this point before the first horse in that heat has reached the winning post, such horse is disqualified from running again in future heats of that race.
This was the horse that ran the whole field out of *distance*. —L'Estrange.
13. in painting, the depicting of distance, as in a landscape.
14. in military usage, space between troops, measured from front to rear.
accessible distances; such distances as may be measured by the application of any linear measure.
angular distance; the angle of separation which the directions of two bodies include. Thus, if the spectator's eye be at any point O, and straight lines be drawn from that point to two objects A and B separated from each other, the angle A O B is called the *angular distance* of the two objects.

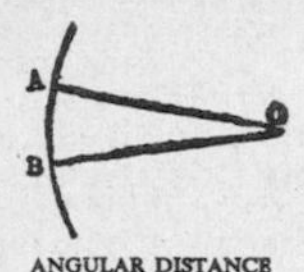

ANGULAR DISTANCE

inaccessible distances; such distances as cannot be measured by the application of any linear measure, but can be measured by means of angles and trigonometrical rules and formulas.
lunar distance; see under *lunar*.
mean distance of a planet; in astronomy, the mean between the aphelion and perihelion distances.
to keep at a distance; to treat aloofly; be reserved or cool toward (someone).
to keep one's distance; to be or remain aloof or reserved.
Syn.—interval, separation, interspace, remoteness, space, length.

dis′tănce, *v.t.*; distanced, *pt., pp.*; distancing, *ppr.* 1. to place or hold at some distance.
2. in racing, to leave behind in a race; to win the race by a great superiority; specifically, to overcome in a race by at least the space between the distance and winning posts.
3. to leave at a great distance behind; to outdo; to excel greatly; to do better or more than.
He *distanced* the most skilful of his contemporaries. —Milner.
4. to cause to appear at a distance; to cause to appear remote or far away.
His peculiar art of *distancing* an object to aggrandize his space. —Miller.

dis′tăn·cy, *n.* distance. [Obs.]

dis′tănt, *a.* 1. separate; apart; having an intervening space of any indefinite extent between.
2. far apart or away; widely separated; remote, as (a) in place; as, a *distant* object appears to be smaller than it actually is; (b) in time, past or future; as, a *distant* age or period of the world; (c) in the line of succession or descent: used indefinitely; as, a *distant* descendant; a *distant* ancestor; (d) in relationship or natural connection or consanguinity; as, a *distant* relation; (e) in kind or nature; hence, not allied; not agreeing with; as, practice very *distant* from principles; (f) in view or prospect; hence, not very likely to be realized; slight; faint; as, a *distant* hope or prospect.
3. away; as, New York is 100 miles *distant*.
4. from or at a distance; remote, or as if remote.
The boy's cry came to her from the field,
More and more *distant*. —Tennyson.
5. indirect; not obvious or plain.
In modest terms and *distant* phrases. —Addison.
6. not cordial; characterized by haughtiness, coldness, indifference, or apathy; reserved.
He passed me with a *distant* bow. —Goldsmith.
Syn.—separate, remote, removed, apart, far, slight, faint, indirect, aloof, haughty, cool.

dis·tan′tiăl (-shăl), *a.* distant. [Obs.]

dis′tănt·ly, *adv.* remotely; at a distance.

dis·tāste′, *n.* 1. aversion; dislike; disrelish: often with *for*; as, a *distaste for* highly seasoned food.
2. discomfort; uneasiness. [Obs.]
Prosperity is not without many fears and *distastes*, and adversity is not without comfort and hopes. —Bacon.
3. displeasure; alienation of affection. [Obs.]
Syn.—disrelish, disinclination, dislike, displeasure, dissatisfaction.

dis·tāste′, *v.t.*; distasted, *pt., pp.*; distasting, *ppr.* 1. to disrelish; to dislike; to have a distaste for; as, to *distaste* drugs. [Obs.]
2. to offend; to disgust; to vex; to displease. [Obs.]

dis·tāste′, *v.i.* to taste bad. [Obs.]

dis·tāste′fụl, *a.* causing distaste; disagreeable; unpleasant; displeasing.

dis·tāste′fụl·ly, *adv.* in a distasteful manner.

dis·tāste′fụl·ness, *n.* disagreeableness; dislike.

dis·tāst′ive, *n.* something distasteful. [Obs.]

dis·tāst′ive, *a.* distasteful. [Obs.]

dis·tās′tūre, *n.* nausea. [Obs.]

dī·stem′ō·nous, *a.* [*di-*, and Gr. *stēmōn*, stamen.] furnished with two stamens.

dis·tem′pẽr, *n.* 1. a bad or unnatural temper.
2. a disproportionate mixture of parts; uneven balance of parts or qualities. [Obs.]
3. disease; malady; indisposition; a mental or physical disorder.
4. an infectious virus disease of young dogs.
5. strangles, a disease of horses.
6. formerly, any of several other infectious diseases of animals, characterized by catarrh, fever, etc.
7. unusual severity of the weather or climate; inclemency. [Obs.]
8. political disorder; tumult.
Syn.—disorder, disease, sickness, malady, indisposition.

dis·tem′pẽr, *v.t.*; distempered, *pt., pp.*; distempering, *ppr.* [ME. *distemperen*; OFr. *destemprer*; LL. *distemperare*, to derange, disorder; L. *dis-* priv., and *temperare*, to temper.]
1. to disease; to disorder; to derange the functions of, as the body or mind.
2. to disturb; to ruffle; to deprive of even temper.
3. to make disaffected, ill-humored, or malignant.
4. to make drunk. [Obs.]

dis·tem′pẽr, *v.t.* [It. *distemperare*, to dissolve or mix with liquid.]
1. to mix (colors or pigments) with water and egg yolks, or size, or some other binding medium.
2. to paint with such a mixture.

dis·tem′pẽr, *n.* 1. a method of painting using distempered pigment, as in mural decoration.
2. distempered paint.
3. painting done in or with distemper.

dis·tem′pẽr·ănce, *n.* distemperature. [Obs.]

dis·tem′pẽr·āte, *a.* 1. immoderate. [Obs.]
2. having distemper. [Obs.]

dis·tem′pẽr·āte·ly, *adv.* in a distemperate manner. [Obs.]

dis·tem′pẽr·ȧ·tūre, *n.* 1. intemperateness; excess of heat or cold, or of other qualities of the weather; as, the *distemperature* of the air or climate. [Rare.]
2. violent tumult; confusion; disorder. [Archaic.]
3. a disordered condition of mind or body. [Archaic.]

dis·tem′pẽr·ment, *n.* a state of being distempered. [Obs.]

dis·tend′, *v.t.* and *v.i.*; distended, *pt., pp.*; distending, *ppr.* [L. *distendere*, to stretch asunder; *dis-*, apart, and *tendere*, to stretch.]
1. to stretch or spread in all directions; to dilate; to enlarge; to expand; to swell, as by pressure from within.
2. to lengthen out in one direction; to extend; to stretch out.

dis·ten·si·bil′i·ty, *n.* the quality or capacity of being distensible.

dis·ten′si·ble, *a.* capable of being distended or dilated.

dis·ten′sion, *n.* same as *distention*.

dis·ten′sive, *a.* distensible; capable of distention.

dis·tent′, *a.* spread; distended.

dis·tent′, *n.* breadth. [Obs.]

dis·ten′tion, *n.* [L. *distentio*, from *distendere*, to stretch apart, distend.] the act of distending; the act of stretching in breadth or in all directions; also, the state of being distended; as, the *distention* of the lungs or bowels.

dis·tẽr′, *v.t.* to banish from a country. [Obs.]

dis·tẽr′mi·nāte, *a.* [L. *disterminatus*.] separated by bounds. [Obs.]

dis·tẽr·mi·nā′tion, *n.* separation. [Obs.]

dis′thēne, *n.* [*di-*, and Gr. *sthenos*, strength.] cyanite: so called because its crystals have the property of being electrified both positively and negatively.

dis·thrōne′, *v.t.* to dethrone.

dis·thrōn′īze, *v.t.* to dethrone. [Obs.]

dis′tịch, *n.* [L. *distichon*; Gr. *distichon*, a distich, from *distichos*, having two rows; *di-*, two, and *stichos*, a row, rank.] a couplet; a couple of verses, or poetic lines, regarded as a unit.

dis′tịch·ous, dis′tịch, *a.* having two rows, or disposed in two rows; specifically, in botany, placed opposite upon the axis in two vertical rows, as certain leaves.

dis′tịch·ous·ly, *adv.* in a distichous manner.

dis·till′, dis·til′, *v.i.*; distilled, *pt., pp.*; distilling, *ppr.* [ME. *distillen*; OFr. *distiller*; L. *distillare*, to drop, to trickle down; *de-*, down, and *stillare*, to drop, from *stilla*, a drop.]
1. to drip; to fall in drops.

Soft showers *distilled*, and suns grew warm in vain. —Pope.
2. to flow gently or in a small stream.
The Euphrates *distilleth* out of the mountains of Armenia. —Raleigh.
3. to use a still; to practice distillation.
4. to undergo distillation.

dis·till′, dis·til′, *v.t.* 1. to let fall in drops; to throw down in drops.
The dew which on the tender grass
The evening had *distilled*. —Drayton.
2. to obtain or extract by the process of distillation; as, to *distill* brandy from wine.
3. to rectify, purify, or refine by or as by distillation; as, to *distill* molasses; to *distill* water.
4. to dissolve or melt. [Rare.]
Swords by the lightning's subtle force *distilled*. —Addison.

dis·till′ȧ·ble, *a.* that may be distilled; fit for distillation.

dis′til·lāte (*or* dis-til′), *n.* the result of distillation; liquid obtained by distilling.

dis·til·lā′tion, *n.* 1. a distilling.
2. the process of first heating a mixture to separate the more volatile from the less volatile parts, and then cooling and condensing the resulting vapor so as to produce a more nearly pure or refined substance: nonvolatile impurities remain in the residue.
3. anything distilled; distillate.
4. the essence of anything.
fractional distillation; see under *fractional*.

dis·til′lȧ·tō·ry, *a.* of or used for distilling; as, *distillatory* vessels.

dis·til′lȧ·tō·ry, *n.* a still or other apparatus for distillation. [Obs.]

dis·tilled′, *a.* produced by distilling.

dis·till′ẽr, *n.* 1. a person or apparatus that distills.
2. a person, company, etc. in the business of making alcoholic liquors produced by distillation.

dis·till′ẽr·y, *n.*; *pl.* **dis·till′ẽr·ies,** 1. a place where distilling is carried on.
2. an establishment or industrial plant where distilled alcoholic liquors are made.
3. the process of distilling. [Obs.]

dis·till′ment, dis·til′ment, *n.* distillation.

dis·tinct′, *a.* [ME. *distinct*; OFr. *distinct*, from L. *distinctus*, pp. of *distinguere*, to distinguish.]
1. not alike; different.
2. not the same; separate; individual.
3. clearly marked off; clear; plain.
4. well-defined; unmistakable; definite.
5. marked; decorated; variegated. [Poetic.]
Distinct with eyes. —Milton.
Syn.—separate, different, disjoined, disunited, well-marked, clear, plain, obvious.

dis·tinct′, *v.t.* to distinguish. [Obs.]

dis·tinc′tion, *n.* [L. *distinctio*, from *distinguere*, to distinguish.]
1. the act of separating or distinguishing; separation; division.
Standards and gonfalons . . . for *distinction* serve. —Milton.
2. a quality, mark, or feature of difference; that which makes or keeps distinct; as, the only *distinction* between the two is the color.
If he does really think that there is no *distinction* between virtue and vice, why, sir, when he leaves our houses, let us count our spoons. —Boswell.
3. difference regarded; regard to distinguishing characteristics or circumstances, as in the phrase, *without distinction*, promiscuously, indiscriminately, all together, alike.
Maids, women, wives, *without distinction*, fall. —Dryden.
4. the power of distinguishing in what respect things differ; discrimination; discernment; judgment.
She (Nature) left the eye *distinction*, to cull out
The one from the other.—Beau. and Fl.
5. eminence; superiority; fame; the state of getting special recognition or honor; as, men who are eminent for their talents, services, or worth are called men of *distinction*.
6. that which confers or marks eminence or special recognition.
Loaded with literary *distinctions*. —Macaulay.
7. the quality that makes one seem superior or worthy of special recognition or honor; as, he fought with *distinction*.
Syn.—division, difference, separation, discernment, discrimination, rank, note, eminence.

dis·tinc′tive, *a.* 1. that marks distinction or difference; distinguishing from others; characteristic; as, *distinctive* names or titles.
2. having the power to distinguish and discern. [Rare.]

dis·tinc′tive·ly, *adv.* with distinction; plainly.

dis·tinc′tive·ness, *n.* state of being distinctive; individuality.

dis·tinct′ly, *adv.* 1. separately. [Obs.]
2. with distinctness; clearly; without the blending of one part or thing with another; as, a proposition *distinctly* understood; a figure *distinctly* defined.
Syn.—clearly, explicitly, definitely, precisely, plainly, obviously.

dis·tinct′ness, *n.* 1. the quality or state of being distinct; a separation or difference that prevents confusion of parts or things; as, the *distinctness* of two ideas or of distant objects.
2. nice discrimination; clearness; precision; as, he stated his arguments with great *distinctness*.

dis·tin·gué′ (dēs-taṅ-gā′), *a.*; *fem.* **dis·tin·guée′** (-gā′), [Fr.] having an air of distinction; distinguished.

dis·tin′guish (-gwish), *v.t.*; distinguished, *pt.*, *pp.*; distinguishing, *ppr.* [ME. *distingwen*; L. *distinguere*, to separate, divide, distinguish.]
1. to indicate difference in by some external mark; to set apart as distinct; as, the farmer *distinguishes* his sheep by marking their ears.
2. to perceive or recognize the individuality of; to note (one thing) as differing from another by some mark or quality; to characterize.
3. to know or ascertain difference in by use of the senses or perceptions; to recognize clearly.
4. to classify or divide by any mark or quality which constitutes difference; to separate by definitions; as, we *distinguish* sounds into high and low, soft and harsh, lively and grave.
5. to separate from others by some mark of honor or preference; to make famous or eminent; as, he *distinguished* himself in chemistry.

dis·tin′guish, *v.i.* 1. to make a distinction; to find or show the difference (often with *between* or *among*); as, a judge will *distinguish between* cases apparently similar.
2. to become distinct or distinguishable; to become differentiated. [Obs.]

dis·tin′guish·ȧ·ble, *a.* 1. capable of being distinguished; that may be separated, perceived, known, or made known, by points of difference; as, a tree at a distance is *distinguishable* from a shrub.
2. worthy of note or special regard. [Obs.]

dis·tin′guish·ȧ·ble·ness, *n.* the state or quality of being distinguishable.

dis·tin′guish·ȧ·bly, *adv.* so as to be distinguished.

dis·tin′guished (-gwisht), *a.* 1. separated or known by a mark of difference, or by different qualities. [Obs.]
2. separated from others by superior or extraordinary qualities; hence, eminent; extraordinary; noted; famous; celebrated; as, *distinguished* men, *distinguished* talents, and *distinguished* services.
3. having an air of distinction.
Distinguished Flying Cross; (a) a decoration given by the United States for heroism or extraordinary achievement in aerial flight against the enemy: instituted in 1917; (b) a similar decoration given by the British government to members of the Royal Air Force.
Distinguished Service Cross; (a) a bronze cross awarded in the United States Army for extraordinary heroism in battle; (b) in England, a British Royal Navy silver cross awarded to naval men below the rank of lieutenant commander for distinguished service against the enemy.
Distinguished Service Medal; (a) a bronze medal awarded in the armed forces of the United States for meritorious service in a duty of great responsibility; (b) in England, a bronze medal awarded to enlisted men in the British Royal Navy or Marines for distinguished service in time of war.
Distinguished Service Order; in England, a gold cross and enameled white ribbon, instituted in 1886, awarded to officers in the Army, Navy, and Royal Air Force for distinguished service in their own particular line of duty.
Syn.—eminent, conspicuous, celebrated, illustrious.—A man is *eminent* when he stands high as compared with those around him; *conspicuous* when he is in a position so as to be easily and generally seen and observed; *distinguished* when he has something which makes him stand apart from others in the public view; *celebrated* when he is widely spoken of with honor and respect; *illustrious* when a splendor is thrown around him which confers the highest dignity.

dis·tin′guished·ly (-gwisht-), *adv.* in a distinguished manner.

dis·tin′guish·ẽr, *n.* one who or that which distinguishes.

dis·tin′guish·ing, *a.* constituting a difference or distinction; distinctive; characteristic; as, the *distinguishing* colors of a bird.
distinguishing pennant; a signaling pennant used to designate a certain ship.

dis·tin′guish·ing·ly, *adv.* with distinction; with some mark of preference.

dis·tin′guish·ment, *n.* distinction; observation of difference. [Obs.]

dis·tī′tle, *v.t.* to deprive of right or title. [Obs.]

Dis′tō·mȧ, *n.* [L., from Gr. *distomos*, two-mouthed; *di-*, two, and *stoma*, a mouth.]
1. a genus of trematode or suctorial parasitical worms or flukes, inhabiting various parts in different animals. *Distoma hepaticum*, or the common liver fluke, is the best known.
2. [d–] any worm of this genus.

dī·stom′ȧ·tous, *a.* of or pertaining to the *Distoma*.

dis·tort′, *v.t.*; distorted, *pt.*, *pp.*; distorting, *ppr.* [L. *distortus*, pp. of *distorquere*, to twist, to turn different ways, to untwist.]
1. to twist out of natural or regular shape; to change the usual shape or appearance of; as, to *distort* the features.
2. to twist mentally or morally.
Wrath and malice, envy and revenge *distort* the understanding. —Tillotson.
3. to alter from the true meaning; to misrepresent; to misstate; to pervert; as, you *distort* the facts.

dis·tort′, *a.* distorted. [Obs.]

dis·tort′ẽr, *n.* one who or that which distorts.

dis·tor′tion, *n.* [L. *distortio*, from *distorquere*, to turn, twist.]
1. the act of distorting; a twisting out of regular shape; a twisting or writhing motion; as, the *distortions* of the face or body.
2. the state of being distorted, or twisted out of shape; deviation from natural shape or position.
3. a perversion of the true meaning; misstatement; misrepresentation.
These absurdities are all framed by a childish *distortion* of my words. —Wren.
4. anything distorted.

dis·tort′ive, *a.* productive of distortion.

dis·tract′, *a.* distracted; also, separate. [Obs.]

dis·tract′, *v.t.*; distracted *or obs.* distraught, *pt.*, *pp.*; distracting, *ppr.* [ME. *distracten*, to distract, from L. *distractus*, pp. of *distrahere*, to draw apart, pull in different directions, distract.]
1. to draw apart; to pull in different directions and separate. [Obs.]
Distract your army, which doth most consist
Of war-mark'd footmen. —Shak.
2. to turn or draw from any object; to divert from any point toward another point, or toward various other objects; as, to *distract* the attention.
If he cannot avoid the eye of the observer, he hopes to *distract* it by a multiplicity of the object. —South.
3. to draw toward different, conflicting objects; to fill with different considerations; to perplex; to confound; to harass; as, to *distract* the mind with cares; you *distract* me with your clamor.
A thousand external details must be left out as irrelevant and only serving to *distract* and mislead the observer. —Caird.
4. to disorder the reason of; to derange the regular operations of the intellect of; to render insane; to craze.
A poor mad soul, . . . poverty hath *distracted* her. —Shak.

dis·tract′ed, *a.* troubled in mind; also, disordered in intellect.
Syn.—deranged, perplexed, mad, frantic, crazed.

dis·tract′ed·ly, *adv.* in a distracted manner.

dis·tract′ed·ness, *n.* the state of being perplexed; madness.

dis·tract′ẽr, *n.* one who or that which distracts.

dis·tract′ful, *a.* distracting. [Obs.]

dis·tract′i·ble, *a.* that may be distracted.

dis·tract′ile, *a.* in botany, having a connective attached to the filament in a horizontal manner, so as to separate the two anther lobes.

dis·traçt'ing, *a.* tending or serving to distract.

dis·traç'tion, *n.* [ME. *distractioun*; L. *distractio*, from *distrahere*, to pull apart.]

1. a drawing apart; separation. [Obs.]

2. a distracting or being distracted; confusion from multiplicity of objects crowding on the mind and drawing the attention different ways; perplexity.

That ye may attend upon the Lord without *distraction*. —1 Cor. vii. 35.

3. anything that distracts; a cause of confusion; as, political *distractions*.

4. madness; a state of disordered reason; insanity.

5. violent mental excitement; extreme perturbation or agony of mind, as from pain or grief; as, this toothache drives me to *distraction*.

This quiet sail is a noiseless wing
To waft me from *distraction*. —Byron.

6. diversity of direction; separate form. [Obs.]

While he was yet in Rome,
His power went out in such *distractions* as,
Beguiled all spies. —Shak.

7. anything calling the mind away from business, study, care, or the like; anything giving the mind a new and less onerous occupation; a diversion; as, after a spell of hard work I found boating a wholesome *distraction*.

8. in Greek grammar, a doubling of two long vowels or the use of two vowels pronounced nearly alike for one.

9. in French law, a diversion of payments from the usual beneficiary to some other person having equitable title to them.

Syn.—perplexity, disturbance, disorder, dissension, tumult, diversion, derangement, insanity, madness, frenzy, recreation.

dis·traç'tious, *a.* distractive. [Obs.]

dis·traçt'ive, *a.* causing perplexity; distracting; confusing; as, *distractive* cares.

dis·trāin', *v.t.*; distrained, *pt.*, *pp.*; distraining, *ppr.* [ME. *distreynen*, to compel, constrain, from L. *distringere*, to pull asunder, to distract.]

1. to tear asunder; to seize; to confine. [Obs.]

2. in law, to seize and hold (property) as security or indemnity for a debt; as, to *distrain* goods for rent or for an amercement.

dis·trāin', *v.i.* to make a seizure of goods to satisfy a claim.

dis·trāin'ȧ·ble, *a.* that is liable to be taken for distress.

dis·trāin·ee', *n.* [*distrain* and *-ee*.] a person whose goods have been seized as security or indemnity for a debt.

dis·trāin'ŏr, dis·trāin'ẽr, *n.* in law, one who seizes goods for debt or service.

dis·trāint', *n.* in law, a distraining; distress.

dis·trāit' (-trā'), *a.* preoccupied; pensive; abstracted; inattentive.

dis·traught' (-trat'), *a.* [ME. *distrauht*, from L. *distractus*, pp. of *distrahere*, to draw apart.]

1. torn apart; rent. [Obs.]

2. distracted; harassed; bewildered; in a state of perplexity.

3. driven mad; crazed.

dis·traught'ed, *a.* distraught. [Obs.]

dis·trēam', *v.i.* to stream or flow down or over. [Obs.]

Yet o'er that virtuous blush *distreams* a tear. —Shenstone.

dis·tress', *n.* [ME. *distresse*; OFr. *destresse*, distress, constraint.]

1. the state of being distressed; extreme pain; anguish of body or mind; great unhappiness.

2. anything that distresses; affliction.

3. a condition of affliction or wretchedness; danger; calamity; bad straits.

4. oppression; compulsion. [Obs.]

5. in law, (a) distraint; (b) the property distrained.

abuse of distress; in law, wrongful use of the powers of distress.

Syn.—suffering, pain, agony, misery, calamity, misfortune, adversity.

dis·tress', *v.t.*; distressed (-trest'), *pt.*, *pp.*; distressing, *ppr.* [ME. *distressen*; OFr. *destresser*, to restrain, constrain, distress, from L. *distringere*, to pull asunder, distract.]

1. to afflict greatly; to afflict with pain or anguish; to harass; to make miserable, unhappy, anxious, etc.; to trouble.

Distress not the Moabites. —Deut. ii. 9.

We are troubled on every side, yet not *distressed*. —2 Cor. iv. 8.

2. to compel or constrain by pain or suffering.

Men who can neither be *distressed* nor won into a sacrifice of duty. —Hamilton.

3. in law, to distrain.

Syn.—pain, grieve, afflict, harass, trouble, perplex.

dis·tress'ed·ness, *n.* a state of being greatly pained or distressed.

dis·tress'fụl, *a.* 1. inflicting or bringing distress; accompanied by distress; causing distress; as, *distressful* pains, a *distressful* sight.

2. feeling or expressing distress.

dis·tress'fụl·ly, *adv.* in a distressful manner.

dis·tress'ing, *a.* painful; harassing; annoying; causing distress.

dis·tress'ing·ly, *adv.* in a distressing manner.

dis·trib'ū·tȧ·ble, *a.* capable of distribution.

dis·trib'ū·tȧ·ry, *n.* any branch of a river that flows away from the main stream and does not rejoin it, as in the delta of a river: opposed to *tributary*.

dis·trib'ūte, *v.t.*; distributed, *pt.*, *pp.*; distributing, *ppr.* [L. *distributus*, pp. of *distribuere*, to divide, distribute; *dis-*, apart, and *tribuere*, to give, from *tribus*, tribe.]

1. to divide among two or more; to deal out; to give or bestow in parts or portions; to allot; as, Moses *distributed* lands to the tribes of Israel.

Walk your dim cloister, and *distribute* dole. —Tennyson.

2. to scatter or spread out, as over a surface.

3. to put (things) in various distinct places.

4. to dispense; to administer; as, to *distribute* justice. [Archaic.]

5. to divide and arrange according to a classification, as into classes, orders, genera, and species.

6. in printing, (a) to break up and return to their separate compartments (the type used in composed matter or pi); (b) to spread, while being worked, as on a form or roller: said of ink.

7. in law, to apportion (an intestate's property) to those entitled to it.

8. in logic, to employ in its full extent, as a term, so as to refer to every individual denoted.

9. in the postal service, to place (the various pieces of mail) in the proper receptacle.

Syn.—dispense, deal out, apportion, partition, allot, share, assign.

dis·trib'ūte, *v.i.* to make an allotment, distribution, or division.

dis·trib·ū·tee', *n.* in law, one of those to whom an intestate's property is to be apportioned.

dis·trib'ū·tẽr, *n.* one who or that which distributes.

dis·tri·bū'tion, *n.* [L. *distributio*, from *distribuere*, to distribute.]

1. a distributing or being distributed; the act of dividing among a number; allotment in parts or portions; as, the *distribution* of an estate among heirs or children.

2. the manner of being distributed; as, an equal *distribution* of property.

3. the system or process of distributing commodities to consumers.

4. the act of giving in charity; the bestowing in portions.

Of great riches there is no real use except it be in the *distribution*. —Bacon.

5. dispensation; administration to numbers; a rendering to individuals; as, the *distribution* of justice. [Archaic.]

6. the act of separating into distinct parts or classes; classification; systematic arrangement; as, the *distribution* of plants into genera or species.

7. in logic, the application of a universal whole to its several kinds or species.

8. in architecture, the dividing and arranging of the several parts of the building according to some plan.

9. in rhetoric, a division and enumeration of the several qualities of a subject.

10. in printing, (a) the returning of type to its proper compartment in a case; (b) the spreading of ink, as on a disk or rollers.

11. in steam engines, the operation by which steam is admitted into and withdrawn from the cylinder at each stroke of the piston.

12. that which is distributed; portion; share.

Our charitable *distributions*.—Atterbury.

13. in statistics, the arrangement of a set of numbers classified according to some property, as frequency, or to some other criterion, as time or location.

geographical distribution; in botany and zoology, that branch of the respective sciences which treats of the distribution of plants and animals over the surface of the earth.

Syn.—apportionment, allotment, partition, arrangement, classification, dispensation, disposal.

dis·tri·bū'tion·ăl, *a.* relating to distribution.

dis·trib'ū·tive, *a.* 1. that distributes or tends to distribute; that divides and assigns in portions; that deals to each his proper share; as, *distributive* justice.

2. relating to distribution.

3. referring to each member of a group regarded individually.

4. in logic, distributed in a given proposition: said of a term.

5. expressing separation, distribution, or division; specifically, in grammar, taking individually the persons or things that make a number; as, *each* is a *distributive* adjective.

6. in mathematics, of the principle in multiplication that allows the multiplier to be used separately with each term of the multiplicand.

dis·trib'ū·tive, *n.* in grammar, a distributive word or expression, as *each* or *every*.

dis·trib'ū·tive·ly, *adv.* in a distributive manner or sense; singly; individually.

dis·trib'ū·tive·ness, *n.* the state or quality of being distributive.

dis·trib'ū·tŏr, *n.* 1. one who or that which distributes.

2. in printing, (a) a roller to facilitate the distribution of ink; (b) a machine to effect type distribution.

3. an agent or business firm that distributes goods to consumers.

4. a device for distributing electric current to the spark plugs of a gasoline engine so that they fire in proper order.

dis·trib'ū·tŏr·ship″, *n.* a franchise held by a distributor.

dis'triçt, *n.* [Fr. *district*; LL. *districtus*, in feudal law a territory within which a lord had the right to administer jurisdiction, a district; from L. *districtus*, pp. of *distringere*, to stretch or draw in different directions, to distrain; *dis-*, apart, and *stringere*, to draw.]

1. a geographical or political division made for a specific purpose; as, a school *district*.

2. any region; part of a country, city, etc.; as, the business *district*.

Congressional district; see under *congressional*.

district attorney; a lawyer elected or appointed to represent the people within a certain district to serve as prosecutor for the state in criminal cases.

district court; see under *court*.

district judge; the judge of a district court.

district school; a school for the pupils of a certain district.

Syn.—division, quarter, locality, province, tract, region, country.

dis'triçt, *v.t.*; districted, *pt.*, *pp.*; districting, *ppr.* to divide into districts or limited portions of territory; as, legislatures *district* states for the choice of representatives.

dis'triçt, *a.* stringent; exacting. [Obs.]

dis·trin'gas, *n.* [L., lit., that you may distrain, from 2d pers. sing. pres. subj. of *distringere*, to distrain.] in law, a writ commanding the sheriff to distrain a person for debt.

dis·trust', *n.* 1. doubt; suspicion; lack of confidence, faith, or reliance; as, *distrust* mars many pleasures.

2. loss of confidence; discredit. [Rare.]

Syn.—diffidence, suspicion, doubt, skepticism.

dis·trust', *v.t.*, distrusted, *pt.*, *pp.*; distrusting, *ppr.* to doubt or suspect the truth, fidelity, firmness, or sincerity of; to have no trust, faith, or confidence in; as, we may often *distrust* our own firmness.

dis·trust'ẽr, *n.* one who distrusts.

dis·trust'fụl, *a.* distrusting; doubting.

distrustful of; suspicious of; having no confidence in.

dis·trust'fụl·ly, *adv.* in a distrustful manner.

dis·trust'fụl·ness, *n.* the state of being distrustful; lack of confidence.

dis·trust'ing·ly, *adv.* suspiciously.

dis·trust'less, *a.* free from distrust. [Obs.]

dis·tūne', *v.t.* to put out of tune. [Obs.]

dis·tŭrb', *v.t.*; disturbed, *pt.*, *pp.*; disturbing, *ppr.* [ME. *distorben*; L. *disturbare*, to drive asunder, tear in pieces; *dis-*, apart, and *turbare*, to disorder, throw into confusion.]

1. to stir; to move; to discompose; to excite from a state of rest or tranquillity; to disquiet.

2. to make uneasy or anxious; to agitate the mind of; to move the passions of; to ruffle.

3. to move from any regular course or operation; to interrupt regular order of; to make irregular; as, don't *disturb* my things.

4. to break in on; interrupt; interfere with.
5. to inconvenience; as, please don't *disturb* yourself.

dis·tŭrb′, *n.* confusion; disorder; disturbance. [Obs.]

dis·tŭrb′ănce, *n.* [ME. *disturbance*; OFr. *destourbance*, from *destourber*; L. *disturbare*, to disturb.]
1. a disturbing or being disturbed; a stirring or excitement; any disquiet or interruption of peace; as, to move without *disturbance*.
2. interruption of a settled state of things; disorder; tumult; as, the *disturbances* of war.
3. the state of being worried, troubled, or anxious; agitation; excitement of passion; perturbation; disorder of thoughts.

They can survey a variety of complicated ideas, without fatigue or *disturbance*. —Watts.

4. anything that disturbs.
5. in law, the hindering or disquieting of a person in the lawful and peaceable enjoyment of his right; the interruption of a right; as, the *disturbance* of a franchise.

dis·tŭr·bā′tion, *n.* disturbance. [Obs.]

dis·tŭrb′ẽr, *n.* 1. one who or that which disturbs or disquiets.
2. in law, one that interferes with another's peaceable enjoyment of his right.

dis·tŭrn′, *v.t.* to turn aside. [Obs.]

dis′tȳle, *n.* [*di-*, and Gr. *stylos*, column.] a portico having two columns.

dis′tȳle, *a.* pertaining to a two-columned portico.

dī·sul′fāte, *n.* [*di-* and *sulfate.*]
1. a salt of disulfuric acid.
2. a chemical compound containing two sulfate groups per molecule.
3. a bisulfate.

dī·sul′fīde, *n.* [*di-* and *sulfide.*] a chemical compound in which two sulfur atoms are united with a single radical or with a single atom of an element; as, carbon *disulfide*, CS_2.

dī·sul′fū·ret, *n.* a disulfide.

dī·sul·fū′riç ac′id, an acid, $H_2S_2O_7$, whose molecule is composed of two molecules of sulfuric acid minus one molecule of water: also called *pyrosulfuric acid*.

dis·ū′ni·form, *a.* not uniform.

dis·ŭn′iŏn (-yun), *n.* 1. a breaking of a tie or bond; separation.
2. absence of unity; dissension; disagreement; discord.

dis·ŭn′iŏn·ist, *n.* 1. a person who advocates or tries to cause disunion.
2. a person who advocated secession of some State or States from the United States (during the Civil War period).

dis·ū·nīte′, *v.t.*; disunited, *pt.*, *pp.*; disuniting, *ppr.* 1. to separate; to disjoin; to part; as, to *disunite* particles of matter.
2. to set at variance; to interrupt the harmony of; to make disagree; as, to *disunite* a delegation.

dis·ū·nīte′, *v.i.* to come apart; to become separate.

dis·ū·nīt′ẽr, *n.* one who or that which disjoins.

dis·ū′ni·ty, *n.* a state of separation; disunion.

dis·ūs′āġe, *n.* gradual cessation of use or custom; neglect of use, exercise, or practice; disuse. [Rare.]

dis·ūṣe′, *v.t.*; disused, *pt.*, *pp.*; disusing, *ppr.*
1. to cease to use.
2. to disaccustom: with *from*, *in*, or *to*; as, *disused to* toils. [Obs.]

dis·ūse′, *n.* the fact or state of being or becoming disused; cessation of use, practice, or exercise; as, the limbs lose their strength by *disuse*.

dis·ū·til′i·ty, *n.* a lack of utility; quality of being harmful; inconvenience.

dis·ū′til·īze, *v.t.* to deprive of usefulness.

dis·val·ū·ā′tion, *n.* disesteem; disreputation. [Obs.]

dis·val′ūe, *v.t.* to undervalue; to disesteem; to regard as of no value. [Rare.]

dis·val′ūe, *n.* disesteem; disregard. [Obs.]

dis·van·tā′ġeous (-jus), *a.* disadvantageous. [Obs.]

dis·vel′ŏp, *v.t.* to develop. [Obs.]

dis·ven′tūre, *n.* a misadventure. [Obs.]

dis·vouch′, *v.t.* to discredit; to contradict. [Obs.]

dis·wạrn′, *v.t.* to dissuade from by previous warning. [Obs.]

dis·wär′ren, *v.t.* in old English law, to rid (land) of the privilege of warren.

dis·wit′ted, *a.* deprived of wits or understanding. [Obs.]

dis·wŏnt′, *v.t.* to rid or deprive of wonted usage. [Obs.]

dis·wŏrk′măn·ship, *n.* bad or defective workmanship. [Obs.]

dis·wŏr′ship, *v.t.* to deprive of reverence; to refuse to revere or worship; to dishonor. [Obs.]

dis·wŏr′ship, *n.* a deprivation or withholding of worship, reverence, or honor. [Obs.]

dis·wŏrth′, *v.t.* to make worthless; to lower in value. [Obs.]

di·syl·lab′iç, *a.* dissyllabic.

di·syl′lȧ·ble, *n.* a dissyllable.

dis·yōke′, *v.t.*; disyoked, *pt.*, *pp.*; disyoking, *ppr.* to take off the yoke of; to unyoke; to free from, or as from, a yoke.

dit, *v.t.* to stop up or close up. [Dial.]

dit, *n.* 1. a word; a sentence; a saying; a decree. [Obs.]
2. a ditty. [Archaic.]

dī′tȧ bärk, [Tagalog *dita*, the name of the tree.] the bitter bark of the devil tree, used for medicinal purposes.

di·tā′tion, *n.* the act of making rich. [Obs.]

ditch (dich), *n.*; *pl.* **ditch′eṣ**, [ME. *diche*; AS. *dic*, a ditch, dike.]
1. a long, narrow trench in the earth made by digging, usually for carrying water; a trench for draining wet land, irrigating the soil, or for making a fence to guard enclosures, etc.
2. a trench for preventing an enemy from approaching a town or fortress: called also a *fosse* or *moat*. It is dug round the rampart or wall between the scarp and counterscarp.
3. any long, hollow channel for water on the earth's surface.

ditch, *v.t.*; ditched (dicht), *pt.*, *pp.*; ditching, *ppr.* 1. to dig a ditch or ditches in; to drain by a ditch.
2. to surround with a ditch.
3. to throw into a ditch; to derail (a train).
4. to desert or get rid of. [Slang.]

ditch, *v.i.* to dig or make a ditch or ditches.

ditch′ẽr, *n.* [ME. *dichere*; AS. *dicere*, a digger, a ditcher, from *dic*, a ditch.]
1. one who digs ditches.
2. a machine for digging ditches or trenches.

ditch′wạ″tẽr, *n.* stagnant, bad water, such as is found in a ditch.

dīte, *v.t.* to prepare; to dight; to make ready. [Obs.]

dī·tē·trag′ō·năl, *a.* [*di-*, and Gr. *tetragōnos*, a four-angled figure; *tetra*, four, and *gōnia*, an angle.] in crystallography, denoting a tetragonal prism, having eight similar faces.

dī·tet·rȧ·hē′drăl, *a.* [*di-*, and Gr. *tetra-*, four, and *hedra*, base.] in crystallography, having the form of a tetrahedral prism with dihedral summits. [Obs.]

di·thē′căl, dī·thē′çous, *a.* [*di-*, and Gr. *thēkē*, a case.] in botany, having two cells or cavities in the ovary.

dī′thē·iṣm, *n.* [*di-*, and Gr. *theos*, god.]
1. the doctrine that there are two supreme gods; dualism.
2. the belief in two universal forces, as of good and of evil.

dī′thē·ist, *n.* one who believes in ditheism; a dualist.

dī·thē·is′tiç, dī·thē·is′tiç·ăl, *a.* of, pertaining to, or characterized by ditheism; dualistic.

dith′ẽr, *n.* great agitation or excitement; a state of distraction.

dith′ẽr, *v.i.* to tremble; to be excited.

dī·thī·on′iç ac′id, an acid, $H_2S_2O_6$, having two sulfur atoms in each molecule and existing only in salts or solutions.

dith′y·ramb (-ram), *n.* [L. *dithyrambus*; Gr. *dithyrambos*, dithyramb.]
1. in ancient Greek poetry, a wild and emotional choric hymn in honor of Dionysus, composed in an elevated style, and sung to the music of the flute.
2. any wildly emotional, enthusiastic song, speech, or writing of an impetuous and irregular character.

dith·y·ram′biç, *a.* 1. pertaining to a dithyramb.
2. wildly emotional or enthusiastic.

dith·y·ram′biç, *n.* a dithyramb.

dī′tion, *n.* rule; power; government. [Obs.]

dī′tion·ā·ry, *a.* and *n.* tributary. [Obs.]

dit′ō·kous, *a.* [Gr. *ditokos*, twin or twice bearing; *di-*, two, and *tokos*, an offspring, from *tiktein*, to bear, bring forth.] in zoology, (a) producing two eggs or young at one time; (b) producing two kinds of young, as certain worms.

dī·tol′yl, *n.* the double radical, $C_{14}H_{14}$, of the hydrocarbon tolyl.

dī′tōne, *n.* [Gr. *ditonon*, a major third; *di-*, two, and *tonos*, tone.] in music, an interval comprehending two major tones.

Dī·trē′mȧ·tȧ, *n.pl.* [L., from Gr. *di-*, two, and *trēma*, a hole.]
1. a family of fishes, the *Ditremidæ*.
2. a group of gastropods having widely separated male and female orifices.

dī·trē′mȧ·tous, *a.* of or pertaining to the *Ditremata*; having two genital apertures.

dī·trē′mid, *n.* any of the *Ditremidæ*.

Dī·trē′mi·dae, *n.pl.* a family of viviparous fishes having an anal and a genital orifice.

dī·trī·çhot′ō·mous, *a.* divided into parts numbering two and three; specifically, in botany, branching two and then three times.

dī·trī′glyph, *n.* [*di-*, and L. *triglyphus*; Gr. *triglyphos*, three-grooved, a triglyph; *treis*, three,

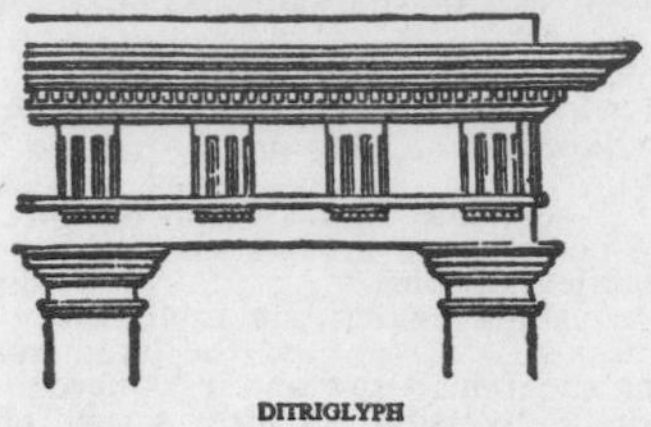

DITRIGLYPH

and *glyphein*, to hollow out.] in architecture, an interval between two columns, admitting two triglyphs in the entablature: used in the Doric order.

dī·trig′ō·năl, *a.* in crystallography, having six sides.

dī·trō·çhē′ăn, *a.* made up of two trochees.

dī·trō′çhee, *n.* [LL. *ditrochæus*; Gr. *ditrochaios*, a double trochee.] in prosody, a double trochee; a foot made up of two trochees.

dit′rō·īte, *n.* [from *Ditro* in Transylvania.] a rock of igneous origin, a nepheline-syenite having sodalite and spinel as constituents.

ditt, *n.* a ditty. [Obs.]

dit·tan′dẽr, *n.* [ME. *ditaundere*, from *ditane*, dittany.] pepperwort, *Lepidium latifolium*, a cruciferous herb found in salt marshes.

dit′tȧ·ny, *n.*; *pl.* **dit′tȧ·nieṣ**, [ME. *ditane*; L. *dictamnum*; Gr. *diktamnon*, the dittany plant, so called from Mount Dicte in Crete, where it grew in abundance.]
1. a pink-flowered mint.
2. a shrubby plant with flowers that give off an inflammable vapor; fraxinella.
3. a plant of the mint family, with oval leaves and clusters of purplish flowers.

dit′tāy, *n.* in Scots law, the matter of charge or ground of indictment against a person accused of a crime; also, the charge itself.

dit′tied (-tid), *a.* sung; adapted to music; as, sweet-*dittied* verse. [Rare or Poet.]

dit′tō, *n.*; *pl.* **dit′tōṣ**, [It. *ditto*; L. *dictum*, a saying, from *dicere*, to say.]
1. the same (as something said or appearing above or before).
2. a duplicate; another of the same.
3. a ditto mark.

dit′tō, *v.t.*; dittoed, *pt.*, *pp.*; dittoing, *ppr.* to repeat; to duplicate; to copy.

dit′tō, *adv.* as before mentioned; in a like manner; as before.

dit′tō·gram, *n.* an unintentional repetition of a letter or letters in writing or copying.

dit·tog′rȧ·phy, *n.* [Gr. *dittos*, *dissos*, double, and *graphein*, to write.] the accidental repetition of a letter or letters in writing or copying.

dit·tol′ō·ġy, *n.* a twofold interpretation or reading.

dit′tō mȧ·çhine′, a machine for duplicating writings or drawings: a trade-mark (*Ditto machine*).

dit′tō märk, a mark (") used in itemized lists or tables to show that a word, figure, or passage above is to be repeated. Example:
4 hrs. overtime Sat.
2 " " Mon.

dit′ty, *n.*; *pl.* **dit′tieṣ**, [ME. *dite*; OFr. *ditē*, a song, a little poem, a story, from L. *dictatum*, a thing dictated.]
1. a short, simple song.

And to the warbling lute soft *ditties* sing. —Sandys.

2. a saying, especially one frequently repeated. [Obs.]

dit′ty, *v.i.* to sing. [Obs.]

dit′ty bag, [from obs. *dutty*, coarse calico.] a small bag used by sailors or soldiers for carrying sewing equipment, toilet articles, etc.

dit′ty box, a ditty bag.

dī·ū′rē·ide, *n.* a compound containing two molecules of urea.

dī·ū·rē′sis, *n.* [Gr. *diourein*, to urinate; *dia-*,

through, and *ourein*, to urinate, from *ouron*, urine.] increase in urine secretion.

dī·ū·ret'iç, *a.* [Gr. *diourētikos*, promoting urine, from *diourein*, to urinate.] increasing the urinary discharge.

dī·ū·ret'iç, *n.* a diuretic drug.

dī·ū·ret'iç·ăl, *a.* diuretic.

dī·ū·ret'iç·ăl·ness, *n.* the state of being diuretical.

dī·ūr'năl, *a.* [ME. *diurnal*; L. *diurnalis*, day by day, from *diurnus*, daily, from *dies*, day.]
1. relating to a day; pertaining to the daytime; as, *diurnal* heat, *diurnal* hours: opposed to *nocturnal*.
2. daily; happening every day; performed in a day; as, a *diurnal* task.
3. performed in twenty-four hours; as, the *diurnal* revolution of the earth.
4. in entomology, living for one day.
5. in botany, opening by day and closing by night, as the morning glory and other flowers.
6. in zoology, active during the day, as certain birds of prey.
diurnal arc; the apparent arc described by heavenly bodies from their rising to their setting.
diurnal circle; see under *circle*.

dī·ūr'năl, *n.* 1. a daybook; a journal. [Archaic.]
2. in zoology, (a) a raptorial bird which flies by day; (b) a lepidopterous insect which is active only during the day.
3. a daily newspaper. [Archaic.]
4. in the Roman Catholic Church, a small book containing the prayers for the canonical hours of the day. [Archaic.]

dī·ūr'năl·ist, *n.* a journalist. [Obs.]

dī·ūr'năl·ly, *adv.* 1. daily; every day.
2. by day; in or during the daytime.

dī·ūr'năl·ness, *n.* the quality of being diurnal.

dī·ūr·nā'tion, *n.* the somnolent state in the daytime of nocturnal animals, as bats, in contrast to their activity at night.

dī·ū·tūr'năl, *a.* [L. *diuturnus*, of long duration, from *diu*, a long time, by day, from *dies*, a day.] lasting; being of long continuance. [Rare.]

dī·ū·tūr'ni·ty, *n.* length of time; long duration. [Rare.]

dī'vä, *n.*; *pl.* **dī'väṣ,** It. **dī've,** [It., from L. *diva*, a goddess, f. of *divus*, a god.] a prima donna; a leading woman singer, especially in grand opera.

dī'vȧ·gāte, *v.i.*; divagated, *pt., pp.*; divagating, *ppr.* [from pp. of L. *divagari*, to wander about, from *dis-*, from, and *vagari*, to wander.]
1. to wander about.
2. to stray from the subject; digress.

dī·vȧ·gā'tion, *n.* a divagating; a digression.

dī'vā·lent (*or* div'ȧ-lent), *a.* [*di-*, and L. *valens* (*-entis*), ppr. of *valere*, to be powerful.]
1. in chemistry, having a valence of two.
2. having two valences.
Also, especially for sense 2, *bivalent*.

di·van', *n.* [Turk. *dīwān*; Per. *dīvān, dīwān*, a council.]
1. in Oriental countries, a royal council or council room.
2. (*or* dī'van), a large, low couch or sofa, usually without arm rests or back.
3. (*or* dī'van), a coffee room, café, or smoking room.
4. a book of poems, especially one containing the works of a single poet.

dī·var'i·çāte, *v.t.*; divaricated, *pt., pp.*; divaricating, *ppr.* [L. *divaricatus*, pp. of *divaricare*, to spread apart.] to branch or spread widely apart.

dī·var'i·çāte, *v.i.* to split into two parts; to fork; to branch.

dī·var'i·çāte, *a.* 1. in botany, branching off, as from a stem or axis, at or almost at a right angle.
2. in zoology, the divisions of any part that spread out widely.

dī·var'i·çāte·ly, *adv.* in a divaricate manner.

dī·var·i·çā'tion, *n.* [L. *divaricare*, to spread apart.]
1. a divaricating; forking; branching apart.
2. a difference of opinion.

dī·var'i·çā·tŏr, *n.* in zoology, a muscle which separates parts, as the one opening the shell of a bivalve.

dīve, *v.i.*; dived *or* dove, *pt.*; dived, *pp.*; diving, *ppr.* [ME. *diven, dyven*; AS. *dyfan*, to dive.]
1. to plunge head first into water; as, to *dive* from a springboard.
2. to go suddenly under water; as, a submarine *dives*.
3. to plunge the hand or body suddenly into a substance or opening; as, he *dived* into his foxhole.
4. to vanish from sight suddenly.
5. in aviation, to make a steep, sudden descent.

dīve, *v.t.* 1. to plunge (a hand, head, etc.) into something.
2. to explore or penetrate by or as by diving.
3. to send (one's airplane) into a dive.

dīve, *n.* 1. a plunge head first into water.
2. any sudden plunge or submersion; as, a *dive* into a net.
3. a cheap, disreputable saloon, etc. [Colloq.]
4. in aviation, a rapid descent.

dīve bomb'ẽr (bom'), an airplane of the bomber type which releases its bombs while diving at the target.

dī·vel'lent, *a.* [L. *divellens* (*-entis*), ppr. of *divellere*, to pull asunder.] drawing asunder; separating. [Rare.]

dīv'ẽr, *n.* 1. one who or that which dives; as, a *diver* for pearls.
2. a person whose occupation is diving or working under water.
3. a bird characterized by its habit of diving, as the grebe, loon, etc.; specifically, the *Colymbidæ*, a family of swimming birds, (*Natatores*). They prey upon fish, which they pursue under water. The leading species are the great northern diver, the red-throated diver, and the black-throated diver.

RED-THROATED DIVER
(*Colymbus septentrionalis*)

dī'vẽrb, *n.* [L. *diverbium*, the dialogue of a comedy; *di-, dis-*, apart, and *verbum*, a word.] a proverb. [Obs.]

dī·vẽr'bẽr·āte, *v.t.* to penetrate or ring through, as sound. [Obs.]

dī·vẽr·bẽr·ā'tion, *n.* a sounding through. [Obs.]

di·vẽrġe', *v.i.*; diverged, *pt., pp.*; diverging, *ppr.* [Mod.L. *divergere*; L. *dis-*, apart, and *vergere*, to turn, incline.]
1. to go in different directions from a common point or from each other: opposed to *converge*; as, the sides of an angle *diverge* from the apex.
2. to differ from a typical form; to vary from a normal state; to deviate.

di·vẽrġe'ment, *n.* the act of diverging.

di·vẽr'ġence, *n.* 1. the act or state of diverging or branching off; a going farther apart; as, the *divergence* of lines.
2. deviation or departure from a norm; difference; as, *divergence* from truth.

di·vẽr'ġen·cy, *n.*; *pl.* **di·vẽr'ġen·cieṣ,** same as *divergence*.

di·vẽr'ġent, di·vẽr'ġing, *a.* 1. departing or going in different directions from each other; as, *divergent* lines, *divergent* paths.
2. disagreeing with or differing from some standard; deviating; variant.

di·vẽr'ġing·ly, *adv.* in a diverging manner.

dī'vẽrṣ, *a.* [ME. *divers*; OFr. *divers*, different, several, from L. *diversus*, pp. of *divertere*, to turn in different directions.]
1. different; various. [Archaic.]
Thou shalt not sow thy vineyard with *divers* seeds. —Deut. xxii. 9.
2. several; sundry; more than one, but not a great number; as, we have *divers* examples of this kind.

dī'vẽrse (*or* di-vẽrs'), *a.* [L. *diversus*, pp. of *divertere*, to turn in different directions.]
1. different; differing.
Four great beasts came up from the sea, *diverse* one from another. —Dan. vii. 3.
2. capable of assuming various and different forms; varied; diversified.
Eloquence is a *diverse* thing. —Jonson.

di·vẽrse', *adv.* in different directions; diversely.

di·vẽrse', *v.i.* to turn aside. [Obs.]

dī'vẽrse·ly (*or* di-vẽrs'ly), *adv.* in different directions or ways; differently; variously.

di·vẽrse'ness, *n.* the quality of being diverse.

di·vẽr·si·fī·ȧ·bil'i·ty, *n.* the quality or state of being diversifiable.

di·vẽr'si·fī·ȧ·ble, *a.* capable of diversification.

di·vẽr″si·fi·çā'tion, *n.* [L. *diversus*, diverse, and *facere*, to make.] the act of diversifying or the state of being diversified; variation; change; as, *diversification* of voice.

di·vẽr'si·fīed, *a.* distinguished by various forms, or by a variety of objects; varied; as, *diversified* tasks.

di·vẽr'si·fī·ẽr, *n.* one who or that which diversifies.

di·vẽr·si·flō'rous, *a.* [L. *diversiflorus*; *diversus*, different, and *flos* (*floris*), a flower.] having two or more kinds of flowers.

di·vẽr·si·fō'li·ous, *a.* [L. *diversus*, different, and *folium*, a leaf.] having leaves which differ in form, color, etc.

di·vẽr'si·fọrm, *a.* [L. *diversus*, different, and *forma*, form.] of a different form; of various forms, or shapes.

di·vẽr'si·fȳ, *v.t.*; diversified, *pt., pp.*; diversifying, *ppr.* [Fr. *diversifier*; ML. *diversificare*, to make different; L. *diversus*, different, and *facere*, to make.] to make different or various in form or quality; to give variety to; to vary.

di·vẽr'ṣion, *n.* 1. the act of turning aside; diverting (*from*); as, the *diversion* of a stream *from* its usual channel.
2. anything that diverts or distracts the attention; hence, a pastime; an amusement.
3. distraction of attention; as, *diversion* of the enemy.
Syn. amusement, entertainment, pastime, recreation, sport.

di·vẽr'ṣion·ăr·y, *a.* having the nature of a diversion; especially, in military usage, serving to distract the enemy from the main point of attack; as, *diversionary* tactics.

di·vẽr'si·ty, *n.*; *pl.* **di·vẽr'si·tieṣ,** [ME. *diversite*; L. *diversitas*, difference, from *divertere*, to turn in different directions.]
1. quality, state, fact, or instance of being diverse; difference; dissimilitude; unlikeness; as, there is a great *diversity* in human constitutions.
2. variety; multiformity; as, a *diversity* of ceremonies in churches.
3. variegation.
Blushing in bright *diversities* of day. —Pope.

dī·vẽr·siv'ō·lent, *a.* [L. *diversus*, different, and *volens* (*-entis*), ppr. of *velle*, to wish.] desiring trouble or differences. [Rare.]

di·vẽr'sō·ry, *a.* tending to divert. [Obs.]

di·vẽr'sō·ry, *n.* [L. *diversorium*, an inn.] an inn by the wayside; a lodging place. [Obs.]

di·vẽrt', *v.t.*; diverted, *pt., pp.*; diverting, *ppr.* [ME. *diverten*; OFr. *divertir*; L. *divertere*, to turn in different directions.]
1. to turn (a person or thing) aside (*from* a course); to deflect; as, to *divert* a river *from* its usual channel; to *divert* appropriated money to other objects.
2. to distract the attention of; hence, to please; to amuse; to entertain; as, children are *diverted* with sports.

di·vẽrt', *v.i.* to turn in another direction; to digress. [Archaic.]

di·vẽrt'ẽr, *n.* one who or that which diverts.

di·vẽrt'i·ble, *a.* capable of diversion.

dī·vẽr'ti·cle, *n.* [L. *diverticulum*, a byway, an inn, from *devertere*, to turn away; *de-*, away, from, and *vertere*, to turn.]
1. a turning; a byway. [Obs.]
2. a diverticulum. [Obs.]

dīv·ẽr·tiç'ū·lȧ, *n.* plural of *diverticulum*.

dīv·ẽr·tiç'ū·lăr, *a.* of or designating a diverticulum.

dīv·ẽr·tiç'ū·lā·ted, *a.* of or having a diverticulum or diverticula.

dīv·ẽr·tiç'ū·lum, *n.*; *pl.* **dīv·ẽr·tiç'ū·lȧ,** [L., from *diverticulum*, a byway.] in anatomy, a pouch or sac opening out from a tubular organ or main cavity.

di·ver·ti·men'tō, *n.*; *pl.* **dī·ver·ti·men'tī,** [It.] any of various light, melodic instrumental compositions in several movements.

di·vẽrt'ing, *a.* that diverts; especially, amusing or entertaining.

di·vẽrt'ing·ly, *adv.* in a diverting manner.

di·vẽrt'ing·ness, *n.* the state or quality of being diverting.

di·vẽrt'iṣe, *v.t.* to divert; to please. [Obs.]

di·vẽr'tiṣe·ment, *n.* a divertissement. [Archaic.]

dī·ver·tïsse·meṅt' (-mäṅ'), *n.* [Fr. *divertissement*, from *divertir*, to divert.]
1. a diversion; amusement.
2. a short ballet or other entertainment between acts of a play or opera; entr'acte.
3. a divertimento.

di·vẽrt′ive, *a.* tending to divert; amusing.
Dī′vēs, *n.* [L., wealthy.]
1. in the Bible, the rich man in the parable: Luke xvi. 19–31.
2. any rich man.
di·vest′, *v.t.*; divested, *pt.*, *pp.*; divesting, *ppr.* [OFr. *devestir*; L. *devestire*, to undress; *de-*, from, and *vestire*, to dress, clothe, from *vestis*, a garment.]
1. to strip (*of* clothing, arms, equippage, etc.): opposed to *invest*; as, to *divest* one *of* his glory.
2. to deprive or dispossess (*of* rank, rights, etc.).
3. in law, to devest.
di·vest′i·ble, *a.* that can be divested.
di·vest′i·tūre, *n.* a divesting or being divested.
di·vest′ment, *n.* divestiture.
di·ves′tūre, *n.* divestiture.
di·vīd′ȧ·ble, *a.* 1. that can be divided.
2. separate; parted. [Obs.]
di·vīd′ănt, *a.* different; separate. [Obs.]
di·vīde′, *v.t.*; divided, *pt.*, *pp.*; dividing, *ppr.* [ME. *dividen*; L. *dividere*, to divide.]
1. to part or separate into pieces; as, to *divide* an apple.
2. to separate into groups; to classify.
3. to cause to be separate; to make or keep separate by or as by a partition or boundary; as, a wall *divides* two houses.
4. to make partition of among a number; to give out in shares; to apportion.
5. to disunite in opinion or interest; to make discordant; to cause disagreement between or among.
There shall be five in one house *divided*, three against two. —Luke xii. 52.
6. in mathematics, (a) to separate into equal parts by a divisor; (b) to be a divisor of.
7. in mechanics, to mark off the divisions of; graduate; gradate.
8. in music, to perform with divisions (sense 12). [Obs.]
Syn.—sever, sunder, cleave, deal out, distribute, share.
di·vīde′, *v.i.* 1. to be or become disunited; to part.
2. to be of different opinion; to hold opposite or contrary views; as, families *divide*.
3. to separate into groups in voting on a question.
4. to share.
di·vīde′, *n.* a watershed; a ridge that divides two drainage areas.
di·vīd′ed, *a.* 1. formed into divisions; parted.
2. in botany, denoting a leaf cut into divisions by incisions extending nearly to the midrib; segmented.
di·vīd′ed·ly, *adv.* separately.
di·vīd′ed pāy′ments, payments in installments.
di′vi·dē et im′pe·rȧ, [L.] divide and rule.
div′i·dend, *n.* [L. *dividendus*, that which is to be divided, gerundive of *dividere*, to divide.]
1. the number or quantity to be divided.
2. a sum or quantity, usually of money, to be divided among stockholders, creditors, members of a co-operative, etc.
3. an individual's share of such a sum or quantity.
4 in insurance, the refund made to the insured from the year's surplus profit.
di·vīd′ẽr, *n.* 1. one who or that which divides.
2. a distributor; one who deals out to each his share.
3. [*pl.*] a pair of small compasses, of which the opening is adjusted by means of a screw and nut, used for dividing lines, describing circles, etc.; compasses.
4. the conical projection at the end of a cutter bar of a reaper or mower separating the standing part from the part to be cut.
di·vīd′ing, *a.* that indicates separation or difference; as, a *dividing* line.
di·vīd′ing·ly, *adv.* by division.
dĭ′vĭ-dĭ′vĭ, *n.* the curled pods of a small tropical American tree, *Cæsalpinia coriaria*, of the pea family: they are astringent and contain tannic and gallic acids used by tanners and dyers; also, the tree itself.

DIVI-DIVI (*Cæsalpinia coriaria*)

di·vid′ū·ăl, *a.* 1. divided; separate.
2. divisible; separable.
3. distributed; shared.
di·vid′ū·ăl·ly, *adv.* by dividing.
di·vid′ū·ous, *a.* divided; divisible. [Rare.]
div·i·nā′tion, *n.* [L. *divinatio*, the faculty of foreseeing, from *divinatus*, pp. of *divinare*, to foresee.]
1. the act of divining; the act or practice of trying to foretell future events or the unknown by occult means.
2. a prophecy; prediction; augury.
3. a successful guess; clever conjecture.
div′i·nā·tŏr, *n.* a diviner. [Obs.]
di·vin′ȧ·tō·ry, *a.* of or by divination.
di·vīne′, *a.* [ME. *divine*; OFr. *divin*; L. *divinus*, divine, inspired, pertaining to a deity, from *divus*, a deity.]
1. of, relating to, or characteristic of God; as, a *divine* nature.
2. appropriated to God or celebrating his praise; holy; sacred; as, *divine* songs, *divine* worship.
3. godlike; heavenly; excellent in the highest degree; extraordinary.
A *divine* sentence is in the lips of the king. —Prov. xvi. 10.
4. devoted to God; religious; sacrosanct.
5. relating to divinity or theology.
6. very pleasing, attractive, etc.: a feminine intensive. [Colloq.]
di·vīne′, *n.* 1. a man skilled in divinity; a theologian.
2. a clergyman.
di·vīne′, *v.t.*; divined, *pt.*, *pp.*; divining, *ppr.* [L. *divinare*, to foresee, divine, from *divinus*, divine, prophetic.]
1. to prophesy; to foretell; to presage.
2. to surmise; to know by intuition; as, I *divined* his meaning in his face.
3. to guess; to conjecture.
di·vīne′, *v.i.* 1. to use or practice divination.
2. to have presages or forebodings.
3. to guess or conjecture.
Syn.—foretell, guess, presage, conjecture, predict, prognosticate, augur.
Di·vīne′ Çom′e·dy, an elaborate narrative poem in Italian, written (1302–1321) by Dante Alighieri: it deals with the author's imaginary journey through Hell, Purgatory, and Paradise.
di·vīne′ly, *adv.* 1. in a divine or godlike manner; in a manner resembling deity.
2. by the agency or influence of God; as, a prophet *divinely* inspired.
3. excellently; in the supreme degree; as, *divinely* brave.
di·vīne′ness, *n.* 1. divinity; participation in the divine nature.
2. excellence in the supreme degree.
di·vīn′ẽr, *n.* 1. one who engages in divination; one who tries to predict events or to reveal the unknown by occult means.
2. a divining rod.
di·vīn′ẽr·ess, *n.* a woman diviner.
di·vīne′ rīght of kings, the supposedly God-given right to rule formerly attributed to monarchs.
dīv′ing, *n.* the art or act of one who or that which dives.
dīv′ing bee′tle, a beetle of any species of the family *Dytiscidæ*, normally living under water.
dīv′ing bell, a large, hollow, bell-shaped apparatus for the purpose of enabling persons to descend and to remain below the surface of water for a length of time, to perform various operations, such as examining the foundations of bridges, blasting rocks, recovering treasure from sunken vessels, etc.: fresh air is injected into it through a flexible pipe by means of forcing pumps.
dīv′ing bōard, a board projecting horizontally over a swimming pool, lake, etc. in such a way that by jumping on the end of it a diver can propel himself farther into the air before plunging into the water.
dīv′ing buck, same as *duikerbok*.
dīv′ing dress, same as *diving suit*.
dīv′ing spī′dẽr, *Argyroneta aquatica*, the water spider.
dīv′ing sūit, a heavy, waterproof garment covering the body, worn by divers working under water: it has a detachable helmet into which air is pumped through a hose.
di·vīn′ing, *n.* the act of a diviner or augur.
di·vīn′ing rod, a forked branch or stick allegedly useful in discovering water, minerals, etc. hidden underground.

DIVING SUIT

di·vin′i·ty, *n.*; *pl.* **di·vin′i·tieṣ**, [ME. *divinite*; L. *divinitas*, a divinity, from *divinus*, divine.]
1. the quality or condition of being divine.
2. a divine being; a god; deity.
3. a divine power or quality; supreme virtue or excellence.
4. the study of religion; theology.
5. a soft, creamy kind of candy.
the Divinity; God; the Lord.
div″i·ni·zā′tion, *n.* the act of making divine; deification.
div′i·nīze, *v.t.*; divinized, *pt.*, *pp.*; divinizing, *ppr.* to make or regard as divine; to deify.
di·viṣ·i·bil′i·ty, *n.* the quality of being divisible.
di·viṣ′i·ble, *a.* [LL. *divisibilis*, divisible, from L. *divisus*, pp. of *dividere*, to divide.]
1. dividable; that can be divided.
2. in mathematics, that can be divided without leaving a remainder.
di·viṣ′i·ble, *n.* that which is divisible.
di·viṣ′i·ble·ness, *n.* divisibility.
di·viṣ′i·bly, *adv.* in a divisible manner.
di·vi′ṣion (-vizh′un), *n.* [ME. *divisioun*; L. *divisio*, a division, separation, from *divisus*, pp. of *dividere*, to divide.]
1. a dividing or being divided; separation.
2. a sharing or apportioning; distribution.
3. a difference of opinion; disagreement.
4. a separation into groups in voting.
5. anything that divides; partition; boundary.
6. anything partitioned off or separated; department; compartment; section; segment.
7. in biology, a group of organisms constituting part of a larger group.
8. in mathematics, the process of finding how many times a number (the *divisor*) is contained in another number (the *dividend*): the number of times constitutes the *quotient*.
9. in military science, a section of an army corps, consisting generally of three regiments and auxiliary troops, under the command of a major general.
10. in naval science, a group of several ships, usually four, under a single commander.
11. in logic, the separation of a genus into species.
12. in music, a florid passage or run, especially as an accompaniment to a ground theme.
cell division; in biology, the division of a cell into two or more cells, each having its own nucleus, occurring in plant or animal development.
Syn.—compartment, section, portion, detachment, separation, partition, difference, discord, disunion.
di·vi′ṣion·ăl, *a.* 1. pertaining to division; noting or making division; as, a *divisional* line.
2. belonging to or connected with a division; as, a *divisional* officer.
di·vi′ṣion·ăl·ly, *adv.* in a divisional manner.
di·vi′ṣion·ā·ry, *a.* divisional.
di·vi′ṣion·ẽr, *n.* one who divides. [Obs.]
di·vi′ṣion sīgn (or **märk**), the symbol (÷), indicating that the preceding number is to be divided by the following number. Example: $8 \div 4 = 2$.
di·vī′sive, *a.* [L. *divisus*, pp. of *dividere*, to divide.]
1. causing or showing division.
2. causing disagreement or dissension.
di·vī′sive·ly, *a.* so as to cause division, separation, or difference.
di·vī′sive·ness, *n.* a tendency toward division or separation.
di·vī′ṣŏr, *n.* [L. *divisor*, a divider.] in mathematics, (a) the number or quantity by which the dividend is divided to produce the quotient; (b) a number or quantity by which another can be divided without leaving a remainder; factor.
common divisor; in mathematics, a number or quantity that divides two or more numbers or quantities without a remainder; factor common to two or more numbers; as, 6 is a *common divisor* of 6, 12, and 36.
di·vōrce′, *n.* [OFr. *divorce*; L. *divortium*, a separation, divorce, from *diversus*, pp. of *divertere*, to turn or go different ways.]
1. in law, a legal dissolution of the bonds of matrimony, or the formal separation of husband and wife by a court.
2. separation; disunion of things closely united.
di·vōrce′, *v.t.*; divorced, *pt.*, *pp.*; divorcing, *ppr.* 1. to dissolve legally a marriage between; separate (one of a married couple) from the other by divorce.

2. to rid oneself of (one's husband or wife) by divorce.
3. to separate; disunite.
4. to take away; to put away.

di·vōrce′, *v.i.* to get a divorce.

di·vor·cé′ (-vōr-sā′), *n.* [Fr.] a divorced man.

di·vōrce′a·ble, *a.* that may or can be divorced.

di·vor·cée′ (-vōr-sā′), *n.* [Fr.] a divorced woman.

di·vōr′cee, *n.* a divorced person.

di·vōrce′ment, *n.* divorce; a divorcing or being divorced.

di·vōr′cẽr, *n.* one who or that which divorces or separates.

di·vōr′ci·ble, *a.* same as *divorceable.*

di·vōr′cive, *a.* causing or leading to divorce.

div′ŏt, *n.* [Scot.] 1. a piece of turf used for roofing, burning, etc.
2. in golf, a piece of turf torn up by a player's club in making a stroke.

dï·vō′tō, *a.* [It. *devout*, from L. *devotus*, pp. of *devovere*, to vow, devote.] in music, devout, grave, solemn.

di·vul′gāte, *a.* published. [Obs.]

di·vul′gāte, *v.t.*; divulgated, *pt., pp.*; divulgating, *ppr.* to divulge.

di·vul′gā·tẽr, *n.* one who divulges.

div·ul·gā′tion, *n.* [LL. *divulgatio*, from L. *divulgare*, to make public.] the act of divulgating.

di·vulġe′, *v.t.*; divulged, *pt., pp.*; divulging, *ppr.* [L. *divulgare*, to make public; *di-*, *dis-*, apart, and *vulgare*, to make public, from *vulgus*, the common people.]
1. to make public; to tell or make known (something private or secret); to reveal; to disclose; as, to *divulge* the proceedings of the cabinet.
2. to declare by a public act; to proclaim. [Rare.]
3. to impart; to give; to confer generally. [Rare.]
Syn.—disclose, reveal, tell, communicate, betray, impart.

di·vulġe′, *v.i.* to become public; to be made known. [Rare.]

di·vulġe′ment, *n.* a divulging or being divulged. [Rare.]

di·vul′ġence, *n.* a divulging, or revealing; disclosure.

di·vul′ġẽr, *n.* one who divulges or reveals.

di·vul′sion, *n.* [L. *divulsio*, a pulling or tearing apart, from *divulsus*, pp. of *divellere*, to tear apart.] a tearing or being torn apart; a rending asunder.

And dire *divulsions* shook the changing world. —Barlow.

di·vul′sive, *a.* pulling asunder; rending.

div′vy, *v.t.* and *v.i.*; divvied, *pt., pp.*; divvying, *ppr.* [clipped form of *divide.*] to share (often with *up.*) [Slang.]

div′vy, *n.*; *pl.* **div′vieṣ,** a share; portion. [Slang.]

di·wan′, *n.* same as *dewan.*

Dix′ie, *n.* [perhaps from *dixie*, popular name for a ten-dollar bank note issued in Louisiana prior to the Civil War: so called from the large *dix* (ten) printed on one side.]
1. the Southern States of the United States, collectively.
2. a song celebrating the South, composed in 1859 by D. D. Emmett: it became popular in the Confederacy during the Civil War.

Dix′ie·land, *a.* in, of, or like the style of jazz associated with New Orleans, characterized by a fast, ragtime tempo.

dix′it, *n.* [L., 3d pers. sing., perf. ind., of *dicere*; see *dictate.*] a statement made without confirmation; dogmatic assertion: also *ipse dixit.*

diz′en (*or* dī′zn), *v.t.*; dizened, *pt., pp.*; dizening, *ppr.* [MD. *disen*, to put flax on a distaff, from L.G. *dise*, bunch of flax.]
1. originally, to furnish with flax or spinning, as a distaff.
2. to dress gaily; to deck out; to bedizen.

dizz, *v.t.* to astonish; to puzzle; to make dizzy. [Rare.]

diz′zärd, diz′ärd, *n.* a blockhead. [Obs.]

diz′zärd·ly, *adv.* in the manner of a dizzard. [Obs.]

diz′zi·ly, *adv.* in a dizzy or dizzying manner.

diz′zi·ness, *n.* giddiness; the state or sensation of being dizzy.

diz′zy, *a.*; *comp.* dizzier; *superl.* dizziest, [ME. *dysy*; AS. *dysig*, stupid, foolish.]
1. feeling giddy or unsteady.
2. causing or likely to cause giddiness; as, a *dizzy* height.
3. confused; bewildered.
4. silly; foolish. [Colloq.]

diz′zy, *v.t.*; dizzied, *pt., pp.*; dizzying, *ppr.* [ME. *desien*; AS. *dysigian*, to be foolish, to confuse, from *dysig*, foolish.] to make dizzy.

diz′zy, *v.i.* to be foolish; to act in a confused manner. [Obs.]

djeb′el (jeb′), *n.* [Fr.; Ar. *jebel.*] a hill: often used in Arabic place names.

djer·eed′, djer·rïd′ (jer-ēd′), *n.* same as *jereed, jerid.*

djinn, djin′nee (jin′), *n.* same as *jinn, jinnee.*

DNA, [*d*eoxyribo*n*ucleic *a*cid.] an essential component of all living matter and a basic material in the chromosomes of the cell nucleus: it transmits the hereditary pattern.

dō, *n.* [It. (perhaps from *dominus*, first word of a Latin hymn): used instead of earlier *ut*, from L. *ut*, that (used as a musical note).] in music, a syllable representing the first or last tone of the diatonic scale: see *solfeggio.*

dö, *v.t.*; did, *pt.*; done, *pp.*; doing, *ppr.* 1. to put or place. [Obs.]
2. to make or cause. [Obs.]
Nothing but death can *do* me to respire. —Spenser.
3. to invest or settle (*on*). [Obs.]
4. to perform (an action, etc.); carry out; fulfill; as, *do* a deed, *do* one's duty.
5. to finish; bring to completion; as, dinner has been *done* for an hour.
6. to cause; bring about; as, it *does* no harm; who *did* this to you?
7. to exert (efforts, etc.); as, *do* your best.
8. to deal with as is required; attend to; as, *do* the ironing; *do* one's nails.
9. to work at; have as one's work or occupation.
10. to work out; solve; as, he *did* the problem.
11. to produce (a play, etc.); as, we *did Hamlet.*
12. to play the role of; as, I *did* Polonius.
13. to cover (distance); as, he *does* a mile in record time.
14. to visit as a sightseer; tour; as, they *did* England in two months.
15. to translate; as, he *did* Horace into English.
16. to give; render; as, he *did* honor to the great dead.
17. to suit; be convenient to; as, this will *do* me very well.
18. to cheat; swindle; as, you've been *done.* [Colloq.]
19. to serve (a jail term). [Colloq.]
to do away with; (a) to get rid of; to dispose of; (b) to destroy; to kill.
to do in; to kill. [Slang.]
to do one proud; to make one have a feeling of pride; also, to do exceedingly well; to achieve success: used with a reflexive pronoun; as, the singer *did herself proud.* [Colloq.]
to do oneself well; to achieve success for oneself.
to do over; to redecorate. [Colloq.]
to do up; (a) to clean and prepare (laundry, etc.); as, the laundry maid *does up* the waists; (b) [Colloq.] to exhaust; as, the work *did me up*; (c) to dress; to arrange; as, she *does up* her hair in the latest fashion; (d) to wrap or tie up in a package; as, *do up* this picture.
to do with; (a) to make use of; to employ; (b) to find helpful.
to have to do with; to have relation with or to; as, he *has* nothing *to do with* us.
Syn.—accomplish, achieve, execute, effect.

dö, *v.i.* 1. to behave; to conduct oneself; as, he *does* well when treated well.
They fear not the Lord, neither *do* they after the law and commandment. —2 Kings xvii. 34.
2. to be active; work; as, *do*, don't talk.
3. to finish: used in the perfect tenses; as, have *done* with dreaming.
4. to get along; fare; as, mother and child are *doing* well.
5. to be adequate or suitable; serve the purpose; as, the black dress will *do.*
to do by; to act toward or for; to behave in respect to or in behalf of.
to do for; (a) to act or provide for; as, he *does* well *for* his children; (b) to ruin; to hurt fatally; as, that shot *did for* him. [Colloq.]
to do without; to manage without; to dispense with.
to have done with; to have no further connection or relation with; to be through with.
to make do; to get along, or manage, with what is available.
As an auxiliary, *do* is used most commonly in forming negative and interrogative sentences; as, *do* you intend to go? *Does* he wish me to come? He *does* not care.—It is also used to express emphasis; as, she is coquettish, but still I *do* love her.—In the imperative it expresses an urgent request or command; as, *do* come; help me, *do*; *do* make haste.—It is also used to form inverted constructions after some adverbs; as, little *did* he realize.—*Do* is also used as a substitute verb; as, I shall probably come, but if I *do* not (come), you must not wait.

dö, *n.* 1. act; deed. [Obs.]
2. bustle; ado. [Rare.]
3. a fraud; a swindle. [Brit. Colloq.]
4. a party. [Brit. Colloq.]

dö′ab, *n.* [Hind. *doab* a section of land between two rivers; *do*, from Sans. *dva*, two, and *ab*, from Sans. *ap*, water, a river.] a section of land between two rivers directly above their confluence.

dōab, *n.* [Ir. *dob*, plaster, mire.] a kind of dark-colored clay found near bogs in Ireland, and used for plastering purposes.

dö′a·ble, *a.* capable of being done.

dö′-ąll, *n.* a general servant; a factotum.

dōat, *v.i.* same as *dote.*

dob′bẽr, *n.* 1. same as *dabchick.*
2. the float on a fisherman's line.

dob′bin, *n.* an old work horse.

dob′by, dob′bie, *n.* [Scot. and Brit. Dial. variant of *Robert.*]
1. a childish old man; a stupid fellow; a dolt.
2. a sprite, sometimes of a malicious nature.
3. a device on a loom for weaving small figures.

dob′by weave, a weave with small, simple patterns.

dob′chick, *n.* dabchick. [Obs.]

Dō′bẽr·măn pin′schẽr (-shẽr), [G.; *Dobermann*, name of the first breeder, and *pinscher*, terrier, from *Pinzgan*, area in northern Austria known for breeding of dogs and horses.] a breed of terrier with short, smooth, dark hair and tan markings.

dō′bie, *n.* same as *doby.*

dō′blȧ, *n.* [OSp., f. of *doblo*, double; L. *duplus*, double; *duo*, two, and *plus*, more.] an obsolete gold coin of Spain.

dō′brȧ, *n.* [Port., from *dobre*, double, from L. *duplus*, double.] any of several obsolete gold coins of Portugal.

dob′sŏn flȳ, [fisherman's term, from the name *Dobson.*] a large insect, *Corydalus cornutus*, with grayish-white wings: the larva (called *hellgrammite*) is used as fishing bait.

dob′ūle, *n.* [L. *dobula.*] a fresh-water fish, *Leuciscus dobula*, allied to the roach, found in European rivers.

dō′by, *n.* and *a.*; *pl.* **dō′bieṣ,** adobe. [Colloq.]

doç, *n.* doctor: often used as a general term of address like *Mac, Bud, Jack*, etc.

dō′cent, *a.* teaching.

dō′cent, *n.* [G., teacher, academic lecturer, from L. *docens*, ppr. of *docere*, to teach.] in some American universities, a teacher or lecturer not on the regular faculty.

Dō·cē′tae, *n.pl.* [LL., from Gr. *Dokētai*, from *dokein*, to seem.] in church history, an early heretical sect of Christians, whose chief tenet was that Christ's body was a mere phantom, or, if real, of celestial origin.

Dō·cet′iç, *a.* pertaining to or of the Docetae; as, *Docetic* doctrine.

Dō·cē′tiṣm, *n.* the doctrines of the Docetae.

Dō·cē′tist, *n.* one of the Docetae.

doçh′mi·aç, *a.* [Gr. *dochmiakos*, from *dochmios*, aslant.] in ancient Greek prosody, consisting of, characterized by, or pertaining to dochmii.

doçh′mi·aç, *n.* a verse or stanza made up of dochmii.

doçh·mī′ȧ·sis, *n.* same as *ancylostomiasis.*

doçh′mi·us, *n.*; *pl.* **doçh′mi·ī,** [L., from Gr. *dochmios*, across, aslant.] in ancient Greek prosody, a foot of five syllables, the first and fourth being short and the others long.

Doçh′mi·us, *n.* a genus of nematoid worms of the family *Strongylidæ.*

doc·i·bil′i·ty, doc′i·ble·ness, *n.* the quality of being docible; teachableness; docility. [Rare.]

doc′i·ble, *a.* [OFr. *docible*; LL. *docibilis*, teachable, from L. *docere*, to teach.] teachable; docile; tractable; easily taught or managed. [Rare.]

doc′ile, *a.* [L. *docilis*, easily taught, from *docere*, to teach.]
1. teachable; easily instructed.
2. tractable; easy to discipline.

dō·cil′i·ty, *n.* [L. *docilitas* (*-atis*), aptness for being taught, from *docilis*, easily taught.] the quality of being docile.

doc′i·mȧ·cy, *n.* same as *docimasy*.

doc·i·mas′tiç, *a.* [Gr. *dokimastikos*, from *dokimastēs*, an assayer, examiner, from *dokimazein*, to test, examine.] proving by experiments; specifically, relating to the assaying of ores or metals.

doc′i·mȧ·sy, doc′i·mȧ·cy, *n.* [Gr. *dokimasia*, an examination, proving, from *dokimazein*, to examine, from *dokimos*, examined, approved, from *dechesthai*, to receive, approve.]
1. the art or practice of assaying ores or metals; metallurgy.
2. the testing of medicines or the ascertaining of facts in physiology.
3. in ancient Greece, a judicial review of candidates for office, applicants for citizenship, etc.

doc·i·mol′ō·ġy, *n.* [Gr. *dokimos*, approved, and *logos*, discourse.] a treatise on the assayer's art.

doc′i·ty, *n.* willingness to be taught; docility. [Dial.]

dock, *n.* [ME. *docke, dokke*; AS. *docce*, dock.] any of several coarse weeds of the buckwheat family, *Polygonaceæ*, especially of the genus *Rumex*, with small, green flowers and large leaves.

dock, *n.* [ME. *doc, dok*; ON. *docker*, a short, stumpy tail, from same base as *dock* (the weed).]
1. the solid part of an animal's tail, excluding the hair.
2. an animal's bobbed tail.
3. a case of leather to cover a horse's docked tail.

dock, *v.t.* [ME. *docken*, from the *n.*]
1. to cut off the end of (a tail, etc.); clip or bob.
2. to shorten the tail of by cutting.
3. to deduct a part from (wages, etc.).
4. to deduct a part from the wages of.

dock, *n.* [from Fl. *docke, dok*, hutch, pen, cage.] the place where the accused stands or sits in court.

dock, *n.* [orig., mud channel made by a vessel's bottom at low tide; hence, fenced-in channel for docking; MD. *docke*, runnel, channel; It. *doccia* or ML. *ductia*, channel, from L. *ductio*, a leading away.]
1. a large, excavated basin equipped with floodgates, used for receiving ships between voyages.
2. a landing pier; wharf.
3. the area of water between two docks.

dock, *v.t.* to bring or pilot (a ship) to a dock.

dock, *v.i.*, to come into a dock.

dock′ăġe, *n.* [*dock* (wharf) and *-age*.]
1. the fee charged for the use of a dock.
2. docking accommodations.
3. the docking of ships.

dock′ăġe, *n.* [*dock*, to cut off, and *-age*.] curtailment; deduction, as of wages.

dock çress, in botany, the nipplewort, *Lapsana communis*.

dock′en, dock′ăn, *n.* the dock (plant). [Brit. Dial.]

dock′ẽr, *n.* a dock worker; a longshoreman.

dock′ẽr, *n.* a person or thing that docks or cuts off.

dock′et, *n.* [merging of *cocket*, a seal, anything sealed or approved, and obs. *doggette*, register, warrant, from It. *doghetta*, small heraldic bend, dim. of *doga*, barrel stave.]
1. a summary, abridged statement, or list of legal decisions.
2. a list of cases to be tried by a law court.
3. any list or summary of things to be done; agenda.
4. a label listing the contents of a package, directions, etc.

dock′et, *v.t.* 1. to enter in a docket.
2. to put a docket on; label; ticket.

dock′mack·ie, *n.* [perhaps via D., from Am. Ind. (Lenape) *dogekumak*.] a North American shrub, *Viburnum acerifolium*, of the honeysuckle family, with maplelike leaves, small clusters of yellow-white flowers, and purple or black berries.

dock′yärd, *n.* a place with docks, machinery, and supplies for repairing or building ships.

doç′maç, *n.* an edible kind of catfish, *Bagrus docmac*, inhabiting the Nile.

Doç·ō·glos′sȧ, *n.pl.* [L., from Gr. *dokos*, a wooden beam or bar, a shaft, and *glōssa*, tongue.] a suborder of marine gastropods, having many beamlike teeth in transverse rows on the radula. It includes the limpets.

doç′quet (-ket), *n.* and *v.* docket. [Obs.]

doç′tŏr, *n.* [ME. *doctour, doctur*, a doctor of medicine, law, or divinity; OFr. *doctour*; L. *doctor*, a teacher, from *docere*, to teach.]
1. a person on whom a university or college has conferred the doctorate: a Doctor of Medicine, Dentistry, Philosophy, Divinity, etc. is properly addressed as *Doctor*.
2. a physician or surgeon (M.D.).
3. a person licensed to practice any of the healing arts, as an osteopath, chiropractor, etc.
4. a witch doctor or medicine man.
5. a makeshift device or apparatus for making emergency repairs.
6. a bright-colored artificial fly used in angling.
7. a teacher. [Rare.]
8. a learned man, especially one of the Schoolmen of the Middle Ages. [Archaic.]

doç′tŏr, *v.t.*; doctored, *pt., pp.*; doctoring, *ppr.*
1. to try to heal; to apply medicine to; as, to *doctor* a child; to *doctor* a headache. [Colloq.]
2. to repair; to mend; to readjust; as, to *doctor* a watch. [Colloq.]
3. to confer the title or degree of doctor upon. [Rare.]
4. to adulterate; to falsify; to tamper with; to change for the purpose of deception; as, to *doctor* butter; to *doctor* accounts. [Colloq.]

doç′tŏr, *v.i.* 1. to practice medicine. [Colloq.]
2. to take medicine, treatments, etc.; to be under a doctor's care.

doç′tŏr·ăl, *a.* 1. of a doctor or doctorate; as, a *doctoral* dissertation.
2. having a doctorate.

doç′tŏr·ăl·ly, *adv.* in the manner of a doctor.

doç′tŏr·āte, *n.* the degree or status of doctor conferred by a university.

doç′tŏr·āte, *v.t.* to make a doctor of by conferring a degree upon. [Rare.]

dŏç′tŏr·ess, *n.* a woman doctor. [Rare.]

doç′tŏr fish, a tropical fish of the genus *Acanthurus*, the surgeon fish: so called from the sharp, lancetlike spines of its tail.

doç′tŏr gum, an aromatic resin of South America: also called *hog gum*.

doç′tŏr·īze, *v.t.* to doctorate. [Rare.]

doç′tŏr·ly, *a.* of, pertaining to, or like a doctor or learned man.

doç′tŏr·ship, *n.* the degree or rank of a doctor.

doç′tress, *n.* see *doctoress*.

doç′tri·nȧ·ble, *a.* of, pertaining to, or constituting doctrine. [Obs.]

doç·tri·nâire′, *n.* [Fr. *doctrinaire*, from L. *doctrina*, doctrine.]
1. one who theorizes without paying sufficient heed to practical considerations; a visionary and unpractical theorist; a visionary.
2. in French history, one of a group of French politicians of moderately liberal principles, who occupied a place in the Chambers after the Restoration of 1815 and advocated the adoption of a constitution similar to that of Great Britain.

doç·tri·nâire′, *a.* characteristic of a doctrinaire; theoretical; impractical; visionary.

doç′tri·năl, *a.* [LL. *doctrinalis*, pertaining to doctrine, from L. *doctrina*, doctrine.]
1. pertaining to doctrine; containing a doctrine or something taught; as, a *doctrinal* observation; a *doctrinal* proposition.
2. pertaining to the act or means of teaching; educational; instructive. [Rare.]

doç′tri·năl, *n.* [*usually in pl.*] something that is a part of doctrine; a tenet.

doç′tri·năl·ly, *adv.* in the form of doctrine or instruction; by way of teaching or positive direction.

doç·tri·nā′ri·ăn, *n.* and *a.* same as *doctrinaire*.

doç′trine, *n.* [ME. *doctrine*; L. *doctrina*, teaching, instruction, from *doctor*, a teacher, instructor; from *docere*, to teach.]
1. something taught; teachings.
2. something taught as the principles or creed of a religion, political party, etc.; tenet or tenets; belief; dogma.
3. the act of teaching; instruction. [Archaic.]

Syn.—dogma, principle, precept, tenet.

doç′ū·drä·mȧ, *n.* [*docu*mentary and *drama*.] a fictionalized dramatization for television of an actual event or about a real person or people.

doç′ū·ment, *n.* [Fr. *document*; L. *documentum*, a lesson, example, proof, from *docere*, to teach.]
1. anything printed, written, etc., relied upon to record or prove something.
2. anything serving as proof.
3. precept; instruction; direction; authoritative dogma. [Obs.]

doç′ū·ment, *v.t.* 1. to provide with a document or documents.
2. to provide (a book, pamphlet, etc.) with references as proof or support of things said in it.
3. to prove or support by reference to documents.

doç·ū·men′tăl, *a.* of a document or documents.

doç″ū·men′tȧ·ry, *a.* 1. consisting of, supported by, contained in, or serving as a document or documents.
2. designating or of a motion picture that records news events or shows social conditions without fictionalization.

doç·ū·men′tȧ·ry, *n.*; *pl.* **doç·ū·men′tȧ·ries,** a documentary motion picture.

doç″ū·men·tā′tion, *n.* 1. the supplying of documents or supporting references; use of documentary evidence.
2. the documents or references thus supplied.

dod, dodd, *v.t.*; dodded, *pt., pp.*; dodding, *ppr.* [ME. *dodden*, to cut off.] to clip or cut off; to poll. [Dial.]

dod′dărt, *n.* a game resembling hockey; also, the stick with which it is played. [Brit. Dial.]

dod·ded, *a.* hornless, as sheep or cattle. [Scot.]

dod′dẽr, *n.* [ME. *doder*; AS. *dodder*, the plant dodder.] any of several parasitic plants of the genus *Cuscuta*, lacking leaves, roots, and chlorophyll: the threadlike stem is equipped with special suckers for drawing nourishment from the host.

dodder grass; the quaking grass, *Briza media*.

LESSER DODDER (*Cuscuta epithymum*)

dod′dẽr, *v.i.*; doddered, *pt., pp.*; doddering, *ppr.* [var. of dial. *dudder*, *dither*; akin to or from AS. *dyderian*, to confuse, delude.]
1. to shake or tremble as from old age.
2. to totter.

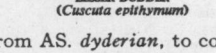

dod′dẽred, *a.* [Dryden's form (influenced by *dodder*) of older *doddard, dotard*, an old decaying oak.]
1. having lost its branches or top because of age, decay, etc.: said of a tree.
2. infirm with age.

dod′dẽr·ing, *a.* trembling, shaky, or tottering, as from old age.

dō′deç·a-, [from L. *dodeca-*; Gr. *dōdeka*, twelve, from *dyo*, two, and *deka*, ten.] a combining form meaning *twelve*, as in *dodeca*ndria: also, before a vowel, *dodec-*.

dō·deç′ȧ·gon, *n.* [*dodeca-*, and Gr. *gōnia*, an angle.] a plane figure bounded by twelve sides and having twelve angles.

Dō″deç·ȧ·ġyn′i·ȧ, *n.pl.* [*dodeca-*, and Gr. *gynē*, a female.] in the Linnaean system, an order of plants having twelve styles or pistils.

dō″deç·ȧ·ġyn′i·ăn, dō·de·çaġ′y·nous, *a.* in botany, having twelve styles.

dō″deç·ȧ·hē′drăl, *a.* pertaining to, or having the form of, a dodecahedron.

dō″deç·ȧ·hē′drŏn, *n.*; *pl.* **dō″deç·ȧ·hē′drŏnṣ, dō″deç·ȧ·hē′drȧ,** [*dodeca-*, and Gr. *hedra*, a seat, base.] a solid figure with twelve plane faces.

DODECAHEDRON

Dō·de·çan′dri·ȧ, *n.pl.* [*dodeca-*, and Gr. *anēr*(*andros*), a male.] in the Linnaean system, a class of plants having from twelve to nineteen stamens.

dō·de·çan′dri·ăn, dō·de·çan′drous, *a.* pertaining to the *Dodecandria*.

dō′de·çāne, *n.* [Gr. *dōdeka*, twelve.] a hydrocarbon of the paraffin series.

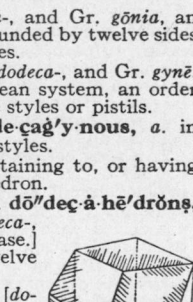

dō′deç·ant, *n.* one of the twelve parts into which the space around a hexagonal crystal is divided by the diametral planes.

dō″deç·ȧ·pet′ăl·ous, *a.* [*dodeca-*, and Gr. *petalon*, a leaf.] in botany, having twelve petals.

dō′de·cärçh, *n.* [*dodeca-*, and Gr. *archos*, a ruler, from *archein*, to rule.] any member of a ruling group of twelve.

dō·deç′ȧ·stȳle, *a.* [*dodeca-*, and Gr. *stylos*, a

column.] in architecture, characterized by twelve columns in front.

dō·deç′ȧ·stȳle, *n.* a portico having twelve columns in front.

dō″deç·ȧ·syl·lab′iç, *a.* containing twelve syllables.

dō″deç·ȧ·syl′lȧ·ble, *n.* [*dodeca-*, and Gr. *syllabē*, a syllable.] a word made up of twelve syllables.

dō″deç·ȧ·tem′ō·ry, *n.* [Gr. *dōdekatēmorion*, a twelfth part; *dōdeka*, twelve, and *morion*, a part.] in astrology, formerly, any of the twelve divisions of the zodiac.

dodġe (doj), *v.i.*; dodged, *pt., pp.*; dodging, *ppr.* [origin uncertain.]
1. to start suddenly aside; to shift suddenly, as to avoid a blow.
2. to use tricks or deceits; to be evasive.

dodġe, *v.t.* 1. to avoid (a blow, etc.) by moving or shifting quickly aside; as, to *dodge* a blow.
2. to evade by cunning, trickery, cleverness, etc.

dodġe, *n.* 1. a dodging.
2. a trick used in cheating or evading.
3. a clever device, plan, etc.

dodġ′ẽr, *n.* 1. one who dodges or evades; also, an artful, crafty fellow.
2. a small, cheap handbill.
3. a cake or bread made of corn meal.

dodġ·ẽr·y, *n.* trickery; craftiness.

dod′i·pōll, dod′dy·pōll, *n.* a blockhead; a dull fellow; a fool. [Obs.]

dod′kin, *n.* [D. *doitkin*, dim. of *duit*, a doit.] a doit, a small coin.

dod′măn, a snail. [Dial.]

dō′dō, *n.* [Port. *doudo*, a dodo, from *doudo*, *doido*, simple, foolish.] a large bird, *Didus ineptus*, now extinct, that had a hooked bill, short neck and legs, and rudimentary wings useless for flying: formerly found on Mauritius.

DODO

Dō·dō·nae′ăn, Dō·dō·nē′ăn, *a.* [L. *Dodonæus*, from *Dodona*; Gr. *Dōdōnē*, Dodona, a city in Epirus.] pertaining to the ancient Grecian city Dodona, or to its celebrated sanctuary and oracle of Zeus.

Dōe, [same word as *doe*; John Doe and Richard Roe were orig. fictitious plaintiff and defendant in a form of ejection action.] a name (*John Doe, Jane Doe*) used in law courts, legal papers, etc. to refer to any person whose name is unknown.

dōe, *n.* a feat. [Obs.]

dōe, *n.*; *pl.* **dōeṣ, dōe,** [ME. *doo*; AS. *dā*; L. *dama, damma*, the doe.] the female of the deer, or of the antelope, rabbit, or almost any other animal the male of which is called a *buck*.

doeg′liç (dĕg′), *a.* pertaining to the doegling.

doeg′ling (dĕg′), *n.* [Faroese.] the piked or rorqual whale, *Balænoptera rostrata*.

dō′ẽr, *n.* [ME. *doer*; AS. *dōere*, from *dōn*, to do.]
1. one who does something or acts in a specified manner; as, a *doer* of good.
2. a person who gets things done; an active or energetic person.

dŏeṣ (duz), *v.* third person singular, present indicative, of the verb *do*.

dōe′skin, *n.* 1. the skin of a female deer.
2. leather made from this.
3. a fine, soft, smooth woolen cloth used for suits, upholstery, etc.

dŏeṣ′n′t (duz′), does not.

dō′est, *v.* archaic second person singular, present indicative, of *do*: used with *thou*, and in auxiliary uses shortened to *dost*.

dō′eth, *v.* archaic third person singular, present indicative, of *do*: in auxiliary uses shortened to *doth*.

doff, *v.t.*; doffed (doft), *pt., pp.*; doffing, *ppr.* [from *do* and *off*.]
1. to take off (clothes, etc.).
2. to remove or lift (one's hat), as in greeting.
3. to strip or divest (oneself). [Obs.]
4. to put or thrust aside; to give up; to get rid of.
5. to strip off by a machine, as in cotton or wool manufacture.

doff, *v.i.* to take off dress; especially, to remove the hat. [Rare.]

dof′fẽr, *n.* a revolving cylinder in a carding machine which doffs, or strips off, the cotton from the cards.

dog (*or* dǫg), *n.*; *pl.* **dogṣ, dog,** [ME. *dog, dogge*; generalized in sense from late, rare AS. *docga, dogga* (usual AS. *hund*, see *hound*), dog of native breed.]
1. any of a large and varied group of domesticated animals related to the fox, wolf, and jackal.
2. the male of any of these animals.
3. a low, contemptible fellow.
4. a prairie dog, dogfish, or other animal thought of as resembling a dog.
5. [from its orig. shape.] an andiron; firedog.
6. a boy or man; as, lucky *dog*, gay *dog*. [Colloq.]
7. [*pl.*] feet. [Slang.]
8. [D–] in astronomy, either of two constellations near Orion, separated from each other by the Milky Way; the Great Dog (*Canis Major*) or the Little Dog (*Canis Minor*).
9. in mechanics, any of several devices for holding or grappling.
10. in meteorology, a parhelion; sundog, seadog, or fogdog.

a dog's age; a comparatively long time; as, I have not seen you for *a dog's age*. [Colloq.]

a dog's life; a wretched, miserable life.

dog eat dog; ruthless and savage competition.

dog in the manger; one who will neither enjoy the use of a thing himself nor let anyone else enjoy it.

every dog has his day; something good or lucky happens to everyone at one time or another.

to give or *throw to the dogs*; to throw away as useless.

to go to the dogs; to deteriorate; to go to pieces.

to let sleeping dogs lie; to let well enough alone; not disturb things as they are for fear of something worse.

to put on the dog; to make a show of being very elegant, wealthy, etc. [Slang.]

dog, *v.t.*; dogged, *pt., pp.*; dogging, *ppr.* 1. to hunt, follow, or track down like a dog.

I have been pursued, *dogged*, and waylaid. —Pope.

2. to hold down with a mechanical dog; as, the log was *dogged* by the movement of a lever.

dog, *adv.* very; completely: used in combination, as, *dog*-tired.

dō′găl, *a.* belonging or pertaining to a doge.

dō·gä′nȧ, *n.* [It.] in Italy, a customhouse or customs duty.

dog āpe, a baboon.

dog′bāne, *n.* [so named because said to be poisonous to dogs.] a perennial plant of the genus *Apocynum*, with clusters of small, pink or white flowers and a milky juice used in medicine.

dog bee, a drone bee.

dog belt, a coal miner's belt, consisting of a leather girdle and chain for drawing small trucks in the lower levels.

dog′ber″ry, *n.*; *pl.* **dog′ber″ries,** 1. the berry or fruit of the European dogwood, the chokeberry, the yellow clintonia, or the mountain ash.
2. in Great Britain, the fruit of certain cranberries.
3. any of these plants.
4. [D–] a stupid, egotistical constable in Shakespeare's *Much Ado About Nothing* (1600).

dog′ber″ry tree, the dogwood.

dog bis′çuit (-kit), 1. a hard biscuit containing ground bones, meat, etc., for feeding dogs.
2. an army field-ration biscuit. [Slang.]

dog′çärt, *n.* 1. a small, light cart drawn by dogs.
2. a small, light, open carriage, usually with two wheels, having two seats arranged back to back: so called because originally it had a box under the seat for a sportsman's dogs.

dog çol′lăr, 1. a collar for a dog.
2. an ornamental neckband sometimes worn by women.

dog dāi′ṣy, the common field daisy.

dog dāyṣ, the period of the year comprising about six weeks of the hottest and most sultry days of July and August, at which period the Dog Star rises and sets with the sun.

dog′drȧw, *n.* the tracking down of an unlawfully wounded deer by the scent of a hound led by hand.

dōġe, *n.* [It. *doge*, from L. *dux* (*ducis*), a leader, from *ducere*, to lead.] the chief magistrate of either of the former republics of Venice and Genoa.

DOGE OF VENICE

dog′-ēar, *n.* a turned-down corner of the leaf of a book.

dog′-ēar, *v.t.* to turn down the corner or corners of (a leaf or leaves in a book).

dog′-ēared, *a.* having the corners of the leaves bent back and soiled by careless usage: said of a book.

dōġe′less, *a.* having no doge.

dog′fāce, *n.* an enlisted man in the army, especially an infantryman. [Slang.]

dog′-fāced (-fāst), *a.* with a face like a dog's.

dog fen′nel, the mayweed.

dog′fīght (-fīt), *n.* a rough, violent fight between, or as between, dogs; specifically, in military usage, combat between fighter planes or tanks at close quarters.

dog′fish, *n.*; *pl.* **dog′fish, dog′fish·eṣ,** 1. any of various small, voracious sharks.
2. any of several other fishes, as the bowfin, or mudfish.

dog fox, a male fox.

dog′ged, *a.* 1. sullen; sour; morose. [Obs.]
2. not giving in readily; persistent; stubborn.

dog′ged·ly, *adv.* in a dogged manner; stubbornly.

dog′ged·ness, *n.* 1. sullenness; moroseness. [Obs.]
2. stubbornness; obstinate persistence; pertinacity.

dog′gẽr, *n.* [ME. *doggere*, from *dog*.] a two-masted boat with a broad beam, used by fishermen in the North Sea.

dog′gẽr, *n.* a concretion of silica and iron found in the Jurassic formation in England.

dog′gẽr·el, dog′grel, *n.* [ME. *dogerel* (Chaucer); prob. from It. *doga*, barrel stave, but influenced by *dog*, as in *dog Latin*.] trivial, inartistic, weakly constructed verse, usually of a burlesque or comic sort; jingle.

dog′gẽr·el, dog′grel, *a.* designating or of doggerel; as, *doggerel* verse or rhyme.

dog′gẽr·y, *n.*; *pl.* **dog′gẽr·ies,** 1. mean or surly behavior like that of a snappish dog.
2. dogs collectively.
3. the rabble; riffraff.

dog′gish, *a.* 1. of or like a dog.
2. snarling; snapping.
3. stylish and showy. [Colloq.]

dog′gish·ly, *adv.* in a doggish manner.

dog′gish·ness, *n.* the quality of being doggish.

dog′-gone, *interj.* [perhaps from *dog* (pox) *on it!*, an imprecation, or perhaps euphemistic remodeling of *God damn*.] damn! darn!: an exclamation used variously to express anger, irritation, surprise, pleasure, etc.

dog′-gone, *v.t.*; dog-goned, *pt., pp.*; dog-goning, *ppr.* to damn: usually in the past participle; as, I'll be *dog-goned* if I'll go. [Colloq.]

dog gràss, a coarse, sharp-bearded grass, *Agropyrum caninum*.

dog grāte, a basket-shaped fire grate supported by firedogs or andirons.

dog′grel, *a.* and *n.* same as *doggerel*.

dog′gy, dog′gie, *n.*; *pl.* **dog′gies,** a little dog: often used as a pet name for any dog.

dog′gy, *a.*; *comp.* doggier; *superl.* doggiest, 1. of or like a dog.
2. stylish and showy. [Colloq.]

dog′head (-hed), *n.* the hammer of a gunlock.

dog′-head″ed, *a.* having a head like that of a dog; as, a *dog-headed* baboon.

dog′-heärt″ed, *a.* unfeeling; cruel; savage; inhuman; pitiless. [Obs.]

dog′hōle, *n.* a low, squalid habitation, fit only for dogs.

dog hook, a wrench or hook used for separating and connecting hose, boring rods, etc.; a kind of iron hook used in handling logs.

dog′house, *n.* a dog's shelter; a kennel.

in the doghouse; in disfavor. [Slang.]

dō′gie, dō′gy, *n.*; *pl.* **dō′gies,** [Texas dial.; also earlier *doughgy*; perhaps from Southwest dial. *dough*, cereal grain still soft and milky before maturity.] in the western United States, a stray or motherless calf.

dog Lat′in, 1. incorrect or ungrammatical Latin.
2. a jargon made up in imitation of Latin.
dog leech, one who treats the diseases of dogs. [Obs.]
dog′-leg ged, *a.* in architecture, having a bend and structure suggesting the shape of a dog's hind leg: said especially of a stairway without a well, in which the upper and under flights are connected by a platform or platforms.
dog let′tẽr, same as *dog's letter.*
dog lī′çhen, the *Peltigera canina,* a plant once supposed to be a specific for hydrophobia.
dog′mȧ, *n.*; *pl.* **dog′mȧș, dog′mȧ·tȧ,** [L. *dogma*; Gr. *dogma,* that which one thinks true, an opinion, decree, from *dokein,* to think, seem.]
1. a doctrine; tenet; belief.
2. doctrines, tenets, or beliefs, collectively.
3. a positive, arrogant assertion of opinion; dogmatic utterance.
4. in theology, a doctrine or body of doctrines formally and authoritatively affirmed.
dog·mat′iç, dog·mat′iç·ăl, *a.* 1. of or like dogma.
2. asserted a priori or without proof.
3. stating opinion in a positive or arrogant manner.
Syn.—imperious, dictatorial, authoritative, arrogant, magisterial, self-opinionated, positive.
dog·mat′iç, *n.* same as *dogmatist.*
dog·mat′iç·ăl·ly, *adv.* positively; in a magisterial manner; arrogantly.
dog·mat′iç·ăl·ness, *n.* the quality of being dogmatic; positiveness.
dog·mȧ·ti′ciăn (-tish′un), *n.* same as *dogmatist.*
dog·mat′içs, *n.pl.* [*construed as sing.*] the study of religious dogmas, especially those of Christianity.
dog′mȧ·tișm, *n.* [LL. *dogmatismus,* from Gr. *dogmatizein,* to lay down a decree, from *dogma,* a decree, dogma.] dogmatic assertion of opinion, usually without reference to evidence.
dog′mȧ·tist, *n.* a person who utters dogmas or is dogmatic.
dog′mȧ·tīze, *v.i.*; dogmatized, *pt., pp.*; dogmatizing, *ppr.* [Fr. *dogmatiser*; ML. *dogmatizare;* Gr. *dozmatizein*; see *dogma.*] to speak or write in a dogmatic manner.
dog′mȧ·tīze, *v.t.* to formulate or express as dogma.
dog′mȧ·tī·zẽr, *n.* one who dogmatizes.
dog nāil, a strong nail with a projection on one side of the head.
dog pärs′ley, a bad-smelling, poisonous herb, *Æthusa cynapium,* resembling parsley.
dog poi′ṣŏn, same as *dog parsley.*
dog′rōse, *n.* a European wild rose, *Rosa canina,* with single, pink flowers and hooked thorns.
dog salm′ŏn (sam′), a salmon of the genus *Oncorhynchus,* found along the Pacific coast of the United States; humpback salmon.
dog's chop, a South African marigold.
dog'ṣ′-ēar, *n.* and *v.t.* dog-ear.
dog's fen′nel, a common weed of disagreeable odor; mayweed.
dog's gràss, same as *dog grass.*
dog shärk, a kind of spotted dogfish, *Scyllium canicula.*
dog′shōre, *n.* one of a number of shores, or pieces of timber, used to hold a ship in place before launching.
dog′skin, *a.* made of the skin of a dog; as, a pair of *dogskin* gloves.
dog sled (*or* **sledġe**), a sled (or sledge) drawn by dogs.
dog′sleep, *n.* 1. pretended sleep.
2. light, fitful sleep like that of a dog.
dog's let′tẽr, [transl. of L. *litera canina.*] the letter R, especially when trilled: so called because of its supposed resemblance to a dog's growl.
dog's mēat, refuse; offal; meat fit only for dogs.
dog's mẽr′çū·ry, a European perennial plant, *Mercurialis perennis.*
dog'ṣ′-tāil, *n.* a coarse kind of grass; yard grass; wire grass.
Dog Stär, 1. Sirius, the brightest star in the constellation Canis Major.
2. Procyon, a bright star in the constellation Canis Minor.
dog′stōne, *n.* a kind of rough stone used for millstones.
dog's tŏngue (tung), same as *hound's tongue.*
dog'ṣ′-tọọth vī′ō·let, same as *dogtooth violet.*
dog tag, 1. an identification tag or license tag for a dog.
2. a military identification tag worn about the neck. [Slang.]
dog tent, same as *shelter tent.*
dog tick, a tick that infests dogs.
dog′tīe, *n.* in architecture, a piece of iron bent at the ends for holding timbers, etc. together.
dog′-tīred, *a.* very tired. [Colloq.]
dog′-tōeș′, *n. sing.* and *pl.* a weed, the common cudweed, *Antennaria plantaginifolia.*
dog′-tŏngue wam·pee′ (-tung), a plant of the arrowhead family found in the southeastern U. S. and Mexico.
dog′tọọth, *n.*; *pl.* **dog′teeth,** 1. a canine tooth; an eyetooth: also *dog tooth.*

DOGTOOTH (molding)

2. an ornamental molding in architecture: so called from its resemblance to the teeth of a dog.
dog′tọọth stär gràss, a grass of Australia used for forage.
dog′tọọth vī′ō·let, 1. an American plant of the lily family, with two mottled leaves and either a yellow or a white flower: it is not related to the violet family: also called *adder's-tongue.*
2. a related similar European plant with a purple flower.
dog town, a colony of prairie dogs.
dog tree, any of a number of European shrubs; the alder, the spindle tree, etc.
dog′trick, *n.* a low, mean trick. [Rare.]
dog′trot, *n.* a slow, easy trot.
dog′vāne, *n.* a vane made of some very light material and set on the weather gunwale of a vessel to indicate the direction of the wind.
dog′wätch, *n.* in nautical usage, either of two duty periods half the length of the normal period, one from 4 to 6 P.M., the other from 6 to 8 P.M.
dog′-wēa″ry, *a.* same as *dog-tired.*
dog whelk, any species of univalve shell of the genus *Nassa.*
dog′wood, *n.* 1. any of various species of *Cornus,* as the *flowering dogwood,* a tree with pink or white flowers early in the spring and clusters of small, red berries in the fall.
2. the wood obtained from any of these trees, much used for manufacturing purposes on account of its hardness.
striped dogwood; a variety of striped maple.
dō′gy, *n.* same as *dogie.*
doiled, *a.* [var. of *dold,* orig. pp. of ME. *dollen,* to make dull.] demented, stupid, foolish, etc. [Scot. and Brit. Dial.]
doi′ly, *n.*; *pl.* **doi′lieș,** [said to be named after a Mr. *Doily* or *Doyley,* a London draper of the latter half of the seventeenth century.]
1. a kind of woolen stuff. [Obs.]
2. a small napkin or mat of linen, paper, etc., used as decoration or protection for a tray, table, or other furniture.
doi′nȧ, *n.*; *pl.* **doi′ne,** [Rumanian *doina.*] a class of Rumanian folk song.
dö′ingș, *n.pl.* 1. things done; deeds; actions; activities.
2. behavior.
doit, *n.* [D. *duit,* a small coin.]
1. a small, obsolete Dutch coin that was worth about ½ cent.
2. anything of trifling value; as, not worth a *doit.*

DOIT

doit′ed, *a.* [var. of *doted,* pp. of *dote.*] foolish, as from old age; senile.
doit′kin, *n.* a doit, or any small coin.
Dō·ket′iç, Dō·kē′tișm, same as *docetic, docetism.*
dokh′mȧ (dok′), *n.* [Per. *dakhma.*] a pit surrounded by a low stone tower with a grated top, on which the Parsees place their dead. The bodies are preyed upon by carnivorous birds until the bones fall into the pit. Also called *tower of silence.*
dok·i·mas′tiç, *a.* same as *docimastic.*
Dŏ′kō, *n.* any member of a tribe of pygmies living south of Ethiopia.
dō·lā′brȧ, *n.*; *pl.* **dō·lā′brae,** [L., from *dolare,* to hew, chip with an ax.] in ancient Rome, an ax, hatchet, or mattock used for chopping or digging.
dō·lab′ri·fọrm, *a.* [L. *dolabra,* an ax, and *forma,* form.] having the form of an ax or hatchet: in botany, applied to certain fleshy leaves, which are straight at the front, tapered at the base, compressed, dilated, rounded, and thinned away at the upper end at the back; in zoology, applied to the foot of certain bivalves.
dōl′ce (-che), *a.* [It., from L. *dulcis,* sweet.]
1. sweet and soft.
2. in music, smooth in performance.
dōl′ce (-che), *n.*; *pl.* **dōl′cī** (-chē), a soft-toned organ stop.
dōl′ce fär nien′te (dōl′che fär nyen′te), [It., (it is) sweet doing nothing.] pleasant idleness.
dōl·ce·men′te (-che-), *adv.* in music, softly and sweetly.
dol′drumș, *n.pl.* [perhaps from *dull,* by analogy with *tantrum.*]
1. low spirits; dull, gloomy, listless feeling.
2. (a) equatorial ocean regions noted for dead calms and light fluctuating winds; (b) the dead calms and light, fluctuating winds characteristic of these regions.
dōle, *n.* [ME. *dol*; OFr. *dol,* from L. *dolere,* to grieve.] grief; sorrow. [Archaic.]
dōle, *n.* [ME. *dole, dale*; AS. *dal,* a division, part.]
1. a giving out of money or food in charity.
2. that which is thus given out; alms.
3. anything given out sparingly.
4. a form of payment by a government to the unemployed, as in England.
5. a person's destiny or lot. [Archaic.]
on the dole; receiving government relief funds.
dōle, *v.t.*; doled, *pt., pp.*; doling, *ppr.* to give sparingly or as a dole: usually with *out*; as, to *dole out* charity.
dōle′fish, *n.* a fisherman's share of a catch.
dōle′fụl, *a.* [ME. *doleful,* from *dol*; OFr. *dol,* sorrow, from L. *dolere,* to feel pain.]
1. sorrowful; expressing grief; as, a *doleful* cry.
2. melancholy; sad; afflicted; as, a *doleful* person.
3. dismal; impressing sorrow; gloomy; as, *doleful* shades.
Syn.—dismal, sorrowful, woeful, cheerless, dolorous.
dōle′fụl·ly, *adv.* in a doleful manner; sorrowfully; dismally; sadly.
dōle′fụl·ness, *n.* sorrow; melancholy; querulousness; gloominess; dismalness.
dō′lent, *a.* sorrowful. [Archaic.]
dol′ẽr·īte, *n.* [Fr., from Gr. *doleros,* deceptive, from *dolos,* deceit.]
1. a coarse-grained variety of basalt.
2. loosely, diabase or any of various other igneous rocks whose composition cannot be analyzed without microscopic examination.
dōle′sŏme, *a.* doleful. [Rare.]
dōle′sŏme·ly, *adv.* in a dismal manner. [Rare.]
dōle′sŏme·ness, *n.* the state of being dismal.
dol·i·chō-, [from Greek *dolichos,* long.] a combining form meaning *long.*
dol″i·chō·ce·phal′iç, dol″i·chō·ceph′ȧ·lous, *a.* [*dolicho-,* and Gr. *kephalē,* head.] having a skull long in proportion to its breadth; having a skull whose width is less than 80% of its length: opposed to *brachycephalic.*
dol″i·chō·ceph′ȧ·ly, dol″i·chō·ceph′ȧ·lișm, *n.* the state of being dolichocephalic.
do′li·ō·fọrm, *a.* [L. *dolium,* a large jar, and *forma,* a form.] like a barrel in form.
Dō·li′ō·lum, *n.* [L. *doliolum,* dim. of *dolium,* a cask, jar.]
1. a genus of free-swimming oceanic tunicates, reproducing with alternation of generation.
2. [d–] any free-swimming oceanic tunicate of this genus.
dŏ′-lit″tle, *n.* one who professes much but accomplishes little. [Colloq.]
Dō′li·um, *n.* [L. *dolium,* a large jar.]
1. a genus of univalve mollusks of large size, including the partridge shell, *Dolium perdix.*
2. [d–] in ancient Rome, an earthenware jar for wine, grain, etc.
doll, *n.* [orig., nickname for *Dorothy.*]
1. a children's toy made to resemble a baby, child, or grown person.

2. a pretty but rather stupid or silly girl or woman.
3. a pretty child.
4. any girl or young woman. [Slang.]

doll, *v.t.* and *v.i.* to dress carefully and stylishly or showily (with *up*). [Slang.]

dol'lăr, *n.* [M.D. *daler*; G. *taler, thaler*, a dollar, shortened form of *Joachimstaler, Joachimsthaler*, so called from *Joachimsthal*, Joachim's dale, in Bohemia, where the silver from which it was coined was first obtained.]
1. the monetary unit of the United States, equal to 100 cents: symbol, **$**, as, **$1.00**.
2. the standard monetary unit of various other countries, as of Canada, Australia, Liberia, Ethiopia, etc.
3. the Mexican peso.
4. any of several monetary units used only in trade, as the British Hong Kong dollar.
5. a coin or piece of paper money of the value of a dollar.
6. a Spanish coin (piece of eight) used in American Revolutionary times. [Obs.]
trade dollar; a silver coin formerly made at the United States mints and intended for use in Oriental trade.

dol″lăr-ȧ-yēar′ man, an expert serving the government for the nominal salary of one dollar, as in time of war.

dol'lăr·dee, *n.* a species of sunfish, common in the United States: also called *blue sunfish*.

dol'lăr di·plō'mȧ·cy, the policy of using the economic power or influence of a government to promote in other countries the business interests of its private citizens, corporations, etc.

dol'lăr·fish, *n.*; *pl.* **dol'lăr·fish, dol'lăr·fish·eṣ,** any of several salt-water food fishes with short compressed bodies and smooth scales.

dol'lŏp, *n.* [origin unknown.]
1. a soft mass or blob, as of some food; lump.
2. a small quantity of liquid; splash, jigger, dash, etc.
3. a measure or amount; as, a *dollop* of wit.

dol'ly, *n.*; *pl.* **dol'lieṣ,** [from *doll.*]
1. a doll; child's term.
2. a stick or board for stirring, used in laundering clothes or washing ore; dasher.
3. a tool used to hold a rivet at one end while a head is hammered out at the other.
4. any of several kinds of low, flat, wheeled frames for transporting heavy objects, as in a factory.
5. in railroading, a narrow-gauge locomotive for yard work.
6. in motion pictures and television, a low, wheeled platform on which the camera is mounted for moving it about the set.

dol'ly, *v.i.* dollied, *pt.*, *pp.*; dollying, *ppr.* to move a dolly forward (*in*), backward (*out*), etc. in photographing or televising the action.

dol'ly, *v.t.* to move (a camera, load, etc.) on a dolly.

dol'ly tub, in mining, the tub in which ore is washed and tossed. [Brit. Dial.]

Dol'ly Vär'den, [from the character of a lively, pretty girl in Dickens' *Barnaby Rudge*.]
1. a dress of sheer figured muslin worn over a bright-colored petticoat.
2. a woman's hat with a large brim, bent down on one side and decorated with flowers.
3. a kind of red-spotted trout found in streams west of the Rocky Mountains: so named from its coloring.

dol'măn, *n.*; *pl.* **dol'mănṣ,** [Fr.; hussar's jacket; Pol. *doloman*, from Turk. *dōlāmān*, long robe.]
1. a long Turkish robe.
2. a hussar's showy, gold-braided jacket worn like a cape with the sleeves hanging free.
3. a woman's coat or wrap with dolman sleeves.

dol'măn sleeve, a kind of sleeve for a woman's coat or dress, tapering from a wide opening at the armhole to a narrow one at the wrist.

dol'men, *n.* [Fr. *dolmen*; Breton *dolmen*, from *dol*, a table.] a prehistoric tomb or monument consisting of a large, flat stone laid across upright stones; cromlech.

DOLMEN

dol'ō·mīte, *n.* [named after the 18th-C. French geologist *Dolomieu*.] rock consisting mainly of magnesium carbonate and calcium carbonate; limestone or marble with much magnesium carbonate in it.

dol·ō·mit'iç, *a.* pertaining to dolomite; of the nature of dolomite.

dol'ō·mīze, *v.t.*; dolomized, *pt.*, *pp.*; dolomizing, *ppr.* to make into dolomite.

dō'lŏr, *n.* [L. *dolor*, pain, grief.] sorrow; grief; lamentation. [Poetic.]
Feast of the Dolors; a Roman Catholic celebration, held on the Friday after Passion Sunday and also on the third Sunday of September, to commemorate the sorrows of the Virgin Mary.

dol·ŏr·if'ĕr·ous, *a.* [L. *dolor*, pain, and *ferre*, to produce.] producing pain. [Rare.]

dol·ŏr·if'iç, *a.* [L. *dolor*, pain, and *facere*, to make.] causing or expressing pain or grief.

dō·lō·rō'sō, *a.* and *adv.* [It., from LL. *dolorosus*, painful, mournful.] in music, with sorrow or plaintive quality.

dol'ŏr·ous, *a.* [ME. *dolerous*; LL. *dolorosus*, painful, mournful.]
1. sad; mournful.
2. painful.

dol'ŏr·ous·ly, *adv.* sorrowfully; in a dolorous manner.

dol'ŏr·ous·ness, *n.* the state or quality of being dolorous.

dō'lŏur, *n.* dolor: British spelling.

dol'phin, *n.* [ME. *dolphyn*; L. *delphinus*; Gr. *delphis*, *delphin*, dolphin.]
1. any of several species, family *Delphinidae*, of cetaceous mammals, characterized by a beaklike snout and conical teeth in the upper jaw.

DOLPHIN (about 8 ft.)

2. either of two swift marine fishes with colors that brighten and change when the fish is taken out of water.
3. in ancient Greece, a mass of lead or iron suspended from the yardarm of a vessel to be suddenly let down upon an enemy's ship.
4. in nautical usage, (a) a spar or buoy, made fast to an anchor, and usually supplied with a ring to enable vessels to ride by it; (b) a mooring post placed at the entrance of a dock.
5. [D–] in astronomy, a northern constellation west of Pegasus: so called from its resemblance to a dolphin: also called *Delphinus*.
6. in heraldry, a heraldic fish, resembling a dolphin.

dol'phin-flow″ĕr, *n.* the larkspur.

dol'phin flȳ, a black aphid, *Aphis fabæ*, destructive to the leaves of the bean plant.

dol'phin strīk'ĕr, a small spar under the bowsprit of a vessel, helping to form a truss which supports the jib boom: also called *martingale*.

dōlt, *n.* [ME. *dold, dult*, from *dul*; AS. *dol*, dull, stupid.] a stupid, slow-witted person; a blockhead.

dōlt, *v.i.* to waste time foolishly; to behave foolishly. [Obs.]

dōlt'ish, *a.* slow-witted; stupid; as, a *doltish* clown.

dōlt'ish·ly, *adv.* in a doltish manner.

dōlt'ish·ness, *n.* stupidity.

dō'lus, *n.* [L. *dolus*; Gr. *dolos*, deceit, treachery.] in law, fraud; deceit practiced maliciously.

dolv'en, obsolete past participle of *delve*.

-dŏm, [ME. and AS., from *dom*, state, condition, power.] a noun-forming suffix meaning: (a) *the rank of, position of, domain of, dominion of*, as in king*dom*, earl*dom*; (b) *the fact of being, state of being*, as in wis*dom*, martyr*dom*; (c) *a total of all who are*, as in official*dom*.

Dom, *n.* [Sp. *don*; L. *dominus*, lord, master.]
1. a title given to certain Roman Catholic monks, priests, or other church dignitaries.
2. a title of respect formerly given by royal decree to gentlemen of Brazil and Portugal: used with the given name.

dom'āġe, *n.* damage. [Obs.]

dō·māin', *n.* [Fr. *domaine*; L. *dominium*, right of ownership, dominion, from *dominus*, lord, master.]
1. dominion; empire; territory under one government or ruler; a commonwealth; as, the vast *domains* of the Russian emperor.
2. possession; estate; the land belonging to one person.
3. in law, immediate or absolute ownership of land; permanent or ultimate ownership; demesne. [Obs.]
4. the sphere or field of activity or influence; as, the *domain* of art or of politics.
eminent domain or *right of eminent domain*; in law, the power of a government over all the property within its limits, by which it is entitled to appropriate, or to authorize the appropriation of, private property for public use, giving just compensation to the owner.
public domain; (a) public lands; (b) the condition of being free from copyright or patent.

dō'măl, *a.* [L. *domus*, a house.] in astrology, pertaining to a house.

dō·mā'ni·ăl, *a.* [Fr. *domanial*, from L. *dominium*, domain.] of or pertaining to a domain or landed estate.

dō'mat·ō·phō·bi·ȧ, *n.* fear of being confined in a house.

dōme, *n.* [OFr. *dome*, a dome, cathedral, cupola, from L. *domus*, house.]
1. a building, especially a stately or majestic building; also, a cathedral or temple. [Poet.]
2. a roof formed by a series of rounded arches or vaults on a round or many-sided base; cupola.
3. anything shaped like a dome; as, (a) the steam chamber of a locomotive; (b) the upper part of a furnace, resembling a hollow hemisphere or small dome.
4. in crystallography, a termination of a prism by two planes meeting in a horizontal edge, like the roof of a house.
5. the hemispherical part of the roof of an astronomical observatory, placed over the telescope so that it rotates, thus allowing any portion of the heavens to be viewed through the instrument which projects through a slit.
6. the head. [Slang.]

dōme, *v.t.*; domed, *pt.*, *pp.*; doming, *ppr.* **1.** to cover with or as with a dome.
2. to form into a dome.

dōme, *v.i.* to have, or take on, the form of a dome; swell out like a dome.

dōme, *n.* and *v.* doom. [Obs.]

Dō·meị' (-mā'), *n.* [Japan., lit., united, from *dō*, same, and *mei*, together, joint.] a Japanese agency for gathering and distributing news.

dōmeṣ'dāy, *n.* same as *doomsday*.

Dōmeṣ'dāy Book, [said to be so named because it spared none and judged all men without bias, like the Last Judgment.] the record of a survey of England made under William the Conqueror in 1086, listing all landowners and showing the value and extent of their holdings: also *Doomsday Book*.

dō·mes'tiç, *a.* [OFr. *domestique*; L. *domesticus*, pertaining to the house, from *domus*, a house, home.]
1. belonging to the house or home; pertaining to one's place of residence and to the family; as, *domestic* life, *domestic* duties.
2. pertaining to one's own country; not foreign; as, *domestic* and foreign issues arose.
3. made or produced in one's own nation or country; native; as, *domestic* manufactures.
4. domesticated; tame; not wild; as, *domestic* animals.
5. home-loving; fond of home and home duties.

dō·mes'tiç, *n.* 1. a domestic worker; maid, cook, butler, etc.
2. [*pl.*] native products.

dō·mes'tiç·ăl, *a.* and *n.* domestic. [Obs.]

dō·mes'tiç·ăl·ly, *adv.* 1. in relation to domestic affairs.
2. in a domestic manner.

dō·mes'ti·çāte, *v.t.*; domesticated, *pt.*, *pp.*; domesticating, *ppr.* [ML. *domesticatus*, pp. of *domesticare*, to tame, to live in a family, from L. *domesticus*, pertaining to a home, domestic, from *domus*, a house.]
1. originally, to cause to be at home.
2. to accustom to home life; make domestic.
3. to cause (animals or plants) to be no longer wild; tame.
4. to civilize.

dō·mes'ti·çāte, *v.i.* to become domestic.

dō·mes·ti·çā'tion, *n.* 1. a domesticating.
2. the fact or state of being domesticated.

dō·mes'ti·çā·tŏr, *n.* one who domesticates.

dō·mes·tic'i·ty, *n.*; *pl.* **dō·mes·tic'i·tieṣ,**
1. home life; family life.
2. devotion to home and family life.
3. [*pl.*] household affairs or duties.

dō·mes'tiç rē·lā'tionṣ çōurt, a municipal

court with jurisdiction over cases involving relations within the family or household, as between husband and wife or parent and child.

dō·mes′tic sci′ence, the study of cooking, sewing, and other household affairs; home economics.

dō·mes′tic wŏrk′ẽr, a person employed to do household work in another's home, as a maid cook, butler, etc.

dom′ett, *n.* an early kind of baize cloth woven with a cotton warp and a woolen filling.

dō′mey·kīte, *n.* [after I. *Domeyko*, a Chilean mineralogist.] a native arsenide of copper, of white or gray color.

dōm′i·căl, dōm′iç, *a.* 1. pertaining to or similar to a dome.

2. having a dome, domes, or domelike structure.

dom′i·cile, dom′i·cil, *n.* [L. *domicilium*, a dwelling, home, from *domus*, a house.]

1. an abode or dwelling; a place of permanent residence; a home; a residence.

2. in law, the place of a person's official or legal residence.

dom′i·cile, *v.t.*; domiciled, *pt.*, *pp.*; domiciling, *ppr.* to establish (oneself or another) in a domicile.

dom′i·cile, *v.i.* to dwell; to reside. [Rare.]

dom·i·cil′i·ā·ry, *a.* [ML. *domiciliarius*, from L. *domicilium*, a home, abode.] pertaining to or connected with a domicile.

domiciliary visit; in law, a visit to a private dwelling, particularly for the purpose of searching it, under authority.

dom·i·cil′i·āte, *v.t.* and *v.i.*; domiciliated, *pt.*, *pp.*; domiciliating, *ppr.* 1. to domicile.

2. to domesticate; to tame. [Obs.]

dom·i·cil·i·ā′tion, *n.* the act of domiciliating or the state of being domiciliated.

dom′i·çul·tūre, *n.* [L. *domus*, house, home, and *cultura*, care, culture.] domestic science. [Rare.]

dom′i·fȳ, *v.t.* [L. *domus*, a house, and *facere*, to make.] in astrology, to divide (the heavens) into twelve houses, in order to make a horoscope. [Obs.]

dom′i·nȧ, *n.*; *pl.* **dom′i·nae,** [L. *domina*, lady, mistress, f. of *dominus*, lord, master.] in old English law, a title given to a lady who held a barony in her own right.

dom′in·ănce, dom′i·năn·cy, *n.* a dominating; a being dominant; control; authority.

dom′i·nănt, *a.* [L. *dominans* (*-antis*), ppr. of *dominari*, to rule.]

1. ruling; prevailing; governing; predominant; exercising authority or influence; as, the *dominant* party or faction.

2. in genetics, designating or relating to that one of any pair of opposite Mendelian characters which, when factors for both are present in the germ plasm, dominates over the other and appears in the organism: opposed to *recessive*: see *Mendel's laws*.

3. in music, of or based upon the fifth tone of a diatonic scale.

dominant estate or *tenement*; in law, the estate or tenement in favor of which a servitude exists over another estate.

dominant owner; one who owns a dominant estate or tenement.

Syn.—controlling, predominant, governing, ruling, prevailing.

dom′i·nănt, *n.* 1. in genetics, (a) a dominant character or factor; (b) an organism having such characters.

2. in music, the fifth note of a diatonic scale.

dom′i·nănt·ly, *adv.* in a dominant manner.

dom′i·nāte, *v.t.* and *v.i.*; dominated, *pt.*, *pp.*; dominating, *ppr.* [L. *dominatus*, pp. of *dominari*, to rule.]

1. to rule; to govern; to predominate over.

2. to tower over (other things); to rise high above (the surroundings, etc.); as, the mountain *dominated* the entire scene; kindness *dominated* his character.

dom·i·nā′tion, *n.* [L. *dominatio*, rule, dominion, despotism, from *dominari*, to rule.]

1. a dominating or being dominated; rule; control; ascendancy.

2. [*pl.*] in theology, the fourth order of angels.

dom′i·nā·tive, *a.* inclined to dominate; governing; imperious.

dom′i·nā·tŏr, *n.* [L. *dominator*, a ruler, from *dominari*, to rule.] one who dominates; a ruler.

dom′i·nē, *n.* same as *dominie*.

dom·i·neer′, *v.i.*; domineered, *pt.*, *pp.*; domineering, *ppr.* [L. *dominari*, to rule, to be master, from *dominus*, master, ruler.] to rule (*over*) in a harsh or arrogant way; bully; tyrannize; impose one's own opinion and wishes.

dom·i·neer′, *v.t.* to govern; to control.

dom·i·neer′ing, *a.* ruling with insolence; arrogant; overbearing; tyrannical; imperious.

dom·i·neer′ing·ly, *adv.* in a domineering manner.

dō·min′iç·ăl, *a.* [ML. *dominicalis*, pertaining to the Lord's day or Sunday, from L. *dominicus*, pertaining to a lord, from *dominus*, lord, master.]

1. pertaining to Jesus as the Lord.

2. connected with or denoting the Lord's day (Sunday).

dominical letter; any of the first seven letters in the alphabet as used in church calendars to indicate Sundays: the letters are assigned to the first seven days of January, and the letter falling to Sunday is the arbitrary symbol for Sunday the rest of the year; as, the *dominical letter* of 1945 was G.

dō·min′iç·ăl, *n.* the Lord's day; Sunday. [Obs.]

Dō·min′i·căn, *n.* [named after St. *Dominic*, 1170–1221, the founder.]

1. in the Roman Catholic Church, a member of an order of mendicant friars and nuns founded in 1215.

2. a native or inhabitant of the Dominican Republic.

Dō·min′i·căn, *a.* 1. belonging or relating to the order of Dominicans or to St. Dominic.

2. of the Dominican Republic.

Dominican tertiaries; the third order of St. Dominic.

Dom′i·nick, *n.* same as *Dominique*.

dom′i·nïe, *n.* [L. *domine*, vocative of *dominus*, a master.]

1. in Scotland, a schoolmaster.

2. (*usually* dō′mi-ni), in the United States, a pastor of the Dutch Reformed Church; hence, [Colloq.] any pastor or clergyman.

dō·min′ion (-yun), *n.* [L. *dominium*, dominion, from *dominus*, master, lord.]

1. sovereign or supreme authority; the power of governing and controlling; domination; sovereignty; control.

2. in law, power to direct, control, use, and dispose of; right of possession and use; as, the private *dominion* of individuals.

3. a governed territory or country.

4. [D–] a self-governing commonwealth of the British Empire.

5. [*pl.*] an order of angels; dominations.

Syn.—authority, government, jurisdiction, territory, region.

Dō·min′ion Day, 1. in Canada, a legal holiday, July 1, celebrating the proclamation of the establishment of the Dominion of Canada in 1867.

2. in New Zealand, a legal holiday, the fourth Monday in September.

dō·min′ion·iṣm, *n.* the status of being a self-governing community, as in the British Empire.

dō·min′ion·ist, *n.* a resident of a dominion.

Dom·i·nïque′ (-nēk′), *n.* [Fr., Dominica.] one of an American breed of domestic chickens with yellow legs and gray, barred plumage: also *Dominick*.

dō·min′i·um, *n.* [L., from *dominus*, lord.] in law, ownership or control of a property or right.

dom′i·nō, *n.*; *pl.* **dom′i·nōeṣ, dom′i·nōṣ,** [Fr. *domino*; It. *domino*, hooded cloak (worn by cathedral canons), from L. *dominus*, lord, master: in reference to the costume of one addressed as "sir."]

1. a long, loose cloak, with a hood, wide sleeves, and a mask, worn at masquerades.

2. a mask or half-mask for the eyes: used at masquerades: formerly worn by ladies when traveling: it is generally black.

3. the wearer of such a cloak or mask.

4. a small, flat, rectangular piece of wood, ivory, bone, or plastic divided into two equal spaces, each of which is either blank or marked with from one to six spots: so called in reference to the blackness of the piece.

5. [*pl., construed as sing.*] a game played with twenty-eight such pieces, which the players must match according to the number of dots on each half.

dom′i·nō the′ō·ry, a postulation that if one country, as in southeastern Asia, should come under Communist control, others would quickly follow, as a row of dominoes standing on edge would fall if the first were pushed.

Dom′i·nus, *n.* [L. *dominus*, lord, master.] the Lord.

Dom′i·nus vō·bis′çum, [L.] the Lord be with you.

dom′i·tȧ·ble, *a.* that can be tamed. [Rare.]

dō′mīte, *n.* [name derived from Puy-de-*Dome*, in Auvergne, France, where it is found.] in mineralogy, a variety of trachyte.

don, *v.t.*; donned, *pt.*, *pp.*; donning, *ppr.* [ME. *don on*; AS. *don on*, lit., to do on.] to put on (a garment, etc.); to dress in (a certain color or material).

don, *n.* [Sp. *don*, Mr., sir, from L. *dominus*, lord, master.]

1. [D–] Mr.; sir: a title of respect, used with the given name, as *Don* Alfonso.

2. a Spanish nobleman or gentleman.

3. a personage of importance; a distinguished man.

4. in England, a head, tutor, or fellow of any college of Oxford or Cambridge. [Colloq.]

Do′ña (dō′nyä), *n.* 1. in Spanish, the feminine of *don*; Lady; Madam: used as a title of respect.

2. [d–] a Spanish lady.

Dō′nȧ, *n.* 1. in Portuguese, Lady; Madam: used as a title of respect.

2. [d–] a Portuguese lady.

dō′nȧ·ble, *a.* that may be given. [Rare.]

Dō′när, *n.* in Germanic mythology, the god of thunder, corresponding to the Norse god Thor.

Dō′nȧ·ry, *n.* [L. *donarium*, a sanctuary, offering, from *donum*, a gift.] a thing given to a sacred use. [Rare.]

don′at, *n.* a grammar. [Obs.]

dō′nāte, *v.t.*; donated, *pt.*, *pp.*; donating, *ppr.* [L. *donatus*, pp. of *donare*, to donate, from *donum*, a gift, from *dare*, to give.] to give; to present; to contribute; to bestow as a gift, especially to some philanthropic or religious cause.

dō·nā′tion, *n.* [L. *donatio* (*-onis*), a giving, from *donatus*, pp. of *donare*, to give.]

1. the act of donating; a granting.

2. that which is given, bestowed, or donated; a gift or grant, as to a charitable organization.

3. in law, the act or contract by which a thing, or the use of it, is transferred to a person or corporation, as a free gift; also, the thing so transferred.

donation party; a party held at the house of some person, usually a minister, each guest bringing with him some gift for the host.

Syn.—grant, benefaction, gratuity, endowment, present, gift.

Don′ȧ·tiṣm, *n.* [ML. *Donatista*, from *Donatus*, Bishop of Casae Nigrae, founder of the sect.] the principles embraced by North African schismatics of the fourth century, called *Donatists*, who considered theirs as the only true church, and the ordinances administered in other churches as invalid.

Don′ȧ·tist, *n.* an adherent of Donatism.

Don′ȧ·tist, Don·ȧ·tist′iç, *a.* pertaining to Donatism.

don′ȧ·tive, *n.* [OFr. *donatif*, from L. *donare*, to give.]

1. a gift; a gratuity; a donation.

The Romans were entertained with shows and *donatives*. —Dryden.

2. in canon law, a benefice given and collated to a person, by the founder or patron, without either presentation, institution, or induction by the ordinary: abolished in 1898.

don′ȧ·tive, *a.* vested or vesting by donation; as, a *donative* advowson.

dō·nā′tŏr, *n.* [L., from *donare*, to give.] a donor.

don′ȧ·tō·ry, *n.*; *pl.* **don′ȧ·tō·rieṣ,** one to whom a donation is given; a donee.

dō′nax, *n.* 1. a species of grass, *Arundo donax*, growing to a great height in southern Europe: its stems are used for fishing rods, etc.

2. [D–] a genus of lamellibranchiate mollusks, of the family *Donacidæ*; the wedge shells.

don·cel′lȧ, *n.* [Sp., a maiden, damsel.] in zoology, any of several brightly colored marine fishes found in West Indian waters and the Straits of Florida.

Don Ços′sack, a member of the eastern branch of the Cossacks, living along the middle and lower parts of the Don.

dŏne (dun), *a.* [*pp.* of *do*.]

1. performed; executed; finished.

2. sufficiently cooked.

done brown; cheated; thoroughly swindled. [Colloq.]

done in; completely exhausted; played out; utterly fatigued. [Colloq.]

to have done with; to cease to have concern or business with.

dō·nee′, *n.* [OFr. *doné, donné*, pp. of *doner, donner*, from L. *donare*, to give, donate.]
1. a person who receives a gift or a donation.
2. the person to whom lands or tenements are given or granted; as, a *donee* in fee tail.

don′et, *n.* same as *donat.*

dong, *n.* [echoic.] a sound imitating or representing that of a large bell.

doñ′gȧ, *n.* [S. Afr.] a deep channel of a river.

Doñ′gō·lȧ leath′ẽr (leth′), [from *Dongola*, province of Anglo-Egyptian Sudan.] a goatskin or calfskin tanned to resemble kid.

dō′ni, *n.* a single-masted trading vessel used on the southern coast of India.

dŏn′jŏn (dun′jun), *n.* [ME. *dongeon*; OFr. *donjon*; LL. *dominio (-onis)*, a dungeon, from L. *dominio (-onis)*, power, from *dominus*, master, lord.] the heavily fortified inner tower or keep of a castle.

Don Jū′ȧn (*also Sp.* hwän), 1. in Spanish legend, a dissolute nobleman and seducer of women, the hero of many poems, plays, and operas.
2. any man who seduces women or has one love affair after another; libertine; rake.

doñ′key (*or* duñ′), *n.*; *pl.* **doñ′keys**, [prob. from *dun*; AS. *dun*; W. *dwn*, dusky, and dim. suffix *-key.*]
1. a small domestic animal resembling the horse but with longer ears and a shorter mane; ass.
2. a stubborn, stupid, or obstinate person.
3. a donkey engine.

doñ′key en′ġine, a small, portable steam engine, especially one used on a ship to lift cargo, etc.

doñ′key pump, an auxiliary steam pump.

doñ′key wŏrk, hard work, esp. if routine or menial.

Don′nȧ, *n.* [It., from L. *domina*, mistress, lady.]
1. Lady; Madam: an Italian title of respect, used with the given name.
2. [d–] an Italian lady.

don′nẽred, don′nărd, *a.* [from Scot. dial. *donner*, to stun, freq. of ME. *donen, donien*, to sound.] stunned; stupefied. [Scot.]

don′nish, *a.* of, characteristic of, or like a university don.

don′nism, *n.* the state or quality of being donnish.

Don′ny·brook Fāir, a fair formerly held once a year in August at Donnybrook, a village near Dublin, Ireland, which became notorious for fighting, drinking, and love-making; hence, any fair or celebration like this.

dō′nŏr, *n.* [L. *donator*, a giver, from *donare*, to give.]
1. one who gives or bestows; one who makes a donation.
2. one who grants an estate; as, a conditional fee may revert to the *donor.*

dö′-nŏth″ing, *a.* idle; inactive; lazy; as, a *do-nothing* policy.

dö′-nŏth″ing·ism, dö′-nŏth″ing·ness, *n.* idleness; inactivity.

Don Quix′ote (kwik′sŏt *or Sp.* kē-hō′tē), 1. a satirical romance by Miguel de Cervantes, published in two parts (1605, 1615).
2. the hero of this romance who tries in a chivalrous but unrealistic way to rescue the oppressed and right the wrongs of the world.

don′ship, *n.* the quality or rank of a don.

dōn′t, 1. do not.
2. does not: in this sense now generally considered a substandard usage.

don′zel, *n.* a squire. [Obs.]

doob grȧss, [Hind. *dūb*; Sans. *dūrvā.*] a kind of pasture grass, *Cynodon dactylon*, widespread in warm countries; Bermuda grass.

doo′dad, *n.* 1. any small object whose name does not readily occur to one; gadget. [Colloq.]
2. a bauble; gimcrack. [Colloq.]

doo′dle, *v.t.*; doodled, *pt., pp.*; doodling, *ppr.* [G. *dudeln*, to play (the bagpipe), hence to trifle, dawdle.]
1. originally, to play (the bagpipe). [Archaic.]
2. to make a fool of; fool. [Dial.]

doo′dle, *v.i.* 1. to move aimlessly or foolishly; dawdle.
2. to scribble aimlessly, especially when the attention is elsewhere; make doodles.

doo′dle, *n.* 1. a foolish person; simpleton.
2. a mark, design, figure, etc. made in aimless scribbling.

doo′dle·bug, *n.* the larva of the ant lion.

doo′dle·sack, *n.* [from G. *dudelsack*, a bagpipe.] a bagpipe.

doo′hick·ey, *n.* [fanciful extension of *do*, as also in *doodad*, etc.] any device; contrivance; gadget: humorous substitute for a name not known or temporarily forgotten. [Colloq.]

dook, *n.* [Scot.] a piece of wood inserted in a brick or stone wall, for holding nails, etc.

dool, *n.* dole. [Obs.]

doo′ly, *n.* [Hind. *dūli*, a litter.] a palanquin, or kind of light litter.

doom, *n.* [ME. and AS. *dom*, lit., what is laid down, judgment, decree.]
1. in history, a statute; decree.
2. a judgment; sentence; condemnation.
3. destiny; fate.
4. tragic fate; ruin or death.
5. Judgment Day.

doom, *v.t.*; doomed, *pt., pp.*; dooming, *ppr.*
1. to judge. [Obs.]
2. to pronounce sentence or judgment on; to condemn; to consign by a decree or sentence; as, the criminal is *doomed* to death.
3. to destine to a tragic fate; as, we are *doomed* to suffer for our sins.
4. to ordain as a penalty.
5. formerly, in New England, to assess taxes upon by estimate, when the owner of property made no statement.

doom, *n.* the doom palm.

doom′āġe, *n.* a penalty or fine for neglect. [Obs.]

doom′ful, *a.* full of destruction.

doom pälm (päm), the gingerbread tree of Africa, *Hyphæne thebaica.* Its fruit, about the size of an apple, is used for food: it has a mealy outer husk or pulp, much like gingerbread in taste: also, *doum palm.*

DOOM PALM
(*Hyphæne thebaica*)

dooms′dāy, *n.* [ME. *domesdai*; AS. *domes dæg*, doomsday or day of doom; *domes*, genit. of *dom*, doom, and *dæg*, day.]
1. the day of the Last Judgment.
2. a day of sentence or condemnation; any day of judgment.

Dooms′dāy Book, same as *Domesday Book.*

dooms′măn, *n.* a judge.

doom′stẽr, *n.* in Scots law, formerly, one who pronounced judgment: he was usually also the executioner.

doon, *n.* [native name.] a tree of Ceylon, *Doona ceylanica*, which yields varnish, resin, and lumber.

dōor, *n.* [ME. *dore, dur*; AS. *dor, duru*, pl. *dura*, door; compare O.H.G. *tor, turi*, D. *deur*, G. *tür*, L. *foris*, Gr. *thyra*, door.]
1. a movable structure for opening or closing the entrance to a building or room, or giving access to a closet, cupboard, etc.: most doors turn on hinges, slide in grooves, or revolve on an axis.
2. the room or building to which a door belongs; as, two *doors* down the hall.
3. anything resembling a door, as the shutter of a cupboard.
4. any opening with a door in it; doorway.
5. passage; means of approach or access; as, an unforgiving temper shuts the *door* to reconciliation.

I am the *door*; by me if any man enter in, he shall be saved. —John x. 9.

in doors; within the house.
next door to; near to; bordering on.
out of doors; out of the house; outdoors.
to lie at one's door; to be chargeable to one; as, if the thing is wrong, the fault *lies at my door.*

dōor′bell, *n.* a bell that rings inside a building or room when an outside push button, lever, etc. is worked by someone wishing to enter.

dōor′cāse, *n.* the frame which encloses a door.

dōor′cheek, *n.* the jamb of a door.

dōor′jamb (-jam), *n.* a vertical piece of wood, etc. constituting the side of a doorway.

dōor′keep″ẽr, *n.* 1. a porter; one who guards the entrance of a house, apartment, etc.
2. a doorman.
3. in the Roman Catholic Church, an ostiary.

dōor′knob (-nob), *n.* a small knob or lever on a door, usually for releasing the latch.

dōor′less, *a.* having no door.

dōor′măn, *n.*; *pl.* **dōor′men**, 1. a man whose work is opening the street door of a public building for those who enter or leave, hailing taxicabs, etc.
2. a doorkeeper.

dōor′mat, *n.* a mat for people to wipe their shoes on before entering a house, room, etc.

dōor′nail, *n.* a large-headed nail used as studding on some doors.
dead as a doornail; dead beyond a doubt.

dōor′plāte, *n.* a plate for a house door, bearing the name of the occupant, the number of the house, etc.

dōor′pōst, *n.* same as *doorjamb.*

dōor′sill, *n.* the sill of a door; a threshold.

dōor′stead (-sted), *n.* a doorway.

dōor′step, *n.* a step that leads from an outer door to a path, lawn, etc.

dōor′stōne, *n.* the stone at a threshold.

dōor′stop, *n.* 1. a weight, spring, etc. used to hold a door open at a desired position or prevent it from closing too forcibly.
2. a thin wooden strip affixed to the frame of a doorway, against which the door closes.

dōor′wāy, *n.* 1. the entrance into a room or building that can be closed by a door.
2. a means of access; as, the *doorway* to China.

dōor′weed, *n.* same as *knotgrass.*

dōor′yärd, *n.* a yard onto which a door of a house opens.

dop, dopp, *n.* [D. *dop*; M.D. *dop, doppe*, a shell, husk, cover.] a device for holding a diamond while it is being cut or polished.

dop, *v.i.* to dip. [Obs.]

dop, *n.* a dip; a curtsy or low bow. [Obs.]

dō′pȧ, *n.* [*d*ihydroxy*p*henyl*a*lanine.] an amino acid that is converted by an enzyme in the blood stream into dopamine: its levorotatory isomer (*L-dopa*) is used as a drug in treating Parkinson's disease.

dō′pȧ·mīne, *n.* [*d*ihydroxy*p*henyl, and *amine.*] an amine essential to normal nerve activity in the brain, an intermediate biochemical product in the synthesis of melanin.

dōpe, *n.* [D. *doop*, sauce, dip, baptism, from *doopen*, to dip, baptize, from *diep*, deep.]
1. any preparation of a thick, liquid, or pasty character: used as a lubricant or absorbent.
2. a dressing, varnish, or filler used as for protecting the cloth covering of airplane wings.
3. a drug used to stimulate race horses.
4. any drug or narcotic. [Slang.]
5. advance information on a race horse's condition. [Slang.]
6. any information; especially, advance information for prediction. [Slang.]
7. a user of narcotics. [Slang.]
8. in photography, a developer.
9. a slow-witted person. [Slang.]
dope fiend; a drug addict. [Slang.]
dope sheet; a publication containing statistical information about race horses, for use in betting on races. [Slang.]

dōpe, *v.t.*; doped (dōpt), *pt., pp.*; doping, *ppr.*
1. to treat with dope.
2. to drug or stupefy.
3. to make out or figure out; also, to predict after analyzing the available information (usually with *out*). [Slang.]

dōpe′y, *a.*; *comp.* dopier; *superl.* dopiest, 1. under the influence of a narcotic. [Slang.]
2. mentally slow or confused; lethargic; stupid. [Slang.]

Dop′pel·gäng·er (dop′l-geng-ẽr), *n.* [G.] a doubleganger.

Dop′pẽr, *n.* [ME. *dopper*; AS. *doppa*, from *doppettan*, to dive, from *deop*, deep.]
1. one of a South African Dutch Calvinistic sect.
2. [d–] a diving bird.

Dop′plẽr ef·fect′, [after Christian *Doppler*

(1803–1853), Austrian mathematician and physicist.] the apparent change of frequency of sound waves or light waves, varying with the relative velocity of the source and the observer: if the source and observer are drawing closer together, the frequency is increased.

dop'plēr·īte, *n.* [named after Christian *Doppler.*] a hydrocarbon of a brownish-black color, found in peat bogs.

dor, *n.* same as *dorbeetle.*

dôr, *n.* a deception, joke, trick, or humbug. [Obs.]

dor, *v.t.* to humbug; to hoax; to trick. [Obs.]

Dō·rä'dō, *n.* [Sp. *dorado*, pp. of *dorar*; LL. *deaurare*, to gild; L. *de*, down, and *aurare*, to overlay with gold, from *aurum*, gold.]
 1. a small southern constellation.
 2. [d–] a large fish resembling the dolphin.

dor'bee"tle, *n.* [from ME. *dore*; AS. *dora*, a beetle, cockchafer; and *beetle.*]
 1. the European dung beetle or cockchafer.
 2. any beetle that flies with a buzzing sound.

dor'bug, *n.* same as *dorbeetle.*

Dor'çās, *n.* [L.; Gr. *dorkas*, gazelle.] in the Bible, a woman who spent her life making clothes for the poor: Acts ix. 36–41.

Dor'çās Sō·cī'e·ty, any of various women's sewing societies for supplying clothes to the poor.

dō·ree', *n.* a fish, the dory.

dor'flȳ, *n.* the dorbeetle.

dor'hawk, dorr'hawk, *n.* the goatsucker of Europe: so called because it lives on dorbeetles.

Dō'ri·ăn, *a.* same as *Doric.*

Dō'ri·ăn, *n.* a native of Doris, an ancient region of Greece; member of a race that formed one of the four main divisions of the ancient Greeks.

Dor'iç, *a.* [L. *Doricus*; Gr. *Dōrikos*, Doric.]
 1. of Doris, an ancient region of Greece, its people, their language, or culture.
 2. designating or relating to the architectural style of Doris, characterized by simplicity of form.
 Doric order; the oldest and plainest of the three orders (Doric, Ionic, Corinthian) of classical Greek architecture: it is characterized by fluted, heavy columns with simple capitals.

DORIC ORDER

Dor'iç, *n.* 1. the Greek dialect of Doris.
 2. the Scottish dialect as contrasted with Standard English.

Dor'i·çişm, Dō'rişm, *n.* a characteristic of the Doric dialect.

Dō'ris, *n.* [LL., from Gr. *doris*, a sacrificial knife.] a genus of gastropods having the gills disposed circularly in a posterior rosette; the sea lemons.

Dor'king, *n.* [name derived from *Dorking*, England.] one of the oldest breeds of domestic fowl, having a large, heavy body, short legs, five toes on each foot, and plumage of varying colors.

dorm, *n.* a dormitory. [Colloq.]

dor'măn·cy, *n.* [OFr. *dormance.*] a dormant state.

dor'mănt, *a.* [ME. *dormant*; L. *dormiens* (-*entis*), ppr. of *dormire*, to sleep.]
 1. sleeping.
 2. as if asleep; quiet; still.
 3. inoperative; inactive.
 4. in biology, torpid in winter; as, *dormant* snakes.
 5. in botany, not vegetating; as, *dormant* plants.
 6. in heraldry, in a sleeping position; as, a lion *dormant.*

LION DORMANT

 dormant partner; same as *silent partner.*
 Syn.—sleeping, slumbering, latent, undeveloped, quiescent, inert.

dor'mănt, *n.* a sleeper, or large beam in the roof of a house, forming a base for other timbers. [Obs. except Dial.]

dor'mēr, *n.* [OFr. *dormeor*; L. *dormitorium*, a sleeping room.] a window set upright in a sloping roof; also, the roofed projection in which this window is set: also *dormer window.*

dor'mēred, *a.* having dormers.

dor'mēr win'dōw, same as *dormer.*

dor'mīce, *n.* pl. of *dormouse.*

dor'mi·tive, *a.* [L. *dormitivus*, from *dormire*, to sleep.] producing sleep or tending to produce sleep; soporific. [Rare.]

dor'mi·tive, *n.* a medicine which promotes sleep; an opiate. [Rare.]

dor'mi·tō·ry, *n.*; *pl.* **dor'mi·tō·ries,** [L. *dormitorium*, a sleeping room, from *dormire*, to sleep.]
 1. a room, building, or part of a building, with sleeping accommodations for a number of people.
 2. a building with many rooms that provide sleeping and living accommodations for a number of people, as in most colleges.
 3. a burial place. [Obs.]

dor'mouse, *n.*; *pl.* **dor'mīce,** [ME. *dormous*, lit., slumber mouse.] a rodent of the family *Myoxidæ*, found in Europe and Asia and sometimes in Africa. They resemble squirrels, live in trees, and are dormant during winter.

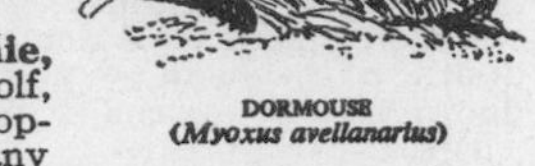

DORMOUSE (*Myoxus avellanarius*)

dor'my, dor'mie, *a.* [Scot.] in golf, ahead of an opponent by as many holes as there remain yet to play: said of a player or a side.

dorn, *n.* [G. *dorn*, a thorn.] the thornback ray.

dor'nick, dor'nock, *n.* [from *Doornik*, Fl. name of Tournai, Belgium, where it was originally made.]
 1. a coarse damask, formerly used for altar cloths and ecclesiastical hangings.

dor'nick, *n.* [Ir. Gael. *dornóg*, Scot. Gael. *doirneag*, from *dorn*, hand.] a stone of a size suitable for throwing.

dorp, *n.* [D.] a small village; a hamlet.

dorr, *n.* same as *dorbeetle.*

dorr'bee·tle, *n.* same as *dorbeetle.*

dor'sȧ, *n.* pl. of *dorsum.*

dor'sad, *adv.* [L. *dorsum*, the back, and *ad*, to, toward.] in anatomy and zoology, toward the back; dorsally.

dor'săl, *a.* [Fr. *dorsal*; LL. *dorsalis*, of or pertaining to the back, from L. *dorsum*, the back.]
 1. in anatomy and zoology, of, pertaining to, or situated on or near the back of an animal or any organ; as, a *dorsal* fin; the *dorsal* aspect of the hand.
 2. in botany, pertaining to the under surface of a leaf.
 dorsal vessel; a long blood vessel lying along the back of an insect and performing the functions of a heart.

dor'săl, *n.* 1. in anatomy, a dorsal vertebra.
 2. in ichthyology, a dorsal fin.
 3. a dossal.

dor'săl·ly, *adv.* on, near, or toward the back; in a dorsal position or direction.

dorse, *n.* [OFr. *dors*, *dos*; L. *dorsum*, the back.]
 1. the back; as, books with rich *dorses.* [Obs.]
 2. a piece of silk, damask, or other rich material, used to cover the back of a chair, or hung behind an altar or within the chancel; especially, a rich hanging covering the back of a chair of state or a throne; a dossal.

dorse, *n.* [G. *dorsch*, a paddock; L.G. *dorsh*, a codfish.] a young cod: once believed to be a distinct species.

dor'sel, *n.* a dossal.

dor'sēr, *n.* a dosser.

Dor'set Horn, any of a breed of large-horned sheep having wool of medium length: originally from Dorsetshire, England.

dor'si-, [from L. *dorsum*, back.] a combining form meaning *of*, *on*, or *along the back*: often identical with *dorso-.*

dor'si·brañch, *a.* and *n.* same as *dorsibranchiate.*

Dor"si·brañ·chi·ā'tȧ, *n.pl.* [*dorsi-*, and L. *branchiæ*, gills.] an order of the *Annelida* in which the branchiae lie along the back. It includes the free marine worms.

dor·si·brañ'chi·āte, *a.* having dorsal branchiae; of or pertaining to the *Dorsibranchiata.*

dor·si·brañ'chi·āte, *n.* one of the *Dorsibranchiata.*

dor·si·çum'bent, *a.* [*dorsi-*, and L. *-cumbens*, ppr. of *-cumbere*, in *incumbere*, to lie down.] lying upon the back.

dor·sif'ēr·ous, *a.* [*dorsi-*, and L. *ferre*, to bear.]
 1. same as *dorsigerous.*
 2. same as *dorsiparous.*

dor'si·fixed (-fixt), *a.* [*dorsi-*, and L. *fixus*, pp. of *figere*, to fix.] attached dorsally: said of anthers, etc.

dor·sig'ēr·ous, *a.* [*dorsi-*, and L. *gerere*, to carry.] in zoology, carrying the young on the back, as certain opossums.

dor·sip'ȧ·rous, *a.* [*dorsi-*, and L. *parere*, to produce.]
 1. in botany, bearing or producing seeds or fruit on the back: applied to ferns or plants of the capillary kind, without stalks.
 2. in zoology, hatching the young upon the back, as the Surinam toad.

dor·si·ven'trăl, *a.* [*dorsi-*, and L. *venter*, belly.]
 1. in botany, having both dorsal and ventral surfaces.
 2. in zoology, dorsoventral.

dor'sō-, [from L. *dorsum*, back.] a combining form meaning: (a) *relating to the back*; (b) *the back and.*

dor·sō·ven'trăl, *a.* 1. in botany, dorsiventral.
 2. in zoology, from the back to the front; from the dorsum to the ventral side.

dor'sū·lum, *n.*; *pl.* **dor'sū·lȧ,** [L., dim. of *dorsum*, the back.] the mesonotum of insects, when large and conspicuous, as in bees.

dor'sum, *n.*; *pl.* **dor'sȧ,** [L., the back.]
 1. in anatomy, the back; also, the back of any part or organ; as, the *dorsum* of the foot.
 2. the ridge of a hill. [Rare.]

dort'y, *a.* [from Scot. dial. *dort*, to sulk, and *-y.*] bad-tempered; sullen. [Scot.]

dō'ry, *n.*; *pl.* **dō'ries,** [Am. Ind. (Central America) *dori*, *duri*, a dugout.] a small, flat-bottomed fishing boat with high sides and considerable sheer of the gunwale.

dō'ry, *n.* [Fr. *dorée*, the dory, lit., gilt, f. of *doré*, pp. of *dorer*; LL. *deaurare*, to gild.]
 1. a small edible fish, *Zeus faber*, found in European seas; the John dory.
 2. any of several fishes related to this, as the wall-eyed pike, *Stizostedion vitreum.*

DORY (*Zeus faber*)

Dō·ryph'ō·rȧ, *n.* [L., from Gr. *doryphoros*, spear-bearing; *dory*, the stem of a tree, a beam, shaft, and *pherein*, to bear.] a genus of beetles which live on and destroy plants: it includes the potato bug.

dō·ryph'ō·rus, *n.*; *pl.* **dō·ryph'ō·rī,** [Gr. *doryphoros*, bearing a spear, from *dory*, a shaft, spear, and *pherein*, to bear, carry.] in classical sculpture, the figure of a man holding a spear.

dos·ȧ·dos' (dō-zȧ-dō'), *adv.* [Fr., lit., back to back.] back to back: used specifically of a figure in a reel or other dance, in which two dancers advance toward each other, pass around each other back to back, and return to their original places.

dos·ȧ·dos', *n.*; *pl.* **dos·ȧ·dos'** (-dōz'), any seat, sofa, carriage, etc. built so that the occupants sit back to back.

dōs'āġe, *n.* 1. in medicine, the act or practice of giving medicine in regular doses.
 2. the amount of medicine in a single dose.
 3. the process of adding to wines, especially to champagnes, anything which will flavor or strengthen it.

dōse, *n.* [Gr. *dosis*, a gift, from *didonai*, to give.]
 1. the quantity of medicine given or prescribed to be taken at one time or at stated intervals.
 2. amount of a remedy, punishment, etc. given or taken at one time; something administered.
 3. any ingredient added to wine, etc. to flavor or strengthen it.
 4. a venereal infection, especially gonorrhea. [Slang.]

dōse, *v.t.*; dosed (dōst), *pt.*, *pp.*; dosing, *ppr.*
 1. to administer (medicine, etc.) in doses.
 2. to give doses to.
 3. to give anything nauseous to.
 4. to add something to (wine, etc.) to flavor or strengthen it.

dōse, *v.i.* to take a dose or doses of medicine.

dō·sim'e·tēr, *n.* [Gr. *dosis*, a gift, dose, and *metron*, measure.] a device used to measure small quantities of liquid, as of doses.

dō·si·met'riç, *a.* pertaining to the measurement of doses.

dō·sim'e·try, *n.* the measurement of liquids as with a dosimeter.

dō·sol'ō·ġy, *n.* [Gr. *dosis*, a dose, and *logos*, description.] the science of measuring medicines into doses.

doss, *n.* a bed, especially in a cheap lodging house. [Brit. Slang.]
doss, *v.i.* to sleep. [Brit. Slang.]
dos'săl, dos'sel, *n.* [OFr. *dossel*; LL. *dorsale*, a canopy, tapestry, from L. *dorsum*, the back.]
1. an ornamental cloth of silk, damask, etc. at the back of the altar or the sides of the chancel of a church.
2. an ornamental upholstery at the back of a chair, throne, etc.
dos'sẽr, *n.* [ME. *dosser*; OFr. *dossier*; LL. *dorserium*, tapestry, a canopy, from L. *dorsum*, the back.]
1. a large basket that can be carried on the back; especially, one of a pair of baskets slung over the back of a pack animal; pannier.
2. a dossal.
dos'sẽr, *n.* one who sleeps at a doss house. [Brit. Slang.]
doss house, a very cheap kind of lodging house. [Brit. Slang.]
dos'si·ẽr (*or* -si-ā), *n.* [Fr., bundle of papers.] a collection of documents recording information about some person or matter.
dos·si·ère' (-ãr'), *n.* [OFr. *dossiere*, a curtain.] that part of a suit of armor which protected the back, extending from the neck to the waist.
dos'sil, dos'sel, *n.* [ME. *dosil*; LL. *docillus*, a spigot, from L. *ducere*, to lead.]
1. a plug; a spigot. [Obs.]
2. a pledget or small piece of cotton or cloth rolled in the form of a cylinder and used for cleaning a wound or sore.
3. in printing, a roll of cloth for cleaning ink from an engraved plate previous to taking an impression from it.
dŏst, *v.* archaic second person singular, present indicative of *do*: used with *thou*.
dot, *n.* [AS. *dott*, a dot, speck, from *dyttan*, to stop up, plug.]
1. a small point or spot made with a pen or other pointed instrument; a speck.
2. a small, round spot.
3. anything resembling a dot.
4. the short sound used in the Morse code of telegraphy, written as a dot: distinguished from *dash*.
5. in mathematics, (a) a decimal point; (b) a symbol of multiplication.
6. in music, (a) a mark after a note or rest, increasing its time value by one-half: two dots increase the time value by three-quarters; (b) a staccato mark.
7. in printing and writing, (a) the mark used above an *i* or *j*: originally a stroke distinguishing *i* from *n*, *m*, *u*, etc.; (b) the similar mark indicating a full stop; period.
dot, *v.t.*; dotted, *pt.*, *pp.*; dotting, *ppr.* 1. to mark with a small dot or spot; as, to *dot* an *i*.
2. to cover with or as with dots; as, a landscape *dotted* with cottages or clumps of trees.
3. to make or form with dots; as, a *dotted* line.
dot, *v.i.* to make a dot or dots.
dot, *n.* [Fr., from L. *dos*, *dotis*, from *dare*, to give.] a woman's dowry at marriage.
dō'tăge, *n.* [ME. *dotage*, from *doten*, *dotien*, to dote.]
1. feebleness or senility; childishness of old age; as, a venerable man, now in his *dotage*.
2. a doting; foolish or excessive fondness.
dō'tăl, *a.* [L. *dotalis*, pertaining to a dowry, from *dos* (*dotis*), a dowry.] of or pertaining to a dowry.
dō'tănt, *n.* same as *dotard*. [Obs.]
dō'tărd, *n.* [ME. *dotard*, from *dotien*, to date.]
1. a person in his dotage; foolish and doddering old person.
2. a decayed tree. [Obs.]
dō'tărd, *a.* 1. foolish; doting; imbecile.
2. decayed, as a tree. [Brit. Dial.]
dō'tărd·ly, *a.* like a dotard; weak; foolish; imbecile.
dō·tā'tion, *n.* [LL. *dotatio* (*-onis*), an act of endowing, from L. *dotare*, to endow, from *dos* (*dotis*), a dowry.] the act of endowing; also, an endowment.
dotch'in (doch'), *n.* [alteration of Chinese *toh*, to measure, and *ching*, to weigh.] a portable steelyard used in China and Japan.
dōte, *v.i.*; doted, *pt.*, *pp.*; doting, *ppr.* [ME. *dotien*, *doten*, to dote.]
1. to be foolish or weak-minded, especially because of old age; show senility.
Time has made you *dote*, and vainly tell
Of arms imagined in your lonely cell.
—Dryden.
2. to be excessively or foolishly fond: with *on* or *upon*; as, to *dote on* one's child; to *dote upon* cherries.
3. to decay; to wither, as a tree. [Obs.]
dōte, *n.* 1. a dowry; a dot. [Obs.]
2. [*pl.*] natural gifts or endowments. [Obs.]
dōte, *n.* an imbecile; a dotard. [Obs.]
dōt'ed, *a.* 1. foolish; silly; stupid. [Obs.]
2. partially decayed, as a tree.
dōte'head (-hed), *n.* one who is given to foolish affections or fancies; a dotard. [Rare.]
dōt'ẽr, *n.* 1. one in his dotage; a senile person.
2. one who is excessively fond; one who dotes: with *on* or *upon*.
dōt'ẽr·y, *n.* the acts, speech, or behavior of a dotard or doter.
dŏth, *v.* archaic third person singular, present indicative, of *do*.
Dō·thid·ē·ā'cē·ae, *n.pl.* [L., from Gr. *dothiēn*, a boil, abscess.] a family of fungi, the spores of which form in asci, having the perithecia immersed in a black or blackish stroma. Some are found on growing plants, others on dead vegetable substances.
doth''i·en·en·te·rī'tis, *n.* [Gr. *dothiēn*, a boil, abscess, and *entera*, intestines.] inflammation of the intestines, characteristic of typhoid fever; also, the fever itself. [Obs.]
dōt'ing, *a.* 1. excessively fond.
2. in botany, doty; decaying from age.
dōt'ing·ly, *adv.* in a doting manner.
dōt'ish, *a.* foolishly fond; imbecile; weak.
dot'kin, *n.* same as *dodkin*.
dot'ted, *a.* marked with, made up of, or covered with dots or dotlike parts.
dot'tel, *n.* same as *dottle*.
dot'tẽr·el, *n.*; *pl.* **dot'tẽr·els** or **dot'tẽr·el,** [ME. *dotrelle*, a dunce, a foolish person, from *dotien*, to dote, to be foolish.]
1. a migratory plover, *Ægialites* or *Eudromias morinellus*, common in Europe and Asia. It derives its name from its apparent stupidity or tameness. Its flesh is considered a great delicacy.
2. any of several related shore birds with a short bill.
3. a person easily duped or deceived. [Dial.]
dot'tle, *n.* [ME. *dottel*, a plug or tap of a vessel; AS. *dott*, a dot, point, from *dyttan*, to plug, stop up.]
1. a stopper; a plug. [Obs.]
2. the caked ash remaining in the bowl of a tobacco pipe after it has been smoked.
dot'trel, *n.* same as *dotterel*.
dot'ty, *a.*; *comp.* dottier; *superl.* dottiest, [from *dot*, a spot.]
1. covered with dots; dotted.
2. feeble; unsteady; shaky. [Colloq.]
3. feeble-minded; mentally weak or queer; crazy. [Colloq.]
dō'ty, *a.*; *comp.* dotier; *superl.* dotiest, [from *dote*.] in botany, discolored and decayed from age.
döu·âne', *n.* [Fr.] a customhouse in France.
döu·â·niẽr', *n.* [Fr.] an officer of the French customs.
dou'ăr, dow'ăr, *n.* [Ar. *daur*, a circle.] a group of Arab tents, arranged in a circle, serving as an enclosure for horses, etc.
Döu·āy' Bī'ble (dọọ-ā'), an English version of the Bible translated from the Latin Vulgate edition for the use of Roman Catholics: the New Testament was published at Reims (1582), the Old Testament at Douai (1609–1610).
dou·blé' (dö-blā'), *a.* [Fr.] in bookbinding, having the inside of the cover lined with leather.
dŏu'ble (dub''l), *a.* [ME. *double*; OFr. *double*; L. *duplus*, double; *duo*, two, and *plenus*, full, from *plere*, to fill.]
1. coupled; composed of two mutual or corresponding parts; as, a *double* chin.
2. twice as much, as many, as large, etc.; containing the same quantity or length repeated.
Take *double* money in your hand.
—Gen. xliii. 12.
3. combining two in one; twofold; as, to hold a *double* office.
4. deceitful; acting two parts; two-faced; deceiving.
And with a *double* heart do they speak.
—Ps. xii. 2.
5. having two layers; folded in two.
6. being of two kinds; dual; as, a *double* standard.
7. having two meanings; ambiguous.
8. designed or made for two; as, a *double* quantity.
9. having a tone an octave lower: said of musical instruments.
10. in botany, having more than one set of petals.
11. of extra weight, size, thickness, strength, etc.; as, a *double* sole; *double* ale.
double bed; a wide bed in which two persons can sleep: the standard width is 54 inches.
double boiler; a cooking utensil made of two pots, one of which is made to fit into the other: food is cooked in the upper pot by the heat of water boiling in the lower.
double indemnity; see under *indemnity*.
double note; in music, a breve.
double play; in baseball, a play by which two men are put out.
double salt; in chemistry, (a) a salt, as sodium potassium tartrate, which in solution produces two different cations or anions; (b) two salts in molecular combination; a compound salt, as alum.
double standard; (a) bimetallism; (b) a code of morals imposing a strict standard of behavior on women, but allowing men greater freedom, especially in matters of sex.
double star; in astronomy, two stars, so near each other that they cannot be distinguished as separate without a telescope.
dŏu'ble (dub''l), *n.* 1. anything twice as much, or twice the number, sum, value, quantity, or length.
If the thief be found, let him pay *double*.
—Ex. xxii. 7.
2. a sharp turn or shift in direction.
3. a trick; a shift; an artifice to deceive.
4. a counterpart; an exact copy; a duplicate; as, he is my *double*.
5. a fold, or the place where a thing is folded; second ply.
6. a substitute actor or singer.
7. a stand-in or substitute, as in motion pictures.
8. beer of more than ordinary strength.
A pot of good *double*. —Shak.
9. in music, (a) a variation; (b) a repetition of words or a refrain in singing; (c) an organ stop that sounds an octave below unison in pitch.
10. [*pl.*] in tennis, etc., a match in which two play on a side.
11. in printing, a doublet.
12. in military usage, double time.
13. in bridge, an instance of doubling an opponent's bid; also, a hand that allows a player to do this.
14. in baseball, a hit on which the batter reaches second base.
15. a twofold victory or defeat.
dŏu'ble, *adv.* 1. twice.
I was *double* their age. —Swift.
2. twofold.
3. two together; in or by pairs.
to see double; to see two images of the same object.
dŏu'ble, *v.t.*; doubled, *pt.*, *pp.*; doubling, *ppr.* [ME. *doublen*; OFr. *doubler*, to double, from L. *duplus*, double.]
1. to fold; as, to *double* the leaf of a book; to *double* down a corner.
2. to increase or extend by adding an equal sum, value, quantity, or length; to multiply by two; as, to *double* a sum of money; to *double* the quantity or size of a thing.
3. to be the double of.
4. to repeat or duplicate; as, to *double* blow on blow.
5. to clench, as the fist (with *up*).
6. in nautical usage, to sail around or by, as a cape, point, etc.
7. in bridge, to increase the point values or the penalties of (an opponent's bid). In auction bridge the increase is double, while in contract bridge it is fixed according to the scoring system.
8. in music, to supply the upper or lower octave to (another part or voice); as, *double* the tenor in brass.
dŏu'ble, *v.i.* 1. to increase to twice the sum, number, value, quantity, or length; to increase or grow to twice as much; to become double; as, a sum of money *doubles* by compound interest in a little while.
2. to enlarge a wager to twice the sum laid.
I am resolved to *double* till I win.
—Dryden.
3. to turn or bend back sharply.
Doubling and turning like a hunted hare.
—Dryden.
4. to play tricks; to use deceit.
5. in printing, to set up the same word or words, unintentionally, a second time.
6. in military usage, to march at double time; as, to *double* across the parade ground.
7. to double the bid of an opponent in auction or in contract bridge.
8. to serve two purposes, serve as a double, etc.
9. in baseball, to hit a double.

to double up; (a) to bend over, as in laughter or pain; (b) to share a room, etc. with someone.
dŏu′ble-a̧ct″ing, *a.* in mechanics, acting or exerting power in two directions, producing a twofold result.
dŏu′ble-bañked (dub′l-bañkt), *a.* having two opposite oars managed by rowers on the same bench, or having two men to the same oar.
dŏu′ble bär, in music, two parallel vertical lines drawn through the staff to indicate the end of a movement.
dŏu′ble-bar′reled, *a.* 1. having two barrels, as a gun.
2. having two uses or purposes.
3. that can be taken in two ways; ambiguous.
dŏu′ble-bāss′, *a.* contrabass.
dŏu′ble bāss, the largest and deepest-toned musical instrument of the violin family: it has a range of more than three octaves.
dŏu′ble bas·so̤on′, a large bassoon pitched an octave lower than the ordinary bassoon.
dŏu′ble bīnd, 1. a situation in which a person is faced with contradictory demands, expectations, etc. so that any action taken will appear to be wrong.
2. any dilemma (sense 2).
dŏu′ble (Black′wa̤ll) hitch, a kind of knot: see *knot*, illus.
dŏu′ble-blīnd, *a.* designating or of a technique or method of evaluating the effects of a drug, course of treatment, etc. in which neither the subjects nor the researchers know who specifically is receiving the drug or treatment under study.
dŏu′ble-breast′ed, *a.* overlapping so as to provide a double thickness of material across the breast, and having a double row of buttons: said of a coat, etc.
dŏu′ble chin, a fold of flesh beneath the chin.
dŏu′ble çross, a double-crossing; treachery. [Slang.]
dŏu′ble-çross, *v.t.*; double-crossed, *pt.*, *pp.*; double-crossing, *ppr.* to betray (a person) by doing the opposite of, or intentionally failing to do, what one has promised; cheat. [Slang.]
dŏu′ble çross′ẽr, one who double-crosses. [Slang.]
dŏu′ble dag′gẽr, a mark (‡) used in printing and writing to indicate a note or cross reference; diesis.
dŏu′ble dāte, a social engagement in which two couples go somewhere or do something together. [Colloq.]
dŏu′ble-dēal′ẽr, *n.* one who is deceitful or tricky; one guilty of duplicity.
dŏu′ble-dēal′ing, *n.* duplicity; the profession of one thing and the practice of another.
dŏu′ble-deck′ẽr, *n.* 1. any structure or vehicle with an upper deck or floor.
2. a sandwich with two layers of filling and three slices of bread. [Colloq.]
dŏu′ble-dig′it, *a.* amounting to ten percent or more; as, *double-digit* inflation.
dŏu′ble dip′ping, the practice of receiving compensation, benefits, etc. from two or more sources in a way regarded as unethical, as from a military pension and also from a government job.
dŏu′ble-dȳed, *a.* 1. twice dyed.
2. thorough; complete; utter; as, a *double-dyed* villain.
dŏu′ble ēa′gle (ē′gl), a gold coin of the United States, worth $20: it is no longer in circulation.
dŏu′ble-edġed′ (-ejd′), *a.* 1. having two cutting edges.
2. cutting both ways: said of an argument which can be applied both for and against the person employing it.
dŏu′ble end′ẽr, anything with its two ends alike, so that it may move or operate in both directions with equal facility.
dŏu′ble-en̄·ten̄′dre (dōb′l-än̄-tän̄′dr), *n.* [Fr. *double*, double, and *entendre*, to understand.]
1. a word or expression having two meanings, especially when one of these has a risqué or indecorous connotation.
2. the use of such a term or terms; ambiguity.
dŏu′ble en′try, see *bookkeeping*.
dŏu′ble ex·pō′ṣūre (-zhūr), 1. the making of two exposures on the same film or plate, either by mistake or for a composite photograph.
2. a photograph made in this way.
dŏu′ble-fāced′ (-fāst′), *a.* 1. having two faces looking in opposite directions, as the Roman god Janus.
2. having both sides or surfaces equally well finished and designed for use.
3. deceitful; hypocritical.
dŏu′ble fēa′tūre, two full-length motion pictures on the same program.
dŏu′ble fīrst, in British universities, (a) one who after a final or honors examination gains a degree in the first class in each of two subjects; (b) a university degree taken with first-class honors in two subjects.
dŏu′ble flōor, a floor constructed with binding and bridging joists.
dŏu′ble·gañg·ẽr, *n.* [G. *doppelegänger*, from *doppel*, double, and *gänger*, goer, walker.] the supposed ghost or wraith of a living person.
dŏu′ble här′ness, 1. a harness for a pair of horses.
2. close association or companionship, as in marriage.
dŏu′ble-head′ed (hed′), *a.* having two heads; as, a *double-headed* eagle in a coat of arms.
dŏu′ble-head′ẽr, *n.* 1. a railroad train drawn by two locomotives.
2. in baseball, two games played in succession by the same two teams on the same day.
dŏu′ble-heärt′ed, *a.* having a false heart; deceitful; treacherous.
dŏu′ble-hung′, *a.* being so suspended as to move up or down with equal ease: said of the two sashes of a window hung with cords and weights.
dŏu′ble-joint′ed, *a.* having joints that permit limbs, fingers, etc. to bend at other than the usual angles.
dŏu′ble-lock′, *v.t.* 1. to fasten with two bolts, or secure with double fastenings.
2. to secure by turning a key or shooting a bolt twice, as in some forms of lock.
dŏu′ble-mīnd′ed, *a.* unsettled; wavering; unstable; undetermined.
dŏu′ble·ness, *n.* 1. the state of being double or doubled.
2. duplicity; deceit.
dŏu′ble-pärk′, *v.t.* and *v.i.* to park (an automobile), usually unlawfully, alongside another that is properly parked next to a curb.
dŏu′ble pneū·mō′ni·ȧ (nū-), pneumonia of both lungs.
dŏu′ble-quick′ (kwik′), *n.* in military usage, a very quick marching step, consisting of 180 steps to the minute: also called *double time*.
dŏu′ble-quick′, *a.* 1. performed in the time of the double-quick.
2. very quick or rapid; as, he disappeared in *double-quick* time.
dŏu′ble-quick′, *adv.* in double-quick step; in double time.
dŏu′ble-quick′, *v.t.* and *v.i.* to march or cause to march in double-quick time.
dŏu′blẽr, *n.* 1. one who or that which doubles.
2. an instrument for augmenting a very small quantity of electricity, so as to make it manifest by sparks or the electrometer.
dŏu′ble-reed′, *a.* designating or of any of a group of wood-wind instruments, as the oboe or bassoon, having two reeds separated by a narrow opening, that are vibrated against each other by the breath.
dŏu′ble-reed′, *n.* a double-reed instrument.
dŏu′ble-rip′pẽr, *n.* a sled used for coasting downhill, composed of two sleds placed one behind the other, united by a long board used for the seat; a bobsled.
dŏu′ble shärp, a symbol (× or ⋇) indicating that a note must be raised two half tones above the natural pitch.
dŏu′ble snīpe, the greater snipe, *Gallinago major*.
dŏu″ble-stop′, *v.i.* to produce two tones at once by drawing the bow over two strings of the violin, etc. at the same time: the strings may or may not be stopped with the fingers, depending upon what tones are desired.
dŏu″ble-stop′, *n.* 1. the two tones produced by double-stopping.
2. the notes showing these.
dŏu′blet (dub′), *n.* [ME. *dublet*, *dobbelet*; OFr. *doublet*, a double stone, a close-fitting garment, dim. of *double*, double.]
1. a close-fitting garment for men, with or without sleeves, covering the body from the neck to a little below the waist. It was introduced from France into England in the fifteenth century and was worn until the time of Charles II.

DOUBLET

2. one of two like things.
3. a pair; a couple.
4. a counterfeit gem composed of two pieces of crystal, with a color between them, so that they have the same appearance as if the whole substance of the crystal were colored.
5. [*pl.*] a pair of dice thrown so that identical sides are uppermost.
6. a simple form of microscope, consisting of a combination of two plano-convex lenses whose focal lengths are in the ratio of three to one, placed with their plane sides toward the object and the lens of shortest focal length next to the object.
7. in linguistics, one of two (or more) words ultimately from the same source, but different in form, and often slightly different in meaning, as *drag* and *draw*.
dŏu′ble tāke, a delayed reaction to some unusual or unexpected situation, statement, etc., in which there is first unthinking acceptance and then a startled and obvious understanding of the true meaning: used especially as a piece of comic business in acting.
dŏu′ble ta̤lk, 1. ambiguous and deceptive talk.
2. meaningless syllables made to sound like talk; gibberish.
dŏu′ble-tēam, *v.t.* [after *team*, *n.* 2.] in sports, to use two players to guard or block (a single opposing player).
dŏu′ble tīme, 1. a rate of payment twice as high as usual, as for overtime on Sundays.
2. a marching cadence of 180 three-foot steps a minute, used in the U.S. Army: normal cadence is 120 steps a minute.
3. double-quick.
4. in music, duple time.
dŏu′ble-tŏngue (-tung), *n.* duplicity. [Obs.]
dŏu′ble-tŏngue, *v.i.* in music, to vibrate the tongue in playing the flute and certain brass instruments, as the cornet, so as to produce staccato tones.
dŏu′ble-tŏngued (-tungd), *a.* not sincere; deceitful.
dŏu′ble·tree, *n.* a crossbar on a vehicle to which the singletrees are attached when two horses are harnessed abreast.
dŏu′ble va̤ult, in architecture, one vault built over another, with a space between the convexity of the one and the concavity of the other.

DOUBLE VAULTS

dŏu′bling, *n.* 1. the act of making double; a repetition; that which is or has been doubled.
2. a shift; an artifice; a turning; as, the *doubling* of a fox.
3. the second distillation of spirits.
4. in heraldry, the lining, as of a mantle.
5. in nautical usage, (a) [*pl.*] the part of a mast between the trestletrees and the cap of the lower spar; (b) the sheathing secured to a ship's side as a protection against chafing by ice, etc., as on arctic whalers.
dŏub·lo̤on′, *n.* [Fr. *doublon*; Sp. *doblón*, a doubloon, from *doblo*, double; from L. *duplus*, double.] a Spanish gold coin, no longer minted. It was originally a double pistole, and varied in value from $5 to $16.
dōu·blūre′, *n.* [Fr., lining, from *double*, double, from L. *duplus*, lit., twofold.] an ornamental lining, as of leather, on the inner side of a book cover.
dŏu′bly, *adv.* 1. twice; to twice the quantity or degree; as, *doubly* wise or good.
2. two at a time.
3. in a deceitful manner; with duplicity [Archaic.]

doubt (dout), *v.i.*; doubted, *pt., pp.*; doubting, *ppr.* [ME. *douten, dowten*; OFr. *douter*, to doubt, fear; L. *dubitare*, to doubt, hesitate, from *duo*, two.]
1. to waver or fluctuate in opinion or belief; to be uncertain or undecided respecting the truth or fact; to be undetermined.
2. to be inclined to disbelief.
3. to hesitate. [Archaic.]

doubt (dout), *v.t.* 1. to question or hold as questionable; to withhold assent from; to feel distrust of.
2. to be inclined to disbelieve; as, I *doubt* the truth of the story.
3. to be fearful, apprehensive, or suspicious of. [Archaic.]

doubt (dout), *n.* 1. uncertainty of mind; unsettled opinion or belief; lack of conviction.
2. a condition of uncertainty.
Thy life shall hang in *doubt* before thee.
—Deut. xxviii. 66.
3. an unsettled point or matter; difficulty.
To every *doubt* your answer is the same.
—Blackmore.
4. apprehension; fear. [Obs.]
beyond doubt; certainly.
in doubt; not certain; not sure.
no doubt; (a) certainly; (b) very likely; probably.
without doubt; certainly.
Syn.—hesitation, mistrust, perplexity, suspense, uncertainty.

doubt'á·ble, *a.* 1. that can be doubted; questionable.
2. redoubtable. [Obs.]

doubt'ănce, *n.* uncertainty. [Obs.]

doubt'ẽr, *n.* one who doubts.

doubt'fụl, *a.* 1. in doubt; ambiguous; not clear in meaning; as, a *doubtful* expression.
2. of uncertain issue; unsure.
Who have sustained one day in *doubtful* fight. —Milton
3. of questionable character; giving rise to doubt or suspicion; as, he employed *doubtful* agents.
4. dubious; not settled in opinion; undetermined; wavering.
5. not secure; suspicious; as we cast a *doubtful* eye. [Obs.]
Syn.—ambiguous, equivocal, dubious, precarious, questionable, uncertain.

doubt'fụl·ly, *adv.* in a doubtful manner; dubiously.

doubt'fụl·ness, *n.* 1. a state of doubt or uncertainty of mind; dubiousness.
2. ambiguity; uncertainty of meaning.
3. uncertainty of event or issue; uncertainty of condition.

doubt'ing, *a.* wavering in mind, hesitating.

doubt'ing·ly, *adv.* in a doubting manner.

doubt'ing Thom'ăs (tom'), [after the apostle *Thomas*, who doubted Jesus' resurrection: John xx. 24–29.] a person who habitually doubts; chronic skeptic.

doubt'less, *a.* free from doubt; confident. [Rare.]

doubt'less, *adv.* 1. without doubt or question; unquestionably; undoubtedly.
2. very likely; probably.

doubt'less·ly, *adv.* unquestionably.

doubt'ous, *a.* doubtful. [Obs.]

döuç, *n.* [Fr.] a monkey having variegated colors, *Pygathrix nemaeus*, found in forested regions of Vietnam.

döuce, *a.* [Scot., from ME. *douce*; OFr. *douce*, f. of *doux*, sweet; L. *dulcis*, sweet.] pleasant; sweet-natured; hospitable. [Scot.]

döu'cet, *n.* [ME., from OFr. *doucet*, sweet, gentle; from L. *dulcis*, sweet.]
1. a pastry; a custard.
2. a testicle of a deer.
3. a kind of flute. [Obs.]
Also *dowcet, dowset.*

döu·cēur', *n.* [Fr. *douceur*; OFr. *doucor*, sweetness, a gift; L. *dulcis*, sweet.]
1. sweetness or charm of manner. [Rare.]
2. a gift; a reward; something given for service done or to be done; especially, a bribe; a tip.

döuçhe, *n.* [Fr., from L. *ductus*, pp. of *ducere*, to lead, bring, conduct.]
1. a jet or stream of liquid applied externally or internally to some part of the body, sometimes for medicinal purposes.
2. a bath or treatment of this kind.
3. a device for douching.

döuçhe, *v.t.* and *v.i.*; douched, *pt., pp.*; douching, *ppr.* to apply a douche to (some part of the body, especially the vagina).

döu'cīne, *n.* [Fr.] a molding, concave above and convex below, serving as a cyma to a cornice; a cyma recta.

döuck'ẽr, *n.* a bird that dips or dives in water; a diver; a ducker. [Obs.]

dōugh (dō), *n.* [ME. *dough, dogh*; AS. *dag.*
1. a mixture of flour, liquid, and other ingredients, worked into a soft, thick mass for baking into bread, pastry, etc.
2. any soft, pastelike mass like this, as potter's clay, etc.
3. money. [Slang.]

dōugh'-bāked (dō'bākt), *a.* not hardened to perfection; soft; imperfectly baked; figuratively, dull-witted; foolish. [Dial.]

dōugh'bīrd, *n.* the curlew of arctic regions, *Numenius borealis.*

dōugh'boy, *n.* 1. a boiled dumpling.
2. a United States infantryman. [Colloq.]

dōugh'fāce, *n.* a timid, easily-influenced politician: used in the United States to designate politicians of the North who were accused of submitting to the slave interests.

dōugh'-fāced (dō'fāst), *a.* easily influenced; pliable.

dōugh'fāce″iṣm, *n.* the character of a doughface; pliability.

dōugh'i·ness, *n.* the state of being doughy.

dōugh'-knēad″ed (dō'nēd″ed), *a.* resembling dough; soft. [Obs.]

dōugh'nut, *n.* a small, usually ring-shaped, cake, made of flour, eggs, and sugar, and fried in deep fat.

dough'ti·ly (dou'), *adv.* in a doughty manner.

dough'ti·ness, *n.* the quality of being doughty; valor; bravery.

dough'ty (dou'), *a.*; *comp.* doughtier; *superl.* doughtiest, [ME. *doughty*; AS. *dohtig, dyhtig*, strong, valiant.] brave; valiant; eminent; noble; illustrious; as, a *doughty* hero: now used humorously with a somewhat archaic flavor.

dōugh'y, *a.*; *comp.* doughier; *superl.* doughiest; like dough; soft, flabby, pasty, etc.

Doug'lăs fīr (dug'), [after David *Douglas* (1798–1834), Scot. botanist in America.] a tall evergreen tree of the pine family, found in the western part of North America and valued for its hard wood: also called *Douglas spruce* (or *pine, hemlock*), *Oregon fir* (or *pine*).

Döu'khō·bọrṣ (dö'kō-), *n.pl.* same as *Dukhobors.*

döu·loç'rȧ·cy, dụ·loç'rȧ·cy, *n.* [Gr. *doulos*, a slave, and *kratein*, to rule.] a government controlled by slaves.

döum, *n.* same as *doom palm.*

döum pälm, same as *doom palm.*

Döu'mä, *n.* same as *Duma.*

doup, *n.* the breech or buttocks; also, the bottom or butt end. [Scot.]

döur, *a.* [ME. *dowre*; L. *durus*, hard.]
1. hard; severe; unyielding. [Scot.]
2. obstinate. [Scot.]
3. sullen; gloomy; forbidding.

döu'rȧ, döu'rȧh, *n.* same as *durra.*

döu·rīne', *n.* [Fr.] a disease of horses and mules, caused by a protozoan and transmitted in copulation.

döu·röu·çöu'li, *n.* [native name.] a small, large-eyed, nocturnal South American monkey, *Aotus trivirgatus*, usually having three lines on the face: also written *durukuli.*

douse, *v.t.*; doused (doust), *pt., pp.*; dousing, *ppr.* [16th-c. slang, prob. from L.G.]
1. originally, to hit forcefully.
2. in nautical usage, to strike or lower in haste; to slacken suddenly; as, *douse* the topsail.
3. to pull off (shoes, clothes, etc.). [Colloq.]
4. to extinguish; to put out (a light or fire) quickly. [Colloq.]
Also spelled *dowse.*

douse, *v.t.*; doused (doust), *pt., pp.*; dousing, *ppr.* [same as preceding *douse*, influenced by *souse.*]
1. to plunge or thrust suddenly into liquid.
2. to drench; to pour water over.
Also spelled *dowse.*

douse, *v.i.* to be immersed or drenched: also spelled *dowse.*

douse, *n.* a blow; a stroke.

dous'ing chock, any of several pieces of timber joined together across the apron and lapped within the inside planking above the upper deck of a vessel.

dous'ing rod, a divining rod.

dout, *v.t.* to put out; to extinguish; to douse. [Obs.]

dout'ẽr, *n.* an extinguisher for candles. [Obs.]

döuze'pẽrṣ, *n.pl.* [OFr. *douze pers*, lit., twelve peers.]
1. in French history, the twelve great peers of the realm.
2. in medieval romance, the twelve great paladins or knights of Charlemagne.

dŏve, *n.* [ME. *dove, douve*, a dove; ON. *dūfa.*]
1. any one of several of the smaller species of birds of the family *Columbidæ*, the pigeons: they are characterized by a full-breasted body, short legs, and a cooing cry. The *dove* is used in poetry as a symbol of peace, gentleness, and purity; in ecclesiastical art, as a symbol of the Holy Spirit.
2. one regarded as gentle, innocent, or beloved.
3. a receptacle shaped like a dove, used in the Middle Ages to contain the Eucharist.
4. an advocate of measures in international affairs designed to avoid or reduce open hostilities: cf. *hawk.*

dōve, *v.* alternative past tense of *dive.*

dŏve çŏl'ŏr, a pinkish-gray color.

dŏve'çōte, dŏve'çot, *n.* a small building or box, raised above the ground, in which pigeons nest; a pigeon house.

dŏve'-eȳed (-īd), *a.* having eyes expressive of tenderness.

dŏve'kie, dŏve'key, *n.* 1. the little auk, *Plautus alle.*
2. the black guillemot.

dŏve'let, *n.* a young or small dove.

dŏve'līke, *a.* having the characteristics of a dove; mild; gentle; pure.

dŏve plant, a tropical American orchid bearing a flower resembling a dove.

Dō'vẽr'ṣ pow'dẽr, see phrase under *powder.*

dŏve'ṣ'-foot, *n.* 1. a small English geranium having a leaf of the shape of a dove's foot.
2. the columbine. [Brit. Dial.]

dŏve'tāil, *n.* 1. a part or thing shaped like a dove's tail; specifically, a projecting, wedge-shaped part (called *tenon*) that fits into a corresponding indentation (called *mortise*) to form a joint.

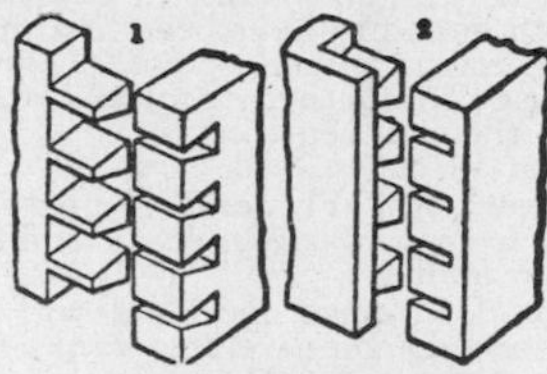

DOVETAIL JOINTS
1. common dovetail 2. lap dovetail

2. a joint thus formed.
dovetail molding; a kind of convex molding resembling a series of dovetails.
dovetail saw; the saw used in cutting dovetails.

dŏve'tāil, *v.t.*; dovetailed, *pt., pp.*; dovetailing, *ppr.* 1. to join or fasten together by means of dovetails.
2. to piece together (facts, etc.) so as to make a logically connected whole.

dŏve'tāil, *v.i.* to fit together closely or logically.

dŏve'tāiled, *a.* having a tail like a dove's; having a dovetail.

dŏve'wood, *n.* the wood of *Alchornea latifolia*, a tree of the spurge family common in Jamaica.

dŏv'ish, *a.* 1. like a dove; innocent. [Rare.]
2. advocating the reduction or avoidance of open hostilities in international affairs.

dow, *n.* same as *dhow.*

dow, *v.t.* to endow. [Obs.]

dow'á·ble, *a.* capable of being endowed; entitled to dower.

dow'á·ġẽr, *n.* [OFr. *douagiere*, from *douage*, a dowry, from *douer*; L. *dotare*, to endow.]
1. a widow with a title or property derived from her dead husband: a title often given to the widows of princes and persons of rank. Thus, the widow of a king is called *queen dowager*, to distinguish her from the wife of her late husband's successor.
2. an elderly woman of wealth and dignity. [Colloq.]

dow'á·ġẽr·iṣm, *n.* the state of being a dowager.

dow'ăr, *n.* see *douar.*

dow'cet, *n.* [OFr. *doucet*, sweet, gentle.] a testicle of a deer; a doucet. [Obs.]

dowd, *n.* [ME. *doude*, a slut.] a dowdy person; especially, a dowdy woman.

dow'di·ly, *adv.* in a dowdy manner.

dow'di·ness, *n.* the state or quality of being dowdy.

dow'dy, *n.*; *pl.* **dow'dieṣ**, a slovenly woman; a slattern.

dow'dy, *a.*; *comp.* dowdier; *superl.* dowdiest,

slovenly; not neat, fashionable, or smart in dress or appearance.

dow′dy·ish, *a.* somewhat dowdy.

dow′el, *n.* [Fr. *douille*, a socket, the barrel of a pistol, a little pipe, from M.H.G. *tübel*; O.H.G. *tupili*, a tap, plug.]

1. a wooden or metallic pin or peg fitted into corresponding holes in two adjacent pieces of wood, stone, etc. to fasten them together.

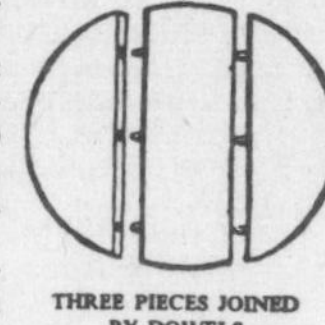
THREE PIECES JOINED BY DOWELS

2. a piece of wood driven into a wall, to which other parts may be nailed; a dook.

dow′el, *v.t.*; doweled *or* dowelled, *pt., pp.*; doweling *or* dowelling, *ppr.* to fasten together or furnish with dowels; as, a cooper *dowels* pieces for the head of a cask.

dow′ẽr, *n.* [ME. *dower, dowere*; OFr. *doaire*; LL. *dotarium*; L. *dos* (*dotis*), a dower.]

1. in law, that portion of a man's estate which his widow inherits for life.

2. the property which a woman brings to her husband at marriage; dowry.

3. a natural endowment, gift, or talent.

dow′ẽr, *v.t.* 1. to furnish with dower.

2. to bestow a talent or power upon.

dow′ẽred, *a.* furnished with dower or a portion.

dow′ẽr·less, *a.* destitute of dower; having no portion or fortune.

dowf, *a.* dull; hollow; also, stupid. [Scot. and Brit. Dial.]

dow′ie, *a.* sad; mournful. [Scot.]

dow′itch·ẽr, *n.* [from Am. Ind. (Algonquian) native name.] a long-legged shore bird, *Limnodromus griseus*, of North America.

dowl, *n.* see *dowle*.

dow′lȧs, *n.* [from *Daoulas*, in France, where the cloth is said to have been first made.]

1. originally, a kind of coarse linen cloth much used in southern Scotland and Yorkshire in the eighteenth century.

2. a heavy calico.

dowle, dowl, *n.* [OFr. *douille*, something soft, downy, from L. *ductilis*, ductile.] fine down; a feather filament.

down, *n.* [ME. *down, downe*, down; prob. of Scand. origin; compare Ice. *dunn*, Sw. *dun*, down.]

1. fine, soft feathers, as on young birds, or covering fowls under the feathers, particularly on the breasts of water fowl, as the duck and swan.

2. soft, fine hair.

The first *down* begins to shade his face. —Dryden.

3. any soft, fine hairy growth, as the soft pubescence upon plants and some fruits or the fine, feathery substance by which seeds are conveyed to a distance by the wind, as in the dandelion and thistle.

down, *v.t.* to cover, stuff, or line with down.

down, *n.* [ME. *doun, down*; AS. *dun*, a hill.]

1. [*usually pl.*] a bank or elevation of sand thrown up by the wind; a dune; a somewhat rounded and grassy hill.

2. [*usually pl.*] an expanse of open, high, grassy land, usually rolling or hilly and used mainly for pasturing sheep.

Seven thousand broad-tailed sheep grazed on his *downs*. —Sandys.

the Downs; (a) a roadstead and rendezvous for shipping in the English channel, near Deal; (b) the treeless, hilly uplands of Kent and Sussex in southeastern England.

down, *adv.* [ME. *down, doun*, down, abbrev. form of *adune*, adown; AS. *adun, adune, ofdune*, from the hill; *a-, of-*, off, from, and *dune*, dat. of *dun*, hill.]

1. from a higher to a lower place; toward the ground.

2. in or on a lower position or level; on the ground.

3. in a direction or place thought of as lower or below; as, *down*town.

4. below the horizon.

5. from an earlier to a later period or person; as, *down* from the Middle Ages.

6. into a low or dejected mental or emotional condition.

7. into a low or prostrate physical condition; as, he came *down* with pneumonia.

8. in an inferior position; in check; as, they held him *down*.

9. to a lower amount or bulk; as, things have come *down* in price.

10. to a heavier consistency; as, to boil *down* a sirup.

11. to a less excited or active condition; as, the waves settled *down*.

12. in a serious or earnest manner; as, get *down* to work.

13. completely; to the full extent; as, loaded *down*.

14. in cash or when bought; as, five dollars *down* and the remainder in installments.

15. in writing; on record; as, take *down* his name.

down, *a.* 1. descending; directed toward a lower position.

2. in a lower place; on the ground.

3. gone, brought, pulled, paid, etc. down.

4. dejected; discouraged.

5. prostrate; ill.

6. in sports, (a) not in play: said of a football; (b) trailing an opponent with reference to the number of points, goals, or strokes; (c) in baseball, put out.

down and out; (a) in boxing, knocked out; (b) in the state of being penniless; friendless, ill, etc.

down in the mouth; dejected; dispirited.

down on (or *upon*); hostile to because of a grievance against; angry or annoyed with. [Colloq.]

down, *prep.* down toward, along, through, into or upon.

down, *v.t.*; downed, *pt., pp.*; downing, *ppr.* to cause to go down; to knock, bring, or get down; to overthrow; to put down; to subdue; to dishearten; to dispirit; as, to *down* proud hearts; to *down* an opponent in argument.

down with; (a) put down; (b) overthrow; do away with: an expression of disfavor.

down, *v.i.* to come, get, or go down; to sink.

down, *n.* 1. a descent.

2. a reverse; misfortune; as, the ups and *downs* of a career.

3. in football, (a) one of four consecutive plays in which the team in possession of the ball must either score or advance the ball a total of at least ten yards in order to keep possession; (b) the declaring of the ball as down, or the play just before this.

down-beăr′, *v.t.* to bear down; to depress. [Rare.]

down′bēat, *n.* in music, the downward stroke of the conductor's hand or baton to indicate the first accent in each measure.

down″bēat, *a.* grimly realistic; depressing. [Colloq.]

down′-bōw, *n.* a stroke on a violin, etc. in which the bow is drawn across the strings from the handle to the tip.

down′ċȧst, *a.* 1. cast downward; directed to the ground; as, a *downcast* eye or look.

2. depressed; dejected; as, *downcast* spirits.

down′ċȧst, *n.* 1. a casting down.

2. sadness; melancholy look.

3. in mining, the ventilating shaft down which the air passes in circulating through a mine.

down′ċȧst·ness, *n.* the state of being downcast; sadness.

down′ċŏme, *n.* 1. a comedown; humiliation; downfall; ruin.

2. a downcomer.

down′ċŏm·ẽr, *n.* the vertical pipe which conducts the waste gases from the top of a close-mouthed blast furnace into hot-blast stoves and boilers: also called *downtake*.

down′drȧft, down′drȧught (-drȧft), *n.* a downward current of air, as in a furnace.

down″-ēast′, *a.* of New England, especially Maine. [Colloq.]

down″-ēast′ẽr, *n.* a native of New England, especially of Maine. [Colloq.]

down′ẽr, *n.* 1. any depressant or sedative, as a tranquilizer, barbiturate, alcoholic drink, etc. [Slang.]

2. something depressing; especially, a depressing experience. [Slang.]

down′fạll, *n.* 1. a falling, especially a sudden or heavy fall, as of rain or snow.

2. ruin; destruction; a sudden fall or ruin; complete failure or overthrow; as, the *downfall* of the Roman Empire.

3. a trap operated when the prey causes a weight to drop.

down′fạll″en, *a.* fallen; ruined.

down′fạll″ing, *a.* descending; falling.

down′grāde, *n.* a downward slope, especially in a road.

on the downgrade; losing success, influence, health, etc.; declining; deteriorating.

down′grāde, *adv.* and *a.* downhill; downward.

down′grāde, *v.t.* to demote to a less skilled job at lower pay.

down′ġȳved, *a.* hanging down like the loose links of fetters. [Obs.]

down′haul, *n.* a rope or series of ropes used to haul down a sail.

down′heärt′ed, *a.* dejected in spirits; discouraged; despondent.

down′hill, *n.* declivity; descent; slope.

down′hill, *a.* descending; sloping downward.

down′hill, *adv.* with a downward tendency; toward the bottom.

to go downhill; to lose success, health, etc.; to decline.

down′-hōme′, *a.* 1. of, from, or associated with a rural, especially Southern, area. [Colloq.]

2. having characteristics associated with rural people; simple, warm, direct, etc. [Colloq].

down′i·ness, *n.* the state or quality of being downy.

Down′ing Street, 1. a short street in Whitehall, London, in which are located the Home, Colonial, and Foreign Offices, and the official residences of the Prime Minister (Number 10) and the Chancellor of the Exchequer.

2. the British government or cabinet.

down′looked (-lookt), *a.* having a downcast countenence; dejected; gloomy; sullen. [Obs.]

down′lȳ″ing, *n.* the time of retiring to rest; time of repose. [Obs.]

down′plāy, *v.t.* to play down; make little of; minimize or remove emphasis from.

down′pōur, *n.* a copious pouring; specifically, a heavy shower of rain.

down′rānge′, *adv.* and *a.* along the course away from the launching site.

down′rīght (-rīt), *adv.* [ME. *downright, dounright, dunriht*; *dun*, down, and *rihte*, right, straight.]

1. straight down; perpendicularly. [Rare.]

2. in plain terms; without ceremony or circumlocution. [Archaic.]

We shall chide *downright*. —Shak.

3. completely; thoroughly.

down′rīght, *a.* 1. absolute; thoroughgoing; as, *downright* madness; *downright* falsehood.

2. plain; artless; unceremonious; blunt; as, he spoke in his *downright* way.

3. straight downward; as, a *downright* blow. [Rare.]

down′rīght·ly, *adv.* plainly; in plain terms; bluntly.

down′rīght·ness, *n.* the state or quality of being downright, or direct and plain.

down′shift, *v.i.* to shift the transmission of a motor vehicle to a lower gear.

down′sit″ting, *n.* the act of sitting down; repose; a resting.

Thou knowest my *downsitting* and mine uprising. —Ps. cxxxix. 2.

down′sīze, *v.t.*; downsized, *pt., pp.*; downsizing, *ppr.* to produce smaller models or styles of; as, to *downsize* automobiles.

down′spout, *n.* a vertical pipe for carrying rain water from a roof gutter to ground level.

down′stāġe′, *adv.* and *a.* at or toward the front of the stage.

down′stāir′, *adv.* and *a.* downstairs. [Rare.]

down′stāirş′, *a.* situated on a lower floor.

down′stāirş′, *n.* a lower floor or floors.

down′stāirş′, *adv.* 1. down the stairs.

2. on or to a lower floor; as, she is now sufficiently recovered to go *downstairs*.

down′strēam′, *adv.* and *a.* in the direction of the current of a stream; down the stream.

down′strōke, *n.* a stroke made with a downward motion; a downward blow.

down′tāke, *n.* 1. see *downcomer*.

2. any pipe, etc. leading downward.

down′thrōw, *n.* 1. in geology and mining, the sinking of a stratum or strata, by which a bed of rock or seam of coal is brought into a lower position than before.

2. the process of throwing down, or the condition of being thrown down; overthrow.

down′tīme, *n.* the time during which a machine, factory, etc. is shut down for repairs or the like.

down′town′, *adv.* to, toward, or in the main business section or geographically lower part of a city or town; as, I am going *downtown*; he works *downtown*.

down′town′, *a.* 1. of, like, or in the main business section of a city; as, a *downtown* street.

2. of or in the geographically lower part of a city or town: opposed to *uptown*.

down′town′, *n.* the main business section of a city or town

down tree, same as *balsa* (sense 1).

down′trod, *a.* downtrodden. [Archaic.]

down′trod″den, *a.* 1. trampled down.

2. oppressed; subjugated; tyrannized over.

The *downtrodden* vassals of perdition. —Milton.

down un′dẽr, Australia or New Zealand. [Colloq.]

down′wȧrd, down′wȧrds, *adv.* [ME. *dounward, duneward*; AS. *aduneweard*; *adune*, adown, down, and *-weard*, -ward.]
1. from a higher place to a lower place, position, state, etc.; as, to move or roll *downward*; to look *downward*.
2. in a course or direction from a head, spring, origin, or source; as, water flows *downward* toward the sea.
3. from an earlier to a later period of time; as, to trace successive generations *downward* from Abraham.

down′wȧrd, *a.* 1. moving or extending from a higher to a lower place; as, a *downward* course; he took his way with *downward* force.
2. from an earlier to a later time.

down′-wäsh, *n.* the air that an airplane wing pushes downward while moving through the air.

down′weed, *n.* the cudweed, *Filago germanica*. [Obs.]

down′weigh (-wā), *v.t.* to press or weigh down.

down′y, *a.* 1. covered with down or nap; as, *downy* wings.
2. covered with pubescence or soft hairs, as a plant.
3. made of soft, fine feathers or hair; as, a *downy* pillow.
4. soft; calm; soothing; as, *downy* sleep.
5. soft and fluffy, resembling down.
6. knowing; cunning; as, a *downy* cove. [Brit. Slang.]

dow′ry, *n.* [ME. *dowrye, dowrie*; OFr. *doaire*; LL. *dotarium*; L. *dos* (*dotis*), a dowry.]
1. the money, goods, or estate which a woman brings to her husband in marriage; the portion given with a wife.
2. a natural talent, gift, or endowment; as, poetry was his *dowry*.
3. a gift given to or for a wife. [Archaic.]
4. a widow's dower. [Archaic.]

dowse, *v.t.* and *v.i.* see *douse*.

dowse, *n.* a blow.

dowse, *v.i.*; dowsed, *pt., pp.*; dowsing, *ppr.* [perh. Corn.] to search for a source of water or minerals with a divining rod.

dows′ẽr, *n.* one who uses a divining rod.

dow′set, *n.* same as *doucet*.

dow′sing rod, [prob. from Corn. merging of G. dial. *deuten*, to declare, with *douse* (to plunge); earlier form *deusing rod*.] a divining rod.

dowve, *n.* a dove. [Obs.]

dow′y, *a.* same as *dowie*.

dox·ō·log′iç·ăl, *a.* pertaining to doxology; giving praise to God.

dox·ol′ō·ġīze, *v.i.* to give glory to God, as in a doxology.

dox·ol′ō·ġy, *n.*; *pl.* **dox·ol′ō·ġieṣ,** [LL. *doxologia*; Gr. *doxologia*, a praising; *doxologos*, giving or uttering praise; *doxa*, praise, opinion, from *dokein*, to think, and *logos*, a word, from *legein*, to speak.] any of several hymns of praise to God; specifically, (a) the *greater doxology*, which begins *Gloria in Excelsis* (glory to God in the highest); (b) the *lesser doxology*, which begins *Gloria Patri* (glory to the Father); (c) a hymn beginning "Praise God from whom all blessings flow."

dox′y, *n.* [from words ending in *-doxy*, as orthodoxy, heterodoxy.] a doctrine, creed, or ism, especially in religion.

dox′y, *n.*; *pl.* **dox′ieṣ,** a loose woman; a prostitute; the mistress of a rogue or vagabond. [Slang.]

doy′en (*or Fr.* dwä-yaṅ′), *n.* [Fr.] the senior in any group, by virtue of length of appointment, age, etc.; the dean.

doy′enne (*or Fr.* dwä-yen′), *n.* [Fr.] feminine of *doyen*.

doy′ley, *n.*; *pl.* **doy′leyṣ,** same as *doily*.

doy′ly, *n.*; *pl.* **doy′lieṣ,** a doily.

dōze, *v.i.*; dozed, *pt., pp.*; dozing, *ppr.* [orig., to stupefy, from L.G.] to sleep lightly or fitfully; nap; be half asleep.
to doze off; to fall into a light sleep.

dōze, *v.t.* 1. to pass or spend (time) in drowsiness or dozing (often with *away* or *out*); as, to *doze away* one's time.
2. to make dull; to stupefy. [Obs.]

dōze, *n.* a light sleep; a slumber.

dŏz′en (duz′n), *n.* [ME. *dozeyn*; OFr. *dozaine*, a dozen; L. *duodecim*, twelve; *duo*, two, and *decem*, ten.] twelve things collectively, usually twelve of a like kind; as, a *dozen* eggs; ten *dozen* collars.
baker's dozen; see under *baker*.

dŏz′enth, *a.* twelfth.

dōz′ẽr, *n.* one who dozes.

dō′zi·ness, *n.* drowsiness; inclination to sleep.

dōz′y, *a.*; *comp.* dozier; *superl.* doziest, 1. drowsy; inclined to sleep; sleepy; sluggish; as, a *dozy* head.
2. decaying; half rotten: used of wood, trees, fruit, etc.

drab, *n.* [Ir. *drabog*, a slut, slattern, from *drab*, a spot, stain; AS. *drabbe*, dregs, lees.]
1. a strumpet; a prostitute.
2. a slatternly woman.

drab, *v.i.*; drabbed, *pt., pp.*; drabbing, *ppr.* to associate with or be a prostitute.

drab, *n.* a kind of wooden box, used in salt works to hold the salt when taken out of the boiling pans.

drab, *n.* [Fr. *drap*, cloth.]
1. a kind of cloth, especially a thick, woolen cloth of a yellowish-brown color.
2. a dull yellowish brown.
3. a quaker moth.

drab, *a.* 1. of a dull yellowish-brown color; as, *drab* cloth.
2. dull; lacking brightness; monotonous.

drab′bẽr, *n.* one who keeps company with drabs. [Obs.]

drab′bet, *n.* a coarse, unbleached linen. [British.]

drab′bish, *a.* having the qualities of a drab; sluttish.

drab′bish, *a.* somewhat of the color of drab.

drab′ble, *v.t.*; drabbled, *pt., pp.*; drabbling, *ppr.* [ME. *drabelen, drablen*, to soil, prob. from AS. *drabbe*, dregs.] to draggle; to make dirty by drawing in mud and water; as, to *drabble* a gown.

drab′ble, *v.i.* 1. to become drabbled.
2. to fish for barbels with a long line and a rod by drawing the line through the water.

drab′lẽr, *n.* a small additional sail, sometimes laced to the bottom of a bonnet on a square sail, in sloops and schooners.

drab′ble-tāil, *n.* an untidy woman; a slattern.

Dra·cae′nȧ, *n.* [LL. *dracæna*, a female dragon; Gr. *drakaina*, f. of *drakōn*, a serpent, dragon.]
1. a genus of trees, family *Liliaceæ*, found in the tropics of the eastern hemisphere, resembling the palms and often attaining large size. The resin, called *dragon's blood*, is obtained from *Dracæna draco*, one of the largest species.
2. [d–] any plant of this or a similar genus.

dra′cănth, *n.* gum tragacanth.

drachm (dram), *n.* a dram or drachma.

drach′mȧ, *n.* [L. *drachma*; Gr. *drachmē*, a drachma, from *drachma*, as much as one can hold in the hand, a handful, from *drasesthai*, to grasp, take by handfuls.]
1. a silver coin among the ancient Greeks, having a different value in different states and at different periods.
2. in ancient Greece, a unit of weight approximately equal to the weight of the coin.
3. in modern Greece, a monetary unit.
4. any of several modern weights or measures.

Drā′cō, *n.* [L. *draco*; Gr. *drakōn*, a serpent, dragon.]
1. a genus of dragon lizards, of the family *Agamidæ*.
2. the Dragon, a constellation of the northern hemisphere, lying partially between the Big Dipper and the Little Dipper.

Drā·cō′ni·ăn, *a.* [L. *Draco* (*-onis*); Gr. *Drakōn*, Draco, from *drakōn*, a dragon.]
1. relating to or like Draco, an Athenian lawgiver of the seventh century B.C.
2. of the severe code of laws in effect in Athens about 621 B.C., drawn up by Draco.
3. [*sometimes* d–] inhumanly cruel or severe; rigorous; inexorable; relentless.
4. [d–] draconic.

Drā·con′iç, *a.* 1. same as *Draconian*.
2. [d–] of or like a dragon.

drā·çon′tiç, *a.* in astronomy, belonging to that space of time in which the moon performs one entire revolution: also written *draconitic*.
draconitic month; the time which the moon takes in making a revolution from a node back to that node.

Drā·çun′çū·lus, *n.* [L., dim. of *draco*, a dragon.]
1. a genus of plants, family *Araceæ*, with a long stalk spotted like a serpent's belly, and pedate leaves. They are natives of southern Europe.
2. [d–] a fish of the genus *Callionymus*; the dragonet.
3. a genus of worms, including *Dracunculus medinensis*, or guinea worm, found in tropical climates, which insinuates itself under the skin of the legs of man, causing a suppurating sore.

drad, *a.* terrible; dreaded. [Obs.]

drȧff, *n.* [ME. *draf*, refuse, chaff; prob. of Celtic origin.] refuse, lees; dregs; the wash given to swine; specifically, the refuse of malt after brewing or distilling, fed to swine.
Still swine eat all the *draff*. —Shak.

drȧff′ish, *a.* worthless.

drȧff′y, *a.* full of, or as if full of, draff, or dregs; like draff; waste; worthless.

drȧft, drȧught (drȧft), *n.* [ME. *draught, draht*, a drawing, pulling, pull, stroke, from AS. *dragan*, to draw, drag, pull.]
1. the act of drawing or pulling, as of a vehicle or load.
2. that which is drawn or the load pulled.
3. a drawing in of a fish net.
Upon the *draught* of a pond not one fish was left. —Hale.
4. the amount of fish caught in one drawing in of the net.
5. a drawing of liquid into the mouth; drinking.
6. the amount taken at one drink.
7. a drink.
8. a drawing into the lungs, as of air or smoke.
9. the air, smoke, etc. drawn in.
10. a drawing, as of beer, from a cask when ordered.
11. a written order from one man, bank, firm, etc. to another directing the payment of money; a bill of exchange; a check.
12. a drawing of money or stock.
13. the choosing or taking of individuals from a group for some special purpose.
14. the taking of qualified persons for compulsory military service.
15. those thus chosen or taken.
16. a drawing or plan of a work to be done; delineation; sketch.
17. the depth of water that a ship draws, or displaces.
18. a writing of any kind as first drawn up; a preliminary suggestion or sketch, to be worked up and finished; as, the first *draft* of a set of resolutions.
19. a current of air, as in a room, heating system, etc.
20. a device for regulating the current of air in a heating system.
21. influence. [Slang.]
22. in mechanics, the taper given to a pattern or die so that the work can be removed easily.
23. the degree of slant given to the furrow of a millstone.
24. a line or border cut along the edge or on the surface of a stone, especially to guide the stonecutter.
25. a deduction made from the gross weight of merchandise to allow for loss from various causes.
26. the area of the openings through which water is discharged from a turbine wheel or through a sluice gate.
27. the act of depleting, or taking away part; a drain; a heavy demand; as, a *draft* upon one's health or resources.
angle of draft; for vehicles or heavy bodies, the angle which the line of direction of the pulling force makes with the plane over which the body is drawn.
forced draft; a strong draft in a furnace, produced by artificial means, as by a blower or the injection of a jet of steam.
natural draft; a draft produced by the exhaustion of the hot air in a furnace or chimney because of the natural tendency of hot air to rise.
on draft; ready to be drawn direct from the cask, without being bottled; as, ale *on draft*.

drȧft, drȧught, *a.* 1. being on draft; drawn direct from the cask as required; as, *draft* beer.
2. relating to or used for drafting or pulling; as, *draft* cattle.

drȧft, drȧught, *v.t.*; drafted, *pt., pp.*; drafting, *ppr.* 1. to choose or take from some special purpose, as compulsory military service, by drawing from a group.
2. to draw off or away.
3. to make a preliminary sketch of or working plans for.
4. in weaving, to draw through the heddles.

drȧft an′i·măl, an animal used for pulling heavy loads.

drȧft bär, 1. a singletree.
2. the bar to which the coupling of a railroad car is attached.

drȧft bōard, an official board of civilians designated to select qualified persons for compulsory service in the United States armed forces.

dräft dodġ′ẽr, a person who avoids or tries to avoid being drafted into the armed forces.
dräft·ee′, *n.* a person drafted, especially one selected for military service.
dräft en′ġine, an engine used for pumping, etc.
dräft′ẽr, *n.* one who drafts.
dräft fũr′năce, a furnace in which forced draft is used.
dräft′i·ly, dräught′i·ly, *adv.* in a drafty manner.
dräft′i·ness, dräught′i·ness, *n.* the condition of being drafty.
dräft net, a dragnet, or hauling net.
dräfts, *n.pl.* checkers; draughts.
dräfts′măn, dräughts′măn, *n.* 1. one who draws plans or designs of structures or machinery.
2. one who draws up written documents, speeches, etc.
3. one who drinks drams; a tippler. [Obs.]
dräfts′măn·ship, dräughts′măn·ship, *n.* the work of a draftsman; skill in drawing, especially architectural or mechanical drawing.
dräft′y, dräught′y, *a.* 1. in, or exposed to, a draft (current of air).
2. letting in, causing, or having a draft or drafts; as, a *drafty* hall.
Great *draughty* rooms. —Yonge.
drag, *v.t.*; dragged, *pt., pp.*; dragging, *ppr.* [ME. *draggen, dragen*; AS. *dragan*, to drag, draw.]
1. to pull; to haul; to draw by force or effort, especially along the ground or other surface; as, to *drag* stone or timber.
2. to pull a grapnel, net, or other device over the bottom of (a river, lake, etc.) in searching for or catching something; dredge.
3. to break (land) by drawing a drag or harrow over it; to harrow.
4. to draw (something) out over a period of time; to continue tediously and painfully.
5. to bring (a subject) into conversation or into a piece of writing, etc. unnecessarily or as if by force.
to drag an anchor; to draw or trail an anchor along the bottom when the anchor will not hold the ship.
to drag on (or *out*); to prolong or be prolonged tediously
Syn.—pull, draw, haul.
drag, *v.i.* 1. to hang so low as to trail on the ground; to be dragged; to be pulled along the ground or other surface.
2. to lag behind.
3. to move slowly; to proceed or be prolonged tediously; as, this business *drags*.
4. to search a river, lake, etc. with a grapnel, net, or other device.
5. to cause the sensation of dragging or tugging; as, a *dragging* fear.
drag, *n.* 1. something dragged or pulled along the ground; specifically, (a) a harrow used for breaking ground; (b) a heavy sledge (vehicle); (c) a large, heavy coach with seats inside and on top.
2. a device used to catch and haul up something under water; grapnel, dragnet, etc.
3. a thing that checks motion, as a brake for retarding the rotation of a carriage wheel; a skid.
4. figuratively, a person or thing forming an obstacle to one's progress or prosperity; anything that hinders or obstructs; as, his brother has been a great *drag* upon him.
5. the amount by which anything drags.
6. the act of dragging; a heavy motion indicative of some impediment; motion effected with slowness and difficulty; as, a heavy *drag* uphill; he had a *drag* in his walk.
7. an object, such as a rough, heavy sledge, used for dragging heavy loads, as stones over the ground.
8. influence. [Slang.]
9. a puff of a cigarette, pipe, etc. [Slang.]
10. a dance. [Slang.]
11. in aeronautics, the resistance to movement brought to bear on an airplane by the air through which it passes.
12. in billiards, a backspin given to the cue ball to cause it to stop upon hitting another ball.
13. in hunting, (a) a trail of scent left by an animal; (b) something dragged over the ground to leave a trail of scent; (c) a hunt over such a trail.
14. the bottom part or section of a founder's molding box.
15. a stonecutter's instrument used for finishing soft stone which has no grit.
16. a kind of floating anchor, usually of spars and sails, to keep a ship's head to the wind or diminish leeway.
17. the difference between the draft of a vessel forward and that aft.
drag′bär, *n.* same as *drawbar*.
drag′bōlt, *n.* a pin used for coupling.
dra·ġée′ (drȧ-zhā′), *n.* [Fr. *dragée*, sugarplum.] a sugar coated candy; also, in pharmacy, any medicine, as a pill, coated with sugar.
drag′gle, *v.t.*; draggled, *pt., pp.*; draggling, *ppr.* [freq. of *drag*.] to make wet and dirty by drawing on the ground, in the mud, or on wet grass; to drabble; to trail.
drag′gle, *v.i.* 1. to be drawn on the ground; to become wet or dirty by being drawn through mud or wet grass.
2. to lag behind; to straggle.
drag′gle·tāil, *n.* a woman who allows her clothes to draggle; a slatternly woman.
drag′gle·tāiled, *a.* slovenly; slatternly; untidy.
drag′hound, *n.* in hunting, a hound trained to follow the scent made by a drag.
drag hunt, a hunt in which a drag, or artificial scent, is used.
drag′līne, *n.* a dragrope or guide rope.
drag liṅk, a link connecting the cranks of two engine shafts.
drag′măn, *n.*; *pl.* **drag′men,** a fisherman who uses a dragnet.
drag′net, *n.* 1. a weighted net to be drawn on the bottom of a river, pond, etc. for catching fish, etc.
2. a net for catching small game.
3. an organized system or network for gathering in or catching people wanted by the authorities, as criminals, etc.
drag′ō·măn, *n.*; *pl.* **drag′ō·măns, drag′ō·men,** [Fr. *dragoman*; Late Gr. *dragoumanos*; Ar. *targumān*, an interpreter, from *targama*, to interpret, explain.] in the Near East, an interpreter or traveler's guide or agent.
drag′ŏn, *n.* [ME. *dragon, dragun*; OFr. *dragon*, a dragon, a standard; L. *draco* (*-onis*); Gr. *drakōn*, a dragon, a serpent, lit., the seeing one, from *derkesthai*, to see.]
1. a mythical monster, usually represented as a sort of winged reptile, with fiery eyes, crested head, and enormous claws, breathing out fire and smoke.
2. a fierce, violent person; especially, a fiercely watchful female guardian; a strict chaperon.
3. a saurian of the genus *Draco*, characterized by the hind ribs extending outward in a nearly straight line, and sustaining an extension of the skin, which forms a kind of wing that enables it to glide from tree to tree. *Draco volans* is about 10 or 12 inches in length, the tail being extremely long in proportion to the body, which is about 4 inches long. Also called *flying dragon* or *flying lizard*.

DRAGON
(*Draco volans*)

4. [D–] a constellation of the northern hemisphere; Draco.
5. a kind of domestic pigeon: also called *dragoon*.
6. formerly, a short musket attached by a swivel to the belt: so named from a representation of a dragon's head at the muzzle.
7. a soldier armed with such a musket; a dragoon.
8. a large serpent or snake. [Archaic.]
9. any of various araceous plants, as the *green dragon* of the genus *Dracunculus*: so called because the stem is mottled like the skin of a snake.
10. in the Authorized Version of the Bible, a word used to translate several Hebrew words now understood to mean *serpent, jackal, Old Serpent* (Satan), etc.
11. in heraldry, a winged animal borne on shields, crests, and supporters.
drag′ŏn, *a.* pertaining to or resembling dragons; fierce; formidable.
drag·ŏ·nāde′, *n.* a dragonnade.
drag′ŏn bēam, in architecture, a beam or piece of timber bisecting the angle formed by the wall plate at corners, used to receive and support the foot of the hip rafter.
drag′ŏn·et, *n.* 1. literally, a little dragon.
2. any of a large group of small, bright-colored sea fishes belonging to the goby family.
drag′ŏn·fish, *n.* same as *dragonet*, sense 2.
drag′ŏn·flȳ, *n.*; *pl.* **drag′ŏn·flīeș,** any of a group of insects having four filmy wings, a long, slender body, and strong, horny mandibles: it flies swiftly and feeds on flies, gnats, etc.

DRAGONFLY

drag′ŏn·head (-hed), *n.* a kind of mint with blue, purple, or white flowers.
drag′ŏn·ish, *a.* dragonlike.
drag·ŏn·nāde′, *n.* [Fr., from *dragon*, dragoon.]
1. the persecution of the French Protestants by the troops of Louis XIV, especially by the dragoons.
2. any persecution or raid in which troops are used.
drag′ŏn·rọọt, *n.* an American plant, *Arisæma dracontium*; green dragon.
drag′ŏn'ș blood (blud), any of several red, resinous substances obtained from various tropical plants and trees, as *Dracæna draco, Daemonorops draco*, etc., used for coloring varnishes and in photoengraving.
drag′ŏn's-head, *n.* 1. a plant of the genus *Dracocephalum*; dragonhead.
2. in astronomy, dragon's head.
drag′ŏn'ș head, 1. the ascending node of a planet or of the moon.
2. dragonhead.
drag′ŏn'ș tāil, the descending node of a planet or of the moon.
drag′ŏn tree, a tall tree of the lily family, *Dracæna draco*, yielding dragon's blood: it grows in the Canary Islands.
drag′ŏn·wŏrt, *n.* a plant belonging to the genus *Artemisia*; also, the snakeweed, *Polygonum bistorta*.
drȧ·gọọn′, *n.* [Fr. *dragon*, a dragoon, a dragon.]
1. originally, a soldier armed with a short musket who served on horseback or on foot; mounted infantryman.
2. a heavily armed cavalryman.
3. a short musket: also called *dragon*. [Obs.]
drȧ·gọọn′, *v.t.*; dragooned, *pt., pp.*; dragooning, *ppr.* 1. to persecute or harass by dragoons.
2. to compel to submit by violent measures; to force (*into* doing something).
The colonies may be influenced to anything, but they can be *dragooned* to nothing. —Price.
drag·ọọn·āde′, *n.* same as *dragonnade*.
drȧ·gọọn′ bĭrd, the umbrella bird of South America, *Cephalopterus ornatus*.
drȧ·gọọn′ẽr, *n.* a dragoon. [Obs.]
drag rāce, a race between hot-rod cars (*dragsters*) to test their rates of acceleration from a complete stop, generally held on a short, straight course (*drag strip*).
drag′rōpe, *n.* 1. a rope that drags or serves to drag something, as pieces of artillery.
2. a rope hung from a balloon or dirigible for use as a variable ballast or mooring line.
drag sāil, drag sheet, a sea anchor for lessening the drift of vessels in heavy gales: it is a kind of floating anchor formed of a square sail kept stretched by metal bars and having a beam attached to it, which serves as a float.
drag strut, any of the internal reinforcing ribs of an airplane wing.
drāil, *v.t.* to trail; to drag. [Obs.]
drāil, *v.i.* 1. to fish by trolling.
2. to be trailed or dragged. [Obs.]
drāin, *v.t.*; drained, *pt., pp.*; draining; *ppr.* [AS. *dreahnian*, to drain, from base of *dryge*, dry.]
1. to draw off (liquid, etc.) gradually.
2. to draw water or any liquid from gradually; to dry or empty in this way; as, the doctor *drained* the abscess.
3. to drink all the liquid from (a cup, glass, etc.).
4. to exhaust gradually; use up slowly: said of strength, resources, etc.
5. to filter.

Salt water, *drained* through twenty vessels of earth, hath become fresh. —Bacon.

Syn.—draw, strain, exhaust, empty, dry.

drāin, *v.i.* 1. to flow off or trickle through gradually; as, let the water *drain* off.
2. to be emptied of liquid by flowing or dropping.
3. to discharge its waters: said of a region; as, Central Europe *drains* into the Danube.

drāin, *n.* 1. a channel or pipe through which water or other liquid flows off; a trench or ditch to carry water from wet land; a watercourse; a sewer; a sink.
2. the act of drawing off or draining; that which gradually exhausts strength, wealth, etc.; as, a *drain* upon one's resources.
3. [*pl.*] the last dregs of anything.
4. in surgery, a tube or other device used to draw off discharge, as from an abscess or a wound.

drāin'ȧ·ble, *a.* capable of being drained.

drāin'ăġe, *n.* 1. the act, process, or method of draining.
2. a system of drains; arrangement of pipes, etc. for carrying off waste matter.
3. that which is drained off.
4. a region or area drained, as by a river.
right of drainage; in law, the right to drain off water in pipes through the estate of another.

drāin'ăġe bā'sin, the land drained by a river system.

drāin'ăġe tūbe, a small tube used to drain a wound or incision.

drāine, *n.* [Fr.] the missel thrush.

drāin'ẽr, *n.* 1. one who lays pipe for draining, makes field drains, etc.
2. a utensil on which articles are placed to drain; a container for drawing off liquid.

drāin'pipe, *n.* a large pipe used to carry off water, sewage, etc.

drāin'tīle, *n.* a tile used in making drains.

drāin trap, any of various devices for preventing the escape of gas, offensive odors, etc. from drains; a chamber in a drain arranged so that the liquid contents prevent the escape of sewer gas, but permit the downward flow of liquids; a trap.

DRAIN TRAPS

drāke, *n.* [ME. *drake*; Ice. *andriki*; M.D. *endtrick*, a male duck; perh. from L. *draco*, a dragon.] a male duck.

drāke, *n.* [ME.; AS. *draca*, from L. *draco*, dragon.]
1. a small cannon of the 17th and 18th centuries.
2. a May fly, used as a fishing bait: also *drake fly*.
3. a dragon. [Archaic.]

drāke'stōne, *n.* a flat stone that may be so thrown upon the surface of the water as to skip along several times before sinking; also, the sport of making such stones skip.

dram, *n.* [ME. *dragme*, a dram; OFr. *dragme*; L. *drachma*; Gr. *drachmē*, an Attic weight, a drachma.]
1. in apothecaries' weight, a unit equal to 60 grains (1/8 ounce): symbol, ʒ.
2. in avoirdupois weight, a unit equal to 27 1/3 grains (1/16 ounce).
3. a fluid dram; 1/128 pint.
4. a small drink of alcoholic liquor.
5. a small quantity of anything.

dram, *v.i.*; drammed, *pt.*, *pp.*; dramming, *ppr.* to drink drams.

dram, *v.t.* to ply with drink.

drä'mȧ, *n.* [LL. *drama*; Gr. *drama*, a deed, act, drama, tragedy, from *dran*, to do.]
1. a literary composition that tells a story, usually of human conflict, by means of dialogue and action, to be performed on the stage by actors; stage play. The principal forms of the *drama* are tragedy and comedy; from modifications or combinations of these result the lyric drama or grand opera, melodrama, tragicomedy, opera bouffe or comic opera, farce, and burlesque.
2. the art or profession of writing, acting, or producing plays; institution of the theater (often with *the*).
3. plays collectively; as, Elizabethan *drama*.
4. a series of events so interesting, vivid, etc. as to resemble those of a play.
5. the quality of being dramatic.

Dram'ȧ·mīne, *n.* a drug used to prevent and relieve seasickness, airsickness, etc.: a trademark.

drȧ·mat'iç, drȧ·mat'iç·ăl, *a.* [LL. *dramaticus*; Gr. *dramatikos*, dramatic, from *drama*, a drama.]
1. of or connected with drama.
2. having the characteristics of a drama, especially conflict; like a play.
3. full of action; highly emotional; vivid, exciting, etc.

drȧ·mat'iç·ăl·ly, *adv.* 1. in a dramatic manner.
2. from the viewpoint of drama.

drȧ·mat'içs, *n.pl.* [*construed as sing.*] 1. the art of performing or producing plays.
2. plays performed and produced by amateurs.

drȧ·mat'iç ten'ŏr, 1. a tenor voice of a lower range and a heavier, more powerful quality than a lyric tenor: it is especially suited to dramatic or heroic roles, as in the operas of Wagner.
2. a singer with such a voice.
Also called *heroic tenor*.

dram'ȧ·tis pẽr·sō'nae, [L., from LL. *dramatis*, genit. of *drama*, a drama, and L. *personæ*, pl. of *persona*, a character.]
1. the characters or actors in a play.
2. a list of these.

dram'ȧ·tist, *n.* the author of a dramatic composition; a writer of plays; a playwright.

dram'ȧ·tī·zȧ·ble, *a.* capable of being dramatized.

dram·ȧ·ti·zā'tion, *n.* 1. a dramatizing.
2. that which is dramatized; dramatized version, as of a novel.

dram'ȧ·tīze, *v.t.*; dramatized, *pt.*, *pp.*; dramatizing, *ppr.* [from LL. *drama*, a drama.]
1. to compose in the form of a drama; to arrange (a story, events, etc.) as a play; to adapt for representation on the stage, screen, etc.: as, to *dramatize* a novel.
2. to look at, interpret, or present (things, actions, oneself, etc.) as though in a play; to regard or show in a dramatic manner; to give dramatic quality to.

dram'ȧ·tīze, *v.i.* to be capable of being dramatized.

dram'ȧ·tūrġe, *n.* same as *dramatist*.

dram·ȧ·tūr'ġiç, *a.* relating to dramaturgy.

dram·ȧ·tūr'ġiç·ăl·ly, *adv.* 1. in a dramaturgic manner.
2. from the viewpoint of dramaturgy.

dram·ȧ·tūr'ġist, *n.* same as *dramatist*.

dram'ȧ·tūr·ġy, *n.* [Fr. *dramaturgie*; Gr. *dramatourgia*, a dramatic composition; *drama*, drama, and *ergon*, work.] the art of writing plays or producing them.

dram'sell″ẽr, *n.* one who sells alcoholic drinks by the glass or dram.

dram'shop, *n.* a saloon or barroom. [Now Rare.]

drañk, *v.* past tense and archaic past participle of *drink*.

drap' d'é·té' (drä' dā-tā'), [Fr.] a thin, twilled woolen cloth.

drāpe, *v.t.*; draped (drāpt), *pt.*, *pp.*; draping, *ppr.* [OFr. *draper*, to make into cloth, from *drap*, cloth; LL. *drappus*, cloth.]
1. to cover, hang, or decorate with or as with cloth or clothes in loose folds.
2. to arrange (a garment, cloth, etc.) artistically in folds or hangings.
3. to make into cloth. [Obs.]

drāpe, *v.i.* 1. to design or arrange drapery.
2. to hang loosely or in loose folds, as drapery.

drāpe, *n.* [Fr. *drap*, cloth.]
1. [*usually in pl.*] cloth hanging in loose folds; drapery; curtain.
2. the manner in which cloth hangs; as, his suit has an English *drape*.

drā'pẽr, *n.* 1. originally, a maker of cloth.
2. a dealer in cloth or dry goods; as, a linen *draper*. [Brit.]

drā'pẽr·ied (-id), *a.* adorned with drapery.

drā'pẽr·y, *n.*; *pl.* **drā'pẽr·ieṣ,** [ME. *draperie*; OFr. *draperie*, drapery, from *drap*, cloth.]
1. cloth; fabric; textile.
2. the business of a draper. [Brit.]
3. hangings or clothing arranged in loose folds.
4. an artistic arrangement of such hangings or clothing, especially in sculpture, painting, etc.
5. [*pl.*] curtains.

drā'pet, *n.* a cloth; a covering. [Obs.]

drap'pie, *n.* a little drop. [Scot.]

dras'tiç, *a.* [Gr. *drastikos*, active, from *dran*, to do, act.]
1. acting with force; severe; harsh; extreme; having a violent effect; as, the police took *drastic* measures.
2. in medicine, powerful; efficacious; as, a *drastic* cathartic.

dras'tiç, *n.* a medicine which speedily and effectually purges.

dras'tiç·ăl·ly, *adv.* in a drastic manner.

dras'ty, *a.* trashy; filthy. [Obs.]

drat, *interj.* [prob. contracted from *'od rot*, from *God rot*.] a mild expletive expressing annoyance, like *confound*, *darn*, etc.

D rā'tion, a United States Army emergency field ration consisting of a specially prepared chocolate bar having a highly concentrated food value: three bars constitute one day's ration.

drat'ted, *a.* darned. [Colloq.]

dråugh (dråf), *n.* draff. [Obs.]

dråught (dråft), *n.*, *a.*, and *v.t.* see *draft*.

dråught'bōard, *n.* a checkerboard. [Brit.]

dråught'house, *n.* a privy. [Obs.]

dråught'i·ly, *adv.* same as *draftily*.

dråught'i·ness, *n.* same as *draftiness*.

dråughts, *n.pl.* the game of checkers: also spelled *drafts*. [Brit.]

dråughts'măn, *n.*; *pl.* **dråughts'men,** 1. a draftsman.
2. any of the pieces used in playing draughts. [Brit.]

dråughts'măn·ship, *n.* same as *draftsmanship*.

dråught'y, *a.*; *comp.* draughtier; *superl.* draughtiest; same as *drafty*.

drāve, *v.* archaic past tense of *drive*.

Drȧ·vid'i·ăn, *n.* [coined by Bishop R. Caldwell from Sans. *Drāvida*, name of a district in southern India.]
1. any member of a group of intermixed races in southern India and southern Ceylon.
2. the family of non-Indo-European languages spoken by these races, including Tamil, Malayalam, Kanarese, Kurukh, Telugu, etc.: it is characterized by a caste classification of nouns, inclusive and exclusive plurals of the pronoun of the first person, and extensive use of verbal auxiliaries.

Drȧ·vid'i·ăn, *a.* of the Dravidians or their languages.

Drȧ·vid'iç, *a.* same as *Dravidian*.

draw, *v.t.*; drew, *pt.*; drawn, *pp.*; drawing, *ppr.* [ME. *drawen*, *drahen*; AS. *dragan*, to draw, drag.]
1. to make move toward one; cause to follow after by exerting physical force; pull; haul; drag; as, a horse *draws* the cart.
2. (a) to pull up, as a sail; (b) to pull down, as a window shade; (c) to pull in, as a dragnet; (d) to pull aside or together, as a curtain.
3. to pull back the drawstring of (a bow).
4. to displace (a specified depth of water) in floating; to need (a specified depth of water) to float in: said of a ship.
5. in billiards, to give backspin to (the cue ball).
6. in cricket, to deflect (the ball) to the side of the field on which the batsman stands, by a slight turn of the bat.
7. to attract; charm; entice.
8. to take into the lungs; breathe in; inhale.
9. to bring forth; elicit; as, his challenge *drew* no reply.
10. to bring about as a result; cause to happen; bring on; as, the airplane *drew* the enemy's fire.
11. in medicine, to cause a flow of (blood, pus, etc.) to some part.
12. to pull out; take out; remove; extract, as a tooth, cork, sword, etc.
13. to take out (a liquid, etc.) by sucking, draining, distilling, seeping, etc.
14. to bring up, as water from a well; cause (liquid) to flow out of an opening, tap, etc.; as, he *drew* a bath, the knife *draws* blood.
15. to take out the viscera of; disembowel.
16. to get or receive from some source; as, he *draws* a good salary.
17. to take out or withdraw (money) held in an account.
18. to write (a check or draft).
19. to extract (a conclusion or inference); deduce.
20. to get or win in a lottery.
21. in card games, (a) to take or get (cards); (b) to cause (a card or cards) to be played out; as, *draw* your opponent's trump.
22. to pull out so as to make longer or larger; stretch; make tense; extend; as, they *drew* the rope tight.
23. to pull out of shape; distort.
24. to stretch, flatten, or shape (metal) by die stamping, hammering, etc.

25. to make metal into (wire) by pulling it through holes.
26. to make (lines, figures, pictures, etc.), as with a pencil, pen, brush, or stylus; delineate; sketch; diagram.
27. to describe.
28. to make (comparisons, etc.); formulate.
to draw and quarter; in medieval history, (a) to execute by tying each arm and leg to a different horse, and then driving the horses in four different directions; (b) to eviscerate after hanging: so used in the phrase *hanged, drawn, and quartered.*
to draw back; to receive back, as duties on goods for exportation.
to draw in; (a) to contract; to bring to a smaller compass; to pull back; as, *to draw in* the reins; (b) to collect; to bring together; (c) to entice, allure, or inveigle; as, *to draw in* others to support a measure.
to draw off; (a) to draw from or away; also, to withdraw; to abstract; as, *to draw off* one's attention; (b) to draw or take from; to cause to flow from; as, *to draw off* wine or cider from a vessel; (c) to extract by distillation.
to draw on; (a) to allure; to entice; to persuade or cause to follow; (b) to occasion; to invite; to bring on; to cause.
to draw oneself up; (a) to assume a straighter posture; stand or sit straight; (b) to bridle.
to draw out; (a) to lengthen; to stretch by force; to extend; (b) to lengthen in time; to protract; to cause to continue; (c) to cause to issue forth; to draw off, as liquor from a cask; (d) to extract, as the spirit of a substance; (e) to call forth; to get (a person) to answer or talk; as, *to draw out* facts from a witness.
to draw over; to persuade or induce to revolt from an opposing party, and to join one's own party; as, some men may be *drawn over* by interest, others by fear.
to draw up; (a) to raise; to lift; to elevate; (b) to arrange in order; to marshal; (c) to compose in due form, as a writing; to draft; as, *to draw up* a deed; *to draw up* a paper; (d) to stop.
Syn.—drag, haul, pull, pluck, tug, delineate, derive.—*Draw* expresses the idea of putting a body in motion from behind oneself or toward oneself; to *drag* is to slowly *draw* something heavy, or to *draw* that which makes resistance; to *haul* is to *drag* with sustained effort. We *draw* a cart; we *drag* a body along the ground; we *haul* a vessel to the shore. To *pull* signifies only an effort to *draw* without the idea of motion; horses *pull* very long sometimes before they can *draw* a heavily laden cart. To *pluck* is to *pull* with a sudden twitch, in order to separate; feathers are *plucked* from birds. To *tug* is to *pull* with strenuous, persistent effort; men *tug* at the oar.

drạw, *v.i.* 1. to draw something (in various senses of the *v.t.*).
2. to be drawn.
3. to move; to come; to approach; as, the day *draws* toward evening.
4. to shrink; to contract.
5. to produce a draft; allow a draft of air, smoke, etc. to move through; as, the chimney *draws* well.
6. in hunting, (a) to track game by following its scent; (b) to move slowly toward the game after pointing: said of hounds.
7. to unsheathe a sword; as, to *draw* and defend oneself.
8. to make a draft or written demand upon a person for payment of a sum of money; as, he *drew* upon me for fifty pounds.
9. to sink or settle in water; as, great ships *draw* deep.
10. in medicine, to cause a flow of blood, pus, etc. to some part.
to draw back; to retire; to move backward; to withdraw.
to draw near or *nigh*; to approach; to come near.
to draw off; to retire; to retreat; as, the company *drew off* by degrees.
to draw on; (a) to advance; to approach; as, the day *draws on*; (b) to gain on; to approach in pursuit; as, the ship *drew on* the flying frigate.
to draw up; to form in regular order; to assume a certain order or arrangement; as, the troops *drew up* in front of the palace.

drạw, *n.* 1. a drawing or being drawn (in various senses).
2. the result of drawing.
3. a thing drawn.
4. that part of a drawbridge which can be drawn up or aside.
5. a drawn game; a tie; a stalemate; the result of a game when neither party gains the advantage; as, the match ended in a *draw*: so called from the former withdrawal of stakes in such a case.
6. a thing that attracts.
7. in card playing, the act of taking a card or cards from the pack or from another person's hand.
8. the game of draw poker. [Colloq.]
9. a land basin that water drains into or through.
to beat to the draw; (a) to draw one's weapon sooner than one's opponent does; (b) to do something sooner than someone else.

drạw'ȧ·ble, *a.* capable of being drawn.

drạw'back, *n.* 1. money or an amount paid back; usually, a certain amount of import duties paid back or remitted to an importer on the exportation of goods previously imported by him, or a certain amount of excise paid back or allowed on the exportation of domestic manufactures.
2. anything that causes loss of advantage or deduction from profit; shortcoming; detriment; disadvantage; hindrance.

drạw'bär, *n.* a strong iron bar projecting from the end of a railroad car for the purpose of receiving the coupling link and pin by which the railroad cars are joined.

drạw'bench, *n.* a machine used in wire drawing: called also *drawing bench.*

drạw'bōlt, *n.* a coupling pin.

drạw'bōre, *n.* in carpentry, a hole pierced through a tenon in such a way that a pin when driven into it will tighten the joint.

drạw'bōre, *v.t.*; drawbored, *pt., pp.*; drawboring, *ppr.* to make a drawbore in.

drạw'boy, *n.* in weaving, a boy who helps a weaver in drawing the heddles to form the pattern of the cloth he is weaving; hence, a mechanical device employed for this purpose.

drạw'bridġe (-brij), *n.* a bridge which can be raised up, let down, or drawn aside, as before the gate of a town or castle, or over a navigable river. Modern drawbridges are generally made to open horizontally.

DRAWBRIDGES

drạw'ċan·sīr, *n.* a blusterer; a braggart: so called from a bullying character in a play, *The Rehearsal*, given in London in the seventeenth century.

drạw'ċan·sīr, *a.* having the characteristics of a braggart; as, a *drawcansir* fellow.

drạw'ċut, *n.* a single cut with a knife or other cutting tool drawn toward the user.

drạw·ee', *n.* one on whom an order, draft, or bill of exchange is drawn.

drạw'ẽr, *n.* 1. one who draws, as one who takes water from a well or liquor from a cask.
2. one who or that which draws or attracts, or has the power of attraction.
3. one who draws a bill of exchange, or an order for the payment of money.
4. a draftsman.
5. a sliding box in a table, bureau, chest, etc., which can be drawn out and then pushed back into place.

drạw'ẽrṣ, *n.pl.* an undergarment for the lower part of the body, sometimes covering the legs; underpants.

drạw'fīle, *v.t.*; drawfiled, *pt., pp.*; drawfiling, *ppr.* to file smooth by drawing the file sidewise instead of lengthwise.

drạw'ġēar, *n.* 1. a harness especially adapted for draft horses.
2. the coupling gear of a railroad car.

drạw'head (-hed), *n.* 1. the flanged head of a drawbar.
2. in spinning, a device in which the slivers are lengthened and receive an additional twist.

drạw'ing, *n.* 1. the act of a person or thing that draws.
2. the art or act of representing something on a surface, by means of lines and shades, as with a pencil, crayon, pen, compasses, etc.; delineation.
3. a sketch, plan, picture, or design made with a pen, crayon, chalk, pencil, etc.
4. a lottery.
a drawing of tea; a small quantity of tea to be steeped.
out of drawing; incorrectly drawn; out of proportion.

drạw'ing aç·çount', 1. an account showing money paid for expenses or as advances on salary, commissions, etc., as to a salesman.
2. the privilege of such an account.

drạw'ing bōard, a flat, smooth board on which paper, canvas, etc. is fastened for making drawings.

drạw'ing ċärd, an entertainer, speaker, show, etc. that normally can be expected to draw a large audience.

drạw'ing knīfe, same as *drawknife.*

drạw'ing pen, a pen with two blades holding ink, used in ruling lines: called also *ruling pen.*

drạw'ing rọọm, 1. a room used for the reception or entertainment of guests or company; a living room or parlor.
2. the company or guests assembled in such a room.
3. a formal reception; as, she was presented at the last *drawing room.*
4. a private compartment on a railroad sleeping car, with accommodations for several people.

drạwk, *n.* [ME. *drauc, drauke.*] darnel; wild oats; also, coarse weeds growing in grain.

drạw'knīfe (-nīf), *n.*; *pl.* **drạw'knīveṣ,** a knife with a handle at each end, usually at right angles to the blade: the user draws it toward him in shaving a surface: also *drawing knife.*

DRAWKNIFE

drạwl, *v.t.* and *v.i.* drawled, *pt., pp.*; drawling, *ppr.* [prob. freq. of *draw.*]
1. to speak slowly, prolonging the syllables.
2. to speak in such a manner that vowels are broken at the points where word pitch changes; as, many Southerners *drawl.*

drạwl, *n.* a manner of speech characterized by slowness and prolongation of syllables.

drạw'latch (-lach), *n.* a housebreaker; a sneak thief. [Obs.]

drạwl'ẽr, *n.* one who drawls.

drạwl'ing·ly, *adv.* with a drawling speech or manner.

drạw'link, *n.* same as *drawbar.*

drạw'lọọm, *n.* a loom on which figured cloth is woven.

drạwn, *v.* past participle of *draw.*

drạwn, *a.* 1. undecided, each party having equal advantage and neither a victory; even; tied; as, a *drawn* battle.
2. pulled out of the sheath.
3. eviscerated; disemboweled; as, a *drawn* chicken.
4. tense; haggard.

drạwn but'tẽr, melted butter, sometimes thickened, used as a sauce.

drạw'net, *n.* a net with wide meshes, used to catch birds.

drạwn wõrk, a kind of ornamental work in which certain threads of a woven fabric, usually linen, are drawn or cut out, and those remaining are embroidered or hemstitched into patterns.

drąw′plāte, *n.* a metal plate having a gradation of conical holes through which wires are drawn to get the desired thickness.

drąw pō′kẽr, a form of poker in which each player is dealt five cards, and unwanted cards (usually not more than three) may be discarded and replacements drawn from the deck before betting begins.

drąw′rod, *n.* a rod connecting two drawbars.

drąw′shāve, *n.* same as *drawknife.*

drąw′spring, *n.* a spring by which a drawbar is connected with a railroad car.

drąw′string, *n.* a string drawn through a hem, as in the waist of a garment or mouth of a bag, to fasten or close it by taking up the fullness.

drąw′tūbe, *n.* a tube sliding within another tube, as in a microscope.

drąw well, a deep well, from which water is drawn by a bucket attached to a long cord.

drāy, *n.* [AS. *dræge,* lit., that which is drawn, from *dragan,* to draw.]
1. a low, strong cart with detachable sides, used for drawing heavy loads.
2. a sledge.

drāy, *v.t.*; drayed, *pt., pp.*; draying, *ppr.* to cart; to carry by means of a dray.

drāy, *v.i.* to drive a dray.

drāy, *n.* [origin obscure.] a squirrel's nest: also written *drey.*

drāy′ȧge, *n.* 1. the use of a dray; the act of transporting by means of a dray.
2. a sum charged or paid for the use of a dray or drays.

drāy çärt, same as *dray.*

drāy hǫrse, a horse used for drawing a dray.

drāy′măn, *n.*; *pl.* **drāy′men,** a man who drives a dray.

draz′el, *n.* [from Scot. *dratch,* to loiter, delay.] a slovenly woman; a slut; a drossel. [Obs.]

dread (dred), *v.t.* and *v.i.*; dreaded, *pt., pp.*; dreading, *ppr.* [ME. *dreden,* to fear; AS. *ondrædan, a-drædan,* to fear, to be afraid of.]
1. to fear intensely; to be in fearful apprehension or expectation of.
2. to regard with awe. [Archaic.]

dread (dred), *n.* 1. great fear and continued alarm in anticipation of impending evil or danger.
2. an overpowering horror or fright; as, a *dread* of snakes.
3. fear mixed with respect and awe.
4. one who or that which is feared or revered.
Let him be your *dread.* —Isa. viii. 13.
5. doubt. [Obs.]

dread, *a.* 1. dreaded or dreadful; terrible; frightful.
2. solemn; awesome; inspiring awe or reverence; as, *dread* sovereign.

dread′ȧ·ble, *a.* of a nature to inspire dread.

dread′ẽr, *n.* one who fears or lives in fear. [Rare.]

dread′fųl, *a.* 1. inspiring great fear; terrible; formidable; as, a *dreadful* storm.
2. awesome; venerable.
How *dreadful* is this place!
—Gen. xxviii. 17.
3. fearful; full of dread. [Obs.]
4. very bad, offensive, disagreeable, etc. [Colloq.]
Syn.—terrible, shocking.

dread′fųl, *n.* a sensational newspaper or periodical; a print chiefly devoted to the narration of stories of criminal life, frightful accidents, etc.; as, he gloated over the penny *dreadfuls.*

dread′fųl·ly, *adv.* 1. in a dreadful manner.
2. very; extremely; as, I am *dreadfully* tired. [Colloq.]

dread′fųl·ness, *n.* terribleness; the quality of being dreadful; frightfulness.

dread′ing·ly, *adv.* with dread or misgiving. [Rare.]

dread′less, *a.* 1. fearless; bold; not intimidated; undaunted; free from fear or terror; intrepid.
2. secure from dread; free from danger; safe. [Obs.]

dread′less, *adv.* doubtless; without fear or doubt. [Obs.]

dread′less·ness, *n.* fearlessness; undauntedness; freedom from fear or terror; boldness.

dread′ly, *a.* dreadful. [Obs.]

dread′ly, *adv.* with dread.

dread′nought, dread′nąught (-nąt), *n.* 1. a thick cloth, with a deep pile, used for warm clothing, or to keep off rain.
2. a garment made of such cloth.
3. a person who fears nothing.
4. [D–] a heavy, armored British battleship built in 1906, the first to have a large battery of 12-inch guns capable of being fired simultaneously in the same direction.
5. any large, powerful, heavily armored battleship of this sort.

drēam, *n.* [ME. *dream, dreem*; in form from AS. *dream,* joy, music (OS. *drōm*); in sense from ON. *draum,* a dream.]
1. a sequence of sensations, images, thoughts, etc. passing through a sleeping person's mind.
2. a fanciful vision or fancy of the conscious mind; daydream; reverie.
3. the state, as of abstraction or reverie, in which such a daydream occurs.
4. a fond hope or aspiration.
5. anything so lovely, charming, transitory, etc. as to seem dreamlike.

drēam, *v.i.*; dreamed *or* dreamt, *pt., pp.*; dreaming, *ppr.* 1. to have dreams.
2. to have daydreams.
3. to have vague notions or any conception (*of*).

drēam, *v.t.* 1. to dream of.
2. to spend in dreaming (with *away* or *out*).
3. to imagine as possible; fancy; suppose.
to dream up; to conceive of, imagine, or devise, as by giving free rein to the imagination. [Colloq.]

drēam′ẽr, *n.* 1. one who dreams.
2. an impractical person; a visionary.
3. a puffbird of the genus *Chelidoptera.*

drēam′fųl, *a.* full of dreams.

drēam′fųl·ly, *adv.* in a dreamy manner.

drēam′i·ly, *adv.* as if in a dream; languidly; in a dreamy manner.

drēam′i·ness, *n.* the quality or state of being dreamy.

drēam′ing·ly, *adv.* in a dreamy manner.

drēam′land, *n.* 1. a place that seems to appear to one in dreams.
2. any lovely but imaginary place.
3. sleep.

drēam′less, *a.* free from dreams.

drēam′less·ly, *adv.* in a dreamless manner.

dreamt, *v.* alternative past tense and past participle of *dream.*

drēam wǒrld, a fanciful, pleasant world such as may be seen in a dream or imagined.

drēam′y, *a.*; *comp.,* dreamier; *superl.* dreamiest, 1. filled with dreams.
2. fond of daydreaming; given to reverie; visionary; impractical; as, a *dreamy* idealist.
3. like something in a dream; shadowy; vague; misty; as, a *dreamy* scene.
4. lulling; soft and soothing; as, a *dreamy* melody.
Syn.—abstracted, absent-minded, oblivious, preoccupied, visionary.

drēar, *n.* gloom; dismalness. [Obs.]

drēar, *a.* [ME. *drery*; AS. *dreorig,* dismal, dreary.] dismal; dreary; melancholy. [Poet.]
A *drear* and dying sound. —Milton.

drēar′i·head (-hed), **drēar′i·hood,** *n.* dreariness. [Archaic.]

drēar′i·ly, *adv.* in a dreary manner; dismally; cheerlessly.

drēar′i·ment, *n.* dreariness.

drēar′i·ness, *n.* the quality or state of being dreary; gloominess; dismalness.

drēar′ing, *n.* grief. [Obs.]

drēar′i·sōme, *a.* exceedingly dreary.

drēar′y, *a.*; *comp.,* drearier; *superl.* dreariest, [ME. *drery, dreri*; AS. *dreorig,* sad, mournful, also bloody, gory, from *dreor,* blood, from *dreosan,* to drip.]
1. dismal; gloomy; dull; cheerless; depressing; as, a *dreary* room.
2. sorrowful; sad. [Archaic.]

drec′che (drech′i), *v.t.* 1. to vex; to trouble; to annoy; to torment. [Obs.]
2. to retard; to delay. [Obs.]

drec′che, *v.i.* to delay. [Obs.]

dredġe (drej), *v.t.*; dredged, *pt., pp.*; dredging, *ppr.* [ME. *dragg,* a mixture of different kinds of grain or pulse; OFr. *dragie,* a kind of digestive powder, sweetmeat; LL. *tragemata*; Gr. *tragēmata,* dried fruits, sweetmeats, from *trogein,* to gnaw, nibble, eat.]
1. to sprinkle flour or some powdered substance on; as, to *dredge* roasting beef.
2. to sprinkle or sift (flour, etc.).

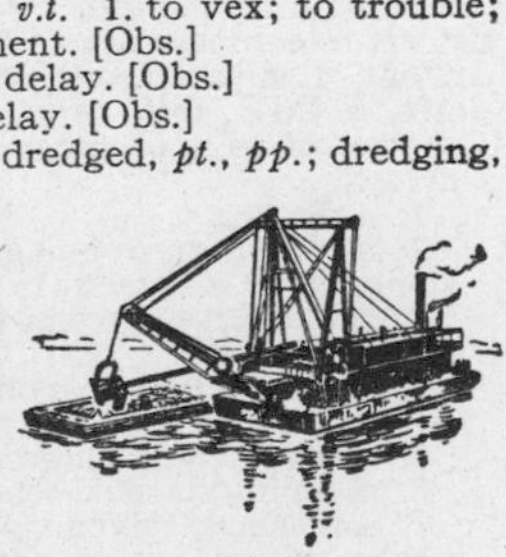

DREDGE

dredġe, *n.* a mixture of grains; especially, oats and barley when sown together.

dredġe, *n.* [from obs. D. *dregghe, dregge,* or from AS. *dragan,* to drag, draw.]
1. a device consisting of a net attached to a frame, dragged along the bottom of a river, bay, etc. to gather shellfish or other things.
2. a dredging machine.

dredġe, *v.t.* 1. to take or catch with a dredge.
2. to make deeper or cleaner with a dredging machine; to widen (a river, a channel, a harbor, etc.) by removing sand, mud, or silt from.

dredġe, *v.i.* to make use of a dredge; as, to *dredge* for oysters.

dredġ′ẽr, *n.* 1. one who uses or operates a dredge.
2. a machine for dredging.
3. a boat or vessel used in dredging for shellfish.

dredġ′ẽr, *n.* a box with a perforated lid used for sprinkling flour, etc.; a dredging box.

dredġ′ing, *n.* the act of sprinkling with flour.

dredġ′ing, *n.* 1. the act or process of using a dredge.
2. that which is brought up by a dredge.

dredġ′ing box, a box with a perforated lid used for sprinkling flour, etc; a dredger.

dredġ′ing mȧ·çhine′, an apparatus used to take up mud, etc., as in deepening or clearing channels, harbors, or river beds.

dree, *v.t.*; dreed, *pt., pp.*; dreeing, *ppr.* [AS. *dreogan,* to bear, suffer, endure.] to suffer; to bear. [Scot. and Archaic.]
to dree one's weird; to endure one's fate. [Scot.]

dree, *v.i.* to be able to do; to endure or continue. [Obs.]

dree, *a.* 1. great; important. [Obs.]
2. tedious; tiresome. [Scot. and Archaic.]

dreg′gi·ness, *n.* fullness of dregs or lees; foulness; feculence.

dreg′gish, *a.* full of dregs; foul; feculent.

dreg′gy, *a.*; *comp.* dreggier; *superl.* dreggiest, full of, having the nature of, or containing dregs or lees; consisting of dregs; foul; muddy; feculent.

dregs, *n.pl.* [ME. *dregges*; ON. *dregg,* dregs, lees.]
1. the sediment of liquids; lees; grounds; feculence; any foreign matter of liquids that goes to the bottom of a vessel.
2. waste or worthless matter; dross; sweepings; refuse; hence, the most worthless part of anything; as, the *dregs* of society.
3. [*sing.*] a small amount remaining; residue.
Syn.—sediment, dross, scum, refuse.

Drei′bųnd (-bųnt), *n.* [G. *drei,* three, and *bund,* an alliance, bond.]
1. a triple alliance.
2. the alliance formed by Germany, Austria-Hungary, and Italy, which lasted from 1882 to 1915.

Dreis′se·nȧ, *n.* the type genus of the *Dreissenidæ.*

Dreis·sen′i·dae, *n.pl.* [L., from Dr. *Dreysen,* of Belgium.] a family of bivalves, having the membranous covering open only for the foot in front of the umbones, and for the siphons at the distal margin: also called *Dreissenacea, Dreisseninæ, Dreissensinæ.*

drench, *v.t.*; drenched, *pt., pp.*; drenching, *ppr.* [ME. *drenchen,* to soak, drench; AS. *drencan,* to give to drink, to drown.]
1. to wet thoroughly; to soak; to fill or cover with water or other liquid.
2. to make (a horse, cow, etc.) drink something, especially medicine.
3. to purge violently.
Syn.—soak, steep, imbrue, saturate, souse, deluge.

drench, *v.i.* to be drowned. [Obs.]

drench, *n.* [ME. *drench*; AS. *drinc,* a drink.]
1. a large dose or draught, especially for a sick animal.
2. a drenching.
3. a thing that drenches; any solution in which a thing is steeped or soaked.

drench′ẽr, *n.* 1. one who or that which drenches.
2. one who gives a drench to a beast.

dreng, *n.* in old English law, a tenant in capite: usually applied to a rent-paying tenant holding in virtue of some service less honorable than knighthood.

dreñ′gȧge, *n.* in old English law, the tenure by which a dreng held land, or the land itself.

drep′ȧ·ni-, [from Gr. *drepanē,* sickle.] a combining form signifying *sickle-shaped, resembling a sickle*; as, *drepani*form.

drep′ȧ·ni·fǫrm, *a.* [*drepani-,* and L. *forma,* form, shape.] shaped like a sickle; falciform.

dre·pā′ni·um, *n.*; *pl.* **dre·pā′ni·ȧ,** in botany, a sickle-shaped cyme.

drep′ȧ·noid, *a.* resembling or shaped like a sickle.

Dreṣ′den, *n.* a fine chinaware or porcelain first made in the early part of the eighteenth century near Dresden, Saxony: also called *Dresden ware.*

dress, *v.t.*; dressed *or* drest, *pt., pp.*; dressing, *ppr.* [ME. *dressen,* to make straight, direct; OFr. *dresser,* to set up, arrange, from L. *directus,* pp. of *dirigere,* to straighten, arrange.]
1. to put clothes on; clothe.
2. to provide with clothing.
3. to decorate; trim; adorn.
4. to arrange a display in; as, he *dresses* store windows.
5. to arrange or do up (the hair).
6. to arrange (troops, etc.) in a straight line or lines.
7. to apply medicines and bandages to (a wound, sore, etc.).
8. to prepare; to put in the condition desired; to make suitable or fit; specifically, (a) to reduce to the proper dimensions, form, and smoothness; as, to *dress* a board or a stone; (b) to clean and draw (a fowl); (c) to cultivate; to till; as, to *dress* a garden; (d) to curry (a horse, leather, etc.).
to dress down; (a) to reprimand; scold; (b) to give a beating to; to thrash. [Colloq.]
to dress ship; to raise the ensign and put up all code flags and bunting on a ship.
to dress up; (a) to dress in formal clothes, or in clothes less informal or more elegant, showy, etc. than one is wearing or usually wears; (b) to arrange in a straight line, as troops.

dress, *v.i.* 1. to get into a straight line; to take up proper alignment; as, look to the right and *dress.*
2. to clothe oneself; to wear clothes; specifically, to dress in formal, conventional, or elegant attire; as, to *dress* for dinner; she loves to *dress.*

dress, *n.* 1. that which is used as the covering or ornament of the body; clothes; garments; clothing; apparel; as, she gives all her thought to *dress.*
2. the usual outer garment worn by women and girls, consisting of a skirt and waist, generally in one garment.
3. formal clothes; as, full *dress.*
4. external covering or appearance.
5. the system of furrows which makes the finish of a millstone.
6. in ornithology, plumage.
Syn.—apparel, raiment, clothing, clothes, vestments, garments, habiliments, accouterments, attire, array, habit.

dress, *a.* 1. of or for dresses; as, *dress* material.
2. worn on formal occasions; as, a *dress* suit.

dress cĩr′çle, a section of seats in a theater or concert hall, usually behind and above the orchestra: so called because formal dress was formerly customary there.

dress cōat, a black or very dark blue coat with tails, part of a man's formal dress.

dress′ẽr, *n.* [Fr. *dressoir.*]
1. a kitchen table or bench on which meat and other things are dressed or prepared for use.
2. a cupboard or set of shelves for dishes and cooking utensils.
3. a chest of drawers for clothes, with a mirror: also called *bureau.*

dress′ẽr, *n.* 1. one who dresses; one who is employed in clothing and adorning another.
2. one who dresses something; one who is employed in preparing, trimming, or adjusting anything.
3. an assistant in a hospital, who dresses wounds, etc.
4. in mechanics, a tool for dressing.
5. in type founding, one employed to dress or finish type.
6. in plumbing, a mallet for bending or straightening lead pipe.
7. one who dresses elegantly or in a certain way; as, a fancy *dresser.*

dress goodṣ, cloth for dresses.

dress′i·ly, *adv.* in a dressy manner.

dress′i·ness, *n.* the state or quality of being dressy.

dress′ing, *n.* 1. raiment; attire.
2. a bandage or medicine applied to a wound or sore.
3. that which is used in preparing land for a crop; manure spread over land.
4. a dressing-down. [Colloq.]
5. in cookery, the stuffing of fowls, pigs, etc.; also, a sauce added to meats, salads, etc.
6. gum, starch, and other substances used in stiffening or preparing silk, linen, and other materials.
7. [*pl.*] in architecture, the moldings round doors, windows, etc.; the stone frames which surround the wall openings in brick buildings.
8. the preparation of ore for smelting.

dress′ing çāse, a box or case fitted with toilet requisites.

dress′ing-down′, *n.* 1. a reprimand; scolding. [Colloq.]
2. a thrashing; beating. [Colloq.]

dress′ing fọr′ceps, forceps used in dressing wounds.

dress′ing gown, a loose robe for wear when one is undressed or lounging.

dress′ing rọọm, 1. a room used in a theater by actors for dressing and making up for their roles.
2. a room in a home in which to make one's toilet, usually connected with a bedroom.

dress′ing tā′ble, a low stand or table with a mirror, for use while putting on cosmetics, etc.

dress′māk″ẽr, *n.* one who makes women's dresses and the like.

dress′māk″ẽr, *a.* designating or of a woman's suit, coat, etc. not cut on severe, mannish lines: distinguished from *tailored.*

dress′māk″ing, *n.* the art, process, occupation, or business of making dresses.

dress pȧ·rāde′, a parade in dress uniform, as of troops on review.

dress rē·hẽars′ăl, a final rehearsal, as of a play, ceremony, or military engagement, performed in exactly the manner in which it is to take place.

dress sūit, a man's formal suit for evening wear.

dress′y, *a.*; *comp.* dressier; *superl.* dressiest. 1. wearing showy, elaborate clothes. [Colloq.]
2. stylish; elegant; smart: said of clothes, parties, etc. [Colloq.]

drev′il, *n.* drivel. [Obs.]

drew, *v.* past tense of *draw.*

drey, *n.* a squirrel's nest; a dray.

dreynt, *v.* obsolete past participle of *drench.*

drib, *v.t.* and *v.i.*; dribbed, *pt., pp.*; dribbing, *ppr.* [from *drip.*] to fall, or let fall, in or as in driblets. [Obs.]

drib, *n.* a drop. [Obs.]

drib′ble, *v.i.*; dribbled, *pt., pp.*; dribbling, *ppr.* [freq. of *drip,* from ME. *drippen, dryppen,* to drip; AS. *dryppan,* to cause to drop.]
1. to fall in small drops or in a quick succession of drops; as, water *dribbles* from the eaves.
2. to slaver; drool.
3. to dribble a ball.

drib′ble, *v.t.* 1. to let fall in drops or driblets.
2. in basketball, to bounce (the ball) or move (the ball) forward by repeated bounces.
3. in soccer, etc., to move (the ball) forward by a rapid succession of short kicks.

drib′ble, *n.* 1. a small drop; driblet; dribbling flow.
2. the act of dribbling a ball.
3. a drizzling rain. [Colloq.]

drib′blẽr, *n.* one who dribbles.

drib′let, drib′blet, *n.* a small amount or part; as, money paid in *driblets.*

drid′dle, *v.i.*; driddled, *pt., pp.*; driddling, *ppr.* to move or act in a feeble or aimless way. [Scot. and Brit. Dial.]

drīe, *v.t.* to dree. [Obs.]

drīed, *v.* past tense and past participle of *dry.*

drīeg̃h (drēkh), *a.* dree. [Scot.]

drī′ẽr, *n.* 1. one who dries, or that which has the quality of drying.
2. a substance added to paint, varnish, or printing ink to make it dry quickly.
3. a mechanical contrivance for drying by heating, blowing, etc.

drī′ẽr, *a.* comparative of *dry.*

drī′est, *a.* superlative of *dry.*

drift, *n.* [ME. *drift, dryft,* an act of driving, a shower of rain or snow, from AS. *drifan,* to drive.]
1. a driving.
2. a drifting; a being driven or carried along, as by a current of air or water.
3. the course on which something is directed.
4. the deviation of a ship or airplane from its path, caused by side currents or winds.
5. a tendency; inclination; trend.
6. meaning; intent; tenor.
7. something driven, as rain, snow, dust, or smoke driven before the wind, or floating matter driven by water currents.
8. a heap of snow, sand, etc. piled up by the wind.
9. in geology, rocks, gravel, sand, etc. carried away from one place and deposited in another by a river or glacier.
10. in mechanics, (a) a tool used for ramming or driving down a heavy object; (b) a tool for enlarging or shaping holes.
11. in mining, a horizontal passageway driven into or along the path of a vein or rock layer.
12. in physical geography, a slow ocean current.
13. in shipbuilding, the difference between the size of a bolt and the hole into which it is to be driven, or between the circumference of a hoop and the circumference of the mast on which it is to be driven.
14. in architecture, the horizontal force which an arch exerts.
drift of the forest; in English law, a roundup of the cattle that are in the forest in order to determine whether the forest is surcharged, whether the cattle are commonable, etc.
Syn.—tendency, direction, motion, tenor, meaning, purport, object, intention, purpose, scope, aim, result, issue, inference, conclusion, end, course.

drift, *v.i.*; drifted, *pt., pp.*; drifting, *ppr.* 1. to accumulate in heaps by the force of wind or water; to be driven into heaps; as, snow or sand *drifts.*
2. to be driven along by or as by a current; as, the ship *drifted* astern; a raft *drifted* ashore.
3. to be carried along by circumstances; to go along aimlessly.
4. in mining, to make a drift; to search for metals or ores.

drift, *v.t.* 1. to drive into heaps; as, a current of wind *drifts* snow or sand.
2. to cover with or as with a drift or drifts; as, the roads were badly *drifted.*
3. in mining, to make or drive a drift in.

drift′ăġe, *n.* 1. that which drifts or is drifted.
2. the deviation from a course due to drifting.
3. a drifting.

drift aṅ′ċhŏr, a drag anchor.

drift′ẽr, *n.* 1. a person or thing that drifts.
2. a boat carrying nets that are allowed to drift with the tide: distinguished from *trawler.*

drift′less, *a.* without direction; aimless.

drift net, a large net used as a gill net.

drift′pïēce, *n.* in shipbuilding, one of the upright or curved pieces of timber that connect the plank sheer and the gunwale.

drift′pin, *n.* same as *drift,* n. 10.

drift′wāy, *n.* 1. a common way for driving cattle in.
2. in nautical usage and in mining, drift.

drift′weed, *n.* seaweed thrown upon the shore by the waves.

drift′wind, *n.* a wind or storm that makes drifts.

drift′wood, *n.* wood drifted or floated by water or washed ashore: often used figuratively; as, human *driftwood.*

drift′y, *a.*; *comp.* driftier; *superl.* driftiest, inclined to drift; full of drifts or heaps, as snow.

drill, *v.t.*; drilled, *pt., pp.*; drilling, *ppr.* [D. *drillen,* to bore, turn round, brandish, train, from M.D. *drille,* a hole.]
1. to pierce with a drill; to bore and make a hole in with or as with a drill.
2. in agriculture, (a) to sow in rows, drills, or channels; as, to *drill* wheat; (b) to sow (a field) in drills; as, the field was *drilled,* not sown broadcast.
3. to teach and train by repeated exercise or repetition of acts.
4. to train in military or physical exercises.
5. to draw on; to entice. [Obs.]

drill, *v.i.* 1. to take part in military, physical, or mental exercises.
2. to sow seed with a drill or in drills.
3. to bore a hole or holes.

drill, *n.* 1. a pointed instrument used for boring holes in metal, wood, stone, etc.; a boring tool that cuts its way as it revolves; also, a drilling machine or drill press.

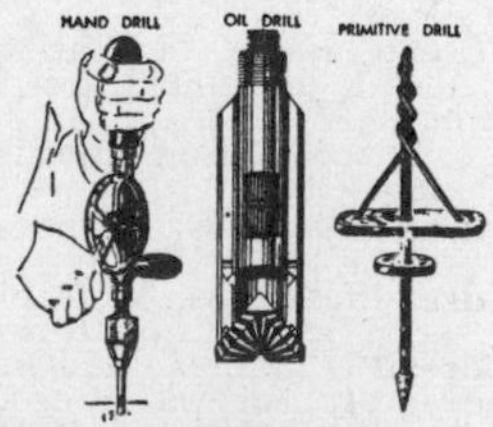

TYPES OF DRILL

2. military or physical exercise and training, especially of a group, as in marching and the manual of arms.
3. the process of training or teaching by making those trained repeat an exercise again and again.
4. the method or style of drilling.
5. in agriculture, a row of seeds planted;

also, the furrow in which the seeds are deposited.

6. a machine for sowing seeds in regular rows; as, a turnip *drill*.

7. *Urosalpinx cinerea*, a marine snail which destroys oysters by boring into their shells and feeding on them.

drill, *v.t.* and *v.i.* to drain; to trickle.

drill, *n.* [earlier *drilling*, from M.H.G. *dril(i)ch*, cloth woven with three threads, from L. *trilix*, three-threaded.] a coarse linen or cotton cloth with a diagonal weave, used for work clothes, etc.

drill, *n.* [probably from Fr. *drill*, a soldier, vigorous fellow.] a baboon native to western Africa, like the mandrill but smaller.

drill bar′rōw, an agricultural drill resembling a wheelbarrow.

drill bōw, a small bow whose string is used for the purpose of rapidly turning a drill.

drill′ẽr, *n.* one who or that which drills.

drill har′rōw, a small drag or harrow for working between drills.

drill′ing, *n.* a kind of coarse linen or cotton cloth; drill.

drill′ing mȧ-chīne′, a machine for operating a drill; a drill press.

drill′mȧs″tẽr, *n.* 1. one who instructs in military drill.

2. one who teaches by drilling.

drill plow, drill plough (plow), a plow which plants and covers seed.

drill press, a machine tool for boring holes in metal, etc.

drill′stock, *n.* in a drilling machine or tool, the holder of the fixed end of a drill.

drī′ly, *adv.* same as *dryly*.

driñk, *v.t.*; drank *or archaic* drunk, *pt.*; drunk *or archaic* drunken, *pp.*; drinking, *ppr.* [ME. *drinken*; AS. *drincan*, to drink.]

1. to take into the mouth and swallow, as liquids; to imbibe; as, to *drink* water or wine.

2. to absorb (liquid or moisture).

3. to swallow the contents of.

4. to drink in honor of; drink a toast to.

5. to take in through the senses, as the ear or eye; to hear; to see; as, to *drink* words or the voice.

I *drink* delicious poison from thy eye.
—Pope.

6. to take in the fumes of; to smoke; as, to *drink* tobacco. [Obs.]

to drink in; to absorb; to take or receive with the senses or the mind.

to drink off; to drink the whole of at a draught; as, *to drink off* a cup of cordial.

to drink to; to drink in honor of; drink a toast to.

to drink up; to drink the whole of.

driñk, *n.* [ME. *drink, drinke*; AS. *drinc*, a drink, from *drincan*, to drink.]

1. any liquid for drinking; a beverage.

2. intoxicating liquor; alcoholic liquor; as, a victim of *drink*.

3. habitual or excessive use of alcoholic liquor.

4. a portion of liquid drunk or for drinking.

5. any body of water; especially, the ocean. [Slang.]

in drink; drunk; tipsy.

driñk′ȧ-ble, *a.* that may be drunk; fit or suitable for drinking.

driñk′ȧ-ble, *n.* [*usually in pl.*] a liquid that may be drunk; a beverage.

driñk′ȧ-ble-ness, *n.* state of being drinkable.

driñk′ẽr, *n.* one who drinks, particularly one who drinks alcoholic liquors to excess or habitually.

driñk′ẽr moth, *Odonestis potatoria*, a large British moth, having long, beaklike palpi.

Driñk′ẽr res′pi-rā-tôr, [after the Am. inventor, Philip *Drinker* (1893–).] an apparatus for inducing artificial respiration over a long period of time: also called *iron lung*.

driñk′ing, *n.* 1. the act of taking into the mouth and swallowing liquids.

2. the practice of drinking to excess.

3. a carousal.

driñk′ing song, a song celebrating the pleasures of drinking alcoholic liquors; song for a drinking party.

driñk′less, *a.* without drink.

drip, *v.i.*; dripped (dript) *or* dript, *pt., pp.*; dripping, *ppr.* [ME. *dryppen*, to drip; AS. *dryppan*, to cause to drop.] to fall in drops; as, water *drips* from eaves.

drip, *v.t.* to let fall in drops.

drip, *n.* 1. a falling in drops; a trickling.

2. moisture or liquid falling in drops.

3. the sound made by liquid falling in drops.

4. in architecture, a flat member of a cornice, sill, etc. projecting so as to throw off water.

5. a person regarded as unpleasant or insipid. [Slang.]

drip coffee; coffee made by pouring boiling water over finely ground coffee grains: usually made in a dripolater.

drip grind; coffee ground for a dripolater, or for drip coffee.

right of drip; in law, an easement or servitude, by which a person has a right to let his drip fall on another person's property.

drip′-drȳ, *a.* designating or of fabrics or garments that dry quickly when hung soaking wet and require little or no ironing.

drip′-drȳ, *v.i.*; drip-dried, *pt., pp.*; drip-drying, *ppr.* to launder as a drip-dry fabric does.

drip′ō-lā-tôr, *n.* [*drip*, and percolator.] a kind of coffeepot in which boiling water poured into the top section seeps slowly through finely ground coffee in the perforated middle section, and then drips into the one below: a trade-mark (*Dripolator*).

drip pan, a dripping pan.

drip′ping, *n.* 1. a falling of a liquid drop by drop.

2. [*usually in pl.*] the fat that drips from meat in roasting.

drip′ping pan, a pan for receiving the fat that drips from meat in roasting.

drip′py, *a.*; *comp.* drippier; *superl.* drippiest, 1. characterized by dripping water, rain, etc.; as, a *drippy* faucet.

2. overly sentimental, stupid, etc. [Slang.]

drip′stōne, *n.* 1. in architecture, a projecting molding or cornice over doorways, windows, etc. to throw off the rain.

2. calcium carbonate, $CaCO_3$, deposited by dripping water in the form of stalactites or stalagmites.

dript, *v.* alternative past tense and past participle of *drip*.

drīve, *v.t.*; drove *or formerly* drave, *pt.*; driven, *pp.*; driving, *ppr.* [ME. *driven, drifen*; AS. *drifan*, to drive, compel to go, urge on, etc.]

1. to impel or urge forward; to force to move; as, we *drive* a nail into wood with a hammer; the wind *drives* a ship on the ocean.

2. to force into or from a state or act; as, ambition *drove* him to crime.

3. to force to work, usually to excess.

4. to force by a blow, thrust, or stroke; to throw, hit, or cast hard and swiftly; as, the batter *drove* the ball into the bleachers.

5. to cause to go through; make penetrate.

6. to make or produce by doing this; as, he *drove* an oil well.

7. to cause to function; to impel or propel as a motive power; as, an engine *drives* the motor boat.

8. to control the movement or direct the course of (an automobile, locomotive, etc.).

9. to take on a drive; to convey (a person) in an automobile or other vehicle; as, to *drive* a person to his door.

10. to urge; to press; as, to *drive* an argument.

11. to carry on with vigor; to prosecute; as, to *drive* a trade.

12. in mining, to dig horizontally.

13. in lumbering, to direct the course of (logs) in a stream.

14. in hunting, (a) to chase (game) from thickets into the clear or into nets, traps, etc.; (b) to cover (an area) in this way.

to drive away; to force to leave; to dispel.

to drive over or *out*; in typesetting, to space out or carry over, as matter being corrected.

drīve, *v.i.* 1. to be impelled; to be moved by force; as, a ship *drives* before the wind.

The hull *drives* on, though mast and sail be torn.
—Byron.

2. to rush and press with violence; as, a storm *drives* against the house.

Fierce Boreas *drove* against his flying sails.
—Dryden.

3. to drive a blow, ball, missile, etc.

4. to be driven; operate: said of an automobile.

5. to go or be conveyed in a vehicle.

6. to operate a motor vehicle.

7. to aim (*at* something); to strive toward; as, we know the end the author is *driving at*.

8. to aim a blow (*at*).

At Anxur's shield he *drove*, and at the blow
Both shield and arm to ground together go.
—Dryden.

drīve, *n.* 1. the act of driving; also, a trip in a vehicle.

2. a road or any place suitable for driving automobiles, etc.

3. in forging and type founding, a matrix formed by a die or punch.

4. a collection of logs to be floated down a river.

5. an effort put forward to achieve some purpose; a campaign.

6. a rounding up of animals for branding, killing, etc.

7. energy; push; as, a person with initiative and *drive*.

8. that which is urgent or pressing; pressure.

9. the apparatus controlling the propulsion of a motor vehicle; as, a gear *drive*.

10. a device that communicates motion to a machine or machine part.

11. in such games as cricket, baseball, tennis, etc., the act of striking or impelling the ball with force; also, the manner in which the ball is driven.

12. a driveway. [Colloq.]

13. in psychology, any of the basic impulses or urges.

drīve′-in′, *a.* designating or of a restaurant, motion-picture theater, bank, etc. designed to render its services to persons who drive up and remain seated in their cars.

drīve′-in′, *n.* such a restaurant, theater, etc.

driv′el, *v.i.*; driveled *or* drivelled, *pt., pp.*; driveling *or* drivelling, *ppr.* [ME. *drivelen*, a variant of *dravelen, drabelen*, to drabble, from AS. *dreflian*, to slobber.]

1. to slaver; to let saliva flow from the mouth.

2. to flow from the mouth like saliva.

3. to speak in a silly or stupid manner; talk childish nonsense.

driv′el, *v.t.* 1. to let run from the mouth.

2. to say in a silly, stupid, or nonsensical manner.

driv′el, *n.* 1. saliva flowing from the mouth.

2. a driveler; a fool; an idiot. [Obs.]

3. foolish talk; senseless utterance; twaddle.

4. a servant; hireling. [Obs.]

Syn.—fatuity, nonsense, trifling, rubbish.

driv′el-ẽr, *n.* one who drivels: also spelled *driveller*.

driv′en, *a.* [past participle of *drive*.]

1. moved along and piled up by the wind; as, *driven* snow.

2. forced into a (specified) condition; as, *driven* mad.

drīv′ẽr, *n.* 1. one who or that which drives.

2. one who drives an automobile, horse, locomotive, etc.

3. one who herds cattle.

4. one who makes his subordinates work hard.

5. a mallet, hammer, tamper, etc.

6. a woodenheaded golf club with little loft, used in hitting the ball from the tee.

7. any machine part that communicates motion to another part.

8. in nautical usage, a large quadrilateral sail.

9. in weaving, a piece of wood which drives the shuttle through the opening in the warp.

the driver's seat; the position of control or dominance.

drīv′ẽr ȧnt, any of several African stinging ants that travel together in large numbers.

drīve shȧft, in an automobile, the metal shaft by means of which the wheels are made to turn: it connects the transmission and the driving mechanism in the rear axle.

drīve′wāy, *n.* a road or passage along which automobiles, etc. may be driven; especially, a path leading from a garage to the street.

drīve well, a well made by driving a pointed tube into the ground until water is reached: also called *driven well*.

drīv′ing, *a.* 1. transmitting force or motion; as, a *driving* belt.

2. moving with force and violence; as, a *driving* rain.

drīv′ing, *n.* 1. the act or process of handling an automobile or other vehicle on the road; as, he is good at *driving*.

2. in golf, the act or style of using a driver.

drīv′ing ax′le (ak′sl), the axle of a driving wheel.

drīv′ing belt, the belt by which machinery is driven by an engine; also, any belt which conveys motion.

drīv′ing box, 1. the journal box of a driving axle.

2. the seat in a carriage occupied by the driver or coachman.

drīv′ing ī′ron (-ŭrn), in golf, a club with an iron head and a nearly straight face.
drīv′ing nōtes, in music, syncopated notes.
drīv′ing rein, a rein attached to the bit rings and held by the driver of the vehicle.
drīv′ing shaft, the shaft upon which a driving wheel rests.
drīv′ing spring, a spring resting upon the box of a driving axle of a locomotive, which bears the weight and aids in deadening shocks.
drīv′ing wheel (hwēl), 1. in machinery, a wheel that communicates motion to another wheel or wheels.
2. one of the large wheels in a locomotive engine fixed upon the crank axle or main-shaft: called also *driver*.
driz′zle, *v.i.*; drizzled, *pt., pp.*; drizzling, *ppr.* [AS. *dreosan*, to fall.] to rain in fine, mistlike drops.
driz′zle, *v.t.* to shed in small drops or particles.
driz′zle, *n.* rain falling in fine, mistlike drops.
driz′zly, *a.* drizzling; characterized by a drizzle.
drof′land, dryf′land, *n.* driftland. [Obs.]
drō′gẽr, *n.* same as *drogher*.
drō′ghẽr (-gẽr), *n.* [prob. native name.]
1. a small West Indian coasting craft, built for carrying goods, having long, light masts and lateen sails.
2. any slow-moving coasting vessel.
drog′măn, drog′ō·măn, *n.* dragoman. [Obs.]
drōgue (drōg), *n.* a buoy attached to the end of a harpoon line.
droil, *v.i.* to work sluggishly or slowly; to plod. [Obs.]
droil, *n.* 1. a drudge. [Obs.]
2. toil; mean work. [Obs.]
droit (*or* Fr. drwä), *n.* [Fr., from OFr. *droit*; LL. *directum*, right, justice, from L. *directus*, right, straight.]
1. a legal right.
2. that to which one has legal claim.
droits of the Admiralty; in English law, the perquisites formerly belonging to the Court of the Admiralty, now paid into the Exchequer.
droi′tū·răl, *a.* in old English law, of a right to property as distinguished from possession.
drōll, *a.*; *comp.* droller; *superl.* drollest, amusing in a quaint way; humorously odd; as, a *droll* fellow.
Syn.—laughable, comical.
drōll, *n.* [OFr. *drolle, draule*, a good fellow, wag; M.D. *drol*, a merry, humorous fellow, a round lump.]
1. a droll or comical person; a jester; a buffoon.
2. a farce or comical exhibition. [Obs.]
drōll, *v.i.* to jest; to play the buffoon.
drōll, *v.t.*; drolled, *pt., pp.*; drolling, *ppr.* 1. to bring about or influence by jesting.
2. to make a jest of. [Rare.]
drōll′ẽr, *n.* a jester; a buffoon. [Obs.]
drōll′ẽr·y, *n.*; *pl.* **drōll′ẽr·ieṣ,** 1. anything quaintly amusing; droll act, remark, etc.
2. the act of joking.
3. a droll quality; quaint humor.
drōll′ish, *a.* somewhat droll.
drōll′ist, *n.* a droll. [Rare.]
drōl′ly, *adv.* in a droll manner.
drō·mae·og′nȧ·thous (-mē-og′nȧ-thus), *a.* [from *dromæus*, generic name of the ostrich, from Gr. *dromaios*, swift-running, and *gnathos*, jaw.] having the bones of the palate similar anatomically to those of the ostrich.
drōme, *n.* [Fr., from Gr. *dromas*, running.] a bird, the crab plover.
-drōme, [from Gr. *dromas*, a runner, from L. *dramein*, to run.] a suffix meaning *running, race course*, as in hippo*drome*, palin*drome*.
drŏm′ē·dā·ry, *n.*; *pl.* **drŏm′ē·dā·rieṣ,** [ME. *dromedarie*; LL. *dromedarius*, a dromedary, from Gr. *dromas*, a running, from *dramein*, to run.]
1. a species of camel, especially the one-humped Arabian camel: it is trained for fast riding.
2. a dromond. [Obs.]
drom′iç, drom′iç·ăl, *a.* [Gr. *dromikos*, good at running, pertaining to a running or race course, from *dromos*, a running, a race course.] of, pertaining to, or characteristic of a dromos.
drom′ond, drom′on, *n.* a large, fast-sailing ship of the Middle Ages.
drom′os, *n.*; *pl.* **drom′oi,** [Gr. *dromos*, a running, a race course, from *dramein*, to run.]
1. in ancient Greece, a course for racing.
2. in archaeology, an avenue, as one leading into a tomb or temple.
-drō′mous, a suffix meaning running, moving, as in cata*dromous*.

drōne, *n.* [ME. *drone, drane*; AS. *dran, dræn*, a drone; prob. imitative of the sound.]

DRONE BEE

1. a male bee, especially a male honey-bee, smaller than the queen bee, but larger than the working bee. The drones have no sting and do no work: after one fertilizes the eggs of the queen bee, it is killed and the rest are driven from the hive.
2. an idler; a sluggard; one who does no work but lives by the work of others.
3. a pilotless airplane whose flight is radio-controlled by an operator in an accompanying craft or on the ground.
drōne, *v.i.*; droned, *pt., pp.*; droning, *ppr.* to live in idleness; loaf.
drōne, *n.* 1. a continuous and monotonous humming or buzzing sound.
2. a bagpipe.
3. its bass pipe.
4. a bass voice or part, sustaining a single low tone.
5. such a tone.
drōne, *v.t.* to utter in a dull, monotonous tone.
drōne, *v.i.*; droned, *pt., pp.*; droning, *ppr.* 1. to talk in a monotonous voice
2. to make a continuous and monotonous humming or buzzing sound; as, the bagpipes *drone* and the drums beat.
drōne bȧss, a bass of one or, at most, two notes.
drōne bee, a male bee; a drone.
drōne fly, *Eristalis tenax*, a fly resembling the drone bee.
drōne′pīpe, *n.* one of the bass pipes of the bagpipe; the drone.
droñ′gō, *n.* [South African.] one of a family of fly-catching birds, with long, forked tails. They inhabit India, the Asiatic islands, and South Africa: also called *drongo shrike*.
drōn′ish, *a.* idle; sluggish; lazy; indolent; inactive; slow.
drōn′ish·ly, *adv.* in a dronish manner.
drōn′ish·ness, *n.* state of being dronish.
droñ′ke·lew, *a.* drunken. [Obs.]
drōn′y, *a.* lazy; sluggish; dronelike.
drook, *v.t.* same as *drouk*.
drool, *v.i.*; drooled, *pt., pp.*; drooling, *ppr.* 1. to let saliva flow from one's mouth; to drivel.
2. to flow from the mouth, as saliva.
3. to speak in a silly or stupid manner; talk childish nonsense. [Slang.]
drool, *v.t.* 1. to let run from the mouth; as, he *drooled* tobacco juice over his chin.
2. to say in a silly, stupid, or nonsensical manner. [Slang.]
drool, *n.* 1. saliva running from the mouth.
2. silly, stupid talk; childish nonsense; twaddle; drivel. [Slang.]
droop, *v.i.*; drooped, *pt., pp.*; drooping, *ppr.* [ME. *droupen*; Ice. *drupa*, to droop.]
1. to sink or hang down; to lean downward, as a body that is weak or languishing.
2. to grow faint; to grow weak; to lose vitality or strength; as, the soldiers *droop* from fatigue.
3. to become dejected or dispirited; to decline.
4. to draw to a close; to proceed downward; as, the day *drooped*.
Syn.—fade, languish, pine, sink.
droop, *v.t.* to let sink or bend down; as, the flowers *drooped* their heads.
droop, *n.* a drooping.
droop′ẽr, *n.* one who or that which droops.
droop′i·ness, *n.* the quality or state of being droopy.
droop′ing·ly, *adv.* in a drooping manner.
droop′y, *a.*; *comp.* droopier; *superl.* droopiest, drooping or tending to droop.
drop, *n.* [ME. *drope*; AS. *dropa*, a drop; O.H.G. *tropfo*; G. *tropfen*; Sw. *droppe*; Ice. *dropi*, a drop.]
1. a small portion of any fluid in a somewhat spherical or pear-shaped form, as when falling; as, a *drop* of water; a *drop* of blood.
2. a thing like a drop in shape, size, etc., as a pendent earring or a small piece of candy.
3. a very small quantity of liquid; as, he had not drunk a *drop*.
4. a very small quantity of anything.
5. in architecture, (a) a gutta; (b) a pendent ornamentation of any kind.
6. anything that projects or falls from a higher position; anything used to bring or let down something else, or cover something; as, (a) a door in a stage or platform; a trap; (b) the part of a gallows on which the convicted person stands before execution, and which is suddenly dropped; (c) a drop curtain; (d) a tube used to convey gas from a fixture to a burner at a lower level; (e) an arrangement for bringing down heavy weights to a vessel's deck; (f) a drop hammer; (g) the movable cover of a keyhole; (h) a slot for depositing letters.
7. the process of falling; an abrupt fall, descent, slump, or decrease; as, a *drop* in prices.
8. the distance between a higher and lower level; depth to which or distance through which anything falls or sinks.
9. in football, a drop kick.
10. [*pl.*] any medicine administered in drops.
11. in nautical usage, the depth of the lowest square sail at its center.
12. a decrease in the potential of an electric current.
at the drop of a hat; (a) at a signal; (b) immediately; at once; without hesitation or reluctance.
drop by drop; drop following drop; little by little.
drop in the bucket; a very small or insignificant quantity.
to get or have the drop on; (a) to get one's gun ready to fire sooner than one's adversary; hence, (b) to forestall another or seize an advantage. [Slang.]
drop, *v.t.*; dropped *or occasionally* dropt, *pt., pp.*; dropping, *ppr.* [ME. *droppen*; AS. *droppan, dropian*, from *dropa*, a drop.]
1. to pour or let fall in drops.
2. to let fall, as any substance; as, to *drop* the anchor; to *drop* a stone.
3. to let go; to dismiss; to lay aside; to leave; to permit to subside; as, to *drop* an affair.
4. to utter slightly, briefly, or casually; to insert indirectly, incidentally, or by way of digression; as, to *drop* a word of suggestion.
5. to send (mail) informally; as, to *drop* a note.
6. to set down and leave (a person or thing) at a specified place; as, the coach *dropped* a passenger at the inn. [Colloq.]
7. to bedrop; to speckle; to variegate; to sprinkle with drops; as, a coat *dropped* with gold.
8. to lower; as, to *drop* the muzzle of a gun.
9. to give birth to: said of animals.
10. to cause to fall, as by wounding or killing.
11. to omit (a letter or letters) in a word.
12. to poach (an egg).
13. to lose (money). [Slang.]
14. in football, (a) to drop-kick (a ball); (b) to make (a goal) in this way.
15. in nautical usage, to outdistance.
drop, *v.i.* 1. to fall in drops, as a liquid.
2. to let drops fall; to drip.
3. to fall; to descend suddenly or abruptly; to come down.
4. to sink to the ground exhausted, wounded, or dead.
5. to fall into a specified state; pass into a less active or less desirable condition; as, she *dropped* off to sleep.
6. to slump; become lower or less, as temperatures, prices, etc.
7. to move down with a current of water or air.
8. to be born: said of animals.
9. to come to an end; to cease; to be neglected and come to nothing; as, let the matter *drop*.
10. to fall short of a mark. [Rare.]
11. to be deep in extent, as a sail.
to drop behind; to be outdistanced; fall behind.
to drop down; in nautical usage, to sail, row, or move down a river or toward the sea.
to drop in; to pay a casual or unexpected visit.
to drop off; (a) to go away or out of sight; (b) to fall asleep. [Colloq.]
to drop out; to stop being a member or participant.
Syn.—distill, fall, decline, descend, faint, droop.
drop bär, in machinery, any bar having a regular descending motion.
drop bot′tŏm, a bottom in a freight car or wagon opening downward to unload earth, coal, etc.
drop çũr′tain (-tin), in theaters, a curtain that can be lowered and raised.

drop fiñ′gẽrș, rods which hold a sheet in place in a printing press.

drop fly, in angling, an artificial fly attached to the leader above another fly at the end.

drop′fọrġe′, *v.t.* to pound (heated metal) between dies with a drop hammer.

drop fọr′ġing, metal forged by a drop hammer.

drop glȧss, a dropper (sense 2).

drop ham′mẽr, 1. a machine for pounding metal into shape, with a heavy weight that is raised and then dropped on the metal.
2. this weight.

drop′-kick, *v.t.* and *v.i.* to give a drop kick to (a football).

drop kick, in football, a kick made by letting the ball drop from the hands and kicking it the instant it rebounds from the ground.

drop lēaf, a hinged board attached to the side of a table to increase its surface area: it hangs down when not in use.

drop′-lēaf, *a.* having a drop leaf.

drop′let, *n.* a little drop.

drop let′tẽr, a letter to be delivered by the office in which it is mailed.

drop′light (-līt), *n.* a light so suspended from a fixture that it can be raised or lowered as desired.

drop′mēal, **drop′mēle**, *adv.* [AS. *dropmælum*; *dropa*, drop, and *mæl*, portion.] by drops. [Obs.]

drop net, 1. a net hanging from a projecting arm to be dropped over a shoal of fish.
2. lace resembling a net.

drop′-off, *n.* 1. a very steep drop.
2. a decline or decrease, as in sales, prices, etc.

drop′-out, *n.* a student who withdraws from school, especially high school, before graduating.

drop′pẽr, *n.* 1. one who or that which drops.
2. a small glass tube with openings at both ends, one reduced, the other usually capped by a hollow rubber piece that is squeezed to draw liquid into the other end or to release it in drops.
3. a harvesting machine that drops the grain for binding.
4. a dog that drops to the ground when it sights game.

drop′ping, *n.* 1. the act of falling or letting fall in drops.
2. that which drops or falls in drops.
3. [*pl.*] dung; manure.

drop′ping bot′tle, a bottle designed to release its contents in drops.

drop′ping·ly, *adv.* in drops.

drop′ping tūbe, same as *dropper*, n. 2.

drop press, 1. a drop hammer.
2. a punch press.

drop shot, 1. shot made by letting molten metal fall in drops to solidify in a container of water below.
2. in tennis, a stroke by which the ball is made to drop just over the net and with very little bounce.

drop shut′tẽr, a camera shutter used for obtaining short exposures: originally, a slide which dropped in front of the lens.

drop′si·căl, *a.* 1. of the nature of dropsy.
2. diseased with or inclined to dropsy.

drop′si·căl·ness, *n.* dropsical condition.

drop′sied (-sid), *a.* affected with dropsy.

drop′stōne, *n.* a stalactite or stalagmite. [Obs.]

drop′sy, *n.* [ME. *dropsie*, *dropesie*; OFr. *idropisie*; L. *hydropisis*, from Gr. *hydrōps*, dropsy, from *hydōr*, water.]
1. edema.
2. a disease produced in some succulent plants by excess of water.

dropt, *v.* occasional past tense and past participle of *drop*.

drop tin, granulated tin formed by pouring molten tin into water.

drop′wīșe, *adv.* by drops.

drop′wõrm, *n.* the caterpillar of any geometrid; a measuring worm.

drop′wõrt, *n.* *Spiræa filipendula*, a tall European plant of the rose family, with fernlike leaves and white or reddish flowers: it resembles the meadowsweet.

Dros′e·rȧ, *n.* [Gr. *droseros*, dewy, from *drosos*, dew, juice.] a genus of the *Droseraceæ*, glandular hairs on the leaves of which secrete a viscid fluid resembling dew, whence the common name of *sundew*.

Dros·e·rā′cē·ae, *n.pl.* [Gr. *droseros*, dewy, from *drosos*, dew, water, juice, and *-aceæ*.] the sundew family, an order of insectivorous plants of which *Drosera* is the typical genus.

dros·e·rā′ceous, *a.* of or like the *Droseraceæ*.

drosh′ky, **dros′ky**, *n.*; *pl.* **drosh′kieș**, **dros′kieș**, [G. *droschke*; Russ. *drozhki*, dim. of *drogi*, a carriage.]

DROSHKY

1. originally, a low, open, four-wheeled vehicle used in Russia, in which the passengers sat astride a narrow bench which connected the front and rear axles.
2. now, any of various other carriages.

drō·som′e·tẽr, *n.* [Gr. *drosos*, dew, and *metron*, a measure.] an instrument for measuring the quantity of dew on a surface in the open air.

drō·soph′i·lȧ, *n.*; *pl.* **drō·soph′i·lae**, [Mod. L., from Gr. *drosos*, dew, liquid, and *philos*, loving]. a small fly used in laboratory experiments in heredity because of its short life cycle and great reproductivity: also called *fruit fly*.

dross, *n.* [ME. *drosse*; AS. *dros*, dregs, from *dreosan*, to fall.]
1. the scum or extraneous matter of metals, formed on the surface in the process of melting; slag; scoria.
2. rust; crust of metals. [Rare.]
3. waste matter; refuse; any worthless matter separated from the better part; impure matter.

dros′sel, *n.* a slut; a dirty wench. [Obs.]

dross′i·ness, *n.* the condition of being drossy.

dross′less, *a.* free from dross.

dross′y, *a.*; *comp.* drossier; *superl.* drossiest, like dross; pertaining to dross; full of dross; impure; worthless; as, *drossy* gold.

droud, *n.* a codfish. [Scot.]

drōugh (drō), *v.* obsolete past tense of *draw*.

drought (drout), *n.* [ME. *drought*, *drowght*, *drougth*, *drugthe*; AS. *drugath*, *drugoth*, dryness; from *dryge*, dry.]
1. dryness; lack of rain or of water.
2. prolonged dryness of the weather which affects the earth and prevents the growth of plants.
3. dryness of the throat and mouth; thirst. [Archaic.]
4. insufficiency; want of something necessary.

drought′i·ness, *n.* a state of drought.

drought′y, *a.* 1. dry; arid; wanting rain.
2. characterized by or suffering from drought.
3. thirsty; dry; wanting drink. [Archaic or Dial.]

drōuk, *v.t.* to drench or soak. [Scot. and Brit. Dial.]

drōu′my, *a.* troubled; muddy. [Obs.]

drouth, *n.* same as *drought*.

drouth′y, *a.* same as *droughty*.

drōve, *v.* past tense of *drive*.

drōve, *n.* [ME. *drove*, *drof*; AS. *draf*, a drove, from *drifan*, to drive.]
1. a number of animals, as oxen, sheep, or swine, driven as a group; flock; herd.
2. a crowd of people in motion.
Where *droves*, as at a city gate, may pass.
—Dryden.
3. a road for driving cattle. [Brit.]
4. a narrow irrigation canal. [Brit.]
5. a drove chisel.
6. the grooved surface made by a drove chisel.

drōve, *v.t.* and *v.i.*; droved, *pt.*, *pp.*; droving, *ppr.* to finish (stone) with a drove chisel.

drōve chiș′el, a broad-faced chisel for smoothing stone.

drō′ven, *v.* obsolete past participle of *drive*.

drō′vẽr, *n.* 1. one who drives cattle or sheep to market.
2. a cattle dealer.
3. a boat driven by the tide. [Obs.]

drōve wõrk, in stonecutting, the grooved surface of finished stone.

drō′vy, *a.* [ME. *drovy*, *drovi*; AS. *drofi*, *drof*, turpid, muddy.] roily; mixed with filthy dregs. [Obs.]

drōw, *v.* past tense of *draw*. [Obs.]

drow, *n.* [Scot.] a tiny elf of a race fabled to dwell in caves and to forge magic metalwork.

drown, *v.t.*; drowned, *pt.*, *pp.*; drowning, *ppr.* [ME. *drownen*, *druncnen*, to drown, sink; AS. *druncnian*, to become drunk, to drown, sink, from *druncen*, pp. of *drincan*, to drink.]
1. to extinguish life in by immersion in water or other liquid.
2. to overflow; to inundate; to flood; to soak; as, to *drown* land.
3. to immerse; to plunge and lose; to cause to disappear; to get rid of; as, to *drown* worries in drink; to *drown* oneself in sensual pleasure.
4. to overwhelm; to overpower; to deaden or muffle (sound, etc.).
My private voice is *drowned* amid the senate. —Addison.
Syn.—sink, immerse, swamp, overwhelm, engulf, deluge, inundate, submerge.

drown, *v.i.* to be suffocated in water or other liquid.

drown′ăġe, *n.* the act of drowning. [Rare.]

drown′ẽr, *n.* one who or that which drowns.

drowșe, *v.i.*; drowsed, *pt.*, *pp.*; drowsing, *ppr.* [AS. *drusan*, *drusian*, to sink, become slow or inactive; *dreosan*, to fall.]
1. to sleep imperfectly or unsoundly; to be sleepy or almost asleep; to doze.
2. to look heavy; to be heavy or dull.

drowșe, *v.t.* 1. to make heavy with sleep; to make dull or sluggish, as with sleep.
2. to spend (time) in drowsing.

drowșe, *n.* the quality or state of being sleepy or almost asleep; a doze.

drow′și·head (-hed), **drow′și·hed**, *n.* drowsiness. [Archaic.]

drow′și·hood, *n.* drowsiness. [Archaic.]

drow′și·ly, *adv.* in a drowsy manner.

drow′și·ness, *n.* the condition of being drowsy.

drow′șy, *a.*; *comp.* drowsier; *superl.* drowsiest,
1. inclined to sleep; being or making sleepy; heavy with sleepiness; lethargic; comatose; soporific.
2. brought on by sleepiness.
3. dull; sluggish; stupid.

drow′șy·head (-hed), *n.* sleepiness. [Archaic.]

drowth, *n.* drought. [Obs.]

drub, *v.t.*; drubbed, *pt.*, *pp.*; drubbing, *ppr.* [Ice. and Sw. *drabba*, to beat, hit; Dan. *dræbe*, to slay; AS. *drepan*, to beat.]
1. to beat with a stick; to thrash; to cudgel.
2. to defeat soundly in a fight, contest, etc.

drub, *v.i.* to strike lightly with the fingers; to thrum; to tap or stamp.

drub, *n.* a blow with a stick or cudgel; a thump; a knock.

drub′bẽr, *n.* one who drubs.

drub′bing, *n.* a sound beating, thrashing, or defeat.

drudġe (druj), *v.i.*; drudged, *pt.*, *pp.*; drudging, *ppr.* [ME. *druggen*, to work hard; Ir. *drugaire*, a slave; Scot. *drug*, a rough pull.] to work hard; to labor with toil and fatigue at tedious, unpleasant, or menial tasks.

drudġe, *v.t.* 1. to pass irksomely; as, he *drudged* away the time.
2. to subject to drudgery.

drudġe, *n.* one who labors at hard, menial, or unpleasant work.

drudġ′ẽr, *n.* a drudge.

drudġ′ẽr, *n.* a dredging box.

drudġ′ẽr·y, *n.* hard, menial, or unpleasant work.

drudġ′ing box, same as *dredging box*.

drudġ′ing·ly, *adv.* in a drudging manner.

drū′ẽr·y, *n.* same as *drury*.

drug, *n.* a drudge. [Obs.]

drug, *v.t.*; drugged, *pt.*, *pp.*; drugging, *ppr.*
1. to put a harmful drug in (a beverage, etc.); as, she *drugged* his food.
2. to give drugs to, especially narcotic drugs or drugs in too great a quantity; hence, to stupefy or poison with or as with a drug.
3. to administer something nauseating to.

drug, *v.i.* 1. to prescribe or administer drugs or medicines, particularly to an excessive degree.
2. to use drugs from habit. [Colloq.]

drug, *n.* [Fr. *drogue*, a drug, stuff; Sp., Port., and It. *droga*, from D. *droog*, dry, any dried substance, as herbs.]
1. any substance used as a medicine or in the preparation of medicines or chemical mixtures: some drugs are poisonous.
2. formerly, any substance used in dyeing.
3. a narcotic, especially one that is habit-forming.
drug on the market; a commodity for which there is little or no demand because the supply is so plentiful.

drug, *n.* same as *drag*, n. 15.

drug ad′dict, a habitual user of narcotics.

drug′gẽr, *n.* a druggist. [Obs.]

drug′get, *n.* [Fr. *droguet*, dim. of *drogue*, stuff, trash.]
1. formerly, a woolen or part-woolen material used for clothing.
2. a coarse fabric used as a floor covering, carpet, lining, etc.
3. a coarse rug from India made of jute or cotton and hair: also *India drugget*.

drug′gist, *n.* [Fr. *droguiste*, from *drogue*, a drug.]

1. a pharmacist; one authorized to fill medical prescriptions.
2. one whose business it is to buy and sell drugs, medical equipment, etc.

drug'less, *a.* without the use of drugs or medicines.

drug'stẽr, *n.* a druggist. [Obs.]

drug'stōre, *n.* a store where medical prescriptions are filled and drugs and medical supplies are sold: most drugstores now also sell cosmetics, tobacco, ice cream, books, etc.

drụ'id, *n.* [Fr. *druide,* from L. *druida,* a druid; Ir. *draoi, druidh,* a magician, sorcerer.]
1. [*often* D–] a priest or soothsayer of a Celtic religious order in ancient Gaul, Britain, and Ireland. The druids possessed some knowledge of geometry, natural philosophy, etc., superintended the affairs of religion and morality, and performed the office of judges: they were influential especially before the Celts were Christianized.
2. [D–] a member of an order known as the United Ancient Order of Druids, founded 1781, in London.

drụ'id·ess, *n.* a woman druid.

drụ·id'iç, drụ·id'iç·ăl, *a.* pertaining to the druids or druidism.

drụ'id·ish, *a.* pertaining to or like druids.

drụ'id·iṣm, *n.* the system of religion, philosophy, and instruction taught by the druids, or their doctrines, rites, and ceremonies.

drum, *n.* [Ir. *druim,* a ridge, a hill.] a long, narrow hill; a ridge; a drumlin.

drum, *n.* [D. *trom;* L.G. *trumme;* D. *trommel, drummel,* a drum; M.H.G. *trumme, trumbe;* O.H.G. *trumba, trumpa,* a trump, trumpet; Dan. *drum,* a boom, a noise. The word is probably of imitative origin.]
1. a percussion instrument in the form of a hollow cylinder or hemisphere covered at the end or ends with a membrane, played by striking with the hands, sticks, etc.
2. the sound produced by beating a drum, or any sound like this.
3. any of various drumlike cylindrical objects.
4. a metal spool or cylinder around which cable, etc. is wound in a machine.
5. a barrellike metal container for oil, etc.
6. in anatomy, (a) the middle ear; (b) the eardrum.
7. in machinery, a cylinder revolving on an axis, for the purpose of turning several small wheels by means of straps passing round its periphery.
8. a quantity packed in the form of a drum; as, a *drum* of figs.
9. sheet iron in the shape of a drum, to receive heat from a stovepipe.
10. in architecture, (a) one of the blocks of which the shaft of a stone column is composed; (b) an upright wall, either circular or polygonal in construction, supporting a dome or cupola.
11. formerly, a noisy, crowded, fashionable, social gathering, as for playing cards; a rout; hence, a tea party.
12. one of several fishes of the family *Sciænidæ* that make a drumming sound, probably by the use of the bones of the pharynx and the resonance of the air bladder.
13. in zoology, (a) the drumlike apparatus of a cicada, by which it produces its song; (b) the resonant hyoid of the howling monkey.

drum, *v.i.;* drummed, *pt., pp.;* drumming, *ppr.*
1. to beat a drum.
2. to beat or tap continually or rhythmically, as with the fingers; as, to *drum* on the table.
3. to beat, as the heart.
4. to make a loud, reverberating sound by quivering the wings: said of the ruffed grouse, etc.

drum, *v.t.* 1. to expel from the army to the accompaniment of the beat of a drum (with *out*); as, *drummed out* of the regiment.
2. to perform on a drum; as, to *drum* the rogue's march.
3. to assemble by beating a drum.
to drum into; to make known to by continued repetition.
to drum up; (a) to summon by or as by beating a drum; (b) to get (business, etc.) by canvassing or soliciting.

drum'bēat, *n.* the sound made by beating a drum.

drum'ble (*or* drum'l), *v.i.* 1. to be slow and inactive; to be sluggish. [Obs.]
2. to speak in a mumbling manner. [Obs.]

drum'fīre, *n.* heavy and continuous gunfire, thought of as resembling drumbeats.

drum'fish, *n.* any of various salt-water and fresh-water fishes that make a drumming noise.

drum'head (-hed), *n.* 1. the membrane stretched over the open end or ends of a drum.
2. the eardrum.
3. the top of a capstan, into which bars are inserted for leverage in turning it.

drum'head cōurt-mär'tiăl (-shăl), a court-martial held in the field for trial of offenses committed during military operations or troop movements: so called because the head of a drum was formerly used as the judges' table.

drum'lin, *n.* [from Ir. *druim,* narrow ridge; and *-lin,* dim. suffix from *-ling.*] a long ridge or oval-shaped hill formed by glacial drift.

drum'loid, *n.* an irregular drumlin.

drum'ly, *a.* turbid; hence, gloomy. [Scot.]

drum mā'jŏr, 1. the chief or first drummer of a regiment; a teacher of drummers. [Obs.]
2. the leader of a drum corps or marching band, or one who precedes it, often whirling a baton into the air and prancing.
3. a noisy social company. [Obs.]

drum'mẽr, *n.* 1. a drum player.
2. a travelling salesman. [Colloq.]
3. one of a certain kind of fish, so called from the noise they make; as, (a) the weakfish; (b) a sculpin of California.
4. *Blatta gigantea,* a large cockroach of tropical America, which drums on wood with its head as a mating call.

Drum'mŏnd līght, [after Thomas *Drummond* (1797–1840), Scot. inventor.] limelight (calcium light).

drum'stick, *n.* 1. the stick with which a drum is beaten.
2. anything in the form of a drumstick; as, the lower joint of a cooked fowl's leg.

drum'stick tree, a tropical tree, *Cassia fistula,* having legumes resembling drumsticks.

drum'wood, *n.* a small tree of the West Indies (*Turpinia occidentalis*).

druñk, *a.* [pp. and archaic pt. of *drink.*]
1. intoxicated; inebriated; overwhelmed or overpowered by alcoholic liquor to the point of losing control over one's faculties.
2. overcome by any powerful emotion; as, *drunk* with joy, happiness, etc.
3. drenched or saturated with moisture or liquid. [Obs.]

druñk, *n.* one who is drunk; also, a drinking spree; as, the officer arrested four *drunks* on a *drunk.* [Slang.]

druñk'ărd, *n.* one given to an excessive use of alcoholic liquor; a person who is often drunk.

druñk'en, *a.* 1. intoxicated; inebriated; habitually drunk.
2. proceeding from intoxication; done in a state of drunkenness; as, a *drunken* quarrel.
3. saturated with liquid or moisture; drenched.

druñk'en·ly, *adv.* in a drunken manner.

druñk'en·ness, *n.* intoxication; inebriation; the quality, habit, or condition of being drunk.

druñk'en·ship, *n.* intoxication. [Obs.]

druñk'ŏ·mē·tẽr, *n.* [*drunk,* and *-o-,* and *-meter.*] a device for testing a sample of exhaled breath to measure the amount of alcohol in the blood.

Drụ·pā'cē·ae, *n.pl.* [L. *drupa;* Gr. *dryppa,* an overripe, wrinkled olive.] a family of *Rosaceæ,* including the plum, cherry, peach, and other similar drupaceous trees.

drụ·pā'ceous, *a.* of, producing, consisting of, or resembling drupes; as, *drupaceous* trees; *drupaceous* fruit.

drụp'ăl, *a.* drupaceous. [Obs.]

drụpe, *n.* [L. *drupa,* Gr. *dryppa,* an overripe olive, from *drypepēs,* ripened on the tree, *drys,* a tree, and *peptein,* to ripen.] a fruit having a fleshy, coriaceous, or fibrous epicarp, without valves, enclosing a nut or stone which contains the kernel or seed proper, as the plum, cherry, apricot, peach, almond, etc.

drụp'el, *n.* a druplet.

drụpe'let, *n.* a small drupe: a loganberry or blackberry consists of many drupelets.

Drụ'ry Lāne, a street in London, famous in the 17th and 18th centuries for its theaters.

drụṣe, *n.* [G.] a geode.

Drụṣe, *n.* [Turk.] a member of a religious sect in Syria, whose creed derived from Moslem, Christian, and Persian sources.

Drụ'ṣi·ăn, Drụ'ṣe·ăn, *a.* of the Druses or their religion.

drụ'ṣy, drụṣed, *a.* studded with small crystals.

drux'y, drux'ey, *a.* spotted with decay; having whitish streaks or spots, as trees.

drȳ, *a.; comp.* drier; *superl.* driest, [ME. *drye, dryge, drige;* AS. *dryge, drige.*]
1. lacking moisture; arid; not moist or damp; lacking the ordinary or average amount of moisture or liquid; specifically, (a) free from juice, sap, or water; not green; as, *dry* wood; *dry* leaves; (b) without tears; as, *dry* eyes; (c) not giving milk or other liquid; as, the cow is *dry;* (d) thirsty; craving drink; as, salt makes me *dry;* (e) not rainy; free from rain or mist; as, *dry* weather; (f) in medicine, characterized by absence of mucous or watery discharge, or of blood; as, *dry* pleurisy; a *dry* cough; (g) in mining, not having or not using water; as, *dry* separation.
2. without butter, jam, etc. on it; as, *dry* toast.
3. solid: opposed to *liquid.*
4. unemotional; plain; matter-of-fact; as, *dry* facts.
5. unfruitful; as, a *dry* interview.
6. devoid of interest; barren; jejune; boring; dull; as, a *dry* lecture; a *dry* subject.
7. devoid of sympathy or cordiality; formal; cold; as, a *dry* reception; a *dry* manner.
8. severe; sarcastic; cynical; sneering; as, a *dry* retort.
9. in art, having a sharp, inflexible preciseness of execution; lacking delicacy or softness of contour or coloring; stiff; formal; hard.
10. having little sugar or sweetness; as, a *dry* wine.
11. in metallurgy, having more oxygen than is desired: said of copper when not thoroughly refined.
12. controlled by or favoring laws prohibiting the sale or use of alcoholic liquors; as, a *dry* district.
not dry behind the ears; immature; inexperienced; naive. [Colloq.]

Syn.—arid, parched, moistureless, dull, tedious, uninteresting.

drȳ, *v.t.* and *v.i.;* dried, *pt., pp.;* drying, *ppr.* [ME. *dryen, drygen;* AS. *drygan, drigan,* to dry; from *dryge, drige,* dry.] to make or become dry.
to dry up; (a) to make or become thoroughly dry; to parch; to wither; (b) [Slang.] to stop talking.

drȳ, *n.; pl.* **drȳṣ,** a person opposed to the use or sale of alcoholic liquors; prohibitionist. [Colloq.]

drȳ'ad, Drȳ'ad, *n.* [L. *dryas* (*-adis*); Gr. *dryas* (*-ados*), a wood nymph, from *drys,* a tree.] in Greek mythology, a nymph living in a tree; a wood nymph.

drȳ·ad'iç, *a.* of or like a dryad.

drȳ āir, air that contains little or no water vapor.

drȳ ā'rē·ȧ, an outside sunken space protecting the foundation of a building from dampness.

drȳ'as, *n.; pl.* **drȳ'ȧ·dēṣ,** a dryad.

drȳ'aṣ·dust, *n.* a very prosaic or dull person.

drȳ'-aṣ-dust, *a.* dull and unimaginative.

drȳ bat'tẽr·y, 1. an electric battery made up of several connected dry cells.
2. a dry cell.

drȳ'-bēat″, *v.t.* to beat until dry; hence, to beat severely. [Obs.]

drȳ bōne, smithsonite, or carbonate of zinc.

drȳ'-bōned″, *a.* having dry, or fleshless, bones; very thin or withered.

drȳ'-brush″, *a.* designating a technique in painting with ink or water color in which as little water as possible is used to transfer the color or ink to the paper.

drȳ cap'i·tăl, in finance, the capital of a corporation whose actual value equals its stated value and is not watered. [Colloq.]

drȳ cas'tŏr, a fat-free beaver skin.

drȳ cell, a voltaic cell either sealed or treated with an absorbent substance so that the contents of the cell cannot be spilled.

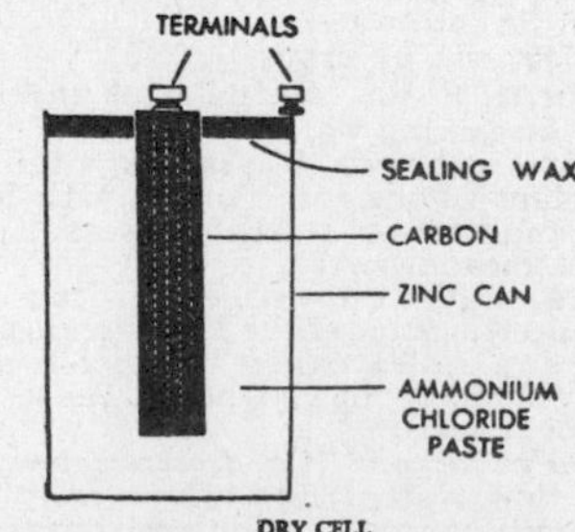

DRY CELL

drȳ'-çlēan', *v.t.* and *v.i.;* dry-cleaned, *pt., pp.;*

dry-cleaning, *ppr.* to clean (garments, etc.) with chemical solvents, such as naphtha or gasoline, instead of water.

drȳ çlēan′ẽr, 1. a solvent such as naphtha, benzine, gasoline, carbon tetrachloride, etc., used in dry cleaning.

2. a person whose business or work is dry cleaning.

drȳ çlēan′ing, a process of cleaning garments and textiles by use of a chemical solvent instead of water.

drȳ′-çleanṣe′ (-klenz′), *v.t.*; dry-cleansed, *pt., pp.*; dry-cleansing, *ppr.* to dry-clean.

drȳ dock, a dock from which the water may be shut or pumped out, used for building and repairing ships.

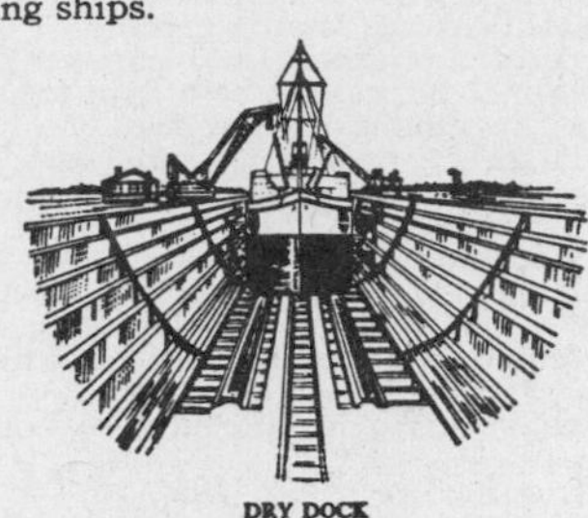

DRY DOCK

drȳ′-dock, *v.t.* and *v.i.* to place in or go into a dry dock.

drȳ′ẽr, *n.* same as *drier.*

drȳ′-eyed (-īd), *a.* not having a tear in the eyes; not weeping.

drȳ′-färm″, *v.i.* and *v.t.* to produce crops on (land) by dry farming.

drȳ färm′ẽr, a farmer who does dry farming.

drȳ färm′ing, farm production where rainfall is scant, without the help of irrigation: it is done by tilling the soil so as to conserve its moisture, and by using crops that are drought-resisting.

drȳ goodṣ, textile fabrics, thread, and similar wares, as distinct from hardware, groceries, etc.

drȳ īce, solid carbon dioxide (CO_2) produced by liquefying carbon dioxide gas by use of high pressure and then suddenly releasing this pressure. It evaporates slowly without becoming a liquid and is used as a refrigerant.

drȳ′ing, *a.* 1. that serves to dry; as, a *drying* wind.

2. quickly becoming dry.

drying oil; oil which has the property of drying rapidly when exposed to the atmosphere: used in preparing paints and varnishes.

drȳ kiln, an enclosed place in which lumber is dried and seasoned by artificial heat.

drȳ ląw, a law prohibiting the manufacture and sale of alcoholic liquors.

drȳ′ly, *adv.* in a dry manner; without emotion; matter-of-factly: also written *drily.*

drȳ meaṣ′ūre (mezh′), a system of measuring the volume of dry things, such as grain, vegetables, etc.; especially, the system in which 2 pints=1 quart, 8 quarts=1 peck, and 4 pecks=1 bushel.

drȳ mul′tūre, in Scots law, a yearly tax levied upon lands to support a mill.

drȳ′ness, *n.* the state or quality of being dry.

drȳ nũrse, a nurse who attends and feeds a child without suckling it: opposed to *wet nurse.*

drȳ′-nũrse″, *v.t.* to be a dry nurse to.

Drȳ·ō·bal′ȧ·nops, *n.* [Gr. *drys,* an oak, *balanos,* an acorn, and *opsis,* appearance.] a genus of resinous evergreen trees which yield camphor oil and Borneo camphor.

drȳ′-pick″, *v.t.* to pluck (poultry) without first loosening the feathers by scalding.

drȳ pīle, a type of voltaic pile made up of several pieces of paper which have been coated with tin or silver on one side and manganese dioxide on the other.

drȳ pīpe, in a boiler, a pipe to keep the water from boiling up into the steam pipe.

drȳ′-plāte′, *a.* denoting the process of photography in which dry plates are used.

drȳ plāte, a photographic plate sensitized to light with a coating that is dried before use.

drȳ point, 1. a needle used by etchers to incise fine lines on a copper plate without employing acid.

2. an engraving made with such a needle, or a print from an engraving so made.

3. the process of making such engravings.

drȳ′-point, *a.* made by means of a dry point.

drȳ rent, in law, a rent reserved without clause of distress. [Obs.]

drȳ rot, 1. a rapid decay of seasoned timber, due to fungi, by which its substance is converted into a dry powder, which issues from minute tubular cavities.

2. a similar fungous disease of plants, fruits, and vegetables.

3. any of various fungi causing such decay.

4. any internal moral or social decay, generally resulting from lack of new or progressive influences.

drȳ′-rot, *v.t.* and *v.i.* to affect with dry rot, or to be affected by it.

drȳ′-rub, *v.t.*; dry-rubbed, *pt., pp.*; dry-rubbing, *ppr.* to rub and cleanse without wetting.

drȳ run, (a) practice in firing small arms or guns without using live ammunition; (b) a rehearsal for any event. [Military Slang.]

drȳ′-sạlt, *v.t.* to salt and dry (meat, etc.) in order to preserve it.

drȳ′sạlt·ẽr, *n.* a dealer in salted or dry meats, pickles, sauces, etc., or in dry goods, paints, drugs, etc. [Brit.]

drȳ′sạlt·ẽr·y, *n.*; *pl.* **drȳ′sạlt·ẽr·ieṣ,** the articles kept by a drysalter, or his warehouse or trade. [Brit.]

drȳ′-shod, *a.* without wetting the feet; with dry feet.

drȳ′-stōne, *a.* built of stone without cement or mortar.

drȳ stōr′āġe, cold storage in which refrigeration is effected by a stream of cold air.

drȳ stōve, a hothouse.

drȳth, *n.* drought. [Obs.]

drȳ vat, a receptacle for dry articles. [Obs.]

drȳ wạll, 1. a wall of rocks or stones with no mortar or cement.

2. a wall constructed of wallboard, plasterboard, etc. without using wet plaster.

drȳ wäsh, laundry washed and dried but not ironed.

D. T.'s (dē′tēz′), delirium tremens. [Slang.]

dū′ad, *n.* [L. *duo,* two.] a group of two; pair; couple.

dū′ăl, *a.* [L. *dualis,* from *duo,* two.]

1. expressing the number two.

2. double; having or consisting of two; twofold; as, the *dual* set of controls in training automobiles.

dū′ăl, *n.* in linguistics, (a) dual number; (b) a word having dual number.

Dual Alliance; the secret alliance between Germany and Austria-Hungary entered into in 1879.

dū′ȧ·lin, *n.* a form of dynamite containing saltpeter, sawdust, and nitroglycerin.

dū′ăl·iṣm, *n.* [L. *dualis,* of two, from *duo,* two.]

1. the state of being divided into or made up of two distinct but related parts; duality.

2. in philosophy, the doctrine that recognizes two radically independent elements, as mind and matter, underlying all known phenomena: opposed to *monism.*

3. in theology, (a) the recognition of two radically different principles in operation, one good, the other bad; (b) the doctrine that man has two natures, physical and spiritual.

4. in chemistry, the theory of Lavoisier that every definite compound consists of two parts having opposite electrical activity.

dū′ăl·ist, *n.* 1. one who upholds dualism.

2. an incumbent of two offices at once. [Rare.]

dū·ăl·is′tiç, *a.* 1. consisting of two; dual.

2. based on or belonging to dualism.

dualistic theory or *system*; same as *dualism,* sense 4.

dū·ăl·is′tiç·ăl·ly, *adv.* 1. in a dualistic manner.

2. from the viewpoint of dualism.

dū·al′i·ty, *n.* [LL. *dualitas,* from *dualis,* of two; *duo,* two.] the state or quality of being dual.

dū′ăl num′bẽr, in some languages, a grammatical number indicating *two, a pair*: distinguished by inflection from *singular* (indicating *one*) and *plural* (indicating *more than two*); the dual occurs regularly in Sanskrit, Old Iranian, Old Irish, etc., with traces in Greek, Gothic, and Anglo-Saxon.

dū′ăl pẽr·sŏn·al′i·ty, in psychology, the abnormal condition of having two different personalities, shown alternately or simultaneously.

dū′ăl-pũr′pŏse, *a.* having, or meant to have, two uses.

dū′ăn, *n.* [Gael.] one of the divisions of a Gaelic poem; also, a poem.

dū′ăr·çhy, *n.* [Gr. *duo,* two, and *archē,* rule.] government by two persons.

dub, *v.t.*; dubbed, *pt., pp.*; dubbing, *ppr.* [ME. *dubben*; AS. *dubban,* to strike, beat; OFr. *duber, aduber,* to equip with arms, prepare.]

1. to hit; strike; thrust; poke.

2. to beat (a drum).

3. to tap (a man) on the shoulder with a sword in conferring knighthood; hence, to invest with the rank of knight.

4. to confer any dignity, title, rank, or appellation upon; to call; to name; to designate.

5. to dress or make smooth; (a) to make (wood, etc.) smooth as by hammering or scraping; (b) to strike with teasels in dressing cloth; (c) to rub a dressing into; as, to *dub* leather; (d) to dress with feathers, etc.; as, to *dub* a fishing fly; (e) to cut or trim the comb and wattles of; as, to *dub* a gamecock for a fight.

6. to be obliged to repeat (a stroke, etc.); bungle (a golf stroke, etc.). [Slang.]

to dub out; to make (an uneven surface) level and ready for plastering by filling in the depressions.

dub, *v.i.* to make a quick noise like a drumbeat.

dub, *n.* 1. a blow. [Rare.]

2. a drumbeat.

3. a clumsy, unskillful player. [Slang.]

4. any clumsy, unskillful person. [Slang.]

dub, *v.t.* [from *double.*] to make a new recording of (a piece of music) by playing the old record: distinguished from *re-press.*

to dub in; in motion pictures, (a) to insert (dialogue, music, etc.) in the sound track; (b) to insert (synchronized dialogue in another language) in place of the original dialogue.

dub, *n.* dialogue, music, etc. inserted in the sound track of a motion picture.

dub, *n.* [Ir. *dob,* mire.] a puddle; a pool. [Scot. and Brit. Dial.]

dụ·bäsh′, *n.* in India, a native interpreter.

dubb, *n.* *Ursus syriacus,* the Syrian bear.

dub′bẽr, *n.* one who or that which dubs.

dub′bẽr, *n.* [E. Ind.] a leather vessel or bottle used in India to hold ghee, oil, etc.

dub′bin, *n.* [from *dubbing.*] a greasy preparation for softening and waterproofing leather: also called *dubbing.*

dub′bing, *n.* 1. the act of conferring knighthood; hence, the giving of any appellation.

2. the act of dressing or making smooth.

3. the material used (a) to dub leather; dubbin; (b) to dress an artificial fly; (c) to dub out a wall for plastering.

dū·bī′e·ty, *n.*; *pl.* **dū·bī′e·tieṣ,** [L. *dubietas,* from *dubius,* doubtful.]

1. the quality of being dubious; doubtfulness.

2. a doubtful thing.

dū·bi·os′i·ty, *n.*; *pl.* **dū·bi·os′i·tieṣ,** same as *dubiety.*

dū′bi·ous, *a.* [L. *dubius,* doubting, uncertain, from *duo,* two.]

1. feeling doubt; hesitating; skeptical.

2. ambiguous; vague; causing doubt; not clear; as, a *dubious* signal.

3. with the outcome undecided or hanging in the balance; as, *dubious* battle.

4. of doubtful propriety; questionable; causing suspicion; as, *dubious* methods.

dū′bi·ous·ly, *adv.* in a dubious manner.

dū′bi·ous·ness, *n.* dubious quality or state.

dū′bi·tȧ·ble, *a.* [L. *dubitabilis,* from *dubitare,* to doubt.] susceptible to doubt; doubtful; uncertain.

dū′bi·tȧ·bly, *adv.* in a dubitable manner; doubtfully.

dū′bi·tăn·cy, *n.* doubt; uncertainty. [Obs.]

dū′bi·tāte, *v.i.* [L. *dubitatus,* pp. of *dubitare,* to doubt.] to doubt. [Rare.]

dū·bi·tā′tion, *n.* [L. *dubitatio,* from *dubitare,* to doubt.] the act of doubting; doubt; hesitation. [Rare.]

dū′bi·tā·tive, *a.* tending to doubt; also, expressing doubt.

dū′bi·tā·tive·ly, *adv.* with doubt.

Dū·boi′si·ȧ, *n.* [named after F. N. A. *Dubois* (1752–1824), French botanist.]

1. in botany, a genus of the *Solanaceæ,* native to Australia.

2. [d–] duboisine.

dū·boi′sine, dū·boi′sin, *n.* in medicine, an alkaloid derived from *Duboisia,* having qualities similar to those of atropine.

dụ·bŏn·nẹt′ (-bŏ-nā′), *n.* [name of Fr. manufacturer.]

1. a kind of fortified French red wine, often served as an apéritif: a trade-mark (*Dubonnet*).

2. a light maroon color, as of this wine.

dụ·bŏn·nẹt′, *a.* of the color of dubonnet.

dū′ca̤l, *a.* [LL. *ducalis*, from L. *dux, ducis*, leader.] pertaining to a duke, or to the estate of a duke; as, a *ducal* coronet.

dū′ca̤l·ly, *adv.* in the manner of a duke.

duç′ăt, *n.* [Fr. *ducat*; LL. *ducatus*, a ducat, duchy, from L. *dux, ducis*, a leader.]
1. any of various coins of silver or gold formerly current in Europe: their values varied from about $.83 to about $2.32.
2. a ticket, especially an admission ticket. [Slang.]

duç·ȧ·tọọn′, *n.* [Fr. *ducaton*; It. *ducatone*, from *ducato*, a ducat.] formerly, a silver coin of Venice.

dù′cẹ (dọọ′chā), *n.* [It.] leader; chief: see *Il Duce*.

duch′ess, *n.* [Fr. *duchesse*, from *duc*, a duke.] the wife or widow of a duke; also, a woman who has the sovereignty of a duchy in her own right.

duch′y, *n.*; *pl.* **duch′ieṣ,** [ME. *duchie, duchee*; OFr. *duchee, duchet*; LL. *ducatus*, the territory of a duke, from L. *dux, ducis*, a leader.] the territory or dominion of a duke or duchess; a dukedom.

duck, *n.* [D. *doek*, linen cloth, light canvas; Ice. *dukr*, cloth.]
1. a cotton or linen cloth lighter than canvas, used for small sails, ticking of beds, etc.
2. [*pl.*] light trousers or other clothing of such cloth. [Colloq.]

duck, *n.*; *pl.* **ducks** or **duck,** 1. any of several swimming birds with a flat bill, short neck and legs, and webbed feet.
2. the female of this bird: distinguished from *drake*.
3. the flesh of a duck as food.
4. a darling; dear. [Colloq.]
5. a person; as, he's a queer *duck*. [Slang.]
6. an amphibious motor vehicle. [Military Slang.]
to make or *play ducks and drakes*; to skip a stone or other flat object along the surface of the water; hence, to risk or squander one's fortune.

duck, *v.t.* and *v.i.*; ducked (dukt), *pt., pp.*; ducking, *ppr.* [ME. *duken, douken*; D. *duiken*; M.H.G. *tuchen*, to duck, dive, stoop.]
1. to dip or plunge into or under water for a moment.
2. to lower, turn, or bend (the head, body, etc.) suddenly, as in avoiding a blow or hiding.
3. to avoid (a task, person, etc.). [Colloq.]
4. to move (*in* or *out*) quickly.

duck, *n.* a ducking.

duck ȧnt, a white Jamaican ant which makes nests in trees.

duck′bill, *n.* an oviparous, burrowing, aquatic mammal, with webbed feet and a bill like that of a duck; the *Ornithorhynchus anatinus*: also called *platypus*.

DUCKBILL (1 1/2 ft. long)

duck′-billed, *a.* having a bill resembling that of a duck.

duck′bōard, *n.* a board or boards forming a slightly raised surface or flooring on a muddy road, wet place, etc.

duck′ẽr, *n.* 1. one who ducks.
2. a diving bird; a dabchick or little grebe.

duck′ẽr, *n.* 1. a person who raises ducks.
2. a duck hunter.

duck′ẽr·y, *n.*; *pl.* **duck′ẽr·ieṣ,** a place for raising ducks.

duck′-foot·ed, *a.* having the hind toe pointing forward, as on a duck's foot: said of fowls.

duck hạwk, 1. the North American peregrine falcon.
2. in England, the marsh harrier, a kind of buzzard.

duck′ing, *n.* the act of plunging, or the state of being plunged, under water; as, to get a *ducking*.

duck′ing, *n.* the sport of hunting ducks as game.

duck′ing stọọl, a stool or chair in which culprits were tied and plunged into water: a form of punishment formerly used in New England for quarrelsome women.

DUCKING STOOL

duck′-leg·ged, *a.* having short legs.

duck′ling, *n.* a young duck.

duck′mēat, *n.* a plant of the genus *Lemna*: also called *duck's meat, duckweed*.

duck mōle, same as *duckbill*.

duck′pinṣ, *n.pl.* [so named when a spectator at the first game said that the pins, on being struck, "flew like ducks."]
1. [*construed as sing.*] a game like bowling or tenpins, played with smaller pins and balls.
2. the pins used in this game.

duck's′ foot, the May apple.

duck snīpe, the willet.

duck′weed, *n.* any of a family of very small flowering plants which float on fresh water like a green scum: so called because eaten by ducks.

duck′y, *a.*; *comp.* duckier; *superl.* duckiest, [early 19th-c. term of endearment; from *duck*, and *-y*.] excellent; delightful, etc. [Slang.]

duçt, *n.* [L. *ductus*, a leading, a conducting, from *ducere*, to lead.]
1. a tube or canal by which a gas, liquid, etc. is conducted or conveyed; specifically, (a) in anatomy, a tubular passage which conveys a fluid, as the blood, lymph, chyle, etc., especially the secretion of a gland; (b) in botany, a large tubular canal or cell; (c) a pipe or conduit with wires or cables running through it.
2. guidance; leading. [Obs.]

duç′ti·ble, *a.* ductile. [Rare.]

duç′tile, *a.* [L. *ductilis*, from *ducere*, to lead.]
1. that can be stretched, drawn, or hammered thin without breaking; not brittle: said of metals.
2. easily molded; plastic; pliant.
3. easily influenced or led; complying; as, the *ductile* minds of youth.

duç′tile·ly, *adv.* in a ductile manner.

duç′tile·ness, *n.* the quality of being ductile.

duç·til′i·ty, *n.* [L. *ductilis*, from *ducere*, to lead.] the quality or condition of being ductile.

duçt′less, *a.* without a duct.

duçt′less gland, any of certain glands, as the thyroid and pituitary, which have no excretory ducts and send their secretions directly into the lymph or blood stream.

duç′tŏr, *n.* [L., from *ducere*, to lead.] in a printing press, a roller which conveys ink from a fountain to another roller.

duç′tūre, *n.* guidance. [Obs.]

dud, *n.* [ult. from D. *dood*, dead.]
1. a shell or bomb that fails to explode when it strikes. [Slang.]
2. an incompetent individual; a person without initiative or energy. [Slang.]

dud′dẽr, *v.t.* to confuse or stun with noise. [Scot. and Brit. Dial.]

dud′dẽr, *v.i.* to tremble; to quake. [Obs.]

dud′dẽr·y, *n.*; *pl.* **dud′dẽr·ieṣ,** a place for the manufacture and sale of woolen cloth. [Dial.]

dud′dy, dud′die, *a.* [from dial. *dud*, coarse cloak, and *-y*.] ragged; tattered. [Scot.]

dūde, *n.* 1. a man too much concerned with his manners and appearance; a fop; a dandy.
2. a city fellow or tourist, especially an Easterner. [Western Slang.]
3. any man or boy. [Slang.]

dū-deen′, *n.* [Ir.] a tobacco pipe of clay having a short, straight stem: written also *dudheen*.

dūde ranch, a ranch or farm operated as a resort for tourists, with horseback riding and similar sports.

dudġ′eŏn, *n.* [W. *dygen*, anger, grudge.] anger; resentment; ill will; discord.

dudġ′eŏn, *n.* [D. *duig*, a stave.]
1. formerly, a wood, perhaps boxwood, used for dagger handles.
2. the handle of a dagger; also, the dagger itself. [Obs.]

dūd′ish, *a.* resembling or having the character of a dude.

dudṣ, *n.pl.* [ME. *dudde*, cloth, cloak.]
1. clothes; clothing. [Slang.]
2. trappings; belongings. [Slang.]

dù′ẹ, *a.* [It.] in music, two.
due corde; two strings: a direction to play the same note on two strings simultaneously, as on the violin.

dūe (dū), *a.* [ME. *due*; OFr. *deu*; Fr. *dû*, pp. of *devoir*, to owe; L. *debere*, to owe.]
1. owed; owed and already matured; as, the note is *due*.
2. proper; fit; suitable; becoming; as, the event was celebrated with *due* solemnities.
3. as much as is required; enough; adequate; as, he will come in *due* time.
4. owing; attributable: followed by *to*; as, his death was *due to* an accident.
5. required or expected to arrive or to have arrived or to be present, before the time specified; as, two mails are now *due*.

dūe, *adv.* directly; exactly, as *due* east.

dūe, *n.* 1. that which is due.
2. just title; right. [Obs.]

dūe, *v.t.* to endue. [Obs.]

dūe bill, a statement in writing given by a debtor to a creditor acknowledging certain indebtedness, but neither payable to his order nor transferable by endorsement.

dūe dāte, the date on which a note, bond, etc. is due.

dūe′fu̇l, *a.* fit; becoming. [Obs.]

dū′el, *n.* [Fr. *duel*; It. *duello*, from L. *duellum*, old form of *bellum*, war, from *duo*, two.]
1. a formal fight between two persons armed with deadly weapons: it is prearranged and witnessed by two others, called *seconds*, one for each combatant.
2. any contest or encounter suggesting such a fight, usually between two persons; as, a verbal *duel*.

dū′el, *v.i.* and *v.t.*; dueled *or* duelled, *pt., pp.*; dueling *or* duelling, *ppr.* to fight a duel with (a person or persons).

dū′el·ẽr, dū′el·lẽr, *n.* a duelist. [Obs.]

dū′el·ing, dū′el·ling, *n.* the act or practice of fighting a duel.

dū′el·ist, dū′el·list, *n.* one who fights, or is an expert at fighting, duels.

dū·el′lō, *n.*; *pl.* **dū·el′lōṣ,** [It.] 1. a duel. [Obs.]
2. the practice or rules of dueling.

duen′de (dwen′de), *n.* [Sp., lit., goblin, spirit.] a special quality or charm that makes one irresistibly attractive.

dū·en′nȧ, *n.* [Sp. *dueña*, from L. *domina*, a mistress, lady.]
1. an elderly woman who has charge of the young unmarried women in a Spanish or Portuguese family.
2. a chaperon or governess.

dūe proc′ess, the course of legal proceedings established by the legal system of a nation or state to protect individual rights and liberties: also called *due process of law*.

dūeṣ, *n.pl.* 1. a fee or tax.
2. the sum of money paid, or to be paid, by a member to an organization, usually for the rights of membership.
to pay one's dues; to earn certain rights, privileges, etc. as by having suffered in struggle. [Slang.]

dū·et′, *n.* [It. *duetto*, from L. *duo*, two.]
1. a piece of music composed for two performers, whether vocal or instrumental.
2. the performers of such a composition.

dụ·et·tī′nō, *n.* [It., dim. of *duetto*, a duet.] a short duet of simple arrangement.

dụ·et′tō, *n.* [It.] a duet.

duff, *v.t.* in Australia, to acquire (stock) by stealing and altering the brands. [Slang.]

duff, *n.* [another form of *dough*, with *gh* sounded as *f*.]
1. a paste or dough made of flour. [Brit. Dial.].
2. a pudding made by boiling flour in a bag.
3. the decaying vegetable matter on the ground in a forest, as leaves, twigs, etc.
4. coal dust or slack.

duf·fȧ·där′, *n.* [E. Ind.] formerly, a noncommissioned officer of the army or police of India.

duf′fel, *n.* [D., from *Duffel*, a town near Antwerp.]
1. a coarse woolen cloth with a thick nap.
2. essential clothing and equipment carried by a woodsman, hunter, or yachtsman.
3. a camper's kit or equipment.

duf′fel bag, a large cloth bag for carrying clothing and personal belongings.

duf′fẽr, *n.* [from Scot. *duffart, doofart*, a dull, stupid fellow.]
1. a person of little wit or ability; an incompetent, awkward, or stupid person.
2. a peddler of cheap jewelry, etc. [Obs.]

duf′fle, *n.* same as *duffel.*
dū·fren′īte, *n.* [after P. A. *Dufrênoy,* French mineralogist.] a hydrous iron phosphate of dark green color.
dug, *v.,* past tense and past participle of *dig.*
dug, *n.* [from same stem as Sw. *dægga,* Dan. *dægge,* to suckle.] the nipple or teat of a female animal.
dụ′gong, *n.* [Malay.] a herbivorous, cetaceous animal of the Indian Ocean, with a tapering body ending in a crescent-shaped or two-lobed fin: also called *sea cow.*
dug′out, *n.* 1. a canoe made by hollowing out a log.
2. a rough structure, primarily an excavation, as in a hillside: often made by digging vertically into the ground and covering the cavity with a rude framework and sod.
3. in baseball, a covered shelter near the diamond for the players to sit in when not at bat or in the field.
dug′wāy, *n.* a road made by digging.
duī′kẽr, *n.*; *pl.* **duī′kẽrș** *or* **duī′kẽr,** [D. *duiker,* a diver; the animal dives into the bush.] a small, horned antelope of South Africa.
duī′kẽr·bok, *n.*; *pl.* **duī′kẽr·bok** *or* **duī′kẽr·boks,** [D. *duiker,* and *bok,* a buck.] a duiker.
duī′kẽr·buck, *n.*; *pl.* **duī′kẽr·buck** *or* **duī′kẽr·bucks,** a duiker.
dūke, *n.* [ME. *duke, duk, duc;* OFr. *duc, dux;* L. *dux,* a leader, general.]
1. a prince who is the ruler of an independent duchy.
2. a nobleman of the highest hereditary rank below that of prince.
3. a chief; a prince. [Obs.]
dūke′dŏm, *n.* 1. the territory of a duke; a duchy.
2. the title or rank of a duke.
dūke′ling, *n.* a little or insignificant duke; also, the child of a duke.
dūkes, *n.pl.* [from *duke,* short for *Duke of York,* used in 19th-c. Eng. rhyming slang for *fork,* hence fingers, hence fist.] the fists or hands. [Slang.]
dūke′ship, *n.* the office or rank of a duke.
Dụ′khŏ·borș (du′kŏ-), *n.pl.* [Russ. *dukhobortsy,* lit., spirit wrestlers; *dukh,* spirit, and *bortsy,* wrestlers.] a Russian religious sect separated from the Orthodox Church in 1785. They have no fixed place or form of worship and no authorized ministry. In the 1890's numbers emigrated to Canada to escape military conscription, which they considered sinful.
Dụ·khŏ·bor′tsy, *n.pl.* same as *Dukhobors.*
dul·çȧ·mā′rȧ, *n.* a plant, the bittersweet.
dul·çȧ·mā′rin, *n.* [L. *dulcis,* sweet, and *amarus,* bitter.] a glucoside derived from *Solanum dulcamara,* the bittersweet.
dulce, *v.t.* to sweeten. [Obs.]
dulce, *a.* [L. *dulcis,* sweet.] sweet; pleasing; gentle. [Obs.]
dulce, *n.* any of various sweet articles, as a bonbon, sweet wine, candied fruit, etc. [Rare.]
dulce′ness, *n.* sweetness. [Obs.]
dul′cet, *a.* [L. *dulcis,* sweet.]
1. sweet to the taste or smell. [Archaic.]
2. sweet to the ear; melodious; harmonious; as, *dulcet* sounds; *dulcet* symphonies.
3. sweet or pleasing to the mind.
dul′cet, *n.* an organ stop of sweet, mellow tone, one octave higher in pitch than the dulciana.
dul·ci·an′ȧ, *n.* [LL., from L. *dulcis,* sweet.] in music, a soft, sweet-toned organ stop like that of a stringed instrument.
dul″ci·fi·çā′tion, *n.* the act of dulcifying.
dul·cif′lū·ous, *a.* [LL. *dulcifluus; dulcis,* sweet, and *fluere,* to flow.] flowing sweetly. [Rare.]
dul′ci·fȳ, *v.t.*; dulcified, *pt., pp.*; dulcifying, *ppr.* [Fr. *dulcifier;* LL. *dulcificare;* L. *dulcis,* sweet, and *-ficare,* from *facere,* to make.]
1. to sweeten. [Rare.]
2. to make pleasant or agreeable; mollify.
dul·cil′ō·quy (-kwi), *n.* softness in speaking. [Obs.]
dul′ci·mẽr, *n.* [OFr. *doulcimer;* It. *dolcemele,* a musical instrument; L. *dulce melos; dulce,* neut. of *dulcis,* sweet, and *melos,* from Gr. *melos,* a song, strain.]

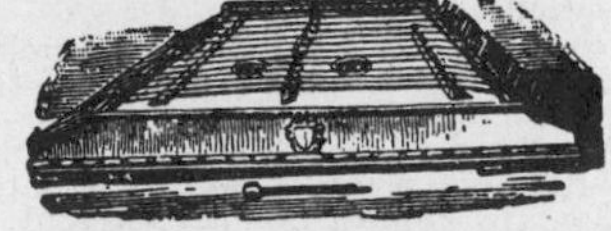
ITALIAN DULCIMER

1. a musical instrument strung with wires which are struck with padded hammers by the player.
2. in the Bible, the psaltry, a kind of harp: Dan. iii. 10.
dul′cin, *n.* same as *dulcitol.*
Dul·cin′ē·ȧ, *n.* [Sp., from *dulce,* sweet; L. *dulcis.*]
1. the plain peasant girl whom Don Quixote imagines to be a beautiful lady and falls in love with.
2. any idealized sweetheart.
dul′ci·tăn, *n.* [*dulcite* and *-an.*] an alcohol, $C_6H_{12}O_6$, derived from dulcitol by heating.
dul′cīte, *n.* same as *dulcitol.*
dul′ci·tōl, *n.* [*dulcite* and *-ol.*] a saccharine, crystalline isomer of mannite, $C_6H_{14}O_6$, found in various plants.
dul′ci·tūde, *n.* [L. *dulcitudo,* from *dulcis,* sweet.] sweetness. [Rare.]
dul′çō·rāte, *v.t.* [LL. *dulcoratus,* pp. of *dulcorare,* to sweeten; L. *dulcis,* sweet.] to sweeten; to make less acrimonious. [Rare.]
dul·çō·rā′tion, *n.* the act of sweetening. [Rare.]
dū′ledġe (-lej), *n.* in mechanics, a peg of wood which joins the ends of the six fellies that form the round of a wheel of a gun carriage.
dū·lī′ȧ, *n.* [LL., from Gr. *douleia,* service, from *doulos,* a slave.] in the Roman Catholic Church, the homage paid to saints and angels: distinguished from *latria.*
dull, *a. comp.* duller; *superl.* dullest, [ME. *dull, dul;* AS. *dol,* foolish, stupid.]
1. stupid; mentally slow; as, a lad of *dull* mind.
2. depressed; sluggish; without life or spirit.

Somewhat *duller* than at first,
I sit (my empty glass reversed.)
—Tennyson.

3. slow of motion; physically slow; sluggish; as, a *dull* stream.
4. lacking sensitivity; unfeeling; as, *dull* to grief.
5. causing boredom; tedious; as, a *dull* party.
6. not felt keenly or sharply; not acute; as, a *dull* headache.
7. slack; as, business is *dull.*
8. not bright; not vivid; dim; as, a *dull* fire; a *dull* light.
9. blunt; not keen or pointed; having a thick edge.

The murderous knife was *dull* and blunt.
—Shak.

10. cloudy; overcast; not clear; not enlivening; as, *dull* weather.
Syn.—stupid, stolid, doltish, sluggish, slow, sleepy, drowsy, lifeless, tiresome, commonplace, uninteresting, prosy, prosaic, blunt, obtuse.
dull, *v.t.* and *v.i.*; dulled, *pt., pp.*; dulling, *ppr.* to make or become dull.
dull, *n.* a snare used to catch fish.
dull, *v.i.* to use a dull in fishing.
dull′ărd, *n.* a stupid person.
dull′ărd, *a.* dull; stupid.
dull′ẽr, *n.* one who or that which dulls.
dull′head (-hed), *n.* a dolt; a blockhead.
dull′ish, *a.* rather dull.
dull′ness, dul′ness, *n.* the state or condition of being dull.
dull′-wit″ted, *a.* having a dull intellect; stupid.
dul′ly, *adv.* in a dull manner.
dụ·loc′ra·cy, *n.* same as *doulocracy.*
dulse, *n.* [Gael. *duileasg.*] a kind of edible seaweed belonging to the suborder *Ceramiaceæ,* the *Rhodymenia palmata:* it has large, red, wedge-shaped fronds.
dul′wil·ly, *n.* a bird, the ring plover. [Brit. Dial.]
dū′ly, *adv.* [from *due* and *-ly.*]
1. properly; fitly; in a suitable or becoming manner.
2. when due; at the right time; on time.
3. as required; sufficiently.
Dụ′mä, Doụ′mä, *n.* the former Russian parliament, set up as a consultative body in 1905 by Czar Nicholas II: ended by the revolution of 1917.
dumb (dum), *a.* [AS. *dumb;* Ice. *dumbr,* mute; D. *dom;* L.G. *dum;* Dan. *dum,* stupid, dull.]
1. lacking the power of speech; not able to make articulate sounds; mute.
2. unwilling to talk; silent; reticent.
3. not accompanied by speech.
4. temporarily speechless, as from fear, grief, etc.
5. producing no sound.
6. not bright; as, a *dumb* white. [Rare.]
7. destitute of some ordinary accompaniment or characteristic; as, a *dumb* barge, without sails; a *dumb* ague, without the usual chills.
8. stupid; moronic. [Colloq.]
dum′bȧ, *n.* [Turk., from Per. *dumb,* tail.] a sheep of the Bokhara and Kirghiz steppe regions of Russia: it is characterized by a fat tail and is valued as a source of astrakhan.
dumb ā′gūe, a form of malarial fever in which the chill and other symptoms are slight or entirely obscured.
dumb′bell, *n.* 1. a weight used for exercise, usually in the form of two metal balls connected by a rigid handle: it is lifted or swung about with the hand to help develop the muscles of the arm, shoulder, and back.
2. a dullard; a stupid person. [Slang.]
dumb çāke, a cake made in silence on St. Mark's eve, by which a girl attempts to learn who is to be her husband.
dumb çāne, a plant, *Dieffenbachia seguine,* growing in the West Indies, which, when chewed, causes swelling of the tongue, and thus produces loss of speech.
dumb çram′bō, a game in which the players are divided into two teams: the first team gives the second a word to guess, the clue being a word that rhymes with it; the second team acts out by dumb show what they think the word is.
dumb′found, *v.t.* same as *dumfound.*
dum′ble·dōre, *n.* 1. a cockchafer. [Brit. Dial.]
2. the bumblebee.
dumb′ly (dum′ly), *adv.* mutely; silently.
dumb′ness, *n.* muteness; silence.
dumb shōw, 1. formerly, a part of a play done in pantomime.
2. gestures without speech.
dumb′-wāit″ẽr, *n.* 1. a small, portable serving stand placed near a dining table.
2. a small, hand-operated elevator with shelves, used for sending food, trash, etc. from one floor to another.
dum′dum, *n.* [from *Dumdum,* arsenal near Calcutta, India.] a soft-nosed bullet that expands when it hits, inflicting a large, jagged wound: also *dumdum bullet.*
dū′mē·tōse, *a.* resembling a bush.
dum′found, *v.t.*; dumfounded, *pt., pp.*; dumfounding, *ppr.* to make speechless by surprising; to amaze; to astonish: also spelled *dumbfound.*
dum′mẽr·ẽr, *n.* one who feigns muteness. [Obs.]
dum′my, *n.*; *pl.* **dum′mieș,** 1. one who is unable to talk; mute: now vulgar in this sense.
2. an actor who plays a nonspeaking part.
3. a dumb-waiter.
4. a figure made in human form, used for displaying clothing, practicing tackling in football, etc.
5. an imitation; sham.
6. a person secretly acting for another while apparently representing his own interests; tool of another.
7. a stupid person. [Slang.]
8. in card games, (a) the declarer's partner, whose hand is exposed on the board and played by the declarer; (b) the hand thus exposed.
9. in printing, the skeleton copy, as of a magazine or book, upon which the format is planned and laid out.
10. a locomotive furnished with condensing engines and, hence, without the noise of escaping steam.
11. a jet from a main, or chief water pipe: so called by firemen.
double dummy; whist with only two players, each having a hand exposed.
dum′my, *a.* 1. silent.
2. imitation; sham.
3. secretly controlled by, or acting as the tool of, another; as, a *dummy* corporation.
4. in card games, played with a dummy.
dū′mōse, dū′mous, *a.* [L. *dumosus,* bushy, from *dumus,* a bramble.] having many bushes and brambles; bushy.
dump, *n.* [prob. from D. *domp,* haze, dullness.]
1. a sad tune or song. [Archaic.]
2. any tune or song. [Archaic.]
3. absence of mind; reverie. [Obs.]
in the dumps; in low spirits; in a depressed or dejected condition.
dump, *v.t.*; dumped, *pt., pp.*; dumping, *ppr.* [ME. *dumpen,* to fall down, throw down; Dan. *dumpe;* Sw. *dimpa,* to fall down suddenly, to rush.]
1. to empty or to unload in a mass; as, to *dump* a load of gravel.
2. in economics, to sell (a large quantity of goods), especially abroad, at a price lower than the domestic market price.

3. to throw away as rubbish; to get rid of.
4. (a) to transfer (data in a computer memory) to another section of storage; (b) to print out (data in a computer memory).
5. in football, to throw (a short pass) into the flat.
to dump on; to treat with contempt; demean. [Slang.]

dump, *v.i.* 1. to fall in a heap or mass.
2. to unload rubbish.
3. to dump commodities.
4. in typesetting, to lift type from a stick when set and put it into a galley, form, etc.
5. to plunge abruptly downward. [Obs.]

dump, *n.* 1. a thump or thud, as of something heavy falling.
2. a place where refuse is deposited; also, the refuse itself; especially, the pile near the mouth of a shaft.
3. (a) a listing of data stored in a computer; (b) a printout of such data.
4. in military usage, a temporary storage place for supplies, as ammunition, food, or clothing, to be distributed in the field.
5. a place that is unpleasant, ugly, uncomfortable, etc. [Slang.]

dump, *n.* [perhaps from *dumpy* (stumpy).]
1. a small, shapeless lump or chunk, as of lead. [Brit.]
2. a crude leaden counter formerly used by boys in playing certain games. [Brit.]
3. a silver coin once used in Australia.

dump'çärt, *n.* a tipcart.

dump'i·ly, *adv.* in a dumpy manner.

dump'i·ness, *n.* the quality or state of being dumpy.

dump'ing, *n.* in economics, a term used to designate the practice of selling goods in large quantities abroad at prices lower than those current at home.

dump'ish, *a.* gloomy; depressed; sad; melancholy. [Rare.]

dump'ish·ly, *adv.* in a dumpish manner.

dump'ling, *n.* [*dump* (shapeless lump), and *-ling.*]
1. a small piece of dough, steamed or boiled and served with meat or soup.
2. a crust of dough filled with fruit and steamed or baked.
3. a short, fat person or animal.

dump'stẽr, *n.* a large, metal trash bin, often of a kind that is emptied, or transported to a dump, by a specially equipped truck: a trade-mark (*Dumpster*).

dump truck, a truck whose contents are unloaded by tilting the truck bed backward with the tail gate open.

dump'y, *a.*; *comp.* dumpier; *superl.* dumpiest, [from *dump, v.*] short and thick; squat; stumpy.

dump'y, *a.*; *comp.* dumpier; *superl.* dumpiest, [see *dump* (sad tune).] melancholy; depressed.

dump'y lev'el, a spirit level having a short telescope with a large aperture, used in surveying.

dun, *a.* [AS. *dun, dunn,* from W. *dwn,* dun, dusky, swarthy.] dull grayish-brown.
dun crow; the hooded crow.
dun diver; the merganser.

dun, *n.* 1. a dull grayish brown.
2. an artificial fly of this color.
3. a May fly.

dun, *v.t.*; dunned, *pt., pp.*; dunning, *ppr.* to give a dun color to.

dun, *v.t.* and *v.i.*; dunned, *pt., pp.*; dunning, *ppr.* [ME. *dunnen*; AS. *dynian,* to make a noise, from *dyne*; Ice. *dynr, duna,* a noise, thunder.] literally, to clamor insistently or repeatedly for payment of (a debt) or from (a debtor).

dun, *n.* 1. a person who duns for payment.
2. an insistent demand for payment of a debt; as, he sent his debtor a *dun*.

dun'bird, *n.* a dun-colored bird; (a) the ruddy duck; (b) the pochard; (c) the female of the scaup duck.

dunce, *n.* [from John *Duns* Scotus, called the "Subtle Doctor," leader of the schoolmen of the 13th c., and opposed to the revival of classical learning. His followers were called *Dunsmen, Duncemen,* and ultimately simply *Dunses, Dunces.* The word came to be applied to any opponent of education, and then to stupid persons in general.]
1. a dull ignorant person.
2. a person who learns more slowly than others.

dunce çap, a cone-shaped hat, sometimes marked D, which children slow at learning were formerly forced to wear in school.

dun'cẽr·y, *n.* dullness; stupidity.

dunch, *v.t.* and *v.i.* to jog or push with the elbow. [Scot. or Brit. Dial.]

dun'ci·çăl, *a.* duncelike.

dun'ci·fȳ, *v.t.* to make stupid. [Rare.]

dun'cish, *a.* rather duncelike. [Rare.]

dun'dẽr, *n.* [Sp. *redundar*; L. *redundare,* to overflow.] lees; dregs; especially, cane-juice dregs.

The use of *dunder* in the making of rum answers the purpose of yeast in the fermentation of flour. —Edwards.

dun'dẽr·head (-hed), *n.* [also early *blunderhead*; D. *donder,* thunder, associated by rhyme with *blunder,* as in Eng. *blunderbuss,* for D. *donderbus,* lit., thunder box.] a stupid person; dunce; numskull.

dun'dẽr-head"ed, *a.* stupid.

dun'dẽr·pāte, *n.* same as *dunderhead.*

dūne, *n.* [Fr. *dune,* from O.D. *duna* (D. *duin*).] a rounded hill or ridge of sand heaped up by the action of the wind.

dūne bug'gy, a small, light automobile generally made from a standard, compact, rear-engine chassis and a prefabricated, often fiberglas body: orig. equipped with wide, low-pressure tires for driving on sand dunes.

dun'fish, *n.* codfish cured by dunning.

dung, *n.* [ME. *dung*; AS. *dung, dyng*; O.H.G. *tunge*; G. *dung,* dung; Dan. *dynge,* a heap, mass.]
1. the excrement of animals; manure.
2. filth.

dung, *v.t.*; dunged, *pt., pp.*; dunging, *ppr.* [ME. *dungen*; AS. *ge-dyngan,* to manure, dung, from *dunge,* dung, manure.]
1. to cover with dung, as in fertilizing.
2. in calico printing, to subject (the fabric) to a solution of cow dung to remove the excess of mordant.

dung, *v.i.* to discharge excrement.

duñ·gȧ·ree', *n.* [Hind. *dungrī.*]
1. a coarse cotton cloth used for tents, sails, work clothing, etc.
2. [*pl.*] work trousers or overalls made of this cloth.

dung bee'tle, any of various beetles, chafers, and scarabs that breed in dung and feed on it.

dun'ġeŏn, *n.* [ME. *dungeon, dongon*; OFr. *dongeon, donjon*; Pr. *donjon*; LL. *domnio,* dungeon, tower, a contr. of *dominio,* domain, possession, from L. *dominus,* lord.] a donion; hence, a prison or place of confinement; especially, a subterranean chamber or other dark and gloomy cell, vault, or prison.

dun'ġeŏn, *v.t.* to confine in a dungeon. [Rare.]

dung flȳ, a dung-eating insect of the family *Scatophagidae.*

dung'fọrk, *n.* a fork, having four or more tines, used in handling dung.

dung'hill, *n.* 1. a heap of dung.
2. anything vile or filthy.
dunghill fowl; the common domestic fowl.

dung'y, *a.*; *comp.* dungier; *superl.* dungiest, full of dung; filthy; vile.

dun'īte, *n.* [named from *Dun* Mountain, New Zealand.] an igneous rock consisting chiefly of chrysolite.

dun·i·was'săl, dun·nie·was'săl, *n.* a gentleman of secondary rank, as a cadet of the nobility. [Scot.]

duñk, *v.t.* and *v.i.*; dunked, *pt., pp.*; dunking, *ppr.* [G. *tunken.*]
1. to dip (bread, cake, etc.) into coffee or other liquid before eating it.
2. to immerse in a liquid for a short time.
3. in basketball, to put (the ball) into the basket by means of a dunk shot.

Duñ'kärds, *n.pl.* Dunkers.

Duñ'kẽrs, *n.pl.* [G. *tunker,* a dipper, from *tunken,* to dip.] a member of a German-American religious sect opposed to military service and the taking of oaths and practicing such rites, as the laying on of hands, washing of the feet before the Eucharist, the kiss of charity, and triple immersion: properly called *Church of the Brethren.*
Seventh-day Dunkers; a sect of Dunkers observing Saturday as their Sabbath.

duñk shot, in basketball, the act of scoring a field goal by leaping up and thrusting the ball down into the basket.

dun'lin, *n.pl.* **dun'lins** or **dun'lin,** from *dunling*; *dun,* dark brown, and dim. *-ling.*] a bird, the red-backed sandpiper.

dun'nāġe, *n.* 1. packing, usually of fagots, loose wood, etc., used about or below a ship's cargo to prevent damage in transit.
2. personal baggage or belongings.

dun'nẽr, *n.* one who duns.

dun'nish, *a.* somewhat dun.

dunn'īte, *n.* a picric acid explosive for projectiles, invented by and named for B. W. *Dunn,* U. S. chemist.

dun'nŏck, *n.* the hedge sparrow. [Brit. Dial.]

dunt, *n.* 1. the staggers, a sheep disease. [Scot. and Brit. Dial.]
2. a stroke; a blow. [Scot. and Brit. Dial.]
3. a wound caused by such a blow. [Scot. and Brit. Dial.]

dunt, *v.t.* and *v.i.* to strike, knock, or jolt with a dunt. [Scot. and Brit. Dial.]

dun'tẽr, *n.* 1. the eider duck. [Scot.]
2. a porpoise. [Scot.]

dun'tẽr gọọse, the eider duck.

dū'ō, *n.*; *pl.* **dū'ōs, dū'ī,** [It.]
1. a duet (especially in sense 2).
2. a pair; couple.

dū'ō-, [from L. *duo,* two.] a combining form meaning *two, double,* as in *duologue.*

dū"ō·dē·cen'ni·ăl, *a.* [L. *duodecim,* twelve.] occurring every twelve years. [Rare.]

dū·ō·dec'i·măl, *a.* [L. *duodecim,* twelve.]
1. relating to twelve or twelfths.
2. consisting of or counting by twelves or powers of twelve.

dū·ō·dec'i·măl, *n.* 1. one twelfth.
2. [*pl.*] in mathematics, a system of numeration with twelve as its base: distinguished from the *decimal* system, which has ten as its base.

dū·ō·dec'i·măl·ly, *adv.* by twelves.

dū·ō·dec'i·mō, *n.*; *pl.* **dū·ō·dec'i·mōs,** [short for L. *in duodecimo,* (in) twelve.]
1. the page size of a book made up of printer's sheets folded into twelve leaves, each leaf being approximately 5 by $7^1/_2$ inches.
2. a book consisting of pages of this size: also called *twelvemo,* and written 12 *mo* or 12°.

dū·ō·dec'i·mō, *a.* consisting of pages of duodecimo.

dū·ō·dē'nȧ, *n.,* pl. of *duodenum.*

dū·ō·dē'năl, *a.* in, of, or relating to the duodenum.

dū·ō·den'ă·ry, *a.* [L. *duodenarius,* containing twelve, from *duodeni,* twelve each.]
1. having to do with twelve; in or increasing by twelves.
2. having to do with duodecimal numeration.

dū"ō·dē·nī'tis, *n.* inflammation of the duodenum.

dū"ō·dē·not'ō·my, *n.* [*duodenum,* and *-tomy,* from Gr. *tomē,* a cutting.] surgical incision into the duodenum.

dū·ō·dē'num, *n.* [from L. *duodeni,* twelve each, so called because its length is about twelve fingers' breadth.] the first section of the small intestine, between the stomach and the jejunum.

dū'ō·grȧph, *n.* in photoengraving, a picture in two shades of the same color, made from two half-tone plates produced by setting the screen at different angles.

dū·ō·lit'ẽr·ăl, *a.* [L. *duo,* two, and *litera,* a letter.] consisting of two letters only; biliteral.

dū'ō·logue (-log), *n.* [L. *duo*; Gr. *dyo,* two, and *logos,* a word, story.] a dialogue for two persons only, especially in a dramatic performance.

duō'mō (dwō'), *n.* [It.] a cathedral.

dū'ō·tōne, *a.* showing a two-tone color effect.

dū'ō·tōne, *n.* a picture having a two-tone color effect.

dū'ō·tȳpe, *n.* in photoengraving, a print produced from two half-tone plates made from the same negative, but etched separately.

dup, *v.t.* [for *do up.*] to open; as, to *dup* a door. [Obs.]

dūp'ȧ·ble, *a.* susceptible of being duped.

dūpe, *n.* [Fr. *dupe,* from OFr. *dupe, duppe,* the hoopoe, a stupid bird.] a person who is easily deceived; one easily led astray or fooled.

dūpe, *v.t.*; duped (dūpt), *pt., pp.*; duping, *ppr.* [Fr. *duper,* to dupe, take in, from *dupe,* one easily taken in.] to deceive; to trick; to cheat.

dūp'ẽr, *n.* one who dupes.

dūp'ẽr·y, *n.*; *pl.* **dūp'ẽr·ies,** a duping or being duped; deception.

dū'pi·ŏn, *n.* [Fr. *doupion*; It. *doppione,* from *doppio*; L. *duplus,* double.] a double cocoon, formed by two silkworms.

dū'ple, *a.* [L. *duplus,* double.]
1. twofold; double.
2. in music, containing an even number of beats (i.e., two or a multiple of two) to the measure: as, *duple* time.
duple ratio; that in which the antecedent term is double the consequent, as of 2 to 1.

dū'plex, *a.* [L. *duplex,* double, twofold; *duo,* two, and *plicare,* to fold.]
1. double; twofold; made up of two parts.
2. in electricity, designating a method of

telegraphy (*duplex telegraphy*) in which one wire is used to transmit two messages simultaneously. The term *duplex* is generic, designating any double use of such a wire; *diplex* and *contraplex* are specific, the former designating simultaneous transmission of two messages in the same direction, and the latter designating opposite simultaneous transmission.

3. in machinery, having two units operating in the same way or simultaneously.

dū'plex, *n.* 1. a duplex apartment or house.
2. either of two small, private compartments forming one unit in a railroad car.

dū'plex, *v.t.* to arrange (a wire, system, etc.) for duplex telegraphy.

dū'plex ȧ·pärt'ment, an apartment with rooms on two floors and a private inner stairway.

dū'plex house, a house consisting of two separate family units.

dū·plex'i·ty, *n.* the quality or state of being duplex.

dū'plex proc'ess, a process for making steel, in which refining of the raw materials is begun in one sort of furnace and finished in another: originally, a Bessemer converter was used for the first stage, and an open hearth furnace for the finishing stage.

dū'pli·cȧ·ble, *a.* that can be duplicated.

dū'pli·çāte, *a.* [L. *duplicatus*, from *duplicare*, to double.]
1. double.
2. having two similar parts.
3. corresponding exactly.
4. designating a way of playing bridge, etc. in which, for comparative scoring, the same hands are played off a second time by players who did not hold them originally.
duplicate proportion or *ratio*; the proportion or ratio of squares. Thus, in geometrical proportion, the first term to the third is said to be in a *duplicate* ratio of the first to the second, or as its square is to the square of the second. Thus, in 2, 4, 8, 16, the ratio of 2 to 8 is a *duplicate* of that of 2 to 4, or as the square of 2 is to the square of 4.

dū'pli·çāte, *n.* 1. another corresponding to the first in all essentials or exactly; a second thing of the same kind; a copy; a transcript; a replica; a facsimile.
2. a counterpart or double.
3. a duplicate game of bridge, etc.
4. in law, one of two or more writings or documents containing the same matter and having equal force and validity; as, a lease made in *duplicate*.
in duplicate; in two precisely similar forms.

dū'pli·çāte, *v.t.*; duplicated, *pt., pp.*; duplicating, *ppr.* [L. *duplicatus*, pp. of *duplicare*, to double.]
1. to double; to make double or twofold.
2. to make an exact copy or copies of.
3. to make, do, or cause to happen again; as, she *duplicated* her former success.

dū'pli·çā·ting mȧ·chïne', a machine for making exact copies of a letter, photograph, drawing, etc.

dū·pli·çā'tion, *n.* 1. a duplicating or being duplicated.
2. a copy; a replica.
3. in botany, chorisis.
4. a doubling; a fold. [Rare.]
5. celebration of the Mass by the same priest twice in one day.

dū'pli·çā·tive, *a.* duplicating.

dū'pli·çā·tŏr, *n.* [LL., doubler, from *duplicare*; see *duplex*.] a machine for making exact copies of written or typewritten matter.

dū'pli·çȧ·tūre, *n.* a doubling or folding, as of the peritoneum. [Rare.]

dū''pli·ci·den'tāte, *a.* [L. *duplex, duplicis*, double, and *dens, dentis*, a tooth.] having a double set of incisors, two in front and two behind, as in the rabbit.

dū·plic'i·ty, *n.*; *pl.* **dū·plic'i·tieṣ,** [Fr. *duplicité*; LL. *duplicitas* (-*atis*), from L. *duplex* (-*icis*), double.]
1. doubleness. [Rare.]
2. hypocritical cunning or deception; the act or practice of exhibiting a different or contrary conduct, or uttering different or contrary sentiments, at different times, in relation to the same thing; double-dealing.
3. in law, the pleading of two or more distinct matters in the same count.

dur, *a.* [G. *dur*, from L. *durus*, hard.] in music, major; as, D *dur*.

dū'rȧ, *n.* [f. of L. *durus*, hard.] in anatomy, the dura mater.

dū·rȧ·bil'i·ty, *n.* [LL. *durabilitas*, from L. *durabilis*, lasting, durable.] the quality of being durable; the power of lasting or continuing in any given state without perishing; as, the *durability* of oak timber.

dū'rȧ·ble, *a.* [L. *durabilis*, from *durare*, to harden; *durus*, hard.]
1. lasting in spite of hard wear or frequent use; as, *durable* cloth.
2. continuing to exist; stable.
3. able to endure. [Archaic.]
Syn.—enduring, lasting, permanent.

dū'rȧ·ble·ness, *n.* power of lasting; durability.

dū'rȧ·bly, *adv.* in a lasting or durable manner; so as to last.

dū'răl, *a.* in anatomy, relating to or derived from the dura mater.

dū·ral'ū·min, *n.* [*dur*able, and *alumin*um.] a strong, lightweight alloy of aluminum with copper, manganese, magnesium, and silicon: a trade-mark (*Duralumin*).

dū'rȧ mā'tēr, [ML., lit., hard mother, transl. of an Ar. term.] the outermost, toughest, and most fibrous of the three membranes covering the brain and spinal cord.

dū·rā'men, *n.* [L., hardness, from *durare*, to harden.] the central layers or heartwood of the trunk or branches of an exogenous tree.

dūr'ănce, *n.* [OFr. *durance*; L. *durans*, ppr. of *durare*, to harden, to last.]
1. imprisonment, especially when long continued.
2. continuance; duration. [Archaic.]
3. durable material of any kind. [Obs.]

dūr'ăn·cy, *n.* continuance; durance. [Obs.]

dūr'ănt, *n.* same as *durance*, sense 3.

dū·ran'tē, *prep.* [L., abl. ppr. of *durare*, to harden, last.] during; as, *durante vita*, during life; *durante bene placito*, during pleasure.

dū·rā'tion, *n.* continuance in time; length of existence; the period during which a thing continues.

dūr'ȧ·tive, *a.* implying or expressing continuance. [Rare.]

dūr'bär, *n.* [Hind. and Per. *darbār*, a ruler's court; *dar*, portal, and *bār*, court.]
1. in India, an official reception or audience held by a native prince, or by a British ruler or governor.
2. the place or hall where this is held.

dūre, *a.* rigorous; hard; stern. [Obs.]

dūre, *v.i.* and *v.t.*; dured, *pt., pp.*; during, *ppr.* [OFr. *durer*; L. *durare*, to harden, last.] to last; to hold on in time or being; to continue; to endure. [Obs. and Dial.]

dūre'ful, *a.* lasting. [Obs.]

dūre'less, *a.* not lasting; fading. [Obs.]

dū'rēne, *n.* [L. *durus*, hard.] a coal-tar derivative, $C_{10}H_{14}$, of crystalline structure.

dū'ress (*or* dū·res'), *n.* [ME. *duresse, duresce*; OFr. *durece, duresse*; L. *duritia*, hardness, harshness, from *durus*, hard.]
1. hardness. [Obs.]
2. constraint; imprisonment; restraint of liberty.
3. compulsion or coercion, as to execute a deed or to commit a misdemeanor.

dū·ress', *v.t.* to place under duress. [Obs.]

dū·ress'ŏr, *n.* in law, one who places another under duress. [Obs.]

du·rez'zȧ (-ret'sȧ), *n.* [It.] in music, harshness of tone or quality.

dūr'fee grass, couch grass.

Dur'gȧ, *n.* [Anglo-Ind.] a Hindu divinity; one of the names given to the consort of Siva, other names being *Devi, Kali, Parvati, Bhavani, Uma*, etc. She is the Amazon champion and protectress of the gods, and is generally represented with ten arms: also spelled *Doorga*.

DURGA

dūr'gan, dūr'gen, *n.* a dwarf; a small-sized person or animal. [Brit. Dial.]

Dūr'hăm (dūr'ăm), *n.* one of a breed of cattle, short-horned and noted as beef producers, coming originally from the county of Durham, England.

dū'ri·ăn, dū'ri·ŏn, *n.* [Malay, from *duri*, thorn.] the oval, edible fruit of an East Indian tree, *Durio zibethinus*; also, the tree itself.

DURIAN (*Durio zibethinus*)

dūr'ing, *prep.* [ME. *duringe*, prep., originally ppr. of *dure*, to last, continue; OFr. *durant*; L. *durare*, to harden, to last; *durus*, hard, lasting.]
1. in or throughout the time or existence of; all through; as, it continued *during* the whole hour.
2. at some point in the entire time of; in the course of; as, he left *during* the lecture.

Dū'ri·ō, *n.* [from Malay *duryon*, the durian.] a genus of trees of the mallow family. *Durio zibethinus*, the durian, is the only species, being a large tree growing in the Malayan Archipelago. The large flowers, of a yellow-green color, are produced on the stem or main branches, and are followed by the edible fruit, which is the size of a man's head.

dū'ri·ty, *n.* [L. *duritas*, hardness, from *durus*, hard.] hardness; firmness.

dūr'măst, *n.* [apparently for *dun mast oak*, dark acorned oak.] a variety of European oak, *Quercus sessiliflora*, valued for its dark, heavy, tough wood.

dūrn, *n.* [Corn. *dorn*, a doorpost.] a supporting mine timber; a gatepost; a doorpost; a window jamb. [Dial.]

dū'rō, *n.*; *pl.* **dū'rōṣ,** [Sp., for *duro peso*, lit., hard peso.] the silver peso, or dollar, of Spain and Spanish America.

Dū'roç-Jēr'ṣey, *n.* any of a breed of large, red hogs: also *Duroc*.

dur'rȧ, *n.* [Ar. *dhurah*.] a variety of grain-producing sorghum; Indian millet: also spelled *doura, dourah*.

dūrst, *v.* archaic past tense of *dare*.

dū·rū·kū'li, *n.* see *douroucouli*.

dū'rum, *n.* [L., neut. of *durus*, hard.] a variety of hard wheat: flour made from it is used in macaroni, spaghetti, etc.

dū·ryl'iç, *a.* of, relating to, or derived from durene.

dū'sack, *n.* [G. *dusak*, from Bohem. *tesak*, a sword.] a kind of rough German cutlass, the blade and hilt being of one piece, used in the sixteenth and seventeenth centuries.

dush, *v.t.* to shove; to strike hard. [Obs.]

dush, *v.i.* to fall hard; to rush. [Obs.]

dusk, *a.* [ME. *dosk, dusk*; AS. *dosc, dox*, dark-colored.] tending to darkness; moderately dark; shadowy; dusky. [Poetic.]

dusk, *n.* 1. the beginning of darkness in the evening; the dark part of twilight; gloaming; as, the *dusk* of the evening.
2. gloom; dusky quality.

dusk, *v.t.* and *v.i.* to make or become dusky or shadowy.

dusk'en, *v.t.* and *v.i.* to dusk. [Rare.]

dusk'i·ly, *adv.* in a dusky manner; dimly.

dusk'i·ness, *n.* a dusky quality or state.

dusk'ish, *a.* moderately dusky; partially obscure.

dusk'ish·ly, *adv.* cloudily; darkly.

dusk'ish·ness, *n.* duskiness.

dusk'y, *a.*; *comp.* duskier; *superl.* duskiest,
1. partially dark or obscure; not luminous; dimly lighted; as, a *dusky* valley.
2. shadowy; swarthy; somewhat dark in color; partially black; dark-colored; not bright; as, a *dusky* brown.
3. gloomy; sad.
dusky duck; *Anas obscura*, the black duck.

dust, *n.* [AS. *dust*; L.G. *dust*; Ice. *dust*, dust; D. *duist*, meal dust; Dan. *dyst*, fine meal.]
1. earth or any other matter so finely powdered and so dry that it is easily suspended in air; anything in the form of a fine powder; as, marble *dust*; also, a cloud of such matter.
2. figuratively, the commotion and confusion accompanying a struggle.

Great contest follows, and much learned *dust*. —Cowper.

3. in cookery, a small amount of some pow-

der dusted upon anything; as, just a *dust* of cinnamon.

4. mortal remains thought of as disintegrating to earth or dust; as, *dust* to *dust*.

5. the grave; as, now shall I sleep in the *dust*.

6. figuratively, a low or humble condition; as, his fame has fallen to the *dust*.

7. anything worthless.

8. refuse, as ashes and rubbish. [Brit.]

9. pollen.

10. tiny gold particles obtained by washing gold deposits.

11. money. [Slang.]

12. a small particle or atom; as, not a *dust* is left. [Rare.]

to bite the dust; to fall in battle; to be defeated.

to kick up or *raise a dust*; to create a commotion or disturbance.

to lick the dust; (a) to fall in battle; to be defeated; (b) to be servile; to grovel.

to make the dust fly; (a) to act energetically; (b) to move swiftly.

to throw dust in (*someone's*) *eyes*; to confuse or deceive (someone), as by misleading answers.

dust, *v.t.*; dusted, *pt., pp.*; dusting, *ppr.* 1. to free from dust; to brush, wipe, beat, or sweep away dust from (often with *off*); as, to *dust* a table or a carpet.

2. to sprinkle with or as with dust; to powder.

3. to sprinkle (powder, etc.) on.

4. to make dusty.

5. to levigate; to make into dust.

dust, *v.i.* 1. to remove dust, especially from furniture, floors, etc.

2. to bathe in dust: said of a bird.

3. to become dusty.

dust'bin, *n.* a container for dust, rubbish, etc.; ash can. [Brit.]

dust bowl, those parts of the Great Plains of the United States where the eroded topsoil of fallow land was blown away by winds so that a vast desert area resulted, largely reclaimed during the administration of Franklin D. Roosevelt: also *Dust Bowl.*

dust brand, a fungus; smut.

dust'ẽr, *n.* 1. a person or thing that dusts.

2. a brush or cloth for removing dust from furniture, etc.

3. a device for dusting a powder on.

4. a device for sprinkling sugar, ground cinnamon, etc.

5. a lightweight coat worn to protect the clothes from dust, as formerly in open automobiles.

dust'i·ly, *adv.* 1. in a dusty manner.

2. with dust.

dust'i·ness, *n.* the state or quality of being dusty.

dust jack'et, a removable paper covering folded around the binding of a book for protection and ornament.

dust'less, *a.* having or causing no dust; as, a *dustless* room, *dustless* chalk.

dust'măn, *n.*; *pl.* **dust'men,** 1. one whose employment is to carry away dirt and rubbish. [Brit.]

2. a character in folklore supposed to make children sleepy by sprinkling dust in their eyes.

dus·to̤o̤r', dus·to̤o̤r'y, *n.* dastur (sense 2).

dust'pan, *n.* a utensil shaped like a short, broad shovel upon which to sweep floor dust, etc.

dust point, a kind of game in which stones were thrown at points placed in a pile of dust.

dust'proof, *a.* keeping out dust; protecting from dust.

dust shot, the smallest size of bird shot.

dust stọrm, a wind storm that sweeps up clouds of dust when passing over an arid region.

dust whirl, dust carried about in a whirl of wind.

dust'y, *a.*; *comp.* dustier; *superl.* dustiest, 1. filled, covered, or sprinkled with dust; clouded with dust.

2. like dust; of the color of dust; as, a *dusty* white; a *dusty* pollen.

dust'y mil'lẽr, 1. a moth miller.

2. *Primula auricula*, the auricula, whose leaves appear floury.

3. *Senecio cineraria*, a grayish foliage plant.

Dutch (duch), *a.* [ME. *Dutche, Duche*; D. *duitsch*, Dutch; O.H.G. *diutisk*, from *diot, diota*, a people, nation.]

1. of the Netherlands, its people, language, or culture.

2. German. [Slang.]

Dutch auction; see under *auction.*

Dutch Belted; any of a breed of dairy cattle that are black with a broad white stripe around the body.

Dutch cheese; see under *cheese.*

Dutch clinker; a long, narrow, hard, yellowish brick made in the Netherlands.

Dutch clover; *Trifolium repens*, white clover.

Dutch courage; courage stimulated by drinking alcoholic liquor; hence, alcoholic liquor. [Colloq.]

Dutch door; a door in two parts, one above the other, each of which can be opened separately.

Dutch foil, Dutch gold, Dutch leaf; same as *Dutch metal.*

Dutch liquid; ethylene dichloride, $C_2H_4Cl_2$, made first in Holland by combining chlorine with ethylene.

Dutch metal; tombac, an alloy of copper and zinc: it is one of the most malleable of copper alloys, used in a thin leaf for decorative work, in place of gold.

Dutch oven; (a) an iron kettle for baking, with a tight-fitting convex lid, on which live coals can be placed; (b) a metal container for roasting meats, etc., with an open side placed so that it is toward the fire; (c) a brick oven whose walls are preheated for cooking.

Dutch rush; *Equisetum hiemale*, the horsetail, or scouring rush.

Dutch treat; a dinner, luncheon, or entertainment at which each participant pays his own expenses. [Colloq.]

Dutch uncle; a person who bluntly and sternly lectures or scolds someone else. [Colloq.]

Dutch, *n.* 1. the language of the Netherlands.

2. German. [Slang.]

3. [*construed as pl.*] the people of the Netherlands.

4. [*construed as pl.*] the German people. [Slang.]

in Dutch; in difficulties or disfavor. [Slang.]

to beat the Dutch; to be very unusual or extraordinary; surpass what has hitherto been considered remarkable. [Slang.]

to go Dutch; to have every participant pay his own expenses. [Colloq.]

dutch, *v.t.* to treat by placing in hot sand, as a quill, to harden and clean.

Dutch'măn, *n.*; *pl.* **Dutch'men,** 1. a native or inhabitant of the Netherlands; Hollander.

2. a Dutch ship.

3. a German. [Slang.]

4. a German ship. [Nautical Slang.]

5. [d–] a wedge or block of wood used to fill a space made by a poorly constructed joint or by the removal of broken or defective material; also, a shim.

Dutch'măn's-breech'es (-brich'ez), *n. sing.* and *pl. Decentra cucullaria*, a low perennial whose flowers have two broad spurs like the legs of baggy breeches.

Dutch'măn's lau'dă·num, *Passiflora murucuja*, a plant of Jamaica, or the narcotic prepared from its flowers.

Dutch'măn's-pīpe, *Aristolochia sipho*, a hardy, woody vine with U-shaped flowers whose calyx resembles a tobacco pipe.

dū'tē·ous, *a.* respectful to those who have authority; obedient; dutiful.

dū'tē·ous·ly, *adv.* in a duteous manner.

dū'tē·ous·ness, *n.* quality of being duteous.

dū'ti·ȧ·ble, *a.* subject to the imposition of duty or tax; as, *dutiable* goods.

dū'tied, *a.* subjected to duties or taxes. [Rare.]

dū'ti·fụl, *a.* 1. performing one's duty or duties; obedient; as, a *dutiful* son or daughter; a *dutiful* subject.

2. expressive of respect or a sense of duty; respectful; required by duty; as, *dutiful* attentions.

Syn.—obedient, compliant, duteous, submissive, docile, respectful, deferential.

dū'ti·fụl·ly, *adv.* in a dutiful manner.

dū'ti·fụl·ness, *n.* dutiful state or quality.

dū'ty, *n.*; *pl.* **dū'ties,** [ME. *ducte, dewtie*; *due, dewe*, due, and *-te, -tie.*]

1. that which a person is bound, by any moral or legal obligation, to pay, do, or perform; conduct owed to one's parents, older people, etc.

2. the moral or legal obligation to follow a certain line of conduct, or to do a certain thing; as, the struggle between *duty* and desire.

3. obedience; submission; also, anything expressing deference or respect; homage; regards; devoir; as, she sends her *duty* in a letter. [Archaic.]

4. any service, labor, function, or office required of any particular person; also, the state of being occupied with such services; as, the *duties* of a motorman; on *duty*.

5. tax, toll, impost, or customs; excise; any sum of money required by government; especially, a sum to be paid on the importation, exportation, or consumption of goods.

6. the performance of a machine as measured by the output of work per unit of fuel. [Brit.]

7. the amount of work that a machine is meant to do; as, a heavy-*duty* tractor.

8. in agriculture, the amount of water needed for irrigation per acre per crop: also *duty of water.*

9. dues; compensation. [Obs.]

off duty; temporarily relieved from one's work.

on duty; at one's assigned work.

to do duty for; to be a substitute for; serve as.

Syn.—obligation, business, function, office.

dū'ty-free', *a.* and *adv.* with no payment of a duty or tax required.

dū·um'vĭr, *n.*; *pl.* **dū·um'vĭrs** or **dū·um'vi·rī,** [L., from *duo*, two, and *vir*, a man.] either of two magistrates in ancient Rome who held office jointly.

dū·um'vi·răl, *a.* pertaining to the duumvirs or duumvirate of Rome.

dū·um'vi·rāte, *n.* [L. *duumviratus*, the office of a *duumvir.*]

1. governmental position or authority held jointly by two men.

2. two men jointly holding such position or authority.

dū·um'vi·rī, *n.*, pl. of *duumvir.*

dụ·vet' (dụ-vā'), *n.* [Fr.] a bedquilt of down.

du̇'ve·tyn, du̇'ve·tyne, du̇'ve·tīne (-tēn), *n.* [from Fr. *duvet*, eider down.] a soft textile with a short, velvety nap, made of wool mixed with some other fiber, as mercerized cotton or spun silk.

dux, *n.*; *pl.* **dū'cēs,** [L.] 1. a leader: applied to the head of a class in certain schools in Scotland.

2. in a fugue, the principal theme or subject, as distinguished from the answer, or *comes.*

duy̆'kẽr·bok, *n.* same as *duiker, duikerbok.*

D valve (dē valv), a valve used on steam engines for opening and closing a passageway, as the cylinder port of a steam engine: so

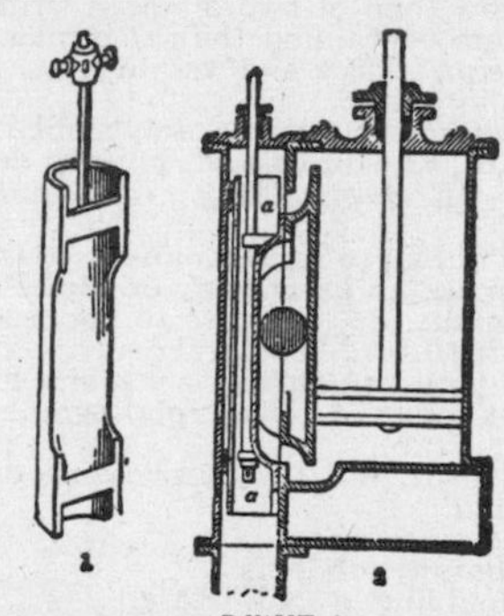

D VALVE
Fig. 1. D valve detached Fig. 2. *a, a,* D valve in place

called from its section resembling the letter **D**. The usual form of the **D** valve is shown in fig. 1, where it is seen detached, and at *a a*, fig. 2, which represents a section of a steam cylinder and nozzles.

dwāle, *n.* [ME. *dwale, dwole*; AS. *dwala, dwola*, error, delusion, heresy.]

1. in heraldry, a sable or black color. [Rare.]

2. the deadly nightshade, *Atropa belladonna.*

3. a sleeping potion. [Obs.]

dwălm, dwäm, *n.* and *v.i.* [AS. *dwolma*, confusion, a chasm.] swoon. [Dial.]

dwang, *n.* in carpentry, a strut between the timbers of a floor to strengthen them.

dwạrf, *n.* [ME. *dwarf, dwerf*; AS. *dweorg, dweorh*, a dwarf.]

1. any human being, animal, or plant which is much below the ordinary size of its species or kind.

2. in folklore, an ugly little being to whom magic powers are attributed.

dwạrf, *v.t.*; dwarfed (dwarft), *pt., pp.*; dwarfing, *ppr.* 1. to hinder from growing to the natural size; to make or keep small; to stunt the growth of.

2. to make smaller.
3. to cause to appear small or petty by contrast; as, the mountain *dwarfs* the foothills.

dwarf, *v.i.* to decrease in dimensions; to become or remain stunted or dwarfed.

dwarf, *a.* below the ordinary size of its species or kind; dwarfed; stunted; diminutive; as, a *dwarf* cedar.
dwarf alder; a small buckthorn tree with leaves like those of an alder.
dwarf chestnut; (a) the chinquapin, a small chestnut tree; (b) its edible nut.
dwarf elder; the danewort.
dwarf wall; in architecture, any wall lower than a single story of a building.

dwarf'ish, *a.* like a dwarf; below the normal stature or size; very small.

dwarf'ish·ly, *adv.* in a dwarfish manner.

dwarf'ish·ness, *n.* smallness of stature.

dwarf'ling, *n.* a very small dwarf.

dwarf'y, *a.* dwarfish. [Rare.]

dwell, *v.i.*; dwelt *or* dwelled, *pt., pp.*; dwelling, *ppr.* [ME. *dwellen*, to linger; AS. *dwellan*, to deceive, hinder, delay; *dwelian*, to err.]
1. to reside; to make one's home; to live; as, he *dwelt* in the valley.
2. to linger or tarry in thought or action; to expatiate: followed by *on* or *upon*; as, he *dwelt upon* her words; to *dwell upon* a note in singing.
3. to continue in any state or condition; as, to *dwell* in harmony.
4. to delay. [Obs.]
Syn.—continue, stay, reside, rest, sojourn, abide, live, exist.

dwell, *n.* in machinery, a momentary cessation of motion in some part of a machine, as in a printing press, when the platen remains stationary a short time in order to produce a better impression.

dwell'ēr, *n.* an inhabitant; a resident in a place.

dwell'ing, *n.* habitation; place of residence; abode; especially, a dwelling house.
Syn.—abode, domicile, habitation, residence.

dwell'ing house, the house, room, apartment, etc. that is one's residence.

dwell'ing plāce, a place of residence; a dwelling.

dwelt, *v.*, alternative past tense and past participle of *dwell.*

dwin'dle, *v.i.*; dwindled, *pt., pp.*; dwindling, *ppr.* [dim. of ME. *dwinen*; D. *dwijnen*, to languish, waste away; Ice. *dvina*; Sw. *tvina*, to languish, cease.]
1. to diminish; to become less; to shrink; to waste or consume away; as, the body *dwindles* in wasting diseases.
2. to degenerate; to sink; to fall away in excellence or usefulness; as, religious societies may *dwindle* into factious clubs.
Syn.—decrease, diminish, fall off, decline, lessen, shrink, waste.

dwin'dle, *v.t.* to diminish; to shrink.

dwin'dle, *n.* progressive decline or degeneration. [Obs.]

dwin'dle·ment, *n.* a decline. [Rare.]

dwīne, *v.i.*; dwined, *pt., pp.*; dwining, *ppr.* [ME. *dwinen*; AS. *dwinan*, to dwindle, pine away; Ice. *dvina*; Sw. *tvina*, to languish.] to languish; to pine away; to fade; to wither. [Archaic or Brit. Dial.]

Dy, in chemistry, dysprosium.

dȳ'ad, *a.* [LL. *dyas, dyadis*; Gr. *dyas, dyados*, two.] consisting of two.

dȳ'ad, *n.* 1. a pair of units considered as one.
2. in chemistry, a bivalent element, atom, or radical.
3. in morphology, a secondary organic unit derived from an aggregate of monads.
4. in biology, a double chromosome resulting from the division of a tetrad; half of a tetrad.

dȳ·ad'iç, *a.* 1. relating to the number two; having two parts or elements; binary.
2. in chemistry, relating to a dyad.
dyadic arithmetic; same as *binary arithmetic* under *binary*.

Dȳ'ak, *n.* [Malay *dayak*, savage.] a member of various related tribes of native inhabitants of the island of Borneo: written also *Dayak*.

dȳ'är·çhy, *n.*; *pl.* **dȳ'är·chieṣ,** 1. same as *diarchy*.
2. in India, the dual form of government established in 1919, which divided governmental functions between the British governor and the provincial governor.

Dȳ'as, *n.* [LL. *dyas*; Gr. *dyas*, two.] in geology, the Permian formation.

dȳ·as'tēr, *n.* same as *diaster*.

dyb'buk (-ăk), *n.* [Heb. *dibbūq*, from *dābhaq*, to cleave, hold to.] in Jewish folklore, the spirit of a dead person that enters the body of a living person and possesses it.

dȳe, *n.* [AS. *deag, deah*, a dye, color.]
1. a color, tint, or hue produced by or as by dyeing.
2. a coloring matter used for dyeing; the solution used in dyeing.
of deepest dye; of the worst or most villainous sort.

dȳe, *v.t.*; dyed, *pt., pp.*; dyeing, *ppr.* [ME. *dyen, deyen*; AS. *deagian, degian*, to dye, color; *deah, deag*, a dye, color.]
1. to stain; to color with or as with a dye.
2. to make (something) a specified color by or as by the use of dye.

dȳe, *v.i.* to absorb or give color to in dyeing; as, silk *dyes* well.

dȳe, *n.* and *v.i.* die. [Obs.]

dȳed'-in-the-wool' (dīd'), *a.* 1. having the yarn dyed before being woven.
2. thoroughgoing; unchangeable.

dȳe'house, *n.* a building in which dyeing is carried on.

dȳe'ing, *n.* the art or practice of coloring fabrics with dyes.

dȳ'ēr, *n.* one whose work or business is dying fabrics.

dȳ'ēr's-brọọm, *n.* a plant, *Genista tinctoria*.

dȳ'ēr's mọss, same as *archil*.

dȳ'ēr's-weed, *n.* 1. a plant of the mignonette family, *Reseda luteola*, which yields various colors according to the mordant used.
2. woad, *Isatis tinctoria*, used in dyeing blue.
3. *Genista tinctoria*, the dyer's-broom.

dȳe'stuff, *n.* any substance constituting or yielding a dye.

dȳe'weed, *n.* the woodwaxen, a small, shrubby plant yielding a yellow dye.

dȳe'wood, *n.* any wood yielding coloring matter for dyeing.

dȳ'ing, *v.* present participle of *die*.

dȳ'ing, *a.* 1. at the point of death; about to die.
2. drawing to a close; about to end; as, a *dying* social order.
3. of or connected with death or dying.

dȳ'ing, *n.* the act or process of ceasing to live or exist.

dȳ'ing·ly, *adv.* in a dying manner.

dȳke, *n.* and *v.t.* same as *dike*.

dȳ'nȧ-, a combining form meaning *power*, as in *dyna*meter: also, before a vowel, *dyn-*.

dȳ·naç·ti·nom'e·tēr, *n.* [Gr. *dynamis*, power, *aktis, aktinos*, a ray, and *metron*, a measure.] an instrument for measuring actinic power, and thus for determining the relative quickness of lenses.

dȳ'nȧ·grȧph, *n.* [Gr. *dynamis*, power, and *graphein*, to write.] an instrument carried in a railway train, which records the speed, condition of track, consumption of fuel, etc.

dȳ'nam-, same as *dynamo-*.

dȳ·nam'e·tēr, *n.* [Gr. *dynamis*, power, and *metron*, a measure.] an instrument for determining the magnifying power of telescopes.

dȳ·nȧ·met'riç, dȳ·nȧ·met'riç·ăl, *a.* pertaining to a dynameter.

dȳ·nam'iç, dȳ·nam'iç·ăl, *a.* [Gr. *dynamikos*, from *dynamis*, power, strength.]
1. pertaining to energy or power in motion; involving or causing energy, motion, action, or change: opposed to *static*.
2. of or relating to dynamics.
3. energetic; vigorous; forceful.
4. relating to or tending toward change.
5. in medicine, functional.
dynamic speaker; a form of loud-speaker operated by an electric coil and a magnetized iron bar.

dȳ·nam'iç, *n.* 1. a motive force.
2. dynamics.

dȳ·nam'iç·ăl·ly, *adv.* in a dynamic way.

dȳ·nam'içs, *n.* [from *dynamic*.]
1. that branch of physics which treats of the action of force on bodies in motion or at rest; kinetics, kinematics, and statics, collectively.
2. the motive and controlling forces, physical and moral, of any kind; also, the study of such forces.
3. that aspect of musical expression which relates to the power, or loudness, of tones.

dȳ'nȧ·miṣm, *n.* [Gr. *dynamis*, power, strength, and *-ism*.]
1. the theory that force or energy, rather than mass or motion, is the basic principle of all phenomena.
2. the quality of being energetic, vigorous, etc.; dynamic quality.

dȳ'nȧ·mist, *n.* one who believes in the theory of dynamism.

dȳ'nȧ·mī·tärd'', *n.* same as *dynamiter*.

dȳ'nȧ·mīte, *n.* [Gr. *dynamis*, power, and *-ite*.] an explosive consisting of an absorbent, as sodium nitrate and wood pulp, saturated with nitroglycerin.

dȳ'nȧ·mīte, *v.t.*; dynamited, *pt., pp.*; dynamiting, *ppr.* 1. to blow up or destroy by the use of dynamite.
2. to charge or prepare for destruction with dynamite.

dȳ'nȧ·mīte gun, an air gun for throwing shells filled with dynamite or other explosives.

dȳ'nȧ·mī·tēr, *n.* one who uses dynamite, especially in terrorist or anarchist activities.

dȳ'nȧ·mī·ting, *n.* the act of destroying by the use of dynamite, especially in terrorist or anarchist activities.

dȳ'nȧ·mī·tiṣm, *n.* the work done by dynamiters.

dȳ''nȧ·mi·zā'tion, *n.* the process of dynamizing medicines.

dȳ'nȧ·mīze, *v.t.*; dynamized, *pt., pp.*; dynamizing, *ppr.* [Gr. *dynamis*, power, and *-ize*.] to increase the strength of (medicines) by certain processes or manipulations, as by shaking, pulverizing, etc.

dȳ·nȧ·mō-, [from Gr. *dynamis*, power.] a combining form meaning *power, strength, energy*, as in *dynamo*graph, *dynamo*geny.

dȳ'nȧ·mō, *n.* [an abbrev. of *dynamo-electric* machine.] a device for converting mechanical energy into electrical energy, usually by expending the mechanical energy in producing a relative periodic motion of a conductor and a surrounding magnetic field.

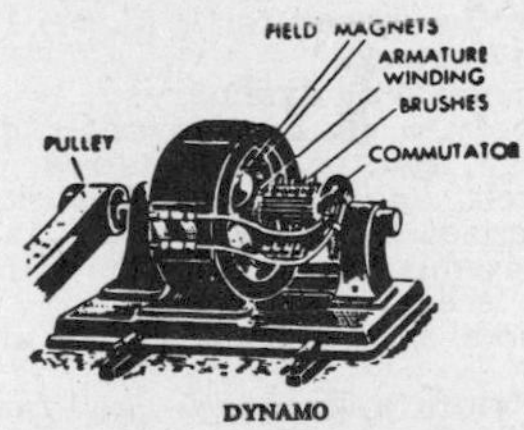

DYNAMO

dȳ'nȧ·mō-ē·leç'triç, *a.* [*dynamo-*, and Gr. *ēlektron*, amber.] of or pertaining to the two kinds of energy, mechanical and electrical, and to the conversion of the one into the other.

dȳ'nȧ·mō-ē·leç'tri·çăl, *a.* same as *dynamo-electric*.

dȳ·nȧ·moġ'e·ny, dȳ''nȧ·mō·ġen'e·sis, *n.* [*dynamo-*, and Gr. *geneia*, genesis, from *gignesthai*, to become, be born.] the exciting of the nerve centers to a higher degree of activity, as by the administration of a nerve tonic.

dȳ·nam'ō·grȧph, *n.* [*dynamo-*, and Gr. *graphein*, to write.] an instrument, variously constructed, for testing, measuring, comparing, and recording the amount of force exerted.

dȳ·nȧ·mom'e·tēr, *n.* [*dynamo-*, and Gr. *metron*, a measure.] an instrument for measuring force or energy.

dȳ''nȧ·mō·met'riç, dȳ''nȧ·mō·met'riç·ăl, *a.* of a dynamometer or dynamometry.

dȳ·nȧ·mom'e·try, *n.* the act or the process of measuring forces at work.

dȳ'nȧ·mō·tŏr, *n.* an electrical generator combining dynamo and motor, for transforming current of one voltage to that of another voltage.

dȳ'năst, *n.* [L. *dynastes*; Gr. *dynastēs*, a lord, ruler, from *dynasthai*, to be able, strong.] a ruler, especially a hereditary ruler.

dȳ·nas'tiç, dȳ·nas'tiç·ăl, *a.* [Gr. *dynastikos*, from *dynastēs*, a lord, ruler.] of or relating to a dynasty.

Dȳ·nas'ti·dae, *n.pl.* [Gr. *dynastēs*, a lord, ruler.] a family of beetles of large size, having hornlike processes: *Dynastes hercules* of South America is the largest known beetle of this family.

dȳ·nas'ti·dăn, *n.* one of the *Dynastidæ*.

dȳ'nas·ty, *n.*; *pl.* **dȳ'nas·tieṣ,** [Gr. *dynasteia*, lordship, rule, from *dynastēs*, a lord, ruler; *dynasthai*, to be able, strong.] a succession of rulers who belong to the same family; also, the period during which a certain family reigns.

dy̅′nȧ·tron, *n.* 1. a four-electrode vacuum tube in which the plate and grid potentials are such that the secondary discharge of electrons from the plate causes a decrease in the plate current simultaneously with an increase in the plate potential: it is often used as an oscillator.

2. a mesotron.

dy̅ne, *n.* [abbrev. of *dynam,* from Gr. *dynamis,* power.] the unit of force which in one second can alter the velocity by one centimeter per second of a mass of one gram: the unit of force in the C.G.S. (metric) system.

dy̅″ō·cae″trī·ȧ·çon″ta·hē′drŏn, *n.* [Gr. *dyo kai triakonta,* thirty-two, and *hedron,* a seat, base.] in geometry, a solid with thirty-two faces.

dy̅·oth′el·iṣm, *n.* [Gr. *dyo,* two, and *thelein,* to will.] the doctrine that the will of Christ was twofold, human and divine.

dy̅·oth′e·līte, *n.* an advocate of dyothelism.

dys-, [from Gr. *dys-,* hard, ill, bad.] a prefix meaning *hard, ill, bad, difficult,* as in *dys*genesis, *dys*nomy.

dys·aes·thē′si·ȧ, *n.* same as *dysesthesia.*

dys·är′thri·ȧ, *n.* [*dys-,* and Gr. *arthron,* a joint.] defective articulation in speaking, resulting from a disease of the central nervous system.

dys·är·thrō′sis, *n.* [*dys-,* and Gr. *arthron,* a joint.] disability or disease of a joint.

dys″çhrō·mȧ·top′si·ȧ, *n.* color blindness; difficulty in distinguishing colors.

dys·çrā′ṣi·ȧ (-zhi-ȧ), *n.* [Gr. *dyskrasia,* bad temperament; *dys-,* bad, and *krasis,* a mixture, from *kerannynai,* to mix.] a diseased condition of the body, marked by general ill health and debility: also written *dyscrasy.*

dys·çrā′siç, *a.* characterized by dyscrasia.

dys′çrȧ·sīte, *n.* [*dys-,* and Gr. *krasis,* a mixture.] a lustrous, grayish mineral made up of antimony and silver.

dys·çrā′sy, *n.* dyscrasia.

dys·en·ter′iç, dys·en·ter′iç·ăl, *a.* 1. pertaining to dysentery.

2. afflicted with dysentery.

dys′en·ter″y, *n.* [L. *dysenteria;* Gr. *dysenteria,* dysentery; *dys-,* bad, and *enteron,* pl. *entera,* the bowels.] any of various intestinal diseases characterized by inflammation, abdominal pain, toxemia, and diarrhea with bloody, mucous feces.

dys·es·thē′ṣi·ȧ, *n.* impairment of any of the senses.

dys·fuñç′tion, *n.* [from *dys-,* and *function.*] in medicine, abnormal, impaired, or incomplete functioning of an organ or part.

dys·ġē·nes′iç, *a.* affected by dysgenesis; relating or pertaining to dysgenesis.

dys·ġen′e·sis, *n.* [*dys-,* and Gr. *genesis,* birth.] lack of fertility; especially, a condition of only partial fertility, as in hybrids which do not breed among themselves, but may with the parent stock. The mule is an example.

dys·ġen′iç, *a.* [*dys-,* and Gr. *genos,* race, family.] in biology, causing deterioration of hereditary qualities: opposed to *eugenic.*

dys·ġen′içs, *n.pl.* [*construed as sing.*] 1. the study of dysgenic trends in a population: opposed to *eugenics.*

2. intermarriage of hereditarily defective individuals.

dys·i·drō′sis, *n.* state of abnormal secretion of sweat; also, a condition in which vesicles form on the palms of the hands and soles of the feet.

dys·lā′li·ȧ, *n.* difficulty in articulation of speech sounds.

dys·lex′i·ȧ, *n.* [*dys-,* and Gr. *lexis,* speech.] loss of power to grasp the meaning of that which is read.

dys·lō′ġi·ȧ, *n.* difficulty in speech caused by impairment in the faculty of reasoning.

dys·lō·ġis′tiç, *a.* [*dys-,* and Gr. *logos,* discourse.] not flattering; disparaging: opposed to *eulogistic.*

dys′lụ·īte, *n.* [*dys-,* and Gr. *lyein,* to loose, dissolve.] a variety of gahnite, or zinc spinel, containing iron and manganese.

dys″men·ŏr·rhē′ȧ (-rē′ȧ), *n.* [*dys-,* and Gr. *mēn,* a month, and *rhoia,* a flowing.] difficult menstruation, often accompanied by pain.

dys″me·rō·ġen′e·sis, *n.* [*dys-,* and Gr. *meros,* part, and *genesis,* birth.] in biology, generation marked by irregularity of constituent parts, differing in function, time of budding, etc.: opposed to *eumerogenesis.*

dys′mẽr·ō·mọrph, *n.* [*dys-,* and Gr. *meros,* part, and *morphē,* shape.] in biology, a form resulting from dysmerogenesis.

dys′nō·my, *n.* [Gr. *dysnomia,* lawlessness, a bad constitution; *dys-,* bad, and *nomos,* law.] bad legislation; the enactment of bad laws. [Rare.]

dys′ō·dīle, *n.* [Gr. *dysōdēs,* ill-smelling; *dys-,* bad, and *ozein,* to smell.] a hydrocarbon of a greenish or yellowish-gray color, in masses composed of thin layers.

dys′ō·dont, *n.* [*dys-,* and Gr. *odous, odontos,* a tooth.] in conchology, monomyarian.

dys·ō′pi·ȧ, dys·op′sy, *n.* [*dys-,* and Gr. *opsis,* view, sight.] dimness of sight.

dys·ō·rex′i·ȧ, *n.* [Gr. *dysorexia,* feebleness of appetite; *dys-,* bad, and *orexis,* appetite.] a lack of appetite.

dys′pȧ·thy, *n.* [Gr. *dyspatheia,* from *dyspathēs,* impatient of suffering, impassive; *dys-,* ill, and *pathos,* feeling.] lack of sympathy or passion.

dys·pep′si·ȧ, *n.* [L. *dyspepsia;* Gr. *dyspepsia,* indigestion, from *dyspeptos; dys-,* bad, and *peptos,* from *peptein,* to soften, cook, digest.] indigestion; impaired digestion.

dys·pep′sy, *n.* dyspepsia. [Now Dial. or Colloq.]

dys·pep′tiç, *n.* a person afflicted with dyspepsia.

dys·pep′tiç, *a.* 1. afflicted with indigestion; as, a *dyspeptic* person.

2. pertaining to or having the characteristics of dyspepsia; as, a *dyspeptic* complaint.

3. taking a morbid view of things; gloomy; grouchy; as, a *dyspeptic* writer.

dys·pep′tiç·ăl, *a.* same as *dyspeptic.*

dys·pep′ti·çăl·ly, *adv.* 1. in the manner of a dyspeptic.

2. with dyspepsia.

dys·phā′ġi·ȧ, dys·phā′ġy, *n.* [*dys-,* and Gr. *phagein,* to eat.] in medicine, difficulty in swallowing.

dys·phā′ṣi·ȧ, *n.* [*dys-,* and Gr. *phasis,* speech.] impairment of the ability to speak or, sometimes, to understand language, as the result of brain injury.

dys·phō′ni·ȧ, *n.* [Gr. *dysphonia; dys-,* bad, and *phōnē,* voice.] difficulty in speaking as a result of a malformation or disease of the organs of speech.

dys·phō′ri·ȧ, *n.* [Gr. *dysphoria; dys-,* hard, and *pherein,* to bear.] in psychology, a generalized feeling of ill-being; especially, an abnormal feeling of anxiety, discontent, physical discomfort, etc.

dysp·nē′ȧ, dysp·noe′ȧ, *n.* [L., from Gr. *dyspnoia; dys-,* hard, and *pnein,* to breathe.] difficult or painful breathing.

dysp·nē′ăl, dysp·noe′ăl, *a.* of dyspnea.

dysp·nē′iç, dysp·noe′iç, *a.* having or caused by dyspnea.

dysp·nō′iç, *a.* same as *dyspneic.*

dys·prō′si·um, *n.* [Mod. L., from Gr. *dysprositos,* difficult of access; *dys-,* hard, and *prositos,* approachable.] a chemical element of the rare-earth group: symbol, Dy; atomic weight, 162.50; atomic number, 66: it is one of the most magnetic of all known substances.

dys″te·lē·ol′ō·ġy, *n.* [coined by Haeckel, from *dys-,* and Gr. *telos,* end, purpose, and *-logia,* from *legein,* to speak.] that branch of physiology which treats of the apparent purposelessness observable in living organisms in connection with rudimentary organs.

dys·thym′iç, *a.* [Gr. *dysthymikos,* from *dysthymia,* despondency, despair; *dys-,* bad, and *thymos,* spirit, courage.] afflicted with chronic melancholy; depressed in spirits.

dys·tō′ci·ȧ (-shi-ȧ), *n.* [Gr. *dystokia; dys-,* hard, and *-tokia,* from *tiktein,* to bear.] painful childbirth; difficult parturition.

dys·tō′pi·ȧ, *n.* [*dys-,* and *utopia.*] a hypothetical place, state, or situation in which conditions and the quality of life are dreadful.

dys′trō·phy, *n.* [*dys-,* and Gr. *trophē,* from *trephein,* to nourish.] abnormal or defective nourishment; unnatural nutrition.

muscular dystrophy; a chronic, noncontagious disease characterized by a progressive wasting of the muscles.

dys·ū′ri·ȧ, dys′ū·ry, *n.* [*dys-,* and Gr. *ouron,* urine.] difficulty or pain in discharging the urine.

dys·ū′riç, *a.* relating to or suffering with dysuria.

dzē′ren, dzē′rŏn, *n.* [Mongolian name.] the Chinese antelope, a swift animal, *Procapra gutturosa,* inhabiting the dry, arid deserts of central Asia, Tibet, China, and southern Siberia.

E

E, e (ē), *n.; pl.* **E′ṣ, e′ṣ, Eṣ, eṣ** (ēz), 1. the fifth letter of the English alphabet: from the Greek *epsilon,* a borrowing from the Phoenician.

2. a sound of E or e.

3. a type or impression for E or e.

4. *a symbol for* the fifth in a sequence or group.

E, e (ē), *a.* 1. of E or e.

2. fifth in a sequence or group.

E, *n.* 1. an object shaped like E.

2. a Roman numeral for 250; with a superior bar (Ē), 250,000.

3. in chemistry, *the symbol for* erbium.

4. in education, (a) a grade fifth in quality, usually equivalent to *condition;* (b) sometimes, a grade first in quality, meaning excellent.

5. in music, (a) the third tone or note in the scale of C major, or the fifth in the scale of A minor; (b) a key, string, etc. producing this tone; (c) the scale having E as the keynote.

6. in physics, *the symbol for,* (a) the modulus of elasticity; (b) electromotive force.

E, *a.* shaped like E.

ē-, a prefix used instead of *ex-* before many consonants, meaning *out, out of, from, without,* as in *eject, egress.*

ēach, *a.* [ME. *eche, ech, ælc, elc;* AS. *ælc; a,* always, and *gelic,* like; G. *jeglich,* each.] every one of two or more considered or treated distinctly from the rest; as, *each* person was called upon to speak.

ēach, *pron.* every one of two or more considered individually; each one; as, *each* did his share; *each* of them heard the remark.

each other; each the other; as, they despise *each other,* that is, *each* despises the *other.*

ēach′where (-hwār), *adv.* everywhere. [Obs.]

ēad′ish, *n.* eddish. [Obs.]

ēa′gẽr, *a.* [ME. *eger, egre;* OFr. *egre, aigre;* L. *acer, acris,* sharp, keen.]

1. keenly desiring; wanting very much; impatient or anxious; ardent; as, the soldiers were *eager* to engage the enemy.

2. sharp; sour; acid. [Obs.]

3. sharp; keen; biting; severe. [Archaic.]

4. brittle; inflexible; not ductile. [Obs.]

Syn.—earnest, fervent, zealous, enthusiastic, vehement, intense, fervid.

ēa′gẽr, *n.* same as *eagre.*

ēa′gẽr·ly, *adv.* in an eager manner; zealously.
ēa′gẽr·ness, *n.* 1. the quality or state of being eager.
2. tartness; sourness. [Obs.]
Syn.—fervor, zeal, ardor, impetuosity, enthusiasm, impatience.
ēa′gle (ē′gl), *n.* [ME. *egle*; OFr. *egle, aigle*; Pr. *aigla*; Sp. *aguila*; It. *aquila*; L. *aquila*, an eagle; f. of *aquilus*, dark-colored, brown.]
1. any of a number of large, strong, flesh-eating birds of prey belonging to the falcon family, noted for their sharp vision and powerful wings.

GOLDEN EAGLE (*Aquila chrysaëtos*)

2. a representation of the eagle, used as a symbol or emblem of a nation, etc.; especially, (a) the military standard of the Roman Empire; (b) the national emblem of the United States; (c) the military insigne of a colonel in the United States armed forces (captain in the United States Navy).
3. a former gold coin of the United States, of the value of ten dollars.
4. [E–] the northern constellation Aquila.
5. a lectern, the design of which is an eagle with outstretched wings supporting the desk on which the book rests.
6. in golf, a score of two strokes under par on a hole with a par of more than three.
ēa′gle-eȳed (-īd), *a.* sharp-sighted as an eagle.
ēa′gle hawk, a South American hawk of the family *Accipitridae.*
ēa′gle owl, the great horned owl of Europe, *Bubo bubo*, or the American *Bubo virginianus.*
ēa′gle rāy, *Myliobatis goodei*, a species of ray; any ray of the family *Myliobatidæ.*
ēa′gless, *n.* a female eagle. [Rare.]
ēa′gle·stōne, *n.* a variety of clay ironstone occurring in hollow nodules about the size of a walnut: so called from the ancient notion that the eagle transported them to her nest to facilitate the laying of her eggs.
ēa′glet, *n.* a young eagle.
ēa′gle vul′tūre, an eaglelike vulture of western Africa, *Gypohierax angolensis.*
ēa′gle·wood, *n.* same as *agallochum.*
ēa′gre (-gẽr), *n.* [Brit. eastern dial. form, prob. with loss of *h-* and originally ME. lowered and lengthened vowel, for western form represented by Early Mod. Eng. *hyger, higre, higer.*] a tidal wave in an estuary: also called *bore.*
eạl′dŏr·măn, eạl′dẽr·măn (ọl′), *n.* an alderman (especially sense 1). [Obs.]
Ēameṣ chāir, [after C. *Eames*, its U.S. designer.] an upholstered swivel chair on rubber mounts.
-ē′ăn, [from L. *-ae-, -e-, -i-* and Gr. *-ai-, -u-* (stem endings of nouns and adjectives); and *-an.*] a suffix meaning *of, belonging to, like,* used to form adjectives and nouns, as Euro*pean*, Aeg*ean*.
ēan, *v.t.* and *v.i.* [AS. *eanian*, to be pregnant.] to yean. [Obs.]
ēan′ling, *n.* a young lamb or kid. [Obs.]
ēar, *n.* [AS. *ear, eare*; D. *oor*; Sw. *öra*; Dan. *ore*; G. *ohr*; L. *auris*, an ear.]
1. the part of the body specialized for the perception of sound; organ of hearing: the human ear consists of (a) the external ear (pinna and external auditory canal); (b) the inner ear (labyrinth), containing the cochlea

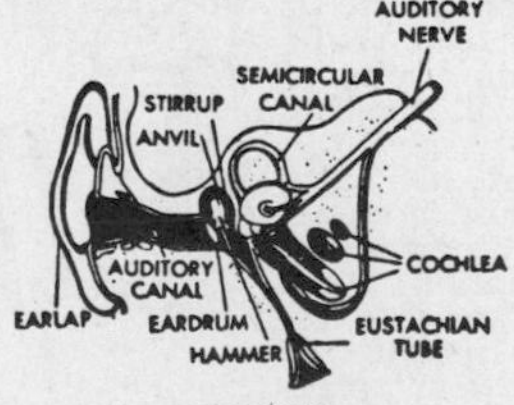

HUMAN EAR

and semicircular canals; and (c) the middle ear (tympanum), a cavity connected to the external ear by the tympanic membrane, to the pharynx by the Eustachian tube, and to the inner ear by a series of three small bones called the *hammer, anvil,* and *stirrup.*
2. the visible, external part of the ear.
3. the sense of hearing; also, the power of distinguishing sounds and judging of harmony; the power of perception of the differences of pitch, rhythm, etc.; as, she has a good *ear* for music.
4. anything resembling an ear; a projecting part from the side of anything; a handle; as, the *ears* of a dish or jug.
5. a favorable hearing; attention; heed; regard.
Give every man thine *ear*. —Shak.
6. in architecture, a crossette.
7. in ornithology, (a) the feathers which cover the external ear passage; (b) a corniplume.
8. in journalism, a small box in either upper corner of the front page of a newspaper, containing weather reports, advertising, etc.
all ears; listening with great attention or eagerness.
to give ear to; to heed; to pay attention to.
to have the ear of; to be in a favorable position to talk to and influence.
to set by the ears; to make strife between; to cause to quarrel.
up to the ears; deeply involved; overwhelmed; as, *up to the ears* in debt.
ēar, *v.t.* to listen to; to hear. [Obs.]
ēar, *v.t.* [ME. *erien*; AS. *erian.*] to plow. [Archaic.]
ēar, *n.* a spike or head of corn or other grain; that part of a cereal plant which bears the seed.
ēar, *v.i.* to sprout ears; to form ears.
ēar′á·ble, *a.* that can be tilled; arable. [Obs.]
ēar′āçhe, *n.* pain in the (middle or inner) ear.
ēar′çoç″kle, *n.* a disease in wheat caused by the presence in the grain of worms belonging to the species *Anguina tritici.*
ēar çonçh, the external ear; the pinna.
ēar′drop, *n.* an ornamental pendant for the ear; an earring.
ēar drops, any of various liquid medicines to be inserted in the ear in drops.
ēar′drum, *n.* in anatomy, the tympanum; also, the tympanic membrane, a thin membrane that separates the middle ear from the external ear and vibrates when struck by sound waves.
ēared, *a.* 1. having ears; having earlike parts or appendages: often used in combination, as, long-*eared.*
2. in biology, auriculate.
ēar′flaps, *n.pl.* two pieces of cloth or fur attached to a cap and turned down to cover the ears in cold weather.
ēar′fụl, *n.* 1. enough or too much of what is heard; as, I got an *earful* of that.
2. important or startling news or gossip.
3. a scolding.
ēar′ing, *n.* in nautical usage, a small rope attached to the cringle of a sail, by which it is bent or reefed; also, a small rope for attaching the upper corner of a sail to the yard or gaff.
ēar′ing, *n.* a plowing of land. [Archaic.]
ēar′ing, *n.* the forming of ears, as in corn.
ẽarl, *n.* [AS. *eorl*, a nobleman of high rank.] a British nobleman, the third in rank, being next below a marquis, and next above a viscount: the wife or widow of an earl is called a *countess.*
Earl Marshal; an officer in Great Britain, the head of the Heralds' College, who has various ceremonial duties.
ēar′lap, *n.* 1. an earflap.
2. the ear lobe.
3. the external ear.
ẽarl′dŏm, *n.* [ME. *erldom*; AS. *eorldom*; *eorl*, earl, and *-dom.*] the jurisdiction, rank, or title of an earl.
ẽarl′duck, *n.* the red-breasted merganser.
ēar′less, *a.* having no ears.
ēar′let, *n.* 1. a small ear.
2. an earring.
ẽar′li·ness, *n.* the state or quality of being early.
ẽarl′ship, *n.* the rank or title of an earl.
ẽar′ly, *adv.* and *a.*; *comp.* earlier; *superl.* earliest. [ME. *erli*; rare AS. *ærlice*, adv., from *ær*, before, and *-lice*, adv. suffix *-ly.*]
1. in advance of some usual or expected time; before the customary time; as, *early* fruit; an *early* harvest; an *early* riser.
2. first; in or near the beginning of a period of time or of some sequence of actions, events, or things; as, an *early* stage of existence; one of his *early* writings.
3. soon to take place; in the near future; as, I shall take an *early* opportunity to inquire into the matter.
4. in the far distant past; in ancient or remote times.
early on; at an early stage; near the beginning.
ẽar′ly bĩrd, a person who arrives early or gets up early in the morning. [Colloq.]
ẽar′ly çor′ăl·rọọt, a small orchid, *Corallorhiza trifida*, found in the eastern U. S.
Ẽar′ly Mod′ẽrn Eng′lish, the English language as spoken and written from about 1450 to about 1750: as compared to Middle English, it is characterized by a sweeping change in the vowel system, whereby the long high vowels were diphthongized, the long mid and low vowels raised, and the short vowels lowered, and by a great increase in vocabulary, based on borrowings from Latin, Greek, and the Romance languages.
ẽar′ly pär′snip, the golden meadow parsnip.
ẽar′ly tril′lĭ·um, the wake-robin.
ēar′märk, *n.* 1. a mark on the ear of a domestic animal by which ownership is made known.
2. any mark for identification; a characteristic; a sign.
ēar′märk, *v.t.* 1. to mark the ears of (livestock) for identification.
2. to set a distinctive or informative mark upon; identify.
3. to set aside or reserve for a special purpose; as, *earmark* these supplies for the army.
ēar-mīnd′ed, *a.* tending to learn and remember in terms of auditory images.
ēar′muffs, *n.pl.* a pair of cloth or fur coverings for the ears, worn in cold weather.
ẽarn, ẽrn, ẽrne, *n.* [AS. *earn*, eagle.] an eagle.
ẽarn, *v.t.*; earned, *pt., pp.*; earning, *ppr.* [ME. *ernen, ernien, earnien*; AS. *earnian*, to earn, merit.]
1. to receive (salary, wages, etc.) for one's labor or service.
2. to get as a result of merit; as, his remarks *earned* him the praise of everyone.
3. to do enough to deserve; get as a consequence; as, she *earned* that spanking.
4. to gain (interest, etc.) as profit.
Syn.—merit, deserve, acquire, gain, attain.
ẽarn, *v.i.* to yearn; also, to grieve; to sorrow. [Obs.]
ẽarn, *v.i.* to curdle, as milk. [Brit. Dial.]
ẽarned run av′ẽr·āġe, in baseball, the average number of earned runs allowed for each nine innings pitched.
ẽar′nest, *a.* [ME. *ernest, eornest*; AS. *eornest, eornost*; D. *ernst*; G. *ernst*, zeal, vigor.]
1. serious and intense; not joking or playful; zealous and sincere; deeply convinced; as, *earnest* in prayer; an *earnest* appeal.
2. intent; fixed.
Their *earnest* eyes were fixed. —Milton.
3. serious; important; not trivial.
Syn.—sincere, eager, urgent, zealous, importunate, fervent, warm.
ẽar′nest, *n.* seriousness; serious intention or conviction; as, it may turn from jest to *earnest.*
in earnest; earnestly; with determination.
ẽar′nest, *v.t.* to be earnest with; to use in earnest. [Obs.]
ẽar′nest, *n.* [W. *ernes*, an earnest, pledge, from *ern*, a pledge; related to Gael. *earlas*, an earnest.]
1. anything which gives assurance, pledge, promise, or indication of what is to follow; token.
2. part of the price of the commodity bargained for, paid by the buyer to the seller to bind the transaction: in full, *earnest money.*
ẽar′nest·fụl, *a.* earnest. [Obs.]
ẽar′nest·ly, *adv.* [ME. *ernestly*; AS. *eornostlice*; *eornost*, earnest, and *lice*, like.] in an earnest manner.
ẽar′nest mŏn′ey, money paid as earnest to bind a bargain or ratify a sale.
ẽar′nest·ness, *n.* the quality or condition of being earnest.
ẽarn′fụl, *a.* [a variant of *yearnful.*] full of anxiety. [Obs.]
ẽarn′ing, *n.* rennet. [Brit. Dial.]
ẽarn′ingṣ, *n.pl.* 1. money gained by labor, services, or performance; wages, salary, etc.
2. money made by an investment or an enterprise; profit.
ēar′phōne, *n.* a receiver for radio, telephone, etc., usually part of a headset; headphone.
ēar′pick, *n.* an instrument for cleansing the ear.
ēar piẽr′cẽr, the earwig.
ēar′rēach, *n.* hearing distance; earshot.
ēar′ring, *n.* an ornament, sometimes provided with a pendant, worn at the ear either by

means of a ring passing through a hole pierced in the lobe or fastened with a screw or clip.

ēar shell, 1. an abalone, a kind of mollusk.
2. its shell, shaped somewhat like the human ear.

ēar'shot, *n.* reach of the ear; especially, the distance at which the unaided human voice may be heard.

ēar'-split"ting, *a.* so loud as to hurt the ears; deafening.

ēarst, *adv.* erst. [Obs.]

ēar stōne, a small, calcareous mass formed in the inner ear of a vertebrate; otolith.

ēarth, *n.* [ME. *erthe, eorthe*; AS. *eorthe*; D. *erde*; O.H.G. *erdha, erda*; Ice. *jordh*; Dan. *jord*; Goth. *airtha*, the earth.]
1. the planet that we live on; terresrial globe: it is the fifth largest planet of the solar system and the third in distance from the sun: diameter, 7,918 mi.; symbol, ⊕.
2. this world, as distinguished from heaven and hell.
3. the land of the earth, as distinguished from air and water; the ground.
4. the soft material of which part of the surface of the globe consists; soil, as distinguished from rock; especially, soil capable of being cultivated.
5. a distinct part of the globe; a country; a region. [Poetic.]
This English *earth*. —Shak.
6. the inhabitants of the earth.
The whole *earth* was of one language. —Gen. xi. 1.
7. (a) the substance of the human body; (b) the human body; (c) human concerns; worldly matters. [Poetic.]
8. the hole of a burrowing animal; a lair.
9. in chemistry, any one of the metallic oxides, formerly classed as elements, which are reduced with difficulty, as baryta, strontia, magnesia, alumina, zirconia, etc.
10. in electricity, the ground forming part of an electric circuit.
Cologne earth; a variety of lignite, or partially fossilized wood, used as a pigment.
down to earth; practical; realistic.
to come back (or *down*) *to earth*; to stop being impractical; return to reality.
to move heaven and earth; to make every effort.
to run to earth; (a) to hunt down; (b) to find by search.

ēarth, *v.t.*; earthed (ẽrtht), *pt., pp.*; earthing, *ppr.* 1. to chase (an animal) into a hole or burrow in the ground.
The fox is *earthed*. —Dryden.
2. to cover (*up*) with earth; to bury.
We *earthed* her in the shades.—B. Jonson.
3. in electricity, to connect with the earth; to ground. [Brit.]

ēarth, *v.i.* to hide in a burrow: said of a fox, etc.

ēarth, *n.* a plowing. [Obs.]

ēarth'bag, *n.* in fortification, a bag filled with earth, used to repair defenses.

ēarth ball, a species of truffle, *Tuber cibarium.*

ēarth bat'tēr·y, a voltaic battery having its elements sunk in the earth to receive its moisture.

ēarth'bōard, *n.* the board of a plow that turns over the earth; the moldboard.

ēarth'born, *a.* 1. born on or of the earth; springing originally from the earth; hence, human; mortal.
2. relating to or arising from earthly objects.
All *earthborn* cares are wrong.—Goldsmith.

ēarth'-bound, ēarth'bound, *a.* 1. confined to or by the earth and earthly things.
2. headed for the earth.

ēarth'bred, *a.* low; abject; groveling.

ēarth chest'nut, the earthnut.

ēarth crab, a mole cricket.

ēarth cur'rent, an electric current flowing through the earth, caused by a difference of potential.

ēarth'din, *n.* an earthquake. [Obs.]

ēarth'drāke, *n.* [AS. *eorth-draca*; *eorthe*, earth, and *draca*, a dragon.] in Anglo-Saxon mythology, a dragon.

ēarth'en, *a.* 1. made of earth; also, made of baked clay; as, an *earthen* vessel.
2. earthly.

ēarth'en-heärt"ed, *a.* having a selfish heart; sordid.

ēarth'en·wāre, *n.* containers, tableware, etc. made of baked clay; also, baked clay.

ēarth'en·wāre, *a.* made of earthenware.

ēarth'fall, *n.* a landslide.

ēarth flax, a fine variety of asbestos, the long, flexible, parallel filaments of which are so delicate as to resemble flax.

ēarth flēa, ēarth flȳ, the chigoe.

ēarth hog, the aardvark: called also *earth pig.*

ēarth house, any one of the underground buildings, known as "Picts' houses," found throughout Scotland.

ēarth'i·ness, *n.* the quality or state of being earthy.

ēarth'līght (-līt), *n.* earthshine.

ēarth'li·ness, *n.* the quality or state of being earthly.

ēarth'ling, *n.* 1. an inhabitant of the earth; a human being.
2. a worldly person; worldling.

ēarth'ly, *a.* 1. pertaining to the earth or to this world; pertaining to the present state of existence; as, *earthly* objects; *earthly* residence.
2. belonging to the earth or world; carnal: opposed to *spiritual* or *heavenly.*
3. made of earth; earthy. [Obs.]
4. possible; conceivable.
What *earthly* benefit can be the result? —Pope.
Syn.—worldly, mundane, groveling, carnal, vile, mean, sordid, corrupt.

ēarth'ly-mīnd"ed, *a.* having a mind devoted to earthly things.

ēarth'mad, *n.* a kind of worm or grub. [Obs.]

ēarth moss, any moss of the genus *Phascum.*

ēarth mŏth'ēr, [*also* E- M-] 1. the planet earth regarded, as in mythology, as the source of all life.
2. any buxom, sensuous woman who is inclined to mother others.

ēarth'mŏv·ēr, *n.* a bulldozer or other large machine for excavating or moving large quantities of earth.

ēarth'nut, *n.* 1. the root, tuber, or underground pod of various plants, as the peanut.
2. an edible underground fungus; truffle.

ēarth pig, same as *earth hog.*

ēarth pitch, a kind of asphalt.

ēarth'quāke (-kwāk), *n.* a quaking, vibratory, or undulating movement of a portion of the earth's crust, produced by underground volcanic forces or by breaking and shifting of rock beneath the surface: earthquakes usually occur in regions where active volcanoes exist: also used figuratively.

ēarth'shāk·ing, *a.* profound or basic in significance, effect, or influence; momentous.

ēarth'shīne, *n.* in astronomy, a faint light visible on the part of the moon not illuminated by the sun, due to the light which the earth reflects on the moon. It is most conspicuous when the illuminated part of the disk is at its smallest, soon after new moon.

ēarth smōke, *Fumaria officinalis*, the plant fumitory.

ēarth'stär, *n.* a fungus of the genus *Geaster*, whose outer layer splits into a starlike form.

ēarth tā'ble, in architecture, a course of stones resting immediately upon the foundation: called also *ground table* or *grass table.*

ēarth'tŏngue (tung), *n.* any one of certain club-shaped fungi of the genus *Geoglossum*, found in lawns and grassy pastures.

ēarth'wȧrd, ēarth'wȧrds, *adv.* toward the earth.

ēarth'wȧrd, *a.* [*earth*, and *-ward.*] toward the earth.

ēarth'wolf (-wulf), *n.* the aardwolf.

ēarth'wŏrk, *n.* 1. in engineering, any operation in which earth has to be removed or filled in, as in cuttings, embankments, etc.
2. in fortification, any construction for defense or attack formed largely of piled-up earth.
3. any construction resembling a military earthwork.

ēarth'wŏrm, *n.* 1. any of various round, segmented, burrowing worms belonging to the class *Oligochaeta*, especially of the genus *Lumbricus*, of which *Lumbricus terrestris* is the best known species.
2. figuratively, a mean, sordid wretch.

ēarth'y, *a.* 1. of or pertaining to earth; consisting of earth; partaking of the nature of earth; terrene; as, *earthy* matter.
2. inhabiting the earth; terrestrial; of this world.
3. (a) gross; not refined; coarse; (b) simple and natural; hearty and unashamed; as, *earthy* humor.
4. in mineralogy, without luster, or dull and roughish to the touch.

ēar trump'et, a trumpet-shaped tube formerly used as a hearing aid by the partially deaf: it funneled the sound into the small end, which was held to the ear.

ēar'wax, *n.* cerumen; the yellowish, waxlike secretion found in the canal of the outer ear.

ēar'wig, *n.* [AS. *eárwicga*; *eáre*, ear, and *wicga*, beetle, worm.]
1. any of a group of insects with thick, short forewings, many-jointed feelers, and a pincerlike part at the tail end, belonging to certain genera of the order *Dermaptera*, especially to the genus *Forficula*, of which *Forficula auricularis* is the commonest species: so called from the baseless notion that these insects creep into a person's ear.
2. in the United States, any of a number of related, small centipedes, especially of the genus *Geophilus.*
3. one who whispers gossip; a prying informer. [Obs.]

ēar'wig, *v.t.*; earwigged, *pt., pp.*; earwigging, *ppr.* to try to influence by whispering gossip or insinuations.

ēar'wit"ness, *n.* one who is able to give testimony to a fact from his own hearing.

ēar'wŏrm, *n.* same as *bollworm.*

ēase, *n.* [ME. *ese, eise*; OFr. *aise, ayse, aize*; It. *agio*, ease.]
1. contentment or comfort, whether of body or mind; freedom from pain, trouble, or annoyance of any kind; tranquillity.
2. facility; readiness; adroitness; freedom from difficulty or great labor.
The mob of gentlemen who wrote with *ease.* —Pope.
3. freedom from constraint, awkwardness, or formality; poise; unaffectedness; as, *ease* of behavior.
4. freedom from poverty; state of being financially comfortable; affluence.
5. rest; leisure; relaxation.
6. satisfaction; relief; accommodation; entertainment. [Obs.]
at ease; (a) in an undisturbed state; free from pain or anxiety; (b) in military usage, in a relaxed position but maintaining attention and silence; also, a command to take such a position.
chapel of ease; see under *chapel.*
to take one's ease; to relax and make oneself comfortable.
Syn.—rest, comfort, tranquillity, restfulness, satisfaction, facility, readiness, easiness.

ēase, *v.t.*; eased, *pt., pp.*; easing, *ppr.* 1. to free from labor or from anything that pains or annoys the body or mind; to give relief to (often with *of*); as, the traveler was *eased of* his burden.
2. to mitigate; to alleviate; to assuage; to allay; to abate or remove in part, as any burden, pain, grief, anxiety, or disturbance.
3. to relieve or release from tension, weight, pressure, or restraint; to make looser (often with *away, down, up,* or *off*); as, to *ease* a rope, sail, etc.
4. to make less difficult; to facilitate.
5. to fit or move by careful shifting, relaxing, etc.; as, they *eased* the piano into place.
to ease the helm (or *rudder*); to put the helm a little to midships in order to relieve the strain on the rudder.
Syn.—relieve, mitigate, alleviate, quiet, tranquilize, pacify, allay, disburden.

ēase, *v.i.* 1. to move or be moved by careful shifting, relaxing, etc.
2. to lessen in tension, speed, pain, etc.

ēase'ful, *a.* affording ease; promoting rest; quiet; peaceful.

ēase'ful·ly, *adv.* with ease or quiet.

ēase'ful·ness, *n.* the state or quality of being easeful.

ēa'sel, *n.* [D. *ezel*; G. *esel*, an ass, a wooden frame, easel.] a stand or frame slightly inclined and having three legs, used to support a canvas, blackboard, etc. on which an artist is working, or to hold a picture on display.

EASEL

ēase'less, *a.* wanting ease.

ēase'ment, *n.* 1. an easing or being eased.
2. convenience; accommodation; that which gives ease, relief, or assistance.
3. in law, any privilege or right which one man has in the land of another, without remuneration or profit, as a right of way, access to water, air, etc.

ēas'i·ly, *adv.* 1. in an easy manner; with ease; without much effort; as, this task may be *easily* performed; that event might have been *easily* foreseen.

2. without pain, anxiety, or disturbance; in tranquillity; as, to pass life well and *easily*.

3. readily; without reluctance.

4. smoothly; quietly; gently; without violent shaking or jolting; as, a carriage moves *easily*.

5. without a doubt; by far; as, she is *easily* the best dancer.

6. very likely; as, the train may *easily* be late.

ēaṣ'i·ness, *n.* 1. the state of being easy to do or get.

2. careless indifference; nonchalance.

3. freedom from stiffness, constraint, effort, or formality; poise; ease of manner; as, *easiness* of style.

ēast, *n.* [ME. *east, æst,* east; AS. *east,* D. *oost, oosten;* O.H.G. *ostan;* G. *ost, osten;* Dan. *ost, osten;* Ice. *austr;* L. *aurora,* for *ausosa,* dawn, the east; Gr. *ēōs, heōs.*]

1. the direction in which sunrise occurs; that point of the horizon lying on the right hand of one facing north.

2. the point of the compass at 90°, in a direction at right angles to that of north and south, and directly opposite west.

3. a region or district in or toward this direction.

4. [E–] the eastern parts of the earth, especially Asia and the nearby islands; the Orient.

down East; (a) New England, especially Maine; (b) in, to, or toward this region. [Colloq.]

the East; the eastern part of the United States; specifically, (a) the part east of the Allegheny Mountains, from Maine through Maryland; (b) the part east of the Mississippi and north of the Ohio.

ēast, *a.* 1. toward, to, of, in, or facing the east; as, the *east* gate; the *east* border; the *east* side.

2. from the east; as, the *east* wind.

3. [E–] designating the eastern part of a continent, country, etc.; as, *East* Africa, *East* Ohio.

4. in ecclesiastical usage, situated in the direction of the altar of a church, looking from the nave.

ēast, *adv.* in an easterly direction; in or toward the east; eastward; as, to steer *east.*

ēast, *v.i.* to move in the direction of the east; to veer toward the east; to orient.

ēast'ȧ·bout, *adv.* in the direction of the east.

ēast'bound', *a.* bound east; going eastward.

ēast bȳ north, the direction, or the point on a mariner's compass, halfway between due east and east-northeast; 11°15′ north of due east.

ēast bȳ south, the direction, or the point on a mariner's compass, halfway between due east and east-southeast; 11°15′ south of due east.

ēast'ẽr, *v.i.* in nautical usage, to veer or shift to the east, as the wind. [Rare.]

Ēas'tẽr, *n.* [ME. *ester, æster;* AS. *eástre, eástran,* a paschal feast, originally a pagan festival in honor of the Goddess of Spring, *Eástre,* held in April.]

1. an annual Christian festival in commemoration of the resurrection of Jesus, held on the first Sunday after the date of the first full moon that occurs on or after March 21.

2. the Sunday on which Easter is held: often called *Easter Sunday.*

Ēas'tẽr dūçe̤ or **of'fẽr·ings̤,** in the Church of England, money paid to the parochial clergy by the parishioners at Easter.

Ēas'tẽr egg, a colored egg or an egg-shaped piece of candy, etc., used as an Easter gift or ornament.

Ēas'tẽr flow'ẽr, *Euphorbia* or *Poinsettia pulcherrima,* a Brazilian shrub of the spurge family, the flowers of which are surrounded by large, brilliant bracts.

Ēas'tẽr gī'ănt, *Polygonum biotorta,* the bistort.

ēast'ẽr·ling, *n.* a native of some country eastward of another; formerly, in England, a trader from the Baltic. [Archaic.]

ēast'ẽr·ly, *a.* 1. coming from the eastward; as, an *easterly* wind.

2. in, of, or toward the east.

ēast'ẽr·ly, *adv.* 1. from the east; as, the wind blew *easterly.*

2. toward the east.

ēast'ẽrn, *a.* [ME. *esterne;* AS. *eastern.*]

1. from the east; as, an *eastern* wind.

2. in, of, toward, or facing the east.

3. [E–] of or characteristic of the East.

ēast'ẽrn, *n.* an easterner.

Ēast'ẽrn Chŭrch, 1. originally, the Christian Church in the Eastern Roman Empire, consisting of the four patriarchates in eastern Europe, western Asia, and Egypt, headed by the Bishops of Constantinople, Alexandria, Antioch, and Jerusalem: distinguished from the *Western Church,* the patriarchate in western Europe and North Africa, headed by the Bishop of Rome.

2. the Orthodox Eastern Church.

3. all Catholics who practice the Eastern rite but acknowledge the supreme authority of the Pope; Uniats.

Ēast'ẽrn Em'pīre, the Byzantine Empire.

ēast'ẽrn·ẽr, *n.* 1. a native or inhabitant of the east.

2. [E–] a native or inhabitant of the eastern part of the United States.

Ēast'ẽrn Hem'i·sphēre, that half of the earth which includes Europe, Africa, Asia, and Australia.

ēast'ẽrn·mōst, *a.* farthest to the east; most eastern.

Ēast'ẽrn Rō'măn Em'pīre, the empire formed by the division of the Roman Empire at the death of Theodosius I in 395 A.D.: it was ended by the Turkish conquest of Constantinople, its capital, in 1453.

Ēast'ẽrn Shōre, the eastern shore of Chesapeake Bay, especially the part in Maryland.

Ēast'ẽrn Stan'dărd Tīme, one of the four standard times in the United States, corresponding to the mean local time of the 75th meridian west of Greenwich, England: it is five hours behind Greenwich time.

Ēas'tẽr·tīde, [*Easter,* and *tide* (time).] the period after Easter, extending in various churches to Ascension Day, Whitsunday, or Trinity Sunday.

Ēast In'di·ȧ Cŏm'pȧ·ny, any of several European companies for exploiting trade with the East Indies, having special trading rights and government support; especially, such an English company, first chartered in 1600 and dissolved in 1874.

Ēast In'di·ȧ·măn, a ship engaged in the East India trade.

Ēast In'di·ăn, 1. pertaining to or belonging to the East Indies, its people, etc.

2. a native or inhabitant of the East Indies.

ēast'ing, *n.* 1. in surveying and in sailing, the distance eastward from a given meridian; the distance gained by a ship on an easterly course.

2. a turning, or veering, to the east.

3. an easterly direction.

ēast'-nŏrth·ēast', *n.* the direction, or the point on a mariner's compass, halfway between due east and northeast; 22°30′ north of due east.

ēast'-nŏrth·ēast', *adv.* and *a.* 1. in or toward the east-northeast.

2. from this direction; as, an *east-northeast* wind.

ēast'-south·ēast', *n.* the direction, or the point on a mariner's compass, halfway between due east and southeast; 22°30′ south of due east.

ēast'-south·ēast', *adv.* and *a.* 1. in or toward the east-southeast.

2. from this direction; as, an *east-southeast* wind.

ēast'wărd, ēast'wărds̤, *adv.* toward the east; in the direction of east.

ēast'wărd, *a.* having a direction toward the east.

ēast'wărd, *n.* an eastward direction, point, or region.

ēast'wărd·ly, *adv.* and *a.* 1. toward the east.

2. from the east; as, an *eastwardly* wind.

ēaṣ'y, *a.; comp.* easier; *superl.* easiest. 1. at ease; being at rest; free from pain, annoyance, anxiety, care, or peevishness; quiet; tranquil; as, an *easy* mind.

2. comfortable; free from want; affording a comfortable living without toil; as, *easy* circumstances.

3. not difficult; not heavy or burdensome; giving or requiring no great labor or exertion; presenting no great obstacles; as, an *easy* task.

4. giving no pain or uneasiness; affording comfort, rest, or relaxation; pleasant; as, an *easy* posture; an *easy* carriage.

5. gentle; moderate; not fast; unhurried; as, a ship under *easy* sail.

6. yielding with little or no resistance; complying; readily influenced; tractable.

He gained their *easy* hearts. —Dryden.

7. not constrained; not stiff, awkward, embarrassed, or formal; as, *easy* manners; an *easy* address.

8. fond of comfort, ease, or idleness.

9. not strict, harsh, or severe; lenient; tolerant.

10. in business, (a) in little demand: said of a commodity; (b) lacking firmness in prices: said of a market; (c) with funds plentiful and interest rates low: said of a money market. Opposed to *tight.*

11. in card games, evenly divided between opponents; as, *easy* aces.

on easy street; well-to-do; in easy circumstances.

to go easy on; (a) to use or consume with restraint; as, *go easy on* the paper; (b) to deal with leniently; as, to *go easy on* traffic violators. [Colloq.]

Syn.—quiet, comfortable, indulgent, facile, lenient, unconstrained, gentle, unconcerned, manageable, not difficult.

ēaṣ'y, *adv.* easily. [Colloq.]

to take it easy; (a) to refrain from anger, violence, haste, etc.; (b) to refrain from hard work; to rest; to relax. Sometimes used as a farewell. [Colloq.]

ēaṣ'y chāir, a cushioned armchair or other lounge chair.

ēaṣ'y·gō'ing, ēaṣ'y-gō'ing, *a.* 1. inclined to take matters in an unworried, unhurried, easy way; good-natured; not strenuous or agitated.

2. having an even, comfortable gait: said of a horse.

ēaṣ'y märk, a person easily duped or taken advantage of. [Colloq.]

ēat, *v.t.;* ate (āt; Brit. et) *or archaic and dial.* eat (et, ēt), *pt.;* eaten *or archaic* eat (et, ēt), *pp.;* eating, *ppr.* [ME. *eten;* AS. *etan;* akin to L. *edere,* G. *essen.*]

1. to put in the mouth, chew, and swallow (food).

2. to use up, devour, destroy, or waste as by eating; consume or ravage (usually with *away* or *up*).

3. to penetrate and destroy, as acid does; corrode.

4. to make by or as by eating; as, termites *eat* their way through wood, acid *ate* holes in my suit.

to eat humble pie; see under *humble pie.*

to eat into; (a) to penetrate and destroy, as acid does; (b) to use up or consume part of.

to eat one's heart out; to brood or feel keenly unhappy for some time over one's sorrows or disappointments.

to eat one's words; to take back what has been uttered; to retract one's assertions.

to eat up; (a) to consume, devour, or use up thoroughly; (b) to engross deeply; as, *eaten up* with curiosity.

Syn.—devour, consume, corrode, wear, gnaw.

ēat, *v.i.* 1. to take food; to feed; to board.

He did *eat* continually at the king's table. —2 Sam. ix. 13.

2. to taste or relish; as, it *eats* like the tenderest beef. [Colloq.]

ēat'ȧ·ble, *a.* fit to be eaten; esculent.

ēat'ȧ·ble, *n.* [*usually in pl.*] anything that may be eaten; that which is fit for food.

ēat'ăge, *n.* food for horses and cattle from aftermath.

ēat'en, past participle of *eat.*

ēat'ẽr, *n.* one who or that which eats.

ēath, *a.* [AS.] easy. [Obs.]

ēath, *adv.* easily. [Obs.]

ēat'ing, *n.* 1. the act of taking food.

2. that which is fit to be eaten; food; as, salmon is good *eating.*

ēat'ing house, a house in which prepared food is sold and served; a restaurant.

ēats, *n.pl.* food; meals. [Colloq.]

eau (ō), *n.; pl.* **eaux** (ō), [Fr., water.] water.

eau de Cologne; same as *cologne.*

eau de Javelle; same as *Javel water.*

eau de vie [Fr., lit., water of life.] brandy.

ēave̤s, *n.pl.; mod. sing.* **ēave,** [orig. sing. now regarded as pl.; AS. *efese, yfese,* eaves, edge; O.H.G. *obisa, opasa,* a porch, hall; G. *oben;* G. dial. *ousch,* a gutter along the eaves.]

1. the edge or edges of the roof of a building, which usually overhang the walls and cast off the water that falls on the roof.

2. figuratively, any projecting rim.

And closing *eaves* of wearied eyes. —Tennyson.

3. margin; edge. [Obs.]

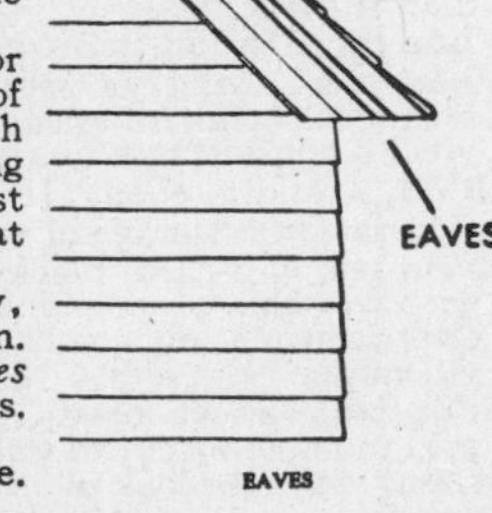

EAVES

ēaveṣ bōard, ēaveṣ ċatch, an arris fillet, or a thick board with a feather edge, nailed across the rafters at the eaves of a roof to raise the course of slates a little: called also *eaves lath.*

ēaveṣ'drop, *n.* [earlier *eavesdrip.*]
1. the water which falls in drops from the eaves of a house.
2. the ground on which it drips.

ēaveṣ'drop, *v.i.* to stand under the eaves or near the windows of a house in order to overhear what is said within doors; hence, to listen secretly to the private conversation of others.

ēaveṣ'drop''pẽr, *n.* one who eavesdrops.

ēaveṣ'drop''ping, *n.* the act of an eavesdropper.

ēaveṣ lath, same as *eaves board.*

ēaveṣ swăl'lōw, 1. a species of swallow that builds a nest of mud under the eaves of houses; the cliff swallow.
2. the house martin.

ēaveṣ trọugh (trọf), a trough or gutter hanging immediately below the eaves of a building to catch the eavesdrop and convey it away.

Eb, in chemistry, erbium.

é·bau·choir' (ā-bō-shwår') *n.* [Fr.] 1. a large chisel used by sculptors to rough-hew their work.
2. a large hatchel, or beating instrument, used by ropemakers.

ebb, *n.* *Emberiza miliaria,* the corn bunting. [Obs.]

ebb, *n.* [AS. *ebbe, ebba*; D. *eb, ebbe*; G. *ebbe,* the falling back of the tide.]
1. the reflux of the tide; the return of tidewater toward the sea: opposed to *flood* or *flow.*
2. a passing backward or away; decline; decay; a falling from a better to a worse state; as, the *ebb* of life; the *ebb* of prosperity.

ebb, *v.i.*; ebbed, *pt., pp.*; ebbing, *ppr.* 1. to flow back; to return, as the water of a tide toward the ocean: opposed to *flow.*
2. to decay; to decline; to return or fall back from a better to a worse state.
Syn.—recede, retire, withdraw, decrease, wane, decline, decay.

ebb, *v.t.* to cause to recede. [Obs.]

ebb an'ċhŏr, the anchor used by a vessel during the ebb tide.

ebb tīde, the reflux of tide water; the outgoing or falling tide: opposed to *flood tide.*

Eb·ē·nā'cē·ae, *n.pl.* [from L. *ebenus,* ebony.] a family of gamopetalous exogens, the ebony family, chiefly inhabiting the tropics: it contains six genera and about two hundred and fifty species, which consist entirely of shrubs or trees, some of large size. *Diospyros* is the largest and most important genus.

eb·ē·nā'ceous, *a.* pertaining to the *Ebenaceæ.*

eb·en·ē'zẽr, *n.* [Heb., stone of help.]
1. any memorial of divine aid.
2. among English dissenters, a chapel or place of worship.

Ē'bi·ō·niṣm, *n.* Ebionitism.

Ē'bī·ō·nīte, *n.* [LL. *Ebionitæ*; Gr. *Ebiōnaioi*; Heb. *ebyonim,* the poor.] one of an early sect of Gnostics who observed the Mosaic law along with the precepts of the Gospel. They denied the divinity of Jesus and rejected many parts of the New Testament.

Ē''bi·ō·nit'iç, *a.* of or pertaining to Ebionitism or the Ebionites.

Ē'bi·ō·nī·tiṣm, *n.* the doctrine or practice of the Ebionites.

eb'lȧ·nin, *n.* same as *pyroxanthin.*

Eb'lis, Ib'lees, *n.* [Ar. *Iblis.*] Satan: the Moslem name.

Ē'bōe, *n.* [W. Ind.] a Negro from Benin.

ē'bōe līght, *Erythroxylon brevipes,* a West Indian shrub.

ē'bōe tọrch'wood, same as *eboe light.*

ē'bōe tree, *Dipteryx eboensis,* a leguminous tree of Central America, the seeds of which yield a considerable quantity of oil.

eb'ŏn, *a.* and *n.* ebony. [Poetic.]

eb'ŏn·ist, *n.* a worker in ebony.

eb'ŏn·īte, *n.* a hard, black rubber, vulcanized with variable proportions of sulfur: used for electric insulation, combs, fountain pens, etc.; vulcanite.

eb'ŏn·īze, *v.t.*; ebonized, *pt., pp.*; ebonizing, *ppr.* to make black; to tinge with the color of ebony; to make look like ebony; as, to *ebonize* wood.

eb'ŏn·y, *n.*; *pl.* **eb'ŏn·ieṣ,** [L. *ebenus*; Gr. *ebenos,* from Heb. *eben,* a stone; so called from its hardness and weight.]
1. a hard, heavy, and durable wood, which takes a fine polish or gloss, and is used for furniture and decorative woodwork. The usual color is black, but red and green varieties are also found. The most valuable is the heartwood of *Diospyros ebenum,* which grows in the flat parts of Ceylon. Other varieties of valuable ebony are obtained from *Diospyros ebenaster* of the East Indies and *Diospyros melanoxylon* of the Coromandel coast in Hindustan. The green ebony of Jamaica, known also as the West Indian or American ebony, is the wood of the leguminous tree *Brya ebenus.*

EBONY (*Diospyros ebenum*)

2. any tree that yields this wood.

eb'ŏn·y, *a.* 1. made of ebony; as, an *ebony* walking stick.
2. like ebony, especially in color; dark; black.

é·boule·ment' (ā-böl-mäṅ'), *n.* [Fr., from *ebouler,* to tumble down.]
1. in fortification, the crumbling or falling of the wall of a fortification.
2. in geology, a sudden landslip in a mountainous region; a landslide.

ē·braç'tē·āte, *a.* [L. *e-* priv., and *bractea,* a thin plate.] in botany, without a bract or bracts.

ē·braç'tē·ō·lāte, *a.* [L., *e-* priv., and *bracteola,* dim. of *bractea,* a thin plate.] in botany, without bractlets.

ē·brī'e·ty, *n.*; *pl.* **ē·brī'e·tieṣ,** [L. *ebrietas,* from *ebrius,* drunken.] drunkenness; intoxication; inebriety.

ę·brĭl·läde' (ā-brē-yäd'), *n.* [Fr.] a check given to a horse, by a sudden jerk of one rein, when he refuses to turn.

ē·bri·os'i·ty, *n.* [L. *ebriositas,* from *ebrius,* drunken.] habitual drunkenness.

ē'bri·ous, *a.* inclined to excessive drinking; given to tippling.

ē·bul'li·āte, *v.i.* [LL. *ebullatus,* pp. of *ebullare,* from L. *ebullire,* to boil up.] to send up bubbles by or as by boiling. [Rare.]

ē·bul'lience (-yens), **ē·bul'lien·cy** (-yen-sy), *n.*
1. an overflow by boiling; a bubbling or boiling up.
2. an overflow of enthusiasm, high spirits, etc.; exuberance.

ē·bul'lient, *a.* 1. bubbling; effervescent; boiling over.
2. overflowing with enthusiasm, high spirits, etc.; showing much exuberance or exhilaration.

ē·bul'li·ō·sçōpe, *n.* [L. *ebullire,* to boil up, and Gr. *skopein,* to view.] an instrument for determining the boiling point of a liquid in order to ascertain the proportion of alcohol in the mixture.

eb·ul·li'tion, *n.* [L. *ebullition,* from *ebullire,* to boil up.]
1. the condition of any liquid when bubbles are rapidly forming in its mass and rising to the surface, as from the application of heat or from chemical activity.
2. a sudden or violent outburst, as of temper or passion.

eb'ūr·ine, *n.* [L. *ebur,* ivory, and *-ine.*] a substance formed of cement and the dust of ivory or of bone.

ē·bũr·nā'tion, *n.* [L. *eburnus,* of ivory, from *ebur,* ivory.] in pathology, the abnormal hardening in a cartilage, bone, or other tissue, so that it resembles ivory in hardness and texture.

ē·bũr'nē·ăn, *a.* made of ivory; of or pertaining to ivory.

ē·bũr''ni·fi·çā'tion, *n.* [L. *eburnus,* of ivory, and *-ficare,* from *facere,* to make.] eburnation.

eb'ūr·nīne, *a.* relating to ivory. [Rare.]

eç-, [L. *ec-,* Gr. *ek-,* from *ex,* out.] a prefix, equivalent to *ex-,* meaning *out of, from,* and used before certain consonants, as in *eclipse, eccentric.*

ē·çal'çȧ·rāte, *a.* [L. *e-* priv., and *calcar,* a spur.] in biology, lacking a spur, or calcar.

Ē·çăr'di·nēṣ, *n.pl.* [L. *e-* priv., and *cardo* (*-inis*), a hinge.] in zoology, an order of hingeless brachiopods, the *Lyopomata.*

ē·çăr'i·nāte, *a.* [L., *e-* priv., and *carina,* a keel.] in zoology, keelless.

é·car·té' (ā-kär-tā'), *n.* [Fr., from *écarter,* to discard, set aside.] a two-handed card game played with thirty-two cards (sevens up through aces), in which the players may discard, and receive other cards from the deck.

ē·çau'dāte, *a.* [L. *e-* priv., and *cauda,* a tail.]
1. in zoology, having no tail; anurous.
2. in botany, having no spur, tail, or tail-like appendage.

Ec·bal'li·um, *n.* [Gr. *ekballein,* to throw out.] a genus of *Cucurbitaceæ,* native to southern Europe and known as the squirting cucumber.

eç'bȧ·sis, *n.* [L., from Gr. *ekbasis,* a going out, issue, event; *ek,* out, and *bainein,* to go.] in rhetoric, a figure in which the orator treats of things according to events and their consequences.

eç·bat'iç, *a.* [from Gr. *ekbainein,* to go out, to issue, *ek,* out, and *bainein,* to go.] in grammar, denoting a mere result or consequence, as distinguished from intention or purpose.

eç·blas·tē'sis, *n.* [Gr. *ekblastēsis,* a shooting or budding out; *ek,* out, and *blastanein,* to sprout.] in botany, the abnormal development of buds in the axils of any of the parts of a flower.

eç'bō·lē, *n.* [Gr. *ekbolē,* a throwing out; *ek,* out, and *ballein,* to throw.] in rhetoric, a digression in which a person is introduced speaking his own words.

eç·bol'iç, *n.* [Gr. *ekballein,* to throw out.] a drug, such as ergot, tending to cause contraction of the uterus in pregnancy and the consequent expulsion of the fetus.

eç·bol'iç, *a.* helping to bring forth the fetus in birth, or causing abortion, by contracting the uterus: said of certain drugs.

eç'bō·line (-lin or -lēn), *n.* [Gr. *ekballein,* to throw out.] an alkaloid constituent of ergot.

eç·ça''lē·ō·bī'ŏn, *n.* [Gr. *ekkalein,* to call out, and *bios,* life.] a contrivance for hatching eggs by artificial heat; an incubator.

eç'cē (*or* ek'e), *interj.* [L.] behold! lo! see!

eç'cē hō'mō, [L.] 1. literally, behold the man: the Vulgate version of Pilate's words when he presented Jesus to the populace before the crucifixion: John xix. 5.
2. a picture or statue of Jesus wearing the crown of thorns.

eç·cen'triç, *n.* [LL. *eccentros,* out of the center, eccentric; Gr. *ekkentros*; *ek,* out, and *kentron,* center.]
1. in ancient astronomy, the supposed orbit of a planet not having the earth (or, later, the sun) precisely in its center.

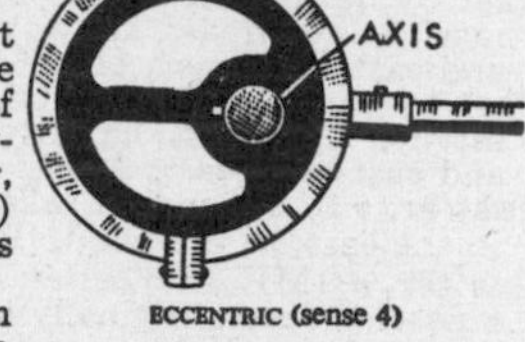

ECCENTRIC (sense 4)

2. in modern astronomy, a great circle tangent to an elliptical orbit at the two extremities of its major axis.
3. a circle or sphere not having the same center as another partly within or around it.
4. a disk set off center on a shaft and revolving inside a strap attached to one end of a rod, thereby converting the circular motion of the shaft into back-and-forth motion of the rod.
5. anyone or anything that acts or operates in an odd or unconventional manner.

eç·cen'triç, *a.* 1. deviating or departing from the center; not having the axis exactly in the center; as, an *eccentric* wheel.
2. in geometry, not having the same center; having different centers: applied to circles and spheres in opposition to *concentric,* having a common center.
3. not exactly circular in shape or motion.
4. irregular; out of the ordinary; capricious.
5. deviating from the norm, as in conduct; odd; whimsical; peculiar; unconventional.
6. not terminating in the same point or directed by the same principle. [Obs.]
7. in forestry, having a trunk lacking in symmetry or regularity of shape.
eccentric anomaly; the angular distance of a planet from its perihelion, as seen from the center of its orbit.
eccentric chuck; in machinery, a lathe chuck in which the position of the center of the piece turned may be changed at will.
eccentric gear; in machinery, (a) the entire apparatus by which an eccentric is utilized; (b) cog wheels which rotate on eccentric axes.
Syn.—anomalous, odd, abnormal, singular, strange, unnatural, peculiar.

eç·cen'triç·ăl, *a.* same as *eccentric.*

eç·cen′triç·ăl·ly, *adv.* with eccentricity; in an eccentric manner.

eç·cen′triç hook, in steam engineering, a journal box in the shape of an inverted U opposite the eccentric strap.

eç·cen·tric′i·ty, *n.*; *pl.* **eç·cen·tric′i·tieş,** 1. the state, quality, or amount of being off center or not concentric.

2. deviation from circular shape.

3. departure or deviation from that which is stated, regular, or usual, as in conduct or manner; oddity; peculiarity; whimsicality; unconventionality; as, the *eccentricity* of a man's genius or conduct.

4. in mathematics, the ratio existing between the distance from any point on a curve of a conic section to the focus and to the directrix.

5. in astronomy, the distance of the center of a planet's orbit from the center of the sun; that is, the distance between the center of an ellipse and its focus. Thus, in the ellipse D E F G, of which A and B are the foci, and C the center, A C or B C is the *eccentricity*.

6. in mechanics, the linear extent of reciprocating motion obtained in an eccentric, which equals the distance between the center of the eccentric and the axis; the throw.

eç·cen′triç rod, the rod attached to the eccentric strap for transferring the motion of the eccentric.

eç·cen′triç strap, the encircling ring clasping the disk of the eccentric, receiving the motion therefrom: called also *eccentric hoop*.

eç·cen·trom′e·tẽr, *n.* [LL. *eccentros*, out of the center, and *metrum*, a measure.] an instrument for determining eccentricity, especially that of a hollow projectile.

eç·ceph·ȧ·lō′sis, *n.* [Gr. *ek*, out, and *kephalē*, head.] in obstetrics, the operation of removing the brain of a fetus in order to accomplish delivery.

eç·chon·drō′mȧ, *n.* [Gr. *ek*, out, and *chondros*, cartilage.] a tumor having its origin in normal cartilage.

eç·çhy·mō′mȧ, *n.*; *pl.* **eç·çhy·mō′mȧ·tȧ,** [Gr. *ek*, out, and *chymos*, juice, from *cheein*, to pour.] in pathology, a swelling of the cellular tissue beneath the skin caused by an effusion of blood; a black-and-blue swelling.

eç·çhy·mō′sis, *n.*; *pl.* **eç·çhy·mō′sēş,** [Gr. *ekchymōsis*, from *ekchymoesthai*, to shed the blood and leave it extravasated under the skin; *ek*, out, and *chymos*, juice, from *cheein*, to pour.]

1. an oozing of blood from a blood vessel into the tissues, as the result of a bruise.

2. a black-and-blue or yellowish mark caused by this.

eç·çhy·mot′iç, *a.* relating to ecchymosis.

eç′cle gràss, in botany, the common butterwort, *Pinguicula vulgaris*. [Brit. Dial.]

eç·clē′ṣi·ȧ, *n.*; *pl.* **eç·clē′ṣi·ae,** [L. *ecclesia*; Gr. *ekklēsia*, an assembly of the people, from *eklētos*, summoned; *ekkalein*, to summon, call out.]

1. the political assembly in the ancient Greek states, at which all free citizens could vote.

2. the members of a church; a congregation.

3. a church building.

eç·clē′ṣi·ăl, *a.* relating to the church; ecclesiastic. [Obs.]

eç·clē′ṣi·ärch, *n.* [LL. *ecclesiarcha*, from Gr. *ekklēsia*, assembly, and *archos*, a ruler.]

1. a ruler of the church, especially one high in authority.

2. a kind of sexton in the Eastern church.

eç·clē′ṣi·ȧst, *n.* [LL. *ecclesiastes*; Gr. *ekklēsiastēs*, a member of an assembly, from *ekklēsia*, an assembly.]

1. an ecclesiastic.

2. [E—] the Book of Ecclesiasticus. [Obs.]

3. a citizen taking part in the ecclesia of ancient Athens. [Rare.]

Eç·clē·ṣi·as′tēş, *n.* [LL., from Gr. *ekklēsiastēs*, a preacher.] a canonical book of the Old Testament, ascribed to Solomon.

eç·clē·ṣi·as′tiç, *n.* a person in orders or one consecrated to the service of a church and the ministry of religion; a clergyman or priest.

eç·clē·ṣi·as′tiç·ăl, eç·clē·ṣi·as′tiç, *a.* [Gr. *ekklēsiastikos*, from *ekklēsia*, an assembly or meeting called out, the church; from *ekkalein*, to call forth or convoke; *ek*, out, and *kalein*, to call.] pertaining or relating to a church, the organization of a church, or the clergy; as, *ecclesiastical* discipline or government; *ecclesiastical* affairs, history, or polity; *ecclesiastical* courts.

Ecclesiastical Commissioners for England; a body of commissioners appointed by Parliament in 1836 to investigate the affairs of the Church of England and to report their condition.

ecclesiastical courts; courts whose business it is to consider all cases pertaining to the discipline of the church.

ecclesiastical law; the law administered by ecclesiastical courts.

ecclesiastical modes; the particular arrangement and disposition of the notes in the musical scale, as formerly appointed and practiced in church service.

Ecclesiastical States; the territory once subject to the pope of Rome as its temporal ruler.

eç·clē·ṣi·as′tiç·ăl·ly, *adv.* in an ecclesiastical manner; in accordance with ecclesiastical usage.

eç·clē·ṣi·as′ti·çiṣm, *n.* 1. ecclesiastical principles, rituals, customs, etc.

2. strong attachment to ecclesiastical forms and usages.

Eç·clē·ṣi·as′ti·çus, *n.* [LL. *ecclesiasticus*, of or belonging to the church; Gr. *ekklēsiastikos*, from *ekklēsia*, an assembly.] a book of proverbs in the Apocrypha, included as canonical in the Douay Bible.

eç·clē·ṣi·ol′ȧ·try, *n.* excessive attachment to and veneration for the forms and ceremonies of the church.

eç·clē″ṣi·ō·loġ′iç·ăl, *a.* belonging to ecclesiology.

eç·clē·ṣi·ol′ō·ġist, *n.* one versed in ecclesiology.

eç·clē·ṣi·ol′ō·ġy, *n.* [Gr. *ekklēsia*, an assembly, a church, and *-logia*, from *legein*, to speak.]

1. the science of church architecture and decoration.

2. the science of church organization and management.

3. a treatise about churches.

eç·cri·nol′ō·ġy, *n.* [Gr. *ekkrinein*, to separate, and *-logia*, from *legein*, to speak.] the branch of physiology which treats of the secretions and excretions of the body.

eç·crit′iç, *n.* [Gr. *ekkritikos*, secretive, from *ekkritos*; from *ek*, out, and *krinein*, to separate.] an eliminative medicine.

eç·cy·ē′sis, *n.* [from Gr. *ekkyein*, to bring forth; *ek*, out, and *kyein*, to be pregnant.] pregnancy occurring outside the uterus.

eç′dẽr·on, *n.* [Gr. *ek*, out, and *deros*, skin.] in histology, the superficial layer of cells upon the skin or upon the mucous membrane; epidermis.

eç·dẽr·on′iç, *a.* pertaining to the ecderon.

eç′dy·sis, *n.*; *pl.* **eç′dy·sēş,** [Gr. *ekdysis*, from *ekdyein*, to get out of, strip off; *ek*, out, and *dyein*, to put on, enter.] the act of shedding or sloughing off dead skin or integument, as by a snake or certain insects.

eç′gō·nine, *n.* in chemistry, an alkaloid base, $C_9H_{15}NO_3$, formed by treating cocaine with hydrochloric acid.

é·chau·guette′ (ā-shō-get′), *n.* [Fr.] a structure devised for the protection of a sentinel, usually a small turret projecting from the wall of a castle.

eçh′e·lon, *n.* [Fr., from *échelle*; OFr. *eschelle*; It. *scala*, from L. *scala*, a ladder.]

1. a steplike formation of units of troops, in which each unit is progressively to the left or right of the one preceding it.

2. any subdivision of a combat force (as an assault *echelon*), or of a headquarters (as a rear *echelon*).

3. any of various formations of ships, aircraft, etc.

4. in optics, an arrangement of plane glass plates put parallel to one another, each overlapping another by the same amount: this apparatus has a high dispersing power and gives a spectrum similar to that obtained from a diffraction grating.

eçh′e·lon, *v.t.* and *v.i.*; echeloned, *pt.*, *pp.*; echeloning, *ppr.* to form or move in echelon.

E·çhid′nȧ, *n.* [L., from Gr. *echidna*, a viper, an adder.]

1. a genus of anteaters of which the echidna is the type.

2. [e—] a small, egg-laying Australian mammal with a long, tapering snout and a sticky tongue: it feeds on ants and is covered with spines: also called *spiny anteater*.

eçh′i·nāte, eçh′i·nā·ted, *a.* [L. *echinatus*, set with prickles, from *echinus*, a hedgehog.] set with prickles; prickly, like a hedgehog; having sharp points; bristled; as, an *echinated* pericarp.

e·çhī′nid, *a.* and *n.* same as *echinoid*.

e·çhin′i·dăn, *n.* a radiate animal, one of the family *Echinoidea*.

e·çhin′i·tăl, *a.* relating to an echinite.

eçh′i·nīte, *n.* [Gr. *echinos*, a hedgehog, and *-ite*.] an echinoid in a fossilized state.

e·çhī′nō-, [from Gr. *echinos*, a sea urchin.] a combining form meaning *prickly*, *spiny*, as in *echino*coccus, *echino*cystis.

E·çhī·nō·çaç′tus, *n.* [*echino-*, and Gr. *kaktos*, a cactus.] a genus of cactaceous plants abounding in Mexico and in the southwestern United States. They are remarkable for the singular forms of their stems. They have showy flowers and are frequently cultivated.

ECHINOCACTUS

e·çhī′nō·çhrōme, *n.* [*echino-*, and Gr. *chrōma*, a color.] a pigment obtained from the bodies of certain echinoderms, usually of a brown or brownish color.

e·çhī·nō·çoç′çus, *n.*; *pl.* **e·çhī·nō·çoç′cī,** [*echino-*, and Gr. *kokkos*, a berry.] a parasitic larva, *Tænia echinococcus*, of a tapeworm found especially in the dog but also in other animals and in man, where it produces fatal tumors in the lungs or liver.

E·çhī·nō·cys′tis, *n.* [*echino-*, and Gr. *kystis*, a bladder.] in botany, a genus of the gourd family, a species of which, *Echinocystis lobata*, grows in the eastern part of the United States.

e·çhī′nō·dẽrm, *n.* [*echino-*, and Gr. *derma*, skin.] one of the *Echinodermata*.

e·çhī·nō·dẽr′măl, *a.* same as *echinodermatous*.

E·çhī·nō·dẽr′mȧ·tȧ, *n.pl.* [from Gr. *echinos*, a hedgehog, sea urchin, and *derma*, skin.] a phylum of the animal kingdom, characterized by a somewhat radial structure and a hard, spiny exoskeleton, including the starfishes and sea urchins.

e·çhī·nō·dẽr′mȧ·tous, *a.* 1. having the characteristics of an echinoderm.

2. of the echinoderms.

e·çhī′noid, *n.* one of the *Echinoidea*.

e·çhī′noid, *a.* of or like the *Echinoidea*.

Eçh·i·noi′dē·ȧ, *n.pl.* [Gr. *echinos*, a hedgehog, sea urchin, and *eidos*, form.] a class of *Echinodermata*; the sea urchins.

eçh·i·nol′ō·ġy, *n.* [*echino-*, and Gr. *-logia*, from *legein*, to speak.] that branch of zoology which treats of the characteristics and classification of echinoderms.

e·çhin′ū·lāte, *a.* [L. *echinus*, a hedgehog.] having a coat of small spines or prickles.

e·çhin′ū·li·fọrm, *a.* [L. *echinus*, a hedgehog, sea urchin, and dim. *-ulus*, and *forma*, form.] in the form of small spines.

e·çhī′nus, *n.*; *pl.* **e·çhī′nī,** [L., from Gr. *echinos*, a hedgehog, sea urchin.]

1. a hedgehog.

2. a sea urchin.

3. [E—] a genus of annuloids, constituting the type of the class *Echinodermata*. The body is covered with a spiny shell. There are various species, several of them edible.

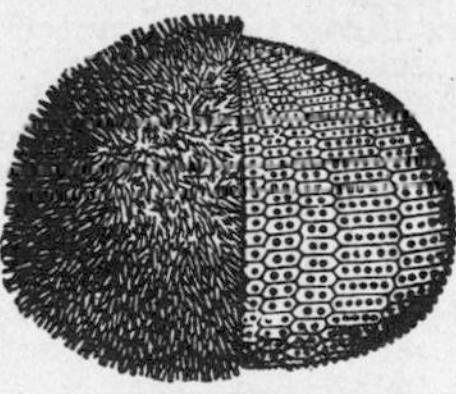

SEA URCHIN (*Echinus esculentus*)

4. in architecture, (a) molding under the abacus of the capital of a Doric column; (b) any of several similar moldings.

Eçh·i·ū·roi′dē·ȧ, *n.pl.* [from Gr. *echis*, *echidos*, an adder, viper, and *oura*, a tail.] an order of worms of the *Gephyrea*.

eçh′ō, *n.*; *pl.* **eçh′ōeş,** [L. *echo*; Gr. *ēchō*, a reverberated sound, an echo; *ēchē*, *ēchos*, a sound, noise; *ēchein*, to sound.]

1. the repeating of a sound, produced by reflection of sound waves from a surface.

2. a sound so produced.

3. any repeating or imitating of the words, style, ideas, etc. of another.

4. a person who repeats or imitates the words, style, ideas, etc. of another.

5. sympathetic response.

6. in bridge and whist, the playing of an informative card in answer to a card led by one's partner.

7. in music, (a) a soft repetition of a phrase; (b) an organ stop for producing the effect of echo.

8. in poetry, the repetition of the terminal syllables of one line at or near the beginning of the next line.

9. [E-] in Greek mythology, a nymph who, for love of Narcissus, pined away until nothing remained of her but her voice.

eçh'ō, *v.i.*; echoed, *pt., pp.*; echoing, *ppr.* 1. to resound with an echo; to reverberate; as, the empty room *echoed*.

2. to be repeated or given back from a surface; as, his voice *echoed* in the hall.

eçh'ō, *v.t.* 1. (a) to repeat (another's words, ideas, etc.); (b) to repeat the words, etc. of (another person).

2. to repeat or reflect (sound) from a surface.

eçh'ō chām'bẽr, a room or device used in recording and broadcasting to increase resonance, produce echo effects, etc.

e·chō'iç, *a.* 1. having the nature of an echo.

2. imitative in sound; onomatopoeic: a term in linguistics used to indicate that a word is formed in approximate imitation of some sound, as *blare, tinkle,* etc.

eçh'ō·işm, *n.* [*echo*, and *-ism.*] formation of words approximately imitating sounds; onomatopoeia.

eçh·ō·lā'li·à, *n.* [Gr. *ēchō*, an echo, and *lalia*, from *lalein*, to babble.] a form of mental disorder in which the patient automatically repeats words heard by or addressed to him.

eçh'ō·less, *a.* giving back no echo; not returning in echo.

ē·chom'e·tẽr, *n.* [Gr. *ēchō*, sound, echo, and *metron*, a measure.] a device used in the measurement of the duration of sounds and in the ascertainment of their ratios and intervals.

ē·chom'e·try, *n.* the art or act of using an echometer.

eçh'ō·stop, *n.* a stop attached to an organ, used by the performer to produce echolike sounds.

eçht, *a.* [G.] genuine; real; authentic.

Ec'i·ton, *n.* [etym. doubtful.] a genus of ants, often known as *army ants* from their practice of marching in large numbers. They are carnivorous and very destructive.

é·clair' (ā-klâr'), *n.* [Fr.] a small, oblong pastry shell filled with flavored custard or whipped cream and covered with frosting.

é·clair·cisse·ment' (ā-klâr-sēs-mäṅ'), *n.* [Fr., from *éclaircir*, to clear up; OFr. *esclarcir*, from L. *clarus*, clear.]

1. a clearing up, as of a disputed or difficult point; clarification; explanation.

2. [E-] the Enlightenment.

eç·lamp'si·à, eç·lamp'sy, *n.* [Gr. *eklampsis*, a shining forth, from *eklampein*, to shine forth; *ek*, out, and *lampein*, to shine.]

1. an attack of convulsions, caused by any of various toxic conditions of the body and occurring especially in the latter stages of pregnancy and in childbirth.

2. an imaginary perception of light flashing in front of the eyes, one of the symptoms of epilepsy. [Obs.]

eç·lamp'tiç, *a.* caused by or suffering from eclampsia.

é·clat' (ā-klä'), *n.* [Fr., from *éclater*, to split, shiver, break forth, shine.]

1. brilliant or conspicuous success.

2. acclaim.

3. (a) brilliance of reputation; fame; renown; (b) notoriety.

eç·leç'tiç, *a.* [Gr. *eklektikos*, from *eklegein*, to select, pick out; *ek*, out, and *legein*, to choose, pick.]

1. choosing; selecting from various systems, doctrines, or sources; adhering to the principles of eclecticism.

2. composed of material gathered from various sources, systems, etc.

Eclectic school; same as *Bolognese school* under *Bolognese*.

eç·leç'tiç, *n.* one who practices eclectic methods in philosophy, science, or art.

eç·leç'tiç·ăl·ly, *adv.* in an eclectic manner.

eç·leç'ti·cişm, *n.* 1. the method or system of an eclectic.

2. the use or upholding of such a method or system.

eç·legm' (-lem'), *n.* [L. *ecligma*; Gr. *ekleigma*, from *ekleichein*, to lick up; *ek*, out, and *leichein*, to lick.] a medicine made by the mixing of oils with sirups. [Obs.]

ē·clipse', *n.* [L. *eclipsis*; Gr. *ekleipsis*, an eclipse, a failing; from *ekleipein*, to leave out, pass over, fail; *ek*, out, and *leipein*, to leave.]

1. the partial or total apparent darkening of the sun when the moon comes between it and the earth (called *solar eclipse*), or of the moon when the earth's shadow is cast upon it (called *lunar eclipse*).

2. any overshadowing or cutting off of light.

3. a temporary obscurity or dulling, as of fame, glory, etc.

annular eclipse; see under *annular*.

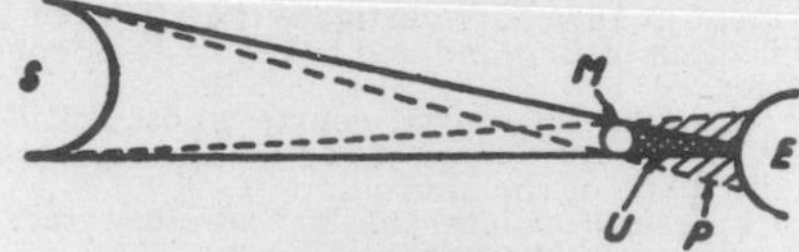

SOLAR ECLIPSE
S, sun; *M*, moon; *E*, earth; *U*, umbra; *P*, penumbra.

ē·clipse', *v.t.*; eclipsed (-klipst'), *pt., pp.*; eclipsing, *ppr.* [ME. *eclipsen*; see the *n.*]

1. to cause an eclipse of; to darken or obscure.

2. to obscure the fame or glory of; overshadow; outshine; surpass; as, Shakespeare *eclipsed* his rivals in the drama.

ē·clipse', *v.i.* to suffer an eclipse. [Poetic.]

ē·clip'sis, *n.* [L., from Gr. *ekleipsis*, an eclipse, a failing.] a leaving out or a suppressing of sounds or words.

ē·clip'tiç, *n.* [ME. *ecliptik*; ML. *ecliptica*; L. (*linea*) *ecliptica*; Gr. *ekleiptikos*, of an eclipse, from *ekleipein*; see *eclipse*.]

1. the sun's apparent annual path, or orbit, or that of the earth as seen from the sun; great circle of the celestial sphere.

2. the plane of the earth's orbit, cutting this circle and inclined at an angle of about 23½ degrees to the celestial equator.

3. a great circle drawn on a terrestrial globe, at the same angle to the terrestrial equator, corresponding to the sun's ecliptic.

ē·clip'tiç, *a.* of eclipses or the ecliptic.

lunar ecliptic limit; the greatest angular distance from the moon's node at which an eclipse of the moon may occur, about 11°.

solar ecliptic limit; the greatest angular distance from the moon's node at which an eclipse of the sun may occur, 18.5°.

ē·clip'tiç·ăl, *a.* same as *ecliptic*.

eç'lō·ġite, *n.* [Gr. *eklogos*, picked out, chosen, from *eklegein*, to pick out, choose.] a metamorphic rock consisting mainly of a green pyroxene, red garnet, and other minerals.

eç'logue (-log), *n.* [Fr. *eclogue*; L. *ecloga*; Gr. *eklogē*, a selection, especially of poems, from *eklegein*, to pick out, choose; *ek*, out, and *legein*, to choose.] a short pastoral poem, usually involving two shepherds conversing with each other; as, the *Eclogues* of Virgil.

ē'çō·cīde, *n.* [from Gr. *oikos*, house; and *-cide*.] the destruction of the environment or of ecosystems, as by the use of defoliants, the emission of pollutants, etc.

ē'çoid, *n.* in anatomy, the colorless framework of a red blood corpuscle.

é·cole' (ā-kọl'), *n.* [Fr.] school.

E. cō'lī, [Mod.L. *E*(*scherichia*) *coli*; T. *Escherich*, G. physician (1857-1911), and L. *coli*, of the colon.] a species of Gram-negative bacteria normally present in the intestines of human beings and all vertebrates and widely used in biological research: its presence in water in certain quantities indicates pollution that can cause diarrhea.

eç·ō·log'iç·ăl, eç·ō·log'iç (*or* ē-kō-), *a.* of or by ecology.

ē·çol'ō·ġist, *n.* an expert in ecology.

ē·çol'ō·ġy, *n.* [from Gr. *oikos*, house; and *-logy*.]

1. the branch of biology that deals with the relations between living organisms and their environment.

2. in sociology, the relationship between the distribution of human groups with reference to material resources, and the consequent social and cultural patterns.

ē·çon·ō·met'riçs, *n.pl.* [*construed as sing.*] [*economy*, and *metrics*.] the use of mathematical and statistical methods in the field of economics to verify and develop economic theories.

ē·çō·nom'iç (*or* ek-ō-), *a.* [L. *œconomicus*; Gr. *oikonomikos*, from *oikonomia*, management of a household or state, the public revenue, from *oikonomos*; *oikos*, house, household, and *nemein*, to distribute, manage.]

1. of the management of the income, expenditures, etc. of a household, private business, community, or government.

2. of the production, distribution, and consumption of wealth.

3. of economics.

4. of the satisfaction of the material needs of people; as, *economic* biology.

ē·çō·nom'iç·ăl (*or* ek-ō-), *a.* 1. not wasting money, time, fuel, etc.; thrifty; as, an *economical* person, an *economical* stove.

2. of economics; economic.

ē·çō·nom'iç·ăl·ly (*or* ek-ō-), *adv.* 1. in an economical manner.

2. from the viewpoint of economics.

ē·çō·nom'iç ġē·og'rà·phy, the branch of geography that deals with the relation of economic conditions to physical geography and natural resources.

ē·çō·nom'içs (*or* ek-ō-), *n.pl.* [*construed as sing.*] [Gr. *ta oikonomika*, the science of household management.] the science that deals with the production, distribution, and consumption of wealth, and with the various related problems of labor, finance, taxation, etc.; political economy.

ē·çon'ō·mist, *n.* 1. an economical or thrifty person.

2. a specialist in economics.

ē·çon″ō·mi·zā'tion, *n.* the act or practice of economizing.

ē·çon'ō·mīze, *v.i.*; economized, *pt., pp.*; economizing, *ppr.* to avoid waste or needless expenditure; to reduce expenses.

ē·çon'ō·mīze, *v.t.* to use or manage with thrift or prudence; as, to *economize* one's income.

ē·çon'ō·mī·zẽr, *n.* 1. one who or that which economizes.

2. any mechanical apparatus that helps save fuel, heat, etc.

ē·çon'ō·my, *n.*; *pl.* **ē·çon'ō·mieş,** [L. *œconomia*; Gr. *oikonomia*, the management of a household or state, the public revenue, from *oikonomos*, a manager, administrator; *oikos*, house, and *nemein*, to distribute, manage.]

1. the management of the income, expenditures, etc. of a household, private business, community, or government.

2. careful management of wealth, resources, etc.; avoidance of waste by careful planning and use; thrift or thrifty use.

3. an instance of this.

4. an orderly management or arrangement of parts; organization or system; as, the *economy* of the human body.

5. a system of producing, distributing, and consuming wealth.

Syn.—frugality, management, thrift.

é·cor·ché' (ā-kọr-shā'), *n.* [Fr., lit., flayed, pp. of *écorcher*, to flay.] a model of a body with the skin completely removed, so as to exhibit the muscular system.

ē·çor'ti·çāte, *a.* [L. *e-* priv., and *corticatus*, from *cortex* (*-icis*), bark, rind.] in botany, without a layer of cortex or corklike tissue: said specifically of certain lichens.

ē'çō·sphēre, *n.* [from Gr. *oikos*, house; and *sphere*.] the zone of the earth, a planet, etc. which contains or is theoretically capable of containing living organisms.

ē·ços'tāte, *a.* [L. *e-* priv., and *costa*, a rib.]

1. in botany, having no central vein or rib: said of a leaf.

2. in zoology, (a) having no ribs; (b) having no ribs attached: said of a vertebra.

ē'çō·sys·tem, *n.* [from Gr. *oikos*, house; and *system*.] a system made up of a community of animals, plants, and bacteria and its interrelated physical and chemical environment.

eç·phō·nē'mà, eç·phō·nē'sis, *n.* [Gr. *ekphōnēma*, from *ekphōnein*, to cry out, pronounce; *ek*, out, and *phōnein*, from *phōnē*, voice, sound.] in rhetoric, a sudden and passionate exclamation.

é·crase·ment' (ā-kräz-mäṅ'), *n.* [Fr., from *écraser*, to crush, bruise.] a surgical operation performed by means of an écraseur.

é·cra·seur' (ā-krà-zẽr'), *n.* [Fr., from *écraser*, to crush, bruise.] a surgical instrument consisting of a looped wire or cord, which is gradually tightened about a part so as to cut it off.

é·cre·visse' (ā-kre-vēs'), *n.* [Fr.] a kind of armor made by fastening overlapping scalelike plates upon a ground of leather.

eç'rü (*or* ā-krü'), *a.* and *n.* [Fr. *écru*, unbleached, raw, from L. *crudus*, raw.] light tan; beige.

ē·crus·tā'ceous, *a.* [L. *e-* priv., and *crusta*, a crust.] without a crustaceous covering: said of thallophytes.

eç'stà·sy, *n.* [LL. *ecstasis*; Gr. *ekstasis*, a being put out of its place, distraction, trance, from *ek*, out, and *histanai*, to place.]

1. a trance, especially one resulting from great religious fervor.

> Whether what we call *ecstasy* be not dreaming with our eyes open, I leave to be examined. —Locke.

2. great joy; rapture; a feeling of delight

that arrests the whole mind; as, to listen with *ecstasy*.

3. a state of being overpowered with emotion, especially joy; the condition of being beside oneself with feeling; as, an *ecstasy* of delight.

4. madness; distraction. [Obs.]

Syn.—delight, rapture, transport, overjoy.

eç'stȧ·sy, *v.t.*; ecstasied, *pt., pp.*; ecstasying, *ppr.* to fill with rapture or enthusiasm.

eç·stat'iç, eç·stat'iç·ăl, *a.* [Gr. *ekstatikos*, from *ekstasis*, ecstasy.]

1. of, having the nature of, or characterized by ecstasy.

2. causing, or caused by, ecstasy.

eç·stat'iç, *n.* a person subject to fits of ecstasy.

eç·stat'iç·ăl·ly, *adv.* in an ecstatic manner.

eçt-, eç·tō-, [from Gr. *ektos*, outside.] a combining form meaning *without, outside, external*: used mainly in forming biological terms, as *ecto*derm, *ecto*zoa.

eç'tad, *adv.* [Gr. *ektos*, outside, and L. *ad*, to.] in anatomy, outward.

eç'tăl, *a.* [Gr. *ektos*, outside, and *-al*.] in anatomy, related to the outside; exterior.

eç·tā'şi·ȧ, *n.* [Gr. *ektasis*, extension, from *ekteinein*; *ek*, out, and *teinein*, to stretch.] in medicine, an enlargement, inflation, or swelling of any hollow organ; as, *ectasia* of the veins.

eç'tȧ·sis, *n.* [LL., from Gr. *ektasis*, extension; *ek*, out, and *teinein*, to stretch.] in prosody, the changing of a syllable from short to long.

eç·ten'tăl, *a.* [Gr. *ektos*, without, and *entos*, within.] in biology, having mutual relation to the ectoderm and the entoderm.

eç'tẽr·on, *n.* same as *ecderon*.

eç·teth'moid, *a.* [*ect-*, and Gr. *ēthmoeidēs*, like a sieve; *ēthmos*, a sieve, and *eidos*, form.] in anatomy, situated outside the ethmoid bone.

eç'thē·sis, *n.* [Gr. *ekthesis*, from *ektithenai*, to put forth, set forth.] the promulgation of a belief by means of a thesis, as [E—], the edict of the Emperor Heraclius forbidding discussion as to the duality of the will of Christ.

eç·thlip'sis, *n.* [LL., from Gr. *ekthlipsis*, a squeezing out, from *ekthlibein*; *ek*, out, and *thlibein*, to squeeze.] in Latin prosody, the elision of the final syllable of a word ending in *m*, when the next word begins with a vowel.

eç·thy̆'mȧ, *n.* [Gr. *ekthyma*, from *ekthyein*, to break out, as tumors; *ek*, out, and *thyein*, to rage, boil.] in medicine, an eruption of the skin in which large, deep-seated pustules form upon broad, inflamed bases.

eç·tō-, same as *ect-*.

eç'tō·blast, *n.* [*ecto-*, and *blast*.] the outer layer of an embryo in the earliest (gastrula) stage; epiblast.

eç·tō·blas'tiç, *a.* of the ectoblast.

eç·tō·bron'çhi·um, *n.*; *pl.* **eç·tō·bron'çhi·ȧ,** [*ecto-*, and Gr. *bronchos*, the windpipe, trachea.] in ornithology, a subdivision of the bronchi lying on the side toward the back of the bird.

eç·tō·çär'di·ȧ, *n.* [*ecto-*, and Gr. *kardia*, heart.] a malformation in which the heart is out of its natural location.

Eç''tō·çär·pā'cē·ae, *n.pl.* [*ecto-*, and Gr. *karpos*, fruit, and *-aceæ*.] a family of algae. They are olive-colored, articulated, filiform, with sporanges either externally attached to the jointed ramuli or formed out of some of the interstitial cells.

eç''tō·çär·pā'ceous, *a.* pertaining to the *Ectocarpaceæ*.

eç·tō·çär'pous, *a.* [*ecto-*, and Gr. *karpos*, fruit.] in zoology, having the sexual organ external to or developed from the ectoderm.

Eç·tō·çär'pus, *n.* [*ecto-*, and Gr. *karpos*, fruit.] a typical genus of algae of the family *Ectocarpaceæ*.

eç·tō·coe'liç, *a.* [*ecto-*, and Gr. *koilion*, a hollow.] lying outside the cavity of the body: said of coelenterates.

eç·tō·çū·nē'i·form, *n.* [*ecto-*, and L. *cuneus*, a wedge, and *forma*, form.] the outer cuneiform tarsal bone: also used adjectively.

eç'tō·cyst, *n.* [*ecto-*, and Gr. *kystis*, a bladder.] in zoology, the external integumentary layer of the *Polyzoa*.

eç'tō·dẽrm, *n.* [*ecto-*, and *-derm*.]

1. the outer layer of cells of an animal embryo in its early stage, from which the nervous system, skin, teeth, etc. are developed.

2. the outer layer of cells of certain organisms, as the coelenterates.

eç·tō·dẽr'măl, eç·tō·dẽr'miç, *a.* belonging or related to the ectoderm.

eç·tō·en'zy̆me, *n.* an enzyme secreted by a cell and acting outside it; exoenzyme.

eç·tō·gen'iç, *a.* [*ecto-*, and *-genic*.] that can be developed outside the host: said of certain parasitic bacteria.

eç·toğ'e·nous, *a.* same as *ectogenic*.

eç·tō·lec'i·thăl, *a.* [*ecto-*, and Gr. *lekithos*, yolk.] in embryology, having, at the beginning of segmentation, the nourishing yolk surrounding the vitellus or formative part of the embryo; as, *ectolecithal* segmentation.

eç'tō·mēre, *n.* [*ecto-*, and Gr. *meros*, part.] in embryology, any of the early cells which eventually form the ectoderm.

eç·tō·mẽr'iç, *a.* of an ectomere.

eç·tō·mor'phiç, *a.* [*ecto-*, and *-morphic*.] designating or of the slender physical type, characterized by predominance of the structures developed from the ectodermal layer of the embryo (i.e., skin, nerves, brain, and sense organs); asthenic: distinguished from *endomorphic*.

-eç'tō·my, [from Gr. *ektomē*, a cutting out, from *ek-*, out, and *temnein*, to cut.] a combining form meaning *a surgical excision of*, as in append*ectomy*, tonsill*ectomy*.

eç·tō·par'ȧ·sīte, *n.* [*ecto-*, and Gr. *parasitos*, a parasite.] a parasite that lives on the outside of an animal, as opposed to *endoparasite*, which lives in the body.

eç''tō·par·ȧ·sit'iç, *a.* pertaining to or resembling an ectoparasite.

eç·tō'pi·ȧ, *n.* [Gr. *ektopios*, *ektopos*, out of place, out of the way; *ek*, out, and *topos*, place.] in pathology, the condition of being out of place: said of an organ; as, *ectopia* of the liver.

eç·top'iç, *a.* pertaining to ectopia; affected by ectopia.

eç·top'iç preg'năn·cy, the abnormal deposit and subsequent development of the fertilized ovum outside the uterus, as in a Fallopian tube.

eç'tō·plasm, *n.* [*ecto-*, and *-plasm*.]

1. in biology, the outer layer of the cytoplasm of a cell: distinguished from *endoplasm*.

2. in spiritualism, the vaporous, luminous substance supposed to emanate from the medium's body during a trance.

eç·tō·plas'miç, *a.* of ectoplasm.

eç·tō·plas'tiç, *a.* same as *ectoplasmic*.

Eç·tō·proç'tȧ, *n.pl.* [*ecto-*, and Gr. *prōktos*, the anus, hinder parts.] an order of polyzoans having the anus placed outside the tentacular disk.

eç'tō·py *n.* see *ectopia*.

eçt·or'găn·işm, *n.* an ectoparasitic organism.

eç'tō·särç, *n.* [*ecto-*, and Gr. *sarx*, *sarkos*, flesh.] the outer layer of certain one-celled animals; the ectoplasm.

eç·tō·skel'e·tŏn, *n.* same as *exoskeleton*.

eç·tō·sō'măl, *a.* pertaining to or resembling the ectosome.

eç'tō·sōme, *n.* [*ecto-*, and Gr. *sōma*, body.] the cortex, or envelope, of a sponge.

eç·tos'tē·ăl, *a.* [*ecto-*, and Gr. *osteon*, a bone.]

1. having relation to extostosis.

2. having relation to the surface of a bone.

eç·tos·tō'sis, *n.* [*ecto-*, and *ostosis*.] formation of bone under the membranous covering of the cartilage, which is either replaced or surrounded by the newly made bone.

eç·tō·zō'iç, *a.* [*ecto-*, and Gr. *zōon*, pl. *zōa*, an animal.] relating to ectoparasites; epizoic.

eç·tō·zō'on, *n.*; *pl.* **eç·tō·zō'ȧ,** an ectoparasite.

eç·trō·mē'li·ȧ, *n.* absence of a limb or limbs.

eç·trō'pi·on, eç·trō'pi·um, *n.* [Gr. *ektropion*, from *ektropos*, turning outward.] an eversion or turning inside out; as, *ectropion* of the lips of a wound.

eç·trot'iç, *a.* [Gr. *ektrōtikos*, from *ektrōsis*, abortion, from *ektitrōskein*, to abort; *ek*, out, and *titrōskein*, *trōein*, to wound, injure.] in medicine, preventive; arresting a disease in its inception.

eç'ty·păl, *a.* of, or having the nature of, an ectype.

eç'ty̆pe, *n.* [L. *ectypus*; Gr. *ektypos*, engraved in relief, formed in outline; *ek*, out, and *typos*, a figure, outline.]

1. a copy; a reproduction of or very close resemblance to an original: opposed to *prototype* and *archetype*.

2. in architecture, a copy in relief or embossed.

eç·ty·pog'rȧ·phy, *n.* [Gr. *ektypos*, wrought in relief, and *-graphia*, from *graphein*, to write.] a method of etching or engraving that leaves the lines in relief instead of being sunk.

é·cu' (ā·kụ'), *n.*; *pl.* **é·cus'** (ā-kụ'), [Fr.]

1. a medieval shield of a mounted soldier.

2. any of various French silver or gold coins, especially a silver crown of the 17th and 18th centuries.

eç·ū·men'iç, oeç·ū·men'iç (ek-), *a.* ecumenical.

eç·ū·men'iç·ăl, oeç·ū·men'iç·ăl (ek-), *a.* [LL. *œcumenicus*; Gr. *oikoumenikos*, of or from the whole world; *oikoumenē* (*gē*), the inhabited (world); f. of ppr. pass. of *oikein*, to dwell, inhabit.]

1. general; universal: used specifically in reference to the Christian Church as a whole.

2. (a) furthering or intended to further the unity or unification of Christian churches; (b) of or having to do with ecumenism.

Ecumenical Bishop; the title assumed by the Pope of Rome.

ecumenical council; see under *council*.

eç''ū·men'i·çişm, *n.* same as *ecumenism*.

eç'ū·men·işm (ek'-), *n.* 1. the ecumenical movement among Christian churches.

2. the principles or practice of promoting cooperation or better understanding among differing religious faiths.

eç'zē·mȧ, *n.* [Gr. *ekzema*, an eruption of the skin, from *ekzein*; *ek*, out, and *zein*, to boil.] a disease of the skin characterized by inflammation, redness, itching, and the formation of vesicles which exude a watery substance that evaporates and leaves the skin covered with crusts; salt rheum; tetter.

eç·zem'ȧ·tous, *a.* 1. having the nature of eczema.

2. having or resulting from eczema.

-ed, (a) a suffix used to form the past tense and past participle of weak verbs, and to form adjectives from nouns or verbs or from other adjectives ending in *-ate*; (b) a suffix added to nouns, meaning *having, provided with, characterized by*.

ē·dā'cious, *a.* [L. *edax* (*-acis*), from *edere*, to eat.] voracious; consuming; devouring.

ē·dăc'i·ty, *n.* [L. *edacitas*, from *edax*, given to eating; from *edere*, to eat.] the state of being edacious; greediness; voracity; ravenousness; rapacity: now humorous.

E'dăm cheeşe, see under *cheese*.

ē·daph'iç, *a.* relating to, or determined by, conditions of the soil.

ed·ȧ·phol'ō·ġy, *n.* the study of soils.

Ed'dȧ, *n.* [ON, *Edda*; prob. akin to ON. *óthr*, poetry.] either of two early Icelandic literary works; (a) the *Prose*, or *Younger*, *Edda* (c. 1230), a summary of Norse mythology with two treatises on the writing of poetry, attributed to Snorri Sturluson; (b) the *Poetic*, or *Elder*, *Edda* (c. 1200), a collection of old Norse poetry.

Ed'diç, Ed·dā'iç, *a.* of or like the Eddas.

ed'dish, *n.* [AS. *edisc*, a pasture, a park for game.] the later pasture, or grass that comes after mowing or reaping: written also *eadish*. [Dial.]

ed'dō, *n.*; *pl.* **ed'dōeş** [prob. from native name in W. Africa.]

1. the edible root of the taro.

2. the root of any of several other related tropical plants.

ed'dy, *n.*; *pl.* **ed'dies,** [ME. *ydy*; prob. from ON. *itha*, an eddy.] a current of air, water, etc. moving against the main current and with a circular motion; little whirlpool or whirlwind.

eddy current; see *Foucault current* under *current*.

ed'dy, *v.i.*; eddied, *pt., pp.*; eddying, *ppr.* to move in an eddy; to whirl.

ed'dy, *v.t.* to cause to move in an eddy. [Rare.]

ę'del·weiss (ā'del-vīs), *n.* [G., from *edel*, noble, precious, and *weiss*, white.] a small plant, *Leontopodium alpinum*, native to the Swiss Alps, having white, woolly leaves arranged in star-shaped clusters with small, yellow flower heads at their center.

ē·dē'mȧ, oe·dē'mȧ, *n.*; *pl.* **ē·dē'mȧ·tȧ, oe·dē'mȧ·tȧ** [Gr. *oidēma*, a swelling, tumor, from *oidein*, to swell.] an abnormal accumulation of fluid in cells, tissues, or cavities of the body, resulting in swelling; dropsy.

ē·dem'ȧ·tōse, oe·dem'ȧ·tōse, *a.* same as *edematous*.

ē·dem'ȧ·tous, oe·dem'ȧ·tous, *a.* [Gr. *oidēma* (*-atos*), a swelling, from *oidein*, to swell.] of, or having the nature of, an edema.

Ē'den, *n.* [LL. *Eden*; Heb. *'ēden*, pleasure.]

1. in the Bible, the first home of Adam and Eve; Paradise.

2. any delightful region or state; a paradise.

Ē·den'iç, *a.* pertaining to or like Eden.

ē'den·īte, *n.* a variety of amphibole containing aluminum.

Ē'den·īze, *v.t.*; Edenized, *pt., pp.*; Edenizing, *ppr.* to transform into an Eden. [Rare.]

ē·den'tăl, *a.* and *n.* same as *edentate.*

ē·den'tăl·ous, *a.* edentate.

Ē·den·tā'tȧ, *n.pl.* [neut. pl. of L. *edentatus,* pp. of *edentare,* to render toothless; *e-,* out, and *dens, dentis,* a tooth.] in zoology, a group of mammals having only molars or no teeth at all, as the sloths, armadillos, and anteaters.

ē·den'tāte, *a.* 1. without teeth.
2. of the *Edentata.*

ē·den'tāte, *n.* an animal of the *Edentata.*

ē·den·tā'tion, *n.* the extraction of teeth. [Obs.]

ē·den'tū·lous, *a.* without teeth.

edġe (ej), *n.* [ME. *egge*; AS. *ecg*; akin to D. *egge,* G. *eck, ecke,* a corner; L. *acer,* sharp.]
1. the sharp border or the thin cutting side of an instrument; as, the *edge* of an ax, razor, knife, sword, or scythe.
2. the abrupt border or margin of anything; the brink; as, the *edge* of the table; the *edge* of a precipice.
3. the border or part adjacent to a line of division; the part nearest some limit; the commencement or early part; the beginning; as, the *edge* of a field; the *edge* of evening.
The new general, unacquainted with his army, and on the *edge* of winter, would not hastily oppose them. —Milton.
4. sharpness, as of mind or appetite; keenness; intenseness; as, the *edge* of appetite or hunger.
Silence and solitude set an *edge* on the genius. —Dryden.
5. keenness; sharpness; acrimony; wounding or irritating power.
Abate the *edge* of traitors. —Shak.
6. advantage; as, you have the *edge* on me. [Colloq.]
on edge; (a) so tense or nervous as to be easily upset; irritable; (b) eager; impatient.
to set the teeth on edge; (a) to cause a tingling or grating sensation in the teeth; (b) to irritate; to provoke.
to take the edge off; to dull the intensity, force, or pleasure of.
Syn.—border, rim, brink, verge, skirt, margin, brim.

edġe, *v.t.*; edged, *pt., pp.*; edging, *ppr.* 1. to sharpen.
2. to furnish with an edge; to form or put an edge on; as, to *edge* a flower bed with box.
3. to exasperate; to embitter. [Obs.]
By such reasonings the simple were blinded and the malicious *edged.* —Hayward.
4. to incite; to provoke; to instigate; to urge on; to egg. [Rare.]
5. to make (one's way) sidewise, as through a crowd.
6. to move little by little or cautiously.
Edging by degrees their chairs forwards, they were in a little time got up close to one another. —Locke.

edġe, *v.i.* 1. to move sidewise.
2. to move gradually or so as not to attract notice; to advance or retire gradually; as, to *edge* along this way.
When one has made a bad bet, it's best to *edge* off. —Colman.

edġe'bōne, *n.* same as *aitchbone.*

edġe'less, *a.* having no sharp edge; blunt; obtuse; unfit for cutting; as, an *edgeless* sword.

edġe'lọng, *adv.* edgewise. [Obs.]

edġe mill, a mill for crushing and triturating by means of a heavy stone rolled round on its edge upon a hard, level, enclosed floor: it is used for grinding oil seeds and for crushing ores.

edġe plāne, a plane for shaping and dressing the edges of boards; also, a tool for trimming and shaping edges of leather.

edġ'ẽr, *n.* one who or that which edges; specifically, a machine for cutting away superfluous parts of timber, such as slabs from a log.

edġe rāil, in railroading, (a) a broad, thin track rail, set with its edge upward: opposed to *flat rail*; (b) a rail placed alongside the main rail at a switch as a guard.

edġe'shot, *a.* dressed on the edges only: said of a board in carpentry.

edġe tọọl, any tool with a sharp edge for cutting, as a chisel or an ax; also, a tool used for sharpening edge tools; more appropriately, an *edging tool.*

edġe'wāyṣ, *adv.* with the edge foremost; on, by, with, or toward the edge.
to get a word in edgeways; to manage to say something oneself in a conversation being monopolized by another or others.

edġe'wīṣe, *adv.* same as *edgeways.*

edġ'ing, *n.* 1. that which is added to the border or which forms the edge, as lace, fringe, or trimming added to a garment for ornament.
2. in horticulture, a row of small plants set along the border of a flower bed.
3. the act of fitting edges, as in carpentry.

edġ'ing·ly, *adv.* shyly; cautiously; mincingly. [Rare.]

edġ'y, *a.* 1. having an edge or edges; sharp.
2. irritable; easily offended; on edge: said of a person.
3. having outlines that are too sharp: said of drawings, paintings, etc.

ed·i·bil'i·ty, *n.* fitness for food; the quality of being edible.

ed'i·ble, *a.* [LL. *edibilis,* from *edere,* to eat.] fit to be eaten; eatable.

ed'i·ble, *n.* [*usually pl.*] anything fit to be eaten; food.
edible snail; any snail that can be eaten, especially one of the genus *Helix.*

ed'i·ble·ness, *n.* edibility; the quality of being suitable for food.

ē'diçt, *n.* [L. *edictum,* from *edicere,* to utter or proclaim; *e-,* out, and *dicere,* to speak.] an official public proclamation or order issued by authority; an order issued by a sovereign to his subjects, as a rule or law requiring obedience.
Edict of Nantes; an edict issued by Henry IV of France, in 1598, giving his Protestant subjects the free exercise of their religion. The revocation of this edict, by Louis XIV, nearly a century later, led to a cruel persecution, which drove most of the Protestants out of the kingdom.
Syn.—decree, proclamation, order, manifesto, announcement, law, command.

ē·diç'tăl, *a.* [LL. *edictalis,* from L. *edictum,* an edict.] having the character of or pertaining to an edict or edicts.

ē·dif'i·cănt, *a.* [L. *ædificans (-antis),* ppr. of *ædificare,* to build.] edifying. [Obs.]

ed"i·fi·çā'tion, *n.* an edifying or being edified; instruction; especially, moral or spiritual instruction or improvement.

ed'i·fi·çā"tō·ry, *a.* [LL. *ædificatorius,* from *ædificator,* a builder.] edifying or intended to edify.

ed'i·fice, *n.* [Fr. *edifice*; L. *ædificium,* a building, from *ædificare,* to build; *ædes, ædis,* a building, temple, and *-ficare,* from *facere,* to make.] a building, especially one of imposing appearance, as a temple, a church, a public building, or a mansion: often used figuratively.

ed·i·fi'ciăl (-fish'ăl), *a.* pertaining to an edifice or structure.

ed'i·fi·ẽr, *n.* one who edifies.

ed'i·fȳ, *v.t.*; edified, *pt., pp.*; edifying, *ppr.* [ME. *edifien, edefien*; L. *ædificare,* to build, erect.]
1. to build; to establish. [Archaic.]
2. to instruct and improve the mind of, particularly morally or spiritually.

ed'i·fȳ, *v.i.* to be improved or enlightened. [Obs.]

ed'i·fȳ·ing, *a.* adapted to instruct and improve; as, an *edifying* discourse.

ed'i·fȳ·ing·ly, *adv.* in an edifying manner.

ed'i·fȳ·ing·ness, *n.* the quality of being edifying.

ē'dīle, *n.* in ancient Rome, an official in charge of buildings, roads, sanitation, public games, etc.

ed'ing·tŏn·īte, *n.* a rare zeolitic mineral which occurs in the cavities of thomsonite near Dumbarton, Scotland: named after a Glasgow mineralogist named *Edington.*

ed'it, *v.t.*; edited, *pt., pp.*; editing, *ppr.* [L. *editus,* pp. of *edere,* to give out, put forth, publish; *e-,* out, and *dare,* to give.]
1. to prepare (an author's works, journals, letters, etc.) for publication, by selection, arrangement, and annotation.
2. to revise and make ready (a manuscript) for publication.
3. to govern the policy of (a newspaper or periodical); decide what is to be printed, etc.

ē·di'tion, *n.* [Fr. *édition*; L. *editio (-onis),* from *edere,* to put forth, publish.]
1. the size, style, or form in which a book is published; as, a pocket *edition.*
2. (a) the total number of copies of a book, newspaper, etc. printed from the same plates, type, etc. and published at about the same time; (b) a single copy of such a printing.
3. the issue of a well-known work distinguished by its editor or publisher; as, the Skeat *edition* of Chaucer.
4. figuratively, a reproduction of anything; as, the boy is a second *edition* of his father.
edition de luxe; a superfine edition, with typography, paper, and binding of the best.

ē·di'tion·ẽr, *n.* an editor. [Obs.]

ē·di'ti·ō prin'ceps (-dish'i-ō), [L.] first edition.

ed'i·tŏr, *n.* [L. *editor,* from *edere,* to put forth, publish.]
1. one who edits.
2. a writer of editorials.

ed·i·tō'ri·ăl, *a.* 1. of an editor or editing; written by an editor.
2. characteristic of an editor or editorial; expressing opinion in the manner of an editor; as, *editorial* comment has no place in news stories.

ed·i·tō'ri·ăl, *n.* an article written by an editor; an article in a newspaper, magazine, etc. explicitly stating opinions of the editor or publisher.

ed·i·tō'ri·ăl·īze, *v.t.* and *v.i.*; editorialized, *pt., pp.*; editorializing, *ppr.* 1. to express editorial opinions about (something).
2. to put editorial opinions into (a newspaper article, etc.).

ed·i·tō'ri·ăl·ly, *adv.* 1. in an editorial manner; as an editor.
2. in or by an editorial or editorials.

ed'i·tŏr in chiēf, *pl.* **ed'i·tŏrṣ in chiēf,** the editor who heads or supervises the editorial staff of a publication.

ed'i·tŏr·ship, *n.* the position, functions, guidance, or authority of an editor.

ed'i·tress, *n.* a woman editor. [Rare.]

Ē'dŏm, *n.* in the Bible, Esau, Jacob's brother.

Ē'dŏm·īte, *n.* in the Bible, a descendant of Edom, or Esau; an Idumean.

Ē'dŏm·īt·ish, *a.* 1. of Edom.
2. characteristic of the Edomites.

Ed"ri·oph·thal'mȧ, *n.pl.* [Gr. *hedraios,* fixed, and *ophthalmos,* the eye.] a group of higher crustaceans whose eyes are fixed and attached at the base instead of being borne upon stalks.

EDRIOPHTHALMA
1. fresh-water shrimp (*Gammarus pulex*); *a,* single eye. 2. head of *Cymothoa*; *b,* cluster of simple eyes

ed"ri·oph·thal'mous, *a.* pertaining to the *Edriophthalma.*

Ed"ū·çȧ·bil'i·ȧ, *n.pl.* [from L. *educare,* to educate.] in old classifications, a superorder of placental mammals whose cerebrum has the distinctive fissure of Sylvius and is considerably larger than the cerebellum, overlapping it as well as the olfactory lobes.

ed"ū·çȧ·bil'i·ăn, *a.* pertaining to the *Educabilia.*

ed"ū·çȧ·bil'i·ty, *n.* capacity for receiving education or of being instructed.

ed'ū·çȧ·ble, *a.* that can be educated or trained.

ed'ū·çāte, *v.t.*; educated, *pt., pp.*; educating, *ppr.* [L. *educatus,* pp. of *educare,* to bring up, rear, or train a child, from *educere*; *e-,* out, and *ducere,* to lead, draw, bring.]
1. to give knowledge or training to; train or develop the knowledge, skill, mind, or character of, especially by formal schooling or study; teach; instruct.
2. to form and develop (one's taste, etc.).
3. to pay for the schooling of (a person).
Syn.—instruct, nurture, discipline, train, teach, develop, ground, school, initiate.

ed'ū·çā·ted, *a.* brought up; instructed; furnished with knowledge or principles; trained; disciplined.

ed·ū·çā'tion, *n.* [L. *educatio,* from *educare,* to educate.]
1. the process of training and developing the knowledge, skill, mind, character, etc., especially by formal schooling; teaching; training.
2. knowledge, ability, etc. thus developed.
3. (a) formal schooling; (b) a kind or stage of this; as, a medical *education,* a high-school *education.*
4. systematic study of the problems, methods, and theories of teaching and learning.
Syn.—instruction, teaching, breeding, cultivation, nurture, training.

ed·ū·çā′tion·ăl, *a.* 1. relating to education.
2. educating; giving instruction or information; as, an *educational* film.

ed·ū·çā′tion·ăl·ly, *adv.* 1. by means of education.
2. from the viewpoint of education.

ed·ū·çā′tion·ist, ed·ū·çā′tion·ăl·ist, *n.* a theorist in or a practical exponent of educational matters.

ed′ū·çā·tive, *a.* 1. relating to educational matters.
2. educating or tending to educate; instructive.

ed′ū·çā·tŏr, *n.* [L. *educator*, a rearer, foster father, pedagogue, from *educare*, to educate.]
1. a person whose work is to educate others; teacher.
2. a specialist in the science of education; authority on educational problems, theories, and methods.

ed′ū·çā·tress, *n.* a woman educator. [Rare.]

ē·dūçe′, *v.t.*; educed (-dūst′), *pt., pp.*; educing, *ppr.* [L. *educere*; *e-*, out, and *ducere*, to lead, draw.]
1. to bring or draw out; to elicit; to evolve.
2. to deduce; to infer from data.

ē·dū′ci·ble, *a.* that can be educed.

ē′duçt, *n.* [L. *eductum*, from *educere*, to lead or draw forth.]
1. something educed.
2. a substance separated unchanged from another substance: distinguished from *product*.

ē·duç′tion, *n.* [L. *eductio* (*-onis*), from *educere*, to lead or bring forth.]
1. an educing.
2. something educed.

ē·duç′tion valve, a valve for the passage of exhaust fluid or steam; an exhaust valve.

ē·duç′tive, *a.* educing or tending to educe.

ē·duç′tŏr, *n.* one who or that which educes.

ē·dul′çō·rāte, *v.t.*; edulcorated, *pt., pp.*; edulcorating, *ppr.* [L. *e-*, out, and *dulcoratus*, pp. of *dulcorare*, to sweeten, from *dulcor*, sweetness; *dulcis*, sweet.]
1. in chemistry, to free from acids or other soluble impurities by washing.
2. to free from acidity or acridity; to soften; to sweeten; to purify.

ē·dul·çō·rā′tion, *n.* the process or action of edulcorating.

ē·dul′çō·rā·tive, *a.* edulcorating.

ē·dul·çō·rā′tŏr, *n.* one who or that which edulcorates; specifically, a device formerly used as a dropping bottle.

ē·dū′li·ous, *a.* edible. [Obs.]

Ed·wạrd′i·ăn, *a.* designating or of the reigns of any of the English kings named Edward; specifically, (a) designating, or in the style of, the architecture of the period of the first three Edwards; (b) of or characteristic of the time of Edward VII, with reference to the literature and art produced then.

Ed·wạrdṣ′i·ȧ, *n.pl.* a typical genus of *Actiniaria*, named after the French naturalist, Henri Milne-Edwards.

Ed·wạrdṣ·ī′i·dae, *n.pl.* in zoology, a division of the *Anthozoa*, of the family *Actiniaria*, of which the *Edwardsia* is the type: the body is divided into eight septa, each of which is reproductive.

ee, *n.* an eye. [Scot.]

But steal me a blink o' your bonny black *ee*.
—Burns.

-ee, [from OFr. pp. ending *-é* masc., *-ée* f.; L. *-atus* masc., *-ata* f.] a noun-forming suffix designating: (a) *the recipient of a specified action, grant, or benefit*, as in appointee, selectee, mortgagee; (b) *a person in a specified condition*, as in absentee, refugee, employee; (c) *a person or thing associated in some way with another*, as in bargee, goatee.

-ee, a suffix forming substandard singulars from nouns ending in *-ese*, as in Chinee, Portugee.

eel, *n.*; *pl.* **eelṣ** or **eel,** [ME. *el*, *ele*; AS. *æl*; D. *aal*; G. *aal*, an eel.]
1. any of a group of fishes with long, slippery, snakelike bodies and no pelvic fins.
2. any of various similar snakelike fishes, including the electric eel and lamprey.

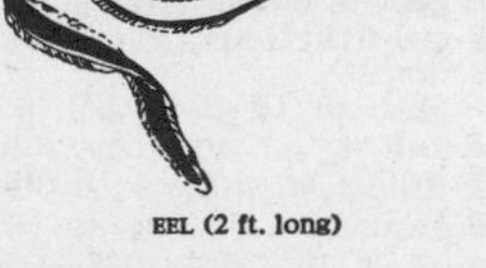
EEL (2 ft. long)

salt eel; a whip made of eelskin; hence, in nautical usage, a rope's end. [Obs.]

eel bȧs′ket, a fisherman's pot, basket, or other receptacle for eels.

eel′buck, *n.* an eelpot or eel basket. [Brit. Dial.]

eel′fāre, *n.* 1. the passage of young eels upstream toward salt water.
2. a brood of eels.

eel fọrk, a spear for catching eels.

eel′grȧss, *n.* a plant, *Zostera marina*, with long, narrow leaves, that grows under water in shallow inlets of the sea, especially of the North Atlantic.

eel′pot, *n.* a boxlike trap for catching eels.

eel′pout, *n.*; *pl.* **eel′pout** or **eel′pouts,** [AS. *ælepute*; *æl*, eel, and *pute*, pout.]
1. any of a group of salt-water fishes resembling the blenny.
2. the burbot, a fresh-water fish of the cod family.

eel shärk, an eel-shaped Japanese shark.

eel′skin, *n.* the skin of an eel.

eel′spēar, *n.* a barbed spear for use in spearing eels.

eel′y, *a.* like an eel; slippery.

een, *n.* obsolete and dialectal pl. of *eye*.

e′en, *adv.* even. [Poetic.]

e′en, *n.* even (evening). [Poetic or Dial.]

e′er (âr *or* ār), *adv.* ever. [Poetic.]

-eer, [from Fr. *-ier*; L. *-arius*.] a suffix used to form: (a) nouns meaning *a person or thing that has to do with*, as auctioneer, engineer; (b) nouns meaning *a person who writes, makes*, etc., as pamphleteer, sonneteer, profiteer: sometimes derogatory; (c) verbs meaning *to have to do with*, as electioneer.

ee′rie, *a.*; *comp.* eerier; *superl.* eeriest, [northern Eng. dial. and Scot.; ME. *eri*, timid.]
1. originally, timid or frightened; uneasy because of superstitious fear.
2. inspiring fear; weird; uncanny.
Also spelled *eery*.

ee′ri·ly, *adv.* in an eerie manner.

ee′ri·ness, *n.* the quality of being eerie.

ee′ry, *a.*; *comp.* eerier; *superl.* eeriest, same as *eerie*.

ef-, same as *ex-*: used before *f*, as in *ef*ferent.

ef′fȧ·ble, *a.* [L. *effabilis*, utterable, from *effari*, to utter, speak out; *ex*, out, and *fari*, to speak.] utterable; that can be uttered or spoken. [Rare.]

ef·fāçe′, *v.t.*; effaced (-fāst′), *pt., pp.*; effacing, *ppr.* [Fr. *effacer*; from L. *ex*, out, and *facies*, form, appearance.]
1. to make disappear as by blotting or rubbing out; to erase, strike, or scratch out, so as to destroy or make illegible; as, to *efface* the letters on a monument; to *efface* a writing.
2. to remove from the mind; to obliterate; as, to *efface* the image of a person in the mind.
3. to cause (oneself) to remain inconspicuous; withdraw (oneself) from notice.
Syn.—erase, obliterate, cancel, expunge, annul, blot out, destroy.

ef·fāçe′ȧ·ble, *a.* capable of being effaced.

ef·fāçe′ment, *n.* an effacing or being effaced.

ef·fa·ré′ (-fȧ-rā′), *a.* [Fr.] in heraldry, denoting an animal represented as rearing on its hind legs, as if it were frightened or enraged.

ef·fas′ci·nāte, *v.t.* [L. *effascinatus*, pp. of *effascinare*, to charm; *ex-*, intens., and *fascinare*, to charm.] to charm; to bewitch. [Obs.]

ef·fas·ci·nā′tion, *n.* fascination. [Obs.]

ef·feçt′, *n.* [L. *effectus*, pp. of *efficere*, to bring to pass, accomplish; *ex*, out, and *facere*, to do.]
1. that which is produced by an operating agent or cause; a result or consequence; as, the *effect* of this war was the breaking up of the kingdom.

Effect is the substance produced, or simple idea introduced into any subject, by the exerting of power. —Locke.

2. the power or ability to produce consequences or results; force; validity; efficacy; as, the obligation is void and of no effect.
3. purport; tenor; import or general intent; as, he made the purchase for his friend and immediately wrote him to that *effect*.
4. influence or action on something; as, the drug had a cathartic *effect*.
5. the combination of color or form in a picture, landscape, etc.; as, cubist *effects* differ from those of impressionists.
6. the impression produced on the mind of the observer or hearer, as by artistic design or manner of speaking, acting, etc.; as, she did that just for *effect*.
7. the condition or fact of being operative or in force; fulfillment (with *in*, *into*, or *to*).
8. [*pl.*] belongings; property; as, household *effects*.
9. in mechanics, the amount of effective work accomplished by a machine during a stated time.
Hall effect; the phenomenon noted as to the effect of the interference of a magnetic field with the onward flow of an electric current.
in effect; (a) in result; actually; in fact; (b) in essence; virtually; (c) in practice; in operation; in force.
of no effect; producing no results; in vain.
Peltier effect; a raising or lowering of temperature at the point where two metals of different powers of electric conductibility come together, dependent upon the direction of the current.
Thomson effect; the production or absorption of heat caused by the flow of an electric current from one point of a conductor to another where the temperature is different.
to give effect to; to put into practice; make operative.
to take effect; to begin to produce results; become operative.
to the effect; with the purport or meaning.
Syn.—consequence, event, issue, meaning, reality, result.

ef·feçt′, *v.t.*; effected, *pt., pp.*; effecting, *ppr.*
1. to bring about; cause to happen; accomplish; produce as a result.
2. to make; produce; construct.
Syn.—accomplish, perform, consummate, achieve, execute.

ef·feçt′ẽr, *n.* one who effects; that which effects; an agent.

ef·feçt′i·ble, *a.* that can be effected.

ef·feç′tion, *n.* an effecting; production.

ef·feç′tive, *a.* [LL. *effectivus*, from *effectus*, pp. of *efficere*, to bring to pass.]
1. having an effect; producing a result.
2. producing a definite or desired result; efficient.
3. operative; active; in effect.
4. making a striking impression; impressive.
5. equipped and ready for combat, as a sailor or ship.
Syn.—cogent, influential, forcible, potent, conclusive, convincing.

ef·feçt′ive, *n.* [*usually in pl.*] a member or unit of the armed forces equipped and ready for combat.

ef·feçt′ive·ly, *adv.* in an effective manner.

ef·feçt′ive·ness, *n.* the quality of being effective.

ef·feçt′less, *a.* without effect; without advantage; useless.

ef·feçt′ŏr, *n.* [L., a producer, from *effectus*; see *effect*.]
1. a muscle, gland, etc. capable of responding to a stimulus, especially to a nerve impulse.
2. that part of a nerve which transmits an impulse to an organ of response.

ef·feç′tū·ăl, *a.* 1. producing the effect desired or intended; having adequate power or force to produce the effect; as, an *effectual* remedy.
2. having legal force; valid.
effectual calling; in Calvinism, the agency of the Holy Ghost, through Christ, in the scheme of salvation.

ef·feç′tū·ăl·ly, *adv.* 1. effectively; efficaciously; in a manner to produce the intended effect; thoroughly; as, the city is *effectually* guarded.
2. actually. [Obs.]

ef·feç′tū·ăl·ness, *n.* the state or quality of being effectual.

ef·feç′tū·āte, *v.t.*; effectuated, *pt., pp.*; effectuating, *ppr.* to bring to pass; to achieve; to accomplish; to cause to happen; to effect.

ef·feç·tū·ā′tion, *n.* an effectuating; accomplishment.

ef·feç′tū·ous, *a.* effectual. [Obs.]

ef·feç′tū·ous·ly, *adv.* effectually. [Obs.]

ef·fem′i·nā·cy, *n.*; *pl.* **ef·fem′i·nā·cieṣ,** 1. the state or quality of being effeminate.
2. an instance of this.

ef·fem′i·nāte, *a.* [L. *effeminatus*, pp. of *effeminare*, to make womanish, from *ex-*, out, and *femina*, a woman.]
1. having the qualities generally attributed to women, as weakness, gentleness, delicacy, etc.; unmanly.
2. characterized by such qualities; weak; soft, decadent, etc.; as, *effeminate* art.
3. womanlike, tender; gentle. [Obs.]

ef·fem′i·nāte, *v.t.* and *v.i.*; effeminated, *pt.*,

pp.; effeminating, *ppr.* to make or become effeminate.

ef·fem′i·nāte·ly, *adv.* 1. in an effeminate manner.

2. by means of a woman; as, *effeminately* vanquished. [Rare.]

ef·fem′i·nāte·ness, *n.* the quality or condition of being effeminate.

ef·fem·i·nā′tion, *n.* the process of becoming or making effeminate.

ef·fen′di, *n.*; *pl.* **ef·fen′diṣ,** [Turk. *efendi*, altered from modern Gr. *aphentēs*; Gr. *authentēs*, a master, ruler.] Sir; Master: a Turkish title of respect.

ef′fĕr·ent, *a.* [L. *efferens* (*-entis*), ppr. of *efferre*, to carry out; *ex*, out, and *ferre*, to bear.] carrying or carried away: said especially of a duct or blood vessel that carries a secretion or blood away from a part, or a nerve that carries impulses away from a nerve center: opposed to *afferent*.

ef′fĕr·ent, *n.* 1. a stream that carries off water from a pond.

2. an efferent nerve, duct, etc.

ef·fĕr·vesce′, *v.i.*; effervesced (-vest′), *pt.*, *pp.*; effervescing, *ppr.* [L. *effervescere*, to boil up, foam up; *ex*, out, and *fervescere*, to begin to boil, from *fervere*, to boil.]

1. to give off gas bubbles, as carbonated beverages; bubble; foam.

2. to come out in bubbles; rise in bubbles in a liquid.

3. to be lively and high-spirited; be vivacious.

ef·fĕr·ves′cence, ef·fĕr·ves′cen·cy, *n.* 1. a bubbling up; foaming.

2. liveliness; high spirits; vivacity; exuberance.

ef·fĕr·ves′cent, *a.* 1. giving off gas bubbles; bubbling up; foaming.

2. lively and high-spirited; vivacious.

ef·fĕr·ves′ci·ble, *a.* that has the quality of effervescing; capable of producing effervescence.

ef·fĕr·ves′cive, *a.* tending to produce effervescence.

ef′fet, *n.* an eft. [Dial.]

ef·fēte′, *a.* [L. *effetus*, that has brought forth, exhausted; *ex*, out, and *fetus*, that has brought forth.] barren; no longer capable of producing, as an animal, a soil, etc.; hence, exhausted; barren; sterile; inefficient through age, use, or decay.

ef·fi·cā′cious, *a.* [L. *efficax* (*-acis*), from *efficere*, to bring to pass, accomplish.] producing the effect intended; having power adequate to the purpose intended; as, an *efficacious* remedy for disease.

ef·fi·cā′cious·ly, *adv.* in an efficacious manner.

ef·fi·cā′cious·ness, *n.* efficacious quality.

ef′fi·cȧ·cy, *n.*; *pl.* **ef′fi·cȧ·cieṣ,** [L. *efficacia*, from *efficere*, to accomplish.] power to produce effects or intended results; effectiveness.

ef·fi′cien·cy (-fish′en-), *n.*, *pl.* **ef′fi·cien·cieṣ,** 1. ability to produce the desired effect with a minimum of effort, expense, or waste; quality or fact of being efficient.

2. the ratio of effective work to the energy expended in producing it, as of a machine; output divided by input.

efficiency engineer; an efficiency expert.

efficiency expert; a person whose work is to increase the efficiency and productivity of a business or industrial plant by finding better methods of performing various operations, cutting down waste, etc.

ef·fi′cient (-fish′ent), *a.* 1. directly producing an effect or result; causative; effective; as, the *efficient* cause.

2. producing the desired effect or result with a minimum of effort, expense, or waste; working well; competent; able; capable.

Syn.—able, capable, effective, competent.

ef·fi′cient, *n.* 1. the agent or cause which produces or causes to exist.

2. a volunteer in the British army who is certified as having a competent knowledge of the duties of the service.

ef·fi′cient·ly, *adv.* in an efficient manner.

ef·fierce′, *v.t.* to make fierce or furious. [Obs.]

ef·fig′i·ăl, *a.* pertaining to an effigy. [Rare.]

ef·fig′i·āte, *v.t.* [LL. *effigiatus*, pp. of *effigiare*, to form, fashion, from *effigies*, an image, likeness.] to form an effigy of. [Rare.]

ef·fig·i·ā′tion, *n.* the act of forming an effigy; also, an effigy. [Rare.]

ef·fig′i·ēṣ, *n.* [L.] an effigy.

ef·fig′ū·rāte, *a.* [L. *ex-* out, and *figuratus*, pp. of *figurare*, to figure; *figura*, a figure.] in botany, having a well-defined form, as opposed to *effuse*: said of lichens.

ef′fi·gy, *n.*; *pl.* **ef′fi·gieṣ,** [L. *effigies*, *effigia*, a copy, image, likeness, from *effingere*; *ex*, out, and *fingere*, to form, fashion.] the image or likeness of a person; representation; portrait; a figure in sculpture, painting, etc.; often, a stuffed figure representing a person who has incurred hatred, commonly hanged or burned in public.

ef·flag′i·tāte, *v.t.* [L. *efflagitatus*, pp. of *efflagitare*, to demand urgently.] to demand earnestly. [Obs.]

ef·flāte′, *v.t.* [L. *efflatus*, pp. of *efflare*; *ex*, out, and *flare*, to blow.] to fill with breath or air. [Rare.]

ef·flā′tion, *n.* an emanation; a puff; also, the act of blowing or puffing. [Rare.]

ef·flō·resce′, *v.i.*; effloresced (-rest′), *pt.*, *pp.*; efflorescing, *ppr.* [L. *efflorescere*, to begin to bloom; incept. from *ex*, out, and *florere*, to blossom; *flos*, *floris*, a flower.]

1. to blossom out; flower.

2. in chemistry, (a) to change from a crystalline to a powdery state through loss of the water of crystallization when exposed to air; (b) to develop a powdery crust as a result of evaporation or chemical change.

ef·flō·res′cence, *n.* 1. a flowering; blooming.

2. the time of flowering.

3. the peak or fulfillment, as of an art or career.

4. in chemistry, (a) the changing of certain crystalline compounds to a whitish powder or powdery crust through loss of their water of crystallization; (b) the powder or crust thus formed.

5. in medicine, an eruption on the skin; rash or other skin lesion.

ef·flō·res′cen·cy, *n.* the quality or condition of being efflorescent. [Obs.]

ef·flō·res′cent, *a.* [L. *efflorescens* (*-entis*), ppr. of *efflorescere*, to begin to blossom.]

1. blossoming; flowering.

2. in chemistry, (a) changing from a crystalline to a powdery state through loss of the water of crystallization when exposed to air; (b) covered with a powdery crust as a result of evaporation or chemical change.

ef·flow′ĕr, *v.t.* [Fr. *effleurer*, to graze, strip the leaves off; *ef-*, L. *ex*, out, and *fleur*; G. *flur*, meadow, plain.] in making leather, to divest (a skin) of its epidermis.

ef′flụ·ence, *n.* [L. *effluens* (*-entis*), ppr. of *effluere*, to flow out.]

1. a flowing out; an emanating.

2. that which flows or issues from any body or substance; emanation; outflow.

ef′flụ·en·cy, *n.* effluence. [Rare.]

ef′flụ·ent, *a.* flowing out or forth.

ef′flụ·ent, *n.* a thing that flows out or forth; specifically, (a) a stream flowing out of a body of water; (b) the outflow of a sewer, sewage tank, etc.

ef·flụ′vi·ȧ, *n.* alternative pl. of *effluvium*.

ef·flụ′vi·ȧ·ble, *a.* that can be emitted in the form of an effluvium. [Obs.]

ef·flụ′vi·ăl, *a.* of, like, or containing effluvia.

ef·flụ′vi·āte, *v.i.* to emit or throw off an effluvium. [Rare.]

ef·flụ·vi·og′rȧ·phy, *n.* the action of a silent electric discharge on a photographic plate.

ef·flụ′vi·um, *n.*; *pl.* **ef·flụ′vi·ȧ, ef·flụ′vi·umṣ,** [L., a flowing out, an outlet, from *effluere*, to flow out; *ex*, out, and *fluere*, to flow.]

1. a real or supposed outflow in the form of a vapor or stream of invisible particles; aura.

2. a disagreeable or noxious vapor or odor.

ef′flux, *n.* [L. *effluxus*, from *effluere*, to flow out.]

1. a flowing out or issuing in a stream; as, an *efflux* of blood from a wound.

2. that which flows out; emanation.

ef·flux′, *v.i.* to run or flow away. [Obs.]

ef·flux′ion (-fluk′shun), *n.* same as *efflux*.

ef·fō′di·ent, *a.* [L. *effodiens* (*-entis*), ppr. of *effodire*, to dig out, dig up.] in zoology, digging; accustomed to dig.

ef·fō·li·ā′tion, *n.* [a variant of *exfoliation*.] the process of losing foliage.

ef·fōrce′, *v.t.* [Fr. *efforcer*; LL. *effortiare*, to force, compel; L. *ex*, out, and *fortis*, strong.] to force; to break through by violence; to ravish. [Obs.]

ef·form′, *v.t.* to fashion; to form. [Rare.]

ef·fọr·mā′tion, *n.* formation. [Rare.]

ef′fọrt, *n.* [Fr. *effort*; LL. *effortiare*, to strengthen, compel; L. *ex*, out, and *fortis*, strong.]

1. the using of energy to get something done; exertion of strength or mental power.

2. a try, especially a hard try; attempt; endeavor.

3. a product or result of working or trying; achievement.

Syn.—attempt, endeavor, trial, essay.

ef·fọrt′, *v.t.* to furnish an auxiliary to. [Obs.]

ef′fọrt·less, *a.* making, requiring, or showing virtually no effort.

ef·fos′sion, *n.* [L. *effossus*, pp. of *effodire*, to dig out.] the act of digging out of the earth. [Rare.]

ef·fran′chiṣe, *v.t.* [OFr. *effranchir*, *esfranchir*, to enfranchise; *es-*, L. *ex*, out, and *franchir*, to free.] to invest with franchises or privileges. [Rare.]

ef·fray′, *v.t.* [Fr. *effrayer*, to frighten.] to frighten. [Obs.]

ef·frē·nā′tion, *n.* [L. *effrenatio* (*-onis*), from *effrenare*, to unbridle; *ex*, out, and *frenare*, to bridle.] unbridled rashness or license; unruliness. [Obs.]

ef·frŏnt′, *v.t.* to inspire with effrontery. [Obs.]

ef·frŏnt′ĕr·y, *n.*; *pl.* **ef·frŏnt′ĕr·ieṣ,** [OFr. *effronterie*, from *effronte*, shameless, L. *effrons* (*-ontis*), putting forth the forehead; barefaced, shameless; *ex*, out, and *frons*, the forehead.] impudence; assurance; shameless boldness; boldness transgressing the bounds of modesty and decorum.

ef·frŏn′tū·ous·ly, *adv.* with effrontery. [Obs.]

ef·fulġe′, *v.t.* and *v.i.*; effulged, *pt.*, *pp.*; effulging, *ppr.* [L. *effulgere*, to shine forth; *ex*, out, and *fulgere*, to shine.] to shine or flash out.

ef·ful′ġence, *n.* a flood of light; great brightness; splendor; as, the *effulgence* of divine glory.

ef·ful′ġent, *a.* shining; bright; splendid; diffusing a flood of light; as, the *effulgent* sun.

ef·ful′ġent·ly, *adv.* in an effulgent manner.

ef·fū·mȧ·bil′i·ty, *n.* the quality of being converted into fumes or vapor. [Obs.]

ef·fūme′, *v.t.* to breathe out (smoke). [Obs.]

ef·fund′, *v.t.* to pour out. [Obs.]

ef·fūṣe′, *v.t.* and *v.i.*; effused, *pt.*, *pp.*; effusing, *ppr.* [L. *effusus*, pp. of *effundere*, to pour forth; *ex*, out, and *fundere*, to pour.]

1. to pour out or forth.

2. to spread; to diffuse.

ef·fūse′, *a.* 1. unrestrained; profuse. [Obs.]

2. in botany, spreading loosely; not having a definite figure: said of a flower.

3. in zoology, having the lips separated by a gap or groove: said of a shell.

ef·fūse′, *n.* an effusion. [Obs.]

ef·fū′ṣion, *n.* [L. *effusio* (*-onis*), from *effundere*, to pour forth.]

1. the act of pouring out; as, the *effusion* of blood, of words, of grace, etc.

2. unrestrained or emotional expression in speech or writing; as, the *effusions* of a youthful poet.

3. demonstrative cordiality of manner; eager welcome; overflowing kindness.

4. in pathology, (a) the escape of any fluid from glands, blood vessels, etc. into body cavities or tissues; (b) the fluid thus effusing.

5. the escape of gases through minute apertures into a vacuum.

ef·fū′sive, *a.* 1. pouring out or forth; overflowing.

2. expressing excessive emotion in an unrestrained manner; overly demonstrative; gushing.

effusive rocks; surface volcanic rocks: distinguished from *intrusive rocks*.

ef·fū′sive·ly, *adv.* in an effusive manner.

ef·fū′sive·ness, *n.* the state or quality of being effusive.

ef′reet, *n.* same as *afrit*.

eft, *n.* [ME. *efte*, *eefte*, *evete*, *ewt*; older, dial., and literary form of *newt*.] a small lizard or newt.

eft, *adv.* [AS. *eft*, *æft*, afterward, again.] again; also, afterwards. [Archaic.]

eft·sọon′, eft·sọonṣ′, *adv.* 1. immediately afterward; forthwith.

2. at frequent intervals; often.

3. again.

[Archaic in all senses.]

ē·gad′, *interj.* a softened or euphemistic form of the oath "by God."

ē′găl, *a.* equal. [Obs.]

ē·gal·i·tär′i·ăn, *a.* and *adv.* same as *equalitarian*.

é·ga·li·té′ (ā-gȧ-lē-tā′), *n.* [Fr.] equality.

ē·gal′i·ty, *n.* equality. [Obs.]

E·ġē′ăn, *a.* same as *Ægean*.

ē′ġence, *n.* [L. *egens* (*-entis*), ppr. of *egere*, to be in want, need.] need; state of want. [Rare.]

ē′ġĕr, *a.* eager. [Obs.]

E·gē′ri·a, *n.* [L.; Gr. *Ēgeria.*]
1. in Roman mythology, a nymph who acted as adviser, and dictated laws, to Numa, second king of Rome.
2. a woman adviser.

ē·gest′, *v.t.*; egested, *pt., pp.*; egesting, ppr. [L. *egestus*, pp. of *egerere*, to bear out, discharge.] to excrete; to pass off, as excrement, perspiration, etc.

ē·ges′tȧ, *n.pl.* [neut. pl. of L. *egestus*, pp. of *egerere*, to throw out, discharge.] any waste matter passed out of the body; excreta.

ē·ges′tion (-jes′chun), *n.* [L. *egestio* (-*onis*), from *egerere*, to bear out, discharge.] the act of egesting; also, egested matter.

ē·ges′tive, *a.* relating to egestion.

egg, *v.t.*; egged, *pt., pp.*; egging, *ppr.* [ME. *eggen*, to incite, urge on; Ice. *eggja*, from *egg*, edge.] to arouse to action; to incite; to urge: usually followed by *on*; as, *egged on* by pride.

egg, *n.* [ME. *egge*; Ice. *egg*; AS. *æg*; Sw. *ägg*; Dan. *æg*, an egg.]
1. the oval body laid by a female bird and by many fishes and reptiles, which contains the germ of a new individual along with food for its development, and is enclosed in a shell or membrane.

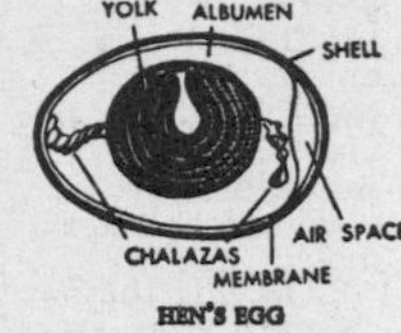

HEN'S EGG

2. a reproductive cell produced by the female; an ovum.
3. a hen's egg, raw or cooked in any way.
4. anything resembling a hen's egg.
5. an origin, germ, or elementary idea.
6. a person; as, he's a good *egg*. [Slang.]
8. an aerial bomb, hand grenade, or torpedo. [Slang.]
egg on one's face; embarrassment due to an obvious blunder. [Colloq.]
to lay an egg; to fail completely: said of a joke, theatrical performance, etc. [Slang.]
to put (or *have*) *all one's eggs in one basket*; to risk all that one has on a single venture, method, etc.

egg, *v.t.* 1. to mix or cover with the yolk or white of eggs, as in cooking.
2. to throw eggs at. [Colloq.]

egg and därt, a decorative molding used in architecture and cabinetwork, consisting of a form shaped like an egg alternating with another form shaped like an arrow, anchor, or tongue: also *egg and anchor, egg and tongue*.

egg ap·pȧ·rā′tus, in botany, a female organ consisting of three cells at the opening of the embryo sac in the higher flowering plants, an egg cell and two sterile cells.

egg ap′ple, the eggplant.

eg′gär, *n.* same as *egger* (a moth).

egg bĩrd, any one of several kinds of sea birds whose eggs have a commerical value.

egg cell, a reproductive cell produced by the female.

egg çōal, any of various sizes of coal between $1^1/_2$ and 4 inches in diameter.

egg crēam, a drink of chocolate syrup, soda water, and milk. [Chiefly New York City.]

egg çup, a special form of cup for holding a soft-boiled egg that is eaten from the shell.

eg′gẽr, *n.* one whose business is the collecting of eggs, as of wild fowl, turtles, etc.

eg′gẽr, *n.* [ME. *eggen*, to incite, urge on.] one who incites.

eg′gẽr, *n.* [origin unknown.] a moth, as any of the two genera, *Eriogaster* or *Lasiocampa*, whose larvae feed on the leaves of trees.

egg foọ yǒng, a Chinese-American dish consisting of eggs beaten and cooked with bean sprouts, onions, minced pork or shrimp, etc.: also called *egg foo young*.

egg′head, *n.* an intellectual: usually a term of contempt or derision as used by anti-intellectuals. [Slang.]

egg′hot, *n.* a warm drink containing eggs, brandy, ale, and sugar.

egg′lẽr, *n.* a collector of or dealer in eggs.

egg′ment, *n.* [ME. *eggement*, from *eggen*, to incite, urge on.] incitement to action; urging.

egg mīte, any of various mites that destroy the eggs of other insects.

egg′nog, *n.* a thick drink composed of egg, milk, and sugar, usually with the addition of a distilled liquor.

egg par′ȧ·sīte, in zoology, a parasitic insect whose eggs are laid in the eggs of other insects.

egg′plȧnt, *n.* a plant allied to the potato and bearing a large, pear-shaped, usually purple-skinned fruit, which is eaten as a vegetable; the *Solanum melongena.*

EGGPLANT
(*Solanum melongena*)

egg rōll, thin, flat egg dough wrapped around minced vegetables, meat, shrimp, etc. in a small roll and fried in deep fat: a Chinese-American dish.

eggs Ben′ē·dict, [origin unknown.] poached eggs served over ham on a split, toasted muffin, topped with hollandaise sauce.

egg′-shāped (-shāpt), *a.* shaped like an egg.

egg′shell, *n.* 1. the brittle outside covering of an egg.
2. a gastropod shaped like an egg.
eggshell china or *porcelain*; an extremely thin variety of porcelain or china.

egg′shell, *a.* 1. fragile and thin, like an eggshell.
2. yellowish-ivory.

egg ûr′chin, any globular sea urchin.

ē′ġis, *n.* same as *aegis.*

eg′lăn·tīne, *n.* [Fr., from OFr. *aiglent*, sweetbrier, hip tree, from L. *aculeus*, a sting, prickle; *acus*, a point, sting.]
1. the sweetbrier, *Rosa eglanteria*: it has pink flowers and a prickly stem.
2. the dogrose or wild rose, *Rosa canina*. *Eglantine* is used in Milton's *l'Allegro* to refer to another flower, probably a honeysuckle, *Lonicera periclymenum.*

eg′len·tere, eg′lăn·tere, *n.* eglantine. [Obs.]

ē·glom′ẽr·āte, *v.t.* [L. *e-*, out, and *glomeratus*, pp. of *glomerare*, to wind up into a ball.] to unwind, as a thread from a ball. [Obs.]

ē′gō (*or* eg′ō), *n.*; *pl.* **ē′gōṣ,** [L. *ego*, I.]
1. the self; the individual as aware of himself.
2. egotism; conceit. [Colloq.]
3. in philosophy, the self, variously conceived as an absolute spiritual substance on which experience is superimposed, the series of acts and mental states introspectively recognized, etc.
4. in psychoanalysis, that part of the psyche which, developing from the id, experiences the external world through the senses, and consciously controls the impulses of the id: distinguished from *superego, id.*

ē″gō·cen′triç, *a.* 1. dwelling upon one's self or upon one's own personal interests almost to the exclusion of everything else; viewing everything in relation to oneself; self-centered.
2. exhibiting an interest in the individual rather than in the group.
3. in philosophy, existing only as conceived in the individual mind: said of the world.

ē″gō·cen′triç, *n.* an egocentric person.

ē″gō·cen·tric′i·ty, *n.* the state or quality of being egocentric.

ē′gō·hood, *n.* personality. [Rare.]

ē·gō′iç·ăl, *a.* of or characteristic of egoism.

ē′gō·iṣm, *n.* 1. the tendency to be self-centered, or to consider only oneself and one's own interests; selfishness.
2. egotism; conceit.
3. in ethics, the doctrine that self-interest is the proper goal of all human actions: opposed to *altruism.*
4. in metaphysics, the opinion of one who thinks everything uncertain except his own existence.

ē′gō·ist, *n.* [Fr. *égoïste*, from L. *ego*, I.]
1. a person who is self-centered or selfish.
2. a conceited person; an egotist.
3. in philosophy, a person who accepts the doctrine of egoism.

ē·gō·is′tiç, ē·gō·is′tiç·ăl, *a.* 1. self-centered or selfish.
2. egotistical; conceited.
3. of an egoist or egoism.

ē·gō·is′tiç·ăl·ly, *adv.* in an egoistic way.

ē·gō′i·ty, *n.* personality. [Rare.]

ē·gō·mā′ni·ȧ, *n.* abnormally excessive egotism.

ē·gō·mā′ni·aç, *n.* a person characterized by egomania.

ē·gō·phon′iç, *a.* same as *aegophonic.*

ē·goph′ō·ny, *n.* same as *aegophony.*

ē′gō·thē·iṣm, *n.* [Gr. *egō*, I, and *theos*, God.] the identification of self with the Deity; self-deification. [Rare.]

ē′gō·tiṣm (*or* eg′ō-), *n.* [L. *ego*, I, and *-tism*, for *-ism.*]
1. constant, excessive reference to oneself in speaking or writing.
2. self-conceit.
3. selfishness; see also *egoism*; the terms are sometimes used interchangeably, but *egotism* is generally considered the more opprobrious term.
Syn.—self-conceit.—*Self-conceit* implies an overweening opinion of oneself; *egotism* stresses the expression of self-conceit in words or actions.

ē′gō·tist, *n.* [L. *ego*, I, and *-tist*, for *-ist.*] a person characterized by egotism.

ē·gō·tis′tiç, ē·gō·tis′tiç·ăl, *a.* 1. showing egotism.
2. pertaining to egotism.

ē·gō·tis′tiç·ăl·ly, *adv.* in an egotistic manner.

ē′gō·tīze, *v.i.*; egotized, *pt., pp.*; egotizing, *ppr.* to act in an egotistic manner.

ē′gō trip, 1. an experience, activity, etc. used for self-fulfillment or self-expression.
2. anything that serves to increase one's vanity, self-conceit, etc.

ē·gran′ū·lōse, *a.* [L. *e-* priv., and *granulum*, dim. of *granum*, a grain.] in botany, without granules.

ē′gre (-gẽr), *a.* eager. [Obs.]

ē·grē′ġious (-jus *or* -ji-us), *a.* [L. *egregius*, lit., chosen or separated from the herd, select, choice, eminent; *e*, out, and *grex, gregis*, herd.]
1. eminent; remarkable; extraordinary; distinguished; as, *egregious* exploits. [Archaic.]
2. outstanding for undesirable qualities; remarkably bad; flagrant; as, an *egregious* mistake.

ē·grē′ġious·ly, *adv.* in an egregious way; as, he is *egregiously* mistaken.

ē·grē′ġious·ness, *n.* state of being egregious.

eg′rē·moigne, *n.* agrimony. [Obs.]

ē′gress, *n.* [L. *egressus*, from *egredi*, to go out; *e*, out, and *gradi*, to step, go.]
1. the act of going out; emergence.
2. a way out; an exit; as, a broad *egress.*
3. the right to go out.
4. in astronomy, the passage of a heavenly body out from behind another.

ē′gress, *v.i.* to depart; to go out.

ē·gres′sion (ē-gresh′un), *n.* [L. *egressio*, from *egredi*, to go out.] the act of going out.

ē·gress′ŏr, *n.* one who goes out. [Rare.]

ē′gret, *n.* [Fr. *aigrette*, a sort of heron, a tuft of feathers.]
1. *pl.* **ē′grets, ē′gret,** any of various herons which have the white feathers on the lower part of the back lengthened and the barbs loose, so that this part of the plumage is very soft and flowing.
2. such a feather: usually *aigrette.*
3. in botany, the flying, feathery, or hairy crown of seeds, as the down of the thistle.
4. in zoology, a variety of monkey found in Java.

eg′ri·mō·ny, *n.* [L. *ægrimonia*, sorrow, anxiety, from *æger*, sick.] mental distress; sorrow. [Obs.]

ẹ·guäl·men′tẹ (-gwäl-), *adv.* [It., from *equale*; L. *æqualis*, equal.] in music, evenly.

ē·gûr′ġi·tāte, *v.t.* [L. *egurgitatus*, pp. of *egurgitare*, to pour out; *e*, out, and *gurgitare*, from *gurges*, a whirlpool.] to emit with a gush, as water from a geyser.

E·gyp′tiăn (-shăn), *a.* [L. *Ægyptius*; Gr. *Aigyptios*, Egyptian, from *Aigyptos*, Egypt.]
1. of Egypt, its people, or their culture.
2. of the Egyptian language.
3. gypsy. [Obs.]
Egyptian architecture; the style of architecture developed and carried to a high state of perfection by the ancient Egyptians and illustrated by some of the oldest structures in existence in the form of pyramids, temples, and monoliths.
Egyptian arum; the taro.
Egyptian bean; the Indian lotus, or its seeds,

which are shaped like beans; also, the hyacinth bean.

Egyptian pound; the gold monetary unit of Egypt, valued at slightly more than a British pound: symbol, £ E.

Egyptian thorn; in botany, a tree, the *Acacia vera*, which yields gum arabic.

E·gyp′tiăn, *n.* 1. a native or inhabitant of Egypt.

2. the Hamitic language of ancient Egypt.

3. a gypsy. [Obs.]

E′gypt·ize, *v.t.* to cause to become, or to claim (something) to be, Egyptian in character, origin, etc. [Rare.]

E·gyp·tol′ō·gẽr, *n.* same as *Egyptologist.*

E·gyp·tō·log′ic·ăl, *a.* relating to Egyptology.

E·gyp·tol′ō·gist, *n.* a student of or expert in Egyptology.

E·gyp·tol′ō·gy, *n.* [Gr. *Aigyptos*, Egypt, and *-logia*, from *legein*, to speak.] the science or study of the ancient language, history, customs, architecture, etc. of Egypt.

eh, *interj.* an exclamation denoting inquiry or slight surprise.

eh′līte (ā′), *n.* [named from *Ehl*, in Austria, where it is found, and *-ite.*] a massive, dark-green, hydrous copper phosphate.

eī′dẽr, *n.* [Ice. *æthr*; Sw. *eider*, an eider, eider duck; Dan. *ederfugl*, eider fowl.]

1. a large species of sea duck of the genus *Somateria*, especially *Somateria mollissima*, which is found on both sides of the North Atlantic: often *eider duck*. Other species are *Somateria mollissima dresseri*, the American eider duck, *Arctonetta fischeri*, the spectacled eider duck, and *Somateria spectabilis*, the king eider duck.

EIDER (*Somateria mollissima*)

2. eider down.

eī′dẽr down, [from ON. *æthar-dun.*] 1. the soft, fine breast feathers, or down, of the eider duck, used as a stuffing for quilts, pillows, etc.

2. a bed quilt stuffed with such feathers.

eī′dẽr yărn, a knitting yarn spun from the wool of the merino sheep.

eī·det′ic, *a.* [Gr. *eidētikos*, constituting a figure, from *eidos*, what is seen, shape.] designating or of mental images that are unusually vivid and almost photographically exact.

eī′dō·grȧph, *n.* [Gr. *eidos*, form, figure, and *graphein*, to write.] an instrument for copying designs, reduced or enlarged in any proportion within certain limits.

eī·dol′ō·clȧst, *n.* an iconoclast.

eī·dō′lon, *n.*; *pl.* **eī·dō′lȧ,** [Gr. *eidōlon*, an image, idol.] a phantom; an image; an apparition.

eigh (ā), *interj.* an exclamatory expression.

eight (āt), *a.* [ME. *eight, eihte, ehte, auhte*; AS. *eahta*; D. *acht*; O.H.G. *ahto*; L.G. *acht*; Sw. *otta*; Ice. *atta*; Goth. *ahtau*; L. *octo*; Gr. *oktō*; Sans. *ashta*, eight.] totaling one more than seven.

eight (āt), *n.* 1. the cardinal number between seven and nine; seven and one.

2. a symbol representing eight units, as 8 or VIII; hence, any curved outline in the shape of the figure 8.

3. any group of eight people or things, as a crew of eight oarsmen.

4. a playing card bearing the number 8 and eight spots of its suit.

eight ball, in the game of pool, a black ball bearing the number eight: in one form of the game, if a player pockets this ball before all the other balls are pocketed, he immediately loses the game.

behind the eight ball; in a very unfavorable position: from having the cue ball directly behind the eight ball in the game of pool, so that the shooter runs the risk of pocketing the eight ball. [Slang.]

eight′een (āt′ēn), *a.* [ME. *eightene, æhtene*; AS. *eahtatyne, eahtatiene*; *eahta*, eight, and *tene, tyn*, ten.] eight and ten, or one more than seventeen; twice nine; as, *eighteen* months.

eight′een, *n.* 1. the cardinal number between seventeen and nineteen; the sum of ten and eight; eighteen units or objects.

2. a symbol representing eighteen units, as 18 or XVIII.

eight·een′mō, *a.* and *n.* octodecimo; 18 mo: a size of book.

eight′eenth, *a.* [AS. *eahtateotha*, eighteenth.]

1. next in order after the seventeenth.

2. being one of eighteen equal divisions of anything.

eight′eenth, *n.* 1. the one following the seventeenth.

2. any of the eighteen equal parts of something; 1/18.

eight′foil, *n.* in heraldry, a plant that has eight leaves: called also *double quatrefoil.*

eight′fōld, *a.* 1. having eight parts.

2. having eight times as much or as many.

eight′fōld, *adv.* eight times the number or quantity.

eighth (ātth), *a.* [ME. *eightethe*; AS. *eahtotha*, eighth.]

1. next in order after the seventh; preceded by seven others in a series; 8th.

2. designating any of eight equal parts into which something is divided.

eighth, *n.* 1. the one following the seventh.

2. one of eight equal parts; 1/8.

3. in music, an octave.

eighth′ly, *adv.* in the eighth place.

eighth nōte, in music, a note which is the eighth part of a whole note: also called *quaver.*

eighth rest, in music, a rest which is the eighth part of a whole rest.

eight′i·eth, *a.* 1. next in order after the seventy-ninth; 80th.

2. designating any of eighty equal parts into which something is divided.

eight′i·eth, *n.* 1. the one following the seventy-ninth.

2. one of eighty equal parts; 1/80.

eight′ling, *n.* in crystallography, a compound or twin crystal composed of eight individuals.

eight′scōre, *a.* and *n.* eight times twenty.

eight′y, *a.* [AS. *eahtatig*; *eahta*, eight, and *-tig*, a form of ten.] eight times ten; fourscore.

eight′y, *n.*; *pl.* **eight′ies,** 1. the cardinal number between seventy-nine and eighty-one.

2. a symbol representing eighty units, as 80 or LXXX.

eigne (ān *or* ā′ne), *a.* [OFr. *aisné, ainsné*; *ains*, before, and *né*, born; L. *ante natus*; *ante*, before, and *natus*, born.]

1. in law, eldest.

2. unalienable; entailed. [Obs.]

eī′kon, *n.* an icon.

ēild, *n.* eld; age. [Obs.]

Eīn·steīn′i·ăn, *a.* pertaining or relating to Albert Einstein (1879–1955), German-born physicist, or to his theories.

eīn·steīn′i·um, *n.* [named after A. *Einstein*: see preceding.] a radioactive element discovered in the debris of the first thermonuclear explosion, but now produced by irradiating plutonium with neutrons: symbol, Es; atomic weight, 252(?); atomic number, 99.

eī′rē·närch, *n.* same as *irenarch.*

eī·ren′ic, *a.* same as *irenic.*

eī·se·gē′sis, *n.*; *pl.* **eī·se·gē′sēs,** [Gr. *eisegesis*, a bringing in; from *eisegeisthai*; *eis*, into, and *hēgeisthai*, to lead, guide.] an improper method of exposition by which the expounder introduces his own ideas into the interpretation of a text: opposed to *exegesis.*

ēi′sel, *n.* [ME. *eisel*; OFr. *aisil*, vinegar.] vinegar. [Obs.]

eis·tedd′fod (ā-steth′vod, es-steth′), *n.*; *pl.* **eis·tedd′fods**; Welsh **eis·tedd·fod′au** (es-teth-vọd′ī), [W., a sitting, session, assembly, from *eistedd*, to sit.] an assembly or session of bards and minstrels held in Wales in ancient times. These meetings were revived in the nineteenth century, and annual meetings for the recitation of prize poems and musical performances are now held under this name.

ēi′thẽr (*or* ī′thẽr), *a.* [ME. *either, eyther, aither*; AS. *ægther*, contr. of *æghwæther*, either, each; *a-*, ever, *ge-*, and *hwæther*, pron., whether.]

1. one or the other (of two); as, *either* side may win; give me *either* orange.

2. each (of two); the one and the other; as, they lined up on *either* bank of the river.

On *either* side one, and Jesus in the midst.
—John xix. 18.

ēi′thẽr, *pron.* one of two; one or the other (of two); as, *either* of them may succeed.

ēi′thẽr, *conj.* 1. a disjunctive conjunction always used as a correlative to and preceding *or*. It implies a choice of alternatives.

Either he is talking, *or* he is pursuing, *or* he is in a journey, *or* peradventure he sleepeth. —1 Kings xviii. 27.

2. or. [Obs.]

Can the fig tree, my brethren, bear olive berries? *either* a vine, figs?—James iii. 12.

ēi′thẽr, *adv.* 1. any more than the other; also (following negative expressions); as, if she doesn't go, he won't *either.*

2. an intensifier in a negative statement, usually in answer to an affirmative; as, "You took it." "I didn't *either!*" [Colloq.]

ē·jac′ū·lāte, *v.t.*; ejaculated, *pt., pp.*; ejaculating, *ppr.* [L. *ejaculatus*, pp. of *ejaculari*, to cast out, throw out; *e*, out, and *jaculari*, from *jaculum*, a dart, missile; *jacere*, to throw.]

1. to eject or discharge (fluids) suddenly.

2. to utter suddenly and vehemently, as an exclamation; as, he *ejaculated* an oath.

ē·jac′ū·lāte, *v.i.* to utter ejaculations; to make sudden and vehement exclamations.

ē·jac·ū·lā′tion, *n.* 1. the act of throwing or darting out. [Obs.]

2. the uttering of a sudden, vehement exclamation; an exclamatory sentence or word.

3. in physiology, the ejection of seminal fluid.

ē·jac′ū·lā·tive, *a.* of, or having the nature of, an ejaculation.

ē·jac′ū·lā·tŏr, *n.* one who or that which ejaculates.

ē·jac′ū·lȧ·tō·ry, *a.* 1. ejaculating; of or for ejaculation; as, the *ejaculatory* ducts of the male.

2. having the nature of an ejaculation; exclamatory; as, *ejaculatory* words.

3. sudden; hasty. [Obs.]

ē·ject′, *v.t.*; ejected, *pt., pp.*; ejecting, *ppr.* [L. *ejectus*, pp. of *ejicere*, to throw out; *e*, out, and *jacere*, to throw.]

1. to throw out; to cast forth; to thrust out; to discharge; as, the chimney *ejects* smoke.

2. to drive out; to expel; as, the heckler was *ejected* from the meeting.

3. in law, to dispossess; to evict; as, to *eject* a tenant.

ē′ject, *n.* something inferred to be in actual existence, as a mental condition or act of another, but which is not accessible to the consciousness of the person making the inference.

ē·jec′tȧ, *n.pl.* [L., pl. of *ejectum*, neut. of *ejectus*, pp. of *ejicere*, to throw out.] refuse; waste matter; ejected matter.

ē·jec·tȧ·men′tȧ, *n.pl.* same as *ejecta.*

ē·jec′tion, *n.* [L. *ejectio*, from *ejicere*, to throw out; cast out.]

1. an ejecting or being ejected.

2. ejected matter.

ē·jec′tion sēat, a seat designed to be ejected with its occupant from an aircraft in an emergency and parachuted to the ground.

ē·jec′tive, *a.* 1. pertaining to or causing ejection.

2. pertaining to or of the nature of an eject.

ē·ject′ment, *n.* 1. an ejecting; a casting out; a dispossession; an expulsion.

2. in law, a writ or action for the recovery of possession of realty from which the owner has been ejected, and for damages for the unlawful detention of the same.

ē·ject′ŏr, *n.* 1. one who or that which ejects.

2. a device wherein a jet of steam or air pumps out a liquid or powdery substance from a place.

3. that device in a breech-loading firearm which withdraws the empty shell from the bore of the gun.

ē·ject′ŏr cŏn·dens′ẽr, in a steam engine, a form of condenser worked by the exhaust steam from the cylinder.

e·ji′dō (ā-hē′thō), *n.* [Sp.] in Spanish and Mexican law, a common used by the people of a town or pueblo.

ē′joọ, *n.* [Malay.] the gomuti.

ej·ū·lā′tion, *n.* [L. *ejulatio*, from *ejulare*, to wail, lament.] outcry; a wailing; lamentation. [Obs.]

ēke, *v.t.*; eked (ēkt), *pt., pp.*; eking, *ppr.* [ME. *eken*; AS. *ecan, ican*; Ice. *auka*; Sw. *öka*; Goth. *aukan*; L. *augere*; Gr. *auxanein*, to increase.] to increase; to enlarge; to lengthen; to protract; to prolong. [Archaic or Dial.]

to eke out; (a) to add something missing to; to supplement; as, he *eked out* his income by writing stories; (b) to manage to make (a living) with difficulty; (c) to use a (supply) frugally.

ēke, *adv.* and *conj.* [AS. *eac*; D. *ook*; G. *auch*; Sw. *och*; Dan. *og*; W. *ac*; L. *ac*, and, also.] also; likewise; in addition. [Archaic.]

ēke, *n.* something added; an addition. [Dial.]

ek′e·bẽrg·īte, *n.* [named after *Ekeberg*, a mineralogist.] a variety of scapolite.

ēke′nāme, *n.* a nickname; an epithet. [Obs.]

ēk′ing, *n.* [from *eke,* to increase.]
1. the act of adding.
2. that which is added; specifically, (a) a piece of wood fitted to make good a deficiency in length, as the end of a knee and the like; (b) the carved work under the lower part of the quarter piece of a vessel at the aft part of the quarter gallery.

ek′lō·ġite, *n.* same as *eclogite.*

el, *n.* 1. [so called because shaped like an L.] an extension or wing at right angles to the main structure; an ell.
2. [from *elevated.*] an elevated railway. [Colloq.]

Ē lä, in music, the highest note in the scale of Guido; hence, the extreme of any quality; any extravagant or hyperbolical saying.

ē·lab′ō·rāte, *v.t.*; elaborated, *pt., pp.*; elaborating, *ppr.* [L. *elaboratus,* pp. of *elaborare,* to work out, labor greatly; *e-,* out, and *laborare,* from *labor,* labor, work.]
1. to produce by effort; to develop with labor.
2. to improve or refine by successive operations; to work out with great care; to work out fully or perfectly in great detail; as, to *elaborate* a work of art.

ē·lab′ō·rāte, *v.i.* to state something in detail; to give additional information; to be more specific (usually with *on* or *upon*).

ē·lab′ō·rāte, *a.* wrought with labor; finished with great diligence; studied; executed with exactness; complicated; painstaking; as, an *elaborate* discourse; an *elaborate* performance.
Syn.—labored, perfected, studied, highly wrought.

ē·lab′ō·rāte·ly, *adv.* in an elaborate manner; with nice regard to exactness.

ē·lab′ō·rāte·ness, *n.* the quality of being elaborate or wrought with great labor.

ē·lab·ō·rā′tion, *n.* 1. the act of elaborating or being elaborated.
2. a thing elaborated.
3. in physiology, the several processes by which the appropriate food of animals and plants is transformed or assimilated so as to render it adapted for the purposes of nutrition.

ē·lab′ō·rā·tive, *a.* serving or tending to elaborate; possessing the power of developing or refining by successive operations, whether of nature or of art; working out with minute attention to details; laboriously bringing to a state of completion or perfection.
elaborative faculty; in psychology, the intellectual power of discerning relations and of viewing objects by means of or in relations; the understanding; the discursive faculty; thought.

ē·lab′ō·rā·tŏr, *n.* one who or that which elaborates.

ē·lab′ō·rā·tō·ry, *a.* elaborating. [Rare.]

ē·lab′ō·rā·tō·ry, *n.* a laboratory. [Obs.]

ē·lā′brāte, *a.* [L. *e-* priv., and *labrum,* a lip.] in entomology, lacking a distinct labrum or lip, as most dipterous insects. [Rare.]

E″lae·ag·nā′cē·ae, *n.pl.* [Gr. *elaiagnos, eleagnos,* a Boetian marsh plant; *elaia,* an olive tree, and *agnos,* equal to *eygos,* a willow tree, and *-aceae.*] in botany, the oleaster family, a small order of apetalous exogens, covered with silvery or brown scales, and having alternate or opposite leaves, and small white or yellow flowers.

ē″lae·ag·nā′ceous, *a.* pertaining or belonging to the *Elæagnaceæ.*

E·lae·ag′nus, *n.* in botany, the typical genus of the *Elæagnaceæ.*

E·lae′is, *n.* [Gr. *elaion,* olive oil, oil, from *elaia,* the olive tree.] in botany, a small genus of palms of Africa and South America. *Elæis guineensis* is an African species which yields an oil used by the natives in cookery and for anointing the body.

ē·lae·ō-, [from Greek *elaion,* olive oil, oil.] a combining form used to signify *relation to* or *connection with oil.*

ē·lae′ō·blȧst, *n.* [*elæo-,* and Gr. *blastos,* a shoot, germ.] in zoology, the urochord of certain of the *Tunicata.*

ē″lae·ō·blas′tiç, *a.* pertaining to the elaeoblast.

E″lae·ō·çär′pus, *n.* [*elæo-,* and Gr. *karpos,* fruit.] a genus of trees and shrubs containing fifty species, natives of India and Australia and the neighboring islands. They have simple leaves and racemes of small flowers. The fruit is oblong or globose, with a rough-shelled nut, surrounded by a fleshy pulp, which is used in curries or pickled like olives.

ē·lae′ō·līte, *n.* [*elæo-,* and Gr. *lithos,* stone.] a coarse, massive variety of nephelite, of a waxy, greasy luster. The predominance of soda in its composition renders its alteration a frequent source of zeolites.

ē·lae′ō·līte sȳ′e·nīte, a syenite containing elaeolite.

ē·lae·om′e·tẽr, ē·lāi·om′e·tẽr, *n.* [*elæo-,* and Gr. *metron,* a measure.] a hydrometer for testing the purity of olive and almond oils, by determining their densities.

ē·lae·op′tēne, ē·lae·op′ten, *n.* [*elæo-,* and Gr. *ptēnos,* winged, fleeting.] the liquid portion of essential oils which does not become solid, as distinguished from the concrete or crystallizable portion called *stearoptene*: written also *elaopten, oleoptene.*

ē·lā′i·dāte, *n.* [*elaidic* and *-ate.*] a salt formed by the union of elaidic acid with a base.

ē·lā·id′iç, *a.* [Gr. *elais* (*-idos*), equal to *elaia,* the olive tree, and *-ic.*] designating or pertaining to a fatty acid, $C_{18}H_{34}O_2$, obtained from oleic acid by adding nitrous or hyponitrous acid.

ē·lā′i·din, ē·lā′i·dine, *n.* [Gr. *elais* (*-idos*), the olive tree, and *-in.*] in chemistry, an ester of elaidic acid.

ē·lā′in, ē·lā′ine, *n.* same as *olein.*

E·lāine′, *n.* in Arthurian legend, any of several women; specifically, (a) Elaine of Astolat, who loved Sir Lancelot; (b) the mother of Sir Galahad.

ē·lāi·od′iç, *a.* [Gr. *elaiōdēs,* oily; *elaion,* olive oil, oil, and *eidos,* form.] derived from castor oil; as, *elaiodic* acid.

ē·lāi·om′e·tẽr, *n.* same as *elaeometer.*

E′lăm·īte, *n.* one living in or a native of Elam, an ancient kingdom, now Khuzistan, Iran.

E′lăm·īte, *a.* of Elam or the Elamites.

E·lăm·it′iç, *n.* the group of languages spoken by the Elamites.

E·lăm·it′iç, *a.* 1. designating or of the languages spoken by the Elamites.
2. Elamite.

ē·lamp′ing, *a.* shining. [Obs.]

é·lan′ (ā-läṅ′), *n.* [Fr., from *élancer,* to dart, hurl.] ardor; enthusiasm; vigor; impetuosity.

ē·lànce′, *v.t.* [Fr. *élancer*; *e-,* L. *e-,* out, and *lancer,* to dart, hurl, from *lance,* a lance.] to throw or shoot; to hurl; to dart. [Poet.]

ē′lănd, *n.* [D. *eland,* an elk.] a large, heavy antelope of Africa, with long, twisted horns; the Cape elk.

el′ȧ·net, *n.* [from Gr. *elaunein,* to drive, set in motion.] a kite belonging to the genus *Elanus.*

é·lan′ vi·tal′ (ā-läṅ′ vē-tȧl′), [Fr., lit., vital force.] in Bergsonian philosophy, the original life force, the creative linking principle in the evolution of all organisms.

ē·lā′ō·līte, *n.* same as *elaeolite.*

ē·lā·op′ten, *n.* same as *elaeoptene.*

el′ȧ·phine, *a.* [Gr. *elaphos,* a deer.] pertaining to the red deer or stag, *Cervus elaphus.*

el′ȧ·phūre, *n.* [Gr. *elaphos,* a deer, and *oura,* a tail.] *Elaphurus davidianus,* a large Chinese deer.

E·lap′i·dae, *n.pl.* a family of venomous serpents typified by the genus *Elaps.*

ē·lap·i·dā′tion, *n.* [L. *elapidatus*; *e-,* out, and *lapidatus,* pp. of *lapidare,* to throw stones; *lapis* (*-idis*), a stone.] a clearing away of stones. [Obs.]

el′ȧ·pine, *a.* pertaining to the *Elapidæ.*

E′laps, *n.* [L. *elops* (*-idis*); Gr. *elops,* a sea fish, serpent.] a genus of venomous snakes, typical of the family *Elapidæ.* Some of the species are called coral snakes, as *Elaps corallina* of Brazil.

ē·lapse′, *v.i.*; elapsed (-lapst′), *pt., pp.*; elapsing, *ppr.* [L. *elapsus,* pp. of *elabi,* to glide away; *e-,* out, and *labi,* to glide, fall.] to slide, slip, or glide away; to pass: used of time; as, two years *elapsed* before he returned.

ē·lap′sion, *n.* the act of elapsing; lapse. [Rare.]

ē·lā′quē·āte, *v.t.* [L. *elaqueatus,* pp. of *elaqueare,* to disentangle; *e-,* out, and *laqueus,* a snare.] to disentangle. [Obs.]

El·ȧ·sip′ō·dȧ, *n.pl.* same as *Elasmapoda.*

e·las′mȧ·pod, *a.* elasmapodous.

e·las′mȧ·pod, *n.* one of the *Elasmapoda.*

El·as·map′ō·dȧ, *n.pl.* [Gr. *elasmos, elasma,* a metal plate, and *pous, podos,* foot.] a group of deep-sea holothurians exhibiting distinct bilateral symmetry.

el·as·map′ō·dous, *a.* pertaining to the *Elasmapoda.*

ē·las′mō·branch, *a.* pertaining to or characteristic of the *Elasmobranchii.*

ē·las′mō·branch, *n.* a member of the *Elasmobranchii.*

ē·las·mō·brañ′chi·ăn, ē·las·mō·brañ′chi·āte, *a.* and *n.* same as *elasmobranch.*

E·las·mō·brañ′chi·ī, *n.pl.* [Gr. *elasmos, elasma,* a metal plate, and *branchia,* gills.] a class of fishes including the sharks, rays, and chimeras, characterized by cartilaginous skeletons, platelike scales, lamelliform gills, and lack of air bladders.

ē·las′mō·saur, *n.* a reptile of the genus *Elasmosaurus.*

E·las·mō·sau′rus, *n.* [Gr. *elasmos, elasma,* a metal plate, and *sauros,* a lizard.] a genus of large fossil American reptiles allied to the plesiosaurs.

ē·las′tiç, *a.* [from Gr. *elaunein,* to drive, set in motion.]
1. having the property of immediately returning to its original size, shape, or position after being stretched, squeezed, flexed, expanded, etc.; flexible; springy; as, a rubber band is *elastic.*
2. possessing the power or quality of recovering from depression or exhaustion; capable of sustaining shocks without permanent injury; as, *elastic* spirits.
3. readily changed to suit circumstances; adaptable; as, *elastic* regulations.
elastic cartilage; cartilage in which the matrix is blended with elastic fibers.
elastic curve; the curve made by a thin elastic rod fixed horizontally at one of its extremities, and weighted at the other.
elastic fluids; fluids which have the property of expanding in all directions on the removal of external pressure, as gases and vapors.
elastic limit; in mechanics, the greatest amount of deformation that a body can stand and still resume its original shape when the strain is removed.
elastic mineral pitch; a brown, massive, elastic variety of bitumen.
elastic tissue; in anatomy, a variety of connective tissue composed of yellow elastic fibers, occurring especially in the walls of arteries and veins.
gum elastic; caoutchouc or India rubber.

ē·las′tiç, *n.* 1. a loosely woven fabric made flexible by strands of rubber running through it.
2. a band, garter, etc. of this material.
3. a rubber band.

ē·las′tiç·ăl, *a.* elastic. [Obs.]

ē·las′tiç·ăl·ly, *adv.* in an elastic manner, by an elastic power; with a spring.

ē·las·tic′i·ty, *n.* 1. the inherent property in bodies by which they recover their former figure or state after the force of external pressure, tension, or distortion has been removed; springiness; as, the *elasticity* of gases.
2. power to resist or overcome depression or mental strain.
3. adaptability.
coefficient of elasticity; the result obtained by dividing a given force or stress exerted upon a body by the resulting strain.

ē·las′ti·cīze, *v.t.*; elasticized, *pt., pp.*; elasticizing, *ppr.* [*elastic* and *-ize.*] to make (fabric) elastic, as by interweaving with rubber strands.

ē·las′tiç·ness, *n.* elasticity. [Rare.]

ē·las′tin, *n.* in chemistry, a substance, elastic when moist, closely resembling albumen except that it is free from sulfur, forming the principal substance of the elastic fiber which is the basic constituent of elastic tissue.

ē·lāte′, *a.* [L. *elatus,* pp. of *efferre,* to bring out, to lift up; *ex,* out, and *ferre,* to bear, to bring.]
1. raised; lifted up. [Archaic.]
2. elated; exalted. [Poetic]
Elate with empty hopes. —Bacon.
Syn.—exalted, proud, delighted, exultant, jubilant, puffed up, overjoyed.

ē·lāte′, *v.t.*; elated, *pt., pp.*; elating, *ppr.* 1. to raise or swell, as the mind or spirits; to make proud, happy, or joyful.
2. to raise; to exalt. [Obs.]

ē·lāt′ed, *a.* [pp. of *elate.*] in high spirits; proud or happy; joyful.

ē·lāt′ed·ly, *adv.* with elation.

ē·lāt′ed·ness, *n.* the state of being elated.

ē·lāte′ment, *n.* elation. [Obs.]

ē·lāt′ẽr, ē·lāt′ŏr, *n.* one who or that which elates.

el′ȧ·tẽr, *n.* [Gr. *elatēr,* a driver, hurler, from *elaunein,* to drive, set in motion.]
1. in botany, (a) one of four elastic filaments attached about the middle of one side of the spores in *Equisetaceæ.* They are curled once or twice round the spore, uncoiling elastically when the spore is discharged; (b) an

elastic spiral filament which aids in the dispersion of the spores, as in liverworts.

2. in entomology, (a) [E–] a genus of beetles comprising over 100 species, typical of the family *Elateridæ*, the click beetles; (b) any beetle of the family *Elateridæ*; (c) an elastic bristle at the end of the abdomen of a podurid, by which it leaps.

3. elasticity. [Obs.]

ē·lat′ẽr·id, *n.* in biology, an elater (the beetle).

ē·lat′ẽr·id, *a.* in biology, of an elater or the elaters.

ē·lat′ẽr·in, ē·lat′ẽr·ine, *n.* [L. *elaterium*, and *-ine*.] the active principle of elaterium, a white, crystalline substance, $C_{20}H_{28}O_6$, a very powerful cathartic.

ē·lat′ẽr·īte, *n.* [Gr. *elatēr*, a driver, and *-ite*.] an elastic mineral hydrocarbon of a blackish-brown color, subtranslucent, and occurring in soft, flexible masses: called also *elastic bitumen* and *mineral caoutchouc*.

el·ȧ·tē′ri·um, *n.* [L., from Gr. *elatērion*, neut. of *elatērios*, driving away.] a cathartic and diuretic substance obtained from the dried juice of the fruit of the *Ecballium elaterium*, or squirting cucumber, and used in the treatment of dropsy.

el″ȧ·tẽr·om′e·tẽr, *n.* [Gr. *elatēr*, a driver, and *metron*, a measure.] an instrument for determining the pressure of a gas; an elatrometer.

el′ȧ·ter·y, *n.* [Gr. *elatērios*, from *elaunein*, to drive, put in motion.] acting force or elasticity; as, the *elatery* of the air. [Obs.]

E·lat·i·nā′cē·ae, *n.pl.* [L. *elatine*; Gr. *elatinē*, a species of toadflax, f. of *elatinos*, from *elatē*, the silver fir.] a family of small polypetalous herbs, the waterwort family, containing only two genera and about twenty species.

ē·lat·i·nā′ceous, *a.* pertaining to the *Elatinaceæ*.

ē·lā′tion, *n.* [L. *elatio*, from *elatus*, pp. of *efferre*, to carry out, lift up; *ex*, out, and *ferre*, to bear.] exaltation; an exultant state of mind; a feeling of pride or joy; high spirits.

Syn.—enthusiasm, rapture, delight, exultation, transport.

ē·lā′tive, *a.* in grammar, lifted up or raised to the highest degree; being of the absolute superlative.

el·ȧ·trom′e·tẽr, *n.* [Gr. *elatēr*, a driver, and *metron*, a measure.] an instrument used in measuring the pressure of confined gases.

ē·lā′yle, *n.* [Gr. *elaion*, olive oil, oil, and *hylē*, matter.] ethylene. [Obs.]

el′bōw, *n.* [ME. *elbowe*; AS. *elboga*, *elnboga*; *eln*, ell, the forearm, and *boga*, a bow.]

1. the junction of the upper arm and forearm; the joint which unites the upper arm with the forearm; especially, the outer part of the curve of a bent arm.

2. anything resembling the bend of the human elbow; specifically, a flexure or angle, as of a wall, building, or road; a sudden turn or bend, as in a river or the seacoast; a jointed piece of pipe bent or turning at an angle; the raised arm of a chair or sofa.

3. in architecture, one of the upright sides which flank any paneled work.

at one's elbow; near at hand; easy to reach.

elbow in the hawse; in nautical usage, the twisting of two cables holding a vessel at anchor, caused by her swinging twice the same way.

out at (the) elbows; having holes in the elbows of one's coat; hence, shabby; reduced in circumstances; poverty-stricken.

to crook (or *bend*) *the elbow*; to drink; to become intoxicated. [Slang.]

to rub elbows with; to associate or mingle with (famous or prominent people, etc.).

up to the elbows; wholly engaged; very busy (*in* work, etc.).

el′bōw, *v.t.*; elbowed, *pt.*, *pp.*; elbowing, *ppr.* to push with or as with the elbow; as, he *elbowed* his way through; to *elbow* people aside.

el′bōw, *v.i.* 1. to jut into an angle; to project; to bend.

2. to use the elbows so as to jostle; to push one's way; to be rudely self-assertive.

el′bōw·bōard, *n.* the inner sill of a window.

el′bōw·chāir, *n.* a chair with arms to support the elbows; an armchair.

el′bōw grēase, vigorous physical effort; hard work. [Colloq.]

el′bōw·room, *n.* room to extend the elbows on each side; hence, freedom from confinement; room for motion or action; ample space or scope.

el′bōw scis′ṣōrṣ, scissors having a bend in the blade or shank.

el·çā′jȧ, *n.* [Ar.] a tree of Arabia, *Trichilia emetica*, the fruit of which is used in the preparation of an ointment.

El·cē′sȧ·īte, *n.* one of a sect of Gnostics which arose among the early Asiatic Christians in the reign of the emperor Trajan. The name is derived from Elcesai, the leader of the sect.

el′chi, el′chee, *n.* [Turk. and Per.] an ambassador or envoy.

eld, *a.* old. [Archaic.]

eld, *n.* [ME. *eld*, *ylde*; AS. *yldu*, *oeld*, from *eald*, old.]

1. old age; decrepitude. [Archaic.]

2. ancient times; former ages; antiquity. [Archaic.]

eld, *v.i.* to become aged. [Obs.]

eld, *v.t.* to make old. [Obs.]

eld′ẽr, *a.* [ME. *elder*, *eldre*; AS. *eldra*, *yldra*, comp. of *eald*, old.]

1. older; senior; having lived a longer time; born, produced, or formed before something else; as, the *elder* brother.

2. pertaining to earlier times; earlier; former; ancient; as, in the *elder* days of art.

3. superior in rank, position, validity, etc.

elder hand; in card playing, the hand that has by right the priority in leading.

eld′ẽr, *n.* [AS. *ealdor*, an elder, parent, ancestor, chief, from *eald*, old.]

1. one who is older than another or others.

2. an ancestor; forefather; predecessor.

Carry your head as your *elders* have done before you. —L'Estrange.

3. an aged person.

4. an older person with some authority or dignity in a tribe or community.

5. any of certain leaders in a church organization, as in the Presbyterian Church.

el′dẽr, *n.* [ME. *elder*, *eldre*, *ellern*, *eller*; AS. *ellen*, elder.]

1. in botany, any shrub or tree of the genus *Sambucus*, of the honeysuckle family, bearing large corymbs of white or pink flowers and red or black berries. The common North American elder bush or elder tree is *Sambucus canadensis*.

2. any of various similar, unrelated plants.

el′dẽr·ber″ry, *n.* 1. the elder (tree).

2. the berry, or drupe, of the elder, having a sweetish acid taste.

eld′ẽr·ish, *a.* somewhat old. [Rare.]

eld′ẽr·ly, *a.* somewhat old; advanced beyond middle age; approaching old age; as, *elderly* people.

eld′ẽr·ship, *n.* 1. the state of being older; seniority.

2. the office or duties of an elder in a church.

3. a body of elders; a presbytery.

eld′ẽr stātes′măn, 1. formerly, in Japan, any of a number of retired statesmen who served informally as a group of advisors to the emperor.

2. any elderly retired statesman who continues to be consulted on governmental matters.

el′dẽr·wŏrt, *n.* a European dwarf elder: called also *danewort*.

eld′est, *a.* [ME. *eldest*, *ealdeste*; AS. *yldesta*, superl. of *eald*, old.] oldest; especially, first-born or oldest surviving; as, the *eldest* son or daughter.

eldest hand; the first player in cards, or the one to the left of the dealer.

el′ding, *n.* [Ice. *elding*, from *eldr*, fire.] rubbish; also, fuel. [Brit. Dial.]

El Dō·rä′dō, [Sp., the golden region.]

1. an imaginary region in the interior of South America, supposed to surpass all others in the richness of its productions, especially gold, gems, etc.: it was the object of much search by early Spanish explorers.

2. any region or source of great abundance.

el′dritch, *a.* hideous; ghastly; wild; demoniacal; as, an *eldritch* shriek, an *eldritch* laugh. [Scot.]

Ē·lē·at′iç, *a.* [L. *Eleaticus*, from *Elea* (Velia), ancient Greek colony in Italy.] designating or of an ancient Greek school of philosophy, centering in Elea during the fifth and sixth centuries B. C., which held that the singular and unchangeable "Being" was the only reality and that plurality, change, and motion were only illusory: Parmenides and Zeno were its outstanding adherents.

Ē·lē·at′iç, *n.* an Eleatic philosopher.

el·ē·çam·pāne′, *n.* [LL. *inula campana*; L. *inula*; Gr. *helenion*, elecampane; LL. *campana*, from L. *campus*, field.]

1. *Inula helenium*, a hardy, perennial, composite plant with large clusters of yellow flowers.

2. a candy made from the root of this plant.

ELECAMPANE (*Inula helenium*)

ē·leçt′, *v.t.*; elected, *pt.*, *pp.*; electing, *ppr.* [L. *electus*, pp. of *eligere*, to pick out, choose; *e-*, out, and *legere*, to pick, choose, select.]

1. generally, to pick out; to select from two or more; to choose; to determine in favor of.

2. to select or choose (a person) for some office by voting; as, to *elect* a representative by ballot or viva voce.

3. in theology, to designate, choose, or select for eternal salvation: used only in the passive with *God* as the implied subject.

Syn.—choose, select, prefer, adopt.

ē·leçt′, *a.* 1. chosen; taken by preference from two or more.

2. in theology, chosen by God for salvation and eternal life.

3. chosen, but not yet inaugurated or invested with office; as, mayor-*elect*.

ē·leçt′, *n.* one who is elect.

the elect; (a) persons belonging to a specially privileged group; (b) in theology, those chosen by God for salvation and eternal life.

ē·leçt′ănt, *n.* one having the power of choosing. [Obs.]

ē·leç′tȧ·ry, *n.* an electuary. [Obs.]

ē·leç′ti·cişm, *n.* ecleticism. [Rare.]

ē·leç′tion, *n.* [L. *electio*, from *eligere*, to choose, select.]

1. the act of choosing; choice.

2. the act of choosing a person to fill an office or position by vote.

3. choice; power to choose; free will; liberty to act or not; discrimination; as, it leaves him no *election* in the matter.

4. in theology, divine choice by God, by which persons are distinguished as objects of mercy, become subjects of grace, are sanctified, and prepared for eternal life in heaven; predestination.

5. the elect. [Rare.]

6. in law, the choice between two rights mutually inconsistent or alternative.

ē·leç·tion·eer′, *v.i.*; electioneered, *pt.*, *pp.*; electioneering, *ppr.* to work for the success of a candidate, political party, issue, etc. in an election.

ē·leç·tion·eer′ẽr, *n.* one who electioneers.

ē·leçt′ive, *a.* 1. dependent on choice; bestowed, filled, or passing by election; as, an office is *elective*.

2. chosen by election.

3. pertaining to or consisting in choice or right of choosing; as, *elective* franchise.

4. having the authority or power of choice; as, an *elective* act.

5. that may be chosen but is not required; optional; as, an *elective* study in a university.

ē·leçt′ive, *n.* an optional course or subject in a school or college curriculum.

ē·leçt′ive af·fin′i·ty, a tendency to combine chemically with a certain substance or substances rather than with another or others.

ē·leçt′ive·ly, *adv.* by choice; with preference.

ē·leçt′ŏr, *n.* [L. *elector*, a chooser, from *eligere*, to choose, select.]

1. one who elects, or one who has the right of choice; a person who has, by law or constitution, the right of voting; a qualified voter.

2. a member of the electoral college.

3. [*usually* E–] [transl. of G. *kurfürst*, lit., choosing prince.] any of the princes of the Holy Roman Empire who took part in the election of the emperor.

ē·leçt′ŏr·ăl, *a.* 1. of an election or electors.

2. made up of electors; as, an *electoral* college.

ē·leçt′ŏr·ăl çol′leġe, an assembly elected by the voters to perform the formal duty of electing the president and the vice-president of the United States: the electors of each State, equal in number to its members in Congress, are expected to cast their votes for the candidates selected by the popular vote in their State.

ē·leçt·ŏr·al′i·ty, *n.* an electorate. [Obs.]

ē·leçt′ŏr·āte, *n.* 1. the rank of an elector in the Holy Roman Empire; also, the territory of such elector.

2. all those qualified to vote in an election.
3. a division or district of voters; an electoral district.

ē·leçt′ŏr·ess, ē·leçt′ress, *n.* the wife or widow of an elector of the Holy Roman Empire.

ē·leç·tō′ri·ăl, *a.* electoral.

ē·leçt′ŏr·ship, *n.* the office or functions of an elector.

Ē·leç′trȧ, *n.* [L., from Gr. *Elektra*, a feminine proper name.]
1. in Greek legend, (a) the daughter of Agamemnon and Clytemnestra: she persuaded her brother, Orestes, to kill their mother and their mother's lover, who together had murdered Agamemnon; (b) one of the Pleiades.
2. in astronomy, a bright star in the Pleiades.

Ē·leç′trȧ çom′plex, in psychoanalysis, the unconscious tendency of a daughter to be attached to her father and hostile toward her mother: see *Oedipus complex*.

ē·leç′tre (-tẽr), **ē·leç′tẽr,** *n.* electrum. [Obs.]

ē·leç·trep′e·tẽr, *n.* [Gr. *ēlektron*, amber, and *trepein*, to turn.] a commutator.

ē·leçt′ress, *n.* see *electoress*.

ē·leç′triç, *n.* 1. a nonconductor of electricity, as glass, amber, etc., which can be used to store or excite an electrical charge.
2. a train, etc. operated by electricity.

ē·leç′triç, *a.* [L. *electrum*; Gr. *ēlektron*, amber.]
1. of, charged with, or conveying electricity; as, an *electric* wire.
2. producing, or produced by, electricity; as, an *electric* generator.
3. operated by electricity; as, an *electric* iron.
4. electrifying; magnetic; exciting; tense.

electric action; a scheme of connections for playing an organ by electrically operating the stops and pedals so that the performer can be at a distance from the organ.

electric adhesion; adhesion caused by the attraction of electrostatic charges of opposite kind.

electric alarm; an alarm operated or controlled by the making or breaking or the change of resistance of an electric circuit, such as a burglar alarm, a thermostat, or a fire alarm.

electric apparatus; the instruments, machinery, and appliances used in electrical measurements, in producing and utilizing electric charges and currents, and in the study of electrical phenomena.

electric appliances; household articles operated by electricity or depending on electricity for their usefulness, as the electric clock, electric heater, etc.

electric atmosphere; same as *aura*, sense 3.

electric battery; same as *battery*, sense 12.

electric burner; a small electric heating plate set in a stand and used as a stove for heating and cooking.

electric candle; two parallel carbons insulated by some heat-resisting material, as kaolin: an alternating current passed in and out of the blunt end of the carbons forms a voltaic arc at the pointed ends: also called *Jablochkoff candle*.

electric cat or *catfish*; a fish found in African waters, capable of giving severe electric shocks.

electric cell; see *cell*, n. 9.

electric chair; (a) an apparatus in the form of a chair, used in electrocuting criminals; hence, (b) [Colloq.] the death sentence or punishment by electrocution; as, he got the *electric chair*.

electric chimes; chimes rung by being struck by hammers oscillating under the influence of electric attraction and repulsion.

electric clock; a clock operated or regulated by an electric motor.

electric column; a voltaic pile.

electric current; a flow of electricity along a conductor in a closed circuit and in one direction or in periodically reversed directions. The current may manifest itself in several ways, as by producing heat, chemical reactions, light, mechanical forces, or magnetic attraction or repulsion. The amount of current is equal, for direct currents, to the difference of potential in volts divided by the resistance in ohms, and is measured in amperes, one ampere being equal to one coulomb per second. For alternating currents, the effects of induction must be taken into account.

electric displacement; the movement of electricity through or in a dielectric subjected to an electric field of force.

electric dogfish; a marine fish, the stargazer, occurring along the Atlantic coast of the United States, and said to have electrical properties.

electric dyeing; a process of dyeing in which the chemical compounds used are decomposed by an electric current.

electric eel; a South American fish of the genus *Gymnotus*, found in fresh water, resembling an eel, and having an organ in its tail capable of giving severe electric shocks.

electric energy; the energy possessed by a system because of electric charges resident in or of currents flowing in the system. The energy of a charged body equals one-half the charge times the potential of the body.

electric expansion; the increase in volume of a body incident to its electrification.

electric explorer; an apparatus making use of induced currents for locating metallic substances in an unmetallic medium, particularly the human body.

electric eye; a photoelectric cell: used for controlling various sorts of apparatus, as for opening doors, etc.

electric fan; a ventilating or blowing fan, driven by an electric motor.

electric field; any space in which the effects of static electricity are discernible.

electric fish; any fish capable of communicating an electric shock.

electric fluid; a theoretical fluid, formerly postulated to account for electric phenomena.

electric fog; a fog accompanied by an electrically charged atmosphere.

electric force; the force of attraction or repulsion exerted by electrically charged bodies.

electric furnace; an electrically heated furnace used in the reduction of ore, manufacture of carbides, etc.

electric guitar; a kind of guitar whose tones are transmitted to an amplifier and loudspeaker through an electrical pickup attached to the bridge.

electric heat; heat generated in a circuit by current electricity.

electric heater; an apparatus that radiates heat generated by the passage of an electric current through a resisting material.

electric indicator; any electrically controlled automatic indicator, as an electric pressure gauge, etc.

electric iron; an electrically heated instrument used for pressing or smoothing.

electric jar; a Leyden jar or condenser.

electric lamp; an apparatus used for lighting in which matter is made luminous by electrical energy.

electric light; the light given off by a conductor, such as a carbon arc or a tungsten filament in an electric light bulb, which, due to its high resistance, becomes incandescent when an electric current is passed through it.

electric lock; an electrically controlled lock.

electric machine; a machine for generating electrical charges or currents, usually a machine for producing static or frictional electric charges, such as the Holtz and the Wimshurst machines. When the generation of a powerful continuous current of electricity is required, a dynamo, driven by steam or water power is used, thus converting mechanical energy into electrical energy by means of electromagnetic induction.

electric main; the principal or trunk conductor or wire of an electric lighting or power circuit.

electric meter; an instrument for measuring the current flowing in, the electromotive force applied to, or the power used in a circuit, as an ammeter, a wattmeter, or a voltmeter.

electric motor; a machine very similar to and often identical in construction with a dynamo, to which an electric current is led and by which the electrical energy of the current is converted into mechanical energy. Practically, it is a dynamo reversed in operation and turned by the magnetic effect of the current.

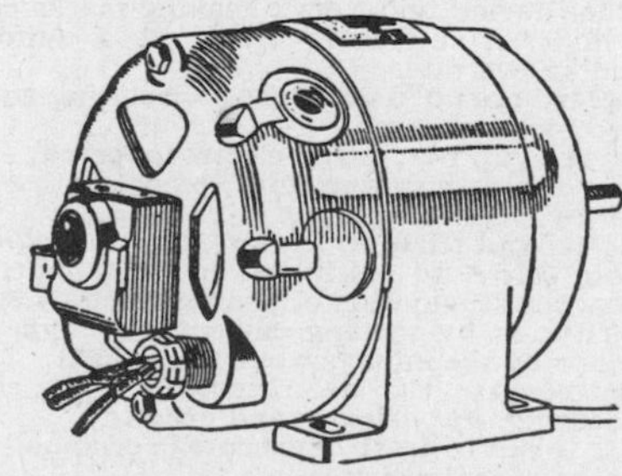

ELECTRIC MOTOR

electric needle; a high-frequency electrode in the form of a needle, used in surgery to cut through tissue, searing it at the same time to prevent bleeding.

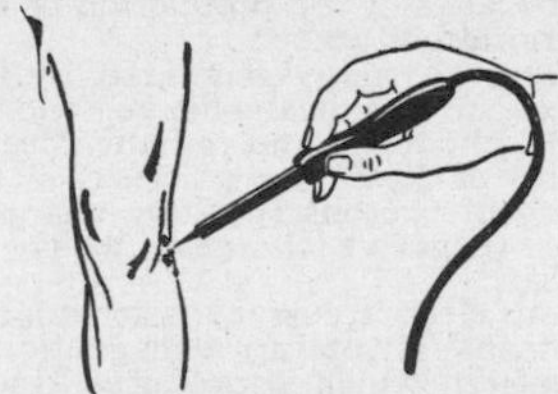

ELECTRIC NEEDLE

electric organ; a musical instrument resembling an organ, but producing tones by means of vacuum tubes instead of pipes.

electric oscillations; alternating currents of very high frequencies.

electric osmosis; the transfer of a substance through a porous wall by an electric current, as the action on various electrodes placed in porous cups in electric batteries, in which the metal particles are transferred through the porous walls and deposited on the cathode.

electric pen; a pen or pointed style, the point of which is rapidly reciprocated by a small solenoid or similar electric device and is thereby enabled to make fine perforations, transferring to another sheet any writing or picture that is to be reproduced or manifolded.

electric pulse; a periodic variation in strength of a current, without any reversal of direction of flow: not an alternation or oscillation.

electric radiation; the radiation of electric energy by wave motion.

electric railway; a railway on which the rolling stock is moved by electric motors commonly supplied by a current taken off a circuit contiguous and parallel to the line.

electric ray; any of a group of rays (fish) capable of giving an electric shock: also called *torpedo*.

electric refrigeration; cooling obtained by the use of an electric refrigerator.

electric refrigerator; a refrigerator in which an electric motor provides the power for a mechanical cooling apparatus.

electric regulator; an apparatus for controlling the speed or the current generation in electric machines.

electric steel; steel made or refined in an electric furnace.

electric stress; force due to the attractions or repulsions of electric charges.

electric tension; the difference of potential; the electromotive force; the voltage.

electric thermometer; a thermometer indicating changes in temperature by the variation of the resistance of a conductor produced by the changes of temperature; also, a thermopile used to indicate differences or variations of temperature.

electric typewriter; a typewriter having keys which, when touched by the fingers, close an electric circuit that employs an electromagnet to force the type against the inked typewriter ribbon.

electric units; the magnitudes of electrical quantities adopted as standards or units for measurement or reference, as the coulomb, the unit of charge, etc.

electric varnish; an insulating varnish.

electric wave; a periodic oscillation of an electric charge having the character of a wave motion, by means of which electrical energy is transmitted through space; an electromagnetic wave.

electric welding; the process of welding metals, in which the welding heat is produced by an electric current passing through the junction of the pieces to be welded. The heat is localized at the welding points owing to the resistance produced by the gap in the circuit.

ē·leç′tri·çăl, *a.* 1. electric.
2. connected with the science or application of electricity; as, an *electrical* engineer.

ē·leç′triç·ăl·ly, *adv.* by or with electricity.

ē·leç′triç·ăl·ness, *n.* the state, condition, or quality of being electrical.

electrical transcription; in radio broadcasting, (a) a large, long-playing phonograph record for recording programs; (b) the use of such records for broadcasting.

ē·leç·tri′ciăn (-trish′ăn), *n.* 1. originally, one versed in the science of electricity; an investigator of the laws governing electricity.

2. one who invents, manufactures, constructs, installs, or repairs electrical apparatus.

ē·leç·tric′i·ty, *n.* [Gr. *ēlektron*, amber. So named because of the production of electricity by friction of amber.

1. a form of energy generated by friction, induction, or chemical change, and having magnetic, chemical, and radiant effects: it is a property of the basic particles of all matter, consisting of protons (positive charges) and electrons (negative charges), which attract each other.

2. (a) an electric current; a stream of moving electrons: it sets up a magnetic field of force through which it produces kinetic energy; (b) static electricity; a charge of stationary particles: it sets up a field of force having potential energy.

Static electricity, so called because the charge is at rest, is produced by friction, by pressure, by heating, and by electrostatic induction. This is the form in which electricity was first known.

Voltaic or current electricity involves the transfer of quantities of electricity along the conducting circuit. Currents are produced by chemical decompositions going on in a cell, by the movement of a conductor in a magnetic field, by the heating of the junction of two dissimilar metals, and by the inductive action of a varying current in one conducting circuit on another circuit in the neighborhood of the first.

Like electric charges repel each other, and unlike charges attract each other. A positive charge induces a negative charge in a neighboring unelectrified object and therefore attracts that object. Similarly, a negative charge produces a positive induced charge.

3. that branch of physics which treats of the laws and phenomena of electricity.

4. electric current supplied as a public utility for lighting, heating, etc.

5. a state of strong emotional tension, anticipation, etc.; as, her entrance created *electricity* in the room.

animal electricity; see under *animal*.

atmospheric electricity; electricity present, induced, or generated in the atmosphere.

dynamical electricity; current, or voltaic, electricity.

excitation of electricity; the production of an electric condition by one of various methods, for example, by rubbing a rod of glass with silk.

Faradaic electricity or *currents*; electrical currents produced by the inductive action of other currents: so called after Faraday, the discoverer of current induction.

frictional electricity; static electricity.

galvanic electricity; an electric current.

organic electricity; electricity developed in living organisms by processes taking place within the organism and incident to its life.

resinous electricity; negative electricity.

vitreous electricity; positive electricity.

ē·leç′triçs, *n.* electricity as a branch of science.

ē·leç′tri·çūte, *v.t.* same as *electrocute*.

ē·leç·tri·çu′tion, *n.* same as *electrocution*.

ē·leç·trif′ẽr·ous, *a.* that can transmit electricity.

ē·leç′tri·fī·ȧ·ble, *a.* capable of receiving or being charged with electricity.

ē·leç″tri·fi·çā′tion, *n.* 1. an electrifying or being electrified.

2. all the installation and equipment required for electrifying.

ē·leç′tri·fī·ẽr, *n.* a person or thing that electrifies.

ē·leç′tri·fȳ, *v.t.*; electrified, *pt.*, *pp.*; electrifying, *ppr.* [*electric*, and L. *-ficare*, from *facere*, to make.]

1. to charge with electricity; to cause to become filled with electricity; as, to *electrify* a storage cell.

2. to affect by the transmission of electricity; to shock by an electric current.

3. to excite suddenly and intensely; to arouse to intense activity; to startle or to surprise, especially by something very inspiring or intensely interesting; to thrill; as, the dispatch reporting the relief of Mafeking *electrified* all England.

4. to equip for the use of electricity.

ē·leç′trine, *a.* [LL. *electrinus*; Gr. *ēlektrinos*, made of amber or electrum, from *ēlektron*, amber.]

1. pertaining to or made of amber. [Obs.]

2. made of electrum. [Obs.]

ē·leç′trīze, *v.t.*; electrized, *pt.*, *pp.*; electrizing, *ppr.* to electrify: also written *electrise*.

ē·leç′tri·zẽr, *n.* one who or that which electrizes.

ē·leç′trō, *v.t.*; electroed, *pt.*, *pp.*; electroing, *ppr.* [abbrev. of *electro*type.] to electrotype.

ē·leç′trō, *n.*; *pl.* **ē·leç′trōṣ,** 1. an electrotype.

2. an electroplate.

ē·leç·trō-, [from Greek *ēlektron*, amber.] a combining form meaning: (a) *electric*, as in *electro*magnet; (b) *electrically*, as in *electro*cute; (c) *electricity*, as in *electro*statics; (d) *electrolysis*, as in *electro*deposit.

ē·leç″trō·ȧ·nal′y·sis, *n.* analysis by means of electrolysis.

ē·leç″trō·bal·lis′tiç, *a.* relating to or performed by electroballistics.

ē·leç″trō·bal·lis′tiçs, *n.* the science of measuring the velocity of a projectile between various points of its trajectory by making it cut wire screens which are placed at those points and form part of an electric circuit. Cutting the screen breaks the circuit and the instant of break is recorded on a chronograph placed on the circuit, thus fixing the instant of passage through each screen.

ē·leç′trō·bȧth, *n.* the solution used in electroplating or electrotyping.

ē·leç″trō·bī·ō·log′iç·ăl, *a.* of or pertaining to electrobiology.

ē·leç″trō·bī·ol′ō·ġist, *n.* a person skilled in electrobiology.

ē·leç″trō·bī·ol′ō·ġy, *n.* the branch of biology which treats of electrical manifestations in living organisms.

ē·leç″trō·bī·os′çō·py, *n.* [*electro-*, and Gr. *bios*, life, and *skopein*, to view.] the testing of the muscles for contractions by passing an electric current through them: done, mainly, to determine whether life is or is not present.

ē·leç′trō·bronze, *n.* an article of metal (usually iron) electroplated with bronze.

ē·leç′trō·bronze, *v.t.* to make an electrobronze of.

ē·leç″trō·cap·il·lar′i·ty, *n.* that branch of physics which treats of the changes in capillarity which are produced by electric forces.

ē·leç·trō·çap′il·lā·ry, *a.* of or relating to electrocapillarity.

ē·leç″trō·çär′di·ō·gram, *n.* [*electro-*, and *cardiogram*.] the tracing produced by an electrocardiograph.

ē·leç″trō·çär′di·ō·gràph, *n.* [*electro-*, and *cardiograph*.] an instrument used to make graphic records of the changes in electric potential produced by the contractions of the heart.

ē·leç″trō·çär·di·ō·graph′iç, *a.* pertaining to or recorded by an electrocardiograph.

ē·leç″trō·çär·di·og′rȧ·phy, *n.* the study of the contractions of the heart by means of an electrocardiograph.

ē·leç·trō·çau′tẽr·y, *n.* the operation of cauterizing with an electrically heated wire.

ē·leç″trō·çhem′iç·ăl, *a.* of or pertaining to electrochemistry.

electrochemical series; a tabulation of the elements, such that each element is electropositive to all placed after it and electronegative to all preceding it.

ē·leç″trō·çhem′is·try, *n.* the science which treats of electricity in relation to chemical processes.

ē·leç″trō·çhron′ō·gràph, *n.* [*electro-*, and Gr. *chronos*, time, and *graphein*, to write.] an instrument for accurately recording the instant of any one or more occurrences and the elapsed time between such records. The time records are made by the making or breaking of a current or circuit, with a clock pendulum or other device, and a style making marks on a cylindrical surface revolving at a uniform and known rate.

ē·leç″trō·çhron″ō·gràph′iç, *a.* relating to an electrochronograph.

ē·leç·trō·çop′pẽr, *v.t.*; electrocoppered, *pt.*, *pp.*; electrocoppering, *ppr.* to coat with copper by electrodeposition.

ē·leç′trō·çul·tūre, *n.* [*electro-*, and L. *cultura*, from *colere*, to cultivate.] in plant cultivation, the stimulation of plant growth by electricity, as by sending currents through the soil or by the influence of electric light.

ē·leç′trō·çūte, *v.t.*; electrocuted, *pt.*, *pp.*; electrocuting, *ppr.* [*electro-* and exe*cute*.]

1. to put to death or execute (a criminal) by means of electricity.

2. to kill accidentally by electricity.

ē·leç·trō·çū′tion, ē·leç·tri·çū′tion, *n.* the act of putting to death by means of an electric current.

ē·leç′trōde, *n.* [*electro-*, and Gr. *hodos*, path, way.] either of the two terminals of an electric source, such as a battery: the positive electrode is called the anode, the negative electrode, the cathode.

ē·leç″trō·dē·poṣ·it, *v.t.* to deposit (a metal) electrolytically.

ē·leç″trō·dē·poṣ′it, *n.* a deposit made by an electric current, as in electroplating.

ē·leç″trō·dī·al′y·sis, *n.* the rapid removal of undesired ions from solution by the application of a direct current to electrodes inserted into a dialysis system.

ē·leç″trō·dȳ·nam′iç, ē·leç″trō·dȳ·nam′iç·ăl, *a.* 1. of electrodynamics.

2. of electricity in motion.

electrodynamic speaker; in radiotelegraphy, a loud-speaker in which the coil carrying the audio-frequency current is fastened to a movable disk, so that both the disk and coil vibrate with the changes in current.

ē·leç″trō·dȳ·nam′içs, *n.pl.* [*construed as sing.*], [*electro-*, and Gr. *dynamikos*, powerful, from *dynamis*, power.] the branch of physics dealing with the phenomena of electric currents and associated magnetic forces.

ē·leç″trō·dȳ·nȧ·mom′e·tẽr, *n.* [*electro-*, and Gr. *dynamis*, power, and *metron*, a measure.] an instrument for measuring the strength of an electric current by means of the interaction between the different parts of a single circuit carrying the current.

ē·leç″trō·en·ceph′ȧ·lō·gram″, *n.* a tracing showing the changes in electric potential produced by the brain.

ē·leç″trō·en·grāv′ing, *n.* the process of engraving by means of electricity.

ē·leç″trō-etch′ing, *n.* a method of etching upon metals by electrolytic action.

ē·leç·trō·ġen′e·sis, ē·leç·troġ′e·ny, *n.* [*electro-*, and the root of Gr. *gignesthai*, to produce.] in physiology, a tetanic state or condition produced in the muscles of the limbs by the passage of an electric current along the spinal cord or nerves.

ē·leç·trō·ġen′iç, *a.* in physiology, of or relating to electrogenesis; as, an *electrogenic* state.

ē·leç″trō·gild′ing, *n.* the gilding of a metallic surface by means of electricity.

ē·leç′trō·gilt, *a.* gilded by means of electricity.

ē·leç′trō·gràph, *n.* [*electro-*, and Gr. *graphein*, to write.]

1. the graphic record made by an electrometer or other device for recording the action of electricity.

2. an electrical device for etching or engraving plates.

3. a telegraphic instrument for transmitting photographs, drawings, etc.

4. the transmitted picture; wirephoto.

ē·leç·trog′rȧ·phy, *n.* 1. galvanography.

2. the reproduction of an engraving by electrodeposition.

ē·lec′trō·jet, *n.* a narrow, high-velocity stream of electric energy that girdles the earth in the ionosphere above the magnetic equator.

ē·leç″trō·ki·net′iç, *a.* of or relating to electrokinetics.

ē·leç″trō·ki·net′içs, *n.* [*electro-*, and Gr. *kinētikos*, from *kinein*, to move.] the branch of electrodynamics treating of electricity in motion, or electric currents, and the forces producing or controlling them: opposed to *electrostatics*.

ē·leç·trō·liēr′, *n.* [*electro-*, and chande*lier*.] a chandelier or fixture for electric lamps.

ē·leç·trō·log′iç, ē·leç·trō·log′iç·ăl, *a.* of or pertaining to electrology.

ē·leç·trol′ō·ġy, *n.* [*electro-*, and Gr. *-logia*, from *legein*, to speak.] the branch of physics treating of electricity.

ē·leç″trō·lū″mi·nes′cence, *n.* the emission of nonincandescent light by certain substances when acted upon by an alternating electric field.

ē·leç·trol′y·sis, *n.* [*electro-*, and Gr. *lysis*, a loosing, from *lyein*, to loose.]

1. the decomposition into ions of a chemical compound in solution by the action of an electric current passing through the solution.

2. the removal of unwanted hair from the body by destroying the hair roots with an electrified needle.

ē·leç′trō·lȳte, *n.* [*electro-*, and *-lyte*.] any substance which in solution is dissociated into ions and is thus made capable of conducting an electric current: when an electric current is passed through an electrolyte, a gas is generated or a solid deposited at the electrodes.

ē·leç·trō·lyt′iç, ē·leç·trō·lyt′iç·ăl, *a.* 1. produced by or pertaining to electrolysis.
2. of or containing an electrolyte.

ē·leç·trō·lyt′i·çăl·ly, *adv.* by electrolysis.

ē·leç·trō·lȳ′zȧ·ble, *a.* capable of being decomposed by an electric current.

ē·leç″trō·ly·zā′tion, *n.* the act or process of electrolyzing.

ē·leç′trō·lȳze, *v.t.*; electrolyzed, *pt., pp.*; electrolyzing, *ppr.* to subject to, or decompose by, electrolysis.

ē·leç·trō·mag′net, *n.* a core of magnetizable substance, such as soft iron, placed within a coil or helix of wire through which an electric current is passed. This magnetizes the core by induction, but the magnetic state thus induced persists during the passage of the current only, and disappears almost wholly with its cessation.

ELECTROMAGNET

ē·leç″trō·mag·net′iç, *a.* 1. of, relating to, or produced by electromagnetism.
2. of or produced by an electromagnet.
electromagnetic engine; an engine in which the motive power is electromagnetic in character, as an electric motor.
electromagnetic speaker; a loud-speaker in which the coil carrying the audio-frequency current is stationary.
electromagnetic stress; stress existing in magnetic fields.
electromagnetic wave; in radio, television, etc., a wave of electric energy radiated into space from an antenna.

ē·leç·trō·mag·net′i·çăl·ly, *adv.* by means of an electromagnet or electromagnetism.

ē·leç·trō·mag·net′içs, *n.* electromagnetism, sense 2.

ē·leç·trō·mag′net·işm, *n.* 1. magnetism produced by an electric current.
2. the branch of physics that deals with the relations between electricity and magnetism.

ē·leç·trō·met′ăl·lũr·ġy, *n.* the branch of metallurgy having to do with the use of electricity for producing heat in smelting, refining, etc., or for separating metals from their ores by electrolysis, or for electroplating.

ē·leç·trom′e·tẽr, *n.* [*electro-*, and Gr. *metron*, a measure.] an instrument for detecting or measuring differences of potential by the effects of electrostatic forces.
absolute electrometer; an electrometer in which the forces of electrostatic attraction or repulsion can be directly measured or indicated.
balanced or *attracted-disk electrometer*; see *balance electrometer*.

ē·leç·trō·met′riç, ē·leç·trō·met′riç·ăl, *a.* of or relating to electrometry or an electrometer; as, an *electrometric* indication.

ē·leç·trom′e·try, *n.* the science or process of making electrical measurements, especially by means of an electrometer.

ē·leç·trō·mō′tion, *n.* 1. the motion of an electric current.
2. motion produced by electric power.

ē·leç·trō·mō′tive, *a.* 1. producing an electric current through differences in potential.
2. relating to electromotive force or electromotion.
back electromotive force; the electromotive force in a circuit opposed to the impressed electromotive force: it is caused by the inductive effect of the current, or by the tendency of the products of electrolytic decomposition to reunite.
electromotive force; the force that can alter the motion of electricity, measured in terms of the energy per unit charge imparted to electricity passing through the source of this force.
impressed electromotive force; the electromotive force due to some outside source, as a dynamo or battery, applied to a circuit or branch of the circuit.

ē·leç·trō·mō′tŏr, *n.* 1. any source of electricity; an apparatus for generating an electric current, as a voltaic cell.
2. a machine or apparatus that transforms electrical into mechanical energy; an electric motor.

ē·leç·trō·mus′çū·lăr, *a.* relating to the action of electricity on the muscles.

ē·leç′tron, *n.* [Gr. *ēlektron*, amber.]
1. electrum.
2. any of the nonnuclear, negatively charged particles that form a part of all atoms, each carrying one negative charge 1.6 x 10^{-19} coulombs in size: the mass of an electron is about $^1/_{1800}$ of that of a proton, and the number of electrons circulating around a nucleus is equal to the number of positive charges on the nucleus.

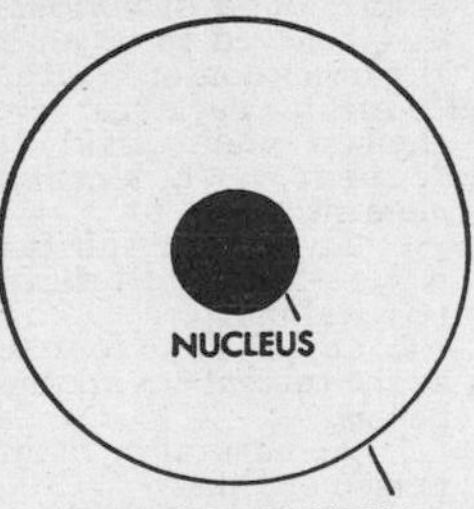

ELECTRON
(diagram of hydrogen atom)

ē·leç·trō·neg′ȧ·tive, *a.* 1. in physics and chemistry, having a negative electrical charge; tending to pass to the positive electrode, or anode, in electrolysis, by the law that opposite charges attract one another.
2. acid; negative; nonmetallic.

ē·leç·trō·neg′ȧ·tive, *n.* a substance that is electronegative.

ē·leç′tron gun, the part of a cathode-ray tube that collects, focuses, and emits the electrons.

ē·leç·tron′iç, *a.* 1. of an electron or electrons.
2. operated, operating, produced, or done by the action of electrons.

ē·leç·tron′iç brāin, any of various calculators, computers, etc. operated electronically.

ē·leç·tron′iç mū′siç, music in which the sounds are originated, organized, or altered by electronic devices, and arranged and recorded on tape for presentation.

ē·leç·tron′içs, *n.pl.* [*construed as sing.*] the branch of physics which is concerned with the phenomena of electronic action in vacuums and gases, and with the use of vacuum tubes, photoelectric cells, etc.

ē·leç′tron mī′çrō·sçōpe, an instrument for focusing rays of electrons, rather than light rays, to form an enlarged image of the object: it is much more powerful than any optical microscope.

ē·leç′tron op′tiçs, the branch of electronics having to do with the control of electron rays by means of electric and magnetic fields, which act upon the rays in the same way that lenses act on light rays.

ē·leç′tron tel′ē·sçōpe, an instrument using a cathode-ray tube to form a visible image of infrared rays brought into focus from a distant object by optical lenses.

ē·leç′tron tūbe, a type of vacuum tube whose functioning is largely dependent on the motion of electrons, as an X-ray tube.

ē·leç′tron-vōlt, *n.* a unit of energy equal to that of an electron falling unimpeded through a potential difference of one volt.

ē·leç·trō·op′tiçs, *n.* electron optics.

ē·leç·trō·path′iç, *a.* of or by electropathy.

ē·leç·trop′ȧ·thy, *n.* [*electro-*, and Gr. *pathos*, suffering.] same as *electrotherapeutics*.

ē·leç′trō·phōne, *n.* [*electro-*, and Gr. *phōnē*, sound.] a device for producing sound by means of electric currents.

ē·leç″trō·phō·rē′sis, *n.* cataphoresis.

Ē·leç·trō·phor′i·dae, *n.pl.* [*electro-*, and Gr. *pherein*, to bear.] a family of fishes, the electric eels.

ē·leç·troph′ō·rous, *a.* electriferous.

ē·leç·troph′ō·rus, *n.*; *pl.* **ē·leç·troph′ō·rī,** [*electro-*, and Gr. *pherein*, to bear.] an apparatus consisting of an insulated disk of resin, shellac, etc. and a metal plate, used in generating static electricity by induction.

ē·leç″trō·phyṣ″i·ō·log′iç·ăl, *a.* relating to electrophysiology.

ē·leç″trō·phyṣ·i·ol′ō·ġy, *n.* that branch of physiology which treats of electrical phenomena produced by or in living organisms.

ē·leç′trō·plāte, *v.t.*; electroplated, *pt., pp.*; electroplating, *ppr.* to cover electrolytically with a coating of metal.

ē·leç′trō·plāte, *n.* that which has been electroplated; especially, silver-plated tableware.

ē·leç′trō·plā·tẽr, *n.* one who electroplates.

ē·leç′trō·plā·ting, *n.* the process or art of plating electrolytically.

ē·leç·trō·poi′ŏn, *n.* [*electro-*, and Gr. *poiōn*, ppr. of *poiein*, to make.] an electrolyte for certain electric batteries, made of potassium dichromate, water, and sulfuric acid.

ē·leç·trō·pō′lăr, *a.* having electric polarity; negatively electrified at one end, or on one surface, and positively at the other: applied to an electrical conductor.

ē·leç·trō·pos′i·tive, *a.* 1. having a positive electrical charge; tending to pass to the negative electrode, or cathode, in electrolysis.
2. basic; metallic; positive.

ē·leç·trō·poṣ′i·tive, *n.* an electropositive substance.

ē·leç·trō·punç′tūre, ē·leç″trō·punç·tū·rā′tion, *n.* in surgery, the application of galvanic currents by inserting needles into the affected part.

ē·leç′trō·sçōpe, *n.* [*electro-*, and Gr. *skopein*, to view.] an instrument for detecting very small charges of electricity, and indicating whether they are positive or negative, as by the divergence of strips of gold leaf.

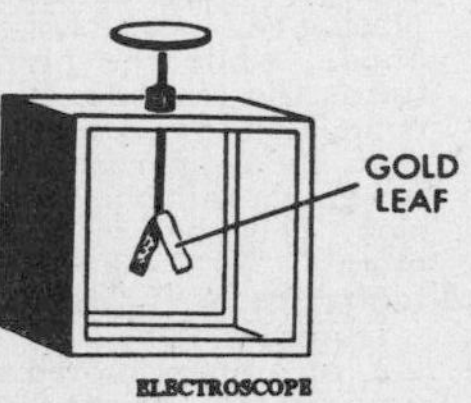

ELECTROSCOPE

ē·leç·trō·sçop′iç, *a.* relating to, measured by, or capable of being detected by, an electroscope.

ē·leç·trō·stat′iç, *a.* of electrostatics; relating to electricity in a state of rest or to stationary electric particles.
electrostatic flux; the transfer of energy through space between two charged bodies.
electrostatic measure; measure of static electricity based on the attraction or repulsion of electrically charged objects.
electrostatic stress; the force exerted by tension existing near any electrically charged body.

ē·leç·trō·stat′içs, *n. pl.* [*construed as sing.*] [*electro-*, and Gr. *statikos*, causing to stand, from *histanai*, to stand.] the branch of electrical science which treats of the properties and effects of electricity at rest, or static electricity.

ē·leç′trō·steel, *n.* steel produced in electric crucibles.

ē·leç·trō·stē′rē·ō·tȳpe, *n.* see *electrotype*.

ē·leç·trō·steth′ō·graph, *n.* [*electro-*, and *stethograph*.] an instrument used in recording heart sounds or cardiac vibrations, which are projected on a viewing screen.

ē·leç·trō·sũr′ġẽr·y, *n.* in surgery, the use of electrically operated instruments to cut through tissues or destroy them.

ē·leç·trō·syn′thē·sis, *n.* in chemistry, synthesis produced by means of an electric current.

ē·leç·trō·teçh′niç·ăl, *a.* of or pertaining to electrotechnics.

ē·leç·trō·teçh′niçs, *n.* the science that deals with the practical application of electricity in the industrial arts.

ē·leç″trō·ther·ȧ·peū′tiç, *a.* relating to electrotherapeutics.

ē·leç″trō·ther·ȧ·peū′ti·çăl, *a.* electrotherapeutic.

ē·leç″trō·ther·ȧ·peū′tiçs, *n. pl.* [*construed as sing.*] in medicine, the application of electricity in disease; electropathy.

ē·leç·trō·ther′ȧ·py, *n.* electrotherapeutics.

ē·leç·trō·thẽr′măl, *a.* using, relating to, or generating heat from electric energy.

ē·leç·trō·thẽr′miçs, *n.pl.* [*construed as sing.*] the branch of science which deals with the direct transformation of electric energy and heat, as in the heating chamber of certain rockets.

ē·leç·trō·thẽr′măn·cy, *n.* electrothermics.

ē·leç·trō·thẽr′mō·stat, *n.* a thermostat operating with electricity.

ē·leç·trō·ton′iç, *a.* in physiology, of or pertaining to electrotonus.

ē·leç·trot′ō·nīze, *v.t.* electrotonized, *pt., pp.* electrotonizing, *ppr.* to produce electrotonus in.

ē·leç·trot′ō·nus, ē·leç″trō·tō·nic′i·ty, *n.* [*electro-*, and Gr. *tonos*, tension.] in physiology, a changed state of a nerve produced during the passage of an electric current through any part of it.

ē·leç·trot′rō·pişm, *n.* [*electro-*, and Gr. *tropos*, from *trepein*, to turn.] in biology, the tropistic effect produced by electricity on vegetable organisms.

ē·leç′trō·tȳpe, *n.* [*electro-*, and Gr. *typos*, figure, image.]
1. a metal facsimile of a plate made by electroplating a wax impression of the original plate.
2. a print made from such a plate.

ē·leç′trō·tȳpe, *v.t.*; electrotyped, *pt., pp.*; electrotyping, *ppr.* to produce an electrotype of;

to duplicate by means of an electrotype; as, to *electrotype* a form.

ē·leç′trō·tȳpe, *v.i.* to make electrotypes.

ē·leç′trō·tȳ·pēr, *n.* one who electrotypes.

ē·leç·trō·typ′iç, *a.* 1. using, having the nature of, or relating to an electrotype.

2. of electrotypy.

ē·leç′trō·tȳ·py, *n.* the process or art of producing electrotypes. A matrix is made by pouring melted wax into a shallow molding case and impressing the cake thus formed with the surface to be duplicated. The matrix is coated with graphite, then suspended in a bath of copper sulfate acting as an electroplating cell in which a copper plate forms the anode, while the plumbago of the matrix forms the cathode. When the electrodes are connected to the terminals of a source of current, the copper is deposited on the cathode, forming a thin shell covering the wax impression. This shell is then backed with molten metal.

ē·leç′trum, *n.* [L., from Gr. *ēlektron*, amber.]

1. amber. [Obs.]

2. an amber-colored alloy of gold and silver, used by the ancient Greeks for coins.

3. an alloy of copper, nickel, and zinc, used for keys, tableware, etc.: also called *German silver, nickel silver.*

ē·leç′tū·ȧ·ry, *n.*; *pl.* **ē·leç′tū·ȧ·rieș,** [LL. *electuarium, electarium*, from Gr. *ekleikton*, from *ekleichein*, to lick up; *ek*, out, and *leichein*, to lick.] a medicine composed of drugs mixed with honey or sirup to form a paste.

el·ee·mos′y·nā·ri·ly, *adv.* in an eleemosynary manner.

el·ee·mos′y·nā·ry, *a.* [LL. *eleemosynarius*, pertaining to alms, one who receives or gives alms, from *eleemosyna*; Gr. *eleēmosynē*, alms.]

1. charitable; of or for charity or alms.

2. supported by or dependent on charity.

3. given by charity; gratuitous; free.

el·ee·mos′y·nā·ry, *n.*; *pl.* **el·ee·mos′y·nā·rieș,** one who lives on alms. [Obs.]

el′ē·gănce, *n.* 1. the state or quality of being elegant; dignified richness and grace, as of manner, language, dress, design, style, etc.

2. that which is elegant.

el′ē·găn·cy, *n.*; *pl.* **el′ē·găn·cieș,** elegance.

el′ē·gănt, *a.* [L. *elegans* (*-antis*), luxurious, choice, fine, from *eligere*, to choose, select.]

1. characterized by dignified richness and grace, as of manner, dress, design, style, etc.; luxurious or opulent in a restrained, tasteful manner.

2. characterized by a sense of propriety or refinement; fastidious in manners and tastes.

3. excellent; fine; first-rate. [Colloq.]

el′ē·gănt·ly, *adv.* in a manner to please; with elegance; with beauty; with pleasing propriety; as, a composition *elegantly* written.

el·ē·gī′aç (*or* ē·lē′gi·aç), *a.* [LL. *elegiacus*; Gr. *elegeiakos*, from *elēgeia, elegeion*, an elegy.]

1. of or composed in dactylic hexameter couplets, the second line (sometimes called a pentameter) having only an accented syllable in the third and sixth feet: the form was used for Greek and Latin elegies and various other lyric poems. Scansion:

/˘˘ | /˘˘ | /˘˘ | /˘˘ | /˘˘ | /˘
/˘˘ | /˘˘ | / | /˘˘ | /˘˘ | / |

2. of, like, or fit for an elegy.

3. sad; mournful; plaintive.

el·ē·gī′aç, *n.* 1. an elegiac couplet.

2. [*pl.*] a series of such couplets; a poem or poems written in such couplets.

el·ē·gī′ȧ·căl, *a.* elegiac.

el″ē·gī·am′bus, *n.*; *pl.* **el″ē·gī·am′bī,** [Gr. *elegeion*, an elegy, and *iambos*, iambus.] a compound form of versification in which a line consists of seven syllables (two dactyls and one long syllable) and an iambic dimeter.

el″ē·gī·og′rȧ·phẽr, *n.* [Gr. *elegeiographos*; *elegeion*, an elegy, and *graphein*, to write.] a writer of elegiac verse. [Obs.]

el′ē·gist, *n.* a writer of elegies.

ē·lē′git, *n.* [L., he has chosen; 3rd pers. sing. perf. ind. of *eligere*, to choose, select.] a writ of execution by which a defendant's goods are appraised and delivered to the plaintiff until his claim is satisfied.

el′ē·gīze, *v.t.*; elegized, *pt., pp.*; elegizing, *ppr.* to commemorate or lament as in an elegy.

el′ē·gīze, *v.i.* to write elegies.

el′ē·gy, *n.*; *pl.* **el′ē·gieș,** [Fr. *élégie*; L. *elegia*; Gr. *elegeia*, from *elegos*, a lament.]

1. a poem of lament and praise for the dead, as Shelley's "Adonais."

2. any poem in elegiac verse.

3. a poem written in a mournfully contemplative tone; as, Gray's "*Elegy* in a Country Churchyard."

ē·lē′i·din, *n.* [Gr. *elaia*, olive oil, oil.] a substance found in various parts of the epidermis, believed to be an intermediate stage in the formation of keratin.

el′ē·me, *a.* [Turk.] gathered by hand; hence, of the best quality: said of fruit; as, *eleme* figs.

el′ē·ment, *n.* [L. *elementum*, a first principle, element.]

1. any of four substances—earth, air, fire, water—formerly believed to constitute all physical matter.

2. any of these four substances thought of as the natural environment of a class of living beings.

3. the natural or fitting environment for a person or thing.

4. a component, feature, or principle of something; basic part.

5. in chemistry, any substance that cannot be separated into different substances except by nuclear disintegration: all matter is composed of such substances.

6. [*pl.*] the bread and wine used in the Eucharist.

7. in electricity, (a) either of a pair of metallic substances that act together in an electrolyte to produce electricity; (b) a positive or negative electrode; (c) the working part of an electrical appliance; as, the heating *element* of an iron.

8. in mathematics, (a) an infinitesimal part of any magnitude; differential; (b) the point, line, etc. that generates a line, surface, etc.

9. in military aviation, the basic unit of an air force, consisting of one or more aircraft: it is a subdivision of a flight.

in one's element; in a situation, surroundings, etc. suited to one.

the elements; (a) the first or basic principles; rudiments; (b) wind, rain, etc.; forces of the atmosphere.

el′ē·ment, *v.t.* to compound of elements or first principles. [Obs.]

el·ē·men′tăl, *a.* 1. of any or all of the four elements (earth, air, fire, and water) believed in by ancient philosophers.

2. of or like natural forces; characteristic of the physical universe.

3. basic and powerful; primal; as, hunger and sex are *elemental* drives.

4. of first principles; elementary; basic; rudimentary; simple.

5. being an essential part or parts.

6. in chemistry, of an element; not a compound.

el·ē·men′tăl·ișm, *n.* worship of the elements as deities.

el″ē·men·tal′i·ty, *n.* composition of principles or ingredients.

el·ē·men′tăl·ly, *adv.* according to elements; in an elemental sense. [Obs.]

el·ē·men′tăr, *a.* elementary. [Obs.]

el·ē·men′tȧ·ri·ly, *adv.* in an elementary manner.

el·ē·men′tȧ·ri·ness, *n.* the state or quality of being elementary.

el″ē·men·tar′i·ty, *n.* elementariness. [Obs.]

el·ē·men′tȧ·ry, *a.* [L. *elementarius*, pertaining to an element; *elementum*, element.]

1. elemental.

2. of first principles; of the rudiments or fundamentals of something; introductory.

3. consisting of one chemical element; not a compound.

4. of a chemical element or elements.

Syn.—physical, material, natural, primary, rudimental, simple, inchoate, component, constituent, ultimate.

el·ē·men′tȧ·ry pär′ti·çle, a particle smaller than an atom, which is not a composite of other particles but is capable of independent existence, as a neutron, proton, electron, etc.

el·ē·men′tȧ·ry sçhool, 1. in educational systems having no junior high school, a school of eight grades, where basic subjects are taught.

2. in educational systems having a junior high school, a similar school of six grades.

Also called *grade school, grammar school.*

el″ē·men·tā′tion, *n.* instruction in primary principles. [Obs.]

el·ē·men′toid, *a.* like an element; having the nature of a simple elementary substance.

el′ē·mi, *n.* [prob. of Ar. origin.] a resin used in the manufacture of varnishes, plasters, and medicinal ointments, and obtained from the bark of the *Canarium* and *Amyris*, genera related to the myrrh family: also *gum elemi.*

el′ē·min, *n.* [*elemi* and *-in.*] either of two derivatives of various elemis, one crystalline, the other oily.

ē·lençh′, *n.* [L. *elenchus*; Gr. *elenchos*, from *elenchein*, to cross-examine, for the purpose

TABLE OF CHEMICAL ELEMENTS

Elements	Symbol	Atomic No.	Atomic Weight*
actinium	Ac	89	227(?)
aluminum	Al	13	26.9815
americium	Am	95	243.13
antimony	Sb	51	121.75
argon	Ar	18	39.948
arsenic	As	33	74.9216
astatine	At	85	210(?)
barium	Ba	56	137.34
berkelium	Bk	97	248(?)
beryllium	Be	4	9.0122
bismuth	Bi	83	208.980
boron	B	5	10.811
bromine	Br	35	79.909
cadmium	Cd	48	112.40
calcium	Ca	20	40.08
californium	Cf	98	251(?)
carbon	C	6	12.01115
cerium	Ce	58	140.12
cesium	Cs	55	132.905
chlorine	Cl	17	35.453
chromium	Cr	24	51.996
cobalt	Co	27	58.9332
copper	Cu	29	63.546
curium	Cm	96	247(?)
dysprosium	Dy	66	162.50
einsteinium	Es	99	252(?)
erbium	Er	68	167.28
europium	Eu	63	151.96
fermium	Fm	100	257(?)
fluorine	F	9	18.9984
francium	Fr	87	223(?)
gadolinium	Gd	64	157.25
gallium	Ga	31	69.72
germanium	Ge	32	72.59
gold	Au	79	196.967
hafnium	Hf	72	178.49
helium	He	2	4.0026
holmium	Ho	67	164.930
hydrogen	H	1	1.00797
indium	In	49	114.82
iodine	I	53	126.9044
iridium	Ir	77	192.2
iron	Fe	26	55.847
krypton	Kr	36	83.80
lanthanum	La	57	138.91
lawrencium	Lr	103	256(?)
lead	Pb	82	207.19
lithium	Li	3	6.939
lutetium	Lu	71	174.97
magnesium	Mg	12	24.312
manganese	Mn	25	54.9380
mendelevium	Md	101	258(?)
mercury	Hg	80	200.59
molybdenum	Mo	42	95.94
neodymium	Nd	60	144.24
neon	Ne	10	20.183
neptunium	Np	93	237.00
nickel	Ni	28	58.71
niobium	Nb	41	92.906
nitrogen	N	7	14.0067
nobelium	No	102	255(?)
osmium	Os	76	190.2
oxygen	O	8	15.9994
palladium	Pd	46	106.4
phosphorus	P	15	30.9738
platinum	Pt	78	195.09
plutonium	Pu	94	239.05
polonium	Po	84	210.05
potassium	K	19	39.102
praseodymium	Pr	59	140.907
promethium	Pm	61	145(?)
protactinium	Pa	91	231.10
radium	Ra	88	226.00
radon	Rn	86	222.00
rhenium	Re	75	186.2
rhodium	Rh	45	102.905
rubidium	Rb	37	85.47
ruthenium	Ru	44	101.07
samarium	Sm	62	150.35
scandium	Sc	21	44.956
selenium	Se	34	78.96
silicon	Si	14	28.086
silver	Ag	47	107.868
sodium	Na	11	22.9898
strontium	Sr	38	87.62
sulfur	S	16	32.064
tantalum	Ta	73	180.948
technetium	Tc	43	97(?)
tellurium	Te	52	127.60
terbium	Tb	65	158.924
thallium	Tl	81	204.37
thorium	Th	90	232.038
thulium	Tm	69	168.934
tin	Sn	50	118.69
titanium	Ti	22	47.90
tungsten	W	74	183.85
uranium	U	92	238.03
vanadium	V	23	50.942
xenon	Xe	54	131.30
ytterbium	Yb	70	173.04
yttrium	Y	39	88.905
zinc	Zn	30	65.37
zirconium	Zr	40	91.22

* International Atomic Weights. Carbon at 12 is the standard.

of refuting, to refute.] a fallacious argument which is apt to deceive under the appearance of truth; a sophism.

ē·leñ′çhiç, ē·leñ′çhiç·ăl, *a.* pertaining to an elenchus.

ē·leñ′çhiç·ăl·ly, *adv.* by means of an elenchus.

ē·leñ′çhīze, *v.i.* to dispute by using elenchi.

ē·leñçh′tiç, ē·leñçh′tiç·ăl, *a.* elenctic.

ē·leñ′çhus, *n.*; *pl.* **ē·leñ′çhī,** [L.; Gr. *elenchos*, cross-examination, disproof, refutation.]

1. an elench.

2. in logic, a syllogism that refutes a proposition by proving the direct contrary of its conclusion.

ē·leñç′tiç, *a.* [Gr. *elenktikos*, fond of cross-examining, critical.] in logic, (a) of elenchus; refuting; (b) of cross-examination.

el′enġe, *a.* [ME. *elenge*; AS. *ellende*, foreign, strange; G. *elend*, miserable.] troubled; filled with sorrow. [Obs.]

el′enġe·ness, *n.* misery; loneliness. [Obs.]

Ē·lē·oçh′ȧ·ris, *n.* [Gr. *elos*, genit. *eleos*, low ground by rivers, marsh, and *chairein*, to rejoice.] a widely distributed genus of sedgelike plants, comprising about eighty species, commonly known as spike rushes, because of the appearance of the stalks.

el′ē·phăn·sy, *n.* [L. *elephantia*, from *elephans*, an elephant.] elephantiasis. [Obs.]

el′ē·phănt, *n.* [L. *elephantus* or *elephas*, *elephantis*; Gr. *elephas*, *elephantos*, an elephant, ivory; perhaps from Heb. *eleph*, an ox.]

1. a huge, thick-skinned, almost hairless mammal, the largest of extant four-footed animals, with a long, flexible snout (called a trunk) and two ivory tusks growing out of the upper jaw. Two existing species are *Elephas indicus* (the Indian elephant) and *Elephas africanus* (the African elephant). The former is characterized by a high, concave forehead, and small ears and tusks which are usually present in the male only. The tusks and ears are much larger in the African elephant, its forehead is convex, and both sexes have tusks.

HEAD OF AFRICAN ELEPHANT
(*Elephas africanus*)

HEAD OF INDIAN ELEPHANT
(*Elephas indicus*)

2. ivory; the tusk of the elephant. [Obs.]

el′ē·phănt ap′ple, an East Indian tree, *Feronia elephantum*, belonging to the *Rutaceæ*, having an edible fruit like the orange; also, the fruit.

el′ē·phănt bee′tle, any of a group of beetles of the genus *Goliathus*, native to Africa.

el′ē·phănt bīrd, a gigantic fossil bird, similar to the ostrich, found in Madagascar, of the genus *Æpyornis*.

el′ē·phănt çreep′ẽr, a creeper, *Argyreia speciosa*, allied to the morning-glory, which runs to the tops of trees: it bears large, rose-colored flowers, and is native to both the Indies.

el′ē·phănt fish, a fish, *Callorhynchus antarcticus*, with a projection of the snout like a proboscis, belonging to the order *Chimæra*.

el′ē·phănt grȧss, a plant native to southern Asia and southern Europe, *Typha elephantina*, considered a congener of the common cattail.

el·ē·phan′ti·aç, *a.* affected with or characteristic of elephantiasis.

el″ē·phăn·tī′ȧ·sis, *n.* [Gr. *elephantiasis*, a skin disease, from *elephas* (*-antos*), an elephant.] a chronic disease of the skin characterized by the enlargement of certain parts of the body, especially the legs and genitals, and by the hardening and ulceration of the surrounding skin: it is caused by small, threadlike worms (*filariae*) which obstruct the lymphatic glands.

El·ē·phan′ti·dae, *n.pl.* [L. *elephas* (*-antis*), an elephant, and *-idæ*.] a family of mammals of which the elephant, *Elephas*, is the type.

el·ē·phan′tine, *a.* [L. *elephantinus*, from *elephas* (*-antis*), an elephant.]

1. pertaining to an elephant or elephants.

2. like an elephant in size or gait; huge, heavy, slow, clumsy, ungainly, etc.

3. in ancient Rome, designating certain books in which the Romans registered the transactions of the senate, magistrates, emperors, and generals: so called because made of ivory.

el′ē·phănt leg, elephantiasis.

el′ē·phănt mouse, a species of jumping or kangaroo mice, one of the African *Insectivora*, with a proboscislike snout: also called *elephant shrew*.

el·ē·phan′toid, el″ē·phan·toid′ăl, *a.* [Gr. *elephas* (*-antos*), an elephant, and *eidos*, form.] similar to an elephant in appearance or habits.

El·ē·phan′tō·pus, *n.* [Gr. *elephantopous*, ivory-footed; *elephas* (*-antos*), an elephant, ivory, and *pous*, a foot.] a genus of herblike plants, native to America and belonging to the aster family.

el·ē·phan′tous, *a.* [L. *elephantiasis*, and *-ous*.] resembling or of the nature of elephantiasis; as, an *elephantous* skin disease.

el′ē·phănt sēal, a seal, sometimes attaining a length of twenty feet, of the subfamily *Cystophorinæ*, genus *Macrorhinus*, the male of which has a proboscislike snout; the sea elephant.

el′ē·phănt's ēar, in botany, a species of the genus *Begonia*, so named because of its large, ornamental leaves.

el′ē·phănt's foot, 1. any of several species of *Elephantopus*.

2. a vine of the yam family, with a large root somewhat resembling an elephant's foot.

el′ē·phănt shrew, same as *elephant mouse*.

el′ē·phănt's tusk, a mollusk, *Dentalium arcuatum*, whose curved tubular shell resembles an elephant's tusk.

El·eū·sin′i·ȧ, *n.pl.* [Gr. *Eleusinia*, neut. pl. of *Eleusinios*, pertaining to *Eleusis* (*-inos*), Eleusis.] the Eleusinian mysteries.

El·eū·sin′i·ăn, *a.* relating to Eleusis, a city in ancient Greece.

El·eū·sin′i·ăn mys′tẽr·ieş, secret religious rites of ancient Greece, celebrated every spring at Eleusis in honor of Demeter and Persephone: they symbolized the annual death and resurrection of vegetation.

el·eū·thē′ri·ăn, *a.* [Gr. *eleutherios*, like a free man, frank, freely giving, from *eleutheros*, free.] giving freedom; liberating: applied to Zeus, as a liberator of slaves.

e·leū″thẽr·ō·mā′ni·ȧ, *n.* [Gr. *eleutheros*, free, and *mania*, madness.] a mania for freedom.

e·leū″thẽr·ō·mā′ni·aç, *n.* one whose zeal for freedom appears to be a mania.

e·leū″thẽr·ō·mā′ni·aç, *a.* having a mania for freedom.

e·leū″thẽr·ō·pet′ăl·ous, *a.* [Gr. *eleutheros*, free, and *petalon*, a leaf.] having the petals free or noncoherent.

el′ē·vāte, *v.t.*; elevated, *pt.*, *pp.*; elevating, *ppr.* [L. *elevatus*, pp. of *elevare*, to raise, lift up; *e-*, out, and *levare*, to make light, lift, from *levis*, light.]

1. to lift or raise from a lower to a higher place; as, to *elevate* a machine or a house.

2. to promote; to raise to a higher rank or position.

3. to improve; to refine; to ennoble; as, to *elevate* the standard of morals.

4. to cheer; to animate; to excite; to raise in spirit.

5. to raise the pitch or volume of; to make louder; as, to *elevate* the voice.

6. to intoxicate slightly or make tipsy. [Colloq.]

Syn.—raise, hoist, exalt, erect, elate, cheer, animate.

el′ē·vā·ted, *a.* 1. raised; lifted up; high.

2. exalted; dignified; noble; lofty.

3. high-spirited; joyful; elated.

el′ē·vā·ted, *n.* an elevated railway. [Colloq.]

el′ē·vā·ted·ness, *n.* the state of being elevated.

el′ē·vā·ted rāil′wāy, a railway elevated above a street on a framework so that the street is left free for traffic.

el·ē·vā′ti·ō (-shi-ō), *n.* [L., from *elevare*, to raise, make light.] formerly, in music, (a) any liturgical composition rendered during the elevation of the Host; (b) the raising of a melody above the common compass in medieval music.

el·ē·vā′tion *n.* [L. *elevatio* (*-onis*), from *elevare*, to raise, make light.]

1. an elevating or being elevated.

2. the act of raising to a higher intellectual or moral level; as, the *elevation* of character, morals, art, or education.

3. a high or elevated place above the surface of the earth; high or rising ground; as, an *elevation* on a prairie.

4. in astronomy, the angular distance of a celestial body above the horizon; altitude; as, the *elevation* of a planet.

5. in drawing, a projection of a building or other structure in a vertical plane; as, a front *elevation* of a temple.

6. in dialing, the angle made by the style with the substylar line.

7. in gunnery, the angle between the axis of a gun and the line of sight; the movement of the axis of a gun in a vertical plane.

8. in geography, the height of any land surface above sea level; altitude.

angle of elevation; the angle made by an ascending line with a horizontal plane.

el′ē·vā·tŏr, *n.* [LL. *elevator*, one who raises up, a deliverer, from L. *elevare*, to raise up, make light.]

1. one who or that which lifts, raises, or conveys anything.

2. a mechanical device of various designs, usually an endless chain or belt, with a series of buckets or scoops, for transferring materials from lower to higher levels.

3. a machine for hoisting or lowering goods or people by means of a suspended cage or car; also, the cage or car itself: in British usage, a *lift*.

4. a warehouse, often cylindrical, for storing, hoisting, and discharging grain; granary.

5. a movable airfoil like a horizontal rudder, usually hinged to the tail section of an aircraft, for making the craft go up or down.

6. in anatomy, a muscle which serves to elevate some organ or part, as the eyelid.

7. in dentistry, an instrument for removing roots of teeth.

8. in surgery, an instrument for raising a depressed part, as of a fractured bone.

el′ē·vā·tō·ry, *a.* [from LL. *elevator*, one who raises up.] tending to raise, or having power to elevate; as, *elevatory* tendencies.

ē·lev′en, *a.* [ME. *elleven*; AS. *endleofan*, eleven; *an*, one, and *-lif*, remainder, as in Goth. *twalif*, AS. *twelf*, twelve.] consisting of ten and one; totaling one more than ten; as, *eleven* dollars.

ē·lev′en, *n.* 1. the cardinal number between ten and twelve.

2. a symbol representing the number, as XI or 11.

3. a team in the games of football or cricket, numbering eleven players.

ē·lev′en·fōld, *a.* 1. having eleven parts.

2. having eleven times as much or as many.

ē·lev′en·fōld, *adv.* eleven times as much or as many.

ē·lev′enth, *a.* 1. the next in order to the tenth; as, the *eleventh* chapter.

2. relating to one of the eleven equal parts into which a thing may be divided; as, the *eleventh* part of an estate.

ē·lev′enth, *n.* 1. the one following the tenth.

2. any of the eleven equal parts of something; $^1/_{11}$.

3. in music, the interval consisting of an octave and a fourth.

elf, *n.*; *pl.* **elveş,** [AS. *ælf*, *ylf*; Ice. *alfr*; Sw. *alf*, *elva*, an elf.]

1. in folklore, a diminutive, wandering sprite or fairy; an imaginary being supposed to exercise magic powers and haunt woods and hills.

2. a diminutive person; a dwarf.

3. a mischievous child.

elf, *v.t.* to entangle (hair). [Rare.]

elf ar′rōw, an arrowhead of flint: called also *elf bolt*, *elf dart*.

elf chīld, a child thought to have been left by elves in place of one stolen; a changeling.

elf dock, the elecampane.

elf fire, the ignis fatuus.

elf′in, *a.* relating or pertaining to elves.

elf′in, *n.* 1. an elf.

2. a butterfly of the genus *Incisalia*.

elf′ish, *a.* resembling an elf.

elf′ish·ly, *adv.* in an elfish manner.
elf′ish·ness, *n.* the quality of resembling an elf.
elf′kin, *n.* a little elf.
elf′land, *n.* the land of elves or fairies.
elf′lock, *n.* hair twisted into knots, as if by elves.
elf owl, a small owl, *Micrathene whitneyi*, of Arizona, California, and Mexico.
El′gin mär′bles, a group of ancient sculptured marbles, named after the Earl of Elgin, who removed them from the temple of Minerva and other buildings in Athens. The marbles consist chiefly of statues and casts now deposited in the British Museum.
Ē′lī, *n.* in the Bible, a high priest of Israel and teacher of Samuel. I Sam. iii.
Ē·lī′ăs, *n.* in the Bible, Elijah: Greek form of the name.
ē·lic′it, *v.t.*; elicited, *pt., pp.*; eliciting, *ppr.* [L. *elicitus*, pp. of *elicere*, to draw out; *e-*, out, and *lacere*, to entice.]
1. to draw out; to bring to light; to deduce by reason or argument; as, to *elicit* truth by discussion.
2. to draw forth; to evoke; as, his irony *elicited* an angry reply.
ē·lic′it, *a.* in philosophy, brought from possibility into real existence. [Obs.]
ē·lic′i·tāte, *v.t.* to elicit. [Obs.]
ē·lic·i·tā′tion, *n.* the act of eliciting or being elicited.
ē·līde′, *v.t.*; elided, *pt., pp.*; eliding, *ppr.* [L. *elidere*, to strike out, to break in pieces.]
1. to break or dash in pieces; to crush. [Obs.]
2. to leave out; to suppress.
3. to leave out or slur over (a vowel, syllable, etc.) in pronunciation to prevent hiatus, as in *th' everlasting hills.*
e·līd′i·ble, *a.* that can be elided.
el″i·ġi·bil′i·ty, 1. the quality or state of being eligible.
2. *pl.* **el″i·ġi·bil′i·ties,** [*usually in pl.*] a quality that makes eligible.
el′i·ġi·ble, *a.* [OFr. *eligible*, from L. *eligere*, to choose, select.] fit to be chosen; worthy of choice; legally or morally qualified; suitable; desirable.
el′i·ġi·ble, *n.* an eligible person.
el′i·ġi·ble·ness, *n.* fitness to be chosen in preference to another; suitableness; desirableness.
el′i·ġi·bly, *adv.* in an eligible manner.
E′li·hū, *n.* [Heb. *elihu*, lit., my God is he.] in the Bible, the youngest of the four men who visited Job in his affliction. Job xxxii–xxxvii.
Ē·lī′jăh, *n.* [Heb. *'ēlīyāhū*, lit., Jehovah is God.] in the Bible, a prophet of Israel in the ninth century B. C. I Kings xvii–xix, II Kings ii. 1–11.
el′i·māte, *v.t.* [L. *elimatus*, pp. of *elimare*, to file, polish; *e-*, out, and *limare*, from *lima*, a file.] to make smooth. [Obs.]
ē·lim′i·nănt, *n.* [L. *eliminans* (*-antis*), ppr. of *eliminare*, to turn out of doors, banish.] in mathematics, the result obtained by the elimination of *n* variables between *n* homogeneous equations of any degree; the resultant of two quantics.
ē·lim′i·nāte, *v.t.*; eliminated, *pt., pp.*; eliminating, *ppr.* [L. *eliminatus*, pp. of *eliminare*, to turn out of doors, banish; *e-*, out, and *limen* (*-inis*), the threshold, door.]
1. to thrust out of doors. [Obs.]
2. to expel; to thrust out; to discharge, or throw off; to get rid of.
3. to leave out of consideration; to reject; to omit.
4. in physiology, to expel (waste products) from the body; as, the kidneys *eliminate* uric acid.
5. in algebra, to get rid of (an unknown quantity) by combining equations.
ē·lim·i·nā′tion, *n.* an eliminating or being eliminated.
ē·lim′i·nā·tive, *a.* carrying on the process of elimination; tending to eliminate.
ē·lim′i·nā·tŏr, *n.* a person or thing that eliminates.
ē·lim′i·nȧ·tō″ry, *a.* eliminating.
ē·liñ′guāte (-gwāt), *v.t.*; elinguated; *pt., pp.*; elinguating, *ppr.* [L. *elinguatus*, pp. of *elinguare*, to deprive of the tongue.] to remove the tongue from. [Obs.]
ē·liñ·guā′tion (-gwā′), *n.* the act of elinguating. [Obs.]
ē·liñ′guid (-gwid), *a.* tongue-tied; not having the power of speech. [Obs.]
el′i·quāte, *v.t.* [L. *eliquatus*, pp. of *eliquare*, to clarify, strain, cause to flow; *e-*, out, and *liquare*, to melt.] in metallurgy, to separate by heat, as an ore from a metal; to smelt.
el·i·quā′tion, *n.* [L. *eliquare*, to melt, clarify, or strain.] in metallurgy, the operation by which a more fusible substance is separated from one that is less so by means of a degree of heat sufficient to melt the one and not the other, as an alloy of copper and lead.
Ē·lis′ȧ·beth, *n.* in the Bible, the mother of John the Baptist and a kinswoman of Mary. Luke i.
Ē·lī′shȧ, *n.* [Heb. *elīshā'*, lit., God is salvation.] in the Bible, a prophet of Israel, ordained by Elijah as his successor. I Kings xix. 16, 19; II Kings ii.
ē·li′sion, *n.* [L., *elisio*, from *elidere*, to strike off; *e-*, out, and *lædere*, to strike.] an eliding or being elided; specifically, in pronunciation, the cutting off or suppression of a vowel at the end of a word, for the sake of sound or measure, when the next word begins with a vowel, e.g., th' embattled plain, th' empyreal sphere.
e·lī′sŏr, *n.* [OFr. *eliseor, eliseur*, a chooser, from *elire*, L. *eligere*, to choose, select.] in law, a sheriff's substitute for returning a jury. In case, on account of their personal interest in the suit, an objection shall lie to the sheriff or the coroners, the venire facias shall be directed to two clerks of the court, or to two persons of the county, named by the court and sworn, who shall return the jury.
e·lite′, é·lite (i-lēt′ *or* ā-lēt′), *n.* [Fr., from *élite*, choice, select; pp. of *élire*; L. *eligere*, to pick out, choose.]
1. [*also construed as pl.*] the choice or most carefully selected part of a group, as of a society or profession.
2. a size of type for typewriters, equivalent to 10-point.
Ē·lite′ Guärd, same as *Schutzstaffel.*
ē·lix′āte, *v.t.* to extract by boiling. [Obs.]
el·ix·ā′tion, *n.* 1. the act of boiling or stewing; also, digestion. [Obs.]
2. in pharmacy, the extraction of ingredients by boiling or stewing. [Obs.]
ē·lix′ir, *n.* [OFr. *elixir*; Sp. *elixir*; Port. *elexir*, from Ar. *el iksīr*, the philosopher's stone; *el, al*, the, and *iksīr*, philosopher's stone; prob. from Gr. *xēros*, dry.]
1. in pharmacy, a tincture or medicine consisting of a sweetened alcoholic solution of a small quantity of the drug or drugs thus compounded.
2. a hypothetical substance sought for by medieval alchemists to change base metals into gold or to prolong life indefinitely: also called *philosopher's stone, elixir of life.*
3. the quintessence; the underlying principle. [Rare.]
4. a remedy for all ailments; panacea; cure-all.
Ē·liz·ȧ·bē′thăn, *a.* of or characteristic of the time when Elizabeth I was queen of England; as, *Elizabethan* architecture; the *Elizabethan* playwrights.
Ē·liz·ȧ·bē′thăn, *n.* an English contemporary of the Elizabethan era in general, especially an author or statesman.
Ē·liz·ȧ·bē′thăn son′net, a Shakespearean sonnet.
elk, *n.* [AS. *elch*; Ice. *-elgr*; M.H.G. *elch*; O.H.G. *elaho, elho*, elk.]
1. a large, mooselike deer of northern Europe and Asia, with broad antlers.
2. the wapiti, a North American deer.
3. a light, flexible leather of horsehide, calf, etc.
elk-horn fern; a fern whose fronds resemble the horns of an elk.
Irish elk; an extinct deer with very large antlers. Its remains are frequently found in the peat bogs of Ireland.

ELK
(*Cervus alces*)

elk, *n.* 1. the wild swan of Europe, *Cygnus ferus*: written also *elke.* [Brit. Dial.]
2. in botany, a species of yew from which bows were made. [Obs.]
elk bärk, the bark of the *Magnolia glauca*; also, the tree itself.
El·kē′sȧ·īte, *n.* same as *Elcesaite.*
elk′nut, *n.* the nut of the *Pyrularia oleifera*; also, the shrub bearing the nut.
elk tree, the *Oxydendrum arboreum*, of the heath family; called also *sorrel tree.*
elk′wood, *n.* the wood of the *Magnolia umbrella* of the United States.
ell, *n.* 1. the letter L.
2. something shaped like an L; specifically, (a) an extension or wing at right angles to the main structure; (b) an L-shaped joint of piping or tubing.
ell, *n.* [ME. *elle, elne*; AS. *eln*, an ell; D. *el, elle*; L. *ulna*, the forearm, elbow, an ell.] a former measure, of different lengths in different countries, used chiefly for measuring cloth. The English ell was forty-five inches. The Flemish ell was twenty-seven inches or three-quarters of a yard.
el′lȧ·chick, *n.* [Nisqualli Ind. *el-la-chick.*] a large edible fresh-water tortoise found on the Pacific coast of the United States.
el·laġ′iç, *a.* [Fr., from *galle*, gall, with the letters transposed.] related to or derived from nutgalls; bitter and astringent.
ellagic acid; a weak, insipid acid, $C_{14}H_6O_8$, obtained from gallnuts.
el′lē·bōre, *n.* hellebore. [Obs.]
el·leb′ō·rin, *n.* an acrid resinous substance found in the winter hellebore, *Helleborus hiemalis.*
el′leck, *n.* the *Trigla cuculus* or cuckoo fish. [Brit.]
El·lē′ri·ăn, *n.* [named from Elias *Eller*, the founder of the sect.] one of a German sect of Millenarians, founded in the early part of the eighteenth century: called also *Ronsdorfer.*
el·lipse′, *n.* [L. *ellipsis*; Gr. *elleipsis*, a want, defect, ellipsis, from *elleipein*, to leave in, fall short; *en*, in, and *leipein*, to leave.] in geometry, the path of a point that moves so that the sum of its distances from two fixed points (called *foci*) is constant; a closed curve produced when a cone is cut by a plane inclined obliquely to the axis and not touching the base.

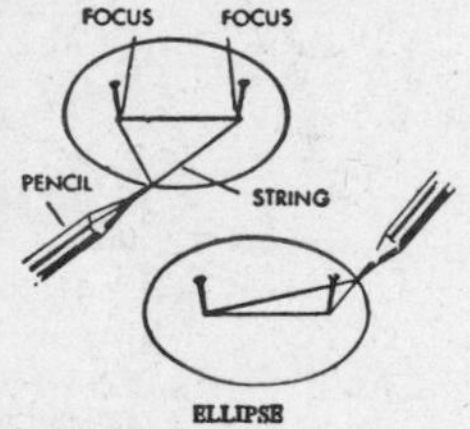

ELLIPSE

el·lip′sis, *n.*; *pl.* **el·lip′sēs,** [L. *ellipsis*; Gr. *elleipsis*, a falling short, omission; from *elleipein*; *en*, in, and *leipein*, to leave.]
1. in grammar, the omission of a word or words necessary for complete construction but understood in the context. Example: "If (it is) possible, (you) come early."
2. in writing and printing, a mark (. . . or ***) indicating an omission of words or letters.
el·lip′sō·gràph, *n.* [Gr. *elleipsis*, an ellipse, and *graphein*, to write.] an instrument to describe an ellipse by continued motion: called also *trammel.*
el·lip′soid, *n.* [Gr. *elleipsis*, an ellipse, and *eidos*, form.] in geometry, a solid figure, all plane sections of which are ellipses or circles; also, the surface of such a solid.
ellipsoid of revolution; a solid figure generated by the rotation of an ellipse about one of its axes. When the rotation is about the major axis the figure is a prolate spheroid; when about the minor axis, an oblate spheroid.
el·lip′soid, *a.* of or shaped like an ellipsoid.
el·lip·soi′dăl, *a.* pertaining to an ellipsoid; having the form of an ellipsoid.
el·lip′tiç·ăl, el·lip′tiç, *a.* [Gr. *elleiptikos*, elliptical, defective, from *elleipsis*, a falling short, defect, ellipse.]
1. pertaining to an ellipse; having the form of an ellipse; as, the planets move in *elliptical* orbits, having the sun in one focus.
2. in grammar, having a part omitted; characterized by ellipsis; as, an *elliptical* phrase.
elliptic compasses; an instrument devised for describing ellipses.
el·lip′tiç·ăl·ly, *adv.* 1. according to the form of an ellipse.
2. with the use of ellipsis; as, *elliptically* expressed.
el·lip·tic′i·ty, *n.* 1. the condition of being elliptical; an elliptical form.
2. the degree of deviation of an ellipse, el-

liptical orbit, etc. from circular form, or of a spheroid from spherical form; as, the *ellipticity* of the earth.

el·lip'tiç-lan'cē·ō·lāte, *a.* having the form of a narrow ellipse with sharp angles at the extremities of the major axis: said of a leaf.

el·lip'tō·grȧph, *n.* same as *ellipsograph*.

ell'wänd, el'wänd, *n.* a stick for measuring, having the length of an ell.

elm, *n.* [AS. *elm* or *ulm treou*; D. *olm*; G. *ulme*, elm tree; L. *ulmus*, elm tree.]

1. any tree of the genus *Ulmus*. The elms are tall, hardy shade trees, growing largely in the North Temperate Zone.

2. the hard, heavy wood of any of these trees.

winged elm; the American *Ulmus alata*, whose younger branches have bark with corky, winglike projections. The wood is fine-grained and valuable because of its resistance to splitting.

elm bee'tle, any beetle that feeds upon the leaves or bark of the elm, as the *Galeruca calmariensis* and the *Galeruca xanthomelæna*.

elm bōr'ēr, any of various beetles whose larvae damage the elm by boring under the bark and into the wood, especially the *Saperda tridentata*.

elm'en, *a.* of or belonging to elms. [Obs.]

elm mọth, any moth the larvae of which feed upon the foliage of elm trees, notably the geometer or span worm, *Eugonia subsignaria*.

El'mō's fīre, same as *St. Elmo's fire*.

elm sạw'flȳ, the *Cimbex americana*, a large sawfly whose larvae feed upon the foliage of the elm.

elm'y, *a.* abounding in elms.

el·ō·çā'tion, *n.* [L. *elocare*; *e-*, out, and *locare*, to place, hire out.]

1. a removal from the usual place of residence. [Obs.]

2. departure from the usual mood; an ecstasy. [Obs.]

ē·loç'ū·lãr, *a.* unicellular; not divided into separate cells.

el·ō·çū'tion, *n.* [L. *elocutio* (*-onis*), from *eloqui*, to speak out, utter.]

1. the art of public speaking or declaiming: often associated with a studied or artificial style of speaking.

2. the manner or method of public reading or speaking; as, his *elocution* was poor.

3. the act of speaking; utterance. [Rare.]

4. eloquence. [Obs.]

el·ō·çū'tion·ȧ·ry, *a.* 1. pertaining to elocution, or containing it.

2. artificial or declamatory.

el·ō·çū'tion·ist, *n.* one who is skilled in elocution; also, one who teaches elocution.

é·loge' (ā-lōzh'), *n.* [Fr., from L. *elogium*, a short observation, an inscription on a tombstone, from Gr. *logos*, discourse.] a panegyric on the dead; a eulogy: usually applied to the oration upon the death of a member of the Academy in France.

el'ō·ġist, *n.* a eulogist. [Obs.]

el'ō·ġy, ē·lō'ġi·um, *n.* praise bestowed on a person or thing; panegyric; an éloge.

El'ō·him, *n.pl.* [Heb. *elōhīm*, pl. of *eloah*, God.] God: Hebrew name used in parts of the Old Testament.

El'ō·hist, *n.* the author of those parts of the Hexateuch in which *Elohim* is used instead of *Yahweh* as the name for God.

El·ō·his'tiç, *a.* 1. of or written by the Elohist.

2. designating those parts of the Old Testament in which *Elohim* is used instead of *Yahweh* as the name for God.

ē·loign', ē·loin', *v.t.* [OFr. *eloigner*; LL. *elongare*, to remove, keep aloof; *e-*, out, and *longus*, long.]

1. to carry away (property).

2. in law, to remove (private property) beyond the jurisdiction of a sheriff, etc.

ē·loign'āte, ē·loin'āte, *v.t.* to eloign. [Obs.]

ē·loign'ment, ē·loin'ment, *n.* removal to a distance; also, distance.[Obs.]

ē·lọng', *v.t.* to put far off; to retard. [Obs.]

ē·lọn'gāte, *v.t.*; elongated, *pt. pp.*; elongating, *ppr.* [LL. *elongatus*, pp. of *elongare*, to remove, keep aloof, protract; *e-*, out, and *longus*, long.]

1. to lengthen; to extend.

2. to remove farther off. [Obs.]

ē·lọn'gāte, *v.i.* to recede; particularly, to recede apparently from the sun, as a planet in its orbit.

ē·lọn'gāte, *a.* 1. lengthened; extended.

2. in botany, long and narrow, as certain leaves.

ē·lọn·gā'tion, *n.* 1. the act of stretching or lengthening; the state of being extended; as, the *elongation* of a wire by stretching.

2. something elongated; extension; continuation.

3. in astronomy, the distance of a planet from the sun, measured in degrees; as, the *elongation* of Venus or Mercury.

4. departure; removal; recession. [Obs.]

ē·lōpe', *v.i.*; eloped (-lōpt'), *pt., pp.*; eloping, *ppr.* [from D. *ontloopen*, to run away; *ont-*, away, and *loopen*, to run.]

1. to run away secretly; especially, to leave one's home to marry a lover.

2. to run away; to escape; to abscond.

ē·lōpe'ment, *n.* the act of eloping.

ē·lōp'ēr, *n.* a person who elopes.

E'lops, *n.* [Gr. *elops*, *ellops*, a kind of sea fish, a serpent.] a genus of fishes inhabiting the seas of America and the West Indies.

el'ō·quence (-kwens), *n.* [Fr. *éloquence*, from L. *eloquentia*, from *eloqui*, to speak out.]

1. speech or writing that is vivid, forceful, fluent, graceful, and persuasive.

2. (a) the art or manner of such speech or writing; (b) the power to persuade with speech or writing.

el'ō·quent, *a.* 1. having, or characteristic of, eloquence; fluent, forceful, and persuasive.

2. expressing or manifesting vividly or impressively; as, an *eloquent* pause; an *eloquent* glance.

el'ō·quent·ly, *adv.* with eloquence; in an eloquent manner.

el'rich, *a.* same as *eldritch*.

else, *a.* or *pron.* [AS. *elles*, otherwise, in another manner, besides; originally, a genit. sing. from an adj. signifying "other," as in *ele land*, another land.]

1. other; different; as, do you expect anything *else?*

2. in addition; more; as, is there anything *else?*

Else follows the word modified.

else, *adv.* 1. otherwise; in the other case; if the fact were different; as, thou desirest not sacrifice, *else* would I give it.

2. if not; as, study, (or) *else* you will fail.

el'sen, el'sin, *n.* an awl, especially one used by a shoemaker. [Brit. Dial.]

else'where (-hwãr), *adv.* in any other place; somewhere else; as, these trees are not to be found *elsewhere*.

else'whith''ēr (-hwith''ēr), *adv.* to another or any other place; in another direction; as, he was compelled to go *elsewhither* for it.

else'wīse, *adv.* in some other way.

ē·lū'ci·dāte, *v.t.*; elucidated, *pt., pp.*; elucidating, *ppr.* [LL. *elucidatus*, pp. of *elucidare*, to make light or clear; L. *e-*, out, and *lucidus*, light, clear, from *lux*, light.] to make clear or manifest; to explain; to remove obscurity from and render intelligible; to illustrate; as, an example will *elucidate* the subject.

ē·lū·ci·dā'tion, *n.* the act of elucidating; explanation; exposition; illustration.

ē·lū'ci·dā·tive, *a.* making clear; fitted for elucidation.

ē·lū'ci·dā·tŏr, *n.* one who elucidates.

ē·lū'ci·dȧ·tō·ry, *a.* serving to elucidate.

ē·luç'tāte, *v.i.* [L. *eluctatus*, pp. of *eluctari*, to struggle out.] to escape by struggling; to struggle forth. [Obs.]

ē·luç·tā'tion, *n.* the act of bursting forth; escape from any difficulty. [Obs.]

ē·lū'çū·brāte, *v.i.* to lucubrate. [Obs.]

ē·lū·çū·brā'tion, *n.* lucubration. [Obs.]

ē·lūde', *v.t.*; eluded, *pt., pp.*; eluding, *ppr.* [L. *eludere*, to finish play, parry a blow, frustrate, deceive; *e-*, out, and *ludere*, to play.]

1. to escape; to evade; to avoid by artifice, stratagem, wiles, deceit, or dexterity; as, to *elude* an enemy; to *elude* the sight; to *elude* detection.

Me gentle Delia beckons from the plain,
Then, hid in shades, *eludes* her eager swain.
—Pope.

2. to escape detection by; evade; baffle; as, the point that you're trying to make *eludes* me.

Syn.—escape, avoid, baffle, shun, evade, parry, fence, mock, frustrate.

ē·lūd'i·ble, *a.* capable of being eluded.

E·lul', *n.* [Heb., from *alal*, to reap, harvest.] the twelfth month of the Jewish year.

ē·lum'bā·ted, *a.* [L. *elumbis*, weakened in the loins; *e-*, out, and *lumbus*, loin.] weakened in the loins. [Rare.]

ē·lus·çā'tion, *n.* [LL. *eluscare*, to make one-eyed; L. *e-*, out, and *luscus*, one-eyed.] defective eyesight; purblindness. [Obs.]

ē·lū'sion, *n.* [L. *elusio*, from *eludere*, to parry a blow, deceive.] an escape by artifice or deception; evasion; the act of eluding.

ē·lū'sive, *a.* 1. practicing elusion; tending to elude.

Elusive of the bridal day, she gives
Fond hopes to all, and all with hopes deceives.
—Pope.

2. hard to grasp or retain mentally; baffling.

ē·lū'sive·ly, *adv.* in an elusive manner.

ē·lū'sive·ness, *n.* the state of being elusive.

ē·lū'sō·ri·ness, *n.* the state of being elusory.

ē·lū'sō·ry, *a.* elusive: said especially of mental impressions.

ē·lūte', *v.t.* [L. *elutus*, pp. of *eluere*, to wash off; *e-*, out, off, and *luere*, to wash.] to cleanse. [Rare.]

ē·lū'tion, *n.* the removal of soluble matter by washing with water, as in refining sugar by washing the calcium sucrate.

ē·lū'tri·āte, *v.t.*; elutriated, *pt., pp.*; elutriating, *ppr.* [L. *elutriatus*, pp. of *elutriare*, to wash out, rack off, from *eluere*, to wash out.]

1. to purify by washing and straining; to decant.

2. to separate the lighter particles from the heavier particles of by washing.

ē·lū·tri·ā'tion, *n.* the act of elutriating.

ē·lux'āte, *v.t.*; eluxated, *pt., pp.*; eluxating, *ppr.* [L. *e-*, out, and *luxatus*, pp. of *luxare*, to dislocate.] to disjoint; to dislocate. [Rare.]

ē·lux·ā'tion, *n.* the dislocation of a bone; luxation. [Rare.]

el'văn, *n.* [Corn.] in mineralogy, a dikelike formation found in Cornwall, England, generally among the granites and running parallel with the tin lodes.

el'văn, *a.* elfin.

el'văn·īte, *n.* same as *elvan*.

el·văn·it'iç, *a.* of or pertaining to elvan.

elve, *n.* an elf. [Obs.]

el'vēr, *n.* a young eel; a young conger or sea eel.

elveṣ, *n.*, pl. of *elf*.

elv'ish, *a.* same as *elfish*.

elv'ish·ly, *adv.* elfishly.

el'wänd, *n.* same as *ellwand*.

el·y·dor'iç, *a.* [Gr. *elaion*, olive oil, oil, and *hydōr*, water.] painted with oil and water colors; as, *elydoric* painting.

Ē·ly'ṣiăn, *a.* in or pertaining to Elysium; hence, yielding the highest pleasures; delightful; happy; blissful; as, *Elysian* fields.

Ē·ly'ṣiăn fieldṣ, Elysium.

Ē·ly'ṣium, *n.* [L. *Elysium*; Gr. *Ēlysion* (*pedion*), Elysian plain, the plain of the departed, from *elysis*, a variant of *eleusis*, from *eleusesthai*, fut. of *elthein*, to go or come.]

1. in Greek mythology, a place assigned to virtuous people after death; the Elysian fields.

2. any place or condition of ideal bliss or complete happiness; paradise.

el'y·tr-, el'y·trō-, [from Gr. *elytron*, a cover, covering, case, sheath.] a combining form meaning *of* or *connected with the vagina*.

el'y·trȧ, *n.*, pl. of *elytron* and *elytrum*.

el'y·trăl, *a.* pertaining to an elytron.

e·lyt'ri·fọrm, *a.* [from *elytron*, and L. *forma*, form.] having the form of an elytron or wing sheath.

el'y·trin, *n.* [*elytrum* and *-ine*.] the white compound forming the base of the hard integuments of crustaceans and certain insects; chitin.

el'y·trō·cēle, *n.* [*elytr-*, and Gr. *kēlē*, a tumor.] same as *colpocele*.

el'y·troid, *a.* [*elytr-*, and Gr. *eidos*, form.] similar to a sheath; elytriform.

el'y·tron, *n.*; *pl.* **el'y·trȧ,** [Mod. L.; Gr. *elytron*, a covering, sheath, from *elyein*, to roll round, to wrap up.] either of the front pair of modified wings in certain insects, which act as protective covering for the rear wings; wing cover.

el'y·trō·plas·ty, *n.* [*elytro-*, and Gr. *plassein*, to form.] vaginal surgery.

el''y·trop·tō'sis, *n.* [*elytro-*, and Gr. *ptōsis*, a fall.] prolapse of the vagina.

el·y·tror'rhȧ·phy, *n.* [*elytro-*, and Gr. *hraphē*, a seam, suture, from *hraptein*, to sew.] same as *colporrhaphy*.

el·y·trot'ō·my, *n.* [*elytro-*, and Gr. *tomē*, a cutting.] a cutting into or through the walls of the vagina.

el'y·trum, *n.*; *pl.* **el'y·trȧ,** same as *elytron*.

El'ze·vīr, *a.* 1. relating to books printed and published by the Elzevir family of Leyden and Amsterdam, who were celebrated for their fine work, from 1583 to 1680.

2. designating the Elzevir type face.

El'ze·vīr, *n.* a small type face, with fine uprights and diagonals and heavy tops and bottoms, introduced by the Elzevirs.

em, *n.* [AS. *em*; L. *em*, the name of the letter *M*.]

1. the thirteenth letter in the alphabet; M or m.

2. in printing, formerly the letter M of any given font, now a square of any size of type, used as a unit of measure, as of column width; especially, an em pica, equal to about $^1/_6$ of an inch.

'em, *pron.* [a contraction of ME. *hem*, them.] them; as, we have seen *'em*. [Colloq.]

em-, a prefix often used for *en-* before bilabial consonants (*p, b, m*).

ē·mac'ẽr·āte, *v.t.* [L. *emaceratus*; *e-*, out, and *macerare*, to make soft, weaken.] to make lean. [Obs.]

ē·mac·ẽr·ā'tion, *n.* a making lean; emaciation. [Obs.]

ē·mā'ci·āte (-shi-āt), *v.i.*; emaciated, *pt.*, *pp.*; emaciating, *ppr.* [L. *emaciatus*, pp. of *emaciare*, to make lean, cause to waste away; *e-*, out, and *macere*, to be lean; *macies*, leanness.] to lose flesh gradually; to waste away.

ē·mā'ci·āte, *v.t.* to cause to lose flesh or weight; to cause to become abnormally lean; as, sorrow, anxiety, and disease ofen *emaciate* the most robust bodies.

ē·mā'ci·āte, *a.* emaciated.

ē·mā'ci·āt·ed, *a.* abnormally lean; wasted away, as from starvation or disease.

ē·mā·ci·ā'tion, *n.* 1. an emaciating; wasting away.

2. abnormal leanness, caused by starvation, disease, etc.

ē·maç'ū·lāte, *v.t.* to remove spots from; to make clean or pure. [Obs.]

ē·maç·ū·lā'tion, *n.* [L. *emaculare*, from *e-*, out, and *macula*, a spot.] the act or operation of freeing from spots and making clean or pure. [Obs.]

em·ȧ·jä'guȧ (-gwȧ), *n.* [Sp. Am.] a tropical shrub of both hemispheres, growing abundantly in moist places. It is remarkable for the strength of its fiber, which is used for making ropes and paper. Also written *majagua*.

em'ȧ·nănt, *a.* [L. *emanans* (*-antis*), ppr. of *emanare*, to flow out, arise; *e-*, out, and *manare*, to flow.] issuing from something else; flowing forth.

em'ȧ·nāte, *v.i.*; emanated, *pt.*, *pp.*; emanating, *ppr.* [L. *emanatus*, pp. of *emanare*, to flow out, arise; *e-*, out, and *manare*, to flow.] to issue from a source; to flow forth; as, light *emanates* from the sun.

em'ȧ·nāte, *v.t.* to send forth; to emit. [Rare.]

em·ȧ·nā'tion, *n.* 1. the act of emanating; a coming forth.

2. that which issues, flows, or proceeds from any source; a thing emitted; as, light is an *emanation* from the sun.

3. the theory that all things have their being, not from the conscious direct action or will of God, but as issuing from the divine essence.

4. in chemistry, a gas given off by some radioactive substance.

em·ȧ·nā'tion·iṣm, *n.* belief in the theory of emanation.

em'ȧ·nā·tist, *n.* a believer in the theory of emanation.

em'ȧ·nā·tive, *a.* emanating or tending to emanate; having to do with emanation.

em'ȧ·nā·tive·ly, *adv.* in the manner of an emanation; by means of an emanation.

em'ȧ·nā·tō·ry, *a.* of the nature of an emanation; emanative.

ē·man'ci·pāte, *v.t.*; emancipated, *pt.*, *pp.*; emancipating, *ppr.* [L. *emancipatus*, pp. of *emancipare*, *emancupare*, to emancipate; *e-*, out, and *mancipare*, to deliver up or make over as property, by means of a formal act called *mancipium*, from *manceps*, a purchaser, contractor; *manus*, hand, and *capere*, to take.]

1. to set free from servitude or slavery; to liberate; to restore from bondage to freedom; as, to *emancipate* a slave.

2. to free from restraint of any kind; to liberate from subjection, controlling power, or influence; as, to *emancipate* one from prejudices or error.

3. in ancient Rome, to set free, as a son from the control of his father, giving him the privilege of managing his affairs as if he were of age.

ē·man'ci·pāte, *a.* emancipated.

ē·man·ci·pā'tion, *n.* the act of setting free from slavery, servitude, or restraint; deliverance from bondage or controlling influence; liberation; as, the *emancipation* of slaves by their proprietors.

Emancipation Proclamation; the proclamation issued by President Lincoln in September, 1862, effective January 1, 1863, by which the Negroes held in slavery in the Confederate States, then in rebellion against the United States, were declared to be thenceforward free. The proclamation was subsequently confirmed by the thirteenth amendment to the Constitution, which finally emancipated all Negroes held as slaves throughout the United States.

Syn.—manumission, deliverance, liberation, freedom, release, enfranchisement.

ē·man·ci·pā'tion·ist, *n.* an advocate of the emancipation of slaves.

ē·man'ci·pā·tŏr, *n.* [LL. *emancipator*, from L. *emancipare*, to emancipate.] one who emancipates.

ē·man'ci·pȧ·tō·ry, *a.* relating to emancipation; having the effect of emancipating.

ē·man'ci·pist, *n.* in Australia, a convict who has been set free.

ē·mär'ġi·nāte, *v.t.*; emarginated, *pt.*, *pp.*; emarginating, *ppr.* [L. *emarginatus*, pp. of *emarginare*, to deprive of the edge; *e-*, out, and *margo* (*-inis*), edge, margin.] to take away the margin of.

ē·mär'ġi·nāte, ē·mär'ġi·nā·ted, *a.* 1. having a notched margin or tip: said of a leaf or a wing.

2. in mineralogy, having all the edges of the primitive form truncated.

ē·mär'ġi·nāte·ly, *adv.* in the form of notches or interrupted margins.

ē·mär·ġi·nā'tion, *n.* the state of being emarginate or notched.

ē·mas'çū·lāte, *v.t.*; emasculated, *pt.*, *pp.*; emasculating, *ppr.* [L. *emasculatus*, pp. of *emasculare*; *e-*, out, and *masculus*, male.]

1. to castrate; to remove the testicles of.

2. to deprive of masculine strength or vigor; to weaken; to make effeminate.

Women *emasculate* a monarch's reign.
—Dryden.

3. to take away the stamens of, as a flower.

ē·mas'çū·lāte, *a.* deprived of vigor or virility.

ē·mas·çū·lā'tion, *n.* 1. the act of depriving of testicles; castration.

2. the act of depriving of vigor or strength; unmanly weakness.

ē·mas'çū·lā·tŏr, *n.* a person or thing that emasculates.

ē·mas'çū·lȧ·tō·ry, *a.* emasculating; depriving of vigor.

em·bāce', *v.t.* to embase. [Obs.]

em·bāle', *v.t.* to make up into a bundle, bale, or package; to pack.

em·bạll', *v.t.* to encircle or embrace. [Obs.]

em·bälm' (-bäm'), *v.t.*; embalmed, *pt.*, *pp.*; embalming, *ppr.* [OFr. *embaumer*, *embausmer*; LL. *imbalsamare*, from L. *in*, in, and *balsamum*, balsam, balm.]

1. to keep (a dead body) from decaying by treating it with various chemicals, usually after removing the viscera, etc.

2. to preserve in memory.

3. to perfume; make fragrant.

em·bälm'ẽr, *n.* one who embalms.

em·bälm'ment, *n.* act of embalming or state of being embalmed.

em·bank', *v.t.*; embanked (-bankt'), *pt.*, *pp.*; embanking, *ppr.* to protect, support, or enclose with a bank of earth, rubble, etc.; to defend by banks, mounds, or dikes.

em·bank'ment, *n.* 1. the act or process of embanking.

2. a bank (of earth, rubble, etc.) used to keep back water, hold up a roadway, etc.

em·bär', *v.t.*; embarred, *pt.*, *pp.*; embarring, *ppr.* [OFr. *embarrer*, *enbarrer*, to bar, bar in.]

1. to bar in; to confine; to imprison.

Where fast *embarred* in mighty brazen wall.
—Spenser.

2. to stop; to hinder; to block up.

He *embarred* all further trade. —Bacon.

em·bär·çā'tion, *n.* same as *embarkation*.

em·bärġe', *v.t.* to place on a barge. [Obs.]

em·bär'gō, *n.*; *pl.* **em·bär'gōeṣ,** [Sp. *embargo*, from *embargar*, to arrest, seize, from L. *in*, in, on, and *barra*, a bar.]

1. a government order prohibiting the entry or departure of commercial ships at its ports, especially as a war measure.

2. any restriction imposed on commerce by law; especially, a prohibition of trade in a particular commodity.

3. restriction; restraint; prohibition.

civil embargo; an embargo laid on the ships of citizens by their own government.

hostile embargo; an embargo laid on the ships of an enemy.

em·bär'gō, *v.t.*; embargoed, *pt.*, *pp.*; embargoing, *ppr.* to put an embargo upon.

em·bärk', *v.t.*; embarked (-bärkt'), *pt.*, *pp.*; embarking, *ppr.* [Fr. *embarquer*; Sp. *embarcar*; L. *in*, in, and LL. *barca*, a bark.]

1. to put on board a ship; as, the general *embarked* his troops.

2. to take on board: said of a ship.

3. to engage (a person) or invest (money, etc.) in an enterprise; as, this projector *embarked* his friends in the expedition.

em·bärk', *v.i.* 1. to go on board a ship; as, the troops *embarked* for Lisbon.

2. to begin a journey.

3. to engage in any business; to undertake; to invest; as, the young man *embarked* rashly in speculation and was ruined.

em·bär·kā'tion, *n.* 1. the act of embarking.

2. that which is embarked; as, an *embarkation* of Jesuits.

em·bärk'ment, *n.* [OFr. *embarquement*, from *embarquer*, to embark.] the act of embarking.

em·bar'răss, *v.t.*; embarrassed (-răst), *pt.*, *pp.*; embarrassing, *ppr.* [Fr. *embarrasser*, to encumber, obstruct; It. *imbarazzare*, to embarrass; *em-*, L. *in*, in, and Pr. *barras*, a bar.]

1. to cause to feel self-conscious, confused, and ill at ease; disconcert; fluster.

2. to hinder; impede; cause difficulties to.

3. to cause to be in debt; cause financial difficulties to.

4. to complicate; make more difficult.

Syn.—puzzle, perplex, disconcert, hamper.

em·bar'răss, *n.* 1. an obstruction to navigation in a stream, caused by the lodging of driftwood, trunks of trees, etc. [Dial.]

2. embarrassment. [Obs.]

em·bar'răss·ing, *a.* that embarrasses.

em·bar'răss·ment, *n.* 1. an embarrassing or being embarrassed.

2. a thing that embarrasses.

em·bāse', *v.t.* to lower in value; to degrade; to debase. [Obs.]

em·bāse'ment, *n.* act of degrading; debasement. [Obs.]

em'băs·sāde, *n.* an embassy. [Obs.]

em·bas'sȧ·dŏr, *n.* same as *ambassador*.

em·bas·sȧ·dō'ri·ăl, *a.* same as *ambassadorial*.

em·bas'sȧ·dress, *n.* same as *ambassadress*.

em'băs·sāġe, *n.* embassy. [Archaic.]

em'băs·sy, *n.*; *pl.* **em'băs·sieṣ,** [OFr. *embascée*, *ambassée*; LL. *ambasciata*, from *ambasciare*, *ambactiare*, to go on a mission, from L. *ambactus*, a dependent, vassal.]

1. the position, functions, or business of an ambassador.

2. the sending of ambassadors.

3. the official residence or offices of an ambassador in a foreign country: also called *legation*.

4. an ambassador and his staff.

5. a person or group sent on an official mission to a foreign government.

6. any important or official mission, errand, or message.

em·bas'tărd·īze, *v.t.* to render illegitimate. [Obs.]

em·bāthe', *v.t.* to bathe.

em·bat'tle, *v.t.* embattled, *pt.*, *pp.*; embattling, *ppr.* [ME. *embatailen*, from *en-*, in, and *batelment*, battlement.] to provide with battlements; to build battlements on.

em·bat'tle, *v.t.* [ME. *embatailen*, *embatelen*; OFr. *embataillier*, to array for battle; *en-*, L. *in*, in, and *bataille*, battle.]

1. to prepare, array, or set in line for battle. [Rare, except in pp.]

2. to fortify.

em·bat'tle, *v.i.* to be ranged in order of battle. [Obs.]

em·bat'tled (-tld), *a.* 1. arrayed in order of battle.

2. furnished with battlements; in heraldry, having the outline resembling a battlement, as an ordinary.

3. having been the place of battle; as, an *embattled* plain or field.

A FESSE EMBATTLED

embattled molding; in architecture, a molding having indentations like those of a battlement.

em·bat'tle·ment, *n.* same as *battlement*.

em·bāy', *v.t.* embayed; *pt.*, *pp.*; embaying, *ppr.* 1. to put or force (a boat, etc.) into a bay for protection or shelter.

EMBATTLED MOLDING

2. to shut in; enclose or surround, as in a bay.

3. to form (a shore) into bays.

em·bāy′ment, *n.* 1. a forming into a bay.
2. a bay or a formation resembling a bay.

em·bēam′, *v.t.* to cause to beam. [Rare.]

em·bed′, im·bed′, *v.t.*; embedded, *pt.*, *pp.*; embedding, *ppr.* 1. to set (flowers, etc.) in earth.
2. to set or fix firmly in a surrounding mass; as, the knife was *embedded* in the wood.
3. to fix in the mind, memory, etc.

em·bed′ment, *n.* the act of embedding or the state of being embedded.

em·bel′lish, *v.t.*; embellished (-lisht), *pt.*, *pp.*; embellishing, *ppr.* [ME. *embelisshen, embelisen*, from OFr. *embellir*; It. *imbellire*; L. *in*, in, and *bellus*, beautiful, fair.]
1. to improve the appearance of; to adorn; to beautify; to decorate; to make beautiful or elegant by ornaments; as, to *embellish* a garden with shrubs and flowers.
2. to improve (a story, etc.) by adding details, often of a fictitious kind; to touch up.
Syn.—beautify, adorn, ornament, illustrate, decorate.

em·bel′lish·ẽr, *n.* one who embellishes.

em·bel′lish·ment, *n.* 1. an embellishing or being embellished; ornamentation.
2. something that embellishes; specifically, (a) an ornament; decoration; (b) a detail or touch, often fictitious, added to improve a story, etc.

em′bẽr, *n.* [ME. *eymbre, eymery*, pl. *emmeres, emeres*; AS. *æmergean*, pl. *æmyrian*; Ice. *eimyrja*, an ember.]
1. a glowing piece of coal, wood, peat, etc. from a fire; especially, such a piece smoldering among ashes.
2. [*pl.*] the smoldering remains of a fire; ashes with glowing pieces of coal, etc. still among them.

em′bẽr, *a.* [ME. *ymber*; AS. *ymbren, ymbryne*, a running around, a circuit; *ymbe*, around, and *ryne*, from *rinnan*, to run.] designating or of three days (called *Ember days*) set aside for prayer and fasting in a specified week of each of the four seasons of the year: observed in the Roman Catholic, Anglican, and certain other churches.

em′bẽr·gọọse, *n.*; *pl.* **em′bẽr·geese,** a web-footed bird of the genus *Urinator*; the great northern diver, *Urinator imber*; the loon.

em′bẽr·ing, *n.* an Ember day. [Obs.]

Em′bẽr week, any of the four weeks in which Ember days occur, viz., the first week after the first Sunday in Lent, the first after Whitsuntide, the first after September 14th, and the first after December 13th.

em·bez′zle, *v.t.*; embezzled, *pt.*, *pp.*; embezzling, *ppr.* [Anglo-Fr. *embesiler*; OFr. *embesillier*, from *en-*, and *besillier*, to destroy.]
1. to appropriate fraudulently to one's own use (what is entrusted to one's care and management); as, it is not uncommon for men entrusted with public money to *embezzle* it.
2. to waste; to dissipate in extravagance. [Obs.]

When thou hast *embezzled* all thy store.
—Dryden.

Syn.—appropriate, peculate, misappropriate, misuse, purloin.

em·bez′zle·ment, *n.* an embezzling; theft or the act of fraudulently appropriating money or goods entrusted to one's care and management; as, the *embezzlements* of public money.

em·bez′zlẽr, *n.* one who embezzles.

em·bil′lōw, *v.i.* to swell and rise like billows on the sea. [Rare.]

em·bi·ot′ō·çoid, *n.* [Gr. *embios*, in life, living, and *tiktein*, to bring forth, and *eidos*, form.] one of a large family of viviparous fishes found on the Californian coast, called surf fishes.

em·bit′tẽr, *v.t.*; embittered, *pt.*, *pp.*; embittering, *ppr.* 1. to make bitter; to make resentful or morose.
2. to make more bitter; to exacerbate; to aggravate.

em·bit′tẽr·ment, *n.* an embittering or being embittered.

em·blȧnch′, *v.t.* to make white. [Obs.]

em·blāze′, *v.t.*; emblazed, *pt.*, *pp.*; emblazing, *ppr.* [*em-*, and *blaze* (a flame).]
1. to light up; to illuminate.
2. to set on fire; to kindle.

em·blāze′, *v.t.* [*em-*, and *blaze* (to proclaim).] to emblazon.

em·blā′zŏn, *v.t.*; emblazoned, *pt.*, *pp.*; emblazoning, *ppr.* 1. to adorn (*with* figures of heraldry or ensigns armorial).
2. to deck in glaring colors; to display brilliantly; to make resplendent.
3. to celebrate; to spread the fame of; to praise; to extol.

We find Augustus *emblazoned* by the poets.
—Hakewill.

em·blā′zŏn·ẽr, *n.* one who emblazons.

em·blā′zŏn·ing, *n.* the act or art of adorning with ensigns armorial.

em·blā′zŏn·ment, *n.* 1. an emblazoning or being emblazoned.
2. a thing emblazoned.

em·blā′zŏn·ry, *n.*; *pl.* **em·blā′zŏn·rieṣ,** 1. heraldic decoration; emblazoning.
2. any brilliant decoration or display.

em′blem, *n.* [L. *emblema* (*-atis*), raised ornaments on vessels; Gr. *emblēma*, an insertion, from *emballein*; *en*, in, and *ballein*, to throw, put.]
1. inlay; inlaid or mosaic work. [Obs.]
2. formerly, a picture with a motto or verses, allegorically suggesting some moral truth.
3. a visible symbol of a thing, idea, class of people, etc.; object or representation that stands for or suggests something else; as, the cross is an *emblem* of Christianity.
4. a sign, badge, or device.
Syn.—symbol, type, token, sign, semblance, similitude.

em′blem, *v.t.* to emblematize. [Rare.]

em·blem·at′iç, em·blem·at′iç·ăl, *a.* pertaining to, containing, or serving as an emblem; symbolic; as, a crown is *emblematic* of royalty.

em·blem·at′iç·ăl·ly, *adv.* by way or means of emblems; in the manner of emblems; by way of allusive representation.

em·blem·at′i·cīze, *v.t.* to transform into an emblem [Rare.]

em·blem′ȧ·tist, *n.* a person who makes or designs emblems.

em·blem′ȧ·tīze, *v.t.*; emblematized, *pt.*, *pp.*; emblematizing, *ppr.* 1. to be an emblem of; to symbolize.
2. to represent by or as by an emblem.

em′blē·ments, *n.pl.* [OFr. *emblaement, emblaiement*, crop, harvest, from *emblaer, emblaier*, from LL. *imbladare*, to sow with grain; L. *in*, in, and *bladum*, grain.] in law, (a) growing crops; (b) the profits from such crops.

em′blem·īze, *v.t.*; emblemized, *pt.*, *pp.*; emblemizing, *ppr.* to emblematize. [Rare.]

em′bliç, *n.* [name in the Moluccas.] the fruit of an East Indian tree, *Phyllanthus emblica*, used, when dried, for dyeing and tanning, under the name *myrobalan*.

em·blọọm′, *v.t.*; embloomed, *pt.*, *pp.*; emblooming, *ppr.* to cover or enrich with bloom. [Obs.]

em·blos′sŏm, *v.t.* to cover or enrich with blossoms.

em·bod′i·ẽr, *n.* one who or that which embodies.

em·bod′i·ment, *n.* 1. an embodying or being embodied.
2. that in which some idea, quality, etc. is embodied; concrete expression or incarnation of some idea, quality, etc.; as, she is the *embodiment* of virtue.
3. anything embodied.

em·bod′y, *v.t.*; embodied, *pt.*, *pp.*; embodying, *ppr.* 1. to give bodily form to; to incarnate; to make corporeal; to invest with matter; as, to *embody* the soul or spirit; a form *embodied*.
2. to give definite, tangible, or visible form to; to make concrete; as, his speech *embodied* democratic ideals.
3. to collect and include (material) in a book, system, statute, etc.
4. to make (something) part of an organized whole; incorporate; as, our ideas are *embodied* in the committee's report.
Syn.—methodize, systematize, codify, incorporate, aggregate, integrate, compact, introduce, enlist, combine, comprehend.

em·bod′y, *v.i.* to unite in a body, mass, or collection; to coalesce. [Rare.]

em·bōgue′ (-bōg′), *v.i.* [Sp. *embocar*, to enter by the mouth; It. *imboccare*, to feed, instruct; L. *in*, in, and *bucca*, the cheek.] to disembogue. [Obs.]

em·bō′guing (-bō′ging), *n.* the place where a river empties into the sea. [Obs.]

em·boil′, *v.i.* to swell with rage. [Obs.]

em·boil′, *v.t.* to cause to swell with rage; to excite uncontrollable rage in. [Obs.]

em·boîte′ment (oṅ-bwot′moṅ), *n.* [Fr., a jointing, fitting in, from *emboiter*, to joint, fit in; OFr. *emboister*, to enclose, fasten up; *en*, in, and *boist*, a box.] in biology, the former doctrine that generation proceeds from an original single germ which contains the germs of all future existences encased one within another.

em·bōld′en, *v.t.*; emboldened, *pt.*, *pp.*; emboldening, *ppr.* to give boldness or courage to; to encourage.

em·bōld′en·ẽr, *n.* one who emboldens.

em·bō·leç′tō·my, *n.* the removal of an embolus by surgery.

em·bol′iç, *a.* 1. of or caused by embolism or an embolus.
2. in embryology, pushing or growing inward, as an invagination.

em′bō·liṣm, *n.* 1. intercalation; the insertion of a day or other period of time into a calendar, as in leap year.
2. the time intercalated.
3. in medicine, (a) the obstruction in a blood vessel caused by the presence of an embolus too large to pass through it; (b) loosely, an embolus.

em·bō·liṣ′măl, *a.* same as *embolismic*. [Obs.]

em·bō·liṣ′miç, em·bō·liṣ′miç·ăl, *a.* related to embolism; affected by embolism; as, the *embolismic* year.

em′bō·līte, *n.* [Gr. *embolē*, from *emballein*, to throw in, insert, and *-ite*.] a grayish-green mineral containing both chloride and bromide of silver.

em·bō′li·um, *n.* [Gr. *embolion*, something thrown in.] a part of the margin of the anterior wing in certain *Hemiptera*.

em′bō·lus, *n.*; *pl.* **em′bō·lī,** [L., from Gr. *embolos*, anything put in, a wedge, from *emballein*; *en*, in, and *ballein*, to throw, cast.]
1. something inserted or acting in another; that which thrusts or drives, as a piston.
2. in medicine, any foreign matter, as a blood clot or air bubble, carried in the blood stream.

em′bō·ly, *n.* [Gr. *embolē*, an insertion.] in embryology, development in a segmentation sphere by the movement of one of its sides inward to form a gastrula.

em·bon·point′ (oṅ-bọṅ-pwaṅ′), *n.* [Fr.] plumpness of body or person; stoutness; corpulence.

em·bọr′dẽr, *v.t.* to adorn with a border.

em·bọṣ′ŏm (-bụz′), *v.t.*; embosomed, *pt.*, *pp.*; embosoming, *ppr.* 1. to take to one's bosom; embrace; cherish.
2. to enclose protectively; surround; shelter.

em·boss′, *v.t.*; embossed (-bost′), *pt.*, *pp.*; embossing, *ppr.* [OFr. *embosser*, to swell up, rise in bunches; *en*, in, on, and *bosse*, a bunch, protuberance.]
1. to decorate or cover with designs, patterns, etc. raised above the surface.
2. to carve, raise, or print (a design, etc.) so that it is raised above the surface; to raise in relief.
3. to embellish; to ornament.

em·boss′, *v.t.* [Fr. *emboîter*, for *emboister*, from *boîte, boiste*, a box.] to enclose, as in a box; to include; to cover. [Obs.]

em·boss′, *v.t.* [It. *imboscare*, from *bosco*, a wood.]
1. to enclose in a wood; to conceal in a thicket. [Obs.]
2. to drive (an animal) hard in hunting. [Obs.]

em·bossed′ (-bost′), *a.* 1. formed or covered with bosses or raised figures.
2. carved or raised in relief.
3. enlarged by swelling; puffed out. [Obs.]

em·boss′ẽr, *n.* 1. one who embosses.
2. an instrument, die, or press for embossing.

em·boss′ing, *n.* the formation of ornamental figures in relief; also, the figures thus formed.

em·boss′ment, *n.* 1. an embossing or being embossed.
2. something embossed; figure or design carved or molded in relief.
3. a bulge.

em·bot′tle, *v.t.*; embottled, *pt.*, *pp.*; embottling, *ppr.* to put into a bottle; to bottle; to include or confine in a bottle. [Rare.]

em·böu·çhure′ (oṅ-bö-shụr′), *n.* [Fr.] 1. a mouth or aperture, as of a river, cannon, etc.
2. the opening out of a river valley into flat ground.
3. in music, the mouthpiece of a wind instrument; also, the fitting of the lips and tongue to the mouthpiece in playing a wind instrument.

em·bōw′, *v.t.* to bend into the form of an arch or bow; as, a dolphin *embowed* on the shield. [Archaic except in pp.]

em·bow′el, *v.t.*; emboweled *or* embowelled, *pt.*, *pp.*; emboweling *or* embowelling, *ppr.* 1. to sink or enclose in another substance; to embed. [Obs.]
2. to disembowel. [Rare.]

em·bow′el·ẽr, *n.* one who disembowels.

em·bow′el·ment, *n.* the act of disemboweling; evisceration. [Rare.]

em·bow′ẽr, *v.i.*; embowered, *pt., pp.*; embowering, *ppr.* to lodge or rest in a bower.

em·bow′ẽr, *v.t.* to enclose or shelter in or as in a bower.

em·bōwl′, *v.t.* to make into the shape of a bowl. [Obs.]

em·box′, *v.t.* to shut up in a box; to furnish with a box.

em·brāce′, *v.t.*; embraced (-brāst′), *pt., pp.*; embracing, *ppr.* [OFr. *embracer*; It. *imbracciare*; LL. *imbrachiare*, to take in the arms, embrace; L. *in*, in, and *brachium*, arm.]

1. to take, clasp, or enclose in the arms; to press to the bosom, in token of affection; to hug.

Paul called to him the disciples and *embraced* them. —Acts xx. 1.

2. to accept readily; avail oneself of; as, he *embraced* the opportunity.

3. to take up; enter upon; adopt; as, he *embraced* a new profession.

4. to encircle; surround; enclose.

5. to include; comprise; contain.

6. to take in mentally; perceive; as, his glance *embraced* the scene.

Syn.—clasp, encircle, hug, comprehend, accept, contain, espouse.

em·brāce′, *v.i.* to join in an embrace.

em·brāce′, *n.* an embracing; a hug.

em·brāce′, *v.t.* [OFr. *embracer, embraser*, to set on fire, incite, instigate; *en*, in, and *braise*, live coals.] in law, to attempt illegally to influence or instruct (a jury).

em·brāce′ment, *n.* 1. a clasp in the arms; a hug; embrace.

2. willing acceptance. [Obs.]

em·brāce′ŏr, em·brā′cẽr, *n.* [OFr. *embraceor, embraseor*, from *embracer, embraser*, to set on fire, incite, instigate.] in law, a person guilty of embracery.

em·brā′cẽr, *n.* the person who embraces.

em·brā′cẽr·y, *n.* in law, an illegal attempt to influence or instruct a jury.

em·brāid′, *v.t.* to put up in braids, as the hair. [Obs.]

em·brāil′, *v.t.* to haul up by brails. [Rare.]

em·branch′ment, *n.* ramification, as of a tree or a river.

em·braṅ′gle, *v.t.*; embrangled, *pt., pp.*; embrangling, *ppr.* to mix up in confusion; to make complicated; to bewilder.

em·braṅ′gle·ment, *n.* an embrangling or being embrangled.

em·brā′ṣūre (-zhũr), *n.* an embrace. [Obs.]

em·brā′ṣūre (-zhũr), *n.* [Fr., from OFr. *embraser*, to skew, or splay the jambs of a door or window; *en*, in, on, and *braser*, to skew.]

1. an opening in a wall or parapet, through which cannon are pointed and discharged.

EMBRASURE

2. in architecture, the enlargement of the aperture of a door or window, on the inside of the wall, as for admitting more light.

em·brāve′, *v.t.* 1. to embellish; to make showy. [Obs.]

2. to inspire with bravery; to make bold. [Obs.]

em·brawn′, *v.t.* to make muscular; to impart strength to. [Obs.]

em·brēathe′ment, *n.* the act of inspiration in breathing. [Rare.]

em·brew′, *v.t.* to imbrue. [Obs.]

em·bright′, *v.t.* to brighten. [Obs.]

em·broad′en, *v.t.* to make broader. [Rare.]

em′brō·cāte, *v.t.*; embrocated, *pt., pp.*; embrocating, *ppr.* [LL. *embrocatus*, pp. of *embrocare*, to foment.] in surgery and medicine, to moisten and rub, as a diseased part of the body, with a liquid substance, as with spirit, oil, etc.

em·brō·cā′tion, *n.* 1. an embrocating.

2. the liquid or lotion with which an affected part is rubbed or washed; a kind of liniment.

em·brōgl′iō (-brōl′yō), *n.* same as *imbroglio*.

em·broid′ẽr, *v.t.*; embroidered, *pt., pp.*; embroidering, *ppr.* [OFr. *embroder*; *em-* (L. *in*), in, and *broder*, to broider, from *bord*, LL. *bordus*, a border, margin.]

1. to border with ornamental needlework or figures; to adorn with raised figures of needlework, as cloth, stuffs, or muslin.

2. to make (a design, etc.) on fabric with needlework.

3. figuratively, to attach ornamental additions to; hence, to exaggerate, especially in narrative; as, the story comes out beautifully *embroidered*.

em·broid′ẽr·ẽr, *n.* one who embroiders.

em·broid′ẽr·y, *n.*; *pl.* **em·broid′ẽr·ieṣ,** [ME. *embrouderie*, from OFr. *embroder*.]

1. the art or work of ornamenting fabric with needlework; embroidering.

2. embroidered work or fabric; ornamental needlework.

3. embellishment, as of a story.

em·broil′, *v.t.*; embroiled, *pt., pp.*; embroiling, *ppr.* [OFr. *embroillir, embrouillir*, to become troubled, confused.]

1. to confuse (affairs, etc.); to mix up; to muddle; to entangle.

The Christian antiquities at Rome are *embroiled* with fable and legend. —Addison.

2. to cause (a person, government, etc.) to take part in a quarrel or fight; to involve.

The royal house *embroiled* in civil war. —Dryden.

em·broil′, *n.* embroilment. [Obs.]

em·broil′ẽr, *n.* one who instigates or promotes embroilments.

em·broil′ment, *n.* [OFr. *embrouillement*, from *embrouiller*, to embroil.] an embroiling or being embroiled.

em·bronze′, *v.t.*; embronzed, *pt., pp.*; embronzing, *ppr.* to make a statue or figure of in bronze.

em·brown′, *v.t.*; embrowned, *pt., pp.*; embrowning, *ppr.* 1. to make brown or dark-colored.

2. to make dark, dim, or obscure; to render dusky.

em·brụe′, *v.t.*; embrued, *pt., pp.*; embruing, *ppr.* same as *imbrue*.

em·brụte′, *v.t.*; embruted, *pt., pp.*; embruting, *ppr.* same as *imbrute*.

em·bry-, embryo-.

em·bry·eç′tō·my, *n.* the surgical removal of an embryo, especially in cases of pregnancy outside of the uterus.

em·bry·ō-, [from Gr. *embryon*, an embryo, fetus.] a combining form meaning *of an embryo* or *fetus*, as in *embryo*logy.

em′bry·ō, *n.*; *pl.* **em′bry·ōṣ,** [Gr. *embryon*, the embryo, fetus, a thing newly born, neut. of *embryos*, growing in; *en*, in, and *bryein*, to swell, be full.]

1. an animal in the earliest stages of its development in the uterus: the human organism in the first three months after conception is called an *embryo*, thereafter a *fetus*.

2. (a) an early or undeveloped stage of something; (b) anything in such a stage.

3. the rudimentary plant contained in a seed.

em′bry·ō, *a.* same as *embryonic*.

embryo bud; a bud located at an unusual place on a plant, as under the bark, fitted to develop when normal buds are accidentally destroyed: called also *adventitious bud*.

em·bry·oç′tō·ny, *n.* [*embryo-*, and Gr. *-ktonia*, from *kteinein*, to kill.] the production of abortion by the destruction of the embryo.

em″bry·ō·ġen′e·sis, *n.* same as *embryogeny*.

em″bry·ō·ġe·net′iç, *a.* of embryogeny.

em″bry·ō·ġen′iç, *a.* same as *embryogenetic*.

em·bry·oġ′e·ny, *n.* [*embryo-*, and Gr. *-geneia*, from *-genēs*, producing.]

1. the formation and development of the embryo.

2. the study of this.

em·bry·og′rȧ·phy, *n.* [*embryo-*, and Gr. *-graphia*, from *graphein*, to write.] a description or treatise on embryos and their development.

em″bry·ō·loġ′iç·ăl, em″bry·ō·loġ′iç, *a.* relating to embryology.

em·bry·ol′ō·ġist, *n.* one who is skilled in the science of embryology.

em·bry·ol′ō·ġy, *n.* [*embryo-*, and Gr. *-logia*, from *legein*, to speak.] a branch of biology dealing with the formation and development of embryos.

em′bry·ŏn, *n.* an embryo: used technically. [Rare.]

em′bry·ō·năl, em′bry·ous, *a.* related to an embryo.

em′bry·ō·nāte, *a.* embryonated. [Obs.]

em′bry·ō·nā·ted, *a.* containing an embryo.

em·bry·on′iç, *a.* 1. of or like an embryo.

2. in an early stage; undeveloped; rudimentary.

embryonic sac; an embryo sac.

em″bry·ō·nif′ẽr·ous, *a.* bearing an embryo. [Rare.]

em·bry·on′i·form, *a.* shaped like an embryo.

Em·bry·oph′y·tȧ, *n.pl.* [*embryo-*, and Gr. *phyton* (pl. *phyta*), a plant.] a subdivision of the vegetable kingdom according to Engler and Prantl, embracing all plants having vascular tissue and produced through embryonic generation.

em″bry·ō·plas′tiç, *a.* [*embryo-*, and Gr. *plastos*, from *plassein*, to form.] helping in the formation of an embryo.

em′bry·ō saç, [*embryo-*, and L. *saccus*, a sac.] in botany, a thin-walled cell in the central part of a seed, where the egg undergoes development after fertilization.

em′bry·ō·sçōpe, *n.* [*embryo-*, and Gr. *skopein*, to view.] an optical instrument for observing the formation and development of embryos in eggs.

em·bry·ot′e·gȧ, *n.*; *pl.* **em·bry·ot′e·gae,** [*embryo-*, and Gr. *tegos*, a roof.] a kind of hard lid or cap covering part of the embryo in some seeds before germination, and pushed off by the growth of the radicle.

em·bry·ot′iç, *a.* embryonic. [Rare.]

em·bry·ot′ō·my, *n.* [*embryo-*, and Gr. *tomē*, a cutting.] a dissecting of the fetus in the womb to facilitate its removal when normal delivery is impossible.

em′bry·ous, *a.* embryonic. [Rare.]

em″bū·ī′ȧ, *n.* [Port.] a tree of the genus *Nectandra*, native to Brazil: the wood is much used in building and cabinetmaking.

em·bulk′, *v.t.* to effect an increase of in bulk. [Rare.]

em·bũrse′, *v.t.* same as *imburse*.

em·bus′, *v.t.* to put on a motor vehicle, as passengers, or troops.

em·bus′, *v.i.* to board a motor vehicle.

em·busk′, *v.t.* to tie with a busk.

em·bus·qué′ (äṅ-bụs-kā′), *n.* [Fr., lit., in ambush or in hiding.] a shirker; a slacker.

em·bus′y (-biz′i), *v.t.* to employ. [Obs.]

em′cee′, *v.t.* and *v.i.*; emceed, *pt., pp.*; emceeing, *ppr.* [from *M.C.*, Master of Ceremonies.], to act as master of ceremonies for (a radio program, etc.). [Slang.]

em′cee′, *n.* a master of ceremonies. [Slang.]

ēme, *n.* an uncle. [Obs.]

e·meer′, *n.* same as *emir*.

e·meer′āte, *n.* same as *emirate*.

ē·mend′, *v.t.* emended, *pt., pp.*; emending, *ppr.* [L. *emendare*, to correct, amend; *e-*, out, and *menda, mendum*, a fault, blemish.] to correct or improve; specifically, to make scholarly corrections in (a literary text, etc.); suggest a different reading for (a passage, etc.).

ē·mend′ȧ·ble, *a.* [L. *emendabilis*, from *emendare*, to correct, amend.] capable of being emended or corrected.

ē′men·dāte, *v.t.* emendated, *pt., pp.*; emendating, *ppr.* to emend (a text).

ē·men·dā′tion, *n.* [L. *emendatio*, from *emendare*, to correct, amend.]

1. an emending.

2. an alteration for the better; correction of an error or fault; as, the last edition of the book contains many *emendations*.

ē′men·dā·tŏr, *n.* one who emendates.

ē·mend′ȧ·tō·ry, *a.* relating to emendation or correction.

ē·mend′ẽr, *n.* one who emends.

ē·men′di·çāte, *v.t.* [L. *emendicatus*, pp. of *emendicare*, to obtain by begging.] to obtain by begging. [Obs.]

em′ẽr·ăld, *n.* [ME. *emeraude*; OFr. *esmeraude, esmeralde*; L. *smaragdus*; Gr. *smaragdos, maragdos*, a precious stone supposed to be the *emerald*.]

1. a precious stone of the beryl variety, of a rich green color and highly valued, ranking with the diamond and ruby as one of the most costly gems.

2. a similar variety of corundum.

3. a rich, bright green color.

4. a printing type, in size between nonpareil and minion, about $6\frac{1}{2}$ point.

em′ẽr·ăld, *a.* 1. having the characteristics of an emerald; especially of a typical green.

2. made of or with an emerald or emeralds.

emerald copper; a silicate of copper, crystalline and emerald in color: called also *dioptase*.

emerald green; a vivid light green pigment obtained from aceto arsenite of copper and used in oil paints or water colors: sometimes also used adjectively.

Emerald Isle; Ireland: probably so called with reference to the green of the landscape, from Drennan's song "Erin" (1795).

emerald nickel; a green incrustation of carbonate of nickel; zaratite.

emerald spodumene; an emerald-green variety of spodumene or lithia emerald, found in North Carolina: also called *hiddenite*.

em′ẽr·ăld fish, a goby, *Gobionellus oceanicus*, found in the West Indies and the Gulf of Mexico, and distinguished by the bright green and blue color at the root of the tongue.

em′ẽr·ăld·ine, *n.* a green dyestuff produced by subjecting goods treated with aniline black to some kind of acid before the black color is fully set.

em′ẽr·ăld moth, a moth, grass-green in color, of the genus *Hipparchus.*

ē·mẽrġe′, *v.i.*; emerged, *pt., pp.*; emerging, *ppr.* [L. *emergere,* to rise out, rise up; *e-,* out, and *mergere,* to dip, immerse.] to rise out of a fluid or other covering; to come forth from concealment or obscurity; to appear; to come into view; to become visible, apparent, or known; as, to *emerge* from the sea; the sun *emerges* from the eclipse; the deer *emerged* from the dusk; the people *emerged* from savagery.

ē·mẽr′ġence, *n.* [L. *emergens* (*-entis*), ppr. of *emergere,* to rise up, rise out.]

1. an emerging.

2. in botany, any of various outgrowths coming from the tissue beneath the epidermis, as a rose thorn.

ē·mẽr′ġen·cy, *n.*; *pl.* **ē·mẽr′ġen·cieṣ,** a sudden or unexpected occurrence or combination of occurrences demanding prompt action; urgent necessity; as, she could do it in an *emergency.*

Syn.—exigency, crisis, strait, necessity, urgency.

ē·mẽr′ġen·cy, *a.* for use in case of sudden necessity; as, an *emergency* brake.

ē·mẽr′ġent, *a.* 1. emerging.

2. arising unexpectedly or as a new development.

emergent year; the date from which time is historically computed; the first year of an epoch; as, the *emergent year* of the United States is 1776; the birth of Christ marks the *emergent year* of Christianity.

ē·mẽr′ġent·ly, *adv.* in an emergent manner.

ē·mẽr′ġent·ness, *n.* the condition or quality of being emergent. [Rare.]

em′ẽr·il, *n.* emery. [Obs.]

ē·mer′it·ed, *a.* honorably retired from public and active service after having served the full term: an obsolete form of *emeritus.*

ē·mer′i·tus, *a.* [L., having served one's time as a soldier, from *emereri,* to serve out one's time; *e-,* out, and *mereri,* to serve, earn, merit.] retired from long, active service on account of age or infirmity, but retaining one's rank or title; as, professor *emeritus.*

ē·mer′i·tus, *n.*; *pl.* **ē·mer′i·tī,** one who has been honorably discharged from public service: usually applied to a member of a profession.

em′ẽr·odṣ, *n.pl.* [OFr. *emmeroide;* L. *hæmorrhois,* a hemorrhoid.] hemorrhoids; piles. [Archaic.]

ē·mẽrsed′ (-mẽrst′), *a.* [L. *emersus,* pp. of *emergere,* to rise up, rise out.]

1. having emerged above the surface.

2. in botany, standing above surrounding water, as the leaves of certain aquatic plants.

ē·mẽr′sion, *n.* [from L. *emergere,* to come forth, rise out; *e-,* out, and *mergere,* to dip, merge.]

1. an emerging; an emergence.

2. in astronomy, the reappearance of a heavenly body after an eclipse; as, the *emersion* of the moon from the shadow of the earth; also, the time of reappearance; the reappearance of a star which has been hidden by the effulgence of the sun's light.

em′ẽr·y, *n.*; *pl.* **em′ẽr·ieṣ,** [OFr. *emeril,* emery; It. *smeriglio,* from Gr. *smyris, smiris,* emery.] a massive variety of corundum, in structure finely granular, its color varying from a deep gray to a bluish or blackish gray, sometimes brownish: it is used in polishing metals and hard stones.

em′ẽr·y bag, a small bag filled with emery and used for cleaning and sharpening needles.

em′ẽr·y bōard, a small, flat stick coated with powdered emery, used as a manicuring instrument.

em′ẽr·y çloth, em′ẽr·y pā′pẽr, cloth or paper coated with glue and emery dust and used for polishing and cleaning metal.

em′ẽr·y wheel, a polishing and grinding wheel made of emery or covered with emery: called also *buff wheel* and *glazer.*

em′e·sis, *n.* [Gr. *emesis,* a vomiting, from *emeein,* to vomit.] a vomiting.

ē·met′iç, ē·met′iç·ăl, *a.* [L. *emeticus;* Gr. *emetikos,* causing vomiting, from *emeein,* to vomit.] inducing to vomit; causing the stomach to discharge its contents by the esophagus and mouth.

ē·met′iç, *n.* a medicine or other substance that causes vomiting.

ē·met′iç·ăl·ly, *adv.* in such a manner as to cause vomiting.

em′e·tīne, em′e·tin, *n.* [*emetic,* and *-ine.*] an alkaloid, $C_{29}H_{40}N_2O_4$, obtained from ipecac root, used as an expectorant and an emetic.

em′e·tō·çȧ·thär″tiç, *a.* causing both vomiting and purging simultaneously.

em·e·tol′ō·ġy, *n.* [Gr. *emetos,* a vomiting, and *-logia,* from *legein,* to speak.] that branch of medicine which deals with emesis and emetics.

em″e·tō·mor′phi·ȧ, *n.* same as *apomorphine.*

ē′meū, ē′mew, *n.* see *emu.*

é·meute′ (ā-mu̇t′; Eng. i-mūt′), *n.* [Fr.] an insurrection; a popular uprising.

em·fōrth′, *prep.* [ME., contr. of *evenforth.*] in accordance with. [Obs.]

em·gal′lȧ, *n.* [native name.] the South African wart hog.

-ē′mi·a, [Mod. L., from Gr. *-aimia,* from *haima,* blood.] a suffix meaning *a* (specified) *condition* or *disease of the blood,* as in leuk*emia*: also spelled *-aemia.*

em′i·çănt, *a.* [L. *emicans* (*-antis*), ppr. of *emicare,* to break forth, spring out; *e-,* out, and *micare,* to sparkle, quiver.] flashing forth like sparks. [Obs.]

em·i·çā′tion, *n.* a sparkling; a flying off in small particles, as from heated iron or fermenting liquors. [Obs.]

ē·miç′tion, *n.* [L. *e-,* out, and *mictio,* from *mingere,* to urinate.]

1. the discharging of urine.

2. urine.

ē·miç′tō·ry, *a.* promoting a urinary flow; diuretic.

ē·miç′tō·ry, *n.* that which promotes a flow of urine; a diuretic.

em′i·grănt, *a.* [L. *emigrans* (*-antis*), ppr. of *emigrare,* to emigrate.]

1. emigrating.

2. of emigrants or emigration.

em′i·grănt, *n.* one who emigrates.

em′i·grāte, *v.i.*; emigrated, *pt., pp.*; emigrating, *ppr.* [L. *emigratus,* pp. of *emigrare,* to move away, depart from a place; *e-,* out, and *migrare,* to move, depart.] to leave one country, state, or region and settle in another; to remove from one country or state to another, for the purpose of residence: opposed to *immigrate;* as, Germans, Swiss, Irish, and Scotch *emigrated* in great numbers to America.

em·i·grā′tion, *n.* 1. an emigrating.

2. emigrants taken collectively; a body of emigrants.

em·i·grā′tion·ăl, *a.* pertaining to emigration.

em·i·grā′tion·ist, *n.* one who is in favor of or helps emigration.

em′i·grā·tŏr, *n.* an emigrant.

é·mi·gré′ (ā-mē-grā′; Eng. em′i-grā), *n.*; *pl.* **é·mi·grés′** (-grā′; Eng. -grāz) ,[Fr.; pp. of *émigrer;* L. *emigrare;* see *emigrate.*]

1. an emigrant.

2. a Royalist who fled from France during the French Revolution.

3. an opponent of the Soviet regime who fled from the Soviet Union after the revolution of 1918.

em′i·nence, *n.* [L. *eminentia,* from *eminens* (*-entis*), excellent, prominent, ppr. of *eminere,* to stand out, project.]

1. a high or lofty place, thing, etc., as a hill.

> The temple of honor ought to be seated on an *eminence.* —Burke.

2. superiority in rank, position, character, achievement, etc.; greatness; celebrity.

3. [E–] in the Roman Catholic Church, a title of honor given to cardinals.

4. in anatomy, a raised area, usually on the surface of a bone.

em′i·nen·cy, *n.*; *pl.* **em′i·nen·cieṣ,** 1. eminence. [Obs.]

2. prominence; relative importance.

em′i·nent, *a.* [L. *eminens* (*-entis*), ppr. of *eminere,* to stand out, project.]

1. rising above other things or places; high; lofty; as, an *eminent* place.

2. projecting; prominent; protruding.

3. standing high by comparison with others; renowned; exalted; distinguished.

4. outstanding; remarkable; noteworthy; as, a man of *eminent* good sense.

eminent domain; see under *domain.*

Syn.—famous, illustrious, celebrated, noted, distinguished.

em′i·nent·ly, *adv.* in an eminent manner or degree; notably; conspicuously; as, to be *eminently* learned or useful.

ē·mïr′, ē·meer′, *n.* [Ar. *amīr, emīr,* a commander, ruler, prince.]

1. an Arabian ruler, prince, or military commander.

2. a title given Mohammed's descendants through his daughter Fatima.

3. a Turkish honorary title.

ē·mïr′āte, *n.* the rule or jurisdiction of an emir.

ē·mïr′ship, *n.* the office held by an emir.

em′is·sā·ry, *n.*; *pl.* **em′is·sā·rieṣ,** [L. *emissarius,* from *emittere,* to send out; *e-,* out, and *mittere,* to send.]

1. a person or agent, especially a secret agent, sent on a specific mission.

2. an outlet, duct, or channel.

Syn.—spy, scout.—An *emissary* differs from a *spy.* A *spy* in war is one who enters an enemy's camp or territory to learn the condition of the enemy; an *emissary* may be a secret agent employed not only to detect the schemes of an opposing party, but to influence their councils. A *spy* in war must be concealed, or he suffers death; an *emissary* may in some cases be known as the agent of an adversary, without incurring similar hazard. A *scout* is concerned with military operations only, has an official standing in the service, and, if captured, is dealt with as an honorable prisoner-of-war.

em′is·sā·ry, *a.* 1. of, or serving as, an emissary or emissaries.

2. in anatomy, applying to ducts which emit fluids or serve as connecting canals; as, *emissary* veins.

em′is·sā·ry·ship, *n.* office or rank of an emissary.

ē·mis′sile, *a.* in zoology, capable of protrusion.

ē·mis′sion (-mish′un), *n.* [L. *emissio,* from *emittere,* to send out.]

1. the act of emitting; as, the *emission* of light from the sun; the *emission* of odors from plants.

2. the act of sending abroad, or into circulation, as notes of a state or of a private corporation; as, the *emission* of bills of credit or treasury notes.

3. that which is emitted; discharge; emanation.

4. in medicine, a discharge of fluid from the body; especially, an involuntary discharge of semen.

emission theory; Newton's theory of light: see *corpuscular theory* under *corpuscular.*

em·is·si′tious (-sish′us), *a.* [L. *emissitius,* from *emittere,* to send out.] looking or narrowly examining; prying. [Obs.]

ē·mis′sive, *a.* emitting or having the power to emit.

em·is·siv′i·ty, *n.* 1. rate at which emission takes place.

2. capacity or tendency to emit.

ē·mit′, *v.t.*; emitted, *pt., pp.*; emitting, *ppr.* [L. *emittere,* to send out; *e-,* out, and *mittere,* to send.]

1. to send forth; to throw or give out; as, fire *emits* heat; the sun and moon *emit* light; animal bodies *emit* perspiration.

2. to let fly; to discharge; to dart or shoot; as, to *emit* an arrow. [Rare.]

3. to issue forth, as an order or decree. [Rare.]

4. to issue, as notes or bills of credit; to print and send into circulation.

5. to utter (sounds, etc.).

ē·mit′tent, *a.* [L. *emittens,* ppr. of *emittere,* to send out.] sending out or forth.

em·man′tle, *v.t.* to immantle. [Obs.]

Em·man′ū·el, *n.* the Messiah: a variant of *Immanuel* (God with us).

em·mär′ble, *v.t.* to work in marble; to decorate with or turn into marble.

em·men′ȧ·gogue (-gog), *n.* [Fr. *emmenagogue;* Gr. *emmēna,* menses, neut. pl. of *emmēnos,* monthly, and *agogos,* a leading, drawing forth, from *agein,* to lead.] in medicine, anything used to assist and promote the menstrual discharges.

em·men·i·op′ȧ·thy, *n.* [Gr. *emmēna,* menses, and *-patheia,* from *pathos,* suffering.] disordered or faulty menstruation.

em·me·nol′ō·ġy, *n.* [Gr. *emmēna,* monthly, menses, and *-logia,* from *legein,* to speak.] that division or branch of medicine dealing with menstruation, its disorders, and their causes.

em′mens·ite, *n.* a picric acid explosive for projectiles, invented by S. H. *Emmens,* American chemist.

em′met, *n.* an ant. [Archaic.]

em·me·trō′pi·ȧ, *n.* [Gr. *emmetros,* in measure, measured; *en,* in, and *metros,* measure, and *ōps, ōpos,* eye.] the normal power of optic refraction, whereby light is brought to a focus exactly on the retina with the eye relaxed.

em·me·trop′iç, *a.* of or pertaining to the normal refractive condition of the eye.
em·met′rō·py, *n.* same as *emmetropia*.
em·mew′, *v.t.* [*em-* (L. *in*, in), and *mew*, a cage.] to mew; imprison; confine; coop up. [Obs.]
em′ō·din, *n.* a crystalline substance, reddish-yellow in color, found especially in rhubarb root and buckthorn bark.
em·ŏl·les′cence, *n.* [L. *emollescens*, softening, ppr. of *emollescere*; *e-*, out, and *mollescere*, freq. of *mollire*, to soften.] in metallurgy, that degree of softness in a fusible body which alters its shape; the first or lowest degree of fusibility.
ē·mol′li·āte, *v.t.*; emolliated, *pt.*, *pp.*; emolliating, *ppr.* [from L. *emollire*, to soften.] to soften; to render effeminate. [Rare.]
ē·mol′lient, *n.* [L. *emolliens* (*-entis*), ppr. of *emollire*, to soften; *e-*, out, and *mollire*, to soften, from *mollis*, soft.] a preparation or medicine that has a softening or soothing effect on surface tissues.
ē·mol′lient, *a.* softening; soothing; making supple; acting as an emollient.
em·ŏl·li′tion, *n.* the act of softening or relaxing. [Obs.]
ē·mol′ū·ment, *n.* [L. *emolumentum*, gain, profit, advantage, from *emolire*, to accomplish, effect; *e-*, out, and *molire*, to exert oneself.]
1. the profit arising from office or employment; that which is received as a compensation for services; payment received for work; wages; salary; fees.
2. advantage; gain in general. [Obs.]
ē·mol·ū·men′tăl, *a.* producing profit; useful; profitable; advantageous. [Rare.]
ē·mŏng′, ē·mŏngst′, *prep.* among. [Obs.]
ē·mōte′, *v.i.*; emoted, *pt.*, *pp.*; emoting, *ppr.* [from *emotion*, by analogy with *devote*, etc.] to conduct oneself in an emotional or theatrical manner; to behave as though acting an emotional role: often used humorously. [Colloq.]
ē·mō′tion, *n.* [from L. *emovere*, to move out, stir up, agitate; *e-*, out, and *movere*, to move.]
1. strong, generalized feeling; psychical excitement.
2. any specific feeling; any of various complex reactions with both psychical and physical manifestations, as love, hate, fear, anger, etc.
Syn.—agitation, perturbation, commotion, excitement, disturbance, feeling.
ē·mō′tion·ăl, *a.* 1. pertaining to emotion or the emotions; characterized by emotion.
2. appealing to the emotions; of a nature to move the feelings or passions; moving; touching.
3. easily aroused to emotion; excitable; easily moved; as, an *emotional* nature.
4. showing emotion.
ē·mō′tion·ăl·iṣm, *n.* 1. emotional character.
2. the tendency to be emotional or to show emotion quickly and easily.
3. display of emotion.
4. an appeal to emotion, especially to sway an audience to some belief.
ē·mō′tion·ăl·ist, *n.* 1. a very emotional person.
2. one who practices the art of exciting emotions in others, as in oratory, art, etc.
ē·mō·tion·al′i·ty, *n.* the quality or condition of being emotional.
ē·mō′tion·ăl·īze, *v.t.*; emotionalized, *pt.*, *pp.*; emotionalizing, *ppr.* to render emotional; to excite the feelings of; to give an emotional character to.
ē·mō′tion·ăl·ly, *adv.* 1. in an emotional manner.
2. with reference to the emotions.
ē·mō′tioned, *a.* affected by emotion. [Rare.]
ē·mō′tive, *a.* characterized by, expressing, or producing emotion; emotional.
ē·mōve′, *v.t.* to excite; arouse. [Obs.]
em·paes′tiç (-pes′), **em·pes′tiç, em·pāis′tiç**, *a.* [Gr. *empaistikē* (supply *technē*, art), from *empaiein*, to strike in, emboss; *en*, in, and *paiein*, to stamp.] of, relating to, or characterized by embossed work.
em·pāir′, *v.t.* to impair. [Obs.]
em·pāle′, *v.t.*; empaled, *pt.*, *pp.*; empaling, *ppr.* to impale.
em·pāle′ment, *n.* same as *impalement*.
em·pan′el, *n.* impanel. [Obs.]
em·pan′el, *v.t.*; empaneled *or* empanelled, *pt.*, *pp.*; empaneling *or* empanelling, *ppr.* 1. to enter the name or names of on a jury list.
2. to choose (a jury) from such a list.
Also spelled *impanel*.
em·pan′ō·ply, *v.t.*; empanoplied, *pt.*, *pp.*; empanoplying, *ppr.* to invest with a panoply.
em·par′ȧ·dīse, *v.t.* same as *imparadise*.
em·pärk′, *v.t.* same as *impark*.
em·pasm′, *n.* [from Gr. *empassein*, to sprinkle in or on; *en*, in, and *passein*, to sprinkle.] a perfumed powder used to conceal the odor of the body.
em·pas′sion, *v.t.* same as *impassion*.
em′pȧ·thy, *n.* [from Gr. *empatheia*, affection, passion, from *en-*, in, and *pathos*, feeling.]
1. the projection of one's own personality into the personality of another in order to understand him better; intellectual identification of oneself with another.
2. the projection of one's own personality into an object, with the attribution to the object of one's own emotions, responses, etc.: also called *pathetic fallacy*.
em·pawn′, *v.t.* to impawn. [Obs.]
em·pēach′, *v.t.* to impeach. [Obs.]
em·pēarl′, *v.t.* same as *impearl*.
em′pen·nȧġe (*or* äṅ-pe-nȧzh′), *n.* [Fr., from *empenner*, to feather an arrow, from *em-*, in, and *penne*, a feather.] the stabilizing tail assembly of an airplane, consisting of vertical and horizontal airfoils, and including the fin, rudder, stabilizer, and elevator.
em·pēo′ple, *v.t.* to form into a people or community. [Rare.]
em′pẽr·ess, *n.* empress. [Obs.]
em·per′il, *v.t.* to imperil. [Obs.]
em·per′ish, *v.t.* to impair. [Obs.]
em′pẽr·ŏr, *n.* [ME. *emperour*; OFr. *empereor*; L. *imperator*, a commander-in-chief, ruler, emperor, from *imperare*, to command; *in*, in, and *perare*, to prepare.]
1. a sovereign or supreme monarch of an empire.
2. any of various large butterflies.
emperor of Japan; an edible fish found in the seas of southern Japan, characterized by its brilliant color; the *Holacanthus imperator*: called also *emperor fish*.
purple emperor; a butterfly of Great Britain, large and beautifully spotted.
em′pẽr·ŏr fish, see *emperor of Japan* under *emperor*.
em′pẽr·ŏr goose, a large goose with transversely barred plumage and white crown, found in Alaskan waters; the *Philacte canagica*.
em′pẽr·ŏr moth, any of several moths with transparent spots on their wings, as the American cecropia moth, *Platysamia cecropia*.
em′pẽr·ŏr pen′guin (-gwin), the largest known penguin; the great king penguin, *Aptenodytes patagonica*.
em′pẽr·ŏr·ship, *n.* the position, rank, or reign of an emperor.
em′pẽr·y, *n.*; *pl.* **em′pẽr·ieṣ**, [ME. *emperie*; OFr. *emperie*, from *emperer*, to rule; L. *imperare*, to command.]
1. the sovereignty of an emperor; empire. [Poetic.]
2. broad dominion or authority. [Poetic.]
Em·pe·trā′cē·ae, *n.pl.* a small family of low-growing evergreen shrubs.
em·pe·trā′ceous, *a.* pertaining to the *Empetraceæ*.
Em′pe·trum, *n.* [Gr. *empetron*, a rock plant; neut. of *empetros*, growing on the rocks; *en*, in, on, and *petros*, a rock.] a genus of plants growing in mountainous regions. The crowberry is the fruit of the *Empetrum nigrum*.
em′phȧ·sis, *n.*; *pl.* **em′phȧ·sēṣ**, [L., from Gr. *emphasis*, an appearing in, outward appearance, from *emphainein*, to show forth; *en*, in, and *phainein*, to show, from *phasis*, appearance.]
1. force of expression, thought, feeling, action, etc.; as, sincerity gives *emphasis* to his contention.
2. special stress given to a syllable, word, phrase, etc. in speaking.
3. special attention given to something so as to make it stand out; importance; stress; weight; as, too much *emphasis* was placed on athletics.
em′phȧ·sīze, *v.t.*; emphasized, *pt.*, *pp.*; emphasizing, *ppr.* to give force or emphasis to; to stress; as, to *emphasize* a thought.
em·phat′iç, em·phat′iç·ăl, *a.* 1. forcible; impressive; strong; as, an *emphatic* voice, tone, or pronunciation; *emphatic* reasoning.
2. using emphasis in speaking, etc.
3. expressed, felt, or done with emphasis.
Syn.—earnest, forcible, strong, energetic, impressive, positive.
em·phat′iç·ăl·ly, *adv.* with emphasis; strongly; forcibly; in a striking manner.
em·phat′iç·ăl·ness, *n.* the quality of emphasis. [Rare.]
em·phren′ṣy, *v.t.* to madden; to render frantic and desperate. [Obs.]
em·phy·sē′mȧ, *n.* [Gr. *emphysēma*, an inflation, from *emphysān*, to inflate, blow in; *en*, in, and *physān*, to blow.]
1. an abnormal swelling of body tissues caused by the accumulation of air; especially, such a swelling of the alveoli or of the tissue connecting the alveoli in the lungs.
2. heaves, a disease of horses.
em·phy·sem′ȧ·tous, *a.* of or pertaining to emphysema; also, having emphysema.
em·phy·teū′sis, *n.* [LL., from Gr. *emphyteusis*, lit., an implanting, from *emphyteuein*, to implant, from *emphyein*; *en*, in, and *phyein*, to produce.] in civil law, a kind of perpetual lease of real estate upon condition of taking care of and paying the taxes upon the land.
em·phy·teū′tȧ, *n.* a holder of an estate under emphyteutic contract.
em·phy·teū′tiç, *a.* held by an emphyteusis; as, *emphyteutic* lands.
em·piērce′, *v.t.* to pierce; to penetrate. [Obs.]
em·pīght′ (-pīte′), *a.* fixed; fastened; placed. [Obs.]
em′pīre, *n.* [OFr. *empire*; L. *imperium*, command, sovereignty, dominion, realm, empire, from *imperare*, to command, order; *in*, in, and *parare*, to order.]
1. supreme power in governing; dominion; sovereignty; absolute power or authority; as, no nation can rightfully claim the *empire* of the ocean.
2. government by an emperor or empress.
3. the period during which such government prevails.
4. a state uniting many territories and peoples under one ruler.
5. the territories, regions, or countries under the jurisdiction and dominion of an emperor or empress.
the Empire; a specified or understood empire; especially, (a) the British Empire; (b) the Holy Roman Empire; (c) the first French Empire, under Napoleon.
Em′pīre, *a.* of or characteristic of the first French Empire (1804–1815), under Napoleon; specifically, (a) designating a style of furniture of this period, characterized by rectangular massiveness, swelling curves, and the use of heavy textiles and bronze ornamentation; (b) designating a gown fashioned in the style of the period, with a short waist, décolleté bodice, flowing skirt, and short, puffed sleeves.
Em′pīre Dāy, May 24, Queen Victoria's birthday, celebrated as a holiday throughout the British Empire.
Em′pīre Stāte, New York State.
em·pir′iç, *n.* [L. *empiricus*; Gr. *empeirikos*, experienced, from *empeiria*, experience; *en*, in, and *peira*, a trial, attempt.]
1. one who enters a practice without a regular professional education and the proper experience; a quack.
2. a person who is ignorant of scientific principles and relies solely on practical experience.
em·pir′iç·ăl, em·pir′iç, *a.* 1. relying or based solely on experiments or experience; as, the *empirical* method.
2. relying or based on practical experience without reference to scientific principles; as, an *empirical* remedy.
em·pir′iç·ăl·ly, *adv.* in an empirical manner; by experiment; according to experience.
em·pir′i·ciṣm, *n.* 1. dependence of a person on his own experience and observation, disregarding theory, reasoning, and science.
2. the practice of medicine without a medical education; hence, quackery; charlatanism.

> Shudder to destroy life, either by the naked knife or by the surer and safer medium of *empiricism*. —Dwight.

3. in philosophy, the theory that sensory experience is the only source of knowledge.
em·pir′i·cist, *n.* one who practices empiricism or believes in the philosophical theory of empiricism; an empiric.
em·plāce′, *v.t.* to put in position; to place; to determine emplacement of. [Rare.]
em·plāce′ment, *n.* 1. the assigning or appointing of a definite place; fixing upon a locality, place, or ground.
2. in military science, the prepared position from which a heavy gun is fired.
em·plas′tẽr, *n.* and *v.* plaster. [Obs.]
em·plas′tiç, *a.* [Gr. *emplastikos*, stopping the pores, clogging, from *emplassein*, to plaster up, daub over.] viscous; glutinous; adhesive; fit to be applied as a plaster; as, *emplastic* applications.

em·plas·trā′tion, *n.* 1. the act of grafting. [Obs.]
2. the act of applying a plaster.

em·plēad′, *v.t.* to implead. [Obs.]

em·pleç′tīte, *n.* [Gr. *emplektos*, inwoven, and *-ite*.] in chemistry, a combination of copper and bismuth with sulfur ($CuBiS_2$) of a tin-white luster, which crystallizes in the orthorhombic system.

em·pleç′ton, *n.* [L., from Gr. *emplekton*, neut. of *emplektos*, interwoven, from *emplekein*, to inweave; *en*, in, and *plekein*, to weave.] in ancient architecture, a method of constructing walls with squared stones outside, and with rough stones in the interior.

em·plōre′, *v.t.* to implore. [Obs.]

em·ploy′, *v.t.*; employed, *pt.*, *pp.*; employing, *ppr.* [OFr. *employer*, *emploier*; L. *implicare*, to infold, engage; *in*, in, and *plicare*, to fold.]
1. to occupy the time, attention, and labor of; to keep busy or at work; as, we *employ* our hands in labor.
2. to use; to make use of; as, we *employ* pens in writing, and arithmetic in keeping accounts.
3. to provide work and pay for; as, public works *employ* thousands of men.
4. to engage in one's service; to hire; as, the president *employed* an envoy to negotiate a treaty.
5. to occupy; to apply or devote to an object; as, to *employ* time.
Syn.—use, hire, occupy, devote, busy, engage, commission.

em·ploy′, *n.* the state of being employed; paid service; employment.

em·ploy′a·ble, *a.* that can be employed; specifically, (a) physically or mentally fit to be hired for work; (b) meeting the minimum requirements for a specified kind of work or position of employment.

em·ploy′ee, em·ploy′ē (*or* em-ploy-ē′), *n.* [Fr. *employé*, f. *employée*, one employed, from *employer*, to employ, engage.] one who is hired by another, or by a business firm, etc., to work for wages or salary: also spelled *employé*.

em·ploy′ẽr, *n.* one who employs; one who uses; one who engages or keeps in service.

em·ploy′ment, *n.* 1. the act of employing or the state of being employed.
2. work; occupation; business; that at which one is employed; as, agricultural *employments*, mechanical *employments*.
Syn.—business, calling, occupation, engagement, trade, profession, vocation.

em·plūme′, *v.t.*; emplumed, *pt.*, *pp.*; empluming, *ppr.* to grace or ornament with plumes.

em·plunġe′, *v.t.* to plunge. [Obs.]

em·pō′di·um, *n.*; *pl.* **em·pō′di·a,** [Gr. *en*, in, and *pous*, *podos*, a foot.] an imperfect claw or hook (called sometimes a *spurious claw*) between the true claws of certain kinds of insects.

em·poi′ṣŏn, *v.t.* 1. to make poisonous; taint or corrupt.
2. to embitter; envenom.

em·poi′ṣŏn′, *n.* poison. [Obs.]

em·poi′ṣŏn·ment, *n.* the act of poisoning. [Obs.]

em·pō·ret′iç, em·pō·ret′iç·al, *a.* [L. *emporeticus*; Gr. *emporeutikos*, mercantile, commercial, from *emporeuesthai*, to trade, traffic.] relating to trade. [Obs.]

em·pō′ri·um, *n.*; *pl.* **em·pō′ri·umṣ** or **em·pō′ri·a,** [L., from Gr. *emporion*, a trading place, mart, from *emporia*, trade, commerce, from *emporos*, a traveler; *en*, in, and *poros*, way.]
1. a place of commerce; a trading center; a market place.
2. a large store for the sale of a variety of goods.

em·pov′ẽr·ish, *v.t.* to impoverish. [Obs.]

em·pow′ẽr, *v.t.*; empowered, *pt.*, *pp.*; empowering, *ppr.* 1. to give power or authority to; to authorize; as, the president is *empowered* to veto legislation.
2. to give ability to; to enable; as, science *empowers* men to control natural forces more effectively.
Also spelled *impower*.
Syn.—authorize, license, commission, delegate, warrant.

em′press, *n.* [ME. *empresse*, *emperesse*; OFr. *empereis*, *emperesse*; L. *imperatrix*, f. of *imperator*, a commander, ruler.]
1. the wife of an emperor.
2. a woman who governs an empire; a woman invested with imperial power or sovereignty.
3. a woman with great power or influence; as, the *empress* of his heart.
empress cloth; a woolen cloth for women's wear, with a finely corded surface, resembling merino.

em·presse′ment (oṅ-pres′moṅ), *n.* [Fr.] demonstrative earnestness; extreme cordiality.

em·print′, *n.* and *v.* imprint. [Obs.]

em·prīṣe′, em·prīze′, *n.* [ME. *emprise*; OFr. *emprise*, from *emprendre*, to undertake, from L. *in*, in, and *prehendere*, *prendere*, to take, seize.]
1. an undertaking; an enterprise. [Archaic.]
2. prowess or daring. [Archaic.]

em·prīṣe′, em·prīze′, *v.t.* to undertake. [Obs.]

em·prīṣ′ing, *a.* full of adventure; very daring. [Obs.]

em·priṣ′ŏn, *v.t.* to imprison. [Obs.]

em·pros·thot′ō·nos, *n.* [Gr. *emprosthotonos*, *emprosthen*, forward, in front, and *teinein*, to stretch.] in pathology, a state of the body in which it is drawn forward through muscular spasm.

empt, *v.t.* to empty. [Dial.]

emp′ti·ẽr, *n.* one who or that which empties.

emp′ti·ness, *n.* 1. a state of being empty; a state of containing nothing; absence of matter; as, the *emptiness* of a vessel.
2. void space; vacuity; vacuum.
3. want of solidity or substance.
4. want of intellect or knowledge; lack of sense.

emp′tion, *n.* [L. *emptio*, from *emere*, to buy.]
1. the act of buying; a purchasing. [Rare.]
2. that which is bought. [Obs.]

emp′tion·al, *a.* purchasable.

emp′tŏr, *n.* [L., from *emere*, to buy.] in law, a buyer.

emp′ty, *a.*; *comp.* emptier; *superl.* emptiest, [ME. *empty*, *emti*; AS. *oemtig*, *oemetig*, from *æmta*, *æmetta*, leisure, rest.]
1. containing nothing; evacuated; void of contents; as, an *empty* chest, *empty* space, an *empty* purse.
2. having no one in it; unoccupied; vacant; as, an *empty* house.
3. meaningless; insincere; vain; as, *empty* promises.
4. unsubstantial; unsatisfactory; worthless; as, *empty* pleasures.
5. not supplied; having nothing to carry; bare.

They beat him, and sent him away *empty*.
—Mark xii. 3.

6. hungry. [Colloq.]

My falcon now is sharp and passing *empty*.
—Shak.

Syn.—hollow, unfilled, unfurnished, unoccupied, vacant, barren, bare, fruitless, meaningless, vacated, weak, silly, senseless, unsatisfying.

emp′ty, *n.*; *pl.* **emp′tieṣ,** an empty freight car, packing case, bottle, barrel, box, etc.; as, returned *empties*.

emp′ty, *v.t.*; emptied, *pt.*, *pp.*; emptying, *ppr.* [ME. *empten*; AS. *æmtian*, from *æmetta*, leisure.]
1. to make empty; to make void or destitute; to deprive of contents; as, to *empty* a vessel; to *empty* an auditorium.
2. to pour out or remove (the contents) of something; as, rivers *empty* themselves into the ocean.
3. to transfer (the contents) *into* something else.

emp′ty, *v.i.* 1. to pour out or discharge its contents; as, the Connecticut river *empties* into the Sound.
2. to become empty.

emp′ty-hand″ed, *a.* bringing or carrying away nothing.

emp′ty-head″ed (-hed″), *a.* frivolous and stupid; silly and ignorant.

emp′ty·ing, *n.* 1. the act of making empty.
2. that which is emptied out.

emp′ty·sis, *n.* in medicine, a discharge of blood from the mouth; hemoptysis.

em·pûr′ple, *v.t.*; empurpled, *pt.*, *pp.*; empurpling, *ppr.* to make purple.

Em·pū′sa, *n.* [from Gr. *empousa*, a hobgoblin.] in botany, a genus of parasitic fungi infesting the bodies and causing the death of insects. *Empusa muscæ* is parasitic upon the common housefly.

em·puz′zle, *v.t.* to puzzle. [Obs.]

em·py·ē′ma, *n.* [Gr. *empyēma*, from *empyein*, to suppurate, from *empyos*; *en*, in, and *pyon*, pus.] the accumulation of pus in a body cavity, especially in the cavity containing the lungs.

em·py·ē′sis, *n.* [Gr. *empyēsis*, suppuration, from *empyein*, to suppurate.] in pathology, an eruption of pustules on the skin.

em·pyr′ē·al, *n.* same as *empyrean*.

em·pyr′ē·al, *a.* [L. *empyrius*, *empyreus*; Gr. *empyrios*, *empyros*, fiery, in fire; *en*, in, and *pyr*, fire.]
1. formed of pure fire or light.
2. of the empyrean; heavenly; sublime.

Go, soar with Plato to the *empyreal* sphere.
—Pope.

em·py·rē′an, *a.* empyreal.

em·py·rē′an, *n.* 1. the highest heaven; specifically, (a) among the ancients, the sphere of pure light or fire; (b) among Christian poets, the abode of God.
2. the sky; the celestial vault; firmament.

em·py·reū′ma, *n.* [Gr. *empyreuma*, from *empyreuein*, to set on fire, kindle, from *empyros*; *en*, in, on, and *pyr*, fire.] in chemistry, burnt smell, the odor of animal or vegetable substances when burned in close vessels.

em″py·reū·mat′iç, em″py·reū·mat′iç·al, *a.* pertaining to empyreuma.
empyreumatic oil; an oil obtained by decomposing organic substances by means of heat.

em·py·reū′ma·tīze, *v.t.* to burn so as to produce an empyreuma.

em·pyr′iç·al, *a.* pertaining to combustion or combustibility. [Rare.]

em·py·rō′sis, *n.* [Gr. *empyrōsis*, from *empyroein*, *empyrenein*, to set on fire.] a general fire; a conflagration. [Obs.]

em′rodṣ, *n.pl.* hemorrhoids. [Obs.]

ē′mū, *n.* [prob. from Port. *ema*, a crane.] a large cursorial bird, *Dromaius novæ-hollandiæ*, found in Australia. It stands higher than the cassowary, from which it differs in having the head and neck feathered. Written also *emeu*.

EMU (6 ft. high)
(*Dromaius novæ-hollandiæ*)

em′ū·la·ble, *a.* worthy of emulation. [Rare.]

em′ū·lāte, *v.t.*; emulated, *pt.*, *pp.*; emulating, *ppr.* [L. *æmulatus*, pp. of *æmulari*, to try to equal or excel another, from *æmulus*, trying to equal or excel.]
1. to strive to equal or excel.
2. to rival successfully.

Thine eye would *emulate* the diamond.
—Shak.

em′ū·lāte, *a.* ambitious. [Obs.]

em·ū·lā′tion, *n.* 1. an emulating.
2. desire or ambition to equal or surpass.
3. (a) ambitious rivalry; (b) envious dislike. [Obs.]
Syn. competition, rivalry.—*Competition* is the struggle of two or more persons for the same object, usually in accordance with certain rules; *emulation* is an ardent desire for superiority arising from competition, but not implying, of necessity, any improper feeling; *rivalry* is a personal contest, and involves, usually, envy, resentment, or detraction.

em′ū·lā·tive, *a.* of, characterized by, or resulting from emulation; as, an *emulative* student.

em′ū·lā·tive·ly, *adv.* in an emulative manner.

em′ū·lā·tŏr, *n.* [L., from *æmulari*, to try to equal or excel.] one who emulates; a rival; a competitor.

em′ū·lā·tress, *n.* a woman who emulates. [Rare.]

em′ūle, *v.t.* to emulate. [Obs.]

ē·mulġe′, *v.t.* to drain. [Obs.]

ē·mul′ġent, *a.* [L. *emulgens* (*-entis*), ppr. of *emulgere*, to milk out, drain out; *e-*, out, and *mulgere*, to milk.] in anatomy, milking or draining out: said of the renal arteries, which supply the kidneys with blood; as, the *emulgent* veins return the blood, after the urine is secreted.

ē·mul′ġent, *n.* 1. an emulgent vessel or vein.
2. a medicine which excites the flow of bile.

em′ū·lous, *a.* [L. *æmulus*, trying to equal or excel.]
1. desirous or eager to equal or excel; as, *emulous* of another's example or virtues.

2. jealous; envious. [Obs.]
3. emulative.

em′ū·lous·ly, *adv.* with desire of equaling or excelling.

em′ū·lous·ness, *n.* the quality of being emulous.

ē·mul′siç, *a.* in chemistry, pertaining to or derived from emulsin.

ē·mul′si·fȳ, *v.t.* and *v.i.*; emulsified, *pt., pp.*; emulsifying, *ppr.* to form into an emulsion.

ē·mul′sin, *n.* [L. *emulsus*, pp. of *emulgere*, to milk or drain out.] an albuminous or caseous substance of which the white part both of sweet and bitter almonds chiefly consists.

ē·mul′sion, *n.* [OFr. *emulsion*, from L. *emulgere*, to milk or drain out.] a fluid, as milk, formed by the suspension of a very finely divided oily or resinous liquid in another liquid; specifically, (a) in pharmacy, a preparation of an oily substance held in suspension in a watery liquid by means of a gummy substance; as, an *emulsion* of cod-liver oil; (b) in photography, a suspension of a salt of silver in gelatin or collodion, used to coat plates and film.

ē·mul′sive, *a.* 1. having the nature of an emulsion.
2. capable of emulsifying.

ē·munç′tō·ry, *n.* and *a.* [LL. *emunctorium*, a pair of snuffers, from L. *emungere*, to wipe or blow the nose, to cleanse; *e-*, out, and *mungere*, to blow the nose.] any part of the body which serves to carry off waste products, as the kidneys, skin, etc.

ē·munç′tō·ry, *a.* performing the function of discharging waste products; excretory.

em·us·çā′tion, *n.* [L. *emuscare*, to clear from moss; *e-*, out, and *muscus*, moss.] a freeing from moss. [Rare.]

ē′mū wren (ren), an Australian bird, *Stipiturus malachurus*, of the family *Sylviadæ*, so named from the tail feathers being loosely barbed and bearing some resemblance to those of the emu.

ē′myd, *n.* a member of the family *Emydidæ*.

Ē·myd′i·dae, *n.pl.* [Gr. *emys*, the water tortoise, and *eidos*, resemblance.] a subfamily of chelonian reptiles, including the fresh-water tortoises or terrapins.

en-, [ME. *en-*; OFr. *en-*; L. *in-*, from prep. *in*, in, into.] a prefix, used to form verbs from nouns, adjectives, and other verbs, meaning: (a) *to put into* or *on*, as in *en*throne; *to cover* or *wrap with*, as in *en*robe: prefixed to nouns; (b) *to make, make into* or *like, cause to be*, as in *en*danger, *en*feeble: prefixed to nouns or adjectives; (c) *in* or *into*, as in *en*close, *en*liven: prefixed to verbs. *En-* often has the force of an intensifier, as in *en*liven, *en*courage. Many words beginning *en-* are also spelled *in-*, (e.g., *en*quire, *in*quire). See also *em-*.

en-, [Gr. *en-*, from prep. *en*, in.] a prefix meaning *in*, used chiefly in Greek derivatives, as *en*demic.

-en, [AS. *-an*.] a suffix used to form the plurals of some nouns; as, ox*en*, brethr*en*.

-en, [ME. *-en, -e*, AS. *-an, -ian*.] a suffix used to form verbs, usually transitive, meaning (a) *to become* or *cause to be*: added to adjectives, as in dark*en*, weak*en*; (b) *to come to have, to cause to have*: added to nouns, as in height*en*, heart*en*, strength*en*.

-en, [from ME. *-en*, AS. *-en*.] a suffix used in the formation of adjectives from concrete nouns; as, wood, wood*en*; gold, gold*en*.

-en, [from ME. *-en*, AS. *-en*.] a feminine suffix used in such words as vix*en*.

-en, [from AS. *-en*.] a suffix used as the termination of the past participle of many strong verbs; as, broke, brok*en*; trod, trodd*en*.

-en, [from AS. *-en*.] a suffix used to form diminutives, as in chick*en*.

en, *n.* 1. the fourteenth letter of the English alphabet, *N, n.*
2. in printing, a space half as wide as an em: used as a unit of measurement.

en·ā′ble, *v.t.*; enabled, *pt., pp.*; enabling, *ppr.* 1. to make able; to provide with means, opportunity, power, or authority (*to* do something).
2. to make possible or effective. [Obs.]

en·ā′ble·ment, *n.* the act of enabling. [Rare.]

en·açt′, *v.t.*; enacted, *pt., pp.*; enacting, *ppr.* 1. to decree; to establish; to make (a bill, etc.) into a law; to pass (a law).
2. to do; to accomplish: usually in the passive; as, the place where the shooting was *enacted*.
3. to represent in or as in a play; to act out; as, to *enact* Hamlet.

en·açt′, *n.* purpose; determination. [Obs.]

en·açt′ive, *a.* enacting or having power to enact.

en·açt′ment, *n.* 1. the passing of a bill into a law; the act of voting, decreeing, and giving validity to a law.
2. a statute; a law enacted; an act; a decree.
3. the acting of a part or representation of a character in a play.

en·açt′ŏr, *n.* 1. one who enacts or passes a law.
2. one who enacts anything.

en·açt′ō·ry, *a.* relating to the establishment of a law; especially, conferring new powers or creating new duties not before existing.

en·aç′tūre, *n.* 1. purpose; effect. [Obs.]
2. fulfillment. [Obs.]

en·al′i·ō·saur, *n.* a member of the *Enaliosauria*.

En·al″i·ō·sau′ri·ȧ, *n.pl.* [Gr. *enalios*, living in the sea; *en*, in, and *hals*, the sea, and *sauros*, a lizard.] a group of fossil marine reptiles of great size, including the ichthyosaurus.

en·al″i·ō·sau′ri·ăn, *a.* relating to the *Enaliosauria*.

en·al″i·ō·sau′ri·ăn, *n.* same as *enaliosaur*.

e·nal′lȧ·gē, *n.* [L. *enallage*; Gr. *enallagē*, an interchange, from *enallassein*; *en*, in, and *allassein*, to change, from *allos*, other.] in grammar, a substitution of one gender, number, case, person, tense, mode, or voice of the same word for another.

em·am′bush, *v.t.* to hide in ambush; to place in ambush. [Obs.]

en·am′el, *v.t.*; enameled *or* enamelled, *pt., pp.*; enameling *or* enamelling, *ppr.* [ME. *enamelen*; OFr. *enamailler, enameler*; *en-*, in, on, and *esmailler*, to enamel, from *esmail*, enamel.]
1. to paint in enamel; to lay enamel into or upon; to decorate by means of enamel; also, to give an enamellike surface to; as, to *enamel* a vase, to *enamel* paper.
2. to decorate in various colors, as if with enamel.
3. to coat with a cosmetic resembling enamel; as, to *enamel* the face.

en·am′el, *v.i.* to practice the art of enameling or the use of enamel.

en·am′el, *n.* 1. a glassy, colored, opaque substance fused to surfaces of metals, glass, and pottery as an ornamental or protective coating.
2. any smooth, hard, glossy coating or surface like enamel.
3. that which is enameled; as, this vase is a choice *enamel*.
4. a lacquer or varnish for leather, cardboard, paper, etc., usually applied with the aid of heat.
5. the smooth, hard substance which covers the crown of a tooth, overlying the dentine.
6. a form of cosmetic coating for the skin of the face.
7. liquid nail polish that produces a smooth, hard, glossy surface.

en·am′el·ăr, en·am′el·lăr, *a.* consisting of enamel; resembling enamel; smooth; glossy.

en·am′el cell, one of the cells of the enamel of the teeth.

en·am′el·ẽr, en·am′el·lẽr, *n.* one who or that which enamels.

en·am′el·ing, *n.* the act or art of laying on enamels.

en·am′el·ist, *n.* one who enamels.

en·am′el ọr′găn, in a developing tooth, the layer of enamel cells which, with its adjacent tissues, forms a cap over the dentine.

en·am′el pāint′ing, painting done with enamel colors and subjected to intense heat for the purpose of fixing it.

en·am′el·wāre, *n.* kitchen utensils, etc. made of enameled metal.

en·am′ŏr, en·am′oŭr, *v.t.* [OFr. *enamourer, enamorer*; LL. *inamorari*, to be in love; L. *in*, in, and *amor*, love.] to fill with love and desire; to charm; to captivate; as, to be *enamoured* of a lady; to be *enamoured* with books or science.

Syn.—captivate, fascinate, enslave, charm, endear, bewitch, enchain.

en·am′ŏr·ment, en·am′oŭr·ment, *n.* the state of being enamored.

en·an·thē′mȧ, *n.* [Gr. *en*, in, and *anthēma*, an eruption.] in medicine, an eruption on a mucous membrane: distinguished from *exanthema*, an eruption of the skin.

en·an·them′ȧ·tous, *a.* relating to enanthema.

ē·nan·thyl′iç, *a.* same as *oenanthylic*.

e·nan·ti·ō-, [from Gr. *enantios*, opposite.] a combining form meaning *opposite*, as in *enantio*pathic.

e·nan″ti·ō·mọr′phiç, *a.* same as *enantiomorphous*.

e·nan″ti·ō·mọr′phous, *a.* [*enantio-*, and Gr. *morphē*, form.] in crystallography, related to each other as the right hand to the left: said of certain hemihedral crystals.

e·nan″ti·ō·path′iç, *a.* in medicine, serving to bring about an opposite pathological condition.

e·nan·ti·op′ȧ·thy, *n.* [*enantio-*, and Gr. *-patheia*, from *pathos*, feeling, affection.] allopathy: opposed to homeopathy.

e·nan·ti·ō′sis, *n.* [Gr. *enantiōsis*, contradiction, opposition, from *enantios*, opposite, contrary; *en*, in, and *antios*, opposite, from *anti*, against.] in rhetoric, a figure of speech by which what is meant to be conveyed in the affirmative is stated in the negative, and vice versa; as, he didn't drink it—oh no! He is a wonderfully good man—oh yes!

en·ärch′, *v.t.*, to arch. [Obs.]

en·ärched′ (-ärcht′), *a.* in heraldry, combined with or supported by an arch; arched.

CHEVRON ENARCHED

en·är′ġīte, *n.* [Gr. *enargēs*, visible, distinct; *en*, in, and *argos*, bright, and *-ite*.] an iron-black or grayish-black mineral, orthorhombic in crystallization, composed chiefly of copper, arsenic, and sulfur, but usually containing a little antimony and zinc, and sometimes silver.

en·ärme′, *n.* [OFr., from *enarmer*, to provide with straps.] the strap for fastening a shield to the arm.

en·ar·rā′tion, *n.* [L. *enarratio*, from *enarrare*, to relate in detail.] recital; relation; account; exposition. [Obs.]

en ar·rière′ (äṅ nȧ-ryãr′), [Fr.] 1. in the rear; behind.
2. in arrears.

en·är·thrō′di·ȧ, *n.* same as *enarthrosis*.

en·är·thrō′di·ăl, *a.* pertaining to enarthrosis.

en·är·thrō′sis, *n.* [Gr. *enarthrōsis*, from *enarthros*, jointed; *en*, in, and *arthron*, a joint.] in anatomy, a ball-and-socket joint; a joint which consists in the insertion of the round end of a bone in the cuplike cavity of another, forming a joint movable in every direction.

ē·nas′cent, *a.* [L. *enascens* (*-entis*), ppr. of *enasci*, to spring up, arise; *e-*, out, and *nasci*, to be born.] coming into existence; incipient. [Obs.]

ē·nȧ·tā′tion, *n.* [from L. *enatatus*, pp. of *enatare*, to swim out; *e-*, out, and *natare*, to swim.] a swimming out; escape by swimming. [Obs.]

ē·nāte′, *a.* 1. growing out.
2. related through the mother.

ē·nā′tion, *n.* [from L. *enatus*, pp. of *enasci*, to spring up.]
1. in botany, an abnormal growth of an organ or of an excrescence upon any part of a plant.
2. maternal relationship.

ē·naun′tẽr, *conj.* [for ME. *in aunter*, peradventure.] lest that. [Obs.]

en a·vant′ (äṅ nȧ-väṅ′), [Fr.] forward; onward: used chiefly as a command.

ē·nav′i·gāte, *v.t.* [L. *enavigatus*, pp. of *enavigare*, to sail out.] to sail out or over. [Obs.]

en·bībe′, *v.t.* to imbibe. [Obs.]

en bloc (*or Fr.* oṅ blok), [Fr.] in block; in a lump; as a whole; all together; as, the tickets were sold *en bloc*.

en·cae′ni·ȧ, *n.* [ME. *encennia*; L.; Gr. *enkainia*, from *en-*, in, and *kainos*, new.]
1. an anniversary festival commemorating the founding of a city, church, etc.
2. [E—] in England, the annual ceremony commemorating the founding of Oxford University.

en·çāġe′, *v.t.*; encaged, *pt., pp.*; encaging, *ppr.* [Fr. *encager*; *en-*, in, and *cage*, a cage.] to shut up or confine in a cage, to coop: also written *incage*.

en·çal′en·dăr, *v.t.*; encalendared, *pt., pp.*; encalendaring, *ppr.* to register in a calendar, as the saints of the Roman Catholic Church.

en·çamp′, *v.i.*; encamped (-kampt′), *pt., pp.*; encamping, *ppr.* to make, and stay in, a camp.

en·çamp′, *v.t.* 1. to form into a camp; to make into a camp.
2. to put in a camp.

Bid him *encamp* his soldiers. —Shak.

en·çamp′ment, *n.* 1. an encamping or being encamped.
2. a camp or camp site.

en·çañ′kẽr, *v.t.* to corrode; to canker. [Rare.]

en·çap′sū·lāte, *v.t.*; encapsulated, *pt., pp.*; encapsulating, *ppr.* to enclose in a capsule.

en·çap·sū·lā′tion, *n.* the act of enclosing in a capsule.

en·çap′sūle, *v.t.* same as *encapsulate*.

en·çär′nȧl·ize, *v.t.*; encarnalized, *pt., pp.*; encarnalizing, *ppr.* to make carnal; to carnalize; also, to incarnate.

en·çär′pi·um, *n.*; *pl.* **en·çär′pi·ȧ,** [Gr. *enkarpios*, containing seed; *en*, in, and *karpos*, fruit.] a sporophore.

en·çär′pus, *n.* [Gr. *enkarpos*, containing fruit; *en*, in, and *karpos*, fruit.] in architecture, a festoonlike ornament, bearing fruit, flowers, leaves, etc.

en·çāse′, *v.t.* 1. to cover completely; to enclose.
2. to put into a case or cases.
Also spelled *incase*.

en·çāse′ment, *n.* same as *incasement*.

en·çash′, *v.t.*; encashed, *pt., pp.*; encashing, *ppr.* to cash; to convert into cash, as a note, draft, etc. [Brit.]

en·çash′ment, *n.* the payment in cash of a note, draft, etc.; the act of encashing. [Brit.]

en cas′se·rōle (*or Fr.* äṅ kȧs-rọl′), [Fr.] (baked and served) in a casserole.

en·çau′mȧ, *n.* [Gr. *enkauma*, from *enkaiein*, to burn in; *en*, in, and *kaiein*, to burn.] a mark left upon the skin by a burn; also, an ulcerous condition of the cornea.

en·çaus′tiç, *a.* [L. *encausticus*; Gr. *enkaustikos*, from *enkaustos*, burnt in; from *enkaiein*, to burn in.] burnt in; done by a process of burning in; prepared by heat; as, *encaustic* tile.
encaustic painting; a kind of painting in which, by heating or burning in wax, the colors are rendered permanent.
encaustic tile; a tile made of clay and stamped in relief, decorated, glazed, and burned to hardness: much used in the ornamentation of walls and pavements.

en·çaus′tiç, *n.* a method of painting or decorating in which colors in wax are fused with hot irons.

en·çāve′, *v.t.*; encaved, *pt., pp.*; encaving, *ppr.* to hide in a cave or recess: also written *incave*.

-ence, [from Fr. *-ence*, L. *-entia*.] a suffix used in the formation of abstract nouns corresponding to adjectives ending in *-ent*, and signifying *action, state, quality*, or *that which relates to the action* or *state*, as in emergence, diligence, excell*ence*.

eṅ·ceinte′ (oṅ-saṅt′), *n.* [Fr., from *enceinte*, pp. of *enceindre*, from L. *incingere*, to gird about, surround.] in fortification, enclosure; the wall or rampart which surrounds a place, sometimes composed of bastions and curtains; the enclosure of a town or of a convent, castle, or cathedral; also, the place so enclosed.

eṅ·ceinte′ (oṅ-saṅt′), *a.* pregnant; with child.

En·cel′ȧ·dus, *n.* [L., Gr. *Enkelados*.] in Greek mythology, a giant with a hundred arms, who fought against the gods: he was killed by Zeus and buried beneath Mt. Etna.

en·cense′, *v.t.* and *v.i.* to incense. [Obs.]

en·ce·phal-, see *encephalo-*.

en·ceph·ȧ·lal′gi·ȧ, *n.* [*encephal-*, and Gr. *algos*, pain.] a pain in the head.

en·ce·phal′iç, *a.* of or pertaining to the brain.

en·ceph·ȧ·lit′iç, *a.* pertaining to or afflicted with encephalitis.

en·ceph·ȧ·li′tis, *n.* [Gr. *enkephalos*, the brain, and *-itis*.] inflammation of the brain.

en″ceph·ȧ·li′tis le·thär′gi·çȧ, sleeping sickness.

en·ceph·ȧ·lō-, [from Gr. *enkephalos*, the brain.] a combining form used in anatomy and medicine, meaning *of* or *related to the brain*, as in *encephalo*coele: also, before a vowel, *encephal-*, as in *encephal*itis.

en·ceph′ȧ·lō·cēle, *n.* [*encephalo-*, and Gr. *kēlē*, a tumor.] hernia of the brain.

en·ceph′ȧ·lō·coele (-sēl), *n.* [*encephalo-*, and Gr. *koilos*, hollow.] the cavity within the cranium.

en·ceph′ȧ·lō·gràph″, *n.* an X-ray photograph of the brain.

en·ceph′ȧ·loid, *a.* [*encephalo-*, and Gr. *eidos*, form.] resembling brain tissue.
encephaloid cancer, a soft, malignant cancer which in form, consistency, and appearance resembles the matter of the brain.

en·ceph′ȧ·loid, *n.* soft carcinoma.

en·ceph·ȧ·lol′ō·ġy, *n.* [*encephalo-*, and Gr. *-logia*, from *legein*, to speak.] the science of the brain.

en·ceph·ȧ·lō′mȧ, *n.*; *pl.* **en·ceph·ȧ·lō′mȧ·tȧ, en·ceph·ȧ·lō′mȧṣ,** 1. a tumor of the brain.
2. a hernia of the brain.

en·ceph′ȧ·lon, *n.*; *pl.* **en·ceph′ȧ·lȧ,** [Gr. *enkephalos*, the brain, properly an adj., within the head; *en*, in, and *kephalē*, head.] the brain.

en·ceph″ȧ·lō·path′i·ȧ, *n.* [*encephalo-*, and Gr. *pathos*, suffering.] any disease of the brain.

en·ceph·ȧ·lop′ȧ·thy, *n.* same as *encephalopathia*.

en·ceph′ȧ·los, *n.* same as *encephalon*.

en·ceph·ȧ·lot′ō·my, *n.* [*encephalo-*, and Gr. *tomē*, a cutting.] dissection of the brain.

en·ceph′ȧ·lous, *a.* [Gr. *enkephalos*, within the head; *en*, in, and *kephalē*, head.] having a head: applied to certain mollusks.

en·chāin′, *v.t.*; enchained, *pt., pp.*; enchaining, *ppr.* [OFr. *enchainer*; Pr. *encadenar*; It. *incatenare*, to enchain; from L. *in*, in, and *catenare*, to chain; *catena*, a chain.]
1. to fasten with a chain; to bind or hold with chains.
2. to hold fast; to captivate; as, to *enchain* the attention.
3. to link together; to connect. [Obs.]

en·chāin′ment, *n.* the act of enchaining or state of being enchained.

en·chāir′, *v.t.*; enchaired, *pt., pp.*; enchairing, *ppr.* to seat in a chair.

en·chan′nel, *v.t.*; enchanneled, *pt., pp.*; enchanneling, *ppr.* to cause to flow in a channel; as, to *enchannel* the stagnant waters of a marsh.

en·chȧnt′, *v.t.*; enchanted, *pt., pp.*; enchanting, *ppr.* [OFr. *enchanter*, *encanter*; Pr. *encantar*; It. *incantare*; L. *incantare*, to bewitch, enchant, to mutter in a magic formula; *in*, in, and *cantare*, to sing.]
1. to cast a spell over, as by magic; to bewitch.

And now about the caldron sing,
Like elves and fairies in a ring,
Enchanting all that you put in. —Shak.

2. to delight in the highest degree; to charm; to entrance; as, the description *enchants* me; we were *enchanted* with the music.
Syn.—charm, fascinate, bewitch, entrance, captivate, enrapture, ravish.

en·chȧnt′ed, *a.* 1. bewitched; charmed; fascinated.
2. invested with magical powers.

en·chȧnt′ẽr, *n.* 1. one who enchants; a sorcerer or magician; one who practices enchantment.
2. one who charms or delights.
enchanter's nightshade; any plant of the genus *Circæa*, found in damp, shady woods in the Northern Hemisphere.

en·chȧnt′ing, *a.* 1. charming; irresistibly attractive; as, an *enchanting* face; *enchanting* music.
2. bewitching; fascinating.

en·chȧnt′ing·ly, *adv.* in a charming manner; delightfully.

en·chȧnt′ment, *n.* 1. the act of casting a spell over; the use of magic to charm.
2. the state of being under the influence of a magic spell or charm.
3. a magic spell or charm.
4. something that charms or delights greatly.
5. great delight or pleasure.
Syn.—magic, spell, witchery, fascination, charm, captivation, allurement, incantation, sorcery.

en·chȧnt′ress, *n.* 1. a sorceress; a woman who uses magic arts or spells.
2. a woman who fascinates or charms.

en·chärġe′, *n.* an injunction; a charge. [Obs.]

en·chärġe′, *v.t.* to give in charge or trust. [Rare.]

en·chāse′, *v.t.*; enchased (-chāst′), *pt., pp*; enchasing, *ppr.* [Fr. *enchâsser*, to enchase; *en-*, in, and *châsse*, a frame.]
1. to encase or enclose so as to be held fast, but not concealed; to place in a setting.
2. to adorn by embossed work; to enrich or beautify by some design or figure in low relief, as a watchcase.
3. to engrave or carve (designs, etc.).

en·chās′ẽr, *n.* one who enchases.

en·chās′ten (-chās′n), *v.t.* to chasten; to chastise. [Rare.]

en·chē′ṣọn, en·chēa′ṣọn, *n.* [ME. *encheson*, *ancheson*, from OFr. *achaison*, from L. *occasio*, occasion, cause, from *incidere*, to happen, chance.] cause; occasion. [Obs.]

en·chest′, *v.t.* to put into a chest. [Obs.]

en·chi·lä′dä, *n.* [Sp., from *en-*, in, and *chile*, chili, and *-ada*, -ade.] a Mexican dish flavored with chili.

eṅ·chī·rid′i·ŏn, *n.* [LL., from Gr. *encheiridion*, a handbook, neut. of *encheiridios*, in the hand; *en*, in, and *cheir*, hand.] a manual; a handbook.

Eṅ·chō′dus, *n.* [Gr. *enchos*, a spear, and *odous*, a tooth.] a genus of scomberoid fossil fishes found in the chalk formation: so called from their spear-shaped teeth.

eṅ·ċhon·drō′mȧ, *n.*; *pl.* **eṅ·ċhon·drō′mȧ·tȧ, eṅ·ċhon·drō′mȧṣ,** [Gr. *en*, in, and *chondros*, a cartilage, and *-oma*.] a cartilaginous tumor.

eṅ·ċhon·drom′ȧ·tous, *a.* 1. of or like an enchondroma.
2. having an enchondroma.

eṅ·ċhō′ri·ăl, eṅ·ċhor′iç, *a.* [LL. *enchorius*; Gr. *enchorios*, in or belonging to the country; *en*, in, and *chōra*, country.] belonging to or used in a country; native; common: used especially to designate the popular, or demotic, writing of ancient Egypt.

eṅ·ċhy·lē′mȧ, *n.* [Gr. *enchein*, to pour in (*en*, in, and root *chy-*, to pour), and *lemma*, a thing received.] a fluid substance filling the cell body and the nucleus.

eṅ·ċhym′ȧ·tous, *a.* distended by infusion: applied to glandular epithelial cells.

en·cī′nȧ, *n.* [Sp., from LL. *ilicina*, holm oak, from L. *ilex*, kind of oak.] the live oak, especially the California live oak.

en·ciṅç′tūre, *n.* an encircling band or belt; a cincture.

en·ciṅç′tūre, *v.t.*; encinctured, *pt., pp.*; encincturing, *ppr.* to surround with or as with a girdle or belt; to encompass; as, the lake is *encinctured* by a dense forest.

en·cin′dẽred, *a.* burned to cinders.

en·cīr′çle, *v.t.*; encircled, *pt., pp.*; encircling, *ppr.* 1. to form a circle about; to enclose or surround; as, luminous rings *encircle* Saturn.
2. to move in a circle around; as, the army *encircled* the city.

en·cīr′çle·ment, *n.* an encircling or being encircled.

en·cīr′çlet, *n.* a small circle; a ring. [Obs.]

en·çlasp′, *v.t.*; enclasped, *pt., pp.*; enclasping, *ppr.* to clasp; to embrace.

en′çlāve (*or Fr. pron.* oṅ-kläv′), *n.* [Fr., from *enclaver*, to enclose.] foreign territory surrounded by a specified country; as, East Prussia was an *enclave* of Poland.

en·çlāve′, *v.t.*; enclaved, *pt., pp.*; enclaving, *ppr.* [ME. *enclaven*; OFr. *enclaver*, to enclose, lock in; LL. *inclavare*; L. *in*, and *clavis*, a key.] to surround or enclose (a place or country) with the territories of another country.

en·çlāve′ment, *n.* the condition of being an enclave.

en·çlit′iç, en·çlit′iç·ăl, *a.* [LL. *encliticus*; Gr. *enklitikos*, enclitic, leaning on, from *enklinein*, to lean toward, incline; *en*, in, and *klinein*, to lean.] in grammar, dependent for its stress on the preceding word: said of a word that has lost its stress in combination (e.g., *man* in lay*man*).

en·çlit′iç, *n.* in grammar, an enclitic word or particle.

en·çlit′iç·ăl·ly, *adv.* in an enclitic manner.

en·çlois′tẽr, *v.t.*; encloistered, *pt., pp.*; encloistering, *ppr.* [OFr. *enclostrer*, from *en-*, in, and *cloistrer*, to enclose, from *cloistre*, an enclosure.] to shut up, as in a cloister; to cloister; to immure. [Obs.]

en·çlōṣe′, *v.t.*; enclosed, *pt., pp.*; enclosing, *ppr.* [ME. *enclosen*; OFr. *enclos*, pp. of *enclore*, to enclose; L. *inclusus*, pp. of *includere*, to enclose; *in*, in, and *claudere*, to shut.]
1. to surround; to shut in; to hem in; to fence in; to confine on all sides; as, to *enclose* a field with a fence.
2. to put into a receptacle.
3. to insert in an envelope, wrapper, etc. together with a letter.
4. to contain.
Also spelled *inclose*.

en·çlō′ṣūre (-zhūr), *n.* [OFr., from *enclos*, pp. of *enclore*, to enclose; and *-ure*.]
1. an enclosing or being enclosed.
2. something that encloses, as a fence, wall, etc.
3. something enclosed; specifically, (a) an enclosed place or area; (b) a document, money, etc. enclosed with a letter.
Also spelled *inclosure*.

en·çlōthe′, *v.t.*; enclothed *or* enclad, *pt., pp.*; enclothing, *ppr.* to clothe.

en·çloud′, *v.t.*; enclouded, *pt., pp.*; enclouding, *ppr.* to obscure with a cloud or clouds; to darken.

en·çō·lụre′ (oṅ-kō-lụr′), *n.* [Fr. *encolure*, the neck and shoulders.] a horse's mane.

en·çō′mi·ast, *n.* [Gr. *enkōmiastēs*, from *enkōmiazein*, to praise, from *enkōmion*, a hymn in honor of a victor, a song of praise.] one who praises another; a panegyrist; one who utters or writes commendations or encomiums.

en·çō·mi·as′tiç, en·çō·mi·as′tiç·ăl, *a.* 1. of an encomiast.
2. of or like an encomium; eulogistic.

en·çō·mi·as′tiç·ăl·ly, *adv.* in an encomiastic manner.

en·çō′mi·um, *n.*; *pl.* **en·çō′mi·umṣ, en·çō′-**

mi·ȧ, [L. *encomium*; Gr. *enkōmion*, a hymn in honor of a victor, a song of praise; neut. of *enkōmios*; *en*, in, and *kōmos*, a revel.] a formal expression of high praise; panegyric; eulogy; elaborate commendation; as, men are quite as willing to receive as to bestow *encomiums*.

Syn.—eulogy, panegyric, praise, laudation.

en·cŏm′pȧss, *v.t.*; encompassed (-păst), *pt.*, *pp.*; encompassing, *ppr.* 1. to encircle; to surround; as, a ring *encompasses* the finger.

2. to contain; to include.

3. to go or sail round; as, Drake *encompassed* the globe. [Obs.]

Syn.—encircle, enclose, surround, include, environ, invest, hem in, shut up.

en·cŏm′pȧss·ment, *n.* an encompassing or being encompassed.

eṅ′çōre (oṅ′kōr), *interj.* [Fr. *encore*; It. *ancora*, yet, still, again, from L. *in hanc horam*, to this hour.] again; once more: used by the auditors and spectators of plays and other performances when they call for a repetition of a particular part.

eṅ′çōre (oṅ′kōr), *n.* 1. a demand by the audience, shown by continued applause, for the repetition of a piece of music, etc., or for further performance or another appearance of the performer or performers.

2. the repetition, further performance, etc. in answer to such a demand.

3. the piece of music, etc. performed in answer to such a demand.

4. the performance of something added to the regular program.

eṅ·çōre′ (oṅ-kōr′), *v.t.*; encored, *pt.*, *pp.*; encoring, *ppr.* to call for a repetition of, as a song; to call for the return of, as a singer.

en·çoun′tẽr, *v.t.*; encountered, *pt.*, *pp.*; encountering, *ppr.* [ME. *encontren*; OFr. *encontrer*, from L. *in*, in, and *contra*, against.]

1. to meet face to face; particularly, to meet suddenly or unexpectedly.

2. to meet in opposition or in a hostile manner; to rush against in conflict; to engage with in battle; as, two armies *encounter* each other.

3. to come upon; to light upon; to meet with; as, to *encounter* obstacles.

4. to oppose; to oppugn; to go counter to; to contest. [Obs.]

en·çoun′tẽr, *v.i.* 1. to meet face to face; to meet unexpectedly.

2. to meet in opposition; to come together in combat; to fight; to conflict.

If thou *encounter* with the boar.—Shak.

3. to meet in debate. [Obs.]

en·çoun′tẽr, *n.* 1. a meeting, particularly a sudden or accidental meeting of two or more persons or bodies.

To shun the *encounter* of the vulgar crowd.
—Pope.

2. a meeting in contest; a single combat; a fight; a conflict; a skirmish; a battle; specifically, a fight between a small number of men, or an accidental meeting and fighting of detachments, rather than a set battle or general engagement.

3. in physics, the mutual approach of the rapidly moving molecules of a gaseous body, at the point of their sudden deflection: so called in the kinetic theory of gases.

Syn.—attack, assault, combat, engagement, meeting, onset.

en·çoun′tẽr, *a.* designating or of a small group that meets for a kind of therapy in personal interrelations, involving a release of inhibitions, an open exchange of intimate feelings, etc.

en·çoun′tẽr·ẽr, *n.* 1. one who encounters; an opponent; an antagonist.

2. one who seeks encounters; one who is ready to accost another.

O, these *encounterers*, so glib of tongue.
—Shak.

en·çour′ăġe, *v.t.*; encouraged, *pt.*, *pp.*; encouraging, *ppr.* [OFr. *encouragier*, *encourager*, to encourage; *en*, in, and *courage*, courage, valor.]

1. to give courage to; to give confidence to; to inspire with courage, spirit, or strength of mind; to embolden; to animate; to incite.

2. to help; to give support to; to be favorable to; to foster.

Syn.—cheer, urge, impel, stimulate, instigate, comfort, promote, advance, forward.

en·çour′ăġe·ment, *n.* [OFr. *encoragement*, encouragement, from *encoragier*, *encourager*, to encourage.]

1. an encouraging or being encouraged.

2. that which encourages.

en·çour′ăġ·ẽr, *n.* one who or that which encourages, incites, or stimulates to action; one who supplies incitements, either by counsel, reward, or means of execution.

The pope is a master of polite learning and a great *encourager* of arts. —Addison.

en·çour′ăġ·ing, *a.* 1. inspiring with hope and confidence; exciting courage.

2. furnishing ground to hope for success; as, an *encouraging* prospect.

Syn.—cheering, animating, emboldening.

en·çour′ăġ·ing çard, in bridge, a card of higher value than necessary, played to a lead by one's partner to encourage repetition of a lead in the same suit as the one being played.

en·çour′ăġ·ing·ly, *adv.* in a manner to give courage or hope of success.

en·cowl′, *v.t.* to invest with a cowl, as a monk.

en·crā′dle, *v.t.* to lay in a cradle.

En′crȧ·tīte, *n.* [LL. *Encratitæ*; Gr. *enkratitai*, pl. of *enkratitēs*, self-disciplined, being in possession of power; *en*, in. and *kratos*, power.] in early church history, one of a sect that abjured marriage and the use of wine and meat: also called *Continent*.

en·crēase′, *v.t.* and *v.i.* same as *increase*.

en·crim′sŏn, *v.t.* to make crimson.

en′cri·năl, en·crin′iç, *a.* relating to encrinites; containing encrinites, as certain kinds of limestone.

en·crin′i·tăl, *a.* same as *incrinal*.

en′cri·nīte, *n.* [Gr. *en*, in, and *krinon*, a lily.] in paleontology, (a) a fossil crinoid, a spiny sea invertebrate; (b) occasionally, any crinoid.

en·cri·nit′iç, en·cri·nit′iç·ăl, *a.* same as *encrinal*.

En′cri·nus, *n.* [Gr. *en*, in, and *krinon*, a lily.]

1. a genus of fossil crinoids.

2. [e–] any encrinite.

en·crisped′ (-krispt′), *a.* curled; formed in curls. [Rare.]

en·crōach′, *v.i.*; encroached (-krōcht′), *pt.*, *pp.*; encroaching, *ppr.* [ME. *encrochen*; OFr. *encrochier*, *encrocher*, *encrocier*, to seize upon, to take; *en*, in, and *croc*, a hook.]

1. to trespass or intrude (*on* or *upon* the rights, property, etc. of another).

2. to advance beyond the proper, original, or customary limits; to make inroads (*on* or *upon*).

Syn.—infringe, trespass, invade, intrude.

en·crōach′, *n.* encroachment. [Obs.]

en·crōach′ẽr, *n.* one who or that which encroaches; one who lessens or limits an object, as a right or privilege, by narrowing its boundaries.

en·crōach′ing·ly, *adv.* by way of encroachment.

en·crōach′ment, *n.* 1. an encroaching.

2. something gained by encroaching.

en·crust′, *v.t.* 1. to cover or line with a crust.

2. to decorate richly and heavily, as with jewels.

en·crust′, *v.i.* to form, or form into, a crust.

en·crust′ment, *n.* incrustation.

en·cuï·rȧssed′ (-kwē-răst′), *a.* in zoology, having a covering like a cuirass; cuirassed; loricate.

en·cum′bẽr, *v.t.*; encumbered, *pt.*, *pp.*; encumbering, *ppr.* [ME. *encombren*; OFr. *encombrer*; *en-*, in, and *combrer*, to hinder, from LL. *cumbrus*, a heap, from L. *cumulus*, a hill.]

1. to hold back the motion or action of, as with a burden; hinder; hamper.

2. to load or fill in such a way as to obstruct: block up; obstruct.

3. to burden; to load or weigh down, as with claims, debts, etc.

Also spelled *incumber*.

en·cum′bẽr·ing·ly, *adv.* in a manner to encumber or impede.

en·cum′bẽr·ment, *n.* the act of encumbering; obstruction. [Rare.]

en·cum′brănce, *n.* [OFr. *encombrance*, from *encombrer*, to encumber.]

1. a load; anything that impedes action, or renders it difficult and laborious; a hindrance; an obstruction; an impediment.

2. in law, a lien or claim on an estate; a legal claim on an estate, for the discharge of which the estate is liable.

3. a family charge; a dependent; particularly, a child or children; as, a widow without *encumbrances*. [Rare.]

Also spelled *incumbrance*.

Syn.—clog, burden, hindrance, impediment, load.

en·cum′brăn·cẽr, *n.* in law, one who has an encumbrance or a legal claim on an estate: also spelled *incumbrancer*.

en·cŭr′tain (-tin), *v.t.* to enclose or drape with curtains or as with curtains.

-en·cy, [L. *-entia*.] a suffix equivalent to *-ence*, used to form abstract nouns corresponding to adjectives ending in *-ent*. It means *act*, *fact*, *quality*, *state*, *result*, or *degree*, as in depend*ency*, emerg*ency*, effici*ency*.

en·cyç′li·căl, en·cyç′liç, *a.* [L. *encyclios*; Gr. *enkyklios*, in a circle, general, common; *en*, in, and *kyklos*, a circle.] for general circulation.

en·cyç′li·căl, en·cyç′liç, *n.* in the Roman Catholic Church, a letter sent by the Pope to the clergy, having to do with church matters.

en·cȳ·clō·pē′di·ȧ, en·cȳ·clō·pae′di·ȧ, *n.* [Gr. *enkyklopaideia*, for *enkyklios paideia*, instruction in the circle of the arts and sciences; *enkyklios*, in a circle, general, and *paideia*, education, from *paideuein*, to educate, bring up a child, from *pais*, *paidos*, a child.]

1. the circle of arts and sciences; a general system of instruction or knowledge. [Rare.]

2. a book or set of books giving information on all branches of knowledge, generally in articles alphabetically arranged.

3. a similar work giving information on one field of knowledge.

en·cȳ″clō·pē·dī′ȧ·căl, en·cȳ·clō·pae·dī′ȧ·căl, *a.* same as *encyclopedic*.

en·cȳ·clō·pē′di·ăn, en·cȳ·clō·pae′di·ăn, *a.* same as *encyclopedic*.

en·cȳ·clō·pē′diç, en·cȳ·clō·pae′diç, *a.* 1. relating to or resembling an encyclopedia.

2. comprehending or treating of a wide range of subjects; comprehensive in scope.

en·cȳ·clō·pē′diç·ăl, en·cȳ·clō·pae′diç·ăl, *a.* same as *encyclopedic*.

en·cȳ·clō·pē′dişm, en·cȳ·clō·pae′dişm, *n.*

1. the art or act of writing or compiling encyclopedias; the possession of broad and varied knowledge; extensive learning.

2. [E–] the doctrines or work of the French Encyclopedists.

en·cȳ·clō·pē′dist, en·cȳ·clō·pae′dist, *n.* 1. the compiler of an encyclopedia or one who assists in such compilation.

2. one whose knowledge includes a great variety of subjects.

3. [E–] in French history, one of the collaborators in the French Encyclopedia, published in the latter half of the eighteenth century. They were the chief exponents of the advanced ideas of their period.

en·cyst′, *v.t.* and *v.i.* encysted, *pt.*, *pp.*; encysting, *ppr.* to enclose or become enclosed in a cyst, capsule, or sac.

en·cys·tā′tion, *n.* same as *encystment*.

en·cyst′ed, *a.* enclosed in a cyst or vesicle; as, an *encysted* tumor.

en·cyst′ment, *n.* the act or process of encysting or the state of being encysted.

end, *n.* [ME. *ende*, *eende*; AS. *ende*; D. *einde*, *eind*; O.H.G. *enti*; G. *ende*; Ice. *endir*, *endi*; Sw. *ände*; Goth. *andeis*; Sans. *anta*, end, limit, border.]

1. a limit or limiting part; boundary; point of beginning or stopping.

2. the last part of anything; final point; finish; completion; conclusion.

3. the part at, toward, or near either of the extremities of anything; tip.

4. consequence; issue; result; outcome; upshot.

The *end* of those things is death.
—Rom. vi. 21.

5. close of life; death; decease; destruction; also, the cause or manner of death; a destroyer.

Unblamed through life, lamented in thy *end*. —Pope.

And award
Either of you to be the other's *end*.—Shak.

6. a fragment or broken piece; a scrap; that which is left; as, candle *ends*.

7. the ultimate point or thing at which one aims or directs his views; the object intended to be reached or accomplished by any action or scheme; purpose; scope; aim; drift; as, private *ends*, public *ends*.

The *end* of all is an action, not a thought, though it were of the noblest.—Carlyle.

8. in spinning, a loose, untwisted ribbon of cotton or wool; a sliver.

9. the reason for being; final cause.

10. in football, a player at either end of the line of scrimmage; also, the position played by him; as, right *end*, left *end*.

an end; on end; upright; erect; as, his hair stands *an end*.

at loose ends; [orig. nautical, with reference to rope.] (a) in an unsettled or indefinite condition; (b) in a disorganized or confused condition.

at one's wit's end; in such a position that one does not know what further to do.

end for end; with the ends, or the position, reversed.

end on; with the end foremost; not sideways.
end to end; in a line so that the ends touch or meet.
in the end; at the end; finally.
no end; a great deal; very much or many. [Colloq.]
on end; (a) standing erect; upright; as, place the log *on end*; (b) continuously; as, he spoke for two hours *on end*.
to make an end of; (a) to finish; to stop; (b) to do away with.
to make both ends meet; (a) to keep one's expenditure within one's income; (b) to manage merely to exist on one's income.
to put an end to; to terminate or destroy.
Syn.—extremity, close, cessation, finish, sequel, termination.

end, *v.t.*; ended, *pt., pp.*; ending, *ppr.* [ME. *enden, endien*; AS. *endian*; D. *einden*; G. *enden*; Ice. *enda*, to end.]
1. to finish; to close; to conclude; to terminate; as, to *end* a controversy; to *end* a war.
On the seventh day God *ended* his work. —Gen. ii. 2.
2. to destroy; to put to death. [Obs.]
3. to complete or to be at the end of; as, that *ends* my task; the cane is *ended* by a ferrule.

end, *v.i.* 1. to come to an end; to cease; to terminate; to close; to conclude; as, the discourse *ended* with impressive words.
All's well that *ends* well. —Shak.
2. to die. [Rare.]

end'ȧ·ble, *a.* capable of being ended; terminable.

end'-ąll, *n.* 1. the end of everything.
2. that which ends everything.

en·dam'ăġe, *v.t.* to bring loss or damage to; to harm; to injure; to prejudice.
The trial hath *endamaged* thee no way. —Milton.

en·dam'ăġe·ment, *n.* damage; loss; injury.

en·dam'ni·fȳ, *v.t.* to injure; to impair; to cause loss to; to damnify. [Rare.]

en·dȧ·moe'bȧ, en·dȧ·mē'bȧ, *n.* [from *endo-*, and *amoeba*.] any of a large group of amoebas, some species of which are found as parasites in the internal organs of man and certain other animals, causing amoebic dysentery and some other diseases.

en·dān'ġẽr, *v.t.*; endangered, *pt., pp.*; endangering, *ppr.* 1. to put in hazard; to bring into danger or peril; to expose to loss or injury; as, we dread anything that *endangers* our life, our peace, or our happiness.
2. to incur the hazard of. [Obs.]
Syn.—imperil, expose, peril, jeopardize, hazard, risk.

en·dān'ġẽred spē'ciēş (-shēz), a species of animal or plant that is in danger of becoming extinct.

en·dān'ġẽr·ment, *n.* hazard; danger.

en·därk', *v.t.* to darken. [Obs.]

en·das·pid'ē·ăn, *a.* [Gr. *endon*, within, and *aspis* (*-idos*), a shield.] in ornithology, having the anterior scutellae lapped around the inner side of the tarsus, but deficient on the outer side.

end bulb, any of the bulbous end organs of sensory nerves.

en·dēar', *v.t.*; endeared, *pt., pp.*; endearing, *ppr.* 1. to make dear; to make more beloved; to bind by ties of affection and love.
2. to raise the price of. [Obs.]

en·dēar'ed·ly, *adv.* with affection; in an endearing manner; dearly. [Obs.]

en·dēar'ed·ness, *n.* the state of being endeared. [Obs.]

en·dēar'ing, *a.* making dear or more beloved.

en·dēar'ing·ly, *adv.* in an endearing or affectionate manner.

en·dēar'ment, *n.* 1. an endearing or being endeared; affection.
2. an expression of affection; a caress.
3. something that endears.

en·deav'ŏr, (-dev'), *v.i.* [ME. *endever*, from *en-*, en-, and *dever, devor*, from OFr. *deveir* (Fr. *devoir*), duty: from the use of these words in such expressions as *se mettre en deveir*, to try to do, to set about; *deveir* from L. *debere*, to owe, to be under obligation.] to try hard; to exert effort; to make an earnest attempt; to strive.

en·deav'ŏr, *v.t.* to try to achieve; to attempt. [Archaic.]

en·deav'ŏr, *n.* an earnest attempt; an effort to accomplish something.

en·deav'ŏr·ẽr, *n.* one who makes an effort or attempt.

en·deav'ŏr·ment, *n.* endeavor. [Obs.]

en·deav'our, *v.i., v.t.,* and *n.* endeavor: British spelling.

en·deç'ȧ·gon, *n.* same as *hendecagon*.

en·de·çağ'y·nous, *a.* same as *hendecagynous*.

en'dē·çāne, *n.* same as *hendecane*.

en·deç·ȧ·phyl'lous, *a.* same as *hendecaphyllous*.

en·deiç'tiç, *a.* [Gr. *endeiktikos*, from *endeiknynai*, to point out, give proof; *en*, in, and *deiknynai*, to point out.] showing; exhibiting; as, an *endeictic* dialogue, in the Platonic philosophy, is one that exhibits a specimen of skill.

en·dē'mi·ăl, *a.* endemic. [Rare.]

en·dem'iç, en·dem'iç·ăl, *a.* [Gr. *endēmios*, equal to *endēmos*, native, belonging to a people; *en*, in, and *dēmos*, the people.]
1. prevalent in or restricted to a particular nation, region, locality, or group; indigenous; as, an *endemic* plant, an *endemic* disease.
2. native; not introduced or naturalized.

en·dem'iç, *n.* a disease of an endemic nature.

en·dem'iç·ăl·ly, *adv.* in an endemic manner.

en·dem·i·ol'ō·ġy, *n.* [Gr. *endēmios*, native, belonging to the people, and *-logia*, from *legein*, to speak.] the branch of medicine dealing with endemic diseases.

en·den·i·zā'tion, *n.* the act or ceremony of naturalization. [Obs.]

en·den'īze, *v.t.* to endenizen. [Obs.]

en·den'i·zen, *v.t.* [*en-*, and *denizen*, from OFr. *denzein*, one living within.] to naturalize. [Rare.]

end'ẽr, *n.* one who or that which ends or finishes.

en·dẽr·mat'iç, *a.* same as *endermic*.

en·dẽr'miç, *a.* [Gr. *en*, in, and *derma*, the skin.] in medicine, applied to the skin and acting by absorption through it.
endermic method; the method of medical treatment in which the medicine enters the system through the skin.

en·dẽr'miç·ăl·ly, *adv.* in medicine, according to the endermic method.

en'de·ron, *n.* [Gr. *en*, in, and *deros*, the skin.] in anatomy, the dermis, or true skin, and the corresponding deep part of the mucous membrane, as distinguished from the epidermis.

en·de·ron'iç, *a.* pertaining to the enderon.

en dés·ha·bil·lé' (äṅ dā-zȧ-bē-yā'), [Fr., in undress.]
1. partly undressed.
2. dressed in a robe, negligee, etc.

end flȳ, a bobfly.

en·dī'ȧ·demed (-demd), *a.* diademed. [Rare.]

en·dīct' (-dīt'), *v.t.* to indict. [Obs.]

en·dīct'ment (-dīt'), *n.* indictment. [Obs.]

end'ing, *n.* [AS. *endung*; see *end*, v.]
1. an end; specifically, (a) the last part; finish; conclusion; (b) death.
2. in grammar, the final letter or letters added to a word or word base to make a derivative or inflectional form; as, *-ed* is the *ending* in *wanted*.

en·dīte', *v.t.* to indite. [Obs.]

en'dīte, *n.* [Gr. *endon*, within, and *-ite*.] in zoology, an appendage on the inner side of the limbs of some crustaceans.

en'dīve (*or* än'dēv), *n.* [Fr. *endive*; Sp. *endibia*; LL. *intiba*, from L. *intibus, intybus*, endive.]
1. a plant, *Cichorium endivia*, natural order *Compositæ*, with ragged, curly leaves which are used in salads, etc.; also called *escarole*.
2. a kind of chicory whose long leaves are blanched for use in salads.

end lēaf, an end paper.

end'less, *a.* 1. without end; having no end or conclusion; eternal; infinite; as, an *endless* line; *endless* bliss.
2. lasting too long; seemingly without end; incessant; continual; interminable; as, *endless* praise; *endless* clamor.
3. with the ends joined to form a closed ring that can move continuously over wheels, etc.; as, an *endless* chain.
endless screw; a screw, the thread of which gears into a wheel with skew teeth, the obliquity corresponding to the angle of pitch of the screw. It is generally used as a means of producing slow motion in the adjustments of machines, rather than for transmitting any great amount of power.

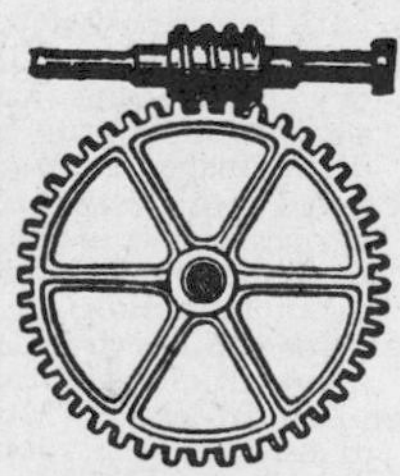
ENDLESS SCREW AND WHEEL

Syn.—boundless, unending, interminable, infinite, imperishable, eternal, unceasing, undying, unlimited, continual, uninterrupted.

end'less·ly, *adv.* in an endless manner.

end'less·ness, *n.* the quality or state of being endless.

end'lơng, *adv.* 1. lengthwise.
2. on end.

end man, 1. any man at the end of a line or row of men.
2. in a minstrel show, the performer at each end of the first row, who tells jokes with the help of the interlocutor.

end'mōst, *a.* at or nearest to the end; last; farthest; remotest.

en·dō-, end-, [from Gr. *endon*, within.] a combining form meaning *within, inside*, as in *endocrine*; *endocardium*.

en'dō·blȧst, *n.* [*endo-*, and Gr. *blastos*, a germ.] the endoderm; hypoblast.

en·dō·blas'tiç, *a.* pertaining to the endoblast.

en·dō·çär'di·ăl, en·dō·çär'di·aç, *a.* [*endo-*, and Gr. *kardia*, heart.]
1. relating to the endocardium.
2. generated within the heart; situated within the heart.

en″dō·çär·dī'tis, *n.* [*endo-*, and Gr. *kardia*, heart, and *-itis*.] inflammation of the endocardium.

en·dō·çär'di·um, *n.* the thin endothelial membrane which lines the cavities of the heart.

en'dō·çärp, *n.* [*endo-*, and Gr. *karpos*, fruit.] in botany, the inner layer of the pericarp, when its texture differs from the outer layer. It may be hard and stony, as in the plum and peach, membranous, as in the apple, or fleshy, as in the orange.

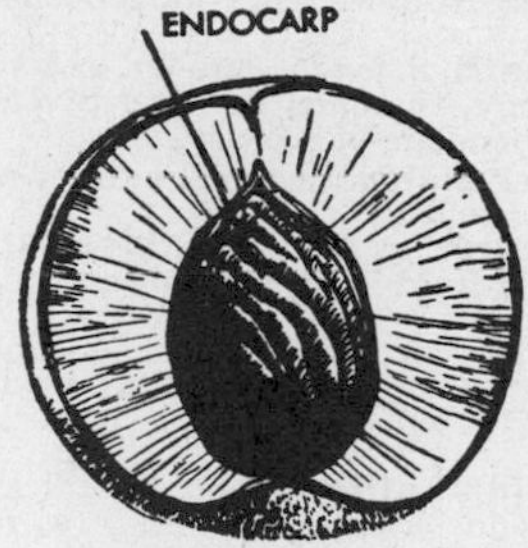

ENDOCARP OF PEACH

en·dō·çhon'drăl, *a.* [*endo-*, and Gr. *chondros*, cartilage, and *-al*.] situated or developing within cartilage.

en·dō·çhō'ri·on, *n.* [*endo-*, and Gr. *chorion*, a membrane, the chorion.] the layer of the allantois, lining the chorion.

en'dō·çhrōme, *n.* [*endo-*, and Gr. *chrōma*, color.] in botany, the coloring matter, other than green, in plant cells.

en·dō·coe'lăr (-sē'), *a.* situated on the inner wall, or visceral side, of the body cavity.

en'dō·çōne, *n.* [*endo-*, and Gr. *kōnos*, a cone.] one of the internal conical sheaths of certain cephalopods.

en·dō·çrā'ni·ăl, *a.* within the cranium; pertaining to the endocranium.

en·dō·çrā'ni·um, *n.* [*endo-*, and Gr. *kranion*, the skull.] the inner surface of the cranium.

en'dō·çrin, *n.* same as *endocrine*.

en·dō·çrī'năl, *a.* same as *endocrinous*.

en'dō·çrīne, (*or* -krin), *a.* [from *endo-*, and Gr. *krinein*, to separate.]
1. designating or of any gland producing one or more internal secretions that are carried by the blood or lymph to some part whose functions they regulate or control.
2. designating or of such a secretion.

en'dō·çrīne (*or* -krin), *n.* any endocrine gland or its secretions: the thyroid, adrenal, and pituitary glands are endocrines.

en·dō·çrin'iç, *a.* same as *endocrinous*.

en″dō·çrī·nol'ō·ġy, *n.* the science or study of the endocrine glands and the internal secretions of the body.

en·dō·çrin″ō·path'iç, *a.* relating to endocrinopathy.

en″dō·çrin·op'ȧ·thy, *n.* any disease caused by a disturbance in the function of the endocrine glands.

en·dōç'rin·ous, *a.* relating to an endocrine gland or its secretion.

en·doç'trine, *v.t.* to teach; to indoctrinate. [Obs.]

en'dō·cyst, *n.* [*endo-*, and Gr. *kystis*, a bladder.] the inner layer of the cell of a polyzoan.

en'dō·dẽrm, *n.* [*endo-*, and Gr. *derma*, skin.] the inner layer of cells of the embryo, from which is formed the lining of the digestive tract and of other internal organs; endoblast; hypoblast.

en·dō·dẽr′măl, en·dō·dẽr′miç, *a.* pertaining to the endoderm.

en·dō·dẽr′mis, *n.* in botany, a layer of cells forming a sheath around a fibrovascular bundle.

en·dō·en′zȳme, *n.* an enzyme that functions within the cell.

en·dog′ȧ·mous, en·dō·gam′iç, *a.* [*endo-*, and Gr. *gamos*, marriage.]
 1. of endogamy.
 2. practicing endogamy.

en·dog′ȧ·my, *n.* [*endo-*, and *-gamy*.] the custom of marrying only within one's own tribe or social group; inbreeding: opposed to *exogamy*.

en′dō·ġen, *n.* [*endo-*, and *-gen*: so called because the stems were formerly believed to grow from within.] any plant that grows by adding tissue irregularly throughout the stem; monocotyledon: distinguished from *exogen*.

en·dō·ġen′e·sis, *n.* same as *endogeny*.

en″dō·ġē·net′iç, *a.* endogenous.

en·doġ′e·nous, *a.* 1. developing from within; originating internally.
 2. in biology, growing or developing from or on the inside.
 3. in physiology and biochemistry, of the anabolism of cells.

en·doġ′e·nous·ly, *adv.* in biology, in an endogenous manner.

en·doġ′e·ny, *n.* [*endo-*, and *-geny*.] in biology, a growing from within; endogenous formation of cells.

en′dog·nath, *n.* [*endo-*, and Gr. *gnathos*, a jaw.] in zoology, the chief or inner division of the oral appendage of a crustacean.

en·dog′nȧ·thăl, *a.* in zoology, of or relating to the endognath.

en′dō·lymph, *n.* [*endo-*, and *lymph*.] in anatomy, the fluid in the membranous labyrinth of the ear.

en″dō·lym·phan′ġi·ăl, *a.* [*endo-*, and L. *lympha*, water, and Gr. *angeion*, a vessel.] in anatomy, situated or included in a lymphatic vessel.

en″dō·lym·phat′iç, *a.* [*endo-*, and L. *lympha*, water, and *-atic*.] in anatomy, (a) relating to or enclosing endolymph; (b) situated or included in a lymphatic vessel.

en·dō·mer′sion, *n.* see *endomersion objective* under *objective*.

en″dō·mē·trī′tis, *n.* [*endo-*, and Gr. *mētra*, womb, and *-itis*.] in medicine, an inflammatory condition of the endometrium.

en·dō·mē′tri·um, *n.* [*endo-*, and Gr. *mētra*, the womb.] in anatomy, the inner lining of the uterus.

en′dō·mọrph, *n.* [*endo-*, and Gr. *morphē*, form.] in mineralogy, a mineral, especially a crystal, enclosed within another.

en·dō·mọr′phiç, *a.* 1. of an endomorph.
 2. of or caused by endomorphism.
 3. designating or of the abdominal physical type, characterized by predominance of the structures developed from the endodermal layer of the embryo (i.e., the internal organs): distinguished from *ectomorphic*.

en·dō·mọr′phiṣm, *n.* 1. the state or fact of being endomorphic.
 2. structural change caused in an intrusive rock by the action of the surrounding rock.

en·dō·mys′i·um, *n.* [*endo-*, and Gr. *mys*, a muscle.] in anatomy, the tissue connecting muscular fibers.

en·dō·neū′ri·um, *n.* [*endo-*, and Gr. *neuron*, a nerve.] in anatomy, tissue connecting nerve fibers.

en·dō·par′ȧ·sīte, *n.* [*endo-*, and Gr. *parasitos*, a parasite.] any parasite that inhabits the internal organs of animals; hookworm, tapeworm, endamoeba, etc.

en″dō·par·ȧ·sit′iç, *a.* of or relating to endoparasites.

en·dō·path′iç, *a.* [*endo-*, and Gr. *pathos*, suffering.] in medicine, relating to diseases arising from internal causes; autopathic.

en″dō·pe·rid′i·um, *n.*; *pl.* **en″dō·pe·rid′i·ȧ,** [*endo-*, and *peridium*, from Gr. *peri*, around, and dim. *-idion*.] in botany, the inner of two peridia, as distinguished from *exoperidium*

en′dō·phragm (-fram), *n.* [*endo-*, and Gr. *phragma*, a fence.] in zoology, a horny partition in the thorax of some *Crustacea*.

en·dō·phrag′măl (-frag′), *a.* of or relating to the endophragm.

en·doph′yl·lous, *a.* [*endo-*, and Gr. *phyllon*, a leaf.] evolved from inside a leaf or sheath.

en′dō·phȳte, *n.* [*endo-*, and Gr. *phyton*, a plant.] in botany, any plant that grows within another plant.

en·dō·phyt′iç, *a.* of or pertaining to an endophyte.

en·doph′y·tous, *a.* [*endo-*, and Gr. *phyton*, a plant.] in zoology, fitted for penetrating and for living within plant tissues, as some insects and their larvae.

en′dō·plaṣm, *n.* [*endo-*, and Gr. *plasma*, a thing formed, from *plassein*, to form, mold.] in biology, the inner part of the cytoplasm of a cell: distinguished from *ectoplasm*.

en·dō·plaṣ′mȧ, *n.* same as *endoplasm*.

en·dō·plaṣ′miç, *a.* of endoplasm.

en′dō·plȧst, *n.* [*endo-*, and Gr. *plastos*, formed.] in protozoan life, a cell nucleus.

en·dō·plas′tron, *n.* same as *entoplastron*.

en·dō·plas′tūle, *n.* [*endo-*, and Gr. *plastos*, formed, molded, and dim. *-ule*.] in biology, among the higher *Protozoa* (as the amoebas), that which corresponds to the nucleolus in a metazoic cell.

en·dō·pleū′rȧ, *n.*; *pl.* **en·dō·pleū′rae,** [*endo-*, and Gr. *pleura*, rib, side.] in botany, the innermost covering of a seed.

en·dō·pleū′rīte, *n.* in zoology, among certain crustaceans, a part of the apodeme.

en·dop′ō·dīte, *n.* in zoology, the inner or principal branch of an ambulatory appendage of a crustacean.

En·dō·proç′tȧ, *n.pl.* same as *Entoprocta*.

en·dō·proç′tous, *a.* same as *entoproctous*.

end ọr′găn, any specialized structure at the peripheral end of nerve fibers having either sensory or motor functions.

en·dọr′phin, *n.* [*endo*genous and mo*rphine*.] any of several peptides secreted in the brain, that have a pain-relieving effect like that of morphine.

en·dọrs′ȧ·ble, *a.* that can be endorsed: also spelled *indorsable*.

en·dọrse′, *v.t.*; endorsed, *pt.*, *pp.*; endorsing, *ppr.* [with altered sp. after L., from ME. *endossen*; OFr. *endosser*, from ML. *indorsare*, from L. *in*, on, upon, and *dorsum*, the back.]
 1. to write on the back of (a document); specifically, (a) to sign one's name as payee on the back of (a check, money order, etc.); (b) to make (a check, etc.) payable to another person by thus signing one's name and adding "payable to the order of —" on the back.
 2. to give support or approval to; sanction; as, civic leaders have *endorsed* the housing project.
 Also spelled *indorse*.

en·dọrse′, *n.* in heraldry, a palelike subordinary much narrower than a pale.

en·dọr·see′, *n.* the person to whom a check, note, etc. is made over by endorsement.

en·dọrse′ment, *n.* 1. the act of writing on the back of a check, note, etc.
 2. something written on the back of a check, note, etc., as the signature of a payee, by which money or property is made over to someone.
 3. a change, as of coverage or beneficiary, written on or added to an insurance policy, and signed by an agent of the insurer.
 4. approval; sanction.
 Also spelled *indorsement*.

en·dọrs′ẽr, *n.* one who endorses: also spelled *indorser*.

en′dō·säṙç, *n.* [*endo-*, and Gr. *sarx*, *sarkos*, flesh.] the endoplasm of certain protozoa.

en′dō·sçōpe, *n.* [*endo-*, and Gr. *skopein*, to view.] an instrument used for examining the inside of a hollow organ of the body, as the rectum or bladder.

en·dŏs′çō·py, *n.* the examination of hollow organs of the body by means of an endoscope.

en·dō·skel′e·tăl, *a.* belonging to or associated with the endoskeleton.

en·dō·skel′e·tŏn, *n.* [*endo-*, and Gr. *skeleton*, a dry body.] the internal bony supporting structure, or true skeleton, in vertebrates: distinguished from *exoskeleton*.

en·dos·mom′e·tẽr, *n.* [*endo-*, and Gr. *ōsmos*, a thrusting, impulsion, and *metron*, a measure.] an instrument to measure the rapidity of endosmotic action.

en·dos·mō·met′riç, *a.* pertaining to measurements of endosmotic action.

en·dos·mō′sis, *n.* [Mod. L., *end-*, and *osmosis*.] in osmosis, the more rapid diffusion of the less dense fluid through the semipermeable membrane to mingle with the more dense: opposed to *exosmosis*.

en·dos·mot′iç, *a.* relating to endosmosis.

en′dō·sōme, *n.* [*endo-*, and Gr. *sōma*, body.] in zoology, the inner layer of certain sponges.

en′dō·spẽrm, *n.* [*endo-*, and Gr. *sperma*, seed.] the nourishment for the embryo, which surrounds the embryo in the seed of a plant.

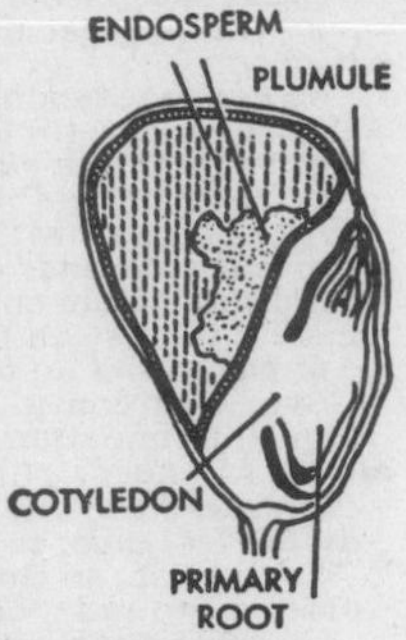

ENDOSPERM
PLUMULE
COTYLEDON
PRIMARY ROOT

ENDOSPERM (of grain of corn)

en·dō·spẽr′miç, *a.* relating to the endosperm; of the nature of the endosperm.

en′dō·spōre, *n.* [*endo-*, and Gr. *sporos*, a sowing, seed.]
 1. in bacteriology, an asexual spore formed within a special spore case.
 2. in botany, the endosporium.

en·dō·spō′ri·um, *n.*; *pl.* **en·dō·spō′ri·ȧ,** [Mod. L.; see *endo-* and *spore*.] the inner layer of the covering of a spore.

en·dō·spọr′ous, *a.* having spores contained in a spore case.

en·doss′, *v.t.* [Fr. *endosser*, to put on the back, endorse; *en*, in, and *dos*, back, from L. *dorsum*, back.] to endorse. [Obs.]

en·dos′tē·ȧ, *n.* pl. of *endosteum*.

en·dos′tē·ăl, *a.* 1. relating to endostosis or the endosteum.
 2. situated inside the bone.

en·dō·stẽr′nīte, *n.* [*endo-*, and Gr. *sternon*, the breast, chest, and *-ite*.] any of the parts of the endothorax of crustaceans and insects originating in the intersternal membrane.

en·dō·stẽr′num, *n.* [*endo-*, and Gr. *sternon*, the breast, chest.] same as *entosternum*.

en·dos′tē·um, *n.*; *pl.* **en·dos′tē·ȧ,** [Mod. L., from *end-*, and Gr. *osteon*, a bone.] the vascular connective tissue lining the marrow cavities of bones.

en·dos′tō·mȧ, *n.* [*endo-*, and Gr. *stoma*, mouth.] in zoology, a posterior plate which supports the labrum in some crustaceans.

en′dō·stōme, *n.* [*endo-*, and Gr. *stoma*, the mouth.]
 1. in botany, (a) the opening through the inner integument of an ovule; (b) the inner peristome of a moss.
 2. in zoology, same as *endostoma*.

en·dos·tō′sis, *n.* [*endo-*, and Gr. *osteon*, a bone, and *-osis*.] the formation of bone within cartilage.

en·dos′trȧ·çum, *n.* [*endo-*, and Gr. *ostrakon*, a shell.] in zoology, the inner layer of a crustacean's exoskeleton.

en′dō·stȳle, *n.* [*endo-*, and Gr. *stylos*, a pillar.] in zoology, a longitudinal fold of the endoderm projecting into the blood cavity of an ascidian.

en·dō·thē′çȧ, *n.*; *pl.* **en·dō·thē′cae,** [*endo-*, and Gr. *thēkē*, a case, chest.] the hard substance making up the lining of the visceral chamber of a coral.

en·dō·thē′çăl, *a.* of or pertaining to the endotheca.

en·dō·thē′ci·um, *n.* [*endo-*, and Gr. *thēkē*, a case, chest.] in botany, (a) a mass of cells in the center of a rudimentary capsule of a moss; (b) the interior lining of an anther cell.

en·dō·thē′li·ăl, *a.* pertaining to the endothelium.

en·dō·thē′li·oid, *a.* of or like the endothelium.

en″dō·thē·li·ō′mȧ, *n.* [*endo-*, and Gr. *thēlē*, nipple, and *ōma*, a tumor.] a tumor originating in or resembling the structure of endothelium.

en·dō·thē′li·um, *n.*; *pl.* **en·dō·thē′li·ȧ,** [Mod. L., from *endo-*, and Gr. *thēlē*, nipple.] the layer of squamous cells lining the inside of blood and lymph vessels, of the heart, and of some other closed cavities.

en·doth′e·loid, *a.* same as *endothelioid*.

en·dō·thẽr′mal, *a.* same as *endothermic*.

en·dō·thẽr′miç, *a.* [*endo-*, and Gr. *thermē*, heat, and *-ic*.] relating to or designating chemical reaction in which heat is absorbed: opposed to *exothermic*.

en·dō·thō′rax, *n.* [*endo-*, and Gr. *thōrax*, a breastplate, chest.] in zoology, the internal processes of the sternal plate in an insect or a crustacean.

en·dō·tox′in, *n.* [*endo-*, and *toxin*.] any of a group of toxic substances found in certain disease-producing bacteria and liberated by the disintegration of the bacterial cell: they harm certain tissue cells.

en·dow′, *v.t.*; endowed, *pt., pp.*; endowing, *ppr.* [ME. *endowen*; OFr. *endouer*; *en-*, in, and *douer*, to endow, from L. *dotare*, to give.]
1. to furnish with a dower. [Obs.]
2. to provide with some talent, quality, etc.; as, he was *endowed* with courage.
3. to give money or property so as to provide an income for the support of (a college, hospital, etc.); bequeath.

en·dow′ẽr, *v.t.* to endow; to enrich with a portion. [Obs.]

en·dow′ẽr, *n.* one who endows.

en·dow′ment, *n.* 1. an endowing.
2. that with which something is endowed; bequest; gift; as, the *endowments* of a church, hospital, or college.
3. that which is given or bestowed on the person or mind; gift of nature; talent; ability.
Syn.—gift, provision, benefit, benefaction, capacity, attainment, qualification.

en·dow′ment pol′i·cy, an insurance policy by which a stated amount is paid to the insured after the period of time specified in the contract, or to the beneficiaries in case the insured dies within the time specified.

En·dō·zō′ȧ, *n.pl.* [*endo-*, and Gr. *zōon*, pl. *zōa*, an animal.] same as *Entozoa*.

en·dō·zō′iç, *a.* same as *entozoic*.

end pā′pẽr, a folded sheet of paper one half of which is pasted to the inside of either cover of a book, the other half forming the first (or last) page of the book: also called *end leaf*.

end plāte, in anatomy, a kind of expansion of tissue connecting a muscle with the terminal of a motor nerve.

end plāy, in machinery, space allowed for movement endways.

end prod′uçt, the final result of any series of changes, processes, or chemical reactions.

en·drudġe′ (-druj′), *v.t.* to make a drudge or slave of. [Obs.]

end stōne, one of the jewels in a timepiece against which a pivot abuts.

end tā′ble, a small table to be placed at either end of a sofa, beside a chair, etc.

en·dūe′, *v.t.*; endued, *pt., pp.*; enduing, *ppr.* [ME. *endewen*; OFr. *enduire*; L. *inducere*, to lead in; *in-*, in, and *ducere*, to lead.]
1. to put on; clothe; cover. [Rare.]
2. to provide (*with* something); specifically, to endow (*with* qualities, talents, etc.).
Also spelled *indue*.

en·dūe′, *v.t.* [OFr. *enduire, induire*, to bring in, cover, digest.] to digest: said of birds, especially of hawks.

en·dūe′ment, *n.* endowment.

en·dūr′ȧ·ble, *a.* that can be endured; bearable.

en·dūr′ȧ·ble·ness, *n.* the state or quality of being endurable.

en·dūr′ȧ·bly, *adv.* in an endurable manner.

en·dūr′ănce, *n.* 1. an enduring.
2. the power of enduring; specifically, (a) ability to last, continue, or remain; (b) ability to stand pain, distress, fatigue, etc.; fortitude.
3. that which is endured; hardship. [Rare.]
4. duration.
Syn.—fortitude, patience, resignation, sufferance.

en·dūr′ănt, *a.* having ability to endure suffering, pain, disappointment, etc. [Rare.]

en·dūre′, *v.t.*; endured, *pt., pp.*; enduring, *ppr.* [ME. *enduren*; OFr. *endurer*, to bear, last, from L. *indurare*; *in-*, in, and *durare*, to harden, to hold out, last, from *durus*, hard.]
1. to stand (pain, fatigue, etc.); bear; undergo.
2. to put up with; tolerate.
Also spelled *indure*.

en·dūre′, *v.i.* 1. to last; continue; remain.
2. to bear pain, etc. without flinching; hold out.
Also spelled *indure*.
Syn.—bear, continue.

en·dūr′ẽr, *n.* one who or that which endures.

en·dūr′ing, *a.* 1. having the capacity for remaining or continuing; durable; not to be destroyed; as, an *enduring* monument.
2. long-suffering.

en·dūr′ing·ly, *adv.* for a long time; permanently.

en·dūr′ing·ness, *n.* the quality or state of enduring; permanence; lastingness.

end′wāyṣ, end′wīṣe, *adv.* 1. on end; erectly; in an upright position.
2. with the end forward.
3. lengthwise.
4. end to end.

en′dy·mȧ, *n.* same as *ependyma*.

en′dy·mal, *a.* same as *ependymal*.

En·dym′i·ŏn, *n.* [L.; Gr. *Endymiōn*.] in Greek legend, a beautiful young shepherd loved by Selene and caressed by her as he slept.

en′dy·sis, *n.*; *pl.* **en′dy·sēṣ,** [Gr. *endysis*, a putting on, entering into, from *endyein*, to put on, get into.] in biology, the growth of new plumage, hair, or scales: opposed to *ecdysis*.

-ene, [from L. *-enus*, adj. suffix.] a suffix used (a) to form names of certain hydrocarbons, especially those which belong to the olefin or ethylene series; as in ethyl*ene*, benz*ene*; (b) to form commercial names for some products.

Ē·nē′id, *n.* same as *Æneid*.

en′e·mȧ, *n.* [Gr. *enema*, an injection, from *enienai*, to send in; *en-*, in, and *hienai*, to send.]
1. a liquid injected into the rectum either as a purgative or a medicine; clyster.
2. the injection of such a liquid.
3. the apparatus used for this.

en′e·my, *n.*; *pl.* **en′e·mieṣ,** [ME. *enemi*; OFr. *enemi*; L. *inimicus*, unfriendly, hostile (as substantive, an enemy); *in-*, not, and *amicus*, a friend.]
1. a person who hates another, and wishes or tries to injure him; a person hostile to an idea, cause, etc.; adversary; foe.
2. (a) a nation or force hostile to another; (b) troops, fleet, ship, member, etc. of a hostile nation.
3. anything hostile or injurious.

en′e·my, *a.* 1. of an enemy; of a hostile nation.
2. hostile; opposed. [Obs.]

en′e·my āl′ien (-yen), an alien residing or interned in a country with which his own country is at war.

en·ep·i·dẽr′miç, *a.* [Gr. *en*, in, and *epidermis*, the outer skin; *epi*, upon, and *derma*, skin, and *-ic*.] in medicine, applied to or laid on the skin; as, *enepidermic* treatment.

en·ẽr·ġē′sis, *n.* [Mod. L., from Gr. *energein*, to be in action: see *energy*.] in botany, the process by which energy is liberated through catabolic action in the cell.

en·ẽr·get′iç, *a.* [Gr. *energētikos*, from *energein*, to be in action, from *energēs, energos*, working, active; *en-*, in, and *ergon*, work.] characterized by or exhibiting energy; operating with force, vigor, and effect; forcible; powerful; efficacious; as, an *energetic* man, *energetic* methods.

en·ẽr·get′iç·ăl, *a.* energetic.

en·ẽr·get′iç·ăl·ly, *adv.* in an energetic manner; with energy and effect.

en·ẽr·get′iç·ăl·ness, *n.* the quality or state of being energetic.

en·ẽr·get′içs, *n.pl.* [*construed as sing.*] the science that deals with the laws of energy.

en·ẽr′ġiç, *a.* having or exhibiting energy. [Rare.]

en′ẽr·ġīze, *v.t.*; energized, *pt., pp.*; energizing, *ppr.* to give energy to; to activate; as, to *energize* the will.

en′ẽr·ġīze, *v.i.* to act energetically; to show energy; to be active.

en′ẽr·ġī·zẽr, *n.* an agent or means of imparting or increasing energy.

en′ẽr·ġī·zing, *a.* capable of giving energy, force, or vigor.

en·ẽr·gū′men, *n.* [L. *energumenus*; Gr. *energoumenos*, ppr. pass. of *energein*, to effect, work on.]
1. a person supposedly possessed by an evil spirit; demoniac.
2. a fanatic; enthusiast.

en′ẽr·ġy, *n.*; *pl.* **en′ẽr·ġieṣ,** [LL. *energia*; Gr. *energeia*, action, operation, energy, from *energēs, energos*, active, at work; *en-*, in, and *ergon*, work.]
1. strength of expression; force of utterance; life; spirit; emphasis.
2. internal or inherent power; potential forces; capacity for vigorous action.
3. [*pl.*] such powers, especially in action; as, apply all your *energies* to the cause.
4. effectual operation; efficacy; strength or force producing the effect.
5. (a) those resources, as petroleum, coal, gas, wind, water, nuclear fuel, and sunlight, from which energy in the form of electricity, heat, etc. can be produced; (b) the available supply of such usable resources; as, an *energy* shortage.
6. in physics, the capacity for doing work and overcoming resistance: see *kinetic energy, potential energy*.
conservation of energy; see under *conservation*.
degradation of energy; see under *degradation*.
energy of rotation; in physics, the energy imparted to a body in giving it rotary motion, measurable by the work it will do in coming to rest.
Syn.—force, vigor.—With *energy* is connected the idea of activity; with *force* that of capability; with *vigor* that of health.

en′ẽr·vāte, *v.t.*; enervated, *pt., pp.*; enervating, *ppr.* [L. *enervatus*, pp. of *enervare*, to deprive of nerves or sinews, to weaken; *e-*, out, and *nervus*, a nerve, sinew.]
1. to deprive of nerve, force, or strength; to weaken physically, mentally, or morally; to render feeble.
2. to cut the nerves of; as, to *enervate* a horse. [Obs.]
Syn.—debilitate, weaken, enfeeble.

ē·nẽr′vāte, *a.* weakened; weak; without strength or force.

en·ẽr·vā′tion, *n.* [LL. *enervatio*, from *enervare*, to weaken.] an enervating or being enervated.

ē·nẽr′vā·tive, *a.* having a tendency to enervate; weakening.

ē·nẽr′vā·tŏr, *n.* that which enervates.

ē·nẽrve′, *v.t.* to weaken; to enervate. [Obs.]

ē·nẽrv′ous, *a.* lacking vigor; enervated; nerveless. [Obs.]

en·fāce′, *v.t.*; enfaced (-fāst′), *pt., pp.*; enfacing, *ppr.* to write or print on the face of (a note, check, draft, or other negotiable paper).

en·fāce′ment, *n.* something written or printed on the face of a document.

en·fam′ine, *v.t.* and *v.i.* to famish. [Obs.]

en·fam′ish, *v.t.* to famish. [Obs.]

eṅ·fȧṅts′ pẽr·dụs′ (äṅ-fäṅ′ per-dụ′), [Fr., lit., lost children.] a forlorn hope: military term, applied to troops in a hopelessly dangerous position.

eṅ·fȧṅt′ ter·rī′ble (äṅ-fäṅ′ te-rē′bl), [Fr., lit., terrible child.]
1. an unmanageable, mischievous child.
2. a person who causes trouble by making frank, bold remarks at the wrong times.

en·feçt′, *a.* to infect. [Obs.]

en·fee′ble, *v.t.*; enfeebled, *pt., pp.*; enfeebling, *ppr.* [ME. *enfeblen*; OFr. *enfeblir*, to enfeeble; *en-*, in, and *feble*, feeble.] to make feeble; to deprive of strength; to weaken; to debilitate; to enervate.

en·fee′ble·ment, *n.* the act of weakening; enervation.

en·fee′blẽr, *n.* one who or that which enfeebles.

en·fee′blish, *v.t.* to weaken. [Obs.]

en·feoff′ (-fef′), *v.t.*; enfeoffed (-feft′), *pt., pp.*; enfeoffing, *ppr.* [OFr. *enfeofer, enfeffer*; *en-*, L. *in*, in, and *feffer*, to invest with a fief.]
1. in law, to invest with an estate held in fee.
2. to surrender or give up. [Obs.]

en·feoff′ment (-fef′), *n.* 1. an enfeoffing or being enfeoffed.
2. a deed or instrument that enfeoffs.
3. a fief.
4. the possession of a fief.

en·fes′tẽr, *v.i.* to gather pus.

en·fet′tẽr, *v.t.*; enfettered, *pt., pp.*; enfettering, *ppr.* to fetter; to bind in or as in fetters.

en·fē′vẽr, *v.t.* to excite fever in. [Rare.]

en·fiērce′, *v.t.* to make fierce. [Obs.]

en·fi·lāde′, *n.* [Fr. *enfiler*, to thread, string, rake with fire, from *en-* (L. *in*), in, and *fil* (L. *filum*), a thread.]
1. gunfire directed from either flank along the length of a column or line of troops.
2. a disposition or placement of troops that makes them vulnerable to such fire.

en·fi·lāde′, *v.t.*; enfiladed, *pt., pp.*; enfilading, *ppr.* to sweep (a column, etc.) with gunfire along its length.

en·fīled′, *a.* [Fr. *enfiler*, to thread, string, rake.] in heraldry, some object which is held impaled, as a head, a coronet, etc.

eṅ·fiṅ′ (äṅ-faṅ′), *adv.* [Fr., lit., in the end.] lastly; at last; finally.

en·fīre′, *v.t.* to inflame; to set on fire. [Obs.]

en·flesh′, *v.t.* to put flesh upon. [Rare.]

eṅ·fleu·rȧġe′ (äṅ-flẽ-räzh′), *n.* [Fr.] the manufacture of perfumes by exposing odorless fixed oils to the exhalations of certain flowers.

en·flow′ẽr, *v.t.*; enflowered, *pt., pp.*; enflowering, *ppr.* to cover or decorate with flowers. [Poet.]

en·fōld′, *v.t.* 1. to wrap in folds; wrap up.
2. to embrace.
Also spelled *infold*.

en·fōld′ment, *n.* an enfolding or being enfolded.

en·fonced′ (-fonst′), *a.* [Fr. *enfoncer*, to sink, to drive into.] deeply sunken. [Rare.]

en·fōrce′, *v.t.*; enforced (-fōrst′), *pt., pp.*; enforcing, *ppr.* [ME. *enforcen*; OFr. *enforcer, enforcier*; LL. *infortiare*, to strengthen.]
1. to give strength to; to strengthen; to invigorate.
2. to make or gain by force; to force; to compel; as, to *enforce* a passage.
3. to put into action by violence; to drive. [Obs.]
Stones *enforced* from the old Assyrian slings. —Shak.
4. to urge with energy; to give force to; to impress on the mind; as, to *enforce* remarks or arguments.
5. to impose by force; as, don't *enforce* your will on the child.
6. to compel observance of; as, to *enforce* the laws.
Syn.—urge, compel, require, exact, exert, strain, execute, drive, constrain.

en·fōrce′, *v.i.* to struggle. [Obs.]

en·fōrce′, *n.* force; strength; power. [Obs.]

en·fōrce′a·ble, *a.* that can be enforced.

en·fōrced′ (-fōrst′), *a.* strengthened; gained by force; compelled.

en·fōr′ced·ly, *adv.* by violence; not by choice.

en·fōrce′ment, *n.* an enforcing or being enforced.

en·fōr′cẽr, *n.* one who enforces.

en·fōr′ci·ble, *a.* enforceable.

en·fōr′cive, *a.* having the quality of enforcing. [Obs.]

en·fōr′cive·ly, *adv.* with compulsion. [Obs.]

en·for′est, *v.t.*; enforested, *pt., pp.*; enforesting, *ppr.* [LL. *inforestare*, to convert into a forest.] to convert or transform into a forest. [Obs.]

en·form′, *v.t.* to inform. [Obs.]

en·foul′dẽred, *a.* mixed with lightning. [Obs.]

en·frāme′, *v.t.* to furnish with a frame.

en·fran′chīse, *v.t.*; enfranchised, *pt., pp.*; enfranchising, *ppr.* [OFr. *enfranchiss-*, stem of *enfranchir*, to set free, enfranchise; *en-*, in, and *franchir*, to set free.]
1. to set free; to liberate from slavery, bondage, legal obligation, etc.
2. to give political privileges or rights to (a city or town).
3. to give a franchise to; to admit to citizenship, especially to the right to vote.
4. to naturalize; to receive as a denizen; as, to *enfranchise* foreign words.

en·fran′chise·ment, *n.* an enfranchising or being enfranchised.
enfranchisement of copyhold lands; in old English law, conversion of copyhold tenements into freeholds.

en·fran′chis·ẽr, *n.* one who enfranchises.

en·free′, *v.t.* to release from captivity or slavery. [Obs.]

en·free′dŏm, *v.t.* to invest with freedom. [Obs.]

en·freeze′, *v.t.* to freeze. [Obs.]

en·gāge′, *v.t.*; engaged, *pt., pp.*; engaging, *ppr.* [OFr. *engager*; It. *ingaggiare*; LL. *invadiare*, to pledge, engage; *in*, in, and *vadium*, a pledge.]
1. originally, to give or assign as security for a debt, etc.
2. to bind (oneself) by a promise; pledge; as, she *engaged* herself to do the job.
3. to bind by a promise of marriage; betroth; as, he became *engaged* to a childhood sweetheart.
4. to arrange for the services of; hire; employ; as, he *engaged* Smith as his lawyer.
5. to arrange for the use of; reserve; as, he *engaged* a hotel room.
6. to entangle.
7. to draw into; involve; as, *engage* him in conversation.
8. to attract and hold (the attention, etc.).
9. to employ the efforts, thoughts, etc. of; keep busy; occupy; as, reading *engages* all my spare time.
10. to enter into conflict with (the enemy).
11. to mesh together; to interlock with so as to produce motion, as one cogwheel with another.
Syn.—employ, hire, retain, reserve.

en·gāge′, *v.i.* 1. to pledge oneself; promise; undertake; agree; as, don't *engage* to do it unless you have time.
2. to occupy or involve oneself; take part; be active; as, she *engaged* in dramatics.
3. to encounter; to begin to fight; to enter into conflict; as, the armies *engaged* in a battle.
4. in mechanics, to articulate, interlock, or mesh, as the teeth of cogwheels.
5. in fencing, to touch and cross blades with one's opponent.

en·gāged′, *a.* 1. pledged.
2. pledged in marriage; betrothed.
3. occupied; busy; employed; without leisure.
4. joined in conflict; involved in combat, as troops.
5. in mechanics, geared together; interlocked.
6. attached to or partly set into (a wall, etc.); as, *engaged* columns.

ENGAGED COLUMN

en·gā′ġed·ly, *adv.* with earnestness; with attachment.

en·gā′ġed·ness, *n.* the state of being seriously and earnestly occupied; zeal; animation.

en·gāge′ment, *n.* 1. the act of engaging, in any of its meanings.
2. the state of being engaged, in any of its meanings.
3. a promise; a pledge.
4. a promise of marriage; betrothal.
5. an arrangement to go somewhere, do something, meet someone, etc.; appointment; obligation.
6. occupation; employment or period of employment.
7. employment in fighting; a conflict; battle.
8. [*usually pl.*] in business, financial obligations; commitments.
9. in mechanics, an interlocking or being in gear; the state of fitting and working together of parts so that motion of one produces motion of another.
10. something that engages.

en·gā′ġẽr, *n.* one who enters into an engagement or contract.

en·gā′ġing, *a.* winning; attractive; tending to draw the attention or the affections; pleasing; as, *engaging* manners.

en·gā′ġing·ly, *adv.* in a manner to win the affections.

en·gā′ġing·ness, *n.* the state of being attractive or agreeable.

en·gal′lănt, *v.t.* to make a gallant of. [Obs.]

en·ġāol′ (-jāl′), *v.t.* to imprison. [Obs.]

en·gär′boil, *v.t.* to disorder. [Obs.]

en̈ gärde (äṅ), [Fr.] in fencing, on guard: the opening position in which the fencer is prepared either to attack or defend.

en·gär′lănd, *v.t.* to put a garland or garlands on or around.

en·gar′ri·sŏn, *v.t.*; engarrisoned, *pt., pp.*; engarrisoning, *ppr.* to furnish with a garrison; to defend or protect by a garrison.

en·gas′tri·myth, *n.* [Gr. *engastrimythos*, a ventriloquist; *en-*, in, *gastri*, dat. of *gastēr*, belly, and *mythos*, speech.] a ventriloquist. [Obs.]

en·ġen′dẽr, *v.t.*; engendered, *pt., pp.*; engendering, *ppr.* [OFr. *engendrer*; Pr. *engendrar, engenrar*; It. *ingenerare*; L. *ingenerare*, to beget; *in-*, in, and *generare*, from *genus*, birth, race.]
1. to produce by sexual union; to beget. [Rare.]
2. to produce; to cause to exist; to bring about; as, pity *engendered* love.

en·ġen′dẽr, *v.i.* 1. to be caused or produced; to be brought into existence.
2. to copulate. [Obs.]

en·ġen′dẽr·ẽr, *n.* one who or that which engenders.

en·ġen′drūre, *n.* [OFr. *engendrure*, from *engendrer*, to beget.]
1. the act of engendering. [Obs.]
2. ancestry; direct lineage. [Obs.]

en·gild′, *v.t.* to gild; to brighten.

en′ġine, *n.* [OFr. *engin, enging, engeng*, natural ability, artifice, mechanical contrivance; It. *ingegno*; L. *ingenium*, natural ability, genius; *in-*, in, and the root of *gignere*, to produce.]
1. natural skill; talent. [Obs.]
2. any agent, means, or instrument used to accomplish a purpose. [Archaic.]
3. any machine that uses energy to develop mechanical power; especially, a machine for starting motion in some other machine.
4. a railroad locomotive.
5. any instrument or machine; apparatus; as, *engines* of warfare, *engines* of torture.
agricultural engine; a portable engine used to run a threshing machine or other farm machinery.
binary engine; a steam engine having two sets of cylinders, the exhaust of one vaporizing a fluid furnishing pressure for the other.
Corliss engine; a steam engine having an automatic drop cutoff, regulated by a wrist plate controlling four plug valves.
cycloidal engine; a lathe for producing on a plate the intricate curved lines seen on currency, watch cases, etc.
pony engine; a small locomotive.
wildcat engine; a locomotive engine having no regular schedule and running without cars attached, sent out on special tasks.

en′ġine, *v.t.*; engined, *pt., pp.*; engining, *ppr.*
1. to fit out with an engine.
2. to employ war engines against. [Obs.]
3. to torture with an engine. [Obs.]

en′ġine drī′vẽr, a locomotive engineer. [Brit.]

en·ġi·neer′, *n.* [ME. *enginer*; OFr. *engigneur*; It. *ingegner*; LL. *ingeniarius*, one who makes or uses an engine, from *ingenium*, an engine, mechanical contrivance.]
1. one educated, skilled, or occupied in any of the various branches of engineering; as, an electrical *engineer*.
2. one who operates an engine, especially the driver of a railroad locomotive.
3. in military science, a member of that branch of the army which is concerned with the construction and demolition of bridges, roads, and fortifications, the laying and sapping of mines, etc.
4. a person who makes engines. [Rare.]

en·ġi·neer′, *v.t.*; engineered, *pt., pp.*; engineering, *ppr.* 1. to plan, construct, or manage as an engineer.
2. to contrive; manage skillfully; superintend; guide (a measure, action, etc. *through*).

en·ġi·neer′ing, *n.* 1. the planning, designing, construction, or management of machinery, roads, bridges, buildings, fortifications, waterways, etc.; science, profession, or work of an engineer.
2. a maneuvering or managing.
chemical engineering; the science or profession of applying chemistry to industrial uses.
civil engineering; the branch of engineering relating to the design and building of highways, bridges, waterworks, harbors, railroads, canals, and other kinds of fixed public works.
hydraulic engineering; the science and art of planning, constructing, and managing waterworks and all utilities employing hydraulic machinery, such as dams, locks, levees, etc.
marine engineering; the science relating to the construction and operation of marine engines.
mechanical engineering; the science that relates to the invention, construction, and adjustment of all kinds of machinery.
military engineering; the science of planning and constructing military works, such as bridges, roads, landing fields, etc.
mining engineering; the science of excavating and utilizing ore.
sanitary engineering; the branch of civil engineering having to do with water supply, draining, and sewage.
steam engineering; the science relating to the construction and use of steam engines and related parts, appliances, or machines.

en′ġine house, a building in which fire engines are housed.

en′ġine lāthe, an intricate lathe used chiefly for screw cutting.

en′ġine·măn, *n.*; *pl.* **en′ġine·men**, a man who operates an engine, especially a stationary engine.

en′ġine·ry, *n.* 1. the art of constructing or managing military engines, or artillery. [Obs.]
2. military engines in general; instruments of war. [Obs.]
3. machinery: engines collectively. [Rare.]

en′ġine shăft, a mine shaft in which the pumping machinery is housed.

en′ġine tŭrn′ing, the act of using a cycloidal engine, or the ornamentation so produced on metal, as on some watch cases, consisting of finely engraved lines radiating from a center.

en′ġi·nous, *a.* [ME. *enginous*; OFr. *engignos*; L. *ingeniosus*, ingenious, from *ingenium*, natural ability.]
1. relating to an engine or to mechanical construction. [Obs.]
2. of an inventive nature; skillful in devising. [Obs.]

en·gird′, *v.t.*; engirt *or* engirded, *pt., pp.*; engirding, *ppr.* to surround; to encircle; to encompass; to gird.

en·gir′dle, *v.t.*; engirdled, *pt., pp.*; engirdling, *ppr.* to encompass; to girdle.

en′ġi·sçōpe, *n.* see *engyscope*.

en·glā′ciăl (-shăl), *a.* in geology, resting within the flow of a glacier; imbedded in the ice of a glacier; as, *englacial* rocks.

Eṅg′land·ẽr (iṅ′gland-), *n.* a native of England.

Eṅg′lish (iṅ′glish), *a.* [ME. *English, Englisch*;

AS. *Englisc*, from *Engle*, *Angle*, Engles, Angles, a Germanic people who settled in Britain.]
1. of England, its people, culture, language, etc.
2. of their language.
English bond; see *bond*, n. 13.
English breakfast tea; a kind of black tea of superior quality.
English daisy; the common daisy.
English horn; a double-reed instrument of the woodwind family, similar to the oboe but larger and a fifth lower in pitch.
English setter; a breed of setter having a flat, white, long-haired coat with black, yellow, or orange spots, and feathery hair on the legs and tail.
English sonnet; see *Shakespearean sonnet*.
English sparrow; the common street sparrow, a small brownish-gray European finch now found extensively in North America.
English walnut; (a) an Asiatic walnut tree now grown in Europe and North America; (b) its nut.

ENGLISH HORN

Eng'lish, *n.* 1. the people of England.
2. the language of the English, spoken also in the United States and most parts of the British Empire.
3. the English language of a specific period or place; as, American *English*, Old *English*, Middle *English*.
4. a characteristic way of using this language; as, the professor's *English* was pedantic.
5. a school course or class in the English language or its literature.
6. the English equivalent of a word in a foreign language; the English translation; as, *Charles* is the *English* of the German *Karl*.
7. in printing, a size of type (14 point) between great primer and pica.
8. [*sometimes* e-] in billiards, bowling, etc., a spinning motion given to a ball, as by striking it on one side.
Eng'lish, *v.t.*; Englished (-glisht), *pt.*, *pp.*; Englishing, *ppr.* 1. to translate into the English language.
2. to apply the principles of English pronunciation, spelling, etc. to; Anglicize, as a foreign word.
3. [*sometimes* e-] in billiards, bowling, etc., to give a spinning motion to (a ball), as by striking it on one side.
Eng'lish·a·ble, *a.* translatable into the English language.
Eng'lish·ism, *n.* 1. a characteristic or the characteristics of the English people.
2. an idiom of British English; Briticism.
3. an attachment to English ways and things.
Eng'lish·măn, *n.*; *pl.* **Eng'lish·men**, 1. a native or inhabitant of England, especially a man.
2. a person of English ancestry, especially a man, as in Canada, Australia, etc.
3. an English ship.
Eng'lish·măn's tie, a kind of knot: see *knot*, illus.
Eng'lish·ry, *n.* 1. the state or fact of being English by birth.
2. a group of people of English descent; especially, the English in Ireland: now chiefly a historical term.
Eng'lish·wom″ăn (-woom″), *n.*; *pl.* **Eng'lish-wom″en** (-wim″), 1. a woman who is a native or inhabitant of England.
2. a woman of English ancestry, as in Canada, Australia, etc.
en·gloom', *v.t.* to make gloomy.
en·glūe', *v.t.*; englued, *pt.*, *pp.*; engluing, *ppr.* to fasten close together; to join firmly, as with glue. [Obs.]
en·glut', *v.t.* 1. to swallow. [Archaic.]
2. to fill; to glut. [Archaic.]
en·gōre', *v.t.* 1. to pierce; to gore. [Obs.]
2. to cause to become bloody.
en·gorge', *v.t.*; engorged, *pt.*, *pp.*; engorging, *ppr.* [Fr. *engorger*, from *en-*, in, and *gorge*, the throat.]
1. to gorge; to glut.
2. to swallow; to devour; to swallow with greediness or in large quantities.
3. in medicine, to congest (a blood vessel, tissue, etc.) with blood or other fluid.
en·gorge', *v.i.* to devour greedily; to feed with eagerness or voracity.
en·gorged', *a.* 1. swallowed in a greedy manner; taken in with voracity.
2. in medicine, choked with blood or other liquid.
en·gorge'ment, *n.* an engorging or being engorged.
en·gōuled', *a.* in heraldry, engoulee.
en·gou·lée' (äṅ-gö-lā'), *a.* [Fr. *engouler*, to gobble up, swallow; *en-*, in, and OFr. *goule*, throat.] in heraldry, swallowed in part; held by the jaws of anything: also used of an ordinary having its two ends resting in the mouths of animals.
en·gråff', *v.t.* to engraft. [Obs.]
en·gråff'ment, *n.* engraftment. [Obs.]
en·gråft', *v.t.* 1. to insert (a shoot or graft from one tree or plant) into another for propagation; graft.
2. to implant; establish firmly; as, patriotism was *engrafted* in his soul.
Also *ingraft*.
en·gråf·tā'tion, en·gråft'ment, *n.* the act of engrafting; also, the thing engrafted.
en·grāil', *v.t.*; engrailed, *pt.*, *pp.*; engrailing, *ppr.* [Fr. *engrêler*, to engrail.]
1. to indent (an edge or line) with concave, curved notches.
2. to decorate with such an indented edge or outline.
en·grāiled', *a.* 1. variegated; spotted. [Obs.]
2. having an indented outline.
3. in heraldry, indented in a series of curves with the points outward.
en·grāil'ment, *n.* 1. an engrailing or being engrailed.
2. the engrailed inner edge of a medal or coin.

A BEND ENGRAILED

en·grāin', *v.t.* [ME. *engreinen*; OFr. *engrainer*, to dye scarlet, from *en-*, in, and *graine*, seed, cochineal dye.]
1. to ingrain.
2. to grain or color in imitation of wood.
en'gram, *n.* [*en-*, and *-gram*.]
1. in biology, a permanent change produced by a stimulus in the protoplasm of a tissue.
2. in psychology, a permanent effect produced in the psyche as a result of stimulation: it serves as the basis for memory.
en·grap'ple, *v.i.* see *grapple*.
en·gråsp', *v.t.* see *grasp*.
en·grāve', *v.t.*; engraved, *pt.*; engraved, *or archaic* engraven, *pp.*; engraving, *ppr.* [OFr. *engraver*, to engrave; *en-*, in, and *graver*, to engrave, impress.]
1. to carve into (a surface); to cut, as metal, stone, or other hard substance, with a chisel or graver; to cut or etch figures, letters, or devices, on or in; to mark by incisions.

> Thou shalt *engrave* the two stones with the names of the children of Israel.
> —Ex. xxviii. 11.

2. to imprint; to impress deeply; to infix; to make a deep or permanent impression on (the mind or memory), as though by engraving.
3. to cut or etch (a picture, letters, etc.) into a metal plate, wooden block, etc. for printing.
4. to print by means of such a plate, block, etc.
en·grāve', *v.t.* to inter. [Obs.]
en·grāve'ment, *n.* engraved work; act of engraving.
en·grāv'ẽr, *n.* one who engraves; a cutter of letters, figures, or devices, on metal plates, wooden blocks, etc. for printing.
en·grāv'ẽr·y, *n.* the work of an engraver. [Obs.]
en·grāv'ing, *n.* 1. the art of cutting designs, writing, etc. on any hard substance, as stone, metal, or wood.
2. the act, process, or art of cutting or etching designs or letters on metal plates, wooden blocks, etc. for printing.
3. that which is engraved; an engraved plate, design, etc.
4. a printed impression made from an engraved surface.
en·grieve', *v.t.* to grieve. [Obs.]
en·grōss', *v.t.*; engrossed (-grōst'), *pt.*, *pp.*; engrossing, *ppr.* [ME. *engrossen*; OFr. *engrossir*, *engroisser*; hyp. LL. *ingrossiare*, to make large, write large; L. *in*, in, and *grossus*, large.]
1. to make thick or gross; to thicken. [Obs.]
2. to make larger; to increase in bulk. [Obs.]
3. to write or copy in a large, bold handwriting; as, to *engross* a legal document.
4. to express formally or in legal form.
5. to take the entire attention of; occupy wholly; absorb; as, worldly cares *engross* the attention of most men.
6. to take all of; to take or assume in undue quantities or degrees; as, to *engross* power.
7. to buy a part or the whole of (any commodity) with a view to controlling its price; to corner; to monopolize. [Archaic.]
en·grōss'ẽr, *n.* 1. a penman whose specialty is engrossing.
2. one who corners a product with a view of raising the price. [Archaic.]
en·grōss'ing, *a.* taking one's entire attention; very interesting; absorbing.
en·grōss'ing hand, a bold, shaded, rounded handwriting employed in transcribing legal documents.
en·grōss'ment, *n.* 1. the act of engrossing; a being engrossed.
2. something engrossed, as a document.
en·guärd', *v.t.* to guard.
en·gulf', *v.t.*; engulfed (-gulft'), *pt.*, *pp.*; engulfing, *ppr.* [OFr. *engolfer*, to engulf, from L. *in*, in, and LL. *golfus*, *gulfus*, a gulf.]
1. to swallow up or overwhelm completely; to absorb.
2. to plunge, as into a gulf.
Also written *ingulf*.
en·gulf'ment, *n.* a swallowing up: also written *ingulfment*.
en'gy·scōpe, *n.* [Gr. *engys*, near, and *skopein*, to view.] a kind of reflecting microscope.
en·hā'lō, *v.t.*; enhaloed, *pt.*, *pp.*; enhaloing, *ppr.* to provide with a halo.
en·hånce', *v.t.*; enhanced, *pt.*, *pp.*; enhancing, *ppr.* [ME. *enhansen*; Anglo-Fr. *enhauncer*; prob. from OFr. *enhaucer*, *enhaucier*; hyp. LL. *inaltiare*, from *in-*, in, and hyp. *altiare*, to raise, from L. *altus*, high.]
1. to raise; to lift. [Obs.]
2. to make greater, as in cost, value, attractiveness, etc.; heighten; intensify; augment.

> Experience of want *enhances* the value of plenty.
> —L'Estrange.

en·hånce', *v.i.* to rise; to increase. [Archaic.]
en·hånced', *a.* 1. made greater; heightened; intensified.
2. in heraldry, placed higher than usual on the shield.
en·hånce'ment, *n.* the state or quality of being enhanced; rise; increase; augmentation.
en·hån'cẽr, *n.* one who or that which enhances.
en·här'bŏr, *v.t.* to find shelter in; to harbor. [Obs.]
en·härd'en, *v.t.* to harden; to make hard. [Obs.]
en·här·mon'iç, *a.* [Gr. *enarmonikos*, in accord, in harmony.]
1. (a) designating or of a musical interval less than a half step; (b) designating a quarter step in early Greek music.
2. designating a scale containing such intervals: distinguished from *chromatic scale*, *diatonic scale*.
3. relating to tones nearly identical in pitch, as E♭ and D♯, produced by the same key on a keyed instrument.
4. designating a change of modulation in notation without change in sound of the given tone.
en·här·mon'iç·ăl·ly, *adv.* in enharmonic style.
en·heärt'en, *v.t.* to encourage. [Rare.]
en·hedge' (-hej'), *v.t.* to encircle with or as with a hedge. [Rare.]
en·hort', *v.t.* [L. *inhortari*, to incite, instigate.] to uplift; to inspire with hope. [Obs.]
en·hun'gẽr, *v.t.* to cause to be hungry. [Rare.]
en·hȳ'drīte, *n.* [Gr. *enydros*, containing water, and *-ite*.] a mineral enclosing water in a small cavity.
en·hȳ'dros, *n.* a chalcedonic enhydrite.
en·hȳ'drous, *a.* [Gr. *enydros*, in water, living in water.] containing water within: said of certain crystals.
E'nid, *n.* [Celt., lit., spotless purity.] in Arthurian legend, the wife of Geraint: she was a model of constancy, loyalty, and patience.
ē·nig'mȧ, *n.* [L. *ænigma*; Gr. *ainigma* (*-atos*), a riddle, dark saying, from *ainissesthai*, to speak darkly, speak in riddles, from *ainos*, a tale, story.]
1. a perplexing statement; riddle.
2. a perplexing, baffling, or seemingly inexplicable matter, person, etc.

ē·nig·mat′iç, ē·nig·mat′iç·ăl, *a.* of or like an enigma; perplexing; baffling; obscure.

ē·nig·mat′iç·ăl·ly, *adv.* in an enigmatic manner.

ē·nig′mȧ·tist, *n.* a maker or speaker in enigmas. [Obs.]

ē·nig′mȧ·tīze, *v.i.* to utter or form enigmas; to deal in riddles.

ē·nig·mȧ·tog′rȧ·phy, *n.* [Gr. *ainigma* (*-atos*), a riddle, and *-graphia*, from *graphein*, to write.] the art of making enigmas.

ē·nig·mȧ·tol′ō·gy, *n.* [Gr. *ainigma* (*-atos*), a riddle, and *-logia*, from *legein*, to speak.] the science of solving enigmas.

en·īsle′ (-īl′), *v.t.*; enisled, *pt., pp.*; enisling, *ppr.* 1. to make (something) into or like an island.

2. to place on or as on an island; isolate. Also *inisle.*

en·jāil′, *v.t.*; enjailed, *pt., pp.*; enjailing, *ppr.* to imprison by putting in jail.

en·jamb′ment, en·jambe′ment (-jam′), *n.* [Fr. *enjambement*, from *enjamber*, to encroach, from *en-*, in, and *jambe*, leg.] in prosody, the running on of a sentence from one couplet or line into the next without pause at the line end.

en·join′, *v.t.*; enjoined, *pt., pp.*; enjoining, *ppr.* [ME. *enjoinen, enjoynen*; OFr. *enjoindre*; L. *injungere*, to join or fasten into, to charge, lay upon; *in-*, in, and *jungere*, to join.]

1. to order; to urge or impose with authority; to command; as, a parent *enjoins* on his children the duty of obedience.

2. in law, to forbid; to stop or prohibit, especially by legal injunction; as, the company was *enjoined* from using false advertising.

en·join′ẽr, *n.* one who enjoins.

en·join′ment, *n.* direction; command; the act of enjoining.

en·joy′, *v.t.*; enjoyed, *pt., pp.*; enjoying, *ppr.* [ME. *enjoyen*; OFr. *enjoier, enjoer*, to give, receive with joy; *en-*, in, and *joie*, joy.]

1. to feel or perceive with pleasure; to take pleasure or satisfaction from; to relish; as, we *enjoy* the conversation of friends.

I could *enjoy* the pangs of death,
And smile in agony. —Addison.

2. to have, possess, and use with satisfaction; to have, hold, or occupy, as a good or profitable thing, or as something desirable; as, we *enjoy* many privileges.

That the children of Israel may *enjoy* every man the inheritance of his fathers.
—Num. xxxvi. 8.

3. to have sexual intercourse with. [Obs.]

to enjoy oneself; to feel pleasure; to have a good time.

en·joy′, *v.i.* to enjoy oneself.

en·joy′ȧ·ble, *a.* capable of being enjoyed or giving enjoyment.

en·joy′ȧ·bly, *adv.* in an enjoyable manner.

en·joy′ẽr, *n.* one who enjoys.

en·joy′ment, *n.* 1. an enjoying; specifically, (a) having the use or benefit of something; having as one's lot or advantage; (b) having or experiencing with joy; getting pleasure from.

2. something enjoyed.

3. pleasure; gratification; happiness; joy.

en·ken′nel, *v.t.* to place in a kennel. [Obs.]

en·kẽr′chiēf, *v.t.*; enkerchiefed (-chēft), *pt., pp.*; enkerchiefing, *ppr.* to cover with or to enfold in a kerchief.

en·kin′dle, *v.t.*; enkindled, *pt., pp.*; enkindling, *ppr.* 1. to kindle; to set on fire; to inflame.

2. to excite; to arouse (passions, etc.).

en·lāce′, *v.t.*; enlaced (-lāst′), *pt., pp.*; enlacing, *ppr.* [ME. *enlacen*; OFr. *enlacer*, to interlace, infold; It. *inlacciare*, to ensnare, entangle; from L. *in-*, in, and *laqueus*, a noose, snare.]

1. to encircle with or as with lace; to lace; to enfold.

2. to entangle; to interlace.

3. to cover with or as with lace.

en·lāce′ment, *n.* the state of being enlaced or the act of enlacing; an encircling; a surrounding.

en·lärd′, *v.t.* to cover with lard or grease; to baste. [Obs.]

en·lärge′, *v.t.* and *v.i.*; enlarged, *pt., pp.*; enlarging, *ppr.* [ME. *enlargen*; OFr. *enlargier*; *en-*, in, and *large*, large.]

1. to make or become greater in quantity or dimensions; to extend in limits, breadth, or size; to expand; to broaden; as, every one desires to *enlarge* his possessions.

God shall *enlarge* Japhet. —Gen. ix. 27.

2. in photography, to reproduce or be capable of being reproduced on a larger scale.

to enlarge on (or *upon*); to speak or write at greater length or in greater detail about; expatiate on.

en·lärged′, *a.* expanded; dilated; swollen.

en·lär′ged·ly, *adv.* with enlargement.

en·lär′ged·ness, *n.* the state of being enlarged.

en·lärge′ment, *n.* 1. an enlarging or being enlarged.

2. something that enlarges by being added; as, the index is an *enlargement* to the book.

3. a reproduction, as of a photograph, on a larger scale.

en·lär′gẽr, *n.* one who or that which enlarges.

en·lāy′, *v.t.* same as *inlay.*

en·lēague′ (-lēg′), *v.t.* to unite, as in a league.

en·length′en, *v.t.* to make longer. [Obs.]

en·lev′en, *n.* eleven. [Obs.]

en·līght′ (-līt′), *v.t.* to illuminate; to enlighten. [Obs.]

en·līght′en, *v.t.*; enlightened, *pt., pp.*; enlightening, *ppr.* 1. to give light to; to give clearer views to; to illuminate; to instruct; to enable to see or comprehend truth; to free from ignorance, prejudice, or superstition.

2. to inform; give clarification to (a person) as to meanings, intentions, etc.

3. to light up. [Archaic.]

Syn.—illuminate, inform, instruct.

en·līght′en·ẽr (-līt′n-ẽr), *n.* one who or that which enlightens.

en·līght′en·ment, *n.* the act of enlightening or the state of being enlightened.

the Enlightenment; an 18th-century European philosophical movement characterized by rationalism, an impetus toward learning, and a spirit of skepticism and empiricism in social and political thought.

en·limn′ (-lim′), *v.t.* to embellish with illuminated letters or figures, as a book. [Obs.]

en·liñk′, *v.t.* to chain together; to connect.

en·list′, *v.t.*; enlisted, *pt., pp.*; enlisting, *ppr.* 1. to enroll for service in some branch of the armed forces.

2. to win the support of; get the help or services of; as, we'll *enlist* him in our movement.

3. to get (the help, support, etc. of someone); as, we'll *enlist* his aid in our cause.

Syn.—enter, register, enroll, incorporate, embody, interest.

en·list′, *v.i.* 1. to join some branch of the armed forces (often with *in*).

2. to join or support a cause or movement (with *in*).

en·list′ed man, any man in the armed forces who is not a commissioned or warrant officer.

en·list′ment, *n.* 1. the act of enlisting or the state of being enlisted.

2. the period of time for which one enlists.

en·līve′, *v.t.* to animate. [Obs.]

en·līv′en, *v.t.*; enlivened, *pt., pp.*; enlivening, *ppr.* 1. to give action or motion to; to make vigorous or active; as, fresh fuel *enlivens* a fire.

2. to give spirit or vivacity to; to animate; to make cheerful.

Syn.—cheer, rouse, exhilarate, inspire, invigorate.

en·līv′en·ẽr, *n.* one who or that which enlivens.

en·lock′, *v.t.* to lock up.

en·lū′mine, *v.t.* to illumine; to enlighten. [Obs.]

en·lūte′, *v.t.* [ME. *enluten*: *en-*, and L. *lutum*, mud, clay.] to cover or coat with mud or clay; to lute. [Obs.]

en·mär′ble, *v.t.* to make like marble. [Obs.]

eṅ masse′ (oṅ mas′). [Fr. lit., in mass.] as a body; all together.

en·mesh′, *v.t.*; enmeshed (-mesht′), *pt., pp.*; enmeshing, *ppr.* to net; to entangle; to entrap: also spelled *inmesh.*

en·mew′, *v.t.* same as *emmew.*

en·mist′, *v.t.*; enmisted, *pt., pp.*; enmisting, *ppr.* to surround with mist.

en′mi·ty, *n.*; *pl.* **en′mi·tieṣ,** [ME. *enmyte, enemyte*; OFr. *enemite, ennemite*, from L. *inimicus*, an enemy] the attitude or feelings of an enemy or enemies; hostility; antagonism.

en·mossed′ (-mọst′), *a.* covered with moss.

en·mōve′, *v.t.* to inmove. [Obs.]

en·muf′fle, *v.t.* to muffle up. [Rare.]

en·nē·ȧ-, [from Gr. *ennea*, nine.] a combining form meaning *nine*, as in *enneagon.*

en″nē·ȧ·çon·tȧ·hē′drăl, *a.* [Gr. *enenēkonta*, ninety, and *hedra*, a seat, base.] having ninety faces.

en′nē·ad, *n.* [Gr. *enneas* (*-ados*), from *ennea*, nine.] a series or group of nine objects; a division of a work containing nine books.

the Enneads; the works, in six books of nine chapters each, of Plotinus, the philosopher, published by Porphyry, his pupil.

en′nē·ȧ·gon, *n.* [*ennea-*, and Gr. *gōnia*, an angle.] in geometry, a plane figure, with nine sides and nine angles; a nonagon.

en·nē·ag′ō·năl, *a.* of or belonging to an enneagon; having nine sides and nine angles.

en·nē·ag′y·nous, *a.* [*ennea-*, and Gr. *gynē*, a woman.] in botany, bearing nine pistils.

en″nē·ȧ·hē′drăl, *a.* [*ennea-*, and Gr. *hedra*, a seat, base.] of, or having the form of, an enneahedron.

en″nē·ȧ·hē′drŏn, en″nē·ȧ·hē′dri·ȧ, *n.* [*ennea-*, and Gr. *hedra*, a seat, base.] a solid figure having nine plane surfaces.

En·nē·an′dri·ȧ, *n.* [*ennea-*, and Gr. *anēr, andros*, a man.] in botany, a class of plants having nine stamens: so classified by Linnaeus.

en·nē·an′dri·ăn, en·nē·an′drous, *a.* [*ennea-*, and Gr. *anēr, andros*, a man.] having nine stamens.

en″nē·ȧ·pet′ăl·ous, *a.* [*ennea-*, and Gr. *petalon*, a leaf.] having nine petals.

en·nē·aph′yl·lous, *a.* having nine leaves or leaflets.

en″nē·ȧ·spẽr′mous, *a.* [*ennea-*, and Gr. *sperma*, a seed.] nine-seeded.

en·nē·at′iç·ăl, en·nē·at′iç, *a.* [Gr. *ennea*, nine.] occurring every ninth time, day, year, etc.; every ninth one of a series.

enneatical day; every ninth day of the course or period of a disease.

enneatical year; every ninth year of a person's life.

en·new′, *v.t.* to make new. [Obs.]

en·niche′, *v.t.* to put in a niche. [Rare.]

en·nō′ble, *v.t.*; ennobled, *pt., pp.*; ennobling, *ppr.* [Fr. *ennoblir*; *en-*, in, and *noble*, noble.]

1. to raise to the rank of nobleman; to raise to nobility; as, to *ennoble* a commoner.

2. to dignify; to exalt; to elevate in degree, qualities, or excellence.

What can *ennoble* sots, or slaves, or cowards? —Pope.

3. to make famous or illustrious. [Obs.]

en·nō′ble·ment, *n.* 1. the act of ennobling or the state of being ennobled.

2. that which ennobles or exalts; excellence; nobility; dignity. [Obs.]

en·nō′blẽr, *n.* one who or that which ennobles.

en′nuï (än′wē; Fr. äṅ-nwē′), *n.*; *pl.* **en′nuiṣ** (än′wēz; Fr. äṅ-nwē′), [Fr.; OFr. *ennoier*, to annoy; L. *inodiare*, from *in odio*, in aversion, at enmity.] weariness and dissatisfaction resulting from inactivity or lack of interest; boredom.

en·nuy·é′ (äṅ-nwē-yā′), *a.* [Fr., pp. of *ennuyer*, to affect with ennui.] suffering with ennui; wearied; bored.

en·nuy·é′, *n.* one suffering from ennui.

Ē′nŏçh, *n.* [Gr. *Enōch*; Heb. *ḥānōkh*, lit., dedicated.] in the Bible, (a) the eldest son of Cain. Gen. iv. 17; (b) the father of Methuselah. Gen. v. 21.

ē·nōd′ăl, *a.* having no node or nodes, as a plant.

ē·nō·dā′tion, *n.* [L. *enodatio*, from *enodare*, to clear from knots; *e-*, out, and *nodus*, a knot.]

1. the act or operation of clearing of knots, or of untying. [Obs.]

2. solution of a difficulty. [Obs.]

ē·nōde′, *a.* without knots or joints. [Obs.]

ē·nōde′, *v.t.* 1. to clear of knots. [Obs.]

2. to solve (a problem); to make clear. [Obs.]

ē·noint′, *v.t.* to anoint. [Obs.]

ē·nom′ō·tärçh, *n.* [Gr. *enōmotarchēs*, from *enōmotia*, an enomoty, and *archein*, to rule.] the commander of an enomoty.

ē·nom′ō·ty, *n.* [Gr. *enōmotia*, lit., a sworn band, from *enōmotos*, sworn, bound by oath; from *en*, in, and *omnynai*, to swear.] in ancient Greece, the smallest division of the Spartan army, twenty-five to thirty-six oath-bound soldiers.

En′ō·plȧ, *n.pl.* [Gr. *enoplos*, in armor; *en*, in, and *hopla*, arms.] a suborder of nemertean worms, having a spinal or platelike armature in the proboscis.

en′ō·plan, *a.* of or relating to the *Enopla.*

en′ō·plan, *n.* one of the *Enopla.*

en·op′trō·man·cy, *n.* [Gr. *enoptron*, mirror, and *manteia*, divination.] divination by the use of a mirror.

ē·nọrm′, *a.* abnormal; wicked. [Obs.]

ē·nọr′mi·ty, *n.*; *pl.* **ē·nọr′mi·tieṣ,** [L. *enormitas*, irregularity, unusual size, from *enormis*, out of rule, irregular; *e-*, out, and *norma*, rule.]

1. the condition or quality of being monstrous, or outrageous, especially the quality of being extremely wicked; as, the *enormity* of atrocious crime or of flagrant villainy.

2. a monstrous or outrageous act; a very wicked crime.

3. the state of being excessively or abnormally large; vastness or immensity. [Rare.]

ē-nọr′mous, *a.* [L. *enormis*; *e-*, out of, and *norma*, rule.]
1. immense in size; far exceeding the usual measure or rule; gigantic; abnormally large.
2. outrageously wicked; heinous; monstrous; atrocious. [Archaic.]
Syn.—immense, excessive, huge, vast.

ē-nọr′mous·ly, *adv.* to an enormous extent; excessively; beyond measure; as, an opinion *enormously* absurd.

ē-nọr′mous·ness, *n.* the state of being enormous or excessive.

en·ọr′thō·trōpe, *n.* [Gr. *en*, in, and *orthos*, straight, and *trepein*, to turn.] a card on various parts of which are drawn, in apparent confusion, parts of figures, which form complete figures or pictures when the card is rapidly revolved.

en·os·tō′sis, *n.*; *pl.* **en·os·tō′sēs,** [from Gr. *en*, in, *osteon*, bone, and *-osis*.] a tumor within a bone.

ē-nough′ (-nuf′), *a.* [ME. *enogh*, *enoh*, *enow*; AS. *genoh*, from *geneah*, it suffices.] satisfying the need or desire; adequate; sufficient.

How many hired servants of my father's have bread *enough* and to spare!
—Luke xv. 17.

ē-nough′, *n.* a sufficiency; the amount or number needed or desired; as, we have *enough* of this sort of cloth.

And Esau said, I have *enough*, my brother.
—Gen. xxxiii. 9.

ē-nough′, *adv.* 1. sufficiently; in a quantity or degree that satisfies or is equal to the desires or wants.

Ye have dwelt long *enough* in this mount.
—Deut. i. 6.

2. fully; quite; as, he is ready *enough* to embrace the offer.
3. in a tolerable or reasonable degree; just adequately; fairly; as, he played well *enough*.

ē-nough′, *interj.* no more! that's enough!

ē-nounce′, *v.t.*; enounced (-nounst′), *pt.*, *pp.*; enouncing, *ppr.* [Fr. *énoncer*, from L. *enunciare*, *enuntiare*, to say out, declare; *e-*, out, and *nuntiare*, to speak, declare.]
1. to state publicly or formally; proclaim.
2. to speak; utter; enunciate; pronounce.

ē-now′, *a.*, *n.*, and *adv.* [ME. *ynoghe*, *inou*; AS. *genog*, orig. form of *genoh*, enough.] enough. [Archaic.]

en pȧs·sänt′ (äṅ pȧ-säṅ′), [Fr.] in passing; incidentally; by the way: used, in chess, of the capture of an opponent's pawn, which has taken its first move of two squares, by one's own pawn that dominates the first of those squares.

en·pā′trŏn, *v.t.* to act as a patron toward. [Obs.]

en·phȳ·tot′iç, *a.* [from *en-*, and Gr. *phyton*, a plant.] affecting certain plants of an area at regular intervals: said of various plant diseases.

en·plāne′, *v.i.* to go aboard an airplane.

en·quēre′ (-kwēr′), *v.i.* to inquire. [Obs.]

en·quīre′, *v.t.* and *v.i.*; enquired, *pt.*, *pp.*; enquiring, *ppr.* to inquire.

en·quīr′ēr, *n.* same as *inquirer*.

en·quīr′y, *n.*; *pl.* **en·quīr′ies,** same as *inquiry*.

en·rāce′, *v.t.* to implant. [Obs.]

en·rāġe′, *v.t.*; enraged, *pt.*, *pp.*; enraging, *ppr.* [OFr. *enrager*, to rave, rage; *en-*, in, and *rage*, rage.] to excite rage in; to make very angry; to make furious.
Syn.—anger, inflame, exasperate, infuriate.

en·rāġe′ment, *n.* the act of enraging or the state of being enraged.

en·rāil′, *v.t.* to enclose with railing. [Obs.]

en·rānġe′, *v.t.* 1. to arrange. [Obs.]
2. to range; traverse; travel over. [Obs.]

en·rank′, *v.t.* to place in ranks or order.

eṅ rȧp·pọrt′ (äṅ rȧ-pọr′), [Fr.] in harmony; in sympathy; in accord.

en·rapt′, *a.* enraptured; rapt.

en·rap′tūre, *v.t.*; enraptured, *pt.*, *pp.*; enrapturing, *ppr.* to fill with pleasure; to delight greatly; to entrance; to enchant.

en·rav′ish, *v.t.* to enrapture.

en·rav′ish·ing·ly, *adv.* in an enravishing manner.

en·rav′ish·ment, *n.* rapture.

en·reġ′is·tēr, *v.t.* to enter in register; to enroll or record.

en rè′gle (äṅ reg′l), [Fr.] according to rule; in order.

eṅ rē·traite′ (äṅ rē-tret′), [Fr.] in retreat; in retirement.

en·rheum′ (-rūm′), *v.i.* and *v.t.* to affect with rheum. [Obs.]

en·rich′, *v.t.*; enriched (-richt′), *pt.*, *pp.*; enriching, *ppr.* [ME. *enrichen*; OFr. *enrichier*, *enrichir*; *en-*, in, and *riche*, rich.]
1. to make rich or richer; to give more wealth to; as, agriculture, commerce, and manufactures *enrich* a nation.
2. to fertilize (soil).
3. to supply with anything splendid or ornamental; to decorate; to adorn; as, to *enrich* a painting with elegant drapery.
4. to give greater value or importance to; as, music has *enriched* my life.
5. to add vitamins, minerals, etc. to (bread, etc.) to increase the food value.

en·rich′ēr, *n.* one who or that which enriches.

en·rich′ment, *n.* 1. an enriching or being enriched.
2. something that enriches.

en·ridġe′ (-rij′), *v.t.* to form into ridges. [Obs.]

en·ring′, *v.t.* to encircle; to enclose.

en·rīp′en, *v.t.* to ripen. [Obs.]

en·rīve′, *v.t.* to rive; to cleave. [Obs.]

en·rōbe′, *v.t.*; enrobed, *pt.*, *pp.*; enrobing, *ppr.* to clothe with a robe; to dress.

en·rock′ment, *n.* a mass of large stones thrown into the water to form the base of a pier, breakwater, etc.

en·rōll′, en·rōl′, *v.t.*; enrolled, *pt.*, *pp.*; enrolling, *ppr.* [ME. *enrollen*; OFr. *enroller*, from LL. *inrotulare*, to write in a roll; L. *in*, in, and *rotulus*, a wheel.]
1. to write in a roll or register; to enter in a list; hence, to enlist; as, they *enrolled* his name; he *enrolled* himself for service.
2. to accept as a member; to make (a person) a member.
3. to roll up; to wrap up. [Rare.]
4. to inscribe (a document); to engross. [Obs.]

en·rōll′ēr, *n.* one who enrolls or registers.

en·rōll′ment, en·rōl′ment, *n.* 1. an enrolling or being enrolled.
2. a list of those enrolled.
3. the number of those enrolled.

en·root′, *v.t.* to fix by the root; to fix fast; to implant firmly or deeply.

en·round′, *v.t.* to surround. [Obs.]

en rŏute (än rōt′; Fr. äṅ), [Fr.] on the way; along the way.

ens *n.*; *pl.* **en′ti·a,** (-shi-a), [L. *ens*, *entis*, a being or thing.]
1. in philosophy, abstract being; existence, in the most general sense; also, that which has being, either concrete or abstract.
2. power; virtue; efficacy; essence. [Obs.]

en·sāfe′, *v.t.* to make safe. [Obs.]

en·sam′ple, *n.* [It. *esempio*; L. *exemplum*.] an example. [Archaic.]

en·sam′ple, *v.t.* to exemplify; to show by example. [Obs.]

en·san′guine (-gwin), *v.t.*; ensanguined, *pt.*, *pp.*; ensanguining, *ppr.* to stain or cover with blood; to make bloody; as, an *ensanguined* field.

en′sāte, *a.* [L. *ensis*, a sword.] having sword-shaped leaves.

en·sçāle′, *v.t.* to cover with or as with scales. [Rare.]

en·sçhed′ūle, *v.t.* to insert in a schedule. [Obs.]

en·sçonce′, *v.t.*: ensconced, *pt.*, *pp.*; ensconcing, *ppr.* [*en-*, and *sconce* (small fortification).]
1. to cover or shelter; to protect; to hide.
2. to place comfortably, snugly, or securely; as, he *ensconced* himself on the sofa.

en·sēal′, *v.t.* to seal; to fix a seal on; hence, to confirm. [Obs.]

en·sēam′, in·sēam′, *v.t.* to sew up. [Rare.]

en·sēam′, *v.t.* to cover with or as with grease. [Obs.]

en·sēar′, *v.t.* to sear; to cauterize. [Obs.]

en·sēarch′, *v.i.* and *v.t.* to search. [Obs.]

en·seel′, *v.t.* to seel, as a hawk. [Obs.]

en·sem′ble (än-säm′bl; Fr. äṅ-säṅ′bl), *n.* [OFr. *ensemble*; LL. *insimul*, at the same time; *in*, in, and *simul*, at the same time.]
1. all the parts of anything taken together so that each part is considered only in relation to the whole; the general effect, as of a whole work of art.
2. a whole costume; a costume of matching parts.
3. in music, (a) the performance together of all the instruments of an orchestra or of all the voices in a chorus; (b) a small group of musicians playing or singing together; (c) the instruments or voices constituting such a group.
4. in the theater, (a) the entire company; (b) their appearance together on the stage.
5. in mathematics, an aggregate or collection of elements or points connected by a series of relations.
tout ensemble; the appearance or effect as a whole.

en·sem′ble, *a.* pertaining to an ensemble; constituting an ensemble; rendered by an ensemble.

en·sem′ble, *adv.* all together; simultaneously.

en·sep′ul·çhēr, en·sep′ul·çhre (-kēr), *v.t.* to put into a sepulcher; to entomb.

en·sē′tē, *n.* [Eth.] the *Musa ensete*, a plant closely allied to the banana. It produces a large leaf, some specimens measuring 18 feet by $3^1/_2$ feet. Only the flower stalks are edible.

en·shel′tēr, *v.t.* to shelter.

en·shiēld′, *v.t.* to shield; to cover.

en·shrīne′, *v.t.*; enshrined, *pt.*, *pp.*; enshrining, *ppr.* to enclose in or as in a shrine; hence, to cherish; to hold as sacred.

en·shroud′, *v.t.*; enshrouded, *pt.*, *pp.*; enshrouding, *ppr.* to cover as with a shroud; to hide; to veil; to obscure.

ENSIFORM LEAF

en′si·form, *a.* [L. *ensis*, sword, and *forma*, form.] having the shape of a sword; xiphoid; as, an *ensiform* leaf.
ensiform cartilage; in anatomy, the somewhat sword-shaped process at the lower extremity of the sternum: also called *ensiform process* and *xiphisternum*.

en′sīgn (en′sīn), *n.* [OFr. *ensigne*, *enseigne*, from L. *insigna*, a standard, badge; L. *insigne*, neut. of *insignis*, distinguished by a mark, remarkable.]
1. a badge, symbol, or token of office or authority.
2. a flag or banner, especially a military or naval banner.
3. in the British Army, formerly, a commissioned officer who served as standard-bearer.
4. (en′sin), [after Fr. *enseigne de vaisseau*, ship's ensign, midshipman.] in the United States Navy, a commissioned officer of the lowest rank, corresponding to a second lieutenant in the Army.
5. a signal or sign. [Obs.]

en′sīgn, *v.t.*; ensigned, *pt.*, *pp.*; ensigning, *ppr.* [ME. *ensignen*; OFr. *ensigner*, *en seigner*, from LL. *insignare*, to mark, indicate.]
1. to give some distinguishing mark to; in heraldry, to distinguish (a charge) by placing over it a crown or some other honorable emblem.
2. to point out as by an ensign. [Obs.]

ENSIGNED CHARGE

en′sīgn·beār′ēr, he who carries the ensign.

en′sīgn·cy, *n.*; *pl.* **en′sīgn·cieṣ,** same as *ensignship*.

en′sīgn·ship, *n.* the rank or position of an ensign in the armed forces.

en′si·lāġe, *n.* [Fr. *ensilage*; *en-*, in, and *silo*, from Sp. *silo*, a silo, from L. *sirus*, Gr. *siros*, *seiros*, a pit to keep corn in, an underground pit.] the operation and method of preserving green fodder (clover, millet, green cornstalks, etc.), by packing it in a silo; also, the fodder thus preserved; silage.

en′si·lāġe, *v.t.*; ensilaged, *pt.*, *pp.*; ensilaging, *ppr.* to ensile.

en′sīle, *v.t.*; ensiled, *pt.*, *pp.*; ensiling, *ppr.* [Sp. *ensilar*, to preserve grain in a place underground; *en-*, in, and *silo*, a silo, underground pit.] to store (fodder) in a silo for preservation.

en·skȳ′, *v.t.* to place among the stars; to render immortal. [Poet.]

en·slāve′, *v.i.*; enslaved, *pt.*, *pp.*; enslaving, *ppr.* to reduce to slavery or bondage; to deprive of liberty and subject to the will of a master; hence, figuratively, to reduce to subjection; to dominate; to subjugate; as, men are often *enslaved* by their passions.

en·slāv′ed·ness, *n.* state of being enslaved.

en·slāve′ment, *n.* the state of being in slavery; bondage; servitude; also, the act of enslaving.

en·slāv′ēr, *n.* one who enslaves.

en·snāre′, *v.t.*; ensnared, *pt.*, *pp.*; ensnaring, *ppr.* to entrap; to catch in or as in a snare: also *insnare*.

en·snār′ēr, *n.* one who ensnares: also *insnarer*.

en·snārl′, *v.t.* to entangle.

en·sō′bēr, *v.t.* to make sober. [Obs.]

en·sor′cell, en·sor′cel, *v.t.* [OFr. *ensorceler*, to bewitch; *en-*, in, and *sorceler*, to bewitch.] to practice the art of a sorcerer upon; to bewitch.

en·sōul′, *v.t.* 1. to take or put into the soul.
2. to endow with a soul.
Also *insoul*.

en·sphēre′, *v.t.*; ensphered, *pt.*, *pp.*; ensphering, *ppr.* 1. to enclose in or as in a sphere.
 2. to make into a sphere.
 Also *insphere.*

en·stamp′, *v.t.* to impress as with a stamp; to impress deeply.

en·stāte′, *v.t.* same as *instate.*

en′stȧ·tīte, *n.* [Gr. *enstates*, an adversary; *en*, in, and *histanai*, to stand, and *-ite.*] in mineralogy, a magnesium silicate of various colors from gray to brown, of orthorhombic crystallization, but occurring also massive and fibrous.

en·stȧ·tit′iç, *a.* of or like enstatite.

en·stōre′, *v.t.* to restore; to repeat. [Obs.]

en·stȳle′, *v.t.* to style; to name; to call. [Obs.]

en·sū′ȧ·ble, *a.* following as a consequence. [Obs.]

en·sūe′, *v.t.*; ensued, *pt.*, *pp.*; ensuing, *ppr.* [ME. *ensuen*; OFr. *ensuer*; L. *insequi*, to follow upon; *in*, in, on, and *sequi*, to follow.] to follow; to pursue. [Obs.]
 Seek peace, and *ensue* it. —1 Pet. iii. 11.

en·sūe′, *v.i.* 1. to follow as a consequence; to result.
 2. to follow in a train of events or course of time; to succeed; to come afterward; as, he spoke, and silence *ensued*; the *ensuing* age or years.

eñ suīte (äṅ swēt′), [Fr.] in or forming a connected series, as rooms; following one another in order.

en·sūre′ (*or* -shoor′), *v.t.* and *v.i.*; ensured, *pt.*, *pp.*; ensuring, *ppr.* same as *insure.*

en·sūr′ēr (*or* -shoor′), *n.* same as *insurer.*

en·swāthe′, *v.t.* to swathe; to wrap or bind in or as in a bandage: also *inswathe.*

en·swāthe′ment, *n.* the act of enswathing or the condition of being enswathed: also *inswathement.*

en·sweep′, *v.t.* to sweep over rapidly.

-ent, [from OFr. *-ent*, L. *-en(t)s*, a ppr. suffix of verbs of 2d, 3d, and 4th conjugations.] a suffix used to form: (a) adjectives from verbs, corresponding to the present participles, as insist*ent*; (b) nouns of agency from verbs, as superintend*ent*, solv*ent*. See also *-ant.*

en·tab′lȧ·tūre, *n.* [OFr. *entablature*, from *entabler*; LL. *intabulare*, to construct a basis; L. *in*, in, on, and *tabulatum*, a flooring, floor.] in architecture, a horizontal superstructure supported by columns and composed of architrave, frieze, and cornice.

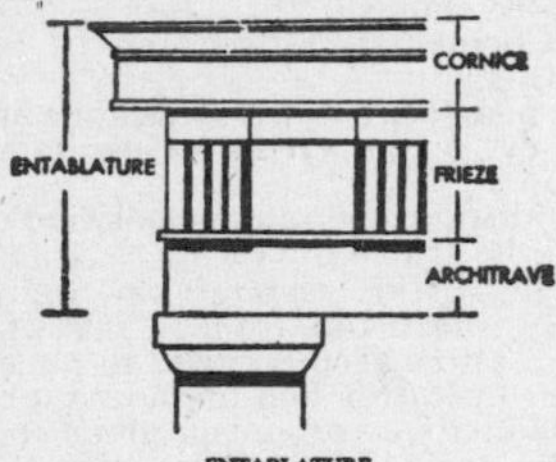

ENTABLATURE

en·tā′ble·ment, *n.* 1. an entablature.
 2. the platform or series of platforms directly beneath a statue and on top of the dado and the base.

en·taç′kle, *v.t.* to supply with tackle. [Obs.]

en′tad, *adv.* [Gr. *entos*, within, and L. *-ad*, toward.] in anatomy, in an inward direction; toward the interior of an organ or body: opposed to *ectad.*

en·tāil′, *v.t.*; entailed, *pt.*, *pp.*; entailing, *ppr.* [ME. *entailen*; LL. *intaliare*, to cut into, carve; L. *in*, in, and LL. *taliare*, to cut, carve.]
 1. in law, to limit the inheritance of (property) to a specific line of heirs in such a way that it can never be legally transferred.
 2. to cause or require as a necessary consequence; involve; necessitate; as, the plan *entails* work.
 3. to carve, as in ornamental work. [Obs.]

en·tāil′, *n.* 1. an entailing or being entailed.
 2. that which is entailed, as an inheritance.
 3. necessary sequence, as the order of descent for an entailed inheritance.
 4. delicately carved ornamentation; intaglio. [Obs.]

en·tāil′ment, *n.* the act of entailing or the state of being entailed; also, the estate entailed.

en′tăl, *a.* [Gr. *entos*, within, and *-al.*] in anatomy, of or having reference to the interior of a body or organ: opposed to *ectal.*

en·tāme′, *v.t.* to tame; to subdue. [Obs.]

en·tȧ·moe′bȧ, *n.*; *pl.* **en·tȧ·moe′bae, en·tȧ·moe′bȧṣ**, an endamoeba: also spelled *entameba.*

en·tañ′gle, *v.t.*; entangled, *pt.*, *pp.*; entangling, *ppr.* 1. to involve in or as in a tangle; to catch, as in a net, vine, etc., so that escape is difficult; ensnare.
 2. to involve in difficulty; confuse; perplex.
 3. to cause to be tangled; complicate.

en·tañ′gle·ment, *n.* 1. an entangling or being entangled.
 2. anything that entangles; an obstruction; a snare; a complication.

en·tañ′glēr, *n.* one who entangles.

en·tā′si·ȧ, *n.* same as *entasis*, n. 2.

en′tȧ·sis, *n.* [Gr. *entasis*, a stretching, distention, from *enteinein*, to stretch; *en*, in, and *teinein*, to stretch.]
 1. in architecture, the almost imperceptible convex swelling in the shaft of a column.
 2. in pathology, the rigidity of tonic spasm, as in tetanus; also, a disease having such symptom.

en·tas′tiç, *a.* [from Gr. *entasis*, a stretching, from *enteinein*, to stretch.] relating to or involving entasis.

en·tel′e·çhy, *n.*; *pl.* **en·tel′e·çhieṣ**, [L. *entelechia*; Gr. *entelecheia*, actuality, from *en telei echein*; *en*, in, *telei*, dat. of *telos*, end, completion, and *echein*, to hold.] in Aristotelian philosophy, complete actuality: distinguished from *potentiality.*

en·tel′lus, *n.* [from Gr. *entellein*, to command, enjoin; *en*, in, and *tellein*, to make to arise.] an East Indian bearded sacred monkey, *Semnopithecus entellus.* It has yellowish fur, a face of a violet tinge, and a long and powerful tail, not prehensile.

en·tend′, *v.t.* to intend. [Obs.]

en·ten′dēr, *v.t.* to treat with tenderness or kindness; also, to mollify, to soften. [Obs.]

en·tente′ (äṅ-tänt′), *n.* [Fr.] 1. an agreement or understanding, as between nations.
 2. the parties to this.
 entente cordiale; cordial understanding; friendly agreement, especially between two governments; specifically, the *Entente Cordiale* signed between Great Britain and France, in 1904, adjusting disputes over Egypt, Morocco, etc.
 Little Entente; a political and economic alliance between Czechoslovakia, Yugoslavia, and Romania: it was established between Czechoslovakia and Yugoslavia in 1920, and Romania joined these two countries in a treaty signed August 23, 1921. By extension, the countries which form this alliance are often referred to as the *Little Entente.*
 Triple Entente; an alliance between France, Great Britain, and Russia, which grew out of the *Entente Cordiale* between France and Great Britain and the Dual Alliance between France and Russia (1890–93). The *Triple Entente* came to an end when the Bolshevist Revolution in Russia (1917) took place. By extension, the nations which formed this entente are often referred to as the *Triple Entente.*

en′tēr, *v.t.*; entered, *pt.*, *pp.*; entering, *ppr.* [ME. *entren*; L. *intrare*, to go into, enter, from *intro*, into the inside, within.]
 1. to come or go into in any manner whatever; to pass into the inside or interior of; to penetrate; to pierce; as, to *enter* a house; the river *enters* the sea; the bullet *entered* his body.
 2. to advance into, in progress; as, a youth has *entered* his tenth year; to *enter* a new era.
 3. to begin (a business, employment, or service); to engage in; to join; to become a member of; as, to *enter* the army; to *enter* college.
 4. to admit or introduce; to initiate; as, to *enter* one into a secret. [Archaic.]
 5. to cause to enter; to put or set in; to insert; as, to *enter* a wedge.
 6. to set down in writing, as in a book; to enroll; to inscribe; as, the clerk *entered* the account.
 7. to report at the customhouse, as a vessel on arrival in port, by delivering a manifest; as, to *enter* a ship or her cargo.
 8. in law, (a) to go in or upon and take possession of, as lands; (b) to place upon the records of a court; as, to *enter* a rule, an appearance, etc.; (c) to file the necessary particulars to secure pre-emption rights to (public land); (d) to file in order to obtain copyright protection, as a literary production.
 9. to cause the name of to be proposed; to offer for entry; to enroll; as, to *enter* a pupil in school; to *enter* an exhibit or an animal for a prize.

en′tēr, *v.i.* 1. to go or come into some place; to make or effect an entry or entrance.
 2. specifically, to make an entrance on stage; as, *enter* King Dodo, laughing.
 3. to pierce; to penetrate.
 entering edge; same as *leading edge.*
 to enter into; (a) to get into the inside or interior of; to penetrate; as, water *enters into* a ship; (b) to engage in; as, *to enter into* business; (c) to be or become initiated in; as, they *entered into* a taste of magnificence; (d) to deal with or treat, as a subject, by discussion, argument, and the like; to make inquiry or scrutiny into; as, *to enter into* the merits of the case; (e) to be an ingredient in; to form a constituent part of; as, lead *enters into* the composition of pewter.
 to enter on or *upon*; to begin; to commence.

en·tēr-, see *entero-.*

en″tēr·ad·ē·nog′rȧ·phy, *n.* [*enter-*, and Gr. *adēn*, a gland, and *-graphia*, from *graphein*, to write.] a treatise on intestinal glands.

en″tēr·ad·ē·nol′ō·ġy, *n.* [*enter-*, and Gr. *adēn*, a gland, and *-logia*, from *legein*, to speak.] that part of anatomy dealing with intestinal glands.

en·tēr·al′ġi·ȧ, *n.* [*enter-*, and Gr. *algos*, pain.] enteric neuralgia.

en′tēr·āte, *a.* [Gr. *enteron*, an intestine, and *-ate.*] having an alimentary canal.

en′tēr·ēr, *n.* one who enters.

en·ter′iç, *a.* [Gr. *enteron*, an intestine, and *-ic.*] of, belonging to, or affecting the intestines; intestinal; also, enterate.
 enteric fever; typhoid fever.

en·te·rī′tis, *n.* [Gr. *enteron*, an intestine, and *-itis.*] an inflammation of the intestine, especially the small intestine.

en·tēr·mēte′, *v.i.* and *v.t.* to meddle. [Obs.]

en·tēr·ō-, [Gr. *enteron*, an intestine] a combining form used in medicine and anatomy to indicate *connection with* or *relation to the intestines*, as in *entero*coele, *entero*pathy. Before vowels *entero-* becomes *enter-.*

en′tēr·ō·cēle, *n.* [*entero-*, and Gr. *kēlē*, tumor.] in surgery, a hernia that contains a part of the intestine.

en′tēr·ō·coele (-sēl), *n.* [*entero-*, and Gr. *koilos*, hollow.] a perivisceral body cavity especially of an actinozoan.

en·tēr·ō·çō·lī′tis, *n.* [*entero-*, and *colitis.*] inflammation of the colon and the small intestine.

en·tēr·og′rȧ·phy, *n.* [*entero-*, and Gr. *-graphia*, from *graphein*, to write.] a treatise on the intestines.

en′tēr·ō·līte, en′tēr·ō·lith, *n.* [*entero-*, and Gr. *lithos*, a stone.] a concretion in the intestines.

en·tēr·ol′ō·ġy, *n.* [*entero-*, and Gr. *-logia*, from *legein*, to speak.] a treatise on the intestines.

en′te·ron, *n.* [Gr. *enteron*, an intestine.] the alimentary canal.

en·tēr·op′ȧ·thy, *n.* [*entero-*, and Gr. *pathos*, suffering.] any intestinal disease.

en′tēr·ō·plas″ty, *n.* [*entero-*, and Gr. *plastos*, from *plassein*, to form, mold.] a plastic operation for the restoration of an injured intestine.

En″te·rop·neū̇s′tȧ, *n.pl.* [*entero-*, and Gr. *pnein*, to breathe.] a group or class of animals allied to the tunicates and comprising *Balanoglossus* as the sole genus.

en·tēr·os′tō·my, *n.*; *pl.* **en·tēr·os′tō·mieṣ**, [*entero-*, and *-stomy.*] the surgical operation of making an artificial opening into the intestine through the abdominal wall, as for drainage.

en·tēr·ot′ō·my, *n.* [*entero-*, and Gr. *tomē*, a cutting.]
 1. intestinal dissection.
 2. a cutting into an intestine.

en″tēr·ō·zō′on, en″tēr·ō·zō′ăn, *n.* an entozoon.

en·tēr·pär′lănce, *n.* [Fr. *entre*, between, and *parler*, to speak.] parley; mutual talk or conversation; conference. [Obs.]

en·tēr·plēad′, *v.i.* to interplead. [Obs.]

en′tēr·prīṣe, *n.* [Fr., from *entreprendre*, to undertake; *entre*, in or between, and *prendre*, to take; *prise*, a taking.]
 1. an undertaking; a project.
 2. a bold, hard, dangerous, or important undertaking.
 3. willingness to venture on such undertakings; readiness to take risks or try something untried; energy and initiative.
 4. the carrying on of projects; participation in undertakings.
 Syn.—adventure, undertaking, venture.

en′tẽr·prīṣe, *v.t.* 1. to undertake; to begin and attempt to perform. [Archaic.]
2. to attack. [Obs.]

en′tẽr·prīṣe, *v.i.* to venture. [Obs.]

en′tẽr·prī·ṣẽr, *n.* an entrepreneur.

en′tẽr·prī·ṣing, *a.* bold or forward to undertake new projects; resolute, active, or prompt to attempt great or untried schemes; full of energy and initiative.
Syn.—active, bold, daring, adventurous, speculative, dashing, venturesome.

en′tẽr·prī·ṣing·ly, *adv.* in an enterprising manner.

en·tẽr·tāin′, *v.t.*; entertained, *pt., pp.*; entertaining, *ppr.* [Fr. *entretenir*; LL. *intertenere*, to entertain; L. *inter*, among, between, and *tenere*, to hold.]
1. to receive into the house and treat with hospitality; to show hospitality to; as, to *entertain* a guest.
2. to take or receive into one's service; to hire. [Obs.]
3. to engage the attention of, with anything that causes the time to pass pleasantly, as conversation, music, or the like; to divert; to please; to amuse.
4. to receive or admit with a view to consider and decide; to take into consideration; as, to *entertain* a proposal.
5. to keep, hold, or maintain in the mind; to harbor; to cherish; as, to *entertain* charitable sentiments.
6. to keep up; to continue. [Archaic.]
7. to cause to pass pleasantly; to while away; as, to *entertain* the irksome hours. [Obs.]
8. to maintain. [Obs.]
9. to engage or encounter in combat. [Obs.]
Syn.—harbor, maintain, foster, receive, recreate, amuse.

en·tẽr·tāin′, *v.i.* to receive guests; to furnish entertainment.

en·tẽr·tāin′, *n.* entertainment. [Obs.]

en·tẽr·tāin′ẽr, *n.* one who entertains; especially, one whose work is singing, dancing, etc., as at nightclubs.

en·tẽr·tāin′ing, *a.* pleasing; amusing; diverting; interesting.

en·tẽr·tāin′ing·ly, *adv.* in an entertaining way.

en·tẽr·tāin′ing·ness, *n.* the quality of entertaining.

en·tẽr·tāin′ment, *n.* [OFr. *entretenement*, from LL. *intertenementum*, from *intertenere*, to entertain.]
1. an entertaining or being entertained; specifically, (a) amusement; (b) hospitality given or received; (c) the consideration of an idea, etc.; (d) a keeping in mind.
2. something that entertains; an interesting, diverting, or amusing thing, as a show or performance.
3. reception; admission. [Rare.]
4. the state of being in pay or service. [Obs.]
Syn.—amusement, diversion, recreation, pastime.

en·tẽr·tāke′, *v.t.* to entertain. [Obs.]

en·tẽr·tis′sūed (-tish′ūd), *a.* intertissued. [Obs.]

en′thē·ăl, en′thē·ăn, *a.* [L. *entheus*; Gr. *entheos*, inspired; *en*, in, and *theos*, god.] divinely inspired. [Obs.]

en′thē·aṣm, *n.* inspiration. [Obs.]

en·thē·as′tiç, *a.* [Gr. *entheastikos*, from *entheos*, inspired; *en*, in, and *theos*, god.] marked by entheasm.

en·thē·as′tiç·ăl·ly, *adv.* in an entheastic manner.

en′thē·āte, en′thē·at, *a.* entheal. [Obs.]

en·thel·min′thȧ, en·thel·min′thēṣ, *n.pl.* the intestinal worms taken collectively.

en·thel·min′thiç, *a.* of or like the enthelmintha.

en·thet′iç, *a.* [Gr. *enthetikos*, fit for planting, from *enthetos*, verbal adj. of *entithenai*; *en*, in, and *tithenai*, to put.] in medicine, coming from without; propagated by inoculation; introduced by infection; exogenous; as, a contagious disease is *enthetic*.

en·thrạll′, en·thrạl′, *v.t.*; enthralled, *pt., pp.*; enthralling, *ppr.* [*en-*, and *thrall*.]
1. to make a slave of; enslave.
2. to put or hold under strong influence; captivate; enchant; fascinate.
Also spelled *inthrall, inthral.*

en·thrạll′ment, en·thrạl′ment, *n.* 1. the act of enthralling or the condition of being enthralled.
2. that which enthralls.

en·thrill′, *v.t.* to pierce. [Obs.]

en·thrōne′, *v.t.*; enthroned, *pt., pp.*; enthroning, *ppr.* 1. to place on a throne, as a king or bishop; to make a king or bishop of.
2. to accord the highest place to; revere; exalt.
Also spelled *inthrone.*

en·thrōne′ment, *n.* an enthroning or being enthroned.

en·thrōn·i·zā′tion, *n.* same as *enthronement.*

en·thrōn′īze, *v.t.*; enthronized, *pt., pp.*; enthronizing, *ppr.* same as *enthrone.*

en·thūṣe′, *v.t.* and *v.i.*; enthused, *pt., pp.*; enthusing, *ppr.* [back-formation from *enthusiasm.*]
1. to make or become enthusiastic. [Colloq.]
2. to show or cause to show enthusiasm. [Colloq.]

en·thū′ṣi·aṣm, *n.* [Gr. *enthousiasmos*, inspiration, enthusiasm, from *enthousiazein*, to be inspired, to be possessed by a god, to inspire; from *enthous, entheos*, possessed by a god; *en*, in, and *theos*, god.]
1. originally, supernatural inspiration or possession; inspired prophetic or poetic ecstasy.
2. intense or eager interest; zeal; fervor.
3. something arousing such interest or zeal.
4. religious frenzy. [Archaic.]

en·thū′ṣi·ȧst, *n.* [Gr. *enthousiastēs*, from *enthousiazein*, to be inspired.]
1. one who is full of enthusiasm.
2. a religious zealot, fanatic, or visionary.

en·thū·ṣi·as′tiç, en·thū·si·as′tiç·ăl, *a.* 1. having or showing enthusiasm; ardent.
2. of, or having the nature of, enthusiasm.

en·thū·ṣi·as′tiç·ăl·ly, *adv.* in an enthusiastic manner; with enthusiasm.

en″thy·mē·mat′iç, en″thy·mē·mat′iç·ăl, *a.* pertaining to or including an enthymeme.

en′thy·mēme, *n.* [L. *enthymema*; Gr. *enthymema*, a thought, argument, from *enthymeisthai*, to consider, keep in mind; *en*, in, and *thymos*, mind.]
1. originally, in Aristotle, an argument from probabilities.
2. in logic, an argument in which one of the premises or, sometimes, the conclusion is not expressed but implied.

en·tīce′, *v.t.*; enticed (-tīst′), *pt., pp.*; enticing, *ppr.* [ME. *enticen, entisen*; OFr. *enticer, enticher*, to excite, entice.] to allure; to lead on by exciting hope of reward or pleasure; to tempt.
Syn.—allure, inveigle.

en·tīce′ȧ·ble, *a.* susceptible of being enticed.

en·tīce′ment, *n.* 1. an enticing or being enticed.
2. something that entices; an allurement.

en·tī′cẽr, *n.* one who entices.

en·tī′cing, *a.* alluring; tempting; inviting.

en·tī′cing·ly, *adv.* in an enticing manner.

en·tīer′ty, *n.* entirety. [Obs.]

en′ti·fȳ, *v.t.* [L. *ens, entis*, a thing, and *-ficare*, from *facere*, to make.] to consider as, or cause to become, an entity. [Rare.]

en·tīre′, *a.* [ME. *entyre*; OFr. *entier*; L. *integer*, whole, untouched, undiminished.]
1. whole; undivided; unbroken; complete in all its parts; undiminished; full; perfect; not mutilated; having all normal elements; as, not an article was left *entire*; *entire* confidence.
2. being wholly of one piece; undivided; continuous.
3. in biology, not divided; (a) without branches; (b) without an opening in the edge, as a leaf; (c) of one piece, as a fin; (d) uncastrated, as a horse.
4. in full strength; unalloyed; unqualified; pure; sincere; faithful; unfeigned. [Obs.]
5. interior. [Obs.]

en·tīre′, *n.* 1. the whole; entirety.
2. porter; stout. [Brit.]
3. a stallion.

en·tīre′ly, *adv.* 1. wholly; completely; fully; unreservedly.
2. solely; only.

en·tīre′ness, *n.* 1. the state of being entire; completeness; totality; entirety.
2. closeness; intimacy; unity. [Obs.]

en·tīre′ty, *n.*; *pl.* **en·tīre′ties,** 1. the state or fact of being entire; wholeness; completeness; entireness; as, *entirety* of interest.
2. an entire thing; whole; total.
3. in law, undivided or sole possession.
in its entirety; as a whole; completely.

en′ti·tā·tive, *a.* considered by itself as an entity or independent existence. [Rare.]

en′ti·tā·tive·ly, *adv.* as abstract existence. [Rare.]

en·tī′tle, *v.t.*; entitled, *pt., pp.*; entitling, *ppr.* [ME. *entitlen*; OFr. *entituler*; LL. *intitulare*, to give title or name to; L. *in*, in, and *titulus*, a title.]
1. to give a title to; to give a name or appellation to.
2. to honor or dignify by a title.
3. to qualify (a person) *to* do something; to give a claim to; to give a right to demand or receive; as, his labor *entitles* him to his wages.
4. to assign or appropriate as by giving a title. [Obs.]
5. to ascribe. [Obs.]
Also spelled *intitle.*

en·tit′ūle, *v.t.* intitule. [Obs.]

en′ti·ty, *n.*; *pl.* **en′ti·tieṣ,** [LL. *entitas*, from L. *ens, entis*, being, ppr. of *esse*, to be.]
1. being; existence.
2. a thing that has real and individual existence, in reality or in the mind; anything real in itself.
3. essence; essential nature. [Rare.]

en·tō-, [Greek *entos*, within.] a combining form meaning *within* or *inner*, as in *ento*phyte: also, before a vowel, *ent-*.

en′tō·blȧst, *n.* [*ento-*, and Gr. *blastos*, a shoot, germ.] same as *endoderm.*

en·tō·bran′çhi·āte, *a.* [*ento-*, and Gr. *branchia*, gills.] having the gills entirely internal.

en·tō·bron′çhi·um, *n.*; *pl.* **en·tō·bron′çhi·ȧ,** [*ento-*, and Gr. *bronchos*, the windpipe.] in zoology, a ventral branch of a bird's bronchus.

en′tō·cēle, *n.* [*ento-*, and Gr. *kēlē*, a rupture.] in pathology, displacement of an internal organ; internal hernia.

en″tō·çū·nē′i·fọrm, *n.* [*ento-*, and L. *cuneus*, a wedge, and *forma*, form.] in anatomy, the innermost of the three tapering or wedge-shaped bones of the tarsus.

en′tō·dẽrm, *n.* same as *endoderm.*

en·tō·dẽr′măl, en·tō·dẽr′miç, *a.* same as *endodermal.*

en·tō·gas′triç, *a.* [*ento-*, and Gr. *gastēr, gastros*, stomach.] of or relating to the inside of the gastric cavity.
entogastric gemmation or *proliferation*; a process of asexual multiplication seen in certain *Discophora*, in which budding occurs within the gastric cavity.

en·toġ′e·nous, *a.* same as *endogenous.*

en·tō·glos′săl, *a.* [*ento-*, and Gr. *glōssa*, the tongue.] inside the tongue: said of the glossohyal bone.

en·tō·glos′săl, *n.* the glossohyal bone.

en·tömb′ (-töm′), *v.t.*; entombed, *pt., pp.*; entombing, *ppr.* 1. to deposit in a tomb or grave; to bury; to inter.
2. to be a tomb for.
Also spelled *intomb.*

en·tömb′ment, *n.* an entombing or being entombed.

en′tō·mēre, *n.* [*ento-*, and Gr. *meros*, a part.] in embryology, the more granular portion of a mammalian ovum, becoming the inner portion in the process of development.

en·tom′iç, en·tom′iç·ăl, *a.* [Gr. *entomon*, an insect.] relating to insects; entomological.

en′tō·mō-, en′tom-, [from Gr. *entomon*, an insect.] a combining form meaning *insect, insects*, as in *entomo*phagous, *entomo*logy.

en·tō·moġ′e·nous, *a.* growing in or upon insects: said of certain fungi.

en′tō·moid, *a.* [Gr. *entomon*, an insect, and *eidos*, form.] like an insect. [Rare.]

en′tō·moid, *n.* a thing, as a leaf, with the appearance of an insect. [Rare.]

en·tom′ō·lin, *n.* same as *chitin.*

en·tom′ō·līte, *n.* a fossil considered to be that of an insect. [Obs.]

en″tō·mō·loġ′iç·ăl, en″tō·mō·loġ′iç, *a.* pertaining to entomology.

en″tō·mō·loġ′iç·ăl·ly, *adv.* according to entomology.

en·tō·mol′ō·ġist, *n.* a student of or specialist in entomology.

en·tō·mol′ō·ġīze, *v.i.*; entomologized, *pt., pp.*; entomologizing, *ppr.* to collect insects for scientific study; to study entomology.

en·tō·mol′ō·ġy, *n.*; *pl.* **en·tō·mol′ō·ġieṣ,** [*entomo-*, and Gr. *-logia*, from *legein*, to speak.]
1. the branch of zoology that deals with insects.
2. a systematic treatise on insects.

En·tō·moph′ȧ·gȧ, *n.pl.* [*entomo-*, and Gr. *phagein*, to eat.] insect eaters: formerly applied to genera of parasitic hymenopters, edentates, and marsupials.

en·tō·moph′ȧ·găn, *a.* of or pertaining to the *Entomophaga.*

en·tō·moph′ȧ·găn, *n.* a member of the *Entomophaga.*

en·tō·moph′ȧ·gous, *a.* insectivorous; entomophagan.

en·tō·moph′i·lous, *a.* [*entomo-*, and Gr. *philos*, loving.] depending chiefly upon insects for fertilization: said of certain flowers.

En″tō·moph·thō·rā′cē·ae, *n.pl.* [*entomo-*, and Gr. *phthora*, destruction, from *phtheirein*, to destroy.] a family of fungi commonly parasitic upon and destructive to insects.

en·tō·moph′y·tous, *a.* [*entomo-*, and Gr. *phyton*, a plant.] same as *entomogenous*.

En·tō·mos′trȧ·çȧ, *n.pl.* [*entom-*, and Gr. *ostrakon*, an earthen vessel, a shell.] a main division of *Crustacea*, including, according to Huxley's system, the *Cirripedia*, *Copepoda*, *Branchiopoda*, and *Ostracoda*.

en·tō·mos′trȧ·çăn, *a.* of or pertaining to the *Entomostraca*.

en·tō·mos′trȧ·çăn, *n.* a member of the *Entomostraca*.

en·tō·mos′trȧ·çous, *a.* entomostracan.

en″tō·mō·tax′y, *n.* [*entomo-*, and Gr. *taxis*, arrangement.] the art of arranging and preserving entomological specimens. [Rare.]

en·tō·mot′ō·mist, *n.* one who dissects insects.

en·tō·mot′ō·my, *n.* [*entomo-*, and Gr. *tomē*, a cutting.] in zoology, the art or science of dissecting insects.

en·ton′iç, *a.* [Gr. *entonos*, stretched, strung, from *enteinein*, to stretch, strain tight; *en*, in, and *teinein*, to stretch.] in pathology, strained; having violent action or abnormal tension.

en·tō·par′ȧ·sīte, *n.* a parasite living within its host: opposed to *ectoparasite*.

en″tō·pe·riph′ẽr·ăl, *a.* [*ento-*, and Gr. *peripthereia*, periphery; *peri*, around, and *pherein*, to bear.] in physiology, arising or developing within the body's periphery.

en′tō·phȳte, *n.* [*ento-*, and Gr. *phyton*, a plant.] a plant that lives inside the body of another plant or of an animal.

en·tō·phyt′iç, *a.* of, like, caused by, or characteristic of entophytes.

en′tō·plaṣm, *n.* same as *endoplasm*.

en·tō·plas′trŏn, *n.*; *pl.* **en·tō·plas′trȧ,** [*ento-*, and LL. *plastra*, a thin plate of metal.] the median and anterior piece of the ventral part of the shell of a turtle or tortoise.

En·tō·proç′tȧ, *n.pl.* [*ento-*, and Gr. *prōktos*, the anus.] a group of polyzoans having the anus close to the mouth and within the tentacles of the lophophore.

en·tō·proç′tous, *a.* pertaining to or having the characteristics of the *Entoprocta*.

ent·op′tiç, *a.* [*ent-*, and Gr. *optikos*, pertaining to sight.] of or relating to the interior of the eye.

ent·op′tiçs, *n.* the science of the internal phenomena of the eye.

ent·or′găn·iṣm, *n.* an internal parasite.

en·tor·ti·lā′tion, *n.* [Fr. *entortiller*, to twist; *en-*, in, *tortiller*, from L. *torquere*, to twist.] a turning into a circle. [Obs.]

en·tō·stẽr′năl, *a.* [*ento-*, and Gr. *sternon*, the breast, chest.] pertaining to the entosternum.

en·tō·stẽr′nīte, *n.* a cartilaginous plate developed internally as a support for muscles, as in some crustaceans.

en·tō·stẽr′num, *n.* 1. one or all of the internal processes of an insect's sternum.

2. an entoplastron.

en·tos′thō·blȧst, *n.* [Gr. *entosthe*, from within, and *blastos*, a bud, germ.] in biology, a granule inside of the nucleolus of a cell.

en·tō·thō′rax, *n.* same as *endothorax*.

ent·ot′iç, *a.* [*ento-*, and Gr. *ous*, *ōtos*, the ear.] of or relating to the inside of the ear.

eṅ·töu·räġe′ (äṅ-tō-räzh′), *n.* [Fr., from *entourer*, to surround; from *en tour*, around; *en*, in, and *tour*, round.]

1. surroundings; environment.

2. a group of associates or attendants; retinue.

en·tō·zō′ȧ, *n.* plural of *entozoon*.

en·tō·zō′ăn, *n.* same as *entozoon*.

en·tō·zō′ăn, en·tō·zō′ăl, *a.* of the entozoa.

en·tō·zō′iç, *a.* 1. in botany, living inside animals, usually as a parasite: said of certain fungi, etc.

2. in zoology, living inside another animal: said especially of certain intestinal worms.

en″tō·zō·ol′ō·ġist, *n.* a student of internal parasitology.

en·tō·zō′on, *n.*; *pl.* **en·tō·zō′ȧ,** [*ento-*, and Gr. *zōon*, an animal.] an animal parasite, especially an intestinal worm, living inside another animal.

en·tr′acte′ (äṅ-trakt′), *n.* [Fr., from *entre*, between, and *acte*, an act.]

1. the interval between two acts of a play, opera, etc.; intermission.

2. a musical selection, dance, etc. performed during this interval.

en·trāil′, *v.t.* [*en-*, and Fr. *treiller*, to lattice, trellis.] to interweave. [Obs.]

en·trāil′, *n.* a coil. [Obs.]

en′trāilṣ, *n. pl.* [ME. *entrailes*; OFr. *entrailles*; LL. *intralia*, from L. *interaneum*, pl. *interanea*, intestine; *interaneus*, inward, interior, from *inter*, between, among.]

1. the inner organs of men or animals; specifically, the intestines; viscera; guts.

2. the inner parts of a thing. [Rare.]

en·trāin′, *v.i.* and *v.t.*; entrained, *pt.*, *pp.*; entraining, *ppr.* to go or cause to go aboard a railroad train.

en·trāin′, *v.t.* to draw after oneself. [Rare.]

en·tram′mel, *v.t.* to trammel; to entangle. [Rare.]

en′trănce, *n.* [OFr. *entrance*, from *entrant*; L. *intrans (-antis)*, ppr. of *intrare*, to enter, from *intro*, to the inside, within.]

1. the act or point of entering; as, the *entrance* of a person into a house.

His own door being shut against his *entrance*. —Shak.

2. the power or liberty of entering; admission.

Truth is sure to find an *entrance* and a welcome too. —South.

3. the doorway, gateway, passage, or avenue by which a place may be entered.

And wisdom at one *entrance* quite shut out. —Milton.

4. commencement; beginning. [Obs.]

This is that which, at first *entrance*, balks and cools them. —Locke.

5. the bow of a vessel, or the forebody under the load water line: opposed to *run*.

Syn.—ingress, entry, admission, admittance, doorway, gateway.

en·trȧnce′, *v.t.*; entranced, *pt.*, *pp.*; entrancing, *ppr.* 1. to put into a trance.

2. to put into an ecstasy; to delight; to charm; to enrapture; to enchant.

I stood *entranced*, and had no room for thought. —Dryden.

en·trȧnce′ment, *n.* 1. an entrancing or being entranced.

2. something that entrances.

en′trănt, *n.* [Fr.; OFr.; see **entrance, n.**]

1. a person who enters.

2. a person entering a profession, an organization, etc.

3. a participant in a contest or competition.

en′trănt, *a.* entering; that enters.

en·trap′, *v.t.*; entrapped (-trapt′), *pt.*, *pp.*; entrapping, *ppr.* [OFr. *entraper*, *entrapper*, to catch in a trap; *en-*, in, and *trape*, a trap.]

1. to catch in or as in a trap.

2. to catch by artifice; to involve in difficulties or distresses; to ensnare; as, we are *entrapped* by the devices of evil men.

Syn.—decoy, lure, inveigle, ensnare.

en·trēat′, *v.t.*; entreated, *pt.*, *pp.*; entreating, *ppr.* [ME. *entreten*, to treat or deal with, to beseech; OFr. *entraiter*, to treat of, entertain; *en-*, in, and *traiter*, to treat.]

1. to ask earnestly; to beseech; to beg; to implore; to supplicate; to solicit pressingly.

Isaac *entreated* Jehovah for his wife. —Gen. xxv. 21.

2. to prevail on by prayer or solicitation; also, to induce. [Obs.]

It were a fruitless attempt to appease a power whom no prayers could *entreat*. —Rogers.

3. to treat; to deal with. [Archaic.]

I will cause the enemy to *entreat* thee well. —Jer. xv. 11.

Also spelled *intreat*.

Syn.—beg, implore, beseech, solicit.

en·trēat′, *v.i.* 1. to make an earnest petition or request.

The Janizaries *entreated* for them, as valiant men. —Knowles.

2. to offer a treaty. [Obs.]

3. to treat; to discourse. [Obs.]

en·trēat′, *n.* entreaty. [Obs.]

en·trēat′ȧ·ble, *a.* that may be entreated, or is soon entreated. [Obs.]

en·trēat′ănce, *n.* entreaty; solicitation. [Obs.]

en·trēat′ẽr, *n.* one who entreats.

en·trēat′fụl, *a.* of an entreating disposition. [Obs.]

en·trēat′ing·ly, *adv.* in an entreating manner.

en·trēat′ive, *a.* pleading; characterized by entreaty. [Obs.]

en·trēat′ment, *n.* entreaty. [Obs.]

en·trēat′y, *n.*; *pl.* **en·trēat′ieṣ,** 1. urgent prayer; earnest petition; pressing solicitation; supplication.

The poor useth *entreaties*; but the rich answereth roughly. —Prov. xviii. 23.

2. treatment; amusement. [Obs.]

Syn.—solicitation, importunity, supplication, prayer.

en·trē·chȧt′ (äṅ-trē-shä′), *n.* [Fr., from It. *(capriola) intrecciata*, intricate (leap), from *intrecciare*, from *in-*, in, and *treccia*, a pleat.] in ballet, a leap straight upward in which the dancer crosses his legs and strikes his heels together, usually several times.

en·tre·côte′ (än-trȧ-kōt′), *n.* [Fr.] boned rib steak.

en′tree, en′trée (än′trā; Fr. äṅ-trā′), *n.* [Fr. *entrée*; f. pp. of *entrer*; OFr. *entrer*; L. *intrare*, from *intra*, within, inside.]

1. the right, permission, or freedom to enter; access.

2. the main course of a meal.

3. formerly, and still in some countries, a dish served before the roast or between the main courses, as between the fish and the meat.

4. in music, the opening number, especially of a ballet or opera.

en′tre·mets (än′tre-mā; Fr. äṅ-trē-mā′), *n.*; *pl.* **en′tre·mets** (-māz; Fr. -mā′), [Fr. *entre*, between, and *mets*, a dish, mess.] a dish served between the main courses or as a side dish.

en·trench′, *v.t.* [*en-*, and *trench*, after Fr. *retrancher*.]

1. to surround or fortify with a trench or trenches.

2. to establish securely: used in the passive voice or with a reflexive pronoun; as, the right to trial by jury is *entrenched* in our legal system.

Also spelled *intrench*.

en·trench′, *v.i.* to encroach; infringe; trespass: also spelled *intrench*.

en·trench′ment, *n.* 1. an entrenching or being entrenched.

2. a trench or system of trenches, usually fortified with mounds of earth, rubble, etc.

3. any fortification or defense.

eṅ tre nöus (äṅ″tr nō′), [Fr., lit., between us.] between ourselves; confidentially.

en′tre·pôt (än′tre-pō; Fr. äṅ-trē-pō′), *n.* [Fr., from L. *interpositum*, neut. of *interpositus*, pp. of *interponere*, to place between; *inter*, between, and *ponere*, to place.]

1. a warehouse or place for the storage of goods.

2. a distributing point for goods, as a seaport or large inland city.

en·tre·prē·nēur′ (än-tr-prē-nẽr′), *n.* [Fr., from *entreprendre*, to undertake.] one who organizes and directs a business undertaking, assuming the risk for the sake of the profit; also, the originator or manager of public entertainments, or of a musical enterprise.

en′tre·sol (-tẽr-; Fr. äṅ-tr-sol′), *n.* [Fr. *entre*, between, and *sol*, ground.] a mezzanine, especially a half story just above the ground floor, as in some hotels and department stores.

en′trō·çhăl, *a.* relating to or made of entrochites; as, *entrochal* marble.

en′trō·çhīte, *n.* [Gr. *en*, in, and *trochos*, a wheel, and *-ite*.] a wheellike joint of a fossil crinoid or encrinite.

en·trō′pi on, en·trō′pi·um, *n.* introversion or turning inward of the edge of the eyelid.

en′trō·py, *n.* [G. *entropie*, arbitrary use (by R.J.E. *Clausius*, 1822–88, Ger. physicist) of Gr. *entropē*, a turning toward, as if from *en(ergie)*, and Gr. *tropē*, a turning.]

1. a thermodynamic measure of the amount of energy unavailable for useful work in a system undergoing change.

2. a measure of the degree of disorder in a substance or a system: entropy always increases and available energy diminishes in a closed system, as the universe.

3. in information theory and computer science, a measure of the information content of a message evaluated as to its uncertainty.

en·trust′, *v.t.* 1. to trust; charge or invest with a trust or duty; as, he *entrusted* his friend with the property.

2. to assign the care of; turn over for safekeeping; as, *entrust* your key to me.

Also spelled *intrust*.

en′try, *n.*; *pl.* **en′trieṣ,** [ME. *entree*; OFr. *entree*; Pr. *intrada*; LL. *intrata*, entry, entrance, f. pp. of L. *intrare*, to enter, from *intro*, to the inside, within.]

1. the passage by which persons enter; a hall; a vestibule; an entryway.

2. the act of entering; entrance; ingress; as, the *entry* of a person into a house or city.

3. the act of committing to writing, or of recording in a book; as, make an *entry* of every sale; also, a thing thus recorded.

4. the exhibition or depositing of a ship's papers at the customhouse; the registration of a ship or cargo.

5. the act of entering and taking possession of lands or other estate.
6. the putting upon record of any action, decree, or order in court.
7. the going into or upon the premises of another wrongfully or feloniously.
8. one entered in a race, competition, etc.; an entrant.
9. (a) a term defined, or a person, place, abbreviation, etc. identified, in a dictionary; (b) the heading under which an encyclopedia article is entered.

en′try·wāy, *n.* a way or passage by which to enter.

en·twīne′, *v.t.* and *v.i.* entwined, *pt., pp.*; entwining, *ppr.* to twine, weave, or twist together or around: also spelled *intwine.*

en·twīne′ment, *n.* a twisting round; union.

en·twist′, *v.t.* 1. to twist together or in (*with*).
2. to make into a twist.
Also spelled *intwist.*

ē·nū′clē·āte, *v.t.*; enucleated, *pt., pp.*; enucleating, *ppr.* [L. *enucleatus*, pp. of *enucleare*, to take out the kernel, to explain; *e-*, out, and *nucleus*, a kernel.]
1. to extract (a kernel, etc.) from a shell or husk.
2. to make clear; explain.
3. in biology, to remove the nucleus of.
4. in surgery, to remove (a tumor, etc.) as a whole from its enclosing sac.

ē·nū′clē·āte, *a.* enucleated.

ē·nū·clē·ā′tion, *n.* an enucleating or being enucleated.

ē·nū′clē·ā·tŏr, *n.* a person or thing that enucleates.

ē·nū′mẽr·āte, *v.t.*; enumerated, *pt., pp.*; enumerating, *ppr.* [L. *enumeratus*, pp. of *enumerare*, to count over, count out; *e-*, out, and *numerare*, to count, from *numerus*, a number.]
1. to count; to count one by one.
2. to name one by one; to specify, as in a list.
Syn.—specify, name, number, recount, detail, reckon, compute, calculate, call over.

ē·nū·mẽr·ā′tion, *n.* [L. *numerus*, number.]
1. the act of counting or numbering.
2. a detailed list; an account of a number of things, in which mention is made of every particular article.
3. in rhetoric, a part of a peroration, in which the orator recapitulates the principal points of the discourse or argument.

ē·nū′mẽr·ā·tive, *a.* 1. enumerating.
2. of enumeration.

ē·nū′mẽr·ā·tŏr, *n.* one who enumerates.

ē·nun′ci·ȧ·ble (-shi-ȧ-bl), *a.* that can be enunciated.

ē·nun′ci·āte, *v.t.*; enunciated, *pt., pp.*; enunciating, *ppr.* [L. *enunciatus*, pp. of *enunciare*, properly *enuntiare*, to say out, declare; *e-*, out, and *nuntiare*, to announce, from *nuntius*, a messenger.]
1. to state definitely.
2. to announce; proclaim.
3. to pronounce (words); especially, to pronounce clearly and distinctly.

ē·nun′ci·āte, *v.i.* to pronounce words; to articulate.

ē·nun·ci·ā′tion, *n.* 1. an enunciating or being enunciated.
2. an announcement; a declaration; open proclamation; public attestation; as, the *enunciation* of doctrines.
3. the manner of enunciating words; articulation; as, his *enunciation* is very distinct.

ē·nun′ci·ȧ·tive, *a.* 1. enunciating; declaratory.
2. pertaining to enunciation.

ē·nun′ci·ȧ·tive·ly, *adv.* declaratively.

ē·nun′ci·ā·tŏr, *n.* [LL. *enunciator*, properly *enuntiator*, from L. *enuntiare*, to speak out, declare.] one who enunciates.

ē·nun′ci·ȧ·tō·ry, *a.* same as *enunciative.*

en·ūre′, *v.t.* and *v.i.* same as *inure.*

en·ū·rē′sis, *n.* [from Gr. *enourein*, to make water in; *en-*, in, and *ourein*, from *ouron*, urine.] involuntary discharge of urine.

en·vas′săl, *v.t.* to reduce to vassalage. [Obs.]

en·vēi′gle, *v.t.* to inveigle. [Obs.]

en·vel′ŏp, *v.t.*; enveloped (-upt), *pt., pp.*; enveloping, *ppr.* [OFr. *envoluper, enveloper*; Pr. *envolopar*, to wrap up, envelop.] 1. to cover, as by wrapping or folding; to enwrap; to invest with or as with a covering.
2. to surround.
3. to conceal; to hide; to obscure.

en′vel·ōpe, en·vel′ŏp, *n.* [Fr. *enveloppe*, from *envelopper* (OFr. *enveloper*); see *envelop.*]
1. a thing that envelops; wrapper; covering.
2. a folded paper container for letters, etc., usually with a gummed flap for sealing.
3. the outer covering of a dirigible or balloon.
4. the bag that contains the gas in a dirigible or balloon.
5. in astronomy, a cloudy mass surrounding the head of a comet on the side toward the sun.
6. in biology, any enclosing membrane, skin, or shell.
7. in botany, any surrounding structure, as the calyx.
8. in geometry, the locus of the ultimate intersections of a series of curves or surfaces.
9. in fortification, a work of earth in the form of a parapet or of a small rampart with a parapet, raised to cover some weak part of the works.

en·vel′ŏp·ment, *n.* 1. an enveloping or being enveloped.
2. that which envelops; a wrapper; a covering.

en·ven′ŏm, *v.t.*; envenomed, *pt., pp.*; envenoming, *ppr.* [ME. *envenimen*; OFr. *envenimer*, from LL. *invenenare*, to poison, envenom; L. *in*, in, and *venenum*, poison, venom.]
1. to put venom or poison on or into; to make dangerous or deadly by poison; as, an *envenomed* arrow; an *envenomed* potion.
2. to fill with hate; to embitter.
The *envenomed* tongue of calumny.
—Smollett.

en·vẽr′meil (-mil), *v.t.* [OFr. *envermeillir*, to make red; *en-*, in, and *vermeil*, vermilion.] to dye red; to give a red color to. [Obs.]

en′vi·ȧ·ble, *a.* [Fr. *enviable*, from *envier*, to envy.] to be envied or desired.

en′vi·ȧ·ble·ness, *n.* the state or quality of being enviable.

en′vi·ȧ·bly, *adv.* in an enviable manner.

en′vi·ẽr, *n.* one who envies.

en′vi·ous, *a.* [ME. *envious, envius*; OFr. *envios*; Sp. *envidioso*; It. *invidioso*; from L. *invidiosus*, envious, exciting envy, from *invidia*, envy.]
1. feeling, showing, or resulting from envy.
Be not thou *envious* against evil men.
—Prov. xxiv. 1.
2. characterized by envy; as, an *envious* disposition.
3. enviable. [Obs.]
4. watchful; cautious; jealous. [Obs.]
5. emulous. [Obs.]
6. spiteful. [Obs.]

en′vi·ous·ly, *adv.* in an envious manner; with envy; spitefully.

en′vi·ous·ness, *n.* the quality or state of being envious.

en·vī′rŏn, *v.t.*; environed, *pt., pp.*; environing, *ppr.* [ME. *environen, envirounen*; OFr. *environer, envirouner*, to surround, from *environ*, around, about.] to surround; to encompass; to encircle; to hem in; to involve; to envelop.
With mountains round about *environed.*
—Spenser.

en·vī′rŏn·ment, *n.* [Fr. *environnement*, from *environner*, to surround.]
1. a surrounding or being surrounded.
2. something that surrounds; surroundings.
3. all the conditions, circumstances, and influences surrounding, and affecting the development of, an organism or group of organisms: often contrasted with *heredity.*

en·vī·rŏn·men′tăl, *a.* of environment.

en·vī·rŏn·men′tăl·ist, *n.* a person working to solve environmental problems, such as air and water pollution, the exhaustion of natural resources, uncontrolled population growth, etc.

en·vī′rŏnṣ (*or* en′vi-), *n.pl.* [ME. *enviroun* (sing.); OFr. *environ*, from *en-*, in, and *viron*, a circuit, from *virer*, to turn.] the districts surrounding a town or city; suburbs; vicinity.

en·viṣ′ăġe, *v.t.*; envisaged, *pt., pp.*; envisaging, *ppr.* [Fr. *envisager*, to envisage; *en-*, in, and *visage*, visage.]
1. to look in the face of; to face.
2. to form an image of in the mind; to visualize.

en·viṣ′ăġe·ment, *n.* an envisaging or being envisaged.

en·vi′ṣion, *v.t.* [*en-*, and *vision.*] to imagine (something not yet in existence); picture in the mind.

en·vol′ūme, *v.t.* to form into or incorporate with a volume. [Rare.]

en·vol′upe, *v.t.* envelop. [Obs.]

en′voy, *n.* [Fr. *envoyé*, a messenger, one sent, pp. of *envoyer*, to send; It. *inviare*, L. *in*, in, on, and *via*, way.]
1. a messenger; agent.
2. an agent sent by a government or ruler to transact diplomatic business: an envoy ranks just below an ambassador.

en′voy, *n.* [ME. *envoye*; OFr. *envoy*, lit., a sending, from *envoier*, to send; see *envoy* (messenger).]
1. originally, a dedication or postscript to a poem, essay, or book, directing it to a specific person's attention.
2. a concluding stanza added to a ballade and some other verse forms.
Often *l'envoi, l'envoy.*

en′voy·ship, *n.* the office of an envoy.

en′vy, *n.*; *pl.* **en′vieṣ,** [ME. *envy, envie*; OFr. *envie*; Sp. *envidia*; L. *invidia*, hatred, ill will, from *invidus*, having hatred or ill will, from *invidere*, to look askance at; *in*, in, upon, and *videre*, to look, see.]
1. a feeling of discontent and ill will because of another's advantages, possessions, etc.; resentful dislike of another who has something desirable.
2. desire for some advantage or possession belonging to another.
3. an object of envious feeling; as, he (or his fortune) was the *envy* of all.
4. malice; malignity. [Obs.]
5. public odium; ill repute. [Obs.]

en′vy, *v.t.*; envied, *pt., pp.*; envying, *ppr.* [ME. *envien*; OFr. *envier*, to envy.]
1. to feel envy toward; to look upon with envy; to resent (another) for excellence or superiority in any way, and to be desirous of acquiring it; as, to *envy* a wealthy man.
2. to feel envy on account of: to look grudgingly upon, as the advantages possessed by another; to regard with a covetous spirit; as, he *envies* your superior knowledge; they *envy* his advancement.
3. to injure; to do harm to. [Obs.]
4. to oppose; to hate. [Obs.]

en′vy, *v.i.* 1. to feel or show envy. [Obs.]
2. to show malice. [Obs.]

en·wall′, *v.t.* same as *inwall.*

en·wăl′lōw, *v.t.* to wallow.

en·wheel′, *v.t.* to inwheel. [Obs.]

en·wīd′en, *v.t.* to make wider.

en·wīnd′, *v.t.* to encircle.

en·wom′ăn (-wụm′), *v.t.* to endow with the qualities of woman; to make womanish. [Rare.]

en·wömb′ (-wöm′), *v.t.* 1. to make pregnant. [Obs.]
2. to bury; to hide or enclose in or as in a womb.

en·wrap′ (-rap′), *v.t.* to wrap; to envelop: also *inwrap.*

en·wrap′ment, *n.* an enwrapping or being enwrapped: also *inwrapment.*

en·wrēathe′, *v.t.* to encircle or surround with or as with a wreath: also *inwreathe.*

en·zōne′, *v.t.* to encompass; to encircle.

en·zō·ot′iç, *a.* [Gr. *en*, in, among, and *zōon*, an animal.] affecting animals in a certain area, climate, or season: said of diseases.

en·zō·ot′iç, *n.* an enzootic disease.

en′zym, *n.* an enzyme.

en·zȳ·mat′iç (*or* en-zi-), *a.* of, like, or derived from an enzyme or enzymes.

en′zȳme (*or* -zim), *n.* [G. *enzym*; L.Gr. *enzymos*, leavened, from Gr. *en-*, in, and *zymē*, leaven.]
1. any of various organic substances that are produced in plant and animal cells and cause changes in other substances by catalytic action; as, pepsin is a digestive *enzyme.*
2. in ecclesiastical usage, leavened bread.

en·zȳ·mō′sis, *n.* see *zymolysis.*

en·zȳ·mot′iç, *a.* [L.Gr. *enzymos*, leavened, fermented; Gr. *en*, in, and *zymē*, leaven.] relating to the enzymes.

ē′ō-, [from Gr. *ēōs*, dawn, morning.] a prefix used in forming terms in paleontology, geology, etc., meaning *early, of an early period of time*, as in *Eocene.*

ē·ō′an, *a.* [L. *eous*; Gr. *ēōos*, from *ēōs*, dawn.] of or pertaining to the dawn; eastern; auroral.

Ē′ō·cēne, *a.* [*eo-* and Gr. *kainos*, new.] designating or of the earliest epoch of the Tertiary Period in the Cenozoic Era, during which mammals became the dominant animals.
the Eocene; the Eocene Epoch or its rocks.

Ē·ō·gae′ȧ, *n.* [Gr. *ēōs*, dawn, and *gaia*, earth.] in zoogeography, a division comprising the African, South American, Australian, and New Zealand regions. [Rare.]

Ē·ō·gae′ăn, *a.* pertaining to Eogaea. [Rare.]

Ē·ō·hip′pus, *n.* [*eo-*, and Gr. *hippos*, horse.] in paleontology, a genus of *Equidæ*, the extinct, prehistoric ancestor of the modern horse: they were of small size, had on the fore feet four toes with a rudimentary thumb, and on the hind ones three toes, and were found in the Lower Eocene of New Mexico.

Ē·ō′li·ăn, *a.* and *n.* see *Aeolian.*

Ē·ol′iç, *a.* and *n.* see *Aeolic.*

ę·ō·lienne′ (ā-ō-lyen′), *n.* [Fr., orig., f. of *éolien*, aeolian: so named from its lightness.] a cloth of silk and wool or silk and cotton, like poplin but lighter.

ē·ō·lī′nȧ, *n.* see *aeolina.*

ē·ol′i·pīle, ē·ol′i·pȳle, *n.* see *æolipile.*

Ē′ō·lis, *n.* see *Aeolis.*

ē′ō·lith, *n.* [*eo-*, and *-lith.*] any of the crude stone tools used in the early part of the Stone Age.

ē·ō·lith′iç, *a.* [*eo-*, and Gr. *lithos*, stone.] in archaeology, pertaining to that early stage of human culture in which crude stone tools were first used.

ē′ŏn, ae′ŏn, *n.* [LL. *æon*, from Gr. *aiōn*, an age, lifetime.] a period of immense duration; an extremely long, unlimited period of time; an age; a cycle; eternity.

ē·ō′ni·ăn, ae·ō′ni·ăn, *a.* [Gr. *aiōnios*, from *aiōn*, an age, lifetime.] lasting for eons; everlasting; eternal.

ē·on′iç, ae·on′iç, *a.* eternal; everlasting.

ē′ō nō′mi·nē, [L.] by that name.

ē′ō·phȳte, *n.* [*eo-*, and Gr. *phyton*, a plant.] in paleontology, a mark or impression found in Eozoic rocks.

ē·ō·phyt′iç, *a.* pertaining to eophytes.

Ē′os, *n.* [Gr. *ēōs*, dawn.] in Greek mythology, the goddess of the dawn, corresponding to the Roman Aurora.

ē′ō·sin, *n.* [Gr. *ēōs*, dawn, and *-in.*]

1. an acid dye produced by the action of bromine on fluorescein suspended in glacial acetic acid. It is rose-colored and is used as a stain in histology and as an acid-base indicator.

2. any of various other red dyes.

ē′ō·sine, *n.* eosin.

ē·ō·sin′iç, *a.* pertaining to or containing eosin.

ē·ō·sin′ō·phil, *a.* [*eosin*, and Gr. *philos*, loving.] readily stained by eosin.

ē·os′phō·rīte, *n.* [Gr. *heōsphoros*, morn-bringing; *ēōs*, dawn, and *-phoros*, from *pherein*, to bear, and *-ite.*] a hydrous phosphate of aluminum and manganese, crystallizing in the orthorhombic system.

-ē·ous, [L. *-eus* and *-ous.*] an adjectival suffix meaning *having the nature of, like*, as in beaut*eous.*

Ē·ō·zō′iç, *a.* [*eo-*, and Gr. *zōē*, life.] of or pertaining to the oldest or pre-Paleozoic system of fossiliferous rocks, such as the Laurentian and Huronian of Canada.

ē·ō·zō′on, *n.* [*eo-*, and Gr. *zōon*, an animal.] a formation formerly supposed to be a fossil foraminifer, found in the Laurentian rocks of Canada and other regions.

ē·ō·zō′on·ăl, *a.* pertaining to an eozoon.

ep-, see *epi-.*

Ep″ȧ·çri·dā′cē·ae, *n.pl.* [Gr. *epi*, upon, and *akron*, top.] a family of monopetalous exogens, very closely allied to the *Ericaceæ*, chiefly native to Australia.

ep″ȧ·çri·dā′ceous, *a.* pertaining to the *Epacridaceæ.*

Ep′ȧ·çris, *n.* [Gr. *epi*, upon, and *akron*, top.] a genus of shrubby plants, chiefly native to Australia, typical of the *Epacridaceæ.*

ē′paçt, *n.* [LL. *epacta*, from Gr. *epakte*, f. of *epaktos*, brought in, intercalated.]

1. in chronology, the moon's age at the commencement of the calendar year, or the number of days by which the last new moon has preceded the beginning of the year.

2. the period of about eleven days by which the solar year exceeds the lunar year of twelve months: also called *annual epact.*

3. the excess of a calendar month over a lunar month: also called *menstrual epact, monthly epact.*

ē·paç′tăl, *a.* [Gr. *epaktos*, brought in, intercalated.] in anatomy, intercalary; additional; supernumerary.

ep·ȧ·gō′gē, *n.* [LL. *epagoge*; Gr. *epagōgē*, a bringing to or in, from *epagein*; *epi*, to, on, and *agein*, to bring, lead.] in logic and rhetoric, oratorical induction; a figure of speech which consists in demonstrating and proving universal propositions by particulars.

ep·ȧ·gog′iç, *a.* pertaining to epagoge.

ē·pā·lē·ā′ceous, *a.* [L. *e-* priv., and *palea*, chaff.] in botany, without chaffy scales.

ē·pal′pāte, *a.* in entomology, having no palpi.

ep·an″ȧ·di·plō′sis, *n.* [LL., from Gr. *epanadiplōsis*, a doubling, repetition, from *epanadiploun*; *epi*, upon, and *anadiploun*, to double.] in rhetoric, a figure by which a sentence ends with the same word with which it begins; as, "*Rejoice* in the Lord alway; and again I say, *Rejoice.*"

ep″an·ȧ·lep′sis, *n.* [Gr. *epanalēpsis*, a repetition, regaining, from *epanalambanein*, to take up again, repeat; *epi*, upon, and *analambanein*, to take up.] in rhetoric, a figure by which the same word or phrase is repeated after other words have intervened.

ep·ȧ·naph′ō·rȧ, *n.* [L., from Gr. *epanaphora*, a reference, repetition, from *epanapherein*; *epi*, upon, and *anapherein*, to bring back.] in rhetoric, a figure of speech which consists in the repetition of a word or phrase at the beginning of successive clauses; anaphora.

ep·ȧ·nas′trō·phē, *n.* [Gr. *epanastrophē*, a return, from *epanastrephein*; *epi*, upon, and *anastrephein*, to turn back.] in rhetoric, a figure by which the speaker makes the end of one clause the beginning of the next; anadiplosis.

ep·an′ō·dos, *n.* [Gr., a rising up, return, recapitulation; *epi*, upon, and *anodos*, a way up.] in rhetoric, (a) a figure in which a sentence or phrase is repeated in inverse order; (b) the return to the principal heads or to the proper subject of a discourse after a digression.

ep·an′ō·dy, *n.* [Gr. *epanodos*, a return.] peloria.

ep″an·or·thō′sis, *n.* [LL., from Gr. *epanorthōsis*, a correction, from *epi*, upon, and *anorthoun*, to set up again; *ana*, up, and *orthoun*, from *orthos*, straight.] in rhetoric, a figure by which a person recalls something just said in order to substitute something stronger or more fitting; as, Most *brave* act. *Brave*, did I say? Most *heroic* act.

ep·an′thous, *a.* [*ep-*, and Gr. *anthos*, a flower.] in botany, growing upon flowers, as certain fungi.

ē·pap′il·lāte, *a.* without papillae.

ē·pap′pōse, *a.* [L. *e-* priv., and Gr. *pappos*, down.] in botany, without pappi: said of certain composite flowers.

ep′ärçh, *n.* [Gr. *eparchos*, from *epi*, upon, and *archein*, to rule.]

1. the governor of a province in ancient Greece.

2. the governor of an eparchy in modern Greece.

3. in the Orthodox Eastern Church, a metropolitan or bishop.

ep·är′çhi·ăl, *a.* of an eparch or eparchy.

ep′ärçh·y, *n.* [Gr. *eparchia*, from *eparchos*, a ruler, commander.]

1. in ancient Greece, a province, prefecture, or territory under the jurisdiction of an eparch or governor.

2. in modern Greece, a political subdivision of a nomarchy or province.

3. in the Orthodox Eastern Church, a diocese.

ep·är·tē′ri·ăl, *a.* [*ep-*, and L. *arteria*, an artery.] in anatomy, located above an artery.

e·pąule′, *n.* [Fr. *épaule*, the shoulder.] in fortification, the shoulder of a bastion or the angle made by the face and flank.

e·pąule′ment, *n.* same as *epaulment.*

ep′ąu·let, ep′ąu·lette, *n.* [Fr., dim. of *épaule*, the shoulder.]

1. a shoulder ornament for certain uniforms, especially military uniforms.

2. any similar ornament, as on a woman's dress.

ep′ąu·let·ed, ep′ąu·let·ted, *a.* furnished with epaulets.

é·pau·lière′ (ā-pō-lyār′), *n.* [Fr., from *épaule*, the shoulder.] in medieval armor, a shoulder plate, either of one piece or composed of several successive plates. It was fastened by laces or points to the sleeve of the hauberk.

ÉPAULIÈRE

e·pąul′ment, e·pąule′ment, *n.* [Fr. *épaulement*, from *épaule*, a shoulder, support.] in fortification, a mass of earth, or embankment, for protecting the guns in a battery both in front and on either flank.

ep·ax′ăl, *a.* same as *epaxial.*

ep·ax′i·ăl, *a.* [*ep-*, and L. *axis*, an axis.] in anatomy, upon, above, or on the dorsal side of an axis: opposed to *hypaxial.*

e·pęe′ (-pā′), *n.* [Fr.; OFr. *espee*; L. *spatha*, broad, flat instrument, broad two-edged sword without a point; Gr. *spathē*, any broad blade.] a sword, especially a thin, pointed sword without a cutting edge, like a foil but heavier and more rigid, used in fencing: also spelled *épée.*

e·pęe′ist, *n.* a person who fences with an epee: also spelled *épéeist.*

Ē·peī′rȧ, *n.* [from Gr. *epi*, upon, and *eiros*, wool.] a genus of spiders typical of the family *Epeiridæ*. *Epeira diadema* is the common garden spider.

Ē·peī′ri·dae, *n.pl.* a family of spiders of which *Epeira* is the typical genus.

ē·peī·rō·gen′ē·sis, *n.* epeirogeny.

ē·peī·rō·gen′iç, ē·peī″rō·gē·net′iç, *a.* [Gr. *ēpeiros*, mainland, and *genesis*, origin, birth.] in geology, of epeirogeny: also spelled *epirogenic.*

ep·eī·rog′e·ny, *n.* [Gr. *ēpeiros*, mainland, and *-geneia*, production.] in geology, the changes in the earth's surface by which the great continental elevations and depressions of the earth's crust are formed: also spelled *epirogeny.*

ep·en′cē·phăl, *n.* epencephalon. [Rare.]

ep·en·cē·phal′iç, *a.* [*ep-*, and Gr. *enkephalos*, the brain.]

1. of or pertaining to the epencephalon.

2. occipital.

ep·en·ceph′ȧ·lon, *n.* [*ep-*, and Gr. *enkephalos*, the brain.]

1. the front part of the most posterior primary vesicle of an embryo's brain: it develops into the pons and part of the cerebellum.

2. the cerebellum. [Rare.]

ep·en′dy·mȧ, *n.* [Gr. *ependyma*, an upper garment, from *ependyein*; *epi*, upon, and *endyein*, to put on.] in anatomy, the membrane lining the cerebral ventricles and the central canal of the spinal cord.

ep·en′dy·mal, *a.* pertaining to the ependyma; as, *ependymal* tissue.

ep·en′dy·mis, *n.* ependyma.

ep·en·dy·mī′tis, *n.* in pathology, inflammation of the ependyma.

ep·en′dy·tēş, *n.* [Gr.] 1. in the Orthodox Eastern Church, the outer altar cloth.

2. formerly, a monk's outer mantle of skins.

ep·ē·net′iç, *a.* [from Gr. *epainetikos*, from *epainein*, to praise; *epi*, upon, and *ainein*, from *ainos*, a tale, praise.] laudatory; bestowing praise. [Obs.]

ep·en′thē·sis, *n.* [Gr. *epenthesis*, an insertion, from *epentithesthai*; *epi*, upon, and *entithesthai*, to put in; *en*, in, and *tithesthai*, to put, place.]

1. in grammar, the insertion or development of an unhistorical sound or syllable in a word to make its pronunciation easier, as the *b* in *mumble* (from ME. *momelen*).

2. any such letter or syllable so occurring.

ep·en·thet′iç, *a.* of, or having the nature of, epenthesis.

ē·pergne′ (ē-pẽrn′ *or* ā-pärn′), *n.* [Fr.] an ornamental stand or dish with sections for fruit, cookies, candy, etc., used as a centerpiece for a dining table.

EPERGNE

é·per′lan (ā-per-län′), *n.* [Fr.] the European smelt.

ep·ex·ē·gē′sis, *n.* [Gr. *epexēgēsis*, a detailed account, from *epexēgeisthai*, to recount in detail; *epi*, upon, and *exēgeisthai*, to lead, point out.] additional explanation; further clarification, as by the addition of a word or words.

ep·ex·ē·get′iç, *a.* of the nature of or pertaining to epexegesis.

ep·ex·ē·get′iç·ăl, *a.* epexegetic.

ep·ex·ē·get′iç·ăl·ly, *adv.* by epexegesis.

eph-, epi-.

ē′phăh, ē′phȧ, *n.* [Heb.] an ancient Hebrew dry measure, equivalent to a bath or about 37 quarts.

e·phē′biç, *a.* [L. *ephebicus*; Gr. *ephebikos.*] of, or having the nature of, an ephebus.

e·phē′bos, *n.*; *pl.* **e·phē′boi,** an ephebus.

e·phē′bus, *n.*; *pl.* **e·phē′bī,** [L., Gr. *ephēbos*, from *epi-*, at, upon, and *hēbē*, early manhood.] in ancient Greece, a youth who had just become a citizen.

E·phē′drȧ, *n.* [from Gr. *ephedra*, a setting by or at a thing; *epi*, upon, and *hedra*, a seat.] a genus of gnetaceous shrubs found in certain desert regions of Asia and America.

e·phed′rine, e·phed′rin (*or* ef′ē-drēn), *n.* a mydriatic alkaloid, $C_{10}H_{15}NO$, found in species of *Ephedra*, used in conditions of low blood pressure, shock, hemorrhage, hay fever and asthma: it causes constriction of the swollen or inflamed blood vessels.

e·phem'ẽr·ȧ, *n.*; *pl.* **e·fem'ẽr·ȧṣ, e·fem'ẽr·ae,** [Gr. *ephēmeros*, for the day, short-lived; *epi*, upon, and *hēmera*, a day.]

1. [E-] in entomology, a genus of insects in which are included the May flies or dayflies of the family *Ephemeridæ*.

2. an insect of the genus *Ephemera* and allied genera.

3. anything having a very short life.

e·phem'ẽr·ăl, *a.* [Gr. *ephēmeros*, for the day, short-lived; *epi*, upon, at, and *hēmera*, day.]

1. diurnal; beginning and ending in a day; continuing or existing one day only.

2. short-lived; existing or continuing for a short time only; transitory; as, *ephemeral* glory.

Syn.—transient, evanescent, fleeting, fugitive, momentary.

e·phem'ẽr·ăl, *n.* anything which has but a brief existence, as certain insects, plants, etc.

e·phem·ẽr·al'i·ty, *n.* the state or quality of being ephemeral.

e·phem'ẽr·ăn, *a.* and *n.* ephemeral. [Obs.]

e·phem'ẽr·id, *n.* in entomology, an insect belonging to the family *Ephemeridæ*.

Eph·ē·mer'i·dae, *n.pl.* a family of insects with gauzy wings, which take their name from the short duration of their lives in the perfect state, as the May fly and dayfly. In the state of larvae and pupae they are aquatic and may exist for two or three years.

eph·ē·mer'i·dēṣ, *n.* pl. of *ephemeris*.

e·phem·ẽr·id'i·ăn, *a.* relating to an ephemeris.

eph·ē·mē'ri·ī, *n.* pl. of *ephemerius*.

e·phem·e·rī'nous, *a.* relating to the *Ephemeridæ*.

e·phem'ẽr·is, *n.*; *pl.* **eph·ē·mer'i·dēṣ,** [L. *ephemeris*; Gr. *ephēmeris*, a diary, calendar, from *ephēmeros*, for the day, daily; *epi*, upon, at, and *hēmera*, day.]

1. a journal or account of daily transactions; a diary. [Obs.]

2. an almanac; a calendar. [Obs.]

3. (a) a collection of tables or data showing the positions of the planets or heavenly bodies for every day of a given period; (b) an astronomical almanac containing such tables.

4. an ephemerid. [Rare.]

e·phem'ẽr·ist, *n.* 1. one who studies the daily motions and positions of the planets. [Obs.]

2. one who uses an ephemeris. [Obs.]

eph·ē·mē'ri·us, *n.*; *pl.* **eph·ē·mē'ri·ī,** [Gr. *ephēmerios*, of or for the day, serving for the day.] in the Orthodox Eastern Church, (a) the priest whose turn it is to officiate; (b) a parish priest; (c) a domestic chaplain; (d) a monastic officer whose duty it is to prepare, elevate, and distribute the loaf used at the ceremony known as the *elevation of the Panagia*.

e·phem'ẽr·ō·morph, *n.* [Gr. *ephēmeros*, of or for a day, short-lived, and *morphē*, form.] any of the lowest forms of life which cannot be definitely classified as animal or vegetable.

e·phem'ẽr·on, *n.*, *pl.* **e·phem'ẽr·ȧ,** [Gr. *ephēmeron*, a short-lived insect, from *ephēmeros*, for the day.] anything which lasts or lives but for a day or for a very short time, especially a May fly, or ephemerid.

e·phem'ẽr·ous, *a.* ephemeral.

E·phē'ṣiăn, (-zhăn), *a.* of or relating to the ancient Ionian city, Ephesus, in Asia Minor, or its people.

E·phē'ṣiăn, *n.* 1. a native or resident of Ephesus.

2. a jovial fellow. [Obs.]

E·phē'ṣiănṣ, *n.pl.* [*construed as sing.*] the Epistle to the Ephesians, a book of the New Testament which was a message from the Apostle Paul to the Christians of Ephesus.

eph·i·al'tēṣ, *n.* [Gr. *ephialtēs*, a nightmare, from *epi*, upon, and *iallein*, to send, throw.] a nightmare.

eph·i·drō'sis, *n.* [Gr. *ephidrōsis*; *epi*, upon, and *hidrōsis*, perspiration, from *hidroein*, to sweat.] in pathology, excessive perspiration.

eph·ip'pi·ăl, *a.* relating to an ephippium.

eph·ip'pi·um, *n.* [L., from Gr. *ephippion*, saddle cloth, *epi*, upon, and *hippos*, horse.]

1. in anatomy, the pituitary fossa of the sphenoid bone.

2. in zoology, a saddle-shaped receptacle on the back of the *Cladocera*, in which the winter eggs are deposited.

eph'od, *n.* [LL. *ephod*; Heb. *ēphōd*, from *āphad*, to put on.] in Jewish antiquity, a richly embroidered outer vestment worn by priests.

eph'ŏr, *n.*; *pl.* **eph'ŏrṣ** or **eph'ō·rī,** [L. *ephorus*; Gr. *ephoros*, an overseer, from *ephoran*; *epi*, upon, and *horan*, to see.]

1. in ancient Greece, a magistrate; especially, one of five magistrates chosen by the people of Sparta as a check on the regal power.

2. in modern Greece, any of various government officials.

eph'ŏr·ăl, *a.* of or relating to an ephor.

eph'ŏr·ăl·ty, *n.* the office or term of office of an ephor.

E'phrā·im (*or* -fri-), *n.* [LL.; Gr. *Ephraim*; Heb. *ephrayim*, lit., very fruitful.] in the Bible, (a) the younger son of Joseph; (b) the tribe of Israel descended from him; hence, (c) the kingdom of Israel.

E'phrā·im·īte, *n.* a descendant of Ephraim; a member of the tribe of Ephraim.

Eph"thi·ȧ·nū'rȧ, *n.* [prob. from Gr. *phthinein*, *phthiein*, to dwindle away, wane, and *oura*, a tail.] a genus of small Australian warblers characterized by diminutive tails.

eph'thi·ȧ·nūre, *n.* one of the *Ephthianura*.

Eph'y·drȧ, *n.* [from Gr. *ephydros*, living on the water; *epi*, on, upon, and *hydōr*, water.] a genus of dipterous insects, the brine flies.

é·pi' (ā-pē'), *n.* [Fr., an ear of corn, spike, cluster.] a light finial to ornament the apex of a roof or to form the termination of a spire.

ep'i-, [from Gr. *epi*, at, on, upon, besides, etc.] a prefix meaning *on, upon, up to, over, on the outside, anterior, beside, besides, among*: *epi-* becomes *ep-* before a vowel, and *eph-* in an aspirated word, as in *eph*emeral.

ep'i·blȧst, *n.* [*epi-*, and Gr. *blastos*, a bud, shoot.]

1. in embryology, the external or upper layer of the blastoderm; the ectoderm.

2. in botany, a small transverse plate found on some grasses.

ep"i·blas·tē'mȧ, *n.*; *pl.* **ep"i·blas·tē'mȧ·tȧ,** [*epi-*, and Gr. *blastēma*, a bud, sprout.] in botany, a superficial outgrowth from any part of a plant.

ep·i·blē'mȧ, *n.* [Gr. *epiblēma*, a cover, patch, from *epiballein*, to throw over; *epi*, upon, and *ballein*, to throw.] in botany, the imperfectly formed epidermis which supplies the place of the true epidermis in submerged plants and on the extremities of growing roots.

ē·pib'ō·lē, *n.* 1. in rhetoric, epanaphora.

2. same as *epiboly*.

ep·i·bol'iç, *a.* [from Gr. *epiballein*, to throw over, add to; *epi*, upon, and *ballein*, to throw.] of, pertaining to, or characteristic of epiboly.

ē·pib'ō·liṣm, *n.* epiboly.

ē·pib'ō·ly, *n.* in embryology, the growth of a group of cells around another group, resulting from the more rapid division of the former.

ep·i·bran'çhi·ăl, *a.* [*epi-*, and Gr. *branchia*, gills.] pertaining to the segment above the ceratobranchial bone in a branchial arch.

ep'iç, *a.* [L. *epicus*; Gr. *epikos*, an epic, from *epos*, a word, speech, tale, song, epic.]

1. of an epic.

2. having the nature of an epic; specifically, (a) heroic; grand; majestic; imposing; (b) dealing with or characterized by events of historical or legendary importance.

ep'iç, *n.* 1. a long narrative poem about the deeds of a traditional or historical hero or heroes of high station; typically, (a) a poem like the *Iliad* and *Odyssey*, with a background of warfare and the supernatural, a dignified style, and certain formal characteristics of structure (plunging *in medias res*, catalogue passages, invocations of the muse, etc.); *classical epic*; (b) a poem like Milton's *Paradise Lost* or Tasso's *Jerusalem Delivered*, in which such structure and conventions are applied to later or different materials; *art epic*; *literary epic*; (c) a poem like *Beowulf*, the *Nibelungenlied*, and the *Chanson de Roland*, considered as expressing the early ideals, character, and traditions of a people or nation as the *Iliad* and *Odyssey* expressed those of the Greeks; *folk epic*; *national epic*.

2. any long narrative poem regarded as having the style, structure, and importance of an epic; as, Dante's *Divine Comedy* is the *epic* of the Ages of Faith.

3. a prose narrative, play, motion picture, etc. regarded as having the qualities of an epic.

4. a series of events regarded as a proper subject for an epic.

ep'i·çăl, *a.* epic.

ep'iç·ăl·ly, *adv.* in the style of an epic.

ep·i·çȧ'lyx, *n.*; *pl.* **ep·i·çȧ'ly·cēṣ,** [*epi-*, and Gr. *kalyx*, a cup, calyx.] in botany, a ring of leaflets at the base of certain flowers, resembling an extra outer calyx, formed either of sepals or bracts, as in mallow and potentilla.

EPICALYX

EPICALYX

ep·i·çan'thiç, *a.* pertaining to an epicanthus.

ep·i·çan'thus, *n.* [Mod. L., from *epi-*, and Gr. *kanthos*, the corner of the eye.] a small fold of skin sometimes covering the inner corner of the eye.

EPICANTHUS

EPICANTHUS

ep·i·çär'di·ăl, ep·i·çär'-di·aç, *a.* of or pertaining to the epicardium.

ep·i·çär'di·um, *n.* [*epi-*, and Gr. *kardia*, heart.] in anatomy, the innermost layer of the pericardium, united with the substance of the heart and constituting its outer surface.

ep·i·çar'i·dan, *n.* [*epi-*, and Gr. *karis* (*-idos*), a shrimp.] one of a family of isopodous crustaceans which are parasitic upon shrimps.

ep'i·çärp, *n.* [*epi-*, and Gr. *karpos*, fruit.] in botany, the outer skin of fruits, the fleshy substance or edible portion being termed the *mesocarp*, and the inner portion the *endocarp*.

ep'i·çēde, ep'i·çed, *n.* a funeral song or discourse.

ep·i·çē'di·ȧ, *n.* pl. of *epicedium*.

ep·i·çē'di·ăl, *a.* epicedian.

ep·i·çē'di·ăn, *a.* elegiac; mournful.

ep·i·çē'di·ăn, *n.* an epicedium. [Obs.]

ep·i·çē'di·um, *n.*; *pl.* **ep·i·çē'di·ȧ,** [LL. *epicedium*; Gr. *epikēdeion*, a dirge, neut. of *epikēdeios*, of or for a funeral; *epi*, on, upon, and *kēdos*, care, sorrow, mourning for one dead.] a funeral song or ode; a dirge.

ep'i·çēne, *a.* [LL. *epicænus*; Gr. *epikoinos*, common; *epi*, upon, to, and *koinos*, common.]

1. belonging to, having the characteristics of, or common to both sexes.

2. in grammar, designating a noun that has but one form of gender, either the masculine or feminine, to indicate an animal of either sex, as Gr. *bous* for the ox and cow.

3. sexless.

The literary prigs *epicene*. —J. Wilson.

ep'i·çēne, *n.* 1. in grammar, a noun the gender of which is common, including both sexes.

2. an epicene person.

ep'i·cen·tẽr, *n.* [Gr. *epikentros*, on the center-point; *epi*, upon, and *kentron*, center.]

1. in geology, the area on the surface of the earth directly above the focus or place of origin of an earthquake.

2. a focal point.

Also spelled *epicentre*.

ep·i·cen'trăl, *a.* 1. in anatomy, situated upon the centrum of a vertebra.

2. of an epicenter.

ep·i·cen'trum, *n.*; *pl.* **ep·i·cen'trȧ,** same as *epicenter*.

ep"i·ce·ras'tiç, *a.* [Gr. *epikerastikos*, tempering the humors, from *epikerannynai*; *epi*, upon, to, and *kerannynai*, to mix.] lenient; assuaging. [Obs.]

ep"i·çheī·rē'mȧ, *n.*; *pl.* **ep"i·çheī·rē'mȧ·tȧ,** [Gr. *epicheirēma*, from *epicheirein*, to undertake, attempt; *epi*, upon, and *cheir*, the hand.] in logic, a syllogism having the truth of one or both of its premises confirmed by a proposition annexed (called a prosyllogism), so that an abridged compound argument is formed.

ep'i·çhīle, *n.* same as *epichilium*.

ep·i·çhil'i·um, *n.*; *pl.* **ep·i·çhil'i·ȧ,** [Gr. *epi-cheilēs*; *epi*, upon, and *cheilos*, lip, brim.] in botany, the terminal portion of the lip of an orchid.

ep·i·çhor'dăl, *a.* [*epi-*, and Gr. *chordē*, chord.] in anatomy, situated above or upon the notochord, as certain brain segments.

ep·i·chō'ri·ăl, *a.* [Gr. *epichōrios*, in or of the country; *epi*, in, and *chōra*, country.] pertaining to the country; rustic; rural.

ep·i·çleī'di·um, *n.* same as *epiclidium*.

ep·i·çlē'sis, *n.* [Gr. *epiklēsis*, a calling upon, invocation, from *epikalein*; *epi*, upon, and *kalein*, to call.] in the celebration of the Eucharist, that part of the prayer of consecration in which the Holy Ghost is invoked.

ep·i·çlī′di·um, *n.*; *pl.* **ep·i·çlī′di·ȧ**, [from Gr. *epi*, upon, and *kleidion*, dim. of *kleis*, a key.] in ornithology, a distention or separate ossification of the scapular end of the clavicle.

ep·i·çlī′năl, *a.* [Gr. *epi*, upon, and *klinē*, a couch, bed, from *klinein*, to recline.] in botany, placed upon the disk or receptacle of a flower.

ep′i·coele (-sēl), *n.* 1. in anatomy, the epicoelia.
2. in zoology, a cavity around the viscera, formed by the invagination of the ectoderm, as in ascidians.

ep·i·coe′li·ȧ, *n.*; *pl.* **ep·i·coe′li·ae**, [from Gr. *epi*, upon, in addition to, and *koilia*, belly, from *koilos*, hollow.] in anatomy, the cavity of the epencephalon, or the upper part of the fourth ventricle of the brain.

ep·i·coe′lous, *a.* of, pertaining to, or possessing an epicoele.

ep′i·coene (-sēn), *a.* see *epicene*.

ep·i·çol′iç, *a.* [Gr. *epi*, upon, and *kolon*, the colon.] in anatomy, relating to that part of the abdomen which is over the colon.

ep·i·çon′dy·lăr, *a.* pertaining to or characteristic of the epicondyle.

ep·i·çon′dyle, *n.* [from Gr. *epi*, upon, and *kondylos*, a knuckle.] in anatomy, an eminence upon the humeral condyle.

ep·i·çor′ȧ·çoid, *n.* a bone or cartilage of the coracoid in certain animals.

ep·i·çor′ŏl·līne, *a.* [*epi-*, and L. *corolla*, a little crown or garland.] in botany, inserted upon the corolla.

ep·i·çot′yl, *n.* [Gr. *epi*, on, upon, and *kotylēdōn*, a cup-shaped hollow.] in botany, the stem of an embryo or seedling just above the cotyledons.

ep·i·çot·y·lē′dŏn·ā·ry, *a.* pertaining to the epicotyl; situated just above the cotyledons.

ep·i·çrā′ni·ȧ, *n.* pl. of *epicranium*.

ep·i·çrā′ni·ăl, *a.* in anatomy, of or pertaining to the epicranium; situated upon the cranium or skull.

ep·i·çrā′ni·um, *n.*; *pl.* **ep·i·çrā′ni·ȧ**, [*epi-*, and Gr. *kranion*, the cranium.]
1. the structures covering the cranium.
2. in zoology, the largest dorsal sclerite of an insect's head.

ē·piç′ri·sis, *n.*; *pl.* **ē·piç′ri·sēș**, [Gr. *epikrisis*, determination, from *epikrinein*, to give judgment on, decide; *epi*, upon, and *krinein*, to judge, separate.] a detailed criticism of a book, paper, etc.

ep·i·çrit′iç, *a.* [Gr. *epikritikos*, determinative, from *epikrisis*, determination, from *epikrinein*, to judge; *epi*, upon, and *krinein*, to judge.] designating or of the nerve fibers in the skin that transmit the sensations of touch and temperature.

Ep·iç·tē′tiăn, *a.* pertaining to Epictetus, a Greek Stoic philosopher in the time of the Roman emperor Domitian.

ep′i·çūre, *n.* 1. [E—] a follower of Epicurus, an Epicurean. [Obs.]
2. a person who enjoys and has a discriminating taste for foods and liquors.
3. a person who is especially fond of luxury and sensuous pleasure.

Ep″i·çū·rē′ăn, *a.* [L. *Epicureus*; Gr. *Epikoureios*, from *Epikouros*, Epicurus.]
1. pertaining to Epicurus, 342?–270 B.C., an ancient Greek philosopher, or to his teachings.
2. [e–] fond of luxury and sensuous pleasure, especially that of eating and drinking.
3. [e–] suited to or characteristic of an epicure.

Ep″i·çū·rē′ăn, *n.* 1. a follower of Epicurus or Epicureanism.
2. [e–] an epicure.

Ep″i·çū·rē′ăn·ișm, *n.* 1. the philosophy of Epicurus or his school, which held that the goal of man should be a life of pleasure regulated by morality, temperance, serenity, and cultural development.
2. adherence to or practice of this philosophy.
3. [e–] epicurism.

ep′i·çūre·ly, *adv.* luxuriously. [Obs.]

ep″i·çū·rē′ous, *a.* epicurean. [Obs.]

ep′i·çū·rișm, *n.* [Fr. *épicurisme*, from L. *Epicurus*, Epicurus.]
1. the tastes, habits, or outlook of an epicure.
2. [E–] Epicureanism.

ep′i·çū·rīze, *v.i.*; epicurized, *pt.*, *pp.*; epicurizing, *ppr.* 1. to feed or indulge like an epicure; to feast.
2. [E–] to profess the doctrines of Epicurus.

ep′i·cȳ·çle, *n.* [LL. *epicyclus*; Gr. *epikyklos*, an epicycle; *epi*, upon, and *kyklos*, a circle.]
1. a circle, whose center moves along the circumference of a greater circle: said chiefly of the orbit described by a planet.
2. in geometry, a circle that rolls around either the interior or exterior of the circumference of another circle.

ep·i·cȳ′çliç, *a.* of or pertaining to an epicycle or epicycles.
epicyclic train; a system of cogwheels, belt pulleys, etc. in which at least one wheel axis moves around the circumference of another fixed or moving axis, permitting an unusual velocity ratio with relative simplicity of parts.

ep·i·cȳ′çli·căl, *a.* same as *epicyclic*.

ep·i·cȳ′çloid, *n.* [Gr. *epikyklos*, an epicycle, and *eidos*, form.] in geometry, a curve generated by a point on the circumference of a circle that rolls around the outside of another circle.

ep″i·cy·çloid′ăl, *a.* pertaining to an epicycloid or having its form or nature.
epicycloidal wheel; a wheel of an epicyclic train.

EPICYCLOIDAL WHEEL

ep″i·cȳ·ē′māte, *a.* [*epi-*, and Gr. *kyēma*, an embryo.] in embryology, having the embryo resting upon a large yolk and not enclosed by a blastodermic vesicle, as fishes and amphibians.

ep·i·deiç′tiç, *a.* see *epidictic*.

ep·i·deiç′tiç·ăl, *a.* see *epidictical*.

ep·i·dem′iç, *a.* [Gr. *epidēmios*, *epidēmos*, among the people, general; *epi*, upon, and *dēmos*, people.] common to or affecting many people in a community at the same time; prevalent; widespread: said of contagious disease.

ep·i·dem′iç, *n.* 1. a disease prevalent in a locality; an epidemic disease; also, the rapid spreading of such a disease.
2. anything that rapidly affects great numbers or is generally prevalent; as, an *epidemic* of patriotic ardor; an *epidemic* of terror.

ep·i·dem′iç·ăl, *a.* epidemic; characteristic of an epidemic.

ep·i·dem′iç·ăl·ly, *adv.* in an epidemic manner.

ep·i·dem′iç en·ceph·ȧ·lī′tis, sleeping sickness.

ep·i·dē·mi·og′rȧ·phy, *n.* [Gr. *epidēmios*, among the people, epidemic, and *-graphia*, from *graphein*, to write.] a treatise on or description of epidemic diseases.

ep·i·dē″mi·ō·loġ′iç·ăl, *a.* pertaining to epidemiology.

ep·i·dē″mi·ō·loġ′iç·ăl·ly, *adv.* in an epidemiological manner.

ep·i·dē·mi·ol′ō·ġist, *n.* one who makes a study of epidemiology.

ep·i·dē·mi·ol′ō·ġy, *n.* [Gr. *epidēmios*, among the people, epidemic, and *-logia*, from *legein*, to speak.] the science which investigates the causes and control of epidemic diseases.

ep′i·dem·y, *n.* an epidemic. [Obs.]

ep·i·den′drăl, *a.* [*epi-*, and Gr. *dendron*, a tree.] growing or existing upon trees.

Ep·i·den′drum, *n.* [from Gr. *epi*, upon, and *dendron*, a tree.] a large genus of tropical American orchids, most of the species of which are epiphytic, growing on trees. The stems are often pseudobulbs, and the leaves are strap-shaped and leathery. The flowers are very handsome, and a large number of the species are in cultivation.

ep′i·dẽrm, *n.* the epidermis.

ep·i·dẽr′măl, *a.* epidermic; pertaining to or like the epidermis.

ep″i·dẽr·mat′iç, *a.* same as *epidermal*.

ep·i·dẽr′mȧ·toid, *a.* same as *epidermoid*.

ep·i·dẽr′mē·ous, *a.* epidermic.

ep·i·dẽr′miç, *a.* pertaining to or like the dermis; epidermal.

ep·i·dẽr′miç·ăl, *a.* epidermic.

ep·i·dẽr′mi·dăl, *a.* epidermal.

ep·i·dẽr′mis, *n.* [LL. *epidermis*; Gr. *epidermis* (*-idos*), the outer skin; *epi*, upon, and *derma*, skin.]
1. the outermost layer of the skin in vertebrates, having no blood vessels and consisting of several layers of cells, covering the dermis.
2. in botany, the outermost layer of cells covering seed plants and ferns.
3. the outer layer of the shells of many mollusks.
4. any of various other integuments.

ep·i·dẽr′moid, *a.* like, or having the nature of, epidermis.

ep·i·dẽr′mōse, *n.* same as *keratin*.

ep·i·dẽr′mous, *a.* epidermal.

ē·pi·dī′ȧ·sçōpe, *n.* a mechanical device for projecting images of opaque and transparent objects upon a screen.

ep·i·diç′tiç, **ep·i·deiç′tiç**, *a.* [L. *epidicticus*, declamatory; Gr. *epideiktikos*, from *epideiknynai*, to display, show, demonstrate; *epi*, upon, and *deiknynai*, to show, point out.] serving to display, exhibit, or explain; demonstrative: applied to oratory.

ep·i·diç′tiç·ăl, **ep·i·deiç′tiç·ăl**, *a.* same as *epidictic*.

ep·i·did′y·măl, *a.* relating to the epididymis.

ep·i·did′y·mis, *n.*; *pl.* **ep″i·di·dym′i·deș**, [Gr. *epididymis*, the epididymis; *epi*, upon, and *didymos*, a testicle.] a long, oval-shaped structure attached to the rear upper surface of each testicle, consisting mainly of the excretory ducts of the testicles.

ep·i·did·y·mī′tis, *n.* [Gr. *epididymis*, the epididymis, and *-itis*.] inflammation of the epididymis.

ep·i·dī′ō·rīte, *n.* [*epi-*, and *diorite*.] a variety of diorite containing fibrous hornblende.

ep·i·dī·ọr·thō′sis, *n.* [Gr.] same as *epanorthosis*.

ep·i·dō′sīte (*or* e-pid′ō-), *n.* [Gr. *epidosis*, a giving besides, increase, and *-ite*.] a rock the chief constituent of which is epidote.

ep′i·dōte, *n.* [Fr. *épidote*, from Gr. *epididonai*, to give besides, increase.] a mineral of a green or gray color, vitreous luster, and partial transparency, crystallizing in the monoclinic system, but also occurring fibrous and granular. It is a silicate of aluminium, calcium, and iron. The epidote group includes zoisite, allanite, and piedmontite.

ep·i·dot′iç, *a.* pertaining to, resembling, or containing epidote.

ep·i·fō′çal, *a.* over the focus, or center of disturbance, of an earthquake.

Ep·i·gae′ȧ, *n.* [Gr. *epigaios*, upon the earth; *epi*, upon, and *gaia*, poet. form of *gē*, earth.] a genus of shrubs of the heath family. *Epigæa repens*, the trailing arbutus, is also called the Mayflower.

ep·i·gae′ăl, *a.* same as *epigeal*.

ep·i·gae′ous, *a.* same as *epigeous*.

ep·i·gam′iç, *a.* [Gr. *epigamos*, marriageable; *epi*, upon, for, and *gamos*, marriage.] serving to attract the other sex in the breeding season: applied to the coloration of birds and animals.

ep·i·gas′trăl, *a.* in anatomy, epigastric.

ep″i·gas·tral′ġi·ȧ, *n.* [Gr. *epigastrion*, epigastrium, and *algos*, pain.] in medicine, pain in the epigastrium.

ep·i·gas′tri·ăl, *a.* epigastric.

ep·i·gas′triç, *a.* [Gr. *epi*, upon, and *gastēr*, *gastros*, stomach, and *-ic*.] pertaining to or located within the epigastrium; as, an *epigastric* artery or vein.

ep·i·gas′tri·um, *n.* [Gr. *epigastrion*, neut. of *epigastrios*, over the stomach; *epi*, upon, and *gastēr*, *gastros*, stomach.]
1. in anatomy, the upper middle part of the abdomen, including the area over and in front of the stomach; the epigastric region.
2. in entomology, the lower side of the middle segment and of the posterior segment of the thorax in certain insects.

ep·i·ġē′ăl, *a.* 1. same as *epigeous*.
2. in entomology, living near the ground, as certain insects.

ep·i·ġē′ăn, *a.* same as *epigeal*.

ep′i·ġee, *n.* same as *perigee*.

ep′i·ġēne, *a.* [*epi-*, and Gr. *gignesthai*, to produce.]
1. in geology, formed or originating on the surface of the earth: opposed to *hypogene*; as, *epigene* rocks.
2. in crystallography, foreign; unnatural; unusual: said of forms of crystals not natural to the substances in which they are found.

ep·i·ġen′e·sis, *n.* [*epi-*, and Gr. *genesis*, birth, descent.]

1. in biology, the theory that the germ cell is structureless and that the embryo develops as a new creation through the action of the environment on the protoplasm: opposed to *preformation.*

2. in geology, metamorphism.

3. in medicine, the appearance of a secondary or auxiliary symptom; also, a secondary symptom.

ep·i·ġen′e·sist, *n.* one who supports the theory of epigenesis.

ep″i·ġē·net′iç, *a.* of or relating to epigenesis.

ep″i·ġē·net′iç·ăl·ly, *adv.* in an epigenetic manner.

ē·piġ′e·nous, *a.* [from Gr. *epi*, upon, and *gignesthai*, to beget, be born.] in botany, growing upon the surface, especially the upper surface of a part, as fungi on leaves.

ep·i·ġē′ous, *a.* [Gr. *epigaios*, on the earth; *epi*, upon, and *gaia*, poet. form of *gē*, earth.] in botany, growing on or above the ground; specifically, directed above ground after germination; as, *epigeous* plants.

ep·i·ġē′um, *n.* perigee. [Obs.]

ep·i·glot, *n.* the epiglottis. [Obs.]

ep·i·glot′tiç, *a.* relating to the epiglottis.

ep″i·glot·tid′ē·ăn, *a.* epiglottic.

ep·i·glot′tis, *n.* [Gr. *epiglōttis*; *epi*, upon, and *glōtta, glōssa*, the tongue.]

1. in anatomy, a cartilaginous structure behind the tongue, which covers the opening of the windpipe during the act of swallowing and thus prevents food and drink from entering the larynx.

2. in zoology, (a) the epistoma of a polyzoan; (b) the epipharynx of an insect.

EPIGLOTTIS

WINDPIPE

EPIGLOTTIS

ē·pig′nȧ·thous, *a.* [*epi-*, and Gr. *gnathos*, the jaw.] in ornithology, hook-billed; having the upper mandible curved downward over the lower, as parrots, gulls, etc.

ē·pig′ō·năl, *a.* [*epi-*, and Gr. *gonē*, seed, generation.] in anatomy, located upon a gonad; as, *epigonal* tissue.

ep″i·gō·nā′ti·on, *n.* [Gr. *epigonation*; *epi*, upon, to, and *gony*, the knee.] in the Orthodox Eastern Church, a diamond-shaped piece of some stiff material which forms part of the dress of bishops while officiating. It hangs from the girdle on the right side as low as the knee.

ep′i·gōne, *n.* a descendant; an heir; a successor; especially, an unworthy or inferior one.

E·pig′ō·nī, *n.pl.*; *sing.* **E·pig′ō·nus,** [L., from Gr. *epigonos*, born after, from *epi*, upon, after, and *gignesthai*, to be born.] in Greek mythology, the sons or descendants of the princes who fought against Thebes under Adrastus, king of Argos.

ep′i·gram, *n.* [L. *epigramma*; Gr. *epigramma*, an inscription, epigram, from *epigraphein*; *epi*, upon, *graphein*, to write.]

1. a poetical inscription. [Obs.]

2. a short poem with a witty or satirical point.

3. any terse, witty, pointed statement, often antithetical. Example: "Crying is the refuge of plain women, but the ruin of pretty ones."

4. the use of epigrams.

ep″i·gram·mat′iç, *a.* [L. *epigrammaticus*; Gr. *epigrammatikos*, from *epigramma* (*-atos*), an inscription, epigram.]

1. writing epigrams; as, an *epigrammatic* poet.

2. like an epigram; concise; pointed; witty; as, *epigrammatic* style or wit.

3. of or full of epigram or epigrams.

ep″i·gram·mat′iç·ăl, *a.* epigrammatic.

ep″i·gram·mat′iç·ăl·ly, *adv.* in an epigrammatic manner.

ep·i·gram′mȧ·tism, *n.* the use of epigrams; epigrammatic style or manner.

ep·i·gram′mȧ·tist, *n.* one who composes epigrams.

ep·i·gram′mȧ·tīze, *v.t.*; epigrammatized, *pt., pp.*; epigrammatizing, *ppr.* [Gr. *epigrammatizein*, from *epigramma* (*-atos*), an inscription, *epigram.*] to represent or express by epigrams; to deal with in an epigram.

ep·i·gram′mȧ·tīze, *v.i.* to make epigrams; to write or speak epigrammatically.

ep·i·gram′mȧ·tī·zẽr, *n.* an epigrammatist.

ep′i·gram·mist, *n.* same as *epigrammatist.*

ep′i·grȧph, *n.* [Gr. *epigraphē*, an inscription, from *epigraphein*, to write upon.]

1. an inscription on a building, tomb, monument, statue, etc.

2. a motto or quotation at the beginning of a book, chapter, etc.

ē·pig′rȧ·phẽr, same as *epigraphist.*

ep·i·graph′iç, ep·i·graph′iç·ăl, *a.* of or pertaining to an epigraph or epigraphy.

ep·i·graph′iç s, *n.* the science of inscriptions.

ē·pig′rȧ·phist, *n.* one versed in epigraphy.

ē·pig′rȧ·phy, *n.* 1. inscriptions collectively.

2. the study that deals with deciphering, interpreting, and classifying inscriptions, especially ancient inscriptions.

ē·pig′y·nous, *a.* in botany, growing upon the top of the ovary or seeming to do so, as petals, sepals, and stamens.

EPIGYNOUS STAMENS

ē·pig′y·ny, *n.* the fact or quality of being epigynous.

Ep·i·hip′pus, *n.* a genus of ancestral horses of the upper Eocene, having a prominent middle toe on each foot.

ep·i·hȳ′ăl, *a.* [*epi-*, and *hyoid.*] pertaining to the stylohyoid ligaments.

ep·i·hȳ′ăl, *n.* one of the stylohyoid ligaments constituting part of the lower or visceral arches.

ep·i·lā′brum, *n.*; *pl.* **ep·i·lā′brȧ,** [L., from Gr. *epi*, upon, and L. *labrum*, lip.] in entomology, a sclerite running transversely on each side of the labrum of a myriapod.

ep′i·lāte, *v.t.*; epilated, *pt., pp.*; epilating, *ppr.* [L. *e, ex*, out of, from, and *pilus*, a hair.] to remove (hair), as by destroying the roots.

ep·i·lā′tion, *n.* the process of removing hair by the roots.

ē·pil′ȧ·tō·ry, *a.* capable of removing hair.

ē·pil′ȧ·tō·ry, *n.* a substance or device for removing hair; a depilatory.

ep′i·lep·sy, *n.* [Gr. *epilēpsia, epilēpsis*, lit., a seizure, epilepsy, from *epilambanein*, to seize upon.] a chronic disease of the nervous system, characterized by convulsions and, often, unconsciousness: also called *falling sickness.*

ep·i·lep′tiç, *a.* 1. of, like, or having the nature of epilepsy.

2. having epilepsy.

ep·i·lep′tiç, *n.* one affected with epilepsy.

ep·i·lep′ti·çăl, *a.* same as *epileptic.*

ep·i·lep′ti·çăl·ly, *adv.* in the manner of an epileptic.

ep·i·lep′ti·form, *a.* [Gr. *epilepsis*, epilepsy, and L. *forma*, form.] resembling epilepsy.

ep″i·lep·toġ′e·nous, *a.* [Gr. *epilēptos*, lit., caught, suffering from epilepsy, and *-genēs*, producing.] producing epilepsy.

ep·i·lep′toid, *a.* [Gr. *epilepsis*, epilepsy, and *eidos*, resemblance.] of the nature of epilepsy; resembling epilepsy.

ep″i·lō·gā′tion, *n.* an epilogue. [Obs.]

ep·i·loġ′iç, ep·i·loġ′iç·ăl, *a.* of or relating to an epilogue.

ē·pil′ō·ġism, *n.* [Gr. *epilogismos*, a reckoning over, from *epilogizesthai*, to reckon over; *epi*, upon, over, and *logizesthai*, to consider, reckon, from *logos*, a description, reckoning.] computation; enumeration. [Obs.]

ep″i·lō·ġis′tiç, *a.* pertaining to an epilogue; of the nature of an epilogue.

ē·pil′ō·ġīze, *v.i.* epilogized, *pt., pp.*; epilogizing, *ppr.* to speak an epilogue.

ē·pil′ō·ġīze, *v.t.* to add an epilogue to.

ep′i·logue (-log), **ep′i·log,** *n.* [Fr. *épilogue*; L. *epilogus*; Gr. *epilogos*, a conclusion, *epilogue*, peroration, from *epilegein*, to say in addition, add; *epi*, upon, and *legein*, to say, speak.]

1. a closing section added to a novel, play, etc., providing further comment, interpretation, or information.

2. in the drama, a short speech or poem addressed to the spectators by one of the actors, after the conclusion of the play; also, the actor or actors who speak this.

ep′i·lō·guīze (-gīz), *v.t.* and *v.i.* to epilogize. [Obs.]

Ep″i·mȧ·chī′nae, *n.pl.* [L., from Gr. *epimachos*, assailable, easy to attack; *epi*, on, upon, and *machesthai*, to fight, from *machē*, a battle.] a subfamily of plumed oscine birds, including birds of paradise.

e·pim′ȧ·çus, *n.* [Gr. *epimachos*, equipped for battle.] a heraldic griffinlike monster.

ep″i·mȧ·nik′i·on, *n.*; *pl.* **ep″i·mȧ·nik′i·ȧ,** [Gr. *epi*, upon, and *manikion*, the sleeve, from L. *manica*, the sleeve, from *manus*, the hand.] in the Orthodox Eastern Church, a sort of removable sleeve.

ep·i·mē′rȧ, *n.* pl. of *epimeron.*

ep·i·mē′răl, *a.* of or relating to the epimera.

ep′i·mēre, *n.* [*epi-*, and Gr. *meros*, part, share.] in biology, a transverse axial segment.

ep·i·mē′ron, *n.*; *pl.* **ep·i·mē′rȧ,** one of the lateral pieces of the dorsal arc of the somite of a crustacean.

Ep·i·mē′theūs, *n.* [L.; Gr. *Epimētheus*, lit., "Afterthinker."] in Greek mythology, a Titan, the brother of Prometheus and husband of Pandora: he was given the task, by the gods, of making man and the animals, and distributing the various faculties to them.

ep·i·myș′i·um, *n.* [L., from Gr. *epi*, upon, and *mys*, a muscle.] the enclosing membrane of a muscle.

ep·i·nā′os, *n.* [*epi-*, and Gr. *naos*, a temple.] in ancient architecture, an opening or space in the rear of the cella; a rear vestibule.

ep·i·nas′tiç, *a.* growing faster on the upper than on the under side, as a leaf.

ep′i·nas·ty, *n.* [*epi-*, and Gr. *nastos*, pressed close, solid, from *nassein*, to press or squeeze close.] in botany, the curvature of a part produced by a growth more rapid on its upper than on its under side, as in the leaves of many plants.

ep·i·neph′rine (*or* rēn), **ep·i·neph′rin,** *n.* [from *epi-*, and Gr. *nephros*, kidney; and *-ine.*] a hormone, $C_9H_{13}NO_3$, secreted by the medulla of the adrenal gland, that stimulates the heart, increases muscular strength and endurance, etc.: it is extracted from animal adrenal glands or prepared synthetically for therapeutic use.

ep·i·neū′răl, *a.* [*epi-*, and Gr. *neuron*, a nerve.] in anatomy, arising from or attached to a neural arch.

ep·i·neū′răl, *n.* one of the spines of a neural arch.

ep·i·neū′ri·um, *n.* [L., from Gr. *epi*, upon, and *neuron*, a nerve.] the layer of connective tissue surrounding a peripheral nerve.

ep·iṅ·glette′, *n.* [Fr. *épinglette*, a primer, a priming wire, a pricker, from OFr. *espingle*; L. *spinula*, dim. of *spina*, a thorn, spine.] in military usage, a needle or piercer for opening the cartridge of a cannon before priming.

ep·i·ni′ciăn (-nish′ăn), **ep·i·ni′ciăl** (-nish′ăl), *a.* [Gr. *epinikios*, of victory; *epi*, upon, and *nikē*, victory.] celebrating victory or triumph.

ep·i·ni′cion, *n.* a song of triumph. [Obs.]

ē·pi·or′nis, *n.* same as *aepyornis.*

ep·i·ō′tiç, *a.* [*epi-*, and Gr. *ous, ōtis*, ear.] in anatomy, situated above the ear.

ep·i·ō′tiç, *n.* the outer and upper element of the bone of the internal ear.

ep″i·pe·dom′e·try, *n.* the mensuration of figures standing on the same base. [Obs.]

ep″i·pe·riph′ẽr·ăl, *a.* [*epi-*, and Gr. *periphereia*, a circumference, from *peripherein*, to carry round; *peri*, around, and *pherein*, to bear.] designating sensations produced by external stimuli.

ep·i·pet′ăl·ous, *a.* [*epi-*, and Gr. *petalon*, a leaf.] borne upon the petals of a flower.

ē·piph′ȧ·ny, *n.* [ME. *epyphany*, LL. *epiphania*; Gr. *epiphaneia*, an appearance, from *epiphainein*, to show forth, manifest; *epi*, upon, and *phainein*, to show.]

1. an appearance or apparition of a deity or other supernatural being.

2. [E—] the yearly festival celebrated on the sixth day of January, the twelfth day after Christmas, in commemoration of the revealing of Jesus as the Christ to the Gentiles in the persons of the Magi at Bethlehem: sometimes called *Twelfth Night.*

3. (a) a moment of sudden intuitive understanding; flash of insight; (b) a scene, experience, etc. that occasions such a moment.

ep·i·phar·yn·ġē′ăl, *a.* in anatomy, of, pertaining to, or indicating an epipharynx.

ep·i·phar·yn·ġē′ăl, *n.* an epipharyngeal bone or cartilage.

ep·i·phar′ynx, *n.* [*epi-*, and Gr. *pharynx*, throat.] in entomology, a lobe under the labrum of an insect covering the opening of the gullet.

ep″i·phē·nom′e·non, *n.*; *pl.* **ep″i·phē·nom′e·nȧ,** [*epi-*, and Gr. *phainomenon*, a phenomenon, from *phainein*, to appear.]

1. a phenomenon that occurs with and seems to result from another.

2. in medicine, a secondary or additional occurrence in the course of a disease.

ep·i·phloe′ō·dăl, (-flē′), **ep″i·phloe·od′iç,** *a.* [*epi-*, and Gr. *phloios*, bark.] in botany, living and growing upon the surface of bark.

ep·i·phloe′um, *n.* [L., from Gr. *epi*, upon, and *phloios*, bark.] in botany, the exterior part of bark.

e·piph′ō·nem, *n.* epiphonema. [Rare.]

ep″i·phō·nē′mȧ, *n.* [L., from Gr. *epiphōnēma*, an exclamation; *epi*, upon, and *phōnein*, to speak, from *phōnē*, voice, sound.] in oratory, an exclamatory sentence or striking reflection, at the end of a passage or discourse.

ē·piph′ō·rȧ, *n.* [L., from Gr. *epiphora*, a bringing to or upon, an addition, from *epipherein*, to bring to or upon.]

1. a condition in which the tears, from increased secretion or some disease of the lachrymal passage, accumulate in the eye and trickle over the cheek.

2. in rhetoric, the repetition of a word or phrase at the end of several sentences or stanzas.

ep′i·phragm (-fram), *n.* [L., from Gr. *epiphragma*, a covering, lid, from *epiphrassein*, to block up.]

1. in zoology, a kind of lid with a mucous interior lining with which a land mollusk closes the opening of its shell during seasons of inactivity, as in hibernation or threatened danger.

2. in botany, a thecal covering in some of the lower orders of plants.

ep·i·phyl·lō·spėr′mous, *a.* [*epi-*, and Gr. *phyllon*, a leaf, and *sperma*, seed.] in botany, bearing the seeds on the back of the leaves, as ferns. [Obs.]

e·piph′yl·lous, *a.* [*epi-*, and Gr. *phyllon*, a leaf.] in botany, inserted upon the leaf.

Ep·i·phyl′lum, *n.* [L., from Gr. *epi*, upon, and *phyllon*, a leaf.] a Brazilian genus of cactaceous plants having jointed stems and petals united in a tube: cultivated for their showy pink or red flowers.

ep·i·phyṣ′ē·ăl, ep·i·phyṣ′i·ăl, *a.* of or pertaining to an epiphysis.

ē·piph′y·sis, *n.*; *pl.* **ē·piph′y·sēṣ,** [L., from Gr. *epiphysis*, an outgrowth, from *epiphyein*, to grow upon.]

1. in anatomy, (a) that part of a bone which is at first separated from the main part by cartilage, but later fuses with it by ossification; (b) the pineal body.

2. in zoology, a tibial spur of a lepidopter.

ē·piph·y·sī′tis, *n.* inflammation of an epiphysis.

ē·piph′y·tăl, *a.* pertaining to an epiphyte.

ep′i·phȳte, *n.* [L., from Gr. *epi*, upon, and *phyton*, a plant, from *phyein*, to grow.]

1. a nonparasitic plant that grows on another plant but gets its nourishment from the air, as certain orchids, mosses, and lichens; an air plant.

2. a fungus that is a parasite on an animal.

ep·i·phyt′iç, ep·i·phyt′iç·ăl, *a.* having the nature of an epiphyte.

ep·i·phȳ·tot′iç, *a.* [from *epi-*, and Gr. *phyton*, a plant; and *-otic*.] epidemic among plants.

ep′i·plaṣm, *n.* [L., from Gr. *epi*, upon, and *plasma*, anything formed, from *plassein*, to form.] in botany, the protoplasm left in the spore case of certain fungi after the spores are formed.

ep·i·plas′trŏn, *n.*; *pl.* **ep·i·plas′trȧ,** [*epi-*, and L. *plastron*, the plastron.] in anatomy, either of the first pair of plates in the plastron of a turtle.

ep″i·plē·rō′sis, *n.* unnatural fullness causing distention, as of the stomach or rectum.

ep·i·pleū′rȧ, *n.*; *pl.* **ep·i·pleū′rae,** [L., from Gr. *epi*, upon, and *pleura*, a rib.] in zoology, (a) a bony process on the rib of a bird or of a fish; (b) a portion near the inflexed margin of the elytron of a beetle.

ep·i·pleū′răl, *a.* 1. of or relating to an epipleura.

2. inserted on a pleural element, as on a rib.

ep·i·pleū′răl, *n.* an epipleura.

ep·i·plex′is, *n.* [LL., from Gr. *epiplēxis*, chastisement, blame, from *epiplēssein*, to chastise, blame, lit., to strike at; *epi*, upon, and *plēssein*, to strike.] in rhetoric, a figure by which a person seeks to convince and move by a kind of upbraiding.

ē·pip′lō·cē, *n.* [LL., from Gr. *epiplokē*, a plaiting together, from *epiplekein*, to plait together; *epi*, upon, and *plekein*, to plait, twist.] a figure of rhetoric by which one striking circumstance is added in due gradation to another; as, he not only spared his enemies, but continued them in employment; not only continued them, but advanced them.

ē·pip′lō·cēle, *n.* [Gr. *epiploon*, the caul, and *kēlē*, a tumor.] in medicine, hernia of the omentum.

ep·i·plō′iç, *a.* pertaining to the caul, or great omentum.

ē·pip′lō·on, *n.*; *pl.* **ē·pip′lō·ȧ,** [Gr. *epiploon*, the caul.] the caul, or great omentum.

ep·i·pō′di·ȧ, *n.* pl. of *epipodium*.

ep·i·pō′di·ăl, *a.* 1. in anatomy, of or relating to the epipodialia.

2. in zoology, of or relating to the epipodium.

ep·i·pō·di·ā′li·ȧ, *n.pl.* [L., from Gr. *epipodios*, upon the feet; *epi*, upon, and *pous*, *podos*, foot.] in anatomy, the radius, ulna, tibia, and fibula, taken collectively.

ē·pip′ō·dīte, *n.* [*epi-*, and Gr. *pous*, *podos*, foot.] a process developed upon the basal joint of the anterior limbs of certain crustacea.

ep·i·pō′di·um, *n.*; *pl.* **ep·i·pō′di·ȧ,** [L., from Gr. *epipodios*, upon the feet; *epi*, upon, and *pous*, *podos*, foot.] in zoology, a muscular lobe developed from the lateral and upper surfaces of the foot of some mollusks.

ep·i·pol′iç, *a.* fluorescent.

ē·pip′ō·liṣm, *n.* fluorescence.

ē·pip′ō·līze, *v.t.* to make fluorescent.

ep·ip·ter′iç, *a.* [*epi-*, and Gr. *pteron*, a wing.] in anatomy, designating a bone rarely found in the human skull at the end of the great wing of the sphenoid.

ep·ip·ter′iç, *n.* an epipteric bone.

ē·pip′tėr·ous, *a.* [*epi-*, and Gr. *pteron*, a wing.] in botany, a fruit or seed which is furnished with a broad margin or wing where it terminates.

ep·ip·ter′y·goid, *a.* [*epi-*, and Gr. *pterygoeidēs*, winglike, feathery; *pteryx*, wing, and *eidos*, form.] lying above the pterygoid bone.

ep·ip·ter′y·goid, *n.* a bone or cartilage in the pterygoid region.

ep·i·pū′biç, *a.* above the pubis; pertaining to the epipubis.

ep·i·pū′bis, *n.*; *pl.* **ep·i·pū′bēṣ,** [*epi-*, and L. *pubis*, the pubis.] bony or cartilaginous matter lying in front of the pubis.

ep·i·rhī′zous, *a.* [*epi-*, and Gr. *rhiza*, root.] in botany, growing on a root.

ē·pī·rō·ġen′iç, *a.* same as *epeirogenic*.

ep·ī·roġ′e·ny, *n.* same as *epeirogeny*.

ē·pis′çō·pȧ·cy, *n.*; *pl.* **ē·pis′çō·pȧ·cieṣ,** [LL. *episcopatus*, the office of a bishop, from *episcopus*, a bishop; Gr. *episkopos*, an overseer, watcher, from *episkopein*, to look upon, examine; *epi*, upon, and *skopein*, to look.]

1. government of the church by bishops; that form of ecclesiastical government in which diocesan bishops are established, as distinct from and superior to priests or presbyters; government of the church by three distinct orders of ministers—deacons, priests, and bishops.

2. the position, rank, or term of office of a bishop; episcopate.

3. bishops collectively.

ē·pis′çō·păl, *a.* 1. belonging to, vested in, or governed by bishops; characteristic of or pertaining to a bishop or bishops; as, *episcopal* authority.

2. [E–] designating or of any of various churches based upon episcopacy, particularly the Protestant Episcopal or the Anglican Church.

ē·pis·çō·pā′li·ăn, *a.* 1. of or governed by bishops.

2. [E–] Episcopal.

ē·pis·çō·pā′li·ăn, *n.* 1. one who belongs to an episcopal church or adheres to the episcopal form of church government and discipline.

2. [E–] a member of the Protestant Episcopal Church.

Ē·pis·çō·pā′li·ăn·iṣm, *n.* the beliefs and ritual of the Episcopalians.

ē·pis′çō·păl·iṣm, *n.* the theory or doctrine that the authority to govern a church rests in a body of bishops and not in any individual: it was rejected by the Vatican Council of the Roman Catholic Church in 1870.

ē·pis′çō·păl·ly, *adv.* by episcopal authority; in an episcopal manner.

ē·pis′çō·pănt, *n.* a bishop. [Obs.]

ē·pis·çō·pā′ri·ăn, *a.* episcopal. [Rare.]

ē·pis′çō·pāte, *n.* [LL. *episcopatus*, the office and dignity of a bishop, from *episcopus*, a bishop.]

1. a bishopric; the position, rank, or term of office of a bishop.

2. a bishop's see.

3. bishops collectively.

ē·pis′çō·pāte, *v.i.* to act as a bishop; to fill the office of a bishop. [Obs.]

ē·pis′çō·pȧ·tūre, *n.* 1. a bishop's see.

2. bishops collectively.

ē·pis′çō·pi·cīde, *n.* [LL. *episcopus*, a bishop, and L. *cædere*, to kill.] the killing of a bishop.

ē·pis′çō·pīze, *v.t.*; episcopized, *pt.*, *pp.*; episcopizing, *ppr.* [from LL. *episcopus*, a bishop.]

1. to consecrate as a bishop.

2. to convert to Episcopalianism.

ē·pis′çō·py, *n.* 1. survey; superintendence. [Obs.]

2. episcopacy. [Obs.]

ep·i·sep′ăl·ous, *a.* [*epi-*, and L. *sepalum*, a sepal.] in botany, situated on or adnate to the sepals: said of stamens.

ep·i·skel′e·tăl, *a.* [*epi-*, and Gr. *skeleton*, a dry body.] having the origin outside of the internal skeleton: said of muscles.

ep·i·sō′dăl, *a.* same as *episodic*.

ep′i·sōde, *n*, [Gr. *epeisodion*, an addition, episode, neut. of *epeisodios*, following upon the entrance, coming in besides; *epi*, besides, and *eisodos*, an entrance, from *eis*, into, and *hodos*, a way, road.]

1. the part of an ancient Greek tragedy between two choral songs: it corresponds to an act.

2. in a novel, poem, etc., any part of the story, or a digression, that is complete in itself; an incident.

3. any event or series of events complete in itself but forming part of a larger one; as, an *episode* in the war.

4. any installment of a serialized story or drama.

5. in music, any incidental passage between repetitions of the main theme, especially in a fugue or rondo.

ep·i·sod′iç, ep·i·sod′iç·ăl, *a.* 1. pertaining to an episode; having the nature of an episode; incidental.

2. divided into episodes.

ep·i·sod′iç·ăl·ly, *adv.* in an episodic manner; in episodes.

ep·i·spā′di·as, *n.* [L., from Gr. *epi*, upon, and *spān*, to draw.] a malformation in which the urethal opening is on top of the penis.

ep·i·spas′tiç, *a.* [Gr. *epispastikos*, drawing to oneself, adapted, from *epispastos*, drawn upon oneself, from *epispān*, to draw upon.] in medicine, causing a serous discharge or blistering.

ep·i·spas′tiç, *n.* a blistering agent; a vesicant.

ep′i·spėrm, *n.* [*epi-*, and Gr. *sperma*, a seed.] in botany, the testa or outer integument of a seed.

ep·i·spėr′miç, *a.* of or relating to the episperm.

ep′i·spōre, *n.* [*epi-*, and Gr. *sporos*, seed.] in botany, the outer integument of lichen spores.

ep·i·stax′is, *n.* [L., from Gr. *epistazein*, to bleed at the nose; *epi*, upon, and *stazein*, to fall in drops.] hemorrhage from the nose; nosebleed.

ē·pis″tē·mō·loġ′i·căl, *a.* having to do with epistemology.

ē·pis·tē·mol′ō·ġy, *n.* [Gr. *epistēmē*, knowledge, and *logos*, discourse.] the theory or science that investigates the origin, nature, methods, and limits of knowledge.

ep·i·stėr′năl, *a.* of or relating to the episternum.

ep·i·stėr′num, *n.*; *pl.* **ep·i·stėr′nȧ,** [L., from Gr. *epi*, upon, and *sternon*, breast.]

1. the uppermost part of the sternum in mammals; the manubrium.

2. the bone between the clavicles and in front of the sternum in certain vertebrates; the interclavicle.

ep·i·stil′bīte, *n.* [*epi-*, and *stilbite*.] a white, translucent mineral of the zeolite group, a crystalline hydrous silicate of aluminium, sodium, and calcium.

ē·pis′tle (ē-pis′l), *n.* [ME. *epistle*; AS. *epistol*; L. *epistola*, *epistula*; Gr. *epistolē*, a letter, message, from *epistellein*, to send to.]

1. a letter, especially one in a formal, dignified, or studied style: now used humorously.

2. [E–] (a) in the New Testament, any of the letters written by an Apostle; (b) a selection, usually from these Epistles, read as part of Mass, Communion, etc. in various churches.

epistle side; the side to the left of the priest or the right of the congregation when the two are face to face.

ē·pis′tle, *v.t.* to write in a letter. [Obs.]

ē·pis′tlėr, *n.* 1. a writer of epistles.

2. one who reads the Epistle in a church service.

ē·pis′tō·lăr, *a.* [LL. *epistolarius*, of or belonging to an epistle, from L. *epistola*, *epistula*, a letter, epistle.] epistolary. [Obs.]

ē·pis′tō·lȧ·ry, *a.* 1. pertaining to epistles, or

letters; suitable to letters and correspondence; as, an *epistolary* style.

2. contained in letters; carried on by letters; as, an *epistolary* correspondence.

ē·pis'tō·lā·ry, *n.* a book of Epistles.

ep·is·tō'lē·ăn, *n.* a letter writer. [Rare.]

ē·pis'tō·lēr, *n.* same as *epistler*.

ē·pis'tō·let, *n.* a short epistle or letter.

ep·is·tol'iç, ep·is·tol'iç·ăl, *a.* epistolary. [Obs.]

ē·pis'tō·līze, *v.i.* to write epistles, or letters.

ē·pis'tō·lī·zēr, *n.* a writer of epistles.

ē·pis"tō·lō·graph'iç, *a.* [Gr. *epistolographikos*, pertaining to or used in writing letters; *epistolē*, a letter, and *graphein*, to write.] used in the writing of letters: applied to the demotic characters of the Egyptians.

ē·pis·tō·log'rȧ·phy, *n.* [Gr. *epistolē*, a letter, and *graphein*, to write.] the art or practice of writing letters.

ep'i·stōme, ep·i·stō'mȧ, *n.* [L., from Gr. *epi*, upon, and *stoma*, mouth.] in zoology, (a) the space between the antennae and the mouth in crustaceous animals; (b) the clypeus of a dipteral insect.

e·pis'trō·phē, *n.* [LL. *epistrophe*; Gr. *epistrophē*, a turning about, from *epistrephein*, to turn about.]

1. in rhetoric, a figure in which several successive sentences (or clauses) end with the same word or phrase; as, faith is a good guide, reason is a better guide, truth is the best guide.

2. in botany, the system governing the disposition of chloroplasts upon a leaf surface in diffuse light.

ep·i·strō'phē·ăl, *a.* 1. in botany, relating to epistrophe.

2. in anatomy, relating to the epistropheus.

epi·strō'phē·us, *n.* the second cervical vertebra.

ep·i·stroph'iç, *a.* of or pertaining to epistrophe.

ē·pis'trō·phy, *n.* [Gr. *epistrophē*, a turning about; *epi*, upon, and *strephein*, to turn.] in botany, a return to or toward a normal state from an abnormal.

ep·i·stȳ'lăr, *a.* of or designating an epistyle.

ep'i·stȳle, *n.* [L. *epistylium*; Gr. *epistylon*, an epistyle; *epi*, upon, and *stylos*, a column.] in architecture, an architrave.

ep·i·syl'lō·ġism, *n.* [*epi-*, and Gr. *syllogismos*, syllogism.] a syllogism partly made up of a premise which was a proposition or conclusion of a syllogism preceding, called the prosyllogism.

ep'i·taph, *n.* [ME. *epitaphe*; OFr. *epitaphe*; L. *epitaphium*, a eulogy; Gr. *epitaphios*, at the tomb, *epitaphios logos*, a funeral oration; *epi*, upon, at, and *taphos*, a tomb, from *thaptein*, to bury.]

1. an inscription on a monument, in honor or memory of a dead person.

> A splendid funeral, a towering monument—
> it may be a lying *epitaph*. —Sprague.

2. a short composition in prose or verse, written as a tribute to a dead person.

ep'i·taph·ēr, *n.* one who writes epitaphs.

ep·i·taph'i·ăl, ep·i·taph'i·ăn, *a.* of, pertaining to, or of the nature of an epitaph.

ep·i·taph'iç, *a.* epitaphial.

ep'i·taph·ist, *n.* an epitapher.

e·pit'ȧ·sis, *n.* [Gr. *epitasis*, a stretching, straining; *epitasis*, from *epiteinein*, to stretch upon or over, to increase.]

1. that part of a play which embraces the main action and leads on to the catastrophe: opposed to *protasis*.

2. in medicine, the paroxysm, or period of violence, of a fever or a disease.

ep"i·thȧ·lam'iç, *a.* of or pertaining to an epithalamium.

ep"i·thȧ·lā'mi·ŏn, *n.*; *pl.* **ep"i·thȧ·lā'mi·ȧ,** [from Mod. L. and Gr.; Gr. *epithalamion*.] an epithalamium.

ep"i·thȧ·lā'mi·um, *n.*; *pl.* **ep"i·thȧ·lā'mi·umṣ, ep"i·thȧ·lā'mi·ȧ,** [L. *epithalamium*, from Gr. *epithalamios*, nuptial; *epi*, at, and *thalamos*, bride chamber.] a nuptial song or poem, in praise of a bride or bridegroom, or of both.

ep·i·thal'ȧ·my, *n.* same as *epithalamium*.

ep·i·thal'line, *a.* [*epi-*, and Gr. *thallos*, a branch.] in botany, borne on the thallus.

ep·i·thē'çȧ, *n.* [L., from Gr. *epi*, upon, and *thēkē*, a case, sheath.] in zoology, a continuous layer surrounding the theca in some corals.

ep·i·thē'ci·um, *n.*; *pl.* **ep·i·thē'ci·ȧ,** [L., from Gr. *epi*, upon, and *thēkē*, a case, sheath.] in botany, the outside of the fruiting disk, as in certain fungi and lichens.

ep·i·thē'li·ăl, *a.* of or pertaining to the epithelium; as, *epithelial* cells or scales.

ep·i·thē'li·oid, *a.* resembling epithelium.

ep·i·thē·li·ō'mȧ, *n.*; *pl.* **ep"i·thē·li·ō'mȧ·tȧ, ep"i·thē·li·ō'mȧṣ,** [Mod. L., from *epithelium*, and *-oma*.] a malignant tumor of epithelial cells, particularly of the skin, mouth, larynx, or urinary bladder.

ep·i·thē'li·um, *n.*; *pl.* **ep·i·thē'li·umṣ, ep·i·thē'li·ȧ,** [L., from Gr. *epi*, upon, and *thēlē*, nipple, teat.]

1. in anatomy, cellular tissue that covers surfaces, forms glands, and lines most cavities of the body: it consists of one or several layers of cells with only little intercellular material.

2. in botany, an epidermis consisting of young thin-sided cells, filled with homogeneous, transparent, colorless sap.

ep'i·them, ep·i·thē'mȧ, *n.* [LL. *epithema*, a poultice; Gr. *epithēma*, anything put on, a cover, lid, from *epitithenai*, to put or lay upon.]

1. in medicine, any external application to the body, other than a salve, ointment, or plaster.

2. an outgrowth of hornlike matter on a bird's beak. [Rare.]

e·pith'e·sis, *n.* [L., from Gr. *epithesis*, a laying on, an addition; *epi*, upon, and *tithenai*, to place, put.] same as *paragoge*.

ep'i·thet, *n.* [L. *epitheton*; Gr. *epitheton*, an epithet, from *epitithenai*, to put on; *epi*, on, upon, and *tithenai*, to put.]

1. an adjective, noun, or phrase expressing some characteristic quality of the thing to which it is applied, or an attributive expressing some quality ascribed to it; as, a *verdant* lawn; a *brilliant* appearance; a *just* man; an *accurate* description.

2. a descriptive name or title applied to a person; as, Ivan *the Terrible*.

ep'i·thet, *v.t.* to describe by epithets. [Rare.]

ep·i·thet'iç·ăl, ep·i·thet'iç, *a.* 1. pertaining to an epithet or epithets.

2. containing or consisting of epithets.

ep"i·thȳ·met'iç, ep"i·thȳ·met'iç·ăl, *a.* [Gr. *epithymētikos*, desiring, lusting after, from *epithymein*, to set one's heart on, desire eagerly.] pertaining to the sexual passion; sensual. [Obs.]

ē·pit'ō·mā·tŏr, *n.* an epitomist. [Rare.]

ē·pit'ō·mē, *n.* [L. *epitome*; Gr. *epitomē*, an abridgment, from *epitemnein*, to cut short, cut upon; *epi*, upon, and *temnein*, to cut.]

1. a brief summary or abstract of a book, report, incident, etc.; a compendium containing the substance or principal matters of something.

> *Epitomes* are helpful to the memory.
> —Wotton.

2. a part or thing that is representative or typical of the characteristics or general quality of the whole.

> The Church of St. Mark's itself is an *epitome* of the changes of Venetian architecture. —Ruskin.

Syn.—abridgment, abstract, compend, compendium, summary, synopsis.

ē·pit'ō·mist, *n.* an epitomizer.

ē·pit'ō·mīze, *v.t.*; epitomized, *pt.*, *pp.*; epitomizing, *ppr.* 1. to make or be an epitome of.

> The author they cite and *epitomize*.—Boyle.

2. to diminish, as by cutting off something; to curtail. [Obs.]

> We have *epitomized* many words to the detriment of our tongue. —Addison.

Syn.—abridge, reduce, abstract, condense, summarize.

ē·pit'ō·mī·zēr, *n.* one who epitomizes.

ep·i·triçh'i·um, *n.* [L., from Gr. *epi*, upon, and *trichion*, dim. of *thrix*, *thrichos*, hair.] an outer epidermal layer of the fetus of some animals, above that from which the hair grows.

ep'i·trīte, *n.* [LL. *epitritos*; Gr. *epitritos*, one and one-third; *epi*, upon, and *tritos*, a third.] in prosody, a foot consisting of three long syllables and one short one, and called first, second, third, or fourth epitrite, according as the short syllable is the first, second, third, or fourth; as, sălūtāntēs, cōncĭtātī, intercălāns, incāntārĕ.

ep·i·troçh'lē·ȧ, *n.* [L., from Gr. *epi*, upon, and *trochlia*, a pulley.] in anatomy, the internal condyle of the humerus.

ep·i·troçh'lē·ăr, *a.* pertaining to the epitrochlea.

ep·i·trō'çhoid, *n.* [*epi-*, and Gr. *trochos*, a wheel, and *eidos*, form.] in geometry, the curve traced by a point in the plane of a circle which rolls on the outside of a fixed circle.

e·pit'rō·pē, *n.* [LL., from Gr. *epitropē*, a reference, from *epitrepein*, to turn over; *epi*, upon, and *trepein*, to turn.] in rhetoric, concession; a figure by which something is granted, often ironically, with a view to obtaining an advantage.

ep·i·ū'răl, *a.* and *n.* same as *epural*.

e·pix'y·lous, *a.* [*epi-*, and Gr. *xylon*, wood.] in botany, having growth upon wood, as fungous plants.

ep·i·zeūx'is, *n.* [LL., from Gr. *epizeuxis*, a joining together, the repetition of a word, from *epizeugnynai*, to fasten or join together.] in rhetoric, the repetition of a word for emphasis.

ep·i·zō'a, *n.pl.* [L., from Gr. *epi*, upon, and *zōon*, an animal.] any of various parasitic animals which live externally upon the bodies of other animals.

ep·i·zō'ăn, *n.* an epizoon.

ep·i·zō'iç, *a.* externally parasitic upon animals, as some fungi or lice.

ep·i·zō'on, *n.* sing. of *epizoa*.

ep"i·zō·ot'iç, *a.* [Fr. *épizootique*, from *épizootie*, epizooty, from Gr. *epi*, upon, and *zōon*, animal.] designating a disease temporarily prevalent among many animals.

ep"i·zō·ot'iç, *n.* an epizootic disease.

ep·i·zō'ō·ty, *n.* an epizootic disease.

ē plūr'i·bus ū'num, [L.] out of many, one: motto of the United States.

ep'oçh (*or* ē'pok), *n.* [LL. *epocha*; Gr. *epochē*, a check, cessation, pause, from *epechein*, to hold in, check.]

1. the beginning of a new and important period in the history of anything; as, the invention of radio marked an *epoch* in communication.

2. a period of time considered in terms of noteworthy and characteristic events, developments, persons, etc.; as, an *epoch* of social revolution.

3. in astronomy, (a) an arbitrary date for which are given the relative data determining the position of a heavenly body; (b) the position of the heavenly body at that time.

4. in geology, a subdivision of a geological period; as, the Eocene *Epoch*.

Syn.—age, century, cycle, date, era, period, time.

ep'ō·çhȧ, *n.* an epoch. [Archaic.]

ep'ō·çhăl, *a.* relating to an epoch; of the character of an epoch.

ep'oçh-māk·ing, *a.* beginning a new epoch; causing new trends or important developments.

ep'ōde, *n.* [OFr. *epode*; L. *epodos*; Gr. *epōdos*, an epode; *epi*, upon, to, and *aeidein*, to sing, from *ōdē*, a song, ode.] in lyric poetry, (a) the third or last part of the ode; that which follows the strophe and antistrophes; (b) a style of lyric poem, after Archilochus, the Greek satirist, characterized by a short line following a longer one: it was used by Horace.

e·pod'iç, *a.* pertaining to or resembling an epode.

ē·pol'li·çāte, *a.* [L. *epollicatus*; *e-* priv., and *pollex*, thumb.] in zoology, having the thumb or the hind toe lacking.

ep·ō·nyçh'i·um, *n.* [L., from Gr. *epi*, upon, and *onyx*, *onychos*, nail.]

1. the thickened disk of epidermis preceding the formation of a nail on the fingers and toes of a fetus.

2. the thinned epidermal layer at the sides and base of the nail.

ep'ō·nym, *n.* [Gr. *epōnymos*, given as a name, surnamed; *epi*, upon, and *onyma*, a name.]

1. a real or mythical person from whose name the name of a nation, institution, etc. is derived or is supposed to have been derived; as, William *Penn* is the eponym of *Penn*sylvania.

2. (a) a person whose name has become closely associated with some period, movement, theory, etc.; (b) the name applied to the period, etc., as *Elizabethan* or *Einsteinian*.

ep'ō·nyme, *n.* an eponym. [Obs.]

ep·ō·nym'iç, *a.* eponymous.

e·pon'y·mist, *n.* an eponymous person, as an ancestor.

e·pon'y·mous, *a.* 1. of or relating to an eponym.

> Every country, every autonomous town, nay even many a hamlet, thus had its *eponymous* hero. —Cox.

2. giving one's name to a people, nation, etc.; as, an *eponymous* founder.

e·pon'y·my, *n.* [Gr. *epōnymia*, a surname.] the derivation of a name from an eponym.

ep·ō·oph'ō·ron, *n.* same as *parovarium*.

ep·ō·pee', ep·ō·poe'iȧ (-yȧ), *n.* [L. *epopœia*; Gr. *epopoiia*, epic poetry; *epos*, an epic, and *poiein*, to make.]

1. an epic poem.
2. epic poetry.
3. the history, action, or fable which makes the subject of an epic poem.

ep′opt, *n.* [L. *epopta*, Gr. *epoptēs*, one initiated in the mysteries, a spectator.] an initiate in the Eleusinian mysteries.

ep·op′tiç, *a.* pertaining to an epopt.

ep′os, *n.* [L.; Gr. *epos*; see *epic*.]
1. epic poetry.
2. a primitive epic poem, handed down by word of mouth.
3. a series of epic events.

ep·ox′y (e-pok′sē), *a.* [*ep-*, and *oxygen*.] designating or of a compound in which an oxygen atom is joined to two carbon atoms in a chain to form a bridge; specifically, designating a resin, containing epoxy groups, that polymerizes spontaneously when mixed with a phenol, forming a strong, hard, resistant adhesive used in glues, enamel coatings, etc.

ep·ox′y, *n.*; *pl.* **ep·ox′ieṣ,** an epoxy resin.

ep′si·lon, *n.* [Gr.; *e*, e, and *psilon*, plain, simple.] the fifth letter of the Greek alphabet, corresponding to English *E*, *e*.

ep′sŏm·īte, *n.* native Epsom salt.

Ep′sŏm sạlts (or **sạlt**), [from *Epsom*, England, famous for its mineral waters.] a white, crystalline salt, magnesium sulfate, $MgSO_4 \cdot 7H_2O$, used chiefly as a cathartic.

ep′ū·lā·ry, *a.* [L. *epularis*, from *epulum*, a feast.] pertaining to a feast or banquet.

ep·ū·lā′tion, *n.* a feasting.

e·pū′lis, *n.*; *pl.* **e·pū′li·dēṣ,** [L., from Gr. *epoulis*, a gumboil; *epi*, upon, and *oulon*, the gum.] a tumor of the alveolar processes of the jaws.

ep′ū·lōse, *a.* feasting to excess. [Obs.]

ep·ū·lō′sis, *n.* [L., from Gr. *epoulōsis*, a cicatrization; *epi*, upon, and *oulousthai*, to be scarred over, from *oulē*, a wound.] in medicine, the formation of a scar in the process of healing.

ep·ū·los′i·ty, *n.* a feasting to excess. [Obs.]

ep·ū·lot′iç, *a.* [Gr. *epoulōtikos*, promoting cicatrization, from *epoulousthai*, to cicatrize.] having a healing or cicatrizing power.

ep·ū·lot′iç, *n.* a medicine or application which tends to heal wounds.

ē·pū′pil·lāte, *a.* [*e-* priv., and L. *pupilla*, pupil.] having no pupil: used in entomology of a color spot without a central dot.

e·pū′răl, *a.* [*epi-*, and Gr. *oura*, tail.] borne dorsally on the tail.

e·pū′răl, *n.* a bone on the dorsal side of the tail.

ep·ū·rā′tion, *n.* [L. *e-* intens., and *puratus*, pp. of *purare*, to purify.] the act of purifying. [Rare.]

ē·pūre′, *n.* [Fr., a draft, working drawing, from *épurer*, to purify, clarify; L. *e-*, out, from, and *purare*, to purify.] in architecture, the plan of a building, or part of a building, traced on a wall or floor, on the same scale as that of the work to be constructed.

Ep′wŏrth Lēague, an American organization of young people of the Methodist Episcopal Church, founded in 1889, to promote personal evangelism and intelligent Bible study.

ē·py·or′nis, *n.* see *Aepyornis*.

eq·uȧ·bil′i·ty (ek-wȧ- *or* ē-kwȧ-), *n.* [L. *æquabilitas*, from *æquabilis*, equable.] the condition or quality of being equable.

eq′uȧ·ble (ek′wȧ- *or* ē′kwȧ-), *a.* [L. *æquabilis*, from *æquare*, to make equal, from *æquus*, equal.]
1. characterized by uniformity, invariableness, or evenness; equal and uniform at all times; steady; as, an *equable* temperature.
2. even; tranquil; serene; as, an *equable* temperament.

Syn.—uniform, regular, proportionate, even.

eq′uȧ·ble·ness, *n.* same as *equability*.

eq′uȧ·bly, *adv.* in an equable manner.

ē′quăl (-kwăl), *a.* [ME. *equal*; OFr. *equal*; L. *æqualis*, equal, from *æquus*, plain, even, flat.]
1. of the same quantity, size, number, value, degree, intensity, etc.
2. having the same rights, privileges, ability, rank, etc. (with *to* or *with*); as, I am *equal with* him in skill.
3. evenly proportioned; balanced or uniform in effect or operation.
4. level; smooth and flat. [Archaic.]
5. equable. [Obs.]
6. impartial; fair; just. [Archaic.]

Equal and unconcerned, I look on all.
—Dryden.

7. of the same interest or concern; of like importance, rank, or dignity. [Now Rare.]

They who are not disposed to receive them may let them alone or reject them; it is *equal* to me. —Cheyne.

8. *equal to*; having the necessary ability, strength, power, capacity, or courage for.

Syn.—even, equable, uniform, unvarying, adequate, proportionate, commensurate, fair, just, equitable.—*Equal* is said of degree, quantity, number, and dimensions, as *equal* in years; *even* is said of the surface and position of bodies; a board is made *even* with another board. *Even* and *equable* are applied to the same object in regard to itself; *like* or *alike* is applied to two or more objects in regard to each other; *uniform* is said either of one object in regard to itself or of many objects in regard to one another.

ē′quăl, *n.* 1. a person, thing, or quantity not inferior or superior to another; specifically, one having the same or a similar age, rank, status, quality, value, etc.

Those who were once his *equals*, envy and defame him. —Addison.

2. the state of being equal; equality. [Obs.]

ē′quăl, *v.t.*; equaled *or* equalled, *pt.*, *pp.*; equaling *or* equalling, *ppr.* 1. to make equal; to make of the same quantity, dimensions, or quality; to equalize. [Archaic.]
2. to be equal to; to be adequate to; to be commensurate with.

On me, whose all not *equals* Edward's moiety. —Shak.

3. to rise to the same state, rank, estimation, or excellence with; to become equal to; as, few commanders *equal* Washington in fame.

What delights can *equal* those
That stir the spirit's inner deeps?
—Tennyson.

4. to make equivalent to; to recompense fully; to answer in full proportion.

Who answer'd all her cares, and *equall'd* all her love. —Dryden.

ē″quăl·i·tā′ri·ăn, *a.* of, or holding, the belief that all men should have equal political and social rights.

ē″quăl·i·tā′ri·ăn, *n.* a person who holds the belief that all men should have equal political and social rights.

ē·quăl′i·ty, *n.*; *pl.* **ē·quăl′i·tieṣ,** [ME. *egalite*; OFr. *egalite*, *équalité*; L. *æqualitas*, equality, from *æqualis*, equal.]
1. the state of being equal; likeness in magnitude or dimensions, value, qualities, degree, and the like; the state of being neither superior nor inferior; as, the *equality* of men; an *equality* of rights.
2. evenness; uniformity; sameness in state or continued course; as, an *equality* of temper.
3. evenness; plainness; uniformity; as, an *equality* of surface. [Now Rare.]
4. in mathematics, a comparison of two quantities which are in effect equal, though differently expressed or represented, usually denoted by two parallel lines, =.

ē″quăl·i·zā′tion, *n.* the act of equalizing or state of being equalized.

ē′quăl·īze, *v.t.*; equalized, *pt.*, *pp.*; equalizing, *ppr.* 1. to make equal; to cause to be equal in amount or degree; as, to *equalize* accounts.
2. to make uniform.
3. to be equal to; to equal. [Obs.]

Syn.—adjust, arrange, balance, neutralize.

ē′quăl·ī·zẽr, *n.* 1. a person who equalizes.
2. a thing that equalizes; especially, an electrical conductor of low resistance, used to equalize voltages.

ē′quăl·ī·zing bär, in mechanics, any leverlike bar used to equalize strain, as a device to distribute weight equally in a passenger coach or engine.

ē′quăl·ly, *adv.* in an equal manner; in or to an equal extent or degree; uniformly; impartially.

ē′quăl mark (or **sign**), the arithmetical sign (=), indicating that the terms on either side of the sign are equal; as, $2 + 2 = 4$.

ē′quăl·ness, *n.* equality; evenness.

ē·quañ′gū·lăr, *a.* equiangular. [Rare.]

ē·quȧ·nim′i·ty (*or* ek′wȧ-), *n.* [L. *æquanimitas*, evenness of mind; *æquus*, even, equal, and *animus*, mind.] evenness of mind; calm temper or firmness of mind; composure.

ē·quan′i·mous, *a.* possessing equanimity.

ē′quănt, *n.* [L. *æquans* (*-antis*), ppr. of *æquare*, to make equal.] in ancient astronomy, an imaginary circle used for determining the motions of the planets.

ē·quāte′, *v.t.*; equated, *pt.*, *pp.*; equating, *ppr.* [L. *æquatus*, ppr. of *æquare*, to make equal.]
1. in mathematics, to state or express the equality of; put in the form of an equation.
2. to make equal or equivalent; treat, regard, or express as equal or equivalent.

ē·quā′tion (-zhun *or* -shun), *n.* [ME. *equacion*; L. *æquatio* (*-onis*), an equalizing, from *æquare*, to make equal.]
1. an equating or being equated.
2. (a) variation in computation due to personal errors in observation, judgment, etc., or the correction to compensate for this: in full, *personal equation*; (b) the amount of such error or correction, as in astronomical computations.
3. in chemistry, an expression in which symbols and formulas are used to represent a chemical reaction; as, $H_2SO_4 + 2NaCl = 2HCl + Na_2SO_4$.
4. in mathematics, a proposition asserting the equality of two quantities and expressed by the sign = between them; an expression of the same quantity in two dissimilar but equal terms; as, $a + b = c$.
5. in astronomy, the correction or quantity to be added to or subtracted from the mean position of a heavenly body to obtain the true position; more generally, the correction arising from any erroneous supposition whatever.

absolute equation; see under *absolute*.

equation clock or *watch*; a clock (or watch) showing the difference between mean solar and apparent solar time.

equation of a curve; in mathematics, an equation giving an expression of the relation of the co-ordinates of every point in the curve.

equation of equinoxes; in astronomy, the difference between the mean and apparent places of the equinox.

equation of the center; in astronomy, the difference between the true and the mean anomaly of a planet.

equation of time; in astronomy, the difference between mean and apparent time, or the reduction of apparent unequal time or motion of the sun or a planet to equable and mean time or motion.

ē·quā′tion·ăl, *a.* denoting an equation or the use of equations.

ē·quā′tŏr, *n.* [ME. *equator*; LL. *æquator*, the equator, from L. *æquare*, to make equal.]
1. an imaginary circle around the earth equally distant at all points from both the North Pole and the South Pole: it divides the earth's surface into the Northern Hemisphere and the Southern Hemisphere.
2. any circle that divides a sphere or other body into two equal and symmetrical parts.
3. in astronomy, the imaginary circle formed by the intersection of the plane of the earth's equator with the observed celestial sphere: in full, *celestial equator*.

magnetic equator; a line on which a dipping needle carried along it remains horizontal: also called the *aclinic line*.

ē·quȧ·tō′ri·ăl (*or* ek-wȧ-), *a.* 1. of or near the earth's equator.
2. of an equator.
3. like or characteristic of conditions near the earth's equator; as, *equatorial* heat.

ē·quȧ·tō′ri·ăl, *n.* a telescope mounted in such a way as to have two axes of motion, one (called *polar axis*) parallel to the earth's axis, the other (called *declination axis*) perpendicular to it: by rotation on the polar axis it can follow the apparent motion of a heavenly body.

ē·quȧ·tō′ri·ăl·ly, *adv.* so as to have the motion of an equatorial; in a line with the equator.

eq′uẽr·ry (ek′wẽr-), *n.*; *pl.* **eq′uẽr·rieṣ,** [Fr. *ecurie*; OFr. *escuyrie*; LL. *scuria*, a stable, from O.H.G. *sciura*, a shed.]
1. formerly, an officer in charge of the horses of a royal or noble household.
2. a personal attendant on some member of the king's family, as in England.

eq′ue·ry, *n.* same as *equerry*.

ē·ques′tri·ăn, *a.* [L. *equester* (*-tris*), pertaining to a horse or horseman, equestrian, from *eques*, a horseman, from *equus*, a horse.]
1. pertaining to horses, horsemen, horseback riding, or horsemanship; performed with horses; as, *equestrian* feats.
2. representing a person on horseback; as, an *equestrian* statue.
3. of or pertaining to the Roman equites, or knights; as, the *equestrian* order.

ē·ques′tri·ăn, *n.* a rider or circus performer on horseback.

ē·ques′tri·ăn·iṣm, *n.* the performance of an equestrian; horsemanship.

ē·ques·tri·enne′, *n.* [from *equestrian*, and Fr. f. suffix *-enne*.] a girl or woman who rides or performs on horseback.

e·qui-, [from Latin *æquus*, equal.] a combining form meaning *equal*, *equally*, as in *equi*valent, *equi*distant.

ē·qui·aṅ′gū·lär, *a.* [*equi-*, and L. *angulus*, an angle.] having all angles equal.

ē·qui·bal′ănce, *n.* [*equi-*, and *balance*.] equal weight; equilibrium.

ē·qui·bal′ănce, *v.t.* to have equal weight with (something); to counterbalance. [Rare.]

ē·qui·çrū′răl, *a.* [*equi-*, and L. *crus* (*cruris*), leg.] having legs of equal length; isosceles; as, an *equicrural* triangle.

ē′qui·çrūre, *a.* equicrural. [Obs.]

Eq′ui·dae (ek′wi-dē), *n.pl.* a family of mammals, the horse family, consisting of a single extant genus, *Equus*.

ē·qui·dif′fẽr·ent, *a.* [*equi-*, and L. *differens* (*-entis*), ppr. of *differre*, to carry different ways, to be different.] having equal differences.

ē·qui·dis′tănce, *n.* equal distance.

ē·qui·dis′tănt, *a.* [*equi-*, and L. *distans* (*-antis*), ppr. of *distare*, to stand apart, to be distant.] being at an equal distance from some point or thing.

ē·qui·dis′tănt·ly, *adv.* at an equal distance.

ē″qui·dī·ūr′năl, *a.* [*equi-*, and L. *diurnus*, daily.] at the time when day and night are equal.

ē′qui·fọrm, *a.* [L. *æquiformis*, uniform; *æquus*, equal, and *forma*, shape.] having the same form; uniform. [Rare.]

ē·qui·fọr′mi·ty, *n.* uniform equality. [Rare.]

ē·qui·lat′ẽr·ăl, *a.* [LL. *æquilateralis*; L. *æquus*, equal, and *latus*, side.] having all the sides equal; as, an *equilateral* triangle.

equilateral hyperbola; a hyperbola which has the two axes equal to one another, the asymptotes forming a right angle.

equilateral shell; a shell in which a transverse line, drawn through the apex of the umbo, divides the valve equally and symmetrically.

EQUILATERAL TRIANGLE

ē·qui·lat′ẽr·ăl, *n.* 1. a side exactly corresponding to another or others in length.

2. a figure of equal sides.

ē·qui·lī′brănt (*or* ē-quil′i-brănt), *n.* [*equi-*, and L. *librans* (*-antis*), ppr. of *librare*, to poise.] in physics, a force (or forces) keeping or tending to keep another force (or forces) in equilibrium.

ē·qui·lī′brāte (*or* ē-quil′i-), *v.t.* and *v.i.*; equilibrated, *pt.*, *pp.*; equilibrating, *ppr.* [*equi-*, and L. *libratus*, ppr. of *librare*, to poise, weigh out.] to balance or counterbalance; to bring into or be in equilibrium.

ē·qui·lī·brā′tion (*or* ē-quil′i-), *n.* an equilibrating or being equilibrated.

ē·qui·lī′brā·tŏr (*or* ē-quil′i-), *n.* any of many devices used to maintain or restore equilibrium.

ē·qui·lib′ri·ous, *a.* equally poised.

ē·qui·lib′ri·ous·ly, *adv.* in equal poise.

ē·qui·lī′brist (*or* ē-quil′i-brist), *n.* one who keeps his balance in unnatural positions and hazardous movements, as a tightrope walker.

ē·qui·lib′ri·ty, *n.* [L. *æquilibritas* (*-tatis*), from *æquilibris*, evenly balanced; *æquus*, equal, and *libra*, a balance.] equilibrium. [Rare.]

ē·qui·lib′ri·um, *n.* [L. *æquilibrium*, an even balance, a level, from *æquilibris*, evenly balanced; *æquus*, even, equal, and *libra*, a balance.]

1. a state of balance or equality between opposing forces.

2. a state of balance or adjustment of conflicting desires, interests, etc.

3. equal balancing of the mind between motives or reasons; a state of indifference or of doubt, when the mind is suspended in indecision between different motives or the different forces of evidence.

4. in chemistry, the stage in a reversible chemical change at which the products of the forward or direct reaction are consumed by the reverse reaction at the same rate as they are formed.

5. in radioactivity, the stage of a radioactive material at which the rate of disintegration and the rate of formation are equal.

ē′qui·lōbed, *a.* [*equi-*, and L. *lobus*, lobe.] in botany, having equal lobes or divisions, as a leaf.

ē″qui·mō·leç′ū·lär, *a.* having an equal number of molecules.

ē″qui·mō·men′tăl, *a.* [*equi-*, and L. *momentum*, moment.] in physics, having the moments of inertia equal.

ē·qui·mul′ti·ple (-pl), *a.* [*equi-*, and L. *multiplex* (*-plicis*), manifold.] multiplied by the same number or quantity.

ē·qui·mul′ti·ple, *n.* in mathematics, a product arising from the multiplication of two or more quantities by the same number or quantity. Hence, *equimultiples* of any numbers or quantities are always in the same ratio to each other as the simple numbers or quantities before multiplication. If 6 and 9 are multiplied by 4, the *equimultiples*, 24 and 36, will be to each other as 6 to 9.

ē·quī′năl, *a.* equine. [Obs.]

ē′quīne, *a.* [L. *equinus*, from *equus*, a horse.] of, pertaining to, or resembling a horse.

ē·qui·nec′es·sā·ry, *a.* [*equi-*, and L. *necessarius*, necessary.] necessary or needful in the same degree. [Rare.]

ē·quin′i·ȧ, *n.* [L., from *equinus*, pertaining to a horse, from *equus*, a horse.] same as *glanders*.

ē·qui·noç′tiăl (-shăl), *a.* [ME. *equinoctial*; L. *æquinoctialis*, from *æquinoctium*, the equinox; *æquus*, equal, and *nox*, night.]

1. pertaining to the equinoxes or to either of the equinoxes.

2. pertaining to the regions or climate of the equinoctial circle or equator; equatorial; as, *equinoctial* heat; an *equinoctial* sun.

3. occurring at or about the time of the equinox, when day and night are equal in length.

equinoctial circle (or *line*); the celestial equator: when the sun crosses it, the days and nights are equally long in all parts of the earth.

equinoctial colure; the meridian which passes through the equinoctial points.

equinoctial point; either of the equinoxes (sense 2).

equinoctial time; time reckoned from a fixed instant common to all the world, that is, the instant when the sun passes the mean vernal equinoctial point.

ē·qui·noç′tiăl, *n.* 1. the equinoctial line.

2. a severe storm or gale which usually occurs at or near the equinox, erroneously supposed to be the result of the sun's crossing the equator.

ē·qui·noç′tiăl·ly, *adv.* in the direction of the equinoctial.

ē′qui·nox, *n.* [Fr. *équinoxe*; L. *æquinoctium*, the equinox; *æquus*, equal, and *nox*, night.]

1. the precise time when the sun crosses the equator, making the day and night everywhere of equal length. The vernal equinox occurs about the 21st of March, and the autumnal equinox about the 22d of September.

2. either of the two points on the celestial equator where the sun crosses it on these dates: also called *equinoctial point*.

3. an equinoctial gale or storm. [Obs.]

ē·quip′, *v.t.*; equipped (-kwipt′), *pt.*, *pp.*; equipping, *ppr.* [OFr. *equiper*, *esquiper*, to put in order, equip; Ice. *skipa*, to place in order, to arrange.]

1. to dress (oneself) for a certain purpose; to array; to accouter; as, to *equip* a person with a suit of clothes.

2. to furnish with the necessities for an undertaking; to fit out; as, the soldiers were *equipped* for battle.

3. to prepare for some particular duty or service, whether physically or mentally; to furnish with qualifications; to train; as, a man well *equipped* for the ministry.

Syn.—accouter, fit out, dress, furnish, adorn.

eq′ui·pāġe, *n.* [OFr. *equipage*, from *equiper*, to equip.]

1. the furnishings, accessories, or outfit of a ship, army, expedition, etc.; equipment.

2. a carriage, especially one with horses and liveried servants.

3. (a) toilet articles; (b) a case for these. [Archaic.]

4. retinue; train; following, as of a person of rank. [Archaic.]

ē·quip′ȧ·rȧ·ble, *a.* comparable. [Obs.]

ē·quip′ȧ·rănce, ē·quip′ȧ·răn·cy, *n.* in logic, a state of equality; equivalence. [Rare.]

ē·quip′ȧ·rāte, *v.t.* [L. *æquiparatus*, pp. of *æquiparare*, to put on a level, compare; *æquus*, equal, and *parare*, to make ready.]

1. to compare. [Obs.]

2. to reduce to a level; to make or regard as equal. [Obs.]

ē·quip′e·dăl, *a.* [LL. *æquipedus*, equal-footed; L. *æquus*, equal, and *pes*, *pedis*, foot.] in zoology, equal-footed; having the pairs of feet equal.

ē·qui·pend′en·cy, *n.* [*equi-*, and L. *pendere*, to hang.] the act or state of hanging in equipoise or of not being inclined or determined either way; an unbiased condition. [Obs.]

ē·quip′ment, *n.* 1. an equipping or being equipped.

2. whatever a person, group, or thing is equipped with; furnishings; outfit.

3. in transportation, cars, trucks, etc.; rolling stock, as distinguished from stationary property.

ē′qui·poiṣe (*or* ek′wi-), *n.* [*equi-*, and *poise*.]

1. equal distribution of weight; hence, equilibrium; a state in which the two ends or sides of a thing are balanced: figuratively applied to moral, social, or political interests or forces.

Our little lives are kept in *equipoise*
By opposite attractions and desires.
—Longfellow.

2. counterpoise; counterbalance.

ē·qui·pol′lence, ē·qui·pol′len·cy, *n.* [ME. *equipolence*; LL. *æquipollens* (*-entis*), having equal power; L. *æquus*, equal, and *pollens*, ppr. of *pollere*, to be strong.]

1. equality of force, value, meaning, etc.

2. in logic, an equivalence between two or more propositions, as when two propositions signify the same thing, though differently expressed.

ē·qui·pol′lent, *a.* [ME. *equipolent*; OFr. *equipolent*; LL. *æquipollens*, having equal power; *æquus*, equal, and *pollens*, ppr. of *pollere*, to be strong.]

1. equal in force, weight, validity, etc.

2. equivalent in meaning or result.

ē·qui·pol′lent·ly, *adv.* in an equipollent manner.

ē·qui·pon′dẽr·ănce, ē·qui·pon′dẽr·ăn·cy, *n.* equality of weight; equilibrium; balance.

ē·qui·pon′dẽr·ănt, *a.* [ML. *æquiponderans*, ppr. of *æquiponderare*, from L. *æquus*, equal, and *ponderare*, to weigh.] of the same weight; evenly balanced (often with *to* or *with*).

ē·qui·pon′dẽr·āte, *v.i.*; equiponderated, *pt.*, *pp.*; equiponderating, *ppr.* [*equi-*, and L. *ponderatus*, pp. of *ponderare*, to weigh.] to be equal in weight; to weigh as much as another thing.

ē·qui·pon′dẽr·āte, *v.i.* 1. to make evenly balanced.

2. to counterbalance.

ē·qui·pon′dẽr·ous, *a.* having the same or equal weight. [Obs.]

ē·qui·pon′di·ous, *a.* having equal weight on both sides. [Obs.]

ē″qui·pō·ten′tiăl (-shăl), *a.* [*equi-*, and L. *potentia*, power.]

1. having equal potentiality or power.

2. in physics, of the same potential.

equipotential surface; a surface having equal potential at all points.

ē·qui·rō′tăl, *a.* [*equi-*, and L. *rota*, a wheel.] having wheels of the same size or diameter, as a machine. [Rare.]

Ē″qui·sē·tā′cē·ae, *n.pl.* [L., from *equus*, horse, and *sæta*, a bristle.] a family of vascular, cryptogamous plants, with jointed hollow stems; the horsetail family.

ē″qui·sē·tā′ceous, *a.* in botany, pertaining to the family *Equisetaceæ*.

Eq·ui·sē′tum (ek-wi-), *n.* [L., from *equus*, a horse, and *seta*, *sæta*, a bristle.]

1. a genus of flowerless plants with hard, jointed stems, the horsetails, being the sole genus of the family *Equisetaceæ*. The cuticle abounds in siliceous cells, on which account the stems of some species are used for polishing wood: called also *Dutch rush* and *scouring rush*.

2. [e—] any plant of this genus.

EQUISETUM

ē·qui·sō′nănce, *n.* an equal sounding: a name by which the Greeks distinguished the consonances of the octave and double octave.

ē·qui·sō′nănt, *a.* [*equi-*, and L. *sonans*, ppr. of *sonare*, to sound.] in music, sounding equally, in unison or in octaves.

eq′ui·tȧ·ble (ek′wi-), *a.* [Fr. *équitable*, from L. *æquitas*, equality, from *æquus*, equal.]

1. possessing or exhibiting equity; equal in regard to the rights of persons; distributing equal justice; giving each his due; assigning to one or more what law or justice demands; just; impartial; as, an *equitable* judge, an *equitable* decision, an *equitable* distribution of an estate.

2. in law, (a) having to do with equity, as distinguished from common or statute law; (b) valid in equity.

Syn.—fair, honest, impartial, just, reasonable.

eq′ui·tȧ·ble·ness, *n.* the quality, state, or condition of being equitable.

eq′ui·tȧ·bly, *adv.* in an equitable manner; according to the principles of equity; justly; impartially; as, the laws should be *equitably* administered.

ē″qui·tan·ġen′tiăl, *a.* [*equi-*, and L. *tangens* (*-entis*), ppr. of *tangere*, to touch.] in geometry, having a tangent equal to a constant line: applied to a curve.

eq′ui·tănt (ek′wi-), *a.* [L. *equitans* (*-antis*), ppr. of *equitare*, to ride, from *eques*, a horseman, from *equus*, a horse.]

1. mounted or sitting upon a horse; riding on horseback. [Rare.]

2. in botany, overlapping: said of leaves whose bases overlap the leaves within or above them, as in the iris.

eq·ui·tā′tion, *n.* [L. *equitatio* (*-onis*), from *equitatus*, pp. of *equitare*, to ride.] the act or art of riding on horseback; horsemanship.

ē·qui·tem·pō·rā′nē·ous, *a.* [*equi-*, and L. *tempus*, time.] equal in or occupying the same time lengths. [Obs.]

eq′ui·tēș (ek′wi-) *n.pl.* [L., pl. of *eques*, a horseman, from *equus*, a horse.] members of a specially privileged class of citizens in ancient Rome, from which the cavalry was formed; equestrian order of knights.

eq′ui·ty (ek′wi-ti), *n.*; *pl.* **eq′ui·tieș,** [ME. *equitee*; OFr. *equite*; L. *æquitas* (*-atis*), equality, from *æquus*, equal.]

1. justice; impartiality; the giving or desiring to give to each man his due.

> With righteousness shall he judge the world, and the people with *equity*.—Ps. xcviii. 9.

2. anything that is fair or equitable.

3. the value of property beyond the total amount owed on it.

4. in law, (a) resort to general principles of fairness and justice whenever existing law is inadequate; (b) a system of rules and doctrines, as in the United States, supplementing common and statute law and superseding such law when it proves inadequate for just settlement; (c) an equitable right or claim; (d) an equity of redemption.

equity of redemption; the right of a mortgagor to redeem his forfeited estate by payment of capital and interest within a reasonable time: it is granted by a court of equity.

Syn.—justice, fairness, right, impartiality, honesty, uprightness.

ē·quiv′ȧ·lence, *n.* [ML. *æquivalentia*, from LL. *æquivalens* (*-entis*), ppr. of *æquivalere*, to have equal power; L. *æquus*, equal, and *valere*, to be strong.]

1. the condition of being equivalent; equality of value, quantity, signification, force, etc.; as, take the goods and give an *equivalence* in corn.

2. in chemistry, equality of combining capacity; the principle that different weights of different substances are equivalent in chemical reactions.

equivalence of force; the doctrine that force of one kind becomes transformed into force of another kind of the same value.

ē·quiv′ȧ·len·cy, *n.* same as *equivalence*.

ē·quiv′ȧ·lent, *a.* [LL. *æquivalens* (*-entis*), ppr. of *æquivalere*, to have equal power; L. *æquus*, equal and *valere*, to be strong.]

1. equal in value, quantity, force, power, effect, excellence, meaning, etc.; interchangeable; as, circumstantial evidence may be almost *equivalent* to full proof.

2. in geology, contemporaneous in origin; corresponding in position in the scale of rocks; as, the *equivalent* strata of different countries.

3. in chemistry, having the same valence.

4. in geometry, equal in area, volume, etc., but not of the same shape.

ē·quiv′ȧ·lent, *n.* 1. that which is equal in value, quantity, force, meaning, etc. to something else.

2. in chemistry, the quantity by weight (of a substance) that combines with one gram of hydrogen or eight grams of oxygen.

3. in geology, a stratum or series of strata in one district formed contemporaneously with another in a different region.

mechanical equivalent of heat; in physics, the amount of mechanical energy which, when transformed into heat, is equivalent to one heat unit. Joule's experiments gave 772 footpounds as the energy equivalent to that expended in raising the temperature of one pound of water 1° F.

ē·quiv′ȧ·lent, *v.t.* to make equivalent to; to furnish an equivalent for; to equal. [Rare.]

ē·quiv′ȧ·lent·ly, *adv.* in an equivalent manner.

ē·qui·val′ūe, *v.t.* to put the same or an equal value upon; to rate as equal. [Rare.]

ē′qui·valve, *n.* a bivalve in which the valves are of equal size and form.

ē′qui·valve, ē′qui·valved, *a.* [*equi-*, and L. *valva*, the leaf of a door.] having valves equal in size and form, as certain bivalve shells.

ē·quiv′ō·ċȧ·cy, *n.* equivocalness.

ē·quiv′ō·ċăl, *a.* [LL. *æquivocus*, of like sound; L. *æquus*, equal, and *vox* (*vocis*), voice.]

1. being of doubtful signification; capable of being understood in different senses; capable of a double interpretation; purposely vague, misleading, or ambiguous; as, *equivocal* words, terms, or senses.

> The beauties of Shakspere are not of so dim or *equivocal* a nature as to be visible only to learned eyes. —Jeffrey.

2. uncertain; undecided; doubtful; as, an *equivocal* outcome.

3. suspicious; questionable; as, *equivocal* morality.

equivocal chord; in music, a chord common to two or more keys and used in transitions from one key to another.

equivocal generation; spontaneous generation.

Syn.—ambiguous, doubtful, dubious, uncertain, vague, obscure.—An expression is *ambiguous* when different parts of it can be so construed as to bring out a diversity of meanings. It is *equivocal* when its ambiguity is deliberately intended to mislead or confuse.

ē·quiv′ō·ċăl, *n.* a word or term of doubtful meaning, or capable of different interpretations.

ē·quiv′ō·ċăl·ly, *adv.* in an equivocal manner; ambiguously.

ē·quiv′ō·ċăl·ness, *n.* the state of being equivocal; ambiguity; double meaning.

ē·quiv′ō·ċāte, *v.i.*; equivocated, *pt.*, *pp.*; equivocating, *ppr.* [LL. *æquivocatus*, pp. of *æquivocari*, to have the same sound, to be called by the same name; L. *æquivocus*, of like sound; *æquus*, equal, and *vox* (*vocis*), voice, sound.] to express one's opinions equivocally or in terms which admit of different senses, in order to deceive or mislead; to be purposely ambiguous; to hedge.

Syn.—prevaricate, quibble, shuffle, evade.

ē·quiv′ō·ċāte, *v.t.* to render equivocal. [Rare.]

> He *equivocated* his vow by a mental reservation. —Sir G. Buck.

ē·quiv·ō·ċā′tion, *n.* [LL. *æquivocatio* (*-onis*), from *æquivocari*, to have the same sound.]

1. ambiguity of speech; the use of words or expressions that are susceptible of a double signification, with a view to mislead; prevarication; as, hypocrites are often guilty of *equivocation*.

2. an equivocal, or ambiguous expression.

3. in logic, a fallacy arising from the use or employment of a word of uncertain or doubtful meaning.

Syn.—evasion, shift, subterfuge, prevarication, quibble.

ē·quiv′ō·ċā·tŏr, *n.* one who equivocates.

ē·quiv′ō·ċā·tō·ry, *a.* characterized by equivocation.

eq′ui·vōque, eq′ui·vōke (ek′wi-vōk), *n.* [Fr. *équivoque*; L. *æquivocus*, of like sound, ambiguous; *æquus*, equal, and *vox* (*vocis*), voice.]

1. an ambiguous expression or phrase.

2. (a) a pun; (b) punning.

3. verbal ambiguity; double meaning.

ē·quiv′ō·rous, *a.* [L. *equus*, horse, and *vorare*, to devour.] feeding or subsisting on horseflesh.

ē′quoid, *a.* [L. *equus*, a horse, and Gr. *eidos*, resemblance.] pertaining to the *Equidæ*; belonging to the horse family; equine.

Ē·quū′lē·us, *n.* [L., dim. of *equus*, a horse.] a very small constellation on the equator.

Ē′quus (ē′kwus), *n.* [L., a horse.] the typical genus of animals of the family *Equidæ*: the horse is *Equus caballus*.

ēr, *interj.* a conventionalized expression of the sound often made by a speaker when hesitating briefly; a vocalized pause.

-ēr, 1. [ME. *-er* (*e*); AS. *-ere.*] a suffix (a) added to nouns meaning *a person having to do with*, as in hatt*er*, cottag*er*; (b) added to place names, meaning *a person living in*, as in New York*er*; (c) in colloquial usage, added to nouns, noun compounds, and noun phrases, meaning *a thing or action connected with*, as in din*er*, double-head*er*; (d) added to verbs, meaning *a person or thing that*, as in spray*er*, roll*er*.

2. [ME. *-re*, *-er*; AS. *-ra.*] a suffix added to many adjectives and adverbs to form the comparative degree, as in lat*er*, great*er*.

3. [ME.; Anglo-Fr. inf. suffix.] a suffix added to verb bases in legal language, meaning *the action of — ing*, as in demurr*er*, waiv*er*.

4. [ME. *-ren*, *-rien*; AS. *-rian*, freq. suffix.] a suffix added to verbs and verb bases, meaning *repeatedly*, as in flick*er*, patt*er*.

Er, in chemistry, erbium.

ē′rȧ, *n.*; *pl.* **ē′rȧș,** [LL. *æra*, an era; earlier use, counters, the items of account, from pl. of L. *æs* (*æris*), brass.]

1. a system of reckoning time by numbering the years from some important occurrence or given point of time; as, the Christian *Era* is dated from approximately four years after Jesus' birth.

2. an event or date that marks the beginning of a new or important period in the history of something.

3. a period of time measured from some important occurrence or date.

4. a period of time considered in terms of noteworthy and characteristic events, developments, men, etc.; as, an *era* of progress.

5. any of the five main divisions of geological time; as, the Paleozoic *Era*.

ē·rā′di·āte, *v.i.* and *v.t.*; eradiated, *pt.*, *pp.*; eradiating, *ppr.* [L. *e-*, from, and *radiatus*, pp. of *radiare*, to radiate, from *radius*, a beam, ray.] to radiate; to shoot out, as rays of light.

ē·rā·di·ā′tion, *n.* emission, as of rays or beams of light.

ē·rad′i·ċȧ·ble, *a.* capable of being eradicated.

ē·rad′i·ċāte, *v.t.*; eradicated, *pt.*, *pp.*; eradicating, *ppr.* [L. *eradicatus*, pp. of *eradicare*, to root out; *e-*, from, out, and *radix* (*-icis*), root.]

1. to pull up by the roots; to destroy at the roots; to root out; to extirpate; as, to *eradicate* weeds.

2. to destroy thoroughly; to get rid of; to wipe out; to extirpate; as, to *eradicate* errors, false principles, vice, or disease.

Syn.—uproot, exterminate, destroy, annihilate.

ē·rad·i·ċā′tion, *n.* [L. *eradicatio* (*-onis*), from *eradicare*, to root out; *e-*, out, and *radix*, root.] an eradicating or being eradicated; extirpation; excision; total destruction.

ē·rad′i·ċā·tive, *a.* eradicating or tending to eradicate.

ē·rad′i·ċā·tive, *n.* a medicine or course of medical treatment that effects a radical cure

ē·rad′i·ċā·tŏr, *n.* one who or that which eradicates: chemical ink removers are called *eradicators*.

ē·ra·diç′ū·lōse, *a.* [L. *e-* priv., and *radicula*, dim. of *radix*, root.] in botany, having no rootlets.

Ē·ran′the·mum, *n.* [L., from Gr. *ēr*, spring, and *anthos*, a flower.] a genus of acanthaceous plants, chiefly tropical, some of whose species are occasionally seen in hothouses.

ē·rās′ȧ·ble, *a.* capable of being erased.

ē·rāse′, *v.t.*; erased (ē-rāst′), *pt.*, *pp.*; erasing, *ppr.* [L. *erasus*, pp. of *eradere*, to scratch out.]

1. to rub or scrape out, as letters or characters written, engraved, or painted; to efface; to blot out; to expunge; as, to *erase* a word or a name.

2. to remove or destroy all marks of; to obliterate, as from the mind.

> All ideas of rectitude and justice are *erased* from his mind. —Burke.

3. to kill. [Slang.]

4. to destroy to the foundation; to raze; as, to *erase* a town.

Syn.—abrade, efface, blot out, obliterate, expunge, cancel, destroy.

ē·rāsed′ (-rāst′), *a.* 1. rubbed or scratched out; obliterated; effaced.

A LION'S HEAD ERASED

2. in heraldry, represented as if forcibly torn off, leaving the separated parts jagged and uneven, as distinguished from *couped*, cut straight across.

ē·rāse′ment, *n.* the act of erasing; a rubbing out; expunction; obliteration; also, an instance of this.

ē·rās′ēr, *n.* a thing that erases; specifically, a device made of rubber, for erasing marks made with ink or pencil, or a pad of felt or cloth, for removing chalk marks from a blackboard.

ē·rā′șion, *n.* [from L. *erasus*, pp. of *eradere*, to erase.]

1. an erasing.

2. in surgery, the removal of diseased tissue by scraping with a curette.

Ē·raș′mi·ăn, *a.* pertaining to Erasmus, a Dutch scholar of the sixteenth century, or to his ideas.

Ē·raș′mi·ăn, *n.* an adherent of Erasmus, especially one who advocates the system of Greek pronunciation which he devised.

Ē·ras′tiăn (-chăn), *a.* of or supporting Thomas Erastus, German-Swiss theologian and physician (1524–1583), or his doctrines, especially that advocating the supreme authority of the state in church matters.

Ē·ras′tiăn, *n.* 1. a follower of Thomas Erastus or his doctrines.

Ē·ras′tiăn·iṣm, *n.* the principles of the Erastians.

ē·rā′sūre (-shūr), *n.* 1. the act of erasing; a scratching out; obliteration.

2. that which has been erased, scratched out, or obliterated; an erased word, mark, etc.

3. the place where a word or letter has been erased.

4. the act of razing or destroying to the foundation; total destruction; as, the *erasure* of cities.

Ẽr′ȧ·tive, *a.* pertaining to Erato, one of the Muses.

Er′ȧ·tō, *n.* [L., from Gr. *Eratō*, lit., the Lovely, from *eratos*, beloved, from *erān*, to love.] in classical mythology, one of the Muses. She presided over lyric, especially amatory, poetry, and is generally represented with the lyre in the left hand and the plectrum in the right in the act of playing.

ẽr′bi·ȧ, *n.* [L., from *erbium*.] in chemistry, the oxide of erbium, a white or pale rose-colored powder.

ẽr′bi·um, *n.* [Mod. L. from *Ytterby*, in Sweden, where gadolinite, the mineral which contains this substance, is found.] a metallic chemical element of the rare-earth group: symbol, Er, E; atomic weight, 167.2; atomic number, 68.

ERATO

ẽrd, *n.* [ME. *erd*, *eard*; AS. *eard*, earth, land.] the earth. [Obs.]

ẽrd shrew, the shrewmouse, *Sorex vulgaris.*

ere (âr), *adv.* [ME. *ere*, *er*; AS. *ær*, before, sooner.] early; soon; previously; before; formerly. [Obs. or Scot.]

ere, *prep.* before (in time). [Archaic or Poet.]

Our fruitful Nile
Flow'd *ere* the wonted season. —Dryden.

ere long; soon; before long.
ere now; formerly; before this time.

ere, *conj.* sooner than; rather than. [Archaic or Poet.]

ēre, *v.t.* to plow; to ear. [Obs.]

Er′e·bus, *n.* in Greek mythology, (a) the son of Chaos, who married his sister Night and was the father of Light and Day; (b) the dark place under the earth through which the dead passed before entering Hades.

The motions of his spirit are dull as night,
And his affections dark as *Erebus*.—Shak.

Er·eçh·tī′tēṣ, *n.* [L., from Gr. *erechthitēs*, the senecio or groundsel, from *erechthein*, to rend, break.] a small genus of composite plants found in America, Australia, and New Zealand. The fireweed, *Erechtites hieracifolia*, is the only species in the United States.

ē·reçt′, *a.* [L. *erectus*, pp. of *erigere*, to set up; out, up, and *regere*, to make straight.]

1. upright or in a perpendicular posture; vertical; as, he stood *erect*.

2. directed upward; raised; uplifted.

His piercing eyes *erect* appear to view
Superior worlds, and look all nature through. —Pope.

3. bristling; stiff: said of hair, etc.

4. intent; alert; vigilant; as, *erect* attention of mind. [Archaic.]

5. in heraldry, upright in position; elevated vertically, as the heads of serpents, the tips of birds' wings, etc.

ē·rect′, *v.t.*; erected, *pt.*, *pp.*; erecting, *ppr.* 1. to raise and set in an upright or perpendicular position, or nearly so; to set upright; to raise up; as, to *erect* a pole or flagstaff.

2. (a) to raise, as a building; to construct; to build; as, to *erect* a house or a church; to *erect* a fort; (b) to put together the component parts of, as of a locomotive, a printing press, a dynamo, or other machine; to assemble.

3. to set up; to cause to arise; as, they *erected* arbitrary social barriers.

4. to set up or establish anew; to found; to form; as, to *erect* a kingdom or commonwealth; to *erect* a new system or theory. [Archaic.]

5. to raise from a low position; to elevate; to exalt; to lift up. [Obs.]

6. to excite; to animate; to encourage. [Obs.]

7. to set forth, as an assertion, consequence, or conclusion from premises; to propound.

8. in geometry, to construct or draw (a perpendicular, figure, etc.) upon a base line.

9. in physiology, to cause to become swollen and hard by being filled with blood.

Syn.—raise, set up, elevate, build, construct, found, establish, institute.

ē·reçt′, *v.i.* 1. to take an upright position; to rise. [Obs.]

2. in physiology, to become swollen and hard by being filled with blood.

ē·reçt′ȧ·ble, *a.* capable of being erected; erectile; as, an *erectable* feather.

ē·reçt′ẽr, *n.* one who or that which erects; one who raises or builds.

ē·reç′tile, *a.* capable of being erected; susceptible of erection; erectable.

erectile tissue; in anatomy, a tissue consisting of a network of expansile capillaries that under stimulus become engorged with blood and cause erection of the part.

ē·reç·til′i·ty, *n.* the quality of being erectile or capable of erection.

ē·reç′tion, *n.* [L. *erectio* (*-onis*), from *erectus*, pp. of *erigere*, to erect.]

1. the act of erecting; the act of setting up or of setting in an upright position.

2. the act of raising or building, as an edifice or fortification; as, the *erection* of a wall or of a house; also, the act of putting together component parts, as of a machine.

3. the state of being raised, built, or elevated; as, the church fell immediately after its *erection*.

4. establishment; settlement; formation; as the *erection* of a commonwealth or of a new system. [Archaic.]

5. exaltation of sentiments. [Obs.]

6. the act of rousing excitement; as, the *erection* of the spirits. [Obs.]

7. anything erected; a building of any kind.

8. in physiology, a becoming or being hard and swollen by filling with blood: said of erectile tissue.

ē·reç′tive, *a.* setting upright; raising.

ē·reçt′ly, *adv.* in an erect posture or manner.

ē·reçt′ness, *n.* the state, quality, or fact of being erect.

ē·reç·tō·pā′tent, *a.* [L. *erectus*, erect, and *patens* (*-entis*), open, spreading.]

1. in botany, having a position intermediate between erect and spreading.

2. in entomology, having the primary wings erect and the secondary horizontal.

ē·reç′tŏr, *n.* [L., from *erectus*, pp. of *erigere*, to erect.]

1. one who or that which erects or raises.

2. in anatomy, a muscle that causes the erection of any part.

3. in optics, an attachment to a compound microscope, telescope, or other instrument, which causes a second inversion of the image, so that the object viewed is presented in an erect or normal position.

ere·lŏng′ (âr-), *adv.* before long; soon; ere long. [Archaic or Poet.]

The world *erelong* a world of tears must weep. —Milton.

er″e·mȧ·çau′sis, *n.* [L., from Gr. *ērema*, slowly, and *kausis*, a burning, from *kaiein*, to burn.] a slow combustion or oxidation of organic matter in the presence of air and water.

e·rē′miç, *a.* [Gr. *eēremos*, desert, from *erēmia*, a desert.] pertaining to or living in dry, sandy places or deserts: used chiefly in zoology.

er′ē·mit·ăġe, *n.* [Obs.] see *hermitage*.

er′ē·mīte, *n.* [LL. *eremita*; Gr. *erēmitēs*, a hermit, from *erēmia*, a desert; from *erēmos*, desolate, lonely.] a hermit; a religious recluse.

er·ē·mit′iç, er·ē·mit′iç·ăl, *a.* [LL. *eremiticus*, like a hermit, from Gr. *erēmitēs*, a hermit.] pertaining to an eremite; having the nature or character of an eremite; living in solitude or in seclusion from the world.

er′ē·mī·tish, *a.* eremitic.

er′ē·mit·iṣm, *n.* the state of an eremite; seclusion from social life.

E·rē·mō·brȳ′ȧ, *n.pl.* [L., from Gr. *erēmos*, desolate, solitary, and *bryon*, a kind of seaweed.] in botany, a group of ferns whose fronds are produced laterally on and articulated with the rootstalk.

e·rē·mō·brȳ′oid, *a.* pertaining to the *Eremobrya*.

er′ē·nȧçh, *n.* [Ir. *airchinneach*; LL. *archidiaconus*, an archdeacon of the early Catholic church; Gr. *archos*, a ruler, and *diakonos*, a deacon.] an ecclesiastic of the early Irish church analogous to an archdeacon.

ere·now′ (âr-), *adv.* before now; heretofore; ere now. [Archaic or Poetic.]

ē·rep′tion, *n.* [L. *ereptio* (*-onis*), from *ereptus*, pp. of *eripere*, to snatch or take away by force.] a taking or snatching away by force.

e·reth′iç, *a.* [Gr. *erethein*, to excite.] pertaining to erethism; excitable.

er′e·thiṣm, *n.* [Gr. *erethismos*, a stirring up, from *erethizein*, to excite, irritate.] in physiology, extreme irritability or sensitivity of any organ or tissue. [Rare.]

er·e·this′tiç, *a.* relating to erethism.

ere′whīle′, ere′whīleṣ′ (âr′), *adv.* a short time ago; a little while before; heretofore. [Archaic.]

I am as fair now as I was *erewhile*.—Shak.

ẽrf, *n.*; *pl.* **ẽr′ven,** [D.] in South Africa, a piece of garden ground, usually about one-half an acre in extent.

ẽrg, *n.* [Gr. *ergon*, work.] in physics, the unit of work or energy in the metric system, being the amount of work done by one dyne acting through a distance of one centimeter.

ẽrg′ăl, *n.* [Gr. *ergon*, work.] in physics, the potential energy.

Ẽr·gȧ·sil′i·dae, *n.pl.* [L., from Gr. *ergasia*, work, daily labor.] a family of parasitic crustaceans of the order *Siphonostomata*. The females of the typical genus *Ergasilus* are parasitic upon the gills of fishes, and those of the genus *Nicothoë* upon the gills of lobsters.

ẽr·gȧ·toç′rȧ·cy, *n.* rule by the workers.

ẽrg′mē″tẽr, *n.* [Gr. *ergon*, work, and *metron*, a measure.] in physics, a device for measuring energy in ergs.

ẽr′gō, *adv.* and *conj.* [L., therefore.] therefore; consequently; hence: used in logic to introduce the conclusion of a syllogism.

ẽr′gō·grȧph, *n.* [from Gr. *ergon*, work; and *-graph*.] an instrument for measuring and recording the amount of work done in muscular exertion: used especially for measuring the rate of fatigue.

ẽr·gom′e·tẽr, *n.* [Gr. *ergon*, work, and *metron*, a measure.] a device or instrument for measuring the amount of energy used or work done; a dynamometer.

ẽr·gō·met′riç, *a.* pertaining to an ergometer.

ẽr′gon, *n.* 1. same as *erg*.

2. work, in terms of its equivalent in heat.

ẽr·gos′tẽr·ōl, *n.* [from *ergot*, and *sterol*.] an alcohol, $C_{28}H_{44}O$, of high molecular weight, formerly prepared from ergot but now chiefly from yeast: when exposed to ultraviolet rays it produces a vitamin (D_1) used to prevent or cure rickets.

ẽr′gŏt, *n.* [Fr. *ergot*, *argot*, a spur, stub of a branch, disease of cereal grasses.]

1. in farriery, a stub, like a piece of soft horn, about the size of a chestnut, situated under the tuft of the fetlock.

2. a growth on the grains of rye, other cereal plants, and some grasses, caused by the attack of a fungus called *Claviceps purpurea*. When the diseased rye of this kind is used for food, it sometimes causes a kind of gangrene.

3. the plant disease in which ergots occur.

4. the fungus causing this disease.

5. the dried fungus, used as a drug to stop bleeding and to contract muscles, as of the uterus during labor.

6. in anatomy, the hippocampus minor of the brain.

ẽr′gŏt·ed, *a.* ergotized.

ẽr·got′iç, *a.* pertaining to or derived from ergot; as, *ergotic* acid.

ẽr′gō·tine, ẽr′gō·tin, *n.* [Fr. *ergotine*.]

1. in chemistry, the active principle of the ergot of rye. It is obtained as a brown powder having a pungent and bitter taste.

2. an extract of ergot.

ẽr·got′i·nine, *n.* an alkaloid obtained from ergot.

ẽr′gō·tiṣm, *n.* [Fr. *ergotisme*, from L. *ergo*.] a logical inference; a conclusion. [Rare.]

ẽr′gŏt·iṣm, *n.* 1. the formation of ergot in plants.

2. in medicine, the diseased condition following the prolonged use of ergot or of ergotized rye in food: it occurs in two forms, the convulsive and the gangrenous.

ẽr′gŏt·īzed, *a.* affected with ergot; as, *ergotized* rye.

ē′ri·ȧ, ē′ri, *n.* the wild silkworm of Assam, which feeds on the castor oil bean.

er′i·ạch, *n.* eric. [Obs.]

Ē′ri·ăn, *a.* relating to or designating Lake Erie or its shores.

Erian age; in geology, the Devonian age. [Rare.]

er'iç, *n.* [Ir. *eiric.*] in old Irish law, a pecuniary recompense or blood fine paid by a murderer to the relatives or family of the murdered person: also written *eriach, erick.*

E·rī'çȧ, *n.* [L., from Gr. *ereikē, erikē,* heath.]

1. the heaths, a large genus of branched rigid shrubs, family *Ericaceæ.*

2. [e–] a plant of this genus.

ERICA (*Erica herbacea*)

Er·i·çā'cē·ae, *n.pl.* a family of exogens, deriving its name from the genus *Erica.* It also contains *Azalea, Rhododendron, Kalmia, Arbutus, Andromeda,* and many other genera.

er·i·çā'ceous, *a.* [Gr. *ereikē, erikē,* the heath.] pertaining to the *Ericaceæ,* or the heath family of plants.

er·i·cē'tăl, *a.* of or pertaining to the genus *Erica*; composed of heaths.

er·i·cin'e·ous, *a.* ericaceous.

e·ri'ci·us, *n.* [L., a hedgehog.] a hedgehog.

e·riç'ō·lin, *n.* [Gr. *ereikē, erikē,* the heath.] in chemistry, a bitter yellow glucoside, found in many of the *Ericaceæ.*

Ē·rid'ȧ·nus, *n.* [L., from Gr. *Ēridanos,* the name of a mythical river.] a southern constellation, the River, containing Achernar, a star of the first magnitude.

Ēr'ie (ēr'i), *n.*; *pl.* **Ēr'ie, Ēr'ieṣ,** [short for Am. Ind. (Huron) *Erieehronous,* the Erie, apparently from *eri'e,* at the place of the cat.] a member of a tribe of Iroquoian Indians who lived in an area east and southeast of Lake Erie.

Ē·rig'e·ron, *n.* [L., from Gr. *ērigerōn,* the groundsel, lit., early old man, so named from its hoary down; *ēri,* early, and *gerōn,* an old man.] a genus of carduaceous plants having asterlike rayed flower heads of white, rose, or violet.

er'i·gi·ble, *a.* capable of being erected. [Rare.]

Er'in (*or* ē'rin), *n.* [O.Ir. *Ērinn,* dat. of *Ēriu,* Eire.] Ireland. [Poetic.]

er·i·nā'ceous, *a.* [L. *erinaceus,* a hedgehog.] pertaining to the hedgehog family; resembling a hedgehog.

e·rin'ē·um, *n.*; *pl.* **e·rin'ē·ȧ,** [L., from Gr. *erineos,* woolly, from *erion,* wool.] any of numerous abnormal growths on the leaves of trees and shrubs, formerly supposed to be due to fungi, but now known to be caused by attacks of mites.

e·riñ'gō, *n.* see *eryngo.*

Er'in gō bragh (brä), Erin (Ireland) forever: the war cry of the ancient Irish.

er'i·nīte, *n.* an emerald-green arsenate of copper, found in Ireland.

Ē·rin'ys, *n.*; *pl.* **Ē·rin'y·ēṣ,** [L., from Gr. *Erinys,* an avenging deity.] in Greek mythology, one of the Furies: written also *Erinnys.*

Ē''ri·ō·den'drŏn, *n.* [Gr. *erion,* wool, and *dendron,* a tree.] the genus of plants comprising the silk-cotton trees: also called *Ceiba.*

E·ri·og'ō·num, *n.* [L., from Gr. *erion,* wool, and *gony,* the knee.] a large genus of plants or herbs, family *Polygonaceæ,* comprising about 160 species, most of which are found in and are characteristic of western United States. They are chiefly low herbs or woody-based perennials, having small, clustered flowers.

ē·ri·om'e·tẽr, *n.* [Gr. *erion,* wool, and *metron,* a measure.] an optical instrument for measuring small diameters, as of minute particles or fibers, by observing the diameter of the colored rings produced by the diffraction of the light in which the objects are viewed.

Ē'ris (*or* er'is), *n.* [L.; Gr. *Eris.*] in Greek mythology, the goddess of strife and discord.

E·ris'tȧ·lis, *n.* [L., name first used by Latreille in 1804.] a genus of flies or dipterous insects with rattail larvae or maggots feeding in manure or decaying vegetable substances: it includes the drone flies.

er·is'tiç, er·is'tiç·ăl, *a.* [Gr. *eristikos,* given to strife or dispute, from *erizein,* to strive, dispute, from *eris,* strife.]

1. pertaining to dispute, argument, or controversy.

2. argumentative; controversial.

er·is'tiç, *n.* 1. a disputant; a controversialist.

2. the art of disputation.

Er·i·trē'ăn, *a.* of Eritrea, in eastern Africa, or its people.

Er·i·trē'ăn, *n.* a native or inhabitant of Eritrea.

ẽrke, *a.* weary. [Obs.]

ẽrl'king, *n.* [G. *erl könig,* elf king.] in German folklore, a spirit who does mischief and evil, especially to children.

ẽrme, *v.i.* to grieve; to lament. [Obs.]

ẽr'mē·lin, ẽr'mi·lin, *n.* ermine. [Archaic.]

ẽr'mine, *n.* [ME. *ermin*; OFr. *ermin*; M.H.G. *hermelin*; O.H.G. *harmo,* the ermine.]

1. any of several weasels found in the northern parts of Europe, Asia, and America, whose fur is brown in the summer but white with a black-tipped tail in winter: also called *stoat.*

ERMINE (15 in. long)

2. the fur of the ermine, as prepared for ornamental purposes, by having the black of the tail inserted at regular intervals so that it contrasts with the pure white of the rest of the fur.

3. the office, rank, functions, or dignity of a judge: from his state robe being, in England and elsewhere, ornamented or bordered with ermine.

I call upon the judges to interpose the purity of their *ermine,* to save us from this pollution. —Lord Chatham.

4. in heraldry, one of the furs, represented by black, triangular spots on a white ground.

ERMINE

ẽr'mine, *v.t.*; ermined, *pt., pp.*; ermining, *ppr.* 1. to clothe or adorn with or as with ermine.

2. to advance to a position of dignity or honor, as to a judgeship.

er·mi·né' (ẽr-mi-nā'), *a.* in heraldry, composed of four ermine spots, as a cross.

ẽr'mined, *a.* 1. clothed with ermine.

2. trimmed with the fur of the ermine.

ERMINES

ẽr'mine moth, 1. a moth of the family *Yponomeutidæ*: so called from its black and white spotted covering, resembling the fur of the ermine.

2. one of various arctiid moths, as the buff ermine, *Arctia lubricipeda,* or the water ermine, *Arctia urticæ.*

ẽr'mineṣ, *n.* in heraldry, a black field marked by white spots, the reverse of ermine.

ERMINITES

ẽr'min·ītes, *n.* in heraldry, a bearing like ermine, but with a single red hair on each side of the ermine spots.

ẽr'mi·noiṣ, *n.* [Fr., from OFr. *ermin,* ermine.] in heraldry, a fur represented by a gold field with black spots.

ERMINOIS

ẽr'mit, *n.* a recluse; a hermit. [Obs.]

ẽrne, ẽrn, *n.* a kind of eagle that lives near the sea; a sea eagle: also written *earn.*

ẽr'nest, *a.* and *n.* earnest. [Obs.]

ẽr'nest·fụl, *a.* full of earnestness; serious. [Obs.]

ē·rōde', *v.t.*; eroded, *pt., pp.*; eroding, *ppr.* [L. *erodere,* to gnaw away; *e-,* from, off, and *rodere,* to gnaw.]

1. to gnaw into; to eat into; to wear away; to disintegrate; as, acid *erodes* metal.

2. in geology, to form by wearing away or smoothing down gradually: used of the action of floods, glaciers, etc. in shaping the earth's surface.

ē·rōde', *v.i.* to become worn away.

ē·rōd'ed, *a.* 1. eaten away; corroded; appearing as if gnawed.

2. in botany and zoology, having the edge irregularly jagged or denticulated, as a leaf or an insect's wing.

ē·rōd'ent, *a.* [L. *erodens* (*-entis*), ppr. of *erodere,* to gnaw.] caustic; having a tendency to eat away; erosive: said of certain drugs.

ē·rōd'ent, *n.* an erosive substance; a caustic.

Ē·rō'di·um, *n.* [L., from Gr. *erōdios,* the heron.] a genus of plants, closely allied to *Geranium,* of which there are about 50 species, including the *heron's-bill* or *stork's-bill.*

er'ō·gāte, *v.t.*; erogated, *pt., pp.*; erogating, *ppr.* to pay out; to give; to spend. [Obs.]

er·ō·gā'tion, *n.* the act of erogating. [Obs.]

ē·rog'e·nous, *a.* [Gr. *erōs,* love, and *-genēs,* producing.] causing erotic sensation; producing or tending to produce sexual desire: applied especially to those zones, or parts, of the body the stimulation of which tends to arouse sexual desire.

-er·ọọ', [prob. from *buckaroo*; use apparently encouraged by double talk.] a humorous slang suffix.

Ē'ros, *n.* [L., from Gr. *Erōs,* Cupid, the god of love, from *erōs,* love, from *erān,* to love.] in Greek mythology, the god of love, son of Aphrodite: the Greek equivalent of the Roman Cupid.

ē·rōse', *a.* [L. *erosus,* pp. of *erodere,* to gnaw off; *e-,* off, and *rodere,* to gnaw.]

1. uneven; irregular, as if eaten or gnawed away.

2. in botany and zoology, having small irregular notches in the margin, as if gnawed, as a leaf or an insect's wing.

ē·rōse'ly, *adv.* irregularly; jaggedly.

ē·rō'ṣion, *n.* [L. *erosio* (*-onis*), from *erosus,* pp. of *erodere,* to gnaw off.]

1. the act or operation of eating or wearing away, or of being worn away or eroded.

2. in medicine, the gradual wearing away, as of the teeth, by chemical action.

3. in geology, the wearing away of the earth's surface, as by floods, glaciers, waves, wind, or any natural process.

erosion theory; in geology, the theory that valleys are due to the wearing influences of water and ice, chiefly in the form of glaciers, as opposed to the theory which regards them as the result of fissures in the earth's crust produced by strains during its upheaval.

ē·rō'sive, *a.* [L. *erosus,* pp. of *erodere,* to gnaw off.] having the property of eating away or eroding; causing erosion.

ē·ros'trāte, *a.* [L. *e-* priv., and *rostratus,* beaked, from *rostrum,* a beak.] in botany, without a beak.

er''ō·tē·mat'iç, *a.* [Gr. *erōtēmatikos,* interrogative, from *erōtēma,* a question, from *erōtān,* to ask.] in rhetoric, using questions.

er'ō·tēme, *n.* [LL. *erotema*; Gr. *erōtēma,* a question, from *erōtān,* to ask.] the mark of interrogation; the question mark (?). [Rare.]

er·ō·tē'sis, *n.* [L., from Gr. *erōtēsis,* a questioning, from *erōtān,* to question.] in rhetoric, a figure of speech by which the speaker implies a strong affirmative, or more frequently a strong negative, under the form of an interrogation, as in the following lines:

Must we but weep o'er days more blest?
Must we but blush? Our fathers bled.
—Byron.

er·ō·tet'iç, *a.* [Gr. *erōtētikos,* skilled in questioning, from *erōtān,* to question.] interrogatory.

ē·rot'iç, ē·rot'iç·ăl, *a.* [Gr. *erōtikos,* from *erōs* (*erōtos*), love.] pertaining to or prompted by sexual feelings or desires; treating of sexual love; amatory; amorous; tending to excite sexual desire.

ē·rot'iç, *n.* 1. a person abnormally sensitive to sexual stimulation.

2. an erotic poem.

ē·rot'i·çȧ, *n.pl.* erotic books, pictures, etc.

ē·rot'iç·ăl·ly, *adv.* in an erotic manner.

ē·rot'i·ciṣm, *n.* 1. erotic character, quality, or tendency; as, the *eroticism* of poetry or novels.

2. sexual instincts and behavior.

3. preoccupation with sex.

er'ō·tiṣm, *n.* eroticism (especially in sense 2).

ē·rō·tō·mā'ni·ȧ, *n.* [L., from Gr. *erōtomania,* raving love; *erōs,* love, and *mania,* madness.] excessive or uncontrollable sexual passion.

ē·rō·tō·mā'ni·aç, *n.* one who has erotomania.

ẽrr, *v.i.*; erred, *pt., pp.*; erring, *ppr.* [ME. *erren*; OFr. *errer*; L. *errare,* to wander.]

1. to wander from the right way; to deviate from the true course; to do wrong; to deviate from the path of duty; to fail morally; as, we have *erred* and strayed like lost sheep.

2. to blunder; to be mistaken or wrong; to fall into error.

3. to wander; to ramble; to go astray. [Obs.]

ẽr'rȧ·ble, *a.* having a tendency to err; fallible.

ẽr'rȧ·ble·ness, *n.* liability to fault or error.

er'rȧ·bund, *a.* [L. *errabundus,* wandering, from *errare,* to wander.] wandering; erratic. [Rare.]

er'răn·cy, *n.* 1. the state of being in error; the condition of containing errors.

2. a tendency or liability to fall into error; fallibility.

er′rănd, *n.* [ME. *erende*; AS. *ærende*, an errand, message.]
1. a verbal message; a communication to be made to some person at a distance. [Archaic.]
2. a trip to carry a message or do a definite thing; especially, a short trip to do a thing for someone else.
3. the thing to be done on such a trip; purpose or object for which one is sent.
a fool's errand; a foolish or futile enterprise.

er′rănt, *a.* [ME. *erraunt*; OFr. *errant*, a wanderer, a knight errant, from *errans* (*-antis*), ppr. of *errare*, to wander.]
1. wandering; roving; rambling: applied particularly to knights (*knights-errant*) who, in the Middle Ages, wandered about to seek adventures.
2. in zoology, of or pertaining to the *Errantia*.
3. deviating from the regular course; erring; wrong.
4. itinerant: formerly applied to judges who traveled on a circuit.
5. notorious; manifest; arrant. [Obs.]

er′rănt, *n.* a wanderer; a knight errant.

Er·ran′ti·ȧ (-shi-ȧ), *n.pl.* [L., from *errans* (*-antis*), ppr. of *errare*, to wander.] a former classification of free-swimming annelids.

er′rănt·ry, *n.* [from L. *errans* (*-antis*), ppr. of *errare*, to wander.]
1. a wandering; a roving or rambling about. [Rare.]
After a short space of *errantry* upon the seas, he got safe back to Dunkirk.—Addison.
2. the condition or way of life of a knight errant; spirit or deeds of chivalry.

er·rā′tȧ, *n.*, pl. of *erratum*: used chiefly of errors in printing.

er·rat′iç, *a.* [ME. *erratik*; OFr. *erratique*; L. *erraticus*, wandering, from *errare*, to wander.]
1. wandering; having no certain course; roving about without a fixed destination; irregular.
2. moving; not fixed or stationary: formerly applied to the planets as distinguished from the fixed stars.
3. irregular; mutable; moving from point to point, as rheumatic pains.
4. deviating from the conventional or usual course; queer; eccentric.
5. in geology, designating a boulder or rock formation transported some distance from its original source, as by a glacier.
Syn.—desultory, aberrant, abnormal, flighty, changeful, capricious, unreliable.

er·rat′iç, *n.* 1. a vagabond. [Obs.]
2. an eccentric or unconventional person.
3. in geology, a boulder or rock which has been conveyed from its original site, as by a glacier, and deposited at a distance; an erratic boulder.

er·rat′iç·ăl·ly, *adv.* without rule, order, or established method; irregularly.

er·rat′iç·ăl·ness, *n.* the state of being erratic.

er·rā′tion, *n.* a wandering. [Obs.]

er·rā′tum, *n.*; *pl.* **er·rā′tȧ,** [L. *erratum*, neut. of *erratus*, pp. of *errare*, to wander.] an error or mistake in writing or printing. The list of the errata of a book is usually printed at the beginning or end, with references indicating the pages and lines in which they occur.
A single *erratum* may knock out the brains of a whole passage. —Cowper.

er′rhīne (-rīn), *a.* [Gr. *errhinon*, errhine, from *en-*, in, and *rhis*, *rhinos*, nose.] affecting the nose or designed to be snuffed into the nose; increasing discharges from the nose and, hence, causing sneezing.

er′rhīne, *n.* an errhine medicine.

ẽrr′ing, *a.* that errs or has erred.

er·rō′nē·ous, *a.* [L. *erroneus*, wandering about, from *errare*, to wander.]
1. wandering; roving; unsettled; devious; irregular. [Obs.]
2. misguided; misled; deviating, by mistake, from the truth; as, destroy not the *erroneous* with the malicious. [Obs.]
3. containing or based on error; wrong; false; mistaken; liable to mislead; as, an *erroneous* opinion; *erroneous* doctrine.

er·rō′nē·ous·ly, *adv.* by mistake; not rightly; falsely.

er·rō′nē·ous·ness, *n.* the state of being erroneous, wrong, or false; deviation from truth or right.

er′rŏr, *n.* [ME. *errour*, *arrore*; OFr. *error*; L. *error*, a wandering or straying about, a mistake, fault, error, from *errare*, to wander.]
1. the state of believing what is untrue, incorrect, or wrong.
2. a mistake in judgment; a wrong belief; an incorrect opinion; a misapprehension.
He was guilty of no *error*. —Brougham.
3. something incorrectly done through ignorance or carelessness; an inaccuracy; an oversight; falsity; as, a clerical *error*; an *error* in a declaration.
4. a transgression of law or duty; a mistake in conduct; a moral fault; transgression.
If it were thine *error* or thy crime,
I care no longer. —Tennyson.
5. in law, a mistake in the proceedings of a court of record either in fact or in law, frequently of such a nature as to entitle the unsuccessful party to have the case reviewed.
6. a wandering; excursion; irregular course. [Obs.]
7. the difference between the approximated or computed result of any operation and the true value, as in mathematics: called also *true error*.
8. in baseball, any misplay (by a member of the team in the field) of a chance that should have resulted in an out for the team at bat, or that permits a runner to advance: a passed ball and a wild pitch are not classed as errors.
error of a clock; in astronomy, the difference between the time indicated by a clock and the true time.
law of error; a law which connects the relative magnitudes of errors with their frequency.
writ of error; an original judicial writ or order, which lies after judgment in an action at law, in a court of record, under which an appellate court may review the proceedings of an inferior court as to questions of law only, apparent in the record, including exceptions noted and filed.
Syn.—mistake, blunder, fallacy, bull, fault, oversight, failure, delusion, sin.

er′rŏr·fụl, *a.* abounding in mistakes; full of errors.

er′rŏr·ist, *n.* one who errs or who encourages error.

ẽrs, *n.* [Fr. *ers*, from L. *ervum*, the bitter vetch.] the bitter vetch.

er·ṡätz′ (-zäts′), *n.* and *a.* [G., lit., replacement, from *ersetzen*, to replace, from *setzen*, to set, to place.] substitute: the word usually suggests inferior quality.

Ẽrse, *n.* and *a.* [Scot. var. of *Irish*.] 1. formerly, Scottish Gaelic.
2. in linguistics, Irish Gaelic.

ẽrsh, ẽarsh, *n.* [a contr. form of *eddish*, from AS. *edisc*, aftermath.] stubble of grain. [Dial.]

ẽrst, *adv.* [ME. *erst*; AS. *ærest*, first.]
1. first; at first; at the beginning; originally. [Obs.]
2. once; formerly; long ago. [Archaic.]
He pensive oft reviews the mighty dead
That erst have trod this desolated ground. —Langhorn.
3. before; till then or now; hitherto. [Archaic.]

ẽrst, *a.* first. [Obs.]

ẽrst′whīle (-hwīl), *adv.* at one time; formerly. [Archaic.]

ẽrst′whīle, *a.* former; as, an *erstwhile* friend.

er·ụ·bes′cence, er·ụ·bes′cen·cy, *n.* [LL. *erubescentia*, blushing, from L. *erubescens* (*-entis*), ppr. of *erubescere*, to blush; *e-*, out, and *rubescere*, to grow red, from *ruber*, red.] a becoming red; redness of the skin or surface of anything; a blushing.

er·ụ·bes′cent, *a.* growing red or reddish; blushing.

er·ụ·bes′cīte, *n.* same as *bornite*.

ē·rụ′çȧ, *n.*; *pl.* **ē·rụ′cae,** [L. *eruca*, a caterpillar.]
1. an insect in the larval state; a caterpillar.
2. [E—] a genus of plants, family *Cruciferæ*, found in the mountains of Europe and central Asia. *Eruca sativa* is the garden rocket, which, when young and tender, is used as a salad.

ē·rụ′ciç, *a.* pertaining to or derived from plants of the genus *Eruca*.
erucic acid; a crystalline compound obtained from rape seed, mustard oil, etc.

ē·rụ′ci·fọrm, *a.* [L. *eruca*, a caterpillar, and *forma*, form.] in entomology, having the form of a caterpillar, as the larva of the sawfly.

ē·ruçt′, *v.t.* and *v.i.* same as *eructate*.

ē·ruç′tāte, *v.t.* and *v.i.* [L. *eructare*, to belch or vomit forth; *e-*, out, and *ructare*, to belch.] to belch; to cast forth or eject, as wind from the stomach.
Aetna in times past hath *eructated* such huge goblets of fire. —Howell.

ē·ruç·tā′tion, *n.* [LL. *eructatio* (*-onis*), a belching, from L. *eructare*, to belch.]
1. the act of belching.
2. that which is belched up.

er′ụ·dīte, *a.* [L. *eruditus*, learned, pp. of *erudire*, to instruct; *e-*, out, and *rudis*, rude.] having extensive knowledge; learned; deeply read; scholarly.

er′ụ·dīte, *n.* a learned person.

er′ụ·dīte·ly, *adv.* with erudition; learnedly.

er′ụ·dīte·ness, *n.* the quality of being erudite.

er·ụ·di′tion, *n.* [L. *eruditio* (*-onis*), an instructing, from *erudire*, to instruct.] learning; scholarship; knowledge gained by study and reading; particularly, learning in literature, history, antiquity, and languages, as distinct from the sciences.
Syn.—learning, lore, knowledge, scholarship, cognition.

er′ụ·gāte, *a.* [L. *erugatus*, pp. of *erugare*, to clear from wrinkles; *e-*, from, and *ruga*, wrinkle.] freed from wrinkles; smoothed; smooth. [Rare.]

ē·rū′ġi·nous, *a.* same as *aeruginous*.

ē·rupt′, *v.i.*; erupted, *pt.*, *pp.*; erupting, *ppr.* [L. *eruptus*, pp. of *erumpere*, to break out, burst forth; *e-*, out, and *rumpere*, to break.]
1. to burst forth or out, as lava from a volcano.
2. to throw forth lava, water, steam, etc.; as, geysers and volcanoes *erupt*.
3. to break out in a rash.
4. to break through the gum and become visible: said of new teeth.

ē·rupt′, *v.t.* to cause to burst forth; to throw forth; to eject.

ē·rup′tion, *n.* [L. *eruptio* (*-onis*), from *erumpere*, to break out.]
1. the act of breaking or bursting forth or out, as flames and lava from a volcano.
2. a throwing forth of lava, water, steam, etc.
3. a sudden outburst, as of emotion or social discontent.
4. in medicine, (a) a breaking out in a rash; (b) a rash.

ē·rup′tion·ăl, *a.* eruptive.

ē·rup′tive, *a.* 1. erupting or tending to erupt.
2. in medicine, attended with skin eruption or rash, or producing it; as, an *eruptive* fever.
3. produced by eruption; as, *eruptive* rocks, such as the igneous or volcanic.

ē·rup′tive, *n.* in geology, any rock or mineral produced by volcanic eruption.

-er·y, [ME. *-erie*; OFr. *-erie*, from LL. *-aria*.] a suffix used to form nouns from verbs or other nouns, meaning (a) *a place to*, as in tann*ery*, brew*ery*; (b) *a place for*, as in nunn*ery*, vin*ery*; (c) *the practice, act,* or *occupation of*, as in surg*ery*, robb*ery*; (d) *the product* or *goods of*, as in pott*ery*, millin*ery*; (e) *a collection of*, as in jewel*ry*, crock*ery*; (f) *the state* or *condition of*, as in drudg*ery*, slav*ery*. Also spelled *-ry*.

Er·y·man′thi·an, *a.* [L. *Erymanthius*.] in Greek mythology, (a) of Mount Erymanthus, a mountain between Arcadia and Achaia; (b) designating a savage boar that lived there and was later captured by Hercules in performance of the third of his twelve labors.

Ē·ryn′ġi·um, *n.* [L., from *eryngion*; Gr. *ēryngion*, a sort of thistle.] a genus of perennial herbs, family *Umbelliferæ*, with broad, spiny, grayish-blue leaves and pale-blue flowers. The roots of *Eryngium maritimum*, a European species, were formerly candied as a sweetmeat, and were believed to possess strong aphrodisiac properties.

ē·ryn′gō, *n.* 1. a plant of the genus *Eryngium*.
2. the candied root of the *Eryngium*. [Obs.]
Also spelled *eringo*.

er·y·sip′e·lăs, *n.* [OFr. *erysipele*; L. *erysipelas*; Gr. *erysipelas*, erysipelas; *erythros*, red, and *pella*, skin.] an acute infectious disease of the skin or mucous membranes characterized by inflammation of the skin, accompanied with fever: it is caused by any of several kinds of streptococcus.

er″y·si·pel′ȧ·toid, *a.* [Gr. *erysipelas*, erysipelas, and *eidos*, form.] resembling erysipelas.

er″y·si·pel′ȧ·tous, *a.* resembling or having erysipelas.

er·y·sip′e·lous, *a.* same as *erysipelatous*.

er·y·thē′mȧ, *n.* [L., from Gr. *erythēma*, a redness of the skin, from *erythainein*, *erythrainein*, to redden, blush, from *erythros*, red.] an abnormal redness of some portion of the skin resulting from capillary congestion.

er·y·them′ȧ·tous, er″y·thē·mat′iç, *a.* pertaining to or characterized by erythema.

er·y·thē′miç, *a.* same as *erythematous*.

e·ryth′r-, same as *erythro-*.

Er·y·thrae′ȧ, *n.* [L., from Gr. *erythraia*, f. of

erythraios, erythros, red.] a genus of annual herbs of the family *Gentianaceæ.*

er·y·thrē′ăn, er·y·thrae′ăn, *a.* of a red color.

ē·ryth′riç, *a.* [Gr. *erythros,* red.] pertaining to erythrin.

ē·ryth′riç ac′id, an acid obtained from *Roccella tinctoria* and other lichens, which possesses the property of forming red coloring matter in contact with air and ammonia.

ē·ryth′rin, *n.* same as *erythric acid.*

Er·y·thrī′nȧ, *n.* [L., from Gr. *erythros,* red.] a genus of tropical leguminous trees (*coral trees*), with trifoliate leaves and clusters of large, usually bright red flowers.

ē·ryth′riṣm, *n.* [Gr. *erythros,* red.] excessive or abnormal redness, especially of the hair of mammals or the feathers of birds.

ē·ryth′rīte, *n.* [Gr. *erythros,* red.]
1. erythritol.
2. a rose-red, hydrous arsenate of cobalt occurring in crystalline forms; cobalt bloom.

ē·ryth′ri·tōl, *n.* [from *erythr-,* and *-ite,* and *-ol:* so named because found in an alkaloid obtained from plants of the genus *Erythrina.*] a sweet, colorless, crystalline compound, $CH_2OH(CHOH)_2CH_2OH$, obtained from some lichens and algae.

ē·ryth′rō-, [from Gr. *erythros,* red.] a combining form meaning: (a) *red,* as in *erythro*cyte, *erythro*phyll; (b) *erythrocyte,* as in *erythro*blast: also, before a vowel, *erythr-.*

ē·ryth′rō·blast, *n.* [*erythro-,* and Gr. *blastos,* a bud.] one of the small nucleated cells normally contained in the marrow of bones, from which the erythrocytes develop.

ē·ryth″rō·blas·tō′sis, *n.* an increase in the number of erythroblasts in the fetus, believed to result from the mixture of the Rh positive factor of one parent with the Rh negative of the other.

ē·ryth·rō·çăr′pous, *a.* [*erythro-,* and Gr. *karpos,* fruit.] bearing red fruit, as certain lichens.

ē·ryth·rō·çhrō′iç, *a.* [*erythro-,* and Gr. *chroa,* color.] exhibiting excessive or abnormal redness in plumage or hair, as certain birds and mammals.

ē·ryth·rō·çhrō′iṣm, *n.* the condition of being erythrochroic.

ē·ryth′rō·çȳte, *n.* [*erythro-,* and Gr. *kytos,* cavity.] a red blood corpuscle: it is a very small, circular disk with both faces concave, and contains hemoglobin, which carries oxygen to the body tissues.

ē·ryth″rō·cy·tom′e·tẽr, *n.* a device for counting red blood corpuscles.

ē·ryth·rō·dex′trine, ē·ryth·rō·dex′trin, *n.* [*erythro-* and *dextrine.*] a variety or modification of dextrine, which is colored red or reddish-brown by iodine.

er′y·throid, *a.* [Gr. *erythros,* red, and *eidos,* form.] red or reddish in color.

er′y·thrōl, *n.* same as *erythritol.*

er·y·thrō′lē·in, *n.* a red compound contained in litmus.

ē·ryth·rō·lit′min, *n.* [*erythro-,* and L. *litmus.*] a red, crystalline compound contained in litmus.

ē·ryth″rō·me·lal′ġi·ȧ, *n.* [*erythro-,* and Gr. *melas,* black, and *algos,* pain.] in pathology, a disorder of the feet or hands characterized by burning pains and purplish coloration.

ē·ryth·rō·mȳ′sin, *n.* [*erythro-,* and strepto*mycin.*] an antibiotic isolated from a soil bacterium (*Streptomyces erythreus*), used in treating various bacterial diseases.

Er·y·thrō′ni·um, *n.* [L., from Gr. *erythronion,* a kind of plant, from *erythros,* red.] a genus of liliaceous plants native to temperate regions, including the dogtooth violet.

ē·ryth·rō·phlē′ine, *n.* a colorless crystalline alkaloid obtained from sassy bark.

ē·ryth′rō·phyll, ē·ryth′rō·phyl, *n.* [*erythro-,* and Gr. *phyllon,* a leaf.] in botany, the red coloring matter of certain leaves in autumn.

er·y·throph′yl·lin, *n.* same as *erythrophyll.*

ē·ryth′rō·sçōpe, *n.* [*erythro-,* and Gr. *skopein,* to view.] an optical device of very simple construction, made by overlapping two plates of glass, one blue, the other yellow. The plates absorb some rays and transmit others, green foliage appearing red when viewed through these glasses, while the effects of light and shade remain.

ē·ryth′rō·sin, *n.* [Gr. *erythros,* red.]
1. a red coloring matter obtained from fluorescein by the action of iodine.
2. a red compound produced from tyrosin by oxidation.

er·y·thrō′sis, *n.* [L., from Gr. *erythros,* red.] in pathology, a condition characterized by a reddish discoloration of the skin and mucous membrane.

Er″y·throx·yl′ē·ae, *n.pl.* [*erythro-,* and Gr. *xylon,* wood.] a family of shrubs or small trees which have alternate stipulate leaves, small pallid flowers, and drupaceous fruit.

Er·y·throx′y·lon, *n.* the principal genus of the family *Erythroxyleæ.* It contains about thirty species, native chiefly to tropical America. *Erythroxylon coca,* the most important of the species, yields coca and cocaine.

ē·ryth′rō·zȳme, *n.* [*erythro-,* and Gr. *zymē,* leaven.] a fermentative substance of madder, which can cause the decomposition of rubian.

es-, [ME. *es-, as-;* OFr. *es-, as-,* from L. *ex-,* from *ex,* out, out of.] a modification of the Latin prefix *ex-,* found in French and other Romance languages, as in *es*cheat, *es*coffier.

-es, a suffix used: (a) [ME.; AS. *-as,* pl. inflection of masc. nouns.] to form the plural of some nouns, as in fish*es:* also *-s, -'s;* (b) [ME.; AS. *-es,* genit. inflection of masc. and neut. nouns.] to form the third person singular, present indicative, of verbs, as in (he) kiss*es:* also *-s;* (c) [ME.; Northumbrian AS. *-s,* third person sing., pres. tense inflection of verbs.] formerly, to form the possessive case of nouns, as in God*es,* Wedn*es*day (*Woden's day*): now written *'s.*

Ē′sau (ē′sọ), *n.* [L.; Gr. *Ēsau;* Heb. *'esāu,* lit., hairy.] in the Bible the son of Isaac and Rebekah, who sold his birthright to his younger twin brother, Jacob. Gen. xxv. 21–34, xxvii.

es″çȧ·drille′, *n.* [Fr. *escadrille,* small fleet.]
1. a naval unit, usually of eight warships.
2. in the French armed forces of World War I, an airplane unit, usually consisting of six planes with their men and equipment.

es′çȧ·lāde, *n.* [Fr.; Sp. *escalada,* from *escalar,* to climb, from L. *scala,* ladder.] the act of scaling or climbing the walls of a fortified place by ladders.

es′çȧ·lāde, *v.t.;* escaladed, *pt., pp.;* escalading, *ppr.* to scale; to mount and pass or enter by means of ladders; as, to *escalade* a wall.

es′cȧ·lād″ẽr, *n.* one who makes an attack by means of an escalade.

es′çȧ·lāte, *v.i.;* escalated, *pt., pp.;* escalating, *ppr.* 1. to rise on or as on an escalator.
2. to expand step by step, as from a limited or local conflict into a general, especially nuclear, war.
3. to grow or increase rapidly, often to the point of becoming unmanageable, as prices or wages.

es′çȧ·lāte, *v.t.* to cause to escalate.

es′çȧ·lā·tŏr, *n.* [Fr. *escalader,* to scale; *escalier,* a staircase, flight of stairs, from L. *scala,* a ladder.] a moving stairway consisting of treads linked in an endless belt, used in department stores, subway stations, etc.

es′cȧ·lā·tŏr çlauṣe, a clause in a contract between an employer and a labor union providing for increases or decreases in pay, as in accordance with fluctuations in the cost of living.

Es·çal·lō′ni·ȧ, *n.* [L., from *Escallon,* a Spanish traveler in South America.] a genus of trees or shrubs, family *Saxifragaceæ,* native to South America.

es·çăl′ŏp, es·çăl′lŏp, *n.* [OFr. *escalope,* a shell.]
1. the scallop, a mollusk that has a ribbed shell with a wavy edge.
2. a decorative curve resembling that of a scallop shell.

es·çăl′ŏp, es·çăl′lŏp, *v.t.* 1. to trim in curves.
2. to bake with crumbs or in a cream sauce.

es·çăl′ŏped, es·çăl′lŏped, *a.* 1. cut or formed in the figure of a scallop; scalloped.
2. in heraldry, covered, as an escutcheon, with waving curved lines, resembling the outlines of scallop shells.

ESCALLOPED SHIELD

es·çam′bi·ō, *n.* [It. *escambio, scambio,* exchange.] in English law, a writ formerly granted to merchants to empower them to draw bills of exchange on persons abroad.

es·çāp′ȧ·ble, *a.* that may be escaped; avoidable.

es·çȧ·pāde′, *n.* [OFr. *escapade,* a prank, trick, from It. *scappata,* a flight, prank, escape.]
1. an escaping or breaking loose from restraint or confining rules.
2. a prank; a wild adventure.

es·çāpe′, *v.i.* escaped (-kāpt′), *pt., pp.;* escaping, *ppr.* [ME. *escapen;* OFr. *escaper,* to escape; LL. *ex capa,* out of cape; L. *ex,* out of, and LL. *capa,* cape, cloak.]
1. to get free; get away; break loose, as from a prison.
2. to avoid an illness, accident, pain, etc.; as, two were killed, but he *escaped.*
3. to flow, drain, or leak away; as, water *escapes* rapidly from the drainpipe.
4. to slip away; disappear; as, the image *escaped* from her memory.

es·çāpe′, *v.t.* 1. to get away from; flee.
2. to avoid; manage to keep away from; as, he *escaped* punishment.
3. to come from involuntarily or unintentionally; as, a scream *escaped* his lips.
4. to slip away from; be missed, unperceived, or forgotten by; as, the exact date *escapes* me.

Syn.—elude, evade, avoid, shun, decamp, flee, depart, abscond, break away.

es·çāpe′, *n.* 1. an escaping.
2. the state of having escaped.
3. a means or way of escape.
4. excuse; subterfuge; evasion. [Obs.]
5. in law, an evasion of legal restraint or of custody without due course of law.
6. sally; flight; irregularity; escapade. [Obs.]
Rome will despise her for this foul *escape.*
—Shak.
7. that which escapes attention; oversight; mistake. [Obs.]
8. in botany, a garden plant growing wild.
9. leakage or loss of various kinds, as of gas from a main, steam from a valve, etc.
10. a temporary mental release from reality; as, movies are an *escape.*

es·çāpe′, *a.* 1. giving temporary mental release from reality.
2. giving a basis for evading a claim, responsibility, etc.
3. making escape possible; as, an *escape* hatch.

es·çāp·ēe′, *n.* a person who has escaped, especially from confinement.

es·çāpe′ment, *n.* [Fr. *échappement.*]
1. the act of escaping or means of escape. [Rare.]
2. the part in a clock or watch that controls the speed and regularity of the balance wheel or pendulum, and thereby of the entire mechanism, by the movement of a notched wheel, one tooth of which is permitted to escape from the detaining catch at a time.
3. the mechanism in typewriters that regulates the horizontal movement of the carriage.

ESCAPEMENT (of clock)

es·çāpe pīpe, a pipe for carrying away any waste fluid.

es·çāp′ẽr, *n.* one who or that which escapes.

es·çāpe′ wheel, the notched wheel in the escapement of a watch or clock.

es·çāp′iṣm, *n.* 1. a tendency to escape from reality, the responsibilities and routine of real life, etc., especially by unrealistic imaginative activity.
2. behavior characterized by this tendency.
3. literature, art, etc. expressing, catering to, or providing an outlet for this tendency.

es·çāp′ist, *a.* characterized by escapism.

es·çāp′ist, *n.* a person whose behavior, writing, etc. is escapist.

es·çăr′buñ·çle, *n.* in heraldry, a carbuncle.

es·çăr·gōt′ (-gō′), *n.* [Fr.] a snail, especially an edible variety.

es′çȧ·rōle, *n.* [Fr.; ML. *escariola,* from L. *escarius,* pertaining to food, fit for eating, from *esca,* food.] a kind of endive, a plant whose leaves are used in salads.

es·çărp′, *n.* [Fr. *escarpe,* from *escarper,* to cut steep.] a scarp; escarpment.

es·çărp′, *v.t.;* escarped (-kärpt′), *pt., pp.;* escarping, *ppr.* in fortification, to slope; to make into a steep slope; to give a steep slope to.

es·çărp′ment, *n.* 1. ground formed into a steep slope as part of a fortification.

2. the precipitous side of any hill or rock; the abrupt face of a high ridge of land; a cliff.

-esce, [L. *-escere.*] a suffix used to form verbs that designate an action just begun or still incomplete, as coal*esce*; such verbs are called *inceptive* or *inchoative.*

-es′cence, [L. *-escentia*, from *-escens*; see *-escent.*] a noun suffix corresponding to the adjective suffix *-escent*, as in opal*escence*, obsol*escence.*

-es′cent, [L. *-escens, -escentis*, ppr. ending of inceptive and inchoative verbs in *-escere.*] an adjective suffix meaning *starting to be, being*, or *becoming* (as indicated), as in convale*scent*, obsol*escent.*

esch·ȧ·lot′, *n.* [Fr. *eschallotte*; OFr. *eschalotte*, var., from *eschalogne*, scallion.] a small onion.

es′chăr, *n.* [Gr. *eschara*, a fireplace, a scab or scar caused by a burn.] a dry scab that forms as the result of a burn or of action by some corrosive substance.

es′chăr, *n.* same as *esker.*

Es′chȧ·rȧ, *n.* [L., from Gr. *eschara*, a scar, scab.] a genus of calcareous zoophytes belonging to the class *Bryozoa* or *Polyzoa.*

es′chȧ·rine, *a.* pertaining to or resembling the genus *Eschara.*

es′chȧ·roid, *a.* same as *escharine.*

es·chȧ·rot′iç, *a.* caustic; producing or having the power of forming an eschar.

es·chȧ·rot′iç, *n.* [Gr. *escharōtikos*, forming a scar, from *escharoun*, to form a scar, from *eschara*, a scar.] a caustic or corrosive substance.

es″chȧ·tō·loġ′iç, es″chȧ·tō·loġ′iç·ăl, *a.* pertaining to eschatology.

es·chȧ·tol′ō·ġist, *n.* a student of eschatology.

es·chȧ·tol′ō·ġy, *n.* [Gr. *eschatos*, furthest, and *logos*, discourse.]

1. the branch of theology dealing with the last or final things, as death, judgment, immortality, etc.

2. the doctrines concerning these.

es·chaunġe′, *n.* exchange. [Obs.]

es·chēat′, *n.* [ME. *eschete*; OFr. *eschet*, lit., that which falls to one, rent, spoil, from pp. of *eschevir*, to fall to one's share, from LL. *excadere*, to fall upon; L. *ex*, out, and *cadere*, to fall.]

1. in England, the reverting of property to the crown when there are no legal heirs.

2. in feudal law, the reverting of property to the lord of the manor when there are no legal heirs.

3. in the United States, the reverting of property to the government when there are no legal heirs.

4. escheated property.

5. escheatage.

es·chēat′, *v.i.*; escheated, *pt., pp.*; escheating, *ppr.* [OFr. *escheoiter*, to receive an escheat.] to revert or fall back by escheat.

es·chēat′, *v.t.* to cause to escheat; to confiscate; also, to forfeit.

The ninepence with which the little girl was to have been rewarded, being *escheated* to the Kenwigs family. —Dickens.

es·chēat′ȧ·ble, *a.* liable to escheat.

es·chēat′ăġe, *n.* the right of succeeding to an escheat.

es·chēat′ŏr, *n.* in England, an officer formerly appointed in every county to look after the escheats of the sovereign and certify them into the treasury.

es·chew′, *v.t.*; eschewed, *pt., pp.*; eschewing, *ppr.* [ME. *eschewen*; OFr. *eschuer*, to avoid, shun; O.H.G. *sciuhen*, to frighten, shun.]

1. to escape from; to avoid. [Obs.]

He who obeys, destruction shall *eschew.* —Sandys.

2. to avoid; to shun; to stay away from.

Let us *eschew* these vulgar fineries of style. —Mathews.

es·chew′ăl, *n.* an eschewing.

es·chew′ănce, *n.* avoidance.

es·chew′ẽr, *n.* one who eschews.

es·chew′ment, *n.* the act of eschewing. [Rare.]

Esch·scholtz′i·ȧ (e-shōlts′i-ȧ), *n.* [L., after Dr. von *Eschscholtz*, a German naturalist.] a small genus of plants, family *Papaveraceæ* of western North America, of which the California poppy is the best known species.

es′chy·nīte, *n.* same as *aeschynite.*

es·çlan′dre (-dẽr), *n.* [Fr.] notoriety; disturbance; a disgraceful occurrence or scene.

es·çlȧ·väġe′ (-väzh′), *n.* [Fr. *esclavage*, slavery.] a necklace worn by women in the middle of the eighteenth century: probably so named from the resemblance of its festoons to the chains of a slave.

es·çō·pet′, es·çō·pette′, *n.* [Sp. *escopeta*, a firelock, a gun; It. *schioppetto*, dim. of *schioppo*, a gun, musket.] a short rifle, or carbine.

Es·çō′ri·ăl, *n.* [Sp. *escorial*, lit., place where a mine has been exhausted, from *escoria*; L. *scoria*, dross, rubbish.] a huge granite structure near Madrid, built in the 16th century by Philip II of Spain: it encloses a monastery, palace, tomb, etc.: also *Escurial.*

es′çort, *n.* [Fr. *escorte*; It. *scorta*, an escort, guide; L. *ex*, out, and *corrigere*, to set right, correct.]

1. one or more persons (or ships, airplanes, etc.) accompanying another or others to give protection or show honor.

2. a man or boy accompanying a woman or girl in public.

3. accompaniment as an escort.

es·çort′, *v.t.*; escorted, *pt., pp.*; escorting, *ppr.* [Fr. *escorter*; It. *scortare*, to escort.] to go with as an escort; accompany to protect or show honor or courtesy to.

Syn.—accompany, attend, go with, convoy, conduct.

es·çot′, *v.t.* to pay the reckoning for. [Obs.]

es·çout′, *n.* a scout. [Obs.]

es·çrībe′, *v.t.*; escribed, *pt., pp.*; escribing, *ppr.* [L. *e-*, out, from, and *scribere*, to write.] to draw (a circle) so as to touch one side of a triangle outside of the triangle, and the extensions of the other two sides.

es′çript, *n.* a manuscript. [Obs.]

es·çri·toire′ (-twor′), *n.* [Fr. *écritoire*; OFr. *escriptoire*, a writing desk, a writing room; LL. *scriptorium*, a writing room, from L. *scribere*, to write.] a writing desk or table: sometimes called *secretary.*

es·çri·tō′ri·ăl, *a.* pertaining to an escritoire.

es·çrod′, *n.* a young cod.

es·çrōll′, es·çrōl′, *n.* a scroll. [Obs.]

es′çrōw, *n.* [OFr. *escroue*, a roll of writings, a bond, scroll.]

1. in law, a written agreement, as a bond or deed, delivered to a third person, to hold till some condition is performed.

2. the custody of an instrument so deposited.

es′çū·ăġe, *n.* [OFr. *escuage*, from *escu*, a shield.] in feudal law, a kind of tenure by knight service, by which a tenant was bound to follow his lord to war.

es·çū·de′rō, *n.* [Sp., from LL. *scutarius*, a shield bearer, from L. *scutum*, a shield.] a shield bearer; an esquire; hence, an attendant upon a person of rank; a lady's page.

es·çū′dō, *n.*; *pl.* **es·çū′dōs̩,** [Sp. *escudo*, a shield, a gold coin, from L. *scutum*, a shield.]

1. any of several obsolete coins of Spain, Portugal, and their former colonies.

2. (a) the gold monetary unit of Portugal, equal to 100 centavos; (b) a Portuguese coin of this value.

Es·çū·lā′pi·ăn, *a.* and *n.* same as *Aesculapian.*

Es·çū·lā′pi·us, *n.* same as *Aesculapius.*

es′çū·lent, *a.* [L. *esculentus*, good to eat, from *esca*, food, from *edere*, to eat.] eatable; fit to be used by man for food; edible; as, *esculent* plants; *esculent* fish.

es′çū·lent, *n.* something that is eatable; that which is or may be safely eaten by man; specifically, an edible vegetable.

es·çū′liç, *a.* [L. *æsculus*, the tallest species of oak.] pertaining to or derived from the horse chestnut; as, *esculic* acid.

es′çū·lin, *n.* [L. *æsculus*, the winter oak.] a crystalline bitter compound derived from the bark of the horse chestnut, *Æsculus hippocastanum.*

Es·çū′ri·ăl, *n.* same as *Escorial.*

es·çutch′eŏn (-kuch′un), *n.* [OFr. *escusson*, an escutcheon, from *escu*, *escut*; L. *scutum*, a shield.]

1. the shield or shield-shaped surface on which a coat of arms is represented; the shield of a family; the picture of ensigns armorial; the symbol of one's birth and dignity.

ESCUTCHEON (Elizabeth, Queen of Henry VII)

2. something shaped like an escutcheon; specifically, (a) the panel on a ship's stern bearing the name; (b) in carpentry, a plate for protecting or ornamenting the keyhole of a door, or to which the handle is attached; a scutcheon; (c) in zoology, the depression behind the beak of a bivalve mollusk; (d) a shieldlike marking upon the rump of certain animals, as cattle, deer, etc., defined by the color or texture of the hair.

a blot on one's escutcheon; a stain on one's honor; disgrace to one's reputation.

escutcheon of pretense; in heraldry, the small shield bearing the coat of arms of an heiress placed in the center of her husband's shield, instead of being impaled with his coat of arms.

es·çutch′eŏned, *a.* having a coat of arms or ensign.

ē·sçū′tel·lāte, *a.* in entomology, not having an apparent scutellum. [Rare.]

Es̩′drăs, *n.* [Gr. *Esdras*, Ezra.]

1. either of two books about Ezra in the Protestant Apocrypha.

2. either of two books of the Old Testament, Ezra and Nehemiah: in the *Douay Bible* they are called *1* and *2 Esdras.*

-ēs̩e (*or* ēs), [OFr. *-eis*; L. *-ensis.*]

1. a suffix used to form adjectives meaning: (a) *of* (a country or place), as in Portug*uese*, Javan*ese*; (b) *in the language* or *dialect of*, as in Chin*ese*, Canton*ese*; (c) *in the style of*, as in Carlyl*ese*, journal*ese.*

2. a suffix used to form nouns corresponding to these adjectives, meaning: (a) *a native* or *inhabitant of*; (b) *the language* or *dialect of*; (c) *the style of.*

-ēs̩e, [from *-ase.*] in biochemistry, a suffix added to the name of a substance, meaning *acted upon by a synthetic enzyme*, as in Cela*nese.*

ēs̩e, *n.* ease; pleasure. [Obs.]

ēs̩e′ment, *n.* casement; relief. [Obs.]

es·em·plas′tiç, *a.* [Gr. *es*, into, *hen*, neut. of *heis*, one, and *plastikos*, skillful in molding, from *plassein*, to mold, form.] molding, shaping, or fashioning into one. [Rare.]

ē·sep′tāte, *a.* [L. *e-* priv., and *septum*, a partition.] in botany and zoology, without partitions or septa.

es′ẽr·ine, *n.* [*esere*, native African name for the plant, and *-ine.*] a resinous alkaloid obtained from the Calabar bean: used in ophthalmic surgery for its effect in contracting the pupil: called also *physostigmine.*

ē·sex′ū·ăl, *a.* asexual. [Rare.]

es·guärd′, *n.* escort; guard. [Obs.]

es′kẽr, es′kăr, *n.* [Ir. *eiscir*, a ridge.] a long, winding, narrow ridge of sand and gravel, probably deposited by a stream flowing in or under glacial ice.

Es·ki·mau′ăn (-mō′), *a.* Eskimoan.

Es′ki·mō, Es′qui·mau (-ki-mō), *n.*; *pl.* **Es′ki·mōs̩, Es′qui·maux** (-ki-mō), [Dan. *Eskimo*, from Am. Ind. *Eskimatsic*, *Askimeg*, eaters of raw flesh.]

1. a member of a race inhabiting Greenland, the Arctic and Hudson Bay coasts of North America, the Labrador coast, Alaska, and the northeastern tip of Asia.

2. the language of the Eskimos, comprising a number of closely related dialects now classified as members of the Eskimo-Aleut language group.

Es′ki·mō, Es′qui·mau, *a.* of or pertaining to the Eskimos or their language.

Es·ki·mō′ăn, *a.* of the Eskimos, their language, or culture.

Es′ki·mō dog, a strong breed of dog native to Greenland and Labrador, with a bushy tail and grayish, shaggy fur: it is used by the Eskimos to pull sleds.

ESKIMO DOG
(20 in. high)

es·loin′, *v.t.* [Fr. *éloigner*; OFr. *esloignier*, to remove.] to remove; to withdraw. [Obs.]

es′nē·cy, *n.* [OFr. *ainsneece*, the right of the firstborn, from LL. *antenatus*, firstborn; L. *ante*, before, and *natus*, pp. of *nasci*, to be born.] in old English law, the right of the eldest coparcener, in the case where an estate descends to daughters jointly for want of a male heir, of making the first choice in the division of the inheritance.

ē·sod′iç, *a.* [Gr. *eis*, into, and *hodos*, a way.] in physiology, conducting impulses to the spinal cord: said of certain nerves.

ē·soph′ȧ·găl, *a.* same as *esophageal.*

ē·sō·phaġ′ē·ăl, ē·sō·phaġ′ē·ăn, *a.* in anatomy, pertaining to the esophagus.

ē·soph·ȧ·got′ō·my, *n.* [Gr. *oisophagos*, gullet, and *tomē*, a cutting.] in surgery, an incision into the esophagus for the purpose of removing any foreign substance that obstructs the passage: written also *oesophagotomy*.

ē·soph′ȧ·gus, *n.* [L. *œsophagus*, from Gr. *oisophagos*, the gullet, lit., the passage for food; *oisein*, fut. inf. of *pherein*, to carry, and *phagein*, to eat.] the gullet; the canal through which food and drink pass from the pharynx to the stomach: written also *oesophagus*.

Ē·sō′pi·ăn, Ē·sop′iç, see *Aesopian, Aesopic*.

es·ō·ter′iç, es·ō·ter′iç·ăl, *a.* [Gr. *esōterikos*, from *esōteros*, inner, comp. of *esō*, within.]
1. taught only to a select number, and not intended for the general body of disciples; designed for and understood only by the initiated: said of ideas, doctrines, literature, etc.
2. characterized by secrecy; private; confidential.
Apposed to *exoteric*.

es·ō·ter′iç, *n.* 1. a person who has been initiated in esoteric rites.
2. a treatise on esoterics; esoteric doctrine or philosophy.

es·ō·ter′i·çȧ, *n.pl.* esoteric facts or things.

es·ō·ter′iç·ăl·ly, *adv.* in an esoteric manner.

es·ō·ter′i·çiṣm, *n.* esoteric practices, principles, or beliefs.

es·ō·ter′içs, *n.* mysterious or secret doctrines.

es′ō·ter·iṣm, *n.* same as *esotericism*.

es′ō·ter·y, *n.* [Gr. *esōteros*, inner.] mystery secrecy.

es·ō·trō′pi·ȧ, *n.* [Mod.L., from Gr. *esō*, within, and Mod.L. *-tropia*, -tropy.] a condition in which only one eye fixes on an object while the other turns inward, producing the appearance of cross-eye.

E′sox, *n.* [L. *esox*, a pike.] a genus of elongated, fresh-water fishes including the northern pike, the muskellunge, etc.

es′pȧ·don, *n.* [Sp., a sword; L. *spatha*; Gr. *spathē*, a broadsword.]
1. a long, two-handled sword, formerly used by foot soldiers.
2. the swordfish.

es·pal′iēr (-yẽr), *n.* [Fr. *espalier*; It. *spalliera*, a support for the shoulders, from *spalla*, the shoulder, from L. *spatula*, a broad piece, a blade.]
1. a latticework or trellis on which fruit trees and ornamental shrubs are trained to grow flat.
2. a tree or row of trees trained on such a latticework.

es·pal′iēr, *v.t.*; espaliered, *pt., pp.*; espaliering, *ppr.* 1. to train as or on an espalier.

ESPALIER

2. to provide with an espalier.

es·pär′cet, *n.* [Fr. *esparcette*; Sp. *esparceta*, sainfoin, from L. *spargere*, to scatter.] a kind of sainfoin, *Onobrychis viciaefolia*.

es·pär′tō, *n.* [Sp. *esparto*; L. *spartum*; Gr. *sparton, spartos*, a kind of broom.] either of two species of long, coarse, pliant and wiry grass, *Stipa tenacissima* and *Lygeum spartum*, found in the southern provinces of Spain and in Algeria: used to make paper, cordage, shoes, matting, baskets, nets, mattresses, sacks, etc.: also *esparto grass*.

es·pau·lière′ (-pō·lyâr′), *n.* [Fr.] same as *epaulière*.

es·pe′ciăl (-pesh′ăl), *a.* [ME. *especial*; OFr. *especial*; L. *specialis*, individual, particular, from *species*, kind.] special; particular; outstanding; exceptional.
Abraham, the *especial* friend of God. —Barrow.

es·pe′ciăl·ly, *adv.* in an especial manner; principally; chiefly; particularly; to a marked degree; unusually.
Syn.—chiefly, mainly, particularly, principally, specially.

es·pe′ciăl·ness, *n.* the state of being especial. [Rare.]

es′pe·rănce, *n.* [Fr.] hope. [Obs.]

Es·pē·răn′tō, *n.* [after pseudonym of Dr. L. L. Zamenhof, who invented the language (1887), lit. (in Esperanto), one who hopes, ult. from L. *sperare*, to hope.] an artificial language for international (chiefly European) use, based on word bases common to the main European languages: it has self-evident parts of speech (all nouns end in *-o*, all adjectives in *-a*, etc.), a single and regular conjugation of verbs, a few simplified inflections, phonetic spelling, accented penults, etc.

es·pī′ăl, *n.* [ME. *espiaile*, from *espien*; OFr. *espier*.]
1. a spy. [Obs.]
2. the act of espying or being espied; observation.
3. discovery.

es·pī′ẽr, *n.* [ME. *aspiere*, from *espien*, to spy.] one who espies, or watches like a spy.

es·pi·nel′, *n.* a kind of ruby; spinel. [Obs.]

es′pi·ō·năġe (-nij; *Fr. pron.* es″pi-ō-näzh′), *n.* [Fr. *espionnage*, from *espion*; It. *spione*, a spy.]
1. spying.
2. the use of spies, especially for military purposes.

es·plȧ·nāde′, *n.* [OFr. *esplanade*, from *esplaner*, to make level; L. *explanare*, to level.]
1. the level or sloping, open space separating the citadel of a fortification and the first houses of the town, so as to leave attackers exposed to fire.
2. any open, level space near a town; especially, a public walk or roadway, often along the seaside; promenade.

es·pleeṣ′, *n.pl.* [OFr. *esples*; LL. *expleta*, the products of land, from L. *expletus*, pp. of *explere*, to fill up.] in law, the products or profits of land, as hay, herbage, corn, rents, etc.

es·pouṣ′ăġe, *n.* espousal. [Obs.]

es·pouṣ′ăl, *n.* [ME. *espousaile*; OFr. *espousailles* (pl.); L. *sponsalia*, a betrothal, from *sponsus*, f. *sponsa*, one betrothed, pp. of *spondere*, to betroth.]
1. [*usually pl.*] (a) a betrothal or betrothal ceremony; (b) a marriage or wedding.
2. an espousing (of some cause, idea, etc.); adoption or advocacy.

es·pouṣe′, *v.t.*; espoused, *pt., pp.*; espousing, *ppr.* [ME. *espousen*; OFr. *espouser*; LL. *sponsare*, to betroth; L. *spondere*, to betroth.]
1. to give in marriage; to betroth; as, the king *espoused* his daughter to a foreign prince.
2. to take in marriage or as a spouse; to marry; to wed: generally said of a man.
3. to make oneself a participator in; to become a partisan in; to adopt, advocate, or support (some cause, idea, etc.).

es·pouṣe′, *n.* a spouse. [Obs.]

es·pouṣe′ment, *n.* the act of espousing or the state of being espoused.

es·pouṣ′ẽr, *n.* one who espouses.

es·pres·si′vō, *a.* and *adv.* [It.] in music, expressive; with ardent expression; expressively: a direction to the performer.

es·pres′sō, *n.*; *pl.* **es·pres′sōṣ,** [It. (*caffè*) *espresso*, pressed-out (coffee), pp. of *esprimere*, to press out, express, from L. *exprimere*, to express.] coffee prepared in a special machine from finely ground coffee beans, through which steam under high pressure is forced.

es·priñ′găl, es·priñ′găld, *n.* a medieval military engine, used to throw stones, etc.

es·prit′ (-prē′), *n.* [Fr.] 1. spirit.
2. lively intelligence or wit.

es·prit′ de corpṣ′ (-kọr′), [Fr., lit., spirit of a body (of persons).] group spirit; sense of pride, honor, etc. in common interests and activities, as of those in the same profession, group, or undertaking.

es·pȳ′, *v.t.*; espied, *pt., pp.*; espying, *ppr.* [ME. *espyen*, to see at a distance; OFr. *espier*; prob. from O.H.G. *spēhon*, to spy.]
1. to catch sight of; make out; spy; descry.
2. to examine and keep watch upon. [Obs.]
He sends angels to *espy* us in all our ways. —Jer. Taylor.
Syn.—discern, descry, observe, discover, detect, see, perceive.

es·pȳ′, *v.i.* to look about; to watch; to spy.

es·pȳ′, *n.*; *pl.* **es·pieṣ′** (-pīṣ′), a spy; a scout; also, espial; espionage. [Obs.]

es·pȳ′ing·ly, *adv.* in a spying manner. [Obs.]

ē·squā′māte, *a.* [L. *e-* priv., and *squama*, scale.] in zoology, having no scales.

ē·squam′ū·lōse, *a.* in botany, having no squamulae, or minute scales.

-esque, [Fr. *-esque*; It. *-esco*; O.H.G. *-isc.*] a suffix used to form adjectives, meaning: (a) *in the manner* or *style of*, as in Roman*esque*, Dant*esque*: some adjectives so formed are also used as nouns, as arab*esque*, burl*esque*; (b) *having the quality of, like*, as in pictur*esque*.

Es′qui·mau (-ki-mō), *n.* and *a.* see *Eskimo*.

es·quīre′, *n.* [OFr. *esquier*, an esquire, shield-bearer; LL. *scutarius*, a squire, shield-bearer; L. *scutum*, a shield.]
1. formerly, a candidate for knighthood, acting as a shield-bearer and attendant for a knight.
2. in England, a member of the gentry next in degree below a knight, given to the younger sons of noblemen, officers of the king's courts and household, counselors at law, sheriffs, army and navy officers, etc.
3. [E–] a title of courtesy placed after a man's surname and corresponding, more ceremoniously, to *Mr*.
4. a landed country gentleman.
5. a man who attends or escorts a woman in public; escort.

es·quīre′, *v.t.*; esquired, *pt., pp.*; esquiring, *ppr.*
1. to attend (a knight) as esquire.
2. to raise to the rank of esquire.
3. to address as Esquire.
4. to escort (a woman or girl).

es·quisse′ (-kēs′), *n.* [Fr.] the preliminary sketch of a picture or model of a statue.

ess, *n.*; *pl.* **ess′eṣ,** 1. the letter S, s.
2. something shaped like an S.

-ess, [ME. *-esse, -isse*; L. *-issa*; Gr. *-issa*.] a suffix added to a masculine noun to form a feminine noun, as in lion*ess*, author*ess*: in nouns of agent ending *-tor* or *-ter*, the vowel is usually dropped before the addition of *-ess* (e.g., actr*ess*).

es·say′, *v.t.*; essayed, *pt., pp.*; essaying, *ppr.* [ME. *assayen*; OFr. *essayer*, to try, attempt.]
1. to try; to attempt; to endeavor; to make an effort to perform.
Then in my madness I *essay'd* the door:
It gave. —Tennyson.
2. to make experiment of; to test the quality of; to try out.
3. to assay (metals). [Obs.]

es′sāy, *n.* [ME. *assay*; OFr. *essai*, a trial, attempt, from LL. *exagium*, a trial of weight, from Gr. *exagion*, a weighing.]
1. (a) a trial; attempt; (b) a trying or testing; endeavor.
2. a short literary composition dealing with a single subject, usually from a personal point of view and without attempting completeness.
3. an assay of a metal. [Obs.]
Syn.—attempt, trial, endeavor, effort, treatise, dissertation, paper, tract.

es·sāy′ẽr, *n.* one who essays.

es′sāy·ist, *n.* a writer of an essay or of essays.

es′se, *n.* [L., to be.] being; existence; essence.

es′sence, *n.* [Fr. *essence*; L. *essentia*, the being or essence of a thing, from *esse*, to be.]
1. something that is, or exists; entity.
2. that which makes something what it is; intrinsic, fundamental nature (of something); essential being.
3. a substance that keeps, in concentrated form, the flavor, fragrance, or other properties of the plant, drug, food, etc. from which it is extracted; essential oil.
4. a solution of such a substance or oil in alcohol.
5. a perfume.
6. in philosophy, that which constitutes the inward nature of anything, underlying its manifestations; true substance.

es′sence, *v.t.*; essenced (-senst), *pt., pp.*; essencing, *ppr.* to perfume; to scent.

Es·sēne′, *n.* [LL. *Esseni*; Gr. *Essenoi*, the Essenes.] a member of an ancient Jewish sect of ascetics and mystics, which existed from the second century B. C. to the second century A. D., practicing abstinence and general strictness of living.

Es′sē·niṣm, *n.* the teachings and customs of the Essenes.

es·sen′tiăl (-shăl), *a.* [LL. *essentialis*, from L. *essentia*, the essence.]
1. of or constituting the intrinsic, fundamental nature of something; basic; inherent; as, there is an *essential* difference between fascism and communism.
2. absolute; complete; perfect; pure; as, *essential* happiness.
3. necessary to make a thing what it is; indispensable; requisite; as, water is *essential* to life.
Judgment is more *essential* to a general than courage. —Denham.
4. containing, or having the properties of, a concentrated extract of a plant, drug, food, etc.; as, an *essential* oil.

5. in medicine, idiopathic; not symptomatic: said of a disease.

6. in music, indispensable: said of tones which constitute a chord and are independent of passing tones.

essential oil; any volatile oil which gives a distinctive odor, flavor, etc. to, and is distilled or expressed from, flowers, fruits, or plants: much used in perfumery.

Syn.—necessary, requisite, indispensable, vital, leading, inherent, radical.

es·sen′tiăl, *n.* 1. existence; being. [Obs.]

2. something necessary or fundamental; indispensable, inherent or basic feature or principle; as, the *essentials* of religion.

es·sen·ti·al′i·ty (-shi-al′), *n.*; *pl.* **es·sen·ti·al′i·tieș,** essential quality, fact, or thing.

es·sen′tiăl·ly, *adv.* in essence or essentials; in a characteristic manner.

es·sen′tiăl·ness, *n.* same as *essentiality*.

es·sen′ti·āte (-shi-), *v.t.* and *v.i.*; essentiated, *pt.*, *pp.*; essentiating, *ppr.* to make or become the essence or being of. [Obs.]

ess′ling, *n.* a young salmon. [Brit. Dial.]

es·soin′, es·soign′ (-soin′), *n.* [ME. *essoyne*; OFr. *essoine*, an excuse, exemption; *es-*, from, and *soin*, care; L. *exonerare*, to relieve from a burden; *ex*, from, and *onus*, burden.]

1. in English law, the alleging of an excuse for one who is summoned to appear in court and who neglects to appear on the day specified.

2. excuse; exemption. [Obs.]

es·soin′, *v.t.* in English law, to excuse for nonappearance in court.

es·soin′ẽr, *n.* in law, one who essoins; an attorney who sufficiently excuses the absence of someone.

es′sō·nīte, *n.* a dark-brown kind of garnet: also called *hessonite, cinnamon stone*.

ēst, *n.*, *a.*, and *adv.* [ME.] east. [Obs.]

-est, [ME. *-est*; AS. *-est, -ost, -ast*, superl. suffix of adjectives and adverbs.] a suffix used to form the superlative degree of most adjectives and adverbs of one or two syllables, as in great*est*, soon*est*.

-est, [ME. *-est*; AS. *-est*, 2d pers. sing., pres. tense inflection.] a suffix used to form the archaic second person singular, present indicative, of verbs, as in go*est*: also *-st*.

es·tab′lish, *v.t.*; established (-lisht), *pt.*, *pp.*; establishing, *ppr.* [ME. *establissen*; OFr. *establir*; L. *stabilire*, to make stable, from *stabilis*, stable.]

1. to make steadfast, firm, or stable; to settle on a firm or permanent basis; to set or fix unalterably.

2. to order, ordain, or appoint (officials, laws, etc.) permanently.

3. to confirm or ratify (what has previously been instituted, settled, or ordained). [Obs.]

4. to found permanently; to institute or settle; to set up (a government, nation, business, etc.); as, to *establish* a colony or an empire.

5. to settle in a secure or favorable office or position; to set up in business or a profession: often with reflexive pronoun; as, the father *established* his son as a merchant; the enemy *established themselves* in the citadel.

6. to make a state institution of (a church).

7. to set up a precedent, theory, reputation, etc. permanently; to cause to be accepted or recognized.

8. to prove; demonstrate; vindicate; as, the plantiff *established* his case.

9. in card games, to win control of (a suit) so that one is sure of taking all the remaining tricks.

Syn.—plant, fix, settle, found, organize, confirm, institute, prove, substantiate, constitute.

es·tab′lished chŭrch, a church officially recognized by the government and supported as a national institution; specifically, [E- C-] the Church of England.

es·tab′lish·ẽr, *n.* one who establishes, ordains, or confirms.

es·tab′lish·ment, *n.* [OFr. *establissement*, from *establis* to establish.]

1. the act of establishing.

2. the state of being established; settlement.

3. a thing established.

4. a settled regulation; system of laws; constitution of government.

5. a fixed or stated allowance for subsistence; income; salary.

6. a permanent civil or military force or organization, such as a fixed garrison or a local government.

7. that form of doctrine and church government established and endowed by the legislature in any country.

8. the place where a person is settled for residence or for transacting business; a person's residence and everything connected with it, as furniture, servants, grounds, etc.; a public or private institution.

the Establishment; (a) the Church of England; (b) the Presbyterian Church of Scotland; (c) in England, a complex consisting of the church, the royal family, and the plutocracy, regarded as holding the chief measure of power and influence; (d) the ruling inner circle of any nation, institution, etc.

es·tab″lish·men·tā′ri·ăn, *n.* one who supports the doctrine of establishment in religion, or belongs to an established church.

es·tȧ·çāde′, *n.* [Fr. *estacade*; Sp. *estacada*, a paling, palisade, from *estacar*, to stake in; from *estaca*, a stake.] a palisade, stockade, or dike set with piles in a sea, river, etc. to check the approach of an enemy.

es·tȧ·fette′, es·tȧ·fet′, *n.* [Fr. *estafette*; It. *staffetta*, a courier, from *staffa*, a stirrup; from O.H.G. *stapfo, staffo*, a step.] a courier on horseback.

es·tȧ·mi·nẹt′ (-nā′), *n.* [Fr.] a café or coffeehouse.

es·tän′ci·ä, *n.* [Sp.] a large estate, especially a cattle ranch, in Spanish America.

es·tän·ci·ẹ′rō, *n.* [Sp.] the owner or overseer of an estancia; a Spanish-American cattle raiser.

es·tāte′, *n.* [ME. *estat*; OFr. *estat*; L. *status*, a state, condition, from *stare*, to stand.]

1. condition or stage of life; state; situation.

Whose life in low *estate* began.—Tennyson.

2. formerly, especially in feudal times, any of the three social classes having specific political powers: the first estate was the Lords Spiritual (clergy), the second estate the Lords Temporal (nobility), and the third estate the Commons (bourgeoisie).

3. rank; quality; the degree of a person's wealth, influence, etc.; also, display of wealth; pomp. [Archaic.]

Who hath not heard of the greatness of your *estate?* —Sidney.

4. fortune; possessions; capital; property in general.

5. the assets and liabilities of a dead or bankrupt person.

6. landed property; individually owned piece of land containing a residence: it is usually large and maintained by great wealth.

7. in law, the degree, nature, extent, and quality of interest or ownership that one has in land, etc.

8. the state; the body politic; the commonwealth; the public; public interest. [Obs.]

9. a person of high rank. [Obs.]

the fourth estate; journalism or journalists: see *estate*, sense 2.

es·tāte′, *v.t.*; estated, *pt.*, *pp.*; estating, *ppr.* 1. to settle an estate upon; to endow with an estate or other property. [Obs.]

2. to give as a possession; to bestow. [Obs.]

All the revenue that was old Sir Rowland's
will I *estate* upon you. —Shak.

es·tāte′ly, *a.* stately. [Obs.]

Es·tātes′-Gen′ẽr·ăl, *n.* the legislature of France before 1789, to which each of the three estates (clergy, nobility, and bourgeoisie) sent representatives.

es·teem′, *v.t.*; esteemed, *pt.*, *pp.*; esteeming, *ppr.* [Fr. *estimer*; L. *æstimare*, to value, consider, estimate.]

1. originally, to set a value on, whether high or low; to estimate; to value.

They that despise me shall be lightly *esteemed.* —1 Sam. ii. 30.

2. to prize; to set a high value on; to have a high regard for or a favorable opinion of; as, ability is always *esteemed*.

3. to consider; to regard; to reckon; to deem; as, I *esteem* this theory useless.

Syn.—appreciate, prize, regard, respect, revere, value, think, account, deem, consider.

es·teem′, *v.i.* to consider the value; to form an estimate: with *of*. [Obs.]

es·teem′, *n.* 1. estimation; opinion; as, this man is worthless in my *esteem*. [Archaic.]

2. high estimation; great regard; favorable opinion; as, he was held in high *esteem*.

3. valuation; estimation of worth. [Obs.]

Syn.—estimate, estimation, respect, regard, honor, admiration, reverence, veneration.

es·teem′ȧ·ble, *a.* worthy of esteem; estimable. [Rare.]

es·teem′ẽr, *n.* one who esteems; one who sets a high value on anything.

A proud *esteemer* of his own parts.—Locke.

es′tẽr, *n.* [G.; synthesis of *äther*, ether, and *säure*, acid.] an organic compound, comparable to an inorganic salt, formed by the reaction of an acid and an alcohol: the organic radical of the alcohol replaces the acid hydrogen of the acid: formerly called *compound ether*.

es′tẽr·āse, *n.* any of a group of enzymes by whose action the hydrolysis of esters is accelerated.

es·tẽr′i·fȳ, *v.t.* and *v.i.*; esterified, *pt.*, *pp.*; esterifying, *ppr.* to change into an ester: said of an acid.

es″thē·mȧ·tol′ō·ġy, *n.* see *aesthematology*.

Es′thẽr (-tẽr), *n.* [L.; Heb. *estēr*; prob. from Bab. *Ishtar*, Ishtar.]

1. in the Bible, the Jewish wife of the Persian king Ahasuerus (Xerxes): she saved her people from slaughter by Haman.

2. the book of the Old Testament that tells her story.

es·thē′siȧ, *n.* the ability to feel sensations: also spelled *aesthesia*.

es·thē′si·ō·ġen, *n.* same as *aesthesiogen*.

es·thē·si·ol′ō·ġy, *n.* same as *aesthesiology*.

es·thē·si·om′e·tẽr, *n.* see *aesthesiometer*.

es·thē′sis, *n.* see *aethesis*.

es′thēte, *n.* 1. a person highly sensitive to art and beauty.

2. a person who exaggerates the value of artistic sensitivity or makes a cult of art and beauty; believer in art for art's sake.

Also spelled *aesthete*.

es·thet′iç, *a.* 1. of esthetics.

2. of beauty.

3. sensitive to art and beauty; showing good taste; artistic.

Also spelled *aesthetic*.

es·thet′iç·ăl, *a.* esthetic: also spelled *aesthetical*.

es·thet′iç·ăl·ly, *adv.* 1. in an esthetic manner.

2. from the point of view of esthetics.

Also spelled *aesthetically*.

es·the·ti′ciăn, *a.* an expert or specialist in esthetics: also spelled *aesthetician*.

es·thet′i·cișm, *n.* 1. esthetic doctrine; cult of beauty, art, and good taste.

2. sensitivity to art and beauty.

Also spelled *aestheticism*.

es·thet′içs, *n. pl.* [*construed as sing.*] the study or philosophy of beauty; theory of the fine arts and of people's responses to them: also spelled *aesthetics*.

es·thē·tol′ō·ġy, *n.* [Gr. *aisthētos*, perceptible, and *logos*, description.] the science dealing with the nature, history, and development of the fine arts.

Es·thō′ni·ăn (*or* -tō′), *a.* and *n.* Estonian.

es″thō·phyș·i·ol′ō·ġy, *n.* see *aesthophysiology*.

es·tif′ẽr·ous, aes·tif′ẽr·ous, *a.* [L. *æstus*, heat, and *ferre*, to produce.] producing heat. [Rare.]

es′ti·mȧ·ble, *a.* [Fr. *estimable*; L. *æstimabilis*, worthy of estimation, from *æstimare*, to estimate, value.]

1. capable of being estimated or valued; calculable; as, *estimable* damage.

2. valuable; worth a great price. [Archaic.]

A pound of man's flesh, taken from a man,
Is not so *estimable.* —Shak.

3. worthy of esteem or respect; deserving good opinion or high value; as, an *estimable* friend.

es′ti·mȧ·ble·ness, *n.* the quality of deserving esteem or regard.

es′ti·mȧ·bly, *adv.* in an estimable manner.

es′ti·māte, *v.t.*; estimated, *pt.*, *pp.*; estimating, *ppr.* [L. *æstimatus*, pp. of *æstimare*, to esteem, value.]

1. to form an opinion or judgment about; to gauge.

2. to form a rough judgment regarding the value, size, weight, degree, extent, quantity, etc. of; to rate by a rough calculation; to fix the worth of, compute, or calculate approximately; to reckon.

Syn.—calculate, value, compute, rate, appraise, measure, reckon, esteem, count, number.

es′ti·māte, *v.i.* to make an estimate or estimates.

es′ti·mȧte (*or* -māt), *n.* 1. a rough calculation of size, value, etc.; especially, an approximate computation of the probable cost of a piece of work, made by a person undertaking to do the work.

2. a written statement of this.

3. an opinion or judgment.

Syn.—esteem, estimation.—*Estimate* supposes an exercise of judgment in determining the amount, value, importance, or magnitude of things; *esteem* is an opinion made up of respect and high regard; *estimation*, properly the act of appraising or evaluating, is used in the sense of both *esteem* and *estimate*.

es·ti·mā′tion, *n.* [ME. *estymacyon*; L. *æstimatio* (-*onis*), a valuation, from *æstimare*, to value, esteem.]

1. the act of estimating.

2. calculation; computation; an opinion or judgment of the worth, extent, or quantity of anything; as, an *estimation* of distance, an *estimation* of moral qualities.

3. esteem; regard; favorable opinion; respect.

I shall have *estimation* among the multitude, and honor with the elders. —Wisdom.

4. conjecture; supposition; surmise. [Obs.]

Syn.—supposition, computation, estimate, calculation, appraisement, honor, regard, esteem.

es′ti·mā·tive, *a.* 1. estimating, or having the power of estimating, comparing, or judging.

2. serving as an estimate.

3. pertaining to or based on an estimate. [Obs.]

es′ti·mā·tŏr, *n.* [L. *æstimator*, from *æstimare*, to value, estimate.] one who estimates, or appraises.

ē·stip′ū·lāte, *a.* exstipulate.

es′ti·vāġe, *n.* [Fr., from *estiver*; L. *stipare*, to pack.] a method of pressing or screwing the cargo into a vessel by means of capstan machinery.

es′ti·văl, aes′ti·văl (es′), *a.* [LL. *æstivalis*, from L. *æstivus*, pertaining to summer, from *æstas*, summer.] pertaining to summer.

es′ti·vāte, *v.i.*; estivated, *pt.*, *pp.*; estivating, *ppr.* [L. *æstivatus*, pp. of *æstivare*, to spend the summer.]

1. to pass or spend the summer.

2. to spend the summer in a dormant condition: opposed to *hibernate*.

Also spelled *æstivate*.

es·ti·vā′tion, aes·ti·vā′tion, *n.* 1. the act of or a place for passing the summer. [Obs.]

2. in botany, the arrangement of the petals within a flower bud before it opens; prefloration.

FORMS OF ESTIVATION
1. involute; 2. revolute; 3. obvolute; 4. convolute; 5. supervolute; 6. induplicate; 7. conduplicate; 8. plaited; 9. imbricated; 10. equitant; 11. valvate; 12. circinate; 13. twisted; 14. alternative; 15. vexillary; 16. cochlear; 17. quincunx; 18. contorted; 19. curvative; 20. equitant.

3. in zoology, the habit or state of sleep of certain animals in summer, as land snails or mollusks.

est mō′dus in rē′bus, [L.] there is a measure in things; temperance is a virtue: a quotation from Horace.

es′toç, *n.* [OFr., from G. *stock*, a stock.] a short sword worn at the girdle by mounted soldiers: an early form of rapier.

es·tō·çāde′, *n.* [Fr., a sword thrust, from *estoc*, a sword.] a thrust with an estoc; also, an estoc or thrusting sword. [Obs.]

es·toile′ (-twol′), *n.* [OFr., from L. *stella*, a star.] in heraldry, a star with six, eight, or more waved points: written also *étoile*.

ESTOILE

Es·tō′ni·ăn, *a.* of Estonia, its people, their language, or culture: also *Esthonian*.

Es·tō′ni·ăn, *n.* 1. a native or inhabitant of Estonia.

2. the Finno-Ugric language of the Estonians.

Also *Esthonian*.

es·top′, *v.t.*; estopped (-topt′), *pt.*, *pp.*; estopping, *ppr.* [OFr. *estoper*; hyp. LL. *stuppare*, to stop with tow, cram, from L. *stuppa*, oakum, tow.]

1. in law, to impede or bar by estoppel.

A man shall always be *estopped* by his own deed, or not permitted to aver or prove anything in contradiction to what he has once solemnly avowed. —Blackstone.

2. originally, to stop up.

3. to bar; to stop; to obstruct; to prevent.

es·top′pāġe, *n.* [from *estop*, and *-age*.] an estopping or being estopped; stoppage.

es·top′pel, *n.* [prob. from OFr. *estoupail*, stopper, bung, from *estoper*.]

1. in law, the prevention of a person from making an affirmation or denial because it is contrary to a previous affirmation or denial that he has made.

2. stoppage; prohibition.

es·tō′vẽrș, *n.pl.* [OFr. *estover*, *estovoir*, necessity, need, a substantive use of the inf. *estover*, *estovoir*, to be necessary.] in law, necessaries or supplies, such as a reasonable allowance out of lands or goods for the use of a tenant, alimony for a divorced wife, etc.

es·trāde′, *n.* [Fr., from Sp. *estrado*, a drawing room, from L. *stratum*, a pavement, floor, bed or couch covering, neut. of *stratus*, pp. of *sternere*, to strew.] an elevated part of the floor of a room; a platform.

es·trȧ·dī′ōl (*or* -ol), *n.* a crystalline, estrogenic substance, having the formula $C_{18}H_{24}O_2$: it is obtained from ovarian fluid, the urine of pregnant mares, etc.

es·trānġe′, *v.t.*; estranged, *pt.*, *pp.*; estranging, *ppr.* [OFr. *estranger*, to alienate, from *estrange*, strange; L. *extraneus*, foreign, from *extra*, beyond, without.]

1. to keep at a distance; to withdraw or remove, as from usual surroundings or associates; to cease to frequent and be familiar with.

2. to alienate; to divert from its original use or possessor; to apply to a purpose foreign to its original or customary one.

They have *estranged* this place and burnt incense in it unto other gods.—Jer. xix. 4.

3. to alienate the affections of; to turn (a person) from an affectionate or friendly attitude to an indifferent, unfriendly, or hostile one; to separate.

I do not know, to this hour, what it is that has *estranged* him from me. —Pope.

es·trān′ġed·ness, *n.* the state of being estranged.

es·trānġe′ment, *n.* the act of estranging or state of being estranged; alienation; a keeping at a distance; removal; as, an *estrangement* of affection.

es·trān′ġẽr, *n.* one who estranges.

es·tran′gle, *v.t.* to strangle. [Obs.]

es·trȧ·pāde′, *n.* [Fr., from OFr. *strappare*, to pull, break.] the action of a horse, when, to get rid of the rider, he rears, plunges, and kicks furiously.

es·trāy′, *n.* [Anglo-Fr. *estraie*, pp. of *estraier*, to stray.]

1. any person or thing out of its usual place.

2. in law, a stray and unclaimed domestic animal.

es·trāy′, *v.i.* to stray. [Archaic.]

es′tre (-tẽr), *n.* 1. a place. [Obs.]

2. [*pl.*] divisions or inner parts of a building. [Obs.]

es·trēat′, *n.* [Anglo-Fr. *estret*, an abstract, extract, from OFr. *estraite*, from LL. *extracta*, from pp. of L. *extrahere*, to draw out; *ex*, out, from, and *trahere*, to draw.] in law, a true copy or duplicate of an original writing, especially of amercements or penalties levied by a court.

es·trēat′, *v.t.*; estreated, *pt.*, *pp.*; estreating, *ppr.* in law, (a) to extract or copy from records of a court of law for purposes of prosecution; (b) to take as a levy, fine, etc.

es·trēpe′, *v.i.*; estreped (-trēpt′), *pt.*, *pp.*; estreping, *ppr.* [OFr. *estreper*, to waste, destroy; L. *extirpare*, to uproot; *ex*, from, and *stirps*, root.] in law, to commit waste or destruction, as by stripping trees of their branches, lands of their trees, houses, etc.

es·trēpe′ment, *n.* [OFr. *estrepement*, spoil, waste, from *estreper*, to waste.] in law, waste; a stripping of land by a tenant, causing loss to the owner.

es′trich, es′tridġe, *n.* the ostrich.

es′trin (*or* ēs′), *n.* estrone: also spelled *oestrin*. [Rare.]

es′trī·ōl, *n.* a female sex hormone, $C_{18}H_{24}O_3$, used to treat conditions of estrogen deficiency, especially in menopause; theelol.

es′trō, *n.* [L. *æstrus*; Gr. *oistros*, a gadfly.] irresistible impulse; ardor; inspiration.

es′trō·ġen, *n.* any of several estrus-producing compounds, as estriol and estrone.

es·trō·ġen′iç, *a.* 1. of estrogen.

2. of or producing estrus.

es′trōne, *n.* [from *estrus*, and *-one*.] a female sex hormone, $C_{18}H_{22}O_2$, injected into the muscles to treat conditions of estrogen deficiency; theelin: it is more active than estriol.

es′trous (*or* ēs′), *a.* of, or having the characteristics of, estrus: also spelled *oestrous*.

es′trụ·ăl (*or* ēs′), *a.* estrous: also spelled *oestrual*.

es′trụ·āte (*or* ēs′), *v.i.* to be in heat; to rut: also spelled *oestruate*.

es·trụ·ā′tion (*or* ēs-), *n.* the fact or state of being under the influence of estrus; rut: also spelled *oestruation*.

es′trum (*or* ēs′), *n.* estrus: also spelled *oestrum*.

es′trus (*or* ēs′), *n.* [L. *œstrus*, gadfly, frenzy; Gr. *oistros*, gadfly, sting, frenzy.]

1. a strong impulse; overwhelming desire; frenzy.

2. the sexual excitement, or heat, of female mammals, corresponding to *rut* in males.

3. the period of this, characterized by sexual desire and changes in the sex organs.

Also spelled *oestrus*.

es·tū·ăr′i·ăl, *a.* of an estuary.

es′tū·ȧ·rine, *a.* formed or deposited in an estuary.

es′tū·ăr·y, *n.*; *pl.* **es′tū·ăr·ieș,** [L. *æstuarium*, part of the seacoast over which the tide ebbs and flows, from *æstus*, the tide.]

1. a boiling spring. [Obs.]

2. an inlet or arm of the sea; a frith or firth; especially, the wide mouth of a river, where the tide meets the current.

es′tū·āte, *v.i.* see *aestuate*.

es·tū·ā′tion, *n.* see *aestuation*.

es·tụ′fȧ, *n.* [Sp., a stove, a warm room.] a heated assembly room or council chamber, usually wholly or partly underground, used by the Pueblo Indians as a general meeting place and, formerly, for religious purposes; a kiva.

es′tūre, *n.* aesture. [Obs.]

ē·sū′ri·ence, ē·sū′ri·en·cy, *n.* hunger; greed; voracity.

ē·sū′ri·ent, *a.* [L. *esuriens* (-*entis*), ppr. of *esurire*, to be hungry.] hungry; voracious; greedy.

ē·sū′ri·ent, *n.* a hungry or greedy person.

eș′ū·rine, *a.* eating; corroding. [Obs.]

eș′ū·rine, *n.* in medicine, a substance, acid to the taste, used to promote appetite or cause hunger. [Obs.]

et, [L., or Fr., from L.] and.

-et, [ME. *-et*; OFr. *-et*, masc., *-ete*, f.] a suffix added to nouns, meaning *little*, as in rivul*et*, isl*et*: it has lost its diminutive force in most words, as in bull*et*, hatch*et*, pock*et*, pull*et*, sonn*et*.

Et, et, in chemistry, ethyl.

ẹ′tȧ, *n.* the seventh letter of the Greek alphabet, corresponding in sound to English *a*, as in *fate*: in English transliteration, it is shown as *ē*.

ē·tääç′, *n.* the blaubok.

ẹ′tȧ·cism, *n.* [from the Gr. letter *η*, *ēta*.] the pronunciation of *eta*, the seventh letter of the Greek alphabet, like *a* in *fate*.

ẹ′tȧ·cist, *n.* one who practices or favors etacism.

é·ta·gère′ (ā-tȧ-zhār′), *n.* [Fr., from *étager*, to elevate by stories or stages, from *étage*, a story.] a piece of furniture with several shelves one above another, as a sideboard, a whatnot, etc.

et a′li·bī, [L.] and elsewhere.

et ā′li·ī, [L.] and others.

et′ȧ·mïne, *n.* [Fr. *étamine*.] a loosely woven cotton or worsted cloth, similar to bunting or voile.

etaoin shrdlu, two sequences of letters on a linotype machine: if the machine jams, the entire slug may drop, so that these sequences may accidentally appear in print.

é·tape′ (ā-), *n.* [Fr.] 1. a public warehouse for goods.

2. a halting place; specifically, a place where troops encamp after a day's march.

3. the length of a day's march.

4. an allowance of provisions, forage, etc. for troops at temporary stopping places during a march.

5. in Russia, a prisonlike building with a stockaded yard, for the temporary confinement and shelter of convicts or exiles in transit under guard.

É·tat′ Ma·jor′ (ā-tä′ ma-zhọr′), [Fr.] the staff of an army or a regiment; the general staff.

et cet′ẽr·ȧ, et caet′ẽr·ȧ, [L., and other things; *et*, and, and *cetera*, nom. pl. neut. of *ceterus*, other, another.] and others of the like kind;

and so forth; and so on: generally used when a number of individuals of a class have been specified, to indicate that more of the same sort might have been mentioned, but for shortness have been omitted; as, stimulants comprise brandy, rum, whisky, wine, beer, *et cetera.*

et·cet′ẽr·ȧṣ, *n.pl.* additional things; odds and ends; customary extras.

Come we to full points here, and are *etceteras* nothing? —Shak.

etch, *n.* eddish. [Obs.]

etch, *v.t.*; etched (echt), *pt., pp.*; etching, *ppr.* [D. *etsen*; G. *ätzen*, to feed, corrode, from M.H.G. *etzen*, to cause to eat.]

1. to make (a drawing, design, etc.) on metal, glass, etc. by the action of an acid: usually done by coating the surface with wax and letting acid eat into the lines or areas laid bare with a special needle.

2. to engrave (a metal plate, glass, etc.) in this way, for use in printing such drawings or designs.

3. to produce (designs, etc.) by this process.

etch, *v.i.* to practice etching; to produce etchings.

etch′ẽr, *n.* one who or that which etches.

etch′ing, *n.* 1. the act, art, process, or practice of producing drawings or designs on plates of metal, glass, etc. by the action of acid.

2. an etched plate, drawing, or design.

3. a print made from an etched plate.

etch′ing ground, the wax or coating with which plates to be etched are covered.

etch′ing nee′dle, an instrument of steel with a fine point, for tracing outlines, etc., in etching.

etch′ing stitch, in needlework, a stitch in outline embroidery.

Ē·tē′ō·clēṣ, *n.* in Greek legend, a son of Oedipus and Jocasta.

ē·tē·os′tiç, *n.* [Gr. *etos*, a year, and *stichos*, a line, verse.] a chronogram. [Obs.]

ē·tẽr′mi·nȧ·ble, *a.* interminable; without end. [Obs.]

ē·tẽrn′, *a.* same as *eterne.*

ē·tẽr′nȧl, *a.* [ME. *eternal*; OFr. *eternel*; LL. *æternalis*; L. *æternus*, eternal, everlasting, from *ævum*, an age.]

1. without beginning or end; existing through all time; everlasting.

2. timeless.

3. perpetual; ceaseless; never stopping; continued without intermission.

And fires *eternal* in thy temple shine. —Dryden.

4. unchangeable; existing at all times without change; always true or valid; as, *eternal* truth.

5. seeming never to stop; happening very often; appearing endless; perpetual; unceasing; continued without intermission; as, *eternal* chatter.

the Eternal City; Rome.

Syn.—endless, everlasting, boundless, immortal, infinite, interminable, perpetual. That is properly *eternal* which has neither beginning nor end; that is *endless* which has a beginning, but no end; that which is *everlasting* has neither interruption nor cessation.

ē·tẽr′nȧl, *n.* 1. [E–] an appellation of God: used with the definite article.

The law whereby the *Eternal* himself doth work. —Hooker.

2. that which is everlasting.

All godlike passion for *eternals* quenched. —Young.

3. eternity. [Obs.]

ē·tẽr′nȧl·ist, *n.* one who holds the existence of the world or of matter to be from eternity.

ē·tẽr′nȧl·īze, *v.t.*; eternalized, *pt., pp.*; eternalizing, *ppr.* to make eternal; to eternize.

ē·tẽr′nȧl·ly, *adv.* 1. continuing through eternity; for all time; without beginning or end.

2. always.

3. continuously; without stopping; constantly.

ē·tẽrne′, *a.* eternal. [Archaic or Poet.]

ē·tẽr′ni·fȳ, *v.t.* to make eternal. [Obs.]

ē·tẽr′ni·ty, *n.*; *pl.* **ē·tẽr′ni·tieṣ,** [ME. *eternite*; OFr. *eternité*; L. *æternitas (-atis)*, eternity, from *æternus*, eternal.]

1. the fact, condition, or quality of being eternal; duration or continuance without beginning or end.

2. infinite time; time without beginning or end.

The narrow isthmus 'twixt two boundless seas,

The past, the future, two *eternities.*—Moore.

3. a long period of time that seems endless; as, an *eternity* of waiting.

4. the endless time after death; hence, future life; immortality.

ē·tẽr·ni·zā′tion, *n.* an eternizing or being eternized.

ē·tẽr′nīze, *v.t.*; eternized, *pt., pp.*; eternizing, *ppr.* [Fr. *éterniser*, from L. *æternus*, eternal.]

1. to make eternal; to make endless.

2. to prolong the existence or duration of indefinitely; to perpetuate; as, to *eternize* woe.

3. to make famous forever; to immortalize.

ē·tē′siăn (-zhăn), *a.* [L. *etesius*; Gr. *etēsios*, lasting a year, yearly, from *etos*, a year.] recurring every year; annual: said of certain Mediterranean winds that blow from the northwest for several weeks every summer.

eth, *n.* same as *edh.*

-eth, [expanded form from ME. *-the.*] a suffix used in forming ordinal numerals from bases ending in a vowel, as in fort*ieth.*

-eth, [ME. *-(e)th*; AS. *-(a)th.*] archaic ending of the third person singular, present indicative, of verbs, as in ask*eth*, bring*eth.*

eth′al, *n.* [*eth*er and *al*cohol.] a solid, fusible substance obtained from spermaceti.

eth′āne, *n.* [from *ether*, and *-ane.*] an odorless, colorless, gaseous hydrocarbon, CH_3CH_3, of the methane series: it is found in natural gas and illuminating gas, and is used as a refrigerant.

Eth′ȧ·nim, *n.* [Heb.] Tishri: the early Hebrew name.

eth′ȧ·nōl, *n.* [from *ethane*, and *-ol.*] ethyl alcohol.

eth′el, *a.* noble. [Obs.]

eth′el·ing, *n.* see *atheling.*

eth′ēne, *n.* same as *ethylene.*

ē·then′iç, *a.* pertaining to ethene, or ethylene.

eth′ē·nyl, *n.* same as *vinyl.*

Ē·thē·os′tō·mȧ, *n.* [L., from Gr. *ēthein*, to strain, and *stoma*, mouth.] a genus of small fresh-water fishes, the darters.

ē·thē·os′tō·moid, *a.* pertaining to the *Etheostoma.*

ē·thē·os′tō·moid, *n.* any of the *Etheostoma.*

ē′thẽr, *n.* [L. *æther*; Gr. *aithēr*, the upper, purer air, ether, from *aithein*, to kindle, burn.]

1. an imaginary substance regarded by the ancients as filling all space beyond the sphere of the moon, and making up the stars and planets.

2. the upper regions of space; clear sky.

3. the air. [Rare.]

4. in chemistry, any of a class of organic compounds that are oxides of hydrocarbon radicals; specifically, a volatile, colorless, highly inflammable liquid, $(C_2H_5)_2O$, with an aromatic odor, prepared by the reaction of sulfuric acid and ethyl alcohol: it is used as an anesthetic and a solvent for resins and fats: also called *diethyl ether.*

5. in physics, a hypothetical invisible substance postulated (in older theory) as pervading space and serving as the medium for the transmission of light waves and other forms of radiant energy.

Also spelled *aether* (in senses 1, 2, 3).

compound ether; an ester.

ē·thē′rē·ăl, *a.* [L. *ætherius*; Gr. *aitherios*, pertaining to the ether, high in the air, ethereal, from *aithēr*, ether.]

1. of or like the ether, or upper regions of space.

2. very light; airy; delicate; as, the *ethereal* grace of her dancing.

3. heavenly; celestial; not earthly.

4. in chemistry, of or pertaining to ether; as, *ethereal* salts.

Also spelled *aethereal.*

ethereal extract; an extract made by means of a solvent containing ether.

ethereal oil; a volatile oil.

ethereal oil of wine; a heavy, yellow liquid consisting of equal volumes of heavy oil of wine and of stronger ether: called also *heavy oil of wine.*

ē·thē′rē·ăl·iṣm, *n.* ethereality.

ē·thē·rē·al′i·ty, *n.* the quality of being ethereal.

ē·thē″rē·ăl·i·zā′tion, *n.* the act or process of etherealizing, or the state of being etherealized.

ē·thē′rē·ăl·īze, *v.t.*; etherealized, *pt., pp.*; etherealizing, *ppr.* 1. to convert into ether; to etherify. [Rare.]

2. to make, or treat as being, ethereal.

ē·thē′rē·ăl·ly, *adv.* in an ethereal manner.

ē·thē′rē·ăl·ness, *n.* the quality of being ethereal.

ē·thē′rē·ous, *a.* composed of ether, or upper regions of space; ethereal.

ē″thẽr·i·fi·çā′tion, *n.* the act or process of forming ether.

ē′thẽr·i·form, *a.* having the form of ether.

ē′thẽr·i·fȳ, *v.t.*; etherified, *pt., pp.*; etherifying, *ppr.* [L. *æther*, ether, and *facere*, to make.] to change (an alcohol) into ether.

ē′thẽr·in, *n.* ethylin. [Obs.]

ē′thẽr·iṣm, *n.* in medicine, the condition resulting from the inhalation of ether as an anesthetic.

ē″thẽr·i·zā′tion, *n.* 1. in medicine, the act or process of administering ether to a patient.

2. the state or condition of the system when subjected to the influence of ether.

ē′thẽr·īze, *v.t.*; etherized, *pt., pp.*; etherizing, *ppr.* 1. to etherify; to convert into ether.

2. to cause to inhale ether fumes so as to make unconscious; to anesthetize with ether.

eth′iç, *n.* [Fr. *éthique*; L. *ethica*; Gr. *ēthikē (technē)*, ethical (art); see *ethical.*] ethics or a system of ethics.

eth′iç, *a.* ethical.

eth′iç·ăl, *a.* [LL. *ethicus*; Gr. *ēthikos*, ethical, moral, from *ēthos*, character, custom, a man's normal state.]

1. having to do with ethics or morality; of or conforming to moral standards.

2. conforming to the standards of conduct of a given profession; as, it is not *ethical* for a judge to hear a case involving his own interests.

ethical dative; in grammar, the dative of a first or second personal pronoun interjected to imply a degree of interest or sympathetic concern.

eth′iç·ăl·ly, *adv.* 1. in an ethical manner.

2. according to ethics.

eth′i·cist, *n.* a student of or an authority or writer upon ethics.

eth′i·cīze, *v.t.*; ethicized, *pt., pp.*; ethicizing, *ppr.* to make, or regard as, ethical.

eth′içs, *n.pl.* 1. [*construed as sing.*] the study of standards of conduct and moral judgment; moral philosophy.

2. [*construed as sing.*] a treatise on this study; a book about morals.

3. the system or code of morals of a particular philosopher, religion, group, profession, etc.

eth′īde, *n.* in chemistry, any binary compound of ethyl.

eth′i·dēne, *n.* ethylidene.

eth′īne, *n.* acetylene.

eth·i·on′iç, *a.* [*ethylene*, and Gr. *theion*, sulfur.] pertaining to a combination of a radical of the ethylene group with a sulfur acid.

ethionic acid; a dibasic acid (ethylene sulfonic acid), found only in aqueous solution.

Ē′thi·op, *n.* and *a.* same as *Ethiopian.*

Ē·thi·ō′pi·ăn, *a.* of Ethiopia, its people, culture, or Semitic language.

Ē·thi·ō′pi·ăn, *n.* 1. a native or inhabitant of Ethiopia.

2. loosely, a Negro.

3. Ethiopic.

Ē·thi·ō′pi·ăn lil′y, the calla lily.

Ē·thi·op′iç, *a.* 1. same as *Ethiopian.*

2. of the Semitic language of the Ethiopians.

Ē·thi·op′iç, *n.* the Semitic language of the Ethiopians. It has a Christian literature and is now used only in the services of the Abyssinian church.

ē′thi·ops, *n.* same as *æthiops.*

eth·mo-, [Gr. *ēthmos*, sieve, from *ēthein*, to strain.] a combining form used in medical and anatomical words to indicate *connection with* or *nearness to the ethmoid bone.*

eth′moid, eth·moid′ăl, *a.* [Gr. *ēthmoeidēs*, from *ēthmos*, strainer, sieve (from *ētheein*, to strain), and *eidos*, form.]

1. like a sieve.

2. designating or of the perforated bone or bones at the front part of the base of the skull, forming part of the septum and walls of the nasal cavity: the olfactory nerves pass through the perforations.

eth′moid, *n.* an ethmoid bone.

eth·mō·tũr′bi·năl, *a.* [*ethmo-*, and L. *turbo (-inis)*, a top.] turbinated or scroll-like; pertaining to the ethmoturbinal.

eth·mō·tũr′bi·năl, *n.* one of the two lateral masses of the ethmoid; the light, spongy bone of which the ethmoid consists for the most part, known as the *superior* and *middle turbinate* bones.

eth′närch, *n.* [Gr. *ethnarchēs*, from *ethnos*, a nation, people, and *archein*, to rule.] the governor of a province or people.

eth′närch·y, *n.* the office or authority of an ethnarch; also, the province under his rule.

eth′niç, *n.* 1. a heathen; a pagan. [Obs.]
2. a member of an ethnic group, especially a member of a minority or nationality group that is part of a larger community.

eth′niç, eth′niç·ăl, *a.* [Fr. *ethnique*; L. *ethnicas*; Gr. *ethnikos*, national, foreign, from *ethnos*, a company, people, nation.]
1. heathen; pagan; pertaining to nations or groups neither Christian nor Jewish.
2. designating or of any of the basic divisions or groups of mankind, as distinguished by customs, characteristics, language, etc.; ethnological.

eth′niç·ăl·ly, *adv.* according to ethnic groups or characteristics.

eth′ni·cişm, *n.* heathenism; paganism. [Obs.]

eth·nic′i·ty, *n.* ethnic classification or affiliation.

eth′nō-, [from Gr. *ethnos*, nation.] a combining form meaning *race, peoples*, as in *ethno*centrism, *ethno*logy: also, before a vowel, *ethn-*.

eth·nō·cen′trişm, *n.* [from *ethno-*, and *center*, and *-ism*.] the emotional attitude that one's own race, nation, or culture is superior to all others.

eth·noġ′e·ny, *n.* [*ethno-* and *-geny*.]
1. that branch of ethnology which deals with the origin of the various races or nations.
2. racial origin.

eth·noġ′rȧ·phēr, *n.* a student of or authority on ethnography.

eth·nō·graph′iç, eth·nō·graph′iç·al, *a.* pertaining to ethnography.

eth·nō·graph′iç·ăl·ly, *adv.* 1. by ethnography.
2. from the viewpoint of ethnography.

eth·noġ′rȧ·phist, *n.* an ethnographer.

eth·noġ′rȧ·phy, *n.* [*ethno-* and *-graphy*.] the branch of anthropology that deals descriptively with specific cultures, especially those of primitive peoples or groups.

eth·nō·loġ′iç·ăl, eth·nō·loġ′iç, *a.* relating to ethnology.

eth·nō·loġ′iç·ăl·ly, *adv.* 1. by ethnology.
2. from the viewpoint of ethnology.

eth·nol′ō·ġist, *n.* a student of or a specialist in ethnology.

eth·nol′ō·ġy, *n.* [*ethno-* and *-logy*.] the branch of anthropology that deals with the comparative cultures of various peoples, including their distribution, folkways, etc.

eth·nō·mū·şi·çol′ō·ġy, *n.* [*ethno-*, and *musicology*.]
1. the study of the music of a particular region and its social and cultural implications.
2. the comparative study of the music of different cultural groups.

eth·ō·loġ′iç, eth·ō·loġ′iç·ăl, *a.* treating of or pertaining to ethics or morality.

ē·thol′ō·ġist, *n.* one who writes on the subject of manners and morality.

ē·thol′ō·ġy, *n.* [L. *ethologia*; Gr. *ēthologia*, a depicting of character; *ēthos*, custom, character, and *logos*, description, from *legein*, to speak.] a treatise on morality; the science of ethics, especially applied ethics.

ē′thos, *n.* [Gr. *ēthos*, an accustomed place or habitation; hence, habit, custom, character.]
1. the characteristic and distinguishing attitudes, habits, etc. of a racial, political, occupational, or other group.
2. the universal or objective elements in a work of art, as distinguished from the emotional or subjective elements: opposed to *pathos*.

eth′yl, *n.* [from *ether* and *-yl*.]
1. the monovalent hydrocarbon radical CH_3CH_2, which forms the base of common alcohol, ether, and many other compounds: symbol, Et, et (no period).
2. (a) tetraethyl lead, $Pb(C_2H_5)_4$, a poisonous, colorless lead compound: a trade-mark (*Ethyl*); (b) any of various gasolines or motor fuels that contain tetraethyl lead to increase power and prevent knocking.

eth′yl, *a.* containing ethyl (sense 1) or tetraethyl lead.

eth′yl al′çō·hol, common alcohol.

eth·yl·am′ine, *n.* a volatile liquid, $C_2H_5 \cdot NH_2$, characterized by an ammoniacal odor.

eth′yl·āte, *v.t.*; ethylated, *pt., pp.*; ethylating, *ppr.* to compound with one or more ethyl groups.

eth′yl·āte, *n.* [*ethyl* and *-ate*.] a compound formed by the replacement of the hydrogen atom in the hydroxyl group of ethyl alcohol by an active metal.

eth′yl·ēne, *n.* [*ethyl* and *-ene*.] a colorless, inflammable, gaseous hydrocarbon of the olefin series, $CH_2{:}CH_2$, with a disagreeable odor: it is obtained from natural or coal gas, by the action of sulfuric acid on alcohol, etc., and is used as a fuel and anesthetic, and in hastening the ripening of fruits: also called *ethene*.
ethylene series; in chemistry, a series of hydrocarbons of which ethylene is the type.

eth′yl·ēne glȳ′çol, the simplest polyhydric alcohol, $OH \cdot CH_2 \cdot CH_2 \cdot OH$.

e·thyl′iç, *a.* containing, relating to, or derived from ethyl.

e·thyl′i·dēne, *n.* a hydrocarbon radical without symmetry of chemical structure, having two units of combining power. It has the same elements as ethylene.

eth′yl·in, *n.* any of the various complex ethers of glycerin and ethyl.

eth′yl ox′īde, diethyl ether.

eth″yl·sul·fū′riç, *a.* containing or relating to ethyl and sulfuric acid.
ethylsulfuric acid; a thick liquid compound of sulfuric acid and alcohol.

ē′ti·ō·lāte, *v.i.*; etiolated, *pt., pp.*; etiolating, *ppr.* [Fr. *etioler*, to blanch, from OFr. *estioler*, to become slender or puny, from *tieule*, tile, from L. *tegula*, a tile, from *tegere*, to cover.
1. to become white or whiter; to be whitened by excluding the light of the sun, as plants.
2. in medicine, to become pale or of a sickly color from sickness or from exclusion of light.

ē′ti·ō·lāte, *v.t.* to blanch; to whiten, as plants, by excluding the sun's rays.

ē′ti·ō·lā·ted, ē′ti·ō·lāte, *a.* blanched; whitened by excluding the sun's rays.

ē·ti·ō·lā′tion, *n.* 1. in gardening, rendering plants white, crisp, and tender, by excluding light from them; also, the condition of a plant so treated.
2. in medicine, paleness or a sickly color caused by disease or exclusion from light.

ē″ti·o·loġ′iç·ăl, *a.* of (an) etiology.

ē″ti·ō·loġ′iç·ăl·ly, *adv.* in an etiological manner.

ē·ti·ol′ō·ġy, *n.*; *pl.* **ē·ti·ol′ō·ġieş,** [LL. *ætiologia*; Gr. *aitologia*, from *aitia*, cause, and *logia*, description.]
1. the assignment of a cause; as, the *etiology* of a folkway.
2. the science of causes or origins.
3. science or theory of the causes or origins of diseases.
Also spelled *aetiology*.

et′i·quette (-ket), *n.* [Fr. *étiquette*, a ticket, label.]
1. the forms, manners, and ceremonies established by convention as acceptable or required in society, in a profession, or in official life.
2. the rules for such forms, manners, and ceremonies.
3. a label. [Rare.]

et′nȧ, *n.* [L. *Ætna*; Gr. *Aitnē*, a volcano in Sicily.] a lamp for heating or vaporizing liquids: it consists of a cup set in a saucer in which alcohol is burned.

Et·nē′ăn, *a.* pertaining to Etna, a volcanic mountain in Sicily: spelled also *Ætnean*.

é·toile′ (ā-twol′), *n.* 1. same as *estoile*.
2. a figure shaped like a star, used in embroidery.

E′tŏn çōat, an Eton jacket.

E′tŏn çol′lăr, 1. a broad, white linen collar worn with an Eton jacket.
2. a collar resembling this.

E·tō′ni·ăn, *a.* of or pertaining to Eton, England, or Eton College, a private preparatory school for boys at Eton.

E·tō′ni·ăn, *n.* one who is or has been a student at Eton College.

E′tŏn jack′et, 1. a boys' short, waist-length jacket with broad lapels, left open in front: worn by students at Eton.
2. a similar jacket, as worn by girls and women.

ETON COLLAR AND JACKET

E·trū′ri·ăn, *a.* and *n.* same as *Etruscan*.

E·trus′căn, *a.* [L. *Etruscus*, Etrurian, from *Etruria*, Etruria.] of Etruria, its people, their language, or culture.

E·trus′căn, *n.* 1. a native or inhabitant of Etruria.
2. the language of the Etruscans.

et sē′quens, [L.] and the following.

et sē·quen′tēş, [L.] and those that follow.

et sē·quen′ti·ȧ (-shi-ȧ), [L.] and those that follow.

-ette, [Fr., fem. of *-et*.] a suffix used to form nouns, meaning (a) *little*, as in dinette, statuette; (b) *female*, as in suffragette; (c) *a substitute for*, as in leatherette.

et′tēr pīke, same as *Adder pike*.

et′tle, *v.t.* to expect; to conjecture; to try. [Dial.]

et′tle, *v.i.* [Scot., from Ice. *ætla*, to think, suppose.]
1. to take aim; hence, to aspire; to be ambitious; to direct one's course. [Dial.]
2. to make an attempt. [Dial.]

et′tle, *n.* intention; aim. [Scot.]

et tū, Brū′te!, and you (too), Brutus!: said to be Julius Caesar's words on seeing his friend Brutus among his assassins: used as a reproachful exclamation implying betrayal.

é′tude (ā′tūd, -tūd′), *n.* [Fr., from L. *studium*, study.]
1. a study.
2. a musical composition for a solo instrument, designed to give practice in some special point of technique, but often performed for its artistic worth.

é·tui′ (ā-twē′), *n.* [Fr.] a small case or box for carrying implements for needlework and toilet articles.

et·wee′, *n.* same as *étui*.

et′ym, *n.* [Rare.] same as *etymon*.

e·tym′iç, *a.* pertaining to the etymon.

et·y·mol′ō·ġēr, *n.* an etymologist.

et″y·mō·loġ′iç·ăl, et″y·mō·loġ′iç, *a.* [LL. *etymologicus*; Gr. *etymologikos*, belonging to etymology, from *etymologia*, etymology.] pertaining to etymology or the derivation of words; according to or by means of etymology.

et″y·mō·loġ′iç·ăl·ly, *adv.* by or according to etymology or its principles.

et″y·mō·loġ′i·çon, *n.* [L., from Gr. *etymologikon*, neut. of *etymologikos*, etymological.] a book in which the etymologies of words are traced; a treatise on the derivation of words.

et·y·mol′ō·ġist, *n.* one versed in etymology; one who studies or teaches the origin or history of words.

et·y·mol′ō·ġīze, *v.t.* and *v.i.*; etymologized, *pt., pp.*; etymologizing, *ppr.* to trace the etymology of; to give the etymology of or to suggest an etymology for (a word or words).

et·y·mol′ō·ġy, *n.*; *pl.* **et·y·mol′ō·ġieş,** [Fr. *étymologie*; L. *etymologia*; Gr. *etymologia*, the true account and analysis of a word; *etymos*, the true literal sense of a word, neut. of *etymos*, true, and *logos*, description, from *legein*, to speak.]
1. the origin and development of a word; tracing a word back as far as possible, generally by the methods of comparative linguistics.
2. an account of this: in this dictionary etymologies are given in brackets following the part-of-speech label.
3. the branch of linguistics that deals with the origin and development of words.
4. in grammar, that division which treats of the various inflections and modifications of words and shows how they are formed from their simple roots.

et′y·mon, *n.* [L. *etymon*; Gr. *etymon*, the true literal sense of a word, etymology, neut. of *etymos*, true.] an original root or primitive word; also, its original signification or root meaning.

ē·typ′iç, ē·typ′iç·ăl, *a.* [L. *e-* priv., and *typus*, a figure, image, from Gr. *typos*, an impression, type, from *typtein*, to beat, strike.] in biology, unconformable to or diverging from the normal type.

eū-, [from Greek *eu-*, well.] a prefix signifying *good, well*, as in *eu*logy: opposed to *dys-*, ill or bad.

Eu, in chemistry, europium.

eū·çāine′, *n.* [from *eu-* and *cocaine*.] either of two synthetic alkaloids, alpha-eucaine, $C_{19}H_{27}NO_4$, and beta-eucaine, $C_{15}H_{21}NO_2$, made from piperidine: their hypochlorides have been used as local anesthetics.

eū·çāi′rīte, *n.* see *eukairite*.

eū′çȧ·lin, eū′çȧ·lyn, *n.* [from *eucalyptus*.] in chemistry, a nonfermentable kind of sirupy substance, obtained by the fermentation of melitose, the sugar of eucalyptus.

eū′cȧ·lypt, *n.* any plant of the genus *Eucalyptus*; a eucalyptus tree.

eū·cȧ·lyp′tē·ōl, *n.* [from *eucalyptus*, and *-ol.*] a crystalline compound made from eucalyptus oil: it is used as an intestinal antiseptic.

eū·cȧ·lyp′tiç, *a.* pertaining to the genus *Eucalyptus* or to any of its species.

eū·cȧ·lyp′tōle, eū·cȧ·lyp′tōl, *n.* [*eucalyptus*, and *-ole, -ol.*] cineole, a liquid found in certain essential oils.

Eū·cȧ·lyp′tus, *n.* [L., from Gr. *eu-*, well, and *kalyptein*, to cover, conceal.]
1. an important genus of subtropical, evergreen trees of the myrtle family, native to and abundant in Australia. Many of the species are valued for their timber or for the gums and oil which they yield.

BRANCH OF EUCALYPTUS TREE

2. [e–] *pl.* **eū·cȧ·lyp′tus·eṣ, eū·cȧ·lyp′tī,** any tree of this genus.

eū·cȧ·lyp′tus oil, an essential oil derived from eucalyptus leaves, used as an antiseptic and disinfectant.

eū·çar′y·ōte, *n.* same as *eukaryote.*

Eū·ceph′ȧ·lȧ, *n.pl.* [L., from Gr. *eu-*, well, and *kephalē*, head.] in entomology, a group of long-legged, slender, two-winged insects, the larvae of which have distinct heads, as crane-flies.

eū·ceph′ȧ·lous, *a.* having a distinct head; specifically, pertaining to the *Eucephala.*

Eū′chȧ·ris, *n.* [L., from Gr. *eucharis*, agreeable; *eu*, well, and *charis*, grace.]
1. in botany, a genus of amaryllidaceous plants found in the mountains of South America, *Eucharis grandiflora* being widely cultivated for its large white flowers.
2. [e–] any plant of this genus.

Eū′chȧ·rist, *n.* [LL. *eucharistia*; Gr. *eucharistia*, thankfulness, gratitude, from *eucharistos*, grateful, thankful; *eu-*, well, and *charizesthai*, to show favor to, from *charis*, favor.]
1. the sacrament of the Lord's Supper; Holy Communion; the sacrifice of the Mass.
2. either or both of the consecrated elements, bread and wine, which are used in the sacrament.
3. [e–] the act of giving solemn thanks. [Obs.]

Eū·chȧ·ris′tiç, Eū·chȧ·ris′tiç·ăl, *a.* 1. [e–] containing expressions of thanks. [Obs.]
2. pertaining to the Eucharist or sacrament of the Lord's Supper.

Eū′çhīte, *n.* [L.Gr. *euchitēs*, from Gr. *euchē*, prayer, from *euchesthai*, to pray.] a member of a sect of Christians which arose in Syria, Mesopotamia, and other eastern countries in the fourth century. They were characterized by their rejection of all sacraments, their ascetic lives, and their dependence upon the presence of the Holy Spirit in answer to prayer.

eū·çhlō′riç, eū′çhlōre, *a.* of a distinct green color: of or pertaining to euchlorine.

eū·chlō′rine, *n.* [Gr. *eu-*, well, and *chlōros*, greenish.] a highly explosive gas obtained by subjecting potassium chlorate to the action of hydrochloric acid: it is locally antiseptic.

eū·çhō·lō′ġi·on, *n.*; *pl.* **eū·çhō·lō′ġi·ȧ,** same as *euchology.*

eū·çhol′o·ġy, *n.*; *pl.* **eū·çhol′ō·ġieṣ,** [L.Gr. *euchologion*, a prayer book; Gr. *euchē*, a prayer, and *logos*, a discourse, from *legein*, to speak.] in the Orthodox Eastern Church, the formulary of prayers; the ritual in which is prescribed the order of ceremonies, sacraments, and ordinances.

eū′çhre (-kẽr), *n.* [etym. unknown; compare G. *juchs*, a joke.]
1. a game of cards for two, three, or four players, played with the thirty-two highest cards of the pack, all the cards below seven except the ace being removed. The highest trump card is the knave, the next the knave of corresponding color, these two being called respectively the right bower and the left bower. Sometimes an additional card, called the joker, is used, which card is then the highest of all.
2. a euchring or being euchred.

eū′çhre, *v.t.*; euchred, *pt., pp.*; euchring, *ppr.*
1. to gain an advantage of two points over (an opponent at euchre) by his failure to take three tricks.
2. to defeat; to outplay; to get the better of; to outwit, as in scheming (often with *out*). [Colloq.]

eū·çhrō′iç, *a.* [Gr. *euchroos*, well-colored; *eu-*, well, and *chroa*, color; see *euchrone.*] designating or of a colorless crystalline acid obtained by heating paramide with an alkali.

eū′çhrō·īte, *n.* in mineralogy, a hydrous arsenate of copper, transparent, brittle, and of a light emerald-green color.

eū′çhrōne, *n.* in chemistry, a dark-blue, soluble substance precipitated by the reduction of euchroic acid.

eū′çhy·my, *n.* [Gr. *euchymia*, goodness of flavor, from *euchymos*, well-flavored; *eu-*, well, and *chymos*, juice.] in medicine, a healthy state of the blood and other fluids of the body. [Obs.]

eū′çlāse, *n.* [from *eu-*, and Gr. *klasis*, a breaking, from *klān*, to break: so named from breaking easily.] a crystalline silicate of aluminum and beryllium, $HBeAlSiO_5$, colored pale green or, sometimes, blue: it is used as a gem.

Eū′çlid, *n.* a treatise on geometry (Euclid's *Elements*) written in the third century B. C. by Euclid, a Greek mathematician; hence, Euclidean geometry.

Eū·çlid′ē·ăn, Eū·çlid′i·ăn, *a.* [L. *Euclides*; Gr. *Eukleidēs*, Euclid.] of Euclid or his geometric principles.

eū′çōne, *a.* [Gr. *eu-*, well, and *kōnos*, a cone.] having crystal cones, as the compound eyes of insects.

Eū·çō·pep′ō·dȧ, *n.pl.* a group of minute entomostracans, including the *Copepoda.*

eū′çrȧ·sy, *n.* [Gr. *eukrasia*, a good mixture or temperature, from *eukratos*, well-tempered; *eu-*, well, and *kerannynai*, to mix.] in medicine, such a due or well-proportioned mixture of qualities in bodies as to constitute health or soundness.

eūç′tiç·ăl, *a.* containing acts of supplication. [Obs.]

eū·dae′mŏn, eū·dē′mŏn, *n.* [Gr. *eudaimōn*, having a good genius, prosperous; *eu-*, well, and *daimōn*, genius, spirit.]
1. a good angel or spirit.
2. in astrology, the eleventh house: so called on account of its signifying favorable happenings.

eū·dae·mō′ni·ȧ, *n.* [Gr. *eudaimonia*, happiness, from *eu-*, good, and *daimōn*, one's demon, fate, soul.] happiness; specifically, in Aristotle's philosophy, happiness, the main universal goal, derived from a life of activity governed by reason.

eū·dae·mon′iç, eū·dae·mon′iç·al, *a.* conducive to happiness.

eū·dae·mon′içs, *n.* same as *eudaemonism.*

eū·dae′mŏn·işm, *n.* [Gr. *eudaimonizein*, to think or call happy, from *eudaimōn*, prosperous, happy.] the doctrine of happiness, or the system of ethics that considers the moral value of actions in terms of their ability to produce happiness.

eū·dae′mŏn·ist, *n.* an adherent of the doctrine of eudemonism.

eū·dae·mŏn·is′tiç, *a.* pertaining to eudemonism.

eū·dī′ȧ·lȳte, *n.* [Gr. *eudialytos*, easy to break up or dissolve; *eu-*, well, easy, and *dialytos*, capable of dissolution, from *dialyein*, to dissolve; *dia*, through, and *lyein*, to loosen.] a mineral of a brownish-red color found in Greenland, and containing lime, soda, and iron in combination with zirconium, silica, tantalum, manganese, and other elements.

eū·di·om′e·tẽr, *n.* [Gr. *eudios*, fine, calm, and *metron*, a measure.]
1. originally, an instrument for measuring the amount of oxygen in the air.
2. an instrument for measuring and analyzing gases.

eū″di·ō·met′riç, eū″di·ō·met′riç·ăl, *a.* pertaining to a eudiometer or to eudiometry; performed or ascertained by a eudiometer; as, *eudiometric* experiments or results.

eū·di·om′e·try, *n.* the analysis of gases by means of a eudiometer.

eū·di·pleū′răl, *a.* [Gr. *eu-*, well, *dis*, two, and *pleura*, side.] in biology, having symmetry in two lateral parts, as the wings of a bird.

Eū′dist, *n.* [Fr. *Eudiste.*] a member of a Roman Catholic missionary order, the Congregation of Jesus and Mary, founded by Jean Eudes, a French priest, in 1643.

Eū·dox′i·ăn, *n.* one of a sect of heretics of the fourth century who were followers of Eudoxius, bishop of Constantinople, an extreme Arian in his views.

eū·em′ẽr·işm, eū·em′ẽr·ist, etc. same as *euhemerism, euhemerist,* etc.

eū′ġē, *interj.* [Gr. *euge*, good!] well done! well said! an exclamation of approval. [Obs.]

eū·ġen′e·sis, *n.* [L., from Gr. *eu-*, well and *genesis*, origin, birth.] in biology, the state or characteristic of being prolific; fertility, especially in the production of hybrid young.

Eū·ġē′ni·ȧ, *n.* [named in honor of Prince *Eugene* of Savoy.] a genus of tropical trees and shrubs of the family *Myrtaceæ.* It contains a large number of species, the most important of which is the allspice or pimento. *Eugenia acris* is the wild clove.

eū·ġen′iç, *a.* of, pertaining to, or derived from cloves.
eugenic acid; same as *eugenol.*

eū·ġen′iç, *a.* [Gr. *eugenēs*, well born; *eu-*, well, and *genos*, race, family.] improving, or relating to the improvement of, the race; relating to the bearing of healthy offspring.

eū·ġen′iç·ăl·ly, *adv.* 1. in a eugenic manner.
2. by or according to eugenics.

eū·ġen′i·cist, *n.* a specialist in or advocate of eugenics.

eū·ġen′içs, *n.pl.* [*construed as sing.*], [Gr. *eugenēs* (see *eugenic*); and *-ics.*] the science that deals with the improvement of races and breeds, especially the human race, through the control of hereditary factors.

eū′ġē·nin, *n.* a substance, $C_{10}H_{12}O_2$, which is an isomer of eugenol.

eū′ġe·nişm, *n.* the collective or combined influences that are best adapted to improve the native qualities of a people.

eū′ġe·nist, *n.* a specialist in eugenics.

eū′ġe·nōl, *n.* [from Mod. L. *Eugenia*, a genus of tropical trees; and *-ol.*] a colorless, aromatic liquid compound, $C_{10}H_{12}O_2$, found in various essential oils, as oil of cloves: it is used as the source of other aromatic compounds and as an antiseptic in dentistry.

eū′ġe·ny, *n.* nobleness of birth. [Obs.]

eūgh (ū), *n.* yew. [Obs.]

Eū·glē′nȧ, *n.* the type genus of the family *Euglenidæ.*

Eū·glen′i·dae, *n.pl.* [L., from Gr. *eu-*, well, and *glēnē*, the pupil of the eye.] a large family of infusorians with brilliant endoplasm, usually green.

eū·glē′noid, *a.* of, pertaining to, or resembling infusorians of the family *Euglenidæ.*

eū·glē′noid, *n.* one of the *Euglenidæ.*

Eū′gū·bine, Eū·gū′bi·ăn, *a.* [It. *Eugubbio*; L. *Iguvium*, a city of Umbria.] of or belonging to ancient Eugubium (now Gubbio), in Italy, or to certain tablets or tables, seven in number, discovered there in 1444.

eū·här·mon′iç, *a.* [Gr. *eu-*, well, and *harmonikos*, harmonic.] producing perfectly concordant sounds, as opposed to sounds produced by tempered instruments.

eū·hem′ẽr·işm, *n.* [L. *Euhemerus*; Gr. *Euēmeros*, a Greek philosopher of the 4th century B. C.] the doctrine that polytheistic mythology arose exclusively, or in the main, out of the deification of dead heroes; the system of mythological interpretation which regards the myths as founded on traditional accounts of real people and events.

eū·hem′ẽr·ist, *n.* one who believes in euhemerism.

eū·hem·ẽr·is′tiç, eū·hem′ẽr·ist, *a.* of or based on euhemerism.

eū·hem·ẽr·is′tiç·ăl·ly, *adv.* after the manner of the euhemerists; rationalistically.

eū·hem′ẽr·īze, *v.t.*; euhemerized, *pt., pp.*; euhemerizing, *ppr.* to treat or explain in the manner of the euhemerists; to treat or explain rationalistically; as, to *euhemerize* a myth, or to explain it as being founded on a basis of history.

eū·hem′ẽr·ize, *v.i.*; euhemerized, *pt., pp.*; euhemerizing, *ppr.* to believe in or practice euhemerism; to treat or explain myths euhemeristically.

eū·kāi′rīte, eū·çāi′rīte, *n.* [named by Berzelius on account of its opportune discovery, from Gr. *eukairos*, timely, opportune; *eu-*, well, and *kairos*, time, season.] a mineral of a shining lead-gray color and granular structure, consisting chiefly of selenium, copper, and silver.

eū·kar′y·ōte, *n.* [Gr. *eu-*, good, and *karyōtis*, a date, from *karyon*, a nut.] an organism made up of cells with true nuclei that divide by mitosis.

eū·kar·y·ot′iç, *a.* of or having to do with eukaryotes.

eū′lȧ·chon, *n.* same as *candlefish*, sense 2.

Eū·lē′ri·ăn, *a.* relating to or formulated by the Swiss mathematician Euler (1707–1783), as *Eulerian* constant, equation, etc.

eū·lō′gi·ȧ, *n.*; *pl.* **eū·lō′gi·ae,** [LL., from Gr. *eulogia*, praise, blessing, eulogy; *eu-*, well, and *legein*, to speak.] in the early church, originally, the Eucharist; later, the part of the elements of the Eucharist sent to the sick, or from one bishop or church to another, as a symbol of Christian love and fellowship; still later, unconsecrated bread not used in the Communion service, but blessed and given as a substitute for the Eucharist to the noncommunicants, as in the Orthodox Eastern Church at the present day. Also called *antidoron*.

eū·log′iç, eū·log′iç·ăl, *a.* eulogistic. [Rare.]

eū·log′iç·ăl·ly, *adv.* eulogistically. [Rare.]

eū′lō·gist, *n.* one who eulogizes.

eū·lō·gis′tiç, eū·lō·gis′tiç·ăl, *a.* of or expressing eulogy; laudatory; commendatory; full of praise.

eū·lō·gis′tiç·ăl·ly, *adv.* in a eulogistic manner.

eū·lō′gi·um, *n.*; *pl.* **eū·lō′gi·ums, eū·lō′gi·ȧ,** same as *eulogy*.

eū′lō·gīze, *v.t.*; eulogized, *pt., pp.*; eulogizing, *ppr.* to praise highly; to compose a eulogy about; to speak or write in commendation of; to extol in speech or writing.

eū′lō·gy, *n.*; *pl.* **eū′lō·gieṣ,** [LL. *eulogia*; Gr. *eulogia*, good or fine language, eulogy, praise; *eu-*, good, and *logos*, discourse, from *legein*, to speak.]

1. a speech or writing in praise of a person, event, or thing; especially, a formal speech or statement praising a dead person.

2. high praise; commendation.

Syn.—encomium, panegyric, tribute.

eū′ly·tīte, eū′ly·tine, *n.* [Gr. *eulytos*, easy to dissolve; *eu-*, well, and *lyein*, to loose, dissolve.] a mineral consisting chiefly of silicate of bismuth.

Eū·men′i·dēṣ, *n.pl.* [L., from Gr. *Eumenidēs*, lit., the gracious ones, from *eumenēs*, well-disposed, gracious; *eu-*, well, and *menos*, mind, temper.] in Greek mythology, the Furies, or Erinyes: so called through fear of offending them.

eū″mẽr·ō·gen′e·sis, *n.* [L., from Gr. *eu-*, well, *meros*, part, and *genesis*, birth, descent.] in biology, that particular kind of generation or development by unit parts, as in the tapeworm, in which each part is a repetition of the one preceding: opposed to *dysmerogenesis*.

eū′mẽr·ō·morph, *n.* [Gr. *eu-*, well, *meros*, part, and *morphē*, shape, form.] an organic form produced by eumerogenesis.

Eū·my·cē′tēṣ, *n.pl.* a class of the Thallophyta, in which are included all the true fungi, as distinguished from seaweeds or algae.

Eū·nō′mi·ăn, *a.* [LL. *Eunomius*; Gr. *Eunomios*, Eunomius.] pertaining to Eunomius or to his teachings.

Eū·nō′mi·ăn, *n.* a disciple of Eunomius, an extreme Arian of the fourth century.

eū′nō·my, *n.* [Gr. *eunomia*, good order, from *eunomos*, well-ordered; *eu-*, well, and *nomos*, law.] equal law, or a well-adjusted constitution of government.

eū′nuçh, *n.* [L. *eunuchus*; Gr. *eunouchos*, a chamberlain, a eunuch; *eunē*, bed, and *echein*, to have, hold.]

1. a castrated man in charge of an Oriental harem or employed as a chamberlain or officer by an Oriental potentate.

2. any castrated man.

eū′nuçh·iṣm, *n.* the state of being a eunuch.

eū′ō·nym, *n.* a good name; a name that is suitable.

eū·on′y·min, *n.* in medicine, a bitter substance derived from the *Euonymus europæus*, or spindle tree, and used as a laxative.

Eū·on′y·mus, *n.* [L., from *euonymos*; Gr. *euōnymos*, the spindle tree, lit., well-named; *eu-*, well, and *onoma*, name.]

1. a genus of shrubs or trees, of the order *Celastraceæ*, containing about fifty species, natives of the temperate regions of the Northern Hemisphere.

2. [e–] the bark of certain species of this genus, used in medicine.

3. [e–] any tree or shrub of this genus. Also spelled *evonymus*.

Eū·or′ni·thēṣ, *n.pl.* [L., from Gr. *eu-*, well, and *ornis* (*ornithos*), a bird.] a division containing all the living kinds of birds except the penguins, the tinamous, and the ratite forms.

eū·oṣ′mīte, *n.* [Gr. *eu-*, well, and *osmē*, a smell.] a brownish-yellow fossil resin which derives its name from the strong, spicy odor it emits when heated.

eū′pȧ·thy, *n.* right feeling. [Obs.]

eū·pat′ō·rine, *n.* an alkaloid obtained from *Eupatorium cannabinum*, or hemp agrimony.

Eū·pȧ·tō′ri·um, *n.* [L. *eupatorium*; Gr. *eupatōrion*, agrimony, from Mithridates *Eupator*, king of Pontus, who first used it as a medicine.]

1. an extensive genus of perennial herbs, chiefly natives of America, of the family *Compositæ*.

2. any plant of this genus, including the mistflower, joe-pye weed, snakeroot, boneset, etc.

eū′pȧ·tō·ry, *n.* a plant of the genus *Eupatorium*.

eū·pat′rid (*or* ū′pȧ-trid), *n.*; *pl.* **eū·pat′ri·dae, eū·pat′ridṣ,** [Gr. *eupatridēs*, from *eu-*, well, good, and *pater*, father.] [*also* E–] any of the hereditary aristocrats of ancient Athens and other Greek states, who were the lawmakers and administrators.

eū′pȧ·trid, *a.* of the eupatridae.

eū·pep′si·ȧ, eū·pep′sy, *n.* [L., from Gr. *eupeptos*, easy of digestion; *eu-*, well, and *peptein*, *pessein*, to digest.] good digestion.

eū·pep′tiç, *a.* 1. of or having good digestion: opposed to *dyspeptic*.

2. aiding digestion.

eū′phē·miṣm, *n.* [Gr. *euphēmismos*, the use of an auspicious word for an inauspicious one, from *euphēmizein*, to use a good or auspicious word for an evil or inauspicious, from *euphēmos*, of good sound or omen; *eu-*, good, and *phēmē*, voice, from *phanai*, to speak.]

1. the use of a word or phrase that is less expressive or direct but considered less distasteful, less offensive, etc. than another.

2. a word or phrase so substituted; as, "she is at rest" is a *euphemism* for "she is dead."

eū′phē·mist, *n.* a user of euphemisms.

eū·phē·mis′tiç, eū·phē·mis′tiç·ăl, *a.* of, containing, having the nature of, or intended as euphemism.

eū·phē·mis′tiç·ăl·ly, *adv.* in a euphemistic manner; by euphemism.

eū′phē·mīze, *v.t.* and *v.i.*; euphemized, *pt., pp.*; euphemizing, *ppr.* [Gr. *euphēmizein*, to use an auspicious for an inauspicious word.] to speak or write of (something) euphemistically.

eū·phō′nē, *n.* [Gr. *euphōnos*, sweet-voiced, musical; *eu-*, good, and *phōnē*, voice.] in organ building, a stop producing a peculiarly sweet and subdued tone.

eū·phon′iç, eū·phon′iç·ăl, *a.* 1. of euphony.

2. euphonious.

eū·phō′ni·ous, *a.* characterized by euphony; having a pleasant sound; harmonious.

eū·phō′ni·ous·ly, *adv.* with euphony; harmoniously.

eū′phō·niṣm, *n.* an agreeable sound or combination of sounds.

eū·phō′ni·um, *n.* [Mod. L., from Gr. *euphōnos*, sweet-voiced, musical.] a brass-wind instrument, now rarely used, resembling the tuba but having a slightly higher range and more mellow tone.

eū′phō·nīze, *v.t.*; euphonized, *pt., pp.*; euphonizing, *ppr.* to make euphonious.

eū′phō·non, *n.* a musical instrument resembling the upright piano in form.

eū′phō·nous, *a.* euphonious. [Rare.]

eū′phō·ny, *n.*; *pl.* **eū′phō·nieṣ,** [LL. *euphonia*; Gr. *euphōnia*, goodness of voice, from *euphōnos*, sweet-voiced, musical; *eu-*, well, and *phōnē*, voice.]

1. the quality of having a pleasing sound; the pleasant effect of a combination of agreeable sounds, as in speech or music.

2. in phonetics, the tendency to make pronunciation easier, as by assimilation, dissimilation, etc., resulting from normal causes of sound change and not from an attempt at pleasanter sound, as formerly believed.

Eū·phor′bi·ȧ, *n.* [L., from Gr. *euphorbion*, an African plant, named from *Euphorbos*, Euphorbus, physician to the king of Mauretania.]

1. a large genus of cactuslike plants of the family *Euphorbiaceæ*, with a thick, milky juice.

2. [e–] any plant of this genus, including the poinsettia, etc.; any of the spurges.

Eū·phor·bi·ā′cē·ae, *n.pl.* an important family of plants, consisting of herbs, shrubs, or very large trees, occurring in all regions of the globe except the arctic. They have an acrid milky juice, and some are poisonous, though the roots of others abound in starch.

eū·phor·bi·ā′ceous, eū·phor′bi·ăl, *a.* of, relating to, or resembling the *Euphorbiaceæ*.

eū·phor′bi·um, *n.* [Gr. *euphorbion*, euphorbium, said to be from *Euphorbus*, physician to Juba, king of Mauretania.] the juice of several species of *Euphorbia*, either exuding naturally or from incisions made in the bark. It is a powerful acrid substance, violently purgative and emetic.

eū·phō′ri·ȧ, eū′phō·ry, *n.* [Mod. L., from Gr. *euphoria*, the power of bearing easily, from *euphoros*, bearing well; *eu-*, well, and *pherein*, to bear.] a feeling of well-being; especially, in psychology, an abnormal feeling of buoyant vigor and health.

eū·phor′iç, *a.* of or characterized by euphoria.

eū·phō′tide, *n.* [Fr. *euphotide*, from Gr. *eu-*, well, and *phōs*, *phōtos*, light.] in mineralogy, a coarse-grained variety of gabbro.

Eū·phrā′si·ȧ, *n.* [L., from Gr. *euphrasia*, delight, good cheer, from *euphrainein*, to delight, cheer; *eu-*, well, and *phrēn*, mind.] a small genus of herbs, of the order *Scrophulariaceæ*, natives of temperate regions.

eū′phrȧ·sy, *n.* the eyebright, *Euphrasia officinalis*.

eū′phrōe, *n.* [from D. *juffrouw*, lit., young woman, from *jong*, young, and *vrouw*, woman.] a long, perforated, cylindrical block to fasten and tighten the ropes supporting an awning on shipboard, a tent, etc.: also spelled *uphroe*.

Eū·phros′y·nē, *n.* [L.; Gr. *Euphrosynē*, from *euphrōn*, cheerful.] in Greek mythology, Joy, one of the three Graces.

eū′phū·iṣm, *n.* [from *Euphues*, a fictitious character in John Lyly's works, from Gr. *euphyēs*, shapely, graceful; *eu-*, well, and *phyē*, growth, from *phyein*, to grow.]

1. the artificial, affected, high-flown style of speaking or writing used by John Lyly and his imitators, characterized by alliteration, balanced sentences, antithesis, farfetched figures of speech, etc.

2. any artificial, high-flown style of speech or writing.

3. an instance of this.

eū′phū·ist, *n.* one who uses euphuism: applied particularly to a class of writers in the age of Elizabeth I, who were noted for their unnatural and high-flown diction.

eū·phū·ist′iç, eū·phū·ist′iç·ăl, *a.* 1. having the nature of euphuism; high-flown, affected, etc.

2. characterized by euphuism.

eū′phū·īze, *v.i.*; euphuized, *pt., pp.*; euphuizing, *ppr.* to speak or write in a euphuistic manner. [Rare.]

eū·pī′on, eū·pī′ōne, *n.* [Gr. *eupiōn*, very fat; *eu-*, well, and *piōn*, fat.] in chemistry, a fragrant, colorless, highly volatile liquid, obtained by the destructive distillation of bones, wood, coal, etc. [Now Rare.]

eū·pit′tōne, *n.* [*eu-*, and *pittacal*, and *-one*.] in chemistry, a yellow crystalline substance, resembling aurin and obtained from the oil of wood tar: also called *eupittonic acid*.

eū·plas′tiç, *a.* [*eu-* and *-plastic*.] in physiology, easily formed into or adapted to the formation of tissue.

eū·plas′tiç, *n.* a euplastic material.

Eū·pleç·tel′lȧ, *n.* a genus typical of the *Euplectellidæ*; *Euplectella aspergillum* is the glass sponge known as Venus's-flower-basket.

Eū·pleç·tel′li·dae, *n.pl.* [L., from Gr. *euplektos*, well-plaited; *eu-*, well, and *plektos*, plaited, from *plekein*, to plait.] a family of siliceous sponges having six-rayed spicules; the glass sponges.

Eū·plex·op′te·rȧ, *n.pl.* [L., from Gr. *eu-*, well, *plekein*, to twist, and *pteron*, a wing.] in entomology, an order of orthopterous insects, varying from the type of their group, having short anterior wings, under which the posterior ones fold. It includes the *Forficulidæ* or *earwigs*.

fāte, fär, fȧst, fąll, finăl, cãre, at; mēte, prẹy, hẽr, met; pīne, marine, bīrd, pin; nōte, mȯve, fọr, atŏm, not; mọọn, book;

eūp·nē′ȧ, eūp·noe′ȧ, *n.* [Mod. L., from Gr. *eu-*, well, and *pnoiē*, breath, from *pnein*, to breathe.] normal respiration: opposed to *dyspnea.*

eū·pyr′i·on, *n.* [L., from Gr. *eu-*, well, and *pyr, pyros*, fire.] any contrivance by which a light may be instantly obtained, as an ordinary match. [Obs.]

Eū·raf′ri·căn, Eū·raf′riç, *a.* [*Europe* and *Africa.*] designating the close physical relation between the continent of Europe and northern Africa: used in geology, biology, ethnology, physiography, etc.: as, a *Eurafric* type of animal or plant; *Eurafrican* climatic conditions, etc.: also called *Mediterranean.*

Eū·raq′ui·lō (-rak′wi-), *n.* same as *Euroclydon.*

Eū·rā′siăn, *a.* 1. of Eurasia.
2. of mixed European and Asiatic descent.

Eū·rā′siăn, *n.* 1. a person of mixed European and Asiatic descent.
2. a member of a people of both Europe and Asia.

Eū·rā·si·at′iç (-shi-), *a.* of Eurasia; Eurasian.

eū·rē′kȧ, *interj.* [Gr., I have found (it), 1st pers. perf. ind. act. of *heuriskein*, to find, discover.]
1. I have found (it): exclamation supposedly uttered by Archimedes when he discovered a way to determine the purity of gold by applying the principle of specific gravity.
2. any exclamation of triumphant achievement, equivalent to "I've got it!"

eū·rhyth′miç, *a.* same as *eurythmic.*

eū·rhyth′miç·ăl, *a.* same as *eurythmical.*

eū·rhyth′miçs, *n.pl.* [*construed as sing.*] same as *eurythmics.*

eū·rhyth′my, *n.* same as *eurythmy.*

eū·rī′pus, *n.*; *pl.* **eū·rī′pī,** [L., from Gr. *euripos*, a strait of the sea where the tide is violent; *eu-*, well, and *rhipē*, a rushing motion, from *rhipein*, to rush.]
1. [E—] a channel between the island of Euboea and Boeotia in Greece, noted for the violent and unpredictable flow of water in both directions.
2. any strait or channel with such a current or tide.

eū′rīte, *n.* [Fr. *eurite*, from Gr. *eurys*, wide.] feldspathic granite, of which feldspar is the principal ingredient; felsite.

Eū′rō·bond, *n.* a corporate bond issued at a fixed rate of interest on an international, usually European, market and repayable in the currency of issue.

Eū·roç′ly·don, *n.* [Gr. *Euroklydōn*; *Euros*, the east wind, and *klydōn*, a wave, billow, from *klyzein*, to dash against. *Euryklydōn* is another reading for *eurykylōn*, a northeast wind.
1. in the Bible, a stormy, northeast wind of the Mediterranean, mentioned in the account of Paul's voyage to Rome: Acts xxvii. 14.
2. any stormy wind.

Eū′rō·dol′lärș, *n.pl.* dollars of the United States circulated among European banks and lending institutions, usually in short-term financing.

Eū·rō′pȧ, *n.* [L.; Gr. *Eurōpē.*] in Greek mythology, a Phoenician princess loved by Zeus: taking on the form of a white bull, he carried her off across the sea to Crete.

Eū·rō·pē′ăn, *a.* of, pertaining to, or connected with Europe, its people, their culture, etc.
European plan; a method of hotel operation in which guests pay a set price per day for lodging and service only, meals being taken à la carte at the hotel restaurant or wherever the guests may choose: distinguished from *American plan.*

Eū·rō·pē′ăn, *n.* a native or inhabitant of Europe.

Eū·rō·pē′ăn·īze, *v.t.*; Europeanized, *pt., pp.*; Europeanizing, *ppr.* to cause to become European, as in habits, dress, culture, scope, etc.

Eū·rō·pē′ō-Ā·si·at′iç (-shi-at′ik), *a.* in phytogeography, Eurasian; palearctic.

eū·rō′pi·um, *n.* [Mod. L., from *Europe*, and *-ium.*] a chemical element of the rare-earth group: symbol, Eu; atomic weight, 151.96; atomic number, 63.

Eū′rus, *n.* [L., from Gr. *Euros*, the east or east-southeast wind.] in Greek mythology, the east wind or the god of the east wind.

eū′ry-, [from Gr. *eurys*, broad.] a combining form, used in scientific terms, meaning *broad, wide*, as in *eury*cephalic.

Eū·ry̆′ȧ·lē, *n.* [*eury-*, and Gr. *halōs*, a threshing floor, a round area.]
1. in botany, a genus of water lilies of India and China, with one species, *Euryale ferox*, the seeds of which are edible.
2. in zoology, the type genus of the *Euryalidæ.*

Eū·ry·al′i·dae, *n.pl.* a family of brittle stars or sand stars, of the class *Ophiuroidea*, having branching rays.

eū″ry·ce·phal′iç, eū·ry·ceph′ȧ·lous, *a.* [*eury-*, and Gr. *kephalē*, head.] in ethnology, having a broad head.

eū·ryc′ĕr·ous, *a.* [*eury-*, and Gr. *keras*, a horn.] broad-horned.

Eū·ryd′i·cē, *n.* [L.; Gr. *Eurydikē.*] in Greek legend, the wife of Orpheus: after she died, he got permission to bring her back from Hades, but she had to return there when Orpheus broke his agreement with Pluto by turning to see whether she was following him.

eū·ryg′nȧ·thous, *a.* [*eury-*, and Gr. *gnathos*, the jaw.] in ethnology, characterized by a broad upper jaw.

eū·ryp′tĕr·id, *n.* any fossil crustacean belonging to the family *Eurypteridæ.*

Eū·ryp·ter′i·dae, *n.pl.* [*eury-*, and Gr. *pteron*, wing.] a family of fossil crustaceans, subclass *Merostomata*, closely allied to the king-crabs. They abounded in the Silurian and Devonian Periods of the Paleozoic Era.

eū·ryp′tĕr·oid, *a.* pertaining to or resembling the *Eurypterus.*

eū·ryp′tĕr·oid, *n.* any species of *Eurypterus.*

Eū·ryp′te·rus, *n.* the type genus of the *Eurypteridæ.*

eū·ryth′miç, eū·rhyth′mic, *a.* 1. characterized by perfect proportion and harmony, or by movement in rhythm.
2. of eurythmics.

eū·ryth′miç·ăl, eū·rhyth′miç·ăl, *a.* same as *eurythmic.*

eū·ryth′miçs, eū·rhyth′miçs, *n.pl.* [*construed as sing.*] the art of performing various bodily movements in rhythm, usually to musical accompaniment.

eū·ryth′my, eū·rhyth′my, *n.* [Gr. *eurythmia*, harmony, from *eurythmos*, rhythmical; *eu-*, well, and *rhythmos*, rhythm.]
1. proportion or motion characterized by harmony.
2. in medicine, the regular beating of the pulse.

Eū·sē′bi·ăn, *a.* of or pertaining to Eusebius, a bishop of Nicomedia in the fourth century, or to his doctrines, which were Arian.

Eū·sē′bi·ăn, *n.* a follower of Eusebius.

eū·spō·ran′ġi·āte, *a.* [Gr. *eu-*, well, *spora*, a seed, and *angeion*, a vessel, receptacle.] having the spore cases produced by a group of cells instead of by a single cell, as certain ferns.

Eū·stā′chi·ăn, *a.* of, pertaining to, or discovered by Eustachio, a famous Italian anatomist and physician of the sixteenth century.
Eustachian catheter; see under *catheter.*
Eustachian tube; a slender tube between the middle ear and the pharynx, which serves to equalize air pressure on both sides of the eardrum.

Eū·stā′thi·ăn, *a.* of or pertaining to Eustathius, an orthodox bishop of Antioch.

Eū·stā′thi·ăn, *n.* 1. one of an orthodox faction in Antioch which, in the fourth century, supported Eustathius, bishop of Antioch, when an attempt was made to replace him by an Arian.
2. one of a sect of the fourth century who lived an ascetic life, following the example of Eustathius, bishop of Sebaste in Pontus.

eū·stat′iç, *a.* [*eu-*, and *static.*] of or pertaining to changes in sea level throughout the world, as because of extensive formation or melting of icecaps.

eū·stō′mȧ·tȧ, *n.pl.* [L., from Gr. *eu-*, well, and *stoma*, mouth.] a division of *Infusoria*, having a well-developed oral aperture, a body less plastic than that of most infusorians, and not more than two flagella.

eū·stom′ȧ·tous, *a.* having a well-developed mouth; specifically, resembling the *Eustomata.*

eū′stȳle, *n.* [Gr. *eustylos*, having goodly pillars; *eu-*, well, and *stylos*, a column, pillar.] same as *intercolumniation.*

eū′tax·y, *n.* [Gr. *eutaxia*, good arrangement.] good or proper arrangement or order.

eū·teç′tiç, *a.* [Gr. *eutēktos*, melting readily; *eu-*, well, and *tēkein*, to melt, fuse.] fusing at the lowest possible temperature.

eū·teç′tiç, *n.* an alloy with a melting point lower than that of any other combination of the same components.

eū·teç′toid, *a.* like a eutectic.

eū·teç′toid, *n.* an alloy like a eutectic, as pearlite.

Eū·tĕr′pē, *n.* [Gr. *Euterpē*, one of the Muses, from *euterpēs*, delightful, charming; *eu-*, well, and *terpein*, to delight, charm.]
1. in Greek mythology, the Muse of music and lyric poetry. She is usually represented with a flute in her hand or with various musical instruments about her.
2. in botany, a genus of South American palms having slender cylindrical stems crowned by a tuft of pinnate leaves, the leaflets narrow, regular, and close together. One of the chief species is the *Euterpe edulis*, or assai palm.

EUTERPE

Eū·tĕr′pē·ăn, *a.* relating to Euterpe; hence, pertaining to music.

eū·tex′i·ȧ, *n.* [L., from Gr. *eutēxia*, being easily melted; *eu-*, well, and *tēkein*, to melt.] the art or process of finding eutectic alloys; also, the quality of melting readily.

eū·thȧ·nā′și·ȧ, *n.* [L., from Gr. *euthanasia*, a painless, happy death; *eu-*, well, and *thanatos*, death.]
1. an easy and painless death; a peaceful manner of dying.
The kindest wish of my friends is *euthanasia.*
—Arbuthnot.
2. act or method of causing death painlessly, so as to end suffering: advocated by some as a way to deal with victims of incurable diseases.

eū·then′içs, *n.pl.* [*construed as sing.*] the science and art of improving races and breeds, especially the human race, through the control of external influences and conditions of environment.

Eū·thy·neū′rȧ, *n.pl.* [L., from Gr. *euthys*, straight, and *neuron*, nerve.] an extensive division of gastropod mollusks having straight visceral nerve loops.

eū·thy·tat′iç, *a.* [L., from Gr. *euthys*, straight, and *tasis*, a stretching, tension, from *teinein*, to stretch.] in physics, pertaining to or characterized by direct or longitudinal stress. [Rare.]

eū′tŏ·ny, *n.* agreeableness or harmony of sound.

eū·troph′iç, *a.* [Gr. *eutrophos*, nourishing; *eu-*, well, and *trephein*, to nourish.] pertaining to or aiding nutrition.

eū·troph′iç, *n.* any agent that promotes nutrition.

eū′trō·phy, *n.* [Gr. *eutrophia*, good nurture, from *eutrophos*, nourishing.] in medicine, healthful nutrition.

eū·trop′iç, *a.* [Gr. *eutropos*, easily turning; *eu-*, well, and *trepein*, to turn.] turning with the sun: said of climbing plants, etc.

Eū·tyçh′i·ăn, *a.* of or pertaining to Eutyches or to his religious doctrines.

Eū·tyçh′i·ăn, *n.* a follower of Eutyches, a monk of Constantinople in the fifth century, who held that the divine and human natures of Christ, after their union, became so blended together as to constitute but one nature.

Eū·tyçh′i·ăn·ism, *n.* the doctrine of Eutyches.

eūx′e·nīte, *n.* [Gr. *euxenos*, hospitable, friendly; *eu-*, well, and *xenos*, a guest, friend.] a brilliant, brownish-black mineral containing yttrium, columbium, uranium, titanium, erbium, and cerium.

ē·vaç′ū·ănt, *a.* [L. *evacuans* (*-antis*), ppr. of *evacuare*, to empty out, evacuate.] causing evacuation, especially of the bowels or stomach; cathartic or emetic.

ē·vaç′ū·ănt, *n.* an evacuant medicine; cathartic or emetic.

ē·vaç′ū·āte, *v.t.*, evacuated, *pt., pp.*; evacuating, *ppr.* [L. *evacuatus*, pp. of *evacuare*, to empty out, purge; *e-*, out, and *vacuare*, to make empty, from *vacuus*, empty.]
1. to make empty; remove the contents of.
2. to discharge (excrement, etc.); void; emit.
3. to move or remove; send away.
4. to give up military occupation of; withdraw from.
5. to make void; to nullify; as, to *evacuate* a marriage or any contract. [Obs.]

ē·vaç′ū·āte, *v.i.* 1. to withdraw, as from a besieged town.
2. to discharge bodily waste, especially feces.

ē·vaç·ū·ā′tion, *n.* 1. an evacuating or being evacuated.
2. in medicine, (a) an emptying or discharging of waste matter, as from the bowels,

urinary bladder, etc.; (b) matter so discharged.

3. a withdrawal of troops from a fortified place, or of civilians from an inhabited area.

ē·vaç′ū·ā·tive, *a.* tending to evacuate.

ē·vaç′ū·ā·tŏr, *n.* one who or that which evacuates.

ē·vaç·ū·ee′, *n.* one who has been evacuated from an area of danger; specifically, one who has been forced to leave an occupied area in time of war.

ē·vād′ȧ·ble, ē·vād′i·ble, *a.* capable of being evaded.

ē·vāde′, *v.i.*; evaded, *pt., pp.*; evading, *ppr.* [Fr. *évader*; L. *evadere*, to pass beyond, escape; *e-*, out, from, and *vadere*, to go.]

1. to escape; get away. [Rare.]

2. to use evasion; be deceitful or clever in avoiding or escaping.

ē·vāde′, *v.t.* 1. to avoid or escape from by deceit or cleverness; keep out of the way of; elude.

2. to avoid doing or answering directly; get around; get out of.

ē·vād′i·ble, *a.* same as *evadable*.

ev·ȧ·gā′tion, *n.* [L. *evagatio* (*-onis*), from *evagari*, to wander forth; *e-*, from, and *vagari*, to wander.] the act of wandering; excursion; a roving or rambling. [Rare.]

ē·vag′i·nȧ·ble, *a.* capable of being evaginated.

ē·vag′i·nāte, *v.t.* and *v.i.*; evaginated, *pt., pp.*; evaginating, *ppr.* [LL. *evaginatus*, pp. of *evaginare*, to unsheath; L. *e-*, from, and *vagina*, a sheath.]

1. to evert; to turn inside out.

2. to protrude by eversion.

ē·vag′i·nāte, *a.* evaginated; protruded.

ē·vag·i·nā′tion, *n.* 1. an evaginating or being evaginated.

2. an evaginated part.

ē′văl, *a.* relating to time or an age. [Obs.]

ē·val′ū·āte, *v.t.*; evaluated, *pt., pp.*; evaluating, *ppr.* [Fr. *évaluer*, to value; L. *e-*, from, and *valere*, to be strong, to be worth.]

1. to determine the worth of; to find the amount or value of; to appraise.

2. in mathematics, to determine the numerical value of; to express in numbers.

ē·val·ū·ā′tion, *n.* 1. an evaluating or being evaluated.

2. valuation.

ev·ȧ·nesce′, *v.i.*; evanesced (-nest′), *pt., pp.*; evanescing, *ppr.* [L. *evanescere*, to vanish away; *e-*, out, and *vanescere*, to vanish.] to disappear; to vanish away; to fade away gradually.

ev·ȧ·nes′cence, *n.* 1. a vanishing; the act of fading away; a gradual departure from sight or possession, either by removal to a distance or by dissipation, as vapor.

2. a tendency to fade from sight; transitoriness.

ev·ȧ·nes′cent, *a.* [L. *evanescens* (*-entis*), ppr. of *evanescere*, to vanish away.] vanishing; fleeting; passing away; liable to dissipation, like vapor; as, the pleasures and joys of life are *evanescent*.

The difference between right and wrong, in some petty cases, is almost *evanescent*.
—Wollaston.

ev·ȧ·nes′cent·ly, *adv.* in an evanescent manner.

ē·van′gel, *n.* [ME. *evangile*; OFr. *evangile*; LL. *evangelium*, the gospel; New Testament Gr. *euangelion*, good news, the gospel, from Gr. *euangelos*, bringing good news; *eu-*, well, and *angelos*, a messenger.]

1. the Gospel or [E–], any one of the four Gospels.

2. good tidings.

3. an evangelist.

ē·van·ġel′i·ăn, *a.* rendering thanks for receiving good news. [Rare.]

ē·van·ġel′iç, *a.* same as *evangelical*.

ē·van·ġel′iç·ăl, *a.* [LL. *evangelicus*, from Gr. *euangelikos*, of or for the gospel or glad tidings, from *euangelion*, the gospel, good tidings; *eu-*, well, and *angelos*, a messenger.]

1. contained in the Gospels, or first four books of the New Testament; as, *evangelical* history.

2. of those Protestant churches, as the Methodist and Baptist, that emphasize the salvation by faith in the atonement of Jesus, and reject the efficacy of the sacraments and good works alone: also called *orthodox*.

3. of the Low Church party in the Church of England.

4. evangelistic.

Evangelical Alliance; an association of evangelical Christians belonging to various churches and countries, formed in 1846 to concentrate the strength of Protestantism.

Evangelical Union; a religious sect founded in Scotland in 1843 by the Rev. James Morison of Kilmarnock.

ē·van·ġel′iç·ăl, *n.* one who belongs to an evangelical church.

ē·van·ġel′iç·ăl·işm, *n.* adherence to evangelical doctrines; also, such doctrines.

ē·van·ġel′iç·ăl·ly, *adv.* in an evangelical manner.

ē·van·ġel′iç·ăl·ness, *n.* the state of being evangelical.

ē·van·ġel′i·cişm, *n.* evangelicalism.

ē·van·ġe·lic′i·ty, *n.* the quality of being evangelical; evangelicism.

ē·van′ġel·işm, *n.* 1. a preaching of, or zealous effort to spread, the Gospel, as in revival meetings.

2. the work of an evangelist.

3. evangelicalism.

ē·van′ġel·ist, *n.* [ME. *evangeliste*; OFr. *evangeliste*; New Testament Gr. *euangelistēs*, a preacher of the gospel, one of the writers of the Gospels, from *euangelizesthai*, to preach the gospel, from Gr. *eu-*, well, and *angelos*, a messenger.]

1. [E–] any of the four writers of the Gospels; Matthew, Mark, Luke, or John.

2. a preacher of the Gospel, especially a traveling preacher; a revivalist; a missionary.

3. in the Mormon Church, a patriarch.

ē·van·ġel·is′tȧ·ry, *n.* a selection of passages from the Gospels; specifically, a book containing such passages, used in the Orthodox Eastern and Roman Catholic churches.

ē·van·ġel·is′tiç, *a.* pertaining to an evangelist or any of the Evangelists; also, evangelical.

ē·van·ġel·is′ti·căl·ly, *adv.* in an evangelistic manner; by or according to evangelism.

ē·van″ġel·i·zā′tion, *n.* the act of evangelizing or the state of being evangelized.

ē·van′ġel·ize, *v.t.*; evangelized, *pt., pp.*; evangelizing, *ppr.* [ME. *evangelizen*; OFr. *evangelizer*; LL. *evangelizare*; New Testament Gr. *euangelizesthai*, to preach the gospel, from Gr. *eu-*, good, and *angelos*, a messenger.] to instruct in the Gospel; to preach the Gospel to; also, to convert to Christianity.

ē·van′ġel·ize, *v.i.* to preach the gospel; to act as an evangelist.

ē·van′ġel·y, *n.* good tidings. [Obs.]

ē·van′ġile, *n.* same as *evangel*.

ē·van′id, *a.* faint; weak; evanescent; liable to vanish or disappear; as, an *evanid* color or smell. [Obs.]

Ev·ȧ·nī′i·dae, *n.pl.* [L., from Gr. *euanios*, bearing trouble easily; *eu-*, well, and *ania*, trouble.] a family of parasitic insects belonging to the order *Hymenoptera*.

ē·van′ish, *v.i.* [L. *evanescere*, to vanish.] to vanish; to disappear; to escape from sight or perception. [Poet.]

ē·van′ish·ment, *n.* a vanishing; disappearance. [Poet.]

ē·vap″ō·rȧ·bil′i·ty, *n.* the quality of being evaporable.

ē·vap′ō·rȧ·ble, *a.* capable of being evaporated.

ē·vap′ō·rāte, *v.i.*; evaporated, *pt., pp.*; evaporating, *ppr.* [L. *evaporatus*, pp. of *evaporare*, to disperse in vapor; *e-*, from, and *vaporare*, to emit vapor, from *vapor*, vapor.]

1. to pass off in vapor, as a fluid; to become vapor; to change from a liquid to a gaseous condition.

2. to give off vapor.

3. to disappear like vapor; to vanish, as, the spirit of a writer often *evaporates* in translating.

ē·vap′ō·rāte, *v.t.* 1. to change or convert from a solid or liquid state into a vapor; to cause to pass into a gaseous state or condition; to vaporize.

2. to remove moisture from (milk, vegetables, fruits, etc.) by heating or drying so as to get a concentrated product.

ē·vap′ō·rāte, *a.* evaporated. [Rare.]

ē·vap′ō·rāt·ed milk, canned, unsweetened milk thickened by evaporation: distinguished from *condensed milk*.

ē·vap·ō·rā′tion, *n.* [L. *evaporatio* (*-onis*), evaporation, from *evaporatus*, pp. of *evaporare*, to evaporate.]

1. the act or process of converting or being converted from a solid or liquid state into a vapor or gas.

2. the act or process of concentrating or drying by removing moisture; as, the *evaporation* of fruit.

3. the result or product of evaporating.

ē·vap′ō·rā·tive, *a.* pertaining to or producing evaporation.

ē·vap′ō·rā·tŏr, *n.* anything used for evaporating; specifically, an apparatus for removing the moisture from food.

ē·vap·ō·rom′e·tēr, *n.* [L. *evaporare*, to evaporate, and *metron*, a measure.] an instrument for determining the quantity of a fluid evaporated in a given time; an atmometer.

ē·vā′si·ble, *a.* evadable.

ē·vā′şion, *n.* [L. *evasio* (*-onis*), from *evasus*, pp. of *evadere*, to evade; *e-*, from, and *vadere*, to go.]

1. an avoiding of a duty, question, fact, etc. by deceit or cleverness.

2. the means of doing this; excuse; subterfuge; equivocation; artifice.

Thou by *evasions* thy crime uncoverest more.
—Milton.

Syn.—sophistry, subterfuge, prevarication, equivocation, artifice.

ē·vā′sive, *a.* 1. tending or seeking to evade; using evasion or artifice to avoid; equivocating; as, he is too *evasive*.

2. containing evasion; artfully contrived to elude; elusive; as, an *evasive* answer.

ē·vā′sive·ly, *adv.* in an evasive manner; elusively.

ē·vā′sive·ness, *n.* the quality or state of being evasive.

Eve, *n.* [ME.; AS. *Efe*, LL. *Eva*, *Heva*; Heb. *hawwāh*, lit., perhaps, life.] in the Bible, Adam's wife, the first woman: Gen. iii. 20.

ēve, *n.* [ME. *even*, *eve*; AS. *æven*, eve.]

1. evening. [Poet.]

Winter, oft, at *eve* resumes the breeze.
—Thomson.

2. the evening or day before a holiday; as, Christmas *eve*.

3. the period just preceding some event; as, the *eve* of a battle.

ēve′chŭrr, *n.* the nightjar or goatsucker, *Caprimulgus europæus*.

ē·veç′tion, *n.* [L. *evectio* (*-onis*), a carrying away or out, from *evectus*, pp. of *evehere*, to carry out; *e-*, out, from, and *vehere*, to carry.]

1. a carrying out or away; also, a lifting up; exaltation. [Obs.]

2. in astronomy, a periodical inequality in the movements of the moon in its orbit, caused by the attraction of the sun.

ē′ven, *n.* evening. [Poet. or Dial.]

ē′ven, *a.* [ME. *even*, *evin*; AS. *efen*, even, smooth.]

1. level; smooth; flat; not rough or waving; as, an *even* tract of land; an *even* surface.

2. tranquil; serene; placid; calm; not easily ruffled or disturbed; as, an *even* temper.

3. level (*with*); parallel to; in the same place or line; as, *even with* the floor.

4. equally balanced; as, both sides were *even*.

5. capable of being divided into two equal parts without a remainder· opposed to *odd*; as, 4, 6, 8, 10 are *even* numbers.

6. whole; exact; as, five dollars *even*.

7. equal or identical in number, quantity, degree, etc.

8. not irregular; not varying; uniform; constant; as, an *even* tempo.

9. owing and being owed nothing.

10. revenged for a wrong, insult, etc.

11. just; equitable; fair; as, an *even* exchange.

12. pure; flawless. [Obs.]

13. clear; plain. [Obs.]

on an even keel; in the position of the keel of a ship when it draws the same water abaft as forward, or when it is upright or not inclined to either side.

Syn.—equal, level, plain, smooth, uniform.

ē′ven, *v.t.*; evened, *pt., pp.*; evening, *ppr.* [ME. *evenen*, *efnen*; AS. *efnian*, to make even, to compare, from *efen*, adj. even.]

1. to make even or level; to level; to lay smooth.

2. to balance, as accounts.

3. to liken; to compare; to use as an equal. [Obs.]

ē′ven, *v.i.* to be equal.

ē′ven, *adv.* [ME. *even*; AS. *efne*, even, exactly, quite, from *efen*, even, used as an adjective.]

1. *used as an intensive or emphatic particle* (a) *emphasizing the limit of what is possible or probable*: though it may seem improbable; moreover; indeed; fully; as, *even* unto death, *even* a fool could understand; (b) *emphasizing precise correspondence*: exactly; precisely; just; in no other way but; as, it happened *even* as I expected; (c) *emphasizing coincidence, concurrence, or simultaneity*: just as; while; as, *even* as he spoke, I left; (d) *emphasizing a comparison*: still; yet; as, his error

was *even* worse; (e) [Archaic.] *emphasizing identity*: namely; particularly; as, one there was, *even* John.
2. in a smooth manner; showing regularity; evenly; as, the soldiers marched *even*. [Obs.]
3. in an even manner. [Obs.]
even if; though; despite the fact that.
ē·vēne′, *v.i.* to happen. [Obs.]
ē′ven·ēr, *n.* 1. one who or that which evens.
2. an equalizer in the form of a lever to govern the power applied: commonly applied to a doubletree.
3. in weaving, an appliance to spread the yarn on the beam.
ē′ven·fall, *n.* the first part of the evening; twilight. [Poet.]
ē′ven·hand, *n.* equality of rank. [Obs.]
ē′ven·hand″ed, *a.* impartial; equitable; just.
ē′ven·hand″ed·ly, *adv.* in an evenhanded manner.
ē′ven·hand″ed·ness, *n.* the state of being evenhanded.
ē′ven·ing, *n.* [ME. *evening*; AS. *æfnung*, evening, from *æfen*, even, eve.]
1. the last part of the day; close of the day and early part of night; period between sunset or the last meal of the day and bedtime.
2. in some parts of the South, in rural areas, and in parts of England, the period from noon through sunset and twilight.
3. a part of the night spent in a specified way; as, a musical *evening*.
4. the decline or latter part of anything; as, the *evening* of power; the *evening* of life.
ē′ven·ing, *a.* in, for, or of the evening.
ē′ven·ing dress (or **clōthes**), formal clothes worn on formal occasions in the evening and at night.
ē′ven·ing flow′ēr, in botany, any plant of the genus *Hesperantha*, common to South Africa, characterized by fragrant flowers which open in the evening.
ē′ven·ing gown, a woman's evening dress, usually long and décolleté.
ē′ven·ing grōs′bēak, a night-singing bird, *Coccothraustes vespertina*, common in North America.
ē′ven·ing prāyer (prâr), same as *evensong*.
ē′ven·ing prim′rōse, an erect, biennial herb, *Œnothera biennis*, having yellow or white flowers opening in the evening.
ē′ven·ing stär, a bright planet, usually Venus, that can be seen in the western sky soon after sunset: also called *Vesper*, *Hesperus*.
ē′ven·ly, *adv.* [ME. *evenly*, *evenliche*; AS. *efenlice*, evenly.]
1. with an even, level, or smooth surface; without roughness, elevations, or depressions; as, things *evenly* spread.
2. equally; uniformly; as, *evenly* balanced.
3. in a level position; horizontally.
4. impartially; without bias.
ē′ven-mind″ed, *a.* characterized by evenness of temper or equanimity.
ē′ven·ness, *n.* [ME. *evennes*; AS. *efennys*, evenness, equality, from *efen*, even.] the state or quality of being even.
ē′ven·sọng, *n.* 1. a song or hymn to be sung in the evening.
2. in the Church of England, a form of worship to be said or sung in the evening; evening prayer.
3. in the Roman Catholic Church, vespers.
4. evening. [Archaic.]
ē·vent′, *n.* [L. *eventus*, *eventum*, an event, occurrence, from *evenire*, to happen; *e-*, out, and *venire*, to come.]
1. that which comes, arrives, or happens, especially an incident of importance; as, the course of *events*.
2. a consequence, a result; an outcome.
3 any one of a series of contests or items in a program; as, the automobile race is the next *event*.
Syn.—incident, occurrence, issue, result, consequence.
ē·vent′, *v.i.* to happen. [Obs.]
ē′ven-tem″pēred (-pērd), *a.* not quickly angered or excited; placid; calm.
ē·ven′tēr·āte, *v.t.*, to rip open; to disembowel. [Obs.]
ē·vent′fụl, *a.* 1. full of outstanding events or incidents; as, an *eventful* period of history.
2. having an important outcome; momentous; as, an *eventful* conversation.
Syn.—important, critical, stirring, notable.
ē′ven·tīde, *n.* evening. [Archaic or Poet.]
ē·ven′ti·lāte, *v.t.* 1. to winnow; to fan. [Obs.]
2. to discuss. [Obs.]
ē·ven·ti·lā′tion, *n.* 1. the act of fanning; ventilation. [Obs.]
2. discussion. [Obs.]
ē·vent′less, *a.* lacking events or excitement; monotonous; uninteresting.
Ēv·en·tog′nȧ·thī, *n.pl.* [L., from Gr. *eu-*, well, *entos*, within, and *gnathos*, the jaw.] a group of teleost fishes found in fresh water, including the carps, chubs, etc.
ēv·en·tog′nȧ·thous, *a.* of or pertaining to the *Eventognathi*.
ē·ven·trā′tion, *n.* [L. *e-*, out, from, and *venter* (*-tris*), the belly.] in pathology, (a) evisceration; (b) the escape or protrusion of part of the viscera through a rupture in the abdominal wall.
ē·ven′tū·ăl, *a.* [L. *eventus*, an event.]
1. coming or happening as a consequence or result of anything; final; ultimate; as, *eventual* victory.
2. contingent; depending on future events or conditions.
ē·ven·tū·al′i·ty, *n.*; *pl.* **ē·ven·tū·al′i·tieṣ**, 1. a possible event, outcome, or condition; contingency; as, we must be ready for any *eventualities*.
2. in phrenology, the faculty of remembering the sequence of occurrences or events.
ē·ven′tū·ăl·ly, *adv.* in the end; finally; ultimately.
ē·ven′tū·āte, *v.i.*; eventuated, *pt.*, *pp.*; eventuating, *ppr.* [L. *eventus*, event, and *-ate*.] to happen in the end; to result (often with *in*).
ē·ven·tū·ā′tion, *n.* the act or condition of eventuating.
ev′ēr, *adv.* [ME. *ever*, *evere*; AS. *æfre*, ever.]
1. at any time; at any period or point of time; as, have you *ever* seen the city of Paris, or shall you *ever* see it?
2. at all times; always; continually; as, *ever* fair.
3. repeatedly.
4. at all; by any chance; in any case; as, if it *ever* starts, we can go.
Ever is also used colloquially as an intensifier; as, was she *ever* tired!
ever and anon; at one time and another; now and then. [Archaic.]
ever so; extremely; very; as, *ever so* good. [Colloq.]
for ever and a day; forever.
or ever; before; as, *or ever* the silver cord be loosed. [Archaic.]
ev″ēr-dūr′ing, *a.* enduring forever; everlasting.
ev′ēr·glāde, *n.* a region of low, spongy land, usually flooded with water and covered with tall grass; swampland.
ev′ēr·green, *a.* having green leaves throughout the year; as, the pine is an *evergreen* tree: opposed to *deciduous*.
ev′ēr·green, *n.* 1 a plant that retains its leaves through all the seasons, as the conifers, holly, etc.
2. [*pl.*] the twigs and branches of any evergreen species, used for ornamentation.

EVERGREEN TREE

ev′ēr·ich, *a.* every. [Obs.]
ev″ēr·ich·ōn′, *pron.* every one. [Obs.]
ev·ēr·lȧst′ing, *a.* 1. lasting forever; eternal; immortal.
2. perpetual; continuing indefinitely or during the present state of things; durable; as, the *everlasting* hills.
3. going on too long; seeming never to stop; tiresome; as, *everlasting* disputes.
ev·ēr·lȧst′ing, *n.* 1. eternity.
2. any of various plants, from the permanence of the color and form of their dry flowers, as cudweeds, immortelles, etc.
3. a stout, ribbed woolen cloth; lasting.
the Everlasting; God.
ev·ēr·lȧst′ing·ly, *adv.* 1. in an everlasting manner.
2. very; excessively. [Colloq.]
ev·ēr·lȧst′ing·ness, *n.* the state of being everlasting.
ev·ēr·liv′ing, *a.* living without end; eternal.
ev·ēr·mōre′, *adv.* always; eternally; at all times; as, happy *evermore*: used also as a substantive, as, for *evermore*.
Ē·vēr′ni·ȧ, *n.* [L., from Gr. *euernēs*, sprouting well; *eu-*, well, and *ernos*, a sprout.] a small genus of lichens.
ē·vērse′, *v.t.* to overthrow or subvert. [Obs.]
ē·vēr′si·ble, *a.* that can be everted.
ē·vēr′sion, *n.* [L. *eversio* (*-onis*), an overthrowing, from *eversus*, pp. of *evertere*, to overthrow.]
1. an overthrowing; destruction. [Obs.]
2. a turning or rolling backward or inside out.
eversion of the eyelids; ectropion, a condition in which the eyelids are turned outward, so as to expose the red internal tunic.
ē·vēr′sive, *a.* designed or tending to evert; subversive. [Obs.]
ē·vērt′, *v.t.* [L. *evertere*, to overthrow; *e-*, out, from, and *vertere*, to turn.]
1. to overturn; to overthrow. [Obs.]
2. to cause to turn inside out.
ē·vēr′tē·brăl, *a.* [L. *e-* priv., and *vertebra*, vertebra.] not vertebral in origin or character, as the anterior portion of the skull.
Ē·vēr·tē·brā′tȧ, *n.pl.* same as *invertebrata*.
ē·vēr′tē·brāte, *a* and *n.* same as *invertebrate*.
ē·vēr′tŏr, *n.* a muscle that everts a part, especially the foot.
ev′ēr·y, *a.* [ME. *every*, *everi*; AS. *æfre ælc*.]
1. all, as of the items or individuals constituting an aggregate, considered separately; each, taken as part of an aggregate.
2. all possible; as, he was given *every* chance to do the job.
3. each interval of (a specified number or time); as, he arrives *every* three days.
every bit; in all points; fully; quite; as, that is *every bit* as good.
every each; every one. [Obs.]
every now and then; from time to time; now and then.
every other; each alternate; as, *every other* Saturday was a holiday.
ev′ēr·y, *pron.* each; everyone. [Obs.]
ev′ēr·y·bod″y, *n.* every person; everyone.
ev′ēr·y·dāy, *a.* 1 daily; as, one's *everyday* routine.
2. suitable for every ordinary day; as, *everyday* shoes.
3. usual; common; as, an *everyday* occurrence.
ev′ēr·y·one (-wun), *pron.* everybody; every person.
ev′ēr·y one, 1. everyone.
2. every person or thing.
ev′ēr·y·thing, *n.* 1. every thing; all things; all; as, *everything* in human life is interesting.
2. all things pertinent.
3. that which is of the greatest value or importance; as, a good reputation is *everything* to a woman.
ev′ēr·y·when, *adv.* at every point in time; always.
ev′ēr·y·where (-hwâr), *adv.* [ME. *everihwar*, everywhere, *ever*, *evere*, ever, and *ihwar*, everywhere, from AS. *gehwær*, everywhere.] in every place; in all places.
ev′ēr·y·where″ness, *n.* omnipresence. [Rare.]
ev′ēr·y·whith″ēr, *adv.* in or to every place or direction. [Rare.]
ē·ves′ti·gāte, *v.t.* to investigate. [Obs.]
ev′et, *n.* [AS. *efete*, a newt.] an eft; a newt.
ē·vi′brāte, *v.i.* to vibrate. [Obs.]
ē·viçt′, *v.t.*; evicted, *pt.*, *pp.*; evicting, *ppr.* [L. *evictus*, pp. of *evincere*, to overcome, prevail; *e-*, from, and *vincere*, to conquer.]
1. to put (a tenant) out by a judicial process or course of legal proceedings; to expel from lands or tenements by law.
2. in law, formerly, to recover (property) through court judgment or superior claim.
3. to convince; to prove. [Obs.]
4. to expel by force.
ē·viç′tion, *n.* [LL. *evictio* (*-onis*), from L. *evictus*, pp. of *evincere*, to evict.]
1. the act of evicting or the condition of being evicted.
2. proof; conclusive evidence. [Obs.]
ev′i·dence, *n.* [ME. *evidence*; OFr. *evidence*, evidence; L. *evidentia*, clearness, from *evidens* (*-entis*), clear, evident; *e-*, from, and *videre*, to see.]
1. the condition of being evident.
2. something that makes another thing evident; indication; sign.
3. something that tends to prove; ground for belief.
4. in law, (a) something legally presented before a court, as a statement of a witness, an object, etc., which bears on or establishes the point in question: distinguished from *testimony* and *proof*; (b) a person who presents testimony; witness; as, state's *evidence*.
in evidence; plain; visible; conspicuous; as, his nose was very much *in evidence*.
king's or *queen's evidence*; in English law, state's evidence.

state's evidence; (a) the evidence offered by the state in prosecuting criminal cases; (b) a person who gives testimony against accomplices in a crime of which he himself is guilty.

Syn.—proof, witness, testimony, affirmation, demonstration, certainty.

ev'i·dence, *v.t.*; evidenced (-denst), *pt., pp.*; evidencing, *ppr.* 1. to indicate; to make clear.

2. to support by testimony; to attest.

ev'i·den·cẽr, *n.* a witness. [Obs.]

ev'i·dent, *a.* [ME. *evident*; OFr. *evident*; L. *evidens* (-*entis*), visible, clear; *e-*, out, and *videre*, to see.] plain; easy to see or perceive; apparent; as, the guilt of an offender cannot always be made *evident*.

Syn.—plain, visible, conspicuous, manifest, obvious, clear, palpable, apparent, discernible.

ev·i·den'tiăl (-shăl), *a.* 1. of the nature of, or affording, evidence.

2. of, serving as, or based on evidence.

ev·i·den'tiăl·ly, *adv.* in an evidential manner.

ev·i·den'ti·ă·ry (-shi-) *a.* same as *evidential*.

ev'i·dent·ly, *adv.* in an evident manner; clearly; obviously; plainly; manifestly.

ev'i·dent·ness, *n.* the state or quality of being evident.

ē·vig'i·lāte, *v.i.* to watch attentively. [Obs.]

ē·vig·i·lā'tion, *n.* a waking or watching. [Obs.]

ē'vil, *a.* [ME. *evel*; AS. *yfel*, evil.]

1. having bad moral qualities; sinful; bad; wicked; corrupt; perverse; as, *evil* thoughts; *evil* deeds.

2. causing pain or trouble; harmful; injurious.

3. threatening or bringing misfortune; unlucky; disastrous; unfortunate; as, an *evil* hour.

4. caused by or considered as being caused by immorality; as, an *evil* name; *evil* fame.

the evil eye; a supposed power superstitiously ascribed in former times to certain persons, by means of which they could injure whomever they looked at.

the Evil One; the *Devil*.

Syn.—mischievous, pernicious, injurious, hurtful, destructive, noxious, baneful, baleful, wicked, bad, corrupt, perverse, vile, base, wrong, vicious, calamitous.

ē'vil, *n.* [ME. *evel*; AS. *yfel*, evil.]

1. anything that causes displeasure, injury, pain, suffering, etc.

2. moral depravity; wickedness; anything morally bad or wrong.

3. king's evil, a skin disease. [Obs.]

the social evil; prostitution.

ē'vil, *adv.* [ME. *evill*; AS. *yfele*, in an evil manner.] not well; ill; in an evil manner; unfortunately; injuriously; unkindly.

ē'vil·dö''ẽr, *n.* one who does evil.

ē'vil-dö''ing, ē'vil·dö''ing, *n.* a doing of evil.

ē'vil eye (ī), the supposed power of harming others by merely looking at them, superstitiously attributed to some people.

ē'vil-eyed (-īd), *a.* possessing or believed to possess the evil eye; also, looking with envy, jealousy, or hostility.

ē'vil-fā''vŏred, *a.* having a bad countenance or appearance; ill-favored.

ē'vil-fā''vŏred·ness, *n.* the state of being evil-favored.

ē'vil·ly, *adv.* in an evil manner.

ē'vil-mīnd'ed, *a.* having an evil mind or disposition; specifically, (a) malicious; wicked; (b) putting an evil interpretation on innocent things; salacious; prurient.

ē'vil-mīnd'ed·ness, *n.* the state or quality of being evil-minded.

ē'vil·ness, *n.* the state or quality of being evil.

ē·vince', *v.t.*; evinced (-vinst'), *pt., pp.*; evincing, *ppr.* [L. *evincere*, to conquer, overcome; *e-*, from, out, and *vincere*, to conquer.]

1. to show in a clear manner; to indicate; to manifest; to make evident; especially, to show that one has (a quality, feeling, etc.); as, to evince a desire; to *evince* stupidity.

2. to conquer; to overcome. [Obs.]

ē·vince'ment, *n.* the act of evincing. [Rare.]

ē·vin'ci·ble, *a.* capable of being evinced; demonstrable.

ē·vin'ci·bly, *adv.* in an evincible manner.

ē·vin'cive, *a.* tending or having the power to evince.

ē'vi·rāte, *v.t.* to emasculate. [Obs.]

ev·i·rā'tion, *n.* castration. [Obs.]

ē·vis'cẽr·āte, *v.t.*; eviscerated, *pt., pp.*; eviscerating, *ppr.* [L. *evisceratus*, pp. of *eviscerare*, to deprive of the entrails.]

1. to disembowel; to take out the entrails of.

2. to deprive of an essential part; to take away the force, significance, etc. of.

ē·vis·cẽr·ā'tion, *n.* the act of eviscerating or the state of being eviscerated.

ev'i·tȧ·ble, *a.* [L. *evitabilis*, avoidable, from *evitare*, to shun, avoid.] capable of being avoided; avoidable.

ev'i·tāte, *v.t.* to avoid. [Obs.]

ev·i·tā'tion, *n.* an avoiding. [Obs.]

ē·vīte', *v.t.* to shun; to avoid. [Archaic.]

ev·i·tẽr'năl, *a.* enduring forever; eternal. [Obs.]

ev·i·tẽr'năl·ly, *adv.* eternally. [Obs.]

ev·i·tẽr'ni·ty, *n.* eternity. [Obs.]

ē·vit'tāte, *a.* [L. *e-* priv., and *vitta*, a band, fillet.] in botany, having no vittae, as the fruit of certain plants.

ev'ō·çȧ·ble, *a.* that can be called forth.

ev'ō·çāte, *v.t.*; evocated, *pt., pp.*; evocating, *ppr.* to evoke; to call forth. [Rare.]

ev·ō·çā'tion, *n.* [L. *evocatio* (-*onis*), a calling out or forth, from *evocatus*, pp. of *evocare*, to call out or forth.]

1. a calling forth; an evoking; a summons.

2. in civil law, the removal of a case from a lower to a higher court.

ē·vō'çȧ·tive (*or* ē-vok'ȧ-), *a.* evoking or tending to evoke.

ev'ō·çā·tŏr, *n.* [L.] one who evokes.

ē·vōke', *v.t.*; evoked (-vōkt'), *pt., pp.*; evoking, *ppr.* [L. *evocare*, to call forth, summon; *e-*, out, from, and *vocare*, to call.]

1. to call forth; to summon; to bring out; to elicit, as a response, etc.

2. to call from one tribunal to another. [Rare.]

ev·ō·lat'iç, ev·ō·lat'iç·ăl, *a.* apt to fly away. [Obs.]

ev·ō·lā'tion, *n.* the act of flying away. [Obs.]

ev'ō·lūte, *n.* [L. *evolutus*, pp. of *evolvere*, to unroll, unfold; *e-*, out, from, and *volvere*, to roll.] in geometry, a curve that is either the locus of the center of curvature of another curve (called the *involute*), or the envelope of the perpendiculars, or normals, of the involute.

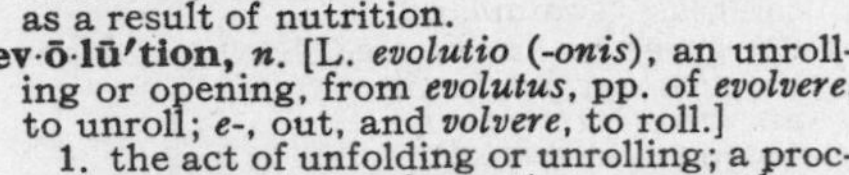

EVOLUTE
ABC, evolute of ADC

ev''ō·lū·til'i·ty, *n.* in biology, the capability of an organism to exhibit change in structure, size, etc. as a result of nutrition.

ev·ō·lū'tion, *n.* [L. *evolutio* (-*onis*), an unrolling or opening, from *evolutus*, pp. of *evolvere*, to unroll; *e-*, out, and *volvere*, to roll.]

1. the act of unfolding or unrolling; a process of development, formation, or growth.

2. a thing or series of things unrolled, unfolded, or evolved; as, the *evolution* of ages.

3. in mathematics, (a) the unfolding or opening of a curve, making it describe an involute; (b) the extraction of the root from a given power: the reverse of *involution*.

4. a change of position, especially in accordance with some definite plan; specifically, (a) in military usage, the doubling of ranks or files, wheeling, countermarching, or other motion by which the disposition of troops is changed; (b) in naval usage, the change of form and disposition of a fleet or the movements of a single vessel during maneuvers.

5. (a) a movement that is part of a series or pattern; (b) a pattern produced, or seemingly produced, by such a series of movements; as, the *evolutions* of a fancy skater.

6. a setting free; giving off; emission or disengaging.

7. in biology, (a) the development of a species, organism, or organ from its original or rudimentary state to its present or completed state; phylogeny or ontogeny; (b) the obsolete theory that the germ cell contains the fully developed individual in miniature form; the theory of preformation; (c) the theory, now generally accepted, that all species of plants and animals developed from earlier forms by hereditary transmission of slight variations in successive generations.

ev·ō·lū'tion·ăl, *a.* same as *evolutionary*.

ev·ō·lū'tion·ȧ·ry, *a.* 1. pertaining to evolution; developmental.

2. in accordance with the theory of evolution.

3. of or by evolutions.

ev·ō·lū'tion·işm, *n.* the theory of evolution.

ev·ō·lū'tion·ist, *n.* 1. a person who believes in the theory of evolution.

2. a person who believes in the possibility of political and social progress by gradual, peaceful steps.

ev·ō·lū'tion·ist, *a.* 1. of the theory of evolution.

2. of evolutionists.

ē·volve', *v.t.*; evolved, *pt., pp.*; evolving, *ppr.* [L. *evolvere*, to roll out or forth; *e-*, out, and *volvere*, to roll.]

1. to unfold; to open out; to work out; to develop gradually.

2. to set free or give off (gas, heat, etc.); to emit or disengage.

3. to produce or change by evolution.

ē·volve', *v.i.* to develop gradually; to reach a highly developed state by a process of growth and change.

2. to unfold; to become disclosed.

ē·volve'ment, *n.* the act of evolving or the state of being evolved.

ē·volv'ent, *n.* [L. *evolvens* (-*entis*), ppr. of *evolvere*, to evolve.] in mathematics, an involute.

ē·vom'it, *v.t.* to vomit. [Obs.]

ev·ō·mi'tion (-mish'un), *n.* the act of vomiting. [Obs.]

ev·on'y·mus, *n.* same as *euonymus*.

ē·vul'gāte, *v.t.* to publish. [Obs.]

ē·vul·gā'tion, *n.* a divulging. [Obs.]

ē·vul'sion, *n.* [L. *evulsio* (-*onis*), from *evulsus*, pp. of *evellere*, to pull or pluck out.] the act of plucking or pulling out by force.

ew (ū), *n.* yew. [Obs.]

ewe (ū), *n.* [ME. *ewe*; AS. *eowu*, a flock of sheep.] a female sheep.

ewe'-neck'' (ū'nek''), *n.* a thin neck, not arched, as that of some horses.

ewe'-necked'' (ū'nekt''), *a.* having a ewe-neck.

ew'ẽr, *n.* [ME. *ewer*; OFr. *ewere*, a water carrier, a water pitcher, from LL. *aquaria*, a water pitcher, from L. *aquarius*, for water, from *aqua*, water.] a kind of pitcher with a wide spout, especially one used with a basin on washstands.

ew'ẽr·y, *n.* [ME. *ewery*, from OFr. *ewere*, a water pitcher.] formerly, a room where table linen and towels were kept and water placed in ewers for use in the household.

ewt, *n.* a newt. [Obs.]

ex, *prep.* [L.] in business and finance, (a) without; exclusive of; as, *ex* dividend, *ex* interest; (b) out of; free of: *ex warehouse* means "free of charges until removed from the warehouse."

ex, *n.*; *pl.* **ex'eş,** 1. the letter X, x.

2. something shaped like an X.

ex- (*or* egz), [from L. *ex*, Gr. *ex*, out, from.]

1. a prefix meaning: (a) *forth, from, out*, as in *ex*pel, *ex*ert, *ex*coriate; (b) *beyond*, as in *ex*cess; (c) *away from, out of*, as in *ex*propriate, *ex*patriate; (d) *thoroughly*, as in *ex*terminate; (e) *upward*, as in *ex*alt; (f) *without, not having*, as in *ex*animate. It appears as *ef-* before *f*, as in *ef*face; *e-* before *b, d, g, h, l, m, n, r*, and *v*, as in *e*duce, *e*gress, *e*lect, *e*mit, etc.; often *ec-*, before *c* or *s*, as in *ec*centric, *ec*stasy; and in many words of French origin, *es-*, as in *es*cape.

2. [orig. from L. phrases like *ex consule, ex magistro*.] a prefix meaning *former, previous, previously*, used to form hyphenated compounds with nouns denoting position, rank, occupation, status, etc., as in *ex*-president, *ex*-convict, etc.

ex-, exo-.

ex·ac'ẽr·bāte (egz-), *v.t.*; exacerbated, *pt., pp.* exacerbating, *ppr.* [L. *exacerbatus*, pp. of *exacerbare*, to exasperate, make angry; *ex-* intens., and *acerbus*, bitter, harsh, sour.]

1. to irritate; to exasperate; to annoy; to embitter.

2. to make more intense or sharp; to aggravate (disease, pain, annoyance, etc.).

ex·ac·ẽr·bā'tion, *n.* [LL. *exacerbatio* (-*onis*), from L. *exacerbatus*, pp. of *exacerbare*, to irritate; *ex-* intens., and *acerbus*, bitter.]

1. the act of exacerbating or the state of being exacerbated.

2. intensification or aggravation, as of a disease, pain, etc.

ex·ac·ẽr·bes'cence (egz-), *n.* exacerbation. [Obs.]

ex·ac·ẽr·vā'tion, *n.* the act of heaping up. [Obs.]

ex·ac'i·nāte (egz-), *v.t.* [L. *ex-* priv., and *acinus*, a berry, the seed of a berry.] to remove a kernel from. [Rare.]

ex·ac·i·nā'tion, *n.* the act of taking out the kernel. [Rare.]

ex·act' (egz-), *a.* [L. *exactus*, precise, accurate, from pp. of *exigere*, to drive out, to measure, determine.]

1. correct; accurate; precise; correctly adjusted; not differing in the least from a stand-

ard; true; actual; as, an *exact* representation; the *exact* time; the *exact* amount; that was the *exact* statement.

2. methodical; careful; not negligent; observing strict method, rule, or order; punctual; as, a man *exact* in business affairs; he is *exact* in keeping an appointment.

3. characterized by exactness; definite; precisely thought out or stated; as, an *exact* demonstration.

We took as *exact* a survey as we could. —Maundrell.

4. strict; severe; rigorous; as, an *exact* disciplinarian.

Syn.—accurate, correct, careful, methodical, precise, nice.

ex·act′, *v.t.*; exacted, *pt.*, *pp.*; exacting, *ppr.* [OFr. *exacter*; LL. *exactare*, freq. of L. *exigere*, to drive out or from, to demand, measure, examine; *ex*, out, from, and *agere*, to drive.]

1. to force or compel to be paid; to extort (with *from* or *of*).

2. to demand and get by authority or force; to insist on (with *from* or *of*).

3. to require; call for; make necessary.

Syn.—demand, enforce, enjoin, extort.

ex·act′, *v.i.* to practice exaction. [Obs.]

ex·ac′tȧ, *n.* [from Am. Sp. *quiniela*, *exacta*; *quiniela*, a form of betting on horse races, in which one wins by picking the first two finishers, in whichever order they finish, and *exacta*, exact.] same as *perfecta*.

ex·act′ẽr, *n.* one who exacts.

ex·act′ing, *a.* 1. unreasonably severe in requirements; oppressive; characterized by exaction; as, an *exacting* master.

2. demanding great care, patience, effort, etc.; arduous; as, *exacting* duties, an *exacting* occupation.

ex·act′ing·ly, *adv.* in an exacting manner.

ex·act′ing·ness, *n.* the quality of being exacting.

ex·ac′tion, *n.* [L. *exactio* (*-onis*), a driving out, expelling, a tax, tribute, from *exactus*, pp. of *exigere*, to drive out, demand, exact.]

1. an exacting, as of strength, money, time, etc.; the act of demanding with authority and compelling to pay or yield; a levying or drawing from by force; a driving to compliance; as, the *exaction* of tribute or of obedience.

2. an excessive demand; extortion.

3. that which is exacted; an enforced fee, tax, etc.

ex·act′i·tūde, *n.* [Fr. *exactitude*, from L. *exactus*, exact.] the quality of being exact; exactness; accuracy.

ex·act′ly, *adv.* in an exact manner; correctly; accurately; precisely; strictly: also used as an affirmative reply, equivalent to "I agree," "quite true."

ex·act′ness, *n.* the quality or condition of being exact.

ex·act′ŏr, *n.* [ME. *exactour*; L. *exactor*, a driver out, expeller, from *exactus*, pp. of *exigere*, to drive out.] one who exacts; demands.

ex·ag′ġẽr·āte (egz-), *v.t.*; exaggerated, *pt.*, *pp.*; exaggerating, *ppr.* [L. *exaggeratus*, pp. of *exaggerare*, to heap up, increase, exaggerate; *ex*, out, up, and *aggerare*, to heap up, from *agger*, a heap, mound.]

1. to heap on; to accumulate. [Obs.]

2. to enlarge beyond the truth; to represent (something) as greater than it is; to magnify beyond the fact; to overstate; as, to *exaggerate* a story.

3. to increase or enlarge to an abnormal degree; overemphasize; intensify.

Syn.—amplify, enlarge, heighten, magnify, overstate, stretch.

ex·ag′ġẽr·āte, *v.i.* to practice exaggeration; to amplify beyond fact in thought or description.

ex·ag′ġẽr·ā·ted, *a.* enlarged beyond the truth; unduly magnified.

ex·ag′ġẽr·ā·ted·ly, *adv.* to an exaggerated degree.

ex·ag′ġẽr·ā·ting·ly, *adv.* in an exaggerated manner.

ex·ag·ġẽr·ā′tion, *n.* 1. a heaping together; heap; accumulation. [Obs.]

2. the act of exaggerating or the state of being exaggerated; a representation of things beyond the truth; hyperbolical representation.

3. a thing that is exaggerated; especially, an overstatement or hyperbole.

ex·ag′ġẽr·ȧ·tive, *a.* inclined to exaggerate; characterized by exaggeration.

ex·ag′ġẽr·ȧ·tive·ly, *adv.* in an exaggerative manner.

ex·ag′ġẽr·ā·tŏr, *n.* [LL. *exaggerator*, from L. *exaggerare*, to heap up, increase, enlarge.] one who or that which exaggerates.

ex·ag′ġẽr·ȧ·tō·ry, *a.* containing exaggeration.

ex·ag′i·tāte (egz-), *v.t.* to shake violently; to agitate. [Obs.]

ex·ag·i·tā′tion (egz-), *n.* agitation. [Obs.]

ex·ā′lāte, *a.* [L. *ex-* priv., and *alatus*, winged, from *ala*, a wing.] in botany, without wings.

ex·al·bū′mi·nōse, *a.* exalbuminous.

ex·al·bū′mi·nous, *a.* [L. *ex-* priv., and *albumen*, albumen, from *albus*, white.] in botany, without albumen: said of seeds.

ex·ạlt′ (egz-), *v.t.*; exalted, *pt.*, *pp.*; exalting, *ppr.* [OFr. *exalter*; L. *exaltare*, to lift up, raise, exalt; *ex*, out, up, and *altus*, high.]

1. to raise high; to elevate: now archaic in the physical sense.

Exalt thy towery head. —Pope.

2. to elevate in power, wealth, rank, or dignity; to promote; as, to *exalt* one to a high position.

3. to elevate with joy, pride, or confidence; to elate.

4. to elevate in estimation and praise; to magnify; to praise; to extol.

Exalt ye the Lord. —Ps. xcix. 5.

5. to heighten or intensify the effect of (colors, etc.).

6. in alchemy, to purify; to refine. [Obs.]

Syn.—elevate, heighten, raise, promote, extol, magnify.

ex′ạl·tāte (eks′), *a.* exalted. [Obs.]

ex·ạl·tā′tion (egs-), *n.* [ME. *exaltacioun*; LL. *exaltatio* (*-onis*), an elevation, from L. *exaltare*, to lift up, exalt.]

1. the act of exalting or the state of being exalted.

2. a feeling of great or excessive joy, pride, power, etc.; elation; rapture.

3. in alchemy, the refinement of bodies or their qualities and virtues. [Obs.]

4. in astrology, the situation of a planet in the zodiac in which it was supposed its powers were at the highest.

ex·ạlt′ed, *a.* raised to a lofty height; elevated; extolled; magnified; refined; dignified; sublime.

ex·ạlt′ed·ly, *adv.* in an exalted manner.

ex·ạlt′ed·ness, *n.* the state of being exalted.

ex·ạlt′ẽr, *n.* one who or that which exalts.

ex·ạlt′ment, *n.* exaltation. [Obs.]

ex·am′ (egz-), *n.* an examination. [Colloq.]

ex·ā′men, *n.* in ecclesiastical usage, examination.

ex·am′e·tẽr, *n.* a hexameter. [Obs.]

ex·am″i·nȧ·bil′i·ty (egz-), *n.* the quality of being examinable.

ex·am′i·nȧ·ble, *a.* capable of being examined.

ex·am′i·nȧnt, *n.* 1. one who is to be examined. [Obs.]

2. an examiner; one who examines.

ex·am′i·nate, *n.* a person who is being or has been examined.

ex·am·i·nā′tion, *n.* [L. *examinatio* (*-onis*), from *examinare*, to weigh, examine, from *examen*, the tongue of a balance.]

1. the act of examining or the state of being examined; search or inquiry, with a view to ascertain the truth or the real state of things; inspection; scrutiny; testing; as, an *examination* of a house or a ship; the *examination* of a theory.

Nothing that is self-evident can be the proper subject of *examination*.—South.

2. means or method of examining.

3. a set of questions asked or answers given in testing; a test.

examination in chief or *direct examination*; in law, the examination of a witness by the one who has put him on the stand, as distinguished from *cross-examination*, which is made by the opposing side.

Syn.—inquiry, investigation, search, scrutiny, study, inspection, inquisition.

ex·am·i·nā′tion·ȧl, *a.* pertaining to examination.

ex·am·i·nā′tion·iṣm, *n.* the practice of relying entirely upon examinations as tests of qualifications, ability, etc.

ex·am·i·nā′tion pā′pẽr, a paper on which are written or printed the questions to be answered in a written examination; also, the paper containing the answers to such questions.

ex·am′i·nā·tŏr, *n.* an examiner. [Rare.]

ex·am′ine, *v.t.*; examined, *pt.*, *pp.*; examining, *ppr.* [ME. *examinen*; OFr. *examiner*; L. *examinare*, to weigh, ponder, examine, from *examen*, the tongue of a balance, from *exigere*, to measure, weigh, examine; *ex*, out, and *agere*, to weigh.]

1. to inspect or observe carefully; to look into the state of; to view in all aspects in order to find out the facts, physical condition, etc. of; to scrutinize; to investigate; to inquire into; as, to *examine* a ship to know whether she is seaworthy; to *examine* a document.

Examine their counsels and their cares. —Shak.

2. to inquire into the qualifications, capabilities, knowledge, or progress of, by questioning carefully; as, to *examine* a candidate for a degree; to *examine* a witness.

Syn.—weigh, investigate, test, scrutinize, criticize, study, discuss, search, try, explore, inspect, observe.

ex·am·i·nee′, *n.* one who is being examined; a candidate for examination.

ex·am′in·ẽr, *n.* one who examines, tries, or inspects; one who interrogates; especially, a person appointed to conduct an examination; as, an *examiner* in a university.

ex·am′in·ẽr·ship, *n.* the office of an examiner.

ex·am′in·ing, *a.* having power to examine; appointed to examine; as, an *examining* committee.

ex′ăm·plȧ·ry (egz′), *a.* exemplary. [Obs.]

ex·am′ple (egz-), *n.* [ME. *example*; L. *exemplum*, that which is taken out of a larger quantity, a sample, an example, from *eximere*, to take out; *ex*, out, and *emere*, to buy.]

1. something selected to show the character or quality of the rest; a sample; a specimen.

2. a person or thing worthy of imitation; a copy or model; one who or that which is proposed or is proper to be imitated.

I have given you an *example*, that ye should do as I have done to you.—John xiii. 15.

3. an instance of something to be avoided; a case that serves as a warning or caution; as, they made an *example* of the thief.

4. an instance serving for illustration of a principle or method; a particular case or problem illustrating a general rule, method, or truth; as, the principles of trigonometry and the rules of grammar are illustrated by *examples*.

Syn.—instance, pattern, model, sample, precedent, prototype, standard, specimen, warning.

ex·am′ple, *v.t.* to exemplify. [Obs. except in the passive.]

ex·am′ple·less, *a.* without example. [Rare.]

ex·an′gui·ous (eks-an′gwi-us), *a.* exsanguinous. [Obs.]

ex·an′gū·lous, *a.* [L. *ex-* priv., and *angulus*, a corner.] having no corners or angles. [Rare.]

ex·an′i·māte (egz-), *a.* [L. *exanimatus*, pp. of *exanimare*, to deprive of life or breath; *ex-* priv., and *anima*, life.]

1. spiritless; disheartened; depressed in spirits.

2. dead; inanimate.

ex·an′i·māte, *v.t.* 1. to deprive of life. [Rare.]

2. to dishearten; to discourage. [Rare.]

ex·an·i·mā′tion, *n.* [L. *exanimatio* (*-onis*), from *exanimare*, to deprive of breath, life, or strength.] deprivation of life or of spirits. [Rare.]

ex·an′i·mous, *a.* lifeless; dead. [Obs.]

ex·an′nū·lāte, *a.* [L. *ex-* priv., and *annulus*, or *anulus*, a ring.] in botany, without a ring: applied to those ferns in which the sporangium is without the elastic ring or annulus.

ex·an′them, *n.* same as *exanthema*.

ex·an·thē′mȧ, *n.*; *pl.* **ex·an·them′ȧ·tȧ**, [LL., from Gr. *exanthēma*, an efflorescence, eruption, from *exanthein*, to bloom, blossom; *ex*, out, and *anthein*, to flower, from *anthos*, a flower.]

1. a skin eruption or rash occurring in certain infectious diseases, as scarlet fever.

2. an infectious disease characterized by such eruptions.

ex·an·thē·mat′iç, *a.* exanthematous.

ex″an·thē″mȧ·tol′ō·ġy, *n.* [Gr. *exanthēma*, an eruption, and *logos*, description, from *legein*, to speak.] in medicine, the study of the exanthemata.

ex·an·them′ȧ·tous, *a.* in medicine, of the nature of or characterized by exanthema.

ex·ant′lāte, *v.t.* to draw out; to exhaust. [Obs.]

ex·ant·lā′tion, *n.* the act of drawing out; exhaustion. [Obs.]

ex′ȧ·rāte, *v.t.* [L. *exaratus*, pp. of *exarare*, to plow up; *ex*, out, up, and *arare*, to plow.] to plow; hence, to mark as if by a plow; to write; to engrave. [Obs.]

ex·ȧ·rā′tion, *n.* the act of plowing; hence, the act of marking as with a plow; writing; engraving. [Obs.]

ex′ärch, *n.* [LL. *exarchus*; Gr. *exarchos*, a beginner, a leader, chief, from *exarchein*, to begin, lead off; *ex*, off, from, and *archein*, to rule.]

1. a prefect or governor of an outlying province in the Byzantine empire.

2. the supreme head of the independent Orthodox Church of Bulgaria.

3. in the Orthodox Eastern Church, originally, an archbishop, or patriarch; later, a bishop or other clergyman serving as a patriarch's deputy or legate.

ex'är·chāte, *n.* the office, dignity, administration, or province of an exarch.

ex·ȧ·rē'ō·lāte, *a.* [L. *ex-* priv., and *areola*, dim. of *area*, area.] in botany, not having areolae.

ex·ar'il·lāte, *a.* [L. *ex-* priv., and *arilla*, aril.] in botany, having no aril; as, *exarillate* seeds.

ex·ȧ·ris'tāte, *a.* [L. *ex-* priv., and *arista*, the awn or beard of grain.] in botany, without an arista, awn, or beard.

ex·är·tic'ū·lāte, *v.t.*; exarticulated, *pt., pp.*; exarticulating, *ppr.* [L. *ex-* priv., and *articulatus*, pp. of *articulare*, to divide into joints, from *articulus*, dim. of *artus*, a joint.]

1. to put out of joint; to luxate.

2. in surgery, to amputate at a joint.

ex·är·tic'ū·lāte, *a.* in zoology, without articulation; not jointed; composed of a single joint.

ex·är·tic·ū·lā'tion, *n.* 1. luxation; the dislocation of a joint.

2. in surgery, amputation at a joint.

ex·as'pĕr·āte (egz-), *v.t.*, exasperated, *pt., pp.*; exasperating, *ppr.* [L. *exasperatus*, pp. of *exasperare*, to irritate; *ex*, out, from, and *asperare*, to roughen, from *asper*, rough.]

1. to anger; to irritate to a high degree; to provoke to rage; to enrage; to excite the anger of; to vex; to infuriate; as, to *exasperate* a person.

2. to aggravate; to intensify (a feeling, disease, etc.); as, to *exasperate* enmity.

Syn.—anger, enrage, irritate, inflame, incense, nettle, provoke, chafe.

ex·as'pĕr·āte, *a.* 1. exasperated.

2. in botany, covered with short, rigid points; rough.

ex·as'pĕr·ā·tĕr, *n.* one who exasperates.

ex·as·pĕr·ā'tion, *n.* [LL. *exasperatio* (*-onis*), from L. *exasperare*, to roughen, irritate.] the act of exasperating or the state of being exasperated; great irritation or annoyance.

Ex·as·pid'ē·ae, *n.pl.* [L., from Gr. *ex*, from, and *aspis*, *aspidos*, a shield.] a group of passerine birds, embracing several South American families, and having exaspidean tarsi.

ex·as·pid'ē·ăn, *a.* in ornithology, having the anterior scutes overlapping the tarsus around the outside, but deficient on the inside.

ex·auc'tŏr·āte (egz-), **ex·au'thŏr·āte,** *v.t.* to dismiss from service; to deprive of an office or dignity. [Obs.]

ex·auc·tŏr·ā'tion, ex·au·thŏr·ā'tion, *n.* dismissal from service; deprivation; the removal of a person from an office or dignity. [Obs.]

ex·au'gū·rāte (egz-), *v.t.* [L. *exauguratus*, pp. of *exaugurare*, to profane; *ex*, out, and *augurare*, to consecrate by auguries, from *augur*, an augur.] in ancient Rome, to change from sacred to secular; to desecrate; to secularize.

ex·au·gū·rā'tion, *n.* in ancient Rome, the act of exaugurating; secularization.

ex·au'thŏr·īze (egz-), *v.t.* to deprive of authority. [Obs.]

ex·cal'cȧ·rāte, *a.* [L. *ex-* priv., and *calcar*, a spur.] in biology, without calcars; ecalcarate.

ex·cal'cē·āte, *v.t.* to deprive of shoes; to make barefooted. [Obs.]

ex·cal·cē·ā'tion, *n.* the act of excalceating, or depriving of shoes. [Obs.]

ex·cal·fac'tion, *n.* the act of making warm; calefaction. [Obs.]

ex·cal·fac'tive, *a.* excalfactory. [Obs.]

ex·cal·fac'tō·ry, *a.* tending to heat; warming. [Obs.]

Ex·cal'i·bŭr, *n.* in Arthurian legend, King Arthur's sword: in one version of the legend, he drew it out of a stone; in another, it was given to him by Vivian, the Lady of the Lake.

ex·camb', ex·cam'bie, *v.t.* [LL. *excambiare*, to exchange.] in Scots law, to exchange: applied specifically to the exchange of land.

ex·cam'bi·ā·tŏr, *n.* one employed to exchange lands; a broker.

ex·cam'bi·on, *n.* [LL. *excambium*, an exchange.] in Scots law, exchange; barter; specifically, the contract by which one piece of land is exchanged for another.

ex·can·des'cence, ex·can·des'cen·cy, *n.* [L. *excandescentia*, growing anger, from *excandescere*, to take fire, to burn; *ex*, out, and *candescere*, to begin to burn, incept. of *candere*, to shine, glitter.]

1. a growing hot; a white heat; a glowing heat. [Rare.]

2. violent anger. [Obs.]

ex·can·des'cent, *a.* white with heat. [Rare.]

ex·can·tā'tion, *n.* disenchantment by a countercharm. [Obs.]

ex·cär'nāte, *v.t.*; excarnated, *pt., pp.*; excarnating, *ppr.* [LL. *excarnatus*, pp. of *excarnare*, to deprive of flesh; L. *ex-* priv., and *caro* (*carnis*), flesh.] to deprive or clear of flesh. [Rare.]

ex·cär'nāte, *a.* divested of flesh. [Rare.]

ex·cär·nā'tion, *n.* [L. *ex-* priv., and *caro* (*carnis*), flesh.] the act of divesting of flesh or the state of being divested of flesh: opposed to *incarnation*. [Rare.]

ex·cär'ni·fi·cāte, *v.t.*; excarnificated, *pt., pp.*; excarnificating, *ppr.* [L. *excarnificatus*, pp. of *excarnificare*, to strip of flesh.] to deprive of flesh. [Obs.]

ex·cär''ni·fi·cā'tion, *n.* the act of depriving of flesh. [Obs.]

ex cȧ·thē'drȧ, [L., lit., from the chair.] with authority, as of a rank or office; from the seat of authority; as, the Pope spoke *ex cathedra.*

ex·cau'dāte, *a.* [L. *ex-* priv., and *cauda*, tail.] in zoology, without a tail; tailless.

ex'cȧ·vāte, *v.t.*; excavated, *pt., pp.*; excavating, *ppr.* [L. *excavatus*, pp. of *excavare*, to hollow out; *ex*, out, and *cavare*, to make hollow, from *cavus*, hollow.]

1. to hollow out; to make a hole or cavity in, as by scooping, digging, or cutting.

2. to expose or uncover by digging; to unearth; as, to *excavate* a cannon from the ruins of a fort.

3. to form by scooping or hollowing out, or by penetrating into any substance and removing the material; as, to *excavate* a tunnel.

4. to dig out; to remove (earth, soil, etc.).

ex·cȧ·vā'tion, *n.* 1. an excavating or being excavated.

2. a hollow or a cavity formed by removing the interior substance; as, many animals burrow in *excavations* of their own forming.

3. in engineering, an open cutting, as in a railway, in distinction from a tunnel.

4. something unearthed by excavating.

ex'cȧ·vā·tŏr, *n.* 1. one who or that which excavates.

2. a machine for excavating, as a dredging machine or digging machine.

3. a dentist's instrument for removing decayed matter from a tooth preparatory to filling it.

ex·cāve', *v.t.* to excavate. [Rare.]

ex·cē'cāte, *v.t.* to make blind. [Obs.]

ex·cē·cā'tion, *n.* the act of making blind. [Obs.]

ex·cēd'ent, *n.* excess. [Rare.]

ex·ceed', *v.t.*; exceeded, *pt., pp.*; exceeding, *ppr.* [ME. *exceden*; L. *excedere*, to go out, go beyond; *ex*, out, beyond, and *cedere*, to go.]

1. to be or go beyond (the given or supposed limit, measure, or quantity); as, he *exceeded* the speed limit.

2. to surpass; to be more or greater than; to outdo; as, the concert *exceeded* our expectations; he *exceeds* me in weight.

> To be nameless in worthy deeds *exceeds* an infamous history. —Sir T. Browne.

Syn.—excel, outdo, surpass, outstrip, outvie, transcend.

ex·ceed', *v.i.* 1. to go too far; to pass the proper bounds.

2. to surpass others, as in a quality or quantity; to be outstanding.

ex·ceed'ȧ·ble, *a.* capable of exceeding. [Obs.]

ex·ceed'ĕr, *n.* one who exceeds.

ex·ceed'ing, *a.* great in extent, quantity, or duration; unusually large; surpassing; extraordinary.

> Cities were built an *exceeding* space of time before the great flood. —Raleigh.

ex·ceed'ing, *adv.* exceedingly. [Archaic.]

ex·ceed'ing·ly, *adv.* to a very great degree; in a degree beyond what is usual; greatly; extraordinarily; extremely.

ex·ceed'ing·ness, *n.* greatness in quantity, extent, or duration. [Obs.]

ex·cel', *v.t.* and *v.i.*; excelled, *pt., pp.*; excelling, *ppr.* [OFr. *exceller*; L. *excellere*, to raise, elevate, surpass, excel.] to be better or greater than, or superior to (another or others); as, he *excels* in wit.

> *Excelling* others, these were great;
> Thou, greater still, must these *excel.*—Prior.
> It was in description and meditation that Byron *excelled.* —Macaulay.

ex'cel·lence, *n.* [ME. *excellense*; L. *excellentia*, superiority, excellence, from *excellens* (*-entis*), ppr. of *excellere*, to surpass, excel.]

1. the state of possessing good qualities in an unusual or eminent degree; the fact or condition of excelling in anything; superiority.

2. any valuable quality; something in which a person or thing excels; anything highly laudable, meritorious, or virtuous in persons, or valuable and esteemed in things.

> Contentment is a moral *excellence.* —Spurgeon.

3. [E—] Excellency.

Syn.—eminence, goodness, superiority, worth, perfection, greatness.

ex'cel·len·cy, *n.*; *pl.* **ex'cel·len·cies,** 1. [E—] a title of honor applied to various persons of high position, as an ambassador, bishop, governor, etc. (with *His*, *Her*, or *Your*).

2. excellence (in senses 1 and 2). [Archaic.]

ex'cel·lent, *a.* 1. possessing excellence; unusually good of its kind; remarkable for good qualities; of great worth; superior; as, an *excellent* citizen, an *excellent* book, an *excellent* idea, *excellent* fruit.

2. excelling; surpassing. [Archaic.]

> Elizabeth was an *excellent* hypocrite. —Hume.

Syn.—admirable, transcendent, prime, superior, sterling, worthy, choice.

ex'cel·lent, *adv.* excellently; exceedingly. [Obs.]

ex'cel·lent·ly, *adv.* 1. in an excellent manner; to an eminent degree; in a manner to please or command esteem.

2. exceedingly; surpassingly. [Obs.]

ex·cel'si·or, *a.* and *interj.* [L. *excelsior*, comp. of *excelsus*, lofty, high, pp. of *excellere*, to elevate, excel.] more lofty; higher; always upward: used as a trade-mark and as a motto, as on the seal of the State of New York.

ex·cel'si·ŏr, *n.* 1. a kind of stuffing or packing material for mattresses, sofas, chairs, etc., consisting of fine, curled shavings of wood.

2. a size of type, 3 point.

ex·cen'trăl, *a.* [L. *ex*, from, and *centrum*, center.] in botany, out of the center.

ex·cen'tric, ex·cen'tric·ăl, etc. same as *eccentric*, etc.

ex·cept', *v.t.*; excepted, *pt., pp.*; excepting, *ppr.* [ME. *excepten*; L. *exceptare*, to take out, except; *ex*, out, and *capere* to take.]

1. to omit from consideration; to exclude; to make an exception of; to take or leave out; as, of the thirty persons present, we must *except* two.

2. to object to; to take exception to. [Obs.]

ex·cept', *v.i.* to object; to take exception (with *against* or *to*); as, I *except against* his statement; his lawyers *except to* the witness.

ex·cept', *prep.* [ME. *except*, from L. *exceptus*, pp. of *excipere*, to take out, except.] leaving out; other than; but.

> I could see nothing *except* the sky.—Swift.

Syn.—excepting, save, but.

ex·cept', *conj.* if it be not that; unless. [Archaic.]

> I will not let thee go, *except* thou bless me. —Gen. xxxii. 26.

ex·cept'ănt, *a.* implying exception.

ex·cept'ing, *prep.* except; leaving out; excluding.

ex·cept'ing, *conj.* unless; except. [Archaic.]

ex·cep'tion, *n.* [L. *exceptio* (*-onis*), from *exceptus*, pp. of *excipere*, to take out, except.]

1. an excepting or being excepted; an excluding, as from a number designated, or from a description; exclusion; as, all voted for the bill, with the *exception* of five.

2. that which is excepted, excluded, or separated from others in a general description; the person or thing specified as distinct or not included; a case to which a rule, general principle, etc. does not apply.

> The *exceptions* do not destroy the authority of the rule. —Macaulay.

3. a person or thing different from others of the same class; anything deviating from the usual pattern or course.

4. an objection; that which is or may be offered in opposition to a rule, proposition, statement, or allegation. [Archaic.]

> I will answer what *exceptions* he can have against our account. —Bentley.

5. in law, (a) a denial of anything alleged and considered valid by the other side, either in point of law or in pleading, or a denial of a matter alleged in bar to an action, or a denial of the sufficiency of an answer; (b) a clause by which the grantor of a deed excepts something before granted; (c) a formal objection to

a ruling or decision of a judge during a trial, noting a claim of error.

bill of exceptions; in law, a statement of exceptions or objections to the rulings or decisions of a judge presiding at a trial, to be referred for consideration and decision to a superior court, or to a full bench.

the exception proves the rule; the exception tests the rule: often used to mean "the exception establishes the rule."

to take exception; (a) to object; to demur; (b) to resent; to feel offended.

ex·cep′tion·ȧ·ble, *a.* liable to exception or objection.

ex·cep′tion·ȧ·ble·ness, *n.* the quality of being exceptionable.

ex·cep′tion·ȧ·bly, *adv.* in an exceptionable manner.

ex·cep′tion·ăl, *a.* relating to or forming an exception; out of the ordinary course; unusual; uncommon; extraordinary; as, *exceptional* talent.

Syn.—rare, peculiar, uncommon, irregular, unusual, abnormal.

ex·cep′tion·ăl·ism, *n.* the fact or state of being an exception to some rule or general principle.

ex·cep·tion·al′i·ty, *n.* the quality of being exceptional.

ex·cep′tion·ăl·ly, *adv.* in an exceptional manner.

ex·cep′tion·ăl·ness, *n.* exceptionality.

ex·cep′tion·ẽr, *n.* one who takes exceptions; one who objects. [Obs.]

ex·cep′tion·less, *a.* without exception; unexceptionable.

ex·cep′tious, *a.* captious; disposed or apt to cavil, or take exceptions. [Obs.]

ex·cep′tious·ness, *n.* disposition to cavil. [Obs.]

ex·cept′ive, *a.* 1. of, containing, or forming an exception.

A particular and *exceptive* law. —Milton.

2. inclined to take exception; captious.

ex·cept′less, *a.* making no exception; extending to all. [Obs.]

ex·cept′ŏr, *n.* one who takes exceptions or makes objections. [Obs.]

ex·cer′ē·brāte, *v.t.* to remove or beat out the brains of. [Obs.]

ex·cer·ē·brā′tion, *n.* [LL. *excerebratus*, pp. of *excerebrare*, to deprive of brains; L. *ex-* priv., and *cerebrum*, the brain.]

1. the act of removing or beating out the brains.

2. in surgery, the removal of the brain from the head of the fetus to facilitate delivery.

ex·cer′ē·brōse, *a.* [L. *ex-* priv., and *cerebrum*, the brain.] having no brains. [Rare.]

ex·cērn′, *v.t.* [L. *excernere*, to sift out, separate; *ex*, out, and *cernere*, to sift, separate.] to excrete. [Obs.]

ex·cērn′ent, *a.* pertaining to or effecting excretion. [Obs.]

ex·cērp′, *v.t.* to excerpt. [Obs.]

ex·cērpt′, *v.t.*; excerpted, *pt., pp.*; excerpting, *ppr.* [L. *excerptus*, pp. of *excerpere*, to pick out, choose; *ex*, out, and *carpere*, to pick, pluck.] to make extracts from (a book, etc.); to cite, quote, take out, or select (passages from a book, etc.).

ex′cērpt, *n.* an extract; a passage selected or quoted from a book, article, etc.

ex·cērp′tȧ, *n.pl.* [L., neut. pl. of *excerptum*, an extract.] excerpts; passages extracted. [Rare.]

ex·cērp′tion, *n.* 1. the act of excerpting or state of being excerpted.

2. that which is excerpted.

ex·cērp′tive, *a.* excerpting; choosing.

ex·cērp′tŏr, *n.* one who makes excerpts; a selector; a culler.

ex·cess′, *n.* [ME. *exces*; L. *excessus*, a departure, a going beyond, from *excessus*, pp. of *excedere*, to go beyond, exceed; *ex*, beyond, and *cedere*, to go.]

1. action or conduct that goes beyond the usual, reasonable, or lawful limit.

2. intemperance; immoderation; overindulgence.

3. an amount or quantity greater than is necessary, desirable, usable, etc.; too much; superfluity.

4. the amount or degree by which one thing is greater or more than another; remainder; surplus.

in excess of; more than.

spherical excess; the excess of the sum of the three angles of a spherical triangle over two right angles, or 180 degrees.

to excess; to too great an extent or degree; too much.

ex′cess (*or* ek-ses′), *a.* above the usual, standard, or specified number or amount; extra; surplus.

excess baggage; baggage in excess of the amount specified to be carried without charge by a train, ship, etc.

excess fare; an extra sum of money paid by a passenger on a train, ship, etc. who desires to travel beyond the point specified on his original ticket, or who desires a higher class of accommodation.

ex·ces′sive, *a.* [LL. *excessivus*, immoderate, from L. *excessus*, pp. of *excedere*, to exceed.] beyond any given degree, measure, or limit, or beyond the usual measure or proportion; characterized by excess; immoderate; inordinate; abnormal; as, *excessive* bulk, *excessive* indulgence.

Dark with *excessive* bright thy skirts appear. —Milton.

Syn.—extreme, superfluous, exorbitant, immoderate, inordinate, extravagant, superabundant, undue, abnormal.

ex·ces′sive·ly, *adv.* in an extreme degree; to an excessive extent; beyond measure; unduly.

ex·ces′sive·ness, *n.* the state or quality of being excessive; excess.

ex′cess-prof′its tax, a tax on business profits that are greater than the statistical average of profits over a certain period of years.

ex·chānge′, *n.* [ME. *eschange*; LL. *excambium*, exchange, from *excambiare*, to exchange; L. *ex*, out, and *cambiare*, to change.]

1. the act of giving one thing or commodity for another; barter; trade; the act of parting with something in return for an equivalent.

O spare her life and in *exchange* take mine. —Dryden.

2. the act of giving and receiving reciprocally; as, an *exchange* of greetings.

3. the substituting of one thing for another; as, the *exchange* of tears for smiles.

4. the thing given in return for something received, or received in return for what is given.

5. a place for exchanging; a place where the merchants, brokers, and bankers of a city meet to transact business at certain hours; as, a stock *exchange*.

6. a central office, or a system operated by it, providing telephone communication in a community or in part of a city: usually identified by some assigned call name.

7. in commerce and finance, (a) the payment of debts by negotiable drafts or bills of exchange, without actual transfer of money; (b) a bill of exchange; (c) a fee paid for settling accounts or collecting a draft, bill of exchange, etc.; (d) an exchanging of a sum of money of one country or of a depreciated issue for the equivalent in the money of another country or of a current issue; (e) the rate of exchange; value of one currency in terms of the other; difference in value between currencies; (f) [*pl.*] the checks, drafts, etc. presented for exchange and settlement between banks in a clearinghouse.

8. in law, a contract by which parties agree to exchange one thing for another.

arbitration of exchange; see under *arbitration*.

bill of exchange; see under *bill*.

par of exchange; the established value of the coin or standard value of one country expressed in the coin or standard value of another.

private branch exchange; a telephone system installed for an organization in order to provide for telephonic communication between persons within the organization as well as with outside telephones: it consists of a switchboard and a number of telephones.

theory of exchanges; a theory, introduced by Prevost, for explaining the equilibrium of temperature of any body. It is founded on the supposition that the quantity of heat which a body diffuses by radiation is equal to the quantity which it receives by radiation from surrounding bodies, and which it absorbs either wholly or in part.

Syn.—intercourse, commerce, dealing, interchange, reciprocity, reciprocation.

ex·chānge′, *v.t.*; exchanged, *pt., pp.*; exchanging, *ppr.* 1. (a) to give, hand over, or transfer (*for* another thing in return); (b) to receive or give another thing for (something returned).

2. to give and receive reciprocally; to give and receive (equivalent or similar things); to interchange; as, they *exchange* gifts at Christmas.

Exchange forgiveness with me, noble Hamlet. —Shak.

3. to part with for a substitute or alternative; as, to *exchange* honor for wealth.

Syn.—change, barter, trade, interchange, swap, commute.

ex·chānge′, *v.i.* 1. to make an exchange; to barter or trade.

2. in finance, to pass or to be taken in exchange or as an equivalent; as, the currency of this country *exchanges* at par.

ex·chānge′, *a.* 1. exchanged; as, an *exchange* student.

2. having to do with exchange; as, an *exchange* broker.

exchange broker; see under *broker*.

ex·chānge·ȧ·bil′i·ty, *n.* the quality or state of being exchangeable.

ex·chānge′ȧ·ble, *a.* 1. capable of being exchanged.

2. ratable by exchange; to be estimated by what may be procured in exchange; as, the *exchangeable* value of goods.

ex·chānge′ȧ·bly, *adv.* in the way of exchange.

ex·chān′ġẽr, *n.* one who exchanges.

ex·chēat′, *n.* escheat. [Obs.]

ex·chēat′ŏr, *n.* an escheator. [Obs.]

ex·cheq′uẽr (eks-chek′), *n.* [ME. *escheker*, lit., a chessboard, a court of revenue, treasury; OFr. *escheker*, a chessboard, from *eschecs*, chess.]

1. [E–] (a) under the Norman kings of England, an administrative and judicial state department in charge of revenue: so called from a table marked into squares, on which accounts of revenue were kept with counters; (b) later, the British Court of Exchequer, which has jurisdiction over finances; (c) [*sometimes* e–] the British state department in charge of the national revenue.

2. the funds in the national treasury.

3. a treasury, as of a country or organization.

4. money in one's possession; funds; finances.

barons of the exchequer; see *baron*, sense 4.

Chancellor of the Exchequer; see under *Chancellor*.

ex·cheq′uẽr, *v.t.*; exchequered, *pt., pp.*; exchequering, *ppr.* to institute a process against (a person) in the Court of Exchequer.

ex·cīde′, *v.t.* [L. *excidere*, to cut out; *ex*, out, and *cædere*, to cut.] to remove by cutting out; to excise.

ex·cip′i·ent, *a.* [L. *excipiens* (*-entis*), ppr. of *excipere*, to take out, except; *ex*, out, and *capere*, to take.] exceptive; objecting. [Rare.]

ex·cip′i·ent, *n.* 1. one who excepts. [Rare.]

2. in pharmacy, any of various inert substances added to a prescription to give the desired consistency or form.

ex′ci·ple, ex′ci·pūle, ex·cip′ū·lum, *n.* [L. *excipulum*, a vessel for receiving liquids, from *excipere*, to take out, receive.] in botany, the part of a thallus which forms a rim or base to the shield of a lichen.

ex·cip′ū·lăr, *a.* pertaining to the exciple in a lichen.

ex·cip′ū·li·fọrm, *a.* resembling an exciple.

ex·cir′cle, *n.* [L. *ex*, out, and *circulus*, a circle.] an escribed circle or the radius of such a circle.

ex·cīṣ′ȧ·ble, *a.* subject to excise; as, whisky is an *excisable* commodity.

ex·cīṣe′ (*or* ek′sīz), *n.* [earlier *accise*; prob. from M.D. *accijs*; OFr. *aceis*, from hyp. LL. *accensus*, from *accensare*, to tax, from L. *ad-*, to, and *census*, a tax.]

1. a tax; a tax or duty imposed on the manufacture, sale, or consumption of certain commodities within a country, as tobacco, spirits, etc.: also *excise tax*.

2. in England, that branch or department of the civil service which is connected with the levying and collecting of such duties.

3. a fee paid for a license to carry on certain occupations, sports, etc.

ex·cīṣe′, *v.t.*; excised, *pt., pp.*; excising, *ppr.*

1. to lay or impose a duty on; to levy an excise on.

2. to force payment of an excise from.

3. to overcharge; to impose upon. [Brit. Dial.]

ex·cīṣe′, *a.* of, pertaining to, or connected with excises.

ex·cīṣe′, *v.t.*; excised, *pt., pp.*; excising, *ppr.* [from L. *excisus*, pp. of *excidere*, to cut off; *ex*, off, and *cædere*, to cut.] to cut out or away; remove, as a tumor.

ex·cīṣe′măn, *n.*; *pl.* **ex·cīṣe′men,** in Great Britain, a government official who collects excises and enforces the laws concerning them.

ex·ci′ṣion, *n.* [L. *excisio* (*-onis*), a destroying, cutting out; *ex*, out, and *cædere*, to cut.]

1. a cutting out or being cut out; removal by or as by cutting.
2. a cutting off from the church; excommunication.

ex·cīt·ȧ·bil′i·ty, *n.* 1. the quality of being easily excited; readiness or proneness to be provoked or moved into action; nervousness.
2. in physiology, the capacity or degree of response to the proper stimulus; irritability.

ex·cīt′ȧ·ble, *a.* 1. capable of being excited; easily stirred up or stimulated; prone to excitement; as, an *excitable* temperament.
2. in physiology, capable of responding to the proper stimulus.

ex·cīt′ănt, *a.* [L. *excitans* (*-antis*), ppr. of *excitare*, to excite.] tending to excite; exciting; stimulating.

ex·cīt′ănt, *n.* [L. *excitans* (*-antis*), ppr. of *excitare*, to excite.] a stimulant.

ex′ci·tāte, *v.t.* to excite. [Obs.]

ex·ci·tā′tion, *n.* [LL. *excitatio* (*-onis*), from L. *excitare*, to excite.]
1. the act of exciting or state of being excited; excitement.
2. in physics, (a) the production of electricity, magnetism, or a magnetic field; (b) the raising of an atom or molecule to an energy state higher than its normal, or ground, state.

ex·cīt′ȧ·tive, *a.* having power to excite; exciting or tending to excite; excitatory.

ex′ci·tā·tŏr, *n.* [LL. *excitator*, from L. *excitare*, to excite.] in electricity, an instrument used to discharge a Leyden jar or other electrical apparatus in such a manner as to protect the operator from the force or effect of the shock.

ex·cīt′ȧ·tō·ry, *a.* tending to excite.

ex·cīte′, *v.t.*; excited, *pt.*, *pp.*; exciting, *ppr.* [ME. *exciten*; OFr. *exciter*; L. *excitare*, to call out or forth, to stimulate, excite; *ex*, out, and pp. of *ciere*, to call, summon.]
1. to put into motion or activity; stir up; as, the injections of adrenalin *excited* the rats.
2. to arouse; call forth; provoke; as, she *excited* his jealousy.
3. to arouse the feelings or passions of; as, the news *excited* us.
4. in electricity, (a) to produce an electric or magnetic field in; (b) to set (an electric current) in motion.
5. in physiology, to produce or increase the response of (an organism, organ, tissue, etc.) to a proper stimulus.
Syn.—incite, arouse, stimulate, kindle, agitate, awaken, irritate, stir up, inflame.—To *excite* is to arouse feelings which were less strong; *incite* is to urge to action corresponding to the feelings awakened.

ex·cīt′ed, *a.* 1. emotionally aroused; agitated.
2. in physics, in a state of excitation.

ex·cī′ted·ly, *adv.* in an excited manner.

ex·cīte′fụl, *a.* calculated to excite; exciting. [Obs.]

ex·cīte′ment, *n.* 1. the act of exciting or the state of being excited; agitation; as, an *excitement* of the people.
2. that which excites or rouses; that which moves, stirs, or induces action.
3. in physiology, a state of increased activity in the body or in any of its organs or parts.

ex·cīt′ẽr, *n.* 1. one who or that which excites.
2. in electricity, a small generator that provides field current for a large dynamo or motor.

ex·cīt′ing, *a.* calling or rousing to action; producing excitement; arousing keen interest, agitation, etc.; stirring; thrilling.
exciting causes; in medicine, causes which tend immediately to produce disease, as distinguished from *predisposing causes*, which make a person susceptible to disease without directly producing it.

ex·cīt′ing·ly, *adv.* in an exciting manner.

ex·cīt′ive, *a.* tending to excite.

ex·cī′tō-, [from L. *excitare*, to excite.] a combining form used in medicine and anatomy to mean *exciting*, as in *excitomotor*.

ex·cī″tō·mō′tŏr, ex·cī″tō·mō′tō·ry, *a.* [*excito-*, and L. *motor*, a mover.] in physiology, exciting or producing motion.

ex·cī″tō·nū′tri·ent, *a.* [*excito-*, and L. *nutriens* (*-entis*), ppr. of *nutrire*, to nourish.] in physiology, stimulating nutrition.

ex·cī′tŏr, *n.* 1. an exciter.
2. in physiology, a nerve which, when stimulated, causes increased activity of the part that it supplies.

ex·cī″tō·sē·crē′tō·ry, *a.* [*excito-*, and L. *secretio* (*-onis*), a dividing, secretion.] in physiology, exciting increased secretion in the glands.

ex·clāim′, *v.t.* and *v.i.*; exclaimed, *pt.*, *pp.*; exclaiming, *ppr.* [L. *exclamare*, to cry out; *ex*, out, and *clamare*, to cry, shout.] to cry out loudly and abruptly; to call out noisily; to protest; to shout or speak suddenly and vehemently, as in surprise, emotion, etc.; to vociferate.

ex·clāim′, *n.* clamor; exclamation. [Archaic.]

ex·clāim′ẽr, *n.* one who cries out or exclaims.

ex·clȧ·mā′tion, *n.* [OFr. *exclamation*; L. *exclamatio* (*-onis*), a calling or crying out, from *exclamare*, to cry out.]
1. outcry; noisy talk; clamor; a vehement, sudden utterance.
2. a word or phrase expressing exclamation; something exclaimed; an interjection.
3. an exclamation mark.

ex·clȧ·mā′tion märk (or **point**), a mark (!) used after a word or sentence in writing or printing to show surprise, strong emotion, etc.: it symbolizes the unusually high pitch and stress heard in actual speech.

ex·clam′ȧ·tive, *a.* containing exclamation.

ex·clam′ȧ·tive·ly, *adv.* in an exclamative manner.

ex·clam′ȧ·tō·ri·ly, *adv.* in an exclamatory manner.

ex·clam′ȧ·tō·ry, *a.* [L. *exclamare*, to cry out, exclaim.] of, using, containing, or expressing exclamation; as, an *exclamatory* phrase.

ex′clāve, *n.* [L. *ex*, out, and *clavis*, a key.] a territory politically a part of a country, but geographically separated from it by being surrounded by foreign territory.

ex·clō′ṣūre (-zhūr), *n.* [from *ex-*, after *enclosure*.] an area protected by various devices against the entrance of animal and insect pests.

ex·clūd′ȧ·ble, *a.* that can be excluded.

ex·clūde′, *v.t.*; excluded, *pt.*, *pp.*; excluding, *ppr.* [ME. *excluden*; L. *excludere*, to shut out; *ex*, out, and *claudere*, to shut.]
1. to refuse to admit, consider, include, etc.; shut out; keep from entering, happening, or being; reject; bar.
2. to put out; force out; expel; banish.
excluded middle or *third*; in logic, one of the laws of negation, according to which there is no individual that does not come under a term or its negative, no third state being possible. The formula is "Everything is either A or not-A."

ex·clūd′ẽr, *n.* one who or that which excludes.

ex·clū′ṣion, *n.* [L. *exclusio* (*-onis*), from *excludere*, to shut out, exclude.]
1. an excluding or being excluded.
2. a thing excluded.
to the exclusion of; so as to keep out, bar, etc.

ex·clū′ṣion·ȧ·ry, *a.* having a tendency to exclude.

ex·clū′ṣion·ẽr, *n.* an exclusionist.

ex·clū′ṣion·iṣm, *n.* the principles or practices of an exclusionist.

ex·clū′ṣion·ist, *n.* one who would preclude another or others from something; specifically, in English history, a member of a group which sought to debar the heirs of Charles II from the throne because they were Roman Catholics.

ex·clū′sive, *a.* [ML. *exclusivus*, from L. *exclusus*, pp. of *excludere*.]
1. excluding all others; shutting out other considerations, happenings, existences, occupations, etc.; as, *vegetable* and *mineral* are *exclusive* terms.
2. having the tendency or power to exclude all others.
3. excluding all but what is specified; as, *only* is an *exclusive* particle.
4. not shared or divided; sole; single; as, an *exclusive* right to sell something.
5. excluding certain people or groups for social or economic reasons.
6. snobbish; undemocratic.
7. charging high prices; as, an *exclusive* shop. [Colloq.]
exclusive of; excluding; not including or allowing for.

ex·clū′sive, *n.* 1. a member of a very select circle of society.
2. anything which excludes.

ex·clū′sive·ly, *adv.* in an exclusive manner; to the exclusion of all others; only; as, it is his, *exclusively*.

ex·clū′sive·ness, *n.* the quality or state of being exclusive.

ex·clū′siv·iṣm, *n.* exclusiveness; exclusionism.

ex·clū′siv·ist, *n.* one who favors or practices any form of exclusiveness or exclusion; an exclusionist.

ex·clū′sō·ry, *a.* [LL. *exclusorius*, from L. *exclusus*, pp. of *excludere*, to shut out, exclude.] capable of excluding.

ex·coct′, *v.t.* to decoct; to obtain by boiling. [Obs.]

ex·coc′tion, *n.* the act of excocting. [Obs.]

ex·cog′i·tāte, *v.t.*; excogitated, *pt.*, *pp.*; excogitating, *ppr.* [L. *excogitatus*, pp. of *excogitare*, to think out, contrive; *ex*, out, and *cogitare*, to think.] to invent; to think out; to devise; to contrive.

ex·cog′i·tāte, *v.i.* to cogitate. [Rare.]

ex·cog·i·tā′tion, *n.* 1. invention; contrivance; an excogitating or being excogitated.
2. a thing excogitated.

ex·cŏm·mūne′, *v.t.* to exclude; to excommunicate. [Obs.]

ex·cŏm·mū′ni·cȧ·ble, *a.* liable to, deserving, or punishable by excommunication.

ex·cŏm·mū′ni·cănt, *n.* one who has been excommunicated.

ex·cŏm·mū′ni·cāte, *v.t.*; excommunicated, *pt.*, *pp.*; excommunicating, *ppr.* [LL. *excommunicatus*, pp. of *excommunicare*, to expel from communion; L. *ex*, out, and *communicare*, to communicate, from *communis*, common.]
1. to expel from communion with a church; to exclude or eject from membership in or the privileges of a church by ecclesiastical authority.
2. to interdict; to forbid or prohibit by making an excommunicable offense of, as the penalty of disobedience. [Obs.]

ex·cŏm·mū′ni·cāte (*or* -kit), *a.* excommunicated.

ex·cŏm·mū′ni·cāte (*or* -kit), *n.* one who is excommunicated.

ex·cŏm·mū·ni·cā′tion, *n.* 1. an excommunicating or being excommunicated.
2. a formal sentence that excommunicates.

ex·cŏm·mū′ni·cȧ·tive, *a.* excommunicating; of or decreeing excommunication.

ex·cŏm·mū′ni·cā·tŏr, *n.* one who excommunicates.

ex·cŏm·mū′ni·cȧ·tō·ry, *a.* pertaining to, decreeing, or causing excommunication.

ex·cŏm·mūn′iŏn (-yun), *n.* excommunication. [Obs.]

ex·cō′ri·ȧ·ble, *a.* capable of being excoriated.

ex·cō′ri·āte, *v.t.*; excoriated, *pt.*, *pp.*; excoriating, *ppr.* [L. *excoriatus*, pp. of *excoriare*, to strip off the skin; L. *ex*, out, off, and *corium*, the skin.]
1. to flay; to strip, scratch, or peel off the skin of; to abrade; to chafe.
2. to denounce strongly.

ex·cō·ri·ā′tion, *n.* 1. an excoriating or being excoriated.
2. an excoriated spot; abrasion; sore.
3. robbery; spoliation; the act of stripping of possessions. [Obs.]

ex·cor′ti·cāte, *v.t.*; excorticated, *pt.*, *pp.*; excorticating, *ppr.* [LL. *excorticatus*, pp. of *excorticare*, to strip off the bark or rind; L. *ex*, off, and *cortex*, *corticis*, bark.] to strip off the bark or rind of, as a tree.

ex·cor·ti·cā′tion, *n.* the act of stripping off bark.

ex·crē·ā′tion, *n.* the act of spitting out. [Obs.]

ex′crē·ment, *n.* [Fr. *excrément*; L. *excrementum*, that which is sifted out, from *excretus*, pp. of *excernere*, to sift out.] matter excreted and ejected; waste matter discharged from the bowels; dung; feces.

ex′crē·ment, *n.* [LL. *excrementum*, from L. *excrescere*, to grow out, to rise.] any natural appendage or outgrowth on the living body, as hair, feathers, etc. [Obs.]

ex·crē·men′tăl, *a.* of, pertaining to, or resembling excrement.

ex″crē·men·ti′tious (-tish′us), **ex″crē·men·ti′tiăl** (-tish′ăl), *a.* of the nature of, pertaining to, or consisting of excrement; excremental.

ex·cres′cence, *n.* [L. *excrescentia*, excrescences, from *excrescere*, to grow out; *ex*, out, and *crescere*, to grow.]
1. a normal outgrowth; natural appendage, as fingernails, hair, etc.
2. an abnormal or disfiguring outgrowth or addition, as a bunion.

ex·cres′cen·cy, *n.*; *pl.* **ex·cres′cen·cieṣ,** 1. an excrescence.
2. the condition of being excrescent.

ex·cres′cent, *a.* 1. growing out of something else in an abnormal manner; forming an excrescence; superfluous.

2. designating or of a sound that has entered a word as a result of the natural position of the vocal organs in pronouncing the contiguous or neighboring sounds, as the *b* in *chamber*: the term *unhistoric* is preferred by linguists.

ex·cres·cen′tiăl, *a.* of, pertaining to, or resembling an excrescence.

ex·crē′tȧ, *n.pl.* [L., neut. pl. of *excretus*, pp. of *excernere*, to separate.] waste matter excreted by the body, as urine and sweat: the term is sometimes applied to feces.

ex·crēte′, *v.t.* and *v.i.*; excreted, *pt.*, *pp.*; excreting, *ppr.* [L. *excretus*, pp. of *excernere*, to sift out, separate.]
1. to separate (waste matter) from the blood or tissue and eliminate from the body, as through the kidneys or sweat glands.
2. in botany, to eliminate (waste matter) from the cells.

ex′crē·tin, *n.* an organic crystalline substance, $C_{20}H_{36}O$, contained in human feces.

ex·crē′tion, *n.* [L. *excretus*, pp. of *excernere*, to separate.]
1. the act or process of excreting.
2. waste matter excreted; sweat, urine, etc.

ex·crē′tive, *a.* excreting or promoting excretion; having the power of separating and ejecting waste matter from the body.

ex′crē·tō·ry, *a.* [LL. *excretorius*, from L. *excretus*, pp. of *excernere*, to separate.] of or for excretion.

ex′crē·tō·ry, *n.* an excretory organ.

ex·crū′ci·ȧ·ble (-shi-ȧ-bl), *a.* liable to torment. [Rare.]

ex·crū′ci·āte (-shi-āt), *v.t.*; excruciated, *pt.*, *pp.*; excruciating, *ppr.* [L. *excruciatus*, pp. of *excruciare*, to torture greatly; *ex-* intens., and *cruciare*, to torture, from *crux*, *crucis*, a cross.]
1. to torture; to inflict intense bodily pain upon.
2. to subject to mental anguish; to torment.

ex·crū′ci·ā·ting, *a.* 1. torturing; causing intense physical or mental pain; unbearably intense; agonizing.
2. excessively elaborate, elegant, or pretentious; as, *excruciating* graciousness. [Colloq.]

ex·crū′ci·āt·ing·ly, *adv.* 1. in an excruciating manner.
2. extremely; unusually; as, *excruciatingly* polite. [Colloq.]

ex·crū·ci·ā′tion, *n.* 1. the act of torturing or the state of being tortured.
2. torture; agony; extreme pain; vexation; anguish.

ex·cū·bā′tion, *n.* [LL. *excubatio* (*-onis*), a watching, keeping watch, from L. *excubare*, to lie or sleep out of doors; *ex*, out, and *cubare*, to lie.] the act of keeping guard. [Obs.]

ex·cul′pȧ·ble, *a.* capable of being exculpated.

ex·cul′pāte, *v.t.*; exculpated, *pt.*, *pp.*; exculpating, *ppr.* [L. *ex*, out, and *culpare*, to blame, from *culpa*, fault.] to clear from a charge or imputation of fault or guilt; to excuse; to vindicate; to declare or prove guiltless.
Syn.—absolve, exonerate, clear, justify, vindicate.

ex·cul·pā′tion, *n.* 1. an exculpating or being exculpated.
2. a thing that exculpates; vindication; evidence of being guiltless.

ex·cul′pȧ·tō·ry, *a.* exculpating or tending to exculpate; excusing; vindicatory.

ex·cūr′, *v.i.* to go to the extreme and beyond proper limits. [Obs.]

ex·cūr′rent, *a.* [L. *excurrens* (*-entis*), ppr. of *excurrere*, to run out, project.]
1. running out or forth.
2. in botany, (a) projecting beyond the tip, as the midrib of certain leaves; (b) having an undivided main stem, as fir trees.
3. in zoology, of ducts, tubes, or passages whose contents flow outward.

ex·cūrse′, *v.i.* and *v.t.*; excursed, *pt.*, *pp.*; excursing, *ppr.* [L. *excursus*, pp. of *excurrere*, to run out or forth; *ex*, out, and *currere*, to run.] to make a digression; to make an excursion.

ex·cūr′ṣion, *n.* [L. *excursio* (*-onis*), a running out or forth, from *excursus*, pp. of *excurrere*, to run out; *ex*, out, and *currere*, to run.]
1. a short trip taken with the intention of returning to the point of departure; short journey for health or pleasure.
2. a round trip (on a train, bus, ship, etc.) at reduced rates, usually with limits set on the time of departure and return.
3. a group taking such a trip or journey.
4. a deviation or digression.
5. a military sortie; raid. [Obs.]
6. in physics, (a) a single movement outward from the mean position in an oscillating or alternating motion; (b) the distance involved in such a movement.

ex·cūr′sion, *a.* for an excursion or excursions; as, *excursion* rates.

ex·cūr′sion·ist, *n.* one who goes on an excursion.

ex·cūr′sive, *a.* 1. having the character of an excursion; as, *excursive* trips.
2. rambling; desultory; as, *excursive* reading.
3. digressive; wandering.

ex·cūr′sive·ly, *adv.* in an excursive manner.

ex·cūr′sive·ness, *n.* the quality of being excursive.

ex·cūr′sus, *n.*; *pl.* **ex·cūr′sus·eṣ** or **ex·cūr′sus,** [L. *excursus*, a running forth, a digression, from *excurrere*, to run out.]
1. a digression, as in a literary work.
2. a dissertation containing a fuller exposition of some important point or topic and appended to a work.

ex·cūr′vāte, ex·cūr′vȧ·ted, *a.* same as *excurved*.

ex·cūrved′, *a.* [L. *ex*, out, and *curvatus*, pp. of *curvare*, to curve, bend.] in zoology, curved outward from the center of a part or organ.

ex·cūṣ′ȧ·ble, *a.* [ME. *excusable*; L. *excusabilis*, from *excusare*, to release from a charge, to excuse.] deserving to be excused; pardonable; justifiable; as, an *excusable* action.

ex·cūṣ′ȧ·ble·ness, *n.* the state or quality of being excusable; pardonableness.

ex·cūṣ′ȧ·bly, *adv.* pardonably; so as to be excusable.

ex·cū·ṣā′tion, *n.* excuse; apology. [Obs.]

ex·cū·ṣā′tŏr, *n.* one who makes or is authorized to make an excuse; an apologist. [Obs.]

ex·cūṣ′ȧ·tō·ry, *a.* making excuse; containing excuse or excuses; apologetic; as, an *excusatory* plea.

ex·cūṣe′, *v.t.*; excused, *pt.*, *pp.*; excusing, *ppr.* [ME. *excusen*; OFr. *excuser*; L. *excusare*, to free from a charge, release, pardon; *ex*, from, and *causa*, a charge.]
1. to try to free (a person) of blame; seek to exonerate.
2. to try to minimize or pardon (a fault); apologize or give reasons for.
3. to consider (an offense or fault) as unimportant; overlook; as, *excuse* my rudeness.
4. to release from an obligation, duty, promise, etc.
5. to permit to leave.
6. to serve as an explanation or justification for; justify; exculpate; absolve; as, his honesty *excuses* his mistake.
to excuse oneself; (a) to ask that one's fault be overlooked; apologize; (b) to ask for permission to leave.
Syn.—pardon, justify, absolve, exonerate, vindicate, forgive, exculpate, extenuate, exempt.

ex·cūse′, *n.* 1. a plea or explanation offered in defense of one's conduct; apology.
2. a release from obligation, duty, etc.
3. that which excuses; that which extenuates or justifies a fault, or is intended to do so.
4. a pretended reason for conduct; pretext.

ex·cūse′less, *a.* having no excuse; inexcusable.

ex·cūṣ′ẽr, *n.* 1. one who offers excuses or pleads for another.
2. one who excuses or forgives another.

ex·cuss′, *v.t.* [L. *excussus*, pp. of *excutere*, to shake out or off; *ex*, out, and *quatere*, to shake.]
1. to shake off. [Obs.]
2. in law, to seize and detain.
3. to discuss; to decipher. [Obs.]

ex·cus′sion, *n.* 1. a seizing by law.
2. the act of excussing; discussion. [Obs.]

ex′ē·at, *n.* [L., lit., let him go, 3rd. pers. sing. pres. subj. act. of *exire*, to go out, depart.]
1. a leave of absence granted a student in English universities.
2. a leave of absence granted by a bishop to a priest who leaves his diocese.

ex′ē·crȧ·ble, *a.* [L. *execrabilis*, from *execrare*, to curse.]
1. deserving to be cursed; very hateful; detestable; abominable; as, an *execrable* wretch.
2. very inferior; of very poor quality.

ex′ē·crȧ·ble·ness, *n.* the state of being execrable.

ex′ē·crȧ·bly, *adv.* in an execrable manner; hatefully; detestably.

ex′ē·crāte, *v.t.*; execrated, *pt.*, *pp.*; execrating, *ppr.* [L. *execratus*, pp. of *execrare*, to curse; *ex*, out, and *sacrare*, to consecrate, from *sacer*, sacred.] to curse; to call down evil upon; hence, to detest utterly; to abhor; to abominate.
Syn.—curse, anathematize, denounce, detest, hate.

ex′ē·crāte, *v.i.* to curse.

ex·ē·crā′tion, *n.* 1. a cursing.
2. a detesting; loathing; abhorrence.
3. a curse; an imprecation.
Cease, gentle queen, these *execrations*.
—Shak.
4. a person or thing cursed or detested.
Syn.—curse, malediction, anathema, imprecation, oath.

ex′ē·crā·tive, *a.* cursing; denunciatory.

ex′ē·crā·tive, *n.* a word or phrase used in cursing.

ex′ē·crā·tive·ly, *adv.* in an execrative manner.

ex′ē·crā·tŏr, *n.* a person who execrates.

ex′ē·crā·tō·ry, *a.* of or characterized by execration.

ex′ē·crȧ·tō·ry, *n.* a formulary of execrations.

ex·eçt′, *v.t.* to exsect. [Obs.]

ex·eç′tion, *n.* exsection. [Obs.]

ex′ē·cū·tȧ·ble, *a.* capable of being executed; that can be done or effected; practicable.

ex·eç′ū·tănt, *n.* [Fr. *exécutant*, ppr. of *exécuter*, to execute.] one who executes or performs; a performer, especially on a musical instrument.

ex′ē·cūte, *v.t.*; executed, *pt.*, *pp.*; executing, *ppr.* [ME. *executen*; OFr. *executer*, to execute, from L. *executus* or *exsecutus*, pp. of *exequi*, or *exsequi*, to follow out, pursue; *ex*, out, and *sequi*, to follow.]
1. to follow out or through; to perform; to do; to fulfill; as, he *executed* the captain's orders.
2. to carry into effect; to administer (laws, etc.).
3. to put to death in accordance with a legally imposed sentence; as, to *execute* a traitor.
4. to kill. [Obs.]
5. in law, to complete or make valid (a writing), as by signing, sealing, and delivering; as, to *execute* a deed or lease.
6. to perform (a musical composition, a part in a play, etc.).
7. to create or produce in accordance with an idea, plan, blueprints, etc.; as, he *executed* a statue in marble.
Syn.—do, perform, accomplish, fulfill, effect, realize, achieve, complete, consummate.

ex′ē·cūte, *v.i.* to perform a musical composition.

ex′ē·cū·tẽr, *n.* one who performs or carries into effect.

ex·ē·cū′tion, *n.* 1. an executing; performance; the act of completing or accomplishing.
The excellence of the subject contributed much to the happiness of the *execution*.
—Dryden.
2. a carrying into effect; administration.
3. a putting to death in accordance with a legally imposed sentence.
4. a producing according to a plan, idea, etc.
5. the manner of doing or producing something.
6. the manner of producing or performing a work of art; the dexterity with which it is accomplished; skill.
7. effective action, especially of a destructive nature; as, the bombs did heavy *execution*.
8. in law, (a) a writ, issued by a court, giving authority to a put a judgment into effect; (b) the act of carrying out the provisions of such a writ; (c) the making valid of a legal instrument, as by signing, sealing, and delivering.

ex·ē·cū′tion·ẽr, *n.* one who executes; one who carries out the death penalty imposed by a court; hangman, headsman, etc.

ex·eç′ū·tive (egz-), *a.* [L. *executus*, pp. of *exequi*, to follow out, execute.]
1. of, capable of, or fit for carrying out duties, functions, etc.; as, *executive* ability.
2. empowered and required to administer (laws, government affairs, etc.); administrative: distinguished from *legislative*, *judicial*.

ex·eç′ū·tive, *n.* 1. a person, group of people, or branch of government empowered and required to administer the laws and affairs of a nation.
2. any person whose function is to administer or manage affairs, as of a corporation, school, etc.

ex·eç′ū·tive·ly, *adv.* in an executive manner.

Ex·eç′ū·tive Man′sion, 1. the White House (in Washington, D.C.), official home of the President of the United States.
2. the official home of the governor of a State.

ex′e·çū·tŏr (ek′si-), *n.* [ME. *executour*; OFr. *executour*; L. *executor, exsecutor,* a performer, accomplisher, from *exequi, exsequi,* to perform, accomplish.]
1. one who executes; a doer; a performer of actions.
2. (ig-zek′) the person appointed to execute a will, or to see it carried into effect.
executor de son tort; one who, without authority, interferes with the goods of a deceased person, by which he subjects himself to the trouble of executorship, without the profits or advantages.

ex·eç·ū·tō′ri·ăl, *a.* pertaining to an executor; executive.

ex·eç′ū·tŏr·ship, *n.* the office of an executor.

ex·eç′ū·tō·ry, *a.* [LL. *exsecutorius,* from L. *exsecutus,* pp. of *exsequi,* to follow out, execute.]
1. executive; administrative.
2. in force; effective, as a law, decree, etc.
3. in law, to be executed or carried into effect at the appropriate time; to take effect on a future contingency; as, an *executory* devise or remainder.

ex·eç′ū·tress, *n.* an executrix. [Rare.]

ex·eç′ū·trix, *n.*; *pl.* **ex·eç′ū·trix·eş, ex·eç·ū·trī′cēş,** a woman executor; a woman appointed to execute a will.

ex·eç′ū·try, *n.* in Scottish law, the estate of a deceased person, passing to an executor's control.

ex′ē·dent, *a.* [L. *exedens* (*-entis*), ppr. of *exedere,* to eat up; *ex,* out, and *edere,* to eat.] eating; as, an *exedent* cancer. [Rare.]

ex′ē·drȧ, ex′hē·drȧ, *n.*; *pl.* **ex′ē·drae, ex′hē·drae,** [L., from Gr. *exedra*; *ex,* out, and *hedra,* a seat.]
1. in ancient Greece, a room, building, or outdoor area with seats, where conversations and discussions were held.
2. a large, semicircular, outdoor bench of wood or stone, usually with a high, solid back.

ex·ē·ġē′sis, *n.*; *pl.* **ex·ē·ġē′sēş,** [L., from Gr. *exēgēsis,* an explanation, from *exēgeisthai,* to show the way, to lead, to explain; *ex,* out, and *hēgeisthai,* to lead, guide, from *agein,* to lead.]
1. the exposition, critical analysis, or interpretation of a word, literary passage, etc., especially of the Bible.
2. in mathematics, the process for finding the root of an equation. [Obs.]

ex′ē·ġēte, *n.* [Gr. *exēgetēs,* a leader, adviser, from *exēgeisthai,* to lead, explain.] one skilled in exegesis.

ex·ē·ġet′iç, ex·ē·ġet′iç·ăl, *a.* pertaining to, or having the nature of, exegesis; explanatory; expository.

ex·ē·ġet′iç·ăl·ly, *adv.* by way of explanation.

ex·ē·ġet′içs, *n.pl.* [*construed as sing.*] the study, art, or practice of exegesis.

ex·ē·ġē′tist, *n.* same as *exegete.*

ex·em′bry·ō·nāte, *a.* [Gr. *ex,* out, and *embryon,* an embryo.] in botany, without an embryo: applied to the spores of cryptogams.

ex·em′plăr (egz-) *n.* [ME. *exemplaire*; LL. *exemplarium,* that which serves as a pattern or model, from L. *exemplum,* a pattern, copy.]
1. a person or thing regarded as worthy of imitation; model; pattern; archetype.
2. a sample; specimen; example.
3. a copy, especially of a book or writing.

ex·em′plăr, *a.* exemplary. [Obs.]
exemplar proposition; in logic, a proposition that states something to be true of one or more examples of a class, regarded as representative of the entire class.

ex·em′plȧ·ri·ly, *adv.* in an exemplary manner.

ex·em′plȧ·ri·ness, *n.* the state or quality of being exemplary.

ex·em·plar′i·ty (eks-), *n.* exemplariness. [Rare.]

ex·em′plȧ·ry (egz-), *a.* 1. serving as a pattern or model for imitation; worthy of imitation; as, an *exemplary* life.
2. serving as a warning or deterrent; as, *exemplary* punishment.
3. serving as a sample, instance, type, etc.; typical.
Syn.—laudable, praiseworthy, honorable, meritorious, worthy, excellent.

ex·em′plȧ·ry, *n.* examplar. [Obs.]

ex·em′plȧ·ry dam′ăġ·eş, in law, damages beyond the actual loss, imposed as a punishment.

ex·em′pli·fī·ȧ·ble, *a.* capable of being exemplified.

ex·em″pli·fi·çā′tion, *n.* [LL. *exemplificatio* (*-onis*), from *exemplificare,* to exemplify.]
1. the act of exemplifying; a showing or illustrating by example.
2. that which exemplifies; an illustration or example, as of a theory, principle, etc.
3. in law, a legally attested or certified copy; as, an *exemplification* of a record, deed, or letters patent.

ex·em′pli·fī·ẽr, *n.* one who exemplifies.

ex·em′pli·fȳ (egz-), *v.t.*; exemplified, *pt., pp.*; exemplifying, *ppr.* [LL. *exemplificare,* to show by example; L. *exemplum,* example, and *facere,* to make.]
1. to show or illustrate by example; to serve as an example of; as, the life of Jesus *exemplified* his doctrines and precepts.
2. to copy; to transcribe; to take an attested copy of (a document, etc.) under seal.
3. to prove or show by an attested copy.

ex·em′plī grā′ti·ȧ (egz-em′plī grā′shi-ȧ), [L., lit., for the sake of example.] for example; for instance.

ex·em′plum (egz-), *n.*; *pl.* **ex·em′plȧ,** [L.]
1. an example; illustration.
2. a moralized tale or anecdote, especially as used to illustrate the text of a medieval sermon.

ex·empt′ (egz-), *v.t.*; exempted, *pt., pp.*; exempting, *ppr.* [ME. *exempten*; L. *eximere,* to take out, deliver, set free; *ex,* out, and *emere,* to take, buy.]
1. to free or permit to be free from a rule or obligation to which others are subject; to excuse; to release; as, to *exempt* one from military duty.
2. to remove; to set aside or away. [Obs.]

ex·empt′, *a.* 1. free from a rule, obligation, etc. to which others are subject; excused; released.
2. left out, omitted, or excluded; not included. [Now Rare.]

His dreadful imprecation hear;
'Tis laid on all, not any one *exempt.*
—Lee and Dryden.

Syn.—free, excused, released, liberated, privileged, absolved.

ex·empt′, *n.* 1. one who is exempted.
2. in England, any of four officers of the yeomen of the royal guard; an exon.

ex·empt′i·ble, *a.* deserving or qualified to be exempted.

ex·emp′tion, *n.* [L. *exemptio* (*-onis*), a taking out, from *exemptus,* pp. of *eximere,* to take out, exempt.]
1. the act of exempting.
2. the state of being exempt; freedom or release from a liability, obligation, etc.; immunity; privilege; as, *exemption* from feudal servitude.

The Roman laws gave particular *exemptions*
to such as built ships or traded in corn.
—Arbuthnot.

3. in the Roman Catholic Church, a dispensation occasionally granted by the Pope to clergymen, and, more rarely, to laymen, to exempt them from the authority of their ordinaries.
Syn.—freedom, immunity, privilege, prerogative.

ex·emp·ti′tious (-tish′us), *a.* separable; capable of being exempted. [Obs.]

ex·en′tẽr·āte, *v.t.*; exenterated, *pt., pp.*; exenterating, *ppr.* [L. *exenteratus,* pp. of *exenterare*; Gr. *exenterizein,* to eviscerate, disembowel; *ex,* out, and *entera,* bowels, vitals.]
1. to take out the bowels or entrails of; to disembowel; to eviscerate: now only figurative. [Rare.]
2. in surgery, to take out (an organ).

ex·en·tẽr·ā′tion, *n.* the act of taking out the bowels; evisceration. [Rare.]

ex·ē·quā′tŭr, *n.* [L., lit., let him perform or follow it out; 3d pers. sing., pres. subj., of *exequi, exsequi,* to follow out, perform.]
1. an official document given to a consul or commercial agent by the government of the country in which he is stationed and authorizing him to perform his duties there.
2. the right granted by secular rulers for the publication of papal bulls, etc.

ex·ē′qui·ăl, *a.* [L. *exequialis, exsequialis,* from *exequiæ, exsequiæ,* the following of a corpse, exequies, from *exsequi,* to follow out.] pertaining to funerals; funereal.

ex·ē′qui·ous, *a.* pertaining to or belonging to exequies. [Rare.]

ex′ē·quy, *n.*; *pl.* **ex′ē·quieş,** [L. *exsequiæ, exequiæ,* nom. pl., lit., the following of a corpse beyond the walls, a funeral procession, funeral rites, from *exsequi, exequi,* to follow out, to accompany to the grave.]
1. [*pl.*] funeral rites; the ceremonies of burial; obsequies.
2. a funeral procession.

ex·ẽr′cent (egz-) *a.* using; practicing; following, as a calling or profession. [Obs.]

ex′ẽr·cī·ṣȧ·ble, *a.* capable of being exercised, used, employed, or exerted.

ex′ẽr·cīṣe, *n.* [ME. *exercise*; L. *exercitium,* exercise, from *exercere,* to drive out, drill, exercise.]
1. active use or operation; employment; as, writing requires the *exercise* of imagination.
2. activity for the purpose of training or developing the body or mind; systematic practice; especially, bodily exertion for the sake of health.
3. [*usually in pl.*] a regular series of movements designed to strengthen or develop some part of the body or some faculty; as, finger *exercises* for the piano.
4. a problem or group of written examples, passages, etc. to be studied and worked out for developing technical skill, as in mathematics, grammar, etc.
5. [*pl.*] a series of ceremonial acts; program of speeches, etc., as at graduation.
exercise bone; a deposit of a hard, bony substance in muscle, tendon, etc., as a result of continual exercise.
Syn.—exertion, use, practice, application, training, employment, drill.

ex′ẽr·cīṣe, *v.t.*; exercised, *pt., pp.*; exercising, *ppr.* 1. to put into action; use; employ; as, he *exercised* self-control.
2. to use habitually; practice; train: used reflexively or in the passive; as, she was *exercised* in virtue.
3. to put into action for the purpose of training or developing, as the body, a muscle, the mind, a mental faculty, etc.
4. to drill (troops).
5. to take up the attention of; especially, to worry; perplex; harass; trouble: used especially in the passive; as, he was greatly *exercised* about the decision.
6. to carry out (duties, etc.); perform; fulfill.
7. to exert, wield, or have (influence, control, authority, etc.).

ex′ẽr·cīṣe, *v.i.* to take exercise; to do exercises.

ex′ẽr·cīṣ·ẽr, *n.* 1. one who exercises.
2. a mechanical apparatus for exercising the muscles.

ex′ẽr·ci·ṣi·ble, *a.* exercisable. [Obs.]

ex·ẽr·ci·tā′tion (egz-), *n.* [ME. *exercitacioun*; L. *exercitatio* (*-onis*), exercise, practice, from *exercitare,* intens. of *exercere,* to exercise.]
1. exercise; practice; use.
2. an essay, oration, etc. that serves as an exercise.

ex·ẽr′ci·tŏr (egz-), *n.* [L. *exercitor,* an exerciser, trainer, from *exercere,* to exercise.] in law, the person entitled to the profits of a ship, whether he is the actual owner or some one else, as the charterer or the captain.

ex·ẽrgue′ (eg-zẽrg′), *n.* [Fr. *exergue,* lit., that which is out of work, the exergue of a coin; Gr. *ex,* out, and *ergon,* work.]
1. the space on a coin or medal between the rim and the bottom of the picture or design: it is often used for the date, place, etc.
2. the inscription in this space.

ex·ẽrt′ (eg-zẽrt′), *v.t.*; exerted, *pt., pp.*; exerting, *ppr.* [L. *exertare, exsertare,* from *exerere, exserere,* to stretch out, put forth; *ex,* out, and *serere,* to join, fasten together.]
1. to thrust forth; to emit; to disclose; to reveal. [Obs.]

Before the gems *exert*
Their feeble heads. —Philips.

2. to put forth energetically; to exercise; to put in action; to bring into active operation; as, to *exert* one's strength, to *exert* one's mind.
3. to put forth; to do or perform. [Now Rare.]

When the will has *exerted* an act of command on any faculty of the soul.—South.

to exert oneself; to put forth effort; to strive.

ex·ẽr′tion, *n.* 1. the act, fact, or process of exerting or straining; the act of putting into motion or action; a striving or struggling.
2. energetic activity; effort; as, the ship was saved by great *exertions* of the crew.

ex·ẽrt′ive, *a.* exerting or tending to exert.

ex·ẽrt′ment, *n.* exertion. [Obs.]

ex·ē′ṣion (egz-), *n.* the act of eating out or through. [Obs.]

ex·es′tū·āte, *v.i.* to boil; to be agitated. [Obs.]

ex·es·tū·ā′tion, *n.* a boiling; ebullition; agitation caused by heat; effervescence. [Obs.]

ex′ē·unt, [L., lit., they go out; 3d pers. pl., pres. ind. of *exire*, to go out.] they go off (the stage): a word used in the text of plays or as a stage direction, to indicate the point in the action when two or more actors leave the stage.

ex′ē·unt om′nēṣ, [L.] all (of the characters who are on stage) go off: a stage direction.

ex fā′ci·ē, [L.] on the face (of a legal document, etc.).

ex·fē·tā′tion, *n.* [L. *ex*, out, and *fœtus*, the fetus.] fetation in some organ other than the uterus.

ex·flect′, *v.t.* [L. *ex*, out, and *flectere*, to turn, bend.] to cause to turn outward. [Rare.]

ex·fō′di·āte, *v.t.* [L. *ex*, out, and *fodire*, to dig.] to take out by digging. [Rare.]

ex·fō′li·āte, *v.t.* and *v.i.*; exfoliated, *pt.*, *pp.*; exfoliating, *ppr.* [LL. *exfoliatus*, pp. of *exfoliare*, to strip of leaves.] to cast off or come off in flakes, scales, or layers, as skin, bark, etc.

ex·fō·li·ā′tion, *n.* 1. an exfoliating or being exfoliated.

2. something exfoliated, as scales, layers of bark, etc.

ex·fō′li·ā·tive, *a.* causing or characterized by exfoliation.

ex·fō′li·ā·tive, *n.* anything which produces or hastens exfoliation.

ex·hāl′à·ble, *a.* that can be exhaled.

ex·hāl′ănt, *a.* having the quality of exhaling or evaporating.

ex·hāl′ănt, *n.* an organ or duct for exhaling.

ex·hà·lā′tion, *n.* 1. an exhaling or being exhaled; expiration or evaporation.

2. that which is exhaled; that which is emitted or which rises in the form of vapor; fumes or steam; emanation; effluvium.

ex·hāle′, *v.i.*; exhaled, *pt.*, *pp.*; exhaling, *ppr.* [Fr. *exhaler*; L. *exhalare*, to breathe out, exhale; *ex*, out, and *halare*, to breathe.]

1. to breathe forth air; to expire.

2. to be given off or rise into the air as vapor; to evaporate.

ex·hāle′, *v.t.* 1. to breathe forth (air or smoke).

2. to give off (vapor, fumes, etc.).

ex·hāle′ment, *n.* exhalation. [Obs.]

ex·hāl′ent, *a.* and *n.* same as *exhalant.*

ex·haust′ (egz-ąst′), *v.t.*; exhausted, *pt.*, *pp.*; exhausting, *ppr.* [LL. *exhaustare*, freq. of L. *exhaurire*, to draw out, drink up; *ex*, out, and *haurire*, to draw, drain.]

1. to draw out or drain off the whole of; to draw out until nothing of the matter drawn is left; as, to *exhaust* the air from a tire.

2. to use or expend the whole of; to consume completely; to cause the loss of; as, to *exhaust* the strength or spirits; to *exhaust* one's patience; to *exhaust* the fertility of the soil.

3. to treat, examine, or discuss exhaustively; to consider thoroughly; as, to *exhaust* a subject or a study.

4. to empty by drawing out the contents; specifically, in chemistry, to remove one or more of the component parts from, by means of solvents.

5. to make weak or worthless; to remove strength or power from; as, he is *exhausted* by his dissipations; the nation was *exhausted* by war.

Syn.—drain, empty, spend, consume, weary, waste.

ex·haust′, *v.i.* to be discharged or let out, as gas or steam from an engine.

ex·haust′, *a.* exhausted. [Obs.]

ex·haust′, *n.* 1. a creating of an outflowing current of air by means of a partial vacuum.

2. an apparatus for doing this, as in getting rid of fumes, dust, stale air, etc.

3. the discharge or release of used steam, gas, etc. from the cylinders of an engine at the end of every working stroke of the pistons.

4. the pipe through which such steam, gas, etc. is released.

5. something given off or let out, as fumes from a gasoline engine.

ex·haust′ dràft, a draft produced by an exhaust fan.

ex·haust′ẽr, *n.* one who or that which exhausts or draws out; specifically, in gas making, one of several devices that prevent back pressure on the retorts.

ex·haust′ fan, a fan that creates a current by forming a partial vacuum.

ex·haust·i·bil′i·ty, *n.* the quality of being exhaustible; capacity for being exhausted.

ex·haust′i·ble, *a.* that can be exhausted.

ex·haust′ing, *a.* causing or tending to cause exhaustion; tiring; fatiguing; as, *exhausting* work.

ex·haus′tion (egz-ąs′chun), *n.* [L. *exhaustus*, pp. of *exhaurire*, to draw off, exhaust.]

1. an exhausting.

2. the state of being exhausted; especially, (a) great fatigue or weariness; (b) the condition of being used up.

3. in mathematics, a method of proving the equality of two magnitudes by showing that if one is supposed either greater or less than the other, there will arise a contradiction.

4. in logic, the method by which a point is proved by showing that any alternative is impossible.

ex·haust′ive, *a.* exhausting or tending to exhaust; specifically, leaving nothing out; complete; thorough; as, *exhaustive* research.

ex·haust′ive·ly, *adv.* in an exhaustive manner; thoroughly.

ex·haust′ive·ness, *n.* the state or quality of being exhaustive.

ex·haust′less, *a.* incapable of being exhausted; inexhaustible; as, an *exhaustless* fund or store.

ex·haust′ment, *n.* exhaustion. [Obs.]

ex·haust′ pīpe, in a steam engine, the pipe which carries the exhaust steam.

ex·haust′ pōrt, in a steam engine, the opening through which the exhaust steam escapes from the cylinder.

ex·haust′ stēam, steam which is discharged after performing its work of producing motion in the piston: called also *exhaust.*

ex·haus′tūre, *n.* exhaustion. [Obs.]

ex′hē·drà, *n.* same as *exedra.*

ex·her′ē·dāte, *v.t.*; exheredated, *pt.*, *pp.*; exheredating, *ppr.* [L. *exheredatus*, pp. of *exheredare*, to disinherit, from *exheres*, disinherited; *ex-* priv., and *heres*, an heir.] to disinherit. [Rare.]

ex·her·ē·dā′tion, ex·he·red·i·tā′tion, *n.* in Roman law, a disinheriting.

ex·hib′it (egz-ib′it), *v.t.*; exhibited, *pt.*, *pp.*; exhibiting, *ppr.* [L. *exhibitus*, pp. of *exhibere*, to hold forth, present; *ex*, out, and *habere*, to hold, have.]

1. to present or expose to view; show; display.

2. to present to public view for entertainment, instruction, advertising, judgment in a competition, etc.

3. to give evidence of; reveal; as, he *exhibited* impatience.

4. in law, to present (a piece of evidence, etc.) officially to a court.

5. in medicine, to administer (a drug, etc.) as a remedy.

ex·hib′it, *v.i.* to put pictures, wares, etc. on public display.

ex·hib′it (egz-ib′it), *n.* 1. any paper produced or presented to a court or to auditors, referees, or arbitrators, as a voucher, or in proof of facts; a voucher or document produced.

2. in law, any document or object produced in court as evidence.

3. any article or number of articles arranged in a public place for show; a display; as, a livestock *exhibit.*

Syn.—exhibition, exposition, fair, showing.

ex·hib′it·ẽr (egz-ib′), *n.* same as *exhibitor.*

ex·hi·bi′tion (eks-i-bish′un), *n.* [LL. *exhibitio* (*-onis*), a handing out, giving up, from L. *exhibere*, to hold forth, present, show.]

1. the act or fact of exhibiting for inspection; a showing or presenting to view; display.

2. the offering, producing, or showing of titles, authorities, or papers of any kind, before a tribunal, in proof of facts.

3. a public show; a display, as of pictures, merchandise, athletic feats, etc. in public.

4. an endowment for the maintenance of scholars in the English universities, not depending on the foundation. [Brit.]

5. in medicine, the act of administering a remedy.

ex·hi·bi′tion·ẽr, *n.* in English universities, one who has a scholarship allowance. [Brit.]

ex·hi·bi′tion·iṣm, *n.* 1. a tendency to call attention to oneself or show off one's talents, skill, etc.

2. in psychology, (a) a tendency to expose parts of the body that are conventionally concealed; (b) an instance of such exposure.

ex·hi·bi′tion·ist, *n.* a person who indulges in exhibitionism.

ex·hib′it·ive (egz-), *a.* serving or tending to exhibit (usually with *of*).

ex·hib′it·ive·ly, *adv.* by representation.

ex·hib′it·ŏr, *n.* one that exhibits; especially, (a) a person, company, etc. that enters an exhibit in a fair, show, competition, etc.; (b) the owner or manager of a motion-picture theater.

ex·hib′it·ō·ry, *a.* 1. exhibiting; showing.

2. of or for exhibition.

ex·hil′à·rănt (egz-il′), *a.* [L. *exhilarans* (*-antis*), ppr. of *exhilarare*, to gladden.] exhilarating.

ex·hil′à·rănt, *n.* that which exhilarates.

ex·hil′à·rāte (egz-il′à-rāte), *v.t.*; exhilarated, *pt.*, *pp.*; exhilarating, *ppr.* [L. *exhilaratus*, pp. of *exhilarare*, to gladden, to make merry; *ex*, out, and *hilarare*, to gladden, from *hilaris*, glad.] to make cheerful or merry; to enliven; to make glad or joyous; to gladden; to cheer; as, good wine *exhilarates* the spirits.

ex·hil′à·rāte, *v.i.* to become cheerful or joyous. [Rare.]

ex·hil′à·rā·ting, *a.* enlivening; giving life and vigor to the spirits; cheering; gladdening.

ex·hil′à·rā·ting·ly, *adv.* in an exhilarating manner.

ex·hil·à·rā′tion, *n.* [LL. *exhilaratio* (*-onis*), a gladdening or enlivening, from L. *exhilaratus*, pp. of *exhilarare*, to gladden.]

1. the act of enlivening the spirits; the act of making glad or cheerful.

2. the state of being enlivened or cheerful; liveliness; animation; high spirits.

ex·hil′à·rā·tive, *a.* exhilarating or tending to exhilarate.

ex·hort′ (egz-ort′), *v.t.*; exhorted, *pt.*, *pp.*; exhorting, *ppr.* [ME. *exhorten*; L. *exhortari*, to exhort; *ex*, out, and *hortari*, to urge, incite.] to incite by words or advice; to animate or urge by arguments to a good deed or to any laudable conduct or course of action; hence, to advise; to warn; to caution.

I *exhort* you to be of good cheer.
—Acts xxvii. 22.

ex·hort′, *v.i.* to deliver exhortation; to use words or arguments to incite to good deeds.

And with many other words did he testify and *exhort.* —Acts ii. 40.

ex·hort′, *n.* exhortation. [Obs.]

ex·hor·tā′tion, *n.* [ME. *exhortacion*; OFr. *exhortation*; L. *exhortatio* (*-onis*), an exhorting, from *exhortari*, to exhort.]

1. the act or practice of exhorting; the act of inciting to laudable deeds; incitement to that which is good or commendable.

2. advice; counsel; admonition; a plea, sermon, etc. that exhorts.

ex·hor′tà·tive, *a.* same as *exhortatory.*

ex′hor·tā·tŏr (eks′), *n.* an exhorter; one who exhorts. [Rare.]

ex·hor′tà·tō·ry (egz-or′), *a.* [LL. *exhortatorius*, from L. *exhortari*, to exhort.] of, or having the nature of, exhortation; meant to exhort; admonitory.

ex·hort′ẽr (egz-ort′ẽr), *n.* one who exhorts or encourages.

ex·hū·mā′tion, *n.* [LL. *exhumatio* (*-onis*), from *exhumare*, to dig up, exhume; L. *ex*, out, and *humus*, the ground.] the act of exhuming; a disinterment.

ex·hūme′, *v.t.*; exhumed, *pt.*, *pp.*; exhuming, *ppr.* [LL. *exhumare*, to dig out of the ground; L. *ex*, out, and *humus*, the ground.]

1. to dig out of the earth from its place of burial; to disinter.

2. to unearth; to disclose; to reveal.

ex·i·gea̋nt′(egz-i-zhoṅ′), **ex·i·gea̋nte′**(-zhoṅt′), *a.* [Fr. *exigeant*, masc., *exigeante*, f., exacting, particular, ppr. of *exiger*; L. *exigere*, to exact.] exacting.

ex′i·ġence (eks′), *n.* same as *exigency.*

ex′i·ġen·cy, *n.*; *pl.* **ex′i·ġen·cieṣ,** [OFr. *exigence*; LL. *exigentia*, necessity, need, from L. *exigens* (*-entis*), ppr. of *exigere*, to drive forth, to exact; *ex*, out, and *agere*, to drive.]

1. the condition or quality of being exigent; urgency; imperative need or want; as, the *exigency* of the times or of business.

2. a situation which demands immediate action, supply, or remedy; as, in the present *exigency*, no time is to be lost.

3. [*pl.*] pressing needs; demands; requirements.

ex′i·ġent, *a.* [L. *exigens* (*-entis*), ppr. of *exigere*, to drive out, drive forth; *ex*, out, and *agere*, to drive.]

1. urgent; critical; pressing; requiring immediate aid or action.

2. requiring more than is reasonable; demanding; exacting.

ex′i·ġent, *n.* 1. an urgent occasion; exigency. [Obs.]

2. in old English law, a writ which required a sheriff to summon a defendant to surrender on pain of outlawry. [Obs.]

ex′i·ġent·ẽr, *n.* in old English law, an officer in the Court of Common Pleas who made out exigents and proclamations in cases of outlawry. [Obs.]

ex′i·ġi·ble, *a.* capable of being exacted; demandable; requirable. [Rare.]

ex·i·gū′i·ty, *n.* [L. *exiguitas* (*-atis*), scantiness, smallness, from *exiguus*, scanty, small.] smallness; scantiness; littleness.

ex·ig′ū·ous (egz-), *a.* [L. *exiguus*, scanty, small.] small; slender; minute; diminutive.

ex·ig′ū·ous·ness, *n.* the state or character of being exiguous. [Rare.]

ex′ïle (eks′ *or* egz′), *n.* [ME. *exil*, *exile*; OFr. *exil*, *essil*; L. *exilium*, *exsilium*, banishment, exile, from *exul*, *exsul*, an exile, one who is banished.]

1. banishment; the state of being expelled from one's native country or place of residence by authority, and forbidden to return, either for a limited time or for life.

2. an abandonment of one's country or removal to a foreign country for residence, either from choice or necessity.

3. one who is banished or expelled from his country by authority; also, one who abandons his country and resides in another.

the Exile; the period in the 6th century B.C. during which the Jews were held in captivity in Babylon.

ex′ïle, *v.t.*; exiled, *pt.*, *pp.*; exiling, *ppr.* to banish, as a person from his country or from a particular jurisdiction, by authority, with a prohibition of return, either for a limited time or for life; to drive away, expel, or transport from one's country.

to exile oneself; to leave one's country with a view not to return.

ex′ïle, *a.* slender; thin; fine. [Obs.]

ex′ïle·ment, *n.* banishment. [Obs.]

ex·il′iç, ex·il′i·ăn, *a.* [L. *exilium*, exile.] of exile, especially the exile of the Jews in Babylon.

ex·i·li′tion, *n.* a sudden springing or leaping out. [Obs.]

ex·il′i·ty, *n.* [L. *exilitas*, from *exilis*, small.] slenderness; fineness; thinness. [Rare.]

ex·im′i·ous, *a.* excellent. [Rare.]

ex·in′ȧ·nïte (egz-), *v.t.* to make empty; to weaken. [Obs.]

ex·in·ȧ·ni′tion, *n.* an emptying or evacuation; hence, privation; loss; destitution.

ex·in·dū′si·āte, *a.* [L. *ex-* priv., and *indusium*, lit., an undergarment; in botany, the indusium.] in botany, not furnished with an indusium: said of ferns.

ex·ist′ (egz-ist′), *v.i.*; existed, *pt.*, *pp.*; existing, *ppr.* [L. *existere*, *exsistere*, to step, or come forth, to stand forth; *ex*, out, and *sistere*, to cause to stand, to set, place, caus. of *stare*, to stand.]

1. to be; to have real existence or being of any kind; as, evils *exist* on every side.

By whom we *exist* and cease to be.—Milton.

2. to live; to have life or animation; as, men cannot *exist* in water, nor fishes on land.

3. to occur; to be present; be (*in* a given condition or place); as, water *exists* in milk.

ex·ist′ence, *n.* [ME. *existence*; OFr. *existence*; LL. *existentia*, existence, from L. *existere*, *exsistere*, to come forth, to exist.]

1. the state of existing; the state or fact of being.

2. life; continuance of being; as, a struggle for *existence*.

3. occurrence; specific manifestation.

4. a manner of existing, being, or living; as, sharecroppers have a poor *existence*.

5. anything which exists; an entity; an actuality.

6. reality; truth; actuality. [Obs.]

Syn.—being, entity, endurance, duration.

ex·ist′en·cy, *n.* existence. [Rare.]

ex·ist′ent, *a.* 1. being; having being or existence.

The eyes and mind are fastened on objects which have no real being, as if they were truly *existent*. —Dryden.

2. existing now; present; immediate.

ex·is·ten′tiăl (egz-is-ten′shăl), *a.* of or based on existence.

ex·is·ten′tiăl·iṣm, *n.* a literary-philosophic cult of nihilism and pessimism, popularized in France after World War II, chiefly by Jean-Paul Sartre: it holds that each man exists as an individual in a purposeless universe, and that he must oppose his hostile environment through the exercise of his free will.

ex·is·ten′tiăl·ly, *adv.* in an existential manner.

ex·ist′ẽr, *n.* one who or that which exists. [Rare.]

ex·ist′i·ble, *a.* capable of existing.

ex·is·ti·mā′tion (egz-), *n.* esteem. [Obs.]

ex′it (eks′ *or* egz′), [L., lit., he goes out; 3rd pers. sing. pres. ind. of *exire*, to go out.] he or she goes out: a direction used in plays, to indicate the point at which an actor is to leave the stage.

ex′it, *n.* [L. *exitus*, a going out, from *exitus*, pp. of *exire*, to go out.]

1. the departure of a player from the stage.

2. any departure; a going out.

3. a way of departure; passage out of a place; as, the building has ten *exits*.

ex·i′tiăl (egz-ish′ăl), **ex·i′tious** (-ish′us), *a.* [L. *exitialis*, destructive, from *exitium*, destruction, ruin.] destructive to life. [Obs.]

ex lī′bris, [L.] 1. from the books (library) of: an inscription followed by the name of the owner, often used on bookplates.

2. a bookplate.

ex′ō-, [from Greek *exō*, without.] a prefix meaning *without*, *outside*, *outer*, *outer part*: used chiefly in scientific words, where it is equivalent to *ecto-* and opposite in meaning to *endo-*, or *ento-*.

ex·ō·cär′di·ȧ, *n.* abnormal position of the heart.

ex·ō·cär′di·ăl, ex·ō·cär′di·aç, *a.* [*exo-*, and Gr. *kardia*, heart.] located outside the heart.

ex′ō·cärp, *n.* [*exo-*, and Gr. *karpos*, fruit.] in botany, the external part or layer of a ripened ovary or fruit; epicarp.

ex·oç·cip′i·tăl, *a.* [L. *ex*, out, and *occiput*, *occipitis*, the back part of the head, the occiput; *ob*, about, and *caput*, head.] of or pertaining to the exoccipitals.

ex·oç·cip′i·tăl, *n.* either of the two lateral bones on each side of the basioccipital, separate in the embryo but co-ossified in the adult of man and other mammals, forming the occipital bone.

ex·ō·chō′ri·on, *n.* [*exo-*, and Gr. *chorion*, skin, leather.] in zoology, the outer coating of the membrane enclosing the egg of an insect.

Ex·ō·coe′tus, *n.* [L., from *exocœtus*, a fish that sleeps on the shore; Gr. *exōkoitos*, sleeping out; *exō*, outside, and *koitē*, bed.] a genus of flying fishes belonging to the family *Exocœtidæ*. The pectoral fins, which are very large, enable them to leap through the air. The best known species are *Exocœtus volitans*, found in the Atlantic, and *Exocœtus exiliens*, in the Mediterranean.

ex·oç′ū·lāte, *v.t.* to put out or destroy the eyes of. [Rare.]

ex·oç·ū·lā′tion, *n.* [L. *exoculare*, to put out the eyes; *ex*, out, and *oculus*, eye.] the act of putting out or destroying the eyes. [Rare.]

ex′ōde, *n.* same as *exodus*.

ex′ōde, *n.* [Fr. *exode*; L. *exodium*, a comic interlude, a conclusion, end; Gr. *exodion*, the finale of a tragedy; neut. of *exodios*, belonging to the end or exit; *ex*, out of, from, and *hodos*, way.]

1. in ancient Greek drama, the conclusion of a play; the catastrophe.

2. in ancient Roman drama, an afterpiece of a farcical or satirical character.

ex′ō·dẽrm, *n.* [*exo-*, and Gr. *derma*, skin.]

1. the outer integument or crust of an insect.

2. in botany, the epidermis.

3. in zoology, the ectoderm.

ex·od′iç, *a.* 1. pertaining to an exodus.

2. in physiology, efferent.

ex′ō·dist, *n.* one who makes an exodus or who emigrates. [Rare.]

ex·ō·don′ti·ȧ (-shi-ȧ), *n.* [Mod.L., from L. *ex*, out, and Gr. *odon*, *odontos*, tooth; and *-ia*.] the branch of dentistry having to do with the extraction of teeth.

ex′ō·dus, *n.* [LL. *Exodus*, the Book of Exodus, from Gr. *exodos*, a going out; *ex*, out, and *hodos*, way.]

1. a journeying forth; a going out; a departure.

2. [E—] the departure from Egypt of the Israelites under the leadership of Moses.

3. [E—] the second book of the Old Testament, which describes this.

ex·ō·en′zȳme, *n.* same as *ectoenzyme*.

ex·of·fi′ciăl (-fish′ăl), *a.* having the authority of an officer; authoritative. [Rare.]

ex of·fi′ci·ō (-fish′i-ō), [L.] by reason of one's office; as, the mayor is, *ex officio*, president of the board of aldermen.

ex·ō·gam′iç, *a.* same as *exogamous*.

ex·og′ȧ·mous, *a.* of, pertaining to, characterized by, or practicing exogamy.

ex·og′ȧ·my, *n.* [*exo-*, and Gr. *gamos*, marriage.] a custom among certain tribes, clans, etc. which prohibits a man from marrying a woman of his own tribe, clan, etc.; outbreeding.

ex′ō·ġen, *n.* [L. *exogenus*; Gr. *exō*, outside, and *-genēs*, producing.] a seed plant that grows by adding layers on its outside; a dicotyledon.

ex″ō·ġē·net′iç, *a.* same as *exogenous*.

ex·oġ′e·nous (eks-), *a.* 1. developing from without; originating externally.

2. in biology, growing or developing from or on the outside.

3. in botany, of the nature of or pertaining to the exogens.

4. in anatomy, growing out from another part: applied to processes which are mere outgrowths of a bone, as a vertebra.

ex′ō·lēte, *a.* worn; faded; also, obsolete. [Obs.]

ex·ō·lū′tion, *n.* relaxation of the nerves. [Obs.]

ex·olve′, *v.t.* to loose. [Obs.]

ex·ō·mol·ō·ġē′sis, *n.* [LL., from Gr. *exomologēsis*, a full confession, from *exomologeisthai*, to confess in full.] a confession in full; a public confession. [Obs.]

ex·om′phȧ·los, ex·om′phȧ·lus, *n.* [L., from Gr. *exomphalos*, having a prominent navel; *ex*, out, and *omphalos*, navel.] in medicine, a navel rupture; umbilical hernia.

ex′ŏn, *n.* in England, a commander of the royal bodyguard; an exempt.

Ex′ŏn, *n.* a native or resident of Exeter, England.

ex·ō·när′thex, *n.* [Mod. Gr. *exōnarthēx*; *exō*, outside, and *narthēx*, the narthex.] in architecture, the outer of two narthexes in a Greek church.

ex·ō′nẽr (egz-), *v.t.* in Scots law, to exonerate.

ex·on′ẽr·āte (egz-on′ẽr-āt), *v.t.*; exonerated, *pt.*, *pp.*; exonerating, *ppr.* [L. *exoneratus*, pp. of *exonerare*, to disburden; *ex-* priv., and *onerare*, to load, from *onus*, *oneris*, a load, burden.]

1. to unload; to disburden. [Obs.]

The vessels *exonerate* themselves into a common duct. —Ray.

2. to relieve, as of a charge or blame resting on one; to clear of an imputation of guilt; to declare or prove blameless.

3. to relieve, as of an obligation, debt, or duty; to discharge of responsibility or liability.

Syn.—absolve, clear, justify, acquit, exculpate, relieve.

ex·on·ẽr·ā′tion, *n.* the act of exonerating or the state of being exonerated.

ex·on′ẽr·ȧ·tive, *a.* freeing from a burden or obligation; tending to absolve.

ex·on′ẽr·ā·tŏr, *n.* [LL. *exonerator*, from L. *exonerare*, to disburden, exonerate.] one who exonerates.

ex·ō·neū′răl, *a.* [*exo-*, and Gr. *neuron*, nerve.] neither included in nor dependent upon the nervous system.

ex·ō·neū′răl·ly, *adv.* in an exoneural manner or situation.

ex·ō·path′iç, *a.* [*exo-*, and Gr. *pathos*, suffering.] in pathology, pertaining to a disease caused by factors outside the organism: opposed to *endopathic* or *autopathic*.

ex″ō·pē·rid′i·um, *n.*; *pl.* **ex″ō·pē·rid′i·ȧ,** [L., from Gr. *exō*, outside, and *pēridion*, dim. of *pēra*, a wallet.] in botany, the outer envelope of a fungus having more than one layer, as in the star fungus.

ex·oph·thal′mi·ȧ, *n.* [L., from Gr. *exophthalmos*, with prominent eyes; *ex*, out, and *ophthalmos*, eye.] a condition in which the eyeball protrudes abnormally, as the result of disease.

ex·oph·thal′miç, *a.* of, pertaining to, affected with, or resembling exophthalmia.

exophthalmic goiter; a disease in which the thyroid gland is swollen, the eyeballs protrude, and the heart palpitates: also called *Graves's* or *Basedow's disease*.

ex·oph·thal′mus, ex·oph·thal′mos, ex·oph·thal′my, *n.* same as *exophthalmia*.

ex·oph′yl·lous, *a.* [*exo-*, and Gr. *phyllon*, a leaf.] in botany, having a naked plumule or one not sheathed in another leaf.

ex′ō·plaṣm (eks′), *n.* [*exo-*, and Gr. *plasma*, anything formed, from *plassein*, to form.] in biology, ectoplasm.

ex·op′ō·dïte, *n.* [*exo-*, and Gr. *pous*, *podos*, foot.] in *Crustacea*, the external one of the two main branches of a limb or appendage.

ex·op·ō·dit′iç, *a.* of or pertaining to the exopodite.

ex·op′tȧ·ble, *a.* [L. *exoptabilis*, desirable, from *exoptare*, to desire.] worthy of being sought after; desirable. [Obs.]

ex′ō·rȧ·ble, *a.* [L. *exorabilis*, easily entreated or moved, from *exorare*, to move by entreaty; *ex*, out, and *orare*, to pray.] susceptible to being moved or persuaded by pleas.

ex′ō·rāte, *v.t.* to obtain by request. [Obs.]

ex·or′bi·tănce (egz-) *n.* [L. *exorbitans* (*-antis*), ppr. of *exorbitare*, to go out of the track; *ex*, out, and *orbita*, track.]

1. a going beyond the rightful or usual limit, as in prices, demands, etc.; extravagance; as, the *exorbitances* of desire, of taxes, or of deportment.

2. lawlessness. [Archaic.]

ex·or′bi·tăn·cy, *n.*; *pl.* **ex·or′bi·tăn·cieṣ,** exorbitance.

ex·or′bi·tănt, *a.* going beyond what is reasonable, proper, just, usual, etc.; excessive; extravagant; enormous; as, *exorbitant* appetites and passions; *exorbitant* taxes.

ex·or′bi·tănt·ly, *adv.* in an exorbitant manner; excessively.

ex′or·ciṣe (eks′), *v.t.*; exorcised, *pt., pp.*; exorcising, *ppr.* [OFr. *exorciser*; LL. *exorcizare*; New Testament Gr. *exorkizein*, to drive away an evil spirit by adjuration, from Gr. *exorkoun*, to swear a person, administer an oath; *ex*, out, and *horkizein*, *horkoun*, to make one swear, from *horkos*, an oath.]

1. to expel or cast out by conjurations, incantations, or religious or magical ceremonies; as, to *exorcise* evil spirits.

2. to free from supposed evil spirits by religious or magical ceremonies; as, to *exorcise* a house.

3. to summon or command (a supposed evil spirit or spirits).

ex′or·cīṣ·ẽr, *n.* one who exorcises.

ex′or·ciṣm, *n.* the expulsion of supposed evil spirits from persons or places by certain adjurations and ceremonies; also, the verbal ceremony or ritual used for this purpose.

ex·or·ciṣ′măl, *a.* of the nature of, pertaining to, or resembling exorcism.

ex′or·cist, *n.* 1. one who exorcises.

2. one of a minor order of both the Orthodox Eastern and Roman Catholic churches.

3. one who conjures up evil spirits. [Obs.]

ex′or·cize, *v.t.*; exorcized, *pt., pp.*; exorcizing, *ppr.* same as *exorcise*.

ex·or′di·ăl (egz-), *a.* pertaining to the exordium of a discourse; introductory.

ex·or′di·um, *n.*; *pl.* **ex·or′di·umṣ, ex·or′di·ȧ,** [L. *exordium*, a beginning, from *exordiri*, to begin, commence.]

1. a beginning.

2. the introductory part of a discourse, treatise, etc.

ex·or·nā′tion (eks-), *n.* ornament; decoration, embellishment. [Rare.]

ex·or′tive, *a.* [L. *exortivus*, pertaining to the rising of the heavenly bodies, from *exortus*, pp. of *exoriri*, to rise out or forth; *ex*, out, and *oriri*, to rise.] relating to the east. [Obs.]

ex·os′çū·lāte, *v.t.* [L. *exosculatus*, ppr. of *exosculari*, to kiss fondly; *ex-*, intens., and *osculari*, to kiss.] to kiss; especially, to kiss heartily. [Obs.]

ex·ō·skel′e·tăl, *a.* relating to the exoskeleton.

ex·ō·skel′e·tŏn, *n.* [L., from Gr. *exō*, outside, and *skeleton*, a dried body, skeleton.] in zoology, the hardened, external supporting structure of an animal, usually composed of a horny, bony, or chitinous substance in the form of plates or scales, as in crustaceans, turtles, and fishes.

ex·os′miç, *a.* same as *exosmotic*.

ex·os·mō′sis, ex′os·mōse, *n.* [L., from Gr. *ex*, out, and *ōsmos*, a thrusting, from *ōthein*, to thrust, push, drive.] in osmosis, the slower diffusion of the more dense fluid through the semipermeable membrane to mingle with the less dense: opposed to *endosmosis*.

ex·os·mot′iç, *a.* relating to exosmosis.

ex′ō·spẽrm, *n.* same as *exospore*.

ex′ō·spōre, *n.* [*exo-*, and Gr. *spora*, a seed.] in botany, the outer covering of a spore; the epispore.

ex·ō·spōr′ous, *a.* [*exo-*, and Gr. *sporos*, a seed, a sowing.] with the spores growing on the outside.

ex·os′sāte, *v.t.* to remove the bones from; to bone. [Obs.]

ex·os·sā′tion, *n.* the act or process of removing the bones or other similar hard substance from; also, the state of having such parts removed. [Obs.]

ex·os′sē·ous, *a.* without bones; boneless. [Obs.]

ex′ō·stōme, *n.* [*exo-*, and Gr. *stoma*, mouth.] in botany, the aperture through the outer integument of an ovule, which together with the endostome completes the foramen.

ex·os·tō′sis, *n.* [L., from Gr. *exō*, outside, and *osteon*, a bone.]

1. an abnormal bony growth on the surface of a bone or tooth.

2. in botany, a knot formed upon the stem or root of a plant.

ex·os·tot′iç, *a.* of the nature of or pertaining to exostosis.

ex·ō·ter′iç, *a.* [LL. *exotericus*; Gr. *exōterikos*, external, from *exō*, outside.]

1. of the outside world; external.

2. not intended for only a chosen few or an inner group of disciples; suitable for outsiders or the uninitiated.

3. that can be understood by the public; popular.

Opposed to *esoteric*.

ex·ō·ter′iç, *n.* one of the general public and not the select few given esoteric instruction; an outsider.

ex·ō·ter′iç·ăl, *a.* same as *exoteric*.

ex·ō·ter′iç·ăl·ly, *adv.* in an exoteric manner.

ex·ō·ter′i·ciṣm, *n.* exoteric doctrines and principles.

ex·ō·ter′içs, *n.* same as *exotericism*.

ex·ō·thē′çȧ, *n.*; *pl.* **ex·ō·thē′cae** (-sē), [L., from Gr. *exō*, outside, and *thēkē*, a case.] the calcareous substance covering the outer wall or the visceral chamber of a coral.

ex·ō·thē′çāte, *a.* having exothecae, as a coral.

ex·ō·thē′ci·um, *n.* [L., from Gr. *exō*, outside, and *thēkē*, a case.] in botany, the outer covering of an anther.

ex·ō·thẽr′miç, *a.* [*exo-*, and Gr. *thermē*, heat.] pertaining to a liberation of heat, as in combustion.

ex·ot′iç (egz-), *a.* [L. *exoticus*; Gr. *exōtikos*, foreign, alien, from *exō*, outside.]

1. foreign; introduced from a foreign country; not native; extraneous; as, an *exotic* plant; an *exotic* term or word.

2. having the charm or fascination of the unfamiliar; strangely beautiful, enticing, etc.

ex·ot′iç, *n.* 1. a foreign or imported thing.

2. a plant that is not native.

ex·ot′iç·ăl, *a.* same as *exotic*.

ex·ot′iç·ăl·ness, *n.* the state or quality of being exotic.

ex·ot′i·ciṣm, *n.* 1. the state or quality of being exotic.

2. anything exotic, as a word or phrase.

ex·ō·tox′in, *n.* any of a group of toxic substances excreted by certain disease-producing bacteria: also called *true toxin*.

ex·pal′pāte, *a.* [L. *ex-* priv., and *palpus*, a feeler, from *palpare*, to stroke, touch softly.] not furnished with palpi or feelers.

ex·pand′, *v.t.*; expanded, *pt., pp.*; expanding, *ppr.* [L. *expandere*, to spread out; *ex*, out, and *pandere*, to spread, extend.]

1. to open; to spread; to unfold; as, a flower *expands* its leaves.

2. to cause to fill more space; to dilate; to enlarge in bulk; to distend; to inflate; as, to *expand* the chest by inspiration.

3. to enlarge in range or scope; to make more comprehensive; to develop in detail; as, to *expand* a discussion.

4. in mathematics, to complete or enlarge by performing operations indicated; as, $(a + b)\ (a - b) = a^2 - b^2$.

Syn.—diffuse, dilate, spread, unfold, swell, enlarge, extend, amplify.

ex·pand′, *v.i.* to become expanded; to open; to spread; to dilate; to extend in bulk or surface; as, metals *expand* by heat.

ex·pand′ed, *a.* in printing, extended.

ex·pand′ẽr, *n.* one who or that which expands; in mechanics, a tool for expanding metal, as for enlarging the opening in the end of a tube or for spreading the lead packing at the joining of iron pipes, so as to make gas-tight joints.

ex·pand′ing, *a.* becoming larger; increasing in dimensions; as, an *expanding* cloud.

expanding bit (or *drill*); in mechanics, a bit (or drill) so made that it can be adjusted to holes of various sizes.

expanding pulley; in mechanics, a pulley made in sections so that its diameter may be varied.

ex·panse′, *n.* [ME. *expans*; L. *expansus*, pp. of *expandere*, to spread out, expand.]

1. a large, open area or unbroken surface; wide extent; great breadth.

2. expansion.

3. the amount of expansion.

ex·panse′, *v.t.* to expand. [Obs.]

ex·pan·si·bil′i·ty, *n.* capacity for expansion; as, the *expansibility* of air.

ex·pan′si·ble, *a.* capable of being expanded or spread; capable of being extended, dilated, or diffused.

Bodies are not *expansible* in proportion to their weight. —Grew.

ex·pan′si·ble·ness, *n.* expansibility.

ex·pan′si·bly, *adv.* in an expansible manner.

ex·pan′sile, *a.* 1. expansible.

2. tending to expand.

3. of or characteristic of expansion.

ex·pan′sion, *n.* [LL. *expansio* (*-onis*), a spreading out, expanding, from L. *expansus*, pp. of *expandere*, to spread out, expand.]

1. the act of expanding or the state of being expanded; enlargement; distention; dilatation.

2. extended surface; extent; amount, degree, or extent to which anything is expanded; wide extent; immensity.

The starred *expansion* of the skies. —Beattie.

3. an expanded thing or part.

4. a development or full treatment, as of a topic.

5. in mechanics, the expanding in volume of gas in the cylinder of an internal-combustion engine after explosion.

6. in mathematics, the development in a fuller form of an expression indicated in a contracted form, as $(a + x)^2 = a^2 + 2ax + x^2$.

7. in a steam engine, the increase in bulk of steam in a cylinder when its communication with the boiler is cut off.

8. in naval architecture, the laying out of the vessel's lines in exact proportions and desired size by enlarging according to mathematical rules the lines of the model or drawing.

ex·pan′sion bōlt, a bolt with an attachment that expands and acts as a wedge as it is screwed inward, used in holes drilled in stone, concrete, etc.

ex·pan′sion çŭrb, a contrivance to counteract expansion or contraction by heat.

ex·pan′sion çŭrve, in a steam engine, the hyberbolic curve that indicates the ratio between the pressure and the volume of expanding gas or vapor in the cylinder.

ex·pan′sion en′ġine, a steam engine in which the supply of steam is cut off before the stroke is complete, the expansive power of the steam admitted being sufficient to complete the stroke.

ex·pan′sion gēar, in a steam engine, the apparatus by which the access of steam to the cylinder is cut off at a given part of the stroke.

ex·pan′sion·iṣm, *n.* the policy of expanding a nation's territory or its sphere or influence, often at the expense of other nations.

ex·pan′sion·ist, *n.* one who believes in or advocates expansionism.

ex·pan′sion joint, in a steam engine, (a) a joint for connecting steam pipes, made with a stuffing box, so as to allow one of them to slide within the enlarged end of the other when the length increases by expansion; (b) an attachment of a boiler in its framing to allow the former to expand without affecting the latter.

ex·pan′sion valve, in a steam engine, a cut-off valve.

ex·pan′sive, *a.* 1. having the power to expand, to spread, or to dilate; having the capacity of being expanded; as, the *expansive* quality of air; the *expansive* atmosphere.

2. widely extended; comprehensive; broadminded; as, *expansive* benevolence.

3. of, or working by means of, expansion.

4. characterized by a free and generous nature; sympathetic; demonstrative; open; as, an *expansive* person.

5. in psychiatry, characterized by expansiveness.

ex·pan′sive·ly, *adv.* in an expansive manner; by means of expansion.

ex·pan′sive·ness, *n.* 1. the state or quality of being expansive.

2. in psychiatry, a state characterized by overestimation of the ego, delusions of grandeur, etc.; megalomania.

ex·pan′sūre, *n.* expanse. [Obs.]

ex pär′tē, [L., lit., from a part; *ex*, out, from, and *parte*, ablative of *pars*, part.] relating to only one part or side; one-sided.

ex·pā′ti·āte (eks-pā′shi-āt), *v.i.*; expatiated, *pt., pp.*; expatiating, *ppr.* [L. *expatiatus*, pp. of *expatiari*, *exspatiari*, to go out of one's course, wander; *ex*, out, and *spatiari*, to walk, roam.]

1. to roam; to rove without prescribed limits; to wander freely.

Bids his free soul *expatiate* in the skies. —Pope.

2. to enlarge in discourse or writing; to elaborate (*on* or *upon*).

ex·pā′ti·āte, *v.t.* to allow to wander at large; to broaden. [Obs.]

ex·pa·ti·ā′tion, *n.* 1. the act of expatiating.
2. a lengthy account of something.

ex·pā′ti·ā·tŏr, *n.* one who expatiates.

ex·pā′ti·ȧ·tō·ry (-shi-ȧ-), *a.* expatiating.

ex·pā′tri·āte, *v.t.* and *v.i.*; expatriated, *pt., pp.*; expatriating, *ppr.* [LL. *expatriatus,* pp. of *expatriare,* to banish; L. *ex,* out of, and *patria,* native country, fatherland, from *pater,* father.]
1. to drive (a person) from his native land; to exile.
2. to withdraw (oneself) from one's native land; to renounce the rights of citizenship where one was born, and become a citizen of another country.

ex·pā·tri·ā′tion, *n.* an expatriating or being expatriated.

ex·pect′, *v.t.*; expected, *pt., pp.*; expecting, *ppr.* [L. *expectare, exspectare,* to look for, await; *ex,* out, and *spectare,* to look.]
1. to wait for. [Obs.]

The guards,
By me encamped on yonder hill, *expect*
Their motion. —Milton.

2. to look for as likely to occur or appear; to anticipate; as, we *expect* a visit that has been promised; we *expected* nothing better.
3. to look for as due, proper, or necessary; as, your bill is due and immediate payment is *expected.*

England *expects* every man to do his duty. —Nelson.

4. to suppose; to presume; to guess; as, I *expect* I did the damage. [Colloq.]
to be expecting; to be pregnant. [Colloq.]
Syn.—anticipate, await, forecast, forebode, wait for, rely on, look for, foresee.

ex·pect′, *v.i.* to wait; to stay. [Obs.]

ex·pect′, *n.* same as *expectation.* [Obs.]

ex·pect′ȧ·ble, *a.* to be expected; that may be expected. [Rare.]

ex·pect′ănce, *n.* same as *expectancy.*

ex·pect′ăn·cy, *n.*; *pl.* **ex·pect′ăn·cies,** [LL. *expectantia,* from L. *expectare, exspectare,* to look for, expect.]
1. an expecting or being expected; expectation.
2. that which is expected, especially on a statistical basis; as, life *expectancy.*
estate in expectancy or *expectant estate*; in law, an estate which one will receive at some future time. It may be either a reversion, a remainder, or an executory interest.

ex·pect′ănt, *a.* 1. expecting; specifically, (a) having or showing expectation; (b) waiting, as for a position, etc.
2. in medicine, designating or of a method of treatment which consists in observing the progress of diseases and removing deranging influences without prescribing active medicines unless absolutely required.
expectant estate; see *estate in expectancy* under *expectancy.*

ex·pect′ănt, *n.* [L. *expectans* (*-antis*), ppr. of *expectare,* to expect.] one who expects something; one who waits in expectation.

ex·pect′ănt·ly, *adv.* in an expectant manner.

ex·pect′ănt mŏth′ẽr, a pregnant woman.

ex·pec·tā′tion, *n.* 1. an expecting or looking forward to an event as about to happen.

The same weakness of mind which indulges absurd *expectations,* produces petulance in disappointment. —Irving.

2. a looking for as due, proper, or necessary.
3. the state of being expected or looked for; the state of being awaited.

Our preparation stands in *expectation.* —Shak.

4. that which is expected; the object of expectation.
5. [*also pl.*] prospect of future good, as of possessions, wealth, and the like.

His magnificent *expectations* made him . . . the best match in Europe. —Prescott.

6. in medicine, expectant treatment.
7. the degree of probability of the occurrence, duration, etc. of something.
expectation of life; the number of years that a person can expect to live after any given age, as indicated by statistics of mortality.
Expectation Week; in church calendars, the week ending with Whitsunday, or the day of Pentecost, the period within which the apostles prayed for and expected the descent of the Holy Ghost.
Syn.—hope.—*Expectation* differs from *hope* in that the latter originates in desire, and may exist with little or no cause for believing that the desired event will arrive, whereas *expectation* is founded on some reasons which render the event probable. *Hope* looks forward to some good; *expectation* looks forward to good or evil.

ex·pect′ȧ·tive, *a.* [L. *expectare, exspectare,* to expect.] of or characterized by expectation.

ex·pect′ȧ·tive, *n.* 1. that which is expected.
2. formerly, in the Roman Catholic Church, the right to a benefice when it should become vacant, granted by the pope or the sovereign; also, the person upon whom the right was conferred.

ex·pect′ed·ly, *adv.* in the expected manner; according to expectation.

ex·pect′ẽr, *n.* one who expects; one who waits for something or for another person.

ex·pect′ing·ly, *adv.* in a state of expectation.

ex·pect′ive, *a.* expectative. [Rare.]

ex·pect′ŏr, *n.* expecter. [Obs.]

ex·pec′tō·rănt, *a.* [L. *expectorans* (*-antis*), ppr. of *expectorare,* to banish from the mind, to expectorate.] pertaining to, causing, or increasing expectoration.

ex·pec′tō·rănt, *n.* any expectorant medicine.

ex·pec′tō·rāte, *v.t.* and *v.i.*; expectorated, *pt., pp.*; expectorating, *ppr.* [L. *expectoratus,* pp. of *expectorare,* to banish from the mind, to expel from the breast; *ex,* out, and *pectus* (*-oris*), breast.]
1. to cough up and spit (phlegm, mucus, etc.).
2. to spit.

ex·pec·tō·rā′tion, *n.* 1. an expectorating.
2. that which is expectorated, as phlegm, etc.

ex·pec′tō·rā·tive, *a.* and *n.* same as *expectorant.*

ex·pēde′, *v.t.* to expedite. [Obs.]

ex·pē′di·āte, *v.t.* to expedite. [Obs.]

ex·pē′di·ence, *n.* same as *expediency.*

ex·pē′di·en·cy, *n.*; *pl.* **ex·pē′di·en·cies,** 1. fitness or suitableness to effect some desired end or the purpose intended; appropriateness to the particular circumstances of the case.
2. that which is the most practical or expedient, taking all the circumstances into account.
3. in ethics, the principle of seeking immediate or selfish gain or advantage at the expense of or without consideration of genuine principle; self-interest.
4. an expedition; adventure. [Obs.]
5. expedition; haste; dispatch. [Obs.]
Syn.—utility, advantage, interest, fitness, propriety.

ex·pē′di·ent, *a.* [L. *expediens* (*-entis*), ppr. of *expedire,* to bring forward, dispatch; *ex,* out, and *pes, pedis,* foot.]
1. useful for effecting a desired result; fit or suitable for the purpose; convenient under the circumstances; advantageous.
2. contributing or tending to contribute to present advantage or self-interest; utilitarian; politic.
3. quick; expeditious. [Obs.]

ex·pē′di·ent, *n.* 1. that which serves to promote or advance; any means which may be employed to accomplish an end; as, let every *expedient* be employed.
2. a makeshift; a resource; means devised or employed in an exigency.

ex·pē·di·en′tiăl (-shăl), *a.* based on or guided by expediency; resulting from expediency or expedients.

ex·pē·di·en′tiăl·ly, *adv.* in an expediential manner, or by expediential means.

ex·pē′di·ent·ly, *adv.* 1. in an expedient manner; suitably; conveniently.
2. hastily; quickly. [Obs.]

ex·ped′i·ment, *n.* 1. in old English law, the whole of a man's goods. [Obs.]
2. an expedient. [Obs.]

ex·ped′i·tāte, *v.t.*; expeditated, *pt., pp.*; expeditating, *ppr.* [LL. *expeditatus,* pp. of *expeditare*; L. *ex,* from, and *pes, pedis,* foot.] formerly, in the forest laws of England, to cut out the balls or claws of, as a dog's forefeet, to prevent it from chasing deer.

ex·ped·i·tā′tion, *n.* the act or process of expeditating, or the state of being expeditated.

ex′pē·dīte, *v.t.*; expedited, *pt., pp.*; expediting, *ppr.* [L. *expeditus,* pp. of *expedire,* lit., to free one caught by the feet, to hasten, dispatch; *ex,* out, and *pes, pedis,* foot.]
1. to hasten; to quicken; to accelerate or make easy the motion or progress of; to facilitate; as, artificial heat may *expedite* the growth of plants.
2. to do quickly.
3. to dispatch; to send forth. [Rare.]
Syn.—hasten, speed, hurry, drive, accelerate, push.

ex′pē·dīte, *a.* 1. quick; ready; prompt; alert; as, *expedite* execution.
2. easy; clear of impediments; unencumbered; as, to make a way plain and *expedite.*
3. convenient.

ex′pē·dīte·ly, *adv.* in an expedite manner.

ex′pē·dīte·ness, *n.* the state or quality of being expedite.

ex′pē·dīt·ẽr, *n.* a person who expedites, especially one employed by an industry, government agency, etc. to expedite urgent or involved projects.

ex·pē·di′tion, *n.* [OFr. *expedition*; L. *expeditio* (*-onis*), a dispatching, from *expedire,* to dispatch.]
1. haste; speed; quickness; dispatch; as, the mail is conveyed with *expedition.*
2. a sending forth or embarking upon a voyage, march, etc. for some definite purpose, as exploration or battle.
3. a journey for such a purpose.
4. the people, ships, equipment, etc. on such a journey.

ex·pē·di′tion·ȧ·ry, *a.* of, pertaining to, or composing an expedition.

ex·pē·di′tion·ist, *n.* one who makes an expedition or goes as one of an expedition.

ex·pē·di′tious (-shus), *a.* done with or characterized by expedition; efficient and speedy; prompt; quick.

ex·pē·di′tious·ly, *adv.* in an expeditious manner; hastily; with celerity or dispatch.

ex·pē·di′tious·ness, *n.* the quality of being expeditious; celerity; quickness.

ex·ped′i·tive, *a.* expeditious. [Obs.]

ex·pel′, *v.t.*; expelled, *pt., pp.*; expelling, *ppr.* [ME. *expellen*; OFr. *expeller*; L. *expellere,* to drive or thrust out; *ex,* out, and *pellere* to thrust, drive.]
1. to drive out; to force to leave; to dismiss forcibly; as, to *expel* a traitor from a country; to *expel* air from the lungs.
2. to dismiss or send away by authority; to deprive of rights, membership, etc.; as, he was *expelled* from school because of misconduct.
3. to reject; to refuse. [Obs.]
4. to exclude; to keep out or off. [Rare.]
Syn.—banish, exile, eject, cast out, oust.

ex·pel′lȧ·ble, *a.* 1. capable of being expelled or driven out.

Acid *expellable* by heat. —Kirwan.

2. subject to expulsion; as, he is not *expellable* from his club on account of his heresy.

ex·pel′lănt, ex·pel′lent, *a.* expelling or tending to expel.

ex·pel′lănt, ex·pel′lent, *n.* an expellant medicine.

ex·pel′lẽr, *n.* one who or that which expels.

ex·pend′, *v.t.*; expended, *pt., pp.*; expending, *ppr.* [L. *expendere,* to weigh out, pay out; *ex,* out, and *pendere,* to weigh.] to disburse; to pay out; to spend; to consume by using; to use up; as, to *expend* money, time, labor, or material.

ex·pend′, *v.i.* 1. to be spent, used, or consumed. [Rare.]
2. to pay out, spend, or disburse money.

ex·pend′ȧ·ble, *a.* 1. that can be expended.
2. in military usage, (a) designating supplies or equipment expected to be used up or destroyed in service and therefore not entered on a certificate of expenditure; hence, (b) designating equipment or men considered replaceable and therefore worth sacrificing to gain an objective.

ex·pend′i·tŏr, *n.* [LL. *expenditor,* from L. *expendere,* to weigh out; *ex,* out, and *pendere,* to weigh.] in old English law, one who was appointed by the commissioners of sewers to pay, disburse, or expend the money collected by taxes for the repair of sewers.

ex·pend′i·tūre, *n.* 1. the act of expending; a spending or using up of money, time, etc.; disbursement; as, a corrupt administration is known by extravagant *expenditures* of public money.
2. the amount of time, money, etc. that is expended; expense.

The receipts and *expenditures* of this extensive country. —Hamilton.

ex·pense′, *n.* [ME. *expense*; OFr. *expense*; LL. *expensa* (supply *pecunia,* money), expense, money spent; L. *expensum,* money spent, neut. of *expensus,* pp. of *expendere,* to expend.]
1. (a) a laying out or expending; the disbursing of money; (b) [Archaic.] employment and consumption, as of time or labor.
2. [*also in pl.*] that which is expended; specifically, money expended; cost; charge; as, a

prudent man limits his *expenses* by his income.

3. [*pl.*] (a) charges met with in carrying out a task, one's work, etc.; (b) money to pay for these charges.

4. cost, with the idea of loss, damage, or sacrifice; as, he did this at the *expense* of his character.

Courting popularity at his party's *expense*. —Brougham.

5. anything which involves or requires great or undue cost; a drain on one's finances; as, sickness is always an *expense*; he was a great *expense* to his father.

at the expense of; (a) with the payment borne by; (b) with the loss of.

Syn.—price, cost, charge, payment, expenditure, outlay.

ex·pense′fu̇l, *a.* costly; expensive. [Obs.]

ex·pense′fu̇l·ly, *adv.* in a costly manner; with great expense. [Obs.]

ex·pense′fu̇l·ness, *n.* expensiveness. [Obs.]

ex·pense′less, *a.* without cost or expense. [Rare.]

ex·pense′ mag′ȧ·zīne, a small magazine of ammunition prepared for immediate use.

ex·pen′sive, *a.* 1. costly; requiring or involving much expense; high-priced; dear; as, an *expensive* dress.

2. given to expense; free in the use of money; extravagant; lavish; as, an *expensive* woman. [Obs.]

ex·pen′sive·ly, *adv.* with great expense; at great cost or charge.

ex·pen′sive·ness, *n.* costliness; the quality of incurring or requiring great expenditures of money; extravagance; as, the *expensiveness* of war is not its greatest evil.

ex·pẽr·ġē·faç′tion, *n.* an awakening or arousing. [Obs.]

ex·pē′ri·ence, *n.* [ME. *experience*; L. *experientia*, a trial, proof, experiment, from *experiens* (*-entis*), ppr. of *experiri*, to try, put to test.]

1. trial, proof, or test. [Obs.]

2. an actual living through an event or events; personally undergoing or observing something or things in general as they occur.

3. anything observed or lived through; as, our trip was a pleasant *experience*.

4. all that has happened to one; everything that one has seen or done; as, it hasn't happened in my *experience*.

5. effect on one of anything or everything that has happened to him; individual reaction to events, feelings, etc.; as, what was your *experience* with the work?

6. (a) activity that includes training, observation or practice, and personal participation; (b) the period of such activity; as, teaching *experience*.

7. knowledge, skill, or practice resulting from this.

8. that feeling which is connected with conversion or regeneration in a spiritual sense.

experience meeting; a meeting, especially among Methodists, for prayer and the relating of religious experiences.

ex·pē′ri·ence, *v.t.*; experienced, *pt.*, *pp.*; experiencing, *ppr.* 1. to have experience of; to undergo; to feel; to meet with; as, we all *experience* pain, sorrow, and pleasure.

2. (a) to exercise; as, to *experience* oneself for hard work; (b) to test. [Obs.]

to experience religion; to be converted.

Syn.—try, feel, undergo, encounter, endure.

ex·pē′ri·enced (-enst), *a.* 1. having had much experience, as in a particular occupation or activity.

2. having learned from experience; made wise, competent, etc. by experience.

ex·pē′ri·en·cẽr, *n.* 1. an experimenter. [Obs.]

2. one who experiences.

ex·pē′ri·ence tā′ble, a table showing life expectancy at given ages, based upon the experience of actuaries.

ex·pē′ri·ent, *a.* experienced. [Obs.]

ex·pē·ri·en′tiăl (-shăl), *a.* acquired from or pertaining to experience; empirical.

Necessary truths are derived from our own thoughts; *experiential* truths are derived from our observation of things about us. —Whewell.

ex·pē·ri·en′tiăl·iṣm, *n.* in philosophy, the theory that experience is the origin and test of all knowledge.

ex·pē·ri·en′tiăl·ist, *n.* one who believes in the doctrine of experientialism.

ex·pē·ri·en′tiăl·ist, *a.* of the nature of or pertaining to experientialism.

ex·pē·ri·en′tiăl·ly, *adv.* by means of experience; empirically.

ex·per′i·ment, *n.* [ME. *experiment*; OFr. *experiment*; L. *experimentum*, a trial, test, from *experiri*, to try, test.]

1. a test or trial of something; specifically, (a) any action or process undertaken to discover something not yet known or to demonstrate something known; (b) something tried to find out whether it will be effective; as, giving students complete freedom to choose their courses is an educational *experiment*.

A political *experiment* cannot be made in a laboratory, nor determined in a few hours. —J. Adams.

2. the conducting of such tests or trials; experimentation.

3. experience. [Obs.]

Michelson-Morley experiment; in physics, an experiment, originally made by A. A. Michelson, American physicist, and E. W. Morley, American chemist, demonstrating that both sections of a divided light ray move at the same velocity in directions perpendicular to each other: deductions from such results indicate that the earth's motion through space does not affect the speed of light, nor is the absolute motion of the earth measurable; this experiment tends to prove the Einstein theory.

ex·per′i·ment, *v.i.*; experimented, *pt.*, *pp.*; experimenting, *ppr.* to make an experiment or experiments: used with *on*, *upon*, *in*, *by*, and *with*; as, scientists *experiment on* natural bodies for the discovery of their qualities, etc.

ex·per′i·ment, *v.t.* to try; also, to establish by trial. [Obs.]

ex·per·i·men′tăl, *a.* [Fr. *experimental*, from L. *experimentum*, an experiment.]

1. of or based on experience rather than theory or authority.

2. based on, tested by, or having the nature of, experiment.

3. for the sake of experiment; testing.

4. tentative.

5. of or used for experiments.

experimental philosophy; philosophy which states nothing as positive truth, but teaches that scientific thought and research will gradually approximate to the truth.

ex·per·i·men′tăl·iṣm, *n.* 1. the theory or practice of depending on experimentation; empiricism.

2. fondness for making experiments.

ex·per·i·men′tăl·ist, *n.* one who makes or is fond of making experiments.

ex·per·i·men′tăl·ize, *v.i.*; experimentalized, *pt.*, *pp.*; experimentalizing, *ppr.* to experiment.

ex·per·i·men′tăl·ly, *adv.* 1. by experiment.

2. as an experiment.

ex·per″i·men·tā′ri·ăn, *a.* experimental. [Obs.]

ex·per″i·men·tā′ri·ăn, *n.* an experimentalist. [Obs.]

ex·per″i·men·tā′tion, *n.* the act, practice, or process of making experiments.

ex·per·i·men′tȧ·tive, *a.* experimental.

ex·per′i·men·tā·tŏr, *n.* an experimenter. [Obs.]

ex·per′i·men·tẽr, *n.* one who makes experiments; one skilled in experiments.

ex·per′i·men·tist, *n.* one who makes experiments; an experimenter.

ex·per·reç′tion, *n.* an awakening from sleep or lethargy; a rousing. [Obs.]

ex′pẽrt (*or* eks-pẽrt′), *a.* [ME. *expert*; OFr. *expert*; L. *expertus*, skilled, experienced, pp. of *experiri*, to try, test.]

1. very skillful; having much training and knowledge in some special field.

2. of or from an expert; as, an *expert* opinion.

ex′pẽrt, *n.* [Fr.] 1. a person who is very skillful or highly trained and informed in some special field.

2. in the United States Army, (a) the highest of the three ratings of proficiency of a rifleman; (b) a soldier with this rating.

Syn.—adroit, clever, dexterous, proficient, ready, skillful, adept, versed, able.

ex·pẽrt′, *v.t.* to experience. [Obs.]

ex″pẽrt·iṣe′, *n.* [Fr.] the skill or knowledge of an expert.

ex·pẽrt′ly, *adv.* in an expert manner.

ex·pẽrt′ness, *n.* skill derived from practice; dexterity; adroitness; as, *expertness* in musical performance, *expertness* in war or in seamanship, *expertness* in reasoning.

ex·pet′i·ble, *a.* worthy of being wished for; desirable. [Obs.]

ex′pi·ȧ·ble, *a.* [OFr. *expiable*, from L. *expiare*, to expiate.] that can be expiated.

ex′pi·āte, *v.t.*; expiated, *pt.*, *pp.*; expiating, *ppr.* [L. *expiatus*, pp. of *expiare*, to make satisfaction or atonement; *ex*, out, and *piare*, to appease, propitiate, from *pius*, devout, pious.]

1. to atone for; to make amends or reparation for (wrongdoing or guilt); to pay the penalty of.

2. to avert by certain observances. [Rare.]

Frequent showers of stones . . . could . . . be *expiated* only by bringing to Rome Cybele. —T. H. Dyer.

ex′pi·āte, *a.* finished; ended. [Obs.]

ex·pi·ā′tion, *n.* 1. the act of atoning for a crime; the act of making amends for wrongdoing or guilt; atonement.

2. the means by which atonement is made; amends.

3. an act by which threatened prodigies were averted. [Obs.]

Upon the birth of such monsters, the Grecians and Romans did use divers sorts of *expiations*. —Hayward.

ex′pi·ȧ·tist, ex′pi·ā·tŏr, *n.* one who expiates.

ex″pi·ȧ·tō′ri·ous, *a.* expiatory. [Obs.]

ex′pi·ȧ·tō·ry, *a.* expiating; intended or serving to expiate; as, an *expiatory* sacrifice.

ex′pi·lāte, *v.t.* to pillage; to plunder; to rob. [Obs.]

ex·pi·lā′tion, *n.* the act of expilating; pillage. [Obs.]

ex′pi·lā·tŏr, *n.* a pillager. [Obs.]

ex·pīr′ȧ·ble, *a.* capable of expiring or coming to an end.

ex·pīr′ănt, *n.* one who is expiring.

ex·pi·rā′tion, *n.* [L. *expiratio* (*-onis*), *exspiratio* (*-onis*), a breathing out, from *expirare*, to breathe out, expire.]

1. the act of breathing out, as of air from the lungs: opposed to *inspiration*.

2. a breathing one's last; a dying.

3. the emission of volatile matter from any substance; evaporation; exhalation; as, the *expiration* of warm air from the earth. [Obs.]

4. cessation; close; end; conclusion; termination of a limited time; as, the *expiration* of a month or year; the *expiration* of a lease; the *expiration* of a contract or agreement.

5. that which is produced by expiring or breathing out; the sound caused by breathing out.

ex·pīr′ȧ·tō·ry, *a.* pertaining to expiration; relating to breathing out air from the lungs.

ex·pīre′, *v.t.*; expired, *pt.*, *pp.*; expiring, *ppr.* [OFr. *expirer*; L. *expirare*, *exspirare*, to breathe out, exhale, expire; *ex*, out, and *spirare*, to breathe.]

1. to breathe out; to expel from the lungs: opposed to *inspire*; as, we *expire* air at every breath.

2. to give off (an odor, vapor, etc.). [Obs.]

3. to conclude. [Obs.]

ex·pīre′, *v.i.* 1. to breathe out air from the lungs: opposed to *inspire*.

2. to breathe one's last breath; to die.

3. to fly out; to be thrown out with force. [Obs.]

The ponderous ball *expires*. —Dryden.

4. to come to an end; to cease; to terminate; to close or conclude, as a given period; as, the lease will *expire* on the first of May.

ex·pī·ree′, *n.* formerly, a convict (specifically, an English convict sent to Australia) who has served his period of punishment.

ex·pīr′ing, *a.* 1. breathing out air from the lungs; also, breathing the last breath; dying; ending; terminating.

2. pertaining to or uttered at the time of dying; as, *expiring* words; *expiring* groans.

ex·pī′ry (*or* eks′pi-), *n.*; *pl.* **ex·pī′rieṣ,** 1. a coming to an end; termination.

We had to leave at the *expiry* of the term. —Lamb.

2. death. [Archaic.]

ex·pis′çāte, *v.t.* [L. *expiscatus*, pp. of *expiscari*, to search out, fish out; *ex*, out, and *piscari*, to fish, from *piscis*, a fish.] to fish out; to discover by artful means or by strict examinations. [Chiefly Scot.]

Expiscating if the renown'd extreme
They force on us will serve their turns. —Chapman.

ex·pis·çā′tion, *n.* the act of expiscating or fishing out; the act of getting at the truth of any matter by strict inquiry and examination. [Chiefly Scot.]

ex·pis′çȧ·tŏr, *n.* one who expiscates. [Chiefly Scot.]

ex·pis′çȧ·tō·ry, *a.* suited or designed to expiscate. [Chiefly Scot.]

ex·plāin′, *v.t.*; explained, *pt.*, *pp.*; explaining, *ppr.* [OFr. *explaner*; L. *explanare*, to flatten, spread out; *ex*, out, and *planare*, to make level, from *planus*, level, plain.]

1. to make plain, clear, or intelligible; to clear of obscurity.
2. to give the meaning or interpretation of; to expound.
3. to account for; to state reasons for.
4. to flatten out; to expand. [Obs.]
to explain away; to state reasons for so as to justify or make understandable.
to explain oneself; (a) to make clear what one means; (b) to give reasons explaining or justifying one's conduct.
Syn.—illustrate, elucidate, interpret, expound.

ex·plāin′, *v.i.* to give an explanation or explanations.

ex·plāin′à·ble, *a.* capable of being cleared of obscurity or of being made plain to the understanding; capable of being interpreted; accountable.

ex·plāin′ēr, *n.* one who explains; an expositor; an interpreter.

ex·plāit′, *v.t.* to explain. [Obs.]

ex′plà·nāte, *a.* in biology, having outward extension in a flat form.

ex·plà·nā′tion, *n.* [L. *explanatio* (*-onis*), a making plain, an explanation, from *explanare*, to explain; *ex*, out, and *planus*, plain.]
1. the act of explaining, expounding, or interpreting; exposition; illustration; interpretation; the act of clearing from obscurity and making intelligible; as, the *explanation* of a passage in Scripture, or of a contract or treaty.
2. that which makes clear, or explains.
3. the sense given a thing by one explaining it; interpretation; meaning.
4. the process of adjusting a misunderstanding by explaining the circumstances; reconciliation.
Syn.—definition, description, exposition, interpretation.

ex·plan′à·tive, *a.* explanatory.

ex·plan′à·tō·ri·ly, *adv.* in an explanatory manner; as an explanation.

ex·plan′à·tō·ri·ness, *n.* the quality of being explanatory.

ex·plan′à·tō·ry, *a.* tending or intended to explain; containing explanation; as, *explanatory* notes.
Syn.—explicit, express.—That which is *explanatory* is added to clear up difficulties or obscurities; that which is *explicit* of itself obviates every difficulty, while that which is *express* requires the language used to be unambiguous.

ex·plăt′, *v.t.* to explain. [Obs.]

ex·plē′tion, *n.* accomplishment; fulfillment. [Obs.]

ex′plē·tive, *n.* [LL. *expletivus*, serving to fill, from L. *expletus*, pp. of *explere*, to fill; *ex*, out, up, and *plere*, to fill.]
1. something which is not necessary, but is added to fill up or to ornament; specifically, in rhetoric and grammar, a word, phrase, etc. which is not necessary for the meaning or construction, but is added for rhetorical, rhythmical, or metrical reasons.
2. a profane interjection; an oath; an imprecation; as, he answered with *expletives*.

ex′plē·tive, *a.* used to fill out a sentence, line, etc.

ex′plē·tive·ly, *adv.* in an expletive manner.

ex′plē·tō·ry, *a.* same as *expletive*.

ex′pli·cà·ble, *a.* [L. *explicabilis*, from *explicare*, to unfold.] that can be explained.

ex′pli·cà·ble·ness, *n.* the state or quality of being explicable.

ex′pli·cāte, *a.* opened; unfolded; explained. [Obs.]

ex′pli·cāte, *v.t.*; explicated, *pt.*, *pp.*; explicating, *ppr.* [L. *explicatus*, pp. of *explicare*, to unfold, spread out; *ex*, out, and *plicare*, to fold.]
1. to unfold; to expand; to open. [Obs.]
2. to unfold the meaning or sense of; to explain; to make clear or explicit (something obscure or implied); to interpret.

ex′pli·cāte, *v.i.* to give an explanation. [Rare.]

ex·pli·cā′tion, *n.* 1. the act of opening or unfolding.
2. the act of explaining; explanation; exposition; interpretation; as, the *explication* of the parables.
3. a detailed account, as of the implications of a statement.

ex′pli·cā·tive, *a.* [from L. *explicatus*, pp. of *explicare*, to unfold, explain.] explicating or tending to explicate; explanatory.

ex′pli·cā·tōr, *n.* [L. *explicator*, from *explicare*, to unfold, explain.] one who unfolds or explains; an expounder.

ex′pli·cā·tō·ry, *a.* explicative; explanatory.

ex·plic′it, *a.* [L. *explicitus*, pp. of *explicare*, to unfold, explain; *ex*, out, and *plicare*, to fold.]
1. plain in language; distinctly expressed; definite; clearly stated; not obscure or ambiguous; express, not merely implied: distinguished from *implicit*.
2. outspoken; saying what is meant with no disguised meaning or reservation: applied to persons; as, he was *explicit* in his terms.
Syn.—express, definite, plain, positive.

ex′pli·cit, [an abbrev. of L. *explicitus* (*est liber*), the book is unfolded or ended; *explicitus*, properly pp. of *explicare*, to unfold, explain.] a word formerly used at the conclusion of books, as *finis* is now used, to indicate the end.

ex·plic′it·ly, *adv.* plainly; expressly; without duplicity; without disguise or reservation of meaning; not by inference or implication; as, he *explicitly* avows his intention.

ex·plic′it·ness, *n.* the quality of being explicit; plainness of language or expression; clearness; direct expression of ideas or intention, without reserve or ambiguity.

ex·plōde′, *v.t.* exploded, *pt.*, *pp.*; exploding, *ppr.* [L. *explodere*, to drive off by clapping; *ex*, off, and *plaudere*, to clap, applaud.]
1. to decry or reject with noise; to express disapprobation of, with noise or sounds of contempt; as, to *explode* a play on the stage. [Obs.]
2. to discredit; to expose as false; to treat with contempt and drive from notice; to drive into disrepute; to reject; as, astrology is an *exploded* science.
3. to make burst with violence and noise; to blow up; to detonate.

The kindled powder *exploded* the ball.
—Blackmore.

4. to cause to change suddenly and violently from a solid to a quickly expanding gas.

ex·plōde′, *v.i.* 1. to be exploded; to burst noisily and violently; to blow up.
2. to break forth noisily; as, he *exploded* with anger at her stupidity.

ex·plōd′ed view (vū), a photograph or drawing showing in proper sequence and relationship the various parts of an assembly, as of a machine.

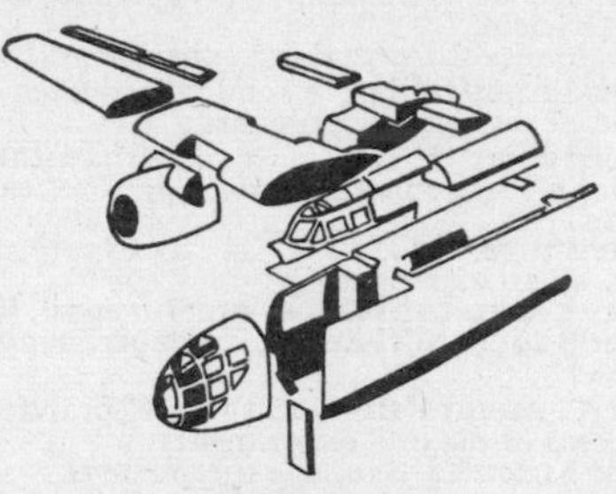

EXPLODED VIEW
(fuselage and wing of airplane)

ex·plōd′ent, *n.* in phonetics, same as *explosive*.

ex·plōd′ēr, *n.* one who or that which explodes.

ex′ploit (*or* eks-ploit′), *n.* [ME. *esploit*; OFr. *esploit*, an exploit, action, deed, from LL. *explicta*, neut. pl., a judicial act, writ, from L. *explicitus*, pp. of *explicare*, to unfold.]
1. a heroic act; a deed of renown or daring; a great or noble achievement.
2. combat; battle; war. [Obs.]

ex·ploit′, *v.t.*; exploited, *pt.*, *pp.*; exploiting, *ppr.* [ME. *esploiten*; OFr. *esploiter*, to perform, dispatch, from LL. *explectare*, to execute, from *explicta*, a judicial act, writ.]
1. to achieve. [Obs.]
2. to make use of; to utilize; to turn to account.
3. to make unethical use of for one's own advantage or profit; to turn selfishly or unfairly to one's own account.
4. in Marxism, to make profit from the labor of (others).

ex·ploi′tăġe, *n.* exploitation.

ex·ploi·tā′tion, *n.* an exploiting or being exploited; especially, the act of utilizing or turning to one's own use.

ex·ploit′à·tive, *a.* 1. exploiting.
2. of exploitation.

ex·ploi′tēr, *v.t.* [Fr.] to exploit. [Rare.]

ex·ploi′tēr, *n.* one who exploits.

ex·ploi′tūre, *n.* the act of exploiting.

ex·plōr′à·ble, *a.* capable of being explored.

ex·plō′rāte, *v.t.* to explore. [Obs.]

ex·plō·rā′tion, *n.* [L. *exploratio* (*-onis*), from *explorare*, to explore.]
1. the act of exploring, or looking into closely; close search; strict or careful examination.
2. the act of traveling for purposes of discovery in regions previously unknown or little known.
3. in medicine, the examination or probing of an organ, wound, etc.

ex·plōr′à·tive, *a.* 1. exploratory.
2. tending to explore.

ex′plō·rā·tōr, *n.* one who explores; one who searches or examines closely. [Rare.]

ex·plōr′à·tō·ry, *a.* of, in, or for exploration.

ex·plōre′, *v.t.*; explored, *pt.*, *pp.*; exploring, *ppr.* [L. *explorare*, to search out, investigate; *ex*, out, and *plorare*, to cry out, wail.]
1. to hunt for; to seek after; to search carefully for. [Obs.]
2. to look into closely; to examine carefully; to investigate.
3. to travel in (a region previously unknown or little known) in order to learn about its natural features, inhabitants, etc.
4. in medicine, to examine or probe (an organ, etc.).
Syn.—examine, pry into, search, seek, scrutinize.

ex·plōre′, *v.i.* to make explorations.

ex·plōre′ment, *n.* the act of exploring; search; trial. [Rare.]

ex·plōr′ēr, *n.* one who or that which explores; specifically, (a) one who explores an unknown or little-known region; (b) an instrument for exploring a wound, etc.

ex·plōr′ing, *a.* engaged in or intended for exploration; as, an *exploring* party.

ex·plō′ṣion, *n.* [L. *explosio* (*-onis*), a driving off by clapping, from *explodere*, to drive off by clapping; *ex*, out, off, and *plaudere*, to clap, applaud.]
1. the act of exploding; a sudden, forcible expansion of a substance, as gunpowder or an elastic fluid, usually accompanied by a loud sound; detonation; as, an *explosion* of dynamite, an *explosion* of fire damp; also, the noise made by exploding.
2. a sudden bursting or flying to pieces as a result of internal pressure; as, the *explosion* of a boiler.
3. a sudden and violent outburst of emotion; a loud breaking forth; as, an *explosion* of anger.
4. in phonetics, the sudden release of breath in the articulation of a plosive.

ex·plō′sive, *a.* 1. of, causing, or having the nature of, an explosion.
2. tending to explode; especially, tending to burst forth noisily.
3. in phonetics, pronounced with a sudden release of breath, as the consonants *b*, *d*, *g*, *k*, *p*, and *t* when used as initial sounds.

ex·plō′sive, *n.* [L. *explosus*, pp. of *explodere*, to explode.]
1. any substance which can explode or cause an explosion; as, gunpowder, nitroglycerin, dynamite, and guncotton are *explosives*.
2. an explosive consonant.

ex·plō′sive·ly, *adv.* in an explosive manner.

ex·pō·li·ā′tion, *n.* a spoiling; a wasting. [Obs.]

ex·pol′ish, *v.t.* to polish carefully. [Obs.]

ex·pōne′, *v.t.* 1. to explain. [Obs.]
2. to represent; to give the characteristics of. [Obs.]
3. to imperil; to expose to danger. [Obs.]

ex·pō′nent, *a.* [L. *exponens* (*-entis*), ppr. of *exponere*, to set forth, indicate; *ex*, out, and *ponere*, to place.] setting forth; explaining; expounding; interpreting.

ex·pō′nent, *n.* 1. a person who sets forth, expounds, or interprets (principles, methods, etc.).
2. a person or thing that is an example or symbol (*of* something).
3. in algebra, a small figure or symbol placed above and at the right of another figure or symbol to show how many times the latter is to be multiplied by itself (e.g., $b^3 = b \times b \times b$).
exponent of a ratio; the quotient arising when the antecedent is divided by the consequent; as, 6 is the *exponent of the ratio* of 30 to 5.

ex·pō·nen′tiăl (-shăl), *a.* in algebra, relating to exponents; especially, involving the variable or unknown quantity as an exponent.
exponential curve; a curve whose nature is defined by means of an exponential equation.
exponential equation; an equation which contains an exponential quantity.
exponential quantity; in algebra, a quantity whose exponent is unknown or variable.
exponential series; a series in which exponential equations and quantities are developed.

ex·pō'ni·ble, *a.* [from L. *exponere*; see *expound.*]
1. needing to be explained.
2. in logic, designating a proposition that needs to be restated for inclusion in a syllogism.

ex·pō'ni·ble, *n.* an exponible proposition.

ex·pōrt', *v.t.*; exported, *pt., pp.*; exporting, *ppr.* [L. *exportare*, to carry out or away; *ex*, out, and *portare*, to carry.] to carry out or away; specifically, in commerce, to send, as produce or goods, from one country to another, especially for purposes of sale; as, to *export* cotton goods, to *export* machinery.

ex'pōrt, *n.* 1. the act or process of exporting; exportation; as, to encourage the *export* of cured meat.
2. that which is exported; goods of any kind sent to a foreign country for sale: usually in the plural; as, our *exports* grow larger year by year.

ex'pōrt, *a.* of exporting or exports; for exportation.

ex·pōrt·à·bil'i·ty, *n.* the state or quality of being exportable.

ex·pōrt'à·ble, *a.* capable of being exported.

ex·pōr·tā'tion, *n.* [L. *exportatio* (*-onis*), a carrying out, exportation, from *exportare*, to carry out.]
1. the act or process of exporting.
2. an export.

ex·pōrt'ēr, *n.* a person or company in the export trade: opposed to *importer*.

ex·pōṣ'ăl, *n.* exposure.

ex·pōṣe', *v.t.*; exposed, *pt., pp.*; exposing, *ppr.* [OFr. *exposer*, from L. *expositus*, pp. of *exponere*, to put or set forth, expose.]
1. to set or cast out; to leave in a place unprotected and uncared for; to abandon; as, among the ancient Greeks, parents *exposed* their unwanted children.
2. to make bare; to uncover; to disclose; as, to *expose* a fraud.
3. to put forward or place in a position to be seen; to exhibit; as, to *expose* goods for sale.
4. to set out to view, as an opinion, set of principles, and the like; to lay open to examination; to promulgate; to interpret; to explain.

Those who seek truth only freely *expose* their principles to the test. —Locke.

5. to make liable; to subject; to place in the way of something to be avoided; as, vanity *exposes* a person to ridicule; this *exposed* him to danger.
6. to hold up to censure by disclosing the faults of; to divulge the crimes of; to show the folly or ignorance of; as, to *expose* a hypocrite or a rogue.
7. in photography, to subject (a sensitized film or plate) to the action of actinic rays.

ex·po·sé' (eks-pō-zā'), *n.* [Fr., pp. of *exposer*, to expose.]
1. a disclosure; specifically, a revelation concerning a person or persons, or a condition of affairs, disagreeable or embarrassing to those involved.
2. a formal and detailed setting forth of the facts of a situation; a demonstration. [Now Rare.]

ex·pōṣed', *a.* 1. laid open; laid bare; unsheltered; uncovered; unprotected; made liable to attack.
2. disclosed.
3. not covered with clothing; indecently or insufficiently clothed.
4. placed in a position or condition favorable to the contracting of disease or contagious infection.

Syn.—liable, subject.

ex·pōṣ'ed·ness, *n.* the state of being exposed, open to attack, or unprotected.

ex·pōṣ'ēr, *n.* one who exposes.

ex·pō·ṣi'tion, *n.* [ME. *expositioun*; OFr. *exposition*; L. *expositio* (*-onis*) a setting forth, narration, from *expositus*, pp. of *exponere*, to set forth, display.]
1. a setting forth of facts, ideas, etc.; detailed explanation.
2. writing or speaking that sets forth or explains: distinguished from *description, narration, argumentation.*
3. a large public exhibition or show, often international in scope.
4. that part of a play, etc. which reveals what has happened before, who the characters are, etc.
5. the first section of certain musical forms, as the sonata, fugue, etc., which introduces the main theme or themes.
6. an exposing or being exposed. [Obs.]

ex·poṣ'i·tive, *a.* [L. *expositus*, pp. of *exponere*, to set forth.] serving to expose or explain; expository; explanatory.

ex·poṣ'i·tŏr, *n.* a person, piece of writing, etc. that expounds or explains; an interpreter.

ex·poṣ'i·tō·ry, *a.* of, containing, or having the nature of, exposition; explanatory.

ex pōst faç'tō, [L., lit., from what is done afterward; *ex*, from, *post*, afterward, and *facto*, ablative of *factus*, pp. of *facere*, to do.] in law, done or made after another thing, but having retroactive effect.

ex post facto law; a law declaring an act penal or criminal which was not illegal at the time it was committed; or raising the grade of an offense, making it greater than it was when committed; or increasing the punishment after the commission of the offense; or altering the rules of evidence, so as to allow different or less evidence to convict the offender than was required when the offense was committed. Such laws are prohibited in the United States by the Constitution.

ex·pos'tū·lāte, *v.i.*; expostulated, *pt., pp.*; expostulating, *ppr.* [L. *expostulatus*, pp. of *expostulare*, to demand vehemently, require; *ex*, out, and *postulare*, to demand.] to reason earnestly (*with* a person) on some impropriety of his conduct, objecting to the wrong he has done or intends, and urging him to desist or to make redress.

The emperor's ambassador *expostulated with* the king that he had broken the league with the emperor. —Hayward.

ex·pos'tū·lāte, *v.t.* to discuss; to examine. [Rare.]

ex·pos·tū·lā'tion, *n.* [L. *expostulatio* (*-onis*), from *expostulare*, to expostulate.]
1. the act of expostulating or reasoning with a person in opposition to his conduct; dissuasion.

Expostulations end well between lovers, but ill between friends. —Spectator.

2. in rhetoric, an address containing expostulation.

ex·pos'tū·lā·tŏr, *n.* one who expostulates.

ex·pos'tū·là·tō·ry, *a.* of or expressing expostulation; as, an *expostulatory* address or debate.

ex·pos'tūre, *n.* exposure. [Obs.]

ex·pō'ṣūre (-zhūr), *n.* 1. an exposing or being exposed (in various senses).
2. the situation of a place in regard to points of the compass, or to a free access of air or light; as, a building has a northern or a southern *exposure*.
3. in photography, (a) the subjection of a sensitized film or plate to the action of actinic rays; (b) a sensitized surface or section of a film for making one picture; (c) the time during which such a surface or film is exposed.

ex·pō'ṣūre mē'tēr, in photography, an instrument for measuring the intensity of light on the subject and thus determining the correct exposure.

ex·pound', *v.t.*; expounded, *pt., pp.*; expounding, *ppr.* [ME. *expounden*; OFr. *expondre*; L. *exponere*, to put forth, expose, expound; *ex*, out, and *ponere*, to put.]
1. to set forth point by point; to state in detail.
2. to explain; to lay open the meaning of; to clear of obscurity; to interpret; as, to *expound* a text of Scripture; to *expound* a law.
3. to lay open; to examine; as, to *expound* the pocket. [Obs.]

ex·pound'ēr, *n.* [ME. *expownere*, from *expounen*, to expound.] one who expounds; an explainer; one who interprets or explains the meaning.

ex·press', *v.t.*; expressed, *pt., pp.*; expressing, *ppr.* [ME. *expressen*; L. *expressus*, pp. of *exprimere*, to press or squeeze out.]
1. to press or squeeze out; to force out or cause to flow by pressure; as, to *express* the juice of grapes or of apples.
2. to get by pressure; elicit by force; extort.
3. to put into words; represent by language; state.
4. to make known; reveal; show; as, his face *expressed* sorrow.
5. to picture, represent, or symbolize in music, art, etc.
6. to show by a sign; symbolize; signify; as, the sign + *expresses* addition.
7. to dispatch, forward, or send by express; as, to *express* a package.

to express oneself; (a) to state one's thoughts; (b) to give expression to one's feelings, imagination, etc., especially in creative or artistic activity.

ex·press', *a.* [ME. *expresse*; L. *expressus*, prominent, distinct, pp. of *exprimere*, to press out, describe.]
1. given in direct terms; not implied or left to inference; clearly expressed; not ambiguous; plain; as, *express* terms; an *express* covenant or agreement.
2. copied; closely resembling; bearing an exact representation.

His face *express*. —Milton.

3. intended or sent for a particular purpose or on a particular errand; as, to send an *express* messenger.
4. [orig., for the *express* purpose of running to one station.] fast, direct, and making few stops; as, an *express* train: distinguished from *local*.
5. characterized by speed or velocity; specifically, (a) for fast driving; as, an *express* highway; (b) high-speed; as, an *express* bullet; (c) for high-speed projectiles; as, an *express* rifle; (d) having to do with railway express, pony express, etc.

ex·press', *adv.* by express.

ex·press', *n.* 1. a special messenger; courier.
2. a message delivered by such a messenger; dispatch sent swiftly.
3. (a) an express train, bus, truck, etc.; (b) an express rifle.
4. the pony express.
5. a method or service for transporting goods or sending money rapidly: express is usually more expensive and faster than freight.
6. the goods transported or money sent by express.
7. any method or means of swift transmission.
8. a business concern operating such a system.
9. a clear or distinct image or representation; an expression. [Obs.]

ex·press'ăge, *n.* 1. the business of carrying by express.
2. the charges made for carrying by express.

ex·press'i·ble, *a.* capable of being expressed.

ex·press'i·bly, *adv.* in an expressible manner.

ex·pres'sion (eks-presh'un), *n.* [L. *expressio* (*-onis*), a pressing out, an expression, from *expressus*, pp. of *exprimere*, to press out, express.]
1. a pressing out or squeezing out, as of juice.
2. a putting into words; a representing in language; a stating.
3. a picturing, representing, or symbolizing in art, music, etc.
4. a manner of expressing; especially, a meaningful and eloquent manner of speaking, singing, etc.; as, she reads with *expression*.
5. a particular word, phrase, or sentence; as, "catch cold" is an idiomatic *expression*.
6. a showing of feeling, character, etc.; as, laughter is often the *expression* of joy.
7. a look, intonation, sign, etc. that conveys meaning or feeling; as, there was a quizzical *expression* on his face.
8. a symbol or set of symbols expressing some algebraic fact, as a quantity or operation.
9. a showing by a symbol, sign, figures, etc.

ex·pres'sion·ăl, *a.* of or pertaining to expression; having the power of expression.

ex·pres'sion·iṣm, *n.* an early 20th-century movement in the arts, especially in drama, characterized by the nonobjective use of symbols, stereotyped characters, stylization, etc. to give objective expression to inner experience.

ex·pres'sion·ist, *a.* of or characterized by expressionism.

ex·pres'sion·ist, *n.* an expressionist artist, writer, etc.

ex·pres·sion·is'tiç, *a.* same as *expressionist*.

ex·pres·sion·is'tiç·ăl·ly, *adv.* in an expressionistic manner.

ex·pres'sion·less, *a.* lacking in expression.

ex·press'ive, *a.* 1. of or characterized by expression.
2. expressing; indicating; serving as a sign; as, a song *expressive* of joy.
3. full of expression; forcible; significant; as, an *expressive* nod.

ex·press'ive·ly, *adv.* in an expressive manner.

ex·press'ive·ness, *n.* the quality of being expressive; the power of expression or representation.

ex·press'ly, *adv.* 1. in an express manner; plainly; in direct terms.
2. on purpose; particularly; especially; as, I wrote for you *expressly*.

ex·press'măn, *n.*; *pl.* **ex·press'men,** one who

is employed by an express company; especially, one who drives a truck for collecting and delivering express packages.

ex·press′ness, *n.* the state of being express.

ex·pres′sō, *n.* same as *espresso.*

ex·press′ ri′fle (-fl), a hunting rifle using a large charge and a light bullet of large caliber, discharged with a high initial velocity: used to kill large game at short range.

ex·press′ trāin, a railroad train designed to carry mail, parcels, or passengers at a high rate of speed, and making but few stops between terminal stations.

ex·pres′sūre, *n.* expression. [Obs.]

ex·press′wāy, *n.* [*express,* and high*way.*] a divided highway for high-speed, through traffic, with full or partial control of access and with grade separations at all or most intersections.

ex′prō·brāte, *v.t.* [L. *exprobratus,* pp. of *exprobrare,* to reproach, upbraid.] to upbraid; to censure; to blame; to condemn. [Rare.]

ex·prō·brā′tion, *n.* the act of charging or censuring reproachfully; reproachful accusation; the act of upbraiding. [Rare.]

ex·prō′brȧ·tive, *a.* upbraiding; expressing reproach. [Rare.]

ex·prō′brȧ·tō·ry, *a.* same as *exprobrative.*

ex·prō·mis′sion (-mish′un), *n.* [L. *expromissus,* pp. of *expromittere,* to promise to pay; *ex,* out, and *promittere,* to promise.] in civil law, the act by which a creditor accepts a new debtor in place of the old debtor, who is discharged.

ex·prō·mis′sŏr, *n.* in civil law, one who becomes bound for the debt of another by substituting himself as principal debtor in his place.

ex·prō′pri·āte, *v.t.*; expropriated, *pt., pp.*; expropriating, *ppr.* [L. *ex,* out, and *proprius,* one's own.]

1. to take (land, property, etc.) from its owner; especially, to take for public use or in the public interest, as by right of eminent domain.

2. to transfer (property) from one person, nation, etc. that owns it to another.

3. to deprive of ownership; dispossess.

ex·prō·pri·ā′tion, *n.* an expropriating or being expropriated.

ex·prō′pri·ā·tŏr, *n.* a person, nation, etc. that expropriates.

ex·pūgn′ (eks-pūn′), *v.t.* to conquer; to take by assault. [Obs.]

ex·pug′nȧ·ble, *a.* [L. *expugnabilis,* from *expugnare,* to take by assault.] capable of being expugned or taken by assault. [Obs.]

ex·pug·nā′tion, *n.* conquest; the act of taking by assault. [Obs.]

ex·pūgn′ẽr (-pūn′), *n.* one who subdues or conquers. [Obs.]

ex·pulse′, *v.t.* to drive out; to expel. [Obs.]

ex·puls′ẽr, *n.* an expeller. [Obs.]

ex·pul′sion, *n.* [L. *expulsio* (*-onis*), a driving out, expulsion, from *expulsus,* pp. of *expellere,* to drive out.]

1. the act of driving out or expelling; as, the *expulsion* of a student from college.

2. the fact or state of being expelled.

ex·pul′sive, *a.* expelling or capable of expelling.

ex·punç′tion, *n.* [LL. *expunctio* (*-onis*), from L. *expunctus,* pp. of *expungere,* to prick or blot out, erase, expunge.] the act of expunging or the state of being expunged.

ex·punge′, *v.t.*; expunged, *pt., pp.*; expunging, *ppr.* [L. *expungere,* to prick or blot out, erase, expunge.] to blot out, as with a pen; to rub out; to efface; to obliterate; to delete; to cancel.

Expunge the whole, or lop the excrescent parts. —Pope.

ex′pũr·gāte, *v.t.*; expurgated, *pt., pp.*; expurgating, *ppr.* [L. *expurgatus,* pp. of *expurgare,* to purge, cleanse; *ex,* out, and *purgare,* to cleanse, purify.]

1. to remove anything considered obscene or otherwise objectionable from (a book, etc.); as, an *expurgated* edition of Shakespeare.

2. to clear; to purge; to cleanse. [Obs.]

ex·pũr·gā′tion, *n.* 1. the act of expurgating or the condition of being expurgated.

2. in astronomy, the emerging of the sun or moon from the umbra after an eclipse. [Obs.]

ex′pũr·gā·tŏr, *n.* one who expurgates.

ex·pũr·gȧ·tō′ri·ăl, *a.* expurgating.

ex·pũr·gȧ·tō′ri·ous, *a.* expurgatory. [Obs.]

ex·pũr′gȧ·tō·ry, *a.* 1. of expurgation.

2. tending to expurgate or purify.

ex·pũrge′, *v.t.* to purge. [Obs.]

ex·quīre′ (eks-kwīr′), *v.t.* to search into or out. [Obs.]

ex′qui·şite (eks′kwi-zit *or* eks-kwi′-), *a.* [ME. *exquisite*; L. *exquisitus,* choice, selected, pp. of *exquirere,* to search out; *ex,* out, and *quærere,* to ask.]

1. very lovely; fine; dainty; delicately beautiful; as, *exquisite* lace.

2. carefully done or elaborately made; as, *exquisite* designing.

3. of highest quality; admirable.

4. highly sensitive; keenly discriminating; fastidious; as, an *exquisite* ear for music.

5. given or characterized by intense emotion; keen; poignant; as, *exquisite* joy or sorrow.

Syn.—choice, rare, refined, delicate, perfect, matchless, intense, consummate.

ex′qui·şite, *n.* one who is overly or affectedly particular as to appearance, taste, etc.; a dandy; a fop; a coxcomb; a dude.

Such an *exquisite* was but a poor companion for a quiet, plain man like me.—Hook.

ex′qui·şite·ly, *adv.* in an exquisite manner; delicately; accurately; with great perfection; intensely; sensitively; as, to feel pain *exquisitely*; a work *exquisitely* finished.

ex′qui·şite·ness, *n.* the quality of being exquisite.

ex·quiş′i·tive, *a.* curious; eager to discover. [Obs.]

ex·quiş′i·tive·ly, *adv.* exquisitely. [Obs.]

ex·san′gui·nāte (eks-san′gwi-), *v.t.*; exsanguinated, *pt., pp.*; exsanguinating, *ppr.* [L. *exsanguinatus,* bloodless; *ex-* priv., and *sanguinare,* to be bloody, from *sanguis,* blood.] to make bloodless; to drain of blood.

ex·san′guine (-gwin), *a.* bloodless; anemic.

ex·san·guin′ē·ous, *a.* same as *exsanguine.*

ex·san·guin′i·ty, *n.* anemia.

ex·san′gui·nous, *a.* [L. *exsanguis,* bloodless.] same as *exsanguine.*

ex·scind′ (eks-sind′), *v.t.*; exscinded, *pt., pp.*; exscinding, *ppr.* [L. *exscindere,* to cut out or tear off; *ex,* out, and *scindere,* to cut, tear.] to cut out; to excise; to extirpate.

ex·sçrībe′, *v.t.* to copy; to transcribe. [Obs.]

ex′sçript, *n.* a copy; a transcript. [Obs.]

ex·sçrip′tũr·ăl, *a.* unscriptural.

ex·sçulp′tāte, *a.* [L. *exsculptus,* pp. of *exsculpere,* to carve out; *ex,* out, and *sculpere,* to carve.] in entomology, covered with irregular and varying longitudinal depressions, as if carved.

ex·sçū′tel·lāte, *a.* same as *escutellate.*

ex·seçt′, *v.t.* [L. *exsectus,* pp. of *exsecare,* to cut out or away; *ex,* out, and *secare,* to cut.] to cut out.

ex·seç′tion, *n.* [L. *exsectio* (*-onis*), from *exsecare,* to cut out or away.] a cutting out or away; specifically, in surgery, an excision.

ex·sẽrt′, *v.t.* [from L. *exsertus,* pp. of *exserere,* to stretch out.] to put forth; to thrust out; to protrude.

ex·sẽrt′ed, ex·sẽrt′, *a.* sticking out; projecting beyond something else; as, *exsert* stamens; *exserted* organs of an animal.

ex·sẽrt′ile, *a.* capable of being thrust out or protruded.

ex·sẽr′tion, *n.* an exserting or being exserted.

ex′-sẽrv′ice, *a.* having formerly been a member of the armed forces.

ex·siç′çănt, *a.* [L. *exsiccans* (*-antis*), ppr. of *exsiccare,* to dry up.] drying; evaporating moisture; having the quality of drying.

ex·siç′çănt, *n.* in medicine, any drug which has drying properties.

ex·siç·çā′tae, *n.pl.* [L., from *exsiccatus,* pp. of *exsiccare,* to dry up.] in botany, dried specimens of plants, especially in a herbarium.

ex′siç·çāte, *v.t.*; exsiccated, *pt., pp.*; exsiccating, *ppr.* [L. *exsiccatus,* pp. of *exsiccare,* to make dry; *ex,* out, and *siccare,* to dry, from *siccus,* dry.] to dry up; to exhaust or evaporate the moisture of.

ex·siç·çā′tion, *n.* an exsiccating or being exsiccated.

ex·siç′çȧ·tive, *a.* tending to make dry.

ex·siç′çȧ·tive, *n.* any preparation which has drying properties.

ex′siç·çā·tŏr, *n.* an apparatus which removes moisture; a desiccator; an evaporator; also, in chemistry, an absorbent.

ex·sil′i·en·cy, *n.* [L. *exsiliens* (*-entis*), ppr. of *exsilire,* to spring or leap forth.] a springing forth. [Rare.]

ex·sō·lū′tion, *n.* relaxation. [Rare.]

ex·spō·li·ā′tion, *n.* spoliation. [Rare].

ex·spū·i′tion, *n.* [L. *exspuitio* (*-onis*), a spitting out, from *exspuere,* to spit out.] a discharge of saliva by spitting. [Rare.]

ex·spū′tō·ry, *a.* [L. *exsputus,* pp. of *exspuere,* to spit out.] spit out; ejected, as if by spitting.

ex·stip′ū·lāte, *a.* [L. *ex-* priv., and *stipula,* a stalk, stem.] in botany, having no stipules.

ex′strō·phy, *n.* [Gr. *ekstrophē,* a dislocation, from *ekstrephein,* to turn aside, overturn; *ek,* out, and *strephein,* to turn.] in pathology, the turning inside out of any organ or part of the body.

ex·suç′çous, *a.* [L. *exsuccus,* from *ex-* priv., and *succus,* juice.] destitute of juice; dry.

ex·suç′tion, *n.* [L. *exsuctus,* pp. of *exsugere,* to suck out; *ex,* out, and *sugere,* to suck.] the act of sucking out.

ex·sū·dā′tion, *n.* same as *exudation.*

ex·suf′flāte, *v.t.*; exsufflated, *pt., pp.*; exsufflating, *ppr.* [LL. *exsufflatus,* pp. of *exsufflare,* to blow away.] to drive away, as an evil spirit, by blowing; to exorcise.

ex·suf·flā′tion, *n.* 1. a blowing out. [Obs.]

2. in ecclesiastical usage, a kind of exorcism performed by blowing.

ex·suf′fli·çāte, *a.* [arbitrary extension of obs. *excufflate,* from LL. *exsufflatus,* pp. of *exsufflare,* to blow away, from L. *ex-,* out, and *sufflare,* to blow.] inflated; puffed up: *Othello,* III, iii. [Obs.]

ex·sū′pẽr·ȧ·ble, *a.* surmountable. [Obs.]

ex·sū′pẽr·ănce, *n.* excess; superiority. [Obs.]

ex·sū′pẽr·ănt, *a.* excelling; surpassing. [Obs.]

ex·sū′pẽr·āte, *v.t.* to excel; to overcome. [Obs.]

ex·sũr′ġent, *a.* [L. *exsurgens* (*-entis*), ppr. of *exsurgere,* to rise up.] rising up.

ex·sus′ci·tāte, *v.t.* to rouse; to excite. [Obs.]

ex·sus·ci·tā′tion, *n.* a stirring up; a rousing. [Obs.]

ex′tȧ·cy, *n.* ecstasy. [Obs.]

ex′tănce, *n.* outward projection. [Obs.]

ex′tăn·cy, *n.* [L. *exstantia, extantia,* from *exstans* (*-antis*), ppr. of *exstare,* to stand out.]

1. the state of rising above others. [Obs.]

2. a part rising above the rest; a projection. [Obs.]

ex′tănt (*or* eks-tant′), *a.* [OFr. *estant,* extant, existing, from L. *extans* (*-antis*), *exstans* (*-antis*), ppr. of *extare, exstare,* to stand out or forth; *ex,* out, and *stare,* to stand.]

1. standing out or above any surface; protruded. [Obs.]

That part of the teeth which is *extant* above the gums. —Ray.

2. still existing; not extinct; not destroyed or lost; as, only a part of the history of Livy is *extant.*

3. conspicuous; evident. [Archaic.]

ex′tȧ·sy, *n.* ecstasy. [Obs.]

ex·tat′iç, *a.* ecstatic. [Obs.]

ex·tem′pō·răl, *a.* extemporaneous. [Archaic.]

ex·tem′pō·răl·ly, *adv.* extemporaneously. [Obs.]

ex·tem·pō·rā′nē·ăn, *a.* extemporaneous. [Obs.]

ex·tem·pō·rā′nē·ous, *a.* [L. *ex,* out, and *tempus* (*-oris*), time.]

1. composed, performed, or uttered offhand, without previous study or preparation; unpremeditated; as, an *extemporaneous* address.

2. in speech classes, etc., spoken with preparation but not written out or memorized: distinguished from *impromptu.*

3. speaking or adept at speaking without preparation.

4. made for the occasion; improvised; as, an *extemporaneous* fireplace.

ex·tem·pō·rā′nē·ous·ly, *adv.* in an extemporaneous manner.

ex·tem·pō·rā′nē·ous·ness, *n.* the quality of being extemporaneous.

ex·tem′pō·rā·ri·ly, *adv.* in an extemporary manner.

ex·tem′pō·rā·ry, *a.* extemporaneous.

ex·tem′pō·rē, *a.* and *adv.* [L., lit., from the moment; *ex,* from, out of, and *tempore,* ablative of *tempus,* time, a period of time, a moment.] without preparation; offhand; impromptu; as, to write or speak *extempore.*

ex·tem′pō·rē, *n.* something spoken or written extemporaneously.

ex·tem′pō·ri·ness, *n.* the state of being extemporary. [Obs.]

ex·tem″pō·ri·zā′tion, *n.* the act of extemporizing; also, something extemporized.

ex·tem′pō·rīze, *v.i., v.t.*; extemporized, *pt., pp.*; extemporizing, *ppr.* 1. to speak, perform, or compose extempore; to improvise.

2. to furnish or contrive (things) in a makeshift way to meet a pressing need.

ex·tem′pō·rī·zẽr, *n.* one who extemporizes.

ex·tend′, *v.t.*; extended, *pt., pp.*; extending, *ppr.* [ME. *extenden*; OFr. *extendre*; L. *extendere,* to stretch out; *ex,* out, and *tendere,* to stretch.]

1. to stretch out in any direction; to carry

forward in length, distance, or time; to spread in breadth; to expand or dilate in size; as, to *extend* lines in surveying; to *extend* roads, limits, bounds.

2. to stretch; to reach forth; as, to *extend* the arm or hand.

3. to expand; to enlarge; to widen; as, to *extend* the capacities or intellectual powers; to *extend* the sphere of usefulness; to *extend* commerce.

4. to continue; to prolong; as, to *extend* the time of payment; to *extend* a furlough.

5. to offer; accord; grant.

6. to stretch or straighten out (a limb of the body): opposed to *flex*.

7. in commerce, to allow a period of time for the payment of (a debt) beyond that originally set.

8. in cooking, to make larger portions of (a scarce or expensive food) by combining with other cheaper foods.

9. in law, (a) in Great Britain, to assess; to value; (b) to seize or levy upon, as by a writ of extent.

Syn.—increase, enlarge, lengthen, protract, stretch, amplify.

ex·tend', *v.i.* to be extended.

ex·tend'ed, *a.* 1. stretched out; spread out.

2. prolonged; continued.

3. enlarged in influence, meaning, scope, effect, etc.; extensive; widespread.

4. in printing, designating type with a wider face than is standard for the height.

ex·tend'ed cāre, nursing care given to convalescents, the disabled, etc. in a facility especially equipped and staffed for the purpose.

ex·tend'ed fam'i·ly, a social unit consisting of parents and children along with other relatives, living in one household and functioning as an integrated family: cf. *nuclear family*.

ex·tend'ed·ly, *adv.* in an extended manner.

ex·tend'ẽr, *n.* one who or that which extends.

ex·tend'i·ble, *a.* 1. capable of being extended.

2. in law, capable of being taken by a writ of extent.

ex·tense', *a.* [L. *extensus*, pp. of *extendere*, to extend.] extended; extensive. [Rare.]

ex·ten·si·bil'i·ty, *n.* the quality or state of being extensible; a capacity for being extended; as, the *extensibility* of a fiber or of a plate of metal.

ex·ten'si·ble, *a.* [Fr. *extensible*, from L. *extendere*, to extend.] capable of being extended.

ex·ten'si·ble·ness, *n.* extensibility.

ex·ten'sile, *a.* 1. capable of being extended.

2. that can be thrust forth, as a claw or tentacle.

ex·ten·sim'e·tẽr, *n.* same as *extensometer*.

ex·ten'sion, *n.* [L. *extensio* (*-onis*), a stretching out, extension, from *extendere*, to extend.]

1. the act of extending.

2. the state of being extended.

3. the amount or degree to which something is or can be extended; range; extent.

4. a branch of a university for students who cannot attend the university proper.

5. an extra telephone connected to the same line as the main telephone.

6. in physics, that property of a body by which it occupies space.

7. in commerce, an agreement on the part of a creditor allowing a debtor further time to pay a debt.

8. in law, a postponement, by agreement of the parties or act of the court, of the time set for any legal procedure.

9. in logic, the extent of the application of a single term; sphere; compass; denotation.

10. in biology, the straightening of a part, as a limb.

11. in surgery, the drawing of a broken limb in a direction from the trunk in order to bring the parts in line.

12. an addition; an annex; a part added to extend; as, the *extension* to the house is finished.

ex·ten'sion·ăl, *a.* having great extent.

ex·ten'sion·ist, *n.* an advocate of extension, as of university extension.

ex·ten'si·ty, *n.* 1. the quality of extension.

2. in psychology, that quality of sensation which permits the perception of space or size.

ex·ten'sive, *a.* 1. having great extent; covering a large area; vast.

2. having a wide scope, effect, influence, etc.; far-reaching; comprehensive.

3. of or characterized by extension.

4. in agriculture, using large areas of land with comparatively little cultivation; as, *extensive* farming: opposed to *intensive*.

5. extensible. [Obs.]

ex·ten'sive·ly, *adv.* widely; largely; to a great extent; as, the story was *extensively* circulated.

ex·ten'sive·ness, *n.* 1. wideness; largeness; extent; as, the *extensiveness* of the ocean.

2. the capacity for being extended. [Obs.]

ex·ten·som'e·tẽr, *n.* [L. *extensus*, pp. of *extendere*, to extend, and *metrum*, measure.] an instrument for measuring the minute degrees of expansion, contraction, or deformation of something.

ex·ten'sŏr, *n.* [LL. *extensor*, a stretcher, used in the sense of one who stretches a victim on the rack, a torturer, from L. *extensus*, pp. of *extendere*, to stretch out.] in anatomy, a muscle that serves to extend or straighten any part of the body, as an arm or a finger: opposed to *flexor*.

EXTENSOR

ex·ten'sūre, *n.* extension; extent. [Rare.]

ex·tent', *a.* extended. [Obs.]

ex·tent', *n.* [ME. *extente*; OFr. *extente*, extent, extension, from L. *extendere*, to extend.]

1. the space, amount, or degree to which a thing is extended; length; breadth; size; as, a great *extent* of country, or of body.

2. scope; limits; comprehensiveness; coverage.

3. an extended space; vast area; as, an *extent* of woodland.

4. in British history, an assessment or valuation, as of land.

5. in law, (a) in Great Britain, a writ (*writ of extent*) by which the person, goods, and property of a debtor could formerly be seized to force payment; (b) seizure by such a writ; (c) in the United States, a writ giving to a creditor temporary ownership of his debtor's property.

Syn.—degree, distance, quantity, space, size.

ex·ten'ū·āte, *v.t.*; extenuated, *pt.*, *pp.*; extenuating, *ppr.* [L. *extenuatus*, pp. of *extenuare*, to make thin, reduce, diminish; *ex*, out, and *tenuare*, to make thin, from *tenuis*, thin.]

1. to make thin, lean, or slender; as, sickness *extenuates* the body. [Obs.]

2. to lessen; to diminish; to weaken.

3. to underrate; to underestimate; to detract from.

4. to lessen or seem to lessen the seriousness of (an offense, guilt, etc.) by giving excuses or serving as an excuse.

ex·ten'ū·āte, *v.i.* to become thin or thinner; to be attenuated. [Rare.]

ex·ten'ū·āte, *a.* thin; slender. [Rare.]

ex·ten'ū·āt·ing cĩr'cum·stan·ces, in law, circumstances that tend to lessen the severity of a crime and its punishment.

ex·ten·ū·ā'tion, *n.* [L. *extenuatio* (*-onis*), a thinning, lessening, from *extenuare*, to make thin.]

1. an extenuating or being extenuated; especially, mitigation, as of the seriousness of a crime, offense, etc.

2. a thing that extenuates; partial excuse.

ex·ten'ū·ā·tive, *a.* same as *extenuatory*.

ex·ten'ū·ā·tŏr, *n.* one who extenuates.

ex·ten'ū·ȧ·tō·ry, *a.* extenuating or tending to extenuate.

ex·tē'ri·ŏr, *a.* [L., comp. of *exter*, *exterus*, the outside.]

1. external; outward; on the outside; outer: opposed to *interior*; as, the *exterior* surface of a concavo-convex lens.

2. originating outside; acting or coming from without; as, *exterior* forces.

3. foreign; relating to foreign nations; as, the *exterior* relations of a state or kingdom.

exterior side; in fortification, the side of an imaginary polygon, upon which the plan of fortification is constructed.

exterior slope; in fortification, that slope of a work which is next outward beyond its superior slope.

ex·tē'ri·ŏr, *n.* 1. an outside or outside surface.

2. outward appearance.

ex·tē'ri·ŏr añ'gle, 1. any of the four angles formed on the outside of two straight lines by a straight line cutting across them.

2. any angle formed by any side of a polygon and the extension of the adjacent side.

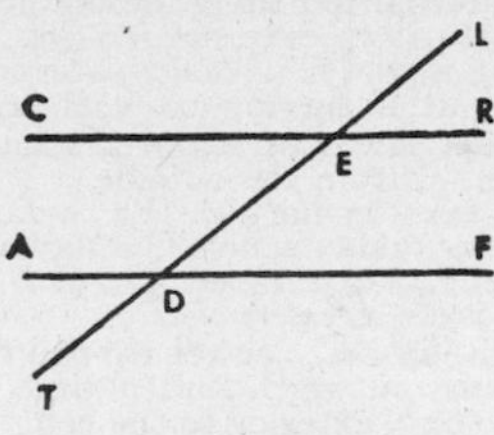

EXTERIOR ANGLES
(CEL, LER, ADT, TDF)

ex·tē·ri·or'i·ty, *n.* the character or fact of being exterior.

ex·tē'ri·ŏr·ly, *adv.* externally.

ex·tẽr'min·ȧ·ble, *a.* capable of being exterminated.

ex·tẽr'mi·nāte, *v.t.*; exterminated, *pt.*, *pp.*; exterminating, *ppr.* [L. *exterminatus*, pp. of *exterminare*, lit., to drive beyond the boundaries, to drive out or away, destroy; *ex*, out, and *terminus*, a boundary.]

1. to drive without the limits or borders; to expel. [Rare.]

2. to destroy completely; to wipe out; to extirpate; as, to *exterminate* weeds or vermin.

3. in algebra, to take away; to cause to disappear; to eliminate; as, to *exterminate* unknown quantities.

Syn.—uproot, abolish, annihilate, destroy, eradicate, extirpate, overthrow.

ex·tẽr·mi·nā'tion, *n.* [LL. *exterminatio* (*-onis*), destruction, from L. *exterminare*, to destroy.]

1. the act of exterminating or the state of being exterminated; total expulsion or destruction; extirpation.

2. in algebra, a taking away; elimination, as of unknown quantities.

ex·tẽr'mi·nā·tive, *a.* same as *exterminatory*.

ex·tẽr'mi·nā·tŏr, *n.* [LL. *exterminator*, a destroyer, from L. *exterminare*, to destroy.] a person or thing that exterminates; specifically, (a) a person whose work or business is exterminating rats, cockroaches, and other vermin; (b) any of various powders, liquids, etc. for exterminating vermin.

ex·tẽr'mi·nȧ·tō·ry, *a.* serving or tending to exterminate.

ex·tẽr'mine, *v.t.* to exterminate. [Obs.]

ex·tẽrn', *a.* [L. *externus*, without, from *exter*, outward.] external; outward; visible; not inherent. [Obs.]

ex'tẽrn (*or* ex-tẽrn'), *n.* 1. a person connected with, but not living in, an institution, as a nonresident doctor in a hospital: opposed to *intern*.

2. the outer or external part; the exterior. [Obs.]

ex·tẽr'năl, *a.* [L. *externus*, outward, external, from *exter*, without.]

1. outward; exterior; as, the *external* surface of a body: opposed to *internal*.

2. on, or for use on, the outside of the body; as, a medicine for *external* use only.

3. outwardly visible; material; existing apart from the mind.

4. originating outside; acting or coming from without; as, an *external* force.

5. for outward appearance or show; superficial; as, *external* deportment.

6. foreign; relating to or connected with foreign nations; as, *external* trade or commerce.

7. in zoology, on the side farthest from the mesial plane; as, the *external* side of a bird's leg.

ex·tẽr'năl, *n.* 1. an outward part; something pertaining to the exterior.

> Adam was then no less glorious in his *externals*; he had a beautiful body, as well as an immortal soul. —South.

2. [*pl.*] outward appearance or behavior; as, the *externals* of religion.

ex·tẽr'năl·ism, *n.* 1. regard for or devotion to externals; specifically, undue devotion to externals, as of religion.

2. in philosophy, phenomenalism.

ex·tẽr·năl·is'tic, *a.* of or pertaining to externalism.

ex·tẽr·nal'i·ty, *n.* 1. the state or quality of being external.

2. *pl.* **ex·tẽr·nal'i·ties**, an external thing.

ex·tẽr"năl·i·zā'tion, *n.* 1. the act of externalizing or the state or condition of being externalized.

2. an externalized thing; embodiment.

ex·tẽr′năl·īze, *v.t.*; externalized, *pt., pp.*; externalizing, *ppr.* 1. to make external.

2. to regard as having external existence.

ex·tẽr′năl·ly, *adv.* in an external manner; outwardly; on or from the outside.

ex·ter·nȧt′ (eks-ter-nȧ′), *n.* [Fr., a day school, from *externe*, a day scholar.] a day school.

ex·tẽr′nīze, *v.t.*; externized, *pt., pp.*; externizing, *ppr.* same as *externalize.*

ex·tẽr·nō·mē′di·ăn, ex·tẽr·nō·mē′di·ăl, *a.* [L. *externus*, outward, and *medius*, middle.] in entomology, exterior to the central line or plane.

ex″tẽr·ō·cep′tive, *a.* [L. *exter*, on the outside; and -*o*, and re*ceptive*.] designating, of, or affected by stimuli from outside the body, as in touching, seeing, smelling, tasting, etc.

ex″tẽr·ō·cep′tŏr, *n.* [Mod. L.] a sense organ or sensory receptor that responds to exteroceptive stimuli.

ex·ter·rā′nē·ous, *a.* [LL. *exterraneus*, of another country; L. *ex*, out, and *terra*, country.] foreign; coming from abroad.

ex″ter·ri·tō′ri·ăl, *a.* [L. *ex*, out, and *territorium*, territory.] outside the territorial limits or jurisdiction of the country, state, etc.; extraterritorial.

ex″ter·ri·tō·ri·al′i·ty, *n.* in law, the condition of being exempt from the laws of the land in which one resides.

ex·tẽr′sion, *n.* [L. *extersus*, pp. of *extergere*, to wipe off, to wipe dry; *ex*, out, and *tergere*, to wipe.] the act of wiping or rubbing out.

ex·till′, *v.i.* to drop or distill from. [Obs.]

ex·til·lā′tion, *n.* the act of distilling from, or falling from in drops. [Obs.]

ex·tim′ū·lāte, *v.t.* to stimulate. [Obs.]

ex·tim·ū·lā′tion, *n.* stimulation. [Obs.]

ex·tinct′, *a.* [L. *extinctus*, *exstinctus*, pp. of *extinguere*, *exstinguere*, to put out, destroy.]

1. extinguished; put out; quenched.

Her weapons blunted, and *extinct* her fires. —Pope.

2. being at an end; having no living descendant; no longer in existence; as, an *extinct* law; the enmity is *extinct*.

ex·tinct′, *v.t.* to put out; to destroy. [Obs.]

ex·tinc′tion, *n.* 1. the act of extinguishing or the state of being extinguished.

2. the fact or state of being or becoming extinct; dying out, as of a race, species of animal, etc.

3. a putting an end to; a coming to an end; destruction; annihilation; as, the *extinction* of a race; the *extinction* of a feud.

ex·tinc′tive, *a.* serving or tending to extinguish.

ex′tine, *n.* [from L. *ext*erus, outside, and *-ine*.] in botany, the outer coat of the pollen grain.

ex·tin′guish (-tin′gwish), *v.t.*; extinguished (-gwisht), *pt., pp.*; extinguishing, *ppr.* [L. *extinguere*, to put out, quench; *ex*, out, and *stinguere*, to quench.]

1. to put out; to quench; to suffocate; as, to *extinguish* fire or flame.

2. to destroy; to put an end to; to cause to die; to wipe out; as, to *extinguish* desire or hope; to *extinguish* a claim or title.

3. to obscure by superior splendor; to eclipse.

4. in law, to nullify.

Syn.—abolish, destroy, extirpate, eradicate, kill, quench, annihilate.

ex·tin′guish·ȧ·ble, *a.* capable of being extinguished.

ex·tin′guish·ẽr, *n.* one who or that which extinguishes; especially, (a) a hollow cone, usually of metal, to be put over the flame of a candle or lamp to extinguish it; (b) any of various kinds of apparatus for extinguishing a fire by spraying chemical liquids, powders, etc.

ex·tin′guish·ment, *n.* the act of putting out or quenching; extinction.

ex·tirp′, *v.t.* to extirpate. [Obs.]

ex·tir′pȧ·ble, *a.* capable of being extirpated.

ex·tir′pāte, *v.t.*; extirpated, *pt., pp.*; extirpating, *ppr.* [L. *extirpatus*, *exstirpatus*, pp. of *extirpare*, *exstirpare*, to root out, eradicate; *ex*, out, and *stirps*, the lower part of a tree, the root.] to pull or pluck up by the roots; to root out; hence, to destroy totally; to exterminate; to abolish; as, to *extirpate* weeds from a field; to *extirpate* a sect.

Syn.—uproot, exterminate, destroy, eradicate, annihilate, abolish.

ex·tir·pā′tion, *n.* [L. *extirpatio* (*-onis*), *exstirpatio* (*-onis*), from *extirpare*, *exstirpare*, to root out, extirpate.] the act of extirpating or the state of being extirpated; total destruction.

ex′tir·pā·tive, *a.* pertaining to or causing extirpation.

ex′tir·pā·tŏr, *n.* one who or that which extirpates.

ex·tir′pȧ·tō·ry, *a.* extirpative.

ex·tir′pẽr, *n.* an extirpator. [Obs.]

ex·tis′pex, *n.*; *pl.* **ex·tis′pi·cēs,** [L., from *exta*, the nobler entrails, and *specere*, to view.] same as *haruspex.*

ex·ti·spi′cious (-spish′us), *a.* relating to the inspection of entrails in order to prognosticate. [Obs.]

ex·tog′e·nous, *a.* same as *exogenous.*

ex·tol′, ex·toll′ (*or* -tōl′), *v.t.*; extolled, *pt., pp.*; extolling, *ppr.* [OFr. *extoller*; L. *extollere*, to raise up, lift up; *ex*, out, up, and *tollere*, to raise.]

1. to raise aloft; to set on high; to elevate. [Obs.]

2. to praise highly; to laud; to eulogize; as, to *extol* virtues, noble exploits, and heroism.

Extol him that rideth upon the heavens by his name Jah. —Ps. lxviii. 4.

Syn.—laud, praise, applaud, commend, magnify, celebrate, glorify.

ex·tol′lẽr, *n.* one who extols; a praiser or eulogist.

ex·tol′ment, ex·toll′ment, *n.* [OFr. *extollement*, from *extoller*, to raise.] the act of extolling; eulogy.

ex·tor′sive, *a.* [L. *extortus*, pp. of *extorquere*, to twist or turn out; *ex*, out, and *torquere*, to turn, twist.] serving to extort; tending to draw from by compulsion. [Rare.]

ex·tor′sive·ly, *adv.* in an extorsive manner; by extortion. [Rare.]

ex·tort′, *v.t.*; extorted, *pt., pp.*; extorting, *ppr.* [L. *extortus*, pp. of *extorquere*, to twist or turn out; *ex*, out, and *torquere*, to twist.] to draw from by force or compulsion; to wrest or wring from by physical force, violence, threats, misuse of authority, or by any illegal means; to exact (money, etc.) *from*; as, conquerors *extort* contributions *from* the vanquished.

ex·tort′, *v.i.* to practice extortion. [Obs.]

ex·tort′, *a.* extortionate. [Obs.]

ex·tort′ẽr, *n.* one who extorts or practices extortion.

ex·tor′tion, *n.* [ME. *extorcioun*; LL. *extorsio* (*-onis*), a wrenching away, from L. *extortus*, pp. of *extorquere*, to wrench away.]

1. the act of extorting; the act or practice of wresting money, etc. from a person by force, threats, misuse of authority, or by any undue exercise of power: sometimes applied to the exaction of too high a price.

2. anything extorted.

Syn.—exaction, overcharge.

ex·tor′tion·ā·ry, *a.* pertaining to or implying extortion.

ex·tor′tion·āte, *a.* 1. characterized by, or having the nature of, extortion.

2. excessive, exorbitant; as, an *extortionate* price.

ex·tor′tion·ẽr, ex·tor′tion·ist, *n.* one who is guilty of extortion.

ex·tor′tion·ous, *a.* extortionate. [Obs.]

ex·tor′tious, *a.* extortionate. [Obs.]

ex·tor′tious·ly, *adv.* in an extortionate manner. [Obs.]

ex·trȧ-, [L. *exter*, *exterus*, on the outside.] a prefix signifying *outside, outside the scope or region of, beyond, more than, besides*, used to form adjectives such as *extra*ordinary.

ex′trȧ, *a.* [from *extraordinary*; also from L. *extra*, additional, extra, from *extra, adv.*, more than, outside.] more, larger, or better than what is stipulated, normal, expected, necessary, or usual; additional; supplementary; as, *extra* compensation, an *extra* edition.

ex′trȧ, *n.* an extra person or thing; specifically, (a) [*often in pl.*] an additional charge; (b) a special edition of a newspaper, put out between regular editions to cover news of unusual interest or importance; (c) something of unusually good quality; (d) an extra worker; (e) in cricket, a run not made from a hit, as a bye; (f) in motion pictures, an actor hired by the day to play a minor part, as a member of a mob scene, etc.

ex′trȧ, *adv.* beyond the usual standard; especially; extraordinarily; unusually; as, you did *extra* well.

ex′trȧ-ax′il·lȧ·ry, ex′trȧ-ax′il·lăr, *a.* in botany, growing from above or below the axils; as, an *extra-axillary* bud.

ex′trȧ·bōld′, *n.* in printing, a style of type heavier than boldface.

ex·trȧ·bran′chi·ăl, *a.* [*extra-*, and Gr. *branchia*, gills.] in anatomy, not located within the branchial arches: said of the cartilages of certain fishes.

ex″trȧ·ca·lic′ū·lăr, *a.* [*extra-*, and L. *calyx*, the calyx.] situated outside the calyculus of a coelenterate.

ex″trȧ·cȧ·non′ic·ăl, *a.* not included among the canonical writings.

ex·trȧ·cap′sū·lăr, ex·trȧ·cap′sū·lȧ·ry, *a.* in anatomy, situated outside a capsule; specifically, of or pertaining to the extracapsularium.

ex″trȧ·cap·sū·lā′ri·um, *n.*; *pl.* **ex″trȧ·cap·sū·lā′ri·ȧ,** [L., from *extra*, beyond, and *capsula*, capsule.] in zoology, that part of a radiolarian which is situated outside of the central capsule.

ex·trȧ·cel′lū·lăr, *a.* [*extra-*, and L. *cella*, a cell.]

1. placed outside a cell.

2. in physiology, existent, developed, or acting outside organic cells; as, *extracellular* digestion.

ex″trȧ-cŏn·densed′, *a.* in printing, designating a style of type narrower than condensed.

ex·tract′, *v.t.*; extracted, *pt., pp.*; extracting, *ppr.* [L. *extractus*, pp. of *extrahere*, to draw or drag out; *ex*, out, and *trahere*, to draw.]

1. to draw out by effort; to pull out; as, to *extract* a tooth; to *extract* a promise from a person.

2. to draw out, as the juices or essence of a substance, by distilling, pressing, or other means; as, to *extract* juice from fruit.

3. to obtain as if by drawing out; to deduce; to derive; to manage to get; as, to *extract* knowledge from a chance acquaintance; to *extract* pleasure from work.

4. to take out or select a part of; to copy out (a passage from a book, etc.).

I have *extracted* out of that pamphlet a few notorious falsehoods. —Swift.

5. in mathematics, to find out (the root of a number or quantity).

ex′tract, *n.* 1. that which is extracted or drawn from something.

2. a passage taken from a book or writing; a quotation; an excerpt.

3. a concentrated form, whether solid, viscid, or liquid, of a food, flavoring, etc.; as, vanilla *extract*.

4. in pharmacy, the substance obtained by treating a drug with some solvent, as ether or alcohol, and then evaporating the preparation.

5. in old chemistry, a principle once supposed to form the basis of all vegetable extracts: called also the *extractive principle.*

6. extraction; descent. [Obs.]

7. in Scots law, a copy, authenticated by the proper officer, of a deed, writing, or other entry, the principal of which is in a public record.

compound extract; in pharmacy, an extract containing the essence of more than one drug.

fluid extract; in pharmacy, a liquid preparation whose volume is equal to a measure of distilled water weighing the same as the amount of drug used.

ex·tract′ȧ·ble, ex·tract′i·ble, *a.* capable of being extracted.

ex·tract′i·form, *a.* [L. *extractus*, pp. of *extrahere*, to draw out, and *forma*, form.] in chemistry, having the characteristics of an extract.

ex·trac′tion, *n.* [L. *extractus*, pp. of *extrahere*, to draw out, extract.]

1. an extracting or a being extracted; as, the *extraction* of a tooth; the *extraction* of a bullet from the body.

2. descent; lineage; derivation of persons from a stock or family; as, he is of French *extraction*.

3. that which is extracted; essence; extract.

ex·tract′ive, *a.* 1. capable of being extracted.

2. tending or serving to extract.

3. of the nature of an extract; extracted.

ex·tract′ive, *n.* 1. an extract.

2. an extractive substance.

3. in chemistry, any one of various substances, such as creatin and xanthin, found in minute quantities in animal tissue.

4. in pharmacy, that portion of an extract which during evaporation becomes insoluble.

ex·tract′ŏr, *n.* [L., from *extractus*, pp. of *extrahere*, to extract.]

1. one who or that which extracts.

2. an evaporator.

3. in surgery, a forceps for extracting substances from the human body.

4. the part of a breech-loading gun that withdraws the cartridge case from the chamber.

5. a metal vessel in which bones are treated to extract glue and gelatin.

6. in Scots law, the official who prepares and authenticates extracts.

ex″trȧ·çŭr·riç′ū·lăr, *a.* not included in the curriculum; not part of the actual course of study (of a college, a university, or a school).

extracurricular activity; an interest or activity pursued by a student, as swimming, football, acting, writing for the school paper, etc., which is not part of the actual course of study leading to the diploma or degree, but which is regarded as an active part of student life.

ex·trȧ·diç′tion·ā·ry, *a.* consisting not in words, but in realities. [Obs.]

ex′trȧ·dīt·ȧ·ble, *a.* 1. liable to extradition; that can be extradited.

2. rendering liable to extradition; as, *extraditable* crimes.

ex′trȧ·dīte, *v.t.*; extradited, *pt.*, *pp.*; extraditing, *ppr.* [L. *ex*, out, and *traditus*, pp. of *tradere*, to give over.]

1. to surrender or give up (an alleged criminal, fugitive, etc.) to the jurisdiction of another nation or state.

2. to obtain the extradition of.

3. to project (a sensation) to a distance from the body by a psychological process; as, when we shake a locked gate and feel the stability of the ends where the hinges, bolts, and locks are, we *extradite* the sensation to that point. [Rare.]

ex·trȧ·di′tion, *n.* [Fr. *extradition*, from L. *ex*, out, and *traditus*, pp. of *tradere*, to give up, give over.]

1. delivery from one state or nation to another of an alleged criminal, fugitive, or prisoner.

2. the projection, by a psychological process, of a sensation to a distance from the body. [Rare.]

extradition treaty; a treaty between two governments regulating the surrender of fugitives from justice, and prescribing the crimes for which they may be extradited.

ex·trā′dos, *n.* [Fr., from L. *extra*, beyond, and *dorsum*, back.] in architecture, the upper or convex surface of an arch or vault; also, the outer curve of a voussoir.

EXTRADOS

EXTRADOS

ex·trā′dosed (-dost), *a.* having an extrados: said of an arch when the curves of the intrados and extrados are concentric and parallel.

ex·trȧ·dō′tăl, *a.* [*extra-*, and L. *dos, dotis*, dowry.] in civil law, not belonging to the dowry: said of a married woman's property.

ex·trȧ·flō′răl, *a.* [*extra-*, and L. *flos, floris*, flower.] in botany, located outside a flower.

ex″trȧ·fō·li·ā′ceous, *a.* [*extra-*, and L. *folium*, a leaf.] in botany, away from the leaves, or inserted in a different place from them; as, *extrafoliaceous* prickles.

ex″trȧ·fō·rā′nē·ous, *a.* [*extra-*, and L. *foris*, a door.] outdoor. [Rare.]

ex·trȧ·ġē′nē·ous, *a.* [*extra-*, and L. *genus*, kind.] belonging to another kind.

ex″trȧ·jụ·di′ciăl (-dish′ăl), *a.* 1. outside or beyond the jurisdiction of a court.

2. out of the ordinary course of legal procedure.

ex″trȧ·jụ·di′ciăl·ly, *adv.* in an extrajudicial manner; in a manner out of the ordinary course of legal proceedings.

ex·trȧ·lē′găl, *a.* outside of legal control or authority.

ex·trȧ·lim′it·ăl, *a.* [*extra-*, and L. *limes, limitis*, limit, boundary.] in zoology, (a) not found within a specified faunal area; as, an *extralimital* species; (b) lying outside a specified part or surface; as, *extralimital* spots on a bird's wing.

ex·trȧ·lim′it·ā·ry, *a.* [*extra-*, and L. *limes*, limit.]

1. being or lying outside the limit or boundary; as, *extralimitary* land.

2. same as *extralimital*.

ex·trȧ·log′iç·ăl, *a.* being outside the domain of logic, when restricted to its syllogistic and subsidiary doctrines without concern as to the truth of reasonings.

ex·trȧ·log′iç·ăl·ly, *adv.* in an extralogical manner.

ex″trȧ·mal·lē′ō·lus, *n.*; *pl.* **ex″trȧ·mal·lē′ō·lī,** [*extra-*, and L. *malleolus*, dim. of *malleus*, a hammer.] in anatomy, the outer malleolus, or projection of the ankle, formed by the lower end of the fibula.

ex·trȧ·mis′sion (-mish′un), *n.* a sending out; emission. [Obs.]

ex·trȧ·mun′dāne, *a.* [LL. *extramundanus*, beyond the world; L. *extra*, beyond, and *mundus*, the world.] beyond the limit of the material or physical world; not of this world; as, *extramundane* beings.

ex·trȧ·mū′răl, *a.* [LL. *extramuranus*, beyond the walls; L. *extra*, beyond, and *murus*, wall.] beyond the walls, as of a fortified city or university; hence, beyond the fixed limits of a place; as, *extramural* residents.

ex·trȧ·nē′i·ty, *n.* the quality of being extraneous or foreign. [Rare.]

ex·trā′nē·ous, *a.* [L. *extraneus*, that which is without, external, from *extra*, without, beyond.]

1. foreign; not belonging or essential to a thing; coming from outside; not intrinsic; as, to separate gold from *extraneous* matter.

2. not belonging to the matter under consideration; not pertinent.

ex·trā′nē·ous·ly, *adv.* in an extraneous manner.

ex·trȧ·nū′çlē·ăr, *a.* [*extra-*, and L. *nucleus*, a kernel.] not included within the nucleus of a cell.

ex″trȧ·oç′ū·lăr, *a.* [*extra-*, and L. *oculus*, an eye.] in entomology, located outside of the eyes: said of the antennae of certain insects.

ex″trȧ·of·fi′ciăl (-fish′ăl), *a.* not within the limits of official duties, rights, etc.

ex·traọr′di·nā·ri·ly, *adv.* in an extraordinary, uncommon, or special manner or degree; exceptionally.

ex·traọr′di·nā·ri·ness, *n.* the quality of being extraordinary; uncommonness.

ex·traọr′di·nā·ry, *a.* [L. *extraordinarius*, out of the common course, rare; *extra*, beyond, and *ordinarius*, ordinary, from *ordo* (*-inis*), a straight line, order.]

1. beyond or out of the common order or method; not in the usual, customary, or regular course; not ordinary; as, *extraordinary* evils require *extraordinary* remedies.

2. exceeding the common degree, limit, measure, etc.; hence, remarkable; exceptional; rare; wonderful; as, the *extraordinary* talents of Shakespeare.

3. (eks-trȧ-ọr′di-nā-ry) outside of the regular staff; for a special purpose or on a particular occasion; having special authority or responsibility; as, an *extraordinary* courier or messenger; an ambassador *extraordinary*.

Syn.—unwonted, uncommon, peculiar, unusual, unprecedented, wonderful, marvelous, prodigious, remarkable.

ex·traọr′di·nā·ry, *n.*; *pl.* **ex·traọr′di·nā·rieṣ,** anything extraordinary or unusual; something exceeding the usual order, kind, or method. [Rare.]

ex″trȧ·pȧ·rō′çhi·ăl, *a.* not within the limits of a parish.

ex′trȧ·pō·lāte″ (*or* eks-trap′ō-lāt), *v.t.* and *v.i.* [*extra*, and inter*polate*.] in statistics, to estimate or infer (a value, quantity, etc. beyond the known range) on the basis of certain variables within the known range, from which the estimated value is assumed to follow; as, sales figures for next year may be *extrapolated* from the known sales figures for preceding years.

ex·trap·ō·lā′tion, *n.* an extrapolating or being extrapolated.

ex″trȧ·prō·fes′sion·ăl (-fesh′un-ăl), *a.* not within the ordinary limits of professional duty or business.

ex″trȧ·prō·vin′ciăl (-shăl), *a.* not within the same province or jurisdiction.

ex·trȧ·reg′ū·lăr, *a.* not comprehended within a rule or rules.

ex·trȧ·sen′sō·ry, *a.* outside the realm of the senses; apart from normal sense perception.

ex″trȧ·stȧ·pē′di·ăl, *a.* [*extra-*, and LL. *stapes*, a stirrup, from O.H.G. *stapf*, step.] in anatomy, situated beyond the stapes: said of part of the axis of the cochlea.

ex″trȧ·stȧ·pē′di·ăl, *n.* that part of the columella of the ear which is extrastapedial.

ex″trȧ·ter·ri·tō′ri·ăl, *a.* 1. outside the territorial limits or jurisdiction of the country, state, etc.

2. of extraterritoriality; as, *extraterritorial* rights.

ex″trȧ·ter·ri·tō·ri·al′i·ty, *n.* 1. freedom from the jurisdiction of the country in which one lives, as in the case of an ambassador or foreign agent.

2. jurisdiction of a country over its citizens in foreign lands.

ex·trȧ·thē′çăl, *a.* [*extra-*, and L. *theca*, from Gr. *thēkē*, a case.] in biology, not included within a theca.

ex·trȧ·trop′iç·ăl, *a.* not within the tropics.

ex·traught′ (-trąt′), *a.* 1. extracted. [Obs.]

2. distracted; frenzied; distraught. [Obs.]

ex″trȧ·ū′tĕr·ine, *a.* situated or occurring outside the uterus: applied to pregnancy in which the fetus is outside the uterus.

ex·trav′ȧ·gănce, *n.* [OFr. *extravagance*; L. *extra*, beyond, and *vagari*, to wander.]

1. a wandering beyond a limit; an excursion or sally from the usual way, course, or limit. [Obs.]

2. a going beyond reasonable or moderate limits in conduct or speech; unreasonable excess.

3. a spending of more than is reasonable or necessary; excessive expenditure; wastefulness.

4. an instance of excess in spending, behavior, or speech.

ex·trav′ȧ·găn·cy, *n.*; *pl.* **ex·trav′ȧ·găn·cieṣ,** extravagance.

ex·trav′ȧ·gănt, *a.* 1. wandering beyond limits or bounds; roving. [Obs.]

2. excessive; exceeding due bounds of reason or moderation; as, the wishes, demands, desires, and passions of men are often *extravagant*.

3. prodigal; profuse in expenditure; spending more than is reasonable or necessary; wasteful; as, an *extravagant* man.

Syn.—prodigal, lavish, profuse.—The idea of immoderation is implied in all these words, but *extravagant* is the most general in its meaning and application. The *extravagant* man spends his money without reason; the *prodigal* man spends it in excesses; one may be *extravagant* with a small sum where it exceeds one's means; one can be *prodigal* only with large sums. *Extravagant* and *prodigal* designate habitual as well as particular actions; *lavish* and *profuse* are more often applied to particular actions, the former to denote an expenditure more or less wasteful or superfluous, the latter to denote an abundant supply.

ex·trav′ȧ·gănt, *n.* 1. one who is extravagant or eccentric. [Obs.]

2. [E—] [*pl.*] certain decretal epistles or constitutions of the popes which were published after the Clementines, but not at first arranged and digested with the other parts of the canon law.

ex·trav′ȧ·gănt·ly, *adv.* in an extravagant manner.

ex·trav·ȧ·gan′zȧ, *n.* [It. *estravaganza*, extravagance.]

1. a literary, musical, or dramatic composition characterized by a loose structure, farce, and fantastic plot development; now, any spectacular and elaborate theatrical production, as certain musical shows.

2. an extravagant flight of feeling or language.

ex·trav′ȧ·gāte, *v.i.*; extravagated, *pt.*, *pp.*; extravagating, *ppr.* 1. to stray; to wander. [Rare.]

2. to wander beyond due limits; to be extravagant. [Rare.]

ex·trav·ȧ·gā′tion, *n.* a wandering beyond limits. [Obs.]

ex·trav′ȧ·sāte, *v.t.* extravasated, *pt.*, *pp.*; extravasating, *ppr.* [*extra-*, and L. *vas*, a vessel.] to let flow or force (blood, etc.) from its normal containers into the surrounding body tissues.

ex·trav′ȧ·sāte, *v.i.* to pass out of the proper vessel, especially by infiltration into the tissues; as, blood *extravasates* around a bruised spot.

ex·trav·ȧ·sā′tion, *n.* 1. the act of extravasating or the state of being extravasated.

2. fluid which has been extravasated; especially, blood that has flowed into the tissues, as from a bruise.

3. in geology, the extrusion of volcanic matter.

ex·trȧ·vas′çū·lăr, *a.* [*extra-*, and L. *vasculum*, dim. of *vas*, a vessel.]

1. not contained in blood and lymph vessels; outside the vascular system.

2. not vascular.

ex·trav′e·nāte, *a.* [*extra-*, and L. *vena*, vein.] let out of the veins. [Obs.]

ex·trȧ·vēr′ṣion, *n.* extroversion (sense 2).

ex′trȧ·vērt, *n.* an extrovert.

ex·trēat′, *n.* extraction. [Obs.]

ex·trēme′, *a.* [OFr. *extreme*; L. *extremus*, last, outermost, superl. of *exter*, outer, outward.]

1. outermost; farthest; at the utmost point, edge, or border; as, the *extreme* verge or point of a thing.

2. going to great lengths; very great or greatest; utmost in degree; of the best or worst that can exist in reality or in imagina-

tion; excessive; immoderate; as, *extreme* pain, grief, or pleasure.
3. last; beyond which there is none; final; as, an *extreme* remedy.
4. radical in opinion, especially in political matters; ultra; advanced.
5. drastic; very severe.
6. in music, augmented; increased by a half step.
extreme and mean ratio; in geometry, the ratio existing between a line and its two segments, when the line is so divided that the whole line is to the greater segment as that segment is to the less.
Syn.—terminal, final, remote, ultimate, utmost, farthest, last, extravagant, immoderate.

ex·trēme′, *n.* 1. either of two things that are as different or far as possible from each other.
2. an extreme degree.
3. an extreme act, expedient, etc.
4. an extreme state or condition; as, an *extreme* of distress.
5. an extreme point; extremity. [Obs.]
6. in logic, (a) the subject or the predicate of a proposition; (b) the major or minor term (as distinguished from the middle term) of a syllogism.
7. in mathematics, (a) the first or last term of a proportion, ratio, or series: opposed to *mean*; (b) the largest or the smallest of three or more magnitudes.
in the extreme; in the highest degree.
to go to extremes; to act or speak in an extreme manner; to be excessive or immoderate.

ex·trēme′less, *a.* having no extremes; infinite.

ex·trēme′ly, *adv.* in the utmost degree; to the utmost point; to a very great degree; exceedingly; as, it is *extremely* hot or cold.

ex·trēme′ unc′tion, in the Roman Catholic Church, the sacrament administered by a priest or bishop to a person who is dying or in danger of death through sickness.

ex·trēm′ism, *n.* the quality or state of going to extremes.

ex·trēm′ist, *n.* 1. a person who goes to extremes.
2. a person who holds extreme, or advanced, views, or advocates extreme measures.

ex·trēm′ist, *a.* of extremism or extremists.

ex·trem′i·ty, *n.*; *pl.* **ex·trem′i·ties,** [L. *extremitas* (*-atis*), the extremity, end, from *extremus*, furthest, extreme.]
1. the outermost or utmost point or part; the end; the limit or border; as, the *extremities* of a country.
2. the most intense kind; the highest, greatest, or furthest degree; as, the *extremity* of cruelty.
3. a state of extreme or utmost necessity, danger, distress, straits, or difficulty; as, a city besieged and reduced to *extremity*.
4. the end of life; dying.
5. [*usually in pl.*] an extreme measure; severe or strong action; as, we must resort to *extremities* when all else fails.
6. [*pl.*] the hands and feet.

ex′tri·cȧ·ble, *a.* capable of being extricated.

ex′tri·cāte, *v.t.*; extricated, *pt.*, *pp.*; extricating, *ppr.* [L. *extricatus*, pp. of *extricare*, to disentangle, extricate; *ex*, out, and *tricæ*, trifles, toys.]
1. to set free; release; disentangle (*from* a net, difficulty, embarrassment, etc.).
2. to cause (a gas, heat, etc.) to be liberated or emitted.
Syn.—disembarrass, disengage, disentangle, liberate, evolve.

ex′tri·cāte, ex′tri·cā·ted, *a.* in entomology, extruded, as the ovipositor of certain insects.

ex·tri·cā′tion, *n.* an extricating or being extricated; a freeing from perplexities; disentanglement, liberation, etc.

ex·trin′sic, ex·trin′sic·ăl, *a.* [L. *extrinsecus*, from without, outer; *exter*, without, and *secus*, otherwise, besides.]
1. not contained in or belonging to the essence or real nature of a body; not inherent; not essential: opposed to *intrinsic*.
2. being, coming, or acting from the outside; external; extraneous.
3. in anatomy, having its origin outside the limits of an organ or limb to which it is partly attached, as certain muscles.
4. in Scots law, irrelevant.

ex·trin·si·cal′i·ty, *n.* the state or quality of being extrinsic.

ex·trin′sic·ăl·ly, *adv.* in an extrinsic manner; externally; from outside.

ex·trin′sic·ăl·ness, *n.* extrinsicality.

ex′trō-, extra- (when opposed to *intro-*).

ex·trō′i·tive, *a.* [L. *extra*, outside, and *ire*, to go.] searching out external matters or things. [Rare.]

ex·trọr′săl, *a.* extrorse.

ex·trọrse′, *a.* [Fr. *extrorse*; L. *extra*, outside, and *versus*, pp. of *vertere*, to turn.]
1. in botany, turned or facing outward or away from the axis of growth: opposed to *introrse*.
2. in zoology, turned outward or away from the median line.

ex·trō·vėr′sion, *n.* [*extra-*, and LL. *versio* (*-onis*), a turning, from L. *vertere*, to turn.]
1. in medicine, the turning inside out of an organ; especially, such a congenital condition of the urinary bladder.
2. in psychology, an attitude in which a person directs his interest to phenomena outside himself rather than to his own experiences and feelings: opposed to *introversion*: also *extraversion*.

ex′trō·vėrt, *n.* in psychology, a person whose interest is more in his environment and in other people than in himself; a person who is active and expressive, or other than introspective: opposed to *introvert*: also *extravert*.

ex·trụde′, *v.t.*; extruded, *pt.*, *pp.*; extruding, *ppr.* [L. *extrudere*, to thrust out or forth; *ex*, out, and *trudere*, to thrust.] to thrust out; to force or press out; to expel; as, plastic material is *extruded* through very small holes to form fibers.

ex·trụde′, *v.i.* to stick out; protrude; project.

ex·trụ′sion, *n.* [L. *extrusus*, pp. of *extrudere*, to thrust out.] the act of extruding or the state of being extruded; expulsion.

ex·trụ′sive, *a.* 1. resulting from or tending toward extrusion; extruding; as, *extrusive* forces.
2. in geology, forced out in a molten condition through the earth's surface; volcanic; as, *extrusive* rock.

ex·tū′bėr·ănce, ex·tū′bėr·ăn·cy, *n.* protuberance. [Obs.]

ex·tū′bėr·ănt, *a.* protuberant. [Obs.]

ex·tū′bėr·āte, *v.i.* to swell; to protrude. [Obs.]

ex·tū·bėr·ā′tion, *n.* protuberance. [Obs.]

ex·tū·mes′cence, *n.* [L. *ex*, out, and *tumescere*, incept. of *tumere*, to swell.] a swelling or rising. [Rare.]

ex·tund′, *v.t.* to beat or squeeze out. [Obs.]

ex·ū′bėr·ănce, ex·ū′bėr·ăn·cy (egz-), *n.* [LL. *exuberantia*, superabundance, from L. *exuberans* (*-antis*), ppr. of *exuberare*, to come forth in abundance.]
1. the state or quality of being exuberant; a great abundance; an overflowing quantity; richness; as, an *exuberance* of fertility or fancy.
2. an instance of this; especially, action or speech showing high spirits.
Syn.—abundance, copiousness, plenty, plenitude, superabundance.

ex·ū′bėr·ănt, *a.* 1. growing profusely; luxuriant; prolific; as, *exuberant* vegetation.
2. overflowing; superabundant; lavish; effusive; as, *exuberant* spirits.
3. overflowing with good health and spirits: said of a person.

ex·ū′bėr·ănt·ly, *adv.* in an exuberant manner.

ex·ū′bėr·āte, *v.i.*; exuberated, *pt.*, *pp.*; exuberating, *ppr.* [L. *exuberatus*, pp. of *exuberare*, to come forth in abundance; *ex*, out, and *uberare*, to be fruitful, from *uber*, an udder.] to abound; to be exuberant. [Rare.]

ex·uc′cous, *a.* exsuccous. [Obs.]

ex′ū·dāte, *n.* matter exuded.

ex′ū·dāte, *v.t.* and *v.i.*; exudated, *pt.*, *pp.*; exudating, *ppr.* to exude.

ex·ū·dā′tion, *n.* 1. the act of exuding or state of being exuded; a discharge of liquid through small openings.
2. that which is exuded, as sweat.

ex·ūde′ (egz-), *v.t.*; exuded, *pt.*, *pp.*; exuding, *ppr.* [L. *exudare*, *exsudare*, to sweat out, exude; *ex*, out, and *sudare*, to sweat.] to discharge in drops, as through small openings or pores; to give out slowly, as moisture; to ooze.

ex·ūde′, *v.i.* to flow slowly or ooze in drops, as from a body through pores or small openings.

ex·ul′cėr·āte (egz-), *v.i.*; exulcerated, *pt.*, *pp.*; exulcerating, *ppr.*; to ulcerate. [Archaic.]

ex·ul′cėr·āte, *a.* ulcerated. [Obs.]

ex·ul·cėr·ā′tion, *n.* ulceration. [Archaic.]

ex·ul′cėr·ȧ·tive, ex·ul′cėr·ȧ·tō·ry, *a.* ulcerous. [Archaic.]

ex·ult′ (egz-), *v.i.*; exulted, *pt.*, *pp.*; exulting, *ppr.* [L. *exultare*, *exsultare*, to leap up, leap for joy; *ex*, out, and *salire*, to leap.]
1. to rejoice greatly; to be jubilant; to glory.
2. to leap up; to leap with joy. [Obs.]

ex·ult′ăn·cy, ex·ult′ănce, *n.* exultation.

ex·ult′ănt, *a.* exulting; triumphant; jubilant.

ex·ul·tā′tion, *n.* [L. *exultatio* (*-onis*), *exsultatio* (*-onis*), a leaping up, rejoicing, from *exultare*, *exsultare*, to leap for joy, exult.] the act of exulting; lively joy at success or victory, or at any advantage gained; great gladness; rapturous delight; triumph.

ex·ult′ing·ly, *adv.* in an exulting manner.

ex·un′dāte, *v.i.* to overflow. [Rare.]

ex·un·dā′tion, *n.* [L. *exundatio* (*-onis*), from *exundare*, to overflow; *ex*, out, and *undare*, to rise in waves, from *unda*, a wave.] an overflowing. [Rare.]

ex′ūrb, *n.* [*ex-*, and sub*urb*: coined (1955) by A.C. Spectorsky (1910–), U.S. author and editor.] a region, generally semirural, beyond the suburbs of a city, inhabited largely by persons in the upper-income group.

ex·ūr′băn·īte, *n.* [coined (1955) by A.C. Spectorsky, from *ex-*, and sub*urbanite*.] a person living in an exurb; especially, one commuting to the city as a business person.

ex·ūr′băn·īte, *a.* of or characteristic of exurbia or exurbanites.

ex·ūr′bi·ȧ, *n.* the exurbs collectively: usually used to connote the pseudo-Bohemianism, exclusivity, etc. regarded as characteristic of exurbanites.

ex·us′ti·ble (egz-), *a.* combustible. [Obs.]

ex·us′tion (egz-), *n.* combustion. [Obs.]

ex·ū″vi·ȧ·bil′i·ty (egz-), *n.* state of being exuviable.

ex·ū′vi·ȧ·ble, *a.* capable of being cast or thrown off in the form of exuviae.

ex·ū′vi·ae (egz-), *n.pl.* [L., that which is stripped or taken off, spoils.]
1. cast skins, shells, or coverings of animals; any parts of animals which are shed or cast off, as the skins of caterpillars, the shells of lobsters, etc.
2. in geology, the fossil shells and other remains which animals have left in the strata of the earth.

ex·ū′vi·ăl, *a.* of the nature of or pertaining to exuviae.

ex·ū′vi·āte, *v.i.* and *v.t.*; exuviated, *pt.*, *pp.*; exuviating, *ppr.* to molt; to cast off (a skin, shell, etc.).

ex·ū·vi·ā′tion, *n.* 1. the act of exuviating.
2. an exuviated covering.

ex-vō′tō, *n.* [L. *ex voto*, lit., from a vow; *ex*, out of, and *voto*, ablative of *votum*, vow.] in the Roman Catholic Church, a votive offering, as a picture or a tablet for a shrine.

-ēy, -y (adjective-forming suffix): used especially after words ending in *y*.

e·yä′let, *n.* [Turk., from Ar. *wali*, *weli*, a governor, lord, master.] formerly, an administrative province of the Turkish empire; a pashalic: now known as a *vilayet*.

ēy′ăs (ī′ăs), *n.* [Fr. *niais*, fresh from the nest, from L. *nidus*, nest.]
1. a young hawk just taken from the nest for training in falconry.
2. an unfledged bird; nestling.

eȳe (ī), *n.* [ME. *eye*, *eghe* (pl. *eyen*, *eghen*); AS. *eage* (pl. *eagan*), eye.]
1. the organ of sight or vision; properly, in vertebrates, the globe or ball movable in the orbit. In all vertebrates, the eye closely resembles that of man, being formed by the combination of two segments from a larger and a smaller sphere. The segment of the lesser sphere forms the anterior part of the eye, and is composed externally of a strong hornlike membrane, the cornea, within which are the aqueous humor and the iris. The iris is a colored muscular membrane, capable of contraction and dilatation, suspended in the aqueous humor, with an opening (the pupil) in the center for the transmission of light. The larger sphere presents three coats, the outermost being the sclerotic, within which is the choroid, and lastly the retina. The last is the sentient coat, and consists of a cuplike expansion of the optic nerve, spread on the black coat, or *pigmentum nigrum*, covering the inner surface of the choroid, The anterior orifice of the choroid is firmly connected to a thick ring of grayish pulpy substance, forming the point at which the sclerotic and cornea without, and the iris within, are united. The

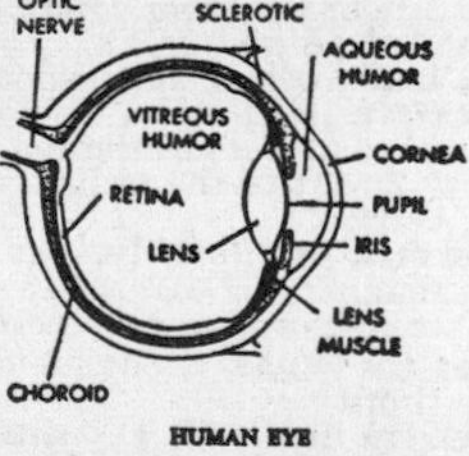

HUMAN EYE

interior sphere is filled with a jellylike, transparent mass, the vitreous humor, immediately in front of which, and just behind the pupil, is the crystalline lens, bearing the same relation to the retina that the lens of a camera does to the sensitive plate.

2. some conspicuous part of the eye or part of its surroundings; (a) the pupil; as, a cat's *eyes* contract; (b) the space or fissure between the eyelids; as, to close the *eyes*; (c) the iris; as, her *eyes* are brown; (d) the orbit of the eye; the socket; as, vacant *eyes* in a skull; (e) the area around the eye, including the eyelids; as, he has a black *eye*; (f) the eyeball.

3. sight; vision.

4. a look; glance; gaze; as, cast your *eye* on this.

5. attention; regard; observation.

6. the power of judging, estimating, discriminating, etc. by eyesight; as, a good *eye* for distances.

7. [*often in pl.*] judgment; opinion; estimation; as, in the *eyes* of the law.

8. anything resembling or suggesting an eye in shape, general appearance, or function; as, (a) the bud or shoot of a plant or tuber; (b) the hole or aperture in a needle to receive the thread; (c) the circular catch of a hook and eye; (d) the loop or ring for fastening the rigging of ships; (e) the center of a target; bull's-eye; (f) the spot on a peacock's tail feather; (g) in architecture, in general, the center of anything; thus, the *eye* of a volute is the circle at its center from which the spiral lines spring; (h) a muscular impression on the inner side of a bivalve, to which the adductor muscle is attached; (i) the hole in the upper millstone through which grain passes; (j) an eyebolt; (k) an opening intended to receive a handle, pin, shaft, etc., as in an adz, wheel, crank, anchor, or the socket of a carriage pole; (l) a loop of metal or thread; (m) an organ sensitive to light, as in certain lower forms of life; (n) a photoelectric cell.

9. a shade of color; a tint; a tinge. [Obs.]

10. anything of supreme brilliance, beauty, importance, or power; as, the sun is the *eye* of day.

Athens, the *eye* of Greece, mother of arts.
—Milton.

11. a calcareous deposit found in the walls of the stomach of crustaceans.

all in one's eye; imaginary; not real. [Slang.]

an eye for an eye; punishment or retaliation similar or equivalent to the injury suffered.

eyes right (or *left*); in military usage, a command to turn the head to the right (or left) while marching, as a salute when passing in review.

half an eye; a hasty or careless glance; imperfect observation.

in the eye of the wind; in nautical usage, in a direction opposite to that of the wind; close to the wind.

in the public eye; (a) much seen in public; (b) often brought to public attention; well-known.

to catch one's eye; to attract one's attention.

to feast one's eyes on; to look at with pleasure or admiration.

to give (a person) the eye; to look at (a person), especially with admiration or invitation. [Slang.]

to have an eye for; to have the ability to notice with discernment and appreciation.

to have an eye to; to watch out for; to attend to; to take care of.

to have (or *keep*) *an eye on*; to watch carefully; to look after; to pay particular attention to.

to keep one's eyes open; to be on the lookout; be watchful.

to make eyes at; to look at lovingly or flirtatiously.

to run one's eye over; to glance over; look at hurriedly.

to see eye to eye; to be in full agreement; hold precisely the same view.

to see with half an eye; to see or understand (something) easily because it is so evident.

to set or *lay* or *clap the eyes on*; to see; to have a sight of.

to shut one's eyes to; to be unwilling to see or think about.

with an eye to; paying attention to; considering.

eȳe, *v.t.*; eyed, *pt., pp.*; eying *or* eyeing, *ppr.* 1. to fix the eye on; to look on; to view; to observe; particularly, to observe or watch narrowly, or with fixed attention.

2. to provide with eyes or holes.

eȳe, *v.i.* to appear; to have an appearance (to the eyes). [Obs.]

eȳe, *n.* a brood; as, an *eye* of pheasants.

eȳe an·i·mal′çūle, a flagellate infusorian, especially one of the family *Euglenidæ*: so called from having a colored spot resembling an eye, at one end.

eȳe′ball, *n.* the ball-shaped part of the eye, enclosed by the socket and eyelids.

eȳe′bär, *n.* in engineering, a bar of steel or iron with an eye at one or both ends.

eȳe′bēam, *n.* a glance of the eye.

eȳe′bōlt, *n.* a bar, or bolt of iron, with an eye at one end.

eȳe′brīght (-brīt), *n.* the *Euphrasia officinalis* of the figwort family, a small European plant with white, yellow, or purple flowers, used in treating diseases of the eye.

eȳe′brow, *n.* 1. the bony arch over each eye.

2. the arch of hair growing on this.

eȳe′cup, *n.* a small cup whose rim is shaped to fit over the eye, used in applying medicine to the eyes or washing them.

eȳed (īd), *a.* 1. having eyes: often used in compounds, as in blue-*eyed*.

2. having markings that look like eyes; spotted.

eȳe′drop, *n.* a tear. [Poet. or Archaic.]

eȳe′flap, *n.* a blinder on a horse's bridle.

eȳe′fụl, *a.* attracting the sight. [Obs.]

eȳe′fụl, *n.* 1. a quantity of something in the eye; as, an *eyeful* of water.

2. as much as can be seen in one glance.

3. a person or thing that looks striking or unusual. [Slang.]

to get an eyeful; (a) to get a good look; (b) to see something very interesting. [Colloq.]

eȳe′glȧnce, *n.* a glance of the eye.

eȳe′glȧss, *n.* 1. a lens to assist sight by correcting any defect of vision; monocle.

2. [*pl.*] a pair of such lenses, usually in a frame: also called *glasses* or, less commonly, *spectacles*.

3. an eyecup.

4. the eyepiece of a telescope, microscope, or similar instrument.

5. the crystalline lens of the eye. [Obs.]

eȳe′hōle, *n.* 1. a peephole.

2. the socket for the eyeball.

3. an opening for receiving a rope, cord, pin, etc.; eyelet.

eȳe′lash, *n.* 1. the line or fringe of hair that edges the eyelid.

2. any of these hairs.

eȳe′less, *a.* lacking eyes; blind.

eȳe′let, *n.* [ME. *oylet*; OFr. *oeillet*, dim. of *oeil*, eye, from L. *oculus*, eye.]

1. a small hole or perforation for receiving a rope, cord, hook, etc.

2. a metal ring or short tube for lining such a hole.

3. a small hole edged by stitching in embroidered work.

4. a peephole or loophole.

5. a small eye; ocellus.

eȳe′let, *v.t.* to make eyelets in; provide with eyelets.

eȳe·let·eer′, *n.* a small, pointed instrument used in making eyelet holes; bodkin.

eȳe′lid, *n.* either of the two movable folds of flesh that cover and uncover the front of the eyeball.

eȳe′-mīnd′ed, *a.* having the tendency to carry on mental processes in association with visual images.

eȳ′en, *n.pl.* eyes. [Archaic and Dial.]

eȳe ō′pen·ẽr, 1. something that causes the eyes to open widely in astonishment or realization, as a striking occurrence or event.

2. a drink of liquor, especially one taken early in the morning. [Slang.]

eȳe′pīece, *n.* in a telescope, microscope, or other optical instrument, the lens or combination of lenses nearest the viewer's eye.

Huygenian eyepiece; a negative eyepiece consisting of two lenses flat on one side and convex on the other, the convex sides being turned away from the eye.

negative eyepiece; an eyepiece in which the rays are focused between the lenses.

positive eyepiece; an eyepiece in which the rays are focused before they reach the lenses.

eȳe′pit, *n.* the eye socket.

eȳ′ẽr, *n.* one who eyes or watches attentively.

eȳe′rēach, *n.* the range of vision; the distance to which one can see.

eȳe′sälve (-säv), *n.* a medicine or ointment for the eye.

eȳe′sẽrv″ănt, *n.* a servant who attends to his duty only when watched, or under the eye of his master or employer. [Archaic.]

eȳe′sẽrv″ice, *n.* 1. service performed only under the observation of an employer.

2. admiring glances.

eȳe shad′ōw, a cosmetic paste of various colors, usually green or blue, applied to the eyelids.

eȳe′shot, *n.* sight; view; glance of the eye; distance that a person can see; range of vision; eyereach.

eȳe′sīght (-sīt), *n.* 1. the range of vision; view; observation.

2. the sense or power of seeing; sight; vision; as, his *eyesight* fails.

eȳe′sōre, *n.* something disagreeable or offensive to the sight.

Mordecai was an *eyesore* to Haman.
—L'Estrange.

eȳe splīce, a splice made by turning the end of a rope back and interlacing it with the rope, forming an end loop, or eye.

eȳe′spot, *n.* 1. one of the rudimentary organs of sight of many invertebrates, consisting of a few pigment cells covering the end of a nerve which is sensitive to light.

2. a spot representing the place of development of the eye in the embryo of higher animals.

3. an ocellus; a spot resembling an eye, as on a peacock's tail.

eȳe′-spot″ted, *a.* marked with spots like eyes.

eȳe′stalk (ī′stąk), *n.* a movable stem or stalk bearing an eye at the end, as in some crustaceans.

eȳe′stōne, *n.* a small, calcareous object with one side flat and the other convex, used for taking cinders, dust, etc. from between the lid and ball of the eye.

eȳe′strāin, *n.* a tired or strained condition of the eye muscles, caused by too much or incorrect use of the eyes, faulty vision, etc.

eȳe′string, *n.* the tendon by which the eye is moved.

eȳ′et, *n.* same as *ait* (isle).

eȳe′tọoth, *n.*; *pl.* **eȳe′teeth,** either of the two pointed teeth in the upper jaw between the bicuspids and the incisors; upper canine tooth.

to cut one's eyeteeth; to become experienced or sophisticated.

eȳe′wäsh, *n.* 1. a lotion for the eyes.

2. (a) nonsense; (b) flattery; (c) something done only to impress an observer.

eȳe′wạ·tẽr, *n.* 1. the natural moisture of the eye.

2. a lotion for the eyes.

eȳe′wiṅk, *n.* 1. a wink, look, or glance.

2. an instant.

eȳe′wiṅk″ẽr, *n.* 1. an eyelash.

2. any foreign particle in the eye that causes blinking.

eȳe′wit″ness, *n.* 1. one who sees or has seen a thing done; one who has personally witnessed an accident, crime, etc.

We were *eyewitnesses* of his majesty.
—2 Pet. i. 16.

2. a person who testifies to what he has seen.

eyght (āt), *n.* same as *ait* (isle).

eyle (āl), *v.t.* and *v.i.* to ail. [Obs.]

eȳ′li·ad, *n.* an amorous look; an ogle. [Obs.]

eyne (īn), *n.*, archaic plural of *eye*.

eȳ′ŏt, *n.* same as *ait* (isle).

eȳ′rȧ (ī′rȧ), *n.* [native South Am. name.] a reddish or chestnut-colored wildcat, *Felis eyra*, ranging from Texas southward into South America. Its body is very long and slender and its legs short, especially the forelegs.

eyre (âr), *n.* [ME. *eyre*; OFr. *erre, oire*, a journey; L. *iter*, a journey.]

1. a journey, tour, or circuit.

2. in English history, a circuit court held by justices in eyre.

justices in eyre; formerly, in England, itinerant judges who rode the circuit to hold courts in the different counties.

ēy′rie, ēy′ry (*or* âr′i), *n.*; *pl.* **ēy′rieṣ,** 1. the nest of an eagle or other bird of prey that builds in a high place.

2. a house or stronghold on a high place.

3. the young (of an eagle, hawk, etc.) in the nest.

Also spelled *aerie*.

eȳ′stẽr, *n.* an oyster. [Obs.]

Ē·zē′ki·el, *n.* 1. a Hebrew prophet who lived among the exiled Jews of Babylonia about 560 B.C.

2. a book of the Old Testament containing his prophetic writings.

Ez′rȧ, *n.* 1. a Hebrew prophet, scribe, and religious reformer of the 5th century B. C.

2. a book of the Old Testament telling of his life and teachings.

F

F, f (ef), *n.*; *pl.* **F's, f's, Fs, fs,** 1. the sixth letter of the English alphabet: a modification of the Old Greek digamma (F), ultimately from the Phoenician.
2. the sound of F or f.
3. a type or impression for F or f.
4. *a symbol for* the sixth in a sequence or group.
5. in genetics, *the symbol for* filial generation.
6. in photography, *the symbol for* F number.

F, *a.* 1. of F or f.
2. sixth in a sequence or group.

F, *n.* 1. an object shaped like F.
2. a medieval Roman numeral for 40: with a superior bar (F̄), 40,000.
3. in chemistry, *the symbol for* fluorine.
4. in education, (a) a grade meaning *failure*; (b) sometimes, a grade third in quality, meaning *fair*.
5. in mathematics, *the symbol for* function.
6. in music, (a) the fourth tone or note in the scale of C major, or the sixth in the scale of A minor; (b) a key, string, etc. producing this tone; (c) the scale having F as the keynote; (d) *a symbol for* the bass clef.
7. in physics, *a symbol for* farad.
8. in printing, *a symbol for* folio.

F, *a.* shaped like F.

fä, *n.* [It.] in music, a syllable representing the fourth tone or subdominant of the diatonic scale.

fa·bā'ceous (-bā'shus), *a.* [L. *fabaceus*, of or consisting of beans, from *faba*, a bean.] of the pea family of plants.

fa·bel'lȧ, *n.*; *pl.* **fa·bel'lae,** [L., dim. of *faba*, a bean.] in anatomy, one of the small bones on the back of the kneejoint or behind the condyle of the femur.

Fā'bi·ăn, *a.* [L. *Fabianus*, of *Fabius*, Roman general of the 3rd c. B.C., who used such a strategy.]
1. using a cautious strategy of delay and avoidance of battle.
2. of the Fabian Society.

Fā'bi·ăn, *n.* a member of the Fabian Society; Fabian socialist.

Fā'bi·ăn·iṣm, *n.* the principles and methods of the Fabian Society.

Fā'bi·ăn Sō·cī'e·ty, an organization of English socialists, established in 1884, aiming to bring about socialism by gradual reforms rather than drastic means.

fā'ble, *n.* [ME. *fable*, OFr. *fable*; L. *fabula*, a narrative, story, from *fari*, to speak.]
1. a fictitious narrative intended to teach some moral truth or precept, in which animals and sometimes inanimate objects are represented as speakers and actors.

Jotham's *fable* of the trees is the oldest extant, and as beautiful as any made since. —Addison.

2. a story or legend invented and developed by imagination or superstition and at one time quite generally believed, but now known to be imaginary; a myth.
3. a story that is not true; a falsehood.
4. the plot, or connected series of events, of a literary work. [Archaic.]

The moral is the first business of the poet; this being formed, he contrives such a design or *fable* as may be most suitable to the moral. —Dryden.

Syn.—allegory, apologue, legend, myth.

fā'ble, *v.i.* and *v.t.*; fabled, *pt.*, *pp.*; fabling, *ppr.* [ME. *fablen*; OFr. *fabler*; L. *fabulare*, to speak, converse, from *fabula*, a fable.] to write or tell (fables, fiction, falsehoods).

Vain now the tales which *fabling* poets tell. —Prior.

fā'bled (-bld), *a.* [pp. of *fable*].
1. told in fables; mythical; legendary.
2. unreal; fictitious; invented.

fā'blēr, *n.* a writer or teller of fables.

fa·bli·au' (-ō'), *n.*; *pl.* **fa·bli·aux'** (-ōz'), [Fr., from OFr. *fabliaus*, from L. *fabella*, dim. of *fabula*, a fable.] in medieval literature, especially French and English literature, a short metrical story, often in eight-syllable lines, telling comic incidents of ordinary life, usually with blunt realism and earthy humor: the genre arose in France in the 12th and 13th centuries.

fab'riç, *n.* [Fr. *fabrique*; L. *fabrica*, a workshop, trade, any product of a trade, fabric, from *faber*, a workman, artisan.]
1. anything made of parts put together; structure; building framework.
2. the style or plan of construction; texture.
3. any woven, knitted, or felted cloth.

fab'riç, *v.t.* to frame; to construct. [Obs.]

fab'ri·çănt, *n.* one who makes or builds; a manufacturer.

fab'ri·çāte, *v.t.*; fabricated, *pt.*, *pp.*; fabricating, *ppr.* [L. *fabricatus*, pp. of *fabricari*, to construct, frame, build, from *fabrica*, any skillful production, a fabric.]
1. to frame; to build; to construct; to make; to manufacture.
2. to make or build as a whole, by connecting its parts; as, to *fabricate* engines.
3. to invent and form; to forge; to devise falsely; as, to *fabricate* a lie or story.

Our books were not *fabricated* with an accommodation to prevailing usages. —Paley.

Syn.—frame, construct, make, manufacture, produce.

fab·ri·çā'tion, *n.* [Fr. *fabrication*; L. *fabricatio* (*-onis*), a making, framing, from *fabricari*, to make.]
1. a fabricating or being fabricated; construction; manufacture.
2. that which is fabricated or manufactured, especially a falsehood or forgery; as, the rumors were mere *fabrications*.

Syn.—fiction, figment, falsehood, fable, invention, untruth.

fab'ri·çā·tŏr, *n.* [L. *fabricator*, a maker, framer, from *fabricari*, to make.] one who constructs or makes; specifically, (a) a maker; a manufacturer; (b) one who invents a fictitious story; a liar.

fab'ri·çā·tress, *n.* a woman fabricator.

fab'ri·koid, *n.* a leatherlike, impervious fabric, having a cloth base covered with a coating of pyroxylin: used in upholstery, bookbinding, and for handbags, pocketbooks, etc.: a trademark (*Fabrikoid*).

fab'rile, *a.* [OFr. *fabrile*; L. *fabrilis*, from *faber*, a workman.] pertaining to a worker in stone, metal, or similar craft, or to his work. [Obs.]

fab'ū·list, *n.* [L. *fabula*, a fable.]
1. one who writes, invents, or tells fables.
2. a liar.

fab'ū·līze, *v.i.* and *v.t.*; fabulized, *pt.*, *pp.*; fabulizing, *ppr.* [L. *fabula*, a fable.] to fable. [Obs.]

fab·ū·los'i·ty, *n.* 1. the quality of being fabulous. [Rare.]
2. a fable. [Obs.]

fab'ū·lous, *a.* [L. *fabulosus*, celebrated in fable, legendary, from *fabula*, a story.]
1. legendary; imaginary; devised; fictitious; as, a *fabulous* story; a *fabulous* description.
2. beyond the limits of belief; exceedingly great; incredible; enormous; immense; as, a *fabulous* sum.
3. given to the telling of fables and legends.

fabulous age; in a nation, the time before the beginning of authentic history; the legendary period.

Syn.—feigned, fictitious, legendary, mythical.

fab'ū·lous·ly, *adv.* in fable or fiction; in a fabulous manner.

fab'ū·lous·ness, *n.* the quality of being fabulous or feigned.

fab'ūr·den, *n.* [OFr. *faux bourdon*.] in music, the simplest or rudest counterpoint; a drone bass; a monotonous refrain or burden. [Obs.]

fa·çade' (-säd'), *n.* [It. *facciata*, the front of a building, from *faccia*, L. *facies*, face.]
1. in architecture, an elevation or exterior face of a building, especially the front or most important face; as, the *façade* of St. Mark's; the *façade* of the Pitti palace.
2. the front part of anything: often used figuratively, with implications of an imposing appearance concealing something inferior.

FACADE (of temple)

fāce, *n.* [ME. *face*; OFr. *face*; L. *facies*, the face, visage, appearance.]
1. in a general sense, the surface of a thing, or the side which presents itself to the view of a spectator; as, the *face* of the earth; the *face* of the waters.

A mist watered the whole *face* of the ground. —Gen. ii. 6.

2. the front part of an animal's head, particularly of the human head, made up of the forehead, eyes, nose, mouth, cheeks, etc.; the visage.
3. the expression of the face as indicative of favor, disfavor, or anger; hence, favor, disfavor, or anger; as, I set my *face* against it.

Therefore came I forth to meet thee, diligently to seek thy *face*, and I have found thee. —Prov. vii. 15.

4. a plane surface of a solid; one of the sides bounding a solid; as, a cube or die has six faces; an octahedron has eight *faces*.
5. the side or surface that is marked, as of a clock, playing card, etc., or finished, as of fabric, leather, etc.
6. confidence; effrontery; boldness; audacity. [Colloq.]

He has the *face* to charge others with false citations. —Tillotson.

7. presence; sight.

There he stood once more before her *face*
Claiming her promise. —Tennyson.

8. the appearance; outward aspect.
9. [from Chin. idiom.] dignity; self-respect; prestige; as, Japan lost *face* by her defeat.
10. the value printed or written on a note: usually *face value*.
11. the topography (of an area).
12. an expressive distortion of the face; grimace. [Colloq.]
13. in law, what is shown by the language of a document, without explanation or addition.
14. in military science, any of the sides of a formation, especially of a square formation.
15. in mineralogy, any surface of a stone or crystal.
16. in typography, (a) the type surface on which a letter is cut; printing part of a letter or plate; (b) the design of type.
17. in commerce, the exact sum expressed on a bill, note, etc., exclusive of interest accrued by law or discount.
18. the edge of any tool which cuts.
19. in mining, especially in coal mining, the end of a working excavation.

 fāte, fär, fȧst, fạll, finăl, cãre, at; mēte, prey, hēr, met; pīne, marīne, bīrd, pin; nōte, mōve, fọr, atŏm, not; mọọn, book;

20. in astrology, one of the thirty-six parts of the zodiac, assigned to one of the planets.

21. in bookbinding, the front edge of a book, as opposed to the *back*.

face down; with the face down; prone, or wrong side up.

face to face; (a) in a confronting attitude; in the actual presence: followed by *with*; as, to have accusers *face to face*; (b) clearly; without the interposition of any other body.

Now we see through a glass, darkly; but then *face to face*. —1 Cor. xiii. 12.

on the face of it; to all appearances; apparently; as, it was a lie *on the face of it*.

to fly in the face of; to dare; to defy.

to make a face; to make a grimace; to distort one's countenance.

to one's face; confronting one; in one's presence; openly and without fear.

to pull (or *wear*) *a long face*; to look sad, glum, disappointed, disapproving, etc.

to put a bold face on; to seem bold or confident about.

to set one's face against; to be determinedly against; disapprove of; resist; oppose.

Syn.—countenance, feature, physiognomy, visage.

fāce, *v.t.*; faced (fāst), *pt., pp.*; facing, *ppr.* 1. to turn, or have the face turned, toward; be in a position opposite to; as, the building *faces* the square.

2. to meet squarely or face to face.

3. to confront with boldness, courage, etc.

I'll *face*
This tempest, and deserve the name of king. —Dryden.

4. to realize and be ready to meet (a condition, fact, etc.).

5. to cover with a new surface.

6. to give a false appearance to; as, alcohol is *faced* with caramel to make it look like whisky.

7. to put a smooth surface on (a stone, tool, etc.).

8. to turn (a card, etc.) with the face up.

9. in military science, to cause (a formation of soldiers) to pivot by giving the appropriate command.

10. in sewing, to add a piece of cloth to (another material) for lining, trimming, etc.

to face down; to disconcert or overcome by a confident, bold manner.

to face it out; to adhere to anything under all circumstances; to persist steadfastly or impudently.

to face the music; to meet the emergency unflinchingly; to meet the consequences, however unpleasant they may be. [Slang.]

to face up to; (a) to face with courage; confront and resist; (b) to realize and be ready to meet (a fact, condition, etc.).

fāce, *v.i.* 1. to carry a false appearance; to play the hypocrite. [Obs.]

2. to turn, or have the face turned, toward a specified thing or person, or in a specified direction.

3. in hockey, lacrosse, etc., to start play by tossing the ball or puck between the two opposing centers (with *off*).

4. in military science, to pivot in a specified direction: usually in the form of a command; as, right *face!*

fāce āche, fāce ā'gūe, in pathology, neuralgia of the face: also called *tic douloureux*.

fāce çārd, any king, queen, or jack in a deck of cards.

fāce'çloth, *n.* 1. a cloth laid over the face of a corpse.

2. a washcloth.

fāce çov'ẽr, in fortifications, an interior glacis placed in the ditch, to prevent damage from the besiegers' fire.

fāced (fāst), *a.* 1. having a face: used in combination; as, two-*faced*, sweet-*faced*.

2. having its upper or outer surface dressed or smoothed; as, a *faced* stone.

3. having a covering or facing, usually of another material; as, a dress *faced* with silk.

fāce guärd, a mask to protect the face, worn by workers in foundries and laboratories, and by participants in certain games.

fāce ham'mẽr, 1. a hammer with a flat face.

2. a large, heavy hammer used in facing stone.

fāce lift'ing, plastic surgery for removing wrinkles, sagging flesh, etc. from the face.

fāce mīte, a mite, *Demodex folliculorum*, parasitic in the hair and sebaceous glands, especially of the nose and ears.

fāce mōld, a pattern used to mark the plank or board out of which are to be cut ornamental band railings, etc.

fāce plāte, 1. a plate used as a standard in testing a plane surface.

2. a plate which shields an object from shock and wear.

3. a disk attached to the revolving spindle of a lathe, to the face of which the piece to be turned is often clamped.

fāce pow'dẽr, a cosmetic powder, as of flesh-colored talc, applied to the face to dull the shine, conceal skin blemishes, etc.

fā'cẽr, *n.* 1. one who is impudent or brazen. [Obs.]

There be no great talkers, nor boasters, nor *facers*. —Latimer.

2. a person or thing that faces.

3. a severe blow in the face; hence, any sudden check that staggers one. [Colloq.]

fac'et, *n.* [Fr. *facette*; OFr. *facete*, dim. of *face*, face.]

1. any of the small, polished plane surfaces of a cut gem.

2. any of a number of sides or aspects, as of a personality.

3. in anatomy, any small, smooth surface on a bone or other hard part.

4. in architecture, the raised plane between the flutes of a column.

5. in zoology, any of the small surfaces of a compound eye, as in some insects.

fac'et, *v.t.*; faceted, *pt., pp.*; faceting, *ppr.* to cut or make facets upon; as, to *facet* a diamond.

fa·cēte', *a.* pleasant; bright; facetious; witty. [Archaic.]

fac'et·ed, *a.* having facets; cut into facets.

fa·cēte'ly, *adv.* in a facete manner. [Obs.]

fa·cēte'ness, *n.* the quality of being facete. [Obs.]

fa·cē'ti·ae (-shi-ē), *n.pl.* [L., from *facetus*, witty.]

1. witty or humorous writings or sayings; witticisms.

2. ribald or coarsely witty books.

fa̤·cē'tious (-sē'shus), *a.* [Fr. *facétieux*, from L. *facetia*, a jest, from *facetus*, elegant, witty.] lightly joking; jocular; jocose, especially at an inappropriate time.

Syn.—witty, jocose.

fa̤·cē'tious·ly, *adv.* in a facetious manner.

fa̤·cē'tious·ness, *n.* the quality of being facetious.

fa·cette', *n.* same as *facet*.

fāce val'ūe, 1. the value printed or written on a bill, bond, etc.

2. the seeming value; as, I took his promise at *face value*.

fāce wheel, same as *crown wheel*.

fā'ciăl (fā'shăl), *a.* [LL. *facialis*, from L. *facies*, face.] of or for the face; as, the *facial* artery, vein, or nerve.

facial angle; the angle made by the intersection of two lines drawn from the base of the nostrils, one to the base of the skull and the other to the most prominent part of the forehead.

FACIAL ANGLE
A. New Guinea native;
B. European woman

facial index; the ratio of the length to the width of the face $\left(\frac{\text{length} \times 100}{\text{width}}\right)$

fā'ciăl, *n.* a treatment for the skin of the face, consisting of the application of astringents and creams, massage, etc. [Colloq.]

fā'ciăl·ly, *adv.* with reference to the face.

fā'ci·end (-shi-), *n.* [from neut. of L. *faciendus*, gerundive of *facere*, to make, do.] in mathematics, the number or factor to be multiplied by another; multiplicand.

fā'cient (-shent), *n.* [L. *faciens* (*-entis*), ppr. of *facere*, to do, make.]

1. a doer; one who does anything.

2. in mathematics, (a) a variable of a quantic; (b) the multiplier.

-fā'cient, [see *facient*.] a suffix used to form adjectives, meaning *making* or *causing to become*, as in lique*facient*.

fā'ci·ēs (-shi-ēz), *n.* [L.] 1. the face.

2. the general aspect or appearance of anything.

facies Hippocratica; the peculiar appearance of the face immediately before death, first described by Hippocrates.

fac'ile, *a.* [Fr. *facile*; L. *facilis*, easy to do, from *facere*, to do, make.]

1. easy to be done or performed; easy; not difficult; performable or attainable with little labor.

Order will render the work *facile* and delightful. —Evelyn.

2. easy to be surmounted or removed; easily conquerable.

The *facile* gates of hell too slightly barred. —Milton.

3. easy in manner; mild; courteous; not haughty, austere, or distant. [Obs.]

I mean she should be courteous, *facile*, sweet. —Jonson.

4. pliant; flexible; easily persuaded or influenced.

Since Adam, and his *facile* consort Eve,
Lost Paradise, deceived by me.—Milton.

5. ready; skillful; dexterous; quick; fluent; as, a *facile* artist, a *facile* pen.

fac'ile·ly, *adv.* in a facile manner; easily.

fac'ile·ness, *n.* the state or quality of being facile.

fa'ci·lē prin'ceps, [L.] easily first or foremost; pre-eminent.

fa̤·cil'i·tāte, *v.t.*; facilitated, *pt., pp.*; facilitating, *ppr.* [Fr. *faciliter*, to facilitate, from L. *facilitas* (*-atis*), facility, from *facilis*, easy.]

1. to make easy or less difficult.

2. to free from difficulty or impediment; to lessen the labor of; as, machinery *facilitates* manual labor.

fa̤·cil·i·tā'tion, *n.* 1. a facilitating.

2. in psychology, increased ease of performance of any action, resulting from the lessening of nerve resistance by the continued successive application of the necessary stimulus: opposed to *inhibition*.

fa̤·cil'i·ty, *n.*; *pl.* **fa̤·cil'i·ties,** [L. *facilitas* (*-atis*), easiness, from *facilis*, easy.]

1. ease of doing or making; freedom from difficulty.

Though *facility* and hope of success might invite some other choice. —Bacon.

2. a ready ability; skill; fluency; dexterity; as, practice gives a wonderful *facility* in executing works of art.

3. pliancy; a tendency to be easygoing, yielding, etc.

It is a great error to take *facility* for good nature. —L'Estrange.

4. easiness of access; complaisance; condescension; affability. [Obs.]

He offers himself to the visits of a friend with *facility*. —South.

5. [*pl.*] the means by which something can be more easily done; conveniences; as, good transportation *facilities*.

Syn.—expertness, readiness.—*Facility* supposes a natural or acquired power of doing something with ease and dexterity; *expertness* is *facility* acquired by long-continued practice; *readiness* emphasizes the promptitude with which anything is done.

fā'cing, *n.* 1. a covering in front for ornament, distinction, protection, defense, or other purpose; as, (a) in architecture, the thin covering of polished stone over an inferior stone, or the layer of plaster or cement on a brick or rough stone wall; (b) in joinery, the woodwork which is fixed round apertures in interiors, to ornament them or to protect the plaster from injury; (c) in engineering, a layer of earth, turf, or stone laid upon the bottom and sloping sides of a canal, railway, reservoir, etc. to protect the exposed surface or to give it a steeper slope; (d) a lining or trimming, often decorative, sewn on the inside or outside edge or part of a dress, coat, etc.; also, any material used for this; (e) [*pl.*] the trimmings, collar, and cuffs of certain military coats.

2. in founding, powder applied to the face of a mold which receives the metal, to give a smooth surface to the casting.

3. [*pl.*] the movement of soldiers in turning round to the right, left, etc.

fā'cing·ly, *adv.* in a facing position.

fa̤·cin'ō·rous, *a.* atrociously wicked. [Obs.]

fa̤·cin'ō·rous·ness, *n.* extreme or atrocious wickedness. [Obs.]

faç'ound, *a.* and *n.* facund. [Obs.]

fac·sim'i·lē, *n.* [L. *factum simile*, made like; *factum*, neut. of *factus*, pp. of *facere*, to make, and *simile*, neut. of *similis*, like.]

1. an exact copy or likeness, as of handwriting.

2. the transmission and reproduction of printed matter by a process involving the use of radio broadcast: the transmitted signals, formed by a photoelectric cell that picks up

the differences in light and dark in the subject matter as it is scanned by a beam of light, are converted into a facsimile of the original matter by a mechanism attached to the radio receiver.

in facsimile; as an exact likeness; in exact reproduction.

fac·sim′i·lē, *a.* 1. of, or having the nature of, facsimile; as, a *facsimile* engraving.

2. producing or intended to produce facsimiles.

facsimile telegraph; a telegraphic apparatus which reproduces at the receiving end messages, pictures, etc. sent at the transmitting end.

fac·sim′i·lē, *v.t.*; facsimiled, *pt., pp.*; facsimileing, *ppr.* to make a facsimile of.

fact, *n.* [L. *factum*, that which is done, a deed, fact, neut. of *factus*, pp. of *facere*, to do, act.]

1. anything done; an act; a deed. [Obs.]

2. a thing that has actually happened or is true; a thing that has been or is.

3. reality; truth; actuality; the state of things as they are.

4. something declared to have happened, or to have existed; the assertion of something as existing or done; as, he depends upon his imagination for his *facts*; there are many false *facts* in his report.

5. in law, something that has taken place, either actually or by supposition, distinguished from a purely legal result.

as a matter of fact; to tell the truth; really: also *in fact, in point of fact.*

fac′tȧ, *n.* pl. of *factum.*

fac′tion, *n.* [Fr. *faction*; L. *factio (-onis)*, a making, doing, company, faction, from *factus*, pp. of *facere*, to do, make.]

1. a number of persons in an organization, having a common end in view; especially, a party within a party, seeking to further its own ends, usually in opposition to the ends or aims of the main body or leadership of the party; a clique.

> By a *faction*, I understand a number of citizens, whether amounting to a majority or minority of the whole, who are united and actuated by some common impulse of passion, or of interest, adverse to the rights of other citizens, or to the permanent and aggregate interests of the community.
> —Madison.

2. partisan conflict within an organization or a country; discord; dissension.

3. in ancient Rome, one of the different troops or companies of combatants in the games of the circus.

fac′tion·ăl, *a.* 1. of a faction or factions; partisan.

2. causing or characterized by faction.

fac′tion·ăl·iṣm, *n.* factional quarreling; a spirit of faction.

fac′tion·ȧ·ry, *a.* factious; zealous; partisan. [Rare.]

fac′tion·ẽr, *n.* one of a faction. [Obs.]

fac′tion·ist, *n.* one who promotes faction.

fac′tious (fak′shus), *a.* [L. *factiosus*, lit., fond of doing, powerful, of or for a party or factions, from *factio (-onis)*, a faction.]

1. producing or tending to produce faction; causing dissension.

2. produced or characterized by faction; as, *factious* tumults; *factious* quarrels.

fac′tious·ly, *adv.* in a factious manner.

fac′tious·ness, *n.* the state or quality of being factious; disposition to cause dissension.

fac·ti′tious (-tish′us), *a.* [L. *facticius*, artificial, factitious, from *factus*, pp. of *facere*, to do.] not natural, genuine, or spontaneous; forced or artificial; as, the *factitious* needs of our era.

fac·ti′tious·ly, *adv.* in a factitious or artificial manner.

fac·ti′tious·ness, *n.* the state or condition of being factitious.

fac′ti·tive, *a.* [L. *factus*, pp. of *facere*, to do.] designating or of a verb that expresses the idea of making, calling, or thinking something to be of a certain character, using a noun, pronoun, or adjective as a complement to its direct object; taking a complementary object. Examples: *make* the dress *short*, *elect* him *president*.

fac′tive, *a.* making; having power to make. [Obs.]

fac′tŏr, *n.* [L. *factor*, a doer, maker, performer, from *facere*, to do, make.]

1. (a) a person who carries on business transactions for another; commission merchant; agent for the sale of goods; (b) a person legally appointed to take care of forfeited or sequestered property; (c) [Scot.] a person who manages an estate for another; steward; bailiff.

2. [from fig. use of 4.] any of the circumstances, conditions, etc. that bring about a result; element or constituent that makes a thing what it is.

3. in biology, a gene.

4. in mathematics, one of the two or more numbers, elements, or quantities which, when when multiplied together, form a given product; as, 7 and 3 are *factors* of 21.

fac′tŏr, *v.t.*; factored, *pt., pp.*; factoring, *ppr.*

1. to manage as an agent; to act as factor for. [Rare.]

2. in mathematics, to resolve into factors.

fac′tŏr·ȧġe, *n.* 1. the business of a factor; buying and selling on commission.

2. the allowance given to a factor by his employer as a compensation for his services: called also a *commission*.

fac′tŏr·ess, *n.* a woman factor. [Rare.]

fac·tō′ri·ăl, *a.* 1. of a factor.

2. pertaining to a factory. [Rare.]

3. in mathematics, of or pertaining to factors or factorials.

fac·tō′ri·ăl, *n.* the product of a given series of consecutive whole numbers beginning with 1; as, the *factorial* of 5 is 1×2×3×4×5, or 120.

fac′tŏr·īze, *v.t.*; factorized, *pt., pp.*; factorizing, *ppr.* 1. in some States, to garnishee or attach the money or effects of.

2. in mathematics, to separate (a product) into factors.

fac′tŏr of sāfe′ty, the ratio of the maximum strength of a piece of material or a part to the probable maximum load to be applied to it.

fac′tŏr·ship, *n.* the position or business of a factor.

fac′tō·ry, *n.*; *pl.* **fac′tō·rieṣ,** [Fr. *factorie*, a factory; LL. *factoria*, from L. *factor*, a doer, maker.]

1. an establishment for the manufacture of goods, including the necessary buildings and machinery; a manufacturing plant.

2. a house or place where factors reside, to transact business for their employers; as, the English merchants have *factories* in the colonies.

3. the body of factors in any place; as, a chaplain to a British *factory*. [Obs.]

fac·tō′tum, *n.* [L. *fac totum*, lit., do everything; *fac*, imper. of *facere*, to do, and *totum*, neut. of *totus*, all, the whole.] a person employed to do all kinds of work; a handy man.

fac′tū·ăl, *a.* 1. pertaining to or consisting of facts.

2. having the nature of fact; real; actual.

fac′tum, *n.*; *pl.* **fac′tȧ,** [L., neut. of *factus*, pp. of *facere*, to do.]

1. in law, an act; a deed accomplished.

2. in law, a deed or a grant or claim which has been sealed.

3. in mathematics, a product. [Obs.]

fac′tūre, *n.* [Fr. *facture*; L. *factura*, a making, from *factus*, pp. of *facere*, to do.]

1. the act or method of making something.

2. the thing made.

fac′ū·lȧ, *n.*; *pl.* **fac′ū·lae,** [L., dim. of *fax* (*facis*), a torch.] a small shining spot on the sun's surface, brighter than the rest of the photosphere.

fac′ū·lăr, *a.* of, pertaining to, or resembling a facula.

fac′ul·tā·tive, *a.* [L. *facultas (-atis)*, faculty, ability.]

1. (a) granting a faculty, or permission; permissive; hence, (b) optional.

2. that may or may not happen; contingent.

3. having to do with a faculty or faculties.

4. in biology, capable of living under conditions other than the usual: said of parasites, etc.

facultative parasite; an organism, usually a fungus, which in its normal state is a saprophyte, but which is capable of developing as a parasite.

fac′ul·tā·tive·ly, *adv.* in a facultative manner.

fac′ul·ty, *n.*; *pl.* **fac′ul·tieṣ,** [ME. *facultee*; OFr. *faculte*; L. *facultas (-atis)*, ability, capability, power, means, from *facul*, *facilis*, easy.]

1. any natural or specialized power of a living organism; as, the *faculty* of seeing, of hearing, of imagining, of remembering.

2. power or ability to do some particular thing; skill derived from practice, or practice aided by nature; habitual skill or ability; dexterity; adroitness; knack; as, he has a remarkable *faculty* for telling a story.

3. formerly, the power to do; ability to perform any action.

4. in ecclesiastical usage, a privilege; a right or power granted to a person by favor or indulgence, to do what by law he may not do; specifically, an authorization by a superior bestowing ecclesiastical rights upon a subordinate: often used in the plural.

5. the individuals constituting a learned profession, or a branch of one, taken collectively.

6. [from L. *facultas*, transl. of Aristotle's *dynamis*, branch of learning.] any of the departments of learning in a university; as, the *faculty* of law, the science *faculty*.

7. all the teachers of a school, college, or university.

8. a power conferred by authority; authorization.

9. what a person is trained to do; trade. [Archaic.]

10. in psychology, any of the powers formerly thought of as composing the mind, such as will, reason, etc.

fac′und, *a.* eloquent; fluent. [Obs.]

fac′und, *n.* eloquence; fluency of speech. [Obs.]

fa·cun′di·ous, *a.* facund. [Obs.]

fa·cun′di·ty, *n.* eloquence; readiness of speech. [Obs.]

fad, *n.* [19th c., from Brit. Midland dial.] a custom, hobby, style, etc. adopted and pursued by many people for a time, with undue zeal; a passing fashion, as in dress, social diversions, etc.; as, her *fad* is collecting old silver; sailor hats are all the *fad* again.

fad′dish, *a.* 1. having the nature of a fad.

2. fond of fads; following fads.

fad′dist, *n.* one who is enthusiastic over a fad or follows fads.

fad′dle, *v.i.* to trifle; to toy; to play. [Brit. Dial.]

fad′dy, *a.* same as *faddish.*

fȧde (fȧd), *a.* [Fr.] stale; insipid; flat; as, a *fade* conversation.

fāde, *v.i.*; faded, *pt., pp.*; fading, *ppr.* [ME. *faden*; OFr. *fader*, to become pale or weak, fade, from *fade*, pale, from L. *fatuus*, foolish, silly.]

1. to wither, as a plant; to lose strength, health, or vigor gradually.

> The flower ripens in its place,
> Ripens, and *fades*, and falls.—Tennyson.

2. to die out; to decay; to perish gradually.

3. to lose freshness, color, or brightness; to tend from a stronger or brighter color to a more faint shade of the same color, or to lose color entirely; to grow dim or indistinct.

4. to disappear gradually.

> Adieu, adieu! my native shore
> *Fades* o'er the waters blue. —Byron.

to fade back; in football, to move back from the line of scrimmage, as in order to throw a forward pass.

to fade in; in motion pictures, radio, and television, to appear gradually; to become more distinct.

to fade out; in motion pictures, radio, and television, to disappear gradually; to become less distinct.

Syn.—fall, fail, decline, sink, droop, dwindle, vanish, change, pale, bleach, etiolate.

fāde, *v.t.* 1. to cause to wither; to wear away; to deprive of color, freshness, or vigor; to dim.

> No winter could his laurels *fade*.
> —Dryden.

2. to meet the bet of; to cover: dice player's term. [Slang.]

fād′ed, *a.* having become less vivid, as color; withered; decayed; vanished.

fād′ed·ly, *adv.* in a faded manner.

fāde′-in″, *n.* in motion pictures, radio, and television, a fading in, or becoming more and more distinct, until the picture or sound is extremely clear.

fāde′less, *a.* unfading.

fāde′less·ly, *adv.* in a fadeless manner.

fāde′-out″, *n.* in motion pictures, radio, and television, the act of fading out, or of becoming less and less distinct, until the picture or sound finally disappears; also, an instance of fading out.

fä′dẽr, *n.* father. [Obs.]

fadġe (faj), *v.i.* [AS. *fegan*, *gefegan*, to fit, to compact.] to suit; to fit; to come close, as the parts of things united; hence, to have one part consistent with another. [Obs.]

fād′ing, *a.* losing color; becoming less vivid; decaying; declining; withering.

fād′ing, *n.* 1. decay; loss of color, freshness, or vigor.

2. in radiotelegraphy, a fluctuation in in-

tensity of the signal received; also, less broadly, a decrease in the intensity of a signal.

fad'ing, *n.* an Irish dance; also, the refrain of a song. [Obs.]

fād'ing·ly, *adv.* in a fading manner.

fād'ing·ness, *n.* decay; liableness to decay.

fad'me, *n.* a fathom. [Obs.]

fād'y, *a.* wearing away; losing color or strength. [Rare.]

fae'căl, *a.* same as *fecal.*

fae'cēs, *n.pl.* same as *feces.*

faeç'ū·là, *n.* same as *fecula.*

fā'ēr·ie, fā'ēr·y (*or* fâr'i), *n.* [var. of *fairy*, first used by Spenser.]

1. fairyland. [Archaic.]

2. fairy. [Archaic.]

Also spelled *faërie, faëry.*

fā'ēr·ie, fā'ēr·y, *a.* fairy: also spelled *faërie, faëry.* [Archaic.]

faf'fle, *v.i.* to stammer. [Obs.]

Fāf'nir (fäv' *or* fäf'), *n.* [ON. *Fāfnir.*] in Norse legend, a giant who, in the form of a dragon, guarded the Nibelung treasure: he was killed by Sigurd.

fag, *v.i.*; fagged, *pt., pp.*; fagging, *ppr.* [earlier form of *flag*, v.; basic sense "to droop."]

1. to drudge; to work hard and become very tired.

2. to act as a fag; to do drudgery for another.

3. to become weary; to fail in strength. [Obs.]

Syn.—work, toil, slave, drudge.

fag, *v.t.* 1. to use or treat (a boy) as a fag; to require or compel (a boy) to do drudgery for one's own benefit.

2. to exhaust; to make weary by labor: usually with *out*; as, he is *fagged out* with his hard study.

fag, *n.* 1. a drudge; specifically, in certain English public schools, as Eton, Harrow, Winchester, and Rugby, a boy who does menial services for another boy of a higher form or class. [Brit. Colloq.]

2. (a) hard, tiring work; anything which wearies and fatigues; a wearisome task; (b) fatigue; weariness. [Brit. Colloq.]

fag, *n.* [etym. uncertain; compare Ice. *flakkia*; O.H.G. *flacken*, to flutter, flag.]

1. a knotty, coarse, or imperfect part in the web of a cloth.

2. the fag end.

fag, *n.* [from *fag end.*] a cigarette. [Slang.]

fag·ā'ceous, *a.* [from Mod. L. *Fagaceæ*, name of the family, from L. *fagus*, beech.] of the beech family of plants, including the beech, oak, and chestnut.

fag end, [*fag* in earlier *n.* sense of "thing hanging loosely."]

1. (a) the last part or coarse end of a piece of cloth; (b) the frayed, untwisted end of a rope.

2. the last and worst part of anything; remnant.

fag'gŏt, *n.* and *v.t.* same as *fagot.*

fag'gŏt·ing, *n.* same as *fagoting.*

Fā'gin, *n.* in Dickens' *Oliver Twist*, an old villain who trains children to be thieves.

Fag·ō·pȳ'rum, *n.* [L., from *fagus*, the beech-tree, and Gr. *pyros*, wheat.] a small genus of annual plants of the buckwheat family, native to central Asia. Two species, *Fagopyrum esculentum*, or common buckwheat, and *Fagopyrum tataricum*, or Indian or Tatarian buckwheat, have been introduced into the United States and are cultivated for food.

fag'ŏt, fag'gŏt, *n.* [ME. *fagott*; OFr. *fagot*, a bundle of sticks, prob. from L. *fax, facis*, a torch.]

1. a bundle of sticks, twigs, or small branches of trees, used for fuel or for filling ditches and other purposes in fortification; a fascine.

2. in metallurgy, a bundle or heap of iron or steel pieces to be worked into bars by hammering or rolling at welding temperature.

3. a person formerly hired to take the place of another at the muster of a military company or to hide deficiency in its number when it was not full. [Obs.]

4. a term of contempt for a dry, shriveled old woman. [Brit. Slang.]

5. the punishment of burning at the stake, as for heresy.

6. a badge representing a fagot, worn on the sleeve in the Middle Ages by those who had recanted heresy, to show the punishment they had so narrowly escaped.

fag'ŏt, fag'gŏt, *v.t.* 1. to make into a fagot; to form fagots of.

2. in sewing, to decorate with fagoting.

fag'ŏt·ing, fag'gŏt·ing, *n.* 1. a decorative stitch made by pulling horizontal threads out of the fabric and tying the cross threads together in bunches.

2. openwork decoration in which the thread is drawn in crisscross stitches across the open seam.

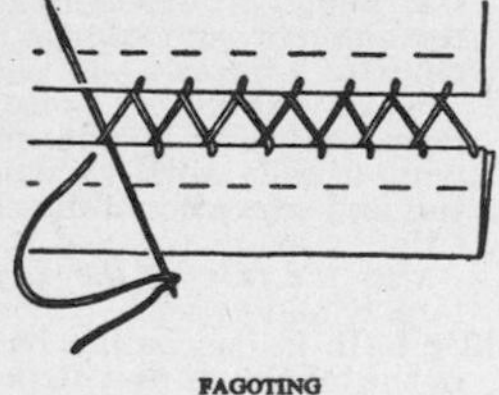

FAGOTING

fag'ŏt ī'ron (ī'ũrn), iron manufactured from fagots.

fa·got'tō, *n.* [It.] the bassoon: so called from its being able to be taken to pieces and made up into a bundle like a small fagot, for convenience of carriage.

fag'ŏt vōte, in Great Britain, a vote procured by the transfer to a person of property under mortgage or otherwise, so as to qualify him for the franchise.

fag'ŏt vōt'ẽr, one who holds or exercises a fagot vote.

Fā'gus, *n.* [L. *fagus*, the beech tree.] a genus of trees, the beeches. There are about twenty species distributed over the temperate regions of the world. They are trees with close, smooth, ash-gray bark, and simple straight-veined leaves.

fā'hăm (fä'ăm), **fā'ăm,** *n.* [native African name.] an orchid, *Angræcum fragrans*, having fragrant leaves from which a tea is made.

Fähl'bănd (fäl'bänt), *n.* [G. *fahl*, pale, and *band*, a band.] a stratum of rock named from the pale, dull color it has from the disintegration of the metallic sulfides contained in it.

Fähl'ẽrz, fähl'ōre, *n.* same as *tetrahedrite.*

fäh'lun·īte, *n.* [named from *Fahlun*, in Sweden.] a hydrous form of iolite.

Fah'ren·heīt (*or* fär'), *a.* [named from Gabriel Daniel *Fahrenheit* (1686–1736), G. physicist who devised the scale.] designating or of a thermometer that places the freezing point of pure water at 32 degrees above zero and the boiling point at 212 degrees above zero, under standard atmospheric pressure.

Fah'ren·heīt (*or* fär'), *n.* the Fahrenheit thermometer or its scale.

fȧ·i·ence' (fȧ-yäṅs'), *n.* [Fr. *faïence*; It. *faenza*, from *Faenza* in Romagna, Italy, the original place of its manufacture.] a fine grade of painted and glazed pottery or porcelain.

fāil, *v.i.*; failed, *pt., pp.*; failing, *ppr.* [ME. *failen*; OFr. *faillir*, to fail, miss; L. *fallere*, to deceive, disappoint.]

1. to become deficient; to be insufficient; to cease to be abundant for supply; to fall short; as, the crops *failed*; our ammunition *failed.*

2. to lose power or strength; to sink; to become weaker; as, the invalid *fails* daily.

3. to miss; not to produce the effect; to miscarry; to be frustrated or disappointed; to be unsuccessful in obtaining a desired end; as, the experiment was made with care, but *failed*; the attack *failed.*

4. to be deficient in a duty, obligation, or expectation; to default; as, he *failed* as a son.

5. to become insolvent or bankrupt; to quit business because of inability to meet one's debts and fulfill one's business obligations.

6. in education, to get a grade of failure; to not pass.

7. to be extinct; to cease; to be entirely wanting; to be no longer produced. [Obs.]

Help, Lord, for the godly man ceaseth; for the faithful *fail* from among the children of men. —Ps. xii. 1.

to fail of; to fail to achieve; to be without.

fāil, *v.t.* 1. to desert; to leave; to abandon; as, fortune never *fails* the brave.

2. to omit or neglect: now rare except with an infinitive; as, he *failed* to go.

The inventive God, who never *fails* his part. —Dryden.

3. to be useless or not helpful to; to be inadequate for; to disappoint.

4. in education, (a) to give a grade of failure to (a pupil); (b) to get a grade of failure in (a subject).

5. not to attain or reach to; to come short of; to fail of. [Obs.]

Though that seat of earthly bliss be *failed.* —Milton.

6. to deceive; to cheat. [Obs.]

fāil, *n.* 1. failure: now only in *without fail*, without failing (to occur, to do something, etc.).

He will *without fail* drive out from before you the Canaanites. —Josh. iii. 10.

2. death. [Obs.]

fāil'ănce, *n.* fault; failure. [Obs.]

fāil'ing, *n.* 1. imperfection; lapse; fault; a weakness; as, tardiness was one of his *failings.*

2. a failure.

Syn.—fault, foible, weakness.—A *fault* is positive, something definite and marked which impairs excellence; a *failing* is negative, some weakness in a man's character, disposition, or habit; a *foible* is a less important weakness, which we overlook or smile at.

fāille (fāl *or* fīl), *n.* [Fr.] a ribbed, soft, plainly woven fabric of silk or rayon, for dresses, etc.

fāil'ūre, *n.* 1. a falling short; deficiency; cessation of supply, or total defect; as, the *failure* of springs or streams; *failure* of rain; *failure* of crops.

2. omission or neglect; a not doing; as, *failure* to obey rules.

3. decay; a weakening; a dying away; as, the *failure* of memory or of sight.

4. a becoming insolvent or bankrupt; as, there were many *failures* that year.

5. a not succeeding in doing or becoming.

6. a person or thing that does not succeed; as, she was an utter *failure* as an actress.

7. in education, (a) a failing to pass; (b) a grade or mark (usually F) indicating a failing to pass.

8. a failing; a slight fault. [Obs.]

fāin, *a.* [ME. *fain, fayn, fæin*; AS. *fægen*, to be glad.]

1. glad; ready. [Archaic and Poet.]

2. content or willing to accept an alternative when the more desirable thing cannot be attained; compelled by circumstances: followed by an infinitive; as, he was *fain to eat* whatever he could get. [Archaic and Poet.]

fāin, *adv.* gladly; with joy or pleasure: used with *would.*

He *would fain* have filled his belly with the husks that the swine did eat. —Luke xv. 16.

fāin, *v.t.* 1. to wish or desire. [Obs.]

2. to make glad. [Obs.]

fāin, *v.i.* to be glad; to rejoice. [Obs.]

fȧi·nāigue' (fȧ-nāg'), *v.i.*; fainaigued, *pt., pp.*; fainaiguing, *ppr.* [clipped form, from *finagle.*]

1. to fail to follow suit in playing cards; renege.

2. to cheat; finagle.

fāi'ne·ănce, *n.* idling; laziness.

fai'né·ant (fā'nē-ănt, *Fr.* fā-nā-äṅ'), *a.* [Fr., from OFr. *faignant*, an idler, orig. ppr. of *faindre*, to feign; altered by association with Fr. *faire*, to do, and *néant*, nothing.] lazy; idle.

fai'né·ant, *n.* a lazy, idle person.

fāint, *a.*; *comp.* fainter; *superl.* faintest, [ME. *faynt, feynt*, weak; OFr. *feint, faint*, feigned, negligent, sluggish, pp. of *feindre, faindre*, to pretend, from L. *fingere*, to touch, handle, feign.]

1. weak; feeble; languid; exhausted; inclined to swoon; as, *faint* with fatigue, hunger, or thirst.

2. weak; not bright or vivid; not clear; dim; indistinct; as, a *faint* color, a *faint* sound, a *faint* recollection.

3. cowardly; timorous; as, a *faint* heart never wins a fair lady.

4. feeble; not vigorous; not active; as, a *faint* resistance, a *faint* exertion.

5. dejected; depressed; dispirited.

My heart is *faint.* —Lam. i. 22.

Syn.—weak, languid, fatigued, unenergetic, timid, irresolute, feeble, exhausted, obscure, half-hearted, dim, pale, faded, inconspicuous.

fāint, *n.* the act of fainting or the state of one who faints; swoon; syncope; a condition of temporary loss of consciousness as a result of an inadequate flow of blood to the brain.

fāint, *v.i.*; fainted, *pt., pp.*; fainting, *ppr.* [ME. *fainten*, from OFr. *feindre*, to feign, work negligently.]

1. to lose sensation and consciousness; to swoon: sometimes with *away*; as, he *fainted* from loss of blood.

On hearing the honor intended her, she *fainted away.* —Guardian.

2. to become feeble; to decline or fail in strength and vigor; to weaken. [Archaic or Poet.]

If I send them away fasting to their own houses, they will *faint* by the way. —Mark viii. 3.

3. to sink into dejection; to lose courage or spirit. [Archaic or Poet.]

Let not your hearts *faint.* —Deut. xx. 3.

4. to decay; to disappear; to vanish; to fade. [Now Rare.]

Gilded clouds, while we gaze on them, *faint* before the eye. —Pope.

fāint, *v.t.* to deject; to depress; to weaken. [Obs.]

fāint'heärt, *n.* a fainthearted person.

fāint'heärt'ed, *a.* cowardly; timorous; dejected; easily depressed, or yielding to fear.

Fear not, neither be *fainthearted.* —Isa. vii. 4.

fāint'heärt'ed·ly, *adv.* in a cowardly manner.

fāint'heärt'ed·ness, *n.* cowardice; timorousness; want of courage.

fāint'ing, *n.* a faint; syncope; a swoon.

fāint'ish, *a.* slightly faint.

fāint'ish·ness, *n.* a slight degree of faintness.

fāint'ling, *a.* timorous. [Obs.]

fāint'ly, *adv.* in a faint manner; feebly; languidly; timorously.

fāint'ness, *n.* the state or quality of being faint; dejection; timorousness; want of strength, brightness, vividness, etc.

fāints, *n.pl.* the crude, impure spirits given off in the first and last stages of the distillation of liquors.

fāint'y, *a.* weak; feeble; languid. [Rare.]

fâir, *a.*; *comp.* fairer; *superl.* fairest, [ME. *fair, fayr*; AS. *fæger*, beautiful, pleasant, fair.]

1. of a light color; not dark or dusky; blond; as, a *fair* complexion; *fair* hair.

2. pleasing to the eye; attractive, lovely, beautiful, or comely; as, a *fair* woman; a *fair* landscape.

Thou art a *fair* woman to look upon. —Gen. xii. 11.

3. free from stain or blemish; unspotted; untarnished; pure; free from anything which might impair the appearance, quality, or character; as, a *fair* character; a *fair* name; a *fair* copy; *fair* water; a *fair* cloth.

4. open; frank; honest; hence, equal; just; equitable; impartial; unprejudiced; as, his offer is *fair*.

5. moderately or passably good; free from serious defects; nearly or fully up to the average; as, he gets a *fair* salary; he has a *fair* reputation.

6. open to attack or access; unobstructed; free from obstacles; distinct; positive; direct; as, a *fair* aim; in *fair* sight; a *fair* view.

7. smooth and even: said of a ship's lines.

8. according to the rules; as, a *fair* defeat.

9. frank; civil; pleasing and courteous.

10. apparently favorable but really false; specious; as, the treacherous friend spoke *fair* words.

11. characterized by favorable conditions; likely; promising; advantageous; as, you are in a *fair* way to promotion; a *fair* subject of ridicule.

12. clear and sunny; unclouded; free from storm or the threat of storm; as, *fair* weather.

13. lawfully hunted; as, *fair* game.

14. of moderately good size; as, a *fair* fortune.

fair and square; with justice and honesty. [Colloq.]

fair to middling; moderately good; passable. [Colloq.]

Syn.—honest, equitable, reasonable, open, frank, clear, impartial, candid, beautiful, just, pure.

fâir, *adv.* [ME. *faire, fayre*; AS. *fægere, fægre*, beautifully, pleasantly, from *fæger*, fair.]

1. politely; frankly; civilly; complaisantly.

2. candidly; honestly; equitably; as, play *fair*.

3. straight; squarely; as, struck *fair* in the face.

4. on good terms; as, to keep *fair* with the world; to stand *fair* with one's companions.

to bid fair; see under *bid*.

fâir, *n.* **1.** beauty. [Archaic.]

2. a woman; especially, a beautiful woman or a beloved one; a sweetheart. [Archaic.]

3. something fair, or good. [Archaic.]

the fair; women collectively; especially, young and beautiful women.

fâir, *v.i.* to clear up; to become clear: said of the weather. [Dial.]

fâir, *v.t.* [ME. *fayren*, to make beautiful; AS. *fægrian*, to become beautiful, *afægrian*, to make beautiful, from *fæger*, beautiful, fair.]

1. to make fair or beautiful. [Obs.]

Fairing the foul with art's false borrow'd face. —Shak.

2. to smooth (timbers, etc.).

fâir, *n.* [ME. *feire, feyre*; OFr. *feire*; LL. *feria*, a fair, a holiday; L. *feriæ*, nom. pl., feast days, holidays.]

1. originally, a gathering of people held at regular intervals for barter and sale of goods.

2. a festival or carnival where there is entertainment and things are sold, often for charity; a bazaar.

3. an exhibition, often competitive, of farm, household, and manufactured products, usually with various amusement facilities and educational displays; a kind of exposition.

after the fair or *the day after the fair*; too late. [Colloq.]

fâir ball, in baseball, a batted ball that stops in the infield, or first strikes the ground there, and does not pass the foul line before first or third base, or that first strikes the ground inside the foul line after passing first or third base: opposed to *foul ball.*

fâir catch, in football, a catch of a kicked ball made after giving the proper signal that no attempt will be made to run with the ball: the opposing players are penalized if they interfere with the catcher.

fâir cop'y, an exact copy of a document after final corrections have been made on it.

fâir em·ploy'ment prac'tic·es, the employment of persons without prejudicial regard to matters that are irrelevant to the work, such as race, religion, sex, etc.

fâir'-fāced (-fāst), *a.* 1. beautiful; having a fair face.

2. two-faced; deceitful; hypocritical in professing affection and kindness; treacherous.

fâir green, in golf, a fairway.

fâir'ground, *n.* an open space where fairs are held.

fâir'-hâired', *a.* 1. having blond hair.

2. favorite; as, the *fair-haired* boy of the family. [Colloq.]

fâir'hood, *n.* fairness; beauty. [Obs.]

fâir'ies' horse, the ragwort, *Senecio jacobæus.*

fâir'ies' tā'ble, 1. the common mushroom, *Agaricus campestris*, and similar fungi.

2. the pennywort, *Hydrocotyle vulgaris.*

fâir'i·ly, *adv.* in a fairylike manner; gracefully.

fâir'ing, *n.* a present, especially one brought from or given at a fair. [Archaic.]

fâir'ing, *n.* [*fair*, v., and *-ing.*] in engineering, an additional part or structure added to an aircraft, etc. to smooth the outline and thus reduce drag.

fâir'ish, *a.* moderately good, well, large, etc.

fâir'-lēad, *n.* [from earlier *fair-leader.*] in nautical usage, a ring block, or piece of wood with holes in it that acts as a guide for the running rigging or a rope, to prevent its being cut or chafed.

fâir'ly, *adv.* [ME. *fayrely*, from *fair*; AS. *fæger*, fair, beautiful.]

1. frankly; honestly; justly; equitably; without disguise, fraud, or prevarication; as, the question was *fairly* stated and argued; let us deal *fairly* with all men.

2. commodiously; conveniently.

3. (a) softly; gently; (b) courteously. [Obs.]

4. beautifully; handsomely.

5. completely; evidently; beyond a doubt; as, his antagonist fought till he was *fairly* winded.

6. moderately; passably; reasonably; as, she sings *fairly* well.

7. clearly; distinctly.

fâir māid, 1. the dried pilchard. [Brit. Dial.]

2. the porgy or scup. [Dial.]

fâir'-māid'-of-Feb'ru·ā·ry, *n.* a flower, the snowdrop.

fâir'-māids-of-Frânce', *n.* one of various flowers, as, (a) *Ranunculus aconitifolius*, the crowfoot; (b) meadow saxifrage; (c) ragged robin.

fâir'-mīnd'ed, *a.* just; upright; unprejudiced; impartial.

fâir'-mīnd'ed·ness, *n.* the quality or character of being fair-minded.

fâir'-nā'tūred, *a.* good-natured; of a pleasant disposition.

fâir'ness, *n.* [ME. *fairnesse*; AS. *fægernes*, from *fæger*, beautiful.] the state, quality, or character of being fair, in any sense of the word.

fâir plāy, an abiding by the rules in sports, games, or any other activity; fairness and honor in dealing with competitors, customers, etc.

fâir sex, women.

fâir'-spō'ken, *a.* speaking or spoken civilly or pleasantly; bland; civil; courteous; plausible.

fâir'wāy, *n.* 1. a navigable channel in a river, bay, etc.

2. in golf, that part of a golf course between the tees and the putting greens where the grass is cut short.

fâir'-weath''ẽr (-weth''), *a.* existing or capable of existing in pleasant weather only; hence, helpful, dependable, etc. only in pleasant, comfortable surroundings; failing in times of distress or need; not willing to make sacrifices; as, a *fair-weather* friend; a *fair-weather* sailor.

fâir'-wŏrld, *n.* prosperity. [Obs.]

fâir'y, *n.*; *pl.* **fâir'ies,** [ME. *fairye, fayry*, enchantment, the fairy folk; OFr. *faerie*, enchantment, from *fae*, a fairy.]

1. an imaginary being or spirit, usually represented as a small, delicate, dainty human being, supposed to have magic powers; a fay: formerly also spelled *faerie, faery, faërie, faëry.*

2. a male homosexual: contemptuous term. [Slang.]

3. (a) an enchantress; (b) fairyland; (c) illusion; magic; (d) fairies collectively. [Obs.]

fâir'y, *a.* 1. of fairies.

2. fairylike; graceful; delicate.

Formerly also spelled *faerie, faery, faërie, faëry.*

fairy beads; in geology, the small, perforated and radiated joints of the fossil *Crinoidea*: sometimes called *St. Cuthbert's beads.*

fairy ring or *circle*; a circle of contrasting color often seen on grass-covered ground, caused by underground fungi: so called because formerly thought to have been made by the dancing of fairies.

fairy tale; (a) a story about fairies, giants, magic deeds, etc.; (b) an unbelievable or untrue story; lie.

fâir'y bîrd, the least tern, *Sterna minuta.* [Brit.]

fâir'y but'tẽr, any of certain fungi, as *Tremella albida* and *Exidia glandulosa*: so called because once believed to be made by the fairies in their dairy.

fâir'y cup, a fungus, *Peziza coccinea*, which is bright red in color and shaped like a cup.

fâir'y fin'gẽr, the foxglove, *Digitalis purpurea.*

fâir'y·land, *n.* 1. the imaginary land or abode of fairies.

2. a lovely, enchanting place.

fâir'y·līke, *a.* of the nature of or resembling a fairy; suited to a fairy; delicate; dainty; as, *fairylike* music.

fâir'y lōaves, fossil sea urchins.

fâir'y mär'tin, an Australian swallow, *Hirundo ariel.*

fâir'y shrimp, the *Chirocephalus diaphanus*, a delicately colored, fresh-water species of phyllopodous crustacean, occurring occasionally in Great Britain.

fâir'y stōne, an echinite. [Brit. Dial.]

fait aç·çom·plī' (fe-tȧ-kon-plē'), [Fr., lit., an accomplished fact.] a thing already done, so that opposition or argument is useless.

fāith, *n.* [ME. *faith, feith*; OFr. *feid*; L. *fides*, faith, belief, trust, from *fidere*, to trust, confide in.]

1. unquestioning belief.

2. unquestioning belief in God, religion, etc.

3. a religion or a system of religious beliefs; as, the Catholic *faith.*

4. anything believed.

5. complete trust, confidence, or reliance; as, children usually have *faith* in their parents.

6. faithfulness; fidelity; loyalty; allegiance to some person or thing.

Her failing, while her *faith* to me remains, I would conceal. —Milton.

7. credibility or truth. [Rare.]

The *faith* of the foregoing narrative. —Mitford.

bad faith; insincerity; dishonesty; duplicity.

good faith; honesty; sincerity.

in faith; indeed; really.

Punic faith; bad faith; infidelity; perfidy: from the popular Roman belief concerning the people of Carthage.

to break faith; (a) to be disloyal to one's beliefs, principles, etc.; (b) to break a promise.

to keep faith; (a) to be loyal to one's beliefs, principles, etc.; (b) to keep a promise.

Syn.—belief, trust, confidence, credence, fidelity, conviction, creed, tenets, doctrine, opinion.

fāith, *interj.* indeed; in faith.

fāith çūre, 1. a method of trying to cure illness by having faith, praying, etc.

2. a cure allegedly caused by such methods.

fāith çūr'ẽr, one who practices, advocates, or believes in faith cure.

fāithed (fātht), *a.* honest; sincere. [Obs.]

fāith'fụl, *a.* 1. full of faith; believing; strong or firm in one's faith, especially religious faith. [Rare.]

Be thou *faithful* to death, and I will give thee a crown of life. —Rev. ii. 10.

2. firmly adhering to duty; of true fidelity,

loyal; true to allegiance; constant in the performance of duties or services; honest; loyal; as, a *faithful* servant.

3. observant of compact, treaties, contracts, vows, or other engagements; true to one's word; reliable; dependable.

4. true; exact; in conformity to the letter and spirit; as, a *faithful* copy.

Syn.—true, firm, attached, loyal, accurate, close, consistent, correspondent, exact, equivalent, stanch, incorruptible.

fāith'fụl, *n.* one who is faithful.

the faithful; (a) the true believers (in any specified religion); (b) the loyal adherents.

fāith'fụl·ly, *adv.* in a faithful manner; loyally; sincerely; honestly; truthfully.

fāith'fụl·ness, *n.* the quality of being faithful; loyalty, constancy in affection; fidelity.

fāith hēal'ẽr, one who tries to cure diseases by prayer and faith.

fāith hēal'ing, faith cure.

fāith'less, *a.* 1. without faith, especially religious faith; without belief in the revealed truths of religion; unbelieving. [Rare.]

O *faithless* generation. —Matt. xvii. 17.

2. not adhering to allegiance or duty; dishonest; disloyal; perfidious; treacherous; as, a *faithless* subject.

3. unreliable; undependable.

4. deceptive.

Yonder *faithless* phantom. —Goldsmith.

fāith'less·ly, *adv.* in a faithless manner.

fāith'less·ness, *n.* the state or quality of being faithless.

fāi'tòur, *n.* [OFr. *faitor*, doer, maker, from L. *factor.*] an imposter; a rogue. [Obs.]

fāke, *n.* [prob. from base of AS. *fæc*, interval.] in nautical usage, one of the circles or windings of a cable or hawser, as it lies in a coil; a single turn or coil.

fāke, *v.t.*; faked (fākt), *pt.*, *pp.*; faking, *ppr.* in nautical usage, to coil in fakes, as a rope, hawser, etc.

fāke, *v.t.* and *v.i.*; faked, *pt.*, *pp.*; faking, *ppr.* [earlier *feague*, *feake*; perhaps from G. *fegen*, to clean, sweep, in 17th-c. thieves' slang.]

1. to make (something) seem real, satisfactory, etc. by any sort of deception; to practice deception by simulating or tampering with (something); counterfeit. [Colloq.]

2. in jazz, to improvise (a chorus, solo passage, etc.). [Colloq.]

to fake a person out; to deceive or outmaneuver a person by a feint, bluff, deceptive act, etc. [Colloq.]

fāke, *n.* anything or anyone not genuine; fraud; counterfeit. [Colloq.]

fāke, *a.* fraudulent; not genuine; sham; false. [Colloq.]

fȧ·keer', *n.* same as *fakir*.

fāk'ẽr, *n.* 1. a person who fakes; fraud; especially, a swindler. [Colloq.]

2. a peddler of trinkets. [Colloq.]

fāk'ing box, in the Lifesaving Service, a box in which ropes or shot lines are coiled in such a way as to prevent tangling or knotting.

fȧ·kïr', *n.* [Ar. *fakir*, *faquir*, a poor man, from *fakr*, *faqr*, poverty.]

1. a member of a Moslem holy sect who lives by begging.

2. any Moslem itinerant beggar, often one claiming to perform miracles.

3. any Hindu ascetic.

fä lä, fȧl lä, 1. syllables used as a refrain in some old songs.

2. a type of part song with this refrain.

fȧ·lä'fel, *n.*; *pl.* **fȧ·lä'fel,** [Ar. *falāfil.*]

1. a small croquette or patty of ground chick-peas and other vegetables, seasoned with spices and deep-fried in oil.

2. a sandwich made by putting one of these in the pocket of a pita.

fa·la·nä'kȧ, *n.* [native name.] a viverrine carnivore, *Eupleres goudotii*, native to Madagascar.

Fā'lanġe (*Sp.* fä-län'hä), *n.* [Sp., lit., phalanx; L. *phalanx*, phalanx.] a fascist organization established in Spain in 1934: it helped to overthrow the republic in the Spanish civil war (1936–1939) and became the only official political party under Franco's regime.

Fȧ·lan'ġist, *n.* a member of the Falange.

Fä·lä'shȧ, *n.* a member of a Hamitic tribe living in Ethiopia and practicing the Jewish religion.

fal'bȧ·lȧ, *n.* [Fr.] a furbelow; flounce; frill.

fal'çāte, *a.* [L. *falcatus*, bent, curved, from *falx* (*falcis*), a sickle.] sickle-shaped; hooked; curved; as, a *falcate* leaf.

fal'çā·ted, *a.* same as *falcate*.

fal·çā'tion, *n.* 1. the state of being falcate. [Obs.]

2. that which is falcate. [Obs.]

fal'chiŏn (*or* -shŏn), *n.* [OFr. *fauchon*, from L. *falx* (*-cis*), a sickle.]

1. a medieval sword with a short, broad, slightly curved blade.

2. any sword. [Poet.]

Fal·cid'i·ăn, *a.* of or pertaining to Publius Falcidius, a Roman tribune in 40 B. C.

Falcidian law; a law, the passage of which was procured by Falcidius, stipulating that at least one fourth of a decedent's estate should go to the heir.

fal'ci·fọrm, *a.* [L. *falx* (*falcis*), a sickle, and *forma*, form.] falcate; in the shape of a sickle; curved; as, *falciform* cartilages.

fạl'çŏn (fạ'kn *or* fal'kŏn), *n.* [ME. *faucon*, *faukon*; OFr. *faucon*, *falcun*; LL. *falco* (*-onis*), a falcon, from L. *falx* (*-cis*), a sickle; perhaps so named from its curved beak and talons.]

PEREGRINE FALCON
(*Falco peregrinus*)

1. any hawk trained to hunt and kill small game, as in the Middle Ages.

2. in zoology, a member of the *Falconinæ*, a subfamily of the *Falconidæ*, characterized by a short, curved, notched beak and long, pointed wings. The species most commonly used in falconry are the gerfalcon, *Falco gyrfalco*, and the peregrine falcon, *Falco peregrinus*. The term *falcon* is restricted by sportsmen to the female; the male, which is smaller and less courageous, is called *tercel*, *tiercel*, or *tercelet*.

3. a small cannon used from the fifteenth to the seventeenth centuries.

fạl'çŏn·ẽr, *n.* [ME. *fauconer*; OFr. *faulconier*; LL. *falconarius*, a falconer, from *falco* (*-onis*), a falcon.]

1. one who breeds and trains falcons for taking game.

2. one who hunts with falcons.

fal'çō·net, *n.* 1. an obsolete type of light cannon.

2. a little falcon; specifically, a finch falcon of the genus *Ierax*, *Hierax*, or *Microhierax*.

3. a shrike of the genus *Falcunculus*.

fạl'çŏn-ġen'tle (fạ'kn), *n.* the female of the European goshawk, *Astur palumbarius*.

Fal·con'i·dae, *n.pl.* [L., from LL. *falco* (*-onis*), a falcon.] a family of raptorial birds, or birds of prey, including the eagles, hawks, and falcons.

Fal·çō·ni'nae, *n.pl.* a subfamily of the *Falconidæ*, comprising the falcons.

fal'çō·nine, *a.* of or pertaining to the family *Falconidæ*.

fal'çō·noid, *a.* pertaining to the *Falconidæ*.

fạl'çŏn·ry (fạ'kn-ry *or* fal'kŏn-ry), *n.* [OFr. *faulconnerie*, from LL. *falco* (*-onis*), a falcon.]

1. the art of training falcons to hunt game.

2. the sport of hunting with falcons.

fal'çō·pẽrn, *n.* a kite falcon.

fal'çū·lȧ, *n.*; *pl.* **fal'çū·lae,** [L., dim. of *falx* (*falcis*), a sickle.] a compressed, curved claw with a sharp point, as that of a cat.

fal'çū·lāte, *a.* shaped like a falcula.

fạld'āge, *n.* [LL. *faldagium*, from AS. *fald*, a fold.]

1. formerly, a right of the lord of a manor to require a tenant to pasture his sheep on the lord's fields, a fold having been provided for them.

2. a fee which a tenant could pay to the lord of a manor in lieu of pasturing his sheep on the lord's fields.

fal'de·ral, fal'de·rol, *n.* [nonsense syllables.]

1. a trifle; gewgaw.

2. mere nonsense.

3. a refrain in some old songs.

Also *folderol*.

fal·det'tȧ, *n.* [It.] an outer silk wrap worn by the women of Malta, combining a hood and cape.

fạld'fee, *n.* a kind of manorial fee.

fạld'ing, *n.* a kind of coarse cloth. [Obs.]

fạl'dis·tō·ry, *n.* a faldstool, or chair used by a bishop. [Obs.]

fạld'stool, *n.* [OFr. *faldestoel*; LL. *faldistolium*; O.H.G. *faltstuol*, lit., a folding stool; *faldan*, to fold, and *stuol*, a chair, stool.]

1. a portable stool or desk used in praying.

FALDSTOOL

2. in the Roman Catholic Church, a backless chair used by a bishop when officiating in a church other than his own, or when not on his throne.

3. in the Anglican Church, a desk at which the litany is read.

Fȧ·lẽr'ni·ăn, *a.* [L. *Falernus*, a mountain in Campania.] of, pertaining to, or coming from a district (Falernus ager) in Campania, Italy, famous in ancient times for its excellent wine.

Fȧ·lẽr'ni·ăn, *n.* the wine made in ancient times in Falernus ager.

fạlk (fạk), *n.* the razor-billed auk, *Alca torda*. [Scot.]

fạll, *v.i.*; fell, *pt.*; fallen, *pp.*; falling, *ppr.* [ME. *fallen*; AS. *feallan*, to fall, from the same root as D. *vallen*; Ice. *falla*, to fall; L. *fallere*, to deceive; Gr. *sphallein*, to cause to fall, to trick.]

1. to come down by the force of gravity; drop; descend.

2. to come down because detached, pushed, dropped, etc.; move down and land forcibly; as, apples *fall* from the tree.

3. to come down suddenly from a standing or sitting position; tumble; topple; become prostrate; as, the child stumbled and *fell*.

4. to be wounded or killed in battle.

A thousand shall *fall* at thy side.—Ps. xci. 7.

5. to come down in ruins; collapse; as, the building *fell*.

6. to hang down; as, the coat *falls* well from the shoulders.

7. to strike; hit; as, the arrow *fell* wide of its mark.

8. to pass from a position, condition, etc. regarded as higher to one regarded as lower.

I beheld Satan as lightning *fall* from heaven. —Luke x. 18.

9. to take a downward direction; as, her glance *fell*, the river *falls* to the sea.

10. to become lower in amount, number, degree, intensity, value, etc.; lessen; as, prices are *falling*, his temperature *fell*.

11. to lose power; be overthrown; as, the government has *fallen*.

Heaven and earth will witness,
If Rome must *fall*, that we are innocent.
—Addison.

12. to lose status, reputation, dignity, etc.

13. to yield to temptation; do wrong; sin; especially (of women), to lose chastity.

14. to be captured or conquered; as, Berlin *fell* to the Allies.

15. to pass into a particular mental or physical state; as, the child *fell* ill.

16. to take on a look of disappointment or dejection; as, her face *fell*.

I have observed of late thy looks are *fallen*. —Addison.

17. to become lower in pitch or volume; as, her voice *fell*.

18. to happen as if by dropping.

19. to take place; occur; as, the meeting *fell* on a Friday.

20. to come by chance, lot, or distribution; as, the prize *fell* to the lucky girl.

It happened this evening that we *fell* into a pleasing walk. —Addison.

21. to come as a right or inheritance; as, the estate *falls* to the widow.

22. to come at a specified place; as, the accent *falls* on the third syllable.

23. to be directed; as, his eye *fell* on a misspelled word.

24. to be spoken; as, the news *fell* from his lips.

25. to be born: said of animals.

26. to be divided (*into*); as, these poems *fall into* two classes.

to fall afoul (or *foul*) *of*; (a) to become entangled with; (b) to have trouble with; (c) [orig. sense.] in nautical usage, to collide with, as a ship.

to fall among; to come among unexpectedly and often against one's wish; as, he *fell among* thieves.

to fall astern; in nautical usage, to move or be driven backward; to recede.

to fall away; (a) to lose flesh; to become lean or emaciated; to pine; (b) to decline gradually; to fade; to languish or become faint; (c) to renounce or desert; to take away friendship, support, etc.

to fall back; to recede; to give way; to withdraw; to retreat.

to fall back on (or *upon*); to have recourse to some support or expedient, generally one formerly tried.

to fall behind; (a) to be outstripped; to lose ground; to be left behind; (b) to be in arrears.

to fall down; (a) to sink to the ground; (b) to prostrate oneself in worship; (c) in nautical usage, to sail toward the mouth of a river; to drift downstream.

to fall down on; to be unsuccessful in; fail in. [Slang.]

to fall flat; to fail to have the desired effect; be completely unsuccessful; as, the joke *fell flat*.

to fall from; to recede from; to depart from, as an agreement or engagement. [Archaic.]

to fall from grace; to lose standing; to backslide; to sin; to lapse in the observance of moral or religious prescriptions.

to fall home; (a) in mechanics, to drop or fall into the place intended; (b) in shipbuilding, to curve or incline inward from the perpendicular: said of the top sides of a ship.

to fall in; (a) to line up in proper formation; (b) to agree; (c) to bend or sink inward; as, the cave *fell in*.

to fall into one's hands; to come into one's possession; to pass into one's control.

to fall in with; (a) to meet by chance; (b) to meet and join; (c) to concur with; to agree with; to comply with; to yield to; as, the measure *falls in with* popular opinion.

to fall off; (a) to withdraw; to separate; as, friends *fall off* in adversity; (b) to perish; to die away; to become disused; as, the custom *fell off*; (c) to drop; as, fruits *fall off* when ripe; (d) to become smaller, less, etc.; (e) to decline; to become worse; (f) in nautical usage, to deviate or depart from the course directed; to fall to leeward.

to fall on (or *upon*); (a) to begin immediately and vigorously; (b) to attack; to assail; (c) to come upon, usually with some degree of suddenness and unexpectedness; to drop on; to descend on; as, fear *fell on* them; (d) to come upon; to discover; as, he *fell on* the plan by chance; (e) to be the duty of; as, the task *fell on* John.

to fall on one's feet; to pass successfully through an adventure or predicament.

to fall out; (a) to quarrel; to begin to contend; to become estranged; (b) to happen; to result; (c) in military usage, to leave or drop out of the ranks.

to fall short; (a) to be deficient; (b) to fail to come up to a standard (with *of*).

to fall through; to fail; to come to nothing; as, his plan *fell through*.

to fall to; (a) to begin; (b) to start attacking; (c) to start eating; (d) to close or move into position by itself.

to fall under; (a) to come under or within the limits of; to become the subject of; (b) to be listed or classified as.

fall, *v.t.* 1. to let fall; to drop. [Obs.]

For every tear he *falls*, a Trojan bleeds.
—Shak.

2. to sink; to depress; as, to raise or *fall* the voice. [Obs.]

3. to diminish; to lessen or lower; as, to *fall* the price of commodities. [Rare.]

4. to bring forth; as, to *fall* lambs. [Rare.]

5. to fell; to cut down; as, to *fall* a tree. [Obs. or Dial.]

6. to throw; to unseat, as a rider. [Rare.]

fall, *n.* 1. the act of dropping or descending from a higher to a lower place by gravity; descent; as, the *fall* of a meteor.

2. the act of dropping or tumbling from a standing or sitting position; as, he was walking on ice and had a *fall*.

3. a hanging down.

4. a downward direction or slope.

5. downfall; capture; overthrow; ruin; as, the *fall* of the Roman Empire.

6. a loss of status, reputation, etc.; a yielding to temptation; a moral lapse; as, the *fall* of Adam.

7. diminution; decrease of price or value; depreciation.

8. in music and oratory, a cadence; as, the *fall* of the voice at the close of a sentence. [Archaic.]

9. [*usually pl.*] water falling over a cliff; a cascade; a waterfall.

10. the outlet or discharge of a river or current of water into an ocean, lake, etc.; as, the *fall* of the Po into the Gulf of Venice.

11. extent of descent; the distance which anything falls; as, the stream has a *fall* of fifty feet to the mile.

12. something that has fallen; also, the amount of what has fallen; as, a ten-inch *fall* of snow.

13. the season when leaves fall; autumn.

14. the act of felling or cutting down; as, the *fall* of timber.

15. (a) a birth: said of animals; (b) the number of animals born at one birth; litter.

16. a broad, turned-down ruff or collar.

17. a piece of cloth hanging from a woman's hat, usually in back; kind of veil.

18. in mechanics, the loose end of a cable or chain of a tackle.

19. in nautical usage, (a) a break in the level of a deck line; (b) [*pl.*] a hoisting apparatus.

20. (a) in wrestling, the act of throwing an opponent on his back so that both shoulders touch the floor; (b) a bout or division of a wrestling match.

21. in botany, an outer and drooping division of the perianth in plants of the genus *Iris*.

22. in astrology, the part of the zodiac opposite the exaltation of a planet.

the Fall of Man or *the Fall*; in Christian theology, the lapse of the human race from a state of innocence into one of innate sinfulness or original sin, owing to the disobedience of Adam and Eve in the Garden of Eden, when they ate the forbidden apple.

the fall of the leaf; autumn; hence, figuratively, the time of decay or of failing power.

to ride for a fall; to behave in a manner likely to cause one trouble or injury.

fall, *a.* of, for, or in the fall, or autumn.

fal·lā'cious, *a.* [L. *fallaciosus*, deceptive, from *fallacia*, deceit, deception, from *fallere*, to deceive.]

1. faulty in logic; producing error or mistake; of the nature of, pertaining to, or embodying a fallacy.

2. misleading and disappointing; deceptive; as, *fallacious* expectations.

Syn.—deceitful, fraudulent, delusive, illusive, sophistical.

fal·lā'cious·ly, *adv.* in a fallacious manner.

fal·lā'cious·ness, *n.* the quality of being fallacious.

fal'là·cy, *n.*; *pl.* **fal'là·cies**, [ME. *fallace*; OFr. *fallace*; L. *fallacia*, deception, from *fallax* (*-acis*), deceitful, from *fallere*, to deceive.]

1. originally, deception.

2. aptness to mislead; being deceptive; delusive quality; as, the *fallacy* of the senses.

3. a false or mistaken idea, opinion, etc.; error.

4. in logic, an argument or proposition apparently sound though really fallacious; a fallacious statement or dogma in which the error is not obvious and which is therefore calculated to deceive or mislead.

Syn.—sophistry, illusion, delusion, sophism.

fal'-lal', *a.* foppish; trifling.

fal'-lal', *n.* a useless piece of finery or frippery.

fal'lax, *n.* a fallacy. [Obs.]

fall'en, *a.* 1. having come down; dropped.

2. prostrate; on the ground.

3. having lost status or moral reputation; degraded.

4. captured; overthrown.

5. ruined; destroyed.

6. dead.

fall'en stär, 1. a species of bluish-green algae of the group *Nostochineæ*, which grow on damp ground.

2. a sea nettle, *Medusa æquorea*. [Brit. Dial.]

fall'ẽr, *n.* 1. one who or that which falls, as the parts of certain machines which perform their work by falling.

2. the hen harrier, *Circus cyaneus*.

fall'fish, *n.* a fresh-water cyprinoid fish, *Semotilus bullaris*, found in the eastern part of North America: also called *chub*.

fall guy (gī), a person made the victim, or left to face the consequences, of a scheme that has miscarried. [Slang.]

fal·li·bil'i·ty, *n.* the quality of being fallible.

fal'li·ble, *a.* [ML. *fallibilis*, liable to err, from L. *fallere*, to deceive.]

1. liable to be mistaken or deceived; as, all men are *fallible*.

2. liable to be inaccurate or erroneous; as, judgment and opinions are *fallible*.

fal'li·bly, *adv.* in a fallible manner.

fall'ing, *a.* descending; dropping; declining; sinking; decreasing in value or volume.

falling band; a broad collar of cambric, linen, lace, etc. turning over upon the shoulders: popular in the seventeenth century.

falling sickness; epilepsy. [Rare.]

falling star; a meteor.

fall'ing, *n.* 1. that which falls or drops; that which sinks; an indentation; a hollow; as, risings and *fallings* in the ground.

2. in pathology, displacement; sinking; as, *falling* of the womb.

fall line, 1. the geographical line indicating the beginning of a plateau, usually marked by many waterfalls and rapids.

2. [F- L-] the line east of the Appalachian Mountains, marking the end of the coastal plains and the beginning of the Piedmont Plateau.

Fal·lō'pi·ăn, *a.* of, pertaining to, or discovered by Gabriel Fallopius, or Fallopio, an Italian anatomist of the sixteenth century.

Fallopian tubes; a pair of slender tubes by which the ova are carried from the ovaries to the uterus: also called *oviducts*.

fall'out″, *n.* the descent to earth of radioactive particles following a nuclear explosion.

fal'lōw, *a.* [ME. *falow*; AS. *fealo*, yellow, pale.] pale-yellow; brownish-yellow.

fal'lōw, *n.* [ME. *falow*, plowed land, from AS. *fealo*, yellow, fallow.]

1. land that has lain a year or more untilled or unseeded, to kill weeds, make the soil richer, etc.; land which has been plowed without being sown.

2. the plowing or tilling of land without sowing it for a season.

green fallow; land made rich and free from weeds by means of some green crop, as turnips or potatoes.

fal'lōw, *a.* 1. left uncultivated or unplanted.

2. untrained; inactive: said of the mind.

fal'lōw, *v.t.* [ME. *falwen*, *falgen*; AS. *fealgian*, from *fealh*, fallow land.] to leave (land) unplanted after plowing.

fal'lōw deer, a European deer, *Cervus dama*, smaller than the red deer, and of a yellowish color spotted with white in the summer. The horns are broader toward the upper part and divide into processes down the outside.

FALLOW DEER (*Cervus dama*)

fal'lōw finch, a small European bird, *Saxicola œnanthe*.

fal'lōw·ist, *n.* one who favors the practice of fallowing land. [Rare.]

fal'lōw·ness, *n.* the state of being fallow.

fal'sā·ry, *n.* a falsifier. [Obs.]

FALLOW FINCH

false, *a.* [ME. *fals*, *false*, untrue, false; OFr. *fals*; L. *falsus*, deceptive, pretended, false, pp. of *fallere*, to deceive.]

1. not true; not conformable to fact; expressing what is contrary to fact or truth; incorrect; wrong; mistaken; as, a *false* report.

2. untruthful; lying; dishonest; uttering what is not true; as, a *false* witness.

3. not well founded; as, a *false* claim.

4. not faithful or loyal; inconstant; deceitful; as, a *false* friend.

5. counterfeit; not genuine or real; artificial; as, *false* teeth.

6. misleading; made or assumed for the purpose of deception; as, *false* tears.

7. not properly so named; deceptively resembling; as, the *false* sunflower.

8. in mechanics, temporary, inessential, or added on for protection, disguise, etc.; as, a desk with a *false* drawer.

9. in music, pitched incorrectly; as, a *false* note.

to put (a person) in a false position; to cause misunderstanding of (a person's) intentions, opinions, etc.

Syn.—untrue, erroneous, fallacious, sophistical, spurious, deceptive, fabricated, bogus, counterfeit, mendacious, sham, mock, unfaithful, dishonorable, faithless, incorrect.

fạlse, *adv.* not truly; not honestly; in a false manner.

to play false or *to play one false*; to act treacherously; to be untrue to one.

fạlse, *v.t.* [ME. *falsien*; OFr. *falser*, to make false, falsify, from L. *falsus*, pp. of *fallere*, to deceive.]

1. to deceive. [Obs.]

2. to violate by lack of veracity. [Obs.]

3. to feign, as a blow. [Obs.]

fạlse ar·rest′, in law, any forceful and unlawful restraint of a person by another.

fạlse bot′tŏm, 1. a bottom (of a box, drawer, etc.) between which and the real bottom there is a secret compartment.

2. the bottom of a whisky glass, etc. raised or narrowed in such a way as to give a deceptive appearance to the true capacity of the glass.

fạlse fāce, a mask; usually, a comical or grotesque mask.

fạlse frụit, same as *pseudocarp*.

fạlse′heärt″ed, fạlse′-heärt, *a.* having a false heart; treacherous; deceitful; perfidious.

fạlse′heärt″ed·ness, *n.* perfidiousness; deceit; treachery.

fạlse′hood, *n.* [ME. *falshod*, from AS. *fals*, fraud, counterfeit, and *hod*, condition; quality.]

1. contrariety to fact or truth; deception; error; falseness; as, the *falsehood* of a report.

2. the telling of lies; lying.

3. a false statement; lie.

4. a false belief, theory, idea, etc.

5. lack of honesty; treachery; deceitfulness; perfidy. [Obs.]

6. a counterfeit; false appearance; imposture. [Obs.]

Syn.—untruth, lie, fabrication, fib, falsity, fiction, fallacy, fraud.

fạlse′ly, *adv.* 1. in a false manner or a manner contrary to truth and fact; not truly; as, to testify *falsely*.

2. treacherously; perfidiously.

Swear unto me that thou wilt not deal *falsely* with me. —Gen. xxi. 23.

3. erroneously; by mistake; incorrectly; as, he quoted the verse *falsely*.

fạlse′ness, *n.* the state or quality of being false.

fạls′ẽr, *n.* a deceiver. [Obs.]

fạl·set′tō, *n.*; *pl.* **fạl·set′tōs̹,** [It. *falsetto*, dim. of *falso*, false, from L. *falsus*, pp. of *fallere*, to deceive.]

1. an artificial way of singing, used especially by tenors, in which the voice is placed in a register much higher than that of the natural voice.

2. the voice used in such singing, usually characterized by a soft, nasal quality.

3. a person singing in falsetto.

fạl·set′tō, *a.* 1. of or singing in falsetto.

2. unnatural; constrained; affected; artificial; as, the book is full of *falsetto* pathos and sentiment. [Rare.]

fạl·set′tō, *adv.* in falsetto.

fạls′ies̹, *n.pl.* pads worn with a brassiere to make the breasts look fuller. [Colloq.]

fạl′si·fī·ȧ·ble, *a.* [OFr. *falsifiable*, from *falsifier*, to falsify.] capable of being falsified.

fạl″si·fi·çā′tion, *n.* [OFr. *falsification*; LL. *falsificatio (-onis)*, the act of falsifying, from *falsificare*, to falsify, L. *falsus*, false, and *facere*, to make.]

1. a falsifying or being falsified.

2. confutation; the act or process of disproving; refutation; as, the *falsification* of a charge.

3. in law, (a) the offense of falsifying a record; (b) in equity, the act of showing an item of a charge to be wrong.

fạl′si·fi·çā·tŏr, *n.* a falsifier.

fạl′si·fī·ẽr, *n.* one who falsifies.

fạl′si·fȳ, *v.t.*; falsified, *pt., pp.*; falsifying, *ppr.* [Fr. *falsifier*; LL. *falsificare*, to make false, corrupt, from L. *falsificus*, that acts falsely, from *falsus* false, and *facere*, to make.]

1. to make false; specifically, (a) to misrepresent; give an untrue or misleading account of; (b) to alter (a record, etc.) fraudulently; (c) to alter from the accepted rule or form; as, a poet sometimes *falsifies* accent.

2. to show to be unfounded or untrue; to disprove; to prove to be false.

3. to violate; to break by falsehood; as, to *falsify* one's faith or word.

4. to feign; as, to *falsify* a blow.

5. in law, to prove to be false, as a judgment; to avoid or defeat.

Syn.—mistake, misinterpret, misrepresent, belie, betray, garble, pervert, misstate.

fạl′si·fȳ, *v.i.* to lie; to tell untruths.

fạls′ĭs̹m, *n.* a clear or self-evident falsity; a statement or assertion, the falsity of which is plainly apparent.

fạl′si·ty, *n.*; *pl.* **fạl′si·ties̹,** [ME. *falsete*, OFr. *fausete*; LL. *falsitas (-atis)*, falsehood, from L. *falsus*, pp. of *fallere*, to deceive.]

1. the condition or quality of being false; specifically, (a) incorrectness; (b) dishonesty; (c) deceitfulness; (d) disloyalty.

2. falsehood; a lie; a false assertion.

Syn.—falsehood, lie, incorrectness, erroneousness, fallaciousness.

Fạl′stạff, Sīr John, in Shakespeare's *Henry IV* (Parts I and II) and *The Merry Wives of Windsor*, a fat, jovial, witty knight, bold and brazen in talk but cowardly on the battlefield.

Fạl·stạff′i·ăn, *a.* of or like Falstaff or his ragged followers; boastful, witty, brazen, etc.

fält′bōat, *n.* [G. *faltboot*, from *falten*, to fold, and *boot*, a boat.] a light, collapsible boat made like a kayak: also *foldboat*.

fạl′tẽr, *v.i.*; faltered, *pt., pp.*; faltering, *ppr.* [ME. *falteren*; OFr. *fauter*, to be deficient, from L. *fallere*, to deceive.]

1. to move uncertainly or unsteadily; totter; stumble.

2. to stumble in speech; speak haltingly; stammer.

3. to act hesitantly; show uncertainty; waver; flinch; as, the front ranks *faltered* before the enemy fire.

4. to lose strength, certainty, etc.; weaken: as, the economy *faltered*.

Syn.—halt, hesitate, hobble, slip, doubt, stammer, stutter, demur, waver, flinch, vacillate.

fạl′tẽr, *v.t.* to utter in a hesitating or stammering manner.

fạl′tẽr, *n.* 1. a faltering.

2. a faltering sound.

fạl′tẽr·ing·ly, *adv.* in a faltering manner.

Fä′luns̹, *n.pl.* [Fr.] in geology, fossiliferous strata in Touraine, France, of the Miocene epoch.

falx, *n.*; *pl.* **fal′cēs̹,** [L., a sickle.]

1. in anatomy and zoology, any part or process which is falcate or falciform; specifically, one of the folds of the dura mater which separate the parts of the brain.

2. in entomology, a chelicera.

fam′ble, *v.i.* to stammer. [Obs.]

fam′ble, *n.* a hand. [Old Slang.]

fāme, *n.* [ME. *fame*; L. *fama*, fame, reputation, from *fari*, to speak; compare Gr. *phēma*, a voice, rumor, reputation, from *phanai*, to speak.]

1. public report or rumor. [Rare or Archaic.]

The *fame* thereof was heard in Pharaoh's house. —Gen. xlv. 16.

2. reputation, especially for good.

3. the state of being well known or much talked about; renown; celebrity.

Syn.—report, rumor, notoriety, celebrity, renown, reputation, credit, honor.

fāme, *v.t.* 1. to make famous. [Archaic.]

2. to tell about widely. [Archaic.]

fāmed, *a.* 1. reported; reputed; popularly believed.

2. widely known; celebrated; renowned (*for* something).

fāme′less, *a.* without renown.

fāme′less·ly, *adv.* in a fameless manner.

Fȧ·meus̹e′ (-müz′), *n.* [Fr., fem. of *fameux*, famous.] a late fall variety of apple.

fȧ·mil′iăl (-yăl), *a.* [from L. *familia*, a family.] of, involving, or common to a family.

fȧ·mil′iăr (-yăr), *a.* [ME. *famylier*; OFr. *familier*; L. *familiaris*, of or pertaining to a household, domestic, from *familia*, household, family.]

1. pertaining to a family; domestic. [Obs.]

2. having, characterized by, or arising from close acquaintance; intimate; not distant; as, a *familiar* friend; on *familiar* terms.

3. closely acquainted; knowing by frequent use or association: followed by *with*; as, he is *familiar with* the classics.

4. too friendly; presumptuous; unduly intimate or bold.

5. well-known; common; ordinary; as, accidents are a *familiar* sight.

6. domesticated: said of animals.

familiar spirit; formerly, a demon or evil spirit believed to act as an intimate servant.

Syn.—intimate, free, unceremonious, affable, common, habitual, near, fraternal, frank, conversant.

fȧ·mil′iăr, *n.* 1. an intimate; a close companion.

All my *familiars* watched for my halting. —Jer. xx. 10.

2. formerly, a demon or evil spirit believed to act as an intimate servant; a familiar spirit. [Obs.]

3. a member of the family; one of the household. [Obs.]

4. in the Court of Inquisition, a person who assisted in apprehending and imprisoning the accused.

5. in the Roman Catholic Church, a member of the household of a bishop, rendering domestic but not menial service.

fȧ·mil·i·ar′i·ty, *n.*; *pl.* **fȧ·mil·i·ar′i·ties̹,** [ME. *familarite*; OFr. *familiarite*; L. *familiaritas*, intimacy, from *familiaris*, familiar.]

1. the state of being familiar; intimacy; close acquaintance; as, their *familiarity* with each other.

2. [*usually in pl.*] conduct warranted only by close friendship; as, his *familiarities* show lack of breeding.

3. free and intimate behavior; absence of formality and ceremony.

4. undue intimacy.

5. close acquaintance (*with* something).

fȧ·mil″iăr·i·zā′tion, *n.* the act or process of making familiar or the state of being familiar.

fȧ·mil′iăr·īze, *v.t.*, familiarized, *pt., pp.*; familiarizing, *ppr.* 1. to make commonly known; as, the war *familiarized* terms like *radar* and *jeep*.

2. to make (another or oneself) accustomed or fully acquainted; as, *familiarize* yourself with the job.

fȧ·mil′iăr·ly, *adv.* in a familiar manner; unceremoniously; without constraint; without formality.

fȧ·mil′iăr·ness, *n.* familiarity. [Rare.]

fȧ·mil′iȧ·ry, *a.* pertaining to a household or family. [Obs.]

Fam′i·lis̹m, *n.* 1. the tenets of the Familists.

2. [f–] the tendency to live in families; fondness for family life; a social system having the family as its unit.

Fam′i·list, *n.* [L. *familia*, a family.]

1. one of a religious sect called the Family of Love which arose in Holland in 1556. They taught that religion consists wholly in love.

2. [f–] the head of a family; a family man. [Rare.]

fam·i·lis′tiç, fam·i·lis′tiç·ăl, *a.* pertaining to Familists or their doctrines.

fam′i·ly, *n.*; *pl.* **fam′i·lies̹,** [L. *familia*, the servants in a household, a household, from *famulus*, a servant, from Oscan *famel*, a servant.]

1. the collective body of persons who live in one house.

2. a father, mother, and their children.

3. the children of the same parents.

4. one's husband (or wife) and children.

5. a group of people related by blood or marriage: relatives.

6. those who descend from one common progenitor; a tribe or race; as, the Israelites were a branch of the *family* of Abraham.

7. descent; lineage.

Go and complain thy *family* is young. —Pope.

8. honorable descent; noble or respectable lineage; as, he is a man of *family*.

9. a collection or union of things having common source or similar features; as, a *family* of languages.

The states of Europe were, by the prevailing maxims of its policy, closely united in one *family*. —E. Everett.

10. a criminal syndicate under a single leader.

11. a commune (n. 5) living in one household, especially under one head.

12. in biology, a subdivision in the classification of plants or animals, ranking above a genus and below an order: family names of plants have the suffix *-aceae*, those of animals, *-idae*.

family Bible; a large Bible with illuminated pages for recording family births, deaths, and marriages.

family circle; (a) a group consisting of the members of a family and intimate friends;

(b) in some theaters, a section in the upper balcony.

family doctor; a doctor, often a general practitioner, who looks after the health of members of a family and keeps their medical histories.

family man; a man having a wife and children dependent upon him; also, a man devoted to his family and home.

family name; a surname.

family of curves or *surfaces*; in geometry, a series of curves or surfaces differing from each other only in the value of one of the constants in the equation of one of them.

Family of Love; see *Familist*, sense 1.

family room; a room in a home, with informal furnishings, used for relaxation and recreation.

family tree; (a) a chart showing the relationship of all the ancestors and descendants in a given family; (b) all the ancestors and descendants in a given family.

Holy Family; the family of which Jesus was a member; specifically, the group comprising Joseph, Mary, and the infant Jesus, a frequent subject in painting.

in a family way; pregnant. [Colloq.]

fam'ine, *n.* [ME. *famine*; OFr. *famine*; LL. *famina*, famine, from L. *fames*, hunger.]

1. an acute and general scarcity of food; dearth; a general want of provisions; also, the time of this.

There was a *famine* in the land. —Gen. xxvi. 1.

2. starvation; great hunger.

3. an acute and general lack of anything.

fam'ine bread (bred), in botany, an arctic lichen, *Umbilicaria arctica*, sometimes used as food.

fam'ine fē'vẽr, typhus fever.

fam'ish, *v.t.*; famished, *pt.*, *pp.*; famishing, *ppr.* [ME. *famen*; OFr. *afamer*, to famish, from L. *ad*, to, and *fames*, hunger.]

1. to starve; to kill or destroy with hunger.

2. to exhaust the strength of, by hunger or thirst.

The pains of *famished* Tantalus he'll feel. —Dryden.

3. to force or constrain by famine or threatened starvation.

He had *famished* Paris into a surrender. —Burke.

fam'ish, *v.i.* 1. to die of hunger.

2. to suffer extreme hunger or thirst; to be exhausted in strength or to come near perishing for want of food or drink.

You are all resolved rather to die than to *famish*. —Shak.

3. to be deprived of anything necessary.

The Lord will not suffer the soul of the righteous to *famish*. —Prov. x. 3.

fam'ish·ment, *n.* a famishing or being famished.

fā'mous, *a.* [ME. *famous*; Fr. *fameux*; L. *famosus*, famed, famous, from *fama*, fame.]

1. celebrated; renowned; much talked of; distinguished; as, *famous* for beauty, wit, etc.

2. excellent; very good; first-rate. [Colloq.]

3. notorious. [Archaic.]

Syn.—renowned, illustrious, celebrated, conspicuous, distinguished, eminent, prominent, noted, notorious.

fā'moused (-must), *a.* renowned. [Obs.]

fā'mous·ly, *adv.* 1. in a famous manner; with great renown or celebrity.

2. unusually or exceeding well; admirably; capitally; as, you did *famously*. [Colloq.]

fā'mous·ness, *n.* renown; fame; celebrity.

fam'ū·lus, *n.*; *pl.* **fam'ū·lī,** [L., a servant.] an assistant or attendant of a medieval scholar or magician.

fan, *n.* [ME. *fan*, *fann*; AS. *fann*, from L. *vannus*, a fan for winnowing grain.]

1. an instrument for producing currents of air for ventilating or cooling; specifically, (a) any flat surface of various materials, as feathers, silk, papier maché, etc., usually mounted on a frame or sticks of ivory, wood, etc., and either permanently expanded or capable of being folded and opened at will; (b) any revolving contrivance of vanes or disks used for blowing a fire, cooling fluids, promoting ventilation, etc.; as, an electric *fan*; (c) a small vane or sail used to keep the large sails of a windmill always at right angles to the wind; (d) an apparatus for regulating or checking, by the resistance of the air to its rapid motion, the velocity of light machinery, as in a clock; (e) an apparatus for regulating the throttle valves of steam engines.

2. something in the form of a fan when spread (a sector of a circle), as a peacock's tail.

3. figuratively, anything that stirs to action or excites an emotion; as, her answer was but a *fan* to his anger.

4. a quintain. [Obs.]

5. an alluvial fan (or cone).

6. a device for separating grain from chaff by throwing the grain into the air so as to cause the chaff to be blown away. [Obs.]

fan window; same as *fanlight*.

fan, *v.t.*; fanned, *pt.*, *pp.*; fanning, *ppr.* 1. to cool and refresh by moving the air with a fan; to blow the air on with a fan; as, to *fan* oneself; the sultan was *fanned* by his slaves.

2. to ventilate; to blow on; to affect by air put in motion; as, to *fan* a fire.

3. to blow away (flies, etc.) with a fan.

4. to move or agitate (air), as with a fan.

5. to separate chaff from and drive it away by a current of air; as, to *fan* wheat.

6. to stir up; to excite; as, her silence *fanned* his disappointment into anger.

7. to spread out into the shape of a fan, or sector of a circle.

8. to separate (grain) from chaff.

9. to spank. [Slang.]

10. to fire (a pistol) several times quickly in succession by slapping the hammer back as with the alternate hand between shots. [Slang.]

11. in baseball, to strike (a batter) out.

fan, *v.i.* 1. to move, as if by a fan.

2. to spread like a fan: often followed by *out*.

3. in baseball, to strike out.

fan, *n.* [probably from *fanatic*.] a person enthusiastic about a specified sport, pastime, or performer; devotee; as, a baseball *fan*, movie *fan*. [Colloq.]

få·nål', *n.* [Fr. *fanal*; It. *fanale*, a signal light; It. dial. *fano*, a lighthouse; L. *pharus*; Gr. *pharos*, a lighthouse.] a beacon light; a ship's lantern; a lighthouse, or the illuminating apparatus in it. [Archaic.]

få·nat'iç, *a.* fanatical.

få·nat'iç, *n.* a fanatical person.

få·nat'iç·ăl, *a.* [L. *fanaticus*, pertaining to a temple, inspired, from *fanum*, a temple.] unreasonably enthusiastic; overly zealous; as, *fanatical* devotion to a cause.

få·nat'iç·ăl·ly, *adv.* in a fanatical manner.

få·nat'iç·ăl·ness, *n.* fanaticism.

få·nat'i·çişm, *n.* excessive and unreasonable enthusiasm or zeal.

få·nat'i·cīze, *v.t.*; fanaticized, *pt.*, *pp.*; fanaticizing, *ppr.* to make fanatical.

få·nat'i·cīze, *v.i.* to become fanatical; to act like a fanatic.

fan blōw'ẽr, a wheel which rotates and produces a current of air.

fan'cied, *a.* imagined; imaginary; unreal; as, a *fancied* wrong.

fan'ci·ẽr, *n.* 1. a person given to fancies.

2. a person with a special interest in the knowledge of something, particularly of the breeding of plants or animals; as, a dog *fancier*.

fan'ci·fụl, *a.* 1. guided by the imagination rather than by reason and experience; subject to the influence of fancy; whimsical; as, a *fanciful* man forms visionary projects.

2. dictated by the fancy; full of wild images; odd; unusual; unique; as, a *fanciful* scheme; a *fanciful* costume.

3. created in the fancy; imaginary; not real; as, a *fanciful* tale.

Syn.—fantastical, visionary, ideal, imaginative, chimerical.

fan'ci·fụl·ly, *adv.* in a fanciful manner.

fan'ci·fụl·ness, *n.* the quality of being fanciful.

fan'ci·less, *a.* without fancy or imagination.

fan'cy, *n.*; *pl.* **fan'cieş,** [ME. *fantasy*; OFr. *fantasie*; LL. *phantasia*, an idea, notion, fancy; Gr. *phantasia*, the look or appearance of a thing, from *phantazein*, to make visible, from *phainein*, to come to light.]

1. (a) originally, imagination in general; (b) decorative, light, whimsical, playful, or capricious imagination: the current literary sense.

2. illusion or delusion.

3. a mental image.

4. an arbitrary idea; notion; caprice; whim.

5. an inclination, liking, or fondness, often temporary.

6. critical taste or judgment in art, dress, etc. [Rare.]

the fancy; the enthusiasts of some sport or hobby, especially boxing; sometimes, any class of people who cultivate a special taste.

Syn.—caprice, conceit, conception, freak, frolic, humor, ideality, image, imagination, inclination, liking, notion, taste, whim.

fan'cy, *a.* 1. based on fancy; capricious; whimsical; fanciful.

2. higher than real value; extravagant; as, a *fancy* price.

3. made or added to please the fancy; ornamental; decorated; not plain; elaborate; as, a *fancy* necktie.

4. of superior skill; intricate and difficult; as, *fancy* diving.

5. of superior quality, and therefore costing more; as, canned goods graded *fancy*.

6. for expensive tastes; as, a *fancy* shop.

7. bred for some special feature or excellence of type: said of animals.

fancy dress; a masquerade costume.

fancy goods; ornamental fabrics or choice articles of show and ornament, as ribbons, embroideries, ties, toilet articles, etc.

fancy man; (a) a man supported by a woman, especially by a prostitute; (b) a man who gambles, especially on horse racing.

fancy woman; (a) a mistress; (b) a prostitute.

fan'cy, *v.t.*; fancied, *pt.*, *pp.*; fancying, *ppr.*

1. to imagine.

He whom I *fancy*, but can ne'er express. —Dryden.

2. to like; to be pleased with; to be fond of; as, he *fancied* her the first time they met.

3. to believe without conviction; to suppose; as, he *fancied* I had wronged him.

4. to breed (animals) for some special feature or excellence of type.

fan'cy, *v.i.* 1. to imagine; to figure to oneself; to believe or suppose without proof.

If our search has reached no farther than simile and metaphor, we rather *fancy* than know. —Locke.

2. to love. [Obs.]

fan'cy dan, [*fancy*, and (prob.) *Dan*, nickname for *Daniel*.] a flashy, ostentatious person, often one who lacks real skill, stamina, etc. [Slang.]

fan'cy-free, *a.* 1. free to fall in love; not married, engaged, etc.

2. carefree.

fan'cy līne, in nautical usage, a line rove through a block at the jaws of a gaff, used as a downhaul.

fan'cy-sick, *a.* love-sick.

fan'cy·wŏrk, *n.* ornamental knitting, crocheting, tatting, embroidery, etc.

fan·dañ'gō, *n.* [Sp., from the African name.]

1. a lively Spanish dance in rhythm varying from slow to quick three-quarter time. It is danced by couples, who hold castanets or sometimes tambourines.

2. music in triple time, suitable for such a dance.

3. a foolish act.

fan'dŏm, *n.* fans collectively, as of a sport or entertainer.

fāne, *n.* [L. *fanum*, a sanctuary, a temple, from *fari*, to speak, consecrate.] a temple or church. [Archaic or Poet.]

From men their cities, and from gods their *fanes*. —Pope.

fāne, *n.* 1. a weathercock; a vane. [Obs.]

2. a flag. [Obs.]

få·nẹ'gå, *n.* [Sp.] the Spanish bushel.

fan'fāre, *n.* [Fr. *fanfare*, a sounding of trumpets; Sp. *fanfarria*, bluster, vaunting, from Ar. *farfār*, talkative.] a flourish of trumpets; also, a noisy or showy display.

fan'fa·ron, *n.* [Fr. *fanfaron*; Sp. *fanfarron*, a blusterer.] a swaggerer; a boaster.

fan·far·on·āde', *n.* 1. boasting talk or action.

2. fanfare.

fan'foot, *n.* a harmless North African lizard, *Ptyodactylus hasselquisti*, whose toes are expanded into round lobes used for adhesion.

fang, *v.t.* [ME. *fangen*, *fongen*; AS. *fon*, to take hold of, seize.]

1. to catch; to seize; to lay hold of; to grip; to clutch. [Obs.]

Destruction *fang* mankind! —Shak.

2. to receive as a guest. [Obs.]

3. to stand sponsor for. [Brit. Dial.]

fang, *n.* [ME. *feng*, a grasping; AS. *feng*, *fang*, booty, a grasping, a seizure, from *gefangen*, pp. of *fon*, to take, seize.]

1. (a) one of the long, pointed teeth with which meat-eating animals seize and tear their prey; canine tooth; (b) one of the long, hollow or grooved teeth through which poisonous snakes inject their venom.

FANGS (of bushmaster)

2. the pointed part of something; tusk; talon.
3. formerly, the root of a tooth.
fanged, *a.* furnished with fangs, or something long and pointed; as, a *fanged* adder.
Chariots *fanged* with scythes. —Philips.
fañ'gle, *v.t.* to fashion. [Obs.]
fañ'gle, *n.* [prob. dim. of AS. *fang, feng,* a taking, a seizure.] something showy and worthless; a gewgaw. [Obs.]
A hatred to *fangles* and the French foolerie of his time. —Wood.
fang'less, *a.* having no fangs; toothless; as, a *fangless* lion.
fan'iŏn (-yŏn), *n.* [OFr. *fanion*; O.H.G. *fano,* a banner.]
1. in military usage, a small flag carried with the baggage of a brigade.
2. a small marking flag for a surveying station.
fan'light (-līt), *n.* a semicircular window, often with sash bars in a fanlike arrangement, over a door or larger window.
fan māil, letters, especially of praise and adulation from strangers, received by a prominent or well-known person.
fan'nel, *n.* [dim. of O.H.G. *fano,* a banner.] same as *fanon.*
fan'nēr, *n.* one who or that which fans; specifically, a fanning mill.
fan'-nērved, *a.* in botany and zoology, having the veins or nerves radiate from a common point, as in a leaf or an insect's wing.
fan'ning mill, fan'ning mȧ·chïne', a blower for removing chaff, husks, dirt, etc. from grain.
fan'ny, *n.* [contraction of *Aunt Fanny,* fanciful euphemism.] the buttocks. [Slang.]
fan'ō, *n.* same as *fanon.*
fan'ŏn, *n.* [ME. *fanone*; OFr. *fanon,* a pendant, the lappet of a miter, from LL. *fano*; O.H.G. *fano,* a banner.] in ecclesiastical usage, (a) a headdress worn by the Pope at Mass; (b) a maniple; (c) the white linen cloth in which the laity make their oblations at the altar.
fan pälm (päm), any palm tree with broad, fan-shaped leaves.
fan shell, a scallop; especially, any bivalve of the genus *Pecten.*
fan'tāil, *n.* 1. any bird of the genus *Rhipidura* of Australia; a fan-tailed flycatcher.
2. a variety of domestic pigeon or a goldfish with a tail in the shape of a fan.
3. a part, tail, or end spread out like an opened fan.
4. in nautical usage, (a) the overhanging portion of the deck on some ships; (b) the part of the main deck at the stern.
fan'tāiled, *a.* having a tail in the shape of a fan.
fan'-tan, *n.* [Chinese *fan,* number of times, and *tan,* apportion.]
1. a Chinese gambling game in which a pile of coins, counters, etc. is covered with a bowl and the players wager as to what the remainder will be after the coins, etc. are counted off in fours.
2. a game of cards that may be played by any number of players, the object being to get rid of all the cards.
fän·tä·ṣï'ȧ (*or* fan-tā'zi-ȧ), *n.* [It., fancy.]
1. a musical composition of no fixed form, with a structure determined by the composer's fancy.
2. a medley of familiar tunes.
fan'tȧ·ṣied, *a.* filled with fancies or imaginations; whimsical.
fan'tȧ·size, *v.t.*; fantasized, *pt., pp.*; fantasizing, *ppr.* [*fantasy,* and *-ize.*] to create or imagine in a fantasy; to have daydreams about.
fan'taṣm, *n.* same as *phantasm.*
fan'tast, *n.* one whose manners, speech, or ideas are fantastic; a visionary.
fan·tas'tiç, *n.* one who is fantastic in any way; an eccentric.
fan·tas'tiç, fan·tas'tiç·ăl, *a.* [OFr. *fantastique*; LL. *phantasticus, fantasticus,* imaginary, from Gr. *phantastikos,* able to present or represent to the mind, from *phantazein,* to make visible.]
1. fanciful; produced or existing only in imagination; imaginary; not real.
2. whimsical; capricious; fanciful; thought of by unrestrained fancy; as, *fantastic* minds; a *fantastic* mistress.
3. odd or strange in appearance; grotesque.
4. seemingly impossible; incredible.
fan·tas·ti·çal'i·ty, *n.* 1. fantasticalness.
2. anything that is fantastic.
fan·tas'tiç·ăl·ly, *adv.* in a fantastic manner.
fan·tas'tiç·ăl·ness, *n.* the state of being fantastic.
fan·tas'ti·ciṣm, *n.* fantasticalness.
fan·tas'tiç·ly, *adv.* fantastically. [Rare.]
fan·tas'tiç·ness, *n.* fantasticalness. [Rare.]
fan·tas'ti·çō, *n.* [It.] a fantastic.
fan'tȧ·sy, phan'tȧ·sy, *n.*; *pl.* **fan'tȧ·sieṣ, phan'tȧ·sieṣ,** [ME. *fantasye, fauntasye*; OFr. *fantasie*; LL. *phantasia,* an idea, notion; Gr. *phantasia,* the look or appearance of a thing.]
1. imagination or fancy; especially, wild, visionary fancy.
2. an unreal mental image; illusion; phantasm.
3. a whim; queer notion; caprice.
4. an imaginative poem, play, etc.
5. in music, a fantasia.
6. in psychology, a mental image, as in a daydream, usually pleasant and with some vague continuity.
fan'tȧ·sy, *v.t.*; fantasied, *pt., pp.*; fantasying, *ppr.* 1. to conceive in the mind; to imagine.
2. in music, to compose or perform, as a fantasia.
3. to fancy; to admire; to have a liking for. [Obs.]
fân·tōc·cï'nï (fân-tō-chē'nē), *n.pl.* [It., pl. of *fantoccio,* a puppet, dwarf, dim. of *fante,* a boy, a servant.]
1. puppets or marionettes.
2. dramatic representations in which puppets are used.
fan'tod, *n.* [prob. from *fan*tastic, and *-od* (origin unknown).] a nervous condition: now usually in the humorous phrase *the fantods,* a state of restless anxiety.
fan'tŏm, *n.* and *a.* same as *phantom.*
fan trā'cēr·y, in architecture, elaborate geometrical carved work which spreads over the surface of a vault, rising from a capital or corbel and diverging like the folds of a fan.

FAN TRACERY

fan'um, *n.* same as *fanon.*
fan vault'ing, vaulting decorated by fan tracery.
fan wheel (hwēl), the wheel of a fan blower.
fan'wïṣe, *adv.* opened out like a folding fan.
fan'wŏrt, *n.* a water plant with submerged, finely divided leaves: it is used in aquariums.
fan'zïne, *n.* [*fan* (devotee), and *magazine.*] a magazine, usually produced by amateurs, devoted to a special-interest group, such as fans of science fiction or comic books.
fap, *a.* fuddled. [Obs.]
fä·quïr' (-kïr'), *n.* same as *fakir.*
fär, *a.*; *comp.* farther; *superl.* farthest: see also *further, furthest.* [ME. *fer, ferr*; AS. *feorr, feor,* far, distant.]
1. distant, in space or time; remote; as, a *far* country; the *far* future.
The nations *far* and near contend in choice. —Dryden.
2. extending a long way; as, a *far* journey.
3. very different in quality or nature.
4. advanced; well along, as in years.
5. more distant; as, the *far* side of a house.
fär, *adv.*; *comp.* farther *or* further; *superl.* farthest *or* furthest. 1. at a great extent or distance of space, time, or degree; as, the *far*-extended ocean; we are separated *far* from each other.
2. to or from a distance in time or position; as, he pushed his researches very *far* into antiquity.
3. in a great proportion; by many degrees; very much; considerably.
Who can find a virtuous woman? for her price is *far* above rubies.—Prov. xxxi. 10.
as far as; (a) to the distance, extent, or degree that; (b) with reference to. [Colloq.]
by far; in a great degree; very much.
far and away; very much; beyond doubt; to a great degree.
far and near; over a wide extent; throughout an entire region; everywhere.
far and wide; widely; everywhere.
far gone; in an advanced state of deterioration.
few and far between; scarce; rare.
from far; from a great distance; from a remote place.
in so far as; to the extent or degree that.
so far; up to this place, time, or degree: also *thus far.*
fär, *n.* a distant place: used in certain phrases, as *from far.*
fär'-ȧ·bout'', *n.* a going out of the way; a wandering; a digression. [Obs.]
far'ad, *n.* [named for Michael *Faraday,* 1791–1867, English physicist.] an electromagnetic unit of capacitance, equal to the amount that permits the storing of one coulomb of charge for each volt of applied potential difference: symbol, F.
far·ȧ·dā'iç, *a.* same as *faradic.*
far'ȧ·dāy, *n.* [named for Michael *Faraday*: see *farad.*] a unit of quantity of electricity which, when passed through an electrolyte, will liberate one gram atomic weight of a univalent element: its value is approximately 96,500 coulombs.
Far'ȧ·dāy'ṣ lạw, in electrolysis, the law that (a) when a current flows through an electrolyte, the amount of chemical action which takes place in a given time is proportional to the total quantity of electricity passed; (b) the weight of the substance liberated at the electrodes by a given quantity of electricity is directly proportional to the atomic weight of the element.
far·ad'iç, *a.* of, pertaining to, producing, or caused by induced electric currents.
far'ȧ·diṣm, *n.* the form of electricity produced by an induced current.
far''ȧ·di·zā'tion, *n.* in medicine, stimulation or treatment with induced electricity.
far'ȧ·dïze, *v.t.*; faradized, *pt., pp.*; faradizing, *ppr.* in medicine, to stimulate or treat, as a muscle, nerve, etc., with induced electricity.
far'an·dōle, fa·ran'dō·lȧ, *n.* [Fr.] a rapid French dance in six-eight time, in which the dancers form in a circle and whirl around, facing in and out alternately; also, the music for such a dance.
fär'ȧ·wāy'', *a.* 1. distant; remote.
2. abstracted; absent-minded; dreamy; pensive; as, a *faraway* look in her eyes.
färce, *v.t.*; farced (färst), *pt., pp.*; farcing, *ppr.* [ME. *farcen*; OFr. *farsir, farcir*; L. *farcire,* to stuff, cram.]
1. to stuff; to fill with mingled ingredients or forcemeat. [Obs.]
2. to fill out as if with stuffing or seasoning; as, he *farced* his play with old jokes.
The first principles of religion should not be *farced* with school points and private tenets. —Sanderson.
3. to fatten.[Obs.]
färce, *n.* [Fr. *farce,* stuffing, a farce, from *farcer,* to stuff; L. *farcire,* to stuff, fill in.]
1. seasoning; stuffing, as that for a fowl.
2. an exaggerated comedy based on broadly humorous situations; play intended only to be funny.
3. broad humor of the kind found in such plays.
4. something absurd or ridiculous; as, his work was just a *farce.*
färce'ment, *n.* stuffing or dressing, as of meat; forcemeat. [Obs.]
fär·cēur', *n.* a joker; also, a writer or actor of farces.
fär'ciăl (-shăl), *a.* same as *farcical* (of a farce).
fär'ci·çăl, *a.* belonging to or of the nature of a farce; appropriate for farce; ludicrous; absurd; burlesque.
They deny the characters to be *farcical,* because they are actually in nature. —Gay.
fär'ci·çăl, *a.* pertaining to farcy, a disease of horses.
fär·ci·çal'i·ty, *n.* 1. the quality of being farcical or ludicrous; absurdity.
2. *pl.* **fär·ci·çal'i·tieṣ,** a farcical action or remark.
fär'ci·çăl·ly, *adv.* in a farcical manner.
fär'ci·çăl·ness, *n.* same as *farcicality.*
fär'ci·līte, *n.* pudding stone. [Obs.]
fär'cin, *n.* same as *farcy.*
fär'cing, *n.* stuffing; forcemeat.
färç'tāte, *a.* [L. *farctus,* stuffed, pp. of *farcire,* to stuff.] in botany, stuffed; crammed or full; without vacuities; not tubular or hollow; as, a *farctate* leaf, stem, or pericarp.

fär′cy, *n.* [LL. *farciminum*, from L. *farcire*, to stuff, cram.] a disease of horses; a form of glanders, attacking the skin and lymphatic glands.

fär′cy bud, a swollen gland, as in farcy.

fārd, *v.t.* to paint, as the face or cheeks; as, a *farded* top. [Obs.]

fārd, *n.* paint, especially rouge. [Obs.]

fär′dāge, *n.* [Fr. *fardage*, from *fardeau*, a load; OFr. *fardel*, a load, probably from Ar. *fardah*, a package.] in nautical usage, dunnage. [Obs.]

fär′del, *n.* a bundle or pack; hence, a burden; misfortune. [Archaic.]

fär′del, *v.t.* to make up in bundles. [Obs.]

fāre, *v.i.*; fared, *pt.*, *pp.*; faring, *ppr.* [ME. *faren*; AS. *faran*, to go, to be in a particular condition, from *ferian*, to carry, convey.]

1. to go; to pass; to move forward; to travel. [Poet.]

So on he *fares*, and to the border comes
Of Eden. —Milton.

2. to be in a specified condition; to be attended with any circumstances or train of events; to go through an experience.

Ill *fares* the land, to hastening ills a prey,
Where wealth accumulates, and men decay.
—Goldsmith.

3. to feed; to be given food and drink; as, we *fared* well, until the crops failed.

4. to happen; to result; as, we shall see how it will *fare* with him.

5. to behave. [Obs.]

fāre, *n.* [ME. *fare*; AS. *faru*, a journey, from *faran*, to go.]

1. the sum paid or due for transportation; as, the *fare* for crossing a river; the *fare* for conveyance in a railroad train.

2. food; diet; as, we had delicious *fare*.

My lord, eat also, though the *fare* is coarse.
—Tennyson.

3. condition of things. [Archaic.]

What *fare*? What news abroad? —Shak.

4. a passenger in a train, bus, taxi, etc.; as, he had not driven far when he was stopped by his *fare*.

5. the quantity of fish taken in a fishing vessel.

6. a journey. [Obs.]

fāre·well′, *interj.* fare well; good-by.

fāre·well′, *n.* 1. a wish of happiness or welfare at parting; parting words.

2. leave; departure.

And takes her *farewell* of the glorious sun.
—Shak.

fāre·well′, *a.* final; parting; last; as, a *farewell* sermon; a *farewell* call.

fär′-fāmed′ (-fāmd′), *a.* widely famous.

fär′fet, *a.* farfetched. [Obs.]

fär′fetch, *v.t.* to bring from far; to draw farfetched conclusions. [Obs.]

fär′fetch, *n.* a deep-laid stratagem. [Obs.]

fär′fetched′ (-fecht′), *a.* 1. brought from a distance. [Archaic.]

2. forced; strained; not naturally resulting or introduced; as, *farfetched* figures of speech.

fär′-flung′, *a.* extending for a great distance.

fär′fōrth, *adv.* far advanced; far. [Obs.]

fȧ·rī′nȧ, *n.* [L. *farina*, ground corn, from *far*, a sort of grain, spelt.]

1. meal or flour; specifically, a soft, tasteless, and commonly white flour, obtained from cereal grains, potatoes, nuts, beans, etc., eaten as a cooked cereal.

2. potato starch or other starch.

3. in botany, formerly, the pollen of flowers.

4. in entomology, a fine, mealy powder found on some insects.

fossil farina; a variety of carbonate of lime, in thin white crusts, light as cotton, and easily reducible to powder.

far·i·nā′ceous, *a.* [LL. *farinaceus*, from L. *farina*, meal.]

1. containing, consisting of, or made from meal or flour; as, a *farinaceous* diet.

2. yielding farina or flour; as, *farinaceous* seeds.

3. like meal; mealy; pertaining to meal; as, a *farinaceous* taste or quality.

4. starchy.

far′i·nōse, *a.* [LL. *farinosus*, mealy, from L. *farina*, meal.]

1. yielding or producing farina.

2. full of meal; mealy.

3. in biology, mealy; covered with a white, powdery substance, as the leaves of some poplars or the wings of certain insects.

fȧ·rin′ū·lent, *a.* same as *farinose*, sense 3.

fär′kle·ber″ry, *n.*; *pl.* **fär′kle·ber″ries,** [etym. uncertain.] a shrub or small tree of the heath family, with large, white flowers and round, black, inedible berries, found in the southern United States.

färl, *v.t.* to furl. [Obs.]

fär′leū, *n.* in Scots law, money paid by tenants in lieu of a heriot.

färm, *n.* [ME. *ferme*, from ML. *firma*, fixed payment, from *firmare*, to fix, from *firmus*, steadfast, stable.]

1. (a) originally, a fixed sum payable at regular intervals, as rent, taxes, etc., or an amount collected in place of taxes, etc.; (b) the letting out, for a fixed amount, of the collection of taxes, with the privilege of keeping all that is collected; (c) the condition of being let out, or farmed out, at a fixed rent.

2. a district of a country leased out by a government for the collection of taxes.

3. a piece of land (with house, barns, etc.) on which crops or animals are raised: originally, such land let out to tenants.

4. something similar to this; as, a tract of water for raising fish is a fish *farm*.

5. in baseball, a minor-league team owned and operated by a major-league team to train young or inexperienced players.

färm, *v.t.*; farmed, *pt.*, *pp.*; farming, *ppr.* 1. to cultivate (land).

2. to collect the taxes and other fees of (a business) on a commission basis or for a fixed amount.

3. to rent (a business, land, etc.) in return for a fixed payment (usually with *out*).

4. to take at a certain rent or rate; to take a lease of.

5. to send (work) from the main shop, office, etc. to workers on the outside (with *out*).

6. to let out the labor of (a convict, etc.) for a fixed amount.

7. to arrange for the care of (children, paupers, etc.).

8. in baseball, to assign to a farm (usually with *out*).

färm, *v.i.* to be a farmer; to engage in agriculture; to cultivate the soil.

färm′ȧ·ble, *a.* capable of being farmed.

färm′ẽr, *n.* [ME. *fermour*, a steward, bailiff; OFr. *fermier*, a farmer, lessee, bailiff, or overseer of a farm.]

1. a tenant; a lessee; one who hires and cultivates a farm; a cultivator of leased ground.

2. one who contracts to collect customs, excise, or other duties by paying a fixed sum to the government for the right to do so.

3. one who earns his living by farming; one who cultivates a farm, whether a tenant or the proprietor; a husbandman; an agriculturist; one who tills the soil.

4. in mining, one who farms the lot and cope of the crown. [Brit.]

farmer's satin; a durable fabric of cotton and wool, having a glossy surface resembling that of satin, used especially for linings.

färm′ẽr·ess, *n.* a woman who farms, or the wife of a farmer.

färm″ẽr·ette′ (-et′), *n.* a girl or woman who owns, works on, or has charge of a farm. [Colloq.]

färm′ẽr-ġen′ẽr·ăl, *n.*; *pl.* **fär′mẽrs-ġen′ẽr·ăl,** [Fr. *fermier général*.] any of the men who farmed certain taxes in France before the Revolution.

Fär′mẽr-Lā′bŏr Pär′ty, 1. a political party in Minnesota, founded in 1919, which favored taxation reforms, social-security legislation, etc.: it merged with the Democratic Party in 1944.

2. a United States political party (1920–1924), which favored nationalization of basic industries and banks.

färm′ẽr·ship, *n.* the occupation of farming; the skill or management of a farmer.

färm′ẽr·y, *n.* the buildings, yards, etc. necessary for the business of a farm. [Rare.]

färm′house, *n.* a house on a farm; the residence of a farmer.

färm′ing, *a.* pertaining to farms or agriculture; as, Iowa is a *farming* state; *farming* machinery.

färm′ing, *n.* 1. the business of cultivating land or employing it for the purposes of husbandry; agriculture.

2. the letting out to farm of land, revenue, etc.

fär′mōst, *a.* most distant or remote. [Rare.]

färm′stead (-sted), *n.* the buildings and land on a farm; a country homestead.

färm′yärd, *n.* the yard surrounding or surrounded by the farm buildings.

fär′ness, *n.* distance, remoteness; the state of being far off.

fā′rō, *n.* [Fr. *pharaon*, perhaps so called from the representation of a *Pharaoh*, the name of the ancient kings of Egypt, upon the back of one of the cards.] a gambling game with cards, in which the players bet on the cards to be turned up from the top of the dealer's pack.

fā′rō bank, an establishment where the game of faro is played; also, the amount risked in the game by the proprietor.

fā′rō box, a metal box from which the cards are dealt in playing faro. It is so contrived that but one card can be removed at a time from a slit at one side, and has a spring which keeps the top card level with the slit.

Fā·rō·ēṣe′, *n. sing.* and *pl.* [Ice. *Færeyskr*, a Faroese, from *Færeyjar*, lit., the sheep islands, the Faeroe islands, from *fær*, sheep.]

1. a native or inhabitant, or the natives and inhabitants collectively, of the Faeroe islands, which lie between the Shetland islands and Iceland.

2. the Norse dialect of the Faeroe islands, akin to Icelandic.

fär′-ọff′, *a.* faraway; remote.

One *far-off* divine event,
To which the whole creation moves.
—Tennyson.

fär′-out′, *a.* very advanced, experimental, or nonconformist. [Colloq.]

fȧr·raġ′i·nous, *a.* [L. *farrago* (*-inis*), mixed fodder for cattle.] formed of various materials; mixed; jumbled; as, a *farraginous speech*. [Rare.]

fȧr·rā′gō, *n.* [L. *farrago* (*-inis*), mixed fodder for cattle, a mixture, medley, from *far*, *farris*, spelt.] a mass composed of various materials confusedly mixed; a medley; a jumble; a hodgepodge.

fär′-rēach′ing, *a.* having a wide range, extent, influence, or effect.

far·rē·ȧ′tion, *n.* same as *confarreation*.

far′ri·ẽr, *n.* [OFr. *ferrier*, a farrier, from L. *ferrarius*, pertaining to iron, a worker with iron, blacksmith, from *ferrum*, iron.]

1. a shoer of horses; a blacksmith.

2. a veterinary, especially one who treats horses. [Obs.]

far′ri·ẽr, *v.i.* to practice as a farrier. [Obs.]

far′ri·ẽr·y, *n.* 1. the art or practice of horseshoeing.

2. the science of preventing or curing the diseases of horses and cattle. [Obs.]

3. a farrier's, or blacksmith's, shop.

far′rōw, *a.* [D. *vaarkoe*, a young cow that has not yet brought forth a calf, a heifer; *var*, *varre*, a bullock; Ice. *farri*, a bullock; AS. *fearr*, a bull.] not bearing a calf in a particular season or year: applied to cows only.

far′rōw, *v.t.* or *v.i.*; farrowed, *pt.*, *pp.*; farrowing, *ppr.* [ME. *fergen*, to bring forth pigs, from AS. *fearh*, a little pig.] to give birth to (a litter of pigs).

far′rōw, *n.* [ME. *faren*, pl., little pigs, from AS. *fearh*, pl. *fearas*, a little pig.]

1. a litter of pigs.

2. a young pig. [Obs.]

far′ry, *n.* a farrow. [Obs.]

färse, *n.* [LL. *farsa*, from L. *farsus*, *fartus*, pp. of *farcire*, to stuff, fill up.] in some English churches before the Reformation, an explanation or paraphrase in English of the text of the epistle read in Latin.

fär′see′ing, *a.* 1. seeing or able to see far.

2. having foresight or forethought; planning ahead; provident.

fär′sīght′ed (-sīt′ed), *a.* 1. able to perceive objects at a distance more clearly than those those near-by; hypermetropic.

2. farseeing; as, a *farsighted* statesman.

fär′sīght′ed·ness, *n.* the state or quality of being farsighted.

fär′thẽr, *a.* comp. of *far*, [ME. *erther*, var. of *further*, substituted for regular *ferrer*, comp; AS. *fyrre*, more remote, farther.]

1. more remote; more distant; as, on the *farther* side.

2. additional; increased; more; as, his *farther* progress was impeded: now usually *further*. *Farther* is often preferred in speaking of distance, *further* in the sense of *additional*, as of time, mention, or treatment.

fär′thẽr, *adv.* comp. of *far*, 1. at or to a greater distance; more remotely; beyond; as, let us look *farther*.

2. to a greater degree or extent.

3. additionally; moreover: in this sense, *further* is generally preferred.

I will disparage her no *farther*, till you are
my witnesses. —Shak.

fär′thẽr, *v.t.* to advance; to further. [Rare.]

fär′thẽr·ănce, *n.* furtherance. [Obs.]

fär′thẽr·mōre, *adv.* furthermore. [Obs.]

fär′thẽr·mōst, *a.* most distant; most remote, farthest.

fär′thest, *a.* superl. of *far,* 1. most distant or remote; as, the *farthest* degree.
2. most extended; longest.

fär′thest, *adv.* superl. of *far,* 1. at or to the greatest distance or most remote point in space or time.
2. to the greatest degree or extent.

fär′thing, *n.* [ME. *ferthing, ferthynge*; AS. *feorthing,* lit., a fourthling, the fourth part of a thing, dim. of *feortha,* fourth.]
1. a small British coin equal to a fourth of a British penny.
2. a division of land. [Obs.]
Thirty acres make a *farthing* land; nine *farthings* a Cornish acre; and four Cornish acres a knight's fee. —Carew.
3. anything very small in amount or value; a trifle; a small quantity. [Obs.]
No *farthing* of grease. —Chaucer.

fär′thin·gāle, *n.* [OFr. *verdugalle, vertugalle,* a farthingale; Sp. *verdugado,* provided with hoops, a farthingale, from *verdugo,* the young shoot of a tree, a rod, hoop, from *verde,* L. *viridis,* green.] a hoop formed of whalebone, etc., used to extend the petticoat, or a skirt or petticoat covering such a hoop, worn by women in the 16th and 17th centuries.

FARTHINGALE

fas′cēs, *n.pl.* [L. *fascis,* pl. *fasces,* a bundle, packet.] in ancient Rome, an ax tied up with a bundle of rods, borne before the chief Roman magistrates as a symbol of their authority: later the symbol of Italian fascism.

fas′cet, *n.* [ME. *faucet*; OFr. *fausset,* a faucet.] in glass manufacturing, (a) a wire basket secured to the end of a rod, for carrying the bottle from the mold to the leer; (b) a rod put into the mouth of the bottle for the same purpose.

fas′ci·ȧ (fash′i-), *n.*; *pl.* **fas′ci·ae,** [L., a band, sash, fillet.]
1. a band; flat strip; fillet.
2. in anatomy, a thin layer of connective tissue covering, supporting, or connecting the muscles or inner organs of the body.
3. in architecture, any flat band with a small projection, as the band of an architrave; also, in brick buildings, the jutting of the bricks beyond the windows in the several stories except the highest.
4. in surgery, a bandage, roller, or ligature.
5. in zoology, a band or belt of color, usually broad and transverse, on the skin, feathers, scales, etc.
6. in music, the sides of a violin.

FASCES

fas′ci·ăl (fash′i-), *a.* pertaining to, consisting of, or composing a fascia.

fas′ci·ăl, *a.* of or relating to the fasces.

fas′ci·āte (fash′i-), *a.* [L. *fasciatus,* pp. of *fasciare,* to swathe, wrap with bands, from *fascia,* a band, fillet.]
1. bound with a band or fillet.
2. in botany, (a) abnormally enlarged and flattened, as some plant stems; (b) growing in a fascicle.
3. in zoology, marked by broad colored bands.

fas′ci·ā·ted, *a.* [L. *fasciatus,* from *fascia,* a bundle, fillet.] fasciate.

fas·ci·ā′tion (fash-i-), *n.* [L. *fascia,* a fillet, band.]
1. the way in which something is bound up.
2. the act of binding up; a bandaging.
3. that which binds; a fascia. [Obs.]
4. in botany, a malformation in plants, in which a stem or branch becomes flattened and widened laterally into the shape of a ribbon.
5. the state of being fasciate.

fas′ci·çle, *n.* [L. *fasciculus,* dim. of *fascis,* a bundle.]
1. a small bundle; specifically, (a) in botany, a small tuft or cluster of fibers, leaves, or flowers; (b) in anatomy, a fasciculus.
2. one of the installments of a book published in parts.

fas′ci·çled, *a.* growing in a fascicle.

fas·ciç′ū·lăr, *a.* same as *fasciculate.*

fas·ciç′ū·lăr·ly, *adv.* same as *fasciculately.*

fas·ciç′ū·lāte, fas·ciç′ū·lā·ted, *a.* [L. *fasciculus,* dim. of *fascis,* a bundle.] formed of, or growing in, clusters or bundles.

fas·ciç′ū·lāte·ly, *adv.* in a fasciculate manner.

fas′ci·çūle, *n.* [Fr., from L. *fasciculus,* dim. of *fascis,* a bundle.]
1. a fasciculus.
2. in entomology, a tuft of close-set hairs.

FASCICULATE ROOT

fas·ciç′ū·līte, *n.* [L. *fasciculus,* a small bundle, and Gr. *lithos,* stone.] a variety of fibrous hornblende of a fasciculate structure.

fas·ciç′ū·lus, *n.*; *pl.* **fas·ciç′ū·lī,** [L., dim. of *fascis,* a bundle.] a small bundle of fibers; specifically, in anatomy, a bundle of nerve fibers in the central nervous system: also *fascicle.*

fas′ci·nāte, *v.t.*; fascinated, *pt., pp.*; fascinating, *ppr.* [L. *fascinatus,* pp. of *fascinare,* to bewitch, charm; Gr. *baskainein,* to bewitch.]
1. originally, to bewitch; to enchant; to put under a spell.
2. to attract or hold motionless, as by a fixed look or by inspiring terror.
3. to charm; to captivate; to attract by delightful qualities.
Syn.—entrance, attract, enrapture, bewitch, enamour.

fas·ci·nā′tion, *n.* [L. *fascinatio* (*-onis*), an enchanting.]
1. the act of fascinating.
2. the state of being fascinated.
3. a fascinating influence; strong attraction; allure; charm.

fas′ci·nā·tŏr, *n.* 1. a person who fascinates.
2. a woman's scarf made of lace, net, yarn, etc., worn around the head and neck.

fas·cīne′, *n.* [Fr. *fascine*; OFr. *fascine*; L. *fascina,* a bundle of sticks, a fagot, from *fascis,* a bundle.] in fortification and engineering, a bundle of sticks bound together, used in raising batteries, in filling ditches, in strengthening ramparts, etc.

FASCINES

fas·cīne′ dwell′ẽr, in archaeology, one of those prehistoric people who built and lived in fascine dwellings.

fas·cīne′ dwell′ing, in archaeology, a lake dwelling of prehistoric times, built upon a foundation of fascines.

fas·cī′ō·lȧ, *n.*; *pl.* **fas·cī′ō·lae,** [L. *fasciola,* dim. of *fascia,* a bandage.] in zoology, a short or narrow band of color.

fas·cī′ō·lăr, *a.* pertaining to a fasciola.

fas′ci·ōle, *n.* 1. same as *fasciola.*
2. one of the bands of modified spines of some sea urchins.

fas′cis, *n.* sing. of *fasces.*

fas′ciṣm (fash′izm *or* fas′), *n.* [It. *fascismo,* from *fascio,* a political group, an organization, a club, from L. *fascis,* a bundle or packet.]
1. [F–] the doctrines, methods, or movement of the Fascisti.
2. [*sometimes* F–] a system of government characterized by rigid one-party dictatorship, forcible suppression of the opposition (unions, other, especially leftist, parties, minority groups, etc.), the retention of private ownership of the means of production under centralized governmental control, belligerent nationalism and racism, glorification of war, etc.: first instituted in Italy in 1922.
3. (a) the political philosophy and movement based on such doctrines and policies; (b) fascist behavior. See also *Nazism.*

Fä·sciṣ′mō (-shēz′), *n.* [It.] fascism.

fas′cist (fash′ist *or* fas′), *n.* 1. [F–] (a) a member of the Fascisti; (b) a member of some similar party; Nazi, Falangist, etc.
2. an advocate of fascism or fascist principles.

fas′cist, *a.* 1. [F–] pertaining to Fascists or Fascism.
2. relating to fascism or fascists; also, adhering to or supporting fascism.

Fȧ·scis′tȧ (fȧ-shis′tȧ; *It.* fä-shē′stä), *n. sing.* a member of the Fascisti.

Fȧ·scis′tī (fȧ-shis′tē; *It.* fä-shē′stē), *n. pl.* an Italian political organization founded at Milan in 1919 by Benito Mussolini, for the ostensible purpose of opposing and suppressing all radical movements in Italy. The members of this organization, known as Black Shirts, made a "march to Rome" in 1922 and established an antidemocratic dictatorship (1922–1943) under the leadership of Mussolini; Fascists.

fȧ·scis′tiç, *a.* fascist.

fȧ·scis′ti·căl·ly, *adv.* in a fascist manner.

fash, *v.t.* and *v.i.* [from OFr. *fascher,* to anger, displease; L. *fastidire,* to feel disgust at, dislike, from *fastidium,* loathing, dislike.] to vex; to annoy; to trouble. [Scot.]

fash, *n.* 1. trouble; vexation. [Scot.]
2. care; pains; attention. [Scot.]

fash′iŏn, *n.* [ME. *facioun*; OFr. *faceon,* fashion, form, outward appearance, from L. *factio* (*-onis*), a making, from *facere,* to make.]
1. the make or form of anything; the state of anything with regard to its external appearance; shape; style; pattern: as, the *fashion* of a hat; the *fashion* of a building; the *fashion* of a ship.
2. kind; sort.
3. the prevailing mode or customary style in dress, speech, conduct, or other things subject to change; especially, the mode or style favored by the dominant circles of society.
4. custom; usage; common practice; something fashionable; as, it is the *fashion* to belong to some fraternal order.
5. way, style, or method of doing or making a thing; as, climbing monkey *fashion*; after the *fashion* of sailors.
6. those people who conform to the fashions of society.
after (or *in*) *a fashion*; to a certain extent; in some manner; not too well; as, she did her work *after a fashion.*
in fashion; fashionable.
out of fashion; not in keeping with prevailing modes.
Syn.—custom, practice, usage, style, manner, mode, way, sort, conventionality.

fash′iŏn, *v.t.*; fashioned, *pt., pp.*; fashioning, *ppr.* 1. to form; to give shape or figure to; to make; to mold.
2. to contrive.
3. to fit; to adapt; to accommodate: with *to.*

fash′iŏn·ȧ·ble, *a.* 1. made according to the prevailing form or mode; stylish; as, a *fashionable* dress.
2. of, characteristic of, or used by people who follow the current style of dress, speech, conduct, etc.
3. capable of being shaped or fashioned. [Obs.]

fash′iŏn·ȧ·ble, *n.* one who conforms to the current styles or fashions; a fashionable person.

fash′iŏn·ȧ·ble·ness, *n.* the state of being fashionable.

fash′iŏn·ȧ·bly, *adv.* in a manner according with fashion, custom, or prevailing practice.

fash′iŏned, *a.* having a certain form or fashion; as, old-*fashioned.*

fash′iŏn·ẽr, *n.* 1. one who fashions or forms anything.
2. a modiste. [Archaic.]

fash′iŏn·ist, *n.* a follower of the modes and fashions.

fash′iŏn·less, *a.* having no fashion.

fash′iŏn·mŏn̄·gẽr, *n.* one who studies and follows the fashions; a fop.

fash′iŏn·mŏn″gẽr·ing, *a.* behaving like a fashionmonger.

fash′iŏn piēce, same as *fashion timber.*

fash′iŏn plāte, 1. an engraving or picture illustrating current fashions in dress.
2. a fashionably dressed person.

fash′iŏn tim′bẽr, one of the hindmost timbers which terminate the breadth and give shape to the stern of a wooden ship.

fas′sā·īte, *n.* [from *Fassa,* in the Tyrol, where it is found.] a mineral, a variety of pyroxene.

fȧst, *v.i.*; fasted, *pt., pp.*; fasting, *ppr.* [ME. *fasten, festen*; AS. *fæstan,* to abstain from food, fast.]
1. to abstain from food beyond the usual time; to go without food; to eat very little or nothing.
2. to abstain from food or from certain kinds of food voluntarily, as in observance of a holy day or as a token of grief, sorrow, repentance, etc.
Thou didst *fast* and weep for the child. —2 Sam. xii. 21.

fȧst, *n.* [ME. *fast, faste*; AS. *fæsten,* a fast, from *fæstan,* to fast.]
1. a state or act of fasting; abstinence from food, either total or partial.
2. the time of fasting, whether a day, week, or longer time.
The *fast* was now already past. —Acts xxvii. 9.
to break (*one's*) *fast*; to take food after a

period of fasting; also, to take the first food of the day after the night's fast; to eat one's breakfast.

fȧst, *a.* [ME.; AS. *faest*; akin to G. *fest*, firm, stable.]

1. not easily moved, firm.
2. firmly fastened.
3. strong; secure against attack; well fortified.
4. loyal; devoted; as, *fast* friends.
5. complete; sound. [Obs. or Dial.]
6. unfading: said of colors.
7. rapid in movement; swift; quick; speedy.
8. permitting or promoting swift movement; as, a *fast* highway.
9. taking or lasting a short time.
10. ahead of time; showing a time in advance of standard; as, a *fast* clock.
11. (a) living in a reckless, wild, dissipated way; (b) having loose morals; promiscuous.
12. glib and deceptive. [Colloq.]
13. in bacteriology, resistant to staining or destruction, as certain bacteria.
14. in photography, having a high shutter speed.

hard and fast; (a) absolutely binding; strictly obligatory; unalterable; as, *hard and fast* rules; a *hard and fast* contract; (b) in nautical usage, firmly grounded; immovable; as, the ship was *hard and fast*.

to make fast; (a) to fasten; to make secure; to close; as, *to make fast* the door; (b) in nautical usage, to belay; as, *to make fast* a rope.

Syn.—firm, secure, fixed, constant, steadfast, stable, unyielding, unswerving, rapid, quick, swift, fleet, speedy, hasty, wild, reckless, gay, dissipated, dissolute.

fȧst, *adv.* [ME. *faste*; AS. *faeste*.]

1. firmly; fixedly.
2. thoroughly; soundly; as, the child was *fast* asleep.
3. rapidly, swiftly, quickly, speedily.
4. in a reckless, dissipated way; wildly.
5. ahead of time.
6. close; near; as, *fast* by the river. [Obs.]

to play fast and loose; to behave with reckless duplicity, insincerity, and inconstancy.

fȧst, *n.* [ME. *fest*; Ice. *festr*, a rope, cord.]

1. that which fastens or holds; specifically, in nautical usage, a rope or chain by which a vessel is moored to a wharf, dock, etc.: named according to the part of the vessel to which it is made fast; as, a bow *fast*.
2. immovable shore ice.

a fast one; a tricky or deceptive act; as, to pull *a fast one*. [Slang.]

fȧst′back, *n.* an automobile body whose roof forms an unbroken curve from windshield to rear bumper.

fȧst dāy, a religious holy day, etc. on which fasting is observed.

fȧs′ten (fȧs′n), *v.t.*; fastened, *pt., pp.*; fastening, *ppr.* [ME. *fastnen, fastnien*; AS. *fæstnian*, to fasten, to confirm, from *fæst*, fast, fixed.]

1. to attach; join; connect.
2. to make fast or secure, as by locking, shutting, buttoning, etc.; to fix firmly in place.
3. to hold, fix, or direct (the attention, gaze, etc.) steadily (*on*).
4. to cause to be connected or attributed; to impute; as, he *fastened* the crime on me.
5. to settle; to clinch; to confirm; as, to *fasten* a bargain.
6. to lay on with strength. [Obs.]

Could he *fasten* a blow, or make a thrust,
when not suffered to approach?
—Dryden.

Syn.—affix, attach, fix, clinch, stick, unite.

fȧs′ten, *v.i.* 1. to become attached or joined.
2. to take hold; cling.

The leech will hardly *fasten* on a fish.
—Brown.

fȧs′ten·ẽr, *n.* one who or that which makes fast or firm.

fȧs′ten·ing, *n.* [ME. *fastnyng*, confirmation, a fastness; AS. *fæstenung*, a fastening.]

1. the act or way of making something fast, or secure.
2. anything that binds and makes fast, or is intended for that purpose; bolt, clasp, hook, lock, button, etc.

fȧst′ẽr, *n.* one who abstains from food.

fȧst-fọọd′, *a.* designating a business, as a hamburger stand, that offers food prepared and served quickly.

fȧst′-hand″ed, *a.* covetous; close-fisted; avaricious. [Obs.]

fas′tī, *n.pl.* [L., from *fastus*, legal, lawful; *fastus dies*, a day on which judgment could be pronounced, from *fas*, divine law, from *fari* to speak.]

1. the Roman calendar, which gave the days for festivals, anniversaries, etc., corresponding to a modern almanac.
2. records or registers of important events.

fas·tid·i·os′i·ty, *n.* fastidiousness. [Rare.]

fas·tid′i·ous, *a.* [L. *fastidiosus*, disdainful, scornful, that feels disgust, from *fastidium*, a loathing, disgust, from *fastus*, disdain, haughtiness, contempt.]

1. difficult to please; rejecting what is common; very critical; suited with difficulty; as, a *fastidious* appetite.
2. daintily refined; easily disgusted.
3. disgusting; loathsome. [Obs.]

Syn.—squeamish, hypercritical, overnice, overparticular, punctilious.—*Fastidious* is applied to one whose taste or feelings are offended by trifling defects or errors, *squeamish* to one who is extremely sensitive to what is unpleasant.

fas·tid′i·ous·ly, *adv.* in a fastidious manner.

fas·tid′i·ous·ness, *n.* the quality of being fastidious.

fas·tig′i·ȧ, *n.* pl. of *fastigium*.

fas·tig′i·āte, fas·tig′i·ā·ted, *a.* [L. *fastigatus*, sloping to a point; *fastigium*, a slope, roof.]

1. narrowing toward the summit, as a sloping roof; pointed.
2. in botany, tapering to a narrow point like a pyramid; having parallel and erect branches, as the Lombardy poplar.
3. in zoology, tapering gradually to an apex; forming a conical bundle.

fas·tig′i·āte·ly, *adv.* in a fastigiate manner.

fas·tig′i·um, *n.*; *pl.* **fas·tig′i·ȧ,** [L.]

1. the summit, apex, or ridge of a house or pediment.
2. the most severe point in an illness.

fȧst′ing dāy, a fast day.

fȧst′ish, *a.* rather fast.

fȧst′ly, *adv.* 1. quickly; rapidly. [Obs.]
2. firmly; surely. [Obs.]

fȧst′ness, *n.* [ME. *fastnesse*, firmness, certainty, a stronghold; AS. *fæstnes*, firmness, a stronghold, from *fæst*, firm, fast, fixed.]

1. the quality or state of being fast.
2. strength; security. [Obs.]

The places of *fastness* are laid open.
—Davies.

3. a stronghold; a fortress or fort; a secure place; as, the enemy retired to their *fastnesses*.
4. closeness; conciseness of style. [Obs.]

fȧst-tạlk′, *v.t.* to persuade with fast, smooth, convincing, but often deceitful talk. [Colloq.]

fȧst tīme, same as *daylight-saving time*.

fas·tū·os′i·ty, *n.* the quality of being fastuous or haughty; ostentation. [Rare.]

fas′tū·ous, *a.* proud; haughty; disdainful.

fas′tū·ous·ly, *adv.* in a fastuous manner.

fat, *a.*; *comp.* fatter; *superl.* fattest, [ME. *fat, fet*; AS. *fæl, fætt*, fat.]

1. (a) containing or full of fat; oily; greasy; (b) having much fat in relation to lean: said of meat.
2. (a) fleshy; plump; (b) too plump; obese.
3. thick, broad.
4. containing something valuable in great quantity; fertile; productive; as, *fat* land.
5. profitable; lucrative; as, a *fat* job.
6. supplied plentifully; ample.
7. dull; stupid; unteachable.

There is little or no sense in the *fat* parts of
any creature, hence the ancients said of
any dull fellow that he had a *fat* wit.
—Johnson.

8. prosperous; affluent.

a fat chance; very little or no chance. [Slang.]

a fat lot; very little or nothing. [Slang.]

Syn.—corpulent, fleshy, pursy, rich, luxuriant, portly, stout, fertile, unctuous, obese.

fat, *n.* 1. an oily, yellow or white substance deposited in the cells of the adipose or cellular membrane, under the skin and in various other parts of animal bodies, and also in vegetable matter, especially in the seeds of certain plants.
2. either animal or vegetable fat used in cookery.
3. fleshiness; plumpness; corpulence.
4. the best or richest part; as, to live on the *fat* of the land.

Abel brought of the *fat* of his flock.
—Gen. iv. 4.

5. work that pays well.
6. in chemistry, a class of glyceryl esters of fatty acids, insoluble in water.

the fat is in the fire; the thing has happened and cannot be prevented.

the fat of the land; the best things obtainable; great luxury.

to chew the fat; to talk together; to chat. [Slang.]

fat, *v.t.* and *v.i.*; fatted, *pt., pp.*; fatting, *ppr.* to make or become fat.

fat, *n.* [ME. *fat, fet*; AS. *fæt*, a vat.]

1. a large tub, cistern, or vessel; a vat. [Obs.]

The *fats* shall overflow with wine and oil.
—Joel ii. 24.

2. an old indefinite measure of capacity, differing for different commodities; thus, a *fat* of grain was a quarter, or eight bushels. [Obs.]

fā′tăl, *a.* [ME. *fatal*; OFr. *fatal*; L. *fatalis*, pertaining to fate, fatal, from *fatum*, fate.]

1. proceeding from fate or destiny; necessary; inevitable. [Obs.]

These things are *fatal* and necessary.
—Tillotson.

2. fateful; decisive; as, the *fatal* day arrived.
3. resulting in death; mortal; as, a *fatal* wound, a *fatal* disease.
4. destructive; ruinous; disastrous.
5. influencing or determining destiny; concerned with fate.

Our acts our angels are, or good or ill,
Our *fatal* shadows that walk by us still.
—Fletcher.

fā′tăl·ism, *n.* [Fr. *fatalisme*, from L. *fatalis*, fatal.]

1. the doctrine that all things are determined by fate, or take place by inevitable necessity.
2. a disposition to accept everything as inevitable and predetermined by fate.

fā′tăl·ist, *n.* one who believes in fatalism; one who maintains that all things happen by inevitable necessity.

fā·tăl·is′tiç, *a.* of, based on, or characterized by fatalism.

fā·tăl·is′ti·căl·ly, *adv.* in a fatalistic manner.

fā·tal′i·ty, *n.*; *pl.* **fā·tal′i·ties,** [Fr. *fatalité*; LL. *fatalitas*, fatal necessity, fatality, from L. *fatalis*, fatal.]

1. the agency of fate or necessity.
2. a fixed, unalterable course of things, independent of any controlling cause; an invincible necessity existing in things themselves.
3. the condition of being fated; subjection to fate.
4. tendency to destruction or danger, or to some critical or hazardous event; an inevitable liability to disaster.
5. a fatal quality; deadliness; deadly effect; as, the *fatality* of any specified disease.
6. an event resulting in death; death; as, accidents in the home cause many *fatalities*.

fā′tăl·ly, *adv.* 1. by decree of fate or destiny; by inevitable necessity or predetermination.
2. mortally; destructively; in death or ruin; as, the encounter ended *fatally*.

fā′tăl·ness, *n.* the quality of being fatal; fatality.

Fä′tȧ Mor·gä′nȧ, [It., lit., fairy Morgan, after Anglo-Fr. *Morgan-le-Fey*.]

1. Morgan le Fay, a fairy in some medieval legends and romances.
2. [f– m–] a mirage, especially one which has been seen in the Strait of Messina, between the coasts of Sicily and Calabria: so called because formerly supposed to be the work of Morgan le Fay.

fat′back, *n.* 1. fat from the back of a hog, usually dried and salted in strips.
2. the menhaden, *Brevoortia tyrannus*.

fat′bīrd, *n.* 1. the guacharo or oilbird, *Steatornis caripensis*. [Dial.]
2. the pectoral sandpiper, *Erolia melanotos* [Dial.]

fat′-brāined, *a.* dull of apprehension.

fat cat, a wealthy, influential person; especially, a heavy contributor to a political party or campaign. [Slang.]

fāte, *n.* [ME. *fate*, fate; L. *fatum*, a prophetic declaration, oracle, from *fatus*, pp. of *fari*, to speak.]

1. the power supposed to determine the outcome of events before they occur; hence, inevitable necessity; destiny depending on a superior cause, and uncontrollable; as, according to the Stoics, every event is determined by *fate*.

Necessity or chance
Approach not me; and what I will is *fate*.
—Milton.

2. something inevitable, supposedly determined by this power.
3. what happens or has happened to a per-

son; lot; fortune; as, it was his *fate* to be a bachelor.
4. final outcome.
5. death; destruction; doom; as, the *fate* of the enterprise was sealed with that first failure.
Yet still he chose the longest way to *fate*.
—Dryden.
6. cause of death. [Rare and Poet.]
With full force his deadly bow he bent,
And feathered *fates* among the mules and sumpters sent. —Dryden.
the Fates; in Greek and Roman mythology, the three goddesses who control human destiny and life: the first (Clotho) spins the thread of life, the second (Lachesis) determines its length, and the third (Atropos) cuts it off.
Syn.—destiny, doom, lot, fortune, death, destruction.

fāte, *v.t.*; fated, *pt., pp.*; fating, *ppr.* to destine. [Obs. except in passive.]

fāt'ed, *a.* 1. decreed by fate; destined; as, he was *fated* to meet a violent end.
Her awkward love indeed was oddly *fated*.
—Prior.
2. destined to destruction; doomed.
3. invested with the power of determining fates. [Obs.]
The *fated* sky
Gives us free scope. —Shak.

fāte'fụl, *a.* 1. revealing what is to come; prophetic.
2. having important consequences; significant; decisive.
3. controlled by or as if by fate.
4. bringing about death or destruction.
The *fateful* steel. —J. Barlow.

fāte'fụl·ly, *adv.* in a fateful manner.

fāte'fụl·ness, *n.* the state or quality of being fateful.

fat'head, *n.* 1. the blackhead or black-headed minnow, *Pimephales promelas*, having a short, round head.
2. a labroid fish, the redfish, *Semicossyphus* or *Pimelometopon pulcher*. It abounds on the coast of California.
3. a stupid person; a blockhead.

fat'head″ed, *a.* dull; heavy-witted; stupid.

fä'thẽr, *n.* [ME. *fader, fadir*; AS. *fæder*; compare G. *vater*, O.H.G. *fatar*, L. *pater*, Gr. *patēr*, Sans. *pitar*, father.]
1. he who begets a child; the nearest male ancestor; a male parent.
The *father* of a fool hath no joy.
—Prov. xvii. 21.
2. a person regarded as a male parent; a protector.
3. [*usually in pl.*] a forefather or forebear; a lineal male ancestor; especially, the progenitor of a race or family; as, Abraham was the *father* of the Israelites.
David slept with his *fathers*.
—1 Kings ii. 10.
4. anyone deserving respect or reverence because of age, position, etc.
5. the oldest member of any profession or body; as, the *father* of the bar.
6. a senator of ancient Rome.
7. [*pl.*] the leaders of a city, assembly, etc.
8. [*often* F–] any of the early Christian religious writers considered reliable authorities on the doctrines and teachings of the Church.
9. in the Roman Catholic Church, (a) any priest; (b) his title.
10. [F–] the Supreme Being; God; in theology, the first person in the Trinity.
Go, ye, therefore, and teach all nations, baptizing them in the name of the *Father*, and of the Son, and of the Holy Spirit.
—Matt. xxviii. 19.
11. one who creates, invents, makes, originates, or composes anything; the author, former, or contriver; a founder, director, or instructor; the first to practice any art; as, Homer is the *father* of epic poetry; Gutenberg is the *father* of printing; the pilgrim *fathers*.
father confessor; (a) a priest who listens to confessions, as in the Roman Catholic Church; (b) a person to whom people habitually tell private matters.
Father in God; a title of a bishop.
Father of His Country; George Washington.
Father of Lies; Satan; the devil.
Father of Medicine; Hippocrates (460?–377? B.C.), a Greek physician.
Father of Waters; the Mississippi River: translation of the Indian name.
Father's Day; the third Sunday in June, a day set aside to honor fathers.
Fathers of the Church; the writers, teachers, and theologians who succeeded the Apostles from the second to the sixth century, such as St. Augustine, St. Athanasius, etc.
Father Time; time personified as a very old man carrying a scythe and an hourglass.
Holy Father; in the Roman Catholic Church, the Pope.
natural father; the father of an illegitimate child.
spiritual father; a father confessor; also, loosely, a religious teacher or one who brings about another's conversion.
to be gathered to one's fathers; to die.

fä″thẽr, *v.t.*; fathered, *pt., pp.*; fathering, *ppr.*
1. to beget; to become the father of.
Cowards *father* cowards, and base things sire base. —Shak.
2. to adopt; to act as a father to; to protect as a father.
3. to originate; found; create; invent; make.
4. to adopt as one's own; to profess or acknowledge oneself to be the author of or responsible for.
Men of wit
Often *fathered* what he writ. —Swift.
5. to ascribe or charge to one as his offspring or production: with *on* or *upon*.
Come, *father* not your lies *upon* me, widow.
—Middleton.

fä'thẽr·hood, *n.* [ME. *fadirhode*, from AS. *fæder*, father, and *had*, state, condition.] the state of being a father; paternity.

fä'thẽr-in-lạw, *n.*; *pl.* **fä'thẽrṣ-in-lạw,** 1. the father of one's husband or wife.
2. a stepfather. [Rare.]

fä'thẽr·land, *n.* [often after G. *vaterland*, fatherland.] one's native land or, sometimes, the land of one's fathers or ancestors.

fä'thẽr-lash″ẽr, *n.* a salt-water fish, *Cottus bubalis*, with a large head and sharp spines.

fä'thẽr·less, *a.* [ME. *faderles*; AS. *fæderleas*, fatherless; *fæder*, father, and *-leas*, -less.]
1. without a living father, or lacking a father's protection; as, a *fatherless* child.
2. not knowing who one's father is.
3. without a known author. [Obs.]

fä'thẽr·less·ness, *n.* the state of being without a father.

fä'thẽr·li·ness, *n.* the quality of being a father; parental kindness, care, and tenderness.

fä″thẽr lọng'legṣ, same as *daddy longlegs*.

fä'thẽr·ly, *a.* [AS. *fæder*, father, and *-lic*, like.]
1. like a kind father in affection and care; tender; paternal; protecting; careful.
2. pertaining or belonging to a father.

fä'thẽr·ly, *adv.* in the manner of a father. [Archaic.]

fä'thẽr·ship, *n.* the state of being a father.

fath'ŏm, *n.*; *pl.* **fath'ŏmṣ** or **fath'ŏm,** [ME. *fathem*, a measure of length about six feet; AS. *fæthm*, the space reached by the arms extended, a measure of length.]
1. a measure of length equal to six feet, used mainly in measuring the depth of water or the length of a rope or cable.
2. mental depth; intellectual reach or scope; penetration; as, a man of *fathom*. [Rare.]

fath'ŏm, *v.t.*; fathomed, *pt., pp.*; fathoming, *ppr.* [ME. *fadomen, fadmen*, to embrace, encompass, from AS. *fæthmian*, to clasp, embrace.]
1. to encompass with the arms extended. [Obs.]
2. to find the bottom or extent of; to sound; to measure the depth of.
3. to reach or penetrate with the mind; to get to the bottom of; to master; to comprehend thoroughly.

fath'ŏm·à·ble, *a.* capable of being fathomed.

fath'ŏm·ẽr, *n.* one who or that which fathoms.

fath'ŏm·less, *a.* 1. having a depth so great that no bottom can be measured; bottomless.
Seas as *fathomless* as wide. —Cowper.
2. incapable of being penetrated by the mind; incomprehensible.

fȧ·tid'iç, fȧ·tid'iç·ăl, *a.* [L. *fatidicus*, prophesying; *fatum*, fate, and *dicere*, to say, speak.] having power to foretell future events; prophetic.
So that the *fatidical* fury spreads wider and wider till at last even Saul must join in it.
—Carlyle.

fȧ·tid'iç·ăl·ly, *adv.* in a fatidic manner.

fȧ·tif'ẽr·ous, *a.* [L. *fatifer*, that brings death; *fatum*, fate, and *ferre*, to bring.] deadly; mortal; destructive. [Rare.]

fat'i·gȧ·ble, *a.* easily fatigued.

fat'i·gāte, *v.t.* to fatigue; to tire. [Obs.]

fat'i·gāte, *a.* fatigued; tired. [Obs.]

fat·i·gā'tion, *n.* fatigue; weariness. [Obs.]

fȧ·tīgue' (-tēg'), *n.* [Fr. *fatigue*, from *fatiguer*; L. *fatigare*, to weary, fatigue.]
1. weariness; physical or mental exhaustion.
2. the cause of weariness; labor; toil; as, the *fatigues* of war.
3. fatigue duty; as, a party of men on *fatigue*.
4. [*pl.*] fatigue clothes.
5. in mechanics, a weakening in metal, wood, etc. caused by repeated or continued vibrations and strains.
6. in physiology, the decreased ability of an organism or one of its parts to function because of prolonged exertion, which causes a toxic decomposition in the muscle and nerve cells.
Syn.—lassitude, weariness, exhaustion, languor, enervation.

fȧ·tīgue', *v.t.*; fatigued, *pt., pp.*; fatiguing, *ppr.* [Fr. *fatiguer*; L. *fatigare*, to weary, tire, fatigue.]
1. to tire out; to weary with labor or any bodily or mental exertion; to harass with toil; to exhaust the strength of.
2. to weaken by continued use.

fȧ·tīgue' çạll, a signal, as a bugle call or drumbeat, summoning soldiers to fatigue duty.

fȧ·tīgue' çlōtheṣ, fȧ·tīgue' dress, clothing of denim or twill worn in doing fatigue duty.

fȧ·tīgue' dū'ty, any labor, other than drill or instruction, assigned to soldiers in training.

fȧ·tīgue' pär'ty, a body of soldiers detailed for fatigue duty.

fȧ·til'ō·quent, *a.* [L. *fatiloquus*, prophesying.] prophetic; prophesying. [Rare.]

Fat'i·mȧ, *n.* Bluebeard's last wife.

Fat'i·mid, *a.* 1. descended from Mohammed's daughter, Fatima.
2. of or characteristic of the Fatimid dynasty or the period during which it was in power.

Fat'i·mid, *n.* a Moslem ruler descended from Fatima and the Caliph Ali: the Fatimids formed a dynasty that ruled over Egyptian Islam and parts of northern Africa (909–1171).

Fat'i·mīte, Fat'i·mīde, *a.* and *n.* [Ar. *Fatimah*, Fatima.] Fatimid.

fȧ·tis'cence, *n.* [L. *fatiscens* (*-entis*), ppr. of *fatiscere*, to open in chinks, gape.] a gaping or opening; a state of being chinky. [Rare.]

fȧ·tis'cent, *a.* opening in chinks; gaping. [Rare.]

fat'-kid″neyed (-nid), *a.* fat; gross: used in contempt. [Rare.]
Peace, ye *fat-kidneyed* rascal! What a brawling dost thou keep! —Shak.

fat'ling, *n.* a lamb, kid, or other young animal, fattened for slaughter.
David sacrificed oxen and *fatlings*.
—2 Sam. vi. 13.

fat'ly, *adv.* grossly; greasily. [Obs.]

fat'ness, *n.* [ME. *fatnes*; AS. *fætnes, fætness*; *fæt*, fat, and *-nes, -ness*.]
1. the quality of being fat; corpulency; fullness of flesh.
Their eyes stand out with *fatness*.
—Ps. lxxiii. 7.
2. unctuousness; sliminess: applied to earth; hence, richness; fertility; fruitfulness.
God give thee of the *fatness* of the earth, and plenty of corn and wine.
—Gen. xxvii. 28.
3. that which gives fertility. [Archaic.]
The clouds dropped *fatness*. —Philips.

fat'sō, *n.* a fat person. [Slang.]

fat'-sol″ū·ble, *a.* soluble in fats.

fat'ten, *v.t.*; fattened, *pt., pp.*; fattening, *ppr.* [AS. *gefætnian*, to fatten.]
1. to make fat, or plump, as by feeding.
2. to make (land) fertile and fruitful.
3. to make richer, larger, etc.; as, he *fattened* his purse by robbing the poor.

fat'ten, *v.i.* to become fat or corpulent; to grow plump, thick, or fleshy.
And villains *fatten* with the brave man's labor. —Otway.

fat'ten·ẽr, *n.* one who or that which fattens; that which gives fatness, richness, or fertility.

fat'ti·ness, *n.* the quality of being fatty; grossness; greasiness.

fat'tish, *a.* somewhat fat.

fat'ty, *a.*; *comp.* fattier; *superl.* fattiest, 1. composed of, containing, or covered with fat.
2. resembling or having the qualities of fat; greasy; as, a *fatty* substance.
fatty acid; any of a series of saturated organic acids having the general formula $C_nH_{2n}O_2$: some occur as glyceryl esters in natural fats.
fatty degeneration; in pathology, the abnormal occurrence of fat particles in tissue cells.

fatty series; a series of paraffin hydrocarbons derived from methane.
fatty tissue; same as *adipose tissue*.
fat'ty, *n.* a fat person. [Colloq.]
fȧ·tū'i·tous, *a.* [L. *fatuitas*, foolishness.] stupid; foolish; fatuous.
fȧ·tū'i·ty, *n.* [L. *fatuitas*, foolishness, from *fatuus*, foolish.]
1. stupidity, especially complacent stupidity; foolishness; folly.
2. something fatuous.
3. idiocy or imbecility. [Rare.]
fat'ū·ous, *a.* [L. *fatuus*, foolish.]
1. complacently stupid or inane; silly; foolish.
2. unreal; illusory. [Rare.]
Thence *fatuous* fires and meteors take their birth. —Denham.
fat'vȧ, fat'vȧh, *n.* same as *fetwa*.
fat'-wit''ted, *a.* dull; stupid.
fau'bourg (fō'boorg), *n.* [Fr., from OFr. *forbourg, forsbourg*, lit., out of town, a suburb.] a suburb or district within a city; as, the *Faubourg* St. Germain of Paris.
fau'căl, *a.* [L. *fauces*, the throat.] pertaining to or produced in the fauces: said of certain vocal sounds.
fau'cēs, *n.pl.* [L., the throat, the gullet.]
1. the passage leading from the back of the mouth into the pharynx.
2. the mouth or opening of the tube of a monopetalous corolla.
3. that portion of the cavity of the first chamber of a shell which may be seen by looking through the aperture.
fau'cet, *n.* [ME. *fauscet*, prob. from OFr. *faulser*, to make a breach in, to falsify, from L. *falsus*, false, pp. of *fallere*, to deceive.] a device with a hand-operated valve for regulating the flow of a liquid from a pipe, barrel, etc.: also called *cock, tap*.
fau'chärd (fō'), *n.* [OFr. *fauchard, faussard*, from *faux*, a scythe, from L. *falx*, a sickle.] a medieval weapon composed of a blade shaped like a scythe, attached to a long handle.
fau'ciăl (-shăl), *a.* relating to the fauces; pharyngeal; faucal.
fau·ci'tis, *n.* [L., from *fauces*, throat.] an inflamed condition of the fauces.
faugh (fạ), *interj.* an exclamation of contempt, disgust, etc.: also spelled *foh*.
fauld, *n.* [Scot.] the working arch or tymp-arch situated above the dam of a blast furnace.
fault, *n.* [ME. *faut, faute*; OFr. *faute, faulte*, a lack, fault, from L. *fallere*, to deceive.]
1. failure to have or do what is required; default; lack. [Obs.]
I could tell to thee, as to one it pleases me, for *fault* of a better, to call my friend. —Shak.
2. something that mars the appearance, character, structure, etc.; a blemish; a flaw; an imperfection.
As patches set upon a little breach,
Discredit more in hiding of the *fault*. —Shak.
3. an error; a deviation from propriety; a slight offense; a neglect of duty; a misdeed.
I do remember my *faults* this day. —Gen. xli. 9.
4. responsibility for something wrong; blame; as, it was her *fault* that they were delayed.
5. in geology, a break in rock strata or veins that causes a section to become dislocated along the line of fracture.

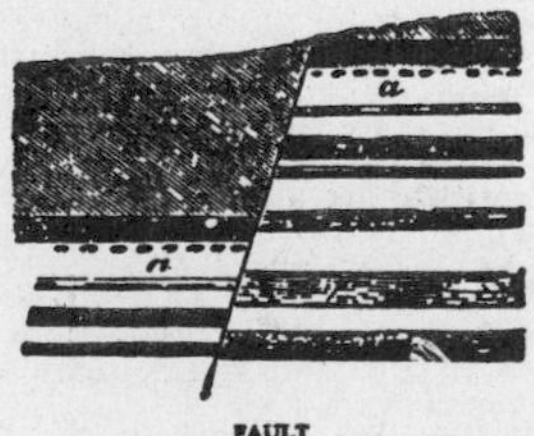

FAULT

6. in hunting, a lost scent; a missing or losing of the trail: said of sporting dogs.
7. in tennis, squash, etc., (a) failure to serve or drive the ball into the proper court; (b) a served ball that does not land in the proper court.
8. in electricity, a defect or point of defect in a circuit which prevents the current from following the intended course.
at fault; (a) in the wrong; worthy of blame; (b) unable to find the scent, as hunting dogs; hence, not knowing what to do; puzzled; thrown off the track.
in fault; guilty of error; in the wrong; deserving blame.
to a fault; too much; excessively.
to find fault; to express blame; to complain; to censure.
to find fault with; to be dissatisfied with; object to; as, *to find fault with* one's friend.
Syn.—blemish, defect, imperfection, flaw, delinquency, misdeed, failing, omission, foible, misdemeanor, weakness.
fault, *v.t.*; faulted, *pt., pp.*; faulting, *ppr.* 1. to charge with a fault; to blame. [Rare.]
2. to lack; to need; to want. [Obs.]
3. in geology, to cause a fault in; as, undulations *faulted* the strata.
fault, *v.i.* 1. to fail; to be wrong; to blunder. [Archaic.]
2. in geology, to develop a fault.
fault block, in geology, a body of rock bounded by faults.
fault'ẽr, *n.* an offender; one who commits a fault. [Obs.]
fault'fīnd''ẽr, *n.* 1. one given to finding fault.
2. in electricity, a device for locating faults.
fault'fīnd''ing, *a.* calling attention to faults; complaining.
fault'fīnd''ing, *n.* the act of pointing out faults; carping criticism.
fault'fụl, *a.* full of faults or sins.
fault'i·ly, *adv.* in a faulty manner.
fault'i·ness, *n.* the quality or condition of being faulty.
fault'ing, *n.* in geology, the act or process of producing faults.
fault'less, *a.* without fault; not defective or imperfect; free from blemish; free from vice; perfect.
Syn.—perfect, blameless, stainless, correct, spotless.
fault'less·ly, *adv.* in a faultless manner.
fault'less·ness, *n.* freedom from faults or defects.
fault līne, in geology, the line of intersection between a fault and another surface.
fault lō'căl·ī·zẽr, in electricity, a piece of equipment used to find breaks in a circuit.
fault rock, the crushed, broken rock found in a fault.
faults'man, *n.* one who corrects and clears up faults or complaints; an adjustor.
fault ter'răce, a topographical condition caused by a nearly equal movement downhill of two parallel faults.
fault vent, a kind of volcanic mouth situated on a fault.
fault'y, *a.*; *comp.* faultier; *superl.* faultiest, [ME. *fauty, fawty*; OFr. *fautif*, faulty, from *faute*, fault.]
1. containing faults, blemishes, or defects; defective; imperfect; as, a *faulty* composition; a *faulty* plan or design; a *faulty* picture.
2. guilty of error; blamable; worthy of censure. [Obs.]
Syn.—incomplete, culpable, blameworthy, reprehensible, censurable.
faun, *n.* [ME. *faun*; L. *Faunus*, Faunus, from *favere*, to be propitious.] in Roman mythology, any of a class of rural deities, differing little from satyrs. They are usually represented as being principally human, but with a short goat's tail, pointed ears, projecting horns, and, sometimes, cloven feet.
Rough satyrs danc'd, and *fauns* with cloven heel
From the glad sound would not be absent long. —Milton.

FAUN

fau'nȧ, *n.*; *pl.* **fau'nȧs, fau'nae,** [L. *Fauna*, a Roman goddess, the sister of Faunus.]
1. the animals or animal life of any stated latitude, region, or age; as, the American *fauna*.
2. a treatise on such animals.
fau'năl, *a.* pertaining to fauna or faunas.
fau'nist, *n.* one who classifies and describes faunas; a naturalist.
fau·nis'tiç, fau·nis'tiç·ăl, *a.* pertaining to fauna or faunas; faunal.
fau·nō·log'iç·ăl, *a.* pertaining to faunology.
fau·nol'ō·gy, *n.* [*fauna*, and Gr. *logos*, a description.] zoogeography.
Fau'nus, *n.* [L.] in Roman mythology, a god of nature, the patron of farming and animals, and a giver of oracles: identified with the Greek Pan.
fau'sen, *n.* a kind of eel. [Obs.]
Faust (foust), *n.* [G. (Dr. Johann Faust), from L. *faustus*, fortunate.] the hero of several medieval legends, an old philosopher who sells his soul to the devil in exchange for knowledge and power: the theme of several literary and operatic works, notably a play by Marlowe, a two-part dramatic poem written by Goethe between 1773 and 1831, and an opera by Gounod based on Goethe's poem.
Faus'tus (fọs'), *n.* Faust: Latin form of the name, used by Marlowe in his poetic drama *The Tragical History of Doctor Faustus* (1593).
faute de mieux' (fōt dē myē'), [Fr.] for want of (something) better.
fau·teuil' (fō-tē'y), *n.* [Fr., from OFr. *faudestueil*; LL. *faldestolium, faldistolium*; O.H.G. *faltstuol*, lit., a folding stool, from *faldan*, to fold, and *stuol*, a chair, seat.]
1. an armchair; an easy chair.
2. the chair of a president or presiding officer.
3. a seat in the French Academy.
fau'tŏr, *n.* a favorer; a patron; one who gives countenance or support. [Obs.]
fau'tress, *n.* a patroness. [Obs.]
fau·vette' (fō-vet'), *n.* [Fr., from *fauve*, fawn-colored.] any of various warblers, as the beccafico. [Archaic.]
fau'vism (fō'vizm), *n.* [Fr. *fauvisme*, from *fauve*, wild beast, orig. adj., fawn-colored.] [*often* F-] a French expressionist movement in painting at the beginning of the twentieth century, involving Matisse, Derain, etc.: it was characterized by bold distortion of form and the use of strong, pure color.
faux päs (fō pä'), [Fr. from *faux*, false, and *pas*, a step.] a social blunder; a tactless act or remark; a breach of good manners.
fȧ'vȧ bēan, [It. *fava*, bean; L. *faba*; and *bean*.] same as *broad bean*.
fa·vag'i·nous, *a.* same as *faveolate*.
fȧ·vel'ȧ, *n.* [Port.] a slum.
fȧ·vel'lȧ, *n.*; *pl.* **fȧ·vel'lae,** [L., from *favus*, a honeycomb.] in botany, a cluster of spores resembling a cystocarp, but formed externally and covered by a gelatinous envelope, as in certain florideous algae.
fav·el·lid'i·um, *n.*; *pl.* **fav·el·lid'i·ȧ,** [L., from *favus*, a honeycomb, and Gr. *eidos*, form, appearance.] in botany, a favella in the frond of florideous algae.
fȧ·vel'loid, *a.* resembling a favella.
fȧ·vē'ō·lāte, *a.* [L. *favus*, a honeycomb.] having cells resembling those of a honeycomb; alveolate.
fȧ·vē'ō·lus, *n.*; *pl.* **fȧ·vē'ō·lī,** [L., from *favus*, a honeycomb.] a small cell resembling a honeycomb.
fȧ·vis'sȧ, *n.*; *pl.* **fȧ·vis'sae,** [L.] in ancient Rome, a crypt; a vault.
fȧ·vō'ni·ăn, *a.* [L. *Favonius*, the west wind, from *favere*, to favor.] pertaining to the west wind; hence, mild; calm; gentle; propitious.
fā'vŏr, *n.* [ME. *favour*; OFr. *favour*; L. *favor*, good will, favor, from *favere*, to be well disposed, to favor.]
1. kind regard; approval; liking; friendly disposition; good will.
His dreadful navy; and his lovely mind,
Gave him the fear and *favor* of mankind. —Waller.
2. help; assistance; disposition to aid, befriend, support, promote, or justify.
3. a kind act or office; kindness done or granted; any act of generosity, good will, etc.; as, he asked a *favor* of her.
4. lenity; mildness or mitigation of punishment.
5. leave; a yielding or concession to another; permission.
But, with your *favor*, I will treat it here. —Dryden.
6. too kind indulgence; unfair partiality.

7. a small gift or present; something bestowed as an evidence of good will; originally, a token of love.

8. a letter; note; communication; as, your *favor* of yesterday's date is at hand.

9. [*pl.*] consent (of a woman) to sexual intimacy; as, Catherine the Great granted her *favors* to many.

10. attractiveness; charm. [Obs.]

challenge to the favor; in law, the challenge of a juror on account of some supposed partiality, by reason of favor or malice, interest, connection, or acquaintance.

in favor; favored; liked.

in favor of; (a) approving; supporting; endorsing; (b) to the advantage of; (c) payable to: said of checks, drafts, etc.

in one's favor; to one's advantage or credit.

out of favor; not favored; not liked.

to find favor; to be regarded with favor; be pleasing to.

fā′vŏr, *v.t.*; favored, *pt.*, *pp.*; favoring, *ppr.* [ME. *favoren*; OFr. *favorer*, to favor, from L. *favor*, a favor, from *favere*, to be well disposed to, to favor.]

1. to regard with kindness; to countenance; to befriend; to encourage.

The lords *favor* thee not. —1 Sam. xxix. 6.

2. to be indulgent or too indulgent toward; be partial to; prefer unfairly.

3. to support; advocate; be for; endorse.

4. to afford advantages for success; to make easier; to help; to assist; to facilitate; as, the darkness *favored* his approach.

5. to do a kindness for.

6. to resemble in features; as, the child *favors* his father.

7. to use gently; to spare; as, the boxer *favored* his injured hand.

fā′vŏr·ȧ·ble, *a.* [ME. *favorable*; OFr. *favorable*; L. *favorabilis*, favored, in favor, from *favere*, to favor.]

1. kind; propitious; friendly; approving.

Lend *favorable* ear to our requests.—Shak.

2. tending to favor or promote; as, conditions *favorable* to population.

3. convenient; advantageous; helpful; as, *favorable* weather.

4. beautiful; well-favored. [Obs.]

fā′vŏr·ȧ·ble·ness, *n.* the state or quality of being favorable.

fā′vŏr·ȧ·bly, *adv.* in a favorable manner.

fā′vŏred, *a.* 1. having a certain appearance; having (specified) features: often used in hyphenated compounds; as, ill-*favored*, well-*favored*, etc.

2. regarded or treated with favor; specifically, (a) provided with advantages; talented; gifted; (b) specially privileged.

fā′vŏred·ly, *adv.* in a favored manner.

fā′vŏred·ness, *n.* the state of being favored.

fā′vŏr·ẽr, *n.* one who or that which favors; one who assists or promotes.

fā′vŏr·ess, *n.* a woman who favors. [Rare.]

fā′vŏr·ing·ly, *adv.* in a manner which shows favor.

fā′vŏr·ite, *n.* [MFr. *favorit*; It. *favorito*, masc., *favorita*, f., a favorite, from *favorire*, to favor; L. *favor*, a favor.]

1. a person or thing regarded with special favor, preference, or affection.

2. a person liked very much and granted special privileges by a king, high official, etc.

A *favorite* has no friend. —Gray.

3. a ringlet or small curl worn by women of the seventeenth and eighteenth centuries.

4. a competitor considered most likely to win.

fā′vŏr·ite, *a.* regarded with special kindness, affection, esteem, or preference; as, a *favorite* author.

favorite son; see under *son*.

fā′vŏr·it·iṣm, *n.* 1. the disposition to favor, aid, or promote the interest of a favorite, or of some person or persons; being unfairly partial.

2. the condition of being favorite.

fā′vŏr·less, *a.* 1. unfavored; not regarded with favor.

2. not favoring; unpropitious. [Obs.]

fa·vōse′, *a.* [L. *favus*, a honeycomb.]

1. honeycombed; resembling a section of a honeycomb.

2. pertaining to or affected with favus, the scalp disease.

fav′ō·sīte, *n.* a fossil of the genus *Favosites*.

Fav·ō·sī′tēṣ, *n.* [L., from *favus*, a honeycomb.] a genus of fossil corals common in Silurian, Devonian, and Carboniferous rocks: so called from the regular polygonal arrangement of their pore cells.

fā′voŭr, *n.* and *v.t.* favor: British spelling: derivatives are similarly spelled (*favoured*, *favourite*, etc.).

fā′vus, *n.* [L., honeycomb.]

1. crusted or honeycombed ringworm, an infectious skin disease chiefly attacking the scalp, characterized by itching and the formation of yellow incrustations about the hair follicles. It is produced by a fungous growth.

2. a tile or slab of marble cut into a hexagonal shape, so as to produce a honeycomb pattern in pavements.

fa̤we, *a.* pleased; gratified; delighted; fain. [Obs.]

fa̤wk′nẽr, *n.* a falconer. [Obs.]

fa̤wn, *n.* [ME. *fawn*, *fawne*; OFr. *faon*, *feon*, a fawn, a young deer, from L. *fetus*, pregnant, offspring.]

1. a young deer; a buck or doe less than one year old.

2. the young of any animal. [Obs.]

3. a pale, yellowish brown, the color of a fawn.

fa̤wn, *a.* having the color of a fawn.

fa̤wn, *v.i.* to bring forth a fawn.

fa̤wn, *v.i.*; fawned, *pt.*, *pp.*; fawning, *ppr.* [ME. *fawnen*, *faunen*, to be glad, receive with joy, fawn like a dog; AS. *fægenian*, to be glad, fawn, from *fægen*, fain, glad.]

1. to court favor or show affection, by frisking about, licking the hand, wagging the tail, etc.: said of a dog.

2. to wheedle; to flatter; to blandish; to act servilely; to cringe and bow to gain favor; as, the courtiers *fawned* on the king.

My love, forbear to *fawn* upon their frowns. —Shak.

fa̤wn, *n.* a servile cringe or bow; flattery. [Obs.]

fa̤wn′ẽr, *n.* one who fawns; one who cringes and flatters.

fa̤wn′ing·ly, *adv.* in a cringing, servile way; flatteringly.

faxed (faxt), *a.* [AS. *feax*, hair.] hairy. [Obs.]

fāy, *v.t.* and *v.i.*; fayed, *pt.*, *pp.*; faying, *ppr.* [ME. *feyen*; AS. *fegan*, to join.] in shipbuilding, to fit closely; to join; as, to *fay* timbers.

faying surface; the face of a metal plate, block, end of a timber, etc. which joins another surface so closely as to leave no space between them.

fāy, *n.* [ME. *fay*; OFr. *fee*, *feie*, *fae*, from L. *fata*, a fairy, *fatum*, fate.] a fairy; an elf.

fāy, *n.* [ME. *fay*, *fey*; OFr. *fei*, faith.] faith: used in oaths; as, by my *fay*. [Archaic.]

fāy, fe̤y, *v.t.* to rid of debris; to clean; to cleanse. [Brit. Dial.]

fāy′ăl·īte, *n.* [named from the island of Fayal.] a black or dark-colored mineral, sometimes iridescent, consisting mainly of silicate of iron.

fȧ·yence′, *n.* same as *faience*.

fāyleṣ, *n.* [perh. from *fail*.] an old game similar to backgammon.

fāze, *v.t.*; fazed, *pt.*, *pp.*; fazing, *ppr.* [form of *feeze*; perh. influenced by Scand.] to disconcert; to nonplus; to disturb; to agitate: also *feaze*, *feeze*. [Colloq.]

F çlef, the bass clef.

Fe, *ferrum*, [L.] in chemistry, iron.

fēa′ber″ry, *n.* the gooseberry. [Brit. Dial.]

fēague (fēg), *v.t.* [prob. from D. *vegen*, to sweep, strike.] to beat or scourge. [Obs.]

fēak, *n.* [AS. *feax*, hair.] a lock or ringlet of hair. [Obs.]

fēak, *v.t.* in falconry, to wipe the beak of (a hawk) after feeding.

fēak, *v.i.* to be uneasy; to be restless from anxiety; to fidget. [Brit. Dial.]

fē′ăl, *a.* [OFr. *feal*, *feyal*, *fedeil*, from L. *fidelis*, faithful, true, from *fides*, faith.] faithful; stanch; loyal; as, tenants swore to be *feal* to their lords.

fē′ăl·ty, *n.*; *pl.* **fē′ăl·tieṣ,** [OFr. *fealte*, *feelte*; L. *fidelitas*, faithfulness, fidelity, from *fidelis*, faithful, trustworthy, from *fides*, faith.]

1. fidelity owed by a tenant or vassal to his feudal lord.

2. fidelity; loyalty; faithfulness. [Archaic or Poet.]

fēar, *n.* [ME. *fere*, *feer*, fear; AS. *fær*, fear, terror.]

1. a feeling of anxiety and agitation caused by the presence or nearness of danger, evil, pain, etc.; timidity; dread; terror; fright; apprehension.

Fear is the passion of our nature which excites us to provide for our security, on the approach of evil. —Rogers.

2. the cause or object of fear; possibility; chance.

The principal *fear* was for the holy temple. —2 Mac. xv. 18.

3. reverence; awe; respectful dread.

4. a feeling of uneasiness; disquiet; anxiety; concern; as, I have a *fear* that you will be late.

for fear of; in order to avoid or prevent; lest.

Syn.—apprehension, misgiving, timidity, trepidation, anxiety, awe, dismay, consternation, alarm, dread, reverence.

fēar, *v.t.*; feared, *pt.*, *pp.*; fearing, *ppr.* [ME. *feren*, *færen*, to frighten, to be afraid; AS. *færan*, to terrify.]

1. to feel a painful apprehension of, as some impending evil; to be afraid of; to dread.

I will *fear* no evil, for thou art with me. —Ps. xxiii. 4.

2. to feel reverence for; to have a reverential awe of; to venerate.

3. to affright; to terrify; to drive away by fear. [Obs.]

4. to have fear for or be solicitous concerning. [Rare.]

5. to expect with misgiving; suspect; as, I *fear* the guests are late.

fēar, *v.i.* 1. to be in apprehension of evil; to be afraid; to feel fear.

2. to be uncertain; to doubt.

If you shall see Cordelia,
As *fear* not but you shall. —Shak.

fēar′ẽr, *n.* one who fears.

fēar′fu̇l, *a.* 1. affected by fear; feeling fear; afraid.

2. terrible; causing fear; frightful; dreadful; awful.

It is a *fearful* thing to fall into the hands of the living God. —Heb. x. 31.

3. showing or resulting from fear; as, a *fearful* look.

4. very bad, offensive, great, etc.; as, a *fearful* liar. [Colloq.]

Syn.—apprehensive, afraid, timid, timorous, pusillanimous, horrible, distressing, shocking, frightful, dreadful, awful, terrible.

fēar′fu̇l·ly, *adv.* 1. to a fearful extent.

2. terribly; dreadfully; in a fearful manner.

3. very much; very; as, he's *fearfully* busy. [Colloq.]

fēar′fu̇l·ness, *n.* 1. the state of being afraid; awe; dread.

2. the quality which causes alarm or fear; as, the *fearfulness* of the thought startled him.

fēar′less, *a.* free from fear; bold; courageous; intrepid; undaunted.

fēar′less·ly, *adv.* without fear; in a bold or courageous manner.

fēar′less·ness, *n.* freedom from fear; courage; boldness; intrepidity.

fēar′no̤ught, fēar′na̤ught (-na̤t), *n.* 1. a heavy woolen cloth used for coats; also, a coat fashioned from such cloth.

2. a person who feels no fear.

fēar′sŏme, *a.* 1. frightful; that induces fear.

2. timid; easy to frighten.

fēa′ṣănce, *n.* [Anglo-Fr. *fesance* (Fr. *faisance*), from *faire*, to do; L. *facere*, to do.] in law, the carrying into effect of a condition, obligation, etc.

fēa·ṣi·bil′i·ty, *n.*; *pl.* **fēa·ṣi·bil′i·tieṣ,** the quality of being feasible, or easy to do; practicability.

fēa′ṣi·ble, *a.* [OFr. *faisable*, that may be done, from *faire*, to make, do.]

1. that may be done, performed, executed, or effected; practicable; possible.

2. likely; reasonable; probable; as, a *feasible* story.

3. that may be used or dealt with successfully; as, land *feasible* for cultivation.

fēa′ṣi·ble·ness, *n.* feasibility; practicability.

fēa′ṣi·bly, *adv.* practicably.

fēast, *n.* [ME. *feeste*, *feste*, *fest*; OFr. *feste*, from L. *festa*, pl. of *festum*, a holiday, festival, feast.]

1. a celebration in commemoration of some great event, or in honor of some distinguished personage; festival, especially a religious festival.

2. a rich and elaborate meal; banquet.

3. anything that gives pleasure because of its abundance or richness; special treat.

immovable feast; a church festival occurring at a fixed date, as Christmas.

movable feast; a church festival which occurs on a specific day of the week succeeding a certain day of the month or phase of the moon. Easter is a movable feast upon which all other movable feasts depend.

Syn.—entertainment, banquet, treat, refreshment, carousal, wassail, festivity, festival, merrymaking, jollification.

fēast, *v.i.*; feasted, *pt., pp.*; feasting, *ppr.* 1. to eat a rich, elaborate meal; to have a feast.
2. to be highly gratified or delighted; as, he *feasted* on the music.

fēast, *v.t.* 1. to entertain at a banquet; to give a feast to; as, he was *feasted* by the king.
2. to delight; to give pleasure to.
Whose taste or smell can bless the *feasted* sense. —Dryden.

fēast dāy, a day for feasting; an ecclesiastical festival.

fēast'ẽr, *n.* one who feasts or gives a feast.

fēast'fụl, *a.* festive; joyful; sumptuous; luxurious.

fēast'fụl·ly, *adv.* festively; luxuriously.

Fēast of Lots, Purim, a Jewish feast.

fēat, *n.* [ME. *feet, fete, faite*; OFr. *fait*, a deed, fact, from L. *factum*, from *facere*, to make, do.] an extraordinary act of strength, skill, daring, etc.; a remarkable deed; an exploit.
Syn.—act, deed, action, exploit, exercise, execution, movement, attainment, performance, achievement.

fēat, *v.t.* to form; to fashion. [Obs.]

fēat, *a.* [ME. *fete, fet*, from OFr. *fait, feit*, made, pp. of *faire*, to do, make; L. *facere*.]
1. fitting; suitable.
2. neat.
3. skillful; adroit.
[Archaic in all senses.]

feath'ẽr (feth'), *n.* [ME. *fether*; AS. *fether*, a feather.]
1. any of the growths which cover the bodies of birds and make up a large part of the wing surface: it consists of a strong, round, horny shaft, partly hollow, from which light, soft, narrow barbs extend to form a thin, flat surface.
2. a feather or featherlike part fastened to the shaft of an arrow to help control its flight.
3. anything like or suggesting a feather or feathers in appearance, lightness, etc.; specifically, (a) a trifle; (b) a fin or rib projecting from a casting for stiffening it; (c) the wake left by submarine's periscope.

FEATHER
BB, barbs (with barbules); D, down; R, shaft; O, opening at end of shaft; P, pith

4. [*pl.*] (a) plumage; (b) attire; dress.
5. kind; nature; class; as, birds of a *feather*.
I am not of that *feather*, to shake off
My friend when he must need me.—Shak.
6. frame of mind; mood; humor; temper; vein.
7. the act of feathering an oar or propeller.
8. a slip, or rib, built longitudinally into a shaft or arbor to strengthen it.
9. a wedge-shaped key placed between two plugs in a hole in a stone, which, when driven into the hole, splits the stone.
10. a thin, wedge-shaped projection on the edge of a board which fits into a groove on the edge of another board; a tongue.
11. a tuft of long, kinky hair which grows on a horse and cannot be made to lie smooth.
12. the fringe of hair along the tail and the back of the legs of some dogs.
13. a plume, sometimes dyed or ornamented, to be worn on a hat.
14. birds collectively; as, fin, fur, and *feather*.
15. an irregular flaw in a precious stone.
a feather in one's cap; an achievement which gives distinction; an accomplishment worthy of pride.
in feather; feathered.
in fine (or *high* or *good*) *feather*; in very good humor, health, or form.
to show the white feather; to show cowardice: from the notion that a white feather in a rooster's tail is a sign of cowardice.

feath'ẽr (feth'), *v.t.*; feathered, *pt., pp.*; feathering, *ppr.* 1. to adorn, fit, cover, or fringe with or as with feathers.
2. to provide (an arrow, etc.) with a feather.
3. to tread, as a cock. [Obs.]
4. to join (boards) by inserting the tongue or feather of one in the corresponding groove of another.
5. to carry (the blade of an oar) in a nearly horizontal position between strokes, so that the water runs off in feathery spray reducing the resistance to the water.
6. to turn (the blade of a propeller) on its shaft so that its leading and trailing edges are nearly parallel with the airplane's line of flight, thus offering minimum resistance or drag when idle.
7. to change the angle of the blades of a helicopter rotor.
8. to give a featheredge to.
to feather one's nest; to grow rich by taking advantage of circumstances.
to tar and feather; to pour heated tar over a person and then cover him with feathers: it is a practice of mob law.

feath'ẽr, *v.i.* 1. to grow feathers; become covered with feathers.
2. to move, grow, or extend like feathers.
3. to look like feathers.
4. to feather an oar or propeller.

feath'ẽr al'um, same as *alunogen*.

feath'ẽr·bed, *a.* designating rules or regulations designed to accomplish featherbedding.

feath'ẽr bed, *v.i.*; featherbedded, *pt., pp.*; featherbedding, *ppr.* to take advantage of such rules.

feath'ẽr bed, a large, heavy quilt thickly filled with feathers or down, used as a mattress.

feath'ẽr·bed·ding, *n.* the practice of limiting work or output in order to provide more jobs and prevent unemployment.

feath'ẽr·bōne, *n.* a substitute for whalebone made from the quills of domestic fowls.

feath'ẽr·brāin, *n.* a featherbrained person.

feath'ẽr·brāined, *a.* giddy; silly; unthinking; frivolous.

feath'ẽr·çut, *n.* a style of hairdressing in which the hair is cut short and unevenly so as to form small, upswept curls with feathery tips.

feath'ẽr drīv'ẽr, one who beats and prepares feathers to make them light or loose. [Obs.]

feath'ẽred, *a.* 1. covered with feathers; as, a bird is a *feathered* animal.
2. winged; fleet.
In *feathered* briefness sails are filled.—Shak.
3. fashioned from or ornamented with feathers; as, a *feathered* shaft.
4. fringed; bordered; margined.
5. having the legs, etc. fringed with hair, as certain breeds of dogs.

feath'ẽr·edġe (-ej), *n.* a very thin edge, as on a board or tool, that can be easily broken or curled.

feath'ẽr·edġed (-ejd), *a.* 1. having a featheredge.
2. having the edges bordered with loops or scallops.

feath'ẽr·few, *n.* feverfew. [Brit. Dial.]

feath'ẽr·foil, *n.* a water plant, genus *Hottonia*: so called from its featherlike leaves.

feath'ẽr grȧss, a grass of the genus *Stipa*, distinguished by its feathered awns.

feath'ẽr·head (-hed), *n.* a frivolous, foolish person; a featherbrain.

feath'ẽr·head"ed, *a.* gay; heedless; featherbrained.

feath'ẽr-heeled, *a.* light-footed; frolicsome; capering.

feath'ẽr·i·ness, *n.* the state or quality of being feathery.

feath'ẽr·ing, *n.* 1. in architecture, a leaflike decoration consisting of many small arcs and foils.
2. in rowing, the uniform turning of the blade of an oar to a horizontal position as it is carried forward for the next stroke.
3. a feathery covering; plumage.
4. an especially delicate and light method of bowing rapid passages on the violin.
5. the act of one who feathers.

feath'ẽr·ing flōat, a float or paddle of a feathering wheel.

feath'ẽr·ing wheel (-hwēl), a paddle wheel whose floats are so arranged as to enter and leave the water edgewise, thus offering little resistance to the water.

feath'ẽr joint, a joint formed by inserting the feather, or tongue, on one board into the groove made to receive it in another.

feath'er kēy, a flat key, or strip, that fits into a groove between parts, as between a shaft and a pulley, so as to allow only relative lengthwise motion of the parts.

feath'ẽr·less, *a.* without feathers; unfledged.

feath'ẽr mẽr'chȧnt, a slacker in time of war. [Slang.]

feath'ẽr ōre, a variety of jamesonite.

feath'ẽr pälm (päm), any palm with featherlike, or pinnate, leaves.

feath'ẽr-pāt"ed, *a.* featherbrained.

feath'ẽr shot, copper which is granulated by being poured molten into cold water: also called *feathered shot*.

feath'ẽr stär, same as *comatula*.

feath'ẽr·stitch, *n.* [so called from resemblance to the arrangement of barbs on a feather.] an embroidery stitch forming a zigzag line.

feath'ẽr·stitch, *v.t.* and *v.i.* to embroider with featherstitches.

feath'ẽr·top grȧss, a European grass with a feathery panicle: called also *wood reed*.

feath'ẽr-vēined, *a.* in botany, designating or of leaves whose veins branch from the midrib to the margin like the parts of a feather, as in the oak and chestnut.

FEATHERSTITCH

feath'ẽr·wēight (-wāt), *n.* 1. any person or thing of comparatively light weight or small size.
2. an unimportant person or thing.
3. a boxer who weighs over 118 but not over 126 pounds.
4. a wrestler who weighs over 123 but not over 134 pounds.
5. the minimum weight that a race horse may carry in a handicap.

feath'ẽr·wēight, *a.* 1. of featherweights.
2. light or trivial.

feath'ẽr·wing, *n.* a plume moth.

feath'ẽr·wood, *n.* a hardwood tree of Australia with wood like hickory.

feath'ẽr·y, *a.* 1. covered with or as with feathers.
2. resembling feathers; soft, light, etc.; as, *feathery* clouds.

fēat'ly, *adv.* 1. suitably; aptly.
2. neatly.
3. skillfully; adroitly.
[Archaic in all senses.]

fēat'ly, *a.* neat; graceful. [Archaic.]

fēat'ness, *n.* dexterity; adroitness; skillfulness. [Archaic.]

fēa'tūre, *n.* [ME. *feture, fetour*; OFr. *faiture*, from L. *factura*, a making, formation, from *facere*, to make.]
1. originally, (a) the make, shape, form, or appearance of a person or thing; (b) attractive appearance; physical beauty.
2. (a) [*pl.*] the form or cast of the face; facial appearance; (b) any of the parts of the face, as the eyes, nose, mouth, etc.
3. a distinct or outstanding part, quality, or characteristic of something; as, the island's chief *feature* was its beauty.
4. a prominently displayed attraction or item, as of an entertainment, store, etc.
5. a special story, article, etc. in a newspaper or magazine, often prominently displayed.
6. a full-length motion picture.

fēa'tūre, *v.t.*, featured, *pt., pp.*; featuring, *ppr.*
1. to portray; represent.
2. to make outstanding or prominent; make a specialty of.
3. to sketch or show the features of.
4. to be a feature of.
5. to imagine; conceive of. [Slang.]

fēa'tūred, *a.* 1. having (a specified type of) facial features.
2. having a certain shape or figure; formed; shaped.
3. given special prominence.

fēa'tūre-length, *a.* full-length: said of a motion picture, magazine article, etc.

fēa'tūre·less, *a.* having no striking, outstanding, or distinctive features.

fēa'tūre·ly, *a.* having marked features; handsome. [Rare.]

fēaze, *v.t.*; feazed, *pt., pp.*; feazing, *ppr.* to faze or feeze.

fēaze, *v.t.* and *v.i.*; feazed, *pt., pp.*; feazing, *ppr.* [prob. from LG. or D.; cf. MD. *vese, veze*, frayed edge.] to untwist; to unravel. [Dial.]

fēaze, *n.* same as *feeze*.

fēaz'ings, *n.pl.* a raveled or ragged rope end.

feb'ri-, [from L. *febris*.] a combining form meaning *fever*, as in *febri*fic, *febri*fuge.

fē·bric'i·ty, *n.* the condition of being feverish.

fē·briç'ū·lōse, *a.* [L. *febriculosus*, from *febri-*

cula, a slight fever, dim. of *febris*, a fever.] having a slight fever.

feb·ri·fā′cient (-shent), *a.* [L. *febris*, a fever, and *faciens* (*-entis*), ppr. of *facere*, to make, do.] causing fever.

feb·ri·fā′cient, *n.* that which produces fever.

fē·brif′ẽr·ous, *a.* [L. *febris*, a fever, and *ferre*, to bear.] causing fever; as, a *febriferous* climate.

fē·brif′iç, *a.* [L. *febris*, a fever, and *-ficus*, from *facere*, to make.] producing fever; feverish.

fē·brif′ū·găl, *a.* mitigating or curing fever.

feb′ri·fūġe, *n.* [L. *febris*, fever, and *fugare*, to drive away.] any substance for reducing or removing fever.

feb′ri·fūġe, *a.* removing or reducing fever.

fē′brile (*or* feb′ril), *a.* [Fr. *fébrile*, from L. *febris*, a fever.]
1. of or characterized by fever; feverish.
2. caused by fever.

Fē·brō′ni·ăn, *a.* relating to the ancient doctrine of Febronianism.

Fē·brō′ni·ăn, *n.* a follower of Febronianism.

Fē·brō′ni·ăn·iṣm, *n.* [from Justinus *Febronius*, a pseudonym of John Nicholas von Hontheim, archbishop of Trèves, in a work on the claims of the pope.] in Roman Catholic theology, a doctrine antagonistic to the admitted claims of the Pope, and asserting the independence of national churches.

Feb′rū·ā·ry, *n.* [L. *Februarius* (*mensis*), originally the month of expiation, from *februa*, a Roman festival of purification, pl. of *februum*, a means of purification.] the second month in the year, introduced into the Roman calendar by Numa, having 28 days in regular years, and 29 days in leap years.

feb·rū·ā′tion, *n.* [L. *februatio* (*-onis*), from *februum*, a means of purification.] purification; a ceremony of purification. [Rare.]

fē′çăl, *a.* [Fr. *fécal*, from L. *fæx*, *fæcis*, dregs.] containing or consisting of dregs, lees, sediment, or excrement: also spelled *faecal*.

fec′che, *v.t.* to fetch. [Obs.]

fē′cēṣ, *n.pl.* [L. *fæces*, pl. of *fæx*, dregs, lees.]
1. excrement; dung.
2. dregs; lees; sediment.
Also spelled *faeces*.

fē′ciăl (-shăl), *a.* same as *fetial*.

fē′ci·fọrk, *n.* [L. *fæces*, dregs, and Eng. *fork*.] in zoology, the anal fork on which feces are carried by some larval insects.

fē′cit, [L.] he (or she) made (it): formerly used on a work of art, along with the name of the maker or designer; as, Stradivarius *fecit*.

feck, *n.* 1. strength; value; vigor.
2. space; quantity; number; as, what *feck* of ground?
3. the greatest part or number; the main part: also *the most feck*.
[Scot. in all senses.]

feck′et, *n.* a waistcoat. [Scot.]

feck′fụl, *a.* powerful; vigorous; sturdy. [Scot.]

feck′fụl·ly, *adv.* powerfully; manfully; ably. [Scot.]

feck′less, *a.* [Scot., from *effectless*; *effect*, and *-less*.]
1. weak; ineffective; spiritless.
2. thoughtless; careless; irresponsible.

feck′ly, *adv.* for the most part; mostly. [Scot.]
Wheel carriages I ha'e but few,
Three carts, an' twa are *feckly* new.—Burns.

feç′ū·là, *n.* [L. *fæcula*, burnt tartar, salt of tartar, dim. of *fæx*, pl. *fæces*, dregs.] starch, especially that obtained from plants by washing down the farinaceous pulp.

feç′ū·lence, feç′ū·len·cy, *n.* [LL. *fæculentia*, from *fæcula*, dim. of *fæx*, pl. *fæces*, dregs.]
1. muddiness; foulness; the quality of being foul with extraneous matter or lees.
2. that which is feculent; lees; sediment; dregs; excrement.

feç′ū·lent, *a.* [L. *fæculentus*, abounding in dregs, impure, from *fæx*, pl. *fæces*, dregs.] foul with extraneous or impure substances; muddy; containing sediment or excrement.

feç′und, *a.* [L. *fecundus*, fruitful, fertile.]
1. fruitful in children; prolific.
2. productive; as, a *fecund* soil.

feç′un·dāte, *v.t.*; fecundated, *pt.*, *pp.*; fecundating, *ppr.* 1. to make fruitful or prolific.
2. in biology, to impregnate; as, the pollen of flowers *fecundates* the stigma.

feç·un·dā′tion, *n.* [L. *fecundatus*, pp. of *fecundare*, to make fertile.] the act of making fruitful or prolific; impregnation.

fe·çun′di·fȳ, *v.t.* [L. *fecundus*, fruitful, and *-ficare*, from *facere*, to make.] to fecundate. [Rare.]

fe·çun′di·ty, *n.* [L. *fecunditas*, from *fecundus*, fruitful, fertile.]
1. fruitfulness; the quality or power of producing offspring in large numbers.
2. the power of germinating; as, the seeds of some plants retain their *fecundity* for many years.
3. fertility; the power of bringing forth in abundance; richness of invention.

fed, *v.* past tense and past participle of *feed*.
fed up; having had enough to become disgusted, bored, or annoyed; surfeited. [Slang.]

fed, *n.* [often F-] a Federal agent or officer. [Slang.]
the Fed; the Federal Reserve System.

fed·ä·yeen′, *n.pl.* [Ar. *fedā'yūn*, lit., those who sacrifice themselves.] Arab irregulars or guerrillas in the Middle East.

fed′dăn, *n.* [Ar. *fadan*, *faddan*, a plow with a yoke of oxen.] a measure of land in Egypt, about one and a quarter English acres.

fed′ẽr·ȧ·cy, *n.*; *pl.* **fed′ẽr·ȧ·cieṣ**, [from LL. *fæderatus*, federate.]
1. an alliance, especially by treaty. [Rare.]
2. a confederacy.

fed′ẽr·ăl, *a.* [Fr. *fédéral*, from L. *fædus* (*-eris*), a league, treaty.]
1. of or formed by a compact; specifically, designating or of a union of states, groups, etc. in which each member agrees to subordinate its power to that of the central authority in common affairs.
2. designating, of, or having to do with a central government of this sort.
3. [*usually* F-] designating, of, or having to do with the central government of the United States.
4. [F-] of or supporting the Federalist Party or its principle of centralized government.
5. [F-] of or supporting the central government of the United States in the Civil War (1861–1865); Union; pro-Union.
Federal Reserve Bank; any of the twelve district banks of the Federal Reserve System.
Federal Reserve System; a centralized banking system in the United States under a Board of Governors (formerly called the *Federal Reserve Board*) with supervisory powers over twelve Federal Reserve Banks, each a central bank for its district, and about 6,000 member banks: it was established in 1913 to develop a currency which would fluctuate with business demands, and to regulate the member banks of each district.

Fed′ẽr·ăl, *n.* 1. same as *Federalist*.
2. a supporter or soldier of the Federal government in the Civil War.

Fed′ẽr·ăl Bū′reau of In·ves″ti·gā′tion, a branch of the United States Department of Justice: it investigates and brings to trial violators of Federal criminal laws, except violators of currency, tax, and postal laws.

Fed′ẽr·ăl Çom·mū·ni·çā′tionṣ Çom·mis′sion, a Federal agency that regulates communication by wire and radio, including the licensing of radio and television stations.

fed′ẽr·ăl·iṣm, *n.* 1. the principles of a federal government.
2. [F-] the principles of the Federalist Party.

fed′ẽr·ăl·ist, *n.* 1. a person who believes in or supports federalism.
2. [F-] a member or supporter of the Federalist Party.
The Federalist; a set of eighty-five articles by Alexander Hamilton, James Madison, and John Jay, published in 1787 and 1788, analyzing the Constitution of the United States and urging its adoption.

fed′ẽr·ăl·ist, *a.* 1. of or supporting federalism.
2. [F-] of or supporting the Federalist Party or its principles.

fed″ẽr·ăl·is′tiç, *a.* federalist.

Fed′ẽr·ăl·ist (or **Fed′ẽr·ăl**) **Pär′ty**, a political party in the United States (1789–1816), led by Alexander Hamilton and John Adams, which advocated the adoption of the Constitution and the establishment of a strong, centralized government.

fed″ẽr·ăl·i·zā′tion, *n.* a federalizing or being federalized.

fed′ẽr·ăl·īze, *v.t.* and *v.i.*; federalized, *pt.*, *pp.*; federalizing, *ppr.* 1. to unite (states, etc.) in a federal union.
2. to put under the authority of a federal government.

Fed′ẽr·ăl Land Banks, twelve banks established in various localities throughout the U. S., under the Farm Loan Act of 1916, to enable farmers to capitalize their holdings through long-time mortgage loans.

fed′ẽr·ăl·ly, *adv.* in a federal manner; jointly.

Fed′ẽr·ăl Rē·ṣẽrve nōte, a note issued by the individual Federal Reserve Banks in various denominations of from 1 to 10,000 dollars, now the prevailing form of United States paper currency in circulation.

Fed′ẽr·ăl Trāde Çom·mis′sion, a Federal agency created in 1915 to investigate unfair methods of competition in business, fraudulent advertising, etc., and to prosecute those guilty of such practices.

fed′ẽr·āte, *a.* [L. *fæderatus*, pp. of *fæderare*, to league together, from *fædus* (*-eris*), a league, treaty.] united by compact under a central government or authority; joined in federation.

fed′ẽr·āte, *v.t.* and *v.i.*; federated, *pt.*, *pp.*; federating, *ppr.* to unite by a compact; to form into a federation.

fed·ẽr·ā′tion, *n.* [Fr. *fédération*; ML. *federatio*, from L. *fæderatus*.]
1. the act of uniting in a league by agreement of each member to subordinate its power to that of the central authority in common affairs.
2. a league; a union.
3. a federal government, as that of the United States.

fed′ẽr·ȧ·tive, *a.* joining in a league; forming, or having the nature of, a federation; as, the *federative* capacity of a nation.

fē·dōr′ȧ, *n.* [Fr., from *Fedora* (1882), play by Sardou.] a soft felt hat with the crown creased lengthwise and a somewhat curved brim.

fee, *n.* [ME. *fee*, *feo*, *fief*, payment; Anglo-Fr. *fee*, *fie* (OFr. *feu*, *fiu*, *fief*); associated with ME. *feo*, *feoh* (from AS. *feoh*), cattle, money, property; called money because cattle were used as a medium of exchange or barter.]
1. originally, (a) heritable land held from a feudal lord in return for service; fief; feudal benefice: also called *feud*; (b) the right to hold such land; (c) payment, service, or homage due to a superior.
2. a payment asked or given for professional services, admissions, licenses, tuition, etc.; charge.
3. a present of money; tip; gratuity.
4. in law, an inheritance in land.
fee simple; ownership (of land) with unrestricted rights of disposition.
fee tail; ownership (of land) limited to a specified class of heirs.
to hold in fee; to own; possess.

fee, *v.t.*; feed, *pt.*, *pp.*; feeing, *ppr.* 1. to pay a fee to.
2. to engage by advancing a sum of money to. [Chiefly Scot.]
3. to hire; to bribe. [Obs.]

fee′ble, *a.* [ME. *feble*, *febul*; OFr. *feble*, *feuble*, *foible*, *flebe*, *floibe*, *floible*, from L. *flebilis*, pass., to be wept over, act., weeping, tearful, from *flere*, to weep.]
1. lacking bodily strength; infirm, as from sickness or old age; debilitated.
2. not full or loud; lacking brightness or vigor; slow; imperfect; as, a *feeble* voice, a *feeble* light.
3. easily broken; frail; as, a *feeble* barrier.
Syn.—wretched, weak, poor, frail, debilitated, dull, forceless, puny, nerveless, enfeebled, enervated, faint, infirm, incomplete, vain, fruitless, scanty, pitiable.

fee′ble, *v.t.* [ME. *feblen*; OFr. *febleier*, *febloier*, to make feeble, from *feble*, feeble.] to weaken; to enfeeble. [Obs.]

fee′ble-mīnd″ed, *a.* 1. subnormal in intelligence: term no longer used in psychology.
2. having a weak will; irresolute. [Rare.]
the feeble-minded; those who are mentally deficient, including morons, imbeciles, and, sometimes, idiots.

fee′ble-mīnd″ed·ness, *n.* the condition of being feeble-minded.

fee′ble·ness, *n.* the state of being feeble in any sense of the word; weakness.

fee′bly, *adv.* weakly; in a feeble manner.

feed, *v.t.*; fed, *pt.*, *pp.*; feeding, *ppr.* [ME. *feden*; AS. *fedan*, to feed, nourish, bring forth, from *foda*, food.]
1. to give food to; to provide food for.
2. to supply or furnish as food; as, the farmer *fed* oats to the horses.
3. to nourish; to sustain; as, the blood *feeds* the body tissue; the news *fed* his anger.
4. to provide (material to be used up); as, *feed* coal to the stove.
5. to provide with material; as, *feed* the stove.
6. to delight; to supply with something desirable; to gratify; as, to *feed* the eye with the beauties of a landscape.
7. in sports, to pass the ball, puck, etc. to

(a player intending to make a shot, try for a goal, etc.).

8. in the theater, to give (an actor) the necessary cue lines.

to feed on (or *upon*); (a) to take as food; be nourished by; (b) to get satisfaction, support, etc. from.

feed, *v.i.* 1. to eat: said principally of animals.

2. to subsist; to live; as, some birds *feed* on seeds and berries.

3. to grow fat. [Brit. Dial.]

4. to support or nourish oneself mentally, as by hope.

5. to flow steadily, as into a machine, for use, processing, etc.

feed, *n.* 1. food given to animals; fodder; pasture.

2. the customary amount of fodder given at one time; as, to carry on a journey two *feeds* of oats.

3. the material supplied to a machine.

4. the part of the machine supplying this material.

5. the supplying of this material.

6. a meal. [Colloq.]

7. in an internal-combustion engine, the system of pipes and tubes, together with the fuel pump or vacuum tank, by means of which the fuel is conveyed from the fuel tank to the carburetor.

differential feed; a device by which a tool, as a lathe, is made to operate with an even, progressive movement.

off one's feed; without appetite for food; somewhat sick: originally said of horses, etc. [Slang.]

feed ā'prŏn, a revolving carrier upon which raw materials, as cotton, wool, etc., are conveyed to and fed into a machine: called also *feed cloth.*

feed'back, *n.* 1. in electronics, the feeding back of part of the output to the input at the proper phase: used in radio to amplify or decrease the strength of a signal.

2. a process in which the factors that produce a result are themselves modified, corrected, strengthened, etc. by that result.

feed'-back, *a.* in electricity, regenerative.

feed bag, a bag filled with grain, fastened over a horse's muzzle for feeding: also called *nose bag.*

to put on the feed bag; to eat a meal. [Slang.]

feed bōard, the inclined plane or table on a folding machine or cylinder press, from which the sheets of paper are fed into the machine.

feed çloth, see *feed apron*

feed dōor, 1. the door of a furnace, through which fuel is fed to the fire.

2. a small sliding door in a grain chute for regulating the quantity of grain to be fed to stock at a time.

feed'ẽr, *n.* 1. a person or thing that feeds; especially, one that supplies material to a machine.

2. anything that supplies or leads into something else, as a stream of water, a railroad, an air route, etc.; subsidiary; tributary.

3. in electricity, a conductor supplying energy to a center from which the energy is distributed into various channels.

4. one who gives food or nourishment; specifically, one who fattens stock for market.

5. one who furnishes incentives; an encourager.

The *feeder* of my riots. —Shak.

6. one who consumes; as, small birds are *feeders* on grain or seeds.

7. in mining, a short cross vein passing into a lode.

8. a trough or vessel to supply food to stock and poultry in proper quantities without waste.

9. one dependent on another, as a servant who is supported by his lord. [Obs.]

feed'head, *n.* 1. a cistern which supplies water by gravity to a steam boiler.

2. in metal founding, an excess of metal above the mold, whose weight forces the molten mass to completely fill the mold: also called *riser* and *deadhead.*

feed'ing, *n.* 1. the act of eating, or of giving to another to eat; also, the act of supplying for consumption, as to a machine, fire, stream, or body of water.

2. feed, or that which furnishes food, particularly for animals; pasture land; as, there is *feeding* there for a thousand sheep.

feed'ing ground, a place to feed animals, or the place where animals habitually feed, either on land or at sea: often used in the plural.

feed mō'tion, the machinery that operates the feed in machines: called also *feed gear.*

feed pump, a steam pump used to force water into a boiler.

feed rack, a rack from which cattle and horses are fed.

feed rod, a speed regulator for a feeding device: called also *feed regulator.*

feed rōll, the roller that feeds material into a machine; as, the *feed roll* of a typewriter, about which the paper is drawn.

feed sçrew (skrö), a long screw which imparts a uniform feed motion to the work in a lathe.

feed wa̤'tẽr, the water fed into a steam boiler.

fee färm, land held in absolute possession and subject to a perpetual fixed rent, without homage or other services.

fee'-fa̤w'-fum', fee'-fō'-fum', *n.* a meaningless expression which, in old fairy tales, is uttered by ogres with murderous intent; hence, gibberish and nonsense intended to delude the ignorant and unsuspecting.

fee fund, in Scots law, the dues of court out of which the clerks and other officers of the court receive their fees.

feel, *v.t.*; felt, *pt., pp.*; feeling, *ppr.* [ME. *felen*; AS. *felan*, to feel, perceive.]

1. to touch or handle in order to become aware of; to examine by touching or handling.

2. to perceive or be aware of through physical sensation; as, he *felt* tears run down his cheeks.

3. to be influenced or moved by; to be sensitive to or emotionally disturbed by.

Would I had never trod this English earth,
Or *felt* the flatteries that grow upon it.
—Shak.

4. to be aware of through intellectual perception; as, I *feel* the weight of his argument.

5. to think; believe; consider.

to feel (a person) out; to find out the opinions or attitude of (a person) by a cautious and indirect approach.

feel, *v.i.* 1. to have physical sensation; to be sentient.

2. to appear to be to the senses, especially to the sense of touch; as, the water *feels* warm.

3. to try to find by touching; grope.

4. to be aware of the condition of being; as, I *feel* sad.

5. to be moved to sympathy, pity, etc.

to feel after; to search for; to seek to find; to seek as a person groping in the dark.

to feel for; (a) to seek to find cautiously or secretly; (b) to sympathize with.

to feel like; to have an inclination or desire for. [Colloq.]

to feel (like) oneself; to feel normally healthy, fit, etc.

to feel up to; to feel capable of. [Colloq.]

feel, *n.* 1. the act of feeling; perception by the senses.

2. sense of touch; perception; sensation.

3. the quality of a thing perceived through touch; as, some rocks have a greasy *feel.*

4. an emotional sensation.

5. instinctive ability or appreciation.

feel'ẽr, *n.* 1. one who or that which feels.

2. a specialized organ of touch in an animal or insect, as a tentacle or antenna.

3. an observation, remark, etc. made, as if casually, to ascertain the views or plans of others.

feel'ing, *a.* 1. expressive of great sensibility; affecting; as, he spoke with *feeling* eloquence.

2. possessing great sensibility; easily moved; as, a *feeling* man; a *feeling* heart.

3. sensibly affected; deep; vivid; as, I had a *feeling* sense of his favors.

feel'ing, *n.* 1. the sense of touch; the sense by which we perceive, through the skin, sensations of contact, pressure, temperature, and pain.

2. the power or faculty of experiencing physical sensation.

3. an awareness; consciousness; sensation; as, a *feeling* of pain.

4. an emotion.

5. [*pl.*] sensitivities; susceptibilities; as, her *feelings* are easily hurt.

6. a kindly, generous attitude; sympathy; pity.

7. (a) an opinion or sentiment; as, it is my *feeling* that events are moving slowly; (b) a premonition; as, I have a *feeling* that something unpleasant will happen.

8. what is attributed to something as a result of one's own impression or emotion; air; atmosphere; as, a great city has a *feeling* of strain and hurry.

9. discriminating and sensitive taste; as, he has a *feeling* for music.

10. the emotional quality in a work of art.

Syn.—sensation, sensibility, consciousness, emotion, sense, impression, conviction, sensitiveness, tenderness, opinion, sentiment, agitation, passion.

feel'ing·ly, *adv.* 1. with expression of great sensibility and strong emotion; as, to speak *feelingly.*

2. so as to be sensibly felt. [Rare.]

These are counselors,
That *feelingly* persuade me what I am.
—Shak.

feer, feere, *n.* same as *fere.*

feeşe, feeze, *n.* a foot race; also, the running start taken before a leap. [Obs.]

fee sim'ple, see under *fee.*

feet, *n.* pl. of *foot.*

on one's feet; (a) in a standing position; (b) firmly established.

to carry (or *sweep*) *off one's feet*; (a) to fill with enthusiasm; (b) to make a deep impression on.

to sit at the feet of; to be an admiring disciple or pupil of.

to stand on one's own feet; to be independent.

feet, *n.* same as *feat.* [Obs.]

fee tāil, [Anglo-Fr. *fee taile*; *fee* (see *fee*) and *taile*, pp. of *taillir*, to cut.] see under *fee.*

feet'less, *a.* lacking feet; as, *feetless* birds.

feeze, *v.t.*; feezed, *pt., pp.*; feezing, *ppr.* to turn; to twist, as a screw; to tighten by screwing down; as, to *feeze* a violin string. [Scot.]

feeze, fēaze, *v.t.* 1. to beat; to frighten; to punish. [Obs.]

2. to disturb; agitate; disconcert. [Colloq.]

feeze, fēaze, *v.i.* to fume; to fret. [Colloq.]

feeze, fēaze, *n.* 1. a rush, hard impact, or rub. [Brit. Dial.]

2. irritable excitement. [Colloq.]

feh, *n.* [Heb.] a variant of peh, the seventeenth letter of the Hebrew alphabet, corresponding to English F, f.

fe̤h'me, fe̤hm·ge·riçh'te, *n.* see *Vehmgerichte.*

fe̤ign (fān), *v.t.*; feigned, *pt., pp.*; feigning, *ppr.* [ME. *feinen*, *feynen*, *feignen*; OFr. *feindre*, *faindre*; Pr. *feigner*; It. *fignere*, from L. *fingere*, to touch, handle, shape.]

1. originally, to form; shape.

2. to make up (a story, excuse, etc.); invent; fabricate.

3. to invent or imagine; to form an idea or conception of.

There are no such things done as thou sayest,
but thou *feignest* them out of thine own
heart. —Neh. vi. 8.

4. to make a false show of; to pretend; to simulate; to counterfeit; as, to *feign* insanity.

fe̤ign, *v.i.* to pretend; to dissemble.

fe̤igned, *a.* 1. fictitious; imagined.

2. pretended; simulated; counterfeit.

feigned issue; in law, a proceeding whereby an action is brought by consent of the parties, to determine some disputed right without the formality of pleading.

fe̤ign'ed·ly, *adv.* in a feigned manner; in pretense; falsely.

fe̤ign'ed·ness, *n.* fiction; pretense; deceit.

fe̤ign'ẽr, *n.* one who feigns; a pretender.

fe̤ign'ing·ly, *adv.* in a false or treacherous manner; feignedly.

fe̤in, fe̤ine, *v.t.* to feign. [Obs.]

fe̤int, *n.* [Fr. *feinte*, a sham, pretense, f. pp. of *feindre*, to feign.]

1. a false show; a sham; a pretense; a stratagem; as, a well-conceived *feint.*

2. a deceptive movement; a pretended blow or attack intended to take the opponent off his guard, as in boxing, fencing, warfare, etc.

fe̤int, *a.* seeming; false; counterfeit. [Obs.]

fe̤int, *v.i.*; feinted, *pt., pp.*; feinting, *ppr.* to make a feint or pretense of attack.

feis (fesh), *n.* [Ir. *feis*, a feast.] a cultural festival of the arts held annually in Ireland or by people of Irish ancestry elsewhere.

feist'y, *a.*; *comp.* feistier; *superl.* feistiest, [from ME. *fīst*, flatus.] full of spirit; specifically, (a) lively, energetic, exuberant, etc.; (b) quarrelsome, aggressive, belligerent, etc. [Colloq. or Dial.]

feld'spär, feld'spath, *n.* [G. *feldspath*, from *feld*, field, and *spath*, *spat*, spar.] any of several crystalline minerals made up mainly of aluminum silicates, usually glassy and moderately hard, found in igneous rocks.

feld·spath'iç, feld·spath'ōse, *a.* containing or resembling feldspar.

fēle, *a.* [AS. *fela*, *feola*, many.] many. [Obs.]

fē·li·cif'iç, *a.* [L. *felix* (*-icis*), happy, and *-ficus*, from *facere*, to make.] causing happiness; giving joy or pleasure.

fē·lic'i·fȳ, *v.t.* to make happy. [Obs.]

fē·lic′i·tāte, *a.* made very happy. [Obs.]

fē·lic′i·tāte, *v.t.*; felicitated, *pt.*, *pp.*; felicitating, *ppr.* [L. *felicitatus*, pp. of *felicitare*, to make happy, from *felix* (*-icis*), happy.]

1. to make happy. [Rare.]

2. to congratulate; to wish joy or pleasure to; as, we *felicitate* our friends on good fortune.

fē·lic·i·tā′tion, *n.* congratulation.

fē·lic′i·tous, *a.* 1. suitable to the occasion; well-chosen; apt and to the point; as, a *felicitous* phrase.

2. having the knack of appropriate and pleasing expression, style, etc.

3. producing felicity; as, a *felicitous* occasion. [Rare.]

Syn.—happy, timely, apropos, successful, opportune, joyous.

fē·lic′i·tous·ly, *adv.* in a felicitous manner; happily; suitably.

fē·lic′i·tous·ness, *n.* the state or condition of being felicitous.

fē·lic′i·ty, *n.*; *pl.* **fē·lic′i·ties,** [ME. *felicitee*; OFr. *felicite*, from L. *felicitas*, happiness, from *felix* (*-icis*), happy.]

1. happiness; perfect content and comfort; bliss.

And, finally, after this life to attain everlasting joy and *felicity*.—Common Prayer.

2. anything which produces happiness or good fortune; a source of satisfaction; as, the *felicities* of a quiet life.

No greater *felicity* can genius attain than that of having purified intellectual pleasure. —Johnson.

3. a faculty of appropriate and pleasing expression in writing, speaking, painting, etc.

4. an apt expression or thought.

fē′lid, *n.* any animal belonging to the cat family, or *Felidæ*.

Fē′li·dae, *n.pl.* [from L. *felis*, properly *feles*, a cat, and *-idæ*.] animals of the cat kind, a family of carnivora. The incisor teeth are equal; the third tooth behind the large canine in either jaw is narrow and sharp, and these, the carnassial or sectorial teeth, work against each other like scissors in cutting flesh; the claws are sheathed and retractile. This family includes the domestic cat, wildcat, lion, tiger, leopard, lynx, jaguar, panther, cheetah, ounce, caracal, serval, ocelot, etc.

fē′līne, *a.* [L. *felinus*, from *feles*, *felis*, a cat.]

1. characteristic of the genus *Felis* or family *Felidæ*; as, *feline* habits.

2. catlike; esp., (a) sly; cruel; treacherous; crafty; stealthy; (b) graceful in a sleek way.

fē′līne, *n.* any animal of the family *Felidæ*.

fē·lin′i·ty, *n.* the quality of being feline.

Fē′lis, *n.* [L. *feles* or *felis*, a cat.] the type genus of the family *Felidæ*.

fell, *v.* past tense of *fall*.

fell, *a.* [ME. *fel*, *fell*; OFr. *fel*, cruel, furious.]

1. cruel; barbarous; inhuman; fierce; savage; ravenous; bloody.

More *fell* than tigers on the Libyan plain. —Pope.

2. causing death; deadly; as, a *fell* plague. [Archaic or Poet.]

3. strong and fiery; keen; biting; sharp; clever; active. [Scot.]

fell, *n.* [ME. *fel*, *fell*; AS. *fel*, *fell*, a skin, hide; O.H.G. *fel*; Ice. *fjall*, *fell*; Sw. *fäll*; Norw. *feld*, a skin, hide.] a skin or hide of an animal.

fell, *n.* [ME. *fel*, *fell*; Ice. *fjall*, *fell*; Dan. *fjæld*, a hill.]

1. a stretch of wasteland; a moor.

2. a barren hill or high, rocky ground. In this sense, it is often incorporated into the names of English and Scottish localities.

fell, *n.* [L. *fel*, gall, bitterness.] anger; melancholy. [Obs.]

fell, *n.* in mining, the smaller fragments of ore which wash through the meshes of a sieve.

fell, *v.t.*; felled, *pt.*, *pp.*; felling, *ppr.* [ME. *fellen*; AS. *fellan*, *fyllan*, to cause to fall, strike down, caus. of *feallan*, to fall.]

1. to cause to fall; knock down; as, the boxer *felled* his opponent with a blow.

2. to cut down (a tree or trees).

3. in sewing, to turn over (the rough edge of a seam) and sew down flat.

fell, *n.* 1. the trees cut down in one season.

2. in sewing, a seam uniting two edges which are folded one over the other and sewed together in this position.

3. in weaving, the end of a web formed by the last weft thread driven up by the lay.

fell′á·ble, *a.* capable of being felled or fit for felling.

fel′läh, *n.*; *pl.* **fel′lähs**; Ar. **fel′läh·in, fel′läh·een,** [Ar. *fellah*, a plowman, peasant, from *falaha*, to cleave the soil, plow.] a peasant or laborer in Egypt or some other countries where Arabic is spoken.

fel·lä′ti·ō, *n.* [Mod.L., from L. *fellatus*, pp. of *fellare*, to suck.] a sexual activity involving oral contact with the male genitals.

fell′ẽr, *n.* a fellow; a man or boy. [Slang or Dial.]

fell′ẽr, *n.* 1. one who hews or knocks down; a device for cutting down trees.

2. a sewing-machine attachment for felling seams.

fell′fãre, *n.* see *fieldfare*.

fell′mŏn·gẽr, *n.* a dealer in fells or hides.

fell′ness, *n.* cruelty; fierce barbarity; rage; absolute ruthlessness.

fel′lōe, *n.* same as *felly*.

fel′lōw, *n.* [ME. *felow*, *felaghe*, a companion, partner, from Ice. *felagi*, a partnership, fellowship; *fe*, property, and *lag*, a laying together, fellowship, from *leggja*, to lay.]

1. originally, a person who shares; partner or accomplice; hence, a companion; an associate; a comrade; a mate.

In youth I had twelve *fellows* like myself. —Ascham.

2. an equal; a person of the same class or rank; peer.

3. either of a pair of similar things used together and suited to each other.

4. (a) a man or boy: often in familiar address; (b) a person; one; as, a *fellow* must eat. [Colloq.]

A *fellow* of infinite jest, of most excellent fancy. —Shak.

5. (a) a person of a lower social class; (b) a coarse, rough man. [Obs.]

Worth makes the man, the want of it the *fellow*. —Pope.

6. a suitor; beau. [Colloq.]

7. a graduate student who holds a fellowship in a university or college.

8. a member of a learned society.

9. a member of a governing body of a college, as at Oxford University. [Brit.]

fel′lōw, *a.* having the same ideas, position, work, etc.; in the same condition; associated; as, *fellow* workers, *fellow* students.

fel′lōw, *v.t.*; fellowed, *pt.*, *pp.*; fellowing, *ppr.*

1. to suit with; to pair with; to match.

2. to associate with; to accompany. [Obs.]

fel′lōw ço̤m′mŏn·ẽr, 1. one who has the same right of common.

2. in Cambridge, Oxford, and Dublin, an undergraduate who commons or dines with the fellows.

fel′lōw·çrȧft, *n.* the second degree in Freemasonry; also, one who has taken this degree.

fel″lōw·feel′, *v.t.* to have a like feeling, as sorrow or joy, with; to feel sympathy with. [Rare.]

fel′lōw feel′ẽr, one who shares another's feelings; one who feels sympathy for another. [Rare.]

fel′lōw feel′ing, a feeling of fellowship or joint interest; sympathy.

fel′lōw·less, *a.* having no equal or associate; peerless; unmatched.

fel′lōw·līke, *a.* like an associate or comrade; companionable; on equal terms. [Obs.]

fel′lōw·ly, *a.* fellowlike; sympathetic. [Rare.]

fel′lōw sẽrv′ănt, each of two or more persons who perform similar tasks for the same employer: an employer cannot ordinarily be held liable for injuries suffered by one servant through the negligence of another.

fel′lōw·ship, *n.* 1. the condition of being an associate; mutual association of persons on equal and friendly terms; communion; companionship; familiar intercourse; intimate familiarity.

Have no *fellowship* with the unfruitful works of darkness. —Eph. v. 11.

Men are made for society and mutual *fellowship*. —Calamy.

2. a mutual sharing, as of experience, activity, interest, etc.; partnership; joint interest; as, *fellowship* in pain.

3. a group of companions or fellows; an association of persons having the same tastes, occupations, or interests; a band; a company.

The great contention of the sea and skies Parted our *fellowship*. —Shak.

4. an endowment, or a sum of money paid from such an endowment, for the support of a graduate student in a university or college.

5. the rank or position of a fellow in a university or college.

fel′lōw·ship, *v.t.*; fellowshipped, *pt.*, *pp.*; fellowshipping, *ppr.* to associate with as a fellow or member of the same church; to admit to fellowship, specifically to Christian fellowship; to unite with in doctrine and discipline.

fel′lōw·ship, *v.i.* to become associated with others, especially in the same church.

fel′lōw trav′el·ẽr, a nonmember who supports or approves the cause of a party, especially the Communist Party.

fel′ly, *adv.* [ME. *felly*, *felli*, *fellich*, fiercely, cruelly.] in a fell manner; cruelly; fiercely; barbarously.

fel′ly, fel′lōe, *n.*; *pl.* **fel′lies, fel′lōes,** [ME. *feli*, *felwe*, *felow*; AS. *felg*, *felge*, a felly, felloe, from AS. *fiolan*, *feolan*, to stick, from the pieces of the rim being put together.]

1. any of the curved pieces of wood which, joined together by dowel pins, form the circumference or circular rim of a wheel into which the spokes are fitted.

2. the rim of a wheel.

fē′lō-de-sē′ (*or* fel′ō-), *n.*; *pl.* **fē′lōs-de-sē′, fel′ō·nēs-de-sē′,** [Anglo-L., lit., felon of (one)self.] in law, suicide or a suicide.

fē′loid, *a.* [L. *feles*, *felis*, a cat, and Gr. *eidos*, form.] of or pertaining to the *Felidæ*; having the characteristics of the cat family.

fel′ŏn, *a.* 1. malignant; fierce; malicious; proceeding from a depraved heart; traitorous; disloyal.

Vain shows of love to vail his *felon* hate. —Pope.

2. wicked; base; criminal.

fel′ŏn, *n.* [ME. *feloun*, *felon*, from *feloun*, wicked, malignant.] a painful, pus-producing infection at the end of a toe or finger, usually occurring near the nail; a deep-seated whitlow.

fel′ŏn, *n.* [ME. *felon*, *feloun*; OFr. *felon*, *fellon*, a wicked person, traitor, from LL. *fello*, *felo*, a traitor, rebel.]

1. in law, a person who has committed a felony; a criminal.

2. a villain. [Rare.]

fel′ŏn·ess, *n.* a woman guilty of a felony.

fē·lō′ni·ous, *a.* 1. wicked; base; criminal.

2. in law, of, like, or constituting a felony; as, *felonious* homicide.

fē·lō′ni·ous·ly, *adv.* in a felonious manner; with the deliberate intention of committing a crime.

fē·lō′ni·ous·ness, *n.* the quality of being felonious.

fel′ŏn·ly, *adv.* feloniously. [Obs.]

fel′ŏ·nous, *a.* wicked; felonious. [Obs.]

fel′ŏn·ous·ly, *adv.* feloniously. [Obs.]

fel′ŏn·ry, *n.* a number of felons, considered collectively; a body of convicts, as in a prison or penal colony.

fel′ŏn·wŏrt, fel′ŏn·wood, *n.* bittersweet.

fel′ŏn·y, *n.*; *pl.* **fel′ŏn·ies,** [ME. *felony*, *felonie*; LL. *felonia*, treason, treachery, from *felo* (*-onis*), a traitor, wicked fellow.]

1. an act of wickedness or treachery. [Obs.]

2. in law, (a) under the feudal system, an offense committed by a vassal, the penalty for which was forfeiture of fief; (b) at common law, one of a limited number of crimes the punishment for which is the forfeiture of land or goods or both (cases of particular heinousness sometimes occasioning additional penalty, even death); (c) in modern usage, a major crime, as murder, arson, rape, etc., for which statute provides a greater punishment than for a misdemeanor.

In many [states] of the United States, *felony* is defined by statute as including all crimes which are punishable by death or imprisonment in the state prison. . . . Many crimes which were not *felonies* at common law are made so by statute, being either expressly declared to be so, or such a penalty being attached to them as to bring them within the meaning of the term. —Smith.

fel′sīte, *n.* [from *fel*spar, and *-ite*.] an igneous rock consisting mainly of feldspar and quartz: also called *felstone*.

fel·sit′iç, *a.* pertaining to or resembling felsite: containing or composed of felsite.

fel′spär, fel′spath, *n.* same as *feldspar*.

fel·spath′iç, *a.* same as *feldspathic*.

fel′stōne, *n.* same as *felsite*.

felt, *v.* past tense and past participle of *feel*.

felt, *n.* [ME. *felt*; AS. *felt*; D. *vilt*; G. *filz*, felt.]

1. a cloth or fabric made of wool, or of wool and fur or hair, the fibers of which are not woven together, but matted or wrought into a compact substance by rolling and pressure, usually with the aid of chemical action, heat, etc.

2. any woven fabric that is partially felted, as by shrinkage or the process of fulling.

3. a strip or piece of felt; also, any article made of felt, particularly a hat.
4. a woven or felted material made of asbestos fibers.
5. skin. [Obs.]

felt, *v.t.*; felted, *pt.*, *pp.*; felting, *ppr.* 1. to mat together, as fibers, so as to form a compact sheet; especially, to make into felt cloth.
2. to jacket or cover over with felt or some similar material; as, to *felt* a steam pipe.

felt, *v.i.* to mat; to become felted.

felt, *a.* made of felt.

felt′ed, *a.* 1. matted as in the process of felting; manufactured into felt.
2. in botany, made up of intertwined or matted filaments.

felt′ẽr, *v.t.* to clot or mat together like felt. [Obs.]

felt grāin, the grain of wood that runs from the outside of the tree toward the center, crossing the annular rings transversely.

felt′ing, *n.* 1. the process of making felt.
2. the various materials used in the manufacture of felt.
3. felted cloth.
4. the splitting or sawing of timber along the felt grain.

felt′wŏrt, *n.* a plant, the mullein.

fel′ty, *a.* feltlike, as in appearance, composition, or feel.

fē·luç′cȧ, *n.* [It. *felucca*; Sp. *feluca*; Ar. *faluka*, from *fulk*, a ship.] a small, narrow ship with two or three masts, propelled by oars or lateen sails or both, used especially along the Mediterranean coasts.

FELUCCA

fel′wŏrt, *n.* any of various species of gentian.

fē′māle, *a.* [ME. and OFr. *femelle*; L. *femella*, dim. of *femina*, a woman.]
1. designating or of the sex that produces ova and bears offspring: opposed to *male*.
2. of, characteristic of, or suitable to members of this sex; feminine.
3. consisting of women or girls.
4. in botany, (a) having a pistil and no stamens; (b) designating or of a reproductive structure or part containing large gametes that can be fertilized by smaller, motile gametes; (c) designating or of any structure or part that produces fruit after it is fertilized.
5. in mechanics, designating or having a hollow part shaped to receive a corresponding inserted part (called *male*): said of a gauge, electric plug, etc.

fē′māle, *n.* a female person, animal, or plant.
female rhyme; same as *feminine rhyme*.
female screw; a concave or internal screw into which a corresponding convex or external screw, called the male, works; a screw nut.

Syn.—feminine, effeminate, womanly.—*Female* is applicable to the sex and to the essential physiological distinctions from the male; *feminine*, to the mental qualities and finer characteristics of women and to the things appropriate to them. *Effeminate*, used chiefly in reference to a man, implies delicacy, softness, or lack of virility.

fē′māl·ist, *n.* one devoted to the female sex; a courter of women; a gallant. [Obs.]

fē′māl·īze, *v.t.*; femalized, *pt.*, *pp.*; femalizing, *ppr.* to make female or feminine.

feme, *n.* [OFr. *feme*, *femme*, from L. *femina*, a woman.]
1. in law, a wife.
2. a woman. [Obs.]
feme covert; in law, a married woman.
feme sole; in law, (a) an unmarried woman; one who has never been married, who is a widow, or who is separated from her husband by divorce; (b) a married woman conducting business or trade or holding property in her own right and responsibility.

fem′ẽr·ell, *n.* [OFr. *fumeraille*, part of a chimney, from *fumer*, to smoke; L. *fumus*, smoke.] in architecture, a lantern or partially open domelike structure erected on the roof of a kitchen, hall, etc., to afford ventilation: written also *fumerell*.

fem′i·cīde, *n.* [L. *femina*, a woman, and *-cidium*, from *cædere*, to kill.] the act of killing a woman.

fem′i·nȧ·cy, *n.*; *pl.* **fem′i·nȧ·cieṣ,** feminine nature.

fem′i·năl, *a.* [from L. *femina*, a woman.] pertaining to a woman; feminine. [Rare.]

fem·i·nal′i·ty, *n.*; *pl.* **fem·i·nal′i·tieṣ,** the state or quality of being female; femininity.

fem′i·nāte, *a.* [L. *feminatus*, from *femina*, a woman.] feminine. [Obs.]

fem·i·nē′i·ty, *n.*; *pl.* **fem·i·nē′i·tieṣ,** [from L. *femineus*, womanly, from *femina*, a woman.]
1. femininity.
2. effeminacy.

fem′i·nine, *a.* [L. *femininus*, from *femina*, a woman.]
1. female; of women or girls.
2. having qualities regarded as characteristic of women and girls, as gentleness, weakness, delicacy, modesty, etc.; womanly.
3. suitable to or characteristic of a woman.
4. effeminate; lacking in manly qualities; womanish: said of men.

Ninus was no man of war at all, but altogether *feminine*. —Raleigh.

5. in grammar, designating or of the gender of words denoting or referring to females or things originally regarded as female.

fem′i·nine, *n.* 1. a female; a woman; the female sex. [Rare.]
2. in grammar, (a) the feminine gender; (b) a word or form in this gender.

fem′i·nine·ly, *adv.* in a feminine manner.

fem′i·nine·ness, *n.* the state or quality of being feminine; female nature.

fem′i·nine rhȳme (rīm), a rhyme of two or, sometimes, three syllables of which only the first is stressed (e.g., fashion, passion; haziness, laziness).

fem·i·nin′i·ty, *n.*; *pl.* **fem·i·nin′i·tieṣ,** [from L. *femininus*, womanly, from *femina*, a woman.]
1. the quality or state of being feminine; womanliness.
2. womankind; women, considered collectively.

fem′i·niṣm, *n.* [from L. *femina*, woman, and *-ism*.]
1. (a) the theory that women should have political, economic, and social rights equal to those of men; (b) the movement to win such rights for women.
2. feminine qualities. [Rare.]

fem′i·nist, *n.* an advocate or supporter of feminism.

fem′i·nist, *a.* of feminism or feminists.

fem′i·nist·iç, *a.* same as *feminist*.

fē·min′i·ty, *n.*; *pl.* **fē·min′i·tieṣ,** the qualities or nature of the female sex; womanliness; also, effeminacy.

fem″i·ni·zā′tion, *n.* the act of making or becoming feminine or womanish.

fem′i·nīze, *v.t.*; feminized, *pt.*, *pp.*; feminizing, *ppr.* [L. *femina*, a woman, and *-ize*.]
1. to make feminine or effeminate.
2. in biology, to cause a male to acquire female characteristics by surgery and gland therapy.

fem′i·nīze, *v.i.* to become feminine or effeminate.

fem′i·nye, *n.* [from OFr. *feminie*, *femmenie*, from *feme*, a woman.] a body of women; particularly [F–] the race of Amazons or their country: also spelled *feminie*. [Archaic.]

femme (fȧm), *n.* [Fr.] a woman or wife.
femme couverte; a married woman.
femme de chambre; a chambermaid; a lady's maid.

fem′ō·rȧ, *n.* alternative plural of *femur*.

fem′ō·răl, *a.* [LL. *femoralis*, from *femur*, the thigh.] of or pertaining to the femur; as, the *femoral* artery, the *femoral* canal.

fem″ō·rō·çau′dăl, *a.* [L. *femur* (*-oris*), the thigh, and *cauda*, a tail.] relating to the femur and the tail, as certain muscles.

fem″ō·rō·tib′i·ăl, *a.* [L. *femur* (*-oris*), the thigh, and *tibia*, the tibia.] pertaining to or situated between the femur and the tibia.

fē′mŭr, *n.*; *pl.* **fē′mŭrṣ, fem′ō·rȧ,** [L. *femur* (*-oris*), the thigh.]
1. in vertebrate animals, the thighbone.
2. in entomology, the third joint of the leg, articulating proximally with the trochanter and distally with the tibia.
3. in architecture, the space between the channels in the triglyph of the Doric order.

fen, *n.* [ME. *fen*, *fenne*; AS. *fen*, *fenn*, a marsh, bog, fen.] low land covered wholly or partially with water but producing sedge, coarse grasses, or other aquatic plants; boggy land; a moor or marsh.

A long canal the muddy *fen* divides. —Addison.

fe·nā′gle, *v.i.* and *v.t.*; fenagled, *pt.*, *pp.*; fenagling, *ppr.* to finagle.

fen′ber″ry, *n.* *Vaccinium oxycoccus*, the small cranberry.

fence, *n.* [ME. *fence*, *fens*, *fense*, a defense, guard, abbrev. of *defense*, *defence*.]
1. a structure erected around or by the side of any open space to prevent passage in or out; especially, a structure enclosing or separating yards, fields, etc. The term is commonly applied to the various forms constructed of posts carrying boards, rails, pickets, or wire, or to iron structures consisting of vertical or horizontal bars or of open work. A wall, hedge, or bank, however, may constitute a fence.
2. a guard; anything to restrain entrance; that which defends from attack, approach, or injury; security; defense. [Archaic.]

A *fence* betwixt us and the victor's wrath. —Addison.

3. the art of self defense, especially by the sword; fencing; skill in fencing or sword play; hence, ability in argument, especially adroitness in sustaining oneself and baffling an opponent's attacks.

I bruised my shin th'other day with playing at sword and dagger with a master of *fence*. —Shak.

4. in machinery, tools, etc., a guard, guide, or gauge, to regulate or restrict movement.
5. a person who buys and sells stolen goods.
6. a place where stolen property is bought and sold.
on the fence; not having chosen to join one side or the other in a controversy.

fence, *v.t.*; fenced (fenst), *pt.*, *pp.*; fencing, *ppr.*
1. to enclose with or as with a fence; to secure by an enclosure; to erect a fence about.
2. to guard; to fortify; to secure from danger or injury.

So much of adder's wisdom I have learnt,
To *fence* my ear against thy sorceries. —Milton.

3. to ward off or parry, as in fencing, argument, or reasoning. [Archaic.]

Reasoning of a very similar character . . . does duty largely as a means of *fencing* off disagreeable conclusions. —Mill.

4. to separate; to divide off; to keep apart; as, to *fence* grainfields from pasture land.
to fence the tables; in the Church of Scotland, to address intending communicants at the Lord's table with words of counsel and admonition.

fence, *v.i.* 1. to practice the art of fencing; to use a sword or foil for the purpose of learning the art of attack and defense; to fight and defend by giving and avoiding blows or thrusts.

They *fence* and push, and, pushing, loudly roar. —Dryden.

2. to avoid giving a direct reply; to parry; to evade.
3. to buy or sell stolen goods.

fence′fụl, *a.* affording defense; as, a *fenceful* weapon.

fence′less, *a.* 1. without a fence; unguarded; open; not closed; as, the *fenceless* ocean.
2. defenseless; having no means of protection.

fence liz′ărd, *Sceloporus undulatus*, the common lizard.

fence mŏnth, in English game laws, the closed season for fishing, etc.

fen′cẽr, *n.* 1. one who makes or repairs fences.
2. one who teaches or practices the art of fencing with sword or foil.
3. a horse good at leaping fences: said generally of a hunter.

fence rọọf, a protective screen or covering. [Obs.]

fence tīme, same as *closed season*.

fen′ci·ble, *a.* capable of being defended or of offering defense; as, a *fencible* castle. [Scot.]

fen′ci·ble, *n.* [*usually in pl.*] a soldier for defense of the country against invasion, and not liable to serve abroad; as, a regiment of *fencibles*. [Archaic.]

fen′cing, *n.* 1. the art of using skillfully a sword or foil in attack or defense.
2. material with which to build a fence.
3. the process of erecting a fence.
4. fences collectively considered, or such fences as may surround the fields on one

estate; as, the storm did great damage to *fencing* throughout this section.

5. in debate, skillful discussion; readiness in repartee; the act of parrying questions, as fencers do thrusts.

fen çrick'et, same as *mole cricket.*

fend, *v.t.*; fended, *pt., pp.*; fending, *ppr.* [ME. *fenden,* abbrev. of *defenden,* to defend.]

1. to defend. [Archaic or Poet.]

2. to keep off; to prevent from entering; to ward off; to shut out; usually followed by *off*; as, to *fend off* blows.

With fern beneath to *fend* the bitter cold. —Dryden.

fend, *v.i.* to act in opposition; to resist; to parry.

to fend for oneself; to manage by oneself; to get along without help.

fend, *n.* a fiend. [Obs.]

fend'ẽr, *n.* one who or that which fends or acts as a defense; any of various mechanical devices of a protective kind; specifically, (a) a screenlike guard against live coals in front of a fireplace; (b) a piece of timber or bundle of rope hung over the side of a vessel to prevent it from being injured in docking; (c) any of the metal frames over the wheels of an automobile or other vehicle to protect against splashing mud, etc.; a mudguard; (d) a device on the front of a streetcar or locomotive to catch or push aside anything on the track; a cowcatcher; (e) the shield of a cultivator, usually of sheet iron, protecting young plants from dirt worked toward them.

fen duck, the shoveler, a species of wild duck found frequently in fens and marshes.

fen'ẽr·āte, *v.t.* [L. *feneratus,* pp. of *fenerare,* to lend on interest, from *fenus,* proceeds, interest.] to put to use, as funds; to lend on interest. [Obs.]

fen·ẽr·ā'tion, *n.* the act of lending on interest. [Obs.]

fen·es·tel'lȧ, *n.* [L., dim. of *fenestra,* a window.] a small window or opening, especially one for displaying relics in an altar.

FENESTELLA

fē·nes'trȧ, *n.*; *pl.* **fē·nes'trae,** [L., a window.]

1. a small windowlike opening, as in the inner wall of the middle ear.

2. in entomology, (a) a hyaline spot, such as is found in the wings of certain butterflies and moths; (b) one of two membrane-covered depressions—supposedly of the nature of simple eyes—near the antennae of cockroaches.

fenestra ovalis; in the human ear, an ovoid opening leading to the cavity of the vestibule.

fenestra rotunda; a smaller opening below the *fenestra ovalis* leading to the cochlea.

fē·nes'trăl, *a.* [from L. *fenestra,* a window.]

1. of a window.

2. of or having a fenestra or fenestrae.

fē·nes'trăl, *n.* a frame fitted with cloth or paper instead of glass, serving as a window.

fē·nes'trāte, *a.* [L. *fenestratus,* pp. of *fenestrare,* to furnish with windows or openings, from *fenestra,* a window.]

1. having a network of openings; irregularly perforated; as, *fenestrate* leaves, in which the cellular tissue does not entirely fill the interstices between the veins.

2. in zoology, having fenestrae.

3. in architecture, same as *fenestrated.*

fē·nes'trā·ted, *a.* 1. having windows; having walls pierced by windows.

2. characterized by having fenestrae; fenestrate.

fen·es·trā'tion, *n.* 1. in architecture, a design in which the windows are arranged to form the principal feature; also, the series or arrangement of windows in a building.

2. the surgical operation of making a fenestra, or perforation, as in the middle ear.

fē·nes'trūle, *n.* [LL. *fenestrula,* dim. of *fenestra,* a window.] in zoology, one of the spaces enclosed by the intersecting branches of *Polyzoa.*

fen'ġīte, *n.* [L. *phengites,* from Gr. *phengitēs,* from *phengos,* light.] a kind of transparent or translucent stone anciently used as glazing in windows.

fen ġoose, the common European wild gray goose; the graylag.

Fē'ni·ăn, *n.* [named from the *Fiann* or *Fianna,* the old militia of Ireland, who were so called from *Finn, Fionn,* a hero of Irish tradition.]

1. any of a group of legendary military heroes of ancient Ireland.

2. a member of a secret Irish revolutionary brotherhood established in New York about 1858 for the purpose of freeing Ireland from English rule.

Fē'ni·ăn, *a.* of the Fenians.

Fē'ni·ăn·iṣm, *n.* the principles, aims, and methods of the Fenians.

feñks, *n.* the ultimate refuse of whale blubber, used as a fertilizer.

fen'land, *n.* marshy land: applied in particular to a district covered with marshes or fens in the middle and eastern parts of England.

fen'neç, *n.* [Ar. *fanak.*] a small, fawn-colored African fox with large ears.

fen'nel, *n.* [ME. *fenel, fenyl*; AS. *fenol, finol,* from L. *feniculum, fæniculum,* dim. of *fenum, fænum,* hay.] a plant of the genus *Fæniculum,* with yellow flowers: its aromatic seeds are used as a seasoning and in medicine.

sweet fennel; a smaller variety than the common fennel. It is used, especially in southern Europe, as a salad herb.

fen'nel·flow·ẽr, *n.* [so named from being confused with the *fennel.*]

1. a hardy herb of the genus Nigella, with blue, yellow, or white flowers: its seeds are often used for seasoning.

2. its flower.

fen'nel wa'tẽr, a liquor prepared from the seeds of the fennel or from oil extracted from the seeds. It is used in medicine.

fen'nish, *a.* same as *fenny.*

fen'ny, *a.* [ME. *fenny*; AS. *fennig, fenneg,* marshy, from *fen, fenn,* marsh, bog.]

1. boggy; marshy; full of fens.

2. growing in fens; as, *fenny* brake.

3. inhabiting marshy ground; as, a *fenny* snake.

Fen'rïr, *n.* [ON.] in Norse mythology, a great wolf, bound by the gods with a magic rope.

Fen'ris-wolf (-woolf), *n.* same as *Fenrir.*

fen'-sucked (-sukt), *a.* drained out of marshes. [Obs.]

fent, *n.* [ME. *fente*; OFr. *fente,* a slit, from *fendre,* L. *findere,* to cleave, split.]

1. an opening left in an article of dress, as in a sleeve or skirt, for convenience in putting on; a placket. [Obs.]

2. a piece of cloth damaged in dyeing or printing. [Brit.]

fen'ū·greek, *n.* [from L. *fenumgræcum, fænum Græcum,* lit., Greek hay; *fænum, fenum,* hay, and *Græcum,* neut. of *Græcus,* Greek.] a plant of the genus *Trigonella,* allied to clover, and cultivated for its seeds, which are used to flavor curry.

feod (fūd), *n.* [var. of *feud.*] an estate held under a feudal lord; a fee; a fief.

feod'ăl, *a.* of feods or feudalism; feudal.

feo·dal'i·ty (fū-), *n.* feudal tenures; the feudal system.

feod'ȧ·ry, *n.* same as *feudary.*

feoff (fef *or* fēf), *v.t.*; feoffed, *pt., pp.*; feoffing, *ppr.* [OFr. *feoffer, fiefer,* from *fief,* a fief.] to give or sell a fief to; to enfeoff.

feoff, *n.* same as *fief.*

feoff·ee', *n.* [OFr. *feoffe,* pp. of *feoffer,* to invest with a fief.] the beneficiary of a feoffment; one to whom land is given as a fief.

feoff'ment, *n.* [OFr. *feoffement,* from *feoffer,* to invest with a fief.] the granting of land as a fief; an enfeoffing; also, the instrument or deed by which corporeal hereditaments are conveyed.

feof'fŏr, feoff'ẽr, *n.* [Anglo-Fr. *feoffour.*] a person granting a feoffment.

-fẽr, [L. *-fer,* from *ferre,* to bear.] a suffix meaning *one that bears* or *produces,* as in coni*fer*: used to form nouns corresponding to adjectives in *-ferous.*

fẽr, *adv.* and *a.* far. [Obs.]

fē·rā'cious, *a.* [L. *ferax* (*-acis*), from *ferre,* to bear.] fruitful; producing abundantly.

fē·rac'i·ty, *n.* [L. *feracitas,* from *ferax* (*-acis*), fruitful.] the quality or state of being feracious; fruitfulness.

Fē'rae, *n.pl.* [L., f. pl. of *ferus,* wild.] an order of mammals, the *Carnivora.*

fē'rae nȧ·tū'rae, [L.] 1. of a wild nature.

2. in law, nondomesticated animals and fowls that are not the private property of anyone.

fē'răl, *a.* [from L. *ferus,* wild.]

1. a term applied to wild animals descended from tame stocks, or to animals having become wild from a state of domestication, or plants from a state of cultivation; as, *feral* pigs.

2. wild by nature; untamed; existing in a state of nature.

3. savage; brutal.

fē'răl, *a.* [L. *feralis,* of or belonging to the dead, from *ferre,* to bear, carry, as in a funeral.]

1. funereal; gloomy.

2. deadly; destructive; mortal.

Fē·rā'li·ȧ, *n.pl.* [L., neut. pl. of *feralis,* of or pertaining to the dead.] a solemn festival held by the Romans on the 21st of February in honor of the dead.

fer"-de-lānce' (-läns'), *n.* [Fr., the iron tip of a lance.] in zoology, a venomous snake of tropical American countries, belonging to the rattlesnake family. It attains a length of from five to seven feet.

fẽrd'ness, *n.* [ME. *ferdnes,* from *ferd,* fear, and *-ness.*] the state of being afraid; fearfulness; fright. [Obs.]

fēre, *n.* [ME. *fere*; AS. (Anglian) *fera,* aphetic form of *gefera*; *ge-,* together, and *-fera,* from base of *faran,* to go.]

1. a companion; a mate. [Archaic.]

2. a husband or wife. [Archaic.]

fēre, *n.* fire. [Obs.]

fēre, *n.* and *v.* fear. [Obs.]

fer'e·tō·ry, *n.*; *pl.* **fer'e·tō·rieṣ,** [L. *feretrum*; Gr. *pheretron,* a bier, litter, from *pherein,* to bear.]

1. a shrine for the relics of saints.

2. a bier.

3. the place in a church where shrines were kept.

FERETORY

fẽr'fōrth, *adv.* farforth. [Obs.]

Fẽr'gus, *n.* in Irish legend, a hero of the army that attacked Cuchulain at Ulster.

fẽr'gu·sŏn·īte, *n.* [named after Robert *Ferguson,* of Scotland.] an ore, of a brownish-black color, consisting of columbic acid and yttria, with some oxide of cerium and zirconia.

fē'ri·ȧ, *n.*; *pl.* **fē'ri·ae,** [LL.] 1. [*pl.*] holidays; festivals.

2. any weekday, especially one not designated by the church as a holiday.

fē'ri·ăl, *a.* [LL. *ferialis,* from *feria,* a holiday.]

1. having to do with a weekday, especially one not a church holiday.

2. having to do with a holiday.

fē·ri·ā'tion, *n.* [from L. *feriari,* to keep holiday, from *feriæ,* holidays.] the act of keeping holiday; cessation from work. [Obs.]

fē'rie, *n.* [OFr. *ferie,* from L. *feriæ,* holidays.] a holiday. [Obs.]

fē'rine, *a.* [L. *ferinus,* from *ferus,* wild.] same as *feral.*

fē'rine, *n.* a wild animal; a savage beast. [Rare.]

fē'rine·ly, *adv.* in the manner of wild beasts.

fē'rine·ness, *n.* wildness; savageness.

Fer·iñ'gi, Fer·iñ'ghee, *n.* [Per. *Farangi*; Ar. *Faranji,* adapted from OFr. *Franc,* a Frank.] in India, a European or a Eurasian, especially one of Portuguese-Indian descent.

Fē'ri·ō, *n.* in logic, one of the valid moods.

Fē·rī'sŏn, *n.* in logic, one of the valid moods.

fer'i·ty, *n.* [L. *feritas,* from *ferus,* wild, savage.] the state or quality of being wild, savage, or untamed.

fẽr'ly, *a.* wonderful; strange. [Obs.]

fẽr'ly, *n.* a wonder; a strange event or object. [Obs.]

fẽr'mȧ·cy, *n.* pharmacy. [Obs.]

fer·mä'tä, *n.* [It.] in music, (a) the holding of a tone or rest beyond its written value, at the discretion of the performer; (b) the sign (𝄐) indicating this. Also called *pause, hold.*

fẽr'ment, *n.* [L. *fermentum,* leaven, yeast, from *fervere,* to boil, be agitated.]

1. that which causes fermentation in other substances, as yeast, bacteria, enzymes, etc.

2. fermentation.

3. a state of excitement; commotion; un-

rest; tumult; agitation; as, to put the emotions in a *ferment*; the people are in a *ferment*.
Subdue and cool the *ferment* of desire.
—Rogers.

fẽr·ment′, *v.t.*; fermented, *pt.*, *pp.*; fermenting, *ppr.* [L. *fermentare*, from *fermentum*, leaven, yeast, from *fervere*, to boil, be agitated.]
1. to cause fermentation in.
2. to excite; to agitate.

fẽr·ment′, *v.i.* 1. to be in the process of fermentation.
2. to seethe; to be in agitation; to be excited; to be disturbed, as by violent emotions or great problems.

fẽr·ment·a̤·bil′i·ty, *n.* capability of being fermented.

fẽr·ment′a̤·ble, *a.* capable of fermentation.

fẽr·ment′ăl, *a.* fermentative. [Obs.]

fẽr·men·tā′tion, *n.* [LL. *fermentatio*, from L. *fermentare*, to ferment, cause to rise, from *fermentum*, yeast, ferment.]
1. the breakdown of complex molecules in organic compounds, caused by the influence of a ferment; as, bacteria cause milk to curdle by *fermentation*.
2. the state of being in high activity or commotion; agitation; excitement; a state of unrest.
An age of violent intellectual *fermentation* and of constant action and reaction.
—Macaulay.
acetous fermentation; see under *acetous*.
alcoholic fermentation; the change which takes place when a saccharine solution is exposed to the action of any of several fungi known as yeast plants. The sugar is converted into carbonic acid and alcohol.
lactic fermentation; the chemical change which takes place in milk in the process of becoming sour, when the sugar of the milk is converted into lactic acid.

fẽr·ment′a̤·tive, *a.* 1. causing or having power to cause fermentation.
2. produced by or consisting in fermentation.

fẽr·ment′a̤·tive·ly, *adv.* in a fermentative manner.

fẽr·ment′a̤·tive·ness, *n.* the state of being fermentative.

fẽr′mẽr·ẽr, *n.* an officer in charge of the infirmary maintained by an abbey, monastery, or similar religious house. [Obs.]

fẽr′me·tūre, *n.* [Fr., from *fermer*, to shut, fasten; L. *firmare*, to make fast.] one of a great variety of devices for closing the bore of a gun which loads at the breech.

fẽr′mil·let, *n.* [OFr.] a buckle or clasp. [Obs.]

fẽr′mi·on, *n.* [after E. *Fermi* (see next entry), and *-on*.] a subatomic particle, as an electron, proton, or neutron, that occurs alone at any one time at a particular energy level.

fẽr′mi·um, *n.* [named after E. *Fermi* (1901–54), American physicist.] a radioactive chemical element produced by intense neutron irradiation of plutonium: symbol, Fm; atomic weight, 257(?); atomic number, 100.

fẽrn, *n.* [ME. *ferne*; AS. *fearn*; G. *farn*, a fern.] any of a large class of shrubby plants called *Filicineae*, having their asexual reproductive cells on the back of the fronds, or leaves, in one-celled spore cases, or sporangia, variously grouped in dots, lines, or masses, and containing but one kind of minute, one-celled, powdery spore. Ferns are cryptogamous plants and abound in humid temperate and tropical regions. In size, they vary from the minute species growing on tree trunks to the giant tree fern of the tropics. They are very abundant as fossil plants. The earliest known forms occur in Devonian rocks, and their remains contribute largely to the formation of the beds of coal.

LADY FERN
(*Athyrium filix-femina*)

Christmas fern; an evergreen fern of North America, *Polystichum acrostichoides*.
climbing fern; a fern, *Lygodium palmatum*, having climbing fronds rising from slender, creeping rootstocks. It overruns low shrubs, the fronds sometimes attaining a length of three feet.
flowering fern; a species, *Osmunda regalis*, common in swamps and wet woods.
scented fern; a species, *Dennstedtia punctilobula*, whose fronds yield an aromatic odor when crushed.
sensitive fern; a fern, *Onoclea sensibilis*, growing in wet places, whose fronds exhibit a tendency to roll up when touched.

fẽrn′ẽr·y, *n.*; *pl.* **fẽrn′ẽr·ieṣ**, a place for cultivating ferns.

fẽrn′gāle, *n.* sweet fern.

fẽrn owl, 1. the goatsucker.
2. the short-eared owl, *Asio flammeus*.

fẽrn seed, the seed, or spores, of fern: formerly supposed to make the person who carried them invisible.

fẽrn′shaw, *n.* a thicket of ferns.

fẽrn′ti·cle, *n.* a freckle. [Brit. Dial.]

fẽrn′y, *a.* abounding in or like ferns.

fē·rō′cious, *a.* [L. *ferox* (-*ocis*), from *ferus*, wild, fierce.]
1. having or exhibiting ferocity, cruelty, savagery, etc.; violently cruel; as, *ferocious* actions or looks.
2. very great; as, a *ferocious* appetite. [Colloq.]
Syn.—fierce, savage, barbarous, untamed, fell, brutal, cruel, sanguinary, bloody.

fē·rō′cious·ly, *adv.* in a ferocious manner.

fē·rō′cious·ness, *n.* same as *ferocity*.

fē·roc′i·ty, *n.* [L. *ferocitas*, from *ferox* (-*ocis*), fierce, bold, savage, from *ferus*, wild.] the quality or condition of being ferocious; fierceness; as, the *ferocity* of barbarians; *ferocity* of countenance.

fer·ō′hẽr, *n.* a tutelary diety of the ancient Persians; also, a symbol, found in various forms on ancient monuments, supposed to represent a deity.

FEROHER

-fẽr·ous, [L. *-fer*, from *ferre*, to bear, and *-ous*.] a suffix meaning *bearing*, *producing*, *yielding*; as, coni*ferous*, auri*ferous*, chyli*ferous*.

fē′rous, *a.* [L. *ferus*, wild, fierce.] fierce; wild; untamable. [Rare.]

fer′răn·dine, *n.* [OFr. *ferrandin*, iron-gray, from L. *ferrum*, iron.] a fabric woven partly of silk and used for garments in the seventeenth century: also spelled *farandine*. [Obs.]

Fer·rä′ra̤, *n.* a claymore or broadsword of excellent quality: named after an Italian swordsmith, Andrea Ferrara.

Fer·rä·rēse′, *a.* of or relating to Ferrara, in Italy, or to the art school once located there.

Fer·rä·rēse′, *n.* a person native to or residing in Ferrara; collectively, all the inhabitants of Ferrara.

fer′ra̤·ry, *n.* [L. *ferraria*, an iron mine, from *ferrum*, iron.] the ironworker's art. [Obs.]

fer′rāte, *n.* a salt formed by combining ferric acid with a base.

fer′rē·ous, *a.* [L. *ferreus*, from *ferrum*, iron.] of or containing iron; also, like iron in hardness, etc.

fẽr′rest, *a.* and *adv.* farthest. [Obs.]

fer′ret, *n.* [ME. *feret*, *ferette*, *forette*, *furette*; OFr. *furet*; LL. *furetus*, a ferret, a dim. of *furo*, a ferret, from L. *fur*, a thief.] an animal of the weasel family, about fourteen inches in length, of a pale yellow color, with red eyes. It is a native of Africa, but has been introduced into Europe and America and is used in catching rabbits, rats, etc.

FERRET
(*Mustela furo*)

fer′ret, *v.t.*; ferreted, *pt.*, *pp.*; ferreting, *ppr.* to drive out of hiding with a ferret; hence, to search for with great care and diligence; to investigate thoroughly; as, to *ferret* out the conspirators.

fer′ret, *v.i.* 1. to hunt with ferrets.
2. to search.

fer′ret, *n.* [It. *fioretto*, a little flower, flowerwork upon silk or embroidery, dim. of *fiore*, a flower.] a kind of narrow ribbon made of wool, cotton, or silk: also called *ferreting*.

fer′ret, *n.* among glassmakers, the iron used to try the melted matter, to see if it is fit to work; also, the iron used to make the rings at the mouths of bottles.

fer′ret·ẽr, *n.* one who hunts with a ferret; also, one who ferrets out secrets.

fer·ret′tō, *n.* [It. *ferretto*, dim. of *ferro*, from L. *ferrum*, iron.] copper calcined with sulfur, used to color glass.

fer′ri-, [from L. *ferrum*, iron.] a combining form meaning *containing ferric iron*.

fer′ri·a̤ge, *n.* the price or fare to be paid at a ferry; also, conveyance over a river or lake in a ferry.

fer′riç, *a.* [from L. *ferrum*, iron.]
1. of, containing, or derived from iron.
2. in chemistry, designating or of iron with a valence higher than two, or compounds containing such iron: distinguished from *ferrous*.
ferric acid; an acid of iron, H_2FeO_4, never obtained in the free state and known only in the form of its salts, the ferrates.
ferric oxide; an oxide of iron, Fe_2O_3, occurring in nature as hematite.

fer·ri·cȳ′a̤·nāte, *n.* same as *ferricyanide*.

fer″ri·cȳ·an′iç ac′id, an acid, $H_3Fe(CN)_6$, obtained by decomposing ferricyanide of lead with sulfuric acid.

fer·ri·cȳ′a̤·nide, *n.* any salt of ferricyanic acid.
potassium ferricyanide; red prussiate of potash, $K_3Fe(CN)_6$, obtained by oxidizing $K_4Fe(CN)_6$ by the action of chlorine.

fer″ri·cȳ·an′ō·gen, *n.* [*ferri-*, and Gr. *kyanos*, a dark blue substance.] a sexivalent radical $(Fe(CN)_6)_2$.

fer′ri·ẽr, *n.* a ferryman; a boatman. [Obs.]

fer·rif′ẽr·ous, *a.* [*ferri-*, and L. *ferre*, to bear.] bearing or containing iron.

fer·ri·prus′si·āte, *n.* same as *ferricyanide*.

fer·ri·prus′siç, *a.* same as *ferricyanic*.

Fer′ris wheel (hwēl), [after George W. G. *Ferris* (1859–1896), Am. engineer who constructed the first one for the World's Fair in Chicago in 1893.] a large upright wheel revolving on a fixed axle and having seats hanging from the frame: used in amusement parks, etc.

FERRIS WHEEL

fer′rīte, *n.* [from L. *ferrum*, iron; and *-ite*.]
1. any yellowish or reddish-brown substance occurring in rocks and containing iron compounds.
2. one of the forms of pure metallic iron, having high magnetic permeability and occurring as a constituent of ordinary iron and steel.
3. any of various compounds in which ferric oxide may be regarded as combined with a more basic metallic oxide, as calcium ferrite, $Ca(FeO_2)_2$.

fer′rō-, [from L. *ferrum*, iron.] a combining form meaning: (a) *iron*, *connection with iron*, as in *ferro*magnetic; (b) *iron and*, as in *ferro*manganese; (c) in chemistry, *containing ferrous iron*, as in *ferro*cyanide.

fer″rō·al·loy′, *n.* any of various alloys of iron used in the manufacture of steel: they are named from the added metal, as ferrochromium, ferromanganese, etc.

fer·rō·çal′cīte, *n.* [*ferro-*, and L. *calx*, *calcis*, lime, and *-ite*.] a kind of calcite which takes on a brown color after exposure, due to the iron contained in it.

fer″rō·chrō′mi·um, *n.* [*ferro-*, and *chrome*.] an alloy of iron and chromium used in making steel.

fer·rō·çon′çrēte, *n.* concrete having an iron or steel framework embedded in it: also called *reinforced concrete, armored concrete.*

fer·rō·cȳ′ȧ·nāte, *n.* a compound of ferrocyanic acid with a base.

fer″rō·cȳ·an′iç, *a.* designating or of an acid, $H_4Fe(CN)_6$, obtained by decomposing a ferrocyanide with sulfuric acid.

fer·rō·cȳ′ȧ·nide, *n.* a salt formed by the union of ferrocyanic acid with a base.
potassium ferrocyanide; yellow prussiate of potash, $K_4Fe(CN)_6$.

fer″rō·mag·nē′siăn, *a.* in mineralogy, having iron and magnesium as constituents.

fer″rō·mag·net′iç, *a.* [*ferro-*, and L. *magneticus*, from *magnes* (*-etis*), a magnet.]
1. formerly, paramagnetic: opposite of *diamagnetic.*
2. highly magnetic, as iron, nickel, etc.: distinguished from *paramagnetic.*

fer·rō·mag′net·ism, *n.* the quality of being ferromagnetic.

fer·rō·mañ′gȧ·nēṣe, *n.* [*ferro-*, and Fr. *manganese*, manganese.] an alloy of iron and manganese, used for making hard steel.

fer·rō·prus′si·āte, *n.* same as *ferrocyanide.*

fer·rō·prus′siç, *a.* same as *ferrocyanic.*

fer·rō·sil′i·cŏn, *n.* a compound of iron and silicon, used in making steel.

fer″rō·sō·fer′riç, *a.* [*ferro-*, and L. *ferrum*, iron.] designating or of the black or magnetic oxide of iron, Fe_3O_4: also known as *magnetite* and *lodestone.*

fer′rō·tȳpe, *n.* [*ferro-*, and Gr. *typos*, impression, image.]
1. a positive photograph taken directly on a thin plate of iron coated with a sensitized film: also called *tintype.*
2. the process of making such photographs.

fer′rous, *a.* [from L. *ferrum*, iron.]
1. of, containing, or derived from iron.
2. in chemistry, designating or of bivalent iron or compounds containing it: distinguished from *ferric.*

fer·rū′ġi·nā·ted, *a.* [from L. *ferruginus*, of the color of iron rust, from *ferrugo* (*-inis*), iron rust, the color of iron rust.] having the color or properties of the rust of iron.

fer·rū·ġi·nā′tion, *n.* the act or process of permeating or coloring with iron ore or iron rust: said of the discoloring of rocks.

fer·rū·ġin′ē·ous, *a.* same as *ferruginous.*

fer·rū′ġi·nous, *a.* [L. *ferruginus*, of the color of iron rust, dusky, from *ferrugo* (*-inis*), iron rust, the color of iron rust, from *ferrum*, iron.]
1. of iron; containing iron; having the nature of iron.
2. having the color of iron rust; reddish-brown.

fer·rū′gō, *n.* [L. *ferrugo*, iron rust, the color of iron rust.] in botany, disease rust. [Obs.]

fer′rule (fer′ụl *or* -ūl), *n.* [formerly *verrel*; OFr. *virole*, an iron ring to put around the end of a staff, from LL. *virola*, a ring, bracelet; L. *viriola*, dim. of *viria*, a bracelet, armlet, from *viere*, to twist, bind around. The spelling of the word was corrupted in imitation of L. *ferrum*, iron.]
1. a metal ring or cap put around the end of a stick, tool, cane, etc. to prevent splitting or to give added strength.
2. in mechanics, a short tube or bushing for tightening a joint.
3. a bushing placed in the end of a flue to expand it.
4. the wooden frame fitted about a slate.

fer′rule, *v.t.*; ferruled, *pt., pp.*; ferruling, *ppr.* to furnish with a ferrule.

fer′ruled, *a.* having a ferrule.

fer·rū′mi·nāte, *v.t.* [L. *ferruminatus*, pp. of *ferruminare*, to cement, solder, from *ferrumen*, cement, solder, from *ferrum*, iron.] to unite by solder; to join together: used of metals. [Rare.]

fer·rū·mi·nā′tion, *n.* the soldering or uniting of metals. [Rare.]

fer′ry, *v.t.*; ferried, *pt., pp.*; ferrying, *ppr.* [ME. *ferien*; AS. *ferian*, to carry, convey, especially in a boat, from *faran*, to go.]
1. to carry or transport across a river or narrow body of water in a boat.
2. to cross (a river, etc.), as on a ferry.
3. to deliver (airplanes) by flying to the destination.

fer′ry, *v.i.* to pass over water in a ferryboat.

fer′ry, *n.*; *pl.* **fer′rieṣ,** 1. a transportation system in which passengers and goods are carried across a river or other narrow body of water.
2. a boat for this purpose.
3. the place or passage where ferryboats cross.
4. the legal right of conveying passengers and goods across a river or other narrow body of water for a fee.
5. the delivery of airplanes from one point to another by flying them.

fer′ry·bōat, *n.* a boat for conveying passengers and goods over streams and other narrow bodies of water.

fer′ry bridġe (brij), 1. a boat to ferry railroad trains across a stream.
2. an adjustable landing platform for a ferry.

fer′ry·măn, *n.*; *pl.* **fer′ry·men,** one who owns, manages, or works on a ferry.

fẽrs, *a.* fierce; furious. [Obs.]

fẽrth, fẽrthe, *a.* fourth. [Obs.]

fẽr′tile, *a.* [L. *fertilis*, fruitful, fertile, from *ferre*, to bear.]
1. fruitful; rich; producing in abundance; prolific; productive; as, a *fertile* valley; a *fertile* variety of fowls; a country *fertile* in explorers.
2. productive in mental achievements; inventive; ingenious; active; having abundant resources; as, a *fertile* imagination.
3. bringing about production; causing or helping fertility; increasing fruitfulness; as, a *fertile* rain.
4. plentiful; produced in large measure; abundant.
5. able to produce young, seeds, fruit, etc.
6. capable of development into a new individual; fertilized; as, *fertile* eggs.
Syn.—fruitful, productive, prolific, fecund, rich, luxuriant.—*Fertile* denotes the power of producing, *fruitful* the act.

fẽr′tile·ly, *adv.* fruitfully.

fẽr′tile·ness, *n.* the state or quality of being fertile; fertility.

fẽr·til′i·tāte, *v.t.* to render fertile; to make productive; to fertilize. [Obs.]

fẽr·til′i·ty, *n.*; *pl.* **fẽr·til′i·tieṣ,** [L. *fertilitas*, from *fertilis*, fruitful, fertile, from *ferre*, to bear.] the quality or state of being fertile; fruitfulness; productiveness.

fẽr′ti·līz·ȧ·ble, *a.* that can be fertilized.

fẽr″ti·li·zā′tion, *n.* 1. the act or process of making fertile or productive; also, the state of being fertilized.
2. in biology, the union of a male and female germ cell; impregnation; specifically, in botany, the application of the pollen to the stigma, and its subsequent action upon the ovules, by means of which a perfect seed containing an embryo is produced; fecundation.
close fertilization; the pollenization of a stigma from the stamens of the same flower: called also *self-fertilization.*

fẽr′ti·līze, *v.t.*; fertilized, *pt., pp.*; fertilizing, *ppr.* 1. to enrich; to make fruitful or productive; as, to *fertilize* the soil.
2. to spread fertilizer on.
3. in biology, to impregnate; specifically, in botany, to pollenize.

fẽr′ti·lī·zẽr, *n.* a person or thing that fertilizes; specifically, (a) any material put on or in the soil to improve the quality or quantity of plant growth, as manure, chemicals, etc.; (b) in botany, something that helps bring about fertilization; as, bees are *fertilizers* of flowers.

fer′ū·lȧ (*or* -ụ-lȧ), *n.*; *pl.* **fer′ū·lae,** [L., the giant fennel, a rod, walking stick.]
1. a staff or rod; a ferule.
2. a staff of authority; a scepter: applied particularly to the scepter of eastern rulers, as those of the Byzantine Empire.
3. [F—] a genus of herbs related to parsley, mostly native to Oriental and Mediterranean countries, a few species, however, being found on the Pacific coast of America. They are large, coarse plants of the family *Umbelliferæ*, having dissected leaves, yellow umbellate flowers, and thick, resinous roots; certain species yield gums of medicinal value, as asafetida and galbanum.
4. any plant of this genus.

fer·ū·lā′ceous, *a.* [L. *ferulaceus*, from *ferula*, the giant fennel, a rod, walking stick.] pertaining to reeds or canes; having a stalk like a reed; reedlike.

fer′ū·lăr, *n.* [from L. *ferula*, a rod, walking stick.] a rod; a ferule. [Obs.]

fer′ule (fer′ụl *or* -ūl), *n.* [L. *ferula*, a rod, walking stick, from *ferire*, to strike.] a ruler or stick used to punish children.

fer′ule, *v.t.*; feruled, *pt., pp.*; feruling, *ppr.* to punish with a ferule.

fer′ule, *n.* same as *ferrule.*

fē·rū′liç, *a.* of, relating to, or obtained from asafetida.

fẽr′vence, *n.* fervency. [Obs.]

fẽr′ven·cy, *n.* [L. *fervens* (*-entis*), ppr. of *fervere*, to boil, glow, rage.] great warmth of feeling; ardor; eagerness; zeal; intense devotion.

fẽr′vent, *a.* 1. hot; burning; glowing; as, a *fervent* summer; *fervent* blood.
2. having or showing great warmth of feeling; ardent; earnest; as, *fervent* zeal, *fervent* piety.

fẽr′vent·ly, *adv.* in a fervent manner.

fẽr′vent·ness, *n.* the state or quality of being fervent; fervency.

fẽr·ves′cent, *a.* [L. *fervescens* (*-entis*), ppr. of *fervescere*, to begin to boil, glow, incept. of *fervere*, to boil, glow.] growing hot.

fẽr′vid, *a.* [L. *fervidus*, from *fervere*, to boil, glow.]
1. very hot; burning; boiling; as, *fervid* heat.
2. impassioned; fervent; as, *fervid* zeal.

fẽr′vid·ly, *adv.* in a fervid manner; earnestly; intensely.

fẽr′vid·ness, *n.* the state or quality of being fervid.

Fer·vi·dọr′ (*Eng.* fũr′vi-dọr), *n.* [Fr., from L. *fervidus*, from *fervere*, to boil.] Thermidor, the eleventh month of the French Revolutionary Calendar.

fẽr′vŏr, *n.* [L. *fervor*, from *fervere*, to boil, grow hot, glow.]
1. intense heat or warmth; as, the *fervor* of a summer's day.
2. intense feeling; ardor; zeal; earnestness; passion.

fẽr′voŭr, *n.* fervor: British spelling.

Fes′cen·nīne, *a.* pertaining to Fescennia (Fescennium), an ancient city in Italy, or to the festivals held there, which were characterized by coarse songs and verses; licentious; scurrilous; vulgar; obscene.

Fes′cen·nīne, *n.* a coarse, licentious song or poem commonly given at nuptial festivals and other celebrations in Fescennia, Rome, and other ancient Italian cities.

fes′çūe, *n.* [ME. *festue, festu*; OFr. *festu*, from L. *festuca*, a stock, straw.]
1. a small stick or other slender object used as a teacher's pointer. [Rare.]
2. any of a group of tough meadow grasses, used for pasture.
3. the plectrum with which the strings of the harp or lyre were struck. [Obs.]
4. the gnomon or style of a sundial. [Obs.]

fes′çūe, *v.t.* to direct or teach with a fescue; to assist in reading by a fescue. [Obs.]

fes′çūe grȧss, same as *fescue* (sense 2).

fess, fesse, *n.* [OFr. *fesse*, a fess, from L. *fascula*, a band.] in heraldry, a horizontal band or girdle comprising the center third of an escutcheon: one of the ordinaries.

FESS

fes′si·tūde, *n.* [from L. *fessus*, weary.] weariness. [Obs.]

fess point, the exact center of an escutcheon.

fess′wīṣe, *adv.* in the position of a fess, or with divisions like those of a fess; horizontally.

fest, *n.* the fist. [Obs.]

-fest, [from G. *fest*, a feast, celebration.] a combining form used in forming colloquial and slang words, meaning *an occasion of much*, as in song*fest*, fun*fest*, slug*fest.*

fes′tăl, *a.* [OFr. *festal*, from L. *festum*, a holiday, feast.] pertaining to a feast or festival; joyous; gay; mirthful.

fes′tăl·ly, *adv.* joyously; mirthfully.

feste, fest, *n.* a feast. [Obs.]

fes′tẽr, *n.* [ME.; OFr. *festre*; L. *fistula*, a pipe, cane.] a small sore producing pus; a pustule.

fes′tẽr, *v.i.*; festered, *pt., pp.*; festering, *ppr.* [ME. *festren, feestren*; OFr. *festrir*, to ulcerate, fester, from *festre*, an ulcer.]
1. to form pus; to suppurate; to ulcerate.
2. to become more and more virulent and fixed; to rankle; to grow embittered.

> Passion and unkindness may give a wound that shall bleed and smart; but it is treachery that makes it *fester.* —South.

3. to decay.

fes′tẽr, *v.t.* 1. to produce ulceration in; to cause to suppurate.
2. to cause to rankle or become bitter; to embitter.

fes′tẽr·ment, *n.* a festering. [Rare.]

fes′ti·nāte, *a.* [L. *festinatus*, pp. of *festinare*, to hasten, from *festinus*, hasty, quick.] hasty; hurried. [Obs.]

fes′ti·nāte·ly, *adv.* hastily. [Obs.]

fes·ti·nā′tion, *n.* [L. *festinatio*, from *festinare*, to make haste.]
1. haste. [Obs.]
2. an involuntary inclination to hurry in walking, especially as a symptom of certain nervous diseases.

Fes·tī′nō, *n.* in logic, one of the valid modes.

fes′ti·văl, *a.* [OFr. *festival*; LL. *festivalis*, from L. *festivus*, festive.] pertaining to a feast; appropriate to or characteristic of a festival or celebration; joyous; mirthful; as, a *festival* entertainment.

fes′ti·văl, *n.* 1. a time or day of feasting or celebration, especially a periodic religious celebration.
The morning trumpets *festival* proclaimed. —Milton.
2. a celebration, entertainment, or series of performances of a certain kind, often held periodically; as, the Bach *festival*.
3. merrymaking; festivity.

fes′tive, *a.* [L. *festivus*, from *festum*, a feast.] of, for, or suitable for a feast or festival; joyous; gay; mirthful.
The glad circle round them yield their souls
To *festive* mirth and wit that knows no gall. —Thomson.

fes′tive·ly, *adv.* in a festive manner.

fes·tiv′i·ty, *n.*; *pl.* **fes·tiv′i·ties,** [L. *festivitas*, from *festum*, a feast.]
1. mirth; joyfulness; gaiety; merriment.
2. a festival.
3. [*pl.*] festive proceedings; things done in celebration.

fes′tiv·ous, *a.* [L. *festivus*, from *festum*, a feast.] pertaining to a feast; joyous. [Rare.]

fes·tọọn′, *n.* [Fr. *feston*, LL. *festo* (*-onis*), a garland, prob. from L. *festum*, a festival.]
1. a chain or garland of flowers, foliage, drapery, etc., suspended so as to form one or more curves.
2. in architecture, etc., a sculptured ornament in imitation of a garland of fruits, leaves, or flowers suspended between two points.

fes·tọọn′, *v.t.*; festooned, *pt.*, *pp.*; festooning, *ppr.* 1. to hang or adorn with festoons.
2. to form into a festoon or festoons.
3. to join by festoons.

fes·tọọn′ẽr·y, *n.* an arrangement of festoons in decoration.

fes·tọọn′y, *a.* belonging to or resembling festoons; consisting of or decorated with festoons.

Fes·tū′cȧ, *n.* [L., a stalk, strawlike weed.] a genus of grasses containing a great number of species, found in the temperate and colder regions of the world. Among them are found some of the best meadow and pasture grasses, as *Festuca elatior* (the meadow fescue) and *Festuca ovina* (the sheep's fescue).

fes′tū·cine, *a.* [L. *festuca*, a stalk, strawlike weed, and *-ine*.] straw-colored.

fes′tū·cous, *a.* [L. *festuca*, a straw.] formed of straw. [Obs.]

fes′tūe, *n.* fescue. [Obs.]

fet, *v.t.* [ME. *fetten*; AS. *fetian*, to bring, fetch.] to fetch; to bring to. [Obs.]

fē′tăl, foe′tăl, *a.* 1. pertaining to a fetus.
2. characteristic of a fetus.

fē·tā′tion, foe·tā′tion, *n.* the development of a fetus; pregnancy; gestation.

fetch, *v.t.*; fetched (fecht), *pt.*, *pp.*; fetching, *ppr.* [ME. *fetchen*, *fecchen*, from AS. *feccan*, to bring, fetch.]
1. to go after and bring back; to get.
We will take . . . men . . . to *fetch* victuals for the people. —Judges xx. 10.
2. to derive; to draw, as from a source.
3. to bring back; to recall; to revive: often used with *to*. [Dial.]
4. to draw (a breath); to heave; as, to *fetch* a sigh.
5. to reach; to attain or come to; to arrive at. [Dial.]
We *fetched* the syren's isle. —Chapman.
6. to bring to a certain state; to draw into a certain place or relation; to cause to come; to produce; to elicit; as, to *fetch* butter by churning.
7. to make or perform; to accomplish or effect; as, to *fetch* a leap or bound. [Dial.]
8. to bring, on sale or in exchange; to obtain as a price; as, wheat *fetches* only seventy-five cents a bushel; a commodity is worth what it will *fetch*.
9. to attract or charm; to captivate or fascinate. [Colloq.]
10. to deliver or deal (a blow, stroke, etc.). [Colloq.]

to fetch a pump; to start the water by priming the pump.
to fetch headway or *sternway*; in nautical usage, to make progress forward or backward. [Obs.]
to fetch out; to bring or draw out; to cause to appear.
to fetch up; to recover or regain, as time or distance lost.

fetch, *v.i.* 1. to go after things and bring them back.
2. to retrieve game: said of hounds.
3. in nautical usage, (a) to take or hold a course; (b) to veer.
to fetch and carry; to perform menial services; to do minor tasks and chores.
to fetch away; in nautical usage, to break away and roll to leeward, as articles on shipboard.
to fetch up; to stop suddenly or to arrive at an unexpected destination, as, having lost our way in the dark, we *fetched up* at Dumfries.

fetch, *n.* 1. a stratagem by which a thing is indirectly brought to pass, or by which one thing seems intended and another is done; a trick; an artifice; as, a *fetch* of wit.
Straight cast about to overreach
The unwary conquerer with a *fetch*. —Hudibras.
2. the act of fetching; the act of laying hold upon, or of drawing in to one.

fetch, *n.* [prob. Anglo-Ir. form of *fetch-life*.] the hallucination of seeing as dead a person who is still alive; a wraith; an apparition.

fetch can′dle, a light seen after nightfall, superstitiously believed to foreshadow a person's death: also called *fetch light*.

fetch′ẽr, *n.* one who fetches.

fetch′ing, *a.* attractive; pretty; charming. [Colloq.]

fete, fête (fāt), *v.t.*; feted *or* fêted, *pt.*, *pp.*; feting *or* fêting, *ppr.* [Fr. *fêter*, to feast, entertain, from *fête*; OFr. *feste*, L. *festum*, a feast, festival.] to feast; to honor with festivities; to entertain sumptuously.

fete, fête (fāt), *n.* [Fr., from OFr. *feste*, a feast, festival.] a festival; an entertainment; especially, a gala entertainment held outdoors.
fête champêtre (shäṅ-pā′tr); a festival or entertainment held in the open air; a garden-party.

fete dāy, a holiday or birthday; especially, a day celebrated in honor of one's patron saint.

fet·e·rī′tȧ, *n.* a grain-yielding sorghum of the southwestern United States, obtained from *Sorghum vulgare*: also called *Sudan durra*.

fē′tiăl (-shăl), *n.*; *pl.* **fē·ti·ā′lēs** (-shi-ā′), [L. *fetialis*, pertaining to the *fetiales*, a college of priests.] in ancient Rome, any of a group of twenty priests who acted as the guardians of the public faith in the matters of declaring war and concluding peace.

fē′tiăl, *a.* of the fetiales or their functions.

fē·ti·ā′lis (-shi-ā′), *n.*; *pl.* **fē·ti·ā′lēs,** same as *fetial*.

fē′tich, etc. see *fetish*, etc.

fē·ti·cī′dăl, foe·ti·cī′dăl, *a.* relating to, or used in the practice of, feticide.

fē′ti·cīde, foe′ti·cīde, *n.* [L. *fetus*, a fetus, and *-cidium*, from *cædere*, to kill.] the killing of a fetus; illegal abortion.

fet′id, *a.* [L. *fetidus*, *fœtidus*, stinking, ill-smelling, from *fetere*, *fœtere*, to stink.] having an offensive smell; having a strong or rancid scent.
Most putrefactions smell either *fetid* or moldy. —Bacon.

fet·id′i·ty, *n.* same as *fetidness*.

fet′id·ness, *n.* the quality of smelling offensive; a fetid quality.

fē·tif′ẽr·ous, *a.* [L. *fetus*, *fœtus*, a fetus, and *ferre*, to bear.] producing young, as animals.

fe·tip′ȧ·rous, *a.* [from *fetus*, and *-parous*.] designating or of animals whose young are born incompletely developed, as marsupials: also spelled *foetiparous*.

fē′tise, fē′tis, *a.* [ME. *fetise*, *fetis*, from OFr. *faitis*, *fetis*, neat, well-made.] neat; trim; graceful; pretty. [Obs.]

fē′tise·ly, *adv.* neatly; adroitly; gracefully; prettily. [Obs.]

fē′tish, fē′tich (*or* fet′ish), *n.* [Fr. *fétiche*; Port. *feitico*, adj. artificial, n. sorcery, charm, from L. *facticius*, *factitius*, artificial, from *facere*, to make.]
1. any object, animate or inanimate, natural or artificial, regarded with a feeling of awe, as having mysterious powers residing in it or as being the representative or habitation of a deity. Among primitive peoples it is usual for each tribe to have a fetish in common, but in addition every individual may have one of his own, to which he offers up prayers.

FETISHES OF DAHOMEY

2. anything to which one gives excessive devotion or blind adoration.
3. in psychiatry, any nonsexual object, such as a foot or a glove, that excites erotic feelings.

fē′tish·ism, fē′tich·ism, *n.* 1. the belief in or worship or adoration of fetishes.
2. unreasoning and blind devotion to any object.
3. in psychiatry, an abnormal condition in which erotic feelings are excited by a nonsexual object, as a foot, glove, etc.

fē′tish·ist, fē′tich·ist, *n.* one who believes in or worships fetishes.

fē·tish·is′tic, fē·tich·is′tic, *a.* pertaining to or marked by fetishism.

fē′tish man, a man credited by savages with supernatural powers; a medicine man.

fet′lock, *n.* [D. *vitlok*, *vitslok*, the pastern of a horse.]
1. a tuft of hair growing on the back of a horse's leg just above the hoof.
2. the part of a horse's leg where this tuft grows; also, the projection of the limb at this joint.
3. a device attached to the leg of a horse in pasture to prevent it from running away or leaping fences.
Also *fetterlock*.

fē′tŏr, *n.* [L. *fetor*, *fœtor*, from *fetere*, to stink.] any strong, offensive smell; stench: also spelled *foetor*.

fet′tẽr, *n.* [ME. *feter*; AS. *fetor*, *feter*, a fetter.]
1. [*usually pl.*] a shackle or a chain for the feet; a chain by which a person or an animal is confined by the feet.
The Philistines bound Samson with *fetters* of brass. —Judges xvi. 21.
2. anything that confines or restrains from motion; a restraint.
Passions too fierce to be in *fetters* bound. —Dryden.

fet′tẽr, *v.t.*; fettered, *pt.*, *pp.*; fettering, *ppr.* [ME. *feteren*, from AS. *gefeterian*, to fetter.]
1. to put in fetters; to shackle or confine the feet of with a chain.
2. to bind; to enchain; to confine; to restrain motion of; to impose restraints on.
Fetter strong madness in a silken thread. —Shak.

fet′tẽr bōne, the great pastern bone of a horse's foot, just below the fetlock joint.

fet′tẽr bush, a shrub of the heath family, found in sandy regions in southern United States. It has thick evergreen leaves and white or pink flowers borne in axillary clusters.

fet′tẽred, *a.* 1. bound or confined by fetters; enchained.
2. in zoology, denoting the feet of animals, when they are stretched backward and appear unfit for walking.

fet′tẽr·ẽr, *n.* one who fetters.

fet′tẽr·less, *a.* free from restraint; unfettered.

fet′tẽr·lock, *n.* 1. a hobble such as is put on a horse to prevent its escape from pasture.
2. in heraldry, a charge within a shackle or fetter.

fet′ti·cus, *n.* the European corn salad, *Valerianella olitoria*: called also *lamb's lettuce*.

fet′tle, *v.t.*; fettled, *pt.*, *pp.*; fettling, *ppr.* [ME. *fetlen*, to make ready.]
1. to repair; to put in right order; to put the finishing touches to. [Dial.]
2. to beat (a person).
3. in metallurgy, to line or cover (the hearth

of a puddling furnace) with ore, silica, or other loose material.

fet′tle, *v.i.* to busy oneself. [Brit. Dial.]

fet′tle, *n.* 1. condition; state; trim; as, the speaker was in fine *fettle.*

2. in metallurgy, the lining for the hearth of a puddling furnace.

fet′tling, *n.* in metallurgy, a loose material, as ore, silica, etc., used to line and protect the hearth of a puddling furnace.

fet·tu̇c·ci′nē (-chē′nē), *n.pl.* [*often construed as sing.*] [It., lit., little ribbons.] broad, flat noodles served with sauce, butter, etc.: also spelled *fettucine, fettucini.*

fē′tus, *n.*; *pl.* **fe′tus·eṣ,** [L. *fetus, fœtus,* a bringing forth, bearing, progeny; adj., pregnant, fruitful.]

1. the unborn young of an animal while still in the uterus or egg, especially in its later stages.

2. in man, the offspring in the womb from the end of the third month of pregnancy until birth: distinguished from *embryo.*

Also spelled *foetus.*

feū, *n.* [OFr. *feu, fieu,* fief.] in Scottish history and law, (a) a fee; a feudal estate; (b) a right to the use and enjoyment of lands, houses, or other heritable subjects in perpetuity in consideration of agricultural services or an annual payment in grain or money, called *feu duty,* and certain other contingent burdens. This was deemed an ignoble tenure, as distinguished from *wardholding,* where the service rendered was purely military, and *blanch-holding,* where it was merely nominal; (c) the land or piece of ground so held.

feū, *v.t.* in Scottish history and law, to grant (land) on feu.

feū′ăr, *n.* a tenant who has his holdings under a feu.

feūd, *n.* [ME. *fede, feide*; AS. *fœhth,* from *fah,* hostile, guilty, outlawed.]

1. enmity; inveterate hatred; mutual aversion. [Obs.]

2. a bitter, deadly quarrel; especially, such a quarrel between clans or families, lasting through several generations.

feūd, *v.i.* to carry on a feud; to quarrel.

feūd, *n.* [LL. *feudum, feodum,* a feud, fief, fee; O.H.G. *fihu, fehu,* cattle, property.] in the feudal system, land held from a lord in return for service given him: also *fee, fief, feoff, feod.*

feū′dăl, *a.* [LL. *feudalis,* feudal, a vassal, from *feudum,* a feud.]

1. of or having to do with land held in feud.

2. of or having to do with feudalism.

feudal system; same as *feudalism.*

feū′dăl, *a.* having to do with a feud, or quarrel.

feū′dăl·iṣm, *n.* the feudal system; the economic, political, and social organization of medieval Europe, in which land, worked by serfs attached to it, was held by vassals in exchange for military and other services given to overlords.

feū′dăl·ist, *n.* a supporter of the feudal system; one versed in feudal law; a feudist.

feū·dăl·is′tiç, *a.* 1. of, or having the nature of, feudalism.

2. inclined toward feudalism.

feū·dal′i·ty, *n.*; *pl.* **feū·dal′i·tieṣ,** 1. the state or quality of being feudal; feudalism.

2. a feudal holding or estate; a fief.

feū·dăl·i·zā′tion, *n.* a feudalizing or being feudalized.

feū′dăl·īze, *v.t.*; feudalized, *pt., pp.*; feudalizing, *ppr.* to make feudal; to establish feudalism in.

feū′dăl·ly, *adv.* 1. according to feudalism.

2. under feudal tenure.

feū′dȧ·ry, *a.* [LL. *feudarius,* from *feudum,* a feud.] pertaining to or devolving on feudal tenure.

feū′dȧ·ry, *n.* 1. one who has holdings under the feudal system; a feudatory.

2. an ancient officer of the court of wards in England: spelled also *feodary.*

feū′dȧ·tā·ry, *n.* and *a.* feudatory. [Obs.]

feū′dȧ·tō·ry, *n.*; *pl.* **feū′dȧ·tō·rieṣ,** [LL. *feudatarius,* from *feudum,* a feud.]

1. a tenant or vassal who holds his lands of a superior on condition of military service; the tenant of a feud or fief.

2. a feud or fief so held.

feū′dȧ·tō·ry, *a.* 1. of the feudal relationship between vassal and lord.

2. owing feudal allegiance (*to*).

feu̧ de joie (zhwä), [Fr., a bonfire, lit., a fire of joy.] a bonfire, or a firing of guns, in token of joy.

feūd′ist, *n.* a participant in a feud, or quarrel.

feūd′ist, *n.* [Fr. *feudiste,* from LL. *feudum,* a feud.]

1. in law, a specialist in feudal law.

2. one holding or letting land under feudal tenure.

Feu̧·illants′ (fu̧-yon′), *n. pl.* a religious order, an offshoot of the Cistercians, founded by Jean de la Barrière: so called from the convent of Feuillans in Languedoc, where it was first established.

feuil·le·morte′ (fu̧-yȧ-mort′), *n.* [Fr., lit., dead leaf.] the color of a faded leaf.

feuil·le·morte′, *a.* of a brown color like that of a fallen or faded leaf.

feuil·le·ton′ (fu̧-yȧ-tōn′), *n.* [Fr., from *feuillet,* a leaf, sheet.]

1. a section of a French newspaper, commonly at the bottom of the page, devoted to criticisms, short stories, or chapters from a serial.

2. an article, story, etc. which appears in this part.

feuil′le·ton·ist (-ton-ist), *n.* one who contributes to the feuilleton.

feuil·le·ton·is′tiç, *a.* ephemeral; shallow; after the style of a feuilleton.

feū′tēr, *v.t.* [ME. *feutre*; OFr. *feutre, fautre, feltre,* a rest for a lance, felt; LL. *flitrum, feltrum,* felt, a pad for a lance.] to make ready by placing in the rest, as a spear: also spelled *fewter.* [Obs.]

feū′tēr·ēr, *n.* a dog keeper: also spelled *fewterer.* [Obs.]

fē′vēr, *n.* [ME. *fever, fevere, fevre*; AS. *fefer, fefor*; Pr. *febre,* from L. *febris,* fever.]

1. a state of abnormally increased body temperature; pyrexia.

2. a disease characterized by a rise in body temperature and by an accelerated pulse, with impaired functions, diminished strength, and often with delirium. Many diseases of which fever is only the leading symptom are designated *fevers*; the principal division of fevers is into *remitting fevers,* which subside or abate at intervals; *intermitting fevers,* which intermit or entirely cease at intervals; and *continued* or *continual fevers,* which neither remit nor intermit.

3. heat; agitation; excitement by anything that strongly affects the emotions; as, this quarrel has set my blood in a *fever.*

Duncan is in his grave;
After life's fitful *fever* he sleeps well.—Shak.

fever and ague; a periodical malarial fever preceded by chills.

fē′vēr, *v.t.*; fevered, *pt., pp.*; fevering, *ppr.* [AS. *feferian,* from *fefer,* fever.] to cause fever in.

fē′vēr, *v.i.* to contract a fever. [Rare.]

fē′vēr bärk, *Alstonia* bark, from which a tonic is prepared.

fē′vēr blis′tēr, a fever sore; a cold sore.

fe′vēr·bu̧sh, *n.* the spicebush or wild allspice, *Lindera benzoin.*

fē′vēr·et, *n.* a slight fever.

fē′vēr·few, *n.* [ME. *fevyrfew, fewerfue*; AS. *feferfuge, feferfugia*; LL. *febrifugia,* a febrifuge; L. *febris,* a fever, and *fugare,* to chase, drive away.] a plant of the aster family, so named from supposed febrifuge qualities. The common feverfew grows to the height of two or three feet, with compound, radiated, white flowers.

fē′vēr flȳ, a dipterous insect, *Dilophus febrilis.*

fē′vēr hēat, a temperature which indicates the presence of fever; hence, a condition marked by stress and excitement.

fē′vēr·ish, *a.* 1. having fever, especially slight fever; as, the patient is *feverish.*

2. characteristic of or marking the presence of fever; as, *feverish* symptoms.

3. causing fever.

4. infested by fever: said of countries.

5. excited; agitated.

fē′vēr·ish·ly, *adv.* in a feverish manner.

fē′vēr·ish·ness, *n.* the state of being feverish.

fē′vēr·nut, *n.* same as *nicker nut.*

fē′vēr·ous, *a.* same as *feverish.*

fē′vēr·ous·ly, *adv.* in a feverish manner. [Obs.]

fē′vēr·ro̤ot, *n.* a plant of the genus *Triosteum,* belonging to the honeysuckle family. It was used by the Indians in the treatment of fevers, and its medicinal qualities are still recognized: called also *feverwort* and *horse gentian.*

fē′vēr sōre, an acute infectious disease caused by a virus and characterized by small blisters of the skin and mucous membranes, especially about the mouth; fever blister; cold sore.

fē′vēr ther′ȧ·py, the treatment of a disease by artificially inducing a rise in bodily temperature to kill or make ineffective the organisms causing the disease.

fē′vēr tree, 1. the blue-gum tree of Australia, considered an efficacious agent against fever.

2. a small rubiaceous tree or shrub of the southern States, which yields the bitter or Georgia bark used as a febrifuge.

fē′vēr·twig, *n.* the climbing bittersweet, *Celastrus scandens.*

fē′vēr·weed, *n.* a plant of the genus *Eryngium,* native to Central America and the West Indies.

fē′vēr·wŏrt, *n.* see *feverroot.*

fē′vēr·y, *a.* affected with fever. [Obs.]

few, *a.*; *comp.* fewer; *superl.* fewest, [ME. *few, fewe, feawe*; AS. *fea,* pl. *feawe,* few; O.H.G. *fo, fao*; Ice. *far*; Sw. *fa*; Goth. *faus*; L. *paucus*; Gr. *pauros,* small, pl. *pauroi,* few.] not many; small in numbers; as, a man of *few* words.

few, *n.* and *pron.* 1. not many; only a limited number: in this sense really an adjective used by ellipsis for a noun, with which the article is omitted; as, *few* cared to listen.

Many be called, but *few* chosen.
—Matt. xx. 16.

2. a small number or quantity; a part of the whole: preceded by an article; as, a *few* of many.

in few; in a few words; shortly; briefly. [Rare.]

Thus Jupiter *in few* unfolds the charge.
—Dryden.

quite a few; a good many; an appreciable or considerable number. [Colloq.]

the few; the minority: contrasted with *the many.*

few′met, *n.* fumet. [Obs.]

few′ness, *n.* smallness of number; paucity.

few′trilṣ, *n.pl.* small articles; knickknacks. [Brit. Dial.]

fe̤y, *v.t.* [D. *veegen*; G. *fegen,* to sweep.] to cleanse; to clear; to clean out. [Obs.]

fe̤y, *n.* faith.

fe̤y, *a.* [ME. *feie, fey*; AS. *fæge,* fated.]

1. fated; doomed to death. [Archaic and Scot.]

2. in an unusually excited or gay state, formerly believed to portend sudden death. [Archaic and Scot.]

fe̤yne, *v.t.* to feign. [Obs.]

fez, *n.*; *pl.* **fez′zeṣ,** [Turk. *fez,* from *Fez,* the city in Morocco, where they were made.] a tapering felt cap, usually red, with a black tassel hanging from the crown: formerly worn by Turkish men.

FEZ

fī, *n.* [arbitrary modification of *fa.*] in music, a syllable representing the tone intermediate between fa and sol of the diatonic scale: see *solfeggio.*

fi·ä′çre (-kẽr), *n.* [Fr., after the Hotel St. Fiacre in Paris.] in France, a small carriage for hire.

fī′ănce, *v.t.*; fianced, *pt., pp.*; fiancing, *ppr.* [Fr. *fiancer,* to betroth.] to betroth. [Obs.]

fi·an·cé′ (fē-äṅ-sā′, fē-äṅ′sā), *n.* [Fr., pp. of *fiancer,* from *fiance,* a promise.] the man to whom a woman is engaged to be married.

fi·an·cée′ (fē-äṅ-sā′, fē-äṅ′sā), *n.* [Fr., fem. pp. of *fiancer*; see *fiancé.*] the woman to whom a man is engaged to be married.

Fī′ăn·nȧ, *n.* the Fenians.

fī′ants, *n.* [Fr. *fiente,* dung.] the dung of a fox, wolf, badger, or certain other animals. [Obs.]

fī′ăr, *n.* 1. the person to whom a property belongs in fee, subject to a life rent. [Scot.]

2. [*pl.*] the price of grain, as fixed, in the counties of Scotland, by the respective sheriffs and a jury. [Scot.]

fi·ȧs′çō, *n.*; *pl.* **fi·ȧs′çoeṣ, fi·ȧs′çōṣ,** [It., lit., a bottle.] a complete failure; action that comes to a ridiculous end.

fī′at, *n.* [L. *fiat,* 3rd pers. sing. pres. subj. of *fieri,* to become, come into existence.]

1. an order issued by legal authority, usually beginning with *fiat* (let it be done); a decree.

2. a sanction; an authorization.

fiat money; paper currency made legal tender by law or fiat, although not backed by gold or silver and not necessarily redeemable in coin.

fī′at lux, [L.] let there be light.

fib, *n.* [origin unknown.] a lie or falsehood about something unimportant; a white lie.

Ask me no questions, and I'll tell you no *fibs*. —Goldsmith.

fib, *v.i.*; fibbed, *pt.*, *pp.*; fibbing, *ppr.* to tell a fib; to speak an untruth.

If you have any mark whereby one may know when you *fib* and when you speak truth, you had best tell it me. —Arbuthnot.

fib′bĕr, *n.* one who tells lies or fibs.

fī′bĕr, fī′bre (-bĕr), *n.* [Fr. *fibre*, from L. *fibra*, a fiber, filament.]

1. a slender, threadlike structure that combines with others to form animal or vegetable tissue.

2. a filament; any threadlike part of a substance, as a filament of spun glass or wool.

3. a threadlike root.

4. a filamentous substance; any substance which may be separated into threads or threadlike structures to be woven or spun; as, hemp *fiber*, asbestos *fiber*.

5. the texture of something; as, a fabric of coarse *fiber*.

6. character; nature; quality; as, a man of strong moral *fiber*.

fibers of Corti; minute, rodlike structures contained within the organ of Corti and essential in the transmission of sound to the cochlear nerve.

vulcanized fiber; paper or other fibrous material treated with a metallic chloride to render it strong and waterproof.

fī′bĕr·bōard″, fī′bre·bōard″, *n.* 1. a building material made of fibers of various substances pressed together to form large sheets or boards: the fibers may be those of wood chips, coarse paper, extracted sugar cane stems, etc.

2. a piece of this material.

fī′bĕred, fī′bred (-bĕrd), *a.* having fibers; composed of fibrous threads.

fī′bĕr-fāced (-fāst), *a.* showing a fiber: applied to paper used in banknotes, etc.

fī′bĕr·glȧs, *n.* finespun filaments of glass made into yarn that is woven into textiles or used in woolly masses as insulation material: a trade-mark (*Fiberglas*).

fī′bĕr·less, *a.* having no fibers; not of a fibrous texture.

fī′bĕr stitch, a stitch employed in the making of pillow lace.

fibr-, same as *fibro-*.

fī·brā′tion, *n.* a fibrous condition; the formation of a fibrous structure.

fī′bri·form, *a.* [L. *fibra*, a fiber, and *forma*, form.] of a structure resembling fiber; fibrous.

fī′bril, *n.* [Fr. *fibrille*, dim. of *fibre*; L. *fibra*, *fiber*.]

1. a small fiber.

2. a root hair.

fī·bril′lȧ, *n.*; *pl.* **fī·bril′lae,** [a dim. from L. *fibra*, a fiber.] same as *fibril*.

fī′bril·lăr, fī′bril·lȧ·ry, *a.* pertaining to fibrils.

fī′bril·lā·ted, fī′bril·lāte, *a.* furnished with fibrils or fibrillae.

fī·bril·lā′tion, *n.* 1. the condition of being fibrillar in structure.

2. a rapid, unco-ordinated series of contractions of the heart muscle, causing weak, irregular, and ineffectual heartbeats.

fī′bril·lōse, *a.* of or like fibrils.

fī′bril·lous, *a.* same as *fibrillose*.

fī′brin, *n.* [L. *fibra*, a fiber, and *-in*.]

1. an elastic, threadlike, insoluble protein formed from fibrinogen by the action of thrombin in the clotting of blood, and forming the network of the clot.

2. a substance resembling this in plant tissues; gluten: often called *plant fibrin*, *vegetable fibrin*.

3. the white fibrous mass remaining after the red corpuscles have been washed from fresh flesh or clotted blood: called also *flesh fibrin*.

fī·bri·nā′tion, *n.* the condition of containing an excessive proportion of fibrin; as, the *fibrination* of the blood in acute rheumatism.

fī′brine, *a.* [L. *fibra*, a fiber, and *-ine*.] having the appearance of fibers; fringed. [Rare.]

fī′bri·nō-, a combining form meaning *fibrin*, as in *fibrino*plastic: also, before a vowel, *fibrin-*.

fī·brin′ō·ġen, *n.* [*fibrino-*, and Gr. *-genēs*, producing.] a blood protein that is converted to fibrin by the action of the enzyme thrombin in the clotting of blood.

fī″brin·ō·ġen′iç, *a.* same as *fibrinogenous*.

fī·bri·nog′e·nous, *a.* 1. of or like fibrinogen.

2. able to form fibrin.

fī″bri·nō·plas′tiç, *a.* similar to or possessed of the qualities of fibrinoplastin.

fī″bri·nō·plas′tin, *n.* [*fibrino-*, and Gr. *plassein*, to form, mold.] same as *globulin*.

fī′bri·nous, *a.* of, like, or having the nature of, fibrin.

fī′brō-, [from L. *fibra*, fiber.] a combining form used in anatomy, physiology, geology, etc., to signify *fibrous matter* or *structure*, as in *fibro*cartilage, *fibro*sis: also, before a vowel, *fibr-*.

fī′brō·blȧst, *n.* [*fibro-*, and Gr. *blastos*, germ.] any cell in the structure of connective tissue.

fī·brō·çär′ti·lāġe, *n.* [*fibro-*, and L. *cartilago*, cartilage.] elastic cartilage.

fī″brō·çär·ti·laġ′i·nous, *a.* pertaining to or composed of fibrocartilage.

fī″brō·çhon·dros′tē·ăl, *a.* [*fibro-*, and Gr. *chondros*, gristle, and *osteon*, bone.] made up of fibrous tissue, cartilage, and bone: said of the human skeleton.

fī′broid, *a.* [*fibr-*, and *-oid*.] like, composed of, or forming fibrous tissue.

fibroid degeneration; a breaking down of normal, healthy tissue into fibroid tissue.

fibroid phthisis; a kind of phthisis which involves the formation of fibroid tissue in the lungs.

fī′broid, *n.* a fibrous tumor.

fī′brō·in, *n.* [*fibro-*, and *-in*.] a white albuminoid of which cobwebs and raw silk are mainly composed.

fī′brō·līte, *n.* [*fibro-*, and Gr. *lithos*, stone.] a mineral of a white or gray color, composed chiefly of aluminum silicate: also called *sillimanite* and *bucholzite*.

fī′brō·mȧ, *n.*; *pl.* **fī·brō′mȧṣ, fī·brō′mȧ·tȧ,** [Mod. L., from *fibr-*, and *-oma*.] a nonmalignant tumor composed largely of fibrous tissue.

fī·brom′ȧ·tous, *a.* of, like, or containing a fibroma.

fī·brō′sis, *n.* [Mod. L., from *fibr-* and *-osis*.] an abnormal increase in the amount of fibrous connective tissue in an organ, part, or tissue.

Fī·brō·spon′ġi·ae, *n.pl.* [*fibro-*, and L. *spongia*, a sponge.] a former classification of sponges with a fibrous skeleton, including the common commercial sponge.

fī′brous, *a.* 1. composed or consisting of fibers; as, a *fibrous* body or substance.

2. of the nature of fibers or filaments; as, *fibrous* roots.

FIBROUS ROOT

fī′brous·ness, *n.* the condition of being of fibrous structure.

fī·brō·vas′çū·lăr, *a.* [*fibro-*, and L. *vasculum*, dim. of *vas*, a vessel.] in botany, composed of woody fiber, or of bundles of fiber and vessels.

fib′stĕr, *n.* one who tells fibs. [Colloq.]

fib′ū·lȧ, *n.*; *pl.* **fib′ū·lae, fib′ū·lȧṣ,** [L. *fibula*, a clasp, buckle, pin; so called because the bone, as it appears in man, is like a clasp.]

1. the long, thin outer bone of the human leg below the knee.

2. a similar bone in the hind leg of animals.

3. in ancient Greece or Rome, a buckle or clasp for fastening garments.

FIBULA
a, fibula; *b*, tibia; *c*, femur; *d*, patella or kneecap

fib′ū·lăr, *a.* in anatomy, of or near the fibula; as, the *fibular* artery.

fib·ū·lā′rē, *n.*; *pl.* **fib·ū·lā′ri·ȧ,** [from L. *fibula*, a clasp, pin, brace.] in anatomy, the outer bone of the proximal row of tarsal bones; in man, the largest of the tarsal bones, articulating with the fibula; the heel bone: called also the *os calcis* or *calcaneus*.

-fiç, [from Fr. and L.; Fr. *-fique*; L. *-ficus*, from unstressed form of *facere*, to make.] an adjectival suffix meaning *making*, *creating*, as in terri*fic*, scienti*fic*.

-fi·çā′tion, [from Fr. and L.; Fr. *-fication*; L. *-ficatio*, from *-ficare*, unstressed combining form of *facere*, to make, do.] a suffix meaning *a making*, *creating*, *causing*, as in calci*fication*, glori*fication*.

fīce, fīse, *n.* any small dog of no distinct breed; a cur; a mongrel. [Dial.]

fiçh′tel·īte, *n.* a mineral resin of greasy feel, white and crystallizable, found in the Fichtelgebirge, Bavaria.

fiçh′ū, *n.* [Fr., from *ficher*, to drive in, pin up; *fiche*, a hook, pin.] a three-cornered lace or muslin cape worn over the shoulders by women.

fiç′kle, *a.* [ME. *fikel*, *fikil*, *fiykel*, from AS. *ficol*, deceitful, untrustworthy.] wavering; inconstant; unstable; of a changeable mind; not firm in opinion or purpose; capricious.

They know how *fickle* common lovers are. —Dryden.

Syn.—fitful, variable, changeable, vacillating, changeful, mutable, inconstant, volatile.

fiç′kle·ness, *n.* a wavering; wavering disposition; inconstancy; changeableness; instability; unsteadiness in opinion or purpose; as, the *fickleness* of lovers.

fiç′kly, *adv.* in a fickle manner. [Rare.]

fī′çō, *n.*; *pl.* **fī′çōeṣ,** [It., a fig.]

1. a worthless trifle.

2. a contemptuous gesture consisting either of thrusting the thumb into the mouth or between two fingers: called also *fig*, or *fig of Spain*. [Obs.]

fī′çoid, *a.* [L. *ficus*, a fig, and Gr. *eidos*, form.] like a fig; ficoidal.

fī·çoid′ăl, *a.* similar to a fig in shape or structure; relating to or characteristic of the order *Ficoideæ*.

Fī·çoi′dē·ae, *n.pl.* [from L. *ficus*, a fig, and Gr. *eidos*, form, and *-eæ*.] a family of annual or perennial herbs, with thick, fleshy leaves and bright flowers borne in clusters. There are numerous species, all natives of the tropics. The typical genus is *Mesembrianthemum*.

fiç′tile, *a.* [L. *fictilis*, from *fingere*, to form, mold, as in clay or wax.]

1. that can be molded; plastic.

2. formed of molded clay.

3. of pottery or ceramics.

fiç′tile·ness, fiç·til′i·ty, *n.* the quality of being fictile; plasticity.

fiç′tion, *n.* [L. *fictio* (*-onis*), from *fingere*, to form, mold, devise.]

1. the act of feigning, inventing, or imagining; as, by the mere *fiction* of the mind.

2. that which is feigned, invented, or imagined; a product of the imagination; an invention; as, the story is a *fiction*.

So also was the *fiction* of those golden apples kept by a dragon, taken from the serpent which tempted Eve. —Raleigh.

3. (a) any literary work portraying imaginary characters and events, as a novel, play, etc.; (b) such works collectively.

4. in law, an assumption made of what is not literally true, for the purpose of passing more rapidly over those parts of the subject which are not disputed and arriving at the points really at issue.

Syn.—fabrication, falsehood, invention, untruth, figment, story.—*Fiction* is opposed to what is real; it may or may not be intended to deceive; a *fabrication* is a *fiction* wrought up for the purpose of deceiving; a *falsehood* requires less invention, being merely a false statement.

fiç′tion·ăl, *a.* relating to or characteristic of fiction; fictitious; imaginary.

fiç′tion·ăl·īze, *v.t.*; fictionalized, *pt.*, *pp.*; fictionalizing, *ppr.* to deal with (historical events, a person's life, etc.) as fiction: also **fiç′tion·īze.**

fiç′tion·ist, *n.* a writer of fiction.

fiç′tious, *a.* fictitious. [Obs.]

fiç·ti′tious (-tish′us), *a.* [L. *fictitius*, *ficticius*, from *fingere*, to form, mold, devise.]

1. of or like fiction; imaginary; not real.

2. counterfeit; false; not genuine; as, *fictitious* fame.

fiç·ti′tious·ly, *adv.* by fiction; falsely; counterfeitly.

fiç·ti′tious·ness, *n.* the quality or state of being fictitious.

fiç′tive, *a.* [Fr. *fictif*.] 1. able to produce fiction.

2. of fiction.

3. imaginary; feigned; sham.

fiç′tŏr, *n.* [L.] one who shapes and fashions; an artist. [Obs.]

Fī′çus, *n.* [L., a fig tree, fig.] a genus of tropical or subtropical trees or shrubs bearing flowers crowded on fleshy receptacles, which in many species, as in the common fig, are edible. The best known species are *Ficus carica*, the common fig; *Ficus bengalensis*, the banian; *Ficus elastica*, the india rubber tree; and *Ficus religiosa*, the pipul tree.

fid, *n.* [Early Mod. Eng. nautical term.] 1. a small, thick lump. [Brit. Dial.]

2. in nautical usage, a square bar of wood or iron, with a shoulder at one end, used to support the topmast.

3. a pin of hard wood or iron, tapering to a point, used to open the strands of a rope in splicing.

4. a bar of wood or metal used to give support to something.

-fid, [L. *-fidus*, split, from base of *findere*, to cleave, divide.] a combining form meaning *separated into* (a specified number of) *parts*, *split*, as in palmati*fid*.

fi·dal′gō, *n.* a Portuguese title of nobility, corresponding to *hidalgo* in Spanish.

fid′dle, *n.* [ME. *fidele, fydyll, fiedele, fithele*; AS. *fithele*; ML. *vidula*; L. *vitula*.]

1. (a) a violin; (b) any instrument of the viol class. Now usually humorous or deprecatory.

2. in nautical usage, a frame or railing on a ship's table to keep dishes, etc. from falling off in rough weather.

fit as a fiddle; in excellent health; physically fit.

to play second fiddle; to take a subordinate position.

fid′dle, *v.i.*; fiddled, *pt., pp.*; fiddling, *ppr.* 1. to play on a violin. [Colloq.]

Themistocles said he could not *fiddle*, but he could make a small town a great city. —Bacon.

2. to fidget; to shift the hands often and do nothing; to toy with an article.

fid′dle, *v.t.* 1. to play (a tune) on the violin. [Colloq.]

2. to waste (time).

fid′dle bee′tle, a Japanese beetle, *Damaster blaptoides*, having a fiddle-shaped body.

fid′dle block, a block used in a ship's rigging, having two sheaves of different sizes, one above the other.

fid′dle bōw, a violin bow.

fid″dle·dee·dee′, *n.* and *interj.* [prob. from *fiddle*, with addition of nonsense syllables.] nonsense: also *fiddle-de-dee*, etc.

fid′dle-fad″dle, *n.* and *interj.* nonsense. [Colloq.]

fid′dle-fad″dle, *a.* trifling; making a bustle about nothing. [Colloq.]

fid′dle-fad″dle, *v.i.*; fiddle-faddled, *pt., pp.*; fiddle-faddling, *ppr.* to trifle; to busy oneself with nothing; to talk trifling nonsense. [Colloq.]

Ye may as easily
Outrun a cloud, driven by a northern blast,
As *fiddle-faddle* so. —Ford.

fid′dle fish, the angel fish: so called from its body being shaped like a fiddle.

fid′dle·head, *n.* a carved decoration on the bow of a ship, over the cutwater, in the form of a volute or scroll, such as that at the head of a violin.

FIDDLEHEAD

fid′dlẽr, *n.* 1. one who plays on a fiddle; a violinist.

2. a fiddler crab.

3. the common English sandpiper: so called from its oscillating movements. In America, the same species is called *teetertail* or *tip-up*.

fid′dlẽr crab, any burrowing crab of the genus *Gelasimus*, having one claw much larger than the other.

FIDDLER CRAB (1 in. across)

fid′dlẽr's green, the heaven to which souls of sailors are regarded as going.

fid′dle-shāped (-shāpt), *a.* shaped like a fiddle.

fid′dle·stick, *n.* 1. a violin bow.

2. an insignificant thing; a mere nothing; a piece of arrant nonsense.

fid′dle·sticks, *interj.* nonsense!

fid′dle·string, *n.* the string of a fiddle, fastened at the ends, and elevated in the middle by a bridge.

fid′dle·wood, *n.* any of several tropical American timber trees of the genus *Citharexylum*, valuable for their hard wood; also, the wood of this tree.

FIDDLE-SHAPED LEAF

fid′dling, *a.* [ppr. of *fiddle*.]

1. that plays the fiddle.

2. trifling; useless; petty.

Fī′dē·ī Dē·fen′sŏr, [L.] Defender of the Faith: one of the titles of the sovereigns of England.

fī·dē·jus′sion (-jush′un), *n.* [LL. *fidejussio* (*-onis*), from *fidejussus*, pp. of *fidejubere*, *fide jubere*, to be surety or bail, lit., confirm by promise.] suretyship; the act of being bound as surety for another.

fī·dē·jus′sŏr, *n.* [LL., from *fidejubere*, to be bond or security.] a surety; one bound for another.

fi·del′i·ty, *n.*; *pl.* **fi·del′i·ties,** [L. *fidelitas*, from *fidelis*, faithful, trusty, from *fides*, faith, trust.]

1. faithfulness; careful and exact observance of duty, or performance of obligations or vows; good faith.

The best security for the *fidelity* of men, is to make interest coincide with duty. —Hamilton.

2. firm adherence to a person or party with which one is united, or to which one is bound; loyalty; as, the *fidelity* of a servant to his master.

3. honesty; veracity. [Obs.]

4. accuracy of reproduction; as, the *fidelity* of a portrait.

Syn.—conscientiousness, trustworthiness, trustiness, fealty, allegiance, constancy, exactness, accuracy, integrity.

Fī′dēs, *n.* [L., faith.] in Roman mythology, the goddess of faith.

fidge (fij), *v.i.* to fidget. [Scot.]

fidg′et (fij′et), *n.* [from obs. *fidge*, to fidget, from ME. *fiken*, from ON. *fikja*, to fidget, hurry about.]

1. the state of being restless, nervous, or uneasy.

2. [*pl.*] restless motions of the body occasioned by nervousness or any bodily or mental discomfort.

3. a restless, nervous, uneasy person.

fidg′et, *v.i.*; fidgeted, *pt., pp.*; fidgeting, *ppr.* to be restless, nervous, or uneasy; make nervous, spasmodic movements; as, she *fidgeted* with her necklace.

fidg′et, *v.t.* to cause to fidget.

fidg′et·i·ness, *n.* the quality or condition of being fidgety.

fidg′et·y, *a.* restless; uneasy; nervous.

Fid′i·ȧ, *n.* [a coined word.]

1. a genus of leaf beetles.

2. [f-] any beetle of this genus.

fi·dic′i·năl, *a.* [L. *fidicinus*, from *fidicen*, a lutist or lyre player.] having reference to stringed musical instruments.

fi·dū′ciăl (-shăl), *a.* [LL. *fiducialis*, from *fiducia*, trust, confidence, from *fidere*, to trust.]

1. based on firm belief or faith; hence, confident; undoubting; firm.

2. of or like a trust; fiduciary.

3. in physics, astronomy, etc., that may be used as a standard of reference for measurement or calculation; as, a *fiducial* point.

fiducial edge; the thin edge (of a ruler).

fi·dū′ciăl·ly, *adv.* in a fiducial manner.

fi·dū′ci·ā·ry (-shi-), *a.* [L. *fiduciarius*, from *fiducia*, trust, a thing held in trust, from *fidere*, to trust.]

1. designating or of a person who holds something in trust for another; of a trustee or trusteeship; as, a *fiduciary* guardian for a minor child.

2. held in trust; as, *fiduciary* property.

3. valuable only because of public confidence and support: said of certain paper money.

fi·dū′ci·ā·ry, *n.*; *pl.* **fi·dū′ci·ā·ries,** 1. one who holds a thing in trust; a trustee.

2. in theology, one who depends for salvation on faith without works; an antinomian. [Obs.]

fī′dus Ā·chā′tēs, [L.] 1. faithful Achates, the companion of Aeneas.

2. a true friend.

fīe, *interj.* [ME. *fi, fy*; OFr. *fi, fy*; L. *fi*, expression of disgust.] shame!: now often used humorously to indicate a pretense of shock or a mild reproach.

fief, *n.* [OFr. *fief, fieu*, from LL. *feudum*, a feud, fief.] in the feudal system, (a) heritable land held from a lord in return for service; feudal benefice; (b) the right to hold such land: also *fee, feud, feoff, feod*.

fiēld, *n.* [ME. *feeld, feld, fild*; AS. *feld*, a field, pasture.]

1. [*often pl.*] a wide stretch of open land; a plain.

2. a piece of cleared land, set off or enclosed, for tillage or pasture; any part of a farm except the garden and appurtenances of the farm buildings; land not covered with wood.

3. a portion of ground designated for a particular purpose; as, a football *field*.

4. an area of land producing some natural resource; as, a gold *field*.

5. any wide, unbroken space; as, a *field* of ice.

6. (a) a battlefield; (b) a battle.

7. (a) an area of military operations; (b) a military area away from the post or headquarters.

8. a realm of knowledge or of special work or opportunity; as, the *field* of television.

9. an area of observation, as in a microscope.

10. the background, as on a flag or coin.

11. in athletics and sports, (a) an area where games or athletic events are held; (b) the part of such an area, usually inside a closed racing track, where contests in the high jump, broad jump, shot-put, pole vault, etc. are held; (c) in baseball, the outfield; (d) all the entrants in a contest; (e) all the active players on the field, as in baseball or football; (f) all the entrants in a contest except the one or ones specified; (g) the team not at bat, as in baseball, cricket, etc.

12. in heraldry, the surface or part of the surface of a shield.

13. in physics, a space within which magnetic or electrical lines of force are active.

to keep the field; to continue activity, as in games, military operations, etc.

to play the field; to take a broad area of operations; not confine one's activities to one object.

to take the field; to begin activity in a game, military operation, etc.

fiēld, *a.* 1. of, in, or for the field or fields.

2. growing in fields; having a field or fields as its habitat.

3. in athletics, of or held on the field: distinguished from *track*.

fiēld, *v.t.*; fielded, *pt., pp.*; fielding, *ppr.* in baseball, cricket, etc., (a) to stop or catch and return (a ball) in play; (b) to put (a player) into a field position.

fiēld, *v.i.* in baseball, cricket, etc., to play in a field position.

fiēld är′my, the largest unit of an army, consisting of two or more corps and usually headed by a lieutenant general: often called *army*.

fiēld är·til′lẽr·y, 1. movable artillery capable of accompanying an army into battle.

2. [F- A-] the branch of the army that uses such artillery: distinguished from *Coast Artillery*.

fiēld baș′il, basil thyme, *Calamintha acinos*.

fiēld bat′tẽr·y, a number of field artillery pieces, usually four, employed as a unit.

fiēld bed, a bed that can be carried into the field; a portable couch or camp bed.

fiēld bīrd, the golden plover. [Dial.]

fiēld book, a book used in surveying, in which the angles, stations, distances, and similar measurements are recorded.

fiēld car′riage (-rij), a gun carriage on which a field gun is transported.

fiēld çŏl′ŏrș, small flags for marking out the positions of squadrons and battalions; also, the flags which mark the position or head quarters of a command while on the march or in camp.

fiēld çorn, a variety of maize used for feeding farm animals.

fiēld′-çor″net, *n.* the magistrate of a township in Cape of Good Hope.

fiēld crick′et, a large European cricket having a louder, more strident chirp than the house cricket.

fiēld dāy, 1. a day devoted to military exercises and display.

2. a day of athletic events and contests.

3. a day spent in outdoor scientific study.

4. a day of pleasantly exciting events or successful activity.

fiēld dog, a dog used for hunting, as a setter, pointer, or retriever.

fiēld drīv′ẽr, a civil officer who takes stray domestic animals to the pound.

fiēld duck, a European duck, the little bustard.

fiēld′ed, *a.* being in the field of battle; encamped.

fiēld′en, *a.* consisting of open tracts of land. [Obs.]

fiēld′ẽr, *n.* in baseball and cricket, a player in the field.

fiēld′ẽr's choice, in baseball, an attempt by a fielder to retire a runner already on base rather than the batter: the batter is not credited with a base hit if he reaches first base safely.

fiēld′fāre, *n.* [ME. *feldfare*; AS. *feldefare*; *felde*, a field, and *faran*, to go, travel.] a European thrush of the genus *Turdus*, about ten inches

FIELDFARE
(*Turdus pilaris*)

in length, the head ash-colored, the back and greater coverts of the wings of a fine, deep chestnut, and the tail black: called also *fellfare*.

fiēld glȧss, 1. a compact, portable, binocular telescope with considerable magnifying power: also called *field glasses*.
2. the lens in a telescope or microscope nearest to the object glass: called also *field lens*.
3. a form of telescope used on shipboard, having an achromatic lens and from three to six joints.

fiēld gōal, 1. in basketball, a basket toss made from play, counting two points.
2. in football, a goal kicked from the field, counting three points.

fiēld gun, a mobile artillery piece for use in the field: also called *fieldpiece*.

fiēld hand, 1. originally, a plantation slave who worked in the fields.
2. now, any hired farm laborer.

fiēld hock′ey, a hockey game played on a field: there are ordinarily eleven players on each side.

fiēld hos′pi·tăl, a temporary military hospital near the combat zone, for emergency treatment.

fiēld īce, ice formed into fields such as float in the polar oceans.

fiēld kāle, same as *charlock*.

fiēld lärk, any of certain small birds; specifically, (a) the meadow lark; (b) the tree pipit or tree lark; (c) the English skylark.

fiēld lenș, same as *field glass*, sense 2.

fiēld mad′dẽr, a European herb, *Sherardia arvensis*, with a prostrate stem spreading from the root, and clusters of small lilac flowers in terminal heads: called also *spurwort*.

fiēld mag′net, the magnet used to create and maintain the magnetic field in a motor or generator.

fiēld mär′shăl, in some European armies, an officer ranking just below the commander in chief.

fiēld mär′shăl·ship, the rank or dignity of a field marshal.

fiēld mär′tin, the kingbird, *Tyrannus tyrannus* or *carolinensis*: called also *bee bird* or *bee martin*.

fiēld mouse, any of several species of mice that live in fields.

fiēld mū′șiç, 1. military musicians, as buglers, drummers, etc.
2. their music.

fiēld of′fi·cẽr, a military officer above the rank of captain and below that of general, as a major, lieutenant colonel, or colonel.
field-officer's court; formerly, in the United States Army, a court-martial presided over by a field officer, subject only to the jurisdiction of garrison and regimental courts.

fiēld of fōrce, in physics, the region under the influence of some force, as gravitational, electrical, etc.

fiēld of hon′ŏr (on′ẽr), 1. originally, a dueling place.
2. a battleground.

fiēld′piēce, *n.* same as *field gun*.

fiēld plŏv′ẽr, 1. the golden plover.
2. the upland plover.

fiēld sal′ăd, same as *fetticus*.

fiēld shōw, a field trial.

fiēldș′măn, *n.*; *pl.* **fiēldș′men,** in cricket, a fielder.

fiēld span′iel (-yel), a breed of spaniels trained to hunt.

fiēld spar′rōw, 1. a sparrow, *Spizella pusilla*, common in the eastern United States.
2. the English hedge sparrow.

fiēld spōrts, 1. sports of the field, as shooting and hunting.
2. athletic events, as pole vaulting, shot-putting, etc., as distinguished from races held on a track.

fiēld stȧff, a pole having a torch at one end with which old-fashioned field guns were touched off.

fiēld trī′ăl, a trial and exhibition of dogs performing in the field, as distinguished from an exhibition indoors, or a bench show.

fiēld trip, a trip away from the classroom to permit the gathering of data at first hand.

fiēld vōle, the short-tailed field mouse.

fiēld wīnd′ing, the winding of a field magnet.

fiēld′wŏrk, *n.* any temporary breastwork, dugout, or other defensive fortification made by troops in the field.

fiēld wŏrk, the work of collecting scientific data in the field, as by a geologist, botanist, etc.

fiēld′wŏrk·ẽr, *n.* a scientist, technician, or student who does field work.

fiēld′y, *a.* open, like a field. [Obs.]

fiēnd, *n.* [ME. *feend*, *feond*; AS. *feond*, an enemy, hater, used of Satan, properly ppr. of *feon*, to hate; L.G. *fijend*, *fijind*; Ice. *fjande*; Dan. *fjende*, an enemy.]
1. an evil spirit; a devil.
O woman! woman! when to ill thy mind
Is bent, all hell contains no fouler *fiend*.
—Pope.
2. an inhumanly wicked person.
3. (a) a person addicted to some activity, habit, etc.; as, a cigarette *fiend*, a bridge *fiend*; (b) a person who is excellent at some activity; as, he's a *fiend* at tennis. [Colloq.]
the Fiend; the Devil; Satan.

fiēnd′fụl, *a.* filled with a fiendish spirit.

fiēnd′fụl·ly, *adv.* in a fiendful manner.

fiēnd′ish, *a.* like or characteristic of a fiend; malicious; inhumanly wicked or cruel.

fiēnd′ish·ly, *adv.* in a fiendish spirit or manner.

fiēnd′ish·ness, *n.* maliciousness.

fiēnd′līke, *a.* resembling a fiend; fiendish.

fiēnd′ly, *a.* extremely malicious; diabolical. [Obs.]

Fī·ē·ras′fẽr, *n.* a genus of fishes having eellike bodies and no ventral fins: most species live parasitically in other marine animals.

fiērce, *a.*; *comp.* fiercer; *superl.* fiercest, [ME. *feirce*, *fers*, *fierse*; OFr. *fers*, *fier*, *fer*, from L. *ferus*, wild, savage.]
1. vehement; violent; furious; rushing; uncontrolled; as, a *fierce* wind.
2. savage; wild; of a violently cruel nature; as, a *fierce* lion.
3. very eager; ardent; intense; as, a man *fierce* for his party.
4. very distasteful, disagreeable, bad, etc. [Slang.]

fiērce′ly, *adv.* in a fierce manner; violently; furiously; as, both sides fought *fiercely*.

fiērce′ness, *n.* the state or quality of being fierce.

fiērd′ing çōurt, [AS. *feorthung*, a fourth part.] an ancient court, so called because four were established within every superior district or hundred. [Obs.]

fī′e·rī fā′ci·as (-shi-as), [L., lit., cause it to be done.] in law, a writ authorizing the proper legal officer to collect a judgment of debt from the property of a person against whom the judgment has been made.

fī′ẽr·i·ly, *adv.* in a fiery manner.

fī′ẽr·i·ness, *n.* the quality or state of being fiery.

fī′ẽr·y, *a.*; *comp.* fierier; *superl.* fieriest, 1. containing or consisting of fire.
2. like fire; glaring, hot, etc.
3. characterized by strong emotion; ardent; spirited; as, *fiery* words.
4. easily stirred up; excitable; as, a *fiery* nature.
5. easily set on fire; inflammable, as coal damp in a mine.
6. inflamed: said of a sore.
7. heated by fire.
The sword which is made *fiery*.
—Hooker.
a fiery cross; (a) in Scotland, a signal sent in ancient times to call a clan to arms. It consisted of a wooden cross, the ends of which had been charred and then dipped in blood; (b) a burning cross, used by the Ku Klux Klan as an emblem or to inspire terror.
Syn.—parched, feverish, ardent, fervid, impetuous, unrestrained, spirited, vehement, irritable, mettlesome, passionate, fierce.

fī·es′tȧ, *n.* [Sp. *fiesta*; ML. *festa*, a feast.]
1. a religious festival; a saint's day.
2. any gala celebration; a holiday celebrated by games, processions, and general merrymaking.

fīfe, *n.* [OFr. *fifre*, a fife; O.H.G. *pfifa*; hyp. ML. *pipa*, a pipe; *pipare*, to play on a pipe, from L. *pipire*, *pipare*, to peep, chirp, as a chicken.] a small instrument resembling a flute, but having a shriller tone. It is used mainly in drum corps and bands to make music for marching.

fīfe, *v.t.* and *v.i.*; fifed (fift), *pt.*, *pp.*; fifing, *ppr.* to play on a fife.

fīf′ẽr, *n.* one who plays on a fife.

fīfe rāil, 1. formerly, the rail on a ship forming the upper fence of the bulwarks on each side of the quarter-deck and poop.
2. the rail around the mainmast to hold belaying pins for the rigging.

fif′teen, *a.* [ME. *fiftene*; AS. *fiftene*, *fiftyne*; *fif*, five, and *ten*, *tyne*, ten.] five more than ten.

fif′teen, *n.* 1. the cardinal number between fourteen and sixteen.
2. a group of fifteen persons or things.
3. the symbol indicating fifteen units; XV; 15.
4. the first point scored on either side in tennis.

fif′teenth, *a.* 1. preceded by fourteen others in a series; 15th.
2. designating any one of the fifteen equal portions of something.

fif′teenth, *n.* 1. the one following the fourteenth.
2. any of the fifteen equal parts of something; 1/15.
3. an ancient tax levied on towns, boroughs, etc. in England, being one-fifteenth part of what each town, etc. had been valued at.
4. in music, (a) an interval of a double octave; (b) a stop tuned a double octave above the open diapason.

fifth, *a.* [ME. *fifthe*, *fifte*; AS. *fifta*, from *fif*, five.]
1. preceded by four others in a series; 5th.
2. designating any of the five equal parts of something.
fifth column; (a) those people in Madrid who gave aid and support to the forces led by Francisco Franco in his uprising against the Spanish republic (1936–1939); (b) any similar group of people who give aid and support to the enemy.
fifth columnist; a member of the fifth column.
fifth nerve; in anatomy, the fifth cranial nerve on either side of the head.
fifth wheel; (a) a horizontal wheellike structure placed on the front axle of a vehicle: upon it the fore part of the body turns freely without tilting; (b) any unnecessary or superfluous person or thing.

fifth, *n.* 1. the one following the fourth.
2. any of the five equal parts of something; 1/5.
3. a fifth of a gallon.
4. in music, (a) an interval of five degrees in a diatonic scale; (b) a tone five degrees above or below a given tone; (c) the combination of two notes separated by this interval; (d) the fifth note of a diatonic scale; dominant.

fifth′ly, *adv.* in the fifth place.

fif′ti·eth, *a.* [ME. *fiftithe*, *fiftugethe*; AS. *fiftigotha*, from *fiftig*, fifty, and *-tha*, *-th*, the ordinal suffix.]
1. preceded by forty-nine others in a series; 50th.
2. designating any of the fifty equal portions of something.

fif′ti·eth, *n.* 1. the one following the forty-ninth.
2. any of fifty equal parts of something; 1/50.

fif′ty, *a.* [ME. *fifty*, *fifti*; AS. *fiftig*; *fif*, five, and *-tig*, ten.] five times ten.

fif′ty, *n.*; *pl.* **fif′tieș,** 1. the cardinal number between forty-nine and fifty-one; ten fives; half of one hundred.
2. the symbol that represents the number; L; 50.
the fifties; the years from fifty through fifty-nine (of a century or a person's age).

fif′ty-fif′ty, *a.* having equal shares; equal; even. [Colloq.]

fif′ty-fif′ty, *adv.* equally. [Colloq.]

fig, *n.* [ME. *fig, fyg*; OFr. *figue, fige*; Pr. *figa*; It. *fico*, from L. *ficus*, a fig tree, fig.]
1. a small, pear-shaped fruit with sweet, pulpy, seed-filled flesh: it is usually dried or preserved for eating.

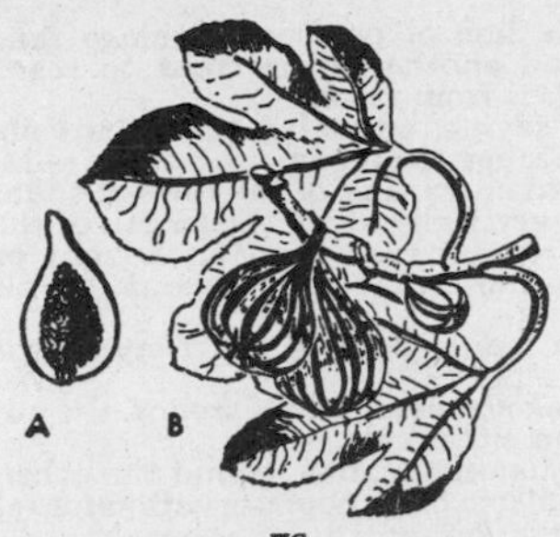

FIG
A, cross section; B, leaves and fruit

2. any of various trees, of the same or a related genus, which bear fruit resembling the true fig.
3. a trifling amount; the least value; as, not worth a *fig*.
4. a fico; a gesture of contempt or disdain made as by placing the thumb between the first and second fingers.
5. a swelling on the frog of a horse's foot.
6. a piece of tobacco; a quid. [Colloq.]
Fig Sunday; Palm Sunday. [Brit. Dial.]
Indian fig; any of several cactaceous plants, especially *Opuntia vulgaris*, or the prickly pear; also, the figlike fruit of such a plant.
Keg fig; same as *Japanese persimmon*.
Pharaoh's fig; the sycamore fig, *Ficus sycomorus*, native to Egypt and Syria. It bears an edible fruit.
red fig; a large, tropical American tree, *Ficus pedunculata*, which spreads like the banian and bears a hard red fruit.
sacred fig; the pipal tree of India.
wild fig; *Clusia flava*, a tropical American shrub.

fig, *v.t.* to insult with ficos, or contemptuous gestures. [Obs.]

fig, *v.t.*; figged, *pt., pp.*; figging, *ppr.* [altered from obs. *feague*, to whip, polish; confused with the contr. for *figure*, prob. from the use of this contracted form in reference to plates in books of fashions.] to dress showily (with *out* or *up*).

fig, *n.* 1. dress; appearance. [Colloq.]
2. shape; condition; as, he was in poor *fig*. [Colloq.]
in full fig; completely dressed or outfitted, especially in a showy manner. [Colloq.]

fig ap'ple, a kind of apple having no core.

fig'ȧ·ry, *n.* a frolic. [Obs.]

fig çake, a preparation of figs and almonds mixed into a hard paste and pressed into cakes.

fig dust, ground oatmeal, used for feeding cage birds.

fig'ēat"ẽr, *n.* 1. a beetle, *Allorhina nitida*, destructive to ripe fruit; the June bug of the southern United States.
2. the European garden warbler or beccafico.

fig'ent, *a.* fidgety; unable to keep quiet. [Obs.]

fig faun, a mythical creature, represented as living in desert places and eating figs.

fig gnat (nat), an insect of the gnat family, injurious to the fig.

fig'gum, *n.* jugglers' tricks. [Obs.]

fight (fīt), *v.i.*; fought (fọt), *pt., pp.*; fighting, *ppr.* [ME. *fighten, fihten, fehten*; AS. *feohtan*, to fight.]
1. to strive or contend for victory; to struggle; to attempt to defeat, subdue, or destroy.

Come and be our captain, that we may *fight* with the children of Ammon.—Judges xi.6.

2. to contend; to try to overcome someone or something; as, to *fight* against jealousy.

fight, *v.t.* 1. to carry on contention with; to struggle against; to try to overcome, as by legislation, argument, etc.
2. to contend with in battle, as with fists, weapons, etc.; as, they *fought* the enemy in two pitched battles.
3. to engage in or carry on (a war, conflict, case, etc.).
4. to gain by struggle; as, he *fought* his way to the top.
5. to cause to fight; to manage (a boxer, gamecock, etc.).
to fight it out; to fight until one side is defeated.
to fight off; to fight to keep away; struggle to avoid.
Syn.—contend, dispute, encounter, oppose, combat, struggle, quarrel, battle.

fight, *n.* [ME. *fight, fiht, feoht*; AS. *feoht*, a fight, battle, from *feohtan*, to fight.]
1. a battle; a combat; a physical struggle.
2. something to screen the combatants in ships. [Obs.]

Up with your *fights* and your nettings prepare. —Dryden.

3. pugnacity; power or inclination to fight; disposition to continue a struggle; as, he still had some *fight* in him.
4. a contest or quarrel of any kind; a struggle; as, a *fight* for supremacy.
Syn.—battle, engagement, skirmish, affair, brush, fray, affray, duel, action, strife, struggle, encounter, combat, contest, conflict.

fight'ẽr, *n.* 1. one that fights or is inclined to fight.
2. a prizefighter; pugilist.
3. a small, light, highly maneuverable airplane for aerial combat: often called *fighter plane*.

fight'ing, *n.* contention; strife; quarrel; battle.

fight'ing, *a.* fitted or trained to fight; qualified to go into battle.
fighting chance; a chance of gaining an object or end only after a hard struggle; as, to have a *fighting chance* of recovery.
fighting crab; same as *fiddler crab*.
fighting sandpiper; the ruff, *Pavoncella* or *Machetes pugnax*, noted for its pugnacity.

fight'ing fish, a small, pugnacious Asiatic fish.

fight'ing·ly, *adv.* in a pugnacious manner.

fight'wīte, *n.* [AS. *fyhtwite*; *feoht*, fight, and *wite*, a fine.] in old English law, a fine imposed upon a person who disturbed the public peace.

fig lēaf, the leaf of a fig tree; also, a thin covering, in allusion to the first covering of Adam and Eve.

What pitiful *fig leaves*, what senseless and ridiculous shifts, are these. —South.

fig mar'i·gōld, any of several plants of the genus *Mesembryanthemum*, with showy flowers of pink or white, found in hot, dry climates.

fig'ment, *n.* [L. *figmentum*, from *fingere*, to make, devise, invent.] an invention; a fictitious story; something made up or imagined; as, these assertions are the *figments* of idle brains.

fig'men·tăl, *a.* having the character of a figment; feigned; unreal; fictitious.

fi'gō, *n.* a fico. [Obs.]

fig'peck"ẽr, *n.* the garden warbler of Europe; a figeater.

fig shell, a sea shell resembling a fig in shape.

fig'ū·lāte, fig'ū·lā·ted, *a.* [L. *figulatus*, pp. of *figulare*, to form, fashion, from *figulus*, a potter.] made of potter's clay; molded; shaped. [Rare.]

fig'ū·line, *a.* [L. *figulinus*, from *figulus*, a potter, from *fingere*, to make, devise.] made of clay or pottery.

fig'ū·line, *n.* potter's clay; also, a piece of pottery or porcelain; small statue.

fig"ūr·ȧ·bil'i·ty, *n.* the quality of being figurable.

fig'ūr·ȧ·ble, *a.* capable of being brought to a certain fixed form or shape; as, lead is *figurable*, but water is not.

fig'ūr·ăl, *a.* 1. represented by figure or delineation; as, *figural* resemblances.
2. in music, figurate.

fig'ū·rant, *n.* [Fr., masc. ppr. of *figurer*, to figure.]
1. one who dances in the ballet.
2. an accessory character on the stage, who figures in its scenes, but has nothing to say; hence, one who figures in any scene without taking a prominent part.

fig·ū·rante', *n.* feminine of *figurant*.

fig'ūr·āte, *a.* [L. *figuratus*, pp. of *figurare*, to form, shape, from *figura*, a figure.]
1. of a certain determinate form; resembling anything of a determinate form. [Rare.]

Plants are all *figurate* and determinate, which inanimate bodies are not.—Bacon.

2. figurative. [Obs.]
3. in music, florid: opposed to *simple*.
figurate numbers; in mathematics, such numbers as do or may represent some geometrical figure. They are formed from any arithmetical series, in which the first term is one and the difference a whole number, by taking the first term and the sums of the first two, first three, first four, etc. as the successive terms of new series, from which another may be formed in like manner, the numbers in the resulting series being such that points representing them are capable of arrangement in different geometrical figures. In the following examples the two lower lines consist of *figurate numbers*, those in the second line being triangular, and those in the third line square:—

1	2	3	4	5	6	etc.
1	3	6	10	15	21	etc.
1	4	9	16	25	36	etc.

fig'ūr·ā·ted, *a.* having a determinate form.

fig'ūr·āte·ly, *adv.* in a figurate manner.

fig·ū·rā'tion, *n.* 1. a forming; a shaping.
2. form; appearance.
3. an ornamenting with or representing by figures or symbols.

fig'ūr·ȧ·tive, *a.* [L. *figurativus*, figurative, from *figuratus*, pp. of *figurare*, to form, fashion.]
1. representing by means of a figure, symbol, or likeness; typical; emblematic.
2. consisting of or employing a rhetorical figure; representing one concept in terms of another that may be thought of as analogous with it; not literal or direct; metaphorical.
3. containing or using figures of speech; as, a description highly *figurative*.
4. in music, figurate.
5. relating to the representation of form or figure through the mediums of drawing, painting, or sculpture.

fig'ūr·ȧ·tive·ly, *adv.* in a figurative manner.

fig'ūr·ȧ·tive·ness, *n.* state of being figurative.

fig'ūre, *n.* [ME. *figure, figoura*; OFr. *figure*; L. *figura*, a form, shape, figure, from *fingere*, to form, shape.]
1. the form of anything; shape; outline; as, flowers have exquisite *figures*.
2. the shape of the human body; human form.
3. a person, especially one seen or thought of in a specified way; as, Roosevelt was one of the greatest *figures* of his time.
4. an illustration; diagram; picture; drawing.
5. a likeness or representation of a person or thing; as, the *figure* of a saint above the door.
6. a design or representation wrought in or printed on a surface, as a textile, paper, sheet metal, etc.; a pattern.
7. in logic, the form of a syllogism with respect to the order or disposition of the middle term.
8. a symbol denoting a number; a digit or the cipher; as, the *figure* 5.
9. [*pl.*] calculation with such symbols; arithmetic; as, she has a poor head for *figures*.
10. in geometry, a surface or space bounded on all sides by lines or planes.
11. a sum of money, either estimated or exact; price; value; as, a conservative *figure*; marked to sell at a low *figure*.
12. in astrology, the horoscope; the diagram of the aspects of the astrological houses.
13. in rhetoric, a figure of speech.
14. in grammar, any deviation from the rules of analogy or syntax; an unusual construction.
15. in dancing, the several steps which the dancer makes in order and cadence, considered as they form certain outlines on the floor.
16. a being of the imagination; a conception of the fancy; a phantasm; an image.

Where beams of warm imagination play,
The memory's soft *figures* fade away.
—Pope.

17. in music, (a) a short theme or group of chords having a single motive; a harmonic phrase; (b) a numeral written upon the bass staff to represent an unwritten chord.
figure-of-eight knot; a kind of knot: see *knot*, illus.
figure of speech; an expression using words in an unusual or nonliteral sense to give beauty or vividness of style; metaphor, personification, simile, litotes, hyperbole, metonymy, synecdoche, etc.; trope.
magnetic figures; the shapes assumed by iron filings about the poles of a magnetic field.
to cut a figure; to attract attention either in admiration or contempt; to make a certain appearance; as, *to cut a* sorry *figure*. [Colloq.]
Syn.—form, mold, shape, outline, condition, appearance, diagram, aspect, likeness, delineation, illustration, pattern, emblem, type, image, metaphor, symbol.

fig'ūre, *v.t.*; figured, *pt., pp.*; figuring, *ppr.*

1. to form or mold into any definite shape; to represent in definite form.

2. to cover or adorn with figures; to ornament with a design; to form figures in by art; to stamp or work with a pattern.

3. to imagine; to represent mentally.

4. to prefigure; to foreshow. [Obs.]

5. in rhetoric, to form figuratively; to use in a sense not literal; to employ metaphors for.

6. to believe; consider; predict. [Colloq.]

7. in music, to indicate chords for (the bass) by writing the appropriate figures next to the notes.

8. to perform the several arithmetical operations on; to compute; as, to *figure* the cost of an article; to *figure* expenses.

to figure in; to add in; include.

to figure on; (a) to count on; to rely on; (b) to consider as part of a scheme or project; to plan on.

to figure out; (a) to solve, as a problem; to compute; (b) to understand; to reason out.

to figure up; to add and find the final amount; to total.

fig'ūre, *v.i.* 1. to appear prominently; to be conspicuous.

2. to scheme or lay plans; to contrive to secure some result; to calculate; as, he is *figuring* to secure the income. [Colloq.]

3. to do arithmetic.

4. to be just as expected or as anticipated. [Colloq.]

fig'ūre çast'ẽr, one who casts horoscopes; an astrologer. [Obs.]

fig'ūre çast'ing, the art of making casts of human or animal figures or of anatomical parts of the human figure to serve as illustrations or models.

fig'ūred, *a.* 1. shaped; formed.

2. represented or shown by a picture, diagram, etc.

3. having a design or pattern.

4. in music, marked with figures representing the appropriate accompanying chords: said of the bass.

5. metaphorical; not to be taken literally; figurative. [Obs.]

6. in heraldry, bearing a likeness of the human face, as a crescent.

figured bass; same as *thorough bass*.

fig'ūre fling'ẽr, a figure caster. [Obs.]

fig'ūre fling'ing, the art of casting horoscopes. [Obs.]

fig'ūre·head, *n.* 1. the figure, statue, or bust on the bow of a ship.

2. a person put in a position of leadership because of his name, rank, importance, etc., but having no real power, authority, or responsibility.

FIGUREHEAD

fig'ūre skāt'ing, ice skating in which the performer traces various elaborate figures on the ice.

fig'ūre stōne, agalmatolite.

fi·gū'ri·ăl, *a.* shown by figures; diagrammed. [Rare.]

fi·gū·rine', *n.* [Fr. *figurine*, dim. of *figure*, a figure.] a small sculptured or molded figure; a statuette.

Tanagra figurines; small figures or figurines made by the ancient Greeks as ornaments and as offerings to the gods. They are found in various places throughout Greece, but the first discovered were from Tanagra.

fig'ūr·ist, *n.* one who makes use of and interprets figurative language.

fig wăsp, any of a family, *Agaontidae*, of small wasps living in certain figs, especially a wasp, *Blastophaga psenes*, active in the pollination of certain cultivated strains.

fig'wŏrt, *n.* any of a group of tall, coarse, strong-smelling plants with small flowers, including the snapdragon, mullein, etc.

Fī'jī, *n.* a native of the Fiji Islands.

Fī·jī'ăn, *a.* pertaining to the Fiji Islands or to their people, language, or culture.

Fī·jī'ăn, *n.* 1. one born in the Fiji Islands.

2. the Melanesian language of the Fijis.

fīke, fȳke, *v.i.* to fidget; to be restless; to be constantly in a state of trivial motion; to be troubled about anything. [Scot.]

fīke, fȳke, *v.t.* to vex; to annoy. [Scot.]

fīke, fȳke, *n.* 1. restlessness or agitation caused by trifling annoyance. [Scot.]

2. any trifling peculiarity in regard to work which causes unnecessary trouble. [Scot.]

fi·lā'ceous, *a.* [from L. *filum*, thread, and *-aceous*.] composed or consisting of threads. [Rare.]

Fi·lă'gō, *n.* [from L. *filum*, thread.] a genus of slender annual herbs covered with a white, cottony substance.

fil'ȧ·ment, *n.* [Fr. *filament*, from L. *filum*, a thread.]

1. a thread; a fiber; specifically, in botany, the threadlike part of the stamen bearing the anther.

2. in electricity, the fine, threadlike wire which is heated to incandescence by an electric current to provide the light source of an incandescent lamp.

3. in electricity or radiotelegraphy, the heated cathode of a vacuum tube from which electrons are emitted.

fil·ȧ·men'tȧ·ry, *a.* formed by a filament or filaments; having the character of a filament.

In the blennies, the forked hake, the forked beard, and some other fishes, the ventral fins are reduced to *filamentary* feelers. —Owen.

fil″ȧ·men·tif'ẽr·ous, *a.* [Fr. *filament*, filament, and L. *ferre*, to bear.] producing threads or filamentous growths.

fil·ȧ·men'toid, *a.* [Fr. *filament*, filament, and Gr. *eidos*, form.] resembling a filament.

fil·ȧ·men'tous, *a.* like a thread; also, consisting of filaments.

fil·ȧ·men'tūle, *n.* [Fr. *filament*, filament, and dim. *-ule*.] any small filament.

fil'an·dẽrṣ, *n.pl.* [Fr. *filandres*, from L. *filum*, a thread.] a disease in hawks, due to the presence of intestinal worms; also, the threadlike worms causing this disease.

fī'lăr, *a.* [from L. *filum*, a thread.] pertaining to a thread: specifically applied to a microscope or other optical instrument having one or more threads or wires stretched across the field of view.

fi·lā'ri·ȧ, *n.*; *pl.* **fi·lā'ri·ae,** [from L. *filum*, a thread.] any of several kinds of threadlike parasitic worms that live in the blood and tissues of vertebrate animals: they are often carried and transmitted by mosquitoes and other invertebrates.

fi·lā'ri·ăl, *a.* of, having the nature of, carrying, or caused by filariae.

fi·lā'ri·ăn, *a.* filarial.

fil·ȧ·rī'ȧ·sis, *n.* [Mod. L.] a diseased condition caused by filarial worms, which are transmitted by mosquitoes and invade lymphatic vessels and lymphoid tissue.

fi·lar'i·form, *a.* [from L. *filum*, a thread, and *forma*, form.]

1. like a thread; filamentous.

2. pertaining to or shaped like filariae.

fī'lāte, *a.* [from L. *filum*, a thread, and *-ate*.] straight, slender, and unbranched, as the antennae of certain dipterous insects.

fil'ȧ·tō·ry, *n.* [LL. *filatorium*, a place for spinning, from L. *filare*, to spin, from *filum*, thread.] a machine which forms or spins threads. [Obs.]

fil'ȧ·tūre, *n.* [LL. *filatura*, the art of spinning, a coarse thread, from L. *filare*, to spin; *filum*, thread.]

1. a drawing out or spinning into threads.

2. the reeling of silk from cocoons.

3. (a) a reel for drawing off silk from cocoons; (b) a place where this is done.

fil'bẽrt, *n.* [ME. *filberde, fylberde, philliberd*; perhaps named from St. *Philibert*, whose feast came in the nutting season.]

1. the fruit of the cultivated *Corylus avellana*, or hazel; the hazelnut.

2. the shrub or low tree yielding this nut.

filch, *v.t.*; filched (filcht), *pt., pp.*; filching, *ppr.* [ME. *filchen*, to steal; perhaps from *felen*, to hide.] to steal (usually something of little value); to pilfer.

Fain would they *filch* that little food away. —Dryden.

filch, *n.* 1. the act of petty thieving; also, the thing taken or the person who filches.

2. a staff with a hook in one end used by thieves in snatching small articles. [Obs. Slang.]

filch'ẽr, *n.* a thief; one who is guilty of petty theft.

filch'ing·ly, *adv.* by pilfering; in a thievish manner.

fīle, *n.* [OFr. *file*, a file, rank, row; LL. *fila*, a string, series, from L. *filum*, a thread.]

1. originally, a thread, line, wire, etc., now, a folder, cabinet, etc., by means of which papers are preserved in due order.

2. an orderly arrangement of papers, cards, etc.; a collection of papers arranged according to date, subject, etc. for the sake of ready reference; as, a *file* of writs; a *file* of newspapers.

3. a roll or list. [Obs.]

Our present musters grow upon the *file*.
To five and twenty thousand men of choice. —Shak.

4. a line of persons or things ranged one behind another, from front to rear: distinguished from *rank*.

So saying, on he led his radiant *files*,
Dazzling the moon. —Milton.

5. in chess, any of the rows of squares running vertically along the length of the board.

6. regular succession of thought or narration; uniform tenor; thread of discourse. [Obs.]

Let me resume the *file* of my narration. —Wotton.

flank file; in a body of troops, the outermost file on either side.

in file; in line, one behind the other.

on file; in orderly preservation for reference; in a file; on record.

fīle, *v.t.*; filed, *pt., pp.*; filing, *ppr.* 1. to arrange, as papers, documents, manuscripts, etc., in order for reference and for preservation.

2. to put (a paper, etc.) in its proper place or order.

3. in law, to place (a legal document) on public record, or among the records of a court.

fīle, *v.i.* to move in a file or line, one after another.

to file off; to wheel and march off in file at right angles to the first line of march.

fīle, *v.t.* [ME. *filen, fylen*, from AS. *afylan*, to make foul, defile.] to soil; to defile; to sully; to pollute. [Archaic.]

fīle, *v.t.* 1. to rub, smooth, sharpen, cut through, grind down, or polish with or as with a file; as, to *file* a wire or the nails.

2. to smooth; to correct; to polish; to urge toward refinement; to improve; as, association with gentlemen *filed* his manners.

fīle, *n.* [ME. *file, fyle*; AS. *feol*, a file.]

1. a steel tool with a rough, ridged surface for smoothing, grinding down, or cutting through something. Files are named either from the nature or number of the cutting faces, the shape of the tool, or the use to which they are put.

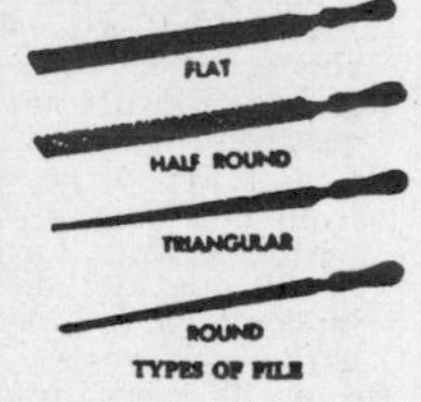

TYPES OF FILE

2. any means used to smooth, polish, or refine, either literally or in a figurative sense.

3. a hard, cunning person; a shrewd person; a deep or artful man; as, a sly old *file*. [Slang.]

4. a cloth for wiping or washing a floor. [Dial.]

5. in entomology, an organ of an insect covered with transverse grooves by means of which stridulation is produced.

bastard file; see under *bastard, a.*

cabinet file; a fine single-cut file used on hardwood.

dead file; a finely cut or smooth file, the grade finer than a smooth file.

second-cut file; a file one grade finer than a bastard, and rougher than a smooth file.

single-cut file; a file cut with only one series of grooves: a coarse *single-cut file* is called a *float*.

smooth file; a file which grades between second-cut and dead.

fīle blank, a piece of steel shaped and ground smooth, ready to be cut into a file.

fīle çlẽrk, a person employed to keep office files in order.

fīle çlōṣ'ẽr, a noncommissioned officer stationed in the rear or on the flank of a company of soldiers to assist in maintaining an exact formation in the ranks.

fīle çut'tẽr, a maker of files.

fīle fīr'ing, firing by infantry one file at a time or one file following another in rapid succession.

fīle'fish, *n.* any of certain fishes, family *Balistidae*, with very small, rough scales.

fīle lēad'ẽr, the soldier at the head of a file; one who leads a file.

fīle märch'ing, the marching of soldiers in files.

fil'e·mot, *n.* [Fr. *feuille-morte*, a dead leaf.] a yellowish-brown color; the color of a faded leaf.

fīl′ẽr, *n.* one who uses a file in cutting, smoothing, or polishing.

fīle shell, any bivalve mollusk of the genus *Pholas*, with a rough shell.

fi·let′ (fi-lā′ *or* fil′ā), *n.* [OFr. *fillet*, a thread, band, from LL. *filetum*, dim. of L. *filum*, a thread.]
 1. a net or lace with a simple pattern on a square mesh background.
 2. a fillet (of fish or meat).

fi·let′ mi·gnōn′ (fi-lā′ min-yōn′), [Fr.] a round cut of lean beefsteak, broiled, usually with mushrooms and bacon.

fil′i·ăl (*or* fil′yăl), *a.* [Fr. *filial*, LL. *filialis*, of a son or daughter, from *filius*, a son, *filia*, a daughter.]
 1. of, suitable to, or due from a son or daughter; as, *filial* love, *filial* duty.
 2. bearing the relation of a child; issuing from as offspring.
 Sprigs of like leaf erect their *filial* heads. —Prior.
 3. in genetics, designating or of any generation following the parental: symbol, F (e.g., F_1 means "first filial," F_2, "second filial," etc.).

fil′i·ăl·ly, *adv.* in a filial manner.

fil′i·āte, *v.t.*; filiated, *pt., pp.*; filiating, *ppr.* 1. to adopt as a foster child.
 2. in law, to fix paternity upon; hence, to assign as the originator of a hitherto anonymous work.
 3. to affiliate.

fil·i·ā′tion, *n.* [Fr. *filiation*; LL. *filiatio* (*-onis*), from *filius*, a son, *filia*, a daughter.]
 1. the state or fact of being a son or daughter; the relation of a son or child to a parent, especially a father: correlative to *paternity*.
 2. adoption.
 3. descent from or as from a parent; derivation; as, the *filiation* of the Romance languages to Latin.
 4. (a) the forming of a new branch or affiliation of a society, etc.; (b) such an affiliated branch.
 5. in law, the determination by a court of the paternity of an illegitimate child.

fil′i·beg, *n.* [Gael. *feileadh-beag*, a small kilt; *feileadh*, a kilt, and *beag*, small, little.] a kilt.

fil′i·bus·tẽr, *v.i.*; filibustered, *pt., pp.*; filibustering, *ppr.* 1. to engage in unauthorized warfare as a freebooter.
 2. to obstruct the passage of a bill by making long speeches, etc.

fil′i·bus·tẽr, *v.t.* to obstruct the passage of (a bill) by making long speeches, etc.

fil′i·bus·tẽr, *n.* [Sp. *filibustero*, from Fr. *flibustier*, *fribustier*, a buccaneer, freebooter; from D. *vrijbuiter*, a freebooter, from *vrij*, free, and *buit*, booty.]
 1. a freebooter or soldier of fortune who engages in unauthorized warfare against a foreign country with which his own country is at peace, in order to enrich himself: first applied to buccaneers in the West Indies who preyed on the Spanish commerce to South America.
 2. a member of a minority group of a legislative body, especially the Senate, who obstructs the passage of a bill by making long speeches, introducing irrelevant issues, etc.
 3. the deliberate obstruction of the passage of a bill by such methods.

fil·i·bus′tẽr·ism, *n.* the methods, acts, or practices of a filibuster.

fil′i·căl, *a.* of or resembling the *Filices* or ferns.

Fil′i·cēs, *n.pl.* [L. *filix*, pl. *filices*, fern.] a large order of cryptogamic plants, the ferns.

fi·lic′iç, *a.* [L. *filix* (*-icis*), a fern.] in chemistry, relating to or produced by ferns; as, *filicic* acid.

fil·i·cīd′ăl, *a.* having to do with filicide.

fil′i·cīde, *n.* [from L. *filius*, son, *filia*, daughter, and *-cidium*, from *cædere*, to kill.]
 1. the act of murdering one's own child.
 2. one who murders his own child.

fi·lic′i·form, *a.* [L. *filix* (*-icis*), a fern, and *forma*, form.] fern-shaped.

Fil·i·cin′ē·ae, *n.pl.* [from L. *filix* (*-icis*), a fern.] the ferns.

fil′i·cīte, *n.* [L. *filix* (*-icis*), a fern, and *-ite*.] a fossil fern or filicoid plant.

fil′i·coid, *a.* [L. *filix* (*-icis*), a fern, and Gr. *eidos*, form.] in botany, fernlike; having the form of ferns or like them in manner of propagation.

fil′i·coid, *n.* a plant resembling a fern.

fil·i·col′ō·gy, *n.* [L. *filix* (*-icis*), a fern, and Gr. *-logia*, from *legein*, to speak.] that branch of botany which deals with ferns.

fi·lī′e·ty, *n.* [LL. *filietas*, from L. *filius*, a son.] the relationship borne by a son to a father; sonship.
 The paternity of A and the *filiety* of B are not two facts, but two modes of expressing the same fact. —J. S. Mill.

fi·lif′ẽr·ous, *a.* [L. *filum*, a thread, and *ferre*, to bear.] producing or bearing threads or threadlike filaments: said of plants and insects.

fil′i·form, *a.* [L. *filum*, a thread, and *forma*, form.] having the form of a thread or filament; slender and of equal thickness from top to bottom; as, a *filiform* style or peduncle.

fi·lig′ẽr·ous, *a.* [L. *filum*, a thread, and *gerere*, to bear.] in zoology, flagellate: applied to infusoria and bacteria.

fil′i·grāin, fil′i·grāne, *n.* [Fr. *filigrane*; It. *filigrana*, a filigree, from L. *filum*, a thread, and *granum*, a grain.] filigree. [Obs.]

fil′i·grāned, *a.* filigreed. [Obs.]

fil′i·gree, *n.* [altered from *filigrain*.]
 1. delicate, lacelike ornamental work of intertwined wire of gold, silver, etc.
 2. any delicate work or figure like this.
 3. anything which is so fanciful, ornamental, or light in structure as to be perishable or of little use.
 Guarantees, he said, were mere *filigree*, pretty to look at, but too brittle to bear the slightest pressure —Macaulay.

fil′i·gree, *a.* pertaining to, resembling, made into, or made of filigree; hence, fanciful; unsubstantial; slight; purely ornamental.

fil′i·gree, *v.t.*; filigreed, *pt., pp.*; filigreeing, *ppr.* to ornament with, or work in, filigree.

fil′i·greed, *a.* ornamented with filigree.

fil′i·gree glȧss, glass into which colored threads have been introduced, which, weaving in and out, produce patterns.

fīl′ing, *n.* [*usually in pl.*] a fragment or particle rubbed off by the act of filing; as, iron *filings*.

Fil·i·ō′quē (-kwē), *n.* [L., lit., and from the Son; *filio*, ablative of *filius*, son, and *que*, the enclitic, and.] the clause of the Nicene Creed stating that the Holy Ghost proceeds from the Son as well as from the Father, it being one of the doctrines serving to separate the Orthodox Eastern Church from the Roman Catholic Church, the former never accepting it.

fil·i·pen′dū·lȧ, *n.* [L. *filum*, a thread, and *pendulus*, hanging, from *pendere*, to hang.] in botany, the true English dropwort, *Spiræa filipendula*.

fil·i·pen′dū·lous, *a.* [L. *filum*, thread, and *pendulus*, hanging, from *pendere*, to hang.] suspended by a thread; specifically, in botany, designating or of tuberous swellings developed in the middle of small, threadlike radicels.

Fil·i·pī′nȧ, *n.* [Sp.] a female native or citizen of the Philippine Islands.

Fil′i·pīne, *a.* Philippine.

Fil·i·pī′nō, *a.* Philippine.

Fil·i·pī′nō, *n.*; *pl.* **Fil·i·pī′nōs,** [Sp.] a native or citizen of the Philippine Islands.

fill, *v.t.*; filled, *pt., pp.*; filling, *ppr.* [ME. *fillen*, *fullen*, *fyllen*; AS. *fyllan*, to fill, make full, from *full*, full.]
 1. to make full; to cause to be occupied to the full capacity of; to supply with as much as can be contained; to place in or pour into until no more can be held; as, to *fill* a bottle; to *fill* a building with people.
 Fill the waterpots with water. And they *filled* them up to the brim. —John ii. 7.
 2. to take up the whole of; to occupy; as, the crowd *filled* the room.
 3. to supply with abundance; to be plentiful in; to pervade; to permeate; to infest.
 Be fruitful, and multiply, and *fill* the waters in the seas. —Gen. i. 22.
 4. to supply with an incumbent; as, to *fill* an office or vacancy.
 5. to hold; to possess and perform the duties of; to officiate in, as an incumbent; as, the president *fills* the office of chief magistrate.
 6. to supply the things needed or called for in (an order, requisition, prescription, etc.).
 7. to close or plug (holes, cracks, etc.).
 8. (a) to feed; (b) to satisfy the hunger of.
 9. to put into a container so as to fill it, or as if to fill it.
 10. to add earth, etc. to (low land) until a required level is reached.
 11. in nautical usage, (a) to swell (a sail); (b) to trim (a yard) so as to catch the wind on the after side of the sail.
 to fill in; (a) to add material sufficient to raise to a given level; as, *to fill in* a ravine; (b) to insert in a blank form; to supply, as missing data; as, *to fill in* particulars; (c) to make complete by inserting or supplying something.
 to fill one in on; to provide one with additional facts, details, etc. of. [Colloq.]
 to fill out; (a) to make fuller, rounder, shaplier, etc.; (b) to make (a document, etc.) complete by inserting or supplying information.
 to fill the bill; to be adequate to the need; to meet the requirements; to be what is desired. [Colloq.]
 to fill up; to make full; to occupy to the entire capacity of; to complete.
 It pours the bliss that *fills up* all the mind. —Pope.

 Syn.—occupy, pervade, make complete, pack, pour, feed, satisfy, satiate, distend, swell.

fill, *v.i.* 1. to grow or become full; to expand to the full capacity; to be satiated; to swell; as, kernels or pea pods *fill* well; sails *fill* in a stiff breeze.
 2. to pour liquid into a cup or glass for drinking.
 In the cup which she hath filled, *fill* to her double. —Rev. xviii. 6.
 to back and fill; see under *back*, v.i.
 to fill away; in nautical language, to brace the yards so that the sails may catch the wind and fill.
 to fill in; to be a substitute.
 to fill out; to become larger, rounder, shaplier, etc.
 to fill up; to grow or become full; as, the channel of the river *fills up* with sand every spring.

fill, *n.* [ME. *fille*, *fulle*, *fylle*; AS. *fyllu*, *fyllo*, fullness, fill.]
 1. all that is needed to make full.
 2. all that is needed to satisfy.
 3. anything that fills or is used to fill a space.
 4. a piece of land artificially raised to a required level, as a railroad embankment.

fill, *n.* [var. of *thill*.] a shaft; a thill. [Dial.]

fil′lȧ·gree, *n.* same as *filigree*.

fïlle (fē′yĕ), *n.* [Fr.] 1. a daughter.
 2. a girl; a maid.
 3. a spinster.
 4. a prostitute.

fïlle de chäm′bre (-shäṅ′br), [Fr.] a chambermaid; a lady's maid.

fïlle de joie′ (-zhwä′), [Fr., lit., daughter of joy.] a prostitute.

filled gōld, brass or other base metal covered with a layer of gold, used as a substitute for solid gold.

filled milk, skimmed milk with vegetable oils added to increase the fat content.

fill′ẽr, *n.* a person or thing that fills; specifically, (a) matter added to some other to increase bulk, as sand in fertilizer; (b) a preparation used to fill in the cracks, grain, etc. of wood before painting or varnishing; (c) the tobacco rolled in the leaf of a cigar; (d) a short, space-filling item in a newspaper; (e) a pad of loose-leaf paper for a notebook; (f) a funnel.

fil′lér (fēl′lăr), *n.* [Hung.] a small Hungarian bronze coin equal to 1/100 of a forint (or, formerly, of a pengö).

fill′ẽr, *n.* a thill horse. [Brit. Dial.]

fil′let, *n.* [OFr. *fillet*, a thread, band, chine of beef, from LL. *filettum*, dim. of L. *filum*, a thread.]
 1. a band; a strip; a ribbon.
 2. a narrow band worn around the head for ornament or to hold the hair in place.
 A belt her waist, a *fillet* binds her hair. —Pope.
 3. (*also pron.* fil′ā) in cookery, a boneless, lean piece of fish or meat. The term is applied specifically to the tenderloin of beef, to the fleshy part of a leg of veal or mutton, to the breast of a chicken, and to a thick, boneless slice of fish.
 Fillet of a fenny snake,
 In the caldron boil and bake. —Shak.
 4. meat rolled together and tied round.
 5. in technology, (a) a strip nailed to a wall to support a shelf; (b) a strip for a door to close against; (c) a band of gold leaf on a picture frame or elsewhere; (d) a strip of metal rolled to a certain size; (e) the thread of a screw; (f) a ring on the muzzle of a gun.
 6. in architecture, a small molding, generally rectangular in section, and having the appearance of a narrow band, used to separate ornaments and moldings; a list; a listel; the ridge between the flutes of a column.

7. in heraldry, a horizontal band on a shield, just below the chief and one-fourth its width.
8. in anatomy, a bundle of nerve fibers; especially, the fibers found at the base of the brain; the lemniscus.
9. in bookbinding, a line impressed on a book cover.
10. [*pl.*] the loins of a horse, beginning at the place where the hinder part of the saddle rests.

fil′let, *v.t.*; filleted, *pt., pp.*; filleting, *ppr.* 1. to bind or decorate with a fillet or little band.
2. (fil′ā, fil-ā′) in cookery, to bone and slice (meat or fish).

fil′let·ing, *n.* 1. the material for making fillets.
2. fillets, collectively.
3. a kind of heavy tape.

fill horse, phill horse, the horse which goes in the shafts; a thill horse. [Dial.]

Thou hast got more hair on thy chin than
Dobbin, my *phill horse*, has on his tail.
—Shak.

fil′li·beg, *n.* same as *filibeg*.

fil′li·bus·tẽr, *n.* same as *filibuster*.

fill′-in, *n.* a person or thing that fills a vacancy or gap, often temporarily.

fill′-in, *a.* of, by, or for a fill-in.

fill′ing, *n.* 1. the act of one who fills or supplies; a becoming or causing to become full.
2. material used for occupying some vacant space, for completing some structure, stopping up a hole, or the like; especially, the gold, amalgam, etc. inserted by a dentist into a prepared cavity in a tooth.
3. the material employed for filling up the outside pores of certain porous woods used for fine work, such as house finishing, cabinet making, etc.
4. the horizontal threads crossing the warp in a woven fabric; the woof.

fill′ing stā′tion, a place where gasoline, oil, services, etc. for automobiles and other motor vehicles are sold at retail: also called *gas* or *gasoline station*.

fil′lip, *n.* [echoic extension of *flip*.]
1. the snap made by a finger which is held down toward the palm by the thumb and then suddenly released.
2. a light blow or tap given in this way.
3. anything that stirs up or arouses; tonic; stimulus.

fil′lip, *v.t.* 1. to jerk or toss with a fillip.
2. to stir up; arouse; stimulate.

fil′lip, *v.i.* to make a fillip.

fil·li·peen′, *n.* same as *philopena*.

fil′lis·tẽr, *n.* 1. a groove, as the rabbet on a sash bar for holding the glass and putty.
2. a kind of plane used for grooving timber or for cutting rabbets.

fil′ly, *n.*; *pl.* **fil′lies,** [Ice. *fylja*, a filly, from *foli*; AS. *fola*, a foal.]
1. a female colt or foal; a young mare.
2. a vivacious young woman or girl. [Colloq.]

film, *n.* [ME. *fylme*; AS. *fylmen*, a film, membrane.]
1. a thin skin; a pellicle; a membrane; a delicate coating or outer layer, partially obscuring that which lies beneath; as, a *film* of gelatin; a *film* of lace.
2. a sheet or roll of a flexible cellulose material covered with a substance sensitive to light and used in taking photographs.
3. a thin veil, haze, or blur, as over the eyes.
4. a motion picture.
5. a delicate thread, as of a cobweb.
film camera; a photographic camera arranged to carry a reel of film: distinguished from a *plate camera*, which carries a limited number of sensitized plates.
film cutter; one who cuts and arranges the strips of film into one continuous chain.
film pack; several sheets of photographic film in a frame that fits in the back of a camera.
film star; an actor or actress having a leading part in motion pictures.
sound film; a motion-picture film which carries a sound track.

film, *v.t.*; filmed, *pt., pp.*; filming, *ppr.* 1. to cover with or as with a film.
2. to take a photograph of.
3. to make a motion picture of; as, they *filmed* the story.

film, *v.i.* 1. to be or become covered with a film.
2. to be filmed or suitable for filming; as, this story won't *film* well.

film′i·ly, *adv.* in a filmy manner; with or through a film.

film′i·ness, *n.* the quality of being filmy.

film′strip, *n.* a length of film containing still photographs, often of illustrations, diagrams, charts, etc., arranged in sequence for projection separately and used as a teaching aid.

film′y, *a.*; *comp.* filmier; *superl.* filmiest. 1. of or like a film; hazy, gauzy, etc.
2. covered with or as with a film; blurred.

fil″ō·plū·mā′ceous, *a.* formed like a filoplume.

fil′ō·plūme, *n.* [L. *filum*, a thread, and *pluma*, a downy feather.] in ornithology, a long, slender, and flexible feather, closely approximating a hair in form, and consisting of a delicate shaft, either destitute of vanes or carrying a few barbs at the tip.

fī′lōse, *a.* [from L. *filum*, a thread.]
1. threadlike.
2. having a threadlike projection.

fil′ō·selle (*or* fil-ō-sel′), *n.* [Fr.] a sort of silk thread resembling floss.

fils (fēs), *n.* [Fr.] a son or a youth: often used like English *Jr.*; as, Dumas *fils*.

fil′tẽr, *n.* [Fr. *filtre*, a filter, from LL. *filtrum*, *feltrum*, felt, fulled wool, this being used for straining liquors.]
1. a device for separating solid particles, impurities, etc. from a fluid by passing it through a porous substance.
2. any porous substance used for this purpose, as sand, charcoal, felt, etc.
3. in physics, (a) a device or substance that passes electric currents of certain frequencies or frequency ranges while preventing the passage of others; (b) a device or substance that partially or completely absorbs certain light rays; as, a color *filter* for a camera lens.

fil′tẽr, *v.t.* [Fr. *filtrer*.]
1. to pass (fluids) through a filter.
2. to remove or separate (solid particles, impurities, etc.) from a fluid by means of a filter.
3. to act as a filter for (electric currents of certain frequencies, etc.).

fil′tẽr, *v.i.* 1. to be filtered.
2. to move or pass slowly; as, the news *filtered* through town.

fil′tẽr, *n.* same as *philter*.

fil″tẽr·ȧ·bil′i·ty, *n.* the quality or state of being filterable.

fil′tẽr·ȧ·ble, *a.* 1. that can be filtered.
2. that goes through a filter.
Also *filtrable*.

fil′tẽr bed, a tank having a sand or gravel bottom, used to filter water, sewage, etc.

fil′tẽr gal′lẽr·y, an underground tunnel or conduit paralleling a stream, to collect water that is filtered through the sand and gravel which cover the bed of the stream.

fil′tẽr·ing, *n.* the act of passing through a filter; percolation: often used in compounds; as, *filtering* funnel.

fil′tẽr pā′pẽr, a porous, unsized paper used in laboratories for filtering liquids.

filth, *n.* [ME. *filthe*, *felthe*, *fulthe*; AS. *fylthe*, filth, foulness, from *ful*, foul.]
1. dirt; any foul matter; anything that soils or defiles; waste matter.
2. moral corruption or something causing it; anything that sullies or defiles the moral character; indecency; obscenity.

Purifying our souls from the dross and *filth*
of sensual delights. —Tillotson.

3. a foul condition. [Obs.]

filth dis·ēase′, in medicine, any disease supposed to arise from drinking impure water or from unsanitary conditions.

filth′i·ly, *adv.* in a filthy manner; foully.

filth′i·ness, *n.* 1. the quality or state of being filthy.
2. that which is filthy; foulness; dirtiness; filth; nastiness; corruption; pollution.

filth′y, *a.*; *comp.* filthier; *superl.* filthiest.
1. full of, or having the nature of, filth; dirty; foul; unclean; nasty; noisome.
2. obscene; morally corrupt; lewd.
3. low; contemptible; mean.

fil·trȧ·bil′i·ty, *n.* filterability.

fil′trȧ·ble, *a.* filterable.

fil′trȧ·ble vī′rus, any virus of ultramicroscopic size, capable of passing through filters that bacteria cannot pass through: some such viruses cause measles, influenza, poliomyelitis, etc.

fil′trāte, *v.t.*; filtrated, *pt., pp.*; filtrating, *ppr.* [LL. *filtratus*, pp. of *filtrare*, to filter.] to filter; to strain.

fil′trāte, *n.* the liquid which has been passed through a filter.

fil·trā′tion, *n.* a filtering or a being filtered.

fil·trā′tion plant, a place where the impurities are removed from a city's or district's water supply, making it fit to drink.

fī′lum, *n.*; *pl.* **fī′lȧ,** [L. *filum*, a thread.]
1. in anatomy, a threadlike structure; a minute fiber.
2. in music, the stem or tail attached to a note.
filum terminale; the slender, gray filament in which the spinal cord terminates.

fim′ble, *n.* [from Fr. (*chanvre*) *femelle*, female hemp.] light summer hemp that bears no seed; the male plants of hemp: also called *fimble hemp*.

fim′bri·ȧ, *n.*; *pl.* **fim′bri·ae,** [LL. *fimbria*, a border, from L. *fimbriæ*, fringe.]
1. a fringe; a band or row of fringing filaments; specifically, (a) [*pl.*] the fringed extremity of a Fallopian tube; (b) the fringe of white filaments surrounding a part of the hippocampus major of the brain.
2. in botany, the dentated or fringelike ring of the operculum of mosses.

fim′bri·ăl, *a.* pertaining to a fimbria.

fim′bri·āte, *a.* [L. *fimbriatus*, fringed, from *fimbria*, a fringe, border.] in botany, fringed; having the margin bordered by filiform processes thicker than hairs.

fim′bri·āte, *v.t.*; fimbriated, *pt., pp.*; fimbriating, *ppr.* to fringe; to put a border on.

fim′bri·ā·ted, *a.* 1. fringed; having a fringed border; fimbriate.
2. in heraldry, ornamented with a narrow border of another tincture.

fim·bri·ā′tion, *n.* 1. the act or process of fimbriating.
2. the condition of being fimbriated.
3. a fringe.

FIMBRIATE PETALS (*Dianthus caryophyllus*)

fim·bril′lȧ, *n.*; *pl.* **fim·bril′lae,** [dim., from L. *fimbra*, a fringe, border.] one of the parts that constitute a minute fringe.

fim·bril′lāte, *a.* composed of fimbrillae.

fim·bril·lif′ẽr·ous, *a.* [*fimbrilla*, dim., from L. *fimbria*, a border, and *ferre*, to bear.] bordered by fimbrillae; fimbrillate.

fim·ē·tā′ri·ous, *a.* [L. *fimetum*, dunghill, from *fimus*, dung.] in botany, growing in or on dung.

fin, *n.* [ME. *finne*, *fynne*; AS. *finn*, a fin; D. *vinne*; L.G. *finne*; Sw. *finne*, a fin; L. *pinna*, fin, wing.]
1. any of several winglike membranous organs on the body of a fish, dolphin, etc., used in swimming, turning, and balancing.
2. anything resembling a fin; as, (a) a finlike part or attachment; (b) the sharp plate in the colter of a plow; (c) in molding, a thin edge on the surface of a casting, caused by the imperfect approximation of two molding boxes, containing each a portion of the mold, the fin being formed by the metal running in between the two parting surfaces; (d) a blade of whalebone; (e) [Slang.] the hand; as, hold up your *fin*; (f) in aeronautics, any fixed or movable airfoil whose chief function is to give stability in flight; (g) in nautical usage, a projection on boats or submarines; also, a fin keel.
3. fish, collectively.
paired fins; the pectoral and ventral fins, which correspond to the hands and feet of erect vertebrates.
unpaired fins; the dorsal, anal, and caudal fins.

fin, *v.t.*; finned, *pt., pp.*; finning, *ppr.* to cut the fins from.

fin, *v.i.* to move the fins, especially in a violent way.

fin, *n.* [from G. (via Yiddish) *fünf*, five.] a five-dollar bill. [Slang.]

fīn′ȧ·ble, *a.* capable of being refined: also spelled *fineable*.

fīn′ȧ·ble, *a.* subject to a fine or penalty: also spelled *fineable*.

fi·nā′gle, *v.i.*; finagled, *pt., pp.*; finagling, *ppr.* [prob. respelling of *Feinagel*, G. mesmerist and whist expert of the Regency.]
1. in card games, to renege; revoke.
2. to use trickery; to be sly or crafty; cheat.

fi·nā′gle, *v.t.* 1. to cheat.
2. to get or manage by trickery, slyness, or craftiness.

fi·nā′glẽr, *n.* a person who finagles.

fī′năl, *a.* [ME. *final*; OFr. *final*; L. *finalis*, from *finis*, end.]
1. pertaining to the end or conclusion; last;

ultimate; as, the *final* issue or event of things; *final* hope; *final* salvation.
2. conclusive; decisive; determinative; as, a *final* judgment.
3. of purpose or result.
Thus we necessarily include, in our idea of organization, the notion of an end, a purpose, a design; or, to use another phrase, a *final* cause. —Whewell.
Syn.—conclusive, ultimate, eventual, last.

fī′năl, *n.* 1. that which is the termination; the last.
2. in the Gregorian scale, the note corresponding to the keynote of the modern scale, being the first tone in the authentic and the fourth from the bottom in the plagal scale.
3. [*pl.*] the last and deciding contest or round of a series of athletic events, tests, etc.; as, twelve players qualified for the *finals*.
4. [*often in pl.*] a final examination. [Colloq.]

fi·nä′le, *n.* [It., from L. *finalis*, from *finis*, end.]
1. the concluding movement or passage of a musical composition.
2. the last scene or feature of an entertainment.
3. the conclusion or last part; end.

fī′năl·ist, *n.* a contestant who participates in the final and deciding contest or contests of a series.

fi·nal′i·ty, *n.* 1. the state of being final; the state of being settled or finally arranged; completeness.
2. *pl.* **fi·nal′i·tieṣ,** anything final or conclusive.
3. in philosophy, the doctrine that nothing exists or was made except for a determinate end; the doctrine of final causes.

fī′năl·īze, *v.t.*; finalized, *pt., pp.*; finalizing, *ppr.* [U.S. neologism.] to make final, to bring to a conclusion.

fī′năl·ly, *adv.* 1. at the end or conclusion; ultimately; lastly; as, the cause is expensive, but we shall *finally* recover.
2. completely; decisively; conclusively.
The enemy was *finally* exterminated. —Davies.

fi·nance′ (*or* fī′), *n.* [ME. *finaunce*, a fine, forfeit; OFr. *finance*, wealth, revenue; LL. *financia*, a money payment, money, from *finare*, to pay a fine or tax, from L. *finis*, end.]
1. the system or science of public revenue and expenditure or of any money matters.
2. [*pl.*] the money resources, income, etc. of a nation, organization, or person.
finance company; a commercial credit company; also, a holding company.

fi·nance′ (*or* fī′), *v.t.*; financed, *pt., pp.*; financing, *ppr.* 1. to have the financial management of; as, to *finance* an arctic expedition; to *finance* a campaign.
2. to supply money for.

fi·nance′ (*or* fī′), *v.i.* to conduct financial operations; to manage finances.

fi·nan′ciăl (-shăl), *a.* pertaining to finance, finances, or financiers; as, *financial* concerns or operations.

fi·nan′ciăl·ist, *n.* a financier. [Colloq.]

fi·nan′ciăl·ly, *adv.* in relation to finance or finances.

fin·an·cīēr′, *n.* [Fr., from *finance*, finance.]
1. a person who engages in financial operations on a large scale.
2. one who is skilled in financial matters or in the principles or system of public revenue.
3. in France before the Revolution, a receiver or farmer of the public revenues.

fin·an·cīēr′, *v.t.* and *v.i.*; financiered, *pt., pp.*; financiering, *ppr.* to act as financier for; to finance.

fīn′ȧ·ry, *n.* a finery (refinery). [Obs.]

fin′back, *n.* a rorqual, a large whalebone whale of the family *Balænopteridæ*, having a prominent dorsal fin. *Sibbaldius tectirostris* is the common finback of the north Atlantic coast, and *Balænoptera velifera* and *Balænoptera davidsoni* are finbacks found in the Pacific: also *finback whale*.

finch, *n.* [ME. *finch*, *fynch*; AS. *finc*, a finch.] any of a large group of small singing birds forming the family *Fringillidæ*, which includes the bunting, canary, cardinal, sparrow, etc. It is often used in compounds to form the names of various fringilline birds; as, bull*finch*, pine*finch*, gold*finch*, chaf*finch*, etc.

fin chāin, a heavy chain having rings on the ends or a ring and a hook, used by whalers in lifting the fore part of a whale.

finch′backed (-bakt), *a.* marked by streaks or blotches, as cattle. [Brit. Dial.]

finched, *a.* same as *finchbacked*.

finch fa̤l′cŏn (fa̤′kn), a falcon of the genus *Hierax*, in size no larger than the finch.

fīnd, *v.t.*; found, *pt., pp.*; finding, *ppr.* [ME. *finden*; AS. *findan*, to find.]
1. to come to; to meet with; to discover, whether unexpectedly or by searching; to obtain, whether by effort or by chance; as, flowers are *found* in the wood; he *found* the coin he sought; to *find* time to visit.
2. to discover by methodical experiment; to ascertain by trial or study; to learn; to perceive; to observe; to detect; as, to *find* the best way to do anything; to *find* the elements in a compound.
3. (a) to recover (something lost); (b) to recover the use of.
4. to consider; think.
5. to reach; attain; as, the blow *found* his chin.
6. to decide; to determine after judicial inquiry; to establish, as facts; to come to or arrive at, as a conclusion; as, to *find* a verdict; to *find* damages; to *find* a true bill.
7. to supply; to furnish; as, to *find* provisions for an expedition.
to find oneself; (a) to be; to fare; as, how do you *find yourself* this morning? (b) to learn what one's real talents and inclinations are, and begin to apply them.
to find out; to unriddle; to solve; to discover; to obtain knowledge of what is hidden; to detect; to bring to light; as, *to find out* a thief or a theft; *to find out* a trick.
Syn.—meet, confront, ascertain, experience, perceive, discover, furnish, supply, invent, recover, attain, observe, detect, arrive at.

fīnd, *v.i.* 1. to decide a question of fact and present the result to the court; as, the jury *finds* for the defendant.
2. in hunting, to locate game; as, the pointer *found* quickly.

fīnd, *n.* a finding; also, something found, especially something of value; as, the excavators of Pompeii have made some great *finds*.

fīnd′ȧ·ble, *a.* capable of being found, discovered, or located.

fīnd′ẽr, *n.* 1. that which or one who finds.
2. in astronomy, a small telescope, attached to a larger one, for the purpose of finding an object more readily for closer view with the more powerful telescope.
3. a small lens attached to a camera to indicate the extent of the field of view and help in adjusting the position of the camera.
4. a graduated slide used to locate objects in the field of a microscope.

fin de siè′cle (faṅ dē syā′kl), [Fr., end of the century.] of or characteristic of the last years of the 19th century: formerly used to refer to progressive ideas and customs, but now generally used to indicate decadence.

fīnd′fa̤ult, *n.* a faultfinder. [Obs.]

fīnd′ing, *n.* 1. discovery; the act of discovering; also, the thing found.
2. maintenance; support; expense. [Obs.]
3. [*pl.*] (a) the tools and materials which some workmen have to furnish in their employment; working supplies; (b) miscellaneous small supplies used by a worker; as, thread, bindings, etc. are *findings* in dressmaking.
4. the conclusion reached after an examination or consideration of facts by a judge, coroner, scholar, etc.

fīnd′ing list, a skeleton catalogue of the contents of a library, designed to facilitate the locating of the volumes.

fin′djăn, fin′ġiăn (fin′jăn), *n.* [Ar.] a small coffee cup used in the Levant, commonly of thin porcelain, without a handle, and supported by an ornamental metal holder, called a zarf: spelled also *fingan*.

fin′dy, *a.* [AS. *findig*, *fyndig*, weighty.] full; heavy; substantial. [Obs.]
A cold May and a windy,
Makes the barn fat and *findy*.
—Old Proverb.

fīne, *a.*; *comp.* finer; *superl.* finest, [ME. *fin*, *fyn*, *fine*; OFr. *fin*, from L. *finitus*, lit., finished, pp. of *finire*, to bound, limit, from *finis*, a limit, bound.]
1. originally, brought to a finish; perfected; hence, in a state of excellence or superiority; elegant; admirable; very good.
2. showy; aiming at effect; ornamented, dressed, or decorated to too great an extent; ostentatious; as, *fine* writing.
3. showing skill or nicety; subtle; discriminating; as, *fine* distinctions.
4. with no impurities; refined.
5. made up of minute particles; not heavy or coarse; as, *fine* dust.
6. small; thin; slender; minute; of very small diameter; as, a *fine* thread; *fine* silk; a *fine* hair.
7. keen; sharp; as, the *fine* edge of a razor.
8. made of delicate constituents or materials; as, *fine* linen or lace.
9. composed of a given proportion of pure metal; as, jewelry 14 carats *fine*.
10. of exceptional character or ability; as, a *fine* teacher.
11. clear and bright: said of the weather.
12. good-looking; handsome; as, a *fine* baby.
13. trained and developed physically to maximum ability: said of athletes, horses, etc.
fine arts; see *art*, n. 2.
fine stuff, a lime solution used as a finishing coat to cover previous coats of coarser plaster.
to sail fine; in nautical usage, to sail close to the wind.
Syn.—beautiful, attractive, showy, dainty, choice, rare, delicate, excellent, polished, slender, minute, thin, suitable, keen.

fīne, *adv.* 1. very well. [Colloq.]
2. in billiards and pool, so that the cue ball touches the object ball lightly on the side in passing and is deflected very little.

fīne, *v.t.* and *v.i.*; fined, *pt., pp.*; fining, *ppr.* [ME. *finen*, to refine, purify, from *fine*, *a.*] to make or become fine or finer.

fīne, *n.* [ME. *fin*, *fyn*, end, end of life, payment in settlement; OFr. *fin*, from L. *finis*, a limit, boundary.]
1. end; conclusion; finish. [Obs.]
2. a sum of money paid to settle a matter; especially, a sum paid by way of penalty for an offense; a pecuniary punishment.
3. in old English law, a conveyance of land, sometimes fictitious; a recorded grant: called also *fine of lands*.
4. in feudal law, a sum of money paid to the lord by his tenant, for permission to alienate or transfer his lands to another.
in fine; (a) in conclusion; (b) in brief.

fīne, *v.t.*, fined, *pt., pp.*; fining, *ppr.* 1. to subject to a pecuniary penalty for an offense or breach of law; to set a fine on by judgment of a court; to punish by fine.
2. to end; to bring to a conclusion; to cause to cease. [Obs.]
Time's office is to *fine* the hate of foes. —Shak.

fīne, *v.i.* [ME. *finen*, to pay a fine; OFr. *finir*, from L. *finire*, to end.]
1. to pay a fine; to pay for a grant, concession, or privilege. [Rare.]
2. to cease; to be ended. [Obs.]

fi′ne, *n.* [It., end.] in music, the end: a direction marking the close of a repeated passage.

fīne′ȧ·ble, *a.* same as *finable*.

fīne ärch, in glass making, a small furnace in which to melt the raw materials for glass.

fīne′-çut′, *a.* cut into small, narrow shreds of equal width: said of tobacco and distinguished from *rough-cut*.

fīne çut, tobacco finely shredded for chewing or smoking.

fīne′-dra̤w′, *v.t.* 1. to sew together (two pieces of cloth, as the edges of a tear) so carefully that the seam cannot be seen.
2. to draw (wire, etc.) out to extreme fineness.
3. to extend (reasoning, etc.) to a high degree of subtleness.

fīne-dra̤wn, *a.* 1. drawn out until very fine, as wire.
2. extremely subtle: said of reasoning, arguments, etc.

fi·neer′, *v.t.* to veneer. [Obs.]

fīne′-grāined′, *a.* having a fine, smooth grain, as some kinds of wood, leather, etc.

fīne′less, *a.* endless; boundless. [Obs.]

fīne′ly, *adv.* in a fine manner; admirably; delicately.

fīne′ness, *n.* 1. the state or quality of being fine.
2. the quantity of pure gold or silver contained in alloys, expressed as fractions of 1,000 or in carats.

fīn′ẽr, *n.* one who refines or purifies. [Brit.]

fīn′ẽr·y, *n.*; *pl.* **fīn′ẽr·ieṣ,** 1. fineness; beauty; attraction; charm. [Rare.]
2. showy articles of dress; gay clothes, jewels, trinkets, and the like.

fīn′ẽr·y, *n.*; *pl.* **fīn′ẽr·ieṣ,** [Fr. *finerie*, from *finer*, to refine.] a refinery where malleable iron or steel is made.

fīne′spun′, *a.* 1. spun or drawn out to extreme fineness; delicate; fragile.
2. extremely subtle.
3. too subtle; not practical.

fi·nesse′, *n.* [Fr. *finesse*, delicacy, nicety, from *fin*, fine.]
  1. skill; adroitness and delicacy of performance.
  2. the ability to handle delicate and difficult situations skillfully and diplomatically.
  3. artifice; stratagem; craft.
  4. in whist, bridge, etc., the act of playing with the view of taking the trick with a lower card while holding a higher card not in sequence with this, in the hope that an intervening card will not be played.
  Syn.—skill, craft, cunning, artifice, deception, maneuver, artfulness, adroitness, subterfuge, machination.

fi·nesse′, *v.t.*; finessed (-nest′), *pt.*, *pp.*; finessing, *ppr.* 1. to change by finesse; bring by finesse (into a certain condition).
  2. in bridge, whist, etc., to make a finesse with (a card).

fi·nesse′, *v.i.* to use or make a finesse.

fīne′still, *v.t.* to distill, as spirit from molasses, treacle, or some preparation of saccharine matter.

fīne′-toothed çōmb (-tötht kōm), a comb with fine, closely set teeth.
  to go over with a fine-toothed comb; to examine very carefully and thoroughly.

fīne′top, *n.* the redtop grass, *Agrostis vulgaris*.

fin′ew (-ū), *n.* moldiness. [Rare.]

fin′ewed, *a.* moldy. [Rare.]

fin′fish, *n.* 1. a finback whale.
  2. a fish having fins, as distinguished from a *shellfish*.

fin′foot, *n.*; *pl.* **fin′foots** or **fin′feet**, any bird of the genus *Heliornis*, allied to the grebes: so called from their feet being lobed.

fin′-foot″ed, *a.* 1. having palmated feet or feet with toes connected by a membrane; web-footed.
  2. having pinnate feet; having a membranous web bordering each toe.

fin′ġent, *a.* [L. *fingens* (*-entis*), ppr. of *fingere*, to form, shape.] forming; shaping; molding; fashioning. [Rare.]

fiṅ′gẽr, *n.* [ME. *finger*; AS. *finger*, a finger.]
  1. any of the five extreme parts of the hand; a digit; also, any of these parts exclusive of the thumb.
  2. the part of a glove covering one of these parts.
  3. a part shaped like or used as a finger; some device which serves the function of a finger.

Fancy, like the *finger* of a clock,
Runs the great circuit, and is still at home.
—Cowper.

  4. a fingerbreadth, a unit of measure ranging from three-quarters of an inch to one inch; also, a unit of measure equal to the length of the adult middle finger, or about four and one-half inches.
  5. in music, ability; skill in playing on a keyed instrument; execution; as, she has a good *finger*.
  6. in mechanics, a projecting part coming into contact with another part and controlling its motion.
  to burn one's fingers; see under *burn*, v.t.
  to have a finger in; to be interested in; to be implicated.
  to have a finger in the pie; (a) to have a share in any concern or act; to participate in the doing of anything; (b) to be meddlesome.
  to have at one's finger ends or *finger tips*; to be quite familiar with; to be able to make available readily.

fiṅ′gẽr, *v.t.*, fingered, *pt.*, *pp.*; fingering, *ppr.*
  1. to handle with the fingers; to touch with the fingers; as, the covetous man delights to *finger* money.
  2. to take; to steal; to pilfer.
  3. to play on, as a musical instrument, by using the fingers; also, to mark (a score) for the guidance of the fingers in playing.
  4. to perform with the fingers; to execute, as delicate manual work.

fiṅ′gẽr, *v.i.* 1. to use the fingers in a certain way on a musical instrument to produce the tune.
  2. to be fingered: said of musical instruments.

fiṅ′gẽr al′phȧ·bet, an alphabet, the letters of which are represented by positions and motions of the hands and fingers: used by deaf mutes.

fiṅ′gẽr-and-tōe′, *n.* a disease, due to a fungus, which attacks the roots of cabbages and turnips, making them hard and inedible.

fiṅ′gẽr bär, a horizontal bar on a mowing or reaping machine, which carries the knives and the fingers between which they slide.

fiṅ′gẽr bōard, the keyboard of a piano, organ, etc.; also, the part of any stringed instrument upon which the strings are pressed by the fingers in order to change the tone.

fiṅ′gẽr bōwl, a bowl or glass to contain water in which the fingers may be rinsed at the conclusion of a meal.

fiṅ′gẽr·breadth (-bredth), *n.* the breadth of a finger, as a measure of length; almost an inch.

fiṅ′gẽr çor′ăl, a variety of coral, *Millepora alcicornis*.

fiṅ′gẽred, *a.* 1. possessing fingers.
  2. soiled or marred by touching.
  3. in botany, (a) fingerlike in form; (b) digitate.
  4. in music, (a) touched or played on, as a keyed, stringed, or holed instrument; (b) marked with figures showing which finger is to be used for producing each note: said of a score; (c) produced by pressing the finger on a particular key, string, or hole, as a note.

fiṅ′gẽr·ẽr, *n.* one who fingers; especially, one who is light-fingered, meddling with or taking that which does not belong to him; a pilferer.

fiṅ′gẽr fẽrn, a variety of European plant of the fern family, especially spleenwort, *Asplenium ceterach*.

fiṅ′gẽr flow′ẽr, the foxglove, *Digitalis purpurea*: so called from its slender, tapering raceme of flowers.

fiṅ′gẽr gråss, a weed, *Panicum sanguinale*, bearing slender, digitate spikes: called also *crab grass*.

fiṅ′gẽr·ing, *n.* 1. the act of touching or handling with the fingers.
  2. in music, (a) a notation on a piece of music showing the proper finger with which to strike each note; (b) act or technique of applying the fingers to the strings, keys, etc. of an instrument to produce the tones.
  3. delicate work made with the fingers.

A shady, fresh, and ripply cove,
Where nested was an arbor, overwove
By many a summer's silent *fingering*.
—Keats.

  4. a coarse woolen yarn used in knitting stockings. [Brit.]

fiṅ′gẽr·ling, *n.* 1. the young salmon; a parr.
  2. any small object.

fiṅ′gẽr märk, a mark, particularly a stain or smudge, left by a finger.

fiṅ′gẽr-märked (-märkt), *a.* having finger marks on it.

fiṅ′gẽr·nāil, *n.* the horny substance on the upper part of the end of a finger: it consists of epithelial cells that develop from a thin layer of the skin.

fiṅ′gẽr nut, in machinery, a nut having winglike projections which may be readily grasped by the fingers in turning.

fiṅ′gẽr plāte, a plate of metal, plastic, etc. around a doorknob or electric light switch to protect against finger marks.

fiṅ′gẽr pōst, a post set up to indicate a direction: often with the figure of a hand and pointing finger on a projecting arm.

fiṅ′gẽr·print, *n.* an impression made by a finger or thumb; particularly, an impression made by the inside of the first joint of the finger, now widely used for identification since its lineation varies with each individual and remains unchanged through life.

FINGERPRINT

fiṅ′gẽr·print, *v.t.* to take the fingerprints of.

fiṅ′gẽr rēad′ing, the use of the fingers to read Braille.

fiṅ′gẽr shell, a marine shell resembling a finger; the piddock.

fiṅ′gẽr shiēld, a shield worn on a finger when sewing to protect it from the needle.

fiṅ′gẽr spŏṅġe, a variety of sponge which branches into finger-shaped lobes.

fiṅ′gẽr·stąll, *n.* a protective covering of rubber, leather, etc. for an injured finger.

fiṅ′gẽr steel, a small steel instrument upon which curriers sharpen their knives.

fiṅ′gẽr tip, 1. the extremity of a finger.
  2. a shield to protect the end of a finger, as from the bowstring in archery.
  to have at one's finger tips; (a) to have available for instant use; (b) to be completely familiar with.
  to one's (or *the*) *finger tips*; entirely; altogether.

fiṅ′gẽr wāve, a loose wave made in a woman's hair by the use of the fingers instead of a curling iron or machine, and without the application of heat.

fin′ġi·ăn, *n.* see *findjan*.

fiṅ′gle-faṅ′gle, *n.* a trifle. [Obs.]

fiṅ′gri·gō, *n.*; *pl.* **fiṅ′gri·gōṣ**, [Jamaica name.] a climbing plant of the genus *Pisonia*, whose fruit is a kind of berry or plum.

fin′i·ăl, *n.* [ME.; *finis*, and *-ial*.]
  1. an ornament at the top of a spire, gable, etc., or at the end of certain structures.
  2. the highest point; apex.

FINIALS

fin′i·çăl, *a.* [from the adj. *fine*.] too particular; too dainty or exacting; fussy; fastidious.
  Syn.—spruce, foppish, fastidious, affected.

fin·i·çal′i·ty, *n.* 1. the state of being finical.
  2. something finical; finicalness. [Rare.]

fin′i·çăl·ly, *adv.* in a finical manner; with extreme nicety.

fin′i·çăl·ness, *n.* extreme nicety in dress or manners; foppishness.

fin′ick·ing, *n.* the quality of being fastidious or of being exacting in trivial matters; fussiness.

fin′ick·ing, fin′ick·y, *a.* same as *finical*.

fi·nif′iç, *a.* [L. *finis*, end, and *-ficus*, from *facere*, to make.] setting a limit; making finite. [Rare.]

fin′i·fȳ, *v.t.* to make fine; to adorn. [Obs.]

fin′i·kin, *a.* same as *finical*.

fīn′ing, *n.* 1. the process of refining or purifying: applied especially to the clarifying of wines, malt liquors, etc.
  2. [*pl.*] the preparation, generally a solution of isinglass or gelatine or white of egg, used to fine or clarify.
  3. the process which cast iron undergoes before puddling; finery.

fī′nis, (*or* fin′is), *n.*; *pl.* **fī′nis·eṣ**, [L.] the end; finish; conclusion: often used at the end of a book or motion picture.

fin′ish, *v.t.*; finished (-isht), *pt.*, *pp.*; finishing, *ppr.* [ME. *finischen*, *finisshen*, from OFr. *finis* (stem of parts *finiss-*), from L. *finire*, to end, from *finis*, end, limit.]
  1. to arrive at the end of; to complete; as, to *finish* the day; to *finish* a journey.
  2. to complete; to perfect; to accomplish; as, to *finish* a house.
  3. to use up; consume entirely.
  4. to remove all blemishes from; perfect; polish.
  5. to reduce to worthlessness; cause to be of no value. [Colloq.]
  6. to put an end to; to disable; to render powerless; to kill; as, to *finish* an opponent. [Colloq.]
  to finish off; (a) to end or complete; (b) to kill or destroy.
  to finish up; (a) to end or complete; (b) to consume all of.
  Syn.—close, complete, end, conclude, perfect, terminate, cease, stop.

fin′ish, *v.i.* 1. to come to an end; cease; die.
  2. to have done; to desist; to stop.
  to finish with; (a) to end or complete; (b) to end relations with; become indifferent to.

fin′ish, *n.* 1. the last part; end.
  2. anything used to finish something else, as polish, wax, etc.
  3. completeness; perfection.
  4. the manner or method of completion.
  5. the way in which the surface, as of furniture, is smoothed, polished, etc.
  6. refinement in manners, speech, etc.; polish in social or cultural matters.
  7. in carpentry, (a) joiner work, as doors, stairs, panels, etc., which completes the interior of a building; (b) high-quality lumber used for this.
  in at the finish; in attendance or activity at the conclusion, as of a contest.

fin′ished (-isht), *a.* 1. ended; concluded.
  2. completed.

3. made perfect; accomplished; excellent.
4. smoothed and polished: said of furniture.
5. reduced to worthlessness; no longer of value.

fin'ish·ẽr, *n.* 1. one who or that which finishes, especially one that adds the final touches to something being made.
2. a decisive blow or happening; that which puts an end to something; as, the rebuke was a *finisher*. [Colloq.]

fin'ish·ing, *a.* last; imparting a polish; marking completion; as, a *finishing* school; a *finishing* press; a *finishing* tool.

fin'ish·ing, *n.* 1. an ending.
2. a completing or perfecting.
3. [*pl.*] the fixtures for lighting, plumbing, etc. in a building.

fin'ish·ing school, a private school for girls which prepares them for life in society, as by teaching music, languages, etc.

fī'nīte, *a.* [L. *finitus*, pp. of *finire*, to end, limit, bound, from *finis*, end, limit.]
1. having measurable or definable limits; not infinite.
2. in grammar, having limits of person, number, and tense: said of a verb that can be used to form the predicate of a sentence.
3. in mathematics, (a) capable of being reached or surpassed by counting: said of numbers; (b) neither infinite nor infinitesimal: said of magnitude.

fī'nīte, *n.* anything that has measurable limits; finite thing.

fī'nīte·ly, *adv.* within limits; to a certain degree only.

fī'nīte·ness, *n.* the condition of being finite; limitation; confinement within certain boundaries; as, the *finiteness* of our natural powers.

fin'i·tūde, *n.* [from L. *finitus*, pp. of *finire*, to end, limit.] the state or quality of being finite; limitation.

The fullness of the creation, and the *finitude* of the creature. —Chalmers.

fink, *n.* [perhaps from the name of a notorious American strikebreaker.] an informer or strikebreaker; especially, a professional strikebreaker.

fin keel, a deep, narrow metal keel, shaped somewhat like a dorsal fin, used on some sailboats to give stability and prevent lateral drift.

Fin'land·ẽr, *n.* a native or inhabitant of Finland; a Finn.

fin'less, *a.* without fins; as, *finless* fish.

fin'let, *n.* a little fin; part of a divided fin, as in a mackerel.

fin'līke, *a.* resembling a fin; as, a *finlike* oar.

Finn, Fin, *n.* 1. a native or inhabitant of Finland; a Finlander.
2. a member of any of the peoples speaking a Finnic language.

fin'năn had'die, fin'năn had'dŏck, smoked haddock.

finned, *a.* having broad edges on either side; possessing a fin or fins.

fin'nẽr, *n.* same as *finback*.

Finn'iç, *a.* 1. Finnish.
2. designating or of the group of languages to which Finnish belongs: see *Finno-Ugric*.

fin'nick·ing, *a.* same as *finicking*.

fin'nick·y, *a.* same as *finicky*.

fin'ni·kin, *n.* same as *finikin*.

Finn'ish, *a.* 1. of Finland.
2. of the Finns, their language, or culture.

Finn'ish, *n.* the language spoken by the Finns, called by themselves *Suomi*.

Fin'nō-, a combining form meaning *Finn* or *Finnish*, as in *Finno*-Ugric.

Fin'nō-Ū'gri·ăn, *a.* and *n.* same as *Finno-Ugric*.

Fin'nō-Ū'griç, *a.* designating or of a subfamily of the Uralic group of languages spoken in northeastern Europe, western Siberia, and Hungary: it includes Finnish, Estonian, Hungarian (Ugric, Magyar), Lapp, etc.

Fin'nō-Ū'griç, *n.* the Finno-Ugric subfamily of languages.

fin'ny, *a.* 1. furnished with fins; as, the *finny* tribes; *finny* prey.
2. like a fin.
3. of fish.
4. containing, harboring, or abounding in fish; as, the *finny* brook; the *finny* deep. [Poet.]

fi·nō'chi·ō, *n.* [It. *finocchio*, from L. *feniculum*, fennel.] a variety of fennel, *Fœniculum dulce*, or sweet fennel, native to southern Europe.

fin'-tōed, *a.* same as *fin-footed*.

fiord, fjord (fyord), *n.* [Dan. and Norw. *fjord*, a frith, bay.] a narrow inlet or arm of the sea bordered by steep cliffs, especially in Norway.

FIORD

fī'ō·rin, *n.* a species of creeping bent grass, *Agrostis vulgaris*, of great value as a meadow grass.

fī'ō·rīte, *n.* [named from Santa *Fiore*, in Tuscany, where it is found.] in mineralogy, a variety of opal occurring in volcanic rocks and formed by the decomposition of siliceous minerals.

fiō·ri·tū'rȧ, *n.*; *pl.* **fiō·ri·tū're,** [It., lit., flowering, flourishing.] musical ornamentation; a musical flourish: commonly used in the plural.

fip'pence, *n.* fivepence.

fip'pen·ny bit, [altered from *fivepenny bit*.] a Spanish or Mexican silver coin worth about six cents, circulated in the United States before 1857.

fip'ple, *n.* [perhaps akin to ON. *Flipi*, horse's lip.] a plug near the mouthpiece of certain wind instruments, as the recorder, to divert the breath in producing the tones.

fip'ple flūte, in music, a type of wind instrument, as the recorder, in which the sound waves are formed inside the pipe after the breath is diverted by a fipple.

fīr, *n.* [ME. *fir*, *fur*, *fyrre*; compare Dan. *fyr*, *fyrr*, and AS. *furh*, in *fuhr-wudu*, fir wood.]
1. the name of several trees of the genus *Abies*, allied to the pines, from which they differ in their leaves growing singly on the stem, and the scales of the cones being smooth, round, and thin. Their timber is valuable, being used in the construction of buildings and for spars and masts of ships.
2. any of various trees of genera allied to *Abies*, as *Pinus*, *Picea*, and *Tsuga*.

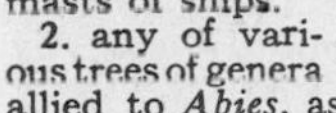

SCOTCH FIR (*Pinus sylvestris*)

3. the wood of any of these trees.
Among the more widely known species of fir are the following: the balsam fir, *Abies balsamea*; the red fir, *Abies magnifica*, *Abies nobilis*, or *Abies amabilis;* the white fir, *Abies grandis*; the spruce fir, *Picea excelsa*; the Scotch fir, *Pinus sylvestris*; and the hemlock fir, *Tsuga Canadensis*.

fīre, *n.* [ME. *fire*, *fir*, *fyre*; AS. *fyr*, fire.]
1. the active principle of burning, characterized by the heat and light of combustion.
2. any combustible body in a state of ignition, or heated to a redness.
3. fuel in a state of combustion, as in a stove, grate, or furnace, on a hearth, or on or in the ground; a mass of material lighted and burning for the sake of the warmth it affords, or for the use of its heat in cooking, etc.

In winter's tedious nights sit by the *fire*
With good old folks. —Shak.

4. the destructive burning of a house or other building, or of a town, forest, etc.; as, a *fire* in a crowded block; the great *fire* of Chicago; a prairie *fire*.
5. light; luster; splendor; anything like a fire in giving light, brilliance, etc.; as, the *fire* of a jewel.

Stars, hide your *fires*! —Shak.

6. ardor; strong feeling, as of love, hate, or anger; violence of passions; as, the *fire* of love.
7. liveliness of imagination; vigor of fancy; intellectual activity; animation; force of sentiment or expression.

And warm the critic with a poet's *fire*. —Pope.

8. torture by burning; hence, trouble; affliction; suffering; severe trial.
9. that which burns and inflames like *fire*; as, the *fire* of the fever burned without ceasing.
10. a spark or a shower of sparks struck out by a blow or friction upon hot iron or from stone.
11. the discharge or firing of firearms or artillery; shooting; as, to run into the *fire* of a masked battery.
12. anything like such a discharge in speed and continuity of action; as, a *fire* of criticism.
between two fires; between two attacks; shot at, criticized, etc. from both sides.
on fire; ignited; inflamed; burning; hence, eager; ardent; zealous.
rapid fire; the firing of the rounds in a firearm in rapid succession.
running fire; the discharge of firearms in rapid succession by one line of troops after another; hence, an uninterrupted succession, as of questions, remarks, or interjections.
to catch fire; to begin burning; to ignite.
to go through fire and water; to undergo great difficulties or dangers.
to hang fire; (a) to fail to fire, or delay in firing: said of a gun; (b) to delay or be delayed; be slow in acting or happening.
to lay a fire; to place fuel ready for starting a fire, as in a fireplace.
to miss fire; (a) to fail to fire, as a gun; (b) to fail in an attempt.
to open fire; (a) to begin to shoot; (b) to begin; to start.
to play with fire; to do something risky.
to set fire to; to make burn; to ignite.
to set on fire; to kindle; to inflame; to excite violent action in.
to set the world on fire; to become very successful, famous, etc.
to strike fire; to make a spark, as with tinder.
to take fire; to become ignited; to begin to burn; hence, to take violent offense; to become enraged; to fly into a passion.
under fire; on the firing line; exposed to the enemy's fire; hence, in the course of being attacked; as, a politician *under fire*.

fīre, *v.t.*; fired, *pt.*, *pp.*; firing, *ppr.* [ME. *firen*, *fyren*, *furen*, to set on fire, expose to fire; AS. *fyrian*, to give warmth to.]
1. to set on fire; to kindle; to apply fire to; to make burn; as, to *fire* a house or chimney; to *fire* a pile.
2. to subject to the action of fire; to expose to an intense heat; to bake in a kiln, as bricks, pottery, etc.
3. to inflame; to excite; to stimulate; as, to *fire* a man with anger or revenge.
4. to animate; to give life or spirit to; as, to *fire* the genius of a poet.
5. to dry by heat.
6. to shoot; to discharge; as, to *fire* a rifle or cannon; to *fire* a torpedo.
7. to cauterize.
8. to illuminate strongly; to make to shine as if on fire; to cause to glow; as, the setting sun *fired* the tree tops.
9. to throw; to hurl; to fling; to turn out; to oust; to eject; as, to *fire* a stone through a window. [Colloq.]
10. to dismiss from a position; to discharge; as, to *fire* an employee. [Colloq.]
11. to provide or supply fuel for; to feed a fire under; as, to *fire* a boiler; coal sufficient to *fire* a furnace during the winter.

fīre, *v.i.* 1. to take fire; to be kindled; to start burning.
2. to tend a fire.
3. to become excited or aroused.
4. to discharge artillery or firearms; as, we *fired* on the enemy at daybreak.
5. to discharge a projectile; as, the gun *fired*.
6. to react in a specified way to firing in a kiln; as, this glaze will *fire* a bright blue.
to fire away; to begin; to start; especially, to start to talk or ask questions. [Colloq.]
to fire up; (a) to start a fire in a furnace, stove, etc.; (b) to become irritated or angry.

fīre ȧ·lärm', 1. a signal to announce the outbreak of a fire.
2. a bell, siren, whistle, etc. to give this signal.

fīre′ärm, *n.* any weapon which expels the charge by the combustion of powder or other explosive; especially, such a weapon small enough to be carried, as a pistol, rifle, etc.

fīre ar′rōw, a dart furnished with some inflammable substance, formerly used in warfare to start fires within an enemy's lines.

fīre′back, *n.* 1. an Asiatic pheasant of the genus *Lophura*, having the plumage of its back of a fiery red color.
2. the back wall of a fireplace or furnace.

fīre′ball, *n.* 1. something resembling a ball of fire, as a kind of lightning.
2. a large, bright meteor.
3. a ball containing material to cause an explosion or a fire: formerly used as a weapon thrown in battle.
4. a vigorous, energetic person. [Colloq.]

fīre bal·loon′, 1. a balloon sent up with fireworks, which are timed to ignite at a certain height.
2. a balloon raised by means of rarefied air, heated by a fire beneath it.

fīre bär, a bar in a grate or furnace, on which the burning coals lie.

fīre′bāse, *n.* a military base in a combat zone from which artillery, rockets, etc. are fired.

fīre bee′tle, 1. a South American beetle, *Pyrophorus noctilucus*, which emits a brilliant phosphorescence from two fenestrae on the thorax: called also *cucujo*.
2. a firefly.

fīre′bīrd, *n.* the Baltimore oriole, *Icterus galbula*; also, the scarlet tanager.

fīre blȧst, a disease of plants and trees, in which they appear as if burnt by fire.

fīre blīght (blīt), a disease of apples, pears, and related fruits which makes them look burnt.

fīre′bōard, *n.* a board used to close a fireplace when not in use.

fīre bōat, a boat equipped with fire-fighting equipment, used along water fronts.

fīre′bomb, *n.* a bomb or missile intended to start a fire; incendiary bomb.

fīre′bomb, *v.t.* to attack, damage, or destroy with a firebomb.

fīre′bōte, *n.* an allowance of fuel to which a tenant of land is entitled. [Obs.]

fīre′box, *n.* 1. the place for the fire in a locomotive engine, stove, etc.
2. a tinderbox. [Obs.]

fīre′brand, *n.* 1. a piece of wood kindled or on fire; a piece of any burning substance.
2. one who inflames factions or causes contention and mischief.

fīre′break, *n.* a strip of land cleared to stop the spread of fire, as in a forest or prairie.

fīre′brick, *n.* a brick made to withstand great heat, used to line fireplaces, furnaces, etc.

fīre bri·gāde′, a body of men organized to fight fires in any particular village, city, or district.

fīre′bug, *n.* a person who deliberately sets fire to buildings, etc.; a pyromaniac; an incendiary. [Colloq.]

fīre clāy, a kind of clay that will resist intense heat, used in making firebricks, furnace linings, etc.

fīre cŏm′pȧ·ny, 1. a company of men equipped with fire-fighting apparatus and organized to extinguish fires.
2. a company which insures property against loss by fire. [Brit.]

fīre′crack″ẽr, *n.* a firework consisting of a paper cylinder enclosing powder, through which a fuse is passed, and exploding with a sharp report upon being ignited: used at celebrations, etc.

fīre′crest, *n.* a small European bird, *Regulus ignicapillus*, having a bright red crest: called also the *fire-crested wren* or *kinglet*.

fīre cross, same as *fiery cross* under *fiery*.

fīre′-cūre, *v.t.* to cure and season (tobacco) over wood fires.

fīre′damp, *n.* a gas, largely methane, formed in coal mines, which is explosive when mixed with a certain proportion of air.

fīre dē·pärt′ment, a municipal department whose work is fighting fires and preventing their occurrence.

fīre′dog, *n.* an andiron; an iron upright for supporting wood in a fireplace.

fīre dōor, a door of metal or other fire-resistant material designed to keep a fire from spreading.

fīre′drāke, *n.* [ME. *firedrake*; AS. *fyrdraca*; *fyr*, fire, and *draca*, a drake, dragon.]
1. in Germanic mythology, a fire-breathing dragon.
2. a meteor; an ignis fatuus; hence, a kind of firework which shoots into the sky. [Obs.]
3. one who toils in the glow of a furnace or fire. [Obs.]

fīre drill, 1. among firemen, practice to improve speed and efficiency in fighting fires, assembling apparatus and equipment, and other techniques necessary in their work.
2. a drill of the occupants of a building, with the object of teaching them the best means of escape in case of fire.
3. a device in use among primitive peoples for producing fire by friction.

fīre′-ēat·ẽr, *n.* 1. one who pretends to eat fire.
2. a hot-tempered, excitable person always ready to quarrel or fight.

fīre en′gīne, 1. a machine for spraying water, chemicals, etc. to extinguish fires: it is often part of a specially designed motor truck.
2. loosely, any motor truck for carrying firemen and equipment to a fire.

fīre es·cāpe′, any device, as a ladder, chute, outside stairway, etc., for escape from a burning building.

fīre ex·tiñ′guish·ẽr (-gwish-), a portable apparatus for use in extinguishing a fire by spraying chemicals on it.

fīre′-fañged, *a.* dried up as by fire: specifically applied to manure which has assumed a baked appearance from the heat evolved during decomposition.

fīre′fīght·ẽr, *n.* a person who helps fight fires; especially, a fireman (sense 1).

fīre′flaught (-flạt), *n.* 1. a flash of lightning, especially when unaccompanied by thunder; heat lightning; a gleam. [Scot.]
2. the aurora borealis. [Dial.]

fīre′flȳ, *n.*; *pl.* **fīre′flīeṣ,** any of several winged beetles whose abdomen glows with a phosphorescent light: the larvae and wingless females are called *glowworms*. With one exception, the fireflies are all coleopterous, and are members of either of two families, the *Elateridæ* and *Lampyridæ*.

FIREFLY (1/2 in. long)

fīre gild′ing, a process of gilding with an amalgam of gold and quicksilver, the latter substance afterward being volatilized by heat, leaving a film of gilt.

fīre′guärd, *n.* a metal screen placed in front of a fireplace.

fīre′hook, *n.* a large iron hook for pulling down burning structures, so as to prevent fire from spreading.

fīre′house, *n.* a fire station.

fīre in·sūr′ănce (-shūr′), insurance whereby an owner of property is insured against loss or damage by fire.

fīre ī′ronṣ (-ūrnz), the irons belonging to a fireplace, as the shovel, tongs, poker, etc.

fīre′less, *a.* without fire.

fīre′less çook′ẽr, an insulated container which when heated stays hot and finishes cooking food placed in it, or keeps the food warm.

fīre′līght, *n.* the light from a fire, especially an open fire.

fīre′lock, *n.* 1. an early type of gunlock in which the priming was ignited by sparks; a wheel lock or flintlock.
2. an early type of musket with such a lock.

fīre māin, a pipe for water to be used in putting out fires.

fīre′măn, *n.*; *pl.* **fīre′men,** 1. a man whose work is to extinguish fires; a member of a fire department.
2. a man who tends the fires of a steam engine, either locomotive, marine, or stationary.
3. one whose special duty it is to examine a coal mine before the workmen enter, to ascertain if fire damp is present.

fīre′-new, *a.* fresh from the forge; brand-new. [Archaic.]

fīre ō′păl, a variety of opal which reflects red and yellow lights.

fīre pan, 1. a pan for holding or carrying fire.
2. in a flintlock, the receptacle for the priming powder.

fīre′plāce, *n.* a place for a fire, especially an open place built in a wall, at the base of a chimney.

fīre′plug, *n.* a street hydrant to which a hose can be attached for fighting fires.

fīre pot, 1. formerly, a pot filled with a burning substance, thrown against an enemy.
2. that part of a stove or furnace which contains the fire.
3. a portable soldering furnace.
4. a crucible.

fīre′pow″ẽr, *n.* in military usage, (a) the effectiveness of a weapon in terms of the accuracy and volume of its fire; (b) the capacity of a given unit to deliver fire.

fīre′proof′, *a.* virtually impossible to set fire to or destroy by fire; very hard to burn.

fīre′proof″, *v.t.* to make fireproof.

fīre′proof″ing, *n.* incombustible material employed to make a structure or substance fireproof; also, the process of making a thing fireproof.

fīr′ẽr, *n.* one who sets fire to anything; an incendiary.

fīre rȧft, a raft loaded with combustibles, used for setting fire to an enemy's ships by being floated among them when on fire.

fīre rōll, a signal, as the beating of a drum or ringing of a bell, to give warning on shipboard of the outbreak of a fire. [Obs.]

fīre′room, *n.* same as *stokehold*.

fīre sāle, a sale at lowered prices of goods damaged in a fire.

fīre screen, a screen to be set in front of a fire to protect against heat or to stop sparks.

fīre set, a set of fire irons with a holder.

fīre set′ting, a process formerly employed by miners for making an opening into a lode. After being heated, the rock was suddenly cooled by water, which caused it to crack open.

fīre ship, a ship filled with materials that will explode and burn when set afire: it is floated among an enemy's ships to destroy them.

fīre′sīde, *n.* a place near the fire or hearth; hence, home; domestic life or family life.

fīre′sīde, *a.* of or at the fireside or domestic circle; intimate; as, *fireside* friends, *fireside* studies.

fīre stā′tion, place where fire engines are kept; engine house.

fīre′stōne, *n.* 1. formerly, flint or iron pyrites used for striking fire.
2. a kind of sandstone which withstands a high degree of heat; a stone which resists the action of fire: used especially of a variety of sandstone in England.

fīre′storm, *n.* an intense fire over a large area, as one initiated by an atomic explosion, that is sustained and spread by the inrushing winds created by the strong draft of rising hot air.

fīre′tāil, *n.* 1. the redstart: also called *fireflirt* and *redtail*.
2. the ruby tail, *Chrysis viridula*; the cuckoo fly.

fīre tow′ẽr, a tower, usually in a forest, where a lookout is posted to watch for fires and give the alarm.

fīre′trap, *n.* a building unsafe in case of fire because it will burn easily or because it lacks adequate exits or fire escapes.

fīre tree, 1. a New Zealand tree, *Metrosideros tomentosa*, which bears red flowers during the winter months.
2. a tree native to Australia, *Nuytsia floribunda*: more commonly called *flame tree*.
3. the Queensland tulip tree.

fīre wall, a fireproof wall to prevent the spread of fire from one room or compartment to the next.

fīre′wārd″en, fīre′wārd, *n.* an official assigned to prevent or fight fire, as in forests, public buildings, etc.

fīre′wa″tẽr, *n.* [Am. Ind. term for whisky, rum, etc.] alcoholic liquor: now humorous.

fīre′weed, *n.* any of various weeds, as the Jimson weed or a coarse, strong-smelling annual plant, *Erechthites hieracifolia*: they grow abundantly on land that has been burned over.

fīre′wood, *n.* wood for fuel.

fīre′wŏrks, *n. pl.* 1. devices, as firecrackers, rockets, sparklers, etc., which are exploded or burned for celebrations or as signals to produce loud noises or brilliant lighting effects.
2. a display of or as of fireworks; a pyrotechnic display.

fīre′wŏrm, *n.* 1. a glowworm.
2. a cranberry vine worm, the larva of the cranberry leaf roller.

fīre wŏr′ship, the worship of fire; particularly, worship of the sun as the most glorious visible object in the universe and also the source of light and heat.

fīre wŏr′ship·ẽr, one who worships fire or the sun.

fīr′ing, *n.* 1. the act of discharging firearms, etc.
2. the application of fire or of a cautery.
3. fuel; firewood or coal.
4. the process of burning or vitrifying bricks, pottery, china, etc., by applying intense heat, as in a kiln.
5. the act of applying fire or of kindling a fire; particularly, the method employed in treating or caring for a fire, the addition of fuel, regulation of dampers, etc.

fīr′ing ī′ron (-ũrn), an instrument used by veterinaries in cauterizing.

fīr′ing līne, 1. the line from which gunfire is, or is intended to be, directed against the enemy.
2. the troops stationed along this line.
3. the front position in any kind of activity.

fīr′ing or′dẽr, the order in which explosions occur in the cylinders of an internal-combustion engine.

fīr′ing pär′ty, same as *firing squad.*

fīr′ing pin, that part in the bolt or breech of a firearm which strikes the primer and explodes the charge.

fīr′ing squäd, a group of soldiers detailed to shoot to death someone so sentenced by a military court, or to fire a volley of shots over the grave at a military funeral.

fĩrk, *v.t.* to beat; to whip; to chastise. [Obs.]

fĩrk, *v.i.* [ME. *ferken, firken,* to take off, carry off; AS. *fercian,* to bring or take away.] to spring; to go off or fly out suddenly. [Obs.]

fĩrk, *n.* a freak; a trick; a whim. [Obs.]

fĩr′kin, *n.* [D. *vier,* four, and *-ken,* -kin.]
1. a measure of capacity equal to the fourth part of a barrel. As the barrels used for various commodities have varied in size, so the firkins have varied: the ale and beer firkin contains nine imperial gallons.
2. a small wooden vessel or cask of indeterminate size, used for butter, soap, etc.

fĩr′lot, *n.* a dry measure formerly used in Scotland. [Scot.]

fĩrm, *a.*; *comp.* firmer; *superl.* firmest, [ME. *ferme;* OFr. *ferm,* from L. *firmus,* steadfast, strong.]
1. closely compressed; compact; hard; solid; as, *firm* flesh; *firm* muscles; a cloth of *firm* texture.
2. fixed; steady; stable; unshaken; not easily moved; as, a *firm* structure.
3. continued steadily; remaining the same; as, a *firm* pressure.
4. unchanging; resolute; constant; as, a *firm* faith.
5. showing determination; positive; as, a *firm* command.
6. in commerce, not rising or falling considerably; steady: said of prices, etc.
to stand firm; to be steadfast in conviction; to remain unchanged by attack, persuasion, etc.
Syn.—strong, robust, close-knit, stanch, steadfast, unyielding, tenacious, unfaltering, resolute, rugged, sturdy, steady.

fĩrm, *v.t.* and *v.i.* 1. to make or become firm.
2. to establish; to confirm. [Archaic.]
And Jove has *firmed* it with an awful nod.
—Dryden.

fĩrm, *n.* [LL. *firma,* a signature, subscription by which a writing was confirmed or rendered valid.] a partnership or association of two or more persons for carrying on a business: distinguished from *corporation:* in the United States and England, a firm is not legally recognized as a person apart from the members forming it.

fĩr′mȧ·ment, *n.* [OFr. *firmament;* L. *firmamentum,* a strengthening, support (LL., the firmament), from *firmare,* to strengthen, from *firmus,* strong, steadfast.]
1. the region of the air; the sky or heavens, viewed poetically as a solid arch or vault.
And God said, Let there be lights in the *firmament.* —Gen. i. 14.
2. established foundation; basis. [Obs.]
Custom is the sanction or the *firmament* of the law. —Jer. Taylor.
3. formerly, in astronomy, the orb of the fixed stars.

fĩr·mȧ·men′tăl, *a.* pertaining to the firmament; celestial; being of the upper regions.

fĩr′măn, *n.*; *pl.* **fĩr′măns,** [Per. *farman,* a mandate, order.] a decree, order, or grant of an Oriental sovereign, as formerly of Turkey, issued for various special purposes, as to insure a traveler protection and assistance; a passport, permit, license, or grant of privileges: written also *firmaun.*

fĩrm′ẽr, *a.* [Fr. *fermoir,* altered, from *formoir,* from *former,* to form.] designating a chisel with a thin blade fixed in a handle.

fĩrm′ẽr, *n.* a firmer chisel.

fĩrm′i·tūde, *n.* [L. *firmitudo,* from *firmus,* steadfast, strong.] strength; solidity. [Obs.]

fĩrm′i·ty, *n.* [L. *firmitas,* from *firmus,* steadfast, strong.] strength; firmness. [Obs.]

fĩrm′less, *a.* shifting; unstable. [Obs.]
Does passion still the *firmless* mind control?
—Pope.

fĩrm′ly, *adv.* 1. solidly; compactly; closely; as, particles of matter *firmly* cohering.
2. steadily; with constancy or fixedness; immovably; steadfastly; as, his resolution is *firmly* fixed.

fĩrm′ness, *n.* 1. closeness or denseness of texture or structure; compactness; hardness; solidity; as, the *firmness* of wood, stone, or cloth.
2. stability; strength; as, the *firmness* of a union or of a federation.
3. steadfastness; constancy; fixedness; as, the *firmness* of a purpose or resolution; the *firmness* of a man or of his courage; *firmness* of mind or soul.
4. certainty; soundness; as, the *firmness* of notions or opinions.
Syn.—constancy, faithfulness, fidelity.
Firmness belongs to the will, and *constancy,* to the affections and principles; the former prevents us from yielding and the latter from fluctuating.

fĩrn, *n.* [G. dial. *firn, firne,* lit., last year's snow.] the coarsely granular snow which will become ice as it moves downward in a glacier, below the line of perpetual snow.
The imperfectly consolidated substance, partly snow and partly ice, is known in Switzerland as névé or *firn.* —Huxley.

fĩr′ring, *n.pl.* in carpentry, same as *furring.*

fĩr′ry, *a.* of or pertaining to firs; formed of fir; abounding in firs.
And oft I heard the tender dove
In *firry* woodlands making moan.
—Tennyson.

fĩrst, *a.* [ME. *first, fyrst, furst;* AS. *fyrst,* from *fore,* before, and superl. *-st, -est.*]
1. advanced before or further than any other in progression; foremost in place; preceding all others in numbers or a progressive series; 1st: used as the ordinal of *one;* as, 1 is the *first* number.
2. preceding all others in the order of time; earliest; as, Adam was the *first* man; George Washington was the *first* president.
3. preceding all others in rank, dignity, or excellence; principal; as, Demosthenes was the *first* orator of Greece.
4. in music, of highest pitch; playing or singing the upper part or the part highest in pitch.
first thing; as the first thing; before anything else.
in the first place; firstly; to begin with.
Syn.—aboriginal, earliest, highest, original, primary, primitive, pristine, primordial.

fĩrst, *adv.* 1. before anything else in the order of time.
Adam was *first* formed, then Eve.
—1. Tim. ii. 13.
2. before all others in place or progression; as, let the officers enter the gate *first.*
3. before anything else in order of proceeding or consideration; as, *first,* let us attend to the examination of the witnesses.
4. before all others in rank; as, he stands or ranks *first* in public estimation.
5. for the first time; as, she *first* saw him at a party.
6. sooner; preferably.
first and last; altogether; throughout; entirely.
first or last; at one time or another; at the beginning or end.

fĩrst, *n.* 1. that which precedes all else; the beginning.
I am Alpha and Omega, the beginning and the end, the *first* and the last.
—Rev. xxii. 13.
2. the one before the second.
3. any person, thing, class, place, etc. that is first.
4. the first day of the month.
5. the first year of a reign, era, etc.
6. [*pl.*] the best quality of merchandise; as, these stockings are *firsts.*
7. the winning place, as in racing.
8. [*usually* F—] in British universities, (a) the highest rank in examinations for honors; (b) a holder of this rank.
9. in music, the highest or leading voice or instrument in an ensemble.

fĩrst′-āid′, *a.* of or used for first aid.

fĩrst āid, emergency treatment given in a case of injury or sudden illness, before regular medical treatment can be obtained.

fĩrst bāse, in baseball, the first position on the diamond, to the right of home plate, which a batter who has hit fairly must reach ahead of the ball.
to get to first base; to accomplish the first step of an undertaking. [Slang.]

fĩrst′-bọrn′, *a.* born first in a family; oldest.

fĩrst′-bọrn′, *n.* the first-born child; the first in the order of birth.

fĩrst çauṣe, 1. a primary or original cause of anything; source.
2. in theology, God as the prime mover.

fĩrst′-çlȧss′, *a.* 1. of the highest class, rank, excellence, etc.; of the best quality.
2. designating or of the best accommodations; as, a *first-class* cabin on a ship.
3. designating or of a class of mail consisting of sealed matter in writing, as letters, and all other matter sealed against ready inspection: such mail carries the highest regular postage rates.

fĩrst′-çlȧss′, *adv.* 1. with the best accommodations; as, we traveled to Europe *first-class.*
2. as or by first-class mail.

fĩrst dāy, Sunday: term used by the Society of Friends (Quakers).

fĩrst es·tāte′, see *estate* (clergy).

fĩrst fiṅ′gẽr, the finger next to the thumb; the index finger.

fĩrst flōor, 1. the ground floor of a building.
2. in Europe and Great Britain, the floor above the ground floor: also sometimes so designated in hotels, etc. in the United States.

fĩrst frūits, 1. the fruit or produce first matured and collected in any season.
2. the first products, results, or profits of any activity; specifically, (a) in old feudal tenures, one year's profit of the land after the death of a tenant, which was paid to the king; (b) in the Church of England, the income of every spiritual benefice for the first year, paid originally to the crown, but now to a board, which applies the money so obtained to the supplementing of the incomes of small benefices.

fĩrst′hand′, *a.* and *adv.* direct; from the first source, as the producer, maker, etc., and without the intervention of agents or intermediaries.

Fĩrst In·tẽr·na′tion·ăl, a working men's association founded in London in 1864 by Karl Marx and Friedrich Engels to spread their philosophy of socialism.

fĩrst lā′dy, the wife of the president of the United States.

fĩrst lieū·ten′ănt, an officer ranking above a second lieutenant and below a captain, as in the United States Army or Marine Corps.

fĩrst′ling, *a.* first produced; as, *firstling* males.

fĩrst′ling, *n.* 1. the first produce or offspring: applied to beasts; as, the *firstlings* of cattle.
2. the thing first thought or done.
The very *firstlings* of my heart shall be
The *firstlings* of my hand. —Shak.

fĩrst′ly, *adv.* first; in the first place; before anything else: used chiefly in enumerating topics.

fĩrst māte, a ship's officer next in rank below the captain.

fĩrst mọrt′gȧġe (mọr′gij), a mortgage having priority over all others as a lien on property.

fĩrst nāme, the Christian or given name.

fĩrst nīght, the opening night of a play, opera, etc.

fĩrst-nīght′ẽr, *n.* a person who regularly attends the opening performances of plays, operas, etc.

fĩrst of·fend′ẽr, a person who has committed a legal offense for the first time.

fĩrst of′fi·cẽr, in nautical usage, a first mate.

fĩrst pā′pẽrṣ, the documents by which an alien makes preliminary application for United States citizenship.

fĩrst pẽr′sọn, that form of a pronoun or verb which refers to the speaker or speakers: in *I* (or *we*) *do, I* (or *we*) and *do* are in the first person.

fĩrst quạr′tẽr, 1. the time of month between new moon and first half-moon.
2. the shape of the moon at this time.

fĩrst′-rāte′, *a.* 1. of the highest class, rank, etc.; of the best quality; as, a *first-rate* scholar or painter.
2. very good; excellent. [Colloq.]

fĩrst′-rāte′, *n.* anything classified as of the

highest rank or excellence; the most powerful of its class; as, this battleship is a *first-rate*.

fĩrst′-rāte′, *adv.* very well. [Colloq.]

Fĩrst Rē·pub′liç, the republic established in France in 1792 after the Revolution, and lasting until the establishment of an Empire by Napoleon in 1804.

fĩrst ser′ġeănt (sär′), in military usage, the highest ranking noncommissioned officer of a company, battery, etc., serving as administrative assistant to the unit commander: eliminated (1948) in the United States Army as a title of rank, but retained as an occupational designation: see *master sergeant*.

fĩrst wătch, in nautical usage, the watch from eight to twelve (midnight); also, the men who keep that watch.

fĩrst wạ′tẽr, the best quality and purest luster: said of diamonds, pearls, etc., but also used figuratively.

fĩrth, *n.* [var. of *frith*.] a narrow inlet or arm of the sea; an estuary.

fĩr tree, same as *fir*.

fisç, *n.* [Fr. *fisc*, from L. *fiscus*, a basket of rushes, money bag, public chest.] the treasury of a prince or state; exchequer. [Rare.]

fis′căl, *a.* [Fr. *fiscal*; LL. *fiscalis*, from L. *fiscus*, a basket of rushes, the state treasury.] 1. pertaining to the public treasury or revenues.

2. financial.

fis′căl, *n.* 1. revenue; the income of a prince or state. [Obs.]

2. a treasurer. [Obs.]

3. in some European countries, a legal official corresponding to public prosecutor: in Scotland, called a *procurator fiscal*.

fis′căl yēar, the twelve-month period between settlements of financial accounts: in the United States the government fiscal year legally ends June 30.

fīse dog, fīce dog, a small dog; a pet.

fis′e·tin, *n.* a yellow crystalline dyestuff obtained from the wood of *Rhus cotinus* or young fustic.

fish, *n.* [Fr. *fiche*, a stake, pin, peg, from *ficher*, to fix; OFr. *fichier*; from L. *figere*, to fasten.] a piece of wood, etc. fastened to another or to a joint to strengthen it.

fish, *v.t.* to strengthen or join by using a fish (a piece of wood, etc.).

fish, *n.*; *pl.* **fish;** in referring to different species, **fish′eṣ,** [ME. *fisch*, *fissh*, *fisc*; AS. *fisc*, fish.]

1. any of a division of vertebrate animals, living in water, breathing by means of permanent gills, and having fins. They have a heart with two cavities, cold blood, a skin usually covered by scales, and an osseous or cartilaginous skeleton.

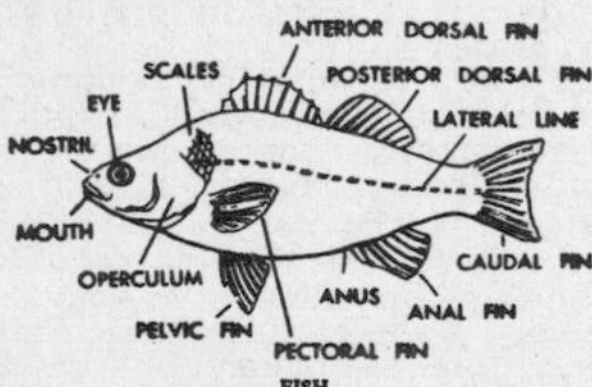

FISH

2. loosely, any of numerous animals whose life is spent entirely or partially in the water, distinguished from a land animal, as certain cetaceans, crustaceans, mollusks, echinoderms, or batrachians.

3. the flesh of fish, used as food.

4. a person thought of as like a fish in being easily lured by bait, lacking intelligence or emotion, etc.; as, the poor *fish* was taken in easily; he's a cold *fish*. [Colloq.]

5. [F–] in astronomy, either of the two groups of stars supposedly outlining a fish and forming the constellation Pisces.

6. in nautical usage, a purchase used to raise the flukes of an anchor up to the gunwale; a fish tackle.

age of fishes; in geology, the Devonian Period.

like a fish out of water; out of one's element; in unfamiliar surroundings; not adapted.

neither fish, flesh, nor fowl (or *nor good red herring*); not anything definite or recognizable.

to drink like a fish; to drink heavily.

to have other fish to fry; to have other affairs engaging one; to have other or more important matters to engross one's attention.

fish, *v.i.*; fished (fisht), *pt.*, *pp.*; fishing, *ppr.* [ME. *fischen*, *fisshen*, *fissen*; AS. *fiscian*, to fish.]

1. to catch or attempt to catch fish; to be employed in taking fish, by any means, as by angling or drawing nets.

2. to attempt or seek to obtain by artifice, or indirectly to seek to draw forth; as, to *fish* for compliments.

to fish in troubled waters; to try to gain something by taking advantage of a confused or troubled situation.

fish, *v.t.* 1. to search by raking or sweeping; to drag.

2. to catch or try to catch fish in; as, we *fished* the stream.

3. to get by fishing.

4. to grope for, find, and bring to view: often with *out* or *up*; as, he *fished* a coin *out* of his pocket.

5. to raise (the anchor) with a fish (n. 6).

to fish for; to search for or try to get, especially by cunning or indirect means.

to fish out; to deplete the stock of fish in (a lake, etc.).

fish, *n.* a counter, used in various games.

fish′ȧ·ble, *a.* containing fish; being suitable for fishing.

fish and chips, small fillets of fish and strips of potato French fried and eaten hot. [Chiefly Brit.]

fish bạll, a fried patty of minced fish, often mixed with mashed potato: also called *fish cake*.

fish bēam, a beam which swells out, usually downward.

fish′-bel″lied, *a.* shaped like a fish's body; swelling out convexly on the under side; as, a *fish-bellied* rail.

fish′ber″ry, *n.* the poisonous berry of *Anamirta paniculata* (*Cocculus indicus*), used to stupefy fish and to permit their capture.

fish′bōlt, *n.* a bolt used to fasten fishplates to rails.

fish′bōne tree, a small tree of New Zealand, *Panax crassifolium*, of the ginseng family, having deeply incised leaves.

fish′bōwl, *n.* a glass bowl in which goldfish, snails, etc. are kept; a small aquarium: also *fish bowl*.

fish çärv′ẽr, an instrument with a broad blade, in shape somewhat resembling a trowel, used to carve and serve fish: called also *fish slice* and *fish trowel*.

fish çrōw, a small, fish-eating crow, *Corvus ossifragus*, found along the eastern coast of the United States.

fish çul′tūre, the hatching and rearing of fish as an industry; pisciculture.

fish dav′it, a spar or iron davit with a block and tackle at the end, formerly used in fishing the anchor.

fish dāy, a day when it is forbidden to eat flesh; a fast day.

fish duck, any merganser.

fish′ẽr, *n.* 1. one who is employed in catching fish; a fisherman.

2. a boat used in fishing.

3. *pl.* **fish′ẽrs, fish′ẽr,** an animal that catches and eats fish; especially, a fish-eating animal of the marten family; the pekan, *Mustela pennanti*. It is found in northern United States and Canada.

fish′ẽr·măn, *n.*; *pl.* **fish′ẽr·men,** 1. a person who fishes for sport or for a living.

2. a ship used in fishing.

fish′ẽr·măn′ṣ bend, a kind of knot: see *knot*, illus.

fish′ẽr·y, *n.*; *pl.* **fish′ẽr·ieṣ,** 1. the business of catching, packing, or selling fish or other products of lakes, rivers, or the sea.

2. a place where fish, etc. are caught; fishing ground.

3. a legal right to catch fish in certain waters or at certain times.

4. a place where fish are bred.

common fishery; the right of taking fish from public waters.

fish′fạll, *n.* the tackle suspended to the fish davit.

fish flour, the flesh of fish, dried and powdered, often used in cookery.

fish′fụl, *a.* abounding with fish; as, a *fishful* pond.

fish fuñ′gus, 1. a red fungus, *Clathrocystis roseopersicina*, seen on salted codfish in warm weather.

2. a fungus, *Saprolegnia ferax*, which causes salmon disease.

fish′gärth, *n.* a garth or weir for the taking and retaining of fish; a fish weir.

fish′gig, *n.* an instrument used for catching fish at sea, consisting of a staff with barbed prongs: spelled also *fizgig* and *fisgig*.

fish glūe, isinglass, a substance prepared from the walls of the air bladders of certain fish.

fish hawk, the *Pandion haliaetus*, the osprey, bald buzzard, or fishing eagle. It feeds principally upon fish which it seizes from the water in its talons.

fish′hook, *n.* 1. a hook, usually barbed, for catching fish.

2. the hook on the end of a fishfall.

fish′i·fȳ, *v.t.*; fishified, *pt.*, *pp.*; fishifying, *ppr.* to change to fish. [Rare.]

fish′i·ly, *adv.* in a fishy manner.

fish′i·ness, *n.* the state or quality of being fishy.

fish′ing, *a.* used or employed in fishery, or by fishermen; as, a *fishing* boat; *fishing* tackle; a *fishing* village.

fish′ing, *n.* 1. the catching of fish for sport or for a living.

2. a place to fish.

fish′ing bañks (or **grounds**), a place where fish are abundant, as off Newfoundland.

fish′ing duck, a fish duck, or merganser.

fish′ing ēa′gle, the osprey.

fish′ing līne, a line used in fishing; a fish line.

fish′ing net, same as *fish net*.

fish′ing rod, a slender pole with an attached line, hook, and, sometimes, a reel, used in fishing.

fish′ing smack, a sloop or similar vessel, manned by fishermen, and employed in sea fishing, especially for cod along the New England coast and northward.

fish′ing taç′kle, the equipment, as hooks, lines, rods, reels, etc., used in fishing.

fish′ing tūbe, a glass tube by means of which small particles are lifted from water.

fish joint, a splice consisting of one or more oblong plates, pieces of steel or wood, bolted to one or both sides of two rails or timbers meeting end to end.

fish ket′tle, a kettle of sufficient length to receive a whole fish.

fish lad′dẽr, a series of steps in the rocks which help fish, especially salmon, to go up a waterfall.

fish′līke, *a.* resembling fish; suggestive or characteristic of fish; fishy.

fish līne, a line, usually with a hook at one end, used in fishing.

fish louse, any of various crustaceans parasitic on fishes.

fish mạw, the air bladder, or sound, of a fish.

fish mēal, dried fish, ground and used as fertilizer or fodder.

fish′mōñ″gẽr, *n.* a dealer in fish.

fish net, a device, consisting in whole or in part of netting, used in the capture of fish.

fish oil, the oil yielded by the bodies of various marine fishes, as the cod, seal, whale, shark, crocodile, grampus, etc.

fish owl, a fish-eating owl, belonging to the genus *Ketupa* or *Scotopelia*. It has rough feet like the fish hawk, which it also resembles in its manner of capturing fish.

fish pēarl, an artificial pearl coated with a preparation made from fish scales.

fish′plāte, *n.* [prob. from Fr. *fiche*, means of fixing, confused with *fish*.] either of a pair of iron or steel plates bolting two rails together lengthwise, as on a railroad.

fish poi′ṣŏn, any of various berries and leaves which cause sickness, stupor, or even death in fish.

fish pōle, same as *fishing rod*.

fish′pond, *n.* a pond where fish are kept or bred.

fish pot, a wicker cage or creel for catching lobsters, crabs, shrimps, etc.

fish′pound, *n.* a submerged net for catching fish; a weir. [Dial.]

fish sauce, a sauce served with fish as an appetizing relish.

fish′skin, *n.* the skin of a fish, especially of sharks, rays, etc., used in the arts under the name *shagreen*.

fish′skin dis·ēase′, same as *ichthyosis*.

fish slīce, same as *fish carver*.

fish slīde, a fish trap set across a current or below a small waterfall to catch fish in the descent: used principally in the southern United States.

fish sound, the air bladder, or air sac, of a fish.

fish stō′ry, an extravagant, highly colored, or exaggerated story; a yarn: so called in reference to the propensity attributed to fishermen to exaggerate the size and weight of their catch. [Colloq.]

fish taç′kle, hook and tackle used for raising the flukes of an anchor to the gunwale of a ship. To this tackle or fall is attached a large iron hook, called the *fishhook*.

fish'tāil, *a.* shaped like a fish's tail, or resembling it in motion.

fishtail burner; a burner from which the blaze issues in the shape of a caudal fin or fishtail.

fish'tāil, *v.i.* to retard the speed of an airplane by swinging the tail from side to side in approaching the ground for a landing. [Colloq.]

fish trow'el, same as *fish carver*.

fish wąrd'en, an officer in charge of fisheries and the enforcement of the fishing laws in his district.

fish'wāy, *n.* an arrangement by which fish may ascend a waterfall or dam: also called *fish ladder*.

fish'wēir, *n.* same as *fishgarth*.

fish'wīfe, *n.*; *pl.* **fish'wīveṣ,** 1. a woman who sells fish.

2. a coarse, scolding woman.

fish'wood, *n.* the Jamaica dogwood tree, *Piscidia erythrina*.

fish'wŏrm, *n.* a worm used for bait in fishing.

fish'y, *a.*; *comp.* fishier; *superl.* fishiest, 1. of or full of fish.

2. inhabited by fish; as, the *fishy* flood.

3. having the qualities of fish; like fish; as, a *fishy* taste or smell.

4. improbable; overdrawn; extravagant; incredible. [Colloq.]

5. dull; without expression; lusterless; as, a *fishy* stare.

6. questionable; suspicious; equivocal; unsound; unreliable; slippery. [Colloq.]

fisk, *v.i.* [ME. *fisken*, to wander about, be in constant motion; Sw. *fjeska*, to fidget.] to run about. [Obs.]

fis'sāte, *a.* deeply cleft; nearly split; marked by depressions or fissures, as the antennae of some insects.

fis'si-, [from L. *fissus*, cleft.] a combining form used in anatomy and biology to signify *cleft*, as in *fissi*dactyl, *fissi*gemmation.

fis·si·daç'tyl, fis·si·daç'tyle, *a.* [*fissi-*, and L. *dactylus*, a finger.] having the digits divided from one another and free.

Fis'si·denṣ, *n.* [*fissi-*, and L. *dens*, *dentis*, a tooth.] a genus of mosses with stems simple, or nearly so, and distichous leaves.

fis''si·ġem·mā'tion, *n.* [*fissi-*, and L. *gemmatus*, pp. of *gemmare*, to put forth buds.] in biology, a method of generation partaking both of gemmation, or budding, and fission.

fis'sile, *a.* [L. *fissilis*, cleft, that may be cleft, from *fissus*, pp. of *findere*, to cleave, split.] that can be split, cleft, or divided in the direction of the grain or of natural joints.

This crystal is a pellucid *fissile* stone. —Newton.

fis·si·liñ'guăl (-gwăl), *a.* [*fissi-*, and L. *lingua*, tongue.] having a forked tongue, like a lizard.

Fis·si·liñ'gui·ȧ (-gwi-), *n.pl.* [*fissi-*, and L. *lingua*, tongue.] a group of the *Lacertilia* or lizards, having the tongue bifid and protrusile.

fis·sil'i·ty, *n.* [L. *fissilis*, that may be cleft, from *fissus*, pp. of *findere*, to cleave.] the quality of being fissile.

fis'sion (fish'un), *n.* [L. *fissio* (*-onis*), from *fissus*, pp. of *findere*, to cleave, split.]

1. a breaking up into parts; a splitting apart; cleavage.

2. in biology, a form of asexual reproduction, found in various simple plants and animals, in which the parent organism divides into two or more parts, each becoming an independent individual.

fis'sion·ȧ·ble, *a.* that can undergo fission; specifically, designating a substance, as uranium, whose nuclei can undergo fission.

fis'sion fuñ'gus, a bacterium; a schizomycete.

fis·si·pal'māte, *a.* [*fissi-*, and L. *palma*, a palm.] having the toes partially joined by a web; semipalmate.

fis·sip'ȧ·riṣm, *n.* reproduction by fission.

fis·si·par'i·ty, *n.* fissiparism.

fis·sip'ȧ·rous, *a.* [*fissi-*, and L. *parere*, to produce.] in biology, reproducing by fission.

fis·sip'ȧ·rous·ly, *adv.* by a fissiparous method; by fission or cell division.

fis·si·pā'tion, *n.* fissiparous reproduction.

fis'si·ped, *a.* [*fissi-*, and L. *pes*, *pedis*, a foot.]

1. having separate toes.

2. relating to the suborder *Fissipedia*.

fis'si·ped, *n.* an animal whose toes are separate or not connected by a membrane.

fis·sip'e·dăl, *a.* same as *fissiped*.

Fis·si·pē'di·ȧ, *n.pl.* [*fissi-*, and L. *pes*, *pedis*, a foot.] a suborder of *Carnivora*, including the dogs, cats, and bears, having fissiped feet adapted for walking.

Fis'si·pēṣ, *n.* [Mod. L., *fissi-*, and L. *pes*, referring to the split flower head.] in botany, a genus of orchids, the only known species being the moccasin flower.

fis·si·ros'trăl, *a.* [*fissi-*, and L. *rostrum*, a beak.]

1. belonging to the *Fissirostres*; characterized by a deeply cleft bill, as swallows, goatsuckers, etc.

2. broad and deeply cleft: said of the beak of certain birds.

Fis·si·ros'trēṣ, *n.pl.* [*fissi-*, and L. *rostrum*, a beak.] a former classification of passerine birds distinguished by having the beak broad and deeply cleft. It includes the swallows, goatsuckers, swifts, martins, etc.

fis'sūr·ăl (fish'ūr-) *a.* relating to a fissure.

fis·sū·rā'tion, *n.* the act of dividing; the state of being divided by fissures.

fis'sūre (fish'ūr), *n.* [L. *fissura*, a cleft, chink, from *findere*, to cleave, split.]

1. a cleft or crack; a narrow chasm made by the parting of any substance; a longitudinal opening; as, the *fissure* of a rock.

2. a dividing or breaking into parts.

3. in anatomy, a deep, narrow sulcus or groove between lobes or parts of an organ, as that dividing the anterior and middle lobes of the cerebrum on each side.

fissure of Rolando; a deep fissure separating the frontal lobe of the cerebrum from the parietal lobe.

fissure of Sylvius; a deep, narrow sulcus or depression dividing the anterior and middle lobes of the cerebrum on each side.

fis'sūre, *v.t.* and *v.i.*; fissured, *pt.*, *pp.*; fissuring, *ppr.* to break into parts; to crack or split apart.

Fis·sū·rel'lȧ, *n.* [dim. from L. *fissura*, a cleft, fissure.] a genus of gastropodous mollusks resembling the limpets in appearance and habits, but differing considerably in structure. The keyhole limpet belongs to this genus.

fis'sūre nee'dle, a spiral needle with which the lips of a wound are sewed together.

fis'sūre vein, a vein of ore deposited in a fissure; a true vein.

fist, *n.* [ME. *fist*, *fyst*, *fust*; AS. *fyst*, a fist.]

1. the hand with the fingers doubled into the palm; a clenched hand.

2. (a) a hand; (b) the grasp; (c) handwriting. [Colloq.]

3. in printing, a sign of a hand with index finger extended (☞), used to call attention to something.

hand over fist; see *hand over hand* under *hand*, n.

fist, *v.t.* 1. to strike with the fist.

2. in nautical usage, to grasp or handle.

fist'ful, *n.* a handful.

fist'iç, *a.* having to do with boxing; fought with the fists; pugilistic; as, *fistic* exploits; *fistic* heroes. [Colloq.]

fist'i·çuffs, *n.pl.* [from *fist*, and *cuff* (a blow).]

1. a fight with the fists; boxing match.

2. blows with the fists; punches.

3. the science of boxing.

fis'ti·nut, *n.* a pistachio nut. [Obs.]

fis·tū'çȧ, *n.* [L., a rammer, beetle.] a kind of pile driver formerly in use.

fis'tū·lȧ, *n.*; *pl.* **fis'tū·lae,** [L., a pipe, cane, ulcer.]

1. a pipe or tube.

2. an abnormal hollow passage from an abscess, cavity, or hollow organ to the skin or to another abscess, cavity, or organ.

3. a gold or silver tube through which the communicants of the early church received the holy wine: it is still used by the Pope.

fis'tū·lăr, *a.* same as *fistulous*.

Fis·tū·lār'i·ȧ, *n.* [L. *fistula*, a pipe, cane, ulcer.]

1. a genus of fishes, characterized by a tubelike snout, with the mouth at the extreme end.

FISTULARIA

2. [f—] a fish of this genus.

fis·tū·lā'ri·oid, *a.* relating to or characteristic of the genus *Fistularia*.

fis'tū·lāte, *v.i.* [L. *fistulatus*, pipe-shaped, furnished with a pipe, from *fistula*, a cane, pipe, ulcer.] to become hollow like a pipe or fistula. [Obs.]

fis'tū·lāte, *v.t.* to make hollow like a pipe. [Obs.]

fis'tūle, *n.* same as *fistula*.

fis'tū·li·fọrm, *a.* [L. *fistula*, a cane, pipe, ulcer, and *forma*, form.] being in round, hollow columns, as a mineral.

Stalactite often occurs *fistuliform*.—Phillips.

Fis·tū·lī'nȧ, *n.* [dim. from L. *fistula*, a cane, pipe, ulcer.] a genus of edible fungi, allied to *Boletus*, found on old oak, walnut, and chestnut trees.

fis'tū·lōse, *a.* same as *fistulous*.

fis'tū·lous, *a.* 1. having the form or nature of a fistula; as, a *fistulous* ulcer.

2. shaped like a pipe or tube.

3. consisting of tubular parts.

fit, *n.* [ME. *fit*, *fyt*, *fytt*; AS. *fit*, a struggle, fight.]

1. any sudden, uncontrollable attack; a paroxysm; as, a *fit* of coughing.

2. (a) a sharp, brief display of feeling; as, a *fit* of anger; (b) a transient mood; as, a *fit* of the blues.

3. a temporary burst of activity; as, he works by *fits*.

4. in medicine, a convulsion; a sudden paroxysm in which the victim loses consciousness.

by fits and starts; in an irregular way; in bursts of activity followed by periods of inactivity.

to have (or *throw*) *a fit*; to become very angry or upset. [Colloq.]

fit, *a.*; *comp.* fitter; *superl.* fittest, [ME. *fit*, *fitte*, *fytte*, meet, suitable.]

1. suitable, convenient; meet; becoming; adapted for a certain end or purpose.

2. proper; right; appropriate.

3. ready; prepared; trained; qualified; as, men of valor *fit* for war.

No man having put his hand to the plow, and looking back, is *fit* for the kingdom of God. —Luke ix. 62.

4. in good physical condition or excellent trim; healthy.

to see fit; to deem just, suitable, or proper.

Syn.—proper, appropriate, expedient, congruous, correspondent, apposite, apt, adapted, prepared, competent, adequate, seemly, befitting, conformable.

fit, *v.t.*; fitted, *pt.*, *pp.*; fitting, *ppr.* 1. to be suitable or adapted to; as, his actions *fit* his words.

2. to be the proper size, shape, etc. for; as, the coat *fits* him.

3. to make or alter so as to fit.

4. to make suitable or qualified.

5. to insert exactly; as, he *fitted* the key in the lock.

6. to equip; to outfit; to furnish with things proper or necessary; as, to *fit* a ship for a long voyage.

to fit out; to furnish; to equip; to supply with necessaries or means; as, *to fit out* a privateer.

to fit up; to prepare; to furnish with things suitable; to make proper for the reception or use of any person; as, *to fit up* a house for a guest.

fit, *v.i.* 1. to be proper or becoming.

2. to suit or be suitable; to be adapted; to be adjusted to the form or size required; as, his coat *fits* very well.

fit, *n.* 1. the condition of fitting or being fitted.

2. the manner of fitting; as, a tight *fit*.

3. anything that fits.

fit, *v.* dialectal past tense and past participle of *fight*.

fit, *n.* [AS. *fitt*, a song.] a short section of a poem, ballad, or song; a canto. [Archaic.]

fitch, *n.*; *pl.* **fitch'eṣ,** the vetch; also, its seed.

fitch, *n.* [D. *vitsche*, *fisse*, *visse*, a polecat.]

1. the fitchew.

2. a fitch brush.

3. the fur or pelt of the fitchew or European polecat.

fitch brush, a fine-pointed brush made from the hair of the fitch, or European polecat. A similar brush of hog's bristles is likewise called by this name.

fitch'é, fitch'ée (fich'ā), *a.* [Fr. *fiché*, pp. of *ficher*, to fix, drive in.] in heraldry, pointed; terminating in a point, as if sharpened; as, a *cross fitché*.

CROSS FITCHÉ

fitched (ficht), *a.* same as *fitché*.

fitch'ẽr, *v.i.*; fitchered, *pt.*, *pp.*; fitchering, *ppr.* in mining, to so operate a drill that it shall stick in the bore hole or become jammed, as in a wedge.

fitch′et, *n.* same as *fitchew.*

fitch′ew, *n.* [ME. *fitchew, fichew;* OFr. *fissiau, fissau;* D. *fisse, visse, vitsche.*]
1. the European polecat.
2. its fur.
Also *fitch, fitchet.*

fitch′y, *a.* same as *fitché.*

fit′fụl, *a.* irregular; spasmodic; capricious; not sustained but variable; as, a man of *fitful* temper; a *fitful* breeze.

fit′fụl·ly, *adv.* irregularly; uncertainly; intermittently; as, the moon shone *fitfully* through the clouds.

fit′fụl·ness, *n.* the state of being fitful; uncertainty; capriciousness.

fith′el, *n.* fiddle. [Obs.]

fit′ly, *adv.* 1. in a fit manner; properly.
2. at the right time.

fit′ment, *n.* something adapted to a purpose; equipment; outfit; the state or act of being fitted. [Obs.]

fit′ness, *n.* 1. suitableness; appropriateness; adaptation; as, the *fitness* of things to their use.

If *fitness* of parts was what constituted the loveliness of form, the actual employment of them would undoubtedly greatly augment it. —Burke.

2. propriety; justness; reasonableness; as, the *fitness* of measures or laws.
3. preparation; qualification; as, a student's *fitness* for college.
4. convenience; the state or quality of being fit.

fit′tȧ·ble, *a.* suitable; adaptable. [Rare.]

fit′ted·ness, *n.* the state of being fitted; fitness. [Rare.]

fit′tẽr, *n.* 1. a person who fits; specifically, (a) a person who alters or adjusts garments to fit; (b) a person who supplies, installs, or adjusts machinery, pipes, etc.
2. a coal broker who sells the coal produced by a particular mine. [Brit.]

fit′tẽr, *n.* a fragment; a flinder; a rag; a flitter. [Obs.]

fit′ting, *a.* suitable; fit; appropriate; becoming.

fit′ting, *n.* 1. an adjustment or trying on of clothes, etc. for fit.
2. something used in an adjustment; as, a pipe *fitting.*
3. [*pl.*] the fixtures, furnishings, or decorations of a house, office, automobile, etc.

fit′ting·ly, *adv.* suitably.

fit′ting·ness, *n.* the state or quality of being suitable or appropriate.

Fit·tō′ni·ȧ, *n.* [named after Sarah and Elizabeth *Fitton,* of England.] in botany, a genus of herbaceous plants of the acanthus family, native to Peru. They are cultivated for the beauty of their brightly colored foliage.

fit′weed, *n.* a plant of the genus *Eryngium,* so called because considered a remedy for hysteria.

fitz- (fits), [OFr. *fiz, filz, fils,* a son.] a prefix meaning *son of,* as in *Fitz*james: formerly used in surnames: more especially applied to the illegitimate offspring of a king, royal prince, or great noble.

five, *a.* [ME. *five, fif;* AS. *fif,* five; L.G. *fif;* O.H.G. *finf;* Sw. *fem;* W. *pump;* L. *quinque;* Gr. *pente;* Lith. *penki;* Sans. *pancha,* five.] four and one added; totaling one more than four.

five, *n.* 1. the cardinal number between four and six; 5; V.
2. anything having five units or members; specifically, (a) a basketball team; (b) a playing card or domino with five spots; (c) [Colloq.] a five-dollar bill.

five′-and-dīme′, *n.* a five-and-ten-cent store.

five′-and-ten′-cent stōre, a store that sells a wide variety of merchandise, originally with many articles priced at five or ten cents: also *five-and-ten:* also called *dime store.*

Five Civ′il·īzed Nā′tionṣ, the Cherokee, Chickasaw, Choctaw, Creek, and Seminole tribes of the Indian Territory (now the eastern part of Oklahoma).

five′-fin″gẽr, *n.* [AS. *fiffingre.*]
1. any of several plants, as the cinquefoil or the oxlip, having leaves with five radiating parts, or flowers with five petals.
2. a starfish with five rays.

five′fōld′, *a.* 1. having five parts.
2. having five times as much or as many.

five′fōld′, *adv.* five times as much or as many.

five hun′dred, a variety of euchre in which the object is to score five hundred points.

five′-lēaf, *n.* cinquefoil; five-finger; five-fingered grass.

five′ling, *n.* a compound crystal composed of five individual parts.

Five Nā′tionṣ, a confederation of Iroquoian Indians, consisting originally of the Mohawks, Oneidas, Onondagas, Cayugas, and Senecas, and later including the Tuscaroras.

fīv′ẽr, *n.* 1. a five-dollar bill.
2. something that scores five in a game.
3. a five-pound note. [Brit.]
[Slang in all senses.]

fiveṣ, *n.* a kind of handball played in England.

fiveṣ, *n.* vives. [Obs.]

fiveṣ çōurt, a place where the game of fives is played.

five′-twen′ty, *a.* relating to the bonds known as five-twenties.

five′-twen′ty, *n.*; *pl.* **five′-twen′tieṣ,** bonds issued by the United States government between 1862 and 1865, bearing six per cent interest, to be redeemed at any time after a period of five years, and payable in twenty years.

Five′-Yēar′ Plan, any of several five-year programs for the development of the socialized industry, agriculture, etc. of the Soviet Union: the first Five-Year Plan was begun in 1928.

fix, *v.t.*; fixed *or* fixt (fikst), *pt., pp.*; fixing, *ppr.* [Fr. *fixer,* from ML. *fixare,* from *fixus,* pp. of *figere,* to fix, fasten, drive in.]
1. to make stable, firm, or secure; to attach or fasten immovably.
2. to establish; to set; to arrange definitely; as, he *fixed* the rent at forty dollars.
3. to set firmly in the mind.
4. to set or direct steadily; to fasten intently; as, he *fixed* his eyes upon the judge.
5. to direct one's eyes steadily at.
6. to transfix; to pierce. [Obs.]
7. to make rigid.
8. to make permanent or lasting; as, color is *fixed* in dyeing.
9. to reach a decision about; find out with certainty; as, the city of Homer's birth has never been *fixed.*
10. to arrange properly; set in order; adjust.
11. to repair; mend.
12. to bank, refuel, and tend (a fire).
13. to prepare and cook (food or meals).
14. to influence the result or action of (a horse race, jury, election, etc.) to one's advantage by bribery, trickery, etc. [Colloq.]
15. to punish; revenge oneself on; get even with. [Colloq.]
16. in chemistry, to make solid or nonvolatile.
17. in photography, to make (a film, slide, etc.) permanent and prevent from fading by washing in a chemical solution.
to fix on (or *upon*); to choose; to settle on.
to fix up; (a) to repair; mend; (b) to arrange properly; set in order; (c) to make arrangements for; take care of. [Colloq.]

fix, *v.i.* 1. to become fixed.

Your kindness banishes your fear,
Resolved to *fix* forever here. —Waller.

2. to prepare or intend; as, I'm *fixing* to go hunting. [Colloq. and Dial.]

fix, *n.* 1. an embarrassing or difficult position; a dilemma, a trying situation; a predicament. [Colloq.]
2. in iron foundries, the material used to line the hearth of a puddling furnace.
3. in aviation, navigation, etc., a position determined from the bearings of two or more known points.
4. a person or situation that can be fixed (sense 14). [Slang.]

fix′ȧ·ble, *a.* that can be fixed, established, or rendered firm.

fix′āte, *v.t.* and *v.i.*; fixated, *pt., pp.*; fixating, *ppr.* [ML. *fixatus,* pp. of *fixare,* from *fixus,* pp. of *figere,* to fix, fasten.]
1. to make or become fixed.
2. in psychology, (a) to direct and focus (the eyes); (b) to direct and focus the eye on (a point).
3. in psychoanalysis, to attach or arrest (one of the component impulses of the libido) at an early stage of psychosexual development.

fix·ā′tion, *n.* 1. (a) a fixing or being fixed; (b) a fixating or being fixated.
2. in chemistry, (a) reduction into a solid or nonvolatile form; (b) the fixing of atmospheric nitrogen.
3. in photography, the treatment of a film, print, etc. to make it permanent.
4. in psychology, (a) the directing and focusing of the eyes on a point; (b) popularly, a morbid preoccupation; obsession.
5. in psychoanalysis, an attaching or arresting of one of the component impulses of the libido at an early stage of psychosexual development.

fix′ȧ·tive, *a.* that can or tends to make permanent, prevent fading, etc.

fix′ȧ·tive, *n.* 1. anything which serves to make colors permanent and unfading, as a mordant.
2. a solution sprayed upon charcoal drawings which fixes them and prevents rubbing.

fixed (fixt), *a.* 1. firm; not movable.
2. established; settled; set; as, a *fixed* price.
3. steady; unmoving; resolute; as, a *fixed* purpose.
4. persisting in the mind, sometimes to the point of delusion, and tending to control the thoughts and action; obsessive; as, a *fixed* idea.
5. in chemistry, (a) nonvolatile; as, *fixed* oils; (b) incorporated into a stable compound from its free state, as atmospheric nitrogen.
fixed air; formerly, carbon dioxide.
fixed capital; see *capital.*
fixed charge; any of certain charges, as taxes, rent, interest, etc., which must be paid, usually at regular intervals, without being changed or shifted, and without reference to the amount of business done.
fixed light; a light emitting steady radiance.
fixed oil; a nonvolatile oil, especially one found in fatty animal tissue and the seeds of some plants.
fixed star; a star whose great distance from the earth makes it appear to keep the same position in relation to other stars.

fix′ed·ly, *adv.* firmly; in a settled or established manner; steadfastly.

fix′ed·ness, *n.* the state of being fixed.

fix′ẽr, *n.* 1. a person or thing that fixes.
2. a person who pays bribes or uses his influence to keep himself or others from being punished for illegal acts. [Colloq.]

fix·id′i·ty, *n.* fixity. [Rare.]

fix′ing, *n.* 1. the act or process of rendering permanent.
2. [*pl.*] furnishings; accessories; trimmings. [Colloq.]

fix′i·ty, *n.* 1. the quality or state of being fixed; steadiness; stability; permanence.
2. *pl.* **fix′i·tieṣ,** anything fixed.

fixt, *v.* poetic past tense and past participle of fix.

fix′tūre, *n.* [from obs. *fixure* (L. *fixura*), after *mixture.*]
1. anything firmly in place.
2. [*usually in pl.*] any of the fittings or furniture of a house, store, etc., attached to the building and considered legally as a part of it; as, bathroom *fixtures.*
3. a person who has been so long in the same place, as a resident or occupant of a situation, that it is difficult to remove him. [Colloq.]

fix′ūre, *n.* fixed condition or position; firmness. [Obs.]

fiz′gig, *n.* 1. a fishgig.
2. a giddy, flirting girl.
3. a kind of firework, made of damp powder, which gives a hissing or fizzing noise when ignited.

fizz, fiz, *n.* [echoic.] 1. a hissing, sputtering sound.
2. a drink, as champagne, soda water, etc. that hisses and bubbles; effervescent drink.
gin fizz; a drink prepared with gin, sugar, bitters, and carbonated water.

fizz, fiz, *v.i.*; fizzed, *pt., pp.*; fizzing, *ppr.* to make a hissing sound.

fiz′zle, *v.i.*; fizzled, *pt., pp.*; fizzling, *ppr.* [echoic.] 1. to fizz; to sputter; to produce a sound similar to that made by liquid poured from a small-necked bottle.
2. to come to nothing, especially after a successful beginning; to result in ignominious failure; to prove a fiasco; to stop short of completion: often followed by *out.* [Colloq.]

fiz′zle, *n.* 1. a hissing or sputtering sound.
2. an attempt that ends in failure; fiasco. [Colloq.]

fiz′zy, *a.*; *comp.* fizzier; *superl.* fizziest, that fizzes; bubbling; effervescent.

fjeld (fyeld), *n.* a barren plateau in Scandinavia.

fjord (fyọrd), same as *fiord.*

Fl, in chemistry, fluorine.

flab′bẽr·gast, *v.t.*; flabbergasted, *pt., pp.*; flabbergasting, *ppr.* [18th-c. slang; prob. from *flabby,* and *aghast.*] to surprise; to amaze; to daze or make speechless. [Colloq.]

flab″bẽr·gas·tā′tion, *n.* the condition of being flabbergasted; a state of utter confusion or bewilderment. [Colloq.]

flab′bi·ly, *adv.* in a flabby manner.

flab′bi·ness, *n.* a flabby quality or state.

flab′by, *a.*; *comp.* flabbier; *superl.* flabbiest, [a variant of *flappy*, from *flap*, to hang loose.]
 1. lacking firmness; limp and soft; flaccid; as, *flabby* muscles.
 2. lacking force; weak.

flā′bel, *n.* [L. *flabellum*, a fan, dim. of *flabrum*, a breeze, from *flare*, to blow.] a fan. [Obs.]

flȧ·bel′lāte, *a.* in biology, having the shape of a fan.

flab·el·lā′tion, *n.* act of cooling as by the use of an electric fan.

flȧ·bel′li·fǫrm, *a.* [L. *flabellum*, a little fan, and *forma*, form.] having the form of a fan; fan-shaped.

flȧ·bel′li·nẽrved, *a.* [L. *flabellum*, a little fan, and *nervus*, nerve.] in botany, having numerous nerves branching in a flabellate manner from a point, as the base of a leaf or petal.

flȧ·bel′lum, *n.*; *pl.* **flȧ·bel′lȧ,** [L., a little fan.]
 1. a fan; specifically, a large fan formed of feathers, ivory, metal, or other material, carried before the Pope and certain other dignitaries on ceremonial occasions.

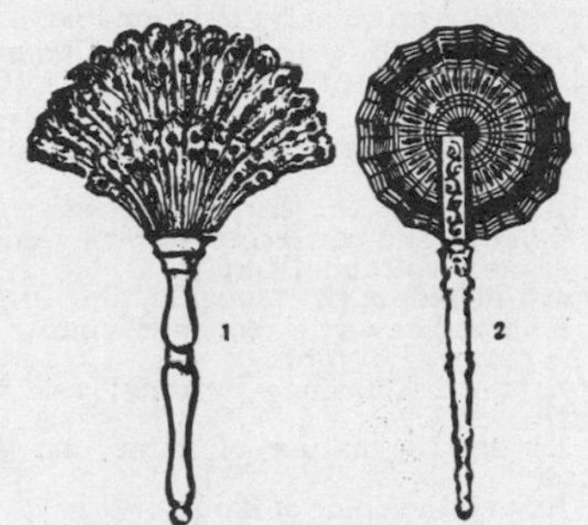

FLABELLA
1. papal flabellum 2. liturgical flabellum

 2. in zoology and botany, a fan-shaped part or structure; especially, an epipodite, a part attached to the maxilliped of certain crustaceans.

flaç′cid, *a.* [L. *flaccidus*, from *flaccus*, flabby.]
 1. hanging in loose folds or wrinkles; soft and limp; flabby; as, *flaccid* muscles.
 2. lacking force; weak; feeble.

flaç·cid′i·ty, *n.* [from L. *flaccidus*, flabby, flaccid.]
 1. the quality or state of being flaccid.
 2. a disease of silkworms caused by the presence of bacteria.

flaç′cid·ly, *adv.* in a flaccid manner.

flaç′cid·ness, *n.* laxity; flaccidity.

flaçhe·rie′, *n.* [Fr.] same as *flaccidity*, sense 2.

flack′ẽr, *v.i.* to flutter as a bird. [Now Dial.]

flack′et, *n.* [ME. *flaket*, *flaget*, from OFr. *flasquet*, *flachet*, dim. of *flasque*, *flache*, a flask.] a barrel-shaped bottle. [Dial.]

flȧ·çọn′, *n.* [Fr.] a small flask or bottle fitted with a stopper, for holding perfume, etc.

Flȧ·cöur′ti·ȧ, *n.* [named after Etienne de *Flacourt*, a French traveler.] the type genus of the family *Flacourtiaceæ*, being a genus of small trees or shrubs found in Asia and Africa, having spinose branches and edible fruit.

flaff, *v.t.* and *v.i.* to flap; to flutter; to crack, as when blown by the wind. [Scot.]

flag, *n.* [of D. or Scand. origin; D. *vlag*; Sw. *flagg*; Dan. *flag*, a flag.]
 1. a piece of cloth or bunting, often attached to a staff, with definite colors, patterns, or symbolic devices, used as a national or state symbol, or to indicate membership in an organization, to signal, etc.; banner; standard; ensign.
 2. [*pl.*] (a) the quills on the second joint of a bird's wing; (b) the long feathers on the leg of a hawk, owl, etc.
 3. the tail of a deer.
 4. the bushy tail of certain hunting dogs, as setters and some hounds.
 black flag; see under *black*.
 flag of truce; a white flag displayed to an enemy to indicate a desire to confer or surrender.
 red flag; (a) the flag symbolizing revolution, revolutionary socialism, etc.: often used figuratively; (b) a danger signal: from the use of a red flag as a signal at railroad crossings; (c) anything that arouses anger.
 service flag; a white flag with a red border displayed during wartime by families and organizations having members in military service: blue stars indicate the number of members in service and gold stars the number killed in service.
 to dip the flag; to salute by lowering the flag and immediately returning it to place. It is done in token of courtesy, welcome, or respect.
 to strike or *lower the flag*; to lower the flag as a sign of surrender; hence, to capitulate; to give up.
 yellow flag; the sanitary or quarantine flag displayed over a ship to indicate the presence of a contagious disease on board.

flag, *v.t.*; flagged, *pt.*, *pp.*; flagging, *ppr.* 1. to decorate or mark with flags.
 2. to signal with or as with a flag; as, he *flagged* the train.
 3. to send (a message) by signaling.
 to flag down; to flag (a train, etc.) as a signal to stop.

flag, *n.* [Early Mod. Eng. *flagge*; ME. *flegge*; Dan. *flæg*, a flag.]
 1. any of several endogenous plants with sword-shaped leaves and purple, blue, yellow, or white flowers, mostly growing in moist places; especially, any plant of the genus *Iris*.
 2. the flower or leaf of any of these plants.
 cooper's flag; the common cattail, or cattail flag, *Typha latifolia*.

flag, *v.i.*; flagged, *pt.*, *pp.*; flagging, *ppr.* [prob. var. of ME. *flacken*, to flutter, influenced by OFr. *flaquir*, to be flaccid, and by echoism.]
 1. to become limp; to droop.
 2. to grow weak; to lose vigor; as, his enthusiasm *flagged*.

flag, *v.t.* 1. to let fall into feebleness; to droop.
 2. to make feeble; to enervate; to exhaust.

flag, *n.* [Ice. *flaga*, a slab of stone, lit., a flake.]
 1. any hard stone split into flat pieces and used for paving.
 2. a piece of this stone.

flag, *v.t.*; flagged, *pt.*, *pp.*; flagging, *ppr.* to lay with flat stones; to pave with flags.

flag çap′tain (-tin), in the British Navy, the captain of a flagship.

Flag Dāy, 1. June 14, the anniversary of the day in 1777, when the United States flag was adopted.
 2. [f– d–] in England, a day when people contribute to some special fund for charity and get small flags in receipt.

flȧ·ġel′lȧ, *n.* alternative plural of *flagellum*.

flaġ′el·lănt, *n.* [L. *flagellans* (-*antis*), ppr. of *flagellare*, to whip, scourge.]
 1. a person who whips; especially, one who whips himself or has himself whipped as a religious discipline or in abnormal eroticism.
 2. [F–] a member of one of the many sects which since the twelfth century have practiced flagellation as a religious discipline.

flaġ′el·lănt, *a.* engaging in flagellation.

flȧ·ġel′lăr, *a.* pertaining to a flagellum.

Flaġ·el·lā′tȧ, *n.pl.* [L., neut. pl. of *flagellatus*, pp. of *flagellare*, to whip, scourge.] a class of protozoans, characterized by long cilialike lashes, or flagella, either distributed over the body, or grouped, as at the anterior end.

flaġ′el·lāte, *v.t.*; flagellated, *pt.*, *pp.*; flagellating, *ppr.* [L. *flagellatus*, pp. of *flagellare*, to whip, scourge, from *flagellum*, a whip, scourge.] to whip; to scourge; to lash, as with a flagellum.

flaġ′el·lāte, *a.* 1. having the form of a flagellum.
 2. having flagella.
 3. pertaining to the *Flagellata*.

flaġ′el·lāt·ed, *a.* same as *flagellate*.

flaġ·el·lā′tion, *n.* a beating or whipping; a flogging; especially, as religious discipline or in abnormal eroticism.

flaġ′el·lā·tŏr, *n.* [LL., from *flagellare*, to whip, scourge.] same as *flagellant*.

flaġ′el·lȧ·tō″ry, *a.* having to do with flagellation.

flaġ·el·lif′ẽr·ous, *a.* [L. *flagellum*, a whip, scourge, and *ferre*, to bear.] in biology, having flagella.

flȧ·ġel′li·fǫrm, *a.* [L. *flagellum*, a whip, and *forma*, form.] shaped like a whiplash or flagellum; long, slender, round, and tapering.

flȧ·ġel′lū·lȧ, *n.*; *pl.* **flȧ·ġel′lū·lae,** [dim. from L. *flagellum*, a whip.] in biology, a spore having one or more flagella.

flȧ·ġel′lum, *n.*; *pl.* **flȧ·ġel′lȧ** or **flȧ·ġel′lums,** [L., a whip, scourge.]
 1. a whip; a scourge.
 2. in botany, (a) a creeping shoot sent out from the bottom of the stem, and giving off leaves and roots; a runner; (b) a whiplike extension bearing undeveloped leaves, found in certain of the *Hepaticæ*.
 3. in zoology, a lashlike appendage found on many infusorians; an appendage to the legs of some crustacea, having some resemblance to a whip, and used as an organ of locomotion; an elongated cilium.
 4. in entomology, the distal portion of a jointed antenna, or all of the antenna beyond the basal joint.

FLAGELLUM (of microorganism)

flaġ·eō·let′, *n.* [OFr. *flageolet*, dim. of *flageol*, *flajeol*, a pipe, flute, dim. from LL. *flauta*, a flute.] a small wind instrument of the fipple flute family, similar to a recorder.

FLAGEOLET

flaġ′eō·let tōneṣ, in music, the harmonic tones on the violin, violoncello, and other stringed instruments.

flag′gi·ness, *n.* laxity; limberness.

flag′ging, *n.* 1. the act of laying with flagstones.
 2. a pavement or sidewalk of flagstones.
 3. flagstones.

flag′ging, *a.* weakening; drooping.

flag′ging·ly, *adv.* weakly; languidly.

flag′gy, *a.* full of flags (the plants).

flag′gy, *a.* of or like flagstone.

flaġ′i·tāte, *v.t.* to importune; to demand imperiously; to urge imperatively. [Rare.]

flȧ·ġi′tious, *a.* [L. *flagitiosus*, from *flagitium*, a shameful or disgraceful act; *flagitare*, to demand, demand fiercely.] shamefully wicked; villainous; atrocious; scandalous; heinous.
 Syn.—shameful, corrupt, flagrant, villainous, atrocious, profligate, felonious, iniquitous, execrable.

flȧ·ġi′tious·ly, *adv.* with extreme wickedness.

flȧ·ġi′tious·ness, *n.* extreme wickedness; villainy.

flag lieū·ten′ănt, an officer who serves under an admiral in a capacity similar to that of an aide-de-camp to a general.

flag′măn, *n.*; *pl.* **flag′men,** 1. a person who carries a flag.
 2. a person whose work is signaling (trains, etc.) with a flag or lantern, as at a railroad crossing.
 3. formerly, a flag officer.

flag of′fi·cẽr, a naval officer in command of a fleet or squadron and hence entitled to display a flag indicating his rank or command.

flag′ŏn, *n.* [ME. *flakon*; OFr. *flacon*, *flascon*; It. *fiascone*, from *fiasca*.]
 1. a container for liquids, usually having a handle, a narrow neck, a spout, and, sometimes, a lid.
 2. the contents of such a container.

flag′pōle, *n.* a pole on which a flag is raised and flown.

flā′grănce, *n.* flagrancy; notoriety; outrage.

flā′grăn·cy, *n.*; *pl.* **flā′grăn·cieṣ,** 1. a burning; great heat; inflammation. [Obs.]
 Lust causeth a *flagrancy* in the eyes.
 —Bacon.
 2. the quality or state of being flagrant.

flā′grănt, *a.* 1. glowing; red; flushed; hence, burning; ardent; eager; as, *flagrant* desires. [Obs.]
 2. happening at the present time; now going on. [Rare.]
 3. flaming into notice; glaring; notorious; scandalous; outrageous; enormous; as, a *flagrant* crime.

flā·gran′tē dē·leç′tō, [L., lit., during the blazing of the crime.] in the very act of committing the crime; red-handed.

flā′grănt·ly, *adv.* notoriously; in a flagrant manner or to a flagrant extent.

flā′grāte, *v.t.* [L. *flagratus*, pp. of *flagrare*, to burn.] to burn. [Obs.]

flȧ·grā′tion, *n.* a burning or conflagration. [Obs.]

flag′rọot, *n.* the root of the sweet flag, *Acorus calamus*. It has a pungent, aromatic flavor.

flag′ship, *n.* the ship that carries the commanding officer of a fleet or squadron, and on which his flag is displayed.

flag′stȧff, *n.* a flagpole.

flag stā′tion, a railroad station at which trains stop only when signaled.

flag′stōne, *n.* a large, flat stone used in paving; a flag.

flag′-wāv·ing, *n.* an effort to arouse intense patriotic or nationalistic feelings by a deliberate appeal to the emotions.

flāil, *n.* [ME. *flail, flayle, flegl*; OFr. *flæl, flaiel*; Pr. *flagel*, from L. *flagellum*, a whip, scourge.]

FLAIL

1. an implement consisting of a free-swinging stick, called a swiple or swingle, tied to the end of another stick, used to thresh grain by hand.

2. an ancient military weapon resembling this, but having the striking part strengthened with an armor of iron or rows of spikes.

flāil′y, *a.* resembling a flail in action. [Obs.]

flāir, *n.* [ME. *flayre*; OFr. *flair*, odor, from *flairer*, to emit an odor, from L. *fragare*, to emit an odor.]

1. odor; savor; smell. [Obs.]
2. keen sense of smell; scent.
3. keen natural discernment.
4. a natural talent or ability; aptitude.
5. a sense of what is stylish and striking. [Colloq.]

flak, *n.* [from G. *F*lieger*a*bwehr*k*anone, antiaircraft gun.]

1. antiaircraft fire.
2. strong, clamorous criticism, opposition, etc.: also *flack.*

flāke, *n.* [ME. *flake, fleke, fleyke*; Ice. *flaki*, a hurdle, a shield of wickerwork for defense.] a light rack or platform used for storing or drying fish, smoked meat, etc.

flāke, *n.* [ME. *flake*; Norw. *flak*, a slice, a piece torn off; Sw. *flaga*, a flake, flaw.]

1. a small, thin mass; as, a *flake* of snow.
2. a thin chip or scale split, cut, or peeled from anything; lamina; fleck; layer; chip.
3. a small particle of combustible matter on fire, separated and flying off.
4. an eccentric, unbalanced, or irrational person. [Slang.]

flāke, *v.t.* and *v.i.*; flaked (flākt), *pt., pp.*; flaking, *ppr.* 1. to form into flakes.

2. to chip or peel off in flakes.
3. to make or become spotted with flakes.

flāke knīfe (nīf), a knife made of a chip of flinty stone, used in prehistoric times.

flāk′ẽr, *n.* 1. a workman who chips flint into flakes.

2. in archaeology, an instrument of bone used to shape flint arrowheads.

flāke stand, the cooling-tub for the worm of a still.

flāke whīte, a white coloring matter made of flakes of white lead.

flāk′i·ly, *adv.* in a flaky manner.

flāk′i·ness, *n.* the state of being flaky.

flāk′y, *a.*; *comp.* flakier; *superl.* flakiest. 1. consisting of or containing flakes.

2. breaking easily into flakes; cleaving off in layers.
3. very eccentric or unconventional. [Slang.]

flam, *n.* [prob. contr. of obs. *flamfew*, a trifle, gewgaw, from OFr. *fanfelue*, a bubble.]

1. a freak or whim. [Obs.]
2. a lie; an illusory pretext; deception.
3. blarney; humbug.

flam, *v.t.*; flammed, *pt., pp.*; flamming, *ppr.* to deceive with falsehood or flattery.

flam·bé′ (floṅ-bā′), *a.* [Fr., pp. of *flamber*, to flame, singe.]

1. in ceramics, having an irregular glaze splashed on the surface.
2. served with a sauce containing brandy, rum, etc. set afire to flame.

flam′beau (flam′bō), *n.*; *pl.* **flam′beaux, flam′beaus** (-bōz), [Fr., from L. *flamma*, a flame.]

1. a flaming torch; formerly one made of thick wicks covered with wax, pitch, etc.
2. a large, ornamental candlestick.
3. a large kettle used for boiling sugar: it is exposed directly to the flames.

flam·boy′ănce, *n.* the quality or state of being flamboyant.

flam·boy′ăn·cy, *n.* same as *flamboyance.*

flam·boy′ănt, *a.* [Fr., ppr. of *flamber*, to flame.]

1. designating or of that style of Gothic architecture in France which was characterized by wavy, flamelike tracery in the windows and florid decoration.
2. blazing; flaming.
3. having a wavy edge, similar to a flame: said of a sword.
4. ornate; too showy.
5. flowery; bombastic; full of exaggerations and figures of speech; as, *flamboyant* speech.

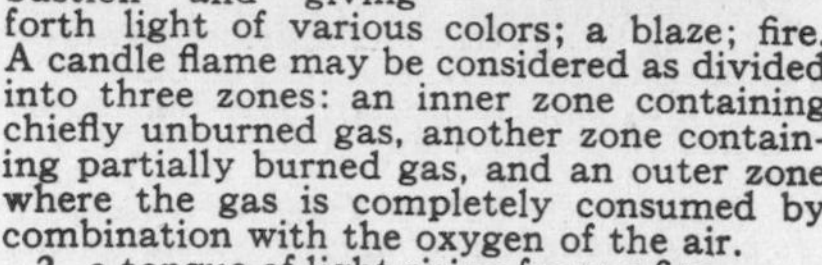

FLAMBOYANT WINDOW

flāme, *n.* [ME. *flambe, flaume, flaumbe*; OFr. *flame, flambe*, from L. *flamma*, a flame, from *flagrare*, to burn.]

1. a stream of vapor or gas undergoing combustion and giving forth light of various colors; a blaze; fire. A candle flame may be considered as divided into three zones: an inner zone containing chiefly unburned gas, another zone containing partially burned gas, and an outer zone where the gas is completely consumed by combination with the oxygen of the air.
2. a tongue of light rising from a fire.
3. the state of burning with a blaze of light.
4. a thing like a flame in heat, brilliance, etc.
5. a strong passion; an intense emotion; a carrying away of the mind by passion, excitement, or anger.
6. one beloved; sweetheart; as, she was my first *flame.* [Slang.]
7. a moth, *Anticlea rubidata.* [Brit.]

oxidizing flame; the tip of the flame from a blowpipe capable of oxidizing metals. It is nonluminous and contains free oxygen at a very high temperature.

reducing flame; the inner luminous portion of the flame from a blowpipe, which will reduce compounds to the metallic state.

flāme, *v.i.*; flamed, *pt., pp.*; flaming, *ppr.* 1. to burn with a blaze of light; burst into flame.

2. to act or be like a flame.
3. to light up with color as if blazing; grow red or hot; as, her face *flamed* with embarrassment.
4. to show intense emotion; become very excited.

to flame up (or *out*); to burst out in or as in flames.

flāme, *v.t.* 1. to burn or heat with flame.

2. to arouse (emotions); inflame. [Poet.]

flāme bridġe, a partition in a fire chamber, nearly as high as the bottom of the boiler, leaving a small space through which the flame and heated gases must pass to the flues.

flāme cell, a cell in which the excretory canal of any flatworm terminates, and into which project minute cilia.

flāme en′ġine, a gas engine. [Obs.]

flāme′flow″ẽr, *n.* a species of the genus *Kniphofia*, or *Tritoma*, native to South Africa. It is a liliaceous plant, having long, grassy leaves, and a raceme of red flowers which change to yellow.

flāme′less, *a.* without flame.

flāme′let, *n.* a little flame.

flā′men, *n.*; *pl.* **flā′mens, flȧ′mi·nēs,** [L.] in ancient Rome, a priest in the service of a particular god. Originally there were three priests so called: the *Flamen Dialis*, consecrated to Jupiter; *Flamen Martialis*, sacred to Mars; and *Flamen Quirinalis*, who superintended the rites of Quirinus or Romulus.

flāme′-of-the-woods, *n.* a rubiaceous shrub, *Ixora coccinea*, native to Asia and the West Indies, but cultivated elsewhere for its showy scarlet flowers.

flāme′out, *n.* the stopping of combustion in a jet engine as a result of some abnormal flight condition.

flāme′proof, *a.* 1. not readily damaged by fire.

2. not catching fire.

flāme rē·aç′tion, a test for certain elements, as copper, by the color they impart to a flame.

flāme′-thrōw′ẽr, *n.* a weapon for shooting a stream of flaming liquid, as oil, at enemy troops and positions.

flāme tree, 1. the Australian fire tree.

2. the *Brachychiton acerifolius* of Australia: so called from its brilliant red flowers.

flȧ·min′ē·ous, *a.* [L. *flaminius*, from *flamen*, a priest.] of or relating to a flamen; flaminical.

flām′ing, *a.* 1. giving forth fire or flames; blazing; illuminating.

2. brilliant; dazzling; flame-colored; like a flame.
3. passionate; ardent; intensely emotional.
4. startling; flagrant.

flām′ing·ly, *adv.* in a flaming manner.

flȧ·miṅ′gō, *n.*; *pl.* **flȧ·miṅ′gōs, flȧ·miṅ′gōes,** [Port. *flamingo, flamengo*; Sp. *flamenco*; associated with *flama*, flame, because of the color.] any of a genus of tropical wading birds called *Phoenicopterus.* The beak is naked, toothed, and bent as if broken; the neck and legs are very long; the feet have the three front toes webbed to the end, and the hind one extremely short; the feathers are colored pink to red.

flȧ·miṅ′gō plant, a tropical plant of the arum family, *Anthurium scherzerianum*, cultivated for its brilliant scarlet flowers.

Flȧ·min′i·ăn, *a.* relating to Caius Flaminius, a Roman censor, or to the public works which were constructed under his censorship.

flȧ·min′i·căl, *a.* pertaining to a Roman flamen.

flam′mȧ·ble, *a.* easily set on fire; that will burn readily or quickly; inflammable.

flam′mē·ous, *a.* [L. *flammeus*, from *flamma*, a flame.] consisting of flame; like flame. [Obs.]

flam·mif′ẽr·ous, *a.* [L. *flammifer*; *flamma*, a flame, and *ferre*, to bear.] producing flame. [Obs.]

flam·miv′ō·mous, *a.* [L. *flammivomus*; *flamma*, a flame, and *vomere*, to vomit.] vomiting flames, as a volcano. [Rare.]

flam′mū·lā·ted, *a.* [L. *flammula*, dim. of *flamma*, a flame.] having a red tinge; ruddy: said of the plumage of birds.

flām′y, *a.* 1. blazing; burning; as, *flamy* breath.

2. having the nature of flame; as, *flamy* matter.
3. having the color of flame.

flaṅ, *n.* [Fr.]

1. a tart filled with cheese, custard, fruit, etc.
2. a piece of shaped metal ready to be made into a coin by the stamp of a die; blank.

flan, *v.i.*; flanned, *pt., pp.*; flanning, *ppr.* to make flaring, as a dish or the jamb of a window. [Brit. Dial.]

flanch, *n.* 1. in mechanics, a flange.

2. in heraldry, a flanched bearing.

flanched (flancht), *a.* in heraldry, having a segment of a circle encroaching on each side of a field.

flaṅ·çō·nāde′, *n.* [Fr., from *flanc*, flank, side.] in fencing, a thrust aimed at the side of an opponent.

flâ·ne·rie′ (flä-ne-rē′), *n.* [Fr.] that which characterizes a flaneur; idle walking; loafing.

flâ·neur′ (flä-nẽr′), *n.* [Fr., a lounger, loiterer, from *flâner*, to lounge.] one who idly saunters without destination or aim; a lounger; a stroller; as, a *flaneur* of the boulevards.

flanġe, *n.* [prob. from OFr. *flangir*, to turn.]

1. a raised or projecting edge, rib, or rim for strength, as in a T-rail; for guidance, as on a rail to keep wheels in place; for connection with some other object, as in some pipes.
2. a tool for making flanges.

FLANGE

flanġe, *v.t.*; flanged, *pt., pp.*; flanging, *ppr.* to form a flange on; to provide with a flange.

flanġe, *v.i.* 1. to extend outward; to flare.

2. to be in the form of a flange.

flanġed, *a.* provided with a flange.

flanġe joint, a joint formed by the union of two flanges, as when two flange pipes are bolted end to end.

flanġe pīpe, a pipe having a flange at each end to form connections.

flan′ġẽr, *n.* 1. one who or that which makes flanges.

2. a device or machine for removing snow from the inside of a rail: used in cleaning railroad tracks.

flanġe rāil, a rail provided with an edge or flange on one side to keep the wheel on the track.

flanġe wheel, any wheel flanged on one or both edges of the rim to prevent its slipping from the rail.

flank, *n.* [ME. *flanke*, the flank; OFr. *flanc*; LL. *flancus*, the side, flank; O.H.G. *hlanca*, *hlanka*, loin, flank, side.]
1. the fleshy side of a person or animal between the ribs and the hip.
2. a cut of beef from this part.
3. loosely, the side of the upper part of the human thigh.
4. the side of anything.
5. the right or left side of an army, or of any division of an army, as of a brigade, regiment, or battalion; also, the territory surrounding either side.
6. in fortification, that part of a bastion which reaches from the curtain to the face.
7. the straight part of the tooth of a gearwheel which receives the impulse.

flank, *a.* of or relating to a flank; as, a *flank* steak, a *flank* attack.

flank, *v.t.*; flanked (flankt), *pt.*, *pp.*; flanking, *ppr.* 1. to form a border of; to be on the side of; as, rocks *flank* the road.
2. to attack the side or flank of (an enemy unit); to place (troops) so as to command or attack the flank.
3. to protect the side of (a friendly unit).
4. to turn the flank of; to pass around the side of (an enemy unit).

flank, *v.i.* to be in a flanking position (with *on* or *upon*).

flank'en, *n.* [Yid., from G. *flanke*, flank.] a cut of beef from the plate, usually boiled and eaten with horseradish.

flank'ēr, *n.* 1. in military science, (a) a fortified position at either flank for protection or attack; (b) any of several men sent out to protect the flanks of a marching column.
2. in hunting, one who beats along the side to keep the quarry within bounds.
3. in football, an offensive back who takes a position closer to the sideline than the rest of the team.

flan'nel, *n.* [earlier *flannen*; prob. from W. *gwlanen*, from *gwlan*, wool.]
1. a soft, lightweight woolen cloth of loose texture.
2. [*pl.*] clothes, especially trousers, of this.
3. flannelette.
4. [*pl.*] heavy woolen underwear. [Colloq.]
Canton or *cotton flannel*; a firm cotton fabric, generally having a long silky nap on one side.

flan'nel, *a.* made or consisting of flannel.
flannel cake; a griddlecake.

flan'nel, *v.t.*; flanneled *or* flannelled, *pt.*, *pp.*; flanneling or flannelling, *ppr.* 1. to wrap or clothe in flannel.
2. to rub with flannel.

flan'neled, *a.* covered or wrapped in flannel.

flan·nel·ette', flan·nel·et', *n.* a soft cotton cloth resembling flannel.

flan'nel·flow'ēr, *n.* 1. the common mullein, *Verbascum thapsus.*
2. the *Macrosiphonia longiflora*, a tropical vine of the dogbane family, having leaves of a flannellike texture and tubular flowers.

flan'nel-mouthed, *a.* 1. speaking thickly, as if one's mouth were full of flannel.
2. smooth-talking in an insincere or deceptive way.

flan'nen, *n.* flannel. [Obs.]

flap, *n.* [ME. *flap*, *flappe*, a stroke, blow, a loose and flexible part of a garment; D. *flap*, a stroke, blow on the ear.]
1. anything broad and flat that hangs loose and is attached at one end; as, the *flap* of a pocket.
2. the motion of anything broad and flat; as, the *flap* of an awning.
3. the sound made by such a movement.
4. a slap.
5. a portion of flesh or skin left after an operation intended to cover the end of a bone or to form a new part.
6. [*pl.*] a disease in the lips of horses.
7. a commotion; stir; fuss. [Slang.]

flap, *v.t.*; flapped, *pt.*, *pp.*; flapping, *ppr.* [ME. *flappen*, to flap, slap; D. *flappen*, to flap; prob. echoic in origin.]
1. to strike with something flat and broad; slap.
2. to move back and forth or up and down as in beating the air, usually with some noise; as, the bird *flapped* its wings.

flap, *v.i.* 1. to be flapping; flutter.
2. to fly by flapping the wings.
3. to hang down as a flap.
4. to become excited or confused. [Slang.]

flap'doo·dle, *n.* nonsense; foolish talk. [Colloq.]

flap'drag"ŏn, *n.* 1. an old game in which the players snatched raisins, plums, etc. from burning liquor and ate them.
2. the raisin, plum, etc. thus caught and eaten.

flap'drag"ŏn, *v.t.* to swallow or devour quickly; to snatch and swallow at a single gulp, as a player at flapdragon.

flap'-ēared, *a.* having broad, flat ears.

flap'jack, *n.* a large pancake; a griddlecake cooked on a griddle over the fire and turned in tossing it up, so that it falls upon the pan with a flap.

flap'pēr, *n.* 1. one who or that which flaps; especially, (a) a flap; (b) a broad fin or flipper; (c) something broad and flat for striking.
2. a young bird or waterfowl just learning to fly: so called from its habit of flapping its wings without rising in the air.
3. a young girl considered bold and unconventional in actions and dress: term popular from about 1910 to 1930. [Colloq.]

flap'pēr skāte, in Great Britain, any of various species of ray.

flap tīle, a tile bent up so as to form an angle or a trough.

flap valve, a hinge valve; a valve that flaps when it closes.

flāre, *v.i.*; flared, *pt.*, *pp.*; flaring, *ppr.* [earlier also *flear*; orig. sense "to flutter"; prob. thieves' slang borrowing of D. *vlederen*, to flutter, or the like.]
1. to blaze up brightly and unsteadily.
2. to signal by flares.
3. to curve or spread outward, as the sides of a ship; bulge.
4. to flutter; to be loose and waving, as a showy thing.

With ribbons pendant *flaring* 'bout her head. —Shak.

to flare up (or *out*); (a) to burst into flame; (b) to become suddenly angry, excited, violent, etc.

flāre, *v.t.* to cause to flare; hence, to signal with flares.

flāre, *n.* 1. a bright unsteady light; a glare.
2. a dazzling light lasting only a little while, used as a signal, to illuminate a landing field, etc.
3. a sudden, brief outburst, as of emotion or sound.
4. a spreading from within outward; a broadening; also, the part of anything which spreads out or widens.
5. in photography, a foggy spot on a film caused by a reflection of light on the lens.

flāre'back, *n.* a flame shooting out backward or otherwise abnormally from a furnace, a cannon, etc.

flāre'-up, *n.* 1. a sudden shooting up and spreading of flame.
2. a sudden, brief display of emotion, violence, etc.

flār'ing, *a.* 1. blazing brightly and unsteadily for a little while.
2. gaudy; lurid.
3. curving or spreading outward.

flār'ing·ly, *adv.* in a flaring manner.

flash, *v.i.*; flashed (flasht), *pt.*, *pp*; flashing, *ppr.* [ME. *flashien*, *flaschen*, to pour, sprinkle; Sw. dial. *flasa*, to burn furiously.]
1. to send out a sudden, brief blaze or light.
2. to be brilliant; sparkle; gleam; as, her eyes *flashed* with anger.
3. to come, move, or pass swiftly and suddenly; to be seen or realized for an instant like a flash of light; as, the automobile *flashed* by; an idea *flashed* through his mind.
Syn.—glitter, gl. ten, gleam.

flash, *v.t.* 1. to send out (light, etc.) in sudden, brief spurts; cause to flash.
2. to send (news, messages, etc.) swiftly or suddenly.
3. to cover (a roof, etc.) with material for weatherproofing.
4. to show briefly or ostentatiously; as, he *flashed* a roll of money. [Colloq.]
5. in glassmaking, (a) to make (glass) into sheets; (b) to put (a colored film of glass) on other glass; (c) to coat with a colored film of glass.
6. to treat (the filament of an incandescent lamp) by flashing.

flash, *n.* 1. a sudden burst of light; a flood of light briefly appearing and disappearing; as, a *flash* of lightning.
2. a sudden, brief display of thought, understanding, feeling, etc.; as, a *flash* of wit.

His companions recollect no instance of premature wit, no striking sentiment, no *flash* of fancy. —Wirt.

3. a short, brief period of time; moment.

The Persians and Macedonians had it for a *flash*. —Bacon.

4. a brief message or item of news sent by telegraph or radio.
5. a gaudy display; showiness.
6. the language of thieves, sharpers, etc.
7. (a) a sudden raising of the water in a channel to help boats over a dam, etc.; (b) the mechanism for this.
8. a preparation containing burnt sugar, used for coloring liquors.
9. anything that flashes or produces a flash.
10. in moving pictures, a view projected on the screen, incidental to, or illustrative of, all or part of the main feature being shown.
flash in the pan; (a) an ineffectual flash of the priming in the pan of a flintlock musket, which fails to explode the charge; (b) a sudden, apparently brilliant effort that fails; (c) a person who fails after such an effort.

flash, *a.* 1. showy; conspicuous; flashy; as, *flash* dress, jewelry, etc.
2. vulgar; offensively conspicuous, especially in dress, as, a *flash* person.
3. of thieves, sharpers, etc.

flash, *n.* [ME. *flasshe*, *flasche*, *flask*; OFr. *flache*, *flasque*, *flac*, a pool, estuary.] a pool. [Brit. Dial.]

flash'-back, *n.* 1. an interruption in the continuity of a story, motion picture, etc. by the narration or portrayal of some earlier episode.
2. the episode so narrated or portrayed.

flash'bōard, *n.* a board placed alongside a dam when the water is low to increase the depth of water.

flash' bulb, *n.* an electric light bulb that gives a brief, dazzling light, used for taking photographs indoors or at night.

flash'çärd, *n.* any of a set of cards with words, numbers, etc. on them, which are flashed one by one before a class for quick response in a drill.

flash'çūbe, *n.* a small, rotating cube containing a flashbulb in each of four sides, designed for taking pictures rapidly with a flash camera.

flash'ēr, *n.* a person or thing that flashes; specifically, (a) a device for causing lights to go on and off intermittently by closing and opening an electric circuit; (b) a beacon, buoy, etc. whose light goes on and off intermittently.

flash flōod (flud), a sudden, violent flood, as after a heavy rain.

flash-for'ward, *n.* 1. an interruption in the continuity of a story, motion picture, etc. by the narration or portrayal of some future episode.
2. such an episode.

flash gun, in photography, a synchronized device that simultaneously sets off a flashbulb and works the camera shutter.

flash'i·ly, *adv.* in a flashy manner.

flash'i·ness, *n.* the quality of being flashy.

flash'ing, *n.* 1. the action of a person or thing that flashes.
2. the sudden raising of water in a channel.
3. in architecture, pieces of lead or other metal let into the joints of a wall, so as to lap over the gutters and keep the rain out; any metal or other material inserted, especially on a roof, to keep the rain out.

flash'light (-līt) *n.* 1. a light that shines in flashes, used for signaling, as in lighthouses, airplane beacons, etc.
2. a portable electric light, usually operated by a small storage battery.
3. a brief, dazzling light for taking photographs at night or indoors.

flash point, the lowest temperature at which the vapor of a volatile oil will ignite with a flash.

flash'y, *a.*; *comp.* flashier; *superl.* flashiest. 1. bright, flashing, or dazzling for a moment; as, *flashy* wit.
2. showy; tawdry; gawdy; as, a *flashy* dress.
3. insipid; vapid; without taste or spirit, as food or drink. [Obs.]

flȧsk, *n.* [Fr. *flasque*; OFr. *flasque*, *flasche*; ML. *flasca*, *flasco*, wine bottle.]
1. any small, bottle-shaped container with a narrow neck, used in laboratories, etc.
2. a small, flattened container for liquor, etc., to be carried in the pocket.
3. a bed in a gun carriage.
4. a frame or box for holding a mold of sand in a foundry.
Erlenmeyer flask; a thin, cone-shaped flask with a flat bottom.
Florence flask; a thin glass flask with a globular body and a long neck, sometimes with a small, flat bottom.

flask'et, *n.* [OFr. *flasquet, flaschet, flachet,* dim. of *flasque,* a flask.]
1. a small flask.
2. a long, shallow basket. [Archaic.]

flat, *a.*; *comp.* flatter; *superl.* flattest. [ME. *flat*; Ice. *flatr*; Sw. *flat*; O.H.G. *flaz,* flat.]
1. having an even surface without risings or indentures, usually horizontal or nearly so; as, a *flat* roof; a *flat* rock.
2. prostrate; lying at full length; not elevated or erect; fallen.

Cease to admire, and beauty's plumes
Fall *flat.* —Milton.

3. having little depth or thickness; broad, even, and thin.
4. tasteless; stale; insipid; as, fruit *flat* to the taste.
5. dull; unanimated; without interest or spirit; as, the sermon was very *flat.*
6. peremptory; absolute; positive; downright; as, he gave the petitioner a *flat* denial.

Thus repulsed, our final hope
Is *flat* despair. —Milton.

7. without much business activity; dull; as, the market is *flat*; stocks are *flat.*
8. without variation; not fluctuating; as, a *flat* rate.
9. not clear or full; blurred; as, a *flat* sound.
10. emptied of air; as, a *flat* tire.
11. in art, (a) designating figures lacking relief or perspective; (b) uniform in tint; (c) without gloss.
12. in grammar, (a) not having the sign *to*: said of an infinitive (e.g., *come* in *make him come home*); (b) not having an inflectional ending: said of a noun used as an adjective (e.g., *orange* in *orange juice*), or of an adverb not having an adverbial ending (e.g., *fast* in *drive fast*).
13. in phonetics, (a) designating or of a vowel sounded with the tongue in a relatively level position (e.g., *a* in *can*); (b) designating or of a voiced consonant.
14. in music, (a) designating a tone a half-step lower than natural; as, B *flat,* a *flat* third; (b) not up to pitch; below the true pitch.
15. completely without money; penniless. [Colloq.]

flat arch; in architecture, an arch which does not rise in a curve, but is covered by a stone or a series of stones fitted to support one another and forming a horizontal roof.

flat cap; in the United States, a paper 14x17 inches, used for writing and for printing.

flat chisel; a chisel used by a sculptor for smoothing.

flat rope; a rope made by plaiting or by braiding rather than by twisting.

Syn.—dull, tame, insipid, vapid, spiritless, level, horizontal, absolute, even, downright, mawkish, tasteless, lifeless.

flat, *adv.* 1. even; exactly; as, he ran 100 yards in 10 seconds *flat.*
2. flatly (in various senses).
3. in a prone or supine position; as, he fell *flat.*
4. bluntly; abruptly.
5. in finance, with no interest.
6. in music, not up to the true pitch.

flat out; (a) at full speed, with maximum effort, etc.; (b) clearly; definitely. [Colloq.]

to fall flat; to fail to accomplish the end in view; to meet with no favor; as, his acting *fell flat.*

flat, *n.* 1. a flat surface or part; as, the flat of the hand.
2. an expanse of level land.
3. a level ground lying at a small depth under the surface of water; a shoal; a shallow; a strand; a sandbank under water.
4. the broad side of a blade.
5. in music, (a) a character (♭) denoting a tone lower by half an interval than another; (b) the tone or note itself designated by such a character; as, the *flat* of B; (c) on the piano keyboard, a key sounding such a note.
6. a boat, broad and flat-bottomed.
7. a straw hat with a low crown and broad brim.
8. a shallow box or container.
9. a flatcar.
10. a piece of theatrical scenery on a flat frame.
11. a deflated tire.
12. [*pl.*] flat-heeled shoes.
13. an apartment or suite of rooms on one floor of a building.
14. in football, the area flanking either end of the offensive line.
15. in mining, any part of a vein of ore lying in a horizontal position.

flat, *v.t.* and *v.i.*; flatted, *pt., pp.*; flatting, *ppr.* to make or become flat.

flat'bed, flat'-bed, *a.* 1. designating or of a truck, trailer, etc. having a bed or platform without sides or stakes.
2. in printing, designating or of a press having a plane or horizontal printing surface.

flat'bōat, *n.* a broad, boxlike boat with a flat bottom, used for carrying freight in shallow waters or on rivers.

flat'-bot''tŏmed, *a.* having a flat bottom, as a boat.

flat'çap, *n.* a cap with a low crown, once much worn in London; hence, a Londoner.

FLATCAPS

flat'çär, *n.* a railroad car without sides or a roof, for carrying some kinds of freight.

flat'fish, *n.* any of various fishes which have a flat body, swim on the side, and have both eyes on one side, including the flounder, turbot, halibut, and sole.

flat'foot, *n.* 1. a condition in which the instep arch of the foot has been flattened.
2. a policeman: so called from the notion that a policeman's feet are flattened by walking his beat. [Slang.]

flat foot, a foot having a flattened instep arch.

flat'-foot''ed, *a.* 1. having feet with flattened instep arches; having flatfoot.
2. designating a manner of walking, with the toes pointed outward, seen in people with flatfoot.
3. downright and firm; plain and uncompromising. [Colloq.]

to catch flat-footed; (a) to catch unprepared to escape; to take by surprise; (b) to catch in the act of committing some offense. [Colloq.]

Flat'head (-hed), *n.* 1. an American Indian of a tribe that lived in northwestern Montana.
2. a Chinook Indian.
3. [f-] an Australian fish, the barramunda.
4. [f-] the puff adder of North America.

flat'head, *a.* having a head flattened artificially by binding a board upon the forehead in childhood, causing the front part of the head to become flat and to slope backward, as practiced by some primitive groups.

flat'-head''ed, *a.* characterized by a flat head; as, a *flat-headed* bolt, nail, or screw.

flat'ī''ron (-ūrn), *n.* a device which, when heated, is used for pressing clothes or cloth: it consists of a handle and a heavy, shaped piece of iron or steel that is flat and smooth on the undersurface.

flā'tive, *a.* [L. *flatus,* pp. of *flare,* to blow.] producing wind; flatulent. [Obs.]

flat knot, a reef knot: see *knot,* illus.

flat'ling, *adv.* [ME.] 1. flatly; at full length. [Archaic.]
2. with the flat side, as of a sword. [Archaic.]

flat'ling, *a.* struck with the flat side; as, a *flatling* blow. [Archaic.]

flat'lings, *adv.* flatling. [Obs.]

flat'long, *adv.* flatling. [Obs.]

flat'ly, *adv.* 1. horizontally; without inclination.
2. evenly; without elevations and depressions.
3. without spirit; dully; frigidly.
4. peremptorily; positively; downright; as, he *flatly* refused his aid.

flat'ness, *n.* 1. evenness of surface; levelness; equality of surface.
2. want of relief or prominence; as, the *flatness* of a figure in sculpture.
3. deadness; vapidness; insipidity; as, the *flatness* of cider or beer.
4. dejection; a low state of the spirits; depression; want of life.
5. dullness; want of point; insipidity; frigidity.

Some of Homer's translators have swelled into fustian, and others sunk into *flatness.* —Pope.

6. dullness or deadness of sound, as opposed to sharpness, clearness, or sonority.

flat sil'vĕr, silver knives, forks, spoons, etc., as distinguished from trays, teapots, etc.

flat'ten, *v.t.*; flattened, *pt., pp.*; flattening, *ppr.*
1. to make flat or flatter; to reduce to an equal or even surface; to level.
2. to beat or knock down to the ground; to lay flat.
3. to make vapid or insipid; to render stale.
4. to depress; to deject, as the spirits; to dispirit.
5. in music, to lower in pitch, especially by a half note.

to flatten a sail; in nautical usage, to extend a sail lengthwise of the vessel, so that its effect is only lateral.

to flatten out; (a) to make flat or flatter by spreading out; (b) in aeronautics, to return (an airplane) to a horizontal position after diving or climbing.

flat'ten, *v.i.* 1. to grow or become flat or flatter.
2. to become prostrate.
3. to level to the ground.

to flatten out; (a) to become flat or flatter by spreading out; (b) in aeronautics, to become horizontal; to level off.

flat'ten·ing ŏv'en, a heated chamber in which hollow glass cylinders, after being split, are laid upon a plane bed for flattening.

flat'tĕr, *v.t.*; flattered, *pt., pp.*; flattering, *ppr.* [Fr. *flatter*; OFr. *flater*; Pr. *flatar,* to pat, stroke, flatter, perhaps from Ice. *flatr,* flat, as if smoothed by the patting of the hand.]
1. to praise too much, untruly, or insincerely.
2. to try to ingratiate oneself, please, or get the favor of, by praise and attention.
3. to make seem more attractive than is so; as, this photographer *flatters* his subjects.
4. to make feel pleased or honored; gratify the vanity of.
5. to please (the eye, ear, etc.).

to flatter oneself; to be pleased with the idea or belief (*that*); delude oneself into thinking (*that*).

flat'tĕr, *v.i.* to use flattery.

flat'tĕr, *n.* 1. a person who flattens something.
2. a die plate for drawing flat strips.
3. a smith's forging tool with a broad, flat face.

flat'tĕr, *a.* comp. of *flat.*

flat'tĕr·ĕr, *n.* one who flatters.

Syn.—sycophant, parasite.

flat'tĕr·ing, *a.* having or exhibiting flattery.

flat'tĕr·ing·ly, *adv.* in a flattering manner; in a manner to flatter.

flat'tĕr·y, *n.*; *pl.* **flat'tĕr·ies,** [ME. *flaterie, flaterye*; OFr. *flaterie,* from *flater,* to flatter.]
1. the act of flattering.
2. excessive, untrue, or insincere praise; exaggerated compliment or attention; blandishment.

Simple pride for *flattery* makes demands. —Pope.

Syn.—adulation, sycophancy, fawning, servility, toadyism, obsequiousness.

flat'test, *a.* superl. of *flat.*

flat'ting, *n.* 1. a method of painting so that the paint dries without gloss.
2. a method of preserving gilding unburnished, by touching it with size.
3. the act or process of making flat, as rolling or hammering metal, flattening glass in an oven, etc.

flat'ting çōat, in painting, a last coat without gloss.

flat'ting fūr'năce, a flattening oven.

flat'ting mill, a mill with rollers for flattening metals.

flat tīre, 1. a tire from which all or most of the air has escaped.
2. a boring, uninteresting person. [Slang.]

flat'tish, *a.* somewhat flat; approaching flatness.

flat'top, flat'-top, *n.* an aircraft carrier. [Slang.]

flat'ū·lence, *n.* 1. gas generated in the stomach and intestines.
2. airiness or emptiness of speech; vanity.

flat'ū·len·cy, *n.* flatulence.

flat'ū·lent, *a.* [from L. *flatus,* pp. of *flare,* to blow.]
1. gaseous; of or affected with gases generated in the stomach and intestines.

2. turgid with gas; as, a *flatulent* tumor. [Obs.]
3. generating or apt to generate gases in the stomach or intestines, as certain foods.
4. empty or windy in speech; vain; puffy; as, a *flatulent* writer; *flatulent* vanity.

flat'ū·lent·ly, *adv.* in a manner characterized by flatulence.

flat'ū·ous, *a.* [from L. *flatus*, pp. of *flare*, to blow.] windy; generating wind. [Obs.]

flā'tus, *n.*; *pl.* **flā'tus·es** or **flā'tus,** [L., a blowing, from *flare*, to blow.]
1. a breath; a puff of wind.
2. gas generated in the stomach or intestines; flatulence.

flat'wāre, *n.* flat table utensils, as knives, forks, and spoons, or plates, platters, etc.

flat'wāys, *adv.* with the flat side foremost, uppermost, or in contact: opposed to *edgeways*.

flat'wīse, *adv.* flatways.

flat'wŏrm, *n.* any of a large group of worms with a flattened, unsegmented body, as the liver fluke and the tapeworm; any platyhelminth or planarian: many flatworms are parasitic.

flaught'ẽr (flat'), *v.t.* to pare or cut from the ground, as turf. [Scot.]

flaught'ẽr, *v.i.* to flutter; to shine fitfully; to flicker. [Scot.]

Flaun'drish, *a.* Flemish. [Obs.]

flaunt, *v.i.*; flaunted, *pt.*, *pp.*; flaunting, *ppr.* [origin doubtful, compare Sw. dial. *flankt*, from *flanka*, to waver, wave about.]
1. to make a gaudy, ostentatious, conspicuous, impudent, or defiant display; as, brazen women *flaunt* through the town.

You *flaunt* about the streets in your new gilt chariot. —Arbuthnot.

2. to flutter or wave freely.

flaunt, *v.t.* to make a showy, proud, defiant, impudent, or offensive display of; as, to *flaunt* a despised emblem.

flaunt, *n.* 1. a flaunting.
2. anything displayed for show. [Rare.]

flaunt'ing·ly, *adv.* in a flaunting way.

flaunt'y, *a.* flaunting; showy. [Rare.]

flȧ·ū·tī'nō, *n.* [It., dim. of *flauto*, a flute.] in music, (a) a small instrument like a flute; a piccolo; (b) a diminutive accordion.

flau'tist, *n.* a person who plays the flute: also *flutist*.

flā·van'i·line, flā·van'i·lin, *n.* [L. *flavus*, yellow; and *aniline*.] in chemistry, a crystalline dyestuff, $C_{16}H_{14}N_2$, a product of coal tar giving a yellow color to fabrics.

flȧ·vē'dō, *n.* [from L. *flavus*, yellow.] in botany, a diseased condition of a plant in which the green parts become yellow.

Flȧ·vē'ri·ȧ, *n.* [from L. *flavus*, yellow.] a genus of tropical American composite plants.

flȧ·ves'cent, *a.* [from L. *flavus*, yellow, and *-escent*.] turning a pale yellow; yellowish.

flā'vin (*or* flav'in), *n.* [from L. *flavus*, yellow.]
1. a complex heterocyclic ketone, $C_{10}H_6N_4O_2$.
2. any of a group of yellow pigments occurring in certain plant and animal products or prepared by synthesis; specifically, riboflavin; lactoflavin.
3. quercetin.

flā'vine (*or* flav'in), *n.* flavin.

flā'vol, *n.* [L. *flavus*, yellow, and *-ol*.] in chemistry, a yellow substance, $C_{14}H_{10}O_2$, derived from anthracene in crystals.

flā'vōne, *n.* 1. in chemistry, a colorless, crystalline compound, $C_{15}H_{10}O_2$, from which various yellow dyes are formed.
2. any derivative of this compound.

flā·vō·prō'tē·in, *n.* any of a group of proteins linked chemically with flavins, especially one that yields riboflavin upon hydrolysis.

flā·vō·pūr'pū·rin, *n.* [L. *flavus*, yellow, and *purpura*, purple, and *-in*.] in chemistry, a dye of the coal-tar series, $C_{14}H_8O_2$, coloring yellow.

flā'vŏr, *n.* [OFr. *flaor*; prob. from L. *flatus*, wind, *fætor*, foul smell.]
1. an odor; smell; aroma.
2. that quality of a substance which gives it a characteristic taste.
3. any substance added to a food to give it a particular taste; flavoring.
4. the characteristic quality of something; distinctive nature; as, the *flavor* of adventure.

Syn.—taste, savor, relish, smack.

flā'vŏr, *v.t.*; flavored, *pt.*, *pp.*; flavoring, *ppr.* to give flavor to; to communicate some quality to, so as to affect the taste or smell; to impart any characteristic quality to.

flā'vored (-vẽrd), *a.* having flavor, especially if distinctive and noticeable.

flā'vŏr·ing, *n.* an essence, extract, etc. used for imparting flavor.

flā'vŏr·ing ex'tract, the odorous and highly flavored principles of certain plants, dissolved in ethyl alcohol.

flā'vŏr·less, *a.* without flavor; tasteless; having no smell or taste.

flā'vŏr·ous, *a.* full of flavor; pleasant to the taste or smell.

flā'vŏr·y, *a.* flavorous.

flā'vŏur, *n.* flavor: British spelling.

flā'vous, *a.* [L. *flavus*, yellow.] yellow. [Obs.]

flaw, *n.* [ME. *flawe*, from Sw. *flaga*, a flake, flaw, break; Dan. *flage*, a flake.]
1. a breach; a crack; a defect made by breaking or splitting; a gap or fissure; a faulty place; as, a *flaw* in a china dish, or in a glass; a *flaw* in a wall.
2. a defect; a fault; an error; as, a *flaw* in reputation; a *flaw* in a will, or in a statute.
3. a falsehood. [Scot.]
4. a disease of the fingernails. [Obs.]

Syn.—blemish, defect, imperfection, breach, break, crack, split, rent.

flaw, *v.t.*; flawed, *pt.*, *pp.*; flawing, *ppr.* 1. to break; to crack.

The brazen caldrons with the frosts are *flawed*. —Dryden.

2. to break; to violate; as, to *flaw* a league. [Rare.]

flaw, *v.i.* to become faulty.

flaw, *n.* [prob. from ON. *flaga*, sudden onset, or cognate D. *vlage*.]
1. a sudden, brief gust of wind, often with rain or snow; squall.
2. a sudden burst of noise and disorder; a tumult; an uproar. [Obs.]

flawed, *a.* defective; having blemishes.

flaw'flow·ẽr, *n.* the European pasqueflower.

flaw'less, *a.* without cracks; without defect; perfect.

flawn, *n.* [ME. *flaun*, *flawn*; OFr. *flaon*; LL. *flado* (*-onis*), from O.H.G *flado*, a flat cake, pancake.] a sort of flat custard or pie. [Archaic.]

flaw'y, *a.*; *comp.* flawier; *superl.* flawiest, 1. full of flaws or cracks; broken; defective; faulty.
2. subject to sudden gusts of wind.

flax, *n.* [ME. *flax*, *flex*; AS. *fleax*, *flex*, flax.]
1. any of several slender, erect plants with delicate blue flowers and narrow leaves: the seeds are used to make linseed oil, and the fibers of the stem are spun into linen thread.
2. the threadlike fibers of these plants, ready for spinning.
3. any of a number of flaxlike plants.

false flax; in botany, a plant, *Camelina sativa*, of the *Cruciferæ*, resembling flax, with pale yellow flowers.

mountain flax; in mineralogy, a very fine, silky variety of asbestos.

native flax; same as *flax plant*.

New Zealand flax; same as *flax plant*.

FLAX (*Linum usitatissimum*) section of plant and seed vessel

flax bĩrd, the scarlet tanager; also, any of various birds feeding upon flaxseeds.

flax brāke, a machine for breaking the dried stems of flax in order to remove them from the fiber.

flax cōmb, a kind of comb with long, sharp steel teeth for removing the woody parts of flax from the fiber; a hatchel.

flax cot'tŏn, a cottonlike form of flax produced by artificial process upon the fiber.

flax'en, *a.* 1. of or made of flax.
2. resembling flax in color; pale-yellow; straw-colored.

flax mill, a mill for manufacturing flax fabrics.

flax plant, in botany, a plant, *Phormium tenax*, of the lily family, whose leaves yield a strong, coarse fiber used for cordage: called also *flax bush* and *New Zealand flax*.

flax pull'ẽr, a machine for uprooting and gathering flax.

flax'seed, *n.* the seed of flax; linseed: it is used in medicine and for making linseed oil.

flax stär, a species of primrose with green flowers.

flax'weed, *n.* *Linaria vulgaris*, the common toadflax; butter and eggs.

flax'y, *a.*; *comp.* flaxier; *superl.* flaxiest, of or like flax; being of a light color; fair.

flāy, *v.t.*; flayed, *pt.*, *pp.*; flaying, *ppr.* [ME. *flean*, *flan*; AS. *flean*; D. *vlaen*, to flay.]
1. to skin; to strip off the skin of, as by whipping.
2. to criticize or scold mercilessly.
3. to rob; plunder; pillage.

flāy'ẽr, *n.* one who strips off the skin.

flēa, *n.* [ME. *flee*, *fle*; AS. *fleah*, *flea*, a flea, prob. from *fleon*, to flee.] any of several small, wingless, jumping insects that are parasitic and bloodsucking.

a flea in one's ear; a sharp, stinging rebuke, rebuff, or hint.

FLEA (1/8 in. long)

flēa'bāne, *n.* a name given to various plants, from their supposed efficacy in driving away fleas. They belong to the genera *Conyza*, *Erigeron*, and *Pulicaria*.

flēa bee'tle, any one of several species of small beetles characterized by strong hind legs used for jumping, as the *Haltica chalybea*, infesting and injuring grapevine.

flēa'bīte, *n.* 1. the bite of a flea.
2. the red spot on the skin caused by the bite of a flea.
3. a trifling wound or pain, or a trifling inconvenience.

flēa'-bit″ten, *a.* 1. bitten by a flea or fleas.
2. infested with fleas.
3. wretched; miserable; decrepit.
4. light-colored with reddish-brown spots: said of horses.

flēak, *n.* a flake. [Obs.]

flēak'ing, *n.* an under layer of reeds in thatching. [Brit. Dial.]

flēa louse, a small insect of the *Psyllidæ* family, resembling the plant louse.

flēam, *n.* [OFr. *flieme*, from LL. *flebotomus*, *phlebotomus*; Gr. *phlebotomon*, a lancet; *phleps*, *phlebos*, a vein, and *temnein*, to cut.] a lancet, or a surgical knife, especially one used for opening veins for letting blood: also called *phlebotome*.

flēam tooth, a tooth, as of a saw, having the form of an isosceles triangle, cutting equally on both sides.

flēam'y, *a.* filled with phlegm. [Obs.]

flēar, *v.t.* and *v.i.* fleer. [Obs.]

flēa'wŏrt, *n.* 1. a European aromatic herb with rough leaves and yellow flowers.
2. a plantain whose seeds, which more or less resemble fleas, are used as a laxative.

flèche (flāsh), *n.* [Fr., an arrow.]
1. in military engineering, a simple, two-faced parapet or other fortification, forming a sharp angle in front and open at the rear.
2. in architecture, a spire; specifically, a spire over the intersection of the nave and the transept in some Gothic churches.

FLÈCHE

fleck, *n.* [Ice. *flekkr*, Sw. *fläcka*, a spot.]
1. a spot; a small colored area; a mark; a speck.
2. a small piece; a particle; a flake.

fleck, *v.t.*; flecked (flekt), *pt.*, *pp.*; flecking, *ppr.* [ME. *flecken*, *flekken*; Ice. *flekka*, to spot, stain, from *flekkr*, a spot, stain.] to cover or sprinkle with flecks; to spot; to variegate; to dapple.

Both *flecked* with white, the true Arcadian strain. —Dryden.

fleck'ẽr, *v.t.* to fleck.

fleck'less, *a.* not flecked; without a stain; hence, clean; innocent; blameless.

flect'ed, *a.* [from L. *flectere*, to bend.] bent: used in heraldry.

flec'tion, *n.* [L. *flectio* (*-onis*), from *flectere*, to bend.]
1. the act of bending, or state of being bent.
2. a bent part or bend.
3. in grammar, inflection.

Also spelled *flexion*.

flec'tion·ăl, *a.* relating to or like flection: also spelled *flexional*.

flec'tŏr, *n.* a flexor. [Rare.]

fled, *v.* past tense and past participle of *flee*.

fledġe (flej), *a.* [ME. *flegge*, *fligge*, able to fly, from AS. *fleogan*, to fly.] feathered; furnished with feathers or wings; able to fly. [Obs.]

fledġe, *v.t.*; fledged, *pt. pp.*; fledging, *ppr.* 1. to rear (a young bird) until it is able to fly.

2. to supply or cover (an arrow, etc.) with feathers.

3. to furnish or cover with a soft covering, as feathers, hair, etc.

fledġe, *v.i.* to become covered with feathers; to become well enough feathered to fly; as, the birds have *fledged* and gone.

fledġ'ling, fledġe'ling, *n.* 1. a young bird just fledged.

2. a young and inexperienced person.

fledġ'ling, fledġe'ling, *a.* raw; inexperienced; unskilled; as, a *fledgling* doctor.

fledġ'y, *a.* covered with feathers or down.

flee, *v.i.*; fled, *pt.*, *pp.*; fleeing, *ppr.* [ME. *flee, fleen, fleon*; AS. *fleon*, to flee.]

1. to run with rapidity, as from danger; to attempt to escape; to hasten from danger or expected evil; as, the enemy *fled* at the first fire.

Arise, take the young child and his mother
and *flee* into Egypt. —Matt. ii. 13.

2. to depart; to leave quickly and suddenly; to hasten away; to disappear; to vanish.

Resist the devil, and he will *flee* from you.
—James iv. 7.

3. to move rapidly; to go swiftly.

flee, *v.t.* to run away or try to escape from; to avoid; to keep at a distance from.

fleece, *n.* [ME. *fleese, flese, fleose*; AS. *fleos, fles*, fleece.]

1. the coat of wool worn by a sheep or other wool-bearing animal.

2. the amount of wool shorn from an animal at one time.

3. any covering of a fleecy character.

4. a soft, warm, napped fabric, used for linings, etc.

5. in manufacturing, a thin delicate layer of wool or cotton fiber gathered upon a cylinder in a carding machine and stripped off by a doffing knife.

fleece, *v.t.*; fleeced (flēst), *pt.*, *pp.*; fleecing, *ppr.* 1. to shear off, as a covering or growth of wool. [Rare.]

2. to shear the fleece from (sheep, etc.).

3. to strip of money, property, etc. by fraud; to rob, cheat, or swindle.

4. to spread over as with wool.

fleeced (flēst), *a.* furnished with a fleece or with fleeces; as, a sheep is well *fleeced*.

fleece'less, *a.* having no fleece.

fleece'-līned, *a.* having the inner surface fleeced.

fleec'ẽr, *n.* one who strips or takes by fraud or trickery.

fleece wool, wool shorn from a living animal, as distinguished from that taken from a dead animal.

fleec'i·ness, *n.* the quality of being fleecy.

flee'cy, *a.*; *comp.* fleecier; *superl.* fleeciest, 1. made of or covered with fleece; woolly; as, a *fleecy* flock.

2. resembling wool or a fleece; soft and light; as, *fleecy* snow; *fleecy* locks.

flē'ẽr, *n.* one who flees or runs away. [Rare.]

fleer, *v.i.*; fleered, *pt.*, *pp.*; fleering, *ppr.* [ME. *flerien, fliren*; Norw. *flira*, to titter, laugh at nothing.]

1. to deride; to sneer; to make a wry face in contempt or scorn; as, to *fleer* and flout.

Covered with an antic face,
To *fleer* and scorn at our solemnity.
—Shak.

2. to leer; to grin with an air of civility. [Obs.]

fleer, *v.t.* to mock; to laugh derisively at.

fleer, *n.* 1. derision or mockery, expressed by words, laughs, or looks.

And mark the *fleers*, the gibes, and notable
scorns. —Shak.

2. a grin of civility. [Obs.]

A sly treacherous *fleer* upon the face of de-
ceivers. —South.

fleer'ẽr, *n.* a mocker; one who fleers.

fleer'ing·ly, *adv.* in a fleering manner.

fleet, *n.* [ME. *fleet*; AS. *fleot*, an arm of the sea, estuary, place where ships float.] a creek, inlet, bay, river, or estuary; an arm of the sea. [Obs. or Dial.]

Fleet marriages; clandestine and often scandalous marriages formerly performed in or near the Fleet Prison, without license or other requisite legal formality, by unscrupulous clergymen. They were forbidden by statute in 1753.

the Fleet; (a) a former small creek in London, now a covered sewer; (b) Fleet Prison, a debtors' prison which stood near this creek.

fleet, *n.* [ME. *fleet, flete, fleot*, a fleet, ship; AS. *fleot*, a ship, from *fleotan*, to float.]

1. (a) a number of warships acting together and under one command, usually in a definite area of operation; as, the Pacific *Fleet* of the Navy; (b) the entire naval force of a country; navy.

2. any group of ships, trucks, buses, airplanes, etc. acting together or under one control.

3. (a) a set of fishing nets, pots, etc. worked together; (b) a single fishing line with 100 hooks.

fleet, *a.*; *comp.* fleeter; *superl.* fleetest, [from the following v.]

1. swift of pace; moving or able to move with rapidity; nimble; light and quick in motion, or moving with lightness and celerity; as, a *fleet* horse or dog.

2. evanescent. [Poet.]

3. light; superficially fruitful; thin; not penetrating deep, as soil. [Brit. Dial.]

fleet, *v.i.*; fleeted, *pt. pp.*; fleeting, *ppr.* [ME. *fleten*; AS. *fleotan*.]

1. originally, to float; swim.

2. to move swiftly; flit; fly.

3. to pass away swiftly; to disappear. [Archaic.]

How all the other passions *fleet* to air!
—Shak.

4. in nautical usage, to change place or position; as, sailors *fleet* forward and aft.

5. to slip, as a cable on the ridges of a capstan.

6. to gutter, as a candle. [Brit. Dial.]

to fleet away; to vanish. [Archaic.]

fleet, *v.t.* [ME. *fleten*, to skim, from AS. *flete, fliete*, cream, skimmings, from *fleotan*, to float.]

1. to skim the surface of; to pass over rapidly; as, a ship that *fleets* the gulf.

2. to cause to pass lightly, or in mirth and joy; as, to *fleet* the time. [Rare.]

3. in nautical usage, to move or cause to move; to cause to change position; as, to *fleet* the crew aft.

fleet'-foot, fleet'-foot·ed, *a.* swift of foot; running or able to run with rapidity.

fleet'ing, *a.* passing rapidly; flying with speed; not durable; as, the *fleeting* hours or moments; *fleeting* pleasures.

Syn.—transient, transitory, brief, ephemeral, evanescent, flitting, fugitive, flying, passing, temporary, vanishing.

fleet'ing·ly, *adv.* in a fleeting manner.

fleet'ings, *n.pl.* curdled milk; curds. [Brit. Dial.]

fleet'ly, *adv.* rapidly; lightly and nimbly; swiftly.

fleet'ness, *n.* swiftness; rapidity; velocity; celerity; speed; as, the *fleetness* of a horse or deer.

Syn.—celerity, quickness, rapidity, velocity, swiftness, speed.

Fleet Street, 1. an old street in London, where many newspaper and printing offices are now located.

2. the London press.

Flem'ing, *n.* 1. a native or inhabitant of Flanders.

2. a Belgian who speaks Flemish.

Flem'ish, *a.* pertaining to Flanders, the Flemings, or their language.

Flemish bond; see *bond*, n. 13.

Flemish brick; a hard, yellowish paving brick.

Flemish coil; a coil of rope like a watch spring.

Flemish eye; in nautical usage, an eye made by dividing the strands of a rope at the end and lapping them over each other.

Flemish horse; the outer short footrope on a topsail yardarm.

Flemish knot; a figure-of-eight knot: see *knot*, illus.

Flemish school; a school of painting originating in Flanders at the beginning of the fifteenth century, Rubens and Van Dyck being among its best-known exponents.

Flem'ish, *n.* the low German language of the Flemings.

the Flemish; the people of Flanders.

flench, *v.t.* to flense.

flense, *v.t.*; flensed (flenst), *pt.*, *pp.*; flensing, *ppr.* [Dan. *flense*; Sw. *flänsa*, to slash, cut up.] to cut up, as a whale, to obtain the blubber or skin.

flesh, *n.* [ME. *flesh, fleisch, flesc*; AS. *flæsc*, flesh.]

1. the soft substance of the body (of a person or animal) between the skin and the bones; especially, the muscular tissue.

2. the pulpy or edible part of fruits and vegetables.

3. the flesh of any animal as food; meat; especially, meat other than fish or fowl.

4. the human body, as distinguished from the soul.

As if this *flesh*, which walls about our life,
Were brass impregnable. —Shak.

5. man in general; mankind; humanity.

She was fairest of all *flesh* on earth,
Guinevere. —Tennyson.

6. human nature, in a good or bad sense; especially, the sensual nature of the human body.

Ye judge after the *flesh*. —John viii. 15.

7. all living beings; as, the way of all *flesh*.

8. the surface of the human body; as, Renoir's technique in painting *flesh*.

9. the usual color of a white person's skin; yellowish pink.

10. kindred; stock; family.

He is our brother, and our *flesh*.
—Gen. xxxvii. 27.

after the flesh; according to outward appearances; carnally; humanly.

flesh and blood; the human body, especially as subject to its natural limitations.

in the flesh; (a) alive; (b) actually present; in person.

one flesh; one person; as, husband and wife become *one flesh*.

one's (own) flesh and blood; a person or persons closely related to one by birth.

flesh, *v.t.*; fleshed (flesht), *pt.*, *pp.*; fleshing, *ppr.* 1. to feed (animals) with flesh so as to incite them to hunt or kill.

2. to prepare for or incite to bloodshed, etc. by a foretaste.

3. to harden; inure.

4. to plunge (a weapon) into flesh.

5. to clothe with flesh.

6. to put flesh on; to fatten.

7. to remove flesh from (a hide).

8. to glut; to satiate; to feed full with flesh or fleshly pleasures.

flesh, *v.i.* to grow fat. [Colloq.]

flesh'brush, *n.* a brush for stimulating circulation in the skin or flesh by friction.

flesh'-cŏl"ŏred, *a.* having the color of the surface of a white person's body; yellowish-pink.

flesh'-ēat"ing, *a.* habitually eating flesh; carnivorous.

fleshed (flesht), *a.* 1. initiated; accustomed; glutted.

2. fat; fleshy.

flesh'ẽr, *n.* 1. a kind of two-handled, blunt-edged knife used for scraping the flesh from hides.

2. one who scrapes the flesh from hides.

3. a butcher. [Scot.]

flesh flēa, the chigoe.

flesh flȳ, an insect that lays its eggs in dead or decaying flesh, as those of the genus *Sarcophaga*: also called *blowfly*.

flesh'hood, *n.* the condition of being an animal or of being a body of flesh.

flesh'i·ness, *n.* the state of being fleshy; abundance of flesh or fat in animals; plumpness; corpulence; grossness.

flesh'ings, *n.pl.* 1. flesh-colored, tight-fitting garments, worn by acrobats, etc.

2. scrapings removed from hides by the flesher.

flesh'less, *a.* destitute of flesh; lean.

flesh'li·ness, *n.* a fleshly state or quality.

flesh'ling, *n.* a person devoted to carnal things. [Obs.]

flesh'ly, *a.* 1. pertaining to the flesh; of the body and its nature; corporeal.

2. fond of bodily pleasures; carnal; worldly; lascivious.

Abstain from *fleshly* lusts. —1 Pet. ii. 11.

3. fleshy.

flesh'ly, *adv.* in a fleshly manner. [Archaic.]

flesh mēat, animal food; the flesh of animals prepared or used for food.

flesh'ment, *n.* eagerness gained by a successful initiation; the state or process of being fleshed. [Rare.]

flesh'mŏn"gẽr, *n.* 1. one who deals in flesh; a butcher. [Obs.]

2. a procurer; a pimp. [Obs.]

flesh'pot, *n.* 1. a pot for cooking meat.

2. [*pl.*] bodily comfort and pleasures; luxury, especially when regarded with envy or longing.

flesh'quāke (-kwāk), *n.* a trembling of the flesh. [Obs.]

flesh tint, the natural color of flesh: a term used in painting.

flesh wŏrm, 1. the larva of a flesh fly; a maggot.

2. the trichina, or spiral threadworm.

flesh wŏund, a wound that does not reach the bones or vital organs.

flesh'y, *a.*; *comp.* fleshier; *superl.* fleshiest. 1. having much flesh; fat; plump; corpulent; as, a *fleshy* thigh; a *fleshy* man.
2. of or like flesh.
3. having a firm pulp; pulpy: said of some fruits.
4. corporeal; pertaining to the bodily nature, as distinguished from the moral. [Obs.]

flet, *v.* obsolete past participle of *fleet.*

fletch, *v.t.* to feather, as an arrow.

fletch, *v.t.* to cut in strips, as fish; to flitch.

fletch'ẽr, *n.* [ME. *fletcher, flecchere*; OFr. *flechier*, an arrow maker, from *fleche*, an arrow.] an arrow maker or featherer; a manufacturer of bows and arrows. [Archaic.]
It is commended by our *fletchers* for bows, next unto yew. —Mortimer.

Fletch'ẽr·ism, fletch'ẽr·ism, *n.* [after Horace *Fletcher* (1849–1919), Am. dietician.] the practice of chewing food slowly and thoroughly, advocated as an aid to digestion.

flēte, *v.t.* and *v.i.* to fleet. [Obs.]

fleth'ẽr, *v.t.* to flatter. [Scot.]

fleūr″-de-lis' (-lē'), *n.*; *pl.* **fleūrs″-de-lis'** (flẽr″-de-lēz'), [Fr., flower of the lily.]
1. the iris (plant or flower).
2. the coat of arms of the former French royal family.
3. in heraldry, an emblem resembling a lily or iris: also *fleur-de-lys, flower-de-luce.*

FLEUR-DE-LIS

fleū·ron', *n.* [Fr., a flower, jewel, from *fleur*, a flower.] in ornamental art, a conventional form of a small flower, usually terminal or apical, but sometimes constituting a member, as the link of a chain.

fleūr'y, *a.* see *flory.*

flew, *v.*, past tense of *fly.*

flew, *n.* a flue (fishing net).

flewed, *a.* having flews; deep-mouthed: said of dogs.

flews, *n.pl.* the large chop or overhanging lip of a deep-mouthed hound or other dog.

flex, *v.t.* and *v.i.*; flexed (flext), *pt., pp.*; flexing, *ppr.* [L. *flexus*, pp. of *flectere*, to bend, curve.]
1. to bend, as the arm.
2. to contract, as a muscle.

flex·an'i·mous, *a.* [L. *flexanimus*, from *flexus*, pp. of *flectere*, to bend, and *animus*, mind.] having power to change the mind. [Obs.]

flex·i·bil'i·ty, *n.* [LL. *flexibilitas*, from L. *flexibilis*, that may be bent or curved.] the quality of being flexible; pliancy; flexibleness; as, the *flexibility* of whalebone.

flex'i·ble, *a.* [L. *flexibilis*, from *flexus*, pp. of *flectere*, to bend, curve.]
1. that may be bent; capable of being turned or forced from a straight line or form without breaking; pliant; yielding to pressure; not stiff; as, a *flexible* rod; a *flexible* plant.
2. capable of yielding to entreaties, arguments, or other moral force; that may be persuaded to compliance; not rigid or obstinate; not inexorable; tractable.
Phocion was no ways *flexible* to the will of the people. —Bacon.
3. that may be adapted or accommodated; adjustable to change; plastic; as, a *flexible* language.
This was a principle more *flexible* to their purpose. —Rogers.
Syn.—pliable, pliant, supple.

flex'i·ble·ness, *n.* the condition or quality of being flexible.

flex'i·bly, *adv.* in a flexible manner.

flex'ile, *a.* [L. *flexilis*, pliant, that may be bent, from *flexus*, pp. of *flectere*, to bend, curve.] flexible; pliant; pliable; easily bent; yielding to power, impulse, or moral force.

flex'iŏn (flek'shun), *n.* [L. *flexio* (-*onis*), from *flexus*, pp. of *flectere*, to bend, curve.] same as *flection.*

flex'iŏn·ăl, *a.* same as *flectional.*

flex'i·tīme, *n.* [*flexi*ble and *time.*] a system allowing individual employees some flexibility in choosing the time, but not the number, of their working hours.

flex'ŏr, *n.* [LL., from L. *flexus*, pp. of *flectere*, to bend.] in anatomy, a muscle that bends a limb or other part of the body: opposed to *extensor.*

flex'tīme, *n.* same as *flexitime.*

flex'ū·ōse, *a.* flexuous.

flex·ū·os'i·ty, *n.* 1. the quality or state of being flexuous.
2. *pl.* **flex·ū·os'i·ties,** a curve or winding.

flex'ū·ous, *a.* [L. *flexuosus*, full of turns, tortuous, from *flexus*, pp. of *flectere*, to bend.]
1. winding; having turns or windings; as, a *flexuous* rivulet.
2. wavering; not steady; as, a *flexuous* flame.
3. in botany, bending or bent; changing its direction in a curve, from joint to joint, from bud to bud, or from flower to flower; as, a *flexuous* branch.

flex'ū·ous·ly, *adv.* in a flexuous manner.

flex'ū·răl, *a.* relating to flexure.

flex'ūre, *n.* [L. *flexura*, a winding.]
1. a winding, curving, flexing, or bending.
2. the part bent; a joint, bend, curve, or fold.
3. the bending of the body; obsequious or servile cringing.
4. in astronomy, the slight bending of an instrument due to its own weight, or the correction of error due to such change.
5. in geology, a bending of a stratum under pressure.
6. the bend of a bird's wing.
7. in mechanics, a strain under which certain plane surfaces are bent or deformed.
8. in geometry, same as *curvature.*

fley, *v.t.* and *v.i.* to frighten; to take fright. [Scot. Dial.]

fley, *n.* a fright. [Scot. Dial.]

Flib'bẽr·ti·gib″bet, Flib'bẽr·di·gib″bet, *n.* 1. the name of a devil. [Obs.]
2. [f–] an imp; one who looks impish.
3. [f–] a person, especially a woman, who chatters constantly.
4. [f–] an irresponsible, flighty person.

flick, *n.* [prob. partly echoic and partly back-formation from *flicker.*]
1. a light, quick stroke or blow, as with a whip; sudden, jerky movement; snap.
2. a light, snapping sound, as of the flick of a whip.
3. a fleck; splotch; streak; dash.

flick, *v.t.* 1. to strike, throw, remove, etc. with a light, quick, snapping stroke.
2. to make a light, quick, snapping stroke with (a whip, etc.).

flick, *v.i.* to move quickly and jerkily; flutter.

flick, *n.* flitch. [Obs.]

flick'ẽr, *v.i.*; flickered, *pt., pp.*; flickering, *ppr.* 1. to flutter; to flap the wings without flying; to strike rapidly with the wings.
And *flickering* on her nest made short essays to sing. —Dryden.
2. to move with a quick, light, wavering motion.
3. to burn or shine unsteadily, as a candle in the wind.

flick'ẽr, *v.t.* to cause to flicker or waver.

flick'ẽr, *n.* 1. a flickering.
2. a dart of flame or light, as in a flickering fire.
3. a brief, passing feeling; as, a *flicker* of fear.
4. [*pl.*] the motion pictures. [Earlier Slang.]

flick'ẽr, *n.* [echoic of the bird's note.] a North American woodpecker, *Colaptes auratus*, characterized by golden-colored wings and a red, crescent-shaped mark on the back of the head: called also *yellowhammer.*

flick'ẽr·ing·ly, *adv.* in a flickering manner.

flick'ẽr·mouse, *n.* the bat; the flittermouse.

flidġe (flij), *a.* fledge. [Obs.]

flidġe, *v.i.* to fledge. [Obs.]

flīed, *v.* past tense and past participle of *fly* (only in reference to baseball: see *fly*, v.i.).

flī'ẽr, *n.* 1. one who or that which flies or flees.
2. a runaway; a fugitive.
3. a bus, train, etc. that has a fast schedule.
4. any step in a straight stairway.
5. a small handbill widely distributed.
6. an aviator.
7. any person or thing capable of great speed; as, he drove a team of *fliers.*
8. a part in machinery that moves rapidly; as, the *flier* of a jack.
9. a reckless venture in speculative business; as, to take a *flier* in stocks. [Slang.]
Also spelled *flyer.*

flīght (flīt), *v.t.* to scare; to cause to flee. [Obs.]

flīght, *n.* [ME. *flight, flyght, fluht*; AS. *flugon*, from *fleon*, to flee.] the act of fleeing; the act of running away from or as from danger or expected evil; hasty departure.
Pray ye that your *flight* be not in the winter. —Matt. xxiv. 20.
to put to flight; to force to run away; make flee.
to take to flight; to run away; flee.

flīght, *v.i.* to take flight in numbers; to migrate, as game birds.

flīght, *n.* [ME. *flight, flyght, fluht*; AS. *flyht*, from *fleogan*, to fly.]
1. the act, manner, or power of flying; volitation; as, the *flight* of birds and insects.
2. the distance flown or that can be flown at one time by an airplane, bird, projectile, etc.
3. a flock or number of beings or things flying through the air together; as, a *flight* of birds, arrows, or bees.
4. (a) a formation of military airplanes in flight; (b) a basic organizational unit of an air force, consisting of a small number of planes of the same type.
5. an airplane scheduled to fly a certain route at a certain time.
6. a trip by airplane.
7. an outburst, mounting, or soaring above the ordinary; lofty elevation and excursion; as, a *flight* of imagination or fancy; a *flight* of ambition.
8. the section of a stairway leading from one landing to the next; as, a *flight* of stairs.
9. in the clapper of a bell, the tail or part below the hammer.
10. the glume or husk of oats, etc. [Brit. Dial.]
11. in angling, tackle that spins the bait around rapidly.
12. in archery, (a) a contest in distance shooting; (b) a special arrow for such shooting: also *flight arrow.*

flīght'ed, *a.* in heraldry, feathered.

flīght'ẽr, *n.* in brewing, a horizontal vane which rotates in a cooler to induce a circular current in the wort.

flīght feath'ẽr (feth'), in ornithology, a stiff feather of a bird's wing.

flīght fọr·mā'tion, the orderly arrangement of two or more airplanes flying together as a unit in close proximity, as for their mutual protection in warfare.

flīght'i·ly, *adv.* in a flighty manner.

flīght'i·ness, *n.* the state or quality of being flighty.

flīght'less, *a.* not able to fly.

flīght of·fi·cẽr, an officer in the United States Air Force ranking just below a second lieutenant.

flīght'shot, *n.* distance which an arrow flies.

flīght'y, *a.* 1. fleeting; swift. [Rare.]
2. given to sudden whims or fancies; unsettled; fickle; frivolous.
3. disordered in mind; somewhat demented.

flim'flam, *n.* [a reduplication of *flam.*]
1. nonsense; rubbish; humbug.
2. a sly trick or deception.

flim'flam, *a.* 1. nonsensical.
2. tricky; deceptive.

flim'flam, *v.t.*; flimflammed, *pt., pp.*; flimflamming, *ppr.* to cheat; to trick; to swindle; to deceive. [Colloq.]

flim'mẽr-ball, *n.* [G. *flimmern*, to glimmer, glitter.] an almost spherical microscopic marine protozoan, covered with delicate swimming organs or cilia.

flim'si·ly, *adv.* in a flimsy manner.

flim'si·ness, *n.* the state or quality of being flimsy; thin, weak texture; weakness; want of substance or solidity.

flim'sy, *a.*; *comp.* flimsier; *superl.* flimsiest. [perhaps from W. *llymsi*, sluggish, spiritless.]
1. thin and easily broken or damaged; fragile; frail.
2. without adequate substance or sense; trivial; ineffectual; as, a *flimsy* excuse.
Syn.—gauzy, poor, thin, transparent, trifling, trivial, inane, slight, superficial, weak, shallow, unsubstantial.

flim'sy, *n.* 1. extremely thin paper, as transfer paper, used by newspaper reporters.
2. copy written on this kind of paper.

flinch, *v.i.*; flinched (flincht), *pt., pp.*; flinching, *ppr.* [a nasalized form of ME. *flecchen*, to flinch, waver.]
1. to draw back, as from a blow or an attack.
2. to draw back from anything difficult, dangerous, or painful; wince; shrink.
3. formerly, in croquet, to let the foot slip when holding a ball under it for a stroke.

flinch, *n.* 1. a flinching; a shrinking.
2. a card game played by building the cards up on the table in a certain order.

flinch'ẽr, *n.* one who flinches or fails.

flinch'ing, *n.* a shrinking or drawing back under pain or difficulty; a flinch.

flinch'ing·ly, *adv.* in a flinching manner.

flin'dẽr, *n.* see *flinders.*

flin'dẽr·mouse, *n.* a flittermouse; a bat. [Dial.]

flin'dẽrs, *n.pl.* [G. *flinder, flinter*, a small piece of shining metal; D. *flenter*, a broken piece.] small pieces or splinters; fragments; as, to break into *flinders*.

fling, *v.t.*; flung, *pt.*, *pp.*; flinging, *ppr.* [ME. *flyngen*, *flengen*, to hurl, rush; Ice. *flengja*, to whip, ride furiously.]

1. to cast, send, or throw from the hand; to hurl; to cast forth with force or suddenness; as, she *flung* her hat aside.

'Tis fate that *flings* the dice; and as she *flings*,
Of kings makes peasants, and of peasants, kings. —Dryden.

2. to put abruptly or violently; as, the crowd was *flung* into confusion.

3. to throw down; overthrow.

4. to move (one's arms, legs, head, etc.) suddenly or impulsively; as, he *flung* his arms about her.

5. to move or enter into hastily and with spirit: used reflexively; as, he *flung* himself into the task.

6. to throw aside; disregard; as, she *flung* caution to the winds.

7. to diffuse; to send forth; to emit; to scatter.

Every beam new transient colors *flings*. —Pope.

to fling about; to scatter in every direction.

to fling away; to reject; to discard; as, *fling away* ambition.

to fling down; (a) to demolish; to ruin; (b) to throw to the ground.

to fling in; to throw in; to make an allowance or deduction for, or not to charge in an account.

to fling off; to baffle in the chase; to defeat of prey; to get rid of.

to fling oneself about; to dash here and there in an agitated manner.

to fling open; to throw open; to open suddenly or with violence; as, *to fling open* a door.

to fling out; to utter sharply or harshly; as, *to fling out* hard words against another.

to fling up; to relinquish; to abandon; as, *to fling up* a situation or an office.

fling, *v.i.* 1. to flounce; to fly into violent and irregular motions; as, the horse began to kick and *fling*.

2. to utter harsh language; to sneer; to upbraid; as, the scold began to flout and *fling*.

3. to rush or spring with violence or haste; to dash; to rush.

fling, *n.* 1. a flinging; a throw; a flounce; a cast from the hand.

2. a gibe; a sneer; a sarcasm; a taunting remark.

I, who love to have a *fling*
Both at senate-house and king. —Swift.

3. a lively dance; as, the Highland *fling*.

4. a brief time of wild actions and unrestrained indulgence in pleasure; as, he had his *fling*.

Give me my *fling*, and let me say my say. —Tennyson.

5. a trial effort; as, he had a fling at working. [Colloq.]

6. a matter of no importance. [Obs.]

England were but a *fling*,
Save for the crooked stick and the gray goose wing. —Old Proverb.

fling'dust, *n.* a streetwalker. [Obs.]

fling'ẽr, *n.* one who flings.

flint, *a.* made or composed of flint; hard and firm, like flint; as, *flint* glass; *flint* wheat; *flint* implements.

flint, *n.* [ME. *flint*; AS. *flint*, flint rock.]

1. a very hard stone, a kind of quartz, which produces sparks when struck against steel: it is usually brown, black, or gray.

2. a piece of this stone, used to start a fire, as material for primitive tools and weapons, etc.

3. anything extremely hard or firm like flint.

to skin a flint; to be guilty of or capable of obtaining money in any mean or hardhearted way.

flint āġe, the Stone Age.

flint brick, a firebrick of hard quality made of pulverized flint.

flint çorn, a variety of Indian corn with very hard kernels.

flint glȧss, a hard, bright kind of glass, distinguished by its containing oxide of lead combined with potassium silicate: used in the manufacture of table glassware, lenses, etc.: named from its formerly having been made from flints.

flint'-heärt"ed, *a.* having a hard, unfeeling heart; cruel.

flint im'plē·ments, tools and weapons made of flint and other hard stones: used by men before they knew how to work with metals and still in use by some primitive peoples.

flint'i·ness, *n.* the quality or state of being flinty; hardness.

flint'lock, *n.* 1. a kind of gunlock in which the priming charge was ignited by a spark from a flint held between the jaws of the cock, or

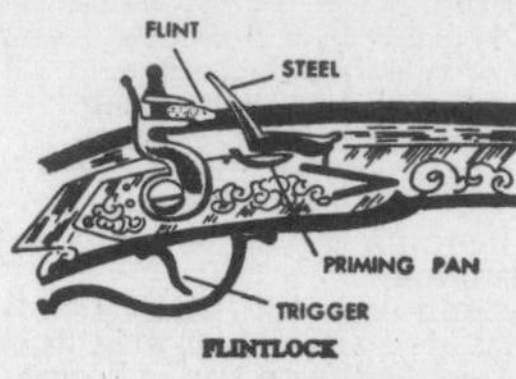

FLINTLOCK

hammer, and struck against a metal plate. It succeeded the matchlock, and was superseded by the percussion lock.

2. an old-fashioned musket equipped with such a lock.

flint mill, a mill for grinding flints.

flint'stōne, *n.* a hard siliceous stone; flint.

flint wąll, a wall containing pieces of broken flints.

flint'wãre, *n.* a kind of earthenware in the manufacture of which ground flints are mixed with the clay.

flint'wood, *n.* the very hard wood of an Australian tree, the mountain ash, *Eucalyptus pilularis*.

flint'y, *a.*; *comp.* flintier; *superl.* flintiest, 1. containing or made of flint; as, a *flinty* rock.

2. like flint; very hard and firm; as, a *flinty* heart.

flip, *n.* a mixed drink composed of ale, beer, cider, etc. and, sometimes, milk and eggs, sweetened, spiced, and heated.

flip, *v.t.*; flipped (flipt), *pt.*, *pp.*; flipping, *ppr.* [echoic.] 1. to toss or move with a quick jerk; flick; fillip; as, *flip* the drawer shut.

2. to toss (a coin, etc.) by snapping with the thumb against the finger.

flip, *v.i.* 1. to make a quick, light stroke, as with the finger or a whip; to snap.

2. to move jerkily.

to flip up; to toss up a coin and see which side will land uppermost, as in determining a choice.

flip, *n.* a flipping; a snap, tap, or jerk.

flip, *a.*; *comp.* flipper; *superl.* flippest, flippant; saucy; pert; impertinent. [Colloq.]

flip dog, an iron used, when heated, to warm flip.

flīpe, *v.t.* to turn inside out, as a stocking in drawing it off. [Brit. and Scot. Dial.]

flip'flap, *adv.* with a flapping noise.

flip'flap, *n.* a continued flapping noise, as of something broad and flat, as a board.

flip'păn·cy, *n.* 1. the quality or state of being flippant, presumptuous, or trifling in speech or conduct; pertness.

2. *pl.* **flip'păn·cieș**, a flippant act or remark.

flip'pănt, *a.* [Ice. *fleipa*, to babble, prattle; *fleipr*, babble, tattle.]

1. of smooth, fluent, and rapid speech; speaking with ease and rapidity; having a voluble tongue; talkative. [Rare.]

2. pert; impertinently talkative; disrespectfully frivolous; saucy; impertinent.

Away with *flippant* epilogues.—Thomson.

Syn.—pert, forward, superficial, saucy, malapert.

flip'pănt, *n.* a person given to flippancy. [Rare.]

flip'pănt·ly, *adv.* in a flippant manner.

flip'pănt·ness, *n.* flippancy.

flip'pẽr, *n.* [from *flip*, v.]

1. a broad, flat part or limb adapted for swimming, as in seals, turtles, whales, etc.

2. the hand. [Slang.]

flīrt, *v.t.*; flirted, *pt.*, *pp.*; flirting, *ppr.* [AS. *fleardian*, to trifle, *fleard*, a foolish thing.]

1. to throw with a jerk or sudden effort or exertion; as, the boys *flirted* water in each other's faces.

2. to move suddenly and jerkily; to wave back and forth with short, quick movements; as, to *flirt* a fan.

3. to jeer or scoff at; to flout. [Obs.]

flīrt, *v.i.* 1. to jeer or gibe; to throw bantering or sarcastic words; to utter contemptuous language. [Obs.]

2. to run and dart about; to move jerkily or unevenly; to be unsteady or fluttering.

3. to play the coquette; to coquet; to make insincere advances; to play at love.

4. to trifle; to play; to toy; as, he *flirted* with the idea of quitting his job.

flīrt, *n.* 1. a sudden jerk; a darting motion; a flutter.

In unfurling the fan are several little *flirts* and vibrations. —Addison.

2. a quick, jerky throw or toss.

3. one who flirts; especially, a girl or woman who plays at love; a coquette.

Several young *flirts* about town had a design to cast us out of the fashionable world. —Addison.

flīrt, *a.* pert; wanton. [Obs.]

flīr·tā'tion, *n.* 1. a quick, sprightly motion. [Obs.]

2. playing at love without serious intentions; flirting; coquetry.

3. a superficial, rather playful love affair.

flīr·tā'tious, *a.* 1. inclined to flirt; given to flirtation.

2. of or characteristic of flirtation.

flīrt'-ġill, *n.* a pert girl; a wanton. [Obs.]

flīrt'i·gig, *n.* a giddy girl. [Dial.]

flīrt'ing·ly, *adv.* in a flirting manner.

flīrt'y, *a.* flirtatious.

flisk, *v.i.* to frisk; to caper. [Obs.]

flisk, *n.* 1. a playful motion; a caper. [Scot.]

2. a whisk broom or brush. [Brit. Dial.]

3. a large-toothed comb. [Brit. Dial.]

flit, *v.t.* 1. to cause to flit or remove; to remove; to dispossess. [Scot. and Brit. Dial.]

2. to move (furnishings, etc.) to other quarters. [Archaic.]

flit, *v.i.*; flitted, *pt.*, *pp.*; flitting, *ppr.* [ME. *flitten*; *flytten*, *flutten*, to move, depart, migrate; Ice. *flytja*; Sw. *flytta*, to remove, carry.]

1. to pass lightly and rapidly; as, memories *flitted* through his mind.

2. to fly with a light, rapid motion; to dart along; to move with celerity through the air; to flutter; as, a bird *flits* away or *flits* in air.

3. to go away. [Dial.]

4. to move from one residence to another, especially by stealth. [Scot. and Brit. Dial.]

5. to be changing or evanescent. [Obs.]

flit, *n.* a flitting; light, rapid movement.

flit, *a.* nimble; quick; swift; fleet. [Obs.]

flitch, *n.*; *pl.* **flitch'eș**, [ME. *flicche*, *fliche*; AS. *flicce*; Ice. *flikki*, a flitch of bacon.]

1. the side of a hog salted and cured; a side of bacon.

2. one of several planks, timbers, or iron plates fastened together side by side to make a large girder or compound beam.

3. a lengthwise strip from the outside of a tree trunk.

4. a thin slice smoked or cut for smoking, as of halibut.

flitch, *v.t.*; flitched (flicht), *pt.*, *pp.*; flitching, *ppr.* to cut into flitches, as a hog.

flīte, *n.* a scolding; a quarrel; a dispute. [Archaic or Dial.]

flīte, *v.i.* and *v.t.* [ME. *fliten*; AS. *flitan*; akin to O.H.G. *flīzan*, to strive.]

1. to quarrel with (a person).

2. to scold.

[Archaic or Dial. in both senses.]

flit'tẽr, *v.t.* and *v.i.* [freq. of *flit*.] to move rapidly and lightly; to flutter. [Chiefly Dial.]

flit'tẽr, *v.i.* to scatter in pieces. [Obs.]

flit'tẽr, *n.* 1. a person or thing that flits.

2. a rag; a tatter.

flit'tẽr·mouse, *n.*; *pl.* **flit'tẽr·mīce**, a bat. [Obs.]

flit'tẽrn, *a.* in tannery, designating or of the bark stripped from young oak trees, which is more valuable than that of old trees.

flit'ti·ness, *n.* unsteadiness; levity; lightness. [Obs.]

flit'ting, *n.* 1. a flying with lightness and speed; a fluttering.

2. a removal from one dwelling to another. [Scot. and Brit. Dial.]

flit'ting·ly, *adv.* in a flitting manner.

flit'ty, *a.* unstable; fluttering. [Obs.]

fliv'vẽr, *n.* a small, cheap automobile, airplane, etc. [Slang.]

fliv'vẽr, *v.i.* to fail. [Slang.]

flix, *n.* down; fur; especially, the down of the beaver.

flix'weed, *n.* hedge mustard.

flō, *n.* [ME. *flo*, *flon*; AS. *flan*, an arrow.] an arrow. [Obs.]

flōat, *n.* [ME. *flote*; AS. *flota*, a boat, ship, from *fleotan*, to float.]

1. anything that stays, or causes something else to stay, on the surface of a liquid; specifically, (a) an air-filled bladder in a fish;

(b) a cork on a fishing line; (c) a floating ball that regulates water level, as in a boiler or tank; (d) a raft; (e) a life preserver; (f) the landing gear on an amphibious airplane.

2. a low, flat, decorated vehicle for carrying exhibits, tableaux, etc. in a parade.

3. [*often pl.*] a row of footlights on a stage.

4. a floating. [Rare.]

5. a flowing; overflowing; flood. [Obs.]

6. a trowel for spreading plaster or cement.

7. a block for polishing marble.

8. an apparatus for tempering steel by a stream of water.

9. a shoemaker's tool for smoothing the inside of a shoe.

10. a coal cart. [Brit.]

11. a low, swinging cart for hauling heavy material.

12. a drag used by farmers for smoothing plowed ground.

13. in mining, fragments of mineral found on the surface.

14. a floating dock or wharf.

15. the act of allowing a currency to float on the market.

flōat, *v.i.*; floated, *pt., pp.*; floating, *ppr.* [ME. *flotien*; AS. *flotian*, to float, swim, from *fleotan*, to float.]

1. to stay on the surface of a fluid; to be buoyed up; as, the ship *floats*.

2. to move or be conveyed on water; as, the raft *floats* down the river.

Three blustering nights, borne by the southern blast,
I *floated*. —Dryden.

3. to drift gently; to move without effort on water, in air, etc.

They stretch their broad plumes and *float* upon the wind. —Pope.

4. to move or drift about vaguely and without purpose; as, idle thoughts *floated* through his mind.

5. to fluctuate freely in relationship to other currencies, as determined by supply and demand: said of a currency.

flōat, *v.t.* 1. (a) to cause to stay on the surface of a liquid; (b) to bring to the surface and cause to stay there.

2. to hold up; to bear; as, enough water to *float* a fleet.

3. to flood.

4. to put into circulation; to place on the market; to start; as, they *floated* a bond issue.

5. to smooth (cement, plaster, etc.).

6. to refine or make (pigments) smooth by grinding them and floating them in a stream of water.

7. to support in business; as, to *float* a company or firm.

8. to allow the exchange value of (a currency) to fluctuate freely in relationship to other currencies.

flōat'ȧ·ble, *a.* capable of being floated.

flōat'ăge, *n.* same as *flotage*.

flōat·ā'tion, *n.* same as *flotation*.

flōat bōard, 1. a board on the rim of an undershot water wheel, which receives the impulse of the stream by which the wheel is driven.

2. one of the paddles of a steamer's paddle wheel.

flōat çāse, an airtight case or drum used in lifting by means of the upward pressure of water.

flōat çop'pēr, minute particles of copper carried away by the action of water.

flōat'ēr, *n.* 1. a person or thing that floats.

2. an instrument for registering the level of a liquid.

3. (a) a voter who is attached to no particular party, especially one whose vote may be purchased; (b) a person who illegally casts a vote at each of several polling places.

4. a person who changes his place of residence or work at frequent intervals; especially, a transient laborer. [Colloq.]

5. [*pl.*] same as *muscae volitantes*.

flōat'-feed, *a.* having the flow of fuel regulated by a float, as some carburetors.

flōat grȧss, any species of grass growing in low, marshy places, as the meadow foxtail, *Alopecurus geniculatus*.

flōat'ing, *a.* 1. that floats.

2. not fixed; not remaining in one place; moving about; as, the *floating* population in wartime industry.

3. in finance, (a) designating an unfunded, short-time debt resulting from current operations and having no specified date for repayment; (b) not permanently invested; used for current expenses; as, *floating* capital.

4. in medicine, displaced, especially downward, from the normal position; as, a *floating* kidney.

floating anchor; a sea anchor; a drag used at sea to keep a ship's head to the wind or prevent drifting.

floating battery; in military usage, a battery mounted upon a float of some kind, as upon a raft or rafts.

floating bridge; (a) a bridge of logs or timber with a floor of plank, supported by water; (b) in military engineering, a kind of double bridge, the upper one projecting beyond the lower one, and capable of being moved forward by pulleys, used for carrying troops over narrow moats in attacking the outworks of a fort; (c) a kind of large steam ferryboat; (d) a pontoon bridge; (e) the movable platform of a ferry dock.

floating dock; a dock that can be lowered in the water for the entrance of a ship, and then raised for use as a dry dock.

floating heart; an aquatic plant of the genus *Limnanthemum*, whose leaves are heart-shaped.

floating island; (a) a floating mass of earth resembling an island; (b) a boiled custard dessert topped with meringue or whipped cream.

floating lever; one of two horizontal brake levers under the center of a railroad car body.

floating light; a lightship.

floating pier; a pier that rises and falls with the tide.

floating ribs; the eleventh and twelfth pairs of ribs, which are not attached to the breastbone or to other ribs; false ribs.

floating screed; a strip of plastering put on to help keep even the thickness of the coat.

floating supply; the supply of stocks, securities, etc. that can be readily bought on the open market.

flōat'ing, *n.* 1. the act of floating.

2. in weaving, a thread of weft which floats, spans, or crosses on the top of several warped threads.

3. in plastering, the second coat of three-coat work.

flōat'ing·ly, *adv.* by floating or as if by floating.

flōat min'ēr·ăl, fragments of ore found at a distance from their native bed or vein, as the result of erosion.

flōat'stōne, *n.* 1. a spongy variety of opal which is light enough to float on water.

2. in bricklaying, a stone employed in smoothing curved work.

flōat valve, a valve regulated by a float.

flōat'y, *a.* buoyant; swimming on the surface; light. [Rare.]

floç, *n.* [from *floccule*.] a very fine, fluffy mass formed by the aggregation of fine suspended particles, as in smoke: also spelled *flock*.

floç'cī, *n.* pl. of *floccus*.

floç·cil·lā'tion, *n.* [from L. *floccus*, a flock of wool.] in pathology, a picking or plucking at the bed clothes by a delirious patient.

floç·çōse', *a.* [LL. *floccosus*, full of flocks of wool, from *floccus*, a flock of wool.]

1. covered with soft wool or hair; flocculent.

2. in botany, covered with tufts of woolly or long, soft hairs; woolly.

floç'çū·lăr, *a.* pertaining to a flocculus.

floç'çū·lāte, *v.i.* and *v.t.*; flocculated, *pt., pp.*; flocculating, *ppr.* [from L. *floccus*, a flock of wool.] to collect in tufts or bunches, as soils, clouds, etc.

floç'çū·lāte, *a.* in entomology, bearing a tuft of stiff and sometimes curly hairs.

floç·çū·lā'tion, *n.* the process of flocculating.

floç'çūle, *n.* [a dim. from L. *floccus*, a flock of wool.] a small detached mass of matter resembling a soft tuft of wool; a floc.

floç'çū·lence, *n.* 1. the state of being flocculent.

2. a peculiar white, waxy excretion of certain insects.

floç'çū·lent, *a.* 1. woolly; fluffy.

2. containing or consisting of small woolly masses.

3. covered with a waxy, woollike substance, as some insects.

4. in chemistry, designating certain precipitates resembling tufts of wool.

floç'çū·lī, *n.* pl. of *flocculus*.

floç'çū·lōse, *a.* flocculent; in botany, floccose.

floç'çū·lus, *n.*; *pl.* **floç'çū·lī,** [dim. from L. *floccus*, a flock of wool.]

1. a small, woolly or hairy tuft.

2. in anatomy, a small, tuftlike lobe on the under side of each half of the cerebellum.

3. a small tuft of hair or feathers; as, the *flocculi* on the legs of an insect.

4. in astronomy, a woolly, cloudlike mass of vapor in the sun's atmosphere.

floç'çus, *n.*; *pl.* **floç'cī,** [L., a flock of wool.]

1. in zoology, a tuft of wool or hair, especially on the end of an animal's tail.

2. [*pl.*] in botany, the fibrous, woollike tufts of hair found sometimes on the sporules of certain fungi.

flock, *n.* [ME. *flock, flok, floc*; AS. *floc, flocc*, a band, company.]

1. a group of certain animals, especially of sheep and goats, living, feeding, etc. together.

2. a group of birds of any kind; as, a *flock* of wild geese, a *flock* of ducks, a *flock* of blackbirds.

3. the members of a church, under a leader figuratively called a *shepherd* or *pastor*.

4. a large number of people or things.

5. the children in one family.

flock, *v.i.*; flocked (flokt), *pt., pp.*; flocking, *ppr.* to assemble or travel in a flock or flocks; to gather in companies or crowds; as, people *flock* together in seasons of disaster; they *flock* to the playhouse.

Syn.—herd, congregate, throng, assemble, crowd.

flock, *n.* [OFr. *floc*; L. *floccus*, a flock or lock of wool.]

1. a lock or tuft of wool or hair.

2. old cloth, rags, wool refuse, and remnants cut and shredded for use in upholstery.

3. the inferior wool fibers added to low-grade fabrics to give weight.

4. a floc.

5. finely powdered wool or cloth used for making flock paper.

flock, *v.t.* to stuff or cover with flock.

flock bed, a bed filled with flocks of wool, or pieces of cloth; a bed stuffed with flock.

A house well furnish'd shall be thine to keep;
And for a *flock bed* I can shear my sheep.
—Dryden.

flock'ling, *n.* a member of a flock. [Obs.]

flock pā'pēr, a kind of wallpaper covered with flock (sense 5): also called *velvet paper*.

flock'y, *a.* abounding with flock or flocks; woolly; flocklike; floccose.

flōe, *n.* [Dan. *is-flage*; Norw. *is-flak*, dial. *is-flok*, an ice floe.]

1. a large, flat field or sheet of floating ice formed at the surface of a sea, etc.

2. a piece of such a field or sheet broken off and floating free.

The whole sea was covered with *floes* varying from a few yards to miles in diameter.
—Moss.

flōe rat, the ringed seal.

flog, *v.t.*; flogged, *pt., pp.*; flogging, *ppr.* [prob. an abbrev. of L. *flagellare*, to whip.]

1. to beat or strike with a strap, stick, or whip; to whip; to lash; as, to *flog* a schoolboy.

2. in fishing, to lash (the water) repeatedly with the line.

3. to beat, in the sense of to surpass; to excel. [Brit. Dial.]

to flog a dead horse; to try to revive interest in a stale subject.

flog'gēr, *n.* 1. one who flogs.

2. a sort of mallet to start the bung of a cask: also called *bung starter*.

flog'ging, *n.* a whipping for punishment; a chastisement.

flog'ging chis'el, a large cold chisel for removing irregularities from castings.

flog'ging ham'mēr, a machinist's heavy hammer for driving a flogging chisel.

flōne, *n.* an arrow. [Obs.]

flong, *v.* obsolete past tense and past participle of *fling*.

flong, *n.* the matrix used in the papier-mâché process of stereotyping, or the paper of which it is composed.

flŏod (flud), *v.t.*; flooded, *pt., pp.*; flooding, *ppr.*

1. to overflow; to inundate; to deluge; as, to *flood* a meadow; the river rose and *flooded* the surrounding country.

2. to cover, fill, or overwhelm like a flood; as, to *flood* the country with cheap literature.

3. to put much or too much water on or in; as, the sprinkler *flooded* the lawn.

flŏod, *v.i.* 1. to rise and overflow; as, the Nile *floods* annually.

2. to come out like a flood; to gush out.

3. to have menstrual or post-partum hemorrhage.

flŏod, *n.* [ME. *flood, flod*; AS. *flod*, flowing water, a river.]

1. an overflowing of water on land usually dry; an inundation; a deluge; as, there is an annual *flood* of the Nile.

2. (a) the flowing of the tide toward the

shore; the rising of the tide: opposed to ebb; (b) the rising tide: also *flood tide.*

3. a great flow or outpouring; as, a *flood* of bank notes, a *flood* of paper currency.

4. a great stream of any fluid or fluidlike substance; as, a *flood* of light, a *flood* of lava.

5. menstrual discharge when excessive.

6. a floodlight. [Colloq.]

7. (a) water, as opposed to land; (b) a large body of water; ocean, sea, lake, or river. [Archaic or Poetic.]

the Flood; the Deluge; the great flood in the days of Noah: Gen. 7.

Syn.—deluge, inundation, abundance, overflow, submergence, superabundance.

flood'āge, *n.* an overflow. [Rare.]

flood an'chŏr, the anchor that holds a ship during the flood tide.

flood çŏn·trōl', the protection of land from floods by the construction of river embankments, soil conservation, reforestation, etc.

flood'ēr, *n.* one who causes a flood.

flood fence, a fence constructed to withstand the force of a flood.

flood'gāte, *n.* 1. a gate in a stream or canal, to control the height and flow of the water; a sluice.

2. anything like this in controlling a flow or an outburst; as, to open the *floodgates* to crime.

flood'ing, *n.* 1. the act of overflowing; inundation.

2. uterine hemorrhage.

flood'līght, *n.* 1. an artificial light of high intensity, usually with a reflector that causes it to shine in a broad beam.

2. such a beam of light.

flood'līght, *v.t.*; floodlighted *or* floodlit, *pt., pp.*; floodlighting, *ppr.* to throw a broad beam of light on; to illuminate by a floodlight.

flood märk, the mark or line to which the tide rises; high-water mark.

flood plāin, in geology, the area in a river valley covered with soil deposited by floods.

flood tīde, the rising tide: opposed to *ebb tide.*

flōor, *v.t.*; floored, *pt., pp.*; flooring, *ppr.* 1. to cover or furnish with a floor; as, to *floor* a house with pine boards.

2. to knock down or lay level with the floor; as, to *floor* an antagonist.

3. (a) to defeat; to put to silence; (b) to puzzle; perplex; confuse. [Colloq.]

4. to finish; to put an end to; as, to *floor* a bottle of wine. [Slang.]

5. to press down to the floor; as, to *floor* an accelerator. [Colloq.]

flōor, *n.* [ME. *floor, flore, flor*; AS. *flor*, a floor.]

1. that part of a building or room on which one walks; the bottom or lower part.

2. the corresponding surface of anything; as, the ocean *floor.*

3. a story in a building; as, the first *floor*, the ground *floor.*

4. a platform of a bridge; also, any similar platform.

5. in legislative bodies, stock exchanges, etc., the part of the house set apart for members; as, the distinguished visitor was admitted to the *floor.*

6. the right to be heard; as, the gentleman from Illinois has the *floor.*

7. in malting, a quantity of grain spread out upon a floor for steeping: also called *piece.*

8. a minimum price level for any commodity.

9. in nautical usage, the flat part of a ship's bottom.

10. in mining, (a) any nearly flat surface on which a deposit lies; (b) a flat, or nearly flat, mass of ore.

flōor'āge, *n.* the area of a floor or floors; floor space; as, the building has a *floorage* of ten thousand square feet.

flōor'çloth, *n.* 1. linoleum, oilcloth, etc. used for covering floors.

2. a cloth used for washing or mopping floors.

flōor çramp, a device for holding strips of flooring in place until they are nailed.

flōor'ēr, *n.* 1. one who makes or lays floors.

2. one who or that which floors, as a blow which floors a person.

3. figuratively, anything which leads to a person's defeat or which overmasters him; as, in the universities, an examination question which a student cannot answer. [Slang.]

flōor ex'ēr·cīşe, in gymnastics, any of several exercises, as cartwheels, handstands, and ballet movements, performed without apparatus.

flōor'head (-hed), *n.* in shipbuilding, an outer end of the floor timbers.

flōor'ing, *n.* 1. a floor.

2. floors collectively.

3. materials for floors.

flōor lēad'ēr, a member of a legislature who is chosen by fellow members of his political party to direct their activities on the floor.

flōor'less, *a.* having no floor.

flōor līght (līt), any opening in a floor for the admission of light.

flōor'man, *n.* 1. a floorwalker.

2. an employee whose duty is to clean, arrange and store goods, hoist loads, etc. on or onto a specified floor of a building.

3. a blacksmith's helper whose work is to remove old shoes, to trim the hoofs, and to nail on new shoes.

flōor plan, 1. in architecture, a scale drawing showing the size and arrangement of rooms, halls, etc. on one floor of a house or other building.

2. in shipbuilding, a drawing representing a waterline section of a ship, and showing the bottom timbers.

flōor'shōw, *n.* an entertainment provided by a night club, café, or other establishment, consisting usually of dancing, singing, and orchestral music.

flōor tim'bēr, one of the timbers on which a floor is laid; in shipbuilding, one of the timbers placed immediately across the keel.

flōor'wąlk''ēr (-wąk''), *n.* a person employed by a department store to walk about, give information, supervise sales, maintain order, prevent or detect thievery, etc.

flọọ'zy, flọọ'zie, *n.*; *pl.* **flọọ'zieş,** 1. a loose, disreputable woman or girl. [Slang.]

2. any woman or girl. [Slang.]

Also spelled *floosy.*

flop, *v.t.*; flopped (flopt), *pt., pp.*; flopping, *ppr.* [a form of *flap.*]

1. to clap or strike, as the wings, the tail, or the flippers; to flap.

2. to cause to fall noisily and clumsily.

3. to turn over suddenly; as, to *flop* a board.

flop, *v.i.* 1. to move or flap around loosely or clumsily, usually with a thud or thuds.

2. to fall or drop in this way; as, he *flopped* wearily into a chair.

3. to make a sudden change.

4. to fail. [Colloq.]

5. to sleep. [Slang.]

to flop over; (a) to turn over heavily or suddenly; (b) to go over to another side or party. [Slang.]

flop, *n.* 1. a flopping.

2. the sound of flopping.

3. a failure. [Colloq.]

4. a place to sleep. [Slang.]

flop, *adv.* with a flop.

flop'house, *n.* a kind of hotel where a night's lodging can be had very cheaply.

flop'ō''vēr, *n.* in television, faulty reception in which the picture appears to move repeatedly up or down the screen.

flop'py, *a.* liable to flop; given to flopping; as, a *floppy* hat. [Colloq.]

flop'py disk, flop'py disç, a small, flexible, relatively inexpensive computer disc for storing data.

Flō'rȧ, *n.* [L. *Flora*, goddess of flowers; *flos, floris*, a flower.]

1. in classical mythology, the goddess of flowers.

2. [f–] *pl.* **flō'rȧş, flō'rae,** the plants of any particular country, region, or period; as, the *flora* of New England: frequently used in association with *fauna*; as, the *fauna* and *flora* of North America.

3. [f–] in botany, a treatise on the species of plants of a region or geological period.

4. one of the small planets or asteroids between the orbits of Mars and Jupiter.

flō'răl, *a.* [L. *floralis*, from *flos, floris*, a flower.]

1. of, made of, or like flowers.

2. [F–] pertaining to Flora; as, *Floral* games.

floral emblem; any flower or plant that is the symbol of a city, country, state, etc.

floral envelope; the perianth, or external covering, of a flower.

Flō·rā'li·ȧ, *n.pl.* in Roman mythology, festive ceremonies held in honor of Flora in the spring.

flō'răl·ly, *adv.* in a floral manner.

flō'ran, *n.* fine-grained tin, either scarcely perceptible in the stone or stamped very small.

Flo·ré·al' (flō-rā-äl'), *n.* [Fr., from L. *floreus*, of flowers, from *flos, floris*, a flower.] the eighth month (April 20–May 19) of the French Revolutionary Calendar, adopted by the First Republic in 1793.

flō'rē·ā·ted, *a.* same as *floriated.*

flor'en, flor'ein, *n.* same as *florin.*

flor'ence, *n.* [from *Florence*, in Italy.]

1. an ancient gold coin of Edward III, value six shillings sterling. [Obs.]

2. a kind of thin silk cloth.

3. [F–] a kind of red wine produced in Tuscany. [Obs.]

Florence flask; see under *flask.*

Flor'en·tīne, *a.* of Florence, Italy, or its people, culture, or art.

Florentine mosaic; a kind of mosaic, often representing natural objects, as leaves and flowers in colors, and laid with precious stones in a surface of black or white marble.

Flor'en·tīne, *n.* 1. a native or inhabitant of Florence.

2. [f–] a kind of silk cloth of fine texture.

3. [f–] a kind of meat or fruit pie baked in a dish, without under crust. [Obs.]

flō·res'cence, *n.* [L. *florescens* (*-entis*), ppr. of *florescere*, to begin to bloom, incept. of *florere*, to bloom, from *flos, floris*, a flower.]

1. a blooming; a blossoming.

2. the condition or period of blooming.

3. a period of success or achievement.

flō·res'cent, *a.* putting forth flowers; blooming.

flō'ret, *n.* [OFr. *floret*, dim. of *flor*, a flower.]

1. a little flower.

2. one of the little flowers in a clustered or compact inflorescence, as in the *Compositæ* or in the spikelet of grasses.

3. a kind of silk floss or yarn.

4. a fencing foil. [Obs.]

flō·rē'tum, *n.* [from L. *flos, floris*, a flower.] a garden for the cultivation and scientific study of flowers.

flō'ri·āge, *n.* [from L. *flos, floris*, a flower, and *-age*.] bloom; blossom. [Obs.]

flō'ri·ā·ted, *a.* having floral decorations.

flor'i·çan, *n.* same as *florikan.*

flō'ri·çōme, *n.* a sponge spicule with rays ending in a bunch of curved branches.

flō·riç'ō·mous, *a.* [LL. *floricomus*; *flos, floris*, a flower, and *coma*, hair of the head.] resembling a floricome.

flō·ri·çul'tūr·ăl, *a.* relating to floriculture.

flō'ri·çul·tūre, *n.* [L. *flos, floris*, a flower, and *cultura*, cultivation.] the cultivation of flowers, especially of decorative flowering plants.

flō·ri·çul'tūr·ist, *n.* an expert in floriculture.

flor'id, *a.* [L. *floridus*, flowery, from *florere*, to bloom, flower.]

1. rosy; ruddy; highly colored: said of the complexion.

2. highly decorated; gaudy; showy; ornate; as, a *florid* passage in music, etc.

3. decorated with flowers; flowery. [Rare.]

Syn.—ruddy, rubicund, flowery, ornate.

Flōr'i·dăn, *a.* and *n.* Floridian.

Flō·rid'ē·ae, *n.pl.* [from L. *floridus*, flowery, from *flos, floris*, a flower.] a subclass of red algae, *Rhodophyceae.*

flō·rid'ē·ous, *a.* relating to the *Florideæ.*

Flō·rid'i·ăn, *a.* of Florida.

Flō·rid'i·ăn, *n.* a native or inhabitant of Florida.

flō·rid'i·ty, *n.* the state or quality of being florid.

flor'id·ly, *adv.* in a florid manner.

flor'id·ness, *n.* 1. brightness or freshness of color or complexion.

2. embellishment; brilliant ornamentation: applied to style.

flō·rif'ēr·ous, *a.* [L. *florifer*; *flos, floris*, a flower, and *ferre*, to bear.] producing flowers; blooming abundantly.

flor''i·fi·çā'tion, *n.* the act, process, or state of flowering.

flō'ri·fọrm, *a.* [L. *flos, floris*, a flower, and *forma*, form.] in the form of a flower.

flor'i·lege, *n.* florilegium. [Obs.]

flor·i·lē'gi·um, *n.*; *pl.* **flor·i·lē'gi·ȧ,** [L. *florilegus*, flower culling; *flos, floris*, a flower, and *legere*, to gather.]

1. the culling or gathering of flowers.

2. a treatise on flowers.

flor'in, *n.* [Fr., from It. *fiorino*, originally a Florentine coin showing a lily, from *fiore*, from L. *flos*, a flower.]

1. originally, a gold coin which first appeared at Florence, Italy, about 1252.

2. an English silver coin equal to two shillings.

3. any of various European silver or gold coins.

flō·ri·pon'di·ō, *n.* [Sp.] a Peruvian plant, *Datura sanguinea.*

flō'rist, *n.* [L. *flos, floris*, a flower, and *-ist*.] a dealer in cultivated and cut flowers; one who raises flowers for sale.

flō·ri·sū′ġent, *a.* [L. *flos, floris,* a flower, and *sugens (-entis),* ppr. of *sugere,* to suck.] sucking flowers: applied to birds and insects which suck honey from flowers.

flō·rọọn′, *n.* [ME. *flouroun,* flowerwork; OFr. *floron,* a flower, jewel, from *flos, floris,* a flower.] a border made ornamental by being worked with flowers; a flower border.

-flō·rous, [L. *-florus,* from *flos, floris,* a flower.] a suffix meaning *having many* or *a* (specified) *number of flowers,* as in multi*florous,* tri*florous.*

flō′rụ·it, [L.] he (or she) flourished: used when dates of birth and death are unknown.

flor′ū·lȧ, *n.*; *pl.* **flor′ū·lae,** [dim. of *flora.*] a small flora, especially of some particular region.

flō̤r′ū·lent, *a.* [L. *florulentus,* flowery.] flowery; blossoming. [Obs.]

flō′ry, *a.* [Fr. *fleuré,* flowered, from *fleur;* L. *flos, floris,* a flower.] in heraldry, bearing flowers: written also *fleury.*

flos′çū·lăr, *a.* [from L. *flosculus,* a little flower, dim. of *flos, floris,* a flower.] in botany, composed of florets; discoid.

flos·çū·lā′ri·ăn, *n.* in zoology, one of a typical genus of rotifers, characterized by ciliated tentacles resembling the florets of a composite flower.

flos′çūle, *n.* [L. *flosculus,* a little flower.] in botany, a single flower of a compound or composite flower; a floret.

flos′çū·lous, *a.* same as *floscular.*

flos fer′rī, [L., flower of iron.] a variety of aragonite, often occurring in veins of iron ore.

flosh, *n.* [perhaps from G. *flösse,* a box in which ore is washed.] a trough in which ore is placed for stamping.

floss, *n.* [OFr. *flosche;* It. *floscia,* soft, flabby, from L. *fluxus,* flowing, loose.]
 1. the rough silk covering a silkworm's cocoon.
 2. the short, downy waste fibers of silk.
 3. a downy or silken substance in the husks and other parts of certain plants, as corn.
 4. untwisted filaments of the finest silk, used in embroidering: also called *floss silk.*

floss hōle, in a blast furnace, an opening for withdrawing slag.

flos″si·fi·çā′tion, *n.* florification. [Rare.]

floss silk, the portions of soft, untwisted silk broken off in the filature of cocoons; floss. It is used chiefly for embroidery and cheap silk fabrics.

floss′y, *a.*; *comp.* flossier; *superl.* flossiest. 1. pertaining to, composed of, or resembling floss; fluffy.
 2. showy; elegant; fancy. [Slang.]

floss′y, *n.* 1. a woman or girl of showy dress and light morals. [Slang.]
 2. any woman or girl. [Slang.]
 Also spelled *flossie.*

flot, *n.* [Scot.] scum; floating grease, as in fatty broth.

flō′tȧ, *n.* [Sp., a fleet.] a fleet; especially, a fleet of Spanish ships which formerly sailed yearly from Cadiz to Vera Cruz, in Mexico, to transport to Spain the products of Spanish America.

flō′tăge, *n.* 1. the act, condition, or power of floating.
 2. anything that floats; especially, floating debris; flotsam.
 Also spelled *floatage.*

flō′tănt, *a.* [Fr. *flottant,* ppr. of *flotter,* to float.] in heraldry, represented as flying, swimming, or floating in air or in water; as, a banner *flotant.*

A BANNER FLOTANT

flō·tā′tion, *n.* 1. the act or condition of floating or launching.
 2. the act of beginning or financing a business by selling an entire issue of bonds, securities, etc.
 3. the act of beginning; a becoming established.
 4. in mining, a method of ore separation in which finely powdered ore is introduced into a bubbling solution to which oils are added: certain minerals float on the surface, and others sink.
 Also spelled *floatation.*
 center of flotation; in shipbuilding, the center of a plane of flotation.
 plane (or *line*) *of flotation;* the plane or line in which the surface of a fluid at rest cuts a body floating in it.
 surface of flotation; in a ship, the surface included by the extreme planes of flotation in rolling and pitching.

flō′tā·tive, *a.* pertaining to flotation.

flōte, *v.* and *n.* float. [Obs.]

flōte, *n.* fleet. [Obs]

flot′ẽr·y, *a.* fluttery. [Obs.]

flō·til′lȧ, *n.* [Sp. *flotilla,* dim. of *flota,* a fleet.] a little fleet or a fleet of small vessels.

flot′săm, *n.* [Anglo-Fr. *floteson;* OFr. *flotaison,* a floating, from *floter,* to float, from AS. *flotian,* to float.] goods lost by shipwreck, and floating on the sea: distinguished from *jetsam.*
 flotsam and jetsam; (a) the wreckage of a ship or its cargo found floating on the sea or washed ashore; (b) miscellaneous trifles or worthless things; (c) transient, unemployed people; drifters; vagrants.

flot′sŏm, flot′sŏn, *n.* flotsam. [Obs.]

flounce, *v.i.*; flounced (flounst), *pt., pp.*; flouncing; *ppr.* [Sw. dial. *flunsa,* to plunge, dip; Norw. *flunsa,* to hurry, work hurriedly.]
 1. to spring, turn, or twist with sudden effort or violence; to jerk; to struggle, as a horse in mire.
 You neither fume, nor fret, nor *flounce.*
 —Swift.
 2. to move with quick flings or turns, as in anger or impatience; as, to *flounce* out of a room.

flounce, *n.* a flouncing.

flounce, *n.* a narrow piece of cloth sewed to a petticoat, frock, or gown, with the lower border loose and spreading; a wide, ornamental ruffle.

flounce, *v.t.*; flounced (flounst), *pt., pp.*; flouncing, *ppr.* to trim with a flounce or flounces.

floun′cing, *n.* material for making flounces; also, a flounce or flounces collectively.

floun′dẽr, *n.*; *pl.* **floun′dẽrṣ, floun′dẽr,** [ME. *flounder, flowndur;* Sw. and Norw. *flundra,* a flounder.]
 1. a flatfish of the family *Pleuronectidæ,* as the plaice.
 2. a tool used in bootmaking to crimp boot fronts.

floun′dẽr, *v.i.*; floundered, *pt., pp.*; floundering, *ppr.* [prob. var. of *founder.*]
 1. to struggle awkwardly to move, as in deep mud or snow; to plunge about in a stumbling manner.
 2. to speak or act in an awkward, confused manner, with hesitation and frequent mistakes.
 Syn.—roll, blunder, bungle, boggle, wallow, tumble.

floun′dẽr, *n.* a floundering.

flour, *n.* [earlier spelling of *flower;* compare Fr. *fleur de farine;* Sp. *flor de la harina,* lit., flower of meal.] the meal of wheat or any other grain finely ground, especially the fine part separated by sifting or grinding; hence, any substance in a fine or powdered condition.
 graham flour; unsifted whole-wheat flour.
 rock flour; fine particles of rock eroded by glacial action.

flour, *v.t.*; floured, *pt., pp.*; flouring, *ppr.* 1. to grind and sift; to convert into flour.
 2. to sprinkle with flour.

flour bee′tle, a beetle living in flour and meal.

flour em′ẽr·y, a powder used for polishing gems, made of corundum or emery.

flour gōld, gold in minute particles, obtained by washing.

flou̇r′ish (flũ′-), *v.i.*; flourished (-isht), *pt., pp.*; flourishing, *ppr.* [ME. *flourishen, flurishen, florischen,* from OFr. *flourir,* to bloom, blossom; from L. *florescere,* incept. of *florere,* to blossom, flower.]
 1. originally, to blossom.
 2. to thrive; to grow luxuriantly; to increase and enlarge, as a healthy growing plant; as, the beech and the maple *flourish* best in a deep, rich, and moist loam.
 3. to be prosperous, to increase in wealth or honor; as, the farmers of the west are *flourishing.*
 4. to be at the peak of development, activity, influence, etc.; to be in one's prime.
 5. to use florid language; to write in an ornamental style.
 They dilate and *flourish* long on little incidents. —Watts.
 6. to make bold strokes in writing; to make large and fanciful lines; as, to *flourish* with the pen.
 7. to make showy, wavy motions, as of the arms.
 8. in music, (a) to play a showy passage; (b) to perform a fanfare, as of trumpets.
 9. to boast; to vaunt; to brag.
 Syn.—prosper, thrive, triumph, brandish, wave.

flou̇r′ish, *v.t.* 1. to adorn with flowers or beautiful figures, either natural or artificial; to ornament with anything showy.
 2. to move or wave in the air by way of show or triumph; to brandish; as, to *flourish* a sword.
 3. to embellish with fine diction; to adorn with rhetorical figures; to grace with ostentatious eloquence. [Obs.]

flou̇r′ish, *n.* 1. a thriving state; success; prosperity. [Rare.]
 2. anything done in a showy or flaunting way.
 3. an ornate musical passage; fanfare.
 4. figures formed by bold, decorative lines or fanciful strokes in writing; as, the *flourishes* about a signature.
 5. a brandishing; the waving of a weapon or other thing; as, the *flourish* of a sword.
 6. a blooming. [Obs.]

flou̇r′ish·ẽr, *n.* one who or that which flourishes.

flou̇r′ish·ing·ly, *adv.* in a flourishing manner.

flou̇r′ish·ing thread (thred), a shiny linen thread for fancywork or mending.

flour mill, 1. a place where grain is ground into flour.
 2. a machine for grinding grain into flour.

flour mīte, a mite that lives in flour.

flour mọth, one of several kinds of moth whose larvae live in and feed upon flour and meal, especially *Ephestia kühniella.*

flour wee′vil, same as *flour beetle.*

flour wŏrm, the larva of insects breeding in flour or meal, especially that of the flour moth.

flour′y, *a.* 1. of flour; also, coated with flour.
 2. like flour in color or texture; powdery or white.

flou̇se, *v.t.* and *v.i.* to splash. [Brit. Dial.]

flout, *v.t.*; flouted, *pt., pp.*; flouting, *ppr.* [Old D. *fluyten;* D. *fluiten,* to play the flute, jeer.] to mock or insult; to treat with contempt.
 He *flouted* us downright. —Shak.

flout, *v.i.* to mock; to sneer; to behave with contempt; to be scornful.
 Fleer and gibe, and laugh and *flout.*
 —Swift.

flout, *n.* a mockery; an insult; a gibe.

flout′ẽr, *n.* one who flouts; a mocker.

flout′ing·ly, *adv.* with flouting; insultingly; disdainfully.

flōw, *v.i.*; flowed, *pt., pp.*; flowing, *ppr.* [ME. *flowen;* AS. *flowan,* to flow.]
 1. to move, as a fluid; to move in a stream, like water; as, the river *flows* to the south.
 2. to move in a way suggestive of a liquid; stream; as, the crowds *flowed* past.
 3. to proceed; to issue; to derive; as, evils *flow* from different sources; wealth *flows* from industry and economy.
 4. to abound; to have in abundance; to be overflowing.
 In that day the mountains shall drop down new wine, and the hills shall *flow* with milk.
 —Joel iii. 18.
 5. (a) to glide along smoothly, without harshness or asperity; as, a *flowing* period; *flowing* numbers; (b) to have smooth and pleasing continuity; as, the lines in this painting *flow.*
 6. to hang loose and waving; as, a *flowing* mantle; *flowing* locks.
 The imperial purple *flowing* in his train.
 Hamilton.
 7. to rise, as the tide: opposed to *ebb;* as, the tide *flows* twice in twenty-four hours.
 8. to have an excessive discharge of blood in menstruation.
 Syn.—stream, issue, progress, glide, course, career, run, float.

flōw, *v.t.* 1. to cover with water; to overflow; to inundate; as, the low grounds along the river are annually *flowed.*
 2. to cover with any liquid, as varnish or glaze; as, a plate *flowed* with collodion.
 3. to cause to flow. [Archaic.]

flōw, *n.* 1. the act or manner of flowing.
 2. a current of rising water; as, the *flow* and ebb of tides.
 3. a stream or anything that flows; as, a *flow* of wealth or immigration into the country.
 4. abundance; copiousness; as, a *flow* of spirits.
 5. the volume of liquid which passes through any given passage in a unit of time; rate of flow.

flōw′ăġe, *n.* 1. the act of flowing, overflowing, or flooding.
 2. a flooded condition.
 3. what flows or overflows.

flōw′-blūe′, *n.* in ceramics, a kind of blue used for an underglaze.

flōw′en, *v.* obsolete past tense plural and past participle of *fly.*

flow′ẽr, *n.* [ME. *flowre, flour, flur*; OFr. *flor, flur, flour,* from L. *flos, floris,* a flower.]

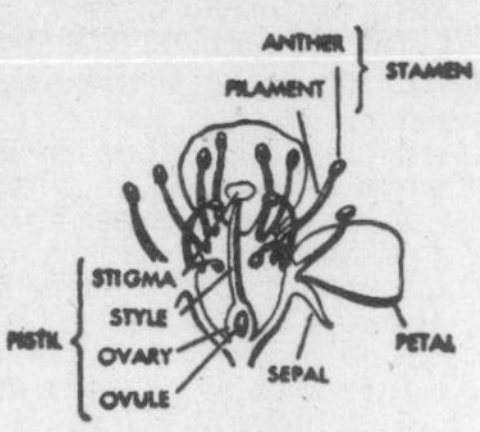

DIAGRAM OF FLOWER

1. in botany, the part of a plant containing or consisting of the organs of reproduction, either together in a monoclinous flower or separate in male and females flowers; especially, this part in seed-producing plants, usually including a surrounding structure of brightly colored leaves or petals; blossom; bloom.

2. a plant cultivated for its blossoms; flowering plant.

3. the best period of a person or thing; time of flourishing.

4. the best or finest part of a thing; the most valuable part; as, young men and women are the *flower* of a nation.

5. something decorative, especially an ornament of style; figure of speech.

6. [*pl.*] in old chemistry, a powdery substance from condensed vapors; as, the *flowers* of sulfur.

7. [*pl.*] the menstrual flow. [Obs.]

fertile or *female flower*; a flower having pistils only.

flower of Bristol; the scarlet lychnis.

flower of Constantinople; the scarlet lychnis.

flower of gold; the goldenrod.

flower of the gods; a South African orchid bearing bright red flowers.

flowers of arsenic; arsenic trioxide.

flowers of benzoin; benzoic acid.

flowers of camphor; powdered camphor which has been prepared by sublimation.

flowers of sulfur; sublimed sulfur.

flowers of wine; a moldlike growth on the surface of fermenting wine.

flow′ẽr, *v.i.*; flowered, *pt., pp.*; flowering, *ppr.* [ME. *flouren*; OFr. *flurir*; L. *florere,* to bloom, blossom.]

1. to blossom; to bloom; as, peach trees *flower* in April, and apple trees in May.

2. to be in the prime and spring of life; to flourish; to be fresh and vigorous.

When *flowered* my youthful spring.
—Spenser.

3. to froth; to ferment gently; to mantle, as new beer. [Obs.]

flow′ẽr, *v.t.* to cover or embellish with figures of flowers; to adorn with flowers.

When the frost *flowers* the whitened window panes. —Arnold.

flow′ẽr·āġe, *n.* the state of flowering; also, flowers collectively.

flow′ẽr an′i·măl, any of the *Anthozoa,* as a sea anemone.

flow′ẽr bed, a space in a garden devoted to the cultivation of flowers.

flow′ẽr bee′tle, one of numerous species of beetles feeding upon flowers, especially those of the genus *Meligethes.*

flow′ẽr bïrd, any bird of the genus *Anthornis,* or honeysuckers.

flow′ẽr bud, the bud which produces a flower, as distinguished from a leaf bud.

flow′ẽr çup, the calyx of a flower; also, the cup-shaped interior of a flower.

flow″ẽr-dē-lūce′, *n.* [from Fr. *fleur de lis,* lit., flower of the lily.]

1. the iris.

2. the fleur-de-lis.

flow′ẽred, *a.* 1. covered with flowers; embellished with flowers; as, a *flowered* gown.

2. bearing or containing flowers.

flow′ẽr·ẽr, *n.* a plant that bears flowers, as distinguished from one cultivated for its foliage.

flow′ẽr·et, *n.* [ME. *flourette*; OFr. *florete, filurette*; LL. *florettus,* from L. *flos, floris,* a flower.] a small flower; also, a floret.

flow′ẽr ġen′tle, a species of amaranth, especially *Amarantus tricolor,* whose foliage is brilliantly colored in yellow, green, and red.

flow′ẽr gïrl, 1. a girl or woman who sells flowers in the streets.

2. a little girl who carries flowers and attends the bride at a wedding.

flow′ẽr head (hed), in botany, a capitulum.

flow′ẽr·i·ly, *adv.* in a flowery manner.

flow′ẽr·i·ness, *n.* the quality or state of being flowery.

flow′ẽr·ing, *a.* 1. blossoming; blooming; having flowers.

2. having conspicuous flowers or blossoms.

flowering fern; a fern of the genus *Osmunda,* family *Osmundaceæ.* It grows in boggy places and wet margins of woods, and derives its name from the upper pinnae of the fronds being transformed into a panicle covered with sporangia.

FLOWERING FERN (*Osmunda regalis*)

flowering plants; plants having stamens and pistils as reproducing organs.

flowering rush; a rushlike aquatic plant, *Butomus umbellatus,* found in Europe and Asia.

flow′ẽr·ing, *n.* 1. the act or state of bearing blossoms, etc.

2. the act of adorning with flowers.

flow′ẽr·less, *a.* 1. having no flowers.

2. in botany, having no reproductive organs.

flow′ẽr·less·ness, *n.* the state or quality of being without flowers.

flow′ẽr-of-an-hour′ (-our′), *n.* the bladder ketmia, *Hibiscus trionum.*

flow′ẽr peck′ẽr, a bird of the family *Dicæidæ* of India and Australia, or of the American family *Cærebidæ,* resembling the hummingbird in plumage and habits.

flow′ẽr·pot, *n.* a porous earthenware pot with a drainage hole in the bottom, used to hold earth for a plant to grow in.

flow′ẽr shōw, an exhibition of flowers.

flow′ẽr stạlk, the stem of a plant that bears the flower or flowers; a peduncle.

flow′ẽr·y, *a.*; *comp.* flowerier; *superl.* floweriest, 1. full of flowers; abounding with blossoms; as, a *flowery* field.

2. adorned with artificial flowers or the figures of flowers; as, a *flowery* pattern.

3. highly embellished with figurative language; florid; as, a *flowery* style.

Flowery Kingdom; China.

flōw′ing, *a.* that flows (in various senses).

flowing battery; an electric battery in which the liquid flows through the cell or cells.

flowing sheets; in nautical usage, sails loosened to the wind, so as to receive it in a direction more nearly perpendicular than when they are close-hauled, although more obliquely than when the vessel is sailing before the wind.

flōw′ing, *n.* the act of running or moving as a fluid.

flōw′ing fũr′nāce, the cupola in which iron is melted in foundries.

flōw′ing·ly, *adv.* in a flowing manner.

flōw′ing·ness, *n.* the quality of being flowing.

flöwk, *n.* a flatfish. [Obs.]

flōwn, *v.* past participle of *fly.*

flōwn, *a.* 1. flushed; excited; exalted.

2. having colors combined or flowing into each other; as, *flown* porcelain.

flōw′sheet, *n.* a diagram showing the materials, operations, etc. involved in a manufacturing process, used in calculating costs: also *flow sheet.*

flū, *n.* influenza. [Colloq.]

flū′āte, *n.* [*flu*or, and *-ate.*] in chemistry, a fluoride. [Obs.]

flū′ȧ·vil, *n.* [perhaps from L. *fluere,* to flow.] in chemistry, a yellow, resinous constituent of gutta-percha, $C_{20}H_{32}O$, extracted by alcohol or some similar solvent.

flū′çăn, flo͝ok′ăn, *n.* [Corn.] in mining, the clayey material in a lode lying between the vein and its surrounding rocks.

fluç·tif′ẽr·ous, *a.* [L. *fluctus,* a wave, and *ferre,* to bear.] producing or tending to produce waves.

fluç·tis′ō·nous, *a.* [L. *fluctus,* a wave, and *sonare,* to sound.] resembling the sound of waves; roaring like the sea.

fluç″tū·ȧ·bil′i·ty, *n.* the quality of being capable of fluctuating.

fluç′tū·ȧn·cy, *n.* tendency to fluctuation. [Rare.]

fluç′tū·ȧnt, *a.* moving like a wave; wavering; unsteady; fluctuating.

fluç′tū·āte, *v.i.*; fluctuated, *pt., pp.*; fluctuating, *ppr.* [L. *fluctuatus,* pp. of *fluctuare,* to waver, rise in waves, from *fluctus,* a flowing, wave, from *fluere,* to flow.]

1. to move back and forth or up and down; rise and fall, as waves.

2. to be continually changing or varying in an irregular way; as, the cost of sugar *fluctuates.*

Syn.—vacillate, vary, waver, oscillate, hesitate.

fluç′tū·āte, *v.t.* to cause to fluctuate; to produce fluctuation in.

fluç·tū·ā′tion, *n.* [L. *fluctuatio* (*-onis*), from *fluctuare,* to waver, rise in waves.]

1. a moving back and forth or up and down; rising and falling, as of waves.

2. continual or irregular variation.

3. in medicine, the wavelike motion of a fluid in a cavity of the body.

fluç′tū·ous, *a.* [L. *fluctuosus,* from *fluctus,* a wave.] abounding in waves; characterized by waves or wavy motions; flowing.

flūe, *n.* [compare OFr. *flue, fluie,* a flowing, from L. *fluere,* to flow.]

1. a tube, pipe, or shaft for the passage of smoke, hot air, gas, etc., as in a chimney.

2. a flue pipe in an organ.

3. the opening or passage for air in such a flue pipe.

flūe, *n.* [Fr. *flou,* light, weak; G. *flau,* weak.] light down, such as rises from cotton, etc.; fluff.

flūe, *n.* [corrupted from *fluke.*] a kind of fluke or barb, as of a harpoon.

flūe, *v.i.*; flued, *pt., pp.*; fluing, *ppr.* to expand or flare out, as the jambs of a window.

flūe, *n.* [ME. *flew*; MD. *vluwe.*] any of various kinds of fishing net: also spelled *flew.*

flūe bridġe (brij), in a reverberating furnace, a low firebrick partition between the flue and the hearth.

flūe′-çūred (-kūrd), *a.* cured or dried by hot air passed through flues: said of tobacco.

flūed, *a.* supplied with a flue or fluke; as, a *flued* harpoon.

flūe ham′mẽr, a hammer used by a cooper for flaring iron hoops to fit a barrel.

flū·el′len, *n.* [prob. from W. *fluellen,* a form of *Llewelyn,* a proper name.] the speedwell, *Veronica officinalis,* a plant of the figwort family.

female fluellen; the toadflax, *Linaria spuria.*

flū′ence, *n.* a flowing. [Obs.]

flū′en·cy, *n.* [Fr. *fluence*; L. *fluentia,* a flowing, fluency, from *fluens* (*-entis*), ppr. of *fluere,* to flow.]

1. the quality of flowing; smoothness; freedom from harshness; as, *fluency* of numbers.

2. the ability to write or speak easily, smoothly, and expressively; readiness or smoothness of speech.

3. affluence; abundance. [Obs.]

flū′ent, *a.* [L. *fluens* (*-entis*), ppr. of *fluere,* to flow.]

1. liquid; flowing.

2. having a flowing motion, or the appearance of flowing; changeable.

Motion being a *fluent* thing. —Ray.

3. ready in the use of words; voluble; speaking or writing with facility and smoothness; as, a *fluent* speaker.

4. flowing; voluble; smooth; as, *fluent* speech; a *fluent* style.

flū′ent, *n.* 1. a stream; a current of water. [Obs.]

2. in mathematics, a variable quantity, considered as continually increasing or diminishing.

flū′ent·ly, *adv.* in a fluent manner.

flū′ent·ness, *n.* the quality of being fluent; fluency.

flūe pīpe, an organ pipe in which the tone is produced by a current of air striking the lip of the mouth, or opening, in the pipe.

flūe stop, in organ building, a stop made up of flue pipes.

flūe′wõrk, *n.* flue stops collectively.

flūe′y, *a.* having the quality of flue or down; flossy.

fluff, *n.* [perh. a merging of *flue* (soft mass) and *puff.*]

1. soft, light down.

2. a loose, soft mass of fur, dust, hair, etc.

3. in the theater, radio, etc., an error in reading lines.

fluff, *v.t.* 1. to shake or pat until loose, feathery, and fluffy.

2. in the theater, radio, etc., to make an error in reading (a word, one's lines, etc.)

fluff, *v.i.* to become fluffy.

fluff′i·ness, *n.* the state of being fluffy.

fluff′y, *a.*; *comp.* fluffier; *superl.* fluffiest, 1. per-

taining to or having the character of fluff; downy.
2. covered with fluff.
Flü'gel·horn (flü'gel-hôrn), *n.* [G.; *flügel*, wing, and *horn*, horn: because of shape.] a brass-wind instrument like the cornet in design but with a tone like that of the French horn.
flū'gel·man, *n.* a fugleman.
flū'id, *a.* [L. *fluidus*, from *fluere*, to flow.]
1. that can flow; not solid; able to move and change shape without separating when under pressure.
2. of a fluid or fluids.
3. like a fluid; that can change rapidly or easily; not settled; mobile or plastic; as, *fluid* beliefs.
flū'id, *n.* any substance that can flow; liquid or gas.
fluid dram (or *drachm*); a liquid measure equal to one-eighth of a fluid ounce or to 3.7 cubic centimeters.
fluid ounce; a liquid measure equal to one-sixteenth of a pint or to 29.57 cubic centimeters.
fluid pressure; pressure of, or like that of, a fluid: it is constant and uniform in every direction.
flū'id·ăl, *a.* fluid.
fluidal structure; in geology, a kind of structure found in igneous rocks, in which the lines of flow of lava are indicated in the forms of crystallization.
flū'id·ex'tract, *n.* in pharmacy, a concentrated fluid preparation of a vegetable drug, containing alcohol either as a preservative or a solvent, and of such strength that one cubic centimeter of the solution is equal in activity to one gram of the dry, powdered drug.
flū·id'iç, *a.* of, or having the nature of, a fluid.
flū·id'i·fȳ, *v.t.*; fluidified; *pt., pp.*; fluidifying, *ppr.* [L. *fluidus*, a fluid, and *-ficare*, from *facere*, to make.] to change to a fluid condition.
flū·id'i·ty, *n.* the quality or state of being capable of flowing; a liquid or gaseous state: opposed to *solidity*.
flū'id·īze, *v.t.*; fluidized, *pt., pp.*; fluidizing, *ppr.* to change to a fluid condition; to fluidify.
flū'id·ness, *n.* the state of being fluid; fluidity.
flū'id·ounce', *n.* a fluid ounce.
flū'i·tănt, *a.* [L. *fluitans* (*-antis*), ppr. of *fluitare*, to float, swim, freq. of *fluere*, to flow.] supported by the buoyancy of a fluid; floating; carried by buoyant force. [Rare.]
flū'kăn, *n.* in mining, flucan.
flūke, *n.* [prob. a form of L.G. *flunk*, *flunke*, a wing, the fluke of an anchor.]
1. either of the two triangular, pointed blades on the arms of an anchor, which fasten in the ground.
2. a lobe or branch of a whale's tail.
3. an instrument for cleaning a hole drilled for blasting.
4. a barb on a harpoon, arrow, lance, etc.
flūke, *n.* 1. a species of flatfish, of the genus *Platessa*, especially a flounder.
2. any of a number of flat, parasitic worms, living especially in sheep's livers.
flūke, *n.* [19th-c. billiard slang; prob. originally "dupe stroke," from slang *fluke*, person easily duped, from *fluke*, flatfish (which is easily caught).]
1. an accidentally good or lucky stroke in billiards, pool, etc. [Slang.]
2. a lucky chance; stroke of luck; as, we won the football game by a *fluke*. [Slang.]
flūke, *v.t.*; fluked (flūkt), *pt., pp.*; fluking, *ppr.* to hit or get by a fluke. [Slang.]
flūke, *v.i.* to make a fluke. [Slang.]
flūke'wŏrm, *n.* same as *fluke* (parasitic worm).
flūke'wŏrt, *n.* a European plant, *Hydrocotyle vulgaris*, once supposed to cause flukes in sheep.
flūk'y, flūk'ey, *a.*; *comp.* flukier; *superl.* flukiest, [from *fluke* (lucky stroke).]
1. resulting from chance; lucky. [Slang.]
2. constantly changing; uncertain; fitful; as, a *fluky* breeze. [Slang.]
flūme, *n.* [ME. *flum*, *flom*, a river, stream; OFr. *flum*; L. *flumen*, a river, stream, from *fluere*, to flow.]
1. an artificial channel, usually an inclined chute or trough, for carrying water to furnish power, transport logs down a mountainside, etc.
2. a narrow gorge or ravine with a stream running through it.
flūme, *v.t.*; flumed, *pt., pp.*; fluming, *ppr.* to send (logs, etc.) down a flume.
flū'mi·nous, *a.* [L. *flumen* (*-inis*), a river.] of or belonging to rivers; abundantly supplied with rivers.
flum'mẽr·y, *n.*; *pl.* **flum'mẽr·ieṣ,** [W. *llymru*, *llymrand*, a kind of food made of oatmeal boiled and soured, from *llymus*, of a sharp quality.]
1. a soft, gelatinous food made of flour or meal; pap.
Milk and *flummery* are very fit for children. —Locke.
2. a sort of soft custard or blancmange.
3. in the manufacture of wheat starch, a jellylike refuse.
4. meaningless compliments or silly talk.
flum'mŏx, *v.t.* [from dial. *flummocks* or thieves' slang.] to confuse; to perplex. [Slang.]
flump, *v.t.* and *v.i.*; flumped, *pt., pp.*; flumping, *ppr.* [imitative word.] to drop or move heavily and noisily.
flump, *n.* the act or sound of flumping.
flung, *v.* past tense and past participle of *fling*.
fluñk, *v.t.*; flunked (fluñkt), *pt., pp.*; flunking, *ppr.* [19th-c. college slang.]
1. to fail in (schoolwork); as, he *flunked* the English examination.
2. to give a mark of *failure* to; to grade as having failed.
3. to cause to fail; as, continued absence will *flunk* a student.
[Colloq. in all senses.]
fluñk, *v.i.* 1. to fail, especially in schoolwork. [Colloq.]
2. to give up; retreat. [Colloq.]
fluñk, *n.* a failure, especially in a recitation or examination; also, a mark or grade of *failure*. [Colloq.]
fluñ'ky, fluñ'key, *n.*; *pl.* **fluñ'kieṣ, fluñ'keyṣ,** [perhaps from Fr. *flanquer*, to flank, run along by the side of, be at one's elbow to render assistance.]
1. a liveried manservant: a term of contempt.
2. a flattering servile person; a toady.
3. a young or inexperienced speculator.
fluñ'ky·iṣm, fluñ'key·iṣm, *n.* the characteristic behavior or spirit of a flunky.
flū'ō-, a combining form meaning *fluorine* or *fluorescent*, as in *fluo*phosphate, *fluo*cerin.
flū'ō, *a.* of or containing fluorine.
flū·ō·bō'rāte, *n.* a compound of fluoboric acid with a base.
flū·ō·bō'riç, *a.* relating to a compound of fluorine and boron.
fluoboric acid; in chemistry, a sirupy acid, HBF_4.
flū·ō·bō'rīde, flū·ō'bō'rid, *n.* [*fluobo*ric and *-ide*.] a salt of fluoboric acid.
flū·ō·cär'bō·nāte, *n.* a double salt or carbon and fluorine.
flū·ō·cē'rine, *n.* fluocerite.
flū·ō·cē'rīte, *n.* [*fluor* and *cerium* and *-ite*.] in mineralogy, a native cerium fluoride.
flū·ō·hȳ'driç, *a.* same as *hydrofluoric*.
flū·ō·phos'phāte, *n.* a phosphate containing fluorine.
flū'ŏr-, same as *fluoro-*.
flū'ŏr, *n.* [LL. *fluor*, a flow, flux, from L. *fluere*, to flow.] fluorite.
fluor albus; leucorrhea.
flū·ŏr·an'thēne, *n.* [*fluor*ene and *phenanthene*.] in chemistry, a coal tar product, $C_{16}H_{10}$.
flū'ŏr·ā·ted, *a.* in chemistry, having fluorine in combination.
flū'ŏr·ēne, *n.* [*fluor*escence and *-ene*.] in chemistry, a product of coal tar, $C_{13}H_{10}$.
flū·ō·resce', *v.i.*; fluoresced (-rest'), *pt., pp.*; fluorescing, *ppr.* to exhibit fluorescence; to be or become fluorescent.
flū·ō·res'cē·in, *n.* [*fluoresce* and *-in*.] a yellowish-red, crystalline compound, $C_{20}H_{12}O_5$, made synthetically from resorcin and phthalic anhydride: an alkaline solution appears green by reflected light and red by transmitted light.
flū·ō·res'cē·ine, *n.* same as *fluorescein*.
flū·ō·res'cence, *n.* [*fluor* and *-escence*.]
1. the property of a substance, such as fluorite, of producing light while it is being acted upon by radiant energy, such as ultraviolet rays or X rays.
2. the production of such light.
3. light so produced.
flū·ō·res'cent, *a.* [*fluor* and *-escent*.] having or resulting from fluorescence.
flū·ō·res'cent lamp, a glass tube coated on the inside with a fluorescent substance that gives off light (*fluorescent light*) when acted upon by a stream of electrons from the cathode.
flū·or'iç, *a.* [*fluor* and *-ic*.] pertaining to fluorine; obtained from fluorine; containing fluorine.
flū'ŏr·īde, flū'ŏr·id, *n.* [*fluor* and *-ide*.] a compound of fluorine with some other element or radical.
flū'ŏr·ine, flū'ŏr·in, *n.* [*fluor* and *-in*, *-ine*: so called because it occurs in fluorite.] a very active chemical element of the halogen family, a corrosive, greenish-yellow gas: symbol, F, Fl; atomic weight, 19.00; atomic number, 9.
flū'ŏr·īte, *n.* [*fluor* and *-ite*.] calcium fluoride, CaF_2, a transparent, crystalline mineral having many colors and perfect cleavage: it is used as a flux, in glassmaking, etc.: also called *fluor*, *fluor spar*.
flū'ō·rō-, a combining form meaning: (a) *fluorine*; (b) *fluorescence*. Also, before a vowel, *fluor-*.
flū·or'ō·fọrm, *n.* [*fluoro-* and *form*yl.] a fluoric gas, CHF_3, differing from chloroform in having fluorine in place of chlorine.
flū'ŏr·oid, *n.* in crystallography, a tetrahexahedral crystal, as in fluorite.
flū·or'ō·sçōpe, *n.* [*fluoro-*, and Gr. *skopein*, to view.] a machine for examining internal structures by viewing the shadows cast on a fluorescent screen by objects or parts through which X rays are directed: the shadows vary in intensity according to the density of the object or part.
flū·or·ō·sçop'iç, *a.* pertaining to fluoroscopy.
flū·ōr·os'çō·py, *n.* [*fluoro-* and Gr. *skopein*, to view.] examination by means of the fluoroscope.
flū'ŏr·ous, *a.* containing fluorine; relating to fluorine.
flū'ŏr spär, [LL. *fluor*, a flow, flux, and AS. *spær*, in *spærstan*, chalkstone.] fluorite.
flū·ō·sil'i·çāte, *n.* [*fluosilic*ic and *-ate*.] a compound of fluosilicic acid with some base.
flū"ō·si·lic'iç, *a.* pertaining to the combination of fluorine and silicon; having fluorine and silicon as constituents.
fluosilicic acid; an acid containing both silicon and fluorine, formed by the combination of hydrogen and silicon with fluoric acid.
flũr'ry, *n.*; *pl.* **flũr'rieṣ,** [Sw. *flurig*, disordered, dissolute.]
1. a sudden blast or gust of wind; a light, temporary breeze.
2. a light snow or rain accompanied by wind.
3. a sudden agitation; commotion, bustle; hurry.
4. the violent movements of a dying whale.
flũr'ry, *v.t.*; flurried, *pt., pp.*; flurrying, *ppr.* to put in agitation; to excite or alarm.
flũrt, *n.* and *v.* flirt. [Obs.]
flush, *v.i.*; flushed (flusht), *pt., pp.*; flushing, *ppr.* [ME. *fluschen*, to fly up suddenly, penetrate.]
1. to flow and spread suddenly; to rush; as, blood *flushes* into the face.
2. to become suddenly red; to blush; as, the cheeks *flush*.
3. to glow.
4. to become cleaned, washed, or emptied out with a sudden flow of water, etc.
5. to start up from cover: said of birds.
flush, *v.t.* 1. to make red suddenly; to cause the blood to rush suddenly into (the face).
Nor *flush* with shame the passing virgin's cheek. —Gay.
2. to elate; to excite; to animate; as, *flushed* with victory.
3. to cleanse by forcing water, etc. through; as, to *flush* the sewers.
4. to drive (birds) from cover; as, to *flush* a covey of quail.
5. to make level or even; as, the mason *flushed* the joint with mortar.
flush, *a.*; *comp.* flusher; *superl.* flushest, 1. fresh; full of vigor; hence, glowing; bright.
2. abundant; abounding; well furnished; prodigal.
3. well supplied, especially with money.
4. lavish; profuse.
5. making an even or unbroken line or surface; adjusted to a margin, edge, etc.; as, the door is *flush* with the walls.
6. direct; full; as, a blow *flush* in the face.
flush, *n.* 1. a sudden and rapid flow, as of water in washing out something.
2. a blush; glow.
3. a sudden feeling of great heat, as in a fever.
4. sudden impulse or excitement; as, a *flush* of joy.
5. bloom; growth; abundance.
6. a term for a number of ducks.

flush, *adv.* 1. in an even manner; so as to be level or in alignment.
2. directly; squarely.

flush, *n.* [Fr. *flux*; L. *fluxus*, a flowing, flow.] a hand of cards all in the same suit: in poker, a flush is just above a straight and below a full house.
bobtail flush; in the game of poker, a hand of four cards of the same suit and one card of an odd suit.
royal flush; in the game ot poker, a straight flush with ace at the head: the highest hand.
straight flush; in the game of poker, a flush in sequence.

flush'bōard, *n.* same as *flashboard.*

flush box, 1. a box placed flush with a street or roadbed and used as an entrance to a conduit containing underground wires.
2. a tank for flushing a water closet, with a float for stopping the flow into the tank as it fills.

flush'ẽr, *n.* 1. the lesser butcher bird of Europe, *Lanius collurio.*
2. one who cleans sewers by flushing.

flush'ing, *n.* 1. a glow of red in the face, as in a fever.
2. in England, heavy shoddy cloth.
3. in weaving, the floating threads which cover the surface of a web.

flush'ing·ly, *adv.* in a flushing manner.

flush'ness, *n.* the quality or condition of being flush.

flush'-riv''et·ed, *a.* having the rivets flush with the surface, as in the hull of an iron ship.

flus'tẽr, *v.t.* and *v.i.*; flustered, *pt., pp.*; flustering, *ppr.* [Ice. *flaustra*, to be flustered, *flaustr*, hurry, fluster.] to make or be confused, nervous, and excited; as, he was *flustered* by the policeman's shouting.

flus'tẽr, *n.* the condition of being flustered.

flus'tẽr·āte, *v.t.*; flusterated, *pt., pp.*; flusterating, *ppr.* to fluster. [Colloq.]

flus·tẽr·ā'tion, *n.* same as *flustration.* [Colloq.]

flus'trāte, *v.t.* to flusterate. [Colloq.]

flus·trā'tion, *n.* the condition of being flustered.

flu̇te, *n.* [Fr. *flute, flûte*; OFr. *fleüte, flaute, flahute*; LL. *flauta*, a flute, from L. *flatus*, a blowing, from *flare*, to blow.]
1. a high-pitched wind instrument consisting of a long, slender tube, played by blowing across a hole near the upper end: by fingering the holes and keys along its length, the player can produce various tones.
2. in architecture, a long, rounded groove in the shaft of a column or pillar; a perpendicular furrow or cavity, cut along the shaft of a column or pilaster.
3. a similar channel in a ruffle of muslin or in other material.
4. one of the several shuttles used in weaving.
5. in bakery, a long, slender breakfast roll.
6. in organ building, a flue stop with the pipes closed to make tones like those of the flute.
7. a tall, slender wine glass.
flûte à bec; a flute with mouthpiece at the end resembling a beak, played like a flageolet.

FLUTE

flu̇te, *v.i.*; fluted, *pt., pp.*; fluting, *ppr.* 1. to play on a flute.
2. to make a flutelike sound.

flu̇te, *v.t.* 1. to form flutes or channels in (a column, etc.); to furnish with a flute or flutes.
2. to sound, as a note or succession of notes, in a flutelike tone.
3. to play on the flute.

flu̇te, *n.* [a corruption of *float.*] a long vessel or boat with flat ribs or floor timbers, round behind and swelled in the middle.
armed en flûte; an armed ship, with her guns in part taken out, as when used as a transport. [Obs.]

flu̇te'bĩrd, *n.* the Australian piping crow.

flu̇te bit, in mechanics, a tool for boring hard woods, such as flutes are made of.

flu̇t'ed, *a.* 1. channeled; furrowed, as a column.
2. in music, flutelike; as, *fluted* notes.

flu̇te'mouth, *n.* a fish with a long, tube-shaped mouth; one of the genus *Aulostoma.*

flu̇t'ẽr, *n.* 1. one who plays on the flute. [Rare.]
2. a person or tool that makes ornamental grooves or flutings.

flu̇te shrīke, a butcherbird of Africa, genus *Laniarius.*

flu̇te stop, an organ stop having a flutelike tone.

flu̇t'ing, *n.* 1. a decoration consisting of long, rounded grooves, as in a column.
2. a groove or grooves, as in a column or ruffle.
3. the act of making such grooves.
4. the act of playing the flute.
5. a whistling, speaking, etc. in a flutelike tone.

FLUTING ON COLUMN

flu̇t'ing ī'ron (-ũrn), an iron with a corrugated surface, for pressing ruffles.

flu̇t'ing mȧ·chïne', 1. a machine for corrugating sheet metal.
2. a machine for making spiral or curved balusters.

flu̇t'ing plāne, in carpentry, a plane for making flutes in wood.

flu̇t'ing sciṣ'ṣōrṣ, a three-tined appliance for crimping fabrics, operated like a pair of scissors.

flu̇t'ist, *n.* a person who plays the flute: also *flautist.*

flut'tẽr, *v.i.*; fluttered, *pt., pp.*; fluttering, *ppr.* [ME. *floteren*; AS. *floterian, flotorian*, to float about.]
1. to move or flap the wings rapidly, without flying or with short flights.

As an eagle stirreth up her nest, *fluttereth* over her young, spreadeth abroad her wings. —Deut. xxxii. 11.

2. to wave or vibrate rapidly and irregularly; as, the flag *fluttered* in the wind.
3. to move about restlessly; to bustle.

No rag, no scrap of all the beau or wit,
That once so *fluttered*, and that once so writ.
—Pope.

4. to move with quick vibrations, flaps, etc.; as, a *fluttering* fan; a *fluttering* sail.
5. to be in a state of tremulous excitement; tremble; quiver.

How long we *fluttered* on the wings of doubtful success. —Howell.

flut'tẽr, *v.t.* 1. to cause to move in quick, irregular motions.
2. to throw into a state of excitement or confusion; to fluster.

flut'tẽr, *n.* 1. quick and irregular motion; vibration; undulation; as, the *flutter* of a fan.
2. a state of excitement or confusion.
3. a condition of the heartbeat in which the contractions are very rapid but regular: in *impure flutter* they are irregular.

flut'tẽr·ẽr, *n.* one who or that which flutters.

flut'tẽr·ing·ly, *adv.* in a fluttering manner.

flut'tẽr kick, a swimming kick in which the legs are moved continually up and down in short, rapid strokes.

flut'tẽr wheel, a kind of water wheel of small diameter with radial paddles against which water strikes at the bottom of a chute, causing rapid rotation with a sound as of fluttering.

flut'tẽr·y, *a.* fluttering or apt to flutter.

flu̇t'y, *a.*; *comp.* flutier; *superl.* flutiest, soft and clear in tone like a flute.

flu̇'vi·ăl, *a.* [L. *fluvialis*, from *fluvius*, a river, stream, from *fluere*, to flow.] belonging to, found in, or produced by rivers; as, a *fluvial* plant.

flu̇'vi·ăl·ist, *n.* one who explains geological phenomena by the action of streams.

flu̇·vi·at'iç, *a.* [L. *fluviaticus*, from *fluvius*, a river.] fluvial.

flu̇'vi·ȧ·tile, *a.* [L. *fluviatilis*, from *fluvius*, a river.] belonging to rivers; existing in rivers; fluvial; as, *fluviatile* strata.

flu̇·viç'ō·line, *a.* [L. *fluvius*, a river, and *colere*, to inhabit.] fluvial.

flu̇·vi·ō-, [L. *fluvius*, a river.] a combining form used in geology to indicate *relation to a river* or *stream.*

flu̇''vi·ō·mȧ·rïne', *a.* [*fluvio-*, and L. *marinus*, of the sea, from *mare*, the sea.] in geology, pertaining to formations made by the action of both river and sea, as in the deposits found at the mouths of rivers.

flu̇''vi·ō·ter·res'tri·ăl, *a.* [*fluvio-*, and L. *terrestris*, of the earth, from *terra*, the earth.] relating to the land and its rivers, as distinguished from the ocean and its beds; as, *fluvioterrestrial* deposits or fossils.

flux, *n.* [ME. *flux*; OFr. *flux*; L. *fluxus*, a flowing, flow, from *fluere*, to flow.]
1. the act of flowing; the motion or passing of a fluid; flow.
2. the moving or passing of anything in continued succession; as, things in this life are in a continual *flux.*
3. a coming in of the tide.
4. any substance or mixture used to promote the fusion of metals or minerals, as alkalis, borax, rosin, etc.
5. fusion; a liquid state from the action of heat. [Rare.]
6. any excessive or unnatural discharge of fluid matter from the body.
7. in physics, the rate of flow of water, heat, electricity, magnetism, etc. over a surface.

flux, *a.* flowing; moving; maintained by a constant succession of parts; inconstant; variable. [Obs.]

flux, *v.t.*; fluxed (fluxt), *pt., pp.*; fluxing, *ppr.* 1. to melt; to fuse; to make fluid.

One part of mineral alkali will *flux* two of silicious earth with effervescence.
—Kirwan.

2. in medicine, to produce an excessive flow or discharge from; to purge.

flux, *v.i.* to flow or stream out. [Archaic.]

flux·ā'tion, *n.* a flowing or passing on. [Obs.]

flux den'si·ty, in physics, the quantity of a fluid or energy emitted per unit of time through a unit of surface area.

flux·i·bil'i·ty, *n.* [LL. *fluxibilitas*, from L. *fluxibilis*, capable of flowing, from *fluere*, to flow.] the quality of being fusible.

flux'i·ble, *a.* [LL. *fluxibilis*, from L. *fluxus*, pp. of *fluere*, to flow.] capable of being melted or fused, as a mineral.

flux'i·ble·ness, *n.* fluxibility.

flux'ile, *a.* [LL. *fluxilis*, fluid, from *fluxus*, pp. of *fluere*, to flow.] fluxible. [Rare.]

flux·il'i·ty, *n.* the quality of being fusible; possibility of being fused or liquefied. [Rare.]

flux'iŏn (fluk'shun), *n.* [L. *fluxio (-onis)*, a flowing, from *fluere*, to flow.]
1. the act of flowing.
2. continuous change.
3. something that flows; discharge.
4. [adopted by Newton.] in mathematics, the rate of continuous change in variable quantities; a differential.
5. in medicine, an unusual flow, as of blood to the brain.

flux'iŏn·ăl, *a.* pertaining to a fluxion or fluxions.

flux'iŏn·ȧ·ry, *a.* fluxional.

flux'iŏn·ist, *n.* one skilled in fluxions.

flux'ive, *a.* flowing; fluid. [Obs.]

flux'ūre, *n.* a flowing or fluid matter. [Obs.]

flȳ, *v.i.*; flew, *pt.*; flown, *pp.*; flying, *ppr.* [ME. *fleyen, flien, fleen, flyen*; AS. *fleogan, fliogan*, to fly.]
1. to move through the air; specifically, (a) to move through the air by using wings, as a bird; (b) to travel through the air in an aircraft; (c) to be propelled through the air, as a bullet.
2. to operate an aircraft.
3. to wave or float in the air, as a flag or kite.
4. to move or pass swiftly or suddenly; as, the door *flew* open.
5. to move suddenly and with violence; as, she *flew* into a rage; the cup broke and *flew* into pieces.
6. to appear to pass swiftly; as, time *flies.*
7. to flee; to run away from danger or evil; to attempt to escape; to escape.

I'll *fly* from shepherds, flocks, and flowery plains. —Pope.

8. to be used up swiftly: said of money, etc.
9. flied, *pt., pp.*; flying, *ppr.* in baseball, to hit a fly.
10. in hawking, to hunt with a hawk.
to fly about; in nautical usage, to change about; to veer: said of the wind.
to fly around; to move about hastily. [Colloq.]
to fly at; to spring toward; to attack.
to fly blind; to pilot an airplane by means of instruments only.
to fly in the face of; (a) [Rare.] to insult; (b) to oppose with violence; to act in direct opposition to.
to fly off; to separate or depart suddenly.
to fly off the handle; to lose one's temper. [Colloq.]
to fly on; to assail suddenly and furiously.

to fly out; (a) to rush out; (b) to burst into a passion; (c) in baseball, to be put out by hitting a fly that is caught by a fielder before it touches the ground.

to let fly; (a) to throw or drive; as, *to let fly* a shower of darts; (b) to direct a verbal attack (at).

flȳ, *v.t.* 1. to run away from; to flee from; to avoid; as, to *fly* the sight of one we hate.

Sleep *flies* the wretch. —Dryden.

2. to cause to move or float in the air; as, to *fly* a kite.
3. to operate (an aircraft).
4. to go over in an aircraft; as, he *flew* the Pacific.
5. to carry or transport in an aircraft.
6. in hawking, to hunt with a hawk.

to fly a kite; to raise cash by exchanging checks, or on accommodation notes.

flȳ, *n.*; *pl.* **flies**, [ME. *flye*; AS. *flyge*, from *fleogan*, to fly.]

1. the act of flying; flight. [Rare.]
2. a flap of cloth that conceals buttons or other fasteners in a garment; especially, such a flap in the front of a pair of trousers.
3. (a) a flap serving as the door of a tent; (b) a piece of fabric serving as an outer or second top on a tent.
4. (a) the width of an extended flag; (b) the part of a flag farthest from the staff.
5. a flywheel.
6. a flyleaf.
7. a hackney carriage. [Brit.]
8. in baseball, a ball batted high in the air within the foul lines.
9. in weaving, a shuttle with wheels driven through the shed by a blow or jerk.
10. in knitting machines, a piece for holding the needle in position while passing through a new loop: also called a *latch*.
11. in spinning, one of the arms that revolve round the bobbin in a spinning frame and twist the yarn as it is wound on the bobbin.
12. that part of a vane which points and shows which way the wind blows.
13. in a theater, a gallery above and behind the proscenium arch, containing overhead lights, machinery for raising and lowering sets, etc.
14. cotton waste.
15. that part of a piano, organ, or similar instrument which covers the keys when not folded or pushed back.

on the fly; (a) while in flight; (b) [Slang.] while in a hurry.

flȳ, *n.*; *pl.* **flies**, [ME. *flie*, *flege*; AS. *fleoge*, *flyge*, from base of *fleogan*, *fliogan*, to fly.]

1. (a) a housefly; (b) any of a large group of insects with two transparent wings, including the housefly, gnat, mosquito, and Mayfly.
2. a device made of feathers, colored silk, etc. to resemble an insect, used as bait in fishing.
3. in printing, (a) formerly, the person whose work was removing sheets from the press as they were printed; (b) a fingered device on the press for removing printed sheets.

fly in the ointment; anything, especially a little thing, that reduces or destroys the value or usefulness of something else.

flȳ, *a.*; *comp.* flier; *superl.* fliest, [orig. thieves' slang; prob. renders D. *vlug* in same sense.]

1. quick; agile; nimble. [Slang.]
2. alert and knowing; sharp. [Slang.]

flȳ a·gar′iç, a common, very poisonous mushroom with an orange-colored cap full of white warts: called also *flybane* and *fly amanita*.

flȳ ash, airborne bits of unburnable ash, especially as a factor in air pollution.

flȳ′a·wāy″, *a.* 1. flying in the wind; streaming; as, *flyaway* hair.
2. flighty.

flȳ′a·wāy″, *n.* 1. a runaway.
2. a flighty person.

flȳ′a·wāy″ grȧss, in botany, a grass of the genus *Agrostis*, characterized by the lightness of its panicle, which is blown about to considerable distances.

flȳ′bāne, *n.* same as *fly agaric*.

flȳ′-bit″ten, *a.* marked by or as if by the bite of flies.

flȳ block, among seamen, a shifting pulley block.

flȳ′blōw, *v.t.* and *v.i.*; flyblew, *pt.*; flyblown, *pp.*; flyblowing, *ppr.* 1. to deposit eggs in (meat, etc.): said of a fly.
2. to contaminate; spoil; taint.

flȳ′blōw, *n.* a blowfly's egg or larva.

flȳ′blōwn, *a.* 1. full of flies' eggs or larvae.
2. contaminated; spoiled; tainted.

flȳ′bōat, *n.* 1. a large, flat-bottomed Dutch boat.
2. a swift-flying sailboat.

flȳ book, a booklike case which holds artificial fishing flies.

flȳ′-bȳ-nīght″, *a.* not trustworthy; financially unsound.

flȳ′-bȳ-nīght″, *n.* a debtor who runs away from his debts.

flȳ′-bȳ-wīre′, *a.* designating or of a control system for an airplane or spacecraft, in which the controls are actuated by electrical impulses, as from a digital computer.

flȳ çap, a cap with a winglike crescent on each side, formerly worn by women.

flȳ′-çast″, *v.i.*; fly-cast, *pt.*, *pp.*; fly-casting, *ppr.* to fish by casting artificial flies, using a lightweight, resilient rod (*fly rod*).

flȳ′çatch″ẽr, *n.* 1. one who or that which catches flies.
2. any of a group of small birds, including the kingbird, pewee, phoebe, and crested flycatcher, that catch insects in flight.
3. any of a number of plants that catch and ingest insects.

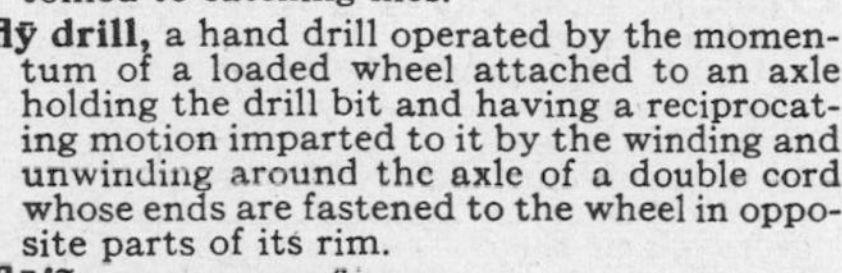

WHITE-COLLARED FLYCATCHER (*Muscicapa albicollis*)

flȳ′-çatch″ing, *a.* fitted for or accustomed to catching flies.

flȳ drill, a hand drill operated by the momentum of a loaded wheel attached to an axle holding the drill bit and having a reciprocating motion imparted to it by the winding and unwinding around the axle of a double cord whose ends are fastened to the wheel in opposite parts of its rim.

flȳ′ẽr, *n.* same as *flier*.

flȳ′-fish, *v.i.*; fly-fished, *pt.*, *pp.*; fly-fishing, *ppr.* to angle with flies, especially artificial flies, as bait.

flȳ′-fish·ing, fishing with flies as bait.

flȳ′flap, *n.* a device used to drive away or to kill flies.

flȳ gŏv′ẽrn·ŏr, in machinery, a governor with fans for regulating speed by air resistance, as in a clock, to regulate the rate of striking.

flȳ hŏn′ey-suç·kle, a plant of the honeysuckle family, of the genus *Lonicera*, from three to five feet in height and bearing honey-colored flowers which produce red berries.

flȳ′ing, *a.* [ppr. of *fly*; cf. AS. *fleogende*, glossing, L. *volucer*.]

1. that flies or can fly.
2. moving as if flying; moving swiftly; fast.
3. like flight through the air.
4. waving or streaming in the air; as, with flags *flying*.
5. hasty and brief; as, a *flying* trip.
6. of or for aircraft or aviators; as, a *flying* field, *flying* suit.

flying adder; a dragonfly.

flying blister; a compress used long enough to irritate the skin.

flying boat; a seaplane; a plane equipped to land on and take off from water.

flying bridge; see under *bridge*.

flying buttress; a buttress connected with a wall at some distance from it by an arch or part of an arch: it serves to resist outward pressure.

FLYING BUTTRESS

flying jib; a small, triangular sail in front of the jib, usually on an extension of the jib boom or bowsprit.

flying jib boom; an addition to the jib boom to accommodate the flying jib.

flying level; in civil engineering, a trial level over the route of an intended canal, road, etc.

flying pinion; the pinion of a fly governor.

flying shot; a shot at an object in motion, as at a bird on the wing.

flying squad; a division or company of men whose work requires them to move with speed from place to place; as, a *flying squad* of detectives.

flying start; (a) the start of a race in which the contestants are already moving when the starting signal is given; (b) any rapid beginning.

to send flying; to set in rapid motion.

flȳ′ing, *n.* the action of a person or thing that flies.

flȳ′ing çŏl′ŏrs̱, 1. flags flying in the air.
2. victory or success.

flȳ′ing çol′umn (-um), a detachment of soldiers lightly equipped for rapid movement and operations independent of the main force.

Flȳ′ing Dutch′măn, 1. a fabled Dutch sailor condemned for his sins to sail the seas until Judgment Day.
2. his ghostlike ship, considered a bad omen by sailors who think they see it. The subject of an opera (1843) by Richard Wagner.

flȳ′ing fiēld, a field prepared for the landing, taking off, and minor servicing of aircraft: distinguished from *airport*.

flȳ′ing fish, any of various fishes, family *Exocoetidae*, whose winglike pectoral fins enable them to glide through the air.

flȳ′ing fox, a large fruit-eating bat with a foxlike head.

flȳ′ing frog, an East Indian tree frog whose long toes fully webbed enable it to glide through the air for short distances.

flȳ′ing gũr′nărd, any of various fishes with winglike fins, capable of flying short distances.

flȳ′ing lē′mũr, an East Indian tree-dwelling mammal of the genus *Galeopithecus*, which has membranes connecting the fore and hind legs and spreading like a parachute when the animal leaps: called also *colugo*.

flȳ′ing mȧ·çhīne′, any aircraft, especially an airplane.

flȳ′ing māre, in wrestling, a throw made by seizing the opponent's wrist, turning, and throwing him over one's back.

flȳ′ing mouse, a small marsupial animal of Australia: called also the *opossum mouse*.

flȳ′ing phȧ·lan′gẽr, a marsupial animal of Australia and New Guinea, capable of leaping like a flying squirrel.

flȳ′ing sau′cẽr, any of various unidentified objects frequently reported since 1947 to have been seen flying at great heights and high speeds, and variously regarded as light phenomena, hallucinations, secret military missiles, etc.

flȳ′ing spī′dẽr, see *ballooning spider* under *ballooning*.

flȳ′ing squid (skwid), in zoology, a cephalopod of the genus *Ommastrephes*, having broad lateral flippers or fins for leaping out of the water.

flȳ′ing squir′rel, any of certain squirrels with winglike folds of skin attached to the legs and body which enable them to make long, gliding leaps.

flȳ′ing wing, an airplane consisting of a single wing of thick section tapered toward the tips and having no fuselage or tail group.

flȳ′lēaf, *n.*; *pl.* **flȳ′lēaves̱** (-lēvz), a blank leaf at the beginning or end of a book.

flȳ mag′gŏt, a larva hatched from the egg of a blowfly.

flȳ′man, *n.* a man who attends to the flies in a theater.

flȳ net, a net to protect animals or people from flies and other insects.

flȳ nut, a nut with flattened wings that can be grasped with the thumb and finger.

flȳ or′çhis, in botany, an orchid whose flowers look like flies.

flȳ′pā·pẽr, *n.* paper smeared with poison or a sticky substance for the purpose of catching or killing flies: also *fly paper*.

flȳ pow′dẽr, any powder poisonous to flies.

flȳ press, a screw press with a heavy rimmed wheel or fly.

flȳ rāil, that part of a table which turns out to support the leaf.

flȳ rod, a very light and flexible fishing rod used when fishing with artificial flies.

flysch, *n.* [Swiss.] in geology, an extensive formation consisting mostly of sandstone, stretching from Switzerland east through the northern Alps as far as Vienna, where it is known as *Vienna sandstone*.

flȳ sheet, a small printed sheet of one page, for distribution by hand; a handbill.

flȳ′snap″pẽr, *n.* in ornithology, (a) a handsome fly-catching bird of southwestern United States and Mexico, the *Phainopepla nitens*; (b) a bird belonging to a genus *Myiarchus* of fly catchers.

flȳ′speck, *n.* 1. the excrementitious stains of flies and insects.
2. any tiny spot.

flȳ′speck, *v.t.*; flyspecked (-spekt), *pt.*, *pp.*; flyspecking, *ppr.* to make flyspecks upon.

flȳ'tāil, *n.* a little net for catching minnows.
flyte, *n.* and *v.* same as *flite.*
flȳ'trap, *n.* 1. a device for catching flies.
2. in botany, a species of sensitive plant called *Venus's flytrap*, the *Dionæa muscipula*, a plant that has the power of seizing insects that light on it.
flȳ'-up-the-çreek', *n.* 1. in ornithology, the little green heron, *Butorides virescens*, common along the streams of the United States: called also *shitepoke*.
2. a fickle or capricious person. [Colloq.]
flȳ'wei̤ght, *n.* a boxer who weighs 112 pounds or less.
flȳ'wei̤ght, *a.* of flyweights.
flȳ'wheel, *n.* a heavy wheel attached to a machine to regulate its speed and uniformity of motion.
fnēṣe, *v.i.* to snort; also, to sneeze. [Obs.]
F num'bẽr, in photography, the measurement of the ratio of a lens diameter to its focal distance: symbol f/, F/, f, F, f:, *f.*: the lower the F number, the shorter the exposure required.
Fō, *n.* [Chinese.] same as *Foh.*
fōal, *n.* [ME. *fole, foile*; AS. *fola*, a foal, colt.] the young of the horse, mule, donkey, etc.; a colt or filly.
foal teeth; a foal's first teeth.
with foal; pregnant: said of the female of the horse kind.
fōal, *v.t.* and *v.i.*; foaled, *pt., pp.*; foaling, *ppr.* to give birth to (a foal).
fōal'foot, *n.* the coltsfoot, *Tussilago farfara*, a plant whose leaf bears a resemblance to a colt's foot.
fōam, *n.* [ME. *fome, foom*; AS. *fam*, foam.]
1. froth; spume; the substance which is formed on the surface of a liquid by fermentation or by violent shaking.
2. something like foam, as the heavy sweat of horses, or frothy saliva.
3. the sea. [Poet.]
fōam, *v.i.*; foamed, *pt., pp.*; foaming, *ppr.* [ME. *fomen*; AS. *fæmen*, to foam, from *fam*, foam.]
1. to froth; to gather foam; as, the billows *foam.*
2. to be in a rage; to be violently agitated.
He *foameth* and gnasheth with his teeth.
—Mark ix. 18.
to foam at the mouth; to be very angry; rage.
fōam, *v.t.* 1. to throw out with rage or violence; with *out.* [Rare.]
Foaming out their own shame.—Jude 13.
2. to cause to foam.
fōam çock, a cock for relieving a steam boiler of foam.
fōam'flow·ẽr, *n.* a small American herb of the saxifrage family, with white flowers that bloom in the spring.
fōam'i·ly, *adv.* in a foamy manner.
fōam'i·ness, *n.* a foamy quality or state.
fōam'ing·ly, *adv.* frothily.
fōam'less, *a.* having no foam.
fōam rub'bẽr, rubber prepared in a firm spongy mass, used in upholstered seats, mattresses, etc.
fōam'y, *a.*; *comp.* foamier; *superl.* foamiest, [ME. *fomy*; AS. *famig*, from *fam*, foam.]
1. foaming or covered with foam.
2. consisting of foam.
3. like foam.
fob, *n.* [prob. from dial. G. *fuppe*, a pocket.]
1. a small pocket in the front of a man's trousers, for carrying a watch, etc.; a watch pocket.
2. a short ribbon or chain attached to a watch and hanging out of such a pocket.
3. any ornament worn at the end of such a ribbon or chain.
fob, *v.t.*; fobbed, *pt., pp.*; fobbing, *ppr.* [from ME. *fobbe, fobbere*, cheater, prob. var. of *foppe* (see *fop*).]
1. to cheat; to trick; to deceive. [Obs.]
2. to abuse; to mistreat. [Obs.]
Also spelled *fub.*
to fob off; (a) to trick or put off (a person) with something second-rate or undesired; (b) to get rid of (something worthless) by deceit or trickery; to palm off.
fob chāin, a ribbon or chain attached at one end to a watch, and at the other to a seal or charm.
fō'çăl, *a.* of or placed at a focus; as, a *focal* point.
focal distance; the distance from the optical center of a lens to the point where the light rays converge; length of the focus: also *focal length.*
focal infection; in medicine and dentistry, a localized infection, as in the tonsils, nasal sinuses, or gums, from which bacterial toxins ultimately attack other and distant organs of the body, reaching them through the blood stream.
focal reaction; in medicine, the reaction brought about in the localized region of a disease or point of infection by administering a test substance.
fō"çăl·i·zā'tion, *n.* a focalizing or being focalized.
fō'çăl·īze, *v.t. and v.i.*; focalized *pt., pp.*, focalizing, *ppr.* 1. to adjust or become adjusted to a focus.
2. in medicine, to limit or be limited to a small area: said of an infection.
fō'çăl length, focal distance.
fō'cī, *n.* alternative plural of *focus.*
fō'cil, *n.* [OFr. *focile*; LL. *focile*, lit., a spindle.] (a) the ulna or tibia, the greater bone of the forearm or leg; (b) the radius or fibula, the lesser bone of the forearm or leg: the former was called *greater focil*, the latter *lesser focil.* [Obs.]
foc'il·lāte, *v.t.* [L. *focillatus*, pp. of *focillare, focillari*, to revive by warmth, cherish, from *focus*, a fireplace.] to furnish with warmth or nourishment. [Obs.]
foc·il·lā'tion, *n.* comfort; support. [Obs.]
fō·cim'e·tẽr, *n.* [L. *focus*, a fireplace, (modern use) focus, and *metrum*, a measure.] in optics, an instrument for determining focal lengths of lenses.
fō·cim'e·try, *n.* the science of using a focimeter.
fō'ç''s'le (fōk'sl), *n.* forecastle: a phonetic spelling.
fō'çus, *n.*; *pl.* **fō'çus·eṣ** or **fō'cī,** [L. *focus*, a fireplace; hearth.]
1. the point where rays of light, heat, etc. or waves of sound come together, or from which they spread or seem to spread; specifically, the point where rays of light reflected by a mirror or refracted by a lens meet (called *real focus*), or the point where they would meet if prolonged backward through the lens or mirror (called *virtual focus*).

LIGHT RAYS — LENS — FOCUS

LIGHT RAYS BROUGHT INTO FOCUS BY LENS

2. the focal distance.
3. an adjustment of this distance to make a clear image; as, he brought the camera into *focus.*
4. any center of activity, attention, etc.
5. a part of the body where an infection is localized or most active.
6. in mathematics, either of two points the sum or difference of whose distances from any point on a curve or conic section is constant.
7. in seismology, the starting point of an earthquake.
aplanatic focus; see under *aplanatic.*
conjugate focus; in optics, one of two focal points, rays from either of which falling upon a lens or a mirror will be focused at the other: the two focal points are *conjugate foci.*
in focus; clear; distinct; sharply defined.
out of focus; indistinct; blurred; not sharply defined.
principal focus; in optics, the focus for solar rays or for any rays that are parallel.
fō'çus, *v.t.*; focused (-kust) *or* focussed, *pt., pp.*; focusing *or* focussing, *ppr.* 1. to bring into focus.
2. to adjust the focal distance of (the eye, a lens, etc.) in order to produce a clear image.
3. to fix on one object or purpose; to concentrate.
fō'çus, *v.i.* to meet at a focus.
fod'dẽr, *n.* an old standard of weight; a fother.
fod'dẽr, *n.* [ME. *fodder, foddur*; AS. *fodor, foddor, foddus*, food, fodder.] dry, coarse food for cattle, horses, and sheep, as hay, straw, etc.
fod'dẽr, *v.t.*; foddered, *pt. pp.*; foddering, *ppr.* to feed with fodder.
fod'dẽr·ẽr, *n.* one who fodders cattle.
fō'di·ent, *a.* [L. *fodiens* (*-entis*), ppr. of *fodere*, to dig, dig up.]
1. digging; throwing up with a spade.
2. adapted for digging or burrowing.
fō'di·ent, *n.* in zoology, a burrower; an animal of the *Fodientia.*
Fō·di·en'ti·ȧ (-shi-ȧ), *n.pl.* [from L. *fodiens* (*-entis*), ppr. of *fodere*, to dig, dig up.] in zoology, a subdivision of edentates having claws fitted for digging and burrowing.
fōe, *n.* [ME. *fo, foo, fa*; AS. *gefah*, an enemy, foe, *ge-* and *feh, fag*, guilty, outlawed.]
1. an enemy; one who maintains personal enmity, hatred, grudge, or malice against another.
2. an enemy in war; one of a nation at war with another; an adversary.
Either three years' famine, or three months to be destroyed before thy *foes.*
—1 Chron. xxi. 12.
3. one who opposes anything in principle; an ill-wisher; an opponent; as, a *foe* to religion; a *foe* to virtue.
4. one who or that which harms or restricts; as, monopoly is a *foe* to low prices.
Syn.—antagonist, adversary, enemy, opponent.
fōe, *v.t.* to treat as an enemy. [Obs.]
foēhn (fẽn), *n.* [G. *föhn, fön*, a warm south wind.] in meteorology, a warm, dry wind blowing down into the valleys of a mountain, especially in the Alps: also spelled *föhn.*
fōe'hood, *n.* enmity. [Obs.]
fōe'măn, *n.*; *pl.* **fōe'men,** an enemy; a foe. [Archaic or Poet.]
Foe·niç'ū·lum (fē-), *n.* [L.] in botany, a genus of plants of the parsley family native to Europe and cultivated for their sweet aromatic foliage; common fennel.
foe'tăl (fē-), *a.* same as *fetal.*
foe·tā'tion, *n.* same as *fetation.*
foe'ti·cīde, *n.* same as *feticide.*
foe'tŏr, *n.* same as *fetor.*
foe'tus, *n.* same as *fetus.*
fog, *n.* [perh. from Dan. *fog*, spray, drift; *snee-fog*, snow falling thick, a snowstorm; Ice. *fok*, spray, snowdrift.]
1. a large mass of water vapor condensed to fine particles, at or just above the earth's surface.
2. a cloud of dust, smoke, etc. obscuring the atmosphere.
3. figuratively, a befuddled state of mind; blurred, bewildered condition.
4. in photography, a blur on a print or film.
fog, *v.t.*; fogged, *pt., pp.*; fogging, *ppr.* 1. to cover or to obscure with fog.
2. to blur; dim; obscure.
3. to confuse; bewilder.
4. in photography, to make blurred.
fog, *v.i.* 1. to become surrounded or covered by fog.
2. to be or become blurred, dimmed, or obscured.
3. in photography, to become foggy, as a negative.
fog, *n.* [ME. *fogge*, grass; W. *ffwg*, dry grass.]
1. a new growth of grass after cutting or grazing.
2. long, rank grass left uncut or ungrazed.
3. moss. [Dial.]
fog, *v.t.* to feed (cattle) on fog.
fog, *v.i.* to act the pettifogger. [Obs.]
fog ȧ·lärm', a device to warn mariners of danger when fog obscures vision.
fog baṅk, a dense mass of fog.
fog bell, a fog alarm consisting of a bell whose ringing gives warning in foggy weather.
fog'bound, *a.* prevented from sailing because of fog.
fog'bōw, *n.* in meteorology, a bow or arch resembling in form a rainbow, but usually white or slightly tinted with a single color, produced by the reflection of light on the globules of fog.
fog'dog, *n.* a bright spot sometimes seen at the horizon in a fog.
fōge, *n.* a smelting furnace for tin. [Brit. Dial.]
fog'eat·ẽr, *n.* a fogdog.
fō'gey, *n.*; *pl.* **fō'geyṣ,** a fogy.
fog'fruit, *n.* a creeping, weedy herb along the banks of rivers, bearing a head of small bluish flowers.
fog'gāġe, *n.* rank or coarse grass not mowed or eaten down in summer or autumn.
fog'gẽr, *n.* one who deals in an underhand way; a pettifogger. [Obs.]
fog'gi·ly, *adv.* with fog; in a foggy manner.
fog'gi·ness, *n.* the state or quality of being foggy.
fog'gy, *a.*; *comp.* foggier; *superl.* foggiest,
1. filled or abounding with fog; misty; murky; as, a *foggy* atmosphere, a *foggy* morning.
2. dim; blurred; clouded.
3. confused; perplexed.
fog'horn, *n.* 1. a horn blown to give warning to ships in a fog.
2. a loud, strident voice.
fō'gie (-gi), *n.* same as *fogy.*
fog'less, *a.* having no fog; as, a *fogless* morning.
fō'gy, *n.*; *pl.* **fō'gieṣ,** a person who is old-fashioned or overly conservative in ideas and actions; as, an old *fogy.*

fō'gy·ish, *a.* of or like a fogy; old-fashioned.
fō'gy·iṣm, *n.* the condition of being a fogy.
fōh, *interj.* an exclamation of abhorrence or contempt; faugh.
Fōh (fō), *n.* the Chinese name of Buddha: also written *Fo* and *Foh-to.*
Fōh'iṣm, *n.* the Buddhism of the Chinese: also spelled *Foism.*
Fōh'ist, *n.* a believer in Foh, or Buddha; an advocate and devotee of Buddhism.
foi'ble, *a.* weak. [Obs.]
foi'ble, *n.* [Fr. *foible, faible,* from OFr. *feble,* feeble, weak.]
1. a small moral weakness, a slight frailty in character.
2. the pointed half of a foil or sword blade: the weaker part.
Syn.—peccadillo, failing, fault, weakness, infirmity, frailty, defect, imperfection.
foil, *v.t.*; foiled, *pt., pp.*; foiling, *ppr.* [ME. *foilen, foylen*; OFr. *fouler,* to trample upon, subdue; LL. *fullare,* to full cloth by trampling or beating, from L. *fullo,* a fuller.]
1. to frustrate; to keep from being successful; baffle; balk; thwart; as, the enemy attempted to pass the river, but was *foiled.*
And by a mortal man at length am *foiled.* —Dryden.
2. in hunting, to make (a scent, trail, etc.) confused, as by trampling, in order to balk the pursuers
foil, *n.* 1. a long, thin fencing sword that has a button at the end covered with leather to prevent injury.
2. the scent or trail of game.
3. the art or sport of fencing with foils.
4. a thwarting. [Archaic.]
5. in wrestling, a throw which is not a complete fall. [Obs.]
to run a foil; to puzzle: from the habit of certain animals of running back over their track to mislead pursuers.

FENCING FOILS

foil, *n.* [ME. *foile*; OFr. *foil, foel, feuill,* a leaf, sheet of paper or metal, from L. *folium,* a leaf.]
1. a leaflike, rounded space or design between cusps or in windows, etc., as in Gothic architecture.
2. a very thin sheet or leaf of metal; as, gold *foil,* tin *foil.*
3. a thin leaf of polished metal placed under a gem to give it brilliance, or under other substances to make them seem precious, as in some jewelry.
4. a person or thing that sets off or enhances another by contrast; as, Laertes is a *foil* to Hamlet.
5. a thin coat of tin, with quicksilver, laid on the back of a looking glass, to cause reflection.
foil, *v.t.* 1. to cover or back with foil.
2. to serve as a contrast to. [Rare.]
3. to decorate (windows, etc.) with foils.
foil'ȧ·ble, *a.* that may be foiled.
foil'ẽr, *n.* one who or that which frustrates or foils.
foil'ing, *n.* foil work in architecture.
foil'ing, *n.* among hunters, the slight mark of a passing deer, etc. on the grass.
foilṣ'măn, *n.*; *pl.* **foilṣ'men,** a fencer who uses a foil.
foin, *v.t.* and *v.i.* [ME. *foynen,* from OFr. *foine,* a pitchfork, fish spear.]
1. to thrust or lunge with a sword or spear. [Archaic.]
2. to prick; to sting. [Archaic.]
foin, *n.* a push; a thrust with a sword or spear. [Archaic.]
foin'ẽr·y, *n.* the act or practice of thrusting in fencing. [Archaic.]
foin'ing·ly, *adv.* in a pushing manner. [Archaic.]
Fo'iṣm (fō'izm), *n.* [from Chin. *Fo,* Buddha.] the Buddhism of China.
foi'ṣŏn, *n.* [OFr. *foison,* from L. *fusio,* an outpouring, abundance.]
1. a plentiful crop; good harvest; plenty. [Archaic.]
2. (a) vitality; strength; ability; (b) [*pl.*] resources. [Obs. or Dial.]
foist, *v.t.*; foisted, *pt., pp.*; foisting, *ppr.* [prob. from dial. D. *vuisten,* to hold in the hand, hence, in dicing, to conceal in the hand, palm off, from *vuist,* a fist.]
1. to put in slyly or stealthily; to insert surreptitiously, as a clause into a contract.
2. to pass off (something false) as genuine (with *on* or *upon*); to impose by fraud; to palm off.
foist, *n.* 1. one who foists or deceives. [Obs.]
2. a foisting; a deception. [Obs.]
foist, *n.* a light and fast-sailing ship. [Obs.]
foist'ẽr, *n.* a rogue; a cheat; a trickster. [Obs.]
foist'ied, *a.* of a musty or moldy character; fusty. [Obs.]
foist'i·ness, *n.* fustiness. [Obs.]
foist'y, *a.* same as *fusty.* [Obs.]
fōld, *v.t.* folded, *pt., pp.*; folding, *ppr.* [ME. *folden, falden*; AS. *fealden,* to fold, wrap up.]
1. to bend or press (something) so that one part is over another; to double up on itself.
2. to draw together and intertwine; as, *fold* your arms.
3. to draw close to the body; as, a bird *folds* its wings.
4. to clasp in the arms; embrace.
5. to wrap up; envelop.
to fold up; to make or become more compact by folding.
fōld, *v.i.* 1. to be or become folded.
2. to fail; be forced to close: said of a play, etc. [Slang.]
to fold up; to fail; be forced to close: said of a play, etc. [Slang.]
fōld, *n.* 1. a folding.
2. a folded part or layer.
3. a mark made by folding.
4. a hollow or crease produced by folded parts or layers.
5. in geology, a rock layer folded by pressure.
fōld, *n.* [ME. *fold, fald*; AS. *fald, falod,* a fold, stall.]
1. a pen or enclosure for sheep; a place where a flock of sheep is kept.
2. a flock of sheep.
3. (a) the members of a church; (b) a church; (c) any group or organization with common interests, aims, etc.
fōld, *v.t.* to gather into a fold, as sheep.
fōld, *v.i.* to be gathered into a fold, as sheep. [Rare.]
-fōld, [ME. *-fold, -fald*; AS. *-feald,* from *faldan,* to fold.] a suffix meaning: (a) *having* (a specified number of) *parts*; (b) (a specified number of) *times as many, as much, as large,* as in ten*fold,* hundred*fold.*
fōld'ăġe, *n.* same as *faldage.*
fōld'bōat, *n.* a faltboat.
fōld'ẽr, *n.* 1. one who or that which folds; specifically, a flat, pointed instrument often of bone, used in folding paper by hand.
2. a sheet of cardboard or heavy paper folded as a holder for papers.
3. a pamphlet or booklet folded but not stitched.
fol'de·rol, *n.* 1. a trifle; gewgaw.
2. mere nonsense.
3. a refrain in some old songs.
Also *falderal, falderol.*
fōld'ing, *n.* 1. a fold; a doubling; the act of making a fold.
2. the keeping of sheep in enclosures on arable land.
folding boat; a jointed boat covered with flexible, waterproof material so as to be folded and carried by tourists or fishermen.
folding chair; a chair with a hinged frame that can be compactly folded for transportation or for storing.
folding doors; a pair of doors with hinged leaves that unfold from either side of a wide doorway and meet in the middle to close it.
fōld'less, *a.* without folds.
fō'li·ȧ, *n.* alternative plural of *folium.*
fō·li·ā'ceous, *a.* [L. *foliaceus,* leafy, of leaves, from *folium,* a leaf.]
1. of or like a leaf of a plant.
2. consisting of leaves or thin layers; having the form of a leaf or plate; as, *foliaceous* spar.
3. having leaves.
fō'li·ăġe, *n.* [OFr. *foillage, feuillage,* from *foille, feuille,* a leaf, from L. *folium,* a leaf.]
1. leaves, as of a plant or tree; mass of leaves; leafage.
2. a decoration consisting of a representation of leaves, flowers, branches, etc.
fō'li·ăġe, *v.t.* to form into the representation of foliage. [Rare.]
fō'li·ăġed, *a.* having foliage: usually in hyphenated compounds; as, dark-*foliaged.*
fō'li·ăġe plant, a plant cultivated for the beauty of its foliage, as the coleus, the begonia, and others.
fō'li·ăr, *a.* [from L. *folium,* a leaf.] of or like a leaf or leaves.
foliar gap; the spreading or opening in the fibers of a stem where a leaf forms.
fō'li·āte, *v.t.*; foliated, *pt., pp.*; foliating, *ppr.* [LL. *foliatus,* pp. of *foliare,* to put forth leaves, from L. *folium,* a leaf.]
1. (a) to divide into thin layers; (b) to beat into foil.
2. to decorate with leaflike layers or ornamentation.
3. to number (the leaves of a book).
fō'li·āte, *v.i.* 1. to separate into layers.
2. to send out leaves.
fō'li·āte, *a.* [L. *foliatus,* leafy, from *folium,* a leaf.]
1. having or covered with leaves.
2. like a leaf or leaves.
foliate curve; in geometry, a folium.
fō'li·ā·ted, *a.* 1. beaten, cast, or otherwise made into a thin plate, as a foil.
2. decorated with ornaments resembling leaves in shape.
3. foiled, as a window; cusped; lobed.
4. covered with a thin foil or amalgam.
5. like or consisting of plates or thin layers; lamellar; as, a *foliated* fracture.
6. in heraldry, having leaves for adornment.
foliated tellurium; same as **nagyagite.**
fō·li·ā'tion, *n.* [from L. *foliare,* to put forth leaves, from *folium,* a leaf.]
1. a growing of or developing into a leaf or leaves; leaf formation.
2. the state of being in leaf.
3. the act or process of beating metal into layers.
4. (a) a splitting into leaflike layers: said of certain minerals and rocks; (b) the property of splitting into such layers; (c) such layers.
5. the process of covering glass with metal foil or some other reflecting substance to make a mirror.
6. the consecutive numbering of leaves, rather than pages, of a book.
7. a leaflike decoration consisting of small arcs or foils.
8. in botany, the way leaves are arranged in the bud; vernation.
fō'li·ȧ·tūre, *n.* 1. leafage; foliage.
2. the state of being beaten into foil.
fō'liç aç'id, [from L. *folium,* a leaf; and *-ic.*] a nitrogenous acid found in green leaves and in certain other plant and animal tissues, believed to be one of the vitamin B complex.
fō·li·i-, [from L. *folium,* a leaf.] a combining form used to mean *relation to a leaf.*
fō·li·iç'ō·lous, *a.* [*folii-,* and L. *colere,* to inhabit.] living and growing upon leaves.
fō·li·if'ẽr·ous, *a.* [*folii-,* and L. *ferre,* to bear.] bearing leaves or leaflike appendages.
fō'li·i·fọrm, *a.* [*folii-,* and L. *forma,* form.] shaped like a leaf.
fol'i·ly, *adv.* [ME. *foly,* foolish.] foolishly. [Obs.]
fō'li·ō (*or* fōl'yō), *n.*; *pl.* **fō'li·ōṣ,** [from L. *folio,* in the phrase *in folio,* in a sheet; *in,* in, and *folio,* abl. of *folium,* a leaf.]
1. a large sheet of paper folded once so that it forms two leaves, or four pages, of a book, manuscript, etc.
2. a book of the largest regular size, formed by folding a sheet of paper once; also, the size of book so made, usually more than 30 centimeters or 11 inches in height.
3. a leaf of a manuscript, book, etc. numbered on only one side.
4. the page number in a book, etc.: even numbers indicate the left, and odd, the right page.
5. the unit of measure of the length of a legal or official document by words per leaf (72 or 90 in England, 100 in the United States).
6. in bookkeeping, a page of a ledger, or facing pages with the same number.
7. a stand or case for loose papers.
in folio; in the form or size of a folio.
fō'li·ō, *v.t.*; folioed, *pt., pp.*; folioing, *ppr.* to page consecutively, as a book or manuscript.
fō'li·ō, *a.* having sheets folded once; of the size of a folio.
folio post; a size of paper, 17 by 22 inches.
fō''li·ō·braṅçh', fō''li·ō·braṅ'çhi·āte, *a.* [L. *folium,* a leaf, and *branchiæ,* gills.] in zoology, having gills in layers like the leaves of a book.
fō'li·ō·lāte, *a.* of or pertaining to small leaves.
fō'li·ōle, *n.* [a dim. from L. *folium,* a leaf.]
1. a leaflet; one of the parts of a compound leaf.
2. in zoology, any leaflike appendage.
fō''li·ō·lif'ẽr·ous, *a.* [*foliole,* dim. from L. *folium,* a leaf, and L. *ferre,* to bear.] bearing small leaves, or folioles.
fō'li·ōse, *a.* [from L. *folium,* a leaf.] in botany, having many leaves; leafy.

fō·li·os′i·ty, *n.* the bulk of a folio.

fō′li·ous, *a.* 1. leafy; thin; unsubstantial.
2. in botany, having leaves; bearing foliage.

-fō′li·ous, [from L. *folium*, a leaf.] a terminal combining form meaning *leaf*, used to form adjectives.

fō′li·ō vẽr′sō, [L.] on the back of the page.

fō′li·um, *n.*; *pl.* **fō′li·ums, fō′li·ȧ,** [L., a leaf.]
1. a thin leaf or plate.
2. in geology, a thin layer or stratum, as in metamorphic rock.
3. in geometry, the part of a curve enclosed by the intersection of two ends at its node; loop.

fōlk (fōk), *n.*; *pl.* **fōlk, fōlks,** [ME. *folk, folc*, people.]
1. a people; tribe; nation; ethnic group.
2. [*pl.*] people; persons; as, *folks* don't agree, town *folk* are not like farmers.
just folks; simple and unassuming; not snobbish; not putting on airs. [Dial. or Colloq.]
(*one's*) *folks*; (one's) family or relatives. [Colloq.]

fōlk, *a.* of or existing among the common people: often distinguished from *art*; as, *folk* ballads differ from art ballads.

fōlk dȧnce, 1. a traditional dance of the common people of a country or region.
2. music for this.

Fōl′ke·ting, Fōl′ke·thing (-ting), *n.* [Dan. *folk*, people, and *ting, thing*, a meeting.]
1. formerly, the lower branch of the Danish legislature.
2. the unicameral legislature of Denmark.

fōlk et·y·mol′ō·ġy, 1. the change that occurs in the form of a word over a period of prolonged usage so as to give it an apparent connection with some other well-known word; as, *cole slaw* becomes *cold slaw* through *folk etymology*.
2. unscientific etymology; popular but incorrect notion of the origin and derivation of a word.
Also called *popular etymology*.

fōlk′land, *n.* [AS. *folcland*; *folc*, the people, and *land*, land.] in old English law, land distributed among the people by the lord of the manor, and held entirely at his will.

fōlk′lōre, *n.* 1. the traditions, beliefs, customs, etc. of a people.
2. the scientific study of these.

fōlk′lōr·ist, *n.* a specialist or expert in folklore.

fōlk med′i·cine, the treatment of disease as practiced traditionally among the common people, involving especially the use of herbs and other natural substances.

fōlk′mo̤o̤t, *n.* [from AS. *folcgemot*; *folc*, the people, and *gemot*, a meeting.] an assembly of the people of a town, country, etc. [Obs.]

fōlk′mōte, fōlk′mōt, *n.* a folkmoot.

fōlk mū′ṣiç, music made and handed down among the common people.

fōlk′-rock, *n.* music with a rhythmic rock-and-roll beat, with words in a folk-song style.

fōlk so̤ng, 1. a song made by a common people and handed down from generation to generation: folk songs are usually of anonymous authorship and often have many versions.
2. a song composed in imitation of this.

fōlk speech, the common, everyday speech of the masses; the vernacular.

fōlk′sy, *a.* 1. of or like the common people. [Colloq.]
2. sociable. [Colloq.]

fōlk tāle, a story, often with legendary or mythical elements, made and handed down among the common people: also *folk story*.

fōlk′wāy, *n.* a way of thinking, feeling, behaving, etc. common to the members of the same social group.

fol′li·çle, *n.* [L. *folliculus*, a small bag, husk, pod, dim. of *follis*, a bellows.
1. in botany, a dry, one-celled seed capsule or pod, which opens along only one side to release its seeds, as a milkweed pod.
2. in anatomy, a small saclike cavity for secretion or excretion; as, a hair *follicle*.
3. in zoology, a cocoon.

fol′li·çle-stim′ū·lāt·ing ho̤r′mōne, a hormone, secreted by the anterior pituitary gland, which stimulates the development of ova in the female and testicular function in the male.

fol·liç′ū·lăr, *a.* 1. of or like a follicle.
2. growing out of a follicle or follicles.

fol·liç′ū·lāte, *a.* having or consisting of a follicle or follicles.

fol·liç′ū·lā·ted, *a.* folliculate.

fol·liç′ū·lin, *n.* same as *estrone*.

fol·liç″ū·lī′tis, *n.* [L. *folliculus*, a small bag, husk, pod, and *-itis*.] in medicine, an inflammation of one or more follicles.

fol·liç′ū·lous, *a.* having or producing follicles.

fol′lieṣ, *n.pl.* [*construed as sing.*] [pl. of *folly*.] a revue: used as part of the title.

fol′li·fu̇l, *a.* full of folly. [Obs.]

fol′lōw, *v.t.*; followed, *pt.*, *pp.*; following, *ppr.* [ME. *folowen, folwen, folgen*; AS. *folgian*, to follow.]
1. to come or go after.
2. to accompany; attend.
3. to go after in order to catch; pursue.
4. to go along; as, *follow* the right road.
5. to come or occur after in time, in a series, etc.
6. to take the place of in rank, position, etc.; as, he *followed* his father as manager.
7. to take up; engage in; as, he *follows* the plumber's trade.
8. to result from; as, disease often *follows* malnutrition.
9. to take as a model; act in accordance with; imitate.
10. to accept the authority of; obey; as, we *followed* the rules of the game.
11. to support or advocate the ideas, opinions, etc. of.
12. to watch or listen to closely; observe; as, she *followed* their conversation intently.
13. to be interested in or attentive to current developments in; as, he *follows* local politics.
14. to understand the continuity or logic of; as, do you *follow* me?
to follow out; to carry out fully.
to follow suit; in card playing, to play a card of the suit led; figuratively, to do as some one else does.
to follow the hounds; to hunt on horseback with hounds.
to follow up; to add to the effectiveness of by doing something more.

fol′lōw, *v.i.* 1. to come, go, or happen after or next after some thing or person in place, sequence, or time; as, you go and I will *follow* later.
2. to attend.
3. to be consequential, as effect to cause.
to follow on; to continue pursuit or endeavor; persevere.
to follow through; (a) to continue and complete a stroke after hitting the ball, as in golf or tennis; (b) to continue and complete an action.
to follow up; (a) to follow closely and persistently; (b) to carry out fully.

fol′lōw, *n.* 1. the act of following.
2. in billiards, a shot that causes the cue ball to continue rolling after striking the ball at which it was aimed: also *follow shot*.

fol′lōw·ẽr, *n.* [ME. *folwere*; AS. *folgere*, from *folgian*, to follow.]
1. one who follows; one who takes another as his guide in doctrines, opinions, or example; an attendant; an adherent; a disciple; as, the *followers* of Plato; the warrior distributed the plunder among his *followers*.

That ye be not slothful, but *followers* of them who through faith and patience inherit the promises. —Heb. vi. 12.

2. a male sweetheart. [Colloq.]
3. a sheet of parchment added to the first sheet of an indenture or other deed.
4. the part (of a machine) that receives motion from another part.
5. (a) the cover of a piston; (b) the cover of a stuffing box.
Syn.—adherent, disciple, partisan.

fol′lōw·ing, *n.* 1. collectively, a group of attendants or followers; those of like opinions and principles of action; as, Lincoln had a large and enthusiastic *following*.
2. an occupation. [Rare.]
the following; (a) the one or ones to be mentioned immediately; (b) what follows; what comes next.

fol′lōw·ing, *a.* 1. that follows; next after.
2. to be mentioned immediately; to be dealt with next; as, the *following* people were chosen.
3. moving in the same direction that a ship is moving: said of the tide or wind.

fol′lōw·ing, *prep.* after; as, *following* dinner he went home.

fol′lōw-through (-thrö), *n.* 1. the act or manner of continuing the swing of a club, racket, etc. to its natural end after striking the ball, as in tennis, golf, baseball, etc.
2. the final part of the stroke after the ball has been hit.

fol′lōw-up, *a.* designating or of anything that follows something else as a repetition or addition; as, *follow-up* visits, a *follow-up* letter.

fol′lōw-up, *n.* 1. a follow-up thing or event.
2. the use of follow-up letters, visits, etc.
3. a following up.

fol′ly, *n.*; *pl.* **fol′lieṣ,** [ME. *folye, folie*; OFr. *folie*, folly, foolishness, from *fol*, a fool.]
1. weakness of intellect; a lack of understanding, sense, or rational conduct.

Here (in newspaper) Fraud and Falsehood labour to deceive.
And *Folly* aids them both, impatient to believe. —Crabbe.

2. any foolish action or belief.
What *folly* 'tis to hazard life for ill.—Shak.
3. a crime. [Archaic.]
4. any foolish and fruitless but expensive undertaking.
Syn.—madness, nonsense, misconduct, imprudence, silliness, foolishness, weakness, absurdity, imbecility.

Fol′sŏm man, [from *Folsom*, New Mexico, where remains have been found.] a member of a race of people believed to have lived in North America at the time of the last glacial age.

Fō′mal·haut, *n.* [Ar. *fom-al-hūt*, mouth of a large fish; *fom*, mouth, and *hūt*, large fish.] a star of the first magnitude in the constellation Piscis Australis.

fō·ment′, *v.t.*; fomented, *pt.*, *pp.*; fomenting, *ppr.* [Fr. *fomenter*; L. *fomentare*, from *fomentum*, a warm application, poultice, from *fovere*, to keep warm.]
1. to apply warm water to; to bathe with warm, medicated lotions, etc.
2. to cherish with heat; to encourage growth of. [Obs.]
3. to stir up; arouse; instigate; incite; as, the unjust tax *fomented* rebellion.
Syn.—excite, encourage, engender, stir up.

fō′ment, *n.* fomentation. [Obs.]

fō·men·tā′tion, *n.* 1. treatment of bodily pain or injury by the application of warm, moist substances.
2. any liquid lotion, compress, etc. so applied.
3. a stirring up; arousing; instigation; incitement.

fō·ment′ẽr, *n.* one who or that which foments; one who or that which encourages or instigates.

fō′mēṣ, *n.*; *pl.* **fō′mi·tēṣ,** [L. *fomes* (*-itis*), kindling wood, tinder, from *fovere*, to warm, keep warm.] any substance that can absorb, hold, and transport infectious germs, as woolen fabrics and other substances.

fon, *n.* [ME. *fon, fonne*; Sw. *fane*, a fool.] a fool; an idiot. [Obs.]

fŏnd (fōṅ), *n.* [Fr. *fond*, from L. *fundus*, bottom.]
1. ground or background, specifically on which lace is worked.
2. foundation; basis; essential nature.
3. supply; fund.

fond, *v.* obsolete past tense of *find*.

fond, *a.*; *comp.* fonder; *superl.* fondest, [ME. *fond*, contr. of *fonned*, foolish, pp. of *fonnen*, to act like a fool.]
1. foolishly naive, credulous, or hopeful; indiscreet; imprudent. [Now Rare.]

Grant I may never prove so *fond*
To trust man on his oath or bond.—Shak.

2. insane; crazed. [Dial.]
3. foolishly tender and loving; doting; too indulgent.
4. affectionate; loving; tender; as, *fond* caresses.
5. cherished with great or unreasoning affection; doted on; as, my *fondest* wish.
6. trifling; valued by folly. [Obs.]
fond of; having a liking or affection for.
Syn.—loving, attached, affectionate, foolish, silly, weak, doting, enamored, devoted.

fond, *v.t.* to treat with great indulgence or tenderness; to caress; to coddle. [Obs.]

fond, *v.i.* to be fond; to be in love. [Obs.]

fon′dănt, *n.* [Fr.] a soft, creamy candy made of sugar, used especially as a filling for other candies.

fon′dle, *v.t.*; fondled, *pt.*, *pp.*; fondling, *ppr.*
1. to treat with tenderness; to caress.
2. to pamper; to coddle. [Obs.]

fon′dlẽr, *n.* one who fondles.

fond′ling, *n.* 1. the act of caressing or treating with tenderness.
2. a person or thing fondled or caressed.
3. a weakling. [Obs.]

fond′ly, *adv.* 1. naively; with simple trust; imprudently.

Fondly we think we merit honor then,
When we but praise ourselves in other men.
—Pope.

2. lovingly; affectionately.
3. foolishly. [Archaic.]

fond'ness, *n.* 1. foolishness; weakness; folly; lack of sense or judgment. [Obs.]
2. foolish tenderness.
3. tender passion; warm affection.

Her *fondness* for a certain earl
Began when I was but a girl. —Swift.

4. strong inclination or propensity; strong appetite or relish; as, *fondness* for peanut butter.
Syn.—attachment, affection, kindness, desire.

fon·dū', *a.* [Fr.] denoting a style of printing calico, wallpaper, etc., in which the colors are blended into each other.

fon'dụe, *n.* [Fr., fem. pp. of *fondre*, to melt.] a dish made of cheese, eggs, etc.

fonṣ et ō·rī'gō, [L.] source and origin.

font, *n.* [Fr. *fonte*, a casting, cast of type, from *fondre*, to cast, found.] in printing, a complete assortment of printing types of one size and style: also *fount*.

font, *n.* [L. *fons*, *fontis*, a fountain, spring.]
1. a bowl, usually of stone, to hold the water used in baptismal services.
2. a basin for the holy water used in symbolic washing on entering certain churches.
3. a fountain or spring. [Poet.]
4. a source; origin; beginning.

FONT WITH COVER

font'ăl, *a.* [LL. *fontalis*, from *fons*, *fontis*, a fount, spring.]
1. of a spring or source; original.
2. baptismal.

fon·tȧ·nel', fon·tȧ·nelle', *n.* [Fr. *fontanelle*, dim. of *fontain*, fountain.]
1. originally, (a) an outlet; (b) [Obs.] an opening in the body for the discharge of secretions.
2. any of the soft, boneless areas in the skull of a baby or young animal, which are later closed up by the formation of bone.

foṅ·tăṅge' (-tonj'), *n.* [named after the Duchesse de *Fontanges*, who introduced the fashion.] a knot of ribbons formerly worn as a headdress; a commode.

fọọd, *n.* [ME. *foode*, *fode*, from AS. *foda*, food.]
1. any substance taken into and assimilated by a plant or animal to keep it alive and enable it to grow; nourishment; nutriment.
2. solid substances of this sort: distinguished from *drink*.
3. a specified kind of food.
4. anything that sustains, nourishes, and augments; whatever helps something to keep active, grow, etc.; as, *food* for thought.

fọọd chāin, in ecology, a sequence (as grass, rabbit, fox) of organisms in a community in which each member feeds on the member below it.

fọọd cȳ'çle, in ecology, all the individual food chains in a community: also *food web*.

fọọd'less, *a.* without food; lacking provisions; barren.

fọọd poi'ṣŏn·ing, 1. the sickness resulting from eating food contaminated by either bacterial toxins or by certain bacteria, often causing vomiting, diarrhea, and prostration.
2. poisoning resulting from naturally poisonous foods, as certain mushrooms, or from chemical contaminants in food.

fọọd proc'es·sŏr, an electrical appliance that can mix, blend, purée, slice, grate, chop, etc. foods rapidly.

fọọd stamp, any of the Federal stamps of various denominations given or sold at less than face value to qualifying unemployed or low-income persons for use in place of cash in buying food.

fọọd'stuff, *n.* any material made into or used as food.

fọọd yolk (yōk), the part of the yolk of an egg that furnishes nourishment for the embryo, as distinguished from the part that produces germination.

fọọl, *n.* [ME. *fool*, *fole*, *fol*; OFr. *fol*, a fool, idiot; LL. *follus*, *follis*, foolish, from L. *follis*, a pair of bellows, windbag, in allusion to the puffed cheeks of a buffoon.]
1. one who is lacking in reason, or the common powers of understanding; an idiot; an imbecile. [Now Rare.]
2. a person with little or no judgment, common sense, wisdom, etc.; a silly person; a simpleton.

Experience keeps a dear school, but *fools*
will learn in no other. —Franklin.

3. a man formerly kept in the household of a nobleman or king to entertain by acting as a clown; professional jester: also *court fool*.
4. a victim of a joke or trick; dupe.
April fool; see under *April*.
feast of fools; a festival held in the Middle Ages at the time of Christmas holidays, the chief feature of which was the choosing of a bishop, an archbishop, or a pope, usually a boy from the choir, who presided and conducted in a mimicking way the ceremonies usually conducted by the dignitary he impersonated.
fool's cap; a cap, usually with bells, formerly worn by a court fool or jester.
fool's errand; a foolish, fruitless errand or adventure; labor performed with no result.
fool's gold; iron or copper pyrites, like gold in color.
fool's paradise; a state of deceptive happiness, based on illusions.
to be no (or *nobody's*) *fool*; to be shrewd and capable.
to play the fool; to act in a ridiculous manner; to do silly things; to clown.

fọọl, *v.i.*; fooled, *pt.*, *pp.*; fooling, *ppr.* [ME. *folen*, *folien*, from OFr. *foler*, *folier*, to be foolish, from *fol*, a fool, idiot.]
1. to act like a fool; to be silly.
2. to joke; to be playful.
to fool around; to do foolish, useless things; to trifle. [Colloq.]

fọọl, *v.t.* 1. to make a fool of; to trick; to dupe; to deceive; to impose on.
2. to infatuate; to make foolish. [Obs.]
to fool away; to spend in trifles, idleness, folly, or without advantage; to squander; as, *to fool away* time or money. [Colloq.]
to fool with; to trifle or meddle with. [Colloq.]

fọọl, *n.* [Early Mod. Eng., kind of trifle (confection); hence, prob. from *fool* (silly person) by analogy with *trifle*.] stewed fruit with cream, especially whipped cream.

fọọl'ẽr·y, *n.*; *pl.* **fọọl'ẽr·ieṣ,** 1. the practice of folly; habitual folly; attention to trifles.
2. an act of folly or weakness; something ridiculous.

fọọl'fish, *n.* same as *filefish*.

fọọl'hăr″di·hood, *n.* the condition characterized by being foolhardy.

fọọl'hăr″di·ly, *adv.* in a foolhardy manner.

fọọl'hăr″di·ness, *n.* the quality of being foolhardy.

fọọl'hăr″dy, *a.*; *comp.* foolhardier; *superl.* foolhardiest, [ME. *folhardi*, *folehardi*; OFr. *fol hardi*, foolishly bold; *fol*, foolish, a fool, and *hardi*, pp. of *hardir*, to make bold.] daring without judgment; rash; foolishly bold and venturesome.
Syn.—rash, precipitate, reckless, venturesome, incautious, headlong

fọọl'ing, *n.* a joking or clowning.

fọọl'ish, *a.* 1. lacking in sense or sound judgment; weak in intellect; unwise; imprudent; acting without judgment or discretion; silly; vain; trifling.

But *foolish* questions avoid.
—2 Tim. ii. 23.

2. ridiculous; despicable.

A *foolish* figure he must make. —Prior.

3. humble; worthless. [Archaic.]
Syn.—absurd, unwise, silly, simple, shallow, brainless, shallow-brained, incautious, weak-minded, imbecile.

fọọl'ish·ly, *adv.* in a foolish manner.

fọọl'ish·ness, *n.* 1. folly; nonsense; the state or quality of being foolish.
2. a foolish action or thing.

The preaching of the cross is to them that
perish *foolishness*. —1 Cor. i. 18.

fọọl'prọọf, *a.* so harmless, simple, or indestructible as not to be mishandled, injured, misunderstood, etc. even by a fool.

fọọls'çap, *n.* [so called from a fool's head and cap being formerly used as a watermark.]
1. any of various sizes of writing paper measuring from 12 by 15 inches to $13^1/_2$ by 17 inches.
2. a fool's cap.

fọọl'ṣ pärs'ley, a nauseating, poisonous European weed resembling parsley, *Æthusa cynapium*.

foot, *n.*; *pl.* **feet,** [ME. *foot*, *fot*; AS. *fot*, a foot; akin to D. *voet*; LG. *foot*; O.H.G. *fuoz*; Dan. *fod*; Sw. *fot*; L. *pes*; Gr. *pous*; Sans. *pad*, a foot, from Sans. root *pad*, to go.]
1. the lower extremity of the leg; the part of the leg, on which a person or animal stands or moves.
2. a thing like a foot in some way; specifically, (a) the part that a thing stands on; base; (b) the lowest part; bottom; as, the *foot* of a page; (c) the last of a series; as, go to the *foot* of the line; (d) the part of a sewing machine that holds the cloth steady.
3. the end of a bed, grave, etc. toward which the feet are directed.
4. *pl.* **foots,** the sediment in a liquid.
5. a group of syllables serving as a unit of meter in verse; especially, such a unit having a specified placement of the stressed or long syllable or syllables, as a trochee, dactyl, spondee, etc.
6. a plan of establishment; fundamental principles. [Obs.]
7. soldiers who march and fight on foot; infantry as distinguished from cavalry.
8. [alternative *pl.* **foot,** generally regarded as substandard.] a linear measure equal to 12 inches, from the approximate length of a human foot; one-third of a yard; 30.48 centimeters.
9. the part of a stocking, boot, etc. which covers the foot.
foot of the fine; formerly, in law, the last part of an acknowledgment of a title of transfer of land.
on foot; (a) standing; (b) walking or running; (c) planned and in course of prosecution; going on.
to have one foot in the grave; to be near death; be very old or ill. [Colloq.]
to put one on his feet; to assist by material aid one who has failed in business, so that he may continue.
to put one's foot down; to be firm; act decisively. [Colloq.]
to put one's foot in it (or *in one's mouth*); to make a blunder that causes one embarrassment or trouble. [Colloq.]
to put the (or *one's*) *best foot forward*; (a) to walk or run at top speed; (b) to make the best possible showing; (c) to try to appear at one's best. [Colloq.]
under foot; (a) on the surface of the ground; on the floor, etc.; (b) in the way; (c) under one's control.

foot, *v.i.*; footed, *pt.*, *pp.*; footing, *ppr.* 1. to dance; to tread to measure or music; to skip.
2. to walk; to go on foot.
3. to proceed; to move along, as a ship.

foot, *v.t.* 1. to kick; to strike with the foot; to spurn. [Obs.]
2. to settle; to establish.
3. to seize and hold with the talons. [Obs.]
4. to walk, dance, or run on, over, or through; tread.
5. to make or put on the foot of (a stocking, etc.).
6. to add (a column of figures) and set down a total.
7. to pay (costs, expenses, etc.); as, he *footed* the bill. [Colloq.]
to foot it; to dance, walk, or run.
to foot up; to add up, as items in a bill.

-foot, a combining form meaning (a specified number of) *feet long*, *high*, *tall*, or *deep*, used to form hyphenated adjectives, as six-*foot*.

foot'ăġe, *n.* the length expressed in feet: said especially of motion-picture film and, in mining, of work that is paid for by the foot.

foot'-and-mouth' dis·ēaṣe', an acute, contagious disease of cattle and deer, caused by a virus and characterized by fever and blisters in the mouth and around the hoofs: it can be transmitted to other domestic animals and man.

foot'bạll, *n.* [ME. (Scots.) *fut ball* (1424).]
1. any of several games played with an inflated leather ball by two teams on a field with goals at each end, the object being to get the ball across the opponents' goal: in *association football*, or *soccer*, the form most closely related to the original, the players are not allowed to use their hands or arms in advancing the ball, which is propelled chiefly by kicking; in *Rugby*, a form popular in England, the play-

ers may kick, throw, or run with the ball, but are not permitted to be in front of it while it is being carried or kicked by a teammate; in *American football*, the elaborated form developed from Rugby, the players may run ahead of the ball for interference, forward passes, etc.
2. (a) the elliptical, inflated ball used in playing American or Rugby football; (b) the spherical, inflated ball used in playing soccer.
3. any issue, problem, etc. that is passed about or shunted from one group to another; as, a political *football*.
foot′bōard, *n.* 1. a board or small platform used for resting or bracing the feet.
2. the board or panel across the foot of a bed.
3. a lever for the foot in operating a machine.
foot′boy, *n.* a young manservant or page.
foot brāke, a brake worked by pressure of the foot, as in an automobile.
foot′breadth (-bredth), *n.* the breadth of a foot.
foot′bridġe (-brij), *n.* a narrow bridge for use by pedestrians only.
foot′-çan″dle, *n.* a unit for measuring illumination: it is equal to the amount of direct light thrown by one international candle on a surface one foot away.
foot′çlọth, *n.* 1. originally, an ornamental cloth put over a horse's back.
2. a carpet; a rug.
foot′ed, *a.* having a foot or feet; especially, having (a specified number or kind of) feet: generally used in hyphenated compounds, as four-*footed*.
-foot′ẽr, a combining form meaning *a person* or *thing* (a specified number of) *feet tall* or *high*: used in hyphenated compounds, as six-*footer*.
foot′fạll, *n.* 1. a footstep.
2. the sound of a footstep or footsteps.
foot fạult, in tennis, failure to keep both feet behind the base line when serving, counted as a point against the server.
foot′gēar, *n.* covering worn on the feet, as shoes, boots, etc.
foot′glōve, *n.* a kind of clothing for the foot. [Obs.]
Foot Guärdṣ, guards for the British sovereign, composed of selected foot soldiers from five infantry regiments.
foot′hạlt, *n.* a disease that attacks the feet of sheep.
foot′hill, *n.* a low hill at or near the foot of a mountain or mountain range.
foot′hōld, *n.* 1. a place to put the feet in standing or climbing.
2. a secure position; as, the rumor had gained a *foothold*.
foot′hook, *n.* same as *futtock*.
foot′hot, *adv.* immediately; in extreme haste. [Obs.]
foot′ing, *n.* 1. the act of moving on the feet; walking, dancing, etc.
2. the act of adding up a column of figures; also, the sum so obtained.
3. a secure place to put the feet; firm foundation to stand on; established place; permanent settlement; foothold; also, a secure placing of the feet.

In ascents, every step gained is a *footing* and help to the next. —Holder.

4. a secure position or basis; foundation.

Taking things on the *footing* of this life only. —Blair.

5. a footprint; a track. [Rare.]

Like *footings* up and down impossible to be traced. —Bacon.

6. a basis for relationship; position in relation to others.

Lived on a *footing* of equality with nobles. —Macaulay.

7. the making of a foot for a stocking, etc.; also, the material used for this.
8. the plain edge of cotton lace without figures.
9. the finer detached fragments of whale-blubber, not wholly deprived of oil.
10. in architecture, the projecting base of a column, pedestal, wall, etc.
foot′ing bēam, in architecture, a tie beam.
foot ī′ron (-ũrn), 1. a step for the foot in entering a carriage.
2. a shackle for the foot of a prisoner. [Obs.]
foot jạw, in zoology, a limb which has been modified into a jawlike organ in crustaceans.
foot kēy, in music, a pedal of an organ.
foot′less, *a.* 1. without a foot or feet.
2. not supported; without basis or substance.
3. clumsy; not skillful or efficient. [Colloq.]
foot lev′el, a kind of level which serves also as a square and foot rule.
foot′lick″ẽr, *n.* a bootlicker; a sycophant; a fawner.
foot′līghts (-līts), *n. pl.* 1. a row of lights along the front of a stage, about on a level with the actors' feet.
2. the theater; the stage; acting as a profession.
foot′ling, *a.* [ppr. of *footle*, to trifle, talk foolishly; altered from dial. *footer*, to trifle.] trivial; trifling; silly and unimportant.
foot′ling, *a.* and *adv.* presenting the feet first.
foot′lock″ẽr, *n.* a small trunk containing the clothing and personal belongings of a soldier, usually kept at the foot of his bed.
foot′-lọọse, *a.* free to go wherever one likes or do as one likes.
foot′măn, *n.*; *pl.* **foot′men,** 1. a soldier who marches and fights on foot; infantryman. [Archaic.]
2. (a) originally, a man who ran on foot beside his master's horse or carriage; (b) a male servant who waits on table, opens the door, accompanies his employer in an automobile or carriage, etc.
3. in entomology, a moth, *Lithosia aurelia*, that resembles a footman in livery.
foot′măn·ship, *n.* the art or faculty of a runner or of a footman.
foot man′tle, a garment once worn to keep the gown clean in riding. [Obs.]
foot′märk, *n.* a footprint.
foot′nōte, *n.* an explanatory note or reference printed at the foot of a page.
foot′nōte, *v.t.* 1. to add a footnote or footnotes to.
2. to add confirmatory evidence to (a statement, etc.).
foot′pace, *n.* 1. a walking pace; normal speed of walking.
2. a step broader than the rest in a flight of stairs; a landing.
3. a raised platform on which the celebrant stands throughout the service of the Mass.
foot′pad, *n.* a highwayman or robber on foot.
foot pāġe, a footboy.
foot′päth, *n.* a narrow path or way for use by pedestrians only.
foot′plāte, *n.* same as *footboard*.
foot pōst, a mailman or messenger that travels on foot.
foot′-pound, *n.* a unit of energy, equal to the amount of energy required to raise a weight of one pound a distance of one foot.
foot′-pound′ăl, a unit of work, equal to the work done when a mass of one pound, accelerating at the rate of one foot per second per second, has moved a distance of one foot.
foot′print, *n.* an impression or mark made by a foot.
foot rāce, an athletic contest in speed on foot.
foot′rāil, *n.* 1. in railroading, a rail with a flange which is wide at the base.
2. any rail or raillike structure for supporting the feet, as under a seat or at the foot of a counter.
foot′rest, *n.* a support to rest the feet on.
foot′rōpe, *n.* in nautical usage, a piece of wire rope stretching along a yard, upon which men stand when reefing or furling: formerly called a *horse*; also, that part of the boltrope to which the lower edge of a sail is sewn.
foot rot, an ulcer in the feet of sheep and cattle.
foot rụle, a ruler, or measuring stick, one foot, or twelve inches, long and usually subdivided into eighths of an inch or less.
foots, *n.pl.* same as *foot*, sense **4.**
foot sçrew, a leveling screw.
foot sōl′diẽr (-jẽr), a soldier who moves and fights largely on foot; an infantryman.
foot′sōre, *a.* having sore and tender feet, as from much walking.
foot′stạlk (-stạk), *n.* 1. the stalk of a flower or stem of a leaf.
2. a stalklike part of an animal, as the muscle by which a barnacle attaches itself.
foot′stạll, *n.* 1. the stirrup of a woman's riding saddle.
2. in architecture, the base of a column.
foot′step, *n.* 1. a person's step.
2. the distance covered in a step.
3. a footprint; the mark or impression of the foot.
4. a footfall; the sound of a step; as, to hear approaching *footsteps*.
5. a step by which to go up or down.
6. in mechanics, a bearing upon which a vertical shaft rotates.
to follow in (*someone's*) *footsteps*; to repeat or imitate (someone's) actions.
foot′stick, *n.* in printing, formerly, a beveled stick placed at the foot of a page or pages in a form to quoin up against.
foot′stōne, *n.* a stone placed at the foot of a grave, to denote the position of the body in the grave: opposed to *headstone*.
foot′stọol, *n.* a low stool for supporting the feet of a seated person.
foot stōve, a small iron box holding live coals, formerly used in carriages, churches, etc., for keeping the feet warm.
foot′-tŏn, *n.* a unit of energy, equal to the amount of energy required to raise a weight of one ton a distance of one foot.
foot tū′bẽr·çle, any of the lateral appendages of worms, resembling a tubercle.
foot valve, a valve at the bottom of a pipe or cylinder opening upward; specifically, the valve in a steam engine opening between the condenser and the air pump.
foot′wāl″ing, *n.* the inside lining of the hull of a ship, extending to the lower deck.
foot′wạll, *n.* in mining, the rock upon which a vein of ore rests.
foot wäsh′ing, an ancient duty of hospitality requiring a host to wash the feet of his guests, and still observed as an ordinance by some Christian churches.
foot′wāy, *n.* 1. a footpath.
2. a sidewalk. [Brit.]
foot′weār, *n.* anything to wear on the feet; shoes, boots, slippers, etc.
foot′wŏrk, *n.* the manner of using the feet, as in boxing, dancing, tennis, football, etc.
foot′wōrn, *a.* 1. worn down by feet; as, a *footworn* pavement.
2. having tired feet, as after a long journey on foot; footsore.
foot′y, *a.* 1. of such a nature as to deposit lees, or foots.
2. low; good-for-nothing. [Slang and Brit. Dial.]
fọọ′zle, *v.t.* and *v.i.*; foozled, *pt.*, *pp.*; foozling, *ppr.* [perh. from G. *fuseln*, to bungle.] to make or do (something) awkwardly; bungle (a stroke in golf, etc.).
fọọ′zle, *n.* 1. a slow, awkward person; a bore. [Colloq.]
2. the act of foozling; an awkward or bungling stroke.
fop, *n.* [ME. *fop*, *foppe*, a fool; G. *fopper*, a jeerer, scoffer.]
1. originally, a foolish person.
2. a vain, affected man who pays too much attention to his clothes, appearance, etc.; a coxcomb; a dandy; a dude.
fop′dọọ″dle, *n.* a fop. [Obs.]
fop′ling, *n.* a petty fop.
fop′pẽr·y, *n.*; *pl.* **fop′pẽr·ieṣ,** 1. the actions, dress, etc. of a fop.

Let not the sound of shallow *foppery* enter
My sober house. —Shak.

2. something foppish.
fop′pish, *a.* of, characteristic of, or fit for a fop; vain and affected.
fop′pish·ly, *adv.* in a foppish manner.
fop′pish·ness, *n.* vanity and extravagance in dress; dandyism.
fọr, *prep.* [ME. *for*; AS. *for*, *fore*, before, for, on account of, through; D. *voor*; Ice. *fyrir*, before; Sw. *för*, before, for; Goth. *faúr*; L. *pro*, before; Gr. *pro*, Sans. *pra*, before, away.]
1. in the place of; instead of; as a substitute or equivalent; as, two apples *for* five cents.

And Joseph gave them bread in exchange *for* horses, and *for* flocks, and *for* the cattle of the herds. —Gen. xlvii. 17.

2. as representative of; on behalf of; as, the attorney did his best *for* his client.
3. in favor of; on the side of; in defense of; as, he fought *for* liberty.
4. suitable to; appropriate or adapted to; as, this vase is *for* flowers.
5. in the direction of; toward; as, the wheel came off and headed *for* the ditch.
6. with the purpose of going to; as, she just left *for* home.
7. with reference or in regard to; as, that is sufficient *for* the present; as *for* me, I am content.
8. in expectation of; in quest of; as expecting or seeking; as, wait *for* the next train; to write *for* money or *for* fame.
9. in honor of or in compliment to; as, the plant was named *for* its discoverer.

10. to the extent or amount of; as, his bond is good *for* ten thousand dollars.

11. at the price or payment of; as, he sold the house for $10,000.

12. to the length, duration, or extent of; throughout; through; as, the movie lasts *for* an hour, the road runs *for* five miles.

13. at (a specified time); as, an appointment *for* two o'clock.

14. meant to be received by or belong to a specified person or thing, or to be used in a specified way; as, flowers *for* a girl, money *for* paying bills.

15. as affecting (a person or thing) in a specified way; as, that will be bad *for* you.

16. notwithstanding; in spite of; as, it is true *for* all that.

17. in search of; as, to look *for* work.

18. because of; on account of; by reason of; as, *for* this reason I cannot go; to howl *for* pain.

19. expressing inclination, tendency, or bent; as, a love *for* art, a taste *for* drink.

20. as an offset to; as, to give blow *for* blow, tit *for* tat.

21. with a view to the use and benefit of; as, to provide *for* a family.

22. in the character of; as being; as, to take one *for* a miser.

23. because of the lack of; as, to be cramped *for* space.

24. in proportion or with reference to; as, the boy is tall *for* his age.

25. with the purpose of being, becoming, or doing something; as, to run *for* governor, a mill *for* sawing lumber.

26. in order; with the purpose; a redundant use of the word, formerly common; as, I came *for* to see you. [Obs. or Vulgar.]

27. before. [Obs.]

for all that; in spite of all that has been said or done.

for (a person or thing) *to*; that (a person or thing) will, should, ought, must, etc.; as, she wrote an order *for* the grocer *to* fill.

O! for; I wish that I had.

fọr, *conj.* [abbrev. of conjunctional phrases, as AS. *for tham*, for this, because, since; *for thy*, for this, therefore; *for thwæm*, wherefore, etc.] because: more formal than *because* and followed by an explanation or reason for what precedes; as, we shall win, *for* fortune is with us.

for why; why; wherefore. [Archaic.]

fọr, *n.* one who is in favor of something, as a legislative measure or proposition; also, what may be said on the affirmative side: opposed to *against*.

fọr-, [ME. *for-*; AS. *for-*, replacing *fer-*, *fær-*.] an Anglo-Saxon and Middle English prefix used chiefly with verbs, meaning: (a) *away*, *apart*, *off*, as in *for*bid, *for*get, *for*go: the original senses are now largely obscured; (b) *very much*, *intensely*, as in *for*weep, *for*frighted.

for′ȧġe, *n.* [ME. *forage*; OFr. *fourage*, forage, pillage, from *forrer*, to forage, from *forre*, *fuerre*, fodder, from L.G. *voder*, food, fodder.]

1. food of any kind for horses and cattle, as hay, corn, oats, etc.; fodder.

2. the act of providing forage; a search for provisions or food.

Col. Mawhood completed his *forage* unmolested. —Marshall.

for′ȧġe, *v.i.*; foraged, *pt.*, *pp.*; foraging, *ppr.*

1. to search for food or provisions.

2. to search for what one needs or wants (with *for* or *about*).

3. to ravage; to feed on spoil. [Obs.]

foraging ant; any of several species of tropical ants characterized by their habit of marching in great armies in quest of food.

for′ȧġe, *v.t.* 1. (a) to get or take food or provisions from; as, the army *foraged* the country round about; (b) to ravage; to plunder.

2. to supply with food or fodder; to feed; as, to *forage* horses.

3. to obtain by foraging; as, we *foraged* a midday meal.

for′ȧġe çap, a small undress cap worn by soldiers.

for′ȧ·ġẽr, *n.* one who or that which forages.

for′ȧ·līte, *n.* [L. *forare*, to bore, and Gr. *lithos*, stone.] in geology, a marking in sandstone, etc., resembling the burrow of a worm.

fō·rā′men, *n.*; *pl.* **fō·ram′i·nȧ, fō·rā′menṣ,** [L., a hole, from *forare*, to bore.]

1. a small opening, as a hole in a bone through which a nerve passes.

2. in botany, the orifice of the coats of the ovule.

foramen magnum; the large opening at the base of the skull through which the lower part of the medulla oblongata passes.

foramen of Monro; in anatomy, the opening between the lateral ventricles of the brain and the third ventricle, admitting the choroid plexus.

foramen of Winslow; in anatomy, an opening connecting the anterior and posterior cavities of the peritoneum.

fō·ram′i·nā·ted, *a.* having little holes; having foramina.

for·ȧ·min′i·fẽr, *n.* in zoology, any of the *Foraminifera*.

Fō·ram·i·nif′e·rȧ, *n.pl.* [L. *foramen* (*-inis*), a hole, and *ferre*, to bear.] an order of *Rhizopoda*, belonging to the subkingdom *Protozoa*, having a shell perforated by pores (foramina) through which slender filaments project.

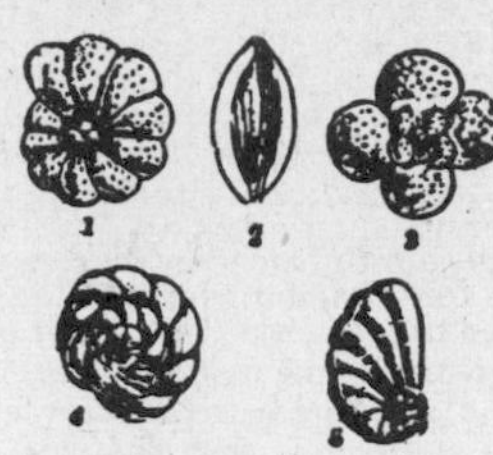

FORAMINIFERA
1. *Planorbulina ugeriana*; 2. *Triloculina tricarinata*; 3. *Globigerina bulloides*; 4. *Rotalia beccarii*; 5. *Nonionina turgida*

fō·ram·i·nif′ẽr·ous, *a.* 1. composed of or pertaining to *Foraminifera*.

2. foraminated.

fō·ram′i·nous, *a.* containing foramina.

fō·ram′i·nūle, *n.* [dim. from L. *foramen* (*-inis*), a hole.] a small foramen.

for·ȧ·min′ū·lous, *a.* foraminulose.

fọr·aṣ·much′, *conj.* inasmuch (followed by *as*).

Forasmuch then *as* we are the offspring of God. —Acts xvii. 29.

for′āy, *v.t.* and *v.i.*; forayed, *pt.*, *pp.*; foraying, *ppr.* to ravage; to plunder; to raid for spoils.

for′āy, *n.* [a form of *forage*.]

1. a sudden or irregular excursion in border warfare, especially one with a view to plunder.

2. the act of foraging.

for′āy·ẽr, *n.* one who engages in forays.

fọrb, *n.* [Gr. *phorbē*, fodder, from *pherbein*, to feed, graze.] a broad-leaved flowering plant, as distinguished from the grasses, sedges, etc.

fọr·bade′, fọr·bad′, *v.* past tense of *forbid*.

fọr·beār′, *v.t.*; forebore *or archaic* forbare, *pt.*; forborne, *pp.*; forbearing, *ppr.* [ME. *forberen*; AS. *forberan*, to abstain from, bear, endure; *for-*, and *beran*, to bear.]

1. to refrain from; to avoid (doing, saying, etc.).

2. to endure; to tolerate. [Archaic or Dial.].

fọr·beār′, *v.i.* 1. to refrain or abstain.

Shall I go against Ramoth Gilead to battle, or shall I *forbear?* —1 Kings xxii. 6.

2. to refuse; to decline.

Whether they will hear, or whether they will *forbear*. —Ezek. ii. 7.

3. to keep oneself in check; to control oneself.

Syn.—abstain, refrain, pause, desist.

for′beār, *n.* same as *forebear*.

fọr·beār′ănce, *n.* 1. the act of forbearing.

2. the quality of being forbearing; self-control; patient restraint.

Have a continent *forbearance*, till the speed of his rage goes slower. —Shak.

3. in law, an extension of time for the payment of a debt.

fọr·beār′ănt, *a.* forbearing.

fọr·beār′ẽr, *n.* one who forbears.

fọr·beār′ing, *a.* patient; long-suffering.

fọr·beār′ing·ly, *adv.* in a forbearing, patient manner.

fọr·bid′, *v.t.*; forbade *or* forbad, *pt.*; forbidding, *ppr.*; forbidden *or archaic* forbid, *pp.* [ME. *forbeden*; AS. *forbeodan*, to forbid, prohibit; *for-*, and *beodan*, to command.]

1. to prohibit; to interdict; to rule against; not permit; as, to *forbid* smoking; to *forbid* the banns of marriage.

2. to command not to enter; to exclude or bar from; as, I have *forbidden* him my house or presence.

3. to make impossible; to prevent; to obstruct; as, an impassable river *forbids* the approach of the army.

A blaze of glory that *forbids* the sight. —Dryden.

4. to challenge. [Obs.]

Syn.—interdict, oppose, prohibit, preclude, debar, restrain.

fọr·bid′, *v.i.* to utter a prohibition; to stand in the way.; as, I would go, but my health *forbids*.

fọr·bid′dănce, *n.* the act of forbidding; prohibition. [Rare.]

fọr·bid′den, *a.* 1. prohibited; interdicted; as, the *forbidden* fruit.

2. hindered; obstructed.

forbidden fruit; (a) in the Bible, the fruit of the tree of knowledge, forbidden to Adam and Eve: Gen. ii. 17.; iii. 3.; (b) something desired but prohibited; (c) in botany, one of several species of *Citrus*, including the fruit of the shaddock, *Citrus grandis*.

fọr·bid′den·ly, *adv.* in a forbidden manner.

fọr·bid′den·ness, *n.* the state of being prohibited.

fọr·bid′dẽr, *n.* one who or that which forbids.

fọr·bid′ding, *a.* repelling approach; repulsive; looking dangerous, threatening, or disagreeable; frightening; as, a *forbidding* aspect.

Syn.—repulsive, deterrent, prohibitory, offensive, disagreeable, odious.

fọr·bid′ding·ly, *adv.* in a forbidding manner.

fọr·bid′ding·ness, *n.* the state or quality of being forbidding; repulsiveness; offense; disagreeableness.

fọr·black′, *a.* [*for-*, intens., and *black*.] extremely black. [Obs.]

fọr·bōre′, *v.* past tense of *forbear*.

fọr·bōrne′, *v.* past participle of *forbear*.

fọr·brụiṣe′, *v.t.* to bruise very much. [Obs.]

fọr·by′, fọr·bye′, *prep.* [ME. *forbi*; see *for* and *by*].

1. close by; near; next to. [Scot. or Archaic.]

2. besides. [Scot. or Archaic.]

fọr·by′, fọr·bye′, *adv.* 1. to one side; aside. [Scot. or Archaic.]

2. past. [Scot. or Archaic.]

3. besides. [Scot. or Archaic.]

fọr·çärve′, *v.t.* to cut through completely. [Obs.]

fōrce, *n.* [Ice. *fors*; Dan. *fos*, a waterfall.] a waterfall: so called from its violence or power. [Brit. Dial.]

fōrce, *v.t.* [an alteration of *farce*.] to fill by stuffing. [Obs.]

fōrce, *v.t.* [OFr. *forcer*, to clip, shear, from *forces*, shears.] to cut off with shears. [Obs.]

fōrce, *n.* [ME. *force*, *fors*; OFr. *force*; LL. *forcia*, *fortia*, from L. *fortis*, strong.]

1. strength; energy; vigor; power.

2. the intensity of power; impetus; as, the *force* of the blow knocked him down.

3. (a) physical power or strength exerted against a person or thing; as, he used *force* in opening the door; (b) the use of physical power to overcome or restrain a person; physical coercion; violence; as, the police resorted to *force* to disperse them.

4. the power of a person to act effectively and vigorously; moral strength; as, *force* of character.

5. the power to control, persuade, influence, etc.; effectiveness.

6. military, naval, or air power.

7. any organized group of soldiers, sailors, etc.

8. any group of people organized for some activity; as, a *sales* force.

9. in law, binding power; validity.

10. in physics, the cause of motion, or of change or stoppage of motion, of a body.

animal force; muscular power.

by force and arms; in law, by force; violently.

in force; (a) in full strength; in full number; (b) in effect; valid; operative.

of force; (a) valid; in force; (b) [Obs.] necessarily.

vital force; see *vital principle*, under *vital*.

Syn.—strength, power, might, energy.

fōrce, *v.t.*; forced (fōrst), *pt.*, *pp.*; forcing, *ppr.* [OFr. *forcier*; LL. *forciare*, *fortiare*, from L. *fortis*, strong, powerful.]

1. to compel; to make (a person or animal) do something by force; as, masters *forced* their slaves to labor.

2. to rape (a woman).

3. (a) to break open, into, or through by force; (b) to make (a way, etc.) by force; (c) to overpower or capture by breaking into, through, etc.; as, we *forced* the enemy's stronghold.

4. to exert to the utmost.

Forcing my strength, and gathering to the shore. —Dryden.

5. to get or take by force; wrest; extort; as, I *forced* the gun from his hand.
6. to drive by, or as by force; cause to move against resistance; impel; as, you may strip the thread if you *force* the bolt; hunger *forced* him to steal.
7. to impose by or as by force (with *on* or *upon*); as, he *forced* his attentions *on* her.
8. to effect or produce by or as by force; produce by unusual or unnatural effort; as, she *forced* a smile.
9. to cause (plants, fruit, etc.) to develop or grow faster by artificial means.
10. (a) to give or add force to; (b) to put in force. [Obs.]
11. in baseball, (a) to cause (a base runner) to be put out at an advanced base by occupying the base behind him; (b) to send (a runner) home to score by walking the batter with the bases full; (c) to cause (a run) to be scored in this way.
12. in card games, (a) to play so as to cause (an opponent) to play a particular card; (b) to cause (a particular card) to be played in this way.
Syn.—coerce, compel, drive, make, necessitate.

fōrce, *v.i.* to endeavor; to strive; to use violence; also, to be of importance. [Obs.]

fōrced (fōrst), *a.* 1. done or brought about by force; not voluntary; compulsory; as, *forced* labor.
2. produced or kept up by unusual effort; not natural; not spontaneous; strained; constrained; as, a *forced* smile.
forced march; in military usage, a long march at a pace faster than usual.
forced sale; a property sale under the authority of a court for payment of a debt; foreclosure sale.
forced vibration; any vibration which differs in rate from the natural or normal because of the action of some outside force.

fōr′ced·ly, *adv.* in a forced manner; by compulsion.

fōr′ced·ness, *n.* the state of being forced.

fōrce feed, a method of pressure lubrication used in internal-combustion engines.

fōrce′fụl, *a.* 1. impelled by violence; driven with force; acting with power.

Against the steed he threw
His *forceful* spear. —Dryden.

2. possessing force; forcible; effective; cogent; as, a *forceful* argument or speech.

fōrce′fụl·ly, *adv.* in a forceful manner.

fōrce′less, *a.* having little or no force; feeble; impotent.

fọrce mȧ·jeūre′ (-zhẽr′), [Fr.]
1. overpowering force.
2. in Roman law, an act of God.

fōrce′mēat, *n.* [alteration of *farce meat*, from Fr. *farcir*, to stuff.] meat chopped fine and highly seasoned, usually used as a stuffing.

fōrce′ment, *n.* a forcing. [Obs.]

fōrce′-out, *n.* in baseball, an out scored against a base runner when he is forced from a base by a teammate's hit and fails to reach the advance base before the ball does.

fọr′ceps, *n.*; *pl.* **fọr′ceps,** rarely **fọr′ceps·eṣ** [L., a pair of tongs, pincers, from *formus*, hot, and *capere*, to take.]
1. small pincers or tongs, used for seizing and holding, and for extracting small objects: used by watchmakers and jewelers, dentists, surgeons, etc.
2. the caudal appendages of certain insects, named from their resemblance to a dentist's forceps.
3. any part or process of an animal body resembling a forceps.

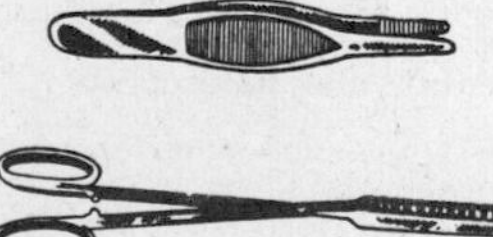

FORCEPS

fōrce pump, a pump with a valveless plunger for forcing a liquid through a pipe, especially for sending water under pressure to a considerable height.

fōr′cẽr, *n.* 1. one who or that which forces, drives, or constrains.
2. the solid piston of a pump; the instrument by which water is driven up a pump under pressure.
3. a small pump worked by hand, used in sinking small pits, draining cellars, etc.

fōr′ci·ble, *a.* 1. having force; forceful; impressive; as, *forcible* words or arguments.
2. done by force; brought about by force; as, a *forcible* abdication or abduction.
forcible detainer; a violent withholding of the lands or goods of another from his possession.
forcible entry; an actual, violent entry into houses or lands without lawful authority.
Syn.—irresistible, cogent, mighty, potent, powerful, strong, effective.

fōr′ci·ble-fee″ble, *a.* apparently vigorous but really feeble; as, a *forcible-feeble* style.

fōr′ci·ble·ness, *n.* the condition or quality of being forcible.

fōr′ci·bly, *adv.* in a forcible manner.

fōr′cing, *n.* the attainment of an end by some process of abnormal development; specifically, (a) in gardening, the art of securing premature vegetation and blooming by means of artificial heat; (b) in wine-making, the fining of wine by artificial methods.

fōr′cing en′ġine, same as *fire engine*.

fōr′cing house, in horticulture, a hothouse for forcing plants.

fōr′cing pit, a pit of wood or masonry, sunk in the earth, for containing fermenting materials to produce bottom heat in forcing plants.

fōr′cing pump, same as *force pump*.

fọr′ci·pǎl, *a.* of the nature of a forceps. [Obs.]

fọr′ci·pāte, *a.* [from L. *forceps* (*-ipis*), a pair of pincers.] formed like a pair of forceps; as, a *forcipate* mouth.

fọr′ci·pā·ted, *a.* forcipate.

fọr·ci·pā′tion, *n.* 1. a pinching with pincers; torture by means of forceps. [Obs.]
2. in zoology, the state or condition of being shaped like forceps; bifurcation.

fọr·cip′ū·lāte, *a.* [a dim. from *forcipate*, from L. *forceps* (*-ipis*), a pair of pincers.] in zoology, relating to an order of echinoderms characterized by small pincerlike dermal appendages.

fōr′cīte, *n.* an explosive substance containing nitroglycerin.

fọr·cut′, *v.t.* to cut through. [Obs.]

fōrd, *n.* [ME. *ford*; AS. *ford*, a ford.]
1. a shallow place in a river or other body of water where it can be passed or crossed by walking or by riding on horseback, in an automobile, etc.
2. a stream to be crossed. [Poet.]

Permit my ghost to pass the Stygian *ford*.
—Dryden.

fōrd, *v.t.*; forded, *pt., pp.*; fording, *ppr.* to pass or cross, as a river or other body of water, at or by way of a ford.

fōrd′ȧ·ble, *a.* that can be forded.

fōrd′ȧ·ble·ness, *n.* the state of being fordable.

fōrd′less, *a.* too deep to be forded; having no ford.

fọr·dö′, *v.t.*; fordid, *pt.*; fordoing, *ppr.*; fordone, *pp.* [ME. *fordon*; AS. *fordon*, to destroy, ruin; *for-* priv., and *don*, to do.]
1. to destroy; to undo; to ruin. [Archaic.]
2. to cause to become exhausted: only in the past participle. [Archaic.]

The heavy plowman snores,
All with weary task *fordone*. —Shak.

Also *foredo*.

fọr·dōne′, *a.* [ME. *fordon*, pp. of *fordon*, to ruin, destroy; AS. *fordon*.] completely exhausted: also spelled *foredone*. [Archaic.]

fọr·drīve′, *v.t.* to drive hither and thither. [Obs.]

fọr·druñk′en, *a.* [AS. *fordruncen*; *for-*, intens., and *druncen*, drunk.] very drunk. [Obs.]

fọr·drȳ′, *v.i.* to dry up. [Obs.]

fọr·dwīne′, *v.i.* [AS. *fordwinan*; *for-*, away, and *dwinan*, to pine.] to waste away. [Obs.]

fōre-, [from AS. *fore-*, *for-*.] a prefix meaning (a) *before in time, place, order*, or *rank*, as in *fore*cast, *fore*noon; (b) *the front part of*, as in *fore*arm, *fore*head.

'fōre, *prep.* before. [Poet.]

fōre, *adv.* [ME.; AS. *fore*.]
1. at, in, or toward the front: now only with reference to the front part, or bow, of a ship, and opposed to *aft*.
2. before, in time; previously. [Obs.]

fōre, *a.* 1. advanced; being in advance of something in motion or progression; as, the *fore* oxen or horses in a team.
2. advanced in time; coming in advance of something; coming first; anterior; preceding; prior; as, the *fore* part of the last century; the *fore* part of the day, week, or year.
3. advanced in order or series; antecedent; as, the *fore* part of a writing or bill.
4. being in front or toward the face: opposed to *back* or *behind*; as, the *fore* part of a garment.
5. at or near the front; as, the *fore* part of a ship or of a coach.
fore boot; in a stagecoach, a compartment under the driver's footboard, for stowing baggage.
fore bow; the front part or pommel of a saddle.
fore sight; in gunnery, that sight of a gun which is nearest to the muzzle, as distinguished from the *rear sight*.

fōre, *n.* [AS. *fore*, before.] the thing or part in front; hence, the foremast of a ship; as, she flew the royal standard at her *fore*.
at the fore; in nautical usage, at the top of the foremast: said of an unfurled flag, etc.
to the fore; (a) to the front; into view; into prominence; (b) at hand; available; (c) alive; still active.

fōre, *prep.* before: used chiefly in oaths. [Obs.]

fōre, *interj.* in golf, a shout warning those ahead that one is about to drive the ball.

fōre·ad·vīṣe′, *v.t.* to advise or counsel before the time of action, or before the event.

fōre·al·leġe′, *v.t.* to allege or cite before.

fōre′-and-ȧft′, *a.* in nautical usage, from the bow to the stern; lengthwise; set lengthwise.

fōre and ȧft, in nautical usage, (a) from the bow to the stern; lengthwise; set lengthwise; (b) at, in, or toward both the bow and the stern.

fōre′-and-ȧf′tẽr, *n.* a schooner, ketch, or other ship with fore-and-aft rig.

fōre·ap·point′, *v.t.* to set, order, or appoint beforehand.

fōre·ap·point′ment, *n.* previous appointment; preordination.

fōre·ärm′, *v.t.*; forearmed, *pt., pp.*; forearming, *ppr.* to arm or prepare for attack or resistance before the time of need.

fōre′ärm, *n.* in anatomy, that part of the arm between the elbow and the wrist.

fōre·ärmed′, *a.* armed beforehand; as, forewarned, *forearmed*.

fōre′bāy, *n.* a deep receptacle at the end of a mill-race, from which the water is admitted to the wheel.

fōre′bēam, *n.* in weaving, the beam on which the web is wound; the breastbeam.

fōre′beār, fọr′beār, *n.* a forefather; an ancestor: usually in the plural; as, the courtly manners of our *forebears*.

fōre·bōde′, *v.t.*; foreboded, *pt., pp.*; foreboding, *ppr.* [AS. *forebodian*; *fore-*, before, and *bodian*, to announce, declare.]
1. to foretell; to portend; to indicate beforehand: usually of something bad or harmful.
2. to foresee; to feel a secret premonition of (something bad or harmful); as, my heart *forebodes* a sad reverse.

fōre·bōde′, *v.i.* to prophesy.
Syn.—augur, betoken, portend, foretell, presage, prognosticate, prophesy.

fōre·bōde′, *n.* foresight; augury. [Obs.]

fōre·bōde′ment, *n.* the act of foreboding.

fōre·bōd′ẽr, *n.* one who forebodes; a prognosticator.

fōre·bōd′ing, *n.* a prediction, portent, or presentiment, especially of something bad or harmful.

fōre·bōd′ing·ly, *adv.* in a foreboding or threatening manner.

fōre′bod″y, *n.*; *pl.* **fōre′bod″ieṣ,** that part of a ship forward of the midship section.

fōre′brāce, *n.* a rope attached to the fore yardarm, to regulate the position of the foresail.

fōre′brāin, *n.* 1. the front part of the brain of an embryo.
2. the part of the fully developed brain evolved from this.

fōre·bȳ′, *adv.* and *prep.* see *forby*.

fōre çab′in, a cabin in the fore part of a ship, with accommodations generally inferior to those of the after cabin or saloon.

fōre′çar″riaġe (-rij), *n.* the part of a four-wheeled vehicle including the fore wheels and parts immediately related.

fōre·çȧst′ (*or* fōr′kȧst), *v.t.*; forecast, *or* forecasted, *pt., pp.*; forecasting, *ppr.* 1. to estimate or calculate in advance; to predict; to prophesy.

It is wisdom to *forecast* consequences.
—L'Estrange.

2. to plan in advance; to foresee.

He shall *forecast* his devices against the strongholds. —Dan. xi. 24.

3. to serve as a prediction or forecast of.

fōre·çȧst′, *v.i.* to form a scheme previously; to contrive something beforehand.

If it happen as I did *forecast*. —Milton.

fōre′ça̤st, *n.* 1. foresight; forethought; as, a man of little *forecast.* [Rare.]
2. a prediction or prophecy, as of the weather.
fōre·ça̤st′ẽr, *n.* one who forecasts.
fōre′ças·tle (fōk′sl; fōr′kȧs-l *is a spelling pronun.*) *n.* [*fore,* and *castle*: so called from the foremost of the two castlelike structures set on the hull of a medieval vessel to command an enemy's decks.]
1. the upper deck of a ship in front of the foremast.
2. the front part of a merchant ship, where the sailors' quarters are located.
Also *fo'c's'le.*
fōre·chō′şen, *a.* pre-elected; chosen beforehand. [Obs.]
fōre′cīt″ed, *a.* cited or quoted before or above.
fōre·clōşe′, *v.t.*; foreclosed, *pt., pp.*; foreclosing, *ppr.* [ME. *forclosen,* from OFr. *forclos,* pp. of *forclore,* to exclude, from *fors* (from L. *foris*), outside, and *clore* (from L. *claudere*), to close.]
1. to shut out; exclude; bar.
The embargo with Spain *foreclosed* this trade. —Carew.
2. to deprive of the right to redeem a mortgage when regular payments have not been kept up.
3. to take away the right to redeem (a mortgage, etc.).
fōre·clōşe′, *v.i.* to foreclose a mortgage, etc.
fōre·clō′şūre (-zhũr), *n.* the foreclosing of a mortgage, etc.
strict foreclosure; in law, a proceeding by which mortgaged property passes directly into the possession of the mortgagee.
fōre·cŏn·cēive′, *v.t.* to preconceive; to conceive beforehand. [Obs.]
fōre′çourse, *n.* the fore mainsail of a square-rigged ship.
fōre′çourt, *n.* 1. a court at the front of a building.
2. in tennis, badminton, etc., the part of the court nearest the net.
fōre·dāte′, *v.t.* to antedate.
fōre′deck, *n.* the fore part of a deck.
fōre·deem′, *v.t.* and *v.i.* to judge in advance; to foretell. [Obs.]
fōre·dē·şīgn′ (-zīn′), *v.t.* to plan beforehand; to forecast.
fōre·dē·tẽr′mine, *v.t.* to decree beforehand.
fōre·dis·pōşe′, *v.t.* to dispose or bestow beforehand. [Rare.]
fōre·dō′, *v.t.* to fordo. [Archaic.]
fōre·dōne′, *a.* fordone. [Archaic.]
fōre·dọọm′, *v.t.* to doom beforehand; to predestinate; to condemn in advance.
Thou art *foredoomed* to view the Stygian state. —Dryden.
fōre′dọọm, *n.* a sentence or judgment in advance; destiny.
fōre′dōor, *n.* the front door of a house. [Brit. Dial.]
fōre′-eld″ẽr, *n.* an ancestor. [Brit. Dial. and Scot.]
fōre′fä″thẽr, *n.* an ancestor; one who precedes another in the line of genealogy in any degree, but usually in a remote degree.
Forefathers' Day; December 22, the anniversary of the landing of the Pilgrims at Plymouth, Massachusetts, in 1620.
fōre·feel′, *v.t.*; forefelt, *pt., pp.*; forefeeling, *ppr.* to feel beforehand; to have a premonition of.
fōre·feel′, *n.* a forefeeling; a premonition. [Rare.]
fōre·feel′ing, *n.* presentiment.
fōre·fence′, *n.* defense in front. [Obs.]
fōre·fend′, *v.t.* to forfend. [Archaic.]
fōre′fiṅ″gẽr, *n.* the finger next to the thumb; the index finger; the first finger.
fōre′foot, *n.* 1. one of the anterior feet of an animal with four or more feet.
2. the meeting point of the keel and the stem of a ship.
fōre′frŏnt, *n.* 1. the extreme front; the foremost part or place; as, the *forefront* of a building.
2. the position of most activity, importance, etc.
fōre′gang″ẽr, *n.* [ME. *foreganger,* a foregoer, forerunner, from AS. *foregangan,* equal to *foregan,* to forego; *fore-,* before, and *gan,* to go.]
1. a predecessor.
2. in whaling, a short piece of rope grafted to the shank of a harpoon, to which the line is attached when the harpoon is used.
fōre·gath′ẽr, *v.i.* same as *forgather.*
fōre′gift, *n.* in English law, a premium paid by a tenant upon taking his lease.

fōre′gïrth, *n.* a girth or strap for the forepart, as of a horse; a martingale.
fōre·gō′, *v.t.* and *v.i.* forewent, *pt.*; foregoing, *ppr.*; foregone, *pp.* 1. to go before in time, place, or degree; to precede.
2. to forgo; to do without.
fōre·gō′ẽr, *n.* [ME. *forgœre,* from *forgan,* to go before.]
1. an ancestor; a progenitor.
2. one who goes before another.
3. one who foregoes.
fōre·gō′ing, *a.* preceding; going before, in time or place; antecedent; as, a *foregoing* period of time; a *foregoing* clause in a writing.
the foregoing; (a) the one or ones previously mentioned; (b) what has already been said or written.
fōre·gọne′, *a.* 1. that has gone before; previous; former.
2. (a) predetermined; known beforehand; confidentially anticipated; (b) inevitable; unavoidable: said of a conclusion.
fōre′ground, *n.* 1. (a) the part of a scene, landscape, etc. nearest to the viewer; (b) the part of a picture represented in perspective as nearest to the viewer.
2. the most noticeable or conspicuous place.
fōre·guess′ (-ges′), *v.t.* to conjecture.
fōre′-gut, *n.* the front part of the alimentary canal in vertebrate embryos: the duodenum, stomach, esophagus, and pharynx develop from it.
fōre′ham″mẽr, *n.* a sledge hammer; the hammer which strikes first.
fōre′hand, *n.* 1. the position in front or above; advantage.
2. the part of a horse in front of the rider.
3. (a) a method of making a forehand stroke, as in tennis; (b) such a stroke.
4. the chief part. [Obs.]
fōre′hand, *a.* 1. foremost; front.
2. designating or of a stroke, as in tennis, made with the palm of the hand turned forward.
3. done sooner than is regular.
And so extenuate the *forehand* sin.—Shak.
fōre′hand″ed, *a.* 1. early; timely; seasonable; as, a *forehanded* care.
2. looking ahead to, or making provision for, the future; thrifty; prudent; as, a *forehanded* farmer.
3. formed in the foreparts.
A substantial, true-bred beast, bravely *forehanded.* —Dryden.
4. in tennis, forehand.
fọre′head (fọr′ed *or* fōr′hed), *n.* [ME. *forhed, forehed, foreheaved*; AS. *foreheafod,* the front part of the head; *for, foran,* before, and *heafod,* head.]
1. the part of the face which extends from the usual line of hair on the top of the head to the eyes; the brow.
2. the front part of anything.
3. impudence; confidence; assurance; audacity; as, to speak with brazen *forehead.* [Obs.]
fōre·hēar′, *v.t.* to be informed of beforehand.
fōre·heärth, *n.* in metallurgy, that part of the hearth of a blast furnace beneath the tymp.
fōre′hōld, *n.* the hold in the forward part of a ship.
fōre′hook, *n.* in ships, a breasthook; a piece of timber placed across the stem, to unite the bows and strengthen the fore part of the ship.
for′eign (-in), *a.* [ME. *forein, foreyn*; OFr. *forain, forein,* from LL. *foraneus,* outside, exterior, from L. *foras,* out of doors.]
1. situated outside one's own country, province, locality, etc.
2. of, from, characteristic of, or dealing with another country or countries; as, a *foreign* language, *foreign* population, *foreign* trade: often opposed to *domestic.*
3. coming from or having to do with another person or thing; not originating in the person or thing specified; not belonging; not characteristic; as, unkindness is *foreign* to his nature.
4. not organically connected; not naturally related: said of substances found in parts of the body or in organisms where they do not naturally occur.
5. excluded; not admitted; held at a distance. [Rare.]
foreign affairs; matters concerning the policy of a country in its relations with other countries.
foreign attachment; see under *attachment.*
foreign bill; an authorization for the payment of a specified sum of money to someone in another state or country: also *foreign bill of exchange, foreign draft.*

foreign exchange; (a) the transfer of credits to a foreign country to settle debts or accounts between residents of the home country and those of the foreign country; (b) foreign bills, collectively.
foreign legion; a military force composed mainly of volunteers from foreign countries; especially, [F- L-] such a French force, based in North Africa.
foreign mission; (a) a religious mission established by foreigners, especially in a non-Christian country; (b) a group of governmental representatives sent on diplomatic or other business to a foreign nation.
foreign office; in some countries, the department of government in charge of foreign affairs.
Syn.—alien, exotic, extraneous, extrinsic, outside, strange.
for′eign-bọrn, *a.* born in some other country; not native.
for′eign-built (-bilt), *a.* built in a foreign country.
for′eign·ẽr, *n.* 1. a person born in or owing allegiance to a foreign country; an alien.
2. loosely or humorously, a person regarded as an outsider or stranger.
3. something, especially a ship, from another country.
for′eign·işm, *n.* 1. the imitation of that which is foreign.
2. any foreign custom, characteristic, idiom, mannerism, etc.
for′eign·ness, *n.* the condition of being foreign; irrelevancy; remoteness; want of relation; as, the *foreignness* of a subject from the main business.
fōre·judġe′ (-juj′), *v.t.*; forejudged, *pt., pp.*; forejudging, *ppr.* 1. to consider or decide before knowing the facts; judge beforehand.
2. to forjudge.
fōre·judġ′ment, *n.* a judgment formed in advance.
fōre·knōw′ (-nō′), *v.t.*; foreknew, *pt.*; foreknowing, *ppr.*; foreknown, *pp.* to have previous knowledge of; to foresee.
Who would the miseries of man *foreknow?* —Dryden.
fōre·knōw′a̤·ble, *a.* that can be foreknown.
fōre·knōw′ẽr, *n.* one who foreknows.
fōre·knōw′ing·ly, *adv.* with foreknowledge.
fōre·knowl′edġe (-nol′ej), *n.* knowledge of a thing before it happens or exists; prescience.
If I foreknew,
Foreknowledge had no influence on their fault. —Milton.
for′el, *n.* [ME. *forel*; OFr. *forel,* a case, sheath, dim. of *forre, fuerre*; LL. *fodrus,* from Goth. *fodr,* a sheath.] a kind of parchment for the cover of books: also written *forrel, forril.*
for′el, *v.t.* to cover or bind with forel. [Obs.]
fōre′lā·dy, *n.* same as *forewoman.*
fōre′lănd, *n.* 1. a promontory or cape; a point of land extending into the sea some distance from the line of the shore; a headland; as, the North and South *Foreland* in Kent, England.
2. a strip of land fronting an embankment or wall of a fortification.
3. land in relation to the territory lying behind it: opposed to *hinterland.*
4. in hydraulic engineering, the land lying between an embankment and the water line.
fōre·lāy′, *v.t.* 1. to lie in wait for; to entrap by ambush: also written *forlay.* [Obs.]
2. to contrive beforehand. [Obs.]
fōre·lēad′ẽr, *n.* one who leads others by his example. [Obs.]
fōre′leg, *n.* either of the front legs of an animal with four or more legs.
fōre·lend′, *v.t.* to lend or give beforehand. [Obs.]
fōre·līe′, *v.i.* to lie in front. [Obs.]
fōre·lift′, *v.t.* to lift up in front. [Obs.]
fōre′lock, *n.* the lock of hair that grows just above the forehead.
to take time by the forelock; to be prompt and vigilant in taking advantage of an opportunity; to act without delay.
fōre′lock, *n.* a cotter pin or linchpin.
fōre′lock, *v.t.* to fasten with a forelock (cotter pin) or forelocks.
fōre′lock bōlt, a bolt in which a forelock is used.
fōre′lock hook, in ropemaking, a device for twisting and uniting the strands of a rope.
fōre·look′, *v.i.* to look beforehand or forward.
fōre′lọọp″ẽr, *n.* in South Africa, one who leads a span of bullocks by means of a rope attached to the horns of the foremost pair.
fōre′măn, *n.*; *pl.* **fōre′men,** [orig., foremost

man, leader.] 1. a man who is chairman and spokesman of a jury.

2. a man in charge of a department or group of workers in a factory, mill, etc.

fōre′măn·ship, *n.* the duties or position of a foreman.

fōre′måst, *n.* the mast of a ship or other vessel which is placed nearest the bow.

fōre′men·tioned, *a.* mentioned before; recited or written in a former part of the same writing or discourse.

fōre′milk, *n.* same as *colostrum.*

fōre′mōst, *a.* [ME. *formest, firmest;* AS. *formest, fyrmest,* foremost, from *forma,* first, a superl. of *for, fore,* fore, before.]

1. first in place or time; most advanced; as, the *foremost* troops of an army.

2. first in rank or importance; leading; as, he held the *foremost* rank.

fōre′mōst, *adv.* first; in the first place; as, to put one's best foot *foremost.*

fōre′mōst·ly, *adv.* foremost. [Obs.]

fōre′mŏth″ẽr, *n.* a woman ancestor.

fōre′nāme, *n.* the name that precedes the family name; a given name; a prenomen, as "John" in the full name of "John Smith."

fōre′nāmed, *a.* 1. named or nominated before.

2. mentioned before in the same writing or discourse.

fōre·nenst′, fōr·nenst′, *prep.* opposite to; over against. [Now Dial.]

fōre′nīght (-nīt), *n.* the fore part of the night. [Scot.]

fōre′noon, *n.* the time from sunrise to noon; morning.

fōre′noon, *a.* of, in, or for the forenoon.

fōre′nō″tice, *n.* notice or information of an event before it happens.

fō·ren′săl, *a.* forensic. [Rare.]

fō·ren′siç, *a.* [from L. *forensis,* public, from *forum,* the market place.]

1. belonging to courts of law; used in courts or legal proceedings; as, a *forensic* term; *forensic* eloquence or disputes.

2. pertaining to or fitted for legal or public argumentation.

forensic medicine; the science concerned with the relations between medicine and law; medical jurisprudence.

fō·ren′siç, *n.* in certain American colleges, as Harvard, an argumentative contest, either oral or written; a debate.

fō·ren′siç·ăl, *a.* forensic. [Obs.]

fō·ren′siç·ăl·ly, *adv.* in a forensic manner; by or with debate.

fōre·or·dāin′, *v.t.*; foreordained, *pt., pp.*; foreordaining, *ppr.* to ordain or appoint beforehand; to preordain; to predestine; to predetermine.

fōre·or′di·nāte, *v.t.*; foreordinated, *pt., pp.*; foreordinating, *ppr.* to foreordain.

fōre·or·di·nā′tion, *n.* previous ordination or appointment; predetermination; predestination.

fōre′pärt, *n.* fore part.

fōre pärt, the part in front; first or early part.

fōre·påssed′, fōre·påst′, *a.* past; bygone. [Rare.]

fōre′paw, *n.* an animal's front paw.

fōre′pēak, *n.* the part of a ship's hold in the angle of the bow.

fōre′piēce, *n.* the dress guard on the front part of a lady's saddle.

fōre plāne, in carpentry, a kind of short jointer used to follow the jack plane in dressing lumber.

fōre′pōst, *n.* an outpost.

fōre·prīze′, *v.t.* to prize or rate beforehand. [Rare.]

fōre·prom′ised (-ist), *a.* promised beforehand; pre-engaged.

fōre′quar·tẽr, *n.* the front half of a side of beef, pork, mutton, etc.

fōre′quōt·ed, *a.* cited before; quoted in a foregoing part of the work.

fōre·ran′, *v.* past tense of *forerun.*

fōre′rañk, *n.* the first rank; the front.

fōre·rēach′, *v.t.*; forereached, *pt., pp.*; forereaching, *ppr.* 1. to overtake; pass, especially in a sailboat.

2. to get an advantage over; get the better of.

fōre·rēach′, *v.i.* 1. to move closer; to gain.

2. to move forward swiftly and suddenly, as a ship.

fōre·rēad′, *v.t.* to signify by tokens beforehand; to predestine. [Obs.]

fōre·rē·cīt′ed, *a.* named or recited before.

fōre·rē·mem′bẽred, *a.* called to mind previously.

fōre rent, in Scotland, rent payable in advance.

fōre′rīght (-rīt), *a.* favorable, as a wind. [Obs.]

fōre′rīght, *adv.* straight forward; onward. [Obs.]

fōre·run′, *v.t.*; foreran, *pt.*; forerunning, *ppr.*; forerun, *pp.* 1. to be the precursor of; to foreshadow; to come before as an earnest of something to follow; to introduce as a harbinger; to herald. [Rare or Archaic.]

Heaviness *foreruns* the good event.
—Shak.

2. to precede; to run before; to go before. [Rare or Archaic.]

3. to forestall. [Rare or Archaic.]

fōre·run′nẽr, *n.* 1. a messenger sent before to announce or prepare the way for another or for something to follow; a harbinger; a herald.

My elder brothers, my *forerunners* came.
—Dryden.

2. an ancestor or predecessor.

3. a prognostic; a sign foreshowing something to follow; as, certain pains in the head, back, and limbs are the *forerunners* of a fever.

4. in navigation, a piece of bunting or some other material attached to a log line to note the limit of drift line.

fōre′said (-sed), *a.* same as *aforesaid.*

fōre′sāil, *n.* 1. the main, square sail on the foremast of a square-rigged ship.

2. the main triangular sail on the mast of a fore-and-aft-rigged ship.

3. [*pl.*] any sails on the foremast or before the mast.

fōre·sāy′, *v.t.* to predict; to foretell. [Now Rare.]

fōre·see′, *v.t.*; foresaw, *pt.*; foreseeing, *ppr.*; foreseen, *pp.* to see beforehand; to see or know (an event) before it happens; to have prescience of; to foreknow.

A prudent man *foreseeth* the evil.
—Prov. xxii. 3.

fōre·see′, *v.i.* to exercise foresight.

fōre·sē′ẽr, *n.* one who foresees or foreknows.

fōre·sēize′, *v.t.* to seize beforehand.

fōre·shad′ōw, *v.t.*; foreshadowed, *pt., pp.*; foreshadowing, *ppr.* to shadow, indicate, or typify beforehand; to prefigure; to presage.

fōre·shad′ōw·ing, *n.* the act of indicating beforehand; anticipation.

fōre′shañk, *n.* 1. the upper part of the front legs of cattle.

2. meat from this part.

fōre′sheet, *n.* 1. one of the ropes used to trim a foresail.

2. [*pl.*] the space in the bows of an open boat.

fōre·shew′, *v.t.* same as *foreshow.*

fōre′ship, *n.* the fore part of a ship; the bow.

fōre′shōre, *n.* the part of a shore between high-water mark and low-water mark.

fōre·short′en, *v.t.*; foreshortened, *pt., pp.*; foreshortening, *ppr.* in drawing, painting, etc., to represent the lines of (an object) as shorter than they actually are in order to give the illusion of proper relative size, in accordance with the principles of perspective.

FORESHORTENED FIGURE

fōre·short′en·ing, *n.* representation in a foreshortened manner.

fōre′shot, *n.* the first running in the distillation of low wines: it is a milky liquid containing much fusel oil.

fōre·shōw′, *v.t.*; foreshowed, *pt.*; foreshowing, *ppr.*; foreshown *or* foreshowed, *pp.* to show beforehand; to prognosticate; to foretell; to prefigure.

Next, like Aurora, Spenser rose,
Whose purple blush the day *foreshows.*
—Denham.

fōre·shōw′ẽr, *n.* one who predicts.

fōre′sīde, *n.* the front or upper side. [Rare or Archaic.]

fōre′sīght (-sīt), *n.* [ME.; prob. after L. *providentia.*]

1. (a) a foreseeing; (b) the power to foresee.

2. a looking forward.

3. thoughtful regard or provision for the future; prudent forethought.

fōre·sīght′ed, *a.* having or indicating foresight.

fōre·sīght′ful, *a.* foresighted. [Rare.]

fōre·sig′ni·fȳ, *v.t.*; foresignified, *pt., pp.*; foresignifying, *ppr.* to signify beforehand; to betoken previously; to foreshow; to typify.

fōre′skin, *n.* the fold of skin that covers the end (*glans*) of the penis and is removed in circumcision; the prepuce.

fōre′skīrt, *n.* the loose and pendulous part of a coat or skirt in front.

fōre·slack′, *v.t.* to forslack. [Obs.]

fōre′sleeve, *n.* the part of a sleeve covering the forearm.

fōre·slōw′, *v.t.* and *v.i.* to delay; hinder; impede. [Obs.]

fōre·spēak′, *v.t.* and *v.i.* 1. to prophesy; to predict; to foretell. [Rare.]

2. to apply for or demand in advance; to bespeak. [Rare.]

fōre·spēak′ing, *n.* a prediction; also, a preface. [Obs.]

fōre′speech, *n.* a preface. [Obs.]

fōre·spent′, *a.* forspent. [Archaic or Poet.]

for′est, *n.* [ME. *forest;* OFr. *forest;* LL. *forestis, foresta, forestum,* a forest, ground, reserved for the chase, from L. *foris, foras,* out of doors, abroad.]

1. a large tract of land covered with trees and underbrush; a woodland: often used figuratively.

2. the trees on such a tract.

3. in Great Britain, a tract of woodland or wasteland, usually the property of the king, preserved for game.

4. in Great Britain, any of certain large tracts of land formerly but not now covered with trees; as, the *Forest* of Dean.

We have many *forests* in England without a stick of timber upon them.
—Wedgwood.

for′est, *a.* relating to or existing in a forest; as, *forest* trees, *forest* gloom.

forest laws; in England, laws for governing and regulating royal forests, especially those in which game was preserved.

for′est, *v.t.*; forested, *pt., pp.*; foresting, *ppr.* to plant with trees; to afforest.

fōre′ståff, *n.* same as *cross-staff* (nautical instrument).

for′est·āġe, *n.* an ancient service paid by foresters to the king; also, the duty paid to foresters.

for′est·ăl, *a.* belonging to or associated with a forest; as, *forestal* privileges.

fōre·stall′, *v.t.*; forestalled, *pt., pp.*; forestalling, *ppr.* [ME. *forstallen,* to stop, obstruct, from AS. *foresteall,* ambush; *fore-,* and *steall,* a standing.]

1. to anticipate; to act in advance of.

What need a man *forestall* his date of grief,
And run to meet what he would most avoid?
—Milton.

2. to hinder or prevent by doing something beforehand.

I will not *forestall* your judgment of the rest.
—Pope.

3. to buy or bargain for (goods of any kind) before they arrive at the market, with intent to sell them at higher prices. This was formerly a penal offense.

4. (a) to deprive by something prior; (b) to intercept; (c) to obstruct by force. [Obs.]

to forestall the market; to interfere in any way with trade so as to cause prices to rise or fall unnaturally, as by buying and holding marketable produce in order to create a scarcity on the market.

fōre·stall′ẽr, *n.* one who forestalls; a person who purchases goods before they come to market, with a view to raise the price.

for·est·ā′tion, *n.* the planting or care of forests; afforestation.

fōre′stāy, *n.* in nautical usage, a rope or wire cable running from the top of the foremast to the bowsprit and serving as a support for the mast.

fōre·stāy′sāil (*or* -sl), *n.* a triangular sail set from the forestay.

for′est·ẽr, *n.* 1. a person trained in forestry.

2. a person in charge of a forest or trees.

3. an inhabitant of a forest.

4. a forest tree. [Rare.]

5. in entomology, any one of several species of moths whose larvae are injurious to forest plants; specifically, the eight-spotted *forester, Alypia octomaculata,* whose caterpillars are destructive to the grapevine.

6. in zoology, the large gray kangaroo, *Macropus giganteus,* of Australia.

Ancient Order of Foresters; a fraternal society founded in England in 1745, and having an American branch established in the United States in 1832.

for'est flȳ, in entomology, any one of several flies which annoy horses and men; specifically, a blood-sucking horsefly, *Hippobosca equina.*

fōre'stick, *n.* the front log of a wood fire.

for'est ōak, any of a group of trees of the genus *Casuarina,* belonging to Australia.

for'est·ry, *n.* 1. the science of cultivating forests and of promoting the growth of forests.

2. systematic forest management for the production of timber, conservation, etc.

3. wooded land; forest land. [Rare.]

fōre'tack·le, *n.* the tackle on the foremast.

fōre'tāste, *n.* a taste beforehand; slight experience of something to be enjoyed, endured, etc. in the future; anticipation.

fōre'tāste', *v.t.*; foretasted, *pt., pp.*; foretasting, *ppr.* to taste beforehand; to have a foretaste of. [Rare.]

fōre·tāst'ēr, *n.* one who tastes beforehand, or has a foretaste of something.

fōre·tēach', *v.t.* to teach beforehand. [Obs.]

fōre·tell', *v.t.*; foretold, *pt., pp.*; foretelling, *ppr.* to tell, announce, or indicate beforehand; to prophesy; to predict.

Syn.—prognosticate, forecast, presage, foretoken, foreshow, forebode.

fōre·tell', *v.i.* to utter prediction or prophecy. [Archaic.]

All the prophets have likewise *foretold* of these days. —Acts iii. 24.

fōre·tell'ēr, *n.* one who foretells, predicts, or prophesies.

fōre·thiñk', *v.t.* 1. to contemplate beforehand; to anticipate in the mind. [Rare.]

The soul of every man
Perpetually does *forethink* thy fall.—Shak.

2. to contrive beforehand. [Obs.]

fōre·thiñk', *v.i.* to think or contrive beforehand. [Obs.]

fōre'thought (-thạt), *n.* 1. a thinking beforehand; anticipation; premeditation.

2. prudent thought for the future; foresight.

fōre'thought, *a.* previously thought; premeditated; aforethought.

fōre'thought·fụl, *a.* having forethought.

fōre'tīme, *n.* time previous to the present; past time.

fōre·tō'ken, *v.t.*; foretokened, *pt., pp.*; foretokening, *ppr.* to be a prophetic sign or omen of; to foreshow; to foreshadow; to prognosticate.

Whilst strange prodigious signs *foretoken* blood. —Daniel.

fōre·tō'ken, *n.* a prognostic; a prophetic sign.

fōre·tōld', *v.* past tense and past participle of *foretell.*

fōre'tọoth, *n.*; *pl.* **fōre'teeth,** one of the teeth in the forepart of the mouth; an incisor.

fōre'top, *n.* 1. the hair on the forepart of a horse's (or, formerly, a person's) head.

2. formerly, that part of a headdress or wig that lay in front.

3. the platform at the head of a ship's foremast.

fōre·top·gal'lănt (*or* fŏr-tȧ-gal'ănt), *a.* designating the parts of a ship just above the foretopmast.

fōre·top'măn, *n.*; *pl.* **fōre·top'men,** a sailor detailed for duty in the foretop.

fōre-top'mȧst, *n.* the mast above the foremast, and at the head of which stands the fore-topgallant mast.

fōre-top'sāil (*or* -sl), *n.* a sail set on the foretopmast, above the foresail.

fọr·ev'ēr, *adv.* [prep. *for,* and adv. *ever.*]

1. throughout eternity; endlessly; for always.

2. constantly; at all times; always.

Syn.—perpetually, continually, always, unceasingly, everlastingly, eternally, endlessly.

fọr·ev'ēr·mōre, *adv.* for always; through time without end: emphatic for *forever.*

fōre·vouched' (-voucht'), *a.* affirmed before; formerly told. [Rare.]

fōre'wărd, *n.* the van; the front. [Obs.]

fōre·wạrn', *v.t.*; forewarned, *pt., pp.*; forewarning, *ppr.* to admonish beforehand; to inform previously; to give previous notice to; to warn in advance.

fōre·went', *v.* past tense of *forego.*

fōre'wind, *n.* a wind that drives a ship forward. [Obs.]

fōre'wit, *n.* 1. one who leads, or wishes to lead, in matters of knowledge or fashion. [Obs.]

2. foresight. [Obs.]

fōre'wit, *v.t.* [ME. *forwiten*; AS. *forewitan,* to foreknow; *fore-,* before, and *witan,* to know.] to know beforehand. [Obs.]

fōre'wom"ăn (-woom"), *n.*; *pl.* **fōre'wom"en** (-wim"), a woman serving as a foreman.

fōre'wŏrd, *n.* [G. *vorwort,* a preface; *vor,* fore, and *wort,* word.] an introduction, preface, or prefatory note.

fōre'wŏrld, *n.* the primeval world.

fōre·wōrn', *a.* worn out. [Archaic.]

fōre'yärd, *n.* the lowest yard on the foremast of a ship.

fọr'feit (-fit), *n.* [ME. *forfet*; OFr. *forfait*; LL. *forisfactum,* a transgression, fault, penalty, neut. pp. of *forisfacere,* to transgress, forfeit, lit., to act beyond; L. *foris,* out of doors, beyond, and *facere,* to do.]

1. a fault; a crime. [Obs.]

2. that which is given up or lost, or the right to which is alienated, by a crime, offense, neglect of duty, or breach of contract; hence, a fine; a penalty; as, he who murders pays the *forfeit* of his life.

3. a thing taken away as a penalty for making some mistake in a game, and redeemable by a specified action.

4. [*pl.*] any game in which such forfeits are taken from players.

5. the act or process of paying a penalty for a crime, fault, mistake, etc.; forfeiture.

Syn.—fine, penalty, damages, amercement, mulct, loss.

fọr'feit, *a.* lost, given up, or taken away as forfeit.

fọr'feit, *v.t.*; forfeited, *pt., pp.*; forfeiting, *ppr.* [ME. *forfeten*; OFr. *forfait,* pp. of *forfaire,* from LL. *forisfacere,* to transgress, forfeit; L. *foris,* out of doors, beyond, and *facere,* to do.] to lose, give up, or be deprived of by some fault, offense, or crime; to lose or alienate the right to possess, by some neglect, crime, etc.; as, to *forfeit* an estate; to *forfeit* the good will of friends.

fọr'feit, *v.i.* to be guilty of a transgression; to fail in keeping an obligation. [Obs.]

fọr'feit·ȧ·ble, *a.* liable to be forfeited; subject to forfeiture.

fọr'feit·ēr, *n.* one who forfeits; one who incurs a penalty, as by forfeiting his bond.

fọr'fei·tūre, *n.* 1. the act of forfeiting; the losing of some right, privilege, estate, honor, office, or property, by an offense, crime, breach of condition, or other act; payment of a penalty or crime.

2. that which is forfeited; a penalty; a forfeit; a fine or mulct.

Syn.—fine, penalty, damage, confiscation, sequestration, amercement.

fọr·fend', *v.t.*; forfended, *pt., pp.*; forfending, *ppr.* [ME. *forfenden*; *for-,* and *fenden,* to fend, keep off.] to fend off; to avert; to prevent; also, to forbid: also written *forefend.* [Archaic.]

Heavens *forfend*! I would not kill thy soul. —Shak.

fọr·fēr'ed, *a.* greatly alarmed; in excessive fear. [Obs.]

fọr'fex, *n.*; *pl.* **fọr'fi·cēṣ,** [L., a pair of shears.] a pair of scissors.

fọr'fi·çāte, *a.* [L. *forfex* (*-icis*), a pair of shears.] having a deep fork, as the tail of a swallow.

fọr·fic'i·fọrm, *a.* [L. *forfex* (*-icis*), a pair of shears, and *forma,* form.] having the form of a pair of scissors.

Fọr·fiç'ū·lȧ, *n.* [L., dim. of *forfex* (*-icis*), a pair of shears.] a genus of insects characterized by forked tails, as the earwigs.

fọr·fiç'ū·lāte, *a.* forficiform.

fọr·gat', *v.* archaic past tense of *forget.*

fọr·gath'ēr, *v.i.* 1. to meet; to convene.

2. to meet by chance; to encounter.

3. to associate or have friendly social relations (*with*).

Also *foregather.*

fọr·gāve', *v.* past tense of *forgive.*

fōrġe, *n.* [ME. *forge*; OFr. *forge,* from L. *fabrica,* a workshop, fabric, from *faber,* a workman, artisan.]

1. a furnace in which iron or other metal is heated to be hammered into form; as, a blacksmith's *forge,* consisting essentially of a bellows and fireplace.

2. a place where metal is heated and hammered or wrought into shape; a smithy.

3. a place where wrought iron is made from pig iron or iron ore.

American forge; a forge for the direct production of iron by subjecting finely crushed ore to a continuous heat.

FORGE

Catalan forge; a forge for making iron directly from its ore.

fōrġe, *v.t.*; forged, *pt., pp.*; forging, *ppr.* [ME. *forgen*; OFr. *forgier, forger*; from L. *fabricari, fabricare,* to make, construct, from *fabrica,* a workshop, from *faber,* a workman, artisan.]

1. to form or shape (metal) by heating and hammering; to beat into any particular shape.

2. to make by or as by this method; to form; to shape; to produce.

Names that the schools *forged,* and put into the mouths of scholars. —Locke.

3. to make falsely; to falsify; to counterfeit; to make in the likeness of something else, with intent to deceive; as, to *forge* coin; to forge a check or a receipt.

fōrġe, *v.i.* 1. to shape metal, as a blacksmith does; to work at a forge.

2. to make an imitation of something for purposes of deception or fraud; to commit forgery.

3. to overreach and click the shoes together: said of a horse.

fōrġe, *v.t.* and *v.i.* [prob. altered from *force.*] to move forward consistently but slowly, as if against difficulties (often with *ahead*).

fōrġe'ȧ·ble, *a.* capable of being forged.

fōrġe cin'dēr, the slag from a forge or blast furnace.

fōrġe'man, *n.* the chief worker at a blacksmith's forge, as distinguished from the striker or hammerman.

fōr'ġēr, *n.* 1. one who works at a forge; one who forges metal.

2. one who counterfeits; a falsifier.

3. one who tells false stories.

fōrġe rōll, one of a system of rolls used in making bars of metal.

fōr'ġēr·y, *n.*; *pl.* **fōr'ġēr·ieṣ,** 1. the act of forging or working metal into shape. [Obs.]

2. the act of forging, fabricating, or producing falsely; especially, the crime of fraudulently making, counterfeiting, or altering any writing, record, instrument, register, note, and the like to deceive, mislead, or defraud; as, the *forgery* of a document or signature.

3. that which is forged, fabricated, falsely or fraudulently devised, or counterfeited.

The writings going under the name of Aristobulus were a *forgery* of the second century. —Waterland.

4. literary invention. [Poet.]

fọr·get', *v.t.*; forgot *or archaic* forgat, *pt.*; forgotten *or* forgot, *pp.*; forgetting, *ppr.* [ME. *forgeten, forgiten*; AS. *forgitan, forgietan,* to forget; *for* priv., and *gitan, gietan,* to get.]

1. to lose the remembrance of; to let go from the memory; to fail to recall; to be unable to remember.

Bless the Lord, O my soul, and *forget* not all his benefits. —Ps. ciii. 2.

2. to fail to do (what one intended) because of carelessness or thoughtlessness; to overlook, omit, or neglect unintentionally; as, she *forgot* to write.

3. to overlook, omit, or neglect intentionally; as, the successful candidate *forgot* the wishes of the voters.

to forget oneself; (a) to say or do something, through lack of self-control, that is not consistent with one's dignity or reputation, as to become angry and abusive upon slight provocation; (b) to be altruistic or unselfish.

Syn.—pretermit, unlearn, overlook, disregard.

fọr·get', *v.i.* to forget things; to be forgetful.

fọr·get'ȧ·ble, *a.* same as *forgettable.*

fọr·get'á·ble·ness, *n.* same as *forgettableness.*

fọr·get'fụl, *a.* 1. apt to forget; having a poor memory.

Bear with me, good boy, I am much *forgetful.* —Shak.

2. heedless; careless; neglectful; inattentive.

Be not *forgetful* to entertain strangers. —Heb. xiii. 2.

3. causing to forget; as, *forgetful* drugs. [Poet.]

fọr·get'fụl·ly, *adv.* in a forgetful manner.

fọr·get'fụl·ness, *n.* 1. the quality of being apt to forget.

2. loss of remembrance or recollection; a ceasing to remember.

A sweet *forgetfulness* of human care. —Pope.

3. neglect; negligence; careless omission; inattention; as, *forgetfulness* of duty.

fōr'ġe·tive, *a.* that may forge or produce; inventive. [Rare.]

fọr·get'-mē-not, *n.* 1. a small European and American plant of the genus *Myosotis,* with hairy leaves and clusters of small, blue or white flowers extensively considered the emblem of faithfulness and friendship.

The sweet *forget-me-nots*
That grow for happy lovers. —Tennyson.

2. any of a number of other plants related or similar to this.

FORGET-ME-NOT (*Myosotis scorpioides*)

fọr·get'tȧ·ble, *a.* that may be forgotten.

fọr·get'tȧ·ble·ness, *n.* the quality of being forgettable.

fọr·get'tẽr, *n.* one who easily forgets.

fọr·get'ting·ly, *adv.* by forgetting or forgetfulness.

fōrġ'ing, *n.* 1. the act of beating into shape.

2. the act of counterfeiting; forgery.

3. the thing forged; a piece of forged work in metal.

fọr·giv'á·ble, *a.* that may be forgiven; pardonable.

fọr·give', *v.t.*; forgave, *pt.*; forgiven, *pp.*; forgiving, *ppr.* [ME. *forgiven, forgifen,* to give up, forgive, remit; AS. *forgiefan, forgifan*; *for-*, away, and *giefan, gifan,* to give.]

1. to give up resentment against or the desire to punish; to stop being angry with; to pardon.

2. to give up all claim to punish or exact penalty for (an offense); to overlook.

3. to cancel or remit, as a debt, fine, or penalty.

Syn.—pardon, absolve, remit, cancel, release.

fọr·give', *v.i.* to show forgiveness; to be inclined to forgive.

fọr·give'ness, *n.* 1. a forgiving or being forgiven; pardon.

2. disposition to pardon; willingness to forgive.

And mild *forgiveness* intercede
To stop the coming blow. —Dryden.

fọr·giv'ẽr, *n.* one who pardons or forgives.

fọr·giv'ing, *a.* disposed to forgive; inclined to overlook offenses; that forgives; as, a *forgiving* temper.

fọr·giv'ing·ly, *adv.* in a forgiving manner.

fọr·giv'ing·ness, *n.* the state of being forgiving.

fọr·gō', *v.t.*; forwent, *pt.*; forgone, *pp.*; forgoing, *ppr.* [ME. *forgon*; AS. *forgan.*]

1. to do without; abstain from; give up.

2. (a) to go past; (b) to overlook; to neglect; (c) to go from; to leave. [Archaic.]

Also *forego.*

fọr·got', *v.* past tense and alternative past participle of *forget.*

fọr·got'ten, *v.* past participle of *forget.*

fọr·hāil', *v.t.* [*for-*, and ME. *halen, halien,* to draw.] to harass or distress. [Obs.]

fō·rin'se·cȧl, *a.* [L. *forinsecus,* from without, on the outside.] foreign; alien. [Obs.]

fọr'int, *n.* [Hung.] the monetary unit of Hungary, equal to about 9 cents in 1947.

fō''ris·fa·mil'i·āte, *v.i.*; forisfamiliated, *pt., pp.*; forisfamiliating, *ppr.* in law, to renounce a legal title to a further share of paternal inheritance; to put oneself out of the family.

fō''ris·fa·mil'i·āte, *v.t.* [LL. *forisfamiliatus,* pp. of *forisfamiliare,* to emancipate; *foris,* outside, and *familia,* family.] in law, to emancipate or free from parental authority; to put (a son) in possession of property in his father's lifetime, either at his own request or with his consent, and thus discharge him from the family.

fō''ris·fa·mil·i·ā'tion, *n.* the act of forisfamiliating or the state of being forisfamiliated.

fọr·judġe' (-juj'), *v.t.* [ME. *forjugen*; OFr. *forjugier,* from *fors,* outside, and *jugier,* to judge.] in law, to expel or dispossess by court judgment: also *forejudge.*

fọrk, *n.* [ME. *fork, forke*; AS. *forc,* from L. *furca,* a fork.]

1. an instrument consisting of a handle with a shank of metal divided into two or more tines or prongs, used for lifting, pitching, spearing, or holding objects; as, to eat with a knife and *fork*; to pitch hay with a *fork.*

2. anything resembling a fork in shape.

3. a division into branches; bifurcation.

4. the point where a river, road, etc. is divided into two or more branches, or where such branches join to form a river, road, etc.

5. one of these branches.

6. an instrument of steel with two prongs, which when set in vibration produces a musical sound, varying in pitch according to the thickness of the metal, the length of the prongs, or their width apart; a tuning fork.

7. a gibbet. [Obs.]

fọrk, *v.i.*; fọrked (fọrkt), *pt., pp.*; forking, *ppr.* to divide into branches; as, the road *forks* here.

fọrk, *v.t.* 1. to raise, spear, or pitch with a fork, as hay.

2. to make into the shape of a fork.

3. in chess, to attack (two chessmen) simultaneously with a knight, etc.

to fork over (or *out, up*); to hand over; to give up; to pay out. [Colloq.]

fọrk bēam, in shipbuilding, a short, forked beam for the support of the deck, as at a hatchway.

fọrk'bēard, *n.* a fish having ventral fins near the head, giving the appearance of a forked beard.

fọrk chuck, an attachment to a turning lathe, so called from that part which screws on the mandrel having on the outer side a square hole in which forked pieces of iron of different sizes, according to the strength required, are placed when in use.

fọrked (fọrkt *or* fọrk'ed), *a.* 1. divided into two or more parts or branches; having a fork or forks; as, a *forked* tongue, *forked* lightning.

2. having prongs: often in hyphenated compounds, as five-*forked.*

3. zigzag; as, *forked* lightning.

fọrk'ed·ly, *adv.* in a forked form.

fọrk'ed·ness, *n.* the state or quality of being forked.

fọrk'head (-hed), *n.* 1. in machinery, the fork at the end of a rod forming part of a knuckle-joint.

2. the barbed head of an arrow. [Obs.]

fọrk'i·ness, *n.* the state or quality of being forked.

fọrk'less, *a.* having no fork: not bifurcated.

fọrk'lift, *n.* a device, usually mounted on a truck (*forklift truck*), for lifting, stacking, etc. heavy objects: it consists typically of projecting prongs that are slid under the load and then raised or lowered.

fọrk'tāil, *n.* 1. a salmon in its fourth year's growth.

2. one of several sparrows with deeply forked tails.

3. the kite: so called because of its forked tail.

fọrk'-tāiled, *a.* having the tail forked, as in the swallow; scissor-tailed.

fork-tailed flycatcher; one of the American tyrant flycatchers, especially *Milvulus tyrannus.*

fork-tailed kite; the swallow-tailed kite, *Elanoides forficatus.*

fork-tailed shrike; a drongo; a shrike of the family *Dicruridæ,* as *Dicrurus forficatus.*

fọrk'y, *a.* forked; furcated; opening into two or more parts; as, a *forky* tongue.

fọr·lāy', *v.t.* same as *forelay.*

fọr·lēave', *v.t.* to leave; to forsake. [Obs.]

fọr·lēse', *v.t.* [AS. *forleósan*; *for-*, intens., and *leósan,* to lose.] to lose. [Obs.]

fọr·let', *v.t.* [AS. *forlætan*; *for-*, away, and *lætan,* to let.] to give over; to abandon. [Obs.]

fọr·līe', *v.i.* to commit fornication. [Obs.]

fọr·līe', *v.t.* to suffocate by lying upon, as a child in bed. [Obs.]

fọr·lọrn', *a.* [ME. *forlorn, forloren*; AS. *forloren,* pp. of *forleósan,* to lose; *for-*, intens., and *leósan,* to lose.]

1. left behind; abandoned; deserted.

For here *forlorn* and lost I tread. —Goldsmith.

2. deprived; bereft.

He went like one that hath been stunned,
And is of sense *forlorn.* —Coleridge.

3. in pitiful condition; wretched; miserable.

4. without hope; desperate.

Syn.—comfortless, helpless, depressed, miserable, wretched, friendless, woebegone, disconsolate, pitiable, abject, destitute, lost, abandoned, forsaken, solitary, hopeless.

fọr·lọrn', *n.* 1. a forlorn person. [Obs.]

2. a forlorn hope; an advanced body of troops; a vanguard.

Our *forlorn* of horse marched within a mile of where the enemy was drawn up. —Cromwell.

fọr·lọrn' hōpe, [altered from D. *verloren hoop,* lit., lost group; *verloren,* pp. of *verliezen,* to lose, and *hoop,* a band.]

1. a group of soldiers detached from the main group for a very dangerous mission.

2. a desperate undertaking; an enterprise with very little chance of success.

3. [through confusion with *hope.*] a faint hope.

fọr·lọrn'ly, *adv.* in a forlorn manner.

fọr·lọrn'ness, *n.* destitution; misery; a forsaken or wretched condition.

-fọrm, [L. *-formis,* from *forma,* a shape, figure.] a suffix meaning: (a) *having the form of, shaped like,* as in cunei*form,* ovi*form*; (b) *having* (a specified number of) *forms,* as in uni*form.*

fọrm, *n.* [ME. *forme, fourme*; OFr. *forme, fourme,* from L. *forma,* shape, figure, image.]

1. the shape or outline of anything; figure; structure, excluding color, texture, and density.

2. the body or figure of a person or animal.

3. anything used to give shape to something else; a mold.

4. the particular way of being that gives something its nature or character; the combination of qualities making something what it is; intrinsic character; as, democracy and autocracy are two *forms* of government.

5. arrangement; especially, orderly arrangement; way that something is put together; pattern; style: distinguished from *content.*

6. a way of doing something; as, his *form* in serving at tennis is good.

7. an established or customary way of acting or behaving; ceremony; ritual; formality.

8. a fixed order of words; formula; as, the *form* of a wedding announcement.

9. a printed document with blank spaces to be filled in; as, an employment application *form.*

10. a particular kind, or type, of a larger group; species or variety; as, man is a *form* of animal life.

11. a condition of mind or body in regard to mental or physical performances of skill, speed, etc.; as, the boxer was in good *form* for the fight.

12. the lair or hiding place of a hare, etc.

13. a long, wooden bench without a back, as formerly in a schoolroom.

14. a grade or class in school.

15. beauty. [Archaic.]

16. in grammar, any of the different appearances of a word in changes of inflection, spelling, or pronunciation; as, *am* is a *form* of the verb *be.*

17. in printing, the type, plates, etc. locked in a frame or chase for printing.

18. likeness; image; exact representation. [Obs.]

He took on him the *form* of a servant. —Phil. ii. 7.

19. in crystallography, the total configuration of planes included under the same symbol.

bad form; conduct not in accord with social custom.

good form; conduct in accord with social custom.

fọrm, *v.t.*; formed, *pt., pp.*; forming, *ppr.* [ME. *formen, fourmen,* from L. *formare,* to shape, fashion, mold, from *forma,* form, shape.]

1. to make, shape, mold, or fashion; to make, as in some particular way; to arrange; as, to *form* an image of clay; to *form* troops into line.

2. to make up; to constitute; to create out of separate elements; as, these men *form* the company.

3. to mold or shape by training and discipline; train; instruct.

4. to develop (habits).

5. to think of; frame in the mind; conceive.

6. to come together into; take the formation of; organize into; as, the boys *formed* lines.

7. in grammar, to make by derivation or by affixes or prefixes; as, to *form* a noun by adding *ness* to an adjective; also, to construct or make up (a sentence, phrase, etc.)

form, *v.i.* 1. to take form; to come into being.

2. to be formed; to assume shape.

3. to take a definite or specific form or shape.

4. to go to or crouch in a form, as a hare.

form'ȧ·ble, *a.* capable of being formed.

form'ăl, *a.* [L. *formalis*, from *forma*, form.]

1. of external form or structure, rather than nature or content; apparent.

2. of the internal form; relating to the character or nature; essential.

3. of or according to prescribed or fixed customs, rules, ceremonies, etc.; as, a *formal* wedding.

4. (a) made or done for outward appearance only; (b) stiff; prim; ceremonious.

5. (a) designated for use or wear at ceremonies, elaborate parties, etc.; as, *formal* dress; (b) requiring clothes of this kind; as, the dance will be *formal*.

6. done or made in orderly, regular fashion; methodical.

7. very regular or orderly in arrangement, pattern, etc.; rigidly symmetrical; as, a *formal* garden.

8. done or made according to the forms that make explicit, definite, valid, etc.; as, a *formal* contract.

9. designating education in schools, colleges, etc.

10. designating or of that level of language usage characterized by expanded vocabulary, complete syntactical constructions, complex sentences, etc.: distinguished from *colloquial* or *informal*.

Syn.—precise, ceremonious, exact, stiff.

form'ăl, *n.* 1. a formal dance or ball.

2. a woman's evening dress.

to go formal; to go dressed in evening clothes. [Colloq.]

for·mal'dē·hȳde, *n.* [*formic* and *aldehyde.*] a colorless, pungent gas, CH_2O, used in solution as a strong disinfectant and preservative.

for'mȧ·lin, *n.* [from *formaldehyde*, and *-in.*] a 40 per cent solution of formaldehyde in water, used as an antiseptic.

form'ăl·işm, *n.* strict or excessive attention to or insistence on outward forms and customs, as in art or religion.

form'ăl·ist, *n.* one who practices formalism.

for·măl·is'tiç, *a.* of or characterized by formalism.

for·mal'i·ty, *n.*; *pl.* **for·mal'i·tieş,** 1. the quality or state of being formal; specifically, (a) a following or observing of prescribed customs, rules, ceremonies, etc.; propriety; (b) careful or too careful attention to order, regularity, precision, or conventionality; stiffness.

2. a formal or conventional act or requirement; ceremony or form, often without practical meaning.

3. external appearance. [Obs.]

4. essence; the quality which makes a thing what it is. [Obs.]

The *formality* of the vow lies in the promise made to God. —Stillingfleet.

5. in philosophy, the manner in which a thing is conceived; a manner in an object importing a relation to the understanding by which it may be distinguished from another object; as, animality and rationality are *formalities*.

Syn.—ceremony, parade, affectation, stateliness, punctiliousness, etiquette.

for″măl·i·zā'tion, *n.* a formalizing or being formalized.

form'ăl·īze, *v.t.*; formalized, *pt.*, *pp.*; formalizing, *ppr.* 1. to give definite form to; to shape.

2. to make formal.

3. to make official, valid, etc. by use of an appropriate form; as, to *formalize* an agreement.

form'ăl·ize, *v.i.* to be formal.

form'ăl log'iç, the branch of logic that studies the validity or correctness of conclusions by investigation of their structural relation to other propositions as evidence.

form'ăl·ly, *adv.* 1. in a formal manner.

2. with regard to form.

for'mat, *n.* [Fr., from L. (*liber*) *formatus*, (a book) formed, pp. of *formare*, to form.] the shape, size, binding, type, paper, and general make-up or arrangement of a book, magazine, etc.

for'māte, *n.* [*form*ic and *-ate.*] a salt composed of formic acid combined with any base.

for·mā'tion, *n.* [L. *formatio* (*-onis*), from *formare*, to form, shape.]

1. the act of forming or making; the act of creating or causing to exist; more generally, the operation of bringing things together, or of shaping and giving form; as, the *formation* of the earth; the *formation* of a constitution.

2. the manner in which a thing is formed; arrangement; structure; order.

3. the thing formed.

4. in geology, a series or group of strata of the same sort of rock or mineral, or having common characteristics.

5. in military usage, an arrangement of troops, ships, airplanes, etc.

form'ȧ·tive, *a.* [from L. *formatus*, pp. of *formare*, to form, shape.]

1. giving form; having the power of giving form; helping to shape, develop, or mold; as, the *formative* arts.

The meanest plant cannot be raised without seeds by any *formative* power residing in the soil. —Bentley.

2. in grammar, serving to form words; as, a termination merely *formative*.

3. relating to formation or development; as, the *formative* period of youth.

form'ȧ·tive, *n.* in grammar, (a) an element, as a prefix or suffix, used with other elements to form words; (b) a word thus formed.

form clȧss, in linguistics, a class made up of words that occur in a distinctive position in constructions and have certain formal features in common, as the form class *noun* in English, made up of all words to which plural and possessive suffixes may be added.

formed, *a.* 1. in astronomy, arranged in groups or constellations: said of stars.

2. in biology, possessing the power of development; organized for formation.

for'me·don, *n.* [OFr., from L. *forma doni*, form of the gift.] in English law, formerly, a writ of right permitting the recovery of entailed property.

for'mel, *n.* [ME. *formel*, *formele*; OFr. *forme*, a female of the falcon or hawk.] the female of the falcon family. [Obs.]

for·mēne', *n.* methane.

form'ẽr, *n.* 1. one who or that which forms.

2. a mechanical device for shaping an article of manufacture; a pattern.

for'mẽr, *a.* [ME. *forme*; AS. *forma*, first; from *for*, *fore*, before, and superl. suffix *-ma*. The comp. suffix *-er* was added on the mistaken supposition that *formest*, foremost, was not a double superlative.]

1. before in time; previous; earlier; past; prior; as, in *former* times.

2. first-mentioned: said of two and opposed to *latter*: often used absolutely (with *the*); as, Jack and Bill are brothers, but the *former* is taller than the latter.

3. near the beginning; preceding; as, the *former* part of a discourse or argument.

4. front; fore. [Obs.]

Syn.—preceding, prior, previous, foregoing.

for·me·ret' (-rā'), *n.* [Fr.] in architecture, the rib which in ribbed vaulting lies next to and in a plane parallel with the wall.

for'mẽr·ly, *adv.* in time past; some time ago; at a former time; as, nations *formerly* made slaves of prisoners taken in war.

Syn.—previously.—*Formerly* means before the present time; *previously*, before some particular event.

form'ful, *a.* creative; imaginative. [Rare.]

form ġē'nus, in biology, a genus composed of similar form species.

for'miç, *a.* [L. *formica*, an ant.]

1. pertaining to ants.

2. designating or of a colorless acid originally obtained from a fluid emitted by red ants when irritated, but now produced commercially from oxalic acid and glycerine: formula, HCO_2H.

For·mī'çȧ, *n.* [arbitrary coinage.] a laminated, heat-resistant thermosetting plastic used for table and sink tops, etc.: a trade-mark.

for'mi·çăn, *a.* resembling an ant.

for'mi·çant, *a.* crawling like an ant; especially, in medicine, designating the pulse when extremely small or scarcely perceptible.

for·mi·çā'ri·ăn, *a.* 1. pertaining to ants.

2. pertaining to ant birds; formicarioid.

for·mi·çā'ri·oid, *a.* of or belonging to the ant birds, *Formicarioideæ*.

for·mi·çā'ri·um, *n.* same as *formicary*.

for'mi·çȧ·ry, *n.* [LL. *formicarium*, an ant hill, from L. *formica*, an ant.] the nest or burrow of a community of ants, often consisting of a mound or a pyramid of earth with various subterranean passages; an ant hill.

for'mi·çāte, *v.i.*; formicated, *pt.*, *pp.*; formicating, *ppr.* [L. *formicatus*, pp. of *formicare*, to crawl, from *formica*, ant.] to crawl or swarm like or with ants.

for'mi·çāte, *a.* [L. *formica*, an ant, and *-ate.*] pertaining to or resembling an ant or ants.

for·mi·çā'tion, *n.* a sensation of the body resembling that made by the creeping of ants on the skin.

for'mi·cid, *a.* resembling or belonging to ants.

for'mi·cid, *n.* an ant or antlike insect.

for'mi·cine, *a.* [L. *formica*, an ant, and *-ine.*] antlike.

for″mi·dȧ·bil'i·ty, *n.* the quality of being formidable.

for'mi·dȧ·ble, *a.* [L. *formidabilis*, from *formidare*, to fear, dread.]

1. exciting fear, apprehension, dread, or awe.

They seemed to fear the *formidable* sight. —Dryden.

2. hard to handle or overcome; as, a *formidable* job.

Syn.—dreadful, terrible, shocking.

for'mi·dȧ·ble·ness, *n.* the quality of being formidable.

for'mi·dȧ·bly, *adv.* in a formidable manner.

for·mid'ō·lōse, *a.* [L. *formidolosus*, from *formidare*, to fear, dread.] filled with dread; greatly afraid. [Obs.]

form'less, *a.* shapeless; without a definite plan or form.

form'less·ly, *adv.* in a formless manner.

form'less·ness, *n.* the quality of lacking form.

form let'tẽr, a letter of standardized form, usually one of a number printed or run off on a duplicating machine, with the date, inside address, special information, etc. filled in separately.

form spē'cieş, a species based upon a single phase of development until a complete cycle furnishes means of correct classification.

for'mū·lȧ, *n.*; *pl.* **for'mū·lȧş, for'mū·lae,** [L., a small pattern, rule, mold, dim. of *forma*, form, shape.]

1. a fixed form of words, especially one that has lost its original meaning or force and is now used only as a conventional or ceremonial expression; as, "Very truly yours" is a *formula* used in letters.

2. any conventional rule or method for doing something, especially when used, applied, or repeated without thought.

3. an exact statement of religious faith or doctrine.

4. a prescription for preparing a medicine, a baby's food, etc.; also, something, especially fortified milk for a baby, prepared according to such a prescription.

5. a set of algebraic symbols expressing a mathematical fact, principle, rule, etc.; as, $A = \pi r^2$ is the *formula* for determining the area of a circle.

6. in chemistry, an expression of the composition of a compound (or a radical, etc.) by a combination of symbols and figures to show the constituents in their exact proportions.

empirical formula; in chemistry, a formula showing the kind of atoms and the number of each kind in any molecule of the substance (e.g. H_2O).

structural formula, *graphic formula*, or *rational formula*; in chemistry, a formula showing the atoms in a molecule and indicating how they are arranged.

for'mū·lăr, *a.* pertaining to a formula.

for″mū·lȧ·ris'tiç, *a.* of a formularizing nature or character.

for″mū·lăr·i·zā'tion, *n.* the act of reducing to a formula; also, anything reduced to a formula.

for'mū·lăr·īze, *v.t.*; formularized, *pt.*, *pp.*; formularizing, *ppr.* to express by means of a formula; to reduce to a formula; to formulate.

for'mū·lȧ·ry, *n.*; *pl.* **for'mū·lȧ·rieş,** [Fr. *formulaire*, from L. *formula*, an established mode of procedure, rule, principle.]

1. a book containing stated and prescribed forms, as of oaths, declarations, prayers, etc.

2. a formula.

3. in pharmacy, a list of medicines with their formulas and directions for compounding them.

for'mū·lȧ·ry, *a.* of, or having the nature of, a formula or formulas.

for'mū·lāte, *v.t.*; formulated, *pt.*, *pp.*; formulating, *ppr.* 1. to reduce to a formula; to express in a formula.

2. to express in a definite or systematic way; as, he *formulated* his theory carefully.

fọr·mū·lā′tion, *n.* 1. the process or act of formulating.

2. a formulated expression.

fọr′mū·lā·tŏr, *n.* one who formulates.

fọr′mūle, *n.* [Fr.] a set or prescribed model; a formula. [Obs.]

fọr″mū·li·zā′tion, *n.* a formulizing.

fọr′mū·līze, *v.t.*; formulized, *pt.*, *pp.*; formulizing, *ppr.* same as *formulate.*

fọr′myl, *n.* [*form*ic and *-yl.*] in chemistry, the radical, HCO, of formic acid.

fŏr·nent′, *prep.* 1. directly opposite to; facing. [Brit. Dial.]

2. in connection with; in regard to. [Obs.]

fọr′ni·çăl, *a.* [L. *fornix* (*-icis*), an arch, vault.] pertaining to the fornix.

fọr′ni·çāte, *a.* [L. *fornicatus*, from *fornix* (*-icis*), an arch, vault.]

1. arched; vaulted like an oven or furnace.

2. in botany, arching over, as a leaf or petal.

fọr′ni·çāte, *v.i.*; fornicated, *pt.*, *pp.*; fornicating, *ppr.* [LL. *fornicatus*, pp. of *fornicari*, to fornicate, from L. *fornix* (*-icis*), a vault, brothel in an underground vault.] to commit fornication.

fọr·ni·çā′tion, *n.* [LL. *fornicatio* (*-onis*), from *fornicari*, to fornicate, from *fornix* (*-icis*), a vault, a brothel in an underground vault.]

1. voluntary sexual intercourse between an unmarried woman and a man, especially an unmarried man: it is generally forbidden by law.

Fornication (is) the act of incontinency in single persons; if either party be married, it is adultery. —Wharton.

2. in the Bible, (a) any unlawful sexual intercourse, including adultery; (b) a forsaking of the true God and worshiping of idols.

fọr·ni·çā′tion, *n.* [L. *fornicatio* (*-onis*), from *fornicatus*, arched, from *fornix* (*-icis*), a vault, arch.] in architecture, the forming of a vault or arch; an arching.

fọr′ni·çā·tŏr, *n.* one who commits fornication.

fọr′ni·çā·tress, *n.* a woman who commits fornication.

fọr′nix, *n.*; *pl.* **fọr′ni·cēs̱,** [L., an arch, vault.]

1. in conchology, the excavated part under the umbo; also, the upper or convex shell in the oyster.

2. in botany, a small elongation on the tube or throat of the corolla.

3. in anatomy, a structure in the brain composed of arched nerve fibers: it is part of the olfactory pathways in the brain.

fọr·ōld′, *a.* of very great age. [Obs.]

fọr·pȧss′, *v.i.* to go by; to pass unnoticed. [Obs.]

fọr·pīne′, *v.i.* to pine or waste away. [Obs.]

fọr·rāy′, *v.t.* to ravage. [Obs.]

fọr·rāy′, *n.* the act of ravaging. [Obs.]

fọr′rel, fọr′ril, fọr′rill, *n.* forel. [Obs.]

fọr·sāke′, *v.t.*; forsook, *pt.*; forsaken, *pp.*; forsaking, *ppr.* [ME. *forsaken*; AS. *forsacan*, to give up, refuse, forsake; *for-*, and *sacan*, to contend, strive.]

1. to leave; to desert; to abandon; as, self-seeking friends and flatterers *forsake* us in adversity.

2. to give up; to renounce (an idea, habit, practice, etc.).

Cease from anger, and *forsake* wrath. —Ps. xxxvii. 8.

Syn.—quit, relinquish, fail, renounce.

fọr·sāk′en, *a.* abandoned; desolate; forlorn.

fọr·sāk′ẽr, *n.* one who forsakes.

fọr·sāy′, *v.t.* [AS. *forsecgan*, to accuse.] to forbid; to renounce. [Obs.]

fọr·shāpe′, *v.t.* [AS. *forscapan*, to transform.] to put out of shape. [Obs.]

fọr·slack′, *v.t.* to delay. [Obs.]

fọr·slōth′, *v.t.* [AS. *forslawian*, to be slow or unwilling.] to suffer loss of by sloth or neglect. [Obs.]

fọr·slōw′, *v.t.* and *v.i.* to defer; to postpone; to be slow; to lag. [Obs.]

fọr·slug′, *v.t.* to suffer loss of through sluggishness. [Obs.]

fọr·sook′, *v.* past tense of *forsake.*

fọr·sọọth′, *adv.* [ME. *forsoothe, forsothe*; AS. *forsoth*; *for*, prep., and *soth*, sooth, truth.] in truth; in fact; certainly; indeed: now only in ironic use. [Archaic.]

A fit man, *forsooth*, to govern a realm! —Hayward.

fọr·spēak′, *v.t.* to bewitch; to harm by too much praise. [Brit. Dial.]

fọr·spent′, *a.* tired out; fatigued. [Archaic or Poet.]

fọr·straught′ (-strąt′), *a.* very much perplexed. [Obs.]

fọr·swăt′, *a.* exhausted by heat and perspiration. [Obs.]

fọr·swēar′, *v.t.*; forswore, *pt.*; forsworn, *pp.*; forswearing, *ppr.* [ME. *forsweren, forswerien*; AS. *forswerian*, to swear falsely; *for-*, and *swerian*, to swear.]

1. to reject or renounce upon oath.

Like innocence, and as serenely bold
As truth, how loudly he *forswears* thy gold!
—Dryden.

2. to deny upon oath.

to forswear oneself; to swear falsely; to perjure oneself.

Syn.—renounce, abjure.

fọr·swēar′, *v.i.* to swear falsely; to commit perjury.

Syn.—perjure.

fọr·swēar′ẽr, *n.* one who forswears.

fọr·swŏnk′, *a.* [AS. *forswincan*, to overwork.] overlabored. [Obs.]

fọr·swōre′, *v.* past tense of *forswear.*

fọr·swōrn′, *v.* past participle of *forswear.*

fọr·swōrn′, *a.* having sworn falsely; perjured.

fọr·swōrn′ness, *n.* the state of being forsworn.

For·syth′i·ȧ, *n.* [named after William *Forsyth* (1737–1804), a British botanist.]

1. a genus of ornamental shrubs with yellow bell-shaped flowers, which appear in early spring before the leaves.

2. any shrub of this genus.

fōrt, *n.* [OFr. *fort*; LL. *fortis*, a fort, stronghold, from L. *fortis*, strong, powerful.]

1. an enclosed place or fortified building for military defense, usually equipped with earthworks, guns, etc.

2. a permanent army post, as distinguished from a temporary training camp.

3. a frontier trading post.

4. see *forte* (strong point).

fōrt′ȧ·lice, *n.* [OFr. *fortelesse, fortelesce*; LL. *fortalitia, fortalitium*, a small fort, from L. *fortis*, strong, powerful.]

1. a small fort or defensive outwork.

2. a fortress. [Archaic.]

fōr′tḛ, *a.* and *adv.* [It., strong, loud.] in music, loud; with force: a direction to the performer.

fōr′tḛ, *n.* in music, a forte note or passage.

fōrte, *n.* [Fr. *fort*, a fort, strong point.]

1. the strong point; the thing that a person does particularly well: formerly also spelled *fort.*

2. the strongest part of the blade of a sword, between the middle and the hilt: opposed to *foible.*

fōr″te·pï·ä′nō, *a.* and *adv.* [It.] in music, loud, then soft: a direction to the performer.

fōr″te·pi·ä′nō, *n.* a pianoforte: the original name.

fōrth, *adv.* [ME. *forth*; AS. *forth*, forth, forward; from *fore*, for, fore, and *-th.*]

1. forward; onward in time; in advance; forward in place or degree; as, one, two, three, and so *forth.*

2. out; into view, as from hiding or obscurity.

3. out; away; beyond the boundary of a place; abroad. [Archaic.]

fōrth, *prep.* out of; out from. [Archaic.]

From *forth* the streets of Pomfret.—Shak.

fōrth′çŏm·ing, *a.* 1. approaching; about to appear; as, the author's *forthcoming* book.

2. available or ready when needed; as, the promised money was not *forthcoming.*

fōrth′çŏm·ing, *n.* a coming forth; an appearing or approaching.

fōrth′gō·ing, *n.* a going forth; a proceeding from.

fōrth′gō·ing, *a.* going forth.

fọr·thiṅk′, *v.t.* to repent of. [Obs.]

fōrth′pu̧t″ting, *n.* 1. a putting forth.

2. a forward disposition; presumption.

fōrth′pu̧t″ting, *a.* that puts forth; also, forward; insistent; bold.

fōrth′rīght (-rīt), *a.* 1. originally, going straight forward.

2. straightforward; direct; frank.

fōrth′rīght, *adv.* 1. straight forward; in a straight direction.

2. immediately; at once.

fōrth′rīght, *n.* a straight path. [Archaic.]

fōrth′rīght·ness, *n.* directness; openness; honesty.

fōrth′wȧrd, *adv.* forward. [Obs.]

fōrth·with′, *adv.* immediately; without delay; directly.

fọr·thȳ′, *adv.* [AS. *for thy*; *for*, prep., and *thy*, instrumental of *thæt*, that.] therefore. [Obs.]

fọr′ti·eth, *a.* [ME. *fowertuthe, fuwertithe*; AS. *feowertigotha*; *feowertig*, forty, and ordinal suffix, *-tha, -th.*]

1. preceded by thirty-nine others in a series; 40th.

2. designating one of the forty equal parts into which anything is or may be divided.

fọr′ti·eth, *n.* 1. the one following the thirty-ninth.

2. any of the forty equal parts of something; $^{1}/_{40}$.

fọr′ti·fī·ȧ·ble, *a.* that can be fortified.

FORTIFICATION

(Interior on the left; exterior on the right): *a a*, Abattis; *b b*, The counterscarp; *c c*, The palisade; *d d*, Scarp; *f f*, Fraise; *f e g g*, The parapet; *h*, Banquette; *i g*, The breastheight

fọr″ti·fi·çā′tion, *n.* 1. the act or science of fortifying.

2. something used in fortifying; especially, a fort or defensive earthwork, wall, etc.

3. a fortified place or position.

4. additional strength; a strengthening in any way.

fọr″ti·fi·çā′tion ag′ăte, a variety of agate exhibiting lines and angles resembling those in a fortification.

fọr′ti·fī·ẽr, *n.* one who or that which fortifies.

fọr′ti·fȳ, *v.t.*; fortified, *pt.*, *pp.*; fortifying, *ppr.* [Fr. *fortifier*; LL. *fortificare*, to strengthen, fortify; from L. *fortis*, strong, and *facere*, to make.]

1. to make strong or stronger; to strengthen physically or structurally.

2. to provide with works of defense; to strengthen and secure by forts, batteries, and fortifications; as, to *fortify* a city.

3. to support; to corroborate; as, he *fortified* his argument with statistics.

4. to add vitamins, minerals, etc. to (bread, etc.) so as to increase the food value.

5. to strengthen (wine, etc.) by adding alcohol.

fọr′ti·fȳ, *v.i.* to build military defenses.

fōr′ti·lāġe, *n.* [a form of *fortalice.*] a little fort; a blockhouse. [Obs.]

fōrt′in, *n.* [Fr.] a little fort; a field fort; a sconce. [Obs.]

fōr′tis, *a.* [L., strong.] in phonetics, strongly articulated; as, a *fortis* stop: opposed to *lenis.*

fōr′tis, *n.* a strongly articulated speech sound, especially a stop: opposed to *lenis.*

fọr·tis′si·mō, *adv.* [It.] in music, very loud.

fọr·tis′si·mō, *n.*; *pl.* **fọr·tis′si·mōs̱, fọr·tis′si·mī,** a passage to be performed fortissimo.

fọr·ti′tion (-tish′un), *n.* a trusting to chance. [Rare.]

fọr′ti·tūde, *n.* [L. *fortitudo*, from *fortis*, strong, powerful.]

1. firm courage; patient endurance of misfortune, pain, etc.

2. physical strength; power of resisting attack. [Obs.]

3. in astrology, any accidental strengthening of the effect of a planet.

fọr·ti·tū′di·nous, *a.* having courage and fortitude.

fōrt′let, *n.* a little fort.

fọrt′nīght (-nīt *or* -nit), *n.* [ME. *fourtenight, fourten night*, fourteen nights.] two weeks. [Chiefly Brit.]

fọrt′nīght·ly, *adv.* once in a fortnight; at intervals of two weeks.

fọrt′nīght·ly, *a.* happening or appearing at two-week intervals.

fọrt′nīght·ly, *n.*; *pl.* **fọrt′nīght·lies̱,** a periodical issued at two-week intervals.

fọr·tread′ (-tred′), *v.t.* to crush by treading upon. [Obs.]

fọr′tress, *n.* [ME. *fortresse*; OFr. *forteresce, fotelesce*; LL. *fortalitia*, a small fort, from L. *fortis*, strong, powerful.]

1. any fortified place; a fort; a stronghold; a place of defense or security.

2. defense; safety; security.

The Lord is my rock and my *fortress.* —Ps. xviii. 2.

fọr′tress, *v.t.*; fortressed (-trest), *pt.*, *pp.*; fortressing, *ppr.* to supply with a fortress; to guard; to fortify.

fọr·tū′it·ism, *n.* the doctrine that happenings from natural causes are accidental and not designed by some higher intelligence.

fọr·tū′i·tous, *a.* [L. *fortuitus,* casual, accidental, from *fors, fortis,* a chance, luck.] accidental; happening by chance.

fọr·tū′i·tous·ly, *adv.* accidentally; by chance.

fọr·tū′i·tous·ness, *n.* the quality of being accidental; chance.

fọr·tū′i·ty, *n.* [from L. *fortuitus,* casual, accidental.] accident: chance.

Fọr·tū′nȧ, *n.* [L., from *fortuna.*] in Roman mythology, the goddess of fortune.

fọr′tū·nāte, *a.* 1. having good luck; lucky.

2. bringing, or coming by, good luck; favorable; auspicious.

Syn.—lucky, fortuitous, prosperous, successful.

fọr′tū·nāte·ly, *adv.* luckily; successfully; by good fortune, or favorable chance.

fọr′tū·nāte·ness, *n.* good luck; success; happiness.

fọr′tūne, *n.* [ME. *fortune;* OFr. *fortune;* L. *fortuna,* chance, hap, fate, fortune.]

1. a fictitious power regarded as bestowing good or evil upon people; luck; chance; fate: often personified.

Though *fortune's* malice overthrow my state. —Shak.

2. the good or evil that is going to happen to one; one's lot, good or bad; especially, one's future lot.

3. good luck; success; prosperity.

His father dying, he was driven to London to seek his *fortune.* —Swift.

4. estate; possessions; wealth; riches; as, a gentleman of small or of large *fortune.*

5. one in possession of or heir to considerable wealth; particularly, a marriageable person of wealth; as, she is a great *fortune.* [Colloq.]

6. in astrology, a fortunate planet: often Jupiter or Venus.

to tell one's fortune; to profess to tell what is going to happen in one's life, as by palmistry, cards, etc.

Syn.—fate, luck, accident, chance, lot, destiny, wealth, possessions.

fọr′tūne, *v.t.* 1. to tell the fortunes of. [Obs.]

2. to provide with wealth. [Rare.]

fọr′tūne, *v.i.* to happen; chance. [Archaic.]

Fọr′tūne 500 (or **1000, 100,** etc.) [from annual listings in *Fortune,* a U.S. magazine.] the 500 (or 1000, 100, etc.) largest U.S. industrial corporations in terms of sales volume.

fọr′tūne hunt′ẽr, one seeking wealth, especially by marrying a rich person.

fọr′tūne·less, *a.* luckless; also, without a fortune.

fọr′tūne·tell″ẽr, *n.* one who professes to forecast the future of others.

fọr′ty, *n.; pl.* **fọr′ties,** [ME. *forti, fourty, feowerti;* AS. *feówertig,* forty; *feówer,* four, and *-tig,* ten.]

1. the cardinal number between thirty-nine and forty-one; 40; XL.

2. in lawn tennis, the third point scored.

the forties; the years from forty through forty-nine (of a century or a person's age).

the roaring forties; the winds prevailing on the Atlantic ocean about the fortieth degree of latitude both north and south and in the Indian and South Pacific oceans.

fọr′ty, *a.* four times ten.

fọr′ty-knot(-not), *n.* a tropical herb of the amaranth family, having many nodes, opposite leaves, and flowers attached directly to the main stem.

fọr′ty-nīn′ẽr, Fọr′ty-Nīn′ẽr, *n.* a person who went to California in the gold rush of 1849. [Colloq.]

fọr′ty winks, a short sleep; nap. [Colloq.]

fō′rum, *n.; pl.* **fō′rums, fō′rȧ,** [L., orig., prob., place boarded off or fenced in; seen also in L. *forus,* gangplank, gaming board.]

1. in Rome, a public place, where causes were judicially tried, and orations delivered to the people; also, a market place.

2. a tribunal; a court.

3. an assembly for the discussion of public matters or current questions.

the Forum; the forum of ancient Rome.

fọr·wāke′, *v.t.* to tire as by loss of sleep. [Obs.]

fọr·wan′dẽr, *v.i.* to wander away; to become weary with wandering. [Archaic.]

fọr′wȧrd, *n.* in basketball, hockey, football, etc., any of the players in the front line or in a front position.

fọr′wȧrd, *v.t.;* forwarded, *pt., pp.;* forwarding, *ppr.* 1. to advance; to promote.

2. to send forward; to transmit; dispatch.

3. to send on to one's new address; as, *forward* her mail to New York.

4. in bookbinding, to prepare (a book) for the finisher by adding the cover, etc.

fọr′wȧrd, *a.* 1. at, toward, or of the front, or fore part.

2. advanced; specifically, (a) ahead of time; early; (b) mentally advanced; precocious; (c) advanced socially, politically, etc.; progressive.

3. moving toward a point in front; onward; advancing.

4. prompt; ready; eager; as, he was *forward* in helping.

5. bold; pushing; presumptuous; pert.

6. of or for the future; as, *forward* buying.

fọr′wȧrd, *adv.* [ME. *forwarde, forwardes;* AS. *foreweard,* forward; *fore,* fore, before, and *-weard,* -ward.]

1. toward the front or a point in front; onward; ahead: opposed to *backward.*

2. toward the future; as, look *forward.*

3. into view or prominence; as, he brought *forward* an opinion.

fọr′wȧrd·ẽr, *n.* 1. one who promotes or advances in progress.

2. one who sends forward or transmits goods; a forwarding agent.

3. in bookbinding, one who does the plain covering of a sewed book and prepares it for the finisher.

fọr′wȧrd·ing, *n.* 1. the act of transmitting or sending forward.

2. in bookbinding, the operation of plain-covering a sewed book, and preparing it for the finisher.

fọr′wȧrd·ly, *adv.* 1. at or toward the front, or fore part.

2. readily; eagerly.

3. boldly; pertly; presumptuously.

fọr′wȧrd·ness, *n.* the quality or state of being forward; specifically, (a) an advanced state of development or progress; (b) readiness; eagerness; (c) boldness; presumption; pertness.

fọr′wȧrd pass, in football, a pass made from behind the line of scrimmage to a teammate in a position toward the opponent's goal.

fọr′wȧrds, *adv.* [ME. *forewardes; foreward* and adv. genit. *-es.*] forward.

fọr·wāste′, *v.t.* to waste. [Obs.]

fọr·wēa′ry, *v.t.* to dispirit; to make very weary. [Obs.]

fọr·weep′, *v.i.* to weep much. [Obs.]

fọr·went′, *v.* past tense of *forgo.*

fọr·whȳ′, *adv.* [ME. *forwhi;* AS. *for hwy,* wherefore; *for* (see *for,* prep.), and *hwy,* instrumental case of *hwæt* (see *what*).] why; wherefore. [Archaic.]

fọr·whȳ′, *conj.* because. [Archaic.]

fọr·wōrn′, *a.* greatly fatigued; exhausted; worn out. [Archaic.]

fọr·yete′, *v.t.* to forget. [Obs.]

fọr·yiēld′, *v.t.* to recompense; to give back. [Obs.]

fọr·zän′dō (fort-sän′dō), *adv.* [It., ppr. of *forzare,* to force.] with force; with stress: in music, a direction to the performer.

fọr·zä′tō (fort-sä′tō), *adv.* forzando.

foss, *n.* [Fr. *fosse;* L. *fossa,* a ditch, trench, f. pp. of *fodere,* to dig.]

1. a ditch, trench, or canal; specifically, the moat around the rampart of a castle.

2. in anatomy, a fossa.

fos′sȧ, *n.; pl.* **fos′sae,** [L., a ditch, trench.] in anatomy, (a) a cavity in a bone, with a large opening; (b) an oval depression in a soft part, as that in the septum of the right auricle of the heart.

fos′sāġe, *n.* in old English law, a duty which the inhabitants of a walled town had to pay for keeping the moat clean.

fos′sak, *n.* a trout of English tidewaters.

Fos·sā′ri·ăn, *n.* [LL. *Fossarii,* pl., from L. *fossa,* a ditch, trench.]

1. in ecclesiastical history, a sect of dissenters who worshiped in ditches and caves in the fifteenth century.

2. [f—] one of the clergy of the fourth century who dug graves.

fosse, *n.* same as *foss.*

fos′set, *n.* a faucet. [Obs.]

fos·sette′, *n.* [Fr., dim. of *fosse,* a ditch, trench.]

1. a little hollow.

2. a dimple.

3. in medicine, a small ulcer of the transparent cornea, the center of which is deep.

fos′sick, *v.i.;* fossicked (-sikt), *pt., pp.;* fossicking, *ppr.* [Brit. Dial. *fossick,* a troublesome fellow.]

1. to be troublesome. [Brit. Dial.]

2. in gold digging, to undermine another's digging; to search for waste gold in relinquished workings, washing places, etc.; hence, to search for any object by which to make gain; as, to *fossick* for clients. [Australia.]

fos′sick·ẽr, *n.* one who works over the waste of gold fields. [Australia.]

fos′sil, *n.* [Fr. *fossile;* L. *fossilis,* dug out, dug up, from *fodere,* to dig up.]

1. originally, any rock or mineral dug out of the earth.

2. any hardened remains or traces of plant or animal life of some previous geological period, preserved in rock formations in the earth's crust.

3. a person who is old-fashioned or has outmoded, fixed ideas. [Colloq.]

fos′sil, *a.* 1. dug out of the earth; as, *fossil* coal; *fossil* salt. [Rare.]

2. resembling or forming a fossil or fossils; as, *fossil* shells, bones, or wood.

3. belonging to the past; unchanged by progress; antiquated.

fossil copal; Highgate resin found in the bed of blue clay at Highgate, near London, a true vegetable gum or resin partly changed by remaining in the earth.

fossil farina; a soft, granular form of lime carbonate resembling meal; rock meal; bergmehl.

fossil ore; fossiliferous ore; specifically, red iron ore or hematite.

fos·sil·if′ẽr·ous, *a.* [L. *fossilis,* dug out, fossil, and *ferre,* to bear.] containing fossils; as, a *fossiliferous* rock or formation.

fos·sil″i·fi·cā′tion, *n.* the act or process of becoming fossilized; also, a fossilized object.

fos′sil·işm, *n.* 1. the scientific study of fossils.

2. the condition of being a fossil or like a fossil.

fos′sil·ist, *n.* an expert on fossils.

fos″sil·i·zā′tion, *n.* 1. a fossilizing or being fossilized.

2. a fossilized thing.

fos′sil·īze, *v.t.;* fossilized, *pt., pp.;* fossilizing, *ppr.* 1. to convert into a fossil or fossils; to petrify; as, to *fossilize* bones or wood.

2. to make out of date, rigid, or incapable of change; as, age has a tendency to *fossilize* men's minds and ideas.

fos′sil·īze, *v.i.* 1. to become or be changed into a fossil.

2. to collect or search for fossils. [Rare.]

fos′sil·īzed, *a.* changed to a fossil; fixed in views and opinions; antiquated.

fos·sil′ō·ġy, fos·sil·ol′ō·ġy, *n.* the scientific study of fossils.

fos′sọr, *n.; pl.* **fos·sō′rēs,** [L., from *fodere,* to dig.] a gravedigger, especially in the early church.

Fos·sō′rēş, *n.pl.* [L., diggers.]

1. a division of hymenopterous insects furnished with a sting in the females, and including the garden wasps, the smooth wasps, the sand wasps, etc.

2. that group of quadrupeds which includes the burrowing moles.

Fos·sō′ri·ȧ, *n.pl.* same as *Fossores.*

fos·sō′ri·ăl, *a.* 1. digging; adapted for digging.

2. of or pertaining to the *Fossores.*

fos·sō′ri·ăl, *n.* [LL. *fossorius,* from L. *fossor,* a digger.] an animal that digs or burrows into the earth to make its home.

fos·sō′ri·ous, *a.* [LL. *fossorius,* from L. *fossor,* a digger.] fossorial.

fos′sū·lȧ, *n.; pl.* **fos′sū·lae,** a little fossa; a small ditch or depression.

fos′sū·lāte, *a.* [L. *fossula,* dim. of *fossa,* ditch, trench, and *-ate.*] having trenches or small grooves.

fos′sūle, *n.* same as *fossula.*

fos′tẽr, *v.t.;* fostered, *pt., pp.;* fostering, *ppr.* [ME. *foster,* from AS. *fostor, foster,* nourishment, rearing, from *foda,* food.]

1. to bring up; rear.

Some say that ravens *foster* forlorn children. —Shak.

2. to help to develop; stimulate; promote; as, hunger *fosters* disease.

3. to cherish; to encourage; harbor fondly in one's mind; as, she *fostered* hopes of becoming an actress.

Syn.—cherish, harbor, indulge.—To *foster* in the mind is to keep with care and positive endeavors; to *cherish* in the mind is to hold dear or set a value upon; to *harbor* is to allow room in the mind, and is generally taken in the worst sense, for giving admission to that which ought to be excluded; to *indulge* in the mind is to give the whole mind to, to make the chief source of pleasure.

fos′tẽr, *v.i.* to be nourished or trained up. [Obs.]

fos′tẽr, *a.* giving, receiving, or sharing affection, care, etc., as if related by blood; having the standing of a specified member of a family but not by birth; as, a *foster* brother.

fos′tẽr, *n.* a foster parent. [Obs.]

fos′tẽr, *n.* a forester. [Obs.]

fos′tẽr·ăge, *n.* 1. the rearing of a foster child.
 2. the state of being a foster child.
 3. the act of giving a child over to foster parents.
 4. a promoting, stimulating, or encouraging.

fos′tẽr bābe, an infant foster child.

fos′tẽr brŏth′ẽr, a boy in his relationship to the child or children of his foster parents.

fos′tẽr chīld, a child reared by anyone other than his mother or father.

fos′tẽr daugh′tẽr (da′tẽr), a girl adopted and reared as one's own daughter.

fos′tẽr ẽarth, earth by which a plant is nourished, though not its native soil.

fos′tẽr·ẽr, *n.* one who fosters.

fos′tẽr fä′thẽr, a man who acts as a father to a child not his own.

fos′tẽr·land, *n.* 1. the land or country which one adopts as a home.
 2. in law, land set apart for the maintenance of a charity.

fos′tẽr·ling, *n.* a foster child.

fos′tẽr·ment, *n.* food; nourishment. [Obs.]

fos′tẽr mŏth′ẽr, a woman who acts as a mother to a child not her own.

fos′tẽr pãr′ent, a foster father or a foster mother.

fos′tẽr sis′tẽr, a girl in her relationship to the child or children of her foster parents.

fos′tẽr sŏn, a boy adopted and reared as one's own son.

fos′tress, *n.* a woman who feeds and cherishes; a nurse.

foth′ẽr, *n.* [AS. *fother, fothur,* a load, wagonload.] an old unit of weight used in weighing lead, lime, etc.; a two-horse load.

foth′ẽr, *v.t.*; fothered, *pt., pp.*; fothering, *ppr.* [prob. from Ice. *fodhra,* to line or fur, from *fodhr,* a lining.] to cover a sail with chopped yarn, oakum, wool, cotton, etc., and, by drawing it over a hole in a vessel, to stop (a leak).

fō′tive, *a.* [from L. *fotus,* pp. of *fovere,* to warm.] nourishing by warmth. [Obs.]

fot′măl, *n.* a former unit of weight for lead, about seventy pounds.

föu·droy′ănt, (*or Fr.* fö-drwȧ-yäṅ′), *a.* [Fr., ppr. of *foudroyer,* to strike by lightning, from *foudre,* lightning; from LL. *fulgere* for L. *fulgur.*] attacking suddenly and severely; fulminant: said of a disease.

föu·gȧde′, *n.* [Fr., from *fouge;* It. *foga,* fury, passion, from L. *fuga,* flight.] formerly in warfare, a little mine charged with powder and covered with stones or earth.

föu·gȧsse′, *n.* same as *fougade.*

fought (fạt), *v.* past tense and past participle of *fight.*

fought′en, *v.* archaic past participle of *fight.*

foul, *a.*; *comp.* fouler; *superl.* foulest, [ME. *foul, ful;* AS. *fūl,* foul, rotten.]
 1. so offensive to the senses as to cause disgust; stinking; loathsome; as, a *foul* odor.
 2. extremely dirty; disgustingly filthy.
 3. full of or covered with dirt or foreign objects; as, a *foul* pipe.
 4. putrid; rotten: said of food.
 5. indecent; obscene; profane; as, *foul* language.
 6. wicked; abominable; as, a *foul* murder.
 7. not clear; stormy; unfavorable; as, *foul* weather, winds, etc.
 8. tangled; caught; jammed; as, a *foul* rope: opposed to *clear.*
 9. not according to the rules of a game; unfair, either by accident or intention.
 10. treacherous; dishonest.
 11. ugly. [Archaic.]
 12. unpleasant, disagreeable, etc. [Colloq.]
 13. in baseball, relating to or having to do with foul balls or foul lines.
 14. in printing, full of errors or changes; as, *foul* copy.
 foul anchor; see under *anchor.*
 foul ball; in baseball, a batted ball that falls outside the foul lines: opposed to *fair ball.*
 foul berth; in navigation, an anchorage in which a ship is likely to foul another ship.
 foul bill of health; among seamen, a certificate stating that a ship hails from a port where contagious disease prevails or that contagion prevails among its crew.
 foul line; (a) in baseball, either of the lines extending from home plate through the outside corners of first base or third base and onward to the end of the outfield; (b) in basketball, the line from which a player makes the free throw or throws granted to him when he is fouled; (c) in bowling, tennis, etc., any of various lines bounding the playing area, outside of which the ball must not be hit, the player must not go, etc.
 foul play; (a) unfair play; action that breaks the rules of the game; (b) treacherous action or violence, as in assault, murder, etc.
 foul shot; in basketball, any of one or more free throws at the basket allowed to a player as a penalty imposed on the opponents for some infraction of the rules: each throw if successful counts for one point.
 foul tip; in baseball, a batted ball barely tipped by the bat and caught by the catcher: it is counted as a strike, and if it is the third strike the batter is out.
 to go (or *fall* or *run*) *foul of;* (a) to collide with and become tangled in; (b) to get into conflict or trouble with.
 to make foul water; in navigation, to sail in water so shallow that the keel of the ship stirs the water and makes it muddy.
 Syn.—defiled, dirty, disgusting, impure, loathsome, noisome, noxious, offensive, nasty, polluted, filthy, unclean, contaminated, coarse, obscene, vulgar.

foul, *v.t.*; fouled, *pt., pp.*; fouling, *ppr.* [ME. *foulen, fulen;* AS. *fylan,* to make foul, from *ful,* foul.]
 1. to make filthy; to defile; to dirty; to soil; as, to *foul* the clothes; to *foul* the face or hands.
 2. to dishonor, disgrace.
 3. to impede; obstruct; specifically, (a) to fill up; encrust; choke; as, grease often *fouls* sink drains; (b) to cover (the bottom of a ship) with impeding growths; (c) to entangle; catch; as, the rope was *fouled* in the shrouds: opposed to *clear;* (d) to collide with.
 4. in games, to make a foul against.
 5. in baseball, to bat (the ball) so that it falls outside the foul lines.
 to foul up; to make a mess of; to make disordered or confused; to entangle or bungle. [Colloq.]

foul, *v.i.* 1. to become dirty.
 2. to be clogged or choked.
 3. to become tangled.
 4. to collide.
 5. to break the rules of a game.
 6. in baseball, (a) to bat the ball so that it falls outside the foul lines; (b) to be retired by a catch of such a ball (with *out*).

foul, *n.* 1. an interference; an act of fouling.
 2. in games and sports, an infraction of the rules.
 3. in baseball, a foul ball.

föu·lärd′, *n.* [Fr.]
 1. a lightweight material of silk, rayon, or silk and cotton, originally brought from India, and usually printed with a small design.
 2. a handkerchief or cravat of this material.

foul brood, a contagious bacterial disease of the larvae of bees, which causes a foul odor.

foul′dẽr, *v.i.* to thunder or flash like lightning. [Obs.]

foul′ly, *adv.* filthily; nastily; hatefully; scandalously, disgracefully; shamefully; unfairly; dishonestly.

foul′märt, *n.* same as *foumart.*

foul′mouthed, *a.* using scurrilous, opprobrious, obscene, or profane language.

foul′ness, *n.* 1. the quality of being foul or filthy; filthiness; defilement.
 2. something foul.

foul′-spō″ken, *a.* slanderous; using foul language.

fou′märt, *n.* [ME. *fulmard, fulmart,* from AS. *ful,* foul, and *mearth,* marten.] the European polecat; the stinking marten.

found, *v.* past tense and past participle of *find.*

found, *v.t.*; founded, *pt., pp.*; founding, *ppr.* [ME. *founden;* OFr. *fonder;* L. *fundare,* to lay the bottom or foundation of a thing, from *fundus,* bottom.]
 1. to lay the basis of; to set for support; to ground; to base; as, this statement is *founded* on facts.
 2. to begin to raise; to begin the construction of; establish; as, to *found* a college or library.
 Syn.—establish, institute, fix, set, build, set up, base, endow, rest, ground, plant, root.

found, *v.i.* to rest or rely; to be based: followed by *on* or *upon.* [Rare.]

found, *v.t.* [Fr. *fondre,* to melt, to cast, from L. *fundo, fusum,* to pour out.]
 1. to melt and pour (metal or materials for glass) into a mold.
 2. to form by melting a metal and pouring it into a mold.

found, *a.* [ME. *funden;* AS. *fundon,* pp. of *findan,* to find.] provided with all the necessaries, especially room and board.

found, *n.* a file having a thin body, used in making combs.

foun·dā′tion, *n.* [ME. *foundacioun, fundacioun;* OFr. *fondation;* LL. *fundatio,* from L. *fundare,* to lay the bottom or foundation of a thing.]
 1. a founding or being founded; establishment.
 2. the establishment of an institution with provision for its upkeep.
 3. a fund invested for a charitable purpose; endowment.
 4. an endowed institution or charity.
 5. the supporting part of a wall, house, etc.; base.
 6. the fundamental principle on which something is founded; basis.
 7. the stiffening or supporting material beneath an outer part, as in a dress.
 8. a foundation garment.
 9. in bee culture, wax inserted in a section as a start for a comb.
 Syn.—institution, establishment, footing, base, basis, origin, ground, groundwork, rudiments.

foun·dā′tion cōurse, same as *base course.*

foun·dā′tion·ẽr, *n.* one who derives support from the funds or foundation of a college or school. [Brit.]

foun·dā′tion gär′ment, a woman's corset or girdle, often with an attached brassiere.

foun·dā′tion·less, *a.* having no foundation.

foun·dā′tion mus′lin, a loosely woven gummed fabric used for stiffening in the manufacture of garments.

foun·dā′tion school, in England, a school established by endowment.

foun·dā′tion stōne, any of the stones constituting the foundation of a building; specifically, a cornerstone.

found′ẽr, *n.* [ME. *founder, fondoure;* OFr. *fondeor, fondour;* Pr. *fundator,* a founder, from L. *fundare,* to found.] one who or that which founds; a builder; an establisher; an originator.
 founder's shares; in law, shares issued to the organizers of a corporation or company: they sometimes carry special privileges.

found′ẽr, *n.* [OFr. *fondeur,* from LL. *fundator,* from L. *fundere,* to pour, found.] a caster; one who casts metals in various forms.

foun′dẽr, *n.* a lameness caused by inflammation within the hoof of a horse.

foun′dẽr, *v.i.*; foundered, *pt., pp.*; foundering, *ppr.* [ME. *foundren,* to founder, cast down; OFr. *fondrer,* to fall in, sink, from *fond,* L. *fundus,* bottom.]
 1. to fill or be filled with water and sink: said of a ship.
 2. to fail; to collapse.
 3. (a) to trip; to fall, as a lame horse; (b) to have founder: said of a horse.

foun′dẽr, *v.t.* 1. to cause inflammation and soreness in the feet of (a horse), so as to disable or lame.
 2. to cause to fill with water and sink: said of a ship.

foun′dẽr·ous, *a.* causing or likely to cause foundering; as, a *founderous* road.

found′ẽr·y, *n.* same as *foundry.*

found′ing, *n.* the art of casting melted metal, according to a given design or pattern.

found′ling, *n.* [ME. *foundling, fundeling,* from *funden,* pp. of *finden,* to find, and dim. *-ling.*] a child found after it has been abandoned by its unknown parents.

found′ling hos′pi·tăl, a hospital for the care of foundlings.

found′ress, *n.* a woman founder. [Rare.]

found′ry, *n.*; *pl.* **found′ries,** 1. a building occupied, fitted, and furnished for casting metals.
 2. metal castings.
 3. the act, process, or work of melting and molding metals; casting.

found′ry ī′ron (-ũrn), iron containing the proper amount of carbon to make it fit for castings.

found′ry lā′dle, a pot-shaped iron vessel for receiving molten metal from the furnace and transferring it to the molds.

found′ry proof, in printing, the final proof before plates are cast.

fount, *n.* a font (of type): British form.

fount, *n.* [L. *fons, fontis*, a fountain.] a fountain or spring; hence, any source of supply.

foun'tain (-tin), *n.* [ME. *fountayne, fontayn*; OFr. *funtaine, fontaine*; LL. *fontana*, from L. *fons, fontis*, a fountain.]

1. a natural spring of water.
2. the head or source of a river.
3. origin; first principle or cause; the source of anything.
4. (a) an artificial spring, jet, or flow of water; (b) the basin, pipes, etc. where this flows; (c) a drinking fountain; bubbler or similar device; (d) a soda fountain.
5. in heraldry, a roundel divided into six spaces by wavy lines across the shield, colored alternately argent and azure.
6. any of various reservoirs or storage places from which something is drawn; as, (a) the barrel of a *fountain* pen; (b) the reserve bulb of a *fountain* inkstand; (c) the cylinder holding the oil in various styles of lamps.

FOUNTAIN

Fountain of Youth; a legendary spring supposed to restore the health and youth of anyone who drank from it: it was sought by Ponce de León and other Spanish explorers in America and the West Indies.

foun'tain·head (-tin-hed), *n.* 1. a spring that is the source of a stream.
2. the primary source of anything.

foun'tain·less, *a.* having no fountain.

foun'tain pen, a pen in which a nib or ball at the end is fed writing fluid from a supply in the reservoir or from a replaceable cartridge in the holder.

foun'tain shell, the conch of the West Indies, *Strombus gigas*.

foun'tain tree, 1. the Indian cedar, *Cedrus deodara*.
2. a Brazilian tree, *Cæsalpinia pluviosa*, the young twigs of which, when shaken, yield a clear drinkable fluid.

fount'ful, *a.* full of springs. [Poet.]

fōur, *a.* [ME. *four, fowr, feower*; AS. *feower*, four.] twice two; totaling one more than three.

fōur, *n.* 1. a cardinal number, one more than three, represented by the symbols 4 or IV.
2. something that has four of anything as its outstanding characteristic, as a playing card or domino marked with four spots.
3. a boat having a crew of four rowers; also, the crew.

four of a kind; in card playing, particularly poker, any four cards dealt having the same denomination.

fōur'bag'gēr, *n.* in baseball, a home run. [Slang.]

four·ché' (för-shā'), *a.* [Fr. *fourché*, from L. *furca*, a fork.] in heraldry, having the ends forked and the forks abruptly terminated, as in a cross.

CROSS FOURCHÉ

four·chette' (-shet'), *n.* [Fr., dim. of *fourche*, a fork.]

1. the wishbone of a bird.
2. the frog of a hoof.
3. a small fold of skin connecting the inner lips (*labia minora*) of the vulva at the lower end.
4. in surgery, an instrument used to raise and support the tongue during the operation of dividing the frenum.
5. in glovemaking, the piece between two adjacent fingers, to which the front and back portions are sewed.

fōur'-çōl·ŏr, *a.* designating or of a process in which printing is done with separate plates in yellow, red, blue, and black, so that any desired color or colors can be produced.

fōur'-çor"nēred, *a.* having four corners.

fōur'-cȳ·çle, *n.* a cycle of four strokes, as in some internal-combustion engines.

fōur'-di·men'sion·ăl, *a.* of or in four dimensions.

Four·drin'i·ēr (foor-), *a.* [after Sealy and Henry *Fourdrinier*, who developed the machine in England early in the 19th century.] designating or of a paper-making machine that produces paper in a continuous strip or roll.

Four·drin'i·ēr, *n.* a Fourdrinier machine.

fōur'-flush, *v.i.*; four-flushed (-flusht), *pt., pp.*; four-flushing, *ppr.* 1. in poker, to draw to fill a bobtail flush and to bet after failing to fill.
2. to bluff. [Slang.]

fōur'-flush, *n.* 1. a bobtail flush.
2. a bluff. [Slang.]

fōur'flush·ēr, *n.* 1. a poker player who four-flushes.
2. a person who bluffs. [Slang.]

fōur'fōld, *a.* [ME. *fourfold, fourfald*; AS. *feowerfeald*; *feower*, four, and *-feald*, -fold.]
1. having four parts.
2. having four times as much or as many.

fōur'foot"ed, *a.* quadruped; having four feet.

Fōur Free'dōmṣ, President Roosevelt's enunciation before Congress, Jan. 6, 1941, of major aims of the United States foreign policy: freedom of speech, freedom of religious worship, freedom from want, and freedom from fear.

föur·gŏn', *n.* [Fr.] a baggage wagon.

fōur'hand"ed, *a.* 1. having four hands or handlike extremities.
2. for four players, as some games.
3. in music, for two performers, as a piano duet.

Fōur'-H' çlub, 4'-H' çlub (-ăch'), [from the aim to improve the *h*ead, *h*ands, *h*eart, and *h*ealth.] a rural youth organization sponsored by the Department of Agriculture, offering instruction in scientific agriculture and home economics.

fōur hun'dred, [popularized by C. J. Allen, New York *Sun* society reporter, from a remark by Ward McAllister: "There are only 400 people in New York that one really knows."] the social set regarded as wealthiest and most exclusive (with *the*).

Föu'ri·ēr·iṣm, *n.* the doctrines of Charles Fourier (1772–1837), French socialist who recommended the reorganization of society into small co-operative communities.

Föu'ri·ēr·ist, *n.* an adherent of or believer in Fourierism.

Föu'ri·ēr·īte, *n.* a Fourierist.

fōur'-in-hand, *n.* 1. a vehicle having one driver for a team of four horses; also, the team so driven.
2. a kind of necktie knotted so that the ends are left hanging.

fōur'-in-hand, *a.* designating or of a four-in-hand.

fōur'-lēaf çlō'vēr, a clover with four leaves, popularly supposed to bring good luck to the finder.

fōur'-let'tēr wŏrd, any of several short words having to do with sex or excrement and generally regarded as objectionable and unprintable.

fōur'ling, *n.* 1. a quadruplet; one of four born at a time.
2. in mineralogy, a four-parted crystal.

föur·neau' (-nō'), *n.*; *pl.* **föur·neaux'** (-nōz'), [Fr., a stove, chamber of a mine.] formerly, in military mining, a powder chamber. [Obs.]

fōur'-ō'çlock", *n.* 1. in botany, an ornamental plant with flowers of various colors which open about four o'clock in the afternoon and close in the morning; *Mirabilis jalapa*: also called *marvel-of-Peru*.
2. the Australian friarbird.

fōur'pence, *n.* 1. a former British silver coin worth about eight cents of United States money.
2. the sum of four pence; four British pennies.

fōur'pen·ny, *a.* 1. costing or valued at fourpence.
2. designating a size of nail: see *-penny*.

fōur'pen·ny, *n.* same as *fourpence*.

fōur'-pōst"ēr, *n.* a large bed having four posts or pillars that sometimes support a canopy or curtains.

fōur'pound·ēr, *n.* a cannon that shoots a four-pound ball.

four·ra·gère' (för-rȧ-zhâr'), *n.* [Fr.] a decoration granted an entire body of troops for bravery in action. It is a braided cord of a designated color, worn around the shoulder seam of the left sleeve of the coat by every member of the unit so decorated.

fōur'sçōre, *a.* four times twenty; eighty.

fōur'sŏme, *a.* of or for four people, as some games.

fōur'sŏme, *n.* 1. a group of four people.
2. in golf, (a) a game involving four players, usually two to a team; (b) the players in such a game.

fōur'squâre (-skwâr), *a.* 1. having four sides and four angles equal; square.
2. unyielding; unhesitating; firm.
3. frank; forthright.

fōur'squâre, *adv.* in a square form; squarely.

fōur'squâre, *n.* a square.

fōur'teen', *a.* [ME. *fourtene, feowertene*; AS. *feówertyne*, fourteen; *feówer*, four, and *teon*, pl. *-tyne*, ten.] four more than ten; twice seven.

fōur'teen', *n.* the cardinal number between thirteen and fifteen; 14 or XIV.

Fōur'teen Points, fourteen conditions set forth by President Wilson in January, 1918, as the basis of a post-war world peace.

fōur'teenth', *a.* [ME. *fourteothe*; AS. *feówerteotha*, from *feówertyne*.]
1. preceded by thirteen others in a series; 14th.
2. designating any of the fourteen equal parts of something.

fōur'teenth', *n.* 1. the one following the thirteenth.
2. any of the fourteen equal parts of something; 1/14.

fōurth, *a.* [AS. *feórtha, feówrtha*; *feówer*, four, and *-tha, -th*, the ordinal suffix.]
1. preceded by three others in a series; the next after the third.
2. describing one of four equal parts of something.

fōurth, *n.* 1. the one following the third.
2. any of the four equal parts of something; 1/4.
3. in music, (a) the tone four degrees above a given tone in a diatonic scale; (b) the interval between these tones; (c) a combination of these tones.

fōurth'-çlȧss', *a.* of the class, rank, excellence, etc. next below the third; specifically, designating or of a class of mail consisting of merchandise or printed matter not first-class or second-class: also called *parcel post*.

fōurth'-çlȧss', *adv.* as or by fourth-class mail.

fōurth di·men'sion, a dimension in addition to those of length, width, and depth: in the theory of relativity, time is regarded as the fourth dimension.

fōurth'ly, *adv.* in the fourth place.

Fōurth of Ju·ly', the holiday celebrating the adoption of the Declaration of Independence on July 4, 1776: also called *Independence Day*.

Fōurth Rē·pub'liç, the republic established in France in 1945, after the liberation in World War II.

fōurth wŏrld, [*often* F- W-] the poorest, most underdeveloped countries of the third world.

fōur'-wāy, *a.* pertaining to four ways; denoting four passages.

four-way cock; a kind of automatic valve used for passing steam alternately to the upper and lower ends of the cylinder and to the condenser, in a steam engine, and for other purposes.

fōur'-wheel, *a.* 1. four-wheeled.
2. affecting four wheels; as, a *four-wheel* drive.

fōur'-wheeled, *a.* having or running on four wheels.

fōur'-wheel"ēr, *n.* a four-wheeled vehicle.

föus'sȧ, *n.* [native name.] a catlike, carnivorous animal of Madagascar, *Cryptoprocta ferox*.

föu'tēr, föu'tre, *n.* [Fr. *foutre*, from L. *futuere*, to have sexual intercourse with.]
1. a despicable fellow.
2. a fig: euphemism for a strong term of contempt. [Obs.]

fō'vē·ȧ, *n.*; *pl.* **fō'vē·ae**, [L.] a pit or shallow depression.

fō'vē·ȧ cen·trā'lis, a small depression in the retina, the point where the vision is most acute.

fō'vē·āte, *a.* [L. *fovea*, a pit, and *-ate*.] pitted; having depressions.

fō·vē'ō·lȧ, *n.*; *pl.* **fō·vē'ō·lae**, [dim. of L. *fovea*, a pit.] a diminutive pit; a small fovea.

fō'vē·ō·lāte, *a.* in botany, marked by minute depressions or pits.

fō'vē·ō·lā·ted, *a.* foveolate.

fō'vē·ōle, *n.* same as *foveola*.

fō·vil'lȧ, *n.*; *pl.* **fō·vil'lae**, [a dim. from L. *fovere*, to warm, cherish.] in botany, the minute powder or semifluid matter contained in the interior of the pollen grain, which is the immediate agent in fertilization.

fowl, *n.*; *pl.* **fowls** or **fowl**, [ME. *fowl, fowel, fugel*; AS. *fugel, fugol*, a fowl; D. *vogel*; Ice. *fugl, fogl*, a fowl, bird.]
1. originally, any bird: used now in combination; as, wild *fowl*.
2. any of the larger domestic birds used as food; specifically, (a) the chicken; (b) the duck, goose, etc.; (c) a full-grown chicken, as distinguished from a springer, etc.
3. the flesh of any of these birds used for food.

fowl, *v.i.*; fowled, *pt., pp.*; fowling, *ppr.* to catch or kill wild birds, either for sport or for food; as, to hunt, fish, and *fowl*.

fowl'ẽr, *n.* a person who hunts, traps, or shoots wild birds.

fow'lẽr·īte, *n.* a zinciferous variety of rhodonite: named after Dr. Samuel Fowler of New Jersey.

Fow'lẽr's sō·lū'tion, a solution of potassium arsenite.

fowl'ing, *n.* the practice of hunting wild fowl.

fowl'ing pie̤ce, a light shotgun for shooting birds.

Fox, *n.* 1. a member of a tribe of Algonquian Indians who lived in Illinois and southwestern Wisconsin.

2. this tribe: merged with the Sac tribe (1760).

fox, *n.*; *pl.* **fox'es** or **fox,** [AS. *fox*, a fox.]

1. (a) any of a group of small, wild, flesh-eating animals of the dog family, with bushy tails and, commonly, reddish-brown fur: the fox is conventionally thought of as sly and crafty; (b) its fur.

FOX (*Vulpes fulva*)

2. the foxfish.

3. a sly, cunning, deceitful person.

4. in nautical usage, a small strand of rope, made by twisting several rope yarns together.

5. a kind of sword. [Obs.]

fox and geese; a game played with pegs or checkers on a chessboard or cross-shaped board; also, any of several games resembling tag.

fox, *v.t.*; foxed (fokst), *pt., pp.*; foxing, *ppr.* 1. to make (beer, etc.) sour by fermenting.

2. [from the color of a fox.] to stain (book leaves, prints, etc.) with reddish-brown or yellowish discolorations.

3. to trick or deceive by slyness or craftiness.

4. to repair (boots, shoes, etc.) with new upper leather.

5. to intoxicate; to stupefy.

fox, *v.i.* 1. to turn sour: said of beer, etc.

2. to become discolored by damp, rust, etc., as timber or paper.

3. to hunt the fox.

4. to act with cunning like a fox. [Now Dial.]

fox bat, same as *flying fox.*

fox bōlt, a bolt having one end split to receive a fox wedge, which, when the bolt is driven in, secures it.

fox brush, the tail of a fox, especially when regarded as the trophy of a fox hunt.

foxed (foxt), *a.* 1. discolored or stained; literally, with marks resembling the color of a fox, as an old book.

2. soured, as beer.

3. tricked.

4. repaired, as shoes.

fox ē'vil, same as *alopecia.*

fox fīre, phosphorescent light given off by decayed wood.

fox'fish, *n.* 1. the fox shark.

2. the gemmous dragonet.

fox'glōve, *n.* [AS. *foxes glofa*, fox's glove.] any of a number of plants of the figwort family, with long spikes full of thimble-like flowers: one species is a source of digitalis.

FOXGLOVE (*Digitalis purpurea*)

fox grāpe, any of several North American varieties of grape, as *Vitis labrusca* and *Vitis rotundifolia.*

fox'hōle, *n.* a hole dug in the ground as a temporary protection for one or two soldiers against enemy gunfire or tanks.

fox'hound, *n.* a hound trained to hunt foxes and other game; a variety of hound having fleetness, great strength, and a keen scent. Its coat is usually white with patches of black and tan.

FOXHOUND

fox'-hunt, *v.i.* to take part in a fox hunt or fox hunts.

fox hunt, a sport in which hunters on horses ride after dogs in pursuit of a fox.

fox hunt'ẽr, one who hunts foxes.

fox hunt'ing, the practice or sport of hunting foxes.

fox'-hunt''ing, *a.* pertaining to or fond of hunting foxes.

fox'i·ly, *adv.* in a foxy manner; slyly.

fox'i·ness, *n.* the quality of being foxy; craft; cunning; shrewdness.

fox'ing, *n.* a piece of leather for repairing or decorating the upper of a shoe.

fox'līke, *a.* resembling a fox; cunning; foxy.

fox shärk, the thresher shark or sea fox, *Alopias vulpinus.*

fox'ship, *n.* the character or qualities of a fox; cunning; foxiness.

fox spar'rōw, a large sparrow of North America: so called from its rusty-red or foxlike color.

fox squir'rel, the largest tree squirrel of eastern North America. It is about twelve inches long, and varies in color from black to shades of red, rusty-brown, and gray.

fox'tāil, *n.* 1. the tail of a fox: also called *fox brush.*

2. in metallurgy, the cinder obtained in the last stage of the charcoal refinery process.

3. any of several tall grasses with long spikes of brushlike flowers.

foxtail wedging; a method of wedging done by inserting into the point of a wooden bolt a thin wedge of hard wood, which, when the bolt reaches the bottom of the hole, splits, expands, and secures it.

fox'tāil gråss, same as *foxtail*, sense 3.

fox ter'ri·ẽr, any of a breed of small, active terriers with a smooth or wire-haired coat, generally white, or white with spots of black and tan, commonly kept in the United States as a housedog or watchdog: they were formerly trained to drive foxes out of hiding.

fox'-trot, *v.i.* 1. to go at a fox trot, or mixed pacing and trotting gait: said of a horse.

2. to dance the fox trot.

fox trot, 1. a slow, mixed gait of a horse in which it trots with the forelegs and paces with the hind legs.

2. a dance in 4/4 time with a variety of steps, both fast and slow.

3. the music for such a dance.

fox wedġe (wej), in carpentry, a wedge used to expand the split end of a fox bolt, to fasten it in a hole or mortise.

fox wolf (-wu̇lf), any of several South American wild dogs which resemble both foxes and wolves.

fox'y, *a.*; *comp.* foxier; *superl.* foxiest, 1. pertaining to foxes; resembling a fox in appearance or character; suggestive of a fox or of cunning; wily; tricky.

Modred's narrow *foxy* face.—Tennyson.

2. having the coarse flavor of the fox grape

3. of the color of the fox; reddish-brown.

4. covered with brownish or yellowish stains, as an old book.

5. attractive, stylish, etc.; specifically, sexually attractive: used especially of women. [Slang.]

foy, *n.* 1. a feast given by or to one who is about to leave on a journey. [Dial.]

2. a feast at the end of a harvest or fishing season. [Dial.]

foy'ẽr (*or Fr.* fwo-yā'), *n.* [Fr., hearth, fireside, lobby, from LL. *focarius*, from L. *focus*, a hearth, fireplace.]

1. an entrance hall or lobby, especially in a theater, hotel, or apartment house.

2. the crucible in a furnace which holds the molten metal.

fō'zi·ness, *n.* the state or quality of being fozy. [Scot.]

fō'zy, *a.* spongy; lacking substance; soft and puffy. [Scot.]

Frä, *n.* [It.] brother: a monk's or friar's title; as, *Fra* Augustine.

frå, *adv.* and *prep.* fro. [Obs.]

frab, *v.i.* and *v.t.* to nag; to plague; to scold; to worry. [Brit. Dial.]

frab'bit, *a.* peevish; cross. [Brit. Dial.]

frab'jous, *a.* [coined by Lewis Carroll in *Through the Looking-Glass.*] splendid; magnificent. [Colloq.]

frä'çås, *n.* [Fr., a crash, disturbance, tumult, from *fracasser*; It. *frassare*, to break in pieces, destroy; *fra*, within, amidst, and *cassare*, from L. *quassare*, intens. of *quatere*, to shake.] a noisy quarrel; a disturbance; a brawl.

frăche, *n.* [perhaps from Fr. *fraiche*, f. of *frais*, fresh.] in glassmaking, an iron pan in which newly formed glass vessels are placed while being annealed.

fraçt'ed, *a.* [L. *fractus*, pp. of *frangere*, to break.] in heraldry, having a part displaced as if broken; as, a chevron *fracted.*

CHEVRON FRACTED

fraç'tion, *n.* [L. *fractio* (-*onis*), a breaking, from *frangere*, to break.]

1. the act of breaking or state of being broken, especially by violence. [Rare.]

2. in ecclesiastical usage, the rite of breaking the bread in the celebration of the Eucharist.

3. a small portion broken off; small part, amount, degree, etc.; a fragment; as, a *fraction* of time.

4. in mathematics, a quantity less than a unit or whole number; any division of a whole number or unit, as 2/5, two-fifths, 1/4, one-fourth: the figure above the line is called the *numerator*, and the figure below the line, the *denominator*. In *decimal fractions*, the denominator is 10, 100, 1000, etc. They are commonly expressed by writing only the numerator with a point before it, by which it is separated from whole numbers; thus, .5, which denotes five-tenths, 5/10, or half of a unit; .25, that is, 25/100, or a fourth part of a unit; also, any quantity expressed in terms of a numerator and denominator, as 13/4.

5. in chemistry, a part separated by fractional crystallization, distillation, etc.

fraç'tion, *vt.* to separate into fractions.

fraç'tion·ăl, *a.* 1. of or pertaining to fractions; constituting a fraction; as, *fractional* currency, *fractional* numbers.

2. fragmentary; small; insignificant; as, a *fractional* part of the audience enjoyed the play.

3. in chemistry, designating or of any of various processes for separating the constituents of a mixture by taking advantage of differences in their solubility, boiling points, etc.; as, *fractional* distillation.

4. in commerce, being less than the unit of transaction, usually 100 shares, in stock exchanges.

fractional crystallization; in chemistry, the separation of different substances by successive solutions and crystallizations.

fractional currency; see under *currency.*

fractional distillation; a method of distillation for separating two liquids which have different boiling points.

fraç'tion·ăl·ly, *adv.* in a fractional manner; by a fraction.

fraç'tion·ăr·y, *a.* 1. fractional.

2. fragmentary.

fraç'tion·āte, *v.t.*; fractionated, *pt., pp.*; fractionating, *ppr.* to separate chemically into fractions by distillation, crystallization, etc.

fraç·tion·ā'tion, *n.* the act or process of fractionating.

fraç'tion·īze, *v.t.* and *v.i.*; fractionized, *pt., pp.*; fractionizing, *ppr.* to divide into fractions.

fraç'tious, *a.* 1. unruly; rebellious; refractory.

2. apt to quarrel; cross; snappish.

Syn.—perverse, cross, irritable, petulant, pettish, waspish, snappish, peevish.

fraç'tious·ly, *adv.* in a fractious manner.

fraç'tious·ness, *n.* the quality of being fractious.

fraç'tō-, [from L. *fractus*, pp. of *frangere*, to break.] a combining form used in hyphenated compounds, meaning *a ragged mass of* (a specified kind of) *cloud*, as in *fracto-stratus.*

fraç·tō-çū'mū·lus, *n.* a mass of small, ragged clouds torn from a cumulus.

fraç·tō-nim'bus, *n.* a mass of ragged, shapeless clouds torn from a nimbus.

fraç·tō-strā'tus, *n.* a ragged cloud in long, threadlike layers, torn from a stratus.

fraç'tūr·ăl, *a.* pertaining to, having the nature of, or caused by a fracture.

fraç'tūre, *n.* [OFr. *fracture*; L. *fractura*, a breaking, a breach, cleft, from *frangere*, to break.]

1. the act or result of breaking.

2. a break; crack; split.
3. a break in a bone or, occasionally, a tear in a cartilage.
4. the texture of the surface of a mineral broken across the normal line of cleavage.

frac'tūre, *v.t.*; fractured, *pt., pp.*; fracturing, *ppr.* to break; to crack; to split; to burst asunder; to separate the continuous parts of; as, to *fracture* a bone.

frac'tūre, *v.i.* to undergo fracture; to break; to crack; to split; as, this stone *fractures* easily.

frāe, *prep.* from. [Scot.]

frāe, *adv.* fro. [Scot.]

fraen'ū·lum, *n.* same as *frenulum.*

frae'num, *n.* same as *frenum.*

Frā·gā'ri·ȧ, *n.* [L. *fraga*, pl., strawberries.] the strawberry genus, a genus of perennial herbs with creeping runners, natural order *Rosaceæ.* Only a few species are known.

frag'ile, *a.* [L. *fragilis*, easily broken, frail, from *frangere*, to break.] brittle; easily broken; weak; liable to fail; easily destroyed; frail; delicate.

The stalk of ivy is tough, and not *fragile.* —Bacon.

Syn.—brittle, frail, frangible, weak.

frag'ile·ly, *adv.* in a fragile manner.

frȧ·gil'i·ty, *n.* [L. *fragilitas*, from *fragilis*, easily broken, frail.] the condition or quality of being fragile; brittleness; weakness; frailness.

frag'ment, *n.* [L. *fragmentum*, a fragment, remnant, from *frangere*, to break.]
1. a part broken off; a piece separated from anything by breaking.

Gather up the *fragments* that remain. —John vi. 12.

2. a detached, isolated, or incomplete part; as, *fragments* of the melody remained in her mind.
3. the part that exists of a literary or other work left incomplete or unfinished; as, this poem is only a *fragment.*

frag·men'tăl, *a.* 1. fragmentary.
2. in geology, designating or of rocks formed of the fragments of rocks that had existed previously; clastic.

frag'men·tā·ri·ly, *adv.* in a fragmentary manner.

frag'men·tā·ri·ness, *n.* the quality or condition of being fragmentary.

frag'men·tā·ry, *a.* composed of fragments; disconnected; incomplete; broken up.

frag·men·tā'tion, *n.* a breaking into fragments.

frag·men·tā'tion bomb (bom), an antipersonnel bomb that scatters the broken, jagged pieces of the bomb case over a wide area when it explodes.

frag'ment·ed, *a.* broken into pieces; existing in fragments.

frag'ment·īze, *v.t.*; fragmentized, *pt., pp.*; fragmentizing, *ppr.* to break into fragments.

frā'gŏr, *n.* a strong, sweet odor. [Obs.]

frā'gŏr, *n.* [L. *fragor*, a breaking, crash, from *frangere*, to break.] a loud, harsh sound; a crash. [Obs.]

frā'grănce, *n.* [L. *fragrantia*, from *fragrans* (*-antis*), fragrant, ppr. of *fragrare*, to emit an odor.]
1. the quality of being fragrant.
2. a sweet smell; a pleasant odor.

frā'grăn·cy, *n.*; *pl.* **frā'grăn·cieṣ,** fragrance. [Rare.]

frā'grănt, *a.* [L. *fragrans* (*-antis*), ppr. of *fragrare*, to emit an odor.] having a pleasant odor; sweet-smelling.

Fragrant the fertile earth
After soft showers. —Milton.

Syn.—odorous, scented, perfumed, balmy, sweet-smelling, aromatic, sweet-scented, odoriferous, spicy.

frā'grănt·ly, *adv.* with sweet scent.

frāil, *a.*; *comp.* frailer; *superl.* frailest. [ME. *freyl, freel*; OFr. *frele*, from L. *fragilis*, easily broken, brittle.]
1. fragile; delicate; easily broken, shattered, damaged, or destroyed; perishable; not firm or durable.

That I may know how *frail* I am. —Ps. xxxix. 4.

2. slender and delicate; not robust; weak.
3. easily tempted; morally weak; liable to sin or misbehave.

Man is *frail* and prone to evil.—Taylor.

Syn.—delicate, weak, fragile, frangible.

frāil, *n.* a woman or girl. [Slang.]

frāil, *n.* [ME. *fraiel, frayle*; OFr. *fraiel*, from ML. *frællum*, a basket.]
1. a rush used for weaving baskets.
2. a flexible basket made of rushes, used in packing dried fruits, as dates, figs, and raisins.
3. the varying quantity of raisins, etc. contained in such a basket, usually 50 or 75 pounds.

frāil'ly, *adv.* weakly; infirmly.

frāil'ness, *n.* weakness; infirmity.

frāil'ty, *n.*; *pl.* **frāil'tieṣ,** 1. the quality or condition of being frail; weakness; especially, moral weakness.

God knows our *frailty*, and pities our weakness. —Locke.

2. a foible or infirmity resulting from some weakness; a fault.

No further seek his merits to disclose,
Or draw his *frailties* from their dread abode. —Gray.

Syn.—frailness, infirmity, failing, foible, imperfection.

frāi'scheūr (frā'shẽr), *n.* [Fr.] freshness; coolness. [Obs.]

frāiṣe, *n.* [Fr. *fraise*, orig., a ruff.]
1. a ruff or high collar.
2. in military usage, a defense consisting of a fence of barbed wire, or, formerly, pointed stakes driven into the ramparts, in a horizontal or inclined position.
3. a grooved tool used by masons for enlarging drill holes.

frāiṣe, froiṣe, *n.* a pancake with bacon in it. [Obs.]

frāiṣe, *v.t.*; fraised, *pt., pp.*; fraising, *ppr.* 1. in stone working, to enlarge (a drill hole) with a fraise.
2. in military usage, to protect with a fraise.

frām'ȧ·ble, *a.* capable of being framed.

fram·bē'ṣi·ȧ, fram·boe'ṣi·ȧ, *n.* [Fr. *framboise*, a raspberry.] in medicine, the yaws, a contagious, tropical disease.

frāme, *v.t.*; framed, *pt., pp.*; framing, *ppr.* [ME. *framen*, to construct, build; AS. *fremman, fremian*, to advance, promote, execute, from *fram*, strong, valiant.]
1. to shape, fashion, or form, usually according to a pattern; to design; as, they *framed* a constitution.
2. to construct; to fit and unite together the several parts of; as, to *frame* a building.
3. to make; to compose; to contrive; to plan; to devise; to invent; to put into words.

For thou art *framed* of the firm truth of valour. —Shak.

4. to utter; as, his lips *framed* the words.
5. to fit, as for a specific use; to regulate; to adjust; to shape; to conform; as, the law was *framed* to equalize the tax burden.
6. to surround or provide with a border, as a picture.
7. to falsify evidence, testimony, etc. beforehand in order to make (a person) appear guilty. [Slang.]

Syn.—adjust, compose, contrive, fabricate, fit, form, invent, plan.

frāme, *v.i.* 1. to shape; to arrange. [Obs.]
2. to contrive. [Obs.]

frāme, *n.* [ME. *frame*, a fabric, structure, advantage, benefit, from AS. *fremu, freme*, profit, advantage.]
1. (a) anything composed of parts fitted together according to a design; (b) any of various machines built on or in a framework.
2. fabric; structure; the main timbers of a structure fitted and joined together for the purpose of supporting and strengthening the whole; framework; as, the *frame* of a house, barn, bridge, or ship; bodily structure; make or build of a person; skeleton.
3. any kind of case or structure made for inserting, enclosing, or supporting things; as, the *frame* of a window, door, picture, or mirror.
4. in printing, a stand to support the cases in which the types are contained.
5. in founding, a kind of ledge enclosing a board, which, being filled with wet sand, serves as a mold for castings.
6. a kind of loom on which linen, silk, etc. is stretched for quilting or embroidering, or on which lace, stockings, and the like are made.
7. an established order or system, especially of government.
8. the way that anything is constructed or put together; organization; form.
9. mood; humor; mental constitution; natural temper or disposition; as, an unhappy *frame* of mind.
10. proper shape; correct form; proportion. [Obs.]

Put your discourse into some *frame.* —Shak.

11. a framing (sense 7). [Slang.]
12. in baseball, an inning. [Colloq.]
13. in bowling, etc., any of the ten divisions of a game, in each of which the pins are set up anew.
14. in motion pictures, each of the small exposures composing a strip of film.
15. in pool, (a) the triangular form in which the balls are set up at the beginning of a game; (b) the balls so set up before the break; (c) the period of play required to pocket all the balls.
16. in shipbuilding, any of the transverse structures that form the ribs of a ship's hull and extend from the gunwale to the bilge or to the keel: called *square frame* when set at a right angle to the vertical plane of keel, and *cant frame* when set at an oblique angle.
17. in television, a single scanning of the field of vision by the televisor.

frā'mē·ȧ, *n.*; *pl.* **frā'mē·ae,** [L.] a long lance or spear used by the early Franks.

frāme house, a house with a wooden framework, usually covered with boards.

frāme of mīnd, mental or emotional state; mood.

frām'ẽr, *n.* one who frames; a maker; a contriver.

frāme saw, a thin saw made rigid by being stretched in a frame.

frāme'-up, *n.* 1. a falsifying of evidence, testimony, etc. to make an innocent person seem guilty. [Colloq.]
2. a surreptitious, underhand arrangement or scheme made beforehand. [Colloq.]

frāme'wŏrk, *n.* 1. a structure, usually rigid, serving to hold the parts of something together or to support something constructed or stretched over or around it; skeletal structure; as, the *framework* of a building.
2. basic structure; constitution; adjusted arrangement; system.

All the *framework* of the land.—Tennyson.

3. work done in a frame.

frām'ing, *n.* 1. the act or style of constructing a frame.
2. a frame, framework, or system of frames.

fram'pōld, *a.* [W. *ffromfol*, passionate.] unruly; peevish; cross; vexatious. [Obs.]

franç, *n.* [Fr., from the device *Francorum rex*, king of the French, on the coin when first struck by King John in 1360.]
1. (a) the monetary unit and a current coin of France, originally equal to 19.3 cents but valued at about 1/4 cent in 1950; (b) an obsolete French coin of gold or silver.
2. (a) the similar monetary unit of Belgium; (b) the similar monetary unit of Switzerland.

fran'chīṣe, *n.* [ME. *franchise*; OFr. *franchise*, freedom, liberty, from *franc*, free.]
1. originally, freedom from some restriction, servitude, etc.
2. a special privilege or right granted by the government, as to be a corporation, operate a public utility, etc.; as, a street railway *franchise.*
3. the district or jurisdiction to which such a privilege extends; the limits of an immunity.
4. the right to vote; suffrage.
5. an asylum or sanctuary, where persons are secure from arrest.
6. frankness; generosity. [Obs.]

fran'chīṣe, *v.t.*; franchised, *pt., pp.*; franchising, *ppr.* [ME. *franchisen, fraunchisen*, from OFr. *franchir*, to make free, from *franc*, free.] to enfranchise; to give liberty to. [Obs.]

fran'chīṣe·ment, *n.* [OFr. *franchisement*, from *franchir*, to make free.] release from burden or restriction; freedom; enfranchisement. [Obs.]

Fran'çiç, *a.* pertaining to the Franks. [Rare.]

fran·cis'çȧ, *n.* [LL., f. of *Franciscus*, Frankish.] a battle-ax used by the ancient Franks, having the head long, curved, and narrow, and set at an obtuse angle to the pole.

Fran·cis'çăn, *a.* [LL. *Franciscus*, a Franciscan; from *Franciscus*, Francis.]
1. of St. Francis of Assisi.
2. designating or of the Roman Catholic order of St. Francis or the Franciscans.

Fran·cis'çăn, *n.* in the Roman Catholic Church, a member of the Franciscan order: also called *Minorites* and *Gray Friars.* The order was founded in Italy, in 1209, by St. Francis of Assisi, and it members devote themselves to missions, preaching, nursing, etc. Their dress is of coarse gray or brown cloth, with cowl, girdle, and sandals. The order is now divided into three independent branches.

fran'ci·um, *n.* [from *France*, and *-ium.*] a metallic chemical element of the alkali group: symbol, Fr; atomic weight, 223 (?); atomic number, 87 (formerly designated as *virginium*).

Fran'cō-, [from LL. *Francus*, a Frank.] a combining form meaning: (a) *Frankish*; (b) *of France, of the French*, as in *Franco*phobe; (c) *France and, the French and*, as in *Franco-*German.

fran'cō·lin, *n.* [Fr. *Francolin*, a francolin; It. *francolino*, from *franco*, free.] any of several African and Asiatic partridges, constituting the genus *Francolinus*.

fran'cō·līte, *n.* a variety of apatite occurring in the Wheal Franco mine in Devonshire, England.

Fran'cō-Prus'siăn War, a war (1870–1871) between France and Prussia that resulted in the defeat of France.

franc-ti"reur' (frän -tē-rūr') *n.*; *pl.* **francs-ti"reur'** (frän -tē-rūr'), [Fr. *franc*, free, and *tireur*, shooter.] any of a group of French irregular soldiers serving variously as light infantry, scouts, etc.

fran'ġent, *a.* [L. *frangens* (*-entis*), ppr. of *frangere*, to break.] causing fractures.

fran·gi·bil'i·ty, *n.* the quality or state of being frangible.

fran'gi·ble, *a.* [OFr. *frangible*, from L. *frangere*, to break.] capable of being broken; breakable; easily broken.

fran'ġi·pāne, *n.* same as *frangipani*.

fran'ġi·pan·i, fran'ġi·pan·ni, *n.* [said to be after a Marquis *Frangipani*, major general under Louis XIV.]

1. any of several tropical American shrubs of the genus *Plumiera* with large, fragrant flowers; especially, the red jasmine, *Plumiera rubra*.

2. a perfume obtained from this flower or imitating its scent.

3. a kind of pastry containing cream, almonds, and sugar.

Also *frangipane*.

fran'gū·lȧ, *n.* [prob. from L. *frangere*, to break; from the brittleness of the stems.] the bark of the alder buckthorn, *Rhamnus frangula*, used as a laxative; also, the alder buckthorn.

fran·gū'liç, fran·gū·lin'iç, *a.* pertaining to frangula.

frangulic acid; a compound obtained from frangulin.

fran'gū·lin, *n.* [*frangula* and *-in.*] in chemistry, a yellow coloring matter contained in the bark of the alder buckthorn and other species of *Rhamnus*.

fran'iŏn, *n.* a paramour. [Obs.]

frank, *n.* [from OFr. *franc*, a pigsty, from *franc*, free, privileged.] a pigpen. [Obs.]

frank, *v.t.* to shut up in a sty, or frank; hence, to fatten. [Obs.]

frank, *n.* the heron. [Brit. Dial.]

frank, *a.*; *comp.* franker; *superl.* frankest, [Fr. *franc*, frank, free, from ML. *francus*, free, at liberty.]

1. open; ingenuous; candid; free in expressing what one thinks or feels.

2. liberal; generous; not niggardly. [Rare.]

3. free; without conditions. [Obs.]

Thy *frank* election make. —Shak.

4. licentious; unrestrained. [Obs.]

5. free from reserve, disguise, or guile; clearly evident; plain; as, *frank* rebellion.

Syn.—artless, candid, honest, ingenuous, plain, open, unreserved, sincere, undisguised.

frank, *v.t.*; franked (frankt), *pt.*, *pp.*; franking, *ppr.* 1. to send (mail) free of postage.

2. to mark (mail) so that it can be sent free.

3. to make easy the coming or going of (a person); allow to pass free of charge.

4. to free; release from; exempt.

frank, *n.* 1. a letter, package, etc. sent under an authorized signature or stamp exempting it from payment of postage or similar charges for service.

2. the signature or stamp so exempting mail from charges.

3. the right or privilege to send mail free.

frank, *v.t.* in carpentry, to form the joint of, as in a window sash where the crosspieces of the frame intersect, by cutting away no more wood than is sufficient to show a miter.

frank, *n.* a frankfurter. [Slang.]

Frank, *n.* [ME.; AS. *Franca.*]

1. a member of the Germanic tribes that established the Frankish Empire, which, at its height (beginning of the 9th century A.D.), extended over what is now France, Germany, and Italy.

2. any native or inhabitant of Europe, especially western Europe: term used by Moslems and Greeks.

frank'al·moin, frank'al·moigne (-moin), *n.* literally, free alms; in English law, a tenure by which a religious corporation might hold lands given to them and their successors forever, on condition of praying for the soul of the donor.

frank chāse, in English law, a right or liberty of free chase.

Frank'en·steīn, *n.* 1. the title character in a novel (1818) by Mary Wollstonecraft Shelley: he is a young medical student who creates a monster that destroys him.

2. any person destroyed by his own creation or invention.

3. (a) popularly, Frankenstein's monster; (b) anything that becomes dangerous to its creator.

frank'ẽr, *n.* one who exercises the privilege of franking mail.

frank fee, in English law, freehold; a holding of lands in fee simple.

frank fẽrm, [ME. *frank*, free, and *ferm*, a farm.] in English law, freehold tenure at a fixed rent.

frank fōld, same as *faldage*.

frank'fũrt·ẽr, frank'fōrt·ẽr, *n.* [G., from *Frankfurt*, Germany.] a smoked sausage of beef or beef and pork, usually enclosed in a membranous casing and made in cylindrical links a few inches long; wiener: also *frankfurt* (or *frankfort*) *sausage*, *frank*.

frank'in·cense, *n.* [ME. *frankincens*, *frankensence*; OFr. *franc encens*; LL. *francum incensum*, lit., pure incense.]

1. a gum resin which burns freely with an aromatic odor and is used as incense. It is obtained from various Asiatic and East African trees of the genus *Boswellia* also called *olibanum*.

2. any gum resin resembling this.

Frank'ish, *a.* of the Franks, their language, or culture.

Frank'ish, *n.* the West Germanic language of the Franks.

frank'lin, *n.* [ME. *franklen*, *frankeleyn*; OFr. *francheleyn*; ML. *francus*, free, frank, and *-ling.*]

1. in England in the 14th and 15th centuries, a landowner of free but not noble birth, ranking just below the gentry.

2. a prosperous farmer who owns much land. [Brit.]

3. a freeman. [Obs.]

Frank·lin'iç, *a.* of or pertaining to Benjamin Franklin (1706–1790).

Franklinic electricity; static electricity.

Frank'lin·iṣm, *n.* static electricity.

frank'lin·īte, *n.* [after *Franklin*, New Jersey, where it is found.] a brilliant black mineral, an oxide of iron, zinc, and manganese.

frank"lin·i·zā'tion, *n.* the application of static electricity in medicine.

Frank'lin stōve, a type of open, iron stove resembling a fireplace, invented by Benjamin Franklin.

frank'ly, *adv.* 1. in a frank manner; without reserve, constraint, or disguise; as, to confess one's faults *frankly*.

2. liberally; freely; generously. [Rare.]

He *frankly* forgave them both. —Luke vii. 42.

Syn.—artlessly, freely, candidly, sincerely, openly, ingenuously, unreservedly, readily, willingly.

frank'mar"riaġe (-rij), *n.* in old English law, an estate of inheritance given to a man and his wife by a close relative of the wife, and descendible to the children of the marriage and their heirs.

frank'ness, *n.* 1. plainness of speech; candor; freedom in communication; openness; ingenuousness; as, he told me his opinion with *frankness*.

2. liberality; bounteousness. [Obs.]

frank'pledġe (-plej), *n.* [Anglo-Fr. *frank-plege* (see *frank, a.*, and *pledge*).]

1. in English history, the system which made each man in a tithing responsible for the actions of other members.

2. a member under this system.

3. the tithing.

fran'tiç, *a.* [ME. *frentik*, *frenetik*; OFr. *frenetique*; L. *phreneticus*, from Gr. *phrenētikos*, *phrenitikos*, mad, suffering from inflammation of the brain, from *phrenitis*, inflammation of the brain, from *phrēn*, mind.]

1. greatly excited by anger, grief, pain, etc.; frenzied.

2. insane. [Archaic.]

Syn.—distracted, infuriate, frenzied, raging.

fran'tiç, *n.* a madman. [Archaic.]

fran'tiç·ăl·ly, *adv.* in a frantic manner.

fran'tiç·ly, *adv.* frantically. [Rare.]

fran'tiç·ness, *n.* condition of being frantic.

frap, *v.t.*; frapped (frapt), *pt.*, *pp.*; frapping, *ppr.* [prob. from OFr. *fraper*, to strike.] in nautical usage, to strengthen or bind together by cables, ropes, etc.; also, to tighten (slack ropes).

frāpe, *n.* a rabble; a crowd. [Obs.]

frap'le, *v.i.* to bluster. [Obs.]

frap'lẽr, *n.* a rowdy; a blusterer. [Obs.]

frap·pé' (fra-pā'), *a.* [Fr., pp. of *frapper*, to strike.] partly frozen; iced; cooled.

frap·pé', *n.* 1. a dessert made of partly frozen beverages, fruit juices, etc.

2. a drink made of some beverage poured over shaved ice.

Frā'ṣẽr·ȧ, *n.* [named after John *Fraser*, botanist, 1750–1817.] a genus of plants of the gentian family, *Gentianaceæ*, containing eight species of erect perennial herbs, native to North America.

frat, *n.* a fraternity, as at a college. [Slang.]

frā'tẽr, *n.* [L., a brother.]

1. a comrade; a brother. [Obs.]

2. a friar. [Obs.]

frā'tẽr, *n.* a dining hall, or refectory, in a monastery. [Obs.]

frȧ·tẽr'năl, *a.* [LL. *fraternalis*, from L. *fraternus*, brotherly, from *frater*, a brother.]

1. of or characteristic of a brother or brothers; brotherly.

2. of or like a fraternal order.

3. designating twins (boys, girls, or boy and girl) developed from separately fertilized ova and thus having hereditary characteristics as different as if they were not twins: distinguished from *identical*.

fraternal insurance; see under **insurance**.

fraternal order (or *society*, *association*); a society, often secret, of members banded together for mutual benefit or for work toward a common goal.

frȧ·tẽr'năl·iṣm, *n.* 1. a fraternal relationship or spirit; brotherliness.

2. the organization and customs of fraternal orders.

frȧ·tẽr'năl·ly, *adv.* in a fraternal manner.

frȧ·tẽr'nāte, *v.i.* [from L. *fraternus*, brotherly.] to fraternize. [Rare.]

fra·tẽr·nā'tion, *n.* fraternization. [Rare.]

frā'tẽr·niṣm, *n.* fraternization. [Rare.]

frȧ·tẽr'ni·ty, *n.*; *pl.* **frȧ·tẽr'ni·tieṣ,** [LL. *fraternitas*, a brotherhood, from L. *fraternus*, brotherly, from *frater*, a brother.]

1. the state or quality of being a brother or brothers; fraternal relationship or spirit; brotherliness.

2. a body of men (or, rarely, women) associated for their common interest, business, or pleasure; a company; a brotherhood; a society; as, a college *fraternity*.

3. a group of people with the same beliefs, profession, occupation, or character; as, the writing *fraternity*.

With what terms of respect knaves and sots will speak of their own *fraternity*. —South.

Syn.—society, association, circle, sodality, league, clan, guild.

frā"tẽr·ni·zā'tion, *n.* a fraternizing.

frat'ẽr·nīze, *v.i.*; fraternized, *pt.*, *pp.*; fraternizing, *ppr.* [Fr. *fraterniser*, from L. *fraternus*, brotherly.]

1. to associate in a brotherly manner; be on friendly terms.

2. to have sexual relations with one of the enemy: said of soldiers in and after World War II. [Colloq.]

frat'ẽr·nīze, *v.t.* to bring into fraternal association or into brotherly sympathy. [Rare.]

frat'ẽr·nīz·ẽr, *n.* one who fraternizes.

frā'tẽr·y, *n.* a frater, or refectory.

frā'tri·āġe, frā'trāġe, *n.* [LL. *fratriagium*, from *fratria*, a fraternity, from L. *frater*, a brother.] a partition of an estate among brothers or coheirs; also, a younger brother's share. [Obs.]

frat'ri·cī·dăl, *a.* 1. pertaining to fratricide.

2. relating to the killing of relatives or fellow-countrymen, as in a civil war.

frat'ri·cīde, *n.* [L. *fratricida*, from *frater*, *fratris*, brother, and -*cidium*, a killing, from *cædere*, to kill.]
1. the act of killing one's own brother or sister.
2. a person who kills his own brother or sister.

Frau, *n.*; *pl.* **Frau'en,** [G.] a married woman; wife: used in Germany as a title corresponding to *Mrs.*

fraud, *n.* [ME. *fraud*, *fraude*; OFr. *fraude*, from L. *fraus*, *fraudis*, a cheating, deceit, error.]
1. (a) deceit; trickery; cheating; (b) in law, intentional deception to cause a person to give up property or some lawful right.

For when success a lover's toil attends,
Few ask if force or *fraud* attained his ends.
—Pope.

2. something said or done to deceive; trick; artifice.
3. a person who deceives or is not what he pretends to be; impostor; cheat. [Colloq.]
actual fraud; a fraud with actual wrongful intent to deceive.
constructive fraud; in law, a fraud that is involved in an act or contract which, though not originating in any actual evil or fraudulent design, has a tendency to deceive or mislead other persons, to violate public or private confidence, or to impair or injure the public interests.
pious fraud; a fraud designed to accomplish a good end; also, colloquially, one who deceives by a false pretense of piety.
statute of frauds; an old English statute designed to prevent frauds by requiring written evidence of important acts or contracts.
Syn.—deceit, artifice, cheat, deception, imposture, imposition, swindle, swindling, treachery, treason.

fraud'ful, *a.* deceitful in making bargains; trickish; treacherous; containing fraud or deceit.

fraud'ful·ly, *adv.* in a fraudful manner.

fraud'less, *a.* free from fraud.

fraud'less·ly, *adv.* in a fraudless manner.

fraud'less·ness, *n.* the state or quality of being fraudless.

fraud'ū·lence, *n.* the quality or state of being fraudulent; deceitfulness; trickery; dishonesty.

fraud'ū·len·cy, *n.* fraudulence.

fraud'ū·lent, *a.* [OFr. *fraudulent*; L. *fraudulentus*, cheating, fraudulent, from *fraus*, *fraudis*, a cheating, trickery, deceit.]
1. deceitful; trickish; given to the use of fraud; as, a *fraudulent* person.
2. containing fraud; founded on fraud; proceeding from fraud; as, a *fraudulent* bargain.
3. treacherous; obtained or performed by artifice.
Syn.—deceiving, cheating, deceptive, deceitful, dishonest.

fraud'ū·lent·ly, *adv.* by fraud; by deceit; by artifice or imposition; designedly.

fraught (frąt), *a.* [ME. *fraught*, *fraght*, a load, cargo, freight, from M.D. *vracht*, a load, cargo, freight; Dan. *fragt*; G. *fracht*, freight, load, lading.] laden; loaded; charged; freighted; filled (followed by *with*); as, a vessel *fraught with* goods, an enterprise *fraught with* danger.

fraught, *n.* a freight; a cargo. [Obs.]

fraught, *v.t.* to load; to fill; to crowd: used only in the past participle.

fraught'äge, *n.* loading; cargo. [Obs.]

Fräu'lein (froi'līn), *n.*; *pl.* **Fräu'lein,** [G.] an unmarried woman: used in Germany as a title corresponding to *Miss.*

Fraun'hō·fẽr līneș, [after Joseph von *Fraunhofer* (1787–1826), Bavarian optician, who first observed and mapped them accurately.] the dark lines visible in the solar spectrum.

frax'in, *n.* [L. *fraxinus*, ash, and -*in*.] a glucoside found in the bark of the common ash tree, *Fraxinus excelsior.*

frax·i·nel'lȧ, *n.* [Mod. L., dim. of L. *fraxinus*, ash tree.] a perennial plant of the rue family, with thick foliage and white flowers: also called *burning bush*, in reference to the fact that its vapor is inflammable on hot nights.

Frax'i·nus, *n.* [L., the ash tree.] a genus of deciduous trees, including the common ash and belonging to the olive family, *Oleaceæ*. The species inhabit the more temperate regions of the northern hemisphere. The common ash of Europe, *Fraxinus excelsior*, yields a heavy, compact wood of great value. Several American species including *Fraxinus americana*, the white ash, are also valuable for their timber.

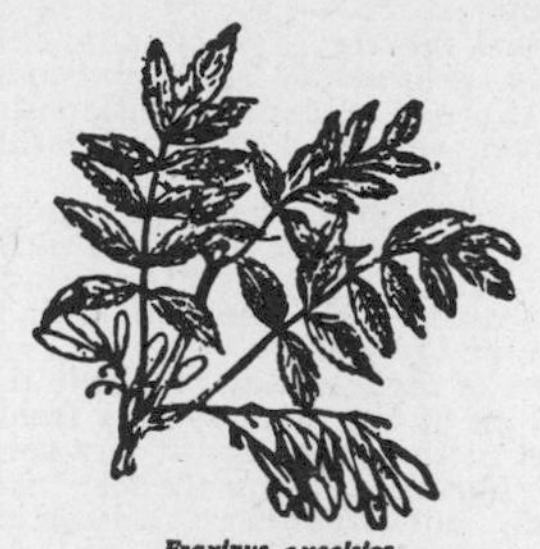
Fraxinus excelsior
common ash

frāy, *n.* [abbrev. of *affray*.]
1. a noisy quarrel; a brawl; an affray.
2. a combat; a battle; also, a single combat or duel.
3. a contest; contention.

frāy, *v.t.* to terrify; to frighten. [Archaic.]

frāy, *v.i.* to quarrel or fight; to brawl. [Archaic.]

frāy, *v.t.* and *v.i.*; frayed, *pt.*, *pp.*; fraying, *ppr.* [OFr. *frayer*, *froyer*; It. *fregare*, from L. *fricare*, to rub.] to make or become worn or ragged by rubbing.

frāy'ing, *n.* peel of a deer's horn.

fraz'zle, *v.t.* and *v.i.*; frazzled, *pt.*, *pp.*; frazzling, *ppr.* [Brit. dial. and U. S.; prob. from L.G.]
1. to wear or become worn to rags or tatters; fray. [Colloq.]
2. to make or become tired or exhausted. [Colloq.]

fraz'zle, *n.* 1. the state of being frazzled. [Colloq.]
2. a worn end; a shred. [Colloq.]

frēak, *n.* [Early Mod. Eng.; perh. via dial. from AS. *frician*, to dance; sense 3 from *freak of nature*, after L. *lusus naturæ*.]
1. a sudden fancy; odd notion; whim.

She is restless and peevish, and sometimes
in a *freak* will instantly change her habitation.
—Spectator.

2. a whimsical nature; capriciousness.
3. any abnormal animal, person, or plant; monstrosity.
4. (a) a user of a specified narcotic, hallucinogen, etc.; as, an acid *freak*; (b) a devotee or buff; as, a rock *freak*; (c) same as *hippie*. [Slang.]
Syn.—whim, fancy, caprice, folly, sport, abnormality, monstrosity.

frēak, *a.* oddly different from what is usual or normal; queer; abnormal.

frēak, *v.t.* [ME. *fraken*, *freken*, to freckle.] to variegate; to checker; to fleck; to streak; to dapple. [Poet.]

Freaked with many a mingled hue.
—Thomson.

frēak, *n.* a fleck or streak. [Poet.]

frēak'ish, *a.* 1. apt to change the mind suddenly; whimsical; capricious.
2. having the nature of a freak; odd; queer.
Syn.—sportive, frisky, whimsical, fanciful, capricious, erratic.

frēak'ish·ly, *adv.* in a freakish manner.

frēak'ish·ness, *n.* capriciousness; whimsicalness.

frēak'y, *a.*; *comp.* freakier; *superl.* freakiest, freakish.

freck'le, *n.* [from ME. *freken*, *fraken*; Ice. *freknur*, a freckle.]
1. a small, yellowish-brown spot on the skin, especially on the face, neck, and hands, usually produced by the action of the sun.
2. any small spot or discoloration.

freck'le, *v.i.*; freckled, *pt.*, *pp.*; freckling, *ppr.* to acquire freckles; as, a skin that *freckles* easily.

freck'le, *v.t.* to cover or mark with freckles; as, the sun *freckled* his face badly.

freck'led (-ld), *a.* spotted; having small, yellowish-brown spots on the skin or surface; as, a *freckled* face or neck, a *freckled* cowslip.

freck'led-fāced (-fāst), *a.* having a face covered with freckles.

freck'led·ness, *n.* the state of being freckled.

freck'ly, *a.* full of freckles; sprinkled with spots.

free, *a.*; *comp.* freer; *superl.* freest, [ME. *free*, *freo*; AS. *freo*, *frio*, *frig*, free.]
1. (a) not under the control of some other person or some arbitrary power; able to act or think without compulsion or arbitrary restriction; having liberty; independent; (b) characterized by or resulting from liberty.
2. (a) having, or existing under, a government that does not impose arbitrary restrictions on the right to speak, assemble, petition, vote, etc.; having political liberty; as, a *free* people; (b) not under control of a foreign government.
3. able to move in any direction; not held, as in chains, etc.; not kept from motion; loose.
4. not held or confined by a court, the police, etc.; acquitted.
5. not held or burdened by obligations, debts, discomforts, etc.; unhindered; unhampered; as, *free* from pain.
6. not confined to the usual rules or patterns; not limited by convention or tradition.
7. not literal; not exact; as, a *free* translation.
8. not held or confined by prejudice or bias.
9. able to choose for itself; not restricted by anything except its own limitations or nature; as, *free* will.
10. not busy; available for other work, use, etc.; as, what time will you be *free?*
11. ready; readily done or made; spontaneous; as, a *free* offer.
12. not constrained or stilted; smooth, easy, and graceful; as, a *free* gait.
13. (a) generous; liberal; lavish; as, a *free* spender; (b) profuse; abundant; copious.
14. frank; straightforward.
15. too frank or familiar in speech, action, etc.; forward; indecorous.
16. without cost or payment; gratis; as, a *free* ticket.
17. not liable to (trade restrictions, etc.); exempt from certain impositions, as, taxes or duties.
18. clear of obstructions; open and unimpeded; as, a *free* road ahead.
19. open to all; as, a *free* market, *free* port.
20. not in contact or connection; not fastened; as, the *free* end of a rope.
21. not united; not combined; as, *free* oxygen.
22. in nautical usage, not opposed; favoring; as, a *free* wind.
23. in phonetics, designating a stress whose position varies in inflected forms of the same word.
free air; air existing without such restraint as is imposed by pressure or friction with the earth's surface; also, less broadly, all of the atmosphere more than 100 feet above the earth.
free alongside ship (or *vessel*); delivered to the dock with freight charges paid by the shipper: said of goods to be hauled by ship.
free and easy; without social restraint or conventionality; informal; unceremonious.
free bond; in chemistry, a unit of valence not employed in forming a compound.
free church; a church in which the sittings are free of charge.
Free Church of Scotland; a large body of Presbyterians that withdrew from the Church of Scotland in 1843, so as to be free from state control.
free city; a city that is an autonomous and independent state: Hamburg, Lübeck, and Bremen were called *free cities* in the Middle Ages because they had no feudal obligations except to the emperor.
free coinage; the system by which a government is legally required to coin for a person, either free or at cost, any gold, silver, or other specified metal that he brings to the mint.
free company; in the Middle Ages, any of the groups of mercenary soldiers (called *free companions*) who fought for whoever hired them.
Free French; in World War II, those Frenchmen who continued resistance against Germany and the French collaborationists after the surrender of France in 1940.
free from (or *of*); (a) lacking; without; (b) released or removed from; (c) beyond; outside of.
free gold; (a) formerly, gold in the United States Treasury above the amount needed to redeem gold certificates; (b) in mining, pure gold.
free goods; goods imported free of duty.

free list; the list of articles or goods not subject to import or export tariff duties; also, a list of persons entitled to free admission (as to an exhibition, a museum, etc.), or entitled to free copies (as of a book).

free on board; delivered (by the seller) aboard the train, ship, etc. at the point of shipment, without further charge to the buyer.

free port; (a) a port open equally to ships of all countries; (b) a port or zone where goods may be unloaded, stored, and reshipped without payment of customs or duties, if they are not imported: also *free zone*.

free services; in the feudal system, services that might be performed by a soldier or freeman, as to serve under his lord in time of war, to contribute money, etc.

free silver; the free coinage of silver, especially at a fixed ratio to the amount of gold coined in the same period.

free socage; in English law, a tenure held in feudal times by services which were certain, free, and honorable.

Free State; any State in which slavery was forbidden before the Civil War.

free throw; same as *foul shot*.

to give (or *have*) *a free hand*; to give (or have) liberty to act according to one's judgment.

to make free with; (a) to use freely; treat as if one owned; (b) to be too familiar with.

to set free; to cause to be free; liberate; release; disengage.

with a free hand; with generosity; lavishly.

free, *adv.* 1. in a free manner; without obstruction, hindrance, obligation, etc.

2. without cost or payment; as, ladies are admitted *free*.

3. in nautical usage, with a favorable wind.

free, *v.t.*; freed, *pt.*, *pp.*; freeing, *ppr.* [ME. *freen*, from AS. *freon*, *freogan*, to free.]

1. to remove any encumbrance or obstruction from; to disengage from; to rid; to strip; to clear; as, to *free* the feet from fetters, to *free* a channel from sand.

2. to set at liberty; to rescue or release from slavery, captivity, authority, obligation, etc.; to loose; as, the prisoner is *freed* from arrest.

3. to exempt from payment of duty, tax, or postage by endorsement; to frank; as, to *free* a letter. [Obs.]

Syn.—clear, deliver, liberate, manumit, ransom, rescue, disenthrall.

free ā'gent, an athlete eligible to play a professional sport who is free to sign a contract with any team with which he can work out an agreement.

free as·sō·ci·ā'tion, in psychoanalysis, the technique of having the patient talk as freely as possible about something, bringing in whatever ideas, memories, etc. are associated with it in his mind: used to discover and clarify repressions.

free bench, formerly, in English law, a widow's dower in a copyhold.

free'biē, free'by (-bē), *n.*; *pl.* **free'bies,** [arbitrary extension of *free*.] something given or gotten free of charge, as a complimentary theater ticket. [Slang.]

free'bōard, *n.* the side of a ship between the rail or gunwale and the water line.

free'boot, *v.i.* to act as a freebooter. [Rare.]

free'boot·ēr, *n.* [D. *vrijbuiter*, from *vrijbuiten*, to plunder; *vrij*, free, and *buit*, plunder.] a pirate; a buccaneer: a plunderer.

free'boot·ing, *n.* plunder; robbery; piracy.

free'boot·y, *n.* pillage or plunder. [Obs.]

free'born, *a.* 1. born free, not in slavery or serfdom.

2. of or fit for such a person or people.

freed'man, *n.*; *pl.* **freed'men,** a man legally freed from slavery or bondage.

free'dŏm, *n.* [ME. *fredom*, freedom; AS. *freodom*; *freo*, free, and *-dom*, -dom.]

1. the state or quality of being free; especially, (a) exemption or liberation from the control of some other person or some arbitrary power; liberty; independence; (b) exemption from arbitrary restrictions on a specified civil right; political liberty; as, *freedom of speech*; (c) exemption or immunity from a specified obligation, discomfort, etc.; as, *freedom* from want; (d) exemption or release from imprisonment; (e) a being able to act, move, use, etc. without hindrance or restraint; (f) a being able of itself to choose or determine action freely; as, *freedom* of the will; (g) ease of movement or performance; facility; (h) a being free from the usual rules, patterns, etc.; boldness of conception or execution; (i) frankness; straightforwardness; (j) an excessive frankness or familiarity.

2. a privilege held by a city, corporation, etc.; franchise.

freedom of the city; (a) originally, citizenship in a city, granted as an honor to nonresidents; (b) now, honorary citizenship in a city, given ceremoniously to distinguished visitors.

freedom of the press; freedom to publish any opinions in newspapers, magazines, books, etc. without government interference or censorship: usually modified to exclude libel, sedition, and obscenity.

freedom of the seas; the principle that merchant ships of any country may freely travel any part of the open seas at any time.

Syn.—liberty, independence, frankness, openness, outspokenness, unrestrictedness.

freed'wom"ăn (-woom"), *n.*; *pl.* **freed'wom"en** (-wim"), a woman legally freed from slavery or bondage.

free en'tēr·prīse, the economic doctrine or practice of permitting private industry to operate with a minimum of control by the government.

free fall, the unchecked fall of a body through the air; specifically, the part of a parachutist's jump before the parachute is opened.

free flight, the flight of a rocket after the fuel supply has been used up or shut off.

free'-fọr-all', *n.* 1. a contest, race, etc. that anyone may enter.

2. a disorganized fight in which many take part; a brawl.

free'-form, *a.* 1. having an irregular, usually curvilinear form or outline.

2. not conforming to the conventional rules of composition, form, etc.; spontaneous, unrestrained, etc.

free'-hand, *a.* drawn, sketched, etc. by hand without the use of instruments, measurements, etc.; as, a *free-hand* drawing.

free'hand·ed, *a.* generous; openhanded.

free'heärt'ed, *a.* 1. open; frank; unreserved.

2. liberal; charitable; generous.

free'heärt'ed·ly, *adv.* unreservedly; liberally.

free'heärt'ed·ness, *n.* frankness; liberality.

free'hōld, *n.* 1. the holding of a piece of land, an office, etc. for life or with the right to pass it on through inheritance.

2. an estate, office, etc. held in this way.

free'hōld, *a.* of or held by freehold.

free'hōld'ēr, *n.* the possessor of a freehold.

chosen freeholder; in New Jersey, one of a governing board that has control of the affairs of a county: in other states called *county commissioner* or *county supervisor*.

free kick, in football, the act of putting the ball in play by a kick which the opponents are restrained from interfering with.

free'-lánce', *a.* of or acting as a free lance.

free'-lánce', *v.i.*; free-lanced, *pt.*, *pp.*; free-lancing, *ppr.* to work as a free lance, as a writer, actor, etc.

free lánce, 1. a medieval soldier who sold his services to any state or military leader; a mercenary.

2. a person who acts according to his principles and is not influenced by any group; an independent.

3. a writer, actor, etc. who is not under contract for regular work but sells his writings or services to any buyer: also called *free-lancer*, *n.*

free liv'ẽr, one who eats and drinks abundantly; one who indulges his appetites freely.

free'-liv'ing, *a.* 1. indulging freely in eating, drinking, and similar pleasures.

2. in biology, living independently of any other organism; not parasitic or symbiotic.

free'lōad·ēr, *n.* a person who habitually imposes on others for free food, lodging, etc.; sponger. [Colloq.]

free lŏve, the principle or practice of sexual relations unrestricted by conventions of marriage, religion, etc.

free lŏv'ẽr, one who practices free love.

free'ly, *adv.* in a free manner; with freedom; without hindrance, restraint, or opposition; as, to move *freely*; to speak *freely*.

> *Freely* ye have received, *freely* give.
> —Matt. x. 8.

Syn.—independently, voluntarily, spontaneously, willingly, readily, liberally, generously, bounteously, munificently, bountifully, abundantly, largely, copiously, plentifully.

free'măn, *n.*; *pl.* **free'men,** 1. one who enjoys liberty, or who is not subject to the will of another; one who is not in slavery or bondage.

2. a citizen; a person who has all civil and political rights in a city or state.

free mär'ket, any market where buying and selling can be carried on without restrictions as to price, etc.

free'mär"tin, *n.* an imperfectly developed female calf, usually sterile, born as the twin of a male.

Free'mā"sŏn, *n.* [from obs. *freemason*, member of a class of skilled itinerant masons: so named prob. from being free to move from town to town, without restraint by local guilds.] a member of an international secret society having as its principles brotherliness, charity, and mutual aid: also called *Free and Accepted Mason*, *Mason*.

free"mȧ·son'iç, *a.* of, pertaining to, or resembling Freemasonry.

> That mysterious undefinable *freemasonic* signal, which passes between women, by which each knows that the other hates her.
> —Thackeray.

Free'mā'sŏn·ry, *n.* 1. the principles, rituals, etc. of Freemasons; Masonry.

2. the Freemasons.

3. [f-] a natural sympathy and understanding among persons with similar experiences.

free'-mill"ing, *a.* easily reduced: said of ores which are reducible without the ordinary process of roasting.

free'-mīnd"ed, *a.* not perplexed; free from care.

free'ness, *n.* 1. the state or quality of being free, unconstrained, unconfined, unencumbered, or unobstructed.

2. openness; unreservedness; frankness; ingenuousness; candor.

3. liberality; generosity; as, *freeness* in giving.

4. gratuitousness; as, the *freeness* of education.

frē'ẽr, *n.* a liberator; one who makes free.

Free'si·ȧ (*or* -zhi-ȧ), *n.* [Mod. L., after E. M. *Fries* (1794–1878), Swed. botanist.]

1. a genus of South African plants of the iris family, *Iridaceæ*, with fragrant white or yellow flowers.

2. [f-] any plant of this genus.

free'-soil', *a.* opposed to the extension of slavery.

free soil, territory in which there is no slavery; especially, any territory in the United States where slavery was prohibited before the Civil War.

Free'-Soil'ẽr, *n.* in United States history, a member of the Free-Soil Party.

Free'-Soil'iṣm, *n.* the principles of the Free-Soil Party.

Free'-Soil' Pär'ty, a former United States political party (1848–1856) that opposed the spread of slavery into the Territories.

free'-spō'ken, *a.* accustomed to speak without reserve; speaking frankly; outspoken.

> One was a *free-spoken* senator. —Bacon.

free'-spō'ken·ness, *n.* the quality of being free-spoken.

free'-stand·ing, *a.* resting on its own support, without attachment or added support.

free'stōne, *n.* 1. a stone, especially sandstone or limestone, that can be cut easily without splitting.

2. a peach, plum, etc. in which the stone, or pit, does not cling to the pulp of the ripened fruit.

free'stōne, *a.* having a pit that does not cling to the pulp of the ripened fruit: said of certain peaches, plums, etc.

free'-swim'ming, *a.* capable of swimming about freely, as certain protozoa.

free'thiñk'ẽr, *n.* a person who forms his opinions about religion independently of tradition, authority, or established belief.

> Atheist is an old-fashioned word. I am a *freethinker*. —Addison.

free'thiñk'ing, *n.* free thought.

free'thiñk'ing, *a.* 1. of freethinkers or free thought.

2. believing in free thought.

free thought (that), opinions about questions of religion formed independently of tradition, authority, or established belief.

free trāde, 1. trade carried on without governmental regulations; especially, international trade conducted without protective tariffs, customs duties, etc.

2. smuggling. [Archaic.]

free'trād'ẽr, one who engages in, advocates, or believes in free trade: also *free trader.*

free ū·ni·vẽr'si·ty, a loosely organized forum for the study in nontraditional ways of subject matter not generally offered in regular university courses.

free vẽrse, verse characterized by much rhythmic variation, new, irregular, or unusual stanzaic forms, and either absence of rhyme or a loose rhyme pattern.

free'wāy, *n.* 1. a multiple-lane divided highway with fully controlled access, as by cloverleafs, for intersecting roads.
2. a highway without toll charges.

free'wheel', *n.* 1. in a bicycle, a device in the rear hub that permits the rear wheel to go on turning when the pedals are stopped.
2. in some automobiles, a device that permits the drive shaft to go on turning when its speed exceeds that of the engine shaft, thus allowing free coasting with the gears engaged.

free'wheel'ing, *n.* 1. a freewheel.
2. the use of a freewheel.

free'wheel'ing, *a.* of, having, or using a freewheel.

free'will', *a.* 1. voluntary; spontaneously given or done.
2. in theology and philosophy, of or holding the doctrine of free will.

free will, 1. the human will regarded as free from restraints, compulsions, or any antecedent conditions; freedom of decision or choice.
2. the doctrine that people have this: opposed to ***determinism.***

freez'a·ble, *a.* capable of being frozen; as, carbon dioxide is *freezable.*

freeze, *v.i.*; froze, *pt.*; frozen, *pp.*; freezing, *ppr.* [ME. *freesen, fresen,* from AS. *freosan.*]
1. to be formed into ice; to be hardened or solidified by cold.
2. to become covered or clogged with ice.
3. to be or become very cold.
4. to become fixed or attached by freezing; as, the automobile tires *froze* to the ground.
5. to die or be damaged by exposure to cold.
6. to become motionless or stiff.
7. to be chilled or made momentarily rigid by a strong, sudden emotion; as, his face *froze* with terror.
8. to become formal, haughty, or unfriendly
to freeze over; to become covered with ice.
to freeze up; figuratively, to assume a frigid and forbidding attitude. [Colloq.]

freeze, *v.t.* 1. to cause to form into ice; to harden or solidify by cold.
2. to cover or clog with ice.
3. to make very cold; to chill.
4. to remove sensation from, as with a local anesthetic.
5. to preserve (food) by rapid refrigeration.
6. to make fixed or attached by freezing.
7. to kill or damage by exposure to cold.
8. to make or keep motionless or stiff.
9. to frighten or discourage by cool behavior, unfriendliness, etc.
10. to make formal, haughty, or unfriendly.
11. (a) to fix (prices, employment, an employee, etc.) at a given level or place by authoritative regulation; (b) to stop consumer production or use of (a critical material), as in wartime; (c) to make (funds, assets, etc.) unavailable to the owners.
to freeze in; to entangle or envelop in ice; as, the ship was *frozen in* for the winter.
to freeze one's blood; to terrify or horrify.
to freeze (on) to; to cling to; hold fast to. [Colloq.]
to freeze out; to keep out or force out by a cold manner, competition, etc. [Colloq.]
to freeze over; to cover with ice.

freeze, *n.* 1. a freezing or being frozen.
2. a period of cold, freezing weather.

freeze'-drȳ, *v.t.*; freeze-dried, *pt., pp.*; freeze-drying, *ppr.* to subject (food, vaccines, etc.) to quick-freezing followed by drying under high vacuum at low temperature: a freeze-dried product, as food, will keep for long periods at room temperature.

freeze frāme, a single frame of a motion picture repeated a number of times so as to stop motion and create the effect of a still photograph for dramatic emphasis.

freeze'-frāme'', *n.* same as *freeze frame.*

freez'ẽr, *n.* 1. a person or device that freezes; especially, a machine for making ice cream and sherbet.
2. a deep freezer.

freez'ing, *a.* very cold; as, a *freezing* atmosphere.

freez'ing, *n.* the process of becoming frozen.

freez'ing·ly, *adv.* in a freezing manner; distantly; coldly.

freez'ing mix'tūre, a mixture of two or more substances, as of salt and snow, which produces intense cold.

freez'ing point, the temperature at which a liquid freezes or becomes solid: the freezing point of water under laboratory conditions is 32° F. or 0° C.

freī·es·lę·ben·īte, *n.* [named after *Freiesleben,* a German mineralogist.] in mineralogy, a bluish-gray sulfide of antimony, lead, and silver, of monoclinic crystallization, brittle, and soft to the touch.

frẹight (frāt), *n.* [Fr. *fret*; D. *vracht*; Dan. *fragt*; G. *fracht,* freight, load, lading.]
1. the cargo, or any part of the cargo, of a ship, railroad car, truck, etc.; lading.
2. the price paid for transporting goods or merchandise by land or sea; as, *freights* are high.
3. a freight train; as, to travel on a *freight.*
4. a method or service for transporting goods, usually bulky goods, by water, land, or air: freight is usually cheaper and slower than express.
5. any load or burden.

frẹight, *v.t.*; freighted, *pt., pp.*; freighting, *ppr.* 1. to load with goods, as a ship, car, or vehicle of any kind, for transporting them from one place to another; as, we *freighted* the ship for Amsterdam.
2. to hire for the transportation of goods.
3. to transport as or send by freight.
4. to load or burden; as, a book *freighted* with learning; to be *freighted* with care.

frẹight'āġe, *n.* 1. the charge for transporting goods or merchandise.
2. freight; cargo; goods transported.
3. the transportation of goods.

frẹight ā'ġent, an employee of a transportation company who receives, forwards, and delivers freight.

frẹight çär, a railroad car especially designed for transporting freight.

frẹight'ẽr, *n.* 1. one who loads a ship.
2. one who receives freighted goods and forwards them to their destination.
3. one who sends goods by freight.
4. a ship for carrying freight; a cargo vessel.

frẹight house, a depot where freight is received and stored until claimed.

frẹight'less, *a.* without freight.

frẹight trāin, a railroad train made up of freight cars.

fremd, *a.* [AS. *fremede,* strange.] strange, foreign, alien, etc. [Obs. or Dial.]

frem'i·tus, *n.*; *pl.* **frem'i·tus,** [L. *fremitus,* from *fremere,* to roar, murmur.] in medicine, a palpable vibration; as, the *fremitus* caused by partial obstruction of the air passages.
vocal fremitus; that fremitus produced by utterance of sounds.

frē'nȧ, *n.* alternative plural of *frenum.*

frē'nāte, *a.* [L. *frenatus,* from *frenum,* a bridle.] having a frenum or frenulum; specifically, in entomology, provided with a delicate organ for attaching the posterior to the anterior wings of an insect, as certain lepidopters.

French, *a.* [ME. *Frenkish, Frensche*; AS. *Fransisc,* from *Franca,* a Frank.] of France, its people, their language, or culture.
French bean; the kidney bean, *Phaseolus vulgaris.*
French berry; same as *Avignon berry.*
French Canadian; (a) a Canadian of French ancestry; (b) same as *Canadian French.*
French casements; same as ***French windows.***
French chalk; see under ***chalk.***
French cleaning; same as ***dry cleaning.***
French cuff; a double cuff on the sleeve of a shirt; a cuff turned back on itself and fastened with a link.
French doors; two adjoining doors that have glass panes from top to bottom and are hinged at opposite sides of a doorway so that they open in the middle.
French dressing; a salad dressing made of vinegar, oil, and various seasonings.
French fried; fried in very hot, deep fat until crisp: French fried potatoes (colloquially called *French fries*) are first cut lengthwise into strips.
French grass; a plant, *Onobrychis sativa,* cultivated and used as fodder.
French heel; a curved high heel on a woman's shoe.
French horn; a brass-wind instrument with three rotary valves and a long, coiled tube ending in a wide, flaring bell: it has a range of 3½ octaves and a mellow tone.

FRENCH HORN

French ice cream; very rich ice cream made with cream and eggs.
French kiss; a passionate kiss with lips parted and tongues touching.
French leave; [from 18th-c. custom, in France, of leaving receptions without taking leave of the host or hostess.] an unauthorized or unceremonious departure; act of leaving secretly or in haste.
French pastry; rich pastry, usually filled with preserved fruit, whipped cream, etc.
French polish; a coating for wood, made of gums dissolved in alcohol; also, the peculiar glossy finish imparted by this polish.
French Provincial; [also **p-**] a style of furniture of or like that of the French provinces, especially in the mid-18th century, often with a white, gold-trimmed finish.
French Revolution; the revolution of the people against the monarchy in France: it began in 1789, resulted in the establishment of a republic, and ended in 1799 with the Consulate under Napoleon.
French Revolutionary Calendar; the official calendar of the first French republic, adopted in 1793 and abolished in 1805: it consisted of twelve months, each containing thirty days and divided into three periods called ***decades,*** with five extra days in the regular year.
French roof; a modified Mansard roof, with a flat, or nearly flat, top.
French seam; a narrow seam sewed on both sides to hide the raw edges of the cloth.
French telephone; an early kind of handset.
French toast; sliced bread dipped in a batter of egg and milk and then fried.
French white; finely pulverized talc.
French windows; a pair of casement windows, usually extending to the floor, that have glass panes from top to bottom and are hinged at opposite sides of a window frame so that they open in the middle.

French, *n.* the Romance (Latinic) language spoken by the French.
the French; the people of France.

French, *v.t.* [often **f-**] 1. to trim the meat from the end of the bone of (a rib chop).
2. to cut (string beans) into long, thin slices before cooking.

French and In'di·ăn Wạr, that part of the Seven Years' War (between England and France) which was fought in America from 1754 to 1763.

French'i·fȳ, *v.t.* and *v.i.*; Frenchified, *pt., pp.*; Frenchifying, *ppr.* to make or become French or like the French in customs, ideas, manners, etc.

french'ing, *n.* a non-parasitic disease of plants, causing the leaves to wither and die.

French'işm, *n.* a characteristic or phrase peculiar to the French or their language.

French'măn, *n.*; *pl.* **French'men,** 1. a native or inhabitant of France, especially a man.
2. a French ship.

French'wom''ăn (-woom''), *n.*; *pl.* **French'wom''en** (-wim''), a woman who is a native or inhabitant of France.

French'y, *a.*; *comp.* Frenchier; *superl.* Frenchiest; of, characteristic of, or like the French.

French'y, *n.*; *pl.* **French'ieş,** a Frenchman or Frenchwoman. [Colloq.]

frend, *n.* friend. [Obs.]

frē·net'iç, frē·net'iç·ăl, *a.* [ME. *frenetik*; L. *phreneticus*; Gr. *phrenētikos,* mad, suffering with inflammation of the brain.] frantic; frenzied: also spelled ***phrenetic, phrenetical.***

frē·net'iç·ăl·ly, *adv.* in a frenetic manner: also spelled *phrenetically.*

fren'ū·lum, *n.*; *pl.* **fren'ū·lȧ,** in anatomy, same as *frenum*: also spelled ***frænulum.***

frē'num, *n.*; *pl.* **frē'numş, frē'nȧ,** [L. *frenum,* a bridle, curb.]
1. a fold of skin or mucous membrane that is attached to a part of the body and checks

or controls its motion, as the fold under the tongue: also spelled *fraenum*.

2. a characteristic ridge upon some insects.

fren'zi·căl, *a.* frenzied. [Obs.]

fren'zied, *a.* wildly excited; frantic.

fren'zied·ly, *adv.* madly; distractedly.

fren'zy, *n.*; *pl.* **fren'zieṣ,** [ME. *frensy, frenesy*; OFr. *frenesie*; L. *phrenesis*, Gr. *phrenitis*, madness, inflammation of the brain, from *phrēn*, mind.] wild excitement; frantic outburst; brief delirium that is almost insanity.

fren'zy, *a.* passionate; madly excited. [Obs.]

fren'zy, *v.t.*; frenzied, *pt., pp.*; frenzying, *ppr.* to fill with frenzy; to make frantic.

frē'on, *n.* [*f*luorine, and *re*frigerant, and *-on* as in *neon*, etc.] a colorless gas, CCl_2F_2, used especially as a refrigerant: a trade-mark (*Freon*).

frē'quence, *n.* [Fr. *fréquence*; L. *frequentia*, a throng, crowd, from *frequens* (*-entis*), crowded.]

1. a crowd; a throng; a concourse; an assembly. [Obs.]

2. same as *frequency*.

frē'quen·cy, *n.*; *pl.* **frē'quen·cieṣ,** 1. originally, (a) the condition of being crowded; (b) a crowd.

2. the fact of occurring often or repeatedly; frequent occurrence.

3. the number of times any action or occurrence is repeated in a given period.

4. in mathematics and statistics, (a) the ratio of the number of actual occurrences to the number of possible occurrences in a given period; (b) the ratio of the number of individuals occurring in a specific class to the total number of individuals under survey.

5. in physics, (a) the number of vibrations or cycles per unit of time; (b) the number of cycles per second of an alternating electric current.

frē'quen·cy mod·ū·lā'tion, 1. the changing of the frequency of the transmitting radio wave in accordance with the sound being broadcast.

2. broadcasting that uses this, characterized by freedom from static and more faithful reproduction of sound.

Distinguished from *amplitude modulation*.

frē'quent, *a.* [Fr. *fréquent*, from L. *frequens* (*-entis*), crowded, repeated.]

1. often seen or done; happening at short intervals; often repeated or occurring; as, we made *frequent* visits to the hospital.

2. accustomed often to practice anything; as, he was *frequent* and loud in his declamations against the revolution.

3. full; crowded; thronged. [Obs.]

4. told often; of common report. [Obs.]

5. constant; habitual.

Syn.—many, repeated, numerous, recurrent, general, continual, usual, common, recurring.

frē·quent', *v.t.*; frequented, *pt., pp.*; frequenting, *ppr.* [Fr. *fréquenter*, from L. *frequentare*, to fill, crowd, visit often, from *frequens*, crowded, frequent, repeated.] to visit often; to be at or in habitually; as, they *frequent* the theater.

He *frequented* the court of Augustus.
—Dryden.

frē·quent'ȧ·ble, *a.* accessible.

frē·quent'ăġe, *n.* the practice of frequenting. [Rare.]

frē·quen·tā'tion, *n.* the act or practice of frequenting.

frē·quent'ȧ·tive, *a.* [LL. *frequentativus*, frequentative, from *frequentare*, to do or make use of frequently.] in grammar, denoting the frequent repetition of an action; as, a *frequentative* verb.

frē·quent'ȧ·tive, *n.* a verb which denotes the frequent occurrence or repetition of an action.

frē·quent'ẽr, *n.* one who frequents; a constant visitor.

frē'quent·ly, *adv.* often; many times; at short intervals; commonly.

frē'quent·ness, *n.* the quality of being frequent or often repeated.

frère (frãr), *n.* [Fr.] 1. a brother. 2. a friar.

fres'cāde, *n.* [OFr. *frescade, fresquade*, from It. *fresco*, fresh, cool.] a cool walk; a shady place.

fres'cō, *n.*; *pl.* **fres'cōes, fres'cōṣ,** [It. *fresco*, fresh, cool, as noun, coolness, freshness, from O.H.G. *frisc*, fresh.]

1. coolness; shade; a cool, refreshing state of the air. [Obs.]

2. the art or technique of painting with water colors on wet plaster.

3. a picture or design painted by the above method.

in fresco; with water colors on wet plaster.

fres'cō, *v.t.*; frescoed, *pt., pp.*; frescoing, *ppr.* to paint in fresco.

fresh, *a.*; *comp.* fresher; *superl.* freshest, [ME. *fresh, fresch*, from AS. *fersc*, fresh; D. *versch*; O.H.G. *frisc*; Ice. *ferskr*; Sw. *frisk*; Dan. *frisk*.]

1. brisk; strong: said of the wind.

2. having the color and appearance of youth; lively; as, a *fresh* complexion.

3. new; recently grown or produced; as, *fresh* vegetables; newly laid; as, *fresh* eggs.

4. recently made or obtained; as, a *fresh* supply of goods from the factory.

5. not impaired by time; not forgotten or obliterated; as, the ideas are *fresh* in my recollection.

6. not salt: said of water.

7. recently drawn; pure and cool; not warm or vapid; as, a glass of *fresh* water.

8. original, spontaneous, and stimulating; as, the conversation was *fresh* and delightful.

9. not tired; vigorous; lively; having new vigor; as, he rose *fresh* for the combat.

10. new; that has lately come or arrived; not known before; as, *fresh* news; *fresh* dispatches.

11. sweet; in a good state; not spoiled, rotten, or stale; as, *fresh* milk.

12. not salted, preserved, pickled, etc.; as, *fresh* meat.

13. unpracticed; inexperienced; not before employed; as, a *fresh* hand on board ship.

14. not worn, soiled, faded, etc.; vivid; bright; clean; as, *fresh* linen.

15. additional; further; as, he made a *fresh* start.

16. designating or of a cow that has newly come into the state of a milker, as after having borne a calf.

fresh out of; having just sold or used up. [Slang.]

Syn.—brisk, strong, vigorous, lively, unimpaired, unfaded, florid, ruddy, new, novel, recent, rare, unpracticed, unaccustomed, unused, inexperienced.

fresh, *a.* [from G. *frech*, bold, impudent.]

1. bold; saucy; impertinent; impudent. [Slang.]

2. drunk; tipsy. [Slang.]

fresh, *n.* 1. a freshet; a stream in overflow.

2. a spring of fresh water flowing into a river or into the ocean.

3. the mingling of fresh water with turbid or with salt water, especially the mingling of the waters of a river or brook with the salt water of a bay or estuary.

4. a freshman. [College Slang.]

fresh'en, *v.t.*; freshened, *pt., pp.*; freshening, *ppr.* 1. to make fresh; to separate from saline particles; as, to *freshen* water, fish, or meat.

2. to refresh; to revive.

3. in nautical usage, to apply new service to (a cable); as, to *freshen* the hawes.

to freshen ballast; to readjust ballast.

to freshen the hawse; to pay out or take in a little of the cable of a vessel at anchor, so as to expose another part of it to the fraying action at the hawse hole.

to freshen the way; to increase the speed, as of a ship in motion.

fresh'en, *v.i.* 1. to grow or become fresh.

2. to have a calf: said of a cow.

3. to come into milk.

fresh'et, *n.* 1. a flood or overflowing of a river, on account of heavy rains or melted snow.

2. a stream or rush of fresh water flowing into the sea.

fresh'-look"ing, *a.* appearing fresh.

fresh'ly, *adv.* 1. in a fresh manner.

2. recently; just now; newly.

fresh'măn, *n.*; *pl.* **fresh'men,** 1. a novice; a beginner.

2. a student of the first year in a college or high school.

3. a person in his first year at any enterprise; as, Senator Smith is a *freshman* in Congress.

fresh'măn, *a.* of or for first-year students; as, the *freshman* curriculum.

Lord! how the seniors knocked about
The *freshman* class of one! —Holmes.

fresh'măn·ship, *n.* the state of a freshman.

fresh'ness, *n.* the condition or quality of being fresh, in any sense of the word.

fresh'-new, *a.* unpracticed. [Obs.]

fresh'-wa"tẽr, *a.* 1. accustomed to sail on fresh water only; as, a *fresh-water* sailor.

2. raw; unskilled; inexperienced; as, *fresh-water* soldiers.

3. in or of the hinterland; inland.

4. somewhat provincial, obscure, etc.; as, a *fresh-water* college.

5. pertaining to, produced by, or living in water that is fresh, or not salt; as, *fresh-water* geological deposits, *fresh-water* fish.

fres·ī'sŏn, *n.* in logic, one of the valid modes.

fret, *n.* a strait. [Obs.]

fret, *v.t.*; fretted, *pt., pp.*; fretting, *ppr.* [ME. *freten*; AS. *fretan*, contr. of *foretan*, to eat up, devour; *for-*, and *etan*, to eat.]

1. to wear away by gnawing, rubbing, chafing, corroding, rusting, etc.; also, to make or form by wearing away.

2. to gnaw; to eat away; as, a worm *frets* the planks of a ship.

3. to agitate; to disturb; to make rough; to cause to ripple; as, to *fret* the surface of water.

4. to tease; to irritate; to vex; to make angry.

Fret not thyself because of evildoers.
—Ps. xxxvii. 1.

5. to devour. [Obs.]

Syn.—chafe, gall, vex, anger, gnaw, corrode, rub, agitate, disturb.

fret, *v.i.* 1. to gnaw (*into, on,* or *upon*).

2. to be worn away; to be corroded, worn, frayed, etc.; as, any substance will in time *fret* away by friction.

3. to be agitated; to become rough or disturbed.

4. to be vexed; to be chafed or irritated; to be annoyed or querulous; to worry.

He *frets*, he fumes, he stares, he stamps the ground. —Dryden.

fret, *n.* 1. the agitation of the surface of a fluid, as when boiling, fermenting, etc.

2. a wearing away.

3. a worn place.

4. irritation; annoyance; worry.

5. in mining, the washed side of a river bank, showing outcroppings by means of which miners are able to locate veins of ore.

6. a cutaneous eruption, as tetter; a chafing, as in the folds of the skin of fat children.

fret, *v.t.*; fretted, *pt., pp.*; fretting, *ppr.* [OFr. *fretter, freter*, to cross, interlace, from *frete*, an iron band, ferrule, from LL. *ferrata*, an iron grating.] to ornament with a fret or fretwork.

fret, *n.* [OFr. *frete*, an iron band, ferrule, from LL. *ferrata*, an iron grating, iron railing, from L. *ferrum*, iron.]

GRECIAN FRETS

1. an ornamental net or network, especially one formerly worn by women as a headdress.

2. an ornamental pattern of small, straight bars intersecting or joining one another at right angles to form a regular design, as for a border.

3. in architecture, an ornamental pattern of this kind in relief; fretwork.

4. in heraldry, a transverse cross interlaced with a hollow, diamond-shaped figure.

fret, *n.* [Fr., a band, a ring, from OFr. *freter*, to make fast.]

1. any of several narrow, lateral ridges fastened across the finger board of a banjo, guitar, mandolin, etc. to regulate the fingering.

2. a caul of gold or silver wire worn by ladies in the middle ages.

fret, *v.t.* to furnish with frets.

fret'fụl, *a.* disposed to fret; ill-humored; peevish; angry; in a state of vexation; as, a *fretful* temper.

Syn.—peevish, cross, captious.—*Peevish* marks the inward spirit, and *fretful* the outward act, while both imply a complaining impatience. *Crossness* is peevishness mingled with vexation or anger.

fret'fụl·ly, *adv.* peevishly; angrily.

fret'fụl·ness, *n.* peevishness; ill-humor; disposition to fret and complain.

fret saw, a saw with a long, narrow, finetoothed blade, for cutting thin wooden boards or metal plates into patterns.

frette, *n.* [Fr., a hoop.] a hoop of steel or wrought iron for strengthening the outside of a cannon or gun.

fret'ted, [past tense and past participle of *fret* (to ornament).] *a.* decorated with frets.

fret'ted, [past tense and past participle of *fret* (to vex).] *a.* 1. away; chafed.

2. worried; anxious; discontented.

fret′ten, *a.* marked; as, pock-*fretten,* marked with the smallpox. [Obs.]

fret′tẽr, *n.* one who or that which frets.

fret′ty, *a.* adorned with or as if with fretwork.

frē′tum, *n.*; *pl.* **frē′tȧ,** [L.] a strait or arm of the sea.

fret′wŏrk, *n.* work adorned with frets; ornamental work with interlacing parts.

Freu′di·ăn (froi′), *a.* of or according to Sigmund Freud or his theories and practices: see *psychoanalysis.*

Freu′di·ăn, *n.* a person who believes in Freud's theories or uses Freud's methods in psychoanalysis.

Freu′di·ăn·ism, *n.* the theories and practices of Sigmund Freud (1856–1939), Viennese psychologist, especially in regard to the causes and treatment of neuroses.

Frey, *n.* [ON. *Freyr.*] in Norse mythology, the god of the crops, fruitfulness, love, peace, and prosperity.

Frey′ȧ (frī′), *n.* in Norse mythology, the goddess of love and beauty, sister of Frey: written also *Frea, Freyia, Freyja.*

Freyr, *n.* Frey.

frī·ȧ·bil′i·ty, *n.* [L. *friabilis,* from *friare,* to rub, crumble.] the quality or state of being friable.

frī′ȧ·ble, *a.* [Fr. *friable*; L. *friabilis,* from *friare,* to rub, crumble.] easily crumbled or pulverized; easily reduced to powder, as pumice.

frī′ȧ·ble·ness, *n.* friability.

frī′ăr, *n.* [from OFr. *frere*; Pr. *fraire, frar*; It. *frate,* from L. *frater,* brother.]

1. in the Roman Catholic Church, a member of any of several religious orders, but especially of one of the four mendicant monastic orders known as the Franciscans, Augustinians, Dominicans, and Carmelites.

2. in printing, any part of a page which has not received a proper impression, and hence is gray or indistinct.

3. any of various small American fishes; silversides; a sand smelt.

4. the friarbird, or leatherhead.

5. the angler, *Lophius piscatorius.* [Ir.]

friar's balsam; an alcoholic solution of benzoin, styrax, tolu balsam, and aloes, used as an application for wounds and ulcers.

frī′ăr·bird, *n.* an Australian bird, *Tropidorhynchus corniculatus,* that eats the honey or nectar from flowers and has a naked, featherless head: also called *leatherhead, poor soldier,* etc.

frī′ăr·ly, *a.* resembling a friar in manner or character; monkish.

frī′ăr's-çap, *n.* the wolfsbane, or monkshood, *Aconitum napellus,* the sepals of which are hooded.

frī′ăr's-çowl, *n.* the wake-robin, *Arum maculatum.*

frī′ăr's-çrown, *n.* the European wool thistle, *Cnicus eriophorus*: called also *friar's-thistle.*

frī′ăr skāte, a sharp-nosed skate, *Raia alba,* of Europe.

frī′ăr's lan′tẽrn, the ignis fatuus or will-o'-the-wisp.

frī′ăr's-this″tle (-this″l), *n.* see *friar's-crown.*

frī′ăr·y, *a.* pertaining to a friar or to a monastery.

frī′ăr·y, *n.* 1. a monastery; a place where friars live.

2. a brotherhood of friars.

frī·ā′tion, *n.* the act of crumbling into small pieces. [Obs.]

frib′ble, *a.* [altered from Fr. *frivole,* perh. under echoic influence.] frivolous; trifling; silly.

frib′ble, *n.* 1. a person who wastes time.

2. any trifling act or thought.

frib′ble, *v.i.*; fribbled, *pt., pp.*; fribbling, *ppr.* 1. to trifle; to waste time or behave in a foolish, frivolous way.

2. to stand or walk unsteadily; to totter. [Obs.]

frib′ble, *v.t.* to deal with in a trifling manner.

frib′blẽr, *n.* a trifler; a fribble.

frib′bling, *a.* foolish; trifling; frivolous.

frī′bŏrg, frī′bŏrgh (-bŭrg), *n.* [AS. *frith-borh,* lit., peace pledge; *frith,* peace, and *borh,* pledge.] same as *frankpledge.*

fri·çăn·deau′ (-dō′), *n.*; *pl.* **fri·çăn·deaux′** (-dōz′), [Fr.] a thick slice of veal or other meat, roasted or stewed and served with a sauce: also written *fricando.*

friç·an·delle′, friç·an·del′, *n.* [Fr.] meat, eggs, spices, etc. rolled into balls and boiled or fried.

friç·ăs·see′, *n.* [Fr., properly f. pp. of *fricasser,* to cut up and fry.] meat cut into pieces, stewed or fried, and served in a sauce of its own gravy.

friç·ăs·see′, *v.t.*; fricasseed, *pt., pp.*; fricasseeing, *ppr.* to cook as a fricassee.

fri·çā′tion, *n.* [L. *fricatio,* from *fricare,* to rub.] the act of rubbing; friction. [Obs.]

friç′ȧ·tive, *a.* [L. *fricatus,* pp. of *fricare,* to rub.] formed and pronounced by forcing the breath through a narrow opening between the teeth, lips, etc.: said of certain consonants, as *f, s, v,* and *z.*

friç′ȧ·tive, *n.* a fricative consonant.

friç′ȧ·trice, *n.* a harlot. [Obs.]

friç′kle, *n.* a bushel basket. [Obs.]

friç′tion, *n.* [Fr. *friction*; L. *frictio,* from *fricare,* to rub.]

1. the rubbing of one body against another.

2. disagreement or conflict because of differences of opinion, temperament, etc.

3. in mechanics, the resistance to motion of two moving objects or surfaces that touch.

4. in medicine, the rubbing of the body so as to stimulate the circulation.

angle of friction; the maximum angle of an inclined plane on which a body will rest without sliding down.

coefficient of friction; the ratio between the force necessary to move one of any two surfaces horizontally over the other, and the pressure between the two surfaces: the *coefficient of friction* for oak and cast-iron is 38:100, or .38.

Syn.—rubbing, grating, attrition, abrasion, contact.

friç′tion·ăl, *a.* of or produced by friction; as, *frictional* electricity.

frictional gearing; wheels which produce motion not by teeth but by friction.

friç′tion·ăl·ly, *adv.* by or with friction.

friç′tion balls, balls placed in a hub or journal to reduce the friction of a revolving axle.

friç′tion brāke, a form of dynamometer; also, a brake operating by friction.

friç′tion chocks, small inclined planes of wood or iron, placed directly behind the wheels of a gun carriage to overcome the force of the recoil.

friç′tion çlutch, in machinery, a clutch, operated by friction, used for connecting machines which need to be frequently engaged and disengaged or which are subject to sudden variations of resistance.

friç′tion çom′pound, same as *friction powder.*

friç′tion çōnes, in machinery, a slip coupling, consisting of two cones *a b,* of which the one *a* is formed on the back of the driving wheel, loose on the driving shaft, and the other *b* forms part of a sliding block (attached to the shaft by a sunk feather) and fits accurately into the interior of that formed on the back of the wheel. The sliding block can be thrown in and out of gear in the ordinary way, by means of a fork *c,* and the transmission of motion depends on the friction of the two conical surfaces. If the load on the machine, which is driven by the second shaft, is suddenly changed, the adhesion between the surfaces of the cones allows them to slip, and thus breakage is avoided.

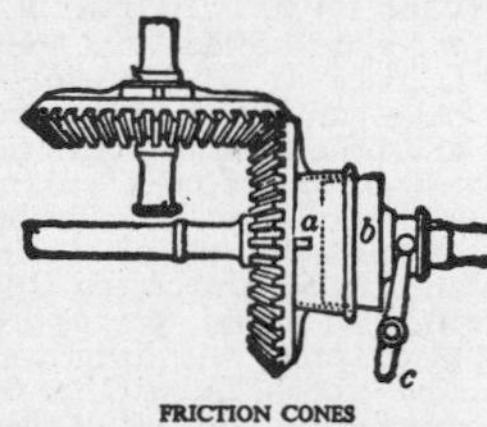

FRICTION CONES

friç′tion gēar, see *frictional gearing* under *frictional.*

friç′tion ham′mẽr, a hammer lifted by the friction of revolving rollers.

friç′tion·less, *a.* having or producing no friction.

friç′tion mȧ·chïne′, a machine which generates frictional electricity.

friç′tion match, a match that lights by friction.

friç′tion mē′tẽr, a device for estimating friction in machinery, as affected by different lubricants.

friç′tion pow′dẽr, a compound, as of antimony and chlorate of potash, that is easily ignited by friction.

friç′tion prīm′ẽr, a device for firing cannon by the friction of a rough wire and friction powder in a tube: called also *friction tube.*

friç′tion tāpe, an adhesive tape for insulating exposed electrical wires: also, *electric tape* or *insulating tape.*

friç′tion tūbe, a friction primer.

friç′tion wheel (hwēl), in machinery, (a) a slip coupling applied in cases where the variations of load are sudden and great, as in dredging machinery, etc. It consists of a strong plain pulley B, keyed on the driving shaft; on the circumference of this a wheel A is fitted, with a series of friction plates *a a a* interposed, and retained in recesses formed in the eye of the wheel. Behind each of these plates a setscrew *b* is inserted, which bears against the back of the plate and can be tightened to regulate the degree of friction required for the ordinary work; should the pressure on the circumference of the wheel A exceed this, the plates slide upon the circumference of the pulley B, which continues to revolve with the shaft, and the wheel itself remains stationary; (b) one of two simple wheels or cylinders intended to assist in diminishing the friction of a horizontal axis. The wheels are simple cylinders *a a,* carried on parallel and independent axes *b b.* They are arranged so as to overlap pair and pair at each end of the main axis *c,* which rests in the angles thus formed by the circumferences. The axis, instead of sliding on a fixed surface, as in ordinary cases, carries round the circumferences of the wheels on which it is supported with the same velocity as it possesses itself, and in consequence the friction of the system is proportionally lessened.

FRICTION WHEEL

FRICTION WHEELS

Frī′dāy, *n.* [ME. *fridai*; AS. *frigedæg,* lit., day of the goddess *Frig,* wife of Wodan, transl. L. *Veneris dies,* Venus' day.]

1. the sixth day of the week.

2. the devoted servant of Robinson Crusoe.

3. a faithful follower or helper: usually *man* (or *girl*) *Friday.*

fridġe (frij), *v.i.* [AS. *frician,* to dance.] to fidget; to frisk about hastily. [Obs.]

frid′stōle, *n.* same as *frithstool.*

fried, *v.* past tense and past participle of *fry.*

fried′çāke, *n.* a small cake fried in deep fat; doughnut or cruller.

friend (frend), *n.* [ME. *frend, freond*; AS. *freond,* properly ppr. of *freon, freogan,* to love.]

1. a person whom one knows well and is fond of; intimate associate; close acquaintance: applied loosely to any associate or acquaintance, or, as a term of address, even to a stranger.

2. a person on the same side in a struggle; ally: opposed to *foe.*

3. a favorer; a supporter or sympathizer; as, a *friend* to commerce; a *friend* to poetry.

4. a lover. [Colloq.]

5. [F—] a member of the Society of Friends; a Quaker.

a friend at court; a person in an influential position who is friendly toward one and able to help him.

Society of Friends; a Christian religious sect founded in England in 1650 by George Fox: the Friends have no formal creed, rites, liturgy, or priesthood, reject violence in human relations, including war, and accord women equal status with men.

to be friends with; to be a friend of.

to make friends with; to become a friend of.

Syn.—associate, companion, acquaintance, familiar, ally, chum, messmate, coadjutor, confidant, adherent.

friend, *v.t.*; friended, *pt., pp.*; friending, *ppr.* to favor; to befriend; to support or aid. [Rare.]

friend′less, *a.* without friends.

friend′līke, *a.* like a friend.

friend′li·ness, *n.* 1. the condition or quality of being friendly; good will.

2. exercise of benevolence or kindness.

friend′ly, *a.*; *comp.* friendlier; *superl.* friendliest. 1. having the disposition of a friend;

kind; like or suitable for a friend, friends, or friendship.

Thou to mankind
Be good and *friendly* still, and oft return.
—Milton.

2. disposed to peace.
3. amicable; as, we are on *friendly* terms.
4. not hostile; as, a *friendly* power or state.
5. favorable; supporting; helpful.
6. desiring friendship.
7. [F–] of the Friends, or Quakers.

Syn.—kind, propitious, helpful, sympathetic, favorable, conciliatory.

friend′ly, *adv.* in the manner of friends; amicably.

friend′ship, *n.* 1. the state of being friends.
2. mutual attachment; intimacy.
3. friendly feeling or attitude.
4. favor; personal kindness.

His *friendships*, still to few confined,
Were always of the middling kind.
—Swift.

5. friendly aid; help; assistance. [Obs.]

Syn.—amity, fellowship, companionship, alliance.

frī′ẽr, *n.* same as *fryer*.

Frīēṣe, *a.* Friesic; Friesian.

Frīēṣe, *n.* a Friesian.

Frīē′ṣiăn, *a.* and *n.* Frisian.

Frīēṣ′iç, *a.* and *n.* Frisian.

frīēze, *n.* [Fr. *frise*; ML. *frisium*, from hyp. Frankish *frisi*, a curl, borders.]
1. a decoration or series of decorations forming an ornamental band around a room, mantel, etc.
2. in architecture, a horizontal band, usually decorated with sculpture, between the architrave and cornice of a building.

frīēze, *n.* [Fr. and M.D. *frise*; akin to preceding entry.] a rough, shaggy woolen cloth used for outer garments since the fourteenth century.

frīēze, *v.t.*; friezed, *pt.*, *pp.*; friezing, *ppr.* 1. to ornament the edge of. [Obs.]
2. to furnish or decorate with a frieze.

frīēze, *v.t.* to furnish with a nap, as cloth; as, a *friezed* garment.

frīēzed (frēzd), *a.* napped; shaggy with nap, as frieze.

frīēz′ẽr, *n.* one who or that which friezes; a machine which friezes cloth.

frig′āte, *n.* [OFr. *fregate*; It. *fregata*, a frigate; prob. contr. of L. *fabricata*, something built or constructed.]
1. a fast, medium-sized sailing warship of the 18th and early 19th centuries, which carried from twenty-eight to sixty guns.
2. any small sailing vessel. [Obs.]

FRIGATE

frig′āte bīrd, a large, strong-winged, tropical sea bird, *Fregata aquila*, that robs other birds of their prey: also called *man-of-war bird* and *frigate pelican*.

frig′āte-built (-bilt), *a.* built like a frigate, in having a quarter-deck and forecastle raised above the main deck.

frig′āte mack′ẽr·el, a marine fish, *Auxis thazard*, abundant in the North Atlantic.

frig·ȧ·tọon′, *n.* [It. *fregatone*, from *fregata*, a frigate.] a Venetian vessel, with a square stern and two masts. [Obs.]

frig·ē·faç′tion, *n.* [L. *frigus*, cold, and *facere*, to make.] the act of making cold. [Obs.]

frig·ē·faç′tive, *a.* having cooling properties. [Obs.]

frig′ẽr·āte, *v.t.* to refrigerate. [Obs.]

Frigg, Frig′gȧ, Frig′ȧ, *n.* [Ice. *Frigg*, goddess of love.] in Norse mythology, the wife of Odin and goddess of heaven, presiding over marriage and the home.

frīght (frīt), *n.* [ME. *frigt*, *freyht*; AS. *fyrhtu*, *fyrhto*, fright; O.H.G. *forhta*; Goth. *faurhtei*, fright.]
1. sudden and violent fear; terror; alarm.
2. anything ugly, peculiar, shocking, or ridiculous; as, she made herself a perfect *fright*. [Colloq.]

Syn.—alarm, panic, consternation, terror.

frīght, *v.t.*; frighted, *pt.*, *pp.*; frighting, *ppr.* to terrify; to scare; to frighten. [Rare and Poet.]

frīght′en (frīt′n), *v.t.*; frightened, *pt.*, *pp.*; frightening, *ppr.* 1. to cause to feel fright; make suddenly afraid; scare; terrify.
2. to make go (*away* or *into* a specified condition) or to force (*out* or *off*) by frightening; as, we *frightened* him *into* confessing.

frīght′en, *v.i.* to become suddenly afraid.

Syn.—daunt, intimidate, scare, affright, alarm, terrify, appall.

frīght′ened, *a.* terrified; filled with fright.

frīght′fụl, *a.* 1. causing fright; terrifying; alarming; as, a *frightful* storm.
2. shocking; disgusting.
3. (a) unpleasant; annoying; (b) great; as, a *frightful* bore. [Colloq.]
4. affected by fright. [Obs.]

Syn.—dreadful, awful, terrible, fearful.

frīght′fụl·ly, *adv.* 1. terribly; dreadfully; in a frightful manner.
2. very. [Colloq.]

frīght′fụl·ness, *n.* the quality of producing fright or of being frightful.

frīght′less, *a.* free from fright.

frīght′ment, *n.* the state of being frightened. [Obs.]

frig′id, *a.* [L. *frigidus*, cold, chill, from *frigere*, to be cold.]
1. extremely cold; wanting heat or warmth; as, a *frigid* climate.
2. lacking warmth of affection; unfeeling; stiff and formal; as, a *frigid* manner.
3. sexually cold; habitually failing to become sexually aroused: said of women.

Frigid Zone; in geography, either of the two zones (*Arctic Zone* and *Antarctic Zone*) lying nearest the earth's poles, each within a circle 23° 30′ from its pole.

Syn.—cold, gelid, apathetic, distant, unfeeling, irresponsive.

frig″id·āire′, *n.* [from L. *frigidarium*, cooling room, from *frigidus*; see *frigid*.] an electric refrigerator: a trade-mark (*Frigidaire*.)

frig″i·dā′ri·um, *n.*; *pl.* **frig″i·dā′ri·ȧ,** [L. neut. of *frigidarius*, of or for cooling, from *frigidus*, cold, chill.]
1. a cooling room in the warm baths of the ancient Romans.
2. a cold-storage room for meats, vegetables, etc.

fri·gid′i·ty, *n.* [LL. *frigiditas*, from *frigidus*, cold, chill.] the quality or state of being frigid.

frig′id·ly, *adv.* in a frigid manner.

frig′id·ness, *n.* coldness; want of heat or vigor.

frig·ō·rif′iç, frig·ō·rif′iç·ăl, *a.* [L. *frigorificus*, cooling, from *frigus* (*-oris*), coolness, cold, and *facere*, to make.] causing cold; freezing or cooling.

frī′jōl, frī′jōle (frē′hōl), *n.*; *pl.* **frī′jōleṣ** (-hōlz *or Sp.* frē-hō′lās), [Sp. *frijol*, *frējol*; prob. from L. *phaselus*; Gr. *phasēlos*, kind of bean, kidney bean.] any bean cultivated for food in Mexico and other Spanish-American countries.

frī·jō·lil′lō (frē-hō-lē′yō), *n.* [Sp., dim. of *frijol*, a kind of bean.] a bean-bearing tree, *Lonchocarpus latifolius*, of Mexico, the West Indies, and the southwestern United States.

frill, *v.i.*; frilled, *pt.*, *pp.*; frilling, *ppr.* [Early MnE. prob. with orig. sense "mesentery of a cow"; perh. from OFr. *fresel*, dim. of *fraise*, mesentery, ruff, influenced in sense by OFr. *friller*, to shiver.] to become frilled or wrinkled: said of a gelatin film in photography when it rises from the plate in ruffles.

frill, *v.t.* 1. to furnish with frills.
2. to form into frills.

frill, *n.* 1. a fold or fringe of hair or feathers around the neck of a bird or animal.
2. any unnecessary ornament; superfluous thing added for show. [Colloq.]
3. an edging or trimming of lace, etc., gathered or pleated and attached at one end but free at the other; ruffle.
4. in photography, the wrinkling of the edge of a film.

frilled, *a.* having a frill or frills.

frill′ing, *n.* 1. frills.
2. material for frills.

frill′-liz″ărd, *n.* a large agamoid lizard, *Chlamydosaurus kingi*, of Australia, which has a membranous fold about its neck, capable of erection in the form of an elaborate frill when the animal is irritated or alarmed: called also *frilled lizard*.

frill′y, *a.*; *comp.* frillier; *superl.* frilliest, 1. full of or covered with frills.
2. like a frill or frills.

frim, *a.* [ME. *frym*; AS. *freme*, a form of *fram*, *from*, bold, strong.] in good condition; flourishing. [Brit. Dial.]

Frī·māire′, *n.* [Fr., from *frimas*, hoar frost, rime, from OFr. *frimer*, to freeze.] the third month in the French revolutionary calendar, instituted in 1793; it began November 21 and ended December 20.

friṅge, *n.* [ME. *fringe*, *frenge*; OFr. *frange*, from L. pl. *fimbriæ*, fringe, border, threads.]
1. a border or trimming of cords or threads; hanging loose or tied in bunches at the top.
2. something resembling a fringe; an open, broken border; an outer edge; as, a *fringe* of trees around a field; a *fringe* of curly hair.
3. in optics, one of the parallel bands resulting from diffraction of light: called also *interference fringe*.
4. in botany, a simple or double row of teeth, bordering the opening of the pod in almost all kinds of mosses.

marginal fringes; the membranous borders, or fringes, along the toes of certain birds.

friṅge, *v.t.*; fringed, *pt.*, *pp.*; fringing, *ppr.* 1. to adorn with fringe or a loose edging.
2. to be a fringe for; line; as, trees *fringed* the lawn.

fringing reef; a coral reef bordering the land.

friṅge, *a.* 1. at the outer edge or border; as, a *fringe* area of television reception.
2. additional; as, *fringe* costs.
3. less important; as, *fringe* industries.

friṅge ben′ē·fit, a payment other than wages or salary made to an employee, as in the form of a pension, vacation, insurance, etc.

friṅged, *a.* bordered with fringe.

fringed gentian; a plant of eastern North America, *Gentiana crinita*, bearing a sky-blue flower with petals delicately fringed.

fringed leaf; a leaf bordered with fine hairs resembling silk fringe.

friṅge′less, *a.* having no fringe.

frin′ġent, *a.* bordering like a fringe; fringing; forming a fringe. [Rare.]

friṅge′pod, *n.* a California plant of the mustard family, *Thysanocarpus laciniatus*, having pods with fringes by means of which they are carried by the wind.

friṅge′tāil, *n.* a breed of ornamental fish having long, fringy fins and tail.

friṅge tree, either of two small trees of the olive family, with fluffy clusters of white flowers, found in the southeastern United States.

friṅge′-tree bärk, the root bark of the fringe tree, dried and used as a medicine.

Frin·ġil′lȧ, *n.* [from L. *fringilla*, *frigilla*, a kind of small bird.] a genus of birds including the European finches.

frin·ġil·lā′ceous, *a.* same as *fringilline*.

Frin·ġil′li·dae, *n.pl.* [from L. *fringilla*, a kind of small bird, and *-idæ*.] the finches, a large family of small, seed-eating birds inhabiting all parts of the globe and belonging to the order *Conirostres*: they have a sharply pointed, conical bill and feet, adapted for perching, with three toes in front and one behind.

frin·ġil′li·form, *a.* like or similar to a finch.

frin·ġil′line, *a.* pertaining to the finches or *Fringillidæ*.

frin·ġil′loid, *a.* same as *fringilline*.

friṅg′y, *a.* 1. like a fringe.
2. having a fringe or fringes.

frip′pẽr, frip′pẽr·ẽr, *n.* [OFr. *fripier*, one who deals in old clothes, from *fripper*, to wear to rags.] one who deals in old clothes. [Obs.]

frip′pẽr·y, *n.*; *pl.* **frip′pẽr·ieṣ,** [OFr. *friperie*, old clothes, from *fripier*, a fripper.]
1. cheap, gaudy clothes; tawdry finery.
2. showy display in dress, manners, speech, etc.; affectation of elegance.
3. cast-off garments; clothes thrown aside after wearing. [Obs.]
4. a place where old clothes are sold. [Obs.]

frip′pẽr·y, *a.* trifling; contemptible.

fri·sé′ (-zā′), *n.* [Fr., from *friser*, to curl.] a type of upholstery fabric having a thick pile consisting of uncut loops or, sometimes, with some loops cut to form a design.

fri·sette′, *n.* [Fr., from *friser*, to curl.] a fringe of curls or fluffy bangs worn on the forehead by women: also spelled *frizette*

frī·ṣeūr′, *n.* [Fr., from *friser*, to curl.] a hairdresser.

Fri′ṣiăn, *a.* of Friesland, the Frisian Islands, their people, or their language.

Fri′ṣiăn, *n.* 1. a native or inhabitant of Friesland or the Frisian Islands.
2. a member of an ancient Teutonic tribe of northern Holland.
3. the Low German, West Germanic language of the Frisians: it is closely related to Old English.

frisk, *v.t.*; frisked (friskt), *pt.*, *pp.*; frisking, *ppr.* [OFr. *frisque*, lively, jolly, gay; Ice. *friskr*; Dan. *frisk*; Sw. *frisk*, fresh.]
1. to leap; to skip; to spring suddenly one way or the other.

The fish fell a-*frisking* in the net.
—L'Estrange.

2. to move in a playful, lively manner.
The *frisking* satyrs on the summits danced.
—Addison.

3. to search (a person) for concealed weapons, stolen articles, etc. by passing the hands quickly over his clothing. [Slang.]

4. to steal something from (a person) thus. [Slang.]

frisk, *a.* lively; brisk; blithe. [Obs.]

frisk, *n.* a frolic; a lively, playful movement; gambol.

frisk'ăl, *n.* a leap or caper. [Obs.]

frisk'ẽr, *n.* one who frisks; an inconstant or unsettled person.

frisk'et, *n.* [Fr. *frisquette*, so called from the frequency of its motion.] in printing, formerly, the light frame hinged to the top of the tympan of a hand press to hold the paper down.

frisk'ful, *a.* brisk; lively.

frisk'i·ly, *adv.* gaily; briskly.

frisk'i·ness, *n.* the quality of being frisky.

frisk'y, *a.* gaily active; frolicsome; gay; lively.

fris'let, *n.* anything frizzled or curled; a small ruffle. [Obs.]

frist, *v.t.* [ME. *frysten, firsten*, to lend, postpone; AS. *firstan*, to give respite to.] to postpone; to postpone the payment of; to give credit for, as goods. [Obs.]

frī·ṣūre', *n.* [Fr., from *friser*, to curl.] a curling and frizzing of the hair; hairdressing.

frit, *v.t.* to waste; to fritter. [Rare.]

frit, fritt, *v.t.*; fritted, *pt., pp.*; fritting, *ppr.* to prepare (materials for glass) by heating; to make into frit.

frit, fritt, *n.* [Fr. *fritte*, from It. *fritta*, frit, pp. of *friggere*, from L. *frigere*, to roast.]

1. the partly fused mixture of sand and fluxes of which glass is made.

2. a partly fused substance used as a basis for certain glazes.

3. a partly fused substance of which soft porcelain is made.

frit'brick, *n.* a mass of frit in the shape of a brick.

frit flȳ, either of two flies of the genus *Oscinis*: an American species, *Oscinis variabilis*, is injurious to clover, and *Oscinis vastator* of Europe damages wheat.

frith, fïrth, *n.* [ME. *firth*, from Ice. *fjördhr*, a frith, bay.]

1. a narrow arm of the sea; a strait; an estuary; the opening of a river into the sea; as, the *Frith* of Clyde; the *Firth* of Forth.

2. a kind of weir for catching fish.

frith, *n.* [ME. *frith*, from AS. *frith*, peace, security, protection.]

1. a forest; a woody place. [Obs.]

2. a small field taken out of a common. [Brit. Dial.]

3. a field which has been taken from woods; a stretch of brush. [Brit. Dial.]

frith'stool, *n.* [AS. *frith-stol*, an asylum, sanctuary.] literally, a stool of peace; among the Anglo-Saxons, a stone chair placed in a church near the altar for the protection of anyone who might seek sanctuary.

frith'y, *a.* woody. [Obs.]

Frit·il·lā'ri·ȧ, *n.* [from L. *fritillus*, a dice box; so called from the shape of the perianth.]

1. in botany, a genus of liliaceous plants with an erect stem bearing a cluster of nodding flowers and surmounted by a tuft of leaves: the largest species has been called *crown imperial*.

2. in zoology, one of several species of nymphalid butterflies.

frit'il·lā·ry, *n.* 1. any of a group of plants of the lily family, with spotted, bell-shaped, drooping flowers.

2. any of a large group of butterflies having wings spotted with many colors.

frit'i·năn·cy, *n.* [from L. *fritinnire*, to twitter, chirp.] a chirping or creaking, as of a cricket. [Obs.]

fritt, *n., v.t.,* and *v.i.* frit.

frit'tẽr, *n.* [ME. *fritoure*, a pancake, from OFr. *friture*, a thing fried, from *frire*, to fry.] a small cake of fried batter, usually containing corn, fruit, or other filling.

frit'tẽr, *v.t.*; frittered, *pt., pp.*; frittering, *ppr.*

1. to cut or break into small pieces, as meat to be fried.

2. to waste (energy, money, time, etc.) bit by bit on trifling or petty things (usually with *away*).

frit'tẽr, *n.* a small piece; fragment; shred. [Rare.]

frit'ting, *n.* the act of making frit.

Fritz, *n.* [World War I slang, from G. nickname for *Friedrich*; Eng. *Frederick*.] a German soldier: usually contemptuous. [Slang.]

friv'ŏl, *v.i.* and *v.t.*; frivoled *or* frivolled, *pt., pp.*; frivoling *or* frivolling, *ppr.* to waste (time) on frivolous or trifling things. [Colloq.]

friv'ō·lism, *n.* frivolity. [Rare.]

fri·vol'i·ty, *n.*; *pl.* **fri·vol'i·tieṣ,** [Fr. *frivolité*, from L. *frivolus*, silly, empty, worthless.]

1. the quality or condition of being frivolous.

2. a frivolous act or thing.

Syn.—lightness, levity, frivolousness, triviality, trifling, puerility.

friv'ō·lous, *a.* [L. *frivolus*, silly, empty, trifling.]

1. trifling; trivial; of little value or importance; not worth notice; as, a *frivolous* argument; a *frivolous* objection or pretext.

2. not properly serious or sensible; silly and light-minded; giddy.

Syn.—trifling, silly, trivial, petty, worthless.

friv'ō·lous·ly, *adv.* in a frivolous manner.

friv'ō·lous·ness, *n.* the quality of being frivolous, trifling, or of very little worth or importance.

friz, *v.t.* and *v.i.*; frizzed, *pt., pp.*; frizzing, *ppr.* [Fr. *friser*, to curl.]

1. to form into small tight curls: said of hair.

2. to form into small, hard knots or tufts: said of the nap of cloth.

3. in making leather, to make soft and of uniform thickness by a process of dressing; to remove the grain from, as skins.

friz, *n.* something frizzed; especially, hair formed into small, tight curls: also spelled *frizz*.

frīze, *n.* frieze. [Obs.]

friz'el, *n.* frizzle. [Obs.]

fri·zette', *n.* [dim. of *friz*.] same as *frisette*.

frizz, *v.t.* and *v.i.* to friz.

frizz, *v.t.* and *v.i.* [from *fry*, with echoic -*zz*.] to fry with a sputtering, hissing noise; to sizzle.

frizz, friz, *n.*; *pl.* **frizz'eṣ,** [ME. *frysen*; OFr. *friser, frizer*, to frizzle, curl.] anything that has been frizzed or made frizzly, as a wig or a tassel.

friz'zing mȧ·ċhïne', a machine for giving fabrics a frizzly surface; also, a machine for dressing lumber by means of a rotating cutter head.

friz'zle, *v.t.* and *v.i.*; frizzled, *pt., pp.*; frizzling, *ppr.* [prob. echoic extension of *fry*, influenced by *sizzle, frazzle, fizzle*, etc.]

1. to make or cause to make a sputtering, hissing noise, as in frying; to sizzle.

2. to make or become crisp by broiling or frying thoroughly.

friz'zle, *v.t.* and *v.i.* [prob. from *friz* (*frieze, freeze*) in earlier sense "raise a nap on cloth," and -*le*, freq. suffix.] to form into small, tight curls; to friz; to crimp.

friz'zle, *n.* 1. a frizz or crisped lock of hair; a small, tight curl.

2. the steel upright part of the pan cover in a flintlock gun, against which the flint strikes to produce sparks.

friz'zlẽr, *n.* one who frizzles.

friz'zly, *a.* full of or covered with small, tight curls; frizzled; as, *frizzly* hair.

friz'zy, *a.* same as *frizzly*.

frō, *adv.* [ME. *fro, fra*; AS. *fra*; Ice. *fra*, prep. from.] from; away; back or backward: now only in *to and fro*; forward and backward.

frō, *prep.* from. [Scot. or Dial.]

frock, *n.* [ME. *frok, froc*; OFr. *froc*, a monk's cowl or habit; Pr. *floc*, from LL. *froccus*, from O.H.G. *froc*, a cloak.]

1. the principal outer garment of a woman or girl; a dress; a gown.

2. an outer robe with large sleeves, worn by monks, friars, etc.

3. the office of a priest, etc.

4. a tunic, mantle, or long coat formerly worn by men.

5. a loose outer garment worn over other clothes; a smock; a shirtlike overall.

6. same as *frock coat*.

7. a woolen jersey worn by sailors as a shirt; as, a Guernsey *frock*.

frock, *v.t.*; frocked (frokt), *pt., pp.*; frocking, *ppr.* to clothe in a frock; hence, to make a monk of.

frock ċōat, a coat, usually double-breasted and with long, full skirts in front and back: worn by men chiefly in the nineteenth century.

frocked (frokt), *a.* clothed in a frock.

frock'less, *a.* without a frock.

frōe, *n.* [perh. shortening of *froward*, in sense "handle turned away."] a wedge-shaped cleaving tool with a handle set into the blade at right angles to the back: also spelled *frow*.

Froē·bel'i·ăn (frē-), *a.* relating to Friedrich Froebel, 1782–1852, a German philosopher, or to the kindergarten system of education, which he founded.

Froē·bel'i·ăn, *n.* one who advocates or teaches by Froebel's system.

frog, *n.* [ME. *frogge*; AS. *frogga*, a frog.]

1. (a) any of a group of small, four-legged, leaping animals with long, powerful hind legs, short forelegs, webbed feet, and no tail: it develops from a tadpole and, when grown, is able to live either in water or on land; (b) an animal resembling this, as a tree frog.

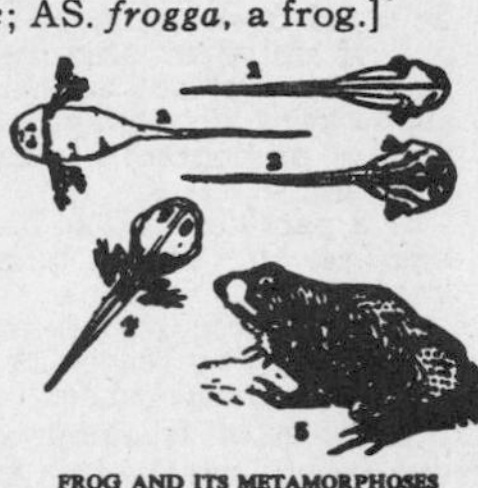

FROG AND ITS METAMORPHOSES

2. a horny growth in the middle of the sole of a horse's foot at some distance from the toe, dividing into two branches and running toward the heel in the form of a fork.

3. a corded or braided looped fastening for a coat or cloak: used as a fastener or for decoration.

4. a scabbard loop.

5. a device on railroad tracks for keeping cars on the proper rails at intersections or switches: so called from its resemblance to the structure of a frog's hind leg.

6. a Frenchman: term of contempt or derision, from the fondness of the French for eating frogs' legs. [Slang.]

frog, *v.t.*; frogged, *pt., pp.*; frogging, *ppr.* to furnish with frogs, as a coat.

frog, *v.i.* to hunt for frogs.

frog'bit, *n.* either of two related plants, *Hydrocharis morsus-ranæ* of Europe and *Limnobium spongia* of the United States: written also *frog's-bit*.

frog cheeṣe, a puffball before it expands and becomes light.

frog'fish, *n.*; *pl.* **frog'fish, frog'fish·eṣ,** any of a number of angler fishes with compressed bodies, large mouths, and flipperlike fins.

frog flȳ, same as *froghopper*.

frog'foot, *n.* same as *duckmeat*.

frogged, *a.* ornamented or fastened with frogs, as a military overcoat.

frog grȧss, a plant of the glasswort family, growing in marshy places near the sea.

frog'gy, *a.*; *comp.* froggier; *superl.* froggiest, of or like a frog; also, abounding in frogs; as, a *froggy* pond.

frog'hop"pẽr, *n.* a homopterous insect, *Aphrophora spumaria*, resembling a frog in the shape of its head, the size and location of its eyes, and its ability to leap. Its larvae are found on plants in frothy masses.

frog lil'y, a yellow lily growing in ponds.

frog'mouth, *n.* one of various species of birds of the family *Podargidæ*, found in the East Indies and related to the goatsuckers.

frol'iç, *a.* [D. *vrolijk*; G. *fröhlich*, from *froh*, joyous, glad, gay.] gay; merry; full of levity; dancing, playing, or frisking about; full of pranks.

The *frolic* wind that breathes the spring.
—Milton.

frol'iç, *n.* 1. a wild prank; a gay trick.

He would be at his *frolic* once again.
—Roscommon.

2. a gay party or game.

3. merriment; gaiety; fun.

Syn.—play, game, sport, festivity, entertainment, gambol, gaiety, lark, spree, merrymaking, prank.

frol'iç, *v.i.*; frolicked, *pt., pp.*; frolicking, *ppr.* to play wild pranks; to play; to make merry.

frol'iç·ful, *a.* frolicsome. [Rare.]

frol'ick·ẽr, *n.* a person who frolics.

frol'ick·y, *a.* frolicsome. [Obs.]

frol'ic·ly, *adv.* with mirth and gaiety. [Obs.]

frol'iç·sŏme, *a.* full of gaiety and mirth; playful; merry; sportive.

frol'iç·sŏme·ly, *adv.* with wild gaiety.

frol'iç·sŏme·ness, *n.* gaiety; merriment.

from, *prep.* [AS. *from, fram*, from, forth.]

1. a particle used to indicate *a point of departure for motion, duration, distance, action, etc.*; *source or beginning of ideas, action, etc.*; (a) beginning at; as, he walked *from* the door; (b) starting with (the first of two named limits); as, I stayed *from* three to six; (c) out of; derived or coming out of; as, he took a comb *from* his pocket; (d) with (a person or thing) as the maker, sender, speaker, teacher, etc.;

as, a letter *from* Mary, facts learned *from* reading.

2. a particle used to indicate *distance, absence, removal, obstruction, exclusion, prevention, freedom*, etc.; (a) at a place not near to; out of contact with; as, keep away *from* me, he is far *from* home; (b) out of the whole of; out of unity or alliance with; as, take two *from* four; (c) out of the possibility or use of; as, he kept me *from* going; (d) out of the possession or control of; as, they released him *from* jail.

3. a particle used to indicate *difference, distinction*, etc.; as not being like; as, he didn't know me *from* Adam.

4. a particle used to indicate *reason, cause, motive, etc.*; by reason of; caused by; because of; as, he trembled *from* fear.

frō′men·ty, *n.* frumenty, a kind of pudding.

from′wȧrd, *prep.* away from. [Obs.]

frond, *n.* [L. *frons, frondis*, a leafy branch, garland of leaves.]

1. the leaflike organ of a fern, differing from a true leaf in that it bears the reproductive cells on its surface.

2. the leaflike part, or shoot, of a lichen, seaweed, etc.

3. a leaf; especially, the compound palm leaf. [Poetic.]

4. in zoology, a leaflike organ of lower animals resembling plants.

frond′āġe, *n.* fronds collectively.

fron·dā′tion, *n.* a lopping of leaves or branches from trees.

Fronde, *n.* [Fr., lit., a sling.] a political party in France, which, during the minority of Louis XIV, opposed the court and Cardinal Mazarin; hence, violent political opposition.

frond′ed, *a.* having fronds.

fron′dent, *a.* [L. *frondens (-entis)*, ppr. of *frondere*, to put forth leaves, from *frons, frondis*, a leafy branch.] covered with foliage.

fron·desce′, *v.i.*; frondesced (-dest′), *pt., pp.*; frondescing, *ppr.* [L. *frondescere*, to become leafy, incept. of *frondere*, to put forth leaves.] to unfold leaves, as plants.

fron·des′cence, *n.* in botany, the process, state, or period of putting forth leaves; also, the foliage put forth.

fron·des′cent, *a.* putting forth new leaves or fronds.

fron·dif′ẽr·ous, *a.* [L. *frons, frondis*, a leafy branch, and *ferre*, to bear.] bearing fronds.

fron·diġ′ẽr·ous, *a.* [L. *frons*, and *gerere*, to bear, carry.] bearing fronds.

frond′let, *n.* a little frond.

fron·dōse′, *a.* bearing fronds; also, like a frond.

fron′dous, *a.* same as *frondose*.

frons, *n.*; *pl.* **fron′tēs**, [L.] the forehead.

frŏnt, *n.* [ME. *front, frunt*; OFr. *front, frunt*; It. *fronte*, from L. *frons, frontis*, the forehead, front.]

1. the forehead; hence, the face; countenance.

His *front* yet threatens, and his frowns command. —Prior.

2. the face as expressive of character, temper, or disposition; as, to put on a bold *front*.

3. impudence; effrontery.

4. the part of something that faces forward or is regarded as facing forward; most important side; fore part.

5. first part; beginning.

6. the place or position directly before the foremost part of a person or thing; as, he stood in *front* of the troops; I passed in *front* of your house.

7. the first or most available bellhop or page, as in a hotel: generally used as a call.

8. the land bordering a lake, ocean, street, etc.

9. a promenade along a body of water.

10. the advanced line, or the whole area, of contact between opposing sides in warfare; combat zone.

11. a broad movement in which different groups are united for the achievement of certain common political or social aims.

12. a person who serves as a public representative of a business, group, etc., usually because of his prestige.

13. a person or group whose work or reputation serves to obscure the real activity or objectives of a business, society, etc.

14. a set of false hair or curls for a lady.

15. a dicky for a shirt.

16. in ecclesiastical usage, a hanging for an altar; a frontal. [Obs.]

17. an appearance, usually pretended or assumed, of social standing, wealth, etc. [Colloq.]

18. in architecture, a face of a building; especially the face with the principal entrance.

19. in meteorology, the boundary between two masses of air that are different, as in density.

frŏnt, *a.* 1. pertaining to the fore part or front; situated in, at, or on the front; as, a *front* door; a *front* room.

2. regarded from the fore part or from a point in front; as, a *front* view.

3. in phonetics, articulated with the front of the tongue; as, *i* (in *bid*) and *e* (in *met*) are *front* vowels.

frŏnt, *v.t.* 1. to face; be opposite to.

2. to be before in place.

3. to meet; confront.

4. to defy; oppose.

5. to supply with a front.

frŏnt, *v.i.* to face in a certain direction; as, the castle *fronted* on the sea.

frŏnt′āġe, *n.* 1. the front part of a building.

2. the direction toward which this faces; exposure.

3. the land between the front edge of a building and the street.

4. (a) the front boundary line of a lot facing a street; (b) the length of this line.

5. land bordering a street, river, lake, etc.

frŏnt′ȧ·ġẽr, *n.* 1. an owner of a frontage.

2. a dweller on a frontier. [Rare.]

fron′tȧl, *a.* 1. of the front; in, on, at, or against the front.

2. of or for the forehead.

fron′tȧl, *n.* the bone of the forehead.

fron′tȧl, *n.* [OFr. *frontel*, a frontlet; LL. *frontale*, an ornament for the forehead; L. pl. *frontalia*, a frontlet.]

1. in medicine, a medicament or preparation to be applied to the forehead. [Obs.]

2. in architecture, (a) a little pediment or frontpiece over a small door or window; (b) a façade.

3. an ornamental band or piece of armor worn on the forehead or over the face.

4. in anatomy, the bone of the forehead.

5. in ecclesiastical usage, an altar covering, formerly of wood or metal, now usually a movable, decorated hanging of ornamental cloth to cover all or part of the front of the altar.

fron′tȧl at·tack′, 1. an attack made against the whole of an enemy's front in a given sector: distinguished from *flanking attack*.

2. any direct attack.

frŏn′tāte, frŏn′tā·ted, *a.* growing broader and broader, as a leaf.

frŏnt′ed, *a.* formed with a front.

frŏn·tiēr′ (*or* fron′), *n.* [OFr. *frontiere*, from LL. *fronteria*, frontier, border of a country, from L. *frons, frontis*, the brow, front.]

1. the border or confine of a country abutting on the territory of another.

2. the part of a settled, civilized country nearest to an unsettled or uncivilized region.

3. any new or incompletely investigated field of learning, thought, etc.: often in the plural, as, the *frontiers* of medicine are still being extended.

frŏn·tiēr′, *a.* of, on, or near the frontier; as, *frontier* garrisons, *frontier* life.

frŏn·tiēr′, *v.t.* to border. [Obs.]

frŏn·tiēr′, *v.i.* to form a boundary, with *on* or *upon*. [Obs.]

frŏn·tiērṣ′mȧn, *n.*; *pl.* **frŏn·tiērṣ′men**, a man who lives on the frontier.

Fron·ti·gnăn′ (-nyoṅ′), *n.* a variety of muscatel wine, named from Frontignan (Hérault), France, where it is produced.

frŏnt′ing·ly, *adv.* in a facing position.

fron′tis·piēce (*or* frun′), *n.* [OFr. *frontispice*, frontispiece, front of a house; LL. *frontispicium*, front of a church, front view; L. *frons, frontis*, front, and *specere*, to view.]

1. in architecture, (a) the principal face of a building; (b) a small pediment over a door, window, etc.

2. formerly, (a) the first page or title page of a book; (b) a preface; foreword.

3. an illustration facing the first page or title page of a book or division of a book.

frŏnt′less, *a.* having no shame or modesty; as, *frontless* vice, *frontless* flattery. [Obs.]

frŏnt′less·ly, *adv.* shamelessly. [Obs.]

frŏnt′let, *n.* [OFr. *frontelet*, a brow band, dim. of *frontel*, a frontlet.]

1. a frontal or brow band; a fillet or band worn on the forehead.

2. the forehead of an animal.

3. the forehead of a bird, when distinguishable by the color or texture of the plumage.

4. an ornamental border for an altar cover.

frŏn′tō-, [from L. *frons, frontis*, forehead, front.] a combining form meaning: (a) *of* or *connected with the frontal bone* or *region and*, as in *fronto*-parietal; (b) *of* or *connected with a meteorological front*, as in *fronto*genesis.

frŏn·tō·gen′e·sis, *n.* the coming into contact of two atmospherically different masses or currents of air, thereby forming a meteorological front and usually causing clouds, rain, snow, etc.

frŏn·tol′y·sis, *n.* the process that tends to destroy a meteorological front, as by mixture or divergence of the frontal air.

fron′ton, *n.* a small pediment; a frontal.

frŏnt′-pāġe, *a.* printed or fit to be printed on the front page of a newspaper; important or sensational.

frŏnt rọom, a room in the front of a house, especially a living room.

frop′pish, *a.* peevish; froward. [Obs.]

frōre, *a.* [ME. *frore, froren*; AS. *froren*, pp. of *freosan*, to freeze.] frozen; frosty. [Archaic or Poetic.]

frō′ry, *a.* 1. frozen. [Obs.]

2. covered with a froth resembling hoarfrost. [Obs.]

frosh, *n.*; *pl.* **frosh**, [from G. *frosch*, lit., a frog, slang term for a first-year student at certain German universities about 1900.] a freshman. [Slang.]

frosh, *n.* [ME. *frosch*; AS. *frox, frosc*.] a frog. [Dial.]

frọst, *n.* [ME. *frost, forst*; AS. *forst, frost*, from *freosan*, to freeze.]

1. the act of freezing or the state of being frozen.

2. that state or temperature of the air which causes the freezing of water; severe cold or freezing weather.

The third day comes a *frost*, a killing *frost*. —Shak.

3. an unsuccessful attempt; especially, a dramatic, musical, or literary failure; as, the last act was a *frost*; the lady's singing proved a *frost*. [Slang.]

4. frozen dew or vapor: called also *hoarfrost*.

Behold the groves that shine with silver *frost*. —Pope.

5. coldness of manner or feeling.

frọst, *v.t.* 1. to cover with frost.

2. to damage, wither, or kill by freezing.

3. to cover with frosting, or icing.

4. to make frostlike in appearance, as some transparent glass.

frọst beãr′ẽr, a cryophorus.

frọst′bird, *n.* the golden plover.

frọst′bīte, *v.t.*; frostbit, *pt.*; frostbitten; *pp.*; frostbiting, *ppr.* to injure the tissues of (a part of the body) by exposure to intense cold; to nip or numb with frost.

frọst′bīte, *n.* injury caused by exposure to intense cold.

frọst′bit″ten, *a.* injured by exposure to intense cold.

frọst blīte, any of various plants of the genus *Atriplex*.

frọst′ed, *a.* 1. covered or whitened with frost.

2. frostbitten; as, *frosted* ears.

3. covered with frosting, or icing.

4. having a surface made to resemble frost, as some nontransparent glass.

frọst′fish, *n.*; *pl.* **frọst′fish, frọst′fish·eṣ**, one of various fish; as, (a) the tomcod; (b) the scabbard fish of New Zealand; (c) the common American smelt.

frọst′flow″ẽr, 1. a small plant of the lily family.

2. its white, star-shaped flower.

3. any of various asters.

frọst grāpe, a kind of wild grape with small, acid fruit.

frọst′i·ly, *adv.* in a frosty manner.

frọst′i·ness, *n.* the state or quality of being frosty.

frọst′ing, *n.* 1. a mixture of sugar, water or other liquid, flavoring, and, sometimes, whites of eggs, etc., for covering a cake; icing.

2. the finish on glass or metal which gives the appearance of fine frost.

3. powdered glass, or the like, used in ornamental work.

frọst lamp, a lamp used in lighthouses to warm the oil in an Argand lamp.

frọst′less, *a.* free from frost; as, a *frostless* winter.

frọst līne, the limit of penetration of frost.

frọst nāil, an ice calk on a horseshoe.

frost'root, *n.* the fleabane, *Erigeron philadelphicus.*

frost smōke, a form of frozen fog resembling smoke seen over bodies of water in extremely cold weather.

frost valve, a secondary valve draining the part of a pipe or hydrant where water is liable to be frozen.

frost'weed, *n.* a plant, *Helianthemum canadenes,* or rockrose: called also *frostwort.*

frost'wŏrk, *n.* 1. the tracery formed by frost on glass, etc.

2. ornamentation like this, as on silver.

frost'wŏrt, *n.* frostweed.

frost'y, *a.*; *comp.* frostier; *superl.* frostiest. 1. cold enough to produce frost; characterized by frost; freezing.

2. covered with or as with frost; as, the grass is *frosty.*

3. cold in manner or feeling; austere; unfriendly.

4. resembling hoarfrost; white; gray-haired; as, a *frosty* head.

5. (a) old; (b) of or like old age.

frōte, *v.t.* [OFr. *froter, frotter,* to rub.] to chafe. [Obs.]

frō'tẽr·ẽr, *n.* one who chafes or frotes. [Obs.]

froth, *n.* [ME. *frothe*; Ice. *frotha,* froth.]

1. spume; foam; the bubbles caused in liquors by fermentation or agitation.

2. foaming saliva caused by disease or great excitement.

3. anything of a light, trifling, or worthless nature, as conversation, ideas, etc.

froth, *v.t.*; frothed (frotht), *pt., pp.*; frothing, *ppr.* 1. to cause to foam.

2. to cover with foam.

3. to spill forth in the form of foam.

froth, *v.i.* to foam; to produce froth; as, the sea *froths*; a horse *froths* at the mouth when heated.

froth'i·ly, *adv.* in a frothy manner.

froth'i·ness, *n.* the state or quality of being frothy.

froth'ing, *n.* rant; empty declamation.

froth in'sect, a froghopper.

froth'less, *a.* free from froth.

froth spit, a kind of white froth on the leaves of plants; cuckoo spit.

froth'y, *a.*; *comp.* frothier; *superl.* frothiest. 1. of, like, or covered with froth; foamy; spumous.

2. soft; not firm or solid. [Obs.]

3. light; trifling; unsubstantial; as, a vain, *frothy* speaker; a *frothy* harangue.

frou'frou, *n.* [Fr.] 1. swish; rustling, as of a silk skirt or dress when the wearer moves.

2. excessive or affected elegance, fanciness, etc. [Colloq.]

frounce, *v.t.* and *v.i.*; frounced (frounst), *pt., pp.*; frouncing, *ppr.* [ME. *frouncen*; OFr. *froncer, fronser,* to fold, gather, wrinkle.]

1. to make or become curled. [Archaic.]

2. to crease; to wrinkle. [Archaic.]

frounce, *n.* 1. a curl or crease; hence, showy display. [Archaic.]

2. a disease in hawks in which spittle gathers as a fringe about the bill. [Obs.]

3. a mass of pimples on the palate of a horse; also, the disease so characterized. [Obs.]

frounce'less, *a.* having no pleat or fold.

frou'zy, frou'sy, *a.* same as *frowzy.*

frow, *n.* [D. *vrouwe*; G. *frau,* a woman, wife, lady.]

1. a Dutch or German woman or wife.

2. an idle, dirty woman; a lazy slattern. [Brit. Dial.]

3. any woman or wife. [Archaic or Rare.]

frōw, *n.* same as *froe.*

frōw, *a.* fragile; crisp; brittle; easily broken. [Brit. Dial.]

frō'wărd, *a.* [ME. *froward*; AS. *framweard*; *fram,* away, from, and *-weard,* -ward.]

1. not willing to yield or comply with what is required or is reasonable; perverse; unyielding; ungovernable; refractory; as, a *froward* child.

They are a very *froward* generation, children in whom is no faith.—Deut. xxxii. 20.

2. adverse; unfavorable. [Obs.]

Syn.—perverse, untoward, wayward, unyielding, ungovernable, refractory, disobedient, petulant, cross, peevish.

frō'wărd·ly, *adv.* perversely.

frō'wărd·ness, *n.* perverseness; disobedience.

frow'ẽr, *n.* same as *froe.*

frown, *v.i.*; frowned, *pt., pp.*; frowning, *ppr.* [ME. *frownen, frounen*; Fr. *froigner,* in *se refroigner,* to knit the brow.]

1. to contract the brows, as in sternness, displeasure, or concentrated thought.

2. to look with displeasure or disapproval (*on* or *upon*).

frown, *v.t.* 1. to silence, subdue, etc. with a disapproving look (with *down*).

2. to express (disapproval, disgust, etc.) by contracting the brows.

frown, *n.* 1. a contracting of the brows in sternness, thought, etc.

His front yet threatens and his *frowns* command. —Prior.

2. any expression of displeasure or disapproval; as, the *frowns* of fortune.

frown'ing·ly, *adv.* sternly; with a look of displeasure, sternness, etc.

frown'y, *a.* scowling; having a frowning look.

frow'y, *a.* musty; rancid; rank. [Obs. or Brit. Dial.]

frow'zi·ly, frow'si·ly, *adv.* in a frowzy manner.

frow'zi·ness, frow'si·ness, *n.* the quality or state of being frowzy.

frow'zy, *a.* [prob. akin to or derived from Brit. dial. *frowsty,* musty.]

1. dirty; in a state of disorder; slovenly; slatternly; as, *frowzy* dress and hair.

2. fetid; musty; rank. [Rare.]

frōze, *v.* past tense of *freeze.*

frō'zen, *v.* past participle of *freeze.*

frō'zen, *a.* 1. congealed by cold; turned into or covered with ice.

2. cold; frosty; chill; subject to severe frost; as, the *frozen* climates of the north.

3. chill or cold in affection; void of sympathy; wanting in feeling or interest; lacking warmth; unsympathetic.

Where *frozen* chastity retires,
Love finds an altar for forbidden fires. —Pope.

4. injured, damaged, or killed by freezing.

5. affected as if turned into ice; as, *frozen* with terror.

6. prohibited in sale or exchange; not marketable because of legal restrictions or unfavorable economic conditions.

7. prohibited from changing to another job or position.

frozen asset; an asset that cannot readily be turned into cash.

frozen credit; credit that is given on a security that cannot instantly be converted into cash; credit on collateral that cannot be sold advantageously at a given time.

frozen custard; a food resembling ice cream, but with less butterfat content and of a looser consistency.

frozen pudding; ice cream made with candied fruit and nuts.

frō'zen·ness, *n.* a state of being frozen.

frub'bish, *v.t.* to furbish. [Obs.]

fruc'ted, *a.* [L. *fructus,* fruit.] in heraldry, bearing fruit, as trees.

fruc·tes'cence, *n.* [L. *fructus,* fruit, and *-escence.*] the time when the fruit of a plant arrives at maturity.

fruc'ti·cist, *n.* [L. *fructus,* fruit, and (-*c*)-*ist.*] one who classes plants in botany by means of their fruit. [Rare.]

Fruc'ti·dor (*or Fr.* frük-tē dor'), *n.* [Fr., from L. *fructus,* fruit.] in the French Revolutionary Calendar adopted by the First Republic, the last month, from August 18 to September 16.

fruc·tif'ẽr·ous, *a.* [L. *fructifer*; *fructus,* fruit, and *ferre,* to bear.] bearing fruit.

fruc"ti·fi·cā'tion, *n.* [from L. *fructificare,* to bear fruit; *fructus,* fruit, and *-ficare,* from *facere,* to make.]

1. the act or process of fructifying or rendering productive of fruit.

2. in botany, (a) the fruit of a plant; (b) the organs which are concerned in the production of the fruit of a plant; (c) [Rare.] the process by which these parts produce fruit.

fruc'ti·fȳ, *v.t.*; fructified, *pt., pp.*; fructifying, *ppr.* [Fr. *fructifier*; L. *fructificare*; *fructus,* fruit, and *-ficare,* from *facere,* to make.] to make fruitful; to render productive; to fertilize; as, to *fructify* the earth.

fruc'ti·fȳ, *v.i.* to bear fruit; to become fruitful.

fruc·tip'ȧ·rous (-rus), *a.* [L. *fructus,* fruit, and *parere,* to produce.] denoting a plant producing several fruits instead of the one which it normally bears.

fruc'tōse (*or* frook'), *n.* [from L. *fructus,* fruit; and *-ose.*] a crystalline sugar, $C_6H_{12}O_6$, found in sweet fruits and in honey: also called *fruit sugar, levulose.*

fruc'tū·ā·ry, *n.*; *pl.* **fruc'tū·ā·ries,** same as *usufructuary.*

fruc·tū·ā'tion, *n.* [L. *fructus* fruit, and *-ation.*] produce; fruit. [Rare.]

fruc'tū·ous, *a.* [ME. *fructuous,* from L. *fructuosus,* abounding in fruit, from *fructus,* fruit.] fruitful; productive.

fruc'tū·ous·ly, *adv.* fruitfully; productively.

fruc'tū·ous·ness, *n.* fruitfulness; productiveness.

fruc'tūre, *n.* [L. *fructus,* fruit, and *-ure.*] use; fruition; enjoyment. [Obs.]

frū'găl, *a.* [OFr. *frugal,* from L. *frugalis,* economical, temperate, pertaining to produce; *frux,* pl. *fruges,* the fruits of the earth.]

1. economical; not spending freely or unnecessarily; saving; sparing; not profuse, prodigal, or lavish.

2. (a) denoting economy; indicating the necessity or desire to save; sparingly provided; as, a *frugal* meal; (b) not costly or luxurious; inexpensive.

frū·gal'i·ty, *n.*; *pl.* **frū·gal'i·ties,** [Fr. *frugalité*; L. *frugalitas,* from *frugalis,* economical, thrifty.] the state or quality of being frugal; prudent economy; prudent or sparing use; thrift.

Without *frugality* none can become rich,
and with it few would be poor. —Johnson.

frū'găl·ly, *adv.* with economy; with good management; in a saving manner.

frū'găl·ness, *n.* same as *frugality.*

frū·gif'ẽr·ous, *a.* [L. *frugifer*; *frux,* pl. *fruges,* the fruits of the earth, and *ferre,* to bear.] producing fruit or grain; fructifying.

Frū·giv'ō·rȧ, *n.pl.* [from L. *frux, frugis,* fruit, and *vorare,* to devour.] a division of the bat family comprising those eating fruit.

frū·giv'ō·rous (-rus), *a.* feeding on fruits.

frūit, *n.* [ME. *fruit, frut*; OFr. *fruit,* from L. *fructus,* enjoyment, means of enjoyment, fruit, produce, profit.]

1. [*usully in pl.*] any plant product, as grain, flax, vegetables, etc.

2. the edible part of a plant or tree, consisting of the seeds and pulpy surrounding tissues: usually distinguished from *vegetable* only when the latter also consists of leaves, root, etc.

3. in botany, the mature ovary of a plant or tree, including the seed, its envelope, and any closely connected parts, as the pit and flesh of a peach, or a pea and its pod.

4. the young of animals or man; offspring; as, the *fruit* of the womb, of the loins, of the body. [Archaic.]

5. that which is produced; effect, result, or consequence, whether advantageous or disadvantageous.

We wish to see you reap the *fruit* of your virtue. —Milton.

aggregate fruit; a fruit formed from a cluster of carpels in one flower, as the raspberry.

collective fruit; see under *collective.*

compound fruit; a collective fruit.

small fruits; strawberries, currants, blackberries, and the like.

spurious fruit; in botany, a pseudocarp.

frūit, *v.t.*; fruited, *pt., pp.*; fruiting, *ppr.* to cause to bear fruit.

frūit, *v.i.* to produce or bear fruit.

frūit'āge, *n.* [OFr. *fruitage,* from *fruit,* fruit, and *-age.*]

1. the bearing of fruit; fruiting.

2. a crop of fruit; fruit collectively; various fruits; fruitery.

With *fruitage* golden-rinded.—Tennyson.

3. a product or consequence; the result of experience, study, or development.

But let me save
This noble *fruitage* of my mind.—Baillie.

frūit bat, a bat of the division *Frugivora.*

frūit bud, the bud that encloses a fructiferous germ.

frūit'cāke, *n.* a rich cake having a large proportion of nuts, preserved fruit, spices, raisins, citron, etc.

frūit crōw, a South American bird of the genus *Chasmorhynchus,* subsisting upon fruit; also, any allied bird.

frūit cup, mixed fruits cut into small pieces and served in a sherbet glass, etc., usually at the beginning of a meal.

frūit dot, the small cluster of sporangia in ferns.

frūit drī'ẽr, an evaporator for fruits and vegetables.

frūit'ẽr, *n.* 1. a person who grows fruit.

2. a tree that bears fruit.

3. a ship for transporting fruit.

frūit'ẽr·ẽr, *n.* [ME. *ffruterer* (with redundant *-er*).]

1. a person who deals in fruit. [Chiefly Brit.]
2. a ship for transporting fruit. [Chiefly Brit.]

fruit'ẽr·y, *n.*; *pl.* **fruit'ẽr·ies,** 1. fruit taken collectively. [Rare.]
2. a repository for fruit. [Obs.]

fruit'es·tere (-tär), *n.* a female fruit dealer. [Obs.]

fruit fly, 1. a small fly of the genus *Drosophila*. Its larvae feed on decaying fruit.
2. any of several other small flies whose larvae feed on fruits and vegetables; as the Mediterranean fruit fly.

fruit'ful, *a.* 1. bearing much fruit.
2. producing much; very productive; prolific; as, *fruitful* soil, a *fruitful* season.
3. producing results; profitable; as, a *fruitful* plan.
4. bearing children; not barren.
Be *fruitful*, and multiply. —Gen. i. 28.
Syn.—prolific, fertile, rich, plenteous, abundant, plentiful.

fruit'ful·ly, *adv.* in a fruitful manner.

fruit'ful·ness, *n.* the quality or condition of being fruitful.

fruit'i·ness, *n.* the quality or condition of being fruity.

fruit'ing, *a.* bearing fruit; pertaining to fruit.

fruit'ing, *n.* the bearing of fruit.

frū·i'tion, *n.* [OFr. *fruition*; L. *fruitio*, enjoyment, from *fruire*, to use, enjoy.]
1. use, accompanied with pleasure, corporeal or intellectual; enjoyment; the pleasure derived from use or possession.
2. [by association with *fruit*.] the bearing of fruit.
3. a coming to fulfillment; realization; as, success was the *fruition* of his years of work.

frū'i·tive, *a.* enjoying.

fruit jär, a large-mouthed, metal-capped, airtight, glass jar or bottle for preserving fruit for domestic uses.

fruit'less, *a.* 1. not bearing fruit; barren; destitute of fruit, increase, or offspring; as, a *fruitless* plant, a *fruitless* union.
2. productive of no advantage or good effect; vain; idle; useless; unprofitable; as, a *fruitless* attempt, a *fruitless* controversy.

fruit'less·ly, *adv.* without any valuable effect; idly; vainly; unprofitably.

fruit'less·ness, *n.* the quality of being vain or unprofitable.

fruit pig'eŏn, any of the pigeons of the genus *Carpophaga*, birds of very brilliant plumage, occurring in India, Australia, etc.

fruit sụ'gär (shụg'ẽr), fructose: also called *levulose*.

fruit tree, a tree bearing edible fruit: applied usually to trees under cultivation.

fruit'wŏrm, *n.* one of numerous larvae injurious to fruit.

fruit'y, *a.*; *comp.* fruitier; *superl.* fruitiest, 1. like fruit in taste or smell; rich in flavor; as, a *fruity* wine.
2. rich in tone; mellow; sonorous; as, a *fruity* voice.
3. rich in interest; spicy; juicy; as, a *fruity* story. [Colloq.]
4. fruitful. [Rare.]

frū·men·tā'ceous, *a.* of, belonging to, or made of a cereal or cereals.

frū·men·tā'ri·ous, *a.* pertaining to wheat or grain. [Rare.]

frū·men·tā'tion, *n.* [L. *frumentatio*, from *frumentari*, to provide grain or corn, from *frumentum*, corn.] in ancient Rome, a largess of grain bestowed on the people, to quiet them when uneasy or turbulent.

frū'men·ty, *n.* [ME. *frumenty, frumentee*; OFr. *frumentee*, from L. *frumentum*, corn.]
1. a dish made of hulled wheat boiled in milk, sweetened, and flavored with cinnamon, etc.
2. wheat. [Obs.]
Also *fromenty, furmenty, furmety.*

frump, *n.* 1. a joke, jeer, or flout. [Obs.]
2. a dowdyish, ill-dressed, and sometimes ill-tempered, woman or, rarely, man.
3. [*pl.*] sulks; sulky mood. [Brit. Dial.]

frump'ish, *a.* dowdy, and sometimes ill-tempered.

frump'y, *a.*; *comp.* frumpier; *superl.* frumpiest, frumpish.

frush, *v.t.* [ME. *frushen*, from OFr. *fruisser, froisser*, to bruise, crush.] to bruise; to crush. [Obs.]

frush, *a.* brittle; easily broken. [Brit. Dial.]

frush, *n.* clatter; uproar; noise. [Obs.]

frush, *n.* [ME. *frosh*; G. *frosh*, a frog.]
1. the part of a horse's foot known as the frog.
2. a disease of a horse's hoof; thrush.

frus'trȧ·ble, *a.* that may be frustrated or defeated. [Obs.]

frus·trā'nē·ous, *a.* vain; useless; unprofitable. [Obs.]

frus'trāte, *v.t.*; frustrated, *pt.*, *pp.*; frustrating, *ppr.* [L. *frustratus*, pp. of *frustrare, frustrari*, to disappoint, deceive, trick, from *frustra*, in vain.]
1. to defeat; to balk; to baffle; to foil; as, he *frustrated* his opponents.
2. to make null; to nullify; to bring to nothing; to render of no effect; as, to *frustrate* a conveyance or deed; to *frustrate* a plan.
3. in psychology, to prevent from gratifying certain impulses and desires, either conscious or unconscious.

frus'trāte, *a.* vain; ineffectual; useless; unprofitable; null; void; of no effect. [Archaic.]

frus'trāte·ly, *adv.* uselessly; in vain. [Obs.]

frus·trā'tion, *n.* [L. *frustratio*, from *frustrare, frustrari*, to disappoint, deceive.]
1. the act of frustrating or the state of being frustrated; disappointment; defeat; as, the *frustration* of one's plans.
2. something that frustrates.

frus'trȧ·tive, *a.* tending to defeat or frustrate.

frus'trȧ·tō·ry, *a.* that makes void; that vacates or renders null; as, a *frustratory* appeal.

frus'tūle, *n.* [LL. *frustulum*, dim. of *frustrum*, a piece, bit.] the hard, two-valved shell of a diatom.

frus'tū·lōse, *a.* made up of small fragments.

frus'tum, *n.*; *pl.* **frus'tums, frus'tȧ,** [L. *frustum*, a bit, a part.]

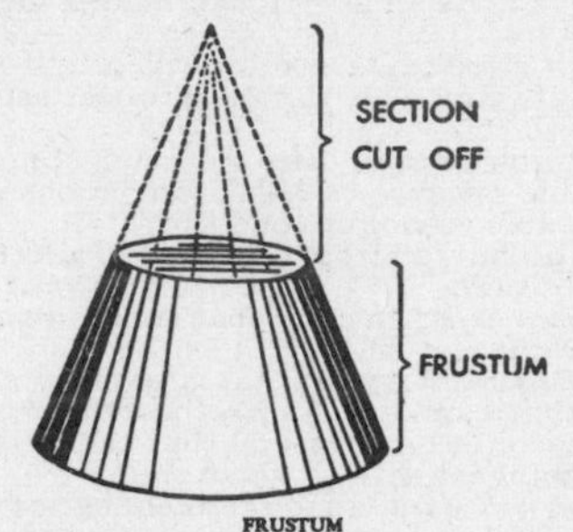

FRUSTUM

1. a piece or part remaining, as the broken shaft of a column. [Rare.]
2. in geometry, the part of a conical or pyramidal solid next the base, left by cutting off the top portion by a plane parallel to the base; also, the part of any solid between two planes which may be either parallel or inclined to each other.

frū·tes'cence, *n.* shrubbiness; frutescent state.

frū·tes'cent, *a.* [from L. *fruticescens* (-*entis*), ppr. of *fruticescere*, to put forth shoots, become shrubby, from *frutex* (-*icis*), a shrub.] in botany, shrubby or becoming shrubby; as, a *frutescent* stem.

frū'tex, *n.* [L.] in botany, a shrub; a plant having a woody, durable stem, but smaller than a tree.

frū'ti·çăl, *a.* shrubby. [Obs.]

frū'ti·çănt, *a.* [L. *fruticans* (-*antis*), ppr. of *fruticare*, to put forth shoots, become bushy.] full of shoots. [Obs.]

frū'ti·çōse, frū'ti·çous, *a.* [L. *fruticosus*, from *frutex* (-*icis*), a bush, shrub.] shrublike; branching like a shrub; as, a *fruticose* stem.

frū·tiç'ū·lōse, *a.* [a dim. from L. *frutex* (-*icis*), a shrub.] pertaining to, resembling, or branching like a small shrub.

frȳ, *v.t.*; fried (frīd), *pt.*, *pp.*; frying, *ppr.* [ME. *fryen, frien*; OFr. *frire*; Pr. *frir, frigir*; It. *friggere*; L. *frigere*, to roast, fry; Gr. *phrygein*, to parch; Sans. *bhrajj*, to roast.]
1. to cook in hot fat or oil over direct heat.
2. to torment; to agitate. [Obs.]

frȳ, *v.i.* 1. to be cooked in hot fat or oil.
2. to seethe; to be agitated. [Obs.]
3. to ferment in the stomach. [Obs.]

frȳ, *n.*; *pl.* **frīes,** 1. a dish of fried food, especially meat.
2. a social gathering, usually outdoors, at which food is fried and eaten; as, a fish *fry*.
3. mental worry or agitation; as, in a continual *fry*. [Colloq.]

frȳ, *n.*; *pl.* **frȳ,** [ME. *frie, fry*; a merging of ON. *frio*, seed, offspring (akin to Goth. *fraiw*) with Anglo-Fr. *frei* (OFr. *froi*, Fr. *frai*), spawn, from the same Gmc. base or from L. *fricare*, to rub.]
1. young fish.
2. small adult fish, especially when in large groups.
3. young; offspring; children.
small fry; (a) children; (b) unimportant people or things.

frȳ'ẽr, frī'ẽr, *n.* 1. one who fries, or that which fries or is fried.
2. food suitable for frying, especially a young chicken.

frȳ'ing, *n.* the act of cooking in hot fat or oil over direct heat.

frȳ'ing pan, a shallow metal pan with a long handle, used for frying food.
out of the frying pan into the fire; from a bad situation into a worse one.

fū, fọọ, *n.* in China, a minor division of a province.

fu', *a.* full; drunk. [Scot.]

fū'ăge, *n.* fumage.

fū'ăr, *n.* see *feuar*.

fub, *v.t.*; fubbed, *pt.*, *pp.*; fubbing, *ppr.* to trick; to cheat.

fub, fubs, *n.* a plump young person. [Obs.]

fub'bẽr·y, *n.* dishonesty; trickery. [Obs.]

fub'by, *a.*; *comp.* fubbier; *superl.* fubbiest, fubsy.

fub'sy, *a.*; *comp.* fubsier; *superl.* fubsiest, [from *fub*, *n.*] fat and squat; plump.

Fū·çā'cē·ae, *n. pl.* a family of dark-colored algae, consisting of olive-colored inarticulate seaweeds, distinguished from the other algae by their organs of reproduction, which consist of archegonia and antheridia, contained in common chambers or conceptacles, united in club-shaped receptacles at the ends or margins of the fronds.

fū·çā'ceous, *a.* of or belonging to the *Fucaceæ*.

fū'çāte, fū'çā·ted, *a.* painted; disguised with paint; also, disguised with false show. [Obs.]

Fụchs, *n.* [G., a fox.] in German universities, a student of the first year; a freshman.

Fụch'si·ȧ (*or, esp. for senses 2 and 3,* fū'shi-ȧ), *n.* [named after Leonard *Fuchs*, a German botanist.]
1. a genus of flowering shrubs, native to South America, Mexico, and New Zealand, family *Onagraceæ*, characterized by having a funnel-shaped, four-parted calyx, four petals set in the mouth of the calyx tube and alternating with its segments, eight exserted stamens, and a long style with a capitate stigma.
2. [f–] any plant of this genus: its flowers are pink, red, or purple.
3. [f–] purplish red.

fūch'si·ȧ (fū'shi-ȧ), *a.* purplish-red.

Fụch'si·ăn, *a.* of or pertaining to I. L. Fuchs (1833–1902), a German authority on mathematics.
Fuchsian group; see under *group*.

fụch'sin, fụch'sine, *n.* [*fuchs*ia and *-in, -ine.*] in chemistry, a purplish-red aniline dye, $C_{20}H_{19}N_3$, occurring in commerce under the names aniline red, magenta, rosaniline, etc.

fū·ciph'ȧ·gous, *a.* fucivorous.

fū·civ'ō·rous, *a.* [L. *fucus*, seaweed, and *vorare*, to eat.] eating or subsisting on seaweed.

fū'çoid, *a.* [L. *fucus*, seaweed, and *eidos*, form.]
1. in botany, belonging to or resembling seaweed, especially the *Fucaceæ*.
2. in geology, marked by traces of fossil fucoids, as certain sandstones.
Also written *fucoidal, fucous.*

fū'çoid, *n.* in botany, a seaweed, especially one of the *Fucaceæ*.

fū·çoid'ăl, *a.* fucoid.

fū'çous, *a.* fucoid.

fū'çus, *n.*; *pl.* **fū'çī, fū'çus·es,** [L., a rock lichen used as a red dye, paint, from Gr. *phykos*, seaweed, rouge.]
1. (a) a kind of paint for the face; (b) any paint or dye; hence, (c) a false show. [Obs.]
2. [F–] a genus of the family *Fucaceæ*, comprising those seaweeds which have flat, leathery fronds.
3. any plant of this genus.

fū'çus, *v.t.* to paint; to rouge. [Obs.]

fū'çū·sol, *n.* [L. *fucus*, seaweed, and *oleum*, oil.] a compound, $C_5H_4O_2$, obtained from seaweed.

fud, *n.* [W. *ffwtog*, a scut, a short tail.] the scut or tail of the hare, cony, etc. [Scot. and Brit. Dial.]

fud, *n.* [from *fud*, a hare's or rabbit's tail.] woolen waste; the refuse of the new wool taken out in the scribbling process, which is mixed with the mungo for use. [Scot. and Brit. Dial.]

fud′dle, *v.t.*; fuddled, *pt., pp.*; fuddling, *ppr.* to muddle, confuse, or stupefy with or as with alcoholic liquor; to befuddle.

fud′dle, *v.i.* to drink to excess. [Rare.]

fud′dle, *n.* 1. liquor; strong drink. [Obs.]
2. a fuddled condition.

fud′dlẽr, *n.* a drunkard.

fud′dy-dud·dy, *n.*; *pl.* **fud′dy-dud·dieṣ,** [prob. reduplicating echoism, suggested by *fuddle* or dial. *fud,* buttocks.].
1. a fussy, critical person. [Slang.]
2. an old-fashioned person. [Slang.]

fudġe (fuj), *v.t.*; fudged, *pt., pp.*; fudging, *ppr.*
1. to poke or prod with a stick. [Brit. Dial.]
2. to make or put together dishonestly or carelessly; to fake.

fudġe, *v.i.* 1. to work unskillfully or at a disadvantage.
2. to refuse to commit oneself or give a direct answer; hedge; as, to *fudge* on an issue.
3. to be dishonest; cheat.

fudġe, *n.* [Pr. Fr. *fuche, feuche*; L.G. *futsh,* exclam., begone!]
1. nonsense; empty talk.
2. a kind of soft candy made of butter, milk, sugar, flavoring, etc.
3. in printing, a short piece of last-minute news or other matter, often printed in color, inserted in a newspaper page.

fudġe, *interj.* nonsense!

fudġe wheel (hwēl), a tool used in shoemaking to ornament sole edges.

Fū·ē′ġi·ăn, *a.* of or relating to Tierra del Fuego, its Indians, or their culture.

Fū·ē′ġi·ăn, *n.* 1. a native or inhabitant of Tierra del Fuego.
2. a member of a tribe of South American Indians who live in Tierra del Fuego.

Fūeh′rẽr (fū′rẽr), *n.* [G.] Führer.

fū′el, *n.* [ME. *fuel, fuelle*; OFr. *fouail, fuail,* from LL. *focalium,* pl. *focalia,* brushwood for fuel, from L. *focus,* fireplace.]
1. any material, as coal, oil, gas, wood, etc., burned to supply heat or power.
2. anything that maintains or intensifies strong feeling, etc.
pressed fuel; any matter too fine for burning while in a powdered state, compressed in blocks as an aid to combustion: called also *artificial fuel.*

fū′el, *v.t.*; fueled *or* fuelled, *pt., pp.*; fueling *or* fuelling, *ppr.* to supply with fuel or combustible matter.

fū′el, *v.i.* to get fuel..

fū′el cell, any of various devices that convert chemical energy directly into electrical energy.

fū′el ē·çon′ō·mī·zẽr, an attachment to a furnace by which waste heat is utilized in warming water entering the boiler.

fū′el·ẽr, fū′el·lẽr, *n.* one who or that which supplies fuel.

fū′el feed′ẽr, a device in a furnace or firebox to supply fuel to a fire as it may be required.

fū′el gas, gas used for fuel, as distinguished from gas used as an illuminant.

fū′el oil, oil used for fuel, as distinguished from oil used as a lubricant or as an illuminant.

fuff, *n.* [imitative.] 1. a puff or pufflike noise; also, a spitting, as of a cat. [Scot.]
2. anger; a fume. [Scot.]

fuff, *v.t.* and *v.i.*; fuffed (fuft), *pt., pp.*; fuffing, *ppr.* to puff. [Scot.]

fuf′fle, *v.t.*; fuffled, *pt., pp.*; fuffling, *ppr.* to dishevel; to disarrange; to muss. [Scot.]

fuff′y, *a.* light; puffy. [Scot.]

fug, *n.* [perh. altered from *fog.*] the heavy air in a closed room, regarded as either oppressive and murky or warm and cozy. [Chiefly Brit.]

fū·gā′cious, *a.* [L. *fugax* (*-acis*), from *fugere,* to flee.]
1. transitory; flying or fleeing away; passing quickly away; fleeting; evanescent.
2. in botany, denoting a part that is soon shed; not permanent, as the corolla of a plant.

fū·gā′cious·ness, *n.* fugacity.

fū·gac′i·ty, *n.* [LL. *fugacitas,* from L. *fuga* (*-acis*), apt to flee, from *fugere,* to flee.] the quality or state of being fugacious.

fū′găl, *a.* of, relating to, or after the style of a fugue.

fū·gä′rä, *n.* [It.] an organ stop giving a tone like a stringed instrument.

fū·gā′tion, *n.* [OFr. *fugation,* from L. *fugare,* to cause to flee, chase.] a hunt; a chase. [Obs.]

-fūġe, [Fr., from L. *fugere,* to flee.] a noun suffix meaning *something that drives away* or *out,* as in febri*fuge,* vermi*fuge.*

fū·ġi·tā′tion, *n.* [L. *fugitatus,* pp. of *fugitare,* freq. of *fugere,* to flee.] in Scots law, the act of a criminal absconding from justice.

fū′ġi·tive, *a.* [Fr. *fugitif*; L. *fugitivus,* from *fugere,* to flee; Gr. *pheugein,* to flee.]
1. fleeing, apt to flee, or having fled, as from danger, justice, etc.

I cannot praise a *fugitive* and cloistered virtue unexercised and unbreathed. —Milton.

Can a *fugitive* daughter enjoy herself while her parents are in tears?—Richardson.

2. staying or lasting but a short time; fleeting; not fixed or durable; evanescent; ephemeral; as, a *fugitive* idea.
3. wandering; vagabond; shifting.
4. of passing or temporary interest, as a literary composition.
Fugitive Slave Law; in United States history, an act of Congress of 1793 or another of 1850, providing for the return of runaway slaves from any State to which they had fled. Both were nullified by the emancipation of all slaves in the United States January 1, 1863.

fū′ġi·tive, *n.* 1. one who flees or has fled from danger, justice, etc.
2. an exile or refugee.

The homage of rebellious *fugitives.* —Dryden.

3. anything that is fleeting or hard to be caught or detained.

Or catch that airy *fugitive* called wit. —Harte.

fū′ġi·tive·ly, *adv.* in a fugitive manner.

fū′ġi·tive·ness, *n.* the state or quality of being fugitive.

fū′gle, *v.i.*, fugled, *pt., pp.*; fugling, *ppr.* [from *fugle*man.]
1. to act as a fugleman; to be the guide or director.
2. to motion in or as in signaling.

fū′gle·măn, *n.*; *pl.* **fū′gle·men,** [G. *flügelmann,* a file leader; *flügel,* a wing, file, and *mann,* a man.]
1. a soldier, especially expert and well drilled, who takes his place in front of a military company as an example or model to the others in their exercises; a file leader.
2. one who takes the initiative in any movement and sets an example for others to follow.

fūgue (fūg), *n.* [Fr.] 1. in music, a polyphonic composition constructed on one or more short subjects or themes, which are harmonized according to the laws of counterpoint, and introduced by the various instruments or voices in succession with various contrapuntal devices.
2. in psychiatry, a state of psychological amnesia during which a patient seems to behave in a conscious and rational way, although upon return to normal consciousness he cannot remember the period of time nor what he did during it; temporary flight from reality.

fū′guist (-gist), *n.* a musician who composes fugues or performs them.

Füh′rer (fū′rẽr), *n.* [G., from *führen,* to lead.] leader: title assumed by Adolf Hitler as head of Nazi Germany (1933–1945): also spelled *Fuehrer.*

-ful (-fool), [from *full, adj.*] a suffix meaning: (a) *full of, characterized by, having,* as in joy*ful,* pain*ful*; (b) *having the qualities of,* as in master*ful*; (c) *having the ability* or *tendency to, apt to,* as in help*ful,* forget*ful*; (d) *the quantity that fills* or *would fill,* as in teaspoon*ful,* hand*ful.*

Fụ′läh, Fụ′lä, *n.*; *pl.* **Fụ′läh, Fụ′lä,** [from native name.]
1. a Moslem people of the Egyptian Sudan, basically Hamitic but with an admixture of Negro stock.
2. their language.
Also *Foolah, Fulbe, Fellatah, Foulah.*

Fụ′läh, Fụ′la, *a.* of or pertaining to the Fulahs.

Fụl′be, *n.* see *Fulah.*

Fụl′brīght″, *a.* [after J. W. *Fulbright* (1905–), U.S. senator from Arkansas.] designating, of, or holding a scholarship or grant in a United States government program for the exchange of United States and foreign scholars, teachers, etc.: the funds are largely derived from the sale of United States surplus property abroad.

Fụl′brīght″, *n.* a Fulbright scholarship, grant, or scholar.

ful′ci·ment, *n.* [L. *fulcimentum,* from *fulcire,* to prop.] a prop; a fulcrum. [Obs.]

ful′crȧ, *n.* alternative plural of *fulcrum.*

ful′çrāte, *a.* [from L. *fulcrum,* a prop, fulcrum, and *-ate.*]
1. in botany, descending to the earth, as a branch or stem.
2. furnished with a fulcrum or fulcrums.

ful′çrum, *v.t.* to supply with or employ as a fulcrum.

ful′çrum, *n.*; *pl.* **ful′çrumṣ, ful′çrȧ,** [L., a bedpost, from *fulcire,* to prop, support.]
1. a prop or support.
2. in mechanics, the support or point of support on which a lever turns in raising or moving something.

PRESSURE
WEIGHT
FULCRUM
FULCRUM OF A LEVER

3. a means of exerting influence, pressure, etc.
4. in botany, an accessory organ of a plant, as a stipule, a bract, a tendril, etc.
5. in zoology, (a) one of a number of spines lying anteriorly on the dorsal, anal, or caudal fin of certain ganoids; (b) the chitinous part of the ligula of a hymenopter.

fụl·fill′, fụl·fil′, *v.t.*; fulfilled, *pt., pp.*; fulfilling, *ppr.* [ME. *fulfillen, fulfyllen*; AS. *fullfyllan*; *full,* full, and *fyllan,* to fill.]
1. to fill to the full; to fill entirely. [Archaic.]
2. to carry out (something promised, desired, expected, predicted, etc.); cause to be or happen.
3. to do (something required); obey.
4. to fill the requirements of; satisfy (a condition); answer (a purpose).
5. to complete; to bring to an end.
to fulfill oneself; to realize completely one's ambitions, potentialities, etc.

Syn.—accomplish, realize.—To *fulfill* is literally to fill quite full, that is, to bring about a full or complete achievement; to *accomplish* is to exert effort and to persevere in order to bring to perfection; to *realize* is to make *real,* namely, whatever has been aimed at.

fụl·fill′ẽr, *n.* one who fulfills or accomplishes.

fụl·fill′ment, fụl·fil′ment, *n.* 1. a fulfilling or being fulfilled.
2. a thing that fulfills.

ful′ġen·cy, *n.* [L. *fulgens* (*-entis*), ppr. of *fulgere,* to flash, gleam, shine.] brightness; splendor; glitter. [Obs.]

ful′ġent, *a.* shining; dazzling; exquisitely bright. [Poet.]

ful′ġent·ly, *adv.* dazzlingly; glitteringly.

ful′gid, *a.* [L. *fulgidus,* from *fulgere,* to shine, gleam.] shining; glittering; dazzling.

ful·gid′i·ty, *n.* splendor. [Rare.]

ful′gŏr, *n.* [L. *fulgor,* lightning, a flash, from *fulgere,* to shine, flash.] splendor; dazzling brightness. [Rare.]

ful′gū·rănt, *a.* [L. *fulgurans* (*-antis*), ppr. of *fulgurare,* to lighten.] like lightning.

ful·gū·rā′tȧ, *n.* [L. *fulguratus,* pp. of *fulgurare,* to flash.] a tube or other appliance used in making an observation of the spectrum of the vapor arising from a liquid through which has been passed a current of electricity.

ful′gū·rāte, *v.i.*; fulgurated, *pt., pp.*; fulgurating, *ppr.* [L. *fulguratus,* pp. of *fulgurare,* to flash.] to give off flashes of or like lightning.

ful′gū·rā·ting, *a.* [L. *fulguratus,* ppr. of *fulgurare,* to lighten.] darting; flashing; sharp and sudden: applied in medicine to pains.

ful·gū·rā′tion, *n.* [L. *fulguratio,* from *fulgurare,* to lighten.]
1. lightning; the act of lightening. [Rare.]
2. the sudden brightening of a fused globule of gold or silver, when the last film of the oxide of lead or copper leaves its surface.

ful′gū·rīte, *n.* [L. *fulgur,* lightning, and *-ite.*] any rocky substance that has been fused or vitrified by lightning; more strictly, a vitrified tube in sand formed by lightning penetrating the solid ground, and fusing a portion of the materials through which it passes.

ful′gū·rous, *a.* [L. *fulgur,* lightning, and *-ous.*] emitting lightning; fulgurant; flashing.

fụl′hăm (fụl′ăm), *n.* see *fullam.*

fū·lig′i·nōse, *a.* fuliginous. [Rare.]

fū·lig·i·nos′i·ty, *n.* sootiness; fuliginous matter; smokiness; gloom.

fū·lig′i·nous, *a.* [L. *fuliginosus,* from *fuligo* (*-inis*), soot.] 1. of, full of, or like soot or smoke; sooty; smoky.
2. dark; gloomy; dusky.

fū·lig′i·nous·ly, *adv.* in a fuliginous manner.

Fū·lig·ū·lī′nae, *n.pl.* [from L. *fulica,* a coot.] a subfamily of the *Anatidæ*; the sea ducks, including the canvasbacks, scoters, eiders, scaups, etc.

fụll, *a.*; *comp.* fuller; *superl.* fullest. [ME. *ful, full*; AS. *ful, full,* full.]

1. having in it all there is space for; holding or containing as much as possible; filled; as, the pail is *full.*
2. having eaten all that one wants.
3. using or occupying all of a given space; as, a *full* load.
4. having a great deal or number of; crowded with; as, a room *full* of people.
5. well supplied, stocked, or provided with; rich or abounding in; as, woods *full* of game.
6. filling the required number, capacity, measure, etc.; complete; as, a *full* dozen.
7. having reached the greatest development, size, extent, intensity, etc.; as, a *full* moon, *full* speed.
8. entirely visible; as, a *full* view.
9. having clearness, volume, and depth; as, a *full* tone
10. plump; round; filled out; chubby; as, a *full* face.
11. with loose, wide folds; with plenty of material; ample; flowing; as, a *full* skirt.
12. (a) greatly affected by emotion, etc.; (b) occupied or engrossed with ideas, thoughts, etc.

full and by; sailing close-hauled, having all the sails full, and lying as near the wind as possible.

full brothers or *sisters*; children of the same father and the same mother.

full cousin; the son or daughter of an aunt or uncle.

full cry; see *in full cry* under *cry.*

full house (or *hand*); in poker, a hand that has three cards of one denomination and a pair of another, as three tens and two queens: it is of less value than four of a kind, but is higher than a flush.

full moon; the moon with its whole disk illuminated, as when opposite to the sun; also, the time when the moon is in this position.

full nelson; in wrestling, a hold in which both arms are placed under the opponent's armpits from behind with the hands pressed against the back of his neck.

full of; (a) filled by or with; (b) having had all that one wants of; (c) occupied or engrossed with.

full time; the normal or standard amount of time required in a given period of work.

fụll, *n.* 1. the greatest measure, extent, state, or degree; as, this instrument answers to the *full*; fed to the *full.*

The swan's down feather,
That stands upon the swell at *full* of tide.
—Shak.

2. that period in the revolution of the moon when it presents to the spectator its whole face illuminated, as it always does when in opposition to the sun.

at the full; at the state or time of fullness.

in full; (a) to, for, or with the full amount, value, etc.; (b) with all the words or letters; not abbreviated or abridged.

fụll, *adv.* 1. quite; to the same degree; without abatement or diminution; equally.

The pawn I proffer shall be *full* as good.
—Dryden.

2. fully; completely; altogether. *Full* is prefixed to other words, chiefly participles, to express utmost extent or degree; as, *full-blown, full-grown,* etc.

I am now *full* resolved. —Shak.

3. directly; straight; exactly; as, he looked him *full* in the face.

Full in the center of the sacred wood.
—Addison.

full many; very many. [Archaic and Poet.]

full well; very well. [Poet.]

fụll, *v.i.* to become full, as the moon.

fụll, *v.t.* to make with loose folds; gather, as a skirt.

fụll, *v.t.* and *v.i.*; fulled, *pt., pp.*; fulling, *ppr.* [ME. *fullen*; OFr. *fuler*, from hyp. LL. *fullare,* to full, from L. *fullo,* cloth fuller.] to clean, shrink, and thicken (cloth) with moisture, heat, and pressure.

fụll ad′mi·răl, in the United States Navy, a four-star admiral, ranking below an Admiral of the Fleet and above a vice-admiral: corresponds to *full general.*

fụll′ăġe, *n.* the price paid for fulling cloth.

fụl′lăm, fụl′hăm (-ăm), *n.* 1. false dice: so named from Fulham, a suburb of London, notorious as a criminal quarter.
2. any sham or make-believe.

fụll′back, *n.* 1. in football, a player whose position is behind the scrimmage line together with, and usually behind, the halfbacks and the quarterback.
2. the position played by a fullback.

fụll bīnd′ing, a bookbinding in which the whole of the sides and back is of leather.

fụll blood (blud), 1. the relationship between brothers and sisters of the same parents.
2. unmixed breed or race.

fụll′-blood″ed, *a.* 1. amply supplied with blood; vigorous; lusty.
2. of unmixed breed or race; thoroughbred.

fụll′-blōwn, *a.* 1. in full bloom; open: said of flowers.
2. fully grown or developed; matured.

fụll′-bod″ied, *a.* having a rich flavor and much strength; as, a *full-bodied* wine.

fụll′-bot″tŏmed, *a.* 1. large and full at the bottom, as a wig.
2. in shipbuilding, having great capacity in the hull.

fụll′-bound, *a.* in bookbinding, having a cover made entirely of leather.

fụll′-dress′, *a.* 1. of full dress; as, a *full-dress* suit.
2. formal; as, a *full-dress* dinner.

fụll dress, formal clothes worn on important or ceremonial occasions; especially, formal evening clothes.

fụll′ẽr, *n.* [ME. *fuller, fullere,* from AS. *fullere,* a fuller; L. *fullo,* a fuller.] one whose occupation is to full cloth.

fụll′ẽr, *n.* [perh. from obs. *full,* to make full, complete, from *full, a.*]
1. a tool used by blacksmiths to hammer grooves into iron.
2. a groove so made.

fụll′ẽr, *v.t.*; fullered, *pt., pp.*; fullering, *ppr.* to stamp a groove or channel in, as with a fuller or swage.

fụll′ẽr's ẽarth, a highly absorbent substance composed of clay and silicious material, either natural or artificial, used for taking grease out of cloth, for refining oil, etc.

fụll′ẽr's hẽrb, *Saponaria officinalis,* a plant formerly used for taking stains out of cloth.

fụll′ẽr's tēa′zel, fụll′ẽr's this′tle (this′l), **fụll′ẽr's weed,** the dried flowerhead of the common teazel, *Dipsacus fullonum.*

fụll′ẽr·y, *n.*; *pl.* **fụll′ẽr·ies,** the place or works where the fulling of cloth is carried on.

fụll·fāce′, *n.* in printing, boldface.

fụll·fāce′, *adv.* with the face turned directly toward the speaker or spectator.

fụll′-fāced (-fāst), *a.* 1. with a full, well-rounded face.
2. with the face turned directly toward the spectator or in a specified direction.

fụll′-fash′iŏned, *a.* knitted to conform to the shape of the foot and leg: said of stockings.

fụll′-fledġed′ (-flejd′), *a.* 1. fully developed or prepared; of full rank or status; as, a *full-fledged* doctor.
2. complete; absolute; as, a *full-fledged* liar. [Colloq.]
3. mature and having full plumage: said of birds.

fụll′-fọrmed, *a.* having full form; matured.

fụll ġen′ẽr·ăl, in the United States Army, a four-star general, ranking below a General of the Army and above a lieutenant general: corresponds to *full admiral.*

fụll′-grōwn, *a.* grown to full size; matured.

fụll′-heärt″ed, *a.* full of courage or confidence.

fụll′-hot, *a.* heated to the limit. [Rare.]

fụll′ing, *n.* the processes by which cloth is fulled.

fụll′ing mill, a mill for fulling cloth by means of pestles or stampers which cleanse it and beat and press it to a close or compact state.

fụll′-leṅgth′, *a.* 1. showing the whole length of an object.
2. showing all of a person's figure: said of a portrait or mirror.
3. of the original, unabridged, or standard length; not shortened; as, a *full-length* novel, *full-length* sofa.

fụll′-manned, *a.* having a complement of men.

fụll′-mouthed, *a.* 1. having a full set of teeth: said of cattle, etc.
2. uttered loudly.

fụll′ness, fụl′ness, *n.* the quality or state of being full (in various senses).

fullness of time; the appointed or allotted time.

fụll′-ọrbed, *a.* having the entire circular face exposed and illuminated; as, the *full-orbed* moon.

fụll ọr′găn, in music, the sounds produced by the pipe organ when all or most of the stops are open, giving the fullest possible volume.

fụll pelt, at top speed.

fụll pitch, in cricket, a ball meant to hit the wicket before hitting the ground.

fụll point, a complete stop.

fụll prō·fes′sŏr, see *professor.*

fụll-rigged′ (-rigd′), *a.* 1. equipped with three or more masts, each mast having its complement of sails: said of a ship.
2. fully equipped.

fụll sāil, 1. the complete number of sails.
2. with every sail set.
3. with the greatest possible speed and energy.

fụll′-sāiled, *a.* in complete readiness; having no hindrance.

fụll stop, a period (punctuation mark).

fụll swing, full activity; operation at full capacity.

fụll tilt, full force; full speed.

fụll′-tīme′, *a.* occupying all of one's time, especially all of one's working day; as, a *full-time* job: opposed to *part-time.*

fụll′-winged, *a.* having complete wings, or large, strong wings.

fụl′ly, *adv.* 1. to the full; completely; entirely; thoroughly.
2. exactly.
3. abundantly; amply.
4. at least; as, there were *fully* 200 people in the room.

fully committed; in law, committed to prison for trial, as distinguished from being previously detained for examination.

Syn.—completely, unreservedly, amply, entirely, wholly, sufficiently, perfectly, plentifully.

ful′măr, *n.* [prob. from ON. *fūll,* foul, unpleasant, and *mār, mōr,* seagull.] a sea fowl, the *Procellaria glacialis,* which inhabits the northern, especially polar, regions, and feeds on the flesh and blubber of dead whales and seals, or other carrion. It is valued for its down, feathers, and oil.

FULMAR (*Procellaria glacialis*)

ful′mi·nănt, *a.* [L. *fulminans* (*-antis*), ppr. of *fulminare,* to lighten.]
1. fulminating.
2. in medicine, developing suddenly and severely, as a disease.

ful′mi·nāte, *v.i.*; fulminated, *pt., pp.*; fulminating, *ppr.* [from L. *fulminatus,* pp. of *fulminare,* to lighten, strike with lightning, from *fulmen,* lightning, thunderbolt.]
1. to thunder and lighten. [Rare.]
2. to explode with sudden violence; detonate.
3. to shout or thunder forth denunciations, decrees, etc.

ful′mi·nāte, *v.t.* 1. to cause to explode.
2. to shout or thunder forth (denunciations, decrees, etc.).

ful′mi·nāte, *n.* 1. in chemistry, a compound of fulminic acid with a base; as, *fulminate* of mercury, which detonates or explodes by percussion, friction, or heat.
2. any highly explosive compound.

ful′mi·nā·ting, *a.* 1. thundering; crackling; exploding; detonating.
2. hurling denunciations, menaces, or censures.

fulminating oil; nitroglycerin: so called for its oiliness.

fulminating powder; see *detonating powder* under *detonating.*

ful·mi·nā′tion, *n.* [L. *fulminatio* (*-onis*), from *fulminare,* to lighten, strike with lightning.]
1. a fulminating or thundering.
2. a violent denunciation by censure or threats, as by papal authority.
3. the explosion of certain chemical preparations; detonation.

ful′mi·nā·tŏr, *n.* one who fulminates.

ful′mi·nȧ·tō·ry, *a.* thundering; striking terror; denouncing.

ful′mine, *v.i.* and *v.t.*; fulmined, *pt., pp.*; fulmining, *ppr.* to fulminate. [Rare.]

ful·min′ē·ous, *a.* same as *fulminous.*

ful·min′iç, *a.* 1. explosive.
2. designating or of an unstable acid, C:N·O·H, that forms highly explosive salts of certain metals, especially of mercury.

ful'mi·nous, *a.* [L. *fulmineus*, from *fulmen*, lightning.] of or like thunder and lightning.

ful·mi·nū'riç, *a.* containing fulminic and cyanuric acids and designating the compound of these two.

fulminuric acid; an acid known by its salts, isomeric with cyanuric acid, $H_3C_3N_3O_3$.

fụl'ness, *n.* same as *fullness*.

ful·sam'iç, *a.* fulsome. [Obs.]

ful'sōme, *a.* [ME. *fulsum*, *fulsom*, full, fat; but influenced by *ful*, *foul*, foul.]

1. disgusting or offensive, especially because of excess or insincerity; as, *fulsome* flattery.

2. [apparent revival of the original sense, obs. since 16th c.] full; ample; abundant.

Syn.—excessive, loathsome, offensive.

ful'sōme·ly, *adv.* rankly; excessively.

ful'sōme·ness, *n.* offensive grossness; excess.

ful'vid, *a.* fulvous. [Rare.]

ful'vous, *a.* [L. *fulvus*, deep yellow, tawny.] tawny; dull reddish-yellow, with a mixture of gray and brown.

ful'wȧ, *n.* [native name.] the butter tree of India, *Bassia butyracea*, and its oil or butter.

fum, *v.i.* [echoic.] to play upon a fiddle. [Obs.]

fū·mā'ceous, *a.* [L. *fumus*, smoke, and *-aceous*.] smoky; hence, pertaining to smoke or smoking; addicted to smoking tobacco. [Rare.]

fū'māġe, *n.* hearth money. [Obs.]

fū'mȧ·rāte, *n.* a salt of fumaric acid.

Fū·mā'ri·ȧ, *n.* [from L. *fumus*, smoke.] a genus of plants of the fumitory family.

fū·mā·ri·ā'ceous, *a.* belonging to the *Fumaria*.

fū·mar'iç, *a.* [from L. *fumus*, fume; and *-ar*, and *-ic*.] designating or of a white, crystalline, unsaturated organic acid, $C_2H_2(COOH)_2$, occurring in Iceland moss, various fungi, and other plants, or produced synthetically from malic acid.

fū'mȧ·rīne, fū'mȧ·rin, *n.* [*fumaria*, and *-ine*, *-in*.] in chemistry, a base obtained from *Fumaria officinalis*, crystallizing in irregular six-sided prisms.

fū'mȧ·rōle, *n.* [It. *fumaruolo*, a fumarole, from LL. *fumariolum*, dim. of *fumarium*, a chimney.] an opening in a volcanic area, from which smoke and gases arise.

fū·mȧ·tō'ri·um, *n.*; *pl.* **fū·mȧ·tō'ri·ȧ,** [Mod. L.] a fumatory.

fū'mȧ·tō·ry, *n.*; *pl.* **fū'mȧ·tō·rieṣ,** [from Mod.L. *fumatorium*, from pp. of L. *fumare*, to smoke, fume.] a place used for fumigating.

fū'mȧ·tō·ry, *a.* of smoke or smoking.

fum'ble, *v.i.* and *v.t.*; fumbled, *pt.*, *pp.*; fumbling, *ppr.* [var. of ME. *famelen*.]

1. to search (*for* a thing) by feeling about awkwardly with the hands; grope clumsily.

2. to handle (a thing) clumsily or unskillfully; bungle.

3. in football, etc., to fail to catch, hold, or handle (the ball) properly.

fum'ble, *n.* 1. a clumsy groping or handling.

2. a failing to catch, hold, or handle the ball properly.

fum'blẽr, *n.* one who fumbles.

fum'bling·ly, *adv.* in a fumbling manner.

fūme, *n.* [ME. *fume*; OFr. *fum*, from L. *fumus*, smoke, steam.]

1. smoke. [Rare.]

2. smoky or vaporous exhalation from anything, especially if offensive or suffocating; exhalation; as, the *fumes* of tobacco.

3. any mental agitation regarded as clouding or affecting the understanding; angry mood; passion. [Rare.]

4. anything like fume in being without substance or fleeting, as an idle conceit.

fūme, *v.i.*; fumed, *pt.*, *pp.*; fuming, *ppr.* [Fr. *fumer*, from L. *fumare*, to smoke, from *fumus*, smoke, steam.]

1. to give off smoke, gas, or vapor.

2. to yield or pass off in fumes.

3. to be in a rage; to be hot with anger.

4. to be stupefied or dulled.

fūme, *v.t.* 1. to smoke; to dry in smoke; to fill with or expose to fumes.

2. to perfume. [Obs.]

3. to disperse or drive away in vapors; as, the heat will *fume* away most of the scent.

4. to flatter excessively.

fūmed ōak, oak wood given a darker color and more distinct markings by exposure to ammonia fumes.

fūme'less, *a.* free from fumes.

fūm'ẽr, *n.* a person or thing that fumes.

fū'mẽr·ell, *n.* a femerel. [Obs.]

fū'met, few'met, *n.* [Fr. *fumier*, dung, from OFr. *femier*, from L. *fimus*, dung.] the dung of deer and kindred animals. [Archaic.]

fū'me·tere (-tār), *n.* a fumitory. [Obs.]

fū·mette', *n.* [Fr. *fumet*, odor, from L. *fumus*, smoke, steam.]

1. the odor from cooking meats.

2. the odor of game kept too long.

fū'mid, *a.* [L. *fumidus*, from *fumus*, smoke, steam.] smoky; vaporous. [Obs.]

fū·mid'i·ty, fū'mid·ness, *n.* smokiness. [Obs.]

fū·mif'ẽr·ous, *a.* [L. *fumifer*; *fumus*, smoke, and *ferre*, to bear.] producing smoke. [Rare.]

fū'mi·fȳ, *v.t.* to fumigate. [Obs.]

fū'mi·gănt, *n.* a substance used in fumigating.

fū'mi·gāte, *v.t.*; fumigated, *pt.*, *pp.*; fumigating, *ppr.* [L. *fumigatus*, pp. of *fumigare*, to smoke, fumigate, from *fumus*, smoke, and *agere*, to do, make.]

1. to expose to the action of fumes, especially in order to disinfect or kill the vermin in.

2. to perfume. [Rare or Archaic.]

fū·mi·gā'tion, *n.* 1. a fumigating or being fumigated.

2. vapors raised by fumigating.

fū'mi·gā·tŏr, *n.* a device for disinfecting by fumigation; also, one using such a device.

fū'mi·gȧ·tō·ry, *a.* having the quality of cleansing by smoke or gas. [Rare.]

fūm'ing, *a.* smoking; emitting vapors; raging.

fūm'ing·ly, *adv.* angrily; in a rage.

fūm'ish, *a.* smoky; hot; choleric. [Obs.]

fūm'ish·ness, *n.* the quality or state of being fumish. [Obs.]

fū'mi·tẽr, *n.* fumitory. [Obs.]

fū'mi·tō·ry, *n.*; *pl.* **fū'mi·tō·rieṣ,** [ME. *fumeter*, *fumetere*, *fumytere*; OFr. *fume terre*, from LL. *fumus terræ*, lit., smoke of the earth; so called from its smell.] any of a group of erect or climbing plants, especially one with clusters of pink or purple flowers, formerly used as a medicine.

fū'mōse, *a.* same as *fumous*.

fū·mos'i·ty, *n.*; *pl.* **fū·mos'i·tieṣ,** 1. the quality of giving off fumes. [Obs.]

2. [*pl.*] eructations. [Obs.]

fūm'ous, *a.* [L. *fumosus*, smoky, from *fumus*, smoke.] producing fumes or smoke; filled with vapor.

fūm'y, *a.*; *comp.* fumier; *superl.* fumiest, producing fumes; full of vapor.

fun, *n.* [from obs. v. *fon* (from ME. *fonnen*), to act foolishly.]

1. lively, gay play or playfulness; merriment; amusement; sport; recreation; joking.

2. a source or cause of amusement or merriment, as an amusing person or thing; as, he's good *fun*.

for (or *in*) *fun*; not seriously; playfully or jokingly.

like fun; by no means; not at all: used to express emphatic negation or doubt. [Slang.]

to make fun of; to ridicule; mock laughingly.

fun, *a.* intended for, or giving, pleasure or amusement; as, a *fun* gift. [Colloq.]

fun, *v.i.*; funned, *pt.*, *pp.*; funning, *ppr.* to make fun; play or joke. [Colloq.]

fū·nam'bū·lāte, *v.i.* [from L. *funis*, a rope, and *ambulatus*, pp. of *ambulare*, to walk.] to walk on a tightrope; to dance on a tightrope.

fū·nam·bū·lā'tion, *n.* dancing or walking on a tightrope.

fū·nam'bū·lȧ·tō·ry, *a.* performing like a ropedancer; pertaining to ropedancing.

fū·nam'bū·list, *n.* [L. *funambulus*, a ropewalker.] a tightrope walker or dancer.

fū·nam'bū·lō, fū·nam'bū·lus, *n.* a funambulist. [Archaic.]

Fū·nā'ri·ȧ, *n.* [LL., f. of *funarius*, of or belonging to a rope, from *funis*, a rope.] a genus of mosses of the family *Bryaceæ*, or true mosses.

fuñç'tion, *n.* [OFr. (Fr. *fonction*); L. *functio*, from pp. of *fungi*, to perform.]

1. the normal or characteristic action of anything; especially, any of the natural, specialized actions of an organ or part of an animal or plant; as, the procreative *function*.

2. a special duty or performance required of a person or thing in the course of work or activity; as, the *function* of a policeman is to protect and assist the public.

3. occupation; employment.

4. a formal ceremony or elaborate social occasion.

5. a thing that depends on and varies with something else.

6. in mathematics, a variable quantity whose value depends on and varies with that of another quantity or quantities.

calculus of functions; see under *calculus*.

Carnot's function; in thermodynamics, a function expressing the ratio of the heat expended to the work it does; the reciprocal of absolute temperature.

continuous function; a quantity whose real values are not affected by the values of its variables between certain given limits.

discontinuous function; see under *discontinuous*.

elliptic function; a function which returns to the same value when its variable changes; a doubly periodic function; the inverse of an elliptic integral.

explicit function; a quantity whose value is expressed directly in terms of another quantity; as, in $x=2y^2$, x is an *explicit function* of y.

implicit function; a quantity whose relation to a variable is not directly expressed, but implied in an equation.

transcendental function; a quantity whose relation to a variable cannot be determined by algebraic processes; as $y=7^x$.

trigonometric function or *circular function*; any function of an arc of a circle or of its angle expressed by a line related thereto; as, in a circle, a line drawn from one extremity of an arc perpendicularly to a radius drawn to its other extremity (radius being unity) is a function of that arc and of the angle it subtends, and is called its sine; other principal functions are cosine, tangent, and cotangent.

vital functions; functions immediately necessary to life, as respiration, digestion, etc.

fuñç'tion, *v.i.*; functioned, *pt.*, *pp.*; functioning, *ppr.* to perform in a required or expected manner; to have some use; to act; to work.

fuñç'tion·ăl, *a.* 1. pertaining to a function or functions.

2. performing a function.

3. in physiology, relating to a special function or to the bodily functions as a whole.

functional disease; in medicine, any derangement of an organ in which there is no apparent degeneration, damage, impairment, or structural change.

functional illiterate; a person whose ability to read is less than that needed for proper functioning in a complex society.

functional shift; the conversion of a linguistic form from one part of speech to another, as the use of a noun as a verb.

fuñç'tion·ăl·iṣm, *n.* theory or practice emphasizing the necessity of adapting the structure or design of anything to its function.

fuñç'tion·ăl·īze, *v.t.* to give or assign a function to.

fuñç'tion·ăl·ly, *adv.* 1. in a functional manner.

2. from the standpoint of function.

fuñç'tion·ā·ry, *n.*; *pl.* **fuñç'tion·ā·rieṣ,** [Fr. *fonctionnaire*, from L. *functio* (*-onis*), function.] one who holds an office or trust; a person who performs a certain function; as, a public *functionary*.

fuñç'tion·āte, *v.i.*; functionated, *pt.*, *pp.*; functionating, *ppr.* to function; officiate.

fuñç'tion·less, *a.* without function.

fuñç'tion wŏrd, a word having little or no lexical meaning but used to show syntactical relation, as an article or conjunction.

fund, *n.* [meaning affected by OFr. *fond*, bottom, ground, stock, capital; from L. *fundus*, bottom, land, estate.]

1. a sum of money, or stock convertible into money, held available for the demands of an individual, company, or corporation engaged in business.

2. a collection of money or an appropriation to be devoted to some specific use; as, a pension *fund*.

3. [*pl.*] money; cash; as, he is out of *funds*.

4. abundance; ample stock or store; as, a *fund* of knowledge.

5. [*pl.*] a permanent government debt on which interest is paid; public securities (with *the*). [Brit.]

fund, *v.t.*; funded, *pt.*, *pp.*; funding, *ppr.* 1. to provide and appropriate a fund for the payment of interest on (a debt).

2. to put or convert into a long-term debt that bears interest.

3. to put in a fund; collect; store.

fund'ȧ·ble, *a.* convertible into a fund or bonds.

fun'dȧ·ment, *n.* [L. *fundamentum*, from *fundare*, to lay the bottom, foundation, from *fundus*, the bottom.]

1. a basic principle; as, the *fundament* of analytics is the conception of position.

2. the buttocks.

3. the anus.

4. foundation. [Obs.]

fun·dȧ·men'tăl, *a.* [ML. *fundamentalis*, from L. *fundamentum*, fundament.]

1. of or forming a foundation or basis; basic; essential.
2. in music, designating or of the lowest, or root, tone of a chord.
3. in physics, designating or of a fundamental.
fundamental bass; in music, the harmonic part consisting of the root tones of the chords.
fundamental colors; primary colors.
fundamental tissue; the tissue of plants, unmodified or only slightly modified.
fundamental tones; tones producing harmonic chords.
Syn.—primary, important, essential.

fun·dȧ·men′tăl, *n.* 1. a leading or primary principle, rule, law, or article, which serves as the groundwork or basis; essential part; as, the *fundamentals* of the Christian faith.
2. in music, the lowest, or root, tone of a chord.
3. in physics, the component having the lowest frequency in a complex vibration; tone produced by the whole of a vibrating body, as distinguished from any of the tones (called *harmonics*) produced by the vibration of any part.

fun″dȧ·men′tăl·iṣm, *n.* 1. [*sometimes* F–] orthodox religious beliefs based on a literal interpretation of the Bible (e.g., complete acceptance of the story of creation as given in Genesis and rejection of the theory of evolution) and regarded as fundamental to the Christian faith.
2. [*sometimes* F–] the movement among some American Protestants emphasizing this belief: opposed to *modernism*.

fun″dȧ·men′tăl·ist, *n.* a person who believes in fundamentalism.

fun″dȧ·men′tăl·ist, *a.* pertaining to fundamentalism or fundamentalists; also, ultraconservative.

fun·dȧ·men′tăl·ly, *adv.* primarily; originally; essentially; at, from, or to the foundation.

fund′ed, *a.* 1. converted into a permanent or long-term debt, or into a loan or bonds payable on demand or at some specified time and bearing regular interest.
2. invested, especially in public funds. [Brit.]
funded debt; the part of a public debt represented by long-term, interest-bearing bonds.

fund′ẽr, *n.* one favoring a sinking fund; one who funds or wishes to fund a public debt; specifically, in Virginia at the close of the Civil War, a person in favor of funding all and not repudiating any part of the debt of the State.

fund′hōld″ẽr, *n.* one who has an investment in public funds. [Brit.]

fun′di, *n.* [native name.] a milletlike grain, *Paspalum exile*, grown in Africa.

fun′di·fọrm, *a.* [L. *funda*, sling, and *forma*, form.] like a sling in form.

fund′ing, *n.* providing funds for the payment of a debt.
funding system; a system of finance or revenue by which provision is made for paying interest on a debt.

fund′less, *a.* without funds.

fun′dus, *n.* [L.] 1. the bottom, rear, or depths of anything.
2. in anatomy, the base of a hollow organ farthest from the opening.

fū·nē′bri·ăl, fū·nē′bri·ous, *a.* [L. *funebris*, from *funus*, *funeris*, a funeral.] pertaining to a funeral; funereal. [Obs.]

fū′nẽr·ăl, *n.* [ME. *funeral*; OFr. *funeral*, *funerail*, from ML. *funeralia*, neut. pl. of *funeralis*, pertaining to a burial, from L. *funus* (*-eris*), a funeral procession, burial.]
1. burial; the ceremony of burying, or otherwise formally disposing of the dead; obsequies.
2. the procession attending the burial of the dead.
3. [*usually pl.*] a discourse or sermon given at a funeral. [Obs.]
4. a disastrous or unwelcome result; a loss; also, a concern or affair; as, his misfortune is not my *funeral*. [Slang.]

fū′nẽr·ăl, *a.* of, pertaining to, or suitable for burial; used at the interment of the dead; as, *funeral* ceremonies.
funeral director; the manager of a funeral home.
funeral home; an establishment containing one or several rooms that may be rented for funeral services or ceremonies.
funeral parlor; same as *funeral home*.
funeral pile; a heap of combustible material on which a dead body is burned; a pyre.

fū′nẽr·ȧ·ry, *a.* of or relating to a funeral or to the interment or cremation of the dead.

fū′nẽr·āte, *v.t.* [L. *funeratus*, pp. of *funerare*, to bury with funeral rites.] to hold a funeral for. [Obs.]

fū·nẽr·ā′tion, *n.* a funeral. [Obs.]

fū·nē′rē·ăl, *a.* suitable to a funeral; pertaining to burial; dismal; mournful; gloomy.

fū·nē′rē·ăl·ly, *adv.* dismally; mournfully.

fuñ·gā′ceous, *a.* of, relating to, or characteristic of a fungus or fungi.

fuñ′găl, *a.* and *n.* fungus.

fuñge, *n.* [from L. *fungus*, a mushroom, a dolt.] a fool; a blockhead. [Obs.]

fun′ġi, *n.* alternative plural of *fungus*.

Fun′ġi, *n.pl.* [L. *fungus*, a mushroom.] in botany, a large group of acotyledonous or cryptogamous plants having no green color. The group includes the mushrooms, toadstools, and microscopic plants growing upon other plants, such as molds, mildew, smut, rust, brand, etc.

FUNGI
1. *Agaricus comatus* (tall cylindrical agaric); 2. *Boletus edulis* (edible boletus); 3. *Morchella esculenta* (roundheaded morel)

Fun′ġi·ȧ, *n.* [from L. *fungus*, a mushroom.] a genus of flat, circular or elliptical corals resembling a mushroom in form.

fun′ġi·ăn, *a.* of or pertaining to the *Fungiidæ*, a family of corals of which *Fungia* is the type genus.

fun′ġi·ăn, *n.* a fungian coral.

fun′ġi·ble, *a.* [LL. *fungibilis*, from *fungi*, to perform, execute.] in law, designating goods, as grain, any unit or part of which can replace another unit, as in discharging a debt; capable of being used in place of another.

fun′ġi·ble, *n.* a fungible thing.

fun′ġiç, *a.* of or obtained from fungi.

fun′ġi·cī·dăl, *a.* serving as a fungicide.

fun′ġi·cīde, *n.* [L. *fungus*, fungus, and *-cida*, from *cædere*, to kill.] any substance that kills fungi or checks the growth of spores.

fun′ġi·fọrm, *a.* [L. *fungus*, a mushroom, and *forma*, form.] having a termination similar to the head of a fungus or mushroom; specifically, in anatomy, designating the papillae of the tongue having a head convex in shape.

fun·ġil′li·fọrm, *a.* [a dim. from L. *fungus*, fungus, and *forma*, form.] fungiform.

fun′ġin, *n.* [*fungus*, and *-in*.] a cellulose of fungi. [Obs.]

fun·ġiv′ō·rous, *a.* [L. *fungus*, a mushroom, and *vorare*, to devour.] feeding on fungi.

fuñ′gō, *a.* [etym. uncertain.] in baseball, designating or of a manner of batting, as for fielding practice, in which the batter himself tosses the ball lightly into the air and hits it as it falls.

fuñ′goid, *a.* [L. *fungus*, a fungus, and Gr. *eidos*, form.] like or characteristic of a fungus.

fuñ′goid, *n.* a fungus.

fuñ·gol′ō·ġist, *n.* a mycologist.

fuñ·gol′ō·ġy, *n.* [L. *fungus*, a mushroom, and *-logia*, from *legein*, to speak.] mycology.

fuñ·gos′i·ty, *n.* 1. a fungous quality or condition.
2. a fungoid excrescence.

fuñ′gous, *a.* [ME. *fungous*; It. *fungoso*, from L. *fungosus*, spongy, from *fungus*, fungus.]
1. of, like, or caused by a fungus or fungi.
2. growing suddenly; not substantial or durable.

fuñ′gus, *n.*; *pl.* **fun′ġī, fuñ′gus·eṣ,** [L.] 1. any plant of the *Fungi*.
2. something that grows suddenly and rapidly like a fungus.
3. in medicine, a spongy, granular growth on the body, sometimes malignant.

fuñ′gus, *a.* same as *fungoid*.

fū′ni·çle, *n.* [L. *funiculus*, dim. of *funis*, a cord, rope.] a small cord or fiber; a funiculus.

fū·niç′ū·lăr, *a.* [L. *funiculus*, dim. of *funis*, a cord.]
1. of, due to, consisting of, or resembling a funiculus or funiculi.
2. of, worked by, or hanging from a rope or cable; as, a *funicular* railway is a mountain railway on which the cars are pulled up and lowered by cables.
funicular action; in mechanics, the force exerted by a cord upon the supports to which its ends are attached, when moved transversely, as in a bowstring.
funicular curve; same as *catenary*.
funicular machine; any of various contrivances intended to illustrate some mechanical principle in statics, consisting mainly of an arrangement of cords and suspended weights.
funicular polygon; in statics, the figure assumed by a string supported at its extremities and acted on by several pressures.

fū·niç′ū·lăr, *n.* a funicular railway.

fū·niç′ū·lāte, *a.* [L. *funiculus*, a small rope, cord, dim. of *funis*, a rope, cord.] having or constituting a funiculus or funiculi.

fū′ni·çūle, *n.* in botany, a funiculus.

fū·niç′ū·lus, *n.*; *pl.* **fū·niç′ū·lī,** [L., a small cord, dim. of *funis*, a cord, rope.]
1. in anatomy, a cord; specifically, (a) the umbilical cord; (b) a bundle of nerve fibers having a sheath of neurilemma; (c) the spermatic cord.
2. in zoology, (a) the chief tendon of the abdomen of an insect; (b) a section of the antenna of an insect between the club and the pedicel.
3. in botany, the slender stalk of an ovule or seed.

fū·nil′i·fọrm, *a.* [from L. *funis*, a rope, and *forma*, form.] in botany, formed of tough, flexible, cordlike fibers, as the roots of some endogens.

fū′nis, *n.* [L., a rope, cord.] the umbilical cord.

fuñk, *n.* [Dan. *funk*, a blow.] a kick; also, ill temper; anger. [Scot.]

fuñk, *v.t.* and *v.i.* to kick; to grow angry. [Scot.]

fuñk, *n.* [prob. from Fl. *fonck*, dismay.]
1. a cowering or flinching through fear; panic.
2. a cowardly or fearful person.
3. a low, depressed mood: also *blue funk*. [Colloq. in all senses.]

fuñk, *v.i.* to be in a funk or panic. [Colloq.]

fuñk, *v.t.* 1. to be afraid of. [Colloq.]
2. to avoid because of fear; shrink from; shirk. [Colloq.]
3. to frighten. [Colloq.]

fuñk, *n.* [compare *funky*.]
1. a musty odor, as of moldy tobacco.
2. funky jazz.

Fuñ′ki·ȧ, *n.* [named after Heinrich Christian *Funck*, German botanist.] a genus of the *Liliaceæ*, the day lilies or plantain lilies of China and Japan, bearing blue or white, fragrant blossoms.

fuñ′ky, *a.*; *comp.* funkier; *superl.* funkiest, in a funk, or panic.

fuñ′ky, *a.*; *comp.* funkier; *superl.* funkiest, [originally Negro argot, literally, smelly, hence musty, earthy, from obs. *funk*, smell, smoke, prob. from Fr. dial. *funkier*, to smoke.] in jazz, having an earthy quality or style derived from early blues.

fun′nel, *n.* [ME. *funelle*, *fonel* (prob. via an OFr. form), from L. *infundibulum*, a funnel, hopper of a mill, from *infundere*, to pour in; *in*, in, and *fundere*, to pour.]
1. an instrument for conveying fluids into small openings, consisting of an inverted hollow cone with a hole at the small end, or a tapering or cylindical tube with a wide, cone-shaped mouth.
2. a thing shaped like a funnel.
3. the shaft or hollow channel of a chimney, through which smoke ascends; especially, the smokestack of a locomotive or steamship.
4. a flue.
5. in nautical usage, a metal ring on a masthead to which the rigging is fitted.
6. in zoology, an infundibulum.

fun′nel, *v.i.* and *v.t.*; funneled *or* funnelled, *pt.*, *pp.*; funneling *or* funnelling, *ppr.* 1. to move or pour through, or as if through, a funnel.
2. to form in the shape of a funnel.
3. to move into a central channel or to a central point.

fun′neled, fun′nelled, *a.* 1. having a funnel.
2. shaped like a funnel.

fun′nel·fọrm, *a.* having the form of a funnel, as certain monopetalous corollas.

fun′nel tūbe, a glass tube with a funnel-shaped top used in chemistry for transferring liquids from one container to another. The top, if shaped to resemble the head of a thistle, is called a *thistle tube*.

FUNNELFORM COROLLA

fun′ni·ly, *adv.* in a funny manner.

fun′ni·ness, *n.* the state or quality of being funny.

fun′ny, *a.*; *comp.* funnier; *superl.* funniest, 1. comical; droll; causing laughter.

2. out of the ordinary; queer; curious; odd; as, a *funny* way to act. [Colloq.]

Syn.—laughable, humorous, facetious, ludicrous, ridiculous.

fun′ny, *n.*; *pl.* **fun′nieș,** [*usually in pl.*] a comic strip. [Colloq.]

fun′ny, *n.*; *pl.* **fun′nieș,** a narrow racing boat, used with a pair of sculls.

fun′ny bōne, the crazy bone; the point at the elbow where the ulnar nerve is only slightly protected and hence sensitive to even a light blow.

fun′ny pā′pẽr, the comic-strip section of a newspaper.

fũr, *n.* [ME. *furre, forre, for*, fur, a pelt, from OFr. *forre, fuerre*, a case, sheath; It. *fodero*; Goth. *fodr*, a sheath.]

1. the thick, soft hair covering the bodies of certain animals.

2. (a) a skin bearing such hair, when stripped and processed for use as material; dressed pelt; (b) [*pl.*] skins of this kind; peltry.

3. a muff, neckpiece, trimming, etc. made of fur; a garment of fur.

4. any furlike or fuzzy coating, as (a) a coat of diseased matter collected on the tongue in illness; (b) the coat or crust formed on the interior of vessels by hard water; (c) the down or fuzz on a peach.

5. collectively, animals yielding fur.

6. in heraldry, one of the three kinds of tinctures.

to make the fur fly; to cause dissension or fighting.

fũr, *a.* pertaining to or made of fur.

fũr, *v.t.*; furred, *pt., pp.*; furring, *ppr.* 1. to line, face, make, trim, or cover with fur.

2. to coat with a deposit.

3. to nail small strips of board on (joists, rafters, etc.), in order to make a level surface for lathing, boarding, etc.

fũr, *v.i.* to become coated with a deposit.

fū·rā′cious, *a.* [L. *furax* (*-acis*), from *furari*, to steal, from *fur*, a thief.] inclined to steal; thievish. [Rare.]

fū·rac′i·ty, *n.* thievishness. [Rare.]

fū′răn, fū′rāne, *n.* [from L. *furfur*, bran; and *-an, -ane*.] a colorless liquid, C_4H_4O, prepared from wood tar, used as a solvent or tanning agent.

fũr′bē·lōw, *n.* [Fr. dial. *farbala*; Sp., Port., It., *falbala*, a furbelow.]

1. a piece of material pleated or puckered, on a gown or petticoat; a flounce or ruffle

2. [*usually pl.*] showy, useless trimming or ornamentation.

fũr′bē·lōw, *v.t.*; furbelowed, *pt., pp.*; furbelowing, *ppr.* to put a furbelow on; to furnish with ornamental frills and flounces.

FURBELOWS

fũr′bish, *v.t.*; furbished, *pt. pp.*; furbishing, *ppr.* [ME. *fourbischen, forbischen*, from OFr. *forbir, fourbir*; O.H.G. *furban*, to clean, polish.]

1. to rub or scour to brightness; to polish; to burnish; as, to *furbish* a sword.

2. to put into usable condition again; renovate (usually with *up*.)

fũr′bish·a·ble, *a.* that can be furbished.

fũr′bish·ẽr, *n.* one who furbishes.

fũr′çāte, fũr′çā·ted, *a.* [ML. *furcatus*, from L. *furca*, a fork.] branching like the prongs of a fork; forked.

fũr′çāte, *v.i.*; furcated, *pt., pp.*; furcating, *ppr.* to branch; to fork.

fũr·çā′tion, *n.* 1. a forking; a branching like the tines of a fork.

2. a forklike part; a branch.

fũr·cel′lāte, *a.* [dim. from L. *furca*, a fork, and *-ate*.] somewhat furcate.

fũr·cif′ẽr·ous, *a.* [L. *furcifer*, yoke-bearer, scoundrel; *furca*, a fork, an instrument of punishment in the form of a fork, and *ferre*, to bear.]

1. villainous. [Rare.]

2. in entomology, having a yokelike or forked process.

Fũr·çrae′ȧ, *n.* [named after A. F. de *Fourcroy*, a French chemist.] a genus of *Amaryllidaceæ*, fibrous plants native to tropical America.

fũr′çū·lȧ, *n.*; *pl.* **fũr′çū·lae,** a small fork or forked process; the wishbone; the furculum.

fũr′çū·lȧr, *a.* having the form of a fork; furcated.

fũr′çū·lum, *n.*; *pl.* **fũr′çū·lȧ,** [a dim. from L. *furca*, a fork.] in anatomy and zoology, any forked part or organ; especially, the wishbone.

fũr′dle, *v.t.*; furdled, *pt., pp.*; furdling, *ppr.* [OFr. *fardel*, dim. of *fard*, a bundle.] to draw up into a bundle. [Obs.]

fũr′fũr, *n.* [L.] 1. dandruff; scurf.

2. [*pl.*] bits of skin; dandruff scales.

fũr·fū·rā′ceous, *a.* [L. *furfuraceus*, from *furfur*, bran, scales on the skin.]

1. scaly; branny; like bran.

2. covered with dandruff; scurfy.

fũr′fũr·ăl, *n.* a colorless, sweet-smelling, oily liquid, $C_5H_4O_2$, produced from corncobs, oat hulls, and other cereal wastes, used to make dyes, lacquers, synthetic resins, etc.

fũr′fū·răn, fũr′fū·rāne, *n.* same as *furan.*

fũr·fū·rā′tion, *n.* [from L. *furfur*, bran, scales on the skin.] the shedding of the scales of the cuticle; desquamation.

fũr′fū·rine, *n.* a white crystalline compound, $C_{15}H_{12}N_2O_3$, obtained from furfurol.

fũr′fũr·ol, *n.* same as *furfural.*

fũr′fū·rous, *a.* [L. *furfurosus*, from *furfur*, bran.] of the nature of bran; furfuraceous.

fū′ri·ăl, *a.* [L. *furialis*, furious, belonging to the Furies, from *furia*, rage, madness.] furious; vehement; harassing. [Obs.]

fū′ri·bund, *a.* [L. *furibundus*, furious, from *furere*, to be mad.] abounding in fury; raging; frenzied. [Rare.]

fū·ri·bun′dăl, *a.* filled with rage. [Obs.]

Fū′rieș, *n.pl.* [L. *Furiæ*, pl. of *furia*, from *furere*, to rage.] in Greek and Roman mythology, the three terrible female spirits with snaky hair (Alecto, Tisiphone, and Megaera) who punished the doers of unavenged crimes: also called *Erinyes, Eumenides.*

fū′ril, *a.* [*fur*furol and benz*il*.] a yellow, crystalline compound, $C_{10}H_6O_4$, a product of the oxidation of furoin.

fū·ril′iç, *a.* of or derived from furil.

fū″ri·ō″sä·men′te, *adv.* [It.] with great agitation; furiously: a musical direction.

fū·ri·ō′sō, *a.* [It., furious.] furious: a musical direction.

fū·ri·ō′sō, *n.* a furious person.

fū′ri·ous, *a.* [ME. *furious*, from L. *furiosus*, full of madness, raging, from *furia*, madness, rage, from *furere*, to be mad.]

1. moving with violence; violently overpowering; as, a *furious* stream, a *furious* attack.

2. raging; violent; full of fury or intense feeling; as, a *furious* animal.

fū′ri·ous·ly, *adv.* in a furious manner.

fū′ri·ous·ness, *n.* the state or quality of being furious.

fũrl, *v.t.*; furled, *pt., pp.*; furling, *ppr.* [prob. from Fr. *ferler*; OFr. *fermlier*; L. *firmum ligare*; *firmum*, firm, and *ligare*, to lay.] to draw up; to wrap or roll (a sail, flag, etc.) close to the yard, stay, or mast, and fasten it by a gasket or cord; to wrap by rolling; as, to *furl* a flag about the staff.

fũrl, *v.i.* to become curled or rolled up.

fũrl, *n.* 1. a roll or coil of something furled.

2. a furling or being furled.

fũr′lọng, *n.* [ME. *furlong*, furlong; AS. *furlang*, a measure, lit., the length of a furrow; *furh*, a furrow, and *lang*, long.] a measure of distance equal to 1/8 of a mile; 40 rods, poles, or perches; 220 yards; 660 feet.

fũr′lough (-lō), *n.* [D. *verlof*, from Dan. *forlov* leave, permission, leave of absence; *for*, for; and *-lov*, Ice. *lov*, leave.] leave of absence; specifically, in military usage, the grant of temporary absence allowed enlisted personnel for a specified period of more than three days.

fũr′lough, *v.t.*; furloughed, *pt., pp.*; furloughing, *ppr.* to furnish with a furlough; to grant a leave of absence to.

fũr′men·ty, fũr′met·y, *n.* same as *frumenty.*

fũr′năce, *n.* [ME. *forneis, fornais*; OFr. *fornais, fornaz*; It. *fornace*, from L. *fornax* (*-acis*), a furnace, kiln, from *fornus, furnus*, an oven.]

1. a structure where heat may be made and maintained for smelting ores, melting metals, consuming combustible substances, heating air, baking pottery, etc.

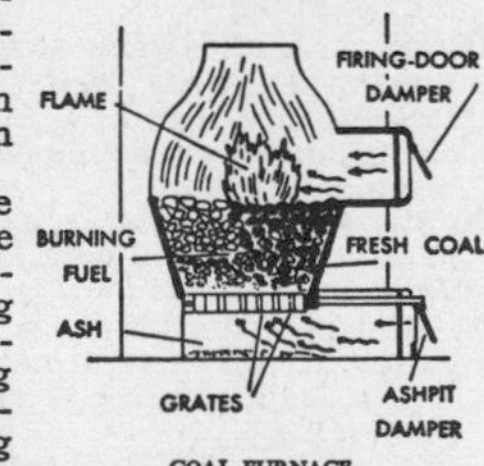

COAL FURNACE

2. any extremely hot place.

3. any place, time, or occasion of severe torture; great trial; as, the *furnace* of affliction.

furnace bridge; a low partition standing vertically in the fire chamber of a furnace for the purpose of deflecting the flame.

furnace cadmium; a substance that accumulates in the chimney of a furnace when smelting zinc-bearing ores.

fũr′năce, *v.t.*; furnaced (-năst), *pt., pp.*; furnacing, *ppr.* to treat by a process in which a furnace is used.

fũr′ni·ment, *n.* [OFr. *fourniment*, from *fournir*, to furnish, supply.] furniture. [Obs.]

fũr′nish, *v.t.*; furnished (-nisht), *pt., pp.*; furnishing, *ppr.* [from OFr. *furniss-*, inflectional base of *furnir, fournir*, to furnish; O.H.G. *frumjan*, to perform, provide, from *fruma*, gain, utility.]

1. to supply with anything wanted or necessary; especially, to put furniture into (a room, etc.).

2. to supply; to provide; to give.

Syn.—supply, provide, equip, afford, yield, bestow, purvey, give.

fũr′nish·ẽr, *n.* one who furnishes.

fũr′nish·ingș, *n.pl.* 1. fixtures or supplies; especially, household furniture and decorations.

2. articles of dress; things to wear.

fũr′ni·tūre, *n.* [Fr. *fourniture*, from *fournir*, to furnish.]

1. originally, a furnishing.

2. the movable things in a room, apartment, etc., which equip it for living, as chairs, sofas, tables, beds, etc.

3. the necessary equipment of a machine, ship, trade, etc.

4. all articles necessary to equip a man and horse, as armor, harness, etc. [Archaic.]

5. in printing, the pieces placed around a page or form of type preparatory to locking it up.

6. an organ stop producing a mixture of tones.

fū′rō·in, *n.* [from *furfurol*.] a colorless, crystalline compound, $C_{10}H_8O_4$.

fū′rọr, *n.* [from Fr. or L.; Fr. *fureur*; L. *furor*, rage, madness.]

1. fury; rage; frenzy.

2. a poetic or religious frenzy.

3. a great, widespread outburst of admiration or enthusiasm; craze; rage.

fụ·rō′re, *n.* same as *furor* (sense 3).

fũrred, *a.* 1. made, trimmed, or lined with fur.

2. having fur: said of an animal.

3. wearing fur.

4. coated with diseased or waste matter.

fũr′ri·ẽr, *n.* [from OFr. *fourreur*, from *fourrer*, to fur.] a dealer in furs; also, one who makes, processes, or repairs fur garments.

fũr′ri·ẽr·y, *n.*; *pl.* **fũr′ri·ẽr·ieș,** 1. furs collectively.

2. the occupation of dealing in furs.

fũr′ri·ness, *n.* the quality or state of being furry.

fũr′ring, *n.* 1. fur used for trimming or lining.

2. the act of trimming, lining, etc. with fur.

3. any furlike deposit, as the furry scale sometimes found in steam boilers or the furry roughness of the tongue in certain diseases; also, the formation of such a deposit.

4. in architecture, (a) the leveling of a floor, wall, etc. or the creating of air spaces with thin strips of wood or metal before adding boards or plaster; (b) the strips thus laid on.

fũr′rōw, *n.* [ME. *forowe, furwe*; AS. *furh*, a furrow; O.H.G., *furuh*; Dan. *fure*; Sw. *fara*; Ice. *for*, a drain.]

1. a narrow groove in the earth made by a plow.

2. anything resembling this, as a deep, narrow rut or track made by a wheel, a deep wrinkle on the face, etc.

3. a plowed field. [Poet.]

fũr′rōw, *v.t.*; furrowed, *pt., pp.*; furrowing, *ppr.* [AS. *furan*, from *furh*, a furrow.]

1. to cut a furrow in; to make furrows in.

2. to cut; to make channels in (the sea); as, to *furrow* the deep.

fũr′rōw, *v.i.* 1. to make furrows.

2. to become wrinkled.

fũr′rōw weed, a weed growing in the sod overturned by a plow.

fũr′ry, *a.*; *comp.* furrier; *superl.* furriest, 1. covered with fur; dressed in fur.

2. consisting of fur.

3. like fur, as in texture.

4. lined or trimmed with fur.

fũr seal, any of several species of seals of the genera *Callorhinus* and *Arctocephalus* of the northern oceans, having fine, soft underfur.

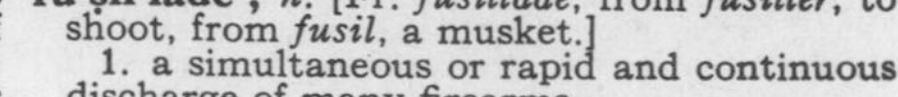

fũr′thẽr, *a.* [ME. *further, forther*; AS. *furthra*, usually regarded as containing the base of AS. *fore*, fore, and the comp. suffix in *af-ter*, *o-ther*, etc.]

1. more remote; more distant or advanced; as, the *further* end of the field. *Further* is now interchangeable with *farther* in this sense, though preference is often given to *farther* in reference to space and to *further* in reference to time, degree, or addition.

2. additional; more, especially in time, degree, or addition; as, we have a *further* reason for our opinion.

What *further* need have we for witnesses?
—Matt. xxvi. 65.

fũr′thẽr, *adv.* [ME. *furthere, forthere*; AS. *furthor*, orig. a neut. acc. of the *a.*]

1. at or to a greater distance; more remotely; beyond; as, seek *further* for innocence.

2. in addition; besides; moreover; as, I say *further* that the evidence is conclusive.

3. to a greater degree or extent.

Further is now generally interchangeable with *farther* in senses one and three, though preference is often given to *farther* in reference to space and *further* in reference to time, degree, or addition.

fũr′thẽr, *v.t.*; furthered, *pt., pp.*; furthering, *ppr.* to help forward; to promote; to cause to advance; to give aid to.

fũr′thẽr·ȧnce, *n.* 1. a helping forward; promotion; advancement.

I know that I shall abide and continue with you all, for your *furtherance* and joy of faith. —Phil. i. 25.

2. something that helps; aid.

fũr′thẽr·ẽr, *n.* one who helps to advance; a promoter; a helper.

fũr′thẽr·mōre, *adv.* moreover; besides; in addition.

fũr′thẽr·mōst, *a.* most remote; furthest.

fũr′thẽr·sŏme, *a.* having the quality of helpfulness.

fũr′thest, *a.* most distant; farthest.

fũr′thest, *adv.* 1. at the greatest distance in space or time.

2. to the greatest degree or extent.

fũr′tive, *a.* [OFr. *furtif*, from L. *furtivus*, stolen, concealed, hidden, from *furtum*, theft, robbery, from *furari*, to steal; *fur*, a thief.] done in a stealthy manner; surreptitious; sly; stealthy.

fũr′tive·ly, *adv.* stealthily.

fū′run̄·cle, *n.* [L. *furunculus*, a thief, pilferer, a boil, dim. of *fur*, a thief.] a small skin abscess; a boil.

fū·run̄′cū·lăr, *a.* [L. *furunculis*, a furuncle, and *-ar.*] relating to boils.

fū·run̄′cū·loid, *a.* [L. *furunculus*, a furuncle, and Gr. *eidos*, form.] resembling a boil.

fū·run̄·cū·lō′sis, *n.* [L. *furunculus*, a furuncle, boil, and *-osis.*] the state of being afflicted with boils.

fū′ry, *n.*; *pl.* **fū′rieṣ,** [ME. *furie*; OFr. *furie*, from L. *furia*, madness, rage, fury.]

1. (a) violent anger; wild rage; (b) a fit of this.

2. violence; vehemence; fierceness.

3. a violent, uncontrollable person, especially a woman.

4. [F–] one of the Furies.

5. frenzy of inspiration. [Archaic.]

fũrze, *n.* [ME. *firs, fyrs*; AS. *fyrs*, furze.] gorse; whin; a thorny evergreen shrub with yellow flowers, common on the plains and hills of Europe; the *Ulex europæus*.

fũrze′chat, *n.* the whinchat, *Pratincola rubetra*, a bird frequenting furze or gorse.

fũrze′ling, *n.* a small bird found in southern England.

fũrz′y, *a.* 1. full of or covered with furze.

2. of or like furze.

fū·ṣāin′, *n.* [Fr., the spindle tree.]

1. a drawing pencil made of charcoal prepared from the wood of the spindle tree.

2. a drawing made with this.

fū′sȧ·rōle, *n.* [Fr. *fusarolle*; It. *fusaruolo*, from *fuso*, L. *fusus*, a spindle, shaft of a column.] in architecture, a molding generally placed under the echinus of columns in the Doric, Ionic, and Corinthian orders.

fus·cā′tion, *n.* a darkening; obscurity. [Obs.]

fus·ces′cent, *a.* [L. *fuscus*, dark, dusky, and *-escent.*] nearly dark brown. [Rare.]

fus′cin, *n.* [L. *fuscus*, dark, dusky, and *-in.*] a brown pigment found in the epithelium of the retina.

fus′çous, *a.* [L. *fuscus*, dark.] brown; of a dark color.

fūṣe, *v.t.*; fused, *pt., pp.*; fusing, *ppr.* [L. *fusus*, pp. of *fundere*, to pour out, shed.]

1. to melt; to liquefy by heat; to make fluid.

2. to unite as if by melting together; to blend; as, America *fuses* the characteristics of various peoples into one.

3. in optics, to blend by bringing the eyes into visual line.

fūṣe, *v.i.* 1. to be melted; to be reduced from a solid to a fluid state by heat.

2. to become united into a mass; to be blended.

3. in optics, to bring the eyes into visual line.

fūṣe, *n.* [It. *fuso*, a cord, tube, casing, from L. *fusus*, hollow spindle or casing.]

1. a narrow tube filled with combustible material or a wick saturated with such material for setting off an explosive charge.

2. any of various other devices for setting off bombs and explosive charges; as, a chemical *fuse*, electrical *fuse*, or percussion *fuse*.

3. in electricity, a wire or strip of easily melted metal placed in a circuit as a safeguard: when the current becomes too strong, the metal melts, thus breaking the circuit.

Also spelled *fuze*.

fū·ṣeau′ (-zō′), *n.* [Fr., a spindle.] a spindle-shaped object of any kind; specifically, the hilt of a sword.

fū·ṣee′, fū·zee′, *n.* [OFr. *fusee*, a spindle full of thread, fusee, from LL. *fusata*, from *fusare*, to use a spindle, from L. *fusus*, a spindle.]

1. a friction match with a large head, intended to burn in a wind.

2. a colored flare used as a railroad signal.

3. in an old-fashioned clock or watch, a grooved cone upon which the cord from the spring container was unwound to equalize the force of the spring.

4. a bony growth on a horse's leg.

5. a figure in the shape of a spindle. [Obs.]

fū·ṣee′, fū·zee′, *n.* [a corruption of Fr. *fusil*, a steel for striking fire, a musket.] a small musket; a fusil. [Obs.]

fūṣe hōle, a hole for the insertion of the fuse in a shell.

fū′ṣel·ăġe (*or* -sel-), *n.* [Fr.; prob. from OFr. *fusel*, dim. of L. *fusus*, a spindle, and *-age.*] the body of an airplane, exclusive of the wings and tail assembly.

fū′ṣel oil (*or* -sel), [G. *fusel*, spirits of an inferior quality.] an oily, acrid, poisonous liquid occurring in alcoholic products that have not been distilled sufficiently to separate the ethyl alcohol from other substances with a low boiling point: it consists generally of a mixture of amyl, butyl, propyl, and isoamyl alcohols: also *fusel*.

fūṣe′-plug, *n.* the plug that holds the fuse and that fills the fuse hole when the shell is charged.

fū·ṣi·bil′i·ty, *n.* 1. the quality of being fusible.

2. the degree to which this quality is present.

fū′ṣi·ble, *a.* [ME. *fusible*; OFr. *fusible*, from L. *fundere*, to pour.] capable of being fused or easily fused.

fusible metal; an alloy, as of lead, tin, and bismuth, compounded in such definite proportions as to melt at a given temperature.

fusible plug; a plug of fusible metal in the plate of a boiler, so placed that it will melt at a temperature too high for safety and allow the steam to escape freely; also, a plug that melts by heat of electrical resistance to guard against excess of current; also, a plug in a system of water pipes, for fire protection of buildings.

fū′ṣi·form, *a.* [L. *fusus*, a spindle, and *forma*, form.] shaped like a spindle; thick, tapering at each end.

fū′ṣil, *a.* [L. *fusilis*, liquid, molten, from *fundere*, to pour.]

1. fusible or fusing. [Rare.]

2. fused; melted.

3. made by melting and molding, or casting; founded.

fū′ṣil, *n.* [Fr. *fusil*, a steel for striking fire, a musket; It. *focile, fucile*; LL. *focile*, a steel for striking fire, from L. *focus*, a fireplace.] an old-fashioned, light musket or firelock resembling a carbine.

fū′ṣil, *n.* [from L. *fusus*, a spindle.] a bearing in heraldry of a rhomboidal figure.

fū′ṣile, *a.* same as *fusil*.

fū·ṣil·eer′, fū·ṣil·iẽr′, *n.* [Fr. *fusilier*, from *fusil*, a musket.]

1. a soldier armed with a fusil. [Obs.]

2. [*pl.*] a title [F—] retained by certain infantry regiments of the British army formerly so armed; as, the Scots *Fusiliers*.

FUSIL

fū·ṣil·lāde′, *n.* [Fr. *fusillade*, from *fusiller*, to shoot, from *fusil*, a musket.]

1. a simultaneous or rapid and continuous discharge of many firearms.

2. something like this; as, a *fusillade* of questions.

fū·ṣil·lāde′, *v.t.*; fusilladed, *pt., pp.*; fusillading, *ppr.* to attack and fight with a fusillade.

fū′ṣion, *n.* [L. *fusio*, from *fundere*, to pour out, melt.]

1. a fusing; a melting or melting together.

2. (a) the union of different things by or as if by melting; a blending; coalition; as, a *fusion* of political parties; (b) the state or fact of being so united.

3. anything made by fusing.

4. in biology, the union of parts usually separated.

5. in optics, the act of bringing the eyes in visual line so that the rays from a single point fall on corresponding localities in each eye and are conveyed to a single visual center, producing the impression of one.

watery fusion; the melting of a crystal in its water of crystallization by heat.

fū′ṣion·iṣm, *n.* in politics, the support of a coalition of parties or factions.

fū′ṣion·ist, *n.* an adherent of fusionism or a participant in a political fusion.

fū′ṣion·ist, *a.* of fusionism or fusionists.

fū′soid, *a.* same as *fusiform*.

fū′sŏme, *a.* handsome; neat; notable. [Brit. Dial.]

fuss, *n.* [17th-c. slang, prob. echoic, used esp. in phr. *keep a fuss with* (now, make a fuss about).]

1. a bustle; unnecessary activity about trivial matters; a nervous, excited state.

2. a fussy person.

Syn.—stir, excitement, tumult, worry, ado, bustle, flurry, fidget.

fuss, *v.i.*; fussed (fust), *pt., pp.*; fussing, *ppr.* to bustle about or worry, especially over trifles.

fuss, *v.t.* to bother or worry with trifling matters; to make uncomfortable. [Colloq.]

fuss′bąll, *n.* same as *fuzzball*.

fuss′-budġ″et, *n.* [*fuss* and *budget*, prob. in sense of "bag, sack."] a fussy person. [Colloq.]

fuss′i·ly, *adv.* with much ado.

fuss′i·ness, *n.* the quality of being fussy.

fuss′ŏck, *n.* a large, fleshy woman. [Brit. Dial.]

fuss′y, *a.*; *comp.* fussier; *superl.* fussiest. 1. habitually fussing; bustling about or worrying over trifles.

2. showing or needing careful attention.

3. full of details, especially if unnecessary or showy.

fust, *v.i.* to become moldy or fusty. [Obs.]

fust, *n.* [OFr. *fusté*, fusty, tasting of the cask, from *fuste*, a cask.] a strong, musty smell. [Brit. Dial.]

fust, *n.* [OFr. *fust, fuist*, a stick, shaft, tree, from L. *fustis*, a knobbed stick, club.] in architecture, the shaft of a column from the astragal to the capital.

fus·tȧ·nelle′, fus·tȧ·nel′lȧ, *n.* [LL. *fustanella*, from *fustianum*, a fustian.] a short white petticoat sometimes worn by men in modern Greece.

fus′tee, fus′tie, *n.* [W. Ind.] the offspring of a white person and an octoroon.

fus′tẽr·iç, *n.* the coloring matter of the shrub fustet.

fus′tet, *n.* [Fr. *fustet*; LL. *fustetus*, a tree, from L. *fustis*, a stick.]

1. the wood of the *Rhus cotinus*, or Venice sumac.

2. the tree itself.

fus′tiăn (-chăn), *n.* [ME. *fustian*; OFr. *fustaine*, from LL. *fustianum, fustanum*, fustian; prob. from *fustis*, wooden stick, transl. of Gr. *xylinon*, wooden.]

1. originally, a coarse cloth of cotton and linen.

2. now, a coarse, twilled cotton stuff, as corduroy, velveteen, etc.

3. an inflated style of talking or writing; bombast; rant; high-sounding nonsense.

fus′tiăn, *a.* 1. made of fustian.

2. pompous; ridiculously tumid; bombastic; pretentious but empty.

fus′tiăn·ist, *n.* one who writes bombast.

fus′tiç, *n.* [Fr. *fustoc*; Sp. *fustoc*, fustic, fustet, from LL. *fustis*, a tree, L. *fustis*, a stick.]

1. a tropical American tree, *Maclura tinctoria*, of the mulberry family, from whose wood a yellow dye is extracted.

2. the dye.

3. any of several other woods from which dyes are extracted.

fus'ti·gāte, *v.t.*; fustigated, *pt., pp.*; fustigating, *ppr.* [L. *fustigatus*, pp. of *fustigare*, to beat with a stick, from *fustis*, a stick.] to beat with a stick or club.

fus·ti·gā'tion, *n.* [L. *fustigatio*, from *fustigare*, to beat with a cudgel, from *fustis*, a stick or club.] punishment by beating with a stick or club, inflicted on freemen in ancient Rome.

fust'i·lug, fust'i·lugs, *n.* a gross, fat, unwieldy person. [Obs.]

fus'tin, *n.* a yellow dyestuff from young fustic.

fust'i·ness, *n.* a fusty state or quality.

fust'y, *a.*; *comp.* fustier; *superl.* fustiest, 1. moldy; musty; ill-smelling; rank; rancid.
 2. not up-to-date; old-fashioned.
 3. melancholy; listless. [Obs.]

futch'ell, *n.* [origin unknown.] in a carriage, a timber that supports the shafts or pole.

fu'thärk, *n.* [from its first six letters: *f, u, th, o (-a), r, c (-k)*.] the runic alphabet: formerly also *futharc, futhorc, futhork*.

fū'tile, *a.* [Fr. *futile*, from L. *futilis*, that easily pours out, from the root of *fundere*, to pour.]
 1. useless; ineffectual; vain.
 2. trifling; of no weight or importance; worthless.
 3. talkative; loquacious; tattling. [Obs.]

fū'tile·ly, *adv.* in a futile manner.

fū·til·i·tăr'i·ăn, *a.* based on or having the belief that everything in life is futile.

fū·til·i·tăr'i·ăn, *n.* a person who believes that everything in life is futile.

fū·til'i·ty, *n.* [L. *futilitas*, emptiness, vanity, from *futilis*, that easily pours out.]
 1. the quality of being useless or ineffectual.
 2. the quality of being frivolous or unimportant.
 3. something futile.
 4. talkativeness; loquaciousness. [Obs.]

fū'til·ous, *a.* worthless; trifling. [Obs.]

fut'tŏck, *n.* [perhaps a corruption of *foot hook*.] one of the upright curved timbers forming the ribs of a wooden ship.

fut'tŏck hoop, a band around a mast for holding the futtock shrouds.

fut'tŏck plāte, one of the iron plates put horizontally around the top of a ship's lower mast to hold the futtock shrouds.

fut'tŏck shrouds, short, stout iron rods connecting the futtock plates with the mast below.

fū'tūr·ăl, *a.* of the future or futures.

fū'tūre, *a.* [ME. *future*; OFr. *futur*, from L. *futurus*, about to be, fut. part. of *esse*, to be.]
 1. that is to be or come; of days, months, or years ahead.
 2. in grammar, indicating time to come; as, the *future* tense of a verb.
 Syn.—forthcoming, coming, advenient, oncoming.

fū'tūre, *n.* 1. time to come; days, months, or years ahead; as, the *future* shall be as the present; in *future*; for the *future*.
 2. what is going to be; what will happen; as, no one can foretell the *future*.
 3. the prospective or potential condition of a person or thing; chance to achieve, succeed, etc.; as, he has a great *future* in politics.
 4. [*pl.*] anything bought or sold to be delivered or received in time to come.
 5. in grammar, (a) the future tense; (b) a verb form in this tense.

fū'tūre·less, *a.* without hope of any better fortune in the future; unfortunate.

fū'tūre life, in religion, the state of the soul after death.

fū'tūre·ly, *adv.* in time to come. [Obs.]

fū'tūre pẽr'fect tense, 1. a tense indicating an action or state as completed in relation to a specified time in the future.
 2. a verb form in this tense (e.g., will have gone, shall have said).

fū'tūre shock, [after the book *Future Shock* (1970) by A. Toffler.] a sudden awareness of one's inaccurate evaluation of the future and the resulting inability to cope with the rapid and myriad changes of modern society.

fū'tūr·ism, *n.* a movement in art, literature, music, etc., shortly before and during World War I, which opposed traditionalism and tried to depict dynamic movement by the elimination of conventional form, balance, and rhythm and by stressing the violence and speed of the machine age.

fū'tūr·ist, *n.* 1. an adherent of futurism.
 2. a person who believes certain Biblical prophecies will be fulfilled in the future.

fū"tūr·is'tic, *a.* of or having to do with the future or futurism.

fū·tū·ri'tion (-rish'un), *n.* the state of being to come or to exist in the future. [Rare.]

fū·tū'ri·ty, *n.*; *pl.* **fū·tū'ri·ties,** 1. future time; time to come.
 2. event or condition to come.
 3. the state of being future.
 4. a futurity race.

fū·tū'ri·ty rāce, a race, usually a horse race, in which the contestants are selected long beforehand.

fū·tū'ri·ty stākes, 1. stakes competed for in a futurity race.
 2. a futurity race.

fūze, *n.* a fuse.

fūze, *v.t.* and *v.i.*; fuzed, *pt., pp.*; fuzing, *ppr.* to fuse.

fū·zee', *n.* a fusee.

fuzz, *n.* fine, light particles of down, wool, etc.; fine hairs or fibers.
 the fuzz; [perh. from *fuss*, in sense "a fussy (i.e., hard to please) person."] a policeman or the police. [Slang.]

fuzz, *v.t.* and *v.i.* to cover or become covered with fuzz.

fuzz'ball, *n.* a large fungus which, when pressed, bursts and scatters a fine dust: called also *giant puffball*.

fuzz'i·ly, *adv.* in a fuzzy manner.

fuzz'i·ness, *n.* the quality or condition of being fuzzy.

fuzz'y, *a.*; *comp.* fuzzier; *superl.* fuzziest, 1. of, like, or covered with fuzz.
 2. not clear; blurred.

-fȳ, [ME. *-fyen, -fien*; OFr. *-fier*; L. *ficare*, from *facere*, to make, do.] a suffix used to form verbs, meaning: (a) *to make, cause to be* or *become*, as in lique*fy*, dei*fy*; (b) *to cause to have, imbue with*, as in digni*fy*, glori*fy*; (c) *to become*, as in emulsi*fy*, putre*fy*.

fȳce, *n.* same as *fice*.

fȳke, *n.* [D. *fuik*, a bow net.] a long bag net used as a fish trap: called also *fyke net*.

fȳke, *n., v.i.* and *v.t.* same as *fike*.

fyl'fot, *n.* [from *fill* and *foot*: so called because used to fill the foot of a colored window.] a heraldic and religious symbol variously used as a secret emblem and also as an ornament: called also *gammadion* and *swastika*.

fyrd, *n.* [AS. *fyrd, fierd, ferd*, an army, expedition.] in Anglo-Saxon history, the national military force, including all males qualified to bear arms.

fyr'dung, *n.* [from AS. *fyrd*, an army, expedition.] in Anglo-Saxon history, the national army, or fyrd, under arms and prepared for war.

fytte, *n.* a fit (division of a long poem). [Obs.]

G

G, g (jē) *n.*; *pl.* **G's, g's, Gs, gs,** 1. the seventh letter of the English alphabet: from the Latin.
 2. a sound of G or g.
 3. a type or impression for G or g.
 4. *a symbol for* the seventh in a sequence or group.

G, g (jē), *a.* 1. of G or g.
 2. seventh in a sequence or group.

G (jē), *n.* 1. a Roman numeral for 400: with a superior bar ($\bar{G}$), 400,000.
 2. [from *grand*, slang term for **$**1,000.] one thousand dollars. [Slang.]
 3. in education, a grade of *good*.
 4. in music, (a) the fifth tone or note in the scale of C major, or the seventh in the scale of A minor; (b) a key, string, etc. producing this tone; (c) the scale having G as the keynote.

G (jē), *a.* shaped like G.
 G clef; the treble clef.

gab, *v.i.*; gabbed, *pt., pp.*; gabbing, *ppr.* [ME. *gabben*, to talk idly, to jest, from Ice. *gabba*, to mock, make game of one.]
 1. to talk much or idly; to chatter. [Colloq.]
 2. to jest; to lie. [Obs.]

gab, *n.* talkativeness; loquaciousness; chatter. [Colloq.]
 gift of (the) gab; the ability to speak fluently; eloquence.

gab, *n.* [Dan. *gab*; Sw. *gap*, the mouth; so called because the *gab* is open to receive whatever is placed within it.] the hook on the eccentric rod of a steam engine, which engages the rockshaft pin.

gab, *v.i.* to project like a tooth or tusk; as, to *gab* from the mouth. [Obs.]

gab, *v.t.* to tell lies. [Obs.]

gab·ăr·dine', *n.* [var. of *gaberdine*.]
 1. a gaberdine.
 2. a woolen sergelike cloth, twilled on one side only and used for suits, coats, etc.
 3. a cotton or rayon cloth resembling woolen gabardine, especially in its weave.

gab'bẽr, *n.* 1. a liar. [Obs.]
 2. one who prates or talks idly. [Colloq.]

gab'ble, *v.i.*; gabbled, *pt., pp.*; gabbling, *ppr.* [from *gab* and *-le*, freq. suffix.]
 1. to prate; to talk fast and incoherently.
 Such a rout, and such a rabble,
 Run to hear Jack Pudding *gabble*.—Swift.
 2. to utter inarticulate sounds with rapidity; as, *gabbling* fowls.

gab'ble, *v.t.* to utter rapidly and incoherently.

gab'ble, *n.* 1. loud or rapid talk without meaning.
 2. inarticulate sounds rapidly uttered, as of fowls.

gab'blẽr, *n.* a prater; a noisy talker; one who utters inarticulate sounds.

gab'bling, *n.* rapid, indistinct utterance; babble.

gab'brō, *n.* [It., from L. *glaber*, bare, smooth.] any of a group of dark, heavy, igneous rocks, composed chiefly of pyroxene and feldspar.

gab'by, *a.*; *comp.* gabbier; *superl.* gabbiest, talkative; inclined to chatter. [Colloq.]

gȧ·belle', *n.* [Fr.; It. *gabella*; Ar. *gabālah*.] a tax levied in certain countries; especially, a tax on salt, levied in France before the Revolution of 1789.

gȧ·belle'man, *n.*; *pl.* **gȧ·belle'men,** a tax-collector; a gabeller. [Rare.]

gȧ·bell'ẽr, *n.* a collector of the gabelle. [Rare.]

gab·ẽr·dïne', *n.* [earlier *gawbardyne*; OFr. *galvardine*, from M.H.G. *walvart*, a pilgrimage.]
 1. a loose coat or cloak of coarse cloth, worn in the Middle Ages, especially by Jews.
 2. gabardine.

gab·ẽr·lun'zie, *n.* [Scot.; printing form of *gaberlunyie*; earlier also *gaberloonie*; prob. from Scot. Gaelic.] a wandering beggar. [Scot.]

gā'bi·ŏn, *n.* [OFr. *gabion*; It. *gabbione*, a large cage, from *gabbia*, coop, from L. *cavea*, a hollow place, a cave, a cage.]
 1. a cylinder of wicker filled with earth or stones, formerly used in building fortifications.
 2. a similar cylinder of metal, used in building dams, foundations, etc.

gā"bi·ŏn·āde', *n.* [Fr. *gabionnade*, from It. *gabbionata*, an intrenchment of gabions, from *gabbione*, a gabion.]
 1. in military engineering, a parapet pro-

tected by gabions, or a work formed chiefly of gabions.

2. in hydraulic engineering, any structure composed of gabions, as a dam sunk in a stream to control the current.

gā′bi·ŏn·ăġe, *n.* an arrangement of gabions as a part of a fortification.

gā′bi·ŏned, *a.* protected by or made of gabions.

gā′ble (-bl), *n.* [ME.; OFr.; prob. from ON. *gaff*, gable.]

1. (a) the triangular wall enclosed by the sloping ends of a ridged roof; (b) popularly, the whole section, including wall, roof, and space enclosed.

2. the end wall of a building, the upper part of which is a gable.

3. a triangular decorative feature in architecture, such as that over a door or window.

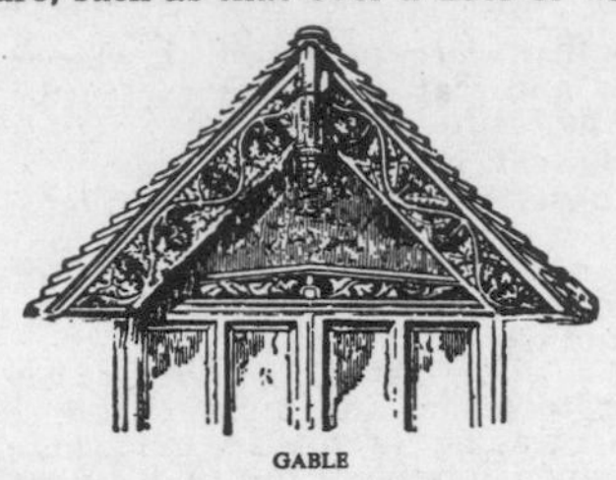

GABLE

gā′ble, *v.t.*; gabled, *pt., pp.*; gabling, *ppr.* to put a gable or gables on.

gā′ble, *v.i.* to be in the form of, or end in, a gable.

gā′ble end, the end of a building which is surmounted by a gable.

gā′ble rọof, in architecture, a ridged roof with a gable at its end or ends.

gā′blet, *n.* a small ornamented gable or canopy formed over a niche or buttress.

gā′ble wạll, the wall on which a gable rests.

gā′ble win′dōw, in architecture, a window in a gable or a window that is gable-shaped at the top.

gab′lock, *n.* [ME. *gaveloc*; AS. *gafeluc*, a spear, a javelin.] the metal spur of a gamecock.

Gā′bri·el, *n.* in the Bible, one of the seven archangels, the angel of the Annunciation and the herald of good news and comfort: Luke i. 26. Dan. viii. ix.

Gā′bri·el·īte, *n.* in ecclesiastical history, an Anabaptist sect founded in 1530 in Pomerania: so called from its founder, Gabriel Scherling.

gā′by, *n.*; *pl.* **gā′bieṣ,** [from Brit. Midland dial.; perh. echoic formation, from *gape, gaup*, after *baby*.] a foolish person; simpleton. [Colloq.]

Gad, *n.* 1. in the Bible, a son of Jacob.

2. a tribe of Israel descended from him.

3. the land where this tribe lived.

Gad, gad, *interj.* a mild oath or expression of surprise, disgust, etc.: a euphemism for *God.*

gad, *n.* [ME. *gad, gadde*; AS. *gad*, a goad.]

1. a sharp-pointed rod or pricking instrument; a goad; the point of a spear or arrowhead.

2. anything that goads; as, the *gad* of poverty.

3. a wedge-shaped bar or ingot of metal.

4. in mining, a metal-pointed punch to break up ore or stone.

5. an instrument of punishment, as a stick or rod. [Colloq.]

under the gad; under compulsion.

upon the gad; upon sudden impulse. [Obs.]

gad, *v.i.*; gadded, *pt., pp.*; gadding, *ppr.* to walk about; to rove or ramble idly or without any fixed purpose; to straggle in growth; to roam abroad for diversion; as, the *gadding* vine; a *gadding* woman.

gad, *v.t.* to get out by the use of gads, as ore.

gad′ȧ·bout, *n.* a person who gads about; one who goes about looking for fun, excitement, etc. [Colloq.]

gad′ȧ·bout, *a.* fond of gadding.

gad′bee, *n.* the gadfly.

gad′bụsh, *n.* in botany, the West Indian mistletoe.

gad′dẽr, *n.* 1. one who gads.

2. in mining, a traveling machine that drills the holes for the gads.

gad′ding, *n.* the act of roving about idly.

gad′ding çär, in mining, the car that carries a gadder.

gad′ding·ly, *adv.* in a gadding manner; rovingly.

gad′dish, *a.* inclined to gad.

gad′dish·ness, *n.* the quality of being gaddish.

gāde, *n.* [LL. *gadus*, the codfish.] in zoology, (a) any fish allied to the family *Gadidæ*, including the cod, hake, rockling, and haddock; (b) in Scotland, the pike.

gad′flȳ, *n., pl.* **gad′flīeṣ,** 1. an insect that goads or stings cattle, as a horsefly.

2. a person who annoys or irritates others.

gadġ′et, *n.* [from engineering jargon; perh. suggested by Scot. *gadge*, form of *gauge*, measuring device, and *-et*, dim. suffix.]

1. any small mechanical contrivance or device.

2. any small object, especially something relatively useless or superfluous.

3. in glassmaking, a spring clip.

Gȧ·dhel′iç (-del′), *adj.* and *n.* Goidelic.

gad′iç, *a.* same as *gadinic.*

gā′did, *n.* [from Mod. L. *Gadidæ*, name of the family, from *gadus*, cod, from Gr. *gados*, kind of fish.] any fish of the cod family, as the cod, haddock, pollack, etc.

Gad′i·dae, *n.pl.* [LL. *gadus*, the cod, from Gr. *gados*, a certain fish.] a family of fishes whose rounded fins are without spines, the cod (*Gadus*) being the type.

gad·in′iç, *a.* pertaining to or derived from the codfish; as, *gadinic* oil.

gad′i·nin, *n.* [LL. *gadus*, cod.] a slightly poisonous substance formed in putrescent fish, particularly codfish.

Gad·i·tā′ni·ăn, *a.* [L. *Gaditanus*, from *Gades*, Cadiz, Spain.] pertaining to the city of Cadiz (ancient Gades), Spain.

gad′ling, *n.* 1. a small gad or spike on armor.

2. one who gads about; a vagabond. [Obs.]

gad′-nāil, *n.* a large nail. [Brit. Dial.]

gā′doid, *a.* [LL. *gadus*, the cod, and Gr. *eidos*, form.] pertaining to the *Gadidæ.*

gā′doid, *n.* a fish of the family *Gadidæ.*

gad·ō·lin′i·ȧ, *n.* [named after Johan *Gadolin*, 18th-c. Finnish chemist.] in chemistry, an oxide of gadolinium.

gad·ō·lin′iç, *a.* pertaining to gadolinium.

gad′ō·lin·īte, *n.* a brown or black silicate mineral, containing some metals of the rare-earth group in combination with iron.

gad·ō·lin′i·um, *n.* a chemical element of the rare-earth group: symbol Gd; atomic weight, 156.9; atomic number 64.

gȧ·drọon′, go·drọon′, *n.* [Fr. *godron*, from *goder*, to crease, pucker.] any of various oval-shaped beadings, flutings, or reedings used to decorate molding, silverware, etc.

gadṣ′măn, *n.*; *pl.* **gadṣ′men,** one who uses a gad; a driver of cattle.

gad′-steel, *n.* a Flemish steel manufactured in the shape of wedges or gads.

gad′ū·in, *n.* [LL. *gadus*, a codfish.] a yellow amorphous compound found in cod-liver oil.

gad′u·ōl, *n.* an alcoholic extract of cod-liver oil.

Gā′dus, *n.* [L., from Gr. *gados*, a fish.] the typical genus of the family *Gadidæ*, including the common cod, the haddock, whiting, hake, ling, etc.

gad′wạll, *n.*; *pl.* **gad′wạllṣ** or **gad′wạll,** a gray duck, *Anas strepera*, living in the northern fresh-water regions of America.

gad·zooks′, *interj.* [from *God's hooks*, nails of the Cross.] a mild oath or expletive. [Archaic.]

> But the money, *gadzooks*, must be paid in an hour. —Prior.

gāe, *v.i.* to go. [Scot.]

gāe, *v.* past tense of *give.* [Scot.]

Ġae′ȧ, *n.* in Greek mythology, the earth personified as a goddess, mother of Uranus, the Titans, etc.; Mother Earth: identified by the Romans with Tellus: also *Gaia, Ge.*

Gaek′wäd (gīk′, jēk′), *n.* Geakwar.

Gaek′wär (gīk′, jēk′), *n.* [Prakrit *Gāekvād*, name of the family (lit., cowherd).] the title of the native prince ruling Baroda, India: also *Gaikwar.*

Gāel, *n.* [contr. from Gael. *Gaidheal.*] a Celt of Scotland, Ireland, or the Isle of Man; especially, a Celt of the Scottish Highlands.

Gāel′iç, *a.* [from Gael. *Gaidhealach.*]

1. of the Gaels.

2. of the Goidelic subfamily of languages or its components; especially, of Scottish Gaelic.

Gāel′iç, *n.* 1. the Goidelic subfamily of languages.

2. one of these languages, especially that of the Scottish Highlands (*Scottish Gaelic*).

gaff, *n.* [ME. and MFr. *gaffe*, prob. of Celt. origin; cf. Ir. *gaf, gafa*, a hook.]

1. a large, strong hook on a pole, or a barbed spear, used in landing large fish.

2. a sharp metal spur fastened to the leg of a gamecock.

3. [earlier in sense of "fair": prob. from fact that visitors were *gaffed* there.] a cheap theater, dance hall, etc. [British Slang.]

4. a spar or pole extending diagonally upward from the after side of a mast and supporting a fore-and-aft sail.

to stand the gaff; to bear up well under difficulties, punishment, ridicule, etc.; to be game. [Slang.]

gaff, *v.t.*; gaffed (gaft), *pt., pp.*; gaffing, *ppr.* 1. to strike or secure with a gaff; as, to *gaff* a salmon.

2. to cheat; hoax; trick. [Brit. Slang.]

gȧffe, *n.* [Fr.] a blunder; faux pas.

gaf′fẽr, *n.* [altered from *godfather.*]

1. an old man, especially one from the country: often used contemptuously or humorously.

2. a foreman of a group of workers. [Brit.]

gaf′fle, *n.* [D. *gaffel*, a fork, pitchfork; AS. *geafl*, a fork.]

1. same as *gaff*, sense 2.

2. a steel lever to bend crossbows. [Archaic.]

gaff″-top′sāil (-sl *or* -sāl), *n.* 1. a light triangular or quadrilateral sail set above a gaff.

2. in zoology, a sea catfish, *Ælurichthys marinus*, having a high and pointed fin on the back.

gag, *v.t.*; gagged, *pt., pp.*; gagging, *ppr.* [ME. *gaggen*; of echoic origin.]

1. to cause to retch or choke.

2. to put something over or into the mouth of, so as to keep from talking, crying out, etc.; hence, to keep (a person) from speaking or expressing himself freely, by intimidation, etc.

> The time was not yet come when eloquence was to be *gagged* and reason to be hoodwinked. —Macaulay.

3. to prevent or limit speech in (a legislative body).

4. to pry or keep open by means of a gag.

> Mouths *gagged* to such a wideness. —Fortescue.

5. in stage slang, to introduce gags into; as, to *gag* a part.

6. in mechanics, to choke or stop up (a valve, etc.).

gag, *v.i.* 1. to retch or choke.

2. to interpolate gags in acting. [Slang.]

gag, *n.* 1. something thrust into or over the mouth to hinder speaking, crying out, etc.

2. a device for holding open the mouth, as in dentistry.

3. figuratively, any restraint upon freedom of speech.

4. a choking mouthful. [Rare.]

5. (a) a joke, especially one with an unexpected turn; (b) a practical joke; hoax or bit of comic business, as on the stage.

6. a serranoid food fish, *Nycteroperca microlepis*, of the Florida and Cuban coast.

7. a strong bit for breaking in a horse.

gag′āte, *n.* jet. [Obs.]

gāġe, *n.* and *v.* same as *gauge.*

gāġe, *n.* [ME. *gage*; OFr. *gage*, a gage, pledge, pawn, from LL. *vadium*; Goth. *wadi*, a surety, pledge, bail.]

1. something deposited or pledged to insure that an obligation will be fulfilled; security.

> The sheriff is commanded to attach him by taking *gage*: that is, certain of his goods, which he shall forfeit if he doth not appear. —Blackstone.

2. the act of pledging or the state of being pledged; security; pawn.

> I was fain to borrow these spurs; I have left my gown in *gage* for them. —B. Jonson.

3. anything thrown down as a token of challenge to combat. Formerly it was customary for the challenger to cast on the ground a glove, a cap, a gauntlet, or the like, which was taken up by the accepter of the challenge.

4. a challenge.

gāġe, *v.t.*; gaged, *pt., pp.*; gaging, *ppr.* 1. to offer as a pledge; to pawn; to give or deposit as a pledge or security; to wage or wager. [Archaic.]

> Against the which, a moiety competent
> Was *gaged* by our king. —Shak.

2. to bind by a pledge; to engage. [Archaic.]

gāġe, *n.* [after Sir William *Gage*, about 1725.] any of several varieties of plum: see *greengage.*

Gā′ġē·ȧ, *n.* [L., after the botanist, Sir Thomas *Gage.*] a genus of small plants of the lily family, found in central Asia and Europe.

găg′ẽr, *n.* same as *gauger.*

găg′gẽr, *n.* 1. one who gags.

2. in molding, a lifter consisting of a light T-shaped piece of iron; also, an iron used to hold in position the core of a mold or to keep the sand of a mold from breaking apart.

gag'gle, *v.i.*; gaggled, *pt., pp.*; gaggling, *ppr.* [echoic; compare D. *gaggelen*, to cackle; Ice. *gagl*, a wild goose.] to make a noise like a goose.

gag'gle, *n.* a flock of geese; hence, a chattering company.

A *gaggle* of geese . . . a *gaggle* of women. —Strutt.

gag man, a man who devises jokes, bits of comic business, etc., as for professional comedians.

gag rein, a rein intended to draw the bit into the corners of the horse's mouth.

gag'root, *n.* a powerful emetic, *Lobelia inflata*: commonly called *Indian tobacco*.

gag rūle (or **law**), a rule or law limiting or preventing discussion; as, in 1836 Congress adopted a *gag rule* to prevent discussion of anything relating to slavery.

gag'tooth, *n.*; *pl.* **gag'teeth,** a tooth which protrudes. [Obs.]

gag'toothed (tootht), *a.* having a gagtooth or gagteeth. [Obs.]

gähn'īte (gän'), *n.* [after J. Gottlieb *Gahn* (1745–1818), a Swedish chemist.] a zinc aluminate, $ZnAl_2O_4$, found as almost opaque crystals of green, brown, or black.

Gāi'à, *n.* Gaea; Ge.

gā'iac (-yak), *n.* same as *guaiac*.

gā·id'ic, *a.* [Gr. *gaia*, earth.] designating or of a colorless, crystalline acid, $C_{16}H_{30}O_2$, derived from and isomeric with hypogeic acid.

gāi'e·ty, *n.*; *pl.* **gāi'e·ties,** [Fr. *gaieté*, gaiety, from *gai*, gay.]

1. the state or quality of being gay; cheerfulness; lively merriment.

2. merrymaking; lively entertainment; festivity.

3. finery; bright appearance; showy display; as, *gaiety* of plumage.

Also spelled *gayety*.

Syn.—animation, vivacity, liveliness, sprightliness, buoyancy.

Gaik'wär, *n.* same as *Gaekwar*.

gāil'lärd, *a.* same as *galliard*.

Gāil·lär'di·à, *n.* [Mod. L., after the Fr. botanist *Gaillard* de Marentonneau.]

1. a genus of American composite plants having large, showy flower heads with yellow or reddish rays and purple disks.

2. [g-] any plant of this genus.

gāil·liärde' (gāl-yärd'), *n.* same as *galliard*.

gāi'ly, *adv.* [ME. *gaily*, *gaili*, from *gay*; OFr. *gai*, gay.]

1. splendidly; brightly; with finery or showiness; as, to be dressed *gaily*.

2. joyfully; merrily; in a gay manner.

Wights, who travel that way daily,
Jog on by his example *gaily*. —Swift.

Also spelled *gayly*.

gāin, *a.* [ME. *gayn*, *gein*, from ON. *gegn*, straight, favorable, helpful.]

1. near; straight: said of roads. [Obs. except Brit. Dial.]

2. ready; well disposed; kindly. [Obs. except. Brit. Dial.]

3. available; convenient. [Obs. except Brit. Dial.]

gāin, *v.t.*; gained, *pt., pp.*; gaining, *ppr.* [ME. *gainen*, *gaynen*, to profit, be of use, from OFr. *gaaignier*, from O.H.G. hyp. *weidanjan*, to work, gain, from *weidenon*, to pasture, from *weide*, pasture.]

1. to obtain by industry or the employment of capital; to get, as profit or advantage; to earn; as, to *gain* a good living; money *gains* six per cent.

What is a man profited, if he shall *gain* the whole world, and lose his own soul? —Matt. xvi. 26.

2. to win; to obtain by effort or merit, as in competition; as, to *gain* a battle or a victory; to *gain* a prize; to *gain* a cause in law.

3. to obtain; to acquire; to procure; to receive; as, to *gain* favor; to *gain* reputation.

4. to obtain as an increase, addition, profit, or advantage; as, to *gain* time; to *gain* ten pounds in weight.

5. to draw into any interest or party; to win to one's side; to conciliate.

To gratify the queen and *gain* the court. —Dryden.

6. to reach; to attain; to arrive at; as, to *gain* the top of a mountain; to *gain* a good harbor.

gained day; the day which a traveler gains in circumnavigating the globe from west to east.

to gain ground; to advance in any undertaking; to prevail; to acquire strength or extent; to increase.

to gain over; to win over to one's side.

to gain the wind; among sailors, to arrive on the windward side of another ship.

Syn.—win, get, acquire, obtain, earn, conquer, master, procure, attain, reach, achieve, realize.—*Gain* implies that we get something by exertion; *win*, that we do it in competition with others.

gāin, *v.i.* to acquire advantage or profit; to improve or advance, as in health, business, etc.; to make progress.

to gain on; (a) to draw nearer to (an opponent in a race, etc.); (b) to make more progress than a competitor.

gāin, *n.* [ME. *gain*, *gein*; OFr. *gain*, *gaaigne*, from *gaaignier*, to cultivate.]

1. an increase; addition; specifically, (a) [*often in pl.*] an increase in wealth, earnings, etc.; profit; winnings; (b) an increase in advantage; improvement. Opposed to *loss*.

But what things were *gain* to me, those I counted loss for Christ. —Philip. iii. 7.

2. the act of getting something; acquisition; accumulation; as, a clear *gain*; a *gain* in speed or weight.

gāin, *n.* [probably from *gain* (increase) with special technical application of sense of "addition."] in carpentry, a joining notch, groove, or mortise.

gāin, *v.t.* in carpentry, to make a notch or groove in; fasten or join by, or fit into, such a groove or notch.

gāin-, [ME. *gain-*; AS. *gegn-*.] a prefix signifying *back, again, against*, as in *gainsay, gainstrive*.

gāin'à·ble, *a.* that can be obtained, reached, won over, or accomplished.

gāin'ăge, *n.* [ME. *gainage*; Anglo-Fr. *gaignage*, from *gaagnier*, to cultivate.]

1. in feudal law, the horses, oxen, wagons, and implements for carrying on tillage.

2. the produce of the land itself, or the profit made by cultivation: also called *wainage*. [Obs.]

gāin'ẽr, *n.* 1. one who gains or obtains profit, interest, or advantage.

2. a fancy dive executed from a front take-off position: the diver performs a back somersault in the air, entering the water feet first.

full gainer; in fancy diving, a *gainer* as distinguished from a *half gainer*.

half gainer; a fancy dive executed from a front take-off position; the diver turns backward in the air, entering the water head first.

gāin'fụl, *a.* producing profit or advantage; advancing interest or happiness; productive of money; adding to the wealth or estate; lucrative.

gāin'fụl·ly, *adv.* with increase of wealth; profitably; advantageously.

gāin'fụl·ness, *n.* profitableness.

gāin'giv·ing, *n.* 1. a misgiving. [Archaic.]

It is but foolery, but it is such a kind of *gaingiving* as would, perhaps, trouble a woman. —Shak.

2. a giving back. [Obs.]

gāin'ing mà·chïne', a machine having a rotating saw, used for cutting gains, grooves, or mortises.

gāin'ing twist, in firearms, a twist or spiral inclination of the grooves, which increases rapidly from the breech toward the muzzle, increasing the rapidity of rotation of the projectile.

gāin'less, *a.* not producing gain; unprofitable; not bringing advantage.

gāin'less·ness, *n.* unprofitableness; want of advantage.

gāin'ly, *adv.* handily; readily; conveniently. [Obs.]

gāin'ly, *a.* [ME. *gaynly*, straight, ready.] handsome; well-formed and graceful; comely; as, a *gainly* youth.

gāin'pāin, *n.* [Fr. *gagne-pain*, lit., bread gainer; from *gagner*, to gain, and *pain*, from L. *panis*, bread.] a sort of gauntlet. [Obs.]

gāin·sāy', *v.t.*; gainsaid, *pt., pp.*; gainsaying, *ppr.* [ME. *geinseggen*; *gein-*, from AS. *gegn*, against, and *seggen*, say.]

1. to deny.

2. to contradict.

3. to speak or act against; oppose; forbid.

gāin'sāy, *n.* a gainsaying.

gāin·sāy'ẽr, *n.* one who contradicts or denies what is alleged; an opposer.

gāin·sāy'ing, *n.* contradiction; opposition; denial.

Gāins'bŏr·ōugh (-bŭr-ō), *n.* any painting by Thomas Gainsborough (1727–1788).

Gāins'bŏr·ōugh hat, a woman's hat with a very wide brim and usually ornamented with two or three large ostrich feathers: patterned after those represented by Gainsborough in his portraits of ladies.

gāin'sŏme, *a.* 1. gainful; bringing gain. [Obs.]

2. comely; well-formed. [Obs.]

'gainst, gainst (genst, gānst), *prep.* against. [Poet.]

gāin'stand, *v.t.* to withstand; oppose; resist. [Obs.]

And seek ye to *gainstand* the faith in God? —Bailey.

gāin'strīve, *v.t.* to resist; withstand; oppose. [Obs.]

The Fates *gainstrive* us not.—Grimoald.

gāir'fowl, *n.* same as *garefowl*.

gāir'ish, gāir'ish·ly, gāir'ish·ness, same as *garish*, etc.

gāit, *n.* [ME. *gate*; *gaite* (N. and Scot.); special application of ON. *gata*, path between hedges, street.]

1. a going; a walk; a march; a way. [Scot.]

2. any of the various foot movements of a horse, as a trot, pace, canter, or gallop.

3. manner of moving on foot; way of walking or running.

Part huge of bulk,
Wallowing unwieldly, enormous in their *gait*. —Milton.

gāit'ed, *a.* having a particular gait or manner of walking: used in hyphenated compounds, as slow-*gaited*, heavy-*gaited*.

gāi'tẽr, *n.* [Fr. *guêtre*.]

1. a cloth or leather covering for the instep and ankle, and, sometimes, the calf of the leg; a spat or legging.

2. a shoe with elastic in the sides and no lacing.

3. formerly, a variety of high-topped shoe.

gāi'tẽr, *v.t.*; gaitered, *pt., pp.*; gaitering, *ppr.* to dress with gaiters.

gāi'tẽr, *n.* the dogwood tree, *Cornus sanguinea*: called also *gaiter tree, gatten tree*, and *gattridge*. [Brit. Dial.]

gal, *n.* a girl. [Slang.]

gā'là (*or* gal'à, *or* gäl'à), *n.* [from Fr. and It.; Fr. *gala*; It. *gala*, from OFr. *gale*, enjoyment, pleasure, prob. from MD. *wale*, riches, wealth; akin to Eng. *weal*.]

1. a festive occasion; festival; celebration.

2. festivity. [Obs.]

in gala; in festive dress.

gā'là, *a.* festive; with festivities and merrymaking; suitable for a festive occasion.

gala day; a day of festivity; a holiday with rejoicings.

ga·lact'-, same as *galacto-*.

ga·lac'tà·gogue (-gog), *n.* [from Gr. *gala*, *galaktos*, milk, and Gr. *agōgos*, leading, from *agein*, to lead.] in medicine, a preparation that stimulates the secretion of milk.

ga·lac'tà·gogue, *a.* that stimulates the secretion of milk.

Ga·lac'ti·à, *n.* [L., from Gr. *gala* (*-aktos*), milk.] a genus of twining plants found chiefly in eastern and southern United States. The flowers are purple and borne in racemes. The common species are called *milk pea*.

ga·lac'tic, *a.* [Gr. *galaktikos*, milky, from *gala* (*-aktos*), milk.]

1. of or obtained from milk; lactic.

2. in astronomy, of the Milky Way, or Galaxy.

3. in medicine, of the flow of milk; helping or increasing the flow of milk.

galactic poles; the two opposite points of the heavens, situated at 90° from the great circle.

ga·lac'tin, ga·lac'tine, *n.* [Gr. *gala* (*-aktos*), milk, and *-ine*.]

1. a milky substance obtained from the sap of the cow tree of South America.

2. an amorphous substance, $C_{54}H_{78}O_{45}N_4$, derived from milk.

3. an amorphous substance, $C_6H_{10}O_5$, obtained from the seeds of leguminous plants.

ga·lac'to-, ga·lact'-, [Gr. *gala* (*-aktos*), milk.] a combining form signifying *milk, milky*, or *containing milk*, as in *galactocele, galactodendron*.

ga·lac'tō·cēle, *n.* [*galacto-*, and Gr. *kēlē*, a tumor.] a tumor of the breast caused by an obstruction of the lacteal glands.

ga·lac·tō·den'drŏn, *n.* [*galacto-*, and Gr. *dendron*, tree.] the cow tree of South America, belonging to the genus *Brosimum*.

ga·lac'toid, *a.* [Gr. *gala* (*-aktos*), milk, and *eidos*, form.] resembling milk.

gal·ac·tom'e·tẽr, *n.* [*galacto-*, and Gr. *metron*, a measure.] an instrument for determining the specific gravity, and hence the richness, of milk; a lactometer.

gal·ac·toph'à·ġist, *n.* [*galacto-*, and Gr. *pha-*

gein, to eat.] one who drinks or feeds on milk.

gal·ac·toph′ȧ·gous, *a.* feeding on milk.

gal·ac·toph′ō·rous, *a.* [Gr. *galaktophoros*, giving milk; *gala* (*-aktos*), milk, and *pherein*, to bear.] producing milk; conveying milk; lactiferous; as, *galactophorous* ducts.

ga·lac″tō·poi·et′iç, *a.* [*galacto-*, and Gr. *poiein*, to make.] tending to increase the flow of milk; causing the secretion of milk.

ga·lac″tō·poi·et′iç, *n.* any substance which tends to increase the secretion and flow of milk.

ga·lac·tor·rhē′ȧ, *n.* [*galacto-*, and Gr. *rhoē*, a flow, from *rhein*, to flow.] in medicine, a continued and excessive flow of milk.

ga·lac′tōse, *n.* [Gr. *gala* (*-aktos*), milk, and *-ose*.] a white, crystalline sugar, $C_6H_{12}O_6$, prepared by the hydrolysis of lactose.

gal·ac·tō′sis, *n.* [Gr. *galaktōsis*, a changing into milk, from *gala* (*-aktos*), milk.] in physiology, the process of secreting or producing milk.

gal·ac·tū′ri·ȧ, *n.* [Gr. *gala* (*-aktos*), milk, and *ouron*, urine.] same as *chyluria*.

Ga·lā′gō, *n.* [from the native name.]

1. a genus of African lemurs. The species, which are nocturnal in their habits, have long hind legs, large eyes, and large membranous ears. The great galago, *Galago crassicaudatus*, is as large as a rabbit. They live in trees, and are sought after as food.

2. [g–] *pl.* **ga·lā′gōṣ**, a member of the genus *Galago*.

gȧ·läh′, *n.* [from the native name.] the pink-breasted cockatoo of Australia.

Gal′ȧ·had, *n.* 1. in late Arthurian legend, a knight who was successful in the quest for the Holy Grail because of his purity and nobility of spirit: he was the son of Lancelot and Elaine.

2. any man regarded as very pure and noble.

gal′ȧ·lith, *n.* [Gr. *gala*, milk; and *-lith*.] an insulating material made from casein.

ga·lañ′găl, ga·lañ′gāle, *n.* same as *galingale*.

Ga·lan′thus, *n.* [Gr. *gala*, milk, and *anthos*, a flower.] a small genus of *Amaryllidaceæ*, represented by the snowdrop, *Galanthus nivalis*, and native to middle and southern Europe. They are herbaceous plants with bulbous roots, narrow leaves, and drooping, white, bell-shaped flowers.

gal′an·tīne, *n.* [OFr. *galentine*; ML. *galatina*, jelly, from L. *gelatus*, pp. of *gelare*, to congeal.] a mold of veal, chicken, or other white meat, boned, seasoned, boiled, and served cold in its own jelly.

ga·lan′ty shōw, [earlier also *galanté*; prob. from It. *galante*, gallant: from the stories portrayed.] a pantomime made by throwing the shadows of puppet figures on a screen or wall.

ga·lȧ·pā′gō, *n.* [Sp., a tortoise.] in medieval military operations, a covering or defense of large wooden shields so placed that the edges overlap, forming a defense similar to the Roman testudo.

gal′ȧ·pee tree, a small tree of the West Indies, *Sciadophyllum brownei*.

gal·ȧ·tē′ȧ, *n.* [after *Galatea*, name of an English warship: the fabric was used to make sailor suits for little boys.] a strong cotton cloth, usually striped, used chiefly for children's clothing.

Ga·lā′tiăn (-shăn), *a.* pertaining to Galatia, or the Galatians.

Ga·lā′tiăn, *n.* [L. *Galatia*; Gr. *Galatia*, Galatia.]

1. a native or inhabitant of Galatia in Asia Minor.

2. [*pl.*] the Epistle to the Galatians, a book of the New Testament which was a message from the Apostle Paul to the Christians of Galatia.

gā′lax, *n.* [Mod. L., from Gr. *gala*, milk: from its white flower.] an evergreen herb with shiny leaves and small, white flowers, found in mountain regions of the southeastern United States: the leaves are often used for wreaths and floral decorations.

gal′ax·y, *n.* [OFr. *galaxie*; L. *galaxias*; Gr. *galaxias*, the Milky Way, from *gala* (*-aktos*), milk.]

1. [*often* G–] the Milky Way, a grouping of millions of stars apparently merging into a luminous band that extends across the sky.

2. *pl.* **gal′ax·ieṣ**, any similar but smaller grouping of stars.

3. (a) an assembly of brilliant or famous people; (b) a brilliant array of things.

gal′bȧ·num, gal′băn, *n.* [L. *galbanum*; Gr. *chalbanē*; Heb. *khelb'nāh*, *chhĕlbenah*, galbanum, from *kheleb*, fatness.] a bitter, bad-smelling Asiatic gum resin, used in medicine and the arts.

gȧlbe, *n.* [Fr.] in art, the contour of the surface of a solid body; specifically, the contour of a vase or urn, a column, etc.

gal′bū·lus, *n.*; *pl.* **gal′bū·lī**, [L., the nut of the cypress tree.] in botany, a cone the scales of which are fleshy and combined into a uniform mass, as the fruit of the juniper.

Gal′chä, *n.* [from the native name.]

1. *pl.* **Gal′chä**, a member of a people living in the Pamirs, west central Asia: also called *Pamiri*.

2. their Iranian language: also called *Pamir*.

gāle, *n.* [prob. from Anglo-N. hyp. *gaul* (ON. *gol*), wind, blast of wind, with softened meaning as in Norw. *gul*, steady wind, moderate gale.]

1. a strong wind, especially one having a velocity between 25 and 75 miles an hour.

2. a breeze. [Poet.]

3. an outburst; as, a *gale* of laughter.

4. a state of pleasant excitement or hilarity. [Colloq.]

gāle, *v.i.* to sing; to cry out. [Obs.]

gāle, *n.* [ME. *gawl*; AS. *gagel*, a myrtle bush.] a hardy plant, *Myrica gale*, growing in Europe, Asia, and America in marshy places: also called *sweet gale*.

gāle, *n.* [ME. *gavel*; AS. *gafol*, tribute, tax.]

1. a periodical payment of rent, duty, interest, or custom; an installment of money. [Brit.]

2. in English law, the right of a free miner to work land for coal or iron in certain districts, as in the Forest of Dean.

gā′lē·ȧ, *n.*; *pl.* **gā′lē·ae**, [L., a helmet.]

1. in botany, the upper lip of an open corolla, or any similar helmetlike part.

2. in zoology, the outer lobe of the maxilla in mandibulate insects.

3. in anatomy, the structure of connective tissue of the scalp uniting the unjoined parts of the occipitfrontalis muscle.

4. in surgery, a kind of bandage which fits over the head.

5. [G–] in paleontology, a genus of sea-hedgehogs or echini, found in fossil form only: they are distinguished by an oval base, from which the shell rises in a vaulted, helmetlike form.

gal′ē·as, *n.* a galleass. [Obs.]

gā′lē·āte, gā′lē·ā·ted, *a.* [L. *galeatus*, pp. of *galeare*, to cover with a helmet, from *galea*, a helmet.]

1. covered with or wearing a helmet; capped by a helmet-shaped part.

2. in botany, having a flower like a helmet; helmet-shaped, as the monkshood and various other aconites.

gāle dāy, day on which rent is due. [Brit.]

gā·lee′, *n.* a miner who holds a gale in crown lands. [Brit. Dial.]

Ga·lē′gȧ, *n.* [Gr. *gala*, milk, and *agein*, to lead, induce.] a genus of tall, smooth, perennial leguminous herbs, mostly natives of the Mediterranean region.

Gā′lē·ī, *n.pl.* [Gr. *galeos*, a kind of shark with marks like a weasel, from *galeē*, a weasel.] a suborder of marine animals including the sharks.

gā′lē·id, *a.* pertaining to the *Galeidæ*.

gā′lē·id, *n.* a shark belonging to the *Galeidæ*.

Gȧ·lē′i·dae, *n.pl.* [*Gale*us and *-idæ*.] a family of small sharks including the dogfishes and topes.

gȧ·lē′i·form, *a.* [L. *galea*, a helmet, and *forma*, form.]

1. resembling a helmet in form.

2. resembling the *Galeidæ*.

gȧ·lē′nȧ, *n.* [L. *galena*, lead ore, the dross of melted lead; Gr. *galēnē*, lit., stillness of the sea, calm, anything that produces tranquillity; hence, an antidote to poison.]

1. in medicine, theriaca; an antidote for poison. [Obs.]

2. native lead sulfide, PbS, a lead-gray mineral with metallic lustre: it is the principal ore of lead, often also containing silver: also called *galenite*.

gȧ·len′iç, gȧ·len′iç·ăl, *a.* pertaining to or containing galena.

Gȧ·len′iç, gȧ·len′iç, *a.* [L. *Galenus*; Gr. *Galenos*, Galen, a physician and medical writer, born at Pergamum, 130 A.D.] relating to Galen or his principles and method of treating diseases; as, the *Galenic* remedies consist of preparation of herbs and roots by infusion, decoction, etc.

Gȧ·len′i·çăl, gȧ·len′i·çăl, *a.* same as *Galenic*.

Gā′len·iṣm, *n.* the doctrines of Galen.

Gā′len·ist, *n.* a follower of Galen in the preparation of medicine and mode of treating diseases.

These *Galenists* were what we should call herb doctors today. —O. W. Holmes.

gȧ·lē′nīte, *n.* same as *galena*, sense 2.

gā′lē·oid, *a.* resembling sharks of the family *Galeidæ*.

Gā″lē·ō·pi·thē′çus, *n.* [L., from Gr. *galeē*, a weasel, and *pithēkos*, an ape.] the flying lemur, a genus of East Indian tree-dwelling mammals related to the *Insectivora*. These animals have the bones of the arm and leg, but not those of the digits, excessively elongated and supporting extensive lateral folds of skin serviceable as a parachute, but not as organs of flight.

Gā·lē·op′sis, *n.* [L., from Gr. *galiopsis*, a nettle; *galeē*, a weasel, and *opsis*, appearance.] in botany, a genus of labiate herbs, native to Great Britain. *Galeopsis tetrahit* is the common hemp-nettle of the United States.

gȧ·lē′rȧ, *n.* [L. *galera*, or *galerum*, a cap, helmet.]

1. in zoology, a weasellike animal, the taira.

2. [G–] the genus of which the taira is the type.

gal·ēr·iç′ū·lāte, *a.* [L. *galericulum*, dim. of *galerum*, a helmetlike covering for the head, cap, from *galea*, a helmet.] covered with or as with a small hat or cap.

gal′ēr·īte, *n.* [L. *galeritus*, one wearing a cap, from *galerus*, *galerum*, a hat or cap.] a fossil echinus of the Chalk formation: so called from its having some resemblance to a hat.

GALERITES

gȧ·lette′, *n.* [Fr.] a thin cake; a buttered roll.

Gȧ·lē′us, *n.* the typical genus of the family *Galeidæ*.

gāle′wōrt, *n.* in botany, same as *gale*.

Gä·lï′bï, *n.* any member of a subdivision of Carib Indians living in the Guianas.

Gȧ·li′ciăn (-lish′un), *a.* 1. of Spanish Galicia, its people, or language.

2. of Polish Galicia or its people.

Gȧ·li′ciăn, *n.* 1. a native or inhabitant of Spanish Galicia.

2. the Portuguese dialect of the Spanish Galicians.

3. a native or inhabitant of Polish Galicia.

Gal·i·lē′ăn, *a.* pertaining or belonging to Galileo, the Italian astronomer and physicist (1564–1642); as, the *Galilean* telescope.

Galilean telescope; a telescope having a concave eyepiece.

Gal·i·lē′ăn, *a.* [L. *Galilæus*; Gr. *Galilaios*, of or pertaining to Galilee, from *Galilaia*, Galilee; Heb. *Galil*, Galilee, lit., a circle.] relating to Galilee, an ancient division of northern Palestine, or its people.

Last came, and last did go,
The pilot of the *Galilean* lake.—Milton.

Gal·i·lē′ăn, *n.* 1. a native or inhabitant of Galilee.

2. in Jewish history, one of a class among the Jews, during the reign of Augustus, who resisted the payment of tribute to Rome.

3. a Christian.

the Galilean; Jesus.

gal′i·lee, *n.* [OFr. *galilee*, from L. *Galilæa*; Gr. *Galilaia*, Galilee, Heb. *Galil*, Galilee, lit., a circle.] a porch or chapel at the west entrance of some medieval churches.

gal·i·mā′ti·ȧs (-shi-us), *n.* [Fr., nonsense, gibberish.] confused speech; jargon; nonsense; confused or nonsensical talk.

She ran into absurdities and a *galimatias* scarce credible. —Fielding.

gal·i·mē′tȧ wood, [a native name.] the wood of the white bully tree, *Dipholis salicifolia*, of the West Indies.

gal′in·gāle, *n.* [ME.; OFr. *galingal*; ML. *galanga*; Ar. *khalanjan*.]

1. the pungent, aromatic root stem of various East Indian plants of the ginger family.

2. a sedge with a pungent root, growing in the south of England; sweet sedge.

Also *galangal*, *galangale*.

gal·iŏn·gee′, *n.* [Turk. *qalyonji*, a man-of-war's-man, a sailor in the navy, from *qalyon*, a man-of-war.] a Turkish sailor.

All that a careless eye could see
In him was some young *Galiongee*.
—Byron.

gal′i·ŏt, gal′li·ŏt, *n.* [OFr. *galiote*; LL. *galeota*, dim. of *galea*, a galley.]

1. a small, swift galley moved both by sails and by oars, having one mast and sixteen or twenty seats for rowers: formerly used on the Mediterranean.

GALIOT

2. a Dutch or Flemish merchant ship with very rounded ribs and flattish bottom, with a mizzenmast placed near the stern, carrying a square mainsail and maintopsail, a forestay to the mainmast (there being no foremast), with forestaysail and jibs.

gal′i·pot, *n.* [Fr.] crude turpentine from certain pine trees of southern Europe: also spelled *gallipot*.

Gā′li·um, *n.* [L. *galion*; Gr. *galion*, galium, used in curdling milk, from *gala*, milk.] an extensive genus of plants belonging to the family *Rubiaceæ*. They have erect square stems, leaves in whorls, and small flowers, usually white. The roots of several species produce a dyestuff.

gall, *n.* [ME. *galle*; AS. *gealla*; perh. from L. *galla*, a gallnut, but prob. connected with OFr. *galle*, an itching, sore (of same origin).]

1. a sore on the skin caused by rubbing or chafing; especially, such a sore on a horse.

2. (a) irritation; annoyance; vexation; (b) a cause of this.

3. a spot worn bare; a flaw or weak spot.

gall, *v.t.*; galled, *pt.*, *pp.*; galling, *ppr.* 1. to wear away by friction; to excoriate; to hurt or break, as the skin, by rubbing or chafing; as, a saddle *galls* the back of a horse.

Tyrant, I well deserve thy *galling* chain.
—Pope.

2. to irritate; to annoy; to vex; to chagrin; as, to be *galled* by sarcasm.

3. to injure; to harass; to annoy; as, the troops were *galled* by the shot of the enemy.

gall, *v.i.* to become sore from rubbing or chafing.

gall, *n.* [OFr. *galle*; L. *galla*, a gallnut.] a tumor on plant tissue caused by irritation due to fungi, insects, or bacteria. The galls of commerce are produced on oak trees by a species

GALL AND GALLFLY
1. gall split to show the cell in which the larva exists; 2. exterior of the gall showing the opening by which the perfect insect escapes

of *Cynips* (gallfly) and have a high tannic acid content. These are also called *gallnuts* and *nutgalls*.

gall, *v.t.* in dyeing, to impregnate with a decoction of gallnuts.

gall, *n.* [ME. *galle*; AS. *gealla*, gall, bile.]

1. a bitter, slightly alkaline, yellowish-green fluid secreted in the glandular substance of the liver and stored in the gall bladder; bile.

2. anything bitter or distasteful; also, bitterness of mind; rancor; malignity.

His daintiest food, his richest wines were all
Turn'd by remorse to bitterness and *gall*.
—Crabbe.

3. the gall bladder.

4. a preparation of ox gall, used in painting.

5. impudence; brazen assurance; audacity. [Colloq.]

6. the scum of molten glass.

gal′lănt, *a.* [OFr. *galant*, gay, brave, ppr. of *galer*, to rejoice, make merry, from *gale*, show, mirth, festivity.]

1. gay; showy; splendid; magnificent; as, *gallant* attire.

2. stately; imposing; grand; as, a *gallant* ship.

3. brave; high-spirited; courageous; heroic; of a noble bearing; as, a *gallant* soldier, a *gallant* foe.

4. [*also* gal-lant′.] showing polite attention to ladies; courteous; chivalrous; courtly; also, having to do with love; amorous.

Syn.—brave, courageous, intrepid, courteous, heroic, fearless, chivalrous, valiant, bold, splendid, showy, gay.

gal′lănt (*or* gal-lant′), *n.* 1. a high-spirited, brave, noble man.

2. a man who is polite and attentive to women.

3. a wooer; a lover; a suitor; also, a paramour.

gal·lant′, *v.t.*; gallanted, *pt.*, *pp.*; gallanting, *ppr.* 1. to court (a woman).

2. to escort or accompany (a woman).

3. to handle with grace or in a modish manner; as, to *gallant* a fan. [Obs.]

gal′lănt·ly, *adv.* 1. in a gallant manner; gaily; showily; as, to be *gallantly* attired.

2. bravely; heroically; as, to fight *gallantly*.

3. [*also* gal-lant′ly.] after the manner of a gallant or wooer.

gal′lănt·ness, *n.* the state or quality of being gallant. [Rare.]

gal′lănt·ry, *n.*; *pl.* **gal′lănt·ries,** [OFr. *galanterie*, from *galant*, gallant.]

1. splendor of appearance; show; magnificence. [Archaic.]

2. bravery; courageousness; heroism; intrepidity; as, the troops entered the fort with great *gallantry*.

3. the behavior of a gallant; courtly manner.

4. [*usually in pl.*] an act or speech characteristic of a gallant.

5. amorous intrigue.

gal′lănt·y shōw, same as *galanty show*.

gall ap′ple, a gallnut; especially, the nut or gall of the gall oak, *Quercus infectoria*.

gal′lāte, *n.* in chemistry, a salt formed by gallic acid combined with a base.

gal′lȧ·tūre, *n.* the chalaza of a bird's egg.

gall blad′dẽr, a membranous sac attached to the liver, in which excess gall or bile is stored and concentrated.

gall duct, a tube or duct by which bile is conveyed.

gal′lē·ass, *n.* [OFr. *galeace*; It. *galeazza*, from *galea*; LL. *galea*, a galley.] a three-masted galley, with guns on each side: it had sails and oars and was used in the Mediterranean during the sixteenth and seventeenth centuries.

galled, *a.* excoriated; denuded; as, a *galled* back; a *galled* tract of land.

Gal·lē′găn, *n.* [Sp. *Gallego*, a native of Galicia, in Spain; L. *Gallæcus*, pl. *Gallæci*, a people in Hispania.] a Galician of Spain, or the Galician language.

gal′lē·in, *n.* [pyro*gall*ol and phthal*ein*.] in chemistry, a crystalline acid, $C_{20}H_{12}O_7$, used in dyeing violet.

gal′lē·ŏn, *n.* [Sp. *galeon*; LL. *galea*, a galley.] a large ship, with three or four decks at the

GALLEON

stern and one or more at the bow: it was used chiefly by the Spaniards of the fifteenth and sixteenth centuries, both as a commercial vessel and a warship.

gal′lē·ŏt, *n.* same as *galiot*.

gall′ẽr, *n.* one who galls, or irritates.

gal′lẽr·ied, *a.* arranged in galleries; having a gallery or galleries.

gal′lẽr·y, *n.*; *pl.* **gal′lẽr·ies,** [OFr. *galerie*, *gallerie*, a long portico, a gallery, prob. from *galerie*, a rejoicing, from *galer*, to rejoice.]

1. a covered walk or porch open at one side or having the roof supported by pillars; colonnade; portico.

2. a long, narrow platform on the outside of a building, above the ground; balcony.

3. a platform or balcony at the quarters or around the stern of an early sailing ship.

4. a platform or projecting upper floor attached to the back wall or sides of a church, theater, etc.; especially, the highest of a series of such platforms in a theater, with the cheapest seats.

5. the cheapest seats in a theater.

6. the people occupying these seats, sometimes regarded as exemplifying popular tastes.

7. popular, or uncultivated, tastes.

8. any group of spectators at a sporting event, legislative meeting, etc.

9. a long, narrow corridor or room.

10. a place or establishment for art exhibitions.

11. a collection of paintings, statues, etc.

12. a place or establishment, originally resembling a gallery (sense 9) for taking photographs, shooting at targets, etc.; as, a shooting *gallery*.

13. a passage underground; (a) in military engineering, a means of communication between parts of a fortification; (b) in mining, a heading or working drift; (c) in zoology, the burrow or other excavation of an animal.

to play to the gallery; (a) in the theater, to act in a manner that will please those in the gallery; hence, (b) to try to win the applause or approval of the public, especially by obvious or easy means.

gal′lẽr·y, *v.t.*; galleried, *pt.*, *pp.*; gallerying, *ppr.* to furnish with a gallery, or balcony.

gal′lẽr·y, *v.i.* to make a gallery, or underground passage.

gal′let, *n.* a chip of stone cut off by a chisel.

gal′let, *v.t.*; galleted, *pt.*, *pp.*; galleting, *ppr.* in masonry, to fill (joints) with gallets.

gal′ley, *n.*; *pl.* **gal′leys,** [ME. *galeye*, *galay*; OFr. *galee*; LL. *galea*, a galley.]

1. in nautical usage, (a) a low, flat-built vessel with one or more rows (banks) of oars, used in ancient times; (b) a low, flat-built vessel with one deck, navigated with sails and oars, formerly common in the Mediterranean, one hundred to two hundred feet in length, having two or three masts and lateen sails, as in the illustration: the oars were usually manned by chained slaves or convicts; (c) a barge of state; specifically, a light, open boat, used on the river Thames by customhouse officers, press gangs, and for pleasure; (d) a large rowboat on British warships, for the captain's use; (e) a ship's kitchen.

GALLEY

2. in printing, (a) a shallow, oblong tray for holding composed type; (b) a galley proof.

gal′ley proof, printer's proof taken from type in a galley to permit correction of errors before the type is made up in pages.

gal′ley slāve, 1. a slave or convict sentenced or compelled to pull an oar on a galley.

2. anyone who must do hard, monotonous work; drudge.

gal′ley-west′, *adv.* completely; into smithereens: only in the phrase *knock galley-west*.

gal′ley·wŏrm, *n.* same as *gallyworm*.

gall′flȳ, *n.*; *pl.* **gall′flies,** an insect, as those of the genus *Cynips*, whose eggs cause galls when deposited on plant stems.

gall gnat (nat), same as *gall midge*.

Gal′lī, *n.* pl. of *Gallus*.

gal·li·am′biç, *a.* pertaining to the galliambus as a form of versification.

gal·li·am′bus, *n.*; *pl.* **gal·li·am′bī,** [L. *galliambus*, a song of the Galli, or priests of Cybele, from *Gallus*, a priest of Cybele, and *iambus*, Gr. *iambos*, an iambic.] a kind of verse consisting of two iambic dimeters catalectic, the last lacking the final syllable.

Gal′li·ăn, *a.* pertaining to Gaul or France; Gallic. [Obs.]

gal′liărd (-yărd), *a.* [ME. and OFr. *gaillard*, thorough, sturdy, gay (prob. by association with *gai*, gay).]
1. valiant; sturdy. [Obs.]
2. lively. [Obs.]

gal′liărd, *n.* 1. a gay, spirited man. [Obs.]
2. a lively French dance in triple time, for two dancers, popular in the 16th and 17th centuries.
3. music for this.

gal′liărd·iṣe, *n.* [Fr.] merriment; excessive gaiety. [Archaic.]

gal′liărd·ness, *n.* gaiety. [Obs.]

gal′li·ass, *n.* same as *galleass*.

Gal′liç, *a.* [L. *Gallicus*, pertaining to Gaul or the Gauls, from *Gallia*, Gaul.]
1. of ancient Gaul or its people.
2. French.

gal′liç, *a.* [Fr. *gallique*, from *galle*; L. *galla*, gallnut.] designating or of an acid, $(OH)_3C_6H_2COOH$, prepared from nutgalls, tannin, etc. and used in the manufacture of inks, dyes, etc.

Gal′li·çăn, *a.* [L. *Gallicus*, from *Gallia*, Gaul.]
1. Gallic.
2. of the Roman Catholic Church in France, especially before 1870.
3. of Gallicanism.

Gal′li·çăn, *n.* 1. a French Roman Catholic.
2. a supporter of Gallicanism.

Gal′li·çăn·iṣm, *n.* the principles enunciated by the French Roman Catholic Church in 1682, claiming limited autonomy.

Gal′li·ciṣm, gal′li·ciṣm, *n.* [Fr. *Gallicisme*, from L. *Gallia*, Gaul.]
1. French idiom or expression, used in another language (e.g., "it gives one furiously to think").
2. French custom, way of thought, etc.

Gal′li·cīze, *v.t.* and *v.i.*; Gallicized, *pt.*, *pp.*; Gallicizing, *ppr.* to make or become French or like the French in thought, language, etc.

gal′li·fọrm, *a.* [L. *gallus*, a cock, and *forma*, form.] belonging to the *Galliformes*.

Gal·li·fọr′mēṣ, *n.pl.* [Mod.L., from L. *gallus*, a cock, and *forma*, form.] in zoology, an order of birds including the common domestic fowl and wild birds of the same order, as chickens, pheasants, turkeys, quail, partridges, etc. They are mostly ground birds, with a heavy body, short wings, and legs adapted to running and scratching for food. They nest on the ground, producing large broods.

gal·li·gas′kinṣ, *n.pl.* [altered from Fr. *garguesque*, from OFr. *garguesque*, *greguesque*; It. *grechesca*, from *Grechesca*, Grecian (hence, orig., "Grecian breeches"); form altered by association with *Gascony* and *galley*.]
1. loosely fitting breeches worn in the 16th and 17th centuries: later applied humorously to any loose breeches.
2. leggings or gaiters. [Brit. Dial.]

gal·li·mau′fry, *n.*; *pl.* **gal·li·mau′frieṣ,** [Fr. *galimafrée*.]
1. a hash made of meat scraps.
2. a hodgepodge; jumbled assortment.

Gal·li·nā′ce·ae, *n.pl.* [L., from *gallinaceus*, pertaining to poultry, from *gallina*, a hen, from *gallus*, a cock.] an order of birds including the domestic fowls; the *Gallinæ*.

gal·li·nā′ceăn (-shun), *a.* same as *gallinaceous*.

gal·li·nā′ceăn, *n.* any gallinaceous bird.

gal·li·nā′ceous, *a.* [L. *gallinaceus*, pertaining to poultry.] resembling common poultry; pheasants, etc.; of or pertaining to the *Galliformes*.

Gal·lī′nae, *n.pl.* [L., from *gallina*, a hen, from *gallus*, a cock.] an order of birds nearly equivalent to the *Galliformes*.

gąll′ing, *a.* irritating; vexatious.

gąll′ing·ly, *adv.* irritatingly.

gal′li·nip·pẽr, *n.* [from *galley*, and *nipper*.] a large mosquito or other insect that can bite or sting painfully.

gal′li·nūle, *n.* [L. *gallinula*, dim. of *gallina*, a hen.] any bird of the genus *Gallinula*, the typical genus of the subfamily *Gallinulinæ*. *Gallinula galeata* is the red-billed mud hen of Florida.

gal′li·ŏt, *n.* same as *galiot*.

gal′li·pot, *n.* [prob. from *galley*, and *pot*; such pots were orig. shipped from Italy.] a small pot or jar of glazed earthenware, especially one used by druggists as a container for medicine.

gal′li·um, *n.* [Mod. L., from L. *Gallia*, Gaul; also a pun on L. *gallus*, a cock, transl. of *Lecoq*, first name of the discoverer, Lecoq de Boisbaudran, 19th-c. Fr. chemist.] a soft, bluish-white, metallic chemical element with an unusually low melting point (29.75° C., or 85.5° F.), used as a substitute for mercury in thermometers, dental amalgam, etc.: symbol, Ga; atomic weight, 69.72; atomic number, 31.

gal′li·vant, *v.i.* [arbitrary elaboration of *gallant*.]
1. to play the gallant or beau; to go about with members of the opposite sex.
2. to go about in search of amusement or excitement; to gad.

gal′li·vat, *n.* a small East Indian vessel with oars and sails, often armed.

gal·liv′ō·rous, *a.* in entomology, gall-devouring: said of the larvae of gall insects.

gal′li·wäsp, *n.* 1. a harmless lizard, genus *Diploglossus*, found in marshes in the West Indies and Central America.
2. a Caribbean lizard fish, *Synodus foetens*.

gal′līze, *v.t.*; gallized, *pt.*, *pp.*; gallizing, *ppr.* in wine making, to add water and sugar to (unfermented grape juice), thereby increasing the quantity of wine produced: after Dr. L. *Gall* of Treves, the originator of the process.

gąll midge, any of several very small flies that produce galls on trees, etc.

gąll mīte, any of various mites (family *Eriophyidæ*) that have only two pairs of legs and produce galls on plants.

gąll′nut, *n.* a nutlike gall, especially on oaks.

Gal′lō-, [L., from *Gallus*, a Gaul.] a combining form meaning: (a) *French*, as in *Gallo*phile; (b) *French and*.

gąll ōak, the oak, *Quercus infectoria*, from which the galls or gallnuts of commerce are obtained.

gal′lō·glȧss, *n.* [Ir. *gallōglach*, servant, heavily armed soldier; *gall* foreigner, and *ōglach*, a youth, servant, soldier.] an armed follower of any of the old Irish chieftains: also spelled *gallowlass*.

Gal·lō·mā′ni·ȧ, *n.* [L. *Gallus*, a Gaul, Frenchman, and *mania*, madness.] extreme admiration for everything of French origin.

Gal·lō·mā′ni·aç, *n.* one who greatly admires all things French.

gal′lŏn, *n.* [ME. *galon*, *galun*; OFr. *galon*; LL. *galo* (*-onis*), *galona*, a gallon.]
1. a dry measure, equal to $^1/_8$ bushel.
2. a liquid measure, equal to four quarts, or eight pints. The United States standard gallon contains 231 cubic inches, or 8.3359 pounds avoirdupois of distilled water at its maximum density with the barometer standing at thirty inches. This is the same as the old English wine gallon. The old English corn gallon contained 272.25 cubic inches and the old ale gallon 282 cubic inches, being the same as the present beer gallon, used to some extent in the United States. The British imperial gallon equals 277.42 cubic inches.
3. any container with a capacity of one gallon.

gal·lọọn′, *n.* [Fr. *galon*, from *galonner*, to braid.]
1. a cotton, silk, or worsted braid or ribbon used for trimming or binding.
2. such braid woven of gold or silver thread.

gal·lọọned′, *a.* furnished or adorned with galloon.

gal′lŏp, *n.* [OFr. *galop*, from *galoper*, to gallop, for *waloper*.]
1. the fastest gait of a horse or other animal, consisting of a succession of leaping strides with all the feet off the ground at one time.
2. a ride on a galloping animal.
3. any fast pace, speedy action, or rapid progression. [Colloq.]

gal′lŏp, *v.i.*; galloped (-lupt), *pt.*, *pp.*; galloping, *ppr.* [ME. *galopen*; OFr. *galoper*, to gallop.]
1. to move or run with leaps or bounds, as a horse; to run or move with speed.
2. to ride with a galloping pace; as, we *galloped* toward the enemy.
3. to move, progress, or act very fast; as, to *gallop* through a book.

gal′lŏp, *v.t.* to cause to gallop; as, to *gallop* a horse.

gal·lō·pāde′, *n.* [Fr. *galopade*, from *galoper*, to gallop.]
1. a lively dance of Hungarian origin.
2. a kind of music appropriate to the dance.

gal·lō·pāde′, *v.i.*; gallopaded, *pt.*, *pp.*; gallopading, *ppr.* to dance a gallopade.

gal′lŏp·ẽr, *n.* 1. a person or animal that gallops.
2. formerly, a light, two-wheeled gun carriage used as a mount for a light cannon.

gal′lŏp·ẽr gun, a light gun mounted on a galloper.

gal′lŏp·ing, *a.* rapid in effect; as, *galloping* consumption.

gal·lō·tan′niç, *a.* in chemistry, pertaining to or derived from the tannin of nutgalls.
gallotannic acid; tannic acid obtained from nutgalls.

gal′lous, *a.* [*gall*ium, and *-ous*.] in chemistry, containing gallium with a valence of two.

gal′lōw, *v.t.* to gally. [Obs.]

Gal′lō·wāy, *n.* 1. a small, hardy horse formerly bred at *Galloway*, Scotland.
2. one of a breed of black and white cattle, originally coming from *Galloway*, Scotland.

gal′lōw·glȧss, *n.* same as *galloglass*.

gal′lōwṣ, *n.*; *pl.* **gal′lōwṣ·eṣ, gal′lōwṣ,** [ME. *gallows*; AS. *galga*, a gallows, gibbet.]
1. an instrument or apparatus on which condemned persons are executed by hanging, usually constructed of two posts with a crossbeam.
2. the punishment of hanging.
3. one who deserves the gallows.
4. [*pl.*] a pair of suspenders. [Colloq.]
5. in printing, a rest for the raised tympan of a hand press. [Obs.]
6. anything resembling a gallows, used for suspending or supporting.

gal′lōwṣ, *a.* fine; dashing; reckless. [Slang.]

gal′lōwṣ, *adv.* to the extreme; very. [Slang.]

gal′lōwṣ bird, one who deserves hanging.

gal′lōwṣ bitts, in nautical usage, a strong frame erected amidships on the deck to hold spare spars: also called *gallows*, *gallows frame*.

gal′lōwṣ frāme, 1. same as *gallows bitts*.
2. a support erected at the mouth of a mining shaft for the hoisting apparatus.

GALLOWS BITTS

gal′lōwṣ hū′mŏr, amused cynicism by one facing disaster; morbid or cynical humor.

gal′lowṣ tree, a gallows.

gąll sick′ness, a disease of cattle, transmitted by ticks.

gąll′stōne, *n.* a biliary concretion, consisting of cholesterol or, occasionally, of calcium salts, sometimes formed in the gall bladder or bile duct: it can obstruct the flow of bile, causing a painful diseased condition.

Gal′lus, *n.*; *pl.* **Gal′lī,** [L., from Gr. *Gallos*, a priest of Cybele.] a priest who had charge of the wild rites attendant upon the worship of Cybele.

Gal′lus, *n.* [L. *gallus*, cock.] a genus of the family *Phasianidæ*, including the domestic fowl.

gal′lus·eṣ, *n.pl.* [from *gallus*, dial. var. of *gallows*.] suspenders; braces. [Colloq.]

gąll′wäsp, *n.* same as *gallfly*.

gal′ly, *v.t.* to scare; to frighten. [Brit. Dial.]

gąll′y, *a.* like gall; bitter as gall.

gal·ly·gas′kinṣ, *n.pl.* same as *galligaskins*.

gal′ly·wŏrm, *n.* one of various worms of *Myriapoda*. having many legs: spelled also *galleyworm*.

ga·loche′, *n.* a galosh. [Obs.]

gȧ·lọọt′, *n.* [orig. naval slang.] a person, especially an awkward, ungainly person: also spelled *galloot*. [Slang.]

gal′ŏp, *n.* [Fr.] 1. a lively dance in $^2/_4$ time, now often forming part of a set of quadrilles.
2. the music for this dance.

gal′ŏp, *v.i.* to dance a galop.

gȧ·lōre′, *adv.* [Ir. *go leor*, enough; *go*, to, and *leor*, sufficient, enough.] plentifully; abundantly; as, money *galore*.

gȧ·lōre′, *n.* abundance. [Rare.]

gȧ·losh′, gȧ·loshe′, *n.* [ME. *galoche*; OFr. *galoche*; LL. *calopedia*, a clog or wooden shoe, from Gr. *kalopodion*, dim. of *kalopous*, a shoemaker's last; *kalon*, wood, and *pous* (*podos*), foot.]
1. originally, (a) a heavy shoe; a clog; (b) any boot or shoe.
2. [*usually in pl.*] any protective overshoe; especially, a high, warmly lined overshoe of rubber and waterproof fabric: also spelled *golosh*, *goloshe*.
3. a high gaiter; a legging extending from the uppers to a point above the ankle

galp, galpe, *v.i.* to gape or yawn. [Obs.]

gąlt, *n.* [Norw. *gald*, hard ground.]
1. a stiff, blue marl, of the Chalk formation. [Brit. Dial.]
2. in geology, a division of the Upper Cretaceous marking its lower boundary.

gȧ·lumph′ (-lumf′), *v.i.* [coined by Lewis Carroll, from *gal*lop, and tri*umph*.] to march or prance along in a self-satisfied, triumphant manner.

gal·van′iç, *a.* 1. of, caused by, or producing an electric current, especially from a battery.
2. stimulating or stimulated as if by electric shock; startling.
galvanic battery; a kind of electric battery in which each cell is made of two elements (as zinc and copper) placed in a liquid (as a solution of chromic acid), whereby a current is produced when the metals are connected by wires in a series circuit.

GALVANIC BATTERY

gal·van′i·căl, *a.* same as *galvanic.*

gal′văn·iṣm, *n.* [It. *galvanismo*, so called from the first investigator in the field, Luigi *Galvani* (1737–1798), professor of anatomy at Bologna.]
1. electric currents or electricity arising from chemical action.
2. the branch of physics treating of this form of electricity.
3. in medicine, treatment of disease by electricity.

gal′vȧ·nist, *n.* an expert in galvanism.

gal″vȧ·ni·zā′tion, *n.* a galvanizing or being galvanized.

gal′vȧ·nīze, *v.t.*; galvanized, *pt., pp.*; galvanizing, *ppr.* 1. to apply an electric current to.
2. to stimulate as if by electric shock; startle; excite.
3. to plate (metal) with zinc, originally by galvanic action.
galvanized iron; iron coated with zinc as a protection against rust.

gal′vȧ·nī·zẽr, *n.* one who or that which galvanizes.

gal′van·ō-, a combining form meaning *galvanic* or *galvanism*, as in *galvano*meter.

gal″văn·ō·çaus′tiç, *a.* [*galvano-*, and Gr. *kaiein*, to burn.] pertaining to galvanic heat employed as a caustic, particularly in electrotherapeutics.

gal″văn·ō·çau′tẽr·y, *n.* [*galvano-*, and Gr. *kautēr*, a burner.] cauterizing with an instrument heated by a galvanic current.

gal·vȧ·nog′ly·phy, *n.* [*galvano-*, and Gr. *glyphein*, to engrave.] a process of making an electroplate for printing by the use of a zinc plate and etching.

gal·van′ō·grȧph, *n.* [*galvano-*, and Gr. *graphein*, to write.] a plate made by the galvanographic process; also, an impression printed from such a plate.

gal″văn·ō·graph′iç, *a.* pertaining to or produced by galvanography.

gal·vȧ·nog′rȧ·phy, *n.* [*galvano-*, and Gr. *graphein*, to write.]
1. same as *electrotyping.*
2. a method of producing plates for copperplate engraving by the galvonoplastic process, without etching.

gal·vȧ·nol′ō·ġist, *n.* one who describes the phenomena of galvanism.

gal·vȧ·nol′ō·ġy, *n.* [*galvano-*, and Gr. *logos*, a description, from *legein*, to speak.] a treatise on galvanism or a description of its phenomena.

gal″văn·ō·mag·net′iç, *a.* same as *electromagnetic.*

gal·vȧ·nom′e·tẽr, *n.* [*galvano-*, and Gr. *metron*, a measure.] an instrument for detecting the existence and determining the strength and direction of an electric current.

gal″văn·ō·met′riç, *a.* 1. relating to or employing a galvanometer or galvanometry.
2. measured by a galvanometer.

gal·vȧ·nom′e·try, *n.* the art of or method employed in measuring the force of electric currents by means of a galvanometer.

gal″văn·ō·plas′tiç, *a.* [*galvano-*, and Gr. *plastos*, formed, molded, from *plassein*, to form, mold.] of or pertaining to galvanoplastics.

gal″văn·ō·plas′tiçs, *n.pl.* [*construed as sing.*] the process of coating things with metal by means of electrolysis; especially, electrotypy.

gal·van′ō·plas·ty, *n.* same as *galvanoplastics.*

gal″văn·ō·punç′tūre, *n.* same as *electropuncture.*

gal·van′ō·sçōpe, *n.* [*galvano-*, and Gr. *skopein*, to view.] an instrument used to determine the presence and indicate the direction of very weak electric currents.

gal″văn·ō·sçop′iç, *a.* relating to or discovered by a galvanoscope.

gal·vȧ·nos′çō·py, *n.* [*galvano-*, and Gr. *skopein*, to view.] the employment of a galvanoscope, especially in medical diagnosis.

gal″văn·ō·thẽr·mom′e·tẽr, *n.* an instrument employed in determining the amount of heat which an electric current generates while passing through various conducting mediums.

gal′văn·ō·thẽr″my, *n.* [from *galvano-*, and Gr. *thermē*, heat.] the production of heat by galvanism, as for medical treatment.

gal·vȧ·not′rō·piṣm, *n.* [*galvano-*, and Gr. *trepein*, to turn.] in botany, the disposition exhibited by growing plants to turn in certain directions when acted upon by an electric current, as to bend toward the positive electrode.

Gal·wē′ġiăn (-jăn), *a.* of Galloway or its people.

Gal·wē′ġiăn, *n.* a native or inhabitant of Galloway.

gal′yak, gal′yaç, *n.* [from word used in Bokhara for a premature lamb, from Russ. *golyak*, bare, naked.] a flat, glossy fur made from the pelts of lambs or kids.

gam, *n.* 1. a school of whales.
2. the exchange of visits between the men on whalers and fishing smacks when they meet at sea and are at leisure.
3. a social visit.

gam, *v.i.*; gammed, *pt., pp.*; gamming, *ppr.* 1. to come together; to congregate: said of whales.
2. to exchange calls and friendly greetings, especially at sea.

gam, *v.t.* to have a social visit with, especially at sea.

gam, *n.* [var. of *gamb.*] a leg; especially, a woman's leg. [Slang.]

gä′mȧ grȧss, [from *Gama*, a cluster of islands in the Maldive group.] a tall, stout grass grown for grazing.

Ga·mā′li·el, *n.* [L.; Gr. *Gamaliel*; Heb. *gamli'el*, lit., reward of God.] in the Bible, (a) a teacher of Saul of Tarsus: Acts v. 34; (b) a ruler of Manasseh: Numb. x. 23.

ga·mash′eṣ, *n.pl.* [OFr. *gamaches*, from *gambe*, leg.] short spatterdashes similar to gaiters; high boots or protective leggings, worn when riding horseback. [Obs.]

gamb, gambe, *n.* [OFr. *gambe*, the leg; LL. *gamba*, a leg, the hoof; Gr. *kampē*, a turn, bend (of a limb).] in heraldry, the leg or shank of a lion or other beast.

gam·bȧ′dō, *n.*; *pl.* **gam·bȧ′dōṣ, gam·bā′dōeṣ,** 1. [Sp. *gambada*; It. *gambata*, a kick, from *gamba*, a leg.] a curvetting leap, by or as by a horse; hence, a prank or antic.
2. [from It. *gamba*, a leg.] a long legging or gaiter attached to a saddle to serve as a stirrup; hence, any long gaiter.
Also *gambade.*

gambe, *n.* same as *gamb.*

gam·beer′, *v.t.*; gambeered, *pt., pp.*; gambeering, *ppr.* [compare Fr. *gambier*, an iron hook.] to gaff fish, particularly mackerel, as they swim alongside a vessel.

gam′be·son, *n.* [ME. *gambeson*; OFr. *gambeson*; LL. *gambeso* (*-onis*), *gambasium*, a gambeson, from O.H.G. *wamba*, belly, stomach.] a quilted or leather tunic stuffed with wool, worn as armor in medieval times.

GAMBESON

gam′bet, *n.* [Fr. *gambette*, a gambet, dim. of OFr. *gambe*, leg.] any of various birds of the genus *Totanus*, especially the large sandpiper *Totanus calidris.*

gam′biẽr, gam′bïr, *n.* [Malay.] an astringent substance extracted from the leaves of *Uncaria gambier*, a shrub growing in the Malayan peninsula. It has medicinal qualities, but is also used in tanning and as a dyestuff.

gam′bist, *n.* a person who plays the viola da gamba.

gam′bit, *n.* [Fr. *gambit*, a gambit, from It. *gambetto*, a tripping up of one's legs, from *gamba*, leg.] one of the openings in chess in which a pawn or other piece is sacrificed for the purpose of gaining an advantageous position.

gam′ble, *v.i.*; gambled, *pt., pp.*; gambling, *ppr.* [freq. of ME. *gamen*, *gamenen*; AS. *gamenian*, to play, game.]
1. to play games of chance for money or other stake.
2. to take a risk in order to gain some advantage.

gam′ble, *v.t.* 1. to lose by betting; to waste; to squander: followed by *away.*
Bankrupts or sots who have *gambled* or slept *away* their estates. —Ames.
2. to bet; to wager.

GAMBIER (*Uncaria gambier*)

gam′ble, *n.* an act which depends upon chance; a risk; an uncertain venture.

gam′blẽr, *n.* a person who gambles or is fond of gambling; especially, one who makes a living by gambling.

gam·bōġe′, *n.* [from *Camboja*, *Cambodia*, a French protectorate in India.]
1. a gum resin produced by several species of trees native to southeastern Asia. It is of a dense, compact texture, and of a reddish-yellow color. It is used chiefly as a pigment, giving a clear yellow color. Taken internally, it is a strong and harsh cathartic.

GAMBOGE (*Garcinia hanburyi*)

2. bright yellow.

gam·bō′ġi·ăn, gam·bō′ġiç, *a.* pertaining to gamboge.

gam′bŏl, *n.* [Fr. *gambade*, a gambol, from It. *gambata*, a kick, from *gamba*, the leg.] a skipping or leaping about in frolic; a skip; a hop; a leap; a sportive prank.

gam′bŏl, *v.i.*; gamboled *or* gambolled, *pt., pp.*; gamboling *or* gambolling, *ppr.* to dance and skip about in play; to frisk; to leap; to start up; to frolic, as children and young animals at play.

gam′brel, *n.* [from It. *gamba*, the leg.]
1. the hock of a horse or similar animal.
2. a stick crooked like a horse's leg, used by butchers for hanging carcasses.
3. a gambrel roof.

gam′brel rọof, a roof with two slopes on each side, the lower steeper than the upper, which form the ridge: also *gambrel.*

GAMBREL ROOF

gam·brọon′, *n.* [etym. doubtful; prob. from *Gombroon*, a Persian seaport from which a large export trade was carried on.] a lightweight twilled fabric of linen or of cotton and worsted mixed, used for lining garments and for summer clothing.

gam′de·bọọ, *n.* [native African name.] a small tree, *Celtis kraussiana*, native to South Africa, yielding a tough timber.

gāme, *n.* [ME. *game*; AS. *gamen*, a game, sport.]
1. any contrivance, arrangement, or contest intended to furnish sport, recreation, or amusement; frolic; play.
2. (a) any specific amusement or sport involving competition under specific rules; as, football and chess are *games*; (b) a single contest in such a competition; as, he went to a basketball *game.*
3. (a) the number of points required for winning; as, the *game* is 25; (b) the score at any given point in a competition; as, at the half the *game* was 7 to 6; (c) that which is gained by winning; victory; win.
4. a set of equipment for a competitive amusement; as, toys and *games* are sold here.
5. the art or quality of playing at any sport; as, he plays a rapid *game* of tennis.

6. any test of skill, courage, or endurance; as, the *game* of life.

7. in certain card games, a point accredited to the player whose hand counts up the highest score.

8. scheme pursued; measures planned; project; as, he saw through my *game*.

This seems to be the present *game* of that crown. —Temple.

9. amorous sport; gallantry. [Obs.]

10. wild birds, fish, or animals which are pursued or killed in sport or for use as food; as, the northern forests are rich in *game*.

11. the flesh of wild birds, fish, or animals served as food.

12. an object of pursuit. [Colloq.]

13. a business or vocation, especially one with an element of risk; as, the stock-market *game*. [Slang.]

big game; (a) large wild animals, as gorillas, elephants, lions, etc., hunted for sport; (b) [Slang.] any important objective difficult or dangerous to pursue.

off one's game; performing poorly.

round game; a card game in which any number of players may participate.

the game is up; all chances for a successful completion are gone: said of enterprises involving risk or danger.

to make game of; to make fun of; make the butt of jokes, teasing, etc.; ridicule.

to play the game; (a) to act according to the rules of a game; (b) to behave as fairness or custom requires. [Colloq.]

Syn.—sport, recreation, pastime, amusement, frolic, diversion, play.

gāme, *a.* 1. having an undaunted spirit; unwilling to admit defeat; full of pluck. [Colloq.]

2. having enough spirit or enthusiasm; ready; as, he's *game* for anything. [Colloq.]

3. pertaining to such animals, wild birds, etc. as are hunted for use as food or for sport.

to die game; to keep one's nerve to the last; to die unconquered in spirit.

gāme, *v.i.*; gamed, *pt.*, *pp.*; gaming, *ppr.* [ME. *gamen*; AS. *gamenian*, to play, game.]

1. to play at any sport or diversion [Dial.]

2. to play for a stake or prize; to use cards, dice, etc. for stakes; to gamble.

gāme, *v.t.* to squander or lose in gambling (with *away*).

gāme, *a.* [also dial. *gammy*; perh. from Fr. dial. *gambi*, limping.] lame; hurt; injured: said especially of a leg. [Colloq.]

gāme bag, a hunter's bag for carrying the game killed.

gāme bīrd, a bird which is hunted for sport or for food.

gāme′çock, *n.* a cock bred or used for cock fighting.

gāme fish, any fish regularly caught for sport, especially any species that fights hard when hooked.

gāme fowl, any one of several breeds of domestic fowl trained for cockfighting.

gāme′keep″ẽr, *n.* a person employed to take care of game birds and animals on public lands or private estates, to prevent poaching, etc.

gāme laws, laws regulating hunting and fishing in order to preserve game.

gāme′ly, *adv.* in a game, or courageous, manner.

gāme′ness, *n.* the quality of being game, or having an unyielding spirit; courage; pluckiness.

There was no doubt about his *gameness*. —Hughes.

gāme plan, 1. the strategy planned before a game, especially a football game.

2. any long-range strategy to reach an objective.

gāme point, 1. the situation in a game, especially tennis, when the next point scored could decide the winner.

2. the winning point.

gāme prē·ṣẽrve′, an area of land in which game, fish, etc. is protected for private use in hunting or fishing.

gāmeṣ′man·ship, *n.* [*game*, and sports*manship*.] skill in handling a situation to one's own advantage by the use of ploys.

gāme′sōme, *a.* gay; sportive; playful; frolicsome.

gāme′sōme·ly, *adv.* merrily; playfully.

gāme′sōme·ness, *n.* sportiveness; merriment.

gāme′stẽr, *n.* a gambler.

gam″e·tan′ġi·um, *n.*; *pl.* **gam″e·tan′ġi·a,** [Mod. L., from Gr. *gametē*, a wife, and *angeion*, a vessel.] the organ or cell of a plant in which gametes are produced.

gam′ēte, *n.* [Gr. *gametē*, a wife, from *gamein*, to marry, from *gamos*, marriage.] a reproductive cell that can unite with another similar one to form the cell that develops into a new individual.

gȧ·met′iç, *a.* of, or having the nature of, a gamete or gametes.

gȧ·mē′tō-, a combining form meaning *gamete*, as in *gameto*phore, *gameto*phyte.

gȧ·mē′tō·cȳte, *n.* a living cell that divides to form gametes.

gȧ·mē′tō·phōre, *n.* that part of a plant bearing the organs that produce gametes.

gȧ·mē′tō·phȳte, *n.* [Gr. *gametē*, a wife, and *phyton*, a plant.] that stage in the development of a thallophytic plant in which the sexual organs are produced.

gāme wạrd′en, an official in charge of enforcing the game laws in a certain area.

gam′iç, *a.* [Gr. *gamikos*, pertaining to marriage, from *gamos*, marriage.] in biology, sexual; also, capable of being developed only through sexual union.

gām′i·ly, *adv.* in a gamy manner; pluckily.

gam′in, *n.* [Fr.] a street urchin or street Arab; a homeless or neglected child left to roam the streets.

gām′i·ness, *n.* the quality of being gamy.

gām′ing, *n.* the act or practice of playing any game for a prize or stake; gambling.

gam′mȧ, *n.* [L. *gamma*; Gr. *gamma*.]

1. the third letter of the Greek alphabet, corresponding to the English *G*, *g*.

2. the symbol for the third in any series.

3. a microgram.

4. a common European noctuid moth, *Plusia gamma*, having on the wing a silvery, Y-shaped spot resembling the Greek gamma.

gam·mā′di·on, *n.*; *pl.* **gam·mā′di·ȧ,** [L.Gr. *gammadion*, from Gr. *gamma*, gamma.] a cross of four capital gammas, especially in the form of a swastika.

gam′mȧ glob′ū·lin, that fraction of blood serum which contains most antibodies, used in the temporary prevention of several infectious diseases, as measles and hepatitis.

gam′mȧ mọth, same as *gamma*, sense 4.

gam′mȧ rāyṣ, one of the three kinds of rays emitted by radioactive substances: they are similar to X rays, but shorter in wave length.

gam′mȧ·rid, *n.* one of the *Gammaridæ*.

Gam·mar′i·dae, *n.pl.* [L. *gammarus*, *cammarus*; Gr. *kammaros*, a kind of lobster, and *-idæ*.] a family of amphipodous crustaceans, typified by the genus *Gammarus*, of which the freshwater shrimp is a species.

gam′mȧ·roid, *a.* pertaining to or having the characteristics of the *Gammaridæ*.

Gam′mȧ·rus, *n.* a genus typical of the family *Gammaridæ*.

gam′mẽr, *n.* [dial. contr. of *grandmother*.] an old woman: often used contemptuously or humorously: correlative of *gaffer*, an old man.

gam′mŏn, *n.* [OFr. *gambon*, from *gambe*, leg.]

1. the bottom end of a side of bacon.

2. the ham of a hog or a side of bacon, smoked or cured.

gam′mŏn, *v.t.*; gammoned, *pt.*, *pp.*; gammoning, *ppr.* to make into bacon; to pickle and dry in smoke.

gam′mŏn, *v.t.* to fasten (a bowsprit) to the stem of a ship, as by iron bands or several turns of a rope.

gam′mŏn, *n.* [ME. *gammen*; AS. *gamen*, game, joy.] in the game of backgammon, a victory for a player when he has thrown off all his men before his opponent has thrown off one.

gam′mŏn, *v.t.* in the game of backgammon, to secure a gammon over.

gam′mŏn, *n.* and *interj.* [prob. from *gammon* (bacon) with jocular allusion, but influenced by *gammon* (game).] nonsense intended to deceive; humbug. [Colloq.]

gam′mŏn, *v.t.* and *v.i.* to talk humbug (to). [Colloq.]

gam′mŏn·ing, *n.* the iron bands or the lashing by which the bowsprit of a vessel is secured to the stem.

gam′mŏn plāte, an iron plate on the stem of a vessel to which the gammon shackles are fastened.

gam′mŏn shaç′kleṣ (-klz), shackles for securing the gammoning.

gam′o-, [from Gr. *gamos*, marriage.] a combining form meaning: (a) *sexually united*, as in *gamo*genesis; (b) *joined*, as in *gamo*sepalous.

gam·ō·ġen′e·sis, *n.* [*gamo-*, and Gr. *genesis*, generation.] reproduction by the uniting of gametes; sexual reproduction.

gam″ō·ġē·net′iç, *a.* pertaining to gamogenesis; produced by gamogenesis.

gam″ō·ġē·net′iç·ăl·ly, *adv.* in a gamogenetic manner.

gam·ō·pet′ăl·ous, *a.* [*gamo-*, and Gr. *petalon*, a leaf.] in botany, having the petals united so as to form a tubelike corolla.

ga·moph′yl·lous, *a.* [*gamo-*, and Gr. *phyllon*, a leaf.] in botany, having a single perianth whorl with coherent leaves; symphyllous: opposed to *apophyllous*.

gam·ō·sep′ăl·ous, *a.* [*gamo-*, and *sepalous*.] in botany, having the sepals united; monosepalous.

-gȧ·mŏus, [from Gr. *gamos*, marriage.] a combining form meaning *marrying*, *uniting sexually*, as in hetero*gamous*, poly*gamous*.

gamp, *n.* a large umbrella: in allusion to the umbrella of Mrs. Gamp in Dickens' novel "Martin Chuzzlewit."

gam′ut, *n.* [ML. *gamma ut*; *gamma*, the gamut, name used by Guido d'Arezzo for the lowest note of his scale, from Gr. *gamma*, the third letter of the Gr. alphabet, and *ut*, from L. *ut*, that, used as a musical note.]

1. in music, (a) the lowest note of the medieval scale, corresponding to modern G below middle C; (b) the complete medieval scale; (c) the entire series of recognized notes in modern music; (d) any complete musical scale, especially the major scale.

2. the entire range or extent of anything.

gām′y, *a.*; *comp.* gamier; *superl.* gamiest, 1. having a strong tangy flavor like that of cooked game.

2. strong in smell or taste; slightly tainted.

3. plucky; high-spirited.

-gȧ·my, [Gr. *-gamia*, from *gamos*, marriage.] a combining form meaning *marriage*, *sexual union*, as in poly*gamy*.

gan, *v.* past tense of *gin*, to begin.

gȧnch, gaunch, *v.t.* [Fr. *gancher*, from *gancio*, a hook.] to impale on sharp stakes or hooks as a method of execution. [Obs.]

gȧnch, gaunch, *n.* the process of executing by ganching. [Obs.]

gan′dẽr, *n.* [ME. *gandre*; AS. *gandra*, the gander.]

1. the male of the goose.

2. a stupid or silly fellow.

3. a look: chiefly in the phrase *take a gander*. [Slang.]

gan′dẽr, *v.i.* to walk leisurely or aimlessly; to saunter. [Colloq.]

Gän′dhi·iṣm, *n.* the theory, doctrine, teachings, belief, or movement of Mohandas K. Gandhi (1869–1948), Hindu reformer and leader, who strongly stressed the efficacy of passive resistance and civil disobedience in the struggle for native independence in India.

gan′dy dȧn′cẽr, [so named from using tools from the *Gandy* Manufacturing Co. (Chicago).] a worker in a railroad section gang. [Slang.]

gä′nef, gä′nof, *n.* [Yiddish, from Heb.] a thief.

Ga·nē′sȧ, *n.* in Hindu mythology, the god of prudence, represented as a man with an elephant's head.

gang, *v.i.* [AS. *gangan*, *gongan*, to go.] to go; to walk. [Scot.]

gang, *n.* [ME. *gang*, a going, a course; AS. *gang*, a going, way.]

1. a going; the act of walking. [Obs.]

2. a number of persons associated together in some way; specifically, (a) a number of workmen or laborers under the supervision of a foreman; as, a *gang* of hod carriers, a *gang* of stokers; (b) an organized group of criminals; (c) a squad of convicts at work; (d) a group of children or youths from the same neighborhood banded together for social reasons.

3. a combination or set of tools or machines of one kind so arranged as to operate together: often used attributively; as, a *gang* plow.

4. as much as one goes for or carries at once. [Scot.]

5. the field or pasture in which animals graze. [Scot.]

gang, *v.i.* to form a gang; to be associated in a gang (often with *up*).

to gang up on; to attack or oppose as a group. [Slang.]

gang, *v.t.* to attack as a gang. [Colloq.]

gang, *n.* same as *gangue*.

gañ′gȧ, *n.* [Sp.] *Pterocles alchata*, a sand grouse.

gang′bōard, *n.* same as *gangplank*.

gang çask, a small cask used for bringing water aboard ships.

gang dāy, [AS. *gangdagas*, gang days; *gang*, a going, and *dæg* (pl. *dagas*), day.] in England, a Rogation day.

gange, *v.t.*; ganged, *pt., pp.*; ganging, *ppr.* to affix (a fishhook) to the ganging of a line.

gang'ẽr, *n.* 1. one who superintends a gang, as the foreman of a gang of laborers.
2. in nautical usage, a chain having one end attached to an anchor and the other to the hawser.

Gan·get'iç, *a.* of or pertaining to the river Ganges; as, the *Gangetic* crocodile.

gang flow'ẽr, the milkwort, *Polygala vulgaris*: so called because it blooms in gang week. [Obs.]

gan'ging, *n.* 1. that part of a fishing line to which the hook is attached, usually of different material from that of the line proper: called also *ganging line*.
2. the act or manner of fastening a fishhook to the ganging of a line.

gan'ging līne, same as *ganging*, sense 1.

gañ'gli·aç, *a.* ganglial.

gañ'gli·ăl, *a.* relating to a ganglion; ganglionic.

gañ'gli·ȧr, *a.* ganglial.

gañ'gli·āte, gañ'gli·ā·ted, *a.* provided with ganglia.

gañ'gli·fọrm, gañ'gli·ō·fọrm, *a.* [Gr. *ganglion*, a tumor, and L. *forma*, form.] having the shape of a ganglion.

gañ·gli·ī'tis, *n.* same as *ganglionitis*.

gañ'gling, *a.* [freq. of *gang*; AS. *gang*, a going, from *gangan*, to go.] thin, tall, and awkward; of loose, lanky build; spindling.

gañ'gli·ō-, a combining form meaning *ganglion*, as in *ganglio*plexus.

gañ'gli·ŏn, *n.*; *pl.* **gañ'gli·ȧ, gañ'gli·ŏnș**, [LL. *ganglion*, from Gr. *ganglion*, a tumor.]
1. in anatomy, (a) a mass of nerve cells serving as a center from which nerve impulses are transmitted; (b) [Obs.] a lymphatic gland.
2. in pathology, a small tumor on a tendon, formed by the elevation of the sheath of the tendon, and the effusion of a viscid fluid into it.
3. a center of force, activity, energy, etc.

gañ'gli·ŏn·ā·ry, *a.* composed of ganglia.

gañ'gli·ŏn cell, a nerve cell characteristic of the ganglia: similar cells are found in other parts of the nervous system.

gañ·gli·on'iç, *a.* pertaining to or of the nature of a ganglion.

gañ·gli·ō·nī'tis, *n.* in pathology, inflammation of a ganglion.

gañ'gli·ŏn·less, *a.* without ganglia: said of a nerve.

gañ·gli·ō·plex'us, *n.* a network of nerve fibers in a ganglion.

gañ'gly, *a.* same as *gangling*.

gang'mȧs"tẽr, *n.* a master or employer of a gang or body of workers.

gang'plañk, *n.* a board or plank forming a temporary bridge for passengers to board or leave a ship: called also *gangboard*.

gang plow, a plow having several shares set in the same frame and operating together so as to make several furrows at the same time.

gañ'grel, *n.* [from ME. *gangen*, AS. *gangan*, to go, walk.]
1. a tall, clumsy fellow. [Scot.]
2. a roving beggar. [Dial. or Archaic.]
3. a child just beginning to walk. [Scot.]

gañ'grel, *a.* vagrant; vagabond. [Dial. or Archaic.]

gañ'grē·nāte, *v.t.* to produce gangrene in; to gangrene. [Obs.]

gañ'grēne, *n.* [OFr. *gangrene*; L. *gangræna*; Gr. *gangraina*, an eating sore, gangrene, from *grainein*, to gnaw, eat.] decay of tissue in a part of the body when the blood supply is obstructed by injury, disease, etc.

gañ'grēne, *v.t.*; gangrened, *pt., pp.*; gangrening, *ppr.* to produce gangrene in.

gañ'grēne, *v.i.* to develop gangrene; to decay.

gañ·grē·nes'cent, *a.* becoming gangrenous.

gañ'grē·nous, *a.* of or having gangrene.

gang sa̤w, a machine consisting of several saws set in the same frame, and acting simultaneously.

gang'stẽr, *n.* a member of a gang, especially of a gang of criminals; hence, any criminal or tough.

gang'tīde, *n.* same as *gang week*.

gangue, *n.* [Fr. *gangue*; Gr. *gang*, a metallic vein, a passage, from AS. *gang*, a going, way.] the commercially worthless minerals associated with economically valuable metallic minerals in a deposit; matrix: also spelled *gang*.

gang'wāy, *n.* 1. a passageway or space through which to enter, leave, or go past.
2. an opening in the bulwarks of a ship by which persons come on board or disembark; also, a gangplank.
3. the part of a vessel on the spar deck, forming a passage along each side, from the quarter-deck to the forecastle.
4. an accommodation ladder.
5. a passageway between rows of seats.
6. an incline for logs, leading from the water to a saw mill.
7. a main level in a mine.
8. in the British House of Commons, a narrow passage running across the house.
to bring to the gangway; formerly, to punish (a seaman) by seizing him and flogging him.

gang'wāy, *interj.* make room! clear the way!

gang'wāy lad'dẽr, a ladder leading down to the water from a ship's gangway.

gang week, Rogation week, when the bounds of parishes were formerly surveyed. [Obs.]

gan'is·tẽr, gan'nis·tẽr, *n.* [G. dial. *ganster*; M.H.G. *ganster*, a spark.] a close-grained, hard sandstone or grit found under certain coal beds: it is used for macadamizing roads, and also for lining metallurgical furnaces and Bessemer converters.

gan'jȧ, *n.* [Hind. *gania*, *ganjha*, the hemp plant.] the dried flowering spikes of the Indian hemp plant, smoked for the intoxicating and narcotic effects.

gan'nen, *n.* in England, a sloping gangway in a coal mine down which coal is carried in tubs or cars running on tracks.

gan'net, *n.* [ME. *gant*; AS. *ganot*, *ganet*, a sea fowl.] the solan goose, *Sula bassana*, of the pelican family.

GANNET (*Sula bassana*)

Gan·ō·ceph'ȧ·lȧ, *n.pl.* [Gr. *ganos*, brightness, and *kephalē*, head.] a group of fossil labyrinthodont amphibians, with horny or ganoid plates covering the head.

gan·ō·ceph'ȧ·lous, *a.* having the characteristic features of the *Ganocephala*.

gȧ'noid, *a.* [Gr. *ganos*, brightness, and *eidos*, appearance.] of or pertaining to the *Ganoidei*.

gȧ'noid, *n.* one of the *Ganoidei*.

gȧ·noid'ăl, *a.* same as *ganoid*.

gȧ·noid'ē·ăn, *a.* and *n.* same as *ganoid*.

Gȧ·noi'dē·ī, *n.pl.* [Gr. *ganos*, brightness, and *eidos*, appearance.] a large subclass of fishes characterized by rows of hard, glossy, enameled scales or plates: the subclass includes the sturgeons, gars, bowfins, and paddlefishes.

gȧ·noid'i·ăn, *a.* and *n.* same as *ganoid*.

gā'nō·in, *n.* [Gr. *ganos*, brightness.] the bony tissue which gives an enamellike appearance to the plates of ganoid fishes and of some labyrinthodonts.

gȧ·nom'ȧ·līte, *n.* [Gr. *ganōma*, brightness, and *lithos*, stone.] a silicate of lead and manganese occurring either massive or in tetragonal crystals.

gä'nŏv (-nŏf), *n.* [Yiddish, from Heb.] a thief: also spelled *ganef*, *ganof*, *gonof*, *gonoph*, etc.

gȧnt'let, ga̤unt'let, *n.* [Sw. *gatlopp*, a running down a lane; *gata*, street or lane, and *lopp*, a course or run.]
1. a former military punishment in which the offender was partly stripped and compelled to run between two rows of men armed with clubs or switches, with which he was struck in passing.
2. a series of difficulties or disagreeable incidents.
3. a section of railroad track over a narrow passage where two lines of track overlap, one rail of each line being within the rails of the other.
to run the gantlet; to undergo the punishment of the gantlet; hence, to run or pass through a course of severe treatment, criticism, or opposition.

Winthrop *ran the gantlet* of daily slights from his neighbors. —Palfrey.

gȧnt'let, ga̤unt'let, *v.t.* to overlap (railroad tracks) so as to make a gantlet.

gȧnt'let, *n.* a glove: see *gauntlet*.

gant'līne, *n.* same as *girtline*.

gant'lōpe, *n.* the gantlet. [Obs.]

gan'try, *n.*; *pl.* **gan'trieș**, [altered from OFr. *gantier*, *chantier*; L. *canterius*, *cantherius*, beast of burden, trellis, rafter; Gr. *kanthēlios*, a pack ass, from *kanthōn*, of same meaning.]
1. a frame on which barrels can be set horizontally.
2. a framework supported at each end so that it spans a distance, used for carrying a traveling crane or displaying railroad signals.
Also *gauntry*, *gantree*.

Gan'y·mēde, *n.* [L. *Ganymedes*; Gr. *Ganymēdēs*.]
1. in Greek mythology, a beautiful youth carried off by Zeus to be the cupbearer to the gods.
2. one of the satellites of the planet Jupiter.

ġāol, *n.* a jail: British spelling.

ġāol'ẽr, *n.* a jailer: British spelling.

gap, *n.* [ME. *gap*, *gappe*; Ice. *gap*, a gap, opening, from *gapa*, to yawn, gape.]
1. a hole or opening, as in a wall or fence, made by breaking or parting.
2. a mountain pass, cleft, or ravine.
3. an interruption of continuity; blank space; hiatus; lacuna.
4. a distance or difference between ideas, natures, etc.; as, there is a *gap* between his thinking and mine.
to stand in the gap; to expose oneself for the protection of something; to make defense against any assailing danger.
to stop a gap; to secure a weak point; to repair a defect; to supply a temporary expedient.

gap, *v.t.*; gapped (gapt), *pt., pp.*; gapping, *ppr.*
1. to indent or notch, as the edge of a knife. [Rare.]
2. to breach; to open a passage through. [Rare.]

gāpe, *v.i.*; gaped (gāpt), *pt., pp.*; gaping, *ppr.* [ME. *gapen*, from Ice. *gapa*, to yawn, gape.]
1. to open the mouth wide, as, (a) indicative of sleepiness, drowsiness, dullness, or indifference, as in yawning; (b) in eager desire for food; as, the young birds were *gaping*; (c) indicative of wonder, surprise, astonishment, or the like; as, the crowd stood *gaping*; (d) expressing earnest desire or expectation; (e) evincing a desire to injure or devour.

They have *gaped* upon me with their mouth. —Job xvi. 10.

2. to open as a gap; to show a fissure or chasm.

May that ground *gape* and swallow me alive. —Shak.

Syn.—yawn, oscitate, stare, gaze.

gāpe, *n.* 1. the act of gaping; specifically, (a) an open-mouthed stare; (b) a yawn.
2. a wide gap or opening.
3. in zoology, the measure of the widest possible opening of a mouth or beak.
the gapes; (a) a fit of yawning or gaping; (b) a disease of young poultry characterized by gaping due to the presence of a nematoid worm, *Syngamus trachealis*, in the windpipe.

gāp'ẽr, *n.* 1. one who gapes.
2. in zoology, (a) a bivalve mollusk, as *Mya truncata*; (b) a broadbill, as *Cymbirhynchus macrorhynchus*, the blue-billed gaper of the East Indies; (c) a serranoid fish, *Serranus cabrilla*.

gāpe'seed, *n.* any object of wonder or astonishment.

gāpes'ing, *n.* the act of gazing about. [Brit. Dial.]

gāpe'wŏrm, *n.* a parasitic roundworm that causes the gapes in young poultry by infesting the larger respiratory passages; *Syngamus trachealis*.

gāp'ing·ly, *adv.* in a gaping manner.

gāp'ing·stock, *n.* one who or that which is an object of open-mouthed wonder or astonishment.

gap lāthe, a lathe which has a gap in its bed so that its swing may be increased: called also *break lathe*.

gap'-tọothed (-tọotht), *a.* having interstices between the teeth.

gāp'y, *a.* having the gapes.

gär, *n.*; *pl.* **gär** or **gärș**, [ME. *gar*, from AS. *gar*, a spear: so called from the pointed snout.] any of a group of marine and fresh-water ganoid fishes characterized by elongated bodies covered with very hard scales, long beaklike snouts, and many sharp teeth: also called *garfish*, *needlefish*.

gär, *v.t.* to cause; to make; to compel. [Scot.]

gȧ·räge' (*or* -räzh'), *n.* [Fr., from *garer*, to protect, preserve; Pr. *garar*; prob. from Frank. *waron*, to watch, protect.]
1. a shelter or storage place for an automobile or automobiles.

2. a business establishment where automobiles are stored, repaired, washed, greased, etc.

gȧ·rāġe′, *v.t.*; garaged, *pt.*, *pp.*; garaging, *ppr.* to put or keep in a garage.

gȧ·rāġe′ sāle, a sale of used or unwanted possessions, as household articles, often held in the garage of a house.

Gar′ȧ·mond, *n.* a style of type based on that designed by Claude Garamond, 16th-century French type founder.

gar′ănce, *n.* [Fr.] *Rubia tinctorum*, the madder.

gȧ·ràn·ceux′ (-sē′), *n.* [Fr., from *garance*, madder.] a product obtained by treating the waste madder of the dyehouses, which still contains a certain quantity of alizarin and other coloring matters, with sulfuric acid, to remove lime, magnesia, etc.

Gar′ănd rī′fle, [after John C. *Garand*, Am. who invented it about 1930.] a semiautomatic, rapid-firing, .30-caliber rifle: the standard infantry weapon of the United States Army in World War II.

gȧ·rañ′găn, *n.* [E. Ind.] *Herpestes javanicus*, a species of mongoose or ichneumon.

gär·ȧ·pä′tȧ, gär·rȧ·pä′tȧ, *n.* [Sp. Am.]
1. any species of tick of the family *Ixodidæ*.
2. *Melophagus ovinus*, the sheep tick.

gar·ȧ·vance′, *n.* [Sp. *garbanzo*, from Basque *garbantzua*, the chick pea; *garau*, grain, and *antzua*, dry.] the chick pea, *Cicer arietinum*.

gärb, *n.* [OFr. *garbe*, gracefulness, from O.H.G. *garawi*, *garaur*, preparation, dress, from *garawen*, to prepare, dress.]
1. clothes; dress, especially an official or other distinguishing dress; fashion or mode of dress; costume; as, the *garb* of a clergyman or judge.

In the *garb* of a barefooted Carmelite.
—Longfellow.

2. outward appearance, form, or covering.
3. fashion; style; manner; mode of doing anything. [Obs.]

Syn.—dress, apparel, clothing, costume, attire, raiment.

gärb, *v.t.*; garbed, *pt.*, *pp.*; garbing, *ppr.* to clothe; to dress.

gärb, gärbe, *n.* [OFr. *garbe*, from O.H.G. *garba*, a sheaf of grain.] a sheaf or bundle, as of grain; in heraldry, a sheaf of any kind of grain, but specifically, a sheaf of wheat: when other than wheat, the kind must be expressed.

gär′bāġe, *n.* [ME. *garbage*, the entrails of fowls; etym. obscure; compare OFr. *garber*, to make fine; *grabeller*, to examine precisely.]
1. offal; the refuse animal or vegetable matter of a kitchen or market; refuse generally.
2. anything worthless or offensive, as obscene writings.

gär′bāġe, *v.t.* to disembowel; to eviscerate. [Obs.]

gär′ble, *v.t.*; garbled; *pt.*, *pp.*; garbling, *ppr.* [OFr. *grabeller*, to examine closely, from Sp. *garbillar*, to sift, from *garbillo*, a coarse sieve, from Ar. *ghirbāl*, a sieve.]
1. to cleanse or sort by sifting. [Rare.]
2. to select the best parts of. [Rare.]
3. to select, suppress, improperly emphasize, or otherwise distort parts of (a story, etc.) in telling, in order to mislead or misrepresent.
4. to confuse or mix up (a quotation, story, etc.) innocently.

Syn.—misrepresent, misquote, mutilate, falsify, pervert.

gär′ble, *n.* 1. anything that has been sifted or from which the coarse parts have been removed. [Obs.]
2. [*pl.*] impurities separated from goods, as spices, drugs, etc.; trash; garblings. [Obs.]

gär′blēr, *n.* one who garbles.

gär′bling, *n.* 1. the act of one who garbles.
2. [*pl.*] same as *garble*, n. 2.

gär′bōard, *n.* [D. *gaarbord*, from *garen* (contr. of *gaderen*, to gather) and *boord*, a board.] in shipbuilding, the first range or strake of planks or plates laid on a ship's bottom next to the keel: called also *garboard strake*, *ground strake*.

gär′boil, *n.* tumult; uproar. [Obs.]

Gär·cin′i·a, *n.* [from Dr. Laurent *Garcin*, a French botanist.] a genus of trees of the gamboge family, found in the tropical regions of Asia and Africa. *Garcinia mangostana* is the mangosteen tree.

gar·çon′ (gȧr-sōṅ′), *n.*; *pl.* **gar·çons′** (gȧr-sōṅ′), [Fr.]
1. a boy, youth, or young man.
2. a waiter or servant.

gärd, *v.* and *n.* guard. [Obs.]

gär′dănt, guär′dănt, *a.* [Fr. *gardant*, ppr. of *garder*, to look, regard.] in heraldry, having the full face turned toward the spectator: said of an animal passant, rampant, etc., used as a bearing.

gärde·bräs′, gärde′brāce, *n.* [Fr. *garde-bras*, arm-guard; *garder*, to guard, and *bras*, arm.] a piece of armor fastened to the elbow plates, and covering the elbow and upper part of the arm: used in the fifteenth century.

GARDEBRAS

gär′den, *n.* [OFr. *gardin*, *jardin*; O.H.G. *garto*, genit. *gartin*, a yard, garden.]
1. a piece of ground for the cultivation of herbs, plants, fruits, flowers, or vegetables: it is usually close to a house.
2. a rich, well-cultivated spot or tract of country; an area of fertile, developed land.

I am arrived for fruitful Lombardy,
The pleasant *garden* of great Italy.
—Shak.

3. [*often pl.*] a place for public enjoyment, planted with trees, flowers, etc., and often having special displays of animal or plant life.

gär′den, *a.* 1. of, for, used in, or grown in a garden.
2. (a) ordinary, commonplace; (b) hardy.
lead (someone) down the garden path; to mislead or deceive (someone).

gär′den, *v.i.*; gardened, *pt.*, *pp.*; gardening, *ppr.* to lay out or to cultivate a garden; to work in a garden.

gär′den, *v.t.* to cultivate as a garden; to make a garden of.

gär′den ȧ·pärt′ments, a complex of low apartment buildings surrounded by lawn.

gär′den bee′tle, a caraboid beetle.

gär′den en′ġine, see *garden pump*.

gär′den·ēr, *n.* [ME. *gardiner*; OFr. *jardinier*; O.H.G. *gartinari*, one who cares for a garden, from *garto*, genit. *gartin*, a garden.]
1. a person who makes, or works in, a garden.
2. a person whose occupation is gardening.

gär′den·ēr bīrd, the New Guinea bowerbird, *Amblyornis inornata*.

gär′den·ēr′ṣ-gär″tērṣ, *n.* *Phalaris arundinacea*, ribbon grass.

gär·den·esque′ (-esk′), *a.* like or resembling a garden.

gär′den flēa, a flea beetle.

gär′den-gāte, *n.* the pansy. [Brit. Dial.]

gär′den glȧss, 1. a globe of dark-colored glass placed on a pedestal as an ornament in gardens.
2. a bell glass used for covering plants.

gär′den house, 1. a summer house in a garden.
2. in the southern United States, a privy.

gär′den hus̱′bȧnd·ry, the raising of garden produce for market.

Gär·dē′ni·ȧ, *n.* [named after Dr. Alexander *Garden* (1730–1791), American botanist.]
1. a genus of trees and shrubs of the madder family, natives of tropical Asia and Africa: the species native to the Cape of Good Hope is well known in cultivation as the Cape jasmine.
2. [g–] a tree or shrub of this genus.
3. [g–] its white or yellowish flower, having fragrant, waxy petals.

gär′den·ing, *n.* the act or occupation of laying out and cultivating gardens; horticulture.

gär′den·less, *a.* destitute of a garden.

gär′den mōld, mold or rich mellow earth suitable for a garden.

Gär′den of the Godṣ, a valley in El Paso County, Colorado, interspersed with isolated rocks eroded into curious imitative forms.

gär′den pär′ty, a party held on a lawn or in a garden.

gär′den plot, a plot of ground used as or suitable for a garden.

gär′den pump, a portable pump used for watering gardens; a garden engine.

gär′den snāil, a European species of snail, *Helix aspersa*.

gär′den spī′dēr, the common name of the spider *Aranea diadema*, from its being found in great numbers in gardens: called also *diadem spider*.

gär′den stand, a stand or frame on which flower pots are placed.

Gär′den Stāte, the State of New Jersey.

gär′den stuff, plants growing in a garden; vegetables for the table.

gär′den sweep, a curving drive through a garden.

gär′den truck, same as *garden stuff*.

gär′den-vȧ·rī′e·ty, *a.* [see *garden*, *a.*, 2 (a).] ordinary; commonplace; as, a *garden-variety* novelist.

gär′den wa̤r′blēr, see *beccafico*.

gär′den wãre, the produce of gardens. [Obs.]

gär′dŏn, *n.* [Fr. and Sp.] a fish of the roach kind, *Leuciscus idus*.

gär·dy·lo͞o′, *n.* [Scot., from Fr. *gare l'eau*, beware of the water.] a cry formerly used in Edinburgh, to warn passers-by to beware of slops thrown from a window.

gãre, *n.* coarse wool growing on the legs of sheep.

gãre′fowl, *n.* [Ice. *geirfugl*.] the great auk, *Alca impennis*; also, the razorbill.

Gar′eth, *n.* [ME., from AS. *Garrath*.] in Arthurian legend, one of the knights of the Round Table, a nephew of King Arthur.

gär′fish, *n.*; *pl.* **gär′fish** or **gär′fish·eṣ,** [ME. *garfysshe*; AS. *gar*, a spear, and *fisc*, fish.] a fish with a long, narrow, beaklike snout; specifically, (a) *Belone vulgaris*, the common garfish of Europe; (b) any one of several species of fishes of the genus *Strongylura*, especially *Strongylura marina*, the common American garfish; (c) any garpike of the genus *Lepidosteus*. Also called *gar*.

COMMON GARFISH (*Belone vulgaris*)

gär′gȧ·līze, *v.t.* to gargle. [Obs.]

gär′gȧ·ney, *n.* [prob. from It. dial. *garganello*, origin prob. echoic of the cry.] a European species of duck, the summer teal, *Anas querquedula*, that lives near fresh water and resembles the American blue-winged teal: called also *cricket teal* and *pied widgeon*.

Gär·gan′tū·ăn, *a.* of or resembling Gargantua, the hero in the satire of Rabelais, who was a giant king; hence, gigantic; huge; prodigious.

gär′gȧ·riṣm, *n.* [LL. *gargarisma*, from Gr. *gargarizein*, to gargle.] a gargle. [Obs.]

gär′get, *n.* [ME. *gargat*; OFr. *gargate*, the throat, dim. of OFr. *gorge*, the throat, from L. *gurges*, a whirlpool.]
1. the throat. [Obs.]
2. a disease of swine or cattle, consisting of a swelling of the throat and the neighboring parts.
3. an inflammation of the udders of cows, ewes, etc.
4. a distemper in hogs.
5. the poke or pokeweed.

gär′gil, *n.* a distemper in geese, which affects the head and often proves fatal. [Now Dial.]

gär′gle, *v.t.*; gargled, *pt.*, *pp.*; gargling, *ppr.* [OFr. *gargouiller*, to gargle, from *gargouille*, the throat, from O.H.G. *gurgula*; L. *gurgulio*, the throat, windpipe.]
1. to wash or rinse, as the throat or mouth, with a liquid kept in motion in the throat by the slow expulsion of air from the lungs.
2. to utter with the sound of gargling.
3. to warble. [Rare.]

gär′gle, *v.i.* to gargle the throat.

gär′gle, *n.* any liquid used for gargling.

gär·gōu·lette′, *n.* same as *gurglet*.

gär′goyle, *n.* [ME. *gargyle*; OFr. *gargoille*, the throat, from L. *gurgulio* (-*onis*), the throat.]
1. a waterspout, usually in the form of an elaborately carved animal or fantastic creature, projecting from the gutter of a building.
2. a projecting ornament (on a building) like a gargoyle in appearance.

GARGOYLE

gar·i·bal′di, *n.* 1. a woman's loose, high-necked blouse with full sleeves, patterned after the shirt worn by the followers of Garibaldi.
2. *Hypsypops rubicundus*, a pomacentrid fish of California, of a red or orange color.

Gar·i·bal′di·ăn, *a.* pertaining to Giuseppe Garibaldi (1807–1882), who strove to bring about the unity and independence of Italy.

Gar·i·bal′di·ăn, *n.* a follower of Garibaldi or an advocate of his policy.

gãr′ish, *a.* [ME. *gauren*; OFr. *garer*, to observe, keep watch, from O.H.G. *waron*, to take heed, guard, from *warjan*, to guard.]
1. gaudy; showy; dazzling; too bright; flashy.
The *garish* blaze of day. —Byron.
2. extravagantly gay; flighty.

gãr′ish·ly, *adv.* in a garish manner; gaudily.

gãr′ish·ness, *n.* the state or quality of being garish.

gär′lănd, *n.* [OFr. *garlande*, a garland; compare O.H.G. *wiara*, an ornament of refined gold, a crown.]
1. a wreath of flowers, leaves, etc., worn on the head or used as decoration.
2. an anthology of poems, songs, etc.
3. in heraldry, a wreath of laurel or oak leaves.
4. in nautical usage, (a) a band or ring of rope used to hoist spars; (b) a kind of net used as a food bag.
5. the principal ornament or thing most prized. [Obs.]
6. a royal crown; a diadem. [Obs.]
7. in mining, a curb set in the wall of a shaft, to carry away any water running down its sides.
8. in architecture, a band of ornamental work round the top of a tower.

gär′lănd, *v.t.*; garlanded, *pt.*, *pp.*; garlanding, *ppr.* to form into or decorate with a garland or garlands.

gär′lănd flow′ẽr, 1. any of several Asiatic species of the genus *Hedychium*, of the ginger family.
2. any of several plants, as *Daphne cneorum*.

gär′lănd·less, *a.* having no garlands.

gär′lănd·ry, *n.* anything made into garlands.

gär′liç, *n.* [ME. *garlek*, *garlec*; AS. *garleác*, garlic, so named from its spearlike leaves; *gar*, a spear, and *leác*, a leek.]
1. a hardy onionlike plant of the lily family, *Allium sativum*, having a bulbous root.
2. the strong-smelling bulb of this plant, made up of small sections called cloves, used as seasoning in meats, salads, etc.
3. a jig or farce popular at the beginning of the seventeenth century. [Obs.]

gär′lick·y, *a.* having the smell or taste of garlic.

gär′liç mus′tärd, a plant of the mustard family, *Sisynbrium alliaria*, having a garlicky odor

gär′liç peãr, a tropical American tree, *Cratæva gynandra*, which bears a fruit that smells like garlic.

gär′liç shrub, 1. a climbing shrub of the West Indies and Guiana, *Adenocalymna alliacea*, having a garlicky odor.
2. any plant of the genus *Petiveria*, belonging to the pokeweed family, especially *Petiveria alliacea*.

gär′liç·wŏrt, *n.* *Alliaria officinalis*, the hedge garlic.

gär′ment, *n.* [ME. *garment*; OFr. *garnement*, from *garnir*, to garnish, adorn.]
1. (a) any article of clothing; (b) [*pl.*] clothes; costume.
2. a covering.

gär′ment, *v.t.* to cover with a garment; to clothe.

gär′ment·less, *a.* having no garment.

gär′men·tūre, *n.* dress; clothes; garments.

gär′nẽr, *n.* [ME. *garner*; OFr. *grenier*; L. *granaria*, neut. pl., a granary, from *granum*, grain.]
1. a granary; a place for storing grain.
2. a store of anything, as of wisdom, thought, etc.

gär′nẽr, *v.t.*; garnered, *pt.*, *pp.*; garnering, *ppr.* to store in or as in a granary; to gather up and save.

gär′nẽr, *v.i.* to accumulate; to become stored up. [Rare.]

gär′net, *n.* [ME. *gernet*; OFr. *grenat*; ML. *granatus*, a garnet, from *granatus*, having seeds, from L. *granum*, a grain, seed: from the resemblance to pomegranate seeds.]
1. a hard, glasslike silicate mineral of various colors: the most precious variety, used as a gem, is of a deep, transparent red.
2. deep red.

gär′net, *n.* [prob. from D. *granaat*, *kranaat*, apparently folk-etymologized forms of Fr. *garant*, fall tackle, from Bret. *garan*, a crane.] in nautical usage, (a) a tackle fixed to the mainstay, and used to hoist the cargo in and out; (b) a clew garnet; (c) a tackle run through a hole in the spar deck of a warship, to assist in handling the guns on the gun deck.

gär′net·ber″ry, *n.* *Ribes rubrum*, the common red currant.

gär′net blende, zinc blende; a native sulfide of zinc.

gär′net hinġe, a hinge resembling the letter **T** laid horizontally; thus, ⊢.

gär·net·if′ẽr·ous, *a.* [LL. *granatus*, the garnet, and L. *ferre*, to bear, bring.] in geology, containing garnets, as a rock matrix.

gär′ni·ẽr·īte, *n.* [from *Garnier*, a French geologist.] in mineralogy, an apple-green silicate of nickel and magnesium.

gär′nish, *v.t.*; garnished (-nisht), *pt.*, *pp.*; garnishing, *ppr.* [ME. *garnischen*; OFr. *garnisant*, ppr. of *garnir*, to defend, warn; compare AS. *wearnian*, to take care, warn; of Germanic origin.]
1. to adorn; to decorate; to embellish; to trim.
All within with flowers was *garnished*. —Spenser.
2. to decorate (food) with something that adds color or flavor; as, a steak is often *garnished* with parsley.
3. in law, to bring garnishment proceedings against (a debtor); to garnishee.
4. to fit with fetters. [Obs. Slang.]
5. to furnish; to supply. [Obs.]

gär′nish, *n.* 1. ornament; something added for embellishment; decoration.
Matter and figure they produce;
For *garnish* this, and that for use.—Prior.
2. in cookery, something placed on or around food to add color or flavor, as parsley or nuts.
3. fetters. [Obs. Slang.]
4. a fee; specifically, a fee formerly extorted from new prisoners by inmates of English jails or by the jailer. [Obs.]

gär′nish bōlt, a bolt having a chamfered or faceted head.

gär′nished (-nisht), *a.* in heraldry, (a) ornamented, as a bearing; (b) armed, as a human limb.

gär·nish·ee′, *n.* in law, a person who has money or other property of a defendant in his possession, and is ordered not to dispose of it pending settlement of the lawsuit.

gär·nish·ee′, *v.t.*; garnisheed, *pt.*, *pp.*; garnisheeing, *ppr.* in law, (a) to attach (a debtor's property, wages, etc.) by the authority of a court, so that it can be used to pay the debt; (b) to order (a person) not to dispose of the defendant's money or property in his possession pending settlement of the lawsuit.

gär′nish·ẽr, *n.* 1. one who garnishes.
2. in law, one who serves garnishment upon another.

gär′nish·ment, *n.* 1. ornament or embellishment.
2. in law, (a) a summons to a person other than the litigants to appear in a lawsuit; (b) a notice ordering a person not to dispose of a defendant's property or money in his possession pending settlement of the lawsuit.

gär′ni·sŏn, *n.* a garrison. [Obs.]

gär′ni·tūre, *n.* [Fr. *garniture*, furniture, supply, from *garnir*, to furnish.] an ornament; decoration; trimming; embellishment.

ga·rọọ′kuh (-ku), *n.* [East Indian.] a vessel used on the Persian gulf for fishing, varying from 50 to 100 feet in length, and having a short keel and a long, overhanging prow and stern.

ga·rọọn′ shell, see *goroon shell*.

ga·rotte′, *n.* and *v.t.* garrote.

gā′rous, *a.* [L. *garum*, pickle.] of or resembling garum.

gär′pīke, *n.* 1. the common garfish, *Belone vulgaris*.
2. any fish of the genus *Lepidosteus* or family *Lepidosteidæ*; a gar.

gar′răn, *n.* [Ir. and Gael. *garran*, *gearran*, a work-horse.] a small horse; a Highland horse; a worn-out horse; a galloway: written also *garron*.

gar′ret, *n.* [ME. *garett*; OFr. *garite*, a watchtower, a lookout, from *garir*, to watch, preserve, from Goth. *warjan*; O.H.G. *werian*, to defend, protect.]
1. the room or rooms just below the roof of a house, especially when unplastered and under a sloping roof; attic.
2. a turret or battlement; a watchtower. [Obs.]

gar′ret, *v.t.* same as *gallet*.

gar′ret·ed, *a.* protected by or provided with a garret or garrets.

gar·ret·eer′, *n.* an inhabitant of a garret; hence, a poor author.

gar′ri·sŏn, *n.* [ME. *garnison*; OFr. *garnison*, provision, supplies for defense, from *garnir*, to provide, supply.]
1. troops stationed in a fort or fortified place.
2. a fort or fortified place with troops, guns, etc.; a military post or station.

gar′ri·sŏn, *v.t.*; garrisoned, *pt.*, *pp.*; garrisoning; *ppr.* 1. to place troops in (a fortress) for defense; to furnish with soldiers; as, to *garrison* a fort or town.
2. to secure or defend by fortresses manned with troops; as, to *garrison* a conquered territory.
3. to place (troops) on duty in a garrison.
garrison cap; a military cap with a round, flat crown and leather visor: distinguished from *overseas cap*.
garrison court-martial; in military science, a part of military legal procedure, now replaced by a special court-martial: see *special court-martial* under *special*.
garrison flag; the largest-sized national flag, 38 feet by 20 feet, which is flown only on special occasions.
garrison prisoner; any military prisoner not a general prisoner; one sentenced or awaiting sentence at a garrison.

Gar·ri·sō′ni·ăn, *n.* in United States history, a believer in and follower of William Lloyd Garrison (1804–1879), abolitionist leader.

Gar·ri·sō′ni·ăn, *a.* pertaining to William Lloyd Garrison.

gar′rŏn, *n.* same as *garran*.

gar′rŏt, *n.* [Fr., from *garrotter*, to tie fast.]
1. in surgery, a means of stopping bleeding by twisting a circular bandage about the part; a tourniquet.
2. an arrow for a crossbow having a square head; a quarrel.

gar′rŏt, *n.* a black and white sea duck, the goldeneye.

gar·rōte′, *n.* [Sp. *garrote*, a cudgel, a strangling by means of an iron collar, from *garra*, a claw, talon, from Breton *gar*, the shank of the leg.]
1. a Spanish method of execution by strangulation with an iron collar tightened by a screw.
2. the iron collar so used.
3. a cord, thong, or length of wire for strangling an enemy outpost or sentry in a surprise attack.
4. (a) a disabling by strangling, as in an attack for robbery; strangulation; (b) strangulation and robbery.
Also written *garotte*, *garrotte*.

gar·rōte′, *v.t.* garroted *or* garrotted, *pt.*, *pp.*; garroting *or* garrotting, *ppr.* 1. to execute or attack with a garrote or by strangling.
2. (a) to disable by strangling, as in an attack for robbery; (b) to strangle and rob.
Also written *garotte*, *garrotte*.

gar·rōt′ẽr, ga·rōt′ẽr, *n.* one who garrotes.

gar·rotte′, *n.* and *v.t.* same as *garrote*.

Gar·rụ·lī′nae, *n.pl.* [L. *garrulus*, chattering, and *-inæ*.] a subfamily of *Corvidæ*, including the jays and magpies.

gar′rụ·line, *a.* pertaining to the *Garrulinæ*.

gar·rụ′li·ty, *n.* [L. *garrulitas*, from *garrulus*, garrulous, from *garrire*, to chatter, talk.] the quality of being garrulous; talkativeness; loquacity.

gar′rụ·lous, *a.* [L. *garrulus*, chattering, prattling, from *garrire*, to chatter, prattle.] talking much, often about unimportant things; loquacious; talkative; prating.
Syn.—talkative, loquacious.—A *garrulous* person indulges in long, prosy talk, with frequent repetitions and lengthened details; *talkative* implies a great desire to talk, and *loquacious*, a great flow of words at command.

gar′rụ·lous·ly, *adv.* in a garrulous manner; chatteringly.

gar′rụ·lous·ness, *n.* talkativeness.

Gar′rụ·lus, *n.* a genus typical of *Garrulinæ*.

gar·rụ′pȧ, *n.* [Sp. Am. name; prob. from Portuguese *garupa*, a crupper.] any of several species of fishes, especially of the genus *Sebastichthys*, found on the coast of California; a rockfish.

Gar′ry·ȧ, *n.* [named after Michael *Garry*, of the Hudson Bay Company.] a genus of opposite-leaved evergreen shrubs of the dogwood family, native to the southwestern United States and the West Indies: *Garrya elliptica* is cultivated in England for ornament.

gär′tẽr, *n.* [ME. *garter*; O.Norm.Fr. *gartier*, a garter, from *garet*, the small of the leg behind the knee, from Bret. *gar, garr*, the shank of the leg.]

1. an elastic band, or a strap suspended from an undergarment, by which a stocking is held in place upon the leg.

2. in heraldry, a bendlet.

3. a tape that is held up for a circus performer to leap over.

4. [G–] (a) the badge of the Order of the Garter, the highest order of British knighthood; (b) the order itself; (c) membership in it.

Garter King-of-Arms; the principal king-of-arms in England, by whom arms are granted and confirmed under the authority of the Earl Marshal.

INSIGNIA OF THE ORDER OF THE GARTER
1. the star; 2. the lesser George; 3. the collar; 4. the George; 5. the garter

Order of the Garter; the highest order of British Knighthood, instituted about 1344 by Edward III, consisting of the sovereign, the Prince of Wales, and 25 knights.

gär′tẽr, *v.t.*; gartered, *pt., pp.*; gartering, *ppr.* to bind with or as with a garter.

gär′tẽr belt, a belt, usually of elastic fabric, with garters suspended from it, worn by women.

gär′tẽr fish, the scabbard fish, a fish of the genus *Lepidopus*.

gär′tẽr snāke, a small, harmless North American snake with yellow stripes, of the genus *Eutænia*: *Eutænia sirtalis* and *Eutænia saurita* are the best-known species.

gärth, *n.* [ME. *garth*; Ice. *garthr*, a yard, court, garden.]

1. a dam or weir for catching fish.

2. an enclosed yard or garden. [Archaic.]

gärth, *n.* a hoop or band. [Brit. Dial.]

ga·rü′bȧ, *n.* [Sp. Am.] a yellow, Brazilian parakeet, *Conurus luteus*.

gā′rum, *n.* [L. *garum, garon*; Gr. *garon*.] a fish sauce prized by the ancient Greeks and Romans.

gär′vie, *n.* [Scot., from Gael. *garbhag*, a sprat, from *garbh*, thick, coarse.] a sprat: called also *garvie herring*. [Scot.]

Gā′ry sçhool sys′tem, a system of school management by which a specified time is devoted to study, to manual training, and to play, with special teachers or supervisors for each division: after Gary, Indiana, where first tried.

gas, *n.* [word invented by the Belgian chemist, Van Helmont (1577–1644), on basis of Gr. *chaos*, chaos.]

1. the fluid form of a substance in which it can expand indefinitely and completely fill its container; form that is neither liquid nor solid; vapor.

2. any mixture of inflammable gases used for lighting or heating.

3. any gas used as an anesthetic, as nitrous oxide.

4. any substance, as phosgene, intentionally dispersed through the atmosphere, as in war, to act as a poison or irritant.

5. (a) gasoline; (b) the accelerator or throttle in an automobile, etc. [Colloq.]

6. empty, idle, or boastful talk. [Slang.]

7. in mining, a mixture of firedamp with air that explodes if ignited.

gas, *v.t.*; gassed (gast), *pt., pp.*; gassing, *ppr.*

1. to supply with gas.

2. to subject to the action of gas.

3. to attack with gas; injure or kill by gas, as in war.

4. to free (lace, net, etc.) from loose filaments by exposing it to many minute jets of gas.

gas, *v.i.* 1. to give off gas.

2. to talk in an empty, idle, or boastful way. [Slang.]

air gas; air charged with a mixture of hydrocarbons.

gas attack; in military science, an offensive in which poisonous gas is used.

laughing gas; nitrous oxide, N_2O, used as an anesthetic, especially in dentistry: so called from the reaction of laughter and exhilaration that inhaling it may produce.

mustard gas; an oily, volatile liquid, $(CH_2ClCH_2)_2S$, used in warfare as a poison gas because of its extremely irritating, blistering, and disabling effects.

natural gas; a mixture of gaseous hydrocarbons, chiefly methane, occurring naturally in the earth in certain places, from which it is piped to cities, etc., to be used as a fuel.

olefiant gas; ethylene: a former name.

tear gas; a gas that causes irritation of the eyes, excessive flow of tears, and temporary blindness.

to step on the gas; (a) to press on the accelerator of an automobile, etc.; (b) to hurry; move or act faster. [Slang.]

gas, *a.* of, using, or operated by gas; as, a *gas* range.

gas·ȧ·liẽr′, *n.* same as *gaselier*.

gas bȧ·cil′lus, a rod-shaped microorganism that infects wounds and causes gas to form in them.

gas′bag, *n.* 1. a bag for holding gas, as in a balloon or dirigible.

2. a bag used for closing a gas main when repairs are being made.

3. a person who talks too much. [Slang.]

gas bat′tẽr·y, in electricity, a voltaic battery in which the elements are hydrogen and oxygen or other gases.

gas black, a dense carbon deposited in gas retorts.

gas blēach′ing, bleaching by the use of sulfur dioxide.

gas bũrn′ẽr, 1. a gas jet.

2. a stove or furnace in which gas is used as fuel.

gas chām′bẽr, a room in which people are put to be killed with poison gas.

gas check, a device designed to prevent the escape of gas at the breech of a firearm.

gas çōal, soft coal from which illuminating gas is made.

gas çŏm′pȧ·ny, a company that supplies gas to a community, generally at a certain rate per 1,000 feet.

Gas′çŏn, *a.* [Fr.] 1. of Gascony, in France, or its people, who were famous for their boastfulness.

2. [g–] boastful; swaggering.

Gas′çŏn, *n.* 1. a native of Gascony.

2. [g–] a boaster; a swaggerer.

gas·çŏn·āde′, *n.* [Fr., from *Gascon*, an inhabitant of Gascony.] a boast or boasting; blustering talk; brag.

gas·çŏn·āde′, *v.i.*; gasconaded, *pt., pp.*; gasconading, *ppr.* to boast; to brag.

gas·çŏn·ād′ẽr, *n.* a boaster.

gas çŏn·dens′ẽr, an apparatus which frees the tar from illuminating gas in its manufacture.

gas·ē′i·ty, *n.* the state or quality of being gaseous.

gas·e·liẽr′, gas·ȧ·liẽr′, *n.* an early kind of chandelier with branches ending in gas jets.

gas en′ġine, an engine in which the explosion of gas in a cylinder drives the piston; internal-combustion engine.

gas′ē·ous, *a.* 1. of, having the nature of, or in the form of gas.

2. figuratively, lacking substance or solidity; flimsy.

Unconnected, *gaseous* information.
—Stephen.

gas′ē·ous·ness, *n.* the state or quality of being gaseous.

gas fit′tẽr, a person whose work is installing and repairing gas pipes and fixtures.

gas fix′tūre, a device that carries gas from the pipe to a jet or burner.

gas fũr′nāce, 1. a furnace that distills gas from coal, etc.

2. a furnace that burns gas as fuel.

gas gañ′grēne, gangrene in which gas bacilli cause the diseased tissues of dirty wounds to become filled with gas and a liquid discharge.

gas glōbe, a hollow globe used as a shade for a gaslight.

gas gŏv′ẽrn·ŏr, any device for the regulation of the flow of gas.

gas gun, a pipe in which gas is exploded in signaling.

gash, *v.t.*; gashed (gasht), *pt., pp.*; gashing, *ppr.* [earlier *garse*; ME. *garsen*; OFr. *garser*.] to make a long, deep cut in; slash.

gash, *n.* [ME. *garse*, from the *v.*] a long, deep cut.

gash, *a.* [perhaps an abbrev. from L. *sagax*, sagacious, wise.]

1. sharp; shrewd; sagacious; having the appearance of sagacity and self-importance. [Scot.]

2. trim; well-dressed. [Scot.]

gash, *v.i.* to gossip; to chatter. [Scot.]

gash, *a.* ghastly. [Scot.]

gash′ful, *a.* full of gashes; hideous. [Obs.]

gas hōld′ẽr, a vessel for storing gas after purification; a gasometer.

gas′house, *n.* a place where gas for heating and lighting is prepared; gasworks: used figuratively to suggest slum areas, roughness, etc.

gash vein, in mining, a vein that does not extend beyond the stratum in which it occurs.

gas″i·fi·çā′tion, *n.* a gasifying or being gasified.

gas′i·fọrm, *a.* [*gas*, and L. *forma*, form.] gaseous; in the form of gas.

gas′i·fȳ, *v.t.* and *v.i.*; gasified, *pt., pp.*; gasifying, *ppr.* [*gas*, and L. *facere*, to make.] to convert into gas.

gas in′di·çā·tŏr, an instrument for indicating the pressure of gas in a pipe, or for showing the presence of firedamp in a mine.

gas jet, 1. a flame of illuminating gas.

2. a nozzle or burner at the end of a gas fixture.

gas′ket, *n.* [prob. from It. *gaschetta*, a rope end.]

1. a piece or ring of rubber, metal, paper, etc. placed around a piston or joint to make it leakproof.

2. in nautical usage, a rope or cord by which a furled sail is tied to the yard.

gas′kin, *n.* [contr. from *galligaskins*.]

1. [*pl.*] galligaskins. [Obs.]

2. the upper part of the hind leg of a horse or similar animal.

gas′king, *n.* a gasket. [Rare.]

gas′līght (-līt), *n.* 1. light produced by the combustion of coal gas.

2. a gas jet or burner.

gas′līght, *a.* of or characteristic of the period of gaslight illumination; as, *gaslight* melodrama.

gas līme, lime used as a filter or purifier for illuminating gas.

gas liq′ūor (lik′ũr), an ammoniacal liquor extracted from coal in the distillation of gas.

gas log, an imitation log in the form of a hollow, perforated cylinder, used as a gas heater in a fireplace.

gas māin, a large underground pipe that conducts gas into smaller pipes leading into houses, factories, etc.

gas′man, *n.*; *pl.* **gas′men,** 1. an employee of a gasworks who regularly reads consumers' gas meters to determine the amount of gas used.

2. a gas fitter.

3. in mining, a person whose work is checking the ventilation and guarding against firedamp.

gas man′tle, a tube of fabric treated with certain incandescent metals and fastened over a gas burner to give off light when heated by the flame.

gas mask, a device worn over the face to prevent the breathing in of poisonous gases by filtering them out of the air.

gas mē′tẽr, an instrument for measuring the quantity of a gas, especially of illuminating gas consumed as fuel.

gas mō′tŏr, a gas engine.

gas′ō-, a combining form meaning *gas*.

gas′ō·ġēne, *n.* same as *gazogene*.

GAS MASK

gas′ō·hol, *n.* [from *gasoline* and *alcohol*.] a mixture of gasoline and alcohol, used as a motor fuel; specifically, a mixture of 90 per cent unleaded gasoline and 10 per cent ethyl alcohol.

gas′ō·līne (*or* gas-ō-līne′), **gas′ō·lēne** (*or* gas-ō-lēne′), *n.* [*gas*, and L. *oleum*, oil, and *-ine*.] a volatile, highly inflammable, colorless liquid obtained by the fractional distillation of petroleum: it is used chiefly as a fuel in internal-combustion engines.

gas·om′e·tẽr, *n.* [*gaso-*, and Gr. *metron*, measure.]

1. a container for holding and measuring gas.

2. a reservoir for gas.

gas·ō·met′riç, *a.* of or pertaining to gasometry, or the measurement of gases.

gasometric analysis; in chemistry, the process of separating and estimating the relative proportions of the elements of a gaseous body.

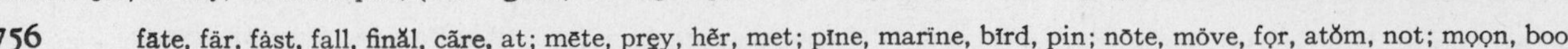

gas·ō·met′riç·ăl, *a.* gasometric.

gas·om′e·try, *n.* the science of measuring gases; especially, the determination of the amount of a gas in a mixture.

gȧsp, *v.i.*; gasped (gȧspt), *pt., pp.*; gasping, *ppr.* [ME. *gaspen, gayspen*, from Ice. *geispa*, to yawn.]

1. to catch the breath suddenly or with effort, as in surprise or in choking.

2. to pant with eagerness; to pant vehemently.

gȧsp, *v.t.* to say or tell with gasps; as, he *gasped* out his story.

gȧsp, *n.* a gasping; catching of the breath with difficulty.

at the last gasp; (a) just before death; (b) just before the end; at the last moment.

gas′pẽr·eau (-ō), *n.* the alewife, a fish of the herring family: French Canadian name.

gas′pẽr·gou, *n.* [compare Fr. *gasparot*, a kind of herring.] the drumfish, a fresh-water fish. [Dial.]

gȧsp′ing·ly, *adv.* with a gasp or with gasps.

gas′pīpe, *n.* same as *gas pipe*.

gas pīpe, a pipe for the conveyance of gas.

gas plant, a plant, *Dictamnus fraxinella*, which gives off an inflammable vapor.

gas rānge, a stove that uses gas as a fuel.

gas reg′ū·lā·tŏr, a gas governor.

gas rē·tort′, a chamber that holds the material from which gas is made.

gas sand, sandstone which yields natural gas.

Gas·sē′ri·ăn, *a.* of or relating to the German physician Gasserius, the discoverer of the ganglion named after him.

Gasserian ganglion; a ganglion at the root of the fifth cranial nerve.

gas shell, an explosive shell filled with poisonous or irritant gas, used in war.

gas′sing, *n.* boasting; empty or pretentious talk. [Slang.]

gas stā′tion, a place for the sale of gasoline, oil, services, etc. for motor vehicles.

gas stōve, a gas range.

gas′sy, *a.*; *comp.* gassier; *superl.* gassiest. 1. full of or containing gas.

2. like gas.

3. full of talk, especially pretentious or boastful talk. [Colloq.]

gȧst, *v.t.* to frighten; to terrify. [Obs.]

gȧst, *n.* a fright. [Obs.]

gas tär, coal tar.

Gas″tẽr·ō·lī·chē′nēṣ, *n.pl.* [L., from Gr. *gastēr*, stomach, and *leichēn*, lichen.] a group of lichens which produce spores in the same way as the *Gasteromycetes*.

Gas″tẽr·ō·mȳ·cē′tēṣ, *n.pl.* [L., from Gr. *gastēr*, stomach, and *mykēs* (-*etos*), mushroom.] an order of fungi represented by the common puffball.

gas″tẽr·ō·mȳ·cē′tous, *a.* pertaining to the *Gasteromycetes*.

gas′tẽr·ō·pod, *n.* and *a.* same as *gastropod*.

Gas·tẽr·op′ō·dȧ, *n.pl.* same as *Gastropoda*.

gas·tẽr·op′ō·dous, *a.* same as *gastropodous*.

gas″tẽr·ō·thē′çȧ, *n.* same as *gastrotheca*.

Gas·tẽr·ot′ri·chȧ, *n.pl.* same as *Gastrotricha*.

gas″tẽr·ō·zō′oid, *n.* same as *gastrozooid*.

gas′tīght (-tīt), *a.* capable of containing or excluding gas; as, a *gastight* flask, a *gastight* stopper.

gȧst′ly, *a.* ghastly. [Obs.]

Gas·tor′nis, *n.* [after *Gaston* Planté, the discoverer, and Gr. *ornis*, a bird.] a genus of fossil ostrichlike birds found in the Paris basin.

gas′tr-, same as *gastro-*.

gas·trae′ȧ, *n.* [L., from Gr. *gastēr*, the stomach.] a hypothetical animal form supposed by Haeckel to have been the ancestor from which all metazoans have descended: it is regarded as similar to the gastrula stage of the metazoan embryo.

gas·trae′um, *n.* [L., from Gr. *gastēr*, the stomach.] in ornithology, the underside of a bird.

gas′trăl, *a.* of or belonging to the stomach; intestinal.

gas·tral′ġi·ȧ, *n.* [L., from Gr. *gastēr*, the stomach, and *algos*, pain.] pain in the stomach or abdomen.

gas trap, a trap to prevent the escape of gas from a sewer.

gas·treç′tō·my, *n.*; *pl.* **gas·treç′tō·mieṣ,** [*gastr-*, and *-ectomy*.] in surgery, the cutting away of a part of the stomach.

gas·trel·çō′sis, *n.* [L., from Gr. *gastēr*, stomach, and *helkōsis*, ulceration, from *helkoun*, to ulcerate, from *helkos*, an ulcer.] stomach ulceration.

gas′triç, *a.* [L. *gaster*; Gr. *gastēr*, stomach.] of, in, or near the stomach.

gastric fever; any fever accompanied by acute disorder of the stomach; severe dyspepsia with fever; enteric fever.

gastric juice; the thin, acid digestive fluid produced by glands in the mucous membrane lining the stomach: it contains enzymes and hydrochloric acid.

gastric ulcer; an ulcer of the lining of the stomach.

gas·tril′ō·quist, *n.* a ventriloquist. [Rare.]

gas·tril′ō·quous, *a.* ventriloquous. [Rare.]

gas·tril′ō·quy, *n.* ventriloquism. [Rare.]

gas′trin, *n.* a hormone that is formed in the stomach and stimulates the production of the gastric juice: it is now regarded as identical with histamine.

gas·trī′tis, *n.* [Mod.L.; *gastr-*, and *-itis*.] inflammation of the stomach, especially of the stomach lining.

gas′trō-, [from Gr. *gastēr*, the stomach.] a combining form meaning: (a) *the stomach*, as in *gastro*enteritis; (b) *the stomach and*, as in *gastro*colic. Also, before a vowel, *gastr-*.

gas′trō·cēle, *n.* [*gastro-*, and Gr. *kēlē*, a tumor.] gastric hernia.

gas·troç·nē′mi·us, *n.* [L., from Gr. *gastēr*, stomach, and *knēmē*, leg.] the large muscle in the calf of the leg.

gas·trō·çol′iç, *a.* [*gastro-*, and Gr. *kōlon*, the colon.] of or attached to the stomach and the transverse colon.

gas′trō·disç, *n.* [*gastro-*, and Gr. *diskos*, a disk.] the germinal disk.

gas″trō·dū·ō·dē′năl, *a.* [*gastro-*, and L. *duodenum*, the duodenum, from *duodeni*, twelve each.] pertaining to both the stomach and the duodenum; as, the *gastroduodenal* artery.

gas″trō·dū″ō·dē·nī′tis, *n.* inflammation of both the duodenum and stomach.

gas·trō·dyn′i·ȧ, *n.* [L., from Gr. *gastēr*, stomach, and *odynē*, pain.] stomach pain; gastralgia.

gas″trō·en·ter′iç, *a.* [*gastro-*, and Gr. *entera*, intestines.] pertaining to both the stomach and the intestines.

gas″trō·en″te·rī′tis, *n.* [*gastro-*, and Gr. *entera*, intestines.] inflammation of the lining of the stomach and the intestines.

gas″trō·ep″i·plō′iç, *a.* [*gastro-*, and Gr. *epiploon*, the caul.] belonging to the stomach and epiploon, or great omentum.

gas″trō·hē·pat′iç, *a.* [*gastro-*, and Gr. *hēpar* (*hēpatos*), the liver.] pertaining to both the stomach and the liver.

gas″trō·hys″tẽr·ot′ō·my, *n.* [*gastro-*, and Gr. *hystera*, the womb, and *tomē*, a cutting.] Caesarean section.

gas′troid, *a.* resembling the stomach. [Rare.]

gas″trō·in·tes′ti·năl, *a.* of the stomach and the intestines.

gas′trō·lith, *n.* [*gastro-*, and Gr. *lithos*, a stone.] in medicine, a stony concretion formed in the stomach.

Gas·trō·lō′bi·um, *n.* [*gastro-*, and Gr. *lobos*, a pod.] a genus of leguminous Australian shrubs with bright-yellow flowers and inflated pods: also called *poison plant* because often fatal to cattle eating it.

gas·trol′ō·ġy, *n.* [*gastro-*, and Gr. *logos*, discourse.] the science of the functions and diseases of the stomach; also, humorously, gastronomy.

gas″trō·mȧ·lā′ci·ȧ, *n.* [L., from Gr. *gastēr*, stomach, and *malakia*, softness, from *malakos*, soft.] softening of the walls of the stomach, occurring usually after death.

gas′trō·man·cy, *n.* [Fr. *gastromantie*, from Gr. *gastēr*, stomach, and *manteia*, divination.] divination by ventriloquial sounds; also, divination by gazing into a crystal ball.

gas·trō·mȳ′cēṣ, *n.* [L., from Gr. *gastēr*, stomach, and *mykēs*, a fungus.] fungoid growths in the stomach.

gas′trō·nōme, gas·tron′ō·mẽr, *n.* [Fr. *gastronome*, from Gr. *gastēr*, stomach, and *nomos*, rule, law.] one who enjoys and has a discriminating taste for foods; an epicure; a judge of the art of cookery.

gas·trō·nom′iç, gas·trō·nom′iç·ăl, *a.* pertaining to gastronomy.

gas·tron′ō·mist, *n.* a gastronome.

gas·tron′ō·my, *n.* [Fr. *gastronomie*; Gr. *gastronomia*, from *gastēr*, stomach, and *nemein*, to regulate, from *nomos*, rule, law.] the art or science of good eating; epicurism.

gas·trop′ȧ·thy, *n.* disease of the stomach.

gas″trō·phō·tog′rȧ·phy, *n.* a method of photographing the inside of the stomach by introducing a small camera into it.

gas·trō·phren′ic, *a.* [*gastro-*, and Gr. *phrēn*, the diaphragm.] pertaining to the stomach and diaphragm.

gas″trō·pneū·mon′iç (-nū-mon′ik), *a.* [*gastro-*, and Gr. *pneumōn*, the lungs.] pertaining to both the stomach and the lungs.

gas′trō·pod, *n.* any of the *Gastropoda*: also *gasteropod*.

gas′trō·pod, *a.* gastropodous: also *gasteropod*.

Gas·trop′ō·dȧ, *n.pl.* [L., from Gr. *gastēr*, stomach, and *podos*, foot.] a class of mollusks having one-piece spiral shells, as the snail, limpet, etc., or no shells at all, as certain slugs: motion is by means of a broad, muscular, ventral disk: also *Gasteropoda*.

gas·trop′ō·dous, *a.* of or like a gastropod: also *gasteropodous*.

gas′trō·pōre, *n.* [*gastro-*, and Gr. *poros*, a pore, a passage.] the pore or orifice of a polypite.

gas·tror′rhȧ·phy, *n.* [*gastro-*, and Gr. *rhaphē*, a seam, from *rhaptein*, to sew.] suture of wounds in the stomach or abdomen.

gas′trō·sçōpe, *n.* [*gastro-*, and Gr. *skopein*, to view.] an instrument for examining the interior of the stomach.

gas·trō·sçop′iç, *a.* pertaining to a gastroscope or gastroscopy.

gas·tros′çō·py, *n.* the inspection of the interior of the stomach with a gastroscope.

gas·trō·splen′iç, *a.* [*gastro-*, and Gr. *splēn*, the spleen.] pertaining to both the stomach and the spleen.

gas′trō·stēġe, *n.* [*gastro-*, and Gr. *stegos*, the roof.] any of the ventral scales of a snake.

gas·tros′tō·my, *n.* [*gastro-*, and Gr. *stoma*, mouth.] an operation by which an artificial opening is made in the stomach for the introduction of food in cases of obstruction of the esophagus.

gas·trō·thē′çȧ, *n.* [*gastro-*, and Gr. *thēkē*, a case.] in entomology, the abdominal case of a pupa: also *gasterotheca*.

gas·trot′ō·my, *n.* [*gastro-*, and Gr. *tomē*, a cutting.] the operation of cutting into or opening the stomach, as for removing gastroliths.

Gas·trot′ri·chȧ, *n.pl.* [Gr. *gastēr*, stomach, and *thrix, trichos*, hair.] a group of worms characterized by ventral cilia.

gas·trō·vas′çū·lăr, *a.* [*gastro-*, and L. *vasculum*, a small vessel.]

1. performing the dual function of digestion and circulation; as, the *gastrovascular* canals of the *Cœlenterata*.

2. of organs with such a dual function.

gas·trox·yn′sis, *n.* [*gastro-*, and Gr. *oxynein*, to make acid.] abnormal acidity of the gastric juices, as in certain forms of nervous dyspepsia.

gas·trō·zō′oid, *n.* [*gastro-*, and Gr. *zōion*, an animal, and *eidos*, form.] a zooid provided with feeding and digestive organs: also *gasterozooid*.

gas′trụ·lȧ, *n.*; *pl.* **gas′trụ·lae,** [L., dim. of *gaster*; Gr. *gastēr*, stomach.] in embryology, a form assumed by the embryo in an early stage of development. It consists essentially of a cuplike body whose walls have two layers, the ectoderm and endoderm, enclosing a central cavity that opens to the outside through the blastopore.

CELLS

GASTRULA

gas′trụ·lăr, *a.* relating to a gastrula or to gastrulation.

gas·trụ·lā′tion, *n.* the process of forming a gastrula.

gas wäsh′ẽr, a device used to remove ammonia from illuminating gas.

gas well, a well from which natural gas is obtained.

gas′wŏrks, *n.* an establishment in which gas for heating and lighting is manufactured; a gashouse.

gat, *v.* archaic past tense of *get*.

gat, *n.* [Scand.] a narrow ship channel between cliffs or sandbanks.

gat, *n.* [from *Gat*ling gun.] a pistol. [Slang.]

gatch, *n.* [Per. *gach*, plaster.] plaster, as used in Persian gatchwork.

gatch′wŏrk, *n.* ornamental work in gatch, or molded plaster.

gāte, *n.* [ME. *gate, gat*; AS. *geat*, a gate, door.]

1. a movable framework or solid structure, especially one that swings on hinges, controlling entrance or exit through an opening in a fence or wall.

2. an opening providing passageway through a fence or wall, with or without such a structure; gateway.

3. any means of entrance or exit; as, the *gate* to one's heart.

4. a mountain gap.
5. a movable barrier, as at a railroad crossing.
6. a structure controlling the flow of water, as in a pipe, canal, etc.
7. (a) the total amount of money received in admission prices to a performance or exhibition; (b) the total number of spectators who pay to see such an event.
8. an aperture in the tumblers of a lock for the passage of the stub.
9. a frame in which a saw is extended to prevent buckling or bending.
to give the gate; to send away; get rid of; dismiss. [Slang.]

gāte, *v.t.*; gated, *pt., pp.*; gating, *ppr.* 1. to furnish with a gate.
2. to confine (a student) to the college grounds. [Brit.]

gāte, *n.* [from AS. *gēotan*, to pour, gush out.]
1. a channel through which molten metal is poured into a mold.
2. the waste part of a casting formed at this channel.

gāte chām′bēr, a recess, as in a wall, which receives a gate when opened.

gāte hook, the hook or part upon which a gate is hung.

gāte′house, *n.* a house beside or over a gate, used as a porter's lodge, etc.

gāte′-leg tā′ble, gāte′-legged tā′ble, see phrase under *table, n.*

gāte′less, *a.* having no gate.

gāte′măn, *n.*; *pl.* **gāte′men,** a man in charge of a gate.

gāte mŏn′ey, money received for admission to an athletic contest, races, etc.

gāte′pōst, *n.* an upright post on which a gate is hinged, or the one to which it is fastened when closed.

gāte valve, a valve with a sliding gate for opening and closing a pipe.

gāte vein, the portal vein. [Obs.]

gāte′wāy, *n.* a way or opening in a wall, fence, etc. fitted with a gate; hence, any means of going in or out; a means of getting at something.

Gath, *n.* [Heb. lit., wine press.] in the Bible, one of the five great cities of the Philistines: II Sam. i. 20.

Gä′thȧ, *n.* [Sans., hymn, psalm.] one of five groups of metrical compositions in the Avesta of the Parsees, attributed to Zoroaster.

gath′ẽr, *v.t.*; gathered, *pt., pp.*; gathering, *ppr.* [ME. *gaderen, gadren*; AS. *gaderian, gædrian*, to gather, from *geador, gader*, together.]
1. to cause to come together; to collect into one place or into one aggregate body; to assemble; to congregate; as, to *gather* an army.
2. to select and take; to cull; to pluck; to separate from others less desired and bring together; to get in, as a harvest; to reap and bring into barns or stores; as, he *gathered* his crop of wheat.
3. to get or collect gradually from various places, sources, etc.; amass; accumulate.
4. to draw (cloth) into fixed pleats or folds along a thread run through it; to pucker; to pleat.
5. to deduce by inference; to collect or learn by observation or reasoning; to conclude; as, from what I hear I *gather* that he was present.
6. to gain, accumulate, or acquire gradually; as, the snowball *gathered* weight by rolling.
7. to take in; as, to *gather* the slack of a sail.
8. to prepare or collect (oneself, one's energies) to meet a situation.
9. to wrinkle (one's brow).
10. in masonry, to narrow suddenly, as a fireplace to meet the dimensions of a flue.
11. in bookbinding, to collect and arrange the parts of (a book, etc.) in regular order for binding.
to gather up; (a) to pick up and assemble; (b) to draw together; make more compact.
to gather way; to start; to begin to move; to acquire motion, as a ship under sail or steam.

gath′ẽr, *v.i.* 1. to collect; to assemble; to unite; to accumulate; as, the clouds *gathered* in the west.
2. to increase; as, the snowball *gathered* as it rolled.
3. to fester; to form pus; to reach the stage of suppuration, as a boil.
4. to become wrinkled: said of a brow.
Syn.—collect, accumulate, amass, assemble, aggregate, group, congregate, suppurate.

gath′ẽr, *n.* 1. a pleat.
2. the forward inclination of the journals on an axle, designed to prevent the wheels from running unevenly.
3. the lower face of the masonry in a fireplace where it narrows to the flue.

gath′ẽr·ȧ·ble, *a.* that can be gathered.

gath′ẽr·ẽr, *n.* 1. one who gathers or collects; as, a news *gatherer*.
2. one who gets in a crop; as, a hay *gatherer*.
3. an attachment on a sewing machine to make gathers in cloth.

gath′ẽr·ing, *n.* 1. the act of collecting or assembling; the act of making a collection, as of money, or of making gathers, as in cloth; the act of collecting and arranging the parts of a book, etc. for binding.
2. what is gathered together; specifically, (a) a crowd; an assemblage; (b) a collection for charity; (c) a series of small pleats in cloth.
3. a festering boil; an abscess.

gath′ẽr·ing çōal, a large piece of coal kept smoldering during the night, in order to start a fire in the morning.

gath′ẽr·ing hoop, a hoop used by coopers for drawing the ends of barrel staves together.

gath′ẽr·ing pal′let, a pallet or lever controlling the operation of the striking mechanism of a clock.

gath′ẽr·ing pēat, 1. a peat serving as a gathering coal.
2. a fiery peat formerly used as a warning signal by the Scottish borderers.

Gat′ling gun, see under *gun*.

gat′-toothed (-tötht), *a.* [etym. and meaning doubtful.] gap-toothed; having open spaces between the teeth. [Obs.]

gaub, *n.* [Hind. *gāb*.] a variety of persimmon tree of the East Indies; also, its astringent fruit.

gauche (gōsh), *a.* [Fr., from MFr. *gauchir*, to become crooked or warped.]
1. left-handed; hence, awkward; tactless; lacking grace, especially social grace.
2. in mathematics, skew; specifically, (a) not in a single plane; twisted; (b) deviating from perfect symmetry by the regular reversal of certain parts.

gau·che·rie′ (gō-she-rē′), *n.* [Fr.] 1. tactlessness; awkwardness.
2. an awkward or tactless act or expression.

Gau′chō, *n.*; *pl.* **Gau′chōs,** [Sp., of Sp. Am. origin.] a cowboy of mixed Indian and Spanish ancestry, living on the South American pampas.

gau′cie, gau′cy, *n.* [origin obscure.] plump; lusty; jolly. [Scot.]

gaud, *n.* [ME. *gaude, gawde*, a jewel, ornament, from L. *gaudium*, gladness, joy.]
1. a worthless or trifling ornament; a trinket; a bauble; as, the *gauds* and vanities of a sumptuous aristocracy.
2. [*pl.*] showy gaities.
3. a jest; trick; sport; fraud. [Obs.]

gaud, *v.i.* to exult; to rejoice. [Obs.]

gaud, *v.t.* to deck gaily; to paint; to adorn with gauds. [Rare.]

gau·de·ā′mus, *n.* [L., lit., let us be joyful: the beginning of a famous medieval student song.] a merrymaking, especially of college students.

gaud′ẽr·y, *n.* finery; gaudy, or ostentatious, appearance, clothes, etc.

gaud′ful, *a.* joyful; showy. [Rare.]

gaud′i·ly, *adv.* in a gaudy manner; showily.

gaud′i·ness, *n.* the quality or condition of being gaudy.

gaud′ish, *a.* gaudy. [Obs.]

gaud′less, *a.* unadorned by gauds. [Rare.]

gaud′y, *a.*; *comp.* gaudier; *superl.* gaudiest, [L. *gaudium*, gladness, joy, from *gaudere*, to rejoice.] showy; outwardly splendid, but lacking in good taste; cheaply brilliant and ornate.

A goldfinch there I saw, with *gaudy* pride
Of painted plumes. —Dryden.

Syn.—tawdry, fine, meretricious, bespangled, glittering, showy, gay, garish.

gaud′y, *n.*; *pl.* **gaud′ies,** [ME. *gaudee*, a bead; LL. *gaudium*, the bead on a rosary, from L. *gaudium*, gladness.]
1. one of the beads in the rosary marking the five joys of the Virgin Mary. [Obs.]
2. one of the tapers burned on an altar in commemoration of the five joys of the Virgin Mary. [Obs.]
3. in England, a feast or festival; especially, an annual college dinner; a gaud day.

gauf′fẽr, *v.t.* and *n.* same as *goffer*.

gauf′fre (gō′fẽr), *n.* [Fr., from OFr. *goffre*, a honeycomb, so called from the gopher's honeycombing the earth.] a gopher.

gāuge, *n.* [OFr. *gauge*, a gauge, a gauging rod, from LL. *gaugia*, the standard measure of a cask.]
1. a standard of measure or scale of measurement; a measure.
2. dimensions; capacity; extent.
3. any device for measuring something, as rainfall, the thickness of wire or metal, the dimensions of a part being machined, the amount of liquid in a container, steam pressure, etc.
4. any means of estimating or judging.
5. the distance between the two rails of a railway: *standard gauge* in most countries is $56^1/_2$ inches: any larger gauge is called *broad* (or *wide*) *gauge*, and any smaller gauge is called *narrow gauge*.
6. the distance between the parallel wheels on opposite sides of a vehicle.
7. the size of the bore of a firearm, especially of a shotgun, as determined by the number per pound of spherical projectiles fitting the bore.
8. in nautical usage, (a) the depth to which a ship with a full cargo is submerged in water; (b) the position of a ship with reference to another ship with a full cargo and to the wind: when to the windward, the ship is said to have the *weather gauge*, when to the leeward, the *lee gauge*.
9. in building, (a) the part of a slate or tile remaining exposed when laid; (b) a row of shingles, slates, etc.
10. in plastering, (a) the quantity of plaster of Paris used with common plaster to accelerate its setting; (b) the composition of plaster of Paris and other materials, used in finishing plastered ceilings, for moldings, etc.
11. in type founding, a piece of hard wood or polished steel, variously notched, used to determine the dimensions of letters.
12. in carpentry, a tool for scoring a line parallel to the straight side of a board, etc.
Also spelled *gage*.

gāuge, *v.t.*; gauged, *pt., pp.*; gauging, *ppr.* 1. to measure accurately by means of a gauge.
2. to measure in respect to proportion, capability, power, etc.; as, I *gauged* his character very accurately.

You shall not *gauge* me
By what we do to night. —Shak.

3. to estimate; judge; appraise.
4. to bring to correct gauge; make conform with a standard.
5. in plastering, to mix (plaster) in the right proportions, depending on the required drying time.
6. to gather (cloth) into folds.
Also spelled *gage*.

gāuge′ȧ·ble, *a.* capable of being gauged or measured.

gāuge çock, a stopcock which indicates the height of liquid in a container.

gāuge çŏn·cus′sion, the jolt caused by the striking of the flanges on the wheels of a railroad car against the rails.

gāuged, *a.* 1. adjusted, fitted, or measured with a gauge.
2. in dressmaking, gathered; puckered; as, a *gauged* skirt.

gāuge dōor, in coal mining, a door in an airway to regulate ventilation.

gāuge glȧss, a vertical tube of strong glass to show the level and condition of the water in a steam boiler.

gāuge knīfe (nīf), a knife the size and depth of whose cut is regulated by a gauge.

gāuge lad′dẽr, a horsing block, used in excavating to lift and support heavy planks designed to form a passageway for wheel barrows.

gāuge lāthe, a wood-turning lathe with edges shaped to a pattern and with a depth of cut regulated by a gauge.

gāuge pin, a pin attached to the platen of a small printing press, to keep the paper in proper position for printing.

gāuge point, the diameter of a cylinder that is one inch in height, and has a capacity equal to a unit of a given measure.

gāu′gẽr, *n.* 1. one who gauges; specifically, one whose business is to ascertain the contents of casks of liquor, etc. to be taxed.
2. a collector of excise taxes.
Also spelled *gager*.

gāu′gẽr·ship, *n.* the office or occupation of a gauger: also spelled *gagership*.

gāuge saw, a saw furnished with a gauge to regulate depth of the cut.

gāuge stuff, in plastering, a compound containing plaster of Paris, used in making cornices, moldings, etc.: also called *gauged stuff*.

gāuge wheel (hwēl), a wheel on the forward

beam end of a plow to regulate the depth of the furrow.

gāu′ging, *n.* the art or method of determining the dimensions or capacity of anything.

Gaul, *n.* [OFr. *Gaule*; L. *Gallus*; Gr. *Gallos*.]
1. any of the Celtic-speaking people of ancient Gaul.
2. a Frenchman.

Gau′leī·tēr (gou′lī-tēr), *n.* [G.] a district leader or administrator under the Nazi regime.

Gaul′ish, *a.* pertaining to Gaul or the Gauls.

Gaul′ish, *n.* the continental branch of the Celtic languages, spoken in ancient Gaul.

Gaul·thē′ri·ȧ, *n.* a genus of shrubs of the heath family, of which the American wintergreen, *Gaultheria procumbens*, is typical, having evergreen leaves and red, edible berries: named after Dr. Gaultier, a Canadian physician; also, [g–] any plant of this genus.

gaum, *v.t.* [Prov. Eng., from AS. *gyman*, *giman*, to care for, heed.] to understand. [Brit. Dial.]

gaum, *v.t.* to daub or smear. [Brit. Dial.]

gäunt, *a.* [ME. *gawnt*, *gawnte*, lean, slender; prob. from Norw. *gand*, a thin pole.]
1. thin and bony; emaciated; hollow-eyed and haggard, as from great hunger or age.
2. looking grim, forbidding, or desolate.

gäunt′let, gȧnt′let, *n.* [OFr. *gantelet*, dim. of *gant*, a glove, from D. *want*, a mitten.]

GAUNTLETS

1. a glove; specifically, in medieval armor, the defensive covering of the hand and wrist.
2. a long glove with a flaring cuff covering the lower part of the arm.
3. the part of such a glove covering the lower part of the arm.
4. in surgery, a form of bandage for the hand.
to take up the gauntlet; (a) to accept a challenge; (b) to undertake the defense of a person, etc.
to throw down the gauntlet; to challenge.

gäunt′let, *n.* a gantlet (form of punishment).

gäunt′let·ed, *a.* having or wearing a gauntlet, or glove.

gäunt′ly, *adv.* leanly; meagerly.

gaun′try, *n.*; *pl.* **gaun′tries,** a gantry.

gaur, gour, *n.* [native E. Ind. name, from Sans. *gaura*, a wild ox.] an East Indian variety of wild cattle similar to the domesticated gayal.

gaure, *v.i.* to gape; to stare; to gaze with open mouth. [Obs.]

gauss, *n.* [after Karl F. *Gauss* (1777–1855), G. mathematician and physicist.] in electricity, a unit used in measuring magnetic induction or magnetic intensity, equal to one line of magnetic force per square centimeter.

Gauss′i·ăn, *a.* named after or discovered by Karl F. Gauss; as, *Gaussian* logarithms.

gauze, *n.* [Fr. *gaze*, gauze, said to be from *Gaza*, in Palestine, where it was first made.]
1. a very thin, light, loosely woven material, usually of silk or cotton: also applied to other material of similar open texture; as, wire *gauze*.
2. a thin mist or haze.

gauze, *a.* made of or like gauze; gauzy.

gauze tree, the lacebark tree, *Lagetta lintearia*, of the West Indies.

gauz′i·ness, *n.* the quality of being gauzy.

gauz′y, *a.*; *comp.* gauzier; *superl.* gauziest; thin, light, and transparent, like gauze; diaphanous.

ga·vāge′ (-väzh′), *n.* [Fr., from *gaver*, to gorge fowls with food in order to fatten them, from *gave*, the crop or craw of a bird.]
1. forced feeding of poultry through a tube, for the purpose of fattening them for market.
2. a similar method of giving nourishment to a patient.

gāve, *v.* past tense of *give*.

gav′el, *v.t.*; gaveled, *pt.*, *pp.*; gaveling, *ppr.* to distribute equally, according to the tenure of gavelkind.

gav′el, *n.* [ME. *gavel*; AS. *gafol*, tribute, tax.] tribute. [Obs.]

gav′el, *n.* [OFr. *gavelle*, a sheaf of corn.] a small unbound parcel of wheat, rye, or other grain, laid together by reapers. [Brit. Dial.]

gav′el, *n.* a gable. [Brit. Dial.]

gav′el, *n.* [use only in U. S. suggests D. or dial. G. origin.]
1. a mason's hammer for breaking off the rough edges of stones.
2. a small mallet rapped on the table by a presiding officer in calling for attention or silence.

gav′el·et, *n.* [from ME. *gavel*; AS. *gafol*, tribute, tax.] in English law, a special writ used for the forfeiture of property because of the withholding of rent or services. [Obs.]

gav′el·kīnd, *n.* [ME. *gavelkynde*, *gavelkende* (orig. Kentish), from *gavel*, tribute, tax, rent, and *kynde*, *kinde*, kind, sort.]
1. formerly, a system of land tenure by which: (a) the property of a man dying intestate was divided equally among his sons; (b) the tenant could dispose of his land by feoffment at the age of fifteen; (c) the land did not escheat upon the conviction of the tenant as a felon.
2. a similar system of land tenure still practiced in Kent and Wales.

gav′e·lock, gav′e·loche, *n.* [ME. *gavelock*; AS. *gafeluc*, a spear or javelin.]
1. a dart; a spear. [Obs.]
2. an iron lever; a crowbar. [Obs.]

gā′vēr·ick, *n.* the red gurnard, a kind of fish.

Gā′vi·ae, *n.pl.* [L. *gavia*, a sea mew.] a group of birds of which gulls are the type.

gā′vi·ăl, *n.* [Hind. *ghariyāl*, a crocodile.] a large Indian crocodile, *Gavialis gangeticus*, having a long, slender snout with a knob on the upper jaw: found chiefly in the Ganges.

Gā·vi·al′i·dae, *n.pl.* a family of crocodiles of which the gavial is the type.

gȧ·votte′, gȧ·vot′, *n.* [Fr. *gavotte*; OFr. *gavote*, a dance of the *Gavots*, name of people of Hautes-Alpes, France, where the dance originated.] a seventeenth-century dance like the minuet, but faster and livelier; also, the music for this, in 4/4 time.

gaw, *n.* a ditch or trench. [Scot.]

Gä′wain (-win), *n.* [prob. from W. *Gwalchmai*; perh. lit., courteous.] in Arthurian legend, a knight of the Round Table, nephew of King Arthur.

gawk, *n.* [ME. *gowke*, a cuckoo, a fool; Ice. *gaukr*, a cuckoo.] a simpleton; a clumsy, stupid fellow.

gawk, *v.i.*, gawked, *pt.*, *pp.*; gawking, *ppr.* to stare like a gawk, in a stupid way. [Colloq.]

gawk′i·ly, *adv.* in a gawky manner.

gawk′i·ness, *n.* the quality of being gawky.

gawk′y, *n.* an awkward, ungainly, or stupid fellow.

gawk′y, *a.* foolish; awkward; clumsy; clownish; ungainly; uncouth.

gāy, *a.* [ME. *gay*; OFr. *gai*; O.H.G. *gahi*, quick, sudden, rash, lively.]
1. joyous and lively; merry; happy; lighthearted.
2. bright; brilliant; as, *gay* colors.
3. given to social life and pleasures; as, a *gay* life.
4. wanton; licentious; as, a *gay* dog.
5. homosexual.
Syn.—merry, lively, blithe, sprightly, sportive, hilarious.

gāy, *n.* a homosexual; especially, a male homosexual.

gāy′ăl (gā′ăl), *n.* [native E. Ind. name.] a species of ox, *Bos frontalis*, found wild in the mountains of northern Burma and Assam, and domesticated in these countries and in the eastern parts of Bengal.

Gä·yȧ·trī′, *n.* [Sans.] a Sanskrit hymn used in the Hindu liturgy.

gāy′bīne, *n.* any one of several showy twining plants of the genus *Ipomæa*.

gaȳ′di·ang, *n.* [native Annamese.] a vessel of Annam with curved decks, somewhat resembling a Chinese junk, and carrying two or three masts and large, triangular sails.

gāy′e·ty, *n.* same as *gaiety*.

gāy′-feath″ēr (-feth″), *n.* the button snakeroot, *Liatris spicata*.

Gāy″lus·sā′ci·ȧ (-shi-a), *n.* [after Joseph *Gay-Lussac*, early 19th-c. French scientist.] a genus of ericaceous shrubs, some deciduous and others evergreen. They have clusters of white or pale green flowers, and black or blue edible fruit, commonly known as huckleberries. They are found in the eastern sections of both North and South America. The common or black huckleberry is the fruit of *Gaylussacia resinosa*.

gāy′lus·sīte, *n.* [after *Gay-Lussac*; see prec. entry.] a white, brittle, glassy sodium-calcium carbonate, found in Peru and in Nevada.

gāy′ly, *adv.* same as *gaily*.

gāy′ness, *n.* gaiety.

Gāy′-Pāy′-Öö′, [from first letters of Russ. *Gosudarstvennoye Politicheskoye Upravlyeniye*, governmental political department.] formerly, the state security police, or secret service, of the Soviet Union, succeeding the Cheka in 1922.

gāy′sŏme, *a.* full of gaiety.

gāy′wings, *n.* a trailing pink wildflower of the eastern United States and Canada.

gāy′you, *n.* [Anglo-Ind.] a narrow, flat-bottomed Annamese fishing boat. It has an outrigger and either two or three masts, and is provided with a movable roof amidships.

GAYYOU

Gȧ·zā′ni·ȧ, *n.* a genus of herbs of the aster family, characterized by large, showy, orange and yellow blossoms, which expand only in bright sunshine. They are native to South Africa and are named after Theodorus Gaza, a medieval Greek scholar of Italy.

gāze, *v.i.*; gazed, *pt.*, *pp.*; gazing, *ppr.* [ME. *gasen*, from Sw. dial. *gasa*, to gaze, stare.] to fix the eyes and look steadily and earnestly; to look with eagerness or curiosity, as in admiration, astonishment, expectancy, or study.

Ye men of Galilee, why stand ye *gazing* up into heaven? —Acts i. 11.

Syn.—gape, stare.—To *gaze* is to look with fixed and prolonged attention, awakened by excited interest or elevated emotion; to *gape* is to look fixedly with feelings of ignorant wonder; to *stare* is to look fixedly with wide-open eyes, as in surprise or curiosity.

gāze, *v.t.* to look at intently. [Poet.]

gāze, *n.* 1. a fixed look; a look of eagerness, wonder, or admiration; a continued look of attention.

With secret *gaze*
Or open admiration him behold.—Milton.

2. the object gazed on; that which causes one to gaze. [Poet.]
at gaze; (a) in stag hunting, in the position assumed by a stag when becoming aware that the dogs are in chase; (b) in heraldry, having the head turned so as to look out from the shield: chiefly used in reference to the figures of a buck, hart, hind, or stag.

STAG AT GAZE

gȧ·zē′bō, *n.*; *pl.* **gȧ·zē′bōs, gȧ·zē′bōes,** [humorously formed from *gaze*, and L. *-ebo*, a fut. ind. 1st pers. sing. ending of a second conjugation verb, meaning lit., I shall gaze.]
1. a summer house affording a fine view.
2. a turret or windowed balcony from which one can gaze at the surrounding scenery.

gāze′hound, *n.* a hound that pursues by sight rather than by scent.

gaz′el, ghaz′ăl, *n.* 1. a piece of Arabic music with a frequent refrain.
2. a form of Persian verse.

Gȧ·zel′lȧ, *n.* the type genus of gazelles: sometimes called *Dorcas*.

gȧ·zelle′, gȧ·zel′, *n.* [OFr. *gazel*, *gazelle*; Ar. *ghazal*, *ghazel*, a gazelle.] a small, swift, graceful antelope of Africa, the Near East, and Asia, with spirally twisted, backward-pointing horns, and large, lustrous soft eyes; especially the *Gazella dorcas* of North Africa.

GAZELLES (*Gazella dorcas*)

Gaz·el·lī′nae, *n.pl.* a group of antelopes of which the gazelle is the type.

gāz′ēr, *n.* one who gazes.

gȧ·zet′, *n.* [It.] a copper coin formerly issued by the Venetian Republic. [Obs.]

gȧ·zette′, *n.* [It. *gazzetta*, a gazette, newspaper, prob. from *gazzetta*, a gazet or small coin, the price paid for the paper; also thought to be from *gazzetta*, a magpie, and to mean a chatterer or tattler.]
1. a newspaper; a printed sheet of paper containing an account of current events: now used mainly in the names of some newspapers.

2. any of several official newspapers of Great Britain, containing announcements and bulletins, as of appointments and promotions in the public service, of public honors awarded, of bankrupts, etc.

ga·zette′, *v.t.*; gazetted, *pt.*, *pp.*; gazetting, *ppr.* to publish, announce, or list in a gazette; hence, to announce formally, as an appointment to the public service.

gaz·et·teer′, *n.* [It. *gazzettiere*, a writer of news, from *gazetta*, a gazette.]
 1. a writer of news for a gazette, or an officer appointed to publish a gazette.
 2. a gazette; a newspaper. [Obs.]
 3. a book containing geographical names and descriptions, alphabetically arranged; a geographical dictionary or index.

gāz′ing·stock, *n.* a person or thing gazed at; an object of curiosity or contempt.

gaz′ō·gēne, *n.* an apparatus for generating gases, especially one for manufacturing aerated water on a small scale for domestic use: also written *gasogene, gasogen.*

ga·zon′, *n.* [Fr., from O.H.G. *waso*, turf, sod.] in fortification, turf used to line parapets and the faces of earthworks. [Obs.]

G çlef, the treble clef.

Gd, in chemistry, *the symbol for* gadolinium.

Gē, *n.* same as *Gaea.*

Ge, in chemistry, *the symbol for* germanium.

gē·ȧ·deph′ȧ·gous, *a.* [Gr. *gē*, the earth, and *adēphagos*, voracious, from *adēn*, enough, and *phagein*, to eat.] pertaining to a group of predaceous beetles living upon the ground, as the carabids.

ġēal, *v.i.* to congeal. [Obs.]

ġēan, *n.* [Fr. *guigne*; OFr. *guisne*; LL. *guindolum*, a kind of cherry; prob. of Slavic origin.] the wild cherry of Europe, *Prunus avium*: its wood is much used for tobacco pipes.

gē″an·ti·clī′năl, *n.* [Gr. *gē*, earth, and *anti*, against, and *klinein*, to slope.] a geanticline.

gē″an·ti·clī′năl, *a.* of, or having the nature of, a geanticline.

gē·an′ti·çline, *n.* in geology, a great upward folding of the earth's crust, often several hundred miles in breadth: opposed to *geosyncline.*

gēar, *n.* [ME. *gere, ger*; AS. *gearwe*, preparation, dress, ornament, from *gearu*, ready, brisk, prompt.]
 1. (a) clothing; apparel; (b) originally, the clothing and equipment of a soldier, knight, etc.
 2. apparatus or equipment for some particular task, as a workman's tools, the rigging of a ship, a harness, etc.
 3. in mechanics, (a) a system of two or more toothed wheels meshed together so that the motion of one is passed on to the others; (b) a gearwheel; (c) adjustment or proper working order; as, out of *gear*; (d) a specific adjustment; as, high *gear* is for greater speed; (e) a part of a mechanism performing a specific function; as, a steering *gear*; (f) the diameter of a hypothetical wheel whose circumference is equal to the distance traveled by a bicycle with one revolution of the pedal.
 4. property; goods; belongings. [Scot.]
 5. business matters; affairs. [Obs.]
 6. any worthless thing; junk; rubbish. [Obs.]
 high gear; (a) in a multiple gear system, the arrangement of gears providing the greatest speed but little power; (b) [Colloq.] high speed.
 in gear; (a) connected to the motor; in adjustment for use; (b) in order.
 low gear; (a) in a multiple gear system, the arrangement of gears providing little speed but great power; (b) [Colloq.] low speed.
 out of gear; (a) not connected to the motor; not in adjustment for use; (b) out of order.
 reverse gear; in a multiple gear system, the arrangement of gears providing reverse, or backward, motion.
 to shift gears; in a multiple gear system, to change from one gear arrangement to another.
 to throw into gear; to set ready to start; to put into motion, as machinery.
 to throw out of gear; to put out of motion, as by turning a lever to disconnect gears.

gēar, *v.t.*; geared, *pt.*, *pp.*; gearing, *ppr.* 1. to harness; to dress; to prepare for operation; to furnish with gear.
 2. in mechanics, (a) to connect by gears; (b) to furnish with gears; (c) to put into gear.

gēar, *v.i.* in machinery, to be in, or come into, gear or operating order; to engage with the connecting parts.

gēar′box, *n.* 1. the unit consisting of the transmission gears in a power-transmission system.
 2. a case enclosing gears to protect them from dirt.

gēar çut′tēr, a machine for cutting gear teeth.

gēar′ing, *n.* 1. harness; dress; gear. [Dial.]
 2. in machinery, a system of gears or other parts by which motion communicated to one portion of a machine is transmitted to another; a train of toothed wheels for transmitting motion.
 3. (a) the fitting of a machine with gears; (b) the manner in which the gears are fitted: there are two main types of gearing, *spur gearing* and *beveled gearing*. In the former the teeth are arranged around either the concave or convex surface of a cylindrical wheel in the direction of radii from the center of the wheel, and are of equal depth throughout. In beveled gearing the teeth are placed upon the exterior periphery of a conical wheel in a direction converging to the apex of the cone, and the depth of the tooth gradually diminishes from the base.

SPUR GEARING

gēar′ing chāin, an endless chain transmitting motion from one toothed wheel to another.

gēar′shift, *n.* a device for connecting any of a number of sets of transmission gears to a motor, etc., or for disconnecting them.

gēar′shift lev′ēr, in machinery, the bar or arm by means of which the various gears are engaged or disengaged.

gēar′wheel, *n.* any wheel having teeth or cogs which act upon the teeth of another wheel to impart or transmit motion: also *gear wheel.*

ġēa′ṣŏn, *a.* rare; uncommon; wonderful. [Obs.]

Gē·as′tēr, *n.* [Gr. *gē*, earth, and *aster*, star.] a genus of gasteromycetous fungi taking the form of stars and lying close to the ground.

ġēat, *n.* [AS. *geotan*, to pour.]
 1. in founding, the hole through which metal is poured into a mold.
 2. in type founding, a lip or spout in the casting ladle.

gē·çär·cin′i·ăn, *n.* [Gr. *gē*, earth, and *karkinos*, a crab.] in zoology, any member of the genus *Gecarcinus*, the land crabs.

geç′çō, *n.* same as *gecko.*

geck, *n.* 1. a dupe; a gull. [Dial.]
 2. a jibe or taunt; derision; scorn. [Scot.]

geck, *v.t.* to cheat, trick, or gull. [Scot. and Brit. Dial.]

geck, *v.i.* to express scorn, derision, or contempt. [Scot. and Brit. Dial.]

geck′ō, *n.*; *pl.* **geck′ōṣ, geck′ōeṣ,** [an imitative word.] any of a group of soft-skinned, insect-eating lizards with a short, stout body, a large head, weak limbs, and suction pads on their feet.

WALL GECKO
(*Gecco fascicularis*)

ged, gedd, *n.* [Ice. *gedda*, a pike, from *gaddr*, *gaddo*, a goad, spike.] a fish, the pike. [Scot. and Brit. Dial.]

ġee, *v.i.*; geed, *pt.*, *pp.*; geeing, *ppr.* to agree; to suit; to fit. [Colloq.]

ġee, *interj.* and *n.* [Early Mod. Eng.] a word of command to a horse, ox, etc. being driven without reins, meaning "turn to the right!" or (usually *gee up*) "go ahead!": also spelled *jee*: opposed to *haw.*

ġee, *v.t.* and *v.i.* 1. to turn to the right.
 2. to evade.
 Also spelled *jee.* Opposed to *haw.*

ġee, *interj.* [euphemistic contraction of *Jesus.*] an exclamation of surprise, etc. [Slang.]

geer, *n.* and *v.* gear. [Obs.]

geese, *n.* pl. of *goose.*

geest, *n.* [L.G. *geest*, sandy, dry, from Old Friesic *gast*, *gest*, dry, barren.] alluvial matter on the surface of land, not of recent origin.

Gē·ez′, Gïz, *n.* [Ethiopic.] the ancient Semitic language of Ethiopia, or Abyssinia, superseded by Amharic.

gee′zēr, *n.* [from dial. *guiser*, a mummer, from *guise.*] an eccentric old man, or, rarely, woman. [Slang.]

ge·fil′te fish, [Yid.; altered from G. *gefüllter fisch*, from *gefüllt*, pp. of *füllen*, to fill, and *fisch*, a fish.] chopped fish, usually a mixture, as of whitefish, pike, and carp, mixed with chopped onion, egg, seasoning, etc., put into a casing of the skin, and boiled, often with vegetables.

Gē·hen′nȧ, *n.* [LL. *Gehenna*; Gr. *Geenna*, *Gaienna*; Heb. *ge-hinnom.*]
 1. in the Bible, the valley of Hinnom, near Jerusalem, where refuse was dumped, perpetual fires being kept up in order to prevent pestilence.
 2. (a) a place of torment and burning; (b) in the New Testament, hell.

> The pleasant valley of Hinnom, Tophet thence
> And black *Gehenna* called, the type of hell.
> —Milton.

ġē′iç, *a.* [Gr. *gē*, the earth.] in chemistry, pertaining to or obtained from the earth or decayed vegetation; as, *geic* acid.

Gei′gēr çoun′tēr, [after Hans *Geiger* (1882–), German physicist who invented it.] an instrument for detecting and counting ionizing particles that pass through it: it consists of a needlelike electrode inside a hollow metallic cylinder filled with gas which, when ionized by the radiation, sets up a current in an electric field.

Gei′ger-Mül′ler coun′tēr (gī′gēr-mul′ēr), an instrument similar to the Geiger counter but with an electrical amplifying system, for detecting radioactivity and measuring its intensity.

Gei′gērṣ, *n.pl.* radioactive particles, etc., as measured by a Geiger counter.

ġē′in, *n.* [Gr. *geinos*, earthy, from *gē*, the earth.] humin; humic acid.

ġei′shä, *n.*; *pl.* **ġei′shä, ġei′shäṣ,** [Japan.] a professional singing and dancing girl of Japan.

Geis′slēr tūbe, [named after the maker, Heinrich *Geissler.*] in electricity, a tube in which a rarefied gas is hermetically sealed. When electricity is discharged through the tube between electrodes, the gas glows its characteristic color: used in spectroscopy, etc.

geī·tō·nog′ȧ·my, *n.* [Gr. *geitōn*, a neighbor, and *gamos*, marriage.] in botany, fertilization of a pistil by pollen from a neighboring flower of the same plant: distinguished from *xenogamy.*

ġel, *n.* [from *gel*atin.] a jellylike substance formed by a colloidal solution in its solid phase: opposed to *sol.*

ġel, *v.i.*; gelled, *pt.*, *pp.*; gelling, *ppr.* to form a gel; to jellify: often used figuratively.

ġel′ȧ·ble, *a.* [L. *gelare*, to freeze.] capable of being congealed.

ġel′ȧ·dȧ, *n.* [native name.] a baboon, *Theropithecus gelada*, found in Abyssinia, notable for the heavy mane of the adult male.

Ge·lā′siăn, *a.* pertaining to or composed by Pope Gelasius (died 496 A.D.), who composed some of the prayers in the Roman liturgy.

ġē·las′tiç, *a.* provoking laughter; risible. [Rare.]

ġē·las′tiç, *n.* something provoking laughter. [Rare.]

ġe·lat″i·fi·çā′tion, *n.* the act of turning to gelatin.

ġel·ȧ·tig′e·nous, *a.* [from *gelatin*, and Gr. *-genēs*, producing.] having the quality of producing gelatin.

ġel′ȧ·tin, ġel′ȧ·tine, *n.* [Fr. *gélatine*, from L. *gelatus*, pp. of *gelare*, to freeze.]
 1. (a) the tasteless, odorless, brittle substance extracted by boiling bones, hoofs, and animal tissues; (b) a similar vegetable substance: gelatin dissolves in hot water, forming a jellylike substance when cool, and is used in the preparation of various foods, medicine capsules, photographic film, etc.
 2. a jelly made with gelatine.
 blasting gelatin; an explosive made of nine parts by weight of nitroglycerin and one of collodion cotton.
 gelatin dynamite; blasting gelatin mixed with a dope, decreasing its explosive power.
 gelatin emulsion; an emulsion of a salt of silver in gelatin for use in photography.

gelatin paper; paper prepared with a coating of gelatin for photographic use.

gelatin process; (a) a copying process by which any matter written or drawn in aniline ink may be transferred to many copies by the use of a gelatin surface kept moist by glycerin, etc. The original, when pressed face down on the moist pad, leaves a stain in the gelatin, and a paper pressed upon that stain receives the copy of the original: the gelatin pad is called a *hectograph*; (b) in photoengraving, a process depending on the variation in solubility caused by the action of light on gelatin containing a bichromate. A print or negative made on such gelatin is treated with water so as to be swelled or washed away in the portions least affected, and from the resulting film a cast is made, as in one process, or the gelatin used for direct printing, as in another process.

ġē·lat′i·nāte, *v.i.*; gelatinated, *pt.*, *pp.*; gelatinating, *ppr.* to be converted into gelatin or into a gelatinous substance.

ġē·lat′i·nāte, *v.t.* to convert into gelatin or into a gelatinous substance.

ġē·lat·i·nā′tion, *n.* the act or process of converting or being turned into gelatin or into a gelatinous substance.

ġel″à·tin·if′ēr·ous, *a.* [*gelatin*, and L. *ferre*, to produce.] producing gelatin; capable of being gelatinized.

ġel·à·tin′i·fọrm, *a.* [*gelatin*, and L. *forma*, form.] having the form of gelatin.

ġē·lat″i·ni·zā′tion, *n.* gelatination.

ġē·lat′i·nīze, *v.i.*; gelatinized, *pt.*, *pp.*; gelatinizing, *ppr.* to gelatinate.

ġē·lat′i·nīze, *v.t.* 1. to change into gelatin or gelatinous matter.

2. in photography, to coat with gelatin.

ġē·lat′i·noid, *a.* [*gelatin*, and Gr. *eidos*, resemblance.] like jelly or gelatin.

ġē·lat′i·noid, *n.* a substance resembling gelatin.

ġē·lat′i·nous, *a.* 1. like jelly; of the character of gelatin; viscous.

2. of or containing gelatin.

ġē·lā′tion, *n.* [L. *gelatio* (*-onis*), a freezing, from *gelare*, to freeze.] the passage of a gas or liquid into a solid state by cooling or freezing; solidification.

geld, gelt, *n.* [AS. *geld*, *gild*, tribute, payment, from *geldan*, *gieldan*, to pay, yield.] a tax paid to the crown by English landholders in the times of the Anglo-Saxon and Norman kings.

geld, *v.t.*; gelded *or* gelt, *pt.*, *pp.*; gelding, *ppr.* [ME. *gelden*, *gilden*, from Ice. *gelda*, to castrate.]

1. to castrate (a horse, etc.); to emasculate.

2. to deprive of any essential part; to weaken.

3. to expurgate, as a book. [Obs.]

geld′à·ble, *a.* capable of being gelded.

geld′à·ble, *a.* liable to taxes. [Obs.]

geld′ēr, *n.* one who castrates animals.

gel′dēr rōṣe, see *guelder-rose*.

geld′ing, *n.* [ME. *gelding*, a eunuch, a castrated horse, from Ice. *geldingr*, a eunuch, from *geldr*, barren.]

1. a castrated horse or other animal.

2. a eunuch; a castrated man. [Archaic.]

ġel′id, *a.* [L. *gelidus*, cool, cold, from *gelu*, frost, cold, from *gelare*, to freeze.] frozen; frosty; very cold.

ġē·lid′i·ty, *n.* the state of being gelid.

ġel′id·ly, *adv.* coldly.

ġel′id·ness, *n.* coldness.

ġel′ly, *n.* jelly. [Obs.]

ġē·los′çō·py, *n.* [Gr. *gelōs*, laughter, and *skopein*, to view.] the observation of laughter as a means of divination of character. [Obs.]

ġē′lōse, *n.* [*gelatin* and *-ose*.] in chemistry, a gelatinlike carbohydrate, $C_6H_{10}O_5$, found in Chinese and Ceylon moss.

ġel·sē′miç, ġel·sē·min′iç, *a.* in chemistry, pertaining to gelsemium.

ġel′se·min, ġel′se·mine, *n.* a very bitter, solid alkaloid derived from *Gelsemium sempervirens*, the yellow jasmine.

Ġel·sē′mi·um, *n.* [It. *gelsomino*, jasmine.]

1. in botany, a genus of evergreen climbing shrubs, having showy, large, fragrant yellow flowers. *Gelsemium sempervirens* is the common yellow jasmine of the southern States.

2. [g–] in medicine, a preparation of the root of the yellow jasmine.

gelt, *n.* geld. [Obs.]

gelt, *n.* a castrated animal; a gelding. [Obs.]

gelt, *n.* tinsel; gilding. [Obs.]

gelt, *v.* alternative past tense and past participle of *geld*.

ġem, *n.* [ME. *gemme*; OFr. *gemme*, a precious stone; It. *gemma*, a precious stone, a bud, from L. *gemma*, a swelling, a bud, a precious stone.]

1. in botany, a bud. [Obs.]

2. a precious or, occasionally, semiprecious stone of any kind, particularly when cut and polished as a jewel.

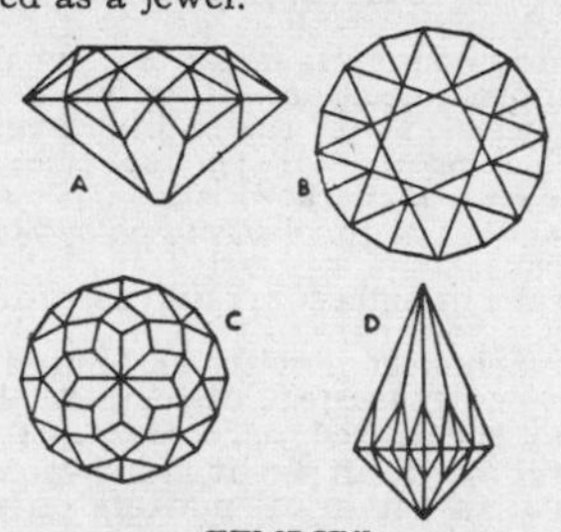

CUTS OF GEMS
A. American (side view); B. American (top view); C. 20th century (top view); D. briolette

3. anything prized for its beauty and value; specifically, anything small and beautiful, rare, perfect, brilliant, or finely wrought; as, a *gem* of a sonnet; a *gem* of eloquence.

4. a moth of the family *Geometridæ*.

5. in England, a size of type intermediate between diamond and brilliant.

6. a kind of muffin.

ġem, *v.t.*; gemmed, *pt.*, *pp.*; gemming, *ppr.* 1. to adorn or set with or as with gems; to bespangle; to bedeck; as, to *gem* a crown; a field *gemmed* with daisies.

A coppice *gemmed* with green and red.
—Tennyson.

2. to bud. [Rare.]

Ge·mä′rà, *n.* [Aram. *gemārā*, completion.] the second division of the Talmud, being a commentary on the preceding part, the Mishna.

Ge·mar′iç, *a.* pertaining to the Gemara.

Ge·mä′rist, *n.* a student of or expert in the Gemara.

ge·mā′tri·à, *n.* [Heb.] a cabalistic method of interpretation of the Hebrew scriptures based upon the numerical value of the letters in the words.

ġem′el, *a.* paired.

ġem′el, *n.* [ME. *gemel*; OFr. *gemel*, a twin, from L. *gemellus*, dim. of *geminus*, a twin.]

1. a twin, or one of twins. [Rare.]

2. in heraldry, either of a pair of bars placed together across a shield.

GEMELS

3. in mechanics, either of two units, as a hook and loop, together forming a hinge: often used attributively; as, *gemel* hinge.

ġem·el·lip′à·rous, *a.* [L. *gemellus*, twin, and *parere*, to produce.] producing twins. [Rare.]

ġem′el ring, a ring composed of two or more separable rings.

ġem′el win′dōw, a window which has two bays.

ġem′i·năl, *n.* a pair. [Obs.]

ġem′i·nāte, *a.* twin; growing or combined in couples or pairs; double; binate.

ġem′i·nāte, *v.t.* [L. *geminatus*, pp. of *geminare*, to double, from *geminus*, twin.] to double; to arrange in pairs.

ġem′i·nāte, *v.i.* to become doubled or paired.

ġem·i·nā′tion, *n.* [L. *geminatio* (*-onis*), a doubling, from *geminare*, to double.] a doubling; duplication; repetition; especially, the doubling of a consonant or consonant sound.

Ġem′i·nī, *n.pl.* [L., twins.]

1. a northern constellation between Cancer and Taurus, containing the stars Castor and Pollux, represented as twins sitting together.

2. the third sign of the Zodiac, entered by the sun about May 21.

3. a form of oath or expletive: now usually altered to *jiminy*.

O *Gemini!* I'd sooner cut my tongue out.
Sheridan.

ġem″i·ni·flō′rous, *a.* [L. *geminus*, double, and *flos* (*floris*), a flower.] in botany, having flowers in pairs.

ġem′i·nous, *a.* geminate.

ġem′mà, *n.*; *pl.* **ġem′mae,** [L., a swelling, bud, gem.]

1. in botany, (a) a leaf bud; (b) a mass of propagative cells in certain mosses and liverworts.

2. in zoology, a budlike outgrowth which becomes entirely or partially separated from the parent body as an independent creature, as in certain of the *Protozoa*.

ġem·mā′ceous, *a.* of, pertaining to, or resembling leaf buds.

ġem′mà·ry, *n.* [ME. *gemmarye*, a gem engraver; LL. *gemmarius*, a gem engraver, jeweler, from L. *gemma*, a gem.]

1. a case for gems; a jewel house; also, gems collectively: also written *gemmery*. [Obs.]

2. a gem engraver. [Obs.]

3. scientific knowledge of gems. [Rare.]

ġem′mà·ry, *a.* pertaining to gems. [Obs.]

ġem′māte, *a.* [L. *gemmatus*, pp. of *gemmare*, to put forth buds.] having or reproducing by means of buds.

ġem′māte, *v.i.*; gemmated, *pt.*, *pp.*; gemmating, *ppr.* in biology, to put forth buds; to have or reproduce by budding.

ġem′mā·ted, *a.* furnished with buds.

ġem·mā′tion, *n.* [L. *gemmatus*, pp. of *gemmare*, to put forth buds.]

1. in botany, the act of budding; the state, form, or construction of the bud of plants.

2. in zoology, the process of reproduction by gemmae; budding.

ġem′mē·ous, *a.* [It. *gemmeus*, pertaining to gems, from *gemma*, a gem.] pertaining to gems; of the nature of gems.

ġem·mif′ēr·ous, *a.* producing buds; specifically, in biology, multiplying by gemmae.

ġem″mi·fi·çā′tion, *n.* [L. *gemma*, a bud, gem, and *facere*, to make.] in biology, the formation of a bud or gemma.

ġem·mi·flō′rāte, *a.* [L. *gemma*, a bud, gem, and *flos* (*floris*), a flower.] having bud-shaped flowers.

ġem′mi·fọrm, *a.* budlike.

ġem′mi·ness, *n.* the quality or state of being gemmy.

ġem·mip′à·rà, ġem·mip′à·rae, *n.pl.* [L., from *gemma*, a bud, gem, and *parere*, to produce.] animals which grow by budding, as the fresh-water polyp, etc.

ġem·mi·par′i·ty, *n.* propagation by budding; the state or quality of being gemmiparous.

ġem·mip′à·rous, *a.* [L. *gemma*, a bud, and *parere*, to bear.] of gemmation; producing buds; reproducing by buds on the body, which mature and fall off into independent animals, as some polyps.

ġem′moid, *a.* [L. *gemma*, a bud, and Gr. *eidos*, resemblance.] like a bud or a gemma.

ġem·mos′i·ty, *n.* the quality of abounding in gems or resembling a gem. [Obs.]

ġem·mū·lā′tion, *n.* same as *gemmation*.

ġem′mūle, *n.* [LL. *gemmula*, dim. of L. *gemma*, a bud.]

1. in botany, a little gemma, or bud.

2. in zoology, a small gemma; especially, in sponges, a germinal mass of spores.

ġem·mū·lif′ēr·ous, *a.* [LL. *gemmula*, a little bud, and L. *ferre*, to bear.] bearing gemmules.

ġem′my, *a.* 1. set with gems.

2. like a gem; glittering.

ge·mōt′, ge·mōte′, *n.* [AS. *gemot*, an assembly.] in Anglo-Saxon history, a meeting: used chiefly in compounds; as, shire *gemot*.

gemṣ, *n.* [G.] the chamois.

gemṣ′bok, *n.* [D., from *gems*, the chamois, and *bok*, a buck.] in zoology, the male of the *Oryx capensis* of South Africa, an antelope with long and nearly straight horns ending in sharp points: called also *kokama*.

gemṣ′họrn, *n.* [G., from *gems*, the chamois, and *horn*, horn.] an organ stop whose hornlike tones are due to tapering metal pipes.

ge̩′mul, *n.* a small deer of South America, *Cariacus chilensis*, having simple forked horns.

ge·müt′lich (ge-mu̇t′likh), *a.* [G.] agreeable; cheerful, cozy, etc.: indicating a general sense of well-being.

-ġen, [Fr. *-gene*; Gr. *-genes*, born, from base of *gignesthai*, to be born, become.] a suffix used to form nouns meaning: (a) *something that produces*, as in oxy*gen*, hydrogen; (b) *something produced* (in a specified way), as in endo*gen*.

ġē′nà, *n.*; *pl.* **ġē′nae,** [L., the cheek.] in zoology, the region between the eye and the mouth; the triangular area which lies between the eye of trilobites and the free margin of the head.

ġe·nappe′, *n.* [from *Genappe*, in Belgium, where it was originally manufactured.] a worsted yarn whose smoothness enables it to be combined with silk in braids, fringes, etc.

ġen·därme′ (zhän-därm′), *n.*; *pl.* **ġen·därmeṣ′,**

[Fr., from pl. *gens d'armes*, men-at-arms, from L. *gens* (*-entis*), a people, nation; *de*, of, from, and *arma*, arms.]

1. a member of a troop of cavalry; a man-at-arms. [Obs.]

2. in France, Belgium, etc., one of the armed police.

3. any policeman: humorous or literary usage.

ġen·därm'ẽr·iē (zhän-), *n.* [Fr.] the French national police collectively, or a similar force: spelled also *gendarmery*.

ġen'dẽr, *n.* [ME.; OFr. *gendre*, with unhistoric *-d-*, from L. *genus, generis*, descent, origin.]

1. in grammar, (a) the classification by which nouns and pronouns (and often accompanying modifiers) are grouped and inflected, or changed in form, in relation to sex or their lack of it: gender is *natural* when, as in English, Persian, and Armenian, animate beings and inanimate things are classified as masculine, feminine, and neuter (e.g., *man*, masc.; *woman*, fem.; *tree*, neut.); gender is *grammatical* when, as in the majority of languages possessing it, beings and things are classified according to remotely animistic, psychological, or formal associations (e.g, Anglo-Saxon *wif*, German *weib*, woman, neut.; Latin *fluvius*, river, masc. [but *flumen*, stream, neut.]; Latin *pirus*, pear tree, fem.): English, now virtually free from noun inflection, shows gender chiefly by pronoun reference; (b) any one of such groupings; (c) any genderlike system of classification, as the caste-system of the Dravidian languages.

2. sex. [Colloq.]

ġen'dẽr, *v.t.*; gendered, *pt., pp.*; gendering, *ppr.* to beget; to engender. [Archaic.]

ġen'dẽr, *v.i.* to copulate; to breed. [Obs.]

ġen'dẽr·less, *a.* without gender.

ġēne, *n.* [Gr. *gen*, to produce.] in genetics, any of the elements by which hereditary characters are transmitted and determined, regarded as a particular state of organization of the chromatin in the chromosome; factor: theoretically each mature reproductive cell carries a gene for every inheritable characteristic, and thus an individual resulting from the union of two such cells receives a set of genes from each of its parents.

ġen"ē·ȧ·ġen'e·sis, *n.* [Gr. *genea*, race, stock, and *genesis*, generation.] a form of alternation of generations.

ġen"ē·ȧ·loġ'iç, ġen"ē·ȧ·loġ'iç·ȧl (*or* jē"nē-), *a.* 1. pertaining to genealogy.

2. tracing a line of descent.

genealogical tree; the genealogy of a family shown in the form of a tree, with roots, stems, and branches.

ġen"ē·ȧ·loġ'iç·ȧl·ly (*or* jē"nē-), *adv.* 1. in a genealogical manner.

2. according to genealogy.

ġen·ē·al'ō·ġist (*or* jē"nē-), *n.* one who traces or studies descents of persons or families; a writer about genealogy.

ġen·ē·al'ō·ġize (*or* jē"nē-), *v.i.* genealogized, *pt., pp.*; genealogizing, *ppr.* to trace or relate genealogy.

ġen·ē·al'ō·ġy (*or* jē"nē-), *n.*; *pl.* **ġen·ē·al'ō·ġieş,** [ME. *genealogie*; OFr. *genealogie*; LL. *genealogia*; Gr. *genealogia*, the tracing of one's descent, genealogy; *genea*, race, stock, and *logos*, a discourse, from *legein*, to speak.]

1. an account or history of the descent of a person or family from an ancestor; enumeration of ancestors and their descendants in the natural order of succession.

2. pedigree; lineage; regular descent of a person or family from a progenitor.

3. genealogical investigation; the science or study of family descent.

ġen'ē·ärch, *n.* [Gr. *genearchēs*, from *genea*, race, family, and *archein*, to rule.] the head of a tribe, clan, or family.

ġē·nēat', *n.* [AS., a companion.] in Anglo-Saxon history, a vassal; one holding land for rent or service.

gé·né·pi' (zhā-nā-pē'), *n.* [Fr.] a sweet absinthe made from two species of Alpine wormwood.

ġen'e·rȧ, *n.* pl. of *genus*.

ġen"ẽr·ȧ·bil'i·ty, *n.* capability of being generated.

ġen'ẽr·ȧ·ble, *a.* [L. *generabilis*, from *generare*, to generate.] capable of being begotten or generated.

ġen'ẽr·ȧl, *a.* [ME. *general*; OFr. *general*, general, common; L. *generalis*, of or belonging to a kind, race, class, general, common, from *genus* (*generis*), kind, class.]

1. of, for, or from the whole or all; not particular; not local; as, a *general* anesthetic, the *general* welfare.

2. of, for, or applying to a whole genus, kind, class, order, or race; as, animal, vegetable, and mineral are the three *general* classifications of matter.

3. existing or occurring extensively; common; widespread; as, there is a *general* unrest in the country.

4. most common; usual; as, what is the *general* pronunciation of that word?

5. concerned with the main or over-all features; lacking in details; not specific; as, these are the *general* characteristics.

6. vague; not precise; as, he spoke in *general* terms.

7. senior or highest in rank; as, the attorney *general*.

8. not connected with or limited to one branch or department of learning, business, etc.; not specialized; as, a *general* store.

general agent; an agent empowered by his principal to act in all matters of a certain kind or in all matters in general.

General Assembly; (a) in some States of the United States, the legislative assembly; (b) the legislative assembly of the United States.

general court-martial; the most formal military court, for judging the gravest offenses: it consists of five or more officers or (since 1948) enlisted men, and can impose the death sentence.

general delivery; (a) delivery of mail at the post office to addressees who call for it; (b) the department of the post office responsible for such delivery.

general election; a final election to choose between the candidates nominated in the primary elections.

general epistle; an epistle written to the entire church; a canonical or catholic epistle.

general headquarters; in military usage, the headquarters of a commanding general in the field.

general issue; an issue taken by a simple denial of an entire charge, or of its substance, as distinguished from a *special issue* raised by denial of a particular part of an allegation.

general officer; any military officer whose rank is superior to that of colonel.

General of the Armies; in the United States Army, the honorary rank given General John J. Pershing on his retirement from active service.

General of the Army; the highest rank in the United States Army, having the insigne of five stars.

general orders; orders issued from military headquarters relating to the entire command.

general paralysis; paresis.

general post office; the main post office of a city or area having branch offices.

general practitioner; a physician who does not specialize in any particular branch of medicine.

general staff; in military usage, a group of specially trained officers who assist the commander of a division or higher unit in planning and supervising military operations.

general store; a store where many sorts of merchandise are sold.

general strike; a strike by workers of an entire trade or industry or of all or many of the industries in a community or country.

general term; a term which is the sign of a general idea.

general verdict; the verdict in a general issue finding simply for the defendant or for the plaintiff.

general warrant; a warrant directed against no particular individual, but suspected persons generally: now illegal.

ġen'ẽr·ȧl, *n.* 1. the whole; the total; that which comprehends all or the chief part: opposed to *particular*.

> In particulars our knowledge begins, and so spreads itself by degrees to *generals*. —Locke.

2. in military usage, (a) a full general: see *full general, lieutenant general, major general, brigadier general, General of the Army*; (b) any general officer: a shortened title; (c) in some foreign armies, an officer ranking immediately below a marshal.

3. the head or chief of an organization more or less military in character; the chief of an order of monks, or of all the houses or congregations established under the same rule; as, the *general* of the Jesuits; the *general* of the Salvation Army.

4. a special form of drum beat for a general assembly of troops or for preparation to march. [Obs.]

5. the public; the populace. [Obs.]

in general; (a) in the main; usually; (b) without specific details; (c) with reference to all spoken of.

ġen'ẽr·ȧl·cy, *n.*; *pl.* **ġen'ẽr·ȧl·cieş,** the rank, commission, tenure of office, or authority of a general.

ġen·e·rā'li·ȧ, *n.pl.* [L., neut. pl. of *generalis*, general.] things in general; general principles or terms.

ġen"ẽr·ȧl·is'si·mō, *n.*; *pl.* **ġen·ẽr·ȧl·is'si·mōş,** [It., superl. of *generale*, general.]

1. in certain countries, the commander in chief of all the armed forces.

2. the commanding officer of several armies in the field.

ġen·ẽr·al'i·ty, *n.*; *pl.* **ġen·ẽr·al'i·tieş,** [Fr. *généralité*; LL. *generalitas* (*-atis*), from L. *generalis*, general.]

1. the quality or state of being general.

2. the main body; the bulk; the greatest part; as, the *generality* of a nation or of mankind.

3. an idea or expression of a general, indefinite, and vague nature; a general statement or principle.

> Let us descend from *generalities* to particulars. —Landor.

ġen'ẽr·ȧl·ī·zȧ·ble, *a.* that can be stated in general terms, or comprehended in a general rule.

ġen"ẽr·ȧl·i·zā'tion, *n.* 1. the act or process of extending from particulars to generals.

2. induction; a general conclusion drawn from specific cases.

> *Generalizations* are apt to be as dangerous as they are tempting. —Lowell.

ġen'ẽr·ȧl·īze, *v.t.*; generalized, *pt., pp.*; generalizing, *ppr.* [Fr. *généraliser*, from L. *generalis*, general.] to make general; especially, (a) to state in terms of a general law or precept; (b) to infer (a general law or precept) from particular instances; (c) to draw, infer, or induce general principles, etc. from; (d) to emphasize the general character rather than specific details of; to make vague; (e) to cause to be widely known or used; to popularize.

ġen'ẽr·ȧl·īze, *v.i.* 1. to formulate general principles or inferences from particulars.

2. to talk in generalities; to make vague or indefinite statements.

ġen'ẽr·ȧl·īzed, *a.* in biology, undifferentiated; synthetic; exhibiting a general type of form or function; not specialized; as, a *generalized* structure.

ġen'ẽr·ȧl·ī·zẽr, *n.* one who generalizes.

ġen'ẽr·ȧl·ly, *adv.* 1. in general; extensively, though not universally; most frequently, but not without exceptions; as, men are *generally* more disposed to censure than to praise.

2. without detail; in the whole taken together.

> *Generally* speaking, they live very quietly. —Addison.

3. in a body; collectively. [Rare.]

> Therefore I counsel that all Israel be *generally* gathered unto thee. —2 Sam. xvii. 11.

4. widely; popularly; extensively; to or by most people; as, it is *generally* believed that he is guilty.

Syn.—usually, ordinarily, commonly, mainly, principally, chiefly.

ġen'ẽr·ȧl·ness, *n.* general quality; commonness.

ġen'ẽr·ȧl·ship, *n.* 1. the office, rank, or person of a general.

2. military skill of a general.

3. judicious tactics; leadership; skill in managing; as, the clever *generalship* of a political leader.

ġen'ẽr·ȧl·ty, *n.* a generality. [Obs.]

ġen'ẽr·ȧnt, *n.* [OFr. *generant*, from L. *generans* (*-antis*), ppr. of *generare*, to beget.]

1. the power that generates; the power or principle that produces; a generator.

2. in mathematics, a generatrix.

ġen'ẽr·āte, *v.t.*; generated, *pt., pp.*; generating, *ppr.* [L. *generatus*, pp. of *generare*, to beget, produce, from *genus* (*-eris*), race, kind.]

1. to beget; to procreate; to propagate; to engender; as, every animal *generates* his own species.

2. to produce; to cause to be; to bring into existence; to form; to originate; as, the dynamo *generates* an electric current; kindness *generates* affection.

3. in mathematics, to trace out or form (a line, plane, figure, or solid) by the motion of a point, line, or plane.

ġen·ẽr·ā′tion, *n.* [L. *generatio* (*-onis*), from *generatus*, pp. of *generare*, to beget.]
1. the act of begetting; reproduction; procreation.
2. production; creation; origination; as, the *generation* of sounds.
3. a single stage or degree in the succession of natural descent; as, father, son, and grandson are three *generations*.
4. the period of time (about thirty years) between the birth of one generation and that of another.
5. all the people born at about the same time or living in the same period of time.
6. in mathematics, the formation of a line, figure, plane, or solid by the motion of a point, line, or plane.
7. in biology, the process by which reproduction is accomplished.
8. a family; a race; a class; any allied group of persons. [Obs.]
spontaneous generation; the supposed creation of living matter from dead or inorganic matter; abiogenesis.

ġen·ẽr·ā′tion·iṣm, *n.* traducianism.

ġen′ẽr·ā·tive, *a.* 1. of the production of offspring; procreative.
2. having the power of producing or originating.

ġen′ẽr·ā·tive gram′măr, a grammatical system consisting of a limited and unchanging set of rules employing a list of symbols and words to generate or describe every possible structure in a language.

ġen′ẽr·ā·tor, *n.* [L. *generator*, from *generare*, to beget, produce.]
1. one who or that which begets, causes, or produces.
2. in music, the principal sound or sounds by which others are produced; the fundamental tone of a series of harmonics or of a chord.
3. a dynamo; any device for transforming mechanical energy into electrical energy.
4. any device for producing a gas or vapor, as an oxygen retort, a steam boiler, etc.
5. in mathematics, a generatrix.

ġen′ẽr·ā·trix, *n.* [L., f. of *generator*, a producer, generator, from *generare*, to produce, generate.]
1. a point, line, or plane whose motion generates a line, plane, figure, or solid.
2. a dynamo.

ġē·ner′iç, *a.* [L. *genus* (*-eris*), race, kind.]
1. of, applied to, or referring to a kind, class, or group; inclusive or general: opposed to *specific*, *special*.
2. in biology, of or characteristic of a genus.

ġē·ner′iç·ăl, *a.* generic. [Rare.]

ġē·ner′iç·ăl·ly, *adv.* with regard to genus; as, an animal *generically* distinct from another.

ġē·ner′iç·ăl·ness, *n.* the quality of being generic.

ġē·ner″i·fi·çā′tion, *n.* [L. *genus* (*-eris*), kind, and *facere*, to make.] in logic, generalization.

ġen·ẽr·os′i·ty, *n.* [Fr. *generosité*; L. *generositas*, nobility, excellence, goodness, from *generosus*, of good and noble birth, noble, from *genus*, race, kind.]
1. the quality of being generous; specifically, (a) nobility of mind; magnanimity; (b) willingness to give or share; a being unselfish.
2. *pl.* **ġen·ẽr·os′i·tieṣ,** a generous act.

ġen′ẽr·ous, *a.* [OFr. *generous*, generous; L. *generosus*, of good and noble birth, excellent, generous, from *genus* (*-eris*), race, kind.]
1. originally, of noble birth.
2. having qualities attributed to people of noble birth; noble-minded; gracious; not mean; magnanimous.
3. willing to give or share; unselfish; bountiful; liberal.
4. large; ample; as, *generous* portions.
5. rich in yield; fertile: said of land, soil, etc.
6. rich, full-flavored, and strong: said of wine.
Syn.—beneficent, bounteous, free, liberal, munificent.

ġen′ẽr·ous·ly, *adv.* in a generous manner; honorably; not meanly; magnanimously; liberally; munificently.

ġen′ẽr·ous·ness, *n.* the quality of being generous; magnanimity; nobleness of mind; liberality; munificence; generosity.

Ġē·nē′si·aç, Ġen·e·sī′ȧ·çăl, *a.* relating to the book of Genesis. [Rare.]

ġē·nē·si·ol′ō·ġy, *n.* [Gr. *genesis*, origin, generation, and *logos*, description, from *legein*, to speak.] systematic knowledge relating to generation.

ġen′e·sis, *n.*; *pl.* **ġen′e·sēṣ,** [L. *genesis*; Gr. *genesis*, birth, origin, from *gignesthai*, to become, to be born.]
1. a beginning; origin; creation; way in which something is formed.
2. [G–] the first book of the Old Testament, containing the history of the creation of the universe, of Adam and Eve, of the Deluge, and of the first patriarchs: so named by those who translated it into Greek.
3. in mathematics, generation. [Obs.]
4. an account of the origin of anything.

-ġen′e·sis, a noun-forming combining form, meaning *origination*, *creation*, *formation*, *evolution* (of something specified), as in parthenogenesis.

ġen′et, *n.* a small-sized, well-proportioned Spanish horse; a jennet.

ġen′et, *n.* [OFr. *genette*; Sp. *gineta*; Ar. *jarnayt*, a genet.]
1. an animal, genus *Genetta*, allied to the civet, and resembling the polecat in appearance: also spelled *genette*.
2. the fur of this animal, or any imitation, as that made from cat skin.

ġē·neth′li·aç, *n.* [Gr. *genethliakos*, belonging to a birthday, from *genethlios*, belonging to one's birth, natal, from *genethlē*, birth, origin, from *gignesthai*, to be born.]
1. a birthday poem. [Obs.]
2. one who is versed in genethialogy. [Obs.]

ġē·neth′li·aç, *a.* pertaining to nativities, as calculated by astrologers; showing the positions of the stars at the birth of any person.

ġē·neth·lī′aç·ăl, *a.* genethliac.

ġē·net′iç, ġē·net′iç·ăl, *a.* [Gr. *genētikos*, having the power of producing generation, from *genesis*, generation.]
1. of the genesis, or origin, of something.
2. of genetics.
3. genic.

ġē·net′iç·ăl·ly, *adv.* 1. with reference to origin, beginning, or genesis.
2. according to the principles of genetics.

ġē·net′iç drift, in evolution, a random fluctuation in the frequency with which a gene appears in a small population, resulting in mutations which, regardless of their adaptive value, become fixed within the group.

ġē·net′i·cist, *n.* a specialist in genetics.

ġē·net′içs, *n.pl.* [*construed as sing.*] [from *genetic.*]
1. the branch of biology that deals with heredity and variation in similar or related animals and plants.
2. the genetic features or constitution of an individual, group, or kind.

Ġē·nē′vȧ, *n.* a city in Switzerland, often the site of international assemblages.
Geneva award; see *Alabama claims*.
Geneva bands; two linen strips hanging from the front of the neck, worn with clerical or academic dress.
Geneva Bible; the English translation of the Bible published in Geneva in 1560, being the first English Bible printed in Roman type, divided into verses, and without the Apocrypha.
Geneva Convention; an agreement signed by the continental powers of Europe at Geneva in 1864 and by Great Britain in 1865, providing for the neutrality of ambulances and hospitals in time of war, and for the protection and immunity from capture of those engaged in succoring the sick and wounded.
Geneva cross; a red Greek cross on a white ground, the emblem adopted by the Geneva Convention to be displayed as a means of protection, in time of war, for persons serving with ambulances, hospitals, etc.
Geneva gown; a long, loose, wide-sleeved black gown, first worn by the Calvinistic clergy of Geneva.

ġē·nē′vȧ, *n.* [Fr. *genièvre*, juniper berry, from L. *juniperus*, the juniper tree.] a liquor distilled from grain or malt, with the addition of juniper berries; Holland gin; gin.

Ġē·nē′văn, *n.* 1. a resident of Geneva.
2. a follower of Calvin.

Ġē·nē′văn, *a.* 1. pertaining to Geneva; Genevese.
2. concerning the doctrines or followers of John Calvin, who established a theocratic state in Geneva; Calvinistic.

Ġē·nē′văn·iṣm, *n.* [so called from the residence of Calvin in Geneva.] Calvinism. [Obs.]

Ġen·e·vēse′, *a.* pertaining to Geneva in Switzerland; Genevan.

Ġen·e·vēse′, *n. sing.* and *pl.* one born or residing in Geneva.

ġen·e·vrette′, *n.* [Fr. *genévrier*, the juniper from *genièvre*, L. *juniperus*, the juniper tree.] a European wine made of wild fruits and flavored with juniper berries.

ġēn′iăl, *a.* [L. *genialis*, pertaining to generation or birth, nuptial, from *genius*, the guardian deity or genius of a person.]
1. contributing to propagation or production; generative; relating to marriage; nuptial. [Rare.]
2. enlivening; contributing to life and growth; supporting life; as, *genial* showers.
3. native; natural. [Obs.]
4. characterized by kindly warmth of disposition and manners; amiable; cordial; sympathetically cheerful; as, a fine, *genial* nature.

The celebrated drinking ode of this *genial* archdeacon. —Warton.

5. relating to or exhibiting genius. [Rare.]

Men of genius have often attached the highest value to their less *genial* works. —Hare.

genial gods; the tutelary deities of the ancient Romans: see *genius*, sense 1.
Syn.—warm, cordial, pleasant, cheering, merry, hearty, revivifying, restorative, inspiriting.

ġē′ni·ăl, *a.* [Gr. *geneion*, chin.] in anatomy, of or relating to the chin; as, a *genial* tubercle.

ġē·ni·al′i·ty, *n.* the quality of being genial; especially, cheerful friendliness; sympathetic cordiality.

ġēn′iăl·ly, *adv.* in a genial manner; cheerfully; cordially.

The spendid sun *genially* warmeth the fertile earth. —Harris.

ġēn′iăl·ness, *n.* the quality of being genial.

ġē·nī′ăn, *a.* pertaining to the chin; genial. [Rare.]

ġen′iç, *a.* of, having the nature of, or caused by a gene or genes; genetic.

-ġen′iç, a combining form used to form adjectives corresponding to nouns ending in *-gen* or *-geny*, as in endo*genic*, phylo*genic*.

ġē·niç′ū·lāte, *v.t.* to form joints or knots in; to bend like a knee joint.

ġē·niç′ū·lāte, ġē·niç′ū·lā·ted, *a.* [L. *geniculatus*, having knee joints, jointed, from *geniculum*, dim. of *genu*, knee.] having a joint or joints like the knee; bent like a knee; as, a *geniculate* stem or peduncle.

ġē·niç·ū·lā′tion, *n.* 1. the state of having knots or joints like a knee.
2. genuflection; kneeling. [Obs.]
3. in anatomy, a geniculate formation.

ġē′nie (-ni), *n.* [OFr. *genie*; L. *genius*, a guardian deity, genius.]
1. disposition; turn of mind. [Rare.]
2. a demon; spirit; jinni.

ġē′ni·ī, *n.* occasional plural of *genius*.

ġē′ni·ō, *n.* [It., from L. *genius*, a genius.] a genius. [Obs.]

ġē″ni·ō·hȳ′oid, *a.* [Gr. *geneion*, chin, and *hyoeides*, hyoid.] in anatomy, connected to the chin and hyoid bone.

Ġen′i·pȧ, *n.* [L., from native W. Ind. name.] a genus of tropical trees of the family *Rubiaceæ*.

ġen′i·pap, *n.* the fruit of the genip tree.

ġen′ip tree, 1. a tree of the genus *Genipa*.
2. a West Indian name for similar trees, the *Melicocca bijuga* and *Hypelate paniculata* of Jamaica.

ġen·i·sä′rō, *n.* [from the native name.] a Nicaraguan tree, *Pithecolobiam saman*, the pods of which are used as food for cattle.

Ġē·nis′tȧ, *n.* [L. *genista*, *genesta*, the broom corn.] a large genus of leguminous plants of which the woadwaxen or dyer's greenweed, *Genista tinctoria*, is probably the best known. It was formerly much used in dyeing, yielding a green color.

ġen·i·tăl, *a.* [ME. *genital*; OFr. *genital*; L. *genitalis*, pertaining to generation or birth, from *genitus*, pp. of *gignere*, to beget.] pertaining to the act or organs of generation.
genital cord; in embryology, a cordlike structure in the fetus of the human species and of most mammals, formed by the union of the Wolffian and Müllerian ducts, and producing the genital passages in both male and female.

ġen·i·tā′li·ȧ, *n.pl.* [L., neut. pl. of *genitalis*, genital.] the genitals.

ġen′i·tălṣ, *n.pl.* the parts of the human body which are the immediate instruments of generation; especially, the external sexual organs.

ġen′i·ting, *n.* same as *jenneting.*

ġen·i·tī′văl, *a.* having genitive form; of or in the genitive case in grammar.

ġen′i·tive, *a.* [L. *genitivus, genetivus,* pertaining to birth or generation; in grammar, the genitive case, from *genitus,* pp. of *gignere,* to beget, produce.] of or in the genitive case.

ġen′i·tive, *n.* 1. the genitive case.
2. a word or construction in the genitive case.
genetive absolute; in Greek grammar, a construction corresponding to the ablative absolute in Latin.

ġen′i·tive çāse, 1. in Latin grammar, a relational case shown by inflection of nouns, pronouns, and adjectives, chiefly expressing possession (L. *liber Petri,* lit., book of Peter, hence Peter's book), material or substance (L. *virga lauri,* twig of laurel), and partition (L. *pars mundi,* part of the world): originally a generic case and almost adjectival in force.
2. in linguistics, loosely, any generic case with functions resembling or thought to resemble those of the Latin genitive; specifically, in English grammar, the possessive case, considered as adjectival by many linguists.

ġen·i·tō-, [from L. *genitus,* pp. of *gignere,* to beget.] a combining form meaning *genital and,* as in *genito*urinary.

ġen″i·tō·çrū′răl, *a.* [*genito-,* and L. *crus, cruris,* the leg.] connected with the thigh and the external genital organs; as, the *genitocrural* nerve.

ġen′i·tŏr, *n.* [L., from *genitus,* pp. of *gignere,* to beget.]
1. one who engenders; a father. [Rare.]
2. [*pl.*] the genital organs. [Obs.]

ġen″i·tō·ū′ri·nā·ry, *a.* [*genito-,* and L. *urina,* urine.] designating or of the genital and urinary organs together.

ġen′i·tūre, *n.* [OFr. *geniture;* L. *genitura,* a begetting, birth, from *genitus,* pp. of *gignere,* to beget.] generation; procreation; birth. [Obs.]

ġēn′ius (-yus), *n.; pl.* for 3, 4, 5, 6 **ġēn′ius·eṣ,** for 1 and 2, **ġē′ni·ī,** [L. *genius,* the guardian deity or spirit of a person, spirit, natural ability, genius, from *gignere* to produce.]
1. (a) [*often* G–] according to ancient Roman belief, a guardian spirit assigned to a person at birth; tutelary deity; hence, (b) [*often* G–] the guardian spirit of any person, place, etc.; (c) either of two spirits, one good and one evil, supposed to influence one's destiny; (d) a person considered as having strong influence over another.

Still had she gazed; but midst the tide
Two angel forms were seen to glide,
The *genii* of the stream. —Gray.

2. a jinni; spirit; demon.
3. particular character or essential spirit of a nation, place, age, language, etc.
4. the peculiar structure of mind with which an individual is endowed; a particular natural talent or aptitude of mind which fits a man in an eminent degree for a certain study or course of life; as, a *genius* for history, for poetry, or painting.

A *genius* for friendship. —Scott.

5. very high intellectual endowment; uncommon powers of intellect, particularly the power of invention or of producing great original works; as, Milton was a man of *genius.*

The true *genius* is a mind of large general powers, accidentally determined to some particular direction. —Johnson.

6. a person having such endowment or ability; as, Shakespeare was a rare *genius.*
Syn.—talent, wisdom, faculty, aptitude, ability, ingenuity, capacity, cleverness.—*Genius* implies superior gifts of nature impelling the mind to exceptional creative or inventive effort in the arts or sciences; *talent* supposes a special aptitude for being molded and directed to specific ends and purposes.

ġē′ni·us lō′cī, [L., lit., the (guardian) spirit of a place.] the general atmosphere of a place.

ġen′ō·blast, *n.* [Gr. *genos,* sex, and *blastos,* germ.] the nucleus of a fertilized ovum.

ġen′ō·cīde, *n.* [Gr. *genos,* race, kind; + *-cide;* first applied to the attempted extermination of the Jews of Nazi Germany.] the systematic killing or extermination of a whole people or nation.

Ġen·ō·ēse′, *n. sing.* and *pl.* one born or resident in Genoa, Italy; the people of Genoa, collectively: also called *Genovese.*

Ġen·ō·ēse′, *a.* pertaining to Genoa, a city of northwestern Italy.

ġen′ō·tȳpe, *n.* [from Gr. *genos,* race, kind; and *type.*]
1. the fundamental constitution of an organism in terms of its hereditary factors.
2. a group of organisms each having the same combination of hereditary traits.

ge·nouil·lère′ (zhē-nö-lyär′), *n.* [Fr., from *génou;* L. *genu,* knee.]
1. in ancient armor, a metal covering for the knee.
2. in fortification, the part of a parapet lying below the sill of an embrasure.

GENOUILLÈRES

-ġe·nous, [*-gen* and *-ous.*] a suffix used to form adjectives derived from nouns ending in *-gen, -geny,* meaning: (a) *producing, generating,* as in nitro*genous;* (b) *produced by, generated in,* as in auto*genous.*

Ġen·ō·vēse′, *a.* and *n.* Genoese.

ġen̓′re (zhon̓′r), *n.* [Fr., kind, genus, from L. *genus, generis,* kind.]
1. a kind; sort; type: said of works of literature, art, etc.
2. genre painting.
genre painting; painting in which subjects from everyday life are treated realistically.

ġen′rō′, *n.* [Japan., lit., first (of the) elders.] in Japan, formerly, a group of retired statesmen assembled to advise the emperor.

ġenṣ, *n.; pl.* **ġen′tēṣ,** [L., orig., that belonging together by birth or descent, from base of *gignere,* to beget, produce.]
1. in ancient Rome, a clan united by descent through the male line from a common ancestor and having both a name and religious observances in common.
2. any tribe or clan; especially, an exogamous group reckoning descent only through the male line.

ġent, *a.* [ME.; OFr.; L. *genitus,* born, pp. of *gignere,* to beget, produce.]
1. of good birth and social standing. [Obs.]
2. pretty; graceful. [Obs.]

ġent, *n.* a gentleman; a man: humorous or vulgar term. [Slang.]

ġen·teel′, *a.* [from Fr. *gentil* (of same origin as *gentle* and *jaunty,* but reborrowed in 16th c.)].
1. formerly, gentlemanly or ladylike; well-bred; refined; polite; elegant; fashionable.
2. excessively, affectedly, or pretentiously well-bred, refined, polite, etc.

ġen·teel′ish, *a.* somewhat genteel.

ġen·teel′ly, *adv.* in a genteel manner.

ġen·teel′ness, *n.* the quality of being genteel.

ġen′tiăn, *n.* [ME. *gencyan;* OFr. *gentiane;* L. *gentiana,* gentian, from *Gentius,* an Illyrian king who was the first to discover its properties.]
1. any of a large group of plants with blue, white, red, or yellow flowers.
2. the bitter root of the yellow gentian, used as a gastrointestinal tonic.

GENTIAN

Ġen·ti·an′ȧ (-shi-an′ȧ), *n.* a large genus of plants typical of the order *Gentianaceæ.*

Ġen″ti·an·ā′cē·ae (-shi-an-ā′sē-ē), *n.pl.* a large order of monopetalous exogens, consisting for the most part of herbaceous plants, with opposite leaves, and yellow, red, blue, or white flowers. The typical genus is *Gentiana.* All have a bitter root, which is employed in medicine.

ġen·tiăn·ā′ceous, *a.* pertaining to the *Gentianaceæ.*

ġen·tiăn·el′lȧ, *n.* [L., from dim. of *gentiana,* gentian.]
1. a kind of blue color.
2. a species of dwarf gentian, *Gentiana acaulis,* native to the Alps.

ġen·ti·an′iç (-shi-), *a.* pertaining to the gentian.

ġen′tiăn·in, *n.* a bitter substance derived from the yellow gentian, *Gentiana lutea.*

ġen′tiăn·ōse, *n.* a substance resembling sugar, derived from the gentian.

ġen′tiăn vī′ō·let, a violet dye used as an antiseptic and as a stain in microscopy.

ġen′tiăn·wŏrt, *n.* any plant of the order *Gentianaceæ.*

ġen′til, *a.* gentle. [Obs.]

ġen′tīle, *n.* [from Fr. and L.; Fr. *gentil;* L. *gentilis,* of the same gens; also, foreigner (in opposition to Roman), pagan, heathen (in opposition to Jew and Christian).]
1. [*also* G–] any person not a Jew.
2. formerly, among Christians, a heathen; pagan.
3. [*also* G–] among Mormons, any person not a Mormon.

ġen′tīle, *a.* 1. [also G–] not Jewish.
2. heathen; pagan.
3. [*also* G–] not Mormon.
4. [*usually* jen′til], of a clan, tribe, people, or nation.
5. [*usually* jen′til], in grammar, designating a nationality or country; as, French is a *gentile* word.

ġen·ti·lesse′, *n.* [ME.; OFr., *gentillise,* from *gentil;* see *gentle.*] the quality of being gentle, or polite; courtesy; good breeding. [Archaic.]

ġen′tīl·ish, *a.* heathenish; pagan. [Obs.]

ġen′tīl·iṣm, *n.* 1. heathenism; paganism.
2. clannishness; tribal feeling.
3. the state of being a gentile.

ġen·ti·li′tious, ġen·ti·li′tiăl (-lish′us, -lish′ăl), *a.* [L. *gentilitius,* pertaining to a clan or gens, from *gentilis,* of or belonging to the same clan or gens, from *gens, gentis,* a clan or gens.]
1. peculiar to a people; national.
2. hereditary.

ġen·til′i·ty, *n.; pl.* **ġen·til′i·tieṣ,** [ME. *gentylete;* OFr. *gentilite,* gentle birth, from L. *gentilitas* (*-atis*), relationship in the same gens, from *gens, gentis,* a gens, clan, tribe.]
1. the quality of being genteel; politeness of manners, graceful behavior; the manners of well-bred people; genteelness: now sometimes ironic.
2. good extraction; dignity of birth. [Rare.]
3. gentry. [Rare.]
4. paganism; heathenism. [Obs.]

ġen′til·īze, *v.i.* 1. to live like a heathen. [Obs.]
2. to play the gentleman. [Obs.]

ġen′til·īze, *v.t.* to cause to be gentle or genteel. [Obs.]

ġen″ti·ō·piç′rin (jen″shi-ō-), *n.* [*gentian,* and Gr. *pikros,* bitter.] a bitter substance derived from gentian root.

ġen′ti·sin, *n.* gentianin.

ġen′tle, *a.; comp.* gentler; *superl.* gentlest, [ME. and OFr. *gentil,* noble, of noble birth; L. *gentilis,* of the same gens.]
1. belonging to a family of social standing; of the upper classes; of good birth.
2. having qualities considered appropriate to those of good birth; refined; polite.
3. noble; chivalrous; as, a *gentle* knight. [Archaic.]
4. generous; kind: in the phrase *gentle reader.*
5. easily handled; tame; as, a *gentle* dog.
6. kindly; serene; patient; as, a *gentle* disposition.
7. mild; moderate; not violent, harsh, or rough; as, a *gentle* tap, a *gentle* rebuke.
8. designating a mild breeze, usually one with a velocity of no more than 12 miles per hour.
9. gradual; as, a *gentle* slope.
the gentle craft (or *art*); (a) fishing; (b) [Obs.] shoemaking.
the gentle sex; women; womankind.
Syn.—tame, mild, meek, placid, pacific, quiet, soft, peaceful, moderate, kind, indulgent.—*Gentle* describes the natural disposition; *tame,* that which is subdued by training; *mild* implies a temper which is, by nature, not easily provoked; *meek,* a spirit which has been schooled to mildness by discipline or suffering.

ġen′tle, *n.* 1. [*usually in pl.*] a gentleman; one born into a family of social standing. [Archaic.]
2. a maggot or larva of the bluebottle fly, used in fishing: so called because soft.
3. a falcon trained for sport.

ġen′tle, *v.t.;* gentled, *pt., pp.;* gentling, *ppr.*
1. to make gentle; to raise from a vulgar condition. [Obs.]
2. to render docile or kind; to soften; to subdue; as, to *gentle* a colt. [Rare.]

ġen′tle·fōlk (-fōk), *n.pl.* persons of good breeding and family: also *gentlefolks.*

ġen′tle-heärt″ed, *a.* having a gentle disposition.

ġen′tle·măn, *n.; pl.* **ġen′tle·men,** [ME. *gentilman* (after OFr. *gentilz hom*); see *gentle* and *man.*]
1. a man of good breeding, kindness, courtesy, and honor; a man having worthy ideals and refinement of thought and action.
2. any man of ordinary respectability and good behavior, regardless of occupation, family, or the like: in the plural, the ordinary courteous form of address to a company of men.

3. a man of good family or good social position; every man above the rank of yeoman, including noblemen; in a more limited sense, a man who without a title bears a coat of arms, or whose ancestors have been freemen; in this sense gentlemen hold a middle rank between the nobility and yeomanry. [Chiefly Hist.]

4. a personal attendant; a valet; as, a gentleman's *gentleman*.

the gentleman from —; in the United States House of Representatives, the member from (a specified State).

ġen′tle-măn-at-ärmṣ′, *n.* in England, one of a band of forty gentlemen, with six officers, who attend the sovereign as a guard on state occasions.

ġen′tle-măn-fär′mẽr, *n.*; *pl.* **ġen′tle-men-fär′mẽrṣ**, a wealthy man who owns and manages a farm, but usually does not work on it.

ġen′tle·măn·līke, *a.* gentlemanly.

ġen′tle·măn·li·ness, *n.* the state or quality of being gentlemanly.

ġen′tle·măn·ly, *a.* pertaining to, like, or becoming a gentleman; polite; courteous; as, *gentlemanly* manners; a *gentlemanly* officer.

ġen′tle·măn of fọr′tūne, an adventurer; specifically, (a) a pirate; (b) a cheating gambler.

ġen′tle·măn'ṣ (or **ġen′tle·men'ṣ**) **á·gree′ment**, an informal, unwritten agreement secured only by the parties' pledge of honor and not legally binding.

ġen′tle·ness, *n.* the quality of being gentle; mildness; tenderness; softness.

ġent′lesse, *n.* gentilesse. [Obs.]

ġen′tle·wom″ăn (-woom″), *n.*; *pl.* **ġen′tle·wom″en** (-wim″), 1. a woman of good family or of good breeding; a woman above the vulgar; a lady.

2. formerly, a woman who attends upon a person of high rank.

ġen′tly, *adv.* 1. in a gentle manner; mildly; tenderly; gradually.

2. after the manner of the gentle of birth; as, *gently* bred.

Ġen·tọọ′, *n.*; *pl.* **Ġen·tọọṣ′**, [Port. *gentio*, a heathen, a gentile.] a Hindu. [Archaic.]

Ġen·tọọ′, *a.* of the Gentoos.

ġen″tri·fi·cā′tion, *n.* a gentrifying or being gentrified.

ġen′tri·fȳ, *v.t.*; gentrified, *pt.*, *pp.*; gentrifying, *ppr.* [from *gentry* and *-fy.*] to convert (an aging area in a city) into a more affluent middle-class neighborhood, as by remodeling or renovating dwellings, resulting in increased property values and in displacement of the poor.

ġen′try, *n.* [ME. *gentry*, *gentrie*, noble or high birth, from OFr. *genterise*, *gentilise*, rank, nobility.]

1. people of refinement, means, and leisure, or of good birth and social standing; especially, in England, the class between the nobility and the yeomanry.

2. any class or group: usually humorous or disparaging; as, the sporting *gentry*.

3. civility; complaisance; courtesy. [Obs.]

4. birth; condition; rank by birth; especially, high rank. [Obs.]

ġen′ty, *a.* neat; trim; slender. [Scot.]

ġē′nū, *n.*; *pl.* **ġen′ū·á**, [L., the knee.] in anatomy, the knee or knee joint; hence, any body with a kneelike angle; as, the *genu* of the corpus callosum.

ġen·ū·fleçt′, *v.i.*; genuflected, *pt.*, *pp.*; genuflecting, *ppr.* [L. *genu*, the knee, and *flectere*, to bend.] to make a genuflection.

ġen·ū·fleç′tion, *n.* [LL. *genuflexio* (*-onis*), from L. *genu*, the knee, and *flectere*, to bend.] the act of bending the knee, as in reverence or worship: also spelled *genuflexion*.

ġen′ū·ine, *a.* [L. *genuinus*, innate, natural, from base of *gignere*, to beget.]

1. of the original stock; purebred.

2. really being what it is said to be; actually coming from the alleged source or origin; real; true; authentic; not counterfeit or artificial.

3. sincere and frank; honest and forthright.

Syn.—natural, real, true, unalloyed, unadulterated, unaffected, veritable, authentic.

ġen′ū·ine·ly, *adv.* in a genuine manner.

ġen′ū·ine·ness, *n.* the quality of being genuine.

ġē′nus, *n.*; *pl.* **ġen′e·rá**, [L. *genus*, birth, origin, descent, race, from *gen*, the root of *gignere*, to beget; Gr. *gignesthai*, to become.]

1. a class; kind; sort.

2. in logic, a class of like objects or ideas, having several subordinate classes, or species.

3. in biology, a classification of plants or animals with common distinguishing characteristics: a genus is the main subdivision of a family and includes one or more species; the genus name is capitalized and precedes the species name, which is not capitalized (e.g., *Homo sapiens*, the scientific name for man).

subaltern genus; in logic, a genus which may become a species of some higher division or classification.

summum genus; in logic, a genus which is the highest; that is, which cannot become a species in a higher genus.

-ġen·y, [Gr. *-geneia.*] a suffix meaning *origin*, *production*, or *development*, as in phylo*geny*.

ġē′ō-, [Gr. *-geō*, from *gaia*, *gē*, the earth.] a combining form meaning *earth*, *of the earth*, as in *geo*centric, *geo*phyte.

ġē·ō·bot′á·ny, *n.* geographical botany.

ġē·ō·cen′triç, ġē·ō·cen′triç·ăl, *a.* [*geo-*, and Gr. *kentron*, center.]

1. measured or viewed as from the center of the earth.

2. having or regarding the earth as a center.

ġē·ō·çhem′is·try, *n.* the science dealing with the chemical composition of the earth's crust.

ġē·ō·çō·rō′ná, *n.* a gaseous belt of ionized hydrogen resembling the sun's corona, surrounding the earth at the limit of the atmosphere.

ġē·oç′rō·nīte, *n.* [*geo-*, and Gr. *Kronos*, Saturn, the alchemistic name of lead.] a crystalline mineral containing lead, antimony, sulfur, and arsenic.

ġē·ō·cyç′liç, *a.* [*geo-*, and Gr. *kyklos*, a circle.]

1. of or relating to the movements of the earth; as, a *geocyclic* diagram.

2. moving round the earth in regular periods.

ġē′ōde, *n.* [Gr. *gaiōdēs*, *geōdēs*, earthlike; *gē*, earth, and *eidos*, form.]

1. a hollow, rounded nodule of rock, the cavity of which is lined with crystals.

2. the cavity of a hollow rock nodule or a similar cavity in bedded rock.

ġē·ō·des′iç, *a.* 1. same as *geodetic* (sense 1): also **ġē·ō·des′i·çăl**.

2. (a) designating the shortest line between two points on a surface, especially a curved surface; (b) of or pertaining to the geometry of such lines.

3. in architecture, having a structurally strong surface made up of short, straight, lightweight bars that form a grid of polygons; as, a *geodesic* dome.

ġē·ō·des′iç, *n.* a geodesic line.

ġē·od′e·sist, *n.* a person skilled in geodesy.

ġē·od′e·sy, *n.* [Gr. *geōdaisia*, the art of mensuration; *gē*, the earth, and *daiein*, to divide.] that part of applied mathematics which has for its object the determination of the magnitude and figure either of the whole earth or of a large portion of its surface, or the locating exactly of points on its surface.

ġē·ō·det′iç, ġē·ō·det′i·çăl, *a.* 1. of or determined by geodesy.

2. same as *geodesic* (sense 2).

ġē·ō·det′i·çăl·ly, *adv.* by or according to geodesy.

ġē·ō·det′içs, *n. pl.* [*construed as sing.*] geodesy.

ġē·od′iç, *a.* of or like a geode.

ġē·ō·dif′e·rous, *a.* bearing or having geodes; as, a *geodiferous* stratum.

ġē′ō·duck, *n.* [Am. Ind.] a very large, burrowing, edible clam, *Panope generosa*, of intertidal beaches of western North America.

ġē·ō·ġen′iç, *a.* of or pertaining to geogeny.

ġē·oġ′e·nous, *a.* [*geo-*, and Gr. *-genēs*, produced.] living in or on the soil, as certain fungi.

ġē·oġ′e·ny, *n.* the study of the origin or genesis of the earth and its formation.

ġē·og·nō′sis, *n.* geognosy. [Rare.]

ġē′og·nost, *n.* [*geo-*, and Gr. *gnōstes*, one who knows.] a person proficient in geognosy.

ġē·og·nos′tiç, ġē·og·nos′tiç·ăl, *a.* relating to geognosy.

ġē·og′nō·sy, *n.* [*geo-*, and Gr. *gnōsis*, knowledge, from *gignōskein*, to know.] the systematic study of the composition of the earth and of the distribution of its various strata and mineral deposits.

ġē·og′rá·phẽr, *n.* one who studies or is versed in geography, or one who compiles a treatise on the subject.

ġē·ō·graph′iç·ăl, ġē·ō·graph′iç, *a.* [LL. *geographicus*; Gr. *geographikos*, of or for geography, from *geōgraphia*, geography.] of or according to geography.

geographical distribution; see under *distribution*.

geographical linguistics; the branch of linguistics which describes the differentiations of languages and dialects within a speech area.

geographical mile; see under *mile*.

geographical variation; a variation of species or variety coincident with or due to variation in geographical location.

ġē·ō·graph′iç·ăl·ly, *adv.* by or according to geography.

ġē·og′rá·phy, *n.*; *pl.* **ġē·og′rá·phieṣ**, [L. *geographia*; Gr. *geōgraphia*, geography; *gē*, the earth, and *graphein*, to write.]

1. the descriptive science dealing with the surface of the earth, its division into continents and countries, and the climate, plants, animals, natural resources, inhabitants, and industries of the various divisions.

2. the physical features, especially the surface features, of a region, area, or place.

3. a book about geography.

ġē′oid, *n.* [Gr. *geoidēs*, *geōdēs*, earthlike; *gē*, the earth, and *eidos*, form, resemblance.] a hypothetical, spheroidal figure of the earth with the entire surface represented as at the mean sea level; the earth as it would be if all parts above mean sea level were removed and all parts below it were filled.

ġē·ō·ī′sō·thẽrm, *n.* [*geo-*, and Gr. *isos*, equal, and *thermē*, heat.] an isogeotherm.

ġē·ol′á·try, *n.* [*geo-*, and Gr. *latreia*, worship.] worship of things terrestrial or of the earth itself. [Rare.]

ġē·ol′ō·ġẽr, ġē·ō·lō′ġi·ăn, *n.* a geologist. [Rare.]

ġē·ō·loġ′iç·ăl, ġē·ō·loġ′iç, *a.* of or according to geology.

ġē·ō·loġ′iç·ăl·ly, *adv.* from a geological viewpoint; by or according to geology.

ġē·ol′ō·ġist, *n.* a student of or specialist in the science of geology.

ġē·ol′ō·ġīze, *v.i.*; geologized, *pt.*, *pp.*; geologizing, *ppr.* to study geology; to make geological investigations or studies of an area, etc.

ġē·ol′ō·ġīze, *v.t.* to study geologically. [Rare.]

ġē·ol′ō·ġy, *n.*; *pl.* **ġē·ol′ō·ġieṣ**, [*geo-*, and Gr. *logos*, a description, from *legein*, to speak.]

1. the science dealing with the structure of the earth's crust and the formation and development of its various layers: it includes the study of individual rock types and early forms of life found as fossils in rocks.

2. the structure of the earth's crust in a given region, area, or place.

3. a book about geology.

ġē·ō·mag·net′iç, *a.* of or pertaining to the magnetic properties of the earth.

ġē·om′á·lişm, *n.* [*geo-*, and Gr. *homalos*, even, level.] in biology, a tendency toward equal lateral development because of gravitation.

ġē′ō·man·cẽr, *n.* one who foretells or divines by geomancy.

ġē′ō·man·cy, *n.* [ME. *geomancie*; OFr. *geomancie*; LL. *geomantia*; Gr. *gē*, the earth, and *manteia*, divination.] a kind of divination by figures or lines formed by a handful of earth cast on the ground, or by dots or points drawn at random.

ġē·ō·man′tiç, ġē·ō·man′tiç·ăl, *a.* pertaining to geomancy.

ġē·om′e·tẽr, *n.* [L. *geometres*; Gr. *geōmetrēs*, a mathematician, geometer; *gē*, the earth, and *metron*, a measure.]

1. one skilled in geometry.

2. in zoology, any moth of the *Geometridæ*.

ġē·om′e·trăl, *a.* pertaining to geometry. [Obs.]

ġē·ō·met′riç, ġē·ō·met′riç·ăl, *a.* [L. *geometricus*; Gr. *geōmetrikos*, belonging to geometry, from *geōmetria*, geometry.]

1. pertaining to geometry; according to the rules or principles of geometry.

2. characterized by or made up of straight lines, triangles, circles, or similar regular forms; as, a *geometric* style; *geometrical* markings of a butterfly's wing.

geometrical construction; in mathematics, construction using only straight lines and circles.

geometrical lathe; see *cycloidal engine* under *engine*.

geometrical pace; five feet in measure.

geometrical plane; the horizontal projective plane in perspective drawing.

geometrical progression; see under *progression*.

geometrical proportion; see under *proportion*.

geometrical radius; the distance from the center of a cogwheel to the pitch line.

geometrical spider; a spider spinning a web more or less circular and intersected by radial lines, as the ordinary garden spider.

geometric stairs; a circular staircase in which the steps are supported at one end by being built into the wall.

geometric decorated style; in architecture, the style of the earlier period of decorated Gothic, in which the tracery and other ornamentation consist entirely of distinct geometrical forms, the principle of verticality and unity by a subordination of parts being fully developed.

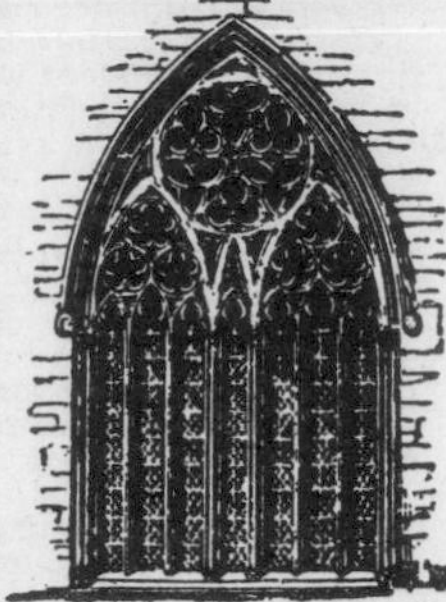
GEOMETRIC DECORATED STYLE

ġē-ō-met'riç-ăl-ly, *adv.* in a geometrical way; by or according to geometry.

ġē″om-e-tri'ciăn (-trish'ăn), *n.* one skilled or specializing in geometry; a geometer.

ġē-om'e-trid, *n.* any moth of the family *Geometridæ*.

ġē-om'e-trid, *a.* of or relating to the *Geometridæ*.

Ġē-ō-met'ri-dae, *n.pl.* [L., from Gr. *geōmetrēs*, earth-measurer, and *eidos*, resemblance.] a family comprising the small moths whose larval forms move by looping their bodies and are known as measuring worms or looping caterpillars.

ġē-om'e-trīze, *v.i.*; geometrized, *pt., pp.*; geometrizing, *ppr.* 1. to work according to the laws of geometry; to perform geometrically.
 2. to study geometry.

ġē-om'e-trīze, *v.t.* to work out geometrically. [Rare.]

ġē-om'e-try, *n.*; *pl.* **ġē-om'e-tries,** [ME. *geometrie, gemetrie*; OFr. *geometrie*; L. *geometria*; Gr. *geōmetria*, the measurement of land, geometry; *gē*, the earth, land, and *metria*, measurement, from *metrein*, to measure.]
 1. the branch of mathematics that deals with points, lines, planes, and solids, and examines their properties, measurement, and mutual relations in space.
 2. a book about geometry.
 descriptive geometry; see under *descriptive*.
 elementary geometry; that branch of the science based upon the methods and axioms of Euclid, the Alexandrian geometer, and dealing only with the properties of the cone and conic sections, the sphere, the cylinder, solids having plane faces, planes, and straight lines.
 higher or *non-Euclidean geometry*; that branch of the science which uses methods other than those of Euclid and assumes his axiom concerning parallel lines not to be true, holding that such lines diverge toward infinity (*hyperbolic geometry*), or converge toward infinity (*elliptic geometry*).

ġē-ō-mor'phiç, *a.* of or pertaining to the shape of the earth or its topographic features.

ġē'ō-mor-phy, *n.* the geographical study of the form of the earth.

ġē-on'ō-my, *n.* [*geo-*, and Gr. *nomos*, law.] the science of the physical laws dealing with the development of the earth.

ġē-ō-phā'ġi-ȧ, ġē-oph'ȧ-ġism, *n.* same as *geophagy*.

ġē-oph'ȧ-ġist, *n.* an earth-eater.

ġē-oph'ȧ-gous, *a.* earth-eating.

ġē-oph'ȧ-ġy, *n.* [*geo-* and *-phagy*.] the eating of earth, either as a psychotic symptom or to make up for lack of food, as in famine areas.

Ġē-oph'i-lȧ, *n.pl.* [L., from Gr. *gē*, earth, and *philos*, loving, from *philein*, to love.] a division of gastropods to which slugs and land snails are assigned in some classifications.

ġē-ō-phys'i-căl, *a.* having to do with geophysics.

ġē-ō-phys'ics, *n.pl.* [*construed as sing.*] the physics of the earth; the science that deals with weather, winds, tides, etc. and their effect on the earth.

ġē'ō-phȳte, *n.* [*geo-*, and *-phyte*.] a plant that grows in earth, especially one with underground buds.

ġē-ō-pol'i-tics, *n.pl.* [*construed as sing.*] [from G. *geopolitik*.] the study of the relation of politics to geography; specifically, the Nazi doctrine of aggressive geographical and political expansion to acquire more living space and promote German domination of the world.

ġē-ō-pon'iç, ġē-ō-pon'iç-ăl, *a.* [Gr. *geōponikos*, of agriculture, from *geōponia*, agriculture, from *geoponos*, a tiller of the earth; *gē*, earth, and *ponos*, work, from *penesthai*, to work, toil.]
 1. of tillage of the earth, or agriculture. [Rare.]
 2. rural; bucolic: humorous usage. [Rare.]

ġē-ō-pon'ics, *n.* agriculture. [Rare.]

ġē-ō-rä'mȧ, *n.* [*geo-*, and Gr. *horama*, a view, from *horan*, to see.] a large, hollow globe or spherical chamber, lined with cloth on which is depicted a general view of the geography of the earth's surface, to be viewed by a spectator from the interior.

ġeor'die, *n.* [nickname for *George*.]
 1. the miner's safety lamp invented by George Stephenson. [Brit. Dial.]
 2. in England, a coal miner; also, a collier sailing on the English coast. [Brit. Dial.]
 3. a guinea bearing an image of St. George. [Brit. and Scot. Dial.]

Ġeorġe, *n.* [Fr. *Georges*; LL. *Georgius*, from Gr. *geōrgos*, a husbandman, farmer; *gē*, the earth, and *ergon*, work.]
 1. a jeweled figure of St. George on horseback slaying the dragon: one of the insignia of the Order of the Garter.

GEORGE (Order of the Garter)

 2. [g–] a brown loaf. [Obs.]

Ġeorġe'-nō″ble, *n.* a gold coin of the time of Henry VIII.

ġeor-ġette' (jor-jet'), *n.* a very thin silk crepe of fine texture and almost transparent, used for women's dresses, blouses, etc.: after Mme. *Georgette* de la Plante, French modiste: also *georgette crepe*.

Ġeor'ġi-ȧ bärk, in botany, the bark of a tree, *Pinckneya pubens*, allied to the cinchona: called also *fever bark* and *Florida quinine*.

Ġeor'ġi-ăn, *a.* 1. (a) of the reigns of George I, II, III, and IV of England (1740–1830); (b) designating or of the artistic style of this period.
 2. of the Georgian S.S.R., its people, language, or culture.
 3. of the State of Georgia.

Ġeor'ġi-ăn, *n.* 1. a native or inhabitant of the Georgian S.S.R.
 2. a native or inhabitant of the State of Georgia.
 3. the language of the Transcaucasian Georgians.

Ġeor'ġi-ȧ pīne, 1. a kind of pine growing in the southern United States, valued for its wood and as a source of turpentine.
 2. its wood.

ġeor'ġiç, *n.* [L. *georgicum* (supply *carmen*, song), a rural song.] a rural poem; a poetical composition on farming or rural life.
 the Georgics; a long poem about farming, by Virgil: it consists of four parts.

ġeor'ġiç, ġeor'ġiç-ăl, *a.* [L. *georgicus*; Gr. *geōrgikos*, agricultural, from *geōrgos*, a husbandman, farmer; *gē*, earth, and *ergon*, work.] relating to rural affairs, agriculture, or husbandry.

Ġeor'ġi-um Sī'dus, [L.] formerly, the planet Uranus: named after George III of England.

ġē-os'cō-py, *n.* [*geo-*, and Gr. *skopein*, to view.] knowledge of the earth, ground, or soil, obtained by inspection.

ġē″ō-sē-len'iç, *a.* [*geo-*, and Gr. *selēnē*, the moon.] of, relating to, or due to the earth and moon as a system; as, *geoselenic* variations.

ġē-ō-stat'iç, *a.* [*geo-*, and Gr. *statikos*, causing to stand, from *histanai*, to stand.]
 1. having to do with pressure of earth or a similar substance.
 2. capable of supporting such pressure, as a kind of arch.

ġē-ō-stat'ics, *n.pl.* [*construed as sing.*] [from *geostatic*.] the branch of physics dealing with the mechanics of the equilibrium of forces in rigid bodies: statics of rigid bodies.

ġē-ō-syn'chrō-nous, *a.* designating or of a satellite or spacecraft in an orbit above the equator, revolving at a rate of speed synchronous with that of the earth's rotation so as, in effect, to be hovering over a point on the earth's surface.

ġē-ō-syn'çline, ġē″ō-syn-çlī'năl, *n.* [*geo-* and *syncline*.] a very large, troughlike depression in the earth's surface: opposed to *geanticline*.

ġē-ō-taç'tiç, *a.* of or influenced by geotaxis.

ġē-ō-tax'is, *n.* [Mod. L.] any movement of a freely moving organism, determined by the force of gravity.

ġē″ō-teç-ton'iç, *a.* [*geo-*, and Gr. *tektōn*, a builder.] pertaining to the earth's structure, especially to the arrangement, structure, distribution, shape, etc. of rocks at the earth's surface.

ġē-ō-thẽr'miç, *a.* [*geo-*, and Gr. *thermos*, heat.] relating to the internal heat of the earth.

ġē″ō-thẽr-mom'e-tẽr, *n.* [*geo-*, and Gr. *thermos*, heat, and *metron*, a measure.] a form of thermometer used to measure temperatures beneath the earth's surface.

ġē-ō-trop'iç, *a.* [*geo-*, and Gr. *tropos*, a turning, from *trepein*, to turn.] growing downward; of, influenced by, having the nature of, or marked by geotropism.

ġē-ot'rō-pism, *n.* [*geo-*, and *-tropism*.] any movement or growth of a living organism in response to the force of gravity: movement toward the center of the earth, as of the roots of plants growing downward, is *positive geotropism*; movement away from the center of the earth, as of shoots extending upward, is *negative geotropism*.

Ġē-phȳ'rē-ȧ, *n.pl.* [L., from Gr. *gephyra*, a mound of earth, a dam, a bridge.] a group of worms comprising the spoonworms, *Sipunculidæ*, and their allies.

ġeph-y-rē'ăn, *n.* a member of the *Gephyrea*.

ġeph-y-rē'ăn, *a.* of or relating to the *Gephyrea*.

ġē'räh, *n.* [Heb., lit., a bean.] the twentieth part of a shekel; specifically, (a) a weight of 13 grains; (b) a silver coin of that weight.

Ġe-raint', *a.* [from Celt.] in Arthurian legend, a knight of the Round Table, husband of Enid.

Ġē-rā-ni-ā'cē-ae, *n.pl.* [L., from *geranium*; Gr. *geranion*, geranium, lit., crane's bill, from *geranos*, a crane.] a family of plants, generally herbaceous, the distinguishing character of which is the growth of fruit composed of five cases, connected with as many flat styles, consolidated round a long conical beak.

ġē-rā-ni-ā'ceous, *a.* of or relating to the *Geraniaceæ*, having flowers with five petals and leaves with many lobes.

ġē-rā'ni-um, *n.* [L., from Gr. *geranion*, geranium, from *geranos*, a crane.]
 1. any of various plants of the genus *Pelargonium* (formerly classed under the genus *Geranium*), commonly cultivated in gardens, as the rose geranium, etc.
 2. any plant of the genus *Geranium*.
 3. [G–] a genus of plants of the *Geraniaceæ*, native to temperate regions throughout the world. They have usually palmately divided leaves and regular flowers, with ten stamens and five carpels, each tipped by a long glabrous awn. The flowers are usually pink or purple and are strong-smelling.

Ġē-rär'di-ȧ, *n.* [named after John *Gerard*, an English herbalist of the 16th century.] a genus of the *Scrophulariaceæ* consisting mostly of root parasites, with flowers rose-colored, purple, or yellow.

ġer-ȧ-tol'ō-gous, *a.* of or relating to geratology.

ġer-ȧ-tol'ō-ġy, *n.* [Gr. *gēras* (*geratos*), old age, and *logos*, discourse, from *legein*, to speak.] the systematic study of degeneration, decadence, and dissolution, as of a species of organisms.

ġẽrbe, *n.* [Fr., a sheaf.]
 1. in heraldry, a garb or sheaf.
 2. in pyrotechnics, a sheaflike firework.

ġẽr'bil, ġẽr'bille, *n.* [Fr. *gerbille*.] a mouselike burrowing rodent of Africa and Asia, having a long tail and long hind limbs, enabling it to leap like a jerboa.

ġēre, *n.* gear. [Obs.]

ġe-rē'fȧ, *n.* in Anglo-Saxon history, a reeve, bailiff, or sheriff. [Obs.]

ġē-ren'dum, *n.*; *pl.* **ġē-ren'dȧ,** [L., neut. of *gerendus*, gerundive of *gerere*, to do, act.] a thing to be done or carried through.

ġẽ'rent, *a.* [L. *gerens* (*-entis*), ppr. of *gerere*, to do, act, perform.] carrying on; managing. [Obs.]

ġē′rent, *n.* [from L. *gerens, gerentis,* ppr. of *gerere,* to bear, conduct.] a person who manages, directs, governs, or rules. [Rare.]

ger′e·nuk, *n.* [Somali *garanug.*] a small antelope, *Litocranius walleri,* of eastern Africa, with a long neck, long legs, and short horns.

ġẽr′fal″cŏn (*or* -fa″kn), *n.* [ME. *gerfaucon;* OFr. *gerfaucon;* LL. *gerofalco, gyrofalco,* a gerfalcon, so named from its circling flight; L. *gyrus,* a circle, and *falco* (*-onis*), a falcon.] a large falcon of northern countries; as, the white or Iceland gerfalcon, *Falco islandus:* also spelled *gyrfalcon.*

ġẽr′ful, *a.* [ME. *gerful, gereful,* from L. *gyrus,* a circle.] changeable in mind; giddy. [Obs.]

ġer·i·ȧ·tri′cian, *n.* a doctor who specializes in geriatrics: also **ġer·i·at′rist.**

ġer·i·at′riçs, *n.pl.* [*construed as sing.*] [from Gr. *geras,* old age; and *-iatrics.*] the branch of medicine that deals with the diseases and hygiene of old age.

gẽr′lănd, gẽr′lŏnd, *n.* a garland. [Obs.]

gẽr′ling, *n.* [prob. for *yearling.*] a salmon on its second return from the sea. [Brit. Dial.]

ġẽrm, *n.* [Fr. *germe,* from L. *germen,* a sprig, offshoot, sprout, bud, germ, embryo.]

1. in biology, the primitive, rudimentary, or embryonic form of an organism; the specific portion of matter from which a new individual is to be developed; seed, bud, etc.

2. a microbe; any microorganism, especially one of the bacteria, causing disease.

3. origin; first principle; rudiment; that from which something can develop or grow; as, the *germ* of human freedom.

ġẽr·māine′, *a.* germane. [Obs.]

ġẽr′măn, *a.* [ME. *germayn, german;* OFr. *germain;* L. *germanus,* children of the same parents, one closely related.]

1. closely related; specifically, (a) having the same parents; as, a brother-*german,* sister-*german;* (b) having the same grandparents on either the father's side or the mother's: a cousin-german is a first cousin.

Brother *german* denotes one who is brother by both the father's and mother's side; cousins *german,* children of brothers or sisters. —Bouvier.

2. germane; relevant; pertinent. [Obs.]

Ġẽr′măn, *a.* [L. *Germanus.*] of, like, or relating to Germany, the Germans, their language, customs, etc.

German knot; a figure-of-eight knot: see *knot,* illus.

German measles; an acute, contagious disease characterized by slight fever, sore throat, pain in the limbs, and small skin eruptions: it resembles measles but is less severe: also called *rubella.*

German paste; a kind of bird food.

German sausage; a large sausage made of spiced, partly cooked meat.

German shepherd dog; a breed of dog somewhat like a wolf in form and size, notable for its intelligence: it was first developed by the Germans and is used in sheepherding, police work, etc.: also called (*German*) *police dog.*

German silver; an alloy of copper, zinc, and nickel, in various proportions, the higher grades having more nickel. It is of a silvery-white color, and is used as a base for plated ware, etc.: also called *nickel silver.*

German text; the modern German black-letter type, somewhat like Old English.

This type is German text

German tinder; a dried fungus used as a combustible; amadou.

Ġẽr′măn, *n.* 1. a native or inhabitant of Germany; a person of German stock.

2. the Germanic language of the Germans, technically called *New High German.*

ġẽr′măn, *n.* [short for *German cotillion.*]

1. a complicated dance for many couples in which partners are changed often; cotillion.

2. a party at which the german is danced.

Ġẽr′măn Bap′tist Breth′ren, a sect of German-American Baptists: also called *Dunkers.*

ġẽr·man′dẽr, *n.* [ME. *germawnder;* OFr. *germandree;* L. *chamædrys;* Gr. *chamaidrys,* from *chamai,* on the ground, and *drys,* a tree.]

1. any of a group of shrubby plants of the mint family, with showy flowers and mintlike leaves.

2. a kind of speedwell, a plant of the figwort family, with long spikes of blue flowers.

ġẽr·māne′, *a.* [L. *germanus,* akin.]

1. closely related; closely connected; relevant; pertinent; appropriate; as, a question *germane* to the case in hand.

2. akin; german.

Ġẽr·man′iç, *a.* [L. *Germanicus,* of the Germans: orig. applied to a particular tribe, prob. Celtic.]

1. of Germany or the Germans; German.

2. designating or of the original language of the German peoples, or its speakers; Teutonic.

3. designating or of the languages descended from this language or their speakers.

Ġẽr·man′iç, *n.* 1. the original language of the German peoples: usually *Primitive Germanic:* also called *Primitive Teutonic.*

2. a principal branch of the Indo-European family of languages, comprising this language and the languages descended from it: these include the extant languages Norwegian, Icelandic, Swedish, Danish (all *North Germanic*), New High German, Yiddish, Plattdeutsch, Dutch, Afrikaans, Flemish, Frisian, Modern English, and Modern Scottish (all *West Germanic*); and the extinct languages Gothic (*East Germanic*), Old Islandic, Old Norwegian, Old Danish, Old Swedish (all *North Germanic*), Old High German, Middle High German, Old Saxon, Middle Low German, Middle Dutch, Old Frisian, Old English, Middle English, and Middle Scottish (all *West Germanic*).

Ġẽr′măn·işm, *n.* 1. an idiom of the German language; an expression derived from or like the German.

2. a German custom, mode of thought, etc.

3. fondness for or imitation of German ways.

Ġẽr′măn·ist, *n.* a student of or specialist in German life or Germanic linguistics and literature.

ġẽr·mā′ni·um, *n.* [L., from *Germania,* Germany.] a rare, grayish-white, metallic chemical element of the carbon family, discovered by Winkler at Freiberg, Germany, in 1886: symbol, Ge; atomic weight, 72.60; atomic number, 32.

Ġẽr′măn·ize, *v.t.;* Germanized, *pt., pp.;* Germanizing, *ppr.* 1. to cause to become German or like the Germans in character, manners, methods, language, or the like.

2. to translate into German.

Ġẽr′măn·ize, *v.i.* to adopt German methods, thought, etc.

Ġẽr·man′ō-, a combining form meaning *German, of Germany, of the Germans,* as in *Germanophobe.*

Ġẽr·man′ō·phīle, *n.* [*Germano-* and *-phile.*] a person who admires or is extremely fond of Germany, its people, customs, influence, etc.

Ġẽr·man′ō·phōbe, *n.* [*Germano-,* and *-phobe.*] a person who hates or fears Germany, its people, customs, influence, etc.

ġẽr·mā′ri·um, *n.* [L., from *germen,* a germ, and *-arium.*] the ovary of a flatworm.

ġẽrm cell, a fertile cell from which a new organism may be developed; egg or sperm cell: opposed to *somatic cell.*

ġẽr′men, *n.;* *pl.* **ġẽr′menş, ġẽr′mi·nȧ,** [L.] a germ: now used only figuratively.

ġẽrm gland, the primitive gland which develops into a testis or an ovary; a gonad.

ġẽr·mi·cī′dăl, *a.* destroying germs.

ġẽr′mi·cīde, *n.* [L. *germen,* a germ, and *cædere,* to kill.] anything used for killing germs, especially bacteria and microorganisms.

ġẽr′mi·çul·tūre, *n.* [L. *germen,* a germ, and *cultura,* culture.] the artificial cultivation of bacteria and other microorganisms.

ġẽr′mi·năl, *a.* [Mod. L. *germinalis,* from L. *germen, germinis.*]

1. of, like, or characteristic of germs or germ cells.

2. in an embryonic stage; in the first stage of growth or development.

germinal disk; (a) a disklike spot in a fertilized ovum in which the first traces of the embryo are visible; (b) the disklike spot on the yolk of an egg where segmentation begins after fertilization.

germinal spot; the nucleolus of an animal germ cell or ovum.

germinal vesicle; (a) in botany, an oösphere; (b) in embryology, the nucleus of an egg before segmentation begins.

Ġẽr′mi năl, *n.* [Fr., from L. *germen,* germ, seed: so named from being the seed month.] the seventh month (March 21 to April 19) of the revolutionary calendar of France, adopted by the First Republic in 1793.

ġẽr′mi·nănt, *a.* [L. *germinans* (*-antis*), ppr. of *germinare,* to sprout forth, bud.] sprouting; germinating.

ġẽr′mi·nāte, *v.i.* and *v.t.;* germinated, *pt., pp.;* germinating, *ppr.* [L. *germinatus,* pp. of *germinare,* to sprout, bud, from *germen,* a sprout, bud.]

1. to sprout or cause to sprout, as from a spore, seed, or bud.

2. to start developing or growing.

ġẽr′mi·nāte, *v.t.* to cause to sprout. [Rare.]

ġẽr·mi·nā′tion, *n.* [ME. *germinacion;* L. *germinatio* (*-onis*), a sprouting forth, budding, from *germinare,* to sprout, bud, from *germen,* a sprout, bud, germ.] a germinating; sprouting; beginning of growth.

ġẽr′mi·nā·tive, *a.* of, causing, or capable of germination.

ġẽr·mi·par′i·ty, *n.* [L. *germen,* a germ, and *parere,* to produce, bring forth.] propagation by the aid of germs or seeds.

ġẽrm lāy′ẽr, any of the three primary layers of cells (ectoderm, endoderm, and mesoderm) from which the various organs and parts of the organism develop by further differentiation.

ġẽrm′less, *a.* free from germs.

ġẽr′mō·ġen, *n.* [L. *germen,* a germ, and Gr. *-genēs,* producing.] a mass of protoplasm, with no cell walls, from which ova are derived.

ġẽr′mŏn, *n.* [Fr.] a fish of the mackerel family; albacore.

ġẽrm plaşm (or **plaş′mȧ**), the substance in germ cells by which hereditary characteristics are believed to be transmitted.

ġẽrm pōre, a pore or opening in the cell wall of a spore or other germ serving as a place of exit for the germ tube.

ġẽrm thē′ō·ry, the theory that infectious diseases are transmitted by specific germs, or microorganisms.

ġẽrm tūbe, a tubular outgrowth from a spore at the time of germination.

ġẽrm′ūle, *n.* an incipient germ.

ġẽrm wạr′fāre, the deliberate contamination of enemy territory with germs in warfare.

gẽrn, *v.i.* to grin. [Scot.]

ġer·ō·çom′iç·ăl, *a.* pertaining to gerocomy. [Rare.]

ġē·roç′ō·my, ġer·ō·çō′mi·ȧ, *n.* [Gr. *gerōn,* an old man, and *komein,* to care for.] the medical science of the treatment of the aged. [Rare.]

ġē·ron′tēş, *n.pl.* [Gr. *gerontes,* pl. of *gerōn,* an old man.] supreme magistrates of the Spartan senate, who were all over sixty.

ġē·ron′tiç, *a.* [Gr. *gerōn,* an old man.] relating to senility; decadent; senile.

ġer·on·toç′rȧ·cy, *n.;* *pl.* **ġer·on·toç′rȧ·cieş,** [Gr. *gerōn,* an old man, and *kratos,* power.]

1. a government controlled by old men.

2. [*pl.*] a governing group composed of old men.

ġer·on·tol′ō·ġy, *n.* [Gr. *geronto-,* from *gerōn,* old man, and *-logy.*] the scientific study of the process of aging and of the problems of aged people.

-ġẽr·ous, [L. *-ger,* from *gerere,* to bear; and *-ous.*] a suffix meaning *producing* or *bearing,* as in denti*gerous.*

ger′ry·man·dẽr, *n.* [from Elbridge *Gerry,* governor of Massachusetts when the method was employed (1812), and *salamander,* from the shape of the redistricted Essex County.] an arrangement of voting districts, intended to favor one political party or candidate.

ger′ry·man·dẽr, *v.t.* 1. to divide (a voting area) in such a way as to give an unfair advantage to one political party.

2. to manipulate unfairly; to falsify to gain advantage.

ger′ry·man·dẽr, *v.i.* to engage in gerrymandering.

ġer′und, *n.* [L. *gerundium,* from *gerere,* to do or carry out.]

1. in Latin, a verbal noun used in all cases but the nominative.

2. in Anglo-Saxon, a dative form of the infinitive with *to* before it; as, *Ic eom to nimanne,* I am to take (or be taken).

3. in English, a verbal noun ending in *-ing:* it has all the uses of the noun but retains certain characteristics of the verb, such as the ability to take an object or an adverbial modifier.

ġē·run′di·ăl, *a.* 1. of or resembling a gerund.

2. used as a gerund.

ġē·run′dive, *n.* [L. *gerundivus,* from *gerere,* to do, act.]

1. a Latin verbal adjective with a typical gerund stem form, used as a future passive participle expressing duty, necessity, fitness, etc. (e.g., *delenda est Carthago,* Carthage must be destroyed).

2. a similar form in any language.

ġē·run′dive, *a.* gerundial.
ġē·run′dive·ly, *adv.* as a gerund or gerundive.
ġē·rū′si·ȧ, ġē·röu′si·ȧ, *n.* [L. *gerusia*; Gr. *gerousia*, from *gerōn*, an old man.] the senate of Sparta and other Dorian states, including all the powers of a state.
ġer·vä′ō, *n.* [native Brazilian name.] a small tropical American shrub of the *Verbenaceæ*, whose leaves are sold in Austria under the name of Brazilian tea.
ġer′y, *a.* variable; fickle. [Obs.]
Ġēr′y·ŏn, *n.* [L.; Gr. *Gēryōn*, or *Gēryonēs*.] in Greek mythology, a winged, three-bodied monster: after killing him, Hercules captured his oxen.
Ġes′ne·rȧ, *n.* a genus of tropical American plants having tuberous rhizomes, opposite leaves, and usually red or orange blossoms.
Ġes·ne·rā′cē·ae, *n.pl.* [L., after Conrad von *Gesner*, a naturalist and scholar of Zurich (1516–1565).] an order of tropical or subtropical herbs or woody plants, comprising nearly a thousand species.
ġes·nēr·ā′ceous, *a.* of or pertaining to the *Gesneraceæ*.
gesse, *v.t.* and *v.i.* to guess. [Obs.]
ġes′sō, *n.* [It., plaster, chalk, from L. *gypsum*, plaster.] in fine arts, plaster of Paris used to prepare a surface for painting or for use in sculpture or bas-reliefs; also, a surface thus prepared.
gesso duro; a durable quality of gesso used for statuettes, bas-reliefs, etc. which are often mounted in a showy frame and tinted to resemble terra cotta.
ġest, ġeste, *n.* [ME. and OFr. *geste*; L. *gesta*, deeds, pl. of pp. of *gerere*, to do, act.]
1. an adventure; deed; exploit.
2. a romantic story of daring adventures, especially one in verse.
ġest, *n.* [Fr. *geste*; L. *gestus*, posture, gesture, from pp. of *gerere*, to bear, behave.]
1. bearing; deportment; carriage. [Archaic.]
2. a gesture. [Archaic.]
Ge·stält′ (ge-shtält′), *n.*; *pl.* **Ge·stäl′ten,** [G. *Gestalt*, form.] in Gestalt psychology, any of the integrated structures or patterns that make up all experience and have specific properties which can neither be derived from the elements of the whole nor considered simply as the sum of these elements.
Ge·stält′ psy·chol′ō·ġy (sī-), a school of psychology, developed in Germany, which affirms that all experience consists of Gestalten, and that the response of an organism to a situation is a complete and unanalyzable whole rather than a sum of the responses to specific elements in the situation.
ġes′tănt, *a.* [L. *gestans* (-*antis*), ppr. of *gestare*, to bear or carry about, freq. of *gerere*, to bear, carry.] pregnant; laden; burdened. [Rare.]
Ge·stä′pō (*or* -shtä′), *n.* popular name for the *Geheime Staatspolizei*, the German state police, organized in 1933 under the Nazi regime to operate against political opposition, and abolished as a result of Germany's defeat in World War II.
Ġes′tȧ Rō·mȧn·ōr′um, literally, the deeds of the Romans, a collection of stories and legends in Latin, which were widely read during the Middle Ages, and used as a source of plots by Chaucer, Shakespeare, etc.
ġes′tāte, *v.t.*; gestated, *pt., pp.*; gestating, *ppr.* [from L. *gestatus*, pp. of *gestare*, to bear, from *gerere*, to bear, carry.] to carry in the uterus during pregnancy.
ġes·tā′tion, *n.* [L. *gestatio* (-*onis*), a bearing, carrying, from *gestare*, to bear or carry about, freq. of *gerere*, to bear, carry.]
1. the act of carrying young in the womb from conception to delivery; pregnancy.
2. the development of a plan in the mind.
3. exercise in which one is borne or carried. [Rare.]
ġes′tȧ·tō·ry, *a.* 1. pertaining to gestation.
2. wearable. [Obs.]
ġes′tiç, *a.* 1. pertaining to deeds; legendary. [Obs.]
2. relating to bodily motion, especially dancing.
ġes′ti·çăl, *a.* gestic.
ġes·tiç ū·lăr, *a.* gesticulatory.
ġes·tiç′ū·lāte, *v.i.*; gesticulated, *pt., pp.*; gesticulating, *ppr.* [L. *gesticulatus*, pp. of *gesticulari*, to make mimic gestures, from *gesticulus*, dim. of *gestus*, a gesture, from *gestus*, pp. of *gerere*, to bear, carry, do.]
1. to make or use gestures to help express one's meaning, as in speaking.
2. to make or use many energetic gestures.
ġes·tiç′ū·lāte, *v.t.* to represent by gesture; to express by gesticulating.
ġes·tiç·ū·lā′tion, *n.* [L. *gesticulatio* (-*onis*), from *gesticulatus*, pp. of *gesticulari*, to gesticulate.]
1. the act of making gestures to express oneself; a gesticulating.
2. a gesture; especially, an energetic gesture.
ġes·tiç′ū·lā·tive, *a.* making, or done with, gestures.
ġes·tiç′ū·lā·tŏr, *n.* one who gesticulates.
ġes·tiç′ū·lȧ·tō·ry, *a.* of or pertaining to gesticulation; representing by gestures.
ġes′tour, *n.* one who narrates gests or adventures; a story teller. [Obs.]
ġes′tūr·ăl, *a.* pertaining to gesture.
ġes′tūre, *n.* [LL. *gestura*, a mode of action, from L. *gestus*, pp. of *gerere*, to bear, carry.]
1. motion of the body, or of part of the body, to express or emphasize ideas, emotions, etc.
2. any action, statement, or characteristic of utterance intended to convey a state of mind, intention, etc.; demonstration of power, principles, etc., often one made only for effect; as, his speech was a *gesture* of friendship.
3. movement of the body or limbs; carriage. [Obs.]
ġes′tūre, *v.t.*; gestured, *pt., pp.*; gesturing, *ppr.* to accompany or enforce with gestures.
ġes′tūre, *v.i.* to make or use a gesture or gestures.
ġes′tūre·less, *a.* without gestures.
ġes′tūre·ment, *n.* the act of making gestures. [Obs.]
Ġe·sund′heit (ge-zoont′hīt), *n.* [G.] (your) health: spoken as a toast or as an expression of good wishes to someone who has just sneezed.
get, *n.* 1. breed; offspring; as, the *get* of a stallion.
2. a begetting.
3. in tennis, etc., a retrieving of a shot seemingly out of reach.
4. a child: used contemptuously. [Scot.]
get, *v.t.*; got *or archaic and dial.* gat, *pt.*; got *or* gotten, *pp.*; getting, *ppr.* [ME. *geten*; ON. *geta*, to obtain, get, beget; AS. *gitan*, *gytan*, to take, obtain, *agitan*, to get.]
1. to come into the state of having (anything); become the owner or receiver of; receive; win; gain; obtain; acquire.
2. to reach; to arrive at; as, we *got* home early.
3. to set up communication with, as on a radio, telephone, etc.; as, did you *get* Paris?
4. (a) to go and bring; (b) to bring; as, go *get* your books.
5. to catch; to capture; to gain hold of.
6. to learn; to commit to memory.
7. to find out or discover to be as the result of experiment or calculation; as, when you add two and two you *get* four.
8. to influence or persuade (a person) to do something; as, please *get* him to leave.
9. to cause (something) to act in a certain way; as, can you *get* the door to shut?
10. (a) to cause to be; as, he *got* his hands dirty; (b) to cause to arrive at; as, *get* this to the printer.
11. to take (oneself) away: often used absolutely.
12. to be sentenced to; as, he *got* ten years.
13. to prepare; as, will you *get* breakfast for us?
14. to give birth to; to procreate; beget: usually said of animals.
15. to be obliged to; to feel a necessity to (with *have* or *has*); as, he has *got* to pass. [Colloq.]
16. to own; to possess (with *have* or *has*); as, he has *got* red hair. [Colloq.]
17. to be or become the master of; especially, (a) to overpower; have complete control of; as, narcotics will *get* him; (b) to puzzle; baffle; as, this problem *gets* me; (c) to take into custody, wound, or kill; (d) in baseball, etc. to put (an opponent) out, as by catching a batted ball.
18. to strike; to hit; as, the blow *got* him in the eye. [Colloq.]
19 to catch the meaning or import of; to understand. [Colloq.]
20. to cause an emotional response in; to irritate, please, thrill, etc.; as, a ride on the roller coaster *gets* me. [Slang.]
21. to notice or observe; as, did you *get* the look on his face? [Slang.]
to get across; to clarify or explain convincingly. [Colloq.]
to get ahead of; to outdo; excel; surpass.
to get around; (a) to circumvent or overcome; (b) to influence, outwit, or gain favor with by cajoling, flattering, etc.
to get at; (a) to approach or reach; (b) to apply oneself to (work, etc.); (c) to find out; ascertain; (d) to influence by bribery or intimidation. [Colloq.]
to get away with; to succeed in doing or taking without being discovered or punished. [Slang.]
to get back; to recover or return.
to get down to; to begin to consider or act on.
to get in; (a) to enter; to join in; (b) to become familiar or closely associated (*with*); (c) to put in.
to get off; (a) to come off, down, or out of; (b) to help to escape sentence or punishment; (c) to lessen the sentence or punishment of; (d) to utter (a joke, retort, etc.); (e) to take off.
to get on; (a) to go on or into; (b) to put on.
to get out; (a) to take out; (b) to issue; publish.
to get out of; (a) to go out from; (b) to escape from or avoid; also, to help to escape from or avoid; (c) to go beyond (sight, etc.); (d) to find out from.
to get over; (a) to recover from; (b) to forget or overlook.
to get to; (a) to succeed in (followed by an infinitive); (b) to succeed in reaching or communicating with; (c) to influence, as by bribery or intimidation. [Colloq.]
to get together; to bring together; accumulate.
to get up; (a) to contrive; arrange; organize; (b) to climb, mount, or reach the top of.
get, *v.i.* 1. to come, go, or arrive (with *from*, *to*, *into*, etc.); as, when do we *get* to New York?
2. to be; become; come to be (doing something); come to be (in a situation, condition, etc.); as, he *got* caught in the rain, *get* in touch with me.
Get is used as a linking verb in idiomatic phrases, and as an informal auxiliary for emphasis in passive construction; as, we *got* beaten yesterday.
to get about; (a) to move from place to place; (b) to go to many social events, places, etc.; (c) to circulate, as news; come to the notice of many.
to get across; (a) to be clear; be understood; (b) to succeed, as in making oneself understood or conveying one's personality to an audience.
to get ahead; to succeed; prosper.
to get along; (a) to proceed; make progress; (b) to leave; go away; (c) to succeed or be fairly successful, as in making a living; (d) to agree; be compatible.
to get around; (a) to move from place to place; (b) to go to many social events, places, etc.; (c) to circulate, as news; to come to the notice of many.
to get away; (a) to go away; leave; (b) to escape; (c) to start, as in a race.
to get back; (a) to return; (b) [Slang.] to retaliate; to get revenge (usually with *at*).
to get by; (a) to pass; (b) [Colloq.] to succeed without being discovered or punished; (c) [Colloq.] to survive; manage.
to get down; to descend; dismount.
to get in; to arrive.
to get it; (a) to understand; (b) to be punished or scolded. [Colloq.]
to get nowhere; to make no progress; to accomplish nothing.
to get off; (a) to leave; to go away; (b) to escape.
to get on; (a) to proceed; to make progress; (b) to grow older; (c) to succeed or be fairly successful, as in making a living; (d) to agree; to be compatible.
to get out; (a) to go out; (b) to leave; to go away; (c) to become no longer a secret.
to get over; to get across (in all senses). [Colloq.]
to get there; to succeed. [Colloq.]
to get through; (a) to finish; (b) to manage to survive.
to get together; (a) to come together; (b) to reach an agreement. [Colloq.]
to get up; (a) to rise (from a chair, from sleep, etc.); (b) to dress elaborately; (c) to advance; make progress.
Syn.—obtain, procure, acquire, secure, gain, win.
get·at′ȧ·ble, *a.* easy to reach or ascertain; accessible.

get'á·wāy, *n.* 1. the act of starting, as in a race.
2. the act of escaping.

Geth·sem'àn·ē, *n.* 1. in the Bible, the garden on the outskirts of Jerusalem, where Jesus wept and prayed and was arrested (Matt. xxvi. 36–50).
2. [*often* g-] any scene or occasion of agony.

get'pen″ny, *n.* that which gains money. [Obs.]

get'tá·ble, *a.* that can be got; obtainable.

get'tẽr, *n.* 1. one who gets, gains, or acquires.
2. one who begets or procreates.

get'tẽr-up, *n.* one who arranges, makes, or contrives anything.

get'tö·geth″ẽr, *n.* an informal social gathering or meeting.

Get'tys·bŭrg Ad·dress', the speech made by President Abraham Lincoln at the dedication of the National Cemetery at Gettysburg, Pa., November 19, 1863, beginning—"Four score and seven years ago our fathers brought forth on this continent a new nation, conceived in liberty, and dedicated to the proposition that all men are created equal."

get'-up, *n.* 1. general arrangement or composition of a thing.
2. costume; outfit; dress.

Gē'um, *n.* [L., the herb bennet, avens; prob. from Gr. *genein*, to taste.] a genus of herbaceous perennials of the family *Rosaceæ*.

ge·vält', ge·väld' (-vält'), *interj.* [from Yid. *g'vald*, lit., violence.] help!: a cry of alarm.

gew'gaw, *n.* [alteration of ME. *giuegoue*, a gewgaw, trifle, perh. from ME. *gawen*, to gape.] a showy trifle; a pretty thing of little worth; a bauble; a trinket.

gew'gaw, *a.* showy without value.

gey, *adv.* considerably; very. [Scot.]

gey̆'sẽr, *n.* [Ice. *geysir*, from *geysa*, to gush, from *gjosa*, gush.]
1. a spring from which hot water, steam, or mud gush out at intervals, frequently to a considerable height in the air: geysers are found in Iceland, New Zealand, and in the Yellowstone region of the United States.
2. a small, gas, hot-water heater of the coil type. [Brit.]

gey̆'sẽr·iç, *a.* pertaining to or resembling a geyser.

gey̆'sẽr·īte, *n.* an opaline mineral deposited on the edges of geysers and hot springs; hydrous silica.

ghar'ry (gar'i), *n.* [Hind. *gari*.] in India, any wheeled vehicle.

ghȧst'ful, *a.* dreary; dismal; fearful. [Obs.]

ghȧst'ful·ly, *adv.* frightfully. [Obs.]

ghȧst'li·ness, *n.* the state or quality of being ghastly.

ghȧst'ly, *a.*; *comp.* ghastlier; *superl.* ghastliest, [ME. *gastly*; AS. *gæstlic*, terrible, from *gæstan*, to frighten, terrify.]
1. horrible; frightful; dreadful; as, a *ghastly* wound.
2. like a ghost; deathlike; pale; as, a *ghastly* face, *ghastly* smiles.
3. very bad; very unpleasant. [Colloq.]
Syn.—deathlike, ghostlike, lurid, cadaverous, pale, pallid, spectral.

ghȧst'ly, *adv.* in a ghastly manner.

ghat, ghaut (gat), *n.* [Hind. *ghat*.]
1. in India, a pass through a mountain.
2. a chain of mountains; especially, either of two ranges bordering the east and west coasts of India.
3. in India, a stairway to a river landing for ritual bathers.
burning ghat; a wide step or space at the head of a ghat, on which the Hindus burn their dead.

ghä·wä'zee, ghä·wä'zī, *n. sing.* and *pl.* [Ar.] female dancers of low caste in Egypt.

ghaz'el (gaz'), *n.* [Ar.] same as *gazel*.

ghä'zī (gä'), *n.* [Ar.] 1. a Moslem hero, especially one who wages war against infidels.
2. [G-] in Turkey, a title of honor meaning "victorious warrior."

Ghē'bẽr, Ghē'bre (gē'bẽr), *n.* [Fr. *guèbre*; Per. *gabr*; prob. from Ar. *kāfir*, infidel.] any of the Zoroastrian fire worshipers who remained in Persia after the Moslem conquest in 637 A.D.

ghee (gē), *n.* [Hind. *ghī*, from Sans. *ghrita*, butter or fat.] in India, the liquid butter remaining when butter from buffalo milk is melted, boiled, and strained.

ghẽr'kin (gẽr'), *n.* [D. *agurkje*; Bohem. *okurka*, a cucumber.]
1. a variety of cucumber bearing small, prickly fruit.
2. the fruit of this plant, used for pickles.
3. the immature fruit of the common cucumber when pickled.
4. in zoology, a sea gherkin.

ghet'tō (get'ō), *n.*; *pl.* **ghet'tōṣ** or **ghet'tī,** [It.] 1. in certain European cities, a section to which Jews are, or were, restricted: the word is also applied, often in an unfriendly sense, to any section (of a city) in which many Jews live.
2. any section of a city in which many members of some national or racial group live, or to which they are restricted.

ghet'tō·īze, *v.t.*; ghettoized, *pt.*, *pp.*; ghettoizing, *ppr.* 1. to restrict to a ghetto.
2. to cause to become a ghetto.

Ghib'el·line (gib'), *n.* [It. *Ghibellino*, for G. *Waiblingen*, an estate in the part of Franconia included under Württemburg, which belonged to the house of Hohenstaufen.] any member of a political party in medieval Italy that favored the German emperors, and opposed the Guelfs, or adherents of the popes.

ghōle (gōl), *n.* ghoul. [Obs.]

ghōst (gōst), *n.* [ME. *gost*, *goost*, *gast*; AS. *gast*, breath, spirit.]
1. originally, spirit; the soul of man; as, to give up the *ghost*, to die.
2. the supposed disembodied spirit of a deceased person; soul or spirit separate from the body, conceived of as appearing to the living as a pale, shadowy apparition.
3. a haunting memory.
4. a faint, shadowy semblance; inkling; slight trace; as, not a *ghost* of a chance.
5. a ghost writer. [Colloq.]
6. in optics and television, an unwanted secondary image or bright spot.
7. [*often* G-] in theology, the Divine Spirit: now only in *Holy Ghost*.

ghōst, *v.t.* 1. to haunt.
2. to be the ghost writer of. [Colloq.]

ghōst, *v.i.* to work as a ghost writer. [Colloq.]

ghōst dȧnce, a North American Indian religious dance, dedicated to the dead, at which the dancers believe ghosts appear.

ghōst'fish, *n.* a pale, whitish variety of *Cryptacanthodes maculatus*, the wrymouth.

ghōst'līke, *a.* like a ghost.

ghōst'li·ness, *n.* the state or quality of being ghostly.

ghōst'ly, *a.* [ME. *gostly*; AS. *gastlic*, of a spirit, spiritual, from *gast*, a specter, breath, spirit.]
1. spectral; supernatural; of, like, or characteristic of a ghost or other apparition.
2. spiritual; relating to the soul or religion; not carnal or secular.

ghōst'ly, *adv.* spectrally; weirdly; spiritually; mystically. [Rare.]

ghōst moth, a nocturnal moth, *Hepialus humuli*, so called from the male being white, and from its habit of hovering in the twilight over one spot.

ghōst·ol'ō·gy, *n.* [*ghost*, and Gr. *-logia*, from *legein*, to speak.] the legendry of supernatural things. [Rare.]

ghōst plant, *Amaranthus graecizans*, the tumbleweed.

ghōst wŏrd, [term invented by W. W. Skeat, 19th-c. Eng. philologist.] a word created through misreading of manuscripts, misunderstanding of grammatical elements, etc. and hence possessing a ghost-existence in a language. Examples: *derring-do*, desperate courage (misunderstanding of ME. *derring do*, lit., daring to do).

ghōst wrīt'ẽr, a person who writes speeches, articles, etc. for another who professes to be the author.

ghoul (gööl), *n.* [Ar. *ghūl*, a demon of the mountains.]
1. in Oriental folklore, an evil being that is supposed to rob graves and feed on the flesh of the dead.
2. a robber of graves.
3. a person who performs horrible acts or enjoys loathsome things.

ghoul'ish, *a.* demoniac; fiendish; like a ghoul.

ghur'ry, ghur'rie (gur'), *n.*; *pl.* **ghur'rieṣ,** [Sans. *ghaṭī*, a water clock.]
1. in India, (a) form of clepsydra; (b) the gong of such an instrument; (c) any kind of clock.
2. (a) among Hindus, the 60th part of a day; 24 minutes; (b) among Anglo-Indians, 60 minutes.

ghyll (gil), *n.* [Ice. *gil*, a ravine.] a gill; a ravine.

G. I. abbreviation for *government issue*: a term first applied to anything issued by the U.S. Army, as supplies, clothing, etc.; later used as an epithet for a soldier, especially an enlisted man, or to describe anything associated with him; as, a *G.I.* haircut.

ġiȧl·lō·lī'nō, *n.* [It. *giallorino*, yellowish, from *giallo*, yellow.] a pigment, Naples yellow.

ġī'ănt, *n.* [ME. *giaunt*; OFr. *geant*; L. *gigas* (*-antis*); Gr. *gigas* (*-antos*), a giant; *gē*, earth, and *genēs*, born.]
1. in Greek mythology, any of a race of huge beings of human form who warred with the gods.
2. any imaginary being of human form but of superhuman size and strength.
3. a person or thing of great size, strength, intellect, etc.

ġī'ănt, *a.* like a giant; extraordinary in size or strength; as, *giant* brothers; a *giant* son.

ġī'ănt cell, same as *osteoclast*.

ġī'ănt çlam, a huge bivalve shell of the family *Tridacnidæ*.

ġī'ănt·ess, *n.* a female giant.

ġī'ănt·ish, *a.* like a giant; very large.

ġī'ănt·iṣm, *n.* same as *gigantism*.

ġī'ănt·īze, *v.i.* to play the giant. [Rare.]

ġī'ănt ket'tle, a huge pothole, as found on the coast of Norway.

ġī'ănt·ly, *a.* giantlike.

ġī'ănt pan'dȧ, a large, black-and-white, bearlike mammal of Tibet: it is almost extinct.

ġī'ănt pow'dẽr, an explosive like dynamite.

ġī'ănt·ry, *n.* the race of giants. [Rare.]

Gī'ănt'ṣ Cauṣe'wāy, a great and unusual formation of columnar basalt on the coast of Antrim, Northern Ireland: there are thousands of vertical columns whose formation is ascribed to a large flow of lava in the Tertiary period: there has been much erosion that has exposed many great cliffs, some of which stand over 500 ft. above sea level.

ġī'ănt·ship, *n.* the state, quality, or character of being a giant.

ġiaour (jour), *n.* [Turk. *gawur*, *jawr*; Per. *gāwr*, an infidel.] a non-Moslem: a name given by Moslems to unbelievers, especially Christians.

ġiär·dī·net'tō, *n.*; *pl.* **ġiär·dī·net'tī,** [It., dim. of *giardino*, garden.] a piece of jewelry decorated with imitations of flowers in precious stones.

gib, *n.* [perh. from OFr. *gibe*, staff.]
1. the hook of gristle that appears on the lower jaw of the male salmon after spawning.
2. an adjustable piece of metal or wood for keeping the moving parts of a machine in place; as, a *gib* and cotter.
gib and key; the fixed wedge and the driving wedge for tightening the strap which holds the brasses at the end of a connecting rod in steam machinery.

gib, *v.t.*; gibbed, *pt.*, *pp.*; gibbing, *ppr.* to secure or fasten with a gib or gibs.

gib, *n.* [short for *Gilbert*, used as a proper name for a cat.]
1. a cat; especially, a tomcat.
2. a castrated cat. [Dial.]

ġib·bär'tas, *n.* [compare L. *gibber*, humpbacked.] a finback or Jupiter whale.

gibbed (gibd), *a.* [from *gibbed cat*, var. of *gib cat* (see *gib*, a cat), but treated as of from an assumed *gib*, to castrate.] castrated: said of a cat.

ġib'bẽr, *v.i.* and *v.t.* [Ice. *gabba*, to mock.] to speak or utter rapidly and inarticulately; chatter unintelligibly.

ġib'bẽr, *n.* unintelligible chatter; gibberish.

ġib'bẽr·ish, *n.* rapid and inarticulate talk; unintelligible chatter; jargon.

ġib'bẽr·ish, *a.* unmeaning; unintelligible; incoherent.

ġib'bet, *n.* [ME. *gibet*; OFr. *gibet*, a gibbet, prob. from *gibet*, a large stick.]
1. a gallows.
2. a structure like a gallows, from which bodies of criminals already executed were hung and exposed to public scorn.
3. the projecting beam of a crane which sustains the pulleys and the weight of goods; a jib.

ġib'bet, *v.t.*; gibbeted *or* gibbetted, *pt.*, *pp.*; gibbeting *or* gibbetting, *ppr.* 1. to execute by hanging.
2. to hang on a gibbet.
3. to expose to ridicule, scorn, infamy, or the like.

gib'bŏn, *n.* [Fr.] a small, slender, long-armed ape of India, southern China, and the East Indies.

gib'bōse, *a.* same as *gibbous*.

gib·bos'i·ty, *n.* 1. the quality or state of being gibbous; protuberance; convexity.

2. *pl.* **gib·bos′i·ties**, a rounded swelling or protuberance.

gib′bous (-bus), *a.* [L. *gibbosus*, humped or hunched, from *gibbus* or *gibba*, a hump.]
1. swelling; protuberant; rounded and bulging.
2. designating the moon when it is in a phase between half-moon and full moon and the curves forming its outline are convex.
3. hunched; humpbacked; crookbacked.

gib′bous·ly, *adv.* in a gibbous or protuberant form.

gib′bous·ness, *n.* the state or quality of being gibbous; also, a protuberance; a round prominence; convexity.

gibbs′īte, *n.* [named after George *Gibbs*, an American mineralogist.] a hydrate of aluminium, a whitish mineral, found in Massachusetts in irregular stalactitic masses.

gib′-çat, *n.* a castrated tomcat. [Dial.]

ġībe, *v.i.*; gibed, *pt.*, *pp.*; gibing, *ppr.* [perh. from OFr. *giber*, to handle roughly.] to cast reproaches and sneering expressions; to rail; to utter taunting, sarcastic words; to flout; to jeer: also spelled *jibe*.

ġībe, *v.t.* to reproach with contemptuous words; to deride; to scoff at: also spelled *jibe*.

ġībe, *n.* an expression of sarcastic scorn; a scoff; a jeer: also spelled *jibe*.
Mark the fleers, the *gibes*, and notable scorns. —Shak.

gib′el, *n.* [G. *gibel*, *giebel*, a kind of carp, from O.H.G. *gebal*, the head.] the Prussian carp, *Carassius vulgaris* or *gibelio*.

ġīb′ēr, *n.* one who utters gibes: also spelled *jiber*.

gib′fish, *n.* a male salmon. [Brit. Dial.]

ġīb′ing·ly, *adv.* in a gibing manner; scornfully: also spelled *jibingly*.

ġib′let, *a.* made of giblets; as, a *giblet* pie.

ġib′let, *n.* [ME. *gibelet*; OFr. *gibelet*, stew made of fowls.]
1. an internal edible part of a fowl, such as the heart, liver, or gizzard, which has been removed before cooking, and is often served separately in a sauce or pie: chiefly used in the plural.
2. [*pl.*] odds and ends. [Dial.]

Ġi·bral′tăr, *n.* rock candy: called also *Gibraltar rock*, in allusion to the Rock of Gibraltar, a fort belonging to Great Britain at the entrance of the Mediterranean.

Gib′sŏn, *n.* [after Hugh *Gibson* (1883–1954), U.S. diplomat.] [*also* g-] a dry martini cocktail served with a tiny pickled onion.

Gib′sŏn ġirl, the American girl of the 1890's as depicted by Charles Dana Gibson.

ġib′staff, *n.* [OFr. *gibbe*, a sort of arm.] a staff to gauge water or to push a boat.

ġī′bus (*Fr.* zhē-bus′), *n.* [Fr.: after the name of the 19th-c. inventor.] an opera hat; a collapsible top hat: also *gibus hat*.

gid, *n.* [from *giddy*, dizzy.] a brain disease of sheep; the staggers.

gid′di·ly, *adv.* in a giddy manner; flightily.

gid′di·ness, *n.* the state or quality of being giddy.
Syn.—flightiness, inconstancy, unsteadiness, levity, thoughtlessness, volatility, fickleness.

gid′dy, *a.*; *comp.* giddier; *superl.* giddiest, [ME. *gidie*, *gedie*, *guydi*; AS. *gydig*, insane.]
1. having a whirling, dazed sensation; having lost the power of preserving balance, and therefore wavering and inclined to fall; dizzy; reeling.
Like music which makes *giddy* the dim brain. —Shelley.
2. causing giddiness or vertigo; rendering dizzy; as, a *giddy* height.
3. turning or circling around very rapidly; whirling.
The *giddy* motion of the whirling mill. —Pope.
4. (a) inconstant; fickle; (b) frivolous; flighty; heedless.

gid′dy, *v.i.*; giddied, *pt.*, *pp.*; giddying, *ppr.* to become giddy; to reel.

gid′dy, *v.t.* to make dizzy or unsteady.

gid′dy·head (-hed), *n.* a person without thought or judgment.

gid′dy-head″ed, *a.* having a giddyhead; heedless; unsteady.

gid′dy-pāced (-pāst), *a.* moving irregularly; reeling; flighty. [Rare.]

gid′dy·pāte, *n.* a giddyhead.

gid′dy-pāt″ed, *a.* giddy-headed.

Gid′ē·ŏn, *n.* in the Bible, a hero of Israel who led his people in the defeat of the Midianites and became a judge of Israel for forty years: Judg. vi. 11 ff.

Gid′ē·ŏn Sō·cī′e·ty, an organization for placing Bibles in hotel rooms, etc., founded in 1899 by a group of commercial travelers.

ġiē, *v.t.* to give. [Scot. and Brit. Dial.]

ġiēr′-ēa″gle, *n.* [D. *gier*, a vulture.] an eagle or bird of the eagle kind, mentioned in Leviticus xi. 18, supposed to be *Neophron percnopterus*, the Egyptian vulture.

gif, *conj.* [AS.] if. [Obs. except Brit. Dial.]

giff′gaff, *n.* give and take; tit for tat; mutual obligation. [Scot. and Brit. Dial.]

gift, *n.* [ME. *gift*, a gift, from AS. *gift*, generally in pl. *gifta*, a marriage, nuptials, from *gifan*, to give.]
1. the act, right, or power of giving or conferring; as, the office is in the *gift* of the mayor.
2. that which is given or bestowed; anything which is voluntarily transferred by one person to another without compensation; a donation; a present.
3. a natural quality or endowment regarded as conferred; talent; as, the *gift* of wit.
4. in law, a voluntary transfer of property without compensation or any consideration: opposed to *sale*.
Syn.—donation, present, benefaction, boon.
to look a gift horse in the mouth; to be critical of something given to one: from the practice of judging a horse's age by its teeth.

gift, *v.t.*; gifted, *pt.*, *pp.*; gifting, *ppr.* 1. to confer as a gift; to give. [Scot.]
2. to endow with a gift or with any power or faculty.

gift′ed, *a.* endowed with a natural ability or aptitude; talented.
Some divinely *gifted* man. —Tennyson.

gift′ed·ness, *n.* the state of being gifted.

gift rōpe, [probably altered from *guess rope*.] in seamen's language, a rope attached to a boat for towing it. [Obs.]

gift′-wrap, *v.t.* to wrap (a gift) attractively, with decorative wrapping, ribbon, etc.

gig, *n.* a dart or harpoon; a fishgig.

gig, *v.i.* to fish with a gig or fishgig.

gig, *v.t.* to spear (a fish) with a gig.

gig, *n.* [ME. *gigge*, whirligig, spinning top; prob. from ON.]
1. a light, two-wheeled, open carriage drawn by one horse.
2. a long, light ship's boat with oars and sail, usually reserved for the commanding officer.
3. a rowboat used in racing.
4. [for *gig mill*.] a machine for raising nap on cloth.
5. any toy that is whirled round in play: specifically, a top or whirligig. [Obs.]

gig, *v.i.*; gigged, *pt.*, *pp.*; gigging, *ppr.* to travel in a gig.

gig, *v.t.* [from a kind of top which, when twirled, threw off a smaller top.] to reproduce another of the same sort. [Obs.]

gig, *n.* [prob. from ME. *gigge* (see *gig*, carriage, etc.) in sense "something light or trivial."]
1. an official record or report of a minor delinquency, as in the army, school, etc.; a demerit. [Slang.]
2. punishment for such a delinquency. [Slang.]

gig, *v.t.*; gigged, *pt.*, *pp.*; gigging, *ppr.* 1. to give a gig to. [Slang.]
2. to punish with a gig. [Slang.]

gig, *n.* [origin unknown.]
1. a gathering of musicians for a session of jazz. [Slang.]
2. a job performing music, especially jazz, often one for a single engagement. [Slang.]
3. any job, performance, or routine; stint. [Slang.]

gig, *v.i.*; gigged, *pt.*, *pp.*; gigging, *ppr.* to have an engagement performing music, especially jazz.

ġī·gant′-, giganto-.

ġī·gan·tē′ăn, *a.* [L. *giganteus*; Gr. *giganteios*, from *gigas* (*-antos*), a giant.] like a giant; gigantic; huge.

ġī·gan·tesque′ (-tesk′), *a.* befitting a giant; characteristic of a giant.

ġī·gan′tiç, *a.* [L. *gigas* (*-antis*), a giant.]
1. of extraordinary size; very large; huge; colossal; enormous; immense.
2. of, like, suitable for, or characteristic of a giant.
A towering specter of *gigantic* mold. —Pope.
Syn.—colossal, enormous, immense, huge.

ġī·gan′tiç·ăl, *a.* gigantic. [Obs.]

ġī·gan′tiç·ăl·ly, *adv.* in a gigantic manner.

ġī·gan′tine, *a.* gigantic; befitting a giant. [Rare.]

ġī·gan′tişm, *n.* [from L. *gigas*, *gigantis*; and *ism*.] abnormal growth of the body, believed to be caused by a disease of the anterior lobe of the pituitary gland: also *giantism*.

ġī·gan′tō-, [from Gr. *gigas*, *gigantos*, a giant.] a combining form signifying *large*, *gigantic*.

ġī·gan′tō·līte, *n.* [*giganto-*, and Gr. *lithos*, a stone.] a variety of pinite, crystallized in six- or twelve-sided prisms.

ġī·gan·tō·loġ′iç·ăl, *a.* pertaining to gigantology.

ġī·gan·tol′ō·ġy, *n.* [*giganto-*, and Gr. *logos*, a description.] an account of or knowledge about giants.

ġī·gan·tom′ȧ·çhy, *n.* [LL. *gigantomachia*; Gr. *gigantomachia*, the battle of the giants; *gigas* (*-antos*), a giant, and *machē*, a battle.]
1. [G-] in Greek mythology, the struggle between the giants and the gods.
2. any war between giants or giant powers.

ġiġe, *n.* a guige. [Obs.]

ġī·ge·lī′rȧ, *n.* [It. *giga*, fiddle, and *lira*, lyre.] a xylophone.

ġī·ġē′ri·um, *n.*; *pl.* **ġī·ġē′ri·ȧ**, [L. *gigeria*, neut. pl., the cooked entrails of poultry.] the gizzard of a bird.

ġig′get, *n.* a gigot. [Obs.]

gig′ging mȧ·çhïne′, a machine for dressing woolen cloth by subjecting it to the action of teazels, the fine hooks of which draw the loose fibers to the surface.

gig′gle, *v.i.*; giggled, *pt.*, *pp.*; giggling, *ppr.* [16th-c.; perh. from M.D. or L.G.; cf. D. *giggelen*, from the base of ME. *gigge*, whirligig (see *gig*, carriage, etc.) and *-le*, freq. suffix.] to laugh with a series of uncontrollable, rapid, high-pitched sounds, suggestive of foolishness, nervousness, etc.; to titter.

gig′gle, *n.* a kind of laugh, with rapid, high-pitched sounds, suggestive of foolishness, nervousness, etc.; a titter.

gig′glēr, *n.* one who giggles or titters.

gig′gly, *a.* given to giggling.

ġig′got, *n.* a gigot. [Obs.]

gig′let, gig′lot, *n.* a wanton; a lascivious girl.

gig mȧ·çhïne′, a gigging machine.

ġi′gō·lō, *n.* [Fr., from *gigolette*, a prostitute, concubine, dim. of *gigole*, tall, thin woman, from *gigue*, long-legged, thin girl, thigh, leg, from *giguer*, to dance, jig, from *gigue*, a fiddle.]
1. a man who is paid to be a dancing partner or escort for women.
2. a man supported by a prostitute.

ġig′ŏt, *n.* [Fr., from OFr. *gigot*, a leg of mutton, dim. of *gigue*, a fiddle.]
1. a leg of mutton, lamb, veal, etc.
2. a small piece of flesh; a slice. [Obs.]
3. a leg-of-mutton sleeve; a sleeve close-fitting from the wrist to the elbow and then flaring out to fullness at the shoulder: also *gigot sleeve*.

gïgue (zhēg), *n.* [Fr.] same as *jig*.

GI Jōe, any man in the United States armed forces; especially, an enlisted soldier of World War II. [Slang.]

Gï′lȧ mon′stēr (hē′lȧ), [from *Gila*, a river in Arizona.] a stout, sluggish, poisonous lizard with a short, stumpy tail and a body covered with beadlike scales arranged in alternating rings of black and orange: it is found in the desert regions of the southwestern United States.

gil′back·ēr, *n.* *Tachysaurus parkeri*, a siluroid fish found on the northern coast of South America.

gil′bērt, *n.* [after William *Gilbert* (1544–1603), English physician and physicist.] the C. G. S. unit for magnetomotive force, equal to 0.7958 ampere turn.

Gil′bēr·ti·ăn, *a.* 1. of Sir William S. Gilbert (1836–1911), English librettist.
2. of, like, or characteristic of his style or humor.

Gil′bērt·ine, *n.* one of a religious order founded in England about 1148, so named from Gilbert, lord of Sempringham, in Lincolnshire.

Gil′bērt·ine, *a.* belonging to the monastic order founded by Gilbert.

gild, *v.t.*; gilded *or* gilt, *pt.*, *pp.*; gilding, *ppr.* [ME. *gilden*; AS. *gyldan*, to overlay with gold, from *gold*, gold.]
1. (a) to overlay with gold, either in leaf or powder, or in amalgam with quicksilver; (b) to coat with a gold color; to cause to appear like gold.
No more the rising sun shall *gild* the morn. —Pope.

2. to illuminate; to brighten; to render bright.

Gild the calm evening of your day.
—Trumbull.

3. to make (something) seem more attractive or more valuable than it is.

gild, *n.* a guild.

gild, *n.* [see *geld.*] a tax. [Obs.]

gild′ẽr, *n.* one who gilds; one whose occupation is to overlay with gold.

gild′ẽr, *n.* a guilder.

gild′hall, *n.* a guildhall.

gild′ing, *n.* 1. the art or practice of overlaying with gold leaf, or with a thin coating of gold.

2. gold, in leaf, powder, or liquid, applied to any surface.

3. that which is laid on in covering with gold; hence, any superficial coating employed to give a better appearance to a thing than is natural to it.

gild′ing met′ăl, a kind of sheet brass rich in copper from which articles to be gilded are made.

gīle, *n.* guile. [Obs.]

ġi·let′ (zhē-lā′), *n.* [Fr., a waistcoat.] a waistcoat or vest; especially, the front of a bodice of a woman's dress resembling a man's vest.

Gil′gȧ·mesh, Gil′gȧ·mish, *n.* [from Bab.] a legendary Babylonian king, hero of an epic (*Gilgamesh Epic*) completed about 2000 B.C. and containing an account of the Biblical Flood.

Ġil′i·ȧ, *n.* [named after Philip *Gil*, a Spanish botanist.] a large genus of plants of the phlox family, native to western United States.

gill, *n.* [ME. *gile, gille*; prob. from Anglo-N.; cf. ON. *gjolnar*, jaws, gills.]

1. the organ for breathing of most animals that live in water, as fish, lobsters, etc.

2. [*often pl.*] (a) a red flap of flesh hanging below the beak of a fowl; wattle; (b) the flesh under and about the chin and lower jaw of a person.

3. [*pl.*] the thin, leaflike, radiating plates on the undersurface of a mushroom.

4. in dressing or spinning flax, a kind of hackle or comb with fine long teeth, used in evenly bunching the fibers.

ġill, *n.* [ME. *gille, gylle*; OFr. *gille*, measure for wine; L. *gillo*, cooling vessel.] a liquid measure, equal to $^{1}/_{4}$ pint.

ġill, *n.* 1. a plant, ground ivy, of the genus *Glechoma*. [Brit. Dial.]

2. malt liquor medicated with ground ivy. [Brit. Dial.]

ġill, *n.* a girl or woman; a sweetheart: from *Gillian*, a woman's name.

Each Jack with his *gill*. —B. Jonson.

ġill, *n.* a pair of wheels and a frame on which timber is conveyed. [Brit. Dial.]

gill, *n.* [ME. *gille, gylle*, from ON. *gil*, a deep, narrow glen.] a woody glen; a place between steep banks, with a rivulet flowing through it; also, a brook. [Brit. Dial.]

ġill, *n.* a leech: also spelled *gell*. [Scot.]

ġill′-āle, *n.* malt liquor flavored with ground ivy.

gill ärch, a branchial arch.

gil·lȧ·rọọ′, *n.* [Ir. *giolla ruadh*; *giolla*, boy, and *ruadh*, red.] a variety of the European trout found in Irish waters, characterized by an exceptionally strong and large stomach.

gill bär, same as *gill arch.*

gill çleft, a branchial cleft; a gill opening.

gill cōmb (kōm), the gill of a mollusk resembling a comb; a ctenidium.

gill çov′ẽr, a bony case covering the gills in fish; the operculum.

gill flap, a gill cover.

gill′flirt, *n.* a wanton girl; a thoughtless, giddy girl. [Archaic.]

gill frāme, in spinning, a device for elongating and leveling the flax; a spreader.

gill fuñ′gus, an agaric.

gill head (hed), a gill frame.

gill house, a place where gill-ale is sold.

gil′li·ăn, *n.* a girl. [Obs.]

gil′lie, gil′ly, *n.*; *pl.* **gil′lieş,** [Scot., from Gael. *gille*, a boy, lad, page.]

1. a boy; a page or menial; in the Scotch Highlands, a male servant, particularly a gamekeeper.

2. [*pl.*] women's sport shoes, cut low and tied with laces that wind about the ankles.

gill lid, the covering of the gills.

gill net, a net so constructed that fish are caught and held in it by the gills when they attempt to escape.

gill ō′pen·ing, the aperture of a fish or other animal by which water is admitted to the gills.

gill plūme, same as *gill comb.*

gill rāk′ẽr, gill rāke, one of the horny filaments within the branchial arch of a fish that protect the gill cavities from injurious substances.

gill slit, same as *gill opening.*

ġil′ly·flow″ẽr, *n.* [altered, from ME. *gilofre, gelofer*; OFr. *gilofre, girofre*, gillyflower; LL. *caryophyllum*; Gr. *karyophyllon*, clove tree, lit., nut leaf, from *karyon*, nut, and *phyllon*, leaf.]

1. any of several plants with clove-scented flowers, including the clove pink, the European wallflower, and the common stock.

2. a variety of apple.

gil′öur, *n.* a guiler. [Obs.]

gilse, *n.* a grilse.

gil′sŏn·īte, *n.* [after S. H. *Gilson*, of Salt Lake City, Utah.] uintaite, a pure asphalt found mainly in Utah.

gilt, *n.* a young female pig. [Brit. Dial.]

gilt, *a.* overlaid with gold leaf or a thin coating of gold; illuminated; adorned; gold-colored.

gilt, *n.* 1. gold or an imitation of gold laid on the surface of a thing; gilding.

2. money. [Rare.]

gilt′-edġe (-ej), *a.* gilt-edged.

gilt′-edġed, *a.* 1. having the edge or edges covered with gold leaf, as the pages of a book.

2. of superlative quality; first-class; of the highest grade or value; as, *gilt-edged* negotiable paper.

gilt′head, *n.* any of a number of sea fishes with gold markings on the head, as the sparoid fish of the Mediterranean or the English cunner.

gilt′tāil, *n.* a worm or larva with a yellow tail, used for bait.

ġim, *a.* neat; spruce; natty. [Brit. Dial.]

ġim′băl, *n.* [OFr. *gemelle*, twin, from L. *gemellus*, dim. of *geminus*, twin, double.]

1. [*pl.*] a device consisting of a pair of rings pivoted on axes at right angles to each other so that one is free to swing within the other: a ship's compass, lantern, etc. will keep a horizontal position when suspended in gimbals.

2. a gemel ring; hence, any quaint contrivance. [Obs.]

ġim′băl joint, a universal joint employing the principle of a gimbal.

ġim′băl ring, the metal support in the center of an upper millstone.

ġim′blet, *n.* a gimlet. [Obs.]

ġim′crack, *a.* [perh. from ME. *gibecrake*, inlaid wood.] showy but cheap and useless.

ġim′crack, *n.* 1. a trivial device or mechanism; a trinket; a cheap, showy, useless thing.

2. a young fop. [Obs.]

ġim′el, *n.* [Heb. *gimel*, lit., camel.] the third letter of the Hebrew alphabet, corresponding to English *G, g.*

ġim′let, *n.* [ME. *gymelot*; OFr. *guinbelet, guimbelet* (Fr. *gibelet*), dim. form, from M.D. *wimpel*, an auger.] a small boring tool with a handle at right angles to a shaft having at the other end a spiral, pointed cutting edge.

ġim′let, *v.t.* 1. to make a hole in with or as with a gimlet.

2. to turn, as a gimlet.

ġim′let eye (ī), 1. a squint eye.

2. a piercing eye.

ġim′let-eyed (-īd), *a.* having a piercing glance; sharp-eyed.

ġim′măl, *n.* 1. a ring formed of two or more interlocked circlets.

2. a gimbal. [Obs.]

ġim′mẽr, *n.* 1. a hinge or clasp. [Brit. Dial.]

2. a gimmal. [Obs.]

ġim′mẽr, *n.* a yearling ewe. [Scot. and Brit. Dial.]

GIMLET

ġim′mick, *n.* [perh. from G. *gemach*, lit., a convenience, via. G. dial. with stress shift.]

1. a secret means of controlling a prize wheel, etc.

2. a trick device used by a magician.

3. anything that tricks or mystifies; deceptive or secret device.

4. any gadget or contrivance whose name is unknown or not recalled.

[Slang in all senses].

gimp, *a.* trim; jimp. [Obs.]

gimp, *v.t.*; gimped, *pt.*, *pp.*; gimping, *ppr.* to jag; indent; notch.

gimp, *n.* [Fr. *guimpe*; OFr. *guimpe, guimple*, a nun's wimple, a wimple, veil, from O.H.G. *wimpal*, a wimple, veil.]

1. a flat trimming or edging usually of cord in an open or braided pattern, sometimes stiffened by wire: used for decorating gowns, furniture, etc.

2. a heavy thread used in the edges of the figures in certain laces.

3. a silk fish line strengthened with a fine wire.

gimp nāil, a small upholsterer's nail for attaching gimp.

ġin, *n.* [abbrev. of *geneva.*]

1. a strong, aromatic alcoholic liquor distilled from rye and other grains and flavored with juniper berries.

2. a similar liquor differently flavored.

3. alcoholic liquors collectively, as a term of reprobation.

gin fizz; see under *fizz.*

gin rickey; a drink made with the juice of a fresh lime, gin, and carbonated water: said to have been named after a Col. Rickey.

ġin, *n.* [ME. *gin, ginne*, ingenuity, contrivance, a machine, engine, abbrev. of *engin, engyn*, an engine.]

1. any of various mechanical devices; specifically, (a) a tripod with pulleys and windlass, used in place of a crane for lifting heavy weights; (b) a machine for driving piles; (c) a machine for separating cotton fibers from the seeds: usually called *cotton gin*; (d) an instrument of torture; (e) a form of windmill pump; (f) in English coal mines, a whim or vertical winch.

2. a trap; a snare.

GIN FOR RAISING HEAVY WEIGHTS

ġin, *v.t.*; ginned, *pt.*, *pp.*; ginning, *ppr.* 1. to clear (cotton) of seeds by the use of a gin.

2. to ensnare by or as by a gin.

gin, *prep.* against (a time specified); by; as, *gin* the morn. [Scot.]

gin, *conj.* [perh. contr. from *given*; perh. influenced by Scot. prep. *gin*, by (a certain time).] if; whether. [Scot.]

gin, *v.t.* and *v.i.*; gan, *pt.*, *pp.*; ginning, *ppr.* [ME. *ginnen*, aphetic form of *beginnen* (to begin) and *onginnen* (AS. *onginnan*, to attempt).] to begin. [Archaic and Poet.]

ġin, *n.* [Australian.] a female native, especially one that is married.

ġin block, a single-wheeled iron or steel tackle block.

ġin′găl, *n.* a jingal.

ġin′ġe·ley, *n.* gingili.

ġin′ġẽr, *n.* [ME. *gingere, gingivere*, partly, from AS. *gingiber, gingifer*, from LL. *zingiber*, and partly, from OFr. *gimgibre, gingimbre*, of the same origin; Gr. *ziggiber-*; Sans. *śṛṅgavēra*, lit., horn body; perh. from Dravidian.]

1. any of a group of tropical herbs of the genus *Zingiber*; especially, *Zingiber officinale*, grown commercially in the East Indies, Africa, and China for its aromatic rootstalk, used for flavoring foods and in medicine.

2. the rootstalk of the ginger plant.

3. the spice made from this.

4. a sandy or reddish color.

5. vigor; spirit. [Colloq.]

GINGER PLANT (*Zingiber officinale*)

ġin′ġẽr, *v.t.* 1. to flavor with ginger.

2. to invigorate; enliven.

ġin′ġẽr āle, an effervescent, nonalcoholic drink flavored with ginger.

ġin′ġẽr beer, a ginger-flavored drink similar to ginger ale, popular in England.

ġin′ġẽr·bread (-bred), *n.* 1. a cake flavored with ginger and molasses.

2. cheap, showy ornamentation, as cheap, fancy carvings on furniture, front porches, etc.

ġin′ġẽr·bread (-bred), *a.* cheap and showy; tawdry; gaudy.

ġin′ġẽr·bread plum, the fruit of the gingerbread tree.

ġin′ġẽr·bread tree, 1. the doom palm.
2. *Parinarium macrophyllum*, an African tree bearing the fruit known as the gingerbread plum.

ġin′ġẽr·bread wŏrk, same as *gingerbread*, sense 2.

ġin′ġẽr gråss, 1. *Andropogon nardus*, an East Indian grass from which an aromatic oil is derived.
2. *Panicum glutinosum*, a coarse, strong grass of the West Indies.

ġin′ġẽr·li·ness, *n.* cautious or fastidious quality.

ġin′ġẽr·ly, *adv.* [*ginger* (perh. from OFr. *genzor*, compar. of *gent*, delicate), and *-ly*.] cautiously; carefully; timidly.

ġin′ġẽr·ly, *a.* cautious; careful; timid.

ġin′ġẽr·snap, *n.* a crisp, spicy cooky flavored with ginger and molasses.

ġin′ġẽr·y, *a.* 1. like or flavored with ginger; spicy; pungent.
2. sandy or reddish in color.

ging′hăm (ging′ăm), *n.* [D. *gingang* (Fr. *guingan*); prob. from Malay *giṅgaṅ*, striped (cloth): transmission to Europe prob. via D.] a yarn-dyed cotton cloth, usually woven in stripes, checks, or plaids: it is used for aprons, house dresses, etc.

ging′hăm, *a.* made of gingham.

ġin′ġi·li, *n.* [Hind. *jinjali*.] 1. sesame seed.
2. the oil of this seed.
Also spelled *gingeli, gingelly.*

ġin·ġī′văl (*or* jin′ji-văl), *a.* [L. *gingivæ*, gums.] of the gums; alveolar.

ġin·ġī′văl, *n.* an alveolar consonant.

ġin·ġi·vī′tis, *n.* [L. *gingivæ*, gums, and *-itis*.] an inflamed condition of the gums.

ging′kō, *n.*; *pl.* **ging′kōes,** a ginkgo.

Giñ·gly·mō′di, *n.pl.* [Gr. *ginglymos*, a hinge, and *eidos*, form.] an order of fishes of the *Ganoidei*.

ġiñ′gly·moid, ġiñ′gly·fọrm, *a.* of or like a ginglymus.

ġiñ·gly·mos′tō·moid, *a.* [Gr. *ginglymos*, a hinge, *stoma*, mouth, and *eidos*, form.] of or like the *Ginglymostomidæ*, a family of sharks in which the lip folds seem to hinge together.

ġiñ′gly·mus, *n.*; *pl.* **ġiñ′gly·mī,** [Gr. *ginglymos*, a hinge-joint.] in anatomy, a hingelike joint; an articulation in which each bone partly receives, and is partly received by, the other, so as to admit only of flexion and extension in one plane, as the elbow joint.

ġin′house, *n.* a building where cotton is ginned.

ġiñk′gō (giñ′kō), *n.*; *pl.* **ġiñk′gōes,** [Japan. *ginko, gingko*, from Chin. *yin-hing*, silver apricot.] a large tree, *Ginkgo biloba*, with fan-shaped leaves and edible yellow fruit, native to northern China and Japan: also *gingko.*

ġin mill, a saloon. [Slang.]

ġinn, *n.* jinn.

ġin′nẽr, *n.* a person who gins cotton.

ġin′net, *n.* a jennet. [Obs.]

ġin′ny çar′riaġe (-rij), [*ginny*, prob. variant of *Jenny*, a personal name.] a small, strong railroad car to carry materials.

ġin rum′my, a card game in which each player is dealt ten cards and alternately draws and discards one at a time until successful in arranging the cards in sets of at least three of the same denomination or sequences of at least three in a suit with a total surplus of not more than ten points, at which time he may lay his cards face upward and end the deal. If a player's surplus is lower than his opponent's, he wins the difference in number of points, but if not, he loses the difference plus a previously fixed penalty. There is a fixed premium for winning each hand, as well as for being able to call "gin" and lay down one's cards without any surplus points.

ġin′seng, *n.* [Chin. *jen shen*.]
1. an herb with a thick, forked, aromatic root: some species are found in China and North America.
2. the root of this plant, used medicinally by the Chinese.

ġin′shop, *n.* a saloon.

Ġiō·çon′dä, Lä (*or* jō-kon′då), *n.* [It., lit., the cheerful one.]
1. a portrait by Leonardo da Vinci, more commonly called *Mona Lisa.*
2. an Italian opera (1876) by Ponchielli.

ġiō·çō′sō, *a.* [It., from L. *jocosus*, playful.] gay; playful: a term used in music.

ġip, *v.t.*; gipped (jipt), *pt., pp.*; gipping, *ppr.* to eviscerate, as fish.

ġip, *n., v.t.* and *v.i.* same as *gyp.*

ġi·pon′, ġi·pöun′, *n.* same as *jupon.*

ġip′sy, *n.*; *pl.* **ġip′sieṣ,** same as *gypsy.*

ġip′sy, *a.* same as *gypsy.*

ġip′sy, *v.i.*; gipsied, *pt., pp.*; gipsying, *ppr.* same as *gypsy.*

ġip′sy hẽrb, mọth, winch, etc., see following *gypsy.*

ġi·raffe′, *n.*; *pl.* **ġi·raffeṣ** or **ġi·raffe,** [Fr. *giraffe*; Sp. Port. *girafa*, from Ar. *zarāf, zarāfa*, a giraffe.]
1. a large, cud-chewing animal of Africa, *Giraffa camelopardalis*, with a very long neck in which the seven vertebrae are elongated, and long legs, the forelegs being of greater length. The giraffe often grows to a height of eighteen feet and is the tallest of existing animals. It has two bony excrescences on its head resembling horns. Its color is usually light fawn marked with darker spots. Also called *camelopard.*
2. [G–] the constellation Camelopard.
3. an eighteenth-century spinet.
4. a special type of car used on inclines in mining, one end being higher than the other.

GIRAFFE
(*Giraffa camelopardalis*)

ġir′ăn·dōle, ġi·ran′dō·lȧ, *n.* [Fr. *girandole*; It. *girandola*, a chandelier, a fire wheel, from *girare*, L. *gyrare*, to turn, from *gyrus*, a circle.]
1. a branched candlestick.
2. a firework rotating while burning.
3. a revolving water jet.
4. a pendant or earring with small stones grouped around a larger one.

ġir′ȧ·sol, ġir′ȧ·sōle, *n.* [Fr. *girasol*, from It. *girasole*, the fire opal, a sunflower; *girare*, to turn, and *sole*, sun; L. *gyrare*, to turn, and *sol, solis*, sun.]
1. a tall sunflower with edible, potatolike roots: usually called *Jerusalem artichoke.* [Rare.]
2. a variety of opal that has a reddish gleam in a bright light; fire opal.
Also spelled *girosol.*

ġird, *n.* 1. a twinge or pang; a sudden spasm which resembles the stroke of a rod or the pressure of a band. [Obs.]
2. a gibe. [Archaic.]

ġĩrd, *v.t.* and *v.i.* [ME. *girden, gerden*, to strike, thrust, smite, from *gerd*; AS. *gyrd*, a rod.]
1. to strike. [Obs.]
2. to taunt; to gibe; to sneer.

ġĩrd, *v.t.*; girt *or* girded, *pt., pp.*; girding, *ppr.* [ME. *girden, gerden*; AS. *gyrdan*, to bind.]
1. to encircle with a belt or band.
2. to fasten with a belt or band.
3. to surround; to encircle; to enclose.
4. to clothe; to dress; to furnish; to equip.
5. to prepare (oneself) for action.

ġĩrd′ẽr, *n.* one who gibes or girds.

ġĩrd′ẽr, *n.* a large beam, usually horizontal, of timber or steel, for supporting the joists of a floor, the framework of a building, the superstructure of a bridge, etc.
bowstring girder; see under *bowstring.*
half-lattice girder; a girder formed by two horizontal beams joined by bars set diagonally without crossing.
lattice girder; a girder consisting of two horizontal beams united by diagonal crossing bars, somewhat resembling wooden latticework.

ġĩrd′ing, *n.* a girdle. [Obs.]

ġĩr′dle, *n.* [ME. *girdel, gerdel*; AS. *gyrdel*, a girdle, from *gyrdan*, to gird.]
1. a band or belt; something drawn round the waist, and tied or buckled; as, a *girdle* of fine linen; a leathern *girdle.*
2. anything that surrounds or encircles.
3. a light, flexible, corsetlike garment, for supporting or molding the waist and hips.
4. the rim of a cut gem.
5. a ring around the trunk of a tree, made by removing bark.
6. the zodiac; also, the equator.
7. a thin stratum of rock in mining.
8. in anatomy, a bony structure to which a limb is attached, as the pelvic *girdle*, formed by the bones of the hips, and the thoracic *girdle*, formed by the clavicles and scapulae.
9. a seaweed of the genus *Laminaria.*

ġĩr′dle, *v.t.*; girdled, *pt., pp.*; girdling, *ppr.*
1. to bind with a belt or sash; to gird.
2. to encircle.
3. to make a circular incision in the bark of (a tree).

ġĩr′dlẽr, *n.* 1. a maker of girdles.
2. a person or thing that girdles, or encircles.
3. a beetle that girdles the twig in which it has laid its eggs: the larva thus has decaying wood for food; as, a twig *girdler*, genus *Oncideres.*

ġĩr′dle·stead (-sted), *n.* the part of the body where the girdle is worn. [Obs.]

ġĩr′dle wheel, a kind of spinning wheel.

ġĩr′kin, *n.* gherkin. [Obs.]

ġĩrl, *n.* [ME. *girle, gerle*, a young person, either girl or boy, from L.G. *gör*, masc., a boy, *göre*, f., a girl.]
1. a female child; hence, any young unmarried woman.
2. a maidservant.
3. a sweetheart. [Colloq.]
4. a woman of any age, married or single.
5. a child. [Obs.]
6. a roebuck less than two years old. [Obs.]

ġĩrl guīde, a member of a British organization (*Girl Guides*) that is like the Girl Scouts.

ġĩrl′hood, *n.* the time or state of being a girl; also, girls collectively.

ġĩrl′ish, *a.* 1. relating to girlhood or to a girl; as, *girlish* hours.
2. resembling or characteristic of girls; suitable for a girl or girlhood; as, *girlish* manners.

ġĩrl′ish·ly, *adv.* in the manner of a girl.

ġĩrl′ish·ness, *n.* the manners of a girl.

ġĩrl sçout, a member of the Girl Scouts.

Ġĩrl Sçouts, an organization founded by Juliette Low in Savannah, Georgia, in 1912 (as *Girl Guides*) to provide healthful, character-building activities for girls.

ġĩrn, *v.i.* to grin. [Obs.]

ġĩrn, *n., v.i.* and *v.t.*, snarl. [Brit. Dial.]

Ġi·ronde′ (*or Fr.* zhē-rōnd′), *n.* [so called because led by deputies from *Gironde*, a department of France on the southwestern coast.] a French political party (1791–1793) that advocated moderate republican principles: it was suppressed by the Jacobins.

Ġi·ron′dist, *n.* a member of the Gironde.

Ġi·ron′dist, *a.* relating to the Gironde or the Girondists.

ġir′ō·sol, *n.* same as *girasol.*

ġir′rŏck, *n.* a species of garfish.

ġĩrt, past tense and past participle of *gird* (to encircle).

ġĩrt, *v.t.* [from *gird*.] 1. to gird; to girdle.
2. to fasten with a girdle, belt, etc.
3. to measure the girth of.

ġĩrt, *v.i.* to measure in girth.

ġĩrt, *n.* same as *girth.*

ġĩrt, *a.* moored by two cables to two anchors placed on opposite sides, to prevent a vessel from swinging.

ġĩrth, *n.* [ME. *girth, gerth*; Ice. *gjördh*, a girdle, girth.]
1. a strap or cinch used in fastening a saddle or load, as upon a horse or mule.
2. the measure of anything cylindrical or resembling a cylinder in form; specifically, the waist measure of a person; as, a man of ample height and *girth.*
3. a girdle.
4. the strap, usually of leather, passing about the pulley in a hand press, which conveys motion to the carriage.

ġĩrth *v.t.* 1. to bind with a girth; to gird.
2. to girdle; to encircle; to surround.

ġĩrth, *v.i.* to measure in girth.

ġĩrt′līne, *n.* a rope used in the process of rigging a ship, to lift the rigging up to the masthead.

ġi·särme′, *n.* [ME.; OFr., from O.H.G. *getisarn*, lit., weeding iron, from *getan*, to weed, and *isarn*, iron.] a battle-ax or halberd with a long shaft, formerly carried by foot soldiers.

ġīṣe, *v.i.* to feed; to pasture. [Obs.]

ġīṣe, *n.* guise. [Obs.]

ġiṣ′el, *n.* a pledge. [Obs.]

ġis′lẽr, *n.* [etym. uncertain.] a parasite of salmon.

ġis·mon′dine, ġis·mon′dīte, *n.* [named after C. G. *Gismondi*, an Italian mineralogist.] a mineral silicate of calcium and aluminum.

ġist, *n.* [OFr. *gist*, abode, lodgings, the point at issue, from 3rd pers. sing. pres. ind. act. of *gesir*, to lie, from L. *jacere*, to lie.]
1. the grounds for action in a lawsuit.
2. the main point of a question; the point on which an action rests; the essence of a matter.

ġist, *n.* [OFr. *giste*, lodging, abode, from *gesir*, to lie; L. *jacere*, to lie.] a place where one sleeps, lodges, or reposes. [Obs.]

git, *v.* to get. [Dial.]

ġi·tä′nō, *n.* [Sp.] a gypsy.

ġīte, *n.* a gown. [Obs.]

gith, *n.* [ME. *gith*; AS. *gith*, the cockle; L. *gith*, the Roman coriander.]
1. the fennelflower.
2. corn cockle.

git′tẽrn, *n.* [ME. *giterne*; OFr. *guiterne*; from L. *cithara*, the guitar; cithara.] an obsolete guitarlike musical instrument; a cithern.

git′tẽrn, *v.i.* to play on a gittern. [Obs.]

ġiust, *n.* a joust. [Obs.]

ġiu̇s·tȧ·men′te, *adv.* [It.] in music, accurately, strictly; exactly.

ġiu̇s′tō, *a.* [It., just, equal, from L. *justus*, just, fair.] in music, in just, equal, correct, or steady time.

give, *v.t.*; gave, *pt.*; given, *pp.*; giving, *ppr.* [ME. *given*, *geven*, from AS. *gifan*, *giefan*, to give.]
1. to turn over the possession or control of to someone without cost or exchange; to hand over as a gift.
2. to hand or pass over; to cause to be in the trust or keeping of someone; to deliver; as, he *gave* the porter his bag to carry; her father *gave* Dorothy in marriage.
3. to hand or pass over in exchange for something else, as money, services, etc.; to sell for a price; to pay; as, I'll *give* you five dollars for the book.
4. to cause to have; to produce in a person or thing; to impart; as, Marlowe *gave* form to Elizabethan drama.
5. to cause to have as an honor or favor; to confer (a title, position, etc.).
6. to let have in answer to a petition; grant; allow; as, God *give* me strength.
7. to be the source, origin, or cause of; produce; supply; as, cows *give* milk.
8. to part with for some cause; to devote to some occupation, pursuit, etc.; as, he *gave* his life for his men.
9. to surrender; yield; concede; as, I'll *give* you that point.
10. to put forward to be taken or not; offer; proffer; as, may I *give* a suggestion?
11. to make (gestures, etc.); as, she *gave* him a cold glance.
12. to utter, emit, or produce (words, etc.); to put in words; communicate; state; as, *give* a reply.
13. to perform; as, they *gave* a concert.
14. to inflict or impose (punishment, sentence, etc.); as, they *gave* him a whipping.
to give away; (a) to make a gift of; donate; bestow; (b) in the marriage ceremony, to give (the bride) to the bridegroom; (c) [Colloq.] to reveal; expose; betray.
to give back; to return; to restore.
to give birth to; to bear; to bring forth, as a child; to be the origin of.
to give forth; to send forth; emit; issue.
to give in; (a) to allow by way of abatement or deduction from a claim; to yield what may be justly demanded; (b) to hand in.
to give it to; to punish; to beat or scold. [Colloq.]
to give line, to give head, to give the reins; to give full liberty to.
to give off; to send forth or out; to emit.
to give out; (a) to utter publicly; to report; to proclaim; to publish; (b) to send forth; (c) to distribute; as, a substance *gives out* steam or odors; (d) to be worn out, spent, or consumed; to fail to last.
to give over; (a) to quit; to cease; to abandon; as, *to give over* a pursuit; (b) to hand over; to turn over.
to give place; to retire to make room for another or for something else.
to give tongue; to bark: said of dogs.
to give up; (a) to resign; to quit; to stop; to cease; as, *to give up* a cause; (b) to surrender; to relinquish; to cede; as, *to give up* a fortress to an enemy; (c) to admit failure and stop trying; (d) to lose hope for; to despair of; (e) to sacrifice; to devote wholly.
to give way; (a) to yield; to withdraw; to make room for; as, inferiors should *give way* to superiors; (b) to fail; to yield to force; to break or fall; to break down; as, the ice *gave way*, and the horses were drowned; the scaffolding *gave way*; (c) in nautical usage, an order to a boat's crew to row after ceasing, or to increase their exertions.

Syn.—confer, grant.—*Give* is generic and includes the other two; *grant* and *confer* include accessory ideas; *confer* adds the idea of condescension or of allowing that which might be withheld; *grant* implies ceremony or the giving to an inferior, and presupposes a request.

give, *v.i.* 1. to yield, as to pressure; as, the earth *gives* under the feet.

Only a sweet and virtuous soul,
Like seasoned timber, never *gives*.
—Herbert.

2. to make gifts; to be in the habit of giving.
3. to be springy; to be resilient.
4. to move; to recede.

Now back he *gives*, then rushes on amain.
—Daniel.

5. to weep; to shed tears. [Obs.]

Whose eyes do never *give*
But through lust and laughter. —Shak.

6. to lead; to open; to afford entrance or view.

A well-worn pathway courted us
To one green wicket in a privet hedge;
This yielding *gave* into a grassy walk.
—Tennyson.

to give in; to go back; to give way; to yield; to confess oneself beaten; to confess oneself inferior to another.
to give in to; to yield assent; to adopt.
to give upon; to front; to look into; as, a gateway *giving upon* a lane: a Gallicism.

give, *n.* 1. capacity to give way; quality of yielding under pressure.
2. a tendency to be springy; resiliency.

give′-ănd-tāke′, *a.* pertaining to the equalization of exchanges.

give′-ănd-tāke′, *n.* 1. an exchange of jesting, wit, or repartee on equal terms.
2. equalization of an exchange.

give′ȧ·wāy, *n.* 1. a game or a method of playing in which the object is to lose tricks. [Colloq.]
2. a betrayal or revelation made accidentally. [Colloq.]
3. anything dispensed or distributed without charge or at low cost to attract buyers, as a toy book given away to children by a store at Christmas time. [Colloq.]

give′ȧ·wāy, *a.* in radio and television, designating a type of program in which prizes are given to contestants, as for answering questions correctly.

giv′en, *v.* past participle of *give*.

giv′en, *a.* 1. inclined; addicted; as, *given* to drinking.
2. known; stated; specified; as, a *given* date.
3. bestowed; presented.
4. in logic and mathematics, taken as a premise; assumed; granted.
5. in law, issued; executed.
given name; the first name, as the baptismal name of a person: distinguished from the surname, or family name.

giv′ẽr, *n.* one who gives; a donor; a bestower; a grantor; one who imparts or distributes.

giv′ing, *n.* 1. the act of conferring, yielding, etc.
2. a gift. [Obs.]

giz′zȧrd, *n.* [ME. *giser*; OFr. *gezier*, *jugier*, the gizzard, from L. *gigeria*, neut. pl., the cooked entrails of poultry.]
1. the second stomach of a bird: it has thick muscular walls and a tough lining for grinding food that has been partially digested in the first stomach.
2. the stomach: humorous usage. [Colloq].
3. in entomology, the proventiculus, a muscular stomach designed for crushing food, often having the walls covered with plates of chitin.
to stick in one's gizzard; to be distasteful to one.

giz′zȧrd shad, any fish of the family *Dorosomidæ*, resembling the common herring.

giz′zȧrd trout, same as *gillaroo*.

glȧ·bel′lȧ, *n.*; *pl.* **glȧ·bel′lae,** [Mod. L., from L. *glabellus*, without hair, from *glaber*, smooth.]
1. in anatomy, the smooth prominence on the forehead between the eyebrows and just above the nose.
2. the frontal portion of a trilobite.

glȧ·bel′lăr, *a.* relating to the glabella.

glȧ·bel′lum, *n.* same as *glabella*.

glā′brāte, *a.* [L. *glabratus*, pp. of *glabrare*, lit., to make smooth, to deprive of hair, from *glaber*, smooth.] in botany and zoology, glabrous.

glā′brē·āte, glā′bri·āte, *v.t.* to cause to become smooth or hairless. [Obs.]

glab′ri·ty, *n.* smoothness; baldness. [Obs.]

glā′brous, *a.* [L. *glaber*, smooth, bald.] smooth; having no hair, down, or fuzz.

gla·cé′ (glȧ-sā′), *a.* [Fr., iced, glazed, pp. of *glacer*, to turn into ice, freeze, from *glace*, L. *glacies*, ice.]
1. having the surface glazed or glossy; glossed; as, *glacé* fruit; *glacé* silk.
2. covered with icing or sugar, as fruits; candied.
3. frozen; iced.

gla·cé′, *v.t.* to cover with icing; to glaze.

glā′ciăl (-shăl), *a.* [L. *glacialis*, icy, frozen, full of ice, from *glacies*, ice.]
1. of ice or glaciers.
2. in geology, of, from, or due to masses of ice, especially in the form of glaciers.
3. in chemistry, having the crystalline appearance of ice at laboratory temperature; as, *glacial* acetic acid.
4. like ice; cold and hard; icy.
glacial epoch; (a) any period of geological time when a large part of the earth was covered with glaciers; (b) the latest of these periods, during the Pleistocene, when a large part of the Northern Hemisphere was covered with glaciers.
glacial period; the period including the glacial epochs; ice age.
glacial theory; the glacier theory.

glā′ciăl·ist, *n.* 1. a student of glaciers and their action.
2. a person who accepts the established theory that certain surface changes of the earth were caused by glaciers.

glā′ciăl·ly, *adv.* by glacial action.

glā′ci·āte (-shi-āt), *v.i.*; glaciated, *pt.*, *pp.*; glaciating, *ppr.* [L. *glaciatus*, pp. of *glaciare*, to turn into ice, freeze.] to turn to ice. [Rare.]

glā′ci·āte, *v.t.* 1. to cover with ice or a glacier; also, to transform into ice.
2. to expose to or change by glacial action.
3. to give a frosted or icelike appearance to.

glā·ci·ā′tion, *n.* a glaciating.

glā′ciẽr (-shẽr), *n.* [Fr. *glacier*, from *glace*, L. *glacies*, ice.] a large mass of ice and snow that forms in areas where the rate of snowfall constantly exceeds the rate at which the snow melts: it moves slowly down a mountain slope or valley until it melts or breaks away.
glacier theory; the theory attributing important geological changes, as the erosion of valleys, the denudation of large portions of the earth's surface, the transportation and deposition of drift or boulder clay, the accumulation of moraines, etc., to the action of glaciers.

glā′ciẽr tā′ble, a rock supported by a column of ice, the surrounding ice, originally as high as the supporting pedestal, having melted away.

glā′ci·ō-, [from L. *glacies*, ice.] a combining form meaning *ice* or *glacier*.

glā″ci·ō·ā′quē·ous (glā″shi-ō-ā′kwē-us), *a.* [*glacio-*, and L. *aqua*, water.] pertaining to or caused by the combined action of ice and water.

glā″ci·ō·log′ic·ăl, *a.* pertaining to glaciology.

glā·ci·ŏl′ō·ġist, *n.* same as *glacialist*.

glā·ci·ŏl′ō·ġy, *n.* [*glacio-*, and Gr. *-logia*, from *legein*, to speak.] the science concerned with the formation of glaciers and icebergs and their action.

glā″ci·ō·nā′tănt, *a.* [*glacio-*, and L. *natans* (*-antis*), ppr. of *natare*, to swim.] pertaining to floating ice or caused by it.

glā′cious, *a.* [OFr. *glacieux*, from L. *glacies*, ice.] like ice; icy. [Obs.]

glā′cis, *n.* [Fr., from OFr. *glacis*, icy, slippery, from L. *glacies*, ice.] a gentle slope or sloping bank; especially, in fortification, a sloping bank so raised as to bring the enemy advancing over it into the most direct line of fire from the fort.

glack, *n.* a defile; a narrow mountain pass. [Scot.]

glad, *a.*; *comp.* gladder; *superl.* gladdest, [ME. *glad*, *gled*; AS. *glæd*, bright, cheerful, shining, glad.]
1. pleased; cheerful; gratified; feeling pleasure, joy, or satisfaction.

He that is *glad* at calamities shall not be unpunished. —Prov. xvii. 5.

2. causing or affording pleasure, joy, or satisfaction; gladdening; joyful.

The *glad* tidings of the kingdom of God.
—Luke viii. 1.

3. pleased; willing; as, I'm *glad* to do it for you.

4. wearing a gay or bright appearance; cheerful; bright; showy; gay.

Glad evening and *glad* morn. —Milton.

Syn.—delighted, gratified, pleased, happy, cheerful, joyous, pleasing.

glad, *v.t.* and *v.i.*; gladded, *pt.*, *pp.*; gladding, *ppr.* to make or become glad; to gladden; to exhilarate. [Archaic.]

Each drinks the juice that *glads* the heart of man. —Pope.

glad, *n.* a gladiolus. [Slang.]

glad′den, *v.t.* and *v.i.*; gladdened, *pt.*, *pp.*; gladdening, *ppr.* [ME. *gladen*; AS. *gladian*, to make glad, from *glæd*, glad.] to make or become glad; to cheer; to please; to exhilarate.

Syn.—please, gratify, rejoice, animate, delight.

glad′dẽr, *n.* one who gladdens or gives joy. [Obs.]

glad′dŏn, *n.* [ME. *gladene, gladine*; AS. *glædene*, a kind of plant; compare L. *gladiolus*, the sword lily.] any of several species of plants of the iris family, especially *Iris fœtidissima*: so called from the swordlike shape of the leaves. [Dial.]

glāde, *n.* [prob. of Scand. origin; compare W. *golead*, a lighting, illumination, from *goleu*, light, clear, AS. *glæd*, bright.]

1. an open space in a wood or forest.

2. an opening in the ice of rivers or lakes, or a place left unfrozen; also, a smooth sheet of ice. [Dial.]

3. an everglade.

glad′en, *n.* same as *gladdon*.

glad eye, an inviting or flirtatious glance: usually in *give* (or *get*) *the glad eye*. [Slang.]

glad′fụl, *a.* full of gladness. [Archaic.]

glad′fụl·ness, *n.* joy; gladness. [Archaic.]

glad hand, cordial welcome. [Slang.]

glad′i·āte, *a.* [L. *gladius*, a sword.] sword-shaped, as the leaf of an iris.

glad′i·ā·tŏr, *n.* [L., from *gladius*, a sword.]

1. in ancient Rome, one of a class of men who fought other men or animals in public for the entertainment of spectators. They were armed with deadly weapons and were slaves, captives, or paid performers.

2. a combatant in general; a disputant.

glad″i·ȧ·tō′ri·ăl, *a.* pertaining to gladiators or to their combats.

glad″i·ȧ·tō′ri·ăn, *a.* gladiatorial. [Obs.]

glad′i·ā·tŏr·ism, *n.* the fighting of gladiators.

glad′i·ā·tŏr·ship, *n.* the conduct, state, or occupation of a gladiator.

glad′i·ȧ·tō·ry, *a.* [L. *gladiatorius*, from *gladiator*, a gladiator.] relating to gladiators. [Obs.]

glad′i·ā·tūre, *n.* gladiatorship. [Obs.]

glad′i·ō·lȧ, *n.* a gladiolus.

glȧ·di·ō′lus (*or* glȧ-dī′ō-lus), *n.*; *pl.* **glȧ·di·ō′lus·es, glȧ·di·ō′lī,** [L. *gladiolus*, the sword lily, a small sword, dim. of *gladius*, a sword.]

1. [G—] an extensive genus of bulbous-rooted plants, of the iris family, found in the warmer parts of Europe and in North Africa, and abundantly in South Africa. They have long sword-shaped leaves and tall spikes of funnel-shaped flowers in various colors.

2. a plant of the genus *Gladiolus*.

3. in anatomy, the middle piece of the sternum; the mesosternum.

glā′di·us, *n.*; *pl.* **glā′di·ī,** [L., a sword.] the horny endoskeleton or pen of a two-gilled cuttlefish.

glad′ly, *adv.* [ME. *gladly, gladliche*; AS. *glædlice*, gladly, from *glæd*, glad.] with pleasure; willingly.

The common people heard him *gladly*. —Mark xii. 37.

glad′ness, *n.* [ME. *gladnesse*; AS. *glædnes*, gladness, from *glæd*, glad]. joy or a moderate degree of joy and exhilaration; pleasure; cheerfulness; the state of being glad.

glad rags, fine or dressy clothes. [Slang.]

glad′ship, *n.* gladness. [Obs.]

glad′sŏme, *a.* 1. pleased; joyful; cheerful.

2. causing joy, pleasure, or cheerfulness; having the appearance of gaiety; pleasing.

glad′sŏme·ly, *adv.* in a gladsome manner.

glad′sŏme·ness, *n.* the state of being gladsome.

Glad′stōne, *n.* [named after William Ewart *Gladstone*, 1809–1898, British statesman.]

1. a roomy, four-wheeled pleasure carriage, with two inside seats, calash top, and seats for driver and footman.

2. a Gladstone bag.

Glad′stōne bag, a traveling bag hinged so that it can open flat into two compartments of equal size.

glad′win, glad′wyn, *n.* same as *gladdon*.

Glag·ō·lit′iç, *a.* [Old Bulg. and Russ. *glagol′*, a word.] of or pertaining to Glagol, an ancient Slavic alphabet, principally used in several Roman Catholic dioceses of Istria and Dalmatia in the psalms, liturgies, and offices of the church.

glāik, *n.* 1. [*usually in pl.*] a deception; a delusion; a trick. [Scot. and Brit. Dial.]

2. a transient gleam or glance. [Scot.]

glāir, *n.* [ME. *glayre, gleire*; OFr. *glaire*, the white of an egg, from L. *clarus*, clear.]

1. the white of an egg used as a varnish to preserve paintings, and as a size in gilding; also, a size or glaze made from this.

2. any viscous, transparent substance resembling the white of an egg.

glāir, *v.t.*; glaired, *pt.*, *pp.*; glairing, *ppr.* to smear with the white of an egg.

glāir′ē·ous, *a.* glairy.

glāir′in, *n.* a substance resembling glair gathering on certain mineral waters.

glāir′y, *a.* like glair; covered with glair.

glāive, *n.* [ME.; OFr., a lance, from L. *gladius*, sword.]

1. a kind of halberd with a swordlike blade. [Archaic.]

2. a sword; especially, a broadsword. [Archaic.]

Also spelled *glave*.

glam′ber″ry, *n.*; *pl.* **glam′ber″ries,** a shrub, *Byrsonima lucida*, valued for its fruit. It grows in southern Florida and the West Indies.

glam′ŏr, *n.* same as *glamour*.

glam′ŏr·ous, *a.* full of glamour; fascinating; alluring.

glam′oūr, *n.* [Scot. var. of *grammar* in sense of *gramarye*, magic.]

1. originally, enchantment; witchcraft; spell; magic.

It had much of *glamour* might
To make a lady seem a knight.—Scott.

2. seemingly mysterious and elusive fascination or allure, as of some person, object, scene, etc.; bewitching charm; delusive enticement: the current sense.

To her soul
All the desert's *glamour* stole.—Whittier.

Also spelled *glamor*.

glam′oūr gĩrl, a young woman whose natural allure is emphasized by cosmetics, dress, etc., as certain actresses and models.

glam′oūr·ous, *a.* same as *glamorous*.

glȧnce, *n.* [G. *glanz*, lit., luster.] any of various ores with a metallic luster: now applied to only a few metallic ores, such as silver glance (argentite) and lead glance (galena).

glance coal; anthracite coal.

glance copper; native copper sulfide.

glȧnce, *v.i.*; glanced (glȧnst), *pt.*, *pp.*; glancing, *ppr.* [from OFr. *glacier*, to slide, slip.]

1. to flash; to gleam.

2. to fly off in an oblique direction; to dart aside; as, the arrow struck the shield and *glanced*; a *glancing* ball or shot.

3. to look with a sudden, rapid directing of the eye; to snatch a momentary or hasty view; as, he *glanced* rapidly over the document.

Then sit again, and sigh, and *glance*. —Suckling.

4. to hint; to make an indirect or passing reference; as, to *glance* at a different subject.

glȧnce, *v.t.* 1. to cause to strike (a surface) at an angle and be deflected.

2. to suggest; to hint.

glȧnce, *n.* 1. a glancing off; a deflected impact.

2. a flash or gleam.

3. a quick glimpse.

glȧn′cing, *a.* shooting; darting; flying off obliquely; as, *glancing* beams; *glancing* shots.

glȧn′cing·ly, *adv.* in a glancing manner.

gland, *n.* [Fr. *glande*; OFr. *glandre*, from L. *glandula*, dim. of *glans, glandis*, an acorn.] any organ that separates certain elements from the blood and secretes them in the form of a substance for the body to use, as adrenalin, or throw off, as urine: there are two kinds of glands, those which have ducts and empty into an organ, as the liver and kidneys, and those without ducts (*ductless glands*), which pass their secretions directly into the blood stream, as the thyroid and adrenals.

gland, *n.* [Fr., from L. *glans*, acorn.]

1. in mechanics, a movable part that compresses the packing on a stuffing box.

2. in aviation, a short tube through a gasbag for the passage of a rope.

glan·dā′ceous, *a.* [L. *glans, glandis*, an acorn.] yellowish-brown; of the color of an acorn.

glan′dăge, *n.* a feeding upon acorns. [Obs.]

glan·dā′ri·ous, *a.* acornlike in shape; glandiform.

glan′dẽred, *a.* having glanders.

glan′dẽr·ous, *a.* having the symptoms of glanders; diseased with glanders.

glan′dẽrs, *n. pl.* [*construed as sing.*], [Fr. *glande*, a gland, from L. *glans, glandis*, an acorn.] a contagious disease of horses, mules, etc., with swelling of the mucous membrane of the nostrils, an increased secretion and discharge of mucus, and enlargement of the glands of the lower jaw. It can be transmitted to man and other animals.

glan′dēs, *n.* pl. of *glans*.

glan·dif′ẽr·ous, *a.* [L. *glandifer*, acorn-bearing; *glans, glandis*, an acorn, and *ferre*, to bear.] bearing acorns. [Rare.]

gland′i·fọrm, *a.* [L. *glans, glandis*, an acorn, and *forma*, form.]

1. in the shape of or resembling a gland.

2. acornlike in shape; glandarious.

glan′dū·lăr, *a.* containing glands; consisting of glands; pertaining to glands.

glan′dū·lăr fē′vẽr, an infectious disease characterized by fever and a generalized swelling of the lymph nodes: also called *infectious mononucleosis*.

glan·dū·lā′tion, *n.* in botany, the situation and structure of the secretory vessels in plants.

glan′dūle, *n.* [L. *glandula*, a kernel, gland, dim. of *glans, glandis*, an acorn.] a small gland.

glan·dū·lif′ẽr·ous, *a.* [L. *glandula*, a gland, and *ferre*, to bear.] bearing glands.

glan′dū·lōse, *a.* glandular.

glan·dū·los′i·ty, *n.* 1. a collection of glands. [Rare.]

2. the quality of being glandulous. [Rare.]

glan′dū·lous, *a.* [L. *glandulosus*, containing kernels or glands, from *glandula*, a gland, kernel, dim. of *glans, glandis*, an acorn.] of, containing, consisting of, or like glands; glandular.

glans, *n.*; *pl.* **glan′dēs,** [L., an acorn.]

1. in botany, a one-celled, compound inferior fruit, with a dry pericarp, as the acorn.

2. the rounded body forming the end of the penis or clitoris.

glans çlī·tor′i·dis, the end of the clitoris, corresponding to the glans penis.

glans pē′nis, the head, or end, of the penis.

glāre, *v.i.*; glared, *pt.*, *pp.*; glaring, *ppr.* [ME. *glaren*, to shine brightly; L.G. *glaren*, to shine brightly, glow, from the same root as AS. *glær*, amber.]

1. to shine with a clear, bright, dazzling light; as, the electric lights *glare* all night.

2. to look with fierce, piercing eyes; to stare.

3. to shine with excessive luster; to be ostentatiously splendid.

She *glares* in balls, front boxes, and the ring. —Pope.

glāre, *v.t.* to give forth or express with a glare.

Every eye *glared* lightning. —Milton.

Syn.—glisten, scintillate, glitter, glister, gleam, sparkle, coruscate, glimmer, flicker.

glāre, *n.* 1. a bright, steady, dazzling light or brilliant reflection, as from sunlight on ice; clear, brilliant luster or splendor that hurts the eyes.

2. a fierce, piercing look; an angry stare.

3. a too bright or showy display.

glāre, *n.* [prob. from *glare*, brightness, as from sunlight on ice.] a smooth, bright, glassy surface, as of ice.

glāre, *a.* having a very smooth, slippery, bright, or glassy surface.

glār′e·ous, *a.* glaireous.

glār′i·ness, *n.* the quality of being glary.

glār′ing, *a.* 1. shining with dazzling luster; steadily bright; as, *glaring* hues.

2. too bright and showy.

3. too obvious to be overlooked; open and bold; easily noticed; as, a *glaring* mistake.

4. staring in a fierce, angry manner; having a hostile, penetrating gaze; as, a *glaring* eye.

glār′ing·ly, *adv.* in a glaring manner.

glār′y, *a.*; *comp.* glarier, *superl.* glariest, glaring; having a dazzling luster.

glār′y, *a.* covered with glare ice; icy.

glȧss, *n.* [ME. *glas, gles*; AS. *glæs*, glass.]

1. a hard, brittle substance, usually transparent or translucent, made by fusing silicates with soda or potash, lime, and, sometimes, various metallic oxides. When heated, it can be made so flexible and ductile that it may be blown, rolled, molded, or otherwise shaped into any desired form, and it can be given almost any color by adding certain metallic oxides or fusible pigments. *Crown glass* is a lime glass without lead; *flint* or *crystal glass* is

a lead glass; *blown glass* is prepared by blowing; *plate glass* is cast and rolled; *spun glass* is drawn out into filaments while ductile; *tempered* or *toughened glass* is hardened by immersion in a hot bath of resin, wax, oil, or other liquid having a high boiling point.
2. any substance like glass in composition or properties.
3. glassware.
4. (a) something made partly or wholly of glass, as a drinking vessel, mirror, lens, telescope, barometer, thermometer, windowpane, etc.; (b) [*pl.*] eyeglasses; (c) [*pl.*] binoculars.
5. the quantity of liquid held by a glass drinking vessel; as, half a *glass*; also, the liquid itself; liquor.
Claude Lorrain glass; see under *mirror*.
Lalique glass; a decorative glassware invented by the French jeweler, René Lalique (born 1860): it is ornamented with figures in relief, usually of birds, animals, flowers, or leaves.
liquid or *soluble glass*; water glass.
glȧss, *v.t.*; glassed (glȧst), *pt., pp.*; glassing, *ppr.* 1. to mirror; to reflect.
2. to enclose in glass.
3. to put into glass jars for preserving.
4. to equip with glass; glaze.
glȧss, *a.* of or made of glass; vitreous; as, a *glass* bottle.
glȧss blō′ẽr, a person or machine that does glass blowing.
glȧss blō′ing, the art or process of shaping molten glass into any desired form by blowing air into a mass of it at the end of a tube.
glȧss çloth, 1. a woven fabric containing glass filaments.
2. an absorbent linen cloth used to wipe glassware or china.
glȧss çrab, a crab of the genus *Scyllarus* or of the genus *Palinurus* in the larval state, being thin as paper, flat, and transparent.
glȧss çut′tẽr, 1. a person whose work is cutting sheets of glass to desired sizes or shapes.
2. a person whose work is inscribing designs on glass.
3. a tool for cutting or inscribing designs on glass.
glȧss çut′ting, 1. the art of cutting sheet glass into panes or other forms.
2. the art of grinding and polishing glassware to produce cut glass.
glȧss′en, *a.* glassy; glazed. [Archaic or Dial.]
glȧss′eȳe, *n.* 1. the walleyed pike, *Stizostedion vitreum*.
2. a species of Jamaican thrush; *Turdus jamaicensis*: so called from the bluish white, pellucid, glasslike iris of its eye.
glȧss′-fāced (-fāst), *a.* having a face that reflects another's feelings like a mirror; as, a *glass-faced* flatterer. [Rare.]
glȧss′fụl, *n.* the amount that will fill a glass.
glȧss gạll, the scum formed on the top of fused glass.
glȧss′house, *n.* 1. a factory or salesroom for glass.
2. a house built mainly of glass, as a hothouse or greenhouse.
glȧss′i·ly, *adv.* in a glassy manner; so as to resemble glass.
glȧss·ine′, *n.* a thin, tough, glazed, nearly transparent paper, made of sulfite pulp, used in window envelopes, etc.
glȧss′i·ness, *n.* the quality or state of being glassy.
Glȧss′īte, *n.* a member of a sect founded in Scotland by John Glass (1695–1773), whose chief tenet was that faith is simply assent to Jesus' teaching. The English and American members are called *Sandemanians*.
glȧss′māk″ẽr, *n.* a person who makes glass.
glȧss′māk·ing, *n.* the art or process of making glass.
glȧss′măn, *n.*; *pl.* **glȧss′men,** 1. a person who sells glassware.
2. a glassmaker.
3. a glazier.
glȧss pā′pẽr, a polishing paper made by sprinkling finely pounded glass on a sheet of paper smeared with a coat of thin glue.
glȧss pot, a vessel used for melting glass.
glȧss′rōpe, *n.* the stem of a species of silicious sponge, *Hyalonema sieboldi*, found in Japan. It consists of long, twisted, silicious fibers which support the body of the sponge.
glȧss snāil, a snail of the genus *Vitrina*, having a translucent shell.
glȧss snāke, a species of legless lizard resembling a snake, and having a brittle tail, as (a) the joint snake, *Ophiosaurus ventralis*, of southern North America; (b) *Pseudopus gracilis* or *Pseudopus pallasi*, of Asia and Europe.
glȧss spŏnġe, a sponge with a silicious or vitreous framework resembling spun glass.
glȧss′wāre, *n.* articles or utensils made of glass.
glȧss′weed, *n.* the glasswort.
glȧss′wŏrk, *n.* 1. the manufacture or ornamentation of glassware, window glass, etc.
2. glassware; anything made of glass.
glȧss′wŏrk″ẽr, *n.* a person who works with glass.
glȧss′wŏrks, *n.pl.* [*construed as sing. or pl.*] a shop or factory where glass is made.
glȧss′wŏrt, *n.* any plant of the genus *Salicornia*, marine herbs having fleshy, leafless stems, growing in salt-water marshes: its ash is rich in soda and was formerly much used in making glass.
glȧss′y, *a.*; *comp.* glassier; *superl.* glassiest, 1. made of glass; vitreous. [Obs.]
2. resembling glass in its properties, as in smoothness, brittleness, or transparency; as, a *glassy* stream.
3. expressionless; fixed; lifeless; as, a *glassy* eye.
In one long, *glassy*, spectral stare,
The enlarging eye is fastened there.
—Whittier.
Syn.—vitreous, smooth, polished, glabrous, brittle, transparent, crystalline, pellucid, limpid, glossy, silken.
Glȧs·wē′ġi·ăn, *a.* of Glasgow.
Glȧs·wē′ġi·ăn, *n.* a native or inhabitant of Glasgow.
glau′bẽr·īte, *n.* [named after Johann Rudolf *Glauber* (1604–1668), a German chemist.] a slightly soluble mineral consisting of sulfate of soda and sulfate of lime, found chiefly in rock salt.
Glau′bẽr sạlt (or **sạlts**), Glauber's salt.
Glau′bẽr's sạlt (or **sạlts**), [see *glauberite*.] sodium sulfate, $Na_2SO_4 \cdot 10H_2O$, a crystalline salt used as a cathartic, etc.
glau·ces′cent, *a.* [L. *glaucus*, Gr. *glaukos*, gleaming, bluish-green.] having a glaucous luster.
glau′cin, *n.* a crystalline alkaloid extracted from plants of the genus *Glaucium*.
Glau′ci·um, *n.* [Gr. *glaukion*, the juice of a plant, prob. the horned poppy, from *glaukos*, bluish-green, gray.] a genus of the *Papaveraceæ*, including the yellow horn poppy.
glau′çō-, [from Gr. *glaukos*, orig., gleaming.] a combining form meaning *bluish-green, silvery*, or *gray*, as in *glauconite*.
glau′çō·dot, *n.* [Gr. *glaukos*, bluish-green, and *dotos*, giving, verbal adj. of *didonai*, to give.] a grayish, tin-white mineral composed of arsenic, cobalt, iron, and sulfur.
glau·çō′mȧ, *n.* [L., from Gr. *glaukōma*, glaucoma, from *glaukos*, a bluish-green.] a disease of the eye, characterized by increased tension within, and hardening of, the eyeball: it leads to a gradual impairment of sight, often resulting in blindness.
glau·çō′mȧ·tous, *a.* of, like, or having glaucoma.
glau′çŏn·īte, *n.* [Gr. *glaukos*, bluish-green.] a granular silicate of potassium and iron, which gives the greenish color to greensand.
glau′çō·phāne, *n.* [Gr. *glaukos*, bluish-green, and *phanos*, bright, from *phanein*, to appear.] a bluish-black mineral, containing sodium and belonging to the hornblende family.
glau·çō′sis, *n.* blindness resulting from glaucoma.
glau′çous, *a.* [L. *glaucus*; Gr. *glaukos*, gleaming, bluish-green.]
1. of a sea-green color; with a green, grayish-blue cast.
2. in botany, covered with a whitish bloom that can be rubbed off, as that of a cabbage leaf.
Glau′çus, *n.* [L.; Gr. *Glaukos*.] in Greek mythology, (a) a fisherman and sailor, supposedly the helmsman of the Argos, who by eating a magic herb became a sea god; (b) the son of Sisyphus, torn to pieces by his own mares; (c) a Lycian prince killed by Ajax in the Trojan War.
glaum, *v.i.* to grope; to reach out gropingly. [Scot.]
Glaux, *n.* [L. *glaux*; Gr. *glaux*, the milk vetch (also an owl), from *glaukos*, gleaming.] a genus of plants, with a single species, *Glaux maritima*, the sea milkwort or black saltwort.
glāve, *n.* a glaive. [Archaic.]
glav′ẽr, *v.i.* to flatter; to wheedle; to chatter. [Obs.]
glav′ẽr·ẽr, *n.* a flatterer. [Obs.]
glāy′mōre, *n.* same as *claymore*.
glāze, *v.t.*; glazed, *pt., pp.*; glazing, *ppr.* [ME. *glasen*, to furnish with glass, cause to shine, from *glas*; AS. *glæs*, glass.]
1. (a) to furnish (a building, etc.) with windows; (b) to furnish (windows, etc.) with glass.
2. to give a hard, smooth, glossy finish to; specifically, (a) to overlay (pottery, etc.) with a substance which gives a glassy finish when fused; (b) to make the surface of (leather, etc.) glossy by polishing, etc.; (c) to cover (food) with a coating of sugar sirup, etc.
3. to cover (the eye) with film.
4. in painting, to place a thin, semitransparent pigment over (a color, surface, etc.), so as to alter the effect.
glāze, *v.i.* to become glassy, glossy, or filmy.
A light on Marmion's visage spread
And fired his *glazing* eye. —Scott.
glāze, *n.* 1. the vitreous coating or glazing of porcelain and fine pottery.
2. anything that glazes.
3. a thin layer of transparent color spread over a painted surface to modify the effect.
4. a jellylike covering formed or spread on meat.
5. a film or coating, as on the eyes.
glāz′en, *a.* resembling glass. [Archaic.]
glāz′ẽr, *n.* 1. one who glazes; specifically, one who glazes pottery; one who imparts a smooth, glassy finish to paper.
2. any tool used for glazing, smoothing, or polishing.
glā′ziẽr, *n.* 1. one whose work is cutting glass.
2. one who glazes pottery.
glā′ziẽr·y, *n.* the work done by a glazier.
glāz′ing, *n.* 1. the act or art of setting glass in windows, etc.
2. the glass set or to be set in windows; as, the *glazing* of a house.
3. a glassy coating; glossy finish.
4. the act of applying a glaze.
5. the vitreous substance applied as glaze.
6. in painting, transparent or semitransparent colors passed thinly over other colors, to modify the effect.
glāz′y, *a.* having a glaze.
glēad, *n.* a gleed; a coal. [Obs.]
glēam, *v.i.* in falconry, to vent refuse matter, as a hawk.
glēam, *n.* [ME. *gleem, glem*; AS. *glæm*, splendor, brightness.]
1. a momentary brightness; flash or beam of light.
2. a faint light.
3. a reflected brightness, as from a polished surface.
4. a brief, faint manifestation, as of hope, understanding, etc.
glēam, *v.i.*; gleamed, *pt., pp.*; gleaming, *ppr.* 1. to shine or reflect with a gleam or gleams
2. to be manifested briefly; to appear or be revealed suddenly.
Syn.—glimmer, glitter.—To *gleam* denotes a faint but distinct emission of light; to *glimmer* describes an indistinct and unsteady light; to *glitter*, a brightness that is intense, but varying.
glēam, *v.t.* to shoot or flash out, as light.
glēam′y, *a.* darting beams of light; gleaming.
glēan, *v.t.* and *v.i.*; gleaned, *pt., pp.*; gleaning, *ppr.* [ME. *glenen*; OFr. *glener*; LL. *glenare*, to glean.]
1. to gather (grain left by reapers).
2. to take the leavings from (a field).
3. to gather (facts, etc.) in small amounts or from places widely scattered by searching here and there.
glēan, *n.* a collection made by gleaning; especially, a handful of grain tied with a band. [Now Dial.]
glēan, *n.* the afterbirth of a domestic animal, as a cow. [Obs.]
glēan′ẽr, *n.* one who gleans.
glēan′ing, *n.* 1. the act of one who gleans.
2. [*usually pl.*] that which is collected by gleaning.
glē′bȧ, *n.*; *pl.* **glē′bae,** [L. *gleba*, *glæba*, a clod.] the tissue enclosed by the peridium of gasteromycetous fungi, containing the spores.

glēbe, *n.* [OFr. *glebe*, a glebe, land belonging to a parsonage, from L. *gleba*, *glæba*, clod, lump of earth.]

1. turf; soil; ground. [Poet.]

Till the glad summons of a genial ray
Unbinds the *glebe*. —Garth.

2. in England, the land belonging to a parish church or ecclesiastical benefice.

glēbe′less, *a.* without glebe.

glē·bos′i·ty, *n.* a glebous condition.

glēb′ous, glēb′y, *a.* [L. *glebosus*, full of clods, from *gleba*, a clod.] turfy; cloddy. [Obs.]

gled, *n.* a glede (bird).

glēde, *n.* [ME. *glede*; AS. *glida*, a kite, lit., a glider, from *glidan*, to glide.] the common kite of Europe, *Milvus ictinus*, a bird of prey.

glēde, *n.* a gleed. [Obs.]

gledġe, *v.i.* to look at anything askance; to squint. [Scot.]

gledġe, *n.* a sly or cunning glance. [Scot.]

Glē·dit′si·ȧ, *n.* [named after J. G. *Gleditsch*, 18th-c. German botanist.] a genus of plants of the order *Leguminosæ*. *Gleditsia triacanthos*, the honey locust, is a large tree native to the United States, where it is commonly cultivated as a shade tree and for ornamental purposes. The stem and branches are covered with hard prickles; the leaves are abruptly once or twice pinnate, and the inconspicuous greenish flowers are borne in small spikes. They are succeeded by long, thin, flat, curved, and often twisted pods, each containing numerous seeds.

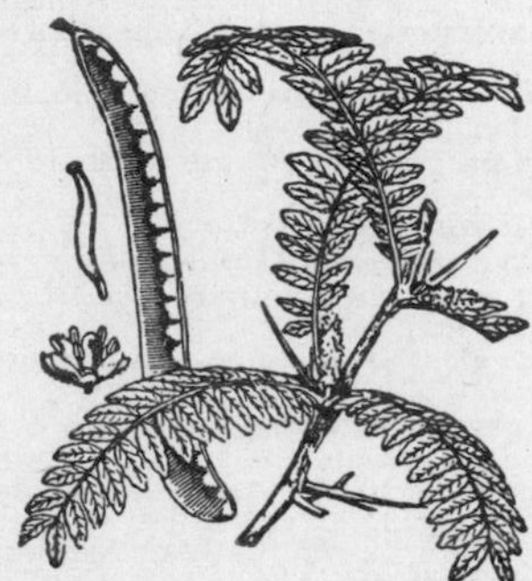

HONEY LOCUST (*Gleditsia triacanthos*)

glee, *n.* [ME. *glee*, *gle*; AS. *gleow*, *gleo*, joy, mirth.]

1. merriment; mirth; gaiety; exhilaration.

2. in music, a vocal composition in three or more solo parts, usually without instrumental accompaniment.

3. music or minstrelsy generally. [Obs.]

glee çlub, in music, a group of singers organized for the purpose of singing part songs.

glee çraft, study or knowledge of music. [Obs.]

gleed, *n.* a glowing coal. [Obs.]

glee′fụl, *a.* full of glee; merry; gay; joyous.

gleek, *n.* 1. a card game for three. [Obs.]

2. three of a kind of anything. [Obs.]

gleek, *n.* 1. a scoff; a trick. [Obs.]

2. an alluring look. [Obs.]

gleek, *v.i.* to make sport; to gibe; to sneer. [Obs.]

glee′măn, *n.*; *pl.* **glee′men,** a singer; a wandering minstrel. [Archaic.]

gleen, *v.i.* to shine; to glisten. [Obs.]

glee′sŏme, *a.* merry; joyous; gleeful.

gleet, *n.* [ME. *glette*; OFr. *glete*, mucus, a flux.]

1. slimy matter; ooze. [Obs. or Scot.]

2. formerly, any morbid discharge from the body.

3. a chronic mucous discharge from the urethra in gonorrhea.

4. a chronic discharge from the nasal cavities of horses, etc.

gleet, *v.i.* 1. to give forth a thin, watery discharge.

2. to flow slowly; to ooze. [Obs.]

gleet′y, *a.* ichorous; thin; watery; limpid.

gleg, *a.* [Ice. *glöggr*, sharp, clever.] keen; acute; alert; quick in perception or action. [Dial. and Scot.]

gleire, gleyre (glãr), *n.* glair. [Obs.]

glen, *n.* [Gael. and Ir. *gleann*, *gleanu*, a valley glen.] a narrow, secluded valley.

Glen·gar′ry, *n.*; *pl.* **Glen·gar′rieṣ,** [from *Glengarry*, valley in Scotland.] [*sometimes* g–] a Scottish cap for men, creased lengthwise across the top and often having short ribbons at the back: also *Glengarry bonnet* (or *cap*).

GLENGARRY

Glen·liv′et, Glen·liv′ăt, *n.* a Scotch whisky: named from the district of its origin, a valley in Banffshire, Scotland.

glē·nō·hū′mēr·ăl, *a.* [Gr. *glēnoeidēs*, like a ball and socket; *glēnē*, a socket, and *eidos*, form, and L. *humerus*, shoulder.] joining the humerus to the glenoid fossa of the scapula.

glē′noid, *a.* [Gr. *glēnoeidēs*, like a ball and socket joint; *glēnē*, a socket, and *eidos*, form.] forming a smooth, shallow cavity or socket for a bone; especially, designating the cavity on the head of the scapula which, together with the head of the humerus, forms the shoulder joint.

glē·noid′ăl, *a.* glenoid. [Rare.]

glent, *n.* and *v.* same as *glint*.

glew, *n.* glue. [Obs.]

gleȳ (glī), *v.i.* [ME. *gleyen*, to shine, glance, squint, from Ice. *glja*, to glitter.] to squint; to gledge. [Scot.]

gleȳ, *adv.* obliquely. [Scot.]

glī′ȧ cell, [Gr. *glia*, glue.] a cell of neuroglia, having many branches.

glī′ȧ·din, *n.* [Gr. *glia*, glue.] a substance obtained from gluten, slightly transparent, brittle, straw-yellow in color, having a slight smell similar to that of honeycomb: also called *glutin*.

glib, *a.* [D. *glibberen*, freq. of *glippen*, to slide; *glibberig*, glib, slippery.]

1. smooth; slippery; as, ice is *glib*. [Dial.]

2. done in a smooth, offhand fashion.

3. (a) speaking or spoken in a smooth, easy manner; facile; fluent; (b) speaking or spoken in a manner too smooth and easy to be convincing.

glib, *n.* [Ir. *glib*; Gael. *glib*, a lock of hair.] a thick, curled head of hair, hanging down over the eyes; also, a man wearing such hair. [Rare.]

glib, *v.t.* to castrate. [Obs.]

glib, *v.t.* to render glib; as, to *glib* the tongue with liquor. [Dial.]

glib′bēr·y, *a.* slippery; fickle; also, voluble. [Obs.]

glib′ly, *adv.* smoothly; volubly.

glib′ness, *n.* the state or quality of being glib.

glid′dēr, glid′dēr·y, *a.* [Prov. Eng., from AS. *glidan*, to glide, slide.] giving uncertain foothold; slippery. [Brit. Dial.]

glīde, *v.i.*; glided, *pt.*, *pp.*; gliding, *ppr.* [ME. *gliden*; AS. *glidan*, to slip, slide, glide.]

1. to flow gently; to move silently and smoothly; to pass along without apparent effort; to move or pass rapidly and with apparent ease; as, a river *glides* along; the boat *glides* over the lake.

2. to move by or pass gradually and unnoticed, as time.

3. to descend slowly in an airplane without using an engine.

4. in music and phonetics, to make a glide.

glīde, *v.t.* to cause to glide.

glīde, *n.* 1. the act or manner of moving smoothly, swiftly, and without labor or obstruction.

2. in music, an even carriage of the voice from tone to tone without a break; a slur.

3. a slow descent in an airplane without using an engine.

4. in phonetics, the incidental, indefinite sound made when the speech organs are passing from the position for one sound to that for another, as in the shift from front (ē) to back (ọọ) in pronouncing (ū).

5. a sliding movement of the foot in waltzing; also, the kind of waltz having this smooth, sliding step.

glīd′ēr, *n.* 1. one who or that which glides.

2. an engineless airplane flown by being manipulated into air currents that keep it aloft.

3. a porch seat suspended in an upright frame so that it can swing back and forth.

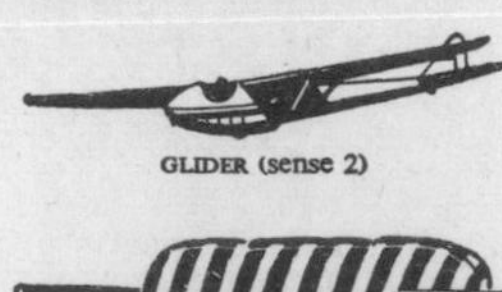

GLIDER (sense 2)

GLIDER (sense 3)

glīd′ēr·pọrt, *n.* in aviation, a port or landing place for gliders.

glīde vow′el, in grammar, a consonantal vowel; a nonsyllabic vowel.

glīde′wŏrt, *n.* [from D. *glidkruid*.] the hemp nettle.

glīd′ing an′gle, the angle formed between the horizon and the downward path of an airplane descending without power.

glīd′ing bōat (bōt), any aircraft capable of landing on and taking off from water; a hydroplane.

glīd′ing joint, in anatomy, a joint which permits of a gliding motion of the surfaces.

glīd′ing mȧ·çhïne′, same as *glider*, sense 2.

glīd′ing plāne, in crystallography, the direction in which a movement of the molecules of a crystal may take place under pressure without fracture.

gliff, *n.* 1. a sudden fright or scare. [Scot. and Brit. Dial.]

2. a short period of time; a moment. [Scot.]

glim, *n.* 1. a light or a candle. [Slang.]

2. an eye; as, he has lost a *glim*. [Slang.]

3. brightness; sheen. [Obs.]

glim′mēr, *v.i.*; glimmered, *pt.*, *pp.*; glimmering, *ppr.* [ME. *glimeren*, from *glim*; AS. *gleomu*, brightness.]

1. to emit feeble or scattered rays of light; to shine faintly; to give a feeble light; as, the morning *glimmers* in the east.

2. to appear or be seen faintly or dimly.

glim′mēr, *n.* 1. a faint light; feeble, scattered rays of light; gleam; shimmer; as, the fading *glimmer* of a lamp; the *glimmer* of pearls.

2. a faint manifestation; a dim perception; a glimpse.

Syn.—gleam, glow, twinkle, flicker.

glim′mēr, *n.* mica.

glim′mēr·ing, *n.* 1. a faint beaming of light.

2. a faint idea; an inkling; a glimpse.

glimpse, *n.* 1. a transitory view; a hasty look; a momentary observation.

2. a transient, sudden shining; a flash of light.

3. a faint, fleeting appearance; an inkling; a glimmer; a trace.

glimpse, *v.i.*; glimpsed (glimst), *pt.*, *pp.*; glimpsing, *ppr.* [ME. *glimsen*, from *glim*; AS. *gleomu*, brightness.]

1. to appear by glimpses. [Archaic or Poet.]

2. to glance; to look or see quickly.

glimpse, *v.t.* to catch a glimpse of; to see momentarily and incompletely; to have a quick view of.

glint, *v.i.*; glinted, *pt.*, *pp.*; glinting, *ppr.* [ME. *glenten*, to shine, gleam; Old Dan. *glinte*, to shine.]

1. to glitter; to gleam; to flash.

2. to peep forth; to glance.

3. to move quickly; to dart.

glint, *v.t.* to cause to gleam or flash; as, their armor *glinted* back the light.

glint, *n.* 1. a gleam or flash of light.

2. a glimpse. [Scot. and Brit. Dial.]

glī·ō′mȧ, *n.*; *pl.* **glī·ō′mȧ·tȧ, glī·ō′mȧṣ,** [Gr. *glia*, glue, and *-oma*.] in pathology, a tumor of the brain, spinal cord, etc., composed of neuroglia.

glī·om′ȧ·tous, *a.* pertaining to, of the nature of, or having a glioma or gliomata.

glī″ō·sär·çō′mȧ, *n.*; *pl.* **glī″ō·sär·çō′mȧ·tȧ,** in pathology, a tumor composed of gliomatous and sarcomatous tissue.

glī·ō′sis, *n.* [Gr. *glia*, glue.] in medicine, a diseased cerebral condition marked by a localized increase of the supporting structure of nervous tissue.

Glī′rēṣ, *n.pl.* [L. *glis*, *gliris*, a dormouse.] same as *Rodentia*.

glī′rine, *a.* of, pertaining to, or like the *Glires*, or *Rodentia*.

glisk, *n.* a gleam; a glimpse. [Scot.]

glis·säde′, *n.* [Fr. *glissade*, from *glisser*, to slide, glide, from O.D. *glitsen*, to slide.]
1. an intentional slide by a mountain climber down a steep slope covered with snow.
2. in ballet dancing, a gliding step to the side.

glis·sade′, *v.i.*; glissaded, *pt.*, *pp.*; glissading, *ppr.* to make a glissade; slide; glide.

glis·san′dō, *n.*; *pl.* **glis·san′dī,** [formed as if It. ppr. equivalent to Fr. *glissant*, ppr. of *glisser*, to slide.]
1. a gliding effect achieved by sounding a series of adjacent tones in rapid succession, as by running a finger over the white keys of a piano.
2. a passage having this effect.

glis·san′dō, *a.* in music, performed with a gliding effect.

glis′ten (glis′n), *v.i.*; glistened, *pt.*, *pp.*; glistening, *ppr.* [ME. *glistnen*; AS. *glisnian*, to glisten, shine.] to shine as if smooth and by reflection of light; to sparkle or scintillate; to gleam with soft, twinkling, or shimmering light.

glis′ten, *n.* shine; sparkle; gleam; glitter.

glis′tẽr, *v.i.* [ME. *glisteren*; prob. from L.G. source.] to shine; to be bright; to sparkle; to be brilliant; to glitter. [Archaic.]
All that *glisters* is not gold. —Shak.

glis′tẽr, *n.* glitter; luster.

glis′tẽr·ing·ly, *adv.* with shining luster.

glitch, *n.* [from G. colloq. *glitsche*, a slip, from *glitschen*, to slip, slide.]
1. a mishap, error, malfunctioning, etc. [Slang.]
2. a sudden, brief change in the rate of radio pulses emitted by a pulsar, theorized to coincide with periods of its rotation.

glit′tẽr, *v.i.*; glittered, *pt.*, *pp.*; glittering, *ppr.* [ME. *gliteren*, *gleteren*; freq. formation; prob. from ON. *glitra*.]
1. to shine; to sparkle with light; to gleam; to glisten; as, a *glittering* sword.
2. to be showy, specious, or striking, and hence, attractive; as, the *glittering* scenes of a court.

glit′tẽr, *n.* 1. brightness; brilliancy; luster; as, the *glitter* of arms.
2. showiness; colorful splendor.

glit′tẽr·ing·ly, *adv.* in a glittering manner; with sparkling luster.

glit′tẽr·y, *a.* having glitter; glittering.

glitz′y, *a.*; *comp.* glitzier; *superl.* glitziest, [prob. via Yid., from G. *glitzern*, to glitter.]
1. having glitter; sparkling; glittery. [Slang.]
2. attracting attention in an ornate or gaudy way; showy; pretentious. [Slang.]

glōam, *v.i.* to grow dark; to get dusky. [Scot.]

glōam, *n.* the gloaming. [Rare.]

glōam′ing, *n.* [ME. *glomyng*; AS. *glomung* from *glom*, twilight; akin to *glowan*, to glow; adopted in literature from Scot. dial.] twilight; the dusk of approaching night.

glōat, *v.i.*; gloated, *pt.*, *pp.*; gloating, *ppr.* [ON. *glotta*, to smile scornfully, to grin.] to gaze or meditate with malicious pleasure, exultation, or avarice (often with *over*).

glō′băl, *a.* 1. spherical; globe-shaped.
2. involving the earth as a whole; worldwide: as, *global* warfare.

glō′bāte, glō′bā·ted, *a.* [L. *globatus*, pp. of *globare*, to make into a ball, from *globus*, a ball, sphere.] having the form of a globe; spherical.

glōbe, *n.* [OFr. *globe*; L. *globus*, a ball, sphere.]
1. any round, ball-shaped thing; a sphere; specifically, (a) the earth; the world; (b) a spherical model of the earth showing the continents, seas, etc.; (c) a similar model of the sky, showing the constellations, etc.
2. anything shaped somewhat like a globe; specifically, (a) a round glass container, as for goldfish; (b) a rounded glass cover for a lamp; (c) an electric light bulb; (d) a small, golden ball used as a symbol of authority.

glōbe, *v.i.* and *v.t.*; globed, *pt.*, *pp.*; globing, *ppr.* to take or cause to take the form of a globe.

glōbe am′ȧ·ranth, a plant of the genus *Gomphrena*, bearing globular heads of purple and white flowers.

glōbe an′i·măl, glōbe an·i·mal′cūle, a protozoan of the genus *Volvox*.

glōbe dāi′sy, a plant, *Globularia vulgaris*.

glōbe′fish, *n.* a fish of the genus *Diodon* or *Tetrodon*, capable of inflating its body into a globular form.

glōbe′flow″ẽr, *n.* a plant of the genus *Trollius*, bearing globular flowers.
Japan globeflower; *Corchorus*.

GLOBEFLOWER (*Trollius europæus*)

glōbe′-shaped (-shāpt), *a.* shaped like a globe.

glōbe sight (sīt), a sight for a rifle, consisting of a small globe set on a pin above the muzzle.

glōbe slāt′ẽr, a crustacean of the genus *Sphæroma*, which rolls itself into globular form.

glōbe this′tle (this′l), a plant of the genus *Echinops*.

glōbe′-trot″tẽr, *n.* a person who travels widely about the world, especially one who does so for pleasure or sightseeing.

glōbe′-trot″ting, *n.* extensive traveling about the world.

glō′bi-, glō′bō-, [from L. *globus*, a ball, sphere.] combining forms meaning *round*, *spherical*, *ball-shaped*.

glō·bif′ẽr·ous, *a.* [*globi-*, and L. *ferre*, to bear.] having a globular terminal.

Glō·big·e·rī′nȧ, *n.* [*globi-*, and L. *gerere*, to carry.] a genus of minute, pelagic foraminifers having globose calcareous shells which form the chief part of the *globigerina ooze*, or soft, chalky mud found on the ocean floor.

glō′bin, *n.* [from L. *globus*, and *-in*.] the protein component of hemoglobin.

glō′boid, *a.* somewhat globular; globate.

glō′boid, *n.* [L. *globus*, a globe, and Gr. *eidos*, form.]
1. a spheroidal mass of calcium-magnesium phosphate found in aleurone.
2. anything spheroidal; a globular body.

glō′bōse, *a.* [L. *globosus*, round as a ball, from *globus*, a ball.] rounded; almost spherical; globular.

glō·bōse′ly, *adv.* in a globose way.

glō·bos′i·ty, *n.* [LL. *globositas*, from L. *globosus*, round as a ball, from *globus*, a ball.] the quality or state of being globose.

glō′bous, *a.* [OFr. *globeux*; L. *globosus*, round as a ball, from *globus*, a ball.] spherical. [Rare.]

glob′ū·lăr, *a.* [L. *globulus*, dim. of *globus*, a ball.]
1. round; spherical; having the form of a ball or sphere.
2. made up of globules.
globular chart; see under *chart*.
globular sailing; sailing on the shortest course between two points, which is on the arc of the great circle passing through them: also called *great-circle sailing*.

Glob·ū·lā′ri·ȧ, *n.* [L. *globulus*, dim. of *globus*, a ball.] a genus of plants which grow in the temperate and warm parts of Europe, including the *globe daisy*.

glob·ū·lar′i·ty, *n.* the quality of being globular; sphericity.

glob′ū·lăr·ly, *adv.* in a spherical form.

glob′ū·lăr·ness, *n.* the quality or state of being globular.

glob′ūle, *n.* [Fr. *globule*; L. *globulus*, a little ball, dim. of *globus*, a ball.]
1. a tiny globe; a small particle of matter, especially of liquid, in a spherical form.
Hailstones have opaque *globules* of snow in their center. —Newton.
2. a minute spherical structure, such as a corpuscle, coccus, spore, etc.
3. a very small pellet or pill, as those used by homeopathic physicians.

glob′ū·let, *n.* a minute globule. [Rare.]

glob·ū·lif′ẽr·ous, *a.* [from *globule*, and *-ferous*.] having or producing globules.

glob·ū·lim′e·tẽr, *n.* [L. *globulus*, dim. of *globus*, a ball, and *metrum*, a measure.] a device for determining the number of red blood corpuscles in the blood.

glob′ū·lin, *n.* [*globule*, and *-in*.] any of a group of albuminous proteins, insoluble in water, found in both animal and vegetable tissue.
serum globulin; in medicine and biochemistry, a globulin obtained from blood serum and cells, some connective tissues, and lymph.

glob′ū·līte, *n.* a spherical mineral form without crystalline structure.

glob′ū·lōse, *a.* globulous.

glob′ū·lous, *a.* [L. *globulus*, dim. of *globus*, a ball.] rounded; globular; having the form of or consisting of globules; spheroidal.

glob′ū·lous·ness, *n.* the state of being globulous.

glōb′y, *a.* round; globelike.

glō·ċhid′i·āte, *a.* [Gr. *glōchis*, an arrow point.] having a barbed tip, as a hair or bristle.

glō·ċhid′i·um, *n.*; *pl.* **glō·ċhid′i·ȧ,** [Gr. *glōchis*, an arrow point.]
1. in zoology, the larva of certain mussels hatched in the gills of the parent.
2. in botany, a barbed hairy appendage of certain heterosporous ferns.

glō′ċhis, *n.*; *pl.* **glō′ċhi·nēs,** [Gr. *glōchis*, *glōchin*, an arrow point.] a glochidiate point, bristle, spine, etc.

glock′en·spiēl (*or* G. glọ′ken-shpēl), *n.* [G., from *glocke*, a bell, and *spiel*, play.] in music, a percussion instrument with flat metal bars, formerly bells or tubes, set in a frame and chromatically tuned to produce bell-like tones when struck with small hammers.

glōde, *v.* obsolete past tense of *glide*.

glōme, *n.* [L. *glomus*, a ball.]
1. in botany, a soredium; a glomerule.
2. one of the prominences at the rear of the frog of a horse's foot.
3. a spool of thread; a ball of yarn. [Obs.]

glom′ẽr·āte, *v.t.*; glomerated, *pt.*, *pp.*; glomerating, *ppr.* [L. *glomeratus*, pp. of *glomerare*, to wind or make into a ball, from *glomus*, a ball of yarn.] to gather or wind into a ball; to collect into a spherical form or mass, as threads. [Obs.]

glom′ẽr·āte, *a.* growing, collected, or arranged in a rounded mass, as glands, flowers, etc.; clustered.

glom·ẽr·ā′tion, *n.* [L. *glomeratio* (*-onis*), from *glomeratus*, pp. of *glomerare*, to form into a ball, from *glomus*, a ball.]
1. the act of forming into a rounded mass; agglomeration or conglomeration.
2. something formed into a rounded mass; a cluster.

glom′ẽr·ūle, *n.* [L. *glomus* (*-eris*), a ball, and *-ule*.]
1. in botany, (a) a dense, globular, cymose cluster of flowers; (b) a mass of adhesive spores in various lichens.
2. in anatomy, a glomerulus.

glō·mer′ū·lus, *n.*; *pl.* **glō·mer′ū·lī,** [a dim. from L. *glomus* (*-eris*), a ball.] in anatomy, a convoluted mass of capillaries, as in the kidney.

glom′ẽr·y, *n.* grammar: a historical form of the word, found in the records of Cambridge University, England; as, a master in *glomery*.

glom·ū·lif′ẽr·ous, *a.* [L. *glomus*, a ball, and *ferre*, to bear.] in biology, having powdery masses on the surface, as certain lichens; having clusters of excrescences.

glon′ō·in, glon′ō·ine, *n.* [*glycerin*, and *oxygen*, and *nitrogen*, and *-in*.] nitroglycerin: especially a solution of this used in medicine.

gloom, *v.i.*; gloomed, *pt.*, *pp.*; glooming, *ppr.* [ME. *gloum*(*b*)*en*; prob. from AS. *glom*, twilight.]
1. to be or look morose, displeased, or dejected.
2. to be or become dark, dim, or dismal.

glọom, *v.t.* to obscure; to darken; to make dismal; to fill with gloom.

glọom, *n.* 1. obscurity; partial or total darkness; thick shade; as, the *gloom* of a forest, the *gloom* of midnight.
2. depression or heaviness of mind; melancholy; sadness; dejection; as, the mind is sunk in *gloom*; a *gloom* overspreads the face.
3. darkness of prospect or aspect; a depressing state of affairs.
4. a dark or gloomy place.
Syn.—darkness, duskiness, obscurity, sadness, depression, dejection, heaviness.

glọom′i·ly, *adv.* in a gloomy manner.

glọom′i·ness, *n.* the state or condition of being gloomy.

glọom′ing, *n.* duskiness; gloaming. [Rare.]

glọomth, *n.* gloominess. [Obs.]

glọom′y, *a.*; *comp.* gloomier; *superl.* gloomiest, 1. overspread with or enveloped in darkness or dimness.
2. melancholy; sad; dejected; morose.
3. causing gloom; dismal; depressing.
Syn.—clouded, dark, depressing, dim, dismal, dull.

glop, *n.* [from perh. *glue* and *slop*.] any soft, gluey substance, thick liquid, etc. [Slang.]

glop′pen, *v.t.* [ME. *glopnen*; ON. *glupna*.] to terrify; alarm; astonish. [Brit. Dial.]

glop′pen, *v.i.* to be terrified or distressed. [Obs.]

glōre, *v.i.* to glare. [Obs.]

Glō′ri·ȧ, *n.* [L., glory.]
1. [*also* g–] (a) glory; praise; a word of worship; (b) any of several Latin hymns in praise of God that begin with this word: see the next two entries; (c) the music for any of these.
2. [g–] a halo or its representation in art.
3. [g–] a cloth of silk and wool, silk and cotton, etc. with a glossy surface, used for umbrellas, etc.

Glō′ri·ȧ in Ex·cel′sis Dē′ō, [L.] glory (be) to God on high: title and first words of the greater doxology.

Glō′ri·ȧ Pā′trī, [L.] glory (be) to the Father: title and first words of the lesser doxology.

glō·ri·ā′tion, *n.* boast; a triumphing. [Obs.]

glō″ri·fi·cā′tion, *n.* [LL. *glorificatio* (*-onis*), from *glorificare*, to glorify; L. *gloria*, glory, and *facere*, to make.]
1. the act of glorifying or state of being glorified.
2. that which glorifies or is used in glorifying; a doxology.
3. a festive occasion; celebration.

glō′ri·fī·ẽr, *n.* a person who glorifies. [Colloq.]

glō′ri·fȳ, *v.t.*; glorified, *pt.*, *pp.*; glorifying, *ppr.* [ME. *glorifien*; OFr. *glorifier*; LL. *glorificare*, to glorify; L. *gloria*, glory, and *facere*, to make.]
1. to make glorious; to give glory to.
2. to exalt and honor in worship.
3. to honor; to praise extravagantly; to extol.
4. to make, or make seem, better, larger, finer, or more beautiful than is actually the case.

glō′ri·ōle, *n.* [L. *gloriola*, dim. of *gloria*, glory.] a halo; a nimbus.

Glō·ri·ō′sȧ, *n.* [f. of L. *gloriosus*, glorious.] in botany, a small genus of climbing lilies bearing red and yellow flowers.

glō·ri·ō′sẽr, *n.* a braggart. [Obs.]

glō·ri·ō′sō, *n.* [It.] a braggart. [Obs.]

glō′ri·ous, *a.* [ME. *glorious*; OFr. *glorios*; L. *gloriosus*, glorious, renowned, boastful.]
1. full of glory; illustrious.
2. giving glory.
3. receiving or deserving glory.
4. splendid; magnificent.
5. very delightful or enjoyable. [Colloq.]

glō′ri·ous·ly, *adv.* in a glorious way.

glō′ri·ous·ness, *n.* the state or quality of being glorious.

glō′ry, *n.*; *pl.* **glō′ries,** [ME. *glory*; OFr. *glorie*; L. *gloria* glory, fame, honor, pride, boasting.]
1. great honor and admiration won by doing something important or valuable; fame; renown.
2. anything bringing this.
3. worship; adoration; praise.
4. the condition of highest achievement, splendor, prosperity, etc.; as, Greece in her *glory*.
5. the highest degree of pleasure, satisfaction, pride, etc.; as, the actress was in her *glory* at the stage door.
6. splendor, magnificence, radiance; as, the *glory* of the Rocky Mountains.
7. heaven or the bliss of heaven.
8. a halo or its representation in art.
gone to glory; dead.
Old Glory; the United States flag; the Stars and Stripes.
Syn.—brightness, radiance, effulgence, honor, fame, celebrity, renown.

glō′ry, *v.i.*; gloried, *pt.*, *pp.*; glorying, *ppr.* [ME. *glorien*; OFr. *glorier*; L. *gloriari*, to glory, boast, from *gloria*, glory, vaunting.]
1. to exult with joy; to rejoice: with *in*.
2. to boast, to be proud of; with *in*; as, to *glory in* one's strength.
Syn.—boast, vaunt.—To *glory* is more particularly the act of the mind, the indulgence of the internal sentiment; to *boast* denotes rather the expression of the sentiment. To *glory* is applied usually to matters of importance, *boast* often to trifling points. To *vaunt* means to proclaim praises aloud, and is taken either in an indifferent or bad sense.

glō′ry hōle, 1. an opening in a furnace, showing the light within.
2. a place, as a drawer, closet, etc., where things are heaped together untidily. [Colloq.]

glō′ry pēa, either of two plants of the genus *Clianthus*, of Australia and New Zealand.

glō′ry tree, a showy, flowering shrub of the tropics, belonging to the genus *Clerodendron*.

glōṣe, *n.* and *v.* same as *gloze*.

glōṣ′ẽr, *n.* same as *glosser*.

gloss, *n.* [ON. *glossi*, a blaze, from *gloa*, to glow.]
1. brightness or luster of a smooth surface; polish; as, the *gloss* of silk.
2. a specious appearance or representation; external show that may deceive.

gloss, *v.t.*; glossed (glost), *pt.*, *pp.*; glossing, *ppr.* 1. to give a polished luster to; to make smooth and shining; as, to *gloss* cloth or silk.
2. to give a specious appearance to; to render plausible; to palliate by specious representation or by minimizing: commonly used with *over*; as, to *gloss over* the facts.

gloss, *v.i.* to become shiny.

gloss, *n.* [ME. *glose*; LL. *glossa*; L. *glossarium*, a foreign or difficult word requiring explanation; from Gr. *glōssa*, the tongue, language.]
1. words of explanation or translation inserted between the lines of a text.
2. a note of comment or explanation accompanying a text, as in a footnote or margin.
3. a collection of such notes; a glossary.
4. a false or misleading explanation.

gloss, *v.i.* 1. to comment; to write or make explanatory remarks; annotate.
2. to make sly remarks; to insinuate.

gloss, *v.t.* 1. to explain; to furnish (a text) with notes of comment or explanation.
2. to interpret falsely.

glos′sȧ, *n.*; *pl.* **glos′sae,** [Gr. *glōssa*, the tongue.] the tongue; specifically, the distal appendage of the lingua of an insect.

glos′săl, *a.* pertaining to the tongue.

glos·san′thrax, *n.* [Gr. *glōssa*, the tongue, and *anthrax*, a carbuncle.] a diseased condition of horses and cattle in which carbuncles affect the mouth and tongue.

glos·sā′ri·ăl, *a.* of, or having the nature of, a glossary.

glos·sā′ri·ăl·ly, *adv.* in the manner of a glossary.

glos′sȧ·rist, *n.* a writer of glosses or a compiler of glossaries.

glos·sā′ri·um, *n.* [Gr. *glōssa*, the tongue.] the labrum or tongue of dipterous insects, as that of the mosquito.

glos′sȧ·ry, *n.*; *pl.* **glos′sȧ·rieṣ,** [LL. *glossarium*, a vocabulary of foreign or antiquated words, from *glossa*; from Gr. *glōssa*, the tongue, word, a foreign or difficult word.] a dictionary or vocabulary explaining words which are obscure, antiquated, local, or foreign; a vocabulary giving the words of a book, author, dialect, science, or art.

Glos·sā′tȧ, *n.pl.* [Gr. *glōssa*, tongue.] the *Lepidoptera*.

glos′sāte, *a.* [Gr. *glōssa*, tongue, and *-ate*.] provided with a glossa, or tongue; also, in entomology, haustellate.

glos·sā′tŏr, *n.* [LL. *glossator*, from *glossare*, to gloss, from *glossa*, a gloss, from Gr. *glōssa*, the tongue.] a writer of glosses.

gloss′ẽr, *n.* a writer of glosses.

gloss′ẽr, *n.* a polisher; one who gives a gloss to something.

glos′siç, *n.* [Gr. *glōssa*, the tongue, a tongue, language, and *-ic*.] a phonetic system of spelling using for each sound the letter or digraph most commonly used in the usual spelling.

gloss′i·ly, *adv.* in a glossy manner.

gloss′i·ness, *n.* a glossy state or quality.

gloss′ist, *n.* a writer of comments.

glos·sit′iç, *a.* of or affected by glossitis.

glos·sī′tis, *n.* [Gr. *glōssa*, the tongue, and *-itis*.] inflammation of the tongue.

gloss′ly, *adv.* like gloss. [Obs.]

glos′sō-, [from Gr. *glōssa*, the tongue.] a combining form meaning, (a) *of the tongue*, as in *glosso*plegia; (b) *the tongue and*, as in *glosso*pharyngeal; (c) *of words or language*, as in *glosso*logy. Also, before a vowel, *gloss-*.

glos″sō·ep·i·glot′tiç, *a.* [*glosso-*, and Gr. *epiglōttis*, the epiglottis.] belonging or relating to both tongue and epiglottis.

glos′sō·grȧph, *n.* a device to record the movements of the tongue in speaking.

glos·sog′rȧ·phẽr, *n.* [Gr. *glōssographos*, from *glōssa*, the tongue, and *graphein*, to write.] a writer or interpreter of glosses.

glos·sō·graph′iç·ăl, *a.* belonging or relating to glossography.

glos·sog′rȧ·phy, *n.* 1. the writing of glosses or glossaries.
2. a treatise on or description of the tongue.

glos·sō·hȳ′ăl, *a.* [*glosso-*, and Gr. *hyoeidēs*, shaped like the letter upsilon (Υ), hyoid; Υ, upsilon, and *eidos*, form.] of or pertaining to the hyoid bone and the tongue.

glos·sō·hȳ′ăl, *n.* the glossohyal cartilage or bone situated anteriorly to the basihyal, as in fishes, birds, etc.

glos·sō·lā′li·ȧ, *n.* [Mod.L., from Gr. *glōsso-* (from *glōssa*, tongue), and *lalia*, a speaking, from *lalein*, to speak, of echoic origin.] an ecstatic or apparently ecstatic utterance of unintelligible speechlike sounds, viewed by some as a manifestation of deep religious experience.

glos·sō·log′iç·ăl, *a.* pertaining to glossology.

glos·sol′ō·ġist, *n.* 1. a glossarist.
2. a philologist.

glos·sol′ō·ġy, *n.* [*glosso-*, and Gr. *-logia*, from *legein*, to speak.]
1. the definition and explanation of terms.
2. linguistics.

glos·soph′ȧ·ġine, *a.* [*glosso-*, and Gr. *phagein*, to eat.] taking food with the tongue, as certain bats, anteaters, and the like.

glos″sō·phar·yn′ġē·ăl, *a.* [*glosso-*, and Gr. *pharynx*, the pharynx.] in anatomy, belonging or relating both to the tongue and the pharynx.

glos″sō·phar·yn′ġē·ăl, *n.* a glossopharyngeal nerve.

glos·soph′ō·rous, *a.* [*glosso-*, and Gr. *-phoros*, from *pherein*, to bear.] provided with a tongue.

glos·sō·plē′ġi·ȧ, *n.* [*glosso-*, and Gr. *plēgē*, a stroke, from *plēssein*, to strike.] in pathology, paralysis of the tongue.

glos·sō·pō′di·um, *n.* [*glosso-*, and Gr. *pous*, *podos*, foot.] in botany, the sheathing base of the leaf of the quillwort, *Isoetes*.

gloss′y, *a.*; *comp.* glossier; *superl.* glossiest,
1. smooth and shining; reflecting luster from a smooth surface; as, *glossy* silk.
2. smooth; plausible; beguiling.

gloss′y, *n.*; *pl.* **gloss′ieṣ,** 1. in photography, a print with a glossy finish.
2. a magazine printed on glossy paper; slick. [Colloq.]

glost ŏv′en, an oven in which glazed pottery is fired.

-glot, [Gr. *-glōttos*, from *glōtta*, var. of *glōssa*, tongue, language.] a combining form meaning *knowledge of* or *communication in* (a specified number of) *languages*, as in poly*glot*, tri*glot*.

glot′tăl, *a.* of or made by the glottis; as, English *h* is produced by a gradual *glottal* narrowing.
glottal stop; a speech sound produced by a momentary complete closure of the glottis: it is commonly heard, often as a variant for medial *t* (in *water*, *bottle*, etc.), in many Scottish and British dialects.

glot′tiç, *a.* glottal.

glot·tid′ē·ăn, *a.* glottic.

glot′tis, *n.*; *pl.* **glot′ti·dēṣ,** [Gr. *glōttis*, the mouth of the windpipe, the glottis, from Attic Gr. *glōtta*, the tongue.] the narrow opening between the vocal cords in the larynx, which, by its expansion and contraction, contributes to the modulation of the voice.

glot″tō·chrō·nol′ō·ġy, *n.* [Mod.L. *glottis*, glottis, from Gr. *glōttis* (see *glottis*), and *chronology*.] a method for estimating the dates when the branches of a family of languages separated from the parent language and from one another.

glot·tō·gon′iç, *a.* [Attic Gr. *glōtta*, the tongue, language, and *gonos*, birth, product.] dealing with the origin of language.

glot·tō·log′iç·ăl, *a.* glossological.

glot·tol′ō·ġist, *n.* a glossologist.

glot·tol′ō·ġy, *n.* glossology.

glout, *v.i.* to scowl; to look sullen. [Scot. Dial.]

glŏve, *n.* [ME. *glove*, *glofe*; AS. *glof*, a glove.]
1. a cover for the hand, with a separate sheath for each finger and the thumb.
2. in sports, (a) a similar covering of padded leather worn by baseball players in the field; (b) a padded mitten worn by boxers: usually *boxing glove*.
to be hand and glove; to be on friendly terms.
to handle with (*kid*) *gloves*; to deal with gently and tactfully.
to put on the gloves; to box. [Colloq.]

glŏve, *v.t.*; gloved, *pt.*, *pp.*; gloving, *ppr.* 1. to supply with gloves.
2. to cover with or as with a glove.
3. to be a glove for.

glŏve çŏm·pärt′ment, a compartment built into the dashboard of an automobile, for miscellaneous articles.

glŏve mŏn′ey, 1. a gratuity given to servants ostensibly to buy them gloves.
2. in England, rewards given to officers of courts, etc.; also, money given by a sheriff of a county in which no offenders were left for

execution to the clerk of assize and the judges' officers.

glŏv′ẽr, *n.* one who makes or sells gloves.

glover's stitch; a stitch used in sewing the seams of gloves; also, a similar stitch (usually called *glover's suture*) used in surgery for sewing up a wound.

glŏve silk, a knitted silk cloth used for gloves, etc.

glŏve sil′vẽr, same as *glove money*.

glōw, *v.i.*; glowed, *pt.*, *pp.*; glowing, *ppr.* [ME. *glowen*; AS. *glowan*, to glow, to be bright, to glitter.]

1. to give off a bright light as a result of great heat; to be incandescent or red-hot.

2. to give out a steady, even light without flame or blaze; as, the harbor lights *glowed*.

3. to be or feel hot; to give out heat.

4. to radiate health or high spirits.

5. to be elated or enlivened by emotion; as, he *glowed* with pride.

6. to show brilliant, conspicuous colors; to be bright; specifically, (a) to be flushed; show red, as from emotion, enthusiasm, etc.: said of the skin; (b) to gleam; flash; light up: said of the eyes; (c) to show great intensity: said of colors.

glōw, *v.t.* to make hot; to cause to flush. [Obs.]

glōw, *n.* 1. light given off as a result of great heat; incandescence.

2. steady, even light without flame or blaze.

3. brilliance, vividness, or intensity of color.

4. brightness of skin color; flush, as from health, emotion, etc.

5. a sensation of warmth and well-being.

6. intensity of emotion; ardor, eagerness, animation, etc.

glōw′bärd, *n.* a glowbird. [Obs.]

glōw′bird, *n.* the glowworm. [Obs.]

glow′ẽr, *v.i.*; glowered, *pt.*, *pp.*; glowering, *ppr.* [from Scot. *glowr*.] to scowl; to stare angrily.

glow′ẽr, *n.* a scowl; a menacing stare.

glōw′flȳ, *n.* a firefly.

glōw′ing·ly, *adv.* in a glowing manner; with great brightness; with ardent zeal or passion.

glōw′lamp, *n.* an incandescent electric lamp.

glōw′wŏrm, *n.* any of a number of wingless insects or insect larvae that give off a phosphorescent light; especially, the wingless female or the larva of the firefly.

Glox·in′i·ȧ, *n.* [Mod. L.; after Benjamin P. *Gloxin*, 18th-c. G. botanist.]

1. a genus of plants of the family *Gesneraceæ*, having large bell-shaped flowers. They are native to tropical America.

2. [g–] a plant of the genus *Gloxinia*.

GLOXINIAS

glōze, *v.t.*; glozed, *pt.*, *pp.*; glozing, *ppr.* [OFr. *gloser*, from *glose*; see *gloss* (explanation).]

1. originally, to make glosses, or comments, on; to explain.

2. to explain away; to gloss (over).

glōze, *v.i.* 1. to make a gloss or glosses; to comment. [Obs.]

2. to fawn or flatter. [Obs.]

glōze, *n.* 1. a gloss; comment. [Archaic or Rare.]

2. flattery. [Archaic or Rare.]

3. specious talk or insincere action. [Archaic or Rare.]

glōz′ẽr, *n.* a flatterer. [Obs.]

glü·cē′mi·ȧ, glü·cae′mi·ȧ, *n.* same as *glycemia*.

glü′ciç, *a.* [Gr. *glykys*, sweet.] of, pertaining to, or derived from glucose.

glucic acid; an acid produced by the action of alkalis or acids on sugar. It is a colorless, amorphous substance, is very soluble in water, attracts rapidly the moisture of the air, and its solution has a decidedly sour taste. All its neutral salts are soluble.

glü·cī′nȧ, *n.* [Gr. *glykys*, sweet.] BeO, the only oxide of the metal glucinum, or beryllium. Pure glucina is white, tasteless, without odor, and insoluble in water but soluble in the liquid fixed alkalis.

glü·cin′iç ac′id, glucic acid.

glü·cin′i·um, *n.* same as *glucinum*.

glü·cī′num, *n.* [Gr. *glykys*, sweet.] beryllium, a metallic chemical element: symbol, Gl: the former name.

glü′cō·gen, *n.* same as *glycogen*.

glü·cō·gen′e·sis, *n.* same as *glycogenesis*.

glü·cō·hē′mi·ȧ, glü·çō·hae′mi·ȧ, *n.* [Gr. *glykys*, sweet, and *haima*, blood.] same as *glycemia*.

glü·çom′e·tẽr, *n.* [Gr. *glykys*, sweet, and *metron*, a measure.] an instrument for measuring the amount of sugar contained in must.

glü·çon′iç, *a.* of or obtained from glucose; maltonic.

gluconic acid; an acid, $C_6H_{12}O_7$, derived from glucose by oxidation.

glü″çō·prō′tē·in, *n.* glycoprotein.

glü′çōse, *n.* [Gr. *glykys*, sweet.]

1. $C_6H_{12}O_6$, a variety of sugar less sweet than cane sugar, occurring naturally in fruits and honey.

2. in chemistry, any one of a class of carbohydrates having the composition $C_6H_{12}O_6$, and of which ordinary glucose is the type.

3. a sirup obtained in the preparation of grape sugar by incomplete hydrolysis of starch in the presence of dilute acid.

glü·ços′iç, *a.* pertaining to or yielding glucose.

glü′çō·sid, *n.* same as *glucoside*.

glü′çō·sīde, *n.* [*glucose* and *-ide*.] any of a class of compounds, either natural or synthetic, which on hydrolysis yield glucose and one or more other substances.

glü″çō·sid′iç, *a.* of or containing glucosides.

glüe, *n.* [ME. *glue*; OFr. *glu*; LL. *glus*, *glutis*, glue; L. *gluten*; Gr. *glia*, glue.]

1. a hard, brittle gelatin made by boiling animal skins, bones, hoofs, etc. to a jelly: when heated in water, it forms a sticky, viscous liquid used to stick things together.

2. any viscous preparation used to stick things together.

glüe, *v.t.*; glued, *pt.*, *pp.*; gluing, *ppr.* to join with glue or a viscous substance; to fasten, as with glue.

glüe, *v.i.* to become firmly or closely united, fixed, or attached.

glüe′pot, *n.* a pot like a double boiler for melting glue: the outer pot, filled with boiling water, causes the glue in the inner one to melt.

glü′ẽr, *n.* one who or that which glues.

glü′ey, *a.*; *comp.* gluier; *superl.* gluiest, 1. like glue; sticky.

2. covered with or full of glue.

glü′ey·ness, *n.* the quality of being gluey.

glug, *v.i.*; glugged, *pt.*, *pp.*; glugging, *ppr.* [echoic.] to make the muffled, gurgling sound of liquid flowing in spurts from a bottle.

glug, *v.t.* to drink, especially by taking large gulps of.

glug, *n.* 1. a glugging sound.

2. a large gulp of liquid.

glü′ish, *a.* having the nature of glue.

glum, *n.* sullenness; gloominess; a frown. [Obs.]

glum, *a.* [Scot. *gloum*, a frown.] gloomy; sullen; morose; depressed.

glum, *v.i.* to look sullen; to be sour of countenance. [Rare.]

glü·mā′ceous, *a.* 1. having glumes.

2. like glumes.

glüme, *n.* [L. *gluma*, a hull or husk, from *glubere*, to bark, cast off the shell.] in botany, the husk or scalelike bract on the axis of the spikelet in grains and grasses.

glü·mif′ẽr·ous, *a.* [L. *gluma*, a husk, hull, and *ferre*, to bear.] bearing a glume or glumes.

glum′ly, *adv.* in a glum manner; moodily.

glum′ness, *n.* sullenness; gloominess.

glump, *v.i.* [a form of *glum*.] to sulk or appear sullen. [Colloq.]

glump′y, *a.* glum; grumpy; sulky. [Colloq.]

glunch, *n.* a look of disdain, anger, or displeasure. [Scot.]

glunch, *a.* sour; frowning. [Scot.]

glü′on, *n.* [*glue* and *-on*.] a quantum of energy or massless particle postulated to carry the force that binds quarks together within subatomic particles.

glut, *v.i.*; glutted, *pt.*, *pp.*; glutting, *ppr.* [ME. *gloten*, *glotten*; OFr. *glotir*, *gloutir*; L. *glutire*, *gluttire*, to devour, gulp down.] to eat like a glutton; to overindulge.

glut, *v.t.* 1. to feed, fill, supply, etc. to excess; surfeit.

2. to flood (the market) with certain goods so that the supply is greater than the demand.

glut, *n.* [ME. *glut*; OFr. *glut*, *glot*, a glutton, from *glotir*, *gloutir*; L. *glutire*, *gluttire*, to swallow.]

1. a glutting or being glutted.

2. a supply of certain goods that is greater than the demand.

3. anything that obstructs passage, as (a) a wooden wedge serving to prevent a cleft from closing in splitting wood; (b) a piece of wood inserted as a fulcrum beneath a thing to be raised; (c) a brickbat which fills up a course.

4. a piece of canvas sewed into the center of a sail near the head, with an eyelet hole in its middle for the becket to go through.

5. the broad-nosed eel, *Anguilla latirostris*.

6. the offal of fish.

7. that which is swallowed. [Obs.]

Syn.—surplus, redundancy, superfluity, overstock.

glü·tȧ·çon′iç, *a.* [*glut*aric, and *aconi*tic, and *-ic*.] in chemistry, designating or of a white crystalline acid, $C_5H_6O_4$.

glü·tae′us, *n.* same as *gluteus*.

glü·tam′iç, *a.* [*glut*en and *-amic*.] designating or of a colorless crystalline acid, $C_5H_9O_4N$, occurring in seeds and beets.

glü′tȧ·mīne, *n.* [*glut*en, and *-amine*.] a crystalline substance, $C_5H_{10}N_2O_3$, found in the leaves and roots of certain plants.

glü·tar′iç, *a.* [*glut*amic and tart*aric*.] designating or of a white, crystalline compound, $C_5H_8O_4$.

glü′tȧ·zin, glü′tȧ·zine, *n.* a crystalline compound derived from pyridine.

glü·tē′ăl, *a.* of or near the gluteus muscles.

glü′ten, *n.* [L., glue.] a gray, sticky, nutritious substance, found in the flour of wheat and other grain, which gives dough its tough, elastic quality.

glü′ten bread (bred), bread made from flour rich in gluten and low in starch: it is eaten by diabetics.

glü′ten·ous, *a.* 1. like gluten.

2. full of gluten.

glü·tē′us, *n.*; *pl.* **glü·tē′ī,** [Mod. L.; Gr. *gloutos*, rump, buttock.] any of the three muscles that form each of the buttocks and act to extend, abduct, and rotate the thigh.

glü′tin, *n.* same as *gliadin*.

glü′ti·nāte, *v.t.* [L. *glutinatus*, pp. of *glutinare*, to glue.] to unite, as with glue.

glü·ti·nā′tion, *n.* the act of uniting, as with glue.

glü′ti·nā·tive, *a.* tenacious.

glü·ti·nos′i·ty, *n.* viscousness.

glü′ti·nous, *a.* [L. *glutinosus*, from *gluten* (*-inis*), glue.

1. gluey, sticky.

2. in botany, having a sticky, moist surface; as, a *glutinous* leaf.

glü′ti·nous·ness, *n.* the quality of being glutinous.

glü·ti′tion (-tish′un), *n.* the act, power, or process of swallowing. [Rare.]

glut′tŏn, *n.* [ME. *gloton*, *glutun*, OFr. *gloton*, *glouton*; L. *gluto*, *glutto*, a glutton, from *glutire*, *gluttire*, to devour.]

1. one who eats too much.

2. one with a great capacity for something; as, a *glutton* for work.

3. a furry, northern animal related to the marten and weasel but larger: the American variety is called *wolverine*.

glut′tŏn, *a.* greedy.

glut′tŏn·ish, *a.* gluttonous.

glut′tŏn·īze, *v.i.* and *v.t.*; gluttonized, *pt.*, *pp.*; gluttonizing, *ppr.* to eat to excess; to eat greedily or too much.

glut′tŏn·ous, *a.* [OFr. *glotonos*, from *gloton*, a glutton.] given to excessive eating; greedy, voracious.

glut′tŏn·ous·ly, *adv.* in a gluttonous manner.

glut′tŏn·ous·ness, *n.* gluttony; the condition of a glutton.

glut′tŏn·y, *n.* [ME. *glotonie*; OFr. *glotonie*, from *gloton*, a glutton.] the habit or act of eating too much.

glȳ·cē′mi·ȧ, glȳ·cae′mi·ȧ, *n.* [Gr. *glykys*, sweet, and *haima*, blood.] the presence of glucose in the blood.

glyc′ẽr·āte, *n.* [*glycer*in and *-ate*.] a salt or ester of glyceric acid.

glyc′ẽr·iç, *a.* [*glycer*in and *-ic*.] of or derived from glycerin.

glyceric acid; a colorless, sirupy acid, $C_3H_6O_4$, derived from glycerin by the action of nitric acid.

glyc′ẽr·id, *n.* glyceride.

glyc′ẽr·ide, *n.* [*glycer*in and *-ide*.] an ester of glycerin, or glycerol, either natural or synthetic.

glyc′ẽr·in, glyc′ẽr·ine, *n.* [Gr. *glykeros*, sweet, and *-in*, *-ine*.] an odorless, colorless, sirupy liquid, $C_3H_5(OH)_3$, prepared by the hydrolysis of fats and oils: it is used as a solvent, skin lotion, food preservative, etc., and in the manufacture of explosives: in chemistry, called *glycerol*.

glyc′ẽr·īte, *n.* [*glycer*in and *-ite*.] in medicine, any preparation having glycerol, or glycerin, as a solvent.

glyc'ẽr·ōl, glyc'ẽr·ōle, *n.* 1. in chemistry, same as *glycerin.*
2. same as *glycerite.*

glyc'ẽr·yl, *n.* [*glycer*in and *-yl.*] the trivalent radical of glycerin, C_3H_5.

glyc'ẽr·yl tri·nī'trāte, nitroglycerin.

glyc'id, glyc'ide, *n.* a compound obtained from certain derivatives of glycerin.

gly·cid'iç, *a.* pertaining to glycid.

gly̆'cin, *n.* same as *glycine.*

gly̆'cīne, *n.* [from G. *glykys*, sweet, and *-ine.*] a sweet, crystalline substance, $NH_2CH_2CO_2H$, obtained by hydrolysis from proteins and having the properties of an amino acid.

gly̆'ço-, [Gr. *glyko-*, from *glykys*, sweet.] a combining form meaning *glycerin, glycerol, glycogen,* as in *glyco*genesis.

gly̆·çō·chō'lāte, *n.* [*glycocol*ic and *-ate.*] a salt or ester of glycocholic acid.

gly̆·çō·çhol'iç, *a.* [Gr. *glykys*, sweet, and *cholē*, gall.] derived from gall; as, *glycocholic* acid.
glycocholic acid; a colorless crystalline acid, $C_{26}H_{43}O_6N$, found in bile.

gly̆'çō·cin, *n.* same as *glycine.*

gly̆'çō·çoll, *n.* [Gr. *glykys*, sweet, and *kolla*, glue.] same as *glycine.*

gly̆'çō·gen, *n.* [Gr. *glykys*, sweet, and *-genēs*, producing.] an insoluble, starchlike substance, $(C_6H_{10}O_5)x$, produced in animal tissues, especially in the liver and muscles, and changed into a simple sugar as the body needs it: also called *animal starch.*

gly̆·çō·gen'e·sis, *n.* the formation of glycogen.

gly̆·çō·gen'iç, *a.* relating to glycogen or glycogenesis.

gly̆·çog'e·ny, *n.* glycogenesis.

gly̆·çō·hē'mi·å, gly̆·çō·hae'mi·å, *n.* same as *glucemia.*

gly̆'çol, *n.* [*glyc*erin and alcoh*ol.*]
1. a colorless, sirupy liquid, $C_2H_4(OH)_2$, prepared by heating any of certain ethylene compounds with an alkali carbonate and used as an antifreeze: more accurately, *ethylene glycol.*
2. any of a group of alcohols of which this compound is the type.

gly̆·çol'iç, *a.* of or containing glycol.
glycolic acid; a crystalline acid, $C_2H_4O_3$, found naturally in unripe grapes or artificially prepared from glycol.

gly̆'çō·lid, gly̆'çōl·lide, *n.* [*glycol*ic and *-id.*] a substance derived from glycolic acid as an amorphous powder by treatment with dry heat.

gly̆·çō·lū'ril, *n.* [*glycol*yl and *ur*ic.] acetylene urea, obtained variously, as by the reaction of urea and oxalic aldehyde with hydrochloric acid.

gly̆'çō·lyl, *n.* [*glycol*ic and *-yl.*] in organic chemistry, the bivalent radical $CO{\cdot}CH_2$, considered to be the essential radical of glycolic acid and many other compounds.

gly̆''çō·nē·ō·gen'e·sis, *n.* [*glyco-* and *neo-* and *-genesis.*] the formation of glycogen.

Gly̆·çō'ni·ăn, *a.* same as *Glyconic.*

Gly̆·çon'iç, *a.* [LL. *Glyconius*; Gr. *Glykōneios*, from *Glycōn*, the inventor of this meter.] pertaining to a verse or meter, consisting of four feet, one dactyl and three trochees.

Gly̆·çon'iç, *n.* a Glyconic verse.

gly̆'çō·nin, *n.* an ointment made by emulsifying glycerin with yolk of egg.

gly̆·çō·prō'tē·id, *n.* a glycoprotein.

gly̆·çō·prō'tē·in, *n.* any of a class of compounds in which a protein is combined with a carbohydrate group: also *glucoprotein.*

gly̆'çōse, *n.* same as *glucose.*

gly̆'çō·sin, gly̆'çō·sine, *n.* [*glyco*l (*-s-*) and *-ine.*] a crystalline compound prepared by treating oxalic aldehyde with ammonia.

gly̆·çō·sū'ri·å, *n.* an abnormal condition in which sugar is excreted in the urine.

gly̆·çō·sū'riç, *a.* of or having glycosuria.

Glyc·yr·rhī'zå (-rī'), *n.* [Gr. *glykyrrhiza*, licorice, from *glykys*, sweet, and *rhiza*, root.]
1. a genus of plants with sweet roots, including the licorice plant, *Glycyrrhiza glabra*, which yields the licorice root of commerce.
2. [g–] in medicine, licorice root.

glyc·yr·rhī'zin (-rī'), *n.* a sweet matter obtained from the root of *Glycyrrhiza glabra*; licorice.

glyn, glynn, *n.* [W. *glyn*, a glen.] a glen: used in Celtic place names.

gly̆·ox'ăl, *n.* [*gly*col and *oxal*ic.] oxalic aldehyde, obtained by slowly oxidizing glycol or acetic aldehyde.

gly̆·ox·al'iç, *a.* pertaining to or derived from glyoxal.

gly̆·ox'å·lin, *n.* [*glyoxal* and *-in.*] a compound derived from glyoxal by the action of ammonia or a cold solution; hence, any compound of a series similarly constituted.

gly̆·ox'im, gly̆·ox'ime, *n.* [*gly*oxal and *-oxim.*] a compound derived from glyoxal by treatment with hydroxylamin; hence, any compound of similar structure.

glyph (glif), *n.* [Gr. *glyphē*, a carving, from *glyphein*, to carve, cut.]
1. a carved figure, either incised or in relief; carved pictograph; hieroglyph.
2. in architecture, a vertical channel or groove.

glyph'iç, *n.* [Gr. *glyphikos*, from *glyphē*, a carving.] a hieroglyphic; a picture or figure implying a word.

glyph'iç, *a.* having to do with a glyph; carved; sculptured.

glyph'ō·gråph, *n.* a plate or print prepared by glyphography.

glyph·ō·gråph'iç, *a.* of or pertaining to glyphography.

gly·phog'rå·phy, *n.* [Gr. *glyphē*, a carving, and *graphein*, to write.] a method of producing a printing plate by engraving on a wax-coated copperplate which is then used to make an electrotype.

glyp'tiç, *a.* [L.Gr. *glyptikos*, from Gr. *glyptos*, fit for carving, carved, from *glyphein*, to carve.]
1. having to do with carving or engraving, especially on gems.
2. in mineralogy, figured.

glyp'tiçs, *n.* the art of engraving figures on precious stones.

glyp'tō·dont, *n.* [Gr. *glyptos*, carved, and *odous, odontos*, a tooth.] an extinct South American mammal of the armadillo family, of the size of an ox and having a carapace composed of a single solid piece.

GLYPTODONT (*Glyptodon clavipes*)

glyp'tō·gråph, *n.* [Gr. *glyptos*, carved, and *graphein*, to write.]
1. a carving on a precious stone or other small object.
2. a gem, seal, etc. so engraved.

glyp·tō·graph'iç, *a.* pertaining to glyptography.

glyp·tog'rå·phy, *n.* the art or study of engraving on precious stones.

glyp'tō·lith, a pebble or stone having facets that have been formed and polished by the action of the weather.

glyp·tō·thē'çå, *n.*; *pl.* **glyp·tō·thē'cae,** [Gr. *glyptos*, carved, *glypton*, a carved image, and *thēkē*, a case, repository.] a building or room for the preservation of works of sculpture.

glys'tẽr, *n.* same as *clyster.*

G'-man, *n.*; *pl.* **G'-men,** [*G*overnment *man.*] an agent of the Federal Bureau of Investigation. [Colloq.]

Gmel'in·å (mel'), *n.* [named after Prof. S. G. *Gmelin*, 18th-c. G. botanist.] an Asiatic genus of plants belonging to the order *Verbenaceæ.*

gmel'in·īte, *n.* [named after Christian G. *Gmelin*, 19th-c. G. chemist.] in mineralogy, a mineral of a white passing into a flesh-red color: it is a hydrated silicate of alumina, lime, and soda.

gnå·phal'i·oid (nå-), *a.* in botany, resembling the genus *Gnaphalium.*

Gnå·phā'li·um (nå-), *n.* [Gr. *gnaphalion*, a downy plant used in stuffing cushions.] a genus of plants of the order *Compositæ*, known by the popular names of *cudweed* and *everlasting.*

gnär, gnärr (när), *v.i.* to growl; to snarl.

gnär, gnärr (när), *n.* [ME. *knarre, gnarre*, a knot.] a knot; specifically, a hard knot on a tree. [Rare.]

gnärl (närl), *v.i.*; gnarled, *pt., pp.*; gnarling, *ppr.* [D. *knorren*; G. *gnarren*; L.G. *knurren, gnurren*, to snarl, growl.] to growl; to snarl.

gnärl, *n.* [a dim. from *gnar.*] a knot on the outside of a tree.
Gnarls without and knots within.
—Landor.

gnärl, *v.t.* to twist; contort; make knotted.

gnärl, *v.i.* to form gnarls.

gnärled, *a.* knotty; full of knots; knobby; twisted; as, the *gnarled* oak.

gnärl'y, *a.* knotty; full of knots; gnarled.

gnash (nash), *v.t.*; gnashed (nasht), *pt., pp.*; gnashing, *ppr.* [ME. *gnasten*, to gnash the teeth; Ice. *gnesta*, to crack; Dan. *knaske*, to crush with the teeth.]
1. to grind or strike (the teeth) together.
2. to grind the teeth upon; bite by grinding the teeth.

gnash, *v.i.* to grind the teeth together, as in rage or pain.
There they him laid
Gnashing for anguish, and despite, and shame. —Milton.

gnash'ing, *n.* a grinding or grating together of the teeth in rage or anguish.
There shall be weeping and *gnashing* of teeth. —Matt. viii. 12.

gnash'ing·ly, *adv.* with gnashing.

gnat (nat), *n.* [ME. *gnat*; AS. *gnæt*, a gnat.]
1. any of several small, two-winged insects of the genus *Culex*, that bite or sting.
2. a mosquito. [Brit.]
to strain at a gnat; to find it hard or impossible to believe or assent to something of trifling importance.

gnat'çatch''ẽr (nat'), *n.* a small American bird of the genus *Polioptila*, related to the kinglets.

gnat flow'ẽr (nat), same as *bee orchis.*

gnat hawk (nat), in zoology, the goatsucker.

gnath'iç (nath'), *a.* [Gr. *gnathos*, a jaw, and *-ic.*] in anatomy, pertaining to the jaw.

gnath'iç in'dex, a measurement of the relative amount of protrusion of the jaw, expressed in terms of the ratio of the distance from the nasion to the basion (arbitrarily taken as 100) to the distance from the basion to the middle point of the alveolar process.

gnå·thid'i·um (nå-), *n.*; *pl.* **gnå·thid'i·å,** [Gr. *gnathos*, a jaw, and dim. *-idion.*] in ornithology, either prong of the naked portion of the lower jaw.

gnā'thi·on (nā'), *n.* [Mod. L., from Gr. *gnathos.*] the lowest point on the median line of the lower jaw.

gnā'thism (nā'), *n.* [Gr. *gnathos*, a jaw, and *-ism.*] the classification of skulls according to measurements of the jaw.

gnath'īte (nath'), *n.* [Gr. *gnathos*, a jaw, and *-ite.*] in zoology, any of the mouth appendages of Arthropoda.

gnā'thō-, [from Gr. *gnathos*, jaw.] a combining form used in zoology, anatomy, etc. to signify *jaw*, as in *Gnatho*stoma, *Gnatho*poda.

gnå·thon'iç, gnå·thon'iç·ăl (nå-), *a.* [L. *Gnatho*, the name of a parasite in the *Eunuchus* of Terence.] flattering; deceitful; fawning.

gnath'ō·pod (nath'), *n.* 1. an animal belonging to the *Gnathopoda.*
2. same as *gnathopodite.*

gnath'ō·pod, *a.* [*gnatho-*, and Gr. *pous, podos*, a foot.] having jawfeet.

Gnå·thop'ō·då (nå-), *n.* [*gnatho-*, and Gr. *pous, podos*, a foot.] in zoology, a division of invertebrates embracing all animals with jawfeet, or appendages performing the functions of locomotion and mastication, as crustaceans.

gnå·thop'ō·dīte (nå-), *n.* [*gnatho-*, and Gr. *pous, podos*, a foot.] in zoology, one of those limbs which, in crustaceans, have been modified into chewing organs.

gnå·thop'ō·dous (nå-), *a.* having jawfeet; pertaining to a gnathopod.

gnå·thos'te·gīte (nå-), *n.* [*gnatho-*, and Gr. *stegos*, a roof, and *-ite.*] in zoology, an expanded maxilliped, or jawfoot, occurring on each side of the mouth of a crustacean, which serves as a cover for the other mouth parts.

Gnå·thos'tō·må (nå-), *n.* [*gnatho-*, and Gr. *stoma* (*-atos*), a mouth.] a division of crustaceans including the branchiopods.

Gnath·ō·stō'må·tå (nath-), *n.pl.* same as *Gnathostoma.*

Gnå·thos'tō·mī (nå-), *n.pl.* a class of vertebrates with functional jaws, including all except the hags, lampreys, and lancelets.

gnath·ō·thē'çå (nath-), *n.*; *pl.* **gnath·ō·thē'cae,** [*gnatho-*, and Gr. *thēkē*, a case, box.] in ornithology, the horny sheath of the lower mandible.

-gnå·thous, [from Gr. *gnathos.*] a combining form meaning *having a* (specified kind of) *jaw*, as in prog*nathous.*

gnat'ling (nat'), *n.* a little gnat.

gnat'snap''pẽr (nat'), *n.* a bird that eats gnats.

gnat'wŏrm (nat'), *n.* the larva of a gnat; a wiggler.

gnaw (nä), *v.t.*; gnawed, *pt.*; gnawed *or* gnawn, *pp.*; gnawing, *ppr.* [ME. *gnawen, gnagen*; AS. *gnagan*, to gnaw.]
1. to cut, bite, and wear away bit by bit with the teeth; as, the rats *gnaw* a board or plank.
2. to make by gnawing.
3. to waste away; to consume; to corrode.
4. to torment, as by constant pain, fear, etc.; harass.
5. to bite in agony or rage; as, to *gnaw* a pen in anger.

gnaw, *v.i.* 1. to bite repeatedly (with *on, away, at*, etc.).
2. to produce an effect of continual biting, consuming, corroding, etc. (with *on, away, at*, etc.); torment.

gnaw'ẽr, *n.* 1. one who or that which gnaws or corrodes.
2. in zoology, any rodent.

gnaw'ing, *n.* 1. a sensation of dull, constant pain or suffering.
2. [*pl.*] pangs, especially of hunger.

gnawn, *v.* alternative past participle of *gnaw*.

gneiss (nīs), *n.* [G.] in mineralogy, a coarse-grained, metamorphic rock composed of quartz, feldspar, and mica, of a structure more or less slaty: if it contains hornblende instead of mica, it is called *syenitic gneiss*.

gneis'siç, *a.* of, like, or composed of gneiss.

gneis'soid, *a.* like gneiss.

gneis'sōse, *a.* like gneiss.

Gnē·tā'cē·ae (nē-), *n.pl.* [from *gnemon* or *gnemo*, the native name in the island of Ternate, and *-aceæ*.] a family of gymnogenous plants, popularly called joint firs, consisting of small trees or shrubs, with flowers arranged in catkins or heads.

gnē·tā'ceous (nē-), *a.* belonging to the *Gnetaceæ*.

gnew, *v.* obsolete past tense of *gnaw*.

gnīde (nīd), *v.t.* [ME. *gniden*; AS. *gnidan*, to rub, break in pieces.] to break in pieces; to pulverize; to rub; to crush. [Obs.]

gnoff, gnof (nof), *n.* [etym. doubtful.] a miser; a churl. [Obs.]

gnōme (nōm), *n.* [Fr. *gnome*, from Gr. *gnōmē*, thought, intelligence; so called from the belief that *gnomes* knew of hidden treasures.
1. in folklore, any of a race of small, misshapen dwarfs supposed to inhabit the inner parts of the earth and to be the guardian of mines, quarries, etc.
2. a small, misshapen person; a dwarf.
3. in zoology, the gnome owl; also, any of several hummingbirds.

gnōme, *n.* [LL. *gnome*, a sentence, maxim; Gr. *gnōmē*, thought, judgment, intelligence, from *gignōskein*, to know.] a brief reflection or maxim; a wise, pithy saying.

gnōme owl, a small owl, *Glaucidium gnoma*: called also *pygmy owl*.

gnom'iç, gnom'iç·ăl (nom'), *a.* [Gr. *gnōmikos*, from *gnōmē*, intelligence, a maxim.]
1. wise and pithy; full of aphorisms.
2. designating or of a writer of aphorisms.
gnomic poets; a group of Greek poets of the 6th and 7th centuries B. C., whose writings were largely gnomic.

gnōm'ish (nōm'), *a.* like a gnome, or dwarf.

gnō·mō·log'iç, gnō·mō·log'iç·ăl (nō-), *a.* pertaining to gnomology.

gnō·mol'ō·gy, *n.* [Gr. *gnōmologia*, a speaking in maxims, a collection of maxims; *gnōmē*, intelligence, a maxim, and *legein*, to speak.] a collection of maxims, precepts, or reflections. [Rare.]

gnō'mon (nō'), *n.* [Gr. *gnōmōn*, one who knows or examines, the index of a sundial, a carpenter's rule, from *gignōskein*, to know.]
1. the metal triangle or pin on a sundial, which, by its shadow, shows the time of day.
2. in astronomy, a style or column erected perpendicular to the horizon: its principal use was to find the meridian altitude of the sun by measuring the length of the shadow.
3. in geometry, the part of a parallelogram remaining after a similar parallelogram has been taken from one of its corners.
4. in an arithmetical series, one of the terms by which polygonal numbers are found.

gnō·mon'iç, gnō·mon'iç·ăl, *a.* 1. of a gnomon, or sundial.
2. of the measurement of time by sundials.
gnomonic projection; a representation of one of the hemispheres of the earth on a flat surface, the pole being the center of that surface, and the point of sight being taken at the center of the sphere.

gnō·mon'iç·ăl·ly, *adv.* according to the principles of the gnomonic projection.

gnō·mon'içs, *n.* [Gr. *gnōmonikē* (supply *technē*, art), the art of dialing; *gnōmonikē*, f. of *gnōmonikos*, pertaining to a gnomon or dial.] the art or science of dialing, or of constructing dials to show the hour of the day by the shadow of a gnomon. [Obs.]

gnō·mon·ol'ō·ġy, *n.* [Gr. *gnōmōn*, a gnomon, and *-logia*, from *legein*, to speak.] a treatise on gnomonics.

-gnō·my, [Gr. *-gnomia*, from *gnōmē*.] a combining form meaning *art* or *science of judging or determining*, as in physio*gnomy*.

gnō'sis, *n.* [Gr. *gnōsis*, knowledge, from *gignōskein*, to know.] superior wisdom; knowledge of mysteries or spiritual truth, such as was claimed to have been mystically acquired by the Gnostics.

-gnō·sis, [from Gr. *gnōsis*, knowledge.] a combining form meaning *knowledge, recognition*, as in dia*gnosis*.

Gnos'tiç (nos'), *a.* [L. *gnosticus*; Gr. *gnōstikos*, knowing, sagacious, from *gignōskein*, to know.]
1. of the Gnostics or Gnosticism.
2. [g-] shrewd; knowing; wise.

Gnos'tiç, *n.* one of a class of rationalists in the early history of the Christian church; also, any believer in Gnosticism.

-gnos·tiç, [from Gr. *gnōstikos*, knowing, from *gnōsis*.] a combining form meaning *of knowledge, of recognition*, as in dia*gnostic*.

gnos'tiç·ăl·ly, *adv.* 1. knowingly. [Colloq.]
2. in the manner or according to the doctrines of the Gnostics.

Gnos'ti·çism, *n.* a system of mystical religious and philosophical doctrines, combining Christianity with Greek and Oriental philosophies, propagated by early Christian sects that were denounced as heretical.

gnos·tic'i·ty, *n.* a gnostic character.

gnō'thi se·au·ton', [Gr. *gnōthi seauton*.] the motto—know thyself: it is inscribed on the temple of Apollo at Delphi.

gnū (nū), *n.* [Hottentot *gnu* or *nju*.] a large African antelope with an oxlike head and horns and a horselike mane and tail: also called *wildebeest*.

GNU (4 1/2 ft. high at shoulder)

gō, *v.i.*; went, *pt.*; gone, *pp.*; going, *ppr.* [ME. *go(n)*, *goon*; AS. *gan*.]
1. to move along; travel; proceed; as, this car can go 90 miles an hour.
2. to be moving; as, who *goes* there?
3. to move; work; operate; as, do you want to see the merry-go-round *go?*
4. to work or operate properly; function in the intended way; as, the motor won't *go*.
5. to behave in a certain way; to gesture, act, or make sounds as specified or shown; as, he *went* like this; the balloon *went* "pop."
6. to take or follow a particular course, line of action, etc.; specifically, (a) to result; turn out; as, the war *went* badly; (b) to be guided, regulated, or directed by a procedure, method, etc.; as, I shall *go* by what you say; (c) to take its course; to proceed; as, how is the evening *going?*
7. to pass: said of time.
8. to pass from person to person; as, a rumor *went* through the office.
9. to be known or accepted; as, she *goes* by the name of Kindsay.
10. to move about or be in a certain condition or state, usually for some time; as, he *goes* in rags.
11. to pass into a certain condition, state, etc.; to become; turn; as, she *went* conservative.
12. to have a certain form, arrangement, etc.; to be expressed, phrased, voiced, or sung; as, how does the old story *go?*
13. to be or act in harmony; to fit in; as, this hat *goes* well with the dress.
14. to put oneself; as, please don't *go* to any trouble.
15. to move off; to leave; depart.
16. to begin to move off, as in a race: used as a command.
17. (a) originally, to leave a court of justice; (b) to continue (unpunished, unrewarded, unrequited, etc.).
18. to cease to have an effect; to come to an end; pass away; as, the pain has *gone*.
19. to die.
20. to be done away with; to be abolished; as, poverty must *go*.
21. to break away; to be carried away or broken off; as, the mast *went* in the storm.
22. to fail; to give way; as, his eyesight will *go* first.
23. to be given up or sacrificed; as, the country house must *go*.
24. to pass into the hands of someone; to come under control of someone; to be allotted or given; as, the prize *goes* to Jean.
25. to be sold at; as, it *went* for $20.
26. to move toward a place or person or in a certain direction; as, when are you *going* to New York?
27. to move out of sight or out of the presence of a person: used as a command.
28. to make regularly scheduled trips to a place or between places; as, this bus *goes* to Canton.
29. (a) to extend, lead, reach, run, etc. to a place; as, this road *goes* to London; (b) to be able to extend or reach; as, the belt won't *go* around his waist.
30. to move toward, enter, or attend and then take part in the activities of, engage in, etc.: (a) additional meaning is conveyed by the use of a noun governed by *to*, or by a participle; as, he *goes to* college, let's *go* swimming; (b) reason for going is indicated by an infinitive, by *and* with a verb, or by a noun governed by *to*; as, he may *go* hang, I'll *go and* find out, he has *gone to* breakfast.
31. to carry one's case, plan, etc. to an authority; as, you must *go* to the president.
32. to turn to a certain activity; to resort to some occupation, etc.; as, do you think they will *go* to war?
33. to carry one's activity to certain lengths; to extend or reach so far in behavior, action, etc.; as, how far did he *go* in his protests?
34. to endure; last; hold out.
35. to have a particular or regular place or position; as, the shirts *go* in the second drawer.
to go about; (a) to take first steps, as in an enterprise; to undertake; (b) in nautical usage, to turn the head of a ship.
to go abroad; to go away from home, as to a foreign country.
to go by; (a) to pass near or beyond; (b) to be overlooked.
to go by the board; to be passed over; to be lost in the confusion.
to go down; (a) to sink or founder; to fail; (b) to be perpetuated, as in history.
to go far; to have much weight, influence, or value.
to go for; (a) to go in search of; (b) to represent; to pass for; (c) to assail personally or otherwise; (d) to be attracted by. [Slang.]
to go hard with; to cause much pain or embarrassment to.
to go in for; to enter or undertake anything with a view to final results; as, *to go in for* golf, honors, politics, etc. [Colloq.]
to go off; (a) to leave; to depart; (b) to explode or be discharged; (c) to happen.
to go on; (a) to proceed; to advance or continue; (b) to be put on or fitted over; (c) in the theater, to make an entrance.
to go one better; to surpass or outdo, as in a contest or rivalry of any kind.
to go out; (a) to be extinguished; (b) to be outdated.
to go over; (a) to cross or traverse; (b) to review; (c) to succeed.
to go through; (a) to sustain to the end; (b) to endure, suffer, or bear.
to go under; (a) to be known by or to pass by (a name, title, etc.); (b) to be overwhelmed or defeated; to perish; to fail, as in business.
to go up; to increase in value or price.
to go with; (a) to accompany; (b) to suit or harmonize with; to agree or coincide with.
to go without; to manage without.
to go without saying; to be taken for granted.
to go wrong; to stray or wander; to fall from virtue.

gō, *v.t.* 1. to contribute or furnish; as, he *went* security for his brother.
2. to wager or bet; as, I'll *go* you a dollar.
3. to tolerate; to put up with. [Slang.]
to go halves: to share equally with another.

gō, *n.*; *pl.* **gōeṣ,** 1. the act of going.
2. something that operates successfully; a success.
3. the power of going; animation; energy. [Colloq.]
4. a state of affairs. [Colloq.]
5. fashion; vogue (with *the*). [Colloq.]
6. an agreement; bargain. [Colloq.]
7. a try; attempt; endeavor. [Colloq.]
8. a quantity given or taken at one time. [Brit. Colloq.]
9. in cribbage, a situation in which a player can lay no card that will not carry the count above 31: the last card played counts one point.
from the word go; from the very beginning.
no go; of no avail; of no use. [Slang.]
on the go; busy; moving about; unsettled. [Colloq.]

gō'ȧ, *n.* [native name.]
1. an antelope, *Procapra picticauda*, native to Tibet.
2. the marsh crocodile.

gōad, *n.* [ME. *gode, god, gad*; AS. *gad*; akin to Lombardic *gaida*, javelin.]
1. a sharp-pointed stick used in driving oxen.
2. any driving impulse; spur.

gōad, *v.t.*; goaded, *pt., pp.*; goading, *ppr.* to drive with or as with a goad; to prick, spur, stimulate; to rouse or incite; as, a people *goaded* by oppression.
That temptation that doth *goad* us on.
—Shak.

gōaf, *n.*; *pl.* **gōaveṣ,** 1. in mining, a section from which the mineral has been almost entirely worked; also, the refuse left from the workings.
2. a grain or hay stack in a barn. [Brit. Dial.]

gō'-ȧ·head' (-hed'), *a.* progressive; energetic; enterprising. [Colloq.]

gōal, *n.* [ME. *gol*, boundary; prob., from hyp. AS. *gal*, inferred from *gælan*, to hinder, impede.]
1. the line or place at which a race is ended; the mark.
Part curb their fiery steeds, or shun the *goal*
With rapid wheels. —Milton.
2. the end or final purpose; the end to which a design tends or which a person aims to reach or accomplish.
Each individual seeks a several *goal*.
—Pope.
3. in certain games, (a) the line, crossbar, or net over or into which the ball or puck must be passed to score; (b) the act of scoring in this way; (c) the score made; (d) a goalkeeper.

gōal'iē, *n.* a goalkeeper. [Colloq.]

gōal'keep''ẽr, *n.* in certain games, a player stationed at a goal to prevent the ball or puck from crossing or entering it: also *goal tender*.

gōal līne, a line representing the goal in various games; especially, in football, either of the two lines, one at each end of the field, across which the ball must be carried or caught for a touchdown.

gōal pōst, either of a pair of upright posts with a crossbar, used as a goal in football, soccer, etc.: in football the ball must be kicked over the crossbar to score a field goal or an extra point after a touchdown.

gō·an'nȧ, *n.* an iguana: an Australian name.

Gō'ȧ pow'dẽr, [from *Goa*, a city of the Malabar Islands.] a bitter powder obtained from a Brazilian tree, *Andira araroba*, and used in medicine.

gōat, *n.* [ME. *gote, goot, gat*; AS. *gat*, a goat.]
1. a horned ruminant quadruped of the genus *Capra*. The horns are hollow, turned backward, rough, and annular on the surface. The male is generally bearded under the chin. Goats are found in all parts of the world, and many varieties are valued for their hair or wool, as the *Cashmere goat*, the *Angora goat*, etc.

CASHMERE GOAT

2. a lecherous man.
3. a person forced to take the blame or punishment for others; scapegoat. [Slang.]
4. [G–] the constellation Capricorn.
to get one's goat; to annoy, anger, or irritate one. [Slang.]

gōat an'tē·lōpe, an antelope of the genus *Nemorhedus*, much like a goat in general appearance.

gōat·ee', *n.* a pointed beard so trimmed that a part of it hangs down from the lower lip or chin, like the beard of a goat.

gōat fig, the wild fig.

gōat'fish, *n.*; *pl.* **gōat'fish** or **gōat'fish·eṣ,** any of several edible fishes of the mullet family, found in tropical waters, with large scales, one or more long barbels attached to the lower jaw, and bright coloration.

gōat'hẽrd, *n.* one who tends goats.

gōat'ish, *a.* 1. resembling a goat in any quality.
2. wanton; lustful; lecherous.

gōat'ish·ly, *adv.* in a goatish manner; lustfully.

gōat'ish·ness, *n.* the quality of being goatish.

gōat mär'jō·răm, wild marjoram.

gōat'milk''ẽr, *n.* the European goatsucker.

gōat mọth, *Cossus ligniperda*, a large moth of a dark color, that feeds on the wood of willows: so called because of its rank odor.

gōat owl, the European goatsucker.

gōats'bāne, *n. Aconitum lycoctonum*, the plant wolfsbane.

gōats'bēard, *n.* 1. any of a group of hardy herbs of the rose family, with spikes of white flowers in clusters.
2. a European plant with yellow or purple flower heads: the root of the purple variety is the vegetable salsify.

gōat's'-chiç'ō·ry, *n.* the fireweed, *Erechtites hieracifolia*.

gōats'foot, *n.* a plant, *Oxalis caprina*, native to South Africa.

gōats'foot çon·vol'vū·lus, the morning-glory found on sea beaches.

gōat's'-hāir, *n.* a formation of short, white, fleecy-looking clouds, said to be a portent of rain.

gōat's'-họrn, *n. Astragalus ægiceras*, a leguminous plant of southern Europe.

gōat'skin, *n.* 1. the skin of a goat or leather made from it.
2. a container for wine, water, etc. made of this leather.

gōat's'-rụe, *n.* a plant, *Galega officinalis*.

gōat's'-thọrn, *n.* any of several thorny leguminous plants of the Levant, as *Astragalus tragacanthus* or *Astragalus poterium*.

gōat'stōne, *n.* a bezoar from a goat.

gōat'suçk''ẽr, *n.* any of various species of nocturnal birds of the genus *Caprimulgus* that feed on insects such as moths, gnats, beetles, etc.: American species include the whippoorwill and nighthawks.

gōat'weed, *n.* 1. the goutweed, *Ægopodium podagraria*.
2. either of two West Indian plants of the figwort family, *Capraria biflora* or *Stemodia durantifolia*.

gōaveṣ, *n.* plural of *goaf*.

gob, *n.* [abbrev. of *gobbet*.] a lump, chunk, or mass, especially of something semiliquid, slimy, etc. [Colloq.]

gob, *n.* the mouth. [Brit. Dial.]

gob, *n.* [origin doubtful.] a sailor of the United States Navy. [Slang.]

gō·bäng', *n.* [Japan. *goban*, a checkerboard.] a Japanese game for two players, played on a checkerboard with colored counters, the object being to place five counters in a row in any direction: also spelled *goban*.

gobbe, *n.* [name in Surinam, South America.] a tropical leguminous plant, *Voandzeia subterranea*, the pods of which are matured beneath the ground. It resembles the peanut.

gob'bet, *n.* [ME. *gobette, gobet*; OFr. *gobet, goubet*, dim. of *gobe*, mouth.]
1. a fragment or bit, especially of raw flesh.
2. a lump; a chunk; a mass.
3. a mouthful.
[Archaic or Rare in all senses.]

gob'bet, *v.t.* to swallow in masses or mouthfuls. [Obs.]

gob'bet·ly, *adv.* in pieces. [Obs.]

gob'bing, *n.* in mining, the refuse thrown back into excavations after the coal is removed.

gob'ble, *v.t.* and *v.i.*; gobbled, *pt., pp.*; gobbling, *ppr.* [prob. echoic freq. from OFr. *gober*, to swallow greedily.]
1. to swallow in large pieces; to swallow hastily.
2. to seize greedily; to acquire graspingly. [Slang.]

gob'ble, *n.* [echoic; var. of *gabble*.] the characteristic throaty noise made by a turkey cock.

gob'ble, *v.i.*; gobbled, *pt., pp.*; gobbling, *ppr.* to make the throaty sound of a turkey.

gob'blẽr, *n.* a turkey cock.

Gob'e·lin (*or Fr. pron.* gō-be-laṅ'), *a.* pertaining to the Gobelins, a French factory in Paris, or designating, of, or like the tapestry or upholstery manufactured there.

Gob'e·lin, *n.* a kind of tapestry made at the Gobelins in France.

gōbe·mōuçhe', *n.* [Fr.] a simpleton; a silly, credulous individual.

gob'et, *n.* a gobbet. [Obs.]

gō'-bē·tween, *n.* one who acts as an intermediary between two parties, as an agent or mediator: often in an unfavorable sense, implying shady dealings.

gō'bi·oid, *a.* [L. *gobius*; Gr. *kōbios*, the gudgeon, and *eidos*, form.]
1. of the family of gobies.
2. pertaining to or resembling a goby.

gō'bi·oid, *n.* a goby; a fish of the genus *Gobius*.

gob'let, *n.* [OFr. *gobelet, goblet*, dim. of *gobel*, a goblet, from LL. *cupellus*, a cup, dim. of L. *cupa*, a tub, cask.]
1. originally, a kind of cup or drinking vessel without a handle.
2. a drinking glass with a base and stem.

gob'lin, *n.* [ME. *gobelyn*; OFr. *gobelin*; ML. *gobelinus*, perh. from *cobalus*; Gr. *kobalos*, a rogue, sprite.] an evil or mischievous spirit, conceived of as ugly or misshapen.

gob'līne, *n.* in nautical usage, a rope leading inward from the martingale; a backrope.

gob'lin·īze, *v.t.*; goblinized, *pt., pp.*; goblinizing, *ppr.* to change into a goblin; to make evil or mischievous like a goblin. [Rare.]

gob'ō·nā·ted, *a.* in heraldry, componé.

gob'o·né (gob'ō-nā), **gō·bō'ny,** *a.* same as *componé*.

gob'stick, *n.* in angling, a device for taking the hook out of a fish's gullet.

gō'by, *n.*; *pl.* **gō'bieṣ** or **gō'by,** [L. *gobio, gobius*, a gudgeon.] any of a group of small, spiny-finned fishes, widely distributed throughout warm and temperate seas: the ventral fins are modified to form a suction disk.

gō'-bȳ, *n.* a passing without recognition; especially, an intentional disregard or slight: usually in *to give* (or *get*) *the go-by*, to slight (or be slighted). [Colloq.]

gō'cärt, *n.* 1. a small framework with casters in which children can learn to walk by pushing themselves along with no danger of falling.
2. a type of light carriage.
3. a small, folding, four-wheeled chair or carriage for a young child to ride in: it can be drawn or pushed by hand.

god, *a.* and *n.* good. [Obs.]

god, *n.* [ME. *god, godd*; AS. *god*, god; akin to L.G. *god*; M.H.G. *got*; Ice. *godh*; Sw. *gud*; Dan. *gud*; Goth. *guth*, god.]
1. any of various beings conceived of as supernatural, immortal, and having special powers over the lives and affairs of people and the course of nature; deity, especially a male deity.
2. [G–] in monotheistic religions, the creator and ruler of the universe, regarded as eternal, infinite, all-powerful, and all-knowing; Supreme Being; Almighty: often used in exclamations, as, good *God! God* almighty!
3. a person or thing that is excessively worshiped and admired; an all-absorbing passion, pursuit, or hobby; something idolized.
Thou *god* of our idolatry, the Press.
—Cowper.
4. an idol.
5. a spectator or auditor in the gallery of a theater.
God willing; if God is willing.
household gods; (a) in Roman mythology, the gods presiding over the household; (b) those things treasured from association with home-life.
the house of God; a house dedicated to the worship of God; a temple; a church.

god, *v.t.* to deify. [Obs.]

god'chīld, *n.*; *pl.* **god'chil''dren,** one for whom a person becomes sponsor at baptism.

God'dam, *n.* [so called from the oath common to Englishmen.] an Englishman: a name given contemptuously by the French.

god'damned, *a.* strongly cursed or damned: used as a curse or strong intensive, often shortened to *goddamn, goddam*.

god'daugh''tẽr (-da''), *n.* a female godchild.

god′dess, *n.* 1. a female deity.
2. a woman of very great charm or beauty, or of surpassing goodness.

gōde, *a.* and *n.* good. [Obs.]

god′et, *n.* [OFr. *godet, goudet,* a tankard.] a tankard. [Obs.]

Gō·dē′ti·ȧ (-shi-ȧ), *n.* [named after M. *Godet,* of Switzerland.] a small genus of plants of the evening primrose family, having purple or pink flowers and growing in the western United States.

gō′-dev″il, *n.* 1. a weight dropped into an oil-well boring to set off a cartridge and thereby start the flow.
2. a kind of flexible plug with scraping branches attached, used for cleaning the pipes of an oil pipe line.
3. a kind of sled, especially one used in logging.

god′fä″thẽr, *n.* [ME. *godfader;* AS. *godfæder; god,* God, and *fæder,* father.]
1. a male godparent.
2. one who gives a name to any person or thing.
These earthly *godfathers* of heaven's lights. —Shak.
3. a juryman: humorous usage. [Obs.]

god′fä″thẽr, *v.t.* to act as godfather to; to take under one's care.

God′-fēar″ing, *a.* [*sometimes* g–] fearing God; hence, reverential; religious.

God′-fọr·säk″en, *a.* 1. [*sometimes* g–] depraved; hopelessly bad.
2. [*sometimes* g–] dreary; desolate. [Colloq.]

God′giv·en, *a.* 1. [*sometimes* g–] given by God.
2. [*sometimes* g–] very welcome; suitable or opportune.

god′head (-hed), *n.* 1. divinity; godship.
2. [G–] God.

god′hood, *n.* the state or quality of being a god; divinity.

Gō·dī′vȧ, *n.* in English legend, the 11th-century patroness of Coventry who rode naked through the streets on a white horse so that her husband would abolish a heavy tax, in accordance with their agreement.

god′less, *a.* 1. impious; wicked.
2. atheistic; having no belief in the existence of God or a god; irreligious.

god′less·ly, *adv.* in a godless manner.

god′less·ness, *n.* the state of being godless.

god′līke, *a.* resembling or suitable to a god or God; divine.

god′līke·ness, *n.* the state of being godlike.

god′li·ly, *adv.* in the manner of a god. [Rare.]

god′li·ness, *n.* piety; the state or quality of being godly.

god′ling, *n.* a relatively unimportant god.

god′ly, *a.*; *comp.* godlier; *superl.* godliest. 1. of or from God; divine. [Archaic.]
2. pious; devout; religious; conformed to God's law; as, a *godly* life.

god′ly, *adv.* piously; righteously. [Archaic.]
All that will live *godly* in Christ Jesus shall suffer persecution. —2 Tim. iii. 12.

god′mŏth″ẽr, *n.* a female godparent.

gō·down′, *n.* [altered from Malay *godoṅ,* warehouse.] in the Orient, a warehouse.

god′pâr″ent, *n.* a person who sponsors a newborn child and assumes responsibility for its faith; godmother or godfather.

gō·drọọn′, *n.* same as *gadroon.*

God′ṣ ā′çre (-kẽr), a burial ground, especially one in a churchyard; cemetery.

god′send, *n.* an unexpected acquisition or piece of good fortune that comes at the opportune moment, as if sent by God.

god′ship, *n.* deity; divinity; the rank or character of a god.

god′smith, *n.* a maker of idols. [Obs.]

god′sŏn, *n.* [ME. *godson, godsone;* AS. *godsunu; god,* God, and *sunu,* son.] a male godchild.

God′speed, *n.* good fortune; success: a wish for the welfare of a person starting on a journey or venture.

god tree, a tree of the West Indies; the *Eriodendron anfractuosum;* the ceiba.

God′wărd, *a.* and *adv.* 1. toward God.
2. in relation or with reference to God.

God′wărdṣ, *adv.* same as *Godward.*

god′wit, *n.* [prob. from AS. *god,* good, and *wiht,* a creature, wight.] a genus of birds, the *limosa,* of the snipe family, having long legs and long, flexible bills.

gō·ẹ·länd′ (-loṅ′), *n.* [Fr.] a white tern, *Gygis candida,* found in the tropics.

gō′ẽr, *n.* 1. one who or that which goes; a runner or walker; as, that horse is a good *goer.*
2. a foot. [Obs.]

goe′thīte (gō′), *n.* [named after the German poet *Goethe.*] a hydrous oxide of iron, $Fe_2O_3{\cdot}H_2O$.

gō′e·ty, *n.* [Gr. *goēteia,* witchcraft, jugglery, from *goēteuein,* to bewitch, from *goēs,* a wizard, sorcerer.] invocation of evil spirits. [Obs.]

gō′fẽr, gō′-fẽr, *n.* [from being asked to *go for* whatever is needed.] an employee who performs minor or menial tasks such as running errands. [Slang.]

goff, *n.* [OFr. *goffe,* dull, blockish.] a foolish clown. [Obs.]

goff, *n.* golf.

gof′fẽr, *v.t.*; goffered, *pt., pp.*; goffering, *ppr.* to crimp, flute, or pleat (cloth, paper, etc.): also *gauffer.*

gof′fẽr, *n.* 1. a goffering iron.
2. a pleating or fluting.
Also *gauffer.*

gof′fẽr·ing, *n.* 1. a pleating, crimping, or fluting.
2. a series of pleats, crimps, or flutes.

gog, *n.* [W. *gog,* activity; rapidity.] haste; ardent desire to go. [Obs.]

Gog and Mā′gog, [Heb. *gōgh, māgōgh.*]
1. in the Bible, representations of the nations that are to war against the kingdom of God under the leadership of Satan. Rev. xx. 8.
2. two huge wooden statues in the Guildhall, London, constructed in 1708 to replace effigies burned in the Great Fire of 1666.

gō′-get′tẽr, *n.* an active and aggressive person who usually gets what he wants. [Slang.]

gog′gle, *v.i.*; goggled, *pt., pp.*; goggling, *ppr.* [ME. *gogelen,* to look asquint, freq. prob. from Ir. and Gael. *gog,* a nod, a slight motion.]
1. (a) to stare with bulging or wide-open eyes; (b) to roll the eyes.
2. (a) to bulge; open wide in a stare; (b) to roll: said of the eyes.

gog′gle, *v.t.* to roll (the eyes).

gog′gle, *a.* full or rolling, as the eyes; staring.

gog′gle, *n.* 1. a strained or affected rolling of the eye.
2. [*pl.*] a kind of spectacles, especially those with side guards to protect the eyes against dust, wind, etc.

gog′gled (-gld), *a.* prominent; staring, as the eye.

gog′gle-eȳe, *n.* 1. a squinting. [Obs.]
2. any of several species of fresh-water fishes found in the Great Lakes and in the waters of the Mississippi Valley: so named from their bulging eyes.

gog′gle-eȳed (-īd), *a.* having bulging, staring, or rolling eyes.

gog′glẽr, *n.* the big-eyed scad, a carangoid fish, widely distributed in tropical seas: also called *goggle-eyed jack.*

gog′let, *n.* a kind of jar or decanter with a long neck, made of porous material for keeping water cool by evaporation: also *gurglet.*

gō′-gō, *a.* [short for *à gogo,* from Fr., in plenty, ad lib., in clover, from *à,* to, and *gogo,* child's word for throat.]
1. of rock-and-roll dancing or dancers or the discothèques, cafés, etc. where such dancing is featured.
2. lively, energetic, up-to-date, etc. [Slang.]

Goi·del′iç, *a.* [from Ir. *Gaedheal;* OIr. *Góidel.*]
1. of the Gaels.
2. designating or of their language.
Also *Gadhelic.*

Goi·del′iç, *n.* the subfamily of the Celtic languages that includes Erse (Irish Gaelic), Scottish Gaelic, and Manx: distinguished from *Brythonic:* also *Gadhelic.*

gō′ing, *n.* 1. the act of leaving or of departure.
2. the period of gestation.
3. the condition of the ground or land as it affects traveling.
4. circumstances affecting progress; working conditions. [Colloq.]

gō′ing, *a.* 1. moving; running; working.
2. conducting its regular business; as, a *going* concern.
3. in existence or available.
going on; nearing or nearly (a specified age or time). [Colloq.]
to be going to; to be about to; be intending to; will or shall.
to get going; to start; begin. [Colloq.]

gō′ing bar′rel, the cylinder containing the mainspring of a timepiece and carrying a toothed wheel for driving the train of wheels.

gō′ing-ō′vẽr, *n.* 1. an inspection or examination, especially a thorough one. [Colloq.]
2. a severe scolding or beating. [Colloq.]

gō′ingṣ-on′, *n.pl.* actions, especially when regarded with disapproval. [Colloq.]

goi′tẽr, goi′tre (-tẽr), *n.* [Fr. *goitre,* from L. *guttur,* throat.]
1. a diseased condition of the thyroid gland characterized by enlargement of the gland, seen as a swelling in the front of the neck.
2. the enlargement or swelling.

goi′tẽred, goi′tred (-tẽrd), *a.* affected with goiter.

goi′trous, *a.* [Fr. *goitreux.*]
1. pertaining to goiter; of the nature of or affected with goiter.
2. designating a geographical area where goiter is prevalent.

gol′ȧ·där, *n.* in East India, one who has charge of a storehouse.

Gol·çon′dȧ, *n.* [named after an ancient city in Hyderabad, India, famous for diamond-cutting in the 16th century.] a place or source of great wealth, as a mine.

gōld, *n.* [ME. *gold, goold, guld;* AS. *gold,* gold.]
1. a heavy, yellow, metallic chemical element with a high degree of ductility and malleability: it is a precious metal and is used in the manufacture of coins, jewelry, alloys, etc.: symbol, Au; atomic weight, 197.2; atomic number, 79.
2. gold coin.
3. money; wealth; riches.
4. that which has any of the qualities of gold, as great value, luster, etc.; as, a heart of *gold.*
5. the bright yellow color of the metal; as, a flower edged with *gold.*
6. in archery, the exact center of the target: so called because marked with gold, or of a gold color; hence, a center shot.
gold lace; lace ornamented with or made of gilt thread.
gold plate; tableware made of gold.
gold standard; (a) a monetary standard solely in terms of gold, in which the basic currency unit is made equal to and redeemable by a specified quantity of gold; (b) the legal weight and fineness of gold used in United States coins before 1934.
green gold; an alloy of gold and silver, as distinguished from red gold.
mosaic gold; (a) ormolu, an alloy of tin, zinc, and copper used for cheap jewelry, picture frames, etc.; (b) a yellow crystalline powder, stannic sulfide, SnS_2, used as a pigment.
old gold; a metallic, dull yellow color.
red gold; an alloy of gold and copper.
rolled gold; a thin plate of gold joined with a plate of inferior metal by rolling.
white gold; gold alloyed with about twenty per cent of platinum, palladium, nickel, etc. to give it a white, platinumlike appearance for use in jewelry.

gōld, *a.* 1. of, made of, like, or containing gold.
2. having the color of gold.
3. secured by or redeemable in gold; based on gold.

gōld′-bēat·en, *a.* gilded. [Obs.]

gōld′bēat·ẽr, *n.* one whose occupation is to beat gold into thin leaves for gilding.
goldbeater's skin; the outer layer of the caecum of an ox, which gold beaters lay between the leaves of the gold while beating it.

gōld′bēat·ing, *n.* the art or process of reducing gold to extremely thin leaves by beating with a hammer.

gōld bee′tle, any of several species of beetles of the genus *Chrysōmela,* order *Chrysōmelidæ,* characterized by their golden color.

gōld′brick, *v.i.* to try to avoid work; to shirk; to loaf. [Military Slang.]

gōld brick, 1. a worthless metal bar or brick gilded to make it appear solid gold and sold as such by swindlers. [Colloq.]
2. anything worthless passed off as genuine or valuable. [Colloq.]
3. a person who tries to avoid work; shirker; loafer. [Military Slang.]

gōld′bug, *n.* same as *gold beetle.*

gōld cẽr·tif′i·çāte, 1. a former United States paper currency redeemable in gold.
2. a United States Treasury note issued to and used only among Federal Reserve Banks: it represents a claim on their gold reserves held by the Treasury.

Gōld Cōast, a district where rich people live; as, the *Gold Coast* of Chicago. [Colloq.]

gōld′çrest, *n.* any of various kinglets or golden-crested birds of the genus *Regulus.*

gōld′çup, *n.* any of various plants of the crowfoot family.

gōld çūre, a method of treatment for alcoholic, morphine, opium, or tobacco habits, in which a fluid containing gold salts is given hypodermically.

gōld dig′gẽr, 1. one engaged in placer mining for gold.

2. a woman who inveigles or entices rich men for purposes of obtaining money or gifts from them. [Slang.]

gōld dig′gings, a gold field devoted to placer mining.

gōld′-dust, *n.* a plant, *Alyssum saxatile*, having golden-yellow flowers; madwort.

gōld dust, gold in very fine particles, the normal state in which it is found in placer mining.

gōld′en, *a.* [ME. *golden, gulden, gylden*; AS. *gylden*, from *gold*, gold.]

1. made of gold; consisting of gold; yielding gold.

2. of the color and luster of gold; bright-yellow.

3. excellent; most valuable; very precious.

4. happy; prosperous and joyful; flourishing.

Golden Age; (a) in Greek and Roman legend, an imaginary early age in which mankind was ideally happy, prosperous, and innocent; (b) [g– a–] the period of greatest progress, prosperity, or cultural achievement, as in a nation's history.

golden balls; the three gilt balls placed in front of a pawnbroker's shop. The golden balls form the Lombardy coat of arms, and were used by the Lombards who settled in London as bankers and moneylenders.

Golden Fleece; (a) in Greek legend, the fleece of gold that hung in the sacred grove at Colchis guarded by a dragon until taken away by Jason and the Argonauts; (b) in heraldry, an order of knighthood established in 1429, the time of its institution by Philip the Good, Duke of Burgundy.

golden number; a number once written in gold in calendars, indicating the year of the lunar cycle.

golden rose; in the Roman Catholic Church, a rose made of gold, which receives the blessing of the Pope on the fourth Sunday of Lent, afterward being presented as a high honor to some worthy member of the church.

golden rule; (a) in arithmetic, the rule of three, or rule of proportion; (b) the rule of doing to others as you would have them do toward you: see Matt. vii. 12., Luke vi. 31.

golden saxifrage; a low-growing herb of the genus *Chrysosplenium*, order *Saxifragaceæ*, annual or perennial, with alternate or opposite crenate leaves and inconspicuous greenish axillary and yellow flowers.

gōld′en as′tẽr, any of a group of hardy plants similar to the daisies, with tall, yellow flower heads.

gōld′en ban′tăm çorn, a variety of sweet corn with bright-yellow kernels on small ears.

gōld′en çȧlf (kȧf), 1. a calf of gold worshiped by the Israelites while Moses was at Mount Sinai: Ex. xxxii. 4.

2. riches regarded as of the greatest importance.

gōld′en chāin, a yellow flowering shrub of the pea family, *Cytisus laburnum*.

gōld′en çlub, a spiked, flowering aquatic plant, *Orontium aquaticum*.

gōld′en ēa′gle, a large, strong eagle found in mountainous districts of the Northern Hemisphere, with brown feathers on the back of its head and neck.

gōld′en·eȳe, *n.*; *pl.* **gōld′en·eȳeṣ, gōld′en·eȳe,** a wild duck with a dark-green back and a white breast, noted for its expert diving and speed in flying.

gōld′en glōw, a tall, hardy North American plant with doubled, yellow, globular flowers.

gōld′en ġoose, a goose in a Greek fable who laid a golden egg each day: its greedy owner, thinking to get all the gold at once, killed the goose, thus losing everything.

Gōld′en Hōrde, [so called from the splendors of their leader's camp.] the Mongol armies that invaded Europe in 1237 and, under the Khans, ruled over Russia for two centuries.

Gōld′en Leġ′end, name given by Caxton to his translation from the French (1483) of the Latin collection of saints' lives originally written by Jacobus de Voragine, bishop of Genoa (1230–1298).

gōld′en·ly, *adv.* in a golden manner; splendidly; delightfully.

gōld′en mēan, [transl. of L. (Horace) *aurea mediocritas*.] the safe, prudent way between extremes; happy medium; moderation.

gōld′en·pērt, *n.* a yellow flowering herb of the figwort family, *Gratiola aurea*.

gōld′en pheaṣ′ănt (fez′), a pheasant of China and Tibet, with brightly colored feathers and a yellow crest.

gōld′en rob′in, the Baltimore oriole.

gōld′en·rod, *n.* any of the plants of the genus *Solidago*, of the order *Compositæ*, having rod-like stems and bright-yellow flowers.

false goldenrod; a plant of the genus *Brachychæta*, closely allied to the genus *Solidago*.

West India goldenrod; an herb of the genus *Neurolæna*, similar to *Solidago*.

white goldenrod; a white-flowered variety of *Solidago*.

gōld′en·rod tree, a shrub, *Bosea yervamora*, a native of the Canary Islands.

gōld′en·sēal, *n.* an American herb of the crowfoot family, with large, round leaves and a thick, yellow rootstock, formerly much used in medicine.

gōld′en wąr′blẽr, a small, yellow American songbird.

gōld′en wed′ding, the fiftieth anniversary of a wedding.

gōld′en·wing, *n.* the yellowhammer.

gōld fẽrn, a fern characterized by a frond sprinkled with a waxy-yellow powder.

gōld fē′vẽr, an excessive desire for digging or otherwise searching for gold; as, the *gold fever* of 1849 in California.

gōld fiēld, a district or region where gold is found.

gōld′-filled′, *a.* made of a base metal overlaid with gold.

gōld′finch, *n.* 1. a common European bird, *Carduelis elegans*, with yellow markings on its wings.

2. any of the small American finches of the genus *Spinus*: the male has a yellow body with black markings.

gōld′fin·ny, *n.*; *pl.* **gōld′fin·nieṣ,** 1. a small, bright-yellow European fish.

2. any of several related sea or fresh-water fishes, as the cunner.

gōld′fish, *n.*; *pl.* **gōld′fish, gōld′fish·eṣ,** a golden-yellow or orange-colored fish of the genus *Cyprinus*, of the size of a minnow: often kept in ponds and fishbowls.

gōld′flow″ẽr, *n.* a composite plant, *Helichrysum stæchas*, characterized by dry, yellow scales.

gōld foil, a thin sheet of gold, thicker than gold leaf.

gōld′ham″mẽr, *n.* the yellowhammer.

gōld′ie, *n.* 1. the English goldfinch.

2. the yellowhammer.

gōld′i·locks, *n.* 1. any of certain plants of the genus *Chrysocoma*, having yellow flowers that grow in tufts at the ends of the stems.

2. a European buttercup.

3. a person with yellow hair.

4. [G–] a little girl in a folk tale who visits the home of three bears.

gōld′in, gōld′ing, *n.* 1. a variety of apple, golden in color.

2. a flower of the genus *Chrysanthemum* that is golden in color.

gōld knobṣ (nobz), the common buttercup: so called from the appearance of the unopened flower.

gōld′-lēaf, *a.* of or decorated with gold leaf.

gōld lēaf, the finest leaf made of gold, thinner than gold foil, used in gilding.

gōld mīne, 1. a mine from which gold ore is obtained.

2. a source of something very valuable or profitable. [Colloq.]

gōld mōle, a small South African mole, characterized by its lustrous fur in varying colors.

gōld nōte, a gold certificate.

gōld′-ŏf-pleaṣ′ūre (-ple′zhũr), *n.* a cruciferous annual European plant, *Camelina sativa*, frequently found in flax fields.

gōld rē·ṣẽrve′, 1. the gold formerly kept in the United States Treasury for redeeming government notes: most of it is now buried at Fort Knox, Kentucky, as a permanent reserve.

2. the quantity of gold in the central or national bank of a country.

gōld rush, a rush of people to territory where gold has recently been discovered, as to California in 1849.

gōld′seed, *n.* dog's-tail grass.

gōld shell, 1. a bivalve, *Anomia ephippium*, found on rocky coasts.

2. a shell holding gold paint for an artist's use.

gōld sīze, a glue used as an adhesive for gold leaf.

gōld′smith, *n.* 1. an artisan who makes vessels and ornaments of gold.

2. a dealer in such articles.

gōld′smith bee′tle, *Cotalpa lanigera*, a large, golden-yellow American beetle that feeds on tree foliage.

gōld stär, a small, gold star of cloth, paper, etc. awarded as a mark of honor in school, etc., or displayed to represent a member of the armed forces killed in the line of duty in wartime.

gōld′-stär mŏth′ẽr, a mother of a member of the armed forces killed in the line of duty in wartime.

gōld stick, a colonel of the British Life Guards or a captain of the gentlemen-at-arms: so called from the gilt rods which they bear when attending the sovereign on state occasions. [Brit.]

gōld′stōne, *n.* glass containing mineral particles and having a glittering, jewellike appearance.

gōld′tāil, *n.* a moth of the genus *Porthesia*, distinguished by an anal tuft of yellow.

gōld′thread (-thred), *n.* a ranunculaceous evergreen plant, *Coptis trifolia*: its yellow roots are used in medicine.

gōld′tit, *n.* the yellow-headed titmouse.

gōld wąsh′ẽr, 1. one who washes away the refuse from gold or from gold ore, as in a cradle.

2. the apparatus used in washing the refuse from gold or from gold ore.

gōld′y·locks, *n.* same as *goldilocks*.

gō′lem, *n.* [Heb., orig., embryo; later, monster.] in Jewish legend, a man artificially created by cabalistic rites; robot; automaton.

gō′let, *n.* the gullet. [Obs.]

golf, *n.* [from D. *kolf*, a club to strike balls with.] an outdoor game, played on a large course with a small, hard rubber ball, and a set of clubs with wooden or metal heads, the object being to drive the ball into a series of variously located four-inch holes (usually nine or eighteen) with the fewest possible strokes.

golf, *v.i.* to play golf.

golf çlub, 1. any of the various clubs with wooden or metal heads and long, slender handles, used in golf.

2. an organization owning and controlling a golf course, clubhouse, etc., for the use of its members.

3. the golf course, clubhouse, etc. operated by by such an organization.

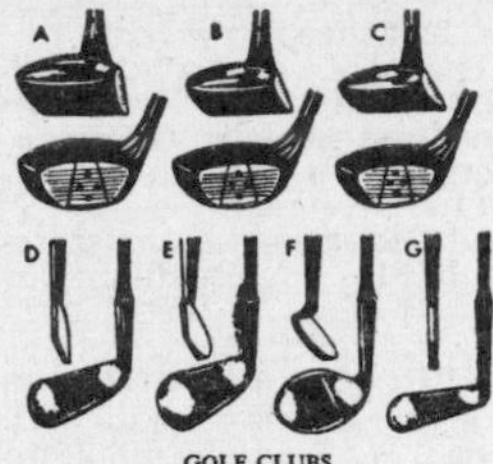

GOLF CLUBS
A, driver; B, brassie; C, spoon; D, mid-iron; E, mashie; F, niblick; G, putter

golf çourse (or **liñks**), a tract of land for playing golf, with tees, greens, fairways, hazards, etc.

golf′ẽr, *n.* one who plays golf.

Gol′gō·thȧ, *n.* [Gr. *Golgotha*; Heb. *gulgoleth*, a skull, the place of a skull.]

1. the place where Jesus was crucified; Calvary: Mark xv. 22.

2. [g–] (a) a burial place; (b) a place of agony or sacrifice.

gōl′iärd (-yărd), *n.* [OFr., glutton, from *gole* (Fr. *gueule*), mouth; L. *gula*, gullet.] any of a class of wandering students of the late Middle Ages who wrote satirical Latin verse and often served as minstrels and jesters.

gōl′iärd·ẽr·y (-yărd-), *n.* a satirical kind of poetry of the Middle Ages.

gōl·iär′diç (-yär′), *a.* of the goliards or their verse.

Gō·lī′ăth, *n.* [LL.; Heb. *golyāth*.] in the Bible, the Philistine giant killed by David with a stone shot from a sling. I Sam. xvii. 4, 49.

gō·lī′ăth bee′tle, [from *Goliath*, the Philistine giant.] any beetle of the genus *Goliathus*, native to Africa and South America, noted for their large size. *Goliathus giganteus* is the typical species.

goll, *n.* a hand; a paw; a claw. [Obs.]

gol′li·wog, gol′li·wogg, *n.* [arbitrary formation; perh. after *polliwog*.]

1. a grotesque black doll used in illustrations by Florence K. Upton for a series of children's books.

2. a grotesque, ugly person.

gol′ly, *interj.* an exclamation of surprise, etc.: a euphemism for *God*.

gō·lōe′-shōe, *n.* see *galosh*.

gō·losh′, gō·loshe′, *n.* same as *galosh*.

Gō′măr·ist, Gō′măr·īte, *n.* a follower of

Francis Gomarus (1563–1641), a Calvinist in Holland.

gom·been′ism, *n.* the practice of borrowing money at high rates of interest. [Irish.]

gom·been′ man, a moneylender demanding a high rate of interest. [Irish.]

gom′bō, *n.* see *gumbo.*

gom·broon′, *n.* [from *Gombroon* (Bandar Abbas), town on the Persian Gulf.] a type of white, semitransparent Persian pottery.

gōme, *n.* [AS. *guma,* a man.] a man. [Obs.]

gōme, *n.* black axle grease.

gō′mẽr, *n.* a measure; omer. [Obs.]

gō′mẽr, *n.* in gunnery, the conelike narrowing of the bore at the breech, in mortars: named for the inventor, Gomer, and first used in the Napoleonic wars.

gom′ẽr·ăl, gom′ẽr·el, gom′ẽr·il, *n.* [perh. from obs. *gome,* a man, and *-erel, -rel,* depreciatory suffix, from OFr. *-erel.*] a simpleton; fool; dolt. [Scot. and N. Eng. Dial.]

gom′me·lin, gom′me·line, *n.* same as *dextrin.*

Gō·mor′răh, Gō·mor′rhȧ, *n.* [Gr. *Gomorrha,* from Heb.]
1. in the Bible, a city destroyed together with a neighboring city, Sodom, by fire from heaven because of the sinfulness of the people: Gen. xix. 24.
2. any wicked city or place.

gom·phī′ȧ·sis, *n.* [Gr. *gomphiasis,* toothache, from *gomphios,* a grinder tooth, molar.] looseness of the teeth, especially the molars.

gom′phō·dont, *a.* [Gr. *gomphos,* a nail, bolt, and *odous, odontos,* a tooth.] in zoology, having teeth in sockets.

gom·phō′sis, *n.* [Gr. *gomphōsis,* a bolting together, from *gomphos,* a bolt, nail.] a form of immovable joint in which a bone or other hard part fits into a socket: teeth fit into the jaw by gomphosis.

Gom·phrē′nȧ, *n.* a genus of tropical plants of the amaranth family, of which the globe amaranth or bachelor's button is a type.

gō·mụ′ti, *n.* [Malay *gumuti.*]
1. a Malayan palm with feathery leaves and a sweet sap from which a crude sugar and palm wine are made: also *gomuti palm.*
2. the wiry fibers from the stalks of its leaves, used in making ropes, etc.

GOMUTI (*Arenga saccharifera*)

gō·mụ′tō, *n.* same as *gomuti.*

-gon, [Gr. *-gōnon,* from *gōnia,* an angle.] a combining form used to form nouns meaning *a figure having* (a specified number of) *angles,* as in penta*gon.*

gon-, see *gono-.*

gon, *v.* obsolete past participle of *go.*

gon′ad, *n.* [from Gr. *gonē,* seed, generation.] in biology, a gland that produces reproductive cells; testis or ovary; a sex gland.

gon′ad·ăl, *a.* of a gonad or gonads.

gon·ad·ec′tō·my, *n.* the excision of a gonad, or sexual gland.

gon″ȧ·dō·trop′iç, *a.* designating or of any substance acting as a stimulant upon the gonads.

gon′ȧ·duçt, *n.* [contr. of *gonad duct.*] an oviduct or seminal duct.

gō·nan′ġi·um, *n.*; *pl.* **gō·nan′ġi·ȧ** or **gō·nan′ġi·umṣ,** in zoology, a receptacle furnishing protection to sexual buds in certain hydroids.

gon·ȧ·poph′y·sis, *n.*; *pl.* **gon·ȧ·poph′y·sēṣ,** [Gr. *gonos,* generation, and *apophysis,* an outgrowth, process.] in entomology, one of the parts making up the external genitals.

Gond, *n.* [from native (Gondi) name.] a member of the Dravidian culture group living in Madhya Pradesh, India.

Gon′di, *n.* [from *Gondi,* name of the principal dialect.]
1. a group of Dravidian dialects spoken in central India.
2. the principal dialect of this group.

gon′dō·lȧ, *n.* [It., ultimately from Romance base *dond-,* to rock.]
1. a long, narrow canalboat with a cabin in the middle and a high, pointed prow and stern, used on the canals of Venice: it is propelled by a pole or one oar at the stern.
2. a flat-bottomed river barge.
3. a gondola car.
4. a cabin suspended under a dirigible or balloon, for holding the motors, instruments, passengers, etc.

GONDOLA

gon′dō·lȧ çär, a railroad freight car with low sides and no top.

gon′dō·let, *n.* [It. *gondoletta,* dim. of *gondola,* a gondola.] a small gondola.

gon dō·liēr′, *n.* [It. *gondoliere,* from *gondola,* a gondola.] a man who rows or poles a gondola.

gọne, *a.* [pp. of *go.*]
1. moved away; departed.
2. ruined.
3. lost.
4. dying; dead.
5. faint; weak.
6. used up; consumed.
7. ago; past.
far gone; (a) much advanced; deeply involved; (b) very tired.
gone on; in love with. [Colloq.]

gọne′ness, *n.* a condition of exhaustion or weakness, as resulting from lack of food; faintness.

gọn′ẽr, *n.* a person or thing that has reached a stage beyond recovery, help, or recall. [Colloq.]

Gon′ẽr·il, *n.* in Shakespeare's *King Lear,* the elder of Lear's two wicked daughters.

gon′fȧ·lŏn, *n.* [It. *gonfalone*; OFr. *gonfanon* (Fr. *gonfalon*); LL. *gonfano, guntfano,* a banner; O.H.G. *gundfano,* a battle standard; *gund, gunt,* a battle, and *gano,* a banner.] a flag or ensign hanging from a crosspiece instead of an upright staff and usually ending in streamers; especially, such a standard used by any of the medieval republics of Italy.

gon″fȧ·lŏn·iēr′, *n.* [from Fr. or It.; Fr. *gonfalonier*; It. *gonfaloniere.*]
1. one who bears a gonfalon; a chief standard bearer.
2. the chief magistrate of any of various Italian republics during the Middle Ages.
3. an officer at Rome who bears the Church standard.
4. the chief officer of any of the sixteen Florentine guilds in the Middle Ages.

gon″fȧ·lŏn·iēr′āte, *n.* the office of a gonfalonier.

gon′fȧ·non, *n.* a gonfalon. [Obs.]

gong, *n.* [AS. *gang,* a going, passage, privy.] a privy; an outdoor toilet. [Obs.]

gong, *n.* [Malay *guṅ,* a gong.]
1. a slightly convex metallic disk that gives a loud, resonant tone when struck.
2. a saucer-shaped bell with a similar tone.

Goṅ·gō·resque′ (-resk′), *a.* pertaining to the Spanish poet Gongora, or resembling his style.

Goṅ′gō·riṣm, *n.* 1. the literary style which characterized the writings of the Spanish poet, Gongora y Argote (d. 1627): its chief features were affected metaphors and strained conceits.
2. any style like this.

gō′ni·ȧ·tīte, *n.* [Gr. *gōnia,* a corner, angle, and *lithos,* stone.] any member of an extinct genus of fossil mollusks, belonging to the dibranchiate cephalopodous mollusks and family of ammonites.

gō′nid, *n.* same as *gonidium.*

gon·i·dan′ġi·um, *n.*; *pl.* **gon·i·dan′ġi·ȧ,** [Gr. *gonē,* generation, seed, and *angeion,* a vessel, receptacle.] in botany, a sporangium in which gonidia are formed.

gō·nid′i·ȧ, *n.* plural of *gonidium.*

gō·nid′i·ăl, *a.* of, relating to, producing, or containing gonidia; as, the *gonidial* grooves of certain anthozoans.

gō·nid′iç, *a.* gonidial.

gō·nid·i·oġ′e·nous, *a.* producing or capable of producing gonidia.

gō·nid′i·ō·phōre, *n.* in botany, a conidiophore.

gō·nid′i·ōse, *a.* having or containing gonidia.

gō·nid′i·um, *n.*; *pl.* **gō·nid′i·ȧ,** [dim. from Gr. *gonē,* seed, generation.]
1. a chlorophyll-bearing, spherical cell in the thallus of lichens, immediately below the surface.
2. a reproductive cell produced asexually in certain algae.

gō·nim′iç, *a.* pertaining to or containing gonimia.

gō·nim′i·um, *n.*; *pl.* **gō·nim′i·ȧ,** [Gr. *gonimos,* productive, fruitful, from *gignesthai,* to produce.] a gonidium of a bluish-green color found in some lichens.

gon′i·mous, *a.* gonimic.

gō′ni·ō-, [from Gr. *gōnia,* an angle.] a combining form meaning *angle,* as in *gonio*metry.

gō·ni·om′e·tẽr, *n.* [Gr. *gōnia,* an angle, corner, and *metron,* a measure.] an instrument for measuring angles, especially of solid bodies.
contact goniometer; a goniometer with two arms that move about the fixed center of a graduated semicircle. When the faces of a crystal are in contact with the arms, a pointer indicates the angle.
reflecting goniometer; a goniometer for measuring the interfacial angles of crystals by reflection.

gō″ni·ō·met′riç, gō″ni·ō·met′riç·ăl, *a.* pertaining to a goniometer or to goniometry.

gō·ni·om′e·try, *n.* [Gr. *gōnia,* an angle, and *metrein,* to measure.] the theory or science of measuring angles.

gō′ni·on, *n.*; *pl.* **gō′ni·ȧ,** [Gr. *gōnia,* an angle, corner.] the point at either angle of the lower jaw.

gō″ni·ō·thē′çȧ, *n.*; *pl.* **gō″ni·ō·thē′cae,** [Gr. *gōnia,* angle, and *thēkē,* a case, box.] in botany, a megasporangium. [Obs.]

gō·ni·ot′rō·pous, *a.* [Gr. *gōnia,* angle, and *tropē,* a turning, from *trepein,* to turn.] in botany, having four corners, with two of the angles lateral, one posterior, and one anterior.

gō·nī′tis, *n.* [Gr. *gony,* knee, and *-itis.*] an inflammatory condition of the knee.

-gō′ni·um, [Mod. L., from Gr. *gonos,* procreation, offspring, semen, seed.] a combining form used to form nouns meaning *a cell* or *structure in which reproductive cells are formed,* as in sporo*gonium.*

gon′o-, [from Gr. *gonos, gonē,* procreation, offspring, semen, seed, from base of *gignesthai,* to be born.] a combining form meaning *reproductive, sexual,* as in *gono*coccus, *gono*phore: also, before a vowel, *gon-.*

gon′ō·blast, *n.* [*gono-,* and Gr. *blastos,* a germ, shoot.] in biology, a germ cell; a reproductive cell.

gon·ō·blas′tid, *n.* in zoology, a gonophore.

gon″ō·blas·tid′i·um, *n.*; *pl.* **gon″ō·blas·tid′i·ȧ,** [*gono-,* and Gr. *blastos,* a germ, shoot, and dim. *-idion.*] in zoology, a blastostyle.

gon·ō·çā′lyx, *n.*; *pl.* **gon·ō·çal′y·cēṣ,** [*gono-,* and Gr. *kalyx,* a cup.] in zoology, the swimming bell of a gonophore.

gon′ō·çhēme, *n.* [*gono-,* and Gr. *ochēma,* a vehicle.] in zoology, a gonophore.

gon·ō·çhō′riṣm, *n.* [*gono-,* and *chōrismos,* separation, from *chōrizein,* to separate.] in biology, differentiation of the sexes; the development of sexual distinction.

gon·ō·çoç′çus, *n.* [*gono-,* and Gr. *kokkos,* grain seed.] the microorganism that causes gonorrhea.

gon′ō·duçt, *n.* same as *gonaduct.*

gō·noe′ci·um (*or* -shi-um), *n.* [*gon-,* and Gr. *oikia,* a house.] in zoology, a reproductive zooid of a polyzoan.

gon′ŏf, gon′ŏph, *n.* [perh. from Heb. *ganābh,* thief.] a thief: also *ganef.*

gon′ō·phōre, *n.* [*gono-,* and Gr. *-phoros,* from *pherein,* to bear.]
1. in zoology, an independent animal cell that produces a hydroid colony by fission, budding, or other asexual means.
2. in botany, an elongated receptacle, lifting the stamens and pistil above the perianth.

gon″ō·poi·et′iç, *a.* [*gono-,* and Gr. *poiētikos,* productive, from *poiein,* to do, make.] in biology, producing reproductive cells.

gon·or·rhē′ȧ, gon·or·rhoe′ȧ, *n.* [LL. *gonorrhœa*; Gr. *gonorrhoia*; *gonos,* seed, semen, and *rhoia,* from *rheein,* to flow.] a venereal disease caused by gonococci, characterized by inflammation of the mucous membrane of the genitourinary tract and a discharge of mucus and pus: it is generally transmitted by sexual intercourse and can seriously affect other mucous membranes, especially those of the eye, as in a baby during childbirth.

gon·or·rhē′ăl, gon·or·rhoe′ăl, *a.* of, caused by, or pertaining to gonorrhea.

gon′ō·sōme, *n.* [*gono-*, and Gr. *sōma*, body.] in zoology, the generative zooids of a hydrozoan, collectively.

gon·ō·thē′çȧ, *n.*; *pl.* **gon·ō·thē′cae,** same as *gonangium.*

gon′ō·tōme, *n.* [*gono-*, and Gr. *tomē*, a cutting, segment.] a segment of a somite in which the reproductive organs develop.

gon·ō·zō′oid, *n.* [*gono-*, and Gr. *zōoeidēs*, like an animal.] in zoology, a reproductive zooid; a gonophore.

gō′ny, *n.*; *pl.* **gō′nieṣ,** 1. a stupid person; a dunce; a booby. [Obs.]
2. in zoology, any of several large pelagic birds; especially, the black-footed albatross, the young of the short-tailed albatross, and the giant fulmar.

-go·ny, [L. *-gonia*; Gr. *-gonia*, from *gignesthai*, to be born.] a suffix used to form nouns meaning *something generated, produced, descended*, etc. as in cosmo*gony*, theo*gony*.

gō·nyd′ē·ăl, *a.* in zoology, of or pertaining to the gonys.

gō′nys, *n.* [Gr. *genys*, chin.] the lower outline of a bird's beak as far as the point where the rami branch.

gon′zō, *a.* [origin unknown.] bizarre, unrestrained, extravagant, etc.; specifically, designating a style of personal journalism so characterized.

goọ, *n.* [symbolic formation; prob. from baby talk.]
1. anything sticky, as glue. [Slang.]
2. anything sticky and sweet. [Slang.]

goọ′bẽr, *n.* [of Afr. origin; said to be from Congo *nguba*.] the peanut, *Arachis hypogæa.*

good, *a.*; *comp.* better; *superl.* best, [ME. *gode*; AS. *god*, good; originally, fit, suitable.]
1. valid; legally firm; sound; not fallacious; genuine; not counterfeit; acceptable; as, a *good* claim, a *good* argument, *good* money.
2. healthy; strong; vigorous; sound; as, *good* eyesight.
3. fresh; unspoiled; uncontaminated; as, *good* eggs.
4. dependable; reliable; right; as, *good* advice.
5. adequate; ample; sufficient; satisfying; as, a *good* meal.
6. morally sound or excellent; specifically, (a) virtuous; (b) pious; (c) kind, benevolent, generous, sympathetic, etc.; (d) well-behaved; dutiful; (e) proper; becoming; as, *good* manners.
7. full; complete; thorough; as, a *good* job of cleaning up.
8. (a) useful; serviceable; suitable to a purpose; effective; efficient; adequate; competent; as, shoes *good* for a year's wear; (b) producing favorable results; beneficial; as, hot lunches are *good* for children.
9. dexterous; clever; able; skilled; expert; as, a *good* mechanic.
10. agreeable, enjoyable, happy, etc.; as, a *good* time, a *good* fellow.
11. honorable; fair; unblemished; unimpeached; as, one's *good* name.
12. *a general intensive, meaning* to a considerable extent, amount, or degree; as, a *good* while ago, a *good* distance, a *good* many.
as good as; virtually; practically; in effect; nearly.
good afternoon, good day, good evening, good morning, good morrow, good night, etc.; salutations of greeting or farewell used for the respective times of day.
good and; (a) very; (b) altogether; entirely. [Colloq.]
good cheap; a good bargain. [Obs.]
good consideration; valuable consideration; also, the ties of blood or of love and affection.
good folk or *good people*; fairies; pixies. [Dial.]
good for; (a) able to survive, endure, or remain in working order for (a specified period of time); (b) worth; (c) able to pay, repay, or give; (d) used to express approval; as, *good for* you!
Good Friday; the last Friday in Lent, the Friday before Easter Sunday, observed in commemoration of the crucifixion of Jesus.
good speed; good luck; success: a farewell denoting a wish for the welfare of a person starting on a journey or venture.
Good Templar; a member of the Society of Good Templars, an association organized for the purpose of promoting temperance.
good turn; a kind act or favor.
in good time; (a) at the right time; promptly; (b) in correct or proper time; (c) in a creditably short time; quickly.
no good; useless; worthless.
to be as good as one's word; to act according to promise.
to hold good; to remain in force; to remain valid; as, the contract *holds good* for a year.
to make good; (a) to carry out, as an offer, etc.; to fulfill; (b) to manage to accomplish; (c) to give or do something as a substitute for; to repay or replace; (d) to be successful; (e) to prove.
Syn.—right, complete, virtuous, sound, benevolent, propitious, serviceable, sufficient, competent, valid, real, considerable, reputable, true, just.

good, *n.* something good; specifically, (a) worth; virtue; merit; as, there is much *good* in him; (b) something contributing to health, welfare, happiness, etc.; benefit; advantage; as, the greatest *good* of the greatest number; (c) something desirable or desired. See also *goods.*
for good, for good and all; for the last time; finally; permanently.
green goods; counterfeit paper money. [Slang.]
the good; (a) those who are good; (b) what is morally good.
to come to no good; to come to a bad end; end in failure, trouble, etc.
to the good; as a profit, benefit, or advantage.
Syn.—boon, benefit, advantage, weal, gain, virtue, prosperity, profit, interest, welfare.

good, *adv.* well; right. [Obs.]

good, *v.t.* to make good. [Obs.]

good, *interj.* an exclamation of satisfaction, pleasure, agreement, etc. In some exclamatory phrases expressing surprise, consternation, etc. (e.g., good gracious! good grief!) *good* is a euphemism for *God.*

Good Book, the Bible (usually with *the*).

good-bȳ′, *interj.* and *n.*; *pl.* **good-bȳṣ′,** [contr. of *God be with ye.*] farewell; adieu.

good-bȳe′, *interj.* and *n.*; *pl.* **good-bȳeṣ′,** same as *good-by.*

good cheer, 1. revelry.
2. good food and drink; feasting.
3. courage.

Good Çon′duçt Med′ăl, in the United States Army, a bronze medal awarded to enlisted men for exemplary behavior, efficiency, and fidelity.

good dēal, 1. a large number or quantity; many or much.
2. very good! [Slang.]

good′-den, *interj.* [contr. of *good even, goode'en.*] good evening. [Obs.]

Goo·dē′ni·ȧ, *n.* [named after Samuel *Goodenough*, Bishop of Exeter.] a genus of the *Goodeniaceæ.*

Good·ē·nī·ā′cē·ae, *n.pl.* a family of Australian shrubs or herbs allied to *Lobelia* family.

good·ē·nī·ā′ceous, *a.* of or like the *Goodeniaceæ.*

good fel′lōw, an agreeable, convivial person.

good″-fel′lōw·ship, *n.* hearty, convivial companionship.

good fōlk (or **pēo′ple**), fairies; pixies. [Dial.]

good′-fọr-nŏth′ing, *a.* useless; of no value or account; shiftless.

good′-fọr-nŏth′ing, *n.* a worthless or useless person.

Good Grāy Pō′et, Walt Whitman (1819–1892), American poet.

good′-heärt″ed, *a.* kind, generous, etc.

good hū′mŏr, a cheerful, agreeable, pleasant mood.

good′-hū′mŏred (-mẽrd), *a.* having or showing good humor; of a cheerful temper.

good′-hū′mŏred·ly, *adv.* in a cheerful way.

good′ing, *n.* a manner of asking alms, wishing good to the donor in return: formerly practiced in England at Christmas.

good′ish, *a.* 1. fairly good; rather good.
2. fairly large; as, a *goodish* distance.

good′-King-Hen′ry, *n.* an herb, *Chenopodium bonus-henricus*, introduced into the United States from Europe, and frequently used as a potherb: also called *allgood, good-King-Harry.*

good′less, *a.* without goods; destitute. [Obs.]

good′li·head (-hed), *n.* goodliness. [Obs.]

good′li·ness, *n.* the quality or condition of being goodly.

good′-look′ing, *a.* handsome or beautiful; pleasing in appearance.

good looks, attractive personal appearance; especially, pleasing facial features.

good′ly, *adv.* finely; well. [Obs.]

good′ly, *a.* 1. pleasing; agreeable; of good quality; fine.
2. graceful; handsome; good-looking.
3. ample; rather large; considerable.
Syn.—pleasant, desirable, excellent fair, comely, considerable.

good′man, *n.*; *pl.* **good′men,** 1. a title equivalent to *Master* or *Mr.*, applied to a man ranking below a gentleman: sometimes used ironically. [Obs.]
2. a husband; the master of a family. [Obs.]

good nā′tūre, a pleasant, agreeable, or kindly disposition; amiability; geniality.

good′-nā′tūred, *a.* having or showing good nature; naturally mild in temper; not easily provoked; amiable.
Syn.—good-tempered, kind, obliging.—*Good-natured* denotes a disposition to please and be pleased; *good-tempered*, a spirit which is not easily ruffled by provocation or other disturbing influences; *kind*, a disposition to make others happy by supplying their wants and granting their requests.

good′-nā′tūred·ly, *adv.* with good nature.

Good Neịgh′bŏr Pol′i·cy, the policy of encouraging friendly political and economic relations between the United States and Latin America: introduced by President Franklin Roosevelt in 1933.

good′ness, *n.* 1. the state or quality of being good; specifically, (a) virtue; excellence; (b) kindness; generosity; benevolence.
2. best part, essence, or valuable property of a thing.

good′ness, *interj.* an exclamation of surprise or wonder: used alone or in various phrases; as, for *goodness'* sake!

good′now, *interj.* an exclamation of wonder or surprise. [Obs.]

goodṣ, *n.pl.* 1. movable personal property.
2. merchandise; wares.
3. fabric; cloth.
4. freight: often used attributively. [Brit.]
the goods; what is required, genuine, or valid. [Slang.]
to deliver the goods; to do or produce the thing required, agreed on, promised, etc.
to get (or *have*) *the goods on*; to discover (or know) something incriminating about. [Slang.]

Good Sȧ·mar′i·tăn, *n.* 1. in the Bible, a person who was the only one to pity and help a traveler who had been beaten and robbed: Luke x. 30–37.
2. anyone who pities or helps another or others unselfishly.

goodṣ en′ġine, a freight engine. [Brit.]

Good Shep′hẽrd (-ẽrd), Jesus: John x. 11.

good′ship, *n.* goodness. [Obs.]

good′-sīzed′, *a.* ample; big or fairly big.

goodṣ shed, a freight warehouse. [Brit.]

goodṣ trāin, a freight train. [Brit.]

goodṣ wag′ŏn, a freight car. [Brit.]

good′-tem′pẽred, *a.* not easily angered; having a good temper; amiable.

good′wīfe, *n.*; *pl.* **good′wīveṣ,** 1. the wife or mistress of a family. [Obs.]
2. a title equivalent to *Mrs.*, applied to a woman ranking below a lady. [Obs.]

good′will′, *n.* good will.

good will, 1. benevolence; friendly disposition.
2. cheerful consent; willingness; readiness.
3. the commercial advantage of any business, due to its established popularity, reputation, patronage, advertising, location, etc., over and beyond its tangible assets.

good′y, *n.*; *pl.* **good′ieṣ,** 1. [*usually in pl.*] something considered very good to eat, as a piece of candy. [Colloq].
2. a person who is weakly or cantingly pious; sanctimonious person: often reduplicated as *goody-goody.* [Colloq.]
3. a kind of fish, the spot.

good′y, *a.* weakly or cantingly pious; sanctimonious: often reduplicated as *goody-goody.* [Colloq.]

good′y, *interj.* a child's exclamation of approval or delight: often reduplicated as *goody-goody.* [Colloq.]

good′y, *n.*; *pl.* **good′ieṣ,** [from *goodwife.*] a woman, especially an old woman or housewife, of lowly social status: formerly used, as in New England, as a title with the surname (e.g., *Goody* Smith).

good′yēar, good′yēarṣ, *n.* a term of indefinite meaning used in oaths. [Obs.]

good'y·ship, *n.* the state or quality of a goody.

goo'ey, *a.* [from *goo.*]
1. sticky, as glue. [Slang.]
2. sticky and sweet. [Slang.]

goof, *n.* [prob. from or akin to ME. *gofisshe, goofish,* foolish.] a stupid, silly, or credulous person. [Slang.]

goof'i·ly, *adv.* in a goofy manner. [Slang.]

goof'i·ness, *n.* the quality or state of being goofy. [Slang.]

goof'y, *a.*; *comp.* goofier; *superl.* goofiest, like or characteristic of a goof; stupid and silly. [Slang.]

goo'gol, *n.* [arbitrarily coined by Edward Kasner, Am. mathematician.]
1. the number 1 followed by 100 zeros.
2. any very large number.

goo'gul, *n.* 1. any of various species of myrrh trees that yield fragrant gums.
2. gum; bdellium.

gook, *n.* a Filipino, Japanese, Korean, etc.: a vulgar, offensive term of hostility and contempt. [Military Slang.]

goom'pain, goom'pa·na, *n.* [E. Ind.] *Odina wodier,* a timber tree of East India; also, its wood or its gum.

goon, *n.* [after a grotesque comic-strip character invented by E.C. Segar (1894–1938).]
1. a person who is awkward, grotesque, stupid, etc. [Slang.]
2. a ruffian or thug, especially one used in breaking a strike, etc. [Slang.]

goop, Goop, *n.* [after the creatures invented by Gelett Burgess (1866–1951).] a silly, ill-mannered, boorish person.

goo'roo, *n.* same as *guru.*

goos·an'dẽr, *n.* [*goose* and *gander.*] the merganser, a fish-eating duck.

goose, *n.* [ME. *goos, gos*; AS. *gos,* a goose.]
1. *pl.* **geese,** rarely **goose,** any of a group of long-necked, web-footed, wild or domestic birds that are like ducks but larger; especially, a female of this group: distinguished from *gander.*
2. the flesh of a goose, used for food.
3. *pl.* **geese,** a silly, stupid person; a simpleton.
4. *pl.* **goos'es,** a tailor's smoothing iron: so called from the resemblance of its handle to the neck of a *goose.*
5. *pl.* **geese,** a game of chance played by two or more persons with counters on a board divided into small compartments. At every fourth or fifth compartment a goose was depicted on the board, and, if the throw of the dice carried the counter of the player on a goose, he might move forward double the actual number thrown. [Obs.]
6. *pl.* **geese,** a player or piece in any of the games of fox and geese.
7. *pl.* **goos'es,** a goosing; a sudden, playful prod in the backside. [Slang.]
the goose hangs high; originally, *the goose honks high,* that is, cries high, as in fair weather; hence, prospects are good. [Slang.]
to cook one's goose; to spoil one's chances, hopes, etc. [Colloq.]

goose, *v.t.*; goosed (gōst), *pt., pp.*; goosing, *ppr.*
1. to hiss at; to condemn by hissing. [Slang.]
2. to prod suddenly and playfully in the backside so as to startle. [Slang.]
3. to feed gasoline to (an engine) in irregular spurts. [Slang.]

goose bär'nȧ·cle, *Lepas anatifera,* a pedunculated barnacle from which the goose was fabled to have originated.

goose'bēak, *n.* a dolphin.

goose'ber"ry (*or* göz'), *n.*; *pl.* **goose'ber"ries,** [OFr. *groselle, groiselle*; Gael. *groiseid,* a gooseberry; W. *grws,* from M.H.G. *krus*; D. *kroes,* crisp, crisped.]
1. a small, sour berry used in making preserves, pies, etc.: it resembles a currant but is larger.
2. the prickly shrub, *Ribes grossularia,* on which it grows.
Barbados gooseberry; *Pereskia aculeata,* a prickly climber bearing edible berries.

goose'bīrd, *n.* the Hudsonian godwit.

goose'cap, *n.* a fool. [Obs.]

goose corn, *Juncus squarrosus,* a kind of rush.

goose egg, 1. an egg of a goose
2. a cipher, or zero, as in a score. [Slang.]

goose'fish, *n.* the angler.

goose flesh, a roughened condition of the skin in which its papillae are erected, caused by shock, cold, etc.

goose'foot, *n.*; *pl.* **goose'foots,** any of a group of plants, including spinach, beets, etc., with large, coarse leaves sometimes shaped like the foot of a goose.

goose grass, 1. *Galium aparine,* cleavers.
2. *Potentilla anserina,* silverweed.
3. *Polygonum aviculare,* doorweed.
4. *Bromus mollis,* soft chess.
5. *Poa annua,* spear grass.

goose'hẽrd, *n.* one who tends geese.

goose mus'sel, a goose barnacle.

goose'neck, *n.* 1. in nautical usage, (a) a swivel of iron fitted to the end of a yard or boom for various purposes; (b) a davit.
2. in machinery, a pipe shaped like the letter S.
3. a hose nozzle with a swivel joint.
4. a flexible rod for supporting a desk lamp, etc.

goose pim'ples (-plz), goose flesh.

goose quill, a quill, or the pen made from a quill, of a goose.

goos'ẽr·y, *n.* 1. a place for keeping geese.
2. silliness or stupidity like that of the goose.

goose skin, 1. a goose's skin.
2. goose flesh.

goose'-step, *v.i.* to march in goose step: often used figuratively.

goose step, 1. the act of marking time by raising the feet alternately without making progress.
2. a marching or parade step that is characterized by its stiffness; especially, the former step of the German infantry, in which the legs are stiff and the knees are unbent.

goose tan'sy, in England, the silverweed: also called *goose grass.*

goose'tŏngue (-tung), *n.* *Achillea ptarmica,* sneezewort.

goose'wing, *n.* 1. one of the clews or lower corners of a ship's mainsail or foresail, when the middle part is furled or tied up.
2. the foresail or the mainsail of a schooner or other two-masted fore-and-aft vessel: when running before the wind these sails are set on opposite sides.
3. a studding sail.

goose'winged, *a.* 1. having a goosewing.
2. relating to a fore-and-aft-rigged vessel, with mainsail set on one side and foresail on the other.

goos'ish, *a.* stupid; like a goose. [Obs.]

goos'y, *a.*; *comp.* goosier; *superl.* goosiest, 1. like or characteristic of a goose; foolish; stupid.
2. (a) easily upset or disturbed by a sudden, playful prod in the backside; (b) nervous; jumpy.
Also spelled *goosey.*

gō'phẽr, *n.* [Fr. *gaufre,* gopher, waffle, honeycomb.]
1. a little quadruped of the genus *Geomys,* as *Geomys bursarius,* having large cheek pouches extending from the mouth to the shoulders, incisors protruding beyond the lips, and broad, molelike forefeet: also *pocket gopher.*

GOPHER (9 in. long)

2. any of several American burrowing squirrels, as *Spermophilus franklini,* the gray gopher; *Spermophilus tridecemlineatus,* the ordinary striped gopher.
3. a species of burrowing land tortoise found in the southern coastal States.
4. the gopher snake.
5. a plow. [Dial.]
6. a waffle. [Brit. Dial.]

gō'phẽr, *v.i.* to burrow; especially, to mine at random or on a small scale.

gō'phẽr drift, same as *gopher hole,* sense 2.

gō'phẽr hōle, 1. the entrance to a gopher's burrow.
2. a prospector's mining drift dug haphazardly.

gō'phẽr snāke, *Spilotes couperi,* a large, nonpoisonous, burrowing snake.

gō'phẽr·wood, *n.* [Heb. *gōpher,* an unknown kind of wood.]
1. in the Bible, the wood used in the building of Noah's ark, believed to be some kind of pine or fir: Gen. vi. 14.
2. *Cladrastis tinctoria,* the yellowwood of the southern United States.

gō'pu·rȧ, *n.* [E. Ind.] in the architecture of the East Indies, either the gateway of a temple or the pyramidal tower above it, sometimes ornamented in a highly intricate manner.

gō·rac'cō, *n.* [E. Ind.] an aromatic tobacco paste smoked in western India.

gō'răl, *n.* [E. Ind.] an animal of the Himalayas like the chamois of Europe, related to the goats and antelopes.

gō'rȧ·my, gōu'rȧ·mi, *n.* [Javanese.] a fresh-water food fish of the genus *Osphromenus,* a native of China and the Malay Archipelago, introduced into the West Indies.

gor'bel·lied, *a.* large-bellied. [Obs.]

gor'bel·ly, *n.* [AS. *gor,* dirt, dung, and *belly.*] a large belly; also, a person having a big belly. [Obs.]

gor'bu·schȧ, *n.* [Russ.] a Pacific coast salmon.

gorce, *n.* [Norm. Fr. *gorse*; OFr. *gorge*; L. *gurges,* a whirlpool, stream.] a pool of water to keep fish in; a weir. [Obs.]

gor'cock, *n.* [from *gorse,* furze or heath.] the moor cock, or male red grouse.

gor'crōw, *n.* [AS. *gor,* dung, dirt, and *crawe,* a crow.] the carrion crow. [Brit. Dial.]

Gor·di·ā'cē·ȧ, *n.* the *Gordiidæ.*

Gor'di·ăn, *a.* of or relating to Gordius, a king of Phrygia, or to the intricate knot tied by him; inextricable; difficult.

Gor'di·ăn knot (not), 1. in Greek legend, a knot tied by King Gordius of Phrygia, which an oracle revealed would be undone only by the future master of Asia: Alexander the Great, failing to untie it, cut the knot with his sword.
2. any perplexing problem.
to cut the Gordian knot; to find a quick, efficient solution for a perplexing problem.

gor'di·ăn, *n.* a hairworm.

Gor·dī'i·dae, *n.pl.* [*gordius* and *-idæ.*] the hairworms, a group of annuloid animals with a long, thin body resembling a horsehair.

Gor'di·us, *n.* [L. *Gordius* (supply *nodus,* a knot), Gordian knot: so called from the knots into which these worms twist their bodies.]
1. a genus of the *Gordiidæ.*
2. [g–] a hairworm of this genus.

Gor·dō'ni·ȧ, *n.* [named after James *Gordon,* a nurseryman of London.]
1. a genus of evergreen shrubs including the loblolly bay and the mountain bay.
2. [g–] a shrub of this genus.

Gor'dŏn set'tẽr, a large hunting dog of a breed characterized by a black, shaggy coat with spots of tan, brown, etc.

gōre, *n.* [ME. *gore,* mud, filth; AS. *gor,* dung, dirt.]
1. blood that is shed or drawn from the body; especially, thick or clotted blood.
2. dirt; mud. [Brit. Dial.]

gōre, *n.* [ME. *gore, gare*; AS. *gara,* an angular point of land, from *gar,* a spear.]
1. a wedge-shaped or triangular piece of cloth sewed into a garment, a sail, etc., to widen it in any part.
2. a triangular piece of land. [Dial.]
3. in heraldry, a charge consisting of two curved lines, one from the sinister chief point, the other from the base middle point, meeting in an acute angle in the middle of the fess point.

GORE
GORE (of skirt)

gōre, *v.t.*; gored; *pt., pp.*; goring, *ppr.* to make or insert a gore or gores in.

gōre, *v.t.*; gored, *pt., pp.*; goring, *ppr.* 1. to stab; to pierce; to penetrate with or as with a pointed instrument, as a spear or the point of a horn.
2. to dig; to hollow out. [Obs.]

gōre'bill, *n.* the garfish. [Brit. Dial.]

gor'fly, *n.*; *pl.* **gor'flies,** [AS. *gor,* dung, and *fly.*] a dung fly. [Brit. Dial.]

gorge, *n.* [ME. *gorge*; OFr. *gorge,* throat, gullet; LL. *gorgia,* a throat, narrow pass; L. *gurges,* a whirlpool, stream.]
1. the throat; the gullet.
2. a gluttonous appetite or meal.
3. the act of eating greedily.
4. what has been swallowed.
5. a feeling of resentment, disgust, anger, etc.
6. the entrance from the rear into a bastion or projecting section of a fortification.
7. a deep, narrow pass between steep heights.
8. in architecture, the narrowest part of the Tuscan and Doric capitals, between the astragal, above the shaft of the column, and the annulets; also, a cavetto or hollow molding.

9. a groove in a pulley.
10. a channel underneath a coping.
11. an obstruction or jam filling a channel or narrow way; as, an ice *gorge.*
12. a gorge hook.
to make one's gorge rise; to cause one to feel nauseated, disgusted, angry, etc.

gorge, *v.t.*; gorged, *pt., pp.*; gorging, *ppr.* [ME. *gorgen*; OFr. *gorger*, to devour greedily, from *gorge*, a throat, gullet.]
1. to swallow; especially, to swallow with greediness, or in large mouthfuls or quantities.
2. to glut; to fill the throat or stomach of; to satiate.

gorge, *v.i.* to feed with greediness; to eat gluttonously.

gorged, *a.* 1. having a gorge or throat.
2. in heraldry, bearing a crown or the like about the neck.
3. overfed; sated.

gorge hook, 1. a fishhook having two barbs leaded together.
2. a prehistoric form of fishing implement made of a slender rod of bone, stone, etc., sharpened at each end and attached to a line at its middle.

gorge'let, *n.* [OFr. *gorgelette*, dim. of *gorge*, a throat.] in ornithology, a gorget.

gor'geous (-jus), *a.* [OFr. *gorgias, gourgias*, gay, gaudy; *gorgias*, ruff for the neck, from *gorge*, throat.]
1. showy; resplendent; splendid; glittering with gay colors; magnificent.
2. beautiful; wonderful; delightful. [Slang.]
Syn.—showy, magnificent, superb, splendid, brilliant.

gor'geous·ly, *adv.* with showy magnificence.

gor'geous·ness, *n.* gorgeous quality or state.

gor·gë·rette', *n.* [OFr., from *gorge*, throat.] a piece of armor made to protect the neck.

gor'gër·in, *n.* [Fr., from *gorgère*, ruff for the throat, from *gorge*.] in architecture, the part of a column just below the top molding or between the shaft and the capital.

gor'get, *n.* [OFr. *gorgette*, from *gorge*, the throat.]
1. a piece of armor for protecting the throat or neck; a kind of breastplate.
2. a collar.
3. a pendent metallic ornament, worn by officers of some armies when on duty.

GORGET

4. a ruff or wimple formerly worn by women.
5. in surgery, a cutting instrument used in lithotomy; also, a concave or cannulated conductor, called a *blunt gorget*.
6. in ornithology, a throat patch, as in many humming birds, marked by a difference in texture or color of the feathers.

gor'get hum'mër, any humming bird, as the rubythroat, genus *Trochilus*.

Gor'gŏn, *n.* [L. *Gorgo* (-*onis*); Gr. *Gorgō* (-*onos*), from *gorgos*, terrible, fierce.]
1. in Greek mythology, any of three sisters with snakes for hair, of terrific aspect, the sight of which turned the beholder to stone. The three were Stheno, Euryale, and Medusa, who was slain by Perseus. Her head set on the shield of Pallas is also sometimes called a *gorgon*.
2. [g–] any ugly, terrifying, or repulsive woman.
3. [g–] the brindled gnu. [Obs.]

Gor'gŏn, *a.* like a Gorgon; very ugly or terrifying; as, a *Gorgon* face.

Gor·gō·nā'cē·ȧ, *n.pl.* same as *Gorgoniaceæ*.

gor·gō·nē'iŏn (-yŏn), *n.*; *pl.* **gor·gō·nē'iȧ,** in architectural sculpture, a mask carved in imitation of a Gorgon's head.

gor·gŏn·esque' (-esk'), *a.* repulsive; gorgonian.

Gor·gō'ni·ȧ, *n.* [L., coral which hardens in the air.] a genus of flexible coral zoophytes, growing in the form of shrubs, twigs, and reticulate fronds. The species are often bright-colored, and among them is the sea fan of the West Indies.

Gor·gō·ni·ā'cē·ae, *n.pl.* [*gorgonia* and *-aceæ*.] an order of *Alcyonaria*, including the sea-shrubs, fan corals, and the red coral of commerce. In all the organism consists of a composite structure made up of numerous polyps supported by a central branched axis formed by secretions from the bases of the polyps.

Gor·gō'ni·ăn, *a.* [Gr. *gorgoneios*, from *Gorgō* (-*onis*), Gorgon.]
1. of or like a Gorgon; pertaining to gorgons.
2. relating to the *Gorgoniaceæ*.

gor·gō'ni·ăn, *n.* one of the *Gorgoniaceæ*.

gor'gŏn·īze, *v.t.* to petrify, as by the sight of a Gorgon; to turn to stone.

gor'gŏn's head (hed), a basket fish.

Gor·gŏn·zō'lȧ, *n.* [from *Gorgonzola*, town in Italy near Milan.] a white Italian pressed cheese like Roquefort in appearance and flavor.

gor'hen, *n.* the female red grouse; the moor hen.

gō·ril'lȧ, *n.* [the Carthaginian navigator Hanno found the name in use in W. Africa in the fifth century B. C. as the native name of a wild creature found there.]
1. the largest and most powerful species of manlike ape, found in equatorial Africa: the adult male is over five feet high and weighs about 500 pounds.
2. (a) a person regarded as like a gorilla in appearance, strength, etc.; (b) a gangster; thug.

GORILLA (5 ft. high)

gor'i·ly, *adv.* in a gory manner.

gor'i·ness, *n.* the quality or condition of being gory.

gōr'ing, *a.* cut gradually sloping, so as to be broader at the clew than at the earing, as a sail.

gorm, *v.t.* to gaum; to smear. [Brit. Dial.]

gor'mȧ, *n.* same as *gormaw*.

gor'mănd, gour'mănd, *n.* [Fr. *gourmand*, a glutton.]
1. a greedy or ravenous eater; a glutton.
2. a gourmet; an epicure.

gor'mănd, gour'mănd, *a.* gluttonous; voracious.

gor'mănd·ẽr, gour'mănd·ẽr, *n.* a gormand. [Obs.]

gor'mănd·ism, gour'mănd·ism, *n.* gluttony.

gor'mănd·īze, gour'mănd·īze, *v.i.* and *v.t.*; gormandized, *pt., pp.*; gormandizing, *ppr.* to eat greedily; to swallow voraciously.

gor'mănd·īz·ẽr, gour'mănd·īz·ẽr, *n.* a greedy, voracious eater; a glutton.

gor'maw, *n.* a cormorant. [Scot.]

gō·roon' shell, a triton or trumpet shell.

gorse, *n.* [ME. *gorst*; AS. *gorst*, gorse, furze.] a low, thick, prickly shrub; furze.

gorse bīrd, a European linnet.

gorse'chat, *n.* the whinchat or linnet.

gorse'duck, *n.* the corncrake.

gorse'hatch, *n.* same as *gorsechat*.

gors'y, *a.* of, full of, or covered with gorse.

gōr'y, *a.* 1. covered with congealed or clotted blood; as, *gory* locks.
2. characterized by much bloodshed; as, a *gory* fight.
3. like gore.

gōr'y dew, bloodlike, gelatinous patches found on damp stones, and consisting of *Palmella cruenta*, a red alga.

gosh, *interj.* an exclamation of surprise, etc.: a euphemism for *God*.

gos'hawk, *n.* [ME. *goshawk, goshauk*; AS. *goshafoc*; *gos*, goose, and *hafoc*, a hawk.] a large, swift, powerful hawk, belonging to the genus *Astur*. The general plumage is a deep brown, the breast and belly white.

Gō'shen, *n.* [Heb. *gōshen*.]
1. in the Bible, the fertile land assigned to the Israelites in Egypt: Gen. xlv. 10.
2. a land of plenty.

gōsh'en·īte, *n.* a colorless beryl named after *Goshen*, Mass., where it is found.

gos'hẽrd, *n.* same as *gooseherd*.

gos'let, *n.* [AS. *gos*, goose, and dim. *-let*.] any of several species of pygmy geese found in India, Africa, and Australia, belonging to the genus *Nettapus*.

gos'ling, *n.* [AS. *gos*, a goose, and dim. *-ling*.]
1. a young goose; a goose not full grown: sometimes used figuratively.
2. a catkin.

gos'pel, *n.* [ME. *godspell, gospel*; AS. *gōdspel*, orig., good spell, good news; intended as transl. of Gr. *euangelion*, good tidings.]
1. the teachings of Jesus and the Apostles.
2. the history of the life and teachings of Jesus.
3. [G–] any of the first four books of the New Testament, ascribed to Matthew, Mark, Luke, and John.
4. [G–] an excerpt from any of these books read in a religious service.
5. a belief or body of beliefs proclaimed or accepted as absolutely true.
6. any doctrine or rule of conduct widely maintained.

gos'pel, *a.* of or accordant with the gospel; as, *gospel* truth.

gos'pel, *v.t.* to instruct in the gospel. [Obs.]

gos'pel·ẽr, gos'pel·lẽr, *n.* [ME. *gospellere*; AS. *godspellere*.]
1. a person who reads the gospel in church services.
2. a person who claims for himself and his sect the sole possession of gospel truth: formerly applied derisively to Puritans, Nonconformists, etc.
3. an evangelist; a writer of a gospel.

gos'pel·īze, *v.t.* 1. to form according to the gospel. [Obs.]
2. to instruct in the gospel; to evangelize. [Rare.]

goss, *n.* gorse.

gos'sȧ·mẽr, *n.* [ME. *gosesomer*, lit., goose summer: with allusion to the warm period in fall (*St. Martin's summer*) when goose is in season and gossamer is chiefly noticed.]
1. a filmy cobweb floating in the air or spread on bushes or grass.
2. a very thin, soft, filmy cloth.
3. (a) a lightweight waterproof cloth; (b) a coat made of this cloth.
4. anything like gossamer.

gos'sȧ·mẽr, *a.* light, thin, and filmy.

gos'sȧ·mẽr spī'dẽr, same as *ballooning spider* under *ballooning*.

gos'sȧ·mẽr·y, *a.* like gossamer; flimsy; unsubstantial.

gos'săn, *n.* [Corn.] reddish rock in the upper portions of a vein of metal: its color is due to oxidized pyrites.

gos·săn·if'ẽr·ous, *a.* containing or yielding gossan.

gos'sat, *n.* the three-bearded rockling, a small British sea fish. [Brit. Dial.]

gos'sib, *n.* a gossip. [Obs.]

gos'sip, *n.* [ME. *gossyp, gossib, godsib*; AS. *godsibb*, a sponsor, lit., God-relative; *god*, God, and *sib*, related.]
1. (a) a godparent; (b) a close friend. [Obs. or Dial.]
2. a person who chatters or repeats idle talk and rumors about others.
3. (a) such talk or rumors; (b) chatter.

gos'sip, *v.i.*; gossiped (-sipt), *pt., pp.*; gossiping, *ppr.* 1. to be a gossip; to indulge in idle talk or rumors about others.
2. to be a companion. [Obs.]

gos'sip, *v.t.* to be sponsor for. [Obs.]

gos'sip·ẽr, *n.* a gossip.

gos'sip·red, *n.* [ME. *gossiprede, godsibrede*, spiritual relationship; *gossip, godsib*; a sponsor, and *-rede*, from AS. *-ræden*, condition.]
1. the mutual relation between sponsors and the person for whom they are sponsors. [Obs.]
2. gossip. [Rare.]

gos'sip·ry, *n.* 1. gossipred. [Obs.]
2. gossip. [Rare.]
3. gossips as a group. [Rare.]

gos'sip·y, *a.* of, full of, or fond of gossip; inclined to be chatty.

gos·soon', *n.* [a corruption of Fr. *garçon*, a boy, attendant.] a boy; also, a servant. [Irish.]

gos'sy·pīne, *a.* [L. *gossypion* and *-ine*.] cottony; like cotton.

Gos·syp'i·um, *n.* [L. *gossypion, gossipion*, the cotton tree.] a genus of the *Malvaceæ*, whose seeds are covered with the fibers that form the cotton of commerce.

got, *v.* past tense and past participle of *get*.

Gō'tȧ·mȧ, *n.* Gautama (Buddha).

gōte, *n.* [O.D. *gote*, a ditch, channel.] a gutter; a sluice. [Brit. Dial.]

gō'tẽr, *n.* a gutter. [Obs.]

Goth, *n.* [LL. *Gothus*, pl. *Gothi*, the Goths.]
1. one of an ancient Germanic tribe or nation which inhabited the shores of the Baltic. Many great hordes of them migrating southward in the second century dispossessed the Romans of Dacia and occupied the coast of the Black Sea from the Don to the Danube. There they divided into two groups, the Visigoths (Western Goths) to the west of the Dnieper, and the Ostrogoths (Eastern Goths) to the east.
2. a barbarian; an uncouth, uncivilized person.

Goth'ăm·īte, *n.* an inhabitant of New York City.

Goth′iç, *a.* [LL. *Gothicus*, from *Gothus*, pl. *Gothi*, the Goths.]
1. pertaining to the Goths or their language.
2. designating or of a style of architecture developed in western Europe between the 12th and 16th centuries and characterized by the use of ribbed vaulting, flying buttresses, pointed arches, steep roofs, etc.
3. [*sometimes* g-] (a) medieval; (b) not classical; (c) barbarous; uncivilized.
4. in literature, using medieval locale, properties, local color, etc., especially to produce an effect of horror and mystery.

Goth′iç, *n.* 1. the East Germanic language of the Goths: it is known chiefly from the Bible translations of Bishop Ulfilas (4th century A.D.) and the vocabulary made by van Busbecq in the Crimea (16th century A.D.).
2. [g-] a style of type without serifs.
THIS LINE IS SET IN GOTHIC.
3. the Gothic style of architecture.

Goth′i·çăl·ly, *adv.* in a Gothic manner; like Gothic.

Goth′iç ärch, a pointed arch.

Goth′i·cişm, *n.* 1. rudeness of manners; barbarity.
2. a Gothic idiom.
3. conformity to the Gothic style of building.

Goth′i·cīze, *v.t.*; Gothicized, *pt., pp.*; Gothicizing, *ppr.* to make Gothic.

gō′thīte, *n.* same as *goethite.*

got′ten, *v.* past participle of *get.*

Göt·ter·däm′mer·ung (gẽt-ẽr-dem′ẽr-oong), *n.* [G., twilight of the gods.]
1. in Germanic mythology, the end of the world; the time when the gods war with their enemies until all are destroyed.
2. an opera by Richard Wagner on this theme.

gouȧçhe (gwȧsh), *n.* [Fr.; It. *guazzo*, water color, spray, liquid splashed about, pool; L. *aqautio*, watering, water, watering place, from *aqua*, water.]
1. a way of painting with opaque colors ground in water and mixed with a preparation of gum.
2. a pigment of this sort.
3. a painting made with such pigments.

göu′bẽr, *n.* same as *goober.*

Göu′dȧ, *n.* [from *Gouda*, Netherlands, city where orig. produced.] a mild cheese made from curds: also *Gouda cheese.*

göu·droṅ′, *n.* [Fr., tar.] a bundle of sticks soaked in pitch, oil, or the like, and used in warfare either for lighting up ditches, etc., or for setting fire to an enemy's works.

gouġe, *n.* [Fr.; LL. *gubia, gulbia*; probably from Celt.]
1. a chisel whose cutting edge is curved, used to cut holes, channels, or grooves in wood or stone, or to cut out forms from leather, etc.
2. a tool used by bookbinders, which forms a curve in gilding.
3. a soft deposit between a vein of ore and its wall.
4. the act of gouging; also, the groove gouged out. [Colloq.]
5. a fraud; a cheat; also, an impostor. [Colloq.]

gouġe, *v.t.*; gouged (goujd), *pt., pp.*; gouging, *ppr.* 1. to scoop out with or as with a gouge.
2. to force out (the eye of a person) with the thumb or finger.
3. to cheat; to defraud. [Colloq.]

gouġe bit, a bit having a curved cutting edge.

gou′ġẽr, *n.* one who or that which gouges, as certain insects.

gouġe shell, a marine shell having a sharp edge.

göu′jon, *n.* [Fr., a gudgeon.] a fish, the mudcat.

göu′lȧsh, *n.* [G. *gulasch*, from Hung. *gulyás*, lit., a shepherd, hence shepherds' food.] a stew made of beef or veal and vegetables seasoned with paprika: also *Hungarian goulash.*

gou′pen, *n.* [ON. *gaupn.*]
1. the hollow of one hand, or of two held together; a handful; a grasp. [Scot.]
2. a small quantity of meal given to the servant in a mill as a perquisite. [Scot.]

gour, *n.* a gaur, or wild ox of India.

gour, *n.* a giaour; an infidel.

Gou′rȧ, *n.* [from native name.]
1. a genus of large crested pigeons of New Guinea and adjacent islands.
2. [g-] one of this genus.

göu′rȧ·mi, *n.* [Javanese.] the goramy, a tropical fresh-water food fish.

gōurd (*or* goord), *n.* [ME.; OFr. *gouorde, gougorde*, from L. *cucurbita.*]
1. any trailing or climbing plant belonging to a family that includes the squash, melon, pumpkin, etc.
2. (a) the bulb-shaped fruit (*bottle gourd*) of one species of this family; (b) any of the ornamental, inedible fruits of related plants.
3. any plant producing such a fruit.
4. the dried, hollowed-out shell of such a fruit, used as a drinking cup, dipper, etc.

göurde, göurd, *n.* [Fr. *gourd*, f. *gourde*, from L. *gurdus*, slow, dull.] the silver monetary unit of Haiti.

gōurd′i·ness, *n.* in farriery, a gourdy condition.

gōurd tree, same as *calabash tree.*

gōurd′wŏrm, *n.* a parasitic worm; specifically, the liver fluke.

gōurd′y, *a.* having swollen legs: said of a horse.

göur′mănd, *n.* see *gormand.*

göur·mẹt′ (-mā′), *n.* [Fr., OFr. *gourmet, groumet*, servant, wine taster, vintner's assistant.] an epicure; a judge of choice foods.

goūr′net, *n.* a gurnard.

goust′y, *a.* dreary; gusty. [Scot.]

gout, *n.* [ME. *goute, gowte*; OFr. *goute, goutte*, a drop, gout; L. *gutta*, a drop: so called from the disease being considered a defluxion.]
1. a disease resulting from a disturbance of the metabolism, characterized by an excess of uric acid in the blood and deposits of uric acid salts in the tissues around the joints, especially of the feet and hands: it causes swelling and severe pain, especially in the big toe.
2. a clot or coagulation; as, *gouts* of blood.
3. a diseased condition of grain due to the gout fly.

goût (gö), *n.* [Fr., from L. *gustus*, taste.] taste; relish.

gout flȳ, a small fly, *Chlorops tæniopus*, the larva of which does much injury to grain, producing gout, or swelling of the stem joints.

gout′i·ly, *adv.* in a gouty manner.

gout′i·ness, *n.* the quality or condition of being gouty.

gout stōne, a concretion chiefly composed of urate of soda, occurring abnormally around the joints, as the result of gout.

gout′weed, gout′wŏrt, *n. Ægopodium podagraria*, a plant of the *Umbelliferæ*, formerly believed to be a specific for gout: called also *ash-weed, herb Gerard*, and *bishop weed.*

gout′y, *a.* 1. diseased with the gout, or subject to the gout; as, a *gouty* person; a *gouty* joint.
2. pertaining to or like the gout.
3. swollen as with the gout.
4. resulting from or causing the gout.
gouty concretion; a gout stone.

gout′y gąll, an excrescence upon the stem of the raspberry, caused by the larva of the beetle *Agrilus ruficollis.*

gŏv′ẽrn (guv′ẽrn), *v.t.*; governed, *pt., pp.*; governing, *ppr.* [ME. *governen, guvernen*; OFr. *guverner*; L. *gubernare*; Gr. *kybernān*, to steer or pilot a ship, direct, command.]
1. to exercise authority over; direct; control; rule; manage.
2. to influence the action or conduct of; guide; sway; as, how is public opinion *governed?*
3. to restrain; hold in check; curb; as, you must *govern* your temper.
4. to regulate the speed (of an automobile, etc.) by means of a governor.
5. to determine; to be a rule or law for; as, the scientific principles *governing* a phenomenon.
6. in grammar, (a) to require (a word) to be in a particular case or mood; (b) to require (a particular case or mood). In English grammar, the term applies to the relationship between a preposition and a following pronoun.

gŏv′ẽrn, *v.i.* to exercise authority; to administer laws.

Syn.—rule, direct, control, moderate, guide, sway, supervise, manage, command, conduct.

gŏv″ẽrn·ȧ·bil′i·ty, *n.* governableness.

gŏv′ẽrn·ȧ·ble, *a.* controllable; manageable; that can be governed.

gŏv′ẽrn·ȧ·ble·ness, *n.* the quality of being controllable.

gŏv′ẽr·nāil, *n.* 1. a helm or rudder. [Obs.]
2. government: also written *governal.* [Obs.]

gŏv′ẽrn·ănce, *n.* [ME. *governance, governaunce*; OFr. *governance, gouvernance*; ML. *gubernantia*, from L. *gubernare*, to govern, pilot.] exercise of authority; control; management; power of government.

gŏv·ẽrn·ȧnte, *n.* [Fr. *gouvernante.*] a governess. [Obs.]

gŏv′ẽrn·ess, *n.* 1. a woman employed in a private home who has the care of instructing and directing children.
2. a woman governor. [Obs.]

gŏv′ẽrn·ment, *n.* [Fr. *gouvernement*, from *gouverner*; L. *gubernare*, to govern.]
1. (a) the exercise of authority over an organization, institution, state, district, etc.; direction; control; rule; management; (b) the right, function, or power of governing.
2. (a) a system of ruling, controlling, etc.; (b) an established system of political administration by which a state, district, etc. is governed.
3. all the people who administer or control the affairs of a state, institution, etc.; administration.
4. any territory which is governed.
5. in grammar, the influence of a word, in regard to construction, over the case or mood of another.

gŏv·ẽrn·men′tăl, *a.* pertaining to government; made by government.

gŏv′ẽrn·ment is′sūe (ish′ū), see *G. I.*

gŏv′ẽrn·ŏr, *n.* [OFr. *governeor, gouvernour*; L. *gubernator*, a pilot, steersman, governor, from *gubernare*, to pilot, steer, direct.]

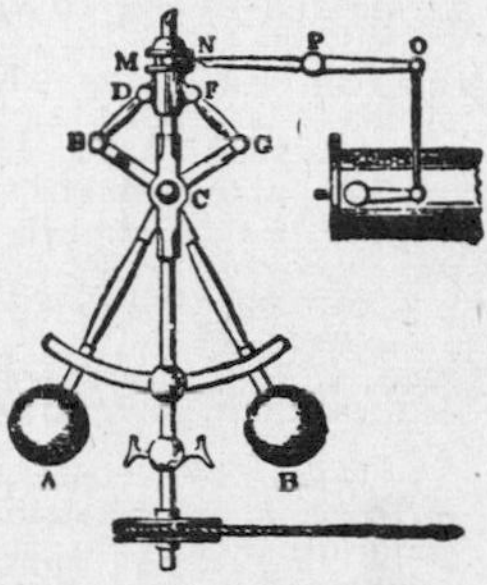

GOVERNOR OF A STEAM ENGINE

1. a person who governs; especially, (a) a person appointed to govern a dependency, province, town, fort, etc.; (b) the elected head of any State of the United States; (c) a person who directs, manages, or helps to direct or manage an organization or institution.
2. a person having authority; especially, one's father: often used as a term of address [Chiefly Brit. Colloq.]
3. a tutor. [Archaic.]
4. a pilot; one who steers a ship. [Obs.]
5. in mechanics, a piece of mechanism by which the speed of a steam engine, turbine, water wheel, or other motor is regulated; more broadly, any regulating device, as one for equalizing the motion of mills and machinery. The common form of governor is shown in the illustration, the centrifugal balls A and B being rotated from the engine and geared with a toggle D E C and F G C pivoted at C and also attached pivotally to the grooved slide M, controlling the lever N O, pivoted at P, which lever in turn regulates the admission of steam into the cylinder.

gŏv′ẽrn·ŏr-ġen′ẽr·ăl, *n.*; *pl.* **gŏv′ẽrn·ŏrş-ġen′ẽr·ăl,** governor general. [Chiefly Brit.]

gŏv′ẽrn·ŏr ġen′ẽr·ăl, *pl.* **gŏv′ẽrn·ŏrş ġen′ẽr·ăl,** a governor who has subordinate or deputy governors under him, as in the British dominions.

gŏv′ẽrn·ŏr·ship, *n.* the position, function, or term of office of a governor.

gow′ăn, *n.* [Scot., from Gael. *gugan*, bud, flower, daisy.]
1. the English daisy. [Scot.]
2. granite rock in a soft or fragile condition.

gow′ăn·y, *a.* decked with gowans. [Scot.]

gowd, *n.* money; gold. [Scot.]

gowd′en, *a.* golden. [Scot.]

gowd′nọọk, *n.* the saury pike, a coast fish. [Scot.]

gowk, *v.t.* to make a fool of. [Scot.]

gowk, *n.* 1. a cuckoo. [Scot.]
2. a silly person. [Scot.]

gowk stọrm, in Scotland, a stiff but short storm, that generally comes about the middle of April when the gowk, or cuckoo, arrives.

gowl, *v.i.* [ME. *goulen, gowlen*; Ice. *gaula*, to low, bellow.] to howl. [Obs.]

gown, *n.* [ME. and OFr. *goune*, from ML. *gunna*, loose robe.]
1. a long, generally loose, outer garment; specifically, (a) a woman's dress; (b) a man's dressing gown; (c) a nightgown; (d) the official dress worn by certain officials, clergymen, scholars, etc., and by students receiving degrees from a university.
2. the members of a college or university, collectively.

gown, *v.t.* to dress in a gown.

gowns'măn, gown'măn, *n.* 1. one whose professional habit is a gown, as a divine or lawyer, and particularly a member of an English university.
2. a civilian.

gow'pen, gow'pin, *n.* same as *goupen.*

goy, *n.*; *pl.* **goy'im,** [Yid.; Heb. *goi,* tribe, nation.] a non-Jew; a gentile.

goz'zărd, *n.* a gooseherd.

Grāaf'i·ăn, *a.* pertaining to or described by Regnier de *Graaf,* 17th-c. Dutch scientist.
graafian follicle (or *vesicle*); a small follicle or sac in the ovary of a mammal in which an ovum matures.

grab, *n.* [Anglo-Ind.] a two-masted ship used on the Malabar coast, having triangular sails.

grab, *v.t.*; grabbed, *pt., pp.*; grabbing, *ppr.* [prob. from M.D., M.L.G. *grabben.*]
1. to seize or snatch suddenly; take roughly and quickly.
2. to get possession of by unscrupulous methods.

grab, *n.* 1. a sudden grasp or seizure; a grabbing.
2. something grabbed.
3. a mechanical device for seizing an object to lift it; as, a *grab* to withdraw tools from a drilled hole.

grab bag, a bag in which various articles are placed to be grabbed sight unseen by a buyer who has paid a fixed price.

grab'bẽr, *n.* one who or that which grabs.

grab'ble, *v.i.*; grabbled, *pt., pp.*; grabbling, *ppr.* [freq. of *grab.*]
1. to grope; to feel with the hands.
2. to sprawl.

grāce, *n.* [OFr. *grace, grasce*; L. *gratia,* favor, esteem, kindness, from *gratus,* pleasing, agreeable.]
1. beauty or charm of form, composition, movement, or expression; elegance with appropriate dignity; as, she danced with much *grace.*
2. an attractive quality, feature, manner, etc.
3. a sense of what is right and proper; decency.
4. (a) disposition to grant something freely; favor; good will; (b) [*pl.*] the condition or fact of being favored; (c) a favor or privilege.
5. mercy; clemency.
6. a period of time granted beyond the date set for the performance of an act or the payment of an obligation; temporary exemption.
7. favor shown by granting such a delay.
8. a short prayer in which blessing is asked, or thanks are given, for a meal.
9. [G–] a title of respect or reverence used in a speaking to or of an archbishop, duke, or duchess, preceded by *His, Her,* or *Your.*
10. in music, a grace note, as an appoggiatura, shake, etc.
11. in theology, (a) the free unmerited love and favor of God; (b) divine influence acting in man to restrain him from sin; (c) a state of reconciliation to God; (d) spiritual instruction, improvement, and edification.
My *grace* is sufficient for thee.
—2 Cor. xii. 9.
12. affectation of elegance; assumption of refinement; as, he laughed at her airs and *graces.*
13. in English universities, an act, vote, or decree of the government of the institution.
14. [*pl.*] a game designed to promote or display grace of motion: it consists in passing a small hoop from one person to another by means of two short sticks.
15. lot; fortune; condition. [Obs.]
16. [*pl.*] thanks. [Obs.]
day of grace; in theology, the time of probation when sinners may obtain forgiveness.
days of grace; the three days after the date of maturity specified in a note which the law allows for its payment.
in the bad graces of; in disfavor with.
in the good graces of; in favor with.
with bad grace; ungracefully; sullenly or reluctantly; as, the apology came *with bad grace.*
with good grace; graciously; gracefully; willingly; as, he made reparation *with good grace.*

grāce, *v.t.*; graced (grāst), *pt., pp.*; gracing, *ppr.* 1. to adorn; to decorate; to lend or add grace to.
Graced with wreaths of victory. —Shak.
2. to dignify; to honor.
3. to supply with heavenly grace.
4. in music, to add grace notes, cadenzas, etc. to; as, to *grace* a melody.

grāce çup, 1. a cup used to drink a toast from after a meal or banquet.
2. the toast.

grāced (grāst), *a.* endowed with grace; graceful; beautiful.

grāce'fụl, *a.* full of or displaying grace or beauty in form, composition, movement, or expression.

grāce'fụl·ly, *adv.* in a graceful manner; with a natural ease and propriety; as, to walk or speak *gracefully.*

grāce'fụl·ness, *n.* beauty with dignity in manner, motion, or countenance; the quality of being graceful.

grāce'less, *a.* 1. lacking any sense of what is right; reprobate.
2. without grace; clumsy or inelegant.

grāce'less·ly, *adv.* without grace.

grāce'less·ness, *n.* the condition or quality of being graceless.

grāce nōte, in music, a note added for embellishment: it is usually printed as a small note just before the note that it embellishes, from which its time value is subtracted.

Grāc'eṣ, *n.pl.* [transl. of L. *Gratiae,* transl. of Gr. *Charites,* pl. of *Charis,* mythological figure personifying grace and beauty.] in Greek mythology, the three sister goddesses who had control over pleasure, charm, elegance, and beauty in human life and in nature: Aglaia (Brilliance), Euphrosyne (Joy), and Thalia (Bloom).

grāce strōke, a finishing touch or stroke; a coup de grace.

grä'cï·äs (grä'thē-äs), *interj.* [Sp.] thanks; thank you.

grac'ile, *a.* 1. slender.
2. gracefully slender.

grac'i·lent, *a.* gracile. [Obs.]

grȧ·cil'i·ty, *n.* the state of being gracile; slenderness; smallness. [Rare.]

grä·ci·ō'sō (-shi-), *n.* [Sp.]
1. in Spanish comedy, a clown.
2. a court favorite. [Archaic.]

grā'cious, *a.* [OFr. *gracios*; L. *gratiosus,* in favor, popular, kind, from *gratia,* favor, grace.]
1. having or showing kindness, courtesy, charm, etc.
2. merciful; compassionate.
3. indulgent or polite to supposed inferiors.
4. having pleasing qualities; attractive. [Archaic.]
5. characterized by or possessing divine grace; virtuous; good.
Gracious in the eyes of God.
—Jer. Taylor.

Syn.—benignant, kind, merciful, mild, compassionate, tender.

grā'cious, *interj.* an expression of surprise.

grā'cious·ly, *adv.* 1. in a gracious or friendly manner; courteously.
2. fortunately; favorably.

grā'cious·ness, *n.* the condition or quality of being gracious.

grac'kle, *n.* [L. *graculus,* the jackdaw: so called from its note.]
1. a bird of the genus *Gracula,* a mina.
2. a bird of America of the family *Icteridæ*; as, the purple *grackle, Quiscalus quiscula;* the rusty *grackle, Scolecophagus carolinus;* the boat-tailed *grackle, Quiscalus major.*

grā'dāte, *v.t.* and *v.i.*; gradated, *pt., pp.*; gradating, *ppr.* [L. *gradatus,* arranged in steps or grades, from *gradus,* a step, grade.] to pass or cause to pass by imperceptible degrees from one to another; shade into one another, as colors.

grā'dāt·ed, *a.* [pp. of *gradate.*] in linguistics, showing the effects of gradation.

grȧ·dā'tion, *n.* [OFr. *gradation*; L. *gradatio* (*-onis*), that which goes up or down by steps, a climax, from *gradatus,* having steps or grades, from *gradus,* a step, grade.]
1. the act or process of forming or arranging in grades, stages, or steps.
2. a gradual change by steps or stages from one condition, quality, etc. to another.
3. a gradual shading of one tint, tone, or color into another.
4. a step, stage, or degree in a graded series; transitional stage; as, there are many *gradations* between good and bad.
5. in geology, the process of wearing away and building up of land by erosion and deposition.
6. in linguistics, the systematic variation seen in the vowels of related bases as conditioned by the presence or absence of stress on the base syllable; as, the vowel variation in *sing, sang, sung* is due to *gradation* in Indo-European.
7. in logic, a regular advancement from step to step, as in an argument.
8. in music, an ascending or descending by a regular succession of chords.
9. in rhetoric, an ascending or descending in terms, as toward a climax.

grā·dā'tion, *v.t.* to form by gradations. [Rare.]

grā·dā'tion·ăl, *a.* of or characterized by gradation.

grad'ȧ·tō·ry, *a.* 1. proceeding step by step. [Rare.]
2. in zoology, fitted for walking; suitable for stepping.

grad'ȧ·tō·ry, *n.* [L. *gradatus,* having steps or grades, from *gradus,* a step.] steps from the cloisters into a church.

grad'dăn, *n.* parched grain of any kind; also, meal ground by hand. [Scot.]

grāde, *n.* [Fr. *grade*; L. *gradus,* a step, degree, rank, from *gradi,* to step, walk.]
1. any of the stages in an orderly, systematic progression; step; degree.
2. (a) a degree in a scale classifying according to quality, rank, worth, etc.; as, these eggs are *grade* A; (b) a group of people of the same rank, merit, worth, etc.
3. the degree of rise or descent of a sloping surface, as of a highway, railroad, etc.
4. a sloping part.
5. (a) one of the divisions by years in a school curriculum: most systems include twelve grades after the kindergarten; (b) the group of pupils in any of these divisions.
6. a mark or rating on an examination, work in a school course, etc.
7. in animal husbandry, an animal with one parent of pure breed.
8. in linguistics, any of the various forms in which the vowel may appear in the base of a word as a result of gradation.
at grade; at the same level, as when two roads cross *at grade.*
the grades; elementary school.
to make the grade; (a) to get to the top of a steep incline; (b) to overcome obstacles and reach a desired goal.
up to grade; with standard quality.

grāde, *v.t.*; graded, *pt., pp.*; grading, *ppr.* 1. to arrange in degrees, ranks, classes, or steps, according to order, series, quality, size, etc.
2. to give a grade, mark, or rating on an examination, work in a school course, etc.
3. to gradate.
4. to make (ground) level or slope (ground) evenly for a roadway, etc.
5. to improve by crossbreeding with a better breed (often with *up*).

grāde, *v.i.* 1. to assume an indicated rank or position in a series; to be of a certain grade.
2. to change gradually; to go through a series of stages.

-grāde, [from L. *gradi,* to walk.] a combining form meaning (a specified manner of) *walking* or *moving,* as in planti*grade.*

grāde çross'ing, the place where a railroad intersects another railroad or a roadway on the same level.

grāde'ly, *a.* decent; orderly. [Brit. Dial.]

grāde'ly, *adv.* decently; orderly. [Brit. Dial.]

grād'ẽr, *n.* 1. one who grades or a device to assist in grading.
2. a pupil in a specified grade at school; as, a fifth *grader.*

grāde sçhọọl, elementary school; grammar school.

grā'di·ent, *a.* [L. *gradiens* (*-entis*), ppr. of *gradi,* to step, walk.]
1. moving by steps; walking; also, adapted for walking or stepping; as, a *gradient* animal.
2. rising or descending by regular degrees of inclination; as, the *gradient* line of a railroad.

grā'di·ent, *n.* 1. the degree of slope in a road, railway, etc.
2. a slope, as of a road or railroad.
3. in physics, (a) the rate of change of temperature, pressure, etc.; (b) a diagram or curve representing this.

grā'di·ent pōst, 1. a post or stake beside a railway indicating by figures the rise or fall in grade.
2. in construction work, a stake marking the level to be maintained; the surface mark.

grā'din, grȧ·dïne', *n.* [Fr., from L. *gradus,* a

step, pace.]
1. one of a series of seats, steps, etc., which rise one after another.
2. a shelf behind an altar, for candlesticks, etc.

grȧ·dïne′, *n.* [Fr.] a sculptor's chisel, having a toothed edge.

grād′ing, *n.* the act of bringing to a grade, as in building a roadway.

grȧ·di′nō, *n.* [It., from L. *gradus*, a grade.] a decoration for the back of an altar; a gradin; a superaltar.

grȧ′dō, *n.* a degree in a scale of music.

grad′ū·ăl, *a.* proceeding by steps or degrees; advancing or occurring little by little; passing from one step to another; regular and slow; as, a *gradual* increase of knowledge; a *gradual* awakening.

grad′ū·ăl, *n.* [LL. *graduale, gradalis*, a book containing hymns and prayers which were originally sung on the steps of a pulpit, from L. *gradus*, a step.]
1. the steps of an altar. [Obs.]
2. a response sung after the Epistle.
3. a book containing choral responses of the Mass.
Gradual Psalm; one of the fifteen psalms (Ps. cxx to cxxxiv inclusive) sung on the steps of the Temple at Jerusalem.

grad·ū·al′i·ty, *n.* regular progression.

grad′ū·ăl·ly, *adv.* 1. by degrees; step by step; little by little.
2. in degree. [Obs.]

grad′ū·ăl·ness, *n.* the state or quality of being gradual.

grad′ū·āte, *v.t.*; graduated, *pt., pp.*; graduating, *ppr.* [LL. *graduatus*, pp. of *graduare*, to honor with a degree, to graduate, from L. *gradus*, a step, degree.]
1. to give a degree or diploma in recognition of the completion of a course of study at a school or college.
2. to mark with degrees for measuring; as, to *graduate* a rule.
3. in chemistry, to bring (fluids) to a certain degree of consistency.
4. to arrange or classify into grades according to size, quality, etc.

grad′ū·āte, *v.i.* 1. to receive a degree or diploma in recognition of the completion of a course of study at a school or college.
2. to pass by degrees; to change gradually.

grad′ū·āte, *n.* 1. one who has received a degree or diploma from a school or college, attesting to the fact that he has completed a course of study.
2. in a laboratory, a vessel having graduated marking, used for measuring liquids, etc.

grad′ū·āte, *a.* 1. having been graduated from a school, college, etc.; being a graduate.
2. of or for graduates; as, *graduate* courses.

grad′ū·ā·ted, *a.* 1. honored with a degree or diploma from some school or college.
2. marked with degrees or regular intervals.
3. in zoology, tapered; said of the tail of a bird where the outer feathers are gradually shortened.
graduated glass, tube, etc.; a glass, tube, etc. with marks on the outside to indicate the amount of the contents at a certain level.

grad′ū·āte school, a division of a university in which instruction is offered in various fields leading to degrees above the bachelor's.

grad′ū·āte·ship, *n.* the state of a graduate.

grad′ū·āte stū′dent, a student working toward an advanced degree at a graduate school.

grad·ū·ā′tion, *n.* [ML. *graduatio (-onis)*, the act of conferring a degree, from *graduare*, to confer a degree, from L. *gradus*, a step, a degree.]
1. a graduating or being graduated from a school or college.
2. the ceremony connected with this; graduation exercises; commencement.
3. a marking of a flask, tube, gauge, etc. with a series of degrees for measuring.
4. one or all of the degrees marked; a degree or scale.
5. an arrangement or classification into grades according to amount, size, quality, etc.
6. the process of bringing a liquid to a certain consistency by evaporation.

grad′ū·ā·tŏr, *n.* 1. an instrument for dividing any line, straight or curved, into small, regular intervals; specifically, (a) a dividing machine; (b) in chemistry, a device for the reduction of a liquid by spreading it out upon a surface.
2. a user of a graduator.

grā′dus, *n.* [from L. *gradus ad Parnassum*, steps to Parnassus, a name for a book on prosody or poetry.]
1. a dictionary of versification for aid in composing poetry, especially in Greek and Latin.
2. in music, graded exercises, each succeeding one more difficult than its predecessor.

grā′dy, *a.* [L. *gradatus*, furnished with steps, from *gradus*, a step.] in heraldry, arranged in or starting from steps; embattled, as an embattled edge.

A BEND GRADY

Grae′ae, *n.pl.* [L.; Gr. *Graiai*, pl. of *graia*, old woman, from *grais*, old; akin to *gerōn*, old man.] in Greek mythology, the three daughters of Phorcus, a sea god: they acted as guards for the Gorgons and had but one eye and one tooth to share among them: also *Graiae*.

Grae′ciṣm, *n.* Grecism.

Grae′cīze, *v.t.* and *v.i.* to Grecize.

Grae′ċō-, Greco-.

Gräf, *n.* [G.] in Germany, Austria, or Sweden, a title of nobility equal to that of an English earl or a French count.

graff, *n.* [ME. *grafe, greive*, a steward, reeve, from Ice. *greifi*, a steward.] a reeve; a steward.

graff, *n.* [ME. *graf*; AS. *græf*, a ditch, grave, from *grafan*, to dig.] a ditch or moat; a grave. [Scot.]

graff, *v.* and *n.* graft. [Obs.]

graff′ăġe, *n.* the slope of a moat or ditch nearest the parapet.

graf′fẽr, *n.* in law, a notary or scrivener. [Obs.]

gräf·fi′tï, *n.pl.*; *sing.* **gräf·fi′tō,** [It., pl. of *graffito*, a scribbling, from *graffiare*, to scratch, scribble, from LL. *graphiare*, to write, from L. *graphium*; Gr. *grapheion*, a style for writing, from *graphein*, to write.] inscriptions and drawings found on rocks or on the walls of ancient ruins.

grȧft, *n.* [ME. *graffe, gryffe*; OFr. *greffe*; LL. *graphiolum*, a small shoot or scion, from L. *graphium*; Gr. *grapheion*, a style for writing, a pencil, from *graphein*, to write.]
1. a small shoot or bud of a tree or plant inserted in another tree or plant, where it continues to grow, becoming a permanent part.

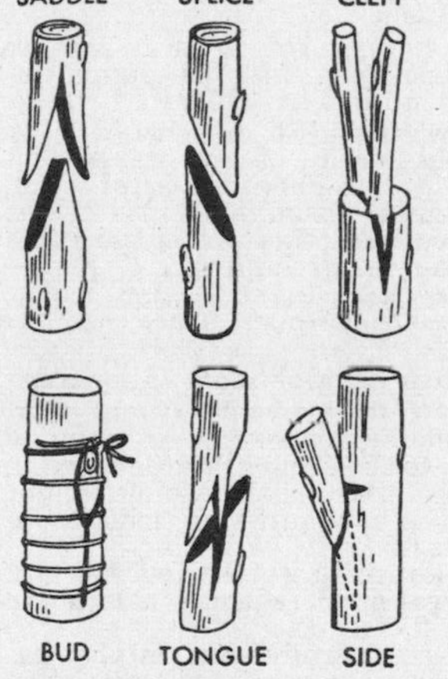

TYPES OF GRAFT

2. the act or process of inserting such a bud or shoot.
3. the place on a plant or tree where such a bud or shoot has been inserted.
4. a tree or plant with such a bud or shoot inserted in it.
5. in surgery, a piece of living tissue joined or to be joined to any part or member of a person or animal where it grows and becomes a permanent part.
6. (a) the act of taking advantage of one's position to gain money, property, etc. dishonestly, as in politics; (b) anything acquired by such illegal methods, as an illicit profit from government business.

grȧft, *v.t.*; grafted, *pt., pp.*; grafting, *ppr.* 1. to insert (a shoot or bud of one plant or tree) as a graft into another plant or tree.
2. to produce (a fruit, flower, etc.) by means of a graft.
3. to obtain (money, etc.) by graft.
4. in surgery, to transplant (a graft).
to graft by approach; in horticulture, to inarch.

grȧft, *v.i.* 1. to be grafted.
2. to make a graft on a plant.
3. to use public office for private gain; to obtain money or property by graft.

grȧft′ăġe, *n.* 1. the act or science of grafting.
2. the state of being grafted.

grȧft′ẽr, *n.* 1. one who inserts scions into or on foreign stocks, or propagates fruit by engrafting.
2. a surgeon who performs the operation of grafting.
3. a dishonest official; a public officer who grafts; a swindler. [Slang.]
4. an instrument used in grafting trees, etc.
5. the tree from which a scion for grafting is cut.

grȧft′ing, *n.* 1. the art, act, or method of inserting grafts.
2. the act of obtaining money illegally, as by a public official who uses his position for the purpose.
3. in carpentry, the joining of two pieces of wood end to end; scarfing.
4. in nautical usage, the manner of weaving over with fine lines, as a block strap, ring bolt, etc.
5. in surgery, the performance of the operation of autoplasty.

grȧft′ing sciṣ′ṣŏrṣ, in surgery, scissors used in autoplasty or skin grafting.

grȧft′ing wax, a substance used in plant or tree grafting to exclude the air and to preserve a new joint, usually made of beeswax, resin, tallow, etc.

grā′hăm (-ăm), *a.* [from Sylvester *Graham* (1794–1851), Am. physician.] designating or made of unsifted, whole-wheat flour; as, *graham* crackers.

Grā′hăm·īte, *n.* a believer in the dietetic system of Sylvester Graham; a vegetarian.

Grā′iae (grā′ē), *n. pl.* Graeae.

grāil, *n.* [OFr. *grael, greel*; LL. *graduale, gradalis*, a service book, a book of prayers and hymns to be used upon the church steps, from L. *gradus*, a step.] a book of offices in the Roman Catholic Church; a gradual.

Grāil, *n.* [OFr. *graal, greal*; LL. *gradalis, gradale*, a flat dish, a shallow vessel, prob. corruption of *cratella*, dim. of L. *crater*, a bowl.] in medieval legend, the Holy Grail, the cup or platter used by Jesus at the Last Supper, and by Joseph of Arimathea to collect drops of blood from Jesus' body at the Crucifixion: the quest of the Grail, which disappeared because its keepers were morally impure, is the subject of Malory's *Morte d'Arthur*, one of Tennyson's *Idylls of the King*, Wagner's *Parsifal*, etc.

grāil, *n.* [OFr. *graile, graille*, fine, small, from L. *gracilis*, slender.] gravel. [Poet.]

grāil, grāille, *n.* a half-round file, single cut, used in making combs.

grāin, *n.* [ME. *greyne*, from OFr. *grein, grain*, a seed, grain (from L. *granum*, a seed, kernel), and *grainne, graine*, seed or grain collectively (from LL. *grana*, fem., orig. pl. of L. *granum*).]
1. a small, hard seed or seedlike fruit, especially that of any cereal plant, as wheat, rice, corn, rye, etc.
2. (a) cereal seeds in general; (b) the seeds of a specific cereal; (c) any plant or plants producing cereal seeds. In Great Britain, commonly called *corn*.
3. a tiny, solid particle, as of salt or sand.
4. a tiny bit; the slightest amount; as, a *grain* of sense.
5. [orig. from the weight of a grain of wheat.] the smallest unit in the system of weights used in the United States and Great Britian, equal to 0.0648 gram: one pound avoirdupois equals 7,000 grains; one pound troy equals 5,760 grains.
6. (a) the arrangement of fibers, layers, or particles of wood, leather, stone, etc.; (b) the markings or texture due to a particular arrangement; (c) paint or other surface finish imitating such markings or texture.
7. (a) that side of a piece of leather from which the hair has been removed; (b) the markings on that side.
8. disposition; nature.
9. (a) kermes or cochineal; (b) a red dye made from either; (c) any fast dye. [Obs.]
10. [*pl.*] the residuum of grain and similar

material left in the mash tub after brewing: also called *draff*.

against the grain; against the direction of the fiber; hence, contrary to one's feelings, nature, wishes, etc.; against one's inclination.

a grain of allowance; a small allowance or indulgence; a small portion to be remitted; something above or below just weight.

grains of paradise; sweet-scented seeds from the African plant *Amomum melegueta*, used in compounding certain liquors and medicines.

in grain; of a lasting color; hence, innate; as, a fool *in grain*.

to dye in grain; to dye in the raw material, as wool or silk before it is manufactured into cloth.

grāin, *v.t.*; grained, *pt., pp.*; graining, *ppr.* 1. to form into grains, as powder, sugar, and the like.

2. to paint so as to give the appearance of the grains or fibers of various woods, marble, etc.

3. in making leather, (a) to cause the grain of (leather) to rise; (b) to produce artificial markings upon, resembling those of a natural leather; (c) to remove the hair from (hides); (d) to soak in a softening liquid, as bate.

4. to produce a dull surface upon; as, to *grain* a stone in lithography.

grāin, *v.i.* 1. to yield fruit or grain. [Obs.]

2. to become granular; to form grains.

grāin, *n.* [ON. *grein*, the branch of a tree.]

1. a branch or subordinate part of a plant; a stem. [Obs.]

2. [*pl.*] an iron instrument with four or more barbed points, and a line attached to it, used at sea for harpooning.

3. a place at which two streams unite; the fork of a river. [Scot. and Brit. Dial.]

grāin'āge, *n.* 1. in 1820, a twenty per cent duty on salt brought to London by aliens: also spelled *granage*. [Obs.]

2. a warty tumor on a horse's leg.

grāin al'cō·hol, ethyl alcohol, especially when made from grain.

grāin bīnd'ẽr, the device on a harvester which binds grain into bundles.

grāine, *n.* [Fr.] silkworm eggs.

grāin el'e·vā·tŏr, a tall building for storing grain.

grāin'ẽr, *n.* one who or that which grains, as (a) one who paints in imitation of the grain of wood, etc.; (b) a tool used to produce such an imitation; (c) a knife to remove hair from hides; (d) bate.

grāin'fiēld, *n.* a field where grain is grown.

grāin'ing, *n.* a fish, the dace.

grāin'ing, *n.* 1. the fork of a stick or tree. [Brit. Dial.]

2. the use of grains in spearing fish.

grāin'ing, *n.* the process of forming a grain or grains; the resulting substance or appearance, as (a) painting in imitation of a grain; (b) indentation; milling, as on a coin; (c) causing a grain on the surface of leather, paper, lithographic stone, etc.; (d) granulation.

grāin'ing bōard, a board used in graining leather, as in impressing a certain pattern upon it.

grāin leath'ẽr (leth'), dressed leather colored on the grain side.

grāin moth, a minute moth of which two species are known, *Tinea granella* and *Gelechia cerealella*, whose larvae are destructive to grain in granaries.

grāin tin, the purest grade of tin.

grāin wee'vil, any weevil destructive to grain in storage, especially *Sitophilus granarius*.

grāin wŏrm, a grain moth's larva.

grāin'y, *a.*; *comp.* grainier; *superl.* graniest, 1. having a clearly defined grain: said of textiles or surfaces, as of wood.

2. full of grain (cereal).

3. consisting of grains; granular.

grāip, *n.* a dungfork. [Scot.]

grāip, *v.t.* to grope; to feel. [Scot.]

grāith, *n.* gear; outfit; equipment. [Scot.]

grāith, *v.t.* to prepare. [Obs.]

gra'kle, *n.* same as *grackle*.

Gral'lae, Gral·là·tō'rēs, *n.pl.* [L. *grallae*, stilts.] orders of birds in the systems of Linnaeus and Vigors, characterized by very long legs, and by the nakedness of the lower part of the tibia, adapting them for wading in water without wetting their feathers. They generally have long necks and long bills. The orders include the cranes, herons, storks, plovers, snipes, rails, coots, etc. Most naturalists have, however, made other classifications, and both terms are obsolescent.

GRALLAE
head and foot: *a*, of bittern; *b*, of crane; *c*, of stork

gral·là·tō'ri·ăl, gral'là·tō·ry, *a.* relating to the *Grallatores*.

gral'liç, *a.* [L. *grallæ*, stilts, crutches.] stilted; relating to the *Grallæ*. [Rare.]

gral'line, *a.* grallic; grallatorial.

gral'line, *n.* a bird of the *Grallæ*.

gral'lŏçh, gral'lŏck, *v.t.* to eviscerate, as a deer.

gral'lŏçh, *n.* the entrails of a deer.

-gram, [from Gr. *gramma*, anything written or drawn, a writing, from *graphein*, to write or draw.] a combining form meaning: (a) *something written* or *drawn*, as in tele*gram*, neuro*gram*; (b) *of* (a specified number of) *grams*, as in kilo*gram*; (c) *of* (a specified fraction of) *a gram*, as in centi*gram*.

gram, gramme, *n.* [Fr. *gramme*, from LL. *gramma*, weight of two oboli, small weight, from Gr. *gramma*, what is written or drawn, letter, writing, from *graphein*, to write, draw.] the basic unit of weight in the metric system, equal to about 1/28 of an ounce (.0022046 pound or 15.4324 grains troy): it was meant to be, and virtually is, the weight of the distilled water at 4° C. contained in a cube whose edge is one-hundredth of a meter.

gram equivalent; the mass of an element to which one gram of hydrogen is chemically equivalent.

gram, *n.* [Port. *grão*, from L. *granum*, a grain.] the chick pea, *Cicer arietinum*, used extensively in India as fodder for horses and cattle.

grä'mà gràss, [Sp.; L. *gramen*, grass.] any of various species of low grasses of the genus *Bouteloua*, as *Bouteloua oligostachya*, the mesquit grass or buffalo grass of Texas, New Mexico, and other western sections.

gram'à·rye, gram'à·ry, *n.* [ME. *gramary*, *gramery*, learning, erudition, magic, *gramere*, grammar.] learning; hence, magic; wizardry. [Obs.]

grà·mash'eș, *n.pl.* same as *gamashes*.

gram a'tŏm, in chemistry, the quantity of an element having a weight in grams numerically equal to the element's atomic weight: a gram atom of sodium, the atomic weight of which is 23, is a quantity of sodium weighing 23 grams.

gram-à·tom'iç weight (wāt), a gram atom.

gram çal ŏ·rie, a small calorie: see *calorie*, sense 1.

gram'-cen'ti·mē·tẽr, *n.* in physics, a unit of mechanical work; the work done when a weight of one gram is raised through the height of one centimeter.

gram dē·gree', the small calorie: see *calorie*, sense 1.

grame, *n.* grief; misery. [Obs.]

grà·mẽr'cy, *interj.* [OFr. *grant merci*, *grand merci*, lit., great thanks.] great thanks; formerly used to express thankfulness with surprise. [Archaic.]

Gram·i·nā'cē·ae, *n.pl.* the *Gramineæ*.

gram·i·nā'ceous, *a.* gramineous.

Grà·min'ē·ae, *n.pl.* [L. *gramineus*, of or pertaining to grass, from *gramen* (*-inis*), grass.] an important group of *Glumaceæ*, the grasses, distributed throughout the globe and comprising about 300 genera and 3500 species.

grà·min'ē·ăl, *a.* gramineous.

grà·min'ē·ous, *a.* [L. *gramineus*, from *gramen* (*-inis*), grass.] grassy; like or pertaining to grass, or to the *Gramineæ*.

gram''i·ni·fō'li·ous, *a.* [L. *gramen* (*-inis*), grass, and *folium*, a leaf.] bearing grasslike leaves.

gram·i·niv'ō·rous, *a.* [L. *gramen* (*-inis*), grass, and *vorare*, to devour.] feeding or subsisting on grass, as cattle.

gram·i·nol'ō·ġy, *n.* [L. *gramen* (*-inis*), grass, and Gr. *-logia*, from *legein*, to speak.] agrostology; science concerning the grasses.

gram'mà·logue (-log), *n.* [Gr. *gramma*, a letter, and *logos*, a word.] in shorthand, a word expressed by a single character or symbol.

gram'măr, *n.* [ME. *gramer*; OFr. *gramaire*; L. *grammatica* (*ars*, art); Gr. *grammatikē technē*, art), grammar, learning, from *gramma*, something written, letter, from *graphein*, to write.]

1. that part of the study of language which deals with the forms and structure of words (morphology) and with their customary arrangement in phrases and sentences (syntax): formerly used to denote all phases of language study (except that of the detailed meaning of words), as centered on morphology and syntax; now often distinguished from the study of pronunciation (*phonology*) and that of word meanings (*semantics*, *semasiology*).

2. the system of word structures and word arrangements of a given language at a given time.

3. a system of rules for speaking and writing a given language, based on the study of its grammar (sense 2) or on some adaptation of Latin grammar.

4. (a) a book containing such rules; (b) a book or treatise on grammar (senses 1 and 2).

5. one's manner of speaking or writing as judged by conventional grammatical rules; as, his *grammar* was poor.

6. (a) the elementary principles of a field of knowledge; (b) a book or treatise on these; a primer.

comparative grammar; the study which regards the resemblances and differences of various languages, classifying them in accordance with their affinities.

gram'măr, *v.i.* to discourse in terms of grammar. [Obs.]

gram·mā'ri·ăn, *n.* [Fr. *grammairien*, from *grammaire*, grammar.]

1. one versed in grammar or the construction of languages; a philologist.

2. one who teaches or writes upon grammar.

gram·mā'ri·ăn·ișm, *n.* the strict observance of grammatical rules and forms; pedantry.

gram'măr·less, *a.* devoid of grammar.

gram'măr sçhọol, 1. an elementary school: the term is variously applied to different school levels, especially to that between the fifth and eighth grades.

2. in England, (a) originally, a school where Latin was taught; (b) a secondary school corresponding to an academic high school in the United States.

gram'mātes, *n.pl.* elements or rudiments of any subject. [Obs.]

gram·mat'iç, *a.* [L. *grammaticus*; Gr. *grammatikos*, versed in letters or grammar (as noun, a grammarian), from *gramma*, a letter, something written, from *graphein*, to write.] belonging to or relating to grammar; dealing with the structure of language; as, a *grammatic* principle.

gram·mat'iç·ăl, *a.* 1. according to the rules of grammar; possessing principles of grammar; as, a *grammatical* construction.

2. relating to grammar; as, a *grammatical* rule.

gram·mat'iç·ăl·ly, *adv.* 1. according to the principles and rules of grammar; as, to write *grammatically*.

2. from the standpoint of grammar.

gram·mat'iç·ăl·ness, *n.* quality of being grammatical, or according to the rules of grammar.

gram·mat'i·ças·tẽr, *n.* [LL. *grammaticaster*, a scribe, notary, from L. *grammaticus*, a grammarian, and *-aster*.] a pedantic or petty grammarian.

gram·mat·i·çā'tion, *n.* a discussion of points in grammar. [Obs.]

gram·mat'i·cișm, *n.* a principle or rule of grammar. [Rare.]

gram·mat'i·cīze, *v.t.* and *v.i.*; grammaticized, *pt., pp.*; grammaticizing, *ppr.* to render grammatical; also, to show one's knowledge or skill in language by discussing grammar.

gram'mà·tist, *n.* a grammarian: generally used disparagingly.

gramme, *n.* a gram.

gram'-mō·leç'ū·lăr weight (wāt), a gram molecule.

gram mol'ē·cūle, in chemistry, the quantity

of an element having a weight in grams numerically equal to the element's molecular weight: also called *mole*.

Gram′-neg′ȧ·tive, *a.* not forming a color precipitate when treated by Gram's method: said of bacteria or tissues that lose the stain after treatment with alcohol.

gram′ō·phōne, *n.* [Gr. *gramma*, a letter, and *phōnē*, a sound.] a trade-mark for a device invented by E. Berliner to record and reproduce sounds. It differs from a phonograph in having a circular disk upon which tracings are made by a recording style, and from which sounds are reproduced by another kind of style attached to the diaphragm of any one of various types of reproducers.

Gram′-poṣ′i·tive, *a.* forming a color precipitate when treated by Gram's method: said of bacteria or tissues that retain the stain after treatment with alcohol.

gram′pus, *n.; pl.* **gram′pus·eṣ,** [earlier *graundepose*, altered (after *grand*), from OFr. *graspeis*, from L. *crassus pisces*; *crassus*, fat, and *pisces*, fish.]
1. a small, black, fierce variety of toothed whale, related to the dolphins.
2. any of several animals related to this.
3. a person who breathes heavily and loudly. [Colloq.]
4. the tongs for handling blooms of wrought iron. [U. S.]

Gram′ṣ meth′ŏd, [after Hans C. J. *Gram* (1853–1938), Dan. physician.] a method of staining bacteria for the purpose of classification.

grȧ·nāde′, grȧ·nā′dō, *n.* a grenade. [Obs.]

gran·ȧ·dil′lȧ, *n.* [Sp. *granadilla*, or *grandilla*, dim. of *granada*, a pomegranate, from L. *granatus*, containing seeds, from *granum*, a seed.]
1. a vine bearing a species of passionflower.
2. the edible fruit of this vine.

gran·ȧ·dil′lȧ tree, *Brya ebenus*, a West Indian tree of the *Leguminosæ* whose wood is the greenish-brown false ebony.

gran·ȧ·dil′lō, *n.* [Sp.] the granadilla tree.

gran′ȧ·ry, *n.*; *pl.* **gran′ȧ·rieṣ,** [L. *granarium*, a granary, from *grana*, pl., grain.]
1. a storehouse or repository for grain after it is threshed; a cornhouse.
2. figuratively, a country or region producing grain in abundance.

gran′ȧ·tīte, *n.* same as *staurolite*.

grand, *n.* a grand piano.
baby grand; the smallest grand piano, of a size used in homes and studios.
concert grand; the largest grand piano, so named because it is used on the concert stage.

grand, *n.* 1. one thousand dollars, a gambler's term. [Slang.]
2. in card playing, a hand or a single round played without a trump suit.

grand, *a.* [ME.; OFr.; L. *grandis*, full-grown, large, great, etc., replacing *magnus* in LL. and Romance languages.]
1. higher in rank, status, or dignity than others having the same title; as, a *grand* duke.
2. great; chief; most important; main; principal; as, the *grand* ballroom.
3. imposing because of size, beauty, and extent; magnificent; as, *grand* scenery.
4. handsome and luxurious; characterized by splendor and display; as, a *grand* banquet.
5. important; distinguished; illustrious.
6. self-important; pretentious; haughty.
7. complete; over-all; comprehensive; as, the *grand* total.
8. admirable; delightful; very satisfactory or good: a general term of approval. [Colloq.]
9. in literature, art, etc., lofty and dignified in expression and treatment.
10. in music, full; complete; as, a *grand* chorus.
Grand Army of the Republic; an organization (1866–1949) of men who were enlisted in the Union army or navy in the Civil War of 1861–1865 and who received honorable discharge: referred to as the *G. A. R.*
grand climacteric; the sixty-third year of a person's life: see *climacteric*.
grand cordon; (a) a ribbon or cordon used to indicate high position in certain orders; also, (b) a person of that degree.
grand cross; (a) the highest degree or rank in certain lodges and orders of knighthood, as in the Order of the Bath; (b) a member of that rank.
grand days; St. John the Baptist's, All Saints', Candlemas, and Ascension days, English holidays observed in the courts and inns of law and chancery; *dies non juridici*.
grand duchess; (a) a grand duke's wife or widow; (b) a female sovereign of a grand duchy; (c) a daughter of a czar of Russia.
grand duchy; the territory ruled by a grand duke or a grand duchess.
grand duke; (a) a sovereign lower in rank than a king and ruling a grand duchy; (b) a brother of a czar of Russia; (c) the eagle owl or great horned owl of Europe.
grand mal; [Fr., lit., great ailment.] an attack of epilepsy in which there are severe convulsions and loss of consciousness: distinguished from *petit mal*.
grand march; a ceremony in which all the guests at a ball march around the ballroom.
Grand Master; the chief or head of a fraternal order, a military order of knighthood, etc.
Grand Mufti; the title of the Moslem leader of the Arabs in Jerusalem.

GRAND PIANO

grand piano; a piano having a large horizontal and harp-shaped case, the top of which may be raised, exposing the strings and the hammers beneath them: used chiefly in studios and concert halls.
grand relief; high relief; alto-rilievo.
grand right and left; in folk dancing, an interweaving of two concentric circles of dancers, one moving clockwise, one counterclockwise, giving right and left hands alternately to successive partners.
grand slam; in bridge, the winning of all the tricks in a deal.
grand tour; (a) a tour of continental Europe formerly taken by young men of the British aristocracy to complete their education; (b) any tour like this.
Syn.—magnificent, dignified, elevated, exalted, great, illustrious, lofty, majestic, superb, pompous.

grand-, [OFr., replacing AS. *ealde-*, ME. *olde-*.] a combining form meaning, in general, *of the generation older than*, as in *grand*father.

gran′dam, gran′dāme, *n.* [Fr. *grande dame*.] a grandmother; an old woman. [Archaic.]

grand′äunt, *n.* the sister of a grandparent; a great-aunt.

grand′chīld, *n.*; *pl.* **grand′chil″dren,** a son's or daughter's child; a child in the second degree of descent.

grand′dad, grand′-dad, *n.* grandfather: an affectionate or children's term: also *grandad*. [Colloq.]

grand′dạugh″tẽr (-dạ″tẽr), *n.* the daughter of a son or daughter.

gran·dee′, *n.* [Sp. and Port. *grande*, a nobleman, from *grande*, great.]
1. in Spain and Portugal, a nobleman of the first rank.
2. any man of high rank or social position; an important personage.

gran·dee′ship, *n.* the rank or estate of a grandee.

gran′deūr (*or* -jūr), *n.* [Fr. *grandeur*, from L. *grandis*, grand.]
1. greatness of position; eminence.
2. splendor; magnificence.
3. moral and intellectual greatness; nobility; dignity.

gran·dev′i·ty, *n.* great age. [Obs.]

grand′fä·thẽr, *n.* 1. the father of one's father or mother: sometimes used as a term of respectful familiarity to any old man.
2. a male ancestor; a forefather.

grand′fä·thẽr çlauṣe, a provision in a State constitution by which a person's right to vote was based on his descent from a voter; in effect, it read: "No person shall vote in this State if he is unable to read and write, unless his father or grandfather was a voter before 1867." Its object was to prevent Negroes from voting in some of the southern States.

grand′fä·thẽr·ly, *a.* 1. of a grandfather.
2. having the characteristics conventionally attributed to a grandfather; kindly; indulgent; benignant.

grand′fä·thẽr′ṣ clock, a large clock with a pendulum contained in a tall, upright case.

grand guärd, a shoulder and breast protection worn on the left side by knights in tournaments.

gran·di·flō′rȧ, *a.* [Mod.L., from L. *grandis*, grand, and *flos* (genit. *floris*), a flower.] bearing large flowers.

gran·di·flō′rȧ, *n.* any of a class of hybrid tea roses with clusters of large to medium-sized flowers on long stems.

gran·dil′ō·quence (-kwens), *n.* the use of high-flown, pompous, bombastic words and expressions.

gran·dil′ō·quent, *a.* [L. *grandis*, grand, and *loquens* (*-entis*), ppr. of *loqui*, to speak.] pompous; bombastic.

gran·dil′ō·quous (-kwus), *a.* [L. *grandiloquus*, from *grandis*, grand, lofty, and *loqui*, to speak.] grandiloquent.

gran′di·ōse, *a.* [Fr. *grandiose*; It. *grandioso*; L. *grandis*, great, grand.]
1. imposing; magnificent; splendid.
2. flaunting; showy; vaunting; pompous.

gran·di·os′i·ty, *n.* [Fr. *grandiosité*; It. *grandiosita*, from *grandioso*, great, grand, from L. *grandis*, grand.] grandiose quality; pomposity.

gran·di·ō′sō, *adv.* [It.] in music, grandly; nobly: a direction to the performer.

grand′ly, *adv.* in a grand or lofty manner.

grand′mäm·mä, grand′mä, *n.* grandmother. [Colloq.]

grand′mȧs′tẽr, *n.* 1. originally a winner of an international chess tournament.
2. any exceptionally skilled chess player.

gräṅd mōṅde (gräṅ mōṅd′), [Fr., lit., great world.] fashionable society.

grand′mŏth·ẽr, *n.* 1. the mother of one's father or mother: sometimes used as a term of respectful familiarity to any old woman.
2. a female ancestor; ancestress.

grand′mŏth·ẽr·ly, *a.* 1. of a grandmother.
2. having the characteristics conventionally attributed to a grandmother; specifically, (a) kindly; indulgent; (b) fussy; interfering.

grand′neph″ew, *n.* the grandson of a brother or sister; a great-nephew

grand′ness, *n.* grandeur; greatness; magnificence.

grand′nïece (-nēs), *n.* the granddaughter of a brother or sister; a great-niece.

Grand Ōld Pär′ty, the Republican Party (of the United States): a name given in 1880.

grand′pä·pä, grand′pä, *n.* grandfather. [Colloq.]

grand′pãr·ent, *n.* a grandfather or a grandmother.

gräṅd prïx (gräṅ prē′), [Fr., lit., great prize.] first prize; highest award in a competition.

grand′sïr, *n.* a grandsire. [Archaic.]

grand′sīre, *n.* 1. a grandfather.
2. a male ancestor.
3. an old man.
[Archaic in all senses.]

grand′sŏn, *n.* the son of a son or daughter.

grand′stand, *n.* the main seating structure for spectators at a sporting event, etc.

grand′stand, *v.i.* to try to gain the applause of an audience by or as by making grandstand plays. [Colloq.]

grand′stand plāy, an unnecessarily snowy play, as in baseball, to get the applause of the spectators. [Colloq.]

grand′uṅ″çle, *n.* a brother of any of one's grandparents; a great-uncle.

grāne, *v.* and *n.* groan. [Scot.]

grāṅġe, *n.* [OFr. *grange*; LL. *granea*, a barn, grange, from L. *granum*, grain, corn.]
1. a farm, with the dwelling house, stables, barns, etc.; particularly, a house or farm at a

distance from other houses or villages; the dwelling of a gentleman-farmer.
2. (a) [G-] an association of farmers for the purpose of promoting the interests of agriculture and for doing away with middlemen or agents intervening between the producer and the consumer. Granges originated in the western United States in 1867. Officially named *Patrons of Husbandry*; (b) any local lodge of this association.
3. the farming establishment and granary of a religious house or of a feudal lord, where, in addition to their own crops, the grain paid as rent and tithes was stored. [Obs.]
4. a granary. [Obs.]

grān'ġẽr, *n.* [OFr. *grangier*, a farmer, from *grange*, a grange.]
1. a member of a grange or the Grange.
2. any farmer.
3. a bailiff or steward of a farm. [Obs.]
4. [*pl.*] stocks or shares in railroads carrying chiefly farm products grown by grangers.

grān'ġẽr·iṣm, *n.* [named after Rev. James *Granger*, the author of a "Biographical History of England," published 1769, which had blank pages to be illustrated by this method.]
1. the practice of using illustrations taken from a number of books to illustrate a work.
2. damage done to a book by clipping such illustrations, etc.

grān'ġẽr·iṣm, *n.* the principles of the Patrons of Husbandry, or grangers.

grān'ġẽr·īte, *n.* one who adds to a book extra illustrations, maps, or the like taken from other books or independently collected.

grān'ġẽr·īze, *v.i.*; grangerized, *pt.*, *pp.*; grangerizing, *ppr.* to practice grangerism.

gran'i-, [from L. *granum*, grain.] a combining form meaning *grain*, as in *grani*vorous.

gra·nif'ẽr·ous, *a.* [L. *granifer*, grain-bearing, *granum*, grain, and *-ferous*.] bearing grain.

gran'i·fọrm, *a.* [L. *granum*, grain, and *-form*.] formed like grains.

gran'ite, *n.* [It. *granito*, granite, lit., grained, pp. of *granire*, to reduce to grains, from *grano*, L. *granum*, a seed, grain.] in geology, a very hard, igneous rock, composed of quartz, feldspar, and mica, or at least of two of these minerals, crystallized together, varying greatly in texture and color.
graphic granite; a species of granite called pegmatite, containing no mica and having the crystals of quartz so arranged that the face of a section of it resembles a tablet covered with Oriental inscriptions.
porphyritic granite; granite in which distinct crystals of feldspar appear embedded in a matrix of finely crystalline structure.
syenitic granite; granite containing hornblende, the chief constituent of syenite: called also *hornblende granite*.

Gran'ite Stāte, a nickname for the State of New Hampshire, on account of its granite hills.

gran'ite·wāre, *n.* 1. ironware covered with an enamel resistant to fire and acids, the enamel having granite tints.
2. a strong pottery of fine quality, which is like ironstone china.
3. pottery mottled to imitate granite.

gra·nit'i-, [from It. *granito*, granite.] a combining form signifying *granite*.

gra·nit'iç, gra·nit'iç·ăl, *a.* 1. pertaining to granite; like granite; having the nature of granite; as, *granitic* texture.
2. consisting of granite; as, *granitic* mountains.

gra·nit''i·fi·cā'tion, *n.* [*graniti-*, and L. *facere*, to make.] the process of being formed into granite.

gra·nit'i·fọrm, *a.* [*graniti-*, and L. *forma*, form.] resembling granite in structure or shape.

gran'i·toid, *a.* resembling granite outwardly or in structure.

grà·niv'ō·rous, *a.* [L. *granum*, grain, and *vorare*, to devour.] feeding or subsisting on grain; as, *granivorous* birds.

gran'nam, *n.* a grandam. [Obs.]

gran'ny, gran'nie, *n.*; *pl.* **gran'nieṣ**, 1. a grandmother.
2. any old woman. [Colloq.]
3. any fussy, exacting person. [Colloq.]
4. a granny knot.

gran'ny knot, gran'ny'ṣ knot (not), a knot like a square knot but with the ends crossed the wrong way, forming an awkward, insecure knot: see *knot*, illus.

gran'ō-, [from L. *granum*, grain.] a combining form meaning: (a) *of* or *like granite*, as in *grano*lithic; (b) *granular*, as in *grano*phyre.

grä'nō, *n.* [It., lit., a grain, from L. *granum*, a grain.] a former bronze Maltese coin, worth a fraction of a cent.

gran·ō'lȧ, *n.* [coined (c. 1870), perh. from L. *granum*, grain, and *-ola*, L. and It. dim. suffix.] a prepared breakfast cereal of rolled oats, wheat germ, sesame seeds, brown sugar or honey, bits of dried fruit or nuts, etc.

gran'ō·lith, *n.* paving stone made up of crushed granite and cement.

gran·ō·lith'iç, *a.* of or made of granolith.

gran'ō·phȳre (-fīr), *n.* [*grano-* and *phyre*.] a pale-colored igneous rock containing quartz and feldspar.

grȧnt, *v.t.*; granted, *pt.*, *pp.*; granting, *ppr.* [ME. *granten*, *graunten*; OFr. *granter*, *graanter*, *craanter*, to promise, assure, yield; LL. *creantare*, to promise, yield, from L. *credens* (*-entis*), ppr. of *credere*, to believe.]
1. to admit as true without proof; to allow; to yield; to concede; as, we take that for *granted* which is supposed to be true.
2. to give in answer to a request; to assent to; to agree to fulfill.
God *granted* him that which he requested.
—1 Chron. iv. 10.
3. (a) to give or confer formally or according to legal procedure; (b) to transfer (the title of a thing) to another by deed or writing; as, the legislature has *granted* all the land.

grȧnt, *v.i.* to consent. [Obs.]

grȧnt, *n.* [OFr. *grant*, *graant*, a promise, assurance, grant, from *granter*, *graanter*, to promise, assure, grant.]
1. the act of granting; a bestowing or conferring.
2. something granted, as property, a tract of land, an exclusive right or power, money from a fund, etc.
3. in law, (a) a conveyance in writing of such things as cannot pass or be transferred by word only, as land, rents, reversions, tithes, etc.; (b) the instrument of such conveyance.
Syn.—present, gift, allowance, stipend.

grȧnt'ȧ·ble, *a.* that may be granted.

grȧn·tee', *n.* in law, a person to whom a grant is made.

grȧnt'ẽr, *n.* one who grants.

grant-in-āid', *n.*; *pl.* **grants-in-āid'**, a grant of funds, as by the Federal government to a State or by a foundation to a writer, scientist, artist, etc., to support a specific program or project.

grȧnt'ŏr, *n.* in law, a person who makes a grant.

grants'măn·ship, *n.* the art or skill of acquiring grants-in-aid.

gran'ū·lăr, *a.* [LL. *granulum*, dim. of L. *granum*, a grain.]
1. containing or consisting of grains or granules: granular eyelids have an inner surface made rough by disease.
2. resembling grains or granules; granulated; as, a stone of *granular* appearance.

gran·ū·lar'i·ty, *n.* the quality or condition of being granular.

gran'ū·lăr·ly, *adv.* in a granular form.

gran'ū·lȧ·ry, *a.* granular.

gran'ū·lāte, *v.t.* and *v.i.*; granulated, *pt.*, *pp.*; granulating, *ppr.* [L. *granum*, a grain.]
1. to form into grains or granules; as, to *granulate* powder or sugar.
2. to raise in small bulges; to make or become rough on the surface.

gran'ū·lā·ted, gran'ū·lāte, *a.* having numerous small elevations, like shagreen; consisting of grains; having the form of grains; granular.
granulated steel; a kind of steel resulting from a process in which pig iron is granulated to furnish the basis of the steel.

gran'ū·lāt·ẽr, *n.* same as *granulator*.

gran·ū·lā'tion, *n.* 1. the act of forming into grains; as, the *granulation* of powder or sugar.
2. the state of being formed into grains.
3. in medicine, (a) the formation of a small, granular mass on a surface, as of a wound that is healing; (b) the mass itself.

gran'ū·lā·tive, *a.* of or characterized by granulation.

gran'ū·lā·tŏr, *n.* a person or thing that granulates.

gran'ūle, *n.* [LL. *granulum*, dim. of L. *granum*, a grain.] a minute grain; also, a small grainlike particle or spot.

gran·ū·lif'ẽr·ous, *a.* [LL. *granulum*, a little grain, and L. *ferre*, to bear.] made up of granulations.

gran'ū·līte, *n.* 1. a granular, crystalline rock containing quartz, feldspar, and occasional dark-red garnets.
2. granite containing biotite and muscovite.

gran·ū·lit'iç, *a.* containing or made of granulite.

gran·ū·lō'mȧ, *n.* [LL. *granulum*, a small grain, and Gr. *-ōma*, tumor.] in medicine, a diseased growth characterized by granulation.

gran'ū·lōse, *a.* same as *granular*.

gran'ū·lōse, *n.* the more soluble part of starch, turned into sugar by the action of enzymes.

gran'ū·lous, *a.* granular.

grāpe, *n.* [OFr. *grape*, *grappe*, a bunch or cluster of grapes, from O.H.G. *chrapho*, a hook, clasp.]
1. any of various small, round, smooth-skinned, juicy fruits, generally purple, red, or green, growing in clusters on a woody vine: grapes are eaten raw, used to make wine, or dried to make raisins: they are classified as berries.
2. any of various vines bearing grapes; grapevine.
3. a dark purplish re l.
4. [*pl.*] (a) a diseased growth on the fetlock of horses, consisting of a cluster of wartlike lumps; (b) bovine tuberculosis.
5. the knob at the butt of a cannon.
6. grapeshot.
chicken grape; a small species of wild grape, *Vitis cordifolia*.
native grape; an evergreen climbing plant of Australia bearing grapes, *Vitis hypoglauca*.
sour grapes; something despised because it cannot be had.
summer grape; a grape, *Vitis æstivalis*, that grows wild in the eastern part of North America.

grāpe çũr·çū'li·ō, a small black weevil whose larva is destructive to the fruit of the grape.

grāpe çūre, the steady and exclusive use of grapes as food in treating a disease.

grāpe diṣ·ēaṣe', a consumptive disease of cattle.

grāpe fẽrn, a thick, fleshy fern, belonging to the genus *Botrychium*.

grāpe'flow''ẽr, *n.* same as *grape hyacinth*.

grāpe'fruit, *n.* [so named because it grows in clusters.]
1. a large, round, edible citrus fruit with a pale-yellow rind, juicy pulp, and a somewhat sour taste.
2. the semitropical evergreen tree that it grows on.

grāpe fuṅ'gus, a mildew that forms on grapevines.

grāpe hop'pẽr, an insect, *Erythroneura comes*, that attacks grapevine leaves.

grāpe hȳ'ȧ·cinth, any of a group of small, hardy bulbs of the lily family, with spikes of small, bell-shaped flowers of blue or white.

grāpe mọth, a moth, as *Polychrosis viteana*, the larva of which feeds upon grapes.

grāp'ẽr·y, *n.*; *pl.* **grāp'ẽr·ieṣ**, a building or enclosure used for the growing of grapes.

grāpe'shot, *n.* a missile formerly discharged from a cannon, intermediate between case shot and solid shot, having much of the destructive spread of the former with somewhat of the range and penetrative force of the latter. A round of grapeshot consisted of three tiers of cast-iron balls arranged, generally three in a tier, between four parallel iron disks connected together by a central wrought-iron pin.

grāpe'stōne, *n.* a seed of the grape.

grāpe su'găr (shu'găr), a simple sugar occurring in many plants and fruits, especially in ripe grapes; dextrose; glucose.

grāpe'vīne, *n.* 1. any of various woody vines bearing grapes.
2. a secret means of spreading or receiving information: also *grapevine telegraph*.
3. a rumor; unfounded report; hearsay.

grāpe wọrm, the larva of the grape moth.

-grȧph, [from Gr. *graphē*, a writing or drawing, from *graphein*, to write or draw.] a combining form meaning *that which writes*, *draws*, or *describes*, or *that which is written* or *drawn*, as in tele*graph*, auto*graph*.

grȧph, *n.* [Gr. *graphē*, a writing, a representation, from *graphein*, to write, draw, represent by lines.]
1. a diagram, as a curve, broken line, series of bars, etc., representing the successive changes in the value of a variable quantity or quantities.
2. in mathematics, a curve or surface showing the locus of a function on a series of coordinates set at right angles to each other.

gràph, *v.t.* to put in the form of or represent by a graph.

graph'ēme, *n.* [*graph*, a spelling, and *-eme* (as in *phoneme*).] all the units or combinations of units representing a single letter of the alphabet, or all those representing a single phoneme.

gra·phē'miç, *a.* of or having to do with a grapheme or graphemes.

gra·phē'miçs, *n.pl.* [*construed as sing.*] the branch of language study dealing with the relationship between speech sounds and the writing system of a language.

-gràph·ẽr, a combining form meaning *a person who writes*, used to form nouns of agent corresponding to nouns ending in *-graph*, *-graphy*, as tele*grapher*, steno*grapher*.

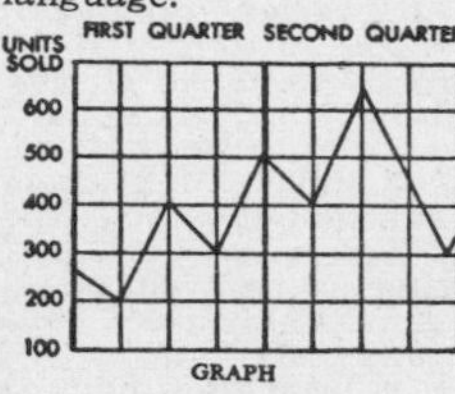

GRAPH

-graph'iç, a combining form used to form adjectives from, or corresponding to, nouns ending in *-graph*, as tele*graphic*, steno*graphic*: also *-graphical*.

graph'iç, graph'iç·ăl, *a.* [L. *graphicus*; Gr. *graphikos*, lit., belonging to painting or drawing, picturesque, writing, from *graphē*, a drawing, a writing, from *graphein*, to represent by means of lines, write.]
1. describing or described in realistic and vivid detail; vivid; lifelike.
2. of the graphic arts.
3. (a) of handwriting; used or expressed in handwriting; (b) written, inscribed, or recorded in letters, etc.
4. having markings that look like written or printed characters: said of minerals.
5. of graphs or diagrams.
6. shown by a graph or graphs.
graphic algebra; a branch of algebra in which the approximate solution of equations is obtained by means of curves and straight lines.
graphic arts; (a) any form of visual artistic representation; especially, painting, drawing, photography, etc.; (b) now, sometimes, only those arts in which impressions are printed from various kinds of blocks or plates, as etching, lithography, dry point, offset, etc.
graphic tellurium; sylvanite.
Syn.—picturesque, illustrative, descriptive, pictorial, forcible, vivid.

graph'iç·ăl·ly, *adv.* in a graphic manner.

graph'iç-ăl·ness, *n.* the condition or quality of being graphic.

graph'iç·ness, *n.* graphicalness.

graph'içs, *n.pl.* [*construed as sing.*] 1. the art of making drawings, as in architecture or engineering, in accordance with mathematical rules.
2. calculation of stresses, etc. from such drawings.

graph·i·ol'ō·ġy, *n.* [Gr. *grapheion*, a style, pencil, and *-logia*, from *legein*, to speak.] the art of writing or delineating.

graph'īte, *n.* [Gr. *graphē*, a writing, from *graphein*, to write, draw, and *-ite*.] one of the forms of carbon: also known as *plumbago* and *black lead*. It has an iron-gray color, metallic luster, granular texture, and is soft and unctuous to the touch. It is used chiefly in the manufacture of pencils, crucibles, lubricants, electrodes, etc.

gra·phit'iç, *a.* relating to, containing, or derived from graphite.
graphitic carbon; carbon found in iron or steel which is considered to be graphite.

graph'i·tīze, *v.t.*; graphitized, *pt.*, *pp.*; graphitizing, *ppr.* 1. to change into graphite by heating or annealing.
2. to put graphite in or on.

graph'i·toid, graph·i·toid'ăl, *a.* [Gr. *graphē*, a writing, and *eidos*, form.] resembling graphite.

graph'o-, [from Gr. *graphē*, a writing, drawing, from *graphein*, to write, draw.] a combining form meaning *writing* or *drawing*, as in *grapho*logy.

graph'ō·līte, *n.* [*grapho-*, and Gr. *lithos*, a stone.] a species of slate suitable for writing on.

gra·phol'ō·ġy, *n.* [*grapho-*, and Gr. *-logia*, from *legein*, to speak.] the study of handwriting, especially as it is supposed to indicate the writer's character, aptitude, etc.

graph·ō·met'riç, graph·ō·met'riç·ăl, *a.* pertaining to or ascertained by a graphometer.

graph·ō·mō'tŏr, *n.* in physiology, of or affecting the movements made in writing.

graph ō·phōne, *n.* [*grapho-*, and Gr. *phōnē*, sound.] an instrument for reproducing recorded sounds; a phonograph: a trade-mark (*Graphophone*).

graph·ō·phon'iç, *a.* relating to the graphophone.

graph'ō·sçōpe, *n.* [*grapho-*, and Gr. *skopein*, to view.] an optical apparatus for magnifying engravings, photographs, etc.

graph'ō·tȳpe, *n.* [*grapho-*, and Gr. *typos*, an impression.] a machine for embossing letters on a thin sheet of metal.

-grà·phy, [from L. *-graphia*; Gr. *-graphia*, writing or drawing, from *graphein*, to represent by means of lines, to write, draw.] a combining form meaning *a writing, drawing, description, discourse, science*, etc., as in bio*graphy*, geo*graphy*.

grap'nel, *n.* [ME. *grapenel*, *grapinel*; OFr. *grapin*, *grappin*, a grapnel, dim. of *grappe*, a hook.]
1. a small anchor, fitted with four or five flukes or claws, used to hold boats or small vessels.

GRAPNEL

2. a grappling iron; a device with a hook or hooks for grasping or holding things.

grap'ple, *n.* [OFr. *grappil*, the grapple on a ship, dim. of *grappe*, a cluster of grapes, from O.H.G. *chrapho*, a hook.]
1. any device for seizing or grasping, as a pair of tongs for lifting blocks of ice.
2. a seizing; grip or hold, as in wrestling.
3. a close fight in which the fighters grip one another.

grap'ple, *v.t.*; grappled, *pt.*, *pp.*; grappling, *ppr.* to seize; to grip and hold; as, to *grapple* an assailant.

grap'ple, *v.i.* 1. to use a grappling iron.
2. to come to grips, as in wrestling; to seize one another.

grap'ple plant, *Harpagophytum*, or *Uncaria procumbens*, a South African plant of the family *Pedaliaceæ*. Its seed vessel has claw-like appendages.

grap'plẽr, *n.* a person or thing that grapples.

grap'ple shot, a shot provided with hinged flukes, and attached to a cable: used to catch in the rigging of a ship in distress, as a life-saving device.

grap'pling, *n.* 1. the act of seizing or laying fast hold on.
2. a grappling iron.

grap'pling ī'ron (-ŭrn) or **hook,** an instrument consisting of an iron bar with several iron claws at one end for grappling and holding things.

grap'soid, *a.* [Gr. *grapsaios*, a crab, and *eidos*, resemblance.] relating to the family *Grapsidæ*.

grap'soid, *n.* a crab of the family *Grapsidæ*.

grap'tō·līte, *n.* [Gr. *graptos*, marked, written, and *lithos*, a stone.] a fossil hydrozoan of the group *Graptoloidea*, found in Silurian rocks.

grāp'y, *a.* pertaining to, composed of, or resembling grapes.

gràsp, *v.t.*; grasped, *pt.*, *pp.*; grasping, *ppr.* [ME. *graspen*, *grapen*, *grapien*, from AS. *grapian*, to grasp, from *grap*, the grasp of the hand.]
1. to seize and hold by clasping or embracing with the fingers or arms.
2. to take hold of eagerly or greedily; seize.
3. to seize mentally; to comprehend; as, to *grasp* the question.
to grasp at; (a) to reach for and try to seize; (b) to take eagerly; to accept with alacrity

gràsp, *n.* 1. the grip or seizure of the hand.
2. possession; hold.
3. reach; the power of seizing.
4. understanding; comprehension; intellectual capacity.
5. the part of a thing to be held or grasped; as, the *grasp* of a sword or of a fishing rod. [Obs.]

gràsp'à·ble, *a.* that may be grasped.

gràsp'ẽr, *n.* one who or that which grasps or seizes.

gràsp'ing, *a.* 1. seizing; embracing; holding.
2. greedy; avaricious.

gràsp'ing·ly, *adv.* 1. in an eager, grasping manner.
2. greedily; avariciously.

gràsp'ing·ness, *n.* the state or quality of being grasping.

gràsp'less, *a.* lacking the power of grasping; as, a *graspless* hand.

gràss, *n.* [ME. *gras*, *gres*; AS. *græs*, grass, herbage.]
1. any of various green plants with blade-like leaves that are eaten by grazing animals: because of their softness and dense growth, grasses are often cultivated for lawns, etc.
2. any of various plants having simple leaves, a stem generally jointed and tubular or with a corklike interior, a husky calyx, called glume, and the seed single, including wheat, rye, oats, barley, sugar cane, etc.
3. ground covered with grass; pasture land or lawn.
4. in mining, the surface at the mine. [Brit.]
5. the season of growing grass; spring.
6. marijuana. [Slang.]
blackseed grass; a tropical grass, *Sporobolus indicus*, found in the southern United States.
dog's-tail grass; a European grass, *Cynosurus cristatus*, valuable for its straw.
grass of Parnassus; a plant of the genus *Parnassia* of the saxifrage family.
Italian rye grass; *Lolium multiflorum*, cultivated for hay and pasture.
to go to grass; (a) to go to pasture; (b) to become worn out, dilapidated, etc.; to decay; to go to ruin; (c) to die; (d) to rest.
to let the grass grow under one's feet; to waste time and opportunity; to procrastinate.

gràss, *v.t.*; grassed (gràst), *pt.*, *pp.*; grassing, *ppr.* 1. to furnish with grass; to grow grass over; as, to *grass* a lawn.
2. to pasture or graze (cattle).
3. to spread out upon grass, as linen for bleaching.
4. to bring or throw down, as game by shooting, or an opponent by a blow; fell.

gràss, *v.i.* to produce grass. [Rare.]

gràs·sā'tion, *n.* [L. *grassatio* (*-onis*), a rioting, from *grassatus*, pp. of *grassari*, to wander about.] a restless wandering about, especially with evil intent. [Rare.]

gràss bàss, the calico bass.

gràss'bīrd, *n.* the sandpiper.

gràss'chat, *n.* the whinchat.

gràss çlọth, a cloth made out of tough grass or ramie fibers.

gràss'çut·tẽr, *n.* 1. a machine for cutting grass; lawnmower.
2. in baseball, a batted ball that skims along the ground. [Colloq.]

gràss finch, a kind of sparrow, *Poecetes gramineus*.

gràss green, the bright, fresh green color of grass.

gràss'-grōwn, *a.* overgrown with grass.

gràss'hop·pẽr, *n.* [ME. *grashopper*; AS. *græshoppa*, *gærshoppa*, a grasshopper; *græs*, grass, and *hoppa*, a hopper, from *hoppian*, to hop, leap.]
1. an orthopterous insect, family *Acrididae*, with very long and slender legs, the thighs of the hind legs being large and adapted to leaping, and large, delicate wings, with the wing covers extending far beyond the abdomen.
2. the connecting lever in a piano communicating motion from the key to the hammer.
3. a light airplane for scouting and observation. [Military Slang.]

gràss'hop·pẽr en'ġine, a steam engine having a walking beam with the fulcrum at one end and the piston rod at the other, its form suggesting a huge grasshopper.

gràss'hop·pẽr lärk (or **wạr'blẽr**), a small song bird of Europe, particularly *Locustella naevia*.

gràss'i·ness, *n.* the state or quality of being grassy.

gràss'land, *n.* land with grass growing on it, kept for pasturage.

gràss'less, *a.* without grass.

gràss mọth, a moth of the genus *Crambus*, found in grass.

gràss owl, an owl, *Tyto longimembris*, of southeastern Asia.

gràss par'à·keet, an Australian parrot, *Melopsittacus undulatus*.

gràss pick'ẽr·el, a small variety of pickerel.

gràss'plot, gràss'plat, *n.* a plot or level spot covered with grass; a lawn.

gràss plŏv'ẽr, the plover found in uplands.

gràss'pol·y, *n.* a species of *Lythrum*, or loosestrife, *Lythrum hyssopifolia*.

gràss por'gy, a fish of the genus *Calamus*, found in the eelgrass of southern Florida.

gràss'quit, *n.* any of the finches of the genus *Tiaris*, found in the American tropics and the West Indies.

gràss'-rọots', *a.* originating among or carried

on by the common people; as, a *grass-roots* political movement. [Colloq.]

gràss snāke, any of several species of small, nonpoisonous snakes that live in swamps and marshes.

gràss snīpe, a large, grayish-brown sandpiper with a pale, streaked, buff-colored breast; the pectoral sandpiper, *Tringa maculata*.

gràss spī′dēr, a spider, *Agalena nævia*, which spins a flat web among grass stems.

gràss spŏnġe, a coarse, flat sponge found off the coast of Florida and in the West Indian islands: called also the *honeycomb sponge*.

gràss tree, 1. an Australian woody plant of the lily family, with grasslike leaves and a spike of flowers: some varieties yield resins used commercially.
2. any of various Australasian trees with grasslike foliage.

gràss vetch, a vetch, *Lathyrus nissolia*: so called from its grasslike leaves.

gràss wid′ōw, 1. a discarded mistress; also, an unmarried woman who has had a child. [Obs.]
2. a woman divorced or otherwise separated from her husband.

gràss wid′ōw·ēr, a man divorced or otherwise separated from his wife.

gràss wrack (rak), the eelgrass, *Zostera marina*, found on the seacoast.

gràss′y, *a.*; *comp.* grassier; *superl.* grassiest. 1. covered with grass; abounding with grass; as, *grassy* fields; *grassy* foreground.
2. of or consisting of grass.
3. resembling grass; green.

gràss′y-green′, *a.* like growing grass in color; bright-green.

grāte, *n.* [ME. *grate*, a trellis, lattice; LL. *grata*, *crata*; L. *cratis*, a hurdle, a kind of basket.]
1. a work or frame composed of parallel or crossbars, with interstices; a kind of latticework, such as is used in windows, doors, etc.; a grating.
2. a frame of iron bars in which coal or other fuel is burned; as, an open *grate*; hence, a fireplace.
3. in mining, a sieve for screening ores.
grate surface; in steam boilers, the area of a grate available for fuel.

grāte, *v.t.*; grated, *pt.*, *pp.*; grating, *ppr.* to provide with a grate or grates.

grāte, *a.* tending to gratify; agreeable. [Obs.]

grāte, *v.t.*; grated, *pt.*, *pp.*; grating, *ppr.* [ME. *graten*; OFr. *grater*; LL. *gratare*, to scrape, scratch, from O.H.G. *chrazzon*, to scrape, scratch.]
1. to rub one thing against another so as to produce a harsh sound.
2. to grind into shreds or particles by rubbing or scraping; as, to *grate* a nutmeg.
3. to offend; to fret; to vex; to irritate; to mortify; as, harsh words *grate* the heart.
4. to grind (the teeth) together with a rasping sound.

grāte, *v.i.* 1. to grind or rub with a harsh scraping or rasping sound.
2. to make a rasping sound; to creak.
3. to have an irritating or annoying effect; as, her voice *grates* on me.

grāt′ed, *a.* worn off or ground to a powder or pulp by grating; as, *grated* horseradish.

grāt′ed, *a.* protected by a grate; furnished with grates; as, a *grated* aperture.

grāte′fụl, *a.* [L. *gratus*, pleasing, agreeable, and *-ful*.]
1. feeling or expressing gratitude; thankful; appreciative.
2. causing gratitude; agreeable; pleasing; acceptable; gratifying; affording pleasure; as, a *grateful* shower of rain.
Syn.—thankful, agreeable, pleasant, refreshing.

grāte′fụl·ly, *adv.* in a grateful, pleasing, or agreeable manner; with gratitude or thankfulness.

grāte′fụl·ness, *n.* the state or quality of being grateful; gratitude.

grāt′ēr, *n.* 1. an instrument or utensil with a rough, indented surface for grating spices, vegetables, cheese, etc.
2. a person or thing that grates.

grȧ·tiç′ū·lāte, *v.t.*; graticulated, *pt.*, *pp.*; graticulating, *ppr.* to divide into squares.

grȧ·tiç·ū·lā′tion, *n.* the division of a design or draft into squares, for the purpose of reducing to smaller, or enlarging to greater, dimensions.

grat′i·çūle, *n.* [Fr. *graticule*, *craticule*, from L. *craticula*, dim. of *cratis*, a hurdle, wickerwork.] a graticulated design, draft, or plan.

grat″i·fi·çā′tion, *n.* [L. *gratificatio* (*-onis*), from *gratificare*, *gratificari*, to gratify, please.]
1. a gratifying or being gratified.
2. that which affords pleasure; satisfaction; delight; as, an accustomed *gratification*.
3. a voluntary reward for services or benefits; gratuity; recompense.
Syn.—enjoyment, satisfaction, comfort, happiness.

grat′i·fīed, *a.* pleased; satisfied.

grat′i·fī·ēr, *n.* one who or that which gratifies or pleases.

grat′i·fȳ, *v.t.*; gratified, *pt.*, *pp.*; gratifying, *ppr.* [Fr. *gratifier*; L. *gratificare*, *gratificari*, to oblige, please, favor; *gratus*, pleasing, agreeable, and *facere*, to make.]
1. to please; to give pleasure to; as, to *gratify* the taste, the appetite, the senses; also, to give in to; to humor; to indulge; as, to *gratify* a child.
2. to reward; to recompense. [Archaic.]
Syn.—indulge, humor, satisfy, please, satiate.—*Gratify* has reference simply to the pleasure communicated; to *indulge* a person implies that something is conceded; to *humor* is to adapt oneself to the varying moods and caprices of others.

grat′i·fȳ·ing, *a.* giving pleasure; affording satisfaction; as, a *gratifying* spectacle.

grat′i·fȳ·ing·ly, *adv.* in a gratifying manner.

grȧ·tin′ (-taṅ′; *Eng.* grat′ăn), *n.* [Fr., from *gratter*, *grater*, to scrape.]
1. the crust of cheese or buttered crumbs over a casserole dish.
2. the dish itself.

grāt′ing, *a.* 1. causing a harsh, rasping sound.
2. sounding harsh and rasping.
3. irritating; annoying.

grāt′ing, *n.* a harsh sound or rubbing.

grāt′ing, *n.* 1. a partition of bars, or latticework of wood or iron; as, the *grating* of a prison or convent.
2. an open cover for the hatches of a ship, resembling latticework; the movable floor of a boat.
3. in optics, same as *diffraction grating* under *diffraction*.

grāt′ing·ly, *adv.* in a grating manner; harshly; offensively.

Grȧ·tī′ō·lȧ, *n.* [L., dim. from L. *gratia*, grace; in allusion to the alleged healing properties of some species.] in botany, a genus of plants of the figwort family, several species of which are native to the United States. The best-known species, *Gratiola officinalis*, hedge hyssop, is used in medicine.

grȧ·tī′ō·lin, *n.* [L. *gratia*, grace, favor, and *-olin*.] in chemistry, a compound derived from *Gratiola officinalis*, hedge hyssop.

grā′tis, *adv.* [L., from *gratia*, favor, kindness.] for nothing; free; without recompense; as, to give a thing *gratis*.

grat′i·tūde, *n.* [Fr. *gratitude*; LL. *gratitudo*, thankfulness, gratitude, from L. *gratus*, pleasing, thankful.] a feeling of thankful appreciation for favors or benefits received; warm, appreciative response to kindness; thankfulness.

grȧ·tū′i·tous, *a.* [L. *gratuitus*, done without pay or profit, free, from *gratia*, favor, kindness.]
1. free; voluntary; not required by justice; granted without obligation, charge, or payment.
2. not required, called for, or warranted by the circumstances; made or done without sufficient cause or reason; as, a *gratuitous* affirmation; a *gratuitous* insult.
gratuitous contract; in law, a contract for the benefit of the person for whom it is made, without a reciprocal promise of benefit to the maker: sometimes called *contract of beneficence*.

grȧ·tū′i·tous·ly, *adv.* in a gratuitous manner; without an equivalent or compensation, or without sufficient cause or reason.

grȧ·tū′i·ty, *n.*; *pl.* **grȧ·tū′i·tieṣ,** [OFr. *gratuite*; LL. *gratuitas*, a free gift, from L. *gratuitus*, free, freely done.]
1. a gift; a donation of money given without compensation.
2. something given in return for service or a favor; a tip.

grat′ū·lȧnt, *a.* [L. *gratulans* (*-antis*), ppr. of *gratulari*, to wish one joy.] congratulatory; expressing joy or gratification.

grat′ū·lāte, *v.t.*; gratulated, *pt.*, *pp.*; gratulating, *ppr.* [from L. *gratulatus*, pp. of *gratulari*, to congratulate, rejoice, from *gratus*, pleasing.] to express joy or gratification at the sight of; congratulate. [Archaic.]

grat′ū·lāte, *v.i.* to express gratification. [Obs.]

grat′ū·lāte, *a.* causing gratification. [Obs.]

grat·ū·lā′tion, *n.* 1. joy; gratification. [Archaic.]
2. an expression of this; congratulation. [Archaic.]

grat′ū·lȧ·tō·ry, *a.* congratulatory. [Archaic.]

grau′pel, *n.* [from G. *graupeln*, to sleet, from *graupelein*, dim. of *graupe*, hulled barley, hail; from Slav.] in meteorology, soft sleet or hail.

grau′wăck·e (grou′väk-e), *n.* [G.] see *graywacke*.

grȧ·vā′men, *n.*; *pl.* **grȧ·vā′mens, grȧ·vam′i·nȧ,** [LL., lit., a burden, trouble, from L. *gravare*, to weigh down, from *gravis*, heavy.]
1. in law, the grievance complained of; the substantial cause of the action.
2. a grievance.

grāve, *v.t.*; graved, *pt.*; graved *or* graven, *pp.*; graving, *ppr.* [ME. *graven*; AS. *grafan*, to dig, bury, carve.]
1. (a) [Obs.] to dig; (b) [Archaic.] to bury.
2. to shape by carving; to carve out; sculpture.
3. to engrave; incise.
4. to impress sharply and clearly; to fix permanently.

grāve, *v.t.* [prob. from OFr. *grave* (Fr. *grève*), beach, coarse sand: ships were orig. beached for cleaning the hulls.] to clean (the hull of a ship) by removing the barnacles, etc. and coating with pitch or tar.

grāve, *a.*; *comp.* graver; *superl.* gravest, [L. *gravis*, heavy, weighty.]
1. requiring serious thought; important; weighty; as, *grave* doubts.
2. of a threatening nature; indicating great danger; ominous; as, a *grave* illness.
3. solemn; sedate; not gay.
4. somber; dull; as, *grave* colors.
5. in music, low or deep in pitch: distinguished from *acute*.
6. in phonetics, having a grave accent.
Syn.—sober, serious, solemn, important, sedate, thoughtful, weighty.

grāve, *n.* [ME. *grave*, *grafe*; AS. *græf*, *graf*, a trench, a grave, from *grafan*, to dig.]
1. a hole in the ground in which to bury a dead body.
2. a burial mound or monument.
3. any place for receiving something dead; as, his bankruptcy was the *grave* of his hopes.
4. death; extinction; as, he does not fear the *grave*.
to have one foot in the grave; to be very ill, old, or infirm; to be near death.
to make one turn in one's grave; to be or do something that would have shocked or strongly displeased one now dead.

grä′ve, *a.* and *adv.* [It.] in music, slow and with solemnity: a direction to the performer.

grāve aç′cent, a mark (`) used to show: (a) in French, the quality of an open *e* (è), as in *chère*, or a distinction in meaning, as in *où*, where (distinguished from *ou*, or); (b) full pronunciation of an ending or syllable normally elided in speech, as in *lovèd*; (c) secondary or weakened stress, as in *týpewrìter*; (d) falling tone or pitch, as in the Chinese language.

grāve′çlōtheṣ, *n.pl.* the clothes or dress in which the dead are interred.

grāve′dig″gēr, *n.* 1. one whose occupation is to dig graves.
2. same as *burying beetle*.

grav′el, *n.* [ME.; OFr. *gravelle*, dim. of *grave* (Fr. *grève*), coarse sand, shingle, seashore.]
1. a loose mixture of pebbles and rock fragments coarser than sand, often mixed with clay, etc.
2. in medicine, a deposit of small concretions that form in the kidneys and may pass through the ureters into the bladder; calculus.
gravel powder; a coarse-grained gunpowder.

grav′el, *v.t.*; graveled *or* gravelled, *pt.*, *pp.*; graveling *or* gravelling, *ppr.* 1. to cover with gravel; as, to *gravel* a walk.
2. to run (a ship or boat) aground on gravel.
3. to puzzle; to stop; to embarrass.
4. to hurt the foot of, as a horse, by gravel lodged under the shoe.
5. to irritate or annoy. [Colloq.]

grav′el-blīnd, *a.* almost completely blind.

grāve′less, *a.* without a grave; unburied.

grav′el·ing, *n.* 1. the act of covering with gravel.
2. a covering of gravel.
3. a young salmon.

grav′el·li·ness, grav′el·i·ness, *n.* a gravelly condition.

grav′el·ly, grav′el·y, *a.* 1. abounding with gravel; consisting of gravel; as, a *gravelly* soil or land.
2. like gravel.

grav′el·root, *n.* in botany, *Eupatorium purpureum*, the joepye weed: also called *stone-root*.

grav′el·stōne, *n.* a calculus; a pebble.

grāve′ly, *adv.* in a grave, solemn manner.

grāv′en, *a.* [alt. pp. of *grave* (to engrave).]
1. engraved; carved; sculptured.
2. sharply and clearly impressed; permanently fixed.
graven image; a carved or shaped image adored as an object of worship; an idol.

grāve′ness, *n.* seriousness; solemnity; sobriety; the quality of being grave.

Grá′ven·stein, *n.* [named after *Gravenstein*, in Schleswig.] a variety of large, yellow apple, streaked with red.

grá·vē′ō·lence, *n.* a rank smell. [Rare.]

grá·vē′ō·lent, *a.* [L. *graveolens* (-*entis*), strong-smelling; *gravis*, heavy, and *olens* (-*entis*), ppr. of *olere*, to smell.] of or having a rank odor. [Rare.]

grāv′ẽr, *n.* [ME. *graver*, *grafer*; AS. *græfere*, a graver, carver, from *grafan*, to dig, grave, carve.]
1. one who carves or engraves; one whose occupation is to cut letters or figures in stone, etc.; a sculptor.
2. an engraving tool; an instrument for graving.

grāv′ẽr·y, *n.* engraving. [Obs.]

grāves, *n.pl.* same as *greaves* (cracklings).

Grāves′ dis·ease′, [after Robert *Graves* (1797–1853), Ir. physician.] exophthalmic goiter.

grāve′stōne, *n.* a tombstone.

grāve′yärd, *n.* a yard or enclosure for the interment of the dead; a cemetery.

grav′ic, *a.* relating to gravitation. [Rare.]

grav′id, *a.* [L. *gravidus*, pregnant, from *gravis*, heavy.] pregnant; with child.

grav′i·dā·ted, *a.* made pregnant; big. [Obs.]

grav·i·dā′tion, *n.* pregnancy. [Obs.]

grá·vid′i·ty, *n.* pregnancy.

grav′i·grāde, *a.* [L. *gravis*, heavy, and *gradi*, to walk.] heavy-footed; of slow movement.

grav′i·grāde, *n.* an animal that walks heavily, as an elephant.

grá·vim′e·tẽr, *n.* [L. *gravis*, heavy, and *metrum*, a measure.] an instrument for determining the specific gravity of bodies, solid or liquid.

grav·i·met′ric, *a.* relating to weight measurement: distinguished from *volumetric*.

grav·i·met′ric·ăl·ly, *adv.* in a gravimetric manner; by means of gravimetry.

grá·vim′e·try, *n.* [from L. *gravis*, heavy; and *-metry*.] the measurement of weight or density.

grāv′ing, *n.* 1. the act of cleaning a ship's bottom.
2. the act of carving or cutting, as in sculpturing. [Archaic.]
graving dock; a dock for holding a ship for graving, or cleaning the bottom, etc.; a dry dock.

grāv′ing piēce, in shipbuilding, a new piece of wood inserted to repair damages.

grav′i·tāte, *v.i.*; gravitated, *pt.*, *pp.*; gravitating, *ppr.* [L. *gravitas* (-*atis*), heaviness, from *gravis*, heavy.]
1. to move or tend to move in accordance with the force of gravity.
2. to sink or fall; to tend to settle at a bottom level, as of a liquid.
3. to be attracted or tend to move (*toward* something or someone).

grav·i·tā′tion, *n.* 1. the fact, act, or effect of gravitating.
2. in physics, the force by which every particle of matter tends to approach every other particle in the universe. Newton's *law of gravitation* is that every body or portion of matter attracts and is attracted directly as its quantity of matter, and inversely as the square of its distance from the attracting body.
3. figuratively, an intellectual or spiritual attraction or tendency toward some condition, activity, or personality.

grav·i·tā′tion·ăl, *a.* of, due to, or relating to gravitation; as, *gravitational* impulses.

grav·i·tā′tion·ăl·ly, *adv.* by or according to gravitation.

grav′i·tā·tive, *a.* 1. causing or inclined to gravitate.
2. caused by or yielding to gravitation.

grav′i·ty, *n.* [L. *gravitas* (-*atis*), weight, heaviness, from *gravis*, heavy.]
1. the state or condition of being grave; especially, (a) solemnity or sedateness of manner or character; earnestness; (b) danger or menace; ominous quality; as, the *gravity* of his illness; (c) seriousness, as of guilt.
2. weight; heaviness; as, specific *gravity*, center of *gravity*.
3. lowness of musical pitch.
4. in physics, gravitation; especially, terrestrial gravitation; the force that tends to draw all bodies in the earth's sphere toward the center of the earth: the rate of acceleration of gravity is approximately 32 feet per second per second.

grá·vūre′, *n.* [Fr., short for *photogravure*.]
1. engraving by means of plates made by a photographic process; photogravure.
2. a plate or print so prepared.

grā′vy, *n.* [ME. *grave*, *gravey*, said to be a misreading of OFr. *grané*, from *grain*, apparently used as a name for cooking ingredients.]
1. the juice given off by meat in cooking.
2. a sauce made by combining this juice with flour, seasoning, etc.
3. easily obtained profit. [Slang.]

grā′vy bōat, a dish for serving gravy: so called from its shape.

grāy, grey, *a.* [ME. *gray*, *grey*; AS. *græg*, gray.]
1. of a color that is a mixture or blend of black and white pigments.
2. (a) darkish; dull; (b) dreary; dismal.
3. having hair that is gray; hence, old.
4. designating any religious order whose members dress in gray; as, the *Gray* Friars.
gray antimony; stibnite.
gray cobalt; smaltite.
gray copper; tetrahedrite.
gray Friar; a member of the Franciscan order.
gray market; a place or system for selling scarce goods secretly at above prevailing prices, a practice considered unethical although legal.
gray matter; (a) grayish nerve tissue of the brain and spinal cord, consisting chiefly of nerve cells, with few nerve fibers: distinguished from *white matter*, which consists chiefly of nerve fibers; (b) [Colloq.] brains; intellectual capacity.
gray mullet; any of a large group of food fishes found mostly in salt water.
gray snapper; a food fish found off the Florida coast.
gray snipe; the dowitcher in winter plumage.
gray squirrel; a large, gray or black squirrel native to the United States.
gray whale; a whalebone whale of the genus *Rachianectes*, formerly common along the California coast.
gray wolf; a large, gray wolf that hunts in packs, native to western North America.

grāy, grey, *n.* 1. a gray color; a mixture of black and white pigments.
2. anything of a gray color, as (a) a badger; (b) a gray duck; (c) a gray horse; (d) a species of salmon; (e) the gray whale; (f) a gray uniform, etc.
3. the twilight of the morning or evening; as, the *gray* of the morning.
4. gray or unbleached fabric or clothing.

grāy, grey, *v.t.*; grayed, *pt.*, *pp.*; graying, *ppr.* to make gray, as the surface of glass by removing the polish; specifically, to print (a photograph) with a ground glass over the negative.

grāy, grey, *v.i.* to become gray; to age.

grāy′back, *n.* any of certain animals having a gray back, as (a) the gray snipe; (b) the gray whale; (c) the red-headed duck; (d) the black-headed duck; (e) an Irish fish, the dab; (f) a body louse; (g) the red-breasted sandpiper. Also spelled *greyback*.

grāy′bēard, *n.* 1. a man with a gray beard; an old man.
2. a large, earthen or stoneware jar or bottle.
Also spelled *greybeard*.

grāy buck, the chikara.

grāy′fish, *n.*; *pl.* **grāy′fish** or **grāy′fish·es,** the smooth or spiny dogfish: also spelled *greyfish*.

grāy′fly̆, *n.* the trumpet fly: also spelled *greyfly*.

grāy′-head′ed (-hed′), *a.* having gray hair; hence, old: also spelled *grey-headed*.

grāy′hound, *n.* [AS. *grighund*.] see *greyhound*.

grāy′ish, *a.* somewhat gray: also spelled *greyish*.

grāy′lag, *n.* [ME. *gray*; AS. *græg*, gray, and W. *llag*, slack, loose, slow, sluggish.] the common wild goose, *Anser ferus*, of Europe, which is thought to be the original of the domestic goose: also spelled *greylag*.

grāy lēaf, in plant pathology, a disease attacking oats growing in certain soils. The blades become blotchy and die early.

grāy′-lēaf pīne, the gray pine, *Pinus sabiniana*.

grāy′ling, *n.*; *pl.* **grāy′ling** or **grāy′lings,**
1. any fish of the genus *Thymallus*. The species are about 16 or 18 inches in length, found in clear, rapid streams, and valued as food.

GRAYLING (*Thymallus vulgaris*)

2. a gray butterfly, *Hipparchia semele*, of Great Britain.

grāy′ness, *n.* the quality of being gray: also spelled *greyness*.

grāy′pāte, grey′pāte, *n.* a young goldfinch in the period before the crimson head feathers appear.

grāy′stōne, grey′stōne, *n.* a grayish or greenish compact rock composed of feldspar and augite and allied to basalt.

grāy′wacke, grey′wacke, *n.* [G. *grauwacke*; *grau*, gray, and *wacke*, stone.] a conglomerate rock consisting of rounded pebbles and sand firmly united.

grāy′weth·ẽr, grey′weth·ẽr, *n.* a kind of stone found in England, bearing a resemblance to a gray sheep: called also *druid stone*, *Saracen stone*, and *sarsen stone*.

grāze, *v.t.*; grazed, *pt.*, *pp.*; grazing, *ppr.* [ME. *grasen*, *gresen*; AS. *grasian*, to graze, from *græs*, grass.]
1. to feed or supply with grass; to furnish pasture for; as, the farmer *grazes* large herds of cattle.
2. to feed on (growing grass, herbage, etc.)
The lambs with wolves shall *graze* the verdant mead. —Pope.
3. to tend while grazing, as cattle; as, Jacob *grazed* Laban's sheep.

grāze, *v.i.* 1. to eat grass; to feed on growing herbage; as, cattle *graze* on the meadows.
2. to supply grass; as, the ground will not *graze* well. [Dial.]

grāze, *v.t.* [prob. from prec. *v.* in orig. sense "to come close to the grass"; some senses influenced by obs. *glace*, to glance off.]
1. to touch or rub lightly in passing.
2. to scrape or scratch (the skin) or the skin of in passing; as, a bullet *grazed* his thigh.

grāze, *v.i.* to scrape, touch, or rub lightly against something in passing.

grāze, *n.* 1. the act of grazing.
2. a slight scratch or scrape caused by grazing.

grāz′ẽr, *n.* an animal that grazes or feeds on growing herbage.

grā′ziẽr, *n.* one who pastures cattle and rears them for market. [Chiefly Brit.]

grāz′ing, *n.* 1. the process of eating growing grass.
2. a pasture.

grä·zi·ō′sō (grät-sē-), *adv.* [It.] in music, gracefully, smoothly, and elegantly: a direction to the performer.

grēase, *n.* [ME. *grese*, *grece*; OFr. *gresse*, *graisse*, grease, fat, from LL. *grassus*, L. *crassus*, fat, thick.]
1. the soft fat of game animals: used in hunting with reference to game in the proper condition for killing; as, a stag in prime (or pride) of *grease*.
2. melted animal fat.
3. any thick, oily substance or lubricant.
4. an inflammation of the skin of a horse's fetlocks, accompanied by an oily discharge.
5. (a) the oily substance in uncleaned wool; (b) an uncleaned fleece or fur.

grēase, *v.t.*; greased, *pt.*, *pp.*; greasing, *ppr.*
1. to smear or lubricate with grease or fat.
2. to bribe; to corrupt or influence with money.
3. to cheat. [Obs.]
4. to transmit to or to affect with the disease of horses called grease.
5. to cause to run smoothly, as if greased.
to grease one's palm; to give one a bribe or tip.

grēase′bush, *n.* greasewood.

grēase cup, a small cup over a bearing in machinery, for containing and supplying grease or oil to lubricate the bearing.

grēase mŏn′key, a mechanic, especially one who works on automobiles or airplanes. [Slang.]

grēase mọth, a moth, *Aglossa pinguinalis*, which in a larval state eats greasy cloth.

grēase pāint, a mixture of grease and coloring matter used by actors in making up for the stage.

grēas′ẽr, *n.* 1. one who or that which greases.
2. a Mexican or Latin American: hostile and contemptuous term. [Slang.]

grēase′wood, *n.* a shrub of the spinach family, very abundant in the alkaline soils of the western United States: also called *greasebush*.

grēas′i·ly, *adv.* in a greasy manner.

grēas′i·ness, *n.* the state of being greasy; oiliness; unctuousness.

grēas′y, *a.*; *comp.* greasier; *superl.* greasiest,
1. containing grease; full of grease; oily; fat; unctuous.
2. smeared or soiled with grease.
3. like grease or oil; slippery; as, a fossil that has a *greasy* feel.
4. affected with the horse disease known as grease.
5. in nautical language, foggy; misty: said of the atmosphere.

grēat, *a.*; *comp.* greater; *superl.* greatest, [ME. *grete, gret*; AS. *great.*]
1. of much more than ordinary size, extent, volume, etc.; especially, (a) designating a thing or group of things larger than others of the same kind; as, the *great* cats are tigers, lions, etc.; the *Great* Lakes; (b) large in number, quantity, etc.; numerous; as, a *great* company; (c) long in duration; as, a *great* while.
2. much higher in some quality or degree; much above the ordinary or average; especially, (a) existing in a high degree; intense; as, a *great* light, *great* pain; (b) very much of a; acting much as (something specified): as, a *great* reader; (c) eminent; important; illustrious; superior; as, a *great* playwright; (d) very impressive or imposing; as, *great* ceremony; (e) having or showing nobility of mind, purpose, etc.; as, a *great* man.
3. of most importance; highest in its class; main; chief; as, the *Great* War.
4. designating a relationship one generation removed; older or younger by one generation: used in hyphenated compounds, as *great*-grandmother.
5. clever; expert; skillful (usually with *at*); as, he is *great at* tennis. [Colloq.]
6. excellent; splendid; fine: a generalized epithet of approval. [Colloq.]
7. pregnant. [Archaic.]
great auk; a large sea bird of the North Atlantic, that was incapable of flight and is now extinct.
Great Basin; a plateau between the Sierra Nevada and the Wasatch Mountains, covering eastern California, western Utah, and most of Nevada: area, 210,000 sq. mi.: many rivers and streams flow into it, forming lakes with no ultimate outlet to the sea.
Great Bear; the constellation Ursa Major: its seven brightest stars form the Big Dipper.
Great Bible; a large Bible prepared under Coverdale in 1539.
great calorie; see *calorie* (sense 2).
Great Charter; see *Magna Charta.*
great circle of a sphere; a circle whose plane passes through the center of the sphere.
great-circle sailing; the navigation of a ship on a great circle of the globe, that is, on the shortest arc between two points.
Great Commoner; nickname used of William Pitt, Henry Clay, Thaddeus Stevens, and William Jennings Bryan.
great Dane; any of a breed of large, powerful dog with short, smooth hair: also *Great Dane.*
Great Divide; (a) a principal mountain watershed; specifically, the Rocky Mountains; (b) death; (c) any important crisis.
great go; the final examination for the bachelor's degree: also *greats.* [Brit. University Slang.]
great gross; twelve gross.
great horned owl; a large North American owl with two prominent tufts of feathers on its head.
Great Lakes; a chain of fresh-water lakes in Canada and the United States, emptying into the St. Lawrence River; Lakes Superior, Michigan, Huron, Erie, Ontario, and, sometimes, St. Clair.
great laurel; a large shrub of the rhododendron family, with thick, oblong, dark-green leaves and delicate, pink flowers in cone-shaped clusters.
Great Mogul; (a) the title of the ruler of the empire established by the Mongols in India in the sixteenth century; (b) [g- m-] a person of importance.
great on; enthusiastic about. [Colloq.]
great organ; the largest and most powerful part of a grand organ, played by a keyboard of its own and forming in many respects an instrument by itself.
Great Powers; the world's most powerful nations.
great primer; a large size of type, 18 point.
Great Schism; the division or conflict in the Roman Catholic Church from 1378 to 1417, when there were two rival popes, one at Avignon, the other at Rome.
Great Sea; the Mediterranean.
great seal; (a) the chief seal of a government; (b) [G– S–] the Lord Chancellor of Great Britain, keeper of the great seal; also, his position.
Great Spirit; the chief god of some North American Indian tribes.
Great Vowel Shift; the complicated series of sound developments (c. 1450 to c. 1830) which changed the vowel system of Middle English into that of Modern English: the Middle English system was characterized by contrasts of short with long vowels and by values of the vowel symbols roughly resembling those found in Modern French and German; overdifferentiation of the Middle English high vowels caused the long vowels to become diphthongs and the short vowels to be lowered in tongue position: also *Great Sound Shift.*
Great War; World War I.
Great Week: in the Orthodox Eastern Church, the week preceding Easter; Holy Week.
Great White Father; the name given by the American Indians to the president of the United States.
Great White Way; the theater section of New York City on Broadway near Times Square: so called because of its brilliant illumination.
great willow herb; a plant of the primrose family, with long leaves and purple flowers in a single spike.
great world; [after Fr. *grand monde.*] fashionable society and its way of life.
Syn.—big, wide, excellent, immense, bulky, majestic, grand, eminent, noble, powerful.

grēat, *n.* 1. the whole; the gross; as, a shipbuilder contracts to build a ship by the *great.*
2. [*pl.*] final examinations for degrees at Oxford University; at Cambridge called *great go.* [Slang.]
the great; those who are great.

grēat′-ȧunt, *n.* a sister of any of one's grandparents; a grandaunt.

grēat′-bel′lied, *a.* pregnant; teeming.

grēat′ċōat, *n.* a heavy overcoat.

grēat′en, *v.t.* and *v.i.* to increase; to make or become great or greater. [Archaic.]

Grēat′ẽr, *a.* designating a large city together with its suburbs; as, *Greater* Cleveland, *Greater* New York.

grēat′-grand′chīld, *n.* the child of a grandson or granddaughter.

grēat′-grand′daugh·tẽr (-dạ), *n.* a daughter of a grandson or granddaughter.

grēat′-grand′fath·ẽr, *n.* the father of a grandfather or grandmother.

grēat′-grand′mŏth·ẽr, *n.* the mother of a grandfather or grandmother.

grēat′-grand′pãr·ent, *n.* a parent of any of one's grandparents.

grēat′-grand′sŏn, *n.* the son of a grandchild.

grēat′-grēat′-, a combining form used with nouns of relationship to indicate *two degrees of removal in an ascending* or *descending scale,* as in *great-great*-grandparent, *great-great*-grandson. Each additional *great-* indicates one further degree of removal.

grēat′heärt′ed, *a.* high-minded; generous; courageous.

grēat·heärt′ed·ness, *n.* high-mindedness; generosity; courage.

grēat′ly, *adv.* 1. in a great degree; much.
I will *greatly* multiply thy sorrow.
—Gen. iii. 16.
2. nobly; illustriously.

grēat′-neph″ew, *n.* a grandson of one's brother or sister; grandnephew.

grēat′ness, *n.* 1. the state or quality of being great; largeness of bulk, dimensions, number, or quantity.
2. breadth of mind; nobility; worth.
Syn.—bulk, size, breadth, nobility, dignity.

grēat′-niēce, *n.* a granddaughter of one's brother or sister; a grandniece.

grēat′-uñ″ċle, *n.* a brother of any of one's grandparents; a granduncle.

grēat un·wäshed′ (-wäsht′), the term of contempt which Edmund Burke (1729–1797), Irish statesman and orator, applied to the working and artisan classes.

Grēat Wạll, the defensive wall (20–30 feet high, 15–20 feet thick, over 1,400 miles long) between Mongolia and China proper, built by the Chinese to keep out invaders: it was begun over 2,000 years ago and completed c. 1600.

grēave, *n.* a grove. [Obs.]

grēave, *v.t.* in nautical usage, to clean the bottom of (a ship); to grave.

grēaveṣ, *n.pl.* [ME. *greves, grayvez*; OFr. *greves,* greaves, pl. of *greve,* the shin.] armor for the legs from the ankle to the knee.

grēaveṣ, *n.pl.* [whaling term from L.G. *greven*; basic sense "coarse elements that will not melt"; base, as in *great, grit.*] cracklings; the sediment of skin, etc. formed when animal fat is melted down for tallow.

grēbe, *n.*; *pl.* **grēbeṣ** or **grēbe,** [Fr. *grèbe.*] any of a group of diving and swimming birds of the loon family, with partly webbed feet and legs set far back on the body.

HORNED GREBE (*Podiceps cornutus*)

Grē′ciăn, *a.* pertaining to Greece; Greek.
Grecian bend; an affected carriage of the body in vogue among women about 1870, when bustles and the wasp waist were fashionable, in which the lower part of the trunk was projected backward and the upper part forward.
Grecian fire; see *Greek fire* under *Greek.*

Grē′ciăn, *n.* [OFr. *Grecien,* from L. *Græcia,* Greece.]
1. a native of Greece; a Greek.
2. a Jew who was Hellenized: so called in Acts vi. 1.
3. a scholar of Greek.

Grē′ciṣm, *n.* 1. an idiom of the Greek language.
2. an imitation of this.
3. the spirit of Greek culture; Hellenism.
Also spelled *Graecism.*

Grē′cīze, *v.t.*; Grecized, *pt., pp.*; Grecizing, *ppr.* 1. to render Grecian; to cause to take Greek character.
2. to translate into Greek.

Grē′cīze, Grē′ciăn·īze, *v.i.* to speak the Greek language; to imitate the Greeks in language, manner, etc.

Grē′ċō-, [from L. *Græcus.*] a combining form meaning: (a) *Greek, Greeks*; (b) *Greek and.* Also spelled *Graeco-.*

Grē″ċō-Rō′măn, *a.* characterized by being partly Greek and partly Roman; pertaining to or influenced by both Greece and Rome; as, *Greco-Roman* art.

greçque (grek), *n.* [Fr., fretwork, f. of *Grec,* Greek.] an ornamental fret of Greek origin. [Archaic.]

gree, *n.* [ME. *gre*; OFr. *gre, gred,* from L. *gratum* neut. of *gratus,* pleasing.]
1. good will. [Archaic.]
2. satisfaction for an injury received: only in *do* (or *make*) *gree.* [Archaic.]

gree, *n.* a step or stair; rank; degree. [Obs.]

gree, *v.i.* to agree. [Obs.]

greece, *n.* a greese. [Obs.]

greed, *n.* [back-formation, from *greedy.*] excessive desire for acquiring or having; desire for more than one needs or deserves; greediness; avarice; cupidity.

greed′i·ly, *adv.* in a greedy manner.

greed′i·ness, *n.* the quality of being greedy.
Syn.—avidity, eagerness, rapacity, voracity, piggishness, gluttony.

greed′y, *a.*; *comp.* greedier; *superl.* greediest, [ME. *gredy, gredi*; AS. *grædig,* greedy, from *græd,* hunger, greed.]
1. wanting to eat and drink too much; ravenous; voracious; gluttonous; as, a lion that is *greedy* of his prey.
2. wanting excessively to have or acquire; desiring more than one needs or deserves; avaricious; covetous; as, *greedy* of gain.
Syn.—gluttonous, voracious, hungry, desirous, avaricious, piggish, insatiable.

gree′gree, *n.* same as *grigri.*

Greek, *a.* [ME. and AS. *Grec, Crec*; L. *Græcus*; Gr. *Graikos*, a Greek.] pertaining to ancient or modern Greece, its people, language, or culture; Grecian; Hellenic.

Greek calends; at no time; never: the Greeks did not have calends.

Greek Catholic; (a) a person belonging to an Orthodox Eastern Church; (b) a Uniat Greek or Byzantine.

Greek (Orthodox) Church; (a) the Orthodox Eastern Church; (b) the established church of Greece, a part of the Orthodox Eastern Church.

Greek cross; a cross with four equal arms at right angles.

Greek Empire; the Byzantine Empire, flourishing from A.D. 395 to 1453.

Greek fire; [from its first use by Greeks of Byzantium.] an incendiary material used in ancient and medieval warfare, said to have burned in water.

Greek-letter fraternity; any American society, especially a student society, whose name is designated by a combination of Greek letters.

Greek rite; the religious ritual of the Orthodox Eastern Church, as distinguished from that of the Roman Catholic Church.

Greek, *n.* 1. a native of Greece, ancient or modern.

2. the language of Greece, ancient or modern.

3. a member of a Greek-letter fraternity. [Slang.]

4. an adventurer. [Slang.]

to be Greek to one; to be incomprehensible or unintelligible to one.

Greek′ish, *a.* peculiar to Greece; somewhat Greek.

Greek′ling, *n.* a little Greek or one of small account.

green, *a.* [ME. *grene*; AS. *grene*, green, from *growan*, to grow.]

1. of the color of foliage and plants when growing; verdant.

2. overspread with or characterized by green foliage; as, a *green* field.

3. keeping the green grass of summer; snowless; mild; as, a *green* December.

4. sickly or bilious, as from illness, fear, etc.

5. fresh; flourishing; undecayed; as, *green* old age.

6. unripe; immature; not arrived at perfection; as, *green* fruit.

7. immature in age; young; inexperienced; raw; as, *green* in age or judgment.

8. easily imposed on or deceived; simple; naive.

9. not dried, seasoned, or cured; unprocessed.

10. fresh; new.

11. jealous. [Colloq.]

green algae; algae in which the chlorophyll predominates.

green blight; a parasitical disease of plants.

green corn; unripe ears of sweet corn, used for cooking and eating.

green crab; the common edible crab, *Carcinides mænas*, of Europe and the United States.

green crop; a crop of green vegetables, as distinguished from a crop of grain, hay, etc.

green earth; a species of mineral earth, used as a pigment; terre verte.

green fire; a composition of sulfur, potassium chlorate, and salts of barium, which on burning gives a greenish flame.

green glass; coarse, ordinary glass of a greenish color, used for bottles, etc.

green hand; a raw and inexperienced person. [Colloq.]

green lead ore; lead chlorophosphate; pyromorphite, a crystalline mineral found in lead veins.

green light; (a) the green phase of a traffic light, indicating permission to go ahead; (b) [Colloq.] authorization to proceed with some undertaking: usually in *to give* (or *get*) *the green light.*

green linnet; a greenfinch.

green manure; (a) a crop of growing plants, as clover, plowed under while still green to fertilize the soil; (b) fresh manure; manure not yet decayed.

green marble; serpentine.

green mineral; malachite; a pigment of carbonate of copper.

green monkey; a long-tailed West African monkey, *Cercopithecus sabaeus*, with greenish hair.

green onion; an immature onion with a long stalk and green leaves, eaten raw as a relish or in salads; scallion.

green pepper; the green immature fruit of the sweet red pepper, eaten as a vegetable.

green sea; a sea or large wave shipped by a vessel in a gale.

green soap; a soft soap made of potash, linseed oil, and alcohol, used in treating skin diseases: so called because originally greenish.

green tea; tea prepared from leaves not fermented before drying: distinguished from *black tea.*

green vitriol; copperas; crystallized ferrous sulfate.

greenware; pottery before it is baked.

green woodpecker; the yaffle, *Picus viridis.*

green, *n.* 1. the color of growing plants; a color composed of blue and yellow rays, which, mixed in different proportions, exhibit a variety of shades; as, apple-*green*, meadow-*green*, leek-*green*, etc.

2. any green pigment or dye.

3. anything colored green, especially clothing; as, the wearing of the *green.*

4. [*pl.*] fresh leaves or branches of trees or other plants, used for ornamentation.

5. [*pl.*] green leafy vegetables, as kale, spinach, etc.

6. a piece of smooth turf on which games are played; as, a golf *green*, a bowling *green.*

7. in golf, (a) the plot of carefully tended turf immediately surrounding each of the holes to facilitate putting; (b) an entire golf course.

brilliant green; a dyestuff derived from coal tar: also called *benzal green.*

Brunswick green; a form of oxychloride of copper; a light-green powder used as a pigment.

copper green; a pigment derived from salts of copper.

emerald green; see under *emerald.*

green with envy; very envious.

Guignet's green; a green coloring matter used and compounded by the French artist Guignet: it is derived from hydrate of chromium and is used in calico printing.

malachite green; a hydrated copper carbonate used as a pigment.

methyl green; a coal-tar dyestuff for cotton, wool, and silk, occurring in commerce as a double zinc salt.

mineral green; malachite.

mountain green; a natural malachite green; green earth.

Paris green; a highly poisonous bright-green powder used as a pigment and as an insecticide: it is a compound of acetate and arsenite of copper: also called *French green, emerald green, Schweinfurt green, Vienna green*, and *mitis green.*

Saxony green; see *cobalt green* under *cobalt.*

Scheele's green; a green coloring matter consisting of copper arsenite: also called *Swedish green.*

the Green; green as the symbol of Irish nationalism; Ireland's national color.

Vienna green; Paris green.

green, *v.t.*; greened, *pt., pp.*; greening, *ppr.* to make green.

green, *v.i.* to become green; to grow green.

green′back, *n.* 1. any piece of United States paper money printed in green ink on the back.

2. an animal with a green back.

Green′back″ẽr, *n.* a member of the Greenback party.

Green′back Pär′ty, the Independent Party, a political party in the United States after the Civil War, advocating government paper money as the only currency.

green′bīrd, *n.* a greenfinch.

green′-blūe′, *n.* the color in the spectrum exactly between primary green and primary blue.

green′bōne, *n.* 1. the garfish, *Belone belone*, from the color of its bones when boiled.

2. the viviparous blenny, or eelpout, *Zoarces viviparus.*

green′brī″ẽr, *n.* in botany, any of various woody, climbing vines of the lily family, with spiny stems.

green brọọm, a plant, *Genista tinctoria*, used in dyeing green.

green′çloth, *n.* in England, formerly, a board or court of justice held in the counting house of the king's household, with power to correct offenders and keep the peace within the precincts of the court.

green drag′ọ̆n, an American wild flower, *Arisæma dracontium*, similar to the jack-in-the-pulpit but with digitate leaves, a very long spadix, and a greenish spathe.

green′ẽr·y, *n.* 1. green plants; verdure.

2. a greenhouse.

green′-eȳed (-īd), *a.* 1. having green eyes.

2. jealous.

the green-eyed monster; jealousy.

green′finch, *n.* 1. the European finch, which has olive-green and yellow feathers: also called *green grosbeak, green linnet, greenbird* etc.

2. the olive-green Texas sparrow.

green′fish, *n.* 1. a pollack or coalfish.

2. the bluefish; the horse mackerel.

green′flȳ, *n.* 1. a louse or aphid that infests plants.

2. a green flesh fly.

green′gāge′, *n.* [after Sir William *Gage*, who introduced it into England from France, c. 1725.] a large plum with golden-green skin and flesh.

green′gill, *n.* 1. an oyster whose gills have been colored green by feeding upon *Confervæ.*

2. the green condition thus caused.

green′grō″cẽr, *n.* a retailer of fresh vegetables and fruits. [Brit.]

green′grō″cẽr·y, *n.*; *pl.* **green′grō″cẽr·ies,** 1. a retail store where fresh vegetables and fruits are sold. [Brit.]

2. [*pl.*] things sold by a greengrocer. [Brit.]

green′head (-hed), *n.* 1. a species of striped bass.

2. the mallard.

3. the golden plover.

4. greenness; immaturity. [Obs.]

green′heärt, *n.* in botany, (a) the *Nectandra rodiœi*, a native of Guiana, the bark of which yields bebeerin, an alkaloid of great value: its timber is highly valued because of its hardness and durability; (b) the *Columbrina ferruginosa*, allied to the buckthorn, the wood having a twisted grain.

green′horn, *n.* [prob. orig. with reference to a young animal with immature horns.]

1. an inexperienced person; beginner; novice.

2. a person easily deceived; dupe.

3. a recently arrived immigrant. [Colloq.] [Humorous or patronizing in all senses.]

green′house, *n.* a house, the roof and sides of which consist largely of glass, for the purpose of cultivating delicate or out-of-season plants, the temperature being kept up by means of artificial heat; a hothouse.

green′ie, *n.* [after the color of a common type.] an amphetamine pill, used as a stimulant. [Slang.]

green′ing, *n.* 1. the process or act of growing green.

2. any of certain varieties of apple of a green color when ripe; as, the Rhode Island *greening.*

green′ing, *n.* [after *The Greening of America* (1970), book by C. Reich.] a becoming more sensitive to basic human values by casting off the commercial and social restrictions of the prevailing culture.

green′ish, *a.* somewhat green; having a tinge of green; as, a *greenish*-yellow.

green′ish·ness, *n.* the quality or state of being greenish.

Green′lănd·ẽr, *n.* one born or residing in Greenland.

green lā′vẽr, an edible seaweed, genus *Ulva*: also called *sea lettuce.*

green leek, a parakeet of the genus *Polytelis*, the scarlet-breasted parrot of Australia.

green′let, *n.* 1. any green-colored vireo; as, the red-eyed *greenlet, Vireo olivaceus.*

2. any similar small green songster.

green′ling, *n.* any of a group of large, flesh-eating fishes with long dorsal fins, living in the North Pacific, especially off the Aleutian Islands.

green′ly, *adv.* with a green color; also, newly, freshly, vigorously, etc.

green′ness, *n.* the state or quality of being green.

green′ŏck·īte, *n.* [after Lord *Greenock*, its discoverer.] a mineral sulfide of cadmium, CdS, crystalline and of an orange-yellow color.

green pow′ẽr, money, as the source of economic power and, hence, social and political power.

green rev·ō·lū′tion, *n.* the simultaneous development of new varieties of food plants and improved agricultural techniques, resulting in greatly increased crop yields.

green′rọọm, *n.* 1. a retiring room for actors and actresses in a theater.

2. a room where new, or green, cloth, pottery, etc. is received.

greens, *n.pl.* see *green*, n. 5.

green'sand, *n.* beds of sand or sandstone, belonging to the Cretaceous period: so called because green earth or glauconite is ordinarily scattered throughout them.

green'sauce, *n.* the field sorrel; also, sour sorrel mixed with sugar and vinegar.

greens fee, a fee paid to play golf on a golf course.

green'shank, *n.* a sandpiper of the genus *Totanus*, having greenish legs and found in Europe.

green'sick"ness, *n.* chlorosis; an anemic disease of young women, which gives the complexion a greenish tinge.

greens'keep"ẽr, *n.* the person in charge of maintaining the turf, bunkers, etc. of a golf course.

green'snāke, *n.* a bright-green, harmless snake of North America.

green stall, a stall on which green vegetables are displayed for sale.

green'stōne, *n.* 1. any stone having a green color, as diorite, melaphyre, and the like.
2. an inferior kind of jade.

green'sward, *n.* turf green with grass.

greenth, *n.* verdure; a green condition. [Rare.]

green'weed, *n.* see *genista.*

Green'wich tīme (gren'ich, grin'ij), mean solar time of the meridian at Greenwich, England, used as the basis for standard time throughout most of the world.

Green'wich Vil'lāge (gren'ich), a section of New York City, on the lower west side of Manhattan, noted as a center for artists, authors, etc.: formerly a village on Manhattan Island.

green'wing, *n.* a teal with green wings.

green'withe, *n.* a climbing orchid of the genus *Vanilla.*

green'wood, *n.* 1. a forest in leaf.
2. wood made green by a certain fungus.

green'y, *a.* green; greenish.

green'y, *n.* 1. the greenfinch.
2. a greenhorn. [Colloq.]

greet, *v.t.*; greeted, *pt.*, *pp.*; greeting, *ppr.* [ME. *greten*; AS. *gretan*, to greet.]
1. to speak or write to with expressions of friendliness, respect, pleasure, etc., as in meeting or by letter; hail; welcome.
2. to meet, receive, address, or acknowledge (a person, utterance, or event) in a specified way; as, the speech was *greeted* with cheers; he was *greeted* by a rifle shot.
3. to come or appear to; make itself manifest to; meet; as, the aroma of coffee *greeted* us.
4. to congratulate. [Obs.]

greet, *v.i.* to meet and salute.

greet, *v.i.* to weep; lament. [Archaic or Dial.]

greet, *n.* salutation; greeting. [Obs.]

greet, *n.* weeping. [Scot.]

greet, *a.* great. [Obs.]

greet'ẽr, *n.* one who greets.

greet'ing, *n.* [ME. *gretinge*; AS. *greting*, from *gretan*, to greet.] 1. salutation; welcome; the act or words of a person who greets.
2. a message of regards from someone absent.

greet'ing, *n.* weeping. [Scot.]

gref'fi·ẽr, *n.* [Fr., from OFr. *greffier*, a scribe; LL. *graphiarius*, a notary, from L. *graphiarius*, pertaining to a style for writing, from *graphium*, a style.] a registrar or recorder.

grē'găl, *a.* [L. *grex, gregis*, a flock.] pertaining to a flock. [Rare.]

grē·gā'ri·ăn, *a.* 1. belonging to the herd; common.
2. gregarious; living in flocks.

Greg·à·rī'nà, *n.* 1. the typical genus of the *Gregarinidæ.*
2. [g–; *pl.* greg-à-rī'nae.] a gregarine.

greg'à·rine, *n.* one of the *Gregarinidæ.*

greg'à·rine, *a.* of or relating to the *Gregarinidæ.*

Greg·à·rin'i·dae, *n.pl.* [L. *gregarius, gregarious*, from *grex, gregis*, a flock.] a group of parasitic protozoans that live in insects, crustaceans, earthworms, etc.

grē·gā'ri·ous, *a.* [L. *gregarius*, belonging to a flock, from *grex, gregis*, a flock, herd.]
1. living in herds or flocks.
2. fond of the company of others; sociable.
3. having to do with a herd, flock, or crowd.
4. in botany, growing in clusters.

grē·gā'ri·ous·ly, *adv.* in a gregarious manner; so as to be gregarious.

grē·gā'ri·ous·ness, *n.* the state or quality of being gregarious.

grège (grāzh), *n.* [Fr., from It. *greggia* (supply *seta*, silk), raw silk, f. of *greggio*, raw, rough.] the color beige or a color between beige and gray.

greg'ō, greg'gō, *n.* in the Levant, a short cloak with a hood.

Grē·gō'ri·ăn, *a.* belonging to, established, or produced by Pope Gregory I or Pope Gregory XIII.

Gregorian calendar; a corrected form of the Julian calendar, introduced by Pope Gregory XIII in 1582 and now used in most countries of the world: it provides for an ordinary year of 365 days and a leap year of 366 days every fourth even year, exclusive of century years, which are leap years only if exactly divisible by 400.

Gregorian chant; a mode of singing or chanting introduced by Pope Gregory I, less monotonous than the Ambrosian, which preceded it; plain song, or plain chant.

Gregorian telescope; the first and most common form of the reflecting telescope, invented by James Gregory (1638–1675), professor of mathematics in the university of St. Andrews.

Gregorian year; a year according to the Gregorian calendar.

greil'lāde, *n.* [etym. unknown.] coarse iron ore used in a Catalan forge.

grei'sen, *n.* [G. *greissen*, to cleave, split.] a crystalline, igneous rock composed chiefly of mica and quartz, in which the feldspar is replaced by fluorspar, tourmaline, tin oxide, rutile, etc.

gre·lōt' (grā-lō'), *n.* [Fr.] a small bell similar to a sleighbell.

grē'mi·ăl, *a.* [LL. *gremialis*, from L. *gremium*, the bosom or lap.] of or pertaining to the lap or bosom. [Rare.]

grē'mi·ăl, *n.* 1. a confidant. [Obs.]
2. a lap cloth worn by a bishop when he sits during the celebration of Mass.

grem'lin, *n.* [Eng. dial., from Fr. dial. *grimelin*, schoolboy, brat, stingy player, dim., from *grimaud*, dunce, scribbler, pedant.]
1. an imaginary small creature whose meddling antics are humorously blamed for the faulty operation of airplanes.
2. such a creature supposed to interfere with the smoothness of any procedure.

grē·nāde', *n.* [OFr. *grenade*, pomegranate, from Sp. *granada*, lit., something containing grains or seeds, a grenade, from L. *granatus*, grained, having seeds, from *granum*, a grain, seed.]
1. a small bomb detonated by a fuse and thrown by hand or fired from a rifle.
2. a glass container to be thrown so that it will break and disperse the chemicals inside: used for putting out fires, spreading tear gas, etc.

rampart grenade; a grenade used by soldiers defending a rampart, for throwing or rolling down upon besiegers.

gren·à·diēr', *n.* [Fr., from Sp. *granadero*, from *granada*, a grenade.]
1. originally, an infantry soldier who carried and threw grenades.
2. a member of a special regiment or corps, as of the Grenadier Guards of the British Army.
3. a bird of brilliant plumage, red above, black below, inhabiting the Cape Colony, and about the size of a sparrow: called also *grenadier grosbeak.*
4. any of a group of deep-sea fishes related to the cod, with a long, tapering tail and soft fins.

gren'à·din, *n.* [Fr. *grenade*, a pomegranate.] a dyestuff containing crude magenta or fuchsin.

gren·à·dīne', *n.* [Fr., dim. of *grenade*, pomegranate.] a sirup made from pomegranate juice, used for flavoring some alcoholic drinks.

gren·à·dīne', *n.* [Fr. *grenadine*, grenadine, dim. of *grenade*, a pomegranate.] a gauzy silk, cotton, wool, or rayon cloth, used for blouses, dresses, curtains, etc.

grē·nā'dō, *n.* a grenade. [Archaic.]

grēne, *a.* and *n.* green. [Obs.]

grès (grā), *n.* [Fr.] sandstone; stoneware.

grès cérame, grès de Flandres; a kind of German stoneware of the Rhine cities.

Gresh'ăm's law, [after the founder of the English Royal Exchange, Sir Thomas *Gresham* (1519–1579), who explained the principle to Queen Elizabeth I in 1558.] the theory that when two or more kinds of money of equal denomination but unequal intrinsic value are in circulation at the same time, the one of greater value will tend to be hoarded or exported; popularly, the principle that bad money will drive good money out of circulation.

gres·sō'ri·ăl, gres·sō'ri·ous, *a.* [L. *gressus*, pp. of *gradi*, to walk.] suited for walking; in ornithology, designating or of birds which have three toes forward (two of which are connected) and one behind.

Gretna Green, a village in Dumfries County, Scotland, just across the English border, famous for its marriages of runaway English couples.

Gre·vil'le·à, *n.* 1. a large genus of Australian trees, with tetramerous flowers and silky leaves: popularly called *silk oaks.*
2. [g–] a tree of this genus.

grew (grů), *v.* past tense of *grow.*

grew'sŏme (grů'sum), *a.* same as *gruesome.*

grew'sŏme·ness, *n.* same as *gruesomeness.*

grey, *a.*, *n.*, *v.t.*, and *v.i.* gray: British spelling.

grey'hound, *n.* [ME. *greyhound, grayhund*; AS. *grighund*, a greyhound.]
1. a tall, slender hound with a narrow, pointed head: the breed is remarkable for the keenness of its sight and its swiftness in running.

GREYHOUND

2. a speedy ocean steamer: in full, *ocean greyhound*: also (rarely) spelled *grayhound.*

grey'lag, *n.* same as *graylag.*

grib'ble, *n.* [prob. dim. from base of *grub.*] a small salt-water crustacean, *Limnoria terebrans*, that bores into timber under water and destroys it.

grīce, *n.* a little pig. [Obs.]

grid, *n.* 1. a grating, gridiron, or other structure with parallel bars.
2. in electricity, a lead plate in a storage battery.
3. an electrode of wire mesh in an electron tube to control the flow of electrons from the filament to the plate.

grid circuit; the part of an electric circuit between the grid and the cathode of an electron tube.

grid condenser; a condenser in series with the grid circuit of an electron tube.

grid current; the flow of electrons between the grid and the cathode of an electron tube.

grid leak; a high resistance placed in the grid circuit of an electron tube to control the grid voltage.

grid, *a.* of football. [Slang.]

grid'dẽr, *n.* a football player. [Slang.]

grid'dle, *n.* [ME. *gridel, gridele*; W. *gredyll*, a griddle, a grate, from LL. *graticula*, a gridiron, from L. *craticula*, dim. of *cratis*, a hurdle.]
1. a heavy plate or pan, broad and shallow, for cooking pancakes, etc.
2. a griddlecake.
3. a miner's wire-bottomed sieve.
4. a stove lid in the form of a grid.

grid'dle, *v.t.*; griddled, *pt.*, *pp.*; griddling, *ppr.* to cook on a griddle.

grid'dle·çāke, a thin, flat cake baked from a batter on a griddle; a pancake.

grīde, *n.* a discordant grating or scraping sound.

grīde, *v.t.* and *v.i.*; grided, *pt.*, *pp.*; griding, *ppr.*
1. to grate or scrape with a grating sound.
2. to pierce or wound. [Obs.]

grid'e·lin, *n.* [Fr. *gris de lin*, flax-gray; *gris*, gray, *de*, of, and *lin*, flax; L. *de*, of, and *linum*, flax.] a color mixed of white and red, or a gray violet: spelled also *gredaline, grizelin.*

grid'ī"ron (-ī"ŭrn), *n.* [ME. *grydyrne, gredirne*, a gridiron, a griddle.]
1. a framework of metal bars or wires for broiling meat or fish; a grille.
2. a frame for supporting ships during repairs, etc.
3. a football field.
4. anything suggesting a gridiron in design.

gridiron pendulum; a compensation pendulum, consisting of parallel bars of different metals, so arranged that the length of the pendulum remains unaltered by changes of temperature.

gridiron valve; a slide valve in which parts arranged somewhat like a gridiron have an equal number of parts similarly arranged in the seat.

grid′lock, *n.* [*grid* and *lock.*] a traffic jam, as at an intersection, in which no vehicle can move in any direction.

grief, *n.* [OFr. *grief*, sorrow, grief, as adj. heavy, grievous, from L. *gravis*, weighty, sad, grievous.]

1. intense emotional suffering caused by loss, misfortune, injury, or evils of any kind; sorrow; regret; as, we experience *grief* when we lose a friend.

2. a cause or the subject of such sorrow.

3. (a) hardships; suffering; pain; (b) a cause of any of these. [Obs.]

to come to grief; to suffer calamity or failure.

grief′ful, *a.* full of grief or sorrow.

grief′less, *a.* without grief.

grief′-strick·en, *a.* stricken with grief; keenly distressed; sorrowful.

griev·a·ble, *a.* lamentable. [Obs.]

griev′ance, *n.* [ME. *grevaunce, grevance*; OFr. *grevance*, an injury, grievance, from *grevant*, ppr. of *grever*, to grieve, afflict.]

1. a circumstance or condition thought to be unjust and ground for complaint or resentment.

2. complaint or resentment, or a ground for this, against a wrong, real or imagined.

3. (a) the inflicting of injury or hardship; (b) a cause of injury or hardship. [Obs.]

grieve, *v.t.*; grieved, *pt., pp.*; grieving, *ppr.* [ME. *greven*; OFr. *grever*; L. *gravare*, to burden, oppress, grieve, from *gravis*, heavy, grievous.]

1. to give pain of mind to; to afflict; to cause to feel grief; to distress.

2. to lament. [Rare.]

3. to harm; injure. [Archaic.]

grieve, *v.i.* to feel deep, acute sorrow or distress; to sorrow; to mourn.

griev′er, *n.* he who or that which grieves.

griev′ing·ly, *adv.* in a grieving manner.

griev′ous, *a.* [ME. *grevous*; OFr. *grevos*; LL. *gravosus*; L. *gravis*, heavy, burdensome, grievous.]

1. causing grief.

2. showing or characterized by grief; as, a *grievous* cry.

3. causing physical suffering; hard to bear; severe; as, *grievous* pain.

4. deplorable; atrocious; as, a *grievous* crime.

griev′ous·ly, *adv.* in a grievous manner.

griev′ous·ness, *n.* the state or quality of being grievous.

griff, *n.* [G. *griff*, a grasp, grip.]

1. grasp. [Obs.]

2. a device in a Jacquard loom to shift the warp threads.

griff, *n.* same as *griffin.*

griff, *n.* a rocky chasm. [Brit. Dial.]

griffe, griff, *n.* [Fr.; Am. Sp. *grifo*, orig., griffin.]

1. the child of a Negro and a mulatto. [Dial.]

2. a mulatto. [Dial.]

3. a person of Negro and American Indian ancestry. [Dial.]

grif·fawn′, *n.* in Ireland, a turf spade having an iron wing on one side of the blade to shape the soft peat, as it is dug from the mass, into square form before drying.

griffe, *n.* [OFr. *griffe*, a claw, nail, talon, from *griffer*, to gripe, grasp, seize, from O.H.G. *grifan*, to grip.] a clawlike ornament at the base of a column.

griffe, *n.* the deposit in new wine soon after bottling.

grif′fin, *n.* [ME. *griffyn*; OFr. *grifon*; LL. *griffus, gryphus*, a griffin, a vulture; L. *gryps*; Gr. *gryps*, a griffin, so called from its hooked beak, from *grypos*, hooked, curved.]

GRIFFIN

1. in mythology, an imaginary animal with the body and hind legs of a lion, and the head and wings of an eagle.

2. a representation of this used in heraldry.

3. a vulture, *Gyps fulvus*, found in the mountainous parts of Europe, North Africa, and Turkey.

4. a close watcher or guard, as of a person; specifically, a chaperon or duenna.

grif′fin, *n.* [prob. from *griffin* (animal), influenced by native word.]

1. an Occidental recently arrived in the East, especially India.

2. a race horse making its first race. [Anglo-Ind.]

grif′fin·age, *n.* in India, the condition of being a griffin or newcomer.

grif′fin·ism, *n.* 1. griffinage; hence, lack of experience.

2. griffinlike vigilance.

grif′fon, *n.* 1. a griffin.

2. one of a breed of wire-haired European dogs, usually of a grayish color, used in hunting game birds.

grif′ter, *n.* [prob. altered from *grafter.*] a petty grafter; one who runs a gambling device at a carnival, resort, etc. [Slang.]

grig, *n.* [ME. *grege*, anything diminutive, dwarf; prob. from ON.]

1. a lively, animated person.

2. a small eel. [Obs. or Dial.]

3. (a) a grasshopper; (b) a cricket. [Obs. or Dial.]

as merry as a grig; a saying supposed generally to have reference to the mirth and cheerfulness ascribed to the grasshopper.

grig, *n.* [W. *grug*, heath.] heather. [Brit. Dial.]

grig′net, *n.* [compare OFr. *perdrix, grignette*, the ordinary partridge.] one of various African birds of the genus *Parisoma.*

gri′gri, *n.* [native word.] an African fetish; a charm or talisman.

grill, *v.t.*; grilled, *pt., pp.*; grilling, *ppr.* [Fr. *griller*, to broil on a gridiron, from *gril*, a gridiron, a grill.]

1. to cook on a gridiron; to broil.

2. to torture by applying heat; hence, to question relentlessly; to cross-examine searchingly.

grill, *v.i.* to be subjected to grilling.

grill, *n.* [Fr. *gril*; OFr. *greil*, a gridiron, *graille* a grate, grating, from L. *craticula*, a gridiron, dim. of *cratis*, wicker work, a hurdle.]

1. a framework of metal bars or wires for broiling meat or fish; a gridiron.

GRILL

2. anything broiled on a gridiron.

3. a grillroom.

grill, *n.* same as *grille.*

gril·lade′, *n.* [Fr., from *griller*, to grill.] broiled meat, or something broiled; also, the act of grilling.

gril′lage, *n.* [Fr., wirework, grating, a frame, from *gril*, a gridiron.] a system of beams laid crosswise to form a foundation for a building in soft soil.

grille, *n.* [Fr., from OFr. *graille*, a grating.] an open grating of wrought iron, bronze, wood, etc., forming a screen to a door, window, or the like: sometimes spelled *grill.*

GRILLE

gril·lé′ (grē-yā′), *a.* [Fr., pp. of *griller*, to grill.]

1. grilled.

2. having a background of crossed parallel bars: said of lace.

grilled, *a.* 1. having a grill.

2. cooked on a grill, or gridiron; broiled.

grill′room, *n.* a restaurant, club, or dining room that makes a specialty of grilled foods.

grill′work, *n.* 1. a grille.

2. something resembling a grille.

gril′ly, *v.t.* to harass. [Obs.]

grilse, *n. pl.* **grilse** or **grils′es,** a young salmon about the time it first returns from the sea to fresh water.

grim, *a.*; *comp.* grimmer; *superl.* grimmest, [ME. *grim, grym*; AS. *grim*, fierce, savage.]

1. fierce; cruel; savage; merciless.

2. hard and unyielding; relentless; stern; resolute; as, *grim* courage.

3. appearing stern, threatening, forbidding, harsh, etc.; as, a *grim* countenance.

4. repellent; uninviting; hideous; as, a *grim* task.

5. dealing with unpleasant subjects; sinister; frightful; ghastly; as, *grim* humor.

Syn.—fierce, ferocious, terrible, hideous, ugly, ghastly, sullen, stern.

gri·mace′, *n.* [Fr., from OFr. *grimace*, a wry face, an ugly look, from *grime*, irritated, vexed, of Teut. origin.]

1. a distortion of the face; a wry or ugly smile or facial expression of pain, contempt, etc., sometimes intended to amuse.

2. an air of affectation; hypocrisy.

gri·mace′, *v.i.*; grimaced (-māst′), *pt., pp.*; grimacing, *ppr.* to distort the features; to make grimaces.

gri·maced′ (-māst′), *a.* distorted; having a crabbed look. [Rare.]

gri·mal′kin, *n.* [earlier *gray malkin* as if from *gray*, and *malkin*, dim. of *Matilda*, etc., as pet name for cat.]

1. a cat; especially, an old female cat.

2. a malicious old woman.

grime, *n.* [ME. *grim*, prob. of Scand. origin, compare Dan. *grime*, a streak, stripe, Sw. dial. *grima*, smut on the face.] dirt, especially sooty dirt, rubbed into a surface, as of the skin.

grime, *v.t.*; grimed, *pt., pp.*; griming, *ppr.* to sully or soil deeply; to make very dirty or grimy.

Grimes Gold′en, [short for *Grimes Golden Pippin*, variety grown (c. 1790) by T. P. *Grimes*, Virginia fruit grower.] an autumn eating apple with a yellow skin: also *Grimes.*

grim′i·ly, *adv.* in a grimy manner.

grim′i·ness, *n.* the condition of being grimy; dirtiness.

grim′ly, *a.* having a hideous or stern look. [Obs.]

grim′ly, *adv.* [ME. *grimly, grymly*; AS. *grimlice*, in a grim manner, from *grim*, grim.]

1. fiercely; ferociously; with a look of fury or ferocity.

2. sourly; sullenly.

grimme, *n.* an antelope, *Cephalophus rufilotus*, of West Africa.

Grimm's law, [after Jakob Grimm's formulation (1822) of parallels noticed by R. K. Rask (1818) and himself.] a systematic statement of consonantal correspondences between Germanic words derived from Indo-European bases containing stop consonants and the cognate words of Indo-European languages other than Germanic: Grimm's original formulation has been amplified by the further discoveries of H. Grassmann (1862) and K. Verner (1876). The part of Grimm's statement immediately affecting English may be summarized thus: (1) Indo-Eur. voiceless stops (p, t, k) = Gmc. voiceless fricatives (f, th, h); hence, L. *p*isc-is (cf. *piscatorial*) = *f*ish, L. *t*en-uis (cf. *tenuous*) = *th*in, Gr. *k*ardia (cf. *cardiac*) = *h*eart. (2) Indo-Eur. voiced aspirated stops (bh, dh, gh) = Gmc. voiced stops (b, d, g) or equivalent fricatives; hence, Sans. *bh*arā-mi, I bear (Gr. *pherō*, L. *fero*; cf. *feretory*) = *b*ear, Sans. *m*ā*dh*u, honey (Gr. *methu*, wine; cf. *methyl*) = mea*d*, L. *h*ost-is (IE. hyp. *ghost-is*; cf. *hostile*) = *g*uest. (3) Indo-Eur. voiced stops (b, d, g) = Gmc. voiceless stops (p, t, k); hence, Gr. *b*urse (cf. *bursar*) = *p*urse, L. e*d*-ere (cf. *edible*) = ea*t*, L. a*g*er (cf. *agriculture*) = a*c*re.

grim′ness, *n.* fierceness of look; sternness; crabbedness.

grim′sir, *n.* a stern, overbearing man. [Obs.]

grim′-the-col′lier (-yẽr), *n.* [so called after a character in an Elizabethan comedy, in allusion to its smutty involucre.] in botany, the orange hawkweed of Europe, *Hieracium aurantiacum*, now found in northeastern United States: called also *king devil.*

grīm'y, *a.*; *comp.* grimier; *superl.* grimiest, covered with or full of grime; very dirty.

grin, *v.i.*; grinned, *pt., pp.*; grinning, *ppr.* [ME. *grinnen*; AS. *grennian*, to show the teeth, snarl, grin.]
1. to smile broadly.
2. to snarl and show the teeth, as a dog.
3. to set the teeth together and open the lips; to show the teeth, as in laughter, scorn, or pain.

grin, *v.t.* to express by grinning.
Grinned horrible a ghastly smile.—Milton.

grin, *n.* 1. the act of grinning.
2. a facial expression resulting from grinning.

grin, *n.* a snare or trap. [Obs.]

grīnd, *v.t.*; ground, *pt., pp.*; grinding, *ppr.* [ME. *grinden*; AS. *grindan*, to grind.]
1. to crush into bits or fine particles between two hard surfaces; to pulverize.
2. to afflict with cruelty, hardship, etc.; crush; oppress; as, a people *ground* by tyranny.
3. to sharpen, shape, or smooth by friction.
4. to press down or together with a crushing, turning motion; to rub harshly or gratingly; as, he *ground* his teeth; she *ground* her heel into the dirt.
5. to operate by turning the crank of; as, to *grind* a coffee mill.
6. to make or produce by grinding.
7. to teach with great effort; as, the boy's teacher had to *grind* the lesson into his head. [Colloq.]
an ax to grind; an object or end of one's own to gain or promote. [Colloq.]

grīnd, *v.i.* 1. to perform the operation of grinding; to move or operate a mill.
2. to be moved or rubbed together, as in the operation of grinding; to grate; as, the *grinding* jaws.
3. to be ground or pulverized by friction; as, corn will not *grind* well before it is dry.
4. to be polished and made smooth by friction; as, glass *grinds* smooth.
5. to be sharpened by grinding; as, steel *grinds* to a fine edge.
6. to perform laborious and unpleasant service; to drudge; to study hard. [Colloq.]

grīnd, *n.* 1. the act of pulverizing, polishing, or sharpening by grinding; also, the sound produced by the act; as, the *grind* of an engine.
2. incessant toil; distasteful labor or study; as, the eternal *grind*. [Colloq.]
3. a student who studies very hard. [Colloq.]

grin·dē'li·ȧ, *n.* [named after H. *Grindel* (1776–1836), a Russian botanist.]
1. a genus of coarse plants with large, yellow flowers.
2. [g–] the dried stems and leaves of some of these plants, used medicinally in the treatment of bronchitis, asthma, and coughs.

grīnd'ẽr, *n.* [ME. *gryndere*, a miller, from AS. *grindan*, to grind.]
1. one who grinds: especially, one whose work is sharpening tools.
2. the instrument of grinding, as a grindstone.
3. (a) a tooth that grinds or chews food; a molar; (b) [*pl.*] [Colloq.] the teeth.
4. an Australian bird, *Seisura inquieta*: also called *restless flycatcher* or *dishwasher*.
5. a bird which makes a noise resembling the sound made in grinding scissors, as the nightjar, *Caprimulgus europæus*: also called *scissor grinder*.
grinder's asthma; a lung disease caused by inhalation of particles thrown from the grinder's wheel.

grīnd'ẽr·y, *n.*; *pl.* **grīnd'ẽr·ies,** 1. a place where grinding is done, as of knives, edge tools, etc.
2. materials used by shoemakers and other workers in leather. [Brit.]

grīnd'ing, *a.* tending to oppress; as, *grinding* taxation.

grīnd'ing, *n.* 1. the act of one who grinds; the action of a grinder.
2. a crushing or grating sound.

grīnd'ing bed, a kind of planing machine for grinding stone slabs, consisting of a moving frame on which the stone lies and passes under a rotating polishing tool.

grīnd'ing bench, in glassmaking, a level stone surface, coated with plaster of Paris, on which a plate of glass is laid to be ground or polished.

grīnd'ing·ly, *adv.* in a grinding manner; oppressively; harshly.

grin'dle, *n.* in zoology, the bowfin or mudfish, *Amia calva*: also called *dogfish, Johnny Grindle.*

grin'dle·stōne, *n.* a grindstone. [Obs.]

grind'let, *n.* a small ditch or drain.

grin'dle·tāil, *n.* a dog with a curling tail. [Obs.]

grīnd'stōne, *n.* [ME. *grindston*, from AS. *grindan*, to grind, and *stan*, a stone.]
1. a flat, circular stone, mounted on a spindle and turned by a winch handle, a treadle, etc., used for grinding or for sharpening tools.
2. a millstone. [Obs.]
to hold one's nose to the grindstone; to keep one at hard, steady labor; to be unremitting in requirements from a person.

grīnd whāle (hwāl), the bottlenose whale.

griñ'gō, *n.*; *pl.* **griñ'gōs,** [Sp., gibberish.] among Spanish-Americans, an Englishman or American: hostile and contemptuous term.

Grin·nel'li·ȧ, *n.* [named after Henry *Grinnell*, a New York merchant.] in botany, a genus of red seaweeds.

grin'nẽr, *n.* one who grins.

grin'ning·ly, *adv.* in a grinning manner.

grint'ing, *n.* grinding. [Obs.]

gri·otte', *n.* [Fr.] a spotted marble of the Pyrenees, with veins varying from dark red to deep green.

grip, *n.* [ME. *grip*; AS. *gripe*, a grasp, a firm hold, from *gripan*, to seize.]
1. the act of taking firmly and holding fast with the hand, teeth, an instrument, etc.; secure grasp; firm hold.
2. the manner in which this is done.
3. any special manner of clasping hands by which members of a secret or fraternal society identify each other as such.
4. the power of grasping firmly; as, his hand has lost its *grip*.
5. the power of understanding; mental grasp.
6. firm control; mastery; as, in the *grip* of disease, get a *grip* on yourself.
7. a mechanical contrivance for clutching or grasping.
8. the part by which a tool, weapon, etc. is grasped in the hand; handle.
9. [prob. from or after D.] a small bag for holding clothes, etc. in traveling; valise.
10. a sudden, intense pain.
11. in a motion-picture studio, a stagehand. [Slang.]
12. in sports, the manner of holding a bat, club, racket, etc.

grip, *v.t.*; gripped, *or* gript, *pt., pp.*; gripping, *ppr.* 1. to take firmly and hold fast with the hand, teeth, an instrument, etc.
2. to give a grip (sense 3) to.
3. to fasten or join firmly (*to*).
4. to get and hold the attention of.
5. to take hold upon; to control (the attention, emotions, etc.).

grip, *v.i.* to get a grip.

grip, *n.* [ME. *grip, grippe*; AS. *gripe*, a burrow.] a small ditch or furrow. [Dial.]

grip, *v.t.* to trench; to drain. [Dial.]

grip, *n.* same as *grippe*.

grip cär, in a cable railroad, the car to which the grip and its means of manipulation are attached.

grīpe, *n.* 1. a griping; clutching.
2. control; mastery.
3. the pressure or pain of something distressing or afflicting.
4. [*pl.*] sudden, sharp pains in the bowels.
5. a handle.
6. a device that grips.
7. a complaint. [Slang.]

grīpe, *v.t.*; griped, *pt., pp.*; griping, *ppr.* [ME. *gripen*; AS. *gripan*, to grasp, seize.]
1. to grasp; pinch; clutch.
2. to distress; oppress; afflict.
3. to cause sudden, sharp pain in the bowels of.
4. to annoy; irritate. [Slang.]

grīpe, *v.i.* 1. to feel sharp pains in the bowels.
2. to get a hold. [Archaic.]
3. to complain; grumble. [Slang.]

grīp'ẽr, *n.* one who or that which gripes.

grīp'ing·ly, *adv.* in a griping manner.

grip'măn, *n.* one who operates a grip: specifically, one who controls the levers of the grip car of a cable train.

grippe, grip, *n.* [Fr., lit., a seizure, from *gripper*, to take hold of, seize.] influenza.

grip'pẽr, *n.* 1. one who or that which grips.
2. in printing, a clutch or clasp that catches a sheet of paper and holds it until printed.
3. in Ireland, a bailiff.

grip'ping, *a.* [ppr. of *grip*.] that grips; holding the attention.

grip'ping·ness, *n.* the state or condition of being gripping.

grip'ple, *n.* a grasp. [Obs.]

grip'ple, *a.* covetous; grasping; greedy. [Dial.]

grip'ple·ness, *n.* the condition of being gripple or greedy. [Dial.]

grip'py, *a.* having the grippe, or influenza. [Colloq.]

grip'sack, *n.* a small, traveling bag; a handbag; a valise; a grip.

gript, *v.* alternative past tense and past participle of *grip*.

grīp'y, *a.* griping; causing or tending to cause gripes.

Grï'quȧ (grē'kwȧ), *n.* a South African mulatto.

grï·saille', *n.* [Fr., from *gris*, gray.]
1. in art, a style of painting in gray monochrome, resembling bas-relief; also, a painting in this style.
2. a kind of fancy dress goods.

grïs'am"bẽr, *n.* [a transposed form.] ambergris. [Obs.]

grise, grïs, *a.* [OFr. *gris*; O.H.G. *gris*, gray.] gray. [Obs.]

grïse, grïs, *n.* gray fur or hair. [Obs.]

Gri·sel'dȧ, *n.* [Fr. or It., from G. *Griseldis, Grishilda*; prob. from O.H.G. *griez*, sand, and *hilda*, battle.]
1. the heroine of various medieval romances, notably the "Clerk's Tale" in Chaucer's *Canterbury Tales*, famous for her meek, long-suffering patience.
2. any patient, meek, long-suffering woman.

gris'ē·ous, *a.* [LL. *griseus*, from O.H.G. *gris*, gray.] mottled gray; gray.

gri·sette', *n.* [Fr., from *gris*, gray; *grisettes* were so called because they formerly wore gowns made of gray woolen cloth.] in France, a shop girl or working girl.

gris'kin, *n.* the lean section of pork loin. [Brit.]

gris'led (-ld), *a.* same as *grizzled*.

gris'li·ness, *n.* the quality or state of being grisly.

gris'ly, *a.*; *comp.* grislier; *superl.* grisliest. [ME. *grisly*; AS. an*grislic*, on*grislic*, horrible, terrible.] frightful; horrible; terrible; as, *grisly* locks; a *grisly* specter.

gris'ly, *a.* same as *gristly*.

grī'sŏn, *n.* [Fr. *grison*, a graybeard, a donkey, from *gris*, gray.] a South American mammal related to, but slightly larger than, a weasel; also, a monkey of South America.

grist, *n.* [ME. *grist, gryst*; AS. *grist*, a grist, lit., a grinding, from *grindan*, to grind.]
1. grain that is to be or has been ground; also, the amount ground at one time; the grain carried to a mill.
Get *grist* to the mill to have plenty in store.
—Tusser.
2. a quantity or lot. [Colloq.]
3. a certain size of rope regulated by the number of the strands.
grist to one's mill; anything that one can use to advantage.

gris'tle (gris'l), *n.* [ME. *gristel, grystyl*; AS. *gristle*, cartilage, from *grist*, a grinding: so called on account of the difficulty of masticating it.] cartilage; a smooth, solid, elastic tissue.

grist'li·ness (gris'), *n.* the quality or condition of being gristly.

gris'tly (gris'li), *a.* 1. like or consisting of gristle; cartilaginous; as, the *gristly* rays of fins.
2. having the nature of gristle.
Also spelled *grisly*.

grist'mill, *n.* a mill for grinding grain; specifically, a mill to which the grain of many customers is brought to be ground separately.

grit, *n.* [ME. *greet, gret*; AS. *greót*, sand, dust.]
1. the coarse part of meal.
2. [*pl.*] oats, wheat, or corn, hulled or coarsely ground.

grit, *n.* [with Early Mod. Eng. vowel shortening from ME. *grete*; AS. *greót*.]
1. rough, hard particles of sand, stone, etc.
2. a hard, coarse sandstone.
3. the texture of stone, with regard to the fineness or coarseness of its grain.
4. firmness; pluck; determined spirit; indomitable courage; invincible will; resolution.
5. [G–] in Canadian politics, a Liberal.

grit, *v.t.*; gritted, *pt., pp.*; gritting, *ppr.* 1. to cover with grit.
2. to grind (the teeth) in anger or determination.

grit, *v.i.* to make a grinding or grating sound, like that of sand under the feet.

grith, *n.* [ME.; AS.; ON., orig., home.]
1. security, protection, or peace, especially

as guaranteed by someone or in some place. [Obs.]
2. a sanctuary. [Obs.]

grit'rock, grit'stōne, *n.* any siliceous rock.

grits, *n.pl.* [ME. *gryttes*; AS. *grytt(e)*.] grain hulled and coarsely ground; especially, coarse hominy.

grit'ti·ly, *adv.* in a gritty manner.

grit'ti·ness, *n.* the quality or state of being gritty.

grit'ty, *a.*; *comp.* grittier; *superl.* grittiest, 1. containing sand or grit; consisting of grit; full of hard particles; sandy.
2. plucky; spirited; courageous.

griv'et, *n.* [Fr., prob. from *gris*, gray, and *vert*, green.] a small African monkey, *Cercopithecus aethiops*, the upper parts of which are of a greenish color and the lower white.

griz'zle, *n.* [ME. *grisel*, *grisell*, an old man, from OFr. *gris*; O.H.G. *gris*, gray.]
1. (a) gray hair; (b) a gray wig.
2. gray; a gray color; a mixture of white and black.

griz'zle, *a.* gray.

griz'zle, *v.t.* and *v.i.*; grizzled, *pt., pp.*; grizzling, *ppr.* to make or become gray.

griz'zle, *v.i.* to fret; to complain. [Brit.]

griz'zled, *a.* 1. gray or streaked with gray.
2. having gray hair.

griz'zly, *a.*; *comp.* grizzlier; *superl.* grizzliest, somewhat gray; grayish.
grizzly bear; see *bear*.

griz'zly, *n.*; *pl.* **griz'zlieṣ,** 1. the grizzly bear.
2. a grating used in hydraulic mining for keeping out the large stones swept down by the current.

grōan, *v.i.*; groaned, *pt., pp.*; groaning, *ppr.* [ME. *gronen*; AS. *granian*, to lament, murmur, groan.]
1. to utter a deep sound expressing pain, distress, or disapproval.
2. to make a sound like this; as, the wind *groans*.
3. to suffer deeply from cruelty, oppression, etc.
4. to be loaded or weighed down.

grōan, *v.t.* to express or utter with a groan or groans; as, the speaker was *groaned* down.

grōan, *n.* a sound made in groaning.
Groans of roaring wind and rain. —Shak.
Syn.—moan, whine, growl, grumble.

grōan'ẽr, *n.* one who groans.

grōan'fụl, *a.* sad; inducing groans.

grōat, *n.* [ME. *grote*, *groote*; L.G. *grote*, O.D. *groot*, a large coin, lit., great.]
1. an old English silver coin equivalent to fourpence.
2. any small or trifling sum.

grōats, *n.pl.* [ME. *grotes*, *groten*; AS. *gratan*, groats.] oats or wheat without the hulls, especially fragments of wheat somewhat larger than grits.

grō'bi·ăn, *n.* [G., from *grob*, coarse, rude.] a person of rude, uncouth, or clownish manners; a boor.

grō'cẽr, *n.* [ME. *grocere*, a corruption of *grosser*, a grocer, a wholesale dealer; OFr. *grossier*, LL. *grossarius*, a wholesale dealer, from *grossus*, great, gross.] a storekeeper who sells food and various household supplies.
grocers' itch; a cutaneous disease caused by mites occurring in sugar and flour.

grō'cẽr·y, *n.*; *pl.* **grō'cẽr·ies,** [OFr. *grosserie*, from LL. *grossarius*, a wholesale dealer.]
1. [*pl.*] the commodities sold by grocers.
2. a grocer's store.
3. the business of a grocer.

grog, *n.* [named after Old *Grog*, the nickname given to Admiral Vernon, who introduced the drink about 1745. He was so called because he wore a grogram cloak.] a mixture of rum and water not sweetened; hence, any kind of alcoholic drink.

grog blos'sŏm, an eruption or redness on the face or nose resulting from the excessive drinking of alcoholic liquor. [Slang.]

grog'gẽr·y, *n.*; *pl.* **grog'gẽr·ieṣ,** a grogshop.

grog'gi·ly, *adv.* in a groggy manner. [Colloq.]

grog'gi·ness, *n.* 1. the quality or condition of being groggy. [Colloq.]
2. in farriery, a tenderness or stiffness in the foot of a horse or weakness in the forelegs, which causes him to move in a hobbling, staggering manner.

grog'gy, *a.*; *comp.* groggier; *superl.* groggiest, 1. drunk; tipsy; intoxicated. [Colloq.]
2. shaky or dizzy, as from a blow, illness, lack of sleep, etc.: current sense. [Colloq.]
3. in farriery, moving in an uneasy, hobbling manner, because of tenderness of the feet.

grog'răm, *n.* [OFr. *gros-grain*; *gros*, coarse gross, and *grain*, grain.]
1. a coarse fabric made of silk, or of silk, worsted, and mohair.
2. an article of clothing made of this.

grog'shop, *n.* a place where alcoholic drinks are sold; a saloon.

groin, *n.* the snout of a swine. [Brit. Dial.]

groin, *n.* [Ice. *grein*, the branch of a tree, a branch, arm, difference.]
1. in anatomy, the depressed part or fold where the abdomen joins either thigh.
2. in architecture, the sharp, curved edge made by the intersection of vaults crossing each other at any angle; also, the rib of wood, stone, etc. covering this edge.
3. a wooden breakwater or frame of woodwork constructed across a beach between low and high water to retain sand or mud thrown up by the tide. [Brit.]

groin, *v.t.*; groined, *pt., pp.*; groining, *ppr.* in architecture, to form into groins; to ornament or furnish with groins.

groined, *a.* having a sharp, curved edge formed by the intersection of two arches, as in a ceiling or roof.

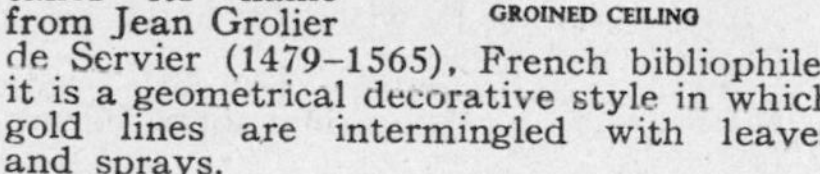
GROINED CEILING

grok, *v.t.* and *v.i.*; grokked, *pt., pp.*; grokking, *ppr.* [coined in a science-fiction novel (1961) by R. A. Heinlein.] to understand thoroughly because of having empathy (with). [Slang.]

Grō'li·ẽr, *a.* designating a style of bookbinding which takes its name from Jean Grolier de Servier (1479–1565), French bibliophile: it is a geometrical decorative style in which gold lines are intermingled with leaves and sprays.

grom'met, *n.* [Fr. *gourmette*, a curb, curb chain; earlier *gromette*, from *gourmer*, to curb.]
1. a ring of rope or metal used to fasten the edge of a sail to its stay, hold an oar in place, etc.
2. a metal eyelet in cloth, leather, etc.
Also *grummet*.

grom'well, *n.* [ME. *gromil*; OFr. *gremil*, prob. from L. *granum*, grain, and *milium*, millet.] any of a group of flowers of the genus *Lithospermum*, with hard, stonelike seeds.

grọọm, *n.* [ME. *grom*, *grome*, a boy, a servant; compare Ice. *gromr*, a man, a servant; etym. doubtful, prob. from AS. *guma*, a man.]
1. a man or boy whose work is tending, feeding, and currying horses.
2. any of a group of officials in charge of particular departments of the British Royal household.
3. a bridegroom.
4. (a) a man; (b) a manservant. [Archaic.]

grọọm, *v.t.*; groomed, *pt., pp.*; grooming, *ppr.* 1. to tend or care for, as a horse; to curry and feed.
2. to cause to appear neat or tidy; as, she *grooms* her child well.
3. to train or develop (a person) for a particular purpose; as, he was *groomed* for political office.

grọọm'ẽr, *n.* one who grooms or that with which one grooms; especially, a mechanical brush for grooming horses.

grọọmṣ'măn, *n.*; *pl.* **grọọmṣ'men,** one who acts as attendant on a bridegroom at the wedding; a best man.

grọọve, *n.* [ME. *grofe*, a pit; D. *groeve*, *groef*, a channel, groove.]
1. a long, narrow furrow or hollow such as is cut by a tool; also, any rut or furrow like this.
2. a habitual course or fixed routine of one's life.
3. in mining, a shaft or pit sunk into the earth. [Brit. Dial.]
4. in anatomy, any narrow furrow, depression, or slit occurring on the surface of an organ, especially of bone.
5. in printing, the hollow on the bottom of type.
in the groove; [said to be from phonograph recording.] performing or performed with smooth, effortless skill: said originally of jazz musicians or music. [Slang.]

grọọve, *v.t.*; grooved, *pt., pp.*; grooving, *ppr.* to cut a groove or grooves in; to furrow.

grọọve, *v.i.* to react in a nonanalytical empathic way to persons, situations, etc. surrounding one.

grọọv'ẽr, *n.* 1. one who or that which cuts a groove.
2. a miner. [Brit. Dial.]

grọọv'ing, *n.* the act or process of cutting or forming a groove; also, a groove or system of grooves.

grọọv'y, *a.*; *comp.* groovier; *superl.* grooviest, [from old slang *in the groove*, working effortlessly.] very pleasing or attractive: a generalized term of approval. [Slang.]

grōpe, *v.i.*; groped, *pt., pp.*; groping, *ppr.* [ME. *gropen*, *gropien*; AS. *grapian*, to grasp, handle, from *grap*, a grip, or grasp, from *gripan*, to seize, grasp.] to search or seek to find something blindly, hesitantly, or uncertainly; to feel one's way, as with the hands.

grōpe, *v.t.* 1. to search out by groping; to feel (one's way).
2. to test; to sound. [Obs.]

grōpe, *n.* a groping.

grōp'ẽr, *n.* one who gropes; one who feels his way or searches by feeling.

grōp'ing·ly, *adv.* in a groping manner.

grōs (grō), *n.* [Fr.] a fabric, usually of silk, of strong texture; as, *gros* de Naples; *gros* de Tours, etc.

grōs'bēak, *n.* any of various birds of the finch family, with a thick, strong, conical bill. The common grosbeak of Europe is *Cocothraustes cocothraustes*. *Ligurinus chloris* is the green grosbeak. American species include the blue grosbeak, *Guiraca cærulea*; the rose-breasted grosbeak, *Pheucticus ludovicianus*, and the black-headed grosbeak, *Pheucticus melanocephalus*.

GROSBEAK

grō'schen (-shun), *n.*; *pl.* **grō'schen,** [G.]
1. in Austria, a bronze coin equal to 1/100 schilling.
2. in Germany, (a) formerly, a small silver coin of varying value; (b) [Colloq.] the 10-pfennig coin.

grōs'grāin (grō'), *a.* [Fr.] having heavy, crosswise cords; as, *grosgrain* silk.

grōs'grāin, *n.* 1. grosgrain silk.
2. a ribbon made of this.

grōss, *a.* [OFr. *gros*, masc., *grosse*, f., big, thick, from LL. *grossus*, thick, big.]
1. too fat; corpulent; overfed; burly; as, a *gross* body.
2. coarse; rough; not fine or delicate; as, *gross* sculpture, *gross* features.
3. rough; vulgar; indelicate; obscene.
The terms which are delicate in one age become *gross* in the next. —Macaulay.
4. very wrong; glaring; flagrant; as, a *gross* mistake, *gross* injustice.
5. thick; dense.
6. not sensitive in perception or feeling; stupid; dull.
Tell her of things that no *gross* ear can hear. —Milton.
7. whole; entire; total; without deductions; as, *gross* income: opposed to *net*.
8. plain; evident; obvious. [Archaic.]
gross national product; the total value of a nation's annual output of goods and services.
gross ton; a unit of weight, equal to 2,240 pounds: also called *long ton*.
gross weight; the weight of merchandise or goods, including the weight of the covering material or containers: distinguished from *net weight*.

grōss, *n.*; *pl.* **grōss'eṣ,** 1. the whole amount; the bulk; the mass; as, the *gross* of the people.
For see the Saxon *gross* begins to move. —Dryden.
2. *pl.* **grōss,** twelve dozen; twelve times twelve; as, a *gross* of bottles, ten *gross*.
in the gross, in gross; (a) in the bulk, or the undivided whole; all parts taken together; (b) wholesale.

grōss, *v.t.* and *v.i.* to make (a specified total amount) before expenses are deducted. [Colloq.]

grōss"i·fi·çā'tion, *n.* [LL. *grossus*, thick, big, and L. *facere*, to make.] the act of making gross; the state of being or becoming gross.

grōss′ly, *adv.* in a gross manner.
grōss′ness, *n.* the state or quality of being gross.
gros·sū·lā′ceous, *a.* [OFr. *groselle*, a gooseberry.] in botany, relating to the gooseberry or currant.
gros′sū·lăr, *a.* [OFr. *groselle, groiselle*, a gooseberry.] pertaining to or resembling a gooseberry; as, *grossular* garnet.
gros′sū·lăr, *n.* a variety of garnet of a green color: called also *grossularite.*
Gros″sū·lā·rī′ē·ae, *n.* [OFr. *groselle, groiselle*, a gooseberry, a currant; prob. from M.H.G. *krus*, curling, crisp.] a family of shrubs resembling the *Saxifragaceæ*, including the gooseberry and currant.
gros′sū·lăr·īte, *n.* grossular.
grōt, grōte, *n.* a groat. [Obs.]
grot, *n.* a grotto. [Poet.]
grō·tesque′ (-tesk′), *a.* [Fr. *grotesque*; It. *grottesco*, odd, extravagant, from *grotta*, a grotto.]
1. in or of a style of painting, sculpture, etc. in which forms of persons and animals are intermingled with foliage, flowers, fruit, etc. in a fantastic design.
2. characterized by distortions or striking incongruities in appearance, shape, manner, etc.; fantastic; bizarre.
3. ludicrously eccentric or strange; ridiculous; absurd.
grō·tesque′, *n.* 1. a grotesque painting, sculpture, etc.
2. grotesque quality, character, or style.
3. a grotesque figure or design.
grō·tesque′ly, *adv.* in a grotesque manner.
grō·tesque′ness, *n.* the state of being grotesque.
grō·tes′quĕr·ie, grō·tes′quĕr·y (-kĕr-), *n.*; *pl.* **grō·tes′quĕr·ieṣ,** 1. a grotesque thing.
2. the quality or state of being grotesque.
3. grotesque paintings, etc. collectively.
Grō′ti·ăn (-shi-), *a.* pertaining to the views of the Dutch scholar and statesman, Hugo Grotius (1583–1645), founder of the modern science of international law.
grot′tō, *n.*; *pl.* **grot′tōeṣ, grot′tōṣ,** [It. *grotta*, a grotto, cave, from LL. *grupta*; L. *crypta*; Gr. *kryptē*, a hidden, underground passage, a crypt, from *kryptos*, hidden, from *kryptein*, to hide.]
1. a cave; a subterranean cavern.
2. a cavelike summerhouse, shrine, etc.
grot′tō·wŏrk, *n.* artificial work in imitation of a natural grotto.
grouch, *n.* 1. one who is sulky or morose; also, the condition of being sulky. [Colloq.]
2. a cause for complaint. [Colloq.]
grouch′i·ly, *adv.* in a grouchy manner. [Colloq.]
grouch′i·ness, *n.* the quality or state of being grouchy. [Colloq.]
grouch′y, *a.*; *comp.* grouchier; *superl.* grouchiest, grumbling; sulky. [Colloq.]
ground, *n.* [ME. *ground*; AS. *grund*, bottom, foundation, soil.]
1. (a) originally, the lowest part, base, or bottom of anything; (b) the bottom of the sea.
2. the solid surface of the earth.
3. the soil of the earth; earth; land; as, he tills the *ground.*
4. any particular piece of land; especially, one set aside for a specified purpose; as, a hunting *ground.*
5. any particular area of reference, discussion, work, etc.; topic; subject; as, let us go over the *ground* again.
6. the distance to a goal, objective, position, etc.
7. [*often pl.*] the logical basis of a conclusion, action, etc.; valid reason, motive, or cause.
8. that on which anything may stand or rest, or be raised or transacted; that from which anything may rise or originate; foundation; basis; groundwork.

To the solid *ground*
Of nature trusts the Mind that builds for aye. —Wordsworth.

9. (a) the surface on which a figure or object is represented; that surface or substance which retains the original color, and to which the other colors are applied to make the representation, as in painting; (b) in sculpture, the flat surface from which the figures rise: said of a work in relief.
10. in etching, a composition spread over the surface of the plate to be etched, to prevent the acid from eating into the plate, except where an opening is made with the point of the etching needle.
11. in music, (a) the ground bass; (b) the plain song; the tune on which descants are raised.
12. formerly, the pit of a theater.
13. in carpentry, a piece of wood fixed to a wall, partition, etc., with its surfaces flush with the plaster, to which the facings or finishings are attached.
14. in electricity, a connection with the ground, as from a wire conveying a current, so as to make the ground a part of the circuit; also, short for *ground circuit, ground terminal, ground wire*, etc.
above ground; alive.
from the ground up; from the first or elementary principles, methods, etc. to the last or most advanced; completely; thoroughly.
happy hunting grounds; the place of happiness after death for hunters or warriors, as conceived by North American Indians.
on delicate ground; in a situation requiring tact.
on firm ground; in a safe situation.
on one's own ground; (a) in a familiar situation; (b) on a subject that one knows well; (c) at home.
on the ground of; because of.
to be on the ground; (a) to be vigilant in watching one's own interests; (b) to be punctual in keeping an engagement.
to break ground; (a) to dig; excavate; (b) to plow; (c) to start building; (d) to start any undertaking; (e) in nautical usage, to be hoisted from its bed: said of an anchor.
to cover ground; (a) to traverse a certain space or distance; (b) to travel; (c) to get a certain amount of work done.
to cut the ground from under one's feet; to deprive of effective defense or argument.
to fall to the ground; to fail; as, the undertaking *fell to the ground.*
to gain ground; (a) to move forward; (b) to make progress; (c) to gain in strength, extent, popularity, etc.
to give ground; to withdraw under attack; retreat; yield.
to hold one's ground; to keep one's position against attack or opposition; not withdraw or retreat.
to lose ground; (a) to fall back; to fail to keep up to the required pace; (b) to lose in strength, popularity, extent, etc.
to run into the ground; to do too long or too often; overdo. [Colloq.]
to shift one's ground; to shift one's position; change one's argument or defense.
to stand one's ground; to maintain one's position; to refuse to yield to opposition; to exhibit a courageous disposition.
to suit one down to the ground; to suit completely. [Colloq.]
to take the ground; to assume a position; as, the Declaration of Independence *takes the ground* that all men are born equal, etc.
ground, *v.i.*; grounded, *pt.*, *pp.*; grounding, *ppr.* 1. to run aground; to strike the bottom and remain fixed: said of a ship.
2. to strike or fall to the ground.
3. in baseball, to be put out on a grounder (usually with *out*).
ground, *v.t.* [ME. *grounden*; AS. *gryndan, agryndan*, to descend, or set, from *grund*, base, foundation.]
1. to lay or set on the ground; to cause to touch the ground.
2. to found; to fix or set, as on a foundation, cause, reason, or principle; as, arguments *grounded* on reason; faith *grounded* on scriptural evidence.
3. to instruct (a person) in first principles; to fix firmly.

Being rooted and *grounded* in love. —Eph. iii. 17.

4. in electricity, to connect (an electrical conductor) with the ground, which becomes part of the circuit; as, to *ground* a wire.
5. to cause (a ship) to run aground.
6. to provide with a background.
7. to found on a firm basis; establish.
8. in aviation, to cause to remain on the ground; keep from flying; as, the plane was *grounded* by bad weather.
ground, *a.* 1. of, on, or near the ground; as, a *ground* room.
2. growing or living in or on the ground.
ground, *v.* past tense and past participle of *grind.*
ground′ăġe, *n.* a fee paid by a ship for the space it occupies while in port.
ground ăir, the air contained in the soil.
ground an′gling, fishing without a float, with a weight placed a few inches from the hook, which is sunk nearly to the bottom.
ground an′nū·ăl, in Scots law, a perpetual leasehold at a fixed annual ground rent.
ground ash, in botany, (a) a slender ash tree or sapling; (b) the goutweed.
ground bāil′iff, in mining, an inspector of mines.
ground bāit, in angling, bait scattered on the water and sinking to the bottom to allure fish to a locality.
ground băss, in music, a short phrase, usually of four to eight measures, running through the bass of an entire movement regardless of variation in the melody.
ground bee′tle, in zoology, any one of many caraboid beetles living on the ground and hiding under stones.
ground′ber″ry, *n.*; *pl.* **ground′ber″rieṣ,** in botany, the plant or the globular red berry of the *Gaultheria procumbens*, or wintergreen.
ground cher′ry, *pl.* **ground cher′rieṣ,** in botany, (a) a herbaceous plant of the nightshade family and of the genus *Physalis*, characterized by a bladderlike calyx, in the cavity of which the fruit is borne; (b) a European shrub of the rose family and of the subgenus *Cerasus*, bearing a small, sour fruit.
ground cir′çuit (-kit), in electricity, a circuit of which the ground is a part.
ground cis′tus, *Rhodothamnus chamæcistus*, a small shrub of Switzerland.
ground çock, a cock having a plug, as of glass or brass, which is ground into its place to secure a tight fit: distinguished from *compression cock.*
ground çol′ŏr, 1. the first coat of paint; base coat.
2. the background color.
ground çŏn·neç′tion, a connection of an electrical circuit to the ground.
ground çrew, a group of people in charge of the maintenance and repair of aircraft.
ground cuck′ọọ, see *chaparral cock.*
ground dŏve, any pigeon of terrestrial habits; as, (a) a bird of the genus *Geopelia* or *Geotrygon*; (b) *Columbigallina passerina*, a dwarfish bird common in the southern States of the United States.
ground′ed·ly, *adv.* in a grounded manner, so as to be firmly fixed.
ground′en, *v.* obsolete past participle of *grind.*
ground′ĕr, *n.* in baseball, cricket, etc., a batted ball that rolls or bounces along the ground.
ground finch, a bird of the genus *Pipilo*, as the towhee bunting.
ground fish, a fish keeping to the bottom of the water, as the cod.
ground flōor, a floor approximately level with the ground.
in on the ground floor; (a) having the same terms and privileges as the original investors: said of someone buying shares of stock after the original issue; (b) in at the beginning (of a business, etc.); hence, (c) in a position of advantage. [Colloq.]
ground fọrm, in grammar and philology, a basic form, as the stem word.
ground fūrze, *Ononis arvensis*, a thorny shrub infesting cultivated land in many parts of Europe: called also *rest harrow.*
ground gāme, running game, as rabbits and hares.
ground glȧss, glass whose surface has been ground so that it diffuses light and is therefore not transparent.
ground grù, ground ice. [Brit. Dial.]
ground hem′lock, *Taxus baccata*, a creeping variety of the common yew.
ground hog, 1. the woodchuck.
2. the *Orycteropus capensis*, a South African anteater.
ground-hog day; February 2, Candlemas Day, when the ground hog is said to come out of hibernation: if he sees his shadow, he will supposedly return to his hole for another six weeks of winter weather.
ground īce, ice formed at the bottom of a river, or other body of water, before it begins to appear on the surface; anchor ice.
ground′ing, *n.* 1. the act or process of founding or establishing; instruction in elementary principles.
2. a design background, as in art or needlework.
3. a finishing of oil and alumina used as an application for wallpaper preparatory to satin finish.

4. a process in which boiled oil is applied to porcelain ware before it is enameled.
5. in marble working, the smoothing of marble by the use of emery.

ground ī'vy, *Glechoma hederacea*, a creeping plant with round, toothed leaves and loose clusters of bluish-purple flowers.

ground joist, a joist of a basement or ground floor.

ground lärk, a bird, the pipit of Europe.

ground lau'rel, the trailing arbutus.

ground'less, *a.* without ground or foundation; baseless; unfounded; as, *groundless* fears.

ground'less·ly, *adv.* in a groundless manner.

ground'less·ness, *n.* the state or quality of being groundless.

ground līne, in geometry and perspective, the line of intersection of the horizontal and vertical planes of projection.

ground'ling, *n.* 1. (a) a fish that lives close to the bottom of the water; (b) an animal that lives on or in the ground; (c) a plant that grows close to the ground; a creeping plant.
2. (a) in the Elizabethan theater, a person who watched the performance from the pit, which had only the ground for a floor; hence, (b) a person lacking critical ability or taste.

ground liv'ẽr·wŏrt, a lichen, *Peltigera canina.*

ground liz'ărd, 1. a skink, *Lygosoma laterale.*
2. a lizard, *Ameiva dorsalis*, very common in Jamaica.

ground loop, an uncontrollable sharp turn sometimes made by an airplane as it taxis before a take-off or after landing.

ground māil, duty paid for the right of having a corpse interred in a churchyard. [Scot.]

ground màss, the matrix in which rock crystals are embedded.

ground mōld, in engineering, a mold or frame by means of which the surface of the ground is worked to any particular form, as in terracing or embanking.

ground niche, in architecture, a niche whose base or seat is on a level with the ground or ground floor.

ground'nut, 1. any of various plants with edible tubers or tuberlike parts, as the peanut.
2. the edible tuber or tuberlike part.

ground par'rŏt, the kakapo, or owl parrot.

ground pēa, the peanut.

ground pēarl, an insect of the West Indies having a shelly covering used by the natives for making necklaces, etc.

ground pig, 1. the aardvark of Africa.
2. a rodent found in Africa, of the genus *Thryonomys.*

ground pig'eŏn, a pigeon of terrestrial habits belonging to the subfamily *Gourinæ.*

ground pīne, 1. any of several kinds of club moss, an evergreen with creeping or underground stems and erect, treelike branches.
2. a European plant that smells like resin.

ground plan, 1. a plan of the ground floor or of any floor of a building, as seen from above: distinguished from *elevation* or *cross section.*
2. a first, fundamental, or basic plan.

ground'plāne, *n.* the horizontal plane of projection in perspective drawing.

ground plāte, 1. in architecture, one of the outermost pieces of framing placed on or near the ground; a groundsill.
2. a bedplate used in soft ground to support railroad ties.
3. a plate of metal sunk in the ground to connect an electric current with the earth.

ground'plot, 1. the ground on which a building is placed.
2. same as *ground plan.*

ground plum, a small herb found in the western United States, bearing purple flowers and a plumlike fruit.

ground rat, the ground pig.

ground rent, rent paid for the privilege of building on another man's land.

ground rōpe, the rope that keeps a trawl net on the bottom.

grounds, *n.pl.* 1. land surrounding or attached to a house or other building; especially, the lawns, gardens, etc. of an estate.
2. the particles that settle to the bottom of a liquid; dregs; sediment; as, coffee *grounds.*
3. basis; foundation; reason; as, *grounds* for divorce.

ground school (sköl), a school at which the fundamentals of airplane construction, design, operation, etc. are taught.

ground sēa, the West Indian name for the swell occurring in a calm and with no other indication of a previous gale: also called *rollers.*

ground'sel, *n.* [ME. *grundeswylie*; AS. *grundeswylige*, from earlier *gundeswelge*, perh. lit., pus swallower, from *gund*, pus, and *swelgan*, to swallow: from use in poultices.] any of a large group of plants of the genus *Senecio*, with yellow, rayed flowers, as the golden ragwort.

ground'sel, ground'sill, *n.* the horizontal timber of a building which lies next to the ground; the ground plate; the sill.

ground slōth, same as *megatherium.*

ground speed, the speed with which an aircraft in flight passes over the ground beneath it.

ground squīr'rel (skwīr'), a burrowing rodent, as the chipmunk, gopher, etc.

ground strōke, a stroke, as in tennis, made in returning the ball after it has struck the ground.

ground sub'stănce, in anatomy, the matrix in which certain cells and tissues are embedded.

ground swell, a violent swelling or rolling of the ocean, caused by a distant storm or earthquake.

ground tāble, same as *earth table.*

ground tac'kle, the anchors, cables, and other tackle used in anchoring a ship.

ground thrush, an ant thrush.

ground tiēr, any row or tier nearest the ground, as of stone in a building or boxes in a theatre.

ground tim'bẽrs, in shipbuilding, the structural timbers forming the framework of a vessel.

ground wa'tẽr, water found underground in porous rock strata and soils, as in a spring.

ground'wāys, *n.pl.* the foundations in a shipbuilding yard, on which keel blocks are laid.

ground wēave, the weave that forms the ground for figured cloth, etc.

ground wīre, in electricity, a wire which is or may be connected to the earth so as to make the earth a part of an electrical circuit.

ground wren (ren), a small California bird.

ground'wŏrk, *n.* the work which forms the foundation of anything; the fundamental part; basis.

gröup, *n.* [Fr. *groupe*; It. *gruppo*, a knot, lump, group; of Germanic origin; compare G. *kropf*, a bunch, a crop.]
1. a number of persons or things gathered closely together and forming a recognizable unit; cluster; aggregation; band; as, a *group* of buildings.
2. a collection of objects or figures forming a design or part of a design.
3. a number of persons or things classified together because of common characteristics, community of interests, etc.
4. in biology, a large number of plants or animals related to each other because of certain similarities.
5. in chemistry, a radical.
6. in the United States Air Force, a unit consisting of four squadrons of the same kind of aircraft.
Fuchsian group; a group of linear transformations, $t = \frac{az + b}{cz + d}$, in which z is an imaginary variable and t an imaginary function of this variable.
Syn.—assemblage, assembly, cluster, collection, clump, bunch, crowd, audience, congregation, meeting, crew, gang, company, throng.

gröup, *v.t.* and *v.i.*; grouped, *pt., pp.*; grouping, *ppr.* [Fr. *grouper.*] to assemble or form into a group or groups.

gröup dy̆·nam'ics, 1. the personal interrelationships among members of a small group.
2. the study of these interrelationships.

gröup'ẽr, *n.*; *pl.* **gröup'ẽrs** or **gröup'er,** any of various tropical food fishes, especially, (a) a basslike fish of the genus *Epinephelus* or *Mycteroperca*; (b) the California rockfish; (c) the triple tail; (d) the hamlet.

gröup'ie, *n.* a girl fan of rock-and-roll groups or other popular personalities, who follows them about, often in the hope of achieving sexual intimacy. [Colloq.]

gröup'ing, *n.* the act or result of arranging in a group; specifically, the art of composing or combining the objects of a picture or piece of sculpture.

gröup in·sūr'ănce, insurance, as life insurance, available to a group of employees, etc. at low premium rates, usually regardless of physical condition or age.

gröup med'i·cine, medical care available to the members of a group, community, state, etc. at a fixed rate, usually annual.

gröup ther'ȧ·py (or **psy̆·chō·ther'ȧ·py**), a form of treatment for a group of patients with similar emotional problems or disorders, as by mutual criticism, psychodrama, etc., usually under a therapist's supervision.

gröup wŏrk, that branch of social work concerned with helping groups or communities of people to advance their individual and collective needs and interests.

grouse, *n.*; *pl.* **grouse,** [etym. uncertain.] any of a group of game birds with a round, plump body, firm, feathered legs, feather-covered nostrils, and mottled feathers, as the ruffed grouse, sage hen, etc.

RED GROUSE (*Lagopus scoticus*)

grouse, *v.i.*; groused, *pt., pp.*; grousing, *ppr.* to hunt or shoot grouse.

grouse, *v.i.* [perh. akin to *grouch* (from OFr. *groucier*) via the OFr. var. *grousser.*] to complain; grumble. [Slang.]

grouse, *n.* 1. a complaint. [Slang.]
2. a person who habitually complains. [Slang.]

grous'ẽr, *n.* a pole or pile, usually pointed and shod with iron, to be driven into the ground as an anchor for a dredging boat, etc.

grout, *n.* [ME. *grout, growte*; AS. *grut*, coarse meal, grout.]
1. (a) coarse meal; (b) [*pl.*] groats.
2. [*usually pl.*] sediment; dregs; grounds. [Brit.]
3. a thin mortar used to fill chinks or cracks.
4. a fine plaster for finishing surfaces.
5. a kind of wild apple.

grout, *v.t.*; grouted, *pt., pp.*; grouting, *ppr.* to place grout in; to make with grout; to use as grout; as, to *grout* a foundation or a walk; to *grout* mortar into crevices.

grout'noll, *n.* a stupid or foolish person; a blockhead. [Obs.]

grout'y, *a.*; *comp.* groutier; *superl.* groutiest, cross; sulky; surly. [Dial.]

grōve, *n.* [ME. *grove*; AS. *graf*, a grove, a small forest.]
1. a group of trees standing together without undergrowth; a small wood.
2. something resembling a wood or trees in a wood.

grov'el (*or* gruv'), *v.i.*; groveled *or* grovelled, *pt., pp.*; groveling *or* grovelling, *ppr.* [from ME. *groveling*, on the face, prostrate, from *grof*, on the face, from Ice. *grufa*, to crouch, grovel.]
1. to lie prone or crawl in a prostrate position, especially abjectly.
2. to behave humbly or abjectly, as before authority; to debase oneself in a servile fashion.
3. to take pleasure in base or mean things; to enjoy what is contemptible.

grov'el·ẽr, grov'el·lẽr, *n.* one who grovels.

grov'el·ing, grov'el·ling, *a.* mean; debased; low.

grōv'y, *a.* pertaining to a grove; frequenting groves; like a grove; abounding in groves.

grōw, *v.i.*; grew, *pt.*; grown, *pp.* growing, *ppr.*; [ME. *growen*; AS. *growan*, to grow, sprout.]
1. to come into being or be produced naturally; sprout; spring up.
2. to exist as living vegetation; thrive; as, orchids do not *grow* in Greenland.
3. to increase in size and develop toward maturity, as a plant or animal does by assimilating food.
4. to increase in size, quantity, or degree, or in some specified manner; as, my troubles are *growing.*
5. to become; turn; as, he *grew* weary.
6. to become attached or united by growth.

7. to advance; to improve; to make progress; as, to *grow* in grace, in knowledge, or in reputation.

8. on a ship, to have a certain position or direction; as, the cables *grow* to port.

to grow on; to have a gradually increasing effect on; to come gradually to seem more important, dear, or admirable to.

to grow out of; (a) to develop from; (b) to outgrow.

to grow up; (a) to advance to full stature or maturity; to become adult; (b) to come to be; develop; arise.

grōw, *v.t.* 1. to cause to grow; to raise, cultivate, or produce; as, to *grow* fruit, cereals, etc.

2. to cover with a growth: used in the passive.

3. to allow to grow; as, he tried to *grow* a mustache.

4. to develop.

grōw'ẽr, *n.* 1. one who raises or grows agricultural products.

2. a plant that grows in a specified way; as, this tree is a rapid *grower*.

grōw'ing pāins, 1. rheumatic pains that sometimes occur in the muscles and joints of growing children: they were formerly attributed to rapid growth.

2. difficulties experienced in the early development of an institution or enterprise.

growl, *v.i.*; growled, *pt.*, *pp.*; growling, *ppr.* [ME. *growlen*, to growl; prob. imitative; compare D. *grollen*, to grumble; G. *grollen*, to be angry; OFr. *grouiller*, to rumble.]

1. to utter an angry, grumbling sound; to make a deep, rumbling, guttural sound in the throat, as a dog does.

2. to speak in a grumbling, surly, ill-tempered tone; to complain; to grumble; as, he *growled* about the price.

3. to rumble, as thunder, cannon, etc.

growl, *v.t.* to express by growling or with a growl; as, he *growled* a reply; to *growl* defiance.

growl, *n.* 1. the low, menacing, throaty sound uttered by an angry dog.

2. a sound resembling this; especially, an inarticulate, angry sound made by a person.

3. a complaint muttered angrily.

growl'ẽr, *n.* 1. one who or that which growls.

2. a fish; (a) the large-mouthed black bass; (b) the grunt.

3. a four-wheeled cab drawn by one horse. [Brit. Colloq.]

4. (a) formerly, a pitcher or pail taken by a customer to a saloon for beer; (b) a keg of beer, equal to 1/8 barrel. [Slang.]

growl'ing·ly, *adv.* in a growling manner.

grōwn, *v.* past participle of *grow*.

grōwn, *a.* 1. having completed its growth; mature; fully developed.

2. covered with a growth.

grōwn'-up', *a.* adult; characteristic of a grownup, or referring to a grownup; as, that child seems to have a *grown-up* attitude.

grōwn'up, *n.* an adult.

grōwth, *n.* 1. a growing or developing; specifically, (a) gradual development toward maturity; (b) origin and development.

2. (a) increase in size, weight, powers, etc.; (b) the amount of this.

3. something that grows or has grown; as, a thick *growth* of grass.

4. a tumor or other abnormal mass of tissue developed in or on the body.

grōwth'fụl, *a.* able to grow. [Rare.]

grōwth họr'mōne, 1. a hormone of the anterior part of the pituitary gland, that promotes normal growth.

2. any of various substances that promote growth, as of plants, beef cattle, etc.

grōwth stock, a stock that is expected to grow in value, chiefly because of the company's policy of retaining much of its profit for expansion, and that pays relatively low dividends.

groyne, *n.* a groin. [Obs.]

grō'zing ī'ron (-ūrn), 1. formerly, a kind of glass cutter having a steel point.

2. a tool for finishing the solder joints of lead pipe.

grub, *v.i.*; grubbed, *pt.*, *pp.*; grubbing, *ppr.* [ME. *grubben*, to dig; prob. of Germanic origin; compare O.H.G. *grubilon*, to grub, dig; AS. *grafan*, to dig.]

1. to dig in the ground.

2. to drudge; to work hard, especially at something menial or tedious.

3. to search about, as among records; to rummage.

4. to eat; to take a meal. [Slang.]

grub, *v.t.* 1. to clear (ground) of roots by digging them up.

2. to dig (roots) out of the ground; to uproot.

3. to feed. [Slang.]

grub, *n.* 1. a larva of a beetle, moth, or other insect: also called *grubworm*.

2. a drudge; a person who works hard at some menial or tedious work.

3. food; something to eat. [Slang.]

grub ax, a mattock: called also *grub hoe*, *grubbing hoe*.

grub'bẽr, *n.* 1. one who grubs.

2. a tool for digging up roots.

3. one who eats; a feeder. [Slang.]

grub'bi·ness, *n.* the quality or state of being grubby.

grub'ble, *v.i.* to feel in the dark, or as a blind man; to grope. [Obs.]

grub'by, *a.*; *comp*. grubbier; *superl*. grubbiest, 1. filthy; dirty; unclean, as if from grubbing.

2. infested with grubs, especially with botfly larvae, as cattle or sheep.

grub'by, *n.* a fish of the genus *Cottus*; a sculpin.

grub hōe, a hoe with a heavy, flat blade for grubbing up roots.

grub hook, a hook drawn by horses and controlled by handles, used for upturning stones, roots, etc.

grub saw, a rough saw for sawing stone.

grub'stāke, *n.* 1. money or supplies advanced to a prospector in return for a share in his findings. [Colloq.]

2. money advanced for any enterprise. [Colloq.]

grub'stāke, *v.t.* to provide with a grubstake. [Colloq.]

Grub'street, *n.* Grub Street.

grub'street, *a.* of or like literary hacks or their work.

Grub Street, 1. originally, the name of a street near Moorfields in London (now called Milton Street), where many literary hacks lived.

2. literary hacks.

grub'wŏrm, *n.* a grub.

grudge, *v.t.*; grudged, *pt.*, *pp.*; grudging, *ppr.* [ME. *gruggen*; OFr. *groucier*, *grouchier*, to murmur, complain, grudge; prob. of Scand. origin; compare Ice. *krytja*, to murmur.]

1. to look upon with envy; to envy (one) the possession of; as, to *grudge* someone a pleasure.

2. to give unwillingly; to begrudge; to permit or grant reluctantly; as, to *grudge* a contribution.

3. to feel or entertain in a malevolent or discontented spirit. [Obs.]

grudge, *v.i.* 1. to murmur; to grumble; to repine; to complain; to be unwilling or reluctant. [Obs.]

Grudge not one against another.
—James v. 9.

2. to feel compunction; to grieve. [Obs.]

grudge, *n.* 1. sullen malice or malevolence; spite; ill will; a cherished dislike; as, an old *grudge*.

2. a reason, cause, or pretext for ill will.

3. unwillingness; reluctance. [Obs.]

4. remorse of conscience. [Obs.]

grudge'fụl, *a.* grudging. [Obs.]

grudg'ẽr, *n.* one who grudges.

grudg'ing·ly, *adv.* unwillingly; with reluctance; in a grudging manner.

grudg'ing·ness, *n.* the state or quality of grudging.

grudg'ings, *n.pl.* coarse meal; grouts. [Obs.]

grū'el, *n.* [ME. *gruel*, *gruwel*; OFr. *gruel*, coarse meal; LL. *grutellum*, dim. of *grutum*, meal; of Germanic origin, compare O.H.G. *gruzzi*, groats.] thin, easily digested broth made by cooking meal in water or milk: it is often fed to invalids.

grū'el, *v.t.*; grueled *or* gruelled, *pt.*, *pp.*; grueling *or* gruelling, *ppr.* to subject to intense strain; to exhaust, as by severe punishment, relentless questioning, etc.

grū'el·ing, **grū'el·ling**, *a.* tormenting; exhausting.

grū'el·ing, **grū'el·ling**, *n.* an experience that has an exhausting effect.

grū'el·ly, *a.* resembling gruel.

grūe'sŏme, **grew'sŏme**, *a.* [from obs. *grue*, to shudder (ME. *gruen*), and *some*; akin to G. *grau sam*, horrible.] causing repulsion or loathing; exciting abhorrence; hideous; horrible; frightful; ugly.

grūe'sŏme·ness, **grew'sŏme·ness**, *n.* the quality of being gruesome.

gruff, *a.*; *comp*. gruffer; *superl*. gruffest, [D. *grof*, coarse, heavy.]

1. of a rough or stern manner, voice, or countenance; sour; surly; severe; rugged; harsh.

2. harsh and throaty; hoarse.

gruff'ly, *adv.* in a gruff manner.

gruff'ness, *n.* the state or quality of being gruff.

gruff'y, *a.*; *comp*. gruffier; *superl*. gruffiest, gruff.

grū'grū, *n.* [prob. native name.]

1. the grub of an insect, *Rhynchophorus palmarum*, which lives in the stems of palm trees and also in the sugar cane, and is regarded as a delicacy by the natives.

2. a tropical American palm with a spiny trunk and feathery leaves: also *grugru palm*.

grum, *a.*; *comp*. grummer; *superl*. grummest, [ME. *grom*, *gram*; AS. *grom*, *gram*, angry, wrathful.]

1. morose; sour; surly. [Rare.]

2. low; deep in the throat; guttural; rumbling; as, a *grum* voice. [Rare.]

grum'ble, *v.i.*; grumbled, *pt.*, *pp.*; grumbling, *ppr.* [M.D. *grommelen*, to murmur, mutter, grunt.]

1. to murmur with discontent; to utter a low, muttering complaint.

2. to rumble; to growl; to make a harsh and heavy sound.

3. to rumble, as thunder.

grum'ble, *v.t.* to utter grumblingly.

grum'ble, *n.* 1. the act of grumbling; a grumbling complaint.

2. a peevish mood: usually in the plural.

3. a rumble.

grum'blẽr, *n.* one who grumbles or murmurs.

grum'bling·ly, *adv.* with grumbling.

grum'bly, *a.*; *comp*. grumblier; *superl*. grumbliest; that grumbles; complaining.

grūme, *n.* [OFr. *grume*, a knot, clot, from L. *grumus*, a little heap.]

1. a thick, sticky fluid. [Rare.]

2. a clot, as of blood. [Rare.]

grum'ly, *adv.* in a grum manner.

grum'met, *n.* same as *grommet*.

grū'mōse, *a.* [from L. *grumus*, little heap; and *-ose*.] in botany, collected in a granular mass.

grū'mous, *a.* 1. resembling or containing grume; thick; clotted; as, *grumous* blood.

2. grumose.

grump'i·ly, *adv.* in a grumpy, surly, or gruff manner.

grump'i·ness, *n.* the quality or state of being grumpy.

grump'ish, *a.* grumpy.

grump'y, *a.*; *comp*. grumpier; *superl*. grumpiest, surly; dissatisfied; gruff; irritable; peevish.

Grun'dy, Mrs., a narrow-minded, puritanical neighbor constantly referred to (but never appearing) in Tom Morton's play *Speed the Plough* (1798) with the question "What will Mrs. Grundy say?": used as a personification of prudishness and narrow-minded conventionality.

Grun'dy·ism, *n.* [from Mrs. *Grundy*.]

1. prudish and narrow-minded conventionality.

2. an instance of this.

grun'gy, *a.*; *comp*. grungier; *superl*. grungiest, [perh. a blend of *grimy*, *dingy*, and *grunt*, childish euphemism for "defecate."] dirty, messy, disreputable, etc.; unpleasant. [Slang.]

grunt, *v.i.*; grunted, *pt.*, *pp.*; grunting, *ppr.* [ME. *grunten*, *gronten*, to grunt, groan; prob. of imitative origin; compare AS. *grunian*, L. *grunnire*, to grunt.]

1. to make a deep, gruff sound in the throat: said of a hog.

2. to make a sound like this, as in annoyance, contempt, effort, etc.

grunt, *v.t.* to express by grunting; as, he *grunted* his disapproval.

grunt, *n.* 1. the deep guttural sound made by a hog.

2. a sound like this, made by a person.

3. any fish of the genera *Hæmulon* or *Orthopristis* that grunts when removed from water: also called *grumbler*, *grunter*, and *pigfish*.

4. a U.S. infantryman in the war in Vietnam. [Slang.]

grunt'ẽr, *n.* 1. one who or that which grunts; specifically, (a) a fish, as the grunt, the gurnard, and others; (b) a hog.

2. an iron rod bent like a hook, used by iron founders.

grunt'ing·ly, *adv.* in a grunting manner.

grun'tle, *v.i.* to grunt; to sulk. [Obs. or Dial.]

grunt'ling, *n.* a young hog.

grup'pō, *n.* [It.] in music, a group; a turn.

Grus, *n.* [L., a crane.] a southern constellation supposedly resembling a crane in shape.

Grū'si·ăn, *a.* [Russ. *Gruziya*, Georgia.] Georgian; relating to Caucasian Georgia.

grutch, *n.* and *v.* grudge. [Obs.]

Gru·yère' (cheese) (grē-yâr'), *n.* [from *Gruyère*, a town in Switzerland.] a light-yellow Swiss cheese, very rich in butterfat, or an American cheese resembling this.

grȳ, *n.* [L. *gry*, a trifle; Gr. *gry*, a grunt.]
1. a measure equal to one-tenth of a line. [Obs.]
2. anything very small. [Rare.]

grȳde, *v.i.* to gride. [Obs.]

Gryl'li·dae, *n.pl.* [L. *gryllus*, a cricket, and *-idæ*.] a family of insects belonging to the order *Orthoptera*; the crickets.

Gryl'lus, *n.* the typical genus of the *Gryllidæ*.

grȳpe, *v.t.* to gripe. [Obs.]

Grȳ·phae'ȧ, *n.* [LL. *gryphus*; L. *gryps*; Gr. *gryps*, a griffin.] a genus of fossil bivalves, allied to the oyster and very abundant in the secondary strata of Europe.

gryph'īte, *n.* crowstone, a fossil shell of *Gryphæa*.

gryph'ŏn, *n.* a griffin (mythical monster).

grȳ·pō'sis, *n.* [Gr. *grypōsis*, a hooking, curving, from *grypos*, hooked, bent.] abnormal inward growth or curvature of the nails.

grȳs'bok, *n.* [D. *grijsbok*; *grijs*, gray, and *bok*, buck.] a South African antelope, *Neotragus melanotis*, about 20 inches high and 3 feet long, of a chestnut color flecked with white.

G string, 1. a loincloth; breechclout.
2. a similar cloth, usually decorated with spangles or tassels, worn by strip-tease dancers.
3. a string tuned to G, as on a violin.

G'-sūit'' (jē'-), *n.* [*G* for *gravity*.] a garment for pilots or astronauts, pressurized to counteract the effects on the body of rapid acceleration or deceleration or of the force of gravity.

guä·chä'rō (gwä-), *n.* [Sp. *guácharo*, sickly, moaning; so named from its cry.] a night bird of South America, of the genus *Steatornis*: the young birds are very plump, and their fat, called *guacharo butter* when rendered, is used for cooking and lighting.

guä'çō, *n.* [S. Am.] 1. a tropical South American plant, *Mikania guaco*, the juice of which is used to treat snake bites, gout, and rheumatism.
2. a Central American plant, *Aristolochia anguicida*, the roots of which are used for the same purpose.

guaī'aç (gwī'), *n.* 1. guaiacum (senses 2 and 3).
2. the tonka bean, the aromatic seed of a tropical South American tree.
3. the tree yielding this.

guaī'aç, *a.* relating to guaiacum.

guaī'ȧ·çōl, *n.* a white, crystalline solid or colorless, oily liquid, $C_6H_4(OH)OCH_3$, prepared from guaiacum or wood creosote and used in medicine and as a chemical reagent.

Guaī'ȧ·çum, Guaī'ō·çum, *n.* [Sp. *guayaco*, from native S. Am. name.]
1. a genus of plants of the order *Zygophyllaceæ*. *Guaiacum officinale*, popularly called *lignum vitæ*, is a native of the warmer parts of America. It is an ornamental tree with blue flowers and pinnate leaves.
2. [g–] the very hard, brownish-green wood of a tree of this genus.
3. [g–] a resin obtained from this tree, used to treat rheumatism, gout, etc.

GUAIACUM
(*Guaiacum officinale*)

guän (gwän), *n.* a South American gallinaceous bird, of the *Penelopinæ*, allied to the curassows.

guä'nȧ, *n.* fabric made from the bark of the West Indian tree *Lagetta lintearia*, or lacebark.

guä'nȧ, *n.* an iguana.

guä·nä'çō, *n.*; *pl.* **guä·nä'çōs** or **guä·nä'çō,** [native S. Am.] the *Auchenia huanaco*, a woolly, reddish-brown animal of the Andes, related to the camel but without humps.

guä·nay' (gwä-nī'), *n.* [Sp., from the native (Quechua) name.] a cormorant of Peru: it is a source of guano.

Guän'çhēs, *n.pl.* the aborigines of the Canary Islands.

guän'i·din, *n.* same as *guanidine*.

guän'i·dīne, *n.* a strongly basic, crystalline substance, $NHC(NH_2)_2$, formed by the oxidation of guanine.

guä·nif'ẽr·ous, *a.* [Sp. *guano*, guano, and L. *ferre*, to bear.] yielding guano.

guä'nin, *n.* same as *guanine*.

guä'nīne, *n.* [from *guano*.] an organic base, $C_5H_5N_5O$, found in the liver, pancreas, etc. of animals and obtained commercially from guano.

guä'nō, *n.* [Sp., from Peruv. *huanu*, dung.]
1. the manure of sea birds, found especially on islands off the coast of Peru: it is used as a fertilizer.
2. any manure, artificial or natural, resembling this, especially that of bats.

guä'ō (gwä'), *n.* a West Indian tree which poisons by contact.

guär (gwär), *n.* [Hind. *guār*.] a leguminous plant of India, now cultivated in the United States for forage.

guä'rȧ, *n.* [Braz.] 1. the scarlet ibis.
2. the maned dog, *Canis jubatus*, of South America.

guä·rä'nȧ, *n.* [Braz.] a preparation made in South America by pounding the seeds of a climbing shrub, *Paullinia sorbilis*, into a paste: it is used as a medicine and as food: called also *guarana bread*.

Guä·rä·nī', *n.*; *pl.* **Guä·rä·nīs', Guä·rä·nī',** [Guarani, lit., warrior.]
1. a member of a tribe of South American Indians who lived in an area between the Paraguay River and the Atlantic.
2. the Tupian language of this tribe, used as a general native vernacular in Paraguay.

guä·rä'nin, guä·rä'nīne, *n.* caffein derived from guarana.

guar·ăn·tee' (gar-), *n.* [OFr. *guarantie*, *garantie*, from *guarantir*, *garantir*, to warrant.]
1. a guaranty (senses 1 and 3).
2. a pledge or assurance; specifically, (a) a pledge that something is as represented and will be replaced if it does not meet specifications; (b) a positive assurance that something will be done in the manner specified.
3. a guarantor.
4. a person who receives a guaranty.
5. something that serves as an assurance of, or promises the happening of, some event; as, the dark clouds were a *guarantee* of rain.

guar·ăn·tee', *v.t.*; guaranteed, *pt.*, *pp.*; guaranteeing, *ppr.* 1. to give a guarantee or guaranty for; as, they *guarantee* their product.
2. to state with confidence; promise; affirm; as, I *guaranteed* that I'd be there.

Syn.—answer for, warrant, guard, insure, obligate.

guar'ăn·tor, *n.* one who makes or gives a guaranty or guarantee.

guar'ăn·ty, *v.t.*; guarantied, *pt.*, *pp.*; guarantying, *ppr.* to guarantee: *guarantee* is the spelling for the verb preferred by lawyers.

guar'ăn·ty, *n.*; *pl.* **guar'ăn·tieş,** [OFr. *garantie*, a guaranty, warranty, from *garant*, *guarant*, *warant*, a warrant, supporter, from O.H.G. *warjan*, to protect.]
1. a pledge to answer for the debt, default, or miscarriage of another who is primarily liable.
2. an agreement that secures the existence or maintenance of something; as, the trade pact was a *guaranty* of increased commerce.
3. something given or held as security.

guä·rä'pō (gwä-), *n.* in the West Indies, a fermented drink made from the juice of the sugar cane.

guärd (gärd), *v.t.*; guarded, *pt.*, *pp.*; guarding, *ppr.* [OFr. *garder*, to keep, from M.H.G. *warten*, to watch.]
1. to keep safe from harm; watch over and protect; defend; shield.
2. to watch over; specifically, (a) to keep from escape or trouble; (b) to hold in check; control; restrain; (c) to supervise entrances and exits through (a door, gate, etc.).
3. to cover (a piece of machinery) with a device to protect the operator.
4. to escort. [Archaic.]
5. to adorn with laces, borders, or bindings, especially as a protection for the edges.
6. to furnish with a guard or guards, as a book, plate, or leaf in bookbinding.
7. to gird. [Obs.]

guärd, *v.i.* 1. to keep watch; take precautions (with *against*).
2. to act as a guard.

guärd, *n.* [ME. *garde*; OFr. *garde*, a guardian, warden, from M.H.G. *warten*, to watch.]
1. the act or duty of guarding; careful watch; wariness; defense; protection.
2. caution; precaution; safeguard.
3. a posture of alert readiness for defense, as in fencing, boxing, etc.
4. any device that protects against injury or loss; specifically, (a) the part of the handle of a sword, knife, or fork that protects the hand; (b) a chain or cord attached to a watch; (c) a ring worn to keep a more valuable ring from slipping off the finger; (d) a safety device, as in machinery.
5. a person or group that guards; specifically, (a) a sentinel or sentry; (b) a railway brakeman or gateman; (c) a person who guards prisoners; (d) [*pl.*] a special unit of troops connected with the household of the British sovereign: also extended to other military units.
6. in basketball, either of the two players whose special duties are defensive.
7. in football, either of the two players at the left and the right of the center.
guard of honor; a guard especially selected to escort an eminent person.
leg-and-foot guard; a (a) device to prevent a horse from interfering; (b) a device to prevent the right leg of an artillery driver from being bruised by the carriage pole.
National Guard; see *National Guard* under *national*.
off one's guard; not vigilant; unprepared.
on one's guard; ready to meet attack; cautious; alert.
to mount guard; in military operations, (a) to muster, inspect, and place a detail of soldiers upon guard; as, we *mounted guard* every day at nine o'clock; (b) to go on guard.
to run the guard; to pass over the line of guards without being detected or arrested, as a spy or a soldier of the camp without a pass.
to stand guard; to do sentry duty.

guärd'ȧ·ble, *a.* that may be guarded.

guärd'ăġe, *n.* wardship. [Obs.]

guärd'ănt, *a.* 1. acting as guardian.
2. in heraldry, designating an animal represented with the face fully turned toward the observer: also spelled *gardant*.

guärd'ănt, *n.* a guardian. [Obs.]

guärd cell, in botany, either of the two concave cells surrounding a pore, as in a fern.

guärd'ed, *a.* 1. defended; protected; accompanied by a guard; kept safe; as, the house is *guarded* on every side.
2. kept from escape or trouble; held in check; supervised.
3. cautious; careful; restrained; as, he was *guarded* in his expressions.
4. serious and of uncertain prognosis; as, a patient in *guarded* condition.
5. in card playing, accompanied by a lower card of the same suit in the same hand: said of the next to the highest card out.

guärd'ed·ly, *adv.* in a guarded manner.

guärd'ed·ness, *n.* caution; circumspection.

guärd'ẽr, *n.* one who guards.

guärd'fish, *n.* the garfish. [Brit. Dial.]

guärd'house, *n.* 1. a building used by the members of a military guard when they are not walking a post.
2. the building where soldiers are confined for breaches of the regulations; hence, any lockup.

guärd'i·ăn, *n.* [OFr. *gardien*, from *garder*, to guard, watch.]
1. one who guards, preserves, or secures; one who protects, cares for, or defends another person, property, etc.; custodian.
2. in law, one who is appointed to take charge of the affairs of a minor, or of any person who is not capable of managing his own affairs.
guardian ad litem; a person appointed by a court to conduct a suit for one under legal incapacity.
guardians of the poor; in England and Ireland, persons elected to manage the poor-law system within a parish or other district.

guärd'i·ăn, *a.* protecting; performing the office of a protector; as, a *guardian* angel, *guardian* care.
Feast of the Guardian Angels; in the Roman Catholic Church, a festival celebrated on October 2.
guardian angel; (a) the angel who, according to some creeds, watches over and guards each human being; hence, (b) anyone who protects or defends another.
guardian spirit; a spirit believed to guard the welfare of a person, family, people, or place.

guärd'i·ăn·ăġe, *n.* guardianship. [Obs.]

guärd'i·ănce, *n.* guardianship. [Obs.]
guärd'i·ăn cell, a guard cell.
guärd'i·ăn·ess, *n.* a female guardian.
guärd'i·ăn·less, *a.* without a guardian.
guärd'i·ăn·ship, *n.* the position, duties, or authority of a guardian.
guärd'less, *a.* without a guard or defense.
guärd lock, a lock to keep the tide from a dock or basin.
guärd mount'ing, the military ceremony of going on guard or of stationing guards.
guärd'rāil, *n.* 1. a safety rail or hand rail, as on a staircase.
2. an extra rail alongside the main rail of a railroad at a crossing, etc., to keep the cars on the track.
guärd ring, a ring which prevents the loss of another ring from one's finger.
guärd'rọom, *n.* 1. the room which a military guard occupies when not walking the post.
2. a place for the temporary confinement of military personnel for minor infractions of regulations or while awaiting court-martial.
guärds, *n.pl.* in European armies, a body of picked men generally regarded as the elite of the troops composing an army, having the special duty of guarding their sovereign, etc.
guärd'ship, *n.* care; protection. [Obs.]
guärd ship, 1. a warship for the protection of the port or harbor in which it is stationed.
2. a ship of a squadron doing guard duty.
guärds'măn, *n.*; *pl.* **guärds'men,** 1. one who guards.
2. a member of a national guard or of any military body called a guard.
guä·rï'bȧ (gwä-), *n.* [Sp. Am.] a howling monkey.
guar'ish (gar'), *v.t.* to heal. [Obs.]
Guär·ner'i·us (gwär-), *n.* a violin made by Giuseppe Guarneri (1687?–1745) of Cremona, Italy, or by some other member of the same family.
guä'sȧ (gwä'), *n.* [Sp.] the jewfish.
guä'vȧ (gwä'), *n.* [Braz. *guayaba.*]
1. one of various species of the genus *Psidium*, especially *Psidium guayava*, a tree of tropical America which bears two varieties of fruit, the pear-shaped or white *guava*, and the apple-shaped or red *guava*.
2. the fruit, used for jelly, preserves, etc.
gua·yu'le (gwä-yọọ'lā), *n.* [Sp.; Nahuatl *quauholli*, from *quauitl*, plant, and *olli*, gum.]
1. the *Parthenium argentatum*, a small shrub of northern Mexico and Texas, cultivated for the rubber obtained from its sap.
2. this rubber: also *guayule rubber*.
gub, *n.* [from *gob*, a lump.]
1. a tooth or projection on a wheel; especially, on a sprocket wheel.
2. a lump. [Obs.]
gū·bẽr·naç'ū·lum, *n.*; *pl.* **gū·bẽr·naç'ū·lȧ,** [L., a rudder, from *gubernare*, to steer.]
1. in anatomy, the conical-shaped cord attached above the lower end of the epididymis, passing below to the bottom of the scrotum, and governing the descent of the testes.
2. in biology, the posterior flagellum in certain protozoans.
gū'bẽr·nănce, *n.* government. [Obs.]
gū'bẽr·nāte, *v.t.* to govern. [Obs.]
gū·bẽr·nā'tion, *n.* government; rule; direction. [Obs.]
gū'bẽr·nā·tive, *a.* governing. [Rare.]
gū''bẽr·nȧ·tō'ri·ăl, *a.* [L. *gubernator*, a helmsman, governor, from *gubernare*, to steer.] of a governor or his office.
gū·ber'ni·yä, *n.* [Russ.] 1. formerly, a territorial subdivision of Russia.
2. a provincial soviet in the Soviet Union.
guck, *n.* [prob. from goo, and m*uck*.] any thick, viscous, sticky or slimy substance. [Slang.]
gud'ġeŏn (guj'ŏn), *n.* [ME. *gojon*; OFr. *goujon*; L. *gobio* (*-onis*); Gr. *kobios*, a kind of fish, a gudgeon.]
1. a small fresh-water fish, *Gobio fluviatilis*, very easily caught, and used for bait.
2. a minnow.
3. one who is easily cheated or ensnared.
4. that which may be gained without ability or merit.
5. a bait.
gud'ġeŏn, *v.t.* to ensnare; to cheat; to dupe.
gud'ġeon, *n.* [ME. *gojon*, *gojone*; OFr. *gojon*, *goujon*, pivot; perh. from *gouge* (a prostitute), with a sexual allusion.]
1. a metal pin or shaft at the end of an axle on which a wheel turns.
2. the socket of a hinge, into which the pin is fitted.
3. the part of a shaft that revolves in a bearing.

Gụd'rụn, *n.* 1. the heroine of an old German saga who is rescued by her lover after many years of suffering.
2. in Norse legend, the daughter of the Nibelung king: she lured Sigurd away from the Valkyrie Brynhild by a magic drink and married him: also *Guthrun*.
gūe, *n.* [Fr. *gueux*.] a rogue. [Obs.]
Guē'bẽr (gē'), *n.* [Per. *gabr*, a fire worshiper, an infidel.] a Gheber; a Zoroastrian.
guel'dẽr-rōse (gel'), **gel'dẽr-rōse,** *n.* [named from its supposed source, *Gelderland*.] the snowball tree, *Viburnum opulus*, especially the cultivated form of that species.
Guelf, Guelph (gwelf), *n.* [It. *Guelfo*, for M.H.G. *Welf*, a family name, from O.H.G. *welf*, a whelp: used as a war-cry of the anti-imperial faction at the battle of Weinsberg (1140).] any member of a political party in medieval Italy that supported the authority of the pope in opposition to the aristocratic party of the Ghibellines.
Guelf'iç, Guelph'iç, *a.* of or belonging to the Guelf family or party.
guē·nōn' (gē-), *n.* any of a large group of long-tailed African monkeys, including the grivet.
guep'ärd (gwep'), **guep'ärde,** *n.* [Fr.] the cheetah.
guẽr'dŏn (gẽr'), *n.* [ME. *guerdon*; OFr. *guerdon*; ML. *widerdonum*, from O.H.G. *widar*, again, against, and L. *donum*, gift.] a reward; a requital; a recompense.
guẽr'dŏn, *v.t.* to reward; to give a guerdon to. [Poetic.]
guẽr'dŏn·ȧ·ble, *a.* [OFr. *guerrdonnable*, from *guerdonner*, to reward.] worthy of reward.
guẽr'dŏn·less, *a.* without reward.
gue'rē·zȧ (ge'), *n.* [from the native African name.] *Colobus guereza*, a large, black-and-white monkey of Abyssinia, having long, soft hair and a bushy tail.
guẽr'īte, *n.* [Fr.] in fortification, a small projecting tower or box of wood at the salient angles of the revetment, to hold a sentry.
Guẽrn'ṣey, *n.* [from *Guernsey*, one of the Channel Islands.]
1. any of a breed of dairy cattle, fawn with white markings.
2. [g–] a knitted woolen shirt or vest.
guer·ril'lȧ (ge-ril'), **gue·ril'lȧ,** *n.* [Sp., skirmishing warfare, dim. of *guerra*, war.]
1. formerly, warfare carried on by guerrillas.
2. any member of a small defensive force of irregular soldiers, usually volunteers, making surprise raids against supply lines, etc. behind the lines of an invading enemy army.
guer·ril'lȧ, *a.* of or by guerrillas.
guess (ges), *v.t.*; guessed (gest), *pt.*, *pp.*; guessing, *ppr.* [ME. *gessen*, to guess; compare Sw. *gissa*, to guess.]
1. to conjecture; to form an opinion or estimate of (something) without means of knowledge; to judge of at random.
2. to judge or form an opinion of (something) from reasons that make a thing probable, but fall short of sufficient evidence; as, from slight circumstances or occasional expressions, one may *guess* an author's meaning.
3. to conjecture rightly; to solve by a correct conjecture; as, to *guess* a riddle.
4. to think; to suppose; to imagine.

Not altogether; better far, I *guess*,
That we do make our entrance several ways.
—Shak.

Syn.—think, reckon, suppose, conjecture, estimate, surmise.
guess (ges), *v.i.* to conjecture; to judge at random; as, we do not know which road to take, but must *guess* at it.
guess, *n.* conjecture; a judgment without any certain evidence or grounds; a surmise.
guess'ȧ·ble, *a.* that can be guessed.
guess'ẽr, *n.* one who guesses.
guess'ing·ly, *adv.* by way of conjecture.
guess'ive, *a.* conjectural. [Obs.]
guess'-rōpe, *n.* a guess-warp.
guess'ti·māte, *n.* [*guess*, and *estimate*.] an estimate based on a guess or conjecture. [Slang.]
guess'ti·māte, *v.t.*; guesstimated, *pt.*, *pp.*; guesstimating, *ppr.* to form a guesstimate of. [Slang.]
guess'-wạrp, *n.* a rope serving to warp a vessel toward a distant object to which the rope is made fast; also, a rope used to secure a boat to another vessel.
guess'wŏrk, *n.* haphazard or conjectural opinion, action, or results; a guess; conjecture.

guest (gest), *n.* [ME. *gest*, *geest*; AS. *giest*, a guest.]
1. a person entertained at the home or table of another; visitor.
2. a person paying for his lodgings, meals, etc. at a hotel or boardinghouse.
3. a person receiving the hospitality of a club, institution, etc. of which he is not a member.
4. an insect or other animal living or breeding in the nest, etc. of another animal.
guest, *v.i.* and *v.t.* to be or entertain a guest.
guest'chām''bẽr, *n.* a room reserved for the use of guests.
guest flȳ, an insect living in a gall made by another insect.
guest house, an inn.
guest rọom, a guest chamber.
guest rōpe, a guess-warp.
guest'wiṣe, *adv.* in the manner of a guest.
Gueux (gē), *n.* [Fr., lit., beggars, scoundrels.] the noblemen and burghers who opposed Philip II in the Netherlands from 1566 on.
guẹ'vï (gwā'), *n.* [S. African.] a duykerbok or pygmy antelope of the genus *Cephalophus*.
guff, *n.* nonsense; idle or foolish talk; sometimes, impudence or impertinence. [Slang.]
guf·faw', *v.i.* to utter a guffaw.
guf·faw', *n.* a loud, coarse burst of laughter.
guf'fẽr, *n.* the eelpout or blenny. [Scot.]
gụ·gal', *n.* [Hind.] the sweet-scented resin of various trees of India, used as incense.
gug'gle, *n.*, *v.i.* and *v.t.* gurgle.
gug'glet, *n.* same as *goglet*.
gūhr, *n.* [G., from *gähren*, *gären*, to ferment.] a loose, earthy deposit from water found in the cavities or clefts of rocks, mostly white, but sometimes red or yellow, from a mixture of clay or ocher.
guī'ȧ·çol, *n.* same as *guaiacol*.
guī'ȧ·çum, *n.* same as *guaiacum*.
guib (gwib), **guī'bȧ,** *n.* *Tragelaphus scriptus*, the West African harnessed antelope, so called from the bars of white on its sides.
guīd'ȧ·ble (gīd'), *a.* that can be guided.
guīd'ănce, *n.* 1. the act of guiding; direction.
2. something that guides.
guīde (gīd), *v.t.*; guided, *pt.*, *pp.*; guiding, *ppr.* [ME. *guiden*, *gyden*; prob. of Gmc. origin; compare AS. *witan*, to know.]
1. to point out the way for; direct on a course; conduct; lead.
2. to direct the course or motion of (a person's hand, a vehicle, etc.) by physical action.
3. to give instruction to; to train.
4. to direct (the policies, action, etc.) of; manage; regulate; govern.
guīde, *n.* [ME. *guide*; OFr. *guis*, a guide.] a person or thing that guides; specifically, (a) a person whose work is conducting strangers or tourists through a region, building, etc.; (b) a part that directs or controls the motion of other parts of a machine; (c) a guidebook; (d) a book giving instruction in the elements of some subject; as, a *guide* to mathematics; (e) in military usage, a soldier at the right front of a column, who regulates its pace and alignment and indicates its route.
guīde bär, one of two parallel bars by which the free end of a piston is made to move in a straight line.
guīde block, one of two blocks attached to the crosshead of an engine, which slide between and are guided by the guide bars.
guīde'bōard, *n.* a board bearing a sign to direct travelers.
guīde'book, *n.* a book containing information concerning places, routes, etc., for the use of tourists.
guīd'ed mis'sile, a military missile whose course toward the target is controlled by radio signals, radar devices, etc.
guīde'less, *a.* having no guide.
guīde'līne, *n.* a standard or principle by which to make a judgment or determine a policy or course of action: also *guide line*.
guīde'pōst, *n.* 1. a signpost for directing travelers.
2. anything that serves as a guide, standard, example, etc.; guideline.
guīde pụl'ley, a pulley which tightens, changes the direction of, or otherwise serves as a guide to a belt.
guīd'ẽr, *n.* one who guides; a guide.
guīde rāil, a guard rail.
guīd'ẽr·ess, *n.* a woman guide. [Obs.]
guīde rōpe, a rope attached to another rope

lifting or dragging a load, to help steady and direct the load.

guid′guid (gwid′gwid), *n.* [imitative.] a rock wren whose cry resembles the yelping of a puppy: called also *barking bird.*

guī′dŏn (gī′), *n.* [Fr.; It. *guidone*, from *guidare*, to guide.]
1. formerly, a small flag or pennant carried by the guide of mounted cavalry.
2. in the United States Army, (a) the identification flag of a unit; (b) a soldier carrying such a flag at the head of the unit: also *guidon bearer.*

guild, gild (gild), *n.* [ME. *gylde, yelde*, etc.; blend of AS. *gyld, gield*, payment, guild, AS. *gegyld*, association (of paying members), ON. *gildi*, guild, guild-feast; all, from base seen in AS. *gieldan*, to pay, make payment.]
1. in medieval times, a union of men in the same craft or trade to uphold standards and protect the members.
2. any association for mutual aid and the promotion of common interests.
3. in plant ecology, any of four groups of parasitic plants (*parasites, saprophytes, epiphytes,* and *lianas*).

guil′dẽr (gil′), *n.* [Early Mod. Eng. *gildren* (ME. *guldren*); altered from D. *gulden*, florin, lit., golden.]
1. a former gold or silver coin of the Netherlands, Germany, or Austria.
2. (a) the unit of currency in the Netherlands; (b) a silver coin of its value.

guild′hall, *n.* 1. a hall where a guild meets.
2. a town hall; specifically, [G-] the hall of the Corporation of the City of London.

guilds′măn (gildz′), *n.*; *pl.* **guilds′men,** a member of a guild.

guild sō′ciăl·ism (-shăl-), a form of socialism proposed in England in the early 20th century, consisting in government ownership of all industries, each to be managed by a guild of workers.

guīle (gīl), *n.* [OFr. *guile, gil*, guile; of Germanic origin.]
1. craft; cunning; artifice; duplicity; deceit.
2. a wile; a trick.

guīle′fụl, *a.* full of or characterized by guile.

guīle′fụl·ly, *adv.* in a guileful manner.

guīle′fụl·ness, *n.* deceitfulness; secret treachery.

guīle′less, *a.* free from guile or deceit; artless.

guīle′less·ly, *adv.* in a guileless manner.

guīle′less·ness, *n.* freedom from guile.

Guïl·lain″-Bär·rẹ′ syn′drōme (gē lan″bä rā′) [after G. *Guillain* and J. *Barré*, 20th-c. Fr. neurologists.] an acute neurological disorder of unknown cause, involving partial paralysis of several muscle groups and occurring rarely after certain viral infections and vaccinations.

guil′le·mot (gil′), *n.* [Fr., dim. of *Guillaume*, William.] any of various narrow-billed arctic diving birds of the auk family.

COMMON GUILLEMOT (*Uria troille*)

guil·lọ̈che′, *n.* [Fr. *guillochis*, from *guillocher*, to ornament with lines, from OIt. *ghiocciare*, to drop, drip; ultimately from L. *gutta*, a drop.] a decorative border design in which two or more lines or bands are interwoven so as to make circular spaces between them.

guil′lō·tïne, *n.* [Fr., from the name of Dr. J. I. *Guillotin*, who advocated its use during the French Revolution in preference to less humane methods.]

GUILLOTINE

1. a machine for beheading persons by the fall of a weighted blade with an oblique edge sliding between upright guides.
2. any of various cutting machines having an oblique-edged blade.
3. in surgery, an instrument for removing the tonsils.

guil·lō·tïne′, *v.t.*; guillotined, *pt., pp.*; guillotining, *ppr.* to behead with the guillotine.

guilt (gilt), *n.* [ME. *gilt*; AS. *gylt*, a fault, offense.]
1. the act or state of having done a wrong or committed an offense; culpability, legal or ethical.
2. conduct that involves guilt; wrongdoing; crime; sin.

guilt′i·ly, *adv.* in a guilty manner.

guilt′i·ness, *n.* the state of being guilty; guilt.

guilt′less, *a.* 1. free from guilt; innocent.
2. without knowledge or experience; ignorant.

Heifers *guiltless* of the yoke. —Pope.

guilt′less·ly, *adv.* without guilt; innocently.

guilt′less·ness, *n.* innocence; freedom from guilt.

guilt′-sick, *a.* sick with guilt; remorseful.

guilt′y, *a.*; *comp.* guiltier; *superl.* guiltiest, [ME. *gilty*; AS. *gyltig*, guilty, from *gylt*, guilt.]
1. having guilt; deserving blame or punishment; culpable.
2. having one's guilt proved; legally judged an offender.
3. showing or conscious of guilt; as, a *guilty* look.
4. of or involving guilt or a sense of guilt; as, a *guilty* conscience.

guim′bärd (gim′), *n.* a jew's-harp. [Obs.]

guimpe (gimp *or* gamp), *n.* [Fr.] a chemisette worn under a pinafore or jumper.

guin′ēa (gin′ē), *n.* 1. formerly, a gold coin of Great Britain, made originally (1663) of gold from Guinea, and last issued in 1813. It was valued at 21 shillings.
2. a guinea fowl.
3. an Italian: hostile and contemptuous term. [Slang.]

Guin′ēa çlọth, a cloth made for export to the West African coast.

guin′ēa çorn, Indian millet, *Sorghum vulgare.*

guin′ēa fowl, a gallinaceous domestic fowl of Africa, of which there are several species, the commonest being the *Numida meleagris.* It is as large as the common domestic hen, and has a colored fleshy horn on each side of the head. Its color is a dark gray, with small, white spots. Also *guinea hen.*

guin′ēa grāins, grains of paradise.

guin′ēa grȧss, a species of African grass, *Panicum jumentorum*, cultivated in the southern United States and used as fodder.

guin′ēa hen, 1. a guinea fowl.
2. a female guinea fowl.

Guin′ēa pep′pẽr, a tree, *Xylopia aethiopica*, of tropical Africa, or its fruits. Also the plant, *Capiscum annum*, or its seeds, from which Cayenne pepper is obtained.

guin′ēa pig, [prob. brought to England by ships plying between England, Guinea, and S. America.]
1. a small, fat mammal of the rat family, with short ears and a short tail: it is domesticated and is often used in biological experiments.
2. any person or thing used in an experiment.

GUINEA PIG (*Cavia cobaya*)

3. any one whose fee is a guinea. [Brit. Slang.]

guin′ēa plum, a West African tree, *Parinarium excelsum*, with long leaves and large terminal bunches of flowers succeeded by a fruit about the size of a plum.

Guin′ēa wŏrm, a species of parasitic threadworm, *Filaria medinensis*, very common in hot countries, and often causing intense pain by forming abscesses beneath the skin of man, dogs, and horses.

Guin′e·vẽr (gwin′), *n.* same as *Guinevere.*

Guin′e·vēre (gwin′), *n.* [from Celt.] in Arthurian legend, the wife of King Arthur and mistress of Sir Lancelot.

guï·pūre′ (gē-), *n.* [Fr.] 1. a kind of gimp.
2. lace without a mesh, but with a distinct pattern held in place by connecting threads.

guï·sȧrme′, *n.* same as *gisarme.*

guīse, *n.* [OFr. *guise*, way, manner, guise, from O.H.G. *wisa*, way, manner.]
1. customary behavior, manner, or carriage. [Archaic.]
2. manner of dress; garb.
3. outward aspect; semblance.
4. a false or deceiving appearance; pretense; as, under the *guise* of friendship he betrayed us.

guīse, *v.t.*; guised, *pt., pp.*; guising, *ppr.* 1. to dress or arrange (*in* a specified manner).
2. to disguise. [Brit. Dial.]

guīse, *v.i.* to go in disguise. [Brit. Dial.]

guīs′ẽr, *n.* a person in disguise, especially a mummer who goes about at Christmas.

gui·tär′ (gi-), *n.* [Fr. *guitare*, from L. *cithara*, Gr. *kithara*, a lyre or lute.] a stringed musical instrument shaped somewhat like a violin, but played by plucking or strumming the strings with the fingers or a plectrum: it usually has three strings of gut and three of silk covered with fine silver wire.

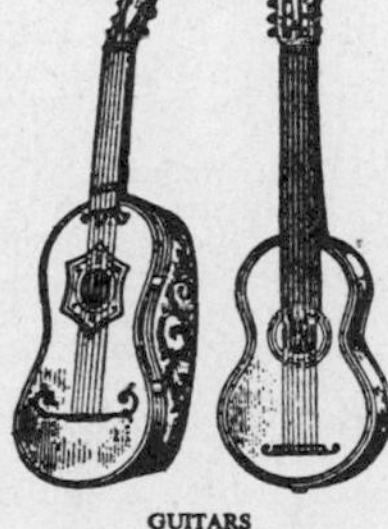

GUITARS

gui·tär′ist, *n.* one who plays a guitar.

guit′guit (gwit′gwit), *n.* the honey creeper, a small, brightly colored bird of tropical America: so called from its note.

Gụj·ä·rä′ti, *n.* the Indo-European, Indic language spoken in the region of the Gujarat States.

gū′lȧ, *n.*; *pl.* **gū′lae,** [L. *gula*, the throat.] the gullet; the throat; (a) the part of the throat next to the chin; (b) in entomology, a plate supporting the submentum.

gụ′läg, *n.* [after "The Gulag Archipelago" by A. Solzhenitsyn, from Russ. acronym for *G(lavnoe) u(pravlenie ispravitel'no-trudovykh) lag(erei)*, Chief Administration of Corrective Labor Camps.]
1. a prison or a forced-labor camp.
2. any place or situation regarded as like such a prison.

gụ·lan′chȧ, *n.* [E. Ind.] *Tinospora cordifolia*, an East Indian climber, whose bitter root is used as a tonic.

gū′lăr, *a.* [L. *gula*, the throat.] pertaining to the throat.

gulch, *n.* [ME. *gulchen*, to swallow greedily, from Norw. *gulka*, to disgorge.] a glutton. [Obs.]

gulch, *v.t.* to swallow greedily. [Obs.]

gulch, *n.* a deep, narrow ravine.

gulch, *n.* a heavy fall. [Brit. Dial.]

gụl′den, *n.* [G., from *gülden*, golden.]
1. any of several gold coins once current in Austria, Germany, and the Netherlands.
2. a guilder (sense 2).

gūles, *n.* [ME. *goules*; OFr. *gueules*, gules, the tincture red, originally pl. of *goule, gole*, the mouth, from L. *gula*, the throat.] in heraldry, red, as a tincture. It is represented in an engraved escutcheon by vertical lines close together.

GULES

gulf, *n.* [OFr. *golfe, goulfe*, a gulf; L.Gr. *kolphos*; Gr. *kolpos*, a fold, the bosom, a bay, or gulf.]
1. a large area of water extending from the ocean or a sea into an indentation of a coast line; as, the *Gulf* of Mexico.
2. an abyss; a deep place in the earth; a chasm; as, the *gulf* of Avernus.
3. a whirlpool; an absorbing eddy.
4. a great interval, space, or degree of separation; a cleavage; as, there is a *gulf* between us.
5. in Cambridge University, the bottom of

the pass list for degrees, in which are placed those students who fail to get honors.

gulf, *v.t.*; gulfed, *pt., pp.*; gulfing, *ppr.* 1. to absorb completely; to swallow up; to engulf.

2. at Cambridge University, to place in the gulf, or at the bottom of a pass list.

gulf'weed, *n.* a coarse seaweed, *Sargassum bacciferum*, which has grape-like air vessels by which it is buoyed up on the surface of the water: found floating in the Gulf Stream and the Sargasso Sea.

GULFWEED (*Sargassum bacciferum*)

gulf'y, *a.* full of whirlpools or gulfs; as, a *gulfy* sea.

gul'gul, *n.* [native E. Ind. name.] in India, a cement made of pounded seashells mixed with oil, which hardens like stone and is put over a ship's bottom so that worms cannot penetrate.

gū·lin'ū·là, *n.* [a dim. from L. *gula*, the throat.] the stage of development of an anthozoan at which the gullet is formed.

gū·lin'ū·lăr, *a.* of or relating to a gulinula.

gull, *n.*; *pl.* **gulls** or **gull,** [ME. *goll*, an unfledged bird, from Ice. *golr*, yellow.]

1. a person easily cheated or misled.

2. a fraud; a cheat; a deception; a trick. [Archaic.]

gull, *v.t.* to cheat; to trick; to dupe.

gull, *n.* [Corn. *gullan*, a gull.] a web-footed, long-winged sea fowl of or closely allied to the genus *Larus*: it has feathers of gray, white, and black. In the larger species, the upper mandible is bent downward at the point.

LESSER BLACK-BACKED GULL (*Larus fuscus*)

gull, *v.t.* to gulp; to swallow. [Obs.]

gull'à·ble, *a.* gullible. [Rare.]

gull'äge, *n.* the act of gulling or state of being gulled. [Obs.]

Gul'làh, *n.* [altered from *Gola* or *Gora*, names of African tribes living in Liberia.]

1. any of a group of Negroes living on the South Carolina and Georgia coast or near-by islands.

2. the English dialect of the Gullahs.

gull'-billed, *a.* having a bill like that of a gull.

gull'ẽr, *n.* a cheat; an impostor. [Obs.]

gull'ẽr·y, *n.* cheat; deception. [Obs.]

gull'ẽr·y, *n.* a breeding place of gulls.

gul'let, *n.* [ME. *golet*; OFr. *goulet*, the throat, a narrow passage, dim. of *gole, goule*; L. *gula*, the throat.]

1. the tube leading from the mouth to the stomach; the esophagus.

2. anything resembling this, as (a) a channel for water; (b) a preparatory cut or channel in excavations, of sufficient width to admit the passage of a temporary track for dump cars; (c) a concave cut in the teeth of some saw blades.

3. the throat or neck.

gul'let, *v.t.* to cut gullets in (a saw).

gul·li·bil'i·ty, *n.* unsuspecting credulity.

gul'li·ble, *a.* easily gulled; credulous: also spelled *gullable*.

gul'li·bly, *adv.* in a gullible manner.

gull'ish, *a.* foolish; stupid.

gull'ish·ness, *n.* foolishness; stupidity.

Gul'li·vẽr's Trav'els, a political and social satire (1726) of 18th-century England by Jonathan Swift, telling of the adventures of the shipwrecked Lemuel Gulliver in four imaginary lands, Lilliput, Brobdingnag, Laputa, and the land of the Houyhnhnms.

gull tēas'ẽr, any bird that torments gulls, as a jager or tern.

gul'ly, *n.*; *pl.* **gul'lies,** [Fr. *goulet*, a narrow entrance, from OFr. *goulet*, the throat, gullet.]

1. a channel or hollow worn in the earth by a current of water; a narrow ravine.

2. a kind of grooved rail. [Brit.]

gul'ly, *v.t.*; gullied, *pt., pp.*; gullying, *ppr.* to make a gully or gullies in.

gul'ly, *n.* a large knife. [Scot. and Brit. Dial.]

gul'ly·gut, *n.* a glutton. [Obs.]

gul'ly·hōle, *n.* an opening into a drain.

gū·los'i·ty, *n.* greediness; voracity. [Obs.]

gulp, *v.t.*; gulped, *pt., pp.*; gulping, *ppr.* [D. *gulpen*, to swallow eagerly.]

1. to swallow hastily, greedily, or in large amounts.

2. to choke back as if swallowing; repress (a sob, etc.).

gulp, *v.i.* to catch the breath in or as in swallowing a large amount.

gulp, *n.* 1. a swallow; also, the amount swallowed at once.

2. a gulping.

gulph, *n.* a gulf. [Obs.]

gum, *n.* [ME. *gumme, goome*, a gum, from AS. *goma*, the palate.] the firm flesh covering the jaws on the inside of the mouth and surrounding the base of the teeth.

gum, *v.t.* to clean and enlarge the spaces between the teeth of; as, to *gum* a worn saw.

gum, *n.* [ME. *gumme, gomme*; OFr. *gomme*; L. *gummi*; Gr. *kommi*, gum.]

1. a sticky substance given off by certain trees and plants, which dries into an uncrystallized, brittle mass soluble in water.

2. any similar plant secretion, as resin.

3. any plant gum processed for use in industry, art, etc.

4. an adhesive, especially on the back of a postage stamp; glue; mucilage.

5. gum elastic; rubber.

6. any gum tree; also, its wood.

7. a part of a hollow gum log used as a beehive, trough, etc. [Dial.]

8. [*pl.*] overshoes or rubbers.

9. chewing gum.

acaroid gum or *gum acaroides*; a gum given off by certain species of *Xanthorrhœa*.

gum ammoniac; ammoniac, a natural gum resin.

gum anime or *animi*; same as *anime*.

gum arabic or *gum acacia*; a gum usually derived from *Acacia arabica* and *Acacia vera*, used in medicine, in the manufacture of candy, etc. The East Indian variety is from *Feronia elephantum*.

gum butea; a gum derived from *Butea frondosa*, used in medicine and the arts.

gum dragon; gum tragacanth.

gum elastic; same as *caoutchouc*.

gum elemi; same as *elemi*.

gum juniper; same as *sandarac* (resin).

gum ladanum; the gum or resin of the *Cistus ladaniferus*.

gum resin; a mixture of resin and gum. The gum resins do not flow naturally from plants, but are mostly extracted by incision, in the form of white, yellow, or red emulsive fluids, which dry and solidify. The most important species are olibanum, galbanum, scammony, gamboge, euphorbium, asafetida, aloes, myrrh, and ammoniac.

gum sandarac; same as *sandarac* (resin).

gum senegal; a gum resembling gum arabic, brought from Senegal, in Africa.

gum tragacanth; a gum obtained from various Asiatic or east European shrubs and trees of the pea family: also *tragacanth*.

gum, *v.t.*; gummed, *pt., pp.*; gumming, *ppr.* to coat, unite, or stiffen with gum.

gum, *v.i.* 1. to secrete or form gum.

2. to become sticky or clogged.

gum an'i·măl, the galago of Senegal, a lemur which feeds upon gums.

gum'bō, *n.* [prob. of Indian or Negro origin.]

1. the okra plant.

2. the edible, sticky pods of this plant.

3. a soup thickened with unripe okra pods.

4. a fine, silty soil of the Western prairies, which becomes sticky and nonporous when wet: also *gumbo soil*.

5. a French patois spoken by Creoles and Negroes in Louisiana and the French West Indies.

Also spelled *gombo*.

gum'boil, *n.* a boil, or abscess, on the gums.

gum'bō lim'bō, *Bursera gummifera*, the West India or Jamaica birch tree. The bark yields cachibou, a resin similar to elemi gum.

gum cis'tus, a European species of rockrose, *Cistus ladaniferus*, yielding a dark-colored resin.

gum'dig·gẽr, *n.* one who digs up the fossil gum or resin from which varnish is made.

gum'drop, *n.* a small piece of candy of a firm, jellylike consistency, made of sweetened gum arabic or gelatin, usually colored, flavored, and covered with sugar.

gum'mȧ, *n.*; *pl.* **gum'mȧ·tȧ, gum'mȧs,** [L. *gummi*, gum.] a syphilitic tumor.

gum'mȧ·tous, *a.* like or relating to a gumma.

gum'mẽr, *n.* a device for increasing the distance between the teeth of a worn saw.

gum·mif'ẽr·ous, *a.* [L. *gummi*, gum, and *ferre*, to bear.] producing gum.

gum'mi·ness, *n.* the state or quality of being gummy.

gum'mīte, *n.* an orange-yellow, gumlike mineral consisting of a complex compound containing uranium, lead, silicon, and oxygen.

gum'mōse, *a.* same as *gummous*.

gum·mō'sis, *n.* the giving off of gummy substances as a result of cell degeneration: a characteristic of certain plant diseases, especially of stone fruits.

gum·mos'i·ty, *n.* gumminess; a viscous or adhesive quality. [Rare.]

gum'mous, *a.* [L. *gummosus*, gummy, from *gummi*, gum.] of the nature or quality of gum.

gum'my, *a.*; *comp.* gummier; *superl.* gummiest, 1. consisting of gum; of the nature of gum; viscous; adhesive; also, covered with or containing gum or viscous matter.

2. yielding gum.

3. puffy; swollen.

gump, *n.* [Ice. *gumpr*, the rump.] a foolish person; a dolt. [Dial.]

gum plant, any of several species of *Grindelia*, the foliage of which is coated with a viscous substance.

gump'tion, *n.* [AS. *gyman*, to understand, heed.]

1. shrewdness in practical matters; common sense. [Colloq.]

2. courage and initiative; enterprise and boldness: the current sense. [Colloq.]

3. the art of preparing colors for painting.

4. meglip.

gum rash, a mild papular eruption, common among children.

gum'shöe, *n.* 1. (a) a rubber overshoe; (b) [*pl.*] sneakers.

2. a detective. [Slang.]

gum'shöe, *v.i.* to go about quietly; to move stealthily. [Slang.]

gum stick, a small piece of some hard substance, as of ivory or coral, used by infants in teething.

gum'-top tree, *Eucalyptus sieberiana*, the Tasmanian and Australian ironbark tree.

gum tree, 1. the black gum, of the genus *Nyssa*, one of the largest trees of the southern United States.

2. *Liquidambar styraciflua*, the sweet gum; a large tree of the witch-hazel family, native to the Atlantic States.

3. any species of the genus *Eucalyptus*, native to Australia.

gum wa̤'tẽr, an aqueous solution of a gum, as of gum arabic.

gum'wood, *n.* wood of any of the gum trees, usually of the genus *Eucalyptus*.

gun, *n.* [ME. *gunne, gonne*, a gun; etym. unknown; compare W. *gwn*, Ir. and Gael. *gunna*, a gun, OFr. *mangonnel*, a machine for throwing stones.]

1. a weapon consisting of a tube of metal, fixed in a stock or mounted on a carriage, from which projectiles are fired by the force of an explosive, usually gunpowder; especially, (a) a cannon, as distinguished from *small arms* and *mortars*; (b) popularly, a rifle, revolver, or pistol.

2. any similar device not discharged by an explosive; as, an air *gun*.

3. anything like a gun in shape or use.

4. the throttle of an engine. [Slang.]

5. the report or discharge of a gun; as, a salute of ten *guns*.

6. one who bears a gun in a hunting party.

7. a kind of jug. [Brit. Dial.]

8. a gauge to establish the width of the plate in rolling plate glass.

BB gun; a form of pneumatic rifle which uses small, round lead shot as the projectile.

Galling gun; an obsolete machine gun having a number of barrels arranged cylindrically, which are fired successively when rotated by means of a crank: invented by Dr. R. J. Gatling, 1818–1903, an American, and first used in the Civil War.

machine gun: an automatic gun, usually mounted and with a cooling apparatus, firing a rapid and continuous stream of bullets fed into it by a belt, clip, or disk.

Quaker gun; a dummy cannon or gun, as of wood: so called from the Quaker opposition to war and militarism.

gun, *v.i.*; gunned, *pt., pp.*; gunning, *ppr.* to shoot; to hunt with a gun.

gun, *v.t.* 1. to open the throttle or press down the accelerator of (an engine) so as to increase the speed. [Slang.]

2. to shoot (a person). [Colloq.]

gun′bōat, *n.* 1. a small armed ship of shallow draft, used to patrol rivers, etc.
2. in coal mines, a small, self-dumping coal car.

gun çar′riaġe (-rij), the carriage or structure on which a gun is mounted, moved, and fired.

gun′çot·tŏn, *n.* a highly explosive substance produced by treating cotton or other forms of cellulose with a mixture of nitric and sulfuric acids.

gun deck, the deck carrying a ship's guns.

gun dog, a dog trained to help a hunter by finding or retrieving game: pointers, setters, and various hounds are used as gun dogs.

gun′fight, *n.* a fight between persons using pistols or revolvers.

gun′fīre, *n.* 1. the firing of a gun or guns.
2. the time set for the ceremonial firing of an artillery piece, as at retreat in the evening.
3. the use of firearms or artillery, as distinguished from other military tactics.

gun′flint, *n.* a piece of flint in the hammer of a flintlock, for striking a spark to set off the charge.

gung hō, [Chin.] work together: slogan of some units of United States Marines in World War II.

gun′jȧh, *n.* same as *ganjah.*

guñk, *n.* [perh. from goo, and *junk.*] any oily, viscous, or thick, messy substance. [Slang.]

gun′lock, *n.* the firing mechanism of a gun.

gun′măn, *n.*; *pl.* **gun′men,** 1. a man armed with a gun, especially for criminal purposes; an armed gangster or thug.
2. a person who makes guns.

gun′-met′ăl, *a.* dark-gray: also *gun-metal gray.*

gun met′ăl, 1. a copper alloy formerly used for making cannon.
2. any of several metals or alloys treated to resemble this.
3. dark gray; the color of tarnished gun metal: also *gun-metal gray.*

gun moll, the mistress or female accomplice of a gunman, or gangster. [Slang.]

Gun′när, *n.* [ON. *Gunnarr,* from *gunnr,* older form of *guthr,* war, battle.] in Norse legend, the brother of Gudrun, husband of Brynhild, and brother-in-law of Sigurd.

gun′nel, *n.* a small, slimy fish of the blenny family, found in the North Atlantic.

gun′nel, *n.* a gunwale.

gun′nẽr, *n.* 1. a soldier, sailor, etc. who fires or helps fire an artillery piece.
2. in the United States Navy, a warrant officer having charge of a ship's guns.
3. a person who uses firearms, especially in hunting.
4. the loon.
5. the sea bream.

gun′nẽr·y, *n.* 1. heavy guns.
2. the science of making and using heavy guns and projectiles.
3. the use or firing of heavy guns.

gun′ning, *n.* the act of hunting or shooting with a gun.

gun′nung, *n. Eucalyptus robusta,* a gum tree of Australia.

gun′ny, *n.*; *pl.* **gun′nieṣ,** [Bengali *gona* or *goni,* a gunny bag.]
1. a strong, coarse fabric made from jute or hemp, used for sacks and bags.
2. a sack or bag made of this: also *gunny sack* (or *bag*).

gun′ny çloth, gunny.

gū·noç′rȧ·cy, *n.* same as *gynecocracy.*

gun pit, an excavated emplacement to protect artillery from enemy fire.

gun plāy, an exchange of shots, as between gunmen and police.

gun′point, *n.* the muzzle of a gun.
at gunpoint; under threat of being shot with a gun.

gun pōrt, a porthole for the muzzle of a gun.

gun′pow″dẽr, *n.* an explosive mixture of saltpeter, sulfur, and charcoal, reduced to fine powder, then granulated and dried, used as a charge in cartridges, shells, etc., for blasting, and in firecrackers.
Gunpowder Plot; in English history, a plot to blow up the Houses of Parliament on Nov. 5, 1605.
gunpowder tea; a fine species of green tea, a carefully picked hyson, the leaves of which are rolled and rounded into pellets.

gun rọọm, 1. quarters on the after portion of the lower gun deck of a British warship, occupied by the junior officers.
2. a room where a collection of guns is kept and displayed.

gun′run·nẽr, *n.* a person who engages in gunrunning.

gun′run·ning, *n.* the smuggling of guns and ammunition into a country.

gun′ship, *n.* a heavily armed helicopter used to support ground troops and assault enemy ground forces.

gun′shot, *n.* 1. the range of a gun; the distance that a projectile from a firearm will carry.
2. the act of firing a gun; the discharge of a gun. [Rare.]
3. shot fired from a gun.

gun′shot, *a.* made by the shot of a gun; as, a *gunshot* wound.

gun′-shȳ, *a.* terrorized at the report of a gun.

gun′smith, *n.* one who makes or repairs small firearms.

gun′smith·ẽr·y, *n.* the business of a gunsmith; the art of making small firearms.

gun′stẽr, *n.* one who uses a gun. [Rare.]

gun′stick, *n.* a rammer or ramrod; a stick or rod to ram down the charge of a musket, etc.

gun′stock, *n.* the wooden handle or butt in which the barrel of a gun is fixed.

gun′stōne, *n.* a cannon ball. [Obs.]

gun taç′kle, the blocks and pulleys affixed to the sides of a gun carriage and the side of a ship, by means of which a gun might be run up to or drawn back from a porthole.

Gun′tẽr's chāin, [named after its inventor, Edmund *Gunter,* 1581–1626, Eng. mathematician.] see *chain,* sense 5.

Gun′tẽr'ṣ līne, in logarithms, (a) a line on Gunter's scale, used for performing the multiplication and division of numbers mechanically by the dividers: called also *line of lines* and *line of numbers*; (b) a sliding scale corresponding to logarithms for performing these operations by inspection without dividers: called also *Gunter's sliding rule.*

Gun′tẽr's quad′rănt (kwod′), a quadrant made of wood, brass, or other substance, a kind of stereographic projection on the plane of the equator, the eye being supposed in one of the poles. It is used to find the hour of the day, the sun's azimuth, etc., and to take the altitude of an object in degrees.

Gun′tẽr'ṣ sçāle, a scale having various lines upon it, both natural and logarithmic, used in solving mechanically problems in navigation and surveying.

Gun′thẽr (-tẽr), *n.* [G., from Germanic *gund-, gunt-,* battle, and *har-,* army.] in the Nibelungenlied, a king of Burgundy, brother of Krienhild and husband of Brunhild.

gun′wāle, gun′nel, *n.* [late ME. *gonne walle*; first applied to bulwarks supporting a ship's guns.]
1. the upper edge of a ship's side; the uppermost wale of a ship, or that piece of timber which extends on either side from the quarterdeck to the forecastle.
2. a piece of timber around the top side of a boat, and having oarlocks for the oars.

gup′py, *n.*; *pl.* **gup′pieṣ,** [after R. J. L. *Guppy,* of Trinidad, who first provided specimens for the British Museum.] a tiny, freshwater fish found in Barbados, Trinidad, and Venezuela: it is often kept in aquariums because of its brilliant coloring.

gũrġe, *n.* a whirlpool. [Rare.]

gũr′ġeŏnṣ, *n.pl.* grudgings; coarse meal. [Obs.]

gũr·gi·tā′tion, *n.* [L. *gurgitare,* to flood, from *gurges* (*-itis*), a whirlpool.] a boiling or surging, as of liquid.

gũr′gle, *v.i.*; gurgled, *pt., pp.*; gurgling, *ppr.* [L. *gurgulio,* the throat, from *gurges,* a whirlpool.]
1. to flow with a bubbling or rippling sound, as water from a narrow-necked bottle.
2. to make a bubbling or rippling sound; as, a baby *gurgles.*

gũr′gle, *v.t.* to utter with a gurgling sound.

gũr′gle, *n.* 1. the act of gurgling.
2. the sound made by a liquid flowing from the narrow mouth of a vessel, or through any narrow opening; the sound made when air is forced through a liquid.

gũr′glet, *n.* same as *goglet.*

gũr′gling·ly, *adv.* in a gurgling manner.

gũr′goyle, *n.* a gargoyle.

gũr′jun, *n.* [E. Ind.] 1. a liquid balsam obtained from East Indian trees of genus *Dipterocarpus,* used in medicine, paints, and varnishes.
2. the tree, *Dipterocarpus alatus,* yielding liquid balsam.

Gũr′kha, *n.* one of a warlike Rajput people, of Hindu faith, living in the mountains of Nepal, Asia.

gũr′nărd, *n.*; *pl.* **gũr′nărdṣ, gũr′nărd,** [ME. *gurnard*; OFr. *gournauld,* a gurnard, from *grogner*; L. *grunnire,* to grunt.] a spiny-finned sea fish having a large head covered with plates of bone, and large, winglike, pectoral fins, each of which has three fingerlike feelers.

GRAY GURNARD (*Trigla gurnardus*)

gũr′net, *n.*; *pl.* **gũr′nets, gũrnet,** gurnard.

gur′rȧh, *n.* [E. Ind.] a kind of plain, coarse India muslin.

gur′ry, *n.* 1. fish offal.
2. the refuse matter from cutting up a whale and trying out the oil.
3. diarrhea. [Obs.]

gur′ry, *n.* [Hind. *garhī,* a small fort.] in India, a small native fort.

gũrt, *n.* in mining, a trench; a gutter.

gũrts, *n.pl.* groats. [Obs.]

gu̇′ru̇, *n.* [Hind., from Sans. *guru,* heavy, weighty, honored.] a Hindu spiritual guide or teacher.

gu̇′ru̇ nut, the kola nut.

gush, *v.i.*; gushed, *pt., pp.*; gushing, *ppr.* [ME. *guschen,* to gush; O.D. *guysen,* to flow out with a gurgling sound; compare Ice. *gusa,* to gush.]
1. to flow out suddenly and plentifully; pour out; spout.
2. to have a sudden, plentiful flow of blood, tears, etc. (often followed by *with*).
3. to express oneself with exaggerated enthusiasm or feeling; talk or write effusively. [Colloq.]

gush, *v.t.* to cause to flow out suddenly and plentifully.

gush, *n.* 1. a sudden, plentiful outflow of a fluid or the like from an enclosed place; also, the fluid, etc. thus emitted; as, a *gush* of melody.
2. a display of exaggerated enthusiasm or feeling; effusive talk or writing. [Colloq.]

gush′ẽr, *n.* 1. one who gushes.
2. anything sending forth a copious stream of liquid; specifically, a drilled oil well which spouts without being pumped.

gush′i·ly, *adv.* in a gushy manner.

gush′i·ness, *n.* the quality of being gushy.

gush′ing, *a.* 1. rushing forth with violence, as a fluid; flowing copiously; as, *gushing* waters.
2. effusive.

gush′ing·ly, *adv.* in a gushing manner.

gush′y, *a.*; *comp.* gushier; *superl.* gushiest, given to or characterized by gush (*n.,* 2); effusive.

gus′set, *n.* [OFr. *gousset,* dim. of *gousse,* a husk, pod.]
1. a piece of chain mail or a metal plate protecting the opening of a joint in a suit of armor.
2. a triangular or specially shaped piece inserted in a garment, glove, etc. to make it stronger or roomier.
3. a triangular metal brace for reinforcing the corner or angle of something.
4. in heraldry, a mark of abatement; a gore.

gus′set, *v.t.* to furnish with a gusset.

gust, *n.* [Ice. *gustr,* a gust, blast, from *gjosa,* to gush, break out.]
1. a sudden, strong rush of air or wind.
2. a sudden burst of rain, smoke, fire, sound, etc.
3. an outburst of laughter, rage, etc.

gust, *n.* [L. *gustus,* a taste.]
1. taste; tasting, or the sense of tasting; the pleasure of tasting; relish; gusto.
2. pleasure; enjoyment.
3. turn of fancy; intellectual taste.
[Archaic in all senses.]

gust, *v.t.* to taste; to have a relish for. [Scot.]

gust′ȧ·ble, *a.* 1. that may be tasted; tastable. [Rare.]
2. pleasant to the taste. [Rare.]

gust′ȧ·ble, *n.* something gustable. [Rare.]

gus·tā′tion, *n.* [L. *gustatio* (*-onis*), from *gustare,* to taste.]
1. the act of tasting.
2. the sense of taste.

gus′tȧ·tive, *a.* gustatory.

gust′ȧ·tō·ry, *a.* pertaining to gust, or taste; as, the *gustatory* qualities of food.

gust′fụl, *a.* gusty; windy; squally.

gust′fụl, *a.* tasteful; well-flavored. [Obs.]

gust′fụl·ness, *n.* relish. [Obs.]

gust′i·ly, *adv.* in a gusty manner.

gust′i·ness, *n.* a gusty quality or state.

gust′less, *a.* tasteless. [Obs.]

gus′tō, *n.*; *pl.* **gus′tōṣ,** [It. and Sp., from L. *gustus*, taste.]

1. taste; liking.

2. keen enjoyment; enthusiastic appreciation; zest; relish.

3. artistic style.

gụs·tō′sō, *a.* and *adv.* [It., from *gusto*, L. *gustus*, taste.] in music, with taste; tastefully: a direction to the performer.

gust′y, *a.*; *comp.* gustier; *superl.* gustiest; subject to sudden blasts of wind; stormy; tempestuous.

Syn.—blustering, squally, stormy, windy.

gut, *n.* [ME. *gutte*; AS. *guttas*, pl., from base of *geotan*, to pour.]

1. [*pl.*] the bowels; entrails: now generally regarded as an indelicate usage.

2. all or part of the alimentary canal; intestine.

3. tough cord made from animal intestines, used for violin strings, surgical sutures, etc.; catgut.

4. the little bag of silk removed from a silkworm before it has spun its cocoon: it is made into strong cord for use in fishing tackle.

5. a narrow passage or gully, as of a stream or path.

6. [*pl.*] the basic, inner or deeper parts. [Colloq.]

7. [*pl.*] (a) pluck; courage; perseverance; (b) impudence; presumptuousness; effrontery; (c) force; power; effectiveness. [Slang.]

hate someone's guts; to hate someone intensely. [Slang.]

gut, *v.t.*; gutted, *pt.*, *pp.*; gutting, *ppr.* 1. to take out the intestines of; to eviscerate.

2. to destroy the interior of, as by fire.

Gụ′ten·bẽrg Bī′ble, a Latin Bible produced at Mainz, Germany, sometime before 1456, reputedly printed by Johannes Gutenberg (1398?–1468). It is generally regarded as the earliest book printed in movable metal type.

Gụth′rụn, *n.* same as *Gudrun*.

gut′less, *a.* lacking courage, daring, perseverance, etc. [Slang.]

guts′y, *a.*; *comp.* gutsier; *superl.* gutsiest, full of guts; daring, courageous, forceful, plucky, etc. [Slang.]

gut′tȧ, *n.*; *pl.* **gut′tae,** [L., a drop.]

1. in pharmacy, a drop.

2. any of a group of small, droplike ornaments on a Doric entablature.

3. in zoology, a droplike spot or marking.

gutta serena; in medicine, same as *amaurosis*.

gut′tȧ, *n.* 1. gutta-percha.

2. the main constituent of gutta-percha, a white, amorphous, gummy substance.

gut′tȧ-pẽr′chȧ, *n.* [Malay *gĕtah*, gum, and *pĕrca*, tree from which it is obtained; form influenced by L. *gutta*, a drop.] a rubberlike substance formed by the milky juice of certain trees of Malaysia, used in electric insulation, dentistry, golf balls, etc.

BRANCH OF GUTTA-PERCHA TREE (*Isonandra gutta*)

gut′tāte, *a.* [L. *guttatus*, from *gutta*, a drop.]

1. spotted, as with drops.

2. in the form of drops.

gut′tā·ted, *a.* guttate.

gut′té (gut′ā), **gut′ty,** *a.* [OFr. *gouté*; L. *guttatus*, spotted, from *gutta*, a drop.] in heraldry, sprinkled with liquid drops.

gut′tẽr, *n.* [ME. *gotere*; OFr. *gutiere*, a channel to receive the drippings from the roof, a gutter, from L. *gutta*, a drop.]

1. a channel for carrying off rain water along or under the eaves of a roof; an eaves trough.

2. a channel or passage for carrying off surface water at the side of a road, street, etc.

3. a channel or groove similar to a gutter, as a groove in cabinetwork, the channel on either side of a bowling alley, etc.

4. in Australia, the bottom of the channel of a river of the Tertiary Period, containing deposits of gold.

5. in printing, the space in a form which produces the inside margins between two printed pages.

6. [*pl.*] mud; mire; dirt. [Scot.]

7. a place or state of living characterized by dirt, poverty, and squalor.

gut′tẽr, *v.t.*; guttered, *pt.*, *pp.*; guttering, *ppr.* 1. to cut or form into narrow channels or grooves, as by the flow of a liquid.

2. to provide with gutters.

3. to carry off, as by a gutter. [Rare.]

gut′tẽr, *v.i.* 1. to flow in a stream.

2. to melt rapidly so that the wax or tallow runs off in channels: said of a candle.

gut′tẽr·ing, *n.* 1. the act of making gutters.

2. material for gutters.

3. a system or set of gutters.

4. the melting and running of wax or tallow on a burning candle.

gut′tẽr·snīpe, *n.* [orig. (Brit. dial.), the common snipe: so called from picking food out of gutters.]

1. a poor, neglected child who spends most of his time in the streets; slum child; street urchin: contemptuous term. [Colloq.]

2. a small bill for advertising purposes: so called because formerly it was pasted to a curbstone.

3. Wilson's snipe, *Gallinago wilsoni*.

gut′tẽr spout, a pipe which carries off the water from a gutter.

gut′ti·fẽr, *n.* [L. *gutta*, drop, and *ferre*, to bear.] a plant that exudes gum or resin.

Gut·tif′e·rae, *n.pl.* [L. *gutta*, a drop, and *ferre*, to bear.] a small order of exogenous trees and shrubs, native to humid, tropical regions: they are generally acrid and yield a yellow gum resin.

gut·tif′ẽr·ăl, *a.* of or pertaining to the *Guttiferæ*; gum-bearing.

gut·tif′ẽr·ous, *a.* yielding gum or resinous substances.

gut′ti·fọrm, *a.* [L. *gutta*, a drop, and *forma*, form.] in the shape of a drop.

gut′tle, *v.t.* and *v.i.*; guttled, *pt.*, *pp.*; guttling, *ppr.* [prob. from *gut*, and *guzzle*.] to eat greedily; gormandize.

gut′tlẽr, *n.* a greedy eater; a glutton.

gut′tū·lȧ, *n.*; *pl.* **gut′tū·lae,** [L., dim. of *gutta*, a drop.] in biology, a small drop or speck of color.

gut′tū·lāte, *a.* marked with small drops.

gut′tū·lous, *a.* in the form of small drops. [Obs.]

gut′tur·ăl, *a.* [L. *guttur*, the throat.]

1. of the throat.

2. loosely, produced in the throat; rasping: said of sounds.

3. characterized by such sounds; as, a *guttural* language.

4. formed by placing the back of the tongue close to or against the soft palate, as the *k* in *keen*; velar.

gut′tur·ăl, *n.* 1. a velar sound.

2. a symbol representing such a sound.

gut′tur·ăl·iṣm, *n.* a guttural manner of speaking.

gut·tur·al′i·ty, *n.* the quality of being guttural.

gut′tur·ăl·īze, *v.t.*; gutturalized, *pt.*, *pp.*; gutturalizing, *ppr.* to utter gutturally.

gut′tur·ăl·ly, *adv.* in a guttural manner.

gut′tur·ăl·ness, *n.* the quality of being guttural.

gut′tur·ine, *a.* pertaining to the throat. [Obs.]

gut′tur·īze, *v.t.* [L. *guttur*, the throat.] to utter in a gutteral manner. [Rare.]

gut′ty, *a.* same as *gutté*.

gut′ty, *a.*; *comp.* guttier; *superl.* guttiest, same as *gutsy*. [Slang.]

gut′wọ̈rt, *n.* a plant of southern Europe, *Globularia alypum*, used as a purgative.

guȳ (gī), *n.* [OFr. *guye*, *guie*, a guide, a crane, from *guier*, to guide.] a rope, chain, rod, etc. used to steady anything.

guȳ, *v.t.*; guyed, *pt.*, *pp.*; guying, *ppr.* [Fr. *guier*, to guide.] to steady, stay, or direct by means of a guy.

guȳ (gī), *n.* [after *Guy* Fawkes (1570–1606), Eng. conspirator executed for his part in the Gunpowder Plot.]

1. in England, an effigy of Guy Fawkes displayed and burned on the anniversary of the Gunpowder Plot.

2. a person whose appearance or dress is odd.

3. a boy or man; fellow; chap. [Slang.]

guȳ, *v.t.* to tease; to ridicule. [Colloq.]

gūze, *n.* [OFr. *gueules*, gules.] in heraldry, a roundlet of sanguine tint, representing an eyeball.

guz′zle, *v.i.* and *v.t.*; guzzled, *pt.*, *pp.*; guzzling, *ppr.* [perh. from OFr. *gosillier*, from *gosier*, throat, from Gallic. *geusiae*, throat.] to drink (or, rarely, eat) greedily or immoderately.

guz′zle, *n.* 1. an insatiable thing or person.

2. a debauch; a drinking bout. [Dial.]

guz′zlẽr, *n.* one who guzzles; an immoderate drinker.

gwyn′i·ad, gwin′i·ad, *n.* [W. *gwyniad*, the fish called whiting, a whitening, from *gwyn*, white.] a fresh-water fish of the whitefish family, *Coregonus pennanti*, abundant in Wales and in many lakes on the continent of Europe: also called *fresh-water herring*, *schelly*, and *powan*.

gȳ′ăl, gȳ′ăll, *n.* same as *gayal*.

gȳ·ăs·çū′tus, *n.* an imaginary animal of gigantic size with legs longer on one side for walking around hills.

ġyb, ġȳbe, *n.* a jib. [Obs.]

ġȳbe, *n.* in nautical usage, a jibe.

ġȳbe, *v.t.* and *v.i.* in nautical usage, to jibe.

ġȳe, *v.t.* to guide. [Obs.]

ġȳle, *n.* [Fr. *guiller*, to ferment.]

1. wort for beer or vinegar.

2. a vat for fermenting beer or vinegar; a wort tub.

3. the amount made at a single brewing.

ġym, *n.* 1. a gymnasium. [Colloq.]

2. a course in gymnastics, athletics, etc., in school or college. [Colloq.]

ġym·khä′nȧ (-kä′), *n.* [Anglo-Ind.; prob. combination of *gymnasium*, and Hind. and Urdu *gēd-khānā*, racket court.]

1. a place where athletic contests or games are held.

2. a sports meet.

ġymn-, see *gymno-*.

ġym·nan′thous, *a.* [*gymn-*, and Gr. *anthos*, flower.] in botany, having neither sepals nor petals; without a perianth.

ġym·nā′ṣi·ȧ, *n.* alternative plural of *gymnasium*.

ġym·nā′ṣi·ärch, *n.* [L. *gymnasiarchus*; Gr. *gymnasiarchos*; *gymnasion*, gymnasium, and *archein*, to rule.] in ancient Greece, one of the officials annually appointed to supervise athletic games, contests, and schools, and paid by the athletes' trainers.

ġym·nā′ṣi·ȧst, *n.* 1. a student in a European Gymnasium.

2. a gymnast.

ġym·nā′ṣi·um, *n.*; *pl.* **ġym·nā′ṣi·umṣ, ġym·nā′ṣi·ȧ,** [L. *gymnasium*; Gr. *gymnasion*, the place where exercises were practiced, from *gymnazein*, to train naked; *gymnos*, naked, stripped.]

1. a place where athletic exercises are performed.

2. [G–] (*G.* gim-nä′zi-oom), in Germany and some other European countries, a secondary school for students preparing to enter a university: name adopted by 15th-century humanists.

3. in ancient Greece, an institution which at first was simply an open place for athletic exercises, but to which were added baths, porticos, and chambers where lectures and the schools of philosophers were held.

ġym′nast, *n.* [Gr. *gymnastēs*, a trainer of athletes, from *gymnazein*, to train in athletic exercises.] one who is skilled in gymnastic exercises.

ġym·nas′tiç, ġym·nas′tiç·ăl, *a.* [L. *gymnasticus*; Gr. *gymnastikos*, from *gymnazein*, to train in athletic exercises.]

1. of physical or athletic exercises or activities.

2. figuratively, relating to mental exercises.

3. athletic. [Rare.]

ġym·nas′tiç, *n.* 1. a gymnast. [Obs.]

2. athletic exercise; athletics.

ġym·nas′tiç·ăl·ly, *adv.* in a gymnastic manner.

ġym·nas′tiçs, *n. pl.* 1. athletic exercises; especially, exercises that can be done in a gymnasium; calisthenics.

2. [*construed as sing.*] the art or sport of such exercises.

ġym′niç, ġym′niç·ăl, *a.* gymnastic; athletic. [Rare.]

ġym′nīte, *n.* [Gr. *gymnos*, bare, naked, and *-ite*; so called from Bare Hills in Maryland, where it is found.] a whitish amorphous mineral; hydrous silicate of magnesia.

ġym′no-, [from Gr. *gymnos*, naked.] a combining form meaning *naked, bare, stripped*, as in *gymno*carpous, *gymno*cyte: also, before a vowel, *gymn-*.

Ġym·nō·blas′tē·ȧ, *n.pl.* [*gymno-*, and Gr. *blas-*

tos, a germ.] a suborder of hydroid polyps with naked buds.

ġym·nō·blas′tiç, *a.* of or characteristic of the *Gymnoblastea.*

ġym·nō·çär′pous, *a.* [*gymno-*, and Gr. *karpos*, fruit.] in botany, having naked fruit.

ġym·nō·cid′i·um, *n.*; *pl.* **ġym·nō·cid′i·ȧ,** [Gr. *gymnos*, naked, and dim. *-idion.*] in botany, the swelling occasionally found at the base of the spore case in urn mosses.

Ġym·noç′lā·dus, *n.* [*gymno-*, and Gr. *klados*, a branch.] a genus of leguminous trees having but one species, *Gymnocladus canadensis*, the Kentucky coffee tree: the wood is hard, compact, and of a fine rose color; the seeds are sometimes used as a substitute for coffee.

Ġym·nō·cō′pȧ, *n.pl.* [*gymno-*, and Gr. *kōpē*, an oar.] a group of *Annelida* whose cephalic appendages only are provided with movable chitinous spines.

ġym·noc′y·tȧ, *n.* [*gymno-*, and Gr. *kytos*, a hollow.] a nucleated cell having no cell wall.

ġym′nō·cȳte, *n.* same as *gymnocyta.*

ġym·nō·cȳ′tōde, *n.* [*gymno-*, and Gr. *kytos*, a hollow, and *eidos*, form.] a nonnucleated cytode without a cell wall.

ġym′nō·dont, *n.* [*gymn-*, and Gr. *odous*, *odontos*, a tooth.] any of a group of fishes, including the globefishes, in which the projecting beak is covered with numerous dental plates.

ġym′nō·gen, *n.* [*gymno-*, and Gr. *-genēs*, producing.] in botany, a gymnosperm.

ġym′nō·ġēne, *n.* [*gymno-*, and Gr. *genys*, chin.] a hawk of the genus *Polyboroides*, found in Africa.

ġym·noġ′e·nous, *a.* [*gymno-*, and Gr. *-genēs*, producing.]
1. in zoology, hatched naked, as certain birds.
2. in botany, with naked seeds; gymnospermous.

Ġym·nō·glos′sȧ, *n.pl.* [*gymno-*, and Gr. *glōssa*, the tongue.] a division of free-swimming modified mollusks in which the radula and jaws are lacking.

Ġym·nō·gram′mē, *n.* [*gymno-*, and Gr. *grammē*, a mark, line.] an extensive genus of ferns, native to warm regions, having the undersurface of the fronds coated with a yellow or silvery powder: also called *gold fern*, *silver fern.*

ġym·noġ′y·nous, *a.* [*gymno-*, and Gr. *gynē*, a female.] in botany, having a naked ovary.

Ġym·nō·lae′mȧ·tȧ, *n.pl.* [*gymno-*, and Gr. *laimos*, the throat.] in zoology, an order of the *Polyzoa*, in which the mouth does not have the valvular structure epistome.

Ġym·nō·nō′tī, *n.pl.* [*gymno-*, and Gr. *nōton*, the back.] a suborder of fishes without dorsal or ventral fins, as the electric eel, *Gymnotus electricus.*

ġym·nō·paed′iç, *a.* [*gymno-*, and Gr. *pais*, *paidos*, boy, child.] in zoology, gymnogenous; hatched naked.

Ġym·nō·phī′ō·nȧ, *n pl.* [*gymn-*, and Gr. *ophis*, a serpent.] an order of tailless amphibians with a long, snakelike body: the limbs are either lacking or rudimentary.

Ġym·noph·thal′mȧ·tȧ, *n.pl.* [*gymn-*, and Gr. *ophthalmos*, the eye.] a family of *Medusæ* (the naked-eyed medusae) having a disk-shaped body, circulating vessels running to the margin, and eye specks either uncovered or lacking.

ġym′nō·plast, *n.* [*gymno-*, and Gr. *plastos*, formed, from *plassein*, to form.] a naked cell or mass of protoplasm.

ġym·nō·rhī′năl, *a.* [*gymno-*, and Gr. *rhis*, *rhinos*, the nose.] in ornithology, having nostrils without feathers.

Ġym·nō·sō′mȧ·tȧ, *n.pl.* [*gymno-*, and Gr. *sōma*, *sōmatos*, the body.] an order of pteropods in which the body is not protected by a shell.

ġym·nos′ō·phist, *n.* [L. *gymnosophistæ*; Gr. *gymnosophistai*, the naked philosophers of India; *gymnos*, naked, and *sophistēs*, a philosopher.]
1. a member of an ancient Hindu sect of ascetics who wore little or no clothing.
2. a person who practices nudism; nudist.

ġym·nos′ō·phy, *n.* the doctrines of the gymnosophists.

ġym′nō·spērm, *n.* [*gymno-*, and Gr. *sperma*, a seed.] any of a large class of plants producing naked seeds, as the conifers.

Ġym·nō·spēr′mae, *n.pl.* in botany, a subdivision of exogens having naked ovules, including the *Cycadaceæ*, *Coniferæ*, and *Gnetaceæ.*

ġym·nō·spēr′măl, *a.* relating to gymnosperms.

ġym·nō·spēr′mous, *a.* of, pertaining to, or resembling the gymnosperms; having naked seeds, or seeds not enclosed in a capsule or ovary.

ġym′nō·spōre, *n.* [*gymno-*, and Gr. *sporos*, a sowing, seed.] in botany, a naked spore.

ġym·nos′pō·rous, *a.* in botany, having naked spores.

ġym·nos′tō·mous, *a.* [*gymno-*, and Gr. *stōma*, a mouth.] in botany, without a peristome, as in certain mosses.

Ġym·not′ō·çȧ, *n.pl.* [*gymno-*, and Gr. *tokos*, offspring, from *tiktein*, *tekein*, to bring forth.] the *Gymnoblastea.*

Ġym·nō′tus, *n.* [Gr. *gymnos*, naked, bare, and *nōton*, the back.]
1. a genus of South American fresh-water fishes including the electric eel, *Gymnotus electricus.*
2. [g-] a fish of this genus.

ġȳn-, (*or* jin; *sometimes* gin), same as *gyno-*.

ġȳn·ae·cē′um, *n.*; *pl.* **ġȳn·ae·cē′ȧ,** [L. *gynæceum*; Gr. *gynaikeion*, the women's apartment, from *gynaikeios*, of or belonging to women, from *gynē*, a woman.]
1. the women's quarters in an ancient Greek or Roman house, which were usually the remotest part of a building, lying beyond an interior court.
2. in botany, a gynoecium.

ġȳ·nae′ciăn, *a.* same as *gynecian.*

ġȳn′ae·cō-, see *gyneco-*.

ġȳn′ae·ō-, see *gyneo-*.

ġȳ·nan′dēr, *n.* a plant of the Linnean class *Gynandria.*

Ġȳ·nan′dri·ȧ, *n.pl.* in the Linnean system of classification, a class of plants whose stamens and pistil are consolidated into a single body.

ġȳ·nan′dri·ăn, *a.* relating to the *Gynandria.*

ġȳ·nan′drō·morph, *n.* an animal having one side male and the other side female.

ġȳ·nan·drō·mor′phişm, *n.* [Gr. *gynē*, a female, and *anēr*, *andros*, a man, male, and *morphē*, form, and *-ism.*] in entomology, the condition of having one side male and the other female.

ġȳ·nan·drō·mor′phous, *a.* characterized by gynandromorphism.

ġȳ·nan′drō·phōre, *n.* [Gr. *gynē*, a female, *anēr*, *andros*, a male, and *pherein*, to bear.] a gynophore bearing stamens as well as pistils, as certain capers.

ġȳ·nan′drous, *a.* [Gr. *gynandros*, of doubtful sex, from *gynē*, a woman, and *anēr*, *andros*, a man.]
1. in botany, having the stamen, or male organ, and pistil, or female organ, united in one column.
2. characterized by gynandry.

ġȳ·nan′dry, *n.* [*gyn-*, and Gr. *anēr*, *andros*, a man.] hermaphroditism.

ġȳ·nan′thēr·ous, *a.* [*gyn-*, and Gr. *anthēros*, flowering, from *anthos*, a flower.] having the stamens converted into pistils, as in certain flowers.

ġȳn′är·çhy, *n.* [*gyn-*, and Gr. *archē*, a government, from *archein*, to rule.] government by a woman or women.

ġȳn′ē-, see *gyneco-*.

ġȳn·ē·cē′um, *n.* same as *gynaeceum.*

ġȳ·nē′ciăn, *a.* [Gr. *gynē*, a woman.] pertaining to women.

ġȳ·nē′ciç, ġȳ·nae′ciç, *a.* [Gr. *gynaikikos*, from *gynē*, a woman.] pertaining to or characteristic of the female sex; female.

ġȳn·ē′ci·um, *n.*; *pl.* **ġȳn·ē′ci·ȧ,** same as *gynaeceum.*

ġȳn′ē·çō- (*or* jin′ē-kō; *sometimes* gī′nē-kō), [Gr. *gynaiko-*, from *gynē*, a woman.] a combining form meaning *woman, female*, as in *gyneco*cracy, *gyneco*logy: words beginning with *gyneco-* may also be spelled *gynaeco-*.

ġȳn·ē·çoç′rȧ·cy, *n.*; *pl.* **ġȳn·ē·çoç′rȧ·cieş,** [Gr. *gynaikokratia*, government by women; *gynē*, a woman, and *kratos*, power, from *kratein*, to rule.] government by a woman or women: also spelled *gynaecocracy.*

ġȳn″ē·çō·loġ′iç, *a.* of gynecology.

ġȳn″ē·çō·loġ·iç·ăl, ġȳn″ae·çō·loġ′iç·ăl, *a.* pertaining to gynecology.

ġȳn·ē·çol′ō·ġist, ġȳn·ae·çol′ō·ġist, *n.* one skilled in gynecology.

ġȳn·ē·çol′ō·ġy, ġȳn·ae·çol′ō·ġy, *n.* [*gyneco-*, and Gr. *-logia*, from *legein*, to speak.] the branch of medicine dealing with the study and treatment of women's diseases, especially of the genitourinary and rectal tracts.

ġȳn·ē′çō·mas·ty, ġȳn·ae′çō·mas·ty, *n.* [*gyneco-*, and Gr. *mastos*, the breast.] abnormal development of the breasts in a male.

ġȳn·ē″çō·mor′phous, *a.* [*gyneco-*, and *-morphous.*] having the form or structural characteristics of a woman or female.

ġȳn″ē·çō·nī′tis, ġȳn″ae·çō·nī′tis, *n.* [Gr. *gynaikōnitis*, a gynaeceum.] a place or apartment reserved for women; a gynaeceum.

ġȳn″ē·çō·path′iç, ġȳn″ae·çō·path′iç, *a.* relating to diseases prevalent among women.

ġȳn·ē·çop′ȧ·thy, ġȳn·ae·çop′ȧ·thy, *n.* [*gyneco-*, and Gr. *pathos*, suffering.] any disease to which women only are subject.

ġȳn′e·ō-, (*or* jin′i-ō), [Gr. *gynaios*, from *gynē*, a woman.] a combining form meaning *woman*: words beginning with *gyneo-* may also be spelled *gynaeo-*.

ġȳn·ē·oç′rȧ·cy, ġȳn·ae·oç′rȧ·cy, *n.* same as *gynecocracy.*

ġȳn·ē·ol′ȧ·try, ġȳn·ae·ol′ȧ·try, *n.* [Gr. *gynē*, a woman, and *latreia*, worship.] excessive fondness for or adoration of women.

ġȳn·ē·phō′bi·ȧ, ġȳn·ae·phō′bi·ȧ, *n.* [*gynē-*, and Gr. *phobos*, fear.] dislike or fear of women; aversion to women.

ġȳn·i·at′riçs, *n.pl.* [*construed as sing.*] [*gyn-* and *-iatrics.*] the branch of medicine dealing with the treatment of women's diseases.

ġȳn·ō- (*or* jin′ō), [from Gr. *gynē*, woman.] a combining form meaning: (a) *woman, female*; (b) *female reproductive organ, ovary, pistil*, as in *gyno*ecium, *gyno*phore. Also, before a vowel, *gyn-*, as in *gyn*archy.

ġȳn′ō·bāse, *n.* [*gyno-*, and Gr. *basis*, base.] an enlargement of the base or receptacle of a flower, supporting the gynoecium.

ġȳn·ō·bā′siç, *a.* characteristic of or pertaining to a gynobase.

ġȳ·noç′rȧ·cy, *n.* gynecocracy.

gyn″ō·dī·oe′cious, *a.* [*gyno-*, and Gr. *di-*, two, and *oikos*, a house.] designating a plant bearing both pistillate and perfect flowers on different individuals.

ġȳ·noe′ci·um, *n.* [*gyno-*, and Gr. *oikos*, house.] the pistils of a flower; the female organ or organs of a flower.

ġȳn″ō·mō·noe′cious, ġȳn″ō·mō·nē′cious, *a.* [*gyno-*, and Gr. *monos*, alone, single, and *oikos*, a house.] having flowers of the female and perfect forms growing on the same plant, but none of the male.

ġȳn′ō·phōre, *n.* [*gyno-*, and Gr. *-phoros*, from *pherein*, to bear.]
1. in botany, a stalk bearing the gynoecium.
2. in zoology, one of the branches bearing the female gonophores of a hydrozoan.

ġȳn·ō·stē′ġi·um, *n.*; *pl.* **ġȳn·ō·stē′ġi·ȧ,** [*gyno-*, and Gr. *stegē*, a roof.] in botany, a covering of any kind of the gynoecium; a perianth.

ġȳn·ō·stē′mi·um, *n.*; *pl.* **ġȳn·ō·stē′mi·ȧ,** [Gr. *gynē*, woman, and *stemon*, warp.] in botany, the column formed by the combining of the stamens and style in orchids.

-ġy·nous, [Mod. L. *-gynus*; Gr. *-gynos*, from *gynē*, a woman.] a combining form meaning: (a) *woman, female*, as in poly*gynous*; (b) *having female organs* or *pistils*, as in mono*gynous*, andro*gynous.*

-ġy·ny, a combining form used to form nouns corresponding to adjectives ending in *-gynous.*

ġyp, *n.* [prob. from *gypsy.*]
1. a swindle; cheat. [Slang.]
2. a swindler. [Slang.]
Also spelled *gip.*

ġyp, *v.t.* and *v.i.*; gypped, *pt.*, *pp.*; gypping, *ppr.* to swindle; cheat. Also spelled *gip.* [Slang.]

ġyp, *n.* [prob. from *gypsy.*] a servant at a college. [Brit.]

ġyp′sē·ous, *a.* [L. *gypseus*, from *gypsum*, gypsum.]
1. like gypsum.
2. containing or consisting of gypsum.

ġyp·sif′ēr·ous, *a.* [L. *gypsum*, gypsum, and *ferre*, to bear.] containing or producing gypsum.

ġyp·soġ′rȧ·phy, *n.* [Gr. *gypsos*, gypsum, and *graphein*, to write, draw.] writing or drawing on gypsum, or the art of engraving on gypsum.

ġyp·soph′i·lȧ, *n.* [Mod. L.; *gypsum* and *-phil.*] any of a group of plants bearing clusters of small white or pink flowers with a delicate fragrance, as babies'-breath.

ġyp′sō·plast, *n.* [Gr. *gypsos*, chalk, gypsum, and *plassein*, to mold.] a cast made of plaster of Paris.

ġyp′sum, *n.* [L. *gypsum*; Gr. *gypsos*, chalk,

gypsum.] a hydrated sulfate of calcium, $CaSO_4 \cdot 2H_2O$: it often occurs in transparent crystals, or crystalline masses, easily splitting into plates, and is then called *selenite*; when white, fine-grained, and translucent, it constitutes *alabaster*; burned to drive off the water, and ground up, it forms *plaster of Paris*.

ġyp′sy, *n.*; *pl.* **ġyp′sieṣ,** [earlier *gypcien*, short for *Egipcien*, Egyptian: so called because thought to have come from Egypt.]
1. [often G–] a member of a wandering Caucasian people with dark skin and black hair, found throughout the world and believed to have originated in India: they are known as musicians, fortune-tellers, etc.
2. [G–] their Indo-European, Indic language, probably based on a dialect of northwestern India; Romany.
3. a person whose appearance or habits are like those of a gypsy.

ġyp′sy, *a.* of or like a gypsy or gypsies.

ġyp′sy, *v.i.*; gypsied, *pt.*, *pp.*; gypsying, *ppr.* to wander or live like a gypsy: also spelled *gipsy*.

ġyp′sy hẽrb (ẽrb), the gypsywort.

ġyp′sy·iṣm, *n.* the conditions or characteristics of gypsy life.

ġyp′sy moth, a European moth, brownish or white, now common in the eastern United States: its larvae feed on leaves, doing much damage to trees and plants.

ġyp′sy winch, a small winch having a ratchet and a pawl and operated by a crank.

ġyp′sy·wŏrt, *n.* any plant of the genus *Lycopus*, family *Labiatæ*. The common gypsywort, or water hoarhound, yields a black dye said to be used by gypsies to make their skin darker.

ġȳ′răl, *a.* [L. *gyrus*, a circle.]
1. whirling; moving in a circular or spiral path.
2. in anatomy, pertaining to a gyrus, or convolution of the brain.

ġȳ′rāte, *a.* 1. winding or going round as in a circle; revolving in a spiral course.
2. in botany, coiled in a circle; circinate.
3. in anatomy, having convolutions.

ġȳ′rāte, *v.i.*; gyrated, *pt.*, *pp.*; gyrating, *ppr.* [L. *gyratus*, pp. of *gyrare*, to turn, whirl, from *gyrus*; Gr. *gyros*, a circle.] to revolve round a central point, as a tornado; to move in a circular or spiral path; to revolve; to whirl.

ġȳ·rā′tion, *n.* [LL. *gyratio* (*-onis*), from L. *gyratus*, pp. of *gyrare*, to turn, from *gyrus*, a circle.]
1. a turning or whirling round; a circular or spiral motion; rotation about an axis.
2. in zoology, a whorl on a spiral univalve shell.
center of gyration; see under *center*.
radius of gyration; the distance between the axis of a rotating body and its center of gyration.
Syn.—circular motion, revolution, rotation.

ġȳ·rā′tŏr, *n.* a person or thing that gyrates.

ġȳ′rā·tō·ry, *a.* moving in a circular or spiral path; whirling; spiraling.

ġȳre, *n.* [L. *gyrus*; Gr. *gyros*, a circle.]
1. a circular or spiral motion; whirl; revolution.
2. a circular or spiral form; vortex.

ġȳre, *v.t.* and *v.i.* to turn round; to whirl. [Rare.]

Ġyr·en·ceph′ȧ·lȧ, *n.pl.* [Gr. *gyros*, a circle, and *enkephalos*, the brain.] one of four subclasses of mammalians which have convoluted cerebra.

ġyr·en·ceph′ȧ·lāte, *a.* gyrencephalous.

ġyr·en·ceph′ȧ·lous, *a.* of or pertaining to the *Gyrencephala*.

ġȳ·rēne′, *n.* [prob. from *GI* (galvanized iron) Marine.] a member of the United States Marine Corps: originally derogatory. [Slang.]

ġyr′fal″çŏn (jũr′fal″ *or* jũr′fa″), **ġẽr′fal″çŏn,** *n.* [ME. *gerfaucon*, from OFr. *gerfaucon*, lit. spear falcon.] any of several large falcons of the arctic regions of Europe, Asia, and America: they are large birds varying in color from dark to almost white.

ġȳ′rī, *n.* pl. of *gyrus*.

ġȳ′rō, *n.* 1. an autogiro. [Colloq.]
2. a gyroscope. [Colloq.]
3. a gyrocompass. [Colloq.]

ġȳ′rō-, [from Gr. *gyros*, a circle.] a combining form meaning: (a) *gyrating*, as in *gyro*scope; (b) *spiral*, as in *gyro*idal; (c) *gyroscope*, as in *gyro*compass.

ġȳ′rō·çŏm″pȧss, a compass consisting mainly of a motor-driven gyroscope whose rotating axis, kept in a horizontal plane, takes a position parallel to the axis of the earth's rotation and thus points to the geographic north pole instead of the magnetic pole.

ġȳ·rog′ō·nīte, *n.* [*gyro-*, and Gr. *gonos*, offspring, seed.] a petrified spiral seed vessel of plants of the genus *Chara*, found in freshwater deposits.

ġȳ·roid′ăl, *a.* [Gr. *gyroeidēs*, like a circle; *gyros*, a circle, and *eidos*, form.] spiral in arrangement or action, as (a) in crystallography, having certain planes arranged spirally, so that they incline all to the right or all to the left of a vertical line; (b) in optics, turning the plane of polarization circularly or spirally to the right or left.

ġyr′ō·man·cy, *n.* [*gyro-*, and Gr. *manteia*, divination.] a kind of divination performed by walking round in a circle or ring.

ġȳ·rom′i·trȧ, *n.* a species of poisonous fungus.

ġȳ′rŏn·ny, ġī′rŏn·ny, *a.* [Fr. *gironne*, from *giron*, a gyron.] in heraldry, designating or of a field that is divided into triangular parts or gyrons of two different tinctures.

GYRONNY

ġȳ′rō·pi·ġeŏn, *n.* a clay pigeon, used as a mark in shooting matches.

ġȳ′rō·pī·lŏt, *n.* an instrument that automatically keeps an airplane flying evenly at the same height on a set course: it consists of two vacuum-driven gyroscopes: also called *automatic pilot*.

ġȳ′rō·plāne, *n.* an aircraft resembling the autogiro: the pitch of the blades of its horizontal propeller can be changed by rotating the blades around their axes.

ġȳ′rō·sçōpe, *n.* [*gyro-*, and Gr. *skopein*, to view.] a wheel mounted in a ring so that its axis is free to turn in any direction: when the wheel is spun rapidly, it will keep its original plane of rotation no matter which way the ring is turned: gyroscopes are used in gyrocompasses and to keep moving ships, airplanes, etc. level.

GYROSCOPE

ġȳ·rō·sçop′iç, *a.* pertaining to the gyroscope or resembling its motion.

ġȳ·rō·sçop′i·çăl·ly, *adv.* by means of a gyroscope.

ġȳ·rōse′, *a.* marked with wavy lines or convolutions.

ġȳ″rō·stā′bil·ī·zẽr, *n.* a motor-driven gyroscope used in an airplane or a ship to reduce the rocking and swaying caused by air currents or rough water.

ġȳ′rō·stat, *n.* [*gyro-*, and Gr. *statikos*, stationary, from *histanai*, to stand.] a gyroscope consisting of a rotating wheel set in a case, used for demonstrating the dynamics of rotating bodies.

ġȳ·rō·stat′iç, *a.* 1. of a gyrostat.
2. of gyrostatics.

ġȳ·rō·stat′içs, *n.* the branch of physics dealing with rotating bodies and their tendency to maintain their plane of rotation.

ġȳ′rō·wheel, *n.* the main rotating flywheel of a gyroscope.

ġȳ′rus, *n.*; *pl.* **ġȳ′rī,** [L., from Gr. *gyros*, a circle, ring.] in anatomy, a convolution, as of the brain.

ġȳve, *n.* [of Celtic origin; compare W. *gefyn*, a fetter, Ir. *geimheal*, chains, fetters.] a shackle, usually for the legs; a fetter: chiefly in the plural. [Archaic.]

ġȳve, *v.t.*; gyved; *pt.*, *pp.*; gyving, *ppr.* to fetter; to shackle; to chain.

H

H, h (āch), *n.*; *pl.* **H's, h's, Hs, hs** (āch′iz),
1. the eighth letter of the English alphabet: from the Greek *eta*, a borrowing from the Phoenician.
2. the sound of H or h, phonetically a rough breathing (aspirate): in English, a glottal fricative in which the glottis gradually narrows toward the position for voicing the following vowel while the tongue and lips assume the position for articulating it; in many words originally from French, as *honor*, *honest*, initial *h* is silent.
3. a type or impression for H or h.
4. *a symbol for* the eighth in a sequence or group.

H, h (āch), *a.* 1. of H or h.
2. eighth in a sequence or group.

H (āch), *n.* 1. an object shaped like H.
2. a Roman numeral for 200: with a superior bar ($\overline{H}$), 200,000.
3. in chemistry, *the symbol for* hydrogen.
4. in music, the German name for the note B natural.
5. in physics, *the symbol for*: (a) henry; (b) the horizontal component of terrestrial magnetism.

H (āch), *a.* shaped like H.

hä, häh, *interj.* [echoic.] an exclamation variously expressing wonder, surprise, anger, triumph, etc.: repeated (*ha-ha*, or *haw-haw*!) it indicates laughter, derision, etc.

hä, häh, *n.* the sound of the exclamation *ha* or of a laugh.

hä, *v.i.* to express hesitation or embarrassment by the interjection *ha*; as, to hum and *ha*.

ha, *v.* a contracted form of *have*. [Now Dial.]

ha, *n.* a hall. [Scot.]

häaf, *n.* [ON. *haf*, high sea, ocean.] deep-sea fishing waters off the Shetland and Orkney Islands.

häaf bōat, a boat used in haaf fishing.

häak, *n.* same as *hake*.

häar, *n.* a fog or mist; a driving east wind, accompanied by mist. [Scot.]

Hȧ·bak′kuk, *n.* [Heb. *ḥabhaqqug*; prob. from *ḥābaq*, to embrace.] in the Bible, (a) a Hebrew prophet of about the seventh century B. C.; (b) a book of the Old Testament containing his prophecies. Also, in the Douay Bible, *Habacuc*.

hä·bȧ·ne̜′rȧ, *n.* [Sp., lit., of *Habana* (Havana).]
1. a slow Cuban dance similar to the tango.
2. the music for this.

hā′bē·ȧs çor′pus, [L., (that) you have the body.] in law, a writ or order requiring that a prisoner be brought before a court at a stated time and place to decide the legality of his detention or imprisonment: the right of *habeas corpus* safeguards one against illegal detention or imprisonment.

Hab·ē·nā′ri·ȧ, *n.* [Mod. L., from L. *habena*, thong.] an extensive genus of terrestrial tuberous-rooted orchids, widely distributed through the temperate and tropical regions of both hemispheres.

hā·ben′dum, *n.*; *pl.* **hā·ben′dȧ,** [L., gerund of *habere*, to have.] the second part of a deed or conveyance (following the premises or first part) or that part which determines the extent of the estate or interest conveyed or granted: so called because it begins with the words "to have and to hold," in the old Latin form *habendum et tenendum*.

hab′ẽr·dash·ẽr, *n.* [ME. *haberdashere*; prob. from Anglo-Fr. *hapertas*, kind of cloth.]

1. a person whose work or business is selling men's furnishings, such as hats, shirts, neckties, handkerchiefs, gloves, etc.

2. a dealer in various small articles, such as ribbons, lace, thread, needles, etc., or, formerly, caps and hats. [Chiefly Brit.]

hab′ẽr·dash·ẽr·y, *n.*; *pl.* **hab′ẽr·dash·ẽr·ieṣ,**
1. things sold by a haberdasher.
2. a haberdasher's shop.

hab′ẽr·dīne, *n.* salted and dried codfish. [Obs.]

hab′ẽr·ġeŏn, *n.* [OFr. *haubergeon*, dim. of *hauberc*, a coat of mail.] a coat of mail or armor to protect the neck and breast, formed of little iron rings united, and descending from the neck to the middle of the body; a short hauberk.

hȧ·bil′ȧ·tō′ry, *a.* [Fr. *habiller*, to clothe.] pertaining to clothes or habiliments; wearing clothes. [Rare.]

hab′ile, *a.* [OFr. *habile*; L. *habilis*, suitable, fit, from *habere*, to have, hold.] able; skillful; handy; clever.

hȧ·bil′i·ment, *n.* [Fr. *habillement*, from *habiller*, to clothe, from *habile*, fit, suitable.] a garment; a piece of clothing: usually in the plural, *habiliments*, denoting dress or attire in general.

hȧ·bil′i·ment·ed, *a.* clothed; furnished with habiliments.

hȧ·bil′i·tāte, *v.t.*; habilitated, *pt.*, *pp.*; habilitating, *ppr.* [LL. *habilitatus*, pp. of *habilitare*, to make suitable, to qualify, from L. *habilis*, suitable, fit.]

1. to clothe; equip; outfit.

2. to furnish (a mine) with equipment and supplies.

hȧ·bil′i·tāte, *v.i.* [from G. *habilitieren*.] to become qualified, as for an office or position: specifically, to qualify for teaching in a German university.

hȧ·bil′i·tāte, *a.* qualified or entitled. [Obs.]

hȧ·bil·i·tā′tion, *n.* [ML. *habilitatio*.] a habilitating or being habilitated.

hȧ·bil′i·tā·tŏr, *n.* one who habilitates; specifically, one who furnishes the equipment for developing mining property.

hȧ·bil′i·ty, *n.* the quality of being habile.

hab′it, *n.* [ME. *habit*; OFr. *habit*; L. *habitus*, condition, appearance, dress, from *habere*, to have, hold.]

1. costume; dress.

2. a particular costume showing rank, status, etc.; specifically, (a) a distinctive religious costume; as, a monk's *habit*; (b) a costume worn for certain occasions; as, a woman's riding *habit*.

3. habitual or characteristic condition of mind or body; disposition; as, a man of healthy *habit*.

4. a thing done often and hence, usually, done easily; practice; custom; act that is acquired and has become automatic.

5. a tendency to perform a certain action or behave in a certain way; usual way of doing; as, he does it out of *habit*.

6. an addiction; as, the alcohol *habit*.

7. in biology, the tendency of a plant or animal to grow in a certain way; characteristic growth; as, a twining *habit*.

Syn.—custom, practice, usage, tendency, garb, costume.

hab′it, *v.t.*; habited, *pt.*, *pp.*; habiting, *ppr.*
1. to dress; to clothe; to array.

They *habited* themselves like rural deities.
—Dryden.

2. to inhabit. [Archaic.]

hab′it, *v.i.* to dwell; to reside. [Obs.]

hab·it·ȧ·bil′i·ty, *n.* habitableness.

hab′it·ȧ·ble, *a.* [OFr. *habitable*; L. *habitabilis*, from *habitare*, to dwell.] capable of being inhabited or dwelt in; capable of sustaining human beings; as, the *habitable* world; some climates are scarcely *habitable*.

hab′it·ȧ·ble·ness, *n.* the state of being habitable.

hab′it·ȧ·bly, *adv.* in a habitable manner.

hab′it·ȧ·çle, *n.* 1. a dwelling; a habitation. [Obs.]

2. an alcove; a niche for a statue. [Obs.]

hab′it·ănce, *n.* dwelling; abode; residence. [Obs.]

hab′it·ăn·cy, *n.* 1. inhabitancy; dwelling; residing.

2. inhabitants collectively; population.

hab′it·ănt, *n.* [Fr. *habitant*; L. *habitans* (*-antis*), ppr. of *habitare*, to dwell.]

1. an inhabitant; a dweller; a resident.

2. (*Fr. pron.* ȧ-bē-toṅ′), a farmer in Canada or Louisiana of French descent: also written *habitan*.

hab′i·tat, *n.* [L.] 1. habitation; the natural abode or locality of an animal, plant, etc.

2. the place where a person or thing is ordinarily found.

hab·i·tā′tion, *n.* [L. *habitatio*, from *habitare*, to dwell, freq. of *habere*, to have, hold.]

1. the act of inhabiting or the state of being inhabited; occupancy.

2. place of abode; a settled dwelling; a house or other place in which to live.

The Lord blesseth the *habitation* of the just.
—Prov. iii. 33.

Syn.—dwelling, abode, house, occupancy.

hȧ·bit′ū·ăl, *a.* [LL. *habitualis*, pertaining to habit or dress, from L. *habitus*, condition, habit, appearance.]

1. formed or acquired by habit, frequent use, or custom; customary; done or caused by habit.

It is the distinguishing mark of *habitual* piety to be grateful for the most common blessings. —Buckminster.

2. being or doing a certain thing by habit; steady; inveterate.

3. usual; frequent; much seen, done, or used.

Syn.—regular, ordinary, perpetual, customary, usual, familiar, accustomed, wonted.

hȧ·bit′ū·ăl·ly, *adv.* in a habitual manner; customarily; by frequent practice or use; as, *habitually* profane; *habitually* kind and benevolent.

hȧ·bit′ū·ăl·ness, *n.* the state or quality of being habitual.

hȧ·bit′ū·āte, *v.t.*; habituated, *pt.*, *pp.*; habituating, *ppr.* [LL. *habituatus*, pp. of *habituare*, to bring into a condition or habit of the body, from L. *habitus*, habit.]

1. to accustom; to make familiar by frequent use or practice; as, men *habituate* themselves to the taste of tobacco.

2. to settle as an inhabitant. [Obs.]

3. to attend or visit often; to frequent. [Colloq.]

hȧ·bit′ū·āte, *a.* inveterate by custom; formed by habit; usual; habitual. [Obs.]

hȧ·bit·ū·ā′tion, *n.* the act of habituating or the state of being habituated.

hab′i·tūde, *n.* [Fr. *habitude*; L. *habitudo*, condition, habit.]

1. habitual or characteristic condition of mind or body; disposition.

2. familiar relation; familiarity. [Obs.]

To write well, one must have frequent *habitudes* with the best company.—Dryden.

3. customary manner or mode of life; repetition of the same acts; custom; habit.

hȧ·bit′u·é (hȧ-bit′ū-ā; *Fr. pron.* ȧ-bē-tü-ā′), *n.* [Fr., properly pp. of *habituer*, to accustom.] a habitual frequenter of any place, especially one of amusement; as, a club *habitué*.

hab′i·tūre, *n.* habitude. [Obs.]

hab′i·tus, *n.* [L.] 1. in natural history, superficial appearance without regard to structure; facies, as of a plant, animal, or mineral.

2. in medicine, constitutional disposition or tendency.

hab′nab, *adv.* at random; by chance; without order or rule; also written *hab or nab*. [Now Dial.]

hab′rō·nēme, *a.* [Gr. *habros*, delicate, and *nēma*, thread.] having the form of fine threads.

hȧ·çhūre′ (*or* hash′ūr), *n.* [Fr., from *hacher*, to chop, from *hache*, ax.] any of a series of short, thin, parallel lines used, especially in mapmaking, to represent a sloping or elevated surface.

hȧ·çhūre′, *v.t.*; hachured, *pt.*, *pp.*; hachuring, *ppr.* to cover with hachures.

hä·ci·en′dȧ, *n.* [Sp., from OSp. *facienda*, employment, estate; L. *facienda*, things to be done, from *facere*, to do.] in Spanish America, (a) a large estate, ranch, plantation, or house in the country; (b) a farm, factory, mine, etc. in the country.

hack, *n.* [originally, a board on which a falcon's meat was put; a form of *hatch*.]

1. a grated frame; specifically, (a) a hatch; a wicker or grated door; (b) a rack from which cattle are fed; (c) a rack on which fish, bacon, cheese, etc. are dried; (d) a set of wooden bars in the tailrace of a mill; (e) a place for drying bricks before they are burned; hence, a row of unburnt bricks laid out to dry.

2. in falconry, the tray from which a young hawk is fed; hence, figuratively, the partial liberty allowed young hawks.

hack, *v.t.* 1. to arrange (unburnt bricks) in rows for drying.

2. in falconry, to allow (a hawk) partial liberty.

hack, *v.t.*; hacked, *pt.*, *pp.*; hacking, *ppr.* [ME. *hacken*, *hakken*; AS. *haccian*, to hew, cut.]

1. to cut or chop irregularly, in a bungling or aimless manner; to mangle with repeated strokes; to notch; as, to *hack* a desk.

2. to utter with stops or catches; to mangle, as language. [Obs.]

3. to dress, as a stone, with a hack hammer.

4. in Rugby football, to kick (another player), especially on the shin.

5. to notch (a tree) in order to release the sap.

6. to break up, as clods of earth.

7. in basketball, to foul by striking the arm of (an opponent who has the ball) with the hand or arm.

8. to deal with or carry out successfully. [Slang.]

to hack it; to carry out or manage something successfully. [Slang.]

hack, *v.i.* 1. to chop or cut in a clumsy or unskillful way; to make a hack or hacks.

2. to give harsh, dry coughs.

3. to stutter; to hesitate in speaking; to stammer. [Obs.]

4. to drudge; to toil slavishly; to work laboriously.

hack, *n.* 1. a gash, slash, or notch; a cut; specifically, a notch made in a tree in blazing a path through a forest.

2. a pickax; a mattock; a hack iron.

3. a dry, broken cough.

4. in Rugby football, a kick on the shin; also, a bruise caused by such a kick.

hack, *n.* [abbrev. of *hackney*.]

1. a horse for hire.

2. a horse for all sorts of work.

3. a saddle-horse.

4. an old, worn-out horse.

5. a person hired to do routine, often dull, writing; literary drudge.

6. a carriage or coach for hire; hence, a taxicab.

7. a hackman.

8. a worker for a political party, usually holding office through patronage, who serves party leaders devotedly and unquestioningly.

hack, *a.* 1. employed as a hack; as, a *hack* writer.

2. done by a hack; as, *hack* work.

3. stale; trite; hackneyed.

hack, *v.t.* to let out for hire, as a horse.

hack, *v.i.* 1. to be exposed or offered to common use for hire.

2. to drudge, as a literary hack.

3. to ride at the ordinary pace of a horse for exercise or pleasure.

4. to drive a taxicab. [Colloq.]

hack′ȧ·mōre, *n.* [compare Sp. *jaquima*, headstall of a halter.] in the western United States, a halter, the nosepiece of which may be so tightened as to serve as a headpiece.

hack′ber″ry, *n.*; *pl.* **hack′ber″rieṣ,** a North American tree, *Celtis occidentalis*, resembling the elm, bearing small, sweet, edible fruit resembling the cherry.

2. a hagberry; a bird cherry.

hack′but, *n.* [Fr. *haquebut*, *haquebute*, from obs. D. *hakebus*; *hake*, *haak*, hook, and *bus*, a gun, gun barrel, lit., box.] an obsolete type of portable firearm with a bent or hooked butt; kind of harquebus: also *hagbut*.

hack′ee, *n.* [so called from the noise it makes.] the chipmunk.

hack′ẽr, *n.* one who or that which hacks; specifically, a tool for notching trees to release the sap.

hack′ẽr·y, *n.* a cart drawn by oxen.

hack ham′mẽr, a tool like an adz with a hammerhead, used in dressing stone.

hack′i·ȧ, *n.* a tree of British Guiana, *Ixora triflorum*, which grows to a height of thirty feet and is valued for its hard wood.

hack′ing, *a.* harsh and dry: said of a cough.

haç′kle, *n.* [orig., *hatchel*; (late) ME. *hakell*, var. of *hechele*: so called from resemblance to a *hatchel*.]

1. (a) any of the long, slender feathers at the neck of a rooster, peacock, pigeon, etc.; (b) such feathers, collectively.

2. in fishing, (a) a tuft of feathers from a rooster's neck, used as the legs of an artificial fly; (b) a hackle fly.

3. [*pl.*] the hairs on a dog's neck and back that bristle, as when it is in danger.

haç′kle, *v.t.*; hackled, *pt., pp.*; hackling, *ppr.*

1. to separate, as the coarse part of flax or hemp from the fine, by drawing through the teeth of a hackle or hatchel.

2. to tear asunder; to cut roughly; to hack.

haç′kle flȳ, an artificial fishing fly with a hackle instead of wings.

haç′kly, *a.*; *comp.* hacklier; *superl.* hackliest.

1. rough; broken, as if hacked.

2. in mineralogy, having fine, short, and sharp points on the surface; as, a *hackly* fracture.

hack′măn, *n.*; *pl.* **hack′men,** the driver of a hack.

hack′mȧ·tack, *n.* [Am. Ind. (Algonquian).]

1. the American larch; tamarack.

2. the juniper.

3. the wood of either of these trees.

4. a natural bend in a tamarack used in boatbuilding for the stem or framing of a boat: also *hackmatack joint.*

hack′ney, *n.* [ME. *hakene, hakenei*, from *Hackney*, England.]

1. a horse for ordinary driving or riding.

2. a carriage for hire.

3. a person hired for dull, monotonous work; drudge.

hack′ney, *a.* 1. let out for hire.

2. much used; trite; as, a *hackney* author or remark.

hack′ney, *v.t.*; hackneyed, *pt., pp.*; hackneying, *ppr.* 1. to exhaust by heavy work, as a horse. [Obs.]

2. to hire out.

3. to make trite by overuse.

hack′ney çōach, a four-wheeled carriage drawn by two horses and seating six persons.

hack′ney çōach′măn, a man who drives a hackney coach.

hack′nēyed, *a.* [pp. of *hackney*.] made trite and commonplace by overuse; as, "raven hair" is a *hackneyed* phrase.

hack′ney·măn, *n.*; *pl.* **hack′ney·men,** a man who lets horses and carriages for hire.

hack′sa̤w, *n.* a hack saw.

hack sa̤w, a saw for cutting metal, consisting of a narrow, fine-toothed blade held in a frame.

HACK SAW

hack′stẽr, *n.* a bully; a ruffian or assassin. [Obs.]

haç′que·tŏn (-ke-), *n.* same as *acton*.

had, *v.* past tense and past participle of *have*.

had′dẽr, *n.* heather. [Scot.]

had′die, *n.* a haddock. [Scot.]

had′dō, *n.* the humpbacked salmon.

had′dŏck, *n.* [ME. *hadok, haddok*; prob. from OFr. *hadot*, kind of salt fish.] a small, edible fish, related to the cod, found off the coasts of Europe and North America.

HADDOCK

hāde, *n.* [probably from dial. *hade*, to incline, slope.]

1. the descent of a hill.

2. in mining, (a) the steep descent of a shaft; (b) the slope of the fracture line between two portions of faulted or dislocated strata; the inclination or deviation of a vein from a vertical direction.

hāde, *v.i.* in mining, to deviate from a perpendicular line of descent; to slope: said of a vein.

Hā′dēş, *n.* [Gr. *Haidēs*.]

1. in Greek mythology, (a) the home of the dead, beneath the earth; (b) the ruler of the underworld: also called *Pluto, Dis*.

2. in the Bible, the state or resting place of the dead: used especially in the Revised Version of the New Testament.

3. [*often* h-] hell: a euphemism. [Colloq.]

Had′ith, *n.* [Ar. *hadith*, tradition.] a legend; a tradition; the appendix to the Koran containing traditions relating to Mohammed.

hadj, *n.* [Ar. *hajj*, a pilgrimage, from *hajja*, to set out, go on a pilgrimage.]

1. the pilgrimage to Mecca that every Moslem is expected to take at least once.

2. any pilgrimage.

hadj′ī, haj′jī, *n.* [Ar. *hājjī*, a form of *hājj*, a pilgrim, from *hajja*, to go on a pilgrimage.]

1. a Moslem who has performed his pilgrimage to Mecca: used as a title of honor.

2. a Christian of the Near East who has visited the Shrine of the Holy Sepulchre in Jerusalem.

Hā′dri·ăn′ş wa̤ll, a masonry wall in the north of England, built by order of the Roman Emperor, Hadrian, about 125 A. D.: it was 75 miles long, from 7 to 10 ft. high, and extended between the Solway and the Tyne.

had′rōme, *n.* [Gr. *hadros*, thick.] in botany, the woody portion of a fibrovascular bundle; the xylem.

Had·rō·sa̤u′rus, *n.* [Gr. *hadros*, thick, and *sauros*, lizard.] a Cretaceous genus of extinct dinosaurian reptiles of higher organization than living reptiles generally, attaining a size of over thirty feet, with a broad ducklike bill containing many small teeth.

hadst, *v.* archaic second person singular, past tense of *have*: used with *thou*.

hāe, *v.t.* to have. [Scot.]

haeç·cē′i·ty (hek-), *n.* [LL. *haecceitas*, thisness, from L. *haec*, f. of *hic*, this.] literally, the quality of being *this*; thisness; the relation of individuality conceived as a positive attribute or essence.

haem-, haem′a·to-, haem′o-, see *hemo-*.

hae′măl, *a.* hemal.

Hae·man′thus, *n.* [*haem-*, and Gr. *anthos*, a flower.] the bloodflower, a genus of South African bulbous plants of the order *Amaryllidaceæ*, so called from the red color of the corolla and involucre of some species.

hae′mat-, hemat-.

hae·mat′i·num, hē·mat′i·non, *n.* [L., from Gr. *haimatinos*, of blood, bloody, from *haima* (-*atos*), blood.] a red, opaque glass known to the ancients and used for mosaics, ornamental vases, etc. It contains no tin and no coloring matter except cupric oxide.

haem′ȧ·tīte, *n.* hematite.

Haem·ȧ·toç′ry·ȧ (hem-), *n.pl.* [*haemato-*, and Gr. *kryos*, cold.] in zoology, a division of vertebrates comprising all cold-blooded species, as amphibians, reptiles, and fishes, as distinguished from the *Haematotherma*.

Haem·ȧ·tō·phi·lī′nȧ, *n.pl.* [*haemato-*, and Gr. *philos*, loving.] the *Desmodontes*, or blood-sucking vampire bats.

Haem″ȧ·tō·thẽr′mȧ, *n.pl.* [*haemato-*, and Gr. *thermos*, warm.] in zoology, a division of vertebrates, comprising all warm-blooded species, as birds and mammals, as distinguished from the *Haematocrya*.

Haem·ȧ·tox′y·lon, *n.* [*haemato-*, and Gr. *xylon*, wood.] a genus of the *Leguminosæ*, having but one species, *Hematoxylon campechianum*, the logwood tree of Central America, from which the logwood of commerce is obtained.

Haem″ō·dō·rā′cē·ae, *n.pl.* [Gr. *haima*, blood, *dōron*, a gift and *-aceae*.] in botany, an order of monocotyledons, consisting of perennials having fibrous roots and sword-shaped leaves with woolly hairs on stems and flowers. The name refers to the red color yielded by the roots of certain species, as *Sanguinaris canadensis*, the redroot of eastern United States.

haem″ō·dō·rā′ceous, *a.* of or like the *Haemodoraceae*.

hae′mō·glō·bin, *n.* hemoglobin.

hae·mō·phil′i·ȧ, *n.* hemophilia.

hae′rēş, *n.*; *pl.* **hae·rē′dēş,** a heres.

hăf, *v.* obsolete past tense of *heave*.

haf′fle, *v.i.*; haffled, *pt., pp.*; haffling, *ppr.* to speak unintelligibly. [Brit. Dial.]

hä′fiz, *n.* [Ar.] a Moslem who can recite the Koran from memory: used as a title of honor.

haf′ni·um, *n.* [Mod. L., from L. *Hafnia*, ancient name of Copenhagen.] a metallic chemical element found with zirconium and somewhat resembling it: symbol, Hf; atomic weight, 178.6; atomic number, 72.

hȧft, *n.* [ME. *haft, heft*; AS. *hæft*, a handle, from the same root as *habban*, to hold.]

1. a handle; especially, the part of a knife, sword, or dagger by which it is held; a hilt.

2. a place of abode or settlement. [Scot.]

hȧft, *v.t.* to set in a haft; to furnish with a handle.

hȧft′ẽr, *n.* a caviler; a wrangler; a debater. [Obs.]

hag, *n.* [ME. *hagge, hegge*, a witch, hag; AS. *hægtes, hægtesse*, a witch, hag.]

1. a repulsive, malevolent old woman.

2. formerly, a witch; a sorceress; a fury.

3. a cartilaginous vertebrate of the *Marsipobranchii*, *Myxine glutinosa*, parasitic on other fishes. It is about five or six inches long and resembles a small eel. It is allied to the lamprey: also called *hagfish*.

4. a phosphorescent appearance on horses' manes or men's hair. [Obs.]

hag, *v.t.* to harass; to torment; to weary. [Obs.]

hag, *n.* 1. a cutting blow; a hack.

2. branches cut for firewood; also, a quantity of wood cut, or to be cut, by one man.

3. a portion of woodland divided for cutting.

4. a quagmire; boggy ground.

[Scot. and Brit. Dial. in all senses.]

Hā′gär, *n.* [Heb. *haghar*, from base prob. akin to Ar. *hajara*, to forsake.] in the Bible, a concubine of Abraham and slave of Abraham's wife Sarah: Hagar fled into the desert with her son Ishmael to escape Sarah's jealous anger: Gen. xvi.

hag′ber″ry, *n.* the bird cherry. [Scot.]

hag′bo̤rn, *a.* born of a hag or witch.

hag′but, *n.* a hackbut.

hag′den, hag′dŏn, *n.* *Puffinus major*, the greater shearwater, a seabird of the north Atlantic: called also *haglet, hag*, and *hagdown*.

Hȧ′gen, *n.* [G.] 1. in the *Nibelungenlied*, Gunther's uncle who murders Siegfried at the bidding of Brunhild.

2. in Wagner's *Götterdämmerung*, the half-brother of Gunther and Gutrune.

hag′fish, *n.*; *pl.* **hag′fish** or **hag′fish·eş,** [from *hag* (a witch).] any of a number of small, eel-like salt-water fishes (*cyclostomes*) with a round, sucking mouth and horny teeth, with which they bore into other fish and devour them.

Hag·gä′dȧ, Hag·gä′dȧh, *n.*; *pl.* **Hag·gä′doth,** [Heb. *haggadah*, from *hagad*, to tell, relate.]

1. [*often* h-] in the Talmud, an anecdote or parable that explains or illustrates some point of law.

2. the part of the Talmud devoted to such narratives.

3. the narrative of the Exodus read at the Seder during the Jewish Passover.

4. a book containing this narrative and the Seder ritual.

hag·gad′iç, *a.* of or pertaining to the Haggada.

hag·gad′i·căl, *a.* same as *haggadic*.

hag·gä′dist, *n.* a haggadic writer or scholar.

Hag′gā·ī, *n.* [Heb. *haggai*, lit., festal.] a book of the Old Testament attributed to Haggai, a Hebrew prophet who lived about 500 B. C.

hag′gărd, *a.* [OFr. *hagard*, wild, strange, unsociable, lit., of the wood, from M.H.G. *hag*, a hedge, wood.]

1. in falconry, designating a hawk captured after reaching maturity.

2. untamed; unruly; wild.

3. (a) wild-eyed; (b) having a wild, wasted, worn look, as from sleeplessness, grief, illness, hunger, etc.; gaunt; drawn.

hag′gărd, *n.* 1. in falconry, a haggard hawk.

2. a hag. [Obs.]

hag′gărd, *n.* [AS. *haga*, hay, and *geard*, yard.] a stackyard. [Brit. Dial.]

hag′gărd·ly, *adv.* in a haggard manner.

hag′ged, *a.* [from *hag*, an old woman.] like a hag. [Obs.]

hag′gis, *n.* [Scot. *hag*, to chop, cut.] a Scottish dish, commonly made of the heart, lungs, and liver of a sheep, minced with suet, onions, oatmeal, salt, and pepper, and boiled in a bag, usually the stomach of a sheep.

hag′gish, *a.* of, like, or resembling a hag.

hag′gish·ly, *adv.* in a haggish manner.

hag′gle, *v.t.*; haggled, *pt., pp.*; haggling, *ppr.* [a freq. of *hack*, to chop, cut.] to notch or cut in an unskillful manner; to mangle; to hack roughly.

hag′gle, *v.i.* to be difficult in bargaining; to argue about terms, price, etc.; to wrangle.

hag′gle, *n.* a haggling.

hag'glẽr, *n.* 1. one who haggles.
2. in England, a huckster.

hag'i·är·chy (*or* hā'ji-), *n.*; *pl.* **hag'i·är·chies**, 1. government by saints or priests.
2. the hierarchy of saints.

hag'i·ō- (*or* hā'ji-), [from Gr. *hagios*, holy.] a prefix meaning *saintly, sacred, holy*, as in *hagiocracy*: also before a vowel, *hagi-*.

hag·i·oc'rȧ·cy, *n.*; *pl.* **hā·gi·oc'rȧ·cies**, [Gr. *hagios*, sacred, and *-kratia*, from *kratein*, to rule.] rule by priests, saints, or others considered holy; theocracy.

Hag·i·og'rȧ·phȧ, *n.pl.* [LL., from Gr. *hagiographa*, neut. pl. of *hagiographos*; *hagios*, sacred, and *graphein*, to write.] the Jewish division of the Old Testament known as the *Ketubim*, or *writings*, including Ruth, Chronicles, Ezra, Nehemiah, Esther, Job, Psalms, Proverbs, Ecclesiastes, Song of Solomon, Lamentations, and Daniel; all of the Old Testament not in the Law or the Prophets.

hag·i·og'rȧ·phȧl, *a.* pertaining to the Hagiographa.

hag·i·og'rȧ·phẽr, *n.* 1. any writer of the Hagiographa.
2. one who writes the lives of saints.
3. any sacred or holy writer.

hag·i·og'rȧ·phist, *n.* same as *hagiographer*.

hag·i·og'rȧ·phy, *n.* [Gr. *hagios*, sacred, and *-graphia*, from *graphein*, to write.]
1. the writing or study of lives of the saints.
2. a book or books containing such lives.

hag·i·ol'ȧ·tẽr, *n.* a person given to hagiolatry; saint-worshiper.

hag·i·ol'ȧ·try, *n.* [Gr. *hagios*, sacred (L. Gr., a saint), and *latreia*, worship.] saint worship; invocation of saints.

hag·i·ol'ō·gẽr, *n.* a writer of or expert in hagiology.

hag·i·ol'ō·gist, *n.* same as *hagiologer*.

hag·i·ol'ō·gy, *n.*; *pl.* **hag·i·ol'ō·gies**, [Gr. *hagios*, sacred (L.Gr., a saint), and *-logia*, from *legein*, to speak.]
1. literature dealing with the lives and legends of the saints; also, a list of saints.
2. a book or collection of saints' lives and legends.

hag'i·ō·scōpe, *n.* [Gr. *hagios*, sacred, and *skopein*, to view.] an opening in an inside wall of a church to afford a view of the high altar from a chapel or side aisle: also called *squint*.

hag'rid''den, *a.* 1. originally, ridden by a witch or hag.
2. obsessed or harassed, as by fears or nightmares.

hag'seed, *n.* the descendant of a hag.

hag'ship, *n.* the state of being a hag or witch.

hag's tooth, in nautical usage, a part of a matting, pointing, etc. which is interwoven with the rest in an erroneous and irregular manner.

hag tā'pẽr, *Verbascum thapsus*, mullein.

Hāgue Trī·bū'năl (hāg), the Permanent Court of Arbitration created by the "International Convention for the Pacific Settlement of International Disputes," founded in 1899 by the International Peace Conference: it was succeeded in 1922 by the Permanent Court of International Justice which, since 1945, selects the nominees for election to the United Nations International Court of Justice.

häh, *interj.* and *n.* ha.

hä'-hä, hä'hä, *n.* [Fr. *haha*.] a fence, wall, etc. set in a ditch around a garden or park so as not to hide the view from within: also *haw-haw*.

Häh·ne·mann'i·ăn, *a.* of or relating to Samuel C. F. Hahnemann, 1755–1843, the German physician who founded homeopathy.

Häh'ne·măn·nism, *n.* Hahnemannian homeopathy.

Haī'dȧ, *n.* 1. any of a tribe of North American Indians of the Queen Charlotte Islands, British Columbia.
2. their isolated language.

haī'ding·ẽr·īte, *n.* [named after Wilhelm von *Haidinger*, an Austrian mineralogist.] an arsenate of calcium, which is white and transparent, with a vitreous luster and white streak.

Haī'duk (hī'), *n.* [Hung. *hajduk*, pl. of *hajdu*, lit., a drover.] one of a class of mercenary Magyar foot soldiers in Hungary.

hāik, *n.* a tramp. [Scot.]

haīk, haīck, *n.* [Ar. *haik*, from *haka*, to weave.] a large piece of woolen or cotton cloth worn by the Arabs over the tunic but under the burnoose.

haī'kwän', *n.* [Chin., lit., sea gate.] Chinese maritime import duties.

hāil, *n.* [ME. *hayle*; AS. *hægel*, *hagol*, hail.]
1. small, rounded pieces of ice that sometimes fall during thunderstorms; frozen raindrops; hailstones.
2. a falling, showering, etc. of hail, or in the manner of hail; as, a *hail* of explosives.

hāil, *v.i.* to pour down hail.

hāil, *v.t.* to pour down in the manner of hail; as, he *hailed* curses upon us.

hāil, *v.t.* [ME. *hailen*, *heylen*, to salute, greet, from *hail*, *heil*, a salutation.]
1. to call; to call to, as a person at a distance, in order to attract attention.
2. to salute; to name by way of tribute.
3. to shout to in greeting, welcome, etc.; to cheer.

hāil, *v.i.* in nautical usage, to call out or signal to a ship.
to hail from; to be from or come from; as, he *hails from* Havana.

hāil, *n.* 1. a hailing; a greeting; a salutation.
2. the distance that a shout will carry; as, he is within *hail*.

hāil, *interj.* an exclamation of tribute, greeting, etc.

hāil, *a.* [ME. *heil*, *heyl*; Ice. *heill*, whole, sound, healthy.] hale; whole; healthy; sound. [Scot.]

hāil Cō·lum'bi·ȧ, [euphemism for *hell*.]
1. a severe beating, punishment, scolding, etc.; as, your mother will give you *hail Columbia* for coming late. [Slang.]
2. boisterous activity; racket; rumpus; as, the children were raising *hail Columbia* in the schoolroom. [Slang.]

hāil fel'lōw, a pleasant companion; a congenial acquaintance: also *hail-fellow*.

hāil fel'lōw well met, congenial, sociable, or friendly, especially in a superficial manner: also *hail-fellow-well-met*.

hāilse, *v.t.* [ME. *hailsen*; Ice. *heilsa*, to greet.] to salute. [Obs.]

hāil'shot, *n.pl.* small shot which scatter like hail. [Obs.]

hāil'stōne, *n.* a particle of hail.

hāil'storm, *n.* a storm in which hail falls.

hāil'y, *a.* of or accompanied by hail.

hāin, *v.t.* to fence off for meadow. [Brit. Dial.]

hāir, *n.* [ME. *here*, *heer*, *her*; AS. *hær*, a hair.]
1. any of the fine, threadlike outgrowths from the skin on an animal or human being.
2. a growth of these; especially, (a) the growth covering the human head; (b) the growth covering all or part of the skin of most mammals.
3. material woven from hair.
4. anything very small in space, margin, degree, etc.

> If the scale turn
> But in the estimation of a *hair*,
> Thou diest. —Shak.

5. in botany, a threadlike growth on a plant.
6. in mechanics, the spring in a hair trigger.
hair of the dog (*that bit one*); a drink of alcoholic liquor taken to cure a hangover. [Colloq.]
not to turn a hair; to remain unaffected by excitement, surprise, fear, etc.
to a hair; exactly; perfectly.
to have (*or get*) *by the short hairs*; to have (or get) completely at one's mercy. [Slang.]
to split hairs; to argue points of no importance; to cavil about trifles; to quibble.

hāir, *a.* 1. made of or with hair.
2. for the care of the hair; as, *hair* tonic.

hāir'bȧll, *n.* a rounded mass of hair often found in the stomach of cows and other ruminants.

hāir'bell, *n.* same as *harebell*.

hāir'bīrd, *n.* same as *chipping sparrow*.

hāir'brāined, *a.* same as *harebrained*.

hāir'breadth, hāir's'breadth (-bredth), *n.* the diameter or breadth of a hair; a very short distance; an extremely small space; sometimes, specifically, the 48th part of an inch.

hāir'breadth, *a.* exceedingly narrow; as, a *hairbreadth* escape.

hāir brown, a clear red-brown color.

hāir'brush, *n.* a brush for the hair.

hāir cell, in anatomy, one of the cells with hairlike projections in the sensitory epithelium of the internal ear.

hāir'cloth, *n.* cloth woven from horsehair or camel's hair: used mainly for covering furniture.

hāir cŏm'păss·es, a pair of compasses provided with a very precise screw adjustment.

hāir'cut, *n.* 1. a cutting or clipping of the hair of the head.
2. the style in which the hair is cut.

hāir di·vī'dẽrs, same as *hair compasses*.

hāir'-dō, *n.* 1. the style in which (a woman's) hair is arranged; coiffure.
2. a hairdressing.

hāir'dress''ẽr, *n.* one whose work is cutting and dressing (women's) hair.

hāir'dress''ing, *n.* 1. the business or work of a hairdresser.
2. the action of dressing hair.

hāir'dress''ing, *a.* of or for dressing the hair.

hāired, *a.* having hair: used in compounds; as, white-*haired*.

hāir'en, *a.* [AS. *hæren*, from *hær*, hair.] of hair. [Obs.]

hāir grȧss, one of several species of slender-stemmed and slender-leaved grasses.

hāir'i·ness, *n.* the state or quality of being hairy.

hāir'less, *a.* lacking hair; bald; as, *hairless* scalps.

hāir'līne, *n.* 1. a line made of hair.
2. a fine line in writing or drawing.
3. a fabric with fine lines woven lengthwise through it; also, one of such lines.
4. the line that defines the scalp, or the outline of the growth of hair on the head, especially of the hair above the forehead.

hāir moss, a moss with hairy calyptra, belonging to the genus *Polytrichum*.

hāir moth, any moth that feeds on fabrics made of hair, as the *Tineola bisselliella*.

hāir net, a net or fine-meshed cap of silk, etc., for keeping a woman's hair in order.

hāir'piēce, *n.* 1. a toupee or wig.
2. a switch of hair, often styled, for a woman's hairdo.

hāir'pin, *n.* a small, usually U-shaped, piece of wire, shell, etc., for keeping the hair or headdress in place.

hāir'pin, *a.* having a sharp and complete turn; U-shaped; as, a road with a *hairpin* bend.

hāir plāte, the iron plate at the back of the hearth of a bloomery fire.

hāir'-rāis·ing, *a.* causing, or thought of as causing, the hair to stand on end; terrifying; horrifying.

hāir salt, [a translation of G. *haar-salz*.] a variety of native Epsom salts.

hāirs'breadth, hāir's'-breadth (-bredth), *n.* and *a.* same as *hairbreadth*.

hāir sēal, an eared non-fur-producing seal.

hāir shīrt, a shirt made of or lined with harsh hair, worn as a penance.

hāir sieve, a strainer with a bottom of hair-cloth.

hāir spāce, in printing, the thinnest piece of metal used in spacing type, equal to about one-half point.

hāir'split''tẽr, *n.* one who makes trivial distinctions; a quibbler.

hāir'split''ting, *a.* making very minute distinctions; quibbling.

hāir'spring, *n.* a slender coiled spring in a watch or clock, which governs the motion of the balance wheel.

hāir'stōne, *n.* same as *sagenite*.

hāir'strēak, *n.* any of a number of small, usually dark-colored butterflies, family *Lycaenidae*, with each hind wing commonly having narrow taillike projections.

hāir'strōke, *n.* a hairline in writing or printing.

hāir'tāil, *n.* a slender-tailed fish of the genus *Trichiurus*, found in warm seas.

hāir trig'gẽr, a trigger so delicately adjusted that it can be sprung with very slight pressure; also, a secondary trigger with which the trigger that discharges the weapon is worked.

hāir'-trig''gẽr, *a.* quick to spring to action; easily moved; as, he has a *hair-trigger* temper.

hāir'wŏrm, *n.* any of a phylum, *Nematomorpha*, of worms parasitic in insects when immature and free-swimming as adults.

hāir'y, *a.*; *comp.* hairier; *superl.* hairiest, 1. overgrown with hair; covered with hair; abounding with hair.
2. of or resembling hair.

hāir'y·bāit, *n.*, the lugworm, genus *Arenicola*.

hāir'y·head (-hed), *n.* the *Lophodytes cucullatus*, or hooded merganser.

hāir'y vetch, a common, annual, leguminous plant, *Vicia villosa*, with hairy foliage and numerous small blue flowers, grown for forage.

Hāi'ti·ȧn (*or* hā'shăn), *a.* pertaining to Haiti, its people, or culture.

Hāi'ti·ȧn, *n.* 1. a native or inhabitant of Haiti.
2. the French dialect spoken by the Haitians.
Also spelled *Haytian*.

hä'jē, *n.* [Ar. *hayya*, a snake.] the Egyptian cobra or asp.

haj'ī, haj'jī, *n.* same as *hadji.*

hāke, *n.*; *pl.* **hāke** or **hākes,** [Norw. *hakefisk,* lit., a hookfish.]
1. a sea fish of the cod family, *Merlucius vulgaris,* the common European *hake,* in shape somewhat resembling the pike.
2. an edible gadoid fish, the silver hake or whiting, *Merlucius bilinearis.*
3. one of several American fishes of the genus *Phycis.*

HAKE (*Merlucius vulgaris*)

hāke, *n.* a drying frame, or feeding frame.

hāke, *v.i.* to go about idly. [Brit. Dial.]

Hā'kē·ȧ, *n.* [named after Baron *Hake,* a German scientist.] a genus of plants found in Australia, including many species, several of which are cultivated, as the native pear, *Hakea acicularis lissosperma,* and the twine bush, *Hakea flexilis.*

hä·keem', *n.* [Ar. *ḥakēm,* wise, learned, hence physician.] in Moslem regions, a doctor; a physician: also spelled *hakim.*

Hä'ken·kreuz (hä'k'n-kroits), *n.* same as *swastika,* sense 2.

hä·kïm', *n.* [Ar. from *hakama,* to govern.]
1. in Moslem countries, a ruler; a judge.
2. a physician.

hak'kȧ, *n.* [Chinese.] in southern China, an immigrant from northern China, against whom there is much prejudice among the natives.

Hä·lä·käh', Hä·lä·chä' (-khä'), *n.*; *pl.* **Hä·lä·kōth', Hä·lä·chōth',** 1. [*often* h–] in the Talmud, any of the laws or ordinances not written down in the Scriptures but based on an oral interpretation of them.
2. the part of the Talmud devoted to such laws and ordinances.

hä'lȧ·kist, hä'lȧ·chist, *n.* a Hebrew judge or scholar who contributed to the Halakah.

hȧ·lā'tion, *n.* in photography, an undesirable spreading or reflection of light on a negative, appearing like a halo around high lights.

hal'bērd, *n.* [OFr. *halebarde*; M.H.G. *helmbarte,* a halberd, an ax with which to split a helmet; *helm,* handle, helve, and *barte,* an ax.]

HALBERDS

1. an ancient military weapon, consisting of a pole or shaft of wood, having a head armed with a steel point and a crosspiece of steel, flat and pointed at both ends, or with a cutting edge at one end and a bent point at the other.
2. in farriery, an extension on the front of a horseshoe to relieve the foot in lameness.
halberd weed; a plant with leaves in the form of a halberd, found in the West Indies, *Neurolæna lobata.*

hal·bērd·iēr', *n.* [OFr. *halebardier,* from *halebarde,* a halberd.] one who is armed with a halberd or carries a halberd as a symbol of office.

hal'bērd-shāped (-shāpt), *a.* having the shape of a halberd.

hal'bērt, *n.* same as *halberd.*

hal'cy·ŏn, *n.* [L. *halcyon, alcyon*; Gr. *alkyōn,* a kingfisher.]
1. in ancient legend, a bird, believed to have been the kingfisher, which was supposed to have a peaceful, calming influence on the sea at the time of the winter solstice.
2. [H-] in zoology, a genus of Australasian kingfishers.

hal'cy·ŏn, *a.* 1. of the kingfisher.
2. calm; quiet; peaceful; undisturbed; happy.
halcyon days; a number of days occurring about the winter solstice, when the weather is calm; hence, days of peace and tranquillity.

hal·cy·ō'ni·ăn, *a.* halcyon; calm.

hal·cy·on'iç, *a.* same as *alcyonic.*

hal'cy·ō·nine, *a.* of or pertaining to the kingfishers of the genus *Halcyon.*

Hal'dăn·ite, *n.* in ecclesiastical history, a follower of the brothers James Alexander and Robert Haldane, who founded an independent evangelical movement in Scotland early in the nineteenth century.

hāle, *a.* [ME. *heil, heyl*; Ice. *heill,* whole, healthy.] sound; healthy; robust, especially as used of an older person; as, a *hale* body.

hāle, *n.* welfare. [Obs.]

hāle, *v.t.*; haled, *pt., pp.*; haling, *ppr.* [ME. *halen, halien*; AS. *holian, geholian,* to acquire, get.]
1. to pull or draw with force; to drag.
2. to force (a person) to go; as, he was *haled* into court.

hāle, *v.i.* to go or come by drawing or pushing.

hā'lēr, *n.* one who hales.

Hā·lē'si·ȧ, *n.* [after Stephen *Hales,* Eng. botanist.] a genus of low trees of the storax family, *Styricaceæ,* of the southern United States, Japan, and China, bearing clusters of white, bell-shaped flowers, which appear before the leaves.

half (håf), *n.*; *pl.* **hålveṣ** (håvz), [ME. *half*; AS. *healf, half,* half.]
1. either part of a thing which is divided into two equal parts; as, *half* a pound; *half* a tract of land; *half* an orange.
2. either of two approximately equal parts; approximately fifty per cent of a mass or number.
3. in basketball, football, etc., either of the two equal periods of the game, between which the players rest.
4. a term of school; a semester. [Colloq.]

hålf, *a.* 1. being either of the two equal parts.
2. being approximately fifty per cent of a mass or number.
3. partial; incomplete; fragmentary; as, *half* knowledge.

hålf, *v.t.* to divide into halves. [Obs.]

hålf, *adv.* 1. to an extent approximately or exactly fifty per cent of the whole.
2. to some extent; as, I was *half* convinced. [Colloq.]
3. by any means; at all: used with *not*; as, he doesn't *half* approve.

hal'fȧ, *n.* same as *alfa.*

hålf'-and-hålf', *n.* 1. something that is half of one thing and half of another; especially, (a) a mixture of equal parts of milk and cream; (b) a mixture of equal parts of porter and ale, beer and stout, etc.
2. something considered to be neither one thing nor another; indeterminate mixture of two things.

hålf'-and-hålf', *a.* combining things equally.

hålf'-and-hålf', *adv.* in two equal parts.

hålf'-āpe, *n.* a lemur.

hålf'back, *n.* in football, either of the two positions back of the line of scrimmage together with the quarterback and fullback. The players occupying the positions are termed *right halfback* and *left halfback.*

hålf'-bāked' (-bākt'), *a.* 1. not properly baked; hence, inexperienced; stupid.
2. not completely planned or thought out; as, a *half-baked* scheme.

hålf'bēak, *n.* a small, long-bodied tropical sea fish somewhat like the gar, with an extended lower jaw suggesting a bird's beak.

hålf bīnd'ing, a style of bookbinding in which the back and corners are covered with leather or other material different from that of the sides.

hålf blood (blud), 1. relation between persons born of the same father or of the same mother, but not of both; as, a brother or sister of the *half blood.*
2. a half-blood.

hålf'-blood, *n.* [based on the obsolete notion that the blood is the medium of heredity.]
1. a person related to another through one parent only.
2. a person born of parents of different races; half-breed.
Also *half blood.*

hålf'-blood, *a.* half-blooded.

hålf'-blood''ed, *a.* 1. having kinship through one parent only.
2. born of parents of different races.
3. in animal husbandry, having a sire or dam of poor pedigree in contrast to that of the other parent.

hålf bōard, in nautical usage, a maneuver of a sailing vessel to the windward by luffing up into the wind.

hålf bo͝ot, a boot that extends halfway up the lower leg.

hålf'-bound, *a.* having the back and corners bound in material different from that of the sides: said of a book.

hålf box, a box that is open at one side.

hålf'-bred, *a.* 1. half-blooded.
2. not well trained in the niceties of polite behavior.

hålf'-breed, *a.* half-blooded.

hålf'-breed, *n.* a person who has parents of different races; especially, the offspring of an American Indian and a white person.

hålf brŏth'ēr, a brother related through one parent only.

hålf'-çȧste, *n.* a half-breed; specifically, the offspring of one European parent and one Asiatic parent.

hålf'-çȧste, *a.* of, or having the position of, a half-caste.

hålf'çock', *v.t.*; halfcocked, *pt., pp.*; halfcocking, *ppr.* to place (the hammer of a gun) at half cock.

hålf çock, the halfway position of the hammer of a firearm, when the trigger is locked and cannot be pulled.
to go off at half cock; (a) to go off too soon: said of a firearm; (b) to speak or act thoughtlessly or too hastily. Also *to go off half cocked.*

hålf'-çracked' (-krakt'), *a.* half-witted; unsound in mind. [Colloq.]

hålf çrown, a British silver coin worth two shillings and sixpence.

hålf deck, 1. a boat shell of the genus *Crepidula.*
2. the deck immediately under the spar deck and next the mainmast.

hålf'-decked (-dekt), *a.* decked over in part.

hålf dol'lăr, 1. a silver coin of the United States and Canada with a value of fifty cents.
2. a half crown. [Brit. Colloq.]

hålf ēa'gle, a gold coin of the United States, worth $5.00: it is no longer current.

hålf'en, *a.* half. [Obs.]

hålf'en·dēal, *adv.* by half. [Obs.]

hålf'-fāced (-fāst), *a.* showing only part of the face.

hålf fish, a half-grown salmon.

hålf gāin'ēr, a back dive made from the stance for a front dive.

hålf'-god, *n.* a demigod.

hålf'heärt''ed, *a.* wanting in spirit, heart, interest or enthusiasm.

hålf'heärt''ed·ly, *adv.* indifferently; without enthusiasm.

hålf·heärt'ed·ness, *n.* lack of enthusiasm; lack of earnestness.

hålf hitch, a knot made by passing the end of the rope around the rope and then through the loop thus made: it is the simplest kind of hitch: see *knot,* illus.

hålf hol'i·dāy, a half of a day for a holiday.

hålf hōṣe, socks, especially knee-length socks.

hålf'-hour' (-our'), *n.* 1. half of an hour; thirty minutes.
2. the point thirty minutes after any given hour.

hålf'-hour', *a.* 1. lasting for thirty minutes.
2. occurring every thirty minutes.

hålf'-hour'ly, *a.* and *adv.* happening or done every half-hour.

hålf'-length, *a.* 1. of half the full or ordinary length.
2. showing a person from the waist up: said of a portrait.

hålf'-length', *n.* a portrait showing only the upper half of the body.

hålf līfe, in nuclear physics, the period required for the disintegration of half of the atoms in a sample of some specific radioactive substance; as, plutonium 238 has a *half life* of about 50 years.

hålf'-måst', *n.* the position of a flag lowered about halfway down its pole or staff as a sign of mourning or a signal of distress.

hålf'-måst', *adv.* about halfway on the staff.

hålf'-måst', *v.t.* to hang (a flag) at half-mast.

hålf'-mo͞on, *n.* 1. the moon at the quarters, when only half its disk is clearly seen.
2. anything in the shape of a half-moon.
3. in fortification, an outwork composed of two faces, forming a salient angle, whose gorge is in the form of a crescent, or half-moon; a ravelin.

hȧlf'-mọọn', *a.* shaped like a half-moon.
hȧlf mọurn'ing, 1. the second period of mourning; also, mourning dress in which gray, lavender, and other subdued shades are used in place of all black.
2. a common butterfly, *Papilio galatea*, having yellow wings with black and white spots.
hȧlf nel'sŏn, in wrestling, a hold in which one arm is placed under the opponent's arm from behind with the hand pressed against the back of his neck.
hȧlf'ness, *n.* the condition of being half.
hȧlf nōte, in music, a minim; a note having one-half the duration of a whole note.
hȧlf'pāce, *n.* [altered from *halpace*, from MFr. *hault pas*, lit., high step.]
1. a raised platform for a throne, altar, etc., usually at the top of steps.
2. a staircase landing, usually between two half flights.
hȧlf pāy, the reduced pay of a retired army or navy officer.
half'pen·ny (hā'pen-i), *n.*; *pl.* **half'pence** (hā'), **half'pen·nieṣ** (hā'), a British bronze coin of the value of half a penny, or two farthings.
half'pen·ny (hā'pen-i), *a.* 1. of the value of a halfpenny.
2. trifling; insignificant.
hȧlf pīke, a pike having a short shaft.
hȧlf pīnt, 1. a liquid or dry measure equal to ¼ quart.
2. a small person. [Slang.]
hȧlf'-pōrt, *n.* in nautical usage, one half of a portlid, for closing portholes.
hȧlf rāy, a line extending from a point in one direction indefinitely.
hȧlf round, a semicircular molding.
hȧlf'-sēaṣ-ō'vẽr, *a.* half-drunk; tipsy. [Slang.]
hȧlf sis'tẽr, a sister related through one parent only.
hȧlf'-sōle, *v.t.* to repair (shoes or boots) by attaching new half soles.
hȧlf sōle, a sole (of a shoe or boot) from the arch to the toe.
hȧlf sov'ẽr·eign (-in), a British gold coin worth ten shillings.
hȧlf'-stȧff, *n.* same as *half-mast*.
hȧlf step, 1. in military usage, a short marching step of fifteen inches (in double time, eighteen inches).
2. in music, the difference in pitch between any two adjacent keys on the piano; half tone; semitone.
hȧlf'-strāined, *a.* half-bred; imperfect. [Rare.]
hȧlf'-swōrd (-sōrd), *n.* half the length of a sword.
hȧlf tīde, the condition or period halfway between flood tide and ebb tide.
hȧlf tim'bẽr, in shipbuilding, one of the timbers in the cant bodies.
hȧlf'-tim''bẽred, *a.* in architecture, denoting a style in which the foundations and principal supports are of timber, and the interstices are filled in with plaster, brick, etc.
hȧlf tint, same as *demitint*.
hȧlf tī'tle, 1. the title of a book, often abbreviated, appearing on the odd page preceding (or sometimes following) the main title page.
2. the title of a subdivision of a book appearing on the odd page immediately preceding that division.
hȧlf'-tōne, *n.* a half tone.
hȧlf'-tōne, *a.* designating, of, or producing half tones.
hȧlf tōne, 1. in art, a tone or shading between light and dark.
2. in music, a half step.
3. in photoengraving, (a) a technique of representing shadings by dots produced by photographing the object from behind a fine screen; (b) a photoengraving so made.
hȧlf'-tŏngue (-tung), *n.* in law, a jury half of one nationality and half of another.
hȧlf'-track, *n.* a heavy truck, armored vehicle, etc. with wheels in front and caterpillar tread on the rear half.
hȧlf'-truth, *n.* a statement or account containing only some of the facts, the rest being purposely left out with the intention of deceiving.
hȧlf'-vol'ley, *v.t.* and *v.i.* to return (a ball) with a half volley.
hȧlf vol'ley, in tennis, cricket, etc., a stroke made by hitting the ball just as it begins to bounce after striking the ground.
hȧlf'wāy, *adv.* 1. at the middle point; at half the distance.
2. incompletely; partially.
3. at all; even remotely; as, he'd win if he were *halfway* good. [Colloq.]
to meet halfway; to be willing to compromise with.
hȧlf'wāy', *a.* 1. equidistant from the extremes; having a center location; midway.
2. incomplete; partial.
halfway covenant; a custom in New England Congregational churches in the middle of the seventeenth century of allowing to moral persons, under certain conditions, all church privileges except admittance to Communion.
halfway house; a stopping place at a point halfway on a journey; an inn or public house midway between two points.
hȧlf'-wit, *n.* 1. a foolish person; a dolt; a blockhead.
2. a person who is feeble-minded, moronic, imbecilic, etc.
hȧlf'-wit''ted, *a.* 1. stupid; silly; foolish.
2. feeble-minded, moronic, imbecilic, etc.
hȧlf'-yēar'ly, *a.* happening twice in a year; semiannual.
hȧlf'-yēar'ly, *adv.* twice in a year; semiannually.
hal·i-, same as *halo-*.
hal'i·but, *n.*; *pl.* **hal'i·but** or **hal'i·buts,** [ME. *haly*, holy, and *butte*, a flounder, plaice, lit., holy flounder: so called because eaten particularly on holidays.] a large, edible flatfish of the genus *Hippoglossus* and family *Pleuronectidæ*, common in the northern seas: it sometimes weighs hundreds of pounds: also *holibut*.

HALIBUT (*Hippoglossus vulgaris*)

Hal''i·chon·drī'i·dae, *n.pl.* [*hali-*, and Gr. *chondros*, cartilage.] an order of sponges having a skeleton of spicule bundles or cemented scattered spicules.
hal'i·çōre, *n.* same as *dugong*.
hal'īde, hal'id, *n.* in chemistry, a compound of a halogen with another element or a radical.
hal'īde, *a.* same as *haloid*.
hal'i·dŏm, hal'i·dōme, *n.* [ME. *halidom*, *haligdom*; AS. *haligdom*, holiness, a sanctuary, sacred relic; *halig*, holy, and *-dom*, -dom.]
1. holiness. [Archaic.]
2. a holy place; a sanctuary. [Archaic.]
3. a thing considered holy; a sacred relic. [Archaic.]
hal·i·eū'tiçs, *n.* [L. *halieutica*; Gr. *halieutika*, pl. of *halieutikos*, pertaining to fishing, from *halieuein*, to fish.] the study of or a treatise on the art of fishing.
hā·li·og'rȧ·phẽr, *n.* one who describes the sea. [Obs.]
hā·li·og'rȧ·phy, *n.* [*hali-*, and Gr. *-graphia*, from *graphein*, to write.] a description of the sea; a treatise on the sea. [Obs.]
Hā·li·ō'tis, *n.* [*hali-*, and Gr. *ous*, *ōtos*, the ear.] a genus of gastropodous mollusks, the ear shells.
hā'li·ō·toid, *a.* relating to or like the genus *Haliotis*; shaped like an ear.
hȧ·lis''tẽr·ē'sis, *n.* a chronic progressive disease during which the bones gradually soften, often resulting in great deformity; osteomalacia: pregnant women are especially prone to it.
hal'īte, *n.* [Gr. *hals*, *halos*, salt, and *-ite*.] native sodium chloride; rock salt.
hal·i·tō'sis, *n.* an offensive odor from the mouth; foul breath.
hal'i·tus, *n.* [L., from *halare*, to breathe.] vapor; breath.
hạlk (hạk), *n.* [ME. *halke*, from AS. *healc*, *healoc*, a hollow.] a corner; a nook. [Obs.]
hạll, *n.* [ME. *halle*, *haule*; AS. *heall*, *heal*, lit., a cover, shelter, from the root of *helan*, to conceal.]
1. originally, (a) the great central room in the dwelling of a king or chieftain, where banquets, games, etc. took place; (b) the dwelling itself.
2. the main dwelling on the estate of a baron, squire, etc.
3. [*sometimes* H–] a building containing public offices or the headquarters of an organization for transacting business, holding meetings, etc.
4. a large public or semipublic room for gatherings, entertainments, dancing, eating, etc.
5. [*sometimes* H–] a college dormitory, classroom, building, eating center, etc.
6. [*sometimes* H–] (a) any of the minor colleges of an English university; (b) the building that houses such a college.
7. a passageway or room between the entrance and the interior of a building; vestibule.
8. a passageway, corridor, or area onto which rooms open.
hạll'ăġe, *n.* a fee paid for goods sold in a hall. [Obs.]
hạll bed'rọọm, a small bedroom off a corridor; especially, a small bedroom at the end of an upstairs corridor.
hal'lē·çret, *n.* same as *allecret*.
hal'lel, *n.* [Heb., praise.] a part of the Jewish religious services consisting of Psalms cxiii to cxviii inclusive, recited or sung on certain feast days.
hal''lē·lụ·iat'iç (-yat'), *a.* [LL. *hallelujaticus* (supply *psalmus*, a psalm), from *hallelujah*, hallelujah.] pertaining to hallelujahs.
hal·lē·lụ'jȧh, hal·lē·lụ'iȧh (-yȧ), *interj.* [LL. *hallelujah*, *alleluiah*; Heb. *halelujāh*, praise ye Jehovah; *halelu*, praise ye, and *Jāh*, a short form of *Jehovah*.] praise (ye) the Lord!
hal·lē·lụ'jȧh, hal·lē·lụ'iȧh, *n.* an exclamation, hymn, or song of praise to God.
Hal'lēy's çom'et, a comet that appears periodically about every 76 years: last appearance, 1910: named after Edmund Halley (1656–1742), English astronomer who computed its orbit, and accurately foretold when it would be seen again in the northern heavens.
hal'liărd, *n.* same as *halyard*.
hal'li·dōme, *n.* same as *halidom*.
hal'li·ẽr, *n.* [from ME. *halen*, to haul.] a kind of net for catching birds.
hạll märk, [so called from Goldsmiths' Hall in London, the seat of the Goldsmiths' Company, by whom stamping is regulated.]
1. in Great Britain, an official stamp of an assay office, on articles of gold or silver, guaranteeing their quality.
2. any evidence of sterling quality or genuineness; as, courtesy is the *hall mark* of a gentleman.
hạll'mōte, *n.* [ME., from *halle*, hall, and *mote*, from AS. *gemot*, a meeting.] a court baron: spelled also *halmote* and *halmot*. [Obs.]
hăl·lō', *interj.*, *n.*, *v.i.* and *v.t.*, same as *hollo*.
Hạll of Fāme, a national institution founded in 1900 by the Council of New York University as a memorial of famous Americans: the names of distinguished Americans to be honored by commemorative tablets are chosen every five years.
hăl·lọọ', *v.t.* and *v.i.*; hallooed, *pt.*, *pp.*; hallooing, *ppr.* [ME. *halowen*, from *halou*, interj.]
1. to shout or call out in order to attract the attention of (a person).
2. to urge on (hounds) by shouting or calling out "halloo."
3. to shout; yell.
hăl·lọọ', *interj.* and *n.* an exclamation used as a call to a person at a distance or as a hunting cry.
hal'lōw, *v.t.*; hallowed, *pt.*, *pp.*; hallowing, *ppr.* [ME. *halowen*, *halwen*, *halgien*; AS. *halgian*, to make holy, from *halig*, holy.]
1. to make holy; to consecrate; to sanctify.
2. to reverence; to honor as sacred; to venerate.
Hal·lōw·een', Hal·lōw·ē'en', *n.* the evening preceding Allhallows, or All Saints' Day: October 31: now usually celebrated with fun-making and masquerading.
hal'lōw·măs, *n.* the feast of All Saints' Day: the former name.
hal·loy'ṣīte, *n.* [named after Dr. d'*Halloy*, a Belgian geologist.] a soft, white, claylike mineral silicate of aluminum.
Hạll·stat'ti·ăn, *a.* [so called from *Hallstatt*, a town in Austria, where many relics of this period are found.] relating to the earliest period of the iron age, at which began the change from the use of bronze to that of iron.
hạll tree, a stand, usually in an entrance hall, with arms or hooks to hold hats, coats, etc.
hal'lū·çăl, *a.* [L. *hallex*, *allex*, the great toe.] of or relating to the great toe.
hal·lū'ci·nāte, *v.t.*; hallucinated, *pt.*, *pp.*; hallucinating, *ppr.* to cause to have hallucinations.
hal·lū'ci·nāte, *v.i.* [L. *hallucinatus*, *allucina-*

tus, pp. of *hallucinari*, *allucinari*, to wander in mind, rave.] to have hallucinations.
hal·lū·ci·nā′tion, *n.* [L. *hallucinatio* (*-onis*), *allucinatio* (*-onis*), from *hallucinari*, *allucinari*, to wander in mind, rave.]
1. the apparent perception of sights, sounds, etc. that are not actually present: it may occur in certain mental disorders.
2. the imaginary object apparently seen, heard, etc.
Distinguished from *delusion*, *illusion*.
hal·lū′ci·nā·tŏr, *n.* [LL., from L. *hallucinari*, to wander in mind.] one who makes mistakes because he is the victim of hallucinations. [Rare.]
hal·lū′ci·nā·tō″ry, *a.* 1. of or characterized by hallucination.
2. producing hallucination.
hal·lū′ci·nō·ġen, *n.* [*hallucin*ation and *-o-* and *-gen.*] a drug or other substance that produces hallucinations.
hal·lū″ci·nō′sis, *n.* a state of mental affliction in which one is subject to hallucinations.
hal′lux, *n.*; *pl.* **hal′lū·cēs̹,** [L. *hallex*, *allex*, the great toe.] the first digit on either of the hind legs of a mammal; especially, in man, the great toe.
hall′wāy, *n.* 1. a passageway or room between the entrance and the interior of a building; vestibule.
2. a passageway; corridor; hall.
ha̤lm (ha̤m), *n.* same as *haulm*.
hal′mȧ, *n.* [Gr. *halma*, from *hallesthai*, to leap.] in ancient Greek athletic contests, the broad jump made with weights in the hands.
hal′mȧ·lille, *n.* [E. Ind.] a hardwood tree, *Berrya amomilla*, closely allied to the linden or lime tree of Europe. It is a native of Ceylon, the Philippines, and Australia.
hā′lō, *n.*; *pl.* **hā′lōs̹, hā′lōes̹,** [L. *halos*, genit. and acc. *halo*; Gr. *halōs*, genit. and acc. *halō*, a threshing floor on which oxen trod in a circular path, the round disk of the sun or moon, a halo around them, from *halein*, to grind.]
1. a ring of light that seems to encircle the sun, moon, or other luminous body: it results from the refraction of light through vapor.
2. a symbolic ring or disk of light shown around the head of a saint, etc., as in pictures; nimbus: often used as a symbol of virtue or innocence.
3. the splendor or glory attributed to a person or thing famed or idealized in legend or history.
hā′lō, *v.t.*; haloed (-lōd), *pt.*, *pp.*; haloing, *ppr.* to surround or encircle with or as with a halo.
hā′lō, *v.i.* to form a halo.
hal′ō-, [from Gr. *hals*, *halos*, salt, hence sea.] a combining form meaning: (a) *of the sea*; (b) *having to do with a salt*, as in *halo*phyte; (c) *having to do with a halogen*.
hal′ō·ġen, *n.* [Gr. *hals*, *halos*, salt, and *-genēs*, producing.] any of the four very active, nonmetallic chemical elements, chlorine, iodine, bromine, and fluorine.
hȧ·loġ′e·nous, *a.* having the nature of a halogen.
hal′oid, *a.* [Gr. *hals*, *halos*, salt, and *eidos*, form.] of or like a binary compound of a halogen with another element or radical.
hal′oid, *n.* a halide.
hal′ō·man·cy, *n.* [*halo-*, and Gr. *manteia*, divination.] divination by the use of salt.
hȧ·loph′i·lous, *a.* [*halo-*, and Gr. *philos*, loving.] salt-loving, as plants native to salty soils.
hal′ō·phȳte, *n.* [*halo-*, and Gr. *phyton*, a plant.] a plant that grows in salt-impregnated soils.
Hal·ō·rā′ġē·ae, *n.pl.* [*halo-*, and Gr. *rhax*, *rhagos*, a berry.] an order of dicotyledons containing a few genera of perennial (rarely annual) terrestrial or aquatic herbs, mostly obscure weeds, natives of ponds or moist places.
hal·ō·sa̤u′ri·ăn, *n.* [*halo-*, and Gr. *sauros*, a lizard.] an extinct marine lizard.
hā′lō·s̱cōpe, *n.* [Gr. *halōs*, a halo, and *skopein*, to view.] a device used to investigate or illustrate the phenomena of halos.
hal·ō·trī′ċhīte, *n.* [*halo-*, and Gr. *thrix*, *trichos*, a hair.] a hydrous sulfate of iron and aluminum found in silky fibrous masses or crystals: its color is yellowish-white.
hȧ·lox′y·lin, *n.* [*halo-*, and Gr. *xylon*, wood.] an explosive composed of charcoal, niter, and yellow prussiate of potash.
ha̤lse, hals, *n.* [ME. *hals*; AS. *heals*, the neck.]
1. the neck or throat. [Obs.]
2. a hawse. [Obs.]
ha̤lse, *v.t.* [AS. *healsian*, to embrace, from *heals*, the neck.]
1. to embrace; to greet. [Obs.]
2. to urge; to entreat. [Obs.]
ha̤lse, *v.t.* [Ice. *halsa*, to clew up a sail, from *hals*, the neck, front sheet of a sail.] to haul; to raise. [Obs.]
hal′sen·ing, *a.* sounding harshly in the throat. [Obs.]
hals′ēr (ha̤s′), *n.* a hawser. [Obs.]
ha̤lt, *v.t.* and *v.i.* to stop; cease or cause to cease, as in marching.
ha̤lt, *n.* [OFr. *halte*, from M.H.G. *halten*, to hold.] a temporary stop, as in marching; a pause.
to call a halt; to order a stop.
ha̤lt, *v.i.* [ME. *halten*; AS. *healtian*, to limp, halt, from *healt*, halt, lame.]
1. to walk with a crippled gait; limp; hobble.
2. to be uncertain; waver; hesitate; as, he *halts* in his speech.
3. to have defects; especially, (a) to be metrically faulty: said of verse; (b) to be illogical: said of argument.
ha̤lt, *a.* lame; crippled; halting; limping. [Archaic.]
ha̤lt, *n.* 1. lameness; a limp. [Archaic.]
2. a sheep disease. [Brit. Dial.]
the halt; those who are lame; cripples.
ha̤lt′ēr, *n.* one who halts or limps.
ha̤l′tēr, *n.* [ME. *halter*, *helter*, *helfter*; AS. *hælfter*, *healfter*, a halter.]
1. a rope or strap and headstall for leading or confining a horse or other animal.
2. a rope for hanging criminals condemned to death; a hangman's noose.
3. execution by hanging.
4. a garment for covering the breast, held up by a cord or loop around the neck, and worn by women and girls to bare the shoulders and back.
ha̤l′tēr, *v.t.*; haltered, *pt.*, *pp.*; haltering, *ppr.*
1. to put a halter on; to fasten with a halter.
2. to hang (a person).
hal′tēr, *n.*; *pl.* **hal·tē′rēs̹,** either of a pair of knobbed, threadlike parts serving as balancing organs in two-winged insects.
ha̤l′tēr·sack, *n.* a knave fit for the gallows. [Obs.]
ha̤lt′ing·ly, *adv.* in a halting way.
hä·lutz′ (khä-), *n.*; *pl.* **hä·lu·tzim′,** [Heb. *haluts*, warrior.] a Jewish pioneer in the agricultural settlements of Israel: also spelled *chalutz*.
häl·väh′, *n.* [Turk. *helwa*; Ar. *halwa*.] a Turkish confection consisting of a paste made of ground sesame seeds and nuts mixed with honey, etc.
hal′vans̹, *n.pl.* in mining, ore of poor quality. [Brit. Dial.]
ha̤lve (ha̤v), *v.t.*; halved, *pt.*, *pp.*; halving, *ppr.* [ME. *halven*, *halfen*, from *half*, a half.]
1. to divide into two equal parts.
2. to share equally (*with* someone); as, he *halved* the winnings *with* me.
3. to reduce by fifty per cent; to reduce to half.
4. to be a half or like a half of. [Rare.]

HALVING (IN JOINERY)

5. to join, as timbers, by lapping or letting into each other. The upper figure represents the simple lap joint, and the lower one the common halving.
6. in golf, to play (a hole, match, etc.) in the same number of strokes as one's opponent.
ha̤lve, *n.* half. [Obs.]
ha̤lved (ha̤vd), *a.* 1. in botany, dimidiate; having or seeming to have one half wanting.
2. in golf, said of a hole when each side or player takes the same number of strokes to make it: a *halved* match is a drawn game.
ha̤lves̹, *n.* plural of *half*.
by halves; (a) halfway; incompletely; imperfectly; (b) halfheartedly.
to go halves; to share expenses, etc. equally.
hal′yȧrd, *n.* [earlier *halier*, from ME. *halien*, to pull; altered by association with *yard*.] one of the ropes or tackles for hoisting or lowering yards, sails, flags, etc.
Hal·y·sī′tēs̹, *n.* [Gr. *halysis*, a chain.] a genus of Paleozoic corals, commonly known as the *chain corals*.
ham, *n.* [AS. *ham*, house, village.] a home, estate, village, or town; a common element in English place names, as Bucking*ham*, Notting*ham*, Dur*ham*, etc.
ham, *n.* [ME. *hamme*, *homme*; AS. *hamm*, the ham.]
1. the part of the leg behind the knee.
2. (a) the back of the thigh; (b) the thigh and the buttock together.
3. the hock or hind leg of a four-legged animal.
4. the upper part of a hog's hind leg, or meat from this, salted, dried, smoked, etc.
5. [from "The *Ham*fat Man," Negro song.] an incompetent actor or performer, especially one who overacts. [Slang.]
6. an amateur radio operator. [Slang.]
Ham, *n.* in the Bible, Noah's second son, traditionally the ancestor of African peoples: Gen. x. 6–20.
ham·ȧ·ċrat′iç, *a.* [Gr. *hama*, together, at the same time, and *kratein*, to rule.] of, or exhibiting, government characterized by mutual action.
ham·ȧ·drȳ′ăd, *n.* [Gr. *hamadryas*, pl. *hamadryades*; *hama*, together with, and *drys*, a tree.]
1. in Greek mythology, a wood nymph, supposed to live and die with the tree to which she was attached.
2. a dog-faced ape or baboon, *Cynocephalus hamadryas*, with long mane and whiskers, a native of Abyssinia.
3. a snake of the genus *Ophiophagus*, large and venomous, resembling a cobra.
ham·ȧ·drȳ′ăs, *n.* the hamadryad or dog-faced ape.
hȧ·mäl′, *n.* [Ar. *hammāl*, a porter, from *hamala*, to carry, bear.]
1. in the Orient, a porter.
2. in India, a man house servant.
Also *hammal*, *hamaul*.
ham·ȧ·mē·li·dā′ceous, *a.* of the *Hamamelideæ*.
Ham″ȧ·mē·lid′ē·ae, *n.pl.* [*hamamelis* (*-id*), and *-eæ*.] an order of dicotyledons, the witch hazels: they consist of small trees or shrubs with alternate, stipulate, feather-veined leaves, and small axillary unisexual flowers: called also *Hamamelidaceæ*.
Ham·ȧ·mē′lis, *n.* [Gr. *hamamēlis*, a kind of medlar or service tree; *hama*, at the same time, and *mēlon*, an apple, any tree fruit.]
1. the typical genus of the *Hamamelideæ*.
2. an astringent fluid extract prepared from *Hamamelis virginiana*, witch hazel.
Hā′măn, *n.* in the Bible, a Persian official who sought the destruction of the Jews but was hanged from his own gallows when his scheming was exposed to King Ahasuerus by Esther: Est. vii.
ham′ärch·y, *n.* [Gr. *hama*, together with, at the same time, and *archein*, to rule.] government in which many heterogeneous elements are organized into a political unit.
ham·är·thrī′tis, *n.* [Gr. *hamarthritis*, gout in all the joints at once; *hama*, at the same time, and *arthritis*, gout.] in medicine, gout in many or all the joints at once.
hȧ·mär·ti·al′ō·ġy, *n.* [Gr. *hamartia*, error, sin, and *-logia*, from *legein*, to speak.] that part of theology which deals with sin; a treatise or discussion concerning sin.
hā′māte, *a.* [L. *hamatus*, furnished with a hook, hooked, from *hamus*, a hook.] hooked; curved into a hook.
hā′mā·ted, *a.* hooked or set with hooks.
hȧ·mā′tum, *n.* [L. *hamatus*, hooked.] the unciform bone of the carpus.
hȧ·ma̤ul′, *n.* a hamal.
ham bee′tle, *Corynetes rufipes*, a beetle, the larva of which attacks cured hams.
ham′ble, *v.t.* [ME. *hamelen*; AS. *hamelian*, to mutilate.]
1. to hamstring. [Obs.]
2. to render (dogs) unfit for hunting by cutting out the balls of the feet. [Obs.]
Ham·ble·tō′ni·ăn, *n.* [name of a famous American stallion (1849–1876).] any of a superior breed of American trotting horses.
Ham′bŭrg, *n.* 1. a European variety of small chicken similar to the Leghorn.
2. a variety of black grape, usually chosen for hothouse growth.
Hamburg lake; a cochineal pigment of a purplish color inclining to crimson.
ham′bŭrg·ēr, *n.* [earlier *Hamburg steak*, after *Hamburg*, Germany.]
1. beef ground and, usually, seasoned.
2. a fried, broiled, or baked patty of such meat; Hamburg steak; Salisbury steak.
3. a sandwich made with such a patty, usually in a round bun.
Ham′bŭrg steăk (stāk), hamburger (senses 1 and 2): also called *hamburger steak*.
hāme, *n.* [ME.; AS. *hama*, a cover, skin; akin

to O.H.G. *hamo*, fishing net, fishhook.] either of the two rigid pieces along the sides of a horse's collar, to which the traces are attached.

hāme, *n.* home. [Scot.]

ham′el, *v.t.* to hamble. [Obs.]

hāme′suck·en, *n.* [Scot., from AS. *hamsocn*, an attack on a man's house; *ham*, home, and *socn*, a seeking.] in Scots law, the offense of beating or assaulting a person in his own house or dwelling place: also written *home-socken, hamesecken*, etc.

hā′mī, *n.* plural of *hamus*.

hā′mi·form, *a.* [L. *hamus*, a hook, and *forma*, form.] hamate; shaped like a hook.

Ham·il·tō′ni·ȧ, *n.* [named after F. Buchanan, the author of some works relating to India, who in late life took the name of *Hamilton*.] a genus of East Indian plants of the order *Rubiaceæ*: the species are shrubs with fragrant flowers which have a funnel-shaped corolla.

Ham·il·tō′ni·ăn, *a.* of, relating to, or characteristic of any person named *Hamilton* or of their methods or ideas, as (a) Sir William Hamilton (1788–1856), a logician and philosopher, of Scotland; (b) Sir William Rowan Hamilton (1805–1865), a mathematician, of Ireland; (c) James Hamilton (1769–1831), teacher of languages in England and America; (d) Alexander Hamilton (1757–1804), first Secretary of the Treasury of the United States, statesman and lawyer.

Ham·il·tō′ni·ăn, *n.* a follower of Alexander Hamilton.

ham·i·nū′rȧ, *n.* [S.Am.] a large South American food fish.

ham·i·ros′trāte, *a.* [L. *hamus*, a hook, and *rostratus*, beaked, from *rostrum*, a beak.] hook-beaked; with a beak like a hook.

hā′mīte, *n.* [L. *hamus*, hook, and *-ite*.] the fossil of an extinct genus of cephalopods: so named from the shell being hooked or bent on itself, instead of being spiral.

Ham′īte, *n.* 1. a person regarded as descended from Ham.

2. a member of any of several dark-skinned peoples native to northern and eastern Africa.

Ham·it′iç, *a.* 1. of or relating to Ham or the Hamites.

2. designating or of a group of African languages related to the Semitic languages and including ancient Egyptian (surviving, from 3400 B. C., as the religious language Coptic), ancient Libyan, the modern Berber dialects, and the Cushitic dialects of Ethiopia and eastern Africa.

ham′let, *n.* *Epinephelus striatus*, a basslike food fish, commonly called the *Nassau grouper*: found from Florida to the southern West Indies.

ham′let, *n.* [ME. *hamlet, hamelet*; OFr. *hamelet*, dim. of *hamel*, a village, a dim. of Germanic origin; compare AS. *ham*, a home.] a small village; a little cluster of houses in the country; especially, in England, one which has no church.

Ham′let, *n.* 1. a famous tragedy by Shakespeare (c. 1602).

2. the hero of this play, a Danish prince who, after many delays, finally avenges the murder of his father, the king, by killing his uncle Claudius, who has murdered the king, usurped the throne, and married Hamlet's mother, Gertrude.

ham′lin·īte, *n.* [named after A. C. *Hamlin*, an American geologist.] a colorless, crystalline phosphate of aluminum and glucinum.

hȧm·mäl′, *n.* a hamal.

ham′mẽr, *v.t.*; hammered, *pt., pp.*; hammering, *ppr.* 1. to beat with or as with a hammer; to pound; as, to *hammer* iron or steel.

2. to make or fasten with a hammer.

3. to drive, force, or shape with or as with hammer blows; as, *hammer* the idea into his head.

to hammer out; (a) to shape, construct, or produce by hammering; (b) to make flat by hammering; (c) to take out by or as by hammering; (d) to develop or work out by careful thought or repeated effort.

ham′mẽr, *v.i.* 1. to work; to be very busy; to labor in contrivance. [Obs.]

Whereon this month I have been *hammering*. —Shak.

2. to strike anything repeatedly with or as with a hammer.

3. to be working or in agitation; to keep up an excited state of feeling. [Obs.]

to hammer (away) at; (a) to work continuously or energetically at; (b) to keep emphasizing or talking about.

ham′mẽr, *n.* [ME. *hamer, homer*; AS. *hamor, homer*, a hammer.]

1. a tool for pounding, usually consisting of a metal head and a handle: one end of the head may be a pronged claw for pulling nails.

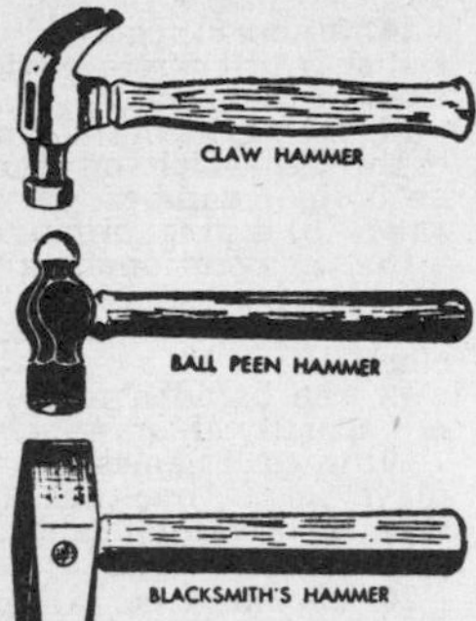

TYPES OF HAMMER

2. a thing like this tool in shape or use; specifically, (a) the mechanism that strikes the firing pin or percussion cap in a firearm; (b) a device for striking a bell or gong; (c) any of the felt-covered mallets that strike against the strings of a piano.

3. the malleus, one of the bones of the middle ear.

4. an auctioneer's gavel.

5. a metal ball weighing twelve or sixteen pounds, hung from a wire handle and thrown for distance in an athletic competition.

6. a drop hammer; triphammer.

hammer and sickle; the emblem of the Communist Party in various countries: it is used on the Soviet flag.

hammer and tongs; [with reference to a blacksmith's work.] with all one's might; very vigorously.

to bring to the hammer; [cf. *n.* 4.] to sell by auction.

under the hammer; [cf. *n.* 4.] for sale at auction.

ham′mẽr·ȧ·ble, *a.* malleable; capable of being shaped by a hammer.

ham′mẽr bēam, a short beam attached to the foot of a principal rafter in a roof, in the place of the tie beam.

ham′mẽr çatch′ẽr, a pad in a piano against which the hammer returns after striking the string.

ham′mẽr·cloth, *n.* [Late ME. *hamerclothe*: perh. so called from its durability.] the cloth which covers the driver's seat in horse-drawn carriages.

ham′mẽr-dressed (-drest), *a.* dressed or prepared with a hammer: especially applied to a building stone which has been dressed with a pointed hammer or pick.

ham′mẽred, *a.* shaped or marked by hammer blows: said of metalwork.

ham′mẽr·ẽr, *n.* 1. one who works with a hammer.

2. the Costa Rican bellbird, *Chasmorhynchus tricarunculatus*.

ham′mẽr·fish, *n.* the hammerhead.

ham′mẽr-härd″en, *v.t.* to make (a metal) hard by hammering it while cold.

ham′mẽr·head, *n.* 1. the head of a hammer.

2. a savage shark of the genus *Sphyrna*, that has a mallet-shaped head with an eye near the center of each end.

3. any of a species, *Hypentelium nigricans*, of small fresh-water fishes of the sucker family; the stone roller.

4. an African bat, *Hypsignathus monstrosus*, that lives on fruit.

5. an African bird related to the herons and storks; the umbrette.

ham′mẽr·ing, *n.* a series of ornamental dents in metalwork made with a hammer.

ham′mẽr·kop, *n.* [S. African.] *Scopus umbretta*, the umbrette.

ham′mẽr·less, *a.* 1. without a hammer.

2. having the hammer or other striking device covered, as some firearms.

ham′mẽr lock, in wrestling, a hold in which one of the opponent's arms is twisted and pressed upward behind his back.

ham′mẽr·măn, *n.*; *pl.* **ham′mẽr·men,** one who works with a hammer, as a blacksmith, a silversmith, etc.

ham′mẽr oys′tẽr, a hammer shell.

ham′mẽr shell, a shell of a bivalve mollusk of the genus *Malleus*, which has hammer-shaped valves.

ham′mẽr tōe, 1. a condition in which the first joint of a toe is permanently bent downward, resulting in a clawlike deformity.

2. such a toe.

ham′mẽr·wŏrt, *n.* the plant pellitory, *Parietaria officinalis*.

ham·mō·çhrȳ′sŏs, *n.* [L., from Gr. *hammochrysos*; *hammos, ammos*, sand, and *chrysos*, gold.] a mineral, containing goldlike particles, mentioned by the ancient Greeks and Romans.

ham′mŏck, *n.* [Sp. *hamaca*, a hammock; of W. Ind. origin.]

SAILOR'S HAMMOCK

1. a hanging bed, consisting of a piece of canvas or netting, about 6 feet long and 3 feet wide, gathered at the ends and suspended by cords and hooks: it is often used on ships.

2. in entomology, a hammocklike case or covering of certain caterpillars.

ham′mŏck, *n.* [var. of hummock.] in the South, a piece of rich land with hardwood trees growing on it.

ham′my, *a.* like or characteristic of a ham (actor). [Slang.]

hā′mōse, hā′mous, *a.* [L. *hamus*, a hook.] in botany, hamate.

ham′pẽr, *n.* 1. a fetter or some instrument that shackles.

2. in nautical usage, necessary but encumbering articles, as a ship's rigging.

ham′pẽr, *v.t.*; hampered, *pt., pp.*; hampering, *ppr.* [prob. same as *hamble, hamel*, from AS. *hamelian*, to mutilate.]

1. to shackle; to entangle; hence, to impede in motion or progress, or to render progress difficult; to hinder; impede; encumber.

They *hamper* and entangle our souls. —Tillotson.

2. to derange or put out of working order, as a piece of mechanism.

ham′pẽr, *n.* in nautical usage, necessary but encumbering articles, as a ship's rigging, etc.

ham′pẽr, *n.* [ME. *hamper*, contr. of *hanaper*, from LL. *hanaperium*, a basket or vessel to keep cups in.] a large basket, usually with a cover.

ham′pẽr, *v.t.* to put into a hamper.

ham′shaç″kle, *v.t.* [*ham* and *shackle*.] to shackle a horse or other animal by drawing the head down and fastening it to a fore leg; hence, to curb; to restrain; to embarrass.

ham′stẽr, *n.* [G. *hamster*, a hamster; O.H.G. *hamastro*, weevil.] a ratlike, burrowing animal of Europe and Asia, family *Cricetidae*, with large cheek pouches in which it carries grain: one variety is used, like the guinea pig, in scientific experiments.

HAMSTER

ham′string, *n.* 1. in human anatomy, a tendon of a thigh muscle at the back of the knee.

2. the tendon above and behind the hock of a quadruped's hind leg.

ham′string, *v.t.*; hamstrung, *pt., pp.*; hamstringing, *ppr.* 1. to cut the hamstring or hamstrings of, so as to lame or disable.

2. to disable; cripple.

ham′ū·lăr, *a.* [L. *hamulus*, dim. of *hamus*, a hook.] like a hook; curved; hamulate.

ham′ū·lāte, *a.* having or resembling a small hook or hooks.

ham′ūle, *n.* a hamulus.

ham′ū·lōse, ham′ū·lous, *a.* hamulate.

ham′ū·lus, *n.*; *pl.* **ham′ū·lī,** [L., dim. of *hamus*, a hook.]

1. in entomology, one of a series of small hooks on the front edge of the lower wings of some of the *Hymenoptera*.

2. in ornithology, a barbicel.

3. in anatomy, a hamular process of a bone.

4. in botany, a hooked bristle or awn in flowers.

hā′mus, *n.*; *pl.* **hā′mī,** [L., a hook.] a hooklet or hook-shaped projection from the front wing of certain lepidopterous insects.

Hän, *n.* an ethnic group of China constituting the majority of the Chinese and distinguished from the Manchus, Mongols, etc.

han′ȧ·pẽr, *n.* [ME. *hamypere*; OFr. *hanapier, hanaper*; LL. *hanaperium*, a basket or vessel for keeping cups in.]

1. a small hamper in which official papers were formerly kept.

2. a repository for money or treasure. [Obs.]

3. formerly, a department of the English Court of Chancery, which received fees for the sealing and enrolling of documents.

hance, hanch, *n.* [ME. *hanche, haunche*; OFr. *hanche, anche, hance*, from O.H.G. *ancha, encha*, the leg, lit., joint or bend.]

1. in architecture, formerly, (a) the lower part, above the springing, of three and four centered arches; (b) a small arch by which a straight lintel is sometimes united to its jamb or impost.

2. [*pl.*] in a ship, falls of the fife rails placed on balusters on the poop and quarter-deck down to the gangway.

han′chi·nol, *n.* [Mex.] *Heimia salicifolia*, a shrub of the order *Lythraceæ*, used as a sudorific and diuretic.

hand, *v.t.*; handed, *pt., pp.*; handing, *ppr.* 1. to give or transmit with or as with the hand; as, *hand* me a book.

2. to lead, guide, or help with the hand; to conduct; as, to *hand* an invalid into a chair.

3. in nautical usage, to furl; to wrap (a sail) close to a yard or mast and fasten it with gaskets.

to hand down; (a) to bequeath, as from father to son, or from predecessor to successor; as, fables are *handed down* from age to age; (b) to announce or deliver (a verdict, etc.)

to hand in; to give; submit.

to hand it to; to give deserved credit to. [Slang.]

to hand out; to distribute; deal out.

to hand over; to give up; to deliver; as, he *handed over* the office to his successor.

to hand round or *around*; to circulate; to spread; to pass from hand to hand; as, *to hand round* a bit of gossip; *to hand round* refreshments.

hand, *n.* [ME. *hand, hond*; AS. *hand, hond*, a hand, from same root as Goth. *hinthan*, to take, seize.]

1. in man, the extremity of the arm, consisting of the palm and five fingers, connected with the arm at the wrist and used for grasp-

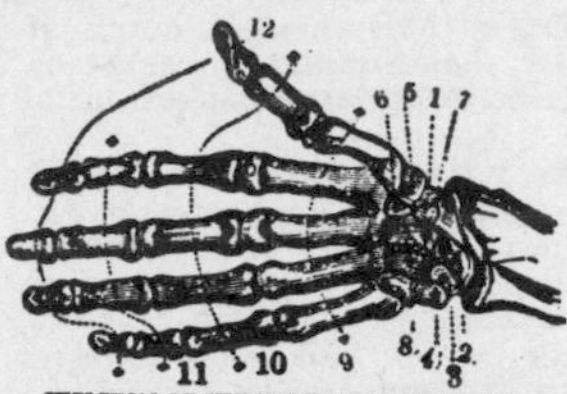

SKELETON OF HUMAN HAND AND WRIST
1. scaphoid bone; 2. semilunar bone; 3. cuneiform bone; 4. pisiform bone; 5. os trapezium; 6. os trapezoides; 7. os magnum; 8. unciform bone; 9. metacarpal bones of thumb and fingers; 10. first row of phalanges of thumb and fingers; 11. second row of phalanges of fingers; 12. third row of phalanges of thumb and fingers

ing or gripping. The human hand is composed of twenty-seven bones; namely, the eight bones of the carpus, or wrist, the five bones of the metacarpus forming the palm, and the fourteen bones or phalanges of the fingers. Of these phalanges the thumb has but two, all the other digits having three each.

2. the corresponding structure in monkeys and some other animals.

3. a side, direction, or position indicated by one hand or the other; either right or left; as, at one's right *hand*.

4. the hand as an instrument for making or producing; as, made by *hand*.

5. the hand as a symbol of its grasping or gripping function; specifically, (a) possession; as, the papers are not in my *hands*; (b) control; power; authority; as, he rules with an iron *hand*; (c) care; charge; supervision; as, the child is in good *hands*; (d) agency; influence; as, one can see his *hand* in the affair; (e) an active part; share; as, take a *hand* in this work.

6. the hand as a symbol of promise; specifically, (a) a clasp or handshake as a pledge of agreement, friendship, etc.; as, give me your *hand* on that; (b) a promise to marry; as, he asked for her *hand*.

7. skill; ability; dexterity; as, this work shows a master's *hand*.

8. manner of doing something; as, he plays with a light *hand*.

9. handwriting.

10. a signature.

11. a clapping of hands; applause; as, they gave the singer a *hand*.

12. assistance; aid; help; as, lend me a *hand*.

13. a person whose chief work is with his hands; especially, one of a staff or crew, as a sailor, farm laborer, etc.

14. a person regarded as having some special skill or characteristic; as, she is quite a *hand* at the piano.

15. (a) a person (or sometimes thing) from or through which something comes: used with an ordinal number; as, he got it at second *hand*; (b) source; origin; authority.

16. a conventional drawing of a hand (☛) used on signposts, etc.

17. an indicator; pointer; as, the *hands* of a clock.

18. the breadth of a hand; handbreadth: now usually about 4 inches.

19. in card games, (a) the cards held by a player at any one time; (b) the conventional number of cards dealt to each player; (c) a player; (d) a round of play.

20. in commerce, (a) a banana cluster; (b) a small tied bundle of tobacco leaves, hemp, etc.

(*at*) *first hand*; from the original source.

at hand; (a) near; close by; (b) ready; prepared.

(*at*) *second hand*; (a) not from the original source; indirectly; (b) not new; previously used.

at the hand of; from; as, mercy *at the hand of* the victor.

by hand; by the use of the hand or hands, not by machinery; as, these clothes were made *by hand*.

from hand to hand; from one to another.

from hand to mouth; spending or consuming immediately what is obtained; with nothing saved for the future.

hand in hand; in union; conjointly; unitedly.

hand over hand; *hand over fist*; easily and in large amounts. [Colloq.]

hand running; one after another; as, three victories *hand running*.

hands down; easily; without effort.

hands off! don't touch! don't interfere!

hands up! raise your hands over your head!: an order given by a person pointing a gun, etc.

hand to hand; in close union, close fight.

heavy hand; severity or oppression.

in hand; (a) in order or control; (b) in possession; (c) being worked on; in process.

note of hand; a promissory note.

on hand; (a) near; (b) available; ready; (c) present.

out of hand; (a) out of control; (b) immediately; (c) over and done with.

to be hand and glove with or *hand in glove with*; to be intimate and familiar with, as a friend or co-worker.

to bite the hand that feeds one; to turn against one's benefactor.

to change hands; to change owners.

to come to hand; to be accepted or received, as a message.

to eat out of one's hand; to be completely dominated by or devoted to one.

to force one's hand; [orig. a whist term.] to force one to act, or declare his intentions, before he is ready.

to get or *have the upper hand*; to obtain or have an advantage over; to surpass.

to have one's hands full; to be extremely busy; to be doing as much as one can.

to hold hands; to hold each other's hand, especially in affection.

to join hands; (a) to become associates; to enter into partnership; (b) to become husband and wife.

to keep one's hand in; to keep in practice in order to retain one's skill.

to lay hands on; (a) to attack, injure, or punish physically; (b) to get hold of; seize; take; (c) to touch with the hands in blessing, ordaining, confirming, etc.

to lend a hand; to give assistance.

to shake hands; to clasp each other's (usually the right) hand as a greeting, pledge, etc.

to show one's hand; [orig. with reference to card playing.] to disclose one's intentions.

to wash one's hands of; to disclaim all responsibility for; to withdraw from participation in; as, *to wash one's hands of* the whole matter.

under the hand of; under the signature and seal of.

hand, *a.* 1. of the hand or hands.

2. controlled by hand; manual.

hand-, an initial combining form meaning *of, with, by* or *for a hand* or *hands*, as in *hand*clasp, *hand*cuff, etc.

hand′bag, *n.* 1. a small container for money, toilet articles, keys, etc., carried by women; a purse.

2. a small case or satchel for use in traveling.

hand′bạll, *n.* 1. a game in which one player strikes a ball against a wall with the hand and an opposing player tries to return it to the wall on the rebound, until one fails to make a proper return.

2. the small rubber ball used in this game.

3. a rubber bulb perforated and used in spraying.

hand′bar″rōw, *n.* 1. a barrow carried with the hands; a litter.

2. a wheelbarrow.

3. a sort of frame used in carrying military supplies.

hand bell, a small bell to be rung by hand instead of by a bell rope.

hand′bill, *n.* a small printed sheet of paper bearing an announcement, etc., to be passed out by hand.

hand′bill, *n.* a kind of pruning knife or hook; a billhook.

hand′book, *n.* 1. a compact reference book on some subject; manual.

2. a guidebook.

3. a book in which bets are recorded, as on horse races.

hand′breadth (-bredth), *n.* a space equal to the breadth of the hand; a palm: now usually about 4 inches.

hand′cär, *n.* a light car used on railways by inspectors or workmen for transportation and for carrying tools, etc., operated manually by means of a crank or a lever with gearing.

hand′cärt, *n.* a small cart, often with only two wheels, pulled or pushed by hand.

hand′clȧsp, *n.* a clasping of hands in greeting, farewell, promise, etc.

hand′clọth, *n.* a handkerchief.

hand′crȧft, *n.* same as *handicraft*.

hand′crȧfts·măn, *n.* same as *handicraftsman*.

hand′cuff, *n.* [*usually in pl.*] either of a pair of connected rings that can be locked about the wrists of a prisoner to keep him from using his hands, or to fasten him to a policeman.

hand′cuff, *v.t.*; handcuffed, *pt., pp.*; handcuffing, *ppr.* to manacle; to restrain with handcuffs.

hand drop, in pathology, a paralyzed condition of the extensor muscles of the hand, the result of blood poisoning: called also *wrist-drop*.

hand′ed, *a.* 1. provided with hands.

2. having the hands joined. [Rare.]

3. having (a specified number or kind of) hands: usually in hyphenated compounds, as left-*handed*, two-*handed*.

4. involving (a specified number of) players; as, three-*handed* bridge.

hand′ẽr, *n.* one who hands or transmits; one who conveys.

hand′fȧst, *n.* 1. a firm hold or grip with or as with the hands. [Archaic.]

2. a clasping of hands to bind a bargain. [Archaic.]

3. a contract, especially of marriage or betrothal. [Archaic.]

hand′fȧst, *a.* 1. (a) betrothed; (b) married. [Archaic.]

2. close-fisted. [Archaic.]

hand′fȧst, *v.t.* [ME. *handfasten, handfesten*; Ice. *handfesta*, to conclude a bargain by shaking hands, betroth; *hönd*, hand, and *festa*, to fasten, pledge.]

1. to betroth or marry by joining hands. [Archaic.]

2. to take hold of with the hand. [Archaic.]

hand′fȧst·ing, *n.* 1. a betrothal. [Archaic.]

2. an obsolete form of irregular or trial marriage ceremonialized by a joining of hands. [Archaic.]

hand′flow″ẽr tree, a large Mexican and Central American tree of the cola-nut family, whose flower stamens are flesh-colored and spread out like the fingers of a hand.

hand′fụl, *n.*; *pl.* **hand′fụls,** 1. as much as the hand will grasp or contain.

2. a small quantity or number; as, a *handful* of men.

3. enough so that more will be too much; plenty.

4. someone or something hard to control. [Colloq.]

5. a handbreadth; a unit of length equal to 4 inches. [Obs.]

hand gal′lŏp, a slow and easy gallop, in which the hand moderates the speed of the horse.

hand gēar, an arrangement for operating a power machine by hand; also, the starting gear of a steam engine.

hand glȧss, 1. a magnifying glass for reading small print, etc.

2. a small mirror with a handle.

3. a protective glass covering for plants.

4. a sandglass used to measure the time in running out the log line on shipboard.

hand grē·nāde′, 1. a small grenade thrown by hand and exploded by a timed fuse or by impact.

2. a glass container full of chemicals, to be thrown at a fire in order to put it out.

hand′grip, *n.* 1. a handclasp; handshake; specifically, a particular handclasp by which members of a fraternal order or secret society greet or recognize each other.

2. a handle, as on a bicycle handle bar.

hand′gun, *n.* any firearm that is held and fired with one hand, as a pistol.

hand′hōld, *n.* 1. a gripping with the hand or hands.

2. a part or thing to take hold of; a hold or support for the hand or hands.

hand′hōle, *n.* a hole through which the hand may be inserted.

hand′i·çap, *v.t.*; handicapped (-kapt), *pt., pp.*; handicapping, *ppr.* 1. to encumber with impediments or disadvantages; to give a handicap to.

2. to place at a disadvantage; to hinder; to impede.

3. to detract from; to weaken; as, excessive egotism *handicaps* a man.

hand′i·çap, *n.* [from *hand in cap*, former kind of lottery game in which winners were penalized.]

1. a restriction or disadvantage in a contest imposed upon a superior competitor, or an allowance of distance, time, or the like given to an inferior contestant, to equalize their chances of winning.

2. a drawback; a hindrance.

3. a contest in which handicaps are given.

hand′i·çap·pēr, *n.* one who fixes handicaps.

hand′i·çrȧft, *n.* [ME. *handcraft*; AS. *handcræft*, a manual occupation; *hand*, hand, and *cræft*, strength, power, skill: the form of the word was influenced by *handiwork*.]

1. manual skill; expertness with the hands.

2. an occupation or art calling for skillful use of the hands, as weaving, pottery, etc.

3. a handicraftsman. [Rare.]

hand′i·çrȧfts·măn, *n.* a man employed in manual occupation; a skilled workman; a craftsman.

hand′i·ly, *adv.* 1. with dexterity or skill; dexterously; adroitly.

2. with ease or convenience.

hand′i·ness, *n.* the quality of being handy; dexterity; adroitness.

hand′ī″ron (-ũrn), *n.* an andiron. [Obs.]

hand′i·wŏrk, *n.* [ME. *handiwerk, handewerc*; AS. *handgeweorc*, work of the hand; *hand*, hand, and *geweorc, weorc*, work.]

1. work done by the hands.

2. that which is made or done with the hands.

3. the result of one's actions; as, this mess is my *handiwork*.

hañ′kēr·chief (hañ′kēr-chif), *n.* [*hand* and *kerchief*.]

1. a piece of cloth, usually linen, cotton, or silk, generally rectangular, carried for the purpose of wiping the face, hands, nose, etc.; a pocket handkerchief.

2. a piece of cloth worn about the neck or the head; kerchief.

hand′-knit, hand′-knit·ted (-nit), *a.* knit by hand.

hand lañ′guȧġe (-gwăj), dactylology; sign language.

han′dle, *v.t.*; handled, *pt., pp.*; handling, *ppr.* [ME. *handlen*; AS. *handlian*, to handle, feel, from *hand*, hand.]

1. to touch; to feel with the hand; to use or hold with the hand.

Handle me, and see; for a spirit hath not flesh and bones. —Luke xxiv. 39.

2. to manage, wield, or manipulate with the hands; as, to *handle* a rifle or an oar.

3. to manage; control; direct.

4. to deal with; as, our office *handles* many requests.

5. to discourse on; to discuss; to manage in writing or speaking; as, the lecturer *handled* his subject with much skill.

6. to behave toward; to treat; as, they *handled* the prisoner roughly.

7. to deal in; to trade in; to buy or sell; as, to *handle* groceries; to *handle* stocks and bonds.

8. to exercise with the hands; to make used to the hands; to train; as, to *handle* a spirited horse.

9. to equip with a handle.

han′dle, *v.i.* 1. to use the hands; to feel with the hands; to work or act by means of the hands.

2. to respond or submit to control; as, the car *handles* well.

han′dle, *n.* [ME. *handel, handyl*; AS. *handle*, a handle, from *handlian*, to handle, feel.]

1. that part of a utensil, tool, etc. which is to be held, turned, lifted, pulled, etc. with the hand.

2. a thing like a handle.

3. that by which something can be taken advantage of for some purpose; occasion.

4. any title attached to a person's name. [Colloq.]

to fly off the handle; to become suddenly or violently angry or excited. [Colloq.]

to get a handle on; to find a means of dealing with, understanding, etc. [Colloq.]

han′dle·ȧ·ble, *a.* capable of being handled.

han′dle bär, [*often in pl.*] 1. a curved or bent metal bar with handles on the ends, for steering a bicycle, motorcycle, etc.

2. a long mustache resembling this. [Colloq.]

han′dlēr, *n.* 1. a person or thing that handles.

2. a boxer's trainer, manager, or second.

hand′less, *a.* without a hand or hands.

han′dling, *n.* [ME. *handlinge, hondlunge*; AS. *handlung*, from *handlian*, to handle, feel.]

1. manipulation; touch; a touching or using with the hand.

2. the act of equipping with handles.

hand′māde, *a.* manufactured by the hand, and not by a machine; as, *handmade* paper.

hand′māid, *n.* a female servant or attendant.

hand′māid″en, *n.* a handmaid. [Archaic.]

hand′māid mọth, *Datana ministra*, a moth of the family *Notodontidae*.

hand′-mē-down, *a.* 1. (a) ready-made; (b) not expensive; not elegant; cheap. [Colloq.]

2. used; secondhand. [Colloq.]

hand′mill, *n.* a mill for grinding grain, pepper, coffee, etc., moved by the hand.

hand ọr′găn, a large music box, similar to a reed organ, played by turning a crank; hurdy-gurdy; barrel organ.

hand′out, *n.* a gift of food, clothing, etc., as to a beggar or tramp.

hand′-picked′ (-pikt′), *a.* 1. picked by hand: said of fruit or vegetables.

2. chosen with care, or for a special purpose: sometimes derogatory; as, a *hand-picked* candidate.

hand′rāil, *n.* a rail serving as a guard or support to be held by the hand, as along a stairway.

hand′saw, *n.* a saw used with one hand.

hand′ṣ′-breadth (-bredth), *n.* a handbreadth.

hand′screw (-skrụ̈), *n.* 1. an engine for raising heavy timbers or weights; a jack.

2. in carpentry, a wooden clamp tightened by hand.

hand′sel, han′sel, *n.* [ME. *hansel, hanselle*; AS. *handselen*; *hand*, hand, and *selen, sylen*, a giving, from *sellen, syllan*, to give.]

1. a present for good luck, as on New Year's or on the launching of a new business.

2. a first payment; specifically, (a) a first installment, as a pledge of future payment; (b) the first money taken in a new business or on any day of business. [Rare.]

3. the first use or specimen of anything, regarded as an indication of what is to follow.

Handsel Monday; the first Monday of the new year, when it was formerly usual in Scotland for servants, children, etc. to receive presents, or handsel.

hand′sel, han′sel, *v.t.*; handseled *or* handselled, *pt., pp.*; handseling *or* handselling, *ppr.*

1. to give a handsel to.

2. to begin or launch with ceremony and gifts; inaugurate.

3. to use, do, etc. for the first time; to be the first to use, etc.

hand′set, *n.* a telephone mouthpiece and receiver mounted together on a handle.

hand′shāke, *n.* a gripping and shaking of each other's hand in greeting, farewell, promise, sealing a bargain, etc.

handṣ′-ọff′, *a.* designating or of a policy, attitude, etc. of not interfering or intervening.

hand′sŏme, *a.*; *comp.* handsomer; *superl.* handsomest. [ME. *handsom, handsum*, easy to handle or use; AS. *hand*, hand, and *-sum*, -some.]

1. (a) moderately large; (b) large; impressive; considerable; as, a *handsome* sum.

2. appropriate; fitting; seemly; proper; gracious; as, it was *handsome* of him to say that.

3. good-looking; of pleasing appearance: said especially of attractiveness that is manly, dignified, or impressive rather than delicate and graceful; as, a *handsome* man, a *handsome* book.

4. dexterous; handy; ready; convenient. [Obs.]

5. characterized by or expressive of liberality or generosity; as, a *handsome* present.

hand′sŏme, *v.t.* to render handsome. [Obs.]

hand′sŏme·ly, *adv.* 1. in a handsome manner.

2. in nautical usage, steadily and carefully; leisurely; as, to lower *handsomely*.

hand′sŏme·ness, *n.* 1. the condition or quality of being handsome.

2. favor; approval.

handṣ′-on′, *a.* designating an activity, training, etc., in which one participates actively.

hand′spīke, *n.* a bar, commonly of wood, used as a lever for various purposes, as in raising weights, heaving about a windlass, etc.

hand′spring, *n.* a gymnastic feat in which the performer turns over in mid-air with one or both hands touching the ground.

hand stamp, a stamp to be used by hand; specifically, a rubber stamp used with a separate ink pad.

hand′-tīght (-tīt), *a.* as tight as can be made by hand; moderately tight.

hand′-tō-hand′, *a.* in close contact; at close quarters: said of fighting.

hand′-tō-mouth′, *a.* characterized by the immediate spending or consuming of what is obtained; with nothing saved for the future.

hand tree, same as *handflower tree*.

hand′wheel, *n.* a small flywheel with, usually, a handle inserted in the rim, used as a crank.

hand′-winged, *a.* having hands developed into something resembling wings; cheiropterous: said of bats.

hand′wŏrk, *n.* work done by the hands, as distinguished from work done by machine.

hand′-wŏrked, hand′-wrought (-wẽrkt, -rạt), *a.* made by hand.

hand′wrīte (-rīt), *v.t.* and *v.i.* to write. [Rare.]

hand′wrīt″ing, *n.* 1. writing done by hand, with pen, pencil, chalk, etc.

2. a style or way of forming letters and words in writing; as, I recognize his *handwriting*.

3. something written by hand; manuscript. [Archaic.]

to see the handwriting on the wall; to see the signs of impending disaster, misfortune, etc.: Dan. v. 5–28.

hand′y, *a.*; *comp.* handier; *superl.* handiest. 1. close at hand; easily reached; conveniently located; accessible.

2. easily used; convenient; saving time or work; as, a *handy* device.

3. easily managed or handled: said of a ship, etc.

4. clever with the hands; deft; adroit.

Syn.—near, convenient, useful, helpful, ready, ingenious.

hand′y-dan′dy, *n.* a children's game in which a small object is shaken between the hands, and then a guess is made as to which hand retains it.

hand′y man, a man employed at various small tasks; doer of odd jobs.

hand′y·wŏrk, *n.* same as *handiwork*.

hang, *v.t.*; hung, *pt., pp.*; hanging, *ppr.*; *for v.t. sense 3 and v.i. sense 4*, hanged *is preferred pt. and pp.* [ME. *hangen*, with form from AS. *hangian* and ON. *hanga*.]

1. to attach to something above with no support from below; suspend.

2. to attach so that motion from the point of attachment is possible; as, a door is *hung* on its hinges so that it can swing.

3. to put to death by tying a rope about the neck and suddenly suspending the body so as to snap the neck or cause strangulation.

4. to fasten (pictures, etc.) to a wall by hooks, wires, etc.

5. to ornament or cover (*with* things suspended); as, she *hung* the room *with* pictures and drapes.

6. to paste (wallpaper) to walls.

7. to exhibit (pictures) in a museum or gallery.

8. to fasten with correct balance, as an ax-head, scythe, etc.

9. to deadlock (a jury), as by withholding one's vote.

hang it; an exclamation of anger or exasperation.

to hang up; (a) to put on a hanger, hook, etc., especially in the proper place; (b) to put a telephone receiver back on the hook; (c) to end a telephone conversation; (d) to delay or suspend the progress of.

hang, *v.i.* 1. to be attached to something above with no support from below; to be suspended.

2. to swing, as on a hinge.

3. to fall or flow, as cloth, a coat, etc.

4. to die by hanging.

5. to incline; lean; droop; bend.

6. to hesitate; to be doubtful or undecided.

7. to exhibit one's pictures in a museum or gallery.

to hang around; to haunt persistently; to loaf around; to idle. [Colloq.]

to hang back; to falter; to be reluctant to advance, as from shyness.

to hang by the eyelids; to hold on by a very slender tenure; to be in a precarious condition.

to hang fire; in a firearm, to fail to explode promptly; hence, to be slow in doing something; to be unsettled.

to hang in the balance; to be doubtful; to be undecided.

to hang on; (a) to retain hold; to hold fast; to refuse to give up; (b) to go on doing; persevere; (c) to depend on; to be contingent on; (d) to lean on; to be supported by; (e) to listen attentively to.

to hang out; (a) to lean out; (b) [Slang.] to reside; also, to spend much of one's time; to frequent.

to hang over; (a) to project over; overhang; (b) to hover over; (c) to loom over; threaten; (d) to be left from a previous time or state.

to hang to; to hold to; to take a firm hold upon.

to hang together; (a) to agree in sentiment and action; (b) to be coherent or consistent; as, the parts of this story do not *hang together*.

hang, *n.* 1. a slope or declivity; amount of slope or declivity; as, the *hang* of a road.

2. the manner or style of hanging; as, the *hang* of drapery.

3. familiarity resulting from practice or aptitude; knack of using or doing; as, to get the *hang* of one's work.

4. underlying thought; main thread; drift; as, the *hang* of a speech.

5. a pause in motion.

6. a bit; as, I don't care a *hang* about it. [Colloq.]

hañ'gär, *n.* [Fr., a shed.] a shed, particularly one for housing aircraft.

hang'bĭrd, *n.* any bird that builds a hanging nest; specifically, an oriole.

hang'bȳ, *n.*; *pl.* **hang'bīeṣ,** a hanger-on; a dependent. [Obs.]

hang'dog, *n.* 1. originally, a person considered fit only for hanging dogs, or to be hanged like a dog.

2. a low, skulking person; sneak.

hang'dog, *a.* of low, skulking, abject character or appearance.

hang'ẽr, *n.* [ME. *hangere.*]

1. a person who hangs things: usually in combination; as, a paper *hanger*.

2. a hangman; executioner.

3. a thing that hangs; especially, a short sword hanging from the belt.

4. a thing on which objects are hung, or by which they can be hung; specifically, (a) a hook, chain, rope, strap, etc. for this purpose; (b) a small frame on which a garment is hung to keep it in shape.

5. in automobiles, a bracket on the spring shackle to hold it to the chassis.

hang'ẽr-on', *n.*; *pl.* **hang'ẽrṣ-on',** a follower or dependent; specifically, (a) a person who attaches himself to another, to some group, etc. although not wanted; (b) a favor-seeker; sycophant; parasite.

hang glīd'ẽr, a large type of kite with a harness in which a person is suspended while gliding through the air on wind currents.

hang glīd'ing, the sport of gliding through the air while suspended from a hang glider.

hang'ing, *n.* 1. the act of suspending or the state of being suspended.

2. execution by the gallows.

3. anything that hangs, as a window curtain, a portier, or a chandelier.

4. [*pl.*] the drapings of the walls of a room.

hang'ing, *a.* 1. attached to something overhead and not supported from below; suspended; pendulous.

2. leaning over; inclining; overhanging.

3. located on a steep slope or slant.

4. unsettled; inconclusive.

5. unhappy; downcast.

6. deserving or causing the death penalty.

7. designating paragraphing in which the first line touches the left margin, the other lines being indented beneath it.

hanging garden; a garden elevated by artificial means, as by pillars, masonry, or terraces; as, the *hanging gardens* of ancient Babylon.

hang'ing but'tress, in architecture, a buttress not standing solid on a foundation, but supported on a corbel: used chiefly as a feature in decoration.

HANGING BUTTRESS

hang'ing mo̤ss, any one of several species of lichen of the genus *Usnea* growing upon rocks and trees: called also *tree moss* and *tree hair*.

hang'ing pōst, the post of a gate or door to which the hinges are fastened.

hang'ing rāil, the strip on a hanging post to which the hinges are attached.

hang'ing stīle, in architecture, the stile in a door frame or window frame holding the hangings, such as hinges, pulleys, etc.

hang'măn, *n.*; *pl.* **hang'men,** a public executioner who hangs convicted criminals.

hang'măn·ship, *n.* the office or duty of a hangman.

hang'nāil, *n.* [altered (by popular association with *hang*), from *agnail*, q.v.] a bit of torn or cracked skin hanging at the side or base of a fingernail.

hang'nest, *n.* a hangbird.

hang'-out, *n.* a place frequented by some person or group. [Slang.]

hang'ō″vẽr, *n.* 1. something remaining from a previous time or state; a survival.

2. headache, nausea, etc., occurring as an aftereffect of drinking much alcoholic liquor.

hang'wọrm, *n.* any of various caterpillars which suspend themselves by a thread.

hañk, *n.* [late ME.; probably from Anglo-N.; cf. ON. *honk*, a coil, skein.]

1. a loop or coil of something flexible.

2. a specific length of coiled thread or yarn; skein: a hank of worsted yarn contains 560 yards; a hank of cotton contains 840 yards.

3. in nautical usage, a ring of wood, metal, or rope on the edge of a staysail, sliding on the controlling stay.

hañk, *v.t.*; hanked, *pt.*, *pp.*; hanking, *ppr.* to form into a hank or hanks.

hañ'kẽr, *v.i.*; hankered, *pt.*, *pp.*; hankering, *ppr.* [Early Mod. Eng.; prob. from D. *hunkeren*, to long for, desire.]

1. to long (*for*) with a keen appetite; to yearn; as, to *hanker for* (or *after*) fruit.

2. to have a strong desire (to do something); as, he's been *hankering* to go.

hañ'kẽr·ing, *n.* a keen appetite that causes uneasiness till it is gratified; vehement desire to possess or enjoy; yearning; craving.

hañ'kẽr·ing·ly, *adv.* longingly.

hañ'key-pañ'key, *n.* same as *hanky-panky*.

hañ'kle, *v.t.* to twist. [Brit. Dial.]

hañks'īte, *n.* in mineralogy, a sulfate and carbonate of sodium, occurring in hexagonal crystals, found in California: named after H.G. *Hanks*, American mineralogist.

hañ'ky-pañ'ky, *n.* [redupl. and dim. formation, from *hand* as in *sleight of hand*.] talk, manipulation, etc. used in or as in tricks of illusion or sleight of hand to fool the observer; trickery; jugglery; deception. [Colloq.]

Han'nȧh, *n.* in the Bible, the mother of Samuel: I Sam. i. 20.

Han·ō·vē'ri·ăn, *a.* 1. relating to Hanover, Germany, or to its citizens.

2. pertaining to the English royal house of Hanover.

Han·ō·vē'ri·ăn, *n.* 1. one of the house of Hanover; also, in English history, an adherent of the house of Hanover.

2. a native or inhabitant of Hanover, Germany.

Han'sȧrd, *n.* the official record of the debates of the British Parliament: so named after the first publisher, Luke *Hansard*.

Han'särd, *n.* a merchant or citizen of one of the Hanse towns.

hanse, *n.* [OFr. *hanse*; M.H.G. *hanse*, an association of merchants; O.H.G. *hanse*, a band of men.]

1. a medieval guild of merchants.

2. the membership fee in this guild.

3. a toll exacted by this guild from nonmembers.

4. [H–] a medieval league of free towns in northern Germany and adjoining countries, formed for economic advancement and protection: the leading members were Bremen, Lübeck, and Hamburg: also called *Hanseatic League*.

Hanse town; any one of the towns embraced in the Hanseatic League.

hanse, *n.* see *hance*.

Han·sē·at'iç, *a.* of the Hanse or the towns that formed it.

han'sel, *n.* and *v.t.* same as *handsel*.

han'sel·in, *n.* a kind of jacket. [Obs.]

Hän'sen's dis·ēase', [after A. *Hansen* (1841-1912), Norw. physician who discovered its causative bacterium.] leprosy.

han'sŏm, *n.* [named after J. A. *Hansom*, its 19th-c. Eng. inventor.] a one-horse covered carriage with two wheels, seating two persons and having an elevated seat behind for the driver.

HANSOM

Hä'nụk·käh, Hä'nụk·kä, *n.* [Heb. *hanūkkāh*, dedication.] a Jewish festival commemorating the rededication of the Temple by Judas Maccabeus in 165 B.C.: also spelled *Chanukah*.

hȧ·nŭm', *n.* [Turk. *khanum*, lady.] a Turkish title of respect for a woman, equivalent to English *Mrs.* or *madam*.

han'ụ·man, *n.* [Sans., lit., having a jaw, from *hanu*, jaw.]

1. in zoology, a sacred monkey of India, *Semnopithecus entellus*: written also *hoonoomaun*.

2. [H–] in Hindu mythology, a god or idol having the characteristics of a monkey.

hap, *n.* [ME. *hap*, *hæp*, *happe*; Ice. *happ*, chance, luck.]

1. that which comes suddenly or unexpectedly; chance; fortune; accident; casual event. [Archaic.]

> Cursed be good *haps*, and cursed be they that build
> Their hopes on *haps*. —Sidney.

2. [*usually in pl.*] an occurrence; happening. [Archaic.]

hap, *v.i.*; happed, *pt.*, *pp.*; happing, *ppr.* [ME. *happen*, from *hap*, *happe*; Ice. *happ*, chance, luck.] to happen; to befall; to come by chance. [Archaic.]

hap, *v.t.* [ME. *happen*, to wrap, cover.] to wrap; to clothe; to cover. [Scot. and Brit. Dial.]

hap'ȧ·lōte, *n.* [Gr. *hapalos*, soft, and *ous*, *ōtos*, ear.] a jumping mouse of Australia about the size of a rat, characterized by long, tapering ears and a tufted tail.

hā'pen·ny, *n.* a halfpenny. [Brit.]

hap'haz″ărd, *n.* chance; accident.

> We take our principles at *haphazard*, on trust. —Locke.

hap″haz'ărd, *a.* not planned; casual; random.

hap″haz'ărd, *adv.* casually; by chance.

häph·tä'räh, *n.*; *pl.* **häph·tä'rōth,** [Heb.] in Jewish synagogue services, the lesson read from the Prophets on every Sabbath and festival of the year, after the reading of the *parashah*, or lesson from the Law.

hap'less, *a.* unlucky; unfortunate; luckless; as, *hapless* youth.

hap'less·ly, *adv.* in a hapless or unlucky manner.

hap'līte, *n.* a mixture of quartz and orthoclase akin to felsite but of crystalline-granular structure, occurring in dikes.

hap'lō-, [from Gr. *haploos*, single, simple.] a combining form meaning *onefold*, *single*, as in *haplo*petalous, *haplo*dont; also, before a vowel, *hapl-*, as in *hapl*oid.

Hap'lō·don, *n.* a genus of rodents, the sewellels.

hap'lō·dont, *a.* [*haplo-*, and *odous*, *odontos*, a tooth.] in zoology, (a) having simple-crowned teeth; (b) relating to the *Haplodontidæ*.

hap'lō·dont, *n.* an animal with simple-crowned teeth; one of the *Haplodontidæ*.

Hap·lō·don'ti·dae, *n.pl.* a family of rodents related to the beavers: the sewellels, *Haplodon*, constitute the sole genus.

hap·log'rȧ·phy, *n.* [*haplo-*, and Gr. *-graphia*, from *graphein*, to write.] the inadvertent omission of one of two or more adjacent and similar letters, syllables, words, phrases, etc. in copying manuscript, as the writing of *haply* for *happily*, etc.; also, a writing containing such omission.

hap'loid, *a.* [*hapl-* and *-oid.*] having the number of chromosomes characteristic of the mature germ cell (half the number of the somatic cell): distinguished from *diploid*.

hap'loid, *n.* a haploid cell or gamete: distinguished from *diploid*.

Hȧ·plō'mī, *n.pl.* [*haplo-*, and Gr. *ōmos*, shoulder.] a division of fishes including the pikes.

hap·lō·pet'ăl·ous, *a.* [*haplo-*, and Gr. *petalon*, a leaf, petal.] in botany, having the petals in a single whorl.

hap·lō'sis, *n.* [*hapl-* and *-osis.*] in biology, a lessening of the number of chromosomes through the division of a diploid cell into two haploids.

hap·lō·stem'ō·nous, *a.* [*haplo-*, and Gr. *stēmōn* (*-onos*), a thread.] in botany, having the stamens in one whorl: written also *aplostemonous*.

hap'ly, *adv.* by hap, luck, accident, or chance; perchance; perhaps. [Archaic.]

hā'p'ŏrth (-pẽrth), *n.* a halfpenny-worth; hence, a small quantity. [Brit. Dial.]

hap'pen, *v.i.*; happened, *pt.*, *pp.*; happening, *ppr.* [ME. *happenen*, *hapnen*, a form of *happen*, from *happe*; Ice. *happ*, chance, luck.]

1. to occur or befall by chance or without plan; to come unexpectedly.

2. to come to pass in the natural order of things; to take place; to occur or befall; as, death *happens* to all of us.

3. to have the luck or occasion; chance; as, she *happened* to know about it.

4. to come by chance (*along*, *by*, *in*, etc.). [Colloq.]

to happen on (or *upon*); to meet or find by chance; to find incidentally.

hap'pen·ing, *n.* something that happens; occurrence; incident; event.

hap'pen·stance, *n.* [*happen* and circum*stance.*] chance occurrence; accidental happening. [Colloq.]

hap'pi·ly, *adv.* 1. in a happy manner or condition; in happy circumstances; as, they lived *happily* ever after.

2. by good fortune; luckily; as, we are *happily* met.

3. appropriately; gracefully; felicitously; aptly; as, his allusions were most *happily* made.

4. haply. [Archaic.]

Syn.—fortunately, contentedly, successfully, felicitously.

hap'pi·ness, *n.* 1. the enjoyment of pleasure without pain; felicity; blessedness; satisfaction.

2. good luck; good fortune.

3. fortuitous elegance; appropriateness.

Syn.—felicity, blessedness, bliss, aptness.

hap'py, *v.t.* to make happy. [Obs.]

hap'py, *a.*; *comp.* happier; *superl.* happiest, [ME. *happy*, from *hap*, *happe*; Ice. *happ*, good luck, chance, hap.]

1. lucky; fortunate; favored by circumstances.

Chemists have been more *happy* in finding experiments than the causes of them. —Boyle.

2. having, showing, or causing a feeling of great pleasure, joy, contentment, etc.; joyous; glad; pleased; satisfied.

He found himself *happiest* in communicating happiness to others. —Wirt.

3. exactly appropriate to the occasion; suitable and clever; felicitous; apt.

One gentleman is *happy* at a reply, another excels in a rejoinder. —Swift.

4. intoxicated or as if intoxicated: sometimes used in hyphenated combinations, as slap-*happy*. [Slang.]

Syn.—lucky, fortunate, felicitous, successful, delighted, joyous, merry, blithesome, prosperous, glad, blissful.

hap'py-gō-luck'y, *a.* taking things as they come; easygoing; unworrying; light-hearted; trusting to luck or chance; as, a *happy-go-lucky* character.

hap'py-gō-luck'y, *adv.* just as may happen; in a haphazard way; by chance.

hä'pu̇·kȧ, *n.* [New Zealand.] a large food fish of New Zealand.

hä'rä-kī'ri, *n.* [Japan., from *hara*, belly, and *kiri*, cutting, cut.] ritual suicide by disembowelment: it is called *seppuku* by the Japanese, and was practiced by high-ranking Japanese in lieu of execution or to avoid disgrace: also *hara-kari*, *harikari*.

hãr'ăm, *n.* a harem.

hȧ·rangue' (-rang'), *n.* [OFr. *harangue*, a public address, from O.H.G. *hring*, a ring, ring of people, arena.] a long, blustering, noisy, or pompous speech; a tirade.

Syn.—speech, oration, declamation, address, tirade.—*Speech* is generic; an *oration* is an elaborate and prepared speech; a *harangue* is a vehement appeal to the passions or a noisy, disputatious address.

hȧ·rangue', *v.i.*; harangued, *pt.*, *pp.*; haranguing, *ppr.* to give a harangue; as, he *harangued* without success.

hȧ·rangue', *v.t.* to address in a harangue; to speak to in an impassioned and forcible manner; as, to *harangue* a political club.

hȧ·rangue'fu̇l, *a.* full of harangue.

hȧ·rang'uẽr (-ẽr), *n.* one who addresses an assembly with vehemence or passion; a noisy declaimer.

hä'rä-nut, *n.* the stone fruit of a plant native to India, *Terminalia citrina*.

har'ăss (*or* hȧ-ras'), *v.t.*; harassed, *pt.*, *pp.*; harassing, *ppr.* [OFr. *harasser*, to tire out, vex.]

1. to weary; to fatigue to excess; to tire with bodily labor; as, to *harass* an army by a long march. [Obs.]

2. to trouble, worry, or torment, as with cares, debts, repeated questions, etc.

3. in military usage, to trouble (the enemy) by constant raids or attacks, continual fire, etc.; harry.

4. to scrape, as in dressing skins.

Syn.—tire, worry, perplex, annoy, irritate.

har'ăss, *n.* 1. waste; devastation. [Obs.]

2. worry; annoyance. [Rare.]

har'ăss·ẽr, *n.* one who harasses.

har'ăss·ment, *n.* 1. the act of harassing, or the condition of being harassed.

2. a thing that harasses.

här'bin·ġẽr, *n.* [ME. *herbergeour*; OFr. *herbergeor*, one who provides a lodging, from *herbergier*, to provide a lodging.]

1. a forerunner; a precursor; one who or that which precedes and gives notice of the arrival of some person or thing.

2. formerly, a royal officer who rode ahead of a traveling court to secure accommodations.

här'bin·ġẽr, *v.t.*; harbingered, *pt.*, *pp.*; harbingering, *ppr.* to act as a harbinger for; to announce; to precede; to presage; to foretell; as, the early flowers *harbinger* spring.

här'bin·ġẽr-ŏf-spring, *n.* an herb of the parsley family, *Erigenia bulbosa*, characterized by early blooming and by flowers having white petals and brownish anthers.

här'bŏr, *n.* [ME. *harbor*, *harber*, *herber*, *herberwe*, *herberge*; Ice. *herbergi*, originally, a shelter for soldiers; *herr*, an army, and *bjarga*, to save, help.]

1. a lodging; a place of entertainment and rest. [Obs.]

For *harbor* at a thousand doors they knocked. —Dryden.

2. a port or haven for ships; a bay or inlet of a sea or large lake in which ships can moor and be sheltered from wind and wave; any navigable water where ships can ride in safety.

3. an asylum; a shelter; a place of safety or refuge, as from storms or danger.

4. in glassworks, a box for holding mixed materials before they are fused.

5. a hiding place of deer; a covert. [Obs.]

close harbor; a harbor with gates at the entrance; a harbor that may be opened or closed at will.

open harbor; a roadstead; an unsheltered harbor.

här'bŏr, *v.t.*; harbored, *pt.*, *pp.*; harboring, *ppr.* 1. to serve as a place of protection to; to house; to shelter; to secrete; as, to *harbor* a thief.

2. to entertain; to hold in the mind; to cherish; as, to *harbor* malice or revenge.

här'bŏr, *v.i.* to lodge or abide for a time; to take shelter, as in a harbor.

This night let's *harbor* here in York. —Shak.

här'bŏr·ȧġe, *n.* 1. a shelter for ships.

2. (a) shelter; (b) lodging.

här'bŏr dūeṣ, certain charges to which a ship or its cargo is subjected for the use of a harbor, moorings, etc.

här'bŏr·ẽr, *n.* one who harbors or shelters.

här'bŏr gas'ket, one of a series of broad but short and well-blacked gaskets, placed at equal distances on the yard of a ship, for showing off a well-furled sail in port.

här'bŏr·less, *a.* without a harbor; destitute of shelter or a lodging.

här'bŏr log, that part of the logbook which contains entries for the period during which a ship is in port.

här'bŏr mȧs'tẽr, the official in charge of enforcing the regulations governing the use of a harbor.

här'bŏr·ōugh (-ō), *n.* an inn; a lodging; a shelter. [Obs.]

här'bŏr·ous, *a.* hospitable; affording shelter. [Obs.]

här'bŏr sēal, the common seal, *Phoca vitulina*.

här'bŏr wätch, a watch kept while a ship is in harbor.

här'bŏur, *n.*, *v.t.* and *v.i.* harbor: British spelling.

här'bŏur·äġe, *n.* harborage: British spelling.

här'brōugh, här'brōw, *n.* harbor. [Obs.]

härd, *a.*; *comp.* harder; *superl.* hardest, [ME. *hard*; AS. *heard*, hard, firm, brave.]

1. firm; solid; compact; not easily penetrated or separated into parts; not yielding to pressure; firm and unyielding to the touch: applied to material bodies, and opposed to *soft*; as, *hard* wood; *hard* flesh; a *hard* apple.

2. made of metal: said of coins.

3. having firm muscles; in good bodily trim; vigorous and robust.

4. showing, or done with, great force or strength; powerful; violent; vigorous; as, a *hard* blow.

5. demanding great physical or mental effort or labor; fatiguing; difficult; specifically, (a) difficult to do; as, *hard* work; (b) difficult to understand, explain, or answer; as, a *hard* question; (c) difficult to deal with; not easily managed or controlled; as, a man *hard* to live with; (d) firmly fastened or tied; as, a *hard* knot. Opposed to *easy*.

6. practical and shrewd; severe in business relations; as, a *hard* customer.

7. causing pain or discomfort; specifically, (a) difficult to endure; trying; exhausting; as, a *hard* life; (b) harsh; severe; stern; as, a *hard* master, *hard* words.

8. very cold, stormy, etc.; inclement; as, a *hard* winter.

9. too clear, bright, or penetrating to be pleasant; as, a *hard* red.

10. having in solution mineral salts that interfere with the lathering and cleansing properties of soap: said of water.

11. containing much alcohol; strong: said of alcoholic liquors.

12. in agriculture, high in gluten content; as, *hard* wheat.

13. in commerce, high and stable: said of a market, prices, etc.

14. in phonetics, (a) popularly, designating *c* and *g* when they are explosive rather than fricative or affricative, as in *cake* and *gun*; (b) voiceless, as the *th* in *thin*. The term is not used in scientific terminology.

15. unfeeling; not easily moved by pity; not susceptible of kindness, mercy, or other tender affections; harsh; severe; obdurate; exacting; as, a *hard* heart, a *hard* landlord.

16. stiff; conventional; constrained; unnatural.

Figures *harder* than the marble itself. —Dryden.

17. zealous; industrious; persevering; energetic; earnest; as, a *hard* worker; a *hard* student.

18. reprobate; bad; as, a *hard* character. [Colloq.]

hard and fast; (a) invariable; unbreakable; strict: said of rules, regulations, etc.; (b) firmly grounded: said of a ship on shore.

hard of hearing; partially deaf.

hard put to it; having considerable difficulty or trouble.

hard up; in great need of something, especially money; in desperate straits. [Colloq.]

in hard condition; in good muscular condition: said of prize fighters, athletes, race horses, etc.

to be hard on; (a) to treat severely; to be harsh toward; (b) to be difficult, unpleasant, or painful for.

Syn.—solid, firm, arduous, difficult, harsh, severe, oppressive.

härd, *adv.* 1. close; near; as, we live *hard* by.
My soul followeth *hard* after thee. —Ps. lxiii. 8.
2. energetically and persistently; steadily and earnestly; as, to work *hard*.
3. with vigor, strength, or violence; as, to hit *hard*.
4. with difficulty: used in hyphenated compounds, as *hard*-earned, *hard*-living.
5. only after a struggle; as, to die *hard*.
6. firmly; tightly; as, to hold on *hard*.
7. so as to be or make firm, solid, or rigid; as, it will freeze *hard*.
8. in nautical usage, with vigor and to the fullest extent: used especially in directions to the helmsman, as, *Hard* alee!
9. so as to raise difficulties or cause pain, trouble, etc.
The question is *hard* set. —Browne.
to go hard with; to cause pain, trouble, or discomfort to.

härd, *n.* 1. the hard part of anything; that which is hard, as the shell of a nut. [Obs.]
2. a hard roadway or path. [Brit. Dial.]
3. [*pl.*] a mixture of alum and salt used by bakers to whiten bread.
4. a ford across a river or a causeway over a swamp. [Brit. Dial.]

härd'back, *n.* a hard-cover book.

härd'bāke, *n.* a kind of sweetmeat of boiled brown sugar or molasses with blanched almonds. [Brit.]

härd'bill, *n.* a grosbeak.

härd'-bit'ten, *a.* 1. originally, that bites hard; tough in fighting: said of dogs.
2. stubborn; tough; enduring; dogged; as, *hard-bitten* soldiers.

härd'bōard, *n.* a boardlike material made in sheets by subjecting fibers from wood chips to pressure and heat.

härd'-boiled', *a.* 1. boiled in water until both the white and yolk solidify: said of eggs.
2. unsentimental; tough; callous. [Colloq.]

härd cash, 1. metal coins.
2. ready money; cash.

härd cī'dẽr, fermented apple juice; alcoholic cider.

härd çōal, anthracite coal.

härd çop'y, a computer printout often supplied along with or instead of a display of data on a fluorescent screen by means of a cathode-ray tube.

härd'-çōre', *a.* 1. constituting or of a hard core.
2. absolute; unqualified.

härd çōre, the firm, unyielding, or unchanging central part or group.

härd drug, any drug, such as heroin or cocaine, that is addictive and potentially very damaging to the body or mind. [Colloq.]

härd'en, *v.t.* and *v.i.*; hardened, *pt.*, *pp.*; hardening, *ppr.* [ME. *hardnen, hardenen*, to make hard.] to make or become hard (in various senses).

Här·den·bẽr'gi·ȧ, *n.* [from Countess *Hardenberg* of Germany.] a genus of leguminous herbs or woody climbing plants, native to Australia. *Hardenbergia monophylla* is sometimes cultivated in greenhouses.

härd'ened, *a.* made hard, or more hard or compact; made unfeeling; made obstinate; confirmed in error or vice.
Syn.—callous, insensible, unfeeling.

härd'en·ẽr, *n.* a person or thing that hardens: specifically, (a) a person who tempers metal tools; (b) a substance used to give a harder film to paint, varnish, etc.

härd'en·ing, *a.* 1. a making or becoming hard.
2. a substance used to harden something.

Här·dē'ri·ăn, *a.* [named after J. J. *Harder*, a Swiss anatomist.] designating a gland of the nictitating membrane in the orbit of the eye in some animals.

härd'-fā"vŏred, *a.* having coarse features.

härd'-fā"vŏred·ness, *n.* coarseness of features.

härd'-fēa"tūred, *a.* having coarse, cruel, stern, or harsh features.

härd'fẽrn, *n.* any fern of the genus *Lomaria*, especially *Lomaria spicant*.

härd'fist'ed, *a.* 1. having hard or strong hands, as a laborer.
2. closefisted; selfish; stingy; niggardly.

härd'-fought (-fọt), *a.* vigorously contested; as, a *hard-fought* battle.

härd'gọọds, *n.pl.* durable goods, such as automobiles, furniture, etc.: also *hard goods*.

härd grȧss, any one of various grasses of several genera, as *Rottbœllia* and *Ægilops*.

härd'hack, *n.* in botany, *Spiræa tomentosa*, a plant of the rose family, with clusters of pink, purple, or white flowers and hairy leaves: it is common in pastures and low grounds.

härd'hand'ed, *a.* 1. having hard hands, as a laborer.
2. severe; tyrannical; ruthless: said of a ruler or rule.

härd hat, 1. a protective helmet worn by construction workers, miners, etc.
2. such a worker. [Slang.]

härd'head (-hed), *n.* 1. clash or collision of heads in contest. [Obs.]
2. an old copper coin of Scotland.
3. in botany, *Centaurea nigra*, the knapweed.
4. in zoology, one of several animals; (a) the gray whale of California; (b) the menhaden; (c) the gray gurnard, *Trigla gurnardus*; (d) the ruddy duck; (e) the salmon trout; (f) the sculpin.
5. a round boulder found among gravel. [Colloq.]
6. a kind of coarse sponge.
7. an alloy left after refining tin.
8. a person who is shrewd and not easily moved.

härd'head'ed, *a.* 1. shrewd and unsentimental; practical; matter-of-fact.
2. stubborn.

härd'head'ed·ness, *n.* shrewdness; practicality; also, stubbornness.

härd'heärt'ed, *a.* cruel; pitiless; unfeeling; inhuman; inexorable.

härd'heärt"ed·ly, *adv.* in a hardhearted or cruel manner.

härd'heärt"ed·ness, *n.* want of feeling or tenderness; cruelty; inhumanity.

här'di·hood, *n.* 1. resolute boldness; bravery; intrepidity; daring.
2. impudence; insolence; effrontery.
It is the society of numbers which gives *hardihood* to iniquity. —Buckminster.
Syn.—audacity, courage, impudence, resolution, boldness, fearlessness, effrontery.

här'di·ly, *adv.* 1. in a hardy manner; with hardiness.
2. certainly; surely. [Obs.]

här'di·ness, *n.* 1. boldness: firm courage; intrepidity; assurance; bravery.
2. capacity for physical endurance; strength.
3. hardship; fatigue. [Obs.]

härd'ish, *a.* rather hard.

härd lā'bŏr, compulsory and continuous physical labor imposed, together with imprisonment, as a punishment for some crimes.

härd'-lā"bŏred, *a.* wrought with severe labor; elaborate; studied; as, a *hard-labored* poem.

härd land'ing, a landing, as of a rocket on the moon, made at relatively high speed, with an impact that may destroy all or much of the equipment.

härd'-līne', *a.* characterized by an aggressive, unyielding position in politics, foreign policy, etc.

härd'ly, *adv.* 1. with difficulty; with great effort.
Recovering *hardly* what he lost before. —Dryden.
2. only just; scarcely; barely: often used ironically or politely to mean "not quite" or "not at all."
3. improbably; not likely.
Hardly shall you find any one so bad, but he desires the credit of being thought good. —South.
4. severely; harshly; oppressively.
Syn.—barely, merely, scarcely, severely.

härd mŏn'ey, coin, as distinguished from paper money.

härd'mouthed, *a.* not sensitive to the bit; not easily governed; as, a *hardmouthed* horse.

härd'ness, *n.* [ME. *hardnesse*; AS. *heardnes*, from *heard*, hard.]
1. firmness; close union of component parts; compactness; solidity; the quality of bodies which resists impression or the separation of their particles: opposed to *softness*.
2. the state or quality of being hard in any sense; as, *hardness* of comprehension, of an undertaking, or of the times.
3. obduracy; impenitence; a confirmed state of wickedness; as, *hardness* of heart.
4. in mineralogy, the quality of bodies which enables them to resist abrasion of their surfaces, the diamond being the hardest body known.
5. the quality imparted to water by reason of holding mineral matter in solution.

härd'-nōsed, *a.* 1. indomitable; tough; stubborn. [Slang.]
2. shrewd and practical. [Slang.]

härd pal'ăte, the bony part of the roof of the mouth, behind the upper teeth.

härd'pan, *n.* 1. a hard layer of earth beneath the soil, composed mainly of clay, and impervious to water.
2. solid, unplowed ground.
3. the hard, underlying part of anything; solid foundation.

härd peār, in botany, a small tree of South Africa, the hard wood of which is used to make musical instruments.

härd rub'bẽr, vulcanized rubber that is firm and comparatively inelastic.

härds, *n.pl.* [ME. *hardes, herdes*, from AS. pl. *heordan*, hards.] the refuse or coarse part of flax or hemp; tow: also *hurds*.

härd sạuce, a sweet, creamy mixture of butter, powdered sugar, and flavoring, served with plum pudding, etc.

härd sell, high-pressure salesmanship.

härd'-set', *a.* 1. in trouble or difficulty.
2. rigid; fixed; firm.
3. stubborn.

härd'-shell, *a.* 1. in zoology, covered with a hard shell; as, a *hard-shell* clam.
2. fixed; immovable as to belief or practice; strict; strait-laced; uncompromising. [Colloq.]

härd'-shelled, *a.* having a shell not recently molted: said of crabs.

härd'ship, *n.* 1. hard circumstances of life.
2. a thing hard to bear; a specific cause of discomfort or suffering, as poverty, pain, etc.
Syn.—trial, burden, privation, affliction.

härd'tack, *n.* large, coarse, hard unleavened bread, traditionally furnished to soldiers or sailors; sea biscuit.

härd'tāil, *n.* a fish, *Caranx chrysos*, or blue runner.

härd'wāre, *n.* 1. articles made of metal, as pots, kettles, saws, knives, nails, etc.
2. heavy military equipment or its parts, especially weapons, vehicles, missiles, etc.
3. (a) apparatus used for controlling spacecraft, etc.; (b) the mechanical, magnetic, and electronic design, structure, and devices of a computer: distinguished from *software*.

härd'wāre·măn, *n.* a maker or seller of hardware.

härd'wood, *n.* 1. any tough, heavy timber with a compact texture.
2. in forestry, wood other than that from a pine, spruce, or other conifer.
3. a tree yielding hardwood.

härd'wood, *a.* made of hardwood; containing trees furnishing hardwood; as, *hardwood* furniture, a *hardwood* forest.

här'dy, *a.*; *comp.* hardier; *superl.* hardiest, [ME. *hardy, hardi*; OFr. *hardi*, hardy, bold, daring, pp. of *hardir*, to make bold; O.H.G. *harti, herti*, hardy.]
1. bold; brave; stout; daring; resolute.
2. strong; firm; compact.
An unwholesome blast may shake in pieces his *hardy* fabric. —South.
3. too bold; full of temerity; rash.
4. inured to fatigue or exposure; robust; vigorous; as, a *hardy* soldier.
5. in gardening, able to survive the winter without special care: said of plants.
Syn.—inured, robust, strong, stouthearted, vigorous, resistant, enduring.

här'dy, *n.* in blacksmithing, a chisellike tool with a square shank set into a hole of the anvil and used for cutting off pieces from iron rods, etc.

här'dy hōle, the hole in an anvil in which a hardy is set.

hāre, *n.*; *pl.* **hāres** or **hāre,** [ME. *hare*; AS. *hara*, a hare.]
1. any of various gnawing mammals, order *Lagomorpha*, with long ears, a short tail, soft fur, a divided upper lip, long hind legs, and hairy soles. The species are numerous and found in most countries, especially those of the Northern Hemisphere.
2. any of the players chased in the game of hare and hounds.
3. [H-] in astronomy, a constellation situated directly under Orion.
Belgian hare; a fancy species of hare bred from Belgian stock for its fur, which is used in making hats, and for its flesh as food.
chief hare, little chief hare; the pika.
first catch your hare; an aphorism to the effect that, before disposing of a thing, you ought to make sure of the possession of it. In

reality the saying arose from a misprint, *catch* being an error for *case*, in the sense of to skin. Properly therefore the direction is, first *case* (skin) your hare, etc.

hare and hounds; a game in which one or two of a party represent hares and the rest hounds, in imitation of the sport of hare-hunting with hounds. The hare or hares set out from the starting place, scattering bits of white paper as they go, the hounds following after an interval and endeavoring to catch them before they reach a point previously determined upon.

mad as a March hare; crazy; eccentric; wild as a hare at breeding time.

hāre′bell, *n.* [ME. *harebelle*; *hare*, a hare, and *belle*, bell.] a slender, delicate plant of the genus *Campanula*, with clusters of blue, bell-shaped flowers; the bluebell.

HAREBELL (*Campanula rotundifolia*)

hāre′brāined, hāre′brāin, *a.* having no more intelligence than a hare; reckless, flighty, giddy, rash, etc.

hāre′brāin, *n.* a harebrained person.

hȧ·reem′, *n.* a harem.

hāre′foot, *n.* 1. a foot resembling that of a hare, slender and extending forward.

2. figuratively, a swift-footed person.

3. a grouse or ptarmigan.

4. same as *hare's-foot*, sense 1.

hāre′-heärt″ed, *a.* timorous; easily frightened.

hāre′hound, *n.* a hound used to hunt hares.

hāre kan·gȧ·roo′, a small kangaroo found in Australia, much like a hare in size and habits.

har′eld, *n.* in zoology, the *Harelda glacialis*, or long-tailed sea duck, valued for its down.

hāre′lip, *n.* 1. a congenital deformity of one or both lips, usually only the upper one, consisting of a cleft like that of a hare's lip: it often results in a speech defect.

2. a lip with such a deformity.

hāre′lipped (-lipt), *a.* having a harelip.

hār′em, *n.* [Turk. *harem*; Ar. *haram*, anything forbidden, a sacred place or thing, from *harama*, to forbid, prohibit.]

1. the division allotted to women in the larger dwelling houses of Moslems.

2. the women, especially the wives and concubines, constituting the household of a Moslem.

3. a place regarded as sacred among Moslems; specifically, either of the two cities Mecca and Medina, from which infidels are excluded.

hȧ·ren′gi·form, *a.* shaped like a herring.

hāre′ṣ′-bāne, *n.* in botany, a species of *Aconitum*, of the crowfoot family; wolf's-bane.

hāre′ṣ′-ēar, *n.* a European plant of the parsley family, genus *Bupleurum*, having a leaf resembling the ear of a hare.

hāre′ṣ′-foot, *n.* 1. a species of red clover, *Trifolium arvense*: also called *harefoot*, *rabbit-foot clover*, and *stone clover*.

2. the corkwood tree of the West Indies and Central America, valued for its lightweight wood, which is used in building boats, rafts, etc.: named from the appearance of the cotton protruding when the boll ripens.

hare's-foot fern; a fern native in the Madeira and Canary Islands, characterized by its gray, hairy rootstocks.

hāre′ṣ′-let″tuce, *n.* the sow thistle, *Sonchus oleraceus*: also called *hare thistle*. [Brit. Dial.]

hāre′ṣ′-pärs″ley, *n.* an umbelliferous European plant, *Anthriscus sylvestris*; the wild chervil.

hāre′ṣ′-tāil, *n.* a grass of the sedge family.

hāre′ṣ′-tāil grȧss, a European grass characterized by a perianth of white cottony fibers resembling a hare's tail.

här′fang, *n.* [Sw. *harfang*, lit., hare-catcher; *hare*, hare, and *fanga*, to catch, seize.] the snowy owl.

hä·ri·ä′li grȧss, the East Indian name of Bermuda grass.

har′i·cōt (-kō), *n.* [Fr., from *harigoter*, to cut to pieces.]

1. a highly seasoned stew of lamb or mutton and vegetables.

2. [said to be from Nahuatl *ayecotli*, bean, but perh. from name of the stew (beans being a constituent?).], (a) the kidney bean; (b) its pod or seed.

har′i·ēr, *n.* same as *harrier*.

hä′ri-kä′ri, *n.* same as *hara-kiri*.

har″i·ō·lā′tion, *n.* [L. *hariolatio* (*-onis*), from *hariolari*, to foretell, from *hariolus*, a soothsayer.] prognostication; soothsaying. [Obs.]

hār′ish, *a.* like a hare.

härk, *v.i.* [ME. *herkien* (akin to G. *horchen*, etc.); perh. from AS. *heorcnian*.] to listen carefully: usually in the imperative, with the effect of an exclamation.

to hark back; (a) to return to an earlier point so as to pick up the scent or trail again; hence, (b) to go back in thought or speech; revert.

härk, *v.t.* to listen to; to hear. [Archaic.]

härk′en, *v.i.* and *v.t.* same as hearken.

härk′en·ēr, *n.* same as *hearkener*.

härl, hąurl, *v.t.* [ME. *harlen*, to drag or scrape.]

1. to drag along with force. [Brit. Dial.]

2. to roughcast, as a wall, with lime. [Brit. Dial.]

3. to entangle; snarl; confuse. [Brit. Dial.]

4. to slit the hind leg of (an animal carcass), for the purpose of suspension or carrying. [Brit. Dial.]

härl, hērl, *n.* [ME. *herle*; prob. from L.G. or D.]

1. any substance made up of filaments, as the combings of flax, hair, etc.

2. a feather barb used in dressing a hook for fly fishing.

Här′leçh, *n.* [named after *Harlech*, in Wales.] in geology, a group of rocks of the Lower Silurian: also called *Harlech grits*.

Här′lē·iăn, *a.* relating to Robert Harley, Earl of Oxford (1661–1724), and Edward Harley (1689–1741), his son; as, the *Harleian* collection in the British Museum, which consists of twenty-two thousand books and manuscripts.

Här′lem, *n.* a section of New York City with a large Negro population.

här′le·quin (-kwin *or* -kin), *a.* 1. comic; ludicrous.

2. of many colors; colorful.

3. [from the resemblance to the slanting eye holes of the mask.] designating eyeglasses with brightly colored frames and slanting, elliptical eyepieces.

harlequin bat; a kind of bat common in India, remarkable for its coloring, pale-tawny brown variegated with white spots.

harlequin beetle; a very large South American longicorn coleopter, *Acrocinus longimanus*, resembling a harlequin in the colors of the elytra, which are gray, red, and black.

harlequin cabbage bug; same as *cabbage bug*.

harlequin caterpillar; the moth *Euchætes egle* in the larval state, characterized by tufts of white, black, and orange.

harlequin duck; an arctic ash-colored duck, the male spotted with white, with eyelids and flanks red.

harlequin flower; in botany, any of the ornamental plants of the genus *Sparaxis*, of the iris family, from South Africa.

harlequin moth; a geometrid moth, *Eufitchia ribearia*, the larva of which feeds on the leaves of the currant and gooseberry: called also *currant moth*, *magpie moth*, and *harlequin*.

harlequin opal; in mineralogy, a precious opal characterized by a play of varied colors on a red or reddish ground.

harlequin snake; a venomous snake, *Elaps fulvius*, of the southern United States, ringed with red and black.

Här′le·quin, *n.* [Fr. *harlequin*, *arlequin*; It. *arlecchino*; OFr. *harlequin*, *hierlekin*, *hellequin*, a demon, spirit, orig. demon huntsman.]

1. in French and Italian comedy and modern pantomime, a traditional clownish character who wears a mask and gay, spangled tights of many colors, and sometimes carries a wooden wand or sword.

2. [h–] anyone who exhibits the characteristics of a stage harlequin; a buffoon; a clownish fellow.

3. [h–] the harlequin duck.

här′le·quin, *v.i.*; harlequined, *pt.*, *pp.*; harlequining, *ppr.* to play the harlequin; to make sport by playing ludicrous tricks.

här″le·quin·āde′, *n.* [Fr. *arlequinade*.]

1. that part of a play or pantomime enacted principally by the harlequin and the clown.

2. buffoonery, or that which resembles the buffoonery of a harlequin; comic pranks.

här′le·quin·ēr·y, *n.* harlequinade.

här′lock, *n.* a plant mentioned by Shakespeare and other Elizabethan writers, not identified, but probably the burdock.

här′lŏt, *n.* [ME. *harlot*, *herlot*; OFr. *harlot*, *herlot*, *arlot*, a vagabond.]

1. a woman who prostitutes her body for hire; a prostitute.

2. a manservant; a churl. [Obs.]

3. a base person; a rogue; a cheat. [Obs.]

här′lŏt, *a.* wanton; lewd; low; base.

här′lŏt, *v.i.* to practice lewdness.

här′lŏt·ry, *n.*; *pl.* **här′lŏt·rieṣ,** 1. the trade or practice of prostitution; habitual or customary lewdness.

2. ribaldry; obscenity. [Obs.]

3. a woman of ill fame. [Archaic.]

4. false show; meretriciousness.

härm, *n.* [ME. *harm*, *herm*; AS. *hearm*, grief, injury.]

1. physical or material injury; hurt; damage; detriment; misfortune.

2. moral wrong; evil; mischief; wickedness.

härm, *v.t.*; harmed, *pt.*, *pp.*; harming, *ppr.* [ME. *harmen*, *hermen*, *harmien*; AS. *hearmian*, to hurt, injure, from *hearm*, grief, injury.] to hurt; to injure; to damage; to inflict harm upon.

här′mȧ·lȧ, *n.* same as *harmel*.

här′mȧ·line, här′mȧ·lin, *n.* [*harmala* and *-in*, *-ine*.] in chemistry, a crystalline alkaloid, $C_{13}H_{14}N_2O$, found in the coverings of harmel seeds.

här·măt·tan′, *n.* [Sp. *harmatán*, from the native (Fanti) name in W. Africa.] an intensely hot, dry wind accompanied by clouds of dust, blowing at intervals from the interior of Africa toward the west coast.

här′mel, *n.* [Ar. *harmal*.] an herb found in Africa and Asia, *Peganum harmala*, possessing a very strong odor, the husks yielding harmaline, and the seeds a vermifuge and disinfectant.

härm′fụl, *a.* causing harm; hurtful.

härm′fụl·ly, *adv.* in a harmful manner.

härm′fụl·ness, *n.* the state or quality of being harmful.

här′mīne, här′min, *n.* in chemistry, a white alkaloid, $C_{13}H_{12}N_2O$, crystalline in form, obtained from harmaline or from harmel seeds.

härm′less, *a.* 1. destitute of power, tendency, or inclination to harm or injure; not hurtful; innocuous; as, *harmless* games, *harmless* drink.

2. unhurt; undamaged; uninjured. [Rare.]

3. in law, free from loss or liability; as, a contract to save one *harmless*.

Syn.—innocent, inoffensive, unoffending, inoxious, innocuous.

härm′less·ly, *adv.* in a harmless manner.

härm′less·ness, *n.* the state or quality of being harmless.

Här·mō′ni·ȧ, *n.* [Gr. *harmonia*, harmony.] in Greek mythology, the daughter of Aphrodite and Ares, and wife of Cadmus: she personified harmony and order.

här·mon′iç, *a.* [L. *harmonicus*; Gr. *harmonikos*, harmonic, from *harmonia*, harmony.]

1. harmonious in feeling or effect; agreeing.

2. in mathematics, designating or of a series of numbers whose reciprocals are in arithmetical progression.

3. in music, (a) of harmony rather than melody or rhythm; (b) of or producing a combination of sounds that is pleasing to the ear; consonant; (c) designating a tone whose rate of vibration is a precise multiple of that of a given fundamental tone.

harmonic interval; in music, the distance between two notes of a chord or between two consonant notes.

harmonic motion; the motion of a point at the foot of a perpendicular dropped from a point moving uniformly in the circumference of a circle, to a fixed diameter of the circle: often called *simple harmonic motion*, as distinguished from the combination of more than one harmonic motion.

harmonic progression; see under *progression*.

harmonic proportion; see under *proportion*.

harmonic triad; in music, the common chord or triad; the chord of a note with its third and fifth.

HARMONIC TRIAD

här·mon′iç, *n.* 1. in music, an overtone, especially one made by lightly stopping a vibrating string at some specified point.

2. in electricity, a voltage or alternating current whose frequency is some integral multiple of the fundamental frequency.

3. in mathematics, any one of several classes of functions.

här·mon′i·çȧ, *n.* [L., fem. of *harmonicus*; see *harmonic*.]

1. a musical instrument consisting of a series of graduated glasses from which tones are produced by rubbing the edges with a wet finger: invented by Benjamin Franklin.
2. a percussion instrument consisting of metal or glass strips which are struck with small mallets.
3. a small wind instrument played with the mouth: it has a series of graduated metal reeds that vibrate and produce tones when air is blown or sucked across them: also called *mouth organ.*

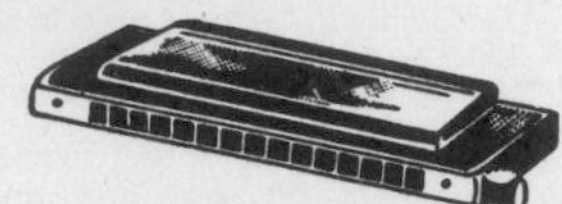

HARMONICA (sense 3)

här·mon′iç·ăl·ly, *adv.* 1. harmoniously. [Archaic.]
2. in mathematics, in harmonic relation or progression.
3. in music, with reference to harmony.

här·mon′i·çŏn, *n.*; *pl.* **här·mon′i·çȧ,** [Gr. *harmonikon,* neut. of *harmonikos,* musical, from *harmonia,* harmony.]
1. a harmonica.
2. a barrel organ in which the tones of various instruments are imitated; an orchestrion.

här·mon′içs, *n.pl.* [*construed as sing.*] the doctrine or science of musical sounds.

här·mō′ni·ous, *a.* [L. *harmonia,* harmony.]
1. adapted to each other; having the parts combined in a proportionate, orderly, or pleasing arrangement; congruous; symmetrical.

God hath made the intellectual world *harmonious* and beautiful without us. —Locke.

2. in music, having tones combined to give a pleasing effect; concordant; consonant; as, *harmonious* sounds are agreeable to the ear.
3. having similar or conforming feelings, ideas, interests, etc.; in accord; as, a *harmonious* family or society.

Syn.—congruous, accordant, proportioned, melodious, musical, dulcet, tuneful, agreeable.

här·mō′ni·ous·ly, *adv.* in a harmonious manner.

här·mō′ni·ous·ness, *n.* the state of being in harmony.

här·mon′i·phon, *n.* [Gr. *harmonia,* harmony, and *phōnē,* sound.] an obsolete wind instrument consisting of a series of free reeds inserted in a tube like a clarinet and played by means of keys like those of an organ.

här′mō·nist, *n.* 1. in music, one skilled in the principles of harmony; a writer of harmony; a musical composer.
2. a poet.
3. a literary scholar who shows the agreement or harmony between corresponding passages of different writers or authors on the same subject.
4. one who harmonizes something.
5. [H-] one of a sect of Protestants from Württemberg, who settled in America in 1803 at Harmony, Pennsylvania. They held their property in common. Also called *Economite* and *Rappist.*

Här′mō·nīte, *n.* same as *Harmonist,* sense 5.

här·mō′ni·um, *n.* [Fr., from L. *harmonia;* see *harmony.*] a small keyboard organ in which the tones are produced by forcing air through metal reeds by means of a bellows operated by pedals.

här″mō·ni·zā′tion, *n.* the act of harmonizing or state of being harmonized.

här′mō·nīze, *v.i.*; harmonized, *pt., pp.*; harmonizing, *ppr.* 1. to agree in action, adaptation, or effect; to agree in sense or purport; as, the arguments *harmonize;* the facts stated by different witnesses *harmonize.*
2. to exist in peace and friendship, as individuals or families.
3. in music, to sing or play in harmony; to agree in sounds or musical effect; as, the tones *harmonize.*

här′mō·nīze, *v.t.* 1. to make harmonious; to cause to agree; to show the harmony or agreement of; to reconcile.
2. to add chords to (a melody) so as to form a harmony; to set accompanying parts to, as an air or melody.

här′mō·nī·zẽr, *n.* one who harmonizes.

här·mō·nom′e·tẽr, *n.* [Gr. *harmonia,* harmony, and *metron,* a measure.] an instrument or monochord for measuring the harmonic relations of sounds.

här′mō·ny, *n.*; *pl.* **här′mō·nieṣ,** [Fr. *harmonie;* L. *harmonia;* Gr. *harmonia,* a fitting together, agreement, from *harmos,* a fitting, joining.]
1. a combination of parts into an orderly or proportionate whole; congruity; as, the *harmony* of the universe.
2. concord or agreement in feeling, action, ideas, interests, etc.; peace and friendship; as, the citizens live in *harmony.*
3. agreement or proportionate arrangement of color, size, shape, etc. that is pleasing to the eye; a fitting well together.
4. an arrangement of parallel passages of different authors, the Scriptures, etc., made so as to bring out corresponding ideas, qualities, etc.
5. agreeable sounds; music.
6. in music, (a) the pleasing combination of two or more tones in a chord; (b) structure in terms of the arrangement, progression, modulation, etc. of chords: distinguished from *melody, rhythm;* (c) the study of this structure.

close harmony; see under *close,* a.

dispersed harmony; harmony in which the tones of the various parts are at wide intervals from each other.

harmony of the spheres; same as *music of the spheres* under *music.*

Syn.—accordance, agreement, amity, concord, congruity, unison, melody.

här′mōst, *n.* [Gr. *harmostēs,* a governor, from *harmozein,* to set in order, arrange.] in ancient Greece, a Spartan governor, regulator, or prefect.

här′mō·tōme, *n.* [Gr. *harmos,* a joint, and *tomē,* a cutting.] in mineralogy, a hydrous silicate of the zeolite group: called also *crossstone,* from the form of its crystals.

härn, *n.* very coarse linen. [Scot.]

här′ness, *n.* [ME. *harneis, harneys;* OFr. *harnas, harnois,* armor; Arm. *harnez,* armor, old iron, from *houarn,* iron.]
1. originally, armor and other military equipment for a man or horse.
2. the leather straps and metal pieces by which a horse, mule, etc. is fastened to a vehicle, plow, or load.

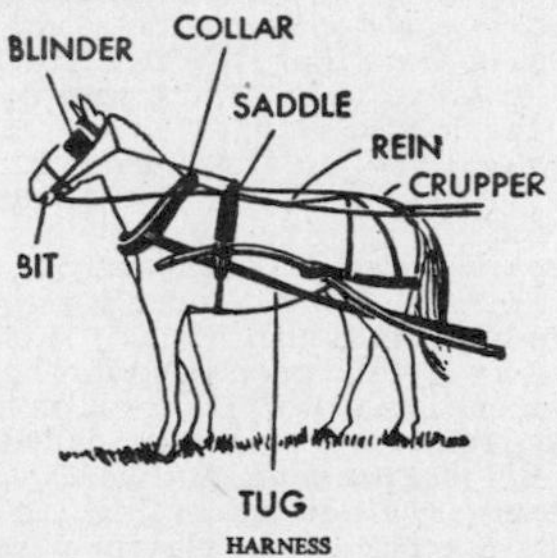

HARNESS

3. any trappings or gear similar to this; specifically, (a) the straps, etc. by which a parachute is fastened to its wearer; (b) a device for raising and lowering the warp threads on a loom.

in double harness; (a) in a harness for two animals pulling the same carriage, plow, etc.; (b) married.

in harness; in or at one's routine work.

här′ness, *v.t.*; harnessed (-nest), *pt., pp.*; harnessing, *ppr.* 1. to dress in armor; to equip with armor for war, as a horseman. [Archaic.]

Harnessed in rugged steel. —Rowe.

2. to equip for draft; to put harness on (a horse, etc.).

Harness the horses. —Jer. xlvi. 4.

3. to equip or furnish for defense. [Obs.]
4. to bring into a condition for working or producing power; as, they *harnessed* the power of the water by building a dam.

här′ness çȧsk, in nautical usage, a cask in which is kept the salt meat for daily use: called also *harness tub.*

här′nessed (-nest), *a.* having marks as if equipped with harness: said of animals.

harnessed antelope; any of several striped African antelopes, as the bushbuck and guib.

här′ness·ẽr, *n.* one who harnesses.

här′ness hitch, a kind of knot: see *knot,* illus.

här′ness mȧk′ẽr, one whose occupation is the making of harness.

härnṣ, *n.pl.* brains. [Scot.]

härp, *n.* [ME. *harpe;* AS. *hearpe,* a harp.]
1. a musical instrument with strings stretched across an open, triangular frame, played by being plucked with the fingers: the modern harp has forty-six strings and a series of foot pedals which permit the playing of half tones.
2. [H-] in astronomy, Lyra, a northern constellation.
3. a harp-shaped object or implement.
4. a coarse grain sieve with wires parallel, bearing some resemblance to a harp. [Scot.]

HARP

5. an Irishman: a vulgar term of prejudice and contempt. [Slang.]
6. same as *harp seal.*

aeolian harp; see under *Æolian.*

härp, *v.i.*; harped (härpt), *pt., pp.*; harping, *ppr.* 1. to play on the harp.
2. to persist in talking or writing tediously or continuously (*on* or *upon* something).

to harp on one string; to dwell tiresomely on one subject or one branch of a subject.

härp, *v.t.* 1. to play, as a tune, upon a harp.
2. to express; to give expression to. [Rare.]

Thou'st *harped* my fear aright. —Shak.

Här′pȧ, *n.* [LL. *harpa,* a harp.] the typical genus of the *Harpidæ.*

härp′ẽr, *n.* 1. a player on the harp.
2. one of several old coins of Ireland with the image of a harp on the reverse side.
3. same as *harp seal.*

Här′pi·dae, *n.pl.* a family of gastropods with longitudinally ribbed shells suggesting the strings of a harp.

härp′ing, *a.* pertaining to the harp; playing on a harp; that harps.

härp′ing, *n.* 1. a continual dwelling on.

Making infinite merriment by *harpings* upon old themes. —Irving.

2. a playing on the harp.

härp′ing ī′ron (-ũrn), a harpoon.

härp′ingṣ, här′pinṣ, *n.pl.* [prob. from Fr *harper,* to grip.]
1. wooden strips or planks on the bow of a ship to give it added strength.
2. wooden pieces used as supports during the construction of a ship.

härp′ist, *n.* one who plays the harp.

här·pọọn′, *n.* [D. *harpoen;* Fr. *harpon,* a grappling iron, harpoon, from *harper,* to gripe, clutch, from *harpe,* a claw, hook; prob. from L. *harpago (-onis);* Gr. *harpage,* a hook, from *harpazein,* to seize.] a spear or javelin with a line attached to it, used to strike and kill whales or any large fishes or sea animals. It consists of a long shank with a broad, flat, triangular head, sharpened at both edges. It is thrown from the hand or fired from a gun.

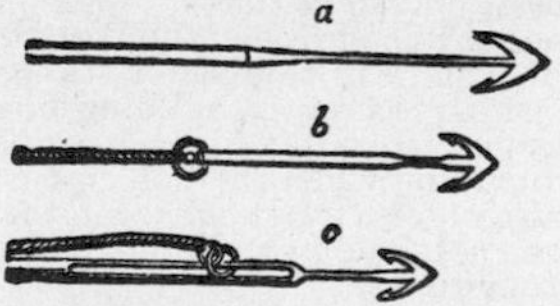

a, HAND HARPOON; *b, c,* GUN HARPOONS

här·pọọn′, *v.t.*; harpooned (-poond), *pt., pp.*; harpooning, *ppr.* to strike, catch, or kill with a harpoon.

här·pọọn′eer, *n.* same as *harpooner.*

här·pọọn′ẽr, *n.* one who casts or directs the harpoon, as at a whale.

här·pọọn′ fọrk, a hayfork consisting of an iron shank having a rope attached to one end and one or two tines to the other, with barbs that close when the tines are driven into the hay.

här·pọọn′ gun, a gun or small cannon, usually mounted on the bow of a whaling boat, for firing a harpoon.

härp′ress, *n.* a woman harper. [Rare.]

härp sēal, in zoology, a seal, *Phoca grænlandica,* of the arctic regions, having on the body a harp-shaped marking: called also *saddler* and *saddleback.*

härp shell, any gastropod shell of the genus *Harpa,* found in tropical seas.

härp′si·çhŏn, *n.* a harpsichord. [Obs.]

härp′si·chord, *n.* [OFr. *harpechorde*; *harpe*, harp, and *chorde*, chord.] a stringed musical instrument with a keyboard, played by the fingers by means of keys operating upon quill points which plucked the strings, making a light, tinkling sound. In form it resembles the modern grand piano, of which it was the precursor.

HARPSICORD

här′pū·la, *n.* [E. Ind.] an East Indian tree of the genus *Harpullia*.

Här·pul′li·a, *n.* a genus of trees found in the tropical parts of Asia, Africa, and Australia, of the family *Sapindaceæ*, including six species, some of which are highly valued for their wood.

Här′py, *n.*; *pl.* **Här′pies,** [OFr. *harpie, harpye*; L. *harpyia*, pl. *harpyiæ*; Gr. *harpyiai*, pl., the harpies, lit., the snatchers, from *harpazein*, to seize, snatch.]

1. in Greek mythology, any of several hideous, filthy, winged monsters with the head and trunk of a woman and the tail, legs, and talons of a bird: they carried off the souls of the dead, seized the food of their victims, etc. The harpies, according to some accounts, were three in number, Aëllo, Ocypete, and Celeno.

HARPY

2. [h–] a harpy eagle.

3. [h–] the *Circus æruginosus*, or marsh harrier, a British species of hawk, allied to the buzzards.

4. [h–] the harpy bat.

5. [h–] any rapacious or ravenous animal or person; an extortioner; a plunderer.

här′py bat, an East Indian fruit bat with nostrils tubular and protuberant.

här′py ēa′gle, a large, short-winged, tropical American eagle, *Thrasaetus harpyia*, with a double crest and a powerful bill and claws.

här′quē·bus, är′quē·bus (-kwē-), *n.* [Fr. *harquebuse, arquebuse*, from OFr. *hacquebuche, hacquebute*, from D. *haakbus*, a gun with a hook; *haak*, a hook, and *bus*, a box, barrel of a gun.] an early type of portable gun, fired by a matchlock and trigger and supported on a hooked staff or forked rest during firing.

här″quē·bus·āde′, *n.* 1. a distilled water applied to a bruise or wound: so called because it was originally used in gunshot wounds.

2. a volley from harquebuses.

här″quē·bus·iēr′, *n.* a soldier armed with a harquebus.

har′rāge, *v.t.* to harry; to harass. [Obs.]

har·ra·teen′, har·a·teen′, *n.* a kind of coarse cloth made of wool.

har′ri·dăn, *n.* [prob. corruption of OFr. *haridelle*, a worn-out horse, jade, from *aride*, dry, withered.] a haggard, disreputable, shrewish old woman.

har′ri·ẽr, *n.* [from *hare* and *-ier*.]

1. any of an English breed of dog, used for hunting hares and rabbits.

2. [*pl.*] the harriers and hunters in a hunt.

3. a cross-country runner.

Originally spelled *harier*.

har′ri·ẽr, *n.* [from *harry*, v.]

1. any person or thing that harries.

2. a hawk of the genus *Circus*, allied to the buzzards, as the marsh harrier, *Circus æruginosus*: also called the *moor buzzard* and *harpy*.

har′rōw, *n.* [ME. *harow, harowe, harwe*; AS. *hearge*, a harrow.]

1. an agricultural implement, usually consisting of a frame of wood or metal set with spikes or sharpened disks. It is drawn over plowed land to level it and break the clods, and to cover seed when sown.

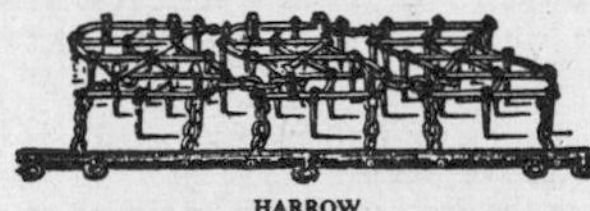
HARROW

2. something causing distress, such as might be inflicted by a harrow: usually in the phrase *under the harrow*.

har′rōw, *v.t.*; harrowed, *pt.*, *pp.*; harrowing, *ppr.* 1. to draw a harrow over for the purpose of breaking clods and leveling the surface, or for covering seed sown; to break or tear with a harrow; as, to *harrow* land.

2. to tear; to lacerate; to cut; to wound; to hurt.

3. to make uncomfortable; to distress; to vex; to torment.

har′rōw, *v.i.* to take harrowing; as, this ground *harrows* well.

har′rōw, *v.t.* to agitate; to harry; to pillage. [Archaic.]

har′rōw, *interj.* [ME. *harrow, haro*; OFr. *haro, harou, harau*, an exclamation, a call for help; OS. *herod*, here, hither, from *her*, here.] an exclamation of sudden distress, surprise, etc. [Obs.]

har′rōw·ẽr, *n.* one who harrows.

har′rōw·ẽr, *n.* one who or that which harrows or ravages, as a harrier hawk. [Archaic.]

har′ry, *v.t.*; harried, *pt.*, *pp.*; harrying, *ppr.* [ME. *haryen, herien, harwen, herwen, hergien*; AS. *hergian*, to ravage, lay waste, from *here*, an army.]

1. to strip; to pillage; to plunder.

2. to harass; to agitate; to torment; to worry.

har′ry, *v.i.* to make a predatory incursion.

härsh, *a.*; *comp.* harsher; *superl.* harshest, [ME. *harsk*; O.Sw. *harsk*, rank, rusty.]

1. unpleasantly sharp or rough; specifically, (a) grating to the ear; discordant; (b) too bright or vivid to the eye; glaring; (c) too strong to the taste; bitter; (d) not smooth to the touch; coarse.

2. unpleasantly crude, abrupt, or strained so as to be offensive to one's mind or feelings.

3. rough, crude, or forbidding in appearance.

4. stern; severe; unfeeling; cruel.

Syn.—austere, rough, stern, morose, rigorous, hard, exacting, severe, acrimonious, sarcastic, cutting, keen, cruel, bitter, ungracious, uncivil, churlish, brutal, ill-tempered.

härsh′ly, *adv.* in a harsh manner.

härsh′ness, *n.* the quality of being harsh in any of its senses.

Syn.—acrimony, tartness, asperity, acerbity, cruelty, churlishness, roughness, sternness, rudeness.

härs′let, *n.* same as *haslet*.

härt, *n.*; *pl.* **härts** or **härt,** [ME. *hart, hert, heort*; AS. *heort, heorot*, a hart, stag.] a stag; a male deer, especially a male red deer when he has passed his fifth year, and the surroyal or crown antler is formed.

hart of ten; a hart with ten tines or branches on his horns.

här′tal, här′tall, *n.* [Hind. *hartāl*.] orpiment.

här·tal′, *n.* [Hind. *hartāl*, from *hāt*, a shop, market, and *tālā*, a lock.] in India, a suspension of work and business, especially as an expression of national mourning or political protest.

härt′beest, *n.*; *pl.* **härt′beests** or **härt′beest,** same as *hartebeest*.

härt′ber″ry, *n.* a kind of European whortleberry, *Vaccinium myrtillus*.

här′te·beest, *n.*; *pl.* **här′te·beests** or **här′te·beest,** [S.Afr. D.; *harte*, hart, and *beest*, beast.] a large, swift South African antelope, the *Alcelaphus caama*, now rare, having a reddish-brown coat with a yellow patch on each haunch, and long horns curved backward at the tips.

härt′en, *v.t.* to hearten. [Obs.]

härt′in, *n.* [Ober*hart* and *-in*.] a fossil resin found with hartite in lignite at Oberhart, Austria.

härt′īte, *n.* [Ober*hart* and *-ite*; so called because found in *Oberhart*, Austria.] a fossil resin resembling hartin.

härt′s′-clō″vẽr, *n.* the yellow sweet clover, *Melilotus officinalis*.

härts′horn, *n.* 1. the antler of the hart or stag, *Cervus elaphus*, formerly much used as a source of ammonia.

2. (a) ammonia in water solution; (b) ammonium carbonate, used in smelling salts; sal volatile.

salt of hartshorn; an impure carbonate of ammonia.

härts′horn plan′tāin, *Plantago coronopus*, a European species of plantain with pinnate leaves.

härt′s′-thorn, *n.* same as *buckthorn*.

härt′s′-tŏngue, härts′tŏngue (-tung), *n.* a fern with long, narrow fronds, found chiefly in Europe and Asia.

härt′s′-trē″foil, *n.* same as *hart's-clover*.

härt′s truf′fles, lycoperdon nuts.

härt′wŏrt, *n.* any of certain umbelliferous plants of the genera *Seseli, Tordylium*, and *Bupleurum*.

hãr′um-scãr′um, *a.* [prob. from *hare*, and *scare*, and *'em*.] wild; reckless; irresponsible; giddy; rash.

hãr′um-scãr′um, *adv.* in a harum-scarum manner.

hãr′um-scãr′um, *n.* a harum-scarum person or action.

ha·rus′pex, *n.*; *pl.* **ha·rus′pi·cēs,** [L., lit., an inspector of entrails.] any of a class of lesser priests and soothsayers in ancient Rome whose business was to inspect the entrails of animals killed in sacrifice, and by them to foretell future events or declare the will of the diety: written also *aruspex* and *haruspice*.

ha·rus′pi·căl, *a.* of or acting as a haruspex.

ha·rus·pi·cā′tion, *n.* haruspicy.

ha·rus′pice, *n.* a haruspex.

ha·rus′pi·cy, *n.* divination by a haruspex.

här′vest, *n.* [ME. *harvest, hervest, herfest*, harvest, autumn; AS. *hærfest*, autumn.]

1. the season of gathering a crop of any kind, especially the time of reaping and gathering matured grain, fruit, vegetables, etc.

2. that which is harvested or ready for harvesting; a crop or crops, as of grain, fruit, etc.

3. the product of labor; reward; fruit or fruits; effects; consequences; results of any conditions or operations; as, the year's *harvest* of books; a *harvest* of woe.

4. the act of harvesting.

här′vest, *v.t.* and *v.i.*; harvested, *pt.*, *pp.*; harvesting, *ppr.* 1. to gather in (a crop, etc.).

2. to gather the crop from (a field).

här′vest bells, a gentian of Europe, *Gentiana pneumonanthe*, blossoming in harvest.

här′vest bug, the chigger, a very small, parasitic larva.

här′vest·ẽr, *n.* one who or that which harvests; specifically, (a) a laborer in harvest; a harvestman; (b) a machine used to harvest crops, as grains, beans, potatoes, etc.; a mechanical reaper.

här′vest fiēld, a field from which a harvest is gathered; a field in which harvesters are at work.

här′vest fish, either of two scombroid fishes of the Atlantic coast of the United States; (a) *Stromateus triacanthus*, or the dollar fish; (b) *Stromateus paru*, found in large numbers at harvest time.

här′vest flȳ, any of various cicadas heard at harvest time.

här′vest hōme, 1. the bringing home of the last harvest load; end of the harvest.

2. a former festival celebrating this.

3. a song sung by harvesters bringing home the last load.

här′vest·less, *a.* without crops; devoid of harvest.

här′vest lord, the head reaper at harvest. [Brit. Dial.]

här′vest louse, same as *harvest bug*.

här′vest·măn, *n.*; *pl.* **här′vest·men,** 1. a laborer in harvest; a reaper.

2. a long-legged spider of the order *Phalangida*, in which the head and abdomen are united in one piece: called also *shepherd spider* and *daddy-longlegs*.

här′vest mīte, same as *harvest bug*.

här′vest moon, the full moon at or about the time of the autumnal equinox, when it rises nearly at the same hour for several days.

här′vest mouse, *Mus minutus*, a very small European species of field mouse, which builds its nest on the stems of wheat or other plants.

här′vest queen (kwēn), an image representing Ceres, formerly carried about on the last day of harvest.

här'vest·ry, *n.* the act or result of harvesting.

här'vest spī'dēr, same as *harvestman,* sense 2.

här'vest tick, same as *harvest bug.*

här'vey·ïze, *v.t.*; harveyized, *pt., pp.*; harveyizing, *ppr.* [named after H. A. *Harvey,* the 19th-c. Am. inventor of the process.] to subject (steel) to a process by which the surface is rendered extremely hard.

has, *v.* the third person singular, present indicative, of *have.*

has'ärd, *n.* hazard. [Obs.]

has'-been, *n.* a person or thing that was formerly popular or effective but is no longer so. [Colloq.]

hash, *v.t.*; hashed (hasht), *pt., pp.*; hashing, *ppr.* [Fr. *hacher,* to chop, mince.]

1. to chop (meat and vegetables) into small pieces for cooking.

2. to make a mess or botch of; to bungle. [Colloq.]

hash, *n.* [OFr. *hachis,* minced meat, from *hacher,* to mince, chop, from G. *hacken,* to hack, cut.]

1. a form of minced food, usually prepared from materials previously cooked, as meat, potatoes, bread crumbs, etc., and recooked by baking or frying.

2. any mixture and second preparation of old matter; a rehash.

3. a sloven; a country clown; a stupid fellow. [Scot.]

4. a hodgepodge; a muddle; a mess.

to make (a) hash of; (a) to bungle; to botch; (b) to destroy or defeat (an opponent, argument, etc.). [Colloq.]

to settle one's hash; to squelch one; to cause one to be silent or inactive. [Colloq.]

hash, *n.* hashish. [Slang.]

hash house, a cheap restaurant. [Slang.]

hash'ish, hash'eesh, *n.* [Ar. *hashish,* dried hemp.]

1. a drug formed from the resin contained in the flowering tops of Indian hemp, *Cannabis sativa*: it is either chewed or smoked for its intoxicating or euphoric effects and has been used in Oriental countries for many centuries.

2. the tender parts of the Indian hemp with their resinous exudations.

hash märk, any of the parallel diagonal stripes worn on the left sleeve of a uniform; service stripe: each stripe indicates the completion of three years' service. [Military Slang.]

Ha·sid'iç, *a.* same as *Chassidic.*

Has'i·dim, *n.pl.*; *sing.* **Has'id,** same as *Chassidim.*

hask, *n.* [W. *hesg,* sedge, rushes.] a basket made of rushes or wicker. [Obs.]

has'let, *n.* [ME. *hastelet*; OFr. *hastellet,* from *haste,* a spit, spear.] the heart, liver, lungs, etc. of a pig or other animal, used for food: also *harslet.*

has'n't, has not.

hȧsp, *n.* [ME. *hasp*; AS. *hæpse,* a hasp, bolt.]

1. a hinged metal fastening for a door, window, lid, book covers, etc.; especially, a clasp that passes over a staple to be fastened by a padlock, hook, pin, etc.

HASP

2. a spindle to wind thread or silk on.

3. a skein of yarn or thread; a quantity of yarn, the fourth part of a spindle.

hȧsp, *v.t.*; hasped (haspt), *pt., pp.*; hasping, *ppr.* [ME. *haspen*; AS. *hæpsian,* from *hæpse,* a hasp, bolt.] to shut or fasten with or as with a hasp.

has'sle, has'sel, *n.* [perh. from dial. *hassle,* to breathe noisily.] a heated discussion; a squabble. [Slang.]

has'sle, *v.i.*; hassled, *pt., pp.*; hassling, *ppr.* to have a hassle. [Colloq.]

has'sle, *v.t.* to annoy, harass, etc. [Slang.]

has'sŏck, *n.* [ME. *hassok,* a coarse grass; AS. *hassuc,* a place where coarse grass grows.]

1. a tussock; a tuft of sedge or coarse grass.

2. a firmly stuffed mat or cushion used as a footstool or seat.

hast, *v.* archaic second person singular, present indicative, of *have*: used with *thou.*

häs'tä lä vïs'tä (äs'), [Sp., lit., until the meeting.] good-by.

has'ta ma·ña'na (äs'tä mä-nyä'nä), [Sp., lit., until tomorrow.] good-by.

has'tāte, *a.* [L. *hasta,* a spear.] spear-shaped; resembling the head of a halberd; triangular, with the angles spreading; as, a *hastate* leaf.

HASTATE LEAF

has'tā·ted, *a.* hastate. [Obs.]

hāste, *n.* [ME. *haste,* haste; AS. *hæst, hœst,* violence.]

1. celerity of motion; speed; swiftness; dispatch; expedition: applied only to voluntary actions.

2. needless or unwise quickness; careless hurrying; as, *haste* makes waste.

I said in my *haste,* All men are liars.
—Ps. cxvi. 11.

3. the state of being urged or pressed by business; urgency; as, I am in great *haste.*

Syn.—hurry, speed, dispatch, nimbleness, rapidity.—*Haste* denotes quickness of action and a strong desire for getting on; *hurry* suggests excitement, bustle, or confusion; *speed* denotes the actual progress which is made; *dispatch,* the promptitude and rapidity with which things are done.

in haste; (a) in a hurry; (b) in too great a hurry; without enough care or thought.

to make haste; to act or go quickly; to hasten.

hāste, *v.t.* and *v.i.* to hurry; to hasten. [Rare.]

I'll *haste* the writer. —Shak.

hās'ten (hās'n), *v.t.*; hastened, *pt., pp.*; hastening, *ppr.* [an extended form of *haste,* v.] to make hurry; to speed up; to drive or urge forward; to push on; to precipitate; to accelerate; to expedite; to hurry; as, to *hasten* one's coming.

hās'ten, *v.i.* to move swiftly; to be rapid in motion; to be speedy or quick; to hurry; as, to *hasten* to a conclusion.

hās'ten·ēr, *n.* 1. one who or that which hastens or urges forward.

2. a haster. [Brit. Dial.]

hās'tēr, *n.* [OFr. *hastier, haster,* a spit, the rack on which a spit turns, from *haste,* a spit.] a metal stand or reflector for confining the heat of the fire to the meat while cooking it.

has·ti·fō'li·ous, *a.* [L. *hasta,* a spear, and *folium,* a leaf.] in botany, having hastate leaves.

has'tile, *a.* [L. *hastile,* the shaft of a spear, from *hasta,* a spear.] hastate.

hās'ti·ly, *adv.* in a hasty manner.

hās'ti·ness, *n.* the state, quality, or condition of being hasty.

hās'ting, *n.* [ppr. of *haste,* v.] an early fruit or vegetable; specifically, in the plural, pease. [Brit. Dial.]

Hās'tings sand, in geology, the middle group of the Wealden formation in England, occurring around Hastings, in Sussex.

Hās'tings sē'ries, a rock strata in Ontario, Canada, corollary to the Grenville series.

hās'tive, *a.* early, as fruit. [Obs.]

has'tlēr, *n.* one who roasts meat. [Obs.]

hās'ty, *a.*; *comp.* hastier; *superl.* hastiest, [ME. *hasty,* from *haste,* haste.]

1. quick; speedy; expeditious; moving or acting with haste: opposed to *slow.*

2. eager; precipitate; rash: opposed to *deliberate.*

3. irritable; short-tempered.

4. early ripe; as, *hasty* fruit. [Obs.]

5. requiring or characterized by quick action; as, a *hasty* departure.

hasty pudding; in the United States, mush; corn-meal mush; in England, mush made of oatmeal or flour.

hat, *n.* [ME. *hat*; AS. *hæt* (pl. *hættas*), a hat.]

1. a covering for the head; a headdress, usually with a crown and brim, made of any of various materials, as felt, silk, wool, straw, etc., and worn to protect the head from the weather, or for ornament: sometimes distinguished from *bonnet, beret, cap,* etc.

HATS

1., 2. time of Henry VIII; 3. time of Mary I; 4. time of Elizabeth I; 5., 6. time of James I and Charles I; 7., 8. time of Commonwealth; 9., 10. time of William III; 11-16. eighteenth century.

2. in the Roman Catholic Church, (a) the official red hat of a cardinal; (b) the rank or position of a cardinal.

3. in tanning, a layer of bark covering hides when soaking in the tan vat.

4. in smelting, a detainer for gases in the tunnel head of a furnace.

Gainsborough hat; a lady's hat with a wide brim, such as those seen in paintings by Gainsborough.

hat in hand; in a humble or obsequious manner; abjectly.

to hang up one's hat; to make oneself at home; to take up one's residence in another's house.

to pass the hat; to ask for money or take up a collection, as at a meeting.

to take one's hat off to; to salute; to congratulate.

to throw one's hat into the ring; (a) to enter a competition; (b) to become a candidate for office.

under one's hat; secret; strictly confidential. [Colloq.]

hāt'ȧ·ble, *a.* same as *hateable.*

hat'band, *n.* a band of cloth around the crown of a hat, just above the brim: a band of black cloth is often worn to show mourning.

hat block, a block or mold on which a hat is shaped and ironed.

hat'box, *n.* a box for carrying or storing a hat or hats.

hatch, *v.t.*; hatched, *pt., pp.*; hatching, *ppr.* [ME. *hacchen, hecchen,* to hatch; compare G. *hecken,* Dan. *hekke,* to hatch.]

1. to produce (young) from eggs by incubation, or by artificial heat.

2. to bring forth young from (an egg or eggs).

3. to contrive or plot; to form by meditation, and bring into being; to originate and produce; to devise; to plan; as, to *hatch* mischief.

hatch, *v.i.* 1. to produce young; as, eggs *hatch.*

2. to emerge from the egg, as an insect, fish, bird, etc.

hatch, *n.* 1. the process of hatching.

2. the brood hatched; that which is hatched.

3. as many chickens, etc. as are produced at one hatching or incubation.

4. the number of eggs put under a fowl or into an incubator for one hatching.

5. an outcome; a result.

hatch, *v.t.* [OFr. *hacher,* to hack; M.H.G. *hacken,* to cut, chop.] to mark or engrave with fine, crossed or parallel lines so as to indicate shading.

hatch, *n.* any of the fine, crossed or parallel lines made by hatching.

hatch, *n.* [ME. *hatche, hacche, hetche, hek, hec,* a half door, wicket (pl. *hacches,* the hatches of a ship); AS. *hæc,* a gate.]

1. the lower half of a door, gate, etc. that has two separately movable halves.

2. (a) a rectangular opening in a ship's deck through which cargo can be lowered; hatchway; (b) a similar opening in the floor or roof of a building.

3. a lid for or as for such an opening; a trap door: such lids were originally gratings.

4. a barrier to regulate the flow of water in a stream; a floodgate.

5. a kind of fishtrap.

6. an opening into a mine. [Rare.]

to be under hatches; to be below deck; hence, to be under confinement or adversity.

hatch, *v.t.* to close or cover with or as with a hatch. [Obs.]

hatch′back, *n.* [from *hatch*, a door, and *back*.] an automobile body with a rear that swings up, providing a wide opening into a storage area.

hatch bōat, a fishing boat with a well for holding fish.

hat′check, *a.* of, for, or working in a checkroom for hats, coats, etc.

hatch′el, *n.* [ME. *hechele, hekele*, a comb for cleaning flax or hemp; compare D. *hekel*, G. *hechel*, a hatchel.] an instrument made of long iron teeth set in a board, for cleaning and dressing flax, hemp, etc.

hatch′el, *v.t.*; hatcheled *or* hatchelled, *pt., pp.*; hatcheling *or* hatchelling, *ppr.* 1. to draw (flax or hemp) through the teeth of a hatchel, for separating the coarse part and broken pieces of the stalk from the fine, fibrous parts.

2. to worry; to tease; to heckle. [Rare.]

hatch′ẽr, *n.* one who or that which hatches; specifically, an incubator.

hatch′ẽr·y, *n.*; *pl.* **hatch′ẽr·ieṣ,** a place for the hatching of eggs, especially those of fish or poultry.

hatch′et, *n.* [ME. *hachet*; OFr. *hachette*, dim. of *hache*, an ax, from G. *hacke*, an ax, from *hacken*, to cut.]

1. a small ax with a short handle, to be used with one hand.

2. a tomahawk.

to bury the hatchet; see under *bury*.

to dig (or *take*) *up the hatchet*; to make war.

hatch′et fāce, a lean, sharp, pointed face.

hatch′et-faced (-fāst), *a.* having a hatchet face.

hatch′et·tin, hatch′et·tine, *n.* [named after Charles *Hatchett*, an English chemist.] a yellowish, semitransparent mineral found in Scotland and Wales: it belongs to the paraffin group of minerals. Also *hatchettite*.

SHINGLING HATCHET

CLAW HATCHET

LATHING HATCHET

TYPES OF HATCHET

hatch′ing, *n.* 1. the drawing or engraving of fine, parallel or crossed lines to show shading.

2. a system of lines for such purpose.

hatch′ment, *n.* [corrupted from *achievement*, which was also spelled *atchievement*, from Fr. *achever*, to finish.] an armorial escutcheon of a dead person: see *achievement*, sense 3.

hatch′wāy, *n.* 1. a rectangular opening in a ship's deck, through which cargo can be lowered.

2. a similar opening, usually covered with a sliding hatch, at the rear of a deckhouse, etc.

3. a similar opening in the floor or roof of a building.

Also *hatch*.

hāte, *v.t.*; hated, *pt., pp.*; hating, *ppr.* [ME. *haten, hatien*; AS. *hatian, hatigian*, to hate.]

1. to dislike greatly; to have a great or extreme aversion to; to detest; to have strong ill will for.

2. to dislike; to wish to avoid; to shrink from; as, he *hates* to work.

Syn.—abhor, detest, loathe, abominate.

hāte, *v.i.* to feel hatred.

hāte, *n.* [ME. *hate, hete*; AS. *hete*, hate.]

1. a strong feeling of dislike or aversion; hatred.

2. a person or thing hated.

hāte′ȧ·ble, *a.* that deserves to be hated.

hāte′fụl, *a.* 1. odious; exciting great dislike, aversion, or disgust.

2. malignant; malevolent; as, *hateful* eyes. [Rare.]

Syn. execrable, abominable, hateful, detestable.

hāte′fụl·ly, *adv.* in a hateful manner.

hāte′fụl·ness, *n.* the quality of being hateful.

hāt′ẽr, *n.* one who hates.

hath, *v.* archaic third person singular, present indicative, of *have*.

hat hon′ŏr (on′), regard shown for a man or woman by taking off the hat.

Hath′ŏr, *n.* in Egyptian mythology, the goddess of love, mirth, and joy, usually represented as having the ears or the head of a cow.

Hath′ŏr çap′i·tăl, in architecture, a capital with faces of Hathor carved on its sides.

Hȧ·thor′iç, *a.* of Hathor or the Hathor capital.

hat′less, *a.* without a hat.

hat mŏn′ey, see *primage*.

hat piēce, a metal protection formerly worn under a hat.

hat′pin, *n.* a long, ornamental pin for fastening a woman's hat to her hair.

hat′rack, *n.* a rack or stand fitted with pegs or hooks, for holding hats, etc.

hā′tred, *n.* [ME. *hatred, hatreden*; *hate*, hate, and *-red, -reden*, from AS. *-rǣden*, signifying state or condition.] great dislike or aversion; hate; enmity; malevolence; intense ill will.

Syn.—antipathy, abhorrence, aversion, detestation, dislike, hostility.

hat′stand, *n.* a hatrack intended to stand on its own base.

hat′tẽr, *v.t.* to harass. [Obs.]

hat′tẽr, *n.* 1. a maker or seller of hats, especially men's hats.

2. in Australia, a miner who has no partner.

mad as a hatter; completely crazy.

hat′ting, *n.* 1. the business of hatmaking.

2. the materials from which hats are made.

hat tree, a stand with arms or hooks to hold hats, coats, etc.

hạu′bẽr·ġeŏn (-jŏn), *n.* a habergeon. [Obs.]

hạu′bẽrk, *n.* [ME. *hauberk, hawberk*; OFr. *hauberc, halberc*, from O.H.G. *halsberc, halsberge*, a protection for the neck, gorget; *hals*, the neck, and *bergan*, to protect, to save.] a medieval coat of armor, usually of chain mail.

hau′ẽr·īte, *n.* [named after F. von *Hauer*, an Austrian geologist.] native manganese sulfide, a reddish-brown or brownish-black isometric metallic mineral of an adamantine luster, generally crystallizing in octahedrons, though sometimes in globular clusters.

hạugh (hạ), *n.* low-lying flat ground on the border of a river. [Brit. Dial. and Scot.]

hạught (hạt), *a.* [acorruption of OFr. *haut, hault*, high, from L. *altus*, high, lofty; the *gh* was probably introduced on the analogy of *high*.] high; elevated; hence, proud; insolent. [Archaic.]

hạugh′ti·ly (hạ′), *adv.* proudly; arrogantly; with contempt or disdain; as, to speak or behave *haughtily*.

hạugh′ti·ness, *n.* the quality of being haughty; arrogance.

Syn.—arrogance, disdain, pride, presumption, contemptuousness. — *Haughtiness* denotes the expression of conscious and proud superiority; *arrogance* is a disposition to claim for oneself more than is justly due, and to enforce it to the utmost; *disdain* stresses the scorn felt for that which is regarded as beneath one.

hạugh′ty, *a.*; *comp.* haughtier; *superl.* haughtiest, [ME. *hautein*; OFr. *hautain*, haughty, proud, from *haut*, high; the *gh* was probably inserted after the analogy of *naughty*.]

1. proud and disdainful; having a high opinion of oneself, with some contempt for others; lofty and arrogant; supercilious.

2. proceeding from excessive pride or pride mingled with contempt; manifesting pride and disdain; as, a *haughty* air or walk; a *haughty* tone.

3. lofty; noble. [Archaic.]

hạul, *v.t.*; hauled, *pt., pp.*; hauling, *ppr.* [ME. *haulen, halen, halien*; AS. *geholian*, to acquire, get.]

1. to pull or draw with force; to drag; as, to *haul* a boat on shore.

2. to transport, convey, or move by wagon, truck, etc.; as, to *haul* wood to one's house.

3. in nautical usage, to change the course of (a ship) by setting the sails.

to haul over the coals; see under *coal*.

to haul the wind; to turn the head of a ship nearer to the point from which the wind blows.

hạul, *v.i.* 1. to pull; tug.

2. to shift direction: said of the wind.

3. to change one's opinion or course of action; as, he *hauled* around to my way of thinking.

4. in nautical usage, to change the course of a ship by trimming sail, usually so as to travel closer to the wind.

to haul off; (a) to alter a ship's course in order to get farther off from any object; (b) to retreat; to withdraw; (c) [Colloq.] to draw the arm back before hitting.

to haul on (or *to, onto*) *the wind*; to haul in sails until they are nearly parallel with the desired course, in order to sail closer to the wind.

to haul up; to sail nearer the direction of the wind.

hạul, *n.* 1. a pulling with force; a violent pull.

2. a draft of a net; as, to catch a hundred fish at a *haul*; also, a place for hauling a seine.

3. that which is gained, won, caught, etc. at one time, as by hauling a net; as, a *haul* of fish.

4. the distance or route over which something is transported; as, a long or a short *haul*.

5. the load or quantity transported.

6. in ropemaking, a bundle of three or four hundred parallel yarns ready for tarring.

hạul′āġe, *n.* 1. the act or operation of hauling.

2. the force used in hauling.

3. the charge made for hauling, as by a railroad.

hạul′ẽr, *n.* one who or that which hauls.

hạulm, hạlm (hạm), *n.* [ME. *halm*; AS. *healm*, halm, straw.]

1. the stalks or stems of cultivated cereals, beans, peas, etc., especially after the crop has been gathered.

2. straw or hay used for thatching roofs, etc.

3. a stem of grass or grain; culm.

hạulse, *n.* a hawse. [Obs.]

hạult, *a.* [OFr. *hault, halt*, from L. *altus*, high, lofty.] haughty. [Obs.]

hạul′yärd, *n.* same as *halyard*.

hạum, *n.* haulm. [Obs.]

häunch, *n.* [ME. *haunche, hanche*; OFr. *hanche, hance, anche*, the haunch; O.H.G. *ancha, encha*, the leg, lit., the joint or bend.]

1. the part of the body including the hip, buttock, and thickest part of the thigh; hindquarter.

2. an animal's loin and leg together; joint of venison, mutton, etc.

3. in architecture, the middle part between the vertex or crown and the springing of an arch: sometimes used to include the spandrel or part of it; the flank.

häunch bōne, the ilium; the hipbone; the innominate bone.

häunched (häncht), *a.* having haunches.

häunt (*or* hạnt), *v.t.*; haunted, *pt., pp.*; haunting, *ppr.* [ME. *haunten, hanten*; OFr. *hanter*, to frequent, resort to.]

1. to frequent; to resort to much or often, or to be much about; to visit (a place) often or continually.

2. to annoy or pester (a person) by constant visiting, following, etc.

3. to appear or recur frequently to; to obsess; as, memories *haunted* her.

4. to be associated with; to fill the atmosphere of; to pervade; as, memories of former gaiety *haunt* the house.

5. to practice; to pursue. [Obs.]

Haunt is often used with a ghost, spirit, etc. as its stated or implied subject.

häunt, *v.i.* to be much about; to be present often.

häunt, *n.* 1. a place to which one frequently resorts; as, a saloon that was the *haunt* of criminals.

2. a lair or feeding place of animals.

3. the habit of resorting to a place. [Obs.]

4. custom; practice. [Obs.]

5. (*also* hant) a ghost. [Dial.]

häunt′ed, *a.* frequently visited or resorted to, especially by apparitions or ghosts.

häunt′ẽr, *n.* one who frequents a particular place.

häunt′ing, *a.* often recurring to the mind; not easily forgotten; as, a *haunting* tune.

hạu′ri·ent, *a.* [L. *hauriens* (*-entis*), ppr. of *haurire*, to draw or drink in.] in heraldry, placed palewise or upright, as if putting the head above water to draw or suck in the air: said of a fish as a bearing.

A SALMON HAURIENT

Hau′sä, Haus′sä, *n.* 1. a Negroid people of Nigeria, Niger, and adjacent areas of the Sudan, numbering over 5,000,000.

2. a member of this people.

3. the language of the Hausa, used as an

international trade language in Negro Africa south of the Sahara.

hau'sen, *n.* [G. *hausen*, a kind of sturgeon.] *Huso huso*, a large sturgeon found in the Black Sea, Caspian Sea, Sea of Azov, etc.

Haus'frau, *n.* [G.] a housewife.

haus'mănn·īte, *n.* [named after J. F. L. *Hausmann*, a 19th-c. German mineralogist.] one of the ores of manganese, having a brownish-black color. It crystallizes in the tetragonal system.

hausse-çol' (hōs-), *n.* [Fr., from *hausser*, to raise, and *col*, neck.] a gorget of plate.

Haus·tel·lā'tȧ, *n.pl.* [L. *haustus*, pp. of *haurire*, to draw in, breathe, swallow.] a very extensive division of insects in which the mouth is furnished with a haustellum, or proboscis adapted for suction. The figures show the form and structure of the haustellum in one of the hawk moths, *Sphingidæ*. Fig. 1 shows the head of the moth with the proboscis extended; figs. 2 and 3 are sections of the proboscis showing its structure, the one (2) viewed from above, the other (3) from beneath.

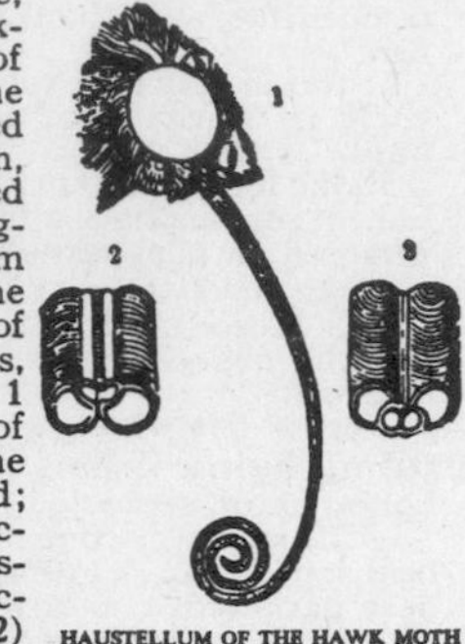

HAUSTELLUM OF THE HAWK MOTH

haus'tel·lāte, *a.* provided with a haustellum or sucker, as certain insects.

haus'tel·lāte, *n.* one of the *Haustellata*.

haus·tel'lous, *a.* haustellate.

haus·tel'lum, *n.*; *pl.* **haus·tel'lȧ,** a tubelike sucking organ, or proboscis, as in various insects.

haus·tō'ri·um, *n.*; *pl.* **haus·tō'ri·ȧ,** [LL., a well, from L. *haustor*, a drawer, from *haurire*, to draw in, breathe in.] a rootlike outgrowth in certain parasitic plants, through which food is absorbed from the host.

haut, *a.* haughty. [Obs.]

haut'boy (hō'boi), *n.* [OFr. *hautbois, haultbois*, lit., high wood; *haut*, high, and *bois*, wood.]

HAUTBOY

1. the oboe, a wind instrument.
2. in botany, a variety of strawberry, *Fragaria moschata*.

haut'boy·ist, *n.* an oboist.

haute çou·ture' (ōt), [Fr., lit., high sewing.] the leading designers and creators of new fashions in clothing for women, or their creations; high fashion.

haute çui·sine' (ōt kwē-zēn'), [Fr., lit., high kitchen.] the preparation of fine food by highly skilled chefs, or the food so prepared.

hau·teur' (hō-tũr'), *n.* [Fr., from *haut*, high, proud.] pride; haughtiness; haughty manner or spirit; snobbery.

haut mōnde (ō mōnd'), [Fr.] high society.

haut päs (ō pä'), [Fr.] a raised step, floor, or platform.

hä'uyne (-win), *n.* [after the French mineralogist, *Haüy*.] a mineral, occurring in grains or small masses, and also in groups of minute, shining crystals. Its color is blue, of various shades. It is found imbedded in volcanic rocks, basalt, phonolite, etc. It is a silicate of aluminum and sodium with sulfate of lime: written also *hauynite*.

Hȧ·van'ȧ, *n.* a cigar made in Havana, or in Cuba, or of Cuban tobacco.

Hav·ăn·ēse', *a.* of or pertaining to Havana, Cuba.

Hav·ăn·ēse', *n. sing.* and *pl.* a native or resident of Havana, Cuba.

have, *v.t.*; had, *pt., pp.*; having, *ppr.* [ME. *haven, habben*; AS. *habban*, to have, hold.]

1. to hold in the hand or in control; own; possess; as, he *has* money.
2. to possess, hold, or contain as a part, characteristic, attribute, or associated feature; as, the week *has* seven days.
3. to be possessed with; to be affected by; as, the children *have* measles.
4. to possess by way of experience; experience; undergo; as, *have* a good time.
5. to possess an understanding of; know; as, Shakespeare is said to have *had* "little Latin and less Greek."
6. to believe, declare, or tell; as, so gossip *has* it.
7. to gain possession, control, or mastery of.
8. to get; take; acquire; as, *have* a drink.
9. to bear or beget (offspring).
10. to perform; to carry on; to engage in; as, we *had* an argument.
11. to cause to; to cause to be; as, please *have* this done at once.
12. to be in a certain relation to; as, we *have* a talkative neighbor beside us.
13. (a) to permit; tolerate; (b) to admit. Used in the negative, as, I won't *have* this nonsense!
14. (a) to hold in a position of disadvantage; as, I *had* my opponent now; (b) to deceive; take in; cheat; as, they've been *had* in that business deal. [Colloq.]

Have is used as an auxiliary with past participles to form phrases expressing completed action, as in the perfect tenses (e.g., I *have* left, I *had* left, I shall *have* left, I would *have* left, etc.), and with infinitives to express obligation or necessity (e.g., we *have* to go). *Have got* often replaces *have*: see *get*. *Have* is conjugated in the present indicative (I) *have*, (he, she, it) *has*, (we, you, they) *have*; in the past indicative (I, he, she, it, we, you, they) *had*. Archaic forms are (thou) *hast, hadst*, (he, she, it) *hath*. The present subjunctive is *have*, the past subjunctive *had*.

to have a care; see under *care*.

to have and to hold; to possess permanently: form used in certain marriage services.

to have at; to attack; strike.

to have done; to stop; get through; finish.

to have it in for; to bear a grudge against. [Colloq.]

to have it out; to settle an issue, disagreement, etc. by fighting or discussion.

to have on; to be wearing; be dressed in.

to have to do with; (a) to be related to or connected with; (b) to be associated with; deal with.

have, *n.* a person or nation with relatively much wealth or rich resources. [Colloq.]

have'lock, *n.* [named after Sir Henry *Havelock* (1795–1857), Eng. general in India.] a light cloth covering for a military cap, falling over the back of the neck for protection against the sun.

hā'ven, *n.* [ME. *haven, havene*; AS. *hæfen, hæfene*, a haven, harbor.]

1. a harbor; a port; a bay, recess, or inlet of the sea, or the mouth of a river which affords good anchorage and a safe station for ships.
2. a shelter; an asylum; a place of safety.

hā'ven, *v.t.* 1. to put (a ship) into port.
2. to provide a haven for; to shelter.

have'-not, *n.* a person or nation with relatively little wealth or poor resources. [Colloq.]

have'n't, have not.

hav'ẽr, *n.* one who has or possesses; a possessor. [Now Rare.]

hā'vẽr, *v.i.* to talk in a silly or incoherent way. [Brit. Dial. and Scot.]

hav'ẽr, *n.* [ME. *haver*; Old L.G. *haboro*, oats.] oats. [Brit. Dial.]

hav'ẽr·el, *n.* one who havers. [Scot.]

hav'er·grȧss, *n.* oat grass.

hā'vẽrs, *interj.* rubbish! nonsense! [Brit.]

hav'ẽr·sack, *n.* [Fr. *haversac*; G. *habersack*, lit., a sack of oats; *haber, hafer*, oats, and *sack*, a sack.]

1. a canvas bag worn on the back or over the shoulder by soldiers and hikers for carrying rations, etc.
2. a gunner's leather bag used for conveying ammunition to a gun. [Obs.]

Hȧ·vẽr'siăn, *a.* of, relating to, or described by Clopton Havers, an English physician of the seventeenth century.

Haversian canal; one of a network of minute canals through which blood vessels pass in bone.

hav'il·där, *n.* [Hind. *hawaldar*; *hawala*, charge, custody, care, and *-dar*, having, possessing.] formerly, in the British Indian armies, a native noncommissioned officer in the native armies of India and Ceylon; a sepoy sergeant.

hav'ing, *n.* that which is had or possessed; goods; property; possession.

Our content is our best *having*. —Shak.

hā'vings, *n.pl.* carriage; behavior in general; manners. [Scot.]

hāv'iŏr, *n.* conduct, behavior. [Obs.]

hav'ŏç, *n.* [earlier esp. in phrase *cry havoc*, to give (an army) the signal for pillage, taking of booty; ME. and Anglo-Fr. *havok*; OFr. *havot*; prob. akin to *hef*, a hook, *haver*, to hook, take; of Gmc. origin.] general destruction or waste; widespread devastation and carnage.

to cry havoc; (a) originally, to give (an army) the signal for pillaging; (b) to warn of great, impending danger.

to play havoc with; to devastate; to destroy; ruin.

hav'ŏç, *v.t.*; havocked, *pt., pp.*; havocking, *ppr.* to destroy; to lay waste. [Obs.]

haw, *interj.* and *n.* a word of command to a horse, ox, etc., meaning "turn to the left!": opposed to *gee*.

haw, *v.t.*; hawed, *pt., pp.*; hawing, *ppr.* to guide to the left, as a horse in driving.

haw, *v.i.* to turn to the left, as a horse in driving.

haw, *v.i.* to hesitate in speaking, as in groping for words; to speak with interruption and hesitation; as, to hem and *haw*.

haw, *interj.* and *n.* a conventionalized expression of the sound made in hesitating utterances: also variously written *er, ur, uh, huh, ah, aw*, etc.

haw, *n.* [ME. *hawe*; AS. *haga*, fruit of *haguthorn*, hawthorn, hence, lit., same word as AS. *haga*, a hedge.]

1. a berry or seed of the hawthorn; the hawthorn.
2. *Viburnum prunifolium*, the black haw, or its fruit.

haw, *n.* 1. a spot or fleck in the eye; especially, a diseased condition of the third eyelid in horses, usually known as the *haws*.
2. the third eyelid, or nictitating membrane: a vestigial organ in mammals, but functional in birds and reptiles.

haw, *n.* [ME. *hawe*; AS. *haga*, an inclosure, a yard, or small field.]

1. a hedge. [Obs.]
2. a small piece of land adjoining a house; a yard; an enclosed piece of land. [Obs.]

Hȧ·wai'iăn (-yăn), *n.* a native or citizen of Hawaii; also, the Polynesian language of the Hawaiians.

Hȧ·wai'iăn, *a.* of or relating to the people of the Hawaiian Islands, or to their language.

haw'finch, *n.* [*haw* (hawthorn), and *finch*.] the common European grosbeak.

haw-haw', *n.* a ha-ha, or sunk fence.

haw'-haw', *n.* and *interj.* see *ha*.

hawk, *n.* [ME. *hauk*; AS. *hafoc, hafuc*, a hawk.]

1. any of an order, *Falconiformes*, of birds of prey, characterized by short, rounded wings, a long tail and legs, and a hooked beak and claws; broadly, any such bird active by day except the vultures and eagles: hawks include the falcons, buzzards, harriers, kites, and caracaras; in a more restricted sense, the term is used of birds belonging to the genera *Accipiter* and *Astur*, typified by the sparrow hawk of Europe and the sharp-shinned hawk and Cooper's hawk of North America.
2. a person regarded as having the preying or grasping nature of a hawk; cheater; swindler.
3. an advocate of all-out war or of measures in international affairs designed to provoke or escalate open hostilities: cf. *dove*.

hawk, *v.t.* and *v.i.*; hawked, *pt., pp.*; hawking, *ppr.* 1. to catch or attempt to catch (birds) by means of hawks trained for the purpose; to practice falconry.
2. to fly at; to attack on the wing, as the hawk does.

hawk, *n.* an audible effort to force up phlegm from the throat.

hawk, *v.i.* [echoic.] to make an audible effort to force up phlegm, etc. from the throat.

hawk, *v.t.* to raise, as phlegm, from the throat, by an audible effort.

hawk, *v.t.* (from *hawker* (peddler).]

1. to sell or offer for sale by shouting in a street or other public place; to peddle.
2. to spread (rumors, etc.).

hawk, *n.* a small, quadrangular board with a handle underneath, used by masons to hold mortar.

hawk'bill, *n.* *Eretmochelys imbricata*, the hawk's-bill tortoise that is the chief source of tortoise shell.

hawk'bit, *n.* 1. any plant of the genus *Hieracium*; a hawkweed.
2. a plant of the genus *Leontodon*, as *Leontodon autumnalis*, or fall dandelion.

hawked (hakt), *a.* curving, like a hawk's bill.

hawk'ẽr, *n.* [prob. from M.L.G. *hoker*, huckster, peddler (D. *heuker*, G. *hoker*), from M.L.G. *hoken*, to crouch (as with a burden, pack, etc.).] one who offers goods for sale by shouting in the street; a peddler; a huckster.

ha̤wk'ẽr, *n.* [AS. *hafecere*, from *hafoc, hafuc*, a hawk.] a person who uses hawks for hunting; a falconer.

Ha̤wk'eȳe, *n.* a native or inhabitant of Iowa, nicknamed the "Hawkeye State." [Colloq.]

ha̤wk'eȳed (-īd), *a.* having a keen eye.

ha̤wk flȳ, a hornet fly: also called *robber fly.*

ha̤wk'ing, *n.* falconry; hunting with hawks.

ha̤wk mọth, a very large moth of the *Sphingidæ*, or sphinxes. The death's-head hawk moth, *Acherontia atropos*, has a marking closely resembling a skull on the upper side of the thorax. All species have a long proboscis to draw the nectar from flowers, and the larvae are usually naked green caterpillars with a caudal spine.

HAWK MOTH (*Sphinx ligustri*)

ha̤wk owl, 1. *Surnia ulula*, a day owl of North America, Asia, and Europe. It resembles a hawk in appearance and habits.

2. any of various other owls, as the snowy owl, the short-eared owl, etc.

ha̤wk's'-bēard, *n.* any of a number of plants of the composite family with red, yellow, or orange flowers.

ha̤wk's'-bill, *n.* 1. a hawkbill.

2. a checking device in the striking movement of clockwork.

Ha̤wk'sha̤w, *n.* [after the character in Tom Taylor's play *The Ticket of Leave Man* (1863).] a detective: humorous term. [Colloq.]

ha̤wk'weed, *n.* any of a group of weedy plants of the composite family, with leaves in flat rosettes and stalks of red, yellow, or orange flowers.

ha̤wm, *v.i.* to idle; to lounge. [Brit. Dial.]

hä'wok, *n.* [N. Am. Indian.] in numismatics, the perforated, disk-shaped, clamshell money of the aborigines of southern California.

ha̤wṣe, *n.* [probably from ON. *hals*, the neck, part of the forecastle or bow of a ship.]

1. that part of the bow of a ship containing the hawseholes, through which the cables run.

2. a hawsehole.

3. the space between the bow of a ship and the anchors.

4. the arrangement of a ship's cables when the ship is moored with both a starboard anchor and a port anchor out from forward.

ha̤wṣe bag, a bag of oakum or the like used to plug hawseholes in a head sea.

ha̤wṣe block, a block of wood used at sea to plug a hawsehole: called also *hawse plug.*

ha̤wṣe bōl'stẽr, a bolster or block of iron or ironed wood placed under a hawsehole to prevent chafing by the cable.

ha̤wṣe box, the hawsehole. [Obs.]

ha̤wse buck'lẽr, an iron plate or hinged shutter for covering the exterior opening of a hawsehole.

ha̤wṣe'hōle, *n.* one of the holes in the bow of a ship through which a cable passes.

ha̤wṣe hook, a breast hook which crosses the hawse timber above the upper deck.

ha̤wṣe piēce, one of the foremost timbers of a ship, through which the hawsehole is cut.

ha̤wṣe'pīpe, *n.* an iron pipe fitted into the hawsehole to prevent the wood from being abraded.

ha̤wṣe plug, a plug used for stopping the hawseholes; a hawse block.

ha̤wṣ'ẽr, *n.* [OFr. *haulseree*, from *haulser, hausser*, to raise, lift; LL. *altiare*, to raise, from L. *altus*, high.] a large rope or small cable, often made of steel, by which a ship is anchored, towed, etc.

ha̤wṣ'er bend, a kind of knot for tying one hawser to another.

ha̤wṣ'ẽr-lāid, *a.* cable-laid.

ha̤wṣe tim'bẽr, an upright in the bow through which a hawsehole is cut.

ha̤wṣe wood, a general name for the hawse timbers.

ha̤wṣ'ing ī'ron (ī'ũrn), a calking iron or chisel.

ha̤wṣ'ing mal'let, a beetle or mallet used in calking.

ha̤w'thọrn, *n.* [ME. *hawethorn*; AS. *hægthorn*, the hawthorn; *haga*, a hedge, haw, and *thorn*, thorn.] any of a group of spiny shrubs and small trees of the genus *Cratægus*, with fragrant flowers of white, pink, or red, and red berries (called haws).

ha̤w'thọrn grōs'bēak, the hawfinch.

hāy, *n.* [ME. *hay, hey*; AS. *hig*, hay, cut grass, also, growing grass.] grass, alfalfa, clover, etc. cut and dried for fodder; grass prepared for preservation.

between hay and grass; between seasons; too late for something and too early for something else. [Colloq.]

hay tea; a decoction used in cattle feed.

not hay; not a trifling amount of money; a considerable sum. [Slang.]

tame hay; hay cut from cultivated grasses.

to hit the hay; to go to bed. [Slang.]

to make hay while the sun shines; to make the best use of time and opportunity.

wild hay; hay cut from wild grass.

hāy, *v.i.*; hayed, *pt., pp.*; haying, *ppr.* to cut or put up grass for hay.

hāy, *n.* [ME. *haye, heye*; AS. *hege*, a hedge, fence, from *haga*, a hedge.]

1. a hedge. [Obs.]

2. a net that encloses the haunt of an animal. [Obs.]

hāy, *n.* [Fr. *haye.*] an old country dance with much winding in and out.

hāy, *v.i.* to lay snares for rabbits. [Obs.]

hāy, *n.* in fencing, a home thrust. [Obs.]

hāy bȧ·cil'lus, a rod-shaped, nonpathogenic bacillus present in hay infusions.

hāy'bird, *n.* 1. the blackcap.

2. the American jacksnipe.

hāy'bōte, *n.* [ME. *haye*, hedge, and *boote*, a fine.] in old English law, an allowance of wood to a tenant for repairing hedges or fences; hedgebote.

hāy'çap, *n.* any covering placed over a haycock to shield it from rain.

hāy'çock, *n.* a conical pile or heap of hay drying in a field.

hāy çōld, hay fever.

hāy fē'vẽr, an acute inflammation of the eyes and upper respiratory tract, characterized by sneezing and sometimes accompanied by fever and asthma: it is an allergic reaction, caused mainly by the pollen of some grasses and trees; polinosis.

hāy'fiēld, *n.* a field in which grass, alfalfa, etc. is grown for hay, or a field on which hay is cured and stored.

hāy'fọrk, *n.* any fork used in handling hay: specifically, a mechanical device for holding a part of a load of hay to be put in a stack or mow.

hāy hook, 1. a hook used for pulling hay from a mow or stack by hand.

2. in heraldry, a hook used as a bearing, sometimes finished with an animal's head.

hāy'ing, *n.* haymaking; the getting in of hay.

hāy'lọft, *n.* the upper story in a barn or stable, used for storing hay.

hāy'māk''ẽr, *n.* 1. one who cuts and dries grass for fodder.

2. a device for curing hay by means of hot air.

3. a kind of dance: called also *haymakers' jig.*

4. a powerful blow with the fist, intended to cause a knockout. [Slang.]

hāy'māk''ing, *n.* the work of cutting grass and curing it for fodder.

hāy'mär·ket, *n.* 1. a place for the sale of hay.

2. [H–] a street in London, known as a theater district.

3. [H–] a square in Chicago, site of a famous demonstration (May 4, 1886) for the eight-hour day.

hāy'mow, *n.* 1. a mow or mass of hay laid up in a barn for preservation.

2. the place in a barn where hay is stored; hayloft.

hāy press, a machine for compressing hay into bales.

hāy'rack, *n.* 1. a sort of frame, generally set on a wagon body, for hauling hay, straw, etc.

2. an open framework at which stock may feed.

hāy'rāke, *n.* a rake for hay.

hāy'rick, *n.* a pile of hay; usually, a long pile for preservation in the open air.

hāy'rīde, *n.* a pleasure ride in a wagon partly filled with hay, by a group on an outing.

hāy'seed, *n.* 1. grass seed shaken from mown hay.

2. bits of chaff and straw from hay.

3. a person having the awkwardness, simplicity, and lack of sophistication regarded as characteristic of people from the country; a rustic: somewhat contemptuous term.

hāy'stack, *n.* a stack or large pile of hay in the open air, laid up for preservation.

hāy'sta̤lk (-sta̤k), *n.* a stalk of hay.

hāy ted'dẽr, a machine for scattering hay so as to expose it to the sun and air. It consists of a pair of wheels supporting a reel carrying bars set with curved tines pointing outward. The reel is rotated by a pinion connected with a spurwheel in the hub of one of the wheels.

HAY TEDDER

hāy'thọrn, *n.* hawthorn.

Hāy'ti·ăn (*or* -shăn), *a.* and *n.* same as *Haitian.*

hāy'wärd, *n.* [ME. *heyward*; AS. *hæigweard*; *haga*, a haw, hedge, and *weard*, keeper.]

1. formerly, an official in charge of fences or hedges around public pastures.

2. an official who impounds stray cattle or other animals.

hāy'wīre, *n.* wire for tying up bales of hay, straw, etc.

hāy'wīre, *a.* [perh. from *haywire camp*, Maine term for logging camp with poor or broken equipment that had to be tied up with haywire.]

1. out of order; disorganized; confused; wrong. [Slang.]

2. crazy: usually in *to go haywire*, to become, or act as if, crazy. [Slang.]

haz'ărd, *n.* [ME. *hazard*, a game of chance; OFr. *hazard*, a game of dice, adventure; perhaps from Ar. *al-zār*, the die.]

1. an early game of chance played with dice, from which craps is derived.

2. chance.

3. risk; peril; danger; jeopardy.

4. something risked. [Archaic.]

5. any obstacle on a golf course, including traps, bunkers, ponds, etc.

6. in court tennis, any of the openings in the court through which a ball may be sent to win a point.

at all hazards; no matter what the risk or danger.

to run the hazard; to risk; to take the chance.

Syn.—chance, risk, venture, danger.

haz'ărd, *v.t.*; hazarded, *pt., pp.*; hazarding, *ppr.* 1. to expose to chance; to put in danger of loss or injury; to venture; to risk; as, to *hazard* one's life to save a friend.

2. to venture to incur or bring on; as, to *hazard* the loss of reputation.

Syn.—risk, venture.

haz'ărd, *v.i.* to take a chance; to run a risk or danger.

haz'ărd·ȧ·ble, *a.* 1. liable to hazard or chance; hazardous; risky. [Obs.]

2. that can be hazarded, or risked.

haz'ărd·ẽr, *n.* 1. one who ventures or puts at stake. [Rare.]

2. one who plays at hazard. [Obs.]

haz'ărd·īze, *n.* a hazardous venture; hazard. [Obs.]

haz'ărd·ous, *a.* 1. dangerous; that exposes to peril or danger of loss or evil; as, a *hazardous* attempt or experiment.

2. of or involving chance.

haz'ărd·ous·ly, *adv.* in a hazardous manner.

haz'ărd·ous·ness, *n.* the state of being attended with danger or risk.

haz'ărd·ry, *n.* rashness; temerity; also, a playing at hazard; gambling. [Obs.]

haz'ărd tā'ble, a table on which hazard is played; any gaming table.

hāze, *n.* [prob. from L.G. dial. as nautical borrowing; ult. connection with AS. *hasu*, gray, is possible, but prob. via L.G. proverb *de hase brouet*, lit., "the hare is brewing," as applied to a mist.]

1. a thin vapor of fog, smoke, dust, etc. in the air.

2. slight confusion or vagueness of mind.

hāze, *v.i.* to be hazy or thick with haze.

hāze, *v.t.*; hazed, *pt., pp.*; hazing, *ppr.* [OFr. *haser*, to irritate, annoy.]

1. in nautical usage, to oppress, punish, or harass by forcing to do hard and unnecessary work.

2. to initiate or discipline (fellow students) by means of horseplay, practical jokes, and tricks, often in the nature of humiliating or painful ordeals.

hā′zel, *n.* [ME. *hasel, hesil*; AS. *hæsel*, the hazel.]
1. any of a group of trees or shrubs of the genus *Corylus*, with edible nuts (called *hazelnuts* or *filberts*).
2. a hazelnut.
3. (a) the wood of this tree or shrub; (b) a stick of this wood.
4. the color of a ripened hazelnut; reddish brown.

hā′zel, *a.* 1. of the hazel tree.
2. of its wood.
3. light reddish-brown; yellowish-brown: hazel eyes are usually flecked with green or gray.

hā′zel çrot′tles, *Sticta pulmonacea*, a lichen yielding a dye for woolen goods.

hāze′less, *a.* devoid of haze.

hā′zel grouse, *Bonasa betulina*, the European ruffed grouse.

hā′zel hen, the hazel grouse.

hā′zel·ly, *a.* 1. of the color hazel.
2. full of, covered with, or abounding in hazels.

hā′zel·nut, *n.* the small, edible, roundish nut of the hazel; the filbert.

hā′zel tree, 1. the common hazel.
2. *Guevina avellana*, a proteaceous evergreen tree of Chile, the tough and elastic wood of which is used in building boats.

hāzel·wŏrt, *n.* in botany, the asarabacca, *Asarum europæum*.

hā′zẽr, *n.* one who hazes.

hā′zi·ly, *adv.* in a hazy manner; vaguely.

hā′zi·ness, *n.* the state of being hazy.

hā′zle, *v.t.* to make dry. [Brit. Dial.]

hā′zy, *a.*; *comp.* hazier; *superl.* haziest, 1. thick with haze; foggy; misty.
A tender *hazy* brightness. —Wordsworth.
2. dim; obscure; not clear; as, to have *hazy* notions about anything.
Syn.—foggy, nebulous, misty, filmy, gauzy, cloudy, murky.

H′-bomb (āch′bom), *n.* hydrogen bomb.

hē, *pron.*; *nom.* he; *poss.* his; *obj.* him; *nom. pl.* they; *poss. pl.* their *or* theirs; *obj. pl.* them. [ME. *he*; AS. *he*.]
1. the masculine singular pronoun of the third person; the man or male being (or, sometimes, the object regarded as male) previously mentioned.
Thy desire shall be to thy husband, and *he* shall rule over thee. —Gen. iii. 16.
2. the person indefinitely; the one; anyone.
He that walketh with wise men shall be wise. —Prov. xiii. 20.
He is often prefixed to the names of animals to designate the male kind; as, a *he*-goat; a *he*-bear.

hē, *n.* a man, boy, or male animal; as, our dog is a *he*.

he̦, *n.* [Heb., lit., window.] the fifth letter of the Hebrew alphabet, roughly corresponding to English *h*.

head (hed), *n.* [ME. *hed, heved*; AS. *heafod*, the head.]
1. (a) the top part of the body in man, the ape, etc., or the front part in most other animals: in higher animals it is a bony structure containing the brain, and including the jaws, eyes, ears, nose, and mouth; (b) the head exclusive of the face.
2. (a) the head as the seat of reason, memory, and imagination; mind; intelligence; as, use your *head*; (b) aptitude; ability; as, he has a *head* for mathematics.
3. the head as a symbol for the individual; person; as, dinner at five dollars a *head*.
4. *pl.* **head**, the head as a unit of counting; as, fifty *head* of cattle.
5. a representation of a head, as in painting or sculpture.
6. the side of a coin with such a representation: also called *heads*: opposed to *tail(s)*.
7. the highest or uppermost part or thing; top; specifically, (a) the top of a page, column of figures, etc.; (b) a printed title at the top of a page, section of writing, etc.; (c) a chief point of discussion; topic of a section, chapter, etc. in a speech or written work; (d) a headline or headlines for a newspaper story; (e) froth floating on newly poured effervescent beverages; as, the *head* on a glass of beer; (f) that end of a cask or drum which is uppermost at any time.
8. the foremost part of a thing; front; specifically, (a) a part associated with the human head; as, the *head* of a bed; (b) the part of a pier farthest from land; (c) the front part of a ship; bow; (d) the front position, as of a column of marching men; (e) either end of something; extremity.
9. the projecting part of something; specifically, (a) the part designed for holding, pushing, striking, etc.; as, the *head* of a pin, the *head* of an arrow; (b) a jutting mass of rock, land, etc., as of a mountain; (c) a point of land; promontory; headland; (d) a projecting place in a boil or other inflammation where pus is about to break through.
10. the membrane stretched across the end of a drum, tambourine, etc.
11. the source of a flowing body of water; beginning of a stream, river, etc.
12. a source of water kept at some height to supply a mill, etc.
13. pressure; as, a *head* of steam.
14. a dominant position; position of leadership or first importance; as, the *head* of the class.
15. a foremost person; leader, ruler, chief, etc.
16. a headmaster.
17. a crisis or culmination; as, things may soon come to a *head*.
18. a toilet. [Nautical Slang.]
19. in botany, (a) a flat or rounded cluster of little flowers, as in the daisy or clover; (b) a large, compact bud; as, a *head* of cabbage; (c) the uppermost part of a plant's foliage; as, the *head* of a tree.
20. in golf, the heavy part of the club; striking part at the end of the stick.
21. in linguistics, that word in a word group which functions grammatically like the entire group.
22. in mining, a heading; drift.
23. in music, the rounded part of a note, at the end of the stem.
by a head; (a) in horse racing, etc., by the length of the animal's head; (b) by a very small margin.
by (or *down by*) *the head*; in nautical usage, with the bow deeper in the water than the stern.
head and shoulders above; definitely superior to.
head over heels; (a) tumbling heels over head; topsy-turvy, as in a somersault; (b) deeply; completely; (c) hurriedly; impetuously; recklessly.
heads up! look out! be careful! [Colloq.]
of the first head; designating a deer at the age when the antlers are first developed.
out of (or *off*) *one's head*; (a) crazy; (b) delirious; raving. [Colloq.]
over one's head; (a) too difficult for one to understand; (b) so that one cannot understand; (c) in spite of one's prior claim; (d) without consulting one; to a higher authority.
to come to a head; (a) to be about to suppurate, as a boil; (b) to culminate.
to give one his head; to let one do as he likes; to give free rein to one.
to go to one's head; (a) to confuse, excite, or intoxicate one; (b) to make one vain or overconfident.
to hang (or *hide*) *one's head*; to lower one's head or conceal one's face in or as in shame.
to keep one's head; to keep one's poise, self-control, etc.; to refrain from becoming excited or flustered.
to keep one's head above water; (a) to remain afloat; to keep from sinking; (b) to keep oneself alive, out of debt, etc.
to lay heads together; to consult or scheme together.
to lose one's head; to lose one's poise, self-control, etc.; to become excited or flustered.
to make head or tail of; to understand: usually in the negative.
to take it into one's head; to conceive the notion, plan, or intention.
to turn one's head; (a) to make one dizzy; (b) to make one vain or overconfident.

head, *a.* 1. most important; principal; commanding; first.
2. to be found at the top or front.
3. striking against the front; as, *head* currents.

head (hed), *v.t.*; headed, *pt.*, *pp.*; heading, *ppr.*
1. to be chief of; command.
2. to lead; precede; as, she *heads* the list.
3. to supply with a head; to shape a head for (a pin, etc.).
4. to behead; decapitate. [Rare.]
5. to trim the higher part from (a tree or plant); poll.
6. to go round the head of; as, they *headed* the stream.
7. to turn or cause to go in a specified direction; as, I *headed* the car for home.
8. in soccer, to hit (the ball) with one's head.
to head off; to get ahead of; intercept; thwart.

head, *v.i.* 1. to originate; to spring; to have its source, as a river.
A broad river, that *heads* in the great Blue Ridge. —Adair.
2. to be directed; to set out; as, how does the ship *head?*
3. to form a head; as, the cabbages *head* early.

-head, -hood, as in god*head*.

head′āçhe, *n.* [ME. *hedake, heavedeche*; AS. *heafodece*.]
1. a continuous pain in the head.
2. a cause of worry, annoyance, or trouble. [Colloq.]

head′āçhe tree, *Premna integrifolia*, a shrub of the vervain family found in Madagascar and the East Indies. Its astringent leaves are used as a remedy for headache.

head′āçhe weed, a shrub, *Hedyosmum nutans*, belonging to the *Chloranthaceæ*, found in Jamaica.

head′āçh·y, *a.* afflicted with a headache; subject to headaches.
He awoke *headachy* and feverish.—Farrar.

head′-and-head′, *adv.* in nautical usage, head on; head to head.

head′band, *n.* 1. a fillet; a band for the head.
2. in bookbinding, the cloth band at each end of the inner back of a book.
3. in printing, an engraved decorative band at the top of a page or at the head of a chapter in a book.

head′band, *v.t.* to put a headband on (the inner back of a book).

head bāy, the water space in a canal directly above the lock.

head bet′ŏ·ny, *Pedicularis canadensis*, the wood betony or lousewort.

head block, in a sawmill, the movable crosspiece of a carriage on which the log rests; a device which supports the log and conveys it to the saw.

head′bōard, *n.* a board forming the head, as of a bed.

head′bŏr″ōugh, head′bŏr″rōw, *n.* [ME. *heedborow, hedborowe*, lit., head pledge.]
1. in England, formerly, the chief of a frankpledge, tithing, or decennary, consisting of ten families: called, in some countries, *borsholder*, and sometimes *tithingman*.
2. in England, a petty constable.

head çāse, in entomology, the integument covering the head of a pupa.

head′chāir, *n.* a chair with a high back provided with some device for supporting the head.

head′cheeşe, *n.* in cookery, parts of the head and feet of hogs, chopped up fine, seasoned, and, after being boiled and jellied, pressed into the form of a cheese.

head′çhūte, *n.* a canvas tube reaching from the head of a ship to the water, through which refuse matter is carried overboard.

head′çloth *n.* 1. a cloth covering for the head.
2. a curtain behind the head of a bed.

head çōal, in England, the upper part of a thick seam of coal worked in separate lifts.

head çrack′ẽr, same as *head spade*.

head′dress, *n.* a covering or ornament for the head; also, any manner of arranging the hair; coiffure.

head′ed, *a.* formed into a head; also, having a heading.

-head′ed, a combining form meaning: (a) *having a* (specified kind of) *head*, as in clear-*headed*; (b) *having* (a specified number of) *heads*, as in two-*headed*.

head′ẽr, *n.* 1. a person or device that puts heads on pins, nails, rivets, etc.
2. a machine that takes off the heads of grain and sends them up an inclined plane into a truck or wagon.
3. a pipe, tube, etc. that connects other pieces to permit the flow of a fluid through them.
4. a headlong fall or dive. [Colloq.]
5. in carpentry, a wooden beam, as in flooring, placed between two long beams with the ends of short beams resting against it.
6. in masonry, a brick or building stone laid across the thickness of a wall with one end toward the face of the wall.
7. one who has charge of a whaleboat.

head′fȧst, *n.* a rope at the head of a ship to fasten it to a wharf or other fixed object.

head′first′, *adv.* with the head foremost; hence, rashly; recklessly.

head′fish, *n.* a sunfish of the genus *Mola.*
head·fōre′mōst, *adv.* headfirst.
head′frāme, *n.* in mining, the frame over the shaft which supports the hoisting gear.
head gāte, the upstream gate of a canal lock; a floodgate of any race or sluice.
head′gēar, *n.* 1. covering or ornament for the head; headdress; hat, cap, etc.
2. the gear of a headframe over the mouth of an excavation.
3. all the parts of a harness for the head of a horse, mule, etc.
4. in nautical usage, the running gear of the sails set forward of the foremast.
head house, in mining, the structure enclosing the headframe which serves to protect it from the weather.
head′-hunt″ẽr, *n.* a savage who practices head-hunting.
head′-hunt″ing, *n.* a custom carried on by certain primitive tribes, as the Dyaks of Borneo, which consists in removing the heads of slain enemies and preserving them as trophies.
head′i·ly, *adv.* in a heady or rash manner; hastily.
head′i·ness, *n.* the condition or quality of being heady.
head′ing, *n.* 1. the act or process of providing with a head.
2. that which stands at the head; title; as, the *heading* of a paper.
3. material for the heads of casks, puncheons, barrels, etc.
4. in masonry, the end of a brick or stone presented outward.
5. in mining, (a) a driftway or passage excavated in the line of an intended tunnel, forming a gullet in which the men work; (b) the place where the work of driving a horizontal passage is being done; (c) the mass of gravel above the head of a sluice in a placer.
6. in sewing, the upper edge of a ruffle, which appears above the line of stitching.
7. homespun cloth. [Dial.]
8. a preparation of equal parts of alum and green vitriol used in brewing to produce a head on liquor.
head′ing chiṣ′el, a chisel used in cutting away the head of a mortise.
head′ing cĩr′çlẽr, a machine used for making heads for barrels, casks, etc.
head′ing çōurse, in architecture, a course which consists entirely of headers, or of stones or bricks laid lengthwise across the thickness of the wall.
head′ing joint, 1. in architecture, a joint of two or more boards at right angles to the fibers.
2. in masonry, a joint between two voussoirs in the same course.
head′ing mȧ·chïne′, 1. a machine by which pins are headed.
2. a reaping machine that cuts off the heads of the grain.
3. a machine for making heads for casks, barrels, etc.
head′ing tool, a tool with which the rod of metal that is used in shaping the heads of nails, bolts, etc. is held.
head kid′ney, in anatomy, the anterior of the three segments of the mesonephros opening into the cloaca. It is the first part of the urogenital system to be differentiated in the vertebrate embryo; the pronephros.
head knee (nē), in shipbuilding, a piece of molded knee timber situated beneath the headrails, and fayed edgewise to the cutwater and stem, for steadying the cutwater.
head knot (not), a knot of ribbons, etc., worn as part of a headdress.
head′lănd, *n.* [ME. *hevedlond*; AS. *heáfod*, head, and *lond*, land.]
1. a cape; a promontory; a point of land projecting from the shore into the sea or other expanse of water.
2. a ridge or strip of unplowed land at the ends of furrows or near a fence.
head′ledġe (-lej), *n.* in shipbuilding, a thwartship piece used in framing the hatchways or ladderways.
head′less, *a.* [ME. *heedless, hevedles*; AS. *hedfodleas.*]
1. having no head; beheaded; as, a *headless* body, r cck, or carcass.
2. lacking a chief or leader.
3. lacking understanding or prudence; rash; stupid; foolish.
head let′tuce, a variety of lettuce, the leaves of which form a compact ball or head.
head′līght (-līt), *n.* 1. a light with a reflector, placed in front of a locomotive, automobile, etc., to light the track or road before it during darkness.
2. a white light carried at the masthead of a steamer when under way at night; a masthead light.
head′līne, *n.* 1. a line at the top of a page in a book, giving the running title, page number, etc.
2. a line or lines of type at the top of a newspaper article, giving a short statement of its contents: the headline is usually in larger type.
3. a rope tied to the head of a horse, cow, etc.
head′līne, *v.t.* and *v.i.* 1. to provide an article with a headline.
2. to give prominence to, as a newspaper article or a vaudeville act.
head līne, in palmistry, that line in the palm which supposedly indicates the qualities of the head.
head′līn″ẽr, *n.* 1. in journalism, one who writes headlines.
2. in the theater, an actor or an act featured on the program in a headline, particularly in vaudeville.
head′lock, *n.* in wrestling, the hold in which one wrestler grips the other by encircling his head with one arm and pressing it against his body.
head′long, *adv.* 1. with the head foremost; as, to fall *headlong.*
2. rashly; recklessly; without deliberation.
He hurries *headlong* to his fate.
—Dryden.
3. hastily; with uncontrolled speed and force.
head′long, *a.* 1. steep; dizzy; precipitous; as, a *headlong* height. [Rare and Poetic.]
2. having the head first; headforemost.
3. moving with uncontrolled speed and force.
4. reckless; impetuous.
head′man, *n.*; *pl.* **head′men,** 1. a leader; chief; often, an overseer; foreman.
2. a headsman; executioner. [Rare.]
head′mȧs·tẽr, *n.* 1. in certain schools, the man in charge of the school; principal.
2. in some colleges, a faculty member residing in and in charge of a residence hall for men.
Also *head master.*
head′mis·tress, *n.* in certain schools, especially schools for girls, the woman in charge of the school; principal: also *head mistress.*
head′mōld, *n.* in architecture, a molding projecting over the head of a window or door.
head′mōld·ing, *n.* a headmold.
head mŏn′ey, 1. a poll tax; a tax per capita.
2. a reward or bounty per head for the capture of prisoners or outlaws.
head′mōst, *a.* most advanced; most forward; first in a line or order of progression; as, the *headmost* ship in a fleet.
head net′ting, an ornamental netting used in merchant ships instead of the fayed planking of the headrails.
head′nōte, *n.* 1. a note placed at the top of a chapter or page.
2. in law, a brief statement placed at the top of a report of a case showing the ruling of the court upon the principles involved therein; a syllabus.
head′-on′, *a.* and *adv.* with the head or front foremost; as, a *head-on* collision.
head′pan, *n.* the brainpan. [Obs.]
head′pen″ny, *n.* a poll tax. [Obs.]
head′phōne, *n.* in radio and telephony, a receiver which is held to the ear by means of a flexible band over the head: generally in plural.
head′piēce, *n.* 1. a helmet, cap, or other covering for the head.
2. an apparatus with headphones, fitting over the head.
3. the head; mind; intellect.
4. in printing, an ornamental design engraved at the beginning of a book, chapter, etc.
head pin, in bowling and tenpins, the pin at the front of a triangle of ten pins.
head′plāte, *n.* 1. a plate covering the breast of the cheeks of a gun carriage.
2. the piece that strengthens the cantle of a saddle.
3. a strip of metal that covers the joints of the top of a carriage.
head′quar″tẽrṣ (-kwar″), *n.pl.* and *sing.* 1. the main office, or center of operations and control, of anyone in command, as in an army, police force, etc.
2. the main office or center of control in any organization.
3. all the people working at such a place.
head′rāce, *n.* a strong current of water; the channel in which water is led to a water wheel: distinguished from *tailrace.*
head′rāil, *n.* in shipbuilding, one of the elliptical rails at the head of a ship.
head′rēach, *v.i.* among seamen, to shoot ahead, as a vessel when brought to the wind and about to be put on the other tack.
head reġ′is·tẽr, the upper register of the voice, in which the higher range of tones is produced.
head′rest, *n.* a support for the head, as on the back of a chair used by dentists, barbers, etc.
head′ring, *n.* a ring worn in the hair by the married men of some Kaffir tribes.
head′room, *n.* in architecture, the clear space below a girder, arch, etc.
head′rōpe, *n.* in nautical usage, that part of a boltrope which terminates any sail on the upper edge, and to which it is sewed.
head′sāil, *n.* any sail set forward of the foremast.
head′set, *n.* 1. in radio and telephony, the combination of receiver and flexible band which is worn on the head; headphones.
2. the combination receiver and transmitter worn by a telephone switchboard operator.
head′shāke, *n.* a significant shake of the head.
head′sheet, *n.* in nautical usage, any one of the sheets of the headsails.
head′ship, *n.* the state or position of being a head or chief; authority; dignity; rule; government.
head′sill, *n.* in sawing, one of the two cross pieces on which the end of the log rests.
head′skin, *n.* a tough substance protecting the case of the sperm whale.
headṣ′măn, *n.*; *pl.* **headṣ′men,** 1. an executioner who cuts off heads.
2. in a colliery, one who removes the coal from the workings to the tramway.
head spāde, a long-handled implement used by whalers for cutting into the head of a whale; a head cracker.
head spin, in wrestling, a method of freeing oneself from a half nelson by suddenly kicking one's feet in the air and twisting around on one's head.
head′spring, *n.* fountainhead; source; origin.
head′stall, *n.* that part of the bridle which fits over the head.
head′stand, *n.* the act of supporting oneself upright on the head with the help of the hands.
head′stick, *n.* 1. in nautical usage, a short, round stick with a hole at each end, through which the headrope of some triangular sails is thrust to prevent its twisting.
2. formerly, in printing, a piece of wood or metal placed at the head of a form between the type and the chase.
head′stock, *n.* in machinery, (a) the framing used to support the gudgeons of a wheel; (b) the frame which supports the revolving spindle in a lathe; (c) the member forming the under frame of a railway car.
head′stōne, *n.* 1. the principal stone in a foundation; the chief or corner stone.
2. the stone marker at the head of a grave.
head stool, a form of pillow once used as a rest for the neck and to protect elaborately dressed hair from being disturbed.
head′strēam, *n.* a stream which forms the source or one of the sources of a river.
head′strong, *a.* 1. determined not to follow orders, advice, etc. but to do as one pleases; self-willed; obstinate.
2. showing such an obstinate determination; as, *headstrong* desire.
Syn.—obstinate, intractable, heady, unruly, stubborn, ungovernable.
head′strong″ness, *n.* obstinacy. [Rare.]
head tax, a poll tax; head money.
head tim′bẽr, in shipbuilding, one of the upright pieces of timber inserted between the upper knee and the curved rail, to support the frame of the head rails.
head′tīre, *n.* dress or attire for the head. [Archaic.]
head tōne, in singing, a tone produced as if in the cavities of the head: distinguished from *chest tone.*
head valve, the upper air-pump valve in a condensing steam engine.
head′wāit′ẽr, *n.* a supervisor of waiters, often

in charge of table reservations, in a restaurant, night club, etc.

head'wărd, head'wărds, *adv.* toward the head.

head'wa"tẽr, *n.* the upper part of a river, near its source, or one of the streams that contribute their waters to form a larger stream: usually in the plural.

head'wāy, *n.* 1. the forward motion of a ship; hence, any kind of progress or advancement.
2. in architecture, headroom.
3. the difference in time or miles between two trains, ships, etc. traveling in the same direction over the same course.

head wind, a wind blowing in the direction directly opposite the course of a ship or aircraft.

head wŏrd, the title word of a paragraph.

head'wŏrk, *n.* 1. mental or intellectual labor.
2. in architecture, the heads and other ornaments on the keystones of arches.
3. [*pl.*] in mining, the headframe with headgear.
4. in engineering, a device to control the quantity of water entering a channel.

head'y, *a.*; *comp.* headier; *superl.* headiest. 1. rash; hasty; precipitate; disposed to rush forward in an enterprise without thought or deliberation.
2. apt to affect the head; inflaming; intoxicating; strong; as, a *heady* wine.

head'yärd, *n.* in nautical usage, one of the yards of a ship's foremast.

hēal, *v.t.* [ME. *helen, hilen*; AS. *helan*, to cover, conceal.] to cover, as a roof with slates, tin, etc. [Brit. Dial.]

hēal, *v.t.*; healed, *pt.*, *pp.*; healing, *ppr.* [ME. *helens*; AS. *hælan*, to heal, make whole, from *hāl*, whole.]
1. to make sound, well, or healthy again; restore to health; as, *heal* the sick.
2. to cure or get rid of (a disease); restore (a wound, sore, etc.) to a healthy condition.
3. to free from grief, troubles, evil, etc.
4. (a) to remedy or get rid of (grief, troubles, etc.); (b) to make up (a breach, differences, etc.); reconcile.
Syn.—cure, remedy, restore.

hēal, *v.i.* 1. to grow sound; to return to a sound state; to get well; as, the wound *heals.*
2. to become scarred or closed: said of a wound.

hēal'ȧ·ble, *a.* capable of being healed. [Rare.]

hēal'all, *n.* in botany, *Prunella vulgaris*, a plant formerly supposed to possess healing properties; also, the horse balm, *Collinsonia canadensis.*

hēald, *n.* same as *heddle.*

hēal'ẽr, *n.* one who or that which heals; specifically, (a) a person who tries to heal through prayer or faith; (b) a remedy.

hēal'ing, *a.* 1. tending to cure; remedial; curative; as, a *healing* medicine; *healing* words; *healing* influence.
2. becoming sound, well, or healthy again.

hēal'ing, *n.* the act or process by which a cure is effected.

hēal'ing hẽrb (ẽrb), the comfrey, *Symphytum officinale.*

hēal'ing·ly, *adv.* in a healing manner.

health (helth), *n.* [ME. *helth*; AS. *hælth*, health, from *hāl*, whole.]
1. physical and mental well-being; soundness; freedom from defect, pain, or disease; normality of mental and physical functions.
Health is something different from strength; it is universal good condition.—Munger.
2. condition of body or mind; as, good or bad *health.*
3. power to heal, restore, or purify. [Rare.]
The tongue of the wise is *health.* —Prov. xii. 18.
4. a toast wishing health and happiness to another; as, to drink one's *health.*
Come, love and *health* to all. —Shak.
health officer; an officer whose duty it is to enforce sanitary rules and regulations.

health fo̤od, food considered to be especially healthful; often, specifically, such food when grown with only animal or vegetable fertilizers and free of chemical additives.

health'fu̇l, *a.* 1. serving to promote health; wholesome; salubrious; salutary; as, a *healthful* air or climate; a *healthful* diet.
2. healthy; sound. [Rare.]

health'fu̇l·ly, *adv.* in a healthful manner; wholesomely.

health'fu̇l·ness, *n.* the state of being healthful.

health'i·ly, *adv.* in a healthy manner or condition.

health'i·ness, *n.* the state or condition of being healthy; soundness; freedom from disease; as, the *healthiness* of an animal or plant.

health in·sūr'ănce (-shūr'), insurance against loss, as of earning capacity, by sickness.

health'less, *a.* 1. infirm; sickly; unhealthy.
2. not conducive to health. [Rare.]

health'less·ness, *n.* the state of being healthless.

health'sŏme, *a.* wholesome. [Rare.]

health'y, *a.*; *comp.* healthier; *superl.* healthiest. 1. being in a sound state; enjoying health; hale; sound; characteristic of health; as, a *healthy* body; a *healthy* color.
2. conducive to health; wholesome; salubrious; as, a *healthy* exercise; a *healthy* climate.
3. showing or resulting from good health; as, a *healthy* appetite.
4. large, vigorous, etc.; as, a *healthy* yell. [Colloq.]
Syn.—salubrious, salutary, sound, wholesome, well, hale, robust, vigorous.

hēam, *n.* [compare AS. cild*hamma*, womb; O.D. *hamme*, the afterbirth.] the afterbirth of an animal. [Obs.]

hēap, *n.* [ME. *heep, heap*; AS. *heáp*, a crowd, or multitude of people, a pile.]
1. a pile or mass; a collection of things lying together in a pile; as, a *heap* of earth or stones.
Huge *heaps* of slain around the body rise. —Dryden.
2. a crowd; a throng: said of persons. [Colloq.]
3. a large quantity; a great many. [Colloq.]
I have noticed a *heap* of things in my life. —R. L. Stevenson.

hēap, *v.t.*; heaped (hēpt), *pt.*, *pp.*; heaping, *ppr.* [ME. *hepen*; AS. *heápian*, to heap, pile together, from *heáp*, a crowd, multitude.]
1. to throw or lay in a heap; to pile; to accumulate; to amass; as, to *heap* stones.
2. to fill full or to overflowing; as, to *heap* a barrel with potatoes.
3. to give in large amounts; as, he *heaped* gifts upon me.

hēap, *v.i.* to accumulate or rise in a heap, or pile.

hēap'ẽr, *n.* one who heaps, piles, or amasses.

hēap'y, *a.* lying in heaps.

hēar, *v.t.*; heard (hẽrd), *pt.*, *pp.*; hearing, *ppr.* [ME. *heren, heeren*; AS. *hiēran*, to hear.]
1. to perceive (sounds) by the ear; to receive an impression of through the auditory nerves of the ear; as, to *hear* a voice; to *hear* words.
O friends! I *hear* the tread of nimble feet. —Milton.
2. to listen to and consider; specifically, (a) to take notice of; pay attention to; as, *hear* this piece of news; (b) to listen to officially; give a formal hearing to; as, he will *hear* your lessons now; (c) to conduct an examination or hearing of (a law case, etc.); try; (d) to consent to; grant; as, he *heard* my entreaty; (e) to be a member of the audience at or of (an opera, radio broadcast, lecture, etc.); (f) to permit to speak; as, I cannot *hear* you now.
3. to be informed of; to be told; to learn.
to hear of; to regard with favor the idea of: always used negatively; as, he would not *hear of* such a thing.
to hear say; to hear a person say; to learn by rumor. [Colloq.]
to hear tell; to hear; to learn. [Dial.]

hēar, *v.i.* 1. to be able to perceive sound; as, he is deaf, he cannot *hear.*
2. to listen; to attend; as, he *hears* with solicitude.
3. to be told; to receive by report; as, so I *hear.*
hear! hear! an exclamatory form of applause used to show approval or agreement with what a speaker is saying.

hẽard, *v.* past tense and past participle of *hear.*

hēar'ẽr, *n.* one who hears; one who attends or listens to what is orally delivered by another; an auditor; one of an audience.

hēar'ing, *n.* 1. the act or process of perceiving sound; also, the faculty or sense by which sound is perceived; one of the five external senses.
Yet in these ears, till *hearing* dies,
One set slow bell will seem to toll. —Tennyson.
2. audience; attention to what is delivered; opportunity to be heard; as, I could not obtain a *hearing.*
3. a judicial investigation or trial, as before a court.
His last offenses to us
Shall have judicious *hearing.* —Shak.
4. extent within which sound, especially that of the human voice, may be heard; as, he was not within *hearing.*

heärk'en, *v.i.* [ME. *herknien, hercnen*; AS. *heorcnean, hercnian, hyrcnian.*] to give careful attention; to listen carefully: also spelled *harken.*

heärk'en, *v.t.* to hear; to pay attention to; to heed: also spelled *harken.* [Archaic.]

heärk'en·ẽr, *n.* one who hearkens; a listener.

hēar'săl, *n.* rehearsal. [Obs.]

hēar'sāy, *n.* report; rumor; common talk; as, the account we have depends on *hearsay.*

hēar'sāy, *a.* having the nature of or based on hearsay.
hearsay evidence; in law, any evidence not based upon the personal knowledge of the witness but known to him only through other persons. Such evidence is usually inadmissable as testimony.

hẽarse, *n.* [ME. *herse, herce*; OFr. *herce*, a harrow, a grated portcullis; L. *hirpex* (-*icis*), a harrow.]
1. (a) a framelike structure above a coffin or tomb, on which to place candles, hangings, etc.; (b) a framework for holding candles at Tenebrae. [Rare.]
2. a bier. [Archaic.]
3. an automobile, or horse-drawn carriage, for conveying the dead to the grave.

hẽarse, *v.t.* to enclose in a hearse. [Obs.]

hẽarse'clo̤th, *n.* a pall; a cloth to cover a coffin or bier.

hẽarse'līke, *a.* suitable to a funeral.

heärt, *n.* [ME. *hart, herte*; AS. *heorte*, heart.]
1. a muscular organ which is the propelling agent of blood in the body, situated in the thorax of vertebrate animals. From this organ the primary arteries arise, and in it the main veins terminate. By its alternate dilatation and contraction the circulation is carried on, the blood being received from the veins, and returned through the arteries. In man, other mammals, and birds, the heart consists of four chambers. Reptiles and amphibians usually have a three-chambered heart, while fishes have two chambers only. The heart of an insect or a spider is a long tube divided into compartments; that of mollusks is two- or three-chambered.

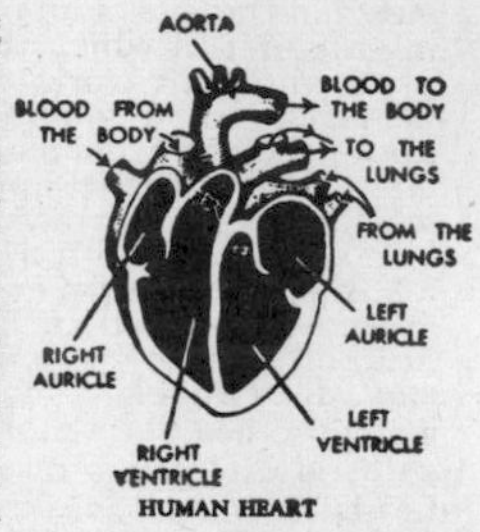

HUMAN HEART

2. the part of the body thought of as containing the heart; breast; bosom.
3. the human heart regarded as the seat of emotions, personality, attributes, etc.; hence, (a) the seat of the emotions: said of the moral side of human nature in contradistinction to the intellectual; as, he was all head and no *heart*; (b) the seat of the will or inclination; disposition; mental tendency; (c) inmost thoughts and feelings; consciousness or conscience; as, I know in my *heart*; (d) any of various humane feelings; love, devotion, sympathy, etc.; (e) mood; feeling; as, I have a heavy *heart*; (f) energy, spirit, resolution, or courage; as, I lost *heart*; to keep up one's *heart.*
4. the inner part of anything; the part nearest the middle or center; as, the *heart* of a country; the *heart* of a tree.
5. the chief part; the vital or most essential part; the real meaning; the core.
6. a person, usually one loved or admirable in some specified way; as, he is a valiant *heart.*
7. strength; power of producing; vigor; fertility; as, to keep the land in *heart.*
8. that which has the shape or form of a heart; especially, a roundish or oval figure or object having an obtuse point at one end and a corresponding indentation or depression at the other: a conventional representation of a heart.
9. secret meaning; real intention.
And then show you the *heart* of my message. —Shak.
10. one of a suit of playing cards marked with the figure of a heart (sense 8) in red; also, [*pl.*] this suit of cards.
11. [*pl.*] in card playing, a game the object of which is to take in as few hearts, in play, as possible.

12. in nautical usage, a wooden block shaped like a heart, through which the lanyards of the stays are rove.

after one's own heart; in accordance with one's desires or ideas; as, a man *after my own heart*.

at heart; in real character or disposition; at bottom; substantially; really; as, he is good *at heart*.

by heart; (a) by memorizing; as, to learn *by heart*; (b) from memory.

heart and hand; with enthusiasm; entirely; as, we are with you *heart and hand*.

heart and soul; with intense earnestness; wholly.

heart of oak; a brave or intrepid person.

to break the heart of; to cause to be overcome with grief or disappointment.

to have at heart; to have an earnest desire for.

to have in the heart; to purpose; to have in design or intention.

to have one's heart in one's mouth; to be greatly frightened or excited.

to lose one's heart; to fall in love.

to set one's heart at rest; to set aside doubts, fears, or worries; to be tranquil or easy in mind.

to set one's heart on; to be very desirous of obtaining or keeping.

to take to heart; (a) to consider seriously; (b) to be troubled or grieved by.

to wear one's heart upon one's sleeve; to expose one's disposition, feelings, or intentions to everyone.

with all one's heart; completely; intensely; earnestly; thoroughly; fully.

Syn.—core, nucleus, kernel, interior, center, character, disposition, courage, hardihood, nature, life, feeling, benevolence.

heärt, *v.t.* to encourage. [Rare.]

heärt, *v.i.* to form a close, compact center, as a plant.

heärt·āche, *n.* sorrow; distress; grief.

heärt at·tack′, any sudden instance of heart failure; especially, a coronary thrombosis.

heärt′bēat, *n.* a pulsation of the heart; hence, a thought or an emotion.

heärt block, in medicine, an abnormal condition in which the auricular and ventricular heart beats occur independently of each other.

heärt bond, in masonry, a kind of bond in which two stones forming the width of a wall have one stone placed over their joint.

heärt′breāk, *n.* overwhelming sorrow or grief.

heärt′breāk″ẽr, *n.* 1. one who or that which breaks hearts.

2. a curl; a lovelock. [Humorous.]

heärt′breāk″ing, *a.* causing great grief or sorrow.

heärt′brō″ken, *a.* deeply disappointed or grieved.

heärt′bûrn, *n.* 1. a burning sensation in the esophagus and stomach, caused by high acidity of the stomach.

2. jealousy; discontent; envy.

heärt′bûrn″ing, *a.* causing discontent.

heärt′bûrn″ing, *n.* 1. heartburn.

2. discontent; jealousy.

heärt çam, in machinery, a wheel or double cam having the form of a heart: it is used for converting a uniform circular motion into a reciprocating alternating motion: called also *heart wheel*.

HEART CAM

heärt cher′ry, a heart-shaped variety of sweet cherry.

heärt çlot, a clot of blood in the heart.

heärt çoç′kle, same as *heart shell*.

heärt′deep, *a.* rooted in the heart.

heärt dis·ēașe′, any diseased condition of the heart, either functional or organic.

heärt′ed, *a.* 1. having a (specified kind of) heart: used in compounds; as, hard-*hearted*, faint-*hearted*, stout-*hearted*, etc.

2. taken to heart; laid up or seated in the heart. [Obs.]

3. having the shape of a heart; cordate. [Rare.]

heärt′en, *v.t.* 1. to encourage; to incite or stimulate the courage of; to strengthen.

Hearten those that fight. —Shak.

2. to restore fertility or strength to; as, to *hearten* land. [Obs.]

heärt′en·ẽr, *n.* one who or that which heartens.

heärt fāil′ūre, the inability of the heart to pump enough blood to maintain an adequate flow to and from the body tissues.

heärt′felt, *a.* deeply felt; sincere; as, *heartfelt* joy or grief.

heärt′-free, *a.* not in love.

heärth, *n.* [ME. *harth, herth*; AS. *heorth*, hearth, fireplace.]

1. the brick, stone, or tiled floor of a fireplace, often extending out into the room.

Fires unrak'd and *hearths* unswept.—Shak.

2. (a) the fireside as the center of family life; (b) the home; family circle.

3. that part of a furnace, stove, or oven on which the fire rests.

4. the fireplace of a blacksmith's forge.

5. in metallurgy, (a) the floor of a reverberatory furnace on which the ore is heated; (b) the lowest part in a blast furnace, through which the melted metal passes into the crucible; (c) a bloomery.

6. the cooking apparatus on board a ship. [Rare.]

7. in soldering, a pan containing charcoal, in which the tools are heated.

heärth cin′dẽr, slag formed in a furnace in which iron is refined.

heärth çrick′et, the common house cricket.

heärt′-heav″i·ness (-hev″), *n.* depression of spirits.

heärt′-heav″y, *a.* sad-hearted; depressed in spirits.

heärth endș, masses of refuse from a furnace in which lead is smelted.

heärth mŏn′ey, hearth tax.

heärth plāte, a plate of cast iron forming the hearth of a refiner's furnace.

heärth′rug, *n.* a rug placed in front of a hearth or fireplace.

heärth′sīde, *n.* 1. the part of a room around a hearth.

2. the home; family circle.

heärth′stōne, *n.* 1. the stone forming a hearth; hence, a fireside; home; the family circle.

2. a soft stone used to clean and whiten floors, doorsteps, etc.

heärth tax, formerly, a tax imposed in England on every hearth in houses paying the church and poor rates: called also *hearth money*.

heärt′i·ly, *adv.* 1. from the heart; with all the heart; with sincerity.

I *heartily* forgive them. —Shak.

2. with zeal; vigorously; as, he *heartily* assisted the prince.

3. with a good appetite and in large amounts; as, he ate *heartily*.

4. completely; fully; very.

Syn.—vigorously, cordially, earnestly, ardently, sincerely, gladly, eagerly.

heärt′i·ness, *n.* the quality or state of being hearty.

heärt′land, *n.* in geopolitics, a political unit dominating an extensive surrounding area that can sustain it agriculturally and industrially and serve as a protective buffer in case of military attack.

heärt′lēaf, *n.* same as *heart trefoil*.

heärt′less, *a.* 1. without a heart.

2. without feeling or affection; cruel; pitiless; as, he treated her in the most *heartless* manner.

3. without courage; spiritless; fainthearted.

Heartless they fought, and quitted soon their ground. —Dryden.

heärt′less·ly, *adv.* in a heartless manner.

heärt′less·ness, *n.* the quality or state of being heartless.

heärt′let, *n.* a little heart.

heärt′ling, *n.* a little heart. [Obs.]

heärt net, the net or pound of a heart seine.

heärt′pēa, *n.* same as *heartseed*.

heärt point, in heraldry, the center point on a shield: also called *fess point*.

heärt′quāke (-kwāk), *n.* trembling of the heart; terror; fear.

heärt′rend″ing, *a.* breaking the heart; overpowering with grief or mental anguish; very distressing.

heärt′-rob″bing, *a.* 1. ecstatic.

2. stealing the heart or affections; winning.

heärts′ēașe, heärt′ș′-ēașe, *n.* 1. ease of heart; tranquillity of mind.

2. any of various plants of the genus *Viola*, particularly *Viola tricolor*, the wild pansy: so called because formerly believed to cure the discomforts of love.

3. any of various other plants, as the wallflower, persicary, or lady's-thumb.

heärt′seed, *n.* any of various plants of the genus *Cardiospermum*, with black seeds, having heart-shaped white scars indicating their point of attachment.

heärt sęine, a weir or fish trap having a heart-shaped pound, which is capable of taking fish under any condition of the tide.

heärt′-shāped (-shāpt), *a.* shaped like a heart; having the form of a heart; cordate.

heärt shell, a mollusk, *Isocardia cor*, having a shell shaped like a heart.

heärt′sick, *a.* sick at heart; deeply depressed; extremely unhappy; despondent.

heärt′sick″en·ing, *a.* tending to become heartsick.

heärt′sick″ness, *n.* sadness; extreme unhappiness.

heärt′sŏme, *a.* 1. heartening; cheering; exhilarating. [Scot.]

2. merry; cheerful; lively. [Scot.]

heärt′sōre, *a.* feeling or showing grief.

heärt′-stir″ring, *a.* exhilarating; inspiring.

heärt′-strick″en, *a.* appalled; dismayed; deeply affected by grief, sorrow, etc.

heärt′string, *n.* a tendon formerly supposed to brace and sustain the heart; hence, [*usually pl.*], strongest affections; most ardent feelings; as, to touch one's *heartstrings*.

heärt′struck, *a.* same as *heart-stricken*.

heärt′throb, *n.* 1. the heartbeat.

2. (a) tender or mawkish emotion: *usually used in the pl.*; (b) a sweetheart. [Slang.]

heärt′-tö-heärt′, *a.* intimate and candid; frank.

heärt trē′foil, *Medicago maculata*, the spotted medic, a leguminous plant having a heart-shaped spot on each leaflet.

heärt wheel (hwēl), same as *heart cam*.

heärt′-whōle (-hōl), *a.* 1. not in love.

2. having courage; undismayed.

3. sincere; genuine; wholehearted.

heärt′wood, *n.* the hard, central part of the trunk of a tree; the duramen.

heärt′wŏrm, *n.* a nematode worm living as a parasite in the blood stream, especially in the heart, of dogs and certain other animals.

heärt′y, *a.*; *comp.* heartier; *superl.* heartiest, 1. proceeding from the heart; sincere; heartfelt; cordial; as, a *hearty* invitation; a *hearty* reception.

2. sound; strong; exhibiting health; healthy; as, a *hearty* man.

3. satisfying and abundant; affording nourishment; as, a *hearty* breakfast.

4. strongly felt; vigorous; not restrained; as, a *hearty* dislike.

5. needing or liking plenty of food; having a good appetite; as, a *hearty* eater.

6. fertile: said of land.

heärt′y, *n.*; *pl.* **heärt′ies,** 1. good fellow; comrade: a form of address used by sailors (usually preceded by *my*); as, pull away, my *hearties*.

2. [*usually in pl.*] a sailor.

heärt yärn, soft yarn in the center of a rope.

hēat, *n.* [ME. *heete, hete*; AS. *hætu*, heat, from *hat*, hot.]

1. the quality of being hot; hotness: in physics, heat is considered a form of energy whose effect is produced by the accelerated vibration of molecules: theoretically, at −273°C, all molecular vibration would stop and there would be no heat.

2. much hotness; great warmth; as, the *heat* of this room is unbearable.

3. degree of hotness or warmth; as, how much *heat* shall I apply?

4. the sensation produced by heat; the sensation experienced when the body is subjected to heat from any source.

5. hot weather or climate; as, the *heat* of the tropics; the *heat* of the day.

6. indication of high temperature, as the condition or color of the body or part of the body; redness; high color; flush.

It has raised animosities in their hearts, and *heats* in their faces. —Addison.

7. the warming of a room, house, etc., as by a stove or furnace; as, his rent includes *heat*, light, and gas.

8. a burning sensation produced by spices, mustard, etc.

9. fever.

10. strong feeling or intensity of feeling; excitement, ardor, anger, zeal, etc.

11. the period or condition of excitement, intensity, stress, etc.; most violent or intense point or stage; as, in the *heat* of battle.

12. a single effort, round, bout, or trial; especially, any of the preliminary rounds of a race, etc., the winners of which compete in the final round.

13. (a) sexual excitement; (b) the period of sexual excitement in animals; rut or estrus.

14. in metallurgy, (a) single heating of

metal, ore, etc. in a furnace or forge; (b) the amount processed in a single heating.

15. (a) intense activity; (b) coercion, as by torture; (c) great pressure, as in criminal investigation. [Slang.]

atomic heat; in chemistry, the result obtained by multiplying the specific heat of an element by its atomic weight.

black heat; the degree to which a metal is heated when its color remains unchanged.

dynamical theory of heat; the theory of heat which assumes it to be a form of molecular energy, and not a kind of matter.

red heat; the temperature to which a metal or other substance is heated when it radiates a red light; also, the state of being at this temperature.

white heat; the degree to which a metal is heated (beyond red heat) when it radiates a white light; also, a state of intense emotion, excitement, etc.

Syn.—warmth, ardor, passion, excitement.

hēat, *v.t.*; heated, *pt.*, *pp.*; heating, *ppr.* [ME. *heten*; AS. *hætan*, to make hot, from *hat*, hot.]

1. to make hot; to communicate heat to, or cause to become warm; as, to *heat* an oven or a furnace; to *heat* iron.

2. to make feverish; to excite; as, to *heat* the blood.

3. to warm with passion or desire; to rouse into action; to animate.

A noble emulation *heats* your breast. —Dryden.

hēat, *v.i.* 1. to grow warm or hot; as, the water *heats* slowly.

2. to become inflamed or excited.

hēat ap′ō·plex·y, sunstroke.

hēat′ed·ly, *adv.* with anger, vehemence, etc.

hēat en′gine, an engine in which heat is transformed into mechanical energy.

hēat′ẽr, *n.* 1. an apparatus for giving heat or warmth; stove, furnace, radiator, etc.: heaters in automobiles use hot water or gasoline.

2. a person whose work is to heat something.

3. in an electron tube, an element set inside the cathode and heated by an electric current so that it indirectly heats the cathode to the temperature at which it will give off electrons.

4. a pistol. [Slang.]

hēat ex·haus′tion (egz-ạs′chun), a form of heatstroke characterized by low body temperature, collapse, and, in severe cases, coma and death: also called *heat prostration*.

hēath, *n.* [ME. *hethe*, *heeth*; AS. *hæth*, the heath plant, a heath.]

1. a tract of open wasteland, especially in the British Isles, covered with heather, low shrubs, etc.; moor.

2. any of various shrubs and plants growing on heaths; especially, any plant of the genus *Erica*, the species of which are widely distributed throughout Europe and South Africa. *Erica*, or *Calluna*, *vulgaris* is used in Great Britain for brooms, thatch, and for heating ovens.

hēath bell, the flower of either of two species of heath, *Erica tetralix* and *Erica cinerea*.

hēath′ber″ry, *n.*; *pl.* **hēath′ber″ries,** any of various berries found on heaths; bilberry, crowberry, etc.

hēath′bīrd, *n.* the black grouse.

hēath′clad, *a.* clothed with heath.

hēath çock, same as *blackcock*.

hēath çorn, the buckwheat, *Polygonum fagopyrum*.

hēath′çup, *n.* *Artanema fimbriatum*, a plant found in the East Indies and Australia. It is cultivated for its large, blue flowers.

hēath cȳ′press, *Lycopodium alpinum*, a species of club moss found in Europe: so called from its resemblance to a miniature cypress tree.

hēa′then, *n.*; *pl.* **hēa′thenṣ, hēa′then,** [ME. *hethen*; AS. *hæthen*, a heathen; a 4th-c. mistranslation of Arm. *hethanos*, heathen, by association with Goth. *haithi*, heath, and misunderstood to mean "wasteland dweller."]

1. one who worships idols or many gods.

2. one who is not a Christian, Jew, or Moslem; also, such people collectively.

3. a person regarded as rude, illiterate, barbarous, or irreligious.

4. originally, and in the Old Testament, a member of any nation or people not worshiping the God of Israel.

hēa′then, *a.* 1. of heathen tribes or culture.

2. pagan.

3. irreligious.

hēa′then·dŏm, *n.* [ME. *hæthendom*; AS. *hæthendom*; *hæthen*, heathen, and *-dom*, -dom.]

1. heathen countries or people.

2. heathen customs and beliefs; heathenism.

hēa′then·esse, *n.* heathenism. [Archaic.]

hēa′then·ish, *a.* 1. of or pertaining to the heathen; as, *heathenish* customs.

2. like or characteristic of the heathen; irreligious; uncivilized.

hēa′then·ish·ly, *adv.* in a heathenish manner.

hēa′then·ish·ness, *n.* the quality or state of being heathenish.

hēa′then·iṣm, *n.* 1. the rites, beliefs, or system of religion of heathens; paganism.

2. manners, morals, and customs regarded as characteristic of heathens; idolatry, barbarity, etc.

hēa′then·īze, *v.t.* and *v.i.*; heathenized, *pt.*, *pp.*; heathenizing, *ppr.* to make or become a heathen or heathenish.

hēa′then·ness, *n.* the state of being heathen.

hēa′then·ry, *n.* heathendom; heathenism.

heath′ẽr (heth′), *n.* [ME. *haddyr*, altered by association with *heath*.]

1. a low-growing plant of the heath family, especially common in the British Isles, with scalelike, overlapping leaves and stalks of small, bell-shaped, purplish-pink flowers.

2. a heath covered with heather.

HEATHER

heath′ẽr, *a.* like heather in color or appearance.

heath′ẽr bell, the bell-shaped flower of the heather.

heath′ẽr grȧss, *Triodia decumbens*, a species of grass growing on heaths.

heath′ẽr·y, *a.* 1. covered with heather.

2. of or like heather.

heath′ẽr·y, *n.* a place where heath grows.

hēath grȧss, same as *heather grass*.

hēath grouse, a European species of grouse, *Tetrao tetrix*: called also *black grouse*.

hēath hen, 1. a female black grouse.

2. a North American grouse related to the prairie chicken.

hēath pēa, *Lathyrus tuberosus*, a leguminous European plant the tubers of which are eaten as a vegetable.

hēath pēat, peat taken from land abounding in heather.

hēath pōult, young of the black grouse.

hēath′wŏrt, *n.* any plant of the heath family.

hēath′y, *a.* 1. of or like heath.

2. covered with heath.

hēat′ing, *a.* tending to impart heat; promoting warmth or heat; as, *heating* medicines or applications.

hēat′ing çoil, a coil of wire which becomes hot when an electrical current is passed through it: the coil is suspended in or wrapped around the substance to be heated.

hēat′ing·ly, *adv.* in a heating manner.

hēat′ing pad, a cloth-covered series of electrical conductors which become warm when an electric current is passed through them: used to warm parts of the body.

hēat′less, *a.* without heat; cold.

hēat līght′ning, lightning without thunder, seen near the horizon, especially on summer evenings: it is believed to be caused by the reflection of distant lightning from clouds.

hēat of fū′ṣion, the amount of heat needed to melt a unit mass of a solid that has just reached the melting temperature.

hēat of vā″pŏr·i·zā′tion, the amount of heat needed to turn one gram of a liquid into a vapor, without a rise in temperature of the liquid.

hēat pump, a device for cooling an enclosed space by pumping hot air out, and for warming it by extracting heat from outdoor air or from a hot-water source and pumping it in.

hēat spot, 1. a freckle.

2. a point on the skin at which the sensation of heat can be produced.

hēat′strōke, *n.* any of several conditions resulting from exposure to excessive heat: see *heat exhaustion*, *sunstroke*.

hēat ū′nit, the unit quantity of heat; the amount of heat required to raise the temperature of a unit mass of water one degree.

hēat wāve, 1. unusually hot weather, resulting from a slowly moving air mass of relatively high temperature.

2. a period of such weather in a particular place.

heaume (hōm), *n.* [Fr.; OFr. *helme*.] a heavy helmet worn in the Middle Ages, covering the entire head and often reaching to the shoulders.

hēave, *v.t.*; heaved *or* hove, *pt.*, *pp.*; heaving, *ppr.* [ME. *heven*; AS. *hebban*, to heave.]

1. to lift; to raise, especially with effort.

2. to lift in this way and throw or cast; as, to *heave* the log.

3. to cause to swell, as the breast.

4. to make (a sigh, groan, etc.) with great effort or pain.

5. in geology, to displace (a stratum or vein) as by the intersection of another stratum or vein.

6. in nautical usage, (a) to raise, haul, pull, move, etc. by pulling with a rope or cable; (b) to cause (a ship) to move in a specified manner or direction.

to heave a cable short; to haul in so much of the cable that the ship is nearly over the anchor.

to heave a ship down; to turn a ship over by means of tackles from the masthead to the shore, for the purpose of cleaning or repairing the bottom.

to heave a ship to; to bring a ship's head to the wind and stop her motion.

to heave taut; to turn a capstan, etc., till the cable becomes taut.

to heave the lead; in nautical usage, to sound with a lead.

to heave the log; in nautical usage, to throw the log into the water to determine the rate of speed.

hēave, *v.i.* 1. to be thrown or raised up; to rise; to bulge out.

2. to rise and fall with rhythmic motions, as the waves of the sea, the lungs in breathing, etc.

3. to pant, as after severe labor or exertion; to breathe hard.

4. to make an effort to vomit; to retch.

5. in nautical usage, (a) to tug or haul (*on* or *at* a cable, rope, etc.); (b) to proceed; move; as, the ship *heaves* into sight.

heave ho! a cry uttered by sailors when hoisting the anchor, etc.

to heave in sight; to appear; to come within sight, as a ship at sea.

hēave, *n.* 1. an upward motion; swell or distention, as of the waves of the sea, of the lungs in breathing, etc.

2. an effort to lift something; a raising.

3. in geology, the horizontal displacement caused by a fault.

heav′en (hev′), *n.* [ME. *heven*; AS. *heofen*, *heofan*, *hefon*, heaven.]

1. [*usually pl.*] the region or expanse which surrounds the earth, in which appear the sun, moon, and stars; the firmament; the sky.

2. [H-] the Supreme Power; God.

3. great happiness; a state of bliss; a sublime or exalted condition; as, a *heaven* on earth.

4. a state of great happiness.

5. in theology, the place where God and his angels are, variously conceived of as the place where the blessed will live after death: often used in exclamations of surprise, protest, etc.; as, *Heavens!*, for *heaven's* sake!, good *heavens!*

6. [*pl.*] the celestial powers collectively; as, the *heavens* are propitious.

heav′en, *v.t.* to make happy, as if placed in heaven; to beatify in the highest degree. [Rare.]

heav′en·li·ness, *n.* the quality or condition of being heavenly.

heav′en·ly, *a.* 1. pertaining to the visible heavens; celestial; as, *heavenly* regions; *heavenly* bliss.

2. resembling heaven; supremely excellent; as, a *heavenly* lyre; a *heavenly* temper.

3. inhabiting heaven; as, a *heavenly* race; the *heavenly* throng.

heav′en·ly, *adv.* 1. in a manner resembling that of heaven.

2. by the influence or agency of heaven; as, a *heavenly*-guided soul.

heav′en·ly-mīnd″ed, *a.* having the affections placed on heaven and on spiritual things; devout.

heav′en·wȧrd, *adv.* and *a.* toward heaven.

heav′en·wȧrdṣ, *adv.* same as *heavenward*.

hēave of′fẽr·ing, in the Levitical law, an offering or oblation to God that was heaved, or lifted up, by the priest.

hēav′ẽr, *n.* 1. one who or that which heaves, or lifts.
2. in nautical usage, a staff or bar used as a lever.

hēaveș, *n.pl.* a respiratory disease of horses, characterized by difficult and laborious respiration, coughing, heaving of the flanks, etc.: also called *broken wind.*

heav′i·ẽr-thăn-āir (hev′), *a.* of or pertaining to air-craft whose weight is greater than that of the air it displaces.

heav′i·ly (hev′), *adv.* 1. in a heavy manner; with great weight; as, *heavily* loaded.
2. grievously; afflictively; oppressively; severely; as, to be *heavily* afflicted.
3. slowly and laboriously; with difficulty; as, to move *heavily*.
That they drave them *heavily*.—Ex. xiv. 25.
4. abundantly; as, *heavily* populated.

heav′i·ness, *n.* [ME. *hevinesse*; AS. *hefignes*, from *hefig*, heavy.] the quality or state of being heavy; dejection; sluggishness; oppression; weight; as, the *heaviness* of an object, the *heaviness* of sorrow.

hēav′ing, *n.* a rising or swell; a panting.

hēav′ing līne, in navigation, a small line having a lead weight at one end: used to catch the hawser on landing.

hēav′ing-līne bend, a clove hitch: see *knot*, illus.

Heav′i·sīde lāy′ẽr (hev′), the Kennelly-Heaviside layer

hēav′y, *a.* afflicted with heaves; as, a *heavy* horse.

heav′y (hev′), *a.*; *comp.* heavier; *superl.* heaviest, [ME. *hevy*; AS. *hefig*, heavy, from *hebban*, to heave, lift.]
1. hard to lift or move because of its weight; weighty.
2. of high specific gravity; of concentrated weight for its size.
3. above the usual or defined weight: said of woolens, silks, certain animals, etc.
4. larger, greater, or more intense than usual or normal; specifically, (a) falling or striking with great force or impact; as, a *heavy* blow; (b) of more than usual quantity; as, a *heavy* vote; (c) violent and intense; rough; as, a *heavy* sea; (d) loud, deep, and resounding; as, *heavy* thunder; (e) thick; coarse; massive; as, *heavy* features; (f) to an unusual extent; operating on a large scale; as, a *heavy* drinker, a *heavy* investor; (g) prolonged and intense; as, *heavy* applause.
5. of great importance; serious; grave; profound; as, a *heavy* responsibility.
6. hard to endure; oppressive; burdensome; distressing; as, *heavy* sorrow.
7. hard to do; difficult; as, *heavy* work.
8. causing grief or sorrow; as, *heavy* news.
9. burdened with grief; sorrowful; depressed; as, a *heavy* heart.
10. burdened with sleep or fatigue; as, *heavy* eyelids.
11. characterized by density, hardness, fullness, etc. suggestive of weight; specifically, (a) hard to digest; as, a *heavy* meal; (b) not leavened properly; doughy; as, a *heavy* cake; (c) remaining in the atmosphere; clinging; penetrating; as, a *heavy* odor; (d) overcast; cloudy; gloomy; lowering; as, a *heavy* sky; (e) hard to work or travel because of mud, sand, clay, etc.; as, a *heavy* road, *heavy* soil.
12. tedious; dull.
13. clumsy; unwieldy; physically awkward; as, a *heavy* walk.
14. steeply inclined; as, a *heavy* grade.
15. in military usage, heavily armed.
16. in the theater, (a) somber; tragic; (b) designating a villain or his role.
heavy metal; see under *metal*.
heavy with child; pregnant.

heav′y, *adv.* heavily: often in hyphenated compounds, as *heavy*-laden.
to hang heavy; to pass tediously; drag.

heav′y, *n.*; *pl.* **heav′ieș,** 1. something heavy.
2. in the theater, (a) a tragic or villainous role; (b) an actor who plays such roles.

heav′y-ärmed, *a.* bearing heavy weapons or armor.

heav′y-dū′ty, *a.* 1. that can resist or withstand great strain, weather, wear, etc.; unusually tough or rugged.
2. having a high tariff rate.

heav′y ẽarth, barium monoxide; baryta.

heav′y-foot′ed, *a.* heavy or clumsy in or as in walking; plodding.

heav′y-hand″ed, *a.* 1. lacking dexterity; without a light touch; tactless.
2. ruling with oppression; cruel; tyrannical.

heav′y-head″ed (-hed″), *a.* thick-headed; dull of apprehension.

heav′y-heärt″ed, *a.* sorrowful; in low spirits.

heav′y hȳ′drō·ġen, the isotope of hydrogen having an atomic weight of slightly more than 2; deuterium: with oxygen it forms heavy water.

heav′y-lăd′en, *a.* 1. laden, or loaded, heavily.
2. heavily burdened with care and trouble; oppressed.

heav′y nī′trō·ġen, the isotope of nitrogen having an atomic weight of 15.

heav′y ox′y·ġen, either of two isotopes of oxygen of atomic weights 17 and 18.

heav′y spär, sulfate of barium; barite; barytes.

heav′y wa̤′tẽr, a compound like water, composed of oxygen and the isotope of hydrogen of atomic weight 2; deuterium oxide, D_2O.

heav′y·wei̥ght (-wāt), *n.* 1. a person or animal weighing much more than average.
2. a boxer or wrestler who weighs 176 pounds or more.
3. a very intelligent, influential, or important person. [Slang.]

heav′y·wei̥ght, *a.* of heavyweights.

heb′dō·mad, *n.* [L. *hebdomas* (*-adis*); Gr. *hebdomas*, the number seven, a week, from *hebdomos*, seventh, from *hepta*, seven.]
1. seven days; a week.
2. in Gnostic philosophy, the sphere of seven; the seven planets and their indwelling spirits; the dominion of the demiurge.

heb·dom′ȧ·dăl, *a.* weekly; consisting of seven days, or occurring every seven days.

heb·dom′ȧ·dăl·ly, *adv.* in weekly periods; by the week; from week to week.

heb·dom′ȧ·dā·ry, *a.* same as *hebdomadal*.

heb·dom′ȧ·dā·ry, *n.* in the Roman Catholic Church, a member of a chapter or convent, whose week it is to officiate at the sacred offices.

heb·dō·mat′iç·ăl, *a.* weekly. [Obs.]

Hē′bē, *n.* [L., from Gr. *Hēbē*, from *hēbē*, youth.]
1. in Greek mythology, the goddess of youth, daughter of Zeus and Hera, cup-bearer of the gods until succeeded by Ganymede, and wife of the deified Hercules, having power to restore the aged to youth and beauty.
2. one of the asteroids, the sixth in the order of discovery.

HEBE

heb′en, *n.* ebony. [Obs.]

heb′e·nŏn, *n.* [perh. var. of *henbane*.] a substance having a poisonous juice.

hē·bē·phrē′ni·ȧ, *n.* [LL., from Gr. *hēbē*, puberty, youth, and *phrēn*, mind.] in psychiatry, a form of dementia praecox appearing at puberty: it is characterized by foolish behavior and rapid deterioration of mentality.

heb′ē·tāte, *v.t.* and *v.i.*; hebetated, *pt.*, *pp.*; hebetating, *ppr.* [L. *hebetatus*, pp. of *hebetare*, to make blunt or dull, from *hebes* (*-etis*), blunt, dull.] to make or become dull or blunt.

heb′ē·tāte, *a.* 1. dull; obtuse; stupid.
2. in botany, having a blunt point, as certain leaves.

heb·ē·tā′tion, *n.* [L. *hebetatio* (*-onis*), from *hebetare*, to make blunt or dull.]
1. the act of making blunt, dull, or stupid.
2. the state of being dulled.

heb′ēte, *a.* dull; stupid. [Rare.]

hē·bet′iç, *a.* [Gr. *hēbētikos*, youthful, from *hēbē*, youth.] in physiology, of or happening at puberty.

heb′ē·tūde, *n.* [L. *hebetudo*, from *hebes* (*-etis*), blunt, dull.] the quality or condition of being dull or lethargic.

heb·ē·tū′di·nous, *a.* [L. *hebetudo* (*-inis*), dullness.] affected with hebetude; lethargic.

Hē·brā′iç, *a.* [LL. *Hebraicus*; Gr. *Hebraïkos*, Hebrew, from *Hebraios*, a Hebrew.] pertaining to or characteristic of the Hebrews, their culture, or language; Hebrew.

Hē·brā′iç·ăl·ly, *adv.* in the manner of the Hebrew language or of the Hebrews.

Hē′brā·ișm, *n.* 1. a Hebrew phrase, idiom, or custom.
2. Hebrew character, thought, or ethical system.
3. Hebrew institutions or practices; Hebrew religion; Judaism.

Hē′brā·ist, *n.* 1. a specialist or expert in the Hebrew language and learning.
2. a follower of Judaism, or the Hebraic ethical system.

Hē·brā·is′tiç, *a.* pertaining to or characteristic of Hebraists or Hebraism.

Hē′brā·īze, *v.t.*; Hebraized, *pt.*, *pp.*; Hebraizing, *ppr.* [Gr. *Hebraïzein*, to speak Hebrew, from *Hebraios*, a Hebrew.] to make Hebrew in character, form, etc.

Hē′brā·īze, *v.i.* to adopt the Hebrew language, customs, ideals, etc.; become Hebrew in character, form, etc.

Hē′brew, *n.* [ME. *Hebrew*; OFr. *hebreu*; LL. *Hebræus*; Gr. *Hebraios*; Aramaic *'ebrāyā*; Heb. *'ibrī*, a Hebrew.]
1. any member of a group of Semitic peoples tracing descent from Abraham, Jacob, and Isaac; Israelite: in modern usage interchangeable with *Jew*.
2. (a) the ancient Semitic language of the Israelites, in which most of the Old Testament was written; (b) the modern form of this language, the official language of Israel.

Hē′brew, *a.* 1. pertaining to Hebrew or the Hebrews.
2. Jewish.

Hē′brew çal′en·dȧr, the Jewish calendar.

Hē′brew·ess, *n.* a Jewess.

Hē′brewș, *n.pl.* [*construed as sing.*] in the Bible, the Epistle to the Hebrews, a book of the New Testament.

Hē·bri′ciăn (-brish′ăn), *n.* one skilled in the Hebrew language; a Hebraist. [Rare.]

Hē·brid′ē·ăn, Hē·brid′i·ăn, *a.* pertaining to the Hebrides Islands, west of Scotland.

Hē·brid′ē·ăn, Hē·brid′i·ăn, *n.* an inhabitant or native of the Hebrides.

Heç′ȧ·tē, *n.* [L. *Hecate*; Gr. *Hekatē*, Hecate.] in Greek mythology, a goddess of the moon, earth, and underground realm of the dead, later regarded as the goddess of sorcery and witchcraft: also spelled *Hekate*.

heç′ȧ·tōmb (-tōm), *n.* [L. *hecatombe*; Gr. *hekatombē*, from *hekaton*, a hundred, and *bous*, ox.]
1. in ancient Greece, a sacrifice of a hundred oxen at one time as an offering to the gods.
2. the sacrifice of any great number at one time; any great slaughter of persons or animals.

heç·ȧ·tom′pe·don, *n.* [Gr. *hekatompedos*, a hundred feet long; *hekaton*, a hundred, and *pous*, *podos*, foot.]
1. an edifice or temple having a length or width of one hundred feet.
2. [H–] the ancient Parthenon at Athens.

heck, *n.* 1. an instrument for catching fish; as, a salmon *heck*.
2. a rack for holding fodder for cattle.
3. a hatch or latch of a door.
4. a door with the upper half latticed or arranged to swing: called also *heck door*.
5. in weaving, a device for separating the warp threads. [Rare.]
[Scot. and Brit. Dial. in senses 1, 2, 3, 4.]

heck, *interj.* [orig. dial. (Lancashire) Eng. (*h*)*eck*, cry of surprise or warning.] an exclamation used as a euphemism for *hell*. [Slang.]

heck′ber″ry, *n.*; *pl.* **heck′ber″rieș,** the small bird cherry of Europe, *Prunus padus*.

heck bōard, the backboard of a cart. [Scot. and Brit. Dial.]

heck box, in weaving, a box holding a set of warp bobbins; a jack. [Scot. and Brit. Dial.]

heck′i·măl, heck′i·mel, *n.* the blue titmouse of Europe, *Parus cæruleus*.

heç′kle, *n.* [ME. *hekele*; D. *hekel*, a heckle.]
1. same as *hatchel*.
2. a feather in a Highlander's bonnet. [Scot.]

heç′kle, *v.t.*; heckled, *pt.*, *pp.*; heckling, *ppr.*
1. to hatchel, as flax.
2. to annoy or confuse (a speaker) by interrupting with questions or taunts.

heç′klẽr, *n.* one who heckles a speaker, etc.

hect-, see *hecto-*.

heç′tāre, *n.* [Fr. *hectare*, from Gr. *hekaton*, a hundred, and L. *area*, area.] a metric measure of surface, equal to 10,000 square meters (100 ares or 2.471 acres).

heç′tiç, *a.* [Fr. *hectique*; Gr. *hektikos*, habitual, hectic, from *hexis*, a permanent condition or habit of the body, from *echein*, to have.]
1. in medicine, a remittent fever, with stages of chilliness, heat, and sweat, variously intermixed, usually present in pulmonary consumption.
2. of, affected with, or characteristic of a

wasting disease, as tuberculosis; consumptive.

3. designating or of the fever accompanying wasting diseases, especially tuberculosis.

4. feverish; fevered; hot; flushed.

5. characterized by confusion, haste, agitation, etc.

heç′tiç, *n.* 1. hectic fever.

2. the flush or pink spot on the cheeks of a person suffering from hectic fever.

3. a person with tuberculosis. [Rare.]

heç′tiç·ăl, *a.* same as *hectic.*

heç′tiç·ăl·ly, *adv.* in a hectic manner.

heç′tō-, [from Gr. *hekaton*, a hundred.] a combining form meaning *a hundred*, as in *hecto*liter, *hecto*graph: also *hekto-* or, before a vowel, *hect-*, *hekt-*.

heç·tō·çot′y·līzed, *a.* changed into a hectocotylus, as an arm of certain cuttlefishes.

heç·tō·çot′y·lus, *n.*; *pl.* **heç·tō·çot′y·lī,** [*hecto-*, and *Gr. kotylē*, a small cup.] one of the arms or tentacles of a male cephalopod which becomes modified as a sexual organ for impregnating the female.

heç′tō·gram, heç′tō·gramme, *n.* [Fr. *hectogramme*, from Gr. *hekaton*, a hundred, and *gramma*, that which is written, a small weight, from *graphein*, to write.] a metric measure of weight, equal to 100 grams (3.527 ounces avoirdupois).

heç′tō·grȧph, *n.* [*hecto-*, and Gr. *graphein*, to write.] an apparatus by means of which written or typed matter or simple line drawings may be reproduced: the material to be copied is written, typed, or drawn upon a carbon-backed sheet, which is then pressed against a glycerin-coated sheet of gelatin: many copies may be made by this method from a single original.

heç′tō·grȧph, *v.t.* to duplicate by means of a hectograph.

heç·tō·graph′iç, *a.* pertaining to a hectograph.

heç′tō·lī·tēr, heç′tō·lī·tre (-tẽr), *n.* [Fr. *hectolitre*, from Gr. *hekaton*, a hundred, and *litra*, a pound.] a metric measure of capacity, equal to 100 liters (26.418 gallons or 2.8378 bushels).

heç′tō·mē·tēr, heç′tō·mē·tre (-tẽr), *n.* [Fr. *hecto-mètre*, from Gr. *hekaton*, a hundred, and *metron*, a measure.] a metric measure of length, equal to 100 meters (109.36 yards).

Heç′tŏr, *n.* [L. *Hector*; Gr. *Hektōr*, lit., holding fast, from *echein*, to hold, have.] in Homer's *Iliad*, a Trojan hero killed by Achilles to avenge the death of Patroclus: he was Priam's son.

heç′tŏr, *n.* [L. *Hector*; Gr. *Hektōr*, Hector: in early popular drama, Hector became the type of a braggart and bully.]

1. a bully; a blustering, turbulent, noisy fellow.

2. one who teases or vexes.

heç′tŏr, *v.t.*; hectored, *pt., pp.*; hectoring, *ppr.* 1. to threaten; to bully; to treat with insolence.

2. to tease; to vex; to torment by words.

heç′tŏr, *v.i.* 1. to play the bully; to bluster; to be turbulent or insolent.

2. to tease; to pester.

heç′tŏr·iṣm, *n.* the disposition or practice of a hector; a bullying. [Rare.]

heç′tŏr·ly, *a.* blustering; insolent. [Rare.]

heç′tō·stere, *n.* [Fr. *hectostère*, from Gr. *hekaton*, a hundred, and *stereos*, solid.] a metric measure of volume, equal to 100 cubic meters (3,531.44 cubic feet).

Heç′ū·bȧ, *n.* in Homer's *Iliad*, the wife of Priam and mother of Hector, Troilus, Paris, and Cassandra.

hē′d, 1. he had.

2. he would.

hed′dle, *n.* [Scand. origin.] any of a series of parallel wires or cords in the harness of a loom, equipped with eyes and used for separating and guiding the warp threads.

hed′dle, *v.t.*; heddled, *pt., pp.*; heddling, *ppr.* in weaving, to pass (the warp thread) through the heddle eye.

hed′dle eȳe, the loop in each heddle through which a warp thread passes.

hed′en·bērg·īte, *n.* [named after Ludwig *Hedenberg*, Swedish chemist, who first analyzed it.] a dark or nearly black cleavable variety of pyroxene, semimetallic in appearance, containing a large proportion of oxide of iron.

Hē·dē·ō′mȧ, *n.* [Gr. *hēdys*, sweet, and *osmē*, odor.] a native American genus of labiate plants bearing fragrant flowers, as *Hedeoma pulegioides*, American pennyroyal.

Hed′e·rȧ, *n.* [L., the ivy.] a genus of woody vines of the ginseng family, including English ivy, *Hedera helix.*

hed·ēr·ā′ceous, *a.* [L. *hederaceus*, from *hedera*, ivy.] pertaining to ivy; like ivy; producing ivy.

hed′ēr·ăl, *a.* composed of ivy; relating to ivy.

hē·der′iç, *a.* relating to or extracted from the ivy.

hederic acid; an acid of the acetylene group contained in the berry and leaf of English ivy, *Hedera helix.*

hed·ēr·if′ēr·ous, *a.* [L. *hedera*, ivy, and *ferre*, to bear.] producing ivy.

hed′ēr·ōse, *a.* [L. *hederosus*, full of ivy, from *hedera*, ivy.] pertaining to or abounding in ivy.

hedġe, *n.* [ME. *hedge*, *hegge*, from AS. *hege*, an enclosure.]

1. a thicket of thorn bushes or other shrubs or small trees, planted around a field to form a fence or in rows to separate plots of cultivated ground.

2. anything serving as a fence or barrier; restriction or defense.

3. a hedging.

hedġe, *a.* 1. of, in, or near a hedge.

2. low or disreputable; furtive; as, a *hedge* love affair.

hedġe, *v.t.*; hedged, *pt., pp.*; hedging, *ppr.* 1. to enclose with a hedge; to fence with a thicket of shrubs or small trees; to separate by a hedge; as, to *hedge* a field or garden.

2. to obstruct with or as with a hedge.

I will *hedge* up thy way with thorns.
—Hos. ii. 6.

3. to surround for defense; to fortify; to surround or encompass as with a barrier (usually with *in*).

4. to try to avoid or lessen loss in (a bet, risk, etc.) by making counterbalancing bets, investments, etc.

hedġe, *v.i.* 1. to hide or protect oneself, as if behind a hedge.

2. to hide behind words; refuse to commit oneself; shilly-shally.

3. to try to avoid or lessen loss by making counterbalancing bets, investments, etc.

hedġe bells, hedge bindweed.

hedġe′ber″ry, *n.* the hagberry.

hedġe bill, hedġ′ing bill, a pruning hook for trimming hedges.

hedġe bīnd′weed, a climbing vine related to the morning-glory.

hedġe fund, a partnership of investors who pool large sums for buying stocks they think will rise in price, at the same time selling shares they think will decline, so as to profit from both the rise and fall in prices.

hedġe gär′liç, a tall, white-flowered weed of the mustard family, with heart-shaped leaves, stiff pods, and the odor of garlic.

hedġe′hog, *n.* 1. (a) an insectivorous quadruped of the genus *Erinaceus*, with a shaggy coat and sharp spines on the back, which bristle and form a hedgelike defense when the animal curls up; (b) any of several other animals resembling the hedgehog, as the porcupine, a similar American animal of a different family.

HEDGEHOG (*Erinaceus europæus*)

2. a leguminous plant of the genus *Medicago*, having spinous pods.

3. a kind of dredging machine, consisting of a series of spades fixed to the periphery of a cylinder and used for loosening mud, silt, etc. on a river bottom, so that it may be carried off by the current.

hedġe′hog çat′ēr·pil·lăr, the bristly larvae of several bombycid moths, which when disturbed roll up like a hedgehog.

hedġe′hog dē·fense′, a method of defensive warfare characterized by the setting up of fortified strong points offering resistance on all sides, thus causing trouble to the enemy even after they have been by-passed: used especially by the Soviet army during the Nazi invasion in World War II.

hedġe′hog fish, the sea hedgehog, *Diodon hystrix.*

hedġe′hog grȧss, a grass with burry spikelets, *Cenchrus tribuloides.*

hedġe′hog pärs′ley, a European herb, *Caucalis daucoides*, having fruit covered with hooked prickles.

hedġe′hog rat, a West Indian rodent having stiff hair interspersed with spines.

hedġe′hog this′tle (this′l), any plant belonging to the cactus family, as the prickly pear, *Opuntia vulgaris.*

hedġe′hop, *v.i.*; hedgehopped, *pt., pp.*; hedgehopping, *ppr.* in aviation, to fly swiftly and very close to the ground, as for spraying insecticide. [Slang.]

hedġe′hop, *v.t.* in aviation, to fly over, swiftly and low. [Slang.]

hedġe hys′sŏp, any of a number of related low-growing plants, as a bitter perennial herb of the genus *Gratiola*, having both emetic and purgative properties.

hedġe mush′ro͞om, an edible mushroom, *Agaricus arvensis*: also called *horse mushroom.*

hedġe mus′tărd, a plant of the genus *Sisymbrium*, formerly much used in medicine.

hedġe net′tle, a nonstinging plant of the genus *Stachys*, of the mint family.

hedġe′pig, *n.* a hedgehog.

hedġe piñk, the soapwort.

hedġe priēst, formerly, any English clergyman with little clerical education; also, in Ireland, formerly, a priest who had been admitted to orders from a hedge school without theological training.

hedġ′ēr, *n.* 1. one who plants or trims hedges.

2. one who hedges in betting, etc.

hedġe′rōw, *n.* a row of shrubs or bushes forming a hedge.

hedġe scho͞ol, in Ireland, formerly, a school held in the open air.

hedġe spar′rōw, in ornithology, *Accentor modularis*, a small, reddish-brown warbler, with white-tipped wings, often frequenting hedges: called also *dunnock, hedge warbler.*

hē·don′iç, *a.* [Gr. *hēdonikos*, from *hēdonē*, pleasure.]

1. pertaining to pleasure.

2. of or related to hedonism or hedonists.

Hedonic sect; a sect of Greek philosophers that placed the highest happiness in pleasure or the gratification of natural desires: called also *Cyrenaic sect.*

hē·don′içs, *n.pl.* [*construed as sing.*] 1. the branch of ethics dealing with the relation of pleasure to duty.

2. the branch of psychology dealing with pleasurable and unpleasurable feelings.

hē′dŏn·iṣm, *n.* [Gr. *hēdonē*, delight, pleasure, from *hēdesthai*, to take delight, enjoy oneself.]

1. in philosophy, the doctrine that pleasure is the principal good and should be the aim of action.

2. in psychology, the theory that a person's actions always have pleasure as their purpose.

3. pleasure-seeking as a way of life.

hē′dŏn·ist, *n.* 1. one who advocates hedonism.

2. a pleasure-seeker; voluptuary.

hē′dŏn·ist, *a.* hedonistic.

hē·dō·nis′tiç, *a.* 1. pertaining to hedonism or hedonists.

2. living a life of pleasure; self-indulgent.

hē·dō·nis′ti·căl·ly, *adv.* in a hedonistic manner.

-hē′drăl, a combining form used to form adjectives corresponding to nouns ending in *-hedron*, as in hexa*hedral.*

-hē′drŏn, [Gr. *-edron*, from *hedra*, a side, face.] a combining form meaning *a geometric figure* or *crystal with a* (specified) *number of surfaces*, as in hexa*hedron.*

hed′y·phāne, *n.* [Gr. *hēdys*, sweet, and *phainesthai*, to shine, appear.] a variety of mimetite.

hee′biē-jee′bieṣ, *n.pl.* [coined by Billy De Beck in his comic strip *Barney Google.*] an attack of nervousness; jitters. [Slang.]

heed, *v.t.*; heeded, *pt., pp.*; heeding, *ppr.* [ME. *heden*; AS. *hedan*, to heed, take care of.] to mind; to regard with care; to take careful notice of; to pay close attention to.

heed, *v.i.* to consider; to be careful; to pay attention; to take notice.

heed, *n.* careful notice; close attention; as, take *heed* of what I say.

With wanton *heed* and giddy cunning.
—Milton.

heed′fụl, *a.* attentive; observing; careful; giving heed; as, *heedful* of advice.

heed′fụl·ly, *adv.* attentively; carefully; cautiously; watchfully.

heed′fụl·ness, *n.* attention; caution; vigilance; circumspection; care.

heed′i·ly, *adv.* cautiously; vigilantly. [Obs.]

heed′i·ness, *n.* attention; caution. [Obs.]

heed′less, *a.* inattentive; careless; not taking heed; unmindful; as, *heedless* of danger.

heed′less·ly, *adv.* carelessly; negligently; inattentively; without care or circumspection.

heed′less·ness, *n.* inattention; carelessness; thoughtlessness; negligence.

heed′y, *a.* heedful. [Obs.]

hee′hạw, *n.* [echoic.]
1. the sound that a donkey makes; bray.
2. a loud, often silly laugh like a bray.

hee′hạw, *v.i.* 1. to bray.
2. to laugh in a loud, often silly way; guffaw.

heel, *v.i.*; heeled, *pt., pp.*; heeling, *ppr.* to incline; to lean to a side: said especially of a ship.

heel, *v.t.* to make (a ship) list.

heel, *n.* 1. the act of heeling.
2. the extent of this.

heel, *n.* [ME. *heel, heele*; AS. *hela, hæla,* heel.]
1. the back part of the human foot, under the ankle and behind the instep.
2. the corresponding part of the hind foot of an animal.
3. figuratively, the whole foot; as, the stag's winged *heel.*
4. the part of any foot covering that covers the heel, as of a stocking, etc.
5. the built-up part of a shoe, supporting the heel.
6. anything suggesting the human heel in location, shape, or function, as the end of a loaf of bread, the rind on cheese, the lower part of a gunstock, the lower end of a ship's mast, a small quantity of liquor left in a bottle, etc.
7. a contemptible or despicable person. [Slang.]
at heel; close to one's heels; just behind.
down at (the) heel; with the heels of one's shoes in need of repair; hence, shabby; seedy; run-down.
heels over head; in somersault fashion; recklessly; as, down they came, *heels over head.*
on (or *upon*) *the heels of*; close behind; immediately following.
out at the heels; having stockings or shoes with holes in the heels; hence, shabby; seedy; run-down.
to cool one's heels; to wait or be kept waiting long and tediously. [Colloq.]
to heel; (a) close to one's heels; just behind; (b) under discipline or control.
to kick up one's heels; to be lively or merry; have fun.
to lay by the heels; (a) to fetter; to shackle; to confine; (b) to overcome; to frustrate; to hinder.
to show one's heels, to show a clean pair of heels; to run away.
to take to one's heels; to flee; to run away.

heel, *v.t.* 1. in cockfighting, to arm (a gamecock) with gaffs.
2. to add a heel to; as, to *heel* a shoe.
3. to follow closely at the rear of; chase.
4. to touch (the floor, etc.) with the heel.
5. in golf, to hit (a ball) with the heel of the club.
6. to equip or supply (a person) with something, especially money: used chiefly in past participle; as, well *heeled.* [Slang.]
to heel in; to cover (plant roots) temporarily with earth in preparation for planting.

heel, *v.i.* 1. to go along at the heels of someone.
2. in dancing, to move the heels rhythmically.

heel′-and-tōe′, *a.* designating or of a walking race or step in which the heel of one foot touches the ground before the toes of the other leave it.

heel′bạll, *n.* a composition of wax and lampblack used in taking impressions of inscriptions, engraved plates, etc., and also in polishing the heels and edges of the soles of shoes.

heel blañk, a piece of leather shaped to form a lift in the heel of a shoe.

heel chāin, the chain that connects the heel of the jib boom with the bowsprit of a ship.

heel çut′tẽr, a tool for cutting layers or lifts for shoe heels.

heeled, *a.* 1. having a heel or heels.
2. (a) having money; (b) armed or provided, especially with a gun. [Slang.]

heel′ẽr, *n.* 1. a fighting cock that strikes well with his heels.
2. a person who puts heels on shoes or boots.
3. a servile supporter of a politician, serving only for personal gain; hanger-on; as, a ward *heeler.* [Colloq.]

heel flȳ, a fly, *Hypoderma lineata,* that attacks the heels of cattle.

heel′ing, *n.* the act of careening, as a ship; heel.

heel′ing er′rŏr, the variation in an iron ship's compass, due to the vessel's heeling.

heel′less, *a.* having no heel or heels.

heel lift, a single layer of leather in a shoe heel; a heel blank.

heel pȧth, the bank or path on the side of a canal opposite the towpath.

heel′piēce, *n.* 1. in medieval armor, a protection surrounding the heel.
2. a piece of leather on the heel of a shoe.
3. any part or piece that by its form, function, etc. suggests a heel.
4. figuratively, the end; the conclusion.

heel′plāte, *n.* 1. a metal plate on the butt of a gunstock.
2. a metal plate attached to a shoe heel to prevent wear.

heel′pōst, *n.* 1. any post forming, or affixed to, the heel or end of something.
2. the post to which a door or gate is hinged.
3. a quoin post of a lock gate.
4. the outer post supporting the partition of a stall in a stable.

heel ring, a ring that holds a scythe blade to the snath.

heel′tap, *n.* 1. a heel lift.
2. a bit of liquor which remains in a glass after drinking.

heel′tap, *v.t.*; heeltapped, *pt., pp.*; heeltapping, *ppr.* to add a piece of leather to the heel of (a shoe).

heel tọọl, a tool that has a heel near the cutting end, used by metal turners.

heft, *n.* a handle; a haft.

heft, *n.* [AS. *hefe,* weight.]
1. heaving; effort. [Obs.]
2. weight; ponderousness. [Colloq.]
3. importance; influence. [Colloq.]
4. the bulk or larger portion of anything. [Colloq.]

heft, *v.t.*; hefted, *pt., pp.*; hefting, *ppr.* 1. to lift; to raise; to heave up. [Colloq.]
2. to try to determine the weight of by lifting. [Colloq.]

heft, *v.i.* to weigh. [Colloq.]

heft, *n.* [G.] a kind of notebook.

heft′y, *a.*; *comp.* heftier; *superl.* heftiest. 1. weighty; heavy. [Colloq.]
2. large and powerful. [Colloq.]

Hē·gē′li·ăn (*or* hā-gā′), *a.* pertaining to Hegel or Hegelianism.

Hē·gē′li·ăn, *n.* a follower of Hegel or his philosophy.

Hē·gē′li·ăn·iṣm, *n.* the philosophy of Hegel, who maintained that every postulate or affirmation (*thesis*) evokes its natural opposite (*antithesis*), and that these two result in a unified whole (*synthesis*), which in turn reacts upon the original thesis.

heġ·ē·mon′iç, heġ·ē·mon′iç·ăl, *a.* [Gr. *hēgemonikos,* pertaining to the leadership, from *hēgemonia,* leadership.] principal; ruling; predominant.

hē·ġem′ō·ny, *n.*; *pl.* **hē·ġem′ō·nieṣ,** [Gr. *hēgemonia,* leadership, chief command, from *hēgemōn,* a leader, from *hēgeisthai,* to lead.] leadership, authority, or influence: usually applied to the political dominance of one state or government in a league or confederation.

hē·ġī′rȧ, *n.* [ML.; Ar. *hijrah,* lit., separation, flight, era of Mohammed, from *hajara,* to leave.]
1. [*often* H–] the forced journey of Mohammed from Mecca to Medina in 622 A.D.: the Moslem era dates from this event.
2. any journey for safety; flight.
Also spelled *hejira.*

hē·gū′men, *n.* [Gr. *hēgoumenos,* ppr. of *hēgeisthai,* to lead.] in the Orthodox Eastern Church, the elected head of a monastery, corresponding to an abbot in the Roman Catholic Church.

hē·gū′me·nē, *n.* [Gr. *hēgoumenē,* f. of *hēgoumenos,* ppr. of *hēgeisthai,* to lead.] in the Orthodox Eastern Church, the head of a nunnery, corresponding to an abbess or prioress in the Roman Catholic Church.

Hei′del·bẽrg man, a type of primitive man, inferred from fossil remains found in 1907 near Heidelberg, Germany: he is believed to have lived between the second and third glacial periods.

heif′ẽr (hef′), *n.* [ME. *hayfare, heckfere,* AS. *heahfore,* a heifer, from *heah,* high, and *fearr,* a bullock.]
1. a young cow that has not borne a calf.
2. a young female terrapin.

heigh (hī), *interj.* an exclamation to attract notice, show pleasure, express astonishment, etc.

heigh′-hō′, *interj.* an exclamation expressing mild astonishment, boredom, disappointment, weariness, etc.

height (hīt), *n.* [ME. *highte, hyghte*; AS. *heathu,* height, a high place.]
1. the topmost point of anything.
2. the highest limit; greatest degree; extreme; climax; culmination; as, the *height* of absurdity.
3. the distance from the bottom to the top.
4. (a) elevation or distance above a given level, as the earth or sea; altitude; (b) elevation (of the sun, a star, etc.) above the horizon, measured in degrees.
5. (a) a relatively great distance from bottom to top; (b) a relatively great distance above a given level.
6. [*often pl.*] a point or place considerably above most others; eminence; elevation; hill.
7. high rank. [Obs.]

height′en, *v.t.*; heightened, *pt., pp.*; heightening, *ppr.* 1. to make higher; to elevate; as, to *heighten* a tower.
2. to increase; to augment; to intensify; to aggravate; as, to *heighten* virtue.

Foreign states have endeavored to *heighten* our confusion. —Addison.

3. to elevate in condition or sentiment; to increase the excellence of; as, to *heighten* one's ambition.

Syn.—exalt, increase, enhance, intensify, vivify, aggravate, raise, exaggerate, amplify.

height′en, *v.i.* to increase; to augment; to become elevated.

Then the captain's color *heightened.* —Tennyson.

height′en·ẽr, *n.* one who or that which heightens.

height-tō-pā′pẽr, *n.* in printing, the standard height of type from face to feet, equal to .9186 of an inch.

heil, *interj.* [G.] greeting! hail!

heil, *v.t.* [G.] to say "heil" to.

Hẹim′däll, *n.* [ON. *Heimdallr.*] in Norse mythology, the watchman of Asgard, city of the gods.

hẹi′min, *n.* [Japan.] in Japan, the plebeian class, including traders, laborers, and artisans.

Heim′lich mȧ·neu′vẽr, (hīm′lik), [after its developer, Dr. H.J. *Heimlich* (1920-), U.S. surgeon.] a technique for saving a person from choking on an object caught in the throat, by applying sudden, sharp pressure to the abdomen just below the rib cage.

hei′nie (hī′nē), *n.* [G. *Heine,* dim. of *Heinrich.*] [*also* H–] a German soldier: term of contempt used especially in World War I. [Slang.]

hẹi′nous (hā′), *a.* [ME. *heinous*; OFr. *haïnos,* odious, hateful, from *hair,* hate.] hateful; odious; atrocious; abominable.

How *heinous* had the fact been, how deserving
Contempt and scorn! —Milton.

Syn.—flagrant, flagitious, atrocious, infamous, nefarious, wicked.—A crime is *heinous* which is so wicked as to arouse the strongest hatred and revulsion; an offense is *flagrant* which is glaringly bad or openly evil; it is *flagitious* if it is grossly or scandalously wicked; a crime is *atrocious* which is extremely or shockingly wrong, bad, evil, cruel, etc.

hẹi′nous·ly, *adv.* in a heinous manner; hatefully; abominably.

hẹi′nous·ness, *n.* the condition or quality of being heinous; odiousness; enormity.

heir (âr), *n.* [ME. *heire, heyre*; OFr. *heir*; L. *heres,* an heir.]
1. a person who inherits or is legally entitled to inherit another's property or title upon the other's death.
2. anyone who inherits any part of an-

other's property, either by the provisions of a will or by the natural action of the law.

3. a person who appears to get some trait from a predecessor or seems to carry on in his tradition.

heir (ãr), *v.t.* to inherit; to succeed to.

One only daughter *heired* the royal state.
—Dryden.

heir ăp·pâr'en·cy, the state or condition of being heir apparent.

heir ap·pâr'ent, *pl.* **heirș ap·pâr'ent,** the heir whose right to a certain property or title cannot be denied if he outlives the ancestor: see *heir presumptive.*

heir'-at-la̤w (ãr'), *n.* one who by the common law succeeds at the death of an ancestor to his lands and tenements.

heir'dŏm (ãr'), *n.* the state of being an heir; succession by inheritance.

heir'ess (ãr'), *n.* a woman or girl who is heir; especially, a woman or girl inheriting or who is expected to inherit great wealth.

heir land, land that is inherited.

heir'less (ãr'), *a.* lacking an heir.

heir'lo͞om (ãr'), *n.* [ME. *heire*; OFr. *heir*; L. *heres*, an heir, and AS. *geloma*, tools, utensils.]

1. a personal chattel which by special custom descends to an heir with the estate.

2. any valuable or interesting piece of personal property which has belonged to a family for a long time; a family relic.

heir prē·șump'tive, *pl.* **heirș prē·șump'tive,** an heir whose right to a certain property or title will be lost if someone more closely related is born before the ancestor dies: see *heir apparent.*

heir'ship (ãr'), *n.* the state, character, or privileges of an heir; right of inheriting; heirdom.

heirship movables; in Scottish law, the best of certain kinds of movables which the heir was formerly entitled to take, besides the heritable estate.

heīst, *n.* [from *hoist.*] a robbery or holdup. [Slang.]

heīst, *v.t.*; heisted, *pt., pp.*; heisting, *ppr.*

1. to rob or steal. [Slang.]

2. to hoist, or lift. [Dial.]

heīst'ẽr, *n.* one who heists, or robs; thief. [Slang.]

hē·jī'rȧ, *n.* same as *hegira.*

Hek'ȧ·tē, *n.* same as *Hecate.*

hek'tō-, hecto-, as in *hekto*gram: also, before a vowel, *hekt-*, as in *hekt*are.

hek'tō·gram, *n.* same as *hectogram.*

hek'tō·grȧph, *n.* and *v.* see *hectograph.*

Hel, *n.* [ON.] 1. in Norse mythology, Loki's daughter, goddess of death and the underworld.

2. the underworld to which the dead not killed in battle were sent.

hel'çoid, *a.* [Gr. *helkos*, a wound, an ulcer, and *eidos*, form.] ulcerous; resembling an ulcer.

hel·çol'ō·ġy, *n.* [Gr. *helkos*, a wound, an ulcer, and *-logia*, from *legein*, to speak.] that branch of pathology which deals with ulcers.

held, *v.* past tense and past participle of *hold.*

Hel'e·nȧ, *n.* [L.Gr. *helenē*, a torch, from *Helenē*, Helen of Troy.] a meteoric light seen about the masts of ships. [Obs.]

Hel'en flow'ẽr, a plant of the genus *Helenium.*

hel'ē·nin, hel'ē·nine, *n.* a substance, C_6H_8O, derived from *Inula helenium*, or elecampane, by the action of alcohol on the fresh root, or by distilling it with water. It crystallizes in white prisms.

He·lē'ni·um, *n.* [Gr. *helenion*, a plant, perh. from Gr. *helix*, twisted, spiral, *helissein*, to turn, to wind.] a genus of herbs of the aster family, having radiate heads and truncate branches, native to North and Central America. *Helenium autumnale*, the sneezeweed, is the best-known species.

Hel'en ŏf Trō̤y, in Greek legend, the beautiful wife of Menelaus, king of Sparta: the Trojan War was started by her elopement with Paris to Troy.

hel'grăm·īte, *n.* see *hellgrammite.*

hē'li-, same as *helio-.*

hē'li·aç, *a.* same as *heliacal.*

hē·lī'ȧ·căl, *a.* [LL. *heliacus*; Gr. *hēliakos*, of or pertaining to the sun, from *hēlios*, the sun.] in astronomy, of or near the sun; solar; specifically, (a) designating the rising of a star when it is first seen again after having been invisible because of its nearness to the sun; (b) designating the last setting of a star before it becomes invisible again.

hē·lī'ȧ·căl·ly, *adv.* in a heliacal manner.

hē″li·an·thā'ceous, *a.* relating to *Helianthus.*

hē·li·an'thin, *n.* [*heli-*, and Gr. *anthos*, a flower.] a coal-tar dye which, when applied to wool or silk, gives it a brilliant orange color: called also *methyl orange.*

hē·li·an'thoid, *a.* pertaining to the *Helianthoidea.*

hē·li·an'thoid, *n.* any of the *Helianthoidea.*

Hē″li·an·thoi'dē·ȧ, *n.pl.* an order of actinozoans; the sea anemones.

hē″li·an·thoi'dē·ăn, *a.* and *n.* same as *helianthoid.*

Hē·li·an'thus, *n.* [*heli-*, and Gr. *anthos*, a flower.] a genus of plants of the aster family, chiefly North American annual or perennial herbs, with rough leaves and large, yellow flowers; the sunflowers.

hel'i·căl, *a.* [Gr. *helix* (*-ikos*), a spiral, tendril.] of or pertaining to a helix; having a spiral form; spiral.

hel'i·căl·ly, *adv.* in a helical manner; spirally.

hel'i·cēș, *n.* alternative plural of *helix.*

Hē·li·chrȳ'sum, *n.* [*heli-*, and Gr. *chrysos*, golden.] a large genus of African and Australian plants of the aster family: the flowers retain their color after they have been dried: also called *everlasting.*

hē·lic'i·fọrm, *a.* having the form of a helix; helical.

hel'i·cin, *n.* a chemical compound, $C_{13}H_{16}O_7$, derived from salicin.

hel'i·cine, *a.* [Gr. *helix* (*-ikos*), a spiral.]

1. relating to the helix of the ear.

2. spiral; coiled.

hel'i·çline, *n.* [*heli-*, and in*cline.*] a ramp which curves as it gradually ascends.

hel'i·çō-, [from Gr. *helix, helikos*, a spiral.] a combining form meaning *spiral, spiral-shaped*, as in *helico*pter: also, before a vowel, *helic-*.

hel'i·çō·grȧph, *n.* [*helico-*, and Gr. *graphein*, to write, draw.] an instrument for drawing spiral lines on a flat surface.

hel·i·çō·ġȳ'rāte, *a.* [*helico-*, and Gr. *gyros*, a ring, circle.] in botany, having an oblique ring, as around the spore cases of *Trichomanes.*

hel'i·çoid, *a.* [Gr. *helikoeidēs*, of winding or spiral form; *helix* (*-ikos*), a spiral, and *eidos*, form.]

1. coiled like a helix; spiral.

2. in zoology, shaped like a snail shell: generally applied to the *Helicidæ*, a family of gastropods.

helicoid cyme; same as *bostryx.*

helicoid dichotomy; in botany, a branching of stems in which the sympodium is made up of branches which are all on one side or the other.

helicoid parabola; in mathematics, the curve which arises when the axis of the common parabola is bent round into the periphery of a circle, and is a line then passing through the extremities of the ordinates, which converge toward the center of the circle.

hel'i·çoid, *n.* in geometry, a surface generated by a straight line moving so that it passes through a fixed helix at all points, as a propeller screw.

hel·i·çoid'ăl, *a.* same as *helicoid.*

hel·i·çom'e·try, *n.* [*helico-*, and Gr. *metron*, a measure.] the art of describing or measuring spirals.

Hel'i·çon, *n.* [Gr. *Helikōn*, Helicon.]

1. a mountain in southern Greece, regarded by the ancient Greeks as the home of the Muses.

2. the supposed origin of poets' creative impulses.

3. [h–] a brass-wind instrument, similar to a bass tuba, consisting of a long tube bent into a circle so that it can be carried over the shoulder.

HELICON

hel·i·çō'ni·ȧ, *n.* a butterfly of tropical America, belonging to the genus *Heliconius.*

Hel·i·çō'ni·ăn, *a.* pertaining to Helicon, a mountain in Greece.

Hel·i·çō'ni·us, *n.* [L. *Heliconius*, of Helicon, from Gr. *Helikōn*, Mt. Helicon.] a genus of tropical American butterflies, typical of the subfamily *Heliconiinæ*, a species of which is found in the southern United States.

hel·i·çō'noid, *a.* pertaining to or resembling butterflies of the genus *Heliconius.*

hel'i·çop″tẽr, *n.* [Fr. *hélicoptère*, from Gr. *helix, helikos*, a spiral, and *pteron*, wing.] a kind of aircraft lifted and moved by a large propeller mounted horizontally above the fuselage: it differs from the autogiro and the gyroplane in that this propeller is turned by motor power and there is no auxiliary vertical propeller for forward motion.

HELICOPTER

hel″i·çō·trē'mȧ, *n.* [*helico-*, and Gr. *trēma*, a hole.] in anatomy, the ear opening at the summit of the cochlea where the two scalae communicate.

hē'li·ō, *n.* 1. a heliogram. [Colloq.]

2. a heliograph. [Colloq.]

hē'li·ō-, [from Gr. *hēlios*, the sun.] a combining form meaning *the sun, bright, radiant*, as in *helio*graph, *helio*centric: also *heli-*.

hē″li·ō·cen'triç, *a.* [*helio-*, and Gr. *kentron*, center.]

1. calculated from, or viewed as from, the center of the sun.

2. having or taking the sun as the center; as, the *heliocentric* theory of the solar system.

heliocentric latitude; the inclination of a line drawn between the center of the sun and the center of a planet to the plane of the ecliptic.

heliocentric longitude; the longitude of a planet as viewed from the sun.

heliocentric place; the place of the ecliptic in which a planet would appear to a spectator if viewed from the center of the sun.

hē″li·ō·cen'triç·ăl, *a.* same as *heliocentric.*

hē″li·ō·cen·tric'i·ty, *n.* the condition of being heliocentric.

hē'li·ō·çhrōme, *n.* [*helio-*, and Gr. *chrōma*, color.] a photograph in natural colors.

hē″li·ō·çhrō'miç, *a.* pertaining to heliochromy.

hē″li·ō·çhrō'mō·tȳpe, *n.* [*helio-*, and Gr. *chrōma*, color, and *typos*, an impression.] a heliochrome.

hē'li·ō·çhrō·my, *n.* the art of producing heliochromes; color photography.

hē'li·ō·dŏn, *n.* [*heli-*, and Gr. *hodos*, path.] in astronomy, an instrument used to show the apparent motion of the sun.

hē'li·ō·ē·leç'triç, *a.* pertaining to electrical phenomena supposedly caused by the sun.

hē'li·ō·en·grāv″ing, *n.* same as *heliogravure.*

hē'li·ō·gram, *n.* [*helio-*, and Gr. *gramma*, writing.] a message sent by means of a heliograph.

hē'li·ō·grȧph, *n.* [*helio-*, and Gr. *graphein*, to write.]

1. formerly, a device for taking photographs of the sun.

2. an instrument for measuring the intensity of sunlight.

3. a photoengraving.

4. a device for sending messages or signaling by flashing the sun's rays from a mirror.

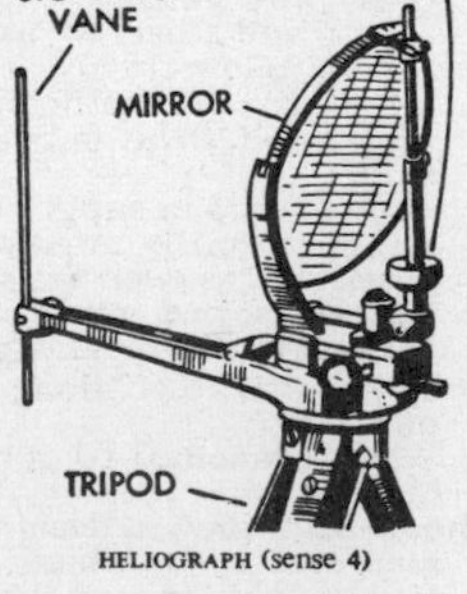

HELIOGRAPH (sense 4)

hē'li·ō·grȧph, *v.t.* and *v.i.*; heliographed, *pt., pp.*; heliographing, *ppr.* to signal or communicate by means of a heliograph.

hē·li·og'rȧ·phẽr, *n.* one who practices or is skilled in heliography.

hē·li·ō·graph'iç, *a.* pertaining to heliography or the heliograph.

hē·li·ō·graph'iç·ăl, *a.* heliographic.

hē·li·og'rȧ·phy, *n.* [*helio-*, and Gr. *graphein*, to write.]

1. the practice, method, or operation of signaling or communicating by means of the heliograph.

2. the art or process of photoengraving.

3. the study of the sun's surface.

hē″li·ō·grȧ·vūre′, *n.* [*helio-*, and Fr. *gravure*, engraving.]
1. photoengraving.
2. a print or plate made by the process of photoengraving.

hē′li·oid, *a.* [Gr. *hēlios*, sun, and *eidos*, form.] like the sun.

hē·li·ol′ȧ·tēr, *n.* [*helio-*, and Gr. *latreuin*, to serve, worship.] a worshiper of the sun.

hē·li·ol′ȧ·try, *n.* [*helio-*, and Gr. *latreia*, worship, from *latreuin*, to serve.] the worship of the sun.

hē′li·ō·līte, *n.* [*helio-*, and Gr. *lithos*, a stone.] same as *sunstone*.

hē·li·ol′ō·ġy, *n.* [*helio-*, and Gr. *-logia*, from *legein*, to speak.] the science dealing with the study of the sun.

hē·li·om′e·tēr, *n.* [*helio-*, and Gr. *metron*, a measure.] an instrument for measuring the angular distance between two stars: it was originally devised for measuring the sun's diameter.

hē″li·ō·met′riç, *a.* pertaining to or determined by means of the heliometer.

hē″li·ō·met′riç·ăl, *a.* heliometric.

hē″li·ō·met′riç·ăl·ly, *adv.* by means of a heliometer.

hē·li·om′e·try, *n.* the art or practice of using a heliometer to determine angular distances between stars.

hē·li·oph′i·lous, *a.* [*helio-*, and Gr. *philos*, loving.] fond of or attracted by the sun, as certain flowers.

hē·li·ō·phō′biç, *a.* [*helio-*, and Gr. *phobeisthai*, to fear.] having an aversion to the sun; shunning the light of the sun.

Hē·li·op′ō·rȧ, *n.* [*helio-*, and Gr. *pōros*, tufa.]
1. the typical genus of the family *Helioporidæ*, or sun corals.
2. [h-] any of the *Heliopora*; a heliopore.

hē′li·ō·pōre, *n.* any species of the genus *Heliopora*; a sun coral.

Hē·li·op′sis, *n.* [*helio-*, and Gr. *opsis*, likeness.] a genus of American plants of the aster family, mostly perennial herbs, with prominent yellow flowers and petioled, opposite leaves.

Hē′li·os, *n.* [Gr. *hēlios*, the sun.] in Greek mythology, the sun god, son of Hyperion.

hē′li·ō·sçōpe, *n.* [*helio-*, and Gr. *skopein*, to view.] a form of telescope fitted for viewing the sun without hurting the eyes, as when made with colored or smoked glasses or with mirrors formed simply of surfaces of transparent glass, which reflect only a small portion of light.

hē·li·ō·sçop′iç, *a.* pertaining to a helioscope.

hē·li·ō′sis, *n.* [Gr. *hēliousthai*, to bask in the sun, from *hēlios*, the sun.]
1. in medicine, (a) treatment of disease by exposure to sunlight; (b) sunstroke.
2. in botany, the presence of burned spots upon leaves resulting from the concentration of the sun's rays through inequalities of the glass of conservatories, or through drops of water resting on the leaves.

hē′li·ō·stat, *n.* [*helio-*, and Gr. *statos*, fixed, from *histanai*, to fix, cause to stand.] an instrument consisting of a mirror slowly revolved by clockwork so as to reflect the rays of the sun continuously in a fixed direction.

hē′li·ō·tax·is, *n.* [Mod. L.; *helio-*, and *-taxis*.] the tendency of certain plants and animals to move or turn under the influence of sunlight.

hē″li·ō·ther′ȧ·py, *n.* the sun cure; the treatment of diseases by exposure to the rays of the sun.

hē·li·oth′id, *a.* pertaining to or characteristic of the *Heliothidæ*.

hē·li·oth′id, *n.* any of the *Heliothidæ*.

Hē·li·oth′i·dae, *n.pl.* [Gr. *hēliōtis*, f. of *hēliōtēs*, of the sun, from *hēlios*, the sun.] a family of noctuid moths.

hē′li·ō·trōpe, *n.* [L. *heliotropium*; Gr. *heliotropion*, a sundial, a plant called the heliotrope; *hēlios*, the sun, and base of *trepein*, to turn.]
1. formerly, a sunflower or other plant whose flowers turn to face the sun.
2. any of a group of plants of the borage family, with fragrant clusters of small, reddish-purple or white flowers.
3. reddish purple.
4. a heliograph (*n.* 4).
5. bloodstone.
false heliotrope; the summer heliotrope.
summer heliotrope; a small shrub, *Tournefortia heliotropoides*, of the borage family.
winter heliotrope; *Petasites fragrans*, a European plant of the aster family.

HELIOTROPE

hē′li·ō·trōpe, *a.* reddish-purple.

hē′li·ō·trō·pēr, *n.* one who has charge of a heliograph at an observing station.

hē·li·ō·trop′iç, *a.* pertaining to, affected by, or characteristic of heliotropism.

hē·li·ō·trop′iç·ăl, *a.* heliotropic.

hē·li·ō·trop′iç·ăl·ly, *adv.* in a heliotropic manner.

hē·li·ot′rō·pişm, *n.* [*helio-*, and Gr. *tropē*, a turning, from *trepein*, to turn.]
1. the tendency of certain plants or other organisms to turn or bend under the influence of light, especially sunlight: *positive heliotropism* causes a turning toward the light: *negative heliotropism* causes a turning away from the light.
2. positive heliotropism.

Hē·li·ō·trō′pi·um, *n.* a genus of plants of the borage family.

hē·li·ot′rō·py, *n.* same as *heliotropism*.

hē′li·ō·tȳpe, *n.* [*helio-*, and Gr. *typos*, an impression.] a picture made by printing directly from a gelatin film exposed under a negative and hardened with chrome alum; also, the process of making such pictures.

hē′li·ō·tȳpe, *a.* pertaining to heliotypy.

hē′li·ō·tȳpe, *v.t.* and *v.i.*; heliotyped, *pt.*, *pp.*; heliotyping, *ppr.* to produce (a picture) by heliotypy.

hē″li·ō·tȳ·pog′rȧ·phy, *n.* [*helio-*, and Gr. *typos*, an impression, and *graphein*, to write, draw.] the art or process of producing phototypes.

hē′li·ō·tȳ·py, *n.* [*helio-*, and Gr. *typos*, an impression.] the art or process of making heliotypes.

Hē″li·ō·zō′ȧ, *n.pl.* [*helio-*, and Gr. *zōon*, an animal.] an order of protozoans of spherical form, with radiolarian skeletons; the sun animalcules.

hē·li·ō·zō′ăn, *n.* any of the *Heliozoa*.

hē·li·ō·zō′ăn, *a.* pertaining to the *Heliozoa*.

hē·li·ō·zō′iç, *a.* heliozoan.

hel′i·pōrt, *n.* [*heli*copter and air*port*.] a field, roof, etc. where helicopters land and take off.

hel·i·spher′iç, *a.* [Gr. *helix* (*-ikos*), a spiral, and *sphaira*, a sphere.] spiral.

hel·i·spher′iç·ăl, *a.* helispheric.

hē′li·um, *n.* [Gr. *hēlios*, the sun.] one of the chemical elements, a very light, inert, colorless gas, used for inflating balloons, dirigibles, etc.: it is preferred to hydrogen for such purposes, although it is slightly heavier, because it is not inflammable: symbol, He; atomic weight, 4.003; atomic number, 2.

hē′lix, *n.*; *pl.* **hē′lix·eş** or **hel′i·çēs,** [L. *helix*, a kind of ivy, a spiral; Gr. *helix* (*-ikos*), a spiral, anything of a spiral shape, from *helissein*, to turn round.]
1. any spiral, either lying in a single plane or, especially, moving around a cone, cylinder, etc., as the thread of a screw.
2. in anatomy, the folded rim of cartilage around the outer ear.
3. in architecture, an ornamental spiral, as a volute on a Corinthian or Ionic capital.
4. in mathematics, a line so curved around a right circular cylinder that it would become a straight line if the cylinder were unfolded into a plane.
5. in zoology, any of a group of spiral-shelled mollusks, including the common snail.

hell, *n.* [ME. *helle*; AS. *hel*, hell, from *helan*, to cover, conceal.]
1. in the Bible, the place where the spirits of the dead are: identified with Sheol and Hades.
2. (a) in Christianity, the place where fallen angels, devils, etc. live and to which sinners and unbelievers go after death for torment and eternal punishment; (b) the people in hell; (c) the powers of evil or darkness.
3. any place or condition of evil, pain, misery, cruelty, etc.
4. any disagreeable experience, as punishment, defeat, etc. [Colloq.]
As profanity *hell* is variously and extensively used, as an interjection expressing irritation, anger, etc. (e.g., oh, *hell*!), as an adverb (e.g., the *hell* with it), and as an intensifier (e.g., *hell*, no!, what the *hell*!).

hē′ll, 1. he will.
2. he shall.

Hel·lad′iç, *a.* designating or of the early peoples living on or around the Greek peninsula; as, the Minoans were a *Helladic* people.

Hel′las, *n.* 1. originally, a district and town in northeastern Greece.
2. Greece: the ancient name. [Now Poet.]

Hel·lȧ·nod′iç, *n.* [Gr. *Hellanodikēs*; *Hellēn* (*-ēnos*), a Greek, and *dikē*, a judgment, decision.] in ancient Greece, a judge or official of games, exercises, or combats.

hell′bend·ēr, *n.* 1. a large, edible salamander, found especially in the Ohio Valley.
2. (a) a prolonged drunken spree or debauch; (b) a drunken, rowdy person. [Slang.]

hell′bent′, *a.* resolved or determined to have or do (with *on* or *for*); recklessly determined. [Slang.]

hell′bọrn, *a.* born of or in hell; hellish in origin or conception.

hell′box, *n.* in printing, a box for damaged type, rules, etc.

hell′bred, *a.* produced in hell.

hell′brọth, *n.* in legend, a mixture used in performing black magic; witch broth.

hell′çat, *n.* 1. a witch; a hag.
2. an evil, spiteful, bad-tempered woman.

hell′-dīv″ēr, *n.* any of several diving birds, as the dabchick.

Hel′lē, *n.* [L.; Gr. *hellē*.] in Greek legend, a girl who, while fleeing with her brother on the ram with the golden fleece, fell off and drowned in the Hellespont.

hel′lē·bōre, *n.* [OFr. *ellebore*; L. *helleborus*, *elleborus*; Gr. *helleboros*, hellebore.]
1. any plant of the genus *Helleborus*.
2. any of a group of plants belonging to the lily family: the white hellebore, or false hellebore, has greenish-white flowers and poisonous roots.
3. the powdered root of the white hellebore, *Veratrum album*, used to destroy lice and caterpillars on growing plants.

hel·lē·bō′rē·in, *n.* [*hellebore* and *-in*.] a crystalline substance obtained from the root of black hellebore and used as a heart stimulant.

hel·leb′ō·rin, *n.* a poisonous glucoside, $C_{36}H_{42}O_6$, obtained from certain hellebore roots: it is a strong purgative.

hel·lē·bō′rine, *n.* [L., from Gr. *helleborinē*, a plant like hellebore, from *helleboros*, hellebore.] an orchid of the genus *Epipactis*, or one of the allied genus *Cephalanthera*.

hel′lē·bō·rişm, *n.* [L. *helleborismus*; Gr. *helleborismos*, from *helleborizein*, to dose with hellebore, from *helleboros*, hellebore.] the medicinal use of hellebore.

hel′lē·bō·rīze, *v.t.* [Gr. *helleborizein*, to dose with hellebore, from *helleboros*, hellebore.] to treat with hellebore, as for insanity.

Hel·lē′bō·rus, *n.* [L. *helleborus*; Gr. *helleboros*, hellebore.] a genus of winter-blooming plants of the family *Ranunculaceæ*, consisting of perennial, low-growing herbs with palmate or pedate leathery leaves and yellowish, greenish, or white flowers shaped like buttercups. *Helleborus orientalis* is the species which produced the black hellebore of the ancients. *Helleborus niger* is the Christmas rose, the poisonous roots of which are used as a heart stimulant.

Hel′len, *n.* [L.; Gr. *Hellēn*.] the legendary ancestor after whom the Hellenes were named.

Hel′lēne, *n.*; *pl.* **Hel′lēneş,** [Gr. *Hellēn* (*-ēnos*).] a citizen or native of ancient or modern Greece; a Greek.

Hel·lē′ni·ăn, *a.* Hellenic.

Hel·len′iç, *a.* [Gr. *Hellēnikos*, from *Hellēn*, a Greek, *Hellēnes*, the Greeks.]
1. pertaining to the Hellenes.
2. of the history, language, or culture of the ancient Greeks.

Hel·len′iç, *n.* 1. the language of ancient Greece.
2. the branch of the Indo-European family of languages to which Greek, in its various dialects and stages of development, belongs.

Hel′len·işm, *n.* [Gr. *Hellēnismos*, imitation of the Greeks, from *Hellēnizein*, to speak Greek.]
1. a Greek phrase, idiom, or custom.
2. the character, thought, culture, or ethical system of ancient Greece.
3. the adoption of the Greek language, customs, etc., as by the Romans.

Hel′len·ist, *n.* [Gr. *Hellēnistēs*, an imitator of the Greeks, from *Hellēnizein*, to speak Greek.]
1. anyone, especially a Jew of the Diaspora, who adopts the Greek language and Greek usages.
2. one skilled in the Greek language and versed in Greek literature.

3. a great admirer of ancient Greek culture, language, etc.

4. any of the Byzantine Greeks of the fifteenth century who helped revive classical learning in Europe.

Hel·lē·nis′tiç, Hel·lē·nis′tiç·ăl, *a.* 1. of or characteristic of Hellenists or Hellenism.

2. of Greek history, language, and culture after the death of Alexander the Great (323 B. C.).

Hel·lē·nis′tiç·ăl·ly, *adv.* in the manner of the Hellenists.

Hel·len·ī·zā′tion, *n.* the act of Hellenizing or the state of being Hellenized.

Hel′len·īze, *v.i.*; Hellenized, *pt., pp.*; Hellenizing, *ppr.* [Gr. *Hellēnizein,* to imitate the Greeks, to speak Greek, from *Hellēnes,* the Greeks.] to adopt the Greek language, customs, ideals, etc.; to become Greek in character, form, etc.

Hel′len·īze, *v.t.* to make Greek, or Hellenistic, in character, form, etc.

hell′ẽr, *n.* a person who is noisy, wild, reckless, etc. [Slang.]

hel′lẽr, *n.*; *pl.* **hel′lẽr,** [G.; M.H.G. *haller, heller,* short for *Haller pfenninc,* penny of Hall (in Swabia).]

1. formerly, (a) a German copper coin, equal to half a pfennig; (b) an Austrian bronze coin, equal to 1/100 of a krone.

2. a small Czechoslovakian coin, equal to 1/100 of a koruna.

Hel·les·pon′tine, *a.* pertaining to the Hellespont.

hell′-fīre, hell′fīre, *n.* [ME. *helle fir*; AS. *hellefyr.*] the fire, hence punishment, of hell.

hell′grăm·mīte, hel′grăm·mīte, *n.* the larva of *Corydalus cornutus,* the dobson, a large neuropteral fly: it is much used as a fish bait.

hell′hag, *n.* an old woman of spiteful or malicious tendencies.

hell′hound, *n.* [ME. and AS. *hellehund.*]

1. a dog of hell, as Cerberus.

2. (a) a fiend; (b) a fiendish, evil person.

hel′li·ẽr, *n.* a tiler; a slater. [Brit. Dial.]

hel′liŏn, *n.* a person fond of deviltry; a mischievous troublemaker. [Colloq.]

hell′ish, *a.* 1. pertaining to hell; also, like hell in qualities; infernal; malignant; wicked; diabolical.

2. very unpleasant; detestable. [Colloq.]

hell′ish·ly, *adv.* in a hellish manner.

hell′ish·ness, *n.* the quality of being hellish.

hell′kīte, *n.* a fiendish, cruel person.

hel·lō′, *interj.* 1. an exclamation of greeting or of response, as in telephoning.

2. an exclamation to attract attention.

3. an exclamation of astonishment or surprise.

hel·lō′, *n.* a saying or shouting of "hello."

hel·lō′, *v.i.* to shout or say "hello"; to call out.

hel·lō′, *v.t.* to say "hello" to.

hell′wărd, *adv.* toward hell.

hell′y, *a.* having the qualities of hell; hellish. [Obs.]

helm, *n.* same as *halm.*

helm, *n.* [ME. *helme*; AS. *helma,* a helm, rudder.]

1. (a) the wheel or tiller by which a ship is steered; (b) the complete steering gear, including the wheel or tiller, rudder, etc.

2. the place or post of direction or management of an organization, enterprise, etc.; as, to be at the *helm* of the administration.

3. a helve; a handle. [Obs.]

helm amidships; the order to keep the rudder fore and aft of the ship.

port the helm; the order to put the helm toward the left side of the ship.

shift the helm; the order to put the helm from port to starboard, or vice versa.

starboard the helm; the order to put the helm to the right side of the ship.

to put the helm down; to push the helm down to the lee side in order to put the ship about or to bring her up to the wind.

to right the helm; to put the helm fore and aft of the ship.

up with the helm; the order to put the helm aweather.

helm, *v.t.* to steer; to guide; to direct.

helm, *n.* [ME. *helm*; AS. *helm,* a protection, a helm.]

1. a helmet. [Poet.]

2. a cloud capping a mountain when the sky is clear. [Brit. Dial.]

helm, *v.t.* [ME. *helmen*; AS. *helmian,* to cover, from *helm,* a covering, a helmet.] to provide with a helmet.

helm′ăġe, *n.* guidance. [Rare.]

hel′met, *n.* [OFr. *healmet,* dim. of *heaume,* a helm, from AS. *helm,* a helm, covering.]

1. a protective covering for the head; specifically, (a) the hoodlike top part of medieval armor, originally made of leather, and afterward strengthened by the addition of bronze and other metals, until finally it was constructed entirely of metal, lined with felt or wadding: helmets were frequently provided with bars and movable flaps to cover the face in battle, and to be opened at other times; (b) the metal head covering worn in modern warfare; (c) the leather head covering used in football; (d) the mesh-faced mask used in fencing; (e) the headpiece of a diver's suit, equipped with air tubes, glass windows, etc.; (f) a fireman's protective hat; (g) a pith hat with a wide brim, worn as a sunshade in hot countries.

TYPES OF HELMET
A. ancient; B. 16th century; C. modern

2. something suggesting such a headpiece in appearance or function, as the arched upper part of the corolla or calyx in certain flowers.

3. in heraldry, the part of a coat of arms which bears the crest.

4. the upper part of a retort.

5. in botany, same as *galea.*

hel′met, *v.t.* to cover or equip with a helmet.

hel′met bee′tle, a beetle of the family *Cassididæ*: so named from its shape.

hel′met bĭrd, a touracou.

hel′met ȼrab, *Limulus longispinus,* a king crab.

hel′met ȼrest, a crested hummingbird of South America, belonging to the genus *Oxypogon.*

hel′met·ed, *a.* 1. wearing or provided with a helmet.

2. shaped like a helmet.

hel′met flow′ẽr, 1. any variety of monkshood.

2. the skullcap.

3. an orchid of South America of the genus *Coryanthes.*

hel′met lĭn′ẽr, a plastic or fiber head covering shaped like and worn under a modern military helmet.

hel′met shell, the shell of a gastropod of the genus *Cassis.* Most of the species are found on tropical shores, but a few are found on the coast of the Mediterranean. Some of the shells attain a large size. *Cassis rufa, Cassis cornuta, Cassis tuberosa,* and others are the material on which shell cameos are usually sculptured.

HELMET SHELL (*Cassis tuberosa*)

hel′minth, *n.* [Gr. *helmins (-inthos),* a worm.] a worm; specifically, a parasitical worm, as the tapeworm or roundworm infesting the intestines.

hel·minth-, hel·min′thō-, [Gr. *helmins (-inthos),* a worm.] combining forms used in botany, zoology, and medicine to signify *a worm* or *pertaining to a worm,* as in *helminthagogue.*

hel·min·thă·goġ′iç, *a.* [*helminth-,* and Gr. *agōgos,* leading, driving, from *agein,* to lead, drive.] anthelmintic.

hel·min′thă·gogue (-gog), *n.* [*helminth-,* and Gr. *agōgos,* leading, driving, from *agein,* to lead, drive.] a vermifuge.

Hel·min′thēs, *n.pl.* [Gr. *helmins (-inthos),* a worm.] a large group of worms, mostly parasitic, including the *Cestoidea, Nematoidea, Trematoidea, Turbellaria,* etc.

hel·min·thī′ă·sis, *n.* [Gr. *helminthiān,* to suffer from worms, from *helmins (-inthos),* a worm.] a disease characterized by or produced by the presence of worms in the body.

hel·min′thiç, *a.* [Gr. *helmins (-inthos),* a worm.] relating to worms; expelling or destroying worms.

hel·min′thiç, *n.* a medicine for expelling worms; a vermicide; a vermifuge; an anthelmintic.

hel·min′thīte, *n.* [Gr. *helmins (-inthos),* a worm.] a long, sinuous mark or track common on the surface of sandstones, believed to be a fossil worm trail.

hel·min′thō-, see *helminth-.*

hel·min′thoid, *a.* [Gr. *helmins (-inthos),* a worm, and *eidos,* form.] wormlike; vermiform.

hel·min·thō·loġ′iç, *a.* pertaining to helminthology.

hel·min·thō·loġ′iç·ăl, *a.* helminthologic.

hel·min·thol′ō·ġist, *n.* one who is versed in helminthology.

hel·min·thol′ō·ġy, *n.* [*helmintho-,* and Gr. *-logia,* from *legein,* to speak.] the scientific study of helminths.

helm′less, *a.* without a helm or steering apparatus.

helmṣ′măn, *n.*; *pl.* **helmṣ′men,** the man at the helm or wheel who steers a ship.

he·lō′bi·ous, *a.* [Gr. *helos,* a marsh, and *bios,* life.] thriving in marshy ground; palustrine.

hē·loc′e·rous, *a.* [Gr. *hēlos,* a stud, nail, and *keras,* horn.] having the characteristics of the *Clavicornia*; clavicorn.

hē′lō·dẽrm, *n.* a lizard of the genus *Heloderma.*

Hē·lō·dẽr′mȧ, *n.* [Gr. *hēlos,* a nail, a stud, a wart or knob, and *derma,* skin.] a genus of venomous lizards of Mexico and the southern United States. *Heloderma suspectum* is the Gila monster; *Heloderma horridum,* a larger species common to Mexico.

Hel′ot (*or* hē′lot), *n.* [L. *Helotæ*; Gr. *Heilōtes,* pl. of *Heilōs,* a Helot, from *Helos,* a town of Laconia whose inhabitants were enslaved by the Spartans.] a serf or slave in ancient Sparta; hence, [h–] any serf or slave.

hel′ot·iṣm, *n.* serfdom or slavery; the condition of a helot.

hel′ot·ry, *n.* helots collectively; also, serfdom or slavery.

help, *v.t.*; helped *or archaic* holp (hōlp), *pt.*; helped *or archaic* holpen (hōl′pn), *or obs.* holp, *pp.*; helping, *ppr.* [ME. *helpen*; AS. *helpan,* to help.]

1. to make it easier for (a person) to do something; aid; assist; specifically, (a) to give (one in need) something necessary, as relief, money, etc.; (b) to do part of the work of; to ease or share the labor of; as, will you *help* me do this problem? (c) to aid in getting (*up, down, in,* etc. or *to, into, out of,* etc.); as, *help* him *into* his coat.

2. to make it easier for (something) to exist, happen, develop, improve, etc.; specifically, (a) to make more effective, larger, intense, etc.; aid the growth of; promote; as, ignorance *helps* war; (b) to cause improvement in; remedy; alleviate; relieve; as, this medicine will *help* your cough.

3. to be responsible for; promote or prevent; as, I can't *help* his bad manners.

4. to keep from; to avoid.

I cannot *help* remarking the resemblance between him and our author. —Pope.

5. to serve; to wait on: said of servants, waiters, clerks, etc.

6. to mend. [Brit. Dial.]

Syn.—assist, aid, succor, relieve.—*Help* is the generic term and may be substituted for the others. We *help* a person to prosecute his work, or *help* him out of a difficulty; we *assist* in order to forward a scheme, or we *assist* a person in the time of his embarrassment; we *aid* a good cause, or we *aid* a person to make his escape; we *succor* a person who is in danger; we *relieve* him in time of distress.

to help forward; to advance by assistance.

to help off; to aid in passing; as, *to help off* time.

to help oneself to; (a) to serve or provide oneself with (food, etc.); (b) to take without asking or being given.

to help out; to aid in getting or doing something.

to help over; to enable to surmount; as, *to help* one *over* a difficulty.

to help up; (a) to assist to erect posture; (b) to promote financially or socially.

help, *v.i.* 1. to give aid; to be co-operative, useful, or beneficial.

A generous present *helps* to persuade, as well as an agreeable person. —Garth.

2. to act as a waiter at table.

help, *n.* [ME. *help*; AS. *help,* from *helpan,* to help.]

 fāte, fär, fȧst, fąll, finăl, cãre, at; mēte, prẹy, hẽr, met; pīne, marïne, bïrd, pin; nōte, mōve, fọr, atŏm, not; mọọn, book;

1. aid; assistance.
2. one who or that which gives assistance; a helper; as, memory is a great *help*.
3. remedy; relief; succor; as, *help* is at hand.
4. (a) a hired helper; as, a domestic servant, farm hand, etc.; (b) hired helpers; employees.
5. a serving of food; helping.

help′ẽr, *n.* one who or that which helps.

help′fu̇l, *a.* rendering aid or assistance; useful.

help′fu̇l·ly, *adv.* in a helpful manner.

help′fu̇l·ness, *n.* assistance; usefulness.

help′ing, *n.* 1. the act of giving help.
2. a portion of food served to one person.

help′less, *a.* 1. without power to help oneself; feeble; weak.
2. without help or protection.
3. incompetent; inefficient.
4. irremediable. [Rare.]
5. unsupplied; destitute; as, *helpless* of necessities. [Rare.]

help′less·ly, *adv.* in a helpless manner.

help′less·ness, *n.* the condition of being helpless.

help′māte, *n.* a companion and helper: usually applied to a wife, sometimes to a husband.

help′meet, *n.* a helpmate.

hel′tẽr-skel′tẽr, *adv.* in haste and confusion; in a disorderly, hurried manner.

hel′tẽr-skel′tẽr, *a.* hurried and confused; disorderly.

hel′tẽr-skel′tẽr, *n.* anything helter-skelter.

helve, *n.* [ME. *helve*; AS. *helf*, a handle.]
1. the handle of a tool, especially of an ax, adz, or hatchet.
2. a tilt hammer; also, the handle of a tilt hammer.

helve, *v.t.*; helved, *pt.*, *pp.*; helving, *ppr.* to furnish with a helve or handle.

Hel·vē′tiăn, *a.* 1. of Helvetia or the Helvetii.
2. Swiss.

Hel·vē′tiăn, *n.* 1. a native or inhabitant of Helvetia.
2. a Swiss.

Hel·vet′iç, *a.* same as *Helvetian*.

Hel·vet′iç, *n.* a Swiss Protestant; an adherent of Zwingli.

Hel·vē′ti·ī (-shi-ī), *n. pl.* [L.] any member of an ancient Celtic people who lived in the western part of what is now Switzerland.

hel′vin, hel′vīte, *n.* [L. *helvus*, light yellow, and *-in*, *-ite*.] a mineral of a yellowish color occurring in regular tetrahedrons, and made up of glucinum, iron, manganese, silica, and sulfur.

hem, *interj.* and *n.* a conventionalized expression of the sound made in clearing the throat to attract attention or show doubt.

hem, *v.i.*; hemmed, *pt.*, *pp.*; hemming, *ppr.*
1. to make the sound of clearing the throat.
2. to pause or hesitate in speaking.

hem, *n.* [ME. *hem*, AS. *hem*, edge, border, from *ham*, an enclosed field.]
1. the border of a fabric, doubled and sewed down to strengthen it and prevent the raveling of the threads.
2. edge; border; margin.

hem, *v.t.*; hemmed, *pt.*, *pp.*; hemming, *ppr.* 1. to form a hem or hems on; to fold and sew down the edge of, as cloth, etc.
2. to encircle; to surround.
3. to confine or restrain: with *in*, *around*, or *about*; as, *hemmed in* by narrow walls.

hēm-, haem- (*or* hem), same as *hemo-*.

hē′mȧ-, hae′mȧ- (*or* hem′ȧ), same as *hemo-*.

hem′ȧ·çhāte, haem′ȧ·çhāte, *n.* [*hema-*, and Gr. *achatēs*, agate.] a variety of quartz marked by spots of red jasper.

hē′mȧ·çhrōme, hae′mȧ·çhrōme, *n.* [*hema-*, and Gr. *chrōma*, color.] the red pigment of the blood.

hem′ȧ·cīte, *n.* [Gr. *haima*, blood.] a composition of blood and vegetable or mineral materials used in the manufacture of small articles, as buttons.

hē′mȧ·çȳte, hae′mȧ·çȳte, *n.* [*hema-*, and Gr. *kytos*, a cavity.] a blood corpuscle.

hē″mȧ·çȳ·tom′e·tẽr, hae″mȧ·çȳ·tom′e·tẽr, *n.* [*hema-*, and Gr. *kytos*, a cavity, and *metron*, a measure.] a device for measuring the number of corpuscles in a definite amount of blood.

hē′mad, hae′mad, *adv.* [Gr. *haima*, blood, and *-ad*.] to or toward the hemal or ventral part of the body.

hē″mȧ·drom′e·tẽr, hae″mȧ·drom′e·tẽr, *n.* [*hema-*, and Gr. *dromos*, a running, and *metron*, a measure.] a device to measure the velocity of arterial blood: also *hemadromometer*.

hē″mȧ·drom′e·try, hae″mȧ·drom′e·try, *n.* measurement of blood velocity: also *hemadromometry*.

hē″mȧ·drom′ō·grȧph, hae″mȧ·drom′ō·grȧph, *n.* [*hema-*, and Gr. *dromos*, a running, and *graphein*, to write.] a device to record blood velocities.

hē″măg·glụ′ti·nāte, hae″măg·glụ′ti·nāte, *v.t.* in immunology, to bring about hemagglutination of.

hē″măg·glụ″ti·nā′tion, hae″măg·glụ″ti·nā′tion, *n.* the agglutination of blood corpuscles.

hē″măg·glụ′ti·nin, hae″măg·glụ′ti·nin, *n.* in immunology, a specific agglutinin, present in blood serum, which causes agglutination of red blood corpuscles.

hē′mȧ·gogue, hae′mȧ·gogue (-gog), *n.* [from *hem-*, and Gr. *agōgos*, leading, from *agein*, to lead.] anything that increases the discharge of blood, as in menstruation.

hē′măl, hae′măl, *a.* [Gr. *haima*, blood.]
1. pertaining to blood.
2. of or upon the side containing the heart and chief blood vessels; in vertebrates, ventral.
hemal arch; the arch formed by the projection anteriorly of the ribs and the sternum from the spinal column.

hē′-man′, *n.*; *pl.* **hē′-men′,** a strong, virile man. [Slang.]

hē″mȧ·poi·ē′sis, hae″mȧ·poi·ē′sis, *n.* same as *hematopoiesis*.

hē″mȧ·poi·et′iç, hae″mȧ·poi·et′iç, *a.* [*hema-*, and Gr. *poiētikos*, capable of making, from *poiein*, to make.] blood-producing.

hē″mȧ·pō·phyṣ′i·ăl, hae″mȧ·pō·phyṣ′i·ăl, *a.* relating to hemapophysis.

hē″mȧ·poph′y·sis, hae″mȧ·poph′y·sis, *n.*; *pl.* **hē″mȧ·poph′y·sēṣ, hae″mȧ·poph′y·sēṣ,** [*hema-*, and Gr. *apophysis*, an outgrowth, a process; *apo*, from, and *phyein*, to grow.] in zoology, the element of either half of a hemal arch that is next to the hemal spine; a costal cartilage.

hē″mȧ·stat′iç, hae″mȧ·stat′iç, *a.* and *n.* same as *hemostatic*.

hē″mȧ·stat′içs, hae″mȧ·stat′içs, *n.* same as *hemostatics*.

hem′at-, haem′at- (*or* hē′mat), same as *hemato-*.

hem″ȧ·tȧ·çhom′e·tẽr, haem″ȧ·tȧ·çhom′e·tẽr, *n.* [*hema-*, and Gr. *tachos*, swiftness, and *metron*, a measure.] a device to measure the velocity of the flow of blood.

hē′mȧ·tal, hae′mȧ·tal, *a.* same as *hemal*.

hē″mȧ·tē′in, hae″mȧ·tē′in, *n.* [Gr. *haima* (*-atos*), blood.] a reddish-brown, crystalline dye, $C_{16}H_{12}O_6$, obtained from logwood extracts by oxidation: also *hematin*.

hē″mȧ·tem′ē·sis, hae″mȧ·tem′ē·sis, *n.* [*hema-*, and Gr. *emein*, to vomit.] in medicine, the ejection of blood by vomiting.

hē′mȧ·thẽrm, hae′mȧ·thẽrm, *n.* [*hema-*, and Gr. *thermē*, heat.] a warm-blooded animal.

hē″mȧ·thẽr′măl, hae″mȧ·thẽr′măl, *a.* in zoology, warm-blooded.

hē″mȧ·thī·drō′sis, hae″mȧ·thī·drō′sis, *n.* [*hema-*, and Gr. *hidrōs*, sweat.] bloody perspiration; blood sweating.

hē·mat′iç, hae·mat′iç, *a.* [Gr. *haimatikos*, of the blood, from *haima* (*-atos*), blood.]
1. of, filled with, or colored like blood.
2. causing a change in the condition of the blood.

hē·mat′iç, hae·mat′iç, *n.* a hematic medicine.

hem′ȧ·tin, haem′ȧ·tin, *n.* [Gr. *haima* (*-atos*), blood, and *-in*.]
1. a dark-brown or blackish substance containing iron, derived from hemoglobin by decomposition.
2. hematein.
3. formerly, heme.

hem·ȧ·tin′iç, *n.* any substance that increases the amount of hemoglobin in the blood.

hem·ȧ·tin′iç, *a.* 1. of hematin.
2. of, filled with, or colored like blood.

hē″mȧ·ti·nom′ē·tẽr, hae″mȧ·ti·nom′ē·tẽr, *n.* a hemoglobinometer.

hē″mȧ·tin·ō·met′riç, hae″mȧ·tin·ō·met′riç, *a.* pertaining to the quantitative determination of hemoglobin in the blood.

hem′ȧ·tīte, haem′ȧ·tīte, *n.* [L. *hæmatites*; Gr. *haimatitēs*, lit., bloodlike, red iron ore, from *haima* (*-atos*), blood.] native anhydrous ferric oxide, Fe_2O_3, an important iron ore: it is brownish red when pulverized.

hem·ȧ·tit′iç, haem·ȧ·tit′iç, *a.* pertaining to hematite, or resembling it; containing hematite.

hem′ȧ·tō-, haem′ȧ·tō- (*or* hē′mȧ-tō), [from Gr. *haima*, *haimatos*, blood.] a combining form meaning *blood*, as in *hematozoon*: also, before a vowel *hemat-*, *haemat-*.

hem·ȧ·tō′biç, haem·ȧ·tō′biç, *a.* hematobious.

hem·ȧ·tō′bi·ous, haem·ȧ·tō′bi·ous, *a.* [*hemato-*, and Gr. *bios*, life.] living as a parasite in blood.

hem′ȧ·tō·blȧst, haem′ȧ·tō·blȧst, *n.* [*hemato-*, and Gr. *blastos*, a germ.] a colorless, circular or oval, lenticular disk in the blood, without hemoglobin, and considered as an immature red blood corpuscle.

hem′ȧ·tō·cēle, haem′ȧ·tō·cēle, *n.* [*hemato-*, and Gr. *kēlē*, a tumor.] a tumor filled with blood.

Hem·ȧ·toç′ry·ȧ, *n.pl.* same as *Hæmatocrya*.

hem″ȧ·tō·çrys′tăl·lin, haem″ȧ·tō·çrys′tăl·lin, *n.* [*hemato-*, and Gr. *krystallos*, ice, crystal, and *-in*.] hemoglobin.

hem′ȧ·tō·cyst, haem′ȧ·tō·cyst, *n.* a cyst filled with blood.

hem″ȧ·tō·ġen′ē·sis, haem″ȧ·tō·ġen′ē·sis, *n.* [*hemato-*, and Gr. *genesis*, generation.] the formation of blood.

hem″ȧ·tō·ġen′iç, haem″ȧ·tō·ġen′iç, *a.* causing or relating to blood formation.

hem·ȧ·toġ′e·nous, haem·ȧ·toġ′e·nous, *a.* [*hemato-*, and Gr. *-genes*, producing.] hematogenic.

hem″ȧ·tō·glob′ū·lin, haem″ȧ·tō·glob′ū·lin, *n.* [*hemato-*, and L. *globulus*, a globe, and *-in*.] hemoglobin.

hē′mȧ·toid, hae′mȧ·toid, *a.* [Gr. *haimatoeidēs*, *haimatōdēs*, bloodlike; *haima* (*-atos*), blood, and *eidos*, form.] bloodlike; bloody.

hē″mȧ·toid′in, hae″mȧ·toid′in, *n.* a crystalline compound often found in extravasated blood. It contains no iron and probably is the same as *bilirubin*.

hem·ȧ·tol′ō·ġy, haem·ȧ·tol′ō·ġy, *n.* [*hemato-*, and Gr. *-logia*, from *legein*, to speak.] the study of the blood and its diseases.

hē″mȧ·tō′mȧ, hae″mȧ·tō′mȧ, *n.*; *pl.* **hē″mȧ·tō′mȧ·tȧ, hē″mȧ·tō′mȧṣ,** [Gr. *haima* (*-atos*), blood, and *-oma*.] a subcutaneous swelling filled with effused blood.

hem″ȧ·tō·per·i·çär′di·um, haem″ȧ·tō·per·i·çär′di·um, *n.* [*hemato-*, and Gr. *perikardion*, the pericardium.] an effusion of blood into the pericardium.

hem″ȧ·tō·phō′bi·ȧ, haem″ȧ·tō·phō′bi·ȧ, *n.* [*hemato-*, and Gr. *-phobia*, from *phobos*, fear.] an abnormal fear upon seeing blood.

hem″ȧ·tō·plas′tiç, haem″ȧ·tō·plas′tiç, *a.* [*hemato-*, and Gr. *plastikos*, plastic, from *plassein*, to mold.] forming blood; productive of blood.

hem″ȧ·tō·poi·ē′sis, haem″ȧ·tō·poi·ē′sis, *n.* [*hemato-*, and Gr. *poiesis*, a making, from *poiein*, to make.] the making of blood; blood formation.

hem″ȧ·tō·pọr′phy·rin, haem″ȧ·tō·pọr′phy·rin, *n.* [*hemato-*, and Gr. *porphyra*, purple, and *-in*.] a derivative of hematin and corresponding substances in invertebrates, produced by decomposition. It contains no iron.

hem′ȧ·tōse, haem′ȧ·tōse, *a.* filled or covered with blood.

hē″mȧ·tō′sin, hae″mȧ·tō′sin, *n.* hematin. [Rare.]

hē″mȧ·tō′sis, hae″mȧ·tō′sis, *n.* [Gr. *haimatōsis*, from *haimatoun*, to make bloody.] blood formation; also, the transformation in the lungs of venous blood into arterial blood.

hem″ȧ·tō·thẽr′măl, haem″ȧ·tō·thẽr′măl, *a.* [*hemato-*, and Gr. *thermos*, warm, from *thermē*, heat.] in zoology, warm-blooded.

hem″ȧ·tō·thō′rax, *n.* [*hemato-*, and Gr. *thōrax*, a breastplate.] hemorrhage into the pleural cavity.

hē″mȧ·tox′y·lin, hae″mȧ·tox′y·lin, *n.* [*hemato-*, and Gr. *xylon*, wood, and *-in*.] a crystalline compound, $C_{16}H_{14}O_6 \cdot 3H_2O$, extracted from logwood and used as an indicator and a stain in microscopy: when oxidized it yields hematein dye.

hem″ȧ·tō·zō′ăn, *n.* same as *hematozoon*.

hem″ȧ·tō·zō′ŏn, *n.*; *pl.* **hem″ȧ·tō·zō′ȧ,** any parasitic animal organism in the blood.

hem·ȧ·tū′ri·ȧ, *n.* [Gr. *haima* (*-atos*), blood, and *ouron*, urine.] a discharge of bloody urine: called also *hematuresis*.

hem′ble, *n.* a shed for cattle; a stable; a hovel. [Brit. Dial.]

hēme, *n.* [shortened from *hematin*.] the nonprotein part of the hemoglobin molecule, containing the pigment: formerly called *hematin*.

hem·el′y·tron, hem·el′y·trum, *n.*; *pl.* **hem·el′y·trȧ,** either of the thickened forewings of certain insects, as the hemipterous insects: also *hemelytrum*, *hemielytron*, *hemielytrum*.

hem″ē·rȧ·lō′pi·ȧ, *n.* [Gr. *hēmera*, day, *alaos*, blind, and *ōps*, *ōpos*, the eye.] the condition of the eyes in which one can see clearly only at night; day blindness: often confused with *nyctalopia*.

hem·ẽr·ō′bi·ăn, *n.* a planipennate insect of the genus *Hemerobius* or related genera.

hē·mer′ō·bid, *a.* of or pertaining to insects of the genus *Hemerobius* and allied genera.

Hem·ẽr·ō′bi·us, *n.* [Gr. *hēmerobios*, living for a day; *hēmera*, a day, and *bios*, life.] a genus of neuropterous insects, the type of the family *Hemerobiidæ*. They are lace-winged flies.

Hem″ē·rō·çal′lis, *n.* [Gr. *hēmerokallis*, a yellow lily that blooms but for a day; *hēmera*, day, and *kalos*, beautiful.] a genus of plants of the lily family, natives of Asia and Europe. *Hemerocallis fulva*, the day lily, is grown in gardens for its showy flowers.

hem′i-, [L. *hemi-*, Gr. *hēmi-*, a half.] a prefix used in many words of Latin and Greek derivation to signify *a half*, as in *hemi*cerebrum, *hemi*cardia.

-hē′mi·ȧ, -emia: words ending with **-*hemia*** may also be spelled *-haemia*.

hem″i·al·bū′min, *n.* see *hemialbumose*.

hem·i·al′bū·mōse, *n.* the most characteristic and most frequently obtained by-product of proteid digestion. It is the forerunner of hemipeptone: called also *hemialbumin*.

hem·i·al′ġi·ȧ, *n.* neuralgic pain in only one side or part of the body, especially of the head.

hem·i·an·aes·thē′si·ȧ, *n.* [*hemi-*, and Gr. *anaisthēsia*, want of perception; *an-* priv., and *aisthanesthai*, to perceive.] in pathology, anesthesia of one lateral half of the body.

hem·i·an·es·thē′siç, hem·i·an·aes·thē′siç, *a.* pertaining to or afflicted with hemianaesthesia.

hem″i·ȧ·nō′pi·ȧ, *n.* hemianopsia.

hem″i·ȧ·nop′si·ȧ, *n.* in pathology, blindness in one half of the visual field. It may affect one eye or both eyes.

hem″i·ȧ·nop′tiç, *a.* pertaining to or afflicted with hemianopsia.

hem·i·at′rō·phy, *n.* in pathology, atrophy confined to one side of the body.

hem′i·branch, *a.* hemibranchiate.

hem′i·branch, *n.* a fish of the order *Hemibranchii*.

hem·i·bran′chi·āte, *a.* pertaining to the *Hemibranchii*; having the branchial apparatus deficient; half-gilled.

Hem·i·bran′chi·ī, *n.pl.* [*hemi-*, and Gr. *branchia*, gills.] an order of fishes having the branchial apparatus incomplete. It includes the sticklebacks and snipefishes.

hē′miç, hae′miç, *a.* of the blood.

hem·i·çär′di·ȧ, *n.* [*hemi-*, and Gr. *kardia*, the heart.] either half, the right or left, of a four-chambered heart.

hem·i·çär′di·aç, *a.* of or pertaining to the hemicardia.

hem′i·çärp, *n.* [*hemi-*, and Gr. *karpos*, fruit.] in botany, one of the halves of a fruit which spontaneously divides into two, as a pea.

hem·i·cer′ē·brăl, *a.* pertaining to a hemicerebrum.

hem·i·cer′ē·brum, *n.*; *pl.* **hem·i·cer′ē·brȧ,** [*hemi-*, and L. *cerebrum*, the brain.] in anatomy, the right or left half of the cerebrum.

hem″i·chō·rē′ȧ, *n.* in pathology, a form of chorea in which the convulsive movements are confined to one side of the body.

hem·i·çol′lin, *n.* [*hemi-*, and Gr. *kolla*, glue, and *-in*.] a peptonelike substance obtained in the formation of semiglutin from gelatin: analogous to semiglutin, but partially soluble in alcohol.

hem·i·crā′ni·ȧ, *n.* [L. *hemicrania*; Gr. *hēmikrania*, a pain on one side of the head or face; *hēmi-*, half, and *kranion*, the skull.] pain in only one side of the head.

hem′i·cȳ·çle, *n.* [Fr. *hémicycle*; L. *hemicyclus*; Gr. *hēmikyklon* or *hēmikyklion*, a semicircle, a semicircular row of seats, from *hēmikyklos* or *hēmikyklios*, semicircular; *hēmi-*, half, and *kyklos*, a circle.]

1. a half-circle; a semicircle.
2. a semicircular arena; a semicircular room or division of a room.

hem·i·çyç′liç, *a.* in botany, designating or of flowers which have the separate portions of the inflorescence arranged in spirals.

hem·i·daç′tyl, hem·i·daç′tyle, *n.* [*hemi-*, and Gr. *daktylos*, a finger.] a flat-toed lizard or gecko of the genus *Hemidactylus*.

Hem·i·daç′tyl·us, *n.* a genus of lizards belonging to the gecko family or flat-toed lizards, which have an oval disk at the base of the toes.

hem″i·dem·i·sem′i·quā·vẽr, *n.* [*hemi-*, and *demi-*, half, and *semi-*, half, and *quaver*.] in music, a sixty-fourth note.

hem·i·dī′tōne, *n.* [*hemi-*, and Gr. *ditonos*, of two tones; *dis*, twice, and *tonos*, a tone.] in Greek music, a minor third.

hem·i·dō·mat′iç, *a.* of or resembling a hemidome.

hem′i·dōme, *n.* in crystallography, a dome parallel to the orthodiagonal: distinguished from *clinodome*.

hem·i·el′y·trum, hem·i·el′y·tron, *n.* same as *hemelytron*.

hem″i·en·ce·phal′iç, *a.* of or pertaining to the hemiencephalon.

hem″i·en·ceph′ȧ·lon, *n.*; *pl.* **hem″i·en·ceph′ȧ·lȧ,** [*hemi-*, and Gr. *enkephalos*, the brain.] in anatomy, a lateral half of the brain.

hē·mig′ȧ·mous, *a.* [*hemi-*, and Gr. *gamos*, marriage.] in botany, having one of the two florets in the same spikelet neuter, and the other unisexual, whether male or female: said of grasses.

hem′i·glyph, *n.* [*hemi-*, and Gr. *glyphē*, a carving.] in architecture, a half channel at the edge of the triglyph tablet in the Doric entablature.

hē·mig′nȧ·thous, *a.* [*hemi-*, and Gr. *gnathos*, jaw.] in ornithology, having one mandible of the beak considerably shorter than the other.

hem·i·hē′drăl, *a.* in crystallography, having only half the number of planes belonging to any particular modification which the law of symmetry requires: said of a crystal.

hem·i·hē′drăl·ly, *adv.* in a hemihedral manner.

hem·i·hē′driç, *a.* hemihedral. [Rare.]

hem·i·hē′drism, *n.* in crystallography, the property or quality of crystallizing in hemihedral forms.

hem·i·hē′dron, *n.* [*hemi-*, and Gr. *hedra*, a seat, base.] in crystallography, a crystal or other solid with but half the proper number of planes, as the tetrahedron.

hem·i·hol·ō·hē′drăl, *a.* [*hemi-*, and Gr. *holos*, whole, and *hedra*, a seat, base.] in crystallography, having half the full number of planes in all the octants.

hem·i·hȳ′drāte, *n.* a hydrate containing half as many molecules of water as of the substance combined with the water.

hem″i·mel·lit′iç, *a.* [*hemi-*, and Gr. *meli*, honey, and *lithos*, stone.] in chemistry, having half the number of carboxyl radicals contained in mellitic acid.

Hem″i·mē·tab′ō·lȧ, *n.pl.* [*hemi-*, and Gr. *metabolē*, a change.] in zoology, those insects which undergo an incomplete metamorphosis.

hem″i·met·ȧ·bol′iç, *a.* in zoology, of or belonging to insects undergoing only an incomplete metamorphosis.

hem·i·mor′phiç, *a.* [*hemi-*, and Gr. *morphē*, form.] in crystallography, designating a crystal with unlike planes at the ends of the same axis.

hem·i·mor′phism, *n.* the property of being hemimorphic.

hem·i·mor′phīte, *n.* calamine: so called because the crystals exhibit hemimorphic characteristics.

hē′min, *n.* [from Gr. *haima*, blood; and *-in*.] a brown, crystalline chloride of heme obtained when blood is treated with hydrochloric acid or glacial acetic acid and sodium chloride: its production by this reaction is evidence of the presence of blood in fluids, stains, etc.

hē·mī′nȧ, *n.*; *pl.* **hē·mī′nae,** [L., from Gr. *hēmina*, a Sicilian measure, from *hēmi-*, *hēmisys*, half.]

1. in ancient Rome, a measure containing half a sextary, or about half a pint English wine measure.
2. in medicine, a former liquid measure.

hē·mī′ō·nus, *n.* same as *dziggetai*.

hem·i·op′si·ȧ, hem·i·op′sy, *n.* same as *hemianopsia*.

hem·i·or′thō·tȳpe, *a.* same as *monoclinic*.

hem·i·pep′tōne, *n.* [*hemi-*, and Gr. *peptikos*, pertaining to digestion, from *peptein*, to cook, digest.] an intermediate compound of peptone, formed before peptone is finally produced, by the gastric and pancreatic juices.

hem·i·plē′ġi·ȧ, *n.* [Mod. L.; after Gr. *hēmiplēx*, *hēmiplēgēs*, stricken on one side; *hēmi-*, half, and *plēssein*, to strike.] paralysis of one side of the body.

hem·i·pleg′iç, *a.* of or having hemiplegia.

hem·i·pleg′iç, *n.* one who has hemiplegia.

hem′i·pod, *a.* [Gr. *hēmipous* (*-podos*), half-footed; *hēmi-*, half, and *pous*, *podos*, foot.] of or pertaining to any bird of the genus *Turnix*.

hem′i·pod, *n.* a hemipod bird.

hem′i·prism, *n.* [*hemi-*, and Gr. *prisma*, a prism.] in crystallography, a prism in the triclinic system of crystallization including only two parallel planes.

hem·i·pris·mat′iç, *a.* pertaining to a hemiprism.

hem·i·prō′tē·in, *n.* [*hemi-*, and *protein*.] in chemistry, a substance supposed to be identical with antialbumid and dyspeptone. It is formed by the heating action of dilute sulfuric acid on albumin.

hē·mip′tẽr, *n.* one of the *Hemiptera*.

Hē·mip′te·rȧ, *n.pl.* [*hemi-*, and Gr. *pteron*, a wing.] a large order of insects, including bedbugs, water bugs, lice, aphids, etc., with piercing and sucking mouth parts: they generally have two pairs of wings, the outer pair thickened toward the base.

hē·mip′tẽr·ăl, *a.* hemipterous.

hē·mip′tẽr·ăn, *n.* one of the *Hemiptera*.

hē·mip′tẽr·ăn, *a.* relating to the *Hemiptera*.

hē·mip′tẽr·ist, *n.* one who makes a collection of or studies the *Hemiptera*.

hē·mip′tẽr·ŏn, *n.* a hemipteran.

hē·mip′tẽr·ous, *a.* of or belonging to the *Hemiptera*.

hem·i·pyr′ȧ·mid, *n.* [*hemi-*, and Gr. *pyramis* (*-idos*), a pyramid.] in crystallography, a pyramid in the monoclinic system of crystallization, including only four parallel planes.

hem″i·py·ram′i·dăl, *a.* pertaining to a hemipyramid.

hem′i·seçt, *v.t.*; hemisected, *pt.*, *pp.*; hemisecting, *ppr.* [*hemi-*, and L. *sectus*, pp. of *sectare*, to cut.] in anatomy, to bisect; to divide into equal right and left parts, or along the mesial plane.

hem·i·seç′tion, *n.* in anatomy, bisection; division into equal right and left parts, or along the mesial plane; also, one of such divisions.

hem′i·spasm, *n.* [*hemi-*, and Gr. *spasmos*, a spasm.] a spasm affecting only one side of the body.

hem′i·sphēre, *n.* [L. *hemisphærium*; Gr. *hēmisphairon*, a hemisphere; *hēmi-*, half, and *sphaira*, a sphere.]

1. half of a sphere or globe; specifically, (a) any of the halves into which the celestial globe is divided by either the celestial equator or the ecliptic; (b) any of the halves of the earth: the earth is divided by the equator into the Northern and Southern Hemispheres and by a meridian into the Eastern Hemisphere (containing Europe, Asia, Africa, and Australia) and the Western Hemisphere (containing the Americas and Oceania); (c) a model or map of any of these halves.
2. the countries and peoples of any of the earth's hemispheres.
3. a sphere of action, knowledge, etc.
4. either lateral half of the cerebrum or cerebellum.

Magdeburg hemispheres; a device consisting of two hemispherical metal cups fitting closely together so as to form a hollow sphere from which, by means of an air pump, the air is exhausted. The instrument was invented by Otto von Guericke at Magdeburg, for the purpose of illustrating by experiment the pressure of the air.

hem·i·spher′iç, *a.* hemispherical.

hem·i·spher′iç·ăl, *a.* pertaining to or formed like a hemisphere; as, a ***hemispherical*** body.

hem·i·sphē′roid, *n.* a half of a spheroid.

hem″i·sphē·roid′ăl, *a.* having the form of a hemispheroid.

hem·i·spher′ūle, *n.* a half-spherule.

hem′i·stich, *n.* [L. *hemistichium*; Gr. *hēmistichion*, a half line; *hēmi-*, half, and *stichos*, a row, line, verse.]

1. half a line of verse, especially the half preceding or following the chief caesura, or rhythmic pause in the middle of a line.
2. an incomplete line of poetry or one shorter than the metrical pattern calls for.

hē·mis′ti·chăl, *a.* pertaining to or made up of hemistichs; as, a ***hemistichal*** division of a verse.

hem·i·sym′me·try, *n.* [*hemi-*, and Gr. *symmetria*, symmetry.] same as ***hemihedrism***.

hem·i·sys′tō·lē, *n.* [*hemi-*, and Gr. *systolē*, a drawing together.] a peculiar kind of irregular action of the heart muscle, in which, with every two beats of the heart, only one beat of the pulse is felt.

hem·i·tẽr′pēne, *n.* [*hemi-*, and *terpene*.] any of a group of isomeric hydrocarbons with the general formula C_5H_8.

hem′i·tōne, *n.* [L. *hemitonium*; Gr. *hēmitonion*, a half tone; *hēmi-*, half, and *tonos*, a tone.] in music, same as *semitone*.

hē·mit′rō·păl, *a.* same as *hemitropous.*

hem′i·trōpe, *a.* [*hemi-*, and Gr. *tropē*, a turning, from *trepein*, to turn.] half-turned; specifically, in mineralogy, designating a crystal formed of two other crystals joined so that corresponding faces are directly opposed.

hem′i·trōpe, *n.* 1. anything hemitropous in structure.
2. in crystallography, a hemitrope crystal.

hem·i·trop′iç, *a.* same as *hemitrope.*

hē·mit′rō·pous, *a.* [*hemi-*, and Gr. *tropē*, a turning, from *trepein*, to turn.]
1. turned half round; half-inverted.
2. in botany, designating an ovule in which the axis of the nucleus is more curved than in an anatropous ovule.

HEMITROPOUS OVULE

hē·mit′rō·py, *n.* the quality or state of being hemitrope.

hem′i·tȳpe, *n.* [*hemi-*, and Gr. *typos*, an impression.] that which is hemitypic, or only partly typical of a given group.

hem·i·typ′iç, *a.* in zoology, only partially typical of a given group, because partaking of the characteristics of some other group.

hem′līne, *n.* 1. the bottom edge, usually hemmed, of a dress, skirt, coat, etc.
2. the height of this edge above the ground.

hem′lock, *n.* [ME. *hemlok*; AS. *hemlic*, *hymelic*, hemlock.]
1. any of a group of poisonous weeds of the carrot family, with small, white flowers and finely divided leaves, especially *Conium maculatum* and species of *Cicuta*. Conium, a powerful sedative, is extracted from hemlock.
2. a poison made from such a weed.
3. any of a group of North American and Asiatic evergreen trees of the pine family, with drooping branches and short, flattened needles: the bark is used in tanning.
4. the wood of the hemlock tree.

HEMLOCK (*Conium maculatum*)

hem′lock pärs′ley, a plant belonging to the genus *Conioselinum*. It resembles hemlock, but is not poisonous.

hem′lock sprūce, same as *hemlock*, sense 3.

hem′mel, *n.* same as *hemble.*

hem′mẽr, *n.* one who or that which hems; specifically, an attachment to a sewing machine for making a hem.

hem′ming, *n.* 1. the act or process of making a hem.
2. the stitching that secures a hem; also, a hem or hems collectively.

hē′mō-, hae′mō- (*or* hem′ō), [from Gr. *haima*, blood.] a combining form meaning *blood*, as in *hemo*globin: also *hem-*, *hema-*.

hē·mō·çhrō′mō·ġen, hae·mō·çhrō′mō·ġen, *n.* [*hemo-*, and Gr. *chrōma*, color, and *-gen.*] any compound of heme with various proteins and other substances.

hē″mō·çhrō·mom′e·tẽr, hae″mō·çhrō·mom′e·tẽr, *n.* [*hemo-*, and Gr. *chrōma*, color, and *metron*, a measure.] an apparatus used in determining the quantity of hemoglobin in fluids.

hē·mō·cȳ′ȧ·nin, hae·mō·cȳ′ȧ·nin, *n.* [*hemo-*, and Gr. *kyanos*, blue, and *-in.*] a coloring matter containing copper, found in the blood of certain invertebrates.

hē″mō·cȳ·tol′y·sis, hae″mō·cȳ·tol′y·sis, *n.* [*hemo-*, and Gr. *kytos*, a hollow vessel, and *lyein*, to loose.] in pathology, dissolution of the blood corpuscles.

hē″mō·cȳ·tō·tryp′sis, hae″mō·cȳ·tō·tryp′sis, *n.* [*hemo-*, and Gr. *kytos*, a hollow vessel, and *tribein*, to rub.] in pathology, a breaking up of the corpuscles of the blood due to pressure.

hē·mō·drom′e·tẽr, hae·mō·drom′e·tẽr, *n.* [*hemo-*, and Gr. *dromos*, a running, course, and *metron*, a measure.] an instrument to measure the velocity of the arterial flow of blood.

hē·mō·drom′ō·grȧph, hae·mō·drom′ō·grȧph, *n.* [*hemo-*, and Gr. *dromos*, a running, a course, and *graphein*, to write.] an instrument that registers automatically the velocity of the blood.

hē·mō·drō·mom′e·tẽr, hae·mō·drō·mom′e·tẽr, *n.* same as *hemodrometer.*

hē·mō·flaġ′el·lāte, hae·mō·flaġ′el·lāte, *n.* any flagellate protozoan parasite in the blood stream.

hē·mō·gas′triç, hae·mō·gas′triç, *a.* [*hemo-*, and Gr. *gastēr*, belly.] relating to the blood and the stomach.

hē·mō·glō′bin, hae·mō·glō′bin (*or* hē′mō·glō-), *n.* [shortened (after *hemo-*) from earlier *haematoglobulin.*] the red coloring matter of the red blood corpuscles, a protein yielding heme and globin on hydrolysis: it carries oxygen from the lungs to the tissues, and carbon dioxide from the tissues to the lungs.

hē·mō·glō·bi·nē′mi·ȧ, hae·mō·glō·bi·nē′mi·ȧ, *n.* [*hemo-*, and L. *globus*, a ball, and Gr. *haima*, blood.] in pathology, a condition in which the hemoglobin is dissolved out of the blood corpuscles and is held in solution in the serum.

hē·mō·glō·bi·nif′ẽr·ous, hae·mō·glō·bi·nif′ẽr·ous, *a.* containing hemoglobin.

hē·mō·glō·bi·nom′e·tẽr, hae·mō·glō·bi·nom′e·tẽr, *n.* [*hemo-*, and L. *globus*, a ball, and *metrum*, a measure.] an instrument for measuring the amount of hemoglobin in the blood; a hemochromometer.

hē·mō·glō·bi·nū′ri·ȧ, hae·mō·glō·bi·nū′ri·ȧ, *n.* [*hemo-*, and L. *globus*, a ball, and Gr. *ouron*, urine.] in pathology, the presence of hemoglobin in the urine, due either to its solution out of the red corpuscles or to disintegration of the red corpuscles.

hē·mō·glob′ū·lin, hae·mō·glob′ū·lin, *n.* same as *hemoglobin.*

hē′moid, hae′moid, *a.* [*hem-*, and *-oid.*] like blood.

hē·mō·leū′çō·cȳte, hae·mō·leū′çō·cȳte, *n.* [*hemo-*, and *leucocyte.*] a white blood corpuscle.

hē·mō·leū′kō·cȳte, hae·mō·leū′kō·cȳte, *n.* same as *hemoleucocyte.*

hē′mō·lymph, hae′mō·lymph, *n.* [*hemo-*, and L. *lympha*, a spring, pure water.] the nutritive fluid, similar to blood or lymph, of some invertebrates.

hē″mō·lym·phat′iç, hae″mō·lym·phat′iç, *a.* pertaining to hemolymph.

hē·mō·lȳ′sin, hae·mō·lȳ′sin, *n.* [from *hemo-*, and Gr. *lysis*, a dissolving; and *-in.*] a substance in the blood serum that causes the destruction of red corpuscles with liberation of hemoglobin into the surrounding fluid: it is sometimes produced by injecting red corpuscles from another individual of the wrong blood group.

hē·mol′y·sis, *n.* [*hemo-*, and *-lysis.*] the destruction of the red corpuscles with liberation of hemoglobin into the surrounding fluid, caused by the presence of hemolysins.

hē·mō·lyt′iç, hae·mō·lyt′iç, *a.* [*hemo-*, and Gr. *lytikos*, destructive, from *lyein*, to loosen.] of, causing, or characterized by hemolysis.

hē′mō·phīle, hae′mō·phīle, *n.* 1. a hemophiliac.
2. a bacterium that grows well in any medium containing hemoglobin.

hē·mō·phil′i·ȧ, hae·mō·phil′i·ȧ, *n.* [*hemo-*, and Gr. *philos*, loving.] a hereditary condition in which the blood fails to clot quickly enough, causing prolonged, uncontrollable bleeding from even the smallest cut: it occurs in males and is transmitted by females.

hē·mō·phil′i·aç, hae·mō·phil′i·aç, *n.* one who has hemophilia.

hē·mō·phil′iç, hae·mō·phil′iç, *a.* 1. of or having hemophilia.
2. growing well in a medium containing hemoglobin: said of certain bacteria.

hē·mop′ty·sis, hae·mop′ty·sis, *n.* [*hemo-*, and Gr. *ptysis*, a spitting, from *ptyein*, to spit.] the spitting of blood from the larynx, trachea, bronchi, or lungs.

hem′or·rhăġe, haem′or·rhăġe, *n.* [L. *hæmorrhagia*; Gr. *haimorrhagia*, a violent bleeding, from *haimorrhagēs*, bleeding violently; *haima*, blood, and *rhēgynai*, to break, burst.] the escape of blood from its vessels; bleeding; especially, heavy bleeding.

hem·or·rhaġ′iç, *a.* of or characterized by hemorrhage.

hem′or·rhoid, haem′or·rhoid (-roid), *n.* [Fr. pl. *hemorrhoides*; L. *haemorrhoidae*; Gr. *haimorrhoides* (*phlebes*), (veins) discharging blood, from *haimorrhoos*, flowing with blood, from *haima*, blood, and *rhein*, to flow.] [*usually in pl.*] a painful swelling or tumor of a vein in the region of the anus, often with bleeding: also called, in the plural, *piles.*

hem·or·rhoid′ăl, haem·or·rhoid′ăl, *a.* pertaining to or affected with hemorrhoids; as, *hemorrhoidal* veins.

hem″or·rhoid·eç′tō·my, haem″or·rhoid·eç′tō·my, *n.* the surgical removal of hemorrhoids.

hē′mō·sçōpe, hae′mō·sçōpe, *n.* [*hemo-*, and Gr. *skopein*, to view.] an instrument used in the spectroscopic examination of the blood, by means of which the thickness of the layer of blood can be regulated: also written *hematoscope.*

hē·mō·spas′tiç, hae·mō·spas′tiç, *a.* [*hemo-*, and Gr. *spān*, to draw.] tending to draw the blood to a part; as, a *hemospastic* agent.

hē·mō·spas′tiç, hae·mō·spas′tiç, *n.* that which draws the blood to a part, as a cupping glass.

hē·mos′tȧ·sis, hae·mos′tȧ·sis, *n.* [Mod. L.; see *hemo-* and *-stasis.*]
1. the stoppage of bleeding.
2. the stoppage of the flow of blood in a vein or artery, as with a tourniquet.
3. stagnation of the blood.

hē′mō·stat, hae′mō·stat, *n.* [from *hemostatic.*] anything used to stop bleeding; specifically, a clamplike instrument used in surgery or a chemical applied to a surface wound.

hē·mō·stat′iç, hae·mō·stat′iç, *a.* [see *hemo-* and *static.*]
1. capable of stopping the flow of blood; styptic.
2. pertaining to stagnation of the blood.

hē·mō·stat′iç, hae·mō·stat′iç, *n.* same as *hemostat.*

hē·mō·stat′içs, hae·mō·stat′içs, *n.* the hydrostatics of the circulatory system.

hē·mō·thō′rax, hae·mō·thō′rax, *n.* same as *hematothorax.*

hē·mō·tox′iç, hae·mō·tox′iç, *a.* of or having to do with a hemotoxin.

hē′mō·tox·in, hae′mō·tox·in, *n.* a toxin capable of destroying erythrocytes.

hemp, *n.* [ME. *hemp*; AS. *henep*, hemp.]
1. a tall Asiatic plant of the genus *Cannabis*, of which *Cannabis sativa* is the only known species. It is an annual herbaceous plant, the fiber of which constitutes the hemp of commerce.
2. the fiber, used to make rope, sailcloth, etc.
3. a drug, especially hashish, made from the flowers and leaves of this plant.
4. any one of various fibers resembling true hemp.
bastard hemp; *Datisca cannabina*, a plant found in western Asia.
Bengal or *Bombay hemp*; *Crotalaria juncea*, an East Indian shrub: also called *sunn.*
Canada hemp; a species of dogbane, *Apocynum cannabinum*: also called *Indian hemp.*
Madras hemp; same as *sunn.*
sisal hemp; see *sisal.*
sunn hemp; see *sunn.*
water hemp; *Acnida cannabina*, a weed of the amaranth family, growing near the eastern coast of the United States.

HEMP (*Cannabis sativa*)

hemp ag′ri·mō·ny, *Eupatorium cannabinum*, a European plant of the aster family, having reddish flowers.

hemp′bush, *n.* *Plagianthus pulchellus*, a plant of the mallow family, growing in Australia and yielding a tough fiber.

hemp′en, *a.* of, like, or made of hemp; as, a *hempen* cord.

hemp net′tle, any plant of the genus *Galeopsis*, belonging to the mint family; especially, a common prickly weed of the United States.

hemp′seed, *n.* the seed of the hemp.

hemp′weed, *n.* 1. the hemp agrimony.
2. seaweed; kelp. [Brit. Dial.]
climbing hempweed; *Mikania scandens*, an American climbing plant of the aster family.

hemp′y, *a.* like hemp.

hem′stitch, *n.* the decorative heading of the inner edge of a hem made by drawing out a few threads running parallel to the hem, and fastening the cross threads by successive stitches.

HEMSTITCH

hem′stitch, *v.t.*; hemstitched (-sticht), *pt.*, *pp.*; hemstitching, *ppr.* to put a hemstitch or hemstitches on.

hen, *n.* [ME. *hen*; AS. *henn*, *hænn*, a hen.]
1. the female of the chicken, or domestic fowl: the male is called a rooster, or cock.
2. the female of various other birds or of certain other animals, as the lobster.
3. a woman. [Slang.]

hen and chick′enṣ, any of various plants with many offshoots, as the houseleek.

hen′bāne, *n.* a coarse, hairy, foul-smelling plant, *Hyoscyamus niger*, of the nightshade family, poisonous to animals, especially fowls: it is used in medicine as a narcotic: also called *hyoscyamus.*

HENBANE (*Hyoscyamus niger*)

hen′bit, *n.* [*hen*, and *bit* (small piece).]
  1. *Lamium amplexicaule*, a labiate weed, the dead nettle.
  2. *Veronica hederæfolia*, the ivy-leaved speedwell.

hence, *adv.* [ME. *hens*, contr. of *hennes*, this, with adverbial genit. *-es*, from AS. *heonan, heona*, hence.]
  1. from this place; away.
  Early to-morrow will we rise, and *hence.* —Shak.
  2. from this time; after now; in the future; as, a year *hence.*
  3. from this life; as, departed *hence.*
  4. as a result; therefore; from this cause or reason, noting a consequence, inference, or deduction.
  Hence different passions more or less inflame,
  As strong or weak, the organs of the frame. —Pope.
  5. from this source or origin.
  All other faces borrowed *hence*
  Their light and grace. —Suckling.

hence, *interj.* depart! go away! get out! *hence with*! away with! take away!

hence, *v.t.* and *v.i.* to send or go away. [Obs.]

hence·fōrth′ (*or* hens′), *adv.* [ME. *hensforth, hennes forth*; AS. *heonan forth*, henceforth.] from this time forward; from now on.
  I never from thy side *henceforth* will stray. —Milton.

hence·fọr′wărd, *adv.* from this time forward; henceforth.

hence·fọr′wărdṣ, *adv.* henceforward. [Obs.]

hench′boy, *n.* a page; a servant. [Obs.]

hench′măn, *n.*; *pl.* **hench′men,** [ME. *hencheman, henshman*, a groom, attendant, from AS. *hengest, hengst*, a horse, and *man*, a man.]
  1. originally, a male attendant; page or squire.
  2. a trusted helper or follower.
  3. a political supporter who works for his own advantage.

hen çlam, 1. same as *surf clam.*
  2. a clam of the genus *Pachyderma*, found on the western coast of the United States.

hen′çọop, *n.* a coop or pen for poultry.

hend, *v.t.* to seize; to lay hold on. [Archaic.]

hend, *a.* 1. clever; handy. [Obs.]
  2. polite; courteous; gentle. [Obs.]
  3. nigh; near at hand; convenient. [Obs.]

hen′deç·ȧ-, [from Gr. *hendeka*, eleven, from *hen*, neut. of *heis*, one, and *deka*, ten.] a combining form meaning *eleven*, as in *hendecahedron, hendecandrous.*

hen·deç·ȧ·çol′iç, *a.* [L.Gr. *hendekakōlos*, of eleven cola; Gr. *hendeka*, eleven, and *kōlon*, a member.] in Greek and Latin prosody, consisting of eleven series or cola; as, a *hendecacolic* period.

hen·deç′ȧ·gon, *n.* [*hendeca-*, and Gr. *gōnia*, an angle.] in geometry, a plane figure of eleven sides and as many angles: written also *endecagon.*

hen·deç·ag′ō·năl, *a.* pertaining to a hendecagon: written also *endecagonal.*

hen·de·çaġ′y·nous, *a.* [*hendeca-*, and Gr. *gynē*, a female.] in botany, having eleven pistils.

hen·deç·ȧ·hē′drăl, *a.* of, or having the form of, a hendecahedron.

hen·deç·ȧ·hē′drŏn, *n.*; *pl.* **hen·deç·ȧ·hē′drŏnṣ, hen·deç·ȧ·hē′drȧ,** [Mod. L.; see *hendeca-* and *-hedron.*] a solid figure with eleven plane surfaces.

hen·dē·çan′drous, *a.* [*hendeca-*, and Gr. *anēr, andros*, a man, a male.] in botany, having eleven stamens.

hen′dē·çāne, *n.* [Gr. *hendeka*, eleven, and *-ane.*] one of the hydrocarbons of the paraffin series, $C_{11}H_{24}$: also written *endecane.*

hen·deç·ȧ·phyl′lous, *a.* in botany, having eleven leaflets: also written *endecaphyllous.*

hen·deç″a·syl·lab′iç, *n.* same as *hendecasyllable.*

hen·deç″ȧ·syl·lab′iç, *a.* pertaining to a hendecasyllable.

hen·deç·ȧ·syl′lȧ·ble, *n.* [Gr. *hendekasyllabos*, eleven-syllabled; *hendeka*, eleven, and *syllabē*, a syllable.] a line of verse having eleven syllables.

hen·deç·ȧ·tō′iç, *a.* [Gr. *hendeka*, eleven.] in chemistry, pertaining to or derived from hendecane; undecylic; as, *hendecatoic* acid.

hen·dī′ȧ·dys, *n.* [Gr. *hen dia dyoin*, one by two; *hen*, neut. of *heis*, one, and *dia*, through, by, and *dyoin*, genit. dual of *dyo*, two.] in rhetoric, a figure of speech in which two nouns connected by *and* are used instead of one noun or a noun and an adjective; as, *deceit and words* for *deceitful words.*

hen′dy, *a.* hend. [Obs.]

hen′ē·quen (-ken), **hen′ē·quin** (-kin), *n.* [Sp. *henequén, jeniquen*, from native (Taino) name in Yucatan.]
  1. fiber obtained from a Central American plant; sisal hemp: it is used for making rope, coarse cloth, etc.
  2. this plant, a kind of agave.

hen′fish, *n.* the sea bream.

hen har′ri·ẽr, a species of hawk of the genus *Circus*; especially, *Circus cyaneus*: so named from its preying on poultry.

hen hawk, any one of certain species of hawks which make poultry their prey, as *Circus cyaneus*, the hen harrier.

hen′-heärt″ed, *a.* having a heart like that of a hen; timid; cowardly; dastardly.

hen′house, *n.*; *pl.* **hen′houṣ·eṣ,** a shelter for poultry.

hen′huṣ″ṣy, *n.* a man who officiously interferes in women's affairs; a cotquean.

hen′i·quen (-ken), *n.* same as *henequen.*

hen′iṣm, *n.* in philosophy, the doctrine that everything is reducible to a single form or principle.

hen louse, a louse attacking poultry or any domesticated bird.

hen mōld, a kind of black spongy soil. [Brit. Dial.]

hen′nȧ, *n.* [Ar. *ḥinnā′.*]
  1. *Lawsonia inermis*, a shrub bearing opposite entire leaves and numerous small, white, fragrant flowers. It is cultivated extensively in Egypt.
  2. a reddish-orange dye made from the leaves of the henna plant; a paste made by a mixture of catechu and powdered henna leaves, used in the East for staining and dyeing fingers and nails, and in the U. S. for tinting the hair auburn.
  3. the color of henna, a reddish brown.

HENNA PLANT (*Lawsonia inermis*)

hen′nȧ, *a.* reddish-brown.

hen′nȧ, *v.t.*; hennaed, *pt., pp.*; hennaing, *ppr.* to tint with henna.

hen′nẽr·y, *n.*; *pl.* **hen′nẽr·ieṣ,** an enclosed place in which fowls are kept or raised.

hen′nes, *adv.* [ME.] hence. [Obs.]

hen′nin, *n.* [OFr.] a headdress worn by French women in the fifteenth century.

hen·ō·ġen′e·sis, hē·noġ′e·ny, *n.* [Gr. *heis, henos*, one, and *genesis*, origin, birth.] same as *ontogeny.*

hen′ō·thē·iṣm, *n.* [Gr. *heis, henos*, one, and *theos*, god.]
  1. a religious doctrine attributing supreme power to one of several divinities in turn.
  2. belief in one god, without denying the existence of others.

hen″ō·thē·is′tiç, *a.* pertaining to henotheism.

hē·not′iç, *a.* [Gr. *henōtikos*, serving to unite, from *henoun*, to unite, from *heis, henos*, one.] reconciling; harmonizing; tending to unite.

hen pär′ty, a party for women only. [Colloq.]

hen′peck, *v.t.*; henpecked, *pt., pp.*; henpecking, *ppr.* to domineer over (one's husband).

hen′pecked, *a.* domineered over by one's wife.

hen plant, *Plantago lanceolata*, a species of plantain, the ribwort; also, *Plantago major*, the common plantain.

Hen·ri·et′tȧ çloth, a fine woolen fabric from which women's dresses are made.

hen′rọost, *n.* a place where domestic fowls roost at night.

hen′ry, *n.*; *pl.* **hen′rieṣ, hen′ryṣ,** [named after Joseph *Henry*, 19th-c. American physicist.] in electricity, the unit by which inductance is measured: it is equal to the inductance of a circuit in which the variation of a current at the rate of one ampere per second induces an electromotive force of one volt.

hen′ṣ′-foot, *n.* an umbelliferous plant, *Caucalis daucoides*, found growing in chalky soils.

hent, *v.t.*; hent, *pt., pp.*; henting, *ppr.* [ME. *henten*; AS. *hentan*, perh. from base of *hand.*] to grasp; to apprehend. [Archaic.]

hent, *n.* a grasping; also, something grasped in the mind; conception; purpose. [Archaic.]

hen′wāre, *n.* same as *badderlocks.*

heṅx′măn, *n.* a henchman. [Obs.]

hē′-ōak′, *n.* same as *beefwood.*

hep, *a.* [perhaps from the drill sergeant's shout (alteration of *step*) marking time for marching troops.] informed; conversant; having knowledge: often with *to*; as, he's *hep to* our trick. [Slang.]

hē′pär, *n.* [Gr. *hēpar*, the liver.]
  1. in homeopathy, calcium sulfide.
  2. in old chemistry, a term applied to any of various compounds of sulfur with the metals, having a brown-red or liver color.

hep′ȧ·rin, *n.* [Gr. *hēpar*, the liver; and *-in.*] a substance found in various body tissues, especially in the liver, injected into the blood to prevent clotting.

hep′at-, same as *hepato-.*

hep·ȧ·tal′ġi·ȧ, *n.* [*hepat-*, and Gr. *algos*, pain.] in pathology, pain affecting the liver.

hep·ȧ·teç′tō·my, *n.* [*hepat-*, and *-ectomy.*] the surgical removal of part or all of the liver.

hē·pat′iç, *a.* [L. *hepaticus*; Gr. *hēpatikos*, of the liver, from *hēpar, hēpatos*, the liver.]
  1. pertaining to or affecting the liver; as, *hepatic* pain.
  2. having the color or shape of the liver.
  3. of the liverworts.
  hepatic air or *gas*; hydrogen sulfide. [Obs.]

hē·pat′iç, *n.* 1. a medicine affecting the liver.
  2. a liverwort.

hē·pat′i·çȧ, *n.* [Mod. L.; see *hepatic*: so named in allusion to its liver-shaped, lobed leaves.]
  1. [H—] a small genus of plants, of the family *Ranunculaceæ*, with three-lobed leaves and small flowers of white, pink, blue, or purple that bloom in the spring.
  2. a plant or flower of this genus.
  3. the common liverwort: a former name.

Hē·pat′i·cae, *n.pl.* a group of cryptogamous plants; the liverworts.

hē·pat′iç·ăl, *a.* hepatic. [Obs.]

hep′ȧ·tīte, *n.* [L. *hepatites*, an unknown precious stone, the liverstone, from Gr. *hēpar, hēpatos*, the liver.] a fetid variety of barite: when heated or rubbed, it exhales a fetid odor, like that of hydrogen sulfide.

hep·ȧ·tī′tis, *n.* [Mod. L.; see *hepato-* and *-itis.*] inflammation of the liver.

hep″ȧ·ti·zā′tion, *n.* 1. in chemistry, the act of impregnating with hydrogen sulfide. [Obs.]
  2. conversion into a substance resembling the liver; as, *hepatization* of the lung.

hep′ȧ·tīze, *v.t.*; hepatized, *pt., pp.*; hepatizing, *ppr.* [Gr. *hēpatizein*, to resemble the liver, from *hēpar, hēpatos*, the liver.]
  1. to impregnate with hydrogen sulfide. [Obs.]
  2. to convert into a substance resembling liver; as, *hepatized* lungs.

hep′ȧ·tō-, [Gr. *hepato-*, from *hēpar, hēpatos*, the liver.] a combining form meaning *the liver*: also, before a vowel, *hepat-*, as in *hepatectomy.*

hē·pat′ō·cēle, *n.* [*hepato-*, and Gr. *kēlē*, tumor.] in pathology, hernia of the liver.

hep″ȧ·tō·cys′tiç, *a.* [*hepato-*, and Gr. *kystis*, the bladder.] in anatomy, pertaining to the liver and gall bladder.

hep″ȧ·tō·gas′triç, *a.* [*hepato-*, and Gr. *gastēr*, the stomach.] in anatomy, pertaining to the liver and stomach.

hep″ȧ·tō·ġen′iç, *a.* [*hepato-*, and Gr. *-genēs*, producing, and *-ic.*] proceeding or produced from the liver.

hep·ȧ·toġ′e·nous, *a.* hepatogenic.

hep·ȧ·tog′rȧ·phy, *n.* [*hepato-*, and Gr. *graphein*, to write.] a description of the liver.

hep″ȧ·tō·li·thī′ȧ·sis, *n.* [*hepato-*, and Gr. *lithi-*

asis, lithiasis, the stone disease, from *lithos*, a stone.] in pathology, a diseased condition characterized by the formation of gallstones in the liver.

hep·ȧ·tol′ō·ġist, *n.* one who studies or specializes in hepatology.

hep·ȧ·tol′ō·ġy, *n.* [*hepato-*, and Gr. *-logia*, from *legein*, to speak.] the branch of medical science dealing with the liver.

hep″ȧ·tō·pañ′crē·ăs, *n.* [*hepato-*, and Gr. *pankreas*, the pancreas.] in zoology, a glandular organ of many invertebrates, usually called the liver.

hep″ȧ·tō·pōr′tăl, *a.* [*hepato-*, and L. *porta*, gate.] in anatomy, relating to the hepatic portal system.

hep″ȧ·tō·rē′năl, *a.* [*hepato-*, and L. *renalis*, pertaining to the kidneys, from *renes*, the kidneys.] in anatomy, pertaining to the liver and the kidneys; as, the *hepatorenal* ligament.

hep″ȧ·tor·rhē′ȧ, hep″ȧ·tor·rhoe′ȧ, *n.* [*hepato-*, and Gr. *rhoia*, a flow, from rhein, to flow.] a diseased flow of bile.

hep·ȧ·tos′cō·py, *n.* [*hepato-*, and Gr. *skopein*, to view.] the practice of divination by inspecting the livers of animals.

hep·ȧ·tot′ō·my, *n.* [*hepato-*, and Gr. *tomē*, a cutting, from *temnein*, to cut.] in surgery, incision into the liver.

hep″ȧ·tō·um·bil′iç·ăl, *a.* [*hepato-*, and L. *umbilicus*, the navel.] relating to the liver and the umbilicus or navel.

hep′çat, *n.* [*hep*, and *cat*, slang for "swing dancer."] a jazz expert or enthusiast. [Slang.]

Hē·phaes′ti·ăn (-fes′), *a.* relating to Hephaestus, the god of fire and metallurgy among the Greeks; hence, relating to metalworking or smithery.

Hē·phaes′tus, *n.* [Gr. *Hēphaistos*.] in Greek mythology, the god of fire and the forge, son of Zeus and Hera: he is identified with the Roman god Vulcan.

Hē·phaïs′tŏs, *n.* same as *Hephaestus*.

hep′pen, *a.* neat; fit; comfortable. [Dial.]

hep′pẽr, *n.* a young salmon; a parr. [Brit. Dial.]

Hep′ple·white, *a.* designating or of a style of furniture designed by George Hepplewhite (?–1786), English cabinetmaker: it is characterized by the use of graceful curves.

hep′tȧ-, [from Gr. *hepta*, seven.] a combining form meaning: (a) *seven*, as in *hepta*gon; (b) in chemistry, *having seven atoms* (or *radicals*) *of a* (specified) *substance*: also, before a vowel, *hept-*.

hep′tȧ·ċhord, *n.* [from Gr. *heptachordos*, seven stringed; *hepta*, seven, and *chordē*, a string, chord.]
1. the interval of a major seventh.
2. a diatonic scale of seven tones.
3. a musical instrument, especially a lyre, with seven strings.

hep·taċh′rō·nous, *a.* [LL. *heptachronus*; Gr. *heptachronos*; *hepta*, seven, and *chronos*, time.] in ancient prosody, heptasemic.

hep·tȧ·col′iç, *a.* [*hepta-*, and Gr. *kōlon*, a limb, member.] in ancient prosody, composed of seven cola or series.

hep′tad, *n.* [Gr. *heptas*, the number seven, from *hepta*, seven.]
1. a series or group of seven.
2. in chemistry, an element or radical with a valence of seven.

hep′tȧ·glot, *n.* [*hepta-*, and Gr. *glōtta*, the tongue, language.] a book in seven languages.

hep′tȧ·glot, *a.* written in seven languages.

hep′tȧ·gon, *n.* [Gr. *heptagōnos*, seven-cornered; *hepta*, seven, and *gōnia*, a corner, an angle.] in geometry, a plane figure with seven sides and seven angles.

hep·tag′ō·năl, *a.* of, or having the form of, a heptagon.

heptagonal numbers; in arithmetic, the numbers 1, 7, 18, 34, etc., the differences of which are an arithmetical progression having a common difference of 5, as the progression 1, 6, 11, 16, etc.

Hep·tȧ·ġyn′i·ȧ, *n.* [*hepta-*, and Gr. *gynē*, a female.] in botany, an order of plants in the Linnaean system of classification, having seven pistils.

hep·tȧ·ġyn′i·ăn, *a.* heptagynous.

hep·taġ′yn·ous, *a.* in botany, having seven pistils.

hep·tȧ·hē′drăl, *a.* of, or having the form of, a heptahedron.

hep·tȧ·hē′drŏn, *n.*; *pl.* **hep·tȧ·hē′drŏnṣ, hep·tȧ·hē′drȧ,** [*hepta-*, and Gr. *hedra*, a seat, base.] in geometry, a solid figure with seven plane surfaces.

hep″tȧ·hex·ȧ·hē′drăl, *a.* [*hepta-*, and Gr. *hex*, six, and *hedra*, a seat, base.] presenting seven ranges of faces one above another, each range containing six faces.

hep·tam′ẽr·ide, *n.* [*hepta-*, and Gr. *meris* (*-idos*), a portion, share, from *meros*, a part.] something consisting of seven parts.

hep·tam′e·rŏn, *n.* [*hepta-*, and Gr. *hēmera*, a day.] a book or treatise containing the transactions of seven days; specifically, [H–], a collection of tales attributed to Queen Margaret of Navarre (1492–1549), in the style of the Decameron of Boccaccio.

hep·tam′ẽr·ous, *a.* [*hepta-*, and Gr. *meros*, a part.] in botany, consisting of seven parts; having its parts in sevens.

hep·tam′e·tẽr, *n.* [*hepta-*, and Gr. *metron*, a measure.] in prosody, a line of verse consisting of seven feet.

hep·tam′e·tẽr, *a.* containing seven metrical feet.

Hep·tan′dri·ȧ, *n.pl.* [*hepta-*, and Gr. *anēr*, *andros*, a male.] in botany, a class of plants in the Linnaean system of classification, having seven stamens.

HEPTANDROUS FLOWER

hep·tan′dri·ăn, *a.* heptandrous.

hep·tan′drous, *a.* having seven stamens.

hep′tāne, *n.* [Gr. *hepta*, seven, and *-ane*.] in chemistry, a liquid hydrocarbon of the paraffin group, contained in petroleum.

hep·tañ′gū·lăr, *a.* [*hepta-*, and L. *angulus*, an angle.] having seven angles.

hep·tȧ·pet′ăl·ous, *a.* [*hepta-*, and Gr. *petalon*, a leaf.] in botany, having seven petals.

hep·taph′yl·lous (*or* -ta-fil′), *a.* [Gr. *heptaphyllos*, seven-leafed; *hepta*, seven, and *phyllon*, a leaf.] in botany, having seven leaves.

hep·tȧ·pod′iç, *a.* in prosody, consisting of or containing seven feet.

hep·tap′ō·dy, *n.* [*hepta-*, and Gr. *pous*, *podos*, a foot.] in prosody, a verse of seven feet; a heptameter.

hep′tärċh, *n.* a ruler of one division of a heptarchy.

hep·tär′ċhiç, *a.* pertaining to a sevenfold government; constituting or consisting of a heptarchy.

hep′tärċh·ist, *n.* same as *heptarch*.

hep′tärċh·y, *n.* [*hepta-*, and Gr. *archē*, a rule, from *archein*, to rule.]
1. (a) a government by seven persons; (b) a state governed by seven persons.
2. a group of seven neighboring or allied kingdoms; as, the *heptarchy* of Anglo-Saxon England (449–828 A. D.), which included the kingdoms of Kent, the South Saxons (Sussex), West Saxons (Wessex), East Saxons (Essex), East Anglia, Mercia, and Northumberland.

hep·tȧ·sē′miç, *a.* [LL. *heptasemos*; Gr. *heptasēmos*; *hepta*, seven, and *sēmeion*, a sign, mark, mora, from *sēma*, a sign.] in ancient prosody, containing seven morae, or units of time; heptachronous.

hep·tȧ·sep′ȧ·lous, *a.* in botany, having seven sepals.

hep·tȧ·spẽr′mous, *a.* [*hepta-*, and Gr. *sperma*, a seed.] in botany, having seven seeds.

hep′tȧ·stiċh, *n.* [*hepta-*, and Gr. *stichos*, a line, verse.] a poem or stanza of seven lines.

hep·tȧ·syl·lab′iç, *a.* [LL. *heptasyllabus*; Gr. *heptasyllabos*; *hepta*, seven, and *syllabē*, a syllable.] in ancient prosody, composed of seven syllables.

Hep′tȧ·teuċh, *n.* [*hepta-*, and Gr. *teuchos*, a tool, a book.] the first seven books of the Old Testament.

hep·tȧ·tom′iç, *a.* same as *heptavalent*.

hep′tȧ·vā·lent, *a.* having a valence of seven; septavalent.

hep′tēne, *n.* same as *heptylene*.

hep′tine (*or* -tēn), *n.* [Gr. *hepta*, seven, and *-ine*.] in chemistry, a hydrocarbon, C_7H_{12}, of the acetylene series.

hep·tō′iç, *a.* [Gr. *hepta*, seven, and *-ic*.] in chemistry, derived from heptane.

hep tree, the hip tree, or dog rose.

hep′tyl, *n.* [*hept-*, and Gr. *hylē*, matter.] in chemistry, the hypothetical radical, C_7H_{15}, of heptane and its derivatives.

hep′tyl·ēne, *n.* [*heptyl* and *-ene*.] in chemistry, a hydrocarbon, C_7H_{14}, of the ethylene series: called also *heptene*.

hep·tyl′iç, *a.* in chemistry, containing or derived from heptyl or heptane.

hẽr, *pron.* [ME. *hire*, *here*, *hure*, genit. and dat. sing.; AS. *hire*, genit. and dat. sing. of *heó*, she.]
1. the possessive form of the personal pronoun *she*, meaning "of, belonging to, or done by her."

She gave also unto *her* husband with her, and he did eat. —Gen. iii. 6.

When used thus, *her* is sometimes called an adjective, or possessive pronominal adjective, agreeing with the following noun. *Her* takes the form *hers* when not followed by the thing possessed.

And what his fortune wanted, *hers* could mend. —Dryden.

2. the objective case of the personal pronoun *she*.

Fear attends *her* not. —Shak.

Her is also used colloquially as a predicate complement with a linking verb (e.g., that's *her*.)

her, *pron.* their. [Obs.]

Hē′rȧ, Hē′rē, *n.* [Gr. *Hēra*; Ionic Gr. *Hērē*, Hera.] in Greek mythology, the supreme goddess of heaven, the wife and sister of Zeus: identified with *Juno* by the Romans.

Hē·raç′lē·ŏn·īte, *n.* in ecclesiastical history, one of an early sect of heretics belonging to the Gnostics, and followers of Heracleon of Alexandria.

Her′ȧ·klēṣ, Her′ȧ·çlēṣ, *n.* Hercules: the Greek name.

her′ăld, *n.* [ME. *herald*; OFr. *heralt*; LL. *haraldus*, *heraldus*, a herald; from O.H.G. *hari*, *heri*, an army, and *waltan*, to rule.]
1. formerly, any of various officials whose duty it was to proclaim war, to challenge to battle, to proclaim peace, and to bear messages from the commander of an army.
2. a proclaimer; a publisher; a messenger; as, the *herald* of another's fame: often used as the name of a newspaper.
3. a forerunner; a precursor; a harbinger.

It was the lark, the *herald* of the morn. —Shak.

4. in medieval times, an officer whose business was to marshal, order, and conduct royal cavalcades, ceremonies at coronations, royal marriages, installations, creations of dukes and other nobles, etc.
5. in England, an official in charge of genealogies, heraldic arms, etc.
6. *Gonoptera libatrix*, a noctuid moth.
7. *Mergus serrator*, the red-breasted merganser.

Heralds' College; an ancient English royal corporation, first instituted by Richard III in 1483. The heralds, the earl marshal, and the kings-at-arms are among its members. Its chief business is the granting of armorial bearings, or coats of arms, and the tracing and preservation of genealogies. Called also *College of Arms*.

her′ăld, *v.t.*; heralded, *pt.*, *pp.*; heralding, *ppr.* to introduce, as by a herald; to act as herald to; to proclaim; to foretell; to announce; to usher in.

her′ăld çrab, a crab, *Huenia heraldica*, so called because its carapace presents a fanciful resemblance to the shield and mantle design used by heraldic painters in depicting coat armor.

he·ral′diç, *a.* pertaining to heralds or heraldry.

he·ral′diç·ăl·ly, *adv.* in a heraldic manner; according to the rules of heraldry.

her′ăld·ry, *n.*; *pl.* **her′ăld·rieṣ,** [from *herald*.]
1. the art or science having to do with coats of arms, genealogies, etc.
2. the function of a herald (sense 5).
3. (a) a coat of arms or heraldic device; (b) coats of arms collectively; armorial bearings.
4. heraldic ceremony or pomp.

her′ăld·ship, *n.* the office of a herald.

her·ȧ·path′īte, *n.* [after W. B. *Herapath*, 19th-c. Eng. chemist.] a salt obtained by dissolving sulfate of quinine in acetic acid, and then adding an alcoholic solution of iodine. It crystallizes in rhomboidal plates, which have a green, metallic luster and polarize light.

her′ąud, *n.* a herald. [Obs.]

hẽrb (ẽrb *or* hẽrb), *n.* [ME. *herbe*, *erbe*; OFr. *herbe*, *erbe*; L. *herba*, grass, herbage, an herb.]
1. any seed plant whose stem withers away to the ground after each season's growth, as distinguished from a tree or shrub whose woody stem lives from year to year.
2. any such plant used as a medicine, sea-

soning, or food: mint, thyme, basil, and sage are herbs.
3. vegetative growth; grass; herbage.

hẽr·bā'ceous, *a.* [L. *herbaceus*, from *herba*, herb.]
1. of, or having the nature of, an herb or herbs.
2. like a green leaf in texture, color, shape, etc.
3. herbivorous. [Obs.]

hẽrb'āġe (ũrb'), *n.* [Fr. *herbage*, from *herbe*, an herb.]
1. herbs collectively, especially those used as pasturage; grass; pasture.
2. the green foliage and juicy stems of herbs.
3. in law, the liberty or right of pasture in the forest or grounds of another man.

hẽrb'āġed (ũrb'), *a.* covered with grass.

hẽrb'ăl, *n.* 1. formerly, a book containing the names and descriptions of herbs or plants.
2. a collection of specimens of plants, dried and preserved. [Obs.]

hẽrb'ăl, *a.* pertaining to herbs.

hẽrb'ăl·iṣm, *n.* the science of herbs.

hẽrb'ăl·ist, *n.* 1. a person who makes collections of herbs.
2. a dealer in medicinal herbs.
3. originally, a descriptive botanist.

hẽrb'ăr, *n.* arbor. [Obs.]

hẽr·bā'ri·ăn, *n.* a herbalist. [Obs.]

hẽrb'ȧ·rist, *n.* a herbalist. [Obs.]

hẽr·bā'ri·um, *n.*; *pl.* **hẽr·bā'ri·umṣ, hẽr·bā'ri·ȧ,** [LL., from L. *herba*, an herb.]
1. a collection of dried plants systematically arranged for botanical study.
2. a room, building, case, etc. for preserving dried specimens of plants.

hẽrb'ȧ·rīze, *v.t.* to herborize. [Archaic.]

Hẽr·bär'ti·ăn, *a.* of J. F. Herbart (1776–1841), German philosopher, or his philosophy of education.

Hẽr·bär'ti·ăn, *n.* a follower of Herbart or his philosophy.

hẽrb'ȧ·ry, *n.*; *pl.* **hẽrb'ȧ·rieṣ,** a garden of herbs.

hẽrb'bāne, *n.* a kind of European broomrape of the genus *Orobanche*, a parasite on plant roots.

hẽrb Bär'bȧ·rȧ, an American and European plant, *Barbared vulgaris*; winter cress.

hẽrb ben'net, a plant of the rose family, with yellow flowers and an aromatic, astringent root; avens.

hẽrb ċär'pen·tẽr, in botany, the selfheal or heal-all, *Prunella vulgaris*, reputed to heal wounds made by tools: also called *carpenter's-herb*.

hẽrb Ċhris'tō·phẽr, any of various plants as baneberry, royal flowering fern, fleabane, meadowsweet, wood betony, etc.

hẽrb doç'tŏr, a doctor who uses chiefly herbs as remedies. [Dial.]

hẽrb'ẽr, *n.* an arbor. [Obs.]

hẽr'bẽrġ·āġe, *n.* a shelter; harborage. [Obs.]

hẽr'bẽ·ġeōur, *n.* a harbinger. [Obs.]

hẽr'bẽrgh, *n.* a harbor. [Obs.]

hẽr·bes'cent, *a.* [L. *herbescens* (*-entis*), ppr. of *herbescere*, to grow into herbs.] growing into herbs. [Rare.]

hẽrb ēve, same as *herb ivy*.

hẽrb frañk'in·cense, a European umbelliferous plant, the laserwort, *Laserpitium latifolium*, having medicinal properties and an aroma like frankincense.

hẽrb Ġer'ärd, the goutweed, *Ægopodium podagraria*.

hẽrb grāce, herb of grace; rue.

hẽr″bi·cīd'ăl, *a.* of or acting as a herbicide.

hẽr'bi·cīde″, *n.* [from L. *herba*, herb; and *-cide*.] any substance used to destroy plants, especially weeds, or to slow down their growth.

hẽr·biç'ō·lous, *a.* [L. *herba*, an herb, and *colere*, to dwell.] existing on herbaceous plants, as fungi. [Rare.]

hẽr·bif'ẽr·ous, *a.* [L. *herba*, an herb, and *ferre*, to bear.] producing herbs; as, a *herbiferous* region.

Hẽr·biv'ō·rȧ, *n.pl.* [L. *herba*, herb, and *vorare*, to devour.] those animals subsisting on herbs or vegetables; the *Ungulata*.

hẽr'bi·vōre, *n.* a herbivorous animal: opposed to *carnivore*.

hẽr·biv'ō·rous, *a.* [L. *herba*, an herb, and *vorare*, to devour.] subsisting on grass or other plants: opposed to *carnivorous*.

hẽrb ī'vy, in botany, (a) the ground pine; (b) the hartshorn plantain; (c) the swine's-cress.

hẽrb'less, *a.* having no herbage.

hẽrb'let, *n.* a small herb.

hẽrb lil'y, any tropical, American amaryllidaceous plant of the genus *Alstrœmeria*.

hẽrb Lōu·ī'ṣȧ, a South American shrub, *Lippia citriodora*, having lemon-scented flowers and leaves; the lemon verbena.

hẽrb Mär'gȧ·ret, the daisy; marguerite; bruisewort.

hẽrb mas'tiç, either of two medicinal plants; (a) a species of Spanish thyme, *Thymus mastichina*; (b) a germander, *Teucrium marum*: also called *cat thyme*.

hẽrb ŏf grāce, any one of three plants: (a) the common rue, *Ruta graveolens*; (b) the hedge hyssop, *Gratiola officinalis*; (c) the European vervain, *Verbena officinalis*.

hẽrb ŏf rē·pent'ănce, same as *herb of grace*.

hẽr'bō·rist, *n.* [Fr. *herboriste*, from *herboriser*, to herborize, from *herbe*, an herb.] a herbalist.

hẽr″bō·ri·zā'tion, *n.* [from *herborize*.]
1. the act of seeking plants in the field; botanical research.
2. [by confusion with *arborization*.] the figuration of plants in mineral substances.

hẽr'bō·rīze, *v.i.*; herborized, *pt.*, *pp.*; herborising, *ppr.* [Fr. *herboriser*, from *herbe*, herb.] to search for plants, or to seek new species of plants, in order to arrange and classify them.

hẽr·bōse', *a.* same as *herbous*.

hẽrb'ous, *a.* [L. *herbosus*, from *herba*, an herb.] abounding with herbs.

hẽrb Par'is, [ML. *herba paris*: perh. after the Trojan *Paris*.] a plant of the lily family, with a single whorl of leaves below a yellowish-green flower.

hẽrb Rob'ẽrt [ME. *herbe robert*; ML. *herba Roberti*: said to be so named from being used to cure a disease known as *Robert's plague* (after *Robert*, Duke of Normandy).] a small plant of the geranium family, growing wild in rocky, moist places: it has red stems, red-stained leaves, and purplish-rose flowers.

hẽrb Sō·phī'ȧ, hedge mustard.

hẽrb trin'i·ty, in botany, (a) the pansy, *Viola tricolor*, bearing a tricolored flower; (b) the liverleaf, *Anemone hepatica*, having a trilobed leaf.

hẽrb twō'pence (tö'), moneywort.

hẽrb'wom″ăn (-woom″), *n.* a woman who sells herbs.

hẽrb'y (ũrb'), *a.* 1. having the nature of or pertaining to herbs.
2. full of or covered with herbs; grassy.

hẽr·cog'ȧ·mous, *a.* in botany, characterized by or pertaining to hercogamy; nonautogamous.

hẽr·cog'ȧ·my, *n.* [Gr. *herkos*, a fence, wall, and *gamos*, marriage.] prevention of autogamy in flowers by abnormal structural development which bars the pollen from the stigmatic chamber.

hẽr·çū'lē·ăn, *a.* [L. *Herculeus*, of or pertaining to Hercules, from *Hercules*, Hercules.]
1. [H–] of Hercules.
2. very great, difficult, or dangerous; requiring the strength or courage of Hercules to encounter or accomplish; as, a *herculean* labor or task.
3. having extraordinary strength or size; as, *herculean* limbs.

Hẽr'çū·lēṣ, *n.* [L., from Gr. *Hēraklēs*, *Hēraklees*, lit., with Hera's glory, Hercules; *Hēra*, Hera, and *kleos*, glory, renown.]
1. a celebrated hero of Greek and Roman mythology, the offspring of Zeus and Alcmene, daughter of Electryon, king of Mycenae. He performed a number of extraordinary feats of strength, particularly the twelve labors imposed on him by Hera.

HERCULES SLAYING THE HYDRA

2. [h–] any very large, strong man.
3. a constellation in the northern hemisphere, near Lyra.

Hercules hammer; a kind of drop hammer.
Hercules powder; a blasting powder or dynamite containing powerful explosives.

Hẽr'çū·lēṣ bee'tle, a South American lamellicorn beetle, *Dynastes hercules*, the male having two projecting horns, the upper being the longer: the largest true insect known, being about six inches long.

Hẽr'çū·lēṣ'-ċlub, *n.* 1. a West Indian tree of the same genus as the prickly ash.
2. a variety of gourd that grows to a large size.
3. the angelica tree.

Hẽr·cyn'i·ăn, *a.* [L. *Hercynia silva*, Hercynian forest.] pertaining to an extensive forest in ancient Germany, the remains of which are in Swabia and on the Harz Mountains.

hẽr'cy·nīte, *n.* [*hercynian*, and *-ite*, so called from its being found in *Hyrcania silva*, the Roman name of the Bohemian forest.] a vitreous mineral containing alumina and iron; iron spinel.

hẽrd, *n.* [ME. *heerde*, *heorde*; AS. *heord*, a herd, flock, a collection of beasts or persons.]
1. a collection or assemblage of large animals feeding, living, or being driven together; a flock; a drove; as, a *herd* of cattle.
2. the common people; a crowd; a rabble: contemptuous term.

hẽrd, *v.t.* and *v.i.* to form into a herd, group, crowd, etc.

hẽrd, *n.* [ME. *herde*, *hirde*, *hurde*; AS. *hirde*, *hierde*, *hyrde*, a herd, a keeper of cattle.] a herdsman: now only in combination; as, a shep*herd*, a goat*herd*, a swine*herd*.

hẽrd, *v.t.*; herded, *pt.*, *pp.*; herding, *ppr.* to tend or drive as a herdsman.

hẽrd'book, *n.* a register containing the pedigrees of choice breeds of cattle.

hẽrd'ẽr, *n.* a herdsman.

hẽr'dẽr·īte, *n.* [named from its discoverer, Baron von *Herder*.] a whitish, crystalline fluophosphate of beryllium and calcium.

hẽrd'ess, *n.* a shepherdess.

hẽrd'groọm, *n.* a keeper of a herd. [Obs.]

hẽr'diç, *n.* [named after its inventor, Peter *Herdic* (1824–1888), of Pennsylvania.] an American carriage having two or four wheels, cranked axle, low-set body, side seats, and back entrance.

hẽrd'măn, *n.* same as *herdsman*.

hẽrd'ṣ'-grȧss, *n.* any of various grasses which are highly esteemed for hay, particularly redtop and timothy.

hẽrdṣ'măn, *n.*; *pl.* **hẽrdṣ'men,** 1. a keeper of herds; one employed in tending or driving herds of cattle.
2. [H–] the constellation Boötes.

hẽrdṣ'wom″ăn (-woom″), *n.* a woman who tends a herd.

hēre, *n.* hair. [Obs.]

hēre, *pron.* her or hers; also, their. [Obs.]

Hē'rē, *n.* same as *Hera*.

hēre, *adv.* [ME. *here*, *heer*, *her*; AS. *her*, here.]
1. at or in this place: often used as an intensive; as, John *here* is a good player.
2. toward, to, or into this place; hither; as, come *here*.
3. at this point in action, speech, etc.; now.
4. on earth; in earthly life.
Opposed to *there*.
here and there; (a) in one place or point and another; (b) hither and thither.
here below; in this life; on the earth.
here goes! an exclamation expressive of decision on starting some act or course of action that requires courage, etc.
neither here nor there; not in this place nor in that; irrelevant; beside the point.

hēre, *interj.* an exclamation used to call attention, introduce a command, answer a roll call, etc.

hēre, *n.* 1. this place; the place where the speaker or writer is.
2. the present; this life or time.

hēre'ȧ·bout, hēre'ȧ·bouts, *adv.* 1. about or near this place; in this general vicinity.
2. about this subject. [Obs.]

hēre·ȧft'ẽr, *adv.* [ME. *herafter*; AS. *heræfter*; *her*, here, and *æfter*, after.]
1. in time to come; in some future time or state; henceforth; as, *hereafter* you must obey.
2. following this, especially in a writing, book, etc.
3. in the state or life after death.

hēre·ȧft'ẽr, *n.* 1. the future.
2. the state or life after death.

hēre·at', *adv.* 1. at this time; when this occurred.
2. at this; by reason of this; as, he was offended *hereat*.

fāte, fär, fȧst, fạll, finăl, cãre, at; mēte, prẹy, hẽr, met; pīne, marīne, bïrd, pin; nōte, möve, fọr, atŏm, not; mọọn, book;

hēre′ȧ·wāy″, *adv.* in this vicinity; hereabout. [Dial.]

hēre-bē′ing, *n.* present existence.

hēre·bȳ′, *adv.* 1. by or through this; by virtue of this; as, *hereby* we became acquainted.
2. near. [Obs.]

he·rē′dēs̤, *n.* plural of *heres.*

hē·red″i·tȧ·bil′i·ty, *n.* condition of being hereditable.

hē·red′i·tȧ·ble, *a.* [LL. *hereditabilis,* from *hereditare,* to inherit, from L. *hereditas (-atis),* an inheriting, from *heres,* an heir.]
1. that may be inherited; inheritable.
2. entitled to inherit. [Obs.]

hē·red′i·tȧ·bly, *adv.* by inheritance; by right of descent.

her·e·dit′ȧ·ment, *n.* [LL. *hereditamentum,* property inherited, from *hereditare,* to inherit, from *heres,* an heir.] in law, any kind of property that may be inherited; lands, tenements, anything corporeal or incorporeal, real, personal, or mixed, that may descend to an heir.
corporeal hereditament; property that is visible and tangible.
incorporeal hereditament; an ideal right, existing in contemplation of law, issuing out of substantial corporeal property, as a right of way, franchise, water right, rent, etc.

hē″red·i·tā′ri·ăn, *n.* one who believes in the biological doctrine of heredity.

hē·red′i·tā·ri·ly, *adv.* by heredity or inheritance; by descent from an ancestor.

hē·red′i·tā·ri·ness, *n.* the quality of being hereditary.

hē·red′i·tā·ry, *a.* [L. *hereditarius,* relating to an inheritance, from *hereditas (-atis),* an inheritance, from *heres (-edis),* an heir.]
1. (a) of, or passed down by, inheritance from an ancestor to a legal heir; ancestral; (b) having title, etc. by inheritance.
2. of or passed down by heredity; designating or of a characteristic transmitted from generation to generation.
3. being such because of emotional attitudes, etc. passed down from ancestors or predecessors; as, our *hereditary* allies.
Syn.—inherited, ancestral, lineal, patrimonial.

hē·red′i·tist, *n.* a person who believes that heredity, rather than environment, determines one's nature and characteristics.

hē·red′i·ty, *n.* [L. *hereditas (-atis),* heirship, from *heres (-edis),* an heir.]
1. that which descends by inheritance; hereditary succession. [Obs.]
2. the transmission from parent to offspring of certain characteristics; tendency of offspring to resemble parents or ancestors.
3. the characteristics transmitted in this way; as, a person's *heredity.*

Her′e·fŏrd, *n.* one of a breed of good working and beef-producing cattle originating in Herefordshire, England, and having a white face and a red body with white markings.

hēre·from′, *adv.* from this; from the foregoing; as, *herefrom* we deduce the conclusion.

hēre·in′, *adv.* 1. in here; in or into this place.
2. in this writing, container, etc.
3. in this matter, detail, etc.

hēre·in·ȧft′ẽr, *adv.* in the part following this part.

hēre″in·bē·fōre′, *adv.* in the part preceding this part.

hēre·in′tö, *adv.* 1. into this place.
2. into this matter, condition, etc.

hẽr′e·mit, hẽr′e·mite, *n.* a hermit. [Obs.]

hẽr·e·mit′iç·ăl, *a.* eremitical. [Obs.]

hēre·of′, *adv.* 1. of this.
2. concerning this.
3. from this; hence. [Archaic.]

hēre·on′, *adv.* on this; hereupon.

hēre·out′, *adv.* out of this place. [Obs.]

hē′rēs̤, *n.*; *pl.* **he·rē′dēs̤,** [L.] in law, an heir: also spelled *haeres.*

hēre′s̤ here is.

her′e·si·ärch, *n.* [LL. *heresiarcha*; Gr. *hairesiarchēs,* the leader of a school; *hairesis,* a sect or school, and *archein,* to lead.] a leader in heresy; the founder or chief of a sect of heretics.

her·e·si·ärch′y, *n.* heresy. [Rare.]

her·e·si·og′rȧ·phẽr, *n.* [Gr. *hairesis,* heresy, and *graphein,* to write.] one who writes on heresies.

her·e·si·og′rȧ·phy, *n.* a treatise on heresy.

her″e·si·ol′ō·ġist, *n.* one versed in heresiology.

her″e·si·ol′ō·ġy, *n.* [Gr. *hairesis,* heresy, and *-logia,* from *legein,* to speak.] the study of heresies, or their history.

hēre′s̤ tö! here's a toast to! I wish success, joy, etc. to!

her′e·sy, *n.*; *pl.* **her′e·sies̤,** [ME. *heresye*; OFr. *heresie*; L. *hæresis,* a school of thought, either philosophical or religious; Gr. *hairesis,* a taking, selection, school, heresy, from *hairein,* to take.]
1. a doctrine, opinion, or set of opinions or principles at variance with established or generally received views or doctrines, as in politics, morality, philosophy, etc.
Duelling, and similar aberrations of honor, a moral *heresy.* —Coleridge.
2. in theology, a doctrine or belief that is contrary to the fundamental doctrine or creed of any particular church; especially, such a belief specifically denounced by the church and regarded as likely to cause schism.
3. the holding of such a belief or opinion.
Syn.—heterodoxy, false doctrine, schism.

her′e·tiç, *n.* [LL. *hæreticus,* of or belonging to heresy, a heretic, from Gr. *hairetikos,* able to choose, heretical, from *hairein,* to take, (in middle voice) to choose.]
1. one who holds heretical opinions; one who holds to a doctrine or opinion contrary to that which is generally accepted or established.
2. in theology, one who holds to a doctrine or opinion that is contrary to the fundamental doctrine or creed of one's church.
A man that is an *heretic,* after the first and second admonition, reject. —Titus iii. 10.

her′e·tiç, *a.* heretical.

hē·ret′i·çăl, *a.* [ML. *hæriticalis.*]
1. of heresy or heretics.
2. containing, characterized by, or having the nature of, heresy.

hē·ret′i·çăl·ly, *adv.* in a heretical manner; with heresy.

hē·ret′i·çāte, *v.t.* [LL. *hæreticatus,* pp. of *hæreticare,* to make a heretic, charge with heresy, from LL. *hæreticus,* a heretic.] to decide to be heresy; to denounce as heretical.

hē·ret·i·çā′tion, *n.* [LL. *hæreticatio (-onis),* from *hæreticare,* to charge with heresy, from *hæreticus,* a heretic.] the act of deciding as heretical.

hē·ret·i·fi·çā′tion, *n.* heretication. [Rare.]

hēre·tö′, *adv.* hereunto; to this place, time, etc.

her′e·toçh, *n.* see *heretoga.*

hēre·tö·fōre′, *adv.* up to this time; formerly; hitherto.

her′e·tog, *n.* see *heretoga.*

her·e·tō′gȧ, *n.* [AS.] in Anglo-Saxon history, the leader or commander of an army, or the commander of the militia in a district.

hēre·un′dẽr, *adv.* under this; in accordance with this.

hēre·un·tö′, *adv.* unto this or this time; hereto.

hēre·up·on′, *adv.* 1. upon this; by reason of this.
2. immediately following this; at once.

hēre·with′ (*or* -with′), *adv.* 1. along with this.
2. by this method or means.

her′i·ŏt, *n.* [ME. *heriet*; AS. *heregeatu,* military equipment, heriot; *here,* army, and *geatwa,* pl., arms, equipment.] in feudal law, a tribute or fine, as the best beast or other chattel, payable to the lord of the fee on the decease of the owner, landholder, or vassal. Originally the heriot consisted of military furniture, or of horses and arms which went to equip the vassal's successor; in modern use, a customary tribute of goods and chattels to the lord of the fee on the decease of the owner of the land.
heriot custom; a heriot depending solely on usage.
heriot service; a heriot due by reservation in a grant or lease of lands.

her′i·ŏt·ȧ·ble, *a.* subject to the payment of a heriot.

hẽr′is·sŏn, *n.* [OFr. *herisson,* a hedgehog, a herisson, from L. *ericius,* a hedgehog.] in fortification, a beam or bar armed with iron spikes pointed outward, and turning on a pivot, used to block up a passage.

her″it·ȧ·bil′i·ty, *n.* the state or quality of being heritable.

her′it·ȧ·ble, *a.* [OFr. *heritable*; LL. *hereditabilis* from L. *hereditas,* inheritance, from *heres (-edis),* an heir.]
1. capable of inheriting or taking by descent.
By the canon law this son shall be legitimate and *heritable.* —Hale.
2. capable of being inherited; inheritable.
heritable rights; in Scots law, rights of an heir; all rights in or connected with land.

her′it·ȧ·bly, *adv.* by way of inheritance; so as to be capable of transmission by inheritance; as, to convey a property *heritably.*

her′it·ăġe, *n.* [OFr. *heritage,* an inheritance, from *heriter*; LL. *hereditare,* to inherit, from L. *hereditas,* inheritance, from *heres,* an heir.]
1. property that is or can be inherited.
2. (a) something handed down from one's ancestors or the past, as a characteristic, a culture, tradition, etc.; (b) the rights, burdens, or status resulting from being born in a certain time or place; birthright.
3. in the Bible, (a) the chosen people of God; Israelites; (b) the Christian church.
As being lords over God's *heritage.* —1 Pet. v. 3.

her′it·ănce, *n.* inheritance; heritage. [Archaic.]

her′it·ŏr, *n.* [Fr. *heretier*; LL. *heritator,* contr. of *hereditator,* from *hereditare,* to inherit.]
1. an inheritor; heir.
2. in Scottish law, the holder of heritable land in a parish.

hẽrl, *n.* [ME. *herle.*]
1. the barb or barbs of a feather with which an artificial fishing fly is trimmed.
2. a fly trimmed with this.

hẽr′ling, hir′ling, *n.* the sea trout. [Scot.]

hẽr′mȧ, *n.*; *pl.* **hẽr′mae, hẽr′maī,** [L.; Gr. *Hermēs,* Hermes.] in ancient Greece, a square pillar of stone topped by a bust or head of Hermes, used as a milestone, signpost, etc.

Hẽr·mā′iç, *a.* [Gr. *Hermoikos,* of or like Hermes, from *Hermēs,* Hermes.] relating to Hermes.

Hẽr·mā′iç·ăl, *a.* Hermaic.

her·män·dăd′ (er-), *n.* [Sp., a brotherhood, from *hermano,* a brother, from L. *germanus,* one closely related, a brother.] in Spanish history, one of the associations formed chiefly for the purpose of resisting the exactions of the nobles. It afterward was recognized as a regular police organization, which has since been superseded by the national gendarmerie.

hẽr″maph·rō·dē′i·ty, *n.* hermaphroditism. [Obs.]

hẽr·maph′rō·dis̤m, *n.* the quality or condition of a hermaphrodite; hermaphroditism.

hẽr·maph′rō·dīte, *n.* [L. *hermaphroditus*; Gr. *hermaphroditos,* a hermaphrodite, so called from *Hermaphroditos,* Hermaphroditus, in Greek legend the son of *Hermes* and *Aphrodite,* who while bathing became united in one body with the nymph Salmacis.]
1. a bisexual being; a being in which the characteristics of both sexes are either really or apparently combined.
2. in biology, an animal having the parts of generation of both male and female, so that reproduction can take place without the union of two individuals, as certain groups of the inferior worms, mollusks, barnacles, etc.
3. in botany, a flower that contains both the stamen and the pistil, or the male and female organs of generation, within the same floral envelope or on the same receptacle.
4. a hermaphrodite brig.

hẽr·maph′rō·dīte, *a.* same as *hermaphroditic.*

hẽr·maph′rō·dīte brig, a two-masted ship with a square-rigged foremast and a fore-and-aft-rigged mainmast.

hẽr·maph·rō·dit′iç, *a.* of, or having the nature of, a hermaphrodite.

hẽr·maph·rō·dit′iç·ăl, *a.* hermaphroditic.

hẽr·maph·rō·dit′iç·ăl·ly, *adv.* after the manner of a hermaphrodite.

hẽr·maph′rō·dīt·is̤m, *n.* the state or quality of being a hermaphrodite; the partial or complete development of male and female sexual organs in one individual.

hẽr·mē·neū′tiç, *a.* [Gr. *hermēneutikos,* of or for interpreting, from *hermēneutēs,* an interpreter, from *hermēneuein,* to interpret, from *Hermēs,* Hermes.] explanatory; interpretative; unfolding the signification; as, *hermeneutic* theology, or the art of expounding the Scriptures.

hẽr·mē·neū′tiç·ăl·ly, *adv.* according to the acknowledged principles of interpretation.

hẽr·mē·neū′tiçs, *n.* the science of interpretation, or of finding the meaning of an author's words and phrases, and explaining it to others; exegesis: particularly applied to the interpretation of the Scriptures.

hẽr·mē·neū′tist, *n.* one versed in hermeneutics. [Rare.]

Hẽr′mēs̤, *n.* [Gr. *Hermēs,* Hermes, the messenger of the gods.]
1. in Greek mythology, a god who served as herald and messenger of the other gods,

identified by the Romans with Mercury and generally pictured with winged shoes and hat, carrying a caduceus: he was also the god of science, eloquence, and cunning, the protector of boundaries and commerce, and guide of departed souls to Hades.

2. [h–] in ancient Greece, a herma, a statue composed of a head, usually that of the god Hermes, placed on a quadrangular pillar, the height of which corresponded to the stature of the human body. Such statues were placed at the doors of houses, in front of temples, near to tombs, at the corners of streets, on high roads as signposts with distances inscribed upon them, and on the boundaries of lands and states.

Hẽr′mēs̱ Tris·me·ġis′tus, [Gr. *Hermēs trismegistos*, lit., Hermes the thrice greatest.] the Greek name for the Egyptian god Thoth, reputed founder of alchemy and other occult sciences: he was, to some extent, identified with Hermes.

hẽr·met′iç, *a.* [L. *Hermes*, from Gr. *Hermēs*, Hermes, as the inventor of occult sciences.]

1. [*usually* H–] relating to Hermes Trismegistus and his lore.

2. magical; alchemical.

3. [from use in alchemy.] completely sealed by fusion, soldering, etc. so that no gas or air can escape or enter; airtight; as, a *hermetic* seal.

Hermetic art; alchemy; chemistry.

Hermetic books; books of the Egyptians, supposedly written by Hermes Trismegistus, which treat of astrology, of universal principles, of the nature and orders of celestial beings, of medicine, and other topics.

hẽr·met′iç·ăl, *a.* hermetic.

hẽr·met′iç·ăl·ly, *adv.* 1. in a hermetic manner; so as to be airtight; as, a vessel *hermetically* sealed or closed.

2. in accordance with the Hermetic books.

hẽr′mit, *n.* [OFr. *hermite, ermite*; LL. *eremita*; Gr. *erēmitēs*, a hermit, from *erēmia*, a solitude, desert place, from *erēmos*, desolate, solitary.]

1. a person who retires from society and lives in solitude, often from religious motives; a recluse; an anchoret.

2. a spiced cooky made with nuts and raisins.

3. a tropical hummingbird.

4. a beadsman; one bound to pray for another. [Obs.]

hẽr′mit·āġe, *n.* [OFr. *hermitage*, a hermitage, from *hermite*; LL. *eremita*; Gr. *erēmitēs*, a hermit.]

1. the habitation of a hermit; a house or hut in which a hermit dwells.

2. a place where a person can live away from other people; a secluded retreat.

3. [H–] a kind of French wine produced from vineyards along the River Rhone: so named from a little hill near Tain in the department of Drôme, where a hermitage formerly existed.

hẽr′mit·ȧ·ry, *n.* a cell occupied by a hermit, annexed to an abbey. [Rare.]

hẽr′mit bīrd, 1. a South American hummingbird of the genus *Phaëthornis*.

2. a South American bird of the genus *Monasa*; a nun bird.

hẽr′mit çrab, a decapod crustacean of the family *Paguridæ*. These crabs take possession of and occupy the castoff univalve shells of various mollusks, carrying this habitation about with them, and changing it for a larger one as they increase in size.

hẽr′mit çrōw, the chough.

hẽr′mit·ess, *n.* a female hermit.

hẽr·mit′iç, hẽr·mit′i·çăl, *a.* of or fit for a hermit; solitary; secluded.

hẽr′mit thrush, a thrush of North America, with a brown body, spotted breast, and reddish-brown tail: it is shy and secluded in habits.

hẽr′mit wa̤r′blẽr, a warbler, *Dendrœca occidentalis*, of western United States.

hẽr·mō·daç′tyl, *n.* [Gr. *hermodaktylos*, lit., Hermes' finger, a plant; *Hermēs*, Hermes, and *daktylos*, finger.] a bulbous root, supposed to be that of the *Colchicum variegatum*, formerly brought from Turkey and at one time much valued as a cathartic.

Hẽr·mō·ġē′nē·ăn, *a.* pertaining to Hermogenes or the doctrines he taught.

Hẽr·mō·ġē′nē·ăn, *n.* one of a sect of ancient heretics, so called from their leader, Hermogenes, who lived near the close of the second century and who held matter to be the fountain of all evil and souls to be formed of corrupt matter.

Hẽr·mō·ġē′ni·ăn, *a.* 1. hermogenean.

2. pertaining to Hermogenianus, a Roman jurist and writer who lived in the fourth century; as, the Gregorian and *Hermogenian* codes.

Hẽr·mō·ġē′ni·ăn, *n.* same as *hermogenean*.

hẽrn, *n.* a heron. [Archaic or Dial.]

Hẽr·nan′di·ȧ, *n.* [named after Dr. *Hernandez*, a Spanish botanist.] a genus of lauraceous East Indian trees containing several species. *Hernandia sonora*, or jack-in-a-box, is so called from the noise made by the wind whistling through its persistent involucels.

HERNANDIA SONORA (Jack-in-a-box)

hẽr·nä′ni, *n.* a variously woven fabric used for making dresses for women; a kind of grenadine.

hẽr′nănt seeds̱, the seeds of *Hernandia ovigera*, imported from India for tanning purposes.

hẽr′ni·ȧ, *n.* [L. *hernia*, a rupture, from Gr. *hernos*, a shoot, sprout.] a protrusion of all or part of an organ through a tear or other abnormal opening in the wall of the containing cavity; especially, the protrusion of part of the intestine through the abdominal muscles: called also *rupture*.

strangulated hernia; a hernia which is so tightly constricted at its neck as to interfere with the circulation of blood and the passage of feces.

hẽr′ni·ăl, *a.* pertaining to or connected with hernia.

hẽr′ni·ō-, a combining form meaning *hernia*, as in *hernio*tomy.

hẽr′ni·oid, *a.* [L. *hernia*, a rupture, hernia, and Gr. *eidos*, form.] like hernia.

hẽr·ni·ol′ō·ġy, *n.* [L. *hernia*, a rupture, hernia, and Gr. *-logia*, from *legein*, to speak.]

1. that branch of surgery which deals with ruptures.

2. a treatise on ruptures.

hẽr·ni·ot′ō·my, *n.* [L. *hernia*, hernia, and Gr. *tomē*, a cutting, from *temnein*, to cut.] in surgery, operation for the repair of hernia.

hẽr′ni·ous, *a.* hernial. [Obs.]

hẽrn′sha̤w, *n.* same as *heronshaw*.

Hē′rō, *n.* in Greek legend, a priestess of Aphrodite at Sestos: her lover, Leander, swam the Hellespont from Abdyos every night to be with her; when he drowned one night, Hero threw herself into the sea.

hē′rō, *n.*; *pl.* **hē′rōes̱,** [OFr. *heroe*; L. *heros*; Gr. *hērōs*, a hero.]

1. in mythology and legend, a man of great strength and courage, favored by the gods and in part descended from them, often regarded as a half-god and worshiped after his death; as, Aeneas and Hector were *heroes* to the ancients.

2. any man admired for his courage, nobility, or exploits, especially in war; as, Washington is a national *hero*.

3. any person admired for his qualities or achievements and regarded as an ideal or model.

4. the central male character in a novel, play, poem, etc., with whom the reader or audience is supposed to sympathize; protagonist: often opposed to *villain*.

5. the central figure in any important event or period, honored for outstanding qualities.

hē′rō·arch·y, *n.* [Gr. *hērōs*, a hero, and *archē*, rule, from *archein*, to rule.] a government of heroes.

Hē·rō′di·ăn, *n.* [LL. *Herodianus*, from *Herodes*; Gr. *Hērōdēs*, Herod.] one of a sect among the Jews in the time of Christ, who were partisans of Herod.

Hē·rō′di·ăn, *a.* pertaining to Herod the Great, king of the Jews, or to the family of Herod or its adherents.

hē·rō′di·ăn, *a.* pertaining to the heron family.

hē·rō′di·ăn, *n.* a bird of the heron family; one of the *Herodiones*.

Hē·rō′di·ī, *n.pl.* same as *Herodiones*.

Hē·rō·di·ō′nēs̱, *n.pl.* [LL. *herodio* (*-onis*); Gr. *herōdios*, a heron.] an order of grallatorial birds, including the herons, storks, ibises, etc.

hē·rō·di·ō′nine, *a.* pertaining to the *Herodiones*.

hē′rō·ess, *n.* a heroine. [Obs.]

hē·rō′iç, *a.* [L. *heroicus*; Gr. *hērōikōs*, pertaining to a hero, from *hērōs*, a hero.]

1. pertaining to, characteristic of, or becoming a hero; brave; bold; intrepid; noble; renowned; as, a *heroic* deed, a *heroic* soldier, *heroic* enterprises.

2. of or characterized by men of godlike strength and courage; as, the *heroic* age.

3. of or about a hero and his deeds; epic; as, a *heroic* poem.

4. exalted; eloquent; high-flown; as, *heroic* words.

5. daring and risky, but used as a last resort; as, *heroic* measures.

6. in art, somewhat larger than life-size but less than colossal; as, a *heroic* statue.

Syn.—brave, courageous, fearless, intrepid, valiant, daring, gallant.

hē·rō′iç, *n.* 1. (a) a heroic poem; (b) [*pl.*] heroic verse.

2. [*pl.*] pretentious, extravagant, or melodramatic talk or action, meant to seem heroic.

hē·rō′iç āġe, the period when the great heroes of a folk or nation, especially of Greece or Rome, are supposed to have lived.

hē·rō′iç·ăl, *a.* same as *heroic*.

hē·rō′iç·ăl·ly, *adv.* in a heroic manner; with valor; bravely; courageously; intrepidly; as, the fort was *heroically* defended.

hē·rō′iç·ăl·ness, *n.* the quality of being heroic; heroism. [Rare.]

hē·rō′iç çou̇p′let, a pair of rhymed lines in iambic pentameter, a verse form used in the late fourteenth century by Chaucer, made the dominant form of English neoclassical verse by Waller, Denham, and Dryden, and perfected in the early eighteenth century by Pope. Example:

"In every work regard the writer's end,
Since none can compass more than they intend."

hē·rō′iç·ly, *adv.* heroically. [Rare.]

hē·rō′iç·ness, *n.* heroicalness. [Rare.]

hē″rō·i·çom′iç, *a.* consisting of the heroic and the ludicrous; denoting high burlesque; as, a *heroicomic* poem.

hē″rō·i·çom′iç·ăl, *a.* same as *heroicomic*.

hē·rō′iç ten′ŏr, 1. a tenor voice with rich, powerful tones.

2. a man with such a voice, especially in opera; a dramatic tenor.

Distinguished from *lyric tenor*.

hē·rō′iç vẽrse, the verse form in which epic poetry is traditionally written, as dactylic hexameter in Greek or Latin, the Alexandrine in French, and iambic pentameter in English.

her′ō·in, *n.* a white, crystalline, odorless, bitter powder, $C_{21}H_{23}NO_5$, derived from morphine: it is a very powerful, habit-forming narcotic whose manufacture and import are now prohibited in the United States: a trade-mark (*Heroin*).

her′ō·ine, *n.* [OFr. *heroine*; L. *heroina*, a female hero, a demigoddess, from Gr. *hērōinē*, a heroine, f. of *hērōinos*, of a hero, from *hērōs*, a hero.]

1. a female hero; a woman of a brave spirit.

2. the principal female character, or the one with whom the hero is in love, in a poem, play, romance, story, or the like.

her′ō·in·iṣm, *n.* the heroin habit.

her′ō·iṣm, *n.* 1. the qualities and actions of a hero or heroine.

2. brave, noble action or trait.

Syn.—courage, fortitude, bravery, valor, intrepidity, gallantry.—*Courage* denotes fearlessness of danger; *fortitude* is passive courage, the habit of bearing up nobly under trials, dangers, and sufferings; *bravery* and *valor* are courage in battle or other conflicts with living opponents; *intrepidity* is firm courage, which does not shrink from the most appalling dangers; *gallantry* is adventurous courage, dashing into the thickest of the fight. *Heroism* may call into exercise all these modifications of courage.

her′ŏn, *n.* [ME. *heroun, heyroun, heiron*; OFr. *hairon*; O.H.G. *heigir*, a heron.] a wading bird of the genus *Ardea*, constituting with the storks and bitterns the family *Ardeidæ*. The species are very numerous, and almost universally spread over the globe, living along marshes and river banks. They are distinguished by having a long, tapered bill cleft beneath the eyes, a compressed body, and long, slender legs naked above the tarsal joint, three toes in front, the two outer united by a membrane. The common heron of Europe is *Ardea cinerea*; the great blue heron of America is *Ardea herodias*.

COMMON EUROPEAN HERON (*Ardea cinerea*)

her'ŏn·ẽr, *n.* a hawk trained to hunt the heron. [Obs.]

her'ŏn·ry, *n.*; *pl.* **her'ŏn·rieṣ,** a place where herons breed.

her'ŏn'ṣ-bill, *n.* a plant of the genus *Erodium*, of the family *Geraniaceæ*: so named because the long-beaked fruit has been fancied to resemble the head and breast of a heron: called also *stork's-bill.*

her'ŏn·sew (-sū), *n.* a heron. [Brit. Dial.]

her'ŏn·shaw, *n.*, a heron. [Brit. Dial.]

hē·rō·ol'ō·ġist, *n.* [Gr. *herōologia*, a tale of heroes; *hērōs*, a hero, and *-logia*, from *legein*, to speak.] one who treats of heroes. [Rare.]

hē'rō·ship, *n.* the character or condition of a hero.

hē'rō wŏr'ship, 1. the worship of heroes, practiced by ancient nations; reverence paid to, or to the memory of, heroes or great men.

2. exaggerated or excessive reverence or admiration for heroes or other important persons.

hẽr'pēṣ, *n.* [L. *herpes*; Gr. *herpēs*, lit., a creeping, the herpes, from *herpein*, to creep.] in pathology, an acute inflammatory virus disease of the skin or mucous membrane, characterized by the eruption of small blisters on the skin and mucous membranes, especially (*herpes zoster*) along the course of a nerve.

hẽr'pēs lā·bi·ā'lis, [L.] a form of herpes; cold sore.

hẽr'pēs zos'tẽr, [L. *herpes* and *zoster*, shingles, from Gr. *zōstēr*, a girdle.] a form of herpes; shingles.

hẽr·pet'iç, *a.* pertaining to or having herpes; resembling herpes or partaking of its nature; as, *herpetic* eruptions.

hẽr·pet'iç·ăl, *a.* herpetic.

hẽr'pe·tiṣm, *n.* in medicine, a tendency to develop herpes or similar cutaneous diseases.

hẽr'pe·toid, *a.* [Gr. *herpeton*, a reptile, and *eidos*, form.] resembling a reptile; as, a *herpetoid* bird.

hẽr"pet·ō·loġ'iç, *a.* pertaining to herpetology.

hẽr"pet·ō·loġ'iç·ăl, *a.* herpetologic.

hẽr"pet·ō·loġ'iç·ăl·ly, *adv.* from a herpetological standpoint.

hẽr·pē·tol'ō·ġist, *n.* a person who studies or specializes in herpetology, or the natural history of reptiles.

hẽr·pē·tol'ō·ġy, *n.* [Gr. *herpeton*, a reptile, and *-logia*, from *legein*, to speak.] the study of reptiles; the natural history of reptiles.

hẽr·pē·tot'ō·mist, *n.* one who dissects reptiles; a student of herpetological anatomy.

hẽr·pē·tot'ō·my, *n.* [Gr. *herpeton*, a reptile, and *tomē*, a cutting, from *temnein*, to cut.] the dissection or anatomy of reptiles.

Herr, *n.*; *pl.* **Herr'en,** [G.; orig. comp. of *hehr*, noble, venerable.] in Germany, a man; gentleman: also used as a title corresponding to *Mr.* or *Sir.*

Herr'en·vọlk (-fọlk), *n.*; *pl.* **Herr'en·völk·er** (-fel-kẽr), [G.] master race: in Nazi ideology, applied to the German people.

her'ring, *n.*; *pl.* **her'ringṣ** or **her'ring,** [ME. *hering*; AS. *hæring*, a herring; prob. from *here*, an army, a post.]

1. a fish of the genus *Clupea*, especially *Clupea harengus*, the common herring of the North Atlantic. Herrings come from high northern latitudes in the spring, and visit the shores of Europe and America in great schools, where they are caught: the adult fish are eaten cooked, dried, salted, or smoked, and the young are canned as sardines.

2. loosely, any related fish, **as the sprat,** pilchard, etc.

her'ring·bōne, *n.* 1. the spine of a herring with the ribs extending from opposite sides in rows of parallel slanting lines.

2. anything made in this pattern, as a kind of cross-stitch, a twill weave, an arrangement of bricks or tiles, etc.

her'ring·bōne, *a.* having the pattern of a herringbone.

herringbone stitch; a kind of cross-stitch used in embroidery and woolen work.

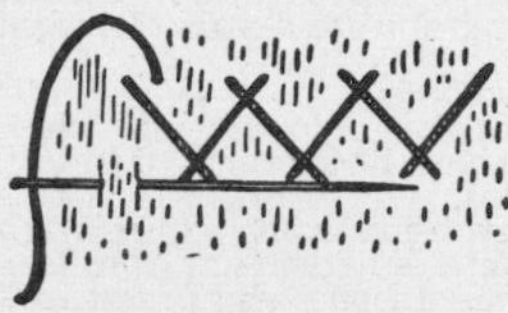

HERRINGBONE STITCH

her'ring·bōne, *v.t.* and *v.i.* to use a herringbone stitch or pattern on.

her'ring buss, a boat of ten or fifteen tons, used in England in the herring fishery.

her'ring gull, a gull such as *Larus argentatus*, that feeds on herrings.

her'ring hog, *Phocæna communis*, the common porpoise.

her'ring king, the ribbon fish: called also *king of the herrings.*

her'ring pond, the ocean, particularly the Atlantic Ocean. [Slang.]

Hẽrrn'hụt·ẽr, *n.* [G. *Herrnhut*, the village of Herrnhut, Saxony, where they settled, on the estate of Nicholas Lewis, count of Zinzendorf, about 1722.] a Moravian.

hẽrṣ, *pron.* [Late ME. *hires*, *hers*, from *hire*, *her*(*e*), *poss. a.*, and *-s* after *his.*] that or those belonging to her: the absolute form of *her*, used without a following noun, often after *of*; as, a friend of *hers*, that book is *hers*, *hers* are better.

hẽr'săll, *n.* rehearsal. [Obs.]

Hẽr'schel, *n.* [named after Sir William *Herschel*, its discoverer.] the planet Uranus.

Hẽr·schē'li·ăn, *a.* pertaining to Sir William Herschel (1738–1822), the English astronomer, or to Sir John Herschel (1792–1871), his son; as, the *Herschelian* telescope.

hẽr'schel·īte, *n.* [named after Sir John *Herschel*, the astronomer.] a mineral allied to chabazite.

hẽrse, *n.* [ME. *herse*, *hers*; OFr. *herce*, a harrow, a portcullis, a triangular candlestick, from L. *hirpex*(*-icis*), a harrow.]

1. in fortification, formerly, (a) a portcullis in the form of a harrow set with iron spikes; (b) a kind of chevaux-de-frise laid in the way or in breaches, with the points up, to obstruct or hinder the march of an enemy.

2. a troop formation formerly used in battle.

3. a framework on which to dry skins.

4. a carriage for bearing corpses to the grave; a hearse. [Obs.]

HERSE, SENSE 5

5. a framework on which lighted candles were placed at funeral ceremonies in the Middle Ages. [Obs.]

6. a grating used for any purpose. [Obs.]

hẽr·self', *pron.* [ME. *hire self*; AS. *hire selfum*, dat. sing. of *hie self.*] a form of the third person singular, feminine pronoun, used: (a) as an intensive; as, she went *herself*; (b) as a reflexive; as, she hurt *herself*; (c) [Irish.] as a subject; as, *herself* will have her tea now; (d) as a quasi-noun meaning "her real, true, or actual self" (e.g., she is not *herself* when she rages like that): in this construction *her* may be considered a possessive pronominal adjective and *self* a noun, and they may be s e parated; as, *her* own sweet *self.*

hẽr'ship, *n.* the stealing of cattle by driving them away. [Scot.]

hẽr'sil·lŏn, *n.* [Fr., from *herse*, a portcullis.] in fortification, formerly, a plank or beam, set with spikes or nails, to retard the march of an enemy.

hẽrtz, *n.*; *pl.* **hẽrtz** or **hẽrtz'eṣ,** [after Heinrich *Hertz*, G. physicist.] the international unit of frequency equal to one cycle per second.

Hẽrtz'i·ăn, *a.* relating to Heinrich Hertz (1857–1894), a German physicist, or to his discoveries; as, the *Hertzian* waves.

Hẽrtz'i·ăn wāveṣ, [after Heinrich *Hertz*, G. physicist.] [*sometimes* h–] radio waves or other electromagnetic radiation resulting from the oscillations of electricity in a conductor.

her'y, *v.t.* to praise; to worship. [Obs.]

hẽr'zog (-tsog), *n.* [G.] formerly, an Austrian or German duke.

hē'ṣ, 1. he is.

2. he has.

Hesh'van, *n.* Cheshvan.

heṣ'i·tănce, *n.* hesitancy.

heṣ'i·tăn·cy, *n.* [L. *hæsitantia*, a stammering, from *hæsitans* (*-antis*), ppr. of *hæsitare*, to hesitate.] the act of hesitating or doubting; slowness in forming decisions; the action or manner of one who hesitates; indecisive deliberation; doubt; vacillation.

Some of them reasoned without doubt or *hesitancy.* —Atterbury.

heṣ'i·tănt, *a.* hesitating; vacillating; doubtful; not ready in deciding or acting; wanting readiness of speech.

He was a man of no quick utterance, but often *hesitant.* —Baxter.

heṣ'i·tănt·ly, *adv.* with hesitancy or doubt.

heṣ'i·tāte, *v.i.*; hesitated, *pt.*, *pp.*; hesitating, *ppr.* [L. *hæsitatus*, pp. of *hæsitare*, to stick fast, hesitate, intens. of *hærere*, to stick, cleave.]

1. to stop or pause respecting decision or action; to be doubtful as to fact, principle, or determination; to be in suspense or uncertainty; to waver; as, he *hesitated* whether to accept the offer or not.

2. to pause; stop momentarily.

3. to be reluctant; not be sure that one should; as, I *hesitate* to ask for a loan.

4. to stammer; to stutter.

Syn.—doubt, falter, pause, scruple, stammer, stutter.

heṣ'i·tāte, *v.t.* to be undecided about; to utter or express with hesitation or reluctance; to insinuate hesitatingly. [Rare.]

Just hint a fault, and *hesitate* dislike.—Pope.

heṣ'i·tāt·ẽr, heṣ'i·tā·tŏr, *n.* one who hesitates.

heṣ'i·tā·ting·ly, *adv.* with hesitation or doubt.

heṣ·i·tā'tion, *n.* [L. *hæsitatio* (*-onis*), from *hæsitare*, to stick fast, hesitate.] a hesitating or feeling hesitant; specifically, (a) indecision; uncertain pausing or delay; (b) a pausing; momentary delay; (c) reluctance; (d) a stammering.

Syn.—hesitancy, wavering, vacillation, uncertainty, doubt, faltering, suspense.

heṣ'i·tā·tive, *a.* characterized by or showing hesitation.

heṣ'i·tā·tō·ry, *a.* hesitating.

hesp, *n.* a measure of two linen thread hanks. [Scot.]

Hes'pẽr, *n.* same as *Hesperus.* [Poet.]

hes·per'e·tin, *n.* a sweetish crystalline compound derived from hesperidin.

Hes·pē'ri·ȧ, *n.* a genus of butterflies, the type of the family *Hesperiidæ.*

Hes·pē'ri·ȧ, *n.* [L.; Gr. *Hesperia*, from *hesperos.*] the Western Land: the ancient Greek name for Italy and the Roman name for Spain.

Hes·pē'ri·ăn, *a.* [L. *hesperius*; Gr. *hesperios*, western, from *hesperos*, western, evening, *Hesperos*, evening star.]

1. of Hesperia.

2. western, occidental.

3. of the Hesperides. [Poet.]

Hes·pē'ri·ăn, *n.* an inhabitant of Hesperia or any western land. [Rare.]

hes·pē'ri·ăn, *n.* any butterfly of the family *Hesperiidæ.*

hes·pē'ri·ăn, *a.* pertaining to the *Hesperiidæ*, a family of lepidopterous insects.

hes'pẽr·id, *n.* a hesperian.

hes'pẽr·id, *a.* pertaining to the *Hesperiidæ*; hesperian.

hes·per'i·dēne, *n.* a variety of terpene obtained from orange oil.

Hes·per'i·dēṣ, *n.pl.* [L., from Gr. *Hesperides*, the Hesperides, from *Hesperos*, Hesperus.] in Greek mythology, (a) the daughters of Hesperus, guardians of the fabulous garden of golden apples, watched over by an enchanted dragon, at the western extremities of the earth. The apples were stolen by Hercules, who slew the dragon; (b) the garden in which the golden apples grew.

Hes·pẽr·id′i·ăn, *a.* pertaining to the Hesperides.

hes·per′i·din, *n.* in chemistry, a crystalline glucoside having the formula $C_{22}H_{26}O_{12}$: it is obtained from unripe citrus fruit.

hes·pẽr·id′i·um, *n.* [from L. *Hesperides*, the Hesperides; so called in allusion to the golden apples of the Hesperides.] in botany, a fleshy fruit with a separable thick envelope, and divided internally into several separable pulpy cells by membranous dissepiments, as the orange or lemon.

Hes·pẽr·ī′i·dae, *n.pl.* [L. *Hesperia*, the west, from *Hesperus*, the evening star.] a family of lepidopterous insects, of which the type is the genus *Hesperia*. These little, large-headed butterflies have a short, jerking kind of flight, and hence they have received the name of *skippers*. *Hesperia sylvanus* and *Thymele alveolus* are typical examples.

Hes·pẽr·or′nis, *n.* [Gr. *hesperos*, western, and *ornis*, a bird.] a genus of large fossil birds with rudimentary wings. Several species have been found in the Cretaceous deposits of North America.

Hes′pẽr·us, *n.* [L., from Gr. *Hesperos*, the evening star.] the evening star, particularly Venus.

Hes′siăn, *a.* relating to Hesse in Germany or its people.

Hessian bit; a kind of jointed bit for bridles.

Hessian boots; tasseled boots reaching almost to the knee, introduced by the Hessian troops, and worn in England in the beginning of the nineteenth century.

Hessian cloth; a coarse cloth manufactured from hemp, used principally for bagging.

Hessian crucible; see under *crucible*.

Hessian fly; a small, two-winged fly, *Cecidomyia destructor*, whose larvae are very destructive to young wheat: so called from the belief that it was brought into America in straw imported for Hessian troops during the Revolution.

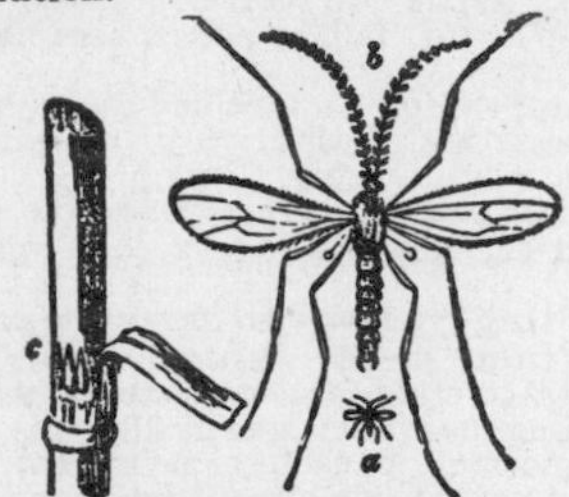

HESSIAN FLY (*Cecidomyia destructor*)
a. male (natural size). *b.* male (magnified). *c.* pupæ fixed on the joint of the wheat stalk.

Hes′siăn, *n.* 1. a native or inhabitant of Hesse, Germany.

2. [*pl.*] hessian boots.

3. [*pl.*] Hessian cloth.

4. any of the Hessian mercenaries who fought for the British in the Revolutionary War.

Hes′si·ăn, *n.* in mathematics, a symmetric determinant whose elements are the second differential coefficients of a rational integral function of two or more variables.

hess′īte, *n.* [after G. H. *Hess* (1802–1850), Swiss chemist; and *-ite.*] in mineralogy, silver telluride, Ag_2Te, found in gray, sectile masses.

hes′sō·nīte, *n.* essonite, a variety of garnet; cinnamon stone.

hest, *n.* [ME. *hest, heste*; AS. *hæs*, a command, from *hatan*, to bid, order, command.]

1. behest; command; precept; injunction; order. [Archaic.]

2. a pledge. [Obs.]

hes′tẽrn, *a.* hesternal. [Obs.]

hes·tẽr′năl, *a.* pertaining to yesterday.

hes·thog′e·nous, *a.* [Gr. *esthēs*, dress, and *-genous.*] in ornithology, covered with down when hatched.

Hes′ti·ȧ, *n.* [Gr. *Hestia.*] in Greek mythology, (a) the goddess of the hearth, identified with the Roman Vesta; (b) one of the nymphs guarding the golden apples of the Hesperides.

Hes′y·chaṣm, *n.* [Gr. *hēsychazein*, to be still or quiet.] the doctrine of the Hesychasts.

Hes′y·chast, *n.* [Gr. *hēsychastēs*, one who leads a quiet, retired life, a hermit, from *hēsychazein*, to be still or quiet, from *hēsychos*, still, quiet.] any member of a sect of mystics begun among the monks at Mt. Athos, Greece, in the fourteenth century, dedicated to quietism.

hes·y·chas′tiç, *a.* [Gr. *hēsychastikos*, quieting, retired, from *hēsychazein*, to be quiet.] expressive of mental serenity; conducing to quietude.

hē·tae′rȧ, hē·taī′rȧ, *n.*; *pl.* **hē·tae′rae, hē·taī′raī,** [Gr. *hetaira*, f. of *hetairos*, a companion.] in ancient Greece, a courtesan or concubine, usually an educated slave.

hē·tae′riṣm, hē·taī′riṣm, *n.* [Gr. *hetairismos*, the practice of a hetaera, from *hetairizein*, to be a hetaera, from *hetaira*, a hetaera or concubine.]

1. concubinage.

2. a system of communal marriage supposed to have been practiced in certain primitive tribes.

hē·tae′rist, hē·taī′rist, *n.* [Gr. *hetairistēs*, one who practices hetaerism, from *hetærizein*, to be a hetaera.] one who practices hetaerism.

hē·tae·ris′tiç, hē·taī·ris′tiç, *a.* pertaining to hetaerism.

het·ae′rō·līte, *n.* [Gr. *hetairos*, a companion, and *lithos*, a stone.] a mineral allied to hausmannite, a zinc-manganese oxide.

hetch′el, *v.t.* and *n.* hatchel. [Obs.]

het′er-, see *hetero-*.

het′ẽr·ȧ·canth, *a.* [*heter-*, and Gr. *akantha*, spine.] in zoology, having asymmetrical dorsal and anal spines.

het·ẽr·ȧ·den′iç, *a.* [*heter-*, and Gr. *adēn*, a gland.] pertaining to or consisting of tissue that is unlike normal glandular tissue, or to glandular tissue occurring in an abnormal place.

het′ẽr·ärçh·y, *n.* the government of an alien. [Obs.]

het″ẽr·ȧ·tom′iç, *a.* [*heter-*, and Gr. *atomos*, an atom.] composed of different kinds of atoms.

het″e·raux·ē′sis (-raks-), *n.* [*heter-*, and Gr. *auxēsis*, increase.] in botany, unequal or unsymmetrical growth of a part of a plant.

het′ẽr·ō-, [Gr. *hetero-*, other, different, from *heteros*, the other (of two).] a combining form meaning *other*, *another*, *different*, as in *heterosexual*: opposed to *homo-*: also, before a vowel, *heter-*.

het″ẽr·ō·blas′tiç, *a.* [*hetero-*, and Gr. *blastos*, a bud, germ.] arising from cells or tissue of a different kind.

het″ẽr·ō·çär′pi·ăn, *a.* heterocarpous.

het″ẽr·ō·çär′piṣm, *n.* [*hetero-*, and Gr. *karpos*, fruit.] in botany, the property of bearing fruit of two sorts or shapes, as in *Amphicarpaea*.

het″ẽr·ō·çär′pous, *a.* [Gr. *heterokarpos*, bearing different fruit; *heteros*, other, different, and *karpos*, fruit.] in botany, bearing fruit of two different kinds.

het″ẽr·ō·cel′lū·lăr, *a.* consisting of dissimilar cells.

het″ẽr·ō·ceph′ȧ·lous, *a.* [*hetero-*, and Gr. *kephalē*, head.] having some heads of male, or staminate, and some of female, or pistillate, flowers, as certain plants of the aster family.

Het·ẽr·oc′e·rȧ, *n.* [*hetero-*, and Gr. *keras*, horn.] a division of *Lepidoptera* including many families; the moths.

het″ẽr·ō·cẽr′çăl, *a.* [*hetero-*, and Gr. *kerkos*, tail.] designating, of, or having a tail fin in which the upper lobe is larger than the lower and contains the upturned end of the spinal column, as in certain fishes.

het′ẽr·ō·cẽr″cy, *n.* the condition of being heterocercal.

het″ẽr·ō·chrō·mat′iç, *a.* [*hetero-* and *-chromatic.*] of, having, or consisting of different or contrasting colors; many-colored: opposed to *homochromatic*.

het′ẽr·ō·chrōme, *a.* heterochromatic.

het″ẽr·ō·chrō′mō·sōme, *n.* an accessory chromosome, present in some germ cells, which passes over intact to only one of the daughter cells instead of being divided between the two; sex chromosome: it is thought to be the factor that determines the organism's sex.

het·ẽr·och′rō·niṣm, *n.* same as *heterochrony*.

het″ẽr·ō·chrō·nis′tiç, *a.* same as *heterochronous*.

het·ẽr·och′rō·nous, *a.* pertaining to heterochrony.

het·ẽr·och′rō·ny, *n.* [Gr. *heterochronos*, of different times; *heteros*, other, different, and *chronos*, time.] in biology, a deviation from the true ontogenetic sequence, with reference to the time of formation of organs or parts.

het′ẽr·ō·çlīne, *a.* [*hetero-*, and Gr. *klinē*, a bed.] same as *heterocephalous*.

het·ẽr·oç′lī·tăl, *a.* see *heteroclite*.

het′ẽr·ō·çlīte, *a.* [LL. *heteroclitus*; Gr. *heteroklitos*, irregularly inflected; *heteros*, other, different, and *klinein*, to bend, incline.] irregular; anomalous; deviating from the standard or norm.

het′ẽr·ō·çlīte, *n.* 1. in grammar, a word which is irregular or anomalous either in declension or conjugation, or which deviates from ordinary forms of inflection in words of a like kind: it is applied especially to nouns irregular in declension.

2. an anomaly. [Rare.]

het″ẽr·ō·çlit′iç, *a.* heteroclite.

het″ẽr·ō·çlit′iç·ăl, *a.* heteroclitic.

het·ẽr·oç′li·tous, *a.* heteroclitic. [Obs.]

het″ẽr·ō·çȳ′cliç, *a.* [*hetero-*, and *cyclic.*] designating or of a cyclic molecular arrangement of atoms of carbon and other elements.

het′ẽr·ō·cyst, *n.* [*hetero-*, and Gr. *kystis*, a bag, pouch.] a very large cell found in certain algae.

het″ẽr·ō·daç′tyl, het″ẽr·ō·daç′tyle, *a.* [*hetero-*, and Gr. *daktylos*, a finger or toe.] in zoology, having the toes irregular, either in regard to number, position, or formation, as in the trogons.

het″ẽr·ō·daç′tyl, het″ẽr·ō·daç′tyle, *n.* a member of the *Heterodactylæ*.

Het″e·rō·daç′ty·lae, *n.pl.* a group of picarian birds having the second toe turned backward, instead of the fourth; the trogons.

het″ẽr·ō·daç′tyl·ous, *a.* 1. same as *heterodactyl*.

2. pertaining to the *Heterodactylæ*.

het′ẽr·ō·dont, *a.* [*hetero-*, and Gr. *odous, odontos*, a tooth.] having teeth of different kinds, as canines, incisors, and molars: distinguished from *homodont*.

het′ẽr·ō·dont, *n.* any animal with different kinds of teeth; a heterodont animal.

het′ẽr·ō·dox, *a.* [Gr. *heterodoxos*, of another or different opinion; *heteros*, other, and *doxa*, opinion.] departing from or opposed to the usual beliefs as established doctrines, especially in religion; inclining toward heresy; unorthodox: opposed to *orthodox*.

het′ẽr·ō·dox, *n.* an opinion contrary to that which is established or generally received. [Obs.]

het′ẽr·ō·dox·ly, *adv.* in a heterodox manner.

het′ẽr·ō·dox·ness, *n.* the state of being heterodox.

het′ẽr·ō·dox·y, *n.* 1. the quality or fact of being heterodox.

2. a heterodox opinion, belief, or doctrine.

het·ẽr·od′rō·mous, *a.* [*hetero-*, and Gr. *dromos*, a running, from *dramein*, to run.] in botany, running in different directions, as leaves on the stem and branches.

het·ẽr·od′rō·my, *n.* in botany, a change in direction of the spiral sequence of leaves on a stem.

het′ẽr·ō·dȳne, *a.* [*hetero-* and *dyne.*] having to do with the combination of radio oscillations of somewhat different frequencies coupled in such a way as to produce beats whose frequency is the difference or sum of the frequencies of the combined oscillations.

het′ẽr·ō·dȳne, *v.t.*; heterodyned, *pt., pp.*, heterodyning, *ppr.* to combine (a series of waves) with a series of a somewhat different frequency, producing beats.

het′ẽr·ō·dȳne, *n.* an accessory generator of radio-frequency voltage.

het·ẽr·oe′cious, *a.* [*heter-*, and Gr. *oikia*, a house.] in biology, living as a parasite on first one host and then another.

het·ẽr·oe′ciṣm, *n.* the parasitism of heteroecious organisms.

het″e·roe·ciṣ′măl, *a.* heteroecious.

het″ẽr·ō·ga·mēte′, *n.* a gamete differentiated sexually or otherwise from another that it unites with, as most male and female gametes: opposed to *isogamete*.

het·ẽr·og′ȧ·mous, *a.* [*hetero-*, and Gr. *gamos*, marriage.]

1. characterized by the uniting of heterogametes.

2. characterized by reproduction in which sexual and asexual generations alternate.

3. characterized by indirect pollination.

4. having flowers in which the stamens and pistils are irregularly arranged.

het·ẽr·og′ȧ·my, *n.* 1. the quality or state of being heterogamous.

2. reproduction in which sexual and asexual generations alternate.

3. indirect pollination.

het·ẽr·ō·gan′gli·āte, *a.* [*hetero-*, and Gr. *ganglion*, ganglion.] possessing a nervous system in which the ganglia are scattered and unsymmetrical, as in the *Mollusca*.

het′ẽr·ō·gēne, *a.* heterogenous.

het″ẽr·ō·gē′nē·ăl, *a.* heterogeneous.

het″ẽr·ō·gē·nē′i·ty, *n.*; *pl.* **het″ẽr·ō·gē·nē′i·ties** [Fr. *hétérogénéité*; ML. *heterogeneitas*.]

1. the quality or condition of being heterogeneous; dissimilarity.

2. a heterogeneous element.

het″ẽr·ō·gē′nē·ous, *a.* [LL. *heterogeneus*; Gr. *heterogenēs*, of different kinds, of different genders; *heteros*, other, different, and *genos*, kind, race, gender.]

1. differing or opposite in structure, quality, etc.; dissimilar; incongruous; foreign.

2. composed of unrelated or unlike elements or parts; varied; miscellaneous.

Opposed to *homogeneous*.

heterogeneous nouns; in grammar, nouns of different genders in the singular and plural numbers; as, *hic locus*, of the masculine gender in the singular, and *hi loci* and *hæc loca*, both masculine and neuter in the plural; *hoc cælum*, neuter in the singular, and *hi cæli*, masculine in the plural.

heterogeneous quantities; in mathematics, quantities incapable of being compared in respect to magnitude.

heterogeneous surds; in mathematics, surds which have different radical signs.

het″ẽr·ō·gē′nē·ous·ly, *adv.* in a heterogeneous manner.

het″ẽr·ō·gē′nē·ous·ness, *n.* heterogeneity.

het″ẽr·ō·gen′e·sis, *n.* [*hetero-*, and Gr. *genesis*, origin, birth.]

1. reproduction in which sexual and asexual generations alternate.

2. reproduction in which the parent bears offspring differing from itself: opposed to *homogenesis*.

3. spontaneous generation.

het″ẽr·ō·gē·net′iç, *a.* pertaining to heterogenesis.

het″ẽr·ō·gen′ic, *a.* [*hetero-*, and *-genic*.] of different origin; not from the same source, individual, or species.

het·ẽr·og′e·nist, *n.* one who believes in the theory of spontaneous generation.

het·ẽr·og′e·nous, *a.* heterogenic.

het·ẽr·og′e·ny, *n.* heterogenesis.

het·ẽr·og′ō·niṣm, *n.* the quality or state of being heterogonous.

het·ẽr·og′ō·nous, *a.* [*hetero-*, and Gr. *gonos*, offspring, generation.]

1. in botany, having two or more kinds of perfect flowers, differing in the length of their stamens and pistils, on the same plant; heterostyled.

2. characterized by reproduction in which sexual and asexual generations alternate.

het·ẽr·og′ō·nous·ly, *adv.* in a heterogonous manner.

het·ẽr·og′ō·ny, *n.* the state of being heterogonous.

het′ẽr·ō·grȧft, *n.* a graft of skin, bone, etc. taken from another individual.

het″ẽr·ō·graph′iç, *a.* pertaining to or characterized by heterography.

het·ẽr·og′rȧ·phy, *n.* [*hetero-*, and Gr. *graphein*, to write.]

1. spelling that differs from current standard usage.

2. spelling, as in modern English, in which the same letter does not always represent the same sound.

het·ẽr·og′y·năl, *a.* heterogynous.

het·ẽr·og′y·nous, *a.* [*hetero-*, and Gr. *gynē*, a woman, a female.] in zoology, having females of two different kinds, one fertile, the other infertile or neuter, as the ants.

het·ẽr·ol′ō·gous, *a.* [*hetero-*, and Gr. *logos*, relation, proportion.]

1. consisting of different elements, or of the same elements in different proportions: opposed to *homologous*.

2. in medicine, differing in structure or form from the normal; as, a *heterologous* tumor is a tumor constituted of a different tissue from that of the part in or on which it is situated.

het·ẽr·ol′ō·ġy, *n.* [*hetero-*, and Gr. *logos*, relation, proportion.] lack or absence of relation or analogy between parts, resulting from their consisting of different elements or deriving from different sources.

het·ẽr·ol′y·sis, *n.* [Mod. L.; see *hetero-* and *-lysis*.] the destruction of cells of one species by lysins or enzymes derived from cells of a different species.

het·ẽr·om′ăl·lous, *a.* [*hetero-*, and Gr. *mallos*, a lock of wool.] in botany, having the leaves or stems turning in different directions, as certain mosses.

Het·e·rom′e·rȧ, *n.pl.* [Gr. *heteromerēs*, unequal; *heteros*, other, different, and *meros*, part.] a division of coleopterous insects comprising those that have five joints in the tarsus of the first and second pair of legs, and only four joints in the tarsus of the third pair.

het·e·rom′e·răn, *n.* one of the *Heteromera*.

het·ẽr·om′ẽr·ous, *a.* [Gr. *heteromerēs*, unequal; *heteros*, different, and *meros*, a part.]

1. in chemistry, composed of different elements, though exhibiting similar properties in certain other respects.

2. in botany, having the parts unequal in number: distinguished from *isomerous*.

3. in zoology, pertaining to the *Heteromera*.

het″ẽr·ō·mē·tab′ō·lous, *a.* [*hetero-*, and Gr. *metabolos*, changeable.] developing with incomplete metamorphosis, as certain insects.

het″ẽr·ō·mọr′phiç, *a.* [Gr. *heteromorphos*, of another form; *heteros*, other, different, and *morphē*, form.]

1. differing from the standard type or form.

2. exhibiting different forms at various stages of development, as insects in the larval and pupal stages.

het″ẽr·ō·mọr′phiṣm, *n.* the quality or state of being heteromorphic; deviation from the standard or normal form.

het″ẽr·ō·mọr′phīte, *n.* a variety of jamesonite; a lead antimony sulfide.

het″ẽr·ō·mọr′phous, *a.* heteromorphic.

het″ẽr·ō·mọr′phy, *n.* in botany, same as *heteromorphism*.

Het″e·rō·mȳ·ā′ri·ȧ, *n.pl.* [*hetero-*, and Gr. *mys*, muscle.] a group of mollusks having unequal adductor muscles.

het″e·rō·mȳ·ā′ri·ăn, *a.* characteristic of the *Heteromyaria*.

het″e·rō·nē′rē·is, *n.* in zoology, a dimorphic sexual form of certain nereidians.

het″ẽr·ō·nom′iç, *a.* [*hetero-*, and Gr. *nomos*, law.] showing a different mode of operation or arrangement: opposed to *isonomic*.

het·ẽr·on′ō·mous, *a.* 1. pertaining or relating to heteronomy; subject to the rule of another: opposed to *autonomous*.

2. in biology, differing in some way from a common type; differentiated or specialized, as parts or organs.

het·ẽr·on′ō·my, *n.* [*hetero-*, and Gr. *nomos*, law.]

1. the state of being subject to the law or authority of another; subordination to authority from without: opposed to *autonomy*.

2. in Kantian philosophy, subjection to the laws or restrictions imposed on man by nature or by his appetites, passions, and desires, and not by reason.

het′ẽr·ō·nym, *n.* [Gr. *heterōnymos*, having a different name; *heteros*, other, different, and *onyma*, name.]

1. a word with the same spelling as another but with a different meaning and pronunciation (e.g., *tear*, a drop of water from the eye, *tear*, to pull apart, rip).

2. a name (of something) in one language that is an exact translation of the name in another language (e.g., German *Fernsprecher*, lit., far speaker, English *telephone*).

het″ẽr·ō·nym′iç, *a.* same as *heteronymous*.

het·ẽr·on′y·mous, *a.* 1. of, or having the nature of, a heteronym.

2. having different names, as a pair of correlatives; as, *son* and *daughter* are *heteronymous*.

3. in optics, designating or of the two crossed images of something seen when the eyes are focused at a point beyond it.

het·ẽr·on′y·mous·ly, *adv.* in a heteronymous manner.

het·ẽr·on′y·my, *n.* the use or relation of heteronyms.

Het″ẽr·ō·öu′si·ăn, *a.* [Gr. *heteroousios*, from *hetero-*, different and *ousia*, essence.] in theology and church history, designating, of, or holding the theory that God the Father and God the Son are different in substance: opposed to *Homoousian*, *Homoiousian*.

Het″ẽr·ō·öu′si·ăn, *n.* an adherent of the Heteroousian theory; Arian.

Het″ẽr·ō·öu′si·ast, *n.* a Heteroousian.

het″ẽr·ō·path′iç, *a.* [*hetero-*, and Gr. *pathos*, suffering.] see *allopathic*.

het·ẽr·op′ȧ·thy, *n.* see *allopathy*.

het″ẽr·ō·pel′mous, *a.* [*hetero-*, and Gr. *pelma*, the sole of the foot.] in ornithology, having each of the two flexor tendons so divided that the flexor hallucis supplies the two posterior toes and the flexor perforans the two anterior toes.

Het·e·roph′ȧ·ġī, *n.pl.* [*hetero-*, and Gr. *phagein*, to eat.] in ornithology, the *altrices*.

het·e·roph′ȧ·gous, *a.* same as *altricial*.

het″ẽr·ō·phā′ṣi·ȧ, *n.* [*hetero-*, and Gr. *phasis*, a saying, from *phanai*, to say, speak.] in pathology, a species of aphasia characterized by the misuse of words.

het·ẽr·ō·phē′miṣm (-fē′mizm *or* -of′ē-mizm), *n.* an example of heterophemy.

het·ẽr·ō·phē′mist (-fē′mist *or* -of′ē-mist), *n.* one who is subject to heterophemy.

het″ẽr·ō·phē·mis′tiç, *a.* pertaining to heterophemy.

het·ẽr·ō·phē′mize, *v.i.*; heterophemized, *pt.*, *pp.*; heterophemizing, *ppr.* to use a heterophemism.

het′ẽr·ō·phē·my (-fē-mi *or* -of′ē-mi), *n.* [*hetero-*, and Gr. *phēmē*, a voice, speech, saying, from *phanai*, to say, speak.] the unconscious saying or writing of one word when another is intended.

het″ẽr·ō·phō′ri·ȧ, *n.* [*hetero-*, and Gr. *-phoria*, from *pherein*, to bear.] in pathology, a relation of the visual lines of the two eyes other than that of parallelism.

het·ẽr·ō·phyl′lous (*or* of′i-lus), *a.* [*hetero-*, and Gr. *phyllon*, a leaf.]

1. in botany, having two different kinds of leaves on the same stem, as *Potamogeton heterophyllus*, which has broad, floating leaves, with narrow leaves submerged in the water.

2. in zoology, having different kinds of foliation or volution of the septal margins.

het″ẽr·ō·plā′ṣi·ȧ, *n.* [*hetero-*, and Gr. *plasis*, a forming, from *plassein*, to form.] in pathology, the presence, in a part of the body, of a tissue that does not belong there normally.

het′ẽr·ō·plaṣm, *n.* same as *heteroplasia*.

het″ẽr·ō·plas′tiç, *a.* [*hetero-*, and Gr. *plastikos*, plastic, from *plassein*, to form.] of or pertaining to heteroplasty.

het′ẽr·ō·plas·ty, *n.* 1. heteroplasia.

2. plastic surgery in which tissue from one individual is grafted onto another.

het′ẽr·ō·pod, *n.* one of the *Heteropoda*.

het′ẽr·ō·pod, *a.* pertaining to or characteristic of the *Heteropoda*; heteropodous.

Het·e·rop′ō·dȧ, *n.pl.* [Gr. *heteropous*, with uneven feet; *heteros*, other, different, and *pous*, *podos*, a foot.] an order of marine mollusks, the most highly organized of the *Gasteropoda*. In this order the foot is compressed into a vertical muscular lamina, serving as a fin, and the gills, when present, are collected into a mass on the back.

het·ẽr·op′ō·dăn, *n.* a heteropod.

het·ẽr·op′ō·dous, *a.* same as *heteropod*.

het″ẽr·ō·pō′lăr, *a.* [*hetero-*, and Gr. *polos*, pole.]

1. having polar correspondence to something other than itself.

2. in biology, having unequal or dissimilar poles, as of the primary axis.

het·ẽr·op′tẽr, *n.* one of the *Heteroptera*.

Het·e·rop′te·rȧ, *n.pl.* [*hetero-*, and Gr. *pteron*, a wing.] a division of hemipterous insects comprising those in which the two pairs of wings are of different consistence, the anterior part being horny or leathery, but generally tipped with membrane.

het·e·rop′te·răn, *n.* a heteropter.

het·e·rop′te·rous, *a.* having wings differentiated; characteristic of the *Heteroptera*.

het·ẽr·op′tiçs, *n.* [*hetero-*, and Gr. *optikos*, optic, from *opsesthai*, to see.] false optics.

het′ẽr·ō·sçōpe, *n.* an apparatus to test heteroscopy.

het″ẽr·os′çō·py, *n.* a difference of vision in the two eyes.

het″ẽr·ō·sex′ū·ăl, *a.* 1. of or characterized by sexual desire for those of the opposite sex: opposed to *homosexual*.

2. in biology, belonging to different sexes, or relating to different sexes.

het″ẽr·ō·sex′ū·ăl, *n.* a heterosexual individual.

het″ẽr·ō·sex″ū·al′i·ty, *n.* 1. a sexual desire for those of the opposite sex.

2. sexual relations between individuals of opposite sex.

Opposed to *homosexuality*.

het·ẽr·ō′sis, *n.* abnormal development and size of animals or plants, produced by crossbreeding.

Het″e·rō·sō′mȧ·tȧ, *n.pl.* [*hetero-*, and Gr. *sōma*, *sōmatos*, body.] a suborder of teleostean fishes, having the body and head not bilaterally symmetrical; the flatfishes.

het″ẽr·ō·som′ȧ·tous (*or* -sō′mȧ-), *a.* pertaining to the *Heterosomata*; having a body bilaterally asymmetrical.

het′ẽr·ō·sōme, *n.* one of the *Heterosomata*.

het″ẽr·ō·sō′mous, *a.* same as *heterosomatous*.

het″ẽr-ō-spōr′iç, *a.* heterosporous.

het″ẽr-ō-spōr′ous, *a.* [*hetero-*, and Gr. *sporos*, seed.] producing more than one kind of asexual spore; especially, producing microspores and megaspores: opposed to *homosporous*.

het″ẽr-ō-stat′iç, *a.* [*hetero-*, and Gr. *statikos*, causing to stand, from *histanai*, to cause to stand.] in electricity, pertaining to an electrometer or any instrument for measuring potential, in which there is electrification independent of that to be tested.

het-ẽr-os′trō-phē, *n.* same as *heterostrophy*.

het″ẽr-ō-stroph′iç, *a.* pertaining to heterostrophy.

het-ẽr-os′trō-phous, *a.* heterostrophic.

het-ẽr-os′trō-phy, *n.* [*hetero-*, and Gr. *strophē*, a turning, from *strephein*, to turn.] the state of being turned in a direction other than the usual one; an opposite turning, as in certain shells.

het′ẽr-ō-stȳled, *a.* [*hetero-*, and Gr. *stylos*, a pillar.] in botany, heterogonous.

het′ẽr-ō-stȳ″ly, *n.* the condition in which flowers on different plants of the same species have styles of different lengths, thereby encouraging cross-pollination.

het″ẽr-ō-taç′tous, *a.* pertaining to or characterized by heterotaxia.

het″ẽr-ō-tax′i-ȧ, *n.* [*hetero-*, and Gr. *-taxia*, from *taxis*, arrangement, from *tassein*, to order, arrange.] arrangement of parts or organs of the body different from that existing in a normal form or type; confused, abnormal, or heterogeneous arrangement or structure.

het″ẽr-ō-tax′iç, *a.* exhibiting heterotaxia.

het″ẽr-ō-tax′is, het′ẽr-ō-tax″y, *n.* same as *heterotaxia*.

het-ẽr-ot′ō-mous, *a.* [*hetero-*, and Gr. *tomē*, a cutting, from *temnein*, to cut.] in mineralogy, having a different cleavage: applied to a variety of feldspar in which the cleavage differs from common feldspar.

het″ẽr-ō-tō′pi-ȧ, *n.* heterotopy.

het″ẽr-ō-top′iç, *a.* same as *heterotopous*.

het″ẽr-ot′ō-pişm, *n.* heterotopy.

het-ẽr-ot′ō-pous, *a.* characterized by heterotopy; misplaced.

het-ẽr-ot′ō-py, *n.* [*hetero-*, and Gr. *topos*, place.]
1. in pathology, a misplacement of normal tissue, especially a congenital malformation of the brain in which masses of gray matter are found transplanted into the white.
2. in biology, a deviation from the true ontogenetic sequence with reference to the place of organs or parts.

Het-e-rot′ri-chȧ, *n.pl.* [*hetero-*, and Gr. *thrix*, *trichos*, hair.] in zoology, an order of ciliate infusorians, comprising some twenty genera, and containing the largest of the species.

het-e-rot′ri-chous, *a.* pertaining to the *Heterotricha*.

het-ẽr-ot′rō-păl, *a.* heterotropous.

het-ẽr-ō-troph′iç, *a.* [from *hetero-* and Gr. *trophikos*, nursing, from *trephein*, to nourish.] obtaining food from organic material; unable to use inorganic matter to form proteins and carbohydrates.

het-ẽr-ot′rō-phy, *n.* [*hetero-*, and Gr. *trophē*, nourishment, from *trephein*, to feed, nourish.] in botany, an irregular method of deriving nutrition; an inability to use inorganic matter to form proteins and carbohydrates: applied especially to certain species of the oak family which have no root hairs and are dependent for nutrition upon a fungus, the hyphae of which surround the roots and perform the functions of root hairs.

het″ẽr-ō-trop′iç, *a.* anisotropic; aeolotropic.

het-ẽr-ot′rō-pous, *a.* [*hetero-*, and Gr. *tropos*, a turning, from *trepein*, to turn.] in botany, having the embryo or ovule oblique or transverse to the axis of the seed.

het″ẽr-ō-typ′iç, *a.* designating or of the first meiotic division of a germ cell.

het″ẽr-ō-typ′iç-ăl, *a.* heterotypic.

het″ẽr-ō-zȳ′gōte, *n.* [*hetero-*, and *zygote*.] in Mendel's theory of heredity, a plant or animal having one or more recessive characteristics and hence not breeding true to type; hybrid: opposed to *homozygote*.

he̱′thing, *n.* contempt; mockery. [Obs.]

het′măn, *n.*; *pl.* **het′măns,** [Pol., from G. *hauptmann*, head or chief man; *haupt*, head, and *mann*, man.]
1. formerly, a Polish military commander.
2. a Cossack chief or leader.

het′măn-āte, *n.* the rule of a hetman.

het′măn-ship, *n.* the office or rank of a hetman.

het up, [*het*, dial. pt. and pp. of *heat*.] excited. [Slang.]

Heū′che-rȧ, *n.* [after J. H. *Heucher*, a German botanist.] a genus of North American perennial plants of the saxifrage family, having round heart-shaped root leaves and a prolonged narrow panicle in small clusters of greenish or purplish flowers.

heūgh (hūkh), *n.* 1. a crag; a precipice; a glen with steep, overhanging sides. [Scot.]
2. a coal mine; a pit. [Scot.]

heū′länd-īte, *n.* [after H. *Heuland*, an English mineralogist.] a hydrated silicate of calcium and aluminum, $CaAl_2Si_6O_{16} \cdot 5H_2O$, occurring as crystals with pearly luster.

heū-ret′iç, *n.* [Gr. *heuretikos*, inventive, from *heuriskein*, to invent, discover.] a branch of logic treating of discovery or invention.

heū-ris′tiç, *a.* [Gr. *heuriskein*, to invent, discover.] helping to discover or learn; specifically, designating a method of education or of computer programming in which the pupil or machine proceeds along empirical lines, using rules of thumb, to find solutions or answers.

heū-ris′tiçs, *n.pl.* 1. heuristic methods.
2. [*construed as sing.*] the art or practice of using heuristic methods or procedures.

hew, *v.t.*; hewed, *pt.*; hewed *or* hewn, *pp.*; hewing, *ppr.*; [ME. *hewen*; AS. *heáwan*, to hew.]
1. to cut or chop with an ax or similar instrument; to hack; to gash.
2. to form or shape with an edged instrument: often with *out*; as, to *hew out* a sepulcher.

Rather polishing old works, than *hewing out* new. —Pope.

3. to chop (a tree) with an ax so as to cause it to fall (usually with *down*).

hew, *v.i.* to make cutting or chopping blows with an ax, knife, etc.

hew, *n.* an instance of hewing. [Obs.]

hew, *n.* color. [Obs.]

hew′ẽr, *n.* one who hews.

hew′hōle, *n.* the green woodpecker.

hewn, *v.* alternative past participle of *hew*.

hewn, *a.* cut or formed by hewing.

hex, *n.* [G. *hexe*, fem., *hexer*, masc.; O.H.G. *hagazussa*, akin to AS. *hægtesse*.]
1. a witch or sorcerer. [Dial.]
2. something supposed to bring bad luck; jinx. [Colloq.]

hex, *v.t.* to bewitch; to jinx. [Colloq.]

hex′ȧ-, [from G. *hex*, six.] a combining form meaning *six*, as in *hexa*gram, *hexa*meter: also, before a vowel, *hex-*.

hex-ȧ-bā′siç, *a.* [*hexa-*, and Gr. *basis*, a base.]
1. in chemistry, designating an acid having six replaceable atoms of hydrogen.
2. containing in each molecule six atoms of a univalent metal or the equivalent in combining capacity.

hex-ȧ-çap′sū-lăr, *a.* [*hexa-*, and L. *capsula*, a box.] in botany, having six capsules.

hex′ȧ-çē, *n.* [*hexa-*, and Gr. *akē*, a point.] a summit of a polyhedron formed by the combination of six faces.

hex-ȧ-chlō′rō-phēne, *n.* [from *hexa-*, and *chloro-*, and *phenol*.] a white, odorless powder, $C_{13}Cl_6H_6O_2$, used in medicine to destroy, or prevent the growth of, bacteria.

hex′ȧ-chord, *n.* [*hexa-*, and Gr. *chordē*, a string, chord.]
1. in Greek music, (a) a diatonic series of six tones; (b) the interval of a major sixth; (c) an instrument having six strings.
2. in music, an interval of four tones and one semitone; a series of six notes.

hex-ach′rō-nous, *a.* [*hexa-*, and Gr. *chronos*, time.] in prosody, having six morae.

hex-ac′id, *a.* in chemistry, designating a base having six atoms replaceable by acids.

hex-ȧ-çol′iç, *a.* [*hexa-*, and Gr. *kōlon*, a member.] in ancient prosody, formed of six cola.

hex-ȧ-çor′ăl-line, *a.* [*hexa-*, and Gr. *korallion*, coral.] having septa consisting of six parts, as corals.

hex-ȧ-çor′ăl-line, *n.* a hexacoralline coral.

hex′açt, *a.* hexactinal.

hex-aç′ti-năl, *a.* [*hex-*, and Gr. *aktis*, *aktinos*, a ray.] in zoology, having six rays.

hex-aç-ti-nel′lid, *a.* [*hex-*, and Gr. *aktis*, *aktinos*, a ray.] in zoology, having siliceous six-rayed spicules: said of certain sponges.

hex-aç-ti-nel′line, *a.* hexactinellid.

Hex-aç-tin′i-ȧ, *n.pl.* [*hex-*, and Gr. *aktis*, *aktinos*, a ray.] in zoology, the *Anthozoa*.

hex-aç-tin′i-ăn, *a.* in zoology, said of certain polyps which have septa in multiples of six.

hex′ad, *a.* [LL. *hexas*; Gr. *hexas*, *hexados*, the number six, from *hex*, six.] in chemistry, having a valence of six.

hex′ad, *n.* 1. in chemistry, an element the atoms of which have a valence of six.
2. a series or group of six.

hex-ȧ-daç′tyl-işm, *n.* the condition or quality of being hexadactylous.

hex-ȧ-daç′tyl-ous, *a.* [*hexa-*, and Gr. *daktylos*, a finger or toe.] having six fingers or toes.

hex-ȧ-deç′āne, *n.* [*hexa-*, and Gr. *deka*, ten; so called because each molecule contains 16 atoms of carbon.] a semisolid hydrocarbon, $C_{16}H_{34}$, derived from petroleum.

hex-ad′iç, *a.* of, or having the nature of, a hexad.

hex-ȧ-em′ẽr-on, *n.* [LL. *hexaemeron*, the six days of the creation; L.Gr. *hexaēmeros*, as adj., of or in six days; *hexa*, six, and *hēmera*, day.]
1. in the Bible, (a) the six-day period of the Creation; (b) a history of this, as in Genesis.
2. a treatise dealing with the Creation.
Also *hexahemeron*, *hexameron*.

hex′ȧ-foil, *a.* six-foiled or six-lobed.

hex′ȧ-gon, *n.* [L. *hexagonum*; Gr. *hexagōnon*, a hexagon, properly neut. of *hexagōnos*, six-cornered; *hex*, six, and *gōnia*, a corner, an angle.] in geometry, a plane figure of six sides and six angles.

hex-ag′ō-năl, *a.* 1. of, or having the form of, a hexagon.
2. having a six-sided base or section: said of a solid figure.
3. in crystallography, designating or of a system having six-sided forms.

hex-ag′ō-năl-ly, *adv.* in the form of a hexagon.

hex′ȧ-gram, *n.* [Gr. *hexa*, six, and *gramma*, a line, letter, writing, from *graphein*, to write.]
1. a six-pointed star formed by extending the sides of a regular hexagon, or by placing one equilateral triangle over another so that corresponding sides intersect.
2. any figure of six lines.
3. one of the sixty-four figures made up of six parallel lines, which form the basis of the Chinese I Ching, or Book of Changes.

Hex-ȧ-gyn′i-ȧ, *n.pl.* [*hexa-*, and Gr. *gynē*, a female.] in botany, an order of plants in the Linnaean system having six styles.

hex-ȧ-gyn′i-ăn, *a.* in botany, having six styles.

hex-ag′y-nous, *a.* hexagynian.

hex-ȧ-hē′drăl, *a.* having the form of a hexahedron; having six plane surfaces.

hex-ȧ-hē′drŏn, *n.*; *pl.* **hex-ȧ-hē′drŏns, hex-ȧ-hē′drȧ,** [*hexa-*, and Gr. *hedra*, a seat, base.] a solid body with six plane surfaces.

hex″a-hem′ẽr-on, *n.* hexaemeron.

hex″a-hȳ′drāte, *n.* a hydrate containing six gram-molecular weights of water per gram-molecular weight of the substance combined with the water.

hex″a-hȳ′driç, *a.* containing six hydroxyl radicals; as, a *hexahydric* alcohol.

hex″ȧ-kis-oç-tȧ-hē′drŏn, *n.* same as *hexoctahedron*.

hex″ȧ-kis-tet-rȧ-hē′drŏn, *n.* same as *hexatetrahedron*.

hex-am′ẽr-on, *n.* hexaemeron.

hex-am′ẽr-ous, *a.* [Gr. *hexamerēs*, of six parts; *hex*, six, and *meros*, a part.] having six parts; specifically, (a) in botany, having the parts of the flower in sixes; (b) in zoology, having the radiating parts of organs arranged in sixes. Also written 6-*merous*.

hex-am′e-tẽr, *n.* [L. *hexameter*; Gr. *hexametros*, of six measures or feet, hexameter; *hex*, six, and *metron*, a measure.]
1. in prosody, a verse of six feet, the first four of which may be either dactyls or spondees, the fifth normally a dactyl, though sometimes a spondee, and the sixth a spondee or trochee.
2. verse consisting of hexameters.

hex-am′e-tẽr, *a.* in prosody, composed of six feet; as, a *hexameter* verse.

hex″ȧ-meth′yl-ēne-tet″rȧ-mine′, *a.* [*hexamethylene*, and *tetramine*.] a crystalline compound, $C_6H_{12}N_4$, used to speed up the vulcanization of rubber and, in medicine, as a urinary antiseptic.

hex-am′e-trăl, *a.* hexametric.

hex-ȧ-met′riç, *a.* 1. of hexameter.
2. arranged in hexameters.

hex-ȧ-met′riç-ăl, *a.* hexametric.

hex-am′e-trist, *n.* one who writes hexameters.

Hex-an′dri-ȧ, *n.pl.* [*hex-*, and Gr. *anēr*, *andros*, a male.] in the Linnaean system of botany, a class of plants having six stamens, which are all of equal or nearly equal length.

hex-an′dri-ăn, *a.* hexandrous.

hex-an′drous, *a.* having six stamens.

hex′āne, *n.* [Gr. *hex*, six, and *-ane*.] in chemistry, any of the five colorless, volatile, liquid hydrocarbons, C_6H_{14}, of the paraffin series.

hex·an′gū·lăr, *a.* [*hex-*, and L. *angulus*, an angle.] having six angles or corners.

hex·ȧ·pär′tīte, *a.* [*hexa-*, and L. *partitus*, pp. of *partire*, to divide.] in architecture, divided by its arching into six parts: said of a vault.

hex·ȧ·pet′ăl·ous, *a.* [*hexa-*, and Gr. *petalon*, a leaf.] in botany, having six petals or flower leaves.

hex·ȧ·phyl′lous, *a.* [*hexa-*, and Gr. *phyllon*, a leaf.] in botany, having six leaves.

hex′ȧ·plȧ, *n.pl.* [*construed as sing.*] [Mod. L.; Gr. *hexapla*, neut. pl. of *hexaploos*, *hexaplous*, sixfold; *hexa*, six, and *-ploos*, -fold.]

1. an edition having six versions arranged in parallel columns.

2. [H-] Origen's edition of the Old Testament.

hex′ȧ·plăr, *a.* containing six columns.

hex′ȧ·pod, *a.* [*hexa-*, and Gr. *pous*, *podos*, a foot.] having six feet.

hex′ȧ·pod, *n.* an invertebrate, six-footed animal; one of the *Hexapoda*.

Hex·ap′ō·dȧ, *n.pl.* [*hexa-*, and Gr. *pous*, *podos*, foot.] the true or six-legged insects.

hex·ap′ō·dăn, *a.* and *n.* same as *hexapod*.

hex·ap′ō·dous, *a.* six-footed; pertaining to the *Hexapoda*.

hex·ap′ō·dy, *n.*; *pl.* **hex·ap′ō·dieṣ,** [Gr. *hexapous*, having six feet; *hex*, six, and *pous*, *podos*, a foot.] in prosody, a line of verse composed of six feet; a hexameter.

hex·ap′tẽr·ous, *a.* [*hexa-*, and Gr. *pteron*, a wing.] in botany, having six parts resembling wings, as a plant.

hex′ärch·y, *n.*; *pl.* **hex′ärch·ieṣ,** a group of six friendly or allied states or governments.

hex·ȧ·sē′miç, *a.* [LL. *hexasemus*; Gr. *hexasēmos*, containing six morae; *hex*, six, and *sēmeion*, a sign, mark, mora.] in ancient prosody, composed of or containing six morae; hexachronous.

hex·ȧ·stem′ō·nous, *a.* [*hexa-*, and Gr. *stēmōn*, warp, a stamen.] in botany, having six stamens.

hex′ȧ·stich, *n.* [L. *hexastichus*; Gr. *hexastichos*, of six lines or rows; *hex*, six, and *stichos*, a row, line, verse.] a stanza or poem composed of six lines.

hex·as′ti·chon, *n.* a hexastich.

hex·as′ti·chous, *a.* [*hexa-*, and Gr. *stichos*, a row, line.] in botany, having parts arranged in six vertical rows.

hex′ȧ·stȳ·lăr, *a.* in architecture, having six columns in front.

hex′ȧ·stȳle, *a.* hexastylar.

hex′ȧ·stȳle, *n.* [L. *hexastylus*; Gr. *hexastylos*, having six columns in front; *hex*, six, and *stylos*, a column.] in architecture, a portico or temple having six columns in front.

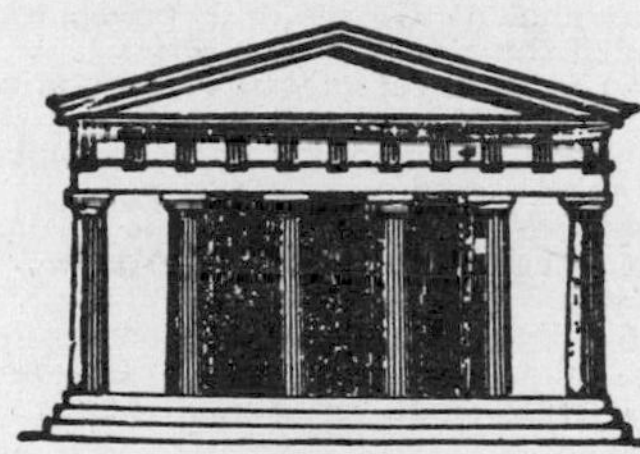

HEXASTYLE

hex″ȧ·syl·lab′iç, *a.* consisting of six syllables.

hex·ȧ·tet·rȧ·hē′drŏn, *n.*; *pl.* **hex·ȧ·tet·rȧ·hē′drȧ,** [*hexa-*, and Gr. *tetra*, four, and *hedra*, a seat, base.] in crystallography, a hemihedron enclosed by twenty-four scalenes.

Hex′ȧ·teūch, *n.* [*hexa-*, and Gr. *teuchos*, a tool, implement, book.] the first six books of the Old Testament.

Hex′ȧ·teūch·ăl, *a.* pertaining to the Hexateuch.

hex·ȧ·tom′iç, *a.* [*hexa-*, and Gr. *atomos*, an atom.] in chemistry, consisting of six atoms: also applied to atoms that are hexavalent, and to alcohols or other compounds having six replaceable hydrogen atoms.

hex·av′ȧ·lent, *a.* [*hexa-*, and L. *valens* (*-entis*), ppr. of *valere*, to have power.]

1. having a valence of six.

2. having six valences: also *sexivalent*.

hex·ax′ōn, *a.* [*hex-*, and Gr. *axōn*, an axle.] having six axes of growth, as a spicule of a sponge.

hex′en·be·ṣen, *n.* [G., from *hexe* and *besen*.] an abnormal growth of shoots at the ends of branches, usually caused by certain fungi; witches'-broom.

hex′ine, *n.* [Gr. *hex*, six, and *-ine*.] in chemistry, a volatile compound, C_6H_{10}, of the acetylene series, derived artificially.

hex·i·ol′ō·ġy, *n.* [Gr. *hexis*, a condition, state, habit, from *echein*, to have, hold, and *-logia*, from *legein*, to speak.] the science dealing with the relation of living beings to their environment.

hex·oç·tȧ·hē′drŏn, *n.* [*hex-*, and Gr. *oktaēdron*, an octahedron; *oktō*, eight, and *hedra*, a seat, base.] a solid contained under forty-eight equal triangular faces.

hex·ō′iç, *a.* in chemistry, relating to or obtained from hexane.

hex′ōne, *n.* [Gr. *hex*, six, and *-one*.] in chemistry, a colorless liquid, $C_6H_{12}O$, used as a solvent for gums, resin, etc.

hex′ōne, *a.* designating a group of organic bases containing six carbon atoms in each molecule, formed by the hydrolysis of proteins.

hex′ō·san, *n.* [from *hexose*, and *-an*.] any of a group of polysaccharides that form hexoses when hydrolyzed.

hex′ōse, *n.* [from *hex-*, and *-ose*.] any of a group of simple sugars containing six carbon atoms in each molecule, as dextrose or fructose.

hex′yl, *n.* [Gr. *hex*, six, and *-yl*.] the hypothetical radical C_6H_{13}, of the hexane series.

hex′yl·ēne, *n.* [*hex-*, and *-yl*, and ethyl*ene*.] in chemistry, one of the ethylene series of hydrocarbons, C_6H_{12}, obtained by distillation from certain coals, and also produced artificially: called also *hexene*.

hex·yl′iç, *a.* relating to or obtained from hexyl or hexane.

hex″yl·reṣ·or′cin·ōl, *n.* [*hexyl*, and *resorcinol*.] a nonpoisonous, pale-yellow, crystalline substance, $C_6H_{13}C_6H_3(OH)_2$, used as an antiseptic and germicide.

hey, *interj.* [ME. *hei*, *hey*; compare D. *hei*; Sw. *hej*.] an exclamation used (a) to express surprise or joy; (b) to attract attention; (c) to incite, as dogs; (d) as an interrogative; as, *hey?* what did you say?

hey′dāy, *interj.* an expression of exultation, surprise, or wonder.

hey′dāy, *n.* [for *high-day*; ME. *hey*, high, and *day*.] the time of greatest health, vigor, beauty, prosperity, etc.; prime.

Hez·e·kī′ăh, *n.* in the Bible, any of several persons of the Old Testament; especially, a king of Judah, contemporary with the prophet Isaiah: 2 Kings xviii—xx.

Hf, in chemistry, hafnium.

Hg, *hydrargyrum*, [L.] in chemistry, mercury.

H′-Hour (āch′our), *n.* in military usage, the exact but unspecified hour at which a military operation is to begin: see also *D-Day*.

hī, *interj.* 1. [contr. from *hiya*, contr. from *how are you?*] an exclamation of greeting.

2. an exclamation used to call attention.

hī·ā′tăl, *a.* of or pertaining to a hiatus.

hī·ā′tăl hẽr′nĭ·ȧ, a hernia of part of the stomach into the opening in the diaphragm through which the esophagus passes: called also *hiatus hernia*.

hī·ā′tus, *n.*; *pl.* **hī·ā′tus·eṣ** or **hī·ā′tus,** [L. *hiatus*, pp. of *hiare*, to gape.]

1. an opening; a gap; a chasm.

2. a slight pause in pronunciation between two successive vowels in adjacent words or syllables, as between the successive *e*'s in *he entered* and *re-enter*.

3. an omission or loss in a manuscript; a lacuna.

hi·bä′chĭ, *n.*; *pl.* **hi·bä′chĭṣ,** [Japan., from *hi*, fire, and *bachi*, bowl.] a charcoal-burning brazier and grill of Japanese design.

Hib·bẽr′ti·ȧ, *n.* [after George *Hibbert*, English botanist.] a genus of plants comprising about seventy species, native to Australia; the rockroses.

hī′bẽr·naç·le, *n.* same as *hibernaculum*, *b & c*.

hī·bẽr·naç′ū·lum, *n.*; *pl.* **hī·bẽr·naç′ū·lȧ,** [L., winter residence, from *hibernare*: see *hibernate*.] any case or covering for protecting an organism during the winter; specifically, (a) a bud or bulb for protecting a plant; (b) a specially modified bud, as in some freshwater polyzoans, that can develop into a colony in the spring; (c) a structure in which a dormant animal passes the winter.

hī·bẽr′năl, *a.* [L. *hibernalis*, from *hiems*, winter.] of winter; wintry.

hī′bẽr·nāte, *v.i.*; hibernated, *pt.*, *pp.*; hibernating, *ppr.* [L. *hibernatus*, pp. of *hibernare*, to pass the winter, from *hibernus*, belonging to winter, from *hiems*, winter.]

1. to spend the winter.

2. to pass the winter in a dormant state, as certain animals: opposed to *aestivate*.

hī·bẽr·nā′tion, *n.* the act, state, or time of hibernating.

Hī·bẽr′ni·ăn, *a.* pertaining to Hibernia (Latin name for *Ireland*) or to its people; Irish. [Poetic.]

Hī·bẽr′ni·ăn, *n.* a native or inhabitant of Ireland. [Poetic.]

Hī·bẽr′ni·ăn·iṣm, *n.* Hibernicism.

Hī·bẽr′ni·ciṣm, *n.* an idiom, characteristic, or custom peculiar to the Irish.

Hī·bẽr′ni·cīze, *v.t.* to make Irish.

hī·bẽr·ni·zā′tion, *n.* hibernation.

Hī·bẽr′nō-Celt′iç, *n.* the Gaelic language of the Irish.

Hī·bẽr′nō-Celt′iç, *a.* pertaining to the Irish Celts.

Hī·bẽr·nol′ō·ġist, *n.* one who studies Hibernology.

Hī·bẽr·nol′ō·ġy, *n.* [L. *Hibernia*, Ireland, and Gr. *-logia*, from *legein*, to speak.] the study of Irish antiquities and history.

Hī·bis′çus, *n.* [L. *hibiscus* or *hibiscum*; Gr. *hibiskos*, the marshmallow.]

1. in botany, an extensive genus of tropical plants, shrubs, and small trees of the mallow family, with large, colorful flowers.

2. [h-] a plant of the genus *Hibiscus*.

hiç′cl·us doç′ti·us, a juggler. [Slang.]

hiç′cup, hiç′cough (-kup), *n.* [Early Mod. Eng. *hikop*, *hickock*, vars. of *hicket*; akin to or from Walloon Fr. *hikett*, from echoic base; *hiccough* is a late sp. after *cough*.]

1. a sudden, involuntary contraction of the diaphragm that closes the glottis at the moment of breathing in.

2. the sharp, quick sound made by this.

hiç′cup, *v.i.*; hiccuped (-kupt), *pt.*, *pp.*; hiccupping, *ppr.* to make a hiccup or hiccups: also *hiccough*.

hiç′cup, *v.t.* to utter with a hiccup or hiccups: also *hiccough*.

hiç et ū·bī′quē, [L.] here and everywhere.

hiç jā′cet, [L.] 1. here lies: inscribed on tombstones.

2. an epitaph.

hick, *n.* [altered from *Richard*.] a person having the awkwardness, simplicity, and lack of sophistication regarded as characteristic of people from the country; rustic; hayseed: somewhat contemptuous term. [Colloq.]

hick, *a.* of or like a hick or hicks. [Colloq.]

hick′ey, *n.* [orig. U.S. dial., prob. for *doohickey*.]

1. a device; gadget; specifically, (a) a tool used for bending pipe; (b) a coupling for electrical fixtures.

2. a pimple or pustule. [Colloq.]

hick joint, in masonry, a joint which is made level with the surface of the mortar.

hick′ō·ry, *n.*; *pl.* **hick′ō·rieṣ,** [Am. Ind. *pohickory*, the hickory tree.]

1. a North American tree of the genus *Carya*, belonging to the walnut family, with large leaves, greenish flowers, and smooth-shelled nuts.

2. the hard, tough wood of the hickory tree.

3. a switch or cane of this wood.

4. the nut of any of the hickory trees: also *hickory nut*.

hick′ō·ry bōr′ẽr, a beetle, the larvae of which infest the bark of the hickory.

hick′ō·ry eū·çȧ·lyp′tus, an Australian tree, *Eucalyptus punctata*, yielding a valuable wood which is used for building and other purposes.

hick′ō·ry ġīr′dlẽr, an American beetle, *Oncideres cingulatus*, which girdles the branches of the hickory.

hick′ō·ry head (hed), the ruddy duck.

hick′ō·ry pīne, *Pinus balfouriana* of the western United States: also, *Pinus pungens* of the eastern United States.

hick′ō·ry shad, 1. the gizzard shad.

2. the fall herring.

Hicks′īte, *n.* one of a sect of Friends or Quakers founded in the United States in 1827 by Elias Hicks, and holding Unitarian doctrines.

hick′wall, *n.* 1. a woodpecker, especially *Picus minor*, the little spotted woodpecker. [Brit. Dial.]

2. *Parus cæruleus*, the little blue titmouse.

hid, *v.* past tense and alternative past participle of *hide*.

hīd′āġe, *n.* [*hide*, a quantity of land, and *-age*.] a tax formerly paid to the kings of England for every hide of land.

hi·dal′gō, *n.*; *pl.* **hi·dal′gōş**, [Sp., contr. of *hijo de algo*, son of something; *hijo*, son, *de*, of, and *algo*, something.] in Spain, a nobleman of secondary rank, below that of a grandee.
hid′den, *v.* past participle of *hide*.
hid′den, *a.* concealed; mysterious; unseen; secret.
hidden fifths or *octaves*; in music, the consecutive fifths or octaves suggested when two voices proceed in similar (not parallel) motion to a fifth or octave.
hid′den·ite, *n.* [after W. E. *Hidden*, Am. mineralogist.] an emerald-green variety of spodumene found in North Carolina and prized as a gem: called also *lithia emerald*.
hid′den·ly, *adv.* in a hidden, secret manner.
hid′den·ness, *n.* the state of being hidden or concealed. [Rare.]
hid′den-veined, *a.* in botany, having concealed veins, as certain leaves; hyphodrome.
hīde, *v.t.*; hid, *pt.*; hidden *or* hid, *pp.*; hiding, *ppr.* [ME. *hiden*, *hyden*; AS. *hydan*, to hide, conceal.]
1. to conceal; to withhold or withdraw from sight; to secrete; as, to *hide* a book; to *hide* a wound.
2. to conceal from the knowledge of others; to keep secret; to suppress.
Tell me now what thou hast done; *hide* it not from me. —Josh. vii. 19.
3. to protect; to keep in safety; to shelter; to remove from danger.
In the time of trouble he shall *hide* me in his pavilion. —Ps. xxvii. 5.
4. to keep from being seen by covering up, obscuring, etc.; to obstruct the view or sight of.
5. to turn away; as, he *hid* his head in shame.
Syn.—conceal, secrete, mask, dissemble, protect, disguise, screen, cover.
hīde, *v.i.* 1. to be or lie out of sight or concealed.
2. to keep oneself out of sight; conceal oneself.
hīde, *n.* [LL. *hida*, from AS. *hid*, *higed*, a certain portion of land for the support of one family, from *hiwan*, a family.] in old English law, a portion of land, varying from 80 to 120 acres.
hīde, *n.* [ME. *hide*, *hyde*; AS. *hyd*, a skin, hide.]
1. the skin of an animal, either raw or dressed: generally applied to the undressed skin of a larger domestic animal, as an ox, horse, etc.
2. the human skin: now humorous or contemptuous. [Colloq.]
neither hide nor hair; nothing whatsoever.
hīde, *v.t.*; hided, *pt.*, *pp.*; hiding, *ppr.* 1. to take the hide off; to skin.
2. to beat severely; thrash; flog. [Colloq.]
hīde′-and-seek′, *n.* a children's game in which some hide themselves and others seek them: also *hide-and-go-seek*.
hīde′bound, *a.* 1. having the skin sticking so closely to the ribs and back as not to be easily loosened or raised: said of animals.
2. having the bark so close or firm that it impedes the growth: said of a tree.
3. obstinate; bigoted; narrow-minded; prejudiced.
4. niggardly; penurious. [Obs.]
hid′ē·ous, *a.* [ME. *hidyous*, *hidous*; OFr. *hidos*, *hisdos*, from L. *hispidus*, rough, shaggy.] horrible to look at, hear, etc.; very ugly; revolting; dreadful.
hid′ē·ous·ly, *adv.* 1. in a hideous manner.
2. to a hideous extent.
hid′ē·ous·ness, *n.* the state or quality of being hideous.
hīde′-out, *n.* a hiding place for gangsters, etc. [Colloq.]
hīd′ẽr, *n.* one who hides or conceals.
hīd′ing, *n.* [ME. *hidinge*.]
1. (a) the act of one that hides; (b) the condition of being hidden: usually in the phrase *in hiding*.
2. a place to hide.
hīd′ing, *n.* a flogging. [Colloq.]
hi·drō′sis, *n.* [Gr. *hidrōsis*, perspiration, from *hidroun*, to perspire, sweat, from *idos*, sweat.] in pathology, (a) perspiration; sweating; (b) abnormally profuse sweating; (c) any skin disease marked by disorder of the sweat glands.
hi·drot′iç, *a.* 1. having to do with sweat.
2. inducing perspiration; sudorific.
hi·drot′iç, *n.* any medicine that induces perspiration; a sudorific.
hīe, *v.i.*; hied, *pt.*, *pp.*; hieing *or* hying, *ppr.* [ME. *hien*, *hyen*; AS. *higian*, to hasten, to strive.] to hasten; to speed: often with a reflexive pronoun.
hīe, *v.t.* to incite; to urge; as, to *hie* on hounds.
hīe, *n.* haste; diligence. [Obs.]
hī′e·māl, *a.* [L. *hiemalis*, of winter, from *hiems*, winter.] belonging to winter; wintry.
hī′e·māte, *v.i.* [L. *hiematus*, pp. of *hiemare*, to pass the winter, from *hiems*, winter.] to winter. [Rare.]
hī·e·mā′tion, *n.* [L. *hiematio* (*-onis*), wintering, from *hiemare*, to pass the winter.] a wintering. [Obs.]
hī′emş, *n.* [L.] winter.
hī′ẽr-, see *hiero-*.
Hī·e·rā′ci·um, *n.* [Gr. *hierakion*, a plant, the hawkweed, from *hierax* (*-akos*), a hawk.] a large genus of plants, the hawkweeds, belonging to the aster family. There are over 300 species widely distributed throughout the temperate regions of the globe, about 25 being known in North America.
hī·ẽr·ā′cō·sphinx, *n.* [Gr. *hierax* (*-akos*), a hawk, and *sphinx*, a sphinx.] an Egyptian sphinx with the head of a hawk.
hī″e·rȧ·pī′çrȧ, *n.* [LL., from Gr. *hiera*, f. of *hieros*, sacred, and *pikra*, f. of *pikros*, sharp, bitter.] a cathartic powder made of pulverized aloes and canella bark.
hī′ẽr·ärçh, *n.* [LL. *hierarcha*; Gr. *hierarchēs*, a steward or keeper of sacred things; *hieros*, sacred, and *archos*, a ruler, from *archein*, to rule, lead.] one who rules or has authority in a religious group or society; a high priest.
hī′ẽr·ärçh·ăl, *a.* pertaining to a hierarch or hierarchy.
hī·ẽr·ärçh′iç, *a.* pertaining to a hierarchy.
hī·ẽr·ärçh′iç·ăl, *a.* hierarchic.
hī·ẽr·ärçh′iç·ăl·ly, *adv.* in a hierarchic manner.
hī′ẽr·ärçh·işm, *n.* hierarchical principles or power; hierarchal character.
The more dominant *hierarchism* of the West. —Milman.
hī′ẽr·ärçh·y, *n.*; *pl.* **hī′ẽr·ärçh·ieş**, [LL. *hierarchia*; Gr. *hierarchia*, the power or rule of a hierarch, from *hierarchēs*, a hierarch.]
1. a system of church government by priests or other clergy in graded ranks.
2. the group of officials in such a system.
3. a group of persons or things arranged in order of rank, grade, class, etc.
4. in theology, (a) any of the three divisions of angels; (b) all the angels.
hī·ẽr·at′iç, *a.* [L. *hieraticus*; Gr. *hieratikos*, of or pertaining to the priest's office, sacerdotal, from *hieros*, sacred.]
1. of or used by priests; priestly; sacerdotal.
2. designating or of the abridged form of cursive hieroglyphic writing once used by Egyptian priests.
hī·ẽr·at′iç·ăl, *a.* hieratic.
hī′ẽr·ō-, [from Gr. *hieros*, sacred, holy.] a combining form meaning *sacred*, *holy*, *consecrated*, etc., as in *hiero*gram, *hiero*latry: also, before a vowel, *hier-*.
hī·ẽr·oç′rȧ·cy, *n.*; *pl.* **hī·ẽr·oç′rȧ·cieş**, [*hiero-*, and Gr. *kratos*, power, from *kratein*, to rule.] government by priests or other clergy; a hierarchy.
hī·ẽr·ō·çrat′iç, *a.* of or characterized by hierocracy.
hī·ẽr·ō·çrat′iç·ăl, *a.* hierocratic.
hī′ẽr·ō·dūle, *n.* [*hiero-*, and Gr. *doulos*, a slave.] in ancient Greece, a slave dedicated to a divinity; a temple slave.
hī′ẽr·ō·glyph, *n.* [Fr. *hieroglyphe*.] a hieroglyphic.
hī′ẽr·ō·glyph, *v.t.* to represent by hieroglyphs. [Rare.]
hī″ẽr·ō·glyph′iç, *a.* [LL. *hieroglyphicus*; Gr. *hieroglyphikos*, hieroglyphic, from *hieroglyphos*, a carver of hieroglyphs; *hieros*, sacred, and *glyphein*, to carve, hollow out.]
1. of, or having the nature of, hieroglyphics.
2. written in hieroglyphics.
3. symbolical; emblematic.
4. hard to read or understand.
hī″ẽr·ō·glyph′iç, *n.* 1. a picture or symbol representing a word, syllable, or sound, used by the ancient Egyptians and others instead of alphabetic letters.
2. [*usually pl.*] a method of writing using hieroglyphics; picture writing.
3. a symbol, sign, etc. hard to understand.
4. [*pl.*] writing hard to read or understand.

EGYPTIAN HIEROGLYPHICS

hī″ẽr·ō·glyph′iç·ăl, *a.* hieroglyphic.
hī″ẽr·ō·glyph′iç·ăl·ly, *adv.* in a hieroglyphic manner.
hī·ẽr·og′ly·phist, *n.* an expert or specialist in interpreting hieroglyphics.
hī′ẽr·ō·gram, *n.* [*hiero-*, and Gr. *gramma*, a writing, from *graphein*, to write.] a writing or symbol of a sacred character.
hī″ẽr·ō·gram·mat′iç, hī″ẽr·ō·gram·mat′iç·ăl, *a.* written in or pertaining to hierograms; relating to sacred writing.
hī″ẽr·ō·gram′mȧ·tist, *n.* a writer of hierograms.
hī·ẽr·og′rȧ·phẽr, *n.* [Gr. *hierographos*, a writer of sacred scripture; *hieros*, sacred, and *graphein*, to write.] a writer of or one versed in hierography.
hī″ẽr·ō·graph′iç, hī″ẽr·ō·graph′iç·ăl, *a.* pertaining to sacred writing.
hī·ẽr·og′rȧ·phy, *n.* sacred writing. [Rare.]
hī·ẽr·ol′ȧ·try, *n.* [*hiero-*, and Gr. *latreia*, worship, from *latreuein*, to worship.] the worship of saints or sacred things. [Rare.]
hī″ẽr·ō·log′iç, hī″ẽr·ō·log′iç·ăl, *a.* pertaining to hierology.
hī·ẽr·ol′ō·ġist, *n.* one versed in hierology.
hī·ẽr·ol′ō·ġy, *n.* [Gr. *hierologia*, sacred or mystical language; *hieros*, sacred, and *-logia*, from *legein*, to speak.] the religious lore and religious literature of a people.
hī′ẽr·ō·man·cy, *n.* [*hiero-*, and Gr. *manteia*, divination.] divination by observing the objects offered in sacrifice.
hī″ẽr·ō·mär′tyr, *n.* [Gr. *hieromartys*; hieros, sacred, and *martys*, *martyr*, a witness, a martyr.] a priest or other person in holy orders who suffers martyrdom.
hī″e·rom·nē′mon, *n.* [Gr. *hieromnēmōn*, lit., mindful of sacred things, from *hieros*, sacred, and *mnēmōn*, mindful, from *mnāsthai*, to remember.]
1. in ancient Greece, a sacred recorder; one of the class of representatives who composed the amphictyonic council.
2. a minister of religion, as at Byzantium.
hī·ẽr·om′ō·naçh, *n.* [Gr. *hieromonachos*; *hieros*, sacred, and *monachos*, a monk.] in the Orthodox Eastern Church, a monk who is also a preist.
hī′ẽr·on, *n.*; *pl.* **hī′ẽr·ȧ**, [Gr. *hieron*, neut. of *hieros*, sacred.] in ancient Greece, a sacred place; a temple; a chapel.
Hī″ẽr·ō·nym′i·ăn, *a.* Hieronymic.
Hī″ẽr·ō·nym′iç, *a.* [from L. *Hieronymus*, Jerome; and *-ic*.] of or done by Saint Jerome.
Hī·ẽr·on′y·mīte, *n.* a member of any of the hermit orders named after Saint Jerome.
hī′ẽr·ō·phant, *n.* [LL. *hierophanta*, *hierophantes*; Gr. *hierophantēs*, a hierophant; *hieros*, sacred, and *phainein*, to show.]
1. in ancient Greece, the priest who expounded the Elusinian mysteries.
2. an interpreter of sacred mysteries and esoteric principles.
hī″ẽr·ō·phan′tiç, *a.* relating to a hierophant or his acts.
hī·ẽr·os′çō·py, *n.* [Gr. *hieroskopia*, divination; *hieros*, sacred, and *skopein*, to view.] hieromancy.
Hī″ẽr·ō·sol′y·mī·tăn, *a.* [LL. *Hierosolymitanus*, of Jerusalem, from L. *Hierosolyma*; Gr. *Hierosolyma*, Jerusalem.] pertaining to Jerusalem.
hī″ẽr·ō·thē′çȧ, *n.*; *pl.* **hī″ẽr·ō·thē′cae**, [Gr. *hierothēkē*; *hieros*, sacred, and *thēkē*, a box.] a receptacle in which sacred things are kept.
hī′ẽr·ūr·ġy, *n.* [Gr. *hierourgia*, religious service, worship.] a holy work or worship.
hī·fȧ·lū′tin, *a.* and *n.* see *highfalutin*.
hī′-fī′, *a.* of or having high fidelity of sound reproduction.
hig′gle, *v.i.*; higgled, *pt.*, *pp.*; higgling, *ppr.* [probably a weakened form of *haggle*.]
1. to carry provisions about and offer them for sale; to peddle.
2. to wrangle; to haggle; to argue about terms, price, etc.
hig′gle·dy-pig′gle·dy, *adv.* [extension of Early Mod. Eng. *higle-pigle*, redupl. formation, prob. after *pig*.] in disorder; in jumbled confusion.
hig′gle·dy-pig′gle·dy, *a.* disorderly; jumbled; confused.
hig′gle·dy-pig′gle·dy, *n.*; *pl.* **hig′gle·dy-pig′gle·dieş**, disorder; jumble; confusion.
hig′glẽr, *n.* a person who higgles.
high (hī), *a.*; *comp.* higher; *superl.* highest, [ME. *hie*, *heigh*, *heh*; AS. *heh*.]

1. lofty; tall; of more than normal height: not used of persons.
2. extending upward a (specified) distance.
3. (a) situated far above the ground or some other level; (b) designating or of highland regions; as, *High* German.
4. reaching to or done from a height; as, a *high* jump, a *high* dive.
5. (a) above other persons or things in rank, position, etc.; most important; (b) above other persons or things in quality, character, etc.; superior; excellent.
6. grave; very serious; as, *high* treason.
7. intellectually advanced; complex; profound: usually in the comparative degree; as, *higher* mathematics.
8. main; principal; chief; as, a *high* priest.
9. greater in size, amount, degree, power, intensity, etc. than usual; as, *high* stakes.
10. expensive; costly.
11. luxurious and extravagant; as, *high* living.
12. haughty; overbearing.
13. advanced to its acme or fullness; fully reached; as, *high* noon.
14. designating or producing tones made by relatively fast vibrations; acute in pitch; sharp; shrill.
15. slightly tainted; having a strong smell; as, this meat is *high*.
16. extreme or inflexible in matters of ceremony, doctrine, etc.
17. hilarious; elated; as, *high* spirits.
18. drunk; intoxicated. [Slang.]
19. in geography, designating a latitude far from the equator.
20. in machinery, of, or in adjustment at, the highest transmission ratio: said of gears.
21. in phonetics, produced with part of the tongue raised toward the roof of the mouth: said of a vowel.

high altar; the chief altar in a cathedral or church.

high and dry; (a) completely out of the reach of water, as a vessel ashore; (b) alone and helpless; stranded.

high and mighty; haughty; overbearing. [Colloq.]

high blower; a horse, with sound lungs, that blows considerably, as when galloping or under excitement.

High Church; the party in the Church of England which supported the high claims to prerogative which were maintained by the Stuarts. The *Low Church* entertained more moderate notions, manifested great enmity to popery, and was inclined to circumscribe the royal prerogatives. The term *High Church*, in the Protestant Episcopal church, is now generally applied to those who exalt the authority and jurisdiction of the church, and attach great value to ecclesiastical dignities and ordinances; the terms *Low-Church party* and *Broad-Church party* are applied to those who hold moderate views in regard to these subjects.

high comedy; comedy appealing to, and reflecting the life of, the upper social classes, characterized by witty, and often sophisticated, dialogue; comedy of manners: now often applied to comedy with serious aims, which seeks to provoke thoughtful amusement.

High Commission Court; in England, an ecclesiastical court created and united to the crown by Queen Elizabeth I in 1559. It was abolished in 1641.

high commissioner; (a) the representative of one country stationed in another; (b) formerly, the representative of the League of Nations in a mandate or protectorate.

high day; a festival day; a holiday.

high explosive; any explosive in which the combustion of the particles is so rapid as to be virtually simultaneous throughout the entire mass, so that it has great shattering effect.

High German; (a) the Germanic dialects spoken in the high regions of central and southern Germany: distinguished from *Low German*; (b) the official and literary form of the German language, technically called *New High German*: it is based principally on the High German dialects of middle Germany.

high hand; the use of arbitrary, arrogant methods; overbearing or dictatorial ways.

high hat; a man's tall, black hat, usually of silk; a top hat.

high jinks; (a) formerly, a Scottish game of forfeits played while drinking; (b) noisy, wild pranks; boisterous merriment.

high jump; an athletic contest in which the contestants jump for height over a horizontal bar set between two upright poles: after each successful trial the bar is raised a little.

high life; the mode of living in fashionable circles; life among the upper ranks of society.

high light; (a) a part on which light is brightest; as, the *high lights* on the cheeks; a part of a painting, photograph, etc. on which light is represented as brightest; also, the representation or effect of such light in a painting, photograph, etc.; (b) the most important, interesting, or outstanding part, scene, etc.

High Mass; in the Roman Catholic Church, a Mass with full ceremonials, music, and incense, celebrated usually at the high altar with a deacon and a subdeacon assisting the celebrant.

high milling; a method of making flour by grinding and sifting the grain a number of times in succession.

high noon; the time when the sun is at the meridian; noon exactly.

high place; in ancient Semitic religions, a temple or other place of worship, usually on a high hill.

high priest, (a) a chief priest; (b) the chief priest of the ancient Jewish priesthood.

high relief; in sculpture, etc., relief in which the figures project half or more than half their natural depth from the background; alto-relievo.

high roller; one who lives extravagantly and recklessly. [Slang.]

high school; (a) in educational systems having no junior high school, a school of four grades offering academic or vocational subjects, attended by students who have completed elementary school; (b) in educational systems having a junior high school, a similar school of three grades.

high seas; that part of the ocean or sea not within the limits of any sovereignty.

high spirits; a happy, cheerful mood; gaiety.

high tea; a meal somewhat more elaborate and served later than the usual tea. [Brit.]

high tide; (a) the highest level to which the tide rises; high water; (b) the time when the tide is at this level; (c) any culminating point or time.

high time; (a) time beyond the proper time but before it is too late; none too soon; (b) [Slang.] a good time; a gay, exciting, enjoyable time.

high treason; treason against the government, state, or ruler: the greatest civil offense.

high water; (a) the utmost flow or the highest elevation of the tide; also, the time when the tide is at its full; (b) the highest level reached by a body of water.

high-water mark; (a) the mark left after high water has receded; (b) the highest point reached in tidal flow, flood, etc.: also used figuratively; as, he has reached the *high-water mark* of success.

high-water shrub; *Iva frutescens*, the marsh elder, a plant of the aster family which grows around the borders of salt marshes on the eastern coast of the United States.

high wine; a distilled spirit in which there is a high percentage of alcohol.

Syn.—elevated, lofty, tall, eminent, exalted, noble, haughty, proud.

hīgh, *adv.* 1. in a high manner.
2. in or to a high level, place, degree, rank, etc.

high and low; everywhere; in every place; as, he searched *high and low*.

to fly high; to have high hopes or ambitions.

hīgh, *n.* 1. a high level, place, etc.
2. an area of high barometric pressure.
3. an arrangement of gears giving the greatest speed.

on high; (a) up in space; high above; (b) in heaven.

The Most High; God; the Almighty.

hīgh, *v.i.* to rise to the greatest elevation, as the tide. [Obs.]

hīgh'bạll, *n.* [sense 1 perh. *high*, and *ball*, bartender's slang for "whisky glass"; perh. influenced by the *v.*]
1. liquor, usually whisky or brandy, mixed with soda water, ginger ale, etc. and served with ice in a tall glass: also *high ball*.
2. a railroad signal, originally a ball hung above the tracks, meaning "go ahead": sometimes used figuratively.

hīgh'bạll, *v.i.* to proceed at great speed. [Slang.]

hīgh'bīnd″ẽr, *n.* 1. a ruffian; a gangster. [Slang.]
2. formerly, any of a gang of criminals from the Chinese section of a city who were believed to hire themselves out as assassins. [Slang.]

hīgh'-blood″ed (-blud″), *a.* of high birth; of noble lineage; highborn.

hīgh'-blōwn, *a.* inflated, as with pride or conceit.

hīgh'bọrn, *a.* of noble birth or extraction.

hīgh'boy, *n.* a high chest of drawers mounted on legs.

hīgh'bred, *a.* 1. of superior stock or breed.
2. possessed of good manners; having the characteristics of good breeding; well-mannered; courteous and cultivated.

hīgh'-brow, hīgh'brow, *a.* a person having or pretending to have highly cultivated, intellectual tastes; an intellectual: usually a term of contempt or derision. [Slang.]

hīgh'-brow, hīgh'brow, *n.* of or fit for a highbrow. [Slang.]

hīgh'-built (hī'-bilt), *a.* of lofty structure.

hīgh'chāir, *n.* a baby's chair with a tray, mounted on long legs.

Hīgh'-Chũrch', *a.* of or like the High Church (see *High Church* under *high*, *a.*); stressing formality and ritual in religious observance.

Hīgh'-chũrch'iṣm, *n.* the principles of the High-Church party.

Hīgh'-chũrch'măn, *n.* one who holds High-Church principles.

Hīgh'-chũrch'măn·ship, *n.* the condition of being a High-churchman.

hīgh'-çlass', *a.* superior; of a very high rating.

hīgh'-çŏl'ŏred, *a.* 1. brilliant or intense in color.
2. red; flushed; florid.
3. vivid.
4. exaggerated; lurid.

hīgh'-em·bowed″, *a.* having lofty arches.

hīgh'ẽr ed·ū·çā'tion, college or university education.

hīgh'ẽr-up', *n.* a person of higher rank or position. [Colloq.]

hīgh·fȧ·lū'tin, hīgh·fȧ·lū'ting, *n.* [perh. altered from *high-flown* or, more prob., from *high-floating*, with insertion of intrusive vowel in ridicule of oratorical speech.] high-flown, pompous language. [Colloq.]

hīgh·fȧ·lū'tin, hīgh·fȧ·lū'ting, *a.* high-flown; pretentious. [Colloq.]

hīgh'-fed, *a.* pampered; fed luxuriously.

hīgh fi·del'i·ty, in radio, sound recording, etc., an approximately exact reproduction of sound achieved by the use of a wide range of sound waves, from 50 to 15,000 (or more) cycles.

hīgh'-fin″ished (-isht), *a.* finished or polished with great care; refined; elaborate.

hīgh'-flā″vŏred, *a.* having a strong flavor.

hīgh'flī'ẽr, hīgh'flȳ'ẽr, *n.* 1. a person or thing that flies high.
2. a person who acts, talks, or thinks in an extravagant, overly ambitious manner.
3. in the eighteenth century, an extreme conservative in politics or in religion.

hīgh'-flōwn', *a.* 1. extravagantly ambitious or aspiring.
2. trying to be eloquent; bombastic; inflated; hyperbolic.

hīgh'flȳ·ing, *a.* extravagant in claims, pretensions, or opinions.

hīgh'-frē'quen·cy, *a.* designating or of an alternating electric current or oscillation with a relatively high frequency, now usually more than 20,000 cycles per second.

hīgh'-gō″, *n.* a drinking bout; a spree; a frolic. [Slang.]

hīgh'-grāde', *a.* pertaining to something superior or highly rated; excellent; as, this is *high-grade* oil.

hīgh'hand'ed, *a.* overbearing; arbitrary; arrogant.

hīgh'-hat', *n.* a person who habitually wears a top hat; hence, an aristocrat; a snob. [Slang.]

hīgh'-hat', *a.* 1. snobbish. [Slang.]
2. elegant; stylish. [Slang.]

hīgh'-hat', *v.t.* and *v.i.* to treat or act snobbishly. [Slang.]

hīgh'-heärt″ed, *a.* full of courage.

hīgh'-heärt″ed·ness, *n.* the quality of being high-hearted.

hīgh'hōld″ẽr, *n.* the flicker, or highhole. [Dial.]

hīgh'hōle, *n.* [altered (through folk etym.) from earlier *hyghwhele*, *highwale*; of echoic origin.] the flicker, a kind of woodpecker. [Dial.]

hīgh'jack, *v.t.*; highjacked, *pt.*, *pp.*; highjacking, *ppr.* to hijack. [Colloq.]

hīgh′jack·ẽr, *n.* a hijacker. [Colloq.]

hīgh′-kēyed′ (-kēd′), *a.* 1. pitched in a high key.
2. full of sensitivity and spirit; high-strung.

hīgh′lănd, *n.* elevated land; a mountainous region: used often as a proper name; as, the *Highlands* of Scotland.

hīgh′lănd·ẽr, *n.* 1. an inhabitant of highlands.
2. [H–] an inhabitant of the Highlands of Scotland: also *Highlandman.*

Hīgh′lănd fling, a lively dance of the Scottish Highlands.

hīgh′lănd·ish, *a.* characterized by high or mountainous land.

Hīgh′lănd·ry, *n.* Highlanders, collectively.

hīgh′līght, *v.t.* 1. to give a high light or high lights to: see *high light* under *high, a.*
2. to give prominence to.

hīgh′-lōw, *n.* a kind of laced shoe reaching to the ankle. [Archaic.]

hīgh′ly, *adv.* 1. in or to a high place. [Rare.]
2. in or to a high office or rank.
3. in or to a high degree; very much; very.
4. with high approval or esteem; favorably.
5. at a high price.

hīgh′-met″tled, *a.* having high spirit; ardent; full of fire; as, a *high-mettled* steed.

hīgh′-mīnd″ed, *a.* 1. proud; arrogant. [Rare.]
2. having or showing high ideals, principles, and feelings.

hīgh′-mīnd″ed·ness, *n.* the state or quality of being high-minded.

hīgh′-muck-ă-muck′, *n.* [*high,* and arbitrary formation (perh. based on dial. *muckle,* great).] a person in a position of importance and authority; especially, one who is always making his authority felt. [Slang.]

hīgh′ness, *n.* 1. the quality or state of being high; height; loftiness.
2. [H–] highest of the nobility: a title used in speaking to or of a member of the royal family, preceded by *His, Her,* or *Your.*

hīgh′-oc̦′tāne, *a.* having a high octane number: said of gasoline.

hīgh′-pälmed (hī′-pämd), *a.* having high and full-grown antlers, as a stag of full growth.

hīgh′pitched′ (-pitcht′), *a.* 1. high in pitch; shrill.
2. lofty; exalted.
3. showing intense feeling; agitated.
4. steep in slope: said of roofs.

hīgh′-pow′ẽred, *a.* very powerful.

hīgh′-pres′sūre (-presh′ẽr), *a.* 1. having, using, or withstanding relatively high pressure.
2. using or applying energetic or strongly persuasive methods or arguments.

hīgh′-pres′sūre, *v.t.* to urge or persuade with high-pressure methods or arguments. [Colloq.]

hīgh′-prīced′ (-prīst′), *a.* costly; expensive.

hīgh′-prin″ci·pled (-pld), *a.* having noble principles.

hīgh′-proof′, *a.* highly rectified; very strongly alcoholic; as, *high-proof* spirits.

hīgh′-rēach′ing, *a.* 1. reaching to a great height.
2. ambitious; aspiring.

hīgh′-rīse′, *a.* designating or of a tall apartment house, office building, etc. of many stories.

hīgh′-rīse′, *n.* a high-rise building.

hīgh′rōad, *n.* 1. a highway; a main road.
2. an easy or direct way.

hīgh rōll′ẽr, [from rolling the dice in gambling.]
1. a person who gambles for very high stakes. [Slang.]
2. a person who spends or invests money freely or recklessly. [Slang.]

hīgh′-sound′ing, *a.* pompous; noisy; ostentatious; as, *high-sounding* words.

hīgh′-spir′it·ed, *a.* full of spirit; lively; fiery; also, courageous; noble.

hīgh′step″pẽr, *n.* a horse that has a high step or that carries itself proudly; hence, a person with a proud or dignified bearing. [Colloq.]

hīgh′-strung′, *a.* [from the tuning of stringed instruments.] highly sensitive; nervous and tense; excitable.

hīght (hīt), *a.* [ME. *highte,* merging AS. *hatte,* pass. pt. with *heht,* act. pt. of *hatan,* to command, order, call.] named; called; as, a maiden *hight* Elaine. [Archaic.]

hīgh′-tāil, hīgh′tāil, *v.i.* and *v.t.* to leave or go in a hurry; scurry off: chiefly in *high-tail it.* [Colloq.]

hīgh′-ten′sion, *a.* having or carrying a high voltage.

hīgh′-test′, *a.* 1. passing severe tests; meeting difficult requirements.
2. having a low boiling point: said of gasoline.

hīgh′-tōned′, *a.* 1. high in tone; high-pitched.
2. characterized by dignity, lofty moral or intellectual quality, high principles, etc.: often used ironically or humorously.
3. of or imitating the manners, attitudes, etc. of the upper classes. [Colloq.]

hīgh′top, *n.* the masthead of a ship. [Obs.]

hīgh′ty-tīgh′ty, *a., n.,* and *interj.* same as *hoity-toity.*

hīgh′wāy, *n.* [ME. *heighwei*; see *high* and *way.*]
1. any road freely open to everyone; a public road.
2. a main road; a thoroughfare.
3. a main route by land or water.
4. a direct way to some objective.

hīgh′wāy·măn, *n.*; *pl.* **hīgh′wāy·men,** one who robs on the public road, or lurks in the highway for the purpose of robbing.

hīgh′-wrought′ (-rọt′), *a.* 1. wrought with exquisite art or skill; elaborate.
2. inflamed to a high degree; as, *high-wrought* passion.

hig′-tā″pẽr, *n.* [AS. *hig,* grass, hay, and *taper,* a taper.] the common mullen, *Verbascum thapsus*: also called *hag-taper, high taper.*

hī′jack, *v.t.* [prob. *hi* (for *high*), and *jack, v.*]
1. to steal (goods in transit, a truck and its contents, etc.) by force. [Colloq.]
2. to steal such goods from (a person) by force. [Colloq.]
3. to cheat, swindle, etc. by or as by the use of force. [Colloq.]
4. to force the pilot of (an aircraft) to fly to a nonscheduled landing point. [Colloq.]
Also spelled *highjack.*

hī′jack·ẽr, *n.* a person who hijacks: also spelled *highjacker.* [Colloq.]

hīke, *v.i.*; hiked, *pt., pp.*; hiking, *ppr.* [from dial. *heik*; prob. akin to *hitch.*] to take a long, vigorous walk; to tramp or march through the country, woods, etc.

hīke, *v.t.* 1. to pull up; hoist; as, *hike* up your pants. [Colloq.]
2. to raise (prices, etc.). [Colloq.]

hīke, *n.* the act of hiking or tramping; a march.

hī′lăr, *a.* of or relating to a hilum.

hi·lā′ri·ous, *a.* [OFr. *hilarious, hilarieux*; L. *hilaris, hilarus*; Gr. *hilaros,* cheerful, glad.] exhilarated and mirthful; jolly; merry.

hi·lā′ri·ous·ly, *adv.* with hilarity.

hi·lar′i·ty, *n.* [OFr. *hilarité*; L. *hilaritas* (*-atis*), from *hilaris,* cheerful, gay.] the state or quality of being hilarious; mirth; merriment.

Hil′ȧ·ry·măs, *n.* the festival of St. Hilary, January 13th.

Hil′dē·brand·ine, *a.* relating to, or resembling Hildebrand, who was Pope Gregory VII (1073–1085), known for his vigorous methods of extending papal authority.

hil′ding, *n.* [prob. from ME. *hilden* (AS. *heldan, hieldan*), to bend down, incline, bow.] a low, base person; a servile wretch. [Archaic.]

hil′ding, *a.* low; base. [Archaic.]

hill, *n.* [ME. *hil, hyl*; AS. *hyll,* a hill.]
1. a natural raised part of the earth's surface, often rounded, smaller than a mountain.
2. a small pile, or mound; as, an ant *hill.*
3. a small mound of soil heaped over and around plants and tubers; as, a *hill* of potatoes.
4. the plants rooted in such a mound.
hill of beans; a very small amount; very little; trifle. [Colloq.]
over the hill; (a) absent without permission; A.W.O.L.; (b) in one's decline.

hill, *v.t.*; hilled, *pt., pp.*; hilling, *ppr.* 1. to form into hills or heaps, as earth.
2. to cover with a hill (sense 3).

hill, *v.i.* to collect or gather into or on a hill.

hill ȧnt, any ant that builds ant hills, *Formica rufa* being the common species.

hill′ber″ry, *n.* the teaberry.

hill′bill·y, *n.* a person who lives in or comes from the mountains or backwoods, especially of the South: somewhat contemptuous term. [Colloq.]

hill′bill·y, *a.* of or characteristic of hillbillies; as, *hillbilly* music. [Colloq.]

hill′bird, *n.* 1. the fieldfare. [Scot.]
2. the Bartramian sandpiper.

hill′ẽr, *n.* a dish used in glazing pottery.

hill fōlk (fōk), the sect otherwise called *Cameronians*; also, the Covenanters in general. [Scot.]

hill′i·ness, *n.* the state of being hilly.

hill′ish, *a.* hilly.

hill mȳ′nȧ, hill mī′nȧ, [*hill,* and Hind. *mainā,* the mynah.] an Asiatic bird of the genu[s] *Gracula,* resembling a starling: it has the abil[-]ity to mimic human speech and is often kep[t] as a pet.

hill′ŏck, *n.* [*hill* and dim. *-ock.*] a small hil[l]

hill pär′tridġe, an Asiatic partridge of the ge[-]nus *Galloperdix.*

hill′sīde, *n.* the side or declivity of a hill.

hill stär, a species of hummingbird.

hill tit, an Asiatic songster of the famil[y] *Liotrichidæ.*

hill′top, *n.* the top of a hill.

hill′wŏrt, *n.* 1. wild thyme.
2. a kind of pennyroyal, *Mentha pulegium*

hill′y, *a.* 1. abounding with hills; rugged uneven, and rolling.
2. like a hill.

hil′sȧh, hil′sȧ, *n.* a fish, *Clupea ilisha,* of th[e] Ganges, highly esteemed as food.

hilt, *n.* [ME. *hilt*; AS. *hilt,* a hilt.] the handle o[r] haft of a sword, dagger, tool, etc.
(*up*) *to the hilt*; thoroughly; entirely.

hilt, *v.t.* to put a hilt on; to set in a hilt.

hilt′ed, *a.* having a hilt.

hī′lum, *n.*; *pl.* **hī′lȧ,** [L. *hilum,* a little thing, a trifle.]
1. same as *hilus.*
2. in botany, (a) a scar on a seed, marking the place where it was attached to the seed stalk; (b) the nucleus in a starch grain.

hī′lus, *n.*; *pl.* **hī′lī,** [Mod.L., var. of *hilum.*] in anatomy, a small notch, recess, or opening, as where vessels and nerves enter an organ.

him, *pron.* [AS. *him,* dat. of *he,* he.]
1. the objective case of *he*: also used colloquially as a predicate complement with a linking verb (e.g., that's *him*).
2. himself; as, he turned *him* to the fray. [Poet.]

Him·ȧ·lā′yăn (*or* hi-mä′lȧ-yăn), *a.* of or relating to the Himalayas, the great range of mountains between India and Tibet.

hi·mat′i·on, *n.*; *pl.* **hi·mat′i·ȧ,** [Gr.] an ancient Greek mantle, usually of woolen cloth, worn as street dress. It often formed the sole garment of men and was used with a tunic by both sexes, folded around the body in various ways. It was generally held in place by the left arm.

Him′ȧ·vat, *n.* [Hind.] in Hindu mythology, the personification of the Himalayan Mountains, the father of Devi.

him·self′, *pron.* [ME. *himself*; from AS. *him selfum,* dat. sing. of nom. *he self,* himself.]
1. an intensive or reflexive form of the third person singular, masculine pronoun. It is generally used along with *he* (or a noun) when a subject; as, *he himself, the man himself,* did so, or *he* did so *himself*; when in the nominative after the verb *to be* it is used either with or without *he* (or a noun); as, it it was *himself* or *he himself.* In the objective it stands alone (as, he hurt *himself*), or with a noun. In Irish dialectal usage it appears as a subject; as, *himself* will have his dinner now.
2. his real, true, or actual self; possession of his natural temper and disposition; as, the man has come to *himself*; let him act *himself.*
by himself; alone; unaccompanied; as, he sits or studies *by himself.*

Him′yăr·īte, *n.* [named from *Himyar,* legendary king of Yemen.]
1. any member of an ancient Arab tribe that lived in southern Arabia.
2. any Arab descended from this tribe.

Him′yăr·īte, Him·yăr·it′ic̦, *a.* of or relating to the Himyarites, their language, culture, etc.

Him·yăr·it′ic̦, *n.* the Himyaritic language.

hin, *n.* [LL., from Gr. *hin,* from Heb. *hīn,* a measure of liquids.] a Hebrew measure of liquids holding about six quarts.

hī′nä·ū tree, [Maori.] *Elæocarpus dentatus,* a New Zealand species of linden bearing an edible fruit.

hīnd, *n.*; *pl.* **hīnds** or **hīnd,** [ME. *hind, hinde*; AS. *hind,* a hind.]
1. the female of the red deer, in and after its third year.
2. the grouper; any fish of the genus *Epinephelus.*

hīnd, *a.*; *comp.* hinder; *superl.* hindmost *or* hindermost, [ME; prob. back-formation from *hinder.*] situated or belonging behind or in the rear; back; rear; as, the *hind* legs of a dog.

hīnd, *n.* [from ME. *hine*; AS. *hina,* earlier *higna, hiwna,* generalized from *genit.* pl. of *higa, hiwa,* member of a household or family.]

1. in northern England and Scotland, a skilled farm worker or servant.
2. a peasant; a rustic.

hīnd′ber″ry, *n.* [so named because supposed to be a favorite food of hinds.] *Rubus idæus,* a wild variety of raspberry.

hīnd′brāin, *n.* in anatomy, the hindmost part of the brain; specifically, (a) the cerebellum, pons, and medulla oblongata; the rhombencephalon; (b) the cerebellum and pons only; the metencephalon; (c) the cerebellum only.

Hin′den·bụrg līne, a line of defense which the Germans placed across northeastern France, in 1916, under General Paul von Hindenburg.

hīnd′ẽr, *a.* [ME. *hindere,* back, from AS. *hinder,* adv., behind.] hind; posterior; back; rear; as, the *hinder* part of a ship.

hin′dẽr, *v.t.*; hindered, *pt., pp.*; hindering, *ppr.* [ME. *hinderen, hindren*; AS. *hindrian,* to hinder, from *hinder,* back, behind.]
1. to make difficult for; to impede; to retard; to check in progression or motion; to obstruct for a time, or to render slow in motion; as, cold *hinders* the growth of plants.
2. to keep back; to restrain; to get in the way of.

hin′dẽr, *v.i.* to interpose obstacles or impediments; as, there is nothing to *hinder.*
Syn.—prevent, impede, obstruct, oppose, delay, retard, clog, embarrass, check, block, thwart, stop, bar, counteract, encumber, inhibit.

hin′dẽr·ănce, *n.* same as *hindrance.*

hin′dẽr·ẽr, *n.* one who or that which hinders.

hīnd′ẽr·mōst, *a.* that coming the very last; hindmost.

hīnd′gut, hīnd′-gut, *n.* the rear or posterior portion of the alimentary canal of an embryo, from which the colon is formed.

hīnd′head (-hed), *n.* the back part of the head; the occiput.

Hin′dī, *n.* [Per. and Hind., from *Hind,* India.]
1. the group of Indo-European, Indic languages spoken in northern India, including Assamese, Bengali, Marathi, Punjabi, Hindustani, etc.
2. a Hindu. [Rare.]

Hin′dī, *a.* of or associated with northern India.

hīnd′mōst, *a.* last; in the rear of all others; superlative of *hind.*

Hin′dọọ, *a.* and *n.*; *pl.* **Hin′dọọṣ,** same as *Hindu.*

Hin′dọọ·iṣm, *n.* same as *Hinduism.*

Hin·dọọ·stä′nī, *a.* and *n.* same as *Hindustani.*

hīnd′quar′tẽr, *n.* either of the two hind legs and loins of a carcass of veal, beef, lamb, etc.

hin′drănce, *n.* [from ME. *hinderen,* AS. *hindrian,* to hinder.]
1. the act of hindering or the condition of being hindered.
2. impediment, obstruction; one who or that which hinders.

hīnd′sīght, *n.* 1. the rear sight of a firearm.
2. ability to see, after the event, what should have been done: opposed to *foresight.*

Hin′dụ, *n.* [Hind. and Per. *Hindū,* an inhabitant of India, from *Hind,* India.]
1. popularly, one of the native race inhabiting Hindustan.
2. an adherent of Hinduism.
3. any member of those peoples of India that speak languages derived from the Indic branch of Indo-European.
Also spelled *Hindoo.*

Hin′dụ, *a.* 1. of the Hindus, their language, culture, etc.
2. of Hinduism.
Also spelled *Hindoo.*

Hin′dụ-Ar′ȧ·biç nū′mẽr·ălṣ, Arabic numerals.

Hin′dụ·iṣm, *n.* any of various forms of modified Brahmanism with additions of Buddhistic and other religious and philosophic ideas. It is the religion and social system of the Hindus.

Hin·dụ·stä′nī, *n.* the most important of the Western Hindi group of languages, used as a trade language throughout India: it contains many words from Persian, Arabic, Turkish, etc., and, as used by Moslems, is also called *Urdu.*

Hin·dụ·stä′nī, *a.* 1. of Hindustan or its people.
2. of Hindustani.

hinġe, *n.* [ME. *henge,* from *hangen, hongen*; AS. *hangian,* to hang.]
1. a joint on which a door, gate, lid, etc. swings.

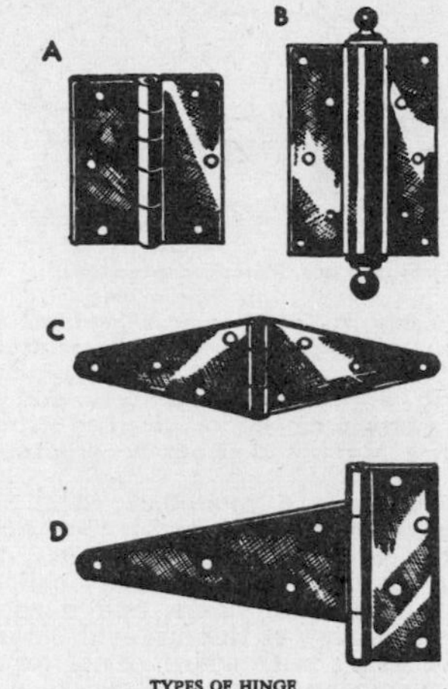

TYPES OF HINGE
A, butt; B, spring; C, strap; D, T hinge

2. a natural joint, as of the bivalve shell of a clam or oyster.
3. that on which anything depends or turns; a pivot; a cardinal principle or point; as, this was the real *hinge* on which the question turned.

hinġe, *v.t.*; hinged, *pt., pp.*; hinging, *ppr.* to furnish with or attach by a hinge or hinges.

hinġe, *v.i.* 1. to stand, depend, or be contingent; as, the question *hinges* on this single point.
2. to hang or swing as on a hinge.

hinġed, *a.* having a hinge or hinges.

hinġe joint, 1. in anatomy, a ginglymus.
2. in mechanics, a joint allowing motion in one plane only.

hinġe′less, *a.* having no hinge.

hin′ny, *n.*; *pl.* **hin′nieṣ,** [L. *hinnus,* from Gr. *ginnos,* a hinny.] the offspring of a stallion and a female donkey: distinguished from *mule.*

hin′ny, *v.i.*; hinnied, *pt., pp.*; hinnying, *ppr.* [ME.; Fr. *hennir*; L. *hinnire,* to neigh.] to whinny; to neigh.

hin′ny, *n.* honey; darling. [Scot. and Brit. Dial.]

hin′oid, *a.* [Gr. *is, inos,* a muscle, nerve, strength, vigor, and *eidos,* form.] having veins which proceed entirely from the midrib of a leaf, and are parallel and undivided, as in the gingerworts.

hinṣ′dȧ·līte, *n.* a mineral related to alunite.

hint, *n.* [Early Mod. Eng., from AS. *henten, hinten,* to seize, grasp.]
1. a slight indication; a faint or indirect suggestion; an intimation; a covert allusion.
2. an occasion; turn; opportunity. [Obs.]
to take a hint; to perceive and act on a hint.

hint, *v.t.* to give a hint of; to suggest indirectly; to intimate.

hint, *v.i.* to make a hint or hints.
to hint at; to suggest indirectly; to intimate.

hin′tẽr·land, *n.* [G., from *hinter,* back, and *land,* land.]
1. the land or district behind that bordering on a coast or river; inland region.
2. an area far from big cities and towns; back country.
3. the inland trade region served by a port.
4. an inland region claimed by the state that owns the coast.

hint′ing·ly, *adv.* in a hinting manner.

hip, *n.* [ME. *hipe, hupe*; AS. *hype,* a hip.]
1. the part of the human body surrounding and including the joint formed by each thighbone and the pelvis; especially, the fleshy part of the upper thigh; the haunch.
2. the corresponding part of an animal's body.
3. in architecture, (a) the external angle at the junction of two sloping sides of a roof; (b) the rafter at such an angle.
4. in engineering, the point of juncture of a sloping end post and the upper chord of a bridge truss.
to have on the hip; to have the advantage over: originally with reference to wrestling.
to smite hip and thigh; to defeat completely.

hip, *v.t.*; hipped (hipt), *pt., pp.*; hipping, *ppr.*
1. to sprain or dislocate the hip of, as a horse.
2. to throw over the hip, as one's opponent in wrestling.
3. to form with a hip, as a roof.

hip, *n.* [ME. *heepe, hepe*; AS. *heópe,* the fruit of the dogrose.] the small, fleshy, ripened fruit of a rosebush.

hip, *interj.* an exclamation used in cheers: usually repeated; as, *hip, hip,* hurray!

hip, *n.* same as *hyp.*

hip′bōne, *n.* 1. the innominate bone.
2. the ilium.
3. the neck of the femur.
Also *hip bone.*

hip gĩr′dle, the pelvic arch.

hip joint, the joint of the hip, a ball-and-socket joint, formed by the reception of the globular head of the femur or thighbone into the socket of the innominate bone.

hip knob (nob), an ornament placed where the hiprafters and ridge of a roof meet.

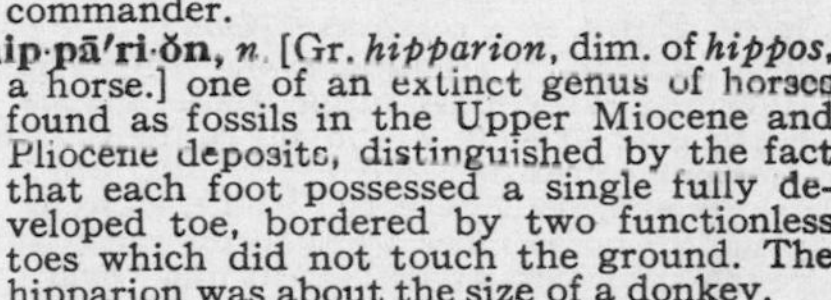
HIP KNOB

hip mōld′ing, in architecture, a kind of molding on the rafter that forms the hip of a roof; sometimes, the back of a hip.

hipp-, same as *hippo-.*

Hip′pȧ, *n.* [Gr. *hippos,* a horse.] a genus of anomurans; the sand bugs or bait bugs.

hip′pärçh, *n.* [Gr. *hipparchos,* from *hippos,* horse, and *archein,* to lead, rule.] in ancient Greece, a cavalry commander.

hip·pā′ri·ŏn, *n.* [Gr. *hipparion,* dim. of *hippos,* a horse.] one of an extinct genus of horses found as fossils in the Upper Miocene and Pliocene deposits, distinguished by the fact that each foot possessed a single fully developed toe, bordered by two functionless toes which did not touch the ground. The hipparion was about the size of a donkey.

Hip·pē·as′trum, *n.* [*hipp-,* and Gr. *astron,* a star.] a genus of the *Amaryllidaceæ,* consisting of bulbous plants popularly known as knight's-star lilies, usually with scarlet, crimson, or deep orange blossoms.

hipped (hipt), *a.* 1. having the hip sprained or dislocated.
2. in architecture, having a hip or hips; as, a *hipped* roof.
3. having hips (of a specified sort): used in hyphenated compounds, as broad-*hipped.*

hipped, *a.* [from *hyp* in *hypochondria.*]
1. in low spirits; melancholy; depressed.
2. offended.
3. obsessed (with *on*).

hip·pi·ā′try, *n.* [*hipp-,* and Gr. *iatreia,* healing, from *iāsthai,* to heal.] the art or practice of treating the diseases of horses.

hip′pie, *n.* any of the young people of the 1960's who, in their alienation from conventional society, have turned variously to mysticism, psychedelic drugs, communal living, experimental arts, etc. [Slang.]

hip′pish, *a.* melancholy; hipped. [Colloq.]

hip′pō-, [from Gr. *hippos,* a horse.] a combining form meaning *horse,* as in *hippophagi.*

hip′pō, *n.*; *pl.* **hip′pōṣ,** a hippopotamus. [Colloq.]

Hip·pō·bos′çȧ, *n.* [*hippo-,* and Gr. *boskein,* to feed.] a genus of parasitic dipterous insects, including the horse tick, *Hippobosca equina.*

hip′pō·çamp, *n.* same as *hippocampus,* sense 2.

hip·pō·çam′păl, *a.* 1. pertaining to the hippocampus of the brain.
2. of or like a hippocampus.

Hip·pō·çam′pus, *n.*; *pl.* **Hip·pō·çam′pī,** [L., a sea horse, from Gr. *hippokampos*; *hippos,* a horse, and *kampos,* a sea monster.]
1. a genus of fishes, closely allied to the *Syngnathidæ* or pipefishes. The upper parts are like the head and neck of a horse in miniature, whence the name *sea horse.* When swimming they maintain a vertical position; also, [h–] a fish of this genus.
2. [h–] in mythology, a creature, half horse, half dolphin, which drew the car of Neptune: also called *hippocamp.*
3. [h–] in anatomy, a ridge along each lateral ventricle of the brain.

HIPPOCAMPUS

hip″pō-cen′taur, *n.* [L. *hippocentaurus*; Gr. *hippokentauros*; *hippos*, horse, and *kentauros*, centaur.] a centaur.

hip′pō-cras, *n.* [Fr., from L. *Hippocrates*; Gr. *Hippokratēs*, Hippocrates, a famous physician.] wine sweetened and flavored with spices, lemon, rosemary, etc., formerly drunk as a cordial.

Hip·pō-crat′iç, *a.* of or belonging to Hippocrates (460?–377? B.C.), a celebrated physician of Greece, regarded as the father of medicine.

Hippocratic face; the expression which the features assume immediately after death, long sickness, excessive hunger, etc.

Hippocratic oath; an oath said to have been imposed by Hippocrates upon his disciples, and which is taken by students about to receive the M.D. degree: it is regarded as a basis for medical ethics.

Hip·poç′rȧ·tiṣm, *n.* the medical doctrines or system of Hippocrates.

Hip′pō-çrēne, *n.* [L., from Gr. *hippos*, a horse, and *krēnē*, a fountain.] in Greek mythology, a spring on Mount Helicon, said to have been produced by a stroke of the hoof of Pegasus, sacred to the Muses; also, its waters, supposed to inspire poets.

hip·pō-çrē′pi·ăn, *a.* [*hippo-*, and Gr. *krēpis*, a boot, shoe.] horseshoe-shaped: a term used of that group of the *Polyzoa* in which the oral tentacles are arranged in a horseshoe-shaped frame.

hip·pō-çrē′pi·ăn, *n.* a polyzoan with tentacles arranged in a horseshoe form.

hip·pō-çrep′i·fọrm, *a.* [*hippo-*, and Gr. *krēpis*, a boot, shoe, and L. *forma*, form.] horseshoe-shaped.

hip′pō-dāme, *n.* a sea horse. [Obs.]

hip′pō-drome, *n.* [L. *hippodromos*; Gr. *hippodromos*, a racecourse, hippodrome; *hippos*, a horse, and *dromos*, a course, running, from *dramein*, to run.]

1. in ancient Greece and Rome, a circus or place for horse races and chariot races, surrounded by tiers of seats built in an oval.

2. an arena or building for a circus, games, etc.

3. a contest, race, etc. in which the result is fraudulently prearranged. [Slang.]

hip′pō-drōme, *v.i.* to conduct or engage in a contest the result of which has been prearranged. [Slang.]

hip′pō-griff, *n.* [Fr. *hippogriffe*, from Gr. *hippos*, a horse, and *gryps*, a griffin.] a mythical monster, whose head and forefeet were those of a griffin and whose hindquarters were those of a horse: also *hippogryph*, *hippogriffin*.

hip′poid, *a.* [Gr. *hippos*, a horse, and *eidos*, form, resemblance.] horselike; having characteristics of a horse.

hip′pō-lith, *n.* [*hippo-*, and Gr. *lithos*, a stone.] a concretion found in the alimentary canals of horses.

hip·pol′ō·ġy, *n.* [*hippo-*, and Gr. *-logia*, from *legein*, to speak.] the study of horses.

Hip·pol′y·tus, *n.* [L.; Gr. *Hippolytos*.] in Greek legend, a son of Theseus: when he rejected the love of his stepmother, Phaedra, she turned Theseus against him by false accusations, and at Theseus' request he was killed by Poseidon, who caused his chariot to overturn.

Hip·pom′ē·nēṣ, *n.* [L.; Gr. *Hippomenēs*.] in Greek legend, a youth who won a race against Atalanta.

hip″pō-pȧ·thol′ō·ġy, *n.* [*hippo-*, and Gr. *pathos*, suffering, and *-logia*, from *legein*, to speak.] the pathology of the horse.

hip·poph′ȧ·ġī, *n.pl.* [Gr. *hippophagos*, horse-eating; *hippos*, horse, and *phagein*, to eat.] those who feed upon horseflesh.

hip·poph′ȧ·ġiṣm, *n.* same as *hippophagy*.

hip·poph′ȧ·ġist, *n.* one who feeds on horseflesh.

hip·poph′ȧ·gous, *a.* eating horseflesh.

hip·poph′ȧ·ġy, *n.* the eating of horseflesh.

hip′pō-phīle, *n.* [*hippo-*, and Gr. *philos*, loving.] one who is especially fond of horses.

hip·pō-pot′ȧ·mus, *n.*; *pl.* **hip·pō-pot′ȧ·mus·eṣ, hip·pō-pot′ȧ·mī, hip·pō-pot′ȧ·mus,** [L. *hippopotamus*; Gr. *hippopotamos*, lit., a river horse; *hippos*, horse, and *potamos*, river.] a large, plant-eating mammal, order *Artiodactyla*, having a square head, a very large muzzle, small eyes and ears, a thick, heavy body, short legs terminated by four toes, a short tail, very thick skin, and no hair, except at the end of the tail: it lives in or near the rivers of Africa.

HIPPOPOTAMUS (*Hippopotamus amphibius*)

hip·pot′ō·my, *n.* [*hippo-*, and Gr. *tomē*, a cutting, from *temnein*, to cut.] the anatomy of the horse.

hip·pū′riç, *a.* [Gr. *hippos*, a horse, and *ouron*, urine.] pertaining to or derived from the urine of a horse and other herbivorous animals.

hippuric acid; a monobasic acid in the urine of horses and other herbivorous animals.

Hip·pū′ris, *n.* [L., from Gr. *hippouris*, decked with a horsetail, also a plant called the mare's-tail; *hippos*, horse, and *oura*, tail.] a genus of plants of the family *Haloragaceæ*, the mare's-tails, with whorls of narrow leaves and inconspicuous flowers. *Hippuris vulgaris* grows in pools and marshes throughout the temperate and cold regions of the globe.

hip′pū-rīte, *n.* [Gr. *hippouris*, horsetailed, and *-ite*.] an extinct bivalve mollusk of the genus *Hippurites*.

-hip′pus, [from Gr. *hippos*, a horse.] a combining form meaning *horse*, as in eo*hippus*.

hip′py, *n.*; *pl.* **hip′pieṣ,** same as *hippie*. [Slang.]

hip rȧft′ẽr, a timber at the angle of a hip roof.

hip roọf, a roof with sloping ends and sides and no gable.

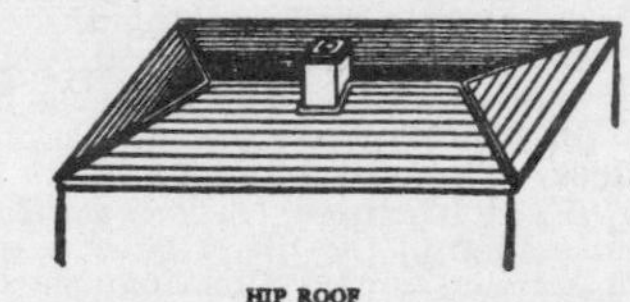

HIP ROOF

hip′shot, *a.* 1. having the hip dislocated.

2. having one hip lower than the other.

hip′stẽr, *n.* [prob. from *hep*, and *-ster*.]

1. a fashionable or stylish person, especially a devotee of modern jazz. [Slang.]

2. same as *beatnik* (a term of the 1950's and early 1960's): cf. *hippie*. [Slang.]

hip tīle, a tile for covering the hips of roofs.

hir′cīne, hir·cī′nous, *a.* [L. *hircinus*, from *hircus*, a goat.] pertaining to or resembling a goat, especially in smell.

hīre, *n.* [ME. *hire*, *hyre*; AS. *hyr*, wages.]

1. the price or compensation paid or contracted to be given for the use of anything, or paid for personal services; wages; rent.

2. a hiring.

for hire, on hire; available for work or use in return for payment.

hīre, *v.t.*; hired, *pt.*, *pp.*; hiring, *ppr.* 1. to get the services of (a person) or the use of (a thing) in return for payment; employ; engage.

2. to give the use of (a thing) in return for payment.

to hire out; to work in return for payment.

hīred gīrl, a maidservant.

hīred man, a gardener, stableman, or farm hand.

hīre′less, *a.* without hire.

hīre′ling, *n.* [ME. *hyrling*; AS. *hyrling*, a hireling; *hyr*, hire, and *-ling*.] one who is hired or who will follow anyone's orders for pay; a mercenary.

hīre′ling, *a.* mercenary; of or like a hireling.

hīr′ẽr, *n.* one who hires.

hīr′ing hạll, an employment office, especially one operated by a union to place its members in jobs in the order of their applications.

hīr′mos, *n.*; *pl.* **hīr′moi,** [LL. *hirmos*; Gr. *eirmos*, a series, context, from *eirein*, to fasten together, join.] in the Orthodox Eastern Church, a stanza or strophe of an ode, used as a model for the rhythm and music of others of the same measure. Also *hirmus*.

hīr′ple, *v.i.* to limp; to hobble. [Scot.]

hīr′sūte (*or* hīr-sūte′), *a.* [L. *hirsutus*, bristly.]

1. hairy; shaggy; set with bristles.

2. in biology, having rough or stiff feathers.

hīr·sūte′ness, *n.* hairiness.

hīr′sūt·iṣm, *n.* a heavy, especially abnormal, growth of hair.

hi·rụ′dine, *a.* [L. *hirudo* (*-inis*), a leech.] relating to leeches.

Hir·ụ·din′ē·ȧ, *n.pl.* [L. *hirudo* (*-inis*), a leech.] a class of annelids provided with a suctorial disk at one or both ends; the leeches.

hi·rụ′din·oid, *a.* of or like a leech; hirudine.

Hi·rụ′dō, *n.* [L.] a genus of the *Hirudinea*, including the common medicinal leech, *Hirudo medicinalis*.

hi·run′dine, *a.* [L. *hirundineus*, from *hirundo* (*-inis*), a swallow.] relating to or like a swallow or swallows (birds).

Hi·run′dō, *n.* [L., a swallow.] a genus of passerine birds, including the barn swallows.

hiṣ, *pron.* [AS. *his*, of him, his, genit. masc. and neut. of *he*.]

1. that or those belonging to him: used without a following noun, often after *of*, as, a friend of *his*, that book is *his*, *his* are better.

2. formerly, the possessive case of *it*.

hiṣ, *possessive pronominal a.* of, belonging to, or done by him.

his′ing·ẽr·īte, *n.* [named after W. *Hisinger* (1766–1852), Swedish mineralogist.] a soft, black iron ore, consisting of silica and iron.

hiṣn, *pron.* a dialectal form of *his*, imitating *mine* or *thine*, used only absolutely; as, this is mine, that is *hisn*.

His·pan′iç, *a.* [L. *Hispanicus*, from *Hispania*, Spain.] belonging to Spain, its language, or people; Spanish.

His·pan′i·ciṣm, *n.* an idiom or mode of speech of the Spanish language.

His·pan′i·cīze, *v.t.* to make Spanish in style.

his′pid, *a.* [L. *hispidus*, rough, bristly.] rough with bristles or minute spines; bristly.

his·pid′i·ty, *n.* the state of being hispid.

his·pid′ū·lous, *a.* having small, short bristles.

hiss, *v.i.*; hissed (hist), *pt.*, *pp.*; hissing, *ppr.* [ME. *hissen*, *hyssen*; of echoic origin.]

1. to make a sound like that of the letter *s* by forcing the breath between the tongue and the upper teeth, especially in contempt or disapproval.

2. to emit any similar sound: said of snakes, geese, steam escaping; etc.

hiss, *v.t.* 1. to condemn or express disapproval by hissing; as, the spectators *hissed* the actor off the stage.

2. to utter hissingly; as, he *hissed* his threats.

3. to force or drive by hissing.

hiss, *n.* a sound like that of a prolonged *s*.

hiss′ing, *n.* 1. a hiss; an expression of scorn or contempt.

2. the occasion or object of scorn and derision.

hiss′ing·ly, *adv.* with a hissing sound.

hist, *interj.* an exclamation to attract attention, call for silence: equivalent to hush! hark!

hist-, same as *histo-*.

his·tam′i·nāse, *n.* [*histamine*, and *-ase*.] an enzyme found in the animal digestive system, capable of inactivating histamine.

his′tȧ·mine, *n.* [from *histidine*, and *amine*], an amine, $C_3H_3N_2 \cdot CH_2 \cdot CH_2 \cdot NH_2$, produced by the decomposition of histidine and found in all organic matter: it is a powerful constrictor of blood vessels and stimulator of gastric secretions.

his′ti·dine, his′ti·din, *n.* [Gr. *histion*, dim. of *histos*; and *-ine*], an amino acid, $C_6H_9N_3O_2$, formed by the hydrolysis of proteins.

his′ti·oid, *a.* histoid.

his·ti·ol′ō·ġy, *n.* same as *histology*.

his·tō-, [from Gr. *histos*, a loom, warp, web, tissue.] a combining form meaning *tissue*, as in *histo*logy: also, before a vowel, *hist-*.

his·tō-çhem′iç·ăl, *a.* pertaining to histochemistry.

his·tō-çhem′is·try, *n.* the study of the chemical components of cells through the use of chemically specific staining reagents.

his·tō-çom·pat·i·bil′i·ty, *n.* a condition of compatibility between the tissues of a graft or transplant and the tissues of the body receiving it.

his′tō-gen, *n.* [*histo-*, and *-gen*.] in botany, a group of cells that give rise to new tissue, such as cambium, phellogen, etc.

his·tō-ġen′e·sis, *n.* [*histo-*, and *-genesis*.] same as *histogeny*.

his·tō-ġē·net′iç, *a.* of or belonging to histogeny; tissue-forming.

his·tō-ġen′iç, *a.* histogenetic.

his·toġ′e·ny, *n.* [*histo-*, and Gr. *-genes*, producing.] the production and growth of organic tissues.

his·tog′rȧ·phẽr, *n.* [*histo-*, and Gr. *graphein*, to write.] a writer of histography.

his·tō·graph′iç, his·tō·graph′iç·ăl, *a.* of or belonging to histography.

his·tog′rȧ·phy, *n.* [*histo-*, and Gr. *-graphia*, from *graphein*, to write.] a treatise upon organic tissues or histogenetic processes.

his′toid, *a.* like the surrounding or normal tissue; as, a *histoid* tumor.

his·tō·log′iç·ăl, his·tō·log′iç, *a.* of histology; dealing with the microscopic structure of the tissues of organic bodies.

his·tō·log′iç·ăl·ly, *adv.* in a histological manner.

his·tol′ō·ġist, *n.* one skilled in histology.

his·tol′ō·ġy, *n.* [*histo-*, and Gr. *-logia*, from *legein*, to speak.]

1. that branch of biology dealing with the microscopic study of the structure of tissues.
2. the tissue structure of an organism or part.

his·tol′y·sis, *n.* [*histo-*, and Gr. *lysis*, a loosing, from *lyein*, to loose.] in biology, the disintegration or dissolution of organic tissue.

his·tō·lyt′iç, *a.* of or belonging to histolysis.

his′ton, *n.* same as *histone*.

his′tōne, *n.* [from Gr. *histos*, and *-one*.] any of a group of simple proteins that yield amino acids on hydrolysis, as the globin of hemoglobin: they are often poisonous when injected into an animal, and prevent the clotting of blood.

his·tō·phys″i·ō·log′iç·ăl, *a.* relating to the physiology of the tissues.

his·tō′ri·ăn, *n.* [OFr. *historien*, from L. *historia*, history.]

1. a writer or compiler of history.
2. an authority on or specialist in history.

his·tō′ri·ā·ted, *a.* decorated with figures of animals, human beings, flowers, etc., as medieval manuscripts.

his·tor′iç, *a.* [L. *historicus*; Gr. *historikos*, from *historia*, history.] historical; especially, famous in history.

his·tor′iç·ăl, *a.* 1. of or concerned with history as a science; as, the *historical* method.

2. providing evidence for a fact of history; serving as a source of history; as, a *historical* document.
3. based on or suggested by people or events of the past; as, a *historical* novel.
4. established by history; not legendary or fictional; authentic; real; factual.
5. showing the development or evolution in proper chronological order; as, a *historical* account.
6. famous in history: now usually *historic*.

historical linguistics; the branch of linguistics which describes the evolution of language structures.

historical painting; a painting dealing with historic events or characters.

historical present; the present tense used in telling about past events: also *historic present*.

his·tor′iç·ăl·ly, *adv.* 1. so as to show the development or evolution in chronological order.

2. according to the facts or principles of history; as history.

his·tor′iç·ăl·ness, *n.* the state of being historical.

his·tō·ric′i·ty, *n.* historical nature or authenticity.

his·tor′i·cīze, *v.t.* and *v.i.* to record; to narrate as history. [Rare.]

his′tō·ried (-rid), *a.* having a history or recorded in history; storied.

his·tō′ri·ẽr, *n.* a historian. [Obs.]

his″tō·ri·ette′, *n.* [Fr., dim. of *histoire*; L. *historia*, history.] a brief history; a short story or narrative.

his·tor′i·fȳ, *v.t.* to relate; to record in history; to chronicle.

his·tō′ri·ō·gràph, *n.* a historiographer. [Obs.]

his·tō·ri·og′rȧ·phẽr, *n.* [Gr. *historia*, history, and *graphein*, to write.]

1. a historian; a writer of history; especially, one appointed to write the history of some institution, country, etc.
2. a specialist in historiography.

his·tō·ri·og′rȧ·phẽr·ship, *n.* the position or rank of historiographer.

his·tō·ri·og′rȧ·phy, *n.* 1. the writing of history.

2. same as *history* (sense 4); specifically, the study of the techniques of historical research and historical writing, the methods of major historians, etc.
3. a body of historical writing.

his·tō·ri·ol′ō·ġy, *n.* [Gr. *historia*, history, and *-logia*, from *legein*, to speak.] a discourse on history; the science of history.

his′tō·rīze, *v.t.* and *v.i.* to chronicle.

his′tō·ry, *n.*; *pl.* **his′tō·rieș,** [L. *historia*; Gr. *historia*, a learning by inquiry, knowledge, a narrative, from *histōr* or *istōr*, knowing, learned, a wise man, from the root of *eidenai*, to know.]

1. an account of what has happened; narrative; story; tale.
2. (a) what has happened in the life or development of a people, country, institution, etc.; (b) a systematic account of this, usually with an analysis and explanation.
3. all recorded events of the past.
4. the branch of knowledge that deals systematically with the past; a recording, analyzing, co-ordinating, and explaining of past events.
5. a known or recorded past; as, this coat has a strange *history*.
6. something that belongs to the past; as, that argument is *history* now.
7. something important enough to be recorded.

to make history; to be or do something important enough to be recorded.

his′tō·ry, *v.t.* to record; to relate; to chronicle. [Obs.]

his′tō·ry piēce, an artistic pictorial representation of any historical event.

his·tot′ō·my, *n.* [*histo-*, and Gr. *tomē*, a cutting.] in surgery, the act of dissecting organic tissues.

his·tō·troph′iç, *a.* [*histo-*, and Gr. *trophē*, nourishment.] tissue building; histogenic.

his′tō·zȳme, *n.* [*histo-*, and Gr. *zymē*, leaven.] an enzyme found in certain organs of animals, that can decompose hippuric acid.

his′tri·ŏn, *n.* [L. *histrio* (*-onis*), a stage player, from Etruscan *hister*, a buffoon.] a player; an actor.

his·tri·on′iç, his·tri·on′iç·ăl, *a.* 1. pertaining to a stage player or to stage playing; theatrical.

2. overacted or overacting; theatrical; melodramatic; artificial; affected.

his·tri·on′iç, *n.* an actor. [Rare.]

his·tri·on′iç·ăl·ly, *adv.* in a histrionic manner.

his·tri·on′i·cișm, *n.* the art of dramatic representation; a theatrical effect.

his·tri·on′içs, *n.pl.* 1. [*construed as sing.*] the art of acting; dramatics.

2. an artificial or affected manner, display of emotion, etc.

his′tri·ō·nișm, *n.* the act or practice of stage players; stage playing; hence, affectation.

hit, *v.t.*; hit, *pt.*, *pp.*; hitting, *ppr.* [ME. *hitten*, *hytten*, to hit, meet with; AS. *hittan*, from Ice. *hitta*, to hit upon, meet with.]

1. to come against, usually with force; strike; as, the car *hit* the tree.
2. to give a blow to; strike; knock.
3. to give (a blow); as, she *hit* him a blow.
4. to strike by throwing, shooting, or otherwise sending a missile; as, he fired and *hit* the deer.
5. to cause (something) to knock, bump, or strike, as in falling, moving, etc. (often with *on* or *against*); as, he *hit* his head *on* the stairs.
6. to affect strongly; distress; injure; as, the Irish were hard *hit* by the potato famine.
7. to come upon by accident or after search; reach; find; light upon; as, he *hit* the right answer.
8. to fall into exact accord with; appeal to; suit; as, the hat *hit* her fancy.
9. in baseball, to get (a specified base hit); as, he *hit* a double.
10. in backgammon, to take up, as a man lying single or uncovered, by moving a man of one's own to its point.

to hit it off; to get along well together; be in harmony; be congenial.

to hit off; (a) to determine; discover; as, *to hit off* a secret; (b) to represent or describe briefly and well; (c) to mimic.

to hit (*out*) *at*; (a) to aim a blow at; try to hit; (b) to attack in words; criticize severely.

hit, *v.i.* 1. to strike; to give a blow or blows.

2. to knock, bump, or strike (usually with *against*).

> If bodies be extension alone, how can they move and *hit* one *against* another?
> —Locke.

3. to fall on by good luck or after search (usually with *upon*).
4. to ignite the combustible mixture in its cylinders: said of an internal-combustion engine.
5. in baseball, to get a base hit.
6. to strike or reach the intended point; to succeed; to suit.

> And millions miss for one that *hits*.
> —Swift.

to hit out; to strike out with the fists.

hit, *n.* 1. a blow that strikes its mark.

2. a collision of one thing with another.
3. an effectively witty or sarcastic remark.
4. a stroke of good fortune.
5. a successful and popular song, book, play, etc.
6. in backgammon, a game won by a player after one or more of his opponent's men have been removed from the board.
7. in baseball, a base hit.

hit or miss; without regard to success or failure; in a haphazard or aimless way.

hit′-and-run′, *a.* hitting and then escaping: usually of an automobile driver who flees from the scene of an accident in which he is involved: also *hit-skip*.

hitch, *v.i.* hitched (hicht), *pt.*, *pp.*; hitching, *ppr.* [ME. *hitchen*, *hytchen*, *hychen*, prob. echoic var. of OFr. *hocier*, to move jerkily.]

1. to move by jerks or with stops; to limp; to hobble; as, to *hitch* along.
2. to become entangled; to be caught or hooked.
3. to hit the feet together in moving: said of a horse.
4. to agree or work well together; as, their ideas do not *hitch*. [Colloq.]
5. to hitchhike. [Slang.]

hitch, *v.t.* 1. to move, pull, or shift with jerks.

2. to fasten with a hook, knot, etc.; unite; tie.
3. to marry: usually in the passive. [Colloq.]

to hitch up; (a) to harness or attach, as a horse to a vehicle; (b) to raise or lift with a jerk.

hitch, *n.* 1. a short, sudden movement or pull; tug; jerk.

2. a hobble; limp.
3. a hindrance; obstacle; obstruction; entanglement.
4. a catching or fastening; thing or part used to connect or join together; catch.
5. a ride in hitchhiking. [Slang.]
6. a period of enlistment. [Military Slang.]
7. in nautical usage, a kind of knot that can be easily undone: see *knot*, illus.

Blackwall hitch; a kind of knot: see *knot*, illus.

without a hitch; smoothly, easily, and successfully.

hitch′hīke, *v.i.*; hitchhiked (-hīkt), *pt.*, *pp.*; hitchhiking, *ppr.* to travel by asking for rides in passing vehicles.

hitch′hīke, *v.t.* to get (a ride) or make (one's way) by hitchhiking.

hitch′hīk·ẽr, *n.* one who obtains, or tries to obtain, rides from passing motorists.

hīthe, *n.* [ME. *hithe*, *hythe*; AS. *hyth*, a port, haven.] a port or small haven: obsolete except in compounds, as in Queen*hithe*.

hith′ẽr, *adv.* [AS. *hider*, *hider*, hither.]

1. to or toward this place; as, to come *hither*.
2. to this point; to this argument or topic; to this end; to this time. [Obs.]

hither and thither; to this place and that; to and fro.

hith′ẽr, *a.* on or toward this side; nearer.

hith′ẽr·mōst, *a.* nearest on this side.

hith′ẽr·tō, *adv.* 1. to this time; till now.

2. hither. [Obs.]

hith′ẽr·wȧrd, *adv.* [AS. *hiderweard*; *hider*, hither, and *-weard*, -ward.] this way; toward this place; hither. [Rare.]

hith′ẽr·wȧrdș, *adv.* hitherward.

Hit′lẽr·ișm, *n.* the fascist program, ideas, and methods of Adolf Hitler and the Nazis.

Hit′lẽr·īte, *n.* a follower of Adolf Hitler; Nazi.

Hit′lẽr·īte, *a.* of or characteristic of Adolf Hitler.

hit man, [from underworld slang *hit*, murder.] a man paid to kill someone; hired murderer. [Slang.]

hit′-ọr-miss′, *a.* haphazard; random.

hit′-skip′, *a.* hit-and-run.

hit′tẽr, *n.* one who hits or strikes.

Hit′tīte, *n.* [LL. *Hethæus* (pl. *Hethæi*), a Hittite; Heb. *khittīm*, Hittites.]

1. a member of an ancient people in Asia Minor and Syria: their rock sculptures and the ruins of their temples are found near Smyrna, in Cappadocia, and Lydia.
2. the language of the Hittites, considered by most authorities to be associated with

Indo-European: it is recorded in divergent cuneiform and hieroglyphic inscriptions.

Hit′tīte, *a.* of the Hittites, their language, or culture.

hīve, *n.* [ME. *hive, hyve*; AS. *hyfe*, a hive.]
1. a box, chest, basket, or other shelter for a colony of domestic bees; beehive.
2. a swarm of bees; the bees of a single colony, inhabiting a hive.
3. a busy swarm or bustling group of people.
4. a place of great bustle and activity.

hīve, *v.t.*; hived, *pt., pp.*; hiving, *ppr.* 1. to put or gather (bees) into a hive.
2. to store up (honey) in a hive.
3. to store up for future use; garner.

hīve, *v.i.* 1. to enter a hive.
2. to live together in or as in a hive.

hīve bee, the common honeybee.

hīve′less, *a.* having no hive.

hīve nest, a group of nests built together or a large nest built and occupied by several pairs of birds in common, as those of the weaver-birds.

hīv′ẽr, *n.* one who collects bees into a hive.

hīveṣ, *n.* [orig. Scot. dial.]
1. croup. [Brit.]
2. urticaria, or nettle rash, and certain other skin allergies, characterized by itching, burning, stinging, and the formation of smooth particles, or wheals, usually red.

hīve vīne, a trailing evergreen herb, *Mitchella repens*, of the madder family: called also *partridgeberry*.

hizz, *v.i.* to hiss. [Rare.]

h′m, *interj.* hem; hum.

Ho, in chemistry, holmium.

hō, *interj.* 1. a call or cry to attract attention or give notice of approach: sometimes used after a destination or direction; as, westward *ho!*
2. an expression of contempt, wonder, mirth, etc.
3. whoa! stop! halt!

hō, *n.* stop; moderation; end. [Obs.]

hō·aç̣t′zin, *n.* same as *hoatzin*.

hōar, *a.* [ME *hore, hoor*; AS. *har*, hoary, gray-haired.]
1. white, gray, or grayish-white.
2. having gray or white hair because very old; hoary; as, a man grave and *hoar*.
3. musty, moldy. [Dial.]

hōar, *n.* 1. hoariness.
2. hoarfrost.

hōar, *v.i.* 1. to become moldy or musty. [Obs.]
2. to grow white with age. [Rare.]

hōard, *n.* [ME. *hord*; AS. *hord*, hoard, store, treasure.]
1. a store, stock, or quantity of anything hidden or kept in reserve; a treasure; as, a *hoard* of provisions for winter, a *hoard* of money.
2. a place in which anything is hoarded. [Obs.]

hōard, *v.t.*; hoarded, *pt., pp.*; hoarding, *ppr.* [ME. *horden*; AS. *hordian*, to hoard, from *hord*, a hoard, treasure.] to collect and lay up; to store secretly; as, to *hoard* gold.

hōard, *v.i.* to collect and form a hoard; to store away; as, she *hoarded* all her life.

hōard′ẽr, *n.* one who lays up a hoard.

hōard′ing, *n.* 1. the act of a person who hoards.
2. something hoarded.

hōard′ing, *n.* [from obs. *hoard*, hoarding; OFr. *hourde*; Frank. *hurda*, a pen, fold.]
1. a temporary wooden fence around a site of building construction or repair. [Brit.]
2. a billboard. [Brit.]
3. in medieval fortification, a wooden structure built above or about the walls of a fortress.

hōared, *a.* moldy; musty. [Obs.]

hōar′frọst, *n.* white frost; white, frozen dew on the ground, leaves, etc.; rime.

hōar′hound, *n.* same as *horehound*.

hōar′i·ness, *n.* the quality or condition of being hoary.

hōarse, *a.* [ME. *hoors, hors*; AS. *has*, hoarse, rough.]
1. having a harsh, rough, husky voice, as when affected with a cold.
2. rough and grating in sound; sounding rough and husky; as, the *hoarse* warning of a foghorn.

Syn.—harsh, grating, discordant, husky, raucous, rough, gruff.

hōarse′ly, *adv.* in a hoarse manner.

hōars′en, *v.t.* and *v.i.* to make or become harsh or hoarse.

hōarse′ness, *n.* [ME. *hoorsnesse*; AS. *hasnes*, from *has*, hoarse.] harshness of voice or sound.

hōar′stōne, *n.* [AS. *har stan*, a hoarstone; *har*, hoar, gray, and *stan*, a stone.] a landmark; a stone used to mark the boundary of an estate. [Brit.]

hōar′y, *a.* 1. white, whitish, or grayish-white; as, the *hoary* willows.
2. having white or gray hair because very old; as, a *hoary* head.
3. very aged; ancient; as, *hoary* fables.
4. moldy, mossy. [Obs.]
5. in botany, grayish-white, caused by very short, dense hairs covering the surface.

hōar′y-head′ed, *a.* having white or gray hair because very old.

hōast, *v.i.* to cough. [Brit. Dial. and Scot.]

hō·at′zin, *n.* [Sp.; Nahuatl *uatzin*.] a crested, olive-colored South American bird: the wings of its young have claws, used in climbing trees: also *hoactzin, hoazin*.

hōax, *n.* [altered from *hocus*.] something done for deception or mockery; especially, some thing meant as a practical joke.

hōax, *v.t.* to deceive with a hoax.

hōax′ẽr, *n.* one who hoaxes.

hō·az′in, *n.* same as *hoatzin*.

hob, *n.* [perh. var. of *hub*.]
1. a ledge at the back or side of a fireplace, on which anything may be placed to be kept warm.
2. a steel mandrel, used as a cutter in making screw-chasing tools.
3. a hardened steel punch used in making dies.
4. the stick, pin, or peg used as a target in quoits, etc.
5. any game in which such a peg is used.

hob, *n.* [orig. familiar form for *Robin* or *Robert*.]
1. a rustic; lout. [Brit. Dial.]
2. [H–] Robin Goodfellow, or Puck.
3. an elf; goblin.
to play (or *raise*) *hob*; to cause mischief; make trouble. [Slang.]

hob′ȧ·nob′, hob′and·nob′, *v.i.* to hobnob.

Hobb′iṣm, *n.* the principles of Thomas Hobbes, a materialistic English philosopher (1588–1679), who believed that a strong government, especially an absolute monarchy, is necessary to control conflicting individual interests and desires.

Hobb′ist, *n.* a follower of Thomas Hobbes.

hob′bit, *n.* [coined in a novel (1938) by J. R. R. Tolkien.] an imaginary being having a very small human form with some rabbitlike qualities, and characterized by sociability, domesticity, and a peace-loving nature.

hob′ble, *v.i.*; hobbled, *pt., pp.*; hobbling, *ppr.* [ME. *hobelen, hoblen*, freq. of *hoppen*, to hop.]
1. to go unsteadily, haltingly, etc.
2. to walk lamely; to limp; to walk with a hitch or hop, or with crutches.

hob′ble, *v.t.* 1. to cause to go haltingly or lamely.
2. to hopple; to impede the movement of (a horse, etc.) by tying two legs together.
3. to perplex. [Obs.]

hob′ble, *n.* 1. an unequal, halting gait; an awkward step; a limp.
2. difficulty; an awkward situation. [Rare.]
3. a hopple; a rope, strap, etc. used to hobble a horse; fetter.

hob′ble-bụsh, *n.* a low-growing honeysuckle, *Viburnum alnifolium*, with wide-spreading branches, dark, wrinkled leaves, clusters of white flowers, and purple berries: also called *American wayfaring tree*.

hob′ble·dē·hoy′, *n.* [prob. based on *hob* (a rustic) with cross associations from *hobble*, Fr. *hober*, to bestir oneself, and *hobereau*, a hobby (hawk).]
1. a youth between boyhood and manhood; adolescent boy.
2. an awkward, clumsy, gawky youth or boy.

hob′blẽr, *n.* one who or that which hobbles.

hob′blẽr, *n.* [ME. *hobler, hobeler*; OFr. *hobeler, hobelier*, from *hobi, hobin*, a small horse.]
1. one who by his tenure was to maintain a hobby, or horse, for military service; one who served as a light-armored soldier on horseback. [Obs.]
2. one who tows a boat, etc., as by a rope along a bank. [Brit. Dial.]

hob′ble skīrt, a woman's skirt which is so narrow below the knees that it hinders the wearer's movements.

hob′bling·ly, *adv.* in a hobbling manner; with a limping, halting step.

hob′bly, *a.* uneven; rough, as a path. [Brit. Dial.]

hob′by, *n.*; *pl.* **hob′bieṣ,** [ME. *hobie, hoby*, OFr. *hobe* from *hober*, to stir, move.] a species of European falcon, *Falco subbuteo*, formerly trained for hawking.

hob′by, *n.*; *pl.* **hob′bieṣ,** [from dim. of *Hob*, familiar form of *Rob*, personal name.]
1. a medium-sized, vigorous horse. [Obs. or Dial.]
2. a hobbyhorse. [Rare.]
3. a subject that a person constantly talks about or returns to. [Rare.]
4. something that a person likes to do or study in his spare time; favorite pastime or avocation.
to ride a hobby; to be excessively devoted to one's favorite pastime or subject.

hob′by·họrse, *n.* [OFr. *hobi*, a horse, hobby, and Eng. *horse*.]
1. (a) a figure of a horse attached to the waist of a person doing a morris dance so that he seems to be riding it; (b) the dancer.
2. a children's toy consisting of a stick with a horse's head.
3. a rocking horse.
4. a hobby; a favorite subject.
5. an early form of bicycle propelled by pushing with the feet along the ground.
6. an imitation horse on a merry-go-round.

hob·by·họrs′iç·ăl, *a.* eccentric; full of whims: used humorously.

hob·by·họrs′iç·ăl·ly, *adv.* whimsically: used humorously.

hob′gob·lin, *n.* [*hob*, a fairy, and *goblin*.]
1. [H–] Robin Goodfellow; Puck.
2. an elf; goblin.
3. a frightening apparition; bogy; bugbear.

hob′līke, *a.* clownish; boorish.

hob′nāil, *n.* 1. a nail with a thick, strong head, used in the soles of heavy shoes.
2. a person who wears hobnailed boots; rustic.

hob′nāil, *v.t.*; hobnailed, *pt., pp.*; hobnailing, *ppr.* 1. to set with hobnails, as a shoe.
2. to trample roughly, as if with hobnailed boots.

hob′nāiled, *a.* 1. set with hobnails; rough.
2. rough; boorish; clumsy, as if wearing hobnailed boots.
hobnailed liver; a form of cirrhosis of the liver marked by a shrunken condition, with hard knobs, like hobnails, on the surface.

hob′nob, *adv.* [AS. *habban*, to have, and *næbban*, for *ne habban*, to not have.] hit or miss; at random.

hob′nob, *v.i.*; hobnobbed, *pt., pp.*; hobnobbing, *ppr.* 1. to drink together or clink glasses in a familiar way.
2. to have familiar associations or relations; to be on close terms (*with* someone); as, he *hobnobs with* all sorts of people.

hob′nob, *n.* a drinking together. [Rare.]

hō′bō, *n.*; *pl.* **hō′bōṣ, hō′bōeṣ,** [19th-c. Americanism; perh. from *ho! beau!*, formerly a call of greeting between vagrants.]
1. a migratory worker: so used by such workers themselves.
2. a vagrant; tramp: often contemptuous. Sometimes shortened to *bo*.

hob ŏr nob, same as *hobnob*.

hō′boy, *n.* same as *hautboy*.

Hob′son's choice, [after Thomas *Hobson* (d. 1631), of Cambridge, England, who owned livery stables and let horses in strict order according to their position near the door.] a choice of taking what is offered or nothing at all.

Hoçh′heim·ẽr, *n.* a white Rhine wine produced at Hochheim, near Mentz, Germany.

hock, *v.t.* and *n.* [in allusion to the game of faro, in which the last card in the box is called *hock*; hence, the last chance, the last resort.] pawn. [Slang.]

hock, *n.* [ME. *hok, hokke, hoc*; AS. *hoc*, mallow.] the hollyhock; also, the mallow. [Obs.]

hock, *n.* originally, Hochheimer; now, any white Rhine wine. [Chiefly Brit.]

hock, *n.* [ME. *houg, hog*, AS. *hoh, ho*, the heel.]
1. the joint bending backward in the hind leg of a horse, ox, etc., corresponding to the human ankle.
2. the corresponding joint in the leg of a fowl.

hock, *v.t.*; hocked, *pt., pp.*; hocking, *ppr.* to hamstring; to disable by cutting the tendons of the hock.

hock′à·mōre, *n.* [altered from *Hochheimer.*] Hochheimer. [Obs.]

Hock′dāy, Hōke′dāy, *n.* [ME. *hokday, hokeday*; *hok,* a corruption of *high, hig,* or *hey,* from AS. *hêah,* high.] a day of feasting and mirth, formerly held in England the second Tuesday after Easter.

hock′ey, *n.* [Early Mod. Eng.; prob. from OFr. *hoquet,* bent stick, crook.]
1. a team game played with curved sticks, the object of each side being to drive a rubber disk or ball into their opponents' goal.
2. a stick with a curved end, with which this game is played: also called *hockey stick.*
field hockey; see under *field.*
ice hockey; the game of hockey, when played on an ice rink, the players wearing ice skates.

hoç′kle, *v.t.*; hockled, *pt., pp.*; hockling, *ppr.* [from *hock,* part of the leg.]
1. to hamstring; to hock.
2. to mow. [Brit. Dial.]

hock′shop, *n.* a pawnshop. [Slang.]

hō′çus, *v.t.*; hocused *or* hocussed (-kust), *pt., pp.*; hocusing *or* hocussing, *ppr.* [abbrev. of *hocus-pocus.*]
1. to cheat, to dupe; to deceive.
2. to drug.
3. to put drugs in (a drink).

hō′çus, *n.* 1. a tricky person; an impostor; also, a magician; a conjurer. [Obs.]
2. liquor that has been drugged.

hō′çus-pō′çus, *n.* [imitation Latin.]
1. a juggler. [Obs.]
2. meaningless words used as a formula by conjurers.
3. a magician's trick or trickery; sleight of hand; legerdemain.
4. any meaningless action or talk meant to draw attention away from some trick or deception.
5. trickery; deception.

hō′çus-pō′çus, *a.* juggling; deceptive; as, a *hocus-pocus* trick.

hō′çus-pō′çus, *v.t.* and *v.i.*; hocus-pocused *or* hocus-pocussed (-kust), *pt., pp.*; hocus-pocusing *or* hocus-pocussing, *ppr.* to trick; dupe. [Colloq.]

hod, *n.* [Fr. *hotte,* a basket for carrying on the back; O.D. *hotte,* a peddler's basket.]
1. a kind of wooden trough for carrying mortar and brick, used in bricklaying: it is fitted with a long handle and is borne on the shoulder.
2. a coal scuttle.
3. a tub for carrying and measuring alewives. [Brit.]
4. a pewterer's blowpipe. [Brit.]

hod çar′ri·ẽr, a worker who carries bricks and mortar in a hod.

hod′den, *n.* [perh. from northern Eng. form of *holden,* pp. of *hold* (perh. because it "holds" natural hue).] a coarse, undyed woolen cloth: a gray variety, made by mixing white and black fleece, is called *hodden gray.* [Scot.]

hod′den, *a.* dressed in hodden; countrified. [Scot.]

hod′dy-dod′dy, *n.* an awkward or foolish person. [Obs.]

Hō′dẽr, *n.* same as *Hodur.*

hodġe′podġe, *n.* [from *hotchpot,* from OFr. *hotchepot,* a mingled mass; O.D. *hutspot,* beef or mutton cut into small pieces and boiled together; *hutsen,* to shake, and *pot,* pot.]
1. a thick stew of various meats and vegetables.
2. a mixed mass; a medley of ingredients.

Hodġ′kin's dis·ēase′, [after Dr. Thomas *Hodgkin* (1798–1866), an English physician who first described it.] a disease characterized by progressive enlargement of the lymph nodes and inflammation of other lymphoid tissues, especially of the spleen.

hō′di·ẽrn, *a.* hodiernal. [Obs.]

hō·di·ẽr′năl, *a.* [L. *hodiernus,* from *hodie,* on this day, contr. of *hoc die,* abl. of *hic dies, hic,* this, and *dies,* day.] of this day; belonging to the present day.

hod′măn, *n.*; *pl.* **hod′men,** a man who carries a hod; a bricklayer's helper; a hod carrier.

hod′măn·dod, *n.* a snail. [Obs.]

hod′ō·graph, *n.* [Gr. *hodos,* way, and *graphein,* to write.] a curve whose radius vector represents the velocity and direction of motion of a moving point.

hō·dom′ē·tẽr, *n.* see *odometer.*

Hō′dŭr, *n.* [ON. *Hothr.*] in Norse mythology, the blind god who unintentionally killed Baldur with a twig of mistletoe given to him by Loki: also spelled *Hoder.*

hōe, *n.* [OFr. *houe, hoe,* from O.H.G. *houwa,* a hoe, from *houwan,* to hew, cut.] a tool for cutting up weeds and loosening the earth in fields and gardens, usually consisting of a thin, flat metal blade set across the end of a long, wooden handle.
Dutch hoe; a hoe having the cutting blade arranged for use by pushing: called also *scuffle hoe, push hoe, thrust hoe.*
horse hoe; a cultivator drawn by a horse.

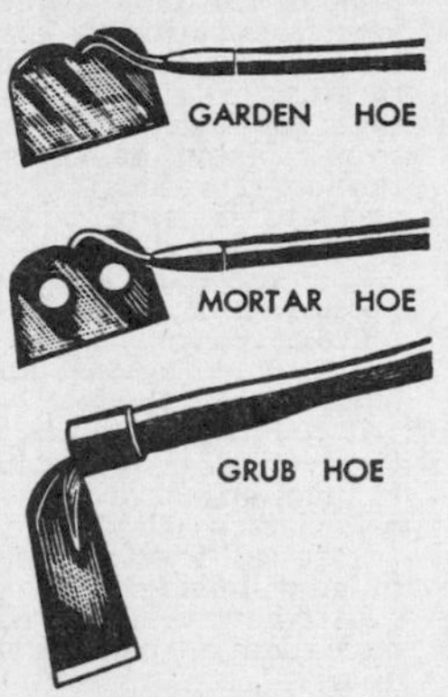

GARDEN HOE
MORTAR HOE
GRUB HOE

TYPES OF HOE

hōe, *v.t.* and *v.i.*; hoed, *pt., pp.*; hoeing, *ppr.* to cut, dig, scrape, cultivate, weed, clean, etc. with a hoe.
a hard (or *long*) *row to hoe*; a difficult or tiresome task to perform.
to hoe one's own row; to do one's own share; to mind one's own business.

hōe′çāke, *n.* a thin bread made of corn meal, water, and salt, originally baked on the blade of a hoe.

hōe′down, *n.* [prob. of U.S. Negro origin; associated with *breakdown* (sense 5).]
1. a lively, rollicking dance, often a square dance.
2. music for this.
3. a party at which hoedowns are danced.

Hoe′nīr (hu′), *n.* [ON.] in Norse mythology, the god who, together with Odin and Loki, created the first man and the first woman.

hog, *n.*; *pl.* **hogs** or **hog,** [ME. *hog, hoge, hogge,* a gelded hog.]
1. a pig; especially, a castrated boar or full-grown pig raised for its meat.
2. by extension, any animal resembling the hog, as the peccary.
3. a greedy, gluttonous, selfish, coarse, or filthy person. [Colloq.]
4. (a) a young sheep not yet shorn; (b) a year-old bullock; (c) a young colt. [Scot. and Brit. Dial.]
5. a kind of scrubbing broom for scraping a ship's bottom under water.
6. in papermaking, an agitator or stirrer in the pulp vat.
hog cholera; see under *cholera.*
hog wild, highly excited; without moderation or restraint. [Colloq.]
to go the whole hog; to go to the limit; to do or accept something fully. [Slang.]

hog, *v.t.*; hogged, *pt., pp.*; hogging, *ppr.* 1. to scrape (a ship's bottom) with a hog.
2. to cut (the hair) short so as to make it bristly; as, to *hog* a horse's mane.
3. (a) to arch (the back) like a hog's; (b) to cause (a ship, keel, etc.) to arch in the center like a hog's back.
4. to grab greedily; take all of or an unfair share of. [Slang.]

hog, *v.i.* to arch in the center so as to resemble a hog's back, as of the keel of a ship.

hō′gan, *n.* [Navaho *qoghan,* house.] the typical dwelling of the Navaho Indians, built of earth walls supported by timbers.

hog ap′ple, the May apple, *Podophyllum peltatum.*

hog′back, *n.* 1. a convex back like that of a hog.
2. a hogframe.
3. a ridge with a sharp crest and abruptly sloping sides, rising above the surrounding level, often formed by the projecting edge of tilted rock strata.

hog çat′ẽr·pil·lăr, the larva of *Darapsa myron* the grapevine sphinx moth, whose head resembles a hog's snout.

hog′chōk″ẽr, *n.* the American sole, *Achirus lineatus*: so called because worthless as food.

hog′çōte, *n.* a shed for swine; a sty. [Obs.]

hog deer, any of various animals; specifically, (a) the axis; (b) *Cervus porcinus,* a spotted deer allied to the axis; (c) the babirussa.

hog fen′nel, sulfurwort.

hog′fish, *n.*; *pl.* **hog′fish, hog′fish·eṣ,** any of various species of fish supposed to look like a hog in some way; specifically, (a) the sailor's-choice; (b) the log perch; (c) the *Lachnolænus maximus,* a labroid West Indian fish; (d) the *Scorpæna scrofa,* a large, red, European fish.

hog′frāme, *n.* in steam ships, a fore-and-aft frame, usually above deck, forming, together with the frame of the vessel, a truss to prevent hogging.

hogged, *a.* arched in the middle: said of a ship when broken, bent, or sprung, as from stranding.

hog′gẽr, *n.* a footless stocking. [Scot. and Brit. Dial.]

hog′gẽr·el, *n.* [dim. of *hog.*] a sheep of the second year.

hog′gẽr pīpe, the upper pipe of a mining pump. [Scot. and Brit. Dial.]

hog′gẽr pump, the uppermost pump in a mine. [Scot. and Brit. Dial.]

hog′gẽr·y, *n.*; *pl.* **hog′gẽr·ieṣ,** 1. a place where hogs are kept.
2. a herd of hogs.
3. behavior considered characteristic of hogs, as living in filth, being greedy, etc.

hog′get, *n.* 1. a young boar of the second year. [Dial.]
2. a colt or sheep over one year old. [Dial.]

hog′gish, *a.* having the qualities of a hog; gluttonous, filthy, mean, or selfish.

hog′gish·ly, *adv.* in a hoggish manner.

hog′gish·ness, *n.* the state or quality of being hoggish; voracious greediness in eating; beastly filthiness; mean selfishness.

hog gum, any of various aromatic resins found in the West Indies.

hog′hẽrd, *n.* a keeper of swine.

hog in är′mŏr, the nine-banded armadillo.

hog louse, a wood louse or sow bug.

hog·mà·nāy′, *n.* [said to be altered from ONorm. Fr. *hoguinané*; altered from OFr. *aguilanneuf*; orig. meaning obscure.] New Year's Eve, when young people go around singing and asking for presents.

hog mēat, the root of a Jamaican herb, the *Boerhaavia decumbens,* used medicinally.

hog mol′ly, 1. the hog sucker.
2. the log perch or hogfish.

hog mul′let, the hog sucker.

hog′nōṣe snāke, the American flathead or puff adder, a small, harmless North American snake with a flat snout and thick body.

hog′nut, *n.* 1. the pignut or brown hickory nut.
2. the earthnut, *Bunium flexuosum.*

hō′gō, *n.* [Fr. *haut goût,* high flavor.] strong flavor or scent. [Obs.]

hog pēa′nut, a vine of the order *Leguminosæ, Amphicarpæa monoica,* whose upper flowers are usually sterile while those at the base ripen a single-seeded pod in the ground or on the surface.

hog′pen, *n.* a hogsty.

hog plum, any of various plants or their fruit; specifically, (a) a plant of the genus *Spondias,* of the West Indies, whose plumlike fruit is fed to hogs; (b) a plant of the genus *Ximenia,* of Florida and the West Indies; called also *wild lime, mountain plum*; (c) the Chickasaw plum, *Prunus angustifolia*; (d) the poisonwood, *Rhus metopium,* of tropical Florida.

hog rat, a Cuban rodent, the hutia.

hog′reeve, *n.* in New England, an officer having the care of stray hogs.

hog′ring, *n.* a metal ring or similar device set in a hog's snout to keep it from rooting up the ground.

hog′ṣ′-back, *n.* anything having the shape of the back of a hog; in geology, a hogback.

hog′ṣ′-bāne, *n.* the sowbane or maple-leaved goosefoot.

hog′ṣ′-bēan, *n.* the henbane.

hog sçōre, in curling, a line drawn across the rink or course at a point one-sixth of the total distance from each tee.

hog′ṣ′-fen″nel, *n.* hog fennel; sulfurwort.

hogṣ′head (-hed), *n.* [ME. *hoggeshed, hoggis hed, hoggeshede,* lit., hog's head; reason for name uncertain.]
1. a liquid measure, especially one equal to 63 gallons (52½ imperial gallons).
2. a large barrel or cask, especially one containing from 100 to 140 gallons.

hog′skin, *n.* tanned leather made of the skin of a hog.

hog snāke, a hognose snake.

hog′stȳ, *n.* a pen or enclosure for hogs.

hog suck′ẽr, a river fish, *Hypentelium nigricans*: also called *hog molly, hog mullet.*

hog′tīe, *v.t.*; hogtied, *pt., pp.*; hogtying *or* hogtieing, *ppr.* 1. to tie the four feet or the hands and feet of.

2. to make incapable of effective action, as if by tying up. [Colloq.]

hog'wăsh, *n.* 1. swill; refuse fed to hogs.
2. empty talk, writing, etc.

hog'weed, *n.* any of various plants regarded as fit for hogs, as the *Ambrosia artemisiæfolia*, ragweed; *Heracleum sphondylium*, the cow parsnip; and *Polygonum aviculare*, doorweed or knotgrass.

hog'wŏrt, *n.* an annual plant, *Croton capitatus*, of the southeastern United States.

hoick, *interj.* hoicks.

hoicks, *v.t.* and *v.i.* to cheer on, as hounds, with or as with the call "hoicks."

hoicks, *interj.* a hunting cry used to urge the hounds.

hoi'den, *n.*, *a.*, and *v.i.* hoyden.

hoi'den·ish, *a.* hoydenish.

hoi pŏl·loi', [Gr., the many.] the common people; the masses: usually patronizing or contemptuous; popularly and redundantly preceded by *the*.

hoișe, *v.t.*; hoised *or* hoist, *pt.*, *pp.*; hoising, *ppr.* to raise; to hoist. [Obs.]

hoist, *v.t.*; hoisted, *pt.*, *pp.*; hoisting, *ppr.* [var. of *hoise*, with unhistoric *-t*; from O.D. *hyssen*, to hoise, hoist.] to raise; to lift or bear upward, especially by a mechanical device, as by means of tackle; as, to *hoist* a sail.

hoist, *v.i.* to be lifted; to rise.

hoist, *n.* 1. the operation of hoisting.
2. an apparatus for raising heavy objects; an elevator or tackle.
3. in nautical usage, (a) the perpendicular height of a flag or sail, as opposed to the *fly*, or breadth from the staff to the outer edge; (b) the middle part of a mast; (c) flags hoisted together as a signal.

hoist'ȧ·wāy'', *n.* a hoist; an elevator. [Colloq.]

hoist bridge, a lift bridge.

hoist'ẽr, *n.* one who or that which hoists.

hoist'wāy, *n.* an opening through which goods may be hoisted, as in a warehouse; an elevator shaft.

hoit, *v.i.* to indulge in noisy mirth; romp; caper. [Obs.]

hoi'ty-toi'ty, *a.* [redupl. of obs. *hoit.*]
1. giddy; flighty; capricious.
2. haughty; arrogant; condescending; patronizing.
3. petulant; fussy; huffy.
Also *highty-tighty*.

hoi'ty-toi'ty, *n.* hoity-toity behavior: also *highty-tighty*.

hoi'ty-toi'ty, *interj.* an exclamation of surprise or disapproval with some degree of contempt or derision: also *highty-tighty*.

Hoity-toity! what have I to do with dreams?
—Congreve.

Hōke'dāy, *n.* see *Hockday*.

hō'kẽr, *n.* [AS. *hocor*, scorn, mockery.] censure; abuse; derision. [Obs.]

hō'kẽr·ly, *adv.* scornfully; abusively. [Obs.]

hō''key·pō'key, *n.* 1. hocus-pocus; trickery.
2. a kind of cheap ice cream sold by street vendors.
Also spelled *hokypoky*.

hō'kum, *n.* [altered from *hocus.*]
1. crudely comic or mawkishly sentimental elements in a play, story, etc., used to gain an immediate emotional response. [Slang.]
2. nonsense; humbug; claptrap; bunk. [Slang.]

hō'ky·pō'ky, *n.* same as *hokeypokey*.

hōl, *a.* whole. [Obs.]

hol·ärç'tiç, *a.* [Gr. *holos*, whole, and *arktikos*, arctic.] completely arctic; relating to the entire arctic regions.

hol·är·thrit'iç, *a.* [Gr. *holos*, whole, and *arthritis.*] affected with arthritis in all the joints.

hol·as·pid'ē·ăn, *a.* [Gr. *holos*, whole, and *aspis* (*-idos*), a shield.] in zoology, having the posterior sheath of the tarsus entire, as the lark.

hol'çad, *n.* [Gr. *holkas* (*-ados*), a ship that is towed, from *helkein*, to draw.] in ancient Greece, a merchant ship.

hōld, *v.t.*; held, *pt.*; held (*archaic* holden), *pp.*; holding, *ppr.* [ME *holden*, *halden*; AS. *healdan*, to hold, keep.]
1. to take and keep with the hands, arms, or other means; to grasp; clutch; seize.
2. to keep from going away; not let escape; as, *hold* the prisoner; will they *hold* the train till we get there?
3. to keep in a certain place or position, or in a specified condition; as, *hold* your head on one side.
4. to restrain or control as by keeping in a certain place; specifically, (a) to keep from falling; to bear the weight of; support; sustain; as, this pillar *holds* the platform; (b) to keep from acting; to keep back; as, *hold* your tongue; (c) to keep from advancing or attacking; (d) to keep from getting an advantage; (e) to get and keep control of; to keep from relaxing; as, the speaker *held* their attention; (f) to keep (a letter, etc.) for delivery at a later time; (g) to keep under obligation; to bind; as, *hold* him to his word.
5. to have and keep as one's own; to be in possession of; own; occupy; as, he *holds* the office of mayor.
6. to keep against an enemy; guard; defend; as, *hold* the fort.
7. to have or conduct together; to carry on (a meeting, conversation, etc.); to perform (a function, service, etc.); as, the college will *hold* classes today.
8. to call together or preside over; as, the judge will *hold* court.
9. to have or keep within itself; contain; to have room or space for; as, this bottle *holds* a quart.
10. to have or keep in the mind.
11. to have an opinion or belief about; to regard; consider; as, I *hold* your statement to be untrue.
12. in law, (a) to decide; abjudge; decree; (b) to bind by contract; (c) to possess by legal title; as, who *holds* the mortgage?
13. in music, to go on sounding (a tone).
14. to wager; to bet. [Archaic.]
to hold back; (a) to restrain; (b) to retain.
to hold down; (a) to keep down or under control; to restrain; (b) [Colloq.] to have and keep (a job).
to hold forth; to offer; to propose.
to hold in; to curb; to restrain; to check.
to hold in hand or *in play*; to have control of; to play with.
to hold off; (a) to keep at a distance; (b) to keep from attacking or doing something.
to hold one's own; to keep one's present condition or position; to lose no advantage.
to hold one's peace; to be silent.
to hold out; (a) to offer; (b) [Slang.] to fail or refuse to give (what is to be given).
to hold over; (a) to postpone consideration of or action on; (b) to keep as a threat or advantage over.
to hold up; (a) to sustain; to lift; (b) to display; to offer as an example; (c) to check; to stop; (d) to stop forcibly and rob; hence, (e) [Colloq.] to overcharge.
to hold water; (a) to check a rowboat's headway by holding the oars steady in the water; (b) to be sound and without leaks; hence, (c) to remain sound, logical, or consistent, as an argument or statement.

hōld, *v.i.* 1. to go on being firm, loyal, etc.; as, *hold* to your resolution.
2. to remain unbroken or unyielding; not give way; as, the rope *held*.
3. to have right or title (usually with *from* or *of*).
4. to be in effect or in force; to be true or valid; as, this principle *holds* in any government.
5. to keep up; to continue; as, the wind *held* from the north.
6. to go no further; to stop oneself; halt: usually in the imperative.
7. to refrain: with *from*.
hold on! hold up! hold hard! halt! stop! wait! [Colloq.]
to hold back; to refrain.
to hold forth; to speak in public; to harangue; to preach; to proclaim.
to hold in; to restrain oneself or one's impulses; as, he could hardly *hold in* from laughing.
to hold off; to remain at a distance.
to hold on; (a) to retain one's hold; (b) to continue; to persist.
to hold out; (a) to last; to endure; to continue; (b) to continue resistance; to stand firm; not yield.
to hold over; (a) to continue in possession, as of an office, after the expiration of some fixed time; (b) to be continued or postponed; as, the matter *holds over*.
to hold together; to be joined; to keep from separating.
to hold up; (a) to last; to endure; to continue; (b) to stop; to delay; to cease.
to hold with; (a) to agree with; (b) to approve of; (c) to side with.

hōld, *n.* [ME. *hold*, *hald*; AS. *heald*, hold, protection, from *healdan*, to hold.]
1. the act or manner of grasping or seizing; grip.
2. a thing to hold or hold on by.
3. a thing for holding or containing something else.
4. a controlling or dominating force; a restraining authority; strong influence; as, his wife has a firm *hold* over him.

The law hath yet another *hold* on you.
—Shak.

5. a prison; a place of confinement.

They laid hands on them, and put them in *hold* unto the next day. —Acts iv. 3.

6. a stronghold; a fortified place; a fort; a castle; a place of security. [Archaic.]
7. in music, the character 𝄐, directing the performer to pause on the note or rest over which it is placed: called also a *pause*.
8. the act or fact of guarding, possessing, keeping in custody, etc. [Obs.]
9. in wrestling, a way of holding or seizing an opponent; as, a scissors *hold*.
to catch hold of; to take; seize; grasp.
to get hold of; (a) to take; seize; grasp; (b) to acquire.
to lay (or *take*) *hold of*; (a) to take; seize; grasp; (b) to get control or possession of.

hōld, *n.* [altered (after *hold*, *v.*), from *hole* or from MD. *hol*, a hole, cave, ship's hold.] the interior of a ship below decks, especially below the lower deck, in which the cargo is carried.

hōld'all, *n.* a large traveling case for carrying clothes, equipment, etc.

hōld'back, *n.* 1. check; restraint; hindrance.
2. the iron or strap on the shaft or pole of a vehicle to which a part of the harness is attached, to enable the animal to back up or to hold back the vehicle when going downhill.

hōld'en, *v.* archaic past participle of *hold*.

hōld'ẽr, *n.* [ME. *holdere.*]
1. a person or thing that holds; specifically, (a) a person who holds, and is legally entitled to payment of, a bill, note, or check; (b) a tenant; (c) a possessor; (d) a device for holding something, as a penholder; (e) a heavy cloth to protect the hands when lifting hot dishes.
2. a canine tooth.
3. a person employed in the hold of a ship.

hōld'ẽr-fọrth, *n.* a haranguer; a preacher.

hōld'fȧst, *n.* 1. any of various contrivances for securing and holding things in place, as a long, flat-headed nail, a catch, a hook, etc.
2. hold; support; a holding fast.
3. a rootlike appendage of a seaweed.

hōld'ing, *n.* 1. the act of keeping or retaining.
2. land, especially a farm, rented from another.
3. [*usually pl.*] property owned, especially stocks or bonds.
4. in certain sports, the act of illegally hindering an opponent, as from using his arms or hands.
5. hold; influence. [Rare.]
6. the burden or chorus of a song. [Obs.]

hōld'ing cŏm'pȧ·ny, in finance, a company that owns, and usually controls, the stocks or securities of other companies.

hōld'ing nōte, in music, a note sustained while other notes are changed.

hōld'out, *n.* in baseball, football, etc., a professional player who has not signed a contract at the regular time because he is insisting upon better terms. [Colloq.]

hōld'ō''vẽr, *n.* a person or thing staying on from a previous period; specifically, a person, as an officeholder or entertainer, who is held over from one term of office, engagement, etc. to another. [Colloq.]

hōld'up, *n.* 1. a stoppage; delay or hindrance.
2. the act of stopping forcibly and robbing.
3. an overcharging. [Colloq.]

hōle, *n.* [ME. *hole*, *hool*, *hol*; AS. *hol*, a hole, cavern, from *hol*, adj., hollow.]
1. a hollow or hollowed-out place; cavity; specifically, (a) an excavation; pit; as, he dug a *hole* in the ground; (b) a small bay or inlet; cove: often in place names; (c) a pool or deep, relatively wide place in a stream; as, a swimming *hole*; (d) an animal's burrow or lair; den.
2. a small, dingy, squalid place; any dirty, badly lighted room, house, etc.
3. a prison cell.
4. (a) an opening in or through anything; break; gap; as, a *hole* in the wall; (b) a tear or rent, as in a garment.
5. a flaw; fault; blemish; defect; as, we found *holes* in his argument.
6. in golf, (a) a small, round, hollow place into which the ball is to be hit; (b) the tee,

fairway, greens, etc. leading to this; as, 18 *holes* of golf.

7. an embarrassing situation or position; a predicament; a scrape; a fix; as, to get into a *hole*. [Colloq.]

a hole to crawl out of; a means of escape; an excuse.

hole high; in golf, as far from the tee as the hole is; even with the hole but not in it.

hole in one; in golf, the act of getting the ball into a hole with one drive from the tee.

in the hole; financially embarrassed or behind: often with a specific sum indicated, as, I'm fifty dollars *in the hole* this month.

the hole; (a) [Colloq.] same as *solitary confinement*; also, a cell used for solitary confinement; (b) in baseball, the area of the infield between the third baseman and the shortstop.

to burn a hole in one's pocket; to make one eager to spend it: said of money.

to crawl into one's hole; to give up an argument; to sneak off. [Colloq.]

to make a hole in; to consume a sizable amount of.

to pick holes in; to pick out errors or flaws in.

hōle, *v.i.*; holed, *pt., pp.*; holing, *ppr.* to go into a hole.

hōle, *v.t.* [ME. *holen, holien*; AS. *holian*, to hollow out, dig a hole, from *hol*, hollow.]

1. to cut, dig, or make a hole or holes in; as, to *hole* a post for the insertion of rails or bars.

2. to put, hit, or drive into a hole; as, to *hole* a ball in pool.

3. to create by making a hole; as, they *holed* a tunnel through the mountain.

4. in mining, (a) to undercut (a coal seam); (b) to connect, as two workings.

to hole out; in golf, to hit the ball into a hole.

to hole up; (a) to hibernate, usually in a hole; (b) to shut oneself in.

hōle, *a.* hollow; empty; hungry. [Brit. Dial.]

hōle, *a.* whole; hale; healthy. [Obs.]

hōle'wŏrt, *n.* same as *hollowwort*.

hōle'y, *a.* having a hole or holes.

hol'i·dāy, *n.* [ME. *holiday, haliday*; AS. *halig dæg*, lit., holy day; *halig*, holy, and *dæg*, day.]

1. a religious festival; holy day: usually *holyday*.

2. a day of freedom from labor; day set aside for leisure and recreation.

3. [*often pl.*] a period of leisure or recreation. [Chiefly Brit.]

4. a day set aside by law or custom for the suspension of business, usually in celebration of some event.

5. in nautical usage, a spot not covered in the operation of applying tar, paint, or whitewash to a ship. [Slang.]

hol'i·dāy, *a.* pertaining to a festival; gay; adapted for or proper to a special occasion; as, the *holiday* spirit.

hō'li·ly, *adv.* piously; with sanctity; in a holy manner; sacredly.

hō'li·ness, *n.* [ME. *holinesse, holynesse, halinesse*; AS. *halignes*, from *halig*, holy.]

1. the quality or state of being holy; purity or integrity of moral character; freedom from sin; sanctity.

2. [H–] a title of the Pope: used with *his* or *your*.

hō'lism, *n.* [*holo-*, and *-ism*.] the view that an organic or integrated whole has a reality independent of and greater than the sum of its parts.

hō·lis'tiç, *a.* pertaining to holism.

hōlk (hōk), *v.t.* to hollow out. [Obs.]

hol'lănd, *n.* a kind of fine linen originally manufactured in Holland, sometimes glazed, used for children's clothing, upholstery, etc.: called *brown holland* when unbleached.

hol'lăn·dāise sauce, [Fr. *hollandaise*, fem. of *hollandais*, of Holland.] a creamy sauce for fish or vegetables, made of butter, egg yolks, vinegar, lemon juice, etc.

Hol'lănd·ēr, *n.* 1. a native or inhabitant of Holland; a Dutchman.

2. [h–] a hard glazed brick: known also as *Dutch clinker*.

Hol'lănd·ish, *a.* of or relating to Holland; Dutch.

Hol'lănds, *n.* gin made in Holland: also *Holland gin*.

hol'lēr, *n.* and *v.* shout; yell. [Colloq.]

hol'lō (*or* hŏl-lō'), *interj.* and *n.*; *pl.* **hol'lōs,**

1. a shout or call, especially to attract a person's attention or stop him, or to urge on hounds in hunting.

2. a shout of greeting or surprise.

Also *hallo, holla, halloa, holloa, hillo, hilloa hullo*.

hol'lō (*or* hŏl-lō'), *v.i.* and *v.t.*; holloed, *pt., pp.*; holloing, *ppr.* 1. to shout at or call out in order to attract the attention of (a person).

2. to urge on (hounds) by shouting or calling out "hollo."

3. to shout or call, as in greeting or surprise.

hol·lōa', *interj.*, *n.*, *v.t.* and *v.i.* same as *hollo*.

hol'lōw, *v.t.* and *v.i.* to hollo.

hol'lōw, *n.* [AS. *holg, holh*, a hole.]

1. a depression or excavation below the general level or in the substance of anything; an empty space in anything; a cavity, natural or artificial; concavity; a cave or cavern; a hole; a groove; a channel; a canal; as, the *hollow* of the hand; the *hollow* of a tree.

2. a valley.

hol'lōw, *v.t.* and *v.i.*; hollowed, *pt., pp.*; hollowing, *ppr.* to make or become hollow.

hol'lōw, *a.* [ME. *holow, holowe, holgh, holg*, hollow, from AS. *holh, holg*, a hollow.]

1. containing an empty space, natural or artificial, within it; not solid; as, a *hollow* tree; a *hollow* tile; a *hollow* sphere.

2. depressed below the surrounding surface; shaped like a cup or bowl; concave.

3. deeply set; sunken; as, *hollow* cheeks.

4. hungry.

5. deep; low; resembling sound reverberated from a cavity; as, a *hollow* roar.

6. not sincere or faithful; false; deceitful; as, a *hollow* heart; a *hollow* friend.

hollow newel; in architecture, the wellhole or opening in the center of winding stairs.

hollow wall; in architecture, a wall built in two thicknesses, leaving a cavity or cavities between, used for ventilation, for insulation, or for saving materials.

HOLLOW WALL

Syn.– empty, concave, faithless, insincere, artificial, unsubstantial, void, flimsy, transparent, senseless, vacant, unsound, false.

hol'lōw, *adv.* in a hollow manner.

to beat all hollow; to beat fully; outdo or surpass by far. [Colloq.]

hol'lōw-eyed, *a.* having deep-set eyes or dark areas under the eyes, as from sickness or lack of sleep.

hol'lōw-heärt''ed, *a.* insincere, deceitful.

hol'lōw·ly, *adv.* insincerely; deceitfully.

hol'lōw·ness, *n.* 1. the state of being hollow.

2. insincerity; deceitfulness; treachery.

hol'lōw root, a plant, *Adoxa moschatellina*, of the *Caprifoliaceæ*; the moschatel.

hol'lōw tīle, hollow units of burned clay used in building walls, etc.

hol'lōw·wŏrt, *n.* *Corydalis cava*, a succulent plant with pink flowers.

hol'lus·chick, *n.*; *pl.* **hol'lus·chick·ie,** in Alaska, a male seal that does not breed.

hōl'ly, *adv.* wholly. [Obs.]

hol'ly, *n.* [ME. *holly, holy*, variant of *holin, holyn*; AS. *holen, holegn*, holly.]

1. a plant of the genus *Ilex*, of several species. The common holly grows from 20 to 30 feet high; the stem is covered with a grayish smooth bark. The leaves are oblong-oval, the edges indented and waved, with sharp thorns terminating each of the points. The flowers grow in clusters, and are succeeded by roundish berries, which turn red in the fall.

HOLLY (*Ilex aquifolium*)

2. the leaves and berries of this plant, used as Christmas ornaments.

3. the holm oak: often called *holly oak*.

hol'ly fērn, a plant, *Aspidium lonchitis*, an evergreen species of shield fern.

hol'ly·hock, *n.* [ME. *holihoc, holihocce*, lit., holy hock; AS. *halig*, holy, and *hoc*, mallow.]

1. a plant of the genus *Althæa*, tall and hardy, with coarse, rounded leaves, a hairy stem, and large, showy flowers of various colors.

2. its flower.

hol'ly ōak, the holm oak, *Quercus ilex*.

hol'ly rōse, a shrub, *Turnera ulmifolia*, with yellow flowers, native to the West Indies.

Hol'ly·wood, *n.* [from *Hollywood*, a section of Los Angeles, California, regarded as the center of the American motion-picture industry.] the American motion-picture industry or its life, world, etc.

hōlm (hōm), *n.* [ME. *holme*, a corruption of AS. *holen*, holly.]

1. the holm oak.

2. the holly. [Dial.]

hōlm, *n.* [AS. *holm*, sea, water, an island.]

1. an islet: often used in place names.

2. a low, flat tract of rich land on the banks of a river; bottoms. [Brit.]

Hōlmes, Shēr'lock (hōmz), a fictitious British detective, famous for his powers of deduction, the main character in many stories by A. Conan Doyle.

hōl'mi·ȧ, *n.* holmium oxide.

hōl'miç, *a.* of or containing trivalent holmium.

hōl'mi·um, *n.* [Mod. L., from *Holmia*, Latinized form of *Stockholm*.] a metallic chemical element of the rare-earth group: symbol, Ho; atomic weight, 164.94; atomic number, 67.

hōlm ōak, 1. a south European evergreen oak, *Quercus ilex*, with hollylike leaves.

2. its wood.

hōlm tree, the holly.

hol'ō-, [from Gr. *holos*, whole.] a combining form meaning *whole, entire*, as in *holo*blast.

hol'ō·blast, *n.* [*holo-*, and Gr. *blastos*, a germ, shoot.] an ovum whose yolk is entirely germinal.

hol·ō·blas'tiç, *a.* entirely germinal; undergoing complete division into segments: said of ova: opposed to *meroblastic*.

hol'ō·çāine, *n.* [*holo-*, and co*caine*.]

1. an organic, crystalline substance, $C_{18}H_{22}O_2N_2$, derived from the coal tars.

2. its hydrochloride, phenacine, used as a local anesthetic, especially in eye operations.

hol'ō·çaust, *n.* [Gr. *holokauston, holokauton*, neut. of *holokaustos, holokautos*, burnt whole; *holos*, whole, and *kaustos* or *kautos*, burnt.]

1. a burnt sacrifice or offering, the whole of which was consumed by fire.

2. complete destruction of people or animals by fire.

3. great or widespread destruction.

the Holocaust; [*also* h-] the systematic destruction of over six million European Jews by the Nazis before and during World War II.

Hol'ō·cēne, *a.* [*holo-*, and *-cene*.] designating or of the Recent epoch of geological time.

Hol·ō·cen'tri·dae, *n.pl.* [*holo-*, and Gr. *kentron*, a point, center.] a family of fishes, the squirrel fishes.

hol·ō·cen'troid, *a.* of the *Holocentridæ*.

Hol·ō·ceph'ȧ·lī, *n.pl.* [*holo-*, and Gr. *kephalē*, head.] a suborder of fishes of the order *Elasmobranchii*, characterized by long jaws encased by dental plates and a cartilaginous endoskeleton.

hol'ō·çrīne (*or* -krin), *a.* [*holo-*, and Gr. *krinein*, to separate.] designating or of a gland whose secretion results from the disintegration of the gland's cells.

hol·ō·çrys'tăl·line, *a.* [*holo-*, and Gr. *krystallinos*, crystalline, from *krystallos*, ice, crystal.] entirely crystalline.

Hol·ō·fēr'nēs, *n.* the general of Nebuchadnezzar's Assyrian army, killed by Judith to save her people: see *Judith*.

hō·log'nȧ·thous, *a.* [*holo-*, and Gr. *gnathos*, jaw.] having the jaw entire, as some land pulmonates.

hol'ō·grȧph, *a.* [*holo-*, and Gr. *graphein*, to write.] wholly written in the handwriting of the person under whose name it appears.

hol'ō·grȧph, *n.* [LL. *holographus*; Gr. *holographos*, entirely autograph; *holos*, whole, entire, and *graphein*, to write.] any holograph writing, as a letter, deed, testament, etc.

hol·ō·graph'iç, *a.* 1. same as *holograph*.

2. of or having to do with holography.

hō·log'rȧ·phy, *n.* [*holo-*, and *-graphy*.] a lensless photographic method that uses laser light to produce three-dimensional images by splitting the laser beam into two beams and recording on a photographic plate the minute interference patterns made by the reference light waves reflected directly from a mirror and the waves modulated when simultaneously reflected from the subject: the virtual image can be reconstructed by shining laser light, white light, etc. through the developed film.

hol·ō·hē'drăl, *a.* [*holo-*, and Gr. *hedra*, a seat, base.] in crystallography, completely symmetrical with respect to planes; having all the similar edges or angles similarly replaced with planes.

hol·ō·hē′driṣm, *n.* the quality of being holohedral.

hol·ō·hē′drŏn, *n.* [*holo-*, and Gr. *hedra*, a seat, base.] a crystalline form in which all the planes required for complete symmetry are present.

hol·ō·hem·i·hē′drăl, *a.* [*holo-*, and Gr. *hēmi*, half, and *hedra*, seat, base.] in crystallography, having half the planes required for complete symmetry present in all sectants.

Hol″ō·mē·tab′ō·lȧ, *n.pl.* [*holo-*, and Gr. *metabolē*, change.] those insects which undergo a complete metamorphosis.

hol″ō·met·ȧ·bol′iç, *a.* passing through a complete series of transformations; undergoing entire metamorphosis, as some insects.

hō·lom′e·tẽr, *n.* [*holo-*, and Gr. *metron*, a measure.] a pantometer or measuring instrument for general use.

hol·ō·mor′phiç, *a.* [*holo-*, and Gr. *morphē*, form.]

1. having the two ends symmetrical in form.

2. in mathematics, having the characteristics of a complete function, as continuity, uniformity, and a finite value for a finite value of the variable.

hol·ō·phō′tăl, *a.* reflecting or refracting rays of light in one unbroken mass without appreciable loss; as, a *holophotal* reflector.

hol′ō·phōte, *n.* [*holo-*, and Gr. *phōs*, *phōtos*, light.] a form of lamp in which almost all the light may be cast in one direction, as in a lighthouse.

hol″ō·phō·tom′e·tẽr, *n.* [*holo-*, and Gr. *phōs*, *phōtos*, light, and *metron*, a measure.] a form of photometer devised to estimate the total light emanating from any source.

hō·loph′rȧ·sis, *n.* [*holo-*, and Gr. *phrasis*, expression.] the use of a single word to convey an entire idea.

hol·ō·phras′tiç, *a.* [*holo-*, and Gr. *phrastikos*, suited for expressing, from *phrazein*, to speak, indicate.] expressing an entire phrase or sentence in one word.

hol·ō·phyt′iç, *a.* [*holo-*, and Gr. *phyton*, a plant.] taking nutrition in the same manner as an ordinary green plant: said of certain infusorians.

hol″ō·plank·ton′iç, *a.* [*holo-*, and Gr. *planktos*, wandering, from *plazein*, to wander.] belonging entirely to the pelagic forms of life; passing their entire existence on the surface of water, as certain gastropods.

hol·op′tiç, *a.* [*holo-*, and Gr. *optikos*, pertaining to sight.] having the eyes close together, as certain dipterous insects.

hol·ō·rhī′năl (-rī′), *a.* [*holo-*, and Gr. *rhis*, *rhinos*, nose.] having the nasal bones only slightly divergent or in actual contact.

hol″ō·sē·ri′ceous (-rish′us), *a.* [Gr. *holosērikos*, all of silk; *holos*, whole, and *sērikos*, silken.] having a complete covering of minute silky hairs.

hol·ō·sid′ẽr·īte, *n.* [Gr. *holosidēros*, all of iron; *holos*, whole, and *sidēros*, iron.] a meteorite containing nothing but metallic iron.

hol·ō·sī′phŏn·āte, *a.* [*holo-*, and Gr. *siphōn*, a tube, pipe.] having the siphon quite tubular, as a class of cephalopods.

hol″ō·spon·dā′iç, *a.* [Gr. *holospondeios*, all of spondees; *holos*, whole, and *spondeios* (supply *pous*, foot), a spondee.] made up wholly of spondees: said of a kind of hexameter.

hō·los′tē·ăn, *a.* of or belonging to the *Holostei*.

hō·los′tē·ăn, *n.* one of the *Holostei*.

Hō·los′tē·ī, *n.pl.* [*holo-*, and Gr. *osteon*, a bone.] that division of the ganoid fishes in which the skeleton is osseous.

hol·ō·ster′iç, *a.* [*holo-*, and Gr. *stereos*, solid.] solid throughout; using no liquid; as, a *holosteric* or aneroid barometer.

Hol·ō·stom′ȧ·tȧ, *n. pl.* [*holo-*, and Gr. *stoma* (*-atos*), mouth.] a division of gastropodous mollusks in which the aperture of the shell is rounded or entire.

hō·los′tō·māte, *a.* holostomatous.

hol·ō·stom′ȧ·tous, *a.* of or like the *Holostomata*; having the shell mouth rounded or entire.

hol′ō·stōme, *n.* 1. a fish of the *Holostomi*.

2. a gastropod of the *Holostomata*.

Hō·los′tō·mī, *n.pl.* [*holo-*, and Gr. *stoma*, mouth.] a division of eellike fishes in which the bones about the mouth are developed.

hō·los′tō·mous, *a.* 1. holostomatous.

2. of or resembling the *Holostomi*.

hol″ō·sym·met′riç, *a.* holohedral.

hol·ō·sym′met·ry, *n.* holohedrism.

hol·ō·thē′çăl, *a.* [*holo-*, and Gr. *thēkē*, a box, case.] having the tarsal sheath undivided; booted: said of certain birds.

hol′ō·thūre, *n.* a holothurian.

hol·ō·thū′ri·ăn, *n.* a member of the *Holothurioidea*.

hol·ō·thū′ri·ăn, *a.* pertaining to the *Holothurioidea*.

Hol·ō·thū·ri·oi′dē·ȧ, *n.pl.* [Gr. *holothourion*, a kind of zoophyte, and *eidos*, form.] the sea cucumbers or sea slugs, a group of echinoderms lacking the calcareous plates typical of the class, but with a leathery integument open at both ends and pierced by orifices through which suctorial feet or ambulacra protrude. They abound in the Asiatic seas, the trepang being a member of the family.

hol·ō·tō′ni·ȧ, *n.* a muscular spasm of the body.

Hō·lot′ri·chȧ, *n.pl.* [*holo-*, and Gr. *thrix*, *trichos*, hair.] a division of *Infusoria* with cilia upon the entire body.

hol′öur, *n.* a fornicator; whoremonger. [Obs.]

hol·ō·zō′iç, *a.* [*holo-*, and Gr. *zōon*, an animal.] entirely and characteristically animal: said of the method of nutrition of certain infusorians.

hōlp, archaic past tense and obsolete past participle of *help*.

hōl′pen, archaic past participle of *help*.

hōl′sŏm, *a.* wholesome. [Obs.]

Hōl′steīn, *n.* [so called because originally from Schleswig-*Holstein* in Prussia.] one of a breed of black-and-white cattle noted for the quantity of milk yielded and also raised for beef.

hōl′stẽr, *n.* [D. *holster*, a pistol case, knapsack.] a leather case for a pistol, carried by a horseman at the fore part of his saddle, or worn at the belt.

hōl′stẽred, *a.* having a holster or holsters.

hōlt, *n.* [ME. *holt*; AS. *holt*, a wood, grove.] a wood or woodland; a tree-covered hillside. [Archaic.]

hōlt, *n.* a hole, burrow, or place of retreat, as (a) a deep place in a river, frequented by fish; (b) a hollowed-out retreat or lodge, as that of an otter. [Dial.]

hōlt, *n.* a hold; a grip. [Dial.]

hō′lus·bō′lus, *adv.* [mock-Latin, from Eng. *whole* and *bolus*.] all at once; in one lump.

hol′we, *a.* hollow. [Obs.]

hō′ly, *a.*; *comp.* holier; *superl.* holiest. [ME. *holy*, *holi*, *halig*; AS. *halig*, holy, sacred.]

1. [*often* H-] belonging to or coming from God; hallowed; consecrated or set apart to a sacred use; having a sacred character or associations; as, the *holy* temple; *holy* vessels; *holy* words.

2. spiritually perfect or pure; free from sin; perfect in a moral sense; as, a *holy* man.

3. deserving reverence or worship.

4. [*often* H-] associated with Jesus and his life; as, the *Holy* Rood.

5. very much of a: a generalized intensive, as, a *holy* terror. [Slang.]

Holy Alliance; an alliance formed in 1815 by the rulers of Russia, Austria, and Prussia to suppress the democratic revolutionary movement in Europe.

Holy Bible; the Bible.

holy bread; bread or a piece of bread consecrated in the Eucharist; hence, the eulogia.

Holy City; (a) a city regarded as sacred by the believers of some religion; as, Jerusalem, Mecca, and Rome are *Holy Cities*; (b) Heaven.

Holy Communion; any of various church rites in which bread and wine are consecrated and received as (symbols of) the body and blood of Jesus; sacrament of the Eucharist, or the Lord's Supper.

Holy Father; a title of the Pope: also *Most Holy Father*.

Holy Ghost; the Holy Spirit.

Holy Ghost plant; the dove plant.

holy herb; vervain.

Holy Innocents' Day; Childermas.

Holy Land; Palestine.

Holy Mother; Mary, mother of Jesus.

Holy Office; in the Roman Catholic Church, a tribunal for the protection of faith and morals, the suppression of heresy, etc.: formerly called *the Inquisition*.

Holy One; God.

Holy Roller; a member of a minor religious sect that expresses religious emotion by making violent movements and sounds during services of worship: humorous or contemptuous term.

Holy Rood; *holy rood*; (a) the cross on which Jesus was crucified; (b) any representation of this; a cross or crucifix symbolizing Christianity, placed over the entrance to the chancel of a church, etc.

Holy Saturday; Saturday before Easter.

Holy Scripture; the Bible.

Holy See; the position, authority, or court of the Pope; Apostolic See.

Holy Sepulcher; the sepulcher at Jerusalem in which the body of Jesus was placed after the Crucifixion.

Holy Spirit; the divine Spirit; the Holy Ghost; the third person in the Trinity.

Holy Synod; the administrative council of any Orthodox church.

Holy Thursday; Ascension day; also, the day before Good Friday; Maundy Thursday.

holy water; water blessed by a priest.

Holy Week; the week preceding Easter Sunday.

Holy Writ; the Bible.

hō′ly, *n.* something holy; a sanctuary.

holy of holies; (a) the innermost part of the Jewish tabernacle and Temple, where the Ark of the Covenant was kept; (b) the bema of an Orthodox Eastern church; (c) any most sacred place.

hō′ly·dāy, *n.* a religious festival; hence, a holiday: also *holy day*.

hō′ly ọr′dẽrṣ, 1. the sacrament or rite of ordination.

2. the rank of an ordained Christian minister or priest.

3. three higher ranks or orders of Christian ministers or priests; specifically, (a) in the Roman Catholic Church, priests, deacons, and subdeacons; (b) in the Anglican Church, bishops, priests, and deacons.

to take holy orders; to be ordained as a Christian minister or priest.

hō′ly·stōne, *n.* [so called because used in scrubbing the decks on Sunday.] a large, flat piece of sandstone used by seamen for cleaning the decks of ships.

hō′ly·stōne, *v.t.* to scrub, as the deck of a vessel, with a sailor's holystone.

hō′ly·tīde, *n.* [*holy*, and *tide*, *n.*] a holy season; day or longer period spent in religious rites or worship.

hom-, homo-.

hom′ȧ·çanth, *a.* [Gr. *homos*, the same, and *akantha*, spine.] having the dorsal and anal spines symmetrical and depressible backward in the same line: said of certain fishes.

hom′ăġe (*or* om′ăj), *n.* [OFr. *homage*, *hommage*; LL. *hominaticum*, a vassal's service, homage, from L. *homo* (*-inis*), a man.]

1. in feudal law, (a) the submission, loyalty, and service which a vassal promised to his lord when first admitted to the land which he held of him in fee; (b) the act of the vassal in making this submission, on being invested with the fee.

2. obeisance; respect paid by external action; reverence; honor: usually with *do* or *pay*.

hom′ăġe, *v.t.*; homaged, *pt.*, *pp.*; homaging, *ppr.* [OFr. *hommager*, to pay homage to, from *hommage*, homage.] to pay respect to by external action; to give reverence to; to profess fealty to. [Obs.]

hom′ăġe·ȧ·ble, *a.* subject to homage. [Obs.]

hom′ȧ·ġẽr, *n.* one who does homage or holds land of another by homage.

hom″ȧ·lō·gon′ȧ·tous, *a.* [Gr. *homalos*, even, equal, and *gony*, *gonatos*, knee.] in ornithology, possessing an ambiens muscle, as the common fowls.

hom″ȧ·lō·graph′ic, *a.* homolographic.

hom·ȧ·loid′ăl, *a.* [Gr. *homalos*, even, level, and *eidos*, form.] flat; resembling a plane; without curvature: said of Euclidean space of any type.

Hom′ȧ·rus, *n.* [Gr. *homarēs*, well-adjusted.] the typical genus of the lobster family.

hō·mat′rō·pine, *n.* [Gr. *homos*, the same, and *atropos*, inflexible.] an alkaloid derived from atropine, which it resembles in properties.

hom·ax·ō′ni·ăl, *a.* [Gr. *homos*, the same, and *axōn*, an axle.] in biology, having equality of axes.

hom·ax·on′iç, *a.* homaxonial.

hom′bre (ọm′), *n.*; *pl.* **hom′breṣ,** [Sp., from L. *homo*, man.] a man; fellow. [Slang.]

hom′bre (om′bẽr), *n.* omber, a card game.

Hom′bŭrg, *n.* [from *Homburg*, Prussia, where first worn.]

1. a man's felt hat with a crown dented from front to back and a stiffened brim turned up slightly at the sides.

2. a woman's hat like this.

hōme, *n.* [ME. *home*, *hoom*, *ham*; AS. *ham*, a home, dwelling.]

1. a dwelling place; the place in which one

resides; the seat of domestic life and interests; specifically, (a) the house, apartment, etc. where one lives or is living temporarily; living quarters; (b) the region, city, state, etc. where one lives.

Home is the sacred refuge of our life.
—Dryden.

2. the place where one was born or reared; one's own city, state, or country; as, let affairs at *home* be well managed by the administration.

3. the place where something is or has been founded, developed, etc.; the seat.

Flandria, by plenty, made the *home* of war.
—Prior.

4. the grave; death.

Man goeth to his long *home*.—Eccles. xii. 5.

5. the place that is the natural environment of an animal, a plant, etc.; as, the *home* of the seal or of the eucalyptus.

6. the abiding place of one's affections; a place where one likes to be; restful or congenial place; as, *home* is where the heart is.

7. a place or institution provided for the needy and the homeless; as, a *home* for orphans or for veterans.

8. the members of a family; household; as, the depression ruined many *homes*.

9. in some games, the place of beginning and ending, as in baseball, cricket, hare and hounds, etc.; the goal or base.

at home; (a) in one's own house, neighborhood, city, or country; (b) as if in one's own home; comfortable; at ease; familiar; (c) willing to receive visitors; (d) a reception at one's home.

hōme, *a.* 1. of home or a home; specifically, (a) of the family, household, etc.; domestic; (b) of one's country, government, etc.; domestic: opposed to *foreign*; (c) of or at the center of activity; of or at headquarters; as, a *home* office.

2. reaching its goal; effective; forceful; to the point.

3. played in the city where the team originates; as, a *home* game.

Home Department; in Great Britain, that department of government relating to the internal affairs of the country, as distinguished from foreign affairs.

home rule; the principle or form of government by which the citizens of a colony, province, city, or country administer their own internal affairs; local self-government; specifically, in British politics, the program of the Irish party advocating a separate parliament for Ireland.

home run; in baseball, a hit driving the ball safely beyond the reach of the opponent fielders and permitting the batter to make a complete circuit of the bases to score a run.

hōme, *adv.* 1. to, at, or toward home or a home; as, go *home*; come *home*.

2. to the place where it belongs; to the point aimed at; as, he drove the nail *home*.

3. to the center or heart of a matter; closely; directly; deeply.

to bring home to; (a) to prove to, impress upon, or make clear to; (b) to fasten the blame for (something) on (someone).

hōme, *v.i.*; homed, *pt., pp.*; homing, *ppr.* 1. to go to one's home.

2. to have a home.

hōme, *v.t.* to send to, put into, or provide with a home.

hō'mē-, homeo-.

hōme'bọrn, *a.* 1. native; natural; domestic; not foreign.

2. having origin at home; relating to home.

hōme'-bound', *a.* bound for home.

hōme'-bred', *a.* 1. bred or reared at home; domestic; native.

2. not cultivated; not polished; not sophisticated; crude.

hōme'-brew' (-brö'), *n.* malt liquor that is brewed at home, or any alcoholic drink that is home-brewed.

hōme'-brewed' (-bröd'), *a.* brewed at home, rather than in a brewery; as, *home-brewed* ale.

hōme'çŏm"ing, *n.* 1. a coming home or homeward; return from travel or after prolonged absence.

2. in many colleges and universities, an annual celebration attended by alumni.

hōme ē·çō·nom'içs, the science and art of homemaking, including nutrition, clothing, budgeting, and child care.

hōme'felt, *a.* felt in one's own heart; as, *homefelt* pleasures.

hōme'-grōwn', *a.* cultivated or grown at home; grown locally; also, domestic, as opposed to *foreign*.

hōme'land, *n.* the country in which one was born or makes one's home.

hōme'less, *a.* without a home.

hōme'līke, *a.* having qualities usually associated with home; comfortable, familiar, friendly, cozy, etc.

hōme'li·ness, *n.* the quality or state of being homely.

hōme'ly, *a.*; *comp.* homelier; *superl.* homeliest. [ME. *homli.*]

1. originally, (a) of the home; domestic; (b) familiar; intimate; (c) fond of home.

2. (a) characteristic of or suitable for home or home life; simple; plain; everyday; as, homely virtues; (b) crude; unpolished.

3. not attractive; plain; ugly.

hōme'māde, *a.* 1. made, or as if made, at home; being of domestic manufacture; made either in a private family or in one's own country.

2. plain; simple; crude.

hōme'māk"ẽr, *n.* a woman who manages a home; housewife.

hōme'māk"ing, *n.* the work of a homemaker; management of a home.

hō'mē·ō-, [Gr. *homoio-*, from *homos*, same.] a combining form meaning *like, the same, similar*, as in *homeo*morphism: also *home-, homoio-*: words beginning with *homeo-* may also be spelled *homoeo-*.

hōme of'fice, 1. the chief or central office of a concern, as opposed to branch offices.

2. [H—O—] in England, the office of the Home Department.

hō"mē·ō·mọr'phism, *n.* [from *homeo*, and Gr. *morphē*, form, and *-ism*.] a close similarity of crystalline forms between substances of different chemical composition.

hō'mē·ō·path, hō'moe·ō·path, *n.* a homeopathist.

hō"mē·ō·path'iç, hō"mē·ō·path'iç·ăl, *a.* 1. pertaining to, according to, belonging to, or practicing homeopathy.

2. containing a very small amount of a drug or other active substance.

hō"mē·ō·path'iç·ăl·ly, *adv.* by or in the method of homeopathy.

hō·mē·op'ȧ·thist, *n.* a believer in homeopathy; a homeopathic practitioner.

hō·mē·op'ȧ·thy, *n.* [Gr. *homoiopatheia*, from *homoiopathes*, having like feelings or affections; *homoios*, like, similar, and *pathos*, feeling, suffering.] the theory or system of curing diseases with very minute doses of medicine which in a healthy person and in large doses would produce a condition like that of the disease treated: opposed to *allopathy*.

hō"mē·ō·stā'sis, *n.* [Mod.L., from *homeo-*, and *stasis*.]

1. in physiology, the tendency to maintain, or the maintenance of, normal, internal stability in an organism by coordinated responses of the organ systems that automatically compensate for environmental changes.

2. any analogous maintenance of stability or equilibrium, as within a social group.

hō"mē·ō·ther'ȧ·py, *n.* [*homeo-* and *therapy*.] the treatment of a disease by giving a substance similar to the agent that caused the disease.

hō"mē·ō·typ'iç, *a.* [*homeo-* and *typic*.] designating the second division of the nuclei of germ cells in meiosis.

hōme plāte, in baseball, the slab that the batter stands beside, across which the pitcher must throw the ball for a strike: it is the last of the four bases that a runner must touch in succession to score a run.

hō'mẽr, *n.* 1. a pigeon trained to return home.

2. in baseball, a home run. [Colloq.]

hō'mẽr, *n.* [Heb. *khōmer*, a homer, a mound, from *khāmar*, to surge up, swell up.] an early Hebrew measure equal to about $6^1/_4$ bushels.

Hō·mer'iç, *a.* [L. *Homericus*; Gr. *Homērikos*, relating to Homer; *Homēros*, Homer.] of, like, or characteristic of the semilegendary Homer, his style, his poems, or the Greek civilization that they describe (c. 1200–800 B.C.).

Homeric laughter; loud, unrestrained laughter.

hōme rọọm, 1. the room where a class in school meets every day to be checked for attendance, receive school bulletins, etc.

2. the students in a specific home room.

hōme'sick, *a.* depressed in spirits or grieved at a separation from home and family; longing for home.

hōme'sick·ness, *n.* in medicine, nostalgia; grief or depression of spirits, occasioned by a separation from one's home or country.

hōme'spun, *a.* 1. spun or wrought at home; of domestic manufacture.

2. plain; unpretentious; homely; not elegant; as, a *homespun* author.

3. made of homespun.

hōme'spun, *n.* 1. cloth made of yarn spun at home.

2. coarse, loosely woven cloth like this.

3. a coarse, unpolished, rustic person. [Obs.]

hōme'stạll, *n.* a homestead. [Obs.]

hōme'stead (-sted), *n.* [AS. *ham*, home, and *stede*, place.]

1. a home; the seat of a family, including the land, house, and outbuildings; especially, a dwelling retained as a home by successive generations.

We can trace them back to a *homestead* on the Rivers Volga and Ural. —Tooke.

2. in law, such a place occupied by the owner and his family and exempted from seizure or forced sale to meet general debts.

3. a 160-acre tract of public land granted by the United States government to a settler to be developed as a farm.

Homestead Act; in the United States, an act of Congress passed in 1862 granting public land not to exceed 160 acres to any citizen or alien intending to become a citizen, to be developed as a farm.

homestead law; in the United States, (a) a law providing for the exemption of a homestead from seizure and sale for debt; (b) same as *Homestead Act*.

hōme'stead, *v.i.* to become a settler on a homestead.

hōme'stead·ẽr, *n.* 1. a person who has a homestead.

2. a settler who holds a homestead granted by the United States government.

hōme'stretch', *n.* 1. the part of a race track between the last turn and the finish line.

2. the final part of any undertaking.

hōme'wărd, *a.* being in the direction of home; as, a *homeward* journey.

hōme'wărd, hōme'wărds, *adv.* toward home; toward one's habitation, or toward one's native country.

hōme'wărd-bound, *a.* bound or directing the course homeward, or to one's native land; returning homeward; as, the *homeward-bound* fleet.

hōme'wŏrk, *n.* 1. work done at home.

2. lessons to be studied or schoolwork to be done outside the classroom.

3. study or research in preparation for some project, activity, etc.: usually in the phrase *to do one's homework*.

hōme'y, *a.*; *comp.* homier; *superl.* homiest, having qualities usually associated with home; comfortable, familiar, cozy, etc.: also spelled *homy*.

hom'i·cī·dăl, *a.* 1. having the nature of, characterized by, or pertaining to homicide.

2. murderous; having a tendency to homicide.

hom'i·cīde, *n.* [OFr. *homicide*; LL. *homicidium*, manslaughter, murder; L. *homo*, man, and *cædere*, to cut, kill.]

1. the killing of one human being by another.

2. a person who kills another; a manslayer.

hom'i·lēte, *n.* [Gr. *homilētēs*, a companion, hearer, from *homilein*, to be in company, converse.] an expert in homiletics; homilist.

hom·i·let'iç, *a.* 1. pertaining to homiletics.

2. having the nature of or characteristic of a homily.

hom·i·let'i·çăl, *a.* homiletic.

hom·i·let'içs, *n.* [Gr. *homilētikos*, of or for conversation, affable, from *homilein*, to be in company, converse, from *homilos*, a gathering, company.]

1. the science that teaches the principles of adapting the discourses of the pulpit to the spiritual benefit of the hearers; the study of sermons.

2. the art of preparing sermons and of preaching.

hom'i·list, *n.* one who writes or preaches homilies; a sermonizer.

hom'i·līte, *n.* in mineralogy, a ferrocalcic borosilicate of a brownish-black color.

hom'i·ly, *n.*; *pl.* **hom'i·lies,** [LL. *homilia*, a sermon, from Gr. *homilia*, intercourse, instruction (L.Gr., a sermon), from *homilos*, an assembly, from *homos*, the same.]

1. a discourse or sermon read or pro-

nounced to an audience, especially one about something in the Bible.

2. a serious admonition or exhortation upon a course of conduct; a tedious, moralizing lecture.

Book of Homilies; in England, a collection of prepared sermons to be used by the inferior clergy, who were not qualified to write homilies.

hōm′ing, *n.* the act of going home or of coming home.

hōm′ing, *a.* [ppr. of *home.*] 1. going home; homeward bound.

2. having to do with guidance homeward or to a goal, target, etc.

hōm′ing pig′eŏn, a pigeon trained to find its way home from distant places, used to carry messages; carrier pigeon.

hom′i·nid, *n.* [from Mod.L. *Hominidae*, from L. *homo*, a man, and *-idae.*] any of a family, *Hominidae*, of two-legged primates including all forms of man, extinct and living.

hom′i·nid, *a.* designating or of the hominids.

hom′i·noid, *n.* [from Mod.L. *Hominoidea*: see *homo*, and *-oidea.*] any of a superfamily, *Hominoidea*, of primates that includes the manlike apes and all forms of man.

hom′i·noid, *a.* of or like man; manlike.

hom′i·ny, *n.* [Am. Ind. *auhuminea*, parched corn.] maize hulled and coarsely broken, prepared for food by being mixed with water and boiled; hulled corn.

hōm′ish, *a.* homelike.

hŏm′mŏck, *n.* same as *hummock.*

hō′mō, *n.*; *pl.* **hom′i·nēs̤,** [L.]

1. man.

2. [H–] the genus of primates comprising modern man (*Homo sapiens*) and several extinct species of man.

hō′mō-, [from Gr. *homos*, the same.] a combining form meaning *same, equal*, as in *homo*carpous: also, before a vowel, *hom-*.

hō·mō·çär′pous, *a.* [*homo-*, and Gr. *karpos*, fruit.] in botany, having similar carpels or fruits, as in the head of a composite flower.

hō·mō·çat·ē·gor′iç, *a.* [*homo-*, and Gr. *katēgoria*, category.] being in the same category.

hō·mō·cen′triç, *a.* [*homo-*, and Gr. *kentron*, a point, center.] having the same center.

hō·mō·cẽr′çăl, *a.* [*homo-*, and Gr. *kerkos*, tail.] in ichthyology, designating, of, or having a tail fin symmetrically attached and developed and the spine ending at or near the center of the base.

hō′mō·cẽr·cy, *n.* in ichthyology, the condition of being homocercal.

hō″mō·çhrō·mat′iç, *a.* of or having one or the same color: opposed to *heterochromatic.*

hō·mō·çhrō′mous, *a.* [*homo-*, and Gr. *chrōma*, color.] homochromatic.

hō·mō·dem′iç, *a.* [*homo-*, and Gr. *dēmos*, district.] in biology, derived from the same undifferentiated aggregate of cells.

hō·mō·dẽr′miç, *a.* in biology, relating to homodermy.

hō′mō·dẽr·my, *n.* [*homo-*, and Gr. *derma*, skin.] in biology, homology with regard to the germinal layers of the skin.

hom′ō·dŏnt, *a.* homo-, and Gr. *odous, odontos*, a tooth.] having a dental armature consisting of similar teeth, as the dolphins: opposite of *heterodont.*

hō·mod′rō·măl, *a.* homodromous.

hō·mod′rō·mous, *a.* [Gr. *homodromos*, running the same course; *homos*, the same, and *dromos*, a course, race, from *dramein*, to run.] in botany, twining in the same direction, that is, to the right or to the left: said of vines or of the arrangement of buds on a branch.

hō·mō·dȳ·nam′iç, *a.* homodynamous.

hō·mō·dȳ′nȧ·mous, *a.* in biology, relating to homodynamy.

hō·mō·dȳ′nȧ·my, *n.* [Gr. *homodynamos*, of like power; *homos*, the same, and *dynamis*, power.] in biology, homology of serial segments.

hō′moe·ō-, same as homeo-.

hō·moe·om′ẽr·ăl, *a.* [Gr. *homœmeros*, consisting of like parts; *homoios*, like, and *meros*, part.] in ancient prosody, relating to a versification in which occur (a) two similar strophes, or (b) two metrically similar systems.

hō″moe·ō·mē′ri·ȧ, *n.* same as *homoeomery.*

hō″moe·ō·mer′iç, hō″mē·ō·mer′iç·ăl, *a.* relating to homoeomery.

hō·moe·om′ẽr·ous, *a.* [*homœo-*, and Gr. *meros*, part.] having parts alike; specifically, in lichenology, having a uniform distribution of gonidia and hyphae over the thallus: written also *homeomerous.*

hō·moe·om′ẽr·y, *n.* [L., from Gr. *homoiomereia*, the state of being homogeneous; *homos*, like, and *meros*, part.] the doctrine of the likeness of parts to the whole as applied to elementary substances.

hō·moe·ō·mor′phism, *n.* [Gr. *homoiomorphos*, of like form; *homoios*, like, and *morphē*, form.] homeomorphism.

hō′moe·ō·path, hō·moe·ō·path′iç, etc. same as *homeopath*, etc.

hō″moe·op·tō′tŏn, *n.* [LL. *homœoptoton*; Gr. *homoioptōtos*, with similar inflection; *homoios*, like, and *ptōsis*, case, inflection.] an old rhetorical figure consisting in the use of the same case endings, inflections, etc. in similar situations, as at the end of phrases.

hō″moe·ō·tē·leū′tŏn, *n.* [LL., from Gr. *homoioteleuton*, rhyme, properly neut. of *homoioteleutos*, having a like ending; *homoios*, like, and *teleutē*, ending, from *telein*, to end.] an old rhetorical figure requiring like-sounding words, syllables, or phrases at the close of a series of sentences or lines.

hō·moe·ō·thẽr′măl, *a.* [*homoeo-*, and Gr. *thermos*, heat.] preserving a uniform temperature regardless of environment: said of the blood of animals.

hō·moe·ō·zō′iç, *a.* [*homoeo-*, and Gr. *zōē*, life.] embracing or marked by similar forms of life; as, *homoeozoic* zones.

hō″mō·e·rot′iç, *a.* of or characterized by homoerotism.

hō·mō·er′ō·tis̤m, *n.* [*homo-* and *erotism.*] sexual desire for a person of the same sex.

hō·mō·fō′căl, *a.* same as *confocal.*

hō·mog′ȧ·mous, *a.* [Gr. *homogamos*, married; *homos*, the same, and *gamos*, marriage.]

1. having flowers all of one sex or all two-sexed.

2. having stamens and pistils that mature at the same time.

hō·mog′ȧ·my, *n.* 1. a homogamous condition.

2. interbreeding in an isolated group of individuals of the same species.

hō·mō·gan′gli·āte, *a.* [*homo-*, and Gr. *ganglion*, a ganglion.] in zoology, characterized by symmetrical arrangement of the ganglia.

hō′mō·ġen, *n.* [Gr. *homogenēs*, of the same race, family, or kind; *homos*, the same, and *genos*, race, family, kind.] in zoology, (a) one of a group having its origin in specifically identical parents; (b) an organ having an origin corresponding to that of an organ in a different class; as, the arm of man is a *homogen* of the wing of a bird.

hō′mō·ġēne, *a.* homogeneous. [Rare.]

hō·mō·ġē′nē·ăl, *a.* homogeneous. [Rare.]

hō″mō·ġē·nē′i·ty, *n.* the character, condition, or quality of being homogeneous.

hō·mō·ġē′nē·ous, *a.* [Gr. *homogenēs*, of the same race, family, or kind; *homos*, the same, and *genos*, race, family, kind.]

1. (a) of the same character, structure, quality, etc.; essentially like; of the same nature; (b) composed of similar or identical elements or parts; uniform. Opposed to *heterogeneous.*

2. in mathematics, (a) of the same kind and therefore capable of being compared in size; (b) having all terms of the same dimensions.

hō·mō·ġen′e·sis, *n.* [*homo-*, and Gr. *genesis*, birth.] in biology, the ordinary or regular course of generation, in which the offspring continues to be like the parent: opposed to *heterogenesis.*

hō″mō·ġē·net′iç, *a.* 1. of, relating to, or denoting homogenesis.

2. of a common origin; characterized by homogeny.

3. in geology, having similar structure, indicating origin through similar agencies.

hō·mog′e·nize, *v.t.*; homogenized, *pt., pp.*; homogenizing, *ppr.* 1. to make homogeneous.

2. to make more uniform throughout in texture, mixture, quality, etc., by breaking down and blending the particles.

hō·mog′e·nized milk, milk in which the fat particles are so finely divided and emulsified that the cream does not separate on standing.

hō·mog′e·nous, *a.* [*homo-*, and Gr. *genos*, race, family, kind.] in biology, having similarity in structure because of common descent.

hō·mog′e·ny, *n.* [Gr. *homogeneia*, community of birth, from *homogenēs*, of the same race or family; *homos*, the same, and *genos*, race, family, kind.] in biology, origin in and descent from a common ancestor, exemplified by certain similar characteristics of structure: opposed to *homoplasy.*

hō·mog′ō·nous, *a.* [*homo-*, and Gr. *gonos*, offspring.] in botany, having the stamens and pistils alike in respect to length and location in all the flowers of individuals of the same species: opposed to heterogonous.

hō·mog′ō·ny, *n.* in botany, the quality or state of being homogonous.

hō′mō·grȧft, *n.* a graft of skin, bone, etc. taken from an individual of the same species.

hom′ō·grȧph, *n.* [Gr. *homographos*, of or with the same letters; *homos*, the same, and *graphein*, to write.] a word of the same spelling as another but derived from a different root and having a different meaning, as, *pine*, to languish, and *pine*, a tree.

hō·mō·grȧph′iç, *a.* relating to homography; specifically, in geometry, noting two figures so related that a point in one has but one corresponding point in the other, and vice versa.

hō·mog′rȧ·phy, *n.* 1. in orthography, the method of using a distinctive character to represent each sound.

2. in geometry, the relation that exists between homographic figures.

hō·moi′ō-, same as *homeo-.*

Hō·moi·ou′si·ăn, *n.* [Gr. *homoiousios*, of like nature or substance; *homoios*, like, and *ousia*, being, from *ousa*, f. of *ōn*, ppr. of *einai*, to be.] in theology and church history, one who believes that the nature of Christ is not identical with, but only similar to, that of the Father, as distinguished from the *Homoousians* and the *Heteroousians.*

Hō·moi·ou′si·ăn, *a.* 1. relating to the Homoiousians or to their doctrines.

2. [h–] having a similar nature.

hō·mol′ō·gāte, *v.t.*; homologated, *pt., pp.*; homologating, *ppr.* [LL. *homologatus*, pp. of *homologare*, from Gr. *homologein*, to agree, assent; *homos*, the same, and *legein*, say, speak.] in law, to approve of; to assent to; to ratify.

hō·mol′ō·gāte, *v.i.* to agree.

hō·mol·ō·gā′tion, *n.* the act of homologating; approval; ratification; specifically, in Scots law, an act by which a person approves of a deed the effect of which is to render that deed, though itself defective, binding.

hō·mō·log′iç, *a.* 1. in geometry, noting two figures in the same plane one of which may be a projection of the other.

2. same as *homologous.*

hō·mō·log′iç·ăl, *a.* pertaining to homology; having a structural affinity.

hō·mō·log′iç·ăl·ly, *adv.* in a homological manner or sense.

hō·mol′ō·ġize, *v.t.*; homologized, *pt., pp.*; homologizing, *ppr.* 1. to render homologous.

2. to demonstrate the existence of homologies in.

hō·mol′ō·ġize, *v.i.* to correspond; to be homologous.

hō·mol′ō·gon, *n.* something that agrees with or is a repetition of another thing; something homologous.

hō″mō·lō·gou′me·nȧ, *n.pl.* [Gr. *homologoumena*, things granted or conceded, properly neut. pl. of *homologoumenos*, ppr. pass. of *homologein*, to agree, admit; *homos*, the same, and *legein*, to speak.] the generally acknowledged books of the New Testament: distinguished from the *antilegomena.*

hō·mol′ō·gous, *a.* [Gr. *homologos*, agreeing, assenting; *homos*, the same, and *legein*, to speak.] having the same relative position, proportion, value, structure, character, etc.; specifically, (a) in geometry, corresponding in relative position and proportion; as, in similar polygons, the corresponding sides, angles, diagonals, etc. are *homologous*; (b) in algebra, having the same relative proportion or value, as the two antecedents or the two consequents of a proportion; (c) in chemistry, designating or of the same chemical type or series, differing by a multiple or arithmetical ratio in certain constituents, while the physical qualities are analogous, with small differences; also, having this relation with another or other compounds of such a series; as, methyl alcohol and ethyl alcohol are *homologous* compounds; (d) in biology, corresponding in type of structure and deriving from a common primitive origin; having like relations to a fundamental type; thus, the human arm, the foreleg of a horse, the wing of a bird, and the swimming paddle of a dolphin or whale, being all composed essentially of the same structural elements, are said to be *homologous*, though they are adapted for quite different functions; (e) in immunology and medicine, having the relationship of a serum and the bacterium from which it is made.

hom″ō·lō·grȧph′iç, *a.* [*homo-*, and Gr. *holos*,

whole, and *graphein*, to write.] maintaining or exhibiting the proper relative proportions of parts; preserving true relations as to size and form.

homolographic projection; that method of laying down portions of the earth's surface on a map or chart so that the different portions of the surfaces delineated have their proper relative size and form.

hom'ō·logue (-log), *n.* [Fr. *homologue*, from Gr. *homologos*, agreeing, assenting.] that which is homologous; that which has the same relative position, proportion, value, or structure; thus, the corresponding sides of similar geometrical figures are *homologues*; an organ agreeing in the plan of its structure with a corresponding organ in a different animal, though differing in function, is a *homologue* of this corresponding organ.

hō·mol'ō·gy, *n.*; *pl.* **hō·mol'ō·gies,** [Gr. *homologia*, agreement, conformity, from *homologos*, agreeing.]

1. the quality or state of being homologous.
2. a homologous correspondence or relationship, as of animal organs, chemical compounds, etc.

general homology; in biology, the general relation or agreement between a part or parts and the basic type.

serial homology; in biology, homology in a series of parts which are repetitions of a typical form.

special homology; in biology, the agreement of a part of an animal with a correspondingly situated part of some other animal.

hō·mol'ō·sine prō·jec'tion, [from Gr. *homalos*, even; and *sine*.] a map of the earth's surface with land areas shown in their proper relative size and form, with a minimum of distortion: it is made by combining two homolographic projections.

HOMOLOSINE PROJECTION

hō·mom'ȧ·lous, *a.* [*homo-*, and Gr. *homalos*, even, level, equal.] in botany, originating all round a stem, as leaves, and all bending or curving round to one side.

hō·mō·mor'phiç, *a.* 1. similar in form and size, as certain chromosomes.

2. relating to or characterized by homomorphism; homomorphous.

hō·mō·mor'phism, *n.* [*homo-*, and Gr. *morphē*, form.]

1. similarity in form.
2. homomorphy.
3. the possession of perfect flowers of a single type or kind.
4. similarity between an insect's larva and its matured form.

hō·mō·mor'phous, *a.* of or characterized by homomorphism.

hō'mō·mor·phy, *n.* [from *homo-*, and Gr. *morphē*, form.] in biology, external resemblance without actual relationship in structure or origin: said of organs or organisms.

hō·mon'ō·mous, *a.* relating to homonomy.

hō·mon'ō·my, *n.* [Gr. *homonomos*, under the same laws; *homos*, the same, and *nomos*, law.] homology; specifically, the homology of parts having a transverse axis.

hom'ō·nym, *n.* [L. *homonymus*; Gr. *homōnymos*, having the same name; *homos*, the same, and *onyma*, *onoma*, name.]

1. a word which agrees with another in pronunciation but differs from it in signification, origin, and, usually, spelling (e.g., *bore* and *boar*).
2. either of two people with the same name; a namesake.

hō·mō·nym'iç, *a.* homonymous.

hō·mon'y·mous, *a.* [L. *homonymus*.]

1. of, or having the nature of, a homonym.
2. having the same name.

hō·mon'y·mous·ly, *adv.* in a homonymous manner.

hō·mon'y·my, *n.* [Gr. *homōnymia*; *homos*, the same, and *onyma*, name.] the quality or condition of being homonymous.

hō·mō·or'găn, *n.* same as *homorgan*.

Hō·mō·ou'si·ăn, *n.* [Gr. *homoousios*, having the same essence; *homos*, the same, and *ousia*, being, substance, from *einai*, to be.] in theology and church history, an adherent of the theory that God the Father and God the Son are identical in substance: opposed to the *Homoiousians* and the *Heteroousians*.

hō·mō·ou'si·ăn, *a.* 1. of the same nature.

2. [H–] pertaining to the Homoousians or their doctrines.

hom'ō·phōne, *n.* [Gr. *homophōnos*, of the same sound or tone; *homos*, the same, and *phōnē*, voice, sound.]

1. any of two or more letters having a sound in common, as *c* and *s*.
2. same as *homonym*.

hom·ō·phon'iç, *a.* 1. in music, (a) formerly, sounding alike; having the same pitch; in unison; (b) having a single voice carrying the melody; monodic; monophonic: opposed to *polyphonic*.

2. homonymous.

hō·moph'ō·nous, *a.* 1. same as *homophonic*, sense 1.

2. in philology, (a) having the same sound but different sense, as *weigh*, *way*; (b) representing the same sound by a different character.

hō·moph'ō·ny, *n.* 1. in phonetics, the quality of a homophone or homophones; sameness of sound.

2. in music, (a) formerly, unison, or music written, sung, or played in unison; (b) music in which a single voice carries the melody, often with an accompaniment in chords; monody; monophony: opposed to *polyphony*.

hō·mō·phyl'iç, *a.* [Gr. *homophylia*, sameness of race; *homos*, the same, and *phylē*, race, family.] in biology, of or pertaining to homophyly.

hō·moph'y·ly, *n.* homology traceable to common ancestry.

hō'mō·plas·my, *n.* [*homo-*, and Gr. *plasma*, anything formed, from *plassein*, to form, mold.] the condition or quality of being related in characteristics which are not derived from common descent but from similarity of environment.

hom'ō·plȧst, *n.* [*homo-*, and Gr. *plastos*, formed, from *plassein*, to form, mold.]

1. in biology, a part agreeing in shape with some other part, but having a distinct nature.
2. anything having a structure like that of another, but of different origin.

hō·mō·plas'tiç, *a.* denoting those homologies which arise in consequence of tissues similar in character being subjected to similar influences. Such homologies may arise between groups whose common ancestry is too remote to be credited with the transmission of the characters.

hō'mō·plas·ty, *n.* in biology, the process of forming homologous tissues.

hō·mop'lȧ·sy, *n.* homology not traceable to common origin: opposed to *homogeny*.

hō·mō·pō'lăr, *a.* [*homo-*, and Gr. *polos*, a pole.] in promorphology, having equal poles: said of organic forms with a definite number of transverse axes.

hō·mō·pol'iç, *a.* homopolar.

hō·mop'tĕr, *n.* a member of the *Homoptera*.

Hō·mop'te·rȧ, *n.pl.* [Mod. L., from Gr., from *homos*, the same, and *pteron*, wing.] in zoology, an order of insects with sucking mouth parts and wings of uniform thickness throughout, including the *Aphidæ*, *Coccidæ*, *Cicadidæ*, *Fulgoridæ*, etc.

HOMOPTERA (*Cicada dlardi*)

hō·mop'tĕr·ăn, *n.* same as *homopter*.

hō·mop'tĕr·ous, *a.* of or pertaining to the *Homoptera*.

hō·mor'găn, *n.* in biology, a similarly organized part or system; a homoplastic part.

Hō'mō sā'pi·ens, [L.] the one and only living species of the genus Homo; man.

hō''mō·sex'ū·ăl, *a.* [*homo-*, and L. *sexualis*, from *sexus*, sex.] of or pertaining to homosexuals or homosexuality; characterized by sexual inclination toward those of the same sex.

hō''mō·sex'ū·ăl, *n.* one whose sexual inclination is toward those of the individual's own sex rather than the opposite sex.

hō''mō·sex''ū·al'i·ty, *n.* 1. sexual desire for those of the same sex.

2. sexual relations between individuals of the same sex.

Opposed to *heterosexuality*.

hō·mō·spōr'ous, *a.* [*homo-*, and Gr. *sporos*, spore, seed.] in botany, having asexual spores of one kind only: opposed to *heterosporous*.

hō'mō·stȳled, *a.* [*homo-*, and Gr. *stylos*, pillar.] in botany, denoting species in which the individuals bear styles of the same length and character: opposed to *heterostyled*.

hō·mō·tax'e·ous, *a.* homotaxial.

hō·mō·tax'i·ăl, *a.* relating to homotaxis.

hō·mō·tax'iç, *a.* relating to homotaxis.

hō·mō·tax'is, *n.* [*homo-*, and Gr. *taxis*, arrangement.] the same arrangement; specifically, in geology, agreement in the arrangement of layers, or in the fossil content, in different localities of strata which occupy the same place or position in the stratified systems, but which may or may not be contemporaneous.

hō'mō·tax·y, *n.* homotaxis.

hō·mō·thẽr'mous, *a.* [*homo-*, and Gr. *thermē*, heat.] in zoology and physiology, having the same degree of bodily temperature at all times.

hō·mot'ō·nous, *a.* [L. *homotonus*; Gr. *homotonos*, of the same tone; *homos*, the same, and *tonos*, tone.] of the same tone; unvarying in tenor.

hō·mot'rō·păl, *a.* homotropous.

hō·mot'rō·pous, *a.* [Gr. *homotropos*, having the same turn; *homos*, the same, and *trepein*, to turn.] turned in the same direction: in botany, said of the radicle of a seed when turned toward the hilum.

hō'mō·tȳ·păl, *a.* homotypic.

hō'mō·tȳpe, *n.* [*homo-*, and Gr. *typos*, impression, form, type.] in biology, an organ or part having a structure agreeing with some fundamental form; as, the foot is a *homotype* of the hand.

hō·mō·typ'iç, *a.* relating to or of the nature of a homotype.

hō·mō·typ'iç·ăl, *a.* homotypic.

hō'mō·tȳ·py, *n.* in biology, correspondence in structure: said of a part with reference to another part in the same individual, as of segments, limbs, vertebrae, etc.

hō''mō·zȳ·gō'sis, *n.* the producing of a homozygote by the union of two gametes of the same strain.

hō·mō·zȳ'gōte, *n.* [*homo-* and *zygote*.] in Mendel's theory of heredity, a plant or animal resulting from the union of gametes with similar characteristics, and hence breeding true to type: opposed to *heterozygote*.

hō·mun'cū·lus, *n.* [L., dim. of *homo*, *hominis*, a man.]

1. a little human being; a dwarf or pygmy.
2. a model of a human being, used for demonstrating anatomy.

hōm'y, *a.*; *comp.* homier; *superl.* homiest; homey. [Colloq.]

hond, *n.* a hand. [Obs.]

Hon·dū'răn, *a.* of Honduras, its people, or culture.

Hon·dū'răn, *n.* a native or inhabitant of Honduras.

hōne, *v.i.*; honed, *pt.*, *pp.*; honing, *ppr.* [Fr. *hogner*, to mutter, murmur, repine.]

1. to pine; to long. [Dial.]
2. to grumble; to moan. [Dial.]

hōne, *n.* [Ice. *hunn*, a knob.] a kind of swelling of the cheek. [Obs.]

hōne, *v.t.* to rub and sharpen on or as on a hone; as, to *hone* a razor; to *hone* a knife on one's shoe.

hōne, *n.* [ME. *hone*, *hoone*; AS. *han*, a stone.] a stone of very fine grit, usually of a slaty composition, used to sharpen cutting tools, especially razors; a whetstone.

hōne slāte, see *polishing slate*.

hon'est (on'), *a.* [ME. *honest*, *onest*; OFr. *honeste*, *honneste*; L. *honestus*, full of honor, virtuous, from *honor*, honor.]

1. originally, (a) honorable; held in respect; (b) respectable, creditable, commendable, seemly, etc.: a generalized epithet of commendation.
2. that will not lie, cheat, or steal; truthful; trustworthy; as, an *honest* man.
3. (a) showing fairness and sincerity; straightforward; free from deceit; as, an *honest* effort; (b) gained or earned by fair methods, not by cheating, lying, or stealing; as, an *honest* living.
4. being what it seems; genuine; pure; as, *honest* wool.
5. frank and open; as, an *honest* face.
6. virtuous; chaste. [Archaic.]

Syn.—truthful, sincere, straightforward, upright, unimpeachable, candid, pure, reliable.

hon'est, *v.t.* to honor. [Obs.]

hon·es·tā'tion, *n.* adornment; grace. [Obs.]

ho·nes′te·tē, ho·nes′te·tee, *n.* honesty. [Obs.]

hon′est·ly (on′), *adv.* 1. in an honest manner; with honesty.

2. truly; really: an intensive; as, *honestly,* I'll do it.

to come honestly by; to come into possession of by honest means.

hōne′stōne, *n.* any variety of stone employed for making hones.

hon′es·ty (on′), *n.* [OFr. *honeste, honneste, oneste*; L. *honestas,* respectability, character, reputation, from *honestus,* honorable.]

1. the state or quality of being honest; specifically, (a) originally, honor; (b) a refraining from lying, cheating, or stealing; a being truthful, trustworthy, or upright; (c) sincerity; fairness; straightforwardness; (d) [Archaic.] chastity.

2. in botany, one of several plants with large purple flowers, as *Lunaria biennis,* common honesty, and *Lunaria rediviva,* perennial honesty: so called because of their semitransparent pods.

Syn.—frankness, integrity, probity, purity, rectitude, sincerity, uprightness.

hōne′wŏrt, *n.* in botany, any of certain plants of the carrot family, as the stone parsley, formerly used as a remedy for hone, a kind of swelling of the cheek.

hŏn′ey, *n.*; *pl.* **hŏn′eys,** [ME. *hony, huny, hunig*; AS. *hunig,* honey.]

1. a sweet, viscid, sirupy substance made by bees as food from the nectar of flowers and deposited in cells of the comb in hives.

2. anything like honey in quality or nature; sweetness.

The king hath found,
Matter against him, that forever mars
The *honey* of his language. —Shak.

3. darling; sweet one; dear: a term of endearment.

hŏn′ey, *a.* 1. of or like honey.

2. dear; sweet.

hŏn′ey, *v.t.*; honeyed *or* honied, *pt., pp.*; honeying, *ppr.* 1. to make sweet or pleasant with or as with honey.

2. to speak sweetly or lovingly to.

3. to flatter.

hŏn′ey, *v.i.* to speak sweetly or lovingly; to be very affectionate, attentive, or coaxing.

hŏn′ey ȧnt, a kind of ant, *Myrmecocystus mexicanus,* inhabiting Mexico and the southwestern United States and living in communities in subterranean galleries. In summer a certain number of these insects store a kind of honey in their abdomens. This is disgorged later and eaten by the others.

hŏn′ey badġ′ẽr, in zoology, the ratel, *Mellivora ratellus*: so named from its fondness for honey.

hŏn′ey bag, the baglike enlargement in the alimentary canal of a bee in which honey is collected and carried.

hŏn′ey bälm (bäm), in botany, a labiate plant of Europe, having large, handsome flowers.

hŏn′ey beăr, 1. the kinkajou.

2. the aswail or sloth bear.

hŏn′ey·bee, *n.* a bee that makes honey; specifically, the hive bee, *Apis mellifica.*

hŏn′ey·ber″ry, *n.*; *pl.* **hŏn′ey·ber″ries,** 1. the berry of *Celtis australis.*

2. the berry of *Melicocca bijuga.*

hŏn′ey·bīrd, *n.* a bird that extracts nectar from flowers; specifically, any one of the *Meliphagidæ* or honey eaters, as *Anthochæra mellivora,* the wattled honey eater.

hŏn′ey blo͝om, in botany, the spreading dogbane, *Apocynum androsæmifolium.*

hŏn′ey bread (bred), in botany, a leguminous tree of the Mediterranean region, bearing sweet, fleshy, edible pods.

hŏn′ey buz′zărd, a bird, *Pernis apivorus,* of the Old World which feeds on the larvae of bees: also called *bee hawk.*

hŏn′ey·çōmb (-kōm), *n.* [AS. *hunigcamb*; *hunig,* honey, and *camb,* comb.]

1. a structure of wax of a firm, close texture, formed by bees into hexagonal cells for repositories of honey and of the eggs which produce their young.

2. anything like this in structure or appearance.

honeycomb bottom; in navigation, a worm-perforated sea bottom: called also *hawse-pipe bottom.*

honeycomb tripe; the mucous membrane of the second stomach of a ruminant, which is divided into small hexagonal cells: called also *honeycomb stomach.*

hŏn′ey·çōmb, *v.t.*; honeycombed (-kōmd), *pt., pp.*; honeycombing, *ppr.* 1. to render like a honeycomb; to fill with openings or holes in the manner of a honeycomb.

2. to permeate or undermine; as, *honeycombed* with intrigue.

hŏn′ey·çōmb, *v.i.* to become full of holes like a honeycomb.

hŏn′ey·çōmb, *a.* of, like, or patterned after a honeycomb.

hŏn′ey·çōmbed, *a.* perforated or formed like a honeycomb; specifically, having little flaws or cells, as cast metal when not solid.

hŏn′ey·çōmb mo͡th, the bee moth.

hŏn′ey·çōmb rā′di·ā″tŏr, a water-cooling device used in internal-combustion engines.

hŏn′ey·çōmb spŏnġe, a grass sponge.

hŏn′ey çreep′ẽr, any of a large group of bright-colored singing birds of tropical and subtropical America.

hŏn′ey·dew, *n.* 1. a sweet fluid exuded from the leaves of some plants in summer.

2. a sweet substance secreted by aphids and other juice-sucking plant insects.

3. a honeydew melon.

hŏn′ey·dew mel′ŏn, a greenish-white muskmelon having a smooth rind and very sweet, green pulp.

hŏn′ey ēat′ẽr, any of a large family of Australasian birds that feed on insects and on honey from flowers: also *honeybird, honeysucker.*

hŏn′eyed (-id), *v.* [ME.] alternative past tense and past participle of *honey.*

hŏn′eyed, *a.* 1. sweetened, covered, or filled with honey.

2. sweet as honey; flattering or affectionate; as, *honeyed* words.

hŏn′ey flow′ẽr, any of the plants of the genus *Melianthus,* native to the Cape of Good Hope: so called from the large amounts of honey contained in the flowers.

hŏn′ey guīde (gīd), a member of either of two groups of small, heavily built, plain-colored birds of Africa, Asia, and the East Indies: they are said to lead men and animals to bees' nests in order to eat the grubs when the honeycombs are taken.

hŏn′ey·less, *a.* destitute of honey.

hŏn′ey lō′çust, a North American tree, *Gleditschia triacanthos,* having strong, spiny branches, featherlike foliage, glossy, flat pods, and wood resembling that of the locust: sometimes called *three-thorned acacia.*

hŏn′ey lō′tus, the white sweet clover, *Melilotus alba.*

hŏn′ey·mo͞on, *n.* 1. formerly, the first month after marriage.

2. the vacation period spent by a newly married couple in travel and recreation.

hŏn′ey·mo͞on, *v.i.*; honeymooned, *pt., pp.*; honeymooning, *ppr.* to have or spend a honeymoon.

Some decent sort of body to *honeymoon* along with me. —Trollope.

hŏn′ey-mouthed, *a.* soft or smooth in speech.

hŏn′ey·pod, *n.* in botany, the pod of the algarroba or mesquite, *Prosopis juliflora*; also, the tree.

hŏn′ey·stōne, *n.* same as *mellite.*

hŏn′ey·suck·ẽr, *n.* same as *honeybird.*

hŏn′ey·suç·kle, *n.* [ME. *honysocle*; AS. *hunisuce*; *hunig,* honey, and *sucan,* to suck.]

1. any of a group of climbing, twining vines of the genus *Lonicera,* with small, fragrant flowers of red, yellow, or white.

2. any of several similar plants with fragrant flowers.

3. clover. [Obs.]

HONEYSUCKLE
(*Lonicera caprifolium*)

hŏn′ey·suç·kle ap′ple, a juicy applelike fungus growing on the branches of *Rhododendron nudiflorum* or azalea; the swamp apple.

hŏn′ey·suç·kle çlō′vẽr, the common white clover, *Trifolium repens.* [Brit. Dial.]

hŏn′ey·suç·kled, *a.* covered with honeysuckles.

hŏn′ey·suç·kle ọr′nȧ·ment, a floral design resembling the honeysuckle, used in painting and relief sculpture; anthemion.

hŏn′ey·suç·kle tree, in botany, an Australian tree of the genus *Banksia,* including several species whose flowers yield honey.

hŏn′ey sug′ăr (shug′), the hard or granulated part of old honey.

hŏn′ey·sweet, *a.* sweet as honey.

hŏn′ey-tŏngued (-tungd), *a.* using soft speech; speaking winningly.

hŏn′ey·wâre, *n.* same as *badderlocks.*

hŏn′ey·wŏrt, *n.* a plant of the genus *Cerinthe,* whose flowers are very attractive to bees.

hong, *n.* [Chinese *hang, hong,* a row, series, a factory.] a warehouse or factory for foreign trade, in China or Japan.

hong merchant; one of a number of Chinese merchants at Canton who formerly had the sole privilege of trading with foreigners.

hong, *v.* obsolete form of *hang.*

hŏn′ied, *a.* [alternative past tense and past participle of *honey.*] honeyed.

ho·ni soit qui mal y pense (ō-nē swȧ′ kē mȧl ē päṅs′), [Fr.] shamed be (anyone) who thinks evil of it: motto of the Order of the Garter.

hoṅk, *n.* [echoic.]

1. the call of a wild goose.

2. any similar sound, as of an automobile horn.

hoṅk, *v.t.* 1. to express by honking.

2. to sound (an automobile horn). [Colloq.]

hoṅk, *v.i.* to make a honking sound.

hoṅk′ẽr, *n.* one who or that which honks; specifically, a wild goose.

hoṅk′y-toṅk, *n.* a cheap, disreputable saloon, cabaret, etc.; dive. [Slang.]

hon′ŏr, hon′ŏur (on′ẽr), *n.* [ME. *honour, honor, onour, onur*; OFr. *honor, hounor, onor, ounour*; L. *honor, honos,* official dignity, repute, esteem.]

1. the esteem due or paid to worth; high estimation; reverence; veneration.

A prophet is not without *honor,* save in his own country. —Matt. xiii. 57.

2. a testimony or token of esteem; any mark of respect or of high estimation by words or actions; as, military *honors,* civil *honors.*

Their funeral *honors* claimed, and asked their quiet graves. —Dryden.

3. dignity; exalted rank or place; distinction; noble appearance.

Godlike erect! with native *honor* clad. —Milton.

4. reputation; good name; as, his *honor* is unsullied.

5. a sense of what is right, just, and true; dignified respect for character, springing from probity, principle, or moral rectitude; scorn of meanness.

6. any particular virtue much valued, as bravery or integrity in men and chastity in women.

If she have forgot *honor* and virtue. —Shak.

7. one who or that which is a source of glory or esteem; he who or that which confers dignity; glory; boast; as, the chancellor is an *honor* to his profession.

8. title or privilege of rank or birth; that which gains for a man consideration, as nobility, knighthood, or other titles.

Restore me to my *honors.* —Shak.

9. that which adorns; ornament; decoration.

The sire then shook the *honors* of his head. —Dryden.

10. in English law, a seigniory of several manors held under one baron or lord paramount.

11. in bridge, etc., any of the four or five highest cards of the trump suit; in a no-trump hand, any of the four aces.

12. in golf, the privilege of driving first from the tee.

13. [H–] a title of address formerly used in addressing or speaking of a person of high rank or office, and still in use with the possessive pronoun when addressing or mentioning certain magistrates, particularly a judge; as, if *His Honor* please; may it please *Your Honor.*

14. [*pl.*] civilities paid, as at an entertainment.

15. [*pl.*] academic and university distinction or pre-eminence; as, he took his degree with *honors* in classics.

affair of honor; a duel; also, a dispute or quarrel resulting in a duel.

code of honor; rules specifying the qualities of honorable conduct, especially in respect to settling differences by dueling.

court of honor; any court convened to decide questions involving a violation of the laws of honor, as, formerly, the courts of chivalry.

debt of honor; a debt, as a bet, for which no security is required or given except that implied by honorable dealing.

honors of war; (a) magnanimous concessions granted to a vanquished enemy, as of marching out from a camp or entrenchments with all the insignia of military etiquette; (b) formal ceremonies accorded to a soldier at the time of his death and burial.

laws of honor; rules established for honorable conduct among gentlemen, formerly recognized and rigidly enforced through public opinion.

on or *upon one's honor*; staking one's good name on the truth of one's statement or the fulfillment of one's promises.

point of honor; a matter affecting a person's honor.

to do honor to; to treat with great consideration; also, to bestow eminence upon one.

to do the honors; (a) to act as host or hostess; (b) to perform certain formal acts of courtesy, such as making introductions, proposing toasts, etc.

to have the honor; to have the opportunity; to be chosen; as, *to have the honor* of introducing a distinguished guest.

word of honor; a pledge which cannot be violated without reflecting upon the honor of the one pledging.

Syn.—respect, nobility, dignity, reputation, spirit, self-respect, renown, esteem.

hon′ŏr (on′), *v.t.*; honored, *pt.*, *pp.*; honoring, *ppr.* [L. *honorare*, to honor, respect, decorate, from *honor*, *honos*, honor, esteem.]

1. to respect greatly; regard highly; esteem.
2. to show great respect or high regard for; treat with deference and courtesy.
3. to worship.
4. to confer an honor on; exalt; ennoble.
5. to accept and pay when due; as, will you *honor* this check?

Syn.—adore, idolize, respect, revere, reverence, venerate, worship, esteem.

hon′ŏr·ȧ·ble (on′), *a.* [L. *honorabilis*, from *honorare*, to honor, esteem.]

1. worthy of being honored; estimable; holding a distinguished rank in society; illustrious or noble.

Many of them believed; also of *honorable* women which were Greeks . . . not a few.
—Acts xvii. 12.

2. actuated by principles of honor or a scrupulous regard to probity, rectitude, or reputation; as, he is an *honorable* man.

3. conferring honor, or procured by noble deeds.

Honorable wounds from battle brought.
—Dryden.

4. consistent with honor or reputation; as, it is not *honorable* to oppress the weak.

5. respected; worthy of respect; regarded with esteem.

Marriage is *honorable* in all.
—Heb. xiii. 4.

6. performed or accompanied with marks of honor or with testimonies of esteem; as, an *honorable* burial.

7. proceeding from an upright and laudable cause, or directed to a just and proper end; not base; characterized by honesty and integrity; as, an *honorable* motive.

Is this proceeding just and *honorable*?
—Shak.

8. not to be disgraced.

Let her descend; . . . my chambers are *honorable*.
—Shak.

9. honest; without hypocrisy or deceit; fair; as, his intentions appear to be *honorable*.

10. an epithet of respect or distinction prefixed to a person's name, commonly given in the United States to one holding or who has held an important public office. In England, this designation is bestowed upon the younger children of earls and the children of viscounts and barons; also, upon persons enjoying trust and honor, and collectively on the House of Commons.

11. becoming men of rank and character, or suited to support men in a station of dignity; as, an *honorable* salary.

Right honorable; a title given to all peers and peeresses of the United Kingdom; to the eldest sons and all the daughters of peers above the rank of viscount; to all privy councilors, and to some civic functionaries, as the lord mayors of London and Dublin.

hon′ŏr·ȧ·ble·ness, *n.* 1. the state of being honorable; eminence; distinction.

2. conformity to the principles of honor, probity, or moral rectitude; fairness.

hon′ŏr·ȧ·bly, *adv.* in an honorable manner; in a manner conferring or consistent with honor.

Syn.—magnanimously, generously, nobly, worthily, justly, equitably, fairly, reputably.

hon·ō·rā′ri·um *n.*; *pl.* **hon·ō·rā′ri·ums, hon·ō·rā′ri·ȧ,** [L. *honorarium* (supply *donum*, gift), neut. of *honorarius*, honorary.]

1. a payment to a professional man for services on which no fee is set or legally obtainable.

2. in England, the fee of a barrister, in allusion to the fact that a barrister cannot enforce payment for services.

hon′ŏr·ȧ·ry, *n.*; *pl.* **hon′ŏr·ȧ·ries,** an honorarium. [Rare.]

hon′ŏr·ȧ·ry, *a.* [L. *honorarius*, relating to or conferring honor, from *honor*, *honos*, esteem, respect.]

1. done or given as an honor; as, an *honorary* degree.
2. designating an office or position held as an honor only, without service or pay.
3. holding such a position or office.
4. depending on one's honor; that cannot be legally enforced or collected: said of debts, etc.

hon′ŏr·ẽr, *n.* one who honors.

hon·ŏr·if′iç, *a.* [L. *honorificus*, from *honor*, and *facere*, to make.] conferring honor; showing respect; as, an *honorific* epithet, title, etc.

hon·ŏr·if′iç, *n.* a complimentary form or phrase for describing or addressing a person or thing that commands respect: used grammatically in Japanese and some other Oriental languages.

hon·ŏr·if′iç·ăl, *a.* honorific.

hon′ŏr·less, *a.* destitute of honor; not honored.

hon′ŏr point, in heraldry, the point between the center and the top of an escutcheon: also called *color point*.

hon′ŏr sys′tem, in various schools and colleges, a system whereby students are trusted to do their work, take examinations, etc. without supervision.

hon′ŏur, *n.* and *v.t.* honor: British spelling.

hont, honte, *n.* and *v.* hunt. [Obs.]

hoọ, *interj.* an exclamation having various shades of meaning, indicating joy, surprise, disdain, etc., according to the manner in which it is uttered.

hoọch, *n.* [contr. of Alaskan Ind. *hoochinoo*, crude alcoholic liquor; perh. var. of *Hutanuwu*, name of a Tlingit tribe.] alcoholic liquor; especially, liquor made or obtained surreptitiously, as during prohibition. [Slang.]

hood, *n.* [from *hoodlum*.] a hoodlum; gangster. [Slang.]

-hood, [ME. *-hode*, *-hod*; AS. *had*, order, condition, character.] a suffix denoting (a) *state*, *quality*, *character*, *condition*, as in child*hood*; (b) *the whole group of* (a specified class, profession, etc.), as in brother*hood*. It is equivalent to *-head* in such words as God*head*.

hood, *n.* [ME. *hood*, *hod*; AS. *hod*, a hood.]

1. one of various kinds of coverings for the head. Hoods are of numerous forms, the simplest being a caplike covering, either tied about the neck or draping the neck and shoulders, sometimes being attached to a cape or jacket.

MONK'S HOOD

2. the folding cover of a carriage or other vehicle, designed to protect the occupants from the sun, rain, etc.

3. in falconry, a close covering fitting the falcon's head when it is not chasing game.

4. anything that resembles a hood in form or use; as, (a) the upper petal or sepal of certain flowers, as monkshood; (b) a low wooden porch leading to the steerage of a ship; (c) the upper part of a galley chimney; (d) the cover of a pump; (e) the covering for a companion hatch, for a mortar, etc.; (f) a piece of tarred canvas put on the ends of standing rigging, etc.; (g) in a chemical laboratory, a fixture shaped like an inverted cone or pyramid for catching and guiding noxious gases into a flue.

5. the metal covering over the engine in automobiles.

6. in shipbuilding, a name given to the foremost and aftermost planks of a ship's bottom, both inside and outside.

7. a fold of cloth worn over the back of the academic gown by a graduate of a college or university: it has distinguishing colors to indicate the wearer's degree or degrees.

8. in zoology, a bird's crest.

hood, *v.t.*; hooded, *pt.*, *pp.*; hooding, *ppr.* 1. to cover with or dress in a hood or a cowl; to put a hood on.

The friar *hooded*, and the monarch crowned.
—Pope.

2. to cover; to blind.

I'll *hood* my eyes. —Shak.

hood′çap, *n.* a species of seal, *Stemmatopus cristatus*, found in the North Atlantic: so called from an appendage on the head, which the male inflates when angry or excited.

hood′ed, *a.* 1. having or covered with a hood.

2. shaped like a hood.

3. in botany, rolled into a cone shape, as the spathe of the jack-in-the-pulpit; cucullate.

4. in zoology, (a) having the head different in color from the body; (b) having a crest like a hood; as, the *hooded* crow; (c) capable of expanding the skin at each side of the neck by movements of the ribs, as the cobra and puffing adder.

hooded crow; a European crow, *Corvus cornix*, gray with black head and wings.

hooded gull; a European gull, *Larus ridibundus*, having a black head.

hooded merganser; a bird of the goose family, characterized by a circular crest of feathers on the head; the *Lophodytes cucullatus*.

hooded seal; same as *hoodcap*.

hooded snake; any snake with a distensible neck, as the asp, cobra, etc.

hood′less, *a.* having no hood.

hoọd′lum, *n.* [orig. used in San Francisco of gangs of toughs employed to beat up the Chinese; said to be from *huddle 'em*, as used by gangs; perh. from *noodlum*, back slang for *Muldoon*, name of gang leader.] a young rowdy, often a member of a gang; street tough; hooligan. [Colloq.]

hood′măn, *n.* the blindfolded person in the game of blindman's buff. [Archaic.]

hood′măn-blind, *n.* blindman's buff. [Archaic.]

hood′mōld, hood′mōld″ing, *n.* in architecture, the upper and projecting molding of the arch over a Gothic door or window.

a a, HOODMOLD

hoọ′doọ, *n.*; *pl.* **hoọ′doọs,** [a variant of *voodoo*.]

1. voodoo.
2. a person or thing that causes bad luck. [Colloq.]
3. bad luck. [Colloq.]

hoọ′doọ, *v.t.* to give or bring bad luck to. [Colloq.]

hood′wink, *v.t.*; hoodwinked (-winkt), *pt.*, *pp.*; hoodwinking, *ppr.* [*hood* and *wink*.]

1. to blind by covering the eyes; to blindfold.

2. to cover; to hide; also, to prevent from seeing.

For the prize I'll bring thee to,
Shall *hoodwink* this mischance. —Shak.

3. to deceive by external appearances or disguise; to impose on.

hood′wŏrt, *n.* an American plant, *Scutellaria lateriflora*: called also *skullcap* and *madweed*.

hood′y, *n.* the hooded crow: called also *hoodie crow*.

hoọ′ey, *interj.* and *n.* nonsense; bunk. [Slang.]

hoọf, *n.*; *pl.* **hoọfs** or rarely **hoọves,** [ME. *hoof*, *hof*; AS. *hof*, a hoof.]

1. the horny substance that covers or terminates the feet of certain animals, as horses, oxen, sheep, goats, deer, etc.; also, the entire foot of such animals.

2. a hoofed animal; a beast.

3. the human foot. [Slang.]

on the hoof; alive; unslaughtered: said of beef cattle.

hoọf, *v.t.* 1. to walk or tramp. [Colloq.]

2. to trample with the hoofs.

3. to dance. [Slang.]

to hoof it; to go afoot; to walk.

hoọf′bēat, *n.* the sound made by the hoof of an animal when it stamps, walks, etc.

hoọf′bound, *a.* having pain in the foot, occasioned by the dryness and contraction of the hoof.

hoọfed (hōft), *a.* furnished with hoofs; ungulate.

hoọf′ẽr, *n.* a professional dancer, especially a tap dancer. [Slang.]

hoọf′less, *a.* without hoofs.

hook, *n.* [ME. *hok*; AS. *hoc*, a hook.]

1. a curved or bent piece of metal, wood, etc., used to catch, hold, or pull something; specifically, (a) a curved piece of wire or bone with a barbed end, for catching fish; (b) a curved piece of metal, wood, etc. fastened to a wall or chain at one end, used to hang things on, raise things up, etc.; as, a coat *hook*; (c) a small metal catch inserted in a loop, or eye, to fasten clothes together; part of a hook and eye; (d) [Nautical Slang.] an anchor.
2. a curved metal implement for cutting grain, etc.; sickle.
3. something shaped like a hook; specifically, (a) a curving cape or headland: used in place names; as, Sandy *Hook*; (b) a bend in a stream.
4. a trap; snare.
5. the stationary part of a hinge, used to hold the pin.
6. in baseball, a curve.
7. in boxing, a short blow delivered with the arm bent at the elbow.
8. in golf, a stroke in which the ball curves to the left of the direction intended.
9. in music, one of the lines at the end of a stem, indicating whether a note is an eighth, sixteenth, etc.

by hook or crook; see under *crook*.
hook and eye; a device for fastening garments, consisting of two small metallic parts, one hooking into the other.
hook-and-ladder company; a company of firemen equipped with a truck holding ladders and long poles with hooks for tearing away parts of a building in order to extinguish fire.
hook, line, and sinker; completely; altogether: originally a fisherman's expression. [Colloq.]
on one's own hook; by oneself; independent of any assistance.

hook, *v.t.*; hooked (hookt), *pt., pp.*; hooking, *ppr.* 1. to attach or fasten with or as with a hook or hook and eye.
2. to take hold of with a hook.
3. to catch with or as with a hook.
4. to catch or deceive by a trick; to swindle.
5. to steal; snatch.
6. to attack or pierce with the horns, as a bull; to gore.
7. to make into the shape of a hook.
8. to work (canvas) by drawing yarn through it with a hook.
9. in baseball, to throw (a ball) so that it curves.
10. in boxing, to hit with a hook.
11. in cricket, to pull.
12. in golf, to drive (a ball) so that it curves to the left of the direction intended.
13. [Labor Union Slang.] to trap (a worker) into becoming a labor spy or informer.

to hook it; to run away. [Slang.]
to hook on; to fasten by or as by a hook.
to hook up; (a) to connect or attach with a hook or hooks; (b) to arrange and connect the parts of (a radio, etc.).

hook, *v.i.* 1. to curve as a hook does; to bend.
2. to be fastened with a hook or hooks.
3. to be caught by a hook.

hook′ȧh, hook′ȧ, *n.* [Ar. *huqqa*, a pipe for smoking, a vase.] an Oriental pipe with a long, flexible tube by means of which the smoke is drawn through water so as to be cooled.

HOOKAH

hook′bill, *n.* any bird with a curved bill.

hook′-billed, *a.* having a curved beak.

hooked (hookt), *a.* 1. bent into the form of a hook; curvated; as, the claws of a beast are *hooked*.
2. furnished with hooks.
3. made with a hook; as, a *hooked* rug.

hook′ed·ness, *n.* the state of being bent like a hook.

hooked rug, a rug made by drawing strips of cloth or yarn back and forth through a canvas or burlap backing.

hook′ẽr, *n.* 1. one who or that which hooks; one who uses a hook, as a fisherman.
2. a pilferer. [Slang.]
3. a strong, copious drink. [Slang.]
4. an undercover operative employed by a labor spy agency, etc. to trap workers into becoming labor spies.

hook′ẽr, *n.* [D. *hoeker*, from *hoek*, a hook.]
1. a small Dutch fishing ship with two masts.
2. an Irish or English fishing smack with one mast.
3. any clumsy, old ship: sailor's term of contempt or affection.

hook′let, *n.* a small hook or hook-shaped organ.

hook′nōse, *n.* a nose curved downward somewhat like a hook; aquiline nose.

hook′-nōsed, *a.* having a hooknose.

hook′um, *n.* [Hind. *hukm*, a command, decree.] in India, an official order.

hook′up, *n.* 1. the arrangement and connection of parts, circuits, etc. in a radio, telephone system, network of radio stations, etc.
2. a connection or alliance between two governments, parties, etc. [Colloq.]

hook′wŏrm, *n.* a small, parasitic roundworm with hooks around the mouth, infesting the small intestine of man and other animals, especially in tropical climates.
hookworm disease; a disease caused by hookworms in the small intestine, characterized by anemia, fever, weakness, and abdominal pain: the larvae enter the body through the skin of the feet, or in contaminated food or drinking water: also called *ancylostomiasis*.

hook′y, *n.* [from *hook it*, to run away.] a truant: used in the phrase, *to play hooky*, to absent oneself from school, etc. without leave. [Slang.]

hook′y, *a.* full of hooks; pertaining to hooks.

hoo′lee, *n.* [Hind. *holī*.] a festival in honor of Krishna, held by Hindus about the time of the vernal equinox, celebrated by singing and dancing.

hoo′li·găn, *n.* [from *Hooligan*, name of an Irish family in Southwark, London.] a young ruffian, especially a member of a street gang; hoodlum.

hoo′li·găn·ism, *n.* the behavior or character of a hooligan; rowdiness; vandalism.

hoo′lock, *n.* [from native name.] a species of gibbon, *Hylobates hoolock*, found in Assam.

hoom, *n.* home. [Obs.]

hoop, *n.* [ME. *hoope, hope*; AS. *hop*, a hoop.]
1. a band of wood or metal used to confine the staves of casks, tubs, etc., or for other similar purposes.
2. a strip of whalebone, steel, etc., used formerly in manufacturing hoop skirts; in the plural, a hoop skirt; as, she wears *hoops*.
3. something resembling a hoop; a ring; anything circular.
4. the quantity of drink between two consecutive hoops in a hooped quart.
5. an old English measure of capacity. [Obs.]
6. the casing around a pair of millstones; also, the band around the rotating millstone.
7. a large, circular band rolled along the ground by children.
8. [*pl.*] thin steel strips folded up into fourteen-foot lengths.
9. in croquet, a wicket or arch.

hoop, *v.t.* 1. to bind or fasten with hoops; as, to *hoop* a barrel or a tub.
2. to clasp; to encircle; to surround.

hoop, *v.i., v.t.*, and *n.* same as *whoop*.

hoop, *n.* same as *hoopoe*.

hoop ash, the North American tree, *Fraxinus nigra*, the tough wood of which is used in making hoops.

hoop′ẽr, *n.* one who hoops casks or tubs; a cooper.

hoop′ẽr, *n.* [from its cry.] *Cygnus columbianus*, the whistling swan of Europe; also, the whooper, *Cygnus cygnus*.

Hoo′pẽr rāt′ing, a rating of the popularity of a radio performer or broadcast, determined by a sample telephone poll of listeners taken during the time of the broadcast, and expressed in terms of millions of listeners: a Hooper rating of 8 means that there are about 8,000,000 listeners.

hoop′ing, *n.* 1. hoops collectively.
2. the material for making hoops.
3. the hoops or rings around the breech of modern guns of large caliber.

hoop′ing cough (kof), same as *whooping cough*.

hoop ī′ron (-ũrn), iron in thin strips from which hoops are made.

hoop′koop plant, hoop′coop plant, [origin unknown.] an Asiatic plant of the bean family, *Lespedeza striata*, naturalized in the southern United States, where it furnishes food for cattle: called also *bush clover*.

hoop′lȧ, *n.* [originally, a stage driver's exclamation.] great excitement; furor; bustle. [Colloq.]

hoop′le, *n.* [dim. of *hoop*.] a child's hoop (sense 7).

hoop lock, the notched fastening of a wooden hoop.

hoop′ōe, hoop′oo, *n.* [OFr. *huppe, hupe*; L. *upupa*, a hoopoe; prob. imitative of its cry.] a brightly-colored European bird of the genus *Upupa*, with a long, curved beak and an erectile crest.

hoop pet′ti·cōat, same as *hoop skirt*.

hoop pīne, a large coniferous tree of Australia, *Araucaria cunninghami*, remarkable for its strong, fine-grained timber and for its edible fruit: called also *Moreton Bay pine*.

hoop pōle, a small young tree cut for making hoops.

hoop skīrt, 1. a framework of hoops fastened together with tapes, worn to spread out a woman's skirt.
2. a skirt worn over this.

hoop snāke, a snake of the southern United States, *Abastor erythrogrammus*, of the family *Colubridae*: named from an erroneous belief that it moves by taking its tail in its mouth and rolling along like a hoop.

hoop tree, a subtropical shrub or tree of the genus *Melia*; the china tree.

hoop wīthe, a shrub of the tropics, whose berries are used in the Philippines as fish poison.

hoo·rāy′, *interj., n., v.t.* and *v.i.* same as *hurrah*.

hoose, hooze, *n.* a disease of cattle affecting the lungs, caused by the presence on the mucous membrane of minute, hairlike worms.

hoose′gow, *n.* [prob. from Sp. *juzgado*, sentenced, from *juzgar*, to judge; L. *judicare*, from *judex*, a judge.] a local jail; a prison; a lockup; a guardhouse. [Slang.]

Hoo′siẽr (-zhẽr), *n.* [prob. specialization of dial. *hoosier*, mountaineer; extension of dial. *hoojee, hoojin*, dirty person, tramp: southern Indiana was largely settled by Kentucky mountaineers.] an inhabitant or a native of Indiana: a nickname.

hoot, *v.i.*; [ME. *houten, huten*; Sw. *huta*; origin echoic.]
1. to utter its characteristic hollow sound: said of an owl.
2. to utter a sound like this.
3. to shout or cry out, especially in scorn or disapproval.

hoot, *v.t.* 1. to express (scorn, disapproval, etc.) by hooting.
2. to express scorn or disapproval of by hooting.
3. to drive or chase away by hooting; as, they *hooted* him out of the room.

hoot, *n.* 1. the sound that an owl makes.
2. any sound like this.
3. a loud shout or cry of scorn or disapproval.
4. something of no worth; as, he doesn't give a *hoot* for your opinion.

hoot, *interj.* an exclamation expressing disappointment, surprise, impatience, or incredulity. [Scot.]

hoot′en·an·ny, *n.*; *pl.* **hoot′en·an·nies,** [orig. in sense of "dingus," "thingumajig"; a fanciful coinage, used also as derogatory epithet; assimilated in form to *Hootin' Annie*.] a meeting of folk singers, especially for public entertainment. [Slang.]

hoot owl, hoot′ing owl, an owl that hoots, particularly the great horned owl: distinguished from *screech owl*.

hoots, *interj.* hoot. [Scot.]

hoove, *n.* [from *heave*.]. a disease in cattle characterized by the excessive inflation of the stomach by gas, caused by eating too much green fodder.

hop, *v.i.*; hopped, *pt., pp.*; hopping, *ppr.* [ME. *hoppen*; AS. *hoppian*, to hop, leap, dance.]
1. to make a short leap or leaps on one foot.
2. to move by leaping or springing on both (or al') feet at once, as a bird, frog, etc.
3. to dance. [Colloq.]
4. to go. [Slang.]
to hop off; in aviation, to leave the ground; to take off. [Colloq.]

hop, *v.t.* 1. to jump over; as, *hop* the hedge.
2. to jump onto; as, *hop* a train.
3. to fly over in an airplane. [Colloq.]
hopping mad; enraged beyond one's self-control. [Colloq.]

hop, *n.* 1. a hopping.
2. a dance, especially an informal one. [Colloq.]
3. a flight in an airplane. [Colloq.]

hop, *n.* [ME. *hoppe*; M.D. *hoppe*, hop.]
1. a climbing vine, *Humulus lupulus*, with cone-shaped, female flowers, differentiated in form from the male flowers.
2. [*pl.*] the dried ripe cones of the female flowers, used for flavoring beer, ale, etc., and in medicine.

HOP (*Humulus lupulus*)

hop, *v.t*; hopped (hopt), *pt.*, *pp.*; hopping, *ppr.* to flavor or treat with hops.

hop, *v.i.* to pick or gather hops.

hop back, a brewer's sieve.

hop′bīne, *n.* the stalk of the hop plant.

hop′bush, *n.* an Australian sapindaceous shrub whose capsules are used in place of hops.

hop çlōv′ẽr, any of a group of clovers with yellow flowers resembling hops, especially *Trifolium procumbens*.

hop dog, a device for removing hop poles. [Brit. Dial.]

hōpe, *n.* 1. an inlet; a small haven or bay; a creek. [Scot. and Brit. Dial.]
2. a sloping plain between ridges of mountains. [Brit. Dial.]

hōpe, *n.* [ME. *hope*; AS. *hopa*, hope, expectation, from *hopian*, to hope.]
1. a desire for some good, accompanied with at least a slight expectation of obtaining it, or a belief that it is obtainable.
2. the object of this.
3. confidence in a future event; the highest degree of well-founded expectation of good.
4. one who or that which furnishes ground for hope, or expectation; as, the *hope* of a nation is its youth.
5. trust; reliance. [Archaic.]
Syn.—expectation, confidence.

hōpe, *v.t.*; hoped (hōpt), *pt.*, *pp.*; hoping, *ppr.* [ME. *hopen*; AS. *hopian*, to hope, look for, expect.]
1. to want and expect.
2. to want very much.

hōpe, *v.i.* 1. to have hope (*for*).
2. to trust or rely. [Archaic.]
to hope against hope; to go on having hope though it seems to be baseless.

hōpe chest, a chest in which a young woman collects linen, clothing, etc. in anticipation of getting married.

hōpe′fụl, *a.* 1. feeling or showing hope; expecting to get what one wants.
2. inspiring or giving hope; as, a *hopeful* sign.

hōpe′fụl, *n.* a young person who seems likely to succeed: used humorously.

hōpe′fụl·ly, *adv.* in a hopeful manner; with hope or confidence.

hōpe′fụl·ness, *n.* the quality or state of being hopeful; promise of good.

hōpe′īte, hō′pīte, *n.* [after T. C. *Hope* (1766–1844), of Edinburgh.] a transparent, light-colored mineral, consisting probably of hydrous zinc phosphate.

hōpe′less, *a.* 1. without hope; despairing.
2. giving no ground for hope; desperate; as, a *hopeless* condition.
Syn.—despondent, despairing, forlorn, desperate, discouraged, irremediable, irreparable.

hōpe′less·ly, *adv.* without hope; in a hopeless manner.

hōpe′less·ness, *n.* the state of being hopeless; despair.

hōp′ẽr, *n.* one who hopes.

Hōpe′well çul′tūre, a prehistoric, mound-building civilization of the Ohio Valley.

hop fac′tŏr, one who deals in hops.

hop flēa bee′tle, *Psylloides punctulata*, a small flealike beetle, destructive to hops.

hop flȳ, an aphid, *Phorodon humuli*, destructive to hops.

hop frog flȳ, a hop froth fly.

hop frọth flȳ, *Aphrophora interrupta*, an insect infesting hopvines.

hop hŏrn′bēam, the American ironwood, *Ostrya virginiana*.

Hō′pi, *n.* [Hopi *Hópitu*, peaceful ones.]
1. a member of a Pueblo tribe of Shoshonean Indians in northeastern Arizona: also called *Moki, Moqui*. They are noted for their complex system of clans and religious ceremonials, their artistry in weaving and dyeing, and their abilities as farmers and herdsmen.
2. their language.

hōp′ing·ly, *adv.* with hope.

hop kiln (kil), an oven for drying hops.

Hop·kin′ṣi·ăn, *a.* of or pertaining to Dr. Samuel Hopkins (1721-1803), a Calvinist of New England, or to his doctrines.

Hop·kin′ṣi·ăn, *n.* an adherent of the theological principles maintained by Dr. Hopkins.

Hop·kin′ṣi·ăn·iṣm, *n.* in theology, the tenets of Dr. Samuel Hopkins, who held most of the Calvinistic doctrines, but rejected the doctrine of original sin.

hop′līte, *n.* [Gr. *hoplitēs*, a heavily armed foot soldier, from *hoplon*, a tool, weapon.] a heavily armed foot soldier of ancient Greece.

hop mil′dew, either of two parasitic fungi, *Sphærotheca humuli* or *Peronoplasmopara humuli*.

hop′-o′-mȳ-thumb′, *n.* a midget; a diminutive person.

hopped up, 1. stimulated by or as by a drug. [Slang.]
2. supercharged: said of an automobile engine, etc. [Slang.]

hop′pẽr, *n.* 1. one who or that which hops.
2. a wooden trough or shoe through which grain passes into a mill; also, a box or frame of boards which receives the grain before it passes into the trough.
3. any contrivance resembling a grain hopper in form or use, as (a) a box which receives apples to conduct them into a crushing mill; (b) a box or funnel for supplying fuel to a furnace, etc.; (c) in glassmaking, a hoppet.
4. the trip of a hammer of a double-action piano.
5. a boat having a compartment with a movable bottom, which opens to discharge the load of refuse, garbage, mud, etc. in deep water: called also *hopper barge*.
6. any hopping insect.

hop′pẽr boy, a rake moving in a circle, used in mills to draw the meal over an opening in the floor, through which it falls.

hop′pẽr çär, a freight car with an open top and a collapsible bottom through which freight can be unloaded.

hop′pẽr çloṣ′et, a toilet with a pan above a trap and a device for flushing.

hop′pẽr çock, the valve that flushes the hopper of a toilet.

hop′pet, *n.* 1. a hand basket.
2. in mining, the dish used by miners to measure ore in.
3. an infant in arms. [Brit. Dial.]

hop pick′ẽr, one who picks hops.

hop pil′lōw, a sack or pillow filled with hops, used as a soporific.

hop′ping, *n.* the act of one who hops or dances.

hop′ping, *n.* a gathering of hops.

hop′ping dick, *Haplocichla aurantia*, a thrush of Jamaica, much resembling the English blackbird.

hop′ple, *v.t.*; hoppled, *pt.*, *pp.*; hoppling, *ppr.* to fetter by tying the feet together; to trammel; to entangle; to hobble.

hop′ple, *n.* [a form of *hobble*.] a fetter for the legs of horses or other animals, when turned out to graze: used chiefly in the plural.

hop′ple·bush, *n.* same as *hobblebush*.

hop pock′et, a sack or bag for holding hops.

hop pōle, a pole inserted at the root of the hop plant for the stem to climb.

hop′py, *a.* 1. full of hops.
2. having a flavor similar to that of hops.

hop′sçotch, *n.* [*hop* (to jump), and *scotch*, a line, scratch.] a children's game in which each player tosses a small stone into one of several compartments of a figure drawn on the ground or pavement and then hops from one compartment to another, picking the stone up or kicking it.

hop tree, *Ptelea trifoliata*, a small rutaceous tree of America, the clustered fruit of which is sometimes used as a substitute for hops.

hop trē′foil, 1. *Trifolium procumbens*, a plant of the bean family: called also *hop clover*.
2. the plant *Medicago lupulina*, greatly resembling yellow clover, and abundant in wastelands and cultivated fields. It is distinguished from trefoil by its twisted legume: called also *hop medick*.

hop′vīne, *n.* the stalk or plant of the hop.

hop′yärd, *n.* a field or enclosure where hops are raised.

Hōr′ae, *n.pl.* [L.; Gr. *Hōrai*.] in Greek mythology, the Hours.

hō′răl, *a.* [LL. *horalis*, from L. *hora*, hour.] relating to an hour or to hours.

hō′răl·ly, *adv.* hourly.

hō·rā′ri·ous, *a.* in botany, enduring only for an hour or two, as the petals of *Cistus*. [Obs.]

hō′rā·ry, *a.* [LL. *horarius*, from L. *hora*, hour.]
1. of an hour or hours.
2. indicating the hours.
3. occurring once every hour; hourly.
4. lasting an hour.

Hō·rā′tiăn, *a.* relating to or resembling the Latin poet Horace, his poetry, or his style.

Hō·rā′ti·us (-shi-us), *n.* in Roman legend, the hero who defended a bridge over the Tiber against the Etruscan army until the Romans had destroyed the bridge, and then swam across the river to safety.

hōrde, *n.* [Fr. *horde*, from Turk. *ordū*, *ordī*, camp.]
1. a nomadic tribe or clan of Mongols.
2. any wandering tribe or group.
3. a crowd; pack; swarm.

hōrde, *v.i.*; horded, *pt.*, *pp.*; hording, *ppr.* to form a horde; to live together like the members of a migratory tribe.

hor·dē·ā′ceous, *a.* [L. *hordeaceus*, from *hordeum*, barley.] resembling barley; of or pertaining to the genus *Hordeum*.

hor′dē·in, *n.* [L. *hordeum*, barley, and *-in*.] in chemistry, a protein constituting about fifty-five per cent of barley meal.

Hor′dē·um, *n.* [L., barley.] a genus of plants of the natural order *Gramineæ*, native to both hemispheres. *Hordeum sativum* is the cultivated barley.

hōre, *a.* hoar. [Obs.]

hōre′hound, *n.* [ME. *horehune*; AS. *harhune*; *har*, hoar, white, and *hune*, horehound.]
1. a bitter plant of the mint family, with white, downy leaves.
2. a bitter juice extracted from its leaves.
3. cough medicine or candy made with this juice.
4. any of various other mints.
Also spelled *hoarhound*.

hō·rī′zōn, *n.* [L. *horizon*; Gr. *horizōn* (supply *kyklos*, circle), the bounding circle, horizon, properly ppr. of *horizein*, to bound, limit, from *horos*, boundary, limit.]
1. the line in which the sky and the earth or sea seem to meet; the boundary line of one's vision on the surface of the earth: called the *sensible*, *visible*, or *apparent horizon*; hence, the limit of one's experience, knowledge, or observation.
2. in astronomy, (a) the plane extending at right angles to the direction of gravity from the eye of the observer to the celestial sphere: called *sensible horizon*; (b) the plane parallel to this plane, passing through the center of the earth; also, the great circle of the celestial sphere whose plane this is: called *astronomical*, *celestial*, or *true horizon*.
3. in geology, a deposit of rock characterized by specific fossils and hence known to have been formed in some particular period.
artificial horizon; see under *artificial*.

hō·rī′zŏn glȧss, in astronomy, one of two small specula on one of the radii of a quadrant or sextant. The one half of the fore glass is silvered, while the other half is transparent, so that an object may be seen directly through it; the back glass is silvered above and below, but in the middle there is a transparent stripe through which the horizon can be seen.

hor·i·zon′tăl, *a.* 1. parallel to the plane of the horizon: opposed to *vertical*.
2. of, relating to, or close to the horizon.
3. measured or contained in a plane of the horizon; as, *horizontal* distance.
4. operating or situated in a level plane; as, a *horizontal* drill; a *horizontal* wheel.
5. flat and even; level.

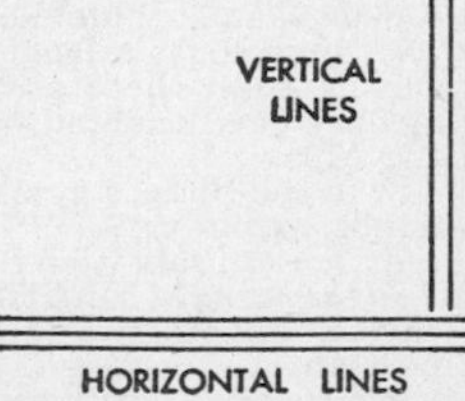

horizontal bar; a smooth, usually round bar, supported horizontally on two upright posts. It is used in gymnastic exercises.
horizontal plane; a plane parallel to the horizon or not inclined to it; in perspective, a plane parallel to the horizon, passing through the center of vision and cutting the perspective plane at right angles.
horizontal projection; a projection made on a plane parallel to the horizon.

hor″i·zon·tal′i·ty, *n.* the state of being horizontal.

hor·i·zon′tăl·ize, *v.t.*; horizontalized, *pt., pp.*; horizontalizing, *ppr.* to arrange or place horizontally.

hor·i·zon′tăl·ly, *adv.* in a horizontal direction or manner.

hor·i·zon′tăl ūn′iŏn (-yun), a labor union whose members all work at the same trade but not necessarily in the same industry; craft union: opposed to *vertical union.*

hor·mō·gō′ni·um, *n.*; *pl.* **hor·mō·gō′ni·à,** [Gr. *hormos*, a cord, chain, and *gonos*, offspring.] in some algae, a chainlike group of reproductive cells.

hor·mog′ō·nous, *a.* like or provided with a hormogonium.

hor·mō′năl, *a.* of, or having the nature of, a hormone.

hor′mōne, *n.* [from Gr. *hormōn*, ppr. of *hormaein*, to stimulate, from *hormē*, impulse.]

1. a chemical substance formed in some organ of the body, as the adrenal glands, the pituitary, etc., and carried to another organ or tissue, where it has a specific effect.

2. a similar substance in plants.

hor·mon′iç, *a.* same as *hormonal.*

horn, *n.* [ME. *horn*; AS. *horn*, horn.]

1. a hard projection growing on the heads of cattle, sheep, and some other hoofed animals, usually projecting to some length, and terminating in a point. In most ruminants the horns have a core of bone surrounded with a sheath of true horn. They are not branched and are never shed.

2. the antler of a deer, which is composed entirely of bone and is shed annually.

3. [*usually pl.*] the symbol of a cuckold: cuckolds are spoken of as wearing horns.

4. a thick and hard form of cuticular substance, as in the scales of reptiles, tortoise shell, birds' beaks, or the nails, claws, and hoofs of animals, especially the dense fibrous substance composing the sheath of the horns of ruminants.

5. anything made of horn, or resembling a horn in shape or use; specifically, (a) a wind instrument of music, originally made of horn; hence, any brass-wind instrument, as the French *horn*; (b) a utensil for holding powder for immediate use, originally made of horn; a powder flask; (c) a drinking cup, originally made of horn; a drinking vessel of any material containing as much as can be swallowed at a draught; a beaker; hence, the contents of such a vessel; (d) a cornucopia; (e) an extremity or point of a crescent-shaped object, as the cusp of the crescent moon; (f) a branch of a subdivided stream; (g) the feeler of an insect, snail, etc.; (h) a tuft of feathers, as on the head of a horned owl; (i) the horny protuberance surmounting the bill of the hornbill; (j) a hornlike process, as in flowers of the milkweed family; (k) the beak of an anvil; (l) the Ionic volute; (m) a projecting corner of an altar; (n) either of two projections on the forward part of a woman's saddle, for supporting the leg; also, the high pommel of a Spanish or half-Spanish saddle, sometimes made of horn; (o) a medieval headdress, or one of its projecting parts, resembling the horn of an ox; (p) in nautical usage, one end of a crosstree; (q) a long projection, frequently of silver or other precious metal, worn on the forehead by natives of many Asiatic countries; (r) a horn-shaped loudspeaker.

6. a device sounded to give a warning; as, a fog *horn*, an automobile *horn*.

7. in geology, a jagged mountain peak resulting from the erosion of several cirques against one headland, as the Matterhorn in the Alps.

8. in the Bible, a symbol of strength, glory, honor, or power.

An horn of salvation for us. —Luke i. 69.

on the horns of a dilemma; having to make a choice between two things, both usually unpleasant.

to blow one's own horn; to praise oneself; to boast. [Colloq.]

to pull (or *draw* or *haul*) *in one's horns*; (a) to hold oneself back; restrain one's impulses, efforts, etc.; (b) to withdraw; recant.

horn, *v.t.* 1. to give horns or a hornlike shape to.

2. to hook; to gore; as, the bull *horned* him.

3. to cuckold. [Archaic.]

horn, *a.* made of horn; as, *horn*-rimmed glasses.

horn al′li·gā·tŏr, leather made from the center back portion of the skin of an alligator.

horn är·rest′ẽr, in electricity, a type of lightning rod in which the end is made of two wires similar to a pair of horns.

horn bär, the crossbar of a carriage.

horn′bēak, *n.* a garfish.

horn′bēam, *n.* [*horn*, and *beam* (tree).]

1. either of two species of trees of the genus *Carpinus* with smooth, gray bark and large clusters of light-green nuts. *Carpinus caroliniana*, called also *blue beech, ironwood*, and *water beech*, is the American hornbeam. The European hornbeam is *Carpinus betulus*, which is known also as *yoke elm, hornbeech, hardbeam*, and *horse beech*.

2. the very hard, white wood of this tree, which takes a hornlike polish; ironwood.

horn′bill, *n.* any of various tropical birds of the *Bucerotidæ*, with partly united toes and a huge, curved bill, often with a bony protuberance on it. The rhinoceros hornbill, *Buceros rhinoceros*, almost the size of a turkey, has a sharp-pointed, slightly curved bill, about ten inches long, and a very large bony protuberance

RHINOCEROS HORNBILL

horn′blende, *n.* [G. *hornblende*; *horn*, horn, and *blende*, blende, an ore of zinc, from *blenden*, to blind, dazzle, deceive.] a black, blackish-green, or dark-brown silicate of calcium and magnesium, usually with iron, manganese, etc.: it is a common mineral found in granite and other igneous rocks. The name *amphibole* is often used to include all the varieties.

horn′blend·iç, *a.* containing or resembling hornblende; pertaining to hornblende.

horn′blōw″ẽr, *n.* one who blows a horn.

horn′book, *n.* 1. formerly, a kind of primer, from which children learned their letters: so called from the transparent horn covering placed over a sheet of parchment, the whole being fixed to a wooden frame with a handle. It generally contained the alphabet in capital and small letters, a table of numbers, and the Lord's Prayer.

2. any elementary treatise or primer.

HORNBOOK

horn′bug, *n.* 1. a large, flat beetle, *Passalus cornutus*, having the head armed with a hornlike prominence.

2. a stag beetle.

horn drum, a wheel used to raise water.

horned, *a.* 1. furnished with or having a horn, horns, or hornlike processes; as, the *horned* moon; a *horned* owl.

2. cuckolded. [Archaic.]

horned adder; the hornsman.

horned bee; *Osmia bicornis*, a species of wild bee having two horns.

horned dace; a fish of the genus *Semotilus*.

horned frog; a frog of South America, *Ceratophrys cornuta*, horned above each eye.

horned grebe; a grebe, *Podiceps cornutus*, which has two thick feather tufts on the head.

horned horse; the gnu.

horned lark; the shore lark.

horned lizard; the horned toad.

horned owl; an owl, *Bubo virginianus*, that grows to large size and has a tuft of feathers projecting in a hornlike manner above each ear.

horned poppy; a horn poppy.

horned pout; a bullhead or catfish.

horned rattlesnake; a rattlesnake, *Crotalus cerastes*, which has two small horns between the eyes.

horned screamer; the kamichi, *Anhima cornuta*.

horned snake; a horned viper.

horned toad; any of several small, scaly, insect-eating lizards of the family *Iguanidæ*, genus *Phrynosoma*, whose body somewhat resembles that of a toad or frog. The body is rough, the tail short, and the head furnished with horny spines. Several species inhabit the arid plains of the southwestern United States and Mexico.

horned viper; a poisonous African snake with a hornlike spine above each eye; cerastes.

horn′ed·ness, *n.* the quality of being horned.

horn′ẽr, *n.* 1. one who works or deals in horn.

2. one who winds or blows the horn.

3. one who cuckolds. [Obs.]

hor′net, *n.* [AS. *hyrnet, hyrnete*, a hornet.] a large wasp of the genus *Vespa*, whose sting gives severe pain. Hornets construct a nest of a coarse, gray, paperlike substance, which is attached to the branches of a tree or placed in a hollow tree. The American hornet is *Vespa maculata*.

to stir up a hornets' nest; to provoke enmity or foster dissensions and strife.

hor′net flȳ, a fly of large size and fierce disposition that preys on bees and other insects.

horn′fish, *n.* 1. the garfish or sea needle.

2. the sauger.

3. the pipefish.

horn flȳ, a small fly of the genus *Hæmatobia*, which clusters about the horns of cattle.

Horn′ie, *n.* Satan. [Scot.]

horn′i·fȳ, *v.t.* 1. to cause to become horny.

2. to cuckold. [Obs.]

hor′ni·ness, *n.* the quality of being horny.

horn′ing, *n.* 1. appearance of the moon when increasing or in the form of a crescent. [Obs.]

2. a charivari; a mock serenade with horns, etc.

letters of horning; in Scots law, a writ under the king's signet issuing at the instance of a creditor against his debtor, commanding him in the king's name to pay or perform within a certain time under pain of being declared a rebel and put in prison.

horn′ish, *a.* somewhat like horn; hard; horny.

horn′ist, *n.* one who plays a horn.

hor·nï′tō, *n.* [Sp., dim. of *horno*, an oven, kiln.] in geology, a fumarole in the form of a small mound, shaped like an oven with a rounded top, common in the volcanic districts of South America.

horn lead (led), in old chemistry, chloride of lead.

horn′less, *a.* having no horns.

horn′-mad, *a.* 1. maddened enough to gore: said of horned animals.

2. furious; mad.

3. mad with jealousy because cuckolded. [Archaic.]

horn mẽr′cū·ry, calomel.

horn ŏf plen′ty, 1. in Greek mythology, the goat horn that suckled Zeus: see *Amalthaea.*

2. a representation in painting, sculpture, etc. of a horn overflowing with fruits, flowers, and grains; cornucopia.

3. an overflowing fullness; abundance.

4. an herb, *Fedia cornucopiæ*, of the valerian family.

5. an ornamental grass of the genus *Cornucopia.*

hor′nō·tīne, *n.* [L. *hornotinus*, of this year.] in ornithology, a bird in its first year. [Rare.]

horn owl, the horned owl.

horn′pīpe, *n.* [ME. *hornpype*, a musical instrument.]

1. an obsolete wind instrument with a bell and mouthpiece made of horn.

2. a lively dance to the music of the hornpipe, formerly popular with sailors.

3. music for this.

horn′plant, *n.* a kind of seaweed, *Ecklonia buccinalis.*

horn plāte, the pedestal or frame for the axle box of a car truck, or a plate in such a frame; an axle guard.

horn pop′py, a plant, *Glaucium luteum*, having glaucous leaves and large, yellow flowers, frequent on sandy seashores.

horn′pout, *n.* the horned pout.

horn quick′sil·vẽr (kwik′), horn mercury; calomel.

horn sil′vẽr, native chloride of silver; cerargyrite.

horn slāte, a gray, siliceous stone. [Obs.]

horns′măn, *n.* 1. one who plays a horn.

2. the plumed viper, *Clotho cornuta*: called also *horned adder* and *puff adder*.

horn snāke, the wampum snake, *Farancia abacura*, having a deep red belly, a blue-black back, and a row of square red spots along the sides.

horn′stōne, *n.* chert, a kind of quartz. [Rare.]

horn′swog·gle, *v.t.*; hornswoggled, *pt., pp.*;

hornswoggling, *ppr.* [fanciful coinage, orig. prob. associated with cuckoldry.] to swindle; humbug; bamboozle. [Slang.]

hor̤n′tāil, *n.* a four-winged insect related to the sawfly: in the adult female the organ for depositing eggs is modified with a horny, taillike extension for cutting into tree trunks, where the eggs are deposited.

hor̤n′thumb (-thum), *n.* a thimble of horn used to protect the thumb of a cutpurse; hence, a cutpurse. [Obs.]

hor̤n′weed, *n.* the hornplant.

hor̤n′wŏrk, *n.* in fortification, an outwork composed of two demibastions joined by a curtain.

hor̤n′wŏrm, *n.* the larval caterpillar of various hawk moths, with a horny growth on the last segment.

hor̤n′wŏrt, *n.* any species of *Ceratophyllum*, growing entirely submerged in lakes and slow-moving streams, with whorls of finely divided leaves.

hor̤n′wrack (-rak), *n.* the sea mat, a polyzoan.

hor̤n′y, *a.*; *comp.* hornier; *superl.* horniest,
1. hard; callous; resembling horn; as, *horny* hands.
2. having horns or projections like horns.
3. consisting of horn or of a hornlike material.

hor̤n′y-hand·ed, *a.* having horny palms; having hands calloused by labor.

hor̤n′y·head (-hed), *n.* a fish, the river chub.

hō·rog′rȧ·phy, *n.* [Gr. *hōrographia*, from *hōrographos*, writing history by seasons or years; *hōra*, hour, and *graphein*, to write.]
1. an account of hours.
2. the art of constructing dials, clocks, or timepieces of any kind.

hor′ō·lōġe, *n.* [OFr. *horologe*; L. *horologium*; Gr. *hōrologion*, an instrument for telling the hour; *hōra*, hour, and *legein*, to tell.] an instrument that indicates the hour of the day; a timepiece; a clock, watch, hourglass, sundial, etc.

hō·rol′ō·ġẽr, *n.* same as *horologist.*

hor·ō·loġ′iç, hor·ō·loġ′iç·ăl, *a.* pertaining to a horologe or to horology.

hor·ō·lō″ġi·og′rȧ·phy, *n.* horography. [Obs.]

hō·rol′ō·ġist, *n.* an expert in horology; a maker of or dealer in timepieces.

Hor̤·ō·lō′ġi·um, *n.* [L.; see *horologe.*] a southern constellation.

hō·rol′ō·ġy, *n.* [from Gr. *hōra*, hour; and *-logy.*] the science or art of measuring time or making timepieces.

hō·rom′e·tẽr, *n.* [Gr. *hōra*, hour, and *metron*, a measure.] a device for measuring time.

hor·ō·met′riç·ăl, *a.* of or pertaining to horometry.

hō·rom′e·try, *n.* [Gr. *hōra*, hour, and *metron*, a measure.] the art or practice of measuring time.

hō·rop′tẽr, *n.* [Gr. *horos*, a boundary, and *optēr*, one who looks, from *optesthai*, to see.] a straight line drawn through the point where the two optic axes meet, and parallel to that which joins the centers of the two eyes or the two pupils; the sum of all points seen single for any given angular position of a person's eyes.

hō·rop·ter′iç, *a.* relating to the horopter.

hor′ō·sçōpe, *n.* [Fr. *horoscope*; L. *horoscopus*; Gr. *hōroskopeion*, from *hōroskopos*, one who observes the hour of birth; *hōra*, hour, and *skopein*, to view.]
1. the position of the planets and stars with relation to one another at a given time, especially at the time of a person's birth, regarded as determining his destiny.
2. a chart of the zodiacal signs and the positions of the planets, etc., by which astrologers profess to tell a person's future.
3. a planisphere invented by John of Padua.
4. a table by which one can tell the length of the days and nights at different places.
to cast a horoscope; to draw up a horoscope so as to calculate the supposed influence of the stars and planets on a person's life.

hor′ō·sçō·pẽr, *n.* one who practices horoscopy; an astrologer.

hō·ros′çō·pist, *n.* same as *horoscoper.*

hō·ros′çō·py, *n.* 1. the art or practice of casting horoscopes.
2. the situation of the planets and stars, especially at the time of a person's birth.

hor·ren′dous, *a.* [L. *horrendus*, from ppr. of *horrere*, to bristle.] fearful; frightful.

hor′rent, *a.* [L. *horrens* (*-entis*), ppr. of *horrere*, to bristle.]
1. bristled; bristling; standing erect like bristles.
2. horrified; shuddering. [Rare.]

hor′ri·ble, *a.* [OFr. *horrible*, *orible*; L. *horribilis*, terrible, dreadful, from *horrere*, to be terrified, to fear.]
1. exciting or tending to excite horror; dreadful; terrible; shocking; hideous; as, a *horrible* story.

A dungeon *horrible* on all sides round. —Milton.

2. very bad; ugly; shocking, unpleasant, etc. [Colloq.]

Syn.—fearful, hideous, terrible.

hor′ri·ble·ness, *n.* the state of being horrible; dreadfulness; terribleness; hideousness.

hor′ri·bly, *adv.* 1. in a horrible manner.
2. to a horrible degree.

hor′rid, *a.* [L. *horridus*, rough, shaggy, bristly, savage, from *horrere*, to bristle.]
1. that can excite horror; dreadful; hideous; shocking; as, a *horrid* spectacle.
2. rough; rugged. [Obs.]

Horrid with fern, and intricate with thorn. —Dryden.

3. very bad, ugly, unpleasant, etc.: the current sense. [Colloq.]

Syn.—horrible, awful, abominable, shocking, unpleasant, disagreeable.

hor′rid·ly, *adv.* in a horrid manner.

hor′rid·ness, *n.* the state of being horrid.

hor·rif′iç, *a.* [L. *horrificus*; *horrere*, to be afraid, to fear, and *facere*, to make.] causing horror; horrifying; horrible.

hor″ri·fi·çā′tion, *n.* 1. the act of horrifying or state of being horrified.
2. that which causes horror.

hor′ri·fy, *v.t.*; horrified, *pt.*, *pp.*; horrifying, *ppr.* [L. *horrificare*, to make rough or terrible, from *horrificus*, causing terror; *horrere*, to be terrified, fear, and *facere*, to make.]
1. to cause to feel horror.

I was *horrified* at the notion. —Hook.

2. to shock greatly. [Colloq.]

hor̤·rip′i·lāte, *v.t.*; horripilated, *pt.*, *pp.*; horripilating, *ppr.* [from L. *horripilatus*, pp. of *horripilare*, to bristle with hairs, from *horrere*, to bristle, and *pilus*, hair.] to produce horripilation.

hor̤·rip′i·lāte, *v.i.* to experience horripilation; bristle or shudder.

hor″rip·i·lā′tion, *n.* [LL. *horripilatio* (*-onis*), from *horripilare*, to bristle with hairs; L. *horrere*, to bristle, and *pilus*, hair.] the erection of the hair of the head or body, resulting from disease, fear, or cold; goose flesh.

hor·ris′ō·nănt, *a.* [L. *horrisonus*, sounding dreadfully; *horrere*, to be terrible, and *sonus*, a sound.] having a terrible sound; sounding dreadfully.

hor·ris′ō·nous, *a.* horrisonant. [Obs.]

hor′rŏr, *n.* [L. *horror*, from *horrere*, to bristle, shake, be afraid.]
1. originally, (a) a bristling; (b) a shuddering.
2. a painful emotion of fear, dread, and abhorrence; a shuddering with terror and loathing; a feeling caused by something frightful and shocking.

An *horror* of great darkness fell upon him. —Gen. xv. 12.

3. strong dislike or aversion; loathing.
4. the quality of causing horror.
5. that which excites fear, loathing, or dread; something that causes intense mental aversion or positive suffering.

And breathes a browner *horror* on the woods. —Pope.

6. something very ugly, bad, disagreeable, etc. [Colloq.]
the horrors; a fit of horror; also, the blues. [Colloq.]

hor′rŏr-strick″en, hor′rŏr-struck, *a.* struck with horror; terrified.

hors de çom·bat′ (o̤r de koṅ-bä′), [Fr., lit., out of the fight.] out of combat; disabled; unable to fight.

hors d'oeu·vre (o̤r dũrv *or* duv), *pl.* **hors d'oeu·vreṣ** (dũrvz *or* duvz), [Fr., lit., outside of work.], [*usually in pl.*] an appetizer, as olives, anchovies, etc., served usually at the beginning of a meal.

hor̤se, *n.*; *pl.* **hor̤s′eṣ** or **hor̤se,** [ME. *hors*; AS. *hors*, a horse.]
1. a large, strong animal, *Equus caballus*, with four legs, solid hoofs, and flowing mane and tail, long ago domesticated for drawing or carrying loads, carrying riders, etc.
2. in zoology, any animal of the family *Equidæ*, including the asses, the quagga, zebra, etc.
3. the full-grown male of the horse; gelding or stallion, as distinguished from a mare.

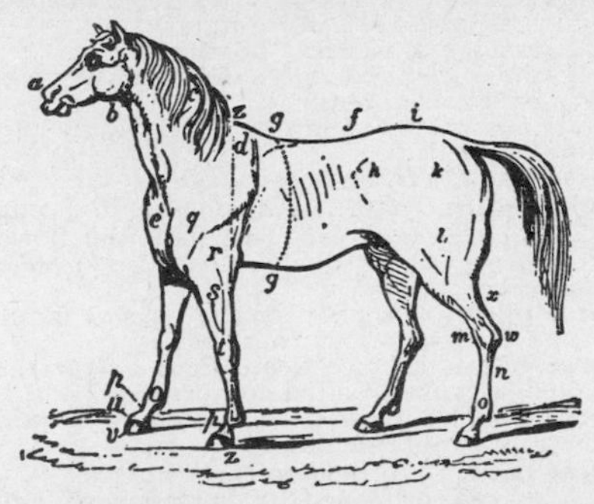

HORSE
a, muzzle; *b*, gullet; *c*, crest; *d*, withers; *e*, chest; *f*, loins; *g g*, girth; *h*, hip, or ilium; *i*, croup; *k*, haunch, or quarters; *l*, thigh; *m*, hock; *n*, shank, or cannon; *o*, fetlock; *p*, pastern; *q*, shoulder bone, or scapula; *r*, elbow; *s*, forearm, or forethigh; *t*, knee; *u*, coronet; *v*, hoof; *w*, point of hock; *x*, hamstring; *z z*, height

4. anything like a horse in that a person sits, rides, or is carried on it.
5. formerly, a wooden frame on which soldiers were made to ride by way of punishment: sometimes called *timber mare.*
6. a frame on legs to support something; specifically, (a) a sawing frame; (b) a clothes-horse.
7. a man: a joking, friendly, or insolent term.
8. in chess, a knight. [Colloq.]
9. a translation used illegitimately by students in the preparation of their work: also called *trot*, *pony.* [Slang.]
10. in gymnastics, a padded block on legs, used for jumping or vaulting.
11. in military usage, mounted troops; cavalry.
12. in mining, a hard part of a rock occurring in the middle of a vein, dividing it into two branches.
13. in nautical usage, a rope extending from the middle to the end of a yard to support the sailors while they loose, reef, or furl the sails; a footrope. [Obs.]
14. work charged for before it is done. [Slang.]
a horse on one; a joke at one's expense. [Slang.]
horned horse; the gnu.
horse of another (or *different*) *color*; an entirely different matter.
to back the wrong horse; (a) to bet on a horse that loses the race; (b) to uphold the losing side.
to be on one's high horse; to speak or act in an overbearing or haughty manner. [Colloq.]
to hold one's horses; to curb one's impatience. [Slang.]
to horse! get on your horse! mount!
to look a gift horse in the mouth; to receive a gift or favor in a critical or exacting spirit: from the practice of determining the age of a horse by inspecting its teeth.
to put the cart before the horse; see under *cart.*
to take horse; (a) to set out to ride on horseback; (b) to be covered, as a mare.
winged horse; Pegasus.

hor̤se, *v.t.*; horsed (hor̤st), *pt.*, *pp.*; horsing, *ppr.*
1. to provide with a horse; to supply a horse or horses for.

. . . Who *horsed* the coach by which he had traveled so many a time. —Thackeray.

2. to sit astride; to bestride. [Rare.]

Leads are filled, and ridges *horsed.* —Shak.

3. to cover (a mare): said of a stallion.
4. to place on the back of a horse; hence, to take on one's own back.
5. to place on a man's back or a wooden horse for the purpose of flogging.
6. to flog.
7. to subject (a person) to horseplay; to make fun of. [Slang.]
8. in nautical usage, to calk, using a horse iron: often with *up*; as, a seam *horsed up* with oakum.

hor̤se, *v.i.* 1. to mount or go on horseback.
2. to be in heat; to rut: said of a mare.

hor̤se, *a.* 1. of a horse or horses.
2. mounted on horses.
3. large, strong, or coarse of its kind; as, *horse*radish.

hor̤se ȧnt, a large ant, *Formica rufa.*

hor̤se är·til′lẽr·y, artillery arranged for rapid

movement, generally accompanying the cavalry, the gunners being also mounted.

hŏrse'back, *n.* 1. the part of a horse's back on which a person sits in riding.
2. a ridge of earth; a hogback.
3. a fissure filled with sand or clay in what was once a coal seam.
on horseback; riding or as if riding on a horse's back.

hŏrse'back, *adv.* on horseback.

hŏrse bälm (bäm), a strong-scented mint, *Collinsonia canadensis*, with yellowish flowers and large, ovate leaves: called also *richweed, stoneroot.*

hŏrse'bāne, *n.* a plant of the parsley family, said to be poisonous to horses.

hŏrse bēan, a large bean, *Faba vulgaris*: so called because it is fed to horses.

hŏrse beech, hurst beech, *Carpinus betulus*, the English hornbeam.

hŏrse bōat, 1. a boat to carry horses.
2. a boat propelled by horsepower. [Obs.]

hŏrse bot, the botfly.

hŏrse box, a car or a section of a vessel arranged for the transportation of horses. [Brit.]

hŏrse'brēak″ẽr, *n.* one who trains horses for use.

hŏrse çāne, a plant, *Ambrosia trifida*, the great ragweed.

hŏrse'çär, *n.* 1. a streetcar drawn by a horse or horses, formerly used in the United States.
2. a car used to transport horses.

hŏrse ças'siȧ (kash'iȧ), an East Indian leguminous plant, *Cassia marginata*, bearing long pods which contain a black cathartic pulp, used as a horse medicine.

hŏrse chest'nut, a large nut, the fruit of *Æsculus hippocastanum*; also, the tree itself.

hŏrse'çlŏth, *n.* a blanketlike covering for a horse's back and loins.

hŏrse çōurs'ẽr, one who keeps horses to race; also, a dealer in horses. [Obs.]

hŏrse çrab, the horseshoe crab.

hŏrse cre·val·lé (kre-vȧl-lā'), a fish, the cavally: so named in South Carolina to distinguish it from the crevallé, a kind of horse mackerel.

hŏrse dev'il, a tumbleweed of the southeastern United States, *Baptisia lanceolata*, one of the *Leguminosæ*: so named because when dried it is blown about and sometimes frightens horses.

hŏrse drench, 1. a dose of horse medicine.
2. a device for giving medicine to a horse.

hŏrse el'dẽr, elecampane.

hŏrse em'met, same as *horse ant.*

hŏrse'finch, *n.* the chaffinch. [Brit. Dial.]

hŏrse'fish, *n.*; *pl.* **hŏrse'fish, hŏrse'fish·eṣ,** a fish, as (a) the moonfish, *Vomer setipinnis*; (b) the sauger; (c) a sea horse.

hŏrse'flesh, *n.* 1. the flesh of a horse, especially as food.
2. horses collectively; as, he has made money in *horseflesh.*
horseflesh ore; bornite, an ore of copper and iron which has a red color when broken.

hŏrse'flȳ, *n.*; *pl.* **hŏrse'flīeṣ,** 1. any of a number of related large flies the female of which sucks the blood of horses, cattle, etc.; gadfly.
2. any of various other flies troublesome to horses, as the botfly.

hŏrse'foot, *n.* 1. in botany, coltsfoot.
2. in zoology, the horseshoe crab.

hŏrse ġen'tiăn, any of a number of weedy plants of the honeysuckle family, with opposite leaves, inconspicuous flowers, and leathery fruit; feverroot.

hŏrse gow'ăn, the oxeye daisy, *Chrysanthemum leucanthemum*; also, the dandelion, *Taraxacum officinalis*, and other plants.

hŏrse gram, a leguminous tropical plant, *Dolichos biflorus*, the pod of which is used in southern India as food for horses and cattle.

Hŏrse Guärdṣ, 1. a guard consisting of a body of cavalry.
2. in England, the cavalry brigade forming the household guard of the English sovereign.
3. the building opposite Whitehall, London, housing this guard and certain departments of the War Office. [Colloq.]

hŏrse'hāir, *n.* 1. the hair of horses, especially that of the mane and tail used for stuffing furniture, cushions, etc.
2. haircloth; the stiff fabric woven of such hair.

hŏrse'hāir, *a.* 1. made of horsehair.
2. covered or stuffed with horsehair.

hŏrse'head (-hed), *n.* 1. any of the moonfishes, *Selene vomer.*
2. a kind of surf duck; the surf scoter.
3. a sea horse.

hŏrse'hēal, hŏrse'heel, *n.* same as *elecampane.*

hŏrse'hīde, *n.* 1. the hide of a horse.
2. leather made from this.

hŏrse'hīde, *a.* made from the hide of a horse.

hŏrse'hoof, *n.*; *pl.* **hŏrse'hoofs,** same as *coltsfoot.*

hŏrse ī'rŏn (-ũrn), in nautical usage, a calking iron held by one workman and struck by another.

hŏrse'jock·ey, *n.* 1. a jockey.
2. one who deals in horses. [Obs.]

hŏrse'knop (-nop), *n.* knapweed, *Centaurea nigra*, especially the black flowerhead of the plant.

hŏrse lat'i·tūdeṣ, either of two belts of calms, light winds, and high barometric pressure, situated at about 30° N. and 30° S. latitude.

hŏrse'läugh (-läf), *n.* a loud, boisterous laugh, usually derisive; a guffaw.

hŏrse'leech, *n.* 1. a large leech said to attach itself to the lips or nostrils of horses and other animals that drink from the water it inhabits.
2. a veterinarian; a farrier. [Archaic.]
3. an importunate beggar.

hŏrse'leech·ẽr·y, *n.* veterinary practice. [Obs.]

hŏrse'less, *a.* having no horse; especially, not needing a horse; self-propelled; as, an automobile was formerly called a *horseless* carriage.

hŏrse lit'tẽr, a kind of wheelless carriage hung on poles borne by two horses.

hŏrse mack'ẽr·el, 1. the largest fish of the mackerel family, the tuna, or tunny.
2. any of various other fishes, as the saurel, cavally, bluefish, etc.

hŏrse'măn, *n.*; *pl.* **hŏrse'men,** 1. a rider on horseback.
2. a cavalryman.
3. a man skilled in riding, training, or handling horses.
4. an inferior variety of carrier pigeon.
5. an ocypodian Brazilian land crab.
6. a fish of the West Indies of the genus *Equetus.*

hŏrse'măn·ship, *n.* the act or art of riding horseback; the art of training and managing horses; equestrian skill.

hŏrse mȧ·rīne', 1. one out of his element, as a horseman would be on board ship.
2. a member of a troop of imaginary marine cavalry.

hŏrse'mint, *n.* 1. a North American species of mint, *Monarda punctata*, with clusters of showy flowers, usually red or purplish.
2. a wild mint of Europe, *Mentha sylvestris.*

hŏrse mus'sel, a large inedible mussel, *Modiolus modiolus.*

hŏrse'nāil, *n.* a horseshoe nail.

hŏrse net'tle, a weed, *Solanum carolinense*, of the nightshade family, with yellow prickles, white or blue flowers, and yellow berries.

hŏrse op'ẽr·ȧ, a motion picture or play about cowboys, cattle rustlers, etc., depicting the wild, adventuresome life supposedly characteristic of the western United States. [Slang.]

hŏrse pis'tŏl, a large pistol formerly carried by men on horseback.

hŏrse'plāy, *n.* rough, boisterous fun.

hŏrse'pond, *n.* a pond for watering horses.

hŏrse pop'py, an umbelliferous plant of Europe, *Seseli hippomarathrum.*

hŏrse'pow″ẽr, *n.* 1. the power exerted by a horse in pulling.
2. a unit for measuring the power of motors or engines, equal to a rate of 33,000 foot-pounds per minute (the force required to raise 33,000 pounds at the rate of one foot per minute).
3. the power of any engine or motor expressed in such standard units.
4. a device for utilizing the pull or weight of a horse in operating machinery.
brake horsepower; the effective horsepower given out by an engine or other motor.
indicated horsepower; the power developed by the cylinders of an engine.

hŏrse'pox, *n.* an acute infectious disease of horses: it is a modified form of smallpox.

hŏrse pũrs'lāne, a plant of the West Indies, *Trianthema monogyna.*

hŏrse rāce, a race by horses; a match of horses in running, trotting, pacing, or steeplechasing.

hŏrse rā'cing, the act or practice of racing with horses.

hŏrse'rad″ish, *n.* 1. a plant of the mustard family, *Cochlearia armoracia*, grown for its pungent, white, fleshy root.
2. a relish made of the grated root of this plant.

hŏrse'rad″ish tree, a tree of Africa and the East Indies, *Moringa pterygosperma*, whose root has a pungent flavor resembling that of horseradish.

hŏrse'rāke, *n.* a large rake drawn by a horse.

hŏrse rough (ruf), an attachment to prevent a horse's shoe from slipping on icy roads.

hŏrse run, a contrivance used to pull loaded cars, wheelbarrows, etc., up a runway from an excavation, by horsepower.

hŏrse sense, good, practical common sense; instinctive shrewdness. [Colloq.]

hŏrse'shöe, *n.* 1. a flat, U-shaped strip of metal fitted to the rim of a horse's hoof for protection, and fastened with nails. The possession of a horseshoe, especially of one found by chance, is superstitiously believed to ward off witchcraft or to bring good luck.
2. anything shaped like a horseshoe, as a curve in a stream or roadway.
3. [*pl.*] a game in which the players toss horseshoes at a stake driven in the ground, the object being to encircle the stake or come as close to it as possible: the stakes in regulation horseshoes are 40 feet apart.
4. the horseshoe crab.
horseshoe bat; a European bat, having the nose leaf shaped like a horseshoe.
horseshoe crab; any of a group of horseshoe-shaped sea animals with a long spinelike tail; a king crab.
horseshoe magnet; a magnet shaped like a horseshoe, having its poles side by side.
horseshoe vetch; a plant of the genus *Hippocrepis*: so named from the shape of its seed pods.

hŏrse'shöe″ing, *n.* the act or work of shoeing horses.

hŏrse'shöe nāil, a heavy, iron nail used to fasten a shoe to a horse's hoof.

hŏrse spŏnġe, a coarse bath sponge, *Spongia equina*, of the Mediterranean.

hŏrse sting'ẽr, a dragon fly. [Brit.]

hŏrse sụg'ăr (shụg'), the sweetleaf tree, *Symplocos tinctoria*, of the southeastern United States: its sweetish leaves are used as fodder for cattle and are also the source of a yellow dye.

hŏrse'tāil, *n.* 1. a horse's tail.
2. a horse's tail as a former Turkish ensign denoting the rank of pasha.
3. any of a number of related rushlike, flowerless plants of the genus *Equisetum* with hollow, jointed stems and scalelike leaves.
4. a fossil bivalve; a hippurite.

hŏrse'tāil tree, a leafless tree of Australia, of the genus *Casuarina.*

hŏrse this'tle (this'l), a thistle of the genus *Cirsium.*

hŏrse tick, a blood-sucking fly; especially, *Hippobosca equina*, a pupiparous dipterous insect which infests horses and cattle; the forest fly.

hŏrse vetch, same as *horseshoe vetch.*

hŏrse'weed, *n.* 1. any of a group of strong-smelling, weedy plants of the mint family, with clusters of small, yellow flowers.
2. a common weed of the composite family.

hŏrse'whip (-hwip), *n.* a whip for driving or managing horses.

hŏrse'whip, *v.t.*; horsewhipped, *pt.*, *pp.*; horsewhipping, *ppr.* to strike with a horsewhip.

hŏrse'wom″ăn (-woom″), *n.*; *pl.* **hŏrse'wom″en** (-wim″), 1. a woman who rides on horseback.
2. a woman skilled in the riding or managing of horses.

hŏrse'wood, *n.* a West Indian tree, *Calliandra comosa*, having showy, deep-red flowers.

hŏrse'wŏrm, *n.* the larva of a botfly.

hŏrse wrañ'glẽr, a herder in charge of a herd of ponies or horses. [Dial.]

hors'ey, *a.* same as *horsy.*

hors'i·ly, *adv.* in a horsy manner.

hors'i·ness, *n.* the state or quality of being horsy.

horst, *n.* [G., orig., thicket, aerie.] in geology, a rased rock mass between two faults.

hors'y, *a.*; *comp.* horsier; *superl.* horsiest, 1. of, having the nature of, or suggesting a horse or horses.
2. connected with or fond of horses, fox hunting, or horse racing; dressing, talking, etc. in the manner of people who are fond of horses, fox hunting, or horse racing.

hŏr·tā'tion, *n.* [L. *hortatio* (-onis), from *hor-*

tari, to urge strongly, incite, freq. of *horiri*, to urge, incite.] the act of exhorting; exhortation. [Rare.]

hor'tȧ·tive, *a.* [L. *hortativus*, from *hortari*, to urge strongly, encourage.] same as *hortatory*.

hor'tȧ·tive, *n.* an exhortation. [Rare.]

hor'tȧ·tō·ry, *a.* [LL. *hortatorius*, from L. *hortator*, an encourager, inciter, from *hortari*, to urge, incite.]
1. giving exhortation or advice.
2. encouraging; inciting; as, a *hortatory* speech.

hor·ten'siăl (-shăl), *a.* [L. *hortensis*, from *hortus*, a garden.] fit for a garden.

hor'ti·cul·tŏr, *n.* [L. *hortus*, a garden, and *cultor*, a tiller.] a horticulturist. [Rare.]

hor·ti·cul'tūr·ăl, *a.* of horticulture.

hor'ti·cul·tūre, *n.* [L. *hortus*, a garden, and *cultura*, culture, from *colere*, to till.] the cultivation of a garden; the art or science of cultivating fruits, flowers, and vegetables.

hor·ti·cul'tūr·ist, *n.* one who is skilled in the art of horticulture; a gardener.

hor'tū·lăn, *a.* [L. *hortulanus*, from *hortus*, a garden.] belonging to a garden.

hor'tus sic'cus, [L.] literally, a dry garden; a classified collection of specimens of plants carefully dried and preserved; a herbarium.

Hō'rus, *n.* in Egyptian mythology, the hawk-headed god of the sun.

hō·san'nȧ, *interj.* and *n.* [Gr. *hōsanna*, from Heb. *hōshī'āh nnā*, lit., save, we pray.] an exclamation or shout of praise to God.

hōse, *n.*; *pl.* **hōse,** archaic **hōs'en,** [ME. *hose*; AS. *hosa*, hose.]
1. formerly, a tight-fitting outer garment covering the hips, legs, and feet, attached to the doublet by cords or ribbons (called *points*), but sometimes extended only to the knees or ankles.
2. [*pl.*] (a) stockings; (b) socks.
3. *pl.* **hōse, hōs'es,** [prob. influenced by D. *hoos*, water pipe, of same origin.] (a) a flexible pipe or tube, used to convey fluids, especially water from a hydrant; (b) such a pipe equipped with a nozzle and attachments; (c) a sheath or sheathing part resembling such a pipe.

hōse, *v.t.*; hosed, *pt.*, *pp.*; hosing, *ppr.* 1. to put water on with a hose; drench or soak with a hose.
2. to beat with a hose. [Slang.]

Hō·sē'ȧ, *n.* a book of the Old Testament containing the writings of Hosea, a Hebrew prophet who lived in the 8th century B.C.

hōse car'riage (-rij), a truck or wagon fitted with a reel or rests to carry the hose of a fire engine: also called *hose cart*.

hōse cŏm'pȧ·ny, a group of firemen who man a hose carriage and handle the hose at fires.

hō'sen, *n.* archaic plural of *hose*.

hō'sier (-zhēr), *n.* a person who makes or sells hosiery or similar knitted or woven goods.

hō'siēr·y, *n.* 1. (a) hose; stockings and socks; (b) other similar knitted or woven goods.
2. the business of a hosier.

hos'pice, *n.* [Fr. *hospice*, from L. *hospitium*, hospitality, an inn, lodging, from *hospes*, a host, guest.]
1. a place of refuge for travelers, especially that belonging to the monks of Saint Bernard in the Alps.
2. a home for the sick or poor.
3. a homelike facility to provide supportive care for terminally ill patients.

hos'pi·tȧ·ble, *a.* [OFr. *hospitable*, from LL. *hospitare*, to receive as a guest, from L. *hospes* (*-itis*), a host, guest.]
1. receiving and entertaining strangers and guests in a friendly, generous manner; kind to strangers and guests; as, a *hospitable* man.
2. proceeding from or indicating hospitality; manifesting generosity; as, a *hospitable* table.
3. liberal and generous in disposition and mind; receptive or open, as to new ideas.

hos'pi·tȧ·ble·ness, *n.* the quality of being hospitable; hospitality.

hos'pi·tȧ·bly, *adv.* with hospitality; in a hospitable manner.

hos'pi·tăl, *n.* [OFr. *hospital*; LL. *hospitale*, a house, inn, from L. *hospitalia*, strangers' apartments, neut. pl. of *hospitalis*, relating to a guest, from *hospes* (*-itis*), a guest, host.]
1. originally, (a) a place of shelter and rest for travelers, etc.; (b) a charitable institution for providing and caring for the aged, infirm, orphaned, etc.: now only in names.
2. an institution where the ill or injured may receive medical, surgical, or psychiatric treatment, nursing, food and lodging, etc. during illness.

hos'pi·tăl, *a.* hospitable. [Obs.]

hos'pi·tăl·ēr, *n.* [OFr. *hospitalier*; ML. *hospitalarius*, from *hospitale*, a house, inn.]
1. a person receiving the care of a hospital. [Rare.]
2. [*usually* H–] a member of one of the charitable societies organized during the Middle Ages to care for the sick, needy, etc., especially a member of a military religious order called the Knights Hospitaler of St. John of Jerusalem.
Also written *hospitaller*.

hos'pi·tăl·ism, *n.* the unsanitary conditions in badly managed hospitals.

hos·pi·tal'i·ty, *n.*; *pl.* **hos·pi·tal'i·ties,** [L. *hospitalitas*, hospitality, from *hospitalis*, relating to a host or guest, from *hospes*, a host, guest.] the act, practice, or quality of receiving and entertaining strangers or guests in a friendly and generous way.

hos"pi·tăl·i·zā'tion, *n.* 1. a hospitalizing or being hospitalized.
2. hospitalization insurance. [Colloq.]
hospitalization insurance; insurance providing hospitalization for the subscriber and, usually, members of his immediate family.

hos'pi·tăl·īze, *v.t.*; hospitalized, *pt.*, *pp.*; hospitalizing, *ppr.* to admit (a patient) to a hospital, or to place in a hospital for treatment.

hos'pi·tāte, *v.t.* to be hospitable to. [Obs.]

hos'pō·dăr, *n.* [Romanian.] a title formerly given to the princes or governors of Moldavia and Wallachia, and, earlier, to the princes of Lithuania and the kings of Poland.

hōst, *n.* [ME. *host*, *ost*; OFr. *host*, a host, army, from L. *hostis*, a stranger, foreigner, foe.] an army; a great number of men ready for war; hence, any great number or multitude.

hōst, *n.* [ME. *host*, *ost*; OFr. *hoste*; L. *hospes* (*-itis*), a host, guest.]
1. a man who entertains guests in his own home or at his own expense; person who initiates or presides over any social gathering.
2. a man who keeps an inn or hotel; innkeeper, landlord, etc.
3. (a) any organism on or in which another (called a *parasite*) lives for nourishment or protection. (b) an individual, especially an embryo, into which a graft is inserted.
4. the person who conducts a radio or television program that features informal conversation, interviews, etc.
to reckon without one's host; to neglect necessary details or facts in making plans or decisions; to make a wrong calculation.

host, *v.i.* to act as a host or hostess.

hōst, *v.t.* to act as a host or hostess to or at.

Hōst, hōst, *n.* [ME. *host*, *hoste*; OF. *hoiste*; L. *hostia*, an animal sacrificed, a victim, from *hostire*, to recompense.] the bread of the Eucharist.

hos'tāge, *n.* [ME. *hostage*, *ostage*; OFr. *hostage*, *ostage*; LL. *hostagium*, *hostaticum*, from *obsidaticus*, the condition of a hostage, from L. *obses*, *obsidis*, a hostage, pledge, security.]
1. a person kept or given as a pledge for the fulfillment of certain agreements.
2. the state of the person thus kept or given.
to give hostages to fortune; to get, be responsible for the care of, or be liable to lose, a wife, children, etc.

hos'tel, *n.* [ME. *hostel*, *ostel*; OFr. *hostel*, *ostel*, from LL. *hospitale*, a large house, an inn, from L. *hospitalis*, of or relating to a guest, from *pes* (*-itis*), a guest.] a lodging place; inn; hostelry; especially, one of a series of supervised shelters (*youth hostels*) used by young people on hikes, etc.

hos'tel·ēr, *n.* an innkeeper; the keeper of a hostel. [Archaic.]

hos'tel·ry, *n.*; *pl.* **hos'tel·ries,** a hotel; an inn; a lodging house.

hōst'ess, *n.* 1. a woman who entertains guests in her own home or at her own expense; often, the wife of a host.
2. (a) a woman who keeps an inn or hotel; (b) a woman married to an innkeeper and sharing some of his duties.
3. (a) a woman whose work is seeing that guests or travelers are comfortable, entertained, etc., as on an airplane; (b) a woman employed in a restaurant to supervise the waitresses, assign guests to tables, etc.; (c) a woman who serves as a paid partner at a public dance hall.
hostess gown; a long, dresslike negligee worn for lounging and entertaining at home.

hōst'ess·ship, *n.* the character or business of a hostess.

hos'tile (*Brit.* -tīl), *a.* [L. *hostilis*, from *hostis*, a foreigner, an enemy.]
1. of or belonging to an enemy; warlike.
2. pertaining to or expressing enmity or opposition; conflicting; antagonistic; inimical.

hos'tile, *n.* an enemy; especially, a North American Indian on the warpath.

hos'tile·ly (*Brit.* -tīl-), *adv.* in a hostile manner.

hos·til'i·ty, *n.*; *pl.* **hos·til'i·ties,** [LL. *hostilitas* (*-atis*), from L. *hostilis*, of or like an enemy; hostile.]
1. a feeling of enmity, ill will, unfriendliness, etc.; antagonism.
2. (a) expression of enmity and ill will; active opposition; hostile act; (b) [*pl.*] a state of war; acts of war; warfare.

hōst'ing, *n.* a muster; the assembling of an armed body. [Obs.]

hos'tlēr, os'tlēr (-lēr), *n.* [contr. of *hosteler*.]
1. a person who takes care of horses at an inn, stable, etc.; groom.
2. a person who services a railroad engine at the end of a run.
3. an innkeeper. [Obs.]

hot, *a.*; *comp.* hotter; *superl.* hottest, [ME. *hot*, *hote*; AS. *hat*, hot.]
1. (a) having much heat; characterized by a temperature higher than that of the human body; (b) characterized by a relatively or abnormally high temperature; very warm: opposed to *cold*.
2. producing a burning sensation in the mouth, throat, etc.; as, *hot* pepper.
3. full of or characterized by any very strong feeling or violent activity; specifically, (a) impetuous; fiery; excitable; as, a *hot* temper; (b) violent; raging; angry; as, a *hot* battle, *hot* words; (c) full of enthusiasm; eagerly intent; ardent; (d) inflamed with sexual desire; lustful; (e) very controversial.
4. (a) following or pressing closely; as, *hot* pursuit; (b) close to what is being sought: said of the seeker.
5. as if heated by friction; specifically, (a) in constant use; as, the news kept the wires *hot*; (b) thrown or batted hard or with great speed: said of a ball; (c) electrically charged, especially with a current of high voltage; as, a *hot* wire; (d) radioactive.
6. that has not had time to lose heat, freshness, currency, etc.; specifically, (a) recently issued or announced; new; as, *hot* news; (b) just arrived; as, *hot* from the front; (c) clear; intense; strong: said of the scent in hunting; (d) recent and seemingly valid; as, a *hot* tip; (e) recently stolen; (f) contraband. [Slang.]
7. excellent; good. [Slang.]
8. in jazz music, (a) designating or of playing characterized by exciting rhythmic and tonal effects, imaginative improvisation, and, often, a fast, driving tempo; (b) designating or of music played in this way.
hot air; empty or pretentious talk or writing. [Slang.]
hot cockles; formerly, a game in which a blindfolded player tried to guess who hit him.
hot cross bun; a bun marked with a cross, eaten especially during Lent.
hot dog; (a) a frankfurter or wiener; (b) a sandwich made of a hot frankfurter or wiener, usually in a soft roll, often served with mustard, catsup, etc. [Colloq.]
hot pants; very brief, tight, outer shorts for women, especially popular in the 1970s.
hot plate; a small gas or electric stove for cooking.
hot pot; meat and potatoes cooked together in a tightly covered pot.
hot rod; an automobile, usually a jalopy, whose motor has been supercharged for high speed. [Slang.]
hot seat; the electric chair. [Slang.]
hot wall; a wall having pipes to conduct heat, so as to speed the growth or ripening of fruit.
hot water; water that is hot, especially when continuously provided as a utility in an apartment, etc.
hot well; the reservoir for hot water from the condenser of a condensing engine.
in hot water; in trouble or difficulty; in an embarrassing situation. [Colloq.]
to get hot; to act, perform, etc. with great spirit or enthusiasm. [Slang.]
to make it hot for; to make things disagreeable, difficult, or uncomfortable for. [Colloq.]
Syn.—burning, fiery, glowing, heated.

hot, *adv.* in a hot manner; hotly.

hot′bed, *n.* 1. a bed of earth heated artificially, as by fermenting manure, and usually covered with glass, for forcing plants or for growing tropical plants in a cool or temperate climate; hence, in a figurative sense, a place which favors rapid growth or development; as, a *hotbed* of sedition.
 2. a platform in a rolling mill used to hold the hot rails, etc., while they cool.

hot′-blood″ed (-blud″), *a.* ardent; excitable; passionate; amatory.

hot′box, *n.* an overheated bearing on an axle or shaft.

hot′-brāined, *a.* hot-headed; impetuous; rash; excitable.

hotch, *v.t.* [Fr. *hocher*, to shake.] to shake or jolt to cause separation, as peas from beans when mixed; to jog. [Scot.]

hotch, *v.i.* to fidget; to be agitated or restless. [Scot.]

hotch′pot, *n.* [ME. *hochepot, hochepoche*; OFr. *hochepot*, from O.D. *hutspot*, a mixture of beef or mutton, hodgepodge.]
 1. a mingled mass; a mixture of many ingredients; a hodgepodge.
 2. in English law, a pooling of property for the purpose of equable division.

hotch′potch, *n.* [from *hotchpot*.]
 1. a thick stew of various meats and vegetables.
 2. a jumbled mixture; medley; mess.
 3. in law, a hotchpot.
 In senses 1 and 2, now usually *hodgepodge*.

hō·tel′, *n.* [Fr. *hôtel*; OFr. *hostel*, from LL. *hospitale*, a large house, an inn.
 1. an establishment or building providing a number of bedrooms, baths, etc., and usually food, for the accommodation of travelers, semipermanent residents, etc.
 2. in France, (a) a dwelling of a person of rank or wealth; a large mansion; (b) a public building.

hô·tel′ de ville (ō-tel′ de vēl), [Fr.] a town hall.

hot′foot, *adv.* hastily. [Colloq.]

hot′foot, *v.i.* to hurry; hasten. [Colloq.]

hot′-foot, *n.* the prank of secretly inserting a match between the sole and upper of a victim's shoe and then lighting it.

hot′head (-hed), *n.* a person with a quick temper.

hot′-head″ed, *a.* 1. quick-tempered; easily made angry.
 2. impetuous; rash; hasty.

hot′house, *n.* 1. a building with the roof and sides of glass, artificially kept warm to shelter tender plants and shrubs; a greenhouse.
 2. any house or room artificially heated to a high temperature; a drying room, as for green pottery.
 3. a bathhouse; also, a brothel. [Obs.]

hot′-liv″ẽred, *a.* irascible; having a violent temper. [Obs.]

hot′ly, *adv.* ardently; vehemently; with heat; fierily; violently; lustfully.

hot′-mouthed, *a.* headstrong; ungovernable, as a horse chafing at the bit. [Obs.]

hot′ness, *n.* the state or quality of being hot; heat; ardor; violence; passion.

hot′-press′, *v.t.* to apply both heat and mechanical pressure to (paper or cloth) for the purpose of giving a smooth, glossy surface.

hot′-press′, *n.* a machine for producing a gloss.

hot′-shọrt, *a.* easily cracked or broken when worked at a red heat: said of metal.

hot′-spir″it·ed, *a.* having a fiery spirit.

hot′spũr, *n.* 1. one who spurs on rashly; a violent, rash, or impetuous person.
 2. a kind of pea of early growth. [Obs.]

hot′spũr, hot′spũrred, *a.* violent; impetuous; rash; headstrong; reckless; hasty. [Obs.]

hot′-tem″pẽred, *a.* having a violent or hasty temper.

Hot′ten·tot, *n.* [S. Afr. D., lit., *hot and tot*, syllables used to imitate clicks characteristic of their language.]
 1. a member of a Negroid race living in South Africa.
 2. the language of the Hottentots, the chief dialect of which is Nama: regarded as forming, together with Bushman, a separate linguistic family.

Hot′ten·tot, *a.* of the Hottentots or their language.
 Hottentot bread; the South African tortoise plant.
 Hottentot breadfruit; Kafir bread.
 Hottentot cherry; a South African plant, *Cassine maurocenia*, yielding a wood used in making musical instruments.

Hot′ten·tot·iṣm, *n.* a characteristic of the Hottentots; especially, a kind of stammering.

hot′tẽr, *v.i.* to move unsteadily; to shiver; to jolt. [Scot.]

hou′dȧh, *n.* same as *howdah*.

Hö̤u′dan, *n.* [from *Houdan*, France, where it originated.] one of a French breed of crested, five-toed chickens with white or black-and-white feathers.

hough (hok), *n.* [see *hock* (joint).] the joint bending backward in the hind leg of a horse, ox, etc., corresponding to the human ankle. [Chiefly Scot.]

hou′let, *n.* a howlet; an owl. [Archaic.]

hōult, *n.* a holt; a wood; a wooded hill. [Obs.]

hound, *n.* [ME. *hound, hund*; AS. *hund*, a dog.]
 1. any of several breeds of large hunting dog characterized by long, drooping ears, short hair, and a deep-throated bark.
 2. any dog.
 3. a contemptible person.
 4. a houndfish.
 5. the old squaw, a duck.

hound, *v.t.*; hounded, *pt., pp.*; hounding, *ppr.* 1. to hunt; to chase; to pursue with or as with hounds; to follow continually; to nag; as, bill collectors *hound* him.
 2. to set on the chase, as a hound; to urge to pursue.

hound, *n.* [from ME. *houn*, from ON. *hūnn*, knob, with unhistoric *-d* after prec. *hound*.]
 1. in shipbuilding, a projection at the masthead for supporting the heel of the topmast and the upper parts of the lower rigging.
 2. a side bar in a vehicle, for increasing the rigidity of the parts connected.

hound′fish, *n.* 1. a shark of the genus *Galeus* or of allied genera; a dogfish.
 2. any of various other fishes, as (a) the garfish, *Tylosurus acus*; (b) the bluefish, *Pomatomus saltatrix*; (c) the Spanish mackerel, *Scomberomorus maculatus*.

hound′ing, *n.* in shipbuilding, a hound, or projection.

hound′ṣ′-tongue (-tung), *n.* a plant of the borage family, genus *Cynoglossum*, with blue flowers and hairy leaves shaped somewhat like a hound's tongue.

hour (our), *n.* [ME. *houre, our, oure, ure*; OFr. *ure, ore*; L. *hora*; Gr. *hōra*, an hour, time, period, season.]
 1. (a) a division of time, one of the twenty-four parts of a day; sixty minutes; (b) one of the twelve points marking the beginning or end of such a division; as, the ninth *hour*.
 2. a point or period of time; specifically, (a) a fixed point or period of time for a particular activity, occasion, etc.; as, the dinner *hour*; (b) an indefinite period of time; as, he spent his happiest *hours* in Paris; (c) the period of time in a classroom; as, the *hour* lasts fifty minutes; (d) [*pl.*] a special period for work, receiving patients, etc.; as, his office *hours* are 2–5; (e) [*pl.*] the usual times for getting up and going to bed; as, he keeps late *hours*.
 3. the time of day as indicated by the timepiece, expressed in hours and minutes; as, the *hour* is 2:30.
 4. a measure of distance set by the normal amount of time passed in traveling it; as, it is two *hours* from New York to Philadelphia by rail.
 5. in astronomy, a sidereal hour; angular unit of right ascension equaling 15° measured along the equinoctial circle.
 6. in ecclesiastical usage, (a) the seven times of the day set aside for prayers; (b) the prayers said at these times.
 after hours; after the regular hours for business, school, etc.
 canonical hours; see under *canonical*.
 hour after hour; every hour.
 hour by hour; each hour.
 of the hour; of this time; of the present.
 one's hour; the time of one's death.
 the small (or *wee*) *hours*; the hours just after midnight.
 to keep good hours; to be at home early; not to be out late or at the usual hours of retiring.

hour an̄′gle, the angular distance, usually measured to the west, between the meridian of the observer and the hour circle passing through a given celestial sphere.

hour cir′çle, in astronomy, any of the twelve great imaginary circles passing through the celestial poles at right angles to the equator.

hour′glȧss, *n.* an instrument having two compartments connected by a narrow neck through which a quantity of sand or other substance requires just an hour to run from the upper to the lower part: similar devices measure any other period of time desired.

HOURGLASS

hour hand, the short hand which indicates the hour on a clock, watch, etc., and moves around the dial once every twelve hours.

hö̤u′ri, *n.* [Per. *ḥūri*, a nymph of paradise.]
 1. a nymph of the Moslem Paradise: in the Koran, the *houris* are represented as most beautiful virgins, endowed with unfading youth.
 2. a seductively beautiful woman.

hour līne, the line on a sundial on which the shadow of the gnomon falls at any hour.

hour′ly, *a.* 1. happening or done every hour; occurring hour by hour.
 2. frequent; often repeated; continual.
 3. done or happening in the course of an hour; as, *hourly* output.

hour′ly (our′), *adv.* 1. every hour; at each succeeding hour.
 2. hour by hour; at any hour.
 3. frequently; continually; as, to signal *hourly*.

hour plāte, the plate of a clock or other timepiece on which the hours are marked; the dial.

Hourṣ, *n.pl.* 1. in Greek mythology, the goddesses of the seasons, justice, order, and peace.
 2. in the Roman Catholic Church, a book containing prayers for certain times of the day.

houṣ′ăge, *n.* a fee for housing goods.

house, *n.*; *pl.* **houṣ′es,** [ME. *hous, hows, hus*; AS. *hus*, a house, prob. from same root as *hydan*, to hide.]
 1. a building for human beings to live in; specifically, (a) the building or part of a building occupied by one family or tenant; dwelling place; (b) a college in a university; (c) an inn; tavern; hotel; (d) a building where a group of people live as a unit; as, a fraternity *house*; (e) a monastery, nunnery, or similar religious establishment.
 2. the people who live in a house, considered as a unit; social group; especially, a family or household.
 3. a family as including kin, ancestors, and descendants, especially a royal or noble family; as, the *House* of Tudor.
 4. something regarded as a house; place that provides shelter, living space, etc.; specifically, (a) the habitation of an animal, as the shell of a mollusk; (b) a building or shelter where animals are kept; as, the monkey *house* in a zoo; (c) a building where things are kept when not in use; as, a carriage *house*; (d) a deckhouse.
 5. any place where something is thought of as living, resting, etc.
 6. (a) a theater; (b) the audience in a theater.
 7. (a) a place of business; (b) a business firm; commercial establishment.
 8. a church, temple, or synagogue.
 9. (a) a building or rooms where a legislative or branch of a legislature meets; (b) a legislative assembly or governing body; as, the *House* of Representatives.
 10. in astrology, (a) one of the twelve parts into which the heavens are divided by great circles through the north and south points of the horizon: used by astrologers in casting horoscopes; (b) a sign of the zodiac considered as the seat of a planet's greatest influence.
 11. a square or division on a chessboard. [Obs.]
 12. the workhouse. [Brit. Colloq.]
 13. the body; the residence of the soul.
 This mortal *house* I'll ruin. —Shak.
 House of Assembly; the lower branch of the legislature of South Africa.
 House of Burgesses; the lower branch of the colonial legislature of Virginia or Maryland.
 house of call; a house where journeymen connected with a particular trade assemble, especially when out of work, and where the unemployed can be reached by those in search of workers.

house of cards; any flimsy, insubstantial structure, plan, etc.

House of Commons; see *commons*, sense 2.

house of correction; see under *correction*.

House of Delegates; the lower branch of the legislature of Maryland, Virginia, or West Virginia.

House of God, of the Lord, of worship, of prayer; a church, temple, or other place of worship.

house of ill fame; a house of prostitution.

House of Keys; the lower, elective branch of the legislature of the Isle of Man: also *Keys*.

House of Lords; see under *lord*.

House of Peers; the upper branch of the legislature of Japan.

House of Representatives; see under *representative*.

lower House; see under *lower*.

on the house; given free, at the expense of the establishment.

the White House; the official residence of the president of the United States at Washington, D. C.; hence, the executive branch of the United States Government.

to bring down the house; to cause very great applause. [Colloq.]

to clean house; (a) to clean and put a house in order; (b) to do away with undesirable conditions.

to keep house; to run a house; to be a housekeeper; to manage the affairs of a house.

to keep to the house; to remain in the house, as on account of illness.

to play house; to pretend to be grown-up people with the customary household duties and routine: a children's phrase. [Colloq.]

to set (or *put*) *one's house in order*; to put one's affairs in order.

upper House; see under *upper*.

Syn.—home, residence, abode, dwelling, domicile, habitation.

house, *v.t.*; housed, *pt.*, *pp.*; housing, *ppr.* [ME. *housen, howsen*; AS. *husian*, to house, from *hus*, house.]

1. to provide a house or lodgings for.
2. to store in a house.
3. to cover, harbor, or shelter by or as if by putting in a house.
4. to drive to a shelter. [Obs.]
5. in nautical usage, to put or stow in a place of safety or security; as, to *house* a sail.

house, *v.i.* 1. to take shelter or lodgings.
2. to abide; to reside.
3. to be situated in an astrological house or region of the heavens.

Where Saturn *houses*. —Dryden.

house ā'ġent, one who looks after the sale, renting, and general care of houses. [Chiefly Brit.]

house'bōat, *n.* 1. a large, flat-bottomed boat with a superstructure resembling a house, usually moored and used as a residence.
2. a motor yacht with particularly commodious living quarters aboard.

house'bōte, *n.* [*house*, and ME. *bot, bote*, amends, reward.] in English law, a sufficient allowance of wood given a tenant to repair the house.

house'break″ẽr, *n.* 1. one who commits the crime of housebreaking.
2. a person who dismantles houses. [Brit.]

house'break″ing, *n.* 1. the act of breaking into another's house to commit theft or some other felony: it is itself a felony.
2. the dismantling of houses. [Brit.]

house'brō·ken, *a.* trained to live in a house (i.e., to defecate and urinate in the proper place): said of a dog, cat, etc.

house'build″ẽr (-bild″), *n.* one in the business of building houses.

house çär, a closed freight car; a boxcar.

house'çärl, *n.* [Late AS. *huscarl*; ON. *hūskarl*, lit., houseman.] a member of the bodyguard or household troops of a Danish or English king or nobleman in late Anglo-Saxon times.

house'çōat, *n.* a woman's long, loose garment for informal wear about the house.

house çrick'et, a European cricket, *Acheta domestica*, that infests houses, especially about fireplaces.

house dog, a watchdog; a dog kept to guard a house.

house'dress, *n.* any relatively inexpensive dress, as of printed cotton, worn in the home while doing housework, etc.

house finch, the purple finch or burion, *Carpodacus frontalis*, of the southwestern United States.

house flag, a flag flown by a merchant ship, indicating the house or firm to which it belongs or is consigned.

house'flȳ, *n.* a two-winged fly, *Musca domestica*, found in and around houses in nearly every country: it feeds on garbage, manure, and food, and is a carrier of typhoid and some other diseases.

house'fụl, *n.* as much or as many as a house will hold or accommodate.

house'hōld, *n.* 1. those who dwell under the same roof and compose a family.
2. the home and its affairs.
3. [H-] the royal household.

house'hōld, *a.* belonging to the house and family; domestic; as, *household* furniture, *household* affairs.

household arts; home economics.

household suffrage or *franchise*; in Great Britain, formerly, the right of householders to vote for members of Parliament.

household troops; troops whose special duty it is to attend a sovereign and guard his palaces.

household word; a word or expression so well known as to be familiar everywhere.

house'hōld″ẽr, *n.* 1. a person who owns or maintains a house as his own.
2. the head of a family or household.

compound householder; see under *compound*.

house'hus″bănd, *n.* a married man whose main occupation is managing a household and performing the domestic chores traditionally done by a housewife.

house'keep″ẽr, *n.* 1. a woman who runs a home, takes care of the housework, etc.
2. one hired to look after the keeping of a house; especially, a female servant who superintends the other servants and manages the domestic affairs of the home.
3. one who remains much at home. [Rare.]
4. a house dog. [Obs.]

house'keep″ing, *a.* domestic; used in a family; as, *housekeeping* commodities.

house'keep″ing, *n.* 1. the work of a housekeeper; management of a house.
2. hospitality. [Obs.]

hou'sel, *n.* [ME. *housel*; AS. *husel*, a sacrifice.] the Eucharist; the sacred bread; also, the act of taking or receiving the sacrament. [Obs.]

hou'sel, *v.t.* [ME. *houselen*; AS. *huslian*, from *husel*, a sacrifice.] to give the Eucharist to. [Obs.]

house'leek, *n.* a plant of the genus *Sempervivum*, often found in Europe growing on the tops of houses, on walls, etc.

house'less, *a.* not having a house or habitation; without shelter; homeless.

house'līne, hous'ing, *n.* among seamen, a small line formed of three strands, used for seizings, etc.

house'māid, *n.* a female servant who does housework.

housemaid's knee; an inflammation of the saclike cavity covering the kneecap, caused by much kneeling.

house mär'tin, the house swallow, *Hirundo urbica*.

house'māte, *n.* one who lives with another in the same house.

house'mŏth·ẽr, *n.* a woman who heads a group of people living together or has charge of a dormitory, sorority house, etc. as chaperon and, often, housekeeper.

house ọr'găn, a periodical published by a business firm for its employees, etc.

house pär'ty, 1. the entertainment of guests overnight or over a period of a few days in a home, usually a country home, or fraternity house, etc.
2. the guests.

house phy·si'ciăn, a resident physician of a hospital, hotel, etc.

house'-rāis·ing, *n.* a gathering of the members of a rural community to help a neighbor build his house or its framework.

house'rọom, *n.* room or accommodation in a house.

house snāke, the milk snake.

house spar'rōw, the common European sparrow, *Passer domesticus*.

house spī'dẽr, a spider that is found around houses, among the most common species being *Pheridium vulgare* and *Pegenaria domestica*.

house'top, *n.* the top of a house; roof.

from the housetops; publicly and widely.

house'wạrm″ing, *n.* a party given by or for someone moving into a new home.

house'wīfe (*for* 2, *usually* huz'if), *n.*; *pl.* **house'wīveṣ** (*for* 2, huz'ivz), 1. (a) a woman who runs a home and takes care of domestic affairs; (b) a woman who runs her own household.
2. a little sewing kit: also called *hussy*.

house'wīfe, house'wīve, *v.t.* and *v.i.* to manage with economy and skill. [Rare.]

house'wīfe·ly, *a.* pertaining to or characteristic of a housewife; economical; domestic.

house'wīfe·ly, *adv.* in the manner of a good housewife.

house'wīf″ẽr·y (*or* huz'if-ri), *n.* the work of a housewife; housekeeping.

house'wŏrk, *n.* the work involved in housekeeping; washing, cleaning, cooking, etc.

house'wrīght (-rīt), *n.* a worker who builds houses.

hous'ing, *n.* 1. the act of sheltering or of putting under cover.
2. shelter or lodging; accommodation in houses, apartments, etc.: often used attributively; as, the *housing* problem.
3. houses collectively.
4. a shelter; covering.
5. in carpentry, the space taken out of one piece to admit the insertion of part of another.
6. in machinery, a support or framework to hold something in position, as a journal box.
7. in nautical usage, the part of the mast below decks.
8. in architecture, a niche for a statue.

hous'ing, *n.* [OFr. *housse*, a short mantle, a cover for a horse.]
1. a blanket over or under a horse's saddle, used originally to keep off dirt, and afterward as an ornamental covering.
2. [*pl.*] the trappings of a horse.
3. a cover attached to the collar or hames of a harness.

hous'ling, *n.* and *a.* same as *houseling*.

houss, *n.* a covering; a housing. [Obs.]

Hous·tō'ni·ȧ, *n.* [named after Dr. William *Houston*, an English botanist.] a genus of low biennial herbs with delicate four-parted blue or white flowers, embracing many species: *Houstonia cærulea* is called *innocence* or *bluet*.

hou'tou, *n.* [from its note.] a South American bird of the genus *Momotus*; a motmot.

houve, *n.* [ME. *houve, howve*; AS. *hufe*, a covering for the head.] a covering for the head; a hood; a cap. [Obs.]

Hou'yhnhnm (-inm), *n.* [prob. coined to represent the whinny of a horse.] one of a race of imaginary beings described by Swift in "Gulliver's Travels" as horses possessing reason, exceptional virtues, and powers of command over the manlike beings called Yahoos.

hōve, *v.* alternative past tense and past participle of *heave*.

hōve, *v.i.* and *v.t.* to rise; to swell; to cause to rise or swell. [Obs.]

hov'el, *n.* [ME. *hovel, hovil*, dim. of AS. *hof*, a house.]
1. an open shed for sheltering cattle or protecting produce, etc. from the weather.
2. a poor cottage; a small mean house.
3. in porcelain manufacturing, a cone-shaped structure of brick around which the ovens or firing kilns are clustered.

hov'el, *v.t.*; hoveled *or* hovelled, *pt.*, *pp.*; hoveling *or* hovelling, *ppr.* 1. to shelter in a hovel.
2. to make in the form of a hovel.

hov'el·ẽr, hov'el·lẽr, *n.* [prob. so called from their use of *hovels* on the shore for shelter.] one engaged in saving life and property from wrecked vessels; also, a vessel used for coasting. [Brit. Dial.]

hov'el·ing, hov'el·ling, *n.* 1. a mode of preventing chimneys from smoking by carrying up two sides higher than those which are less liable to receive strong currents of air, or leaving apertures on all the sides, so that when the wind blows over the top the smoke may escape below.
2. a chimney so constructed.

hō'ven, *v.* obsolete past participle of *heave*.

hŏv'ẽr (*or* hov'), *v.i.*; hovered, *pt.*, *pp.*; hovering, *ppr.* [ME. *hoveren*, freq. of *hoven*, to wait; linger, abide, from AS. *hof*, house.]
1. to hang or remain fluttering in the air; to remain suspended over a place or object; to remain floating in the air (often with *over* or *about*).
2. to linger or wait close by; to move around

(with *near* or *about*); as, a ship *hovering* on the coast.

3. to be in doubt or hesitation; to be irresolute; to waver.

Hovering o'er the paper with her quill. —Shak.

hŏv′ẽr, *v.t.* to shelter by covering with the wings, as a brooding hen.

hŏv′ẽr, *n.* a protection or shelter. [Obs.]

hŏv′ẽr·crȧft, *n.* [*hover*, and air*craft*.] a vehicle which travels across land or water just above a cushion of air provided by a downward jet, as from its engines, propellers, etc.: a trademark (*Hovercraft*).

hŏv′ẽr·ẽr, *n.* one who or that which hovers.

hŏv′ẽr ground, light ground. [Obs.]

hŏv′ẽr hạwk, the kestrel.

hŏv′ẽr·ing·ly, *adv.* in a hovering manner.

how, *adv.* [ME. *how, hough, hwu*; AS. *hu*, how.]

1. in what manner; in what way; by what means.

2. in what state, condition, or plight.

How, and with what reproach, shall I return? —Dryden.

3. for what reason; from what cause; why; as, *how* is it that you don't know?

4. by what name or title.

5. with what meaning; to what effect.

6. to what degree, extent, or amount; as, *how* long shall we suffer these indignities? *how* much better is knowledge than gold?

7. at what price; as, *how* is flour selling?

8. what: usually a request to repeat something said. [Colloq.]

How is also used in exclamations and relative constructions, and as an intensive.

how now? how is that? what is the meaning of this?

how so? how is it so? why?

how then? (a) what is the meaning of this? (b) how else?

how, *interj.* an exclamation of greeting attributed to, and still used humorously in imitation of, American Indians.

how, *n.* the way of doing; manner; method.

how, *n.* 1. any hollow place; the hold of a ship. [Obs.]

2. a glen; a dell; a plain. [Scot.]

how·adj′i, *n.* [Ar. *khawāja*; Per. *kh′āja*, a merchant, rich gentleman.] a merchant or traveler: so called in some parts of the East.

how bē′it, *adv.* 1. however it may be; nevertheless. [Archaic.]

2. although. [Obs.]

Howbeit we must be cast upon a certain island. —Acts xxvii. 26.

how′dȧh, *n.* [Hind. *haudah*, from Ar. *haudaj*, a litter carried by a camel or elephant.] a canopied seat on the back of an elephant or camel, for two or more persons to ride in: also spelled *houdah*.

HOWDAH

how′die, how′dy, *n.* a midwife. [Scot.]

how′-dö-yoū-dö′, how′-d′ye-dö′, *n.* an annoying or awkward situation: usually preceded by *fine, pretty, nice*, etc. [Colloq.]

How dö yoū dö? How is your health?: a conventionalized expression of greeting, used when meeting a person or being introduced.

how′dy, *interj.* a familiar form of greeting; a contraction of *how do ye*, or *how do you* (*do*). [Dial. or Colloq.]

how·e′er′, *adv.* and *conj.* however.

how′el, *n.* [compare Dan. *hövl*, G. *hobel*, a plane.] a plane with a convex sole, used by coopers for smoothing the insides of barrels.

how′el, *v.t.* to smooth with a howel.

how′ell, *n.* the upper stage in a furnace for firing porcelain.

how·ev′ẽr, *adv.* 1. in whatever manner; by whatever means; as, *however* good or bad it may be.

2. to whatever degree or extent.

how·ev′ẽr, *conj.* nevertheless; notwithstanding: yet; still; though: used in a clause or sentence that could properly begin with *but*.

howff, houff, *n.* a haunt; a place of resort. [Scot.]

how′itz·ẽr, *n.* [G. *haubitze*, from Bohem. *haufnice*, a howitzer, originally a sling.] a short cannon with a low muzzle velocity, firing shells in a relatively high trajectory.

HOWITZER

howk, houk, *v.t.* and *v.i.* to dig; to hollow out by digging; to burrow. [Scot.]

how′kẽr, *n.* same as *hooker*.

howl, *v.i.*; howled, *pt., pp.*; howling, *ppr.* [ME. *howlen, houlen*, to howl, an imitative word.]

1. to utter the long, loud, wailing cry of wolves, dogs, etc.

2. to utter a loud, mournful sound, expressive of anger, grief, or distress; to wail.

Howl ye, for the day of the Lord is at hand. —Isa. xiii. 6.

3. to make a similar sound, as the wind.

4. to shout or laugh in scorn, mirth, etc.

howling monkey; any of a group of long-tailed monkeys with a loud, howling cry, found in Central and South America.

one's night to howl; one's time for unrestrained pleasure.

howl, *v.t.*; howled, *pt., pp.*; howling, *ppr.* 1. to utter or speak with a howl or outcry.

2. to drive or effect by howling.

howl down; to render a speaker's words inaudible by uttering howls, catcalls, etc.

howl, *n.* 1. the cry of a dog or wolf, or other like sound.

2. the cry of a human being in anger, grief, etc.

howl′ẽr, *n.* 1. one who howls.

2. a howling monkey.

3. a stupid, ridiculous mistake.

howl′et, *n.* [Fr. *hulotte*, an owl.] an owlet: called also *houlet*. [Archaic.]

howl′ing, *a.* 1. filled with howls or howling beasts; dreary; as, in the *howling* wilderness.

2. that howls.

3. great; as, a *howling* success. [Slang.]

how′līte, *n.* [named after Henry *How*, a Nova Scotian mineralogist.] in mineralogy, a chalky calcium borosilicate.

howm, *n.* a lowland by a waterside; a holm. [Scot.]

how′ry, *a.* dirty; nasty. [Brit. Dial.]

how·sō·ev′ẽr, *adv.* 1. to whatever degree or extent; however.

2. by whatever means; in whatever manner.

how′-tö′, *a.* [from the phrase *how to make* (or *do*) *something*.] giving elementary instruction in some handicraft, hobby, etc.; as, a *how-to* book. [Colloq.]

hox, *v.t.* to hock. [Obs.]

hoy, *n.* [Fl. *hui*, a hoy, a lighter.]

1. a small fore-and-aft rigged vessel resembling a sloop, no longer used.

2. a heavy barge.

hoy, *interj.* [ME.] an exclamation to attract attention, drive hogs, etc.

hoy, *n.* a shout of "hoy."

hoy, *v.t.* to incite; pursue. [Scot.]

Hoy′ȧ, *n.* [named after Thomas *Hoy*, an English gardener.] a genus of tropical climbing shrubs of the milkweed family, cultivated for their gaudy flowers.

hoy′den, *n.* [Early Mod. Eng., orig., awkward man; perh. phonetic sp. of D. *heiden*, heathen; cf. phrase *little heathen*.] a bold, boisterous girl; a tomboy: also spelled *hoiden*.

hoy′den, *a.* bold and boisterous; tomboyish: also spelled *hoiden*.

hoy′den, *v.i.* to behave like a hoyden: also spelled *hoiden*.

hoy′den·ish, *a.* of or like a hoyden; bold and boisterous; tomboyish: also spelled *hoidenish*.

Hoyle (hoil), *n.* a book of rules and instructions for card games, originally compiled and edited by Edmond Hoyle (1672–1769), English authority on card games and chess.

according to Hoyle; according to the rules and regulations; in the prescribed, fair, or correct way.

hoy′măn, *n.* one who navigates a hoy.

Hras′vēlg, *n.* in Scandinavian mythology, the huge eagle that watches by the root of the Tree of the World, to devour the dead.

huȧ·rä′cheṣ (hȧ-rä′chiz; *Sp.* wä-rä′chās), *n. pl.* [Am. Sp.] Mexican sandals, made of straps or woven leather strips.

Huäs′tek (wäs′tek), *n.* [from native name.] an American Indian language of Mexico that constitutes, with its dialect, a distinct branch of the Mayan family of languages.

hub, *n.* [a form of *hob*.]

1. the center part of a wheel.

HUBS OF WHEELS

2. a center of interest, importance, or activity.

3. the hilt of a weapon. [Rare.]

4. a roughness, as in a road. [Rare.]

5. a block used to scotch wheels.

6. a peg or hob at which quoits are pitched.

7. in plumbing, a short pipe for coupling ends.

8. a steel punch for impressing designs on coins, dies, etc.

hub plank; a guard plank along a bridge truss, placed at hub height.

the Hub; a nickname for Boston.

up to the hub; to a great extent; deeply involved; as, a man is in debt *up to the hub*.

hub′-band, *n.* a metal band to protect a wooden hub.

Hub′bīte, *n.* a resident of the Hub, or Boston [Humorous.]

hub′ble, *n.* 1. a small hump.

2. confusion; uproar. [Brit. Dial.]

hub′ble-bub″ble, *n.* [echoic.] 1. an East Indian hookah, or water pipe, with bowl made of a coconut shell, so constructed that the tobacco smoke passes through water, making the noise from which it is named.

2. a continuous sound of bubbling.

3. hubbub; uproar.

HUBBLE-BUBBLE

hub′ble·shōw, *n.* confusion or uproar. [Brit. Dial.]

hub′bly, *a.* filled with hubbles; rough.

hub′bub, *n.* a confused sound of many voices; a tumult; uproar.

hub′by, *n.*; *pl.* **hub′bieṣ,** husband: familiar diminutive. [Colloq.]

hub′by, *a.* having hubs and ruts, as a frozen or sun-baked mud road.

hub′-deep, *a.* having depth equal to the height of a hub; as, the mire is *hub-deep*.

hub′nẽr·īte, *n.* [after Adolf *Hübner*, a German chemist.] in mineralogy, a dark-colored manganese tungstate, $MnWO_4$, isomorphous with wolframite.

hū′bris, *n.* [Gr. *hybris*.] wanton insolence or arrogance resulting from excessive pride or from passion.

Hub′shee, *n.* [Per. *Habshi*, an Abyssinian.] an Abyssinian; an Ethiopian.

huç·ȧ·toon′, *n.* [Fr. *hoqueton*, jacket.] a cotton fabric designed for the African trade.

huçh, hu′çhen, *n.* [G.] a large salmon found in the Danube: called also *bull trout*.

huck, *v.i.* to haggle in trading. [Obs.]

huck, *n.* huckaback. [Colloq.]

huck′ȧ·back, *n.* [Early Mod. Eng. *hugaback, hagabag*, suggest association with *back* or *bag*.] a coarse linen or cotton cloth with a rough surface, used for toweling.

huç′kle, *n.* [a dim. from obs. *huck*, a hip.]

1. the hip.

2. a bunch or projection resembling the hip.

huç′kle·backed (-bakt), *a.* having round shoulders; hunchbacked.

huç′kle·ber″ry, *n.*; *pl.* **huç′kle·ber″rieṣ,** [corruption of *whortleberry*, from AS. *wyrtil*, a small shrub, and *berie*, berry.]

1. any of a number of related shrubs having dark-blue berries resembling blueberries.

2. the fruit of any of these shrubs.

3. loosely, a blueberry.

huç′kle·bōne, *n.* 1. the hipbone.

2. the astragalus or upper anklebone.

huck′stẽr, *n.* [ME. *hokestere*, from or akin to MD. *hokester, hoekster*; prob. from *hoek, hoke*, a corner.]

1. a peddler or hawker of wares, especially of fruits, vegetables, etc.

2. a mean, haggling tradesman; a tricky, mercenary peddler.

3. an advertising man. [Colloq.]

huck′stẽr, *v.t.*; huckstered, *pt., pp.*; huckstering, *ppr.* 1. to peddle; to sell.

2. to bargain in or haggle over.

huck′stẽr·ẽr, *n.* a huckster.

huck′stress, *n.* a female peddler.

hud, *n.* the shell or hull of a nut. [Brit. Dial.]

hud′dle, *v.i.*; huddled, *pt., pp.*; huddling, *ppr.* [orig. (16th c.), to put out of sight; perh. var. of ME. *hoderen* in same sense (from base of *hide*).]

1. to crowd close together; to nestle together in a heap; as, animals *huddle* together from fear or for warmth.

2. to draw or hunch oneself up in a heap.

3. in football, to gather in a huddle.

hud′dle, *v.t.* 1. to crowd close together.

2. to hunch or draw (oneself) up.

3. to do, put, or make hastily and carelessly.

4. to push or thrust in a hurried or disordered manner; as, he *huddled* the children into the automobile.

hud′dle, *n.* 1. a confused crowd or heap of persons or things.

2. confusion; muddle; jumble.

3. in football, a grouping of a team behind the line of scrimmage to receive signals before a play.

4. a private conference; secret discussion. [Slang.]

to go into a huddle; to have a private conference or secret discussion. [Slang.]

hud′dlẽr, *n.* one who huddles or throws things into confusion; a bungler.

hud·dup′, *interj.* a command to a horse, urging him to get up and go forward.

Hū·di·bras′tiç, *a.* like, or in the style of, Samuel Butler's *Hudibras*, a mock-heroic satirical poem (1663–1678) in tetrameter couplets, ridiculing the Puritans.

Hud·sō′ni·ȧ, *n.* a genus of cistaceous plants of the eastern United States, of which the heath is typical.

Hud·sō′ni·ăn, *a.* relating to the explorer Henry Hudson or to the bay or river discovered by him.

Hud′sŏn sēal, the skin or fur of the muskrat dyed to resemble that of the seal.

hūe, *n.* [ME. *hew, hewe*; AS. *hiw, heow*, form, appearance, color.]

1. color.

Painted in heavenly *hues* above.—Byron.

2. a particular variety of a color; shade; tint.

hūe, *n.* [OFr. *hu, hui, heu*, a hunting cry.] a vociferous cry; clamor: now used only in the phrase *hue and cry*.

hue and cry; [Anglo-Norm. *hu e cri.*] (a) originally, a loud shout or cry by those pursuing a felon: all who heard were obliged to join in the pursuit; also, the pursuit itself; (b) any loud outcry or clamor.

hūed, *a.* having some (specified) shade or intensity of color or (a specified number of) colors: used in hyphenated compounds, as rosy-*hued*, many-*hued*.

hūe′less, *a.* without color.

hū′ẽr, *n.* one whose business is to cry out or give an alarm; specifically, a fisherman stationed on a high point to give notice of the approach of a shoal of fish or of their movements.

huff, *n.* 1. a sudden burst of anger, resentment, arrogance, petulance, etc.

2. one swelled with a false opinion of his own value or importance.

Lewd, shallow-brained *huffs* make atheism and contempt of religion the badge of wit. —South.

3. in checkers, the removal of a player's piece from the board after neglect to capture his adversary's piece.

4. a light, puffy pie crust. [Brit. Dial.]

huff, *v.t.*; huffed (huft), *pt., pp.*; huffing, *ppr.* 1. to cause to swell up; to distend or puff up. [Obs.]

2. to treat with arrogance; to show an insolent manner toward.

3. in checkers, to remove from the board, as a forfeited or captured piece.

4. to make angry; offend.

huff, *v.i.* 1. to swell up; to become distended. [Brit. Dial.]

2. to puff up with anger, conceit, or arrogance; hence, to storm; to rave; to bluster.

A *huffing*, shining, flattering, cringing coward. —Otway.

huff′çap, *n.* a swaggerer; a bully. [Obs.]

huff′çap, *a.* swaggering; blustering. [Obs.]

huff′ẽr, *n.* a swaggerer; a blusterer; a huff. [Obs.]

huff′i·ly, *adv.* in a huffy manner.

huff′i·ness, *n.* the state of being huffy.

huff′ing·ly, *adv.* in a petulant manner; swaggeringly. [Rare.]

huff′ish, *a.* 1. peevish; quick-tempered; petulant.

2. inclined to be arrogant. [Obs.]

huff′ish·ly, *adv.* in a huffish manner.

huff′ish·ness, *n.* the state of being huffish.

huff′y, *a.*; *comp.* huffier; *superl.* huffiest. 1. swelled; distended; puffed up; as, the bread is *huffy*. [Obs.]

2. filled with pride, arrogance, or conceit; swaggering. [Obs.]

3. easily offended; touchy.

4. angered or offended.

hug, *v.t.*; hugged, *pt., pp.*; hugging, *ppr.* [prob. via dial., from ON. *hugga*, to comfort, console; akin to AS. *hycgan*, to think.]

1. to put the arms around and hold closely and fondly; to embrace tightly and affectionately.

2. (a) to squeeze tightly between the forelegs: said of a bear; (b) to squeeze tightly with the arms.

3. to cling to or cherish (a belief, opinion, etc.).

4. to keep close to; as, the automobile *hugged* the curb.

hug, *v.i.* to clasp or embrace one another closely.

hug, *n.* 1. a close, affectionate embrace.

2. a tight clasp or hold with the arms, as in wrestling.

3. a bear's squeeze.

hūġe, *a.*; *comp.* huger; *superl.* hugest. [ME. *huge, hoge, hogge, hoghe*, from OFr. *ahoge, ahuge*, great, large, huge.]

1. having an immense bulk; very large or great; enormous; as, a *huge* mountain, a *huge* ox.

2. very great in any respect; possessing some one characteristic in a high degree; as, a *huge* space, a *huge* difference.

He took the *hugest* pains to adorn his big person. —Thackeray.

Syn.—enormous, gigantic, colossal, immense, prodigious.

hūġe′ly, *adv.* very greatly; enormously.

hūġe′ness, *n.* the state or condition of being huge.

hug′gẽr, *n.* one who hugs.

hug′gẽr, *v.t.* and *v.i.* to lie in ambush; to conceal. [Obs.]

hug′gẽr-mug″gẽr, *v.t.* to hush up; to smother or cover up.

hug′gẽr-mug″gẽr, *v.i.* to act in a secret way; to consult secretly.

hug′gẽr-mug″gẽr, *a.* 1. hidden; secret; underhanded. [Archaic.]

2. confused; disordered; muddled.

hug′gẽr-mug″gẽr, *n.* 1. concealment; secrecy. [Archaic.]

2. a confusion; jumble; muddle.

hug′gle, *v.t.* [freq. of *hug.*] to hug; to cuddle; to snuggle. [Obs.]

Hū′gue·not (-ge-), *n.* [Fr.; earlier *eiguenot, eydguenot*, from G. *eidgenosse*, sworn companion, confederate; influenced by Besançon *Hugues*, a Geneva reformer.] any French Protestant of the sixteenth or seventeenth century.

Hū′gue·not·ism, *n.* the doctrines, beliefs, or practices of the Huguenots; French protestantism.

hū′ġy, *a.* vast. [Obs.]

huh, *interj.* an exclamation used to express contempt, derision, surprise, etc., or to ask a question.

hu′iä bĩrd, [native name.] in zoology, a starling of New Zealand, the *Heteralocha acutirostris*: named from its note.

hūke, *n.* [OFr. *huque, hucque*; O.D. *huycke*, a cloak, mantle.] a hooded cape worn in the fifteenth century. [Obs.]

hu′lȧ-hu′lȧ, *n.* [Hawaiian.] a native Hawaiian dance performed by women: also *hula*.

hulch, *n.* a hunch. [Obs.]

hulch′y, *a.* bent; humped. [Obs.]

hulk, *n.* [ME. *hulke*; AS. *hulc*; LL. *hulka, hulca, olca*; Gr. *holkas*, a ship which is towed, a ship of burden.]

1. (a) originally, any ship; (b) a big, unwieldy ship.

2. the body of a ship, especially if old and dismantled.

3. [*usually pl.*] an old, dismantled ship or one specially built and not intended to be seagoing, formerly used as a prison.

4. a big, clumsy person or thing.

hulk, *v.i.* 1. to rise bulkily (usually with *up*).

2. to slouch or lounge about in a heavy, clumsy manner. [Dial.]

hulk, *v.t.*; hulked, *pt., pp.*; hulking, *ppr.* 1. to take out the entrails of; as, to *hulk* a hare. [Rare.]

2. in mining, to remove the loose material lying between the walls of a vein.

hulk′ing, *a.* [ppr. of *hulk.*] big and clumsy; bulky and unwieldy.

hulk′y, *a.* hulking.

hull, *n.* [ME. *hule, hole, hoole*; AS. *hulu*, hull, husk.]

1. the outer covering of a seed or fruit, as the husk of grain, pod of peas, shell of nuts, etc.

2. the calyx of some fruits, as the raspberry, strawberry, etc.

3. any outer covering.

4. the frame or body of a ship, excluding the spars, sails, and rigging.

5. the frame or main body of a flying boat or amphibian, on which it floats when in the water.

hull down; far enough away so that the hull is below the horizon: said of a ship.

hull, *v.t.*; hulled, *pt., pp.*; hulling, *ppr.* 1. to strip off or separate the hull or hulls of; as, to *hull* grain.

2. to pierce the hull of with a shell, torpedo, etc.

hull, *v.i.* to float or drive on the water, like the hull of a ship, without sails. [Obs.]

hul′lȧ·bȧ·lo͞o″, *n.* [echoic duplication based on *hullo, hallo.*] loud noise and confusion; clamor; uproar; hubbub.

hulled, *a.* stripped of the hulls.

hulled corn; corn prepared for food by the removal of the hulls; hominy.

hull′ẽr, *n.* one who or that which hulls; specifically, a hulling machine.

hul·lō′, *interj., n., v.t.* and *v.i.* same as *hello*.

hul′ly, *n.* a wicker eel trap; a perforated box for keeping crabs, etc. in the water. [Brit. Dial.]

hū′lō·thē·ism, hū′lō·ist, *n.* same as *hylotheism, hylotheist*.

hul′vẽr, *n.* [ME. *hulver, holver, hulfere*, holly; ON. *hulfr*, dogwood.] holly, an evergreen shrub or tree. [Now Dial.]

hum, *v.i.*; hummed, *pt., pp.*; humming, *ppr.* [of imitative origin.]

1. to make a low, continuous, murmuring sound like that of a bee, a revolving electric fan, etc.

2. to make a confused, droning sound: as, the room *hummed* with voices.

3. to express approval or dissent by an inarticulate murmur.

4. to sing with closed lips, not saying the words.

5. to be busy or full of activity. [Colloq.]

hum, *v.t.* 1. to sing (a tune, etc.) with the lips closed, not saying the words.

2. to produce an effect on by humming; as, to *hum* a child to sleep.

hum, *n.* 1. any low, inarticulate, monotonous, murmuring, whirring, or buzzing sound, as that made by bees in flight, by a spinning top, or by a crowd of people at a distance; any distant, continuous, confused sound.

2. a low, inarticulate sound uttered by a person as an expression of embarrassment, doubt, pleasure, surprise, or the like; as, *hums* and haws.

3. a strong ale or mixture of ale and spirit. [Obs.]

venous hum; a hum heard in auscultation of a vein, as in anemia.

hum, *n.* a humbug; a hoax. [Colloq.]

hum, *interj.* 1. a conventionalized expression of the sound made when clearing the throat to attract attention or show doubt.

2. a conventionalized expression of a sound made with closed lips to express contempt, surprise, pleasure, etc.

hum, *v.i.* 1. to make a hum (conventionalized expressions).

2. to pause or hesitate in speaking: usually in the phrase *hum and haw*.

hū′măn, *a.* [ME. *humayne*; OFr. *humaine*; L. *humanus*; akin to *homo*, a man, *humus*, soil.]

1. of or characteristic of a person or persons; such as people have.

2. having the form or nature of a person; that is a person; consisting of people.

3. having or showing the qualities characteristic of people.

hū′măn, *n.* a human being.

hū′măn·āte, *a.* made human. [Obs.]

hū·māne′, *a.* [earlier var. of *human*; now usually associated directly with L. *humanus*.]

1. having what are considered the best qualities of mankind; kind, tender, merciful, considerate, etc.

2. civilizing; refining; humanizing; as, *humane* learning.

hū·māne′ly, *adv.* in a humane manner.

hū·māne′ness, *n.* the quality of being humane.

hū′măn·iṣm, *n.* 1. the quality of being human; human nature.

2. any system or way of thought or action concerned with the interests and ideals of people.

3. the study of the humanities.

4. [H–] the intellectual and cultural movement that stemmed from the study of classical Greek and Latin literature and culture during the Middle Ages and was one of the factors giving rise to the Renaissance: it was characterized by an emphasis on human interests rather than on the natural world or religion.

hū′măn·ist, *n.* 1. a student of human nature and human affairs.

2. a student of the humanities.

3. [H–] a student of Latin and Greek culture; especially, any Renaissance scholar who was a follower of Humanism.

hū′măn·ist, *a.* of humanism or the humanities; humanistic.

hū·măn·is′tiç, *a.* of, belonging to, or characterizing humanism, the humanists, the humanities, or humanity.

hū·măn·is′tiç·ăl·ly, *adv.* in a humanistic manner.

hū·man·i·tā′ri·ăn, *n.* 1. a person devoted to promoting the welfare of humanity, especially through the elimination of pain and suffering; a philanthropist.

2. an adherent of humanitarianism (senses 2 and 3).

hū·man·i·tā′ri·ăn, *a.* of, belonging to, or characteristic of humanitarians or humanitarianism; philanthropic.

hū·man·i·tā′ri·ăn·iṣm, *n.* 1. the beliefs or actions of humanitarians (sense 1).

2. in ethics, (a) the doctrine that man's obligations are limited to the welfare of mankind; (b) the doctrine that man may perfect his own nature without the aid of divine grace.

3. in theology, the doctrine that denies the divinity of Jesus.

hū·man′i·ty, *n.*; *pl.* **hū·man′i·tieṣ,** [ME. *humanitye*; OFr. *humanite*; L. *humanitas* (*-atis*), human nature, the condition of being a man, from *humanus*, pertaining to man, from *homo* (*-inis*), a man.]

1. the fact or quality of being human; the peculiar nature of man, by which he is distinguished from other beings.

2. mankind collectively; the human race.

Humanity must perforce prey on itself.
—Shak.

3. the fact or quality of being humane; the kind feelings, dispositions, and sympathies of man; kindness; benevolence.

4. mental cultivation; liberal education; instruction in classical and polite literature. [Archaic.]

5. [*pl.*] human qualities; characteristics of human beings, especially those considered desirable.

the humanities; (a) languages and literature, especially the classical Greek and Latin; (b) the branches of learning concerned with human thought and relations, as distinguished from the sciences; especially, literature and philosophy, and, often, the fine arts, history, etc.

hū·măn·i·zā′tion, *n.* the act of humanizing or the state of being humanized.

hū′măn·īze, *v.t.*; humanized, *pt.*, *pp.*; humanizing, *ppr.* 1. to make humane; to subdue any tendency to cruelty and make kind, merciful, considerate, etc.; civilize; refine.

Was it the business of magic to *humanize*
our natures? —Addison.

2. to make human; to give a human character or expression to; to invest with the character of humanity.

hū′măn·īze, *v.i.* to grow civilized; to become human or humane.

hū′măn·ī·zẽr, *n.* one who or that which humanizes.

hū′măn·kīnd, *n.* the race of man; mankind; the human species.

hū′măn·ly, *adv.* 1. in a human manner.

2. within human ability or knowledge; by human means.

3. according to the experience or knowledge of human beings; from a human viewpoint.

hū′măn·ness, *n.* human condition or quality.

hū′măn·oid, *a.* [*human*, and *-oid*.] nearly human, as in appearance or behavior.

hū′măn·oid, *n.* a nearly human creature; specifically, (a) any of the earliest ancestors of modern man; (b) in science fiction, a living, reasoning creature inhabiting another planet.

hū′māte, *n.* [*humic* and *-ate*.] a salt or ester of humic acid.

hū·mā′tion, *n.* [L. *humatio*, from *humare*, to cover with earth, bury, from *humus*, ground, earth.] interment; burial. [Obs.]

hum′bird, *n.* the hummingbird. [Obs.]

hum′ble, *a.*; *comp.* humbler; *superl.* humblest. [ME. *humble*; OFr. *humble*, *humle*, *humele*; L. *humilis*, low, small, slight, from *humus*, earth, ground.]

1. having or showing a consciousness of one's defects or shortcomings; not proud; not self-assertive; modest.

2. low in condition, rank, or position; lowly; unpretentious; as, a *humble* home.

Syn.—lowly, meek, submissive, unassuming, unobtrusive, unpretending.

hum′ble, *v.t.*; humbled, *pt.*, *pp.*; humbling, *ppr.* 1. to bring down; to lower in condition, rank, or position; to abase; as, the power of Rome was *humbled*.

2. to make humble or lowly in mind; to abase the pride of; to reduce the arrogance and self-dependence of; in a religious sense, to make meek and submissive to the divine will: often used reflexively.

Syn.—humiliate, lower, mortify, disgrace.

hum′ble, hum′mel, *v.t.* [Scot. *hummel*, *hummle*, having no horns.]

1. to break. [Rare.]

2. to break off the awns of (barley). [Scot.]

3. to break off the horns of. [Scot.]

hum′ble, hum′mel, *a.* 1. bruised. [Obs.]

2. without horns; as, a *humble* cow. [Scot.]

hum′ble·bee, *n.* [ME. *humbylbee*, from *hum(b)len*, to keep on humming (from *hummen*, to hum, and *-le*, freq. suffix), and *bee*.] a bumblebee.

hum′ble·ness, *n.* the state or quality of being humble; humility; meekness.

hum′ble pīe, [earlier *umble pie*, from *umbles*, entrails of a deer; ME. and OFr. *nombles*, from L. *lumbulus*, dim. of *lumbus*, loin.] formerly, a pie made of the inner parts of a deer, served to the servants after a hunt.

to eat humble pie; to undergo humiliation, especially that of admitting one's error and apologizing.

hum′ble plant, a sensitive plant, *Mimosa pudica*.

hum′blẽr, *n.* he who or that which humbles; one who reduces pride or mortifies.

hum′bleṣ (-blz), *n.pl.* entrails of a deer: written also *umbles*. [Obs.]

hum′bly, *adv.* 1. in a humble manner; with modest submissiveness; with humility.

Hope *humbly* then; with trembling pinions
soar;
Wait the great teacher, death, and God
adore. —Pope.

2. in a low state or condition.

Hum′bōldt çur′rent (-bōlt), [after Baron Alexander von *Humboldt*; see next entry.] the cold ocean current flowing north along the coasts of Chile and Peru.

hum′bōldt·ine (-bōlt-), *n.* [from Baron Alexander von *Humboldt* (1769–1859), German mineralogist, and *-ine*.] an oxalate of iron occurring in coal.

hum′bug, *n.* [18th-c. slang; orig. reference lost.]

1. (a) something made or done to cheat or deceive; fraud; sham; hoax; (b) misleading, dishonest, or empty talk.

2. a dishonest person; a person who does not live up to his claims; an impostor.

3. a spirit of trickery, deception, etc.

hum′bug, *v.t.*; humbugged, *pt.*, *pp.*; humbugging, *ppr.* to deceive; to dupe; to cheat.

hum′bug, *v.i.* to practice deceit.

hum′bug″gẽr, *n.* one who humbugs.

hum′bug″gẽr·y, *n.* the practice of imposition and fraud; pretense; sham; deception.

hum·ding′ẽr, *n.* [prob. fanciful coinage.] a person or thing considered excellent of its kind. [Slang.]

hum′drum, *a.* [echoic extension of *hum*.] having no variety; dull; monotonous.

hum′drum, *n.* 1. a humdrum person.

2. humdrum talk, routine, etc.; monotony.

hum″dudġ′eŏn, hum″dūr′ġeŏn, *n.* [*hum*, an imposition, and *dudgeon*, anger.] an outcry or complaint about a trifle. [Scot. Slang.]

hū·meçt′, hū·meç′tāte, *v.t.* [L. *humectatus*, pp. of *humectare*, to moisten, wet.] to moisten; to wet; to water. [Rare.]

hū·meç′tănt, *a.* moistening; diluent. [Obs.]

hū·meç′tănt, *n.* a substance added or applied to another to help it retain moisture.

hū·meç·tā′tion, *n.* the act of moistening, wetting, or watering. [Rare.]

hu′mẽr·ăl, *a.* [Mod. L. *humeralis*, from L. *humerus*.]

1. of or near the humerus.

2. of or near the shoulder or shoulders.

humeral veil; in the Roman Catholic Church; a narrow veil worn round the shoulders at Mass by the officiating priest or a subdeacon.

hu″mẽr·ō·ab·dom′i·năl, *a.* relating to the humerus and the abdomen.

hū′me·rus, *n.*; *pl.* **hū′me·rī,** [L. *humerus*, *umerus*, the shoulder, upper part of the arm.]

1. the bone of the upper arm or forelimb, extending from the shoulder to the elbow; also, that part of the arm or limb containing the humerus.

2. the femur of the anterior legs of an insect; the brachium.

3. the subcostal vein of the anterior wings of certain insects of the order *Hymenoptera*.

hum′hum, *n.* [E. Ind.] a kind of plain, coarse Indian cloth, made of cotton.

hū′miç, *a.* [L. *humus*, the earth, soil.] relating to or derived from humus, or mold; as, *humic* acid.

hū′mid, *a.* [L. *humidus*, *umidus*, moist, from *humere*, *umere*, to be moist.] moist, damp; specifically, containing much water vapor; as, *humid* air or atmosphere.

hū·mid″i·fi·çā′tion, *n.* a humidifying or being humidified.

hū·mid′i·fī·ẽr, *n.* anything that humidifies; specifically, a device for keeping air moist.

hū·mid′i·fȳ, *v.t.*; humidified, *pt.*, *pp.*; humidifying, *ppr.* to make humid; to dampen; to moisten.

humidified air; air whose moisture content has been brought to a definite desired percentage.

hū·mid′i·stat, *n.* [*humidity*, and *-stat*.] an automatic device for controlling the extent to which a humidifier or dehumidifier modifies the relative humidity.

hū·mid′i·ty, *n.* [ME. *humidytee*; OFr. *humidite*; L. *humiditas* (*-atis*), dampness, moisture, from *humidus*, damp.]

1. moisture; dampness.

2. the amount or degree of moisture in the air.

relative humidity; the amount of moisture in the air as compared with the amount that the air could contain at the same temperature, expressed as a percentage.

hū′mid·ness, *n.* humidity.

hū′mid·or, *n.* [from *humid*.]

1. a device for keeping the air moist in a tobacco jar, case, etc.: it is often a tube containing moistened sponges.

2. a jar, case, etc. equipped with such a device.

hū′mi·fūse, *a.* [L. *humus*, the ground, and *fusus*, pp. of *fundere*, to pour, spread out.] in botany, trailing along the ground; procumbent; as, a *humifuse* plant.

hū′mi·fȳ, *v.t.*; humified, *pt.*, *pp.*; humifying, *ppr.* [L. *humificare*, *umifacere*, to moisten; *humere*, *umere*, to be moist, and *facere*, to make.] to make moist; to make humid.

hū·mil′i·ănt, *a.* humiliating; mortifying. [Rare.]

hū·mil′i·āte, *v.t.*; humiliated, *pt.*, *pp.*; humiliating, *ppr.* [LL. *humiliatus*, pp. of *humiliare*, to humiliate, from L. *humilis*, humble, lowly.] to humble; to lower the pride or dignity of; to hurt the feelings of by causing to be or seem foolish or contemptible; to mortify.

hū·mil·i·ā′tion, *n.* the act of humiliating or the state of being humiliated.

hū·mil′i·ā·tō·ry, *a.* humiliating or tending to humiliate.

hū·mil′i·ty, *n.*; *pl.* **hū·mil′i·tieṣ,** [OFr. *humilite*; L. *humilitas* (*-atis*), lowness, meanness, baseness, from *humilis*, lowly, humble.]

1. the state or quality of being humble of mind or spirit; absence of pride or self-assertion.

2. [*pl.*] acts of self-abasement.

hū′min, *n.* [*humus* and *-in*.] a dark-colored, bitter compound derived from humus: also called *humic acid*, *gein*, *ulmin*, etc.

hū·mī′rī, *n.* [native name.] a small Brazilian tree, *Humiria floribunda*, yielding balsam.

Hūm′iṣm, *n.* the system of ideas or the teachings of David Hume (1711–1776), Scottish philosopher whose skepticism restricted knowledge to experience of ideas and impressions and denied the possibility of ultimately verifying their truth.

Hū̆m′ist, *n.* a follower of David Hume.

hūm′ite, *n.* [named after Sir Abraham *Hume.*] a variety of chondrodite, a gem of a reddish-brown color and a resinous luster, crystallized in octahedrons, much modified by truncation and bevelment.

hum′mel, *a.* see fourth *humble.*

hum′mel, *v.t.* see third *humble.*

hum′mel·ẽr, *n.* one who or that which hummels; specifically, an instrument or machine for separating the awns of barley from the seed. [Brit. Dial.]

hum′mẽr, *n.* 1. one who or that which hums.
2. a hummingbird.
3. a person or thing surpassing others in liveliness and energy. [Old Slang.]

hum′ming, *n.* a low, buzzing noise.

hum′ming, *a.* 1. producing a low, buzzing noise.
2. having a frothy appearance arising from effervescence; as, *humming* beer. [Colloq.]
3. having great activity or intensity; spirited; agitated; brisk. [Colloq.]

hum′ming·bīrd, *n.* any of a group of very small, brightly colored birds constituting the family *Trochilidæ,* with a long, slender bill and narrow wings that vibrate rapidly and make a humming sound in flight: they feed upon the nectar of flowers and small insects.
hummingbird bush; a leguminous shrub of South America, the flowers of which attract hummingbirds.
hummingbird moth; same as *hawk moth.*

HUMMINGBIRD (*Ornismya ornata*)

hum′mŏck, *n.* [earlier also *hammock*; orig. naut.; perh. from base of *hump,* and nautical *-ock.*]
1. a low, rounded hill; knoll; hillock.
2. a ridge or bump in an ice field.
3. a tract of wooded land, higher than a near-by swamp or marsh.

hum′mŏck·ing, *n.* the forming of hummocks by floating masses of ice pressing against and rising one above another.

hum′mŏck·y, *a.* 1. full of hummocks.
2. like a hummock.

hum′mum, *n.* [Ar. *hammām,* hot bath.] a turkish bath.

hū′mŏr, (*or* ū′), *n.* [OFr. *humor,* from L. *humor,* moisture, from *humere, umere,* to be moist.]
1. originally, any fluid or juice of an animal or plant; especially, any of the four fluids (*cardinal humors*) formerly considered responsible for one's health and disposition; blood, phlegm, choler (yellow bile), or melancholy (black bile).
2. (a) a person's disposition or temperament; (b) a mood; state of mind.
3. whim; fancy; caprice.
4. the quality that makes something seem funny, amusing, or ludicrous; comicality.
5. (a) the ability to perceive, appreciate, or express what is funny, amusing, or ludicrous; (b) the expression of this in speech, writing, or action. Usually distinguished from *wit.*
6. any chronic disease of the skin, supposedly caused by a bad blood condition.
7. any fluid or fluidlike substance of the body; blood, lymph, bile, etc.; as, the aqueous *humor.*
out of humor; vexed; crusty; crabbed.
Syn.—mood, disposition, temper, fancy, caprice, wit, pleasantry.

hū′mŏr (*or* ū′), *v.t.*; humored, *pt., pp.*; humoring, *ppr.* 1. to gratify by yielding to the particular inclination, humor, wish, or desire of; to indulge; to manage by concession or compliance; as, to *humor* the sick, the infirm, and the aged.
2. to adapt oneself to.
Syn.—gratify, indulge, favor, pamper, please.

hū′mŏr·ăl, *a.* [Fr., from L. *humor.*] pertaining to or proceeding from the humors of the body; as, a *humoral* fever.

hū′mŏr·ăl·iṣm, *n.* 1. the state of being humoral.
2. same as *humorism,* sense 1.

hū′mŏr·ăl·ist, *n.* one who believes in the theory of humorism.

hū·mŏr·esque′ (-esk′), *n.* [G. *humoreske,* from L. *humor.*] a light, fanciful, playful, or humorous musical composition; caprice.

hū′mŏr·iṣm, *n.* 1. the obsolete theory that all diseases originate in the humors of the body.
2. the spirit or disposition of a humorist.

hū′mŏr·ist, *n.* 1. one who conducts himself according to his own inclination or bent of mind; one who gratifies his own humor. [Archaic.]
2. one who indulges in humor in speaking or writing; one who is skilled in the literary expression of humor.
3. one who has a well-developed sense of humor; a wag; a droll.
4. a humoralist. [Obs.]

hū·mŏr·is′tiç, *a.* pertaining to a humorist.

hū′mŏr·less, *a.* without humor.

hū′mŏr·ous, *a.* [LL. *humorosus,* moist; also Eng. *humor* and *-ous.*]
1. having or expressing humor; funny; amusing; comical; droll.
2. whimsical; capricious. [Archaic.]
3. (a) moist; (b) humoral. [Obs.]

hū′mŏr·ous·ly, *adv.* 1. capriciously; whimsically; in conformity with one's humor.
We resolve by halves, rashly and *humorously.* —Calamy.
2. wittily; pleasantly; jocosely; in a manner to excite mirth or laughter.

hū′mŏr·ous·ness, *n.* 1. the state or quality of being humorous; a sense of humor; jocularity.
2. fickleness; capriciousness.

hū′mŏr·sŏme, *a.* 1. influenced by the humor of the moment; capricious.
2. odd; humorous; adapted to excite laughter. [Scot. and Brit. Dial.]

hū′mŏur, *n.* and *v.t.* humor: British spelling.

hump, *n.* [17th c.; probably from international nautical usage; cf. L.G. *hump,* a heap, hill.]
1. a rounded, protruding lump, as the fleshy mass on the back of a camel: in man, a hump is caused by a deformity of the spine.
2. a hummock; mound.
3. a fit of melancholy. [Brit. Slang.]

hump, *v.t.* 1. to cause to assume the shape of a hump; to arch; hunch; as, the cat *humped* its back.
2. to exert (oneself). [Slang.]

hump′back, *n.* 1. a humped, deformed back.
2. a humpbacked person.
3. in zoology, (a) a whale of the genus *Megaptera,* having a hump on its back; (b) a species of small salmon of the genus *Oncorhynchus,* of the American Pacific coast.

hump′backed (-bakt), *a.* having a humped back.

humped (humpt), *a.* having a hump or humps; humpbacked.

humph, *interj.* a snorting or grunting sound expressing doubt, surprise, disdain, disgust, etc.

hump′-shōul″dẽred, *a.* having humped shoulders.

Hump′ty Dump′ty, the personified egg of a well-known nursery rhyme, represented as a short, squat person.

hump′y, *a.* 1. having humps; humped.
2. like a hump.

hump′y, *n.*; *pl.* **hump′ieṣ,** [Australian.] a hut.

hum′strum, *n.* an imperfect musical instrument or one out of tune.

hū′mus, *n.* [L., the earth, the ground, the soil.] a brown or black substance resulting from the partial decay of leaves and other vegetable matter; the organic part of the soil.

Hun, *n.* [ME. *Hunne*; AS. *Hune* (akin to ON. *Hunar*), from native name.]
1. a member of a savage Asiatic people who, led by Attila, invaded eastern and central Europe in the 4th and 5th centuries A.D.
2. [h–] any savage or destructive person; vandal: term of contempt applied to German soldiers in World War I.

hunch, *n.* [form of *hump.*]
1. a hump.
2. a chunk; lump; hunk.
3. a feeling that something is going to happen; premonition or suspicion: from the superstition that it brings good luck to touch the back of a hunchback. [Colloq.]

hunch, *v.t.*; hunched (huncht), *pt., pp.*; hunching, *ppr.* to draw (one's body, etc.) into the shape of a hump; form into a hump; as, don't *hunch* your back so.

hunch, *v.i.* to move forward jerkily; push; shove.

hunch′back, *n.* a humpback.

hunch′backed (-bakt), *a.* having a humped back.

hun′dred, *n.* [ME. *hundred, hunderd, hundrith*; AS. *hundred, hundræth,* lit., a count or tale of a hundred.]
1. the cardinal number next above ninety-nine; ten times ten; 100; C.
2. a division of an English county; originally, probably, 100 hides of land.
3. a corresponding division in the early United States, still surviving in Delaware.

hun′dred, *a.* ten times ten; as, a *hundred* men; five *hundred* dollars.

hun′dred çōurt, in England, a court held for the inhabitants of a hundred.

Hun′dred Dāys, the days from March 15 to June 28, 1815, the period between Napoleon's return to France from Elba and his final defeat and abdication.

hun′dred·ẽr, *n.* 1. a resident or freeholder of an English hundred.
2. one having the jurisdiction of a hundred.
3. in English law, a man who may be called to serve on a jury in any controversy respecting land within the hundred to which he belongs.

hun′dred·fōld, *n.* one hundred times the bulk or measure of anything.

hun′dred·fōld, *a.* 1. having a hundred parts.
2. having a hundred times as much or as many.

hun′dred·fōld, *adv.* a hundred times as much or as many: with *a* (or, British, *an*).

hun′dredth, *n.* one of one hundred equal parts of anything.

hun′dredth, *a.* 1. being the last in order of one hundred successive things.
2. consisting of one of one hundred equal parts of anything; the quotient of the division of one tenth by ten; as, the *hundredth* part of an estate.

hun′dred·wẹight, *n.* 1. in the United States, one hundred pounds.
2. formerly and still frequently in England, a weight of 112 pounds, or four quarters, each containing 28 pounds: usually denoted by *cwt.*

hung, *v.* past tense and past participle of *hang.*

Huṅ·gā′ri·ăn, *n.* [LL. *Hungaria,* Hungary, from *Hungari,* the Magyars.] a native or inhabitant of Hungary; a Magyar; also, the Finno-Ugric language of the Hungarians; Magyar.

Huṅ·gā′ri·ăn, *a.* of or relating to Hungary, the Hungarians, or the language of Hungary.

huṅ′gẽr, *n.* [AS. *hunger, hungor,* hunger.]
1. the discomfort, pain, or weakness caused by a need for food.
2. a desire, need, or appetite for food.
3. any strong desire; craving.

huṅ′gẽr, *v.i.*; hungered, *pt., pp.*; hungering, *ppr.* [ME. *hungren, hongren*; AS. *hyngran,* to hunger, from *hunger,* hunger.]
1. to feel hunger; to crave food.
2. to desire with great eagerness; to long (with *for* or *after*).
Blessed are they which do *hunger* and thirst *after* righteousness. —Matt. v. 6.

huṅ′gẽr, *v.t.* to starve; to subject to hunger.

huṅ′gẽr-bit, huṅ′gẽr-bit″ten, *a.* pained, pinched, or weakened by hunger.

huṅ′gẽred, *a.* hungry. [Obs.]

huṅ′gẽr·ẽr, *n.* one who hungers.

huṅ′gẽr flow′ẽr, the whitlow grass, *Draba incana,* growing in poor soils.

huṅ′gẽr·ly, *a.* hungry; wanting food. [Archaic.]

huṅ′gẽr·ly, *adv.* with keen appetite; hungrily. [Archaic.]

huṅ′gẽr-stärved, *a.* starved with hunger. [Obs.]

huṅ′gẽr strīke, a refusal of a prisoner, political leader, etc. to eat until the authorities grant certain demands.

huṅ′gri·ly, *adv.* with keen appetite; voraciously; in a hungry manner.

huṅ′gry, *a.*; *comp.* hungrier; *superl.* hungriest, [ME. *hungry, hungri, hungrig*; AS. *hungrig,* hungry, from *hunger,* hunger.]
1. feeling, having, or showing hunger; specifically, (a) wanting or needing food; (b) craving; eager; as, a *hungry* glance.
2. producing hunger. [Rare.]
3. not fertile; barren: said of soil.

huṅk, *n.* [prob. from Fl. *hunke,* hunk.] a large piece, lump, or slice of bread, meat, etc.; chunk.

huṅk, *n.* [D. *honk,* a post, station, home.] in some children's games, the goal; as, to be on *hunk.* [Dial.]

huṅ′kẽr, *v.i.* [cf. D. *huiken,* ON. *hokra,* to

crouch.] to squat or crouch with the body resting on the calves of the legs. [Scot.]

hun̄'kẽrṣ, *n.pl.* the haunches; the hams. [Scot.]

hun̄ks, *n.*; *pl.* **hun̄ks,** [prob. akin to D. *hondsch*, lit., doggish, stingy, G. *hündisch*.] a stingy, disagreeable, surly person; miser.

hun̄k'y, *n.* [from *Hungarian*.] a person from east central Europe; especially, a person of Hungarian extraction: also *hunkie, hunkey, hunk*: vulgar term of prejudice and contempt. [Slang.]

hun̄k'y, *a.*; *comp.* hunkier; *superl.* hunkiest, [from U.S. local *hunk*, goal, home (in tag and similar games), hence safe place, all right, from D. *honk*, a post, station, goal.]

1. all right; giving satisfaction. [Slang.]

2. even; square. [Slang.]

hun̄k'y-dō'ry, *a.* to one's satisfaction; as it should be. [Slang.]

Hun'nish, *a.* 1. of or like the Huns.

2. barbarous; savage; destructive.

hunt, *v.t.*; hunted, *pt.*, *pp.*; hunting, *ppr.* [ME. *hunten*; AS. *huntian*; prob., from base of *hentan*, to seize.]

1. to chase (game) for food or sport.

2. to search eagerly or carefully for; to try to find.

3. (a) to pursue; chase; drive; (b) to hound; harry; persecute.

4. (a) to go through (a tract of country) in pursuit of game; (b) to search (a place) carefully.

5. to use (dogs or horses) in chasing game.

6. in bell ringing, to change the order of (a bell) in a hunt.

to hunt down; (a) to pursue until successful in catching or killing; (b) to search for until successful in finding.

to hunt up; (a) to hunt for; search for; (b) to find by searching.

hunt, *v.i.* 1. to follow the chase; to go out in pursuit of game or wild animals.

2. to seek by close pursuit; to search (with *after* or *for*).

He *after* honor *hunts*, I *after* love.—Shak.

3. in machinery, to alternate between fast and slow; to run with varying speed.

4. in bell ringing, to shift the place of a bell in its set according to certain rules. When the place of the bell is shifting from first to last, the process is called *hunting up*; when the place is shifting from last to first, it is called *hunting down*.

hunt, *n.* 1. the act of chasing wild animals for the purpose of catching them; a chase.

2. a pack of hounds. [Obs.]

3. a group of people who hunt together.

4. a district covered in hunting.

5. the game secured in the hunt. [Obs.]

6. the act of searching for something; a search; an inquisition.

7. in bell ringing, a series of regularly varying sequences in ringing a group of from five to twelve bells.

hunt'ẽr, *n.* 1. one who hunts.

2. a dog that scents game or is employed in the chase.

3. a horse used in the chase.

4. a watch with a hunting case.

5. in zoology, a hunting spider, or a spider which hunts for its prey.

6. a Jamaican cuckoo, *Hyetornis pluvialis*.

Hun·tē'ri·ăn, *a.* pertaining to or named after (a) John Hunter, Scottish surgeon who lived in the eighteenth century; (b) his brother William, Scottish anatomist.

hunt'ẽr's moon, the full moon after the harvest moon.

hunt'ing, *n.* [AS. *huntung*, verbal n. of *huntian*, to hunt.]

1. the act of a person or animal that hunts.

2. in electricity, the periodic increase and decrease in the speed of a synchronous motor with respect to the current.

hunt'ing, *a.* of or for hunting.

hunt'ing box, a temporary residence occupied for the purpose of hunting; a hunting lodge.

hunt'ing çase, a watchcase provided with a hinged cover to serve as a protection to the crystal: so called from use by foxhunters.

hunt'ing çat, the cheetah.

hunt'ing çog, in machinery, an extra cog in one of two geared wheels, serving to change the order of contact of the teeth, so that the same teeth shall not continually meet.

hunt'ing dog, 1. a dog trained for hunting.

2. a wild dog of South Africa somewhat resembling a hyena.

hunt'ing ground, a district used for hunting.

hunt'ing horn, a horn or bugle used in the chase.

hunt'ing knife (nīf), a large knife used by hunters to skin and cut up game.

hunt'ing leop'ărd (lep'), the cheetah.

hunt'ing lodge (loj), same as *hunting box*.

hunt'ing sēat, same as *hunting box*.

hunt'ing spī'dẽr, a spider that pursues its prey instead of waiting for it in a web; a hunter.

Hun'ting·tŏn's chō·rē'ȧ, [after G. *Huntington* (1851–1916), American physician.] a progressive hereditary chorea, accompanied by increasing mental deterioration.

hunt'ing wätch, a watch with a hunting case; a hunter.

hunt'ress, *n.* 1. a woman who hunts, or follows the chase.

2. a mare used for hunting.

hunts'măn, *n.*; *pl.* **hunts'men,** 1. a hunter. [Chiefly Brit.]

2. the man whose office it is to manage the chase and take charge of the hounds. [Chiefly Brit.]

hunts'măn's-çup, *n.* the sidesaddle flower or pitcher plant, *Sarracenia purpurea*, with large, cuplike leaves and purple or greenish flowers.

hunts'măn·ship, *n.* the art or practice of hunting, or the qualifications of a hunter.

hunts'măn's-horn, *n.* a plant, *Sarracenia flava*, of the southern United States.

hunt's-up', *n.* a rousing tune played on the hunting horn to arouse huntsmen; hence, any call or sound that awakens.

Hū'on pīne, [after the *Huon*, river in Tasmania.] a large tree of Tasmania, *Dacrydium franklinii*, with bright-green scalelike leaves and close-grained wood.

Hụ'pȧ, *n.* 1. any member of a tribe of North American Indians of northwestern California.

2. their Athapascan language.

Hụ'rȧ, *n.* [S. Am. name.] a genus of tropical American plants of the family *Euphorbiaceæ*. *Hura crepitans*, the sandbox tree, is remarkable for the loud report with which its seed vessel bursts, for which reason it is often called the *monkey's dinner bell*.

hūr'den, *n.* a coarse kind of linen. [Obs.]

hūr'dle, *n.* [ME. *hurdel, hyrdle*; AS. *hyrdel*, a hurdle.]

1. a portable frame or structure of twigs, osiers, or sticks, used for temporary fences or enclosures.

2. in England, formerly, a sledge or crate on which criminals were drawn to the place of execution.

3. one of the movable, framelike barriers placed across a racecourse to be leaped by the men or horses contesting in a hurdle race or steeplechase.

4. an obstacle; a difficulty to be overcome.

the hurdles; a race in which the contestants must jump over a series of hurdles.

HURDLE

hūr'dle, *v.t.*; hurdled, *pt.*, *pp.*; hurdling, *ppr.*

1. to enclose or fence off with hurdles.

2. to jump over (a hurdle) in a race.

3. to overcome (an obstacle).

hūr'dle rāce, same as *the hurdles*.

hūrd'lẽr, *n.* a runner who takes part in the hurdles.

hūr'dle·wŏrk, *n.* work resembling a hurdle.

hūrdṣ, *n.pl.* the refuse of flax, jute, hemp, etc.

hūr'dy-gūr'dy, *n.*; *pl.* **hūr'dy-gūr'dieṣ,** [imitative of the sounds made by the instrument.]

1. a boxed, lutelike instrument played by turning a crank attached to a resined wheel that scrapes the strings and produces sound: it is used by street musicians.

2. any musical instrument played by turning a crank; barrel organ.

3. a water wheel driven by a jet of water under pressure.

HURDY-GURDY

hūre, *n.* [OFr.] 1. a cap. [Obs.]

2. in heraldry, the head of an animal.

hūr·kä'rȧ, *n.* [Hind. *harkara*, a messenger, scout; *har*, every, and *kar*, work.] in India, one who carries messages; a native courier: written also *hurkaru* and *hircarrah*.

hūr'kle, *v.i.* to stoop, crouch, or squat. [Obs.]

hūrl, *v.t.*, hurled, *pt.*, *pp.*; hurling, *ppr.* [ME. *hurlen*, contr. of *hurtlen*, to dash against, strike forcibly.]

1. to throw with violence; to drive with great force; as, to *hurl* a stone.

And *hurl* them headlong to their fleet and main. —Pope.

2. to cast down; to overthrow.

3. to utter with vehemence; as, to *hurl* back an answer to a charge.

hūrl, *v.i.* 1. to throw or fling something (*at* a person or thing).

2. to move with force or violence; to rush. [Archaic.]

3. in baseball, to pitch. [Slang.]

4. to play the game called hurling.

5. to be wheeled. [Scot.]

hūrl, *n.* 1. the act of throwing with violence; a violent throw or fling.

2. tumult; riot; commotion. [Obs.]

3. the stick used in the game of hurling.

hūrl'bat, *n.* 1. a whirlbat; an old kind of weapon. [Obs.]

2. a bat used in the game of hurling.

hūrl'ẽr, *n.* one who hurls or who plays at hurling.

hūrl'ey, hūrl'y, *n.* 1. hockey or hurling.

2. a hockey stick.

hūrl'ing, *n.* 1. a throwing with force.

2. a ball game in which opposing sides or parties try to hurl or force a ball through their opponents' goal, or to deposit it at some designated spot at a distance; in Ireland, the game is the same as field hockey.

hūrl'wind, *n.* a whirlwind. [Obs.]

hūr'ly, *n.*; *pl.* **hūr'lieṣ,** uproar; turmoil; confusion.

hūr'ly-būr'ly, *n.*; *pl.* **hūr'ly-būr'lieṣ,** [prob. extended from *hurly*.] a turmoil; uproar; hubbub; confusion.

hūr'ly-būr'ly, *a.* disorderly and confused.

Hū'rŏn, *n.* [Fr., a coarse fellow, ruffian, from *hure*, unkempt head.] a member of a confederation of Iroquoian Indian tribes that lived between Georgian Bay and Lake Ontario, Canada: also called *Wyandot*.

Hū'rŏn, *a.* of the Hurons.

hụ·rä', *interj.*, *n.*, *v.t.* and *v.i.* same as *hurrah*.

hụ·räh', *interj.* [G. *hurra*; Dan. and Sw. *hurra*, hurrah.] an exclamation expressing approval, joy, or exultation.

hụ·räh', *n.* a cheer; a shout of approval, joy, or exultation.

hụ·räh', *v.i.* to cheer; to shout "hurrah."

hụ·räh', *v.t.* to greet, encourage, or applaud with shouts of "hurrah."

hụ·rāy', *interj.*, *n.*, *v.t.* and *v.i.* same as *hurrah*.

hūr'ri·çāne, *n.* [Sp. *huracan*, a hurricane; W. Ind. (Taino) *huracan*.]

1. a violent cyclone with winds moving from 70 to 100 miles an hour, usually accompanied by rain, thunder, and lightning: hurricanes generally occur in the tropics.

2. anything like a hurricane in force and speed; violent outburst.

Syn.—gale, storm, cyclone, tornado.

hūr'ri·çāne bird, the frigate bird.

hūr'ri·çāne deck, the top deck of a passenger ship plying inland waters.

hūr'ri·çāne lamp, 1. an oil lamp or candlestick with a tall glass chimney to keep the flame from being blown out.

2. an electric lamp in imitation of this.

hūr·ri·çā'nō, *n.* a hurricane; a waterspout. [Obs.]

hūr'ried, *a.* 1. hastened; forced to do, move, act, etc. in a hurry.

2. done, carried on, etc. in a hurry; hasty; as, a *hurried* meal.

hūr'ried·ly, *adv.* in a hurried manner.

hūr'ried·ness, *n.* the state of being hurried.

hūr'ri·ẽr, *n.* one who hurries, urges, or impels.

hūr'ry, *v.t.*; hurried, *pt.*, *pp.*; hurrying, *ppr.* [ME. *horien*, to hurry; compare Old Sw. *hurra*, to whirl round, M.H.G. *hurren*, to hurry, Ice. *hurr*, a great noise; prob. ultimately of imitative origin.]

1. to cause to move or act more rapidly or too rapidly; to drive, move, send, force, or carry with haste.

2. to cause to occur or be done more rapidly or too rapidly; to accelerate the preparation or completion of; urge on.

3. to urge or cause to act soon or too soon.
Syn.—hasten, quicken, accelerate, rush, flurry, precipitate.

hũr'ry, *v.i.* to move or act with haste; to move faster than is comfortable or natural; as, the business is urgent; let us *hurry*.

hũr'ry, *n.*; *pl.* **hũr'rieṣ,** 1. a hurrying or being hurried; rush; urgency.
2. eagerness to do, act, go, etc. quickly.
3. tumult; bustle; commotion. [Dial.]
Ambition raises a tumult in the soul, and puts it into a violent *hurry* of thought. —Addison.
Syn.—haste, urgency, bustle, rush.

hũr'ry·ing·ly, *adv.* in a hurrying manner.

hũr'ry-scũr'ry, *n.* an agitated, confused rushing about; disorderly confusion.

hũr'ry-scũr'ry, *v.i.* to hurry and scurry about; to act hurriedly and confusedly.

hũr'ry-scũr'ry, *a.* hurried and confused.

hũr'ry-scũr'ry, *adv.* in a hurried, confused manner.

hũr'ry-skũr'ry, *n.*, *a.*, *adv.*, and *v.i.* same as *hurry-scurry*.

hũrst, *n.* [ME. *hurst, hirst*; AS. *hyrst*, a grove, wood.]
1. a wood or grove: sometimes used in place names, as in Hazle*hurst*.
2. in milling, the frame of a run of millstones.
3. in heraldry, a charge representing a small group of trees.
4. a drift or bank of sand near a river. [Scot.]

hũrt, *v.t.*; hurt, *pt.*, *pp.*; hurting, *ppr.* [ME. *hurlen, hyrten, horten*, to knock, hit, hurt; OFr. *hurter, heurter*, to push, thrust, hit.]
1. to cause physical pain or injury to; to wound or bruise painfully; as, the body is *hurt* by a severe blow.
2. to cause injury, loss, or diminution to; to impair in value, quality, usefulness, beauty, or pleasure; to injure; to damage; to harm.
Virtue may be assailed, but never *hurt*. —Milton.
3. to give mental pain to; to wound the feelings of; to offend.

hũrt, *v.i.* 1. to cause injury, damage, or pain.
2. to give or have the sensation of pain; to be sore; as, my leg *hurts*.

hũrt, *n.* 1. anything that gives pain to the body; a wound, a bruise, or the like.
The pains of sickness and *hurts*. —Locke.
2. injury; loss; damage; detriment.
Why should damage grow to the *hurt* of the kings? —Ezra iv. 22.
3. something that wounds the feelings.
Syn.—wound, bruise, injury, harm, damage, loss, detriment, mischief, bane, disadvantage.

hũrt'ẽr, *n.* one who or that which hurts.

hũrt'ẽr, *n.* 1. in fortification, a timber placed at the interior slope as a revetment to prevent injury to the parapet by the wheels of the gun.
2. [*pl.*] in ordnance, pieces of wood or iron at the front of the chassis to prevent the top carriage from running off when in battery.
3. in vehicles, (a) a butting piece on an axle; (b) a strengthening piece against a shoulder of an axle.

hũrt'fụl, *a.* causing hurt; harmful; as, intemperance is *hurtful* to health.
Syn.—pernicious, destructive, harmful, baneful, prejudicial, detrimental, disadvantageous, mischievous, injurious, noxious.

hũrt'fụl·ly, *adv.* in a hurtful manner.

hũrt'fụl·ness, *n.* the state or quality of being hurtful; injuriousness.

hũr'tle, *v.i.*; hurtled, *pt.*, *pp.*; hurtling, *ppr.* [ME. *hurtlen, hurtelen*, freq. of *hurlen*, to dash, hurl.]
1. to come with a crash; to clash; collide; to dash violently (with *against* or *together*).
2. to make a crashing sound when or as when colliding; to clatter; as, the noise of battle *hurtled* in the air.
3. to move noisily with a crashing or clattering sound; to move violently and swiftly.

hũr'tle, *v.t.* 1. to throw, shoot, fling, or cast with violence; hurl.
2. to dash against; to come into collision with. [Archaic.]

hũr'tle, *n.* a hurtling; collision; clash. [Poetic.]

hũr'tle·ber''ry, *n.*; *pl.* **hũr'tle·ber''rieṣ,** 1. a whortleberry.
2. a huckleberry.

hũrt'less, *a.* 1. harmless; innocent; doing no injury; as, *hurtless* blows.
2. receiving no injury; unharmed.

hũrt'less·ly, *adv.* without harm.

hũrt'less·ness, *n.* harmlessness.

huṣ'bănd, *n.* [ME. *h(o)usbonde*; AS. *husbonda, húsbunda*; *hus*, house, and *bonda, bunda*, master, head of a family, married man.]
1. the male head of a household; one who directs the economy of a family. [Obs.]
2. a tiller of the ground; a husbandman. [Obs.]
3. a man joined to a woman by marriage; a married man: the correlative of *wife*.
4. a manager, as of a household. [Archaic.]
5. a male animal kept for breeding purposes. [Rare.]
6. an agent for the owners of a ship employed to manage it while it is in port, especially to oversee the purchasing of stores, repairs, maintenance, etc.: commonly called *ship's husband*.

huṣ'bănd, *v.t.*; husbanded, *pt.*, *pp.*; husbanding, *ppr.* 1. to direct and manage with frugality; to use with economy; as, a man *husbands* his estate, his means, or his time.
He is conscious how ill he has *husbanded* the great deposit of his Creator.—Rambler.
2. to become, or act as, the husband of.
3. to cultivate (soil or plants). [Obs.]
4. to supply with a husband. [Archaic.]

huṣ'bănd·ȧ·ble, *a.* manageable with economy. [Rare.]

huṣ'bănd·ăġe, *n.* the compensation allowed to a ship's husband.

huṣ'bănd·hood, *n.* the state of being a husband.

huṣ'bănd·less, *a.* having no husband.

huṣ'bănd·ly, *a.* frugal; thrifty. [Rare.]

huṣ'bănd·măn, *n.*; *pl.* **huṣ'bănd·men,** 1. a farmer; a person whose occupation is husbandry. [Archaic or Poetic.]
2. the master of a family. [Obs.]

huṣ'bănd·ry, *n.* 1. originally, management of domestic affairs, resources, etc.
2. frugality; good management; thrift.
3. farming.

hush, *v.t.*; hushed (husht), *pt.*, *pp.*; hushing, *ppr.* [ME. *husshen, hoschen*; of imitative origin.]
1. to still; to silence; to calm; to make quiet; to repress; as, to *hush* the noisy crowd.
My tongue shall *hush* again this storm of war. —Shak.
2. to allay; to calm; to soothe; to lull.
Wilt thou, then,
Hush my cares? —Otway.
to hush up; to suppress; to keep concealed.

hush, *v.i.* to stop making noise; to be or become quiet or silent.

hush, *a.* silent; still; quiet; as, they are *hush* as death. [Archaic.]

hush, *n.* absence of noise; quiet; silence.

hush, *interj.* an exclamation calling for silence.

hush'ȧ·bȳ, *interj.* be still! hush! a word used to lull children to sleep.

hush'ẽr, *n.* an usher. [Obs.]

hush'ing, *n.* in mining, the process of uncovering or washing out minerals by a strong stream of water; flushing.

hush mŏn'ey, a bribe to secure silence; money paid to a person to keep him from telling something.

hush pup'py, [? because orig. used to hush the hunger cries of hunting dogs.] in the southern United States, a small, fried ball of corn meal dough.

husk, *n.* [ME. *husk, huske*, related to O.D. *hulsche*; M.H.G. *huldsche, hulsche*, a husk.]
1. the dry outer covering of certain fruits or seeds of plants; the rind or hull; specifically, in the United States, the covering of the ears of maize or Indian corn; the shuck.
2. the outer or worthless part of anything; waste; refuse; as, the *husks* of religion.
3. the frame of a run of millstones.

husk, *v.t.*; husked (huskt), *pt.*, *pp.*; husking, *ppr.* to remove the husk or husks from.

husk, *n.* the greater dogfish. [Obs.]

husk, *n.* huskiness. [Rare.]

husked (huskt), *a.* 1. stripped of husks.
2. covered with a husk.

husk'ẽr, *n.* 1. one who husks corn.
2. a husking pin.
3. a husking machine.
4. an oyster opener. [Dial.]

husk'i·ly, *adv.* in a husky voice; hoarsely.

hus'ki·ly, *adv.* in a husky manner; with strength or force.

husk'i·ness, *n.* the quality of being husky, or hoarse.

hus'ki·ness, *n.* the quality of being husky, or big and strong.

husk'ing, *n.* 1. the act of stripping off husks.
2. a husking bee.

husk'ing bee, a cornhusking, or gathering of friends or neighbors to assist a farmer in husking corn, usually ending with dancing, feasting, etc.

husk'ing pin, a peg or pin worn on the hand to aid in removing the husks from corn.

husk'y, *a.*; *comp.* huskier; *superl.* huskiest, 1. (a) full of, containing, or consisting of husks; (b) like a husk.
2. dry in the throat; hoarse and rough.

hus'ky, *a.*; *comp.* huskier; *superl.* huskiest, [from *husk* (outer covering).] big and strong; robust; burly.

hus'ky, *n.*; *pl.* **hus'kieṣ,** a husky, or strong, person.

Hus'ky, *n.*; *pl.* **Hus'kieṣ,** [perhaps altered from *Eskimo*.]
1. an Eskimo.
2. the Eskimo language.
3. [*sometimes* h–] an Eskimo dog; a hardy dog used for pulling sleds in the Arctic.

hū'sō, *n.* [O.H.G. *huso*, the huso.] a very large sturgeon, *Acipenser huso*, found in the Black and Caspian Seas.

huṣ·sär', *n.* [Hung. *huszár*; Serb. *husar, gusar*; MGr. *koursarios*; LL. *cursarius*; from *cursa, cursus*, a raid; L. *cursus*, a run, course, from *currere*, to run.]
1. originally, a member of the light cavalry of Hungary or Croatia.
2. now, a member of any European regiment of light-armed cavalry, usually with brilliant dress uniforms.

huṣ'ṣif, *n.* a housewife. [Obs.]

Huss'ite, *n.* a follower of John Huss, the Bohemian reformer, who was burned alive in 1415.

Huss'ite, *a.* of John Huss or his religious ideas.

huṣ'ṣy, *n.*; *pl.* **huṣ'ṣieṣ,** [contr. from ME. *huswife*, housewife.]
1. a woman, especially one of low morals or behavior: contemptuous or playful term.
2. a saucy, pert girl; minx.
3. a small sewing kit. [Dial.]
4. a thrifty woman; a housewife. [Obs.]

hus'tingṣ, *n.pl.* [*usually construed as sing.*] [ME. *husting*; AS. *husting*; Ice. *husthing*, a council called by a king, earl, or guardsman; *hus*, house, and *thing*, an assembly.]
1. originally, (a) a deliberative assembly; (b) a court formerly held in the chief cities of England; especially, a court, which still survives, held within the city of London before the lord mayor, recorder, and sheriffs; (c) the platform in London Guildhall where such a court was formerly held; (d) the temporary platform where candidates for Parliament formerly stood for nomination and spoke.
2. the proceedings at an election.
3. any place where political campaign speeches are made.

hus'tle (hus'l), *v.t.*; hustled, *pt.*, *pp.*; hustling, *ppr.* [D. *hutselen*, freq. of *hutsen, hotsen*, to shake, jolt.]
1. to push or knock about; to shove or jostle in a rude, rough manner.
2. to force in a rough, hurried manner; as, he *hustled* the unwelcome visitors out of the house.
3. to cause to be done quickly or too quickly; hurry.

hus'tle, *v.i.* 1. to push one's way; to move hurriedly.
2. to work or act rapidly or energetically. [Colloq.]

hus'tle, *n.* 1. a hustling; a rough jostling, pushing, or shoving.
2. energetic action; drive; push. [Colloq.]

hus'tlẽr (-lẽr), *n.* one who hustles.

huṣ'wife (huz'if), *n.* a housewife. [Obs.]

huṣ'wife·ly (-if-), *adv.* prudently. [Obs.]

huṣ'wife·ry (-if-), *n.* housewifery. [Obs.]

hut, *n.* [OFr. *hutte, hute*, from O.H.G. *hutta*, a hut, cottage.]
1. a small house, hovel, or cabin; a mean lodge or dwelling; a temporary shelter.
2. the back end of the breech pin of a musket.

hut, *v.t.*; hutted, *pt.*, *pp.*; hutting, *ppr.* to put in or furnish with a hut or huts, as troops encamped in winter quarters.

hut, *v.i.* to live in a hut or huts.
The troops *hutted* for the winter. —Pickering.

hutch, *n.* [ME. *hucche, huche, hoche*; OFr. *huche*, a bin, kneading trough, mill hopper, from LL. *hutica*, a chest.]

1. a chest, bin, box, coop, or pen in which articles may be kept or animals confined; as, a grain *hutch*; a rabbit *hutch*.

2. a hut.

3. in mining, a small car in which ore is brought to the surface; also, a trough in which ore is washed.

4. a measure, two Winchester bushels.

5. the casing of a device for bolting flour.

6. a china cabinet with open shelves on top of drawers and cupboards.

hutch, *v.t.*; hutched, *pt., pp.*; hutching, *ppr.* to store or put in or as in a hutch.

Hutch·in·sō′ni·ăn, *a.* pertaining to John Hutchinson or Mrs. Anne Hutchinson or to their doctrines.

Hutch·in·sō′ni·ăn, *n.* 1. a believer in the opinions of John Hutchinson, of Yorkshire, England, a philosopher and naturalist of the eighteenth century, who rejected Newton's doctrine of gravitation, and maintained that the Old Testament Scriptures embraced a complete system of natural science as well as of theology.

2. in American history, a believer in the antinomian teachings of Mrs. Anne Hutchinson, who lived in the early years of the settlement of Massachusetts.

hū·ti′ȧ, *n.* [Sp., prob. from native name.] a Cuban rodent of the genus *Capromys*.

Hut′tẽr·īte, *n.* [after Jacob *Hutter*, 16th-century Austrian religious reformer, and *-ite*.] any member of a group of Anabaptists, originally from Moravia, who live in settlements in the Dakotas, Montana, and Alberta, Canada, and hold beliefs similar to those of the Mennonites.

Hut·tō′ni·ăn, *a.* in geology, relating to that theory of the earth which was first advanced by Dr. James Hutton (1726–1797), now called the Plutonic theory.

Huy·gē′ni·ăn, *a.* relating to Christian Huygens, a Dutch astronomer and mathematician of the seventeenth century; as, the *Huygenian* eyepiece: written also *Huyghenian*.

huzz, *v.i.* to buzz. [Obs.]

hụz·zä′, *n.* and *interj.* [G. *hussa*, a form of hurrah.] a shout of approval, joy, exultation, etc.: replaced in current usage by *hurrah*.

hụz·zä′, *v.i.* to cheer; to shout "huzza."

hụz·zä′, *v.t.*; huzzaed, *pt., pp.*; huzzaing, *ppr.* to greet, encourage, or applaud with shouts of "huzza."

He was *huzzaed* into the court. —Addison.

hȳ′ȧ·cinth, *n.* [Fr. *hyacinthe*; L. *hyacinthus*; Gr. *hyakinthos*, the hyacinth.]

1. a plant of the genus *Hyacinthus*, belonging to the lily family, with long, narrow leaves and spikes of fragrant, bell-shaped flowers; especially, the cultivated species, *Hyacinthus orientalis*.

2. one of several plants of the same family.

3. (a) the bulb of any of these plants; (b) the flower.

4. a gem; specifically, (a) among the ancients, a blue gem, probably the sapphire; (b) any of the reddish-orange varieties of zircon, garnet, or topaz; jacinth.

5. a water bird with purple feathers.

6. bluish purple.

hȳ′ȧ·cinth bēan, a climbing plant, *Dolichos lablab*, of the bean family.

hȳ·ȧ·cin′thi·ăn, *a.* hyacinthine. [Rare.]

hȳ·ȧ·cin′thine, *a.* [L. *hyacinthinus*; Gr. *hyakinthinos*, from *hyakinthos*, hyacinth.]

1. of or like the hyacinth (gem or flower); made of or adorned with hyacinths.

2. blue or bluish-purple.

3. red-orange.

4. [H–] of or like Hyacinthus.

Hȳ·ȧ·cin′thus, *n.* [L.] 1. in Greek mythology, a youth loved and accidentally slain by Apollo, who caused to grow from his blood a flower bearing the letters AI AI (a Greek cry of sorrow).

2. in botany, a genus of bulbous plants of the lily family, including about thirty species, native to central Europe, Asia, and Africa.

Hȳ′ȧ·dēṣ, *n.pl.* [L. *Hyades*; Gr. *Hyades*; the ancients derived the word from *hyein*, to rain.]

1. in Greek mythology, the daughters of Atlas, placed in the sky by Zeus.

2. in astronomy, a cluster of stars in Taurus, supposed by the ancients to indicate the approach of rainy weather when they rose with the sun.

Hȳ′adṣ, *n.pl.* see *hyades*.

hȳ·ae′nȧ, *n.* same as *hyena*.

hȳ′al-, same as *hyalo-*.

hȳ·ȧ·les′cence, *n.* the act or process of becoming transparent; also, the state of being glassy; glassiness.

hȳ·ȧ·les′cent, *a.* [Gr. *hyalos*, glass, and *-escent.*] becoming hyaline; manifesting hyalescence.

hȳ′ȧ·lin, *n.* [*hyal-*, and *-in.*] any of various translucent, albuminoid substances; especially, such a substance forming the walls of hydatid cysts.

hȳ′ȧ·line, *a.* [Gr. *hyalinos*, glassy, from *hyalos*, glass.] glassy; resembling glass; consisting of glass; crystalline; transparent; as, a *hyaline* cartilage.

hȳ′ȧ·line, *n.* 1. anything transparent or glassy, as the smooth sea or clear sky; specifically, (a) the hyaloid membrane; (b) the hyaline cartilage; (c) hyaloplasm.

2. hyalin.

hȳ′ȧ·line mem′brāne diṣ·ēaṣe′, a disease of newborn infants, a respiratory disorder caused by an abnormal membrane of protein lining the alveoli of the lungs.

hȳ′ȧ·līte, *n.* [Gr. *hyalos*, glass, and *-ite.*] a pellucid variety of opal, sometimes transparent, sometimes whitish and translucent.

hȳ·ȧ·lī′tis, *n.* in pathology, inflammation of the vitreous humor or of the hyaloid membrane of the vitreous humor.

hȳ′al·ō-, [from Gr. *hyalos*, glass.] a combining form used in chemistry, geology, etc. to signify *glass, glassy, transparent*, as in *hyalo*phane, *hyalo*pterous: also, before a vowel, *hyal-*.

hȳ·al′ō·gen, *n.* [*hyalo-*, and *-gen.*] any of the various insoluble, mucoidlike substances found in animal tissue and producing hyalins upon hydrolysis.

hȳ′ȧ·loid, *a.* [*hyalo-*, and Gr. *eidos*, form.] in anatomy, glassy, vitreous, or transparent; hyaline.

hyaloid membrane; a membrane enclosing the vitreous humor of the eye.

Hȳ″ȧ·lō·nē′mȧ, *n.* [*hyalo-*, and Gr. *nema*, thread.] a genus of the class *Hyalospongiae*, the glass sponges.

hȳ·al′ō·phāne, *n.* [*hyalo-*, and Gr. *phainesthai*, to appear.] a monoclinic barium feldspar.

hȳ′ȧ·lō·plaṣm, *n.* [*hyalo-*, and Gr. *plasma*, anything formed, from *plassein*, to form, mold.] the ground substance of the protoplasm of a cell: it is clear and fluid, as distinguished from the granular and reticulate parts.

hȳ·ȧ·lop′tẽr·ous, *a.* [*hyalo-*, and Gr. *pteron*, a wing.] having the wings transparent: said of insects.

hȳ·ȧ·lō·sid′ẽr·īte, *n.* [*hyalo-*, and Gr. *siderītēs*, of iron, from *sidēros*, iron.] a ferruginous variety of olivine.

Hȳ″ȧ·lō·spon′ġi·ae, *n.pl.* [*hyalo-*, and Gr. *spongia*, a sponge.] a class of siliceous sponges in which the skeleton is composed of six-rayed spicules becoming ultimately united together. The species are found at great depths of the ocean.

hȳ″ȧ·lō·tē′kīte, *n.* [*hyalo-*, and Gr. *tēkein*, to melt.] in mineralogy, a white crystalline silicate of lead, barium, and calcium, of a vitreous luster.

hȳ·bẽr′nȧ·çle, *n.* same as *hibernacle*.

Hȳ·blae′ăn, *a.* pertaining to the ancient city of Hybla, in Sicily, famous for the honey produced in the neighboring locality.

hyb′ō·dont, *a.* [Gr. *hybos*, humpbacked, and *odous*, *odontos*, tooth.] pertaining to or resembling a genus, *Hybodus*, of fossil fishes allied to the sharks.

hyb′ō·dont, *n.* a fish of the genus *Hybodus*.

Hyb′ō·dus, *n.* a genus of fossil fishes that prevailed throughout the Triassic and Cretaceous periods. They are allied to the sharks.

hȳ′brid, *n.* [L. *hybrida*, *hibrida*, offspring of tame sow and wild boar.]

1. the offspring of two animals or plants of different races, varieties, species, etc.

2. anything of mixed origin.

3. in linguistics, a word made up of elements from different languages (e.g., *hydroplane, sociology*).

hȳ′brid, *a.* of, or having the nature of, a hybrid.

hȳ′brid·iṣm, *n.* 1. the production of hybrids; crossbreeding; interbreeding.

2. the quality, condition, or fact of being hybrid.

hȳ′brid·ist, *n.* one who hybridizes.

hȳ·brid′i·ty, *n.* the quality or condition of being hybrid.

hȳ′brid·ī·zȧ·ble, *a.* capable of producing a hybrid by crossing with some other species, race, etc.

hȳ″brid·i·zā′tion, *n.* the act of hybridizing or the state of being hybridized.

hȳ′brid·īze, *v.t.;* and *v.i.;* hybridized, *pt., pp.;* hybridizing, *ppr.* to produce or cause to produce hybrids; to interbreed; to cross.

hȳ′brid·ī·zẽr, *n.* one who hybridizes.

hȳd′āġe, *n.* hidage. [Obs.]

hȳ·dan·tō′iç, *a.* relating to hydantoin.

hȳ·dan′tō·in, *n.* [Gr. *hydōr*, water, and *allantoin.*] in chemistry, a sweetish crystalline compound, $C_3H_4N_2O_2$, found in beet juice.

hȳ′dȧ·tid, *n.* [Gr. *hydatis* (*-idos*), a drop of water, a water vesicle, from *hydōr*, *hydatos*, water.] a cyst containing watery fluid and the larvae of a tapeworm, sometimes found in the body of both animals and man.

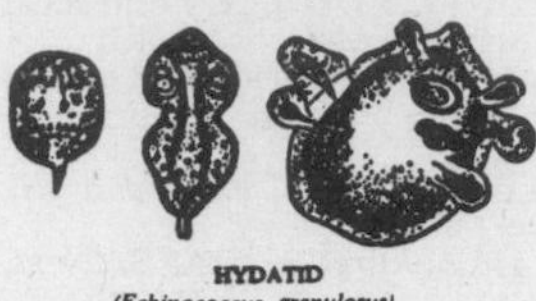

HYDATID
(Echinococcus granulosus)

hydatid of Morgagni; in anatomy, one of the small pedunculated growths found beside the head of the epididymis and formed mainly of connective tissue and blood vessels.

hȳ·dat′i·form, *a.* [Gr. *hydatis* (*-idos*), a water vesicle, and L. *forma*, form.] having the form of a hydatid.

hȳ·dȧ·tiġ′e·nous, *a.* [Gr. *hydatis* (*-idos*), a hydatid, and *-genēs*, producing.] producing or bearing hydatids.

hȳ′dȧ·toid, *a.* and *n.* [Gr. *hydōr*, *hydatos*, water, and *eidos*, form.] like water; aqueous.

hȳ′dȧ·toid, *n.* the aqueous humor of the eye. [Obs.]

hyd·nō·çär′pāte, *a.* a salt or ester of hydnocarpic acid.

hyd·nō·çär′piç, *a.* [from Mod. L. *Hydnocarpus*, name of a genus of trees (from Gr. *hydnon*, edible fungus, and *karpos*, fruit); and *-ic.*] designating or of an acid, $C_{15}H_{27}COOH$, found in the oil of a tree that grows in India and Malaysia, used in treating leprosy.

hydr-, see *hydro-*.

Hȳ′drȧ, *n.*; *pl.*, for 2, 4, 6, and 7, **hȳ′drăṣ, hȳ′drae,** [ME. and OFr. *ydre*; also ME. *ydra*; both from L.; Gr. *hydra*, water serpent.]

TENTACLES
MOUTH
BUD
BUD
HYDRA

1. in Greek mythology, the nine-headed serpent slain by Hercules: when any one of its heads was cut off, it was replaced by two others.

2. [h–] any persistent or ever-increasing evil with many sources and causes.

3. a southern constellation outlining a serpent.

4. [h–] any of a group of very small fresh-water animals, with a tubelike body and a mouth surrounded by tentacles.

5. the genus to which these fresh-water animals belong.

6. [h–] the sexual bud or medusa of a hydroid.

7. [h–] a spirit thermometer having an extended bulb which makes it register quickly.

hȳ·draçh′nid, *n.* [*hydr-*, and Gr. *achnē*, foam.] in zoology, a water mite parasitic upon mollusks, fishes, and water insects.

hȳ·drac′id, *n.* [*hydr-*, and L. *acidus*, sour, sharp.] in chemistry, an acid containing no oxygen, as HCl, H_2S, HCN, etc.

hȳ·drȧ·çryl′iç, *a.* [*hydr-*, and *acrylic.*] designating or of a colorless, crystalline acid, $C_3H_6O_3$, which, when heated, separates into water and acrylic acid.

hȳ·draç·tin′i·ăn, *n.* [*hydr-*, and Gr. *aktis* (*-inos*), a ray.] in zoology, any marine hydroid of the genus *Hydractinia* or kindred genera, usually found growing upon the shells of mollusks and forming a mosslike coating.

hȳ·drae′mi·ȧ, *n.* same as *hydremia*.

hȳ′drȧ·gogue (-gog), *a.* [LL. *hydragogus*; Gr. *hydragōgos*, conducting water, a water carrier; *hydōr*, water, and *agōgos*, leading, from *agein*, to lead.] causing a discharge of water, especially from the intestine.

hȳ'drȧ·gogue, *n.* any cathartic or other substance causing a discharge of water from the intestine.

Hȳ'drȧ·head'ed (-hed-), *a.* having many heads, like the Hydra of Greek mythology; hard to suppress; ever growing in monstrosity: said of evils of all kinds.

hȳ·dram'ide (*or* -īd), *n.* [*hydr-*, and *amide.*] in chemistry, a crystalline substance produced by the action of ammonia on certain aldehydes.

hȳ·dram'ine, *n.* in chemistry, one of a series of organic bases of a viscous nature, produced by the action of ammonia on ethylene oxide.

Hȳ·drañ'ġē·ȧ, *n.* [*hydr-*, and Gr. *angeion*, a vessel.]
1. a genus of shrubs or herbs of the family *Saxifragaceæ*, with opposite leaves and large, showy clusters of white, blue, or pink flowers. The common species, *Hydrangea hortensis*, is a native of China.
2. [h–] a plant of this genus.

hȳ'drȧnt, *n.* [Gr. *hydrainein*, to irrigate, from *hydōr*, water.]
1. a device with suitable valves and a spout by which water is raised and discharged from a water main; a fire plug.
2. a water faucet. [Dial.]

hȳ'dranth, *n.* [*hydr-*, and Gr. *anthos*, a flower.] in zoology, any of the feeding branches (*zooids*) of a hydroid colony.

hȳ·drär'ġil·līte, *n.* [*hydr-*, and Gr. *argillos*, white clay.] a variety of gibbsite.

hȳ·drär'ġy·rāte, *a.* hydrargyric. [Rare.]

hȳ·drär·ġy·rī'ȧ·sis, *n.* same as *hydrargyrism.*

hȳ·drär·ġyr'iç, *a.* [from L. *hydrargyrus* (see *hydrargyrum*); and *-ic.*] of or containing mercury; mercuric.

hȳ·drär'ġy·riṣm, *n.* [from *hydrargyrum*, and *-ism.*] poisoning with mercury; mercurialism.

hȳ·drär'ġy·rum, *n.* [L. *hydrargyrus*; Gr. *hydrargyros*, quicksilver; *hydōr*, water, and *argyros*, silver.] in chemistry, mercury: symbol, Hg (no period).

hȳ·drär·thrō'sis, *n.* [*hydr-*, and Gr. *arthrōsis*, articulation, from *arthron*, joint.] in pathology, the accumulation of a watery deposit in the cavity of a joint.

hȳ·dras'tin, *n.* same as *hydrastine.*

hȳ·dras'tine (*or* -tin), *n.* [from Mod. L. *Hydrastis*, name of the genus of herbs (from Gr. *hydōr*, water); and *-ine.*] a bitter, crystalline alkaloid, $C_{21}H_{21}O_6N$, extracted from the rootstalk of the goldenseal and used in treating dyspepsia, constipation, etc.

hȳ'drāte, *n.* [*hydr-*, and *-ate.*] a compound formed by the chemical combination of water and some other substance; as, plaster of Paris, $2CaSO_4 \cdot H_2O$, is a *hydrate.*

hȳ'drāte, *v.t.* and *v.i.*; hydrated, *pt.*, *pp.*; hydrating *ppr.* 1. to become or cause to become a hydrate.
2. to combine with water.

hȳ'drā·ted, *a.* formed by chemical combination with water.

hȳ·drā'tion, *n.* a hydrating; chemical combination with water to form a hydrate.

hȳ·drau'liç, *a.* [Fr. *hydraulique*; L. *hydraulicus*; Gr. *hydraulikos*, pertaining to a water organ, from *hydraulis, hydraulos*, a water organ, a water pipe; *hydōr*, water, and *aulos*, a tube, pipe.]
1. of hydraulics.
2. operated by the movement and force of liquid; as, a *hydraulic* brake or press.
3. setting or hardening under water; as, *hydraulic* mortar.

hydraulic brake; a brake in which the brake bands are actuated by liquid under pressure.

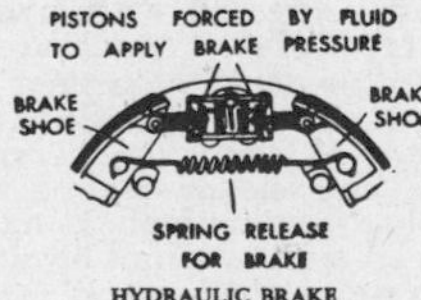

HYDRAULIC BRAKE

hydraulic cement; a cement having the property of becoming hard under water; a cement made of hydraulic lime.

hydraulic elevator; an elevator operated by the pressure or weight of water.

hydraulic lime; a species of lime that hardens in water, used for cementing under water.

hydraulic main; in gasworks, a pipe containing water through which the gas is passed in the process of purification.

hydraulic mining; a method of mining by washing the ore out of the bank with a powerful jet of water, as from a hose.

hydraulic press; a machine in which practical application is made of the well-known principle in hydrostatics that a pressure exerted on any part of the surface of a liquid is transmitted undiminished to every part of the liquid and in all directions. By this apparatus great power is obtained for compressing objects or drawing or lifting great weights.

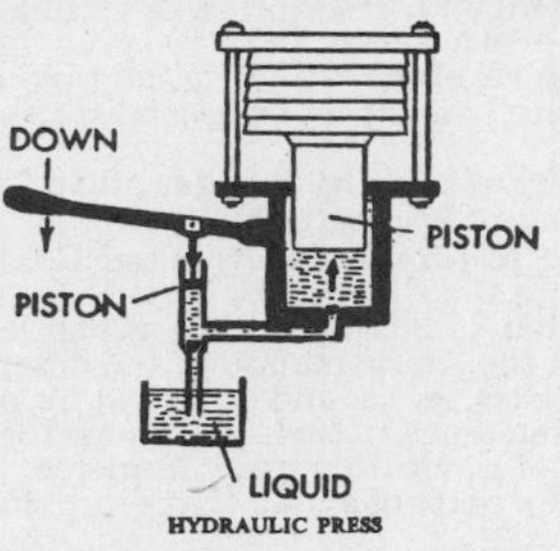

HYDRAULIC PRESS

hydraulic ram; a machine by which the momentum or weight of falling water can be made available for raising a portion of the water to a considerable height.

hydraulic valve; an inverted cup which is lowered over the upturned open end of a pipe, the edge of the cup being submerged in water, forming a water seal and closing the pipe against the passage of air or gases.

hȳ·drau'liç·ȧl, *a.* same as *hydraulic.*

hȳ·drau'liç·ȧl·ly, *adv.* by hydraulic power.

hȳ·drau·lic'i·ty, *n.* the property possessed by certain cements, of solidifying under water.

hȳ·drau'li·çŏn, *n.* [Gr. *hydraulikon* (supply *organon*, organ), a hydraulic organ.] in music, an old form of organ in which water was used to regulate the pressure of the air: also called *hydraulic organ.*

hȳ·drau'lics, *n. pl.* [*construed as sing.*], [from *hydraulic.*] the branch of physics having to do with the mechanical properties of water and other liquids and with the application of these properties in engineering.

hȳ'drȧ·zin, *n.* same as *hydrazine.*

hȳ'drȧ·zīne (*or* -zin), *n.* [*hydr-*, and *az-*, and *-ine.*] a colorless liquid base, NH_2NH_2, which forms a monohydrate $(NH_2NH_2 \cdot H_2O)$ and a series of salts.

hȳ·draz'ō-, [*hydr-*, and *azo-.*] a combining form meaning *containing the group* -HNNH- *combined with two hydrocarbon radicals.*

hȳ·drȧ·zō'āte, *n.* any salt of hydrazoic acid.

hȳ·drȧ·zō'iç, *a.* [*hydr-*, and *azo-*, and *-ic.*] designating or of a colorless, volatile acid, HN_3, from which the hydrazoates are derived.

hȳ·drē'mi·ȧ, *n.* an excess of water in the blood.

hȳ·dren·ceph'ȧ·loid, *a.* same as *hydrocephaloid.*

hȳ·dren'tėr·ō·cēle, *n.* [*hydr-*, and Gr. *enteron*, intestine, and *kēlē*, a tumor.] a hernial tumor, whose contents are intestinal, with the addition of water.

hȳ'dri·ȧ, *n.*; *pl.* **hȳ'dri·ae,** [L., from Gr. *hydria*, a waterpot, from *hydōr*, water.] a large Greek vase, with three handles and a capacious body.

HYDRIA

hȳ'dri·ad, *n.* [Gr. *hydrias* (*-ados*), of or from the water, from *hydōr*, water.] in mythology, a water nymph.

hȳ'driç, *a.* relating to or containing hydrogen.

-hȳ'driç, [see *hydric.*] a combining form used to indicate *the presence of* (a specified number of) *hydroxyl radicals* or *replaceable hydrogen atoms in the molecule*, as in mono*hydric.*

hȳ'drid, *n.* same as *hydride.*

hȳ'drīde, (*or* -drid), *n.* [*hydr-*, and *-ide.*] a compound of hydrogen with either another element or a radical.

hȳ'dri·form, *a.* [L. *hydra*, a hydra, and *forma*, form.] formed like a hydra.

hȳ·drī'ō·dāte, *n.* a salt of hydriodic acid.

hȳ·dri·od'iç, *a.* [*hydr-*, and *iodic.*] designating or of an acid, HI, produced by the direct combination of hydrogen and iodine or by the hydrolysis of phosphorus tri-iodide: it is a colorless gas, readily soluble in water, and forms salts called iodides.

hȳ'drō-, [from Gr. *hydōr*, water.] a combining form meaning (a) *water*, as in *hydro*static, *hydro*meter; (b) in chemistry, *the presence of hydrogen*, as in *hydro*cyanic. Also, before a vowel, *hydr-*.

hȳ·drō'ȧ, *n.* [*hydr-*, and Gr. *ōon*, an egg.] a chronic inflammatory disease of the skin characterized by pustules, vesicles, etc., and intense itching.

hȳ''drō·bȧ·rom'e·tėr, *n.* [*hydro-*, and Gr. *baros*, weight, pressure, and *metron*, a measure.] a device for measuring the depth of sea water by its pressure.

Hȳ·drō·brañ·çhi·ā'tȧ, *n.pl.* [*hydro-*, and Gr. *branchia*, gills.] a division of gastropods, containing species which breathe only water.

hȳ·drō·brañ'çhi·āte, *a.* pertaining to the *Hydrobranchiata*; breathing water only; breathing through gills.

hȳ·drō·brō'māte, *n.* [*hydrobromic* and *-ate.*] a salt of hydrobromic acid.

hȳ·drō·brō'miç, *a.* [*hydro-*, and *bromic.*] designating or of an acid, HBr, produced by the direct combination of hydrogen and bromine or by the hydrolysis of phosphorus tribromide: it is a colorless gas, readily soluble in water, and forms salts called bromides.

hȳ·drō·çär'bŏn, *n.* any compound containing only hydrogen and carbon: benzene and methane are hydrocarbons.

hȳ·drō·çär·bō·nā'ceous, *a.* consisting of or characteristic of a hydrocarbon.

hȳ·drō·çau'lus, *n.*; *pl.* **hȳ·drō·çau'lī,** [*hydro-*, and Gr. *kaulos*, stem.] the main stem of the coenosarc of a hydrozoan.

hȳ'drō·cēle, *n.* [Gr. *hydrokēlē*, hydrocele; *hydōr*, water, and *kēlē*, a tumor.] a collection of watery fluid in a cavity of the body, especially in the scrotum or along the spermatic cord.

hȳ·dro·cel'lū·lōse, *n.* a substance derived from cellulose by the action of hydrochloric acid, and produced in the form of a fine powder.

hȳ''drō·cē·phal'iç, *a.* pertaining to hydrocephalus.

hȳ·drō·ceph'ȧ·loid, *a.* characteristic of or resembling hydrocephalus.

hydrocephaloid disease; a condition of coma sometimes developed in children when in a state of exhaustion following diarrhea.

hȳ·drō·ceph'ȧ·lous, *a.* same as *hydrocephaloid.*

hȳ·drō·ceph'ȧ·lus, *n.* [Mod. L.; Gr. *hydrokephalon*, water in the head; *hydōr*, water, and *kephalē*, head.] a condition characterized by an abnormal increase in the amount of fluid in the cranium, causing enlargement of the head, wasting away of the brain, and loss of mental powers.

hȳ·drō·ceph'ȧ·ly, *n.* same as *hydrocephalus.*

hȳ''drō·cē·ram'iç, *a.* [*hydro-*, and Gr. *keramikos*, from *keramos*, earthenware.] allowing liquids to escape through pores: said of certain kinds of pottery which, by evaporation from their surface, cool the liquids they contain.

Hȳ''drō·çhȧ·rid'ē·ae, *n.pl.* a family of monocotyledonous floating and creeping plants, inhabiting ditches, rivers, and lakes in various parts of the world: written also *Hydrocharidaceæ.*

Hȳ·droçh'ȧ·ris, *n.* [Gr. *hydrocharēs*, delighting in water, *hydōr*, water, and *chairein*, to rejoice.] the typical genus of the *Hydrocharideæ*; the frogbit.

hȳ·drō·çhī'non, *n.* same as *hydroquinone.*

hȳ·drō·çhlō'rāte, *n.* any salt of hydrochloric acid.

hȳ·drō·çhlō'riç, *a.* [*hydro-*, and *chloric.*] designating or of an acid, HCl, produced by the combination of hydrogen and chlorine or by the reaction of salt and sulfuric acid, and existing as a colorless gas or as a colorless solution of this gas in water: it forms salts called chlorides. The aqueous solution of *hydrochloric acid* is also called *muriatic acid.*

hȳ·drō·çhlō'rīde, hȳ·drō·çhlō'rīd (*or* -rid), *n.* a compound of hydrochloric acid and an organic base.

Hȳ·drō·çor·ȧl·lī'nae, *n.pl.* [*hydro-*, and Gr. *korallion*, coral.] a suborder of the *Hydroidea*, similar to the corals.

hȳ''drō·çō·tär'nīne (*or* -nin), *n.* an alkaloid derived from opium.

Hȳ·drō·çot'y·lē, *n.* [*hydro-*, and Gr. *kotylē*, a cavity, cup.] a genus of plants of the order *Umbelliferæ*, the water pennyworts.

hȳ·drō·çȳ'ȧ·nāte, *n.* cyanide. [Obs.]

hȳ''drō·çȳ·an'iç, *a.* [*hydro-*, and *cyanic.*] designating or of a weak, highly poisonous acid,

HCN, produced by the combination of hydrogen and cyanogen, and existing as a colorless liquid with the smell of peach blossoms or bitter almonds: also called *prussic acid.*

hȳ·drō·cȳ′ȧ·nīde (*or* -nid), *n.* a compound of hydrocyanic acid.

hȳ′drō·cyst, *n.* [*hydro-*, and Gr. *kystis*, a bladder.] in zoology, a process, a sort of feeler attached to the coenosarc of the *Physophoridæ*, a family of oceanic *Hydrozoa.*

Hȳ·drō·diç′ty·on, *n.* [*hydro-*, and Gr. *diktyon*, a net.] a genus of green-spored algae, so called because, when full-grown, they resemble a purse composed of a network of threads.

hȳ″drō·dȳ·nam′iç, *a.* [*hydro-*, and Gr. *dynamis*, power, and *-ic.*]

1. having to do with hydrodynamics.

2. of, derived from, or operated by, the action of water, etc. in motion.

hȳ″drō·dȳ·nam′iç·ăl, *a.* same as *hydrodynamic.*

hȳ″drō·dȳ·nam′içs, *n.pl.* [*construed as sing.*] the branch of physics having to do with the motion and action of water and other liquids; dynamics of liquids.

hȳ″drō·dȳ·nȧ·mom′ē·tẽr, *n.* [*hydro-*, and Gr. *dynamis*, power, and *metron*, a measure.] a device to measure the speed of a moving fluid by determining the pressure it exerts.

hȳ″drō·ē·leç′triç, *a.* [*hydro-*, and Gr. *ēlektron*, amber.] producing, or having to do with the production of, electricity by water power or by the friction of water or steam.

hȳ″drō·ē·leç·tric′i·ty, *n.* electricity produced by water power or by the friction of water or steam.

hȳ″drō·ex·traçt′ŏr, *n.* [*hydro-*, and L. *extractus*, pp. of *extrahere*, to draw out.] a centrifugal machine to remove moisture.

hȳ″drō·fer″ri·cȳ·an′iç, *a.* same as *ferricyanic.*

hȳ″drō·fer″rō·cȳ·an′iç, *a.* same as *ferrocyanic.*

hȳ″drō·flū·or′iç, *a.* [*hydro-*, and *fluoric.*] designating or of an acid, H_6F_6, H_4F_4, H_2F_2, or HF (depending on the temperature), produced by the reaction of concentrated sulfuric acid with solid fluorides, and existing as a colorless, fuming, corrosive liquid with a boiling point of 19°C.: it reacts with silicates and is therefore used in etching glass.

hȳ·drō·flū·ō·sil′i·çāte, *n.* same as *fluosilicate.*

hȳ″drō·flū″ō·si·lic′iç, *a.* same as *fluosilicic.*

hȳ′drō·foil, *n.* 1. a winglike surface which, when moved through a liquid, develops forces the direction and magnitude of which depend upon the speed of motion and the position of the foil with respect to the line of movement.

2. any of the winglike structures attached to the hull of some watercraft: at a certain speed the hull is lifted above the water and the craft skims along on the hydrofoils at great speeds.

3. a craft with such hydrofoils.

hȳ′drō·fūġe, *a.* [*hydro-*, and L. *fugare*, to put to flight, from *fugere*, to flee.] shedding water.

hȳ″drō·gal·van′iç, *a.* of, caused by, or belonging to electricity generated by the action of liquids; as, a *hydrogalvanic* current. [Rare.]

hȳ′drō·ġen, *n.* [Fr. *hydrogène*; see *hydro-* and *-gen*: coined in 1787 by the Fr. chemist G. de Morveau, in reference to the generation of water from the combustion of hydrogen.] an inflammable, colorless, odorless, gaseous chemical element, the lightest of all known substances: symbol, H; atomic weight, 1.0080; atomic number, 1.

heavy hydrogen; same as *deuterium.*

hydrogen bomb; an extremely destructive kind of atom bomb operating on the principle of atomic fusion, in which the atoms of a heavy isotope of hydrogen are fused into helium under the extraordinarily intense heat and pressure created by explosion of a nuclear-fission unit in the bomb: also *H-bomb.*

hydrogen bond; a bond formed through a hydrogen atom between an electronegative atom or group and a similar atom or group attached to a different molecule.

hydrogen dioxide; same as *hydrogen peroxide.*

hydrogen ion; the positively charged ion in all acids: symbol, H^+.

hydrogen oxide; water, H_2O.

hydrogen peroxide; an unstable compound, H_2O_2, existing as a slightly blue, sirupy liquid, often used in dilute solution as a bleaching or disinfecting agent.

hydrogen sulfide; an inflammable, poisonous gas, H_2S, with the characteristic odor of rotten eggs.

hȳ′drō·ġen·āte″, *v.t.*; hydrogenated, *pt., pp.*; hydrogenating, *ppr.* to combine with, treat with, or expose to the action of, hydrogen; as, oil is *hydrogenated* to produce a solid fat.

hȳ″drō·ġen·ā′tion, *n.* the process of hydrogenating or the state of being hydrogenated.

hȳ′drō·ġen·īde, hȳ′drō·ġen·īd (*or* -id), *n.* a hydride.

hȳ·drō·ġē′ni·um, *n.* [from *hydrogen.*] hydrogen. [Obs.]

hȳ′drō·ġen·īze, *v.t.*; hydrogenized, *pt., pp.*; hydrogenizing, *ppr.* to hydrogenate.

hȳ·droġ′e·nous, *a.* of or containing hydrogen.

hȳ·drog′nō·sy, *n.* [*hydro-*, and Gr. *gnōsis*, knowledge.] a description of or treatise upon the world's waters.

hȳ·drog′rȧ·phẽr, *n.* [*hydro-*, and Gr. *graphein*, to write.] an expert or specialist in hydrography.

hȳ·drō·graph′iç, hȳ·drō·graph′iç·ăl, *a.* of or relating to hydrography.

hȳ·drog′rȧ·phy, *n.* [*hydro-*, and Gr. *graphein*, to write.]

1. that branch of science which has for its object the study, mapping, and description of seas, lakes, rivers, and other waters, especially with reference to their usefulness for the purposes of navigation and commerce.

2. the parts of a map that represent surface waters.

hȳ·drog′ū·ret, *n.* [*hydrogen* and *-uret.*] a hydride. [Obs.]

hȳ′droid, *a.* [*hydra* and *-oid.*]

1. like a hydra or polyp.

2. of, relating to, or resembling the *Hydroidea* or *Hydrozoa.*

hȳ′droid, *n.* one of the *Hydroidea* or *Hydrozoa*; especially, any of the polyps, which reproduce by budding.

Hȳ·droi′dē·ȧ, *n.pl.* [Gr. *hydroeidēs*, like water; *hydōr*, water, and *eidos*, form.] the typical subclass of *Hydrozoa.* They have an alimentary region provided with an adherent disk and prehensile tentacles.

hȳ″drō·ki·net′iç, *a.* [*hydro-* and *kinetic.*] of the motions of fluids or the forces producing or influencing such motions.

hȳ″drō·ki·net′içs, *n.pl.* [*construed as sing.*], [*hydro-*, and *kinetics.*] the branch of physics having to do with the motions of fluids.

hȳ·drō·loġ′iç, hȳ·drō·loġ′iç·ăl, *a.* pertaining to hydrology.

hȳ·drol′ō·ġist, *n.* an expert in hydrology.

hȳ·drol′ō·ġy, *n.* [*hydro-*, and Gr. *-logia*, from *legein*, to speak.] the science of water, its properties, distribution phenomena, and laws; especially, the study of underground sources of water.

hȳ·drol′y·sis, *n.*; *pl.* **hȳ·drol′y·sēş** [*hydro-*, and *-lysis.*] a chemical reaction in which a compound reacts with the ions of water (H^+ and OH^-) to produce a weak acid, a weak base, or both.

hȳ′drō·lȳte, *n.* any substance undergoing hydrolysis.

hȳ·drō·lyt′iç, *a.* of or causing hydrolysis.

hȳ′drō·lȳze, *v.t.* and *v.i.*; hydrolyzed, *pt., pp.*; hydrolyzing, *ppr.* to undergo or cause to undergo hydrolysis.

hȳ·drō·mag′nē·sīte, *n.* [*hydro-*, *magnesium*, and *-ite.*] a white, chalklike variety of magnesium carbonate.

hȳ′drō·man·cy, *n.* [ME. *idromancie*; L. *hydromantia*; Gr. *hydromanteia*, from *hydōr*, water, and *manteia*, divination.] divination by the observation of water.

hȳ·drō·mā′ni·ȧ, *n.* [*hydro-*, and Gr. *mania*, madness.] in pathology, an abnormal craving for water.

hȳ·drō·man′tiç, *a.* pertaining to hydromancy.

hȳ″drō·mē·çhan′i·çăl, *a.* of hydromechanics.

hȳ″drō·mē·çhan′içs, *n.pl.* [*construed as sing.*] [*hydro-*, and Gr. *mēchanikos*, mechanic, from *mēchanē*, a machine.] the branch of physics having to do with the laws governing the motion and equilibrium of fluids.

hȳ″drō·mē·dū′sȧ, *n.*; *pl.* **hȳ″drō·mē·dū′sae,** a jellyfish (*medusa*) formed from a budding growth on a hydroid.

Hȳ″drō·mē·dū′sae, *n.pl.* [*hydro-*, and Gr. *Medousa*, the Gorgon of classic mythology.] a subclass of hydrozoans comprehending those related to the *Hydra* by reason of reproduction by lateral gemmation.

hȳ′drō·mel, *n.* [L. *hydromel* or *hydromeli*; Gr. *hydromeli*, a kind of mead made of water and honey; *hydōr*, water, and *meli*, honey.] a liquor consisting of honey diluted with water. Before fermentation, it is called simple *hydromel*; after fermentation, it is called vinous *hydromel*, or mead.

hȳ·drō·met·ăl·lŭr′ġiç·ăl, *a.* of or pertaining to hydrometallurgy.

hȳ·drō·met·ăl·lŭr′ġiç·ăl·ly, *adv.* in a hydrometallurgical manner.

hȳ·drō·met′ăl·lŭr·ġy, *n.* [*hydro-*, and Gr. *metallourgos*, working in metals, a miner, *metallon*, a mine, metal, and *ergon*, work.] the act of assaying or reducing ores by washing out the insoluble matter with various liquid reagents; also, any process for this purpose.

hȳ·drō·met·ȧ·mor′phişm, *n.* [*hydro-*, and Gr. *metamorphōsis*, a metamorphosis.] metamorphism of rocks by addition and depletion of material in solution in water.

hȳ·drō·mē′tē·ŏr, *n.* [*hydro-*, and Gr. *meteōron*, a meteor.] any atmospheric phenomenon dependent for its production upon the vapor of water, as rain, hail, snow, etc.

hȳ·drō·mē″tē·ō·ro·loġ′iç·ăl, *a.* of or pertaining to hydrometeorology.

hȳ·drō·mē″tē·ọr·ol′ō·ġy, *n.* [*hydro-*, and Gr. *meteōrologia*, meteorology.] the branch of meteorology which concerns itself with water in the atmosphere in the form of rain, clouds, snow, hail, etc.

hȳ·drom′e·tẽr, *n.* [*hydro-*, and Gr. *metron*, a measure.]

1. in physics, an instrument for determining the specific gravities of liquids. Hydrometers are variously constructed. A very common type consists of a graduated stem of uniform diameter and cross section, a bulb to cause it to float in the fluid, and a weight or counterpoise to cause the stem to stand upright as it floats. On being placed in a liquid it sinks until a certain point on the scale is on a level with the surface of the liquid, and from the reading of the scale at that point the specific gravity of the liquid is ascertained either directly or by a simple calculation.

HYDROMETER

2. an instrument for measuring the flow of water in rivers, conduits, etc.

hȳ·drō·met′riç, hȳ·drō·met′riç·ăl, *a.* 1. pertaining to a hydrometer or to the determination of the specific gravity of fluids.

2. made by a hydrometer; as, *hydrometric* observations.

hydrometric pendulum; an instrument consisting of a hollow ball suspended from the center of a graduated quadrant, and held in a stream to mark by its deflection the velocity of the current.

hȳ·drō·met′rō·grȧph, *n.* [*hydro-*, and Gr. *metron*, a measure, and *graphein*, to write.] an instrument to determine and record the amount of water discharged in a specific time.

hȳ·drom′e·try, *n.* [*hydro-*, and Gr. *metron*, a measure.] measurement of the specific gravity of liquids by the use of a hydrometer.

hȳ·drō·mī′çȧ, *n.* [*hydro-*, and L. *mica*, a crumb, grain.] a substance resembling muscovite in composition, but containing more water. It is a variety of potash mica.

hȳ″drō·mon′ō·plāne, *n.* [*hydro-* and *monoplane.*] an airplane with one main wing, capable of landing on and taking off from water.

hȳ″drō·mō′tŏr, *n.* [*hydro-*, and L. *motor*, from *movere*, to move.] a motor impelled by the reaction of a jet of water.

hȳ′drō·nạut, *n.* [*hydro-*, and *astronaut.*] in the United States Navy, a person trained to operate deep submergence vehicles.

hȳ″drō·neg′ȧ·tive, *a.* [*hydro-*, and *negative.*] in biology, characterized by negative hydrotropism.

hȳ″drō·nē·phrō′sis, *n.* [*hydro-*, and Gr. *nephros*, a kidney, and *-osis.*] a distention of the ureter and the renal pelvis caused by obstruction of the outflow of the urine.

hȳ″drō·nē·phrot′iç, *a.* of or pertaining to hydronephrosis; affected with hydronephrosis.

hȳ′drō·nette, *n.* [Fr.] a small pump or sprinkler designed for use in a garden.

hȳ·dron′iç, *a.* of or having to do with hydronics.

hȳ·dron′içs, *n.pl.* [*construed as sing.*] [*hydr-*, and *electronics.*] the science dealing with electrically controlled systems for heating, cooling, etc. by the forced circulation of liquids or vapors.

hȳ″drō·nī′triç, *a.* [*hydro-* and *nitric.*] pertaining to nitric or hydronitric acids.

Hȳ″drō·pȧ·ras′tȧ·tae, *n.pl.* a religious sect of the early church, the Aquarians.

hȳ′drō·path, *n.* one who practices or believes in hydropathy; a hydropathist.

hȳ·drō·path′iç, hȳ·drō·path′iç·ăl, *a.* of, by, or using hydropathy.

hȳ·drop′ȧ·thist, *n.* one who advocates or practices hydropathy.

hȳ·drop'ȧ·thy, *n.* [*hydro-*, and Gr. *pathos*, suffering, disease.] the treatment of disease by the use of water; specifically, a method of treatment that attempts to cure all diseases by the external or internal use of much water.

hȳ·drō·per·i·çär'di·um, *n.* [*hydro-*, and Gr. *perikardion*, the pericardium.] in pathology, cardiac dropsy.

hȳ"drō·per"i·pneū·mō'ni·ȧ (-nū-), *n.* [*hydro-*, and Gr. *peripneumonia*; *peri*, around, about, and *pneumōn*, the lung.] inflammation of the lungs complicated with dropsy.

hȳ·drō·per"i·tō·nē'um, *n.* [*hydro-*, and Gr. *peritonaion*, peritoneum.] in pathology, dropsy of the peritoneal cavity; ascites.

hȳ'drō·phāne, *n.* [*hydro-*, and Gr. *phanos*, clear.] in mineralogy, an opaque variety of opal that becomes translucent or transparent by immersion in water.

hȳ·droph'ȧ·nous, *a.* [*hydrophane* and *-ous.*] translucent or transparent when wet.

hȳ'drō·phid, *n.* [*hydr-*, and Gr. *ophis*, a snake.] a venomous sea snake of the family *Hydrophidæ*.

hȳ·drō·phō'bi·ȧ, *n.* [LL., from Gr. *hydrophobia*, hydrophobia; *hydōr*, water, and *phobos*, fear.]

1. an abnormal fear of water.
2. [from the symptomatic aversion to, and inability to swallow, water and other liquids.] rabies (especially in man).

hȳ·drō·phō'biç, *a.* [Gr. *hydrophobikos*, from *hydrophobia*, hydrophobia.] of or having hydrophobia.

hȳ'drō·phoid, *a.* pertaining to *Hydrophidæ*, a family of sea snakes.

hȳ'drō·phōne, *n.* [*hydro-*, and *-phone.*]

1. an instrument for detecting, and registering the distance and direction of, sound transmitted through water.
2. an instrument for detecting the flow of water in a pipe.

Hȳ·droph'ō·rȧ, *n.pl.* [Gr. *hydrophoros*, water-bearing; *hydōr*, water, and *pherein*, to bear, carry.] one of the three divisions into which Huxley and other authors divide the *Hydrozoa*, the other two being the *Discophora* and the *Siphonophora*. The members are, in all cases except that of *Hydra*, fixed ramified hydrosomes, on which many hydranths and gonophores are developed.

hȳ'drō·phōre, *n.* [Gr. *hydrophoros*, water-carrying; *hydōr*, water, and *pherein*, to bear.] an instrument for obtaining for examination small quantities of the water of a river, a lake, or an ocean from any specific depth.

Hȳ"drō·phyl·lā'cē·ae, *n.* [*hydro-*, and Gr. *phyllon*, a leaf, and *-aceæ.*] an order of plants known as waterleaves, including nearly 20 genera and 125 species, the majority of which are American.

hȳ"drō·phyl·lā'ceous, *a.* of or relating to the *Hydrophyllaceæ*.

hȳ·drō·phyl'li·um, *n.*; *pl.* **hȳ·drō·phyl'li·ȧ** or **hȳ·drō·phyl'li·umṣ,** [*hydro-*, and Gr. *phyllon*, a leaf.] in zoology, an overlapping transparent appendage or leaflike plate which protects the polypites in some oceanic hydrozoans, as the *Siphonophora*: called also *bract*.

Hȳ·drō·phyl'lum, *n.* [*hydro-*, and Gr. *phyllon*, a leaf.] a genus of American perennial marsh herbs with blue or white flowers, the type of the *Hydrophyllaceæ*, or waterleaf family.

hȳ'drō·phyte, *n.* [*hydro-*, and Gr. *phyton*, a plant.] an aquatic plant; a plant which lives and grows in water or very wet earth.

hȳ·droph·y·tol'ō·ġy, *n.* [*hydro-*, and Gr. *phyton*, a plant, and *-logia*, from *legein*, to speak.] that branch of botany which relates to water plants.

hȳ·droph'y·tŏn, *n.*; *pl.* **hȳ·droph'y·tȧ,** [*hydro-*, and Gr. *phyton*, a plant.] the connective element in a hydroid colony of zooids.

hȳ·droph'y·tous, *a.* characteristic of a hydrophyton.

hȳ·drop'iç, *a.* [L. *hydropicus*; Gr. *hydrōpikos*, dropsical, from *hydrops*, dropsy, from *hydōr*, water.] of or having dropsy; dropsical.

hȳ·drop'iç·ăl, *a.* hydropic.

hȳ·drop'iç·ăl·ly, *adv.* in a hydropical manner.

hȳ'drō·pī·pēr, *n.* [*hydro-*, and L. *piper*, a pepper.] in botany. *Polygonum hydropiper*, a species of knotweed water pepper; smartweed.

hȳ'drō·plāne, *n.* [*hydro-*, and *plane.*]

1. a small, light motorboat with a flat bottom rising in steps to the stern so that it can skim along the water's surface at high speeds.
2. a seaplane.
3. an attachment for an airplane that enables it to glide along on the water.
4. a horizontal rudder used to submerge or raise a submarine.

hȳ'drō·plāne, *v.i.* 1. to drive or ride in a hydroplane.

2. to skim along like a hydroplane.

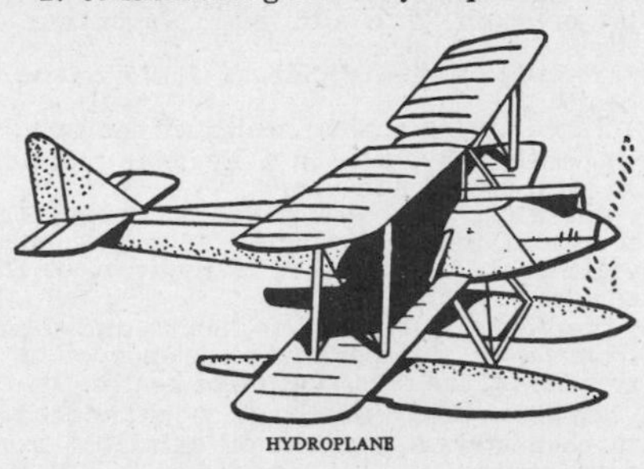

HYDROPLANE

hȳ"drō·plan'ū·lȧ, *n.* [*hydro-*, and L. *planus*, flat.] in zoology, an intermediate larval stage of a coelenterate, occurring between the planula and actinula stages.

hȳ·drō·pneū·mat'iç, *a.* [*hydro-*, and Gr. *pneumatikos*, of or caused by wind or air, from *pneuma*, wind, air.] of, pertaining to, or produced by the action of water and air; involving the combined action of water and air or gas.

hȳ·drō·pon'iç, *a.* of or grown by hydroponics.

hȳ"drō·pon'içs, *n.* [*hydro-*, and Gr. *ponos*, labor.] the science of growing plants in solutions containing the necessary minerals, instead of in soil.

hȳ"drō·pos'i·tive, *a.* in biology, pertaining to or characterized by positive hydrotropism.

hȳ'drō·pot, *n.* [Gr. *hydropotēs*, from *hydōr*, water, and *pinein*, to drink.] one who drinks water; a water drinker.

Hȳ·drop'ō·tēṣ, *n.* [Gr. *hydropotēs*, water drinker.] in zoology, a genus of small, Chinese deer.

hȳ·drō·prō·pul'sion, *n.* [*hydro-*, and E. *propulsion.*] propulsion by means of a hydromotor.

hȳ'drop·sy, *n.* same as *dropsy*.

Hȳ"drop·te·rid'ē·ae, *n.pl.* [*hydro-*, and Gr. *pteris* (*-idos*), a fern.] a class or group of cryptogams including the families *Marsiliaceæ* and *Salviniaceæ*; the water ferns: called also *Rhizocarpeæ*.

hȳ'drō·pult, *n.* [*hydro-*, and L. *catapulta*, a catapult.] a force-pump worked by hand power; a garden pump: written also *hydrapult*.

hȳ·drō·quin'ōl, *n.* hydroquinone.

hȳ"drō·qui·nōne', *n.* [*hydro-* and *quinone.*] a white, crystalline substance, $C_6H_4(OH)_2$, used in medicine and photography.

hȳ·dror'ȧ·chis, hȳ·dror'rhȧ·chis, *n.* [*hydro-*, and Gr. *rhachis*, spine.] in pathology, an abnormal collection of fluid within the spinal column; spinal dropsy.

hȳ·drō·rhī'zȧ, *n.*; *pl.* **hȳ·drō·rhī'zae** or **hȳ·drō·rhī'zȧs,** [*hydro-*, and Gr. *rhiza*, a root.] in zoology, the adherent base or proximal extremity of a hydrozoan.

hȳ·drō·rhī'zăl, *a.* pertaining to or characteristic of a hydrorhiza.

hȳ·dror·rhē'ȧ, hȳ·dror·rhoe'ȧ, *n.* [Gr. *hydrorroia*, a flowing of water; *hydōr*, water, and *rhoia*, from *rhein*, to flow.] in pathology, a discharge of watery fluid.

hȳ'drō·ṣalt, *n.* [*hydro-*, and *salt.*] a salt of a hydracid; also, an acid salt.

hȳ'drō·sçope, *n.* [Gr. *hydroskopion*, a water clock; *hydōr*, water, and *skopein*, to view.]

1. an ancient water clock consisting of a cylindrical graduated tube, from which water slowly escaped through an opening at the bottom, measuring the lapse of time.
2. an instrument for indicating the humidity of the air; a hygroscope. [Obs.]
3. an instrument which makes it possible to examine objects far below the surface of a body of water, consisting of a long tube fitted with various optical instruments at the end.

hȳ'drō·sol, *n.* [*hydro-* and *solution.*] a colloidal dispersion in which water is the dispersing medium.

hȳ'drō·sōle, *n.* a hydrosol.

hȳ·drō·sō'mȧ, *n.*; *pl.* **hȳ·drō·sō'mȧ·tȧ,** [*hydro-*, and Gr. *soma* (*-atos*), body.] in zoology, the entire colony of a hydrozoan: written also *hydrosome*.

hȳ·drō·sō'măl, *a.* of or relating to a hydrosoma.

hȳ·drō·som'ȧ·tous, *a.* of or relating to a hydrosoma.

hȳ'drō·sōme, *n.* same as *hydrosoma*.

hȳ'drō·sphēre, *n.* [*hydro-* and *-sphere.*]

1. all the water on the surface of the earth.
2. the moisture in the atmosphere surrounding the earth.

hȳ'drō·stat, *n.* [Gr. *hydrostatēs*, a hydrostatic balance.]

1. an apparatus for preventing the explosion of a steam boiler.
2. an electrical device for showing or regulating the level of water in a reservoir, etc.

hȳ·drō·stat'iç, hȳ·drō·stat'iç·ăl, *a.* [Gr. *hydrostatēs*, a hydrostatic balance; *hydōr*, water, and *statos*, standing.] relating to hydrostatics; pertaining to or in accordance with the principles of the equilibrium of fluids.

hydrostatic balance; see under *balance*.

hydrostatic paradox; the principle that any quantity of water however small can be made to balance any weight however great.

hydrostatic press; same as ***hydraulic press***: see under *hydraulic*.

hȳ·drō·stat'iç·ăl·ly, *adv.* according to hydrostatics or hydrostatic principles.

hȳ"drō·stȧ·ti'ciăn, *n.* one versed in hydrostatics. [Rare.]

hȳ·drō·stat'içs, *n.pl.* [*construed as sing.*] that branch of physics which has to do with the pressure and equilibrium of water and other liquids; statics of liquids.

hȳ·drō·sul'fīde, *n.* [*hydrogen*, and *sulfide.*] a compound containing the HS radical and some other radical or element, produced by the partial replacement of the hydrogen in hydrogen sulfide: also called *bisulfide*.

hȳ·drō·sul'fīte, *n.* 1. any salt of hydrosulfurous acid; hyposulfite.

2. loosely, sodium hyposulfite, a bleaching agent.

hȳ·drō·sul'fū·ret, *n.* a hydrosulfide. [Obs.]

hȳ·drō·sul'fū·ret·ted, *a.* combined with sulfuretted hydrogen.

hȳ·drō·sul'fūr·ous, *a.* [*hydrogen*, and *sulfurous.*] hyposulfurous.

hȳ·drō·tel'lū·rāte, *n.* [*hydrogen*, *tellurium*, and *-ate.*] a salt formed by the combination of an acid composed of hydrogen and tellurium with a salifiable base.

hȳ·drō·tel·lū'riç, *a.* of or pertaining to, or obtained from, hydrogen and tellurium.

hȳ·drō·thē'çȧ, *n.* [Gr. *hydrothēkē*, a reservoir for water; *hydōr*, water, and *thēkē*, a case, box.] a small chitinous cup, in which each polypite of the *Sertularida* and *Campanularida* is protected.

hȳ·drō·ther·ȧ·peū'tiç, *a.* of hydrotherapeutics, or hydrotherapy.

hȳ·drō·ther·ȧ·peū'tiçs, *n.pl.* [*construed as sing.*] [*hydro-*, and Gr. *therapeutikos*, from *therapeuein*, to attend, serve.] same as *hydrotherapy*.

hȳ·drō·ther'ȧ·py, *n.* the treatment of disease by the internal or external use of water.

hȳ·drō·thēr'măl, *a.* [*hydro-*, and Gr. *thermos*, hot.] of or relating to hot water; especially, having to do with the action of hot water in producing geological changes by dissolving mineral substances and redepositing them when cooled.

hȳ·drō·thō'rax, *n.* [*hydro-*, and Gr. *thōrax*, the chest.] dropsy in the chest; a condition characterized by an abnormal amount of watery fluid in the pleural cavity.

hȳ·drot'iç, *a.* [Gr. *hydrotēs*, moisture, from *hydōr*, water.] causing a discharge of water.

hȳ·drot'iç, *n.* a medicine that removes water or phlegm.

hȳ·drot'iç·ăl, *a.* hydrotic.

hȳ·drō·trop'iç, *a.* of or showing hydrotropism.

hȳ·drot'rō·piṣm, *n.* the tendency of a plant to grow in the direction of moisture.

hȳ'drous, *a.* [Gr. *hydōr*, water, and *-ous.*]

1. watery.
2. containing water, especially water of crystallization, in chemical combination.

hȳ·drox'īde, *n.* [*hydro* and *oxide.*] a compound consisting of an element or radical combined with the hydroxyl radical (OH).

hȳ·drox'y, *a.* hydroxyl.

hȳ·drox'y-, a combining form meaning *hydroxyl*: preferred to *oxy-*.

hȳ·drox·y·kē'tōne, *n.* a ketone containing the hydroxyl radical.

hȳ·drox'yl, *n.* [*hydrogen*, *oxygen*, and *-yl.*] the

monovalent radical OH, present in all hydroxides.

hȳ″drox·yl·am′ine, *n.* [*hydroxyl* and *amine.*] a colorless, odorless base, NH_2OH, used as a reducing agent.

Hȳ·drō·zō′ȧ, *n.pl.* either of the two divisions of *Cœlenterata*, small aquatic and chiefly marine animals having a saclike body consisting of two layers of cells, and a mouth that opens directly into the body cavity.

hȳ·drō·zō′ăn, hȳ·drō·zō′ăl, *a.* pertaining to the hydrozoa.

hȳ·drō·zō′ăn, *n.* an animal of the *Hydrozoa*: hydras, certain jellyfishes, polyps, etc. are hydrozoans.

hȳ·drō·zō′on, *n.*; *pl.* **hȳ·drō·zō′ȧ,** [*hydro-*, and Gr. *zoon*, an animal.] in zoology, any of a class of radiated animals forming with the *Actinozoa* the subkingdom *Cœlenterata*: the *Hydrozoa* are divided into four subclasses—*Hydroidea*, *Siphonophora*, *Discophora*, and *Lucernarida*.

Hȳ′drus, *n.* [Gr. *hydros*, a water snake.]

1. a genus of water snakes, now generally called *Hydrophis*, the type of the family *Hydridæ*.

2. a constellation of the southern hemisphere.

hȳ·ē′măl, *a.* same as *hiemal*.

hȳ′e·māte, *v.i.* same as *hiemate*.

hȳ·e·mā′tion, *n.* same as *hiemation*.

hȳ·ē′nȧ, *n.* [L. *hyæna*; Gr. *hyaina*, a hyena, an animal which has a bristly mane like the hog's from *hys*, a hog.] any of a group of wolflike, flesh-eating animals of Africa and Asia, with a bristly mane, short hind legs, and a characteristic shrill cry: hyenas feed on carrion and are considered cowardly: also spelled *hyaena*.

SPOTTED HYENA

hȳ·ē′nȧ dog, 1. an African animal, *Lycaon pictus*, somewhat resembling a hyena: called also *hunting dog, painted hyena*.

2. an aardwolf. [Obs.]

hȳ·en′i·fọrm, *a.* having the form or characteristics of the hyena or of its family, the *Hyenidæ*.

hȳ·ē′noid, *a.* like a hyena; hyeniform.

hȳ′ē·tăl, *a.* [Gr. *hyetos*, rain, from *hyein*, to rain.] of or relating to rain or its distribution with reference to different regions.

hȳ′ē·tō-, [from Gr. *hyetos*, rain, from *hyein*, to rain.] a combining form meaning *rain, rainfall*, as in *hyeto*graph, *hyeto*logy: also, before a vowel, *hyet-*.

hȳ′ē·tō·gràph, *n.* [*hyeto-*, and Gr. *graphein*, to write.] a chart showing the average annual rainfall.

hȳ″ē·tō·graph′iç, hȳ″ē·tō·graph′iç·ăl, *a.* relating to hyetography.

hȳ·ē·tog′rȧ·phy, *n.* [*hyeto-*, and Gr. *-graphia*, from *graphein*, to write.] the branch of meteorology having to do with the geographical distribution of rainfall.

hȳ·ē·tō·log′iç·ăl, *a.* of hyetology.

hȳ·ē·tol′ō·gy, *n.* [*hyeto-*, and Gr. *-logia*, from *legein*, to speak.] the branch of meteorology which treats of rain, snow, etc.

hȳ·ē·tom′ē·tẽr, *n.* [*hyeto-*, and Gr. *metron*, a measure.] a rain gauge; a device that measures the rainfall at a given place.

hȳ″ē·tō·met′rō·gràph, *n.* [*hyeto-*, and Gr. *metron*, a measure, and *graphein*, to write.] a hyetometer with an attachment for registering the amount of rainfall for each unit of time.

Hȳ·ġē′iȧ (hī-jē′ȧ), *n.* [Gr. *hygieia*, goddess of health, from *hygieia*, health, soundness of body, from *hygiēs*, healthy, sound.]

1. in Greek mythology, the goddess of health, daughter of Aesculapius.

2. one of the small planets or asteroids between the orbits of Mars and Jupiter, discovered in 1849.

Hȳ·ġē′iăn, *a.* 1. relating to Hygeia, the goddess of health.

2. [h–] relating to health and its preservation.

hȳ′ġē·ist, hȳ′ġiē·ist, *n.* a hygienist.

hȳ′ġiēne (*or* -ji-ēn), *n.* [Fr. *hygiène*, from Gr. *hygiainein*, to be sound, healthy, from *hygiēs*, sound, healthy.] the science of health and its maintenance; system of principles for the preservation of health and prevention of disease.

hȳ·ġi·en′iç, hȳ·ġi·en′iç·ăl, *a.* 1. of hygiene or health.

2. promoting health; healthful; sanitary.

hȳ·ġi·en′iç·ăl·ly, *adv.* in a hygienic manner; so as to preserve health.

hȳ·ġi·en′içs, *n.pl.* [*construed as sing.*] the science of health; hygiene; sanitary science.

hȳ′ġi·en·ist, *n.* an expert in hygiene, or the science of health.

hȳ·ġi·ol′ō·ġy, *n.* [Gr. *hygieia*, health, and *-logia*, from *legein*, to speak.] the science of or a treatise on the preservation of health.

hȳ′grine, *n.* [Gr. *hygros*, wet, moist, and *-ine*.] in chemistry, a pungent oil extracted from coca leaves.

hȳ′grō-, [from Gr. *hygros*, wet, moist.] a combining form meaning *wet, moisture*, as in *hygro*meter, *hygro*scope: also, before a vowel, *hygr-*.

hȳ′grō·deīk, *n.* [*hygro-*, and Gr. *deiknynai*, to show, point out.] in physics, a hygrometer fitted with wet and dry bulb thermometers and a gauge which automatically records the relative humidity.

hȳ′grō·gràph, *n.* [*hygro-*, and Gr. *graphein*, to write.] an instrument which registers automatically the variations of atmospheric moisture.

hȳ·grō′mȧ, *n.*; *pl.* **hȳ·grō′mȧ·tȧ, hȳ·grō′mȧṣ,** [*hygro-*, and Gr. *-ōma*, a suffix meaning a tumor.] in medicine, a swelling resulting from a distended cyst or sac filled with serum.

hȳ·grom′ȧ·tous, *a.* like or affected by a hygroma.

hȳ·grom′ē·tẽr, *n.* [*hygro-*, and Gr. *metron*, a measure.] an instrument for measuring humidity.

hȳ·grō·met′riç, hȳ·grō·met′riç·ăl, *a.* 1. pertaining to hygrometry.

2. readily absorbing or attracting moisture from the air, as potash.

hȳ·grom′ē·try, *n.* the branch of physics having to do with measuring the amount of moisture in the air.

hȳ·groph′ȧ·nous, *a.* [*hygro-*, and Gr. *-phanēs*, from *phainein*, to show.] in botany, transparent or watery when moist, and opaque when dry.

hȳ·groph′i·lous, *a.* [*hygro-*, and Gr. *philos*, loving.] flourishing in damp places, as a snail or a water lily.

hȳ′grō·plaṣm, *n.* [*hygro-*, and Gr. *plasma*, anything formed, molded.] in biology, the fluid element of cell protoplasm, as distinguished from stereoplasm.

hȳ′grō·sçōpe, *n.* [*hygro-*, and Gr. *skopein*, to view.] an instrument for recording changes in atmospheric humidity.

hȳ·grō·sçop′iç, hȳ·grō·sçop′iç·ăl, *a.* 1. of, measurable by, or according to a hygroscope.

2. having the property of absorbing or attracting moisture from the air; hygrometric.

hȳ″grō·sçō·pic′i·ty, *n.* the quality of being hygroscopic (sense 2).

hȳ·grō·stat′içs, *n.* [*hygro-*, and Gr. *statikos*, causing to stand, from *histanai*, to cause to stand.] the science of measuring or comparing degrees of moisture.

hȳ′ing, *v.* alternative present participle of *hie*.

hȳke, *n.* a haik. [Obs.]

Hyk′sōs, *n. pl.* [Gr. *Hyksōs*, from Egypt. *Hiq shasu*, chief of the nomadic tribes.] foreign kings of Egypt who formed the XVth and XVIth dynasties (1750?–1580? B.C.): also called *Shepherd Kings*.

hȳl-, see *hylo-*.

hȳ′lȧ, *n.* [Mod. L., from Gr. *hylē*, wood.] a tree frog: loosely called *tree toad*.

hȳ′lae·ō·saụr, *n.* a fossil lizard of the genus *Hylæosaurus*.

Hȳ·lae·ō·saụ′rus, *n.* [Gr. *hylaios*, of the wood or forest, and *sauros*, a lizard.] a genus of gigantic fossil lizards discovered in the Wealden formation of Tilgate Forest in England and characterized by a series of enormous spines, or bony dermal scutes, along the ridge of the back.

hȳ·lär′ċhi·căl, *a.* [Gr. *hylē*, wood, matter, and *archikos*, ruling, from *archein*, to rule.] presiding over matter. [Rare.]

hȳ′lē, *n.* [Gr. *hylē*, wood, matter.] matter: a term used in philosophy.

hȳ′leg, *n.* [Ar.] in astrology, the planet which rules at the time of one's nativity.

hȳ′li·ciṣm, *n.* see *hylism*.

hȳ′li·cist, *n.* [Gr. *hylē*, wood, matter.] a materialist; a believer in the theory of hylism.

Hȳ′li·dae, *n.pl.* [Gr. *hylē*, wood, forest, matter, and *-idæ*.] a family of amphibian vertebrates, distinguished from the true frogs by having dilated disks, or suckers, covered with viscid matter at the tips of their toes, which enable them to climb trees; the tree toads or tree frogs.

hȳ′liṣm, *n.* [Gr. *hylē*, wood, matter.] in metaphysics, a theory which regards matter as the principle of evil: also called *hylicism*.

hȳ′lō-, [from Gr. *hylē*, wood, matter.] a combining form meaning: (a) *wood*, as in *hylo*phagous; (b) *matter, substance*, as in *hylo*zoism. Also, before a vowel, *hyl-*.

hȳ′lō·bāte, *n.* [Gr. *hylobatēs*, one who inhabits or haunts the woods; *hylē*, wood, forest, and *batēs*, one who mounts, from *bainein*, to go.] in zoology, an ape of the genus *Hylobates*; the long-armed ape or gibbon.

Hȳ·lob′ȧ·tēṣ, *n.* a genus of apes including the gibbons.

hȳ·lō′dēṣ, *n.* [Gr. *hylōdēs*, woody, of the wood; *hylē*, wood, and *eidos*, form.] a tree frog, *Hyla pickeringi*, of North America.

hȳ·lō·ġen′e·sis, *n.* [*hylo-*, and Gr. *genesis*, generation.] the origin of matter. [Rare.]

hȳ′loid, *a.* [Gr. *hylē*, wood, and *eidos*, form.] pertaining to the *Hylidæ*, a family of tree toads.

hȳ′loid mem′brāne, a delicate membrane containing the vitreous humor of the eye.

hȳ′lō·ist, *n.* [Gr. *hylē*, wood, matter, and *-ist*.] one who believes matter to be God.

hȳ·lop′ȧ·thiṣm, *n.* [*hylo-*, and Gr. *pathos*, feeling, and *-ism*.] the belief that matter has the faculty of perception and that spirit and matter are retroactive.

hȳ·lop′ȧ·thist, *n.* a believer in hylopathism.

hȳ·loph′ȧ·gous, *a.* [Gr. *hylophagos*, eating wood; *hylē*, wood, and *phagein*, to eat.] feeding on the young shoots of trees, roots, etc., as certain insects.

hȳ′lō·thē·iṣm, *n.* [*hylo-*, and Gr. *theos*, god, and *-ism*.] the doctrine that matter is God, or that there is no God except matter and the universe.

hȳ′lō·thē·ist, *n.* a believer in hylotheism.

hȳ·lot′ō·mous, *a.* [*hylo-*, and Gr. *tomos*, cutting, from *temnein*, to cut.] wood-cutting, as sawflies and certain other insects.

hȳ·lō·zō′iç, *a.* pertaining to hylozoism.

hȳ·lō·zō′iṣm, *n.* [*hylo-*, and Gr. *zōē*, life, and *-ism*.] the doctrine that all matter has life, or that matter and life are inseparable.

hȳ·lō·zō′ist, *n.* one who believes in hylozoism.

Hȳ′men, *n.* [L., from Gr. *Hymēn* (*-enos*), god of marriage.]

1. in ancient mythology, the god of marriage, son of Bacchus and Venus, or of Apollo and Urania.

2. [h–] (a) marriage or the state of marriage; (b) a wedding song or poem.

hȳ′men, *n.* [Gr. *hymēn*, a membrane.]

1. in anatomy, the thin mucous membrane that usually covers part of the opening of the vagina in a virgin.

2. in botany, the fine pellicle which encloses a flower in the bud.

Hȳ·men·ae′ȧ, *n.* [f. of L. *Hymenæus*, relating to Hymen, the god of marriage: so called from the leaf being formed of a pair of leaflets.] a genus of tropical American trees of the natural order *Leguminosæ*, including *Hymenæa courbaril*, the locust tree of the West Indies, valued for its resin and its hard, tough heartwood.

hȳ·men·ē′ăl, hȳ·men·ē′ăn, *a.* [L. *Hymenæus*, relating to the god of marriage, from *Hymen*; Gr. *Hymēn*, Hymen.] pertaining to a wedding or marriage.

hȳ·men·ē′ăl, *n.* a marriage song or poem.

hȳ·mē′ni·ăl, *a.* of or relating to the hymenium.

hȳ·me·niç′ō·lăr, *a.* present in the hymenium.

hȳ·me·nif′ẽr·ous, *a.* [Gr. *hymenion*, a membrane, and L. *ferre*, to bear.] having or developing a hymenium.

hȳ·mē′ni·um, *n.*; *pl.* **hȳ·mē′ni·ȧ, hȳ·mē′ni·umṣ,** [Gr. *hymenion*, dim. of *hymēn*, a membrane.] the fruit-bearing surface of certain fungi, as that of the gills of the mushroom.

hȳ′me·nō-, [from Gr. *hymēn*, membrane.] a combining form meaning *membrane*, as in *hymeno*pter: also, before a vowel, *hymen-*.

hȳ·men·og′e·ny, *n.* [*hymeno-*, and Gr. *-genēs*, producing.] the production of artificial membranes by contact of two fluids, as albumin and fat, when the former gives a coating to the globules of the latter.

hȳ′men·oid, *a.* [Gr. *hymēn*, a membrane, and *eidos*, form.] resembling a hymenium.

hȳ″me·nō·mȳ·cēte′, *n.* any fungus of the *Hymenomycetes.*

Hȳ″me·nō·mȳ·cē′tēș, *n.pl.* [*hymeno-*, and Gr. *mykēs* (pl. *mykētes*), a mushroom.] in some classifications, a subclass of Basidiomycetes, consisting of fungi characterized by having naked reproductive organs, called the hymenium: this subclass contains the *Agaricus*, the *Polyporus*, and the *Tremella*.

hȳ″me·nō·mȳ·cē′toid, *a.* resembling a hymenomycete.

hȳ″me·nō·mȳ·cē′tous, *a.* of or relating to the hymenomycetes.

hȳ·men′ō·phōre, hȳ·men·oph′ō·rum, *n.* [*hymeno-*, and Gr. *-phoros*, from *pherein*, to bear.] that part of a fungus which supports the hymenium.

Hȳ″me·nō·phyl′lum, *n.* [*hymeno-*, and Gr. *phyllon*, a leaf.] a genus of ferns, including a large number of species with filmy pellucid fronds, found chiefly in hot, damp, tropical forests.

hȳ·men·op′tẽr, *n.* any of the *Hymenoptera*.

Hȳ·men·op′te·rȧ, *n.pl.* [Gr. *hymenopteros*, membrane-winged; *hymēn*, a membrane, and *pteron*, wing.] a large, highly specialized order of insects, including wasps, bees, ants, ichneumon flies, etc., which have a biting or sucking mouth and, when winged, four membranous wings.

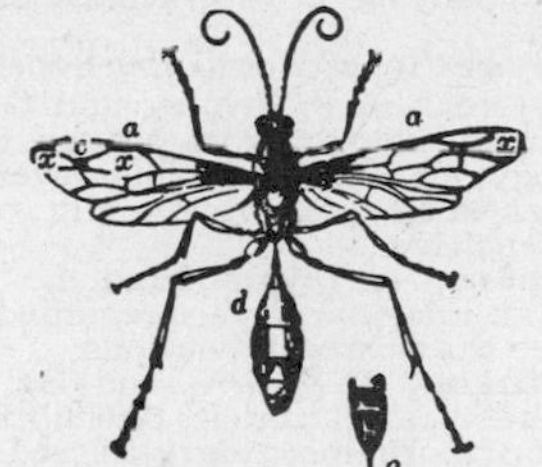

HYMENOPTERA (*Ichneumon grossarlus*)
a, a, stigmata; *c*, marginal, or radial, cell; *x x x*, submarginal, or cubital cells; *d*, pedunculated abdomen; *o*, ovipositor of female

hȳ·men·op′tẽr·ăl, *a.* hymenopterous.

hȳ·men·op′tẽr·ăn, *n.* a hymenopterous insect.

hȳ·men·op′tẽr·ăn, *a.* hymenopterous.

hȳ·men·op′tẽr·on, *n.*; *pl.* **hȳ·men·op′tẽr·ȧ,** a hymenopterous insect.

hȳ·men·op′tẽr·ous, *a.* having the characteristics of the *Hymenoptera*.

hymn (him), *n.* [AS. *hymen, ymen* (pl. *ymnas*); LL. *hymnus*; Gr. *hymnos*, a hymn, festive song, ode.]

1. a song in praise or honor of God, a god, or gods.

2. any song of praise or glorification.

hymn, *v.t.* and *v.i.*; hymned (himd), *pt., pp.*; hymning (him′ing *or* him′ning), *ppr.* to praise in song; to worship by singing hymns.

hym′năl, *n.* [LL. *hymnus*, a hymn, and *-al.*] a collection of hymns, generally for use in public worship; a hymnbook.

hym′năl, *a.* of or using hymns.

hym′nȧ·ry, *n.* a hymnbook. [Rare.]

hymn′book (him′), *n.* a book containing a collection of hymns.

hym′niç, *a.* relating to hymns.

hymn′ing (him′), *n.* the singing of hymns.

hym′nist, *n.* one who composes hymns.

hym′nō·dist, *n.* an expert in hymnody.

hym′nō·dy, *n.* [LL. *hymnodia*; Gr. *hymnoidia*, the singing of a hymn; *hymnos*, a hymn, festive song, and *aeidein*, to sing.]

1. the art or practice of singing hymns.

2. hymnology.

3. hymns collectively.

hym·nog′rȧ·phẽr, *n.* a writer of hymns, or one who writes on the subject of hymns.

hym·nog′rȧ·phy, *n.* [Gr. *hymnos*, a hymn, and *graphein*, to write.] the art of writing hymns.

hym·nol′ō·ġist, *n.* a composer of hymns; also, one versed in hymnology.

hym·nol′ō·ġy, *n.* [Gr. *hymnologia*, the science of hymns, from *hymnologos*, singing hymns, *hymnos*, a hymn, and *-logia*, from *legein*, to speak.]

1. the study of hymns, their use, history, etc.

2. hymns collectively.

3. the writing or composition of hymns.

hȳ′ō-, [from Gr. *hyoeidēs*, shaped like the Gr. letter ϒ, upsilon.] a combining form meaning *of the hyoid bone*: also *hy-*.

hȳ′ō·dont, *n.* in zoology, any fish belonging to the family *Hyodontidæ*.

Hȳ·ō·don′ti·dae, *n.pl.* [*hyo-*, and Gr. *odous, odontos*, a tooth.] a small family of fresh-water fishes; the mooneyes.

hȳ·ō·glos′săl, *a.* [*hyo-*, and Gr. *glōssa*, tongue.] of or relating to the hyoid arch and the tongue; pertaining to the muscle on either side of the tongue joining it to the hyoid bone.

hȳ·ō·glos′sus, *n.* [*hyo-*, and Gr. *glōssa*, tongue.] a flat muscle at either side of the base of the tongue by which the tongue is attached to the hyoid bone.

hȳ′oid, *a.* [Gr. *hyoeidēs*, shaped like the letter ϒ, upsilon; ϒ, upsilon, and *eidos*, form.] designating or of a bone or bones at the base of the tongue, U-shaped in man.

hyoid arch; in anatomy, the branchial arch which joins the tongue on either side to the skull and which includes the hyoid bone.

hyoid bone; the principal element and central part of the hyoid arch.

hȳ′oid, *n.* the hyoid bone or bones.

hȳ·oid′ē·ăl, hȳ·oid′ē·ăn, *a.* same as *hyoid*.

hȳ″ō·man·dib′ū·lăr, *a.* [*hyo-*, and LL. *mandibula*, a jaw.] relating to the hyoid arch and the lower jaw.

hȳ″ō·man·dib′ū·lăr, *n.* the upper part of the hyoid, which in fishes is joined to the skull.

hȳ′ō·men·tăl, *a.* [*hyo-*, and L. *mentum*, the chin.] of or connected with the hyoid bone and the chin or front part of the lower jaw.

hȳ·ō·plas′trŏn, *n.* [*hyo-*, and LL. *plastra*, a thin plate of metal.] either of the second lateral pair of plates in the ventral shield of a turtle: called also *hyosternum*.

hȳ·os′cine, *n.* [*hyoscyamus* and *-ine.*] in chemistry, same as *scopolamine*.

hȳ·os·cȳ′ȧ·min, *n.* same as *hyoscyamine*.

hȳ·os·cȳ′ȧ·mine, *n.* [from L. *hyoscyamus*, henbane, from Gr. *hyoskyamos*, from *hys*, pig, and *kyamos*, bean, and *-ine.*] a colorless, crystalline, very poisonous alkaloid, $C_{17}H_{23}NO_3$, obtained from henbane and other plants of the nightshade family: it is used in medicine as a sedative, hypnotic, etc.

Hȳ·os·cȳ′ȧ·mus, *n.* [L., from Gr. *hyoskyamos*, henbane, lit., hog bean; *hys, hyos*, hog, and *kyamos*, a bean.]

1. a genus of plants of the nightshade family.

2. [h–] any plant of this genus; specifically, henbane.

hȳ·ō·stẽr′năl, *a.* [*hyo-*, and Gr. *sternon*, the breast, chest.]

1. relating to the sternum and the hyoid bone.

2. relating to the hyoplastron of a turtle.

hȳ·ō·stẽr′num, *n.* same as *hyoplastron*.

hȳ·ō·styl′iç, *a.* [*hyo-*, and Gr. *stylos*, a pillar.] having the jaws connected with the cranium by the hyomandibular part of the hyoid arch, as in fishes, not attached to the skull as in mammals.

hyp, *n.* [*often pl.*] a fit of melancholy; hypochondria (usually with *the*). [Obs.; formerly Colloq.]

hyp-, same as *hypo-*.

hyp·ȧ·byss′ăl, *a.* [*hyp-* and *abyssal.*] in geology, consolidated or partly crystalline from fusion at moderate depths underground.

hȳ·pae′thrăl, *a.* [L. *hypæthrus*; Gr. *hypaithros*; *hypo*, under, and *aithēr*, ether, clear sky.] open to the sky; roofless: said of buildings and courts in classical architecture: also spelled *hypethral*.

hyp·al·ġē′si·ȧ, *n.* hypalgia.

hȳ·pal′ġi·ȧ, *n.* [*hyp-*, and Gr. *algos*, pain.] lessened or impaired sensibility to pain.

hȳ·pal′lȧ·ġē, *n.* [Gr. *hypallagē*, an exchange, interchange, from *hypallassein*, to interchange; *hypo*, under, and *allassein*, to change.] in grammar, a figure of speech consisting of an interchange of cases; as, *dare classibus austros*, for *dare classes austris*.

hȳ·pan′thi·um, *n.* [*hyp-*, and Gr. *anthos*, flower.] in botany, a fruit or flower having its axis enlarged under the calyx, as the pear or the calycanthus.

hȳ·pȧ·poph′y·sis *n.*; *pl.* **hȳ·pȧ·poph′y·sēș,** [*hyp-*, and Gr. *apophysis*, sprout, process.] a median outgrowth or process on the ventral side of a vertebra.

hȳ·pär·tē′ri·ăl, *a.* [*hyp-*, and Gr. *artēria*, artery.] situated beneath an artery.

hȳ·pas′pist, *n.* [Gr. *hypaspistēs*, a shield-bearer; *hypo*, under, and *aspis*, a shield.] in ancient Greece, a shield-bearer, especially one of the Macedonian royal guard.

hȳ·pax′i·ăl, *a.* [*hyp-*, and L. *axis*, an axle, axis.] in anatomy, situated beneath the vertebrae.

hȳpe, *n.* 1. hypodermic. [Slang.]

2. a drug addict. [Slang.]

3. deception; especially, loud, exaggerated promotion or publicity. [Slang.]

hȳpe, *v.t.*; hyped, *pt., pp.*; hyping, *ppr.* 1. to stimulate, excite, enliven, etc. artificially, by or as by the injection of a drug: usually with *up*; as, *hyped*-up glamour. [Slang.]

2. to promote or publicize in a sensational way. [Slang.]

hȳ′pẽr-, [Gr., from *hyper*, over, above, concerning.] a prefix meaning: (a) *over, above, more than the normal, excessive*, as in *hyper*critical, *hyper*opia; (b) in chemistry, formerly, *per-*, as in *hyper*oxide. Opposed to *hypo-*.

hȳ·pẽr·ac′id, *a.* excessively acid.

hȳ″pẽr·ȧ·cid′i·ty, *n.* excessive acidity, especially of the gastric juice.

hȳ·pẽr·ae′mi·ȧ, *n.* same as *hyperemia*.

hȳ″pẽr·aes·thē′si·ȧ, *n.* same as *hyperesthesia*.

hȳ″pẽr·al·ġē′si·ȧ, *n.* [*hyper-*, and Gr. *algēsis*, sense of pain.] abnormally high sensitiveness to pain.

hȳ″pẽr·al·ġē′siç, *a.* of or relating to hyperalgesia.

hȳ″pẽr·ap·ō·physʹ′i·ăl, *a.* of, relating to, or like a hyperapophysis.

hȳ″pẽr·ȧ·poph′y·sis, *n.*; *pl.* **hȳ″pẽr·ȧ·poph′y·sēș,** [*hyper-*, and Gr. *apophysis*, a sprout.] a projection on the dorsal side of a neural spine, locking the vertebra with the one next below.

hȳ·pẽr·as′pist, *n.* [Gr. *hyperaspistēs*, one who holds a shield over, a protector; *hyper*, over, and *aspis*, a shield.] in ancient Greek armies, one who held a shield to protect another; hence, a defender. [Obs.]

hȳ″pẽr·bar′iç, *a.* [*hyper-*, and *baric.*]

1. of or having a pressure or specific gravity greater than that within the body tissues or fluids.

2. designating or of a pressurized, usually oxygenated chamber, used in the experimental treatment of various diseases and conditions.

hȳ·pẽr′bȧ·ton, *n.*; *pl.* **hȳ·pẽr′bȧ·tȧ,** [L., from Gr. *hyperbatos*, transposed, from *hyperbainein*, to step over; *hyper*, over, and *bainein*, to go.] in rhetoric, inversion; a transposition or change in the usual grammatical order of words or clauses, as "broad is the way" for "the way is broad."

hȳ·pẽr′bō·lȧ, *n.*; *pl.* **hȳ·pẽr′bō·lȧș,** [Gr. *hyperbolē*, a throwing beyond, excess, from *hyperballein*, to throw beyond; *hyper*, over, beyond, and *ballein*, to throw.] a curve formed by the section of a cone cut by a plane that makes a greater angle with the base than the side of the cone makes.

HYPERBOLA

hȳ·pẽr′bō·lē, *n.* [Gr. *hyperbolē*, a throwing beyond, excess, from *hyperballein*, to throw beyond or over; *hyper*, over, beyond, and *ballein*, to throw.] exaggeration for effect, not meant to be taken literally. Example: This story is as old as time.

hȳ·pẽr·bol′iç, hȳ·pẽr·bol′iç·ăl, *a.* 1. of, or having the form of, a hyperbola.

2. relating to or containing hyperbole; exaggerating or diminishing beyond the fact; exceeding the truth; as, a *hyperbolical* expression.

hyperbolic functions; the mathematic functions of a hyperbola corresponding to the trigonometric functions of a circle, as the hyperbolic sine, secant, etc.

hyperbolic logarithms; the Napierian, or natural, system of logarithms.

hȳ·pẽr·bol′iç·ăl·ly, *adv.* in the form of a hyperbola.

2. with exaggeration; in a hyperbolic manner.

hȳ·pẽr′bō·lism, *n.* 1. the use of hyperbole.

2. a hyperbolic statement.

hȳ·pẽr′bō·list, *n.* one who uses hyperbole.

hȳ·pẽr′bō·līze, *v.t.* and *v.i.*; hyperbolized, *pt.*,

pp.; hyperbolizing, *ppr.* to express with hyperbole.

hȳ·pẽr′bō·loid, *n.* [Gr. *hyperbolē*, a hyperbola, and *eidos*, form.]
1. a quadric surface having one or more of its plane sections hyperbolas; also, a solid having such a surface.
2. a hyperbola of one of the higher orders.

hȳ″pẽr·bō·loi′dăl, *a.* of or resembling a hyperboloid.

hȳ·pẽr·bō′rē·ăn, *a.* [LL. *Hyperboreanus*, from L. *Hyperboreus*; Gr. *hyperboreos*, beyond the north wind; *hyper*, over, beyond, and *boreas*, the north wind.]
1. of the far north.
2. very cold; frigid.
3. [H–] of the Hyperboreans.

hȳ·pẽr·bō′rē·ăn, *n.* 1. [H–] in Greek legend, an inhabitant of a northern region of sunshine and everlasting spring, beyond the mountains of the north wind.
2. a person living in a far northern region.

hȳ·pẽr·cär′bū·ret·ed, *a.* having gaseous hydrocarbons in excess, as water gas.

hȳ″pẽr·cat·ȧ·lec′tic, *a.* [Gr. *hyperkatalēktikos*; *hyper*, over, beyond, and *katalēktikos*, stopping off, incomplete, from *katalēgein*, to cease.] in prosody, having one or two extra syllables beyond the last regular measure.

hȳ·pẽr·chlō′ric, *a.* same as *perchloric.*

hȳ″pẽr·chrō·mā′si·ȧ, *n.* [*hyper-*, and Gr. *chrōma*, color.] abnormal pigmentation of the skin.

hȳ·pẽr·chrō′mȧ·tism, *n.* the state of having abnormally intensified coloration.

hȳ″pẽr·chrō·mȧ·tō′sis, *n.* same as *hyperchromasia.*

hȳ·pẽr·cor′ȧ·coid, *n.* [*hyper-*, and Gr. *korakoeidēs*, shaped like a crow's beak; *korax* (-*akos*), crow, and *eidos*, form.] in ichthyology, the scapula.

hȳ·pẽr·crit′ic, *n.* [*hyper-*, and Gr. *kritikos*, a critic; properly an adj., able to discern or decide, from *krinein*, to decide, judge.] one who is critical beyond measure or reason; an overrigid critic; a captious censor.

hȳ·pẽr·crit′ic, *a.* same as *hypercritical.*

hȳ·pẽr·crit′ic·ăl, *a.* 1. overcritical; critical beyond reason; captious; as, a *hypercritical* reader.
2. excessively exact; as, a *hypercritical* statement.

hȳ·pẽr·crit′ic·ăl·ly, *adv.* in a hypercritical manner.

hȳ·pẽr·crit′i·cism, *n.* excessive rigor of criticism; an exaggerated exercise of the critical faculties.

hȳ·pẽr·crit′i·cīze, *v.t.*; hypercriticized, *pt.*, *pp.*; hypercriticizing, *ppr.* to criticize harshly or with undue severity.

hȳ″pẽr·dū·lī′ȧ, *n.* [*hyper-*, and Gr. *douleia*, service.] the veneration given by Roman Catholics to the Virgin Mary, so called because higher than that given to other saints (which is known as *dulia*), though inferior to *latria*, the worship due to God alone.

hȳ″pẽr·dy·nam′i·ȧ, *n.* [Gr. *hyperdynamos*, of higher power; *hyper*, over, above, and *dynamis*, power.] in medicine, excessive functional energy; overexcitement of nervous or muscular action.

hȳ″pẽr·el·lip′tic, *a.* [*hyper-*, and Gr. *elleiptikos*, defective, from *elleipein*, to leave in, fall short.] in mathematics, beyond or transcending what is elliptic.

hȳ·pẽr·ē′mi·ȧ, *n.* [*hyper-*, and Gr. *haima*, blood.] a congestion of blood in any part of the body.

hȳ·pẽr·ē′mic, *a.* affected with or characterized by hyperemia.

hȳ″pẽr·es·thē′si·ȧ, *n.* [Mod. L., from *hyper-*, and *esthesia*.] an abnormal sensitivity of the skin or some sense organ.

hȳ″pẽr·es·thet′ic, *a.* of or having hyperesthesia.

hȳ″pẽr·eū·tec′tic, *a.* containing more of the lesser component than is present in a eutectic solution or alloy.

hȳ·pẽr·gen′e·sis, *n.* [*hyper-*, and Gr. *genesis*, generation, production.] in medicine, abnormal increase of tissue; overgrowth.

hȳ″pẽr·gē·ō·met′ric, *a.* pertaining to hypergeometry.

hȳ″pẽr·gē·om′e·try, *n.* [*hyper-*, and Gr. *geōmetria*; *gē*, land, the earth, and *metrein*, to measure.] geometry which assumes more than three dimensions of space.

Hȳ′pẽr·gon, *n.* 1. a trade-mark of a lens.
2. [h–] any lens having this trade-mark.

hȳ″pẽr·hē·dō′ni·ȧ, *n.* [*hyper-*, and Gr. *hēdonē*, pleasure.] in medicine, a pathological heightening of pleasurable sensations.

Hȳ″pẽr·i·cā′cē·ae, *n.pl.* [*Hyperic*um and -*aceæ*.] a natural order of plants of which the genus *Hypericum* is the type.

hȳ″pẽr·i·cā′ceous, *a.* of the *Hypericaceæ*.

Hȳ·per′i·cum, *n.* [L., from Gr. *hypereikon*, St.-John's-wort; *hypo*, under, and *ereikē*, heath, heather.]
1. a genus of herbaceous plants, usually with dotted leaves and pentamerous yellow flowers. *Hypericum perforatum*, St.-John's-wort, is one of the most common plants of this genus.
2. [h–] any plant of this genus.

HYPERICUM
(*Hypericum calycinum*)

hȳ·pẽr·i·dē·ā′tion, *n.* [*hyper-*, and Gr. *idea*, idea.] excessive mental activity.

hȳ″pẽr·i·nō′sis, *n.* [*hyper-*, and Gr. *is*, *inos*, strength, fiber.] an abnormally fibrinous state of the blood: opposed to *hypinosis*.

Hȳ·pē′ri·ŏn, *n.* [L.; Gr. *Hyperiōn*.] in Greek mythology, (a) a Titan, son of Uranus and Gaea, and father of the sun god Helios; (b) Helios himself.

hȳ″pẽr·ki·nē′si·ȧ, *n.* same as *hyperkinesis*.

hȳ″pẽr·ki·nē′sis, *n.* [*hyper-*, and Gr. *kinēsis*, movement, from *kinein*, to move.] in medicine, a condition of abnormally increased muscular movement.

hȳ″pẽr·ki·net′ic, *a.* of or characterized by hyperkinesis.

hȳ·pẽr·met·ȧ·mor′phō·sis, *n.* [*hyper-*, and Gr. *metamorphōsis*, a transformation.] in entomology, a kind of metamorphism in which more than the usual number of changes takes place: in some insects the larva itself is more than once completely metamorphosed.

hȳ·pẽr′me·tẽr, *n.* [LL., from Gr. *hypermetros*, going beyond the meter, beyond measure; *hyper*, over, beyond, and *metron*, a measure.] in prosody, a verse containing a redundant syllable.

hȳ·pẽr·met′ric, hȳ·pẽr·met′ric·ăl, *a.* in prosody, having a redundant syllable.

hȳ″pẽr·me·trō′pi·ȧ, hȳ·pẽr·met′rō·py, *n.* [Gr. *hypermetros*, beyond measure, excessive, and *ōps*, *ōpos*, eye.] the condition of being farsighted; abnormal vision in which the rays of light are focused behind the retina so that distant objects are seen more clearly than near ones.

hȳ″pẽr·me·trop′ic, *a.* of or having hypermetropia; farsighted.

hȳ·pẽrm·nē′si·ȧ, *n.* [*hyper-*, and Gr. *mnēsis*, remembrance.] extraordinary power in remembering or recollecting.

Hȳ·pẽrm·nes′trȧ, *n.* in Greek mythology, the only one of the Danaïdes, the fifty daughters of King Danaüs, who did not kill her husband at her father's command.

hȳ″pẽr·myr″i·ō·rä′mȧ, *n.* [*hyper-*, and Gr. *myrios*, countless, and *horama*, a view, from *horān*, to see.] a show or panorama exhibiting many objects or scenes.

hȳ′pẽr·nic, *n.* Nicaraguan dyewood; any red dyewood extract.

Hȳ″pẽr·ō·är′ti·ȧ (-shi-ȧ), *n.pl.* [Gr. *hyperōos*, being above, upper, and *artios*, complete, perfect.] in zoology, an order of marsipobranchiate lampreys having many teeth and the nasal aperture in the top of the head and without connection with the mouth.

hȳ′pẽr·on, *n.* [*hyper-*, and baryon.] any of a class of baryons which are heavier than nucleons.

Hȳ·pẽr·ō′ō·don, *n.* [Gr. *hyperōos*, being above, upper, and *odous*, *odontos*, a tooth.] a genus of beaked whales including the bottlenose whale.

hȳ·pẽr·ō′pi·ȧ, *n.* same as *hypermetropia*.

hȳ·pẽr·op′ic, *a.* of or having hypermetropia.

hȳ″pẽr·ō·rex′i·ȧ, *n.* [*hyper-*, and Gr. *orexis*, desire, appetite, from *oregein*, to reach out, desire.] in medicine, an inordinate craving for food; insatiable appetite; voracity.

hȳ″pẽr·os·tō′sis, *n.*; *pl.* **hȳ″pẽr·os·tō′sēs,** [Mod. L.; *hyper-*, and *ostosis*.] an abnormal increase or thickening of bony tissue.

hȳ″pẽr·os·tot′ic, *a.* of or having hyperostosis.

Hȳ″pẽr·ō·trē′tȧ, Hȳ″pẽr·ō·trē′tī, *n.pl.* [Gr. *hyperōē*, the palate, and *trētos*, perforated.] an order of fishes, including the hagfishes, belonging to the class *Marsipobranchia*.

hȳ·pẽr·ox′īde, *n.* a peroxide. [Obs.]

hȳ·pẽr·ox′y·gen·ā·ted, *a.* containing in combination a supersaturation of oxygen.

hȳ·pẽr·ox·y·mū′ri·āte, *n.* a perchlorate. [Obs.]

hȳ·pẽr·ox·y·mū·ri·at′ic, *a.* perchloric. [Obs.]

hȳ·pẽr·par′ȧ·sīte, *n.* [*hyper-*, and Gr. *parasitos*, eating beside, a parasite.] in biology, a parasite of a parasite, as larvae living in and feeding on other larvae.

hȳ·pẽr·pep′si·ȧ (*or* -shȧ), *n.* [*hyper-*, and Gr. *pepsis*, digestion.] in medicine, a kind of indigestion in which an excessive quantity of chlorides is contained in the gastric fluids.

hȳ·pẽr·phā′si·ȧ (-zhi-), *n.* [*hyper-*, and Gr. *phasis*, a speaking, from *phanai*, to speak.] in medicine, loss of control of the organs of articulation; deranged utterance.

hȳ·pẽr·phys′ic·ăl, *a.* [*hyper-*, and Gr. *physikos*, natural, pertaining to nature, from *physis*, nature.] supernatural; beyond physical laws.

hȳ″pẽr·pi·tū′i·tȧ·rism, *n.* 1. excessive activity of the pituitary gland or its anterior lobe.
2. the condition of excessive skeletal growth caused by this.

hȳ·pẽr·plā′si·ȧ, *n.* [*hyper-*, and Gr. *plasis*, a forming, from *plassein*, to form, mold.] in pathology, excessive formation of tissue; an increase in the size of a tissue or organ owing to an increase in the number of cells.

hȳ·pẽr·plas′ic, *a.* hyperplastic.

hȳ·pẽr·plas′tic, *a.* pertaining to or characterized by hyperplasia.

hȳ·pẽrp·nē′ȧ, *n.* [*hyper-*, and Gr. *pnoē*, *pnoiē*, breath.] panting or abnormally rapid respiration.

hȳ″pẽr·py·ret′ic, *a.* of or having hyperpyrexia.

hȳ″pẽr·py·rex′i·ȧ, *n.* [*hyper-*, and Gr. *pyressein*, to be feverish, from *pyretos*, fever.] in pathology, an abnormally high fever.

hȳ·pẽr·sen′si·tive, *a.* abnormally or excessively sensitive.

hȳ′pẽr·spāce, *n.* [*hyper-*, and L. *spatium*, space.] an imaginary space regarded as having more than three dimensions.

hȳ′pẽr·sthēne, *n.* [*hyper-*, and Gr. *sthenos*, strength: so called from its difficult frangibility.] an orthorhombic, dark-colored, foliated brittle mineral of pearly luster: it is a silicate of iron and magnesium: also called *Labrador hornblende.*

hȳ·pẽr·sthē′ni·ȧ, *n.* [*hyper-*, and Gr. *sthenos*, strength.] in pathology, a condition of abnormal excitement of the vital phenomena.

hȳ·pẽr·sthen′ic, *a.* relating to hypersthenia; overstimulated.

hȳ·pẽr·sthen′ic, *a.* composed of or containing hypersthene.

hȳ·pẽr·sthē′nīte, *n.* a dark-colored granitelike rock composed of hypersthene and labradorite.

hȳ·pẽr·ten′sion, *n.* 1. any abnormally high tension.
2. abnormally high blood pressure, especially in the arteries, or a diseased condition of which this is the chief symptom.

hȳ·pẽr·ten′sive, *a.* of or having high blood pressure.

hȳ·pẽr·ten′sive, *n.* a hypertensive person.

hȳ·pẽr′thē·sis, *n.* [Gr. *hyperthesis*, a passing over, transposition, from *hypertithenai*; *hyper*, over, and *tithenai*, to set, put.] in philology, the removal of a letter from the syllable to which it originally belonged to another syllable immediately preceding or following it; transposition or metathesis; thus, in Greek, *melaina* is used for *melania*.

hȳ·pẽr·thet′ic·ăl, *a.* [Gr. *hyperthetikos*, superlative; *hyper*, over, and *tithenai*, to place.] hyperbolical; superlative. [Obs.]

hȳ·pẽr·thyr′i·ŏn, *n.* [Gr. *hyperthyrion*; *hyper*, over, and *thyra*, door.] in architecture, a cornice over a door or window.

hȳ·pẽr·thȳ′roid, *a.* of, characterized by, or having hyperthyroidism.

hȳ·pẽr·thȳ′roid, *n.* a person having hyperthyroidism.

hȳ·pẽr·thȳ′roid·ism, *n.* 1. excessive activity of the thyroid gland.
2. the condition caused by this or by taking too much thyroid extract, characterized by a rapid pulse, sleeplessness, etc.

hȳ·pẽr·ton′ic, *a.* 1. having abnormally high tension or tone, especially of the muscles.
2. having an osmotic pressure higher than that of an isotonic solution.

hȳ″pẽr·tri·chō′sis, *n.* [*hyper-*, and Gr. *thrix*,

trichos, hair, and *-osis*.] excessive growth of hair of a part or the whole of the body.

hȳ·pẽr·trī·di·men′sion·ăl, *a.* having more than three dimensions.

hȳ·pẽr·troph′iç, *a.* producing or tending to produce hypertrophy; of or pertaining to hypertrophy.

hȳ·pẽr·troph′iç·ăl, *a.* hypertrophic.

hȳ·pẽr′trō·phous, *a.* exhibiting hypertrophy.

hȳ·pẽr′trō·phy, *v.t.* and *v.i.*; hypertrophied, *pt., pp.*; hypertrophying, *ppr.* to increase abnormally in size.

hȳ·pẽr′trō·phy, *n.* [*hyper-*, and Gr. *trophē*, nutrition, from *trephein*, to nourish.]

1. an increase in the size of a tissue or organ independent of the general growth of the body: opposed to *atrophy*.

2. in botany, the excessive development of one part of a plant to the detriment of another.

hȳ·pẽr·typ′iç, *a.* surpassing the type; showing abnormal development of characteristics.

hȳ·pẽr·typ′iç·ăl, *a.* hypertypic.

hȳ·pẽr·ven′ti·lāte, *v.i.* and *v.t.*; hyperventilated, *pt., pp.*; hyperventilating, *ppr.* to undergo or cause to undergo hyperventilation.

hȳ·pẽr·ven·ti·lā′tion, *n.* [*hyper-* and *ventilation*.] extremely rapid or deep breathing that overoxygenates the blood, causing dizziness, fainting, etc.

hȳ″pẽr·vī″tȧ·min·ō′sis, *n.* a disorder resulting from excessive vitamin dosage.

hyp·es·thē′si·ȧ, *n.* [Mod. L.; *hyp-*, and *esthesia*.] impaired power of sensation; especially, diminished sensitivity to touch.

hȳ·pē′thrăl, *a.* same as *hypaethral*.

hȳ′phȧ, *n.*; *pl.* **hȳ′phae,** [Gr. *hyphē*, a weaving, a web, from *hyphainein*, to weave.] any of the threadlike parts making up the mycelium of a fungus.

hȳ′phăl, *a.* in botany, relating to or of the nature of a hypha.

hȳ·phē′mi·ȧ, hȳ·phae′mi·ȧ, *n.* [Gr. *hyphaimos*, suffused with blood, bloodshot; *hypo*, under, and *haima*, blood.]

1. deficiency of blood.

2. extravasation of blood.

hȳ′phen, *n.* [LL., from Gr. *hyphen*, a hyphen, lit., under one; *hypo*, under, and *hen*, neut. acc. of *heis*, one.] a mark (-) used between the parts of a compound word or the syllables of a divided word, as at the end of a line.

hȳ′phen, *v.t.*; hyphened, *pt., pp.*; hyphening, *ppr.* to hyphenate.

hȳ′phen·āte, *n.* an American of foreign birth or origin, as a German-American: sometimes an opprobrious term.

hȳ′phen·āte, *v.t.*; hyphenated, *pt., pp.*; hyphenating, *ppr.* 1. to join or separate by a hyphen.

2. to write or print with a hyphen.

hȳ′phen·āte, *a.* hyphenated.

hȳ·phen·ā′tion, *n.* 1. a hyphenating or being hyphenated.

2. a hyphen.

hȳ·phen′iç, *a.* of or pertaining to the hyphen.

hȳ·phen·i·zā′tion, *n.* hyphenation.

hȳ′phen·īze, *v.t.*; hyphenized, *pt., pp.*, hyphenizing, *ppr.* to hyphenate.

Hȳ″phō·mȳ·cē′tēs̹, *n.pl.* [Gr. *hyphe*, a web, and *mykēs*, *mykētos*, a mushroom.] in botany, a division of fungi with naked spores, often septate, and a floccose thallus. It is composed of microscopic plants growing as molds over dead or living organic substances.

hȳ·phō·mȳ·cē′tous, *a.* pertaining to, relating to, or characteristic of the *Hyphomycetes*, or microscopic vegetable molds; as, *hyphomycetous* fungi.

hȳ′pi-, same as *hypo-*.

hȳ·pid″i·ō·mọr′phiç, *a.* [*hypi-*, and Gr. *idiomorphos*, of particular form; *idios*, particular, and *morphē*, form.] in crystallography, idiomorphic in part.

hȳ·pid″i·ō·mọr′phiç·ăl·ly, *adv.* in a hypidiomorphic manner.

hyp·i·nō′sis, *n.* [*hypi-*, and Gr. *is*, *inos*, strength, fiber.] in pathology, a diminished amount of fibrin in the blood: opposed to *hyperinosis*.

hyp·i·not′iç, *a.* lacking fibrin; characterized by hypinosis.

hypn-, see *hypno-*.

hyp·nȧ·gog′iç, *a.* [*hypn-*, and Gr. *agōgē*, a leading, from *agein*, to lead.] leading to sleep; hypnotic.

hyp′nō-, hypn-, [from Gr. *hypnos*, sleep.] a combining form used to signify *sleep* or *hypnotism*, as in *hypno*phobia, *hypno*genesis.

hyp′nō·bāte, *n.* [*hypno-*, and Gr. *bainein*, to go.] a somnambulist; a sleepwalker.

hyp·nō·bā′ti·ȧ, *n.* somnambulism.

hyp′nō·cyst, *n.* [*hypno-*, and Gr. *kystis*, a bladder.] in biology, a dormant encysted protozoan which does not form spores.

hyp·nō·ġen′e·sis, *n.* [*hypno-*, and Gr. *genesis*, generation, production.] the production of a hypnotic condition.

hyp·nō·ġē·net′iç, *a.* pertaining to or producing the hypnotic trance.

hyp·nō·ġē·net′iç·ăl, *a.* hypnogenetic.

hyp·nō·ġen′iç, *a.* hypnogenetic.

hyp·noġ′e·ny, *n.* hypnogenesis.

hyp′noid, *a.* resembling hypnosis.

hyp·noid′ăl, *a.* hypnoid.

hyp·nō·loġ′iç·ăl, *a.* relating to hypnology.

hyp·nol′ō·ġist, *n.* one versed in hypnology.

hyp·nol′ō·ġy, *n.* [*hypno-*, and Gr. *-logia*, from *legein*, to speak.] the science dealing with sleep and hypnosis.

hyp′nōne, *n.* [Gr. *hypnos*, sleep, and *-one*.], acetophenone, a compound possessing hypnotic properties.

hyp·nō·phō′bi·ȧ, *n.* [*hypno-*, and Gr. *phobos*, fear.] morbid fear of sleep.

Hyp′nos, *n.* in Greek mythology, the god of sleep: identified by the Romans with Somnus.

hyp·nō′sis, *n.*; *pl.* **hyp·nō′sēs̹,** [Gr. *hypnos*, sleep, and *-osis*.] a sleeplike condition psychically induced, usually by another person, in which the subject loses consciousness but responds, with certain limitations, to the suggestions of the hypnotist.

hyp·nō·spō·ranġe′, *n.* same as *hypnosporangium*.

hyp″nō·spō·ran′ġi·um, *n.*; *pl.* **hyp″nō·spō·ran′ġi·ȧ,** [*hypno-*, and Gr. *spora*, a spore, and *angeion*, a cup.] in botany, a sporangium containing or producing hypnospores.

hyp′nō·spōre, *n.* [*hypno-*, and Gr. *spora*, a spore, generation.] in botany, a resting spore; a spore that requires a period of repose, or quiescence, before germinating.

hyp·nō·ther′ȧ·py, *n.* [*hypno-*, and *therapy*.] the treatment of disease by hypnotism.

hyp·not′iç, *a.* [Fr. or L.; Fr. *hypnotique*; L. *hypnoticus*; Gr. *hypnōtikos*, tending to sleep, from *hypnos*, sleep.]

1. causing sleep; soporific.

2. of, having the nature of, or inducing hypnosis.

3. easily hypnotized.

4. under the influence of hypnosis.

hyp·not′iç, *n.* 1. any drug causing sleep; a soporific.

2. a hypnotized person or one easily hypnotized.

hyp·not′iç·ăl·ly, *adv.* 1. in a hypnotic manner.

2. by hypnotism.

hyp′nō·tis̹m, *n.* [Gr. *hypnos*, sleep.]

1. the act or practice of inducing hypnosis.

2. the science of hypnosis.

hyp′nō·tist, *n.* one who hypnotizes.

hyp·nō·tis′tiç, *a.* pertaining to or inducing hypnotism.

hyp·nō·tī′zȧ·ble, *a.* that can be hypnotized.

hyp″nō·ti·zā′tion, *n.* the act of hypnotizing or the condition of being hypnotized.

hyp′nō·tīze, *v.t.*; hypnotized, *pt., pp.*; hypnotizing, *ppr.* 1. to put into a hypnotic state; to make hypnotic.

2. to entrance, as by eloquent speech. [Colloq.]

hyp′nō·tī·zẽr, *n.* one who induces hypnotism.

hyp′nō·toid, *a.* [*hypno-*, and Gr. *eidos*, form.] similar to hypnotism in cause or in effect.

Hyp′num, *n.* [Gr. *hypnon*, moss.] in botany, a very large genus of mosses distributed through all parts of the world.

Hyp′nus, *n.* Hypnos.

hȳ′pō-, [Gr. *hypo-*, from *hypo*, under, less than.] a prefix meaning: (a) *under, beneath, below*, as in *hypo*dermic, *hypo*cycloid; (b) *less than, subordinated to*, as in *hypo*taxis; (c) in chemistry, *having a lower state of oxidation*, as in *hypo*phosphorous. Also, before a vowel, *hyp-*. Opposed to *hyper-*.

hȳ′pō, *n.* 1. a hypodermic. [Colloq.]

2. a hypochondriac. [Slang.]

hȳ′pō, *n.*; *pl.* **hȳ′pōs̹,** in photography, sodium thiosulfate, $Na_2S_2O_3 \cdot 5H_2O$, a colorless, crystalline salt used in solution as a fixing agent.

hȳ·pō·ā′ri·ăn, *a.* in anatomy, relating to a hypoarion.

hȳ·pō·ā′ri·ŏn, *n.*; *pl.* **hȳ·pō·ā′ri·ȧ,** [*hypo-*, and Gr. *ōarion*, dim. of *ōon*, an egg.] one of a pair of oval-shaped ganglia lying beneath the optic lobes of typical fishes.

hȳ′pō·blast, *n.* [*hypo-*, and Gr. *blastos*, a germ, shoot.] in biology, the innermost layer of the blastoderm: called also *endoblast, entoderm, endoderm*, and *hypoderm*.

hȳ·pō·blas′tiç, *a.* pertaining to a hypoblast; endodermal.

hȳ·pob′ō·lē, *n.* [Gr. *hypobolē*, a throwing under, suggesting, from *hypoballein*, to throw under; *hypo*, under, and *ballein*, to throw.] in rhetoric, a mentioning and refuting of arguments in anticipation of them.

hȳ·pō·brañ′ċhi·ăl, *a.* [*hypo-*, and Gr. *branchia*, gills.] situated under the gills.

hȳ·pō·brañ′ċhi·ăl, *n.* a bone or cartilage under the gills of fishes.

hȳ·pō·brō′mīte, *n.* [*hypo-*, and *bromous*, and *-ite*.] in chemistry, a compound containing hypobromous acid.

hȳ·pō·brō′mous, *a.* [*hypo-*, and Gr. *brōmos*, bad-smelling.] in chemistry, designating an unstable acid the salts of which are called hypobromites.

hȳ·pō·bū′li·ȧ, *n.* [*hypo-*, and Gr. *boulē*, will.] deficiency of will power.

hȳ′pō·cärp, hȳ·pō·cär′pi·um, *n.* [*hypo-*, and Gr. *karpos*, fruit.] in botany, the enlargement of the stem or receptacle beneath the fruit.

hȳ·pō·cär·pō·ġē′ăn, *a.* same as *hypogeal*.

hyp′ō·ca̤ust, *n.* [L. *hypocaustum*; Gr. *hypokauston*, a room heated by a furnace below; *hypo*, under, and *kaiein*, to burn.] among the ancient Greeks and Romans, a space below the floor into which hot air was piped from a furnace to warm the rooms.

hȳ″pō·ċhlōr·hȳ′dri·ȧ, [*hypo-*, and Gr. *chlōros*, green, and *hydōr*, water.] in medicine, a condition resulting from a deficiency of hydrochloric acid in the gastric juice.

hȳ·pō·ċhlō′rīte, *n.* [*hypochlorous* and *-ite*.] in chemistry, a salt of hypochlorous acid: calcium hypochlorite is the chief constituent of bleaching powder.

hȳ″pō·ċhlō′rous, *a.* [*hypo-*, and Gr. *chlōros*.] in chemistry, of or pertaining to an unstable acid, HClO, known only in solution and used as a bleaching and oxidizing agent.

hȳ″pō·ċhlōr·ū′ri·ȧ, *n.* in medicine, an abnormal condition marked by low chloride content in the urine.

hyp·ō·ċhon′dri·ȧ, *n.* [LL., from Gr. *hypochondria*, pl. of *hypochondrion*, the soft part of the body below the cartilage and above the navel; *hypo*, under, and *chonaros*, cartilage: so called because the condition was supposed to have its seat in this region.] in medicine, a state of depression and anxiety regarding one's own state of health, often with imaginary illnesses.

hyp·ō·ċhon′dri·aç, hyp″ō·ċhon·drī′ȧ·çăl, *a.* 1. pertaining to or in the region of the hypochondrium.

2. affected, characterized, or produced by hypochondria.

> The *hypochondriac*, melancholy complexion of us islanders. —Berkeley.

3. producing melancholy or low spirits.

hyp·ō·ċhon′dri·aç, *n.* one affected with hypochondria.

hyp″ō·chon·drī′ȧ·çăl, *a.* same as *hypochondriac*.

hyp″ō·ċhon·drī′ȧ·çăl·ly, *adv.* in a hypochondriac manner.

hyp″ō·ċhon·drī′ȧ·çis̹m, *n.* same as *hypochondria*.

hyp″ō·ċhon·drī′ȧ·sis, *n.* same as *hypochondria*.

hyp·ō·ċhon′dri·um, *n.*; *pl.* **hyp·ō·ċhon′dri·ȧ,** [L. *hypochondrium*; Gr. *hypochondrion*; *hypo*, under, and *chondros*, cartilage.] in anatomy, either of the two lateral and superior regions of the abdomen under the cartilages of the false ribs, and to the right and left of the epigastrium.

hyp·ō·ċhon′dry, *n.* same as *hypochondrium*.

hyp′ō·cist, *n.* [Gr. *hypokistis*, a plant growing on the roots of the cistus; *hypo*, under, and *kistos*, the cistus.] an inspissated juice obtained from a plant, *Cytinus hypocistis*: it is used as an astringent.

hyp·ō·çlī′di·um, *n.*; *pl.* **hyp·ō·çlī′di·ȧ,** [*hypo-*, and Gr. *kleidion*, a little key, dim. of *kleis*, a key.] the median process at the junction of the clavicles of a bird, as shown in the wishbone of a chicken: also written *hypocleidium*.

hyp″ō·çō·ris′tiç, *a.* [Gr. *hypokoristikos*; *hypo*, under, and *korizesthai*, to caress.] of, or having the nature of, a pet name, as a diminutive or term of endearment.

hȳ·pō·çot′yl, *n.* [abbrev. of *hypocotyledonous*.] the part of the axis, or stem, below the cotyledons in the embryo of a plant.

hȳ·pō·crā·ter′i·form, *a.* [Gr. *hypokratērion*, the stand of a mixing bowl, and L. *forma*, form.] tubular below, but suddenly expanding into a flat border at the top; salver-shaped.

HYPOCRATERIFORM COROLLA

hȳ″pō·crā·ter·i·mor′phous, *a.* [Gr. *hypokratērion*, the stand of a mixing bowl, and *morphē*, form.] same as *hypocrateriform*.

hy·poc′ri·sy, *n.* [LL. *hypocrisis*; Gr. *hypokrisis*, a reply, acting a part, feigning, from *hypokrinesthai*, to play a part, pretend; *hypo*, under, and *krinesthai*, to contend, dispute.] a feigning to be what one is not; the acting of a false part; a deception as to real character and feeling, especially in regard to morals and religion.

hyp′ō·crite, *n.* [Gr. *hypokritēs*, one who answers, plays a part, a pretender, from *hypokrinesthai*, to answer, play a part; *hypo*, under and *krinesthai*, to dispute, contend.] one who feigns to be what he is not; especially, one who pretends to be pious, virtuous, etc. without really being so.

And the *hypocrite's* hope shall perish.
—Job viii. 13.

hyp′ō·crite·ly, *adv.* deceptively. [Obs.]

hyp·ō·crit′iç, *a.* same as *hypocritical*.

hyp·ō·crit′iç·ăl, *a.* proceeding from hypocrisy; having the qualities of a hypocrite; dissembling.

hyp·ō·crit′iç·ăl·ly, *adv.* in a hypocritical manner.

hyp·ō·çrys′tăl·line, *a.* [*hypo-*, and Gr. *krystallinos*, from *krystallos*, ice, crystal.] having crystals embedded in an amorphous groundmass.

hȳ·pō·cȳ′çloid, *n.* [*hypo-*, and Gr. *kykloeidēs*; *kyklos*, circle, and *eidos*, form.] the line traced by a point on the circumference of a circle rolling on the inner circumference of a stationary circle.

hȳp·ō·daç′ty·lum, *n.*; *pl.* **hȳp·ō·daç′ty·lȧ,** [*hypo-*, and Gr. *dactylos*, a finger, a toe.] the under side of the toe of a bird: opposed to *acrodactylum*, the upper side.

hyp′ō·dẽrm, *n.* same as *hypoblast*.

hȳp·ō·dẽr′mȧ, *n.* [*hypo-*, and Gr. *derma* (*-atos*), skin.]

1. in botany, a layer of strengthening tissue under the epidermis.
2. in zoology, the hypodermis.

hȳp·ō·dẽr′măl, *a.* 1. of the hypoderma or hypodermis.
2. lying under the epidermis.

hyp″ō·dẽr·mat′iç, *a.* same as *hypodermic*.

hyp″ō·dẽr·mat′iç·ăl·ly, *adv.* same as *hypodermically*.

hȳp·ō·dẽr′miç, *a.* [*hypo-*, and Gr. *derma* (*-atos*), skin.]

1. of the parts under the skin.
2. injected under the skin.
3. of the hypodermis.

hȳp·ō·dẽr′miç, *n.* 1. a hypodermic syringe.
2. a hypodermic injection.

hȳp·ō·dẽr′miç·ăl·ly, *adv.* in a hypodermic manner.

hȳp·ō·dẽr′miç in·jeç′tion, the injection of a medicine or drug under the skin.

hȳp·ō·dẽr′miç syr·inge′, a glass syringe attached to a hollow needle (*hypodermic needle*), used for giving hypodermic injections.

hȳp·ō·dẽr′mis, *n.* 1. in annelids, a thick, tough layer under the cuticle.
2. in entomology, the soft lining of the abdominal walls of an insect.
3. in embryology, the hypoblast.

hȳp·ō·eū·teç′tiç, *a.* containing less of the secondary component than is present in the eutectic mixture of the same components.

hȳp·ō·ġae′iç, *a.* [*hypo-*, and Gr. *gē*, the earth.] derived from or belonging to the peanut; as, *hypogaeic* acid.

hȳp·ō·ġae′ous, *a.* hypogeous.

hȳp·ō·gas′triç, *a.* of or relating to the hypogastrium; situated below the stomach.

hȳp·ō·gas′tri·um, *n.*; *pl.* **hȳp·ō·gas′tri·ȧ,** [Gr. *hypogastrion*, the lower belly, neut. of *hypogastrios*, abdominal; *hypo*, under, and *gastēr*, belly.] that part of the abdomen below the umbilical region, especially its central part.

hȳp·ō·ġē′ăl hȳp·ō·ġae′ăl, *a.* [LL. *hypogeus*, *hypogæus*; Gr. *hypogaios*, under the earth, underground; *hypo*, under, and *gē*, *gaia*, earth.] in botany, growing under the ground; pertaining to plants living and fructifying beneath the surface of the ground, as the truffle.

hȳp·ō·ġē′ăn, hȳp·ō·ġae′ăn, *a.* same as *hypogeal*.

hyp′ō·ġēne, *a.* [*hypo-*, and Gr. *-genēs*, from *gignesthai*, to be born.] in geology, formed beneath the surface of the earth: applied to rocks formed and crystallized at great depths beneath the surface: opposed to *epigene*.

hȳ·poġ′ē·nous, *a.* [*hypo-*, and Gr. *-genēs*, from *gignesthai*, to be born.] in botany, growing beneath; attached by growth to the under side: opposed to *epigenous*.

hȳp·ō·ġē′ous, *a.* same as *hypogeal*.

hȳp·ō·ġē′um, *n.* [L., from Gr. *hypogeion*, *hypogaion*, an underground chamber, properly neut. of *hypogeios*, or *hypogaios*, underground; *hypo*, under, and *gē*, or *gaia*, ground, earth.] in architecture, formerly, all the parts of a building which were underground, as the cellar, etc.; a subterranean apartment or passage, as the catacombs or the underground parts of an amphitheater.

hȳp·ō·glos′săl, *a.* [*hypo-*, and Gr. *glōssa*, tongue.] in anatomy, under the tongue; lying or arranged beneath the tongue; specifically, designating or of the motor nerves of the tongue.

hȳp·ō·glos′sis, *n.* [Gr. *hypoglōssis*; *hypo*, under, and *glōssa*, the tongue.]

1. in anatomy, the under part of the tongue; in entomology, a part of the second sclerite in coleopters.
2. in pathology, (a) a tumor under the tongue; (b) a pill, etc. to be dissolved beneath the tongue.

hȳp·ō·glot′tis, *n.* same as *hypoglossis*.

hȳp·ō·glȳ·cē′mi·ȧ, *n.* a deficiency of sugar in the blood.

hȳ·pog′nȧ·thous, *a.* [*hypo-*, and Gr. *gnathos*, jaw.] having the lower jaw or mandible longer than the upper.

hyp′ō·ġyn, *n.* a hypogynous plant.

hȳ·poġ′y·nous, *a.* [*hypo-*, and Gr. *gynē*, a woman, female.] in botany, growing from below the base of the ovary; having all or any of the floral organs situated below the ovary.

hȳ·pōġ′y·ny, *n* the state of being hypogynous.

hȳ·pō·hȳ′ăl, *a.* [*hypo-*, and *hyoid*, and *-al*.] in zoology, relating to a part of the hyoidean arch in the skeleton of fishes; as, a *hypohyal* bone.

hȳ″pō·ki·net′iç, *a.* [*hypo-*, and Gr. *kinētikos*, from *kinein*, to move.] in physiology, having an insufficiency of muscular activity.

hȳ·pō·nas′tiç, *a.* showing the effect of hyponasty.

hȳ′pō·nas·ty, *n.* [*hypo-*, and Gr. *nastos*, close pressed, solid, from *nassein*, to press or squeeze close.] in botany, a condition characterized by more rapid growth on the lower than on the upper side of an organ, causing it to curve upward.

hȳ·pō·nī′trīte, *n.* [*hyponitrous* and *-ite*.] in chemistry, any salt produced by combination with a hyponitrous acid.

hȳ·pō·nī′trous, *a.* [*hypo-*, and *nitrogen*, and *-ous*.] in chemistry, designating chemical compounds containing nitrogen with a lower valence than in nitrous compounds.

hyponitrous acid; an acid, $H_2N_2O_2$, whose salts are produced by reduction from nitrates: it is an active reducing and oxidizing agent.

hyp′ō·nōme, *n.* [Gr. *hyponomē*, an underground passage, properly f. of *hyponomos*, underground; *hypo*, under, and *nemein*, to dwell.] in zoology, the pipe or passage in the structure of a cephalopod, used in swimming by the force of water ejected.

hȳ″pō·phar·yn′ġē·ăl, *a.* [*hypo-*, and Gr. *pharynx*, the throat.] in zoology, pertaining to the lower part of the pharynx, especially of insects.

hȳ·pō·phar′ynx, *n.* [*hypo-*, and Gr. *pharynx*, the throat.] in some insects, a part attached to the lower side of the pharynx, sometimes having a long tonguelike extension.

hȳ·pō·phloe′ō·dăl, *a.* same as *hypophloeodic*.

hȳ″pō·phloe·od′iç, *a.* [*hypo-*, and Gr. *phloios*, bark.] in lichenology, living under the bark of a plant; also, pertaining to tissues beneath the outer bark.

hȳ·pō·phloe′ous, *a.* same as *hypophloeodic*.

hȳ·pō·phos′phāte, *n.* [*hypophosphorous* and *-ate*.] in chemistry, a salt of hypophosphoric acid.

hȳ·pō·phos′phīte, *n.* [*hypophosphorous* and *-ite*.] in chemistry, a salt of hypophosphorous acid.

hȳ″pō·phos·phor′iç, *a.* [*hypophosphorous* and *-ic*.] in chemistry, containing phosphorus with a lower valence than in phosphoric compounds.

hypophosphoric acid; an acid, $H_4P_2O_6$, produced by the slow oxidation of phosphorus in contact with water which holds it in solution.

hȳ·pō·phos′phŏr·ous ac′id, [*hypo-*, and Gr. *phōsphoros*, lit., light bringer; *phōs*, light, and *pherein*, to bear.] an acid, H_3PO_2, obtained from phosphorus: it is a strong reducing agent.

hȳ·poph′y·ġē, [Gr. *hypophygē*, a refuge, recess; *hypo*, under, and *pheugein*, to flee.] in architecture, a feature of the Doric column consisting of a hollow curve beneath a member, as under a capital; an apophyge.

hȳ·pō·phyl′lous, *a.* same as *hypogenous*.

hȳ·pō·phys′i·ăl, *a.* [*hypo-*, and Gr. *physikos*, physical.] in anatomy, relating to the hypophysis.

hȳ·poph′y·sis, *n.*; *pl.* **hȳ·poph′y·sēṣ,** [Gr. *hypophysis*, an undergrowth, process, from *hypophyein*; *hypo*, under, and *phyein*, to make to grow.]

1. the pituitary gland.
2. in mosses, an enlargement in the pedicel at the base of the capsule.
3. in botany, a layer of cells in the embryo of flowering plants, from which the primary root and rootcap originate.

hȳ·pō′pi·ăl, *a.* relating to a hypopus.

hȳ″pō·pi·tū′i·tȧ·riṣm, *n.* 1. deficient activity of the pituitary gland.
2. the condition caused by this, characterized by excessive fat, loss of the sexual urge, wasting away of the external sex organs, and loss of hair.

hȳ·pō·plā′si·ȧ (-zhi-ȧ), *n.* [Mod. L., from *hypo-*, and *-plasia*.] a condition of decreased or arrested growth of an organ or tissue of the body.

hȳ·pō·plas′tiç, *a.* of or characterized by hypoplasia.

hȳ·pō·plas′trŏn, *n.* [*hypo-*, and LL. *plastra*, a thin plate of metal.] the third lateral division in the ventral shell of a turtle.

hȳ·pō·pō′di·um, *n.*; *pl.* **hȳ·pō·pō′di·ȧ,** [Mod. L., from *hypo-*, and *-podium*.] the base of a leaf, including the stalk.

hȳ·pop′ti·lum, *n.*; *pl.* **hȳ·pop′ti·lȧ,** [*hypo-*, and Gr. *ptilon*, a feather.] in ornithology, an additional feather springing from a feather; also, the hyporachis or stem of such a supplementary feather: called also *aftershaft*.

hyp′ō·pus (*or* hī′pō-), *n.* [*hypo-*, and Gr. *pous*, *podos*, a foot.] an immature nymph of certain acaridans.

hȳ·pō·pyġ′i·ăl, *a.* pertaining to the hypopygium.

hȳ·pō·pyġ′i·um, *n.*; *pl.* **hȳ·pō·pyġ′i·ȧ,** [Gr. *hypopygion*, the rump; *hypo*, under, and *pygē*, the buttocks.] in entomology, (a) the clasping organ at the abdominal extremity of certain male dipterous insects; (b) the last visible ventral segment of the abdomen of an insect.

hȳ·pō′py·on, hȳ·pō′py·um, *n.* [Gr. *hypopyon*, a kind of ulcer, properly neut. of *hypopyos*, tending to suppurate; *hypo*, under, and *pyon*, pus.] an accumulation of pus in the cavity between the cornea and the lens of the eye.

hȳ·pō·rȧ·çhid′i·ăn, *a.* pertaining to a hyporachis.

hȳ·pō·rā′çhis, *n.*; *pl.* **hȳ·pō·raçh′i·dēṣ,** [Gr. *hyporrhachis*, the hollow above the hip; *hypo*, under, and *rhachis*, the spine.] in ornithology, (a) the stem of a hypoptilum or aftershaft; (b) the hypoptilum or aftershaft itself.

hȳ″pō·rȧ·dī′ō·lus, *n.*; *pl.* **hȳ″pō·rȧ·dī′ō·lī,** [*hypo-*, and *radiolus*, dim. of L. *radius*, a staff, spoke of a wheel, radius.] a barbule of a hyporadius.

hȳ·pō·rā′di·us, *n.*; *pl.* **hȳ·pō·rā′di·ī,** [*hypo-*, and L. *radius*, a staff, spoke of a wheel, radius.] in ornithology, a barb of an aftershaft.

hyp′ọr·çhem, *n.* same as *hyporcheme*.

hyp·ọr·çhē′mȧ, *n.*; *pl.* **hyp·ọr·çhē′mȧ·tȧ,** same as *hyporcheme*.

hyp″ọr·çhē·mat′iç, *a.* relating to a hyporcheme.

hyp′ọr·çhēme, hyp′ọr·çhem, *n.* [Gr. *hyporchēma*, from *hyporcheisthai*, to dance, with music; *hypo*, under, and *orcheisthai*, to dance.] in ancient Greek drama, a song sung by part of the chorus, accompanied with dancing and dumb show.

hȳ·pō·rhā′çhis, *n.* same as *hyporachis*.

hȳ·pō·scē′ni·um, *n.* [Gr. *hyposkēnion*; *hypo*, under, and *skēnē*, the stage.] a low wall at the front of the stage in the ancient Greek theater.

hȳ·pō·skel′e·tăl, *a.* [*hypo-*, and Gr. *skeleton*, a skeleton, and *-al*.] developed under the axis of the endoskeleton: opposed to episkeletal.

hȳ·pō·spā′di·ȧ, *n.* [Gr. *hypospadios*, one having hypospadia; *hypo*, under, and *spăn*, to draw.] a malformation of the penis in which the opening of the urethra is along the under side: also called *hypospadias*.

hȳ·pos'tȧ·sis, *n.*; *pl.* **hȳ·pos'tȧ·sēs,** [Gr. *hypostasis*, a supporting, foundation, from *hyphistanai*, to set under, pass, to stand under; *hypo*, under, and *histanai*, to stand, make to stand.]

1. in medicine, (a) a deposit; sediment; (b) a settling of blood in the lower parts of the body as a result of a slowing down of the blood flow.

2. in philosophy, the underlying principle or nature; essence; substance.

3. in theology, (a) originally, the unique essence or nature of the Godhead and, therefore, of the three persons of the Trinity; (b) any of the three persons of the Trinity; (c) the personality of Christ as distinguished from his two natures, human and divine.

hȳ·pō·stat'iç, hȳ·pō·stat'iç·ăl, *a.* [Gr. *hypostatikos*, belonging to substance, from *hypostatos*, substantially existing, placed under; *hypo*, under, and *histanai*, to stand, cause to stand.]

1. having to do with substance or essence; essential; elemental.

2. (a) having to do with distinct personality; distinctly personal; (b) having to do with divine personality.

3. masked or suppressed by another factor that is not an allelomorph: said of certain factors in heredity.

4. in medicine, due to hypostasis, or deposition.

hypostatic union; in theology, the union of the two natures or attributes of Christ, the human and the divine.

hȳ·pō·stat'iç·ăl·ly, *adv.* in a hypostatic manner; personally.

hȳ·pos″tȧ·tī·zā'tion, *n.* 1. a hypostatizing or being hypostatized.

2. something hypostatized.

hȳ·pos'tȧ·tīze, *v.t.*; hypostatized, *pt.*, *pp.*; hypostatizing, *ppr.* 1. to make into or consider as a distinct substance; to attribute substantial or personal existence to.

2. to regard as a reality; to assume to be actual.

hȳ·pō·stẽr'num, *n.*; *pl.* **hȳ·pō·stẽr'nȧ,** the hypoplastron.

hȳ·pos'tō·mȧ, *n.*; *pl.* **hȳ·pō·stō'mȧ·tȧ,** [*hypo-*, and Gr. *stoma* (*-atos*), the mouth.] in zoology, the lower part of the mouth; the proboscis, as of crustaceans and hydrozoans.

hȳ·pō·stom'ȧ·tous, *a.* [*hypo-*, and Gr. *stoma* (*-atos*), the mouth.] having the mouth beneath, or on the ventral side, as some infusorians.

hȳ'pō·stōme, *n.* same as *hypostoma*.

hȳ·pos'tō·mous, *a.* same as *hypostomatous*.

hȳ·pos'trō·phē, *n.* [Gr. *hypostrophē*, a turning about, recurrence, from *hypostrephein*, to turn about; *hypo*, under, and *strephein*, to turn.]

1. in medicine, (a) a recumbent patient's turning of his body; (b) a relapse in disease.

2. in rhetoric, a return to the subject after the interjection of a parenthesis.

hȳ'pō·stȳle, *a.* [Gr. *hypostylos*, resting on pillars; *hypo*, under, and *stylos*, a pillar.] in architecture, supported by columns; having columns beneath.

hȳ'pō·stȳle, *n.* a structure in which the ceiling is supported by columns; a covered colonnade.

hȳ·pō·sul'fāte, *n.* a compound of hyposulfuric acid and a base.

hȳ·pō·sul'fīte, *n.* 1. a salt of hyposulfurous acid.

2. sodium hyposulfite, $Na_2S_2O_4$.

3. formerly, and still popularly but incorrectly, sodium thiosulfate, $Na_2S_2O_3$, used as a fixing agent in photography: also called *hypo*.

hȳ″pō·sul·fū'riç, *a.* [*hyposulfurous* and *-ic*.] pertaining to sulfur less highly oxidized than in its sulfuric compounds.

hyposulfuric acid; an acid, $H_2S_2O_6$, known only in its salts and in solution with water.

hȳ″pō·sul·fū'rous, *a.* designating a compound of sulfur with less oxygen than that present in sulfurous acid.

hyposulfurous acid; a dibasic acid, $H_2S_2O_4$, produced by the reduction of sulfurous acid and used as a bleaching and reducing agent.

hȳ·pō·taç'tiç, *a.* relating to hypotaxis.

hȳ·pō·tär'săl, *a.* pertaining to or resembling the hypotarsus.

hȳ·pō·tär'sus, *n.*; *pl.* **hȳ·pō·tär'sī,** [*hypo-*, and Gr. *tarsos*, the flat of the foot.] in ornithology, a process on the back part of the main tarsometatarsal bone: called also *calcaneum*.

hȳ·pō·tax'is, *n.* [Gr. *hypotaxis*, subjection, submission, from *hypotassein*; *hypo*, under, and *tassein*, to arrange.] subordination of arrangement in grammatical construction: opposed to *parataxis*.

hȳ·pot'e·nūse, hȳ·poth'e·nūse, *n.* [LL. *hypotenusa*; Gr. *hypoteinousa*, lit., subtending, properly f. of ppr. of *hypoteinein*, to subtend, to stretch under; *hypo*, under, and *teinein*, to stretch.] in a right-angled triangle, the side opposite the right angle.

a b, HYPOTENUSE

hȳ·pō·thal'lus, *n.*; *pl.* **hȳ·pō·thal'lī,** [*hypo-*, and Gr. *thallos*, a young shoot or branch.] the mass of delicate filaments upon which the thallus of a crustaceous lichen is developed.

hȳ·poth'eç, *n.* [from Fr. and L.; Fr. *hypothèque*; L. *hypotheca*, a pledge, security; Gr. *hypothēkē*, something put under (obligation), pledge, from *hypotithenai*, to put under, pledge.] in law, security or right given to a creditor over a debtor's property without transfer of possession or title.

hȳ·pō·thē'çȧ, *n.* same as *hypothec*.

hȳ·poth'ē·çȧ·ry, *a.* [LL. *hypothecarius*.] of or secured by a hypothec.

hȳ·poth'ē·çāte, *v.t.*; hypothecated, *pt.*, *pp.*; hypothecating *ppr.* [LL. *hypothecatus*, pp. of *hypothecare*, to hypothecate, from *hypotheca*; Gr. *hypothekē*, a pledge, mortgage.]

1. to pledge to a creditor in security for some debt or demand, but without transfer of title or delivery of possession.

2. to put in pawn; to pledge.

hȳ·poth·ē·çā'tion, *n.* 1. (a) a hypathecating or being hypothecated; (b) a claim against hypothecated property.

2. the act of putting in pawn.

3. in maritime law, the act of mortgaging a ship; bottomry.

4. in French law, a lien on real estate, etc., for security of a debt, without giving the creditor possession.

5. in American finance, a lien on personal property, as negotiable securities, given as security for a debt by transferring possession to the creditor.

hȳ·poth'ē·çā·tŏr, *n.* one who hypothecates.

hȳ·pō·thē'ci·ăl, *a.* relating to the hypothecium.

hȳ·pō·thē'ci·um, *n.* [*hypo-*, and Gr. *thēkē*, a case.] in certain fungi, a layer of hyphal tissue beneath the hymenium.

hȳ·poth'ē·när, *a.* [Gr. *hypothenar*; *hypo*, under, and *thenar*, palm.] pertaining to the hypothenar.

hȳ·poth'ē·när, *n.* in anatomy, the fleshy prominence on the palm above the base of the little finger: also called *hypothenar eminence*.

hȳ·poth'ē·nūse, *n.* same as *hypotenuse*.

hȳ·pō·thẽr'măl, *a.* [*hypo-*, and Gr. *thermos*, heat.]

1. lukewarm; tepid.

2. of or characterized by hypothermia.

hȳ·pō·thẽr'mi·ȧ, *n.* [*hypo-*, and Gr. *thermos*, heat.] in medicine, subnormal body temperature.

hȳ·poth'ē·sis, *n.* [Gr. *hypothesis*, groundwork, foundation, supposition, from *hypotithenai*, to place under; *hypo*, under, and *tithenai*, to place.]

1. a supposition; a proposition or principle which is supposed or taken for granted, in order to draw a conclusion or inference for proof of the point in question; something not proved, but assumed for the purpose of argument.

2. a system or theory imagined or assumed to account for what is not understood.

hȳ·poth'ē·sist, *n.* same as *hypothetist*.

hȳ·poth'ē·sīze, *v.i.*; hypothesized, *pt.*, *pp.*; hypothesizing, *ppr.* to make a hypothesis.

hȳ·poth'ē·sīze, *v.t.* to assume; to suppose.

hȳ·pō·thet'iç, hȳ·pō·thet'iç·ăl, *a.* 1. based on, involving, or having the nature of, a hypothesis; assumed; supposed.

2. given to the use of hypotheses; as, a *hypothetical* mind.

3. in logic, conditional; as, a *hypothetical* proposition.

hȳ·pō·thet'iç·ăl·ly, *adv.* in a hypothetical manner or relation; by way of supposition.

hȳ·poth'ē·tist, *n.* one who defends or seeks to establish a hypothesis.

hȳ·pō·thȳ'roid, *a.* of or characterized by hypothyroidism.

hȳ·pō·thȳ'roid·işm, *n.* 1. deficient activity of the thyroid gland.

2. the abnormal condition caused by this, often characterized by sluggishness, goiter, etc.

hȳ·pō·ton'iç, *a.* 1. having abnormally low tension or tone, especially of the muscles.

2. having an osmotic pressure lower than that of an isotonic solution.

hȳ″pō·trȧ·çhē'li·um, *n.* [L., from Gr. *hypotrachēlion*, the lower part of the neck, the neck of a column; *hypo*, under, and *trachēlos*, the neck.] in architecture, the slenderest part of the shaft of a column immediately under the fillet, separating the shaft from the capital; the part which forms the junction of the shaft with its capital.

a, HYPOTRACHELIUM

Hȳ·pot'ri·çhȧ, *n.pl.* [*hypo-*, and Gr. *thrix*, *trichos*, hair.] a division of free-swimming infusorians with cilia on the ventral side only.

hȳ·pō·trō'çhoid, *n.* [*hypo-*, and Gr. *trochos*, a wheel, and *eidos*, form.] a curve traced by a point in a circle rolling upon the inner circumference of a fixed circle.

hȳ·pō·typ'iç, hȳ·pō·typ'iç·ăl, *a.* [*hypo-*, and Gr. *typos*, type.] not developed to the full type; not quite typical.

hȳ″pō·ty·pō'sis, *n.* [Gr. *hypotyposis*, an outline, general representation; *hypo*, under, and *typos*, figure, image.]

1. in rhetoric, animated description; word-picturing.

2. in science, a concise outline of a subject.

hȳ·pō·xan'thine (-zan'), *n.* [Gr. *hypoxanthos*, yellowish-brown, from *hypo*, under, and *xanthos*, yellow, and *-ine*.] a crystalline substance, $C_5H_4N_4O$, present in the muscular tissue of animal bodies and also in some plants: it forms compounds with both acids and bases.

hȳ·pō·zō'iç, *a.* [*hypo-*, and Gr. *zōē*, life.] in geology, designating rocks older than the oldest of those containing evidences of organic life.

hypped (hipt), *a.* see second *hipped*.

hyp'si-, same as *hypso-*.

hyp″si·cē·phal'iç, *a.* [*hypsi-*, and Gr. *kephalē*, head.] showing hypsicephaly; high, as a skull.

hyp·si·ceph'ȧ·ly, *n.* high cranial development, having a vertical index of over 75.

hyp'si·loid, *a.* [Gr. *hypsiloeidēs*, shaped like upsilon; *υ*, upsilon, and *eidos*, form.] shaped like the Greek letter upsilon (*υ*).

Hyp·sis·tā'ri·ăn, *n.* [Gr. *Hypsistarios*, a worshiper of the Most High God, from *hypsistos*, highest, *superl. adj.*, from *hypsi*, *adv.*, on high, aloft.] one of an Asiatic sect in the fourth century whose religious beliefs were derived from Christian, Jewish, and pagan doctrines.

hyp'sō-, hyp'si-, [from Gr. *hypsi*, on high.] a combining form meaning *high* or *height*, as in *hypso*dont, *hypso*phyllum.

hyp'sō·dont, *a.* [*hypso-*, and Gr. *odous*, *odontos*, tooth.] high-toothed; having teeth with comparatively long crowns and short roots.

hyp·sog'rȧ·phy, *n.* [*hypso-*, and Gr. *-graphia*, from *graphein*, to write.]

1. the configuration of a land surface with respect to its different heights; topographic relief.

2. the observation, representation, or description of this.

3. the parts of a map that show this.

4. hypsometry.

hyp·som'e·tẽr, *n.* [*hypso-*, and Gr. *metron*, a measure.] an instrument for computing altitude through atmospheric pressure as determined from the boiling point of a liquid.

hyp·sō·met'riç, hyp·sō·met'ri·căl, *a.* relating to hypsometry.

hyp·som'e·try, *n.* the measuring of altitudes and heights, especially with reference to sea level.

hyp'sō·phyl, hyp'sō·phyll, *n.* any leaf, other than a foliage leaf, borne on a flower stalk: applied especially to involucral leaves, bracts, and the like.

hyp·soph'yl·lā·ry, hyp·soph'yl·lär, *a.* relating to a hypsophyl.

hyp·sō·phyl'lum, *n.*; *pl.* **hyp·sō·phyl'lȧ,** [*hypso-*, and Gr. *phyllon*, a leaf.] a hypsophyl.

hȳ·pū'răl, *a.* [Gr. *hypo*, under, and *oura*, a tail.] situated under the tail: specifically applied to the small bones in fishes supporting the inferior fin rays.

hȳ·rac'id, *n.* a member of the *Hyracoidea*.

hȳ·raç'ō·dont, *a.* [Gr. *hyrax* (*-akos*), the shrew-mouse, and *odous*, *odontos*, tooth.] having molars resembling those of the genera *Hyrax* and *Rhinoceros*.

hy̆'ra·çoid, *a.* pertaining to or characteristic of the *Hyracoidea.*

Hy̆·ra·çoi'dē·a, *n.* [Gr. *hyrax* (*-akos*), the shrewmouse, and *eidos*, form.] an order of small mammals resembling rabbits, with four toes on each forefoot and three on each hind foot, the *Hyracidæ* being the only family and *Hyrax* the only genus; the hyraxes or rock rabbits.

hy̆'rax, *n.* [Gr. *hyrax*, the shrewmouse.] one of the *Hyracoidea*, the species being variously known as *cony, daman, rock rabbit*, etc.

Hyr·çā'ni·ăn, Hyr'çăn, *a.* pertaining to Hyrcania, an ancient province southeast of the Caspian Sea.

hyrst, *n.* same as *hurst.*

hy̆'sŏn, *n.* [Chinese *hi-tchun*, lit., blooming spring or first crop.] a species of green tea from China.

hyson skin; the inferior leaves of hyson tea.

young hyson; the early crop of hyson tea.

hys'sŏp, *n.* [L. *hysopum, hyssopum, hyssopus*; Gr. *hyssōpos* or *hyssōpon*, an aromatic plant, from Heb. *ēzōph*, an aromatic plant.]

1. a labiate plant, *Hyssopus officinalis*, bearing small clusters of blue flowers; the leaves are aromatic and pungent, and are sometimes used in medicine.

2. its flowers.

3. any of several American thistle plants.

4. in the Bible, a plant whose twigs were used for sprinkling water in ancient Jewish religious rites: Psalms li.7.

hys'tẽr-, see *hystero-*.

hys·tẽr·al'gi·ȧ, *n.* [Gr. *hysteralgēs*; *hystera*, the uterus, and *algos*, pain.] neuralgia of the uterus.

hys·tẽr·an'thous, *a.* [Gr. *hysteros*, later, after, and *anthos*, flower.] in botany, putting forth leaves after the opening of the flowers, as willows and poplars.

hys·tẽr·eç'tō·my, *n.* [*hyster-*, and Gr. *ektomē*, a cutting out; *ek*, out, and *temnein*, to cut.] in surgery, the removal of the uterus or part of the uterus from the body by excision.

hys·te·rē'sis, *n.* [Gr. *hysterēsis*, a coming short, deficiency, from *hysterein*, to be behind, come short, from *hysteros*, later, behind.] in physics, the lagging of the effect in a body when the force acting on it is changed; especially, a lag in the changes of magnetization behind the varying magnetizing force.

hys·te·ret'iç, *a.* of, characterized by, or caused by hysteresis.

hys·te·ret'iç çon'stănt, the hysteretic loss in ergs per cubic centimeter per cycle.

hys·te·ret'iç loss, a loss of power in operating electrical devices, caused by magnetic hysteresis.

hys·tē'ri·ȧ, *n.* [Gr. *hystera*, the uterus, womb.]

1. a psychiatric condition variously characterized by emotional excitability, excessive anxiety, sensory and motor disturbances, and the simulation of organic disorders, such as blindness, deafness, etc.

2. any outbreak of wild, uncontrolled excitement or feeling, such as fits of laughing and crying; hysterics.

hys·ter'iç, *n.* 1. [*usually pl., occas. construed as sing.*] a hysterical fit; hysteria (sense 2).

2. a person subject to hysteria.

hys·ter'iç·ăl, hys·ter'iç, *a.* [L. *hystericus*; Gr. *hysterikos*, suffering in the uterus, hysterical, from *hystera*, the uterus, womb: because women seemed to be hysterical more than men, hysteria was attributed by the ancients to disturbances of the uterus.]

1. of or characteristic of hysteria.

2. like or suggestive of hysteria; emotionally uncontrolled and wild.

3. having or subject to hysteria.

hys·ter'içs, *n.* same as *hysteria.*

hys·te·rī'tis, *n.* same as *metritis.*

hys'tẽr·ō-, hys'tẽr-, [from Gr. *hystera*, the uterus, womb.] a combining form meaning *uterus*, or *womb*, as in *hysterodynia*, or *hysteria*, as in *hysteroepilepsy.*

hys''tẽr·ō·çat'ȧ·lep''sy, *n.* hysteria with catalepsy.

hys'tẽr·ō·cēle, *n.* [*hystero-*, and Gr. *kēlē*, a tumor.] hernia involving the uterus.

hys''tẽr·ō·dyn'i·ȧ, *n.* [*hystero-*, and Gr. *odynē*, pain.] uterine pain.

hys''tẽr·ō·ep'i·lep·sy, *n.* [*hystero-*, and Gr. *epilēpsis*, a seizure, attack.] in medicine, a form of hysteria accompanied by epileptic convulsions.

hys''tẽr·ō·ep·i·lep'tiç, *a.* pertaining to or of the nature of hysteroepilepsy.

hys''tẽr·ō·ġen'iç, *a.* [Gr. *hysteros*, later, after, and *-genēs*, producing, from *gignesthai*, to become.] produced afterward; of later origin: applied to intercellular spaces in plants formed in older tissues.

hys''tẽr·ō·ġen'iç, *a.* causing hysteria.

hys·tẽr·oġ'e·ny, *n.* [*hystero-*, and Gr. *-genēs*, producing.] the induction of hysteria.

hys'tẽr·oid, *a.* [*hystero-*, and Gr. *eidos*, form.] resembling hysteria; as, a *hysteroid* disease.

hys'te·ron prot'e·ron, [Gr. *hysteron*, neut. of *hysteros*, latter, following, and *proteron*, neut. of *proteros*, former.]

1. a figure in which the logical order of ideas is reversed; as, "I die, I faint, I fail."

2. in logic, the fallacy of assuming as true, and using as an argument, what is to be proved; begging the question.

hys·tẽr·op'ȧ·thy, *n.* [*hystero-*, and Gr. *pathos*, suffering.] any disease or disorder of the uterus.

Hys·tẽr·oph'y·tȧ, *n.pl.* same as *Fungi.*

hys·tẽr·oph'y·tăl, *a.* pertaining to a hysterophyte or to the *Hysterophyta.*

hys·ter'ō·phyte, *n.* [*hystero-*, and Gr. *phyton*, a plant.] in botany, a plant which springs from and lives upon organic matter; a plant of the order *Hysterophyta*; a fungus or any similar growth.

hys·tẽr·op·tō'sis, *n.* [*hystero-*, and Gr. *ptōsis*, a falling.] falling or inversion of the uterus.

hys·tẽr·ot'ō·my, *n.* [*hystero-*, and Gr. *tomē*, a cutting.]

1. a Caesarean operation.

2. an incision of the uterus.

hys·tri·cī'ȧ·sis, *n.* same as *hystricismus.*

hys'tri·cine, *a.* [L. *hystrix* (*-icis*), a porcupine, and *-ine.*] pertaining to or resembling a porcupine.

hys·tri·cis'mus, hys'tri·cism, *n.* [L. *hystrix* (*-icis*), a porcupine, and *-ismus.*] in pathology, a disease characterized by spinelike processes of the skin; a form of ichthyosis.

hys''tri·çō·mor'phiç, *a.* [L. *hystrix*; Gr. *hystrix* (*-ichos*), a porcupine, and *morphē*, form.] relating to the *Hystricomorpha*, a series of rodents including the porcupines, cavies, agonties, etc.

Hys'trix, *n.* [L. *hystrix*; Gr. *hystrix*, a porcupine.] a genus of rodents having quill-like spines growing among the hairs on certain parts of the body: it includes the old-world porcupines.

I

I, i (ī), *n.*; *pl.* **I's, i's, Is, is** (īz), 1. the ninth letter of the English alphabet: via Latin from the Greek *iota*, a modification of the Phoenician (Semitic *yodh*, a hand). This letter, first dotted in the eleventh century, was not distinguished from *j* until the seventeenth century.

2. a sound of I or i.

3. a type or impression for I or i.

4. *a symbol for* the ninth in a sequence or group.

I, i (ī), *a.* 1. of I or i.

2. ninth in a sequence or group.

I (ī), *n.* 1. an object shaped like I.

2. a Roman numeral for 1: when it is placed after another numeral, a unit is to be added (e.g., VI = V + I, or 6), and when it is placed before another numeral, a unit is to be subtracted (e.g., IV = 4).

3. in astronomy, the inclination of an orbit to the ecliptic.

4. in chemistry, *the symbol for* iodine.

5. in education, a mark of *incomplete*, given in a course not completed by the student.

6. in logic, a particular affirmative proposition.

7. in physics, *the symbol for* (a) density of current; (b) intensity of magnetization; (c) the moment of inertia.

8. in zoology, *the symbol for* incisor.

I (ī), *a.* shaped like I.

I, *pron.*; *pl.* **wē,** [ME. *i, ich, ih*; AS. *ic*, I.] the person speaking or writing: *I* is the nominative case form, *me* the objective, *my* and *mine* the possessive, and *myself* the intensive and reflexive, of the first personal singular pronoun.

I, *n.*; *pl.* **I's,** 1. the pronoun *I* thought of as a word; as, he uses too many "*I's*" in writing.

2. the ego.

ī-, [ME. *i-, y-*; AS. *ge-*.] y-. [Archaic.]

-i·ȧ, [L.; Gr.] a noun-forming suffix used in (a) the names of countries, as in Ind*ia*; (b) the names of diseases, as in pneumon*ia*; (c) the names of classic festivals, as in Lupercal*ia*; (d) Greek and Latin words carried over into English, as in milit*ia*; (e) English plurals of Greek and Latin words, as in paraphernal*ia*; (f) in biology, the names of classes, as in Rept*ilia*; (g) in botany, the generic names of plants, as in Zinn*ia*; (h) in chemistry, the names of alkaloids, as in strychn*ia*: see *-ine.*

-i·ăl, [L. *ialis, -iale.*] an adjective-forming suffix, as in magister*ial*, artific*ial.*

ī·am·ȧ·tol'ō·ġy, *n.* [Gr. *iama*, medicine, and *-logia*, from *legein*, to speak.] in medicine, the science which treats of remedies; materia medica.

ī'amb, *n.* [Fr. *iambe*; L. *iambus*; Gr. *iambos.*] a metrical foot of two syllables, the first unaccented and the other accented, as in English verse, or the first short and the other long, as in Greek and Latin verse. Example: "Tŏ strívė, / tŏ séek, / tŏ fínd, / ănd nót / tŏ yíeld."

ī·am'biç, *a.* [from Fr. or L.; Fr. *iambique*; L. *iambicus*; Gr. *iambikos.*] of or made up of iambs.

ī·am'biç, *n.* 1. an iamb.

2. an iambic verse.

3. a piece of satirical verse written in iambs.

ī·am'biç·ăl, *a.* iambic. [Rare.]

ī·am'biç·ăl·ly, *adv.* in the manner of an iambic.

ī·am'bīze, *v.t.* [Gr. *iambizein*, to assail in iambics, from *iambos*, an iambus.] to satirize in iambic verse. [Rare.]

ī·am'bus, *n.*; *pl.* **ī·am'bus·eș, ī·am'bī,** [L.] an iamb.

-i·ăn, [Fr. *-ien*; L. *ianus*, from *-i-* stem ending, and *-anus.*] -an, as in Grec*ian*, reptil*ian*, etc.

-i·an'ȧ, same as *-ana.*

I·an'thi·nȧ, *n.*; *pl.* **I·an'thi·nae,** [Gr. *ianthinos*, violet-colored; *ion*, violet, and *anthos*, a flower.]

1. a genus of oceanic gastropodous mollusks; the violet snails. They are found in the open sea in the warmer parts of the world. When irritated they pour out a violet secretion to conceal themselves.

2. [i–] a violet snail of the genus *Ianthina.*

iär'ō·vīșe (yär'), *v.t.* iarovised, *pt., pp.*; iarovising, *ppr.* to jarovize.

-ī'ȧ·sis, [from L. *-iasis*, from Gr. *-iasis.*] a combining form meaning: (a) *process* or *condition*; (b) *pathological* or *morbid condition*, as in hypochondr*iasis*, elephant*iasis.*

ī·ā·trȧ·lip'tiç, *a.* [Gr. *iatraleiptēs*, a surgeon

who anoints; *iatros*, a physician, and *aleiptēs*, an anointer, from *aleiphein*, to anoint.] curing by ointments and friction.

iatraliptic method; see *epidermic method* under *epidermic*.

ī·at′riç, *a.* [Gr. *iatrikos*, from *iatros*, a physician, from *iāsthai*, to cure, heal.] relating to medicine or physicians.

ī·at′riç·ăl, *a.* iatric.

-i·at′riçs, a combining form meaning *treatment of disease*, as in ped*iatrics*.

ī·at′rō-, [from Gr. *iatros*, a physician, from *iāsthai*, to heal, cure.] a combining form used in medical terms to signify *medical, medicinal*, as in *iatro*logy, *iatro*physical.

ī·at·rō·çhem′iç·ăl, *a.* of or relating to iatrochemistry.

ī·at·rō·çhem′ist, *n.* a physician who practices iatrochemistry.

ī·at·rō·çhem′is·try, *n.* [*iatro-*, and LL. *chimia*, chemistry, from Gr. *chēmeia*, *chymeia*, an infusion, from *chein*, to pour.] the science of the application of chemistry to medicine; used especially in connection with the theories and doctrines of a medical school in the Netherlands in the seventeenth century, which held chemical action to be the sole essential to the due operation of the vital functions.

ī·à·trol′ō·ġy, *n.* [*iatro-*, and Gr. *-logia*, from *legein*, to speak.] the science of medicine; a treatise on medicine or physicians.

ī·at″rō·math·ē·mat′iç·ăl, *a.* see *iatrophysical*.

ī·at·rō·math″ē·mȧ·ti′ciăn (-tish′ăn), *n.* [*iatro-*, and Gr. *mathēmatikos*, a mathematician.] one of the iatrophysical school of physicians.

ī·at·rō·mē·çhan′iç·ăl, *a.* iatrophysical.

ī·at·rō·phyṣ′iç·ăl, *a.* designating a school of physicians in Italy in the seventeenth century. They sought to explain the functions of the body and the application of remedies by statical and hydraulic laws, and were eager students of anatomy, since they believed it was only by accurate knowledge of all the parts that they could apply their mathematical and dynamical principles.

-ī′à·try, [from Gr. *iatreia*, healing, medical treatment.] a combining form meaning *medical treatment*, or *method of treatment*, as in psych*iatry*, hipp*iatry*.

Ī-bēam, a beam the cross section of which is shaped like the letter I.

Ī·bē′ri·ăn, *n.* 1. any member of an ancient people in Caucasian Iberia, believed to be the ancestors of the Georgians.

2. a native or inhabitant of Iberia, the Spanish-Portuguese peninsula.

3. the language spoken there in ancient times, from which Basque is believed to be derived.

Ī·bē′ri·ăn, *a.* [L. *Iberia*, *Hiberia*; Gr. *Ibēria*, Spain, from *Ibēres*, the inhabitants of Spain.] relating to Iberia in Europe (the Spanish-Portuguese peninsula).

Ī·bē′ri·ăn, *a.* [L. *Iberia*, Iberia, from *Iberes*; Gr. *Ibēres*, the ancient inhabitants of Iberia, in Asia.] relating to ancient Asiatic Iberia, now Georgia in Transcaucasia.

Ī·bē′ris, *n.* [Gr. *iberis*, a kind of pepperwort.] a genus of cruciferous plants, consisting of annual, perennial, and shrubby species, mostly native to the Mediterranean region and the East. Several species are cultivated under the name of *candytuft*.

ī′bex, *n.*; *pl.* **ī′bex·eṣ** or **ib′i·cēṣ**, [L.] any of several varieties of wild goat of Europe, Asia, or Africa, especially that found in the Alps, Apennines, and Pyrenees: the male has large, backward-curved horns.

IBEX (*Capra ibex*)

i·bī′dem, *adv.* [L.] in the same place: used in writing, usually in the contracted form *ib.* or *ibid.*, to show further reference to the book, chapter, etc. cited just before.

-i·bil′i·ty, *pl.* **-i·bil′i·tieṣ**, [L. *-ibilitas*.] a suffix used to form nouns from adjectives ending in *-ible*, as in sens*ibility*.

ī′bis, *n.*; *pl.* **ī′bis·eṣ**, [L., from Gr. *ibis*, the ibis.] any of several large wading birds related to the herons, with long legs and a long, slender, curved bill, found chiefly in tropical regions: the sacred ibis of the Nile is the most common.

SACRED IBIS (*Ibis æthiopica*)

-i·ble, [L. *-ibilis*.] -able: used in forming adjectives derived directly from Latin verbs ending in *-ire* or *-ere*, as divis*ible*, leg*ible*.

ib·n-, [Ar., son (of).] a combining form used as the first element in many hyphenated Arabic names, as in *ibn-Saud*.

Ī′bō, *n.* [from the native name.]

1. *pl.* **I′bo**, a member of a Negroid people living in Nigeria, Africa.

2. the group of West Sudanic dialects spoken by the Ibo.

i·bō′ga·in, i·bō′ga·ine, *n.* an alkaloid obtained from a shrub of Central Africa. Sometimes used as a substitute for cocaine.

Ib′sen·iṣm, *n.* the ideas, aims, and principles of playwriting, etc. characteristic of Henrik Ibsen and his followers.

-iç, [from Fr. or L. or Gr.; Fr. *-ique*; L. *-icus*; Gr. *-ikos*.]

1. a suffix used to form adjectives meaning: (a) *of, having to do with*, as in volcan*ic*, German*ic*; (b) *like, having the nature of, characteristic of*, as in angel*ic*, class*ic*; (c) *produced by, caused by*, as in photograph*ic*, symphon*ic*; (d) *made up of, consisting of, containing*, as in dactyl*ic*, alcohol*ic*; (e) in chemistry, *having a higher valence than is indicated by the suffix -ous*, as in nitr*ic*, phosphor*ic*.

2. a suffix used to form nouns, through the substantive use of adjectives in *-ic*, as in mag*ic*, cosmet*ic*.

Adverbs corresponding to adjectives in *-ic* are formed by adding *-ally* or, less often, *-ly*.

i·çaç′ō, *n.* [Sp.] the cocoa plum.

-i·çal, [LL. *-icalis*, from *-icus*, -ic, and *-alis*, -al.] a suffix corresponding to *-ic*, used to form adjectives from nouns ending in *-ic*, as in phys*ical*, polem*ical*, or from other adjectives ending in *-ic*, as in poet*ical*, com*ical*: such adjectives sometimes have special or differentiated meanings (e.g., histor*ical*, econom*ical*), further removed from the base than those of the corresponding *-ic* forms.

Ī·çā′ri·ăn, *a.* [L. *Icarius*; Gr. *Ikarios*, relating to *Icarus*.]

1. of, like, or belonging to Icarus; hence, adventurous; foolhardy.

2. of, like, or belonging to any place named Icaria, as (a) a deme of Attica; (b) an island near Samos, now Nikaria; (c) a fictitious community described by Etienne Cabet in a romance, Voyage en Icarie.

3. of, like, or belonging to the communistic principles of, or to any of the settlements founded upon the principles of, Cabet.

Ī·çā′ri·ăn, *n.* a native or resident of Icaria or of an Icarian settlement; a follower of Cabet.

Iç′ar·us, *n.* [L.; Gr. *Ikaros*.] in Greek legend, the son of Daedalus: escaping from Crete by flying with wings made by Daedalus, Icarus flew so high that the sun's heat melted the wax by which his wings were fastened, and he fell to his death in the sea.

īce, *n.* [ME. *ise*, *is*, *ys*; AS. *is*, ice.]

1. the glassy, brittle, crystalline form of water made solid by cold; frozen water.

2. a piece, layer, or sheet of this.

3. anything like frozen water in appearance, structure, etc.

4. a frozen dessert, usually made of water, fruit juice, egg white, and sugar.

5. icing· frosting.

6. a diamond or diamonds. [Slang.]

bay ice; ice formed in bays or other inlets of the sea.

on thin ice; in a risky, unsafe situation. [Colloq.]

to break the ice; (a) to make a start by getting over initial difficulties; (b) to make a start toward getting better acquainted and less formal, as by talking to someone just met.

to cut no ice; to have no influence or effect. [Colloq.]

īce, *v.t.*; iced (īst), *pt., pp.*; icing, *ppr.* 1. to change into ice; to freeze.

2. to cover with ice; to apply ice to.

3. to cool by putting ice on, in, or around.

4. to cover (cake, etc.) with icing, or frosting.

īce, *v.i.* to freeze (often with *up* or *over*).

-ice, [ME. *-ice*, *-ise*, *-is*; OFr. *-ice*; L. *-itius*, masc., *-itia*, f., *-itium*, neut.] a suffix meaning *the condition, state*, or *quality of*, as in just*ice*, mal*ice*.

īce āġe, in geology, the glacial epoch.

īce an′çhŏr, in nautical usage, an anchor with one fluke, for securing vessels to ice.

īce ax, a kind of ax used by mountain climbers to cut steps in ice.

īce bag, an ice pack (sense 2).

īce′bērg, *n.* [prob. from D. *ijsberg*, lit., ice mountain.] a great mass of ice broken off from a glacier and floating in the sea.

īce′bērg let′tuce, lettuce that grows in compact heads, with large, crisp, curling leaves.

īce bīrd, a sea bird of arctic regions; especially, the dovekie, or little auk.

īce′blink, *n.* [*ice*, and *blink*, after D. *ijsblink* or Dan. *isblink*.] a luminosity in the sky near the horizon, caused by the reflection of light from an expanse of ice.

īce′bōat, *n.* 1. originally, a light skiff mounted on runners and propelled over ice by sails.

2. now, a light, boatlike frame, often triangular, equipped with runners resembling the blades of skates and propelled by a sail.

3. an icebreaker.

īce′bound, *a.* 1. held fast or surrounded by ice, as a boat.

2. blocked up or made inaccessible by ice, as a coast.

īce′box, *n.* 1. a refrigerator; especially, one in which ice is used for cooling foods.

2. a box or compartment, as in a refrigerator, for containing ice.

īce′break″ēr, *n.* 1. a sturdy boat for breaking a channel through ice.

2. a wedgelike structure for protecting a pier, etc. from floating ice.

īce′çap, *n.* a large, permanent ice sheet with a raised center, especially one covering the top of a mountain, plateau, etc.

īce çhest, a refrigerator.

īce′-çōld′, *a.* having the temperature of ice; freezing cold.

īce çŏm·pärt′ment, the section of a refrigerator or cooling system in which the ice is kept or formed.

īce çrēam, [orig., *iced cream*.] a food consisting of cream, butterfat, or milk, and sometimes eggs, sweetened, flavored, beaten to a uniform consistency, and frozen.

īce′-çrēam′, *a.* made of or with ice cream.

īce′-çrēam′, *n.* ice cream.

ice-cream cone; a cone-shaped wafer holding a scoop of ice cream.

ice-cream freezer; a contrivance used in making ice cream; usually, a can provided with a stirring paddle, which may be rotated in a tub containing ice and salt.

ice-cream soda; a mixture of soda water and ice cream, flavored with fruits, fruit juices, or other ingredients.

īced (īst), *a.* 1. covered or cooled with or as with ice; congealed; frozen.

2. frosted; coated with frosting or icing.

īced frūits, preserved fruits coated with sugar.

īce drops, in botany, transparent growths resembling icicles.

īced tēa, a beverage consisting of brewed tea, sugar, and lemon, chilled with bits or cubes of ice, usually served in tall glasses.

iced-tea spoon; a teaspoon with a long handle, used for stirring iced tea.

īce′fąll, *n.* the fall of masses of ice from an iceberg or glacier.

īce fiēld, an extensive flat mass of floating ice.

īce flōat, an ice floe.

īce flōe, a great mass or sheet of floating ice.

īce foot, [*ice*, and *foot*, after Dan. *isfod*.] a wall of ice along a shore in polar regions, formed between the high and low watermarks by the tide.

īce′-free′, *a.* 1. without ice; not frozen.

2. always without ice; never frozen; as, an *ice-free* harbor.

īce′-glāzed, *a.* glazed or encrusted with ice.

īce hock′ey, the game of hockey played on ice by players wearing skates.

īce′house, *n.* a storehouse designed for the preservation of ice during warm weather.

Ice′land·ẽr, *n.* [ME. *Island,* Iceland.] a native or inhabitant of Iceland.

Ice·lan′diç, *a.* pertaining to Iceland, to its people, or to their culture.

Ice·lan′diç, *n.* 1. the North Germanic language of the people of Iceland.
2. loosely, Old Icelandic, the language of the Icelandic sagas.

Ice′lănd moss, in botany, a species of lichen, *Cetraria islandica,* found in arctic and mountainous regions and used as a food and as a medicine.

Ice′lănd spär, a transparent, colorless calcite, found especially in Iceland: it is used by opticians for making double-refracting prisms.

īce′less, *a.* designating a refrigerator or cooling system that operates by mechanical means; as, an *iceless* refrigerator.

īce′less, *n.* an electric refrigerator. [Colloq.]

īce mȧ·chīne′, a machine for making ice by artificial means.

īce′man, *n.*; *pl.* **īce′men,** 1. a man who is skilled in traveling upon or climbing over ice, as an Alpine climber.
2. a dealer in ice; one who delivers ice to consumers.

īce mȧs′tẽr, one skilled in sailing a ship through the ice of the Arctic Ocean: called also *ice pilot.*

īce nee′dle, in meteorology, a thin piece of ice, so light that it floats in the air in clear, cold weather.

īce pack, 1. a large expanse of broken floating ice, pressed and frozen together.
2. a bag, usually of rubber, used to contain cracked ice for cold applications to reduce swelling, ease pain, etc.

īce pā′pẽr, transparent gelatin in thin sheets, used in copying and transferring writing and designs: also called *papier glacé.*

īce pick, a pointed metal tool for breaking ice.

īce pī′lŏt, an ice master.

īce pitch′ẽr, a pitcher for containing ice water.

īce plant, a plant, *Mesembryanthemum crystallinum,* growing in Mediterranean regions, South Africa, and southern California, having leaves covered with sparkling particles like ice crystals.

īce plow, a sort of plow for cutting grooves in ice in ponds, lakes, etc., with a view to its removal, or to open a passage for boats.

īce′quāke, *n.* the rending crash that accompanies the breaking up of floes of ice.

īce rāin, 1. rain that forms a glaze of ice.
2. sleet.

ī·cē′ry·ȧ, *n.* in zoology, a scale insect of the genus *Icerya,* infesting the orange plant.

īce sạw, a large saw used for cutting through the ice to relieve ships when frozen up, or for cutting blocks of ice for storage, sometimes with a heavy weight attached for the purpose of giving the descending stroke.

īce sheet, a thick layer of ice covering an extensive area for a long period, as in the ice age.

īce spär, a variety of feldspar, the crystals of which resemble ice.

īce stọrm, a rain storm, the drops of which are congealed to ice as soon as they touch any object, as the branch of a tree.

īce tā′ble, a broad expanse of ice.

īce tongṣ, large iron nippers for handling blocks of ice.

īce wạ′tẽr, 1. water from melted ice.
2. water cooled with or as with ice; iced water.

Iç̧h·neū′mi·ȧ, *n.* [Gr. *ichneumōn,* the ichneumon.] a subgenus of *Herpestes,* distinguished from the true ichneumons by having longer limbs and hairy soles.

iç̧h·neū′mŏn, *n.* [L., from Gr. *ichneumōn,* the ichneumon, lit., a tracker, from *ichneuein,* to track out, hunt after, from *ichnos,* a track or footstep.]

EGYPTIAN ICHNEUMON (*Herpestes ichneumon*)

1. a small, weasellike animal (genus *Herpestes*) of India and Africa; a mongoose.
2. the ichneumon fly.

iç̧h·neū′mŏn flȳ, any of a large group of wasplike but stingless insects having wormlike larvae that live as parasites in or on the larvae of other insects.

ICHNEUMON FLY

Iç̧h·neū·mon′i·dae, *n.pl.* [Gr. *ichneumōn,* the ichneumon, and *eidos,* form.] a family of hymenopterous insects, the genera and species of which are very numerous, over 3000 species existing in Europe alone; the ichneumon flies.

iç̧h·neū·mon′i·dăn, *a.* relating to the *Ichneumonidæ.*

iç̧h·neū·mon′i·dēṣ, *n.pl.* the members of the family *Ichneumonidæ.*

iç̧h·neū′mous, *a.* relating to or resembling an ichneumon fly; parasitic.

iç̧h′nīte, *n.* [Gr. *ichnos,* a footprint.] in geology, a fossil footprint.

iç̧h′nō-, [from Gr. *ichnos,* a footprint.] a combining form used in paleontology, etc. to signify *a track, footprint, trace,* as in *ichno*logy.

iç̧h′nō·gràph, *n.* in drawing, a plan, as of a building; a ground plan.

iç̧h·nō·graph′iç, iç̧h·nō·graph′iç·ăl, *a.* pertaining to ichnography; describing a ground plan.

iç̧h·nog′rȧ·phy, *n.* [L. *ichnographia*; Gr. *ichnographia,* a tracing out, a ground plan; *ichnos,* a track, plan, and *graphein,* to write.]
1. a scale drawing of the ground plan of a building; floor plan.
2. the art of drawing such plans.

iç̧h′nō·līte, *n.* [*ichno-,* and Gr. *lithos,* a stone.] a fossil footmark.

iç̧h″nō·li·thol′ō·ġy, *n.* [*ichno-,* and Gr. *lithos,* a stone, and *-logia,* from *legein,* to speak.] ichnology.

iç̧h·nō·loġ′iç·ăl, *a.* of or relating to ichnology.

iç̧h·nol′ō·ġy, *n.* [*ichno-,* and Gr. *-logia,* from *legein,* to speak.] that branch of geology which treats of the fossil footmarks of animals.

ī′ç̧hor, *n.* [Gr. *ichōr,* the blood of the gods, juice, the serum of blood.]
1. in Greek mythology, an ethereal fluid flowing instead of blood in the veins of the gods.

Of course his perspiration was but *ichor,*
Or some such other spiritual liquor.
—Byron.

2. a thin, acrid, watery discharge from a wound or ulcer.

ī′ç̧hor·ous, *a.* like ichor; thin; watery; serous.

ī·ç̧hor·rhae′mi·ȧ, *n.* [Gr. *ichōr,* juice, ichor, *rhein,* to flow, and *haima,* blood.] in pathology, an infected condition of the blood due to the presence of ichorous matter.

iç̧h′thi·din, *n.* [Gr. *ichthys,* a fish, and *-id,* and *in.*] a nitrogenous compound found in the yolk of the immature eggs of cyprinoid fishes.

iç̧h′thin, *n.* [Gr. *ichthys,* a fish, and *-in.*] in physiological chemistry, a substance closely allied to albumen, present in the yolk of the eggs of cartilaginous fishes.

iç̧h′thū·lin, *n.* [Gr. *ichthys,* a fish, and *hylē,* matter, and *-in.*] in chemistry, an albuminous compound, a constituent of the yolks of young eggs of salmon and allied fishes.

iç̧h′thus, *n.* same as *ichthys.*

iç̧h′thy·iç, *a.* [Gr. *ichthys,* a fish.] pertaining to fishes; having the character of a fish.

iç̧h′thy·ō-, iç̧h′thy-, [from Gr. *ichthyo-,* from *ichthys,* a fish.] a combining form meaning *fish* or *fishlike,* as in *ichthyo*latry, *ichythyo*morphous.

iç̧h′thy·ō·çol, iç̧h″thy·ō·çol′lȧ, *n.* [L. *ichthyocolla*; Gr. *ichthyokolla,* fish glue; *ichthys,* a fish, and *kolla,* glue.] fish glue; isinglass.

iç̧h″thy·ō·çop′rō·līte, *n.* [*ichthyo-,* and Gr. *kopros,* dung, and *lithos,* a stone.] in geology, the fossil excrement of fishes.

iç̧h″thy·ō·dor′ū·lite, *n.* [*ichthyo-,* and Gr. *dory,* a spear, and *lithos,* a stone.] the fossil dorsal spine of certain fishes.

iç̧h·thy·og′rȧ·phy, *n.* [*ichthyo-,* and Gr. *graphein,* to write.] a treatise on fishes.

iç̧h′thy·oid, iç̧h·thy·oid′ăl, *a.* [Gr. *ichthys,* a fish, and *eidos,* form.] like a fish.

iç̧h′thy·oid, *n.* formerly, a fishlike vertebrate.

iç̧h′thy·ōl, *n.* [*ichthy-,* and L. *oleum,* oil.] an oleaginous compound derived from a bituminous mineral containing the remains of fossil fishes and used in medicine: a trade-mark (*Ichthyol*).

iç̧h·thy·ol′ȧ·try, *n.* [*ichthyo-,* and Gr. *latreia,* worship.] worship of fishes; also, worship of an ichthyomorphic image.

iç̧h′thy·ō·līte, *n.* [*ichthyo-,* and Gr. *lithos,* a stone.] fossil fish, or the figure or impression of a fish or part of a fish in rock.

iç̧h″thy·ō·loġ′iç, iç̧h″thy·ō·loġ′iç·ăl, *a.* pertaining to ichthylogy.

iç̧h·thy·ol′ō·ġist, *n.* one versed in ichthyology.

iç̧h·thy·ol′ō·ġy, *n.* [*ichthyo-,* and Gr. *-logia,* from *legein,* to speak.]
1. the science of fishes; that part of zoology which treats of fishes, their structure, form, and classification, their habits, uses, etc.
2. *pl.* **iç̧h·thy·ol′ō·ġieṣ,** a treatise on fishes.

iç̧h′thy·ō·man·cy, *n.* [*ichthyo-,* and Gr. *manteia,* a prophesying.] divination by the heads and entrails of fishes.

iç̧h′thy·ō·morph, *n.*; *pl.* **iç̧h″thy·ō·mọr′phȧ,** [*ichthyo-,* and Gr. *morphē,* form.] a triton, salamander, or other urodele.

iç̧h″thy·ō·mor′phiç, iç̧h″thy·ō·mọr′phous, *a.* [*ichthyo-,* and Gr. *morphē,* form.]
1. having the shape of a fish, as certain gods of ancient Assyria and Syria.
2. in zoology, resembling a fish in form and structure; ichthyopsid.

iç̧h·thy·oph′ȧ·ġist, *n.* one who eats or subsists on fish.

iç̧h·thy·oph′ȧ·gous, *a.* [Gr. *ichthyophagos,* eating fish; *ichthys,* a fish, and *phagein,* to eat.] eating or subsisting on fish.

iç̧h′thy·oph·ȧ·ġy, *n.* the practice of eating fish.

iç̧h″thy·oph·thal′mīte, *n.* [*ichthy-,* and Gr. *ophthalmos,* an eye, and *-ite.*] in mineralogy, fish-eye stone; apophyllite.

Iç̧h″thy·oph·thī′rȧ, *n.pl.* [*ichthyo-,* and Gr. *phtheir,* a louse.] in zoology, a group of crustaceans including numerous species that are parasitic on fishes; fish lice.

iç̧h·thy·op′sid, *a.* pertaining to or resembling the *Ichthyopsida.*

iç̧h·thy·op′sid, *n.* one of the *Ichthyopsida.*

Iç̧h·thy·op′si·dȧ, *n.pl.* [*ichthy-,* and Gr. *opsis,* appearance, and *-ida.*] in Huxley's classification, the primary division of *Vertebrata* comprising fishes, fishlike vertebrates, and amphibians.

Iç̧h·thy·op·te·ryġ′i·ȧ, *n.pl.* [*ichthyo-,* and Gr. *pteryx, pterygos,* a wing.] in paleontology, an order of extinct reptiles of the Mesozoic; ichthyosaurs.

Iç̧h·thy·ọr′nis, *n.* [*ichthy-,* and Gr. *ornis,* a bird.] an extinct genus of birds with socketed teeth and biconcave vertebrae, remains of which are found in America in beds of Cretaceous rocks.

ICHTHYORNIS
1. *Ichthyornis dispar*; 2. right jaw, inner view

Iç̧h·thy·ọr′ni·thēṣ, *n.pl.* [*ichthy-,* and Gr. *ornis, ornithos,* a bird.] in ornithology, a group of extinct birds with teeth and biconcave vertebrae, of which *Ichthyornis* is the typical genus.

iç̧h″thy·ọr·nith′iç, iç̧h·thy·ọr′ni·thoid, *a.* relating to or having the characteristics of the Ichthyornithes.

iç̧h′thy·ō·sạur, *n.* one of the order *Ichthyosauria.*

Iç̧h″thy·ō·sạu′ri·ȧ, *n.pl.* [*ichthyo-,* and Gr. *sauros,* a lizard.] in paleontology, an order of gigantic marine reptiles now extinct, shaped somewhat like a whale, with very large head and no obvious neck, a fishlike body, four paddlelike flippers, short biconcave vertebrae, and an extended caudal extremity: called also *Ichthyopterygia, Ichthyosaura,* and *Ichthyosauri.*

iç̧h″thy·ō·sạu′ri·ăn, *a.* relating to the *Ichthyosauria.*

ich″thy·ō·saụ′ri·ăn, *n.* any member of the *Ichthyosauria.*

Ich″thy·ō·saụ′rus, *n.* 1. the typical genus of *Ichthyosauria.*

2. [i–] any species of this genus; an ichthyosaur.

ich·thy·ō′sis, *n.* [Gr. *ichthys,* a fish, and *-osis.*] a disease of the skin, which renders it thick, hard, dry, and scaly: also called *fishskin disease, xeroderma.*

ich·thy·ot′iç, *a.* of, like, or having ichthyosis.

ich·thy·ot′ō·mist, *n.* one who is versed in ichthyotomy.

ich·thy·ot′ō·my, *n.* [*ichthyo-,* and Gr. *tomē,* a cutting, from *temnein,* to cut.] the anatomical structure or the science of the anatomy of fishes.

ich′thys, *n.* [Gr. *ichthys,* a fish.] the representation of a fish found on many seals, rings, urns, tombstones, etc. belonging to the early times of Christianity, and supposed to have a mystical meaning, from each character of the Greek word for fish forming an initial letter of the Greek words for Jesus Christ, Son of God, Saviour.

-i′ciăn, [Fr. *-icien;* see *-ic* and *-ian.*] a suffix used to form nouns meaning *a person engaged in, practicing,* or *specializing in* (a specified field), as in beaut*ician.*

ī′ci·çle, *n.* [ME. *iseickle, isikel, hysehykylle;* AS. *isgicel,* an icicle; *is,* ice, and *gicel,* an icicle.] a tapering, pointed, hanging piece of ice, formed by the freezing of water as it drips; as, *icicles* formed on the eaves of the house.

ī′ci·çled (-kld), *a.* studded with icicles.

ī′ci·ly, *adv.* in an icy manner; very coldly.

ī′ci·ness, *n.* the quality or state of being icy or of being very cold.

ī′cing, *n.* a mixture of sugar, water or other liquid, flavoring, and, sometimes, whites of eggs, etc., for covering a cake; frosting.

i·ci′ ŏn pȧrle′ fran·çais′ (frän-se′), [Fr.] French is spoken here.

-iç′i·ty, [L. *-icitas.*] a suffix used to form nouns from adjectives ending in *-ic,* as in authen*ticity.*

ī′çon, *n.; pl.* **ī′çons, ī′çō·nēs,** [L., from Gr. *eikōn,* an image, figure, likeness.]

1. an image; figure; representation; picture.

2. in the Orthodox Eastern Church, a sacred image or picture of Jesus, Mary, a saint, etc. Also spelled *ikon, eikon.*

ī·çon′iç, ī·çon′iç·ăl, *a.* [L. *iconicus;* Gr. *eikonikos,* copied from life, from *eikōn,* a figure, likeness.]

1. relating to or resembling an icon or image of any kind; as, an *iconic* statue, an *iconic* diagram.

2. conventional; of a fixed style: said of some statues and busts.

ī′çŏn·işm, *n.* [L. *iconismus;* Gr. *eikonismos,* delineation, from *eikonizein,* to delineate, mold into form.] imagery. [Obs.]

ī′çŏn·ize, *v.t.* [Gr. *eikonizein,* to mold into form, from *eikōn,* a figure, likeness.] to make an icon; to represent by an icon. [Rare.]

ī·çon′ō-, [from Gr. *eikōn,* an image, figure.] a combining form meaning *figure, image, likeness,* as in *icono*dule, *icono*graph.

ī′çon′o·claşm, *n.* [*icono-,* and Gr. *klan,* to break.]

1. the act of breaking or destroying images; especially, the destruction of objects of veneration, as pictures and images in churches.

2. the act of attacking or ridiculing traditional and venerated institutions or ideas.

ī·çon′ō·çlast, *n.* [*icono-,* and Gr. *klan,* to break.]

1. a breaker or destroyer of images; a person determinedly hostile to the worship of images.

2. one who makes attacks upon cherished beliefs; one who attacks or ridicules traditional or venerated institutions or ideas regarded by him as erroneous or based on superstition.

3. a member of a group in the Orthodox Eastern Church in the eighth and ninth centuries who denounced the use of icons.

4. a member of a group who engaged in or advocated the destruction of church images in the Netherlands in the sixteenth and seventeenth centuries.

ī·çon·ō·çlas′tiç, *a.* of or characteristic of iconoclasm or iconoclasts; as, *iconoclastic* zeal.

ī·çon′ō·dūle, ī·çon′ō·dū·list, *n.* [*icono-,* and Gr. *douleia,* servitude, from *douleuein,* to be subject to, to serve.] a worshiper of images.

ī·çon′ō·gráph, *n.* [*icono-,* and Gr. *graphein,* to write.] an illustration for a book.

ī·çō·nog′rȧ·phẽr, *n.* one skilled in iconography.

ī·çon·ō·graph′iç, ī·çon·ō·graph′iç·ăl, *a.* of or belonging to iconography; showing by pictures, images, etc.

ī·çō·nog′rȧ·phy, *n.* [Gr. *eikonographia,* a sketch, description, from *eikonographos,* a portrait painter; *eikōn,* a likeness, image, and *graphein,* to write, draw.]

1. that branch of knowledge which treats of the representation of objects by means of images or statues, busts, paintings, mosaic works, engravings on gems or metals, and the like; especially, the study of the portraits of a specific person.

2. the art of pictorial representation or illustration.

3. a series or collection of images.

ī·çō·nol′ȧ·tẽr, *n.* [*icono-,* and Gr. *latreus,* a worshiper, from *latreuein,* to worship.] one who worships images.

ī·çō·nol′ȧ·try, *n.* [*icono-,* and Gr. *latreia,* worship.] the worship of images.

ī·çō·nol′ō·gy, *n.* [*icono-,* and Gr. *-logia,* from *legein,* to speak.]

1. the study of icons, images, or emblematical representations and of their worship.

2. icons collectively.

3. representation by icons or symbols.

ī·çō·nom′ȧ·çhy, *n.* [Gr. *eikōn,* image, and *machē,* battle.] active opposition to icons or other sacred images.

ī·çō·noph′i·list, *n.* [*icono-,* and Gr. *philos,* loving.] a collector or connoisseur of prints, engravings, etc.

ī·çon′ō·sçōpe, *n.* [*icono-* and *-scope.*] an electronic device in a television transmitter, consisting of a vacuum tube enclosing a photosensitive plate on which the image is projected and an electron gun that scans the image with a narrow focused beam: a trade-mark (*Iconoscope*).

ī·çon′ō·stas, *n.* an iconostasis.

ī·çon·ō·stā′si·ŏn, *n.* an iconostasis.

ī·çō·nos′tȧ·sis, *n.* [L.Gr. *eiknostasis;* Gr. *eikōn,* an image, and *stasis,* a standing.] in the Orthodox Eastern Church, the high screen, decorated with icons, which separates the bema and sacristy from the remainder of the church.

ī′çō·sȧ-, ī′çō·si-, [from Gr. *eikosi,* twenty.] a combining form used in mathematics, botany, etc., to signify *twenty;* as in *icosa*hedron, *icosi*tetrahedron: also, before a vowel, *icos-,* as in *icos*andria.

ī″çō·sȧ·hē′drăl, *a.* [*icosa-,* and Gr. *hedra,* a seat, base.] of, or having the form of, an icosahedron.

ī″çō·sȧ·hē′drŏn, *n.; pl.* **ī″çō·sȧ·hē′drȧ,** [Gr. *eikosaedron,* a body with twenty sides; *eikosi,* twenty, and *hedra,* a side, base.] a solid figure with twenty plane surfaces.

regular icosahedron; a regular solid having twenty equilateral triangles for its faces.

Ī·çō·san′dri·ȧ, *n.pl.* [*icos-,* and Gr. *anēr, andros,* a male.] in the Linnean system of botany, a class of plants having twenty or more stamens inserted in the calyx.

ī·çō·san′drous, ī·çō·san′dri·ăn, *a.* pertaining to the *Icosandria;* having twenty or more stamens inserted in the calyx.

ī″çō·si·tet·rȧ·hē′drŏn, *n.* [Gr. *eikosi,* twenty, *tettares,* four, and *hedra,* a seat, base.] a solid figure having twenty-four plane surfaces.

-içs, [see *-ic.*] 1. a suffix used to form plural nouns meaning (a specified) *art* or *science,* as in mathemat*ics*: such nouns are usually construed as singular.

2. a suffix used to form plural nouns meaning (specified) *activities, practice, system, properties,* as in statist*ics*: such nouns are usually construed as plural.

Iç·tē′ri·ȧ, *n.* [Gr. *ikteros,* jaundice, a yellow bird, the sight of which was said to cure the jaundice.] a genus of birds generally included in the warbler family; the chattering flycatchers or yellow-breasted chats of North America.

iç·ter′iç, *a.* [L. *ictericus;* Gr. *ikterikos,* jaundiced, from *ikteros,* jaundice.]

1. of jaundice.

2. affected with jaundice.

3. used in treating jaundice.

iç·ter′iç, *n.* a remedy for jaundice.

iç·ter′iç·ăl, *a.* same as *icteric.*

ic′tẽr·ine, *a.* yellow in coloration, as a bird.

iç·tẽr·i′tious (-rish′us), **iç·tẽr′i·tous,** *a.* [L. *icterus;* Gr. *ikteros,* jaundice.] yellow; having the color of skin affected by the jaundice.

iç′tẽr·oid, *a.* [Gr. *ikteros,* jaundice, and *eidos,* form.] icteritious; also, icterine.

iç′te·rus, *n.* [L., from Gr. *ikteros,* jaundice.]

1. a plant disease in which the leaves become yellow.

2. in pathology, jaundice.

iç′tiç, *a.* [L. *ictus,* a blow.] of, like, or due to a blow; striking; abrupt. [Rare.]

iç′tus, *n.* [L., a blow, stroke, in prosody a beating time, from *ictus,* pp. of *icere,* to strike, hit, beat.]

1. in medicine, a stroke; a beat; a sudden attack, as (a) a paralytic stroke; (b) the beat of the pulse; (c) a fit.

2. in music and prosody, the stress or accent marking the rhythm; the intensity of delivery which distinguishes one syllable or note from others.

ī′cy, *a.; comp.* icier; *superl.* iciest, [AS. *isig,* from *is,* ice, and *-ig, -y.*]

1. having much ice; full of or covered with ice.

2. of ice.

3. like ice; specifically, (a) slippery; (b) very cold; frigid.

4. cold in manner or attitude; unfriendly; aloof.

ī′cy-pēarled, *a.* studded with drops of ice.

I′d, 1. I would.

2. I had.

3. I should.

id, *n.* [L., it; neut. sing. of *is,* he; used as transl. of G. *es,* it.] in psychoanalysis, that part of the psyche which is regarded as the reservoir of the libido and the source of instinctive energy: it is dominated by the pleasure principle and impulsive wishing, and its impulses are controlled through the development of the ego and superego: distinguished from *ego, superego.*

-id, [from L. *-is,* pl. *-ides;* Gr. *-is,* pl. *-ides,* patronymic suffix.] a suffix used to form nouns meaning *a thing belonging to* or *connected with;* specifically, (a) *a meteor that seems to radiate from a* (specified) *constellation,* as in Leon*id;* (b) *an epic poem about* (a specified subject), as in Aene*id.*

-id, [from Fr. or Mod. L.; Fr. *-ide;* Mod. L. *-idae.*] a suffix meaning *an animal belonging to a* (specified) *group,* as in arachn*id.*

-id, [L. *-idus.*] a suffix used in many words of Latin origin, as fet*id,* tep*id, fluid.*

-id, [Fr. *-ide;* L. *-is, -idis;* Gr. *-is, -idos;* also directly from L. or Gr.] a suffix used in certain words of Greek origin, as pyram*id,* orch*id.*

-id, in chemistry, *-ide.*

-i·dȧ, a suffix used in zoology as a termination of names of groups of animals.

-i·dae′, [Mod. L., pl. of L. *-ides;* Gr. *-idēs,* patronymic suffix.]

1. a suffix used in forming the scientific names of zoological families, as Can*idae* (the dog family).

2. a patronymic suffix showing descent from the person or family to whose name it is added; as, the Atr*idae* were the descendants of Atreus.

Ī·dae′ăn, *a.* [L. *Idæus;* Gr. *Idaios,* from *Idē,* Mount Ida.] relating to Mount Ida.

I′dȧ·hō·ăn, *a.* of Idaho.

I′dȧ hō ăn, *n.* a native or inhabitant of Idaho.

Ī·dā′li·ăn, *a.* [L. *Idalius,* from *Idalium;* Gr. *Idalion,* Idalia.] inhabiting or relating to the town of Idalium in Cyprus, which was sacred to the goddess Aphrodite.

ī′dănt, *n.* [formed from *id*: used as an abbrev. of *idioplasma.*] in biology, one of Weismann's groups of pangens; a chromosome.

-īde (*or* -id), a suffix added to part of the name of one of the elements in a binary compound, as in sodium chlor*ide,* hydrogen sulf*ide.*

īde, *n.* [Norw. *id,* small fry.] a fresh-water food fish of the carp family, *Leuciscus idus.*

ī·dē′ȧ, *n.* [L. *idea;* Gr. *idea,* a form, the look or appearance of a thing as opposed to its reality, from *idein,* to see.]

1. a thought; mental conception; mental image; notion.

2. an opinion or belief.

3. a plan; scheme; project; intention; aim.

4. a hazy perception; vague impression; fanciful notion; fancy; inkling.

5. meaning or significance.

6. in music, a theme or figure.

7. in philosophy, according to Plato, a model or archetype of which all real things are but imperfect imitations and from which their existence derives: in modern philosophy, the term is used variously to mean absolute truth, the immediate object of thought, one

of the ultimate principles apprehended by reason, etc.

Syn.—image, impression, conception.

ī·dē′ȧed, ī·dē′ȧ′d, *a.* having or imbued with an idea; as, a one-*ideaed* person.

ī·dē′ăl, *a.* [Fr. *idéal*; LL. *idealis*, existing in idea, ideal, from L. *idea*, an idea.]

1. existing as an idea, model, or archetype; consisting of ideas (sense 5).

2. thought of as perfect or as a perfect model; exactly as one would desire; of a perfect kind.

3. of, or having the nature of, an idea or conception; identifying or illustrating an idea or conception; conceptual.

4. existing only in the mind as an image, fancy, or concept; visionary; imaginary: distinguished from *real, material*.

5. in philosophy, of idealism; idealistic.

Syn.—fanciful, unreal, imaginary, perfect, visionary.

ī·dē′ăl, *n.* 1. a conception embodying perfection.

2. an object which corresponds with such a conception; a perfect model.

3. something that exists only in the mind. *beau ideal*; an imaginary object without fault; a flawless pattern, model, example, or standard.

ī·dē′ȧ·less, *a.* lacking an idea or ideas.

ī·dē′ăl·işm, *n.* [from Fr. *idéalisme* or G. *idealismus.*]

1. behavior or thought based on a conception of things as they should be or as one would wish them to be; idealization.

2. a striving to achieve one's ideals.

3. in art and literature, imaginative treatment that seeks to show the artist's or author's conception of perfection; representation of imagined types or ideals: opposed to *realism*.

4. in philosophy, any of various theories which hold that the objects of perception are actually ideas of the perceiving mind and that it is impossible to know whether reality exists apart from the mind: opposed to *materialism*.

ī·dē′ăl·ist, *n.* 1. a person whose behavior or thought is based on ideals: often used contemptuously to mean an impractical visionary or dreamer.

2. an adherent or practitioner of idealism in art, literature, or philosophy.

ī·dē′ăl·ist, *a.* idealistic.

ī·dē·ăl·ist′iç, *a.* 1. of or characteristic of an idealist.

2. of, characterized by, or based on idealism.

ī·dē·ăl·ist′iç·ăl, *a.* idealistic.

ī·dē·al′i·ty, *n.*; *pl.* **ī·dē·al′i·tieş,** 1. the quality or state of being ideal.

2. [*usually in pl.*] something that is only ideal and has no reality.

3. the ability to conceive ideals.

ī·dē″ăl·i·zā′tion, *n.* 1. an idealizing or being idealized.

2. the result of idealizing.

ī·dē′ăl·īze, *v.i.*; idealized, *pt., pp.*; idealizing, *ppr.* 1. to form an ideal or ideals.

2. to represent things in the manner of an idealist.

ī·dē′ăl·īze, *v.t.* to make ideal; to think of or represent as ideal; to regard or show as perfect or more nearly perfect than is true.

ī·dē′ăl·ī·zẽr, *n.* one who idealizes; one who applies ideals to real objects.

ī·dē′ăl·ly, *adv.* 1. in accordance with an ideal or ideals; in an ideal manner; perfectly.

2. in theory.

ī·dē·ȧ·loġ′iç, *a.* same as *idealogical*.

ī·dē′ȧ·lǫgue (-lǫg), *n.* same as *ideologue*.

ī·dē′āte, *v.t.*; ideated, *pt., pp.*; ideating, *ppr.* to form an idea of; to imagine or conceive.

ī·dē′āte, *v.i.* to form an idea or ideas.

ī·dē′āte, *n.* in philosophy, the external object correlative with an idea.

ī·dē·ā′tion, *n.* the formation of ideas.

ī·dē·ā′tion·ăl, *a.* relating to the formation of ideas; ideative.

ī·dē′ȧ·tive, *a.* same as *ideational*.

i·dée fixe′ (ē-dā fēks′), [Fr.] a fixed idea; obsession.

ī′dem, *pron.* and *a.* [L.] the same; the same as that previously mentioned: abbreviated *id.*

ī·den′tiç, *a.* identical; especially, having exactly the same wording, contents, purpose, etc.: said of diplomatic messages or action by two or more governments.

ī·den′tiç·ăl, *a.* [LL. *identicus*, the same, from L. *identidem*, repeatedly, from *idem*, the same.]

1. the very same; as, the *identical* person.

2. exactly alike or equal; as, an *identical* proposition.

identical equation; in algebra, an equation which may be satisfied by giving any values whatever to the literal quantities.

identical proposition; in logic, a proposition whose subject and predicate are identical in content and extent (e.g., that which is mortal is not immortal).

identical twins; a pair of twins who were developed from a single fertilized ovum: they are always of the same sex and show great similarity in physical appearance.

ī·den′tiç·ăl·ly, *adv.* in an identical manner; with actual sameness.

ī·den′tiç·ăl·ness, *n.* sameness.

ī·den·ti·fī′ȧ·ble, *a.* capable of being identified.

ī·den″ti·fi·çā′tion, *n.* 1. an identifying or being identified.

2. anything by which a person or thing can be identified; as, he used his driver's license as *identification*.

3. in psychoanalysis, an emotional tie unconsciously causing a person to think, feel, and act as he imagines the person with whom he has the tie does.

ī·den′ti·fī·ẽr, *n.* a person or thing that identifies.

ī·den′ti·fȳ, *v.t.*; identified, *pt., pp.*; identifying, *ppr.* [LL. *identicus*, the same, and L. *-ficare*, from *facere*, to make.]

1. to make identical; to consider or treat as the same; as, *identify* your interests with ours.

2. to show to be a certain person or thing; to fix the identity of; to show to be the same as something or someone assumed, described, or claimed.

3. to join or associate closely; as, he has become *identified* with the labor movement.

4. in psychoanalysis, to make identification of (oneself) with someone else: often used absolutely.

5. in biology, to determine the species of.

ī·den′ti·fȳ, *v.i.* 1. to become the same; to combine in interest, purpose, use, etc.

2. to put oneself in another's place, so as to understand and share the other's thoughts, feelings, problems, etc.; sympathize (*with*).

ī·den′tişm, *n.* the philosophical doctrine of Schelling, making subject and object identical: also called *doctrine of identity*.

ī·den′ti·ty, *n.*; *pl.* **ī·den′ti·tieş,** [LL. *identitas*, sameness, from *identicus*, the same, from L. *identidem*, repeatedly, from *idem*, the same.]

1. the condition or fact of being the same in all qualities under consideration; sameness; oneness.

2. (a) the condition or fact of being some specific person or thing; individuality; (b) the condition of being the same as something or someone assumed, described, or claimed.

3. in mathematics, an equation which is true for all permissible sets of values of the variables which appear in it: e.g., $x^2 - y^2 = (x + y)(x - y)$.

ī·den′ti·ty çrī′sis, [coined by Erik Erikson (1902–), American psychoanalyst.] the condition of being uncertain of one's feelings about oneself, especially with regard to character, goals, and origins, occurring especially in adolescence as a result of growing up under disruptive, fast-changing conditions.

id′ē·ō- (*or* ī′dē-ō), [from Fr. or Gr.; Fr. *ideo-*, from Gr. *idea*.] a combining form meaning *idea*, as in ideogram, ideology.

id′ē·ō·gram (*or* ī′dē-), *n.* [*ideo-* and *-gram.*]

1. a graphic symbol representing an object or idea without expressing, as in a phonetic system, the sounds that form its name.

2. a symbol representing an idea rather than a word (e.g., 5, +, =, φ, ¢, ÷).

id′ē·ō·grȧph (*or* ī′dē-), *n.* [*ideo-*, and Gr. *graphein*, to write.] a pictorial representation of an idea or object; an ideogram.

id″ē·ō·graph′iç, id″ē·ō·graph′iç·ăl, *a.* of, or having the nature of, an ideogram or ideography.

id″ē·ō·graph′iç·ăl·ly, *adv.* in an ideographic manner.

id″ē·og′rȧ·phy, *n.* [*ideo-*, and Gr. *-graphia*, from *graphein*, to write.]

1. the use of ideograms to express ideas; graphic representation without the use of names.

2. the study of ideograms.

ī″dē·ō·loġ′iç (*or* id″ē-), *a.* ideological.

ī″dē·ō·loġ′iç·ăl, *a.* pertaining to ideology.

ī″dē·ol′ō·ġist, *n.* 1. a student of or expert in ideology.

2. a person occupied mainly with ideas; idle theorist or visionary.

3. an exponent of a specified ideology; theorist.

ī·dē′ō·lǫgue (-lǫg), *n.* [Fr. *idéologue*, from Gr. *idea*, an idea, and *logos*, a description.] an ideologist.

ī·dē·ol′ō·ġy, *n.* [Fr. *idéologie*; Gr. *idea*, an idea, and *-logia*, from *legein*, to speak.]

1. the study of ideas, their nature and source.

2. the theory that all ideas are derived exclusively through sensation.

3. thinking, speculating, or theorizing, especially when the theory or system of theories is idealistic, abstract, idle, impractical, or farfetched.

4. the doctrines, opinions, or way of thinking of an individual, class, etc.

i′dē·ō·mō″tion, *n.* [*ideo-*, and L. *motus*, motion.] in physiology, unconscious motion made in response to an idea.

i′dē·ō·mō″tŏr, *a.* [*ideo-*, and L. *motor*, a mover.] pertaining to ideomotion.

i′dē·ō·phōne″, *n.* [*ideo-*, and *phone.*] in linguistics, the expression of an idea, as in many African languages, by means of a sound, often reduplicated, that creates an image of an action, object, etc.

īdeş, *n.pl.* [L. *idus*, pl., the ides.] in the ancient Roman calendar, the fifteenth day of March, May, July, and October, and the thirteenth day of the other months.

id est, [L.] that is (to say).

id′i·ō-, [Gr. *idio-*, from *idios*, one's own.] a combining form meaning *one's own, personal, distinct*, as in idiocrasy, idiograph.

id″i·ō·bī·ol′ō·ġy, *n.* [*idio-*, and Gr. *bios*, life, and *-logia*, from *legein*, to speak.] the science of the functions of a particular organism.

id′i·ō·blast, *n.* [*idio-*, and Gr. *blastos*, a bud, offshoot.]

1. in biology, any of the hypothetical units of which a cell is ultimately composed.

2. in botany, an isolated cell differing greatly from the surrounding cells, as a resin cell in pine.

id″i·ō·çrā′sis, *n.* same as *idiocrasy*.

id·i·oç′rȧ·sy, *n.*; *pl.* **id·i·oç′rȧ·sieş,** [Gr. *idiokrasia*, a peculiar temperament; *idios*, one's own, and *krasis*, a mixture, temperament.] an idiosyncrasy.

id″i·ō·çrat′iç, id″i·ō·çrat′iç·ăl, *a.* idiosyncratic.

id′i·ō·cy, *n.*; *pl.* **id′i·ō·cieş,** [from *idiot*, and *-cy* (as *prophecy*, from *prophet*); but compare Gr. *idiōteia*, uncouthness, lack of training.]

1. the state of being an idiot.

2. behavior like that of an idiot; great foolishness or stupidity.

3. an idiotic act or remark.

id″i·ō·cȳ·cloph′ȧ·nous, *a.* [*idio-*, and *kyklos*, a circle, and *-phanēs*, from *phainesthai*, to appear.] same as *idiophanous*.

id″i·ō·ē·leç′triç, *a.* [*idio-*, and Gr. *ēlektron*, amber.] that can be electrified by friction: opposed to *anelectric*.

id′i·ō·grȧph, *n.* [*idio-*, and Gr. *graphein*, to write.] a characteristic signature or writing; one's own private mark; trade-mark.

id″i·ō·graph′iç, id″i·ō·graph′iç·ăl, *a.* belonging to, resembling, or containing an idiograph or idiographs.

id′i·ŏm, *n.* [LL. *idioma*; Gr. *idiōma*, a peculiarity, a peculiar phraseology, an idiom, from *idiousthai*, to make one's own, from *idios*, one's own, private, peculiar.]

1. the language or dialect of a people, region, class, etc.

2. the usual way in which the words of a language are joined together to express thought.

3. an accepted phrase, construction, or expression contrary to the usual patterns of the language or having a meaning different from the literal.

4. the style of expression characteristic of an individual; as, the *idiom* of Carlyle.

5. a characteristic style, as in art or music.

id″i·ō·mat′iç, id″i·ō·mat′iç·ăl, *a.* [Gr. *idiōmatikos*, peculiar, characteristic, from *idioma*, a peculiarity, an idiom.]

1. characteristic of a particular language; in accordance with the particular nature of a language; as, an *idiomatic* phrase.
2. using or having many idioms.
3. of, or having the nature of, an idiom or idioms.

id″i·ō·mat′iç·ăl·ly, *adv.* according to the idiom of a language; in an idiomatic manner.

id″i·ō·mor′phiç, *a.* [*idio-*, and Gr. *morphē*, form.]
1. having a form of its own.
2. in mineralogy, retaining characteristic form against influences tending to change it: said of crystals.

id″i·ō·mor′phous, *a.* same as *idiomorphic.*

id″i·ō·mus′çū·lăr, *a.* [*idio-*, and L. *musculus*, a muscle.] relating to muscular action, especially to a temporary contraction of the muscle upon being struck by a dull implement transverse to its fibers.

id″i·ō·neū·rō′sis, *n.* [*idio-*, and Gr. *neuron*, a nerve.] neurosis arising from disorder in the nerves remote from the nerve centers.

id″i·ō·pȧ·thet′iç, *a.* same as *idiopathic.*

id″i·ō·path′iç, id″i·ō·path′iç·ăl, *a.* relating to, or having the nature of, an idiopathy.

id·i·op′ȧ·thy, *n.* [Gr. *idiopatheia*, feeling for oneself alone, from *idios*, one's own, peculiar, and *pathos*, feeling, suffering.] an independent disease, neither induced by nor related to another disease; a spontaneous or primary disease.

id·i·oph′ȧ·nous, *a.* [*idio-*, and Gr. *-phanēs*, from *phainesthai*, to appear.] designating a form of crystal in which axial interference figures are apparent without the use of a polariscope.

id′i·ō·phōne, *n.* [*idio-* and *-phone.*] any of a class of musical instruments that consist of some elastic material, as wood or metal, capable in itself of producing sound, as the triangle, chimes, or celesta.

id′i·ō·plaşm, *n.* [*idio-*, and Gr. *plasma*, a thing formed, from *plassein*, to form.] the active and characteristic part of cell protoplasm, as distinguished from the nutritive plasma; germ plasm.

id″i·ō·rē·pul′sive, *a.* [*idio-*, and L. *repulsus*, pp. of *repellere*, to drive back, repel.] self-repelling; as, the *idiorepulsive* power of heat.

id′i·ō·sōme, *n.* [*idio-*, and Gr. *sōma*, the body.] in biology, the unit of idioplasm which imparts the hereditary characteristics; an idioblast.

id″i·ō·stat′iç, *a.* [*idio-*, and Gr. *statikos*, static, from *histanai*, to cause to stand.] in electricity, pertaining to a method by which measurements in difference of potential are made without the employment of auxiliary electrification.

id″i·ō·syn′çrȧ·sy, *n.*; *pl.* **id″i·ō·syn′çrȧ·sieş,** [Gr. *idiosynkrasia*; *idios*, one's own, peculiar, and *synkrasis*, a mixing together, tempering, from *synkerannynai*, to mix together; *syn*, together, and *kerannynai*, to mix.]
1. the temperament or mental constitution peculiar to a person or group.
2. any personal peculiarity, mannerism, etc.

id″i·ō·syn·crat′iç, id″i·ō·syn·crat′iç·ăl, *a.* of, characterized by, or resulting from idiosyncrasy.

id″i·ō·syn·crat′iç·ăl·ly, *adv.* in an idiosyncratic manner.

id′i·ŏt, *n.* [OFr. *idiot*, an idiot; L. *idiota*, an ignorant, common person; Gr. *idiōtēs*, one without professional knowledge, an ignorant, common person, from *idiousthai*, to make one's own, from *idios*, one's own, peculiar.]
1. a mentally deficient person with an intelligence quotient of less than 25; person mentally equal or inferior to a child two years old: *idiot* is the lowest classification of mental deficiency, below *imbecile* and *moron.*
2. loosely, a very foolish or stupid person.

id′i·ŏt·cy, *n.* idiocy. [Rare.]

id″i·ō·thal′ȧ·mous, *a.* designating certain lichens having some part, as the fruit, different in color from the thallus.

id″i·ō·thēr′miç, *a.* [*idio-*, and Gr. *thermē*, heat.] heated by itself; requiring no external agent of heat; self-heating.

id·i·ot′iç, id·i·ot′iç·ăl, *a.* [Gr. *idiōtikos*, private, peculiar, rude, from *idiōtēs*, a private citizen, an unlettered, rude person.] of, having the nature of, or characteristic of an idiot; very foolish or stupid.

id·i·ot′iç·ăl·ly, *adv.* in an idiotic manner.

id·i·ot′i·çon, *n.*; *pl.* **id·i·ot′i·çȧ,** [Gr. *idiōtikos*, masc., *idiōtikon*, neut., private, peculiar to oneself.] a dictionary of a particular dialect, or of the words and phrases peculiar to one part of a country.

id′i·ŏt·ish, *a.* idiotic. [Obs.]

id′i·ŏt·işm, *n.* [L. *idiotismus*; Gr. *idiōtismos*, a popular way of speaking, from *idiōtizein*, to use common language, from *idiōtēs*, a private person, from *idios*, one's own, peculiar.]
1. idiocy. [Rare.]
2. idiotic action or behavior.
3. idiom. [Obs.]

id′i·ŏt·īze, *v.i.* to become stupid. [Rare.]

id′i·ŏt·ry, *n.* idiocy. [Rare.]

id′i·ō·tȳpe, *n.* [*idio-*, and Gr. *typos*, type.] in chemistry, a substance that is typical of a class; one of a series having the same characteristics. [Obs.]

id″i·ō·typ′iç, *a.* having the character of an idiotype. [Obs.]

ī′dle, *a.*; *comp.* idler; *superl.* idlest, [ME. *idel*; AS. *idel*, useless, vain, empty.]
1. not engaged in any occupation or employment; unoccupied; inactive; not busy.

Why stand ye here all the day *idle?*
—Matt. xx. 6.

2. slothful; given to rest and ease; not inclined to work; lazy; as, an *idle* fellow.
3. affording leisure; vacant; not occupied; as, *idle* hours.
4. remaining unused; unemployed.

The *idle* spear and shield were high up hung.
—Milton.

5. producing no effect; useless; vain; ineffectual; fruitless; as, *idle* rage.
6. baseless; unfounded; as, *idle* rumors.
7. unfruitful; barren; empty. [Obs.]

Syn.—unoccupied, unemployed, vacant, inactive, sluggish, useless, ineffectual, futile, frivolous, vain, trifling, unprofitable, unimportant.

ī′dle, *v.i.*; idled, *pt., pp.*; idling, *ppr.* [ME. *idlen*; AS. *idlian*, to become useless, from *idel*, idle, useless.]
1. to move slowly or aimlessly; to loaf.
2. to spend time unprofitably; to be unemployed or inactive.
3. to operate slowly without transmitting power: said of machinery; as, the windmill *idled* in the breeze.

ī′dle, *v.t.* 1. to waste (usually with *away*); as, to *idle away* time.

If you have but an hour, will you improve that hour instead of *idling* it *away?*
—Chesterfield.

2. to cause (a motor, etc.) to idle.

ī′dle·head″ed (-hed″), *a.* 1. foolish; unreasonable.
2. delirious; insane. [Obs.]

ī′dle·ness, *n.* [ME. *idelnesse*; AS. *idelnes*, from *idel*, idle.] the state or condition of being idle.

ī′dle-pāt″ed, *a.* idleheaded; stupid. [Obs.]

ī′dle pul′ley, a pulley riding loosely on a shaft, pressing against a belt to guide it or take up the slack.

ī′dlēr, *n.* 1. one who does nothing and wastes time; a lazy person; a sluggard.
2. in nautical usage, a person on board a ship who, because of constant day duty, is not required to keep night watch.
3. in mechanics, an idle wheel or idle pulley.

ī′dless, ī′dlesse, *n.* idleness. [Poetic or Archaic.]

ī′dle wheel (hwēl), a wheel placed between two others to transfer motion from one axis to another without change of direction. If A and B were in contact they would revolve in opposite directions, but because of the intermediate axis of C they revolve in the same direction.

IDLE WHEEL

2. an idle pulley.

ī′dly, *adv.* [ME. *idelliche*; AS. *idellice*, from *idel*, idle.] in an idle manner; lazily; sluggishly; foolishly; uselessly.

Ī′dō, *n.* [an Esperanto affix, used as a complete word, meaning offspring.] an artificial auxiliary language, a modified form of Esperanto.

ī′dō·çrāse, *n.* [Fr., from Gr. *eidos*, form, and *krasis*, mixture.] vesuvianite.

ī′dŏl, *n.* [OFr. *idole*; L. *idolum*, an image, form, specter, apparition; Gr. *eidōlon*, an image, a phantom, from *eidos*, form.]
1. an image of a god, used as an object or instrument of worship: sometimes said of any heathen deity.
2. any object of ardent or excessive devotion or admiration.
3. (a) an image; effigy; (b) anything that has no substance but can be seen, as a shadow or an image in a mirror. [Obs.]
4. in logic, a fallacy.

ī·dō′lȧ, *n.* plural of *idolon.*

ī·dō·las′tēr, ī·dō·las′tre, *n.* an idolater. [Obs.]

ī·dol′ȧ·tēr, *n.* OFr. *idolatre*; LL. *idololatres*; Gr. *eidōlolatrēs*, a worshiper of idols; *eidōlon*, an image, an idol, and *latris*, one hired to serve, a servant, from *latron*, pay, hire.]
1. a worshiper of an idol or idols; one who worships as a deity that which is not God.
2. an adorer; a devoted admirer.

ī·dol′ȧ·tress, *n.* a woman who is an idolater.

ī·dō·lat′riç·ăl, *a.* tending to idolatry.

ī·dol′ȧ·trīze, *v.i.*; idolatrized, *pt., pp.*; idolatrizing, *ppr.* to worship idols.

ī·dol′ȧ·trīze, *v.t.* to adore; to worship; to idolize.

ī·dol′ȧ·trous, *a.* 1. pertaining to idolatry; having the nature of idolatry, or of the worship of false gods.
2. consisting in the worship of idols.
3. consisting of or showing an excessive attachment or reverence; as, an *idolatrous* veneration for antiquity.

ī·dol′ȧ·trous·ly, *adv.* in an idolatrous manner; with excessive reverence.

ī·dol′ȧ·try, *n.*; *pl.* **ī·dol′ȧ·trieş,** [OFr. *idolatrie*; LL. *idolatria*; Gr. *eidōlolatreia*, idolatry; *eidōlon*, an idol, and *latreia*, service.]
1. the worship of idols, images, etc.
2. excessive attachment or veneration for some person or thing; admiration which borders on adoration.

ī′dŏl·ish, *a.* idolatrous. [Obs.]

ī′dŏl·işm, *n.* 1. idolatry.
2. a fallacious notion; false reasoning.

ī′dŏl·ist, *n.* an idolater.

ī·dŏl·i·zā′tion, *n.* an idolizing or being idolized.

ī′dŏl·īze, *v.t.*; idolized, *pt., pp.*; idolizing, *ppr.*
1. to make an idol of; as, the Egyptians *idolized* the ibis.
2. to love to excess; to adore; as, to *idolize* gold, to *idolize* children.

ī′dŏl·īze, *v.i.* to worship idols.

ī′dŏl·ī·zēr, *n.* one who idolizes.

ī·dol′ō·çlast, *n.* [Gr. *eidōlon*, an idol, and *klān*, to break.] one who breaks idols; an iconoclast.

ī·dol·ō·graph′iç·ăl, *a.* [Gr. *eidōlon*, an idol, and *graphein*, to write.] describing or treating of idols.

ī·dō′lon, ī·dō′lum, *n.*; *pl.* **ī·dō′lȧ,** [L. *idolum*; Gr. *eidōlon*, an image, phantom.] a mental image; a false idea; a fallacy; a phantom, a specter.

ī′dŏl·ous, *a.* idolatrous; heathenish. [Obs.]

Ī·dom′ē·neūs, *n.* in Greek legend, a king of Crete who led his subjects against Troy in the Trojan War.

ī·dō′nē·ous, *a.* [L. *idoneus*, fit, proper.] fit; suitable; proper; convenient; adequate. [Rare.]

id·or′găn, *n.* [Gr. *idea*, an idea, and *organon*, an organ.] in biology, an elementary organism ranking below the *Metazoa*; a plastid.

id′ri·ȧ·line, id′ri·ȧ·lin, *n.* a colorless, crystalline compound obtained from idrialite.

id′ri·ȧ·līte, *n.* [*Idria*, Yugoslavia, and *-lite.*] an opaque, greenish or brownish-black mineral obtained from the quicksilver mines of Idria, Yugoslavia.

i·drō′sis, *n.* same as *hidrosis.*

Id·ū·mē′ăn, *a.* [L. *Idumæus*; Gr. *Idoumaios*, from *Idoumaia*; Heb. *Ĕdōm*, Edom, lit., red.] of or pertaining to Idumaea, or Edom, an ancient kingdom in western Asia.

Id·ū·mē′ăn, *n.* a native or inhabitant of ancient Idumaea; an Edomite.

Ī′dūn, *n.* same as *Ithunn.*

ī′dyl, ī′dyll, *n.* [L. *idyllium*; Gr. *eidyllion*, a short, descriptive poem; *eidos*, form, figure, image, and *-yllion*, dim. suffix.]
1. a short poem or prose work describing a simple, pleasant scene of rural, pastoral, or domestic life: the literary tradition of the term goes back to Theocritus, who described pastoral life in Sicily for sophisticated readers of Alexandria.
2. a scene or incident suitable for such a work.
3. an extended narrative poem; as, "The *Idylls* of the King."
4. in music, a simple, pastoral composition.

ī′dyl·ist, ī′dyll·ist, *n.* a writer or composer of idyls.

ī·dyl′liç, ī·dyl′li·çăl, *a.* 1. of or pertaining to an idyl; suitable or fit for an idyl.

2. pleasing and simple; pastoral or picturesque.

ī·dyl′li·çăl·ly, *adv.* in an idyllic manner.

-iē, [earlier form of *-y*; revitalized in back-formation *movie.*] a suffix meaning *small, little,* as in lass*ie*, dogg*ie*: often used to express affection.

-iẽr, [ME. *-ier, -yer, -iere,* from *-ere*; AS. *-ere,* the suffix added to verbs to form nouns of the agent, preceded by *i,* the formative of weak verbs in ME. *-ien,* AS. *-ian.*] a suffix used to form nouns meaning *a person concerned with* (a specified action or thing), as in bombard*ier*, coll*ier*, glaz*ier*.

if, *conj.* [ME. *if, ef*; AS. *gif,* if.]

1. in case that; granting that; supposing that; allowing that.

If thou be the Son of God, command that these stones be made bread.—Matt. iv. 3.

2. whether or not.

She doubts *if* two and two make four. —Prior.

3. although; as, I am innocent, *if* appearances are against me.

4. would that: expressing a wish; as, *if* I had only known!

i′fāith′, indeed; truly. [Obs.]

i·fecks′, *interj.* an exclamation equivalent to *i′faith.* [Obs.]

-if′ẽr·ous, see *-ferous.*

-i·fȳ, see *-fy.*

ig·ȧ·sū′riç, *a.* contained in or obtained from nux vomica, or St. Ignatius's bean.

ig·ȧ·sū′rin, *n.* [Malay *igasura,* the *Strychnos* bean, nux vomica.] a poisonous alkaloid obtained from nux vomica, or St. Ignatius's bean.

Ig′drȧ·sil, Ig′drȧ·syl, Igg′drȧ·sil, *n.* in Norse mythology, Yggdrasill, the tree of the universe.

ig′lọọ, *n.* [Esk. *igdlu,* snow house.]

1. an Eskimo house or hut, dome-shaped and usually built of blocks of packed snow.

IGLOO

2. the excavation that a seal makes in the snow over its breathing hole, for the protection of its young.

Also spelled *iglu.*

ig·nä′rō, *n.* [It., from L. *ignarus,* ignorant.] a blockhead. [Obs.]

Ig·nā′tiăn, *a.* pertaining to St. Ignatius, a Christian martyr.

ig″nē·ō·ā′quē·ous, *a.* [L. *igneus,* of fire, and *aqua,* water.] same as *aqueoigneous.*

ig′nē·ous, *a.* [L. *igneus,* of fire, fiery, from *ignis,* fire.]

1. of, containing, or having the nature of, fire; fiery.

2. produced by the action of fire; specifically, formed by volcanic action or great heat; as, *igneous* rock.

ig·nes′cent, *a.* [L. *ignescens (-entis),* ppr. of *ignescere,* to take fire, to burn, from *ignis,* fire.]

1. bursting into flame.

2. giving off sparks when struck with steel.

ig·nes′cent, *n.* an ignescent substance.

ig′nēṣ fat′ū·ī, plural of *ignis fatuus.*

ig′ni-, [from L. *ignis,* fire.] a combining form meaning *fire,* as in *igni*ferous.

ig·niç′ō·list, *n.* [*igni-,* and L. *colere,* to worship.] a fire worshiper.

ig·nif′ẽr·ous, *a.* [*igni-,* and L. *ferre,* to bear.] producing fire.

ig·nif′lū·ous, *a.* flowing with fire. [Obs.]

ig′ni·fȳ, *v.t.*; ignified, *pt., pp.*; ignifying, *ppr.* [*igni-,* and L. *facere,* to make.] to form into fire. [Rare.]

ig·nig′e·nous, *a.* [L. *ignigenus,* producing fire; *ignis,* fire, and *-genus,* from *gignere,* to produce.] produced by the action of fire.

ig·nip′ō·tent, *a.* [L. *ignipotens (-entis),* ruler of fire; *ignis,* fire, and *potens,* powerful.] having power over fire.

ig·ni·punç′tūre, *n.* [*igni-,* and L. *punctura,* a puncture.] in surgery, puncture with a heated needle or stylus.

ig′nis fat′ū·us; *pl.* **ig′nēṣ fat′ū·ī,** [L. *ignis,* fire, and *fatuus,* foolish.]

1. a light seen at night moving over swamps or marshy places, believed to be caused by the combustion of gases, arising from rotting organic matter: popularly called *will-o'-the-wisp, jack-o'-lantern.*

2. a deceptive hope, goal, or influence; delusion.

ig·nīt′ȧ·ble, *a.* that can be ignited.

ig·nīte′, *v.t.*; ignited, *pt., pp.*; igniting, *ppr.* [L. *ignitus,* pp. of *ignire,* to set on fire, from *ignis,* fire.]

1. to kindle or set on fire.

2. to heat intensely; to make glow with heat.

3. to excite; as, his speech *ignited* the crowd.

ig·nīte′, *v.i.* to catch on fire; to start burning.

ig·nīt′ẽr, *n.* 1. a person or thing that ignites.

2. a device used to set off explosives, as a time exploder for igniting the powder of a torpedo.

ig·nīt′i·ble, *a.* that can be ignited.

ig·ni′tiŏn, *n.* [Fr. *ignition,* from pp. of L. *ignire,* to set on fire.]

1. a setting on fire or catching on fire.

2. the means by which a thing is ignited.

3. in an internal-combustion engine, (a) the igniting of the explosive mixture in the cylinder; (b) the device for doing this.

4. in chemistry, the heating of a compound or mixture to the point of complete combustion or complete chemical change.

ig·nī′tŏr, *n.* [L. *ignitus,* pp. of *ignire,* to set on fire.] an igniter.

ig·nī′tron, *n.* [*igni*te, and elec*tron.*] a type of mercury-arc rectifier tube having a mercury-pool cathode and a single graphite anode: when a current is passed through an igniter rod into the pool, the mercury vapor is ionized and an arc starts between the cathode and anode: it is used chiefly in high-resistance welders.

ig·niv′ō·mous, *a.* [LL. *ignivomus*; L. *ignis,* fire, and *vomere,* to vomit.] vomiting fire; as, an *ignivomous* mountain. [Rare.]

ig·nō·bil′i·ty, *n.* the state or quality of being ignoble; ignobleness.

ig·nō′ble, *a.* [Fr. *ignoble*; L. *ignobilis,* unknown, obscure; *in-,* not, and *nobilis,* known.]

1. of low birth or family; not noble; not illustrious. [Rare.]

2. base; not noble in character or quality; unworthy; mean; as, an *ignoble* motive.

3. in falconry, designating the short-winged falcons which fly after game instead of pouncing.

Syn.—degraded, reproachful, scandalous, infamous, degenerate, mean, base, dishonorable, humble, plebeian, lowly.

ig·nō′ble, *v.t.* to make ignoble; to degrade.

ig·nō′ble·ness, *n.* the state or quality of being ignoble; lack of dignity; meanness.

ig·nō′bly, *adv.* in an ignoble manner.

ig·nō·min′i·ous, *a.* [Fr. *ignominieux*; L. *ignominiosus.*]

1. characterized by or bringing on ignominy; shameful; dishonorable; disgraceful.

2. contemptible; despicable.

3. degrading; humiliating.

Syn.—shameful, scandalous, dishonorable, infamous.

ig·nō·min′i·ous·ly, *adv.* in an ignominious manner; disgracefully; shamefully.

ig′nō·min·y, *n.*; *pl.* **ig′nō·min·ieṣ,** [Fr. *ignominie*; L. *ignominia,* disgrace, dishonor; *in-,* without, and *nomen,* name, renown, reputation.]

1. loss of one's reputation; shame; reproach; dishonor; infamy.

Their generals have been received with honor after their defeat; yours with *ignominy* after conquest. —Addison.

2. disgraceful, shameful, or contemptible quality, behavior, or act.

Syn.—infamy, opprobrium, disgrace.

ig′nō·my, *n.* ignominy. [Archaic.]

ig·nō·rā′mus, *n.*; *pl.* **ig·nō·rā′mus·eṣ,** [L., lit., we take no notice; 1st pers. pl., pres. ind., of *ignorare,* to take no notice, to be ignorant.]

1. originally, the word written by a grand jury on a bill of indictment thrown out for lack of evidence.

2. an ignorant person.

ig′nō·rănce, *n.* [ME.; OFr.; L. *ignorantia.*]

1. the condition or quality of being ignorant; lack of knowledge, education, etc.

2. unwareness (*of*).

ig′nō·rănt, *a.* [OFr. *ignorant*; L. *ignorans (-antis),* ppr. of *ignorare,* to lack knowledge, be ignorant.]

1. lacking knowledge; uninstructed or uninformed; untaught; unenlightened.

2. uninformed (*in*) or unaware (*of*).

Ignorant of guilt, I fear not shame. —Dryden.

3. showing lack of knowledge, education, or experience; caused by ignorance; as, *ignorant* remarks.

4. unwittingly committed. [Obs.]

Syn.—illiterate, unlearned, unlettered, uninformed, untaught, benighted, uneducated, unenlightened.—*Ignorant* denotes lack of knowledge, either as of a single subject or of information in general; *illiterate* refers to an ignorance of letters, or of knowledge acquired by reading and study.

ig′nō·rănt, *n.* a person untaught or uninformed; one unlettered or unskilled. [Obs.]

ig′nō·rănt·iṣm, *n.* same as *obscurantism.*

ig′nō·rănt·ist, *n.* same as *obscurant.*

ig′nō·rănt·ly, *adv.* in an ignorant manner; without knowledge, instruction, or information.

ig·nō·rā′tion, *n.* [L. *ignoratio (-onis),* ignorance, from *ignorare,* to be ignorant.] the state or fact of being ignorant. [Obs.]

ig·nōre′, *v.t.*; ignored, *pt., pp.*; ignoring, *ppr.* [Fr. *ignorer*; L. *ignorare,* to have no knowledge of, to ignore, from *ignarus,* not knowing; *in-,* not, and *gnarus,* knowing.]

1. to be ignorant of. [Obs.]

2. to pass over or by without notice; to act as if one were unacquainted with; to shut the eyes to; to leave out of account; to disregard; as, to *ignore* facts.

3. in law, to reject (a bill of indictment) for lack of evidence.

ig·nōre′ment, *n.* the act of ignoring, or state of being ignored.

Ĭ·gō·rot′, *n.*; *pl.* **Ĭ·gō·rot′, Ĭ·gō·rots′,** [Sp. *Igorrote,* prob. from *Igolot,* name used in certain older records; of Tagalog origin.]

1. a member of any of the Malayan tribes of head-hunters living in Luzon, in the Philippines.

2. their Indonesian language.

Ĭ·gōr·rō′tẹ (-tā), *n.* same as *Igorot.*

I·grāine′, *n.* [cf. OFr. *Iguerne, Igerne*; perh. from Celt.] in Arthurian legend, the mother of King Arthur.

i·guä′nȧ, *n.* [Sp., from the native Haitian name.] any of several large tropical American lizards, usually living in trees.

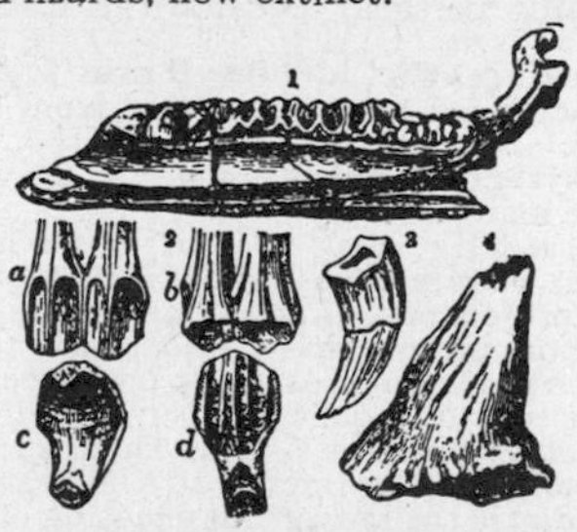

COMMON IGUANA (*Iguana tuberculata*)

i·guä′ni·ăn, *a.* pertaining to the iguana.

i·guä′nid, *n.* one of the *Iguanidæ.*

I·guä′ni·dae, *n.pl.* [Sp. *iguana,* the iguana, and *-idae.*] a family of lacertilian reptiles of which the *iguana* is the type genus.

i·guä′nō·don, *n.* [Mod. L., from *iguana,* and Gr. *-odōn,* -toothed, from *odōn, odontos,* a tooth.] any of a group of very large two-footed lizards, now extinct.

REMAINS OF IGUANODON

1. right side of lower jaw; 2. *a,* two upper molars, external aspect; *b,* do, inner aspect; *c,* external aspect of mature lower molar; *d,* inner aspect of do; 3. fang; 4. horn

i·guä′nō·dont, *a.* having teeth like those of the iguanodon.

i·guä′noid, *a.* [Sp. *iguana,* the iguana, and Gr. *eidos,* form.] pertaining to the *Iguanidæ.*

i·guä′noid, *n.* any member of the *Iguanidæ.*

ih·räm′, *n.* [Ar. *iḥram,* a prohibiting, from *ḥarama,* to forbid.]

1. a costume consisting of one piece of white cotton around the waist and another over the shoulder, worn by Moslem pilgrims to Mecca: while wearing it they are under certain restrictions and rules.

2. a pilgrim who has put on this costume.

3. the restrictions and rules that he must observe.

IHS, [from L. misreading of ΙΗΣ, for which the proper L. form would be IES.] a contraction derived from the Greek ΙΗ(ΣΟΥ)Σ, Jesus, used as a symbol or monogram.

ī'kŏn, *n.* an icon.

il-, (a) in- (not); (b) in- (in). Used before *l*.

-il, see *-ile*.

Il, in chemistry, illinium.

Il'ä, *n.* a Bantu dialect spoken in Northern Rhodesia.

ī'läng-ī'läng, *n.* [Tagalog.]

1. an East Indian tree with fragrant, greenish-yellow flowers.

2. the oil obtained from these flowers, used in perfumes.

Also spelled *ylang-ylang*.

Il Dù'çe (dọọ'chā), [It.; L. *dux, ducis.*] the chief; the leader: title assumed by Benito Mussolini, Fascist head of Italy (1922–1943).

-ile, [from Fr. or L.; Fr. *-il, -ile;* L. *-ilis.*] a suffix meaning *of, having to do with, that can be, like, suitable for,* as in doc*ile*, miss*ile*: sometimes also *-il*, as in civ*il*, foss*il*.

il'ē-, see *ileo-*.

īle, *n.* an ear of corn. [Obs.]

īle, *n.* an aisle. [Obs.]

il'ē-aç, *a.* of the ileum.

il'ē-aç, *a.* of an ileus.

il·ē·ī'tis, *n.* [L. *ilium*, generally in pl. *ilia*, the flank, and *-itis.*] an inflamed condition of the ileum.

il'ē·ō-, [from L. *ileum, ilium,* pl. *ilia*, the groin or flank.] a combining form meaning: (a) *of the ileum,* as in *ileo*stomy; (b) *ileac and*. Also, before a vowel, *ile-*.

il″ē·ō·cae'çăl, *a.* pertaining to the ileum and caecum.

ileocaecal valve; a double fold of mucous membrane preventing passage from the large to the small intestine.

il″ē·ō·çol'iç, *a.* [*ileo-*, and L. *colon*, the colon.] of or relating to the ileum and the colon.

il·ē·os'tō·my, *n.* [*ileo-*, and Gr. *stoma*, mouth, opening.] the surgical operation of making an opening in the ileum.

il″ē·ō·tȳ'phus, *n.* [*ileo-*, and Gr. *typhos*, stupor, the stupor arising from fever.] typhoid fever.

il'ē·um, *n.* [L. *ileum*, or *ilium*, usually in pl. *ilia*, the flank, groin, from Gr. *eilein*, to roll, twist.] in anatomy, the lowest part of the small intestine, opening into the large intestine.

il'ē·us, *n.* [Mod. L.; L. *ileus, ileos;* Gr. *eileos*, colic, from *eilein*, to twist, turn, roll.] an abnormal condition caused by obstruction of the intestines, resulting in severe constipation and pain.

ī'lex, *n.* [L., the holm oak.]

1. a genus of evergreen trees and shrubs of the holly family, many of which are native to Central America, others occurring throughout the tropical and temperate regions of the world.

2. [i–] a tree or shrub of this genus.

3. [i–] the evergreen oak; the holm oak.

il'i·ȧ, *n.* plural of *ilium*.

Il'i·aç, *a.* relating to Ilium, or Troy.

il'i·aç, *a.* [Fr. *iliaque*, in form from LL. *iliacus*, relating to colic, from L. *ileus*, but with meaning as if from L. *ileum, ilium*, pl. *ilia*, the groin, flank.]

1. pertaining to the ileum; ileac. [Obs.]

2. pertaining to the ilium.

iliac arteries; the arteries formed by the bifurcation of the aorta, near the last lumbar vertebra. They divide into the external iliac and hypogastric arteries.

Il'i·ăd, *n.* [L. *Ilias (-adis)*, Gr. *Ilias (-ados)*, the Iliad, from *Ilios, Ilion*, Ilium, a poetical name for Troy, from its founder, *Ilus*, the son of Tros.] a long Greek epic poem, in twenty-four books, about the siege of Troy by the Greeks in the Trojan War: it is ascribed to Homer.

i·lic'iç, *a.* [L. *ilex, ilicis*, the holm oak.] of, obtained from, or relating to the holly and plants of the same genus.

il'i·cin, *n.* [L. *ilex, ilicis*, the holm oak, and *-in.*] a bitter, brownish-yellow crystalline compound obtained from holly, *Ilex aquifolium*.

Il·i·cin'ē·ae, *n.pl.* [L. *ilex, ilicis*, the holm oak, and *-in-*, and *-eæ.*] the *Aquifoliaceæ*, or holly family of plants.

il'i·ō-, [from L. *ilium, ileum*, pl. *ilia*, the flank.] a combining form meaning: (a) *of the ilium;* (b) *iliac and*, as in *ilio*sacral.

il″i·ō·fem'ō·răl, *a.* [*ilio-*, and L. *femur*, the thigh.] of or designating the ilium and the femur.

il″i·ō·lum'băr, *a.* [*ilio-*, and L. *lumbus*, the loin.] of or designating the ilium and the lumbar regions.

Il'i·ŏn, *n.* ancient Troy; Ilium. [Obs.]

il″i·ō·psō'ăs, *n.* [*ilio-*, and Gr. *psoa*, the muscle of the loins.] the great flexor muscle of the hip, constituting the iliac and great psoas muscles, by some anatomists designated as distinct.

il″i·ō·sā'çrăl, *a.* of the ilium and the sacrum.

-il'i·ty, [Fr. *-ilité;* L. *-ilitas.*] a suffix used to form nouns from adjectives (and their derived nouns) ending in *-ile, -il, -able, -ible,* as in imbec*ility*, civ*ility*, ab*ility*, sensib*ility*.

Il'i·um, *n.* ancient Troy.

il'i·um, *n.*; *pl.* **il'i·ȧ,** the uppermost of the three sections of the hipbone.

ī·lix·an'thin, *n.* [L. *ilex*, the holm oak, and Gr. *xanthos*, yellow, and *-in.*] a yellow dye found in the leaves of holly.

ilk, *a.* [ME. *ilke;* AS. *ilc*, the same.] same; like. [Obs.]

ilk, *n.* a family; kind; sort; class; from a misunderstanding of the phrase *of that ilk*. [Colloq.]

of that ilk; (a) in Scotland, of the same name (as the place he owns or from which he comes); as, MacDonald *of that ilk* (i.e., MacDonald of MacDonald); (b) of the same sort or class.

ilk, *pron.* the same. [Obs.]

ilk, il'kȧ, *a.* each. [Scot.]

ill, *a.*; *comp.* worse; *superl.* worst, [ME. *ille;* Ice. *illr*, ill.]

1. characterized by, causing, or tending to cause harm or evil; specifically, (a) morally bad or wrong; evil; as, *ill* repute; (b) causing pain, discomfort, etc.; adverse; as, *ill* fortune; (c) harsh; cruel; not kind or friendly; as, *ill* will; (d) unfavorable; unfortunate; unpropitious; promising trouble; as, *ill* news.

2. not healthy; not well; having a disease; sick; indisposed.

3. not according to rule, custom, desirability, etc.; faulty; incomplete; imperfect; improper; as, *ill* breeding.

ill at ease; uneasy; uncomfortable.

ill blood; hatred; hostility; unfriendliness; enmity.

to go ill with; to be unfortunate for or unfavorable to.

to take ill; to be annoyed or offended at.

Syn.—bad, iniquitous, evil, wicked, sick, ailing, indisposed, poorly.

ill, *n.* 1. wickedness; depravity; evil.

2. misfortune; calamity; evil; disease; pain; whatever annoys or impairs happiness, or prevents success.

ill, *adv.*; *comp.* worse; *superl.* worst, 1. in an ill manner; specifically, (a) badly; wrongly; improperly; imperfectly; (b) harshly; cruelly; unkindly.

2. with difficulty; scarcely; as, he can *ill* afford to refuse.

Ill, prefixed to participles, or to adjectives having the form of past participles, forms many compound words the meanings of which are made apparent by the elements; as, *ill*-fated, *ill*-humored, *ill*-timed, etc.

I'll, 1. I shall.

2. I will.

il·lab'ile, *a.* not liable to fall or err; infallible. [Obs.]

il·lȧ·bil'i·ty, *n.* the quality of being illabile. [Obs.]

ill-ad·vīsed', *a.* showing or resulting from lack of proper consideration or sound advice; unwise.

il·lapse', *n.* [L. *illapsus*, a falling or flowing into, properly pp. of *illabi*, to fall or flow into; *in*, into, and *labi*, to slip, fall.] a gliding in; an entrance of one thing into another.

il·lapse', *v.i.* [L. *illapsus*, pp. of *illabi*, to fall or flow into.] to fall, pass, or glide: usually followed by *into*. [Rare.]

il·lā'quē·ȧ·ble, *a.* capable of being ensnared or illaqueated. [Rare.]

il·lā'quē·āte, *v.t.* [L. *illaqueatus*, pp. of *illaqueare*, to ensnare; *in*, into, and *laqueare*, to snare, from *laqueus*, a snare.] to ensnare, to entrap; to entangle; to catch. [Rare.]

il·lā·quē·ā'tion, *n.* 1. the act of ensnaring. [Rare.]

2. a snare; a noose; a trap. [Rare.]

il·lā'tion, *n.* [LL. *illatio (-onis)*, a carrying in, an inference, from *illatus*, pp. of *inferre*, to carry in; *in*, into, and *ferre*, to carry.]

1. the act of inferring from premises or reasons; inference.

2. that which is inferred; an inference; a deduction; a conclusion.

> Inconsequent *illations* from a false conception of things. —Sir T. Browne.

il'lȧ·tive, *a.* [L. *illativus*, from *illatus*, pp. of *inferre*, to carry in; *in*, into, and *ferre*, to bear.]

1. expressing or introducing an inference: said of words, as *therefore*.

2. of, or having the nature of, an illation; inferential.

3. expressing movement inward; as, the Uralic languages have an *illative* case.

illative conversion; in logic, that conversion or transposition in which the truth of the converse follows from the truth of the proposition given; thus, the proposition "Religion is the truest wisdom," becomes, by *illative conversion*, "The truest wisdom is religion."

il'lȧ·tive, *n.* that which denotes illation or inference; an illative particle.

il'lȧ·tive·ly, *adv.* by inference.

il·laud'ȧ·ble, *a.* [L. *illaudabilis*, not praiseworthy; *in-*, not, and *laudabilis*, praiseworthy.] not laudable; not worthy of approbation or commendation; blameworthy; deserving censure or dispraise.

il·laud'ȧ·bly, *adv.* in an illaudable manner.

il·lȧ·wär'rȧ pälm (päm), [so called from *Illawarra*, a district of Australia in which it grows.] an Australian palm, *Ptychosperma cunninghamii* or *Seaforthia elegans*, with large, feathery fronds.

ill'-bē'ing, *n.* an unhealthy, unhappy, or evil condition: opposed to *well-being*.

ill'-bōd'ing, *a.* inauspicious; unfavorable.

ill'-bred, *a.* not well-bred; rude; unpolished; impolite.

ill breed'ing, the quality or state of being ill-bred.

ill'-çŏn·sid'ēred, *a.* not properly considered; not suitable; not wise.

ill'-dē·fīned', *a.* poorly defined; not clear or definite.

ill'-dis·pōṣed', *a.* 1. having a bad disposition; malicious or malevolent.

2. unfriendly or unfavorable (*toward*).

Il·lec·ē·brā'cē·ae, *n.pl.* [L. *illecebra*, a charm.] a small family of exogenous plants, chiefly consisting of herbaceous weeds, found in the temperate parts of the world. The typical genus is *Illecebrum*, and the order is sometimes called *Paronychiaceæ*.

il·lec·ē·brā'tion, *n.* enticement; allurement. [Obs.]

il·lec'ē·brous, *a.* alluring; full of allurement. [Obs.]

il'leck, *n.* the gemmous dragonet fish, *Callionymus lyra*. [Brit.]

il·lē'găl, *a.* [from Fr. *illégal* or ML. *illegalis;* see *in-* (not) and *legal*.] prohibited by law; against the law; unlawful; illicit; not authorized or sanctioned.

il·lē·gal'i·ty, *n.* 1. the state or quality of being illegal.

2. *pl.* **il·lē·gal'i·tieṣ,** an illegal action.

il·lē'găl·īze, *v.t.*; illegalized, *pt., pp.*; illegalizing, *ppr.* to make illegal or unlawful.

il·lē'găl·ly, *adv.* in an illegal manner; unlawfully; as, a man *illegally* imprisoned.

il·lē'găl·ness, *n.* illegality. [Rare.]

il·leġ·i·bil'i·ty, *n.* the state or quality of being illegible.

il·leġ'i·ble, *a.* [L. *in-* priv., and LL. *legibilis*, legible.] incapable of being read; badly written or printed so that the words cannot be easily read.

il·leġ'i·ble·ness, *n.* illegibility.

il·leġ'i·bly, *adv.* in an illegible manner; as, a letter written *illegibly*.

il·lē·ġit'i·mȧ·cy, *n.* the condition or character of being illegitimate.

il·lē·ġit'i·māte, *a.* [from L. *illegitimus*, not lawful.]

1. born of parents not married to each other; bastard.

2. incorrectly deduced or concluded; not logical.

3. contrary to law or rules; illegal; unlawful.

4. not in keeping with accepted usage: said of words or phrases.

il·lē·ġit'i·māte, *v.t.*; illegitimated, *pt., pp.*; illegitimating, *ppr.* to make illegitimate; to prove to be born out of wedlock; to bastardize.

> The marriage should only be dissolved for the future, without *illegitimating* the issue. —Burnet.

il·lē·ġit'i·māte·ly, *adv.* in an illegitimate manner; unlawfully.

il·lē·ġit·i·mā'tion, *n.* the act of declaring illegitimacy.

il·lē·ġit'i·mȧ·tīze, *v.t.*; illegitimatized, *pt., pp.*; illegitimatizing, *ppr.* to make illegitimate; to illegitimate.

il·lev'i·ȧ·ble, *a.* that cannot be levied. [Obs.]

ill fāme, bad reputation; as, a house of prostitution is sometimes called a house of *ill fame.*

ill'-fāt'ed, *a.* 1. having or certain to have an evil fate or unlucky end.

2. causing misfortune; unlucky.

ill'-fā'vŏred, *a.* 1. ugly; of unpleasant appearance.

Ill-favored and lean-fleshed.—Gen. xli. 3.

2. unpleasant; offensive.

ill'-fā'vŏred-ly, *adv.* in an ill-favored manner.

ill'-fā'vŏred·ness, *n.* the state of being ill-favored.

ill'-found'ed, *a.* not supported by facts or sound reasons.

ill'-got'ten, *a.* obtained by evil, unlawful, or dishonest means; as, *ill-gotten* gains.

ill'-hū'mŏr, *n.* a disagreeable, cross, or sullen mood or state of mind.

ill'-hū'mŏred, *a.* having or showing ill-humor; disagreeable, cross, or sullen.

il·lib'ẽr·ăl, *a.* [Fr. *illiberal;* L. *illiberalis;* see *in-* (not) and *liberal.*]

1. lacking a liberal education or training; without culture; ill-mannered.

2. intolerant; bigoted; narrow-minded.

3. miserly; stingy.

il·lib'ẽr·ăl·iṣm, *n.* same as *illiberality.*

il·lib·ẽr·al'i·ty, *n.* the quality of being illiberal.

il·lib'ẽr·ăl·īze, *v.t.;* illiberalized, *pt., pp.;* illiberalizing, *ppr.* to make illiberal.

il·lib'ẽr·ăl·ly, *adv.* ungenerously; uncharitably; disingenuously; parsimoniously.

il·lib'ẽr·ăl·ness, *n.* illiberality.

il·lic'it, *a.* [Fr. *illicite;* L. *illicitus,* not allowed.] not allowed by law, custom, etc.; unlawful; prohibited; unauthorized; improper.

il·lic'it·ly, *adv.* in an illicit manner.

il·lic'it·ness, *n.* the quality of being illicit.

il·lic'it·ous, *a.* illicit. [Obs.]

Il·lic'i·um, *n.* [from L. *illicere,* to allure, charm.] in botany, a genus of the magnolia family of trees and shrubs whose fruit is used as a spice and whose seeds yield a fragrant oil used in flavoring cordials, being nearly the same as oil of anise.

il·līght'en (-līt'), *v.t.* to enlighten. [Obs.]

il·lim'it·ȧ·ble, *a.* incapable of being limited or bounded; as, the *illimitable* void.

Syn.—boundless, unlimited, vast, infinite, unbounded, immeasurable, limitless.

il·lim'it·ȧ·ble·ness, *n.* the state of being illimitable.

il·lim'it·ȧ·bly, *adv.* 1. without possibility of being bounded.

2. without limits.

il·lim·it·ā'tion, *n.* [L. *in-* priv., and *limitatio* (*-onis*), limitation.] the state of being illimitable.

il·lim'it·ed, *a.* unbounded; interminable.

il·lim'it·ed·ness, *n.* boundlessness; the state of being without limits or restriction.

il·li·ni'tion (-nish'un), *n.* [L. *illinere,* to smear, spread on; *in,* on, and *linere,* to smear, spread.]

1. a thin crust of some extraneous substance formed on minerals. [Rare.]

2. a rubbing in of ointment or liniment; also, that which is rubbed in.

il·lin'i·um, *n.* [Mod. L., after the University of *Illinois,* where research on it was done.] a former name for chemical element 61: see *promethium.*

Il·li·nois' (-noi'), *n.; pl.* **Il·li·nois',** a member of a confederation of Algonquian Indian tribes that lived in Illinois.

Il·li·nois'ăn (-noi'ăn), *a.* of the State of Illinois.

Il·li·nois'ăn, *n.* a native or inhabitant of the State of Illinois.

il·li·quā'tion, *n.* [L. *in,* in, and *liquatio* (*-onis*), a melting, from *liquare,* to melt.] the process of liquefying any substance in a solvent. [Obs.]

il·liq'uid (-lik'wid), *a.* [L. *in-* priv., and *liquidus,* liquid.] in law, not established by any documentary evidence.

ill'ish, *a.* slightly ill. [Rare.]

il·li'ṣiŏn (-lizh'un), *n.* [LL. *illisio* (*-onis*), from L. *illisus,* pp. of *illidere,* to strike against; *in,* on, against, and *lædere,* to strike.] a dashing against or into. [Rare.]

il·lit'ẽr·ȧ·cy, *n.* 1. the state or quality of being illiterate; lack of education or culture; especially, inability to read or write.

2. *pl.* **il·lit'ẽr·ȧ·cies,** a mistake (in writing or speaking) resulting from ignorance.

il·lit'ẽr·ăl, *a.* not literal. [Rare.]

il·lit'ẽr·āte, *a.* [L. *illiteratus,* unlettered, uneducated; *in-* priv., and *litteratus,* marked with letters, educated, from *littera,* a letter.]

1. ignorant; uneducated; especially, unable to read or write.

2. having or showing limited knowledge, experience, or culture, especially in some particular field; as, he is musically *illiterate.*

il·lit'ẽr·āte, *n.* a person who is illiterate; especially, one unable to read or write.

il·lit'ẽr·āte·ly, *adv.* ignorantly.

il·lit'ẽr·āte·ness, *n.* lack of education; illiteracy.

il·lit'ẽr·ȧ·tūre, *n.* illiteracy. [Rare.]

ill'-judġed', *a.* injudicious.

ill'-lived', *a.* living wickedly. [Obs.]

ill'-look'ing, *a.* having a disagreeable appearance; homely.

ill'-man'nẽred, *a.* rude; not polite.

ill nā'tūre, an unpleasant, disagreeable disposition.

ill'-nā'tūred, *a.* habitually bad-tempered; snappish.

ill'-nā'tūred-ly, *adv.* in an ill-natured manner.

ill'-nā'tūred·ness, *n.* the quality of being ill-natured.

ill'ness, *n.* 1. badness; unfavorableness; as, the *illness* of the weather. [Obs.]

2. disease; indisposition; sickness; as, he has recovered from his *illness.*

Syn.—disease, disorder, distemper, indisposition, malady, sickness, ailment.

il·lō·çal'i·ty, *n.* the quality of not being located.

il·loġ'iç·ăl, *a.* 1. ignorant or negligent of the rules of logic or correct reasoning; as, an *illogical* disputant.

2. contrary to the rules of logic or sound reasoning; as, an *illogical* inference.

il·loġ'iç·ăl·ly, *adv.* in a manner contrary to the rules of correct reasoning.

il·loġ'iç·ăl·ness, *n.* faulty reasoning.

ill'-ō'mened, *a.* having unlucky omens.

il·lor'i·çāte, *a.* in zoology, without a protecting cover or lorica.

ill'-spent', *a.* misspent; spent wastefully.

ill'-stärred', *a.* fated to be unfortunate: from astrological notions.

ill'-sūit'ed, *a.* not well-suited; not appropriate.

ill'-tem'pẽred, *a.* of bad temper; morose; crabbed; sour; peevish; fretful.

ill'-tīmed', *a.* done or said at an unsuitable time; inopportune.

ill'-trēat', *v.t.* to treat unkindly, cruelly, or unfairly; to harm; abuse; maltreat.

ill'-trēat'ment, *n.* unkind, cruel, or unfair treatment; abuse: also *ill treatment.*

ill tūrn, 1. an unfriendly, unkind, or malevolent act.

2. a decline in health, wealth, etc.

il·lū'ci·dāte, *v.t.* to elucidate. [Obs.]

il·lūde', *v.t.* [OFr. *illuder;* L. *illudere,* to play with, to make sport of; *in,* in, on, and *ludere,* to play.] to deride; to deceive; to mock. [Obs.]

il·lūme', *v.t.;* illumed, *pt., pp.;* illuming, *ppr.* [OFr. *illumer;* L. *illuminare,* to light up; *in,* on, and *luminare,* to light.] to illumine; to illuminate. [Poet.]

il·lū'mi·nȧ·ble, *a.* [LL. *illuminabilis,* from L. *illuminare,* to light up.] that can be illuminated.

il·lū'mi·nănt, *a.* [L. *illuminans* (*-antis*), ppr. of *illuminare,* to light up, illuminate.] illuminating; giving or producing light.

il·lū'mi·nănt, *n.* that which illuminates or affords light; as, the candle was formerly the chief *illuminant.*

il·lū'mi·nā·ry, *a.* pertaining to illumination; illuminative.

il·lū'mi·nāte, *v.t.;* illuminated, *pt., pp.;* illuminating, *ppr.* [L. *illuminatus,* pp. of *illuminare,* to light up; *in,* on, and *luminare,* to light, from *lumes, luminis,* a light.]

1. to give light to; to light up.

2. (a) to make clear; to explain; elucidate; (b) to inform; instruct; enlighten.

3. to make famous; to make illustrious.

4. to decorate with light; as, they *illuminated* the city for the holiday.

5. (a) to decorate (an initial letter or word) with designs, tracings, etc. of gold, silver, or bright colors; (b) to decorate (a manuscript, page, border, etc.) with such initial letters, miniature pictures, etc.

il·lū'mi·nāte, *v.i.* to make a display by means of lights, as on a festive occasion. [Rare.]

il·lū'mi·nāte, *a.* enlightened; illuminated; made bright. [Archaic.]

il·lū'mi·nāte, *n.* one pretending to have extraordinary knowledge or skill; one of the illuminati.

il·lū·mi·nā'tī, *n.pl.* [L. pl. of *illuminatis,* pp. of *illuminare,* to light up.]

1. in church history, persons who had received baptism: in the ceremony they were given a lighted taper as a symbol of their spiritual enlightenment.

2. [I-] members of a 16th-century Spanish sect who believed that, by mental prayer, they had attained to so perfect a state as to have no need of ordinances, sacraments, and good works.

3. [I-] the members of an anticlerical, deistic, republican society founded in 1776 by Adam Weishaupt, professor of law at Ingolstadt in Bavaria. It was suppressed by the Bavarian government in 1785: called also the *Order of the Illuminati.*

4. persons who profess to have extraordinary knowledge or enlightenment: chiefly a satirical use.

il·lū·mi·nā'tion, *n.* [OFr. *illumination;* LL. *illuminatio* (*-onis*), from L. *illuminare,* to light up, illuminate.]

1. an illuminating or being illuminated; specifically, (a) a lighting up; a supplying of light; (b) clarification; explanation; (c) enlightenment; instruction; (d) decoration with lights; (e) decoration of initial letters, manuscripts, etc. with designs, colors, etc.

2. light; the intensity of light per unit of area.

3. the designs, tracings, etc. used in decorating manuscripts.

4. the lights used in decorating a city, etc.

il·lū'mi·nȧ·tiṣm, *n.* same as *illuminism.*

il·lū'mi·nā·tive, *a.* illuminating or tending to illuminate.

il·lū'mi·nā·tŏr, *n.* [LL. *illuminator,* from L. *illuminare,* to light up, illuminate.]

1. one who or that which illuminates or gives light; specifically, any apparatus for concentrating or reflecting light.

2. one who illuminates manuscripts, pages, etc.

il·lū'mine, *v.t.* and *v.i.;* illumined, *pt., pp.;* illumining, *ppr.* [Fr. *illuminer;* L. *illuminare,* to light up; *in,* in, and *luminare,* to light, from *lumen,* a light.] to illuminate or be illuminated; light up.

il·lū'mi·nẽr, *n.* one who illuminates.

Il·lū'mi·niṣm, *n.* the principles of the Illuminati.

il·lū·mi·nis'tiç, *a.* relating to the Illuminati or to Illuminism.

il·lū'mi·nīze, *v.t.;* illuminized, *pt., pp.;* illuminizing, *ppr.* to initiate into the doctrines or principles of the Illuminati.

il'lū·pi, *n.* [E. Ind.] an East Indian tree, *Bassia longifolia,* of the star apple family, the bark, leaves, and juice of which are used medicinally.

il·lūre', *v.t.* to allure; to entice. [Obs.]

ill'-ūs'āġe, *n.* unfair, unkind, or cruel treatment; abuse: also *ill usage.*

ill'-ūṣe', *v.t.* to use badly; to treat unfairly, unkindly, or cruelly; to abuse.

ill'-ūse', *n.* ill-usage.

il·lū'ṣion, *n.* [L. *illusio* (*-onis*), a mocking, jeering, from *illusus,* pp. of *illudere,* to mock, play with; *in,* on, and *ludere,* to play.]

1. a false idea or conception; a belief or opinion not in accord with the facts.

2. an unreal, deceptive, or misleading appearance or image.

3. a false perception, conception, or interpretation of what one sees, where one is, etc.: in psychology, an abnormal illusion is a *hallucination.*

4. a delicate, gauzy cloth used for veils, etc.; tulle.

Syn.—chimera, deception, delusion, fallacy.

il·lū'ṣion·ȧ·ble, *a.* liable to illusion. [Rare.]

il·lū'ṣion·ăl, *a.* of, or having the nature of, an illusion.

il·lū'ṣion·iṣm, *n.* the theory or doctrine that the material world exists only in illusive sense impressions.

il·lū'ṣion·ist, *n.* 1. a person subject to illusions, or false impressions; a visionary.

2. a person who believes in illusionism.

3. an entertainer who produces illusions; a sleight-of-hand artist.

il·lū'sive, *a.* producing, based on, or having the nature of, illusion; deceptive; unreal.

il·lū'sive·ly, *adv.* in an illusive manner.

il·lū'sive·ness, *n.* deception; false show; the quality of being illusive.

il·lū'sō·ry, *a.* [LL. *illusor,* a mocker, from L. *illusus,* pp. of *illudere,* to mock, illude.] deceiving or intending to deceive, as by false appearances; fallacious; unreal; illusive.

Illusory creations of imagination.

—J. Caird.

il·lus'trȧ·ble, *a.* that can be illustrated. [Obs.]

il'lus·trāte (*or* i-lus'), *v.t.;* illustrated, *pt., pp.;*

illustrating, *ppr.* [L. *illustratus*, pp. of *illustrare*, to light up, illuminate, from *illustris*, clear, bright, lustrous.]

1. (a) to explain; to make clear; (b) to make clear or easily understood by examples, comparisons, etc.; exemplify.

2. (a) to furnish (books, etc.) with explanatory or decorative drawings, designs, or pictures; (b) to explain or decorate: said of pictures, etc.

3. (a) to make luminous; illuminate; (b) to make bright; adorn; (c) to make illustrious. [Obs.]

il·lus′trāte, *a.* famous; renowned; illustrious. [Obs.]

il·lus·trā′tion, *n.* [ME. *illustracione*, from OFr. or L.; OFr. *illustration*; L. *illustratio*.]

1. an illustrating or being illustrated.

2. an example, story, analogy, etc. used to help explain or make something clear.

3. a picture, design, diagram, etc. used to decorate or explain something.

il·lus′trȧ·tive, *a.* 1. tending to illustrate, elucidate, explain, or exemplify; as, an argument or simile *illustrative* of a subject.

2. tending to make glorious or illustrious; honorific. [Obs.]

il·lus′trȧ·tive·ly, *adv.* by way of illustration or elucidation.

il′lus·trā·tŏr (*or* i-lus′), *n.* [LL. *illustrator*, an enlightener, from L. *illustrare*, to light up, illustrate.] a person or thing that illustrates; especially, an artist who makes illustrations for books, magazines, etc.

il·lus′trȧ·tō·ry, *a.* illustrative.

il·lus′tri·ous, *a.* [from ME. *illustre* (from L. *illustris*, clear, conspicuous, distinguished, from *illustrare*), and *-ous*.]

1. possessing luster or brilliancy; luminous; bright; shining.[Obs.]

2. distinguished by greatness, nobleness, etc.; conspicuous; renowned; eminent; as, an *illustrious* magistrate.

3. conferring luster or honor; brilliant; renowned.

Illustrious acts high raptures do infuse. —Waller.

Syn.—renowned, glorious, brilliant, eminent, distinguished, celebrated, conspicuous, noble, famous.

il·lus′tri·ous·ly, *adv.* in an illustrious manner.

il·lus′tri·ous·ness, *n.* the state or quality of being illustrious; greatness; grandeur; glory.

il·lus′trous, *a.* lacking luster. [Obs.]

il·lū·tā′tion, *n.* [L. *in*, in, and *lutum*, mud.] the act of bathing in mud or the sediment of a mineral spring; a mud bath. [Rare.]

ill will, unfriendly feeling; hate; dislike.

ill′-wish′ẽr, *n.* one who wishes ill to another.

il′ly, *adv.* badly; ill: now generally regarded as substandard or dialectal.

Il·lyr′i·ăn, *a.* of Illyria, its people, or culture.

Il·lyr′i·ăn, *n.* 1. a native or inhabitant of Illyria.

2. the ancient language of the Illyrians: it is regarded as a distinct branch of the Indo-European family of languages.

il′men·īte, *n.* [from the *Ilmen* Mountains in the southern Urals, where the mineral was first found.] a lustrous black isomorph of hematite, found as a mineral oxide of iron and titanium.

il′vȧ·īte, *n.* [L. *Ilva*, Elba, and *-ite*.] in mineralogy, a black crystallized mineral composed of iron, calcium, and silica, found on the island of Elba: called also *lievrite* and *yenite*.

I′m, a contraction for *I am*.

im-, an assimilated form of *in-* (not), used before *b*, *m*, and *p*.

im-, an assimilated form of *in-* (in), used before *b*, *m*, and *p*.

im′ăġe, *n.* [OFr. *image*; L. *imago* (*-inis*), an imitation, copy, image.]

1. (a) an imitation or representation of a person or thing, drawn, painted, etc.; especially, a statue; (b) a sculptured figure used as an idol.

2. the visual impression of something produced by reflection from a mirror, refraction through a lens, etc.

3. a person or thing very much like another; a copy; counterpart; likeness.

4. (a) a mental picture of something; conception; idea; impression; (b) the concept of a person, product, institution, etc. held by the general public, often one deliberately created or modified by publicity, advertising, etc.

5. a type; typical example; symbol; embodiment; as, he is the *image* of laziness.

6. a vivid representation; graphic description; as, this play is the *image* of life.

7. a figure of speech, especially a metaphor or simile.

8. in psychoanalysis, a picture or likeness of a person, as of a parent, constructed in the unconscious and remaining there.

real image; in optics, an image formed by the rays themselves proceeding from an object.

virtual image; in optics, an image formed by a prolongation of the rays which proceed from an object.

im′ăġe, *v.t.*; imaged, *pt.*, *pp.*; imaging, *ppr.*

1. to represent or form an image of; to figure; portray; delineate.

2. to reflect; to mirror.

3. to picture in the mind; imagine.

4. to be a symbol or type of; typify.

5. to describe graphically or vividly; to describe with figures of speech.

im′ăġe·ȧ·ble, *a.* that may be imaged. [Rare.]

im′ăġe breāk′ẽr, one who breaks images; an iconoclast.

im′ăġe grāv′ẽr, a carver or sculptor.

im′ăġe·less, *a.* having no image.

im′ȧ·ġẽr, *n.* one who forms images, material or mental. [Obs.]

im′ăġe·ry, *n.*; *pl.* **im′ăġe·rieṣ,** [OFr. *imagerie*, from L. *imago* (*-inis*), an image.]

1. the work of one who makes representations, pictures, or statues; images generally.

Rich carvings, portraitures, and *imagery*. —Dryden.

2. show; appearance. [Obs.]

What can thy *imagery* of sorrow mean? —Prior.

3. forms of the fancy; mental images.

The *imagery* of a melancholic fancy. —Atterbury.

4. in rhetoric, representations in writing or speaking; lively descriptions which impress the images of things on the mind; figures of speech.

I wish there may be in this poem any instance of good *imagery*. —Dryden.

5. form; likeness. [Obs.]

im′ăġe wŏr′ship, the worship of images; idolatry.

im·aġ′i·nȧ·ble, *a.* [Fr. *imaginable*; LL. *imaginabilis*, from L. *imaginari*, to imagine.] capable of being imagined or conceived; as, the point is proved with all *imaginable* clearness.

im·aġ′i·nȧ·ble·ness, *n.* the state of being imaginable.

im·aġ′i·nȧ·bly, *adv.* in an imaginable manner.

im·aġ′i·năl, *a.* [LL. *imaginalis*, figurative, from L. *imago* (*-inis*), a figure, image.]

1. of or pertaining to the imagination. [Rare].

2. using rhetorical figures in discourse.

3. in zoology, of or relating to the imago.

imaginal disks; in zoology, the hypodermic cells retained by certain larvae after separation from the eggs, out of which the wings and legs are formed.

im·aġ′i·nănt, *a.* imagining; conceiving. [Obs.]

im·aġ′i·nănt, *n.* one who is given to imagining things; an imaginer. [Obs.]

im·aġ′i·nãr·i·ly, *adv.* in an imaginary or fanciful manner; in imagination; ideally.

im·aġ′i·nãr·i·ness, *n.* the state of being fancied or imaginary.

im·aġ′i·nãr·y, *a.* [L. *imaginarius*, seeming, fancied, existing in imagination, from *imago* (*-inis*), an image.] existing only in the imagination or fancy; visionary; fancied; not real.

Imaginary ills and fancied tortures. —Addison.

imaginary quantity or *expression*; in mathematics, an algebraic expression or symbol having no assignable arithmetical or numerical meaning or interpretation; the square root of a negative quantity: called also *impossible quantity* or *expression*.

Syn.—unreal, ideal, fanciful, chimerical, visionary.

im·aġ′i·nãr·y, *n.*; *pl.* **im·aġ′i·nãr·ieṣ,** in algebra, an imaginary quantity or expression.

im·aġ·i·nā′tion, *n.* [L. *imaginatio* (*-onis*), imagination, from *imaginari*, to imagine, from *imago* (*-inis*), an image.]

1. (a) the act or power of forming mental images of what is not actually present; (b) the act or power of creating mental images of what has never been actually experienced, or of creating new images or ideas by combining previous experiences; creative power. *Imagination* is often regarded as the more seriously and deeply creative faculty, which perceives the basic resemblances between things, as distinguished from *fancy*, the lighter and more decorative faculty, which perceives superficial resemblances.

The power of the mind to decompose its conceptions, and to recombine the elements of them at its pleasure, is called its faculty of *imagination*. —Taylor.

2. image in the mind; conception; idea.

Sometimes despair darkens all her *imaginations*. —Sir P. Sidney.

3. a foolish notion; empty fancy.

4. the ability to understand and appreciate imaginative creations of others, especially works of art and literature.

5. contrivance; scheme; device; plot. [Archaic.]

Thou hast seen all their vengeance and all their *imaginations* against me. —Lam. iii. 60.

im·aġ·i·nā′tion·ăl, *a.* of or caused by the imagination.

im·aġ·i·nā′tion·ăl·iṣm, *n.* a state of the mind in which the imagination rules.

im·aġ′i·nā·tive, *a.* [OFr. *imaginatif*, from L. *imaginatus*, pp. of *imaginari*, to imagine.]

1. having, using, or showing imagination; having creative or productive talent; able to imagine or fond of imagining.

2. owing existence to or characterized by imagination; as, *imaginative* art; *imaginative* genius.

Syn.—creative, conceptive, ideal, poetical, romantic, inventive, original.

im·aġ′i·nā·tive·ly, *adv.* in a fanciful or imaginative manner.

im·aġ′i·nā·tive·ness, *n.* the state of being imaginative.

im·aġ′ine, *v.t.*; imagined, *pt.*, *pp.*; imagining, *ppr.* [ME. *imaginen*; OFr. *imaginer*, *ymaginer*; L. *imaginari*, to picture oneself, fancy, imagine, from *imago* (*-inis*), a likeness, image.]

1. to form a notion or idea of in the mind; to make a mental image of; to create by the imagination.

2. to conceive in thought; to think; to suppose; guess.

3. to contrive in purpose; to scheme; to devise. [Archaic.]

How long will ye *imagine* mischief against a man? —Ps. lxii. 3.

im·aġ′ine, *v.i.* 1. to conceive; to suppose; to have a notion or idea; as, I cannot *imagine* how it happened.

2. to use the imagination.

im·aġ′in·ẽr, *n.* one who imagines.

im′ăġ·ing, *n.* the forming of an image.

im·aġ′in·ous, *a.* fanciful or imaginative. [Obs.]

im′ăġ·iṣm, *n.* [from *Des imagistes*, title of the first anthology of imagist poetry (1914).] a movement that arose in modern poetry during the years before the end of World War I as a revolt against romanticism: its principles included the use of precise, concrete images, freedom from convention in theme and form, the extensive use of free verse, subject matter drawn from modern life, and the use of suggestion rather than complete statement.

im′ăġ·ist, *n.* any of a group of poets who believed in and practiced imagism (c. 1912–1924): it included Amy Lowell, John Gould Fletcher, etc.

im′ăġ·ist, *a.* of imagism or the imagists.

im·ăġ·is′tiç, *a.* same as *imagist*.

i·mā′gō, *n.*; *pl.* **i·mā′gōeṣ,** [L. *imago* (*-inis*), an image, likeness.]

1. (a) the final, adult, reproductive stage in the development of an insect; (b) an insect in this stage.

2. in psychoanalysis, an image.

i-mäm′, *n.* [Ar. *imām*, a guide, chief, leader, from *amma*, to walk before, precede.]

1. a Moslem priest who performs the regular service of the mosque.

2. [often I-] any of various Moslem leaders with this title, as the Caliph, etc.

Also spelled *imaum*.

IMAM OF A MOSQUE

i·mä′ret, *n.* [Turk.] a hostelry for travelers in Turkey.

i·mäum′, *n.* same as *imam*.

im·bälm′ (-bäm′), *v.t.* same as *embalm*.

im·ban′, *v.t.* [*in-* and *ban*.] to put a ban upon; to excommunicate.

im·band′, *v.t.*; imbanded, *pt.*, *pp.*; imbanding, *ppr.* to form into a band or bands.

im·ban′nẽred, *a.* furnished with banners.

im·bärk′, *v.t.* and *v.i.* same as *embark.*

im·bär·kā′tion, *n.* same as *embarkation.*

im·bärk′ment, *n.* same as *embarkment.*

im·bärn′, *v.t.*; imbarned, *pt.*, *pp.*; imbarning, *ppr.* to put in a barn, as to store. [Obs.]

A fair harvest, well in and *imbarned.* —Herbert.

im·bāse′, *v.t.* same as *embase.*

im′bat, *n.* a breeze that blows off the Mediterranean along the northern shore.

im·bat′tle, *v.t.* to furnish with battlements: usually spelled *embattle.*

im·bat′tled, *a.* same as *embattled.*

im′bē·cile, *a.* [OFr. *imbecile*; L. *imbecillis, imbecillus,* feeble, weak.]
1. weak; feeble; destitute of strength; impotent. [Rare.]
2. mentally feeble; of or showing deficient intellect.
3. very foolish or stupid.

im′bē·cile, *n.* 1. a mentally deficient person with an intelligence quotient ranging from 25 to 50; a person mentally equal to a child between three and eight years old: *imbecile* is the second-lowest classification of mental deficiency, above *idiot* and below *moron.*
2. loosely, a very foolish or stupid person.

im′bē·cile, *v.t.* to weaken. [Obs.]

im·bē·cil′i·tāte, *v.t.*; imbecilitated, *pt.*, *pp.*; imbecilitating, *ppr.* to weaken; to make imbecile.

im·bē·cil′i·ty, *n.* [OFr. *imbecilete*; L. *imbecilitas* (*-atis*), weakness, feebleness of mind or body, from *imbecillis, imbecillus,* weak, feeble.]
1. the state of being an imbecile.
2. behavior like that of an imbecile; great foolishness or stupidity.
3. an imbecile act or remark.

im·bed′, *v.t.* same as *embed.*

im·bel′liç, *a.* [L. *in-* priv., and *bellicus,* warlike.] not warlike or martial. [Obs.]

im·bībe′, *v.t.*; imbibed, *pt.*, *pp.*; imbibing, *ppr.* [L. *imbibere,* to drink in; *in,* in, and *bibere,* to drink.]
1. to drink or drink in.
2. (a) to absorb (moisture); (b) to inhale.
3. to take into the mind and keep, as ideas, principles, etc.

im·bībe′, *v.i.* to drink.

im·bīb′ẽr, *n.* one who or that which imbibes.

im·bi·bi′tion (-bish′un), *n.* the act of imbibing.

im·bit′tẽr, *v.t.* same as *embitter.*

im·bit′tẽr·ment, *n.* same as *embitterment.*

im·blāze′, *v.t.* same as *emblaze.*

im·bod′y, *v.t.* and *v.i.* same as *embody.*

im·bōld′en, *v.t.* same as *embolden.*

im·bon′i·ty, *n.* [LL. *imbonitas,* want of goodness, inconvenience; L. *in-* priv., and *bonitas,* goodness, from *bonus,* good.] lack of goodness. [Obs.]

im·bosk′, *v.t.* [It. *imboscare*; *im-,* in, and *bosco,* a wood.] to conceal, as in bushes; to hide. [Obs.]

im·bosk′, *v.i.* to lie concealed. [Obs.]

im·boṣ′ŏm (-booz′), *v.t.* same as *embosom.*

im·boṣ′tūre, *n.* an embossed ornament. [Obs.]

im·bōw′, *v.t.* same as *embow.*

im·bow′el, *v.t.* same as *embowel.*

im·bow′ẽr, *v.i.* and *v.t.* same as *embower.*

im·brāce′, *v.t.* same as *embrace.*

im·brañ′gle, *v.t.* same as *embrangle.*

im′bri·çāte, im′bri·çā·ted, *a.* [L. *imbricatus,* pp. of *imbricare,* to cover with gutter tiles, to form like a roof or gutter tile, from L. *imbrex* (*-icis*), a gutter tile, from *imber,* rain.]
1. bent or hollowed like a roof or gutter tile.
2. in botany, lying over each other in regular order, like tiles on a roof, as the scales on the cup of some acorns; overlapping each other at the margins, without any involution, as leaves in the bud.
3. in decoration, overlapping, or represented as if overlapping; as, an *imbricated* pattern.

IMBRICATE BUD

im′bri·çāte, *v.t.*; imbricated, *pt.*, *pp.*; imbricating, *ppr.* to place so as to overlap, or to make appear overlapped.

im′bri·çāte, *v.i.* to overlap.

im·bri·çā′tion, *n.* 1. the state of being imbricate; particularly, a real or apparent overlapping, as of shingles.
2. in masonry, a structure, as tiling, wall, or the like, laid so as to break joints.
3. a concavity like that of a gutter tile.

IMBRICATION roof and column

im·brō·çā′dō, *n.* [*im-,* in or on, and Sp. *brocado,* brocade.] cloth of gold or of silver. [Obs.]

im·brōç·çä′tȧ, im·brō·çä′tȧ, *n.* in fencing, a kind of thrust. [Obs.]

im·brōgl′iō (-brōl′yō), *n.* [It., confusion, from *imbrogliare,* to confuse.]
1. a confused heap. [Rare.]
2. an involved and confusing situation; state of confusion and complication.
3. a confused misunderstanding or disagreement; entanglement.

im·brown′, *v.t.* same as *embrown.*

im·brụe′, *v.t.*; imbrued, *pt.*, *pp.*; imbruing, *ppr.* [ME. *imbrowen*; OFr. *embruer,* to give to drink; L. *in-,* in, and *bibere,* to drink.]
1. to wet or moisten; to soak; to drench in a fluid, especially in blood.

Whose arrows in my blood their wings *imbrue.* —Sandys.

2. to soak into. [Obs.]

im·brụ′ment, *n.* the act of imbruing; the condition of being imbrued.

im·brụte′, *v.t.*; imbruted, *pt.*, *pp.*; imbruting, *ppr.* to degrade to the state of a brute; to reduce to brutality.

And mix with bestial slime
This essence to incarnate and *imbrute.*
—Milton.

im·brụte′, *v.i.* to sink to the state of a brute.

im·brụte′ment, *n.* the act of degrading to the level of a brute; also, the state of being thus degraded.

im·būe′, *v.t.*; imbued, *pt.*, *pp.*; imbuing, *ppr.* [OFr. *imbuer*; L. *imbuere,* to wet, soak.]
1. to fill with moisture; to saturate; imbrue.
2. to fill with color; to dye; stain; tinge.
3. to fill (the mind, etc.); permeate; pervade; inspire (*with* principles, feelings, emotions, etc.).

im·būe′ment, *n.* the act of imbuing or the state of being imbued.

im·bũrse′, *v.t.* [L. *in-,* in, and *bursa,* a purse.] to supply or stock with money. [Rare.]

im·bũrse′ment, *n.* the act of supplying with money. [Rare.]

im′id, *n.* same as *imide.*

im·id·az′ōl, *n.* [from *imide,* and *azole.*] a colorless, crystalline base, $C_3H_4N_2$.

im′ide, *n.* [variant of *amide.*] an organic compound containing the divalent radical NH.

i·mī′dō, *a.* of an imide or imides.

i·mī′dō-, a combining form used in chemistry to denote substances which contain the radical NH, called the imido group.

i·mī′dō ac′id, an organic acid formed by the union of one or more acid radicals with a compound of the imido group, in which the hydrogen is replaceable.

i·mid′ō·ġen, *n.* [*imido-* and hydro*gen.*] the divalent radical NH. [Rare.]

i·mīne′, *n.* [arbitrary alteration of *amine.*] a compound containing the divalent radical NH united to alkyl or other nonacid radicals.

i·mī′nō, *a.* of an imine or imines.

i·mī′nō-, [from *imine.*] a combining form meaning of or *containing the divalent radical NH united to alkyl or other nonacid radicals.*

im″i·tȧ·bil′i·ty, *n.* the quality of being imitable.

im′i·tȧ·ble, *a.* [Fr. *imitable*; L. *imitabilis,* from *imitari,* to imitate.]
1. capable of being imitated or copied.
2. worthy of imitation. [Obs.]

im′i·tȧ·ble·ness, *n.* the quality of being imitable.

im′i·tăn·cy, *n.* the tendency to imitate. [Rare.]

im′i·tāte, *v.t.*; imitated, *pt.*, *pp.*; imitating, *ppr.* [L. *imitatus,* pp. of *imitari,* to imitate.]
1. to try to act or be the same as; to follow the example of; as, one should *imitate* the wise.
2. to act the same as; to mimic.
3. to reproduce in form, color, etc.; to make a duplicate of; copy; counterfeit.
4. to be or become like in appearance; look like; resemble; as, glass is made to *imitate* diamonds.
5. to use as a model or pattern.

Syn.—copy, follow, mimic, ape, mock.

im·i·tā′tion, *n.* [L. *imitatio* (*-onis*), imitation, from *imitari,* to imitate.]
1. the act of imitating.

Poetry is an act of *imitation,* that is to say, a representation, counterfeiting, or figuring forth. —Sidney.

2. that which is made or produced as a copy; likeness; resemblance; also, a counterfeit.

Both these arts are not only true *imitations* of nature, but of the best nature. —Dryden.

3. in music, the repetition of essentially the same melodic idea, often with slight changes in rhythm, intervals, etc., by different parts or voices in a polyphonic composition.
4. in biology, mimicry.

im·i·tā′tion, *a.* made to resemble something else, usually something superior or genuine; not real; sham; bogus; as, *imitation* leather.

im·i·tā′tion·ăl, *a.* relating to imitation.

im′i·tā·tive, *a.* [L. *imitatus,* pp. of *imitari,* to imitate.]
1. inclined to imitate or follow in manner; as, man is an *imitative* being.
2. aiming at resemblance; employed in the art of creating resemblances; as, painting is an *imitative* art.
3. formed after a model, pattern, or original.

This temple, less in form, with equal grace,
Was *imitative* of the first in Thrace.
—Dryden.

4. in biology, designating an animal which makes use of imitation, as for concealment.
5. not genuine or real; imitation.
6. approximating in sound the thing signified; echoic: said of words (e.g., *hiss, ripple, clang*).

im′i·tā·tive, *n.* in grammar, a verb that expresses imitation. [Obs.]

im′i·tā·tive·ly, *adv.* in an imitative manner.

im′i·tā·tŏr, *n.* [L. *imitator,* from *imitari,* to imitate.] one who or that which imitates.

im′i·tā·tŏr·ship, *n.* the office or state of an imitator.

im′i·tā·tress, *n.* a female imitator.

im′i·tā·trix, *n.* same as *imitatress.*

im·maç′ū·lāte, *a.* [ME. *immaculate*; L. *immaculatus,* unspotted; *in-* priv., and *maculatus,* pp. of *maculare,* to spot, soil.]
1. perfectly clean; without a spot or stain; unsoiled.
2. perfectly correct; without a flaw, fault, or error.
3. pure; innocent; without sin.

Immaculate Conception; a doctrine of the Roman Catholic Church, that the Virgin Mary was conceived without original sin, proclaimed as a dogma by Pope Pius IX in 1854: sometimes confused with *virgin birth.*

im·maç′ū·lāte·ly, *adv.* in an immaculate manner; with spotless purity.

im·maç′ū·lāte·ness, *n.* the quality or state of being immaculate; spotless purity.

im·māiled′, *a.* wearing mail or armor.

im·mal′lē·ȧ·ble, *a.* not malleable; that cannot be extended by hammering. [Rare.]

im·man′ȧ·çle, *v.t.* to put manacles on; to fetter or confine; to restrain from free action. [Rare.]

im·mȧ·nā′tion, *n.* [L. *in,* into, and *manatus,* pp. of *manare,* to flow.] a flowing or entering in.

im·māne′, *a.* [L. *immanis,* great, large.] vast; huge; very great; formidable; monstrous. [Archaic.]

im·māne′ly, *adv.* monstrously; cruelly.

im′mȧ·nence, im′mȧ·nen·cy, *n.* the state or condition of being immanent.

im′mȧ·nent, *a.* [LL. *immanens* (*-entis*), ppr. of *immanere,* to remain in or near; L. *in,* in, and *manere,* to remain.]
1. living, remaining, or operating within; inherent.
2. in theology, present throughout the universe: said of God.

Im·mā′nēṣ, *n.pl.* [L., pl. of *immanis,* monstrous.] the *Dinornithes*: an earlier name.

im·man′i·fest, *a.* hidden; not visible. [Rare.]

im·man′i·ty, *n.* [L. *immanitas,* hugeness, cruelty, from *immanis,* vast, huge.] monstrosity; the condition of being immane. [Obs.]

im·man′tle, *v.t.* to cover, as with a cloak or mantle.

Im·man′ū·el, Em·man′ū·el, *n.* [LL. *Emmanuel*; Gr. *Emmanouēl*; Heb. *immanuel*, lit., God with us; *im*, with, *anu*, us, and *el*, God.] a name given by Isaiah to the Messiah of his prophecy (Is. vii. 14), often applied to Jesus (Matt. i. 23).

They shall call his name *Emmanuel*. —Matt. i. 23.

im·mär·ces′ci·ble, *a.* [LL. *immarcescibilis*, unfading; L. *in-* priv., and *marcescere*, to wither, fade.] unfading; enduring. [Obs.]

im·mär·ces′ci·bly, *adv.* in an unfading manner. [Obs.]

im·mär′gin·āte, *a.* without margin or border.

im·mär′tiăl (-shăl), *a.* not martial; not warlike. [Rare.]

im·mȧsk′, *v.t.* to cover, as with a mask; to disguise. [Obs.]

im·match′ȧ·ble, *a.* that cannot be matched.

im·mȧ·tē′ri·ăl, *a.* [ME. *immateriel*; ML. *immaterialis*.]

1. not material; not consisting of matter; incorporeal; as, *immaterial* spirits.

2. unimportant; without weight; that does not matter.

im·mȧ·tē′ri·ăl·işm, *n.* the theory or doctrine that material things do not exist objectively but only as mental perceptions.

im·mȧ·tē′ri·ăl·ist, *n.* a believer in immaterialism.

im·mȧ·tē·ri·al′i·ty, *n.* 1. the quality of being immaterial.

2. *pl.* **im·mȧ·tē·ri·al′i·tieş,** something immaterial.

im·mȧ·tē′ri·ăl·īze, *v.t.*; immaterialized, *pt.*, *pp.*; immaterializing, *ppr.* to make immaterial.

im·mȧ·tē′ri·ăl·ly, *adv.* 1. in an immaterial manner.

2. in an unimportant degree.

im·mȧ·tē′ri·ăl·ness, *n.* the state of being immaterial; immateriality.

im·mȧ·tē′ri·āte, *a.* not consisting of matter; immaterial. [Obs.]

im·mȧ·tūre′, *a.* [L. *immaturus*, unripe; *in-* priv., and *maturus*, ripe.]

1. not mature or ripe; not completely grown or developed; as, *immature* fruit.

2. not finished or perfected; incomplete.

3. hasty; too early; coming before the natural time. [Archaic.]

im·mȧ·tūred′, *a.* immature.

im·mȧ·tūre′ly, *adv.* in an immature manner; too soon; before ripeness or completion.

im·mȧ·tūre′ness, *n.* the state of being immature; unripeness; incompleteness.

im·mȧ·tū′ri·ty, *n.* [L. *immaturitas*, from *immaturus*, unripe, immature.] the state or quality of being unripe or incomplete.

im″mē·ȧ·bil′i·ty, *n.* [L. *in-* priv., and *meabilis*, passable, from *meare*, to go.] a lack of the ability to flow or pass through.

im·meaş″ūr·ȧ·bil′i·ty (-mezh″), *n.* the quality of being immeasurable.

im·meaş′ūr·ȧ·ble, *a.* that cannot be measured; immense; boundless; vast; as, an *immeasurable* distance or space.

im·meaş′ūr·ȧ·ble·ness, *n.* the state of being immeasurable.

im·meaş′ūr·ȧ·bly, *adv.* to an extent not to be measured; beyond all measure.

im·meaş′ūred, *a.* not measured; vast.

im·mē·chan′iç·ăl, *a.* not mechanical; unmechanical. [Obs.]

im·mē·chan′iç·ăl·ly, *adv.* unmechanically. [Obs.]

im·mē′di·ȧ·cy, *n.* the quality or state of being immediate.

im·mē′di·āte, *a.* [L. *in-* priv., and LL. *mediatus*, pp. of *mediare*, to divide in the middle, from L. *medius*, middle.] having nothing coming between; with no intermediary; specifically, (a) not separated in space; in direct contact; closest; nearest; also, near; close; adjoining; adjacent; (b) not separated in time; acting or happening at once; instant; of the present; (c) next in order, succession, etc.; next in line; directly or closely related; as, one's *immediate* family; (d) directly affecting; direct; first-hand; as, an *immediate* cause; (e) understood or perceived directly or intuitively; as, an *immediate* inference.

Syn.—proximate, contiguous, present, direct, instant, next, close.

im·mē′di·āte·ly, *adv.* in an immediate manner; specifically, (a) without intervening agency or cause; directly; (b) without delay; at once; instantly.

im·mē′di·āte·ly, *conj.* at the very moment that; as soon as; as, return *immediately* you are done. [Chiefly Brit.]

Syn.—directly, instantly, forthwith, instanter, at once, straightway, right away, right off.

im·mē′di·āte·ness, *n.* the state of being immediate.

im·mē′di·ȧ·tişm, *n.* the quality or state of being immediate; immediateness.

im·med′i·çȧ·ble, *a.* [L. *immedicabilis*; *in-* priv., and *medicabilis*, curable.] that cannot be healed; incurable.

Im′mel·mănn tŭrn, [after Max *Immelmann*, G. ace (1890–1916).] a maneuver in which an airplane is half looped to an upside-down position and then half rolled back to normal, upright flight: used to gain altitude while making a 180-degree change in direction.

im·mē·lō′di·ous, *a.* not melodious.

im·mem′ō·rȧ·ble, *a.* not memorable.

im·mē·mō′ri·ăl, *a.* [ML. *immemorialis*; see *in-* (not) and *memorial*.] extending back beyond memory or record; very old; ancient.

im·mē·mō′ri·ăl·ly, *adv.* in an immemorial manner; beyond memory.

im·mense′, *a.* [Fr. *immense*; L. *immensus*, vast, unmeasured; *in-* priv., and *mensus*, pp. of *metiri*, to measure.]

1. unlimited; unbounded; infinite.

O goodness infinite! goodness *immense*! —Milton.

2. vast in extent; very great in extension or in volume; as, an *immense* distance, *immense* mountain.

3. very good; remarkable for any excellence whatever; as, the picnic was *immense*. [Slang.]

Syn.—huge, gigantic, enormous, colossal, great, mammoth, stupendous, prodigious, vast, immeasurable, boundless.

im·mense′ly, *adv.* vastly; very greatly.

im·mense′ness, *n.* the state or quality of being immense.

im·men′si·ty, *n.* [L. *immensitas* (*-atis*), from *immensus*, unmeasurable.]

1. the state or quality of being immense; unlimited extension; an extent not to be measured; infinity.

By the power we find in ourselves of repeating, as often as we will, any idea of space, we get the idea of *immensity*.—Locke.

2. vastness in extent or bulk; greatness.

im·men′sive, *a.* immeasurable. [Obs.]

im·men″sụ·rȧ·bil′i·ty (-shụ-), *n.* the quality of being immensurable.

im·men′sụ·rȧ·ble (-shụ-), *a.* [LL. *immensurabilis*; L. *in-* priv., and LL. *mensurabilis*, measurable, from L. *mensura*, a measure.] that cannot be measured; immeasurable.

The law of nature—a term of *immensurable* extent. —Ward.

im·men′sụ·rāte, *a.* unmeasured. [Obs.]

im·mẽrd′, *v.t.*; immerded, *pt.*, *pp.*; immerding, *ppr.* [Fr. *emmerder*; L. *in*, on, and *merda*, dung.] to conceal or cover with merd or dung. [Rare.]

im·mẽrġe′, *v.t.*; immerged, *pt.*, *pp.*; immerging, *ppr.* [L. *immergere*; *in*, into, and *mergere*, to dip, plunge.] to plunge into or under a fluid; to immerse.

im·mẽrġe′, *v.i.* to plunge or disappear, as in a liquid.

im·mer′it, *n.* want of worth. [Obs.]

im·mer′it·ed, *a.* unmerited. [Obs.]

im·mer′it·ous, *a.* undeserving. [Obs.]

im·mẽrse′, *v.t.*; immersed, *pt.*, *pp.*; immersing, *ppr.* [L. *immersus*, pp. of *immergere*, to dip, plunge into; *in*, into, and *mergere*, to dip, plunge.]

1. to plunge, drop, or dip into or as if into a liquid, especially so as to cover completely.

2. to baptize by putting the body under water.

3. to plunge into a specified state; to involve or engage deeply; as, he was *immersed* in thought.

im·mẽrse′, *a.* immersed. [Obs.]

im·mẽrsed′ (-mẽrst′), *a.* 1. plunged into or as if into a liquid; deeply engaged; concealed by entering into any medium, as into the light of the sun or the shadow of the earth.

2. in botany, growing under water.

3. in biology, covered by the other organs or parts.

im·mẽrs′i·ble, *a.* [*in-* priv., and L. *mersus*, pp. of *mergere*, to plunge.] that can be immersed.

im·mẽr′sion, *n.* [LL. *immersio* (*-onis*), from L. *immergere*, to dip or plunge into; *in*, into, and *mergere*, to dip, plunge.]

1. the act of immersing or the state of being immersed.

2. a method of Christian baptism by submerging the entire person in water.

3. the state of being engrossed or deeply engaged; as, an *immersion* in the affairs of life.

4. in astronomy, the concealment of one heavenly body behind, or in the shadow of, another: opposed to *emersion*.

5. in microscopy, the process of using a liquid medium between the objective and the object.

immersion lens; in microscopy, an ordinary objective of short focal distance arranged so that when in use a drop of liquid having an index of refraction equal to that of glass occupies a space between it and the cover glass of the slide holding the object.

im·mẽr′sion·ist, *n.* in theology, one who believes and teaches that no baptism but that by immersion is valid.

im·mesh′, *v.t.*; immeshed (-mesht′), *pt.*, *pp.*; immeshing, *ppr.* to entangle in the meshes of a net or in a web; to enmesh.

im·mē·thod′iç·ăl, *a.* having no method; without systematic arrangement; without order or regularity; confused.

im·mē·thod′iç·ăl·ly, *adv.* without order or regularity; irregularly.

im·mē·thod′iç·ăl·ness, *n.* want of method; confusion.

im·meth′ŏd·īze, *v.t.* to free from method; to make unmethodical.

im·met′riç·ăl, *a.* unmetrical; not metrical.

im·mew′, *v.t.* to mew up.

im′mi·grănt, *n.* [L. *immigrans* (*-antis*), ppr. of *immigrare*, to go or remove into, to immigrate.] a person who immigrates.

im′mi·grănt, *a.* immigrating.

im′mi·grāte, *v.i.*; immigrated, *pt.*, *pp.*; immigrating, *ppr.* [L. *immigratus*, pp. of *immigrare*, to go or remove into; *in*, into, and *migrare*, to remove.] to come into a new country, region, or environment in order to settle there: opposed to *emigrate*.

im′mi·grāte, *v.t.* to bring in as an immigrant or immigrants.

im·mi·grā′tion, *n.* [L. *immigrare*, to immigrate.]

1. an immigrating.

2. the number of immigrants during a specified period.

im′mi·nence, *n.* [L. *imminentia*, from *imminens* (*-entis*), ppr. of *imminere*, to project over, overhang, threaten.]

1. the quality or fact of being imminent.

2. something imminent; impending evil, danger, etc.

im′mi·nen·cy, *n.* imminence.

im′mi·nent, *a.* [L. *imminens* (*-entis*), ppr. of *imminere*, to project over, overhang, threaten; *in*, on, and *minere*, to project.]

1. hanging over; projecting from above. [Rare.]

2. appearing as if about to happen; likely to happen without delay; impending: said of misfortune, evil or danger, etc.

Syn.—threatening, menacing.

im′mi·nent·ly, *adv.* in an imminent manner, threateningly.

im·min′gle, *v.t.* and *v.i.*; immingled, *pt.*, *pp.*; immingling, *ppr.* to mix or mingle thoroughly; to blend.

im·mi·nū′tion, *n.* a lessening; diminution; decrease. [Obs.]

im·mis·ci·bil′i·ty, *n.* incapability of mingling or being mixed.

im·mis′ci·ble, *a.* [L. *in-* priv., and LL. *miscibilis*, mixable, from L. *miscere*, to mix.] that cannot be blended or mixed; as, oil and water are *immiscible*.

im·mis′sion (-mish′un), *n.* [L. *immissio* (*-onis*), a letting in, from *immissus*, pp. of *immittere*, to let or send into; *in*, into, and *mittere*, to send.] the act of sending or thrusting in; injection.

im·mit′, *v.t.* [L. *immittere*, to send or let in.] to send in; to inject: opposed to *emit*.

im·mit′i·gȧ·ble, *a.* not mitigable; incapable of being mitigated or appeased.

im·mit′i·gȧ·bly, *adv.* 1. in an immitigable manner.

2. to an unmitigable degree.

im·mix′, *v.t.* and *v.i.* [from *immixt*, mixed in with, assumed to be Eng. pp.] to mix thoroughly.

im·mix′ȧ·ble, *a.* that cannot be thoroughly mixed.

im·mixed′ (-mixt′), *a.* unmixed. [Obs.]

im·mix′tūre, *n.* 1. an immixing.

2. the state or fact of being immixed or involved.

im·mō'bile, *a.* [L. *immobilis*, immovable; *in-* priv., and *mobilis*, movable.]
1. not movable; firmly set or placed; stable.
2. not moving or changing; motionless.

im·mō·bil'i·ty, *n.* [L. *immobilitas*, from *immobilis*, immovable; *in-* priv., and *mobilis*, movable, from *movere*, to move.] the state or quality of being immobile.

im·mō·bi·li·zā'tion, *n.* an immobilizing or being immobilized.

im·mō'bi·līze, *v.t.*; immobilized, *pt.*, *pp.*; immobilizing, *ppr.* 1. to make immobile; to prevent the movement of; to keep in place.
2. to take out of circulation and hold as security for bank notes: said of coin.
3. to prevent the movement of (a limb or joint) with splints or a cast.

im·mod'ẽr·ȧ·cy, *n.* immoderation. [Rare.]

im·mod'ẽr·ăte, *a.* [L. *immoderatus*, unrestrained, without measure; *in-* priv., and *moderatus*, pp. of *moderari*, to restrain, measure.]
1. not moderate; without restraint; too much; unreasonable; excessive; extravagant; as, *immoderate* spending.
2. boundless. [Obs.]
Syn.—inordinate, intemperate, exorbitant, unreasonable.

im·mod'ẽr·ăte·ly, *adv.* in an immoderate manner; excessively; unreasonably.

im·mod'ẽr·ăte·ness, *n.* excess; extravagance; lack of moderation.

im·mod·ẽr·ā'tion, *n.* excess; lack of moderation.

im·mod'est, *a.* [L. *immodestus*, unrestrained; *in-* priv., and *modestus*, restrained, modest.] lacking in the reserve or restraint which decency requires; not modest; specifically, (a) indecent; unchaste; lewd; (b) bold; forward; impudent.
Syn.—indelicate, indecorous, impudent, gross, shameless, unchaste.

im·mod'est·ly, *adv.* in an immodest manner.

im·mod'es·ty, *n.* [L. *immodestia*; *in-* priv., and *modestia*, modesty.] lack of modesty; indecency; lack of delicacy or decent reserve.

im'mō·lāte, *v.t.*; immolated, *pt.*, *pp.*; immolating, *ppr.* [L. *immolatus*, pp. of *immolare*, to sprinkle a victim with sacrificial meal; *in*, on, and *mola*, meal.] to sacrifice; especially, to offer or kill as a sacrifice.

im·mō·lā'tion, *n.* 1. the act of immolating or the state of being immolated.
2. that which is immolated.

im'mō·lā·tŏr, *n.* one who immolates.

im·mō'ment, *a.* trifling. [Obs.]

im·mō·men'tous, *a.* unimportant; not momentous. [Rare.]

im·mor'ăl, *a.* [L. *in-* priv., and *moralis*, moral.] not in conformity with accepted principles of right and wrong behavior; contrary to the moral code of the community; wicked; especially, not in conformity with the accepted standards of proper sexual behavior; unchaste; lewd; licentious; obscene.
Syn.—depraved, wicked, lewd, licentious, vicious, dissolute, profligate.

im·mō·ral'i·ty, *n.* 1. the state or quality of being immoral.
2. immoral behavior.
3. *pl.* **im·mō·ral'i·tieṣ,** an immoral act or practice; vice.

im·mor'ăl·ly, *adv.* in an immoral manner; in violation of morality.

im·mọr'tăl, *a.* [L. *immortalis*, undying, imperishable; *in-* priv., and *mortalis*, mortal.]
1. not mortal; deathless; living forever.
2. of immortal beings or immortality; divine; heavenly; as, an *immortal* vision.
3. lasting as long as this world; enduring; unfading; constant.
4. having lasting fame; remembered forever.
Syn.—imperishable, incorruptible, eternal, deathless, sempiternal, indissoluble, everlasting, perpetual, endless, undying.

im·mọr'tăl, *n.* an immortal being; specifically, (a) [*pl.*] the gods of ancient Greece or Rome; (b) a person having lasting fame.
the Forty Immortals; the members of the French Academy. [Colloq.]

im·mọr'tăl·ist, *n.* one who believes that the soul is immortal.

im·mọr·tal'i·ty, *n.* [ME. *immortalite*; OFr. *immortalite*; L. *immortalitas*, from *immortalis*, immortal.]
1. the condition or quality of being immortal; exemption from death and annihilation; unending existence.
2. exemption from oblivion; enduring fame.

im·mọr''tăl·i·zā'tion, *n.* the act of immortalizing or the state of being immortalized.

im·mọr'tăl·īze, *v.t.*; immortalized, *pt.*, *pp.*; immortalizing, *ppr.* 1. to make immortal.
2. to exempt from oblivion; to perpetuate; to give lasting fame to.
I look for streams *immortalized* in song. —Addison.

im·mọr'tăl·ly, *adv.* in an immortal manner; with exemption from death.

im·mọr·telle', *n.*; *pl.* **im·mọr·telleṣ',** [Fr., f. of *immortel*, undying.] any of various plants whose blossoms keep their color and shape when dried; an everlasting.

im·mọr''ti·fi·cā'tion, *n.* lack of mortification or subjection of the passions. [Obs.]

im·mō'tile, *a.* not motile; stationary; not capable of moving.

im·möv·ȧ·bil'i·ty, *n.* the condition or quality of being immovable; steadfastness.

im·möv'ȧ·ble, *a.* 1. incapable of being moved; fast; firmly fixed.
2. not moving; immobile; motionless; stationary.
3. not to be moved from a purpose; steadfast; fixed; that cannot be induced to change or alter; as, a man who remains *immovable*.
4. that cannot be altered or shaken; unalterable; unchangeable; unyielding; steadfast; as, an *immovable* purpose or resolution.
5. unemotional; impassive; not impressible; not susceptible of compassion or tender feelings; unfeeling.
6. in law, fixed; not liable to be removed; permanent in place; as, an *immovable* estate.

im·möv'ȧ·ble, *n.* that which cannot be moved; specifically, in law, immovable possessions or property, as land, trees, buildings, etc.

im·möv'ȧ·ble·ness, *n.* the state or quality of being immovable.

im·möv'ȧ·bly, *adv.* in an immovable manner; unalterably; unchangeably.

im·mund', *a.* unclean.

im·mun'di·ty, *n.* uncleanness.

im·mūne', *a.* [ME. *immuin*; OFr. *immune*; L. *immunis*, free from public service, exempt; *in-* priv., and *munis*, ready to serve, *munus*, duty, burden, tax.] having immunity; exempt from or protected against something disagreeable or harmful; especially, not susceptible to some specified disease; protected as by inoculation.

im·mūne' bod'y, a substance giving immunity to a specific disease, produced in the blood and lymph of individuals exposed to or inoculated with the antigen causing the disease; antibody.

im·mū'ni·ty, *n.*; *pl.* **im·mū'ni·tieṣ,** [ME. *ynmunite*; OFr. *immunité*; L. *immunitas* (*-atis*), freedom from public service, from *immunis*, free from public service.]
1. freedom or exemption from obligation in any respect; exemption or release from any charge, duty, office, tax, or imposition; as, the *immunities* of the clergy.
2. freedom; as, *immunity* from error.
3. resistance to or protection against a specified disease; power to resist infection.

im·mū·ni·zā'tion, *n.* an immunizing or being immunized.

im'mū·nīze, *v.t.*; immunized, *pt.*, *pp.*; immunizing, *ppr.* to give immunity to, as by inoculation; to make immune.

im·mū'nō-, a combining form meaning *immune, immunity.*

im''mū·nō·as'sāy, *n.* [*immuno-*, and *assay*.] a technique for analyzing, and measuring the concentration of, antibodies, hormones, etc. in the body, used in diagnosing disease, detecting the presence of a tumor or drug, etc.

im·mū·nol'ō·ġy, *n.* [*immuno-* and *-logy*.] the branch of medicine dealing with immunity to disease.

im''mū·nō''rē·aç'tion, *n.* the reaction between an antigen and its antibody in the establishment of immunity.

im''mū·nō''sup·pres'sion, *n.* the inactivation of a specific antibody by various agents, thus permitting the acceptance of a foreign substance, as a transplant, by an organism.

im''mū·nō''ther'ȧ·py, *n.* 1. the treatment of disease or infection by immunization.
2. the process of immunosuppression.

im·mūre', *v.t.*; immured, *pt.*, *pp.*; immuring, *ppr.* [OFr. *emmurrer*; L. *in*, in, and *murus*, a wall.]
1. to enclose within or as within walls; to shut up; to confine.
Thou wert *immured*, restrained, captivated, bound. —Shak.
2. to wall; to surround with walls. [Obs.]
3. to seclude or isolate (oneself); as, he *immured* himself in his books.

im·mūre'ment, *n.* the act of immuring or the state of being immured.

im·mū'ṣiç·ăl, *a.* unmusical.

im·mū·tȧ·bil'i·ty, *n.* [L. *immutabilitas*, from *immutabilis*, unchangeable.] the state or quality of being immutable; unchangeableness; immutableness; invariableness.

im·mū'tȧ·ble, *a.* [L. *immutabilis*; *in-* priv., and *mutabilis*, changeable.] unchangeable; invariable; never changing or varying; not capable or susceptible of change.

im·mū'tȧ·ble·ness, *n.* unchangeableness; immutability.

im·mū'tȧ·bly, *adv.* unchangeably; unalterably; invariably; in an immutable manner.

im'ou pīne, [prob. from native name.] in botany, a tree of the yew family, *Dacrydium cupressinum*, growing in New Zealand and having dense, heavy red wood.

imp, *n.* [ME. *impe*; AS. *impa*, a scion, shoot, twig.]
1. a son; child; offspring; progeny. [Obs.]
A lad of life, an *imp* of fame. —Shak.
2. a devil's offspring; a young demon.
3. a mischievous child.
4. something fastened on, as by splicing, in order to repair, fill out, or lengthen, as a feather in a broken or deficient wing of a falcon. [Archaic.]
5. a graft; a scion; a slip. [Obs.]

imp, *v.t.*; imped, *pt.*, *pp.*; imping, *ppr.* [ME. *impen*, from AS. *impa*, a scion, shoot.]
1. to implant, especially by grafting. [Archaic.]
2. to repair (the wing or tail of a falcon) by grafting on a feather or feathers. [Archaic.]
3. to furnish with wings. [Archaic.]
4. to help out by adding, increasing, enlarging, etc. [Archaic.]

im·pack'ment, *n.* the state of being packed or compressed. [Rare.]

im·paçt', *v.t.*; impacted, *pt.*, *pp.*; impacting, *ppr.* [OFr. *impacter*, to press close together; L. *impactus*, pp. of *impingere*, to strike or thrust against, to strike together.] to force tightly together; to pack; to wedge.

im'paçt, *n.* 1. a striking together; violent contact; collision; also, the single instantaneous blow or stroke communicated from one body in motion to another either in motion or at rest; a forcible momentary touch, contact, or impression.
2. the force of a collision; shock.
3. the power of an event, idea, etc. to produce changes, move the feelings, etc.

im·paçt'ed, *a.* pressed tightly together; driven firmly in; wedged in; especially, firmly lodged in the jaw: said of a tooth unable to erupt because of its abnormal position.

im·paç'tion, *n.* [L. *impactio* (*-onis*), a striking against, from *impingere*, to thrust against or strike.] the act of impacting or the condition of being impacted, wedged, or closely fixed.

im·pāint', *v.t.* to paint; to adorn with colors.

im·pāir', *v.t.*; impaired, *pt.*, *pp.*; impairing, *ppr.* [ME. *empairen*; OFr. *empeirer*, to make worse; L. *in-*, intens., and *pejorare*, to make worse, from *pejor*, worse.] to make worse, less, weaker, etc.; to deteriorate; to diminish in quantity, value, or excellence; to lessen in power; to weaken; to enfeeble.

im·pāir', *v.i.* to become worn out; to deteriorate. [Rare.]

im'pāir, *a.* 1. unsuitable. [Obs.]
2. not paired.

im·pāir', *n.* diminution; decrease; injury. [Obs.]

im·pāir'ẽr, *n.* one who or that which impairs.

im·pāir'ment, *n.* 1. an impairing or being impaired.
2. damage; injury; deterioration.

im·pä'lȧ, *n.*; *pl.* **im·pä'lȧ** or **im·pä'lȧṣ,** [Zulu.] a medium-sized, reddish antelope, *Aepyceros melampus*, of central and southern Africa.

im·pal'ȧ·tȧ·ble, *a.* unpalatable. [Rare.]

im·pāle', *v.t.*; impaled, *pt.*, *pp.*; impaling, *ppr.* [Fr. *empaler*, to impale; L. *in*, on, and *palus*, a pole, stake.]
1. to surround with or as with a palisade; to fence in. [Rare.]
2. (a) to pierce through with, or fix on, something pointed; to transfix; (b) to punish or torture by fixing on a stake thrust through the body.
3. to make helpless, as if fixed on a stake; as, her glance *impaled* him.
4. in heraldry, to join (two coats of arms) side by side on one shield.

im·pāle′ment, *n.* 1. an impaling or being impaled.

2. in heraldry, the division of a shield palewise, especially for placing the arms of two persons side by side.

IMPALEMENT

im·pal′lȧ, *n.* [native name.] the pallah, or roodebok, a South African antelope.

im·pal′lid, *v.t.* to make pallid or pale. [Obs.]

im·pälm′ (-päm′), *v.t.* to grasp; to take in the hand. [Obs.]

im·pal·pȧ·bil′i·ty, *n.* the quality of being impalpable.

im·pal′pȧ·ble, *a.* [L. *in*, not, and *palpare*, to touch.]

1. that cannot be felt; that cannot be perceived by the touch; as, an *impalpable* powder is one so fine that no grit can be felt.

2. too slight or subtle to be readily grasped by the mind; inappreciable.

im·pal′pȧ·bly, *adv.* in an impalpable manner; imperceptibly.

im·pal′sy, *v.t.* to strike with palsy; to paralyze. [Rare.]

im·pā′nāte, *a.* [L. *in*, in, and *panis*, bread.] embodied in bread.

im·pā′nāte, *v.t.* to embody in bread.

im·pȧ·nā′tion, *n.* [ML. *impanatio*, from pp. of *impanare*, to embody in bread, from L. *in-*, in, and *panis*, bread.] the doctrine that the body of Christ is present in the bread and wine of the Eucharist after consecration by the priest, with no actual change in their substance: distinguished from *transubstantiation*.

im·pȧ·nā·tŏr, *n.* [LL., from L. *in*, in, and *panis*, bread.] one who believes in imapanation.

im·pan′el, *v.t.*; impaneled *or* impanelled, *pt.*, *pp.*; impaneling *or* impanelling, *ppr.* to empanel.

im·par′ȧ·dīse, *v.t.*; imparadised, *pt.*, *pp.*; imparadising, *ppr.* 1. to make as happy as though in paradise; to transport; enrapture.

2. to make into a paradise.

im·par′ăl·leled, *a.* unparalleled. [Obs.]

im·pär′dŏn·ȧ·ble, *a.* unpardonable. [Obs.]

im·par·i·dig′i·tāte, *a.* [L. *impar*, unequal, and *digitus*, finger.] odd-toed; odd-fingered; perissodactyl; with an uneven number of digits on a foot or hand.

im·par·i·pin′nāte, *a.* [L. *impar*, unequal, and *pinnatus*, feathered.] pinnate and terminated by a single leaflet; oddly pinnate.

IMPARIPINNATE LEAF

im·par′i·syl·lab′iç, *a.* [L. *impar*, unequal, and *syllaba*, a syllable.] having an unequal number of syllables in various cases; as, *timor*, *timoris*, is an *imparisyllabic* Latin noun.

im·par′i·ty, *n.*; *pl.* **im·par′i·tieş,** [L. *impar*, unequal.]

1. inequality; disproportion; difference of degree, rank, or excellence; incongruity. [Rare.]

2. oddness; indivisibility into equal parts. [Obs.]

im·pärk′, *v.t.*; imparked, *pt.*, *pp.*; imparking, *ppr.* 1. to shut up (animals) in a park.

2. to enclose (land) for a park.

im·pärl′, *v.i.*; imparled, *pt.*, *pp.*; imparling, *ppr.* [OFr. *emparler*, to talk.]

1. to hold mutual discourse. [Obs.]

2. in law, to have license to settle a lawsuit amicably; to have delay for mutual adjustment.

im·pär′lănce, *n.* [OFr. *emparlance*, from *emparler*, to talk.] in law, the license or privilege of a defendant, granted on motion, to have delay of trial, to see if he can settle the matter amicably by talking with the plaintiff; hence, continuance of a suit till another day, or from day to day.

im·pär·sŏn·nee′, *a.* [LL. *impersonatus*; L. *in*, in, and *persona*, person.] presented, instituted, and inducted into a rectory, and in full possession, as a clergyman. [Brit.]

im·pär·sŏn·nee′, *n.* a clergyman imparsonnee.

im·pärt′, *v.t.*; imparted, *pt.*, *pp.*; imparting, *ppr.* [OFr. *empartir*; L. *impertire*, to share with another; *in*, in, and *partire*, to part, divide.]

1. to bestow upon another a share or portion of (anything); to give.

2. to tell; to reveal; to communicate; to make known; as, to *impart* a message.

Syn.—share, give, grant, disclose, divulge, communicate, reveal, confer, tell.

im·pärt′, *v.i.* 1. to bestow a share.

2. to share. [Obs.]

im·pärt′ănce, *n.* communication of a share; grant. [Rare.]

im·pär·tā′tion, *n.* an imparting or being imparted.

im·pärt′ẽr, *n.* one who imparts. [Rare.]

im·pär′tiăl (-shăl), *a.* [L. *in-* priv., and LL. *partialis*, partial, from L. *pars*, *partis*, parts.] not partial; not biased in favor of one party more than another; unprejudiced; disinterested; equitable; just; fair.

im·pär′tiăl·ist, *n.* one who is impartial. [Rare.]

im·pär·ti·al′i·ty (-shi-al′), *n.* the quality or condition of being impartial; freedom from favoritism, bias, or prejudice.

im·pär′tiăl·ly, *adv.* in an impartial manner; without bias of judgment.

im·pär′tiăl·ness, *n.* the state of being impartial.

im·pärt·i·bil′i·ty, *n.* the quality or condition of being impartible.

im·pärt′i·ble, *a.* [L. *impartibilis*; *in-* priv., and *partibilis*, partible, from *pars*, *partis*, a part.] not partible or subject to partition; that cannot be partitioned or divided; indivisible: said of an estate.

im·pärt′i·ble, *a.* [L. *in*, in, and *partire*, to divide.] capable of being imparted, communicated, or bestowed.

im·pärt′i·bly, *adv.* in an impartible manner.

im·pärt′ment, *n.* the act of imparting; also, the thing imparted.

im·pȧss·ȧ·bil′i·ty, *n.* the quality or state of being impassable.

im·pȧss′ȧ·ble, *a.* that cannot be passed, crossed, or traveled over; not admitting a passage; as, an *impassable* road, mountain, or gulf.

im·pȧss′ȧ·ble·ness, *n.* the state of being impassable.

im·pȧss′ȧ·bly, *adv.* in a manner or degree that prevents passing or the power of passing.

im·passe′ (im-pas′ *or* im′pas), *n.*; *pl.* **im·pas′seş,** [Fr.] a blind alley; an impassable road; by extension, a situation that has no solution or affords no escape.

im·pas·si·bil′i·ty, *n.* [LL. *impassibilitas*, from *impassibilis*, not capable of passion, impassible.] the state or quality of being impassible.

im·pas′si·ble, *a.* [ME.; OFr.; LL. *impassibilis*, not capable of passion; L. *in-* priv., and *passibilis*, able to suffer, from *passus*, pp. of *pati*, to suffer, endure.]

1. incapable of pain or suffering; that cannot be affected with pain or uneasiness.

2. apathetic; not revealing emotion or passion.

3. that cannot be injured; invulnerable.

im·pas′si·ble·ness, *n.* the state of being impassible.

im·pas′sion (-pash′un), *v.t.*; impassioned, *pt.*, *pp.*; impassioning, *ppr.* [It. *impassionare*.] to arouse emotionally; to move or affect strongly with passion.

im·pas′sion·ȧ·ble, *a.* easily excited to anger; susceptible of strong emotion.

im·pas′sion·āte, *v.t.*; impassionated, *pt.*, *pp.*; impassionating, *ppr.* [LL. *impassionatus*, strongly affected; L. *in-* intens., and *passio* (*-onis*), passion.] to affect powerfully; to arouse deep feeling in.

im·pas′sion·āte, *a.* impassioned.

im·pas′sion·āte, *a.* [L. *in-* priv., and LL. *passionatus*, passionate, from L. *passio* (*-onis*), passion.] without passion or feeling. [Now Rare.]

im·pas′sioned (-pash′und), *a.* actuated or moved by passion; having or showing strong feeling; passionate; fiery; ardent; as, an *impassioned* speaker or address.

im·pas′sive, *a.* 1. not feeling pain; not suffering; insensible.

2. that cannot be injured; invulnerable.

3. not feeling or showing emotion; placid; calm; serene.

im·pas′sive·ly, *adv.* in an impassive manner.

im·pas′sive·ness, *n.* the state or quality of being impassive.

im·pas·siv′i·ty, *n.* impassiveness.

im·pas·tā′tion, *n.* 1. the act of making into paste.

2. that which is made into paste.

im·pāste′, *v.t.*; impasted, *pt.*, *pp.*; impasting, *ppr.* [It. *impastare*.]

1. to enclose or crust over with paste or a pasty substance.

2. to make a paste or crust of.

3. to apply a thick coat or coats of paint to.

im·pȧs′tō, *n.* [It., from *impastare*, to cover with paste.]

1. painting in which the paint is laid on thickly.

2. paint so laid on.

im·pat′i·ble, *a.* [L. *impatabilis*; *in-* priv., and *pati*, to suffer.]

1. intolerable; that cannot be borne. [Obs.]

2. apathetic; without feeling. [Obs.]

im·pā′tience (-shens), *n.* [OFr. *impacience*; L. *impatientia*, impatience, from *impatiens* (*-entis*), impatient.] lack of patience; specifically, (a) annoyance because of delay, opposition, etc.; (b) restless eagerness to do something, go somewhere, etc.

im·pā′tien·cy, *n.* impatience. [Obs.]

Im·pā′ti·enş (-shi-enz), *n.* [L. *impatiens* (*-entis*), not enduring, impatient.]

1. a genus of plants of the balsam family, with spurred flowers and pods that burst and scatter their seeds when ripe: also called *touch-me-not*, *jewelweed*, *snapweed*, *balsam*.

2. [i—] any plant of this genus.

im·pā′tient (-shent), *a.* [OFr. *impacient*; L. *impatiens* (*-entis*), not enduring or suffering, impatient; *in-* priv., and *patiens* (*-entis*), enduring, patient, ppr. of *pati*, to suffer, endure.]

1. without patience; uneasy or fretful; not enduring evil, opposition, or delay; intolerant; hasty; eager; restless; as, *impatient* at the delay; *impatient* of restraint; *impatient* for a friend's arrival; *impatient* under evils.

2. showing or caused by impatience; as, an *impatient* remark.

3. not to be borne; intolerable. [Obs.]

impatient of; not willing to bear or tolerate; showing dislike for.

Syn.—eager, restless, uneasy, fretful, hasty, peevish, petulant, irritated.

im·pā′tient, *n.* one who is impatient.

im·pā′tient·ly, *adv.* in an impatient manner.

im·pat″rŏn·i·zā′tion, *n.* absolute seigniory or possession; also, the act of bestowing such possession. [Obs.]

im·pat′rŏn·īze, *v.t.*; impatronized, *pt.*, *pp.*; impatronizing, *ppr.* to take possession of. [Obs.]

im·pāve′, *v.t.* to incorporate in a pavement, as a figure in mosaic. [Rare.]

im·pav′id, *a.* [L. *impavidus*, fearless; *in-* priv., and *pavidus*, fearing.] having no fear. [Rare.]

im·pav′id·ly, *adv.* without fear; intrepidly. [Rare.]

im·pawn′, *v.t.*; impawned, *pt.*, *pp.*; impawning, *ppr.* to pawn; to pledge; to deposit as security.

im·pēach′, *v.t.*; impeached (-pēcht), *pt.*, *pp.*; impeaching, *ppr.* [ME. *empechen*; OFr. *empescher*, to hinder; LL. *impedicare*, to fetter, to catch, entangle; L. *in*, in, and *pedica*, a fetter, from *pes*, *pedis*, foot.]

1. to hinder; to impede. [Obs.]

2. to call to account; to challenge or discredit (a person's honor, reputation, etc.).

3. to charge with a crime or misdemeanor; to make charges of misconduct in office against (a public officer) before a competent tribunal; as, to *impeach* a judge.

4. in law, to call in question the reliability of, as a witness or commercial paper.

Syn.—arraign, accuse, indict, discredit, censure, charge with, blame.

im·pēach′, *n.* 1. hindrance. [Obs.]

2. impeachment. [Rare.]

im·pēach·ȧ·bil′i·ty, *n.* the quality of being impeachable.

im·pēach′ȧ·ble, *a.* 1. liable to be impeached.

2. making one liable to be impeached; as, an *impeachable* act.

im·pēach′ẽr, *n.* one who impeaches.

im·pēach′ment, *n.* [OFr. *empeschement*, hindrance, from *empescher*, to hinder.]

1. hindrance; obstruction. [Obs.]

2. censure; accusation; a calling in question the purity of motives or the rectitude of conduct; as, this declaration is no *impeachment* of his motives or of his judgment.

3. an accusation or charge brought against a public officer for misconduct in office. In the United States, it is the right of the House of Representatives to impeach, and of the Senate to try and determine an impeachment of, the chief executive and other Federal officers.

articles of impeachment; see under *article*.

impeachment of waste; in law, an action to restrain a tenant from wasting the property of the owner or to compel him to pay for injury done by waste.

im·pēarl′, *v.t.* and *v.i.*; impearled (-pẽrld), *pt.*, *pp.*; impearling, *ppr.* 1. to form into pearls or pearllike drops.

Dewdrops which the sun
Impearls on every leaf, and every flower.
—Milton.

2. to decorate with pearls or with anything resembling pearls.

The dews of the morning *impearl* every thorn. —Digby.

3. to make pearly.

im·peç·cȧ·bil′i·ty, *n.* the quality of being impeccable.

im·peç′çȧ·ble, *a.* [LL. *impeccabilis*; L. *in-* priv., and *peccare*, to sin.]

1. not liable to sin or wrongdoing; exempt from the possibility of sinning; as, no mere man is *impeccable*.

2. without defect or error; faultless; flawless.

im·peç′çȧ·ble, *n.* an impeccable person.

im·peç′çȧ·bly, *adv.* in an impeccable manner.

im·peç′çăn·cy, im·peç′çănce, *n.* the quality of being impeccant.

im·peç′çănt, *a.* [L. *in-* priv., and *peccans* (*-antis*), ppr. of *peccare*, to sin.] free from sin or wrong; blameless.

im·pē·çū·ni·os′i·ty, *n.* the quality or state of being impecunious or moneyless.

im·pē·çū′ni·ous, *a.* [L. *in-* priv., and *pecunia*, money.] having no money; poor; especially, constantly poor.

im·pēd′ănce, *n.* [from *impede*, and *-ance*.]

1. the apparent resistance in an alternating electrical current, corresponding to the true resistance in a direct current.

2. the ratio of the force per unit area to the volume displacement of a given surface across which sound is being transmitted.

im·pēde′, *v.t.*; impeded, *pt., pp.*; impeding, *ppr.* [L. *impedire*, to entangle, ensnare, lit., to hold the feet; *in*, in, and *pes, pedis*, foot.] to hinder; to stop in progress; to obstruct; to retard; as, to *impede* the progress of troops.

Syn.—hinder, obstruct, check, delay, prevent, embarrass, retard, fetter, hamper.

im·pēd′i·ble, *a.* that can be impeded. [Rare.]

im·ped′i·ment, *n.* [L., *impedimentum*, a hindrance, from *impedire*, to hinder, impede.]

1. an impeding or being impeded.

2. anything that impedes; specifically, (a) a speech defect; stutter, lisp, stammer, etc.; (b) anything preventing the making of a legal contract, especially of a marriage contract.

Syn.—obstacle, difficulty, hindrance.

im·ped′i·ment, *v.t.* to impede. [Obs.]

im·ped·i·men′tȧ, *n.pl.* [L., pl. of *impedimentum*, baggage, a hindrance.] things which impede or hinder progress, as on a trip; encumbrances; specifically, (a) baggage; equipment carried while traveling; (b) the supplies or baggage carried along with an army.

im·ped·i·men′tăl, *a.* of or like an impediment; hindering; obstructing.

im′pē·dīte, *a.* hindered. [Obs.]

im′pē·dīte, *v.t.* to impede. [Rare.]

im·pē·di′tion (-dish′un), *n.* a hindering. [Obs.]

im·ped′i·tive, *a.* [L. *impeditus*, pp. of *impedire*, to hinder.] causing hindrance; of the nature of an impediment.

im·pel′, *v.t.*; impelled, *pt., pp.*; impelling, *ppr.* [L. *impellere*, to drive, push, or strike against, to drive on; *in*, on, and *pellere*, to drive.]

1. to push, move, or drive forward; to propel; as, a ball is *impelled* by the force of powder.

2. to force, compel, or urge; to incite; to constrain; as, a man may be *impelled* by hunger; motives of policy *impel* nations to confederate.

Syn.—actuate, drive, force, push, move, instigate, incite, urge, press, induce.

im·pel′lent, *a.* [L. *impellens* (*-entis*), ppr. of *impellere*, to drive on, impel.] impelling or tending to impel.

im·pel′lent, *n.* anything that impels; motive, inducement, etc.

im·pel′lĕr, *n.* one who or that which impels.

im·pen′, *v.t.*; impenned, *pt., pp.*; impenning, *ppr.* to pen; to shut or enclose in a narrow place. [Rare.]

im·pend′, *v.i.*; impended, *pt., pp.*; impending, *ppr.* [L. *impendere*, to overhang, threaten; *in*, on, and *pendere*, to hang.]

1. to hang or be suspended (*over*); as, a dark cloud *impends over* the land.

2. to be about to happen; to be near at hand; to be imminent; as, an *impending* disaster.

Destruction sure o'er all your heads *impends*. —Pope.

im·pend′, *v.t.* to threaten. [Rare.]

im·pend′ence, im·pend′en·cy, *n.* the stat or quality of being impendent; imminence.

im·pend′ent, *a.* [L. *impendens* (*-entis*), ppr. of *impendere*, to overhang, impend.] hanging over; imminent; threatening; about to happen; impending; as, an *impendent* evil.

im·pend′ing, *a.* 1. hanging over.

2. about to happen; imminent or threatening.

im·pen″ē·trȧ·bil′i·ty, *n.* the condition or quality of being impenetrable.

im·pen′ē·trȧ·ble, *a.* [L. *impenetrabilis*; *in-* priv., and *penetrabilis*, penetrable.]

1. that cannot be penetrated or pierced; not admitting the passage of other bodies; impervious; as, an *impenetrable* shield.

2. that cannot be solved or understood; unfathomable; inscrutable.

3. unreceptive to ideas, impressions, influences, etc.

4. in physics, having the property by which two bodies are prevented from occupying the same space at the same time.

im·pen′ē·trȧ·ble·ness, *n.* impenetrability.

im·pen′ē·trȧ·bly, *adv.* in an impenetrable manner.

im·pen′i·tence, *n.* lack of penitence or repentance; absence of contrition or sorrow for sin; hardness of heart.

He will advance from one degree of *impenitence* to another. —Rogers.

im·pen′i·ten·cy, *n.* same as *impenitence*.

im·pen′i·tent, *a.* [LL. *impænitens*; L. *in-* priv., and *pœnitens* (*-entis*), ppr. of *pænitere*, to repent, from *pæna*, punishment.] not penitent; not repenting of sin; not contrite; without regret, shame, or remorse.

im·pen′i·tent, *n.* one who is impenitent.

im·pen′i·tent·ly, *adv.* without repentance or contrition for sin; obdurately.

im·pen′nāte, *a.* [L. *in-* priv., and *pennatus*, winged.] without feathers or wings; specifically, designating or of a group of nonflying, swimming birds with very short wings covered with feathers resembling scales, as the penguins.

im·pen′nāte, *n.* an impennate bird, as the penguin.

Im·pen′nēṣ, *n.pl.* [L. *in-* priv., and *penna*, a feather, wing.] the penguin group of birds.

im·pen′nous, *a.* [L. *in-* priv., and *penna*, a wing.] in zoology, having no wings. [Obs.]

im·pēo′ple (-pē′), *v.t.* same as *empeople*.

im′pe·rȧnt, *a.* [L. *imperans* (*-antis*), ppr. of *imperare*, to command.] commanding. [Obs.]

im′pe·rāte, *a.* commanded. [Obs.]

im·per·ȧ·tī′văl, *a.* in grammar, relating to the imperative mood.

im·per′ȧ·tive, *a.* [L. *imperativus*, commanding, from *imperare*, to command, order; *in*, in, on, and *parare*, to prepare, order.]

1. having the nature of, or indicating, authority or command; as, an *imperative* gesture.

2. absolutely necessary; urgent; compelling; as, it is *imperative* that I go at once.

3. in grammar, designating or of the mood of a verb that expresses a command, strong request, or exhortation.

Syn.—urgent, irresistible, dictatorial, inexorable, peremptory, compulsory, obligatory, mandatory.

im·per′ȧ·tive, *n.* 1. a command; an order.

2. in grammar, (a) the imperative mood; (b) a verb in this mood.

im·per′ȧ·tive·ly, *adv.* with command; authoritatively.

im·per′ȧ·tive·ness, *n.* the state or quality of being imperative.

im·pē·rā′tŏr, *n.* [L., from *imperare*, to command.] in ancient Rome, (a) during the earlier republic, the title given a victorious general; (b) later, one holding the imperium or power of chief military command; a commander; (c) during the empire, the official title of the supreme ruler or emperor as commander in chief of the armies; emperor.

im·per·ȧ·tō′ri·ăl, *a.* [L. *imperatorius*, from *imperator*, a commander.]

1. commanding.

2. relating to an emperor or to his office.

im·per·ȧ·tō′ri·ăn, *a.* imperatorial. [Obs.]

im·per′ȧ·tō·ry, *a.* imperatorial. [Obs.]

im·pēr·cēiv′ȧ·ble, *a.* imperceptible. [Rare.]

im·pēr·cēiv′ȧ·ble·ness, *n.* imperceptibleness; [Rare.]

im·pēr·cēived′, *a.* same as *unperceived*.

im·pēr·cep·ti·bil′i·ty, *n.* the quality of not being perceptible.

im·pēr·cep′ti·ble, *a.* [LL. *imperceptibilis*; L. *in-* priv., and *perceptibilis*, perceptible.] not plain or distinct to the senses or the mind; especially, so slight, gradual, subtle, etc. as not to be easily perceived; undiscernible; not easily seen or observed; as, *imperceptible* increase by growth.

im·pēr·cep′ti·ble·ness, *n.* the quality of being imperceptible.

im·pēr·cep′ti·bly, *adv.* in an imperceptible manner.

im·pēr·cep′tion, *n.* the absence of perception.

im·pēr·cep′tive, *a.* not perceiving; lacking perception.

im·pēr·cip′i·ent, *a.* not perceiving or not having power to perceive.

im·pēr·di·bil′i·ty, *n.* the state or quality of being imperdible. [Obs.]

im·pēr′di·ble, *a.* that cannot be destroyed or lost. [Obs.]

im·pēr′di·bly, *adv.* in an indestructible manner. [Obs.]

im·pēr′feçt, *a.* [L. *imperfectus*, unfinished; *in-* priv., and *perfectus*, finished, pp. of *perficere*, to finish.]

1. not finished or complete; lacking in something.

2. not perfect; having a defect, fault, or error.

3. in the grammar of certain inflected languages, designating or of the tense of a verb that indicates a past action or state as incomplete, continuous, customary, or going on at the same time as another: "was writing" and "used to write" are forms corresponding to the imperfect tense in languages having such a tense.

4. in music, diminished.

imperfect arch; in architecture, an arch whose curve is less than that of a semicircle.

imperfect cadence; a cadence consisting of the chord of the tonic followed by that of the dominant.

imperfect consonance; in music, the major and minor third and sixth.

imperfect flower; a unisexual flower; a flower lacking either stamens or pistils.

imperfect interval; in music, an interval which does not contain its complement of simple sounds.

imperfect number; a number which is not equal to the sum of its aliquot parts or divisors.

imperfect obligation; a self-imposed obligation or one that the law cannot enforce.

imperfect tense; see *imperfect, a.* (sense 3).

im·pēr′feçt, *n.* in grammar, (a) the imperfect tense; (b) a verb in this tense.

im·pēr′feçt, *v.t.* to render imperfect. [Obs.]

im·pēr·feç·ti·bil′i·ty, *n.* the state of being imperfectible.

im·pēr·feç′ti·ble, *a.* incapable of being perfected.

im·pēr·feç′tion, *n.* [OFr. *imperfection*; LL. *imperfectio* (*-onis*), imperfection, from L. *imperfectus*, imperfect.]

1. the quality or condition of being imperfect.

2. a shortcoming; defect; fault; blemish.

Syn.—blemish, fault, immaturity, incompleteness, failing, deficiency, weakness, fraility.

im·pēr·feç′tive, *a.* in grammar, designating or of an aspect of verbs, as in Russian and other Slavonic languages, expressing incompletion, or continued repetition, of the action.

im·pēr·feç′tive, *n.* 1. the imperfective aspect.

2. a verb in this aspect.

im·pēr′feçt·ly, *adv.* in an imperfect manner or degree; not fully; not entirely; not completely; not in the best manner; not without fault or failure.

im·pēr′feçt·ness, *n.* the state of being imperfect.

im·pēr′fō·rȧ·ble, *a.* incapable of being perforated or bored through.

Im·pēr·fō·rā′tȧ, *n.pl.* in zoology, a division of foraminifers whose exoskeletons are without perforations: opposed to *Perforata*.

im·pēr′fō·rāte, im·pēr′fō·rā·ted, *a.* [L. *in-* priv., and *perforatus*, pp. of *perforare*, to perforate.]

1. having no holes or openings; unpierced.

2. having a straight edge without perforations: said of a postage stamp, etc.

3. in anatomy, lacking the normal opening.

im·pēr′fō·rāte, *n.* an imperforate stamp.

im·pēr·fō·rā′tion, *n.* the state of being imperforate.

im·pē′ri·ăl, *a.* [OFr. *imperial*; L. *imperialis*, pertaining to an empire or emperor, from *imperium*, an empire, command, from *imperare*, to command.]

1. of an empire.

2. of a country having control or sovereign rights over other countries or colonies.

3. of, or having the rank of, an emperor or empress.

4. having supreme authority; sovereign.

5. majestic; august; magnificent.

6. of great size or superior quality.

7. according to the standard of weights and measures fixed by British law.

Imperial Chamber; the sovereign court of the Holy Roman Empire.

Imperial Diet; an assembly of all the states of the Holy Roman Empire.

imperial gallon; the standard British gallon, equal to 277.42 cubic inches or about 1$^1/_5$ United States gallons.

Imperial Guard; the royal guard of the first Napoleon.

im·pē′ri·ăl, *n.* 1. [I–] (a) a supporter of the Holy Roman emperor; (b) a soldier of his troops.

2. a gold coin of the former Russian Empire.

3. (a) the roof or top of a coach; (b) a case or trunk carried on this.

4. an article of great size or superior quality; often a trade name.

5. a size of writing paper measuring 23 by 31 inches (in England, 22 by 30 or 32 inches).

6. [after Napoleon III, who set this fashion.] a pointed tuft of beard on the lower lip and chin.

im·pē′ri·ăl·iṣm, *n.* 1. imperial state, authority, spirit, or system of government.

2. the policy and practice of forming and maintaining an empire; in modern times, it is characterized by a struggle for the control of raw materials and world markets, the subjugation and control of territories, the establishment of colonies, etc.

im·pē′ri·ăl·ist, *n.* 1. [I–] (a) a supporter of the Holy Roman emperor; (b) a soldier of his troops.

2. a supporter of any emperor.

3. a person favoring imperialism.

im·pē·ri·ăl·is′tiç, *a.* 1. of or characteristic of imperialism or imperialists.

2. favoring imperialism.

im·pē·ri·ăl·is′tiç·ăl·ly, *adv.* in an imperialistic manner.

im·pē·ri·al′i·ty, *n.* imperial power, authority, or rank. [Obs.]

im·pē′ri·ăl·īze, *v.t.*; imperialized, *pt., pp.*; imperializing, *ppr.* to bring into the condition of an empire; to endow with imperial qualities or characteristics.

im·pē′ri·ăl·ly, *adv.* in an imperial manner.

im·pē′ri·ăl moth, a large American moth having yellow wings with dark markings.

im·per′il, *v.t.*; imperiled *or* imperilled, *pt., pp.*; imperiling *or* imperilling, *ppr.* to bring into danger; to put in peril.

im·per′il·ment, *n.* the act of endangering; jeopardy; danger; an imperiling.

im·pē′ri·ous, *a.* [L. *imperiosus*, full of command, powerful, from *imperium*, command.]

1. authoritative; commanding with rightful authority.

2. dictatorial; haughty; overbearing; arrogant; domineering; as, an *imperious* tyrant.

3. imperative; urgent; pressing; as, *imperious* appetite.

Syn.—lordly, domineering, commanding, haughty, imperative, overbearing, tyrannical.

im·pē′ri·ous·ly, *adv.* 1. with arrogance of command; with a haughty air of authority; in a domineering manner.

2. with urgency or force not to be opposed.

im·pē′ri·ous·ness, *n.* 1. authority; air of command.

2. arrogance of command; haughtiness.

im·per·ish·ȧ·bil′i·ty, *n.* the quality of being imperishable.

im·per′ish·ȧ·ble, *a.* not subject to decay; not liable to perish; indestructible; enduring permanently; as, an *imperishible* monument, *imperishable* renown.

im·per′ish·ȧ·ble·ness, *n.* the quality of being imperishable.

im·per′ish·ȧ·bly, *adv.* in an imperishable manner.

im·pē′ri·um, *n.*; *pl.* **im·pē′ri·ȧ,** [L., from *imperare*, to command.]

1. in ancient Rome, the authority conferred upon a chief military commander.

2. supreme power; absolute authority or rule; imperial sovereignty; empire.

3. in law, one of the highest powers belonging to an executive, the power to employ all the forces of the state in carrying out its laws.

imperium in imperio; a power within a power; an empire within an empire; a state within a state.

im·pẽr′mȧ·nence, *n.* the fact or condition of being impermanent.

im·pẽr′mȧ·nen·cy, *n.* same as *impermanence.*

im·pẽr′mȧ·nent, *a.* not permanent; not enduring; fleeting; temporary.

im·pẽr″mē·ȧ·bil′i·ty, *n.* the quality or condition of being impermeable.

im·pẽr′mē·ȧ·ble, *a.* not permeable; not permitting passage, especially of fluids; as, rubber is *impermeable* to water.

im·pẽr′mē·ȧ·ble·ness, *n.* the state of being impermeable.

im·pẽr′mē·ȧ·bly, *adv.* in an impermeable manner.

im·pẽr·mis′si·ble, *a.* not to be permitted; that cannot be granted or allowed.

im·pẽr·sçrū′tȧ·ble, *a.* inscrutable. [Obs.]

im·pẽr·sçrū′tȧ·ble·ness, *n.* inscrutability. [Obs.]

im·pẽr′sŏn·ăl, *a.* [L. *in-* priv., and *personalis*, personal.]

1. not personal; specifically, (a) without connection or reference to any particular person; as, an *impersonal* attitude; (b) not existing as a person; as, time is an *impersonal* force.

2. in grammar, designating or of a verb occurring only in the third person singular, in English generally with *it* as the indefinite subject (e.g., "it is snowing").

impersonal verb; in grammar, a verb used without a definite subject, as *it rains.*

im·pẽr′sŏn·ăl, *n.* 1. an impersonal thing. [Rare.]

2. an impersonal verb.

im·pẽr·sŏn·al′i·ty, *n.* 1. the condition or quality of being impersonal.

2. *pl.* **im·pẽr·sŏn·al′i·tieṣ,** an impersonal thing.

im·pẽr′sŏn·ăl·ly, *adv.* in an impersonal manner; not personally.

im·pẽr′sŏn·āte, *v.t.*; impersonated, *pt., pp.*; impersonating, *ppr.* [L. *in*, in, and *persona*, a person.]

1. to represent in the form of a person; personify; embody; as, he *impersonates* the spirit of the people.

2. to act the part of; to take the character of; as, Edwin Booth *impersonated* many of Shakespeare's heroes.

3. to mimic the appearance, behavior, manner, etc. of (a person) for purposes of entertainment.

im·pẽr′sŏn·āte, *a.* embodied in a person; personified.

im·pẽr·sŏn·ā′tion, *n.* the act of impersonating or state of being impersonated; specifically, (a) personification; embodiment; (b) an imitation of another's character or personality.

im·pẽr′sŏn·ā·tŏr, *n.* one who impersonates.

im·pẽr·son″i·fi·çā′tion, *n.* impersonation.

im·pẽr·son′i·fȳ, *v.t.* to impersonate; to personify.

im·pẽr·spi·çū′i·ty, *n.* lack of perspicuity.

im·pẽr·spiç′ū·ous, *a.* [L. *imperspicuus*; *in-* priv., and *perspicuus*, clear.] not perspicuous; not clear; obscure. [Rare.]

im·pẽr·suād′ȧ·ble (-swād′), *a.* not open to persuasion; unyielding.

im·pẽr·suād′ȧ·ble·ness, *n.* the state of being impersuadable.

im·pẽr·suā·si·bil′i·ty (-swā-), *n.* the quality of being impersuasible. [Rare.]

im·pẽr·suā′si·ble, *a.* not to be moved by persuasion; not yielding to arguments. [Rare.]

im·pẽr′ti·nence, *n.* [LL. *impertinentia*, from L. *impertinens* (*-entis*), not belonging or pertaining.]

1. the quality or fact of being impertinent; specifically, (a) lack of pertinence; irrelevance; pointlessness; (b) unsuitabilily; inappropriateness; incongruity ;(c) insolence; impudence.

2. an impertinent act, remark, etc.

3. a trifle; a thing of little or no value.

There are many subtle *impertinences* learnt in schools. —Watts.

im·pẽr′ti·nen·cy, *n.* same as *impertinence.*

im·pẽr′ti·nent, *a.* [L. *impertinens* (*-entis*), not belonging or pertaining; *in-* priv., and *pertinens* (*-entis*), ppr. of *pertinere*, to belong, pertain; *per*, through, and *tenere*, to hold.]

1. not pertaining to the matter in hand; having no bearing on the subject; irrelevant; pointless.

2. not suitable to the circumstances; inappropriate; incongruous.

3. insolent; impudent; rude; intrusive; not showing proper respect or manners; meddling with that with which one has no concern.

Syn.—officious, impudent, insolent, intrusive, irrelevant, meddling.—A person is *officious* who obtrudes his assistance where it is not needed; he is *impertinent* when he intermeddles in things with which he has no concern.

im·pẽr′ti·nent, *n.* an intruder; a meddler; one who interferes in the matters of others.

im·pẽr′ti·nent·ly, *adv.* in an impertinent manner; officiously; intrusively; rudely.

im·pẽr·tran·si·bil′i·ty, *n.* the quality of being impertransible. [Rare.]

im·pẽr·tran′si·ble, *a.* [L. *in-* priv., and *pertransire*, to pass through; *per*, through, and *transire*, to pass.] not to be passed through. [Rare.]

im·pẽr·tũrb·ȧ·bil′i·ty, *n.* the condition or quality of being imperturbable.

im·pẽr·tũrb′ȧ·ble, *a.* [LL. *imperturbabilis*; L. *in-* priv., and *perturbare*, to throw into confusion, disturb; *per*, through, and *turbare*, to disturb.] that cannot be disconcerted, disturbed, or agitated; impassive.

im·pẽr·tũrb′ȧ·bly, *adv.* in an imperturbable manner

im″pẽr·tũr·bā′tion, *n.* freedom from agitation or excitement; serenity; calmness.

im·pẽr·tũrbed′, *a.* unperturbed or not disconcerted.

im·pẽr·vi·ȧ·bil′i·ty, *n.* the quality of being impervious.

im·pẽr′vi·ȧ·ble, *a.* impervious; impermeable.

im·pẽr′vi·ȧ·ble·ness, *n.* imperviousness.

im·pẽr′vi·ous, *a.* [L. *impervius*, impassable; *in-* priv., and *pervius*, passable, from *per*, through, and *via*, way.]

1. incapable of being penetrated or passed through; impenetrable; impermeable; as, a fabric *impervious* to moisture.

2. not affected or influenced by (with *to*); as, a man *impervious to* reason.

im·pẽr′vi·ous·ly, *adv.* in an impervious manner.

im·pẽr′vi·ous·ness, *n.* the state of being impervious.

im′pẽr·y, *n.* empery. [Obs.]

im·pest′, *v.t.* to infect with a plague.

im·pes′tẽr, *v.t.* to vex; to entangle; to embarrass. [Obs.]

im·pē·tig′i·nous, *a.* [L. *impetigo*, a ringworm.]

1. of, or of the nature of, impetigo.

2. having impetigo.

im·pē·tī′gō, *n.* [L., from *impetere*, to rush upon, attack.] any of certain skin diseases characterized by the eruption of pustules; especially, a contagious disease of this kind, caused by staphylococci.

im′pē·trȧ·ble, *a.* 1. that may be obtained by petition. [Obs.]

2. persuasive. [Obs.]

im′pē·trāte, *v.t.* [L. *impetratus*, pp. of *impetrare*, to accomplish, gain by request; *in-* intens., and *patrare*, to accomplish.]

1. to obtain by request or entreaty.

2. to implore. [Rare.]

im·pē·trā′tion, *n.* [OFr. *impetracion*; L. *impetratio* (*-onis*), from *impetrare*, to get, obtain.]

1. the act of obtaining by request or entreaty.

2. in old English law, the obtaining of benefices from the Roman Catholic Church, which belonged to the disposal of the king and other lay patrons of the realm.

im′pē·trā·tive, *a.* obtaining or tending to obtain by entreaty or request; impetrating.

im′pē·trā·tŏr, *n.* one who impetrates.

im′pē·trā·tō·ry, *a.* impetrating; beseeching; containing entreaty.

im·pet·ū·os′i·ty, *n.* [LL. *impetuositas*, from L. *impetuosus*, impetuous.] 1. the state or quality of being impetuous; fury; violence; vehemence.

2. *pl.* **im·pet·ū·os′i·tieṣ,** an impetuous act or feeling.

im·pet′ū·ous, *a.* [L. *impetuosus*, from *impetus*, a rushing upon, from *impetere*, to rush upon; *in*, in, upon, and *petere*, to seek.]

1. rushing with great force and violence; having great impetus; moving rapidly; furious; forcible; fierce; raging; as, an *impetuous* wind, an *impetuous* torrent.

2. acting suddenly with little thought; rash; impulsive.

Syn.—rushing, hasty, precipitate, impulsive, vehement, rash, fiery, passionate, fierce.

im·pet′ū·ous·ly, *adv.* with impetuosity.

im·pet′ū·ous·ness, *n.* the state or quality of being impetuous.

im′pē·tus, *n.*; *pl.* **im′pē·tus·eṣ,** [L., a rushing upon, from *impetere*, to rush upon.]

1. the force with which a body moves

against resistance, resulting from its mass and the velocity at which it is set in motion.

2. anything that stimulates activity; driving force or motive; incentive; impulse.

3. in gunnery, the altitude through which a projectile must fall to acquire a velocity equal to that with which it is discharged from a gun.

Im′pē·ăn pheas′ănt (fez′), a bird, *Lophophorus impeyanus*, found in the colder portions of India. The male is particularly handsome, having a crest and spangled iridescent plumage.

im′phee, *n.* [African.] a sugar cane, *Holcus saccharatus*, found in Africa, resembling the sorghum of the United States.

im′pi, *n.* [Zulu.] a large band of Zulu or Kaffir warriors.

im·piç′tūre, *v.t.* same as *picture.*

im·piērce′, *v.t.* to pierce. [Obs.]

im·piērce′à·ble, *a.* not pierceable. [Obs.]

im·pī′e·ty, *n.*; *pl.* **im·pī′e·tieș,** [L. *impietas*, impiety, from *impius*, impious; *in-* priv., and *pius*, pious.]

1. the state or condition of being impious; irreverence toward God.

2. an impious or irreverent act; as, guilty of numerous *impieties.*

3. a lack of respect toward persons or things to which one should be devoted; undutifulness; as, filial *impiety.*

im·pig′nō·rāte, *v.t.*; impignorated, *pt., pp.*; impignorating; *ppr.* to pledge or pawn. [Obs.]

im·pig·nō·rā′tion, *n.* the act of pawning or the condition of being pawned. [Obs.]

imp′ing, *n.* [verbal noun of *imp*, v.]

1. a graft; the act of grafting.

2. in falconry, repair of a hawk's feathers or wing.

im·pinġe′, *v.i.*; impinged, *pt., pp.*; impinging, *ppr.* [L. *impingere*, to drive into, to thrust, strike at; *in*, in, and *pingere*, to strike.]

1. to fall, strike, dash, clash, or hit (*on, upon*, or *against* something).

The cause of reflection is not the *impinging* of light *on* the solid or impervious parts of bodies. —Newton.

2. to make inroads or encroach (*on* or *upon* the property or rights of another).

im·pinġe′ment, *n.* the act of impinging.

im·pin′ġent, *a.* impinging.

im·pinġ′ẽr, *n.* a person or thing that impinges.

im·piñ′guāte (-gwāt), *v.t.* to fatten; to make fat. [Obs.]

im·piñ·guā′tion, *n.* the process of fattening; also, a fattened state or condition. [Obs.]

im′pi·ous, *a.* [L. *impius*; *in-* priv., and *pius*, devout, reverential.] not pious; wanting piety; specifically, (a) irreverent toward the Supreme Being; irreligious; profane; (b) [Rare.] disrespectful toward persons or things to which one should be devoted.

When vice prevails and *impious* men bear sway. —Addison.

im′pi·ous·ly, *adv.* in an impious manner; profanely; wickedly.

im′pi·ous·ness, *n.* impiety; the condition of being impious.

imp′ish, *a.* of, or having the qualities of, an imp; mischievous.

imp′ish·ly, *adv.* in an impish manner.

im·pit′ē·ous, *a.* pitiless.

im·plā·ċà·bil′i·ty, *n.* [LL. *implacabilitas*, from L. *implacabilis*, implacable.] the condition or quality of being implacable; inexorableness.

im·plā′ċà·ble, *a.* [L. *implacabilis*, unappeasable; *in-* priv., and *placabilis*, appeasable, from *placere*, to appease.]

1. not placable; not to be appeased; that cannot be pacified; inexorable; as, *implacable* malice.

2. not to be relieved, lessened, or assuaged. [Obs.]

Syn.—irreconcilable, unappeasable, relentless, inexorable, vindictive, pitiless, unforgiving.

im·plā′ċà·ble·ness, *n.* implacability.

im·plā′ċà·bly, *adv.* in an implacable manner.

im·plāce′ment, *n.* same as *emplacement.*

im·plā·cen′tăl, *a.* not having a placenta; pertaining to or characteristic of the *Implacentalia.*

im·plā·cen′tăl, *n.* a mammal having no placenta.

Im″plā·cen·tā′li·à, *n.pl.* [L. *in-* priv., and *placenta*, a cake (in anat., placenta), and *-alia.*] a division of mammals not having the placenta developed. It includes the marsupials and monotremes.

im·plā·cen′tāte, *a.* same as *implacental.*

im·plȧnt′, *v.t.* implanted, *pt., pp.*; implanting, *ppr.* [LL. *implantare*, to plant in, to invest; L. *in*, in, and *plantare*, to plant.]

1. to plant firmly or deeply; embed.

2. to fix firmly in the mind; to instill; inculcate.

3. in medicine, to insert (a piece of living tissue) in grafting.

im′plȧnt, *n.* in medicine, (a) an implanted piece of tissue; a graft; (b) a tube of radium or other radioactive substance inserted into, or near, diseased body tissue in the treatment of cancer, etc.

im·plan·tā′tion, *n.* the act of implanting, inculcating, or instilling; also, a being implanted.

im·plạu·ṣi·bil′i·ty, *n.* the quality of being implausible.

im·plạu′ṣi·ble, *a.* not plausible; not having the appearance of truth or credibility and not likely to be believed.

im·plạu′ṣi·ble·ness, *n.* implausibility.

im·plạu′ṣi·bly, *adv.* in an implausible manner.

im·plēach′, *v.t.* to interweave. [Rare.]

im·plēad′, *v.t.*; impleaded, *pt., pp.*; impleading, *ppr.* [ME. *empleden*; OFr. *emplaidier*, to plead, pursue at law; *en-*, in, and *plaidier, pledier*, to plead.]

1. to institute and prosecute a suit against in court; to sue at law.

2. to accuse; to arraign; to impeach.

3. to plead (a cause, etc.).

im·plēad′, *v.i.* 1. to institute legal proceedings; to sue.

2. to plead a cause, etc.

im·plēad′à·ble, *a.* not to be pleaded against or evaded. [Rare.]

im·plēad′ẽr, *n.* one who impleads or prosecutes another; an accuser.

im·plēaș′ing, *a.* unpleasing. [Obs.]

im·pledġe′, *v.t.* to pawn.

im′plē·ment, *n.* [LL. *implementum*, a filling up, from L. *implere*, to fill up; *in*, in, and *plere*, to fill.] something used or needed in a given activity; especially, an instrument, tool, utensil, vessel, or the like; as, the *implements* of trade or of husbandry.

im′plē·ment, *v.t.*; implemented, *pt., pp.*; implementing, *ppr.* 1. to carry into effect; to fulfill; accomplish.

2. to provide with the means for carrying into effect or fulfilling; to give practical effect to.

3. to provide or equip with implements.

im·plē·men′tăl, *a.* pertaining to or in any way connected with implements; characterized by the use of implements; having the nature of an implement; instrumental.

im″plē·men·tā′tion, *n.* an implementing or being implemented.

im·plē′tion, *n.* [LL. *impletio* (*-onis*), from L. *impletus*, pp. of *implere*, to fill up.]

1. the act of filling or the state of being full.

2. that which fills up.

im′plex, *a.* enfolded; intricate; entangled; complicated. [Rare.]

im′plex, *n.* in mathematics, a doubly infinite system of surfaces.

im·plex′iŏn (-plek′shun), *n.* [L. *implexio* (*-onis*), an entwining, from *implexus*, pp. of *implectere*, to entwine; *in*, in, and *plectere*, to twist.] the act of enfolding or involving; also, the state of being involved. [Rare.]

im·plex′ous, *a.* in botany, entangled; interwoven; interlaced. [Rare.].

im·plī′à·ble, *a.* not pliable [Rare.]

im′pli·cāte, *v.t.*; implicated, *pt., pp.*; implicating, *ppr.* [L. *implicatus*, pp. of *implicare*, to enfold, involve; *in*, in, and *plicare*, to fold.]

1. to enfold; to intertwine; to entangle.

2. to imply.

3. to involve; to bring into connection with; to show or prove to be connected or concerned; as, the evidence did not *implicate* the accused person in the conspiracy; to be *implicated* in a plot.

Syn.—entangle, involve.

im·pli·cā′tion, *n.* [L. *implicatio* (*-onis*), an entwining, enfolding, from *implicare*, to enfold, implicate.]

1. the act of implicating or the state of being implicated; entanglement.

2. an implying or being implied.

3. that which is implied, from which an inference may be drawn.

im′pli·cā·tive, *a.* tending to implicate or imply.

im′pli·cā·tive·ly, *adv.* by implication.

im′pli·cā·tō″ry, *a.* implicating.

im·plic′it, *a.* [from Fr. or L.; Fr. *implicite*; L. *implicitus*, pp. of *implicare*, to enfold, involve.]

1. formerly, implicated; entangled.

2. suggested or to be understood though not plainly expressed; implied: distinguished from *explicit.*

3. necessarily or naturally involved though not plainly apparent or expressed; essentially a part or condition; inherent.

4. without reservation or doubt; unquestioning; absolute.

implicit function; see under *function.*

im·plic′it·ly, *adv.* in an implicit manner; so as to be implicit.

im·plic′it·ness, *n.* the state or quality of being implicit.

im·plic′i·ty, *n.* implicitness. [Obs.]

im·plīed′, *a.* involved, suggested, or understood, but not actually expressed; deducible by inference or implication.

im·plī′ed·ly, *adv.* by implication or inference.

im·plōde′, *v.t.* and *v.i.*; imploded, *pt., pp.*; imploding, *ppr.* [formed by substituting *im-* for *ex-* in *explode.*]

1. to burst inward.

2. in phonetics, to pronounce by implosion.

im·plō′dent, *n.* in phonetics, a sound made by implosion.

im·plō·rā′tion, *n.* [L. *imploratio* (*-onis*), from *implorare*, to implore.] earnest supplication: the act of imploring.

im′plō·rā·tŏr, *n.* one who implores. [Obs.]

im·plōr′à·tō·ry, *a.* earnestly imploring; supplicating. [Rare.]

im·plōre′, *v.t.*; implored, *pt., pp.*; imploring, *ppr.* [L. *implorare*, to beseech, entreat; *in-* intens, and *plorare*, to cry out, weep.]

1. to call upon in supplication; to beseech or beg (a person) to do something; to pray to earnestly; to petition with urgency; to entreat.

Imploring all the gods that reign above. —Pope.

2. to ask for earnestly; to beg or pray for; to beseech; as, to *implore* forgiveness.

im·plōre′, *v.i.* to entreat; to beg.

im·plōre′, *n.* earnest supplication. [Obs.]

im·plōr′ẽr, *n.* one who implores.

im·plōr′ing·ly, *adv.* in an imploring manner.

im·plō′ṣion, *n.* [formed by substituting *im-* for *ex-* in *explosion.*]

1. a sudden bursting inward: opposed to *explosion.*

2. in phonetics, a compression of the air in the mouth at the beginning of uttering certain consonants, as *p* or *k.*

im·plō′sive, *a.* produced by implosion.

im·plō′sive, *n.* a sound or consonant produced by implosion.

im·plō′sive·ly, *adv.* by implosion; in an implosive manner.

im·plụmed′, *a.* having no plumes or feathers. [Rare.]

im·plunġe′, *v.t.* to plunge. [Rare.]

im·plụ′vi·um, *n.*; *pl.* **im·plụ′vi·à,** [L. *impluvium* or *inpluvium*, from *impluere*, to rain into; *in*, in, and *pluere*, to rain.] in ancient Roman architecture, a basin in the middle of the atrium or entrance hall, below the compluvium or open space in the roof, to receive the rain.

A. IMPLUVIUM B. COMPLUVIUM

im·plȳ′, *v.t.*; implied, *pt., pp.*; implying, *ppr.* [L. *implicare*, to involve, entangle, enfold; *in*, in, and *plicare*, to fold.]

1. to enfold or entangle; to wrap up. [Obs.]

2. to indicate without saying openly or directly; to hint; suggest; intimate; as, his attitude *implied* boredom.

3. to have as a necessary part, condition, or effect; to contain, include, or involve naturally or necessarily; as, drama *implies* conflict.

Where a malicious act is proved, a malicious intention is *implied.* —Sherlock.

4. to ascribe; to refer. [Obs.]

Syn.—signify, denote, include, betoken, mean, involve.

im·poi′ṣŏn, *v.t.* to empoison. [Obs.]

im·poi′ṣŏn·ment, *n.* empoisonment. [Obs.]

im·pō′lăr·i·ly, im·pō′lăr·ly, *adv.* not according to the direction of the poles. [Obs.]

im·pol′i·cy, *n.* inexpedience; unsuitableness to the end proposed; bad policy.

im·pō·līte′, *a.* [L. *impolitus*, unpolished; *in*-priv., and *politus*, pp. of *polire*, to polish.] not polite; discourteous; uncivil; rude in manners.

im·pō·līte′ly, *adv.* uncivilly; in an impolite manner.

im·pō·līte′ness, *n.* incivility; want of good manners.

im·pol′i·tiç, *a.* not politic; unwise; imprudent; not expedient; as, an *impolitic* measure, an *impolitic* diplomat.

im·pō·lit′i·çăl, *a.* impolitic. [Obs.]

im·pō·lit′i·çăl·ly, *adv.* impoliticly. [Obs.]

im·pol′i·tiç·ly, *adv.* not wisely; not with due prudence; in a manner to injure interests.

im·pol′i·tiç·ness, *n.* the state or quality of being impolitic.

im·pon″dĕr·ȧ·bil′i·ty, *n.* the quality or condition of being imponderable.

im·pon′dĕr·ȧ·ble, *a.* not ponderable; that cannot be weighed or measured.

im·pon′dĕr·ȧ·ble, *n.* [*in*- priv., and LL. *ponderabilis*, that may be weighed.] anything imponderable; in physics, anything supposed to have no weight: used formerly to designate heat, light, electricity, and magnetism: sometimes applied to ether and to spiritual or mental phenomena or agencies.

im·pon′dĕr·ȧ·ble·ness, *n.* the state or quality of being imponderable.

im·pon′dĕr·ous, *a.* imponderable. [Obs.]

im·pon′dĕr·ous·ness, *n.* the state of being imponderous. [Obs.]

im·pōne′, *v.t.*; imponed, *pt., pp.*; imponing, *ppr.* [L. *imponere*, to put or lay on; *in*, on, and *ponere*, to put.]

1. to stake; to wager. [Obs.]

2. to impose. [Obs.]

im·pọọf′, *n.* a South African animal, the eland: called also *impoofo*.

im·pọọn′, *n.* [S. African.] in zoology, the duiker.

im·pọọr′, *v.t.* to impoverish. [Obs.]

im·pō·ros′i·ty, *n.* want of porosity; closeness of texture; compactness excluding pores.

im·pōr′ous, *a.* solid; without pores; very close or compact in texture.

im·pōrt′, *v.t.*; imported, *pt., pp.*; importing, *ppr.* [L. *importare*, to bring in, introduce, bring about; *in*, in, and *portare*, to carry.]

1. to bring (goods) from a foreign country into one's own country in commerce: opposed to *export*; as, we *import* wines from France.

2. to bring in from the outside or introduce into; as, to *import* vigor into one's style.

3. to bear or convey as signification or meaning; to mean; to signify; to imply; as, the term clearly *imports* a thorough understanding.

4. to be of weight, moment, or consequence to; to have a bearing on; to concern.

If I endure it, what *imports* it you?
—Dryden.

Syn.—mean, signify, imply, interest, convey, concern, indicate.

im·pōrt′, *v.i.* to have meaning, importance, or significance; to matter.

im′pōrt, *n.* 1. the act or business of importing goods.

2. that which is imported or brought into a country from another country or state.

3. that which is borne or conveyed by words, actions, or circumstances; meaning; signification; the sense which words are intended to convey to the understanding.

4. importance; weight; consequence.

im·pōrt′ȧ·ble, *a.* capable of being imported.

im·pōrt′ȧ·ble, *a.* [ME. *importable*; LL. *importabilis*, that cannot be borne; L. *in*- priv., and *portabilis*, that can be borne.] intolerable; unendurable. [Obs.]

im·pōrt′ȧ·ble·ness, *n.* the state of being intolerable. [Obs.]

im·pọr′tănce, *n.* [LL. *importantia*, importance, from L. *importans* (*-antis*), ppr. of *importare*, to bring in; *in*, in, and *portare*, to bring.]

1. the state or quality of being important; significance; value; consequence; a bearing on some interest; as, the education of youth is of great *importance* to a free government.

2. weight or consequence in self-estimation; dignity; social standing.

3. import; meaning. [Obs.]

4. an important matter. [Obs.]

5. importunity. [Obs.]

Syn.—consequence, weight, moment.—*Importance* is what things have in themselves; *consequence* is the *importance* of a thing from its consequences; *weight* implies a positively great degree of *importance*; *moment* is that *importance* which a thing has from the power in itself to produce effects, or to determine interests.

im·pọr′tăn·cy, *n.* importance. [Obs.]

im·pọr′tănt, *a.* [LL. *importans* (*-antis*), momentous, important, properly ppr. of L. *importare*, to bring in, introduce.]

1. weighty; momentous; of great consequence, significance, or value.

2. having, or acting as if having, power, authority, influence, high position, etc.; pompous; pretentious; as, an *important* manner.

3. importunate. [Obs.]

Syn.—significant, relevant, considerable, dignified, influential, weighty, momentous, material, grave, essential.

im·pọr′tănt·ly, *adv.* in an important manner.

im·pōr·tā′tion, *n.* [L. *importare*, to bring in, import.]

1. an importing or being imported: opposed to *exportation*.

2. something imported; an import.

3. conveyance. [Obs.]

im·pōrt′ĕr, *n.* one who imports; a merchant, corporation, etc. in the business of importing goods.

im·pọr′tū·nȧ·ble, *a.* unendurable; burdensome. [Obs.]

im·pọr′tū·nȧ·cy, *n.* the act of importuning; persistent solicitation; also, the quality of being importunate.

im·pọr′tū·nāte, *a.* [LL. *importunatus*, pp. of *importunari*, to vex, be troublesome, from L. *importunus*, troublesome.]

1. pressing or urging in request or demand; urgent and persistent in solicitation; refusing to be denied; annoyingly urgent or persistent; as, an *importunate* suitor or petitioner; an *importunate* demand.

2. causing vexation; troublesome. [Obs.]

im·pọr′tū·nāte·ly, *adv.* in an importunate manner.

im·pọr′tū·nāte·ness, *n.* the state or quality of being importunate.

im·pọr′tū·nā·tŏr, *n.* one who importunes.

im·pọr·tūne′, *a.* 1. importunate.

2. inopportune. [Obs.]

3. vexatious. [Obs.]

im·pọr·tūne′, *v.t.* importuned, *pt., pp.*; importuning, *ppr.* [Fr. *importuner*; LL. *importunari*, to be troublesome, vex, from L. *importunus*, without access, troublesome; *in*- priv., and *portus*, a harbor.]

1. to trouble with requests or demands; to urge or entreat persistently or repeatedly.

2. to ask for urgently; to demand. [Rare.]

3. to trouble; to annoy. [Obs.]

4. to impel. [Obs.]

5. to import; to imply. [Obs.]

im·pọr·tūne′, *v.i.* to be importunate; to make persistent demands; to solicit with pertinacity.

im·pọr·tūne′ly, *adv.* with importunity.

im·pọr·tū′nĕr, *n.* one who importunes.

im·pọr·tū′ni·ty, *n.*; *pl.* **im·pọr·tū′ni·tieṣ,** [Fr. *importunité*; L. *importunitas*, unfitness, unsuitableness, from *importunus*, unfit, troublesome.]

1. an importuning or being importunate; pressing solicitation; urgent request; application for a claim or favor which is urged with troublesome frequency or pertinacity.

2. unseasonableness. [Obs.]

im·pōr′tū·ous, *a.* [L. *importuosus*; *in*- priv., and *portuosus*, abounding in harbors, from *portus*, a harbor.] without a port, haven, or harbor. [Obs.]

im·pōṣ′ȧ·ble, *a.* that may be imposed or laid on.

im·pōṣ′ȧ·ble·ness, *n.* the state of being imposable.

im·pōṣe′, *v.t.*; imposed, *pt., pp.*; imposing, *ppr.* [Fr. *imposer*; L. *imponere*, to lay or put on; *in*, on, and *ponere*, to put, place.]

1. to place (a burden, tax, etc. *on* or *upon*); to inflict; force; as, the king *imposed* a tax on the people.

2. to force (oneself, one's presence, etc.) on another or others without right or invitation; to obtrude.

3. to pass off; to palm off; to foist, especially by deception; as, he *imposed* his doctrines upon the confused nation.

4. to arrange (pages of type) in a frame in the proper order of printing.

5. to place; put; deposit. [Archaic.]

6. in ecclesiastical usage, to lay on (the hands), as in ordination or confirmation.

7. to fix on; to impute. [Rare.]

8. to subject by way of punishment. [Obs.]

Impose me to what penance your invention
Can lay upon my sin. —Shak.

to impose on (or *upon*); (a) [Rare.] to make an impression on; to have influence with because of prestige, etc.; (b) to take liberties with; to take advantage of; (c) to get the better of by deceiving; to cheat; defraud.

im·pōṣe′, *n.* command; injunction. [Obs.]

im·pōṣe′ment, *n.* imposition. [Rare.]

im·pōṣ′ĕr, *n.* one who imposes.

im·pōṣ′ing, *a.* making a strong impression because of great size, strength, dignity, etc.; impressive; as, an *imposing* air or manner.

im·pōṣ′ing·ly, *adv.* in an imposing manner.

im·pōṣ′ing·ness, *n.* the condition of being imposing.

im·pōṣ′ing stōne, in printing, a smooth level stone or plate of metal on which pages or columns of type are imposed or forms made up.

im·pō·ṣi′tion (-zish′un), *n.* [Fr. *imposition*; L. *impositio* (*-onis*), a laying upon, application, from *impositus*, pp. of *imponere*, to lay or put upon, impose.]

1. an imposing or imposing on; specifically, (a) the forcing of oneself, one's presence, etc. on another or others without right or invitation; obtrusion; (b) a taking advantage of friendship, etc.; as, it is an *imposition* to ask him to help; (c) in ecclesiastical usage, the laying on of hands, as in ordination or confirmation; (d) the act of laying, putting, or placing on; (e) the act of levying, enjoining, inflicting, and the like; as, the *imposition* of taxes; (f) in printing, the act of arranging the pages of a sheet upon the imposing stone, adjusting the spaces between them, and fastening them into a chase.

2. something imposed; specifically, (a) a tax, fine, etc.; (b) an unjust burden, requirement, etc.; (c) a deception; fraud; (d) [Brit.] in schools, an exercise imposed on students as punishment.

im·pos·si·bil′i·ty, *n.* [OFr. *impossibilité*; LL. *impossibilitas*.]

1. the fact or quality of being impossible.

2. *pl.* **im·pos·si·bil′i·tieṣ,** something impossible.

im·pos′si·ble, *a.* [OFr. *impossible*; L. *impossibilis*, not possible; *in*- priv., and *possibilis*, possible, from *posse*, to be able.]

1. not capable of being, being done, or happening.

2. not capable of being done easily or conveniently; as, it was *impossible* for me to come yesterday.

3. not capable of being endured, used, etc., because disagreeable or unsuitable; as, an *impossible* person.

impossible quantity; see under *imaginary*.

im·pos′si·ble, *n.* an impossibility. [Rare.]

im·pos′si·bly, *adv.* 1. in an impossible manner.

2. to an impossible extent.

im′pōst, *v.t.* [OFr.; LL. *impositus*.] to classify (imported goods) in order to assess the proper taxes.

im′pōst, *n.* [OFr. *impost*, a tax (Fr. *impost*, an impost in architecture); LL. *impositus*, a tax, from L. *impositus*, pp. of *imponere*, to lay upon, impose.]

1. any tax or tribute imposed by authority; particularly, a duty or tax on imported goods, paid or secured by the importer at the time of importation.

2. in architecture, the point where an arch rests on a wall or column, usually marked by horizontal moldings.

A A. SHAFTED IMPOST

im·pos′tŏr, *n.* [LL. *impostor*, a deceiver; L. *impositor*, one who deceives by imposing or applying a name, from *impositus*, pp. of *imponere*, to put upon, impose.] one who imposes on others; a person who assumes a character for the purpose of deception; a deceiver under a false character.

im·pos′tŏr·ship, *n.* the quality or character of an impostor.

im·pos′tress, im·pos′trix, *n.* a woman impostor. [Rare.]

im·pos′trous, *a.* having the nature of an impostor.

im·pos′tū·māte, im·post′hū·māte, *v.i.* and *v.t.* [*impostume* and *-ate.*] to form or affect with an abscess. [Obs.]

im·pos′tū·māte, im·post′hū·māte, *a.* of the character of an abscess; affected with an abscess. [Obs.]

im·pos·tū·mā′tion, im·post·hū·mā′tion, *n.* the act of forming an abscess; also, an abscess; an impostume. [Obs.]

im·pos′tūme, im·post′hūme, *n.* [corruption of *aposteme.*] an abscess; a collection of pus or purulent matter in any part of an animal body. [Rare.]

im·pos′tūme, im·post′hūme, *v.t.* and *v.i.* impostumate. [Obs.]

im·pos′tūre, *n.* [LL. *impostura,* deceit, from L. *impositus,* pp. of *imponere,* to impose upon; *in,* upon, and *ponere,* to put.] deception practiced under a false or assumed character; fraud or imposition by an impostor.

Syn.—deception, cheat, imposition, fraud.

im·pos′tūred, *a.* deceptive; deceitful; like an impostor. [Obs.]

im′pō·tence, *n.* [OFr. *impotence;* L. *impotentia,* want of power, inability; from *impotens* (*-entis*), feeble, weak, impotent.] the quality or condition of being impotent; specifically, (a) lack of physical strength; weakness; (b) lack of effectiveness; helplessness; (c) lack of ability to engage in sexual intercourse: said of males.

im′pō·ten·cy, *n.* same as *impotence.*

im′pō·tent, *a.* [OFr. *impotent;* L. *impotens* (*-entis*), weak, feeble; *in-* priv., and *potens* (*-entis*), powerful, ppr. of *posse,* to be able.]

1. lacking physical strength.

2. ineffective, powerless, or helpless: as, *impotent* rage.

3. unable to engage in sexual intercourse: said of males.

Syn.—weak, powerless, useless, feeble, helpless, nerveless, enfeebled.

im′pō·tent, *n.* one who is impotent.

im′pō·tent·ly, *adv.* weakly; without power.

im·pound′, *v.t.*; impounded, *pt., pp.*; impounding, *ppr.*

1. to shut up (an animal) in a pound.

2. to take into legal custody.

3. to gather and enclose (water) for irrigation, etc.

im·pound′ăge, *n.* the act of impounding or the state of being impounded.

im·pound′ēr, *n.* one who impounds.

im·pov′ēr·ish, *v.t.*; impoverished, *pt., pp.*; impoverishing, *ppr.* [OFr. *empoverir,* to make poor; L. *in,* in, and *pauper,* poor.]

1. to make poor; to reduce to poverty or indigence.

2. to exhaust the strength, richness, or fertility of; to cause to deteriorate.

im·pov′ēr·ish·ēr, *n.* one who or that which impoverishes.

im·pov′ēr·ish·ment, *n.* [OFr. *empoverissement,* from *empovrir,* to make poor, impoverish.]

1. a reducing to poverty; the act of impoverishing or state of being impoverished.

2. something that impoverishes.

im·pow′ēr, *v.t.* same as *empower.*

im·prac″ti·cȧ·bil′i·ty, *n.* 1. the quality of being impracticable.

2. *pl.* **im·prac″ti·cȧ·bil′i·ties,** something impracticable.

im·prac′ti·cȧ·ble, *a.* [*im-* (not) and *practicable.*]

1. not capable of being carried out in practice; as, an *impracticable* plan.

2. not capable of being used; as, an *impracticable* road.

3. not capable of being managed or dealt with; intractable; as, an *impracticable* person.

Syn.—impossible.

im·prac′ti·cȧ·ble·ness, *n.* impracticability.

im·prac′ti·cȧ·bly, *adv.* in a manner or degree not practicable.

Morality not *impracticably* rigid.
—Johnson.

im·prac′ti·căl, *a.* not practical.

im·prac·ti·cal′i·ty, *n.* 1. the quality of being impractical.

2. *pl.* **im·prac·ti·cal′i·ties,** something impractical.

im′prē·cāte, *v.t.*; imprecated, *pt., pp.*; imprecating, *ppr.* [L. *imprecatus,* pp. of *imprecari,* to invoke, pray to; *in,* upon, and *precari,* to pray, from *prex* (*-ecis*), a prayer.]

1. to pray for (evil, misfortune, etc.); to invoke (a curse).

2. to invoke evil upon; to curse. [Rare.]

im·prē·cā′tion, *n.* [L. *imprecatio* (*-onis*), an invoking of evil, a curse, from *imprecari,* to imprecate.] the act of imprecating evil on anyone; also, a curse.

Syn.—curse, malediction, anathema, execration.

im′prē·cȧ·tō·ry, *a.* of, like, or uttering an imprecation.

im·prē·cīse′, *a.* not precise, exact, or definite; vague.

im·prē·ci′sion (-sizh′un), *n.* lack of precision or exactness.

im·prēgn′ (-prēn′), *v.t.* to impregnate. [Obs.]

im·preg·nȧ·bil′i·ty, *n.* the quality of being impregnable.

im·preg′nȧ·ble, *a.* [OFr. *imprenable; in-* priv., and *prenable,* able to be taken, from *prendre,* L. *prehendere,* to take, seize.]

1. not to be stormed or taken by assault; that cannot be reduced by force; able to resist attack; as, an *impregnable* fortress.

2. not to be moved, impressed, or shaken; unyielding; invincible.

The man's affection remains wholly unconcerned and *impregnable.* —South.

im·preg′nȧ·ble, *a.* that can be impregnated.

im·preg′nȧ·ble·ness, *n.* impregnability.

im·preg′nȧ·bly, *adv.* in a manner to resist penetration or assault; in a manner to defy force; as, a place *impregnably* fortified.

im·preg′nănt, *a.* [LL. *imprægnans* (*-antis*), ppr. of *imprægnare,* to impregnate.] impregnating. [Rare.]

im·preg′nănt, *n.* any impregnating agent. [Rare.]

im·preg′nāte, *v.t.*; impregnated, *pt., pp.*; impregnating, *ppr.* [LL. *imprægnatus,* pp. of *imprægnare,* to make pregnant; L. *in,* in, and *prægnans* (*-antis*), pregnant.]

1. to fertilize (an ovum).

2. to make pregnant.

3. to fertilize (land); to make fruitful.

4. to fill or saturate; to cause to be permeated; as, they *impregnated* their clothing with insecticide.

5. to indoctrinate or imbue (*with* ideas, feelings, principles, etc.).

im·preg′nāte, *a.* impregnated.

im·preg·nā′tion, *n.* 1. the act of impregnating; also, the state of becoming impregnated.

2. something that impregnates.

3. complete saturation.

4. in geology, a deposit of ore in small, isolated grains, so as not to form a true vein.

im·preg′nā·tŏr, *n.* a person or thing that impregnates.

im·prē·jū′di·cāte, *a.* not prejudiced; impartial. [Obs.]

im·prē′nȧ·ble, *a.* impregnable. [Obs.]

im·prep·ȧ·rā′tion, *n.* lack of preparation, unreadiness.

im·pre′sȧ, *n.* [It.] a personal device, as on a seal, bookplate, etc.

im·pre·sä′rï·ō, *n.*; *pl.* **im·pre·sä′rï·ōs,** [It., from *impresa,* an enterprise.] the organizer, manager, or director of an opera or ballet company, concert series, etc.

im·prē·scrip·ti·bil′i·ty, *n.* the state of being imprescriptible.

im·prē·scrip′ti·ble, *a.* incapable of being lost, taken away, or revoked; inviolable.

im·prē·scrip′ti·bly, *adv.* in an imprescriptible manner.

im·prēse′, *n.* same as *impresa.*

im·press′, *v.t.*; impressed, *pt., pp.*; impressing, *ppr.* [ME. *impressen;* OFr. *empresser,* to impress; L. *impressus,* pp. of *imprimere,* to press into or upon, stamp, impress; *in,* on, upon, and *premere,* to press.]

1. to use pressure on so as to leave a mark; as, he *impressed* the clay with a die.

2. to mark by using pressure; stamp; imprint.

3. to apply with pressure; as, he *impressed* the die in the clay.

4. to have a considerable effect on the mind or emotions of.

5. to implant firmly on the mind or fix in the memory.

im·press′, *v.i.* to press or crowd about. [Obs.]

im′press, *n.* [LL. *impressus,* a pressing upon, from L. *impressus,* pp. of *imprimere,* to press upon, impress.]

1. a mark or indentation by pressure.

2. the figure or image of anything made by pressure; stamp; likeness.

3. an effect produced on the mind or feelings by some strong influence.

4. an impresa.

im′press, *n.* same as *impressment.*

im·pressed′ (-prest′), *a.* 1. stamped into; printed upon by pressing or stamping.

2. in biology, sunk below the general surface as if stamped, or marked with sunken lines, areas, etc.

im·press·i·bil′i·ty, *n.* the quality of being impressible.

im·press′i·ble, *a.* that can be impressed; impressionable.

im·press′i·ble·ness, *n.* impressibility.

im·press′i·bly, *adv.* in a manner to make impression.

im·pres′sion (-presh′un), *n.* [OFr. *impression;* L. *impressio* (*-onis*), a pressing into or upon, an attack, impression, from *impressus,* pp. of *imprimere,* to press on or into, to impress.]

1. an impressing.

2. a result or effect of impressing; specifically, (a) a mark, imprint, etc. made by physical pressure; (b) an effect produced on the mind or senses by some force or influence; as, his music makes little *impression* on me; (c) the effect produced by any effort or activity; as, our attempt at cleaning made no *impression* on the dirt.

3. a vague notion or feeling; inkling; as, I have the *impression* that he was there.

4. in dentistry, the imprint of the teeth and surrounding tissues in wax or plaster, used as a mold in making dentures.

5. in printing, (a) the pressing of type or plates on paper, etc.; printing; (b) a printed copy; (c) all the copies printed as a single edition.

proof impression; in engraving, an impression taken prior to finishing a block or plate, for the purpose of criticism and final correction.

im·pres″sion·ȧ·bil′i·ty, *n.* the quality of being impressionable.

im·pres′sion·ȧ·ble, *a.* easily affected by impressions; capable of being influenced intellectually, emotionally, or morally; sensitive.

im·pres′sion·ȧ·ble·ness, *n.* impressionability.

im·pres′sion·ăl, *a.* of, or having the nature of, an impression.

im·pres′sion·ism, *n.* a theory and school of art, exemplified by the work of Manet, Monet, Renoir, Degas, Pissarro, etc., whose chief aim is to reproduce only the immediate and over-all impression made by the subject on the artist, without much attention to detail: the term has been extended to literature that similarly seeks to express the immediate impressions of reality on the writer, and to music, as by Debussy and Ravel, which seeks to produce atmospheric effects and suggest impressions by various characteristic devices.

im·pres′sion·ist, *n.* a painter, writer, composer, etc. who practices impressionism.

im·pres′sion·ist, *a.* of or characteristic of impressionism or impressionists.

im·pres·sion·is′tic, *a.* 1. impressionist.

2. conveying a quick or over-all impression.

im·pres′sion·less, *a.* not susceptible; incapable of being impressed.

im·press′ive, *a.* 1. making or tending to make an impression; having the power of affecting, or of exciting the mind or emotions; as, an *impressive* discourse; an *impressive* scene.

2. capable of being impressed; susceptible. [Rare.]

Syn.—forcible, solemn, affecting, imposing, important.

im·press′ive·ly, *adv.* in an impressive manner.

im·press′ive·ness, *n.* the quality of being impressive.

im·press′ment, *n.* [*impress* (to force into service), and *-ment.*] the practice or act of impressing men or property for the use or service of the public.

im·press′ŏr, *n.* one who or that which makes impressions. [Obs.]

im·pres′sūre (-presh′ūr), *n.* an impression.

im′prest, *n.* [It. *impresto,* a loan, from phr. (*dare*) *in prestito,* (to give) in loan; *in,* in, and *prestito,* a loan, from *prestare,* to lend, from L. *præstare,* to become surety for, lit., to stand before; *præ-,* before, and *stare,* to stand.] a loan or advance of money; especially, money advanced to a person from government funds to enable him to carry on some work for the government.

imprest accountant; in English law, a person to whom an imprest is given.

im′prest, *a.* lent; advanced as a loan.

im·prest′, *v.t.*; imprested, *pt., pp.*; impresting, *ppr.* to advance on loan. [Obs.]

im·prev′ȧ·lence, im·prev′ȧ·len·cy, *n.* incapability of prevailing. [Obs.]

im·prē·vent·ȧ·bil′i·ty, *n.* the quality of being impreventable. [Rare.]

im·prē·vent′ȧ·ble, *a.* incapable of being prevented. [Rare.]

im·pri·mā′tūr, *n.* [Mod. L., lit., let it be

pressed upon, or printed, 3rd pers. sing. pres. subj. pass. of L. *imprimere*, to press upon.]
1. license to publish or print a book, article, etc.; especially, sanction given by the Roman Catholic Church.
2. any sanction or approval.

im·prim'ẽr·y, *n.* a print; impression; also, a printing house; art of printing. [Obs.]

im·prīm'ing, *n.* first effort in an undertaking. [Obs.]

im·prī'mis, *adv.* [L., for *in primis*, lit., among the first; *in*, among, and *primis*, abl. pl. of *primus*, first.] in the first place; first in order.

im·print', *v.t.*; imprinted, *pt.*, *pp.*; imprinting, *ppr.* [ME. *emprinten*; OFr. *empreinter*, to stamp, imprint.]
1. to impress; to mark by pressing or stamping; as, a character or device *imprinted* on wax or cloth.
2. to stamp, as letters and words on paper by means of types; to print.
3. to press; as, she *imprinted* a kiss on my forehead.
4. to fix on the mind or memory; to impress; as, let your father's admonitions and instructions be *imprinted* on your mind.

im'print, *n.* [OFr. *empreinte*, an imprint, from *empreint*, pp. of *empreindre*, to impress, stamp, from L. *imprimere*, to press upon, impress.]
1. a mark made by imprinting.
2. a characteristic effect or result; as, the *imprint* of starvation.
3. a publisher's or printer's note on the title page or at the end of a book, giving his name, the time and place of publication, etc.

im·priș'ȯn, *v.t.* [ME. *imprisonen*; OFr. *emprisonner*, to imprison; *en-*, in, and *prison*, a prison.]
1. to put into a prison; to confine in a prison or jail, or to arrest and detain in custody in any place.
2. to confine; to shut up; to restrain or limit in any way.

im·priș'ȯn·ẽr, *n.* one who imprisons another.

im·priș'ȯn·ment, *n.* 1. the act of putting and confining in prison; the act of arresting and detaining in custody.
2. confinement in a place; restraint of liberty to go from place to place at pleasure.
false imprisonment; unlawful imprisonment.

im·prob·ȧ·bil'i·ty, *n.* 1. the quality of being improbable.
2. *pl.* **im·prob·ȧ·bil'i·tieș,** something improbable.

im·prob'ȧ·ble, *a.* [L. *improbabilis*, not deserving of approbation; *in-* priv., and *probabilis*, deserving of approval, from *probare*, to approve.] not likely to be true or to happen; not probable; unlikely.

im·prob'ȧ·ble·ness, *n.* the state of being improbable; improbability.

im·prob'ȧ·bly, *adv.* with little or no probability: now only in *not improbably*.

im'prō·bāte, *v.t.* [L. *improbatus*, pp. of *improbare*, to disapprove; *in* priv., and *probare*, to approve.] to disallow; not to approve. [Obs.]

im·prō·bā'tion, *n.* [L. *improbatio* (-*onis*), from *improbatus*, pp. of *improbare*, to disapprove.]
1. the act of disapproving.
2. in Scots law, the act of disproving the legality or authenticity of a forged document.

im·prō'bȧ·tive, *a.* relating to or of the character of improbation.

im·prō'bȧ·tō·ry, *a.* same as *improbative*.

im·prō'bi·ty, *n.*; *pl.* **im·prō'bi·tieș,** [L. *improbitas* (-*atis*), badness, wickedness, from *improbus*, bad; *in-* priv., and *probus*, good.] lack of probity; dishonesty.

im·prō·fi'cience (-fish'ens), *n.* improficiency.

im·prō·fi'cien·cy (-fish'en-) *n.* lack of proficiency.

im·prof'it·ȧ·ble, *a.* unprofitable. [Obs.]

im·prō·gress'ive, *a.* not progressive.

im·prō·gress'ive·ly, *adv.* not progressively.

im·prō·lif'iç, *a.* not prolific; unfruitful. [Obs.]

im·prō·lif'iç·āte, *v.t.* to impregnate; to fecundate. [Obs.]

im·prompt', *a.* [L. *impromptus*; *in-* priv., and *promptus*, ready, prepared.] lacking promptness; not prepared. [Obs.]

im·promp'tū, *adv.* and *a.* [L. *in promptu*, in readiness; *in*, in, and *promptu*, abl. of *promptus*, readiness, from *promptus*, brought out ready, prompt.] offhand; without previous study; as, a verse uttered or written *impromptu*; an *impromptu* reply.

im·promp'tū, *n.* an impromptu speech, performance, etc.

im·prop'ẽr, *a.* [ME. *improper*; OFr. *impropre*; L. *improprius*, not proper; *in-* priv., and *proprius*, one's own, proper.]
1. not suitable for or consistent with the purpose or circumstances; ill-adapted; unfit.
2. not in accordance with the truth, fact, or rule; wrong; incorrect.
3. contrary to good taste or decency; indecorous.

im·prop'ẽr, *v.t.* to impropriate. [Obs.]

im·prop·ẽr·ā'tion, *n.* the act of reproaching. [Obs.]

im·prop'ẽr fraç'tion, a fraction in which the denominator is less than the numerator (e.g., $^5/_3$).

im·prop'ẽr·ly, *adv.* not properly.

im·prō·pi'tious (-pish'us), *a.* not propitious; unpropitious. [Obs.]

im·prō·pōr'tion·ȧ·ble, *a.* not proportionable. [Obs.]

im·prō·pōr'tion·āte, *a.* not proportionate; not adjusted. [Obs.]

im·prō'pri·āte, *v.t.*; impropriated, *pt.*, *pp.*; impropriating, *ppr.* [LL. *impropriatus*, pp. of *impropriare*, to take as one's own; *in*, in, and *proprius*, one's own.]
1. to appropriate to private use; to take to oneself; as, to *impropriate* thanks to oneself. [Obs.]
2. to transfer (church income or property) to private individuals.

im·prō'pri·āte, *a.* having been impropriated.

im·prō·pri·ā'tion, *n.* 1. an impropriating.
2. anything impropriated.

im·prō'pri·ā·tōr, *n.* one who makes or receives an impropriation.

im·prō·pri·ā'trix, *n.* a woman impropriator.

im·prō·prī'e·ty, *n.*; *pl.* **im·prō·prī'e·tieș,** [Fr. *impropriété*; L. *improprietas* (-*atis*), impropriety, from *improprius*, improper.]
1. the quality of being improper.
2. improper action or behavior.
3. an improper use of a word or phrase (e.g., "borrow" for "lend").

im·pros·per'i·ty, *n.* lack of success or prosperity. [Obs.]

im·pros'pẽr·ous, *a.* [L. *improsper*, not fortunate; *in-* priv., and *prosper*, fortunate.] not prosperous. [Obs.]

im·pros'pẽr·ous·ly, *adv.* unsuccessfully; unprosperously; unfortunately. [Obs.]

im·pros'pẽr·ous·ness, *n.* ill success; lack of prosperity. [Obs.]

im·pröv·ȧ·bil'i·ty, *n.* the state or quality of being improvable.

im·pröv'ȧ·ble, *a.* 1. susceptible of improvement; that can be improved.
I have a fine spread of *improvable* lands. —Addison.
2. that may be used to advantage or for the increase of anything valuable. [Rare.]
The essays of weaker heads afford *improvable* hints to better. —Browne.

im·pröv'ȧ·ble·ness, *n.* the quality of being improvable.

im·pröv'ȧ·bly, *adv.* in a manner that can be improved.

im·pröve', *v.t.*; improved, *pt.*, *pp.*; improving, *ppr.* [*in-* intens., and OFr. *prover*, to test, to show to be sufficient, from L. *probare*, to approve, from *probus*, good.]
1. to make better; to advance in value or good qualities; as, a good education *improves* the mind and the manners.
2. to use or employ to good purpose; to make productive; to turn to profitable account; to use to good advantage.
True policy, as well as good faith, in my opinion, binds us to *improve* the occasion. —Washington.
3. to make (land) more valuable by cultivation, etc.
Syn.—correct, amend, mend, meliorate, heighten, advance.

im·pröve', *v.i.* 1. to grow or become better in quality or condition; as, we are pleased to see our children *improve* in knowledge or strength.
We take care to *improve* in our frugality and diligence. —Atterbury.
2. to increase; to be enhanced; to rise; as, the price of cotton *improves*; or is *improved*.
to improve on or *upon*; to do or make better than.

im·pröve'ment, *n.* 1. an increase or advancement in worth, learning, wisdom, skill, or other excellence; as, the *improvement* of the mind by cultivation.
2. melioration; a making or growing better, or more valuable; as, the *improvement* of the roads; the *improvement* of the breed of horses or cattle.
3. a valuable addition; excellence added or a change for the better: sometimes with *on* or *to*; as, many writers have tried to make *improvements on* Shakespeare.
4. in patent law, an additional device or a change of form or of composition in something already patented.
5. a person or thing representing a higher degree of excellence.
6. instruction; growth in knowledge or refinement; edification; betterment.
I look upon your city as the best place of *improvement*. —South.
7. use or employment to beneficial purposes; a turning to good account; as, the *improvement* of natural advantages.
8. a change or addition to land, property, etc. to make it more valuable, such as a house, fence, garage, etc.
Syn.—betterment, melioration, amendment, advancement, enhancement, progress, proficiency.

im·pröv'ẽr, *n.* one who or that which improves.

im·prō·vīd'ed, *a.* unforeseen; unexpected; not provided against. [Obs.]

im·prov'i·dence, *n.* [LL. *improvidentia*; L. *in-* priv., and *providus*, foresighted.] lack of thrift or providence; failure to provide for the future; neglect of the measures which foresight might dictate for safety or advantage.
Syn.—negligence, prodigality, carelessness, shiftlessness, wastefulness.

im·prov'i·dent, *a.* [L. *in-* priv., and *providus*, foresighted.] lacking foresight and thrift; failing to provide for the future; neglecting the measures which foresight would dictate.
Syn.—wasteful, negligent, shiftless, prodigal.

im·prov·i·den'tiăl·ly (-shăl-), *adv.* improvidently. [Obs.]

im·prov'i·dent·ly, *adv.* in an improvident manner.

im·pröv'ing, *a.* that improves.
improving lease; in Scots law, a kind of lease or extension of lease granted to a tenant as an inducement to him to improve the leased premises.

im·pröv'ing·ly, *adv.* in an improving manner.

im·prov'i·sāte, *a.* improvised. [Rare.]

im·prov'i·sāte, *v.t.* and *v.i.* to improvise; to extemporize. [Rare.]

im·prov·i·șā'tion, *n.* 1. an improvising.
2. something improvised.

im·prov'i·șā·tōr, *n.* one who improvises.

ïm·prō·vï·șä·tō'rẹ, *n.* [It. *improvvisatore*.] same as *improvvisatore*.

im·prov''i·sȧ·tō'ri·ăl, *a.* of, or having the nature of, an improvisator or improvisation.

im·prō·vī'șȧ·tō·ry, *a.* same as *improvisatorial*.

ïm·prō·vï·șä·trï'cẹ (-chā), *n.*; *pl.* **ïm·prō·vï·șä·trï'cï** (-chē), a woman improvisatore.

im'prō·vīșe, *v.t.* and *v.i.* improvised, *pt.*, *pp.*; improvising, *ppr.* [Fr. *improviser*, to improvise, from L. *improvisus*, unforseen; *in-* priv., and *provisus*, pp. of *providere*, to foresee, anticipate.]
1. to compose, or simultaneously compose and perform, sing, etc., on the spur of the moment and without any preparation; extemporize.
2. to make, provide, or do with the tools and materials at hand, usually to fill an unforeseen and immediate need; as, he *improvised* a bed out of leaves.

im'prō·viș·ẽr, *n.* one who improvises.

im·prō·vi'șion (-vizh'un), *n.* improvidence. [Obs.]

im·prō·vī'șō, *a.* [L., on a sudden, abl. of *improvisus*, unforeseen; *in-* priv., and *provisus*, foreseen.] improvised; not previously prepared.

ïm·pröv·vï·șä·tō'rẹ, *n.*; *pl.* **ïm·prōv·vï·șä·tō'rï,** [It.] a performer who improvises poems or songs.

ïm·prōv·vï·șä·trï'cẹ (-chā), *n.*; *pl.* **ïm·prōv·vï·sä·trï'cï** (-chē), [It.] a woman improvvisatore.

im·prü'dence, *n.* [L. *imprudentia*, rashness, want of foresight, from *imprudens* (-*entis*), without foresight, imprudent.]
1. the quality of being imprudent; indiscretion; want of caution, circumspection, or a due regard to the consequences of words to be uttered, or actions to be performed; heedlessness; rashness.
2. imprudent speech or behavior.

im·prü'dent, *a.* [L. *imprudens* (-*entis*), without foresight, imprudent; *in-* priv., and *prudens* (-*entis*), prudent.] lacking in judgment or caution; not prudent; indiscreet; injudicious; not attentive to the consequences of words or actions; rash; heedless.

im·prū′dent·ly, *adv.* in an imprudent manner.

im·pū′bẽr·ăl, *a.* [L. *impubes* (*-eris*); *in-* priv., and *pubes* (*-eris*), grown up.] below the age of puberty; not mature. [Rare.]

im·pū′bẽr·ty, *n.* the state of not having reached puberty.

im′pū·dence, *n.* [OFr. *impudence*; L. *impudentia*, shamelessness, from *impudens* (*-entis*) shameless.]

1. the quality of being impudent; effrontery; assurance characterized by disrespect.

Those clear truths, that either their own evidence forces us to admit, or common experience makes it *impudence* to deny. —Locke.

2. impudent speech or behavior.

Syn.—effrontery, sauciness, boldness, insolence.—*Impudence* refers more especially to the feelings; *effrontery* to some gross and public exhibition of shamelessness; *sauciness* to a sudden outbreak of *impudence*.

im′pū·den·cy, *n.*; *pl.* **im′pū·den·cieṣ,** same as *impudence*.

im′pū·dent, *a.* [ME. *impudent*; L. *impudens* (*-entis*), shameless; *in-* priv., and *pudens* (*-entis*), ashamed.]

1. shameless; immodest. [Obs.]

2. shamelessly bold; saucy; insolent.

When we behold an angel, not to fear
Is to be *impudent*. —Dryden.

Syn.—audacious, brazen, saucy, impertinent, insolent, pert, forward, rude.

im′pū·dent·ly, *adv.* in an impudent manner.

At once assail
With open mouths, and *impudently* rail. —Sandys.

im·pū·dic′i·ty, *n.* [L. *impudicitia*, immodesty; *in-* priv., and *pudicus*, modest.] immodesty; shamelessness.

im·pūgn′ (-pūn′), *v.t.*; impugned, *pt.*, *pp.*; impugning, *ppr.* [OFr. *impugner*; L. *impugnare*, to attack, assail; *in*, on, against, and *pugnare*, to fight.] to oppose or challenge as false; to attack by words or arguments; to contradict; to cast reflections, as upon one's motives.

The truth hereof I will not rashly *impugn*, or overboldly affirm. —Peacham.

im·pūgn′ȧ·ble, *a.* open to attack; questionable as to sincerity or honesty. [Rare.]

im·pug·nā′tion, *n.* an impugning or being impugned.

im·pūgn′ẽr (-pūn′), *n.* one who impugns.

im·pūgn′ment, *n.* the act of making a charge or attack; also, the attack itself.

im·pū′is·sȧnce, *n.* [Fr.] impotence; weakness; lack of power or authority.

im·pū′is·sȧnt, *a.* [Fr.] weak; impotent.

im′pulse, *n.* [L. *impulsus*, a pushing against, a shock, impulse, from *impulsus*, pp. of *impellere*, to push or strike against; *in-*, against, and *pellere*, to push, strike.]

1. (a) an impelling, or driving forward with sudden force; (b) an impelling force; sudden, driving force; push; thrust; impetus; (c) the motion or effect caused by such a force.

2. (a) incitement to action arising from a state of mind or some external stimulus; (b) a sudden inclination to act, without conscious thought; (c) a motive or tendency coming from within.

These were my natural *impulses* for the undertaking. —Dryden.

3. in mechanics, the change in momentum effected by a force, measured by multiplying the average value of the force by the time during which it acts.

4. in physiology, a stimulus transmitted in a muscle or nerve, which causes or inhibits activity in the body.

Syn.—incentive, push, incitement, force, influence, instigation, motive.

im·pulse′, *v.t.* to impel; to incite. [Now Rare.]

im·pul′sion, *n.* [L. *impulsio* (*-onis*), a pushing against, from *impulsus*, pp. of *impellere*, to push against, impel.]

1. an impelling or being impelled.

2. an impelling force.

3. movement or tendency to move resulting from this force; impetus.

4. impulse (sense 2).

im·pul′sive, *a.* 1. impelling; driving forward.

Poor men! poor papers! We and they
Do some *impulsive* force obey.—Prior.

2. (a) acting or given to acting on impulse; as, an *impulsive* person; (b) produced by or resulting from impulse; as, an *impulsive* remark.

3. in mechanics, acting briefly and as a result of impulse.

im·pul′sive, *n.* that which gives an impulse. [Obs.]

im·pul′sive·ly, *adv.* in an impulsive manner.

im·pul′sive·ness, *n.* the state of being impulsive.

im·pul′sŏr, *n.* [L. *impulsor*, from *impellere*, to impel.] one who or that which impels. [Obs.]

im·punc′tāte, *a.* without pits, spots, or holes.

im·punc′tū·ăl, *a.* not punctual. [Rare.]

im·punc·tū·al′i·ty, *n.* lack of punctuality. [Rare.]

im·pūne′, *a.* [L. *impunis*.] not yet punished. [Obs.]

im·pū′ni·ty, *n.* [L. *impunitas*, from *impunis*, free from punishment; *in-* priv., and *pœna*, punishment.] exemption from punishment, penalty, injury, or loss; as, no person should be permitted to violate the laws with *impunity*.

im·pū·rā′tion, *n.* the act of rendering impure; impurity. [Obs.]

im·pūre′, *a.* [L. *impurus*; *in-* priv., and *purus*, pure.]

1. not pure; foul; feculent; mixed or impregnated with foreign matter; adulterated; as, *impure* water or milk.

2. unchaste; lewd; unclean; obscene; as, *impure* actions or language.

3. unclean; not purified according to religious ritual.

4. unclean; soiled; dirty.

5. mixed; having more than one color, tone, style, etc.

6. not idiomatic or grammatical.

Syn.—adulterated, dirty, filthy, coarse, gross, ribald, immodest, vulgar.

im·pūre′, *v.t.* to make foul; to defile. [Obs.]

im·pūre′ly, *adv.* in an impure manner; with impurity.

im·pūre′ness, *n.* [L. *impuritas*, from *impurus*, impure; *in-* priv., and *purus*, pure.] the state of being impure.

im·pū′ri·ty, *n.* [OFr. *impurité*; L. *impuritas*.]

1. the state or quality of being impure.

2. *pl.* **im·pū′ri·tieṣ,** an impure thing or element.

The foul *impurities* that reigned among the monkish clergy. —Atterbury.

im·pũr′ple, *v.t.* same as *empurple*.

im·pūt·ȧ·bil′i·ty, *n.* the quality or state of being attributable.

im·pūt′ȧ·ble, *a.* 1. that can be imputed or charged to a person; chargeable; attributable; as, crimes and errors are *imputable* to those who commit them.

2. accusable; chargeable with a fault. [Obs.]

im·pūt′ȧ·ble·ness, *n.* the state of being imputable.

im·pūt′ȧ·bly, *adv.* in an imputable manner.

im·pū·tā′tion, *n.* [LL. *imputatio* (*-onis*), a charge, an account, from L. *imputatus*, pp. of *imputare*, to charge, impute.]

1. the act of imputing or charging; attribution; as, the *imputation* of faults to someone.

2. charge or attribution of evil; censure; reproach.

Let us be careful to guard ourselves against these groundless *imputations* of our enemies, and to rise above them. —Addison.

3. a fault or crime imputed.

4. in theology, the attributing of personal guilt or righteousness to one or more persons on account of the offense or merits of another.

im·pūt′ȧ·tive, *a.* [LL. *imputativus*, charging, accusatory, from L. *imputare*, to charge, impute.] of, inclined to, or characterized by imputation.

im·pūt′ȧ·tive·ly, *adv.* by imputation.

im·pūte′, *v.t.*; imputed, *pt.*, *pp.*; imputing, *ppr.* [ME. *inputen*; OFr. *emputer* (Fr. *imputer*); L. *imputare*, to set to the account of, impute; *in*, in, to, and *putare*, to estimate, charge, think.]

1. to attribute (something, especially a crime or a fault) to another; to charge with; to ascribe.

2. in theology, to ascribe (good or evil) to a person as coming from another.

3. to reckon; to consider; to regard. [Rare.]

Syn.—count, reckon, attribute, ascribe, charge.

im·pūt′ẽr, *n.* one who imputes or attributes.

im·pū·tres′ci·ble, *a.* not subject to putrefaction or corruption.

in-, [from the prep. *in*; in words of L. origin, from the L. prep. *in*.] a prefix used: (a) to mean *in, into, within, on, toward*, as in *in*breed, *in*fer, *in*duct; (b) as an intensifier in some words of Latin origin, as in *in*stigate. Assimilated in words of Latin origin to *il-* before *l*, as in *il*luminate, *ir-* before *r*, as in *irri*gate, and *im-* before *m*, *p*, and *b*, as in *immi*grate, *im*peach, *im*bibe.

in-, [from L. *in-*.] a prefix meaning *no, not, without, non-*, as in *in*significant: assimilated to *il-* before *l*, as in *il*literate, *ir-* before *r*, as in *ir*responsible, and *im-* before *m*, *p*, and *b*, as in *im*material, *im*possible, *im*becile.

-in, in chemistry, same as *-ine*.

In, in chemistry, indium.

in, *prep.* [ME. *in*, *yn*; AS. *in*, in; with the simple form of *in* there became merged the ME. *inne*, from AS. *inne*, in, within.]

1. contained or enclosed by, inside; within; as, *in* the room, *in* the envelope.

2. wearing; clothed by; as, the lady *in* red.

3. during the course of; as, it was done *in* a day.

4. at, before, or after the end of; as, I'll be with you *in* an hour.

5. perceptible to (a specified sense); as, he is *in* sight.

6. limited by the scope of; as, *in* my opinion.

7. being a member of or worker at; as, he is *in* business.

8. amidst; surrounded by; as, *in* a storm.

9. affected by; having; as, he is *in* trouble.

10. engaged or occupied by; as, *in* a search for truth.

11. with regard to; as concerns; as, weak *in* faith, they vary *in* size.

12. so as to form; as, arranged *in* curls.

13. with; by; using; as, he paints *in* oil, written *in* English.

14. made of; as, it was done *in* wood.

15. because of; for; as, he cried *in* pain.

16. by way of; as, do this *in* my defense.

17. as a part of the capacity or function of; belonging to; as, he didn't have it *in* him.

18. into; as, come *in* the house: *into* is generally preferred in this sense.

In expresses inclusion with relation to space, place, time, state, circumstances, manner, quality, substance, a class, a whole, etc.

in that; because; for the reason that; in view of the fact that.

in the name of; see under *name*.

in, *adv.* [ME. *in*, *inne*; AS. *in*, *inne*, *innan*, in, within.]

1. from a point outside to one inside; as, he went *in*; the ring of hunters closed *in*.

2. so as to be contained by a certain space, condition, or position; as, labor's vote put him *in*.

3. so as to be agreeing with; as, he fell *in* with our plans.

4. so as to form a part of; as, mix cream *in* the sauce.

5. in law, a term used to express the nature of a privilege; as, a tenant is *in* by the lease.

6. in nautical usage, furled; as, the sails are *in*.

in for; certain to have or get (usually an unpleasant experience).

in with; associated with in partnership, friendship; etc.

to have it in for; to hold a grudge against. [Colloq.]

in, *a.* 1. that is in power; as, the *in* group.

2. inner; inside.

3. coming or going inside; inward; as, the *in* door, the *in* boat.

4. profiting to the extent of; as, he is *in* a hundred dollars. [Colloq.]

in, *n.* 1. [*usually in pl.*] a person or thing that is in power, as a team at bat, a party holding office, etc.

2. a place or means of entrance; introduction. [Colloq.]

3. special influence or favor; pull. [Colloq.]

ins and outs; (a) all the complex physical details of a place; hence, (b) all the details and intricacies.

in, *v.t.*; inned, *pt.*, *pp.*; inning, *ppr.* 1. to collect; gather in; as, *in* the hay before it rains. [Dial.]

2. to enclose. [Dial.]

-ī′nȧ, [from L. *-ina*, f. of *-inus*.] a suffix used primarily to form feminine names, titles, occupational designations, etc., as in Christ*ina*, czar*ina*, baller*ina*.

-ī′nȧ, [from L. *-ina*, neut. pl. of the adjective suffix *-inus*.] a suffix used in zoology to form Latin or Latinized names of groups of animals.

in·ȧ·bil′i·ty, *n.* [compare L. *inhabilis*, unfit, unable; *in-* priv., and *habilis*, fit, able.] the quality or state of being unable; lack of sufficient power, capacity, strength, or means to accomplish some end; as, *inability* to purchase a farm.

Syn.—weakness, powerlessness, disability,

incapacity, helplessness, impotence, incapability, incompetence.

in·ā′ble, *v.t.* to enable. [Obs.]

in·ā′ble·ment, *n.* enablement. [Obs.]

in ab·sen′ti·à (-shi-à), [L.] in absence; although not present; as, she received her college degree *in absentia.*

in·ab′sti·nence, *n.* lack of abstinence; a partaking; indulgence of appetite; as, the *inabstinence* of Eve. [Rare.]

in·ab·stract′ed, *a.* not abstracted. [Obs.]

in·à·bū′sive·ly, *adv.* without abuse. [Obs.]

in·aç·cess·i·bil′i·ty, *n.* the quality or state of being inaccessible.

in·aç·cess′i·ble, *a.* [LL. *inaccessibilis,* unapproachable; *in-* priv., and *accessibilis,* approachable, from L. *accessus,* an approach, access.] not accessible; specifically, (a) impossible to reach or enter; (b) that cannot be seen, talked to, influenced, etc.; inapproachable; (c) not obtainable.

in·aç·cess′i·ble·ness, *n.* inaccessibility.

in·aç·cess′i·bly, *adv.* so as to be inaccessible.

in·aç·cord′ănt, *a.* not in accordance; disagreeing; lacking harmony.

in·aç′çū·rà·cy, *n.* 1. the quality of being inaccurate; lack of accuracy.

2. *pl.* **in·aç′çū·rà·cieș,** something inaccurate; an error; mistake.

in·aç′çū·răte, *a.* not accurate; not exact or correct; not according to truth; erroneous; as, an *inaccurate* statement, copy, or transcript.

Syn.—incorrect, erroneous, inexact, faulty, defective, blundering, loose.

in·aç′çū·răte·ly, *adv.* in an inaccurate manner; not according to truth; incorrectly; erroneously.

in·aç·quaint′ănce (-kwānt′), *n.* lack of acquaintance.

in·aç·qui·es′cent (-kwi-), *a.* not acquiescing.

in·aç′tion, *n.* absence of motion or action; inertness or idleness.

in·aç′ti·vāte, *v.t.*; inactivated, *pt., pp.*; inactivating, *ppr.* 1. to make inactive.

2. to cause (a military unit, governmental bureau, etc.) to go out of existence; to dissolve.

3. in biochemistry, to destroy the activity of (a serum) by heat.

in·aç′tive, *a.* [L. *in-* priv., and *activus,* active.]

1. not active; inert; having no power to move; incapable of action.

2. not diligent or industrious; not busy; idle; also, habitually idle; indolent; sluggish; as, an *inactive* official.

3. not affecting the plane of polarized light: said of some isomers of certain optically active crystalline substances.

Syn.—idle, inert, lazy, slothful, sluggish, dull, passive.

in·aç′tive·ly, *adv.* in an inactive manner.

in·aç·tiv′i·ty, *n.* the quality or state of being inactive.

in·aç′tū·āte, *v.t.* to put in action. [Obs.]

in·aç·tū·ā′tion, *n.* operation. [Obs.]

in·ad·ap·tā′tion, *n.* a state of not being adapted or fitted.

in·ad′ē·quà·cy (-kwà-), *n.*; *pl.* **in·ad′ē·quà·cieș,** quality, state, or instance of being inadequate.

in·ad′ē·quăte, *a.* not adequate; not equal to the purpose; insufficient to effect the object; as, *inadequate* power, strength, or resources.

in·ad′ē·quăte·ly, *adv.* not fully or sufficiently; not completely.

in·ad′ē·quăte·ness, *n.* the state of being inadequate; inadequacy; inequality; incompleteness.

in·ad·ē·quā′tion, *n.* lack of exact correspondence. [Archaic.]

in·ad·hēr′ent, *a.* free; not adhering.

in·ad·hē′șion (-zhun), *n.* lack of adhesion.

in·ad·mis·si·bil′i·ty, *n.* the quality of being inadmissible, or not proper to be received; as, the *inadmissibility* of an argument, or of evidence in court.

in·ad·mis′si·ble, *a.* not admissible; not proper to be admitted, allowed, or received; as, *inadmissible* testimony, an *inadmissible* proposition.

in·ad·mis′si·bly, *adv.* 1. in a manner not admissible.

2. to an inadmissible degree.

in·ad·vēr′tence, *n.* 1. the quality or fact of being inadvertent; inattention; negligence; heedlessness; as, many mistakes and some misfortunes arise from *inadvertence.*

2. an instance of this; any oversight, mistake, or fault which proceeds from negligence.

Syn.—oversight, negligence, inattention, carelessness.

in·ad·vēr′ten·cy, *n.*; *pl.* **in·ad·vēr′ten·cieș,** inadvertence.

in·ad·vēr′tent, *a.* 1. not attentive or observant; heedless; careless; negligent.

2. due to oversight; unintentional.

in·ad·vēr′tent·ly, *adv.* heedlessly; carelessly; in an inadvertent manner.

in·ad·viș′à·ble, *a.* not proper to be advised; not wise or prudent.

in·ad·viș′à·ble·ness, *n.* the state of being inadvisable.

-ī′nae, [L. *-inæ,* f. pl. of adjectives in *-inus* in agreement with understood *bestiæ,* animals.] a suffix used in zoology to form Latinized names of subfamilies of animals, as Elephantinæ, Equinæ, etc.

in ae·tēr′num, [L.] to eternity; forever.

in·af·fà·bil′i·ty, *n.* reservedness in conversation; lack of sociability.

in·af′fà·ble, *a.* not affable; reserved.

in·af·feç·tā′tion, *n.* lack of affected manner. [Rare.]

in·af·feçt′ed, *a.* unaffected. [Obs.]

in·āid′à·ble, *a.* that cannot be assisted. [Rare.]

in·āl″ien·à·bil′i·ty (-yen-), *n.* the quality of being inalienable.

in·āl′ien·à·ble, *a.* not alienable; that cannot be legally or justly alienated or transferred to another; as, a minor's *inalienable* estate.

in·āl′ien·à·ble·ness, *n.* the state or quality of being inalienable.

in·āl′ien·à·bly, *adv.* so as to be inalienable.

in·al·i·men′tăl, *a.* affording no nourishment. [Rare.]

in·al″tēr·à·bil′i·ty, *n.* the quality of being inalterable.

in·al′tēr·à·ble, *a.* that cannot be altered or changed; unalterable.

in·al′tēr·à·ble·ness, *n.* the state or quality of being unalterable.

in·al′tēr·à·bly, *adv.* in an unalterable manner.

in·à·mis′si·ble, *a.* [LL. *inamissibilis*; L. *in-* priv., and *amissus,* pp. of *amittere,* to lose.] not liable to be lost. [Rare.]

in·à·mis′si·ble·ness, *n.* the state of not being liable to be lost.

in·am·ō·rä′tà, *n.* [It., f. of *inamorato,* a lover.] a woman beloved; a sweetheart or mistress.

in·am′ō·răte, *a.* [L. *in,* in, and *amor,* love.] inflamed with love.

in·am′ō·răte·ly, *adv.* in an enamored manner.

in·am·ō·rä′tō, *n.* [It., from LL. *inamoratus,* pp. of *inamorare,* to cause to love, from L. *in,* in, and *amor,* love.] a man loved; a woman's lover.

in·à·möv′à·ble, *a.* not subject to removal. [Rare.]

in′-and-in′, *a.* and *adv.* repeatedly with individuals of the same or closely related stocks; as, *in-and-in* breeding.

in′-and-in′, *n.* an old gambling game with dice. [Obs.]

in·āne′, *a.* [L. *inanis,* empty.] 1. empty; void.

2. lacking sense or meaning; senseless; foolish; silly.

in·āne′, *n.* a void space; space beyond the confines of the world.

in·āne′ly, *adv.* in an inane manner; senselessly.

ī·nän′gà, *n.* [New Zealand.] a small fish, *Retropinna richardsoni,* found in the fresh waters of New Zealand.

in·an′gū·lăr, *a.* not angular. [Obs.]

in·an′i·māte, *v.t.* [LL. *inimatus,* pp. of *inimare,* to put life in; L. *in,* in, and *anima,* life.] to animate. [Obs.]

in·an′i·măte, *a.* [L. *inanimatus*; *in-* priv., and *anima,* life.]

1. not animate; not endowed with (animal) life; dead; as, stones and earth are *inanimate* substances; an *inanimate* body.

2. not animated; dull; spiritless.

in·an′i·mā·ted, *a.* inanimate.

in·an′i·măte·ness, *n.* the condition of being inanimate.

in·an·i·mā′tion, *n.* inanimateness.

in·an·i·mā′tion, *n.* the act of animating by the infusion of life. [Obs.]

in·à·ni′tion (-nish′un), *n.* [ME. *in-anisioun*; OFr.; LL. *inanitio (-onis),* emptiness, from L. *inanitus,* pp. of *inanire,* to empty, from *inanis,* empty, void.]

1. the quality or condition of being empty; emptiness.

2. exhaustion from lack of food or an inability to assimilate it.

in·an′i·ty, *n.* [Fr. *inanité*; L. *inanitas,* emptiness, from *inanis,* empty.]

1. emptiness; void space; vacuity.

2. lack of sense; foolishness; frivolousness.

3. *pl.* **in·an′i·tieș,** an inane action or pursuit; a senseless or silly act, remark, etc.

in·an′thēr·āte, *a.* in botany, having no anthers.

in·ap′à·thy, *n.* a condition without apathy. [Rare.]

in·ap·pēal′à·ble, *a.* that cannot be appealed.

in·ap·pēaș′à·ble, *a.* that cannot be appeased.

in·ap·pel·là·bil′i·ty, *n.* the quality of being beyond the power of appeal.

in·ap·pel′là·ble, *a.* beyond the power of appeal; settled finally.

in·ap′pē·tence, *n.* [Fr. *inappétence*; L. *in-* priv., and *appetentia,* appetite.] lack of appetite or desire.

in·ap′pē·ten·cy, *n.* same as *inappetence.*

in·ap′pē·tent, *a.* having or showing inappetence.

in·ap″pli·çà·bil′i·ty, *n.* the quality or condition of not being applicable; unfitness.

in·ap′pli·çà·ble, *a.* not applicable; inappropriate; not suited or suitable to the purpose; as, the argument or the testimony is *inapplicable* to the case.

in·ap′pli·çà·ble·ness, *n.* the quality or condition of being inapplicable.

in·ap′pli·çà·bly, *adv.* in an inapplicable manner.

in·ap·pli·çā′tion, *n.* lack of application; lack of attention or assiduity; negligence; indolence; neglect of study or industry.

in·ap′pō·șite, *a.* not apposite; not fit or suitable; not pertinent; irrelevant; as, an *inapposite* argument.

in·ap′pō·șite·ly, *adv.* not pertinently; not suitably.

in·ap·prē′ci·à·ble (-shi-à-), *a.* [*in-* (not), and appreciable.] too small to be observed or have any value; negligible.

in·ap·prē′ci·à·bly, *adv.* to an inappreciable degree.

in·ap·prē·ci·ā′tion (-shi-), *n.* lack of just valuation.

in·ap·prē′ci·à·tive, *a.* lacking appreciation.

in·ap·prē·hen′si·ble, *a.* not intelligible; that cannot be apprehended, or understood.

in·ap·prē·hen′sion, *n.* lack of apprehension.

in·ap·prē·hen′sive, *a.* 1. lacking the ability to apprehend, or understand.

2. not perceiving danger, trouble, etc.

in·ap·prōach·à·bil′i·ty, *n.* the quality or condition of being inapproachable.

in·ap·prōach′à·ble, *a.* that cannot be approached.

in·ap·prōach′à·bly, *adv.* so as to be inapproachable.

in·ap·prō′pri·ăte, *a.* not appropriate; unsuited; not proper; not belonging to or fitted for.

in·ap·prō′pri·ăte·ly, *adv.* in an inappropriate manner.

in·ap·prō′pri·ăte·ness, *n.* unsuitableness.

in·apt′, *a.* 1. not apt; not suitable; inappropriate.

2. lacking skill or aptitude; awkward.

in·apt′i·tūde, *n.* lack of aptitude; specifically, (a) lack of suitability; (b) lack of skill.

in·apt′ly, *adv.* in an inapt manner.

in·apt′ness, *n.* unfitness.

in·ā′quāte, *a.* [L. *inaquatus,* pp. of *inaquare,* to turn into water; *in,* into, and *aqua,* water.] embodied in water or transformed into water. [Rare.]

in·à·quā′tion, *n.* the state of being inaquate. [Rare.]

in·ar′à·ble, *a.* not arable; not capable of being plowed or tilled.

in·ärch′, *v.t.*; inarched (-ärcht′), *pt., pp.*; inarching, *ppr.* to graft by uniting (a shoot) to another plant while both are growing on their own roots.

in·ärch′ing, *n.* a method of engrafting by which a scion, without being separated from its parent tree, is joined to a stock standing near.

INARCHING

in·ärm′, *v.t.* to surround with or as with the arms; to embrace.

in·är·tiç′ū·lāte, *a.* [LL. *inarticulatus,* not articulate; L. *in-* priv., and *articulatus,* pp. of *articulare,* to divide into joints, articulate.]

1. produced without the normal articulation of understandable speech: said of vocal sounds, as, an *inarticulate* cry.

2. (a) not able to speak; mute; dumb; (b) not able to speak understandably or expressively.

3. unexpressed; as, *inarticulate* passion.

4. in zoology, without joints, segments, hinges, or valves.

in·är·tiç′ū·lāt·ed, *a.* not articulated.

in·är·tiç′ū·lāte·ly, *adv.* in an inarticulate manner.

in·är·tiç′ū·lāte·ness, *n.* the state or condition of being inarticulate.

in·är·tiç·ū·lā′tion, *n.* indistinctness of sounds in speaking.

in·är·ti·fi′ciăl (-fish′ăl), *a.* 1. not artificial; natural.
2. inartistic; unskillful.
3. unaffected; simple.

in·är·ti·fi′ciăl·ly, *adv.* in an inartificial manner.

in·är·ti·fi′ciăl·ness, *n.* the state of being inartificial.

in·är·tis′tic, *a.* not artistic; specifically, (a) not conforming to the standards or principles of art; (b) lacking artistic taste.

in·är·tis′tiç·ăl, *a.* same as *inartistic.*

in·är·tis′tiç·ăl·ly, *adv.* in an inartistic manner.

in·as·much′, *conj.* because; since; seeing that (followed by *as*).

in·at·ten′tion, *n.* 1. failure to give attention; heedlessness; negligence.

Novel lays attract our ravished ears,
But old the mind with *inattention* hears.
—Pope.

2. a heedless or negligent act.

in·at·ten′tive, *a.* not attentive; heedless; careless; negligent; as, an *inattentive* spectator or hearer.

Syn.—heedless, unmindful, unobservant, absent-minded.

in·at·ten′tive·ly, *adv.* without attention; carelessly; heedlessly.

in·at·ten′tive·ness, *n.* the condition of being inattentive.

in·au·di·bil′i·ty, *n.* the quality or condition of being inaudible.

in·au′di·ble, *a.* [LL. *inaudibilis*, not audible; L. *in-* priv., and *audire*, to hear.] not audible; that cannot be heard; as, an *inaudible* voice or sound.

Syn.—low, suppressed, stifled, muffled, still, soundless, silent.

in·au′di·ble·ness, *n.* the condition of being inaudible.

in·au′di·bly, *adv.* so as to be inaudible.

in·au′gūr, *v.t.* to inaugurate. [Now Rare.]

in·au′gū·răl, *a.* pertaining to inauguration or to the ceremonies of inauguration, especially to the address delivered by the officer inaugurated.

in·au′gū·răl, *n.* an inaugural address; as, the *inaugural* delivered by a president of the United States upon the occasion of his accession to office.

in·au′gū·rāte, *v.t.*; inaugurated, *pt., pp.*; inaugurating, *ppr.* [L. *inauguratus*, pp. of *inaugurare*, to practice augury, to take the omens, to consecrate a place or a person by augury; *in*, in, and *augur*, an augur.]
1. to induct (an official) into an office with solemnity or suitable ceremonies; to invest with an office in a formal manner.
2. to initiate formally or ceremoniously, as some important public movement or campaign; as, to *inaugurate* a reform in the methods of transportation.
3. to celebrate formally the first public use of; to dedicate; as, the mayor *inaugurated* the new library.

in·au′gū·rāte, *a.* inaugurated. [Obs.]

in·au·gū·rā′tion, *n.* [LL. *inauguratio* (-*onis*), a beginning, from L. *inaugurare*, to consecrate, to inaugurate.] an inaugurating or being inaugurated.

In·au·gū·rā′tion Dāy, the day on which a newly elected president of the United States is inaugurated: before 1934, March 4, now, January 20, of the year following the election.

in·au′gū·rā·tŏr, *n.* one who inaugurates.

in·au′gū·rȧ·tō·ry, *a.* inaugural. [Rare.]

in·au′rāte, *v.t.* [L. *inauratus*, pp. of *inaurare*, to cover with gold; *in*, on, and *aurare*, to cover with gold, from *aurum*, gold.] to embellish with gold or with gold leaf. [Obs.]

in·au′rāte, *a.* 1. embellished with gold or with gold leaf. [Rare.]
2. in biology, having a metallic luster resembling gold; specifically, describing features of the *Coleoptera*. [Rare.]

in·au·rā′tion, *n.* the act or process of gilding or covering with gold. [Obs.]

in·aus′pi·cāte, *a.* ill-omened. [Obs.]

in·aus·pi′cious (-pish′us), *a.* not auspicious; ill-omened; unfortunate; unlucky; evil; unfavorable.

in·aus·pi′cious·ly, *adv.* in an inauspicious manner.

in·aus·pi′cious·ness, *n.* the state of being inauspicious.

in′bē·ing, *n.* 1. inherent existence.
2. essence; basic nature.

in′blōwn, *a.* having been blown into. [Obs.]

in′bōard, *a.* and *adv.* 1. inside the hull or bulwarks of a ship or boat; as, an *inboard* cargo.
2. in mechanics, inward; toward the inside; as, the stroke of a piston toward the steam chest is the *inboard* stroke.

in′bōard, *n.* a marine motor mounted inboard.

in′bond, *a.* in architecture, having bricks or stones laid as headers, or lengthwise across a wall: opposed to *outbond*, where the brick or stone is laid with its length parallel to the face of the wall. An *inbond* and *outbond* wall is one where the bricks or stones are laid alternately across and in the direction of the face of the wall.

INBOND AND OUTBOND WALL
A, Header B B, Stretchers

in′bo̤rn, *a.* [AS. *inboren.*] present in the organism at birth; innate; natural.

in′bound, *a.* bound toward the place where one is: opposed to *outbound.*

in′breăk, *n.* a break into or inward: opposed to *outbreak.* [Rare.]

in′breăk·ing, *n.* the act of breaking in. [Rare.]

in·brēathe′, *v.t.*; inbreathed, *pt., pp.*; inbreathing, *ppr.* [ME. *inbrethen*; after L. *inspirare.*]
1. to breathe in. [Rare.]
2. to inspire. [Rare.]

in′bred, *a.* 1. inborn.
2. (*often* in-bred′) bred from closely related parents; resulting from inbreeding.

in′breed (*or* in-brēd′), *v.t.*; inbred, *pt., pp.*; inbreeding, *ppr.* 1. to form or develop within.
2. to breed by continual mating of individuals of the same or closely related stocks.

in′bŭrn·ing, *a.* burning fiercely within; as, *inburning* rage, fury, wrath, hatred, zeal, etc.

in′bŭrnt, *a.* burned in, or as if burned in; impressed beyond effacement.

in′bŭrst, *n.* 1. a bursting in, inward, or into.
2. something that bursts in.

in′bȳ, *adv.* toward the center or interior; inward. [Scot.]

in′bȳ, *a.* located near by. [Scot.]

in′bȳ, *prep.* near to. [Scot.]

in′bȳe, *adv., a.,* and *prep.* same as *inby.*

In′cȧ, *n.* [Sp., from Peruvian native (Quechua) *ynca*, prince of the royal family.]
1. any member of a group of Quechuan Indian tribes that dominated ancient Peru until the Spanish conquest: the Incas had a highly developed civilization.
2. a king or other member of the ruling family of these tribes.

in·çāge′, *v.t.* same as *encage.*

in·çal″çū·lȧ·bil′i·ty, *n.* 1. the quality or state of being incalculable.
2. *pl.* **in·çal″çū·lȧ·bil′i·ties,** something incalculable.

in·çal′çū·lȧ·ble, *a.* 1. that cannot be calculated; beyond calculation.
2. too uncertain to be counted on; unpredictable.

in·çal′çū·lȧ·ble·ness, *n.* the quality of being incalculable.

in·çal′çū·lȧ·bly, *adv.* so as to be incalculable.

in·çȧ·les′cence, *n.* a growing warm; incipient or increasing heat. [Rare.]

in·çȧ·les′cen·cy, *n.* same as *incalescence.*

in·çȧ·les′cent, *a.* [L. *incalescens* (-*entis*), ppr. of *incalescere*, to grow warm or hot; *in-* intens., and *calescere*, to become warm.] growing warm; increasing in heat. [Rare.]

in cam′ẽr·ȧ, [L., in chamber.]
1. in a judge's private office rather than in open court.
2. in closed session, as a committee meeting or hearing not open to the public; secretly.

in·cam·ẽr·ā′tion, *n.* [L. *in*, in, and *camera*, chamber.] the act or process of uniting lands, revenues, or other rights to the pope's domain. [Obs.]

In′căn, *a.* of the Incas, their empire, or civilization.

In′căn, *n.* 1. an Inca.
2. Quechua.

in·can·desce′, *v.i.* and *v.t.*; incandesced, *pt., pp.*; incandescing, *ppr.* [L. *incandescere.*] to become or make incandescent.

in·can·des′cence, *n.* a being or becoming incandescent.

in·can·des′cent, *a.* [L. *incandescens* (-*entis*), ppr. of *incandescere*, to become warm or hot, to glow.]
1. glowing with intense heat; red-hot or, especially, white-hot.
2. very bright; shining brilliantly; gleaming.

incandescent lamp; a lamp consisting of a glass globe enclosing a vacuum within which is mounted a filament of conducting material, which is heated to incandescence by an electric current.

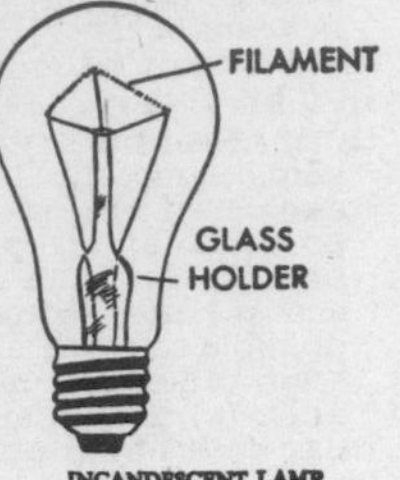

INCANDESCENT LAMP

in·çȧ·nes′cent, *a.* [L. *incanescens* (-*entis*), ppr. of *incanescere*, to become gray; *in*, in, and *canescere*, to become gray, from *canus*, white, hoary.] growing white or gray.

in·çā′nous, *a.* [L. *incanus*, quite gray, hoary; *in*, in, and *canus*, white, hoary.] in botany, covered with soft white hairs: said of leaves or stems.

in·çan·tā′tion, *n.* [LL. *incantatio* (-*onis*), from L. *incantare*, to chant a magic formula; *in*, in, and *cantare*, to sing, chant.]
1. the chanting of magical words or a formula in casting a spell or performing other magic.
2. the words or formula so chanted.
3. any magic or sorcery.

in·çant′ȧ·tō·ry, *a.* of the nature of, or dealing with, incantation.

in·çan′tŏn, *v.t.*; incantoned, *pt., pp.*; incantoning, *ppr.* to form a canton of or to unite with cantons already formed. [Rare.]

in·çā·pȧ·bil′i·ty, *n.* the quality of being incapable; natural incapacity or lack of power; as, the *incapability* of a child to comprehend logical syllogisms.

in·çā′pȧ·ble, *a.* [Fr. *incapable*; LL. *incapabilis*, incapable; L. *in-* priv., and LL. *capabilis*, capable, from L. *capere*, to take.]
1. not capable; lacking the necessary ability, competence, strength, etc.
2. in law, not legally qualified or eligible.

incapable of; (a) not allowing or admitting; not able to accept or experience; as, *incapable of* change; (b) lacking the ability or fitness for; as, *incapable of* sustained thought; (c) not legally qualified for.

Syn.—unqualified, unable, unfitted, weak, incompetent, feeble, disqualified, insufficient.

in·çā′pȧ·ble, *n.* an incapable person, mentally, morally, or physically.

in·çā′pȧ·bly, *adv.* in an incapable manner.

in·çȧ·pā′cious, *a.* [LL. *incapax* (-*acis*), incapable; L. *in-* priv., and *capax* (-*acis*), capable, capacious.] not capacious; not large or spacious; narrow; of small content.

in·çȧ·pā′cious·ness, *n.* narrowness; lack of capacity.

in·çȧ·pac′i·tāte, *v.t.*; incapacitated, *pt., pp.*; incapacitating, *ppr.* 1. to deprive of the normal capacity for doing, performing, knowing, etc.; to make unable or unfit; as, old age and infirmity often *incapacitate* men.
2. to disqualify; to deprive of legal requisites or qualifications.

in·çȧ·pac·i·tā′tion, *n.* the act by which one is incapacitated, or the state of one who is incapacitated.

in·çȧ·pac′i·ty, *n.*; *pl.* **in·çȧ·pac′i·ties,** 1. lack of capacity, power, or fitness, either physical or mental.
2. lack of legal qualification or requisites; disqualification; disability by deprivation of power; as, the *incapacity* of a minor to make contracts.

in·çap′sū·lāte, *v.t.* to encapsulate.

in·çap′sū·lāte, *a.* [L. *in*, in, and *capsula*, a box.] enclosed in a capsule or cyst.

in·çap·sū·lā′tion, *n.* the act of confining in a capsule or the state of being thus confined.

in·çär′cẽr·āte, *v.t.*; incarcerated, *pt., pp.*; incarcerating, *ppr.* [LL. *incarceratus*, pp. of *incarcerare*, to imprison; L. *in*, in, and *carcer*, a prison.]
1. to imprison; to confine in a jail.
2. to confine; to shut up or enclose.

incarcerated hernia; in medicine, a form of hernia which is constricted but not strangulated.

in·çär′cẽr·āte, *a.* imprisoned; confined. [Archaic.]

in·çär·cẽr·ā′tion, *n.* 1. the act of imprisoning or confining; imprisonment; confinement.

2. in surgery, constriction about the neck of a hernial sac.

in·căr′cĕr·ā·tŏr, *n.* one who incarcerates.

in·căr′di·nāte, *v.t.*; incardinated, *pt., pp.*; incardinating, *ppr.* [from the pp. of ML. *incardinare*; from *in-* and LL. *cardinalis*, a cardinal.]

1. to install (a priest, deacon, etc.) in a specified diocese, etc.

2. to make (a person) a cardinal.

in·cărn′, *v.t.* to cover with flesh; to cause to heal over.

in·cărn′, *v.i.* to become covered with flesh; to heal.

in·căr′nȧ·dīne, *a.* [Fr. *incarnadin*; It. *incarnatino*, from *incarnato*; LL. *incarnatus.*]

1. flesh-colored; pink.

2. red; especially, blood-red.

in·căr′nȧ·dīne, *n.* the color of either flesh or blood.

in·căr′nȧ·dīne, *v.t.*; incarnadined, *pt., pp.*; incarnadining, *ppr.* to make incarnadine.

in·căr′nănt, *a.* flesh-producing; wound-healing.

in·căr′nāte, *a.* [LL. *incarnatus*, pp. of *incarnari*, to be made flesh; L. *in*, in, and *caro, carnis*, flesh.]

1. endowed with a human body; in human form; personified; as, he is evil *incarnate.*

2. (a) flesh-colored; pink; (b) red; rosy.

in·căr′nāte, *v.t.*; incarnated, *pt., pp.*; incarnating, *ppr.* 1. to provide with flesh or a body; to embody.

2. to give actual form to; to make real.

3. to be the type or embodiment of (a quality or concept); as, he *incarnates* the courage of the whole race.

in·căr′nāte, *v.i.* to grow flesh, as in the healing of a wound. [Rare.]

in·căr·nā′tion, *n.* [OFr. *incarnatiun*; LL. *incarnatio* (*-onis*), from *incarnari*, to be made flesh; L. *in*, in, and *caro, carnis*, flesh.]

1. endowment with a human body; appearance in human form.

2. [I–] the taking on of human form and nature by Jesus conceived of as the Son of God.

3. any person or animal serving as the embodiment of a god or spirit.

4. any person or thing serving as the type or embodiment of a quality or concept; as, he is the *incarnation* of courage.

in·căr′nȧ·tive, *a.* causing new flesh to grow; healing. [Obs.]

in·căr′nȧ·tive, *n.* a medicine that tends to promote the growth of new flesh in the healing of wounds. [Obs.]

in·çāse′, *v.t.*; incased, *pt., pp.*; incasing, *ppr.* to encase.

in·çāse′ment, *n.* 1. an incasing or being incased.

2. something that incases.

in·çȧsk′, *v.t.*; incasked, *pt., pp.*; incasking, *ppr.* to cover with or as with a casque. [Obs.]

in·çat·ē·nā′tion, *n.* [LL. *incatenatio* (*-onis*), from *incatenare*, to chain together; L. *in*, in, and *catena*, a chain.] the act of linking together.

in·çau′tion, *n.* lack of caution.

in·çau′tious, *a.* not cautious; unwary; not circumspect; heedless; as, *incautious* youth.

in·çau′tious·ly, *adv.* unwarily; heedlessly; without due circumspection.

in·çau′tious·ness, *n.* lack of caution; unwariness.

in′çȧ·vā·ted, *a.* [L. *uncavatus*, pp. of *incavare*, to make hollow; *in*, in, and *cavus*, hollow.] made hollow; bent round or in. [Rare.]

in·çȧ·vā′tion, *n.* 1. the act of making hollow.

2. a hollow; a depression.

in·çāved′, *a.* shut up in a cave.

in·çav′ĕrned, *a.* shut up in a cavern, or as if in a cavern.

in·cēd′ing·ly, *adv.* with majesty. [Rare.]

in·cē·leb′ri·ty, *n.* [L. *in-* priv., and *celeber*, famous.] lack of distinction. [Rare.]

in·cend′, *v.t.* [L. *incendere*, to set on fire; *in*, on, in, and *candere*, to shine, glow, burn.] to inflame; to excite. [Obs.]

in·cen′di·ȧ·rism, *n.* [from *incendiary*, and *-ism.*]

1. the willful destruction of property by fire.

2. the willful stirring up of strife, riot, rebellion, etc.

in·cen′di·ăr·y, *n.*; *pl.* **in·cen′di·ăr·ies,** [L. *incendiarius*, setting on fire, an incendiary, from *incendium*, a fire, from *incendere*, to burn.]

1. a person who willfully destroys property by fire.

2. a person who willfully stirs up strife, riot, rebellion, etc.

3. an incendiary bomb, substance, etc.

in·cen′di·ăr·y, *a.* 1. having to do with the willful destruction of property by fire.

2. causing or designed to cause fires, as certain substances, bombs, etc.

3. willfully stirring up strife, riot, rebellion, etc.

in·cen′di·ous, *a.* incendiary. [Obs.]

in·cen′di·ous·ly, *adv.* in an incendiary manner. [Obs.]

in·cen′sănt, *a.* enraged; ferocious; in heraldry, describing an animal, as a lion or a boar, with flames issuing from the mouth.

in·cen·sā′tion, *n.* incense offering. [Rare.]

in·cense′, *v.t.*; incensed (-senst), *pt., pp.*; incensing, *ppr.* [L. *incensus*, pp. of *incendere*, to set on fire, inflame; *in*, in, on, and *candere*, to shine, glow, burn.]

1. to set fire to. [Obs.]

2. to enkindle or inflame to violent anger; to excite angry passions in; to provoke; to irritate; to exasperate.

in′cense, *n.* [ME. *ansens, encenz*; LL. *incensum*, incense.]

1. any substance producing a pleasant odor when burned: used in some religious ceremonies.

2. the smoke or fragrance from such a substance.

3. any pleasant odor.

4. pleasing attention, praise, or admiration.

in′cense, *v.t.*; incensed, *pt., pp.*; incensing, *ppr.* 1. to make fragrant with or as with incense; to perfume.

2. burn or offer incense to.

in′cense, *v.i.* to burn incense.

in′cense-brēath″ing, *a.* exhaling sweet odors, as of incense.

in·censed′ (-senst′), *a.* 1. inflamed to violent anger; exasperated.

2. in heraldry, depicted as in a rage, with flames issuing from the mouth.

in·cense′ment, *n.* violent irritation of the passions; heat; exasperation. [Rare.]

in·cen′sĕr, *n.* a censer. [Obs.]

in·cen′sion, *n.* [L. *incensio* (*-onis*), from *incensus*, pp. of *incendere*, to set on fire.] the act of kindling; the state of being on fire. [Obs.]

in·cen′sive, *a.* tending to excite or provoke. [Obs.]

in·cen′sŏr, *n.* [LL., from L. *incendere*, to set on fire.] a kindler of anger; an inflamer of passions; one who incites or instigates. [Obs.]

in·cen′sō·ry, *n.*; *pl.* **in·cen′sō·ries,** the vessel in which incense is burnt and offered; a censer.

in·cen′sur·ȧ·ble (-shur-), *a.* not censurable.

in·cen′sur·ȧ·bly, *adv.* in a manner not admitting of censure.

in·cen′tive, *a.* [ME. *incentive*; L. *incentivus*, striking up the tune, from pp. of *incinere*, to sing.] influencing to action; encouraging; stimulating; motivating.

in·cen′tive, *n.* that which influences or encourages to action; motive; spur; stimulus; as, the desire for promotion is often a powerful *incentive* to action.

in·cen′tive·ly, *adv.* incitingly; encouragingly.

in·cept′, *v.i.*; incepted, *pt., pp.*; incepting, *ppr.* [L. *inceptus*, pp. of *incipere*, to take up, to begin; *in*, in, on, and *capere*, to take.] to become qualified for a degree in a university: now used only at Cambridge University, England.

in·cept′, *v.t.* 1. to begin or undertake.

2. to take in; to receive; specifically, to ingest; to intussuscept; as, amoebas *incept* food particles.

in·cep′tion, *n.* [L. *inceptio* (*-onis*), from *inceptus*, pp. of *incipere*, to begin, lit., to take up.]

1. beginning; outset; commencement.

2. the act of receiving. [Rare.]

in·cep′tive, *a.* 1. beginning; introductory; initial.

2. in grammar, expressing the beginning of an action.

in·cep′tive, *n.* an inceptive verb or phrase.

in·cep′tive·ly, *adv.* in an inceptive manner.

in·cep′tŏr, *n.* [LL. *inceptor*, from L. *inceptus*, pp. of *incipere*, to begin.]

1. a beginner; one learning the rudiments. [Rare.]

2. one who incepts at an English university.

in·cĕr·ā′tion, *n.* [L. *inceratus*, pp. of *incerare*, to cover with wax.] the act of covering with wax. [Obs.]

in·cĕr′tain (-tin), *a.* uncertain; doubtful. [Obs.]

in·cĕr′tain·ly, *adv.* uncertainly; doubtfully. [Obs.]

in·cĕr′tain·ty, *n.* uncertainty; doubt. [Obs.]

in·cĕr′ti·tūde, *n.* [Fr. *incertitude*; LL. *incertitudo* (*-inis*), uncertainty, from L. *incertus*, uncertain; *in-* priv., and *certus*, certain.]

1. uncertainty; doubtfulness; doubt.

2. insecurity.

in·ces′sȧ·ble, *a.* unceasing; continual. [Rare.]

in·ces′sȧ·bly, *adv.* continually; unceasingly. [Rare.]

in·ces′săn·cy, *n.* unintermitted continuance; unceasingness.

in·ces′sănt, *a.* [LL. *incessans* (*-antis*); L. *in-* priv., and *cessans* (*-antis*), ppr. of *cessare*, to cease.] unceasing; unintermitted; uninterrupted; continual; as, *incessant* rains; *incessant* clamors.

in·ces′sănt·ly, *adv.* without ceasing; continually.

Syn.—unceasingly, uninterruptedly.

in′cest, *n.* [OFr. *inceste*; L. *incestum*, unchastity, incest, neut. of *incestus*, unclean, unchaste; *in-* priv., and *castus*, chaste.]

1. sexual intercourse between persons too closely related to marry legally.

2. in ecclesiastical usage, spiritual incest.

spiritual incest; (a) in old church law, sexual intercourse between persons who have a spiritual alliance, as because of baptism or confirmation together; (b) the act of holding two benefices, by a vicar or other beneficiary, one of which depends on the collation of the other.

in·ces′tū·ous, *a.* [LL. *incestuosus*, from L. *incestus*, unclean, unchaste.]

1. guilty of incest; as, an *incestuous* person.

2. of or having the nature of incest; as, an *incestuous* connection.

in·ces′tū·ous·ly, *adv.* in an incestuous manner.

in·ces′tū·ous·ness, *n.* the state or quality of being incestuous.

inch, *n.* [ME. *inche, ynche*; AS. *ynce, ince*, an inch, from L. *uncia*, a twelfth part, an inch, an ounce.]

1. a measure of length, equal to $^1/_{12}$ foot (2.54 centimeters): symbol, ″ (e.g., 10″): *square inch* is a measure of surface area; *cubic inch* is a measure of volume or cubic content.

2. a fall (of, rain, snow, etc.) equal to the amount that would cover a surface to the depth of one inch.

3. a unit of pressure as measured by a barometer or manometer, equal to the pressure balanced by the weight of a one-inch column of liquid, usually mercury, in the instrument.

4. a very small amount, degree, or distance; trifle; bit.

by inches; by exceedingly small consecutive movements; gradually; slowly.

every inch; in all respects; thoroughly.

inch by inch; gradually; slowly; by degrees.

within an inch of; not far from; almost to; very near.

within an inch of one's life; almost to one's death; very near to losing one's life.

inch, *a.* being an inch in any dimension; as, an *inch* board; a three-*inch* nail.

inch, *v.t.*; inched (incht), *pt., pp.*; inching, *ppr.* 1. to drive by inches or small degrees.

2. to divide into spaces an inch in width or length.

inch, *v.i.* to move slowly, by or as if by inches; as, to *inch* along.

inch, *n.* [Gael. *innis*, island.] in Scotland and Ireland, an isolated piece of land, as an island or hill.

in·chăm′bĕr, *v.t.*; inchambered, *pt., pp.*; inchambering, *ppr.* to lodge in a chamber. [Rare.]

in·chānge′ȧ·ble, *a.* unchangeable. [Obs.]

in·chȧnt′, *v.t.* to enchant. [Obs.]

in·char′i·tȧ·ble, *a.* uncharitable. [Obs.]

in·char′i·ty, *n.* lack of charity. [Obs.]

in·chāse′, *v.t.* same as *enchase.*

in·chas′ti·ty, *n.* unchastity. [Obs.]

inched (incht), *a.* 1. measured into inches; as, an *inched* rule.

2. being or having a length of (a certain number of) inches; as, a four-*inched* blade: usually written four-*inch*, etc.

in·chest′, *v.t.* to put into or enclose by a chest. [Obs.]

inch′mēal, *adv.* [*inch* and *meal*; cf. *piecemeal.*] by the inch; a little at a time; slowly.

by inchmeal; by small degrees.

in′chō·āte, *a.* [L. *inchoatus*, pp. of *inchoare*, to begin.] begun, but only partially in operation or existence; in existence in an elementary form; rudimentary; as, an *inchoate* idea.

in′chō·āte, *v.t.* to begin.

in·chō·āte·ly, *adv.* incipiently; in an elementary or rudimentary manner.

in·chō·ā′tion, *n.* [LL. *inchoatio* (*-onis*), from L. *inchoare*, to begin.] an early stage or beginning; commencement; inception.

in·chō′ā·tive, *a.* [LL. *inchoativus*, from L. *inchoatus*, pp. of *inchoare*, to begin.]
1. inchoate. [Rare.]
2. in grammar, inceptive; expressing the beginning of an action.

in·chō′ā·tive, *n.* an inceptive verb.

inch′pin, *n.* a deer's sweetbread. [Obs.]

inch′wŏrm, *n.* the larva of a geometrid moth; the measuring worm.

in·çiç′ū·rȧ·ble, *a.* [L. *in-* priv., and *cicurare*, to tame, from *cicur*, tame.] incapable of being tamed. [Obs.]

in·cīde′, *v.i.* to be incident. [Rare.]

in′ci·dence, *n.* [Fr. *incidence*; LL. *incidentia*, a falling upon, from L. *incidens* (*-entis*), ppr. of *incidere*, to fall upon.]
1. the act, fact, or manner of falling upon or influencing.
2. the degree or range of occurrence or effect; extent of influence.
3. in geometry, partial coincidence between two figures, as of a line and a point contained in it.
4. in physics, (a) the falling of a line, or a ray of light, projectile, etc. moving in a line, on a surface; (b) the direction of such falling.
angle of incidence; the angle which a ray of light, falling on any surface, makes with a perpendicular to that surface.
line of incidence; the line in the direction of which a ray meets a surface.

A B, LINE OF INCIDENCE
A B H, ANGLE OF INCIDENCE

in·ci·den′cy, *n.* incidence. [Obs.]

in′ci·dent, *a.* [Fr. *incident*; L. *incidens* (*-entis*), ppr. of *incidere*, to fall upon; *in*, on, and *cadere*, to fall.]
1. falling on; as, an *incident* ray.
2. casual; fortuitous; not in the usual course of things. [Rare.]
3. happening or likely to happen in connection with; as, misfortunes *incident* to the poor.
4. in law, appertaining to or dependent upon something else; as, rights *incident* to one's holdings.

in′ci·dent, *n.* 1. something that happens; event; occurrence.
2. something that happens as a result of or in connection with something more important; minor event or episode, especially one in a novel, play, etc.
3. in law, something incident to something else.
Syn.—circumstance, event, contingency, fact, episode, happening, occurrence.

in·ci·den′tăl, *a.* 1. happening or likely to happen as a result of or in connection with something more important; being an incident; casual.
2. secondary or minor, but usually associated; as, the *incidental* costs of education.
incidental music; music played in connection with the presentation of a play, motion picture, poem, etc. in order to heighten the mood or effect on the audience; mood music.

in·ci·den′tăl, *n.* 1. something incidental.
2. [*pl.*] miscellaneous items or expenses.
3. in music, a grace note, etc. immediately preceding, or included in, a chord to which it does not properly belong.
Syn.—casual, accidental, contingent.

in·ci·den′tăl·ly, *adv.* 1. casually; without intention; accidentally; as, I was *incidentally* present when the conversation took place.
2. by the way: used in introducing a new but related topic.

in·ci·den′tăl·ness, *n.* the condition of being incidental.

in′ci·dent·ly, *adv.* incidentally. [Obs.]

in·cin′ẽr·ȧ·ble, *a.* that may be incinerated. [Rare.]

in·cin′ẽr·āte, *v.t.*; incinerated, *pt.*, *pp.*; incinerating, *ppr.* [LL. *incineratus*, pp. of *incinerare*, to burn to ashes; L. *in*, in, to, and *cinis* (*-eris*), ashes.] to burn to ashes; to consume; to cremate.

in·cin′ẽr·āte, *a.* wholly consumed; incinerated. [Obs.]

in·cin′ẽr·ā·tẽr, *n.* same as *incinerator*.

in·cin·ẽr·ā′tion, *n.* the act of reducing to ashes by combustion.

in·cin′ẽr·ā·tŏr, *n.* 1. a person or thing that incinerates.
2. a furnace for burning refuse and garbage.
3. a crematory.

in·cip′i·ence, in·cip′i·en·cy, *n.* a beginning; the fact or condition of being incipient; first stage.

in·cip′i·ent, *a.* [L. *incipiens* (*-entis*), ppr. of *incipere*, to begin, lit., to take up; L. *in*, in, on, and *capere*, to take.] beginning; commencing; in the first stages of existence; as, the *incipient* stage of a fever.

in·cip′i·ent·ly, *adv.* in an incipient manner.

in′ci·pit, [L.] (here) begins: a word sometimes placed at the beginning of medieval manuscripts.

in′ci·pit, *n.* a beginning.

in·cīr′cle, *v.t.* to encircle. [Obs.]

in·cīr′çlet, *n.* encirclet. [Obs.]

in·cīr·çum·sçrip′ti·ble, *a.* that cannot be circumscribed or limited. [Obs.]

in·cīr·çum·sçrip′tion, *n.* the state of being limitless. [Obs.]

in·cīr·çum·speçt′, *a.* lacking in circumspection. [Obs.]

in·cīr·çum·speç′tion, *n.* lack of circumspection; heedlessness. [Obs.]

in·çīṣe′, *v.t.*; incised, *pt.*, *pp.*; incising, *ppr.* [Fr. *inciser*; L. *incisus*, pp. of *incidere*, to cut into; *in*, into, and *cædere*, to cut.]
1. to cut into with a sharp tool.
2. to make (figures, inscriptions, etc.) by cutting; to engrave; to carve.

in·çīṣed′, *a.* 1. cut or engraved; carved; made by cutting.
2. in botany, with sharp angles between the lobes; as, an *incised* leaf or petal.

in·çīse′ly, *adv.* in the manner of incisions or notches. [Rare.]

in·ci′ṣion (-sizh′un), *n.* [Fr. *incision*; L. *incisio* (*-onis*), lit., a cutting into, from *incisus*, pp. of *incidere*, to cut into, incise.]
1. an incising.
2. a result of incising; a cut; gash.
3. incisive quality.
4. in surgery, a cut made into a tissue or organ.

in·ci′sive, *a.* [Fr. *incisif*, from L. *incisus*, pp. of *incidere*, to cut into.]
1. cutting into.
2. sharp; keen; penetrating; piercing; acute; as, an *incisive* mind, *incisive* language.
3. of an incisor.

in·cī′ṣŏr, *n.* [L. *incisus*, pp. of *incidere*, to cut into.] any of the front teeth, between the canines in either jaw, adapted for cutting.

in·cī′ṣŏr, *a.* incisorial; pertaining to the incisors or incisorial teeth.

in·ci·sō′ri·ăl, *a.* having sharp edges fitted for cutting; as, the *incisorial* teeth.

in·cī′sō·ry, *a.* having the quality of or adapted for cutting.

in·ciṣ′ūre (-sizh′), *n.* [L. *incisura*.] a cut; a place opened by cutting; an incision.

in·cī′tănt, *n.* [L. *incitans* (*-antis*), ppr. of *incitare*, to incite.] that which excites action; an inciting cause.

in·ci·tā′tion, *n.* [L. *incitatio* (*-onis*), from *incitare*, to incite.]
1. the act of inciting or moving to action; incitement.
2. incitement; incentive; motive; that which excites to action.

in·cīt′ȧ·tive, *n.* an inciting agent. [Obs.]

in·cīte′, *v.t.*; incited, *pt.*, *pp.*; inciting, *ppr.* [Fr. *inciter*; L. *incitare*, to arouse, set in motion, hasten, incite; *in*, in, on, and *citare*, to set in motion, urge.] to move to action by persuasion or motives presented; to stir up; to rouse; to spur on; as, to *incite* foes to combat.
Syn.—stimulate, instigate, goad, arouse, animate, encourage, spur, urge, move.

in·cīte′ment, *n.* [L. *incitamentum*, an incentive, from *incitare*, to incite.]
1. the act of inciting.
2. that which incites, or moves to action; motive; incentive; impulse.

From the long records of a distant age,
Derive *incitements* to renew thy rage.
—Pope.

in·cīt′ẽr, *n.* one who or that which incites.

in·cīt′ing·ly, *adv.* so as to excite to action.

in·civ′il, *a.* uncivil. [Obs.]

in·ci·vil′i·ty, *n.*; *pl.* **in·ci·vil′i·tieṣ,** [LL. *incivilitas*, from L. *incivilis*, uncivil; *in-* priv., and *civilis*, civil.]
1. lack of courtesy; rudeness of manners; impoliteness.
2. any act of rudeness or discourtesy.
3. lack of civilization. [Obs.]
Syn.—rudeness, discourtesy, impoliteness, disrespect, unmannerliness.

in·civ″i·lī·zā′tion, *n.* the state of being without civilization; barbarism.

in·civ′il·ly, *adv.* uncivilly; rudely. [Obs.]

in·civ′iṣm, *n.* [Fr. *incivisme*, lack of devotion to the existing government; L. *in-* priv., and *civis*, a citizen.] lack of patriotism or of loyalty to one's country or government.

in·çlȧ·mā′tion, *n.* [L. *inclamatio*.] a crying out. [Obs.]

in·çlau′dent, *a.* failing to close, as a flower. [Rare.]

in′çlȧ·vā·ted, *a.* [LL. *inclavatus*, pp. of *inclavare*, to fasten with a nail; L. *in*, in, and *clavare*, to fasten with a nail, from *clavus*, a nail.] set; fixed firmly. [Obs.]

in′-çlēar″ẽr, *n.* in banking, the clerk who represents his bank at a clearing house: he receives payable paper, balances accounts, etc. [Brit.]

in·çlem′en·cy, *n.* [L. *inclementia*, from *inclemens*, harsh, inclement.]
1. lack of clemency; unmercifulness; harshness.
2. roughness; storminess; severity; as, we were detained by the *inclemency* of the weather.

in·çlem′ent, *a.* [L. *inclemens* (*-entis*), harsh, rude; *in-* priv., and *clemens* (*-entis*), kind.]
1. lacking leniency; unmerciful; harsh; as, an *inclement* person.
2. rough; stormy; as, *inclement* weather.
Syn.—harsh, cruel, unmerciful, severe, stormy, rough, rigorous, unkind, forbidding.

in·çlem′ent·ly, *adv.* in an inclement manner.

in·çlīn′ȧ·ble, *a.* [L. *inclinabilis*, from *inclinare*, to lean upon, incline.]
1. inclined; favorably disposed.
2. that can be inclined.

in·çlīn′ȧ·ble·ness, *n.* the state of being inclinable; inclination. [Obs.]

in·çli·nā′tion, *n.* [ME. *inclinacioun*; L. *inclinatio* (*-onis*), a leaning, inclining, bending, from *inclinare*, to lean upon, incline.]
1. a bending, leaning, or sloping.
2. bend; lean; slope, slant.
3. the extent or degree of incline from a horizontal or vertical position, course, etc.
4. the difference in direction of two lines, planes, or surfaces as measured by the angle between them.
5. (a) a particular disposition or bent of mind; bias; tendency; (b) a liking or preference.
6. any action, practice, or thing toward which one is inclined.
7. the dip of the magnetic needle, or its tendency to incline toward the earth; also, the angle made by the needle with the horizon.
8. the act of decanting liquors by inclining the vessel. [Obs.]
9. a person liked or preferred. [Obs.]
inclination of an orbit; in astronomy, the angle which the plane of an orbit makes with the plane of the ecliptic; as, the *inclination of the orbit* of the earth is 23° 27′.
Syn.—leaning, slope, tendency, disposition, proneness, aptness, predilection, bias, bent, attachment, affection, liking, wish.

in·çli·nā′tion çŏm′păss, same as *inclinometer*.

in·çlīn′ȧ·tō·ri·ly, *adv.* obliquely; with inclination.

in·çlīn·ȧ·tō′ri·um, *n.* an inclinometer.

in·çlīn′ȧ·tō·ry, *a.* tending to incline or lean.

in·çlīne′, *v.i.*; inclined, *pt.*, *pp.*; inclining, *ppr.* [ME. *inclinen*; OFr. *encliner*; L. *inclinare*, to bend down, lean; *in*, on, to, and *clinare*, to lean.]
1. to deviate from a horizontal or vertical position, course, etc.; to lean; to tend; as, converging lines *incline* toward each other.
2. to bend or bow the body or head.
3. to be disposed; to have some wish or desire; to tend, as toward an opinion, course of action, etc.

Their hearts *inclined* to follow Abimelech.
—Jud. ix. 3.

4. to have a preference or liking.

in·çlīne′, *v.t.* 1. to cause to lean; to direct; as, *incline* the column or post to the east.
2. to give a tendency to; to influence; to dispose.

Incline my heart unto thy testimonies.
—Ps. cxix. 36.

3. to bend; to cause to stoop or bow; as, to *incline* the head in acts of reverence.
to incline one's ear; to pay heed; to listen willingly.

in′çlīne, *n.* [ME. *encline*; OFr. *enclin*, an incline, from *encliner*, to incline.] anything that inclines, as an inclined plane, a sloping road, etc.

in·clīned′, *a.* 1. having an inclination; specifically, (a) sloping; leaning; (b) disposed; willing; tending.

2. forming an angle with another line, plane, or body.

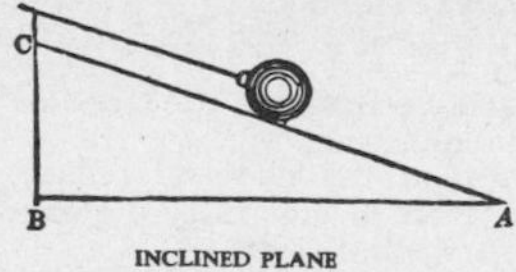

INCLINED PLANE

inclined plane; in mechanics, a plane inclined to the horizon, or forming with a horizontal plane any angle whatever excepting a right angle. In the accompanying figure, A C is the inclined plane; C B is the height of the plane, B A its base, and B A C the angle of inclination.

in·clīn′ẽr, *n.* one who or that which inclines; specifically, an inclined dial.

in·clīn′ing, *a.* inclined; leaning; causing to lean.

in·clīn′ing, *n.* 1. tendency; inclination.

2. a party or faction. [Archaic.]

in·cli·nom′e·tẽr, *n.* [L. *inclinare*, to incline, and *metrum*, a measure.]

1. a magnetic needle free to swing in a vertical plane, used to indicate the direction of the earth's magnetic force.

2. in civil engineering, a device for measuring the inclination of an embankment, declivity, etc.; a clinometer.

3. in aeronautics, an instrument which indicates the angle of an airplane with reference to the horizon; a turn-and-bank indicator.

in·clip′, *v.t.* to enclasp; to enclose; to surround. [Rare.]

in·clois′tẽr, *v.t.*; incloistered, *pt., pp.*; incloistering, *ppr.* to shut up or confine in a cloister.

in·clōṣe′, *v.t.*; inclosed, *pt., pp.*; inclosing, *ppr.* [ME. *inclosen, enclosen.*]

1. to surround; to shut in; to confine on all sides; as, to *inclose* a field with a fence.

2. to put into a receptacle.

3. to insert in an envelope, etc. together with a letter.

4. to contain.

Also spelled *enclose.*

in·clōs′ẽr, *n.* one who or that which incloses.

in·clō′ṣūre (-zhūr), *n.* [var. of *enclosure.*]

1. an inclosing or being inclosed.

2. something that incloses, as a fence, wall, etc.

3. something inclosed; specifically, (a) an inclosed place or area; (b) a document, money, etc. inclosed in an envelope with a letter.

Also spelled *enclosure.*

in·cloud′, *v.t.*; inclouded, *pt., pp.*; inclouding, *ppr.* to darken; to obscure.

in·clūd′á·ble, *a.* that can be included.

in·clūde′, *v.t.*; included, *pt., pp.*; including, *ppr.* [ME. *includen*; L. *includere*, to shut in, include; *in*, in, and *claudere*, to shut, close.]

1. to enclose; to shut up or in.

2. to have as part of a whole; to contain; comprise.

3. to take into account; to consider as part of a whole; to put in a total, category, etc.; as, I *include* the five dollars you owe me.

Syn.—comprise, comprehend, embrace, inclose.

in·clūd′ed, *a.* contained, enclosed, or involved.

included stamens; in botany, short stamens not projecting beyond the margin of the corolla.

in·clūd′i·ble, *a.* same as *includable.*

In·clū′sȧ, *n.pl.* [L., neut. pl. of *inclusus*, pp. of *includere*, to shut in, include.] in zoology, a division of bivalvular mollusks characterized by having the mantle open anteriorly, including shipworms, clams, razor clams, etc.

in·clū′ṣion (-zhun), *n.* [L. *inclusio* (*-onis*), a shutting up, from *inclusus*, pp. of *includere*, to shut in, include.]

1. the act of including or the state of being included.

2. in mineralogy, any foreign matter, whether solid or liquid, enclosed within the mass of a mineral or crystal.

in·clū′ṣion bod′y, in medicine, any of various small particles occurring in the leucocytes in various diseases, especially in scarlet fever.

in·clū′sive, *a.* [L. *inclusus*, pp. of *includere*, to shut in, include.]

1. including or tending to include; especially, taking everything into account; reckoning everything.

2. including the terms, limits, or extremes mentioned; as, a vacation from the first to the tenth *inclusive* is a vacation of ten days.

inclusive of; including; taking into account.

in·clū′sive·ly, *adv.* in an inclusive manner; so as to include or be included.

in·clū′sō·ry, *a.* inclusive. [Rare.]

in·clū′sus, *n.* in church history, a hermit who was shut up voluntarily in a cave or hut.

in·cōach′, *v.t.*; incoached, *pt., pp.*; incoaching, *ppr.* to enclose in a coach. [Rare.]

in·cō·act′, *a.* unconstrained. [Obs.]

in·cō·act′ed, *a.* incoact. [Obs.]

in·cō·ag′ū·lȧ·ble, *a.* that cannot be coagulated.

in·cō·ȧ·les′cence, *n.* the condition or quality of not uniting or blending. [Rare.]

in·coct′ed, *a.* uncooked; hence, indigestible. [Obs.]

in·cō·ẽr′ci·ble, *a.* 1. not to be coerced or compelled; that cannot be forced.

2. in physics, (a) above the critical point of liquefaction by pressure: said of gases; (b) capable of passing through solids: said of radiant energy.

in·cō·ex·ist′ence, *n.* the fact of not existing together. [Rare.]

in·cog′, *a., n.,* and *adv.* incognito. [Colloq.]

in·cog′i·tȧ·ble, *a.* [L. *incogitabilis*, thoughtless, unthinkable; *in-* priv., and *cogitabilis*, thinkable, from *cogitare*, to think.] unthinkable.

in·cog′i·tănce, in·cog′i·tăn·cy, *n.* [L. *incogitantia*, thoughtlessness, from *incogitans* (*-antis*), thoughtless, unthinking.] lack of thought, or of the power of thinking.

in·cog′i·tănt, *a.* [L. *incogitans* (*-antis*), unthinking, thoughtless; *in-* priv., and *cogitans* (*-antis*), ppr. of *cogitare*, to think.] not thinking; thoughtless.

in·cog′i·tănt·ly, *adv.* without consideration; thoughtlessly.

in·cog′i·tā·tive, *a.* not thinking; lacking the power of thought.

in·cog·i·tȧ·tiv′i·ty, *n.* the quality of being without the power of thought.

in·cog′ni·tȧ, *n.*, feminine form of *incognito.*

in·cog′ni·tănt, *a.* illiterate; stupid. [Obs.]

in·cog′ni·tō, *adv.* and *a.* [It.] in disguise; under an assumed name; as, he travels *incognito.*

in·cog′ni·tō, *a.* [It., from L. *incognitus*, unknown; *in-* priv., and *cognitus*, pp. of *cognoscere*, to know.] pertaining to a disguise in person or in character; as, his is an *incognito* character.

in·cog′ni·tō, *n.*; *pl.* **in·cog′ni·tōṣ,** 1. a person who is incognito.

2. (a) the state of being incognito; (b) the disguise assumed.

in·cog′ni·zȧ·ble, *a.* that cannot be recognized, known, or distinguished.

in·cog′ni·zănce, *n.* lack of knowledge or recognition.

in·cog′ni·zănt, *a.* not cognizant (*of*); lacking knowledge or awareness.

in·cog·nos·ci·bil′i·ty, *n.* the quality of being incognizable.

in·cog·nos′ci·ble, *a.* [L. *incognoscibilis*, not to be known; *in-* priv., and *cognoscibilis*, to be known, from *cognoscere*, to know.] same as *incognizable.*

in·cō·hēr′ence, *n.* 1. lack of coherence; a being incoherent.

2. incoherent speech, thought, etc.

in·cō·hēr′en·cy, *n.*; *pl.* **in·cō·hēr′en·cieṣ,** incoherence.

in·cō·hēr′ent, *a.* not coherent; specifically, (a) lacking cohesion; not sticking together; (b) not logically connected; disjointed; rambling; (c) characterized by incoherent speech, thought, etc.

Syn.—unconnected, incongruous, loose, inconsistent.

in·cō·hēr·en·tif′iç, *a.* giving rise to incoherence. [Rare.]

in·cō·hēr′ent·ly, *adv.* in an incoherent manner; without coherence.

in·cō·hēr′ent·ness, *n.* the state of being incoherent.

in·cō·in′ci·dence, *n.* lack of coincidence or agreement. [Rare.]

in·cō·in′ci·dent, *a.* not coincident; not agreeing in time, place, or principle.

in·cō·lū′mi·ty, *n.* safety; security. [Obs.]

in·cŏm′bẽr, *v.t.* to encumber. [Obs.]

in·cŏm·bīn′ing, *a.* not combining or uniting; disagreeing; differing. [Obs.]

in·cŏm·bus·ti·bil′i·ty, *n.* the quality of being incombustible.

in·cŏm·bus′ti·ble, *a.* not combustible; that cannot be burned; fireproof.

in·cŏm·bus′ti·ble, *n.* an incombustible substance.

in·cŏm·bus′ti·ble·ness, *n.* incombustibility; the state of being incombustible.

in·cŏm·bus′ti·bly, *adv.* so as to resist combustion.

in′cŏme, *n.* [ME. *income*; AS. *in*, in, and *cuman*, to come.]

1. a coming in.

2. money periodically received for labor or services; also, money received from the rental of property, the proceeds of business, the profits of commerce, interest on loans, etc.; revenue.

3. in physiology, food taken into the body.

income tax; a tax upon a persons' income, especially on income over and above a specified sum.

in′cŏm·ẽr, *n.* a person or thing that comes in or follows another.

in′cŏm·ing, *a.* 1. coming in; filling up: opposed to *outgoing.*

2. taking possession or coming into a firm or company, as a new tenant or a new member.

3. being next in turn; ensuing. [Scot.]

in′cŏm·ing, *n.* 1. a coming in; as, the *incoming* of a train.

2. whatever comes in; as, the ***incoming*** exceeds the outgoing.

in·com′i·ty, *n.* lack of courtesy, civility, or good manners. [Rare.]

in″cŏm·men″sụ·rȧ·bil′i·ty (-shụ-), *n.* the quality or state of being incommensurable.

in·cŏm·men′sụ·rȧ·ble, *a.* 1. that cannot be measured or compared by the same standard or measure; without a common standard of comparison; as, coins and trees are *incommensurable.*

2. not worthy of comparison.

3. having no common divisor: said of two or more numbers or quantities.

in·cŏm·men′sụ·rȧ·ble, *n.* an incommensurable thing, quantity, etc.

in·cŏm·men′sụ·rȧ·ble·ness, *n.* the state of being incommensurable.

in·cŏm·men′sụ·rȧ·bly, *adv.* 1. in an incommensurable manner.

2. to an incommensurable degree.

in·cŏm·men′sụ·rāte, *a.* not commensurate; specifically, (a) not equal in measure or size; (b) not proportionate; not adequate; as, his ability is *incommensurate* to his work; (c) that cannot be measured or compared by the same standard or measure; incommensurable.

in·cŏm·men′sụ·rāte·ly, *adv.* not in equal or due measure or proportion.

in·cŏm·men′sụ·rāte·ness, *n.* the condition or quality of being incommensurate.

in·cŏm·mis′ci·ble, *a.* [LL. *incommiscibilis*; L. *in-* priv., and LL. *commiscibilis*, mixable, from L. *commiscere*, to mix.] that cannot be mixed. [Rare.]

in·cŏm·mix′tūre, *n.* a state of being unmixed. [Obs.]

in·com′mō·dāte, *v.t.* to incommode. [Obs.]

in·com·mō·dā′tion, *n.* the state of being incommodated. [Obs.]

in·cŏm·mōde′, *v.t.*; incommoded, *pt., pp.*; incommoding, *ppr.* [Fr. *incommoder*; L. *incommodare*, to inconvenience, from *incommodus*, inconvenient; *in-* priv., and *commodus*, convenient.] to inconvenience; to give trouble to; to put out or bother.

in·cŏm·mōde′, *a.* troublesome; inconvenient. [Obs.]

in·cŏm·mōde′, *n.* anything that is troublesome or inconvenient. [Obs.]

in·cŏm·mōde′ment, *n.* inconvenience. [Obs.]

in·cŏm·mō′di·ous, *a.* 1. causing inconvenience; uncomfortable; troublesome.

2. inconveniently small, narrow, etc.

in·cŏm·mō′di·ous·ly, *adv.* in a manner to create inconvenience; inconveniently; unsuitably.

in·cŏm·mō′di·ous·ness, *n.* inconvenience; unsuitableness.

in·cŏm·mod′i·ty, *n.* inconvenience; trouble.

in·cŏm·mū″ni·cȧ·bil′i·ty, *n.* the quality of not being communicable.

in·cŏm·mū′ni·cȧ·ble, *a.* [LL. *incommunicabilis*; L. *in-* priv., and *communicare*, to communicate.] that cannot be communicated or told.

in·cŏm·mū′ni·cȧ·ble·ness, *n.* incommunicability.

in·cŏm·mū′ni·cȧ·bly, *adv.* in an incommunicable manner.

in·cŏm·mū·ni·cä′dō, *a.* [Sp.] unable or not

allowed to communicate; cut off from means of communication; as, the prisoners were held *incommunicado*.

in·çŏm·mū'ni·çā·ted, *a.* not imparted. [Obs.]

in·çŏm·mū'ni·çā·ting, *a.* having no communion with each other. [Obs.]

in·çŏm·mū'ni·çā·tive, *a.* not communicative; not inclined to talk; reserved; reticent.

in·çŏm·mū'ni·çȧ·tive·ly, *adv.* not communicatively.

in·çŏm·mū'ni·çȧ·tive·ness, *n.* the quality of being incommunicative.

in·çŏm·mūt·ȧ·bil'i·ty, *n.* the quality of being incommutable.

in·çŏm·mūt'ȧ·ble, *a.* [L. *incommutabilis*; *in-* priv., and *commutabilis*, changeable.] not to be exchanged or commuted with another.

in·çŏm·mūt'ȧ·ble·ness, *n.* incommutability.

in·çŏm·mūt'ȧ·bly, *adv.* in an incommutable manner.

in·çŏm·paçt', in·çŏm·paçt'ed, *a.* not compact; not having the parts firmly united; not solid.

in·çom''pȧ·rȧ·bil'i·ty, *n.* the quality or state of being incomparable.

in·çom'pȧ·rȧ·ble, *a.* [L. *incomparabilis*, that cannot be equaled; *in-* priv., and *comparabilis*, comparable.] that admits of no comparison with others; specifically, (a) having no basis of comparison; having no characteristics in common; incommensurable; (b) beyond comparison; unequaled; matchless; peerless.

Her words do show her wit *incomparable*. —Shak.

in·çom'pȧ·rȧ·ble·ness, *n.* the quality or state of being incomparable.

in·çom'pȧ·rȧ·bly, *adv.* beyond comparison; in an incomparable manner.

in·çŏm·pāred', *a.* not matched; peerless. [Obs.]

in·çŏm'pȧss, *v.t.* same as *encompass*.

in·çŏm·pas'sion (-pash'un), *n.* lack of compassion. [Obs.]

in·çŏm·pas'sion·āte, *a.* lacking compassion or pity. [Rare.]

in·çŏm·pas'sion·āte·ly, *adv.* without pity or tenderness. [Rare.]

in·çŏm·pas'sion·āte·ness, *n.* lack of pity. [Rare.]

in·çŏm·pat·i·bil'i·ty, *n.* 1. inconsistency; the quality or state of being incompatible; as, there is a permanent *incompatibility* between truth and falsehood.

2. *pl.* **in·çŏm·pat·i·bil'i·tieṣ,** something incompatible.

in·çŏm·pat'i·ble, *a.* 1. inconsistent; that cannot subsist with something else; as, truth and falsehood are essentially *incompatible*.

2. irreconcilably different or disagreeing; incongruous; as, *incompatible* tempers.

3. legally or constitutionally inconsistent; that cannot be united in the same person without violating the law or constitution; as, the offices of a legislator and of a judge are *incompatible*, as they cannot be held at the same time by the same person.

4. in medicine and pharmacy, not suitable for being mixed or used together: said of substances having an undesirable action on each other or on the body.

incompatible terms; in logic, terms which do not admit of combination in thought, as in the phrase "thunderous silence."

in·çŏm·pat'i·ble, *n.* [*usually in pl.*] an incompatible person or thing.

in·çŏm·pat'i·ble·ness, *n.* the quality or state of being incompatible; incompatibility.

in·çŏm·pat'i·bly, *adv.* inconsistently; incongruously.

in·çom'pē·tence, *n.* the quality, state, or fact of being incompetent.

in·çom'pē·ten·cy, *n.* same as *incompetence*.

in·çom'pē·tent, *a.* [LL. *incompetens* (*-entis*), insufficient; *in-* priv., and *competens*, able, sufficient, competent.]

1. without adequate ability, knowledge, fitness, etc.; failing to meet requirements; incapable; unskillful.

2. not legally qualified.

Syn.—disqualified, inefficient, unsuited, unfit, unable, incapable.—*Incompetent* denotes a lack of the requisite qualifications for performing a given act; *incapable* denotes a general lack of ability or power.

in·çom'pē·tent, *n.* an incompetent person; especially, one who is mentally deficient.

in·çom'pē·tent·ly, *adv.* insufficiently; inadequately; not suitably; in an incompetent manner.

in·çŏm·pet·i·bil'i·ty, *n.* incompatibility. [Obs.]

in·çŏm·pet'i·ble, *a.* incompatible. [Obs.]

in·çŏm·plēte', *a.* [LL. *incompletus*; L. *in-* priv., and *completus*, complete.]

1. lacking a part or parts; not whole; not full.

2. not finished; as, the building is *incomplete*.

3. imperfect; not thorough.

4. in botany, lacking any of the floral parts, as the calyx, corolla, stamens, or pistils.

5. designating or of a chemical reaction that is reversible.

in·çŏm·plēte'ly, *adv.* in an unfinished manner; not completely.

in·çŏm·plēte'ness, *n.* an unfinished state; the lack of completeness.

in·çŏm·plē'tion, *n.* the state of being incomplete.

in·çŏm'plex', *a.* not complex; uncompounded; simple.

in·çŏm·plī'ȧ·ble, *a.* not compliable. [Obs.]

in·çŏm·plī'ănce, *n.* refusal to comply; noncompliance; untractableness.

in·çŏm·plī'ăn·cy, *n.* same as *incompliance*.

in·çŏm·plī'ănt, *a.* unyielding; not compliant or pliant.

in·çŏm·plī'ănt·ly, *adv.* not compliantly.

in·çŏm·pōṣed', *a.* disordered; disturbed. [Obs.]

in·çŏm·pōṣ'ed·ly, *adv.* not composedly. [Obs.]

in·çŏm·pōṣ'ed·ness, *n.* lack of composure. [Obs.]

in·çŏm·poṣ'ite, *a.* [L. *incompositus*, not well put together; *in-* priv., and *compositus*, pp. of *componere*, to put together.] uncompounded; simple; not composite.

in·çŏm·pos·si·bil'i·ty, *n.* the quality of being incompossible. [Rare.]

in·çŏm·pos'si·ble, *a.* not possible to be or subsist with something else. [Rare.]

in·çom·prē·hense', *a.* not to be comprehended. [Obs.]

in·çom·prē·hen·si·bil'i·ty, *n.* [LL. *incomprehensibilitas*, from L. *incomprehensibilis*, that may not be laid hold of, incomprehensible.] the quality of being incomprehensible.

in·çom·prē·hen'si·ble, *a.* [ME. *incomprehensibele*; OFr. *incomprehensible*; L. *incomprehensibilis*, that cannot be seized, taken, or comprehended; *in-* priv., and *comprehensibilis*, comprehensible.]

1. that cannot be understood; unintelligible; not comprehensible.

2. illimitable. [Archaic.]

in·çom·prē·hen'si·ble·ness, *n.* incomprehensibility.

in·çom·prē·hen'si·bly, *adv.* in a manner which the mind cannot comprehend or understand; inconcievably.

in·çom·prē·hen'sion, *n.* lack of comprehension or understanding.

in·çom·prē·hen'sive, *a.* 1. not comprehensive; understanding little.

2. not broadly inclusive; restricted.

in·çom·prē·hen'sive·ly, *adv.* in an incomprehensive manner.

in·çom·prē·hen'sive·ness, *n.* that quality which makes a thing incomprehensible.

in·çŏm·press·i·bil'i·ty, *n.* the quality or state of being incompressible.

in·çŏm·press'i·ble, *a.* not to be compressed; resisting compression.

in·çŏm·press'i·ble·ness, *n.* that quality which makes an object incompressible.

in·çŏm·pūt·ȧ·bil'i·ty, *n.* the quality of being incomputable.

in·çŏm·pūt'ȧ·ble, *a.* that cannot be computed.

in·çon·çēal'ȧ·ble, *a.* not concealable; not to be kept secret or out of sight.

in·çon·çēiv·ȧ·bil'i·ty, *n.* the quality of being inconceivable.

in·çon·çēiv'ȧ·ble, *a.* that cannot be conceived; that cannot be thought of, understood, imagined, or believed.

in·çon·çēiv'ȧ·ble·ness, *n.* the quality of being inconceivable; incomprehensibility.

in·çon·çēiv'ȧ·bly, *adv.* 1. in an inconceivable manner.

2. to an inconceivable degree.

in·çon·çep'ti·ble, *a.* inconceivable. [Rare.]

in·çon·çẽrn'ing, *a.* trivial; of little importance. [Obs.]

in·çŏn·cinn', in·çŏn·cinne', *a.* inconcinnous. [Obs.]

in·çŏn·cin'ni·ty, *n.* [L. *inconcinnitas*, inelegance, from *inconcinnus*, inelegant; *in-* priv., and *concinnus*, elegant, graceful.] unsuitableness; lack of proportion.

in·çŏn·cin'nous, *a.* incongruous; unsuitable; disagreeing; not to be reconciled. [Obs.]

in·çon·çlūd'ent, *a.* without a conclusion or consequence. [Obs.]

in·çon·çlūd'ing, *a.* inferring no consequence. [Obs.]

in·çon·çlū'sive, *a.* not closing, concluding, or settling a point in debate, or a doubtful question; not decisive; not final; ineffective; as, *inconclusive* evidence.

in·çon·çlū'sive·ly, *adv.* in an inconclusive manner.

in·çon·çlū'sive·ness, *n.* the state or quality of being inconclusive.

in·çon·çoçt', *a.* inconcocted. [Obs.]

in·çon·çoçt'ed, *a.* not fully digested; not matured; unripened. [Obs.]

in·çon·çoç'tion, *n.* the state of being indigested; unripeness; immaturity. [Obs.]

in·çon'çrēte, *a.* [LL. *inconcretus*, not concrete; L. *in-* priv., and *concretus*, concrete.] lacking concrete characteristics. [Rare.]

in·çon·çũr'ring, *a.* not concurring; not agreeing. [Rare.]

in·çon·çus'si·ble, *a.* [L. *in-* priv., and LL. *concussibilis*, that can be shaken, from L. *concussus*, pp. of *concutere*, to shake.] that cannot be shaken. [Obs.]

in·çon·den·sȧ·bil'i·ty, in·çon·den·si·bil'i·ty, *n.* the quality of being incondensable.

in·çon·den'sȧ·ble, in·çon·den'si·ble, *a.* not capable of condensation; that cannot be condensed.

in·çon'dite, *a.* [L. *inconditus*, without order, irregular; *in-* priv., and *conditus*, put together.]

1. poorly constructed: said of literary works.

2. lacking finish or refinement; unpolished; crude.

in·çon·di'tion·ăl, *a.* without any condition, exception, or limitation; absolute. [Obs.]

in·çon·di'tion·āte, *a.* not limited or restrained by conditions; absolute.

in·çon·fọrm', *a.* that will not conform. [Obs.]

in·çon·fọrm'ȧ·ble, *a.* not conformable.

in·çon·fọrm'i·ty, *n.* lack of conformity; nonconformity.

in·çon·fūṣed', *a.* not confused; distinct. [Rare.]

in·çon·fū'ṣion, *n.* distinctness; lack of confusion. [Obs.]

in·çon·fūt'ȧ·ble, *a.* that cannot be confuted. [Obs.]

in·çon·fūt'ȧ·bly, *adv.* unanswerably. [Obs.]

in·çon·ġēal'ȧ·ble, *a.* not congealable. [Rare.]

in·çon·ġēal'ȧ·ble·ness, *n.* the quality of being incongealable. [Rare.]

in·çon·ġēn'iăl, *a.* not congenial; not of a like nature; unsuitable.

in·çon·ġē·ni·al'i·ty, *n.* unlikeness of nature; unsuitableness.

in·çoñ'grụ·ence, *n.* [LL. *incongruentia*, inconsistency, from L. *incongruens* (*-entis*), inconsistent; *in-* priv., and *congruens*, consistent.] lack of congruence or agreement; incongruity.

in·çoñ'grụ·ent, *a.* 1. not congruent; unsuitable; incongruous.

2. in anatomy, not agreeing in conformation; as, *incongruent* surfaces in a joint.

in·çoñ·grụ'i·ty, *n.* [ML. *incongruitas*, from L. *incongruus*.]

1. the condition, quality, or fact of being incongruous; specifically, (a) lack of harmony or agreement; (b) lack of fitness or appropriateness.

2. *pl.* **in·çoñ·grụ'i·tieṣ,** something incongruous.

in·çoñ'grụ·ous, *a.* [L. *incongruus*, inconsistent; *in-* priv., and *congruus*, consistent.] not congruous; not congruent; specifically, (a) lacking harmony or agreement; incompatible; (b) having inconsistent or inharmonious parts, elements, etc.; (c) not corresponding to what is right, proper, or reasonable; unsuitable; inappropriate.

Syn.—inconsistent, inappropriate, incompatible, unsuitable, disagreeing, inharmonious.

in·çoñ'grụ·ous·ly, *adv.* in an incongruous manner.

in·çoñ'grụ·ous·ness, *n.* the state or quality of being incongruous.

in·çon·neçt'ed, *a.* without connection. [Rare.]

in·çon·neç'tion, *n.* lack of connection; loose, disjointed state. [Obs.]

in·çon·nex'ed·ly, *adv.* without connection. [Obs.]

in·çon·nū' (*or Fr. pron.* aṅ-kọn-nū'), *n.* [Fr., unknown.] the salmon of the Mackenzie River, *Stenodus mackenzii*.

in·çon'scion·ȧ·ble (-shun-), *a.* having no sense of good and evil; unconscionable. [Obs.]

in·çon'scious (-shus), *a.* unconscious. [Rare.]

in·çon·seç'ū·tive, *a.* not consecutive.

fāte, fär, fȧst, fạll, finăl, cãre, at; mēte, prey, hẽr, met; pīne, marine, bïrd, pin; nōte, mŏve, fọr, atŏm, not; mọọn, book;

in·çon·seç'ū·tive·ness, *n.* the state of not succeeding in regular order.

in·çon'sē·quence, *n.* [L. *inconsequentia*, from *inconsequens* (*-entis*), inconsequent.] quality or instance of being inconsequent; lack of logic, logical sequence, or relevance.

in·çon'sē·quent, *a.* [L. *inconsequens* (*-entis*), not consequent; *in-* priv., and *consequens* (*-entis*), ppr. of *consequi*, to follow after.] not consequent; specifically, (a) not following as a result; (b) not following as a logical inference or conclusion; irrelevant; (c) not proceeding in logical sequence; characterized by lack of logic.

in·çon·sē·quen'tiăl (-shăl), *a.* 1. not regularly following from the premises; inconsequent; illogical.
2. not of consequence; not of importance; of little moment.

in·çon·sē·quen'tiăl, *n.* something inconsequential.

in·çon·sē·quen·ti·al'i·ty (-shi-al'), *n.* state of being inconsequential.

in·çon·sē·quen'tiăl·ly, *adv.* in an inconsequential manner; without regular sequence.

in·çon'sē·quent·ness, *n.* the state or quality of being inconsequent.

in·çon·sid'ẽr·ȧ·ble, *a.* not worthy of consideration or notice; unimportant; small; trivial; as, an *inconsiderable* distance.

in·çon·sid'ẽr·ȧ·ble·ness, *n.* the state or quality of being inconsiderable.

in·çon·sid'ẽr·ȧ·bly, *adv.* 1. in an inconsiderable manner.
2. to an inconsiderable degree.

in·çon·sid'ẽr·ȧ·cy, *n.* thoughtlessness; lack of consideration. [Obs.]

in·çon·sid'ẽr·āte, *a.* [L. *inconsideratus*, not considerate; *in-* priv., and *consideratus*, pp. of *considerare*, to look at carefully, to consider.]
1. insufficiently considered; ill-advised.
2. without thought or consideration for others; thoughtless; heedless.
3. of little importance. [Obs.]

in·çon·sid'ẽr·āte·ly, *adv.* in an inconsiderate manner.

in·çon·sid'ẽr·āte·ness, *n.* the state of being inconsiderate.

in·çon·sid·ẽr·ā'tion, *n.* [LL. *inconsideratio* (*-onis*); L. *in-* priv., and *consideratio* (*-onis*), consideration, from *considerare*, to consider.] lack of due consideration; inattention to consequences; also, an inconsiderate act.

in·çon·sist'ence, *n.* inconsistency.

in·çon·sist'en·cy, *n.* 1. the quality or state of being inconsistent.
2. *pl.* **in·çon·sist'en·cieş,** something inconsistent; an inconsistent act, remark, etc.

in·çon·sist'ent, *a.* not consistent; specifically, (a) lacking agreement in kind, nature, form, etc.; not in harmony or accord; incompatible; as, practice *inconsistent* with belief; (b) not uniform; not holding together; self-contradictory; as, an *inconsistent* narrative; (c) not holding to the same principles or practice; changeable; as, *inconsistent* behavior.
Syn.—incongruous, incompatible, incoherent, disagreeing.—Things are *incongruous* when they are not suited to each other, so that their union is unbecoming; *inconsistent* when they are opposed to each other, so as to render it improper or wrong; *incompatible* when they cannot coexist, and it is therefore impossible to unite them. *Inconsistent* refers either to the actions or sentiments of men; *incongruous* to the modes and qualities of things; *incoherent* to speech or thoughts.

in·çon·sist'ent·ly, *adv.* in an inconsistent manner; incongruously; with self-contradiction; without steadiness or uniformity.

in·çon·sist'ent·ness, *n.* inconsistency. [Obs.]

in·çon·sist'ing, *a.* inconsistent. [Obs.]

in·çon·sōl·ȧ·bil'i·ty, *n.* the condition of being inconsolable.

in·çon·sōl'ȧ·ble, *a.* [L. *inconsolabilis*, inconsolable; *in-* priv., and *consolabilis*, consolable, from *consolari*, to console.] not to be consoled; disconsolate; brokenhearted.
Syn.—cheerless, joyless, spiritless, melancholy, gloomy, disconsolate, comfortless, forlorn, heartsick.

in·çon·sōl'ȧ·ble·ness, *n.* the quality or state of being inconsolable.

in·çon·sōl'ȧ·bly, *adv.* in a manner that does not admit of consolation.

in·çon'sō·nănce, *n.* disagreement of sounds; discordance of any kind.

in·çon'sō·năn·cy, *n.* inconsonance. [Obs.]

in·çon'sō·nănt, *a.* [LL. *inconsonans* (*-antis*), unsuitable; L. *in-* priv., and *consonans* (*-antis*), ppr. of *consonare*, to sound together, to agree.] not consonant; not agreeing; discordant.

in·çon'sō·nănt·ly, *adv.* in an inconsonant manner; discordantly.

in·çon·spiç'ū·ous, *a.* [LL. *inconspicuus*; L. *in-* priv., and *conspicuus*, conspicuous.] not easily discernible; scarcely to be perceived by the sight; not conspicuous; attracting little attention; not striking.

in·çon·spiç'ū·ous·ly, *adv.* in an inconspicuous manner.

in·çon·spiç'ū·ous·ness, *n.* the state of being inconspicuous.

in·çon'stănce, *n.* inconstancy. [Obs.]

in·çon'stăn·cy, *n.* [OFr. *inconstance*; L. *inconstantia*, inconstancy, from *inconstans* (*-antis*), inconstant.] the state or quality of being inconstant; especially, (a) lack of firmness in mind or purpose; (b) unsteadiness or fickleness in affections or loyalties; (c) lack of uniformity in nature, value, etc.; irregularity.

in·çon'stănt, *a.* not constant; changeable; specifically, (a) not remaining firm in mind or purpose; (b) unsteady in affections or loyalties; fickle; (c) not uniform in nature, value, etc.; irregular.
Syn.—changeable, fluctuating, variable, mutable, unsteady, unstable, unsettled, vacillating.

in·çon'stănt·ly, *adv.* in an inconstant manner; not steadily.

in·çon·sūm'ȧ·ble, *a.* not to be consumed; that cannot be consumed.

in·çon·sūm'ȧ·bly, *adv.* so as not to be consumable.

in·çon·sum'māte, *a.* [LL. *inconsummatus*, unfinished; L. *in-* priv., and *consummatus*, pp. of *consummare*, to accomplish, finish.] not consummate; not finished; not complete. [Obs.]

in·çon·sum'māte·ness, *n.* state of being incomplete. [Obs.]

in·çon·sump'ti·ble, *a.* not to be spent, wasted, or destroyed. [Obs.]

in·çon·tam'i·nāte, *a.* [L. *incontaminatus*; *in-* priv., and *contaminatus*, pp. of *contaminare*, to defile, contaminate.] not contaminated.

in·çon·tam'i·nāte·ness, *n.* uncorrupted state.

in·çon·ten·tā'tion, *n.* discontentment. [Obs.]

in·çon·test·ȧ·bil'i·ty, *n.* the quality of being incontestable.

in·çon·test'ȧ·ble, *a.* not contestable; not to be disputed; not admitting debate; too clear to be controverted; incontrovertible; as, *incontestable* evidence, truth, or facts.
Syn.—indisputable, unquestionable, unassailable, impregnable, irrefutable.

in·çon·test'ȧ·ble·ness, *n.* the state or quality of being incontestable.

in·çon·test'ȧ·bly, *adv.* in a manner to preclude debate; indisputably; incontrovertibly; indubitably; certainly.

in·çon·test'ed, *a.* uncontested. [Obs.]

in·çon·tig'ū·ous, *a.* [LL. *incontiguus*, that cannot be touched; L. *in-* priv., and *contiguus*, touching.] not contiguous; not adjoining; not touching; separate. [Obs.]

in·çon·tig'ū·ous·ly, *adv.* not contiguously; separately. [Obs.]

in·çon'ti·nence, *n.* [OFr. *incontinence*; L. *incontinentia*, lack of self-control, from *incontinens* (*-entis*), not containing, intemperate; *in-* priv., and *continere*, to contain.]
1. lack of restraint of the passions or appetites; free or uncontrolled indulgence of the passions or appetites; especially, lack of restraint of the sexual appetite; lewdness.
2. incapability of containing, holding, or keeping something.
3. in medicine, the inability of any of the organs to restrain discharges of their contents, so that the discharges are involuntary; as, *incontinence* of urine.

in·çon'ti·nen·cy, *n.* incontinence.

in·çon'ti·nent, *a.* 1. not restraining the passions or appetites, particularly the sexual appetite; indulging lust without restraint; unchaste; lewd.
2. incapable of containing, holding, keeping, etc.; as, *incontinent* of information.
3. unable to restrain a natural discharge, as of urine, from the body.

in·çon'ti·nent, *n.* one who is unchaste.

in·çon'ti·nent, *adv.* immediately; without delay. [Archaic.]

in·çon'ti·nent·ly, *adv.* 1. in an incontinent manner; without due restraint of the passions or appetites; unchastely.
2. immediately; without delay. [Archaic.]

in·çon·traçt'ed, *a.* not contracted; not shortened. [Obs.]

in·çon·trōl'lȧ·ble, *a.* not to be controlled; that cannot be restrained or governed; uncontrollable.

in·çon·trōl'lȧ·bly, *adv.* in a manner that admits of no control; uncontrollably.

in·çon·trō·vẽr·ti·bil'·ity, *n.* the quality of being incontrovertible.

in·çon·trō·vẽr'ti·ble, *a.* that cannot be controverted; undeniable; indisputable; too clear or certain to admit of dispute.

in·çon·trō·vẽr'ti·ble·ness, *n.* the condition of being incontrovertible.

in·çon·trō·vẽr'ti·bly, *adv.* in a manner that precludes debate or controversy; undeniably.

in·çon·vēn'ience (-yens), *n.* [OFr. *inconvenience*; LL. *inconvenientia*, inconvenience, inconsistency, from L. *inconveniens* (*-entis*), unsuitable, inconvenient.]
1. the quality or state of being inconvenient; lack of comfort, ease, etc.; bother; trouble.
2. anything inconvenient.

in·çon·vēn'ience, *v.t.*; inconvenienced (-yenst), *pt., pp.*; inconveniencing, *ppr.* to cause inconvenience to; to cause trouble or bother to; to incommode.
Syn.—annoy, molest, trouble, disturb, embarrass.

in·çon·vēn'ien·cy, *n.* inconvenience.

in·çon·vēn'ient, *a.* [OFr. *inconvenient*; L. *inconveniens* (*-entis*), unsuitable, inconsistent; *in-* priv., and *conveniens* (*-entis*), ppr. of *convenire*, to come together, fit, accord.] not convenient; specifically, (a) not favorable to one's comfort; difficult to do, use, or get to; causing trouble, bother, work, etc.; unhandy; (b) [Obs.] not appropriate.

in·çon·vēn'ient·ly, *adv.* not conveniently; unsuitably; incommodiously; in a manner to give trouble; unseasonably.

in·çon·vẽrs'ȧ·ble, *a.* not inclined to free conversation; incommunicative; unsocial; reserved. [Rare.]

in·çon'vẽr·sănt, *a.* not conversant; not familiar; not versed. [Rare.]

in·çon·vẽrt'ed, *a.* not converted. [Rare.]

in·çon·vẽrt·i·bil'i·ty, *n.* the quality or condition of being inconvertible.

in·çon·vẽrt'i·ble, *a.* [LL. *inconvertibilis*; L. *in-* priv., and LL. *convertibilis*, convertible, from L. *convertere*, to turn about, change.] not convertible; that cannot be changed into or exchanged for something else; as, some paper money is *inconvertible* into silver or gold.

in·çon·vẽrt'i·ble·ness, *n.* the state of being inconvertible.

in·çon·vẽrt'i·bly, *adv.* in an inconvertible manner.

in·çon·vin'ci·ble, *a.* not convincible; that cannot be convinced; not capable of conviction.

in·çon·vin'ci·bly, *adv.* in a manner not admitting of convincing; so as to be inconvincible.

in·çōn'y, *a.* rare, pretty, nice. [Obs.]

in·çō·ọr'di·nāte, *a.* not co-ordinate.

in·çō·ọr·di·nā'tion, *n.* lack of co-ordination.
in-co-ordination of muscular movement; in physiology, irregularity of movement, caused by loss of voluntary control.

in·çor'ō·nāte, *a.* [L. *in*, on, and *coronare*, to crown, from *corona*, a crown.] invested with a crown.

in·çọr'pō·rȧ·ble, *a.* that can be incorporated.

in·çọr'pō·răl, *a.* not consisting of matter or body; immaterial. [Obs.]

in·çọr·pō·ral'i·ty, *n.* the quality of being incorporeal; immateriality. [Obs.]

in·çọr'pō·răl·ly, *adv.* without matter or a body; immaterially. [Obs.]

in·çọr'pō·rāte, *a.* [L. *in-* priv., and *corporatus*, pp. of *corporare*, to form into a body, from *corpus*, a body.]
1. not consisting of matter; not having a material body; incorporeal.
2. not incorporated; not having the character of a corporate body. [Rare.]

in·çọr'pō·rāte, *a.* [L. *incorporatus*, pp. of *incorporare*, to unite in a body, embody; *in*, in, and *corporare*, to form into a body, from *corpus*, a body.]
1. formed or combined into one body or unit; intimately united, joined, or blended.
2. formed into, or combined as part of, a corporation; incorporated.

in·çọr'pō·rāte, *v.t.*; incorporated, *pt., pp.*; incorporating, *ppr.* 1. to combine or join with something already formed; to make part of another thing; to include; embody.

2. to bring together in a single whole; to mix or combine completely; to merge.
3. to admit into a corporation or association as a member.
4. to form (individuals or units) into a legally organized group that acts as one individual; to form into a corporation.
5. to give substantial, material, or physical form to.

in·çor′pō·rāte, *v.i.* to unite or combine into one group or substance; to be mixed, merged, or blended; to form a corporation: usually followed by *with*; as, paints *incorporate with* oil.

in·çor′pō·rā·ted, *a.* 1. combined or united.
2. organized as a legal corporation; as, an *incorporated* town.

in·çor·pō·rā′tion, *n.* [OFr. *incorporation*; LL. *incorporatio* (*-onis*), an incorporating, embodying, from *L. incorporare*, to embody, incorporate.]
1. the act of incorporating or state of being incorporated.
2. a corporation.

in·çor′pō·rā·tive, *a.* characterized by incorporation; having the capacity and tendency to incorporate.

in·çor′pō·rā·tŏr, *n.* 1. a person who incorporates.
2. any of the original members of a corporation, whose names appear in its charter.

in·çor·pō′rē·ăl, *a.* [L. *incorporeus*, without a body; *in-* priv., and *corporeus*, corporeal, from *corpus*, a body.]
1. not consisting of matter; not having a material body or substance; immaterial.
2. of spirits or angels.
3. in law, without physical existence in itself but belonging as a right to a material thing or property, as a patent, copyright, etc.
incorporeal hereditament; see under *hereditament*.

in·çor·pō′rē·ăl·işm, *n.* 1. belief in an incorporeal existence.
2. incorporeal existence; immateriality.

in·çor·pō′rē·ăl·ist, *n.* a believer in an incorporeal existence.

in·çor·pō·rē·al′i·ty, *n.* immateriality; incorporealism.

in·çor·pō′rē·ăl·ly, *adv.* without body; immaterially.

in·çor·pō·rē′i·ty, *n.* 1. the quality or state of being incorporeal; immateriality.
2. *pl.* **in·çor·pō·rē′i·tieş,** an incorporeal entity or attribute.

in·çorpse′, *v.t.* to incorporate. [Obs.]

in·çŏr·reçt′, *a.* [L. *incorrectus*, uncorrected, unimproved; *in-* priv., and *correctus*, pp. of *corrigere*, to correct, improve.]
1. not correct; not exact; not according to a copy or model, or to established rules; untrue; wrong; inaccurate; faulty.
2. not according to law or morality; improper.

in·çŏr·reç′tion, *n.* lack of correction. [Obs.]

in·çŏr·reçt′ly, *adv.* in an incorrect manner; not in accordance with truth or other standard; inaccurately; not exactly; as, a writing *incorrectly* copied; testimony *incorrectly* stated.

in·çŏr·reçt′ness, *n.* lack of conformity to truth or to a standard; inaccuracy.

in·çor·re·spond′ence, *n.* failure to correspond; want of agreement. [Rare.]

in·çor·re·spond′en·cy, *n.* incorrespondence. [Rare.]

in·çor·re·spond′ing, *a.* not corresponding. [Rare.]

in·çor″ri·ġi·bil′i·ty, *n.* the quality of being incorrigible.

in·çor′ri·ġi·ble, *a.* [LL. *incorrigibilis*, from L. *in-* priv., and LL. *corrigibilis*, corrigible, from L. *corrigere*, to correct.] not capable of correction, improvement, or amendment, especially because firmly established, as a bad habit; not to be reformed or redeemed; as, *incorrigible* drunkards.

in·çor′ri·ġi·ble, *n.* one who is bad beyond hope of correction or reform.

in·çor′ri·ġi·ble·ness, *n.* incorrigibility.

in·çor′ri·ġi·bly, *adv.* in an incorrigible manner; so as to be incorrigible.

in·çŏr·rōd′i·ble, *a.* that cannot be corroded.

in·çŏr·rupt′, *a.* [L. *incorruptus*, uninjured; *in-* priv., and *corruptus*, pp. of *corrumpere*, to break up, destroy, corrupt.] not corrupt; specifically, (a) not marred, impaired, or spoiled; (b) morally sound; not defiled, evil, impure, perverted, or depraved; (c) upright; honest; above the power of bribes; (d) containing no errors, alterations, or foreign admixtures: said of languages, texts, etc.

in·çŏr·rupt′ed, *a.* incorrupt. [Obs.]

in·çŏr·rupt·i·bil′i·ty, *n.* the state or quality of being incorruptible.

in·çŏr·rupt′i·ble, *a.* [ME. *incorruptible*; OFr. *incorruptible*; LL. *incorruptibilis*, incorruptible; L. *in-* priv., and LL. *corruptibilis*, corruptible, from L. *corrumpere*, to destroy, corrupt.]
1. that cannot corrupt or decay; not admitting of corruption or destruction.

> Our bodies shall be changed into *incorruptible* and immortal substances. —Wake.

2. that cannot be bribed; inflexibly just and upright.

In·çŏr·rupt′i·ble, *n.* a member of a religious sect in the sixth century, which held the doctrine that Christ suffered only in appearance, as his body was incorruptible and therefore could not feel hunger, distress, or pain.

in·çŏr·rupt′i·ble·ness, *n.* the quality of being incorruptible.

in·çŏr·rupt′i·bly, *adv.* in an incorruptible manner; so as not to admit of corruption or decay.

in·çŏr·rup′tion, *n.* [LL. *incorruptio* (*-onis*), from L. *incorruptus*, not corrupt; *in-* priv., and *corruptus*, pp. of *corrumpere*, to destroy, corrupt.] incapability of being corrupt or corrupted. [Archaic.]

> It is sown in corruption; it is raised in *incorruption*. —1 Cor. xv. 42.

in·çŏr·rupt′ive, *a.* not liable to corruption or decay. [Obs.]

in·çŏr·rupt′ly, *adv.* in an incorrupt manner; purely; without yielding to corrupt influence.

in·çŏr·rupt′ness, *n.* 1. exemption from decay, error, or corruption.
2. purity of mind or manners; probity; integrity; honesty.

in·çras′sāte, *v.t.*; incrassated, *pt.*, *pp.*; incrassating, *ppr.* [LL. *incrassatus*, pp. of *incrassare*, to make thick; L. *in*, in, and *crassare*, to thicken, from *crassus*, thick.]
1. to make thick or thicker; to thicken.
2. in pharmacy, to make (fluids) thicker by the mixture of other substances less fluid, or by evaporation.

in·çras′sāte, *v.i.* to become thick or thicker.

> Acids dissolve or attenuate; alkalis precipitate or *incrassate*.

in·çras′sāte, *a.* 1. in botany and zoology, thickened or becoming thicker.
2. gradually swelling out toward the tip: said of the antennae of insects.

in·çras′sā·ted, *a.* made thick or thicker; incrassate.

in·çras·sā′tion, *n.* 1. the act of thickening or the state of becoming thick or thicker.
2. a thickened growth or formation.

in·çras′sȧ·tive, *a.* having the quality of thickening.

in·çras′sȧ·tive, *n.* that which has the power to thicken.

in·çrēas′ȧ·ble, *a.* that can be increased.

in·çrēas′ȧ·ble·ness, *n.* the state or condition of being increasable.

in·çrēase′, *v.i.*; increased, *pt.*, *pp.*; increasing, *ppr.* [ME. *increassen*; OFr. *encreistre*; L. *increscere*, to increase; *in*, in, on, and *crescere*, to grow.]
1. to become greater in size, quantity, value, degree, etc.; to grow; to augment; as, plants *increase* in size by growing; property *increases* in value.
2. to become greater in numbers by producing offspring; to multiply.

Syn.—enlarge, swell, heighten, dilate, enhance, augment, grow, expand, spread.—*Enlarge* implies a widening of extent; *increase*, an accession in point of size, number, strength, etc.

in·çrēase′, *v.t.* to augment or make greater in size, quantity, number, value, degree, etc.; as, to *increase* wealth; to *increase* value.

in′çrēase, *n.* 1. an increasing or becoming increased; multiplication, as of offspring; augmentation; a growing larger in extent, quantity, number, or value.

> Of the *increase* of his government and peace, there shall be no end. —Isa. ix. 7.

2. the result or amount of increasing or augmentation; that which is added to the original stock; as, the population showed an *increase* of 10 per cent.
3. progeny; issue; offspring.

> All the *increase* of thine house shall die in the flower of their age. —1 Sam. ii. 33.

4. generation. [Obs.]
5. the waxing, as of the moon. [Obs.]

> Seeds, hair, nails, hedges, and herbs will grow soonest, if set or cut in the *increase* of the moon. —Bacon.

on the increase; increasing.

Syn.—addition, accession, augmentation, gain, accretion, enlargement, increment, extension, growth.

in·çrēase′fụl, *a.* abundant in produce. [Rare.]

in·çrēase′ment, *n.* the act or fact of increasing; increase. [Rare.]

in·çrēas′ẽr, *n.* one who or that which increases.

in′çrēase twist, same as *gaining twist*.

in·çrēas′ing·ly, *adv.* more and more; to an ever-increasing degree.

in·çrē·āte′, *v.t.* to create within. [Rare.]

in′çrē·āte, in′çrē·ā·ted, *a.* uncreated; existing eternally; as, a divine being is considered to be *increate*.

in·çred·i·bil′i·ty, *n.* the quality of surpassing belief; also, anything too extraordinary to admit of belief.

in·çred′i·ble, *a.* [L. *incredibilis*; *in-* priv., and *credibilis*, credible, from *credere*, to believe.] that cannot be believed; not to be credited; too extraordinary and improbable to admit of belief.

> Why should it be thought a thing *incredible* with you, that God should raise the dead? —Acts xxvi. 8.

Syn.—unbelievable, fabulous, mythical.

in·çred′i·ble·ness, *n.* incredibility.

in·çred′i·bly, *adv.* in a manner to preclude belief.

in·çred′it·ed, *a.* not believed. [Obs.]

in·çrē·dū′li·ty, *n.* [L. *incredulitas* (*-atis*), from *incredulus*, unbelieving; *in-* priv., and *credulus*, believing.] unwillingness or inability to believe; doubt; skepticism.

in·çred′ū·lous, *a.* 1. not believing; indisposed to admit the truth of what is related; refusing or witholding belief; doubting; skeptical.
2. suggesting or showing disbelief; as, an *incredulous* smile.

in·çred′ū·lous·ly, *adv.* in an incredulous manner.

in·çred′ū·lous·ness, *n.* incredulity.

in′çrē·mȧ·ble, *a.* [OFr. *incremable*; L. *in-* priv., and LL. *cremabilis*, combustible, from L. *cremare*, to burn.] that cannot be burnt. [Obs.]

in′çrē·māte, *v.t.* same as *cremate*.

in·çrē·mā′tion, *n.* same as *cremation*.

in′çrē·ment, *n.* [L. *incrementum*, growth, increase, from *increscere*, to increase; *in*, in, on, and *crescere*, to grow.]
1. increase; a growing in bulk, quantity, number, value, or amount; augmentation; growth; gain.
2. produce; production.
3. matter added; amount of increase.
4. in mathematics, the finite increase of a variable quantity.
5. in rhetoric, a climacteric period.
6. in heraldry, the condition of the waxing moon; represented by a crescent.
method of increments; in mathematics, the method of finite differences in contradistinction to that of fluxions: now called *the calculus of finite differences*.

in·çrē·men′tăl, *a.* of or resulting from an increment or increments.

in′çrē·pāte, *v.t.* to chide; to rebuke. [Obs.]

in·çrē·pā′tion, *n.* a chiding or rebuking; rebuke; reprehension. [Obs.]

in·çres′cence, *n.* an increase by successive additions, as in the growing of a plant.

in·çres′cent, *a.* [L. *increscens* (*-entis*), ppr. of *increscere*, to increase; *in*, in, on, and *crescere*, to grow.]
1. increasing; growing; augmenting; swelling.
2. in heraldry, said of the new moon, with its horns pointing toward the dexter side.

THE MOON IN CRESCENT

in·çrest′, *v.t.* to adorn with a crest. [Rare.]

in·çrē′tion, *n.* [*in* and *secretion*.] in physiology, (a) secretion into the body; (b) a substance, as a hormone, internally secreted.

in·çrim′i·nāte, *v.t.*; incriminated, *pt.*, *pp.*; incriminating, *ppr.* [LL. *incriminatus*, pp. of *incriminare*, to accuse of crime; L. *in*, in, on, and *criminare*, to accuse, from *crimen* (*-inis*), a crime.]
1. to charge with a crime; to accuse.
2. to involve in, or make appear guilty of, a crime or fault.

in·çrim·i·nā′tion, *n.* an incriminating or being incriminated.

in·çrim′i·nā·tŏr, *n.* one who incriminates.

in·çrim′i·nȧ·tō·ry, *a.* incriminating or likely to incriminate; as, *incriminatory* testimony.

in·croy·á′ble (aṅ -krwä-yȧ′bl), *n.* [Fr., lit., incredible.] a French dandy of the period of the Directory.

in·crû·en′tăl, *a.* unbloody; not attended with blood. [Obs.]

in·çrust′, *v.t.*; incrusted, *pt., pp.*; incrusting, *ppr.* [OFr. *encrouster*; L. *incrustare*, to cover with a coat or rind; *in*, in, on, and *crusta*, a crust.]

1. to cover with a crust or with a hard coat; to form a crust on the surface of; as, iron *incrusted* with oxide or rust; a vessel *incrusted* with salt.

2. to decorate elaborately, especially with gems.

in·crus′tāte, *v.t.*; incrustated, *pt., pp.*; incrustating, *ppr.* to incrust. [Rare.]

in·crus·tā′tion, *n.* [LL. *incrustatio* (*-onis*), from L. *incrustare*, to incrust.]

1. an incrusting or being incrusted.

2. a crust; hard outer layer or coating.

3. an elaborate decorative coating, inlay, etc.

in·çrust′ment, *n.* incrustation.

in·crys′tăl·lī·zȧ·ble, *a.* that will not crystallize; that cannot be formed into crystals; uncrystallizable.

in′çū·bāte, *v.t.*; incubated, *pt., pp.*; incubating, *ppr.* [L. *incubatus*, pp. of *incubare*, to lie in or upon; *in*, in, on, and *cubare*, to lie.]

1. to sit on and hatch (eggs).

2. to keep (eggs, embryos, bacteria, etc.) in a favorable environment for hatching or developing.

in′çū·bāte, *v.i.* to go through the process of incubation.

in·çū·bā′tion, *n.* [L. *incubatio* (*-onis*), a lying upon eggs, a brooding, from *incubare*, to lie in or upon; *in*, in, on, and *cubare*, to lie, recline.]

1. an incubating or being incubated.

2. the phase in the development of a disease between the infection and the first appearance of symptoms.

in·çū·bā′tion·ăl, *a.* of incubation.

in′çū·bā·tive, *a.* of or characterized by incubation.

in′çū·bā·tŏr, *n.* [LL. *incubator*, one who lies in a place, from L. *incubare*, to lie upon or in.] a person or thing that incubates; specifically, (a) an artificially heated container for hatching eggs; (b) a similar apparatus in which premature babies are kept for a period; (c) an apparatus for developing bacterial cultures.

in·çū′bȧ·tō·ry, *a.* pertaining to the process of incubation or to the means of incubating; as, the *incubatory* pouch of an ascidian.

in·çūbe′, *v.t.* to establish securely, as if set in a cube. [Obs.]

in·çū′bi·tūre, *n.* incubation. [Obs.]

in′çū·bous, *a.* [L. *incubare*, to lie upon.] in botany, having the leaves arranged so that the upper part of each covers the base of the one above.

in′çū·bus, *n.*; *pl.* **in′çū·bus·eṣ** or **in′çū·bī,** [LL., nightmare, a demon supposed to be the cauṣe of nightmare, from L. *incubare*, to lie upon; *in*, in, upon, and *cubare*, to lie.]

1. a spirit or demon thought in medieval times to lie on sleeping persons, especially women, with whom it sought sexual intercourse: see also *succubus*.

2. a nightmare.

3. anything oppressive; a burden.

in′çū·dăl, *a.* in anatomy, relating to or having an incus.

in·çū′dēṣ, *n.* plural of *incus*.

in·cul′çāte, *v.t.*; inculcated, *pt., pp.*; inculcating, *ppr.* [L. *inculcatus*, pp. of *inculcare*, to tread in, tread down; *in*, in, on, and *calcare*, to trample under foot, from *calx, calcis*, heel.] to impress upon the mind by frequent repetition or insistent urging (often with *on* or *upon*).

Syn.—impress, urge, enforce, infuse, instill, implant, press, teach.

in·cul·çā′tion, *n.* an inculcating or being inculcated.

in·cul′çā·tŏr, *n.* one who inculcates.

in·culk′, *v.t.* to inculcate. [Obs.]

in·culp′, *v.t.* to inculpate. [Obs.]

in·cul′pȧ·ble, *a.* [LL. *inculpabilis*, unblamable; L. *in-* priv., and *culpabilis*, blamable, from *culpa*, fault.] not culpable.

in·cul′pȧ·ble·ness, *n.* unblamableness.

in·cul′pȧ·bly, *adv.* unblamably; without blame or fault.

in·cul′pāte, *v.t.*; inculpated, *pt., pp.*; inculpating, *ppr.* [LL. *inculpatus*, pp. of *inculpare*, to blame; L. *in*, in, on, and *culpa*, fault, blame.] to blame; to incriminate.

in·cul·pā′tion, *n.* an inculpating.

in·cul′pȧ·tō·ry, *a.* inculpating or likely to inculpate.

in·cult′, *a.* [L. *incultus*, uncultivated; *in-* priv., and *cultus*, pp. of *colere*, to till, cultivate.]

1. uncultivated: said of land.

2. unrefined.

[Rare in both senses.]

in·cul′ti·vā·ted, *a.* not cultivated; uncultivated. [Obs.]

in·cul·ti·vā′tion, *n.* neglect or lack of cultivation. [Obs.]

in·cul′tūre, *n.* lack or neglect of cultivation. [Obs.]

in·çum′ben·cy, *n.*; *pl.* **in·çum′ben·cieṣ,**

1. the quality or condition of being incumbent.

2. something incumbent; specifically, (a) a duty or obligation; (b) an overlying weight or mass.

3. (a) the holding and administering of a position; especially, the holding of a church benefice; (b) tenure of office.

in·çum′bent, *a.* [L. *incumbens* (*-entis*), ppr. of *incumbere*, to lay oneself upon, recline or rest upon; *in*, on, and *cubare*, to lie down.]

1. lying, resting, or pressing with its weight on something else.

And when to move the *incumbent* load they try. —Addison.

2. in botany, leaning on or resting against; as, *incumbent* stamens or anthers.

3. resting upon as duty or obligation; imposed and emphatically urging or pressing to performance: used with *upon* or *on*; as, the duties *incumbent upon* a minister.

All men, truly zealous, will perform those good works which are *incumbent on* all Christians. —Sprat.

4. in ornithology, said of the hind toe of a bird when it is on a level with the front toes, so that in walking its entire length touches the ground.

5. impending; imminent.

Syn.—pressing, binding, coercive, urgent, devolving, obligatory.

in·çum′bent, *n.* the person who is in present possession of a benefice or of any office.

in·çum′bent·ly, *adv.* in an incumbent manner.

in·çum′bĕr, *v.t.* same as *encumber*.

in·çum·bi′tion (-bish′un), *n.* the act of sitting or lying in close contact. [Obs.]

in·çum′brănce, *n.* same as *encumbrance*.

in·çum′brăn·cĕr, *n.* same as *encumbrancer*.

in·çū·nab′ū·lȧ, *n. pl.*; *sing.* **in·çū·nab′ū·lum,** [L. *incunabula*, neut. pl., swaddling-clothes, a cradle, origin, beginning; *in*, in, and *cunabula*, neut. pl., a cradle, dim. of *cunæ*, f. pl., a cradle.]

1. the very first stages of anything; infancy; beginnings.

2. early printed books; especially, books printed before 1500.

in·çū·nab′ū·lăr, *a.* of incunabula.

in·çûr′, *v.t.*; incurred, *pt., pp.*; incurring, *ppr.* [L. *incurrere*, to run into, or toward, attack; *in*, in, toward, and *currere*, to run.] to come into, acquire, or meet with (something undesirable), especially through one's own actions; to bring upon oneself.

in·çûr′, *v.i.* to fall; enter. [Obs.]

in·çûr·ȧ·bil′i·ty, *n.* the quality or state of being incurable.

in·çûr′ȧ·ble, *a.* [OFr. *incurable*; LL. *incurabilis*, incurable; L. *in-* priv., and LL. *curabilis*, curable, from L. *curare*, to care for, to cure.]

1. that cannot be cured; not admitting of cure; beyond the power of skill or medicine; as, an *incurable* disease.

2. not admitting remedy or correction; irremediable; remediless; as, *incurable* evils.

Syn.—irredeemable, irreparable, immedicable.

in·çûr′ȧ·ble, *n.* a person having an incurable disease or disorder.

in·çûr′ȧ·ble·ness, *n.* the state or quality of being incurable.

in·çûr′ȧ·bly, *adv.* in an incurable manner; without possibility of cure; beyond remedy or correction.

in·çū·ri·os′i·ty, *n.* same as *incuriousness*.

in·çū′ri·ous, *a.* [L. *incuriosus*, careless; *in-* priv., and *curiosus*, careful.]

1. not curious or inquisitive; uninterested; indifferent.

2. not interesting; lacking novelty.

in·çū′ri·ous·ly, *adv.* without inquisitiveness.

in·çū′ri·ous·ness, *n.* want of curiosity or inquisitiveness.

in·çûr′rence, *n.* an incurring; as, the *incurrence* of guilt.

in·çûr′rent, *a.* [L. *incurrens* (*-entis*), ppr. of *incurrere*, to run into or upon; *in*, into, and *currere*, to run.] characterized by a flowing or running into; as, an *incurrent* flow of water into a river or a lagoon.

in·çûr′sion, *n.* [L. *incursio* (*-onis*), from *incurrere*, to run against or into.]

1. a running in or coming in.

2. an unfriendly entry; invasion; raid.

in·çûr′sive, *a.* making an attack or incursion; invasive.

in·çûr′vāte, *v.t.* and *v.i.*; incurvated, *pt., pp.*; incurvating, *ppr.* [L. *incurvatus*, pp. of *incurvare*, to bend in, curve in; *in*, in, and *curvare*, to bend, curve.] to bend or curve inward.

in·çûr′vāte, *a.* bent or curved inward.

in·çûr·vā′tion, *n.* 1. an incurvating or being incurvated.

2. the act of bowing or bending the body in respect or reverence.

in·çûrve′, *v.t.* and *v.i.*; incurved, *pt., pp.*; incurving, *ppr.* to curve inward.

in·çûrve′, *n.* 1. an incurving.

2. in baseball, a pitched ball that curves toward the batter.

in·çûrved′, *a.* bent; curved or bent inward.

in·çûr′vi·ty, *n.* the state or quality of being bent or crooked; crookedness; a bending inward. [Obs.]

iṅ′çus, *n.*; *pl.* **iṅ·çū′dēs,** [L., an anvil, from *incussus*, pp. of *incudere*, to forge, strike upon.]

1. one of the three small bones in the middle ear: so named from its resemblance to the shape of a blacksmith's anvil.

2. the middle part of the mastax of a rotifer.

in·çūṣe′, *a.* [L. *incusus*, pp. of *incudere*, to forge with a hammer, lit., to pound upon; *in-*, in, on, and *cudere*, to strike, hit.] hammered or pressed in: said of the design on a coin, etc.

in·çūṣe′, *n.* an incused design.

in·çūṣe′, *v.t.*; incused, *pt., pp.*; incusing, *ppr.* [L. *incusus*, pp. of *incudere*, see *incuse, a.*] to make an impression in by stamping, as in a coin.

in′çut, *a.* inserted by cutting in: used, in printing, of notes placed in reserved spaces in the text instead of in the margin or at the bottom of the page.

in·çūte′, *v.t.* to incuse. [Obs.]

in·cyst′, *v.t.* and *v.i.* to encyst. [Obs.]

in·cyst′ed, *a.* encysted. [Obs.]

Ind, *n.* [ME. and OFr. *Inde*; L. *India*.]

1. India. [Poet.]

2. the Indies. [Obs.]

in·dä′bȧ, *n.* [Zulu *in-daba*, subject, matter.] a council or conference among South African tribes.

in′dȧ·gāte, *v.t.* [L. *indagatus*, pp. of *indagare*, to seek.] to seek or search out.

in·dȧ·gā′tion, *n.* the act of searching; search; inquiry; investigation.

in′dȧ·gā·tive, *a.* of a searching character; inquiring.

in′dȧ·gā·tŏr, *n.* a searcher; one who seeks or inquires with diligence. [Now Rare.]

in·dam′ăġe, *v.t.* to endamage. [Obs.]

in′dȧ·min, *n.* indamine.

in′dȧ·mīne, *n.* [prob. from *indigo* and *amine*.] any of a group of organic dyes containing the NH group; especially, phenylene blue, $NH{:}C_6H_4{:}N{\cdot}C_6H_4{\cdot}NH_2$.

in·därt′, *v.t.*; indarted, *pt., pp.*; indarting, *ppr.* to dart in; to thrust or strike in.

in′dȧ·zōl, *n.* [*ind*ol, and *az*ote.] a crystalline nitrogenous compound, $C_7H_6N_2$, formed from a diazo-derivative of cinnamic acid by heating.

inde (ind), *a.* sky-blue. [Obs.]

in·dēar′, *v.i.* to endear. [Obs.]

in·debt′ (-det′), *v.t.* [back-formation from *indebted*.] to make indebted or obligated. [Rare.]

in·debt′ed, *a.* [ME. *endetted*, from LL. *indebitatus*, pp. of *indebitare*, to charge with debt; L. *in*, in, and *debitum*, debt.]

1. being in debt; having incurred a debt; legally obliged to repay for something received.

2. obliged by something received for which gratitude is due.

in·debt′ed·ness, *n.* 1. the state or quality of being indebted.

2. the amount owed; all one's debts.

in·debt′ment, *n.* the state of being indebted.

in·dē′cence, *n.* indecency. [Obs.]

in·dē′cen·cy, *n.* [Fr. *indecence*; L. *indecentia*, unbecomingness, indecency; *in-* priv., and *decens* (*-entis*), decent.]

1. the state or quality of being indecent; lacking in modesty; obscenity in speech or in manner.

2. *pl.* **in·dē′cen·cieṣ,** that which is not decent; an indecent act or statement, etc.

in·dē′cent, *a.* [from Fr. or L.; Fr. *indécent*; L. *indecens.*] not decent; specifically, (a) not proper and fitting; unseemly; improper; (b) morally offensive; immodest; obscene.

Syn.—immodest, filthy, obscene, nasty, impure, foul, shameless, indecorous, unchaste, lewd.

in·dē′cent·ly, *adv.* in an indecent manner.

in·dē·cid′ū·āte, *a.* not deciduate; without a decidua.

in·dē·cid′ū·ous, *a.* [L. *in-* priv., and *deciduus*, falling.] not deciduous; evergreen.

in·dec′i·mȧ·ble, *a.* not liable to the payment of tithes. [Obs.]

in·dē·cī″phĕr·ȧ·bil′i·ty, *n.* the quality or state of being indecipherable.

in·dē·cī′phĕr·ȧ·ble, *a.* that cannot be deciphered; illegible.

in·dē·cī′phĕr·ȧ·bly, *adv.* in a manner not decipherable.

in·dē·ci′ṣion, *n.* lack of decision; an inability to decide or a tendency to change the mind frequently; hesitation or vacillation.

in·dē·cī′sive, *a.* 1. not decisive; not bringing to a final close or ultimate issue; as, an *indecisive* battle.

2. characterized by indecision; unsettled; wavering; vacillating; hesitating.

in·dē·cī′sive·ly, *adv.* in an indecisive, wavering manner.

in·dē·cī′sive·ness, *n.* the state or quality of being undecided; unsettled state.

in·dē·çlīn′ȧ·ble, *a.* [L. *indeclinabilis*, unchangeable, indeclinable; *in-* priv., and *declinabilis*, declinable.] not declinable; having no case inflections; as, *pondo*, in Latin, is an *indeclinable* noun.

in·dē·çlīn′ȧ·ble, *n.* an indeclinable word.

in·dē·çlīn′ȧ·bly, *adv.* without variation or change.

in·dē·çom·pōṣ′ȧ·ble, *a.* not capable of decomposition, or of being resolved into the primary constituent elements.

in·dē·çom·pōṣ′ȧ·ble·ness, *n.* the state or quality of being indecomposable.

in·deç′ō·rous (*or* in-dē-kō′), *a.* [LL. *indecorosus*; L. *indecorus*, unbecoming, inappropriate; *in-* priv., *decorus*, seemly, becoming, decorous.] unbecoming; unseemly; lacking decorum, propriety, good taste, etc.

in·deç′ō·rous·ly, *adv.* in an unbecoming manner.

in·deç′ō·rous·ness, *n.* the state or quality of being indecorous.

in·dē·çō′rum, *n.* [L., neut. of *indecorus*, unbecoming, indecorous.]

1. lack of decorum; lack of propriety, good taste, etc.

2. an indecorous act, remark, etc.

in·deed′, *adv.* [ME. *indede*, in deed, in fact.] certainly; truly; admittedly: often used to give emphasis; as, it is *indeed* warm.

in·deed′, *interj.* an exclamation of surprise, bitterness, doubt, sarcasm, etc.

in·dē·fat″i·gȧ·bil′i·ty, *n.* the state or quality of being indefatigable.

in·dē·fat′i·gȧ·ble, *a.* [L. *indefatigabilis*, that cannot be tired out; *in-* priv., and *defatigare*, to tire out, weary.] not defatigable; not easily exhausted.

Upborne with *indefatigable* wings.
—Milton.

Syn.—untiring, unwearied, assiduous, persistent, sedulous, unremitting, persevering.

in·dē·fat′i·gȧ·ble·ness, *n.* indefatigability.

in·dē·fat′i·gȧ·bly, *adv.* in an indefatigable manner.

in·dē·fēa·ṣi·bil′i·ty, *n.* the quality of being indefeasible.

in·dē·fēa′ṣi·ble, *a.* not defeasible; not to be defeated; not to be made void; as, an *indefeasible* estate.

in·dē·fēa′ṣi·ble·ness, *n.* same as *indefeasibility.*

in·dē·fēa′ṣi·bly, *adv.* in an indefeasible manner.

in·dē·feçt·i·bil′i·ty, *n.* the quality of being indefectible.

in·dē·feçt′i·ble, *a.* 1. unfailing; not liable to defect, failure, or decay.

2. without a fault or blemish; perfect.

in·dē·feçt′ive, *a.* not defective.

in·dē·fen·si·bil′i·ty, *n.* the quality or state of being indefensible.

in·dē·fen′si·ble, *a.* not defensible; incapable of being defended, maintained, or justified.

in·dē·fen′si·ble·ness, *n.* indefensibility.

in·dē·fen′si·bly, *adv.* in an indefensible manner; so as to be indefensible.

in·dē·fen′sive, *a.* having no defense. [Obs.]

in·dē·fi′cien·cy (-fish′en-), *n.* the quality of not being deficient. [Obs.]

in·dē·fi′cient, *a.* not deficient. [Obs.]

in·dē·fīn′ȧ·ble, *a.* not definable; incapable of being defined; inexplicable.

in·dē·fīn′ȧ·bly, *adv.* in an indefinable manner.

in·def′i·nite, *a.* [L. *indefinitus*, indefinite; *in-* priv., and *definitus*, pp. of *definere*, to limit, define.] not definite; specifically, (a) having no exact limits; (b) not precise or clear in meaning; vague; (c) not sharp or clear in outline; blurred; indistinct; (d) not certain or positive; unsure; (e) in botany, of no fixed number, or too many to count: said of the stamens, etc. of certain flowers; (f) in grammar, not limiting or specifying; as, *a* and *an* are *indefinite* articles, *any* is an *indefinite* pronoun.

indefinite proposition; in logic, a proposition which has for its subject a common term without any sign to indicate distribution or nondistribution; as, man is mortal.

indefinite term; in logic, a privative or negative term, in respect of its not defining or marking out an object by a positive attribute; as, an unorganized being.

Syn.—unlimited, undefined, indeterminate, inexact, vague, uncertain, indistinct.

in·def′i·nite·ly, *adv.* in an indefinite manner.

in·def′i·nite·ness, *n.* the quality of being indefinite, indefined, unlimited, etc.

in·dē·fin′i·tūde, *n.* indefiniteness.

in·dē·his′cence, *n.* the quality of being indehiscent.

in·dē·his′cent, *a.* not dehiscent; not opening at maturity to discharge its seeds; as, the apple is an *indehiscent* fruit.

in·dē·leç′tȧ·ble, *a.* not delectable; unpleasant; disagreeable.

in·dē·lib′ĕr·āte, *a.* not deliberate; done or performed without deliberation or consideration; sudden; unpremeditated.

in·dē·lib′ĕr·ā·ted, *a.* unpremeditated. [Obs.]

in·dē·lib′ĕr·āte·ly, *adv.* without deliberation or premeditation.

in·dē·lib·ĕr·ā′tion, *n.* lack of deliberation.

in·del·i·bil′i·ty, *n.* the quality of being indelible.

in·del′i·ble, *a.* [L. *indelibilis*, inperishable; *in-* priv., and *delibilis*, perishable, from *delere*, to destroy.]

1. that cannot be blotted out, washed out, obliterated, etc.; lasting; permanent.

2. leaving an indelible mark; as, *indelible* ink.

Syn.—ineffaceable, persistent, permanent.

in·del′i·ble·ness, *n.* the quality of being indelible.

in·del′i·bly, *adv.* so as to be indelible.

in·del′i·çȧ·cy, *n.* 1. the quality of being indelicate.

2. *pl.* **in·del′i·çȧ·cieṣ,** something indelicate.

in·del′i·çāte, *a.* not delicate; especially, lacking, or offensive to, propriety or modesty.

Syn.—impolite, indecorous, unrefined, rude, immodest, unbecoming, coarse.

in·del′i·çāte·ly, *adv.* in an indelicate manner; indecently; unbecomingly.

in·dem″ni·fi·çā′tion, *n.* 1. the act of indemnifying or state of being indemnified.

2. that which indemnifies; recompense.

in·dem′ni·fī·ēr, *n.* a person or company that indemnifies.

in·dem′ni·fȳ, *v.t.*; indemnified, *pt., pp.*; indemnifying, *ppr.* [L. *indemnis*, unhurt, and *facere*, to make.]

1. to protect against or keep free from loss, damage, etc.; to insure.

2. (a) to repay for what has been lost or damaged; to compensate for a loss, etc.; to reimburse; (b) to redeem or make good (a loss).

in·dem·ni·tee′, *n.* a person who receives, or is entitled to, an indemnity.

in·dem′ni·tŏr, *n.* a person who provides indemnity.

in·dem′ni·ty, *n.*; *pl.* **in·dem′ni·tieṣ,** [Fr. *indemnité*; LL. *indemnitas*, security from loss or damage, from L. *indemnis*, unhurt; *in-* priv., and *damnum*, a hurt, damage.]

1. protection or insurance against loss, damage, etc.

2. legal exemption from penalties or liabilities incurred by one's actions.

3. repayment or reimbursement for loss, damage, etc.; compensation.

act of indemnity; an act or decree for the protection or relief of a person, especially a public officer, who, because of having violated the law in some way, is liable to a penalty.

double indemnity; a clause in life insurance policies providing for the payment of twice the face value of the contract in the case of accidental death.

in·dē·mon·strȧ·bil′i·ty, *n.* the condition or quality of being indemonstrable.

in·dē·mon′strȧ·ble, *a.* not demonstrable; that cannot be proved.

in·dē·mon′strȧ·ble·ness, *n.* the state of being indemonstrable.

in′dēne, *n.* [from *indole*, and *-ene.*] a colorless, oily hydrocarbon, C_9H_8, obtained from coal tar.

in·den·i·zā′tion, *n.* endenization. [Obs.]

in·den′īze, *v.t.* to endenize. [Obs.]

in·den′i·zen, *v.t.* to endenizen. [Rare.]

in·dent′, *v.t.*; indented, *pt., pp.*; indenting, *ppr.* [LL. *indentare*, to notch, to make jagged like a row of teeth; L. *in*, in, and *dens, dentis*, a tooth.]

1. (a) to cut toothlike points into (an edge or border); to notch; (b) to make jagged or zigzag in outline.

2. to sever (a written contract, etc.) along an irregular line, so that the parts may be identified.

3. to write out (a contract, etc.) in duplicate.

4. to indenture.

5. (a) to space (the beginning of a paragraph, the edge of a column of figures, etc.) in from the regular margin; (b) to make an indention in (a paragraph, etc.).

6. (a) to request or order goods from; (b) to make an order for (goods).

in·dent′, *v.i.* 1. to form or be marked by notches, points, or a jagged border.

2. to enter into an indenture, or contract.

3. to space in from the margin; to make an indention.

4. to draw up an order or requisition in duplicate.

5. to run or wind in and out; to move in a zigzag course; to double. [Obs.]

in′dent, *n.* 1. a cut or notch in the margin of anything, or a recess like a notch.

2. an indenture, or written contract.

3. a space in from the margin, indention.

4. an indented line, paragraph, etc.

5. an official requisition or order for goods.

in·dent′, *v.t.* [*in-* (in), and *dent* (slight hollow).]

1. to make a dent, or slight hollow, in.

2. to apply (a mark, etc.) with pressure; to impress; to stamp in.

in′dent, *n.* a dent.

in·den·tā′tion, *n.* 1. the act of indenting or the state of being indented.

2. a notch; a cut in the margin of anything.

3. a dent or slight depression.

4. an indention; a space in from a margin.

in·dent′ed, *a.* 1. cut in the edge into points like teeth; notched; as, an *indented* molding.

2. indentured.

3. in heraldry, notched like a saw; serrated.

in·dent′ed·ly, *adv.* by or with indentions.

in·den·tee′, *a.* in heraldry, having indents not joined to each other, but set apart.

INDENTEE BORDER

in·dent′ing, *n.* an impression like that made by a tooth.

in·den′tion, *n.* [*indent* (to cut) or *indent* (to make a dent in), and *-ion.*]

1. a spacing in from the margin.

2. an empty or blank space left by this.

3. (a) a dent, or slight hollow; (b) the making of a dent.

hanging indention; in printing, a uniform indention of every line of a paragraph except the first, which is of full width and overhangs the others.

in·dent′ment, *n.* indenture. [Obs.]

in·den′tūre, *n.* [OFr. *endenture*; LL. *indentura*, an indenture, from *indentare*, to indent; L. *in*, in, toward, and *dens, dentis*, tooth.]

1. the act of indenting or the state of being indented; indentation.

2. in law, a deed or written agreement between two or more parties: indentures were originally in duplicate, laid together and indented or cut in a waving line, so that the two

papers or parchments corresponded to each other.

3. [*usually pl.*] a contract binding one person to work for another for a given length of time, as an apprentice to a master, or an immigrant to service in a colony.

4. an official, authenticated list, inventory, etc.

in·den′tūre, *v.t.*; indentured, *pt., pp.*; indenturing, *ppr.* 1. to bind by indenture; as, to *indenture* an apprentice.

2. to indent.

in·dē·pend′ence, *n.* 1. the state or quality of being independent; freedom from the influence, control, or determination of another or others; self-maintenance or self-government.

> Let fortune do her worst, whatever she makes us lose, as long as she never makes us lose our honesty and our *independence*. —Pope.

2. income sufficient to make one independent of others.

Declaration of Independence; the formal statement, written by Thomas Jefferson and adopted July 4, 1776 by the Second Continental Congress, declaring the thirteen American colonies free and independent of Great Britain: there were fifty-six signers.

Independence Day; the Fourth of July, the anniversary of the adoption of the Declaration of Independence on July 4, 1776: a legal holiday in the United States.

in·dē·pend′en·cy, *n.*; *pl.* **in·dē·pend′en·cieṣ,** 1. independence.

2. an independent nation, province, etc.

in·dē·pend′ent, *a.* [L. *in-* priv., and *dependens* (*-entis*), ppr. of *dependere*, to depend upon, lit., to hang down from.]

1. not dependent; not subject to the control, influence, or determination of another or others; not subordinate.

2. (a) not depending on another for financial support; (b) large enough to enable one to live without working: said of an income, a fortune, etc.; (c) having an independent income; not needing to work for a living.

3. not subject to bias, persuasion, or influence; not obsequious; self-directing; as, a man of an *independent* mind.

4. free; easy; self-commanding; bold; unconstrained; as, an *independent* air or manner.

5. free from the rule of another; controlling or governing oneself; self-governing.

6. not connected or related to another, to each other, or to a group; separate; as, an *independent* grocer.

7. [I–] pertaining to the Independents.

8. not connected with any party or organization; as, an *independent* voter.

9. in mathematics, that does not depend upon another quantity for its value: said of a quantity or function.

independent of; regardless of; apart from.

Syn.—free, separate, unrestricted, exempt, unconstrained, uncontrolled, clear.

in·dē·pend′ent, *n.* 1. a person who is independent in thinking, action, etc.; specifically, [*often* I–] a person not an adherent of any political party; one who votes as he wishes, without regard to party labels.

2. [I–] (a) a person who believes that a local organized Christian church is or should be self-sufficient and not dependent on external ecclesiastical authority; (b) in England, a Congregationalist.

in·dē·pend′ent çlauṣe, in grammar, a main clause.

in·dē·pend′ent·iṣm, *n.* the principles of any independent party.

in·dē·pend′ent·ly, *adv.* in an independent manner.

in·dep′rȧ·vāte, *a.* undepraved. [Obs.]

in·dep·rē·hen′si·ble, *a.* that cannot be found out. [Obs.]

in·dē·prīv′ȧ·ble, *a.* that cannot be deprived.

in′-depth′, *a.* carefully worked out, detailed, profound, thorough, etc.; as, an *in-depth* study.

in·dē·sçrīb·ȧ·bil′i·ty, *n.* the quality or state of being indescribable.

in·dē·sçrīb′ȧ·ble, *a.* that cannot be described; beyond the power of description.

in·dē·sçrīb′ȧ·bly, *adv.* in an indescribable manner.

in·dē·sçrip′tive, *a.* not descriptive. [Rare.]

in·dē·ṣērt′, *n.* lack of merit or worth. [Rare.]

in·des′i·nent, *a.* [L. *in-* priv., and *desinens* (*-entis*), ppr. of *desinere*, to cease.] not ceasing; perpetual. [Obs.]

in·des′i·nent·ly, *adv.* without cessation. [Obs.]

in·dē·ṣir′ȧ·ble, *a.* undesirable. [Obs.]

in·dē·struç·ti·bil′i·ty, *n.* the quality or condition of being indestructible.

in·dē·struç′ti·ble, *a.* not destructible; that cannot be destroyed.

in·dē·struç′ti·ble·ness, *n.* indestructibility.

in·dē·struç′ti·bly, *adv.* so as to be indestructible.

in·dē·tēr′mi·nȧ·ble, *a.* [LL. *indeterminabilis*, that cannot be defined; L. *in-* priv., and LL. *determinabilis*, that can be defined, from L. *determinare*, to define, limit.] not determinable; specifically, (a) that cannot be decided or settled; (b) that cannot be definitely set down or ascertained.

in·dē·tēr′mi·nȧ·ble·ness, *n.* indeterminancy.

in·dē·tēr′mi·nȧ·bly, *adv.* in an indeterminable manner.

in·dē·tēr′mi·nȧ·cy, *n.* the state or quality of being indeterminate.

in·dē·tēr′mi·nāte, *a.* [LL. *indeterminatus*; L. *in-* priv., and *determinatus*, pp. of *determinare*, to define, determine.]

1. not determinate; specifically, (a) having inexact limits; indefinite; indistinct; vague; as, an *indeterminate* result; (b) unsettled; undecided; inconclusive; (c) irresolute.

2. in botany, (a) racemose; (b) having the floral leaves separate and not overlapping in the bud.

indeterminate analysis; a branch of algebra in which there is always given a greater number of unknown quantities than of independent equations, by reason of which the number of solutions is indefinite.

indeterminate coefficients; in mathematics, a method of analysis invented by Descartes, in which the coefficients are arbitrarily assumed for making calculations.

indeterminate problem; in mathematics, a problem which has an infinite number of solutions, or one in which there are fewer imposed conditions than there are unknown or required results.

indeterminate quantity; in mathematics, a quantity which has no fixed value, but which may be varied in accordance with any proposed condition.

indeterminate series; in mathematics, a series whose terms proceed by the powers of an indeterminate quantity.

in·dē·tēr′mi·nāte·ly, *adv.* in an indeterminate manner; indefinitely.

in·dē·tēr′mi·nāte·ness, *n.* indeterminacy.

in·dē·tēr·mi·nā′tion, *n.* 1. the state or quality of being indeterminate.

2. lack of determination.

in·dē·tēr′mined, *a.* undetermined; unsettled; unfixed.

in·dē·tēr′min·iṣm, *n.* the doctrine that the will is to some degree free, or that one's actions and choices are not altogether determined by a sequence of causes independent of his will.

in·dē·tēr′min·ist, *n.* a person who believes in indeterminism.

in·dē·tēr′min·ist, *a.* of indeterminism or indeterminists.

in·dē·tēr″min·is′tiç, *a.* indeterminist.

in·dē·vōte′, *a.* not devout. [Obs.]

in·dē·vōt′ed, *a.* not devoted. [Obs.]

in·dē·vō′tion, *n.* lack of devotion; absence of devout affections.

in·dē·vout′, *a.* irreligious; not having devout affections.

in·dē·vout′ly, *adv.* without devotion.

in′dex, *n.*; *pl.* **in′dex·eṣ, in′di·cēṣ,** [L. *index*, *indicis*, an informer, discoverer, that which points out, a title, index, from *indicare*, to point out, indicate; *in*, in, to, and *dicare*, to declare.]

1. the index finger; forefinger.

2. a pointer or indicator, as the needle on a dial.

3. a thing that points out; indication; sign; representation; as, performance is an *index* of ability.

4. (a) an alphabetical list of names, subjects, etc. together with page numbers, usually placed at the end of a book or other publication; (b) a list describing the items of a collection and where they may be found; catalogue; as, a library *index*.

5. the relation or proportion of one amount or dimension to another.

6. [I–] (a) the *Index Librorum Prohibitorum*; (b) the *Index Expurgatorius*.

7. a table of contents, preface, prologue, or statement of subject. [Obs.]

8. in mathematics, an exponent.

9. in printing, a sign (☛) calling special attention to certain information; fist.

dental index; a number used to indicate the size of teeth: it is the ratio between the distance from basion to nasion and the distance from the anterior surface of the first premolar to the posterior surface of the last molar.

Index Expurgatorius; formerly, a list of books that the Roman Catholic Church forbade its members to read unless certain passages condemned as dangerous to faith, morality, etc. were deleted or changed.

Index Librorum Prohibitorum; a list of books that the Roman Catholic Church condemns and forbids its members to read (except by special permission) as dangerous to faith, morality, etc.

index of a logarithm; the characteristic or integral part of a logarithm, which precedes it and is always one less than the number of integral figures in the given number.

index of refraction; in optics, the ratio of the sine of the angle of incidence to the sine of the angle of refraction when light is transmitted through a refracting substance.

index rerum; an alphabetical index of topics, memoranda, occurrences, etc.

in′dex, *v. t.*; indexed (-dext), *pt., pp.*; indexing, *ppr.* 1. (a) to make an index of or for; (b) to include in an index.

2. to indicate or give a sign of.

in′dex·ēr, *n.* one who makes an index.

in′dex er′rŏr, a constant error arising from the inaccurate adjustment of the index on mathematical instruments, which must be added to or deducted from all readings taken.

in′dex fiṅ′gēr, the forefinger; the finger next to the thumb.

in′dex glȧss, the mirror attached to the index of a quadrant or a sextant.

in′dex hand, a pointer attached to the mechanism of a watch, clock, or other instrument having a dial or graduated measuring scale.

in·dex′iç·ăl, *a.* having the form or nature of an index; pertaining to an index.

in·dex′iç·ăl·ly, *adv.* in the manner of an index.

in′dex num′bēr, a number used to measure change in prices, wages, employment, production, etc.: it shows percentage variation from an arbitrary standard, usually 100, representing the status at some earlier time.

in′dex plāte, in mechanics, a circular steel plate with holes in it, used for graduating circles or for subdividing wheels for gear-cutting: called also *division plate*.

in·dex·ter′i·ty, *n.* lack of dexterity or readiness in the use of the hands; clumsiness; awkwardness. [Rare.]

In′di·ȧ, *a.* [L. *India*; Gr. *India*, India, from *Indos*, the Indus river.] pertaining to India; Indian; made in or connected with India.

India ink; (a) a black pigment of lampblack mixed with a gelatinous substance: called also *China ink*; (b) a liquid ink made from this.

India matting; a kind of matting made in China and India of grass and reeds.

India paper; (a) a soft, thin paper of a light buff color, made in China, Japan, etc., and used for taking impressions of engravings; (b) a thin, tough, opaque printing paper, used for Bibles, etc.

India proof; a proof taken from an engraved block or plate upon India paper.

India silk; a thin silk fabric woven like cambric.

in·dī′ȧ·dem, *v.t.* to place or set in a diadem.

In′di·ȧ·măn, *n.*; *pl.* **In′di·ȧ·men,** a merchant ship traveling regularly between England and India; especially, a large ship of this sort belonging to the English East India Company.

In′di·ăn, *a.* [LL. *Indianus*, from L. *India*; Gr. *India*, India, from *Indos*, L. *Indus*, the Indus river, from Sans. *sindhu*, a river.]

1. of India or the East Indies, their people, or culture.

2. of the American aboriginal races (American Indians) or the West Indies, or their cultures.

3. of a type used or made by Indians.

4. made of maize, or Indian corn.

Indian bay; in botany, *Persea indica*, a plant of the same genus as the Carolina red bay.

Indian bean; in botany, the catalpa: so called from the shape of its pods.

Indian berry; in botany, *Anamirta paniculata*, of the moonseed family.

Indian bread; (a) bread made from corn meal; (b) a fungus eaten by the American Indians; tuckahoe.

Indian club; a wooden or metallic club shaped like a tenpin, swung in the hand for exercise.

INDIAN CLUB

Indian corn; (a) a kind of grain that grows in kernels on large ears; (b) its ears; (c) its seeds or kernels. Also called *maize* or, in the United States, Canada, and Australia, *corn*.

Indian cress; in botany, the nasturtium, *Tropæolum majus*.

Indian cucumber; in botany, a plant of the lily family, *Medeola virginiana*, having a tuberous white horizontal rootstock with the taste of a cucumber.

Indian currant; in botany, a shrub, *Symphoricarpus vulgaris*, of the honeysuckle family, bearing small, dark-red berries resembling currants.

Indian fig; see under *fig*.

Indian file; single file; (in a) single line, one behind the other: it was the American Indians' way of walking a trail.

Indian fire; a composition of sulfur, niter, and arsenic sulfide, giving a brilliant white light and used in fireworks.

Indian giver; a person who gives something and then asks for it back: from the belief that American Indians expected an equivalent in return when giving something. [Colloq.]

Indian grass; in botany, a kind of coarse grass, *Sorghum nutans*.

Indian hemp; (a) the American dogbane, *Apocynum cannabinum*, a plant with a tough bark formerly used in ropemaking: the root is used in medicine; (b) the common hemp.

Indian jalap; a jalap made from the *Ipomæa turpethum* of East India.

Indian licorice; an Indian shrub of the pea family, with licoricelike roots and poisonous, red and black seeds used for beads, as a weight, and in medicine: also called *jequirity*.

Indian mallow; a plant, *Abutilon avicennæ*, of the mallow family, with soft, velvety leaves and small, orange-yellow flowers.

Indian meal; meal made from Indian corn; corn meal.

Indian-meal moth; same as *meal moth*.

Indian millet; a tall grass whose varieties include durra and broomcorn; grain sorghum.

Indian ox; same as *zebu*.

Indian paint; the juice of the *Sanguinaria canadensis*, or bloodroot.

Indian paintbrush; the painted cup, a plant of the figwort family.

Indian physic; in botany, a plant of the rose family, including two species, *Gillenia trifoliata*, or Bowman's root, and *Gillenia stipulata*, or American ipecac.

Indian pink; in botany, (a) a plant (*Ipomæa quamoclit*) of the *Convolvulaceæ*, native in tropical America but now generally naturalized, characterized by its red or crimson flowers; the cypress vine; (b) the China pink, *Dianthus chinensis*, characterized by large-toothed petals of various colors.

Indian pipe; a leafless wild herb, *Monotropa uniflora*, native to Asia and the United States, with one waxy, pipe-shaped flower on each stem: it is a saprophyte.

Indian plantain; in botany, any one of the species of *Cacalia*, a plant of the composite family.

Indian poke; in botany, a plant, *Veratrum viride*, of the lily family, having yellowish-green flowers turning greener with age; the American white hellebore.

Indian pudding; a steamed pudding made of corn meal, molasses, milk, etc.

Indian red; (a) a yellowish-red iron ore, originally from an island in the Persian Gulf, used in early times as a pigment; (b) a native iron (ferric) oxide used by North American Indians as war paint, and by early American painters.

Indian reed; same as *Indian shot*.

Indian rice; in botany, *Zizania aquatica*, or water oats, a tall and reedlike grass whose seeds were used by American Indians for food.

Indian shot; in botany, a plant (*Canna indica*) of the arrowroot family: named from its hard shot-like seeds.

FRUIT OF INDIAN SHOT

Indian soap; in botany, any tree of the genus *Sapindus*, the fruit of which is used as a substitute for soap; the soapberry tree.

Indian summer; (a) a period of mild, warm, hazy weather following the first frosts of late autumn, especially on the North American continent; (b) the final years of a person's life, regarded as being serene, tranquil, reminiscent, etc.

Indian tobacco; in botany, the *Lobelia inflata*, a hardy weed with spikes of light-blue flowers, growing in the northwestern United States.

Indian turnip; (a) in botany, a plant, *Arisæma triphyllum*, commonly called jack-in-the-pulpit; (b) its root.

Indian wheat; Indian corn. [Obs.]

Indian yellow; a bright-yellow coloring matter.

In′di·ăn, *n.* 1. a native of India or the East Indies.

2. a member of any of the aboriginal races of North America, South America, or the West Indies: originally so named from the belief, held by early explorers, that these regions were part of Asia.

3. popularly, any of the languages spoken by the American Indians.

In″di·ăn·eer′, *n.* an Indiaman. [Rare.]

In·di·an′i·ăn, *a.* of Indiana.

In·di·an′i·ăn, *n.* a native or inhabitant of Indiana; a Hoosier.

In′di·ăn·ist, *n.* a specialist in the history and languages of India.

In′di·ȧ-rub′bẽr, in′di·ȧ-rub′bẽr, *a.* of, or having the characteristics of, India rubber.

India-rubber tree; any tree whose exudations yield India rubber; specifically, the *Ficus elastica* of the East Indies.

In′di·ȧ rub′bẽr, in′di·ȧ rub′bẽr, natural rubber; especially, caoutchouc, crude rubber obtained from latex.

In′diç, *a.* [L. *Indicus*; Gr. *Indikos*.]

1. of India.

2. designating or of a branch of the Indo-European languages, including many of the languages spoken, or formerly spoken, in India.

in′di·çăn, *n.* [from L. *indicum*, indigo; and *-an*.]

1. a glucoside, $C_{14}H_{17}NO_6$, found in a natural state in the indigo plant: it is converted by water and oxygen into indigo.

2. an indigo-forming substance, $C_8H_6NOSO_2OH$, the potassium salt of which is present in animal urine.

in′di·çănt, *a.* [L. *indicans* (*-antis*), ppr. of *indicare*, to point out, indicate.] pointing out; indicating.

in′di·çănt, *n.* anything that points out or indicates.

in′di·çāte, *v.t.*; indicated, *pt.*, *pp.*; indicating, *ppr.* [L. *indicatus*, pp. of *indicare*, to show, indicate; *in*, in, to, and *dicare*, to point out, declare.]

1. to show; to point out; to point to; to direct attention to; as, a weather vane *indicates* the direction of the wind.

2. to be or give a sign or token of; to signify; betoken; intimate; as, thunder *indicates* that a storm is near.

3. to show the need for; to call for; to make necessary; as, in this weather a roaring fire is *indicated*.

4. to show or point out as a cause, nature, treatment, or outcome: said of a disease, etc.

5. to express briefly or generally.

in′di·çā·ted, *a.* manifested by an indicator.

in′di·çāt″ing, *a.* showing, recording, or registering.

indicating caliper; in machinery, a kind of caliper or measuring device equipped with a dial gauge designed to show any error in the size of the work.

indicating control switch; in electricity, a secondary or auxiliary switch which shows either the last operation or the position or both of the device under control.

indicating gauge; in mechanics, a device which gives visual evidence of changes or variations in dimensions or contour.

in·di·çā′tion, *n.* [L. *indicatio* (*-onis*), from *indicare*, to point out, indicate.]

1. the act of indicating.

2. mark; token; sign; symptom; something that indicates, points out, or signifies.

3. in medicine, any symptom or occurrence in a disease, which serves to direct to cause, treatment, etc.

4. the amount or degree registered by an indicator.

in·diç′ȧ·tive, *a.* [LL. *indicativus*; L. *indicare*, to point out, indicate.]

1. giving an indication, suggestion, or intimation; showing; signifying; pointing out.

2. designating or of that mood of a verb used to express an act, state, or occurrence as actual, or to ask a question of fact: it is the usual form of the verb: distinguished from *subjunctive*, *imperative*.

in·diç′ȧ·tive, *n.* 1. the indicative mood.

2. a verb in this mood.

in·diç′ȧ·tive·ly, *adv.* in an indicative manner.

in′di·çā·tŏr, *n.* [LL. *indicator*, one who points out, from L. *indicare*, to point out, indicate.]

1. one who or that which indicates; specifically, (a) any device, as a gauge, dial, register, or pointer, that measures or records and visibly indicates; (b) an instrument which registers the pressure in the cylinder of a steam engine at every instant during the stroke of the piston, the pressure being admitted to the instrument and exerted upon a piston with a lever index supplied with a stylus which rests against a sheet of paper wrapped upon a rotating hollow cylinder.

2. in botany, the Virginia grape fern: its presence was believed to be a sign of ginseng growing nearby.

3. in microscopy, a pointer or index attached to or near the eyepiece for the purpose of locating an object in the field.

4. any of various substances used to indicate the acidity or alkalinity of a solution, the beginning or end of a chemical reaction, the presence of certain substances, etc., by changes in color.

5. a bird, the honey guide; also, [I–] the genus to which it belongs.

indicator telegraph; a telegraph whose signals consist in movements of a magnetic needle over the face of a dial plate.

in′di·çā·tŏr çärd, a card which contains the record made by an indicator of pressure in the cylinder of a steam engine.

in′di·çā·tŏr dī′ȧ·gram, same as *indicator card*.

in′di·çȧ·tō·ry, *a.* indicating; serving to show or make known.

in·di·çā′trix, *n.* 1. in geometry, a curve made by a surface intersecting a plane infinitesimally near to and parallel with a tangent plane.

2. in crystallography, an ellipsoid assumed for the purpose of determining the optical structure of a crystal.

in·di·çā′vit, *n.* [L., lit., he has shown, 3rd pers. sing. perf. ind. act. of *indicare*, to show, indicate.] in English law, a writ of prohibition at the instance of the patron, by which a suit against his incumbent involving tithes can be removed from the ecclesiastical court to the civil courts.

in′dice, *n.* an indication. [Obs.]

in′di·çēṣ, *n.* alternative plural of *index*.

in·di′ci·ȧ (-dish′i-), *n.pl.*; *sing.* **in·di′ci·um,** [L., pl. of *indicium*, a notice, mark, disclosure, discovery, from *index* (*-icis*), an informer, sign, mark.] signs; characteristic marks; indications; tokens; especially, printed markings substituted for the stamps, cancellations, or postmarks, on bulk mail.

in·dic′i·ble, *a.* that cannot be spoken or expressed. [Obs.]

in·diç′ō·līte, *n.* [Gr. *indikon*, indigo, and *lithos*, stone.] in mineralogy, a variety of tourmalin, of an indigo-blue color, sometimes with a tinge of azure or green.

in·dīct′ (-dīt′), *v.t.*; indicted, *pt.*, *pp.*; indicting, *ppr.* [ME. *enditen*, to write down; accuse; Anglo-Fr. and OFr. *enditer*, to accuse, point out, from L. *indicare*, to declare, proclaim, freq. of *indicere*, to declare, accuse; *in*, in, and *dicere*, to speak.] to charge with the commission of a crime; especially, to make formal accusation against on the basis of positive legal evidence: usually said of the action of a grand jury.

in·dīct′ (-dīt′), *v.t.* to indite. [Obs.]

in·diçt′, *v.t.* [L. *indictus*, pp. of *indicere*.] to announce in public. [Obs.]

in·dīct′ȧ·ble (-dīt′), *a.* 1. liable to be indicted; as, an *indictable* offender.

2. subject to be presented by a grand jury; making indictment possible; as, an *indictable* offense.

in·dīct·ee′, *n.* a person indicted.

in·dīct′ēr (-dīt′), *n.* one who indicts.

in·diç′tion, *n.* [LL. *indictio* (*-onis*), a space of fifteen years; L., a proclamation of the imposition of a tax, from *indicere*, to declare, proclaim.]

1. declaration; proclamation. [Rare.]

2. the edict of a Roman emperor fixing the valuation of property for tax purposes at the beginning of each fifteen-year period: it was first made by Constantine in 312 A.D.

3. the tax so levied.

4. (a) a cycle of fifteen years; (b) a particular year in such a cycle.

in·diç′tive, *a.* [LL. *indictivus*, from L. *indictus*, pp. of *indicere*, to declare.] proclaimed; declared. [Obs.]

in·dīct′ment (-dīt′), *n.* [ME. and Anglo-Fr. *enditement*.]

1. an indicting or being indicted.

2. a charge; an accusation; specifically, a formal written accusation charging one or more persons with the commission of a crime, presented by a grand jury to the court when the jury has found, after examining the prosecutor's statement of the charge (*bill of indictment*), that there is a valid case.

in·dīct′ŏr, *n.* in law, the person who presents an indictment.

In′dieș, *n.pl.* the East and West Indies.

in·dif′fẽr·ence, *n.* [Fr. *indifférence*; L. *indifferentia*, from *indifferens* (*-entis*), indifferent, careless.]

1. the quality, state, or fact of being indifferent; specifically, (a) lack of concern, interest, or feeling; apathy; (b) lack of importance, meaning, or worth.

2. impartiality; freedom from prejudice, prepossession, or bias. [Obs.]

Syn.—insensibility, apathy, unconcern.

in·dif′fẽr·en·cy, *n.* same as *indifference*.

in·dif′fẽr·ent, *a.* [OFr. *indifferent*; L. *indifferens* (*-entis*), indifferent, careless; *in-* priv., and *differens* (*-entis*), different, ppr. of *differe*, to carry asunder, to differ; *dis-*, apart, and *ferre*, to carry.]

1. neutral; not inclined to one side, party, or thing more than to another; having or showing no partiality, bias, etc.

2. unconcerned; feeling no interest, concern, or feeling respecting anything; as, it seems to be impossible that a rational being should be *indifferent* to the means of obtaining endless happiness.

> It was a remarkable law of Solon, that any person, who, in the commotions of the republic, remained neuter, or an *indifferent* spectator of the contending parties, should be condemned to perpetual banishment.
> —Addison.

3. of no consequence or importance; immaterial; as, it is *indifferent* which road we take.

4. passable; of a middling state or quality; neither good nor very bad; fair; average.

5. not particularly good; rather poor or bad.

6. inactive; neutral in quality, as a chemical magnet, etc.: chiefly in scientific use.

7. in biology, undifferentiated.

Syn.—neutral, unconcerned, apathetic, disinterested.

in·dif′fẽr·ent, *adv.* indifferently. [Obs.]

in·dif′fẽr·ent·ișm, *n.* 1. the state of being indifferent.

2. the attitude of mind which perceives or acknowledges no difference between the true and the false in religion or philosophy; a kind of agnosticism.

3. in metaphysics, the doctrine of absolute identity.

in·dif′fẽr·ent·ist, *n.* one who believes in or practices indifferentism.

in·dif′fẽr·ent·ly, *adv.* 1. without distinction or preference; as, to offer pardon *indifferently* to all.

2. equally; impartially; without favor, prejudice, or bias.

3. in a neutral state; without concern; without desire or aversion.

> Set honor in one eye and death i' the other,
> And I will look on death *indifferently*.
> —Shak.

4. not well; tolerably; passably; as, *indifferently* well; to be *indifferently* entertained.

in·di·fụl′vin, *n.* [L. *indicum*, indigo, and *fulvus*, of a reddish yellow.] in chemistry, a reddish-yellow resin derived from indican.

in·di·fus′cin, *n.* [L. *indicum*, indigo, and *fuscus*, dusky, and *-in*.] in chemistry, a brown compound, $C_{24}H_{20}N_2O_6$, derived from indican.

in′di·ġen, *n.* same as *indigene*.

in′di·ġence, *n.* [Fr. *indigence*; L. *indigentia*, need, want, from *indigens* (*-entis*), needy, ppr. of *indigere*, to need; Old L. *indu*; L. *in*, in, and *egere*, to need.] the condition of being indigent; penury; poverty; as, many of the human race live in *indigence*.

Syn.—poverty, want, need, penury, destitution, privation.—*Poverty* is generic, denoting a deficiency in the means of living; *indigence* is stronger, implying an absence of the necessaries of life. *Want* and *need* are applied usually to temporary conditions.

in′di·ġen·cy, *n.* indigence. [Obs.]

in′di·ġēne, *n.* [Fr. *indigène*; L. *indigena*, a native.] one born in a country; a native animal or plant.

in·diġ′e·nous, *a.* [LL. *indigenus*; L. *indigena*, born in a country, native, from Old L. *indu*; L. *in*, within, and *gignere*, to bear, produce.]

1. native; born, growing, or produced naturally in a country or region; not exotic; as, corn and cotton are *indigenous* to North America.

2. innate; inherent; inborn.

Syn.—original, native, aboriginal.

in′di·ġent, *a.* [Fr. *indigent*; L. *indigens* (*-entis*), in need; Old L. *indu*; L. *in*, in, and *egere*, to need.]

1. destitute; in poverty; needy; poor.

> Charity consists in relieving the *indigent*.
> —Addison.

2. lacking; destitute (of). [Archaic.]

in′di·ġent·ly, *adv.* in an indigent manner.

in·di·ġest′, *n.* a crude mass. [Obs.]

in·di·ġest′, *a.* without organization; not matured or digested; chaotic. [Obs.]

in·di·ġest′ed, *a.* [L. *indigestus*, unarranged, without order; *in-* priv., and *digestus*, pp. of *digerere*, to distribute, arrange.]

1. not digested; not changed or prepared for nourishing the body; undigested; crude.

2. not well considered; not ordered in the mind.

3. confused; chaotic.

4. not prepared by heat; uncooked.

5. in medicine, not brought to suppuration, as the contents of an abscess or boil; not in a condition ready for healing; as, an *indigested* wound. [Obs.]

in·di·ġest′ed·ness, *n.* the condition or quality of not being digested.

in·di·ġest·i·bil′i·ty, *n.* the condition or quality of being indigestible.

in·di·ġest′i·ble, *a.* [Fr. *indigestible*; LL. *indigestibilis*; L. *in-* priv., and LL. *digestibilis*, digestible, from L. *digerere*, to arrange, digest.] that cannot be digested; not easily digested.

> Such a torrent of *indigestible* similes.
> —Wharton.

in·di·ġest′i·ble·ness, *n.* indigestibility.

in·di·ġest′i·bly, *adv.* so as to be indigestible.

in·di·ġes′tion (-chun), *n.* [LL. *indigestio* (*-onis*); L. *in-* priv., and LL. *digestio* (*-onis*), digestion, from L. *digestus*, pp. of *digerere*, to arrange, digest.] incapability of or difficulty in digesting food; dyspepsia.

in·di·ġest′ive, *a.* 1. having indigestion.

2. likely to cause indigestion.

in·diġ′i·tāte, *v.i.* to interlock like the fingers of one hand with those of another. [Obs.]

in·diġ′i·tāte, *v.t.* to point out with the finger. [Obs.]

in·diġ·i·tā′tion, *n.* the act of pointing out with the finger; indication. [Obs.]

in·di·glū′cin, *n.* [Gr. *indikon*, indigo, and *glykys*, sweet.] a sugarlike compound, $C_6H_{10}O_6$, obtained from indican.

in·dīgn′ (-dīn′), *a.* [Fr. *indigne*; L. *indignus*; *in-* priv., and *dignus*, worthy.]

1. undeserving; unworthy. [Obs. or Poetic.]

2. disgraceful. [Obs. or Poetic.]

in·dig′nănce, *n.* indignation. [Rare.]

in·dig′năn·cy, *n.* indignation. [Rare.]

in·dig′nănt, *a.* [L. *indignans* (*-antis*), ppr. of *indignari*, to consider as unworthy or improper, to be displeased at; *in-* priv., and *dignari*, to deem worthy, from *dignus*, worthy.] affected with indignation; feeling the mingled emotions of anger and scorn or contempt, as when a person is exasperated by unjust, mean, or ungrateful action or treatment.

Syn.—incensed, exasperated, provoked, irate.

in·dig′nănt·ly, *adv.* in an indignant manner.

in·dig·nā′tion, *n.* [OFr. *indignation*; L. *indignatio* (*-onis*), displeasure, indignation, from *indignari*, to consider as unworthy, to be indignant.]

1. anger mingled with contempt, disgust, or abhorrence, caused by disapprobation of something mean, disgraceful, or unjust.

> And when the ten heard it, they were moved with *indignation* against the two brethren.
> —Matt. xx. 24.

2. the effects of anger as manifested in judgment or punishment. [Obs.]

> O, let them (the heavens) hurl down their *indignation*.
> —Shak.

Syn.—anger, resentment, wrath, ire, displeasure, scorn, fury.

in·dig′ni·fȳ, *v.t.* to treat disdainfully, unbecomingly, or unworthily. [Obs.]

in·dig′ni·ty, *n.*; *pl.* **in·dig′ni·tieș,** [L. *indignitas*, unworthiness, vileness, unbecoming behavior, from *indignus*, unworthy; *in-* priv., and *dignus*, worthy.]

1. something that humiliates, insults, or injures the dignity or self-respect; an affront.

2. (a) the quality or state of being unworthy or disgraceful; (b) unworthy or disgraceful conduct; (c) indignation. [Obs.]

Syn.—insult, affront, disrespect, contumely, dishonor.

in·dīgn′ly (-dīn′), *adv.* unworthily. [Obs.].

in′di·gō, *n.*; *pl.* **in′di·gōș, in′di·gōeș,** [Sp. *indigo*; L. *indicum*, indigo; Gr. *indikon* (supply *pharmakon*, dye), indigo, lit., Indian dye, from *Indikos*, Indian, from *India*, India.]

1. a blue dye obtained from certain plants or made synthetically, usually from aniline.

2. any of a group of plants of the pea family that yield indigo: see *indigo plant*.

3. a deep violet-blue, designated by Newton as one of the seven primary colors.

bastard indigo; same as *false indigo* (a).

Chinese indigo; a cruciferous plant, *Isatis indigotica*, of North China.

Egyptian indigo; a leguminous plant, *Tephrosia apollinea*, a native of Egypt. It is narcotic, and yields a fine blue dye.

false indigo; (a) *Amorpha fruticosa*, an American shrub of the bean family; (b) an American plant, *Baptisia australis*, of the bean family: called also *wild indigo* and *blue false indigo*.

indigo brown; a brown, resinous substance found in crude indigo.

indigo carmine; a dyestuff obtained by treating indigo with sulfuric acid.

indigo white; a compound, $C_{16}H_{12}N_2O_2$, obtained by subjecting commercial indigo to the action of reducing agents, such as alkaline fluids containing sulfate of iron, or a mixture of grape sugar, alcohol, and strong soda lye.

in′di·gō ber′ry, the fruit of *Randia aculeata*, a rubiaceous shrub of the West Indies, yielding a blue dye.

in′di·gō bīrd, same as *indigo bunting*.

in′di·gō-blūe′, *n.* indigo blue.

in′di·gō-blūe′, *a.* of indigo blue.

in′di·gō blūe, 1. the coloring matter of indigo; indigotin.

2. the color indigo.

in′di·gō bun′ting, a small finch, *Passerina cyanea*, native to the eastern United States: the male is indigo-blue, the female brown.

in′di·gō çop′pẽr, same as *covellin*.

In·di·gof′e·rȧ, *n.* [*indigo*, and L. *ferre*, to bear.] a large genus of tropical plants of the pea family, indigenous to the warmer parts of Asia, Africa, and America. Some of the species yield indigo.

in′di·gō·ġen, *n.* indigo white. [Obs.]

in′di·goid, *a.* [from *indigo*, and *-oid*.] of a class of dyes that produce a color resembling indigo.

in′di·goid, *n.* a dye that produces a color resembling indigo.

in·dig′ō·līte (*or* in′di·gō-), *n.* same as *indicolite*.

in·di·gom′e·tẽr, *n.* [*indigo*, and Gr. *metron*, a measure.] an instrument for showing the strength of an indigo solution.

in·di·gom′e·try, *n.* the art or method of determining the coloring power of indigo.

in′di·gō plant, a plant of the genus *Indigefera*, from which indigo is obtained. The species most commonly cultivated under this name

INDIGO PLANT (*Indigofera tinctoria*)

is *Indigofera tinctoria*, a native of the East Indies and other parts of Asia, and grown in many parts of Africa and America. It is a shrubby plant about three or four feet high, with narrow pinnate leaves and long, narrow pods. The West Indian indigo is *Indigofera anil*, a short-podded plant. native to the West Indies and the warmer parts of America, and cultivated in Asia and Africa.

in′di·gō snāke, the gopher snake.

in′di·gō·tāte, *n.* [*indigot*ic and *-ate.*] a salt of indigotic acid.

in·di·got′iç, *a.* [*indigot*in and *-ic.*] pertaining to or obtained from indigo.

indigotic acid; an acid obtained by boiling indigo in dilute nitric acid: called also *nitrosalicylic* or *anilic acid.*

in·dig′ō·tin (*or* -di-gō′), *n.* [*indigo*, and *-t-*, and *-in.*] a dark-blue powder with a coppery luster, $C_{16}H_{10}N_2O_2$, the coloring matter and chief ingredient of indigo; indigo blue.

in·di·hū′min, *n.* [L. *indicum*, indigo, and *humus*, earth, soil, and *-in.*] same as *indigo brown* under *indigo.*

in·dil′ȧ·tō·ry, *a.* not dilatory or slow. [Obs.]

in·dil′i·ġence, *n.* lack of diligence. [Obs.]

in·dil′i·ġent, *a.* not diligent; idle; slothful. [Obs.]

in·dil′i·ġent·ly, *adv.* without diligence. [Obs.]

in·di·min′ish·ȧ·ble, *a.* not diminishable. [Rare.]

in′din, *n.* [*indigo* and *-in.*] a crystalline substance, $C_{16}H_{10}N_2O_2$, of a rose color, isomeric with indigo blue.

in·di·reçt′, *a.* [L. *indirectus*; *in-* priv., and *directus*, straight, pp. of *dirigere*, to make straight, mark out.]

1. not straight or rectilinear; deviating from a direct line or course; circuitous; as, an *indirect* route.

2. not tending to a purpose by the shortest or plainest course, or by obvious means; not straight to the point, or to the person or thing aimed at; as, an *indirect* accusation, an *indirect* attack, an *indirect* answer or proposal.

3. not fair or honest; not open; equivocal; tending to mislead or deceive.

Indirect dealing will be discovered one time or other. —Tillotson.

4. not resulting directly or immediately from a cause, but following consequentially and remotely; not direct in descent or derivation; as, *indirect* claims; an *indirect* inheritance.

indirect claims; claims for damages not direct but consequential.

indirect demonstration; see under *demonstration.*

indirect discourse; statement of what a person said, without quoting his exact words: thus, "he said that he would be there" is indirect discourse; "he said, 'I will be there'" is direct discourse; in Latin, *oratio obliqua* and *oratio recta*, respectively.

indirect evidence; in law, inferential or circumstantial evidence.

indirect lighting; a method of artificial illumination whereby light is not cast directly from the light source, but is either diffused or shielded in such a manner that it reaches the eye by reflection from a wall, ceiling, or other surface. The advantage of this type of lighting lies chiefly in the reduction or total absence of glare or shadows.

indirect object; the word or words denoting the person or thing indirectly affected by the action of the verb: it generally names the person or thing to which something is given or for which something is done (e.g., *him* in *give him the ball, do him a favor*).

indirect tax; a tax on manufactured goods, imports, etc. that is paid indirectly by the consumer because it is added to the price.

in·di·reç′tion, *n.* 1. roundabout action, procedure, or means.

2. deceit; dishonesty.

in·di·reçt′ly, *adv.* in an indirect manner; not in a straight line or course; obliquely; not by direct means; not in express terms; unfairly.

Your crown and kingdom *indirectly* held. —Shak.

in·di·reçt′ness, *n.* the condition or quality of being indirect; obliquity; devious course; unfairness; dishonesty.

in·di·rē′tin, *n.* a component of indigo brown, obtained from indican.

in·di·rū′bin, *n.* [L. *indicum*, indigo, and *ruber*, red, and *-in.*] an isomer of indigo blue, $C_{16}H_{10}N_2O_2$, obtained by the decomposition of indican.

in·dis̤·cērn′i·ble (-zērn′), *a.* that cannot be discerned; imperceptible; not discoverable.

in·dis̤·cērn′i·ble·ness, *n.* incapability of being discerned.

in·dis̤·cērn′i·bly, *adv.* in an indiscernible manner.

in·dis·cērp·i·bil′i·ty, *n.* the quality of being indiscerpible. [Obs.]

in·dis·cērp′i·ble, *a.* indiscerptible. [Obs.]

in·dis·cērp′i·ble·ness, *n.* indiscerptibleness. [Obs.]

in·dis·cērp′i·bly, *adv.* indiscerptibly. [Obs.]

in·dis·cērp·ti·bil′i·ty, *n.* the quality of being indiscerptible.

in·dis·cērp′ti·ble, *a.* not discerptible; indivisible.

in·dis·cērp′ti·ble·ness, *n.* indiscerptibility.

in·dis·cērp′ti·bly, *adv.* in an indiscerptible manner.

in·dis′ci·plin·ȧ·ble, *a.* undisciplinable.

in·dis′ci·pline, *n.* lack of discipline or instruction.

in·dis·çŏv′ēr·ȧ·ble, *a.* undiscoverable.

in·dis·çŏv′ēr·y, *n.* lack of discovery. [Obs.]

in·dis·çreet′, *a.* not discreet; lacking discretion, as in speech or action; imprudent; inconsiderate; injudicious.

Syn.—injudicious, inconsiderate, rash, imprudent, hasty, unwise.

in·dis·çreet′ly, *adv.* not discreetly.

in·dis·çreet′ness, *n.* indiscretion.

in·dis·çrēte′, *a.* [L. *indiscretus*, not separated, undistinguished; *in-* priv., and *discretus*, pp. of *discernere*, to separate, distinguish.] not discrete or separated; compact.

in·dis·çre′tion (-kresh′un), *n.* 1. lack of discretion; the state or quality of being indiscreet.

2. an indiscreet action or remark; indiscreet deportment.

Syn.—imprudence, rashness, mistake.

in·dis·çrim′i·nāte, *a.* not discriminate; undistinguishing; not making any distinction; lacking discrimination; indistinguishable; confused; promiscuous.

The *indiscriminate* defense of right and wrong. —Junius.

in·dis·çrim′i·nāte·ly, *adv.* in an indiscriminate manner.

in·dis·çrim′i·nā·ting, *a.* not making any distinction.

in·dis·çrim′i·nā·ting·ly, *adv.* in an indiscriminating manner.

in·dis·çrim·i·nā′tion, *n.* the condition of being indiscriminate; lack of discrimination.

in·dis·çrim′i·nā·tive, *a.* not discriminating.

in·dis·çussed′, *a.* not discussed. [Obs.]

in·dis·pen·sȧ·bil′i·ty, *n.* the quality or state of being indispensable.

in·dis·pen′sȧ·ble, *a.* 1. incapable of being dispensed with; not to be omitted, remitted, or spared; absolutely necessary or requisite; as, air and water are *indispensable* to life.

2. not subject to exemption; not admitting of a dispensation. [Obs.]

Syn.—essential, necessary, requisite, needful, fundamental.

in·dis·pen′sȧ·ble, *n.* an indispensable person or thing.

in·dis·pen′sȧ·ble·ness, *n.* indispensability.

in·dis·pen′sȧ·bly, *adv.* in an indispensable manner.

in·dis·pērsed′ (-pērst′), *a.* not dispersed. [Obs.]

in·dis·pōs̤e′, *v.t.*; indisposed, *pt.*, *pp.*; indisposing, *ppr.* [Fr. *indisposer*, to indispose; L. *in-* priv., and *disponere*, to distribute, dispose.]

1. to disincline; to make averse or unwilling.

They may sometimes *indispose* and irritate the reader. —M. Arnold.

2. to make unable or unfit; to disqualify.

3. to affect with indisposition or illness; to disorder; to make somewhat ill.

It made him rather *indisposed* than sick. —Walton.

in·dis·pōs̤ed′, *a.* 1. slightly ill.

2. unwilling; disinclined.

in·dis·pōs̤′ed·ness, *n.* the condition or quality of being indisposed.

in·dis·pō·s̤i′tion (-zish′un), *n.* [LL. *indispositio* (*-onis*), inappropriateness; L. *in-* priv., and *dispositio* (*-onis*), arrangement, disposition.]

1. the state of being indisposed or disinclined; aversion; dislike; unwillingness; disinclination.

A general *indisposition* toward believing. —Atterbury.

2. slight disorder of the normal functions of the body; slight illness.

in·dis·pū·tȧ·bil′i·ty, *n.* the state or quality of being indisputable.

in·dis·pū′tȧ·ble (*or* -dis′pū-), *a.* [LL. *indisputabilis*; L. *in* priv., and *disputabilis*, disputable, from *disputare*, to dispute.] that cannot be disputed or doubted; incontrovertible; incontestable; too evident to admit of dispute.

Syn.—incontrovertible, indubitable, undeniable, unquestionable, incontestable, undoubted, positive, certain.

in·dis·pū′tȧ·ble·ness, *n.* indisputability.

in·dis·pū′tȧ·bly (*or* -dis′pū-), *adv.* in an indisputable manner; unquestionably.

in·dis·pūt′ed, *a.* undisputed. [Obs.]

in·dis′si·pȧ·ble, *a.* incapable of being dissipated.

in·dis·sol·ū·bil′i·ty, *n.* [Fr. *indissolubilité.*] the quality of being indissoluble.

in·dis·sol′ū·ble, *a.* [L. *indissolubilis*; *in-* priv., and *dissolubilis*, dissoluble, from *dissolvere*, to dissolve.]

1. not capable of being dissolved, melted, decomposed, disintegrated, or liquefied; as, few substances are absolutely *indissoluble* by heat, but many are *indissoluble* in water.

2. not to be broken or rightfully violated; perpetually binding or obligatory; firm; lasting; stable; as, an *indissoluble* league or covenant.

in·dis·sol′ū·ble·ness, *n.* indissolubility.

in·dis·sol′ū·bly, *adv.* in an indissoluble manner.

in·dis̤·s̤olv′ȧ·ble, *a.* same as *indissoluble.* [Rare.]

in·dis̤·s̤olv′ȧ·ble·ness, *n.* indissolubility. [Rare.]

in·dis′tăn·cy, *n.* nearness. [Obs.]

in·dis·tinçt′, *a.* [L. *indistinctus*, obscure, indistinct; *in-* priv., and *distinctus*, pp. of *distinguere*, to point out, distinguish.]

1. not separate or separable; not clearly marked off; not plainly defined.

Indistinct as water is in water. —Shak.

2. not seen or heard clearly; faint; obscure; not clear; blurred; as, an *indistinct* vision, an *indistinct* view.

Syn.—confused, indefinite, indistinguishable, obscure, dim, doubtful, vague, ambiguous.

in·dis·tinç′ti·ble, *a.* indistinguishable. [Obs.]

in·dis·tinç′tion, *n.* lack of distinction; confusion; uncertainty; lack of distinguishableness.

The *indistinction* of many of the same name . . . hath made some doubt.—Browne.

in·dis·tinç′tive, *a.* 1. not distinctive; lacking distinction.

2. making no distinction; incapable of distinguishing.

in·dis·tinç′tive·ness, *n.* the state or quality of being indistinctive.

in·dis·tinçt′ly, *adv.* in an indistinct manner.

in·dis·tinçt′ness, *n.* the condition of being dim, obscure, confused, or indefinite; as, *indistinctness* of letters upon a printed page.

in·dis·tin′guish·ȧ·ble, *a.* that cannot be distinguished or separated; imperceptible.

in·dis·tin′guish·ȧ·bly, *adv.* so as to be indistinguishable.

in·dis·tin′guished (-gwisht), *a.* not distinguished. [Rare.]

in·dis·tŭrb′ănce, *n.* freedom from disturbance; calmness; repose; tranquillity. [Now Rare.]

in·ditch′, *v.t.* to bury in a ditch. [Obs.]

in·dīte′, *v.t.*; indited, *pt.*, *pp.*; inditing, *ppr.* [ME. *enditen*; see *indict*, to accuse.]

1. to express or describe in prose or verse. [Archaic.]

2. to put in writing; to compose and write.

3. to prompt; to dictate. [Obs.]

in·dīte′ment, *n.* 1. an inditing.

2. something indited.

in·dīt′ēr, *n.* one who indites.

in′di·um, *n.* [Mod. L., from L. *indicum*, indigo; and *-ium*: from the two indigo lines in its spectrum.] a rare metallic chemical element, soft, ductile, and silver-white, occurring in some zinc ores: symbol, In; atomic weight, 114.76; atomic number, 49.

in·di·vērt′i·ble, *a.* incapable of being diverted; not to be turned aside.

in·di·vīd′ȧ·ble, *a.* indivisible. [Obs.]

in·di·vīd′ed, *a.* undivided. [Obs.]

in·di·vid′ū·ăl, *a.* [LL. *individualis*; L. *individuus*, indivisible, inseparable; *in-* priv., and *dividuus*, divisible, from *dividere*, to divide.]

1. originally, not divisible; not separable.

2. existing as a single, separate thing or being; single; separate; particular.

3. of, for, or by a single person or thing.

4. relating to or characteristic of a single person or thing.

5. distinguished from others by special characteristics; of a peculiar or striking character; as, an *individual* style.

in·di·vid′ū·ăl, *n.* 1. a single being, or thing of

any kind; a single group when taken as a unit.

2. a person.

3. in biology, a single organism in existence separate from the parent; one of a kind, whether partially or fully developed, as the entire product of a fertilized egg or ovule, or the bud of a plant.

in·di·vid'ū·ăl·işm, *n.* 1. the leading of one's life in one's own way without regard for others.

2. individual character; individuality.

3. an individual peculiarity.

4. the doctrine that individual freedom in economic enterprise should not be restricted by governmental or social regulation; laissez-faire.

5. the doctrine that the state exists for the individual and not the individual for the state.

6. in philosophy, egoism.

in·di·vid'ū·ăl·ist, *n.* a person who practices or believes in individualism (in various senses).

in·di·vid'ū·ăl·ist, *a.* same as *individualistic.*

in·di·vid·ū·ăl·is'tiç, *a.* of individualism or individualists.

in·di·vid·ū·al'i·ty, *n.*; *pl.* **in·di·vid·ū·al'i·tieş,** 1. the sum of the characteristics or qualities that set one person or thing apart from others; individual character.

2. the condition of existing as an individual; separate existence; oneness.

3. a single person or thing; an individual.

4. indivisibility; inseparability. [Obs.]

in·di·vid"ū·ăl·i·zā'tion, *n.* an individualizing or being individualized.

in·di·vid'ū·ăl·īze, *v.t.*; individualized (-īzd), *pt., pp.*; individualizing, *ppr.* 1. to distinguish; to select or mark as an individual, or as different from other persons and things.

2. to consider individually; to specify; to particularize.

in·di·vid'ū·ăl·ī·zẽr, *n.* one who or that which individualizes.

in·di·vid'ū·ăl·ly, *adv.* 1. separately; one at a time; as an individual or individuals; to the exclusion of others; as, ten men will unitedly accomplish what one of them *individually* cannot perform.

2. inseparably; indivisibly. [Obs.]

Omniscience—an attribute *individually* proper to the Godhead. —Hakewill.

3. showing individual characteristics; distinctively.

in·di·vid'ū·āte, *a.* undivided. [Obs.]

in·di·vid'ū·āte, *v.t.*; individuated, *pt., pp.*; individuating, *ppr.* [LL. *individuatus*, pp. of *individuare*, to make individual, from L. *individuus*, individual.]

1. to make individual or distinct; to give individuality to.

2. to distinguish from others of the same species.

in·di·vid·ū·ā'tion, *n.* 1. an individuating or being individuated.

2. the condition of existing as an individual.

in·di·vid'ū·ā·tŏr, *n.* one who or that which dividuates.

in"di·vi·dū'i·ty, *n.* individuality; also, indivisibility. [Obs.]

in·di·vin'i·ty, *n.* lack of divine power. [Obs.]

in·di·viş·i·bil'i·ty, *n.* the state or quality of being indivisible.

in·di·viş'i·ble, *a.* [LL. *indivisibilis*; L. *in-* priv., and LL. *divisibilis*, divisible, from L. *dividere*, to divide.]

1. that cannot be divided, separated, or broken; not separable into parts.

2. in mathematics, that cannot be divided without leaving a remainder.

in·di·viş'i·ble, *n.* anything that cannot be divided.

in·di·viş'i·ble·ness, *n.* indivisibility.

in·di·viş'i·bly, *adv.* so as to be indivisible.

in·di·vi'şion, *n.* a state of being not divided; absence of division.

In'dō-, [Gr., from *Indos*, the Indus, from O. Pers. *Hindu*, India.] a combining form meaning (a) *of India, of Indian* (*Hindu*) *stock*; (b) *of India and.*

In'dō-Ăr'y·ăn (*or* -yăn), *a.* 1. of the Indo-Aryans.

2. designating or of the Indo-European languages of India; Indic.

In'dō-Ăr'y·ăn, *n.* a native of India who speaks an Indo-European language. The term is now seldom used.

In'dō-Chī·nēşe', *a.* 1. of Indo-China, its Mongoloid people, or their culture.

2. Sino-Tibetan: term now seldom used.

in·doc·i·bil'i·ty, *n.* [LL. *indocibilitas*, from *indocibilis*, unteachable; L. *in-* priv., and LL. *docibilis*, teachable, from L. *docere*, to teach.] the quality of being unteachable. [Obs.]

in·doc'i·ble, *a.* unteachable; not capable of being taught, or not easily instructed. [Obs.]

in·doc'i·ble·ness, *n.* indocibility. [Obs.]

in·doc'ile (*or* -dō'cile), *a.* [L. *indocilis*, not teachable; *in-* priv., and *docilis*, teachable, from *docere*, to teach.] not docile; not easy to teach or discipline.

in·dō·cil'i·ty, *n.* [LL. *indocilitas* (*-atis*), from L. *indocilis*, unteachable.] the quality of being indocile.

in·doç'tri·nāte, *v.t.*; indoctrinated, *pt., pp.*; indoctrinating, *ppr.* [L. *in*, in, and *doctrinare*, to teach, from *doctrina*, learning.]

1. to instruct in doctrines, theories, beliefs, or principles.

2. to instruct; to teach.

in·doç·tri·nā'tion, *n.* an indoctrinating or being indoctrinated.

in·doç'tri·nā·tŏr, *n.* a person who indoctrinates.

In'dō-Eñg'lish, *a.* same as *Anglo-Indian.*

In'dō-Eū·rō·pē'ăn, *a.* designating or of a family of languages that includes most of those spoken in Europe and many of those spoken in southwestern Asia and India.

In'dō-Eū·rō·pē'ăn, *n.* 1. the Indo-European family of languages: its principal branches are Indic, Iranian, Armenian, Tokharic, Hellenic, Illyrian, Albanian, Italic, Celtic, Germanic, Baltic, and Slavic.

2. the hypothetical language, reconstructed by modern linguists, from which these languages are thought to have descended.

in'dō·gen, *n.* [*ind*igo and *-gen.*] the complex radical, C_8H_6NO, found in indigo.

in·doğ'e·nide, *n.* any of the derivatives of indogen.

In'dō-Gēr·man'iç, *a.* Indo-European: term now chiefly used by German-trained scholars.

In'dō-Hit'tīte, *n.* according to recent research, the hypothetical language from which the Indo-European and Hittite languages descended: it is divided into two branches, pre-Indo-European languages on the one hand and such languages as Hittite, hieroglyphic Hittite, and Luwian on the other.

in'dō·in, *n.* a synthetic substance resembling indigo.

In'dō-I·rā'ni·ăn, *a.* designating or of the Indic and Iranian branches of the Indo-European family of languages as spoken or formerly spoken in India, Afghanistan, Iran, etc.: the term is now chiefly applied to the status of these languages before Indic and Iranian became dialectically distinct.

in'dōle, in'dŏl, *n.* [from *indigo*, and *phenol.*] a white crystalline compound, C_8H_7N, obtained from indigo and formed as a product of the intestinal putrefaction of proteins: it is used in perfumery, etc.

in'dō·lence, *n.* [L. *indolentia*, freedom from pain; *in-* priv., and *dolens* (*-entis*), ppr. of *dolere*, to feel pain.]

1. freedom from pain or discomfort of body or of mind. [Obs.]

2. quality, condition, or instance of being indolent; habitual idleness; indisposition to labor; laziness.

in'dō·len·cy, *n.* indolence. [Obs.]

in'dō·lent, *a.* [L. *in-* priv., and *dolens* (*-entis*), ppr. of *dolere*, to feel pain, grieve.]

1. habitually idle; disliking or avoiding work; lazy; listless; sluggish; indulging in ease; inactive; idle; as, an *indolent* person, an *indolent* life.

2. in medicine, causing little or no pain; as, an indolent tumor.

in'dō·lent·ly, *adv.* in an indolent manner.

in'dō·lēş, *n.* [L., an inborn or native quality, from Old L. *indu*, within.] natural bent; characteristic qualities and temperament. [Rare.]

in'dō·line, in'dō·lin, *n.* [*ind*igo and phen*ol*, and *-in.*] in chemistry, a crystalline substance, $C_{16}H_{14}N_2$, a polymer of indol.

in·dom'ȧ·ble, *a.* indomitable. [Obs.]

in·dom'i·tȧ·ble, *a.* [L. *in-* priv., and *domitare*, freq. of *domere*, to tame, subdue.] not easily discouraged, defeated, or subdued; unyielding; unconquerable; as, *indomitable* courage or will.

in·dom'i·tȧ·bly, *adv.* 1. in an indomitable manner.

2. to an indomitable degree.

In·dō·nē'siăn, *a.* 1. of Indonesia, its people, etc.

2. designating or of a group of some two hundred Austronesian languages spoken in Indonesia, the Philippines, Java, etc., including Malay, Tagalog, Javanese, etc.

In·dō·nē'siăn, *n.* 1. a member of a light-brown, non-Malay race of Indonesia, the Philippines, Java, etc., apparently of mixed Polynesian and Mongoloid stock.

2. an inhabitant of Indonesia.

3. the Indonesian languages.

in'dōor, *a.* [for earlier *within-door.*]

1. of the inside of a house or building.

2. living, belonging, or carried on in a house or building.

in'dōor bāse'bạll, 1. the game of baseball, adapted for playing in a gymnasium or on a small field: the ball is larger and softer and the base lines shorter than those in baseball proper: also called *softball.*

2. this ball.

in'dōorş, *adv.* into, inside, or within a building or house; as, come *indoors*; he is employed *indoors.*

in·dō·phē'nōl, *n.* [*ind*igo, and *phenol.*] any of a series of synthetic blue dyes derived from quinonimines.

in·dorş'ȧ·ble, *a.* same as *endorsable.*

in·dor·sā'tion, *n.* endorsement. [Scot.]

in·dorse', *v.t.*; indorsed (-dorst), *pt., pp.*; indorsing, *ppr.* to endorse.

in·dorsed' (-dorst'), *a.* same as *endorsed.*

in·dor·see', *n.* same as *endorsee.*

in·dorse'ment, *n.* same as *endorsement.*

in·dorş'ẽr, *n.* same as *endorser.*

in·dow', *v.t.* to endow. [Obs.]

in·dow'ment, *n.* endowment. [Obs.]

in·dox'yl, *n.* [*ind*igo and hydr*oxyl.*] a compound, C_8H_7NO, produced by the hydrolysis of indican and synthesized by several methods: it is important in the synthesis of indigo.

in·dox·yl'iç, *a.* related to indoxyl.

In'drȧ, *n.* [Sans.] a Hindu deity originally representing the sky or heavens, and worshiped in the Vedic period as the supreme god, though he afterward assumed a subordinate place in the Indian pantheon. He is represented in various ways in painting and sculpture, especially with four arms and hands, and riding on an elephant.

INDRA

in'drȧft, in'drạught (-drȧft), *n.* 1. a drawing in; inward pull or attraction.

2. an inward flow, current, or stream.

3. an opening from the sea into the land; an inlet. [Obs.]

in'drạwn', *a.* drawn in; introspective.

in·drench', *v.t.* to overwhelm with water; to drown; to drench. [Obs.]

in'dri, *n.* [Fr.; false use of Malagasy *indry*, behold, mistaken for the name of the animal.] a large animal of the lemur family, *Indris laniger*, native to Madagascar.

in·dū'bi·ous, *a.* not dubious or doubtful; certain.

in·dū'bi·tȧ·ble, *a.* [L. *indubitabilis*; *in-* priv., and *dubitabilis*, doubtful, from *dubitare*, to doubt.] that cannot be doubted; unquestionable; evident.

Syn.—unquestionable, indisputable, undeniable, incontrovertible, irrefragable.

in·dū'bi·tȧ·ble, *n.* an indubitable statement or proposition.

in·dū'bi·tȧ·ble·ness, *n.* the state of being indubitable.

in·dū'bi·tȧ·bly, *adv.* in an indubitable manner; surely; unquestionably; without doubt.

in·dū'bi·tāte, *a.* not questioned; evident; certain. [Obs.]

in·dū'bi·tāte, *v.t.* to call in question; to surround with doubt. [Obs.]

in·dūce', *v.t.*; induced (-dūst'), *pt., pp.*; inducing, *ppr.* [ME. *enducen*; L. *inducere*, to lead or bring in; *in*, in, and *ducere*, to lead.]

1. to lead on to some action, condition, belief, etc., as by persuasion or argument; to prevail on; to incite; to persuade.

2. to produce; to bring on; to cause; as, a fever *induced* by extreme fatigue.

3. to introduce; to bring into view. [Obs.]

4. to put or draw on; to place upon. [Obs.]

5. to reach (a general rule or conclusion) by inference from particular facts.

6. in physics, to bring about (an electric or magnetic effect) in a body by exposing it to the influence or variation of a field of force.

Syn.—actuate, cause, incite, influence, instigate, persuade.

in·dūced′, *a.* caused; brought on; caused by induction.

induced current; in electricity, a current produced in a conductor by a variation in the intensity of the magnetic field through which it passes.

in·dūce′ment, *n.* 1. motive; anything that leads the mind to will or to act; incentive.

If this *inducement* move her not to love,
Send her a letter of thy noble deeds.
—Shak.

2. in law, an explanatory introduction in a pleading.

3. the act of inducing.

Syn.—cause, incitement, motive, reason.

in·dū′cẽr, *n.* one who or that which induces, persuades, or influences.

in·dū′ci·ble, *a.* that can be induced.

in·duçt′, *v.t.*; inducted, *pt., pp.*; inducting, *ppr.* [L. *inductus*, pp. of *inducere*, to lead or bring in; *in*, in, and *ducere*, to lead.]

1. to bring in or introduce; to initiate.

2. to place in a benefice or official position with formality or ceremony; to install.

3. (a) to bring formally into a society or organization; to initiate; (b) to bring formally into the armed forces.

4. in physics, to induce.

in·duç′tănce, *n.* 1. the property of an electric circuit by which a varying current in it produces a varying magnetic field that induces voltages in the same circuit or in a near-by circuit: it is measured in henrys.

2. the capacity of an electric circuit for reacting to a current produced in this way.

3. a circuit, condenser, etc. having inductance.

in·duçt″ee′, *n.* a person inducted or being inducted.

in·duç′tē·ous, *a.* in electricity, made to assume polarity or change of polarity by induction.

in·duç′tile, *a.* not ductile; specifically, (a) that cannot be stretched, drawn, or hammered thin without breaking; (b) not easily molded; not pliant; (c) not easily led; intractable.

in·duç·til′i·ty, *n.* the quality or condition of being inductile.

in·duç′tion, *n.* [OFr. *induction*; L. *inductio* (*-onis*), a leading or bringing into, an introducing.]

1. an inducting or being inducted; installation; introduction; entrance; initiation.

2. an introduction or preface; an introductory scene in a play; a preamble or prologue. [Archaic.]

3. a beginning; commencement. [Obs.]

4. in logic, the process of reasoning or drawing a conclusion from particular facts or individual cases; also, the conclusion reached by such reasoning.

5. an inducing, or bringing about.

6. in physics, the act or process by which an electric or magnetic effect is produced in an electrical conductor or magnetizable body when it is exposed to the influence or variation of a field of force.

electrodynamic induction; the generation of an electric current in a conductor by the influence of another current.

electromagnetic induction; the generation of an electromotive force by the cutting of the magnetic flux, as by a moving conductor in an electric generator.

electrostatic induction; the development of an electrical charge in a body by the influence of a static charge in another body brought close to it, the induced charge being of opposite character to the inducing charge.

magnetic induction; magnetization induced in a magnetizable substance when brought into a magnetic field.

mutual induction; induction which two adjacent circuits produce on each other, due either to variations in the strength of the current in the circuits, or to variations in the distance between the circuits.

Syn.—In *induction* we observe a sufficient number of individual facts, and, on the ground of analogy, extend what is true of them to others of the same class, thus arriving at general principles or laws. In *deduction* we begin with a general truth, and seek to connect it with some individual case by means of a middle term or class of objects known to be equally connected with both. Thus we deduce the specific from the general, attributing to the former the distinctive qualities of the latter.

in·duç′tion·ăl, *a.* pertaining to induction; inductive.

in·duç′tion bal′ănce, an electrical apparatus for the detection of the presence of a metallic substance by the aid of induced currents. It consists essentially of two primary coils of wire placed in the circuit of a battery and microphone. Two small secondary coils are placed near them in the circuit of a telephone, and when the currents induced in them exactly neutralize or balance each other, no sound is heard in the telephone. Should the balance be disturbed as by the introduction of a piece of metal, the telephone is made to emit a sound.

in·duç′tion bridġe, a form of induction balance for measuring the value of electric resistances.

in·duç′tion çoil, a coiled apparatus made up of two coupled circuits: interruptions in the direct current in one circuit produce an alternating current of high potential in the other.

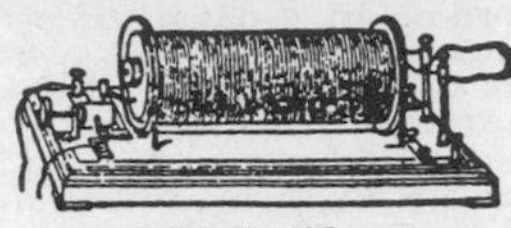

INDUCTION COIL

It consists essentially of two coils wound on a hollow cylinder, within which is a core formed of a bar of soft iron or a bundle of soft iron wires. One of the coils, called the *primary coil*, is connected with the battery by means of an arrangement for establishing and breaking connection with it, so as to produce temporary currents; the other, the *secondary coil*, is wound round the first, but carefully insulated from it, and in it is generated a current by induction every time the current begins or stops in the primary coil. Called also *Ruhmkorff coil* and *inductorium*.

in·duç′tion pīpe, the pipe in a steam engine through which the live steam passes to the cylinder.

in·duç′tion pōrt, in a steam engine, the port which is open for the admission of steam into the cylinder.

in·duç′tion valve, the valve in a steam engine which directs the admission of steam into the cylinder.

in·duç′tive, *a.* [LL. *inductivus*, leading to inferences, serving to induce.]

1. inducing; attractive; persuasive.

2. of, or proceeding by methods of, logical induction; as, *inductive* reasoning.

3. produced by induction.

4. of inductance or electrical or magnetic induction.

5. introductory.

6. in physiology, producing a change or response in an organism.

7. tending to induce or cause. [Obs.]

in·duç′tive·ly, *adv.* by induction or inference.

in·duç·tiv′i·ty, *n.* 1. the property of a substance which determines its capacity for electrical or magnetic induction; inductance.

2. specific inductive capacity.

in·duç·tom′e·tẽr, *n.* [L. *inductio* (*-onis*), induction, and *metrum*, a measure.] an instrument for measuring the degree or rate of electrical induction, or for comparing the specific inductive capacities of various substances.

in·duçt′ŏr, *n.* [L., one who stirs up, a chastiser, lit., one who leads or brings in.]

1. a person who inducts.

2. a thing that inducts; specifically, a part of an electrical apparatus that acts on another, or is acted upon, by induction.

in·duç·tō′ri·um, *n.* same as *induction coil*.

in·duç′tō·sçōpe, *n.* [L. *inductio* (*-onis*), induction, and Gr. *skopein*, to view.] an instrument for detecting magnetic or electrical induction.

in·duç′triç, *a.* in electricity, acting on other bodies by induction. [Obs.]

in·duç′triç·ăl, *a.* inductric. [Obs.]

in·dūe′, *v.t.*; indued, *pt., pp.*; induing, *ppr.* [L. *induere*, to put on, to dress oneself, from Old L. *indu*, L. *in*, in, on.] to endue.

in·dūe′ment, *n.* same as *enduement*.

in·dulġe′, *v.t.*; indulged, *pt., pp.*; indulging, *ppr.* [L. *indulgere*, to be kind or indulgent to.]

1. to yield or satisfy (a desire); to give oneself up to.

2. to gratify the wishes of; to be very lenient with; to humor.

3. to grant as an ecclesiastical indulgence or dispensation to.

4. to grant as a kindness, favor, or privilege. [Obs.]

5. in business, to grant (a person) an extension of time to make payment on a bill or note.

Syn.—gratify, pamper, favor, humor, please.

in·dulġe′, *v.i.* to yield to one's own desires; to indulge oneself (*in* something); as, to *indulge in* sin.

Most men are more willing to *indulge in* easy vices, than to practice laborious virtues.
—Johnson.

in·dulġe′ment, *n.* indulgence. [Rare.]

in·dul′ġence, *n.* [ME. *indulgence*; L. *indulgentia*, indulgence, gentleness, from *indulgens* (*-entis*), ppr. of *indulgere*, to indulge.]

1. an indulging or being indulgent.

2. what is indulged in.

3. an indulging oneself; giving way to one's own desires.

4. a favor or privilege.

If all these gracious *indulgences* are without effect on us, we must perish in our folly.
—Rogers.

5. in business, an extension of time to make payment on a bill or note, granted as a favor.

6. [*sometimes* I–] in English history, the grant of certain religious liberties to Dissenters and Roman Catholics by Charles II and James II.

7. in the Roman Catholic Church, a remission of temporal or purgatorial punishment still due for a sin after the guilt has been forgiven in the sacrament of penance.

in·dul′ġence, *v.t.*; indulgenced, *pt., pp.*; indulgencing, *ppr.* to apply an indulgence to.

in·dul′ġen·cy, *n.* indulgence. [Now Rare.]

in·dul′ġent, *a.* [L. *indulgens* (*-entis*), ppr. of *indulgere*, to indulge.] indulging or inclined to indulge; kind or lenient, often to excess.

Syn.—compliant, forbearing, tender, tolerant, lenient.

in·dul·ġen′tiăl (-shăl), *a.* relating to the indulgences of the Roman Catholic Church. [Obs.]

in·dul′ġent·ly, *adv.* in an indulgent manner; with compliance; mildly; favorably.

in·dul′ġẽr, *n.* one who indulges.

in·dul′ġi·āte, *v.t.* to indulge. [Obs.]

in′dū·lin, *n.* same as *induline*.

in′dū·line (*or* -lin), *n.* [*ind*igo, and *-ule*, and *-ine*.] any of a series of blue or black aniline dyes.

in·dult′, *n.* [LL. *indultum*, an indulgence, neut. of L. *indultus*, pp. of *indulgere*, to indulge.]

1. in canon law, a privilege or special permission to do something otherwise prohibited, granted by ecclesiastical authority, as by the Pope to a bishop, for a specified or unspecified period of time.

2. in Spain, a duty, tax, or custom formerly paid to the king on imported goods.

in·dul′tō, *n.* an indult, or tax.

in′dū·ment, *n.* a garment; covering. [Obs.]

in·dū·men′tum, *n.* [L., a garment, from *induere*, to put on.]

1. in ornithology, plumage.

2. in botany, a hairy covering.

in·dū′nȧ, *n.* [Zulu.] a Zulu leader.

in·dū′pli·cāte, *a.* [L. *in*, in, on, and *duplicatus*, pp. of *duplicare*, to double, from *duplex*, double.] having the edges folded or rolled in, but not overlapping: said of the arrangement of leaves in a leaf bud or of the calyx or corolla in a flower bud.

in·dū·pli·cā′tion, *n.* the state of being induplicate; anything induplicate.

in·dū′pli·cȧ·tive, *a.* same as *induplicate*.

in·dūr′ănce, *n.* endurance. [Obs.]

in′dū·rāte, *v.t.*; indurated, *pt., pp.*; indurating, *ppr.* [L. *induratus*, pp. of *indurare*, to make hard; *in*, in, and *durare*, to harden, from *durus*, hard.]

1. to make hard; to harden; as, extreme heat *indurates* clay.

2. to make unfeeling, callous, or stubborn.

in′dū·rāte, *v.i.* to grow hard; to harden or become hard.

in′dū·rāte, *a.* 1. hardened.

2. made callous, stubborn, obdurate, or unfeeling.

in′dū·rā·ted, *a.* same as *indurate*.

in·dū·rā′tion, *n.* 1. an indurating or being indurated.

2. a hardened mass or formation.

in′dū·rā·tive, *a.* indurating or tending to indurate.

In′dus, *n.* a southern constellation.
in·dū′ṣi·ȧ, *n.* plural of *indusium.*
in·dū′ṣi·ăl, *a.* [from L. *indusium,* a covering.] composed of or containing an indusium or indusia.
indusial limestone; in geology, a fresh-water limestone found in Auvergne, France, mainly composed of the agglomerated indusia of caddis flies.
in·dū′ṣi·āte, *a.* having an indusium.
in·dū′ṣi·ā·ted, *a.* indusiate.
in·dū′ṣi·um, *n.*; *pl.* **in·dū′ṣi·ȧ,** [L., undergarment, tunic; associated with *induere,* to put on, but prob. from Gr. *endysis,* dress, clothing, from *endyein,* to go into, put on.]
1. in anatomy and zoology, (a) any covering membrane, as the amnion; (b) a case enclosing an insect larva.
2. in botany, an outgrowth of the leaf epidermis in ferns, covering the sporangia.
in·dus′tri·ăl, *a.* [from Fr. and ML.; Fr. *industriel*; ML. *industrialis.*]
1. having the nature of or characterized by industry or industries.
2. of, connected with, or resulting from industry or industries.
3. working in industries.
4. of or concerned with people working in industries.
5. for use by industries: said of products.
industrial arts; the technical arts used in industry, especially as a subject for study in schools.
industrial disease; any disease commonly occurring in a particular industry.
industrial exhibition; an exhibition of industrial products.
industrial relations; relations between employers and employees.
Industrial Revolution; [*often* i— r—] the change in social and economic organization resulting from the replacement of hand tools by machine and power tools and the development of large-scale industrial production: applied to this development in England from about 1760 and to similar later changes in other countries.
industrial school; a technical school offering instruction in the manual or industrial arts; especially, such a school to which neglected youths are sent for training.
industrial union; a labor union to which all the workers in a given industry can belong, no matter what their occupation or trade: distinguished from *craft* (or *horizontal*) *union*: also called *vertical union.*
in·dus′tri·ăl, *n.* 1. a person engaged in an industrial pursuit.
2. a stock, bond, etc. of an industrial corporation or enterprise.
in·dus′tri·ăl·iṣm, *n.* social and economic organization characterized by large industries, machine production, concentration of workers in towns and cities, etc.
in·dus′tri·ăl·ist, *n.* a person who owns, controls, or has an important position in the management of an industrial enterprise.
in·dus′tri·ăl·ist, *a.* pertaining to or characterized by industrialism.
in·dus″tri·ăl·i·zā′tion, *n.* an industrializing or being industrialized.
in·dus′tri·ăl·īze, *v.t.*; industrialized, *pt., pp.*; industrializing, *ppr.* 1. to make industrial; to establish or develop industrialism in.
2. to organize as an industry.
in·dus′tri·ăl·ly, *adv.* with reference to industry; in an industrial manner.
In·dus′tri·ăl Wŏrk′ẽrṣ of the Wŏrld, a former international labor organization favoring socialism and the abolition of the wage system: abbreviated *I. W. W.*
in·dus′tri·ous, *a.* [L. *industriosus,* active, diligent, from *industria,* diligence, industry.]
1. originally, characterized by or showing intelligent work; skillful; clever.
2. characterized by earnest, steady effort; hard-working; diligent.
Frugal and *industrious* men are commonly friendly to the established government.
—Temple.
Syn.—busy, active, diligent, laborious, sedulous.
in·dus′tri·ous·ly, *adv.* in an industrious manner.
in·dus′tri·ous·ness, *n.* the quality of being industrious.
in′dus·try, *n.*; *pl.* **in′dus·trieṣ,** [Fr. *industrie*; L. *industria,* diligence, industry, assiduity, from *industrius,* active, industrious.]
1. originally, (a) intelligent work; skill; cleverness; (b) an application of this; device; contrivance.
2. earnest, steady effort; constant diligence in or application to work.
3. systematic work; habitual employment.
4. any branch of trade, business, production, or manufacture; as, the paper *industry,* the motion-picture *industry.*
5. (a) manufacturing productive enterprises as distinguished from agriculture; (b) the owners and managers of industry.
Syn.—activity, diligence, sedulousness, assiduity, laboriousness.
in·dū′tive, *a.* [L. *indutus,* pp. of *induere,* to cover.] in botany, having the usual integumentary covering: applied to seeds. [Rare.]
in·dū′vi·ae, *n.pl.* [L., garments, clothing, from *induere,* to put on.] the withered leaves which remain on the stems of some plants.
in·dū′vi·āte, *a.* in botany, covered with induviae.
in·dwell′, *v.i.*; indwelt, *pt., pp.*; indwelling, *ppr.* to dwell, or live (*in*).
in·dwell′, *v.t.* to dwell in; to inhabit.
in′dwell·ẽr, *n.* an inhabitant.
in′dwell·ing, *a.* dwelling within; remaining, as in the heart; as, *indwelling* sin.
in′dwell·ing, *n.* residence within, as in the heart or soul.
-ine (*variously* īn, in, ēn), a suffix meaning *of, having the nature of, like*: (a) [Fr. *-in, -ine*; L. *-inus,* masc., *-ina,* f., *-inum,* neut.] added to bases of Latin origin to form adjectives, and nouns derived from them, as in aquil*ine,* div*ine*; (b) [L. *-inus*; Gr. *-inos.*] used to form adjectives, as in adamant*ine,* crystall*ine.*
-ine (*variously* in, īn, ēn), a suffix of various sources, used to form feminine nouns; (a) [from L. *-ina,* from Gr. *-inē.*] as in hero*ine*; (b) [from L. *-ina.*] as in Clement*ine*; (c) [from G. *-in,* after Fr. *-ine.*] as in landgrav*ine* and some other German feminine titles.
-ine (in), [Fr. *-ine*; L. *-ina,* suffix of f. abstract nouns.] a suffix used to form certain abstract nouns, as in medic*ine,* doctr*ine.*
-ine (en, in, īn), [arbitrary use of L. *-inus,* masc., *-ina,* f., *n.* and *a.* ending.] (a) a suffix used to form the commercial names of certain products, as in vasel*ine*; (b) a suffix used to form the chemical names of *halogens,* as in brom*ine,* iod*ine*; (c) a suffix used to form the chemical names of *alkaloids* or *nitrogen bases,* as in morph*ine*: also *-in.* The names of neutral substances, as carbohydrates, glucosides, proteins, etc. are formed with *-in* (e.g., inul*in,* amygdal*in,* album*in*).
in·ēarth′, *v.t.* to put into the earth; to inter; to bury. [Poetic.]
in·ē′bri·ȧ·cy, *n.* the habit of becoming intoxicated.
in·ē′bri·ȧnt, *a.* [L. *inebrians* (*-antis*), ppr. of *inebriare,* to intoxicate.] intoxicating.
in·ē′bri·ȧnt, *n.* anything that intoxicates; an intoxicant.
in·ē′bri·āte, *v.t.*; inebriated, *pt., pp.*; inebriating, *ppr.* [L. *inebriatus,* pp. of *inebriare,* to intoxicate; *in* intens., and *ebriare,* to make drunk, from *ebrius,* drunk.]
1. to make drunk; to intoxicate.
2. to disorder the senses of; to stupefy; to excite; to exhilarate.
in·ē′bri·āte, *v.i.* to become intoxicated. [Obs.]
in·ē′bri·āte, *n.* a drunken person, especially a habitual drunkard.
in·ē′bri·āte, *a.* intoxicated; drunk.
in·ē′bri·āt·ed, *a.* drunk; intoxicated.
in·ē·bri·ā′tion, *n.* drunkenness; intoxication; the state of being inebriated.
in·e·bri′e·ty, *n.* drunkenness; intoxication.
in·ē′bri·ous, *a.* [L. *in-* intens., and *ebrius,* drunk.] drunk or partly drunk; producing intoxication. [Rare.]
in·ed·i·bil′i·ty, *n.* the state or quality of being inedible.
in·ed′i·ble, *a.* not edible; not fit to be eaten.
in·ed′it·ed, *a.* unpublished; not edited; as, an *inedited* manuscript.
In·ed″ū·çȧ·bil′i·ȧ, *n.pl.* [L. *in-* priv., and *educare,* to bring up, educate.] a series of mammals having a comparatively small cerebrum, as rodents, edentates, etc.
in·ed″ū·çȧ·bil′i·ăn, *a.* pertaining to the *Ineducabilia.*
in·ed″ū·çȧ·bil′i·ăn, *n.* any of the *Ineducabilia.*
in·ef·fȧ·bil′i·ty, *n.* the quality of being ineffable.
in·ef′fȧ·ble, *a.* [Fr.; L. *ineffabilis*; *in-* priv., and *effabilis,* utterable, from *effari,* to speak out, to utter.]
1. too overwhelming to be expressed or described in words; inexpressible.
2. too awesome or sacred to be spoken; as, God's *ineffable* name.
Syn.—inexpressible, inconceivable, indescribable.
in·ef′fȧ·ble·ness, *n.* unspeakableness; the quality of being ineffable.
in·ef′fȧ·bly, *adv.* so as to be ineffable.
in·ef·fāce′ȧ·ble, *a.* that cannot be effaced; impossible to wipe out or erase; indelible.
in·ef·fāce′ȧ·bly, *adv.* so as to be ineffaceable.
in·ef·feçt′i·ble, *a.* impracticable. [Rare.]
in·ef·feçt′ive, *a.* 1. not effective; not producing the effect intended.
2. not capable of performing satisfactorily; incompetent; inefficient; as, he is *ineffective* in an emergency.
in·ef·feçt′ive·ly, *adv.* in an ineffective manner.
in·ef·feçt′ive·ness, *n.* the quality of being ineffective.
in·ef·feç′tū·ăl, *a.* not producing or not able to produce the desired effect; inefficient; weak; as, an *ineffectual* remedy.
Syn.—fruitless, useless, vain, idle, unavailing, abortive, ineffective.
in·ef·feç·tū·al′i·ty, *n.* ineffectualness; the quality of being ineffectual.
in·ef·feç′tū·ăl·ly, *adv.* in an ineffectual manner.
in·ef·feç′tū·ăl·ness, *n.* lack of effect, or of power to produce it; inefficacy.
in·ef·fẽr·ves′cence, *n.* lack of effervescence; a state of not effervescing.
in·ef·fẽr·ves′cent, *a.* not effervescing.
in·ef·fẽr·ves·ci·bil′i·ty, *n.* the quality of being ineffervescible.
in·ef·fẽr·ves′ci·ble, *a.* not capable of effervescence.
in·ef·fi·çā′cious, *a.* not efficacious; not having power to produce the desired effect: said of medicines, treatments, etc.
in·ef·fi·çā′cious·ly, *adv.* without efficacy or effect.
in·ef·fi·çā′cious·ness, *n.* lack of power to produce the effect, or lack of effect; inefficacy.
in·ef′fi·çȧ·cy, *n.* [LL. *inefficacia,* from L. *inefficax* (*-acis*), ineffectual, inefficacious.] lack of efficacy; lack of power to produce the desired effect; as, the *inefficacy* of medicines or of means.
in·ef·fi′cien·cy (-fish′en-), *n.* the quality, condition, or fact of being inefficient; lack of efficiency.
in·ef·fi′cient, *a.* not efficient; specifically, (a) not producing the desired effect with a minimum use of energy, time, etc.; ineffective; (b) lacking the necessary ability; unskilled; incapable.
in·ef·fi′cient·ly, *adv.* in an inefficient manner.
in·ē·lab′ō·rāte, *a.* not elaborate; not done with care; unfinished as to details.
in·ē·las′tiç, *a.* not elastic; inflexible, rigid, unyielding, unadaptable, etc.
in·ē·las·tic′i·ty, *n.* the quality or condition of being inelastic.
in·el′ē·gănce, *n.* 1. lack of elegance; the quality of being inelegant.
2. something inelegant.
in·el′ē·găn·cy, *n.*; *pl.* **in·el′ē·găn·cieṣ,** inelegance.
in·el′ē·gănt, *a.* not elegant; lacking refinement, good taste, grace, etc.; coarse, crude.
in·el′ē·gănt·ly, *adv.* in an inelegant or unbecoming manner; coarsely; roughly.
in·el″i·gi·bil′i·ty, *n.* the quality, state, or fact of being ineligible; lack of eligibility.
in·el′i·gi·ble, *a.* [LL. *ineligibilis,* that cannot be chosen; L. *in-* priv., and *eligere,* to choose.]
1. not eligible for election to an office.
2. not worthy to be chosen or preferred; not expedient.
in·el′i·gi·bly, *adv.* in an ineligible manner.
in·el′ō·quence, *n.* lack of eloquence.
in·el′ō·quent, *a.* not eloquent; not fluent, forceful, and persuasive.
in·el′ō·quent·ly, *adv.* without eloquence.
in·ē·luç·tȧ·bil′i·ty, *n.* the quality or state of being ineluctable.
in·ē·luç′tȧ·ble, *a.* [L. *ineluctabilis*; *in-* priv., and *eluctabilis,* that may be resisted by struggling, from *eluctari,* to struggle.] not to be resisted by struggling; not to be avoided or escaped; certain; inevitable; as, *ineluctable* fate.
in·ē·luç′tȧ·bly, *adv.* so as to be ineluctable.
in·ē·lūd′i·ble, *a.* that cannot be eluded or escaped; imminent.
in·em′bry·ō·nāte, *a.* not embryonated.
in·ē·nar′rȧ·ble, *a.* that cannot be narrated or told.
in·ē·nū′çlē·ȧ·ble, *a.* [L. *in-* priv., and *enucleatus,* pp. of *enucleare,* to enucleate; *e,* out, and

nucleus, a kernel.] that cannot be removed without cutting; as, an *inenucleable* tumor.

in·ept′, *a.* [L. *ineptus*, unsuitable, stupid; *in-* priv., and *aptus*, suitable, fit.]
1. not apt or fit; unfit; unsuitable.
2. unreasonable; foolish; absurd.
3. awkward; clumsy; inefficient.

In·ep′tī, *n.pl.* [L., pl. of *ineptus*, stupid, inept.] a group of birds typified by the dodo.

in·ept′i·tūde, *n.* 1. the quality of being inept.
2. an inept act, remark, etc.

in·ept′ly, *adv.* unfitly; unsuitably; foolishly.

in·ept′ness, *n.* unfitness; lack of aptitude.

in·eq′uȧ·ble (-ek′wȧ- *or* -ē′kwȧ-), *a.* not equable; lacking in uniformity; as, an *inequable* climate.

in·ē′quăl, *a.* unequal; uneven; various.

in·ē·quäl′i·ty, *n.*; *pl.* **in·ē·quäl′i·tieș**, [MFr. *inequalité*; L. *inæqualitas* (*-atis*), unlikeness.]
1. the quality of being unequal; lack of equality.
2. an instance of lack of equality; specifically, (a) difference or variation in size, amount, rank, quality, social position, etc.; (b) unevenness in surface; lack of levelness; (c) lack of proper proportion; unequal distribution.
3. in mathematics, the relation between two unequal quantities, or an expression of this relationship: also *inequation*. Examples: $a \neq b$ (a is not equal to b), $4 < 7$ (4 is less than 7), $3a > 2b$ (3a is greater than 2b).
4. in astronomy, an irregularity or deviation in the motion of a planet or satellite from its uniform mean motion; also, the extent of such deviation.

in·ē·quā′tion, *n.* in mathematics, an inequality.

in′ē·qui-, [*in-* priv., and *equi-*.] a combining form meaning *not equal, not equally*, as in *inequi*lateral.

in·ē·qui·dis′tȧnt, *a.* not being equally distant.

in·ē·qui·lat′ĕr·ăl, *a.* 1. having unequal sides; not equilateral.
2. in conchology, lacking equality in the anterior and posterior parts of the valve, as in the mussel and oyster.

in·ē·qui·lō′bāte, *a.* in biology, having lobes differing in size or lacking symmetry.

in·eq′ui·tȧ·ble, *a.* not equitable; unfair; not just.

in·eq′ui·tāte, *v.t.* to ride horseback into, upon, or over. [Obs.]

in·eq′ui·ty, *n.* 1. lack of the quality of equity or fairness.
2. *pl.* **in·eq′ui·tieș**, an instance of injustice or unfairness.

in·ē′qui·valve, *a.* having unequal valves, as the shell of an oyster.

in·ē·qui·val′vū·lăr, *a.* inequivalve.

in·ē·rad′i·cȧ·ble, *a.* incapable of being eradicated; too firmly fixed to be rooted out or done away with.

in·ē·rad′i·cȧ·bly, *adv.* so as to be ineradicable.

in·ē·rās′ȧ·ble, *a.* incapable of being erased.

in·ĕr·get′iç, *a.* having no energy. [Obs.]

in·ĕr·get′iç·ăl, *a.* inergetic. [Obs.]

in·ĕr·get′iç·ăl·ly, *adv.* without energy. [Obs.]

in·ĕrm′, *a.* [L. *inermis*, unarmed; *in-* priv., and *arma*, arms.] in botany, unarmed; having no prickles or thorns, as a leaf.

in·ĕr′mous, *a.* same as *inerm*.

in·ĕr·rȧ·bil′i·ty, *n.* the quality or state of being inerrable.

in·ĕr′rȧ·ble, *a.* [LL. *inerrabilis*; L. *in-* priv., and *errare*, to wander, err.] not erring; infallible.

in·ĕr′rȧ·ble·ness, *n.* same as *inerrability*.

in·ĕr′rȧ·bly, *adv.* in an inerrable manner; infallibly.

in·er′răn·cy, *n.* the state or quality of being inerrant.

in·er′rănt, *a.* not erring; making no mistake; infallible.

in·er·rat′iç, *a.* not erratic or wandering; fixed.

in·ĕrr′ing·ly, *adv.* without error, mistake, or deviation.

in·ĕrt′, *a.* [L. *iners* (*-ertis*), without skill or art, idle; *in-* priv., and *ars*, *artis*, skill, art.]
1. having inertia; without power to move or to resist an opposing force.
2. tending to be physically or mentally inactive; dull; slow.
3. with few or no active properties; neutral; as, the *inert* ingredients of a medicine.

Syn.—inactive, sluggish, powerless, lazy, slothful, lifeless, passive.—A man may be *inactive* from mere lack of incentive, but one who is *inert* has something in his constitution or his habits which operates like a weight holding him back from exertion. *Sluggish* is still stronger, implying some defect of physical or mental constitution.

in·ĕr′tiȧ (-shȧ), *n.* [L. *inertia*, lack of art or skill, ignorance, from *iners* (*-ertis*), unskillful, inert.]
1. in physics, the tendency of matter to remain at rest if at rest, or, if moving, to keep moving in the same direction, unless affected by some outside force: symbol, I.
2. a tendency to remain in a fixed condition without change; disinclination to move or act.
3. in medicine, lack of activity, as of the uterus when it ceases to contract in parturition.

in·ĕr′tiăl, *a.* of, or having the nature of, inertia.

in·ĕr′tion, *n.* lack of activity; lack of action or exertion. [Rare.]

in·ĕrt′ly, *adv.* in an inert manner.

in·ĕrt′ness, *n.* the state or quality of being inert.

in·er′ū·dīte, *a.* [L. *ineruditus*; *in-* priv., and *eruditus*, polished.] without erudition.

in·es·çāp′ȧ·ble, *a.* that cannot be escaped; unavoidable; inevitable.

in·es′çāte, *v.t.* to bait; to lay a bait for. [Obs.]

in·es·çā′tion, *n.* the act of baiting. [Obs.]

in·es·çutch′eŏn, *n.* in heraldry, a miniature escutcheon borne upon a shield or escutcheon.

INESCUTCHEON

in es′sē, [L. *in*, in, and *esse*, to be.] in being; actually existing: distinguished from *in posse*, which denotes that a thing is not, but may be.

in·es·sen′tiăl (-shăl), *a.* 1. without essence or existence; immaterial. [Rare.]
2. not essential; not really necessary or important; unessential.

in·es·sen′tiăl, *n.* something inessential.

in·es′ti·mȧ·ble, *a.* [OFr. *inestimable*; L. *inæstimabilis*, not worthy to be esteemed; *in-* priv., and *æstimabilis*, worthy of estimation, from *æstimare*, to value, esteem.]
1. that cannot be estimated or computed; as, an *inestimable* sum of money.
2. too valuable or excellent to be properly measured or appreciated; above all price; as, *inestimable* rights.

in·es′ti·mȧ·bly, *adv.* to an inestimable degree.

in·ē·vā′si·ble, *a.* that cannot be evaded.

in·ev′i·dence, *n.* lack of evidence; obscurity. [Rare.]

in·ev′i·dent, *a.* not evident; not clear or obvious; obscure. [Rare.]

in·ev″i·tȧ·bil′i·ty, *n.* the state, quality, or fact of being inevitable.

in·ev′i·tȧ·ble, *a.* [ME.; L. *inevitabilis*; *in-* priv., and *evitabilis*, avoidable, from *evitare*, to shun, avoid.] that cannot be avoided or evaded; certain to happen; as, to die is the *inevitable* lot of man.

Syn.—certain, unavoidable, necessary.

in·ev′i·tȧ·ble·ness, *n.* the state of being inevitable.

in·ev′i·tȧ·bly, *adv.* so as to be inevitable; unavoidably; certainly.

in·ex·açt′ (-egz-), *a.* not exact; not precisely correct or true.

in·ex·açt′i·tūde, *n.* [Fr.] lack of exactitude; inexactness.

in·ex·açt′ly, *adv.* without exactness; not accurately.

in·ex·açt′ness (-egz-), *n.* incorrectness; lack of precision.

in·ex·cīt·ȧ·bil′i·ty, *n.* the quality or condition of being inexcitable. [Rare.]

in·ex·cīt′ȧ·ble, *a.* that cannot be excited. [Rare.]

in·ex·çūș·ȧ·bil′i·ty, *n.* the quality of being inexcusable.

in·ex·çūș′ȧ·ble, *a.* [L. *inexcusabilis*; *in-* priv., and *excusabilis*, excusable, from *excusare*, to excuse.] that cannot or should not be excused; unpardonable; unjustifiable; as, *inexcusable* folly.

in·ex·çūș′ȧ·ble·ness, *n.* the quality of being inexcusable.

in·ex·çūș′ȧ·bly, *adv.* in an inexcusable manner; so as to be inexcusable.

in·ex′ē·çrȧ·ble, *a.* execrable in the highest degree: apparently so used by Shakespeare. [Obs.]

in·ex·ē·çūt′ȧ·ble, *a.* that cannot be executed or performed.

in·ex·ē·çū′tion, *n.* lack of execution; failure to do something; nonperformance; as, the *inexecution* of a treaty.

in·ex·ĕr′tion (-egz-), *n.* lack of exertion; failure to exert oneself.

in·ex·hāl′ȧ·ble (-eks-), *a.* that cannot be exhaled; not evaporable.

in·ex·hạust′ed (-egz-ạst′), *a.* unexhausted.

in·ex·hạust′ed·ly, *adv.* so as to be unexhausted.

in·ex·hạust·i·bil′i·ty, *n.* the quality or state of being inexhaustible.

in·ex·hạust′i·ble, *a.* that cannot be exhausted; specifically, (a) that cannot be used up or emptied; (b) indefatigable; tireless.

in·ex·hạust′i·ble·ness, *n.* inexhaustibility.

in·ex·hạust′i·bly, *adv.* 1. in an inexhaustible manner.
2. to an inexhaustible degree.

in·ex·hạust′ive, *a.* not to be exhausted or spent.

in·ex·ist′ (-egz-), *v.i.* to exist within something else; to be inherent.

in·ex·ist′ence, *n.* nonexistence.

in·ex·ist′ence, *n.* existence within; inherence. [Rare.]

in·ex·ist′en·cy, *n.* inherence. [Rare.]

in·ex·ist′ent, *a.* not in or having being; not existent.

in·ex·ist′ent, *a.* existing within; inherent. [Rare.]

in·ex″ō·rȧ·bil′i·ty (-eks″), *n.* the quality of being inexorable.

in·ex′ō·rȧ·ble, *a.* [L. *inexorabilis*; *in-* priv., and *exorabilis*, easily entreated, from *exorare*, to entreat, persuade.] that cannot be influenced or moved by entreaty or persuasion; as, an *inexorable* tyrant; an *inexorable* judge.

Syn.—unrelenting, immovable, unchangeable, unyielding, incompassionate, inflexible, implacable, relentless.

in·ex′ō·rȧ·ble·ness, *n.* the quality of being inexorable.

in·ex′ō·rȧ·bly, *adv.* in an inexorable manner.

in·ex·pan′si·ble, *a.* not expansible.

in·ex·peçt′ȧ·ble, *a.* that cannot be expected.

in·ex·peçt′ănt, *a.* without expectation.

in·ex·peç·tā′tion, *n.* absence of expectation.

in·ex·peçt′ed, *a.* not expected. [Obs.]

in·ex·peçt′ed·ly, *adv.* in an unexpected manner. [Obs.]

in·ex·peçt′ed·ness, *n.* absence of expectation. [Obs.]

in·ex·pē′di·ence, *n.* inexpediency.

in·ex·pē′di·en·cy, *n.* the quality or condition of being inexpedient.

in·ex·pē′di·ent, *a.* not expedient; not suitable or practicable for a given situation; inadvisable; unwise; as, whatever tends to retard or defeat success is *inexpedient*.

Syn.—improper, inconvenient, unfit, unsuitable, inappropriate, inadvisable, impolitic.

in·ex·pē′di·ent·ly, *adv.* not expediently; unfitly.

in·ex·pens′ive, *a.* not expensive; costing relatively little; low-priced; cheap.

in·ex·pē′ri·ence, *n.* [LL. *inexperientia*; L. *in-* priv., and *experientia*, experience, from *experiens* (*-entis*), ppr. of *experiri*, to try.] lack of experience or of the knowledge or skill resulting from experience.

in·ex·pē′ri·enced (-enst), *a.* lacking experience or the knowledge or skill resulting from experience.

in·ex·pērt′, *a.* [L. *inexpertus*; *in-* priv., and *expertus*, pp. of *experiri*, to try.]
1. not expert; unskillful; amateurish.
2. lacking in experience. [Obs.]

in·ex·pērt′ness, *n.* lack of expertness.

in·ex′pi·ȧ·ble, *a.* [L. *inexpiabilis*; *in-* priv., and *expiare*, to atone, expiate.]
1. that cannot be expiated or atoned for; as, an *inexpiable* crime or offense.
2. that cannot be mollified or appeased; implacable; as, *inexpiable* hate. [Archaic.]

in·ex′pi·ȧ·ble·ness, *n.* the quality or state of being inexpiable.

in·ex′pi·ȧ·bly, *adv.* in an inexpiable manner.

in·ex′pi·āte, *a.* not expiated. [Rare.]

in·ex·plāin′ȧ·ble, *a.* that cannot be explained; inexplicable.

in·ex′plē·ȧ·bly, *adv.* insatiably. [Obs.]

in·ex″pli·çȧ·bil′i·ty, *n.* the quality or state of being inexplicable.

in·ex′pli·çȧ·ble, *a.* [L. *inexplicabilis*; *in-* priv., and *explicabilis*, explainable, from *explicare*, to set forth, explain.] that cannot be explained, understood, or accounted for; as, an *inexplicable* mystery.

in·ex′pli·çȧ·ble·ness, *n.* the state of being inexplicable.

in·ex′pli·çȧ·bly, *adv.* in an inexplicable manner.

in·ex·plic′it, *a.* not explicit; vague; indefinite; general.

in·ex·plōr′ȧ·ble, *a.* that cannot be explored, searched, or discovered.

in·ex·plō′sive, *a.* not explosive.

in·ex·pō′ṣūre (-zhūr), *n.* the state of not being exposed.

in·ex·press·i·bil′i·ty, *n.* the quality of being inexpressible.

in·ex·press′i·ble, *a.* that cannot be expressed; indescribable or unutterable; as, *inexpressible* grief, joy, or pleasure.

in·ex·press′i·bleṣ, *n.pl.* breeches or trousers: a humorous usage.

in·ex·press′i·bly, *adv.* in an inexpressible manner; so as to be inexpressible.

in·ex·press′ive, *a.* 1. inexpressible. [Archaic.]

2. not expressive; lacking meaning or expression; as, an *inexpressive* face.

in·ex·press′ive·ness, *n.* the state of being inexpressive.

in·ex·pug′nȧ·ble, *a.* [Fr.; L. *inexpugnabilis*; *in-* priv., and *expugnabilis*, that may be subdued by force, from *expugnare*, to subdue by force.] that cannot be defeated by force; unconquerable; unyielding.

in·ex·pug′nȧ·bly, *adv.* so as to be inexpugnable.

in·ex·sū′pẽr·ȧ·ble, *a.* [L. *inexsuperabilis*; *in-* priv., and *exsuperabilis*, surmountable.] that cannot be overcome. [Obs.]

in·ex·tend′ed, *a.* having no extension. [Rare.]

in·ex·ten′si·ble, *a.* not extensible.

in·ex·ten′sion, *n.* lack of extension; unextended state.

in ex·ten′sō, [L.] at full length; unabridged.

in·ex·tẽr′mi·nȧ·ble, *a.* that cannot be exterminated. [Rare.]

in·ex·tinçt′, *a.* unextinguished. [Rare.]

in·ex·tin′gui·ble, *a.* inextinguishable. [Obs.]

in·ex·tin′guish·ȧ·ble, *a.* that cannot be extinguished; unquenchable; as, *inextinguishable* flame, thirst, or desire.

in·ex·tin′guish·ȧ·bly, *adv.* so as to be inextinguishable.

in·ex·tir′pȧ·ble, *a.* [L. *inextirpabilis*; *in-* priv., and *extirpare*, to root out, extirpate.] that cannot be extirpated; not to be uprooted.

in ex·trē′mis, [L., in extremity.] at the point of death.

in·ex″tri·çȧ·bil′i·ty, *n.* the quality or state of being inextricable.

in·ex′tri·çȧ·ble, *a.* [Fr.; L. *inextricabilis*, *in-* priv., and *extricare*, to disentangle, extricate.]

1. that one cannot extricate himself from.

2. that cannot be disentangled or untied.

3. so complicated or involved as to be insolvable.

in·ex′tri·çȧ·ble·ness, *n.* inextricability.

in·ex′tri·çȧ·bly, *adv.* so as to be inextricable.

in·eye′ (-ī′), *v.t.*; ineyed (-īd′), *pt.*, *pp.*; ineyeing, *ppr.* to propagate by budding; to bud. [Obs.]

in·fal′li·bil·ist, *n.* one who believes in infallibility; especially, a believer in the dogma of papal infallibility.

in·fal·li·bil′i·ty, *n.* the state or quality of being infallible.

papal infallibility; in the Roman Catholic Church, the dogma that the Pope, as the supreme pontiff, is divinely guarded from error when speaking officially on matters of faith or of morals: the dogma was promulgated by the Vatican Council in July, 1870.

in·fal′li·ble, *a.* [LL. *infallibilis*; L. *in-* priv., and LL. *fallibilis*, fallible, from L. *fallere*, to deceive, err.]

1. not fallible; not capable of error; never wrong.

2. not liable to fail, go wrong, make a mistake, etc.; dependable; reliable.

3. in the Roman Catholic Church, incapable of error in setting forth doctrine on faith and morals: said especially of the Pope speaking *ex cathedra* (i.e., in his official capacity).

in·fal′li·ble, *n.* an infallible person or thing.

in·fal′li·ble·ness, *n.* infallibility.

in·fal′li·bly, *adv.* in an infallible manner.

in·fāme′, *v.t.* to defame. [Obs.]

in′fȧ·mīze, *v.t.*; infamized, *pt.*, *pp.*; infamizing, *ppr.* to make infamous.

in′fȧ·mous, *a.* [ME.; OFr. *infameux*; LL. *infamosus*, L. *infamis*, of evil report; *in-* priv., and *fama*, report, fame.]

1. having a very bad reputation; notorious; in disgrace or dishonor.

2. causing or deserving a bad reputation; scandalous; outrageous.

3. in law, (a) punishable by imprisonment in a penitentiary: said of certain crimes; (b) guilty of such a crime.

Syn.—wicked, heinous, disgraceful, shameful, execrable, ignominious.

in′fȧ·mous·ly, *adv.* in an infamous manner.

in′fȧ·mous·ness, *n.* the quality of being infamous.

in′fȧ·my, *n.*; *pl.* **in′fȧ·mieṣ,** [Fr. *infamie*; L. *infamia*, ill fame, from *infamis*, of ill report, infamous; *in-* priv., and *fama*, fame.]

1. very bad reputation; notoriety; disgrace; dishonor.

2. the quality of being infamous; great wickedness.

3. an infamous act.

4. in law, loss of character and of certain civil rights sustained by a person convicted of an infamous crime.

Syn.—ignominy, opprobrium. — *Infamy* causes either the person or thing to be ill spoken of; *ignominy* causes the name and the person to be held in contempt; *opprobrium* causes the person to be spoken of in severe terms of reproach.

in′făn·cy, *n.*; *pl.* **in′făn·cieṣ,** [L. *infantia*, inability to speak, infancy, from *infans* (*-antis*), speechless, an infant; *in-* priv., and *fari*, to speak.]

1. the state or period of being an infant; babyhood; very early childhood.

2. the beginning or earliest stage of anything.

3. in law, the state or period of being a minor; period before the age of legal majority, usually twenty-one; minority.

in·fan′dous, *a.* odious beyond the power of expression. [Obs.]

in·fang′thiēf, in·fang′thef, *n.* [AS. *infangenetheóf*; *infangen*, pp. of *infon*, to seize, and *theóf*, a thief.] in old English law, the right of a lord of the manor to deal with acts of petty larceny, etc. committed within his jurisdiction.

in′fănt, *n.* [ME. *enfaunt*; OFr. *enfant*; L. *infans*, *infantis*, adj. not speaking, n. a child infant; *in-* priv., and *fans*, *fantis*, ppr. of *fari*, to speak.]

1. a very young child; a baby.

2. a person in the state of legal infancy; a minor.

in′fănt, *a.* 1. of or for infants or infancy; as, *infant* food.

2. in a very early stage; not mature; as, an *infant* bud, *infant* industries.

in′fănt, *v.t.* to bear (a child, etc.). [Obs.]

in·fan′tȧ, *n.* [Sp. and Port., f. of *infante*, a child, infant.]

1. any daughter of a king of Spain or Portugal.

2 the wife of an infante.

in·fan′tę, *n.* [Sp. and Port.; L. *infans*; see *infant*, *n.*] any son of a king of Spain or Portugal, except the heir to the throne.

in′fănt·hood, *n.* the state or period of infancy. [Rare.]

in·fan′ti·cī·dăl, *a.* pertaining to infanticide.

in·fan′ti·cīde, *n.* [LL. *infanticidium*, the killing of an infant; L. *infans* (*-antis*), an infant, and *cædere*, to kill.] the intentional killing of an infant or infants; child murder.

in·fan′ti·cīde, *n.* [LL. *infanticida*, one who kills an infant.] one who kills an infant.

in′făn·tīle, *a.* [L. *infantilis*, belonging to an infant, from *infans* (*-antis*), an infant.]

1. of infants or infancy.

2. like or characteristic of an infant; babyish; childish or childlike.

3. in the earliest stage of development.

4. in physical geography, designating or of an early stage of development in a period succeeding a change of level caused by uplift.

infantile paralysis; an acute infectious disease, more common in children than adults, caused by a virus inflammation of the gray matter of the spinal cord: it is accompanied by paralysis of various muscle groups that atrophy, resulting, usually, in permanent deformities: also called (*acute anterior*) *poliomyelitis*.

in·fan′ti·liṣm, *n.* an abnormal state in which infantile, or childish, characteristics persist into adult life: it is marked by retarded mental and physical growth and a lack of sexual development.

in′făn·tīne, *a.* [Fr. *infantin*, *enfantin*.] infantile; babyish; childish or childlike.

in′fănt·līke, *a.* like an infant.

in′fănt·ly, *a.* like an infant. [Obs.]

in′făn·try, *n.* [Fr. *infanterie*; Sp. *infanteria*, infantry, from Sp. and Port. *infante*, a very young person, a knight's page, foot soldier, from L. *infans* (*-antis*), a child, infant.]

1. children collectively. [Obs.]

2. foot soldiers collectively; especially, that branch of an army consisting of soldiers trained and equipped to fight on foot.

in′făn·try·măn, *n.*; *pl.* **in′făn·try·men,** a soldier of infantry; a foot soldier.

in·färce′, *v.t.* to stuff; to put out. [Obs.]

in·färçt′, *n.* [L. *infartus*, pp. of *infarcire*, to stuff; *in*, in, and *farcire*, to stuff.] an area of dying or dead tissue resulting from obstruction of the blood vessels normally supplying the part.

in·färçt′ed, *a.* affected by infarction; as, an *infarcted* artery.

in·färç′tion, *n.* the development of an infarct.

in·fash′iŏn·ȧ·ble, *a.* unfashionable. [Obs.]

in·fat′i·gȧ·ble, *a.* indefatigable. [Obs.]

in·fat′ū·āte, *v.t.*; infatuated, *pt.*, *pp.*; infatuating, *ppr.* [L. *infatuatus*, pp. of *infatuare*, to make a fool of; *in-*, intens, and *fatuus*, foolish.]

1. to make foolish; to affect with folly; to weaken the intellectual powers of or to deprive of sound judgment; as, whom the gods intend to destroy they first *infatuate*.

2. to inspire with unreasoning passion or attraction; as, to be *infatuated* with love of gaming.

in·fat′ū·āte, *a.* infatuated.

in·fat′ū·āte, *n.* a person who is infatuated.

in·fat′ū·ā·ted, *a.* 1. foolish; lacking sound judgment.

2. completely carried away by unreasoning passion or attraction.

in·fat′ū·ā·ting, *a.* affecting with folly.

in·fat·ū·ā′tion, *n.* [LL. *infatuatio* (*-onis*), from L. *infatuare*, to infatuate.]

1. an infatuating.

2. the fact or state of being infatuated; unreasoning passion or attraction.

Syn.—folly, madness, intoxication, foolishness, unreason.

in·fąust′, *a.* [L. *infaustus*, unlucky, unfortunate; *in-* priv., and *faustus*, propitious.] not propitious. [Rare.]

in·fąust′ing, *n.* the act of making unlucky. [Obs.]

in·fēa·ṣi·bil′i·ty, *n.* the quality or state of being infeasible.

in·fēa′ṣi·ble, *a.* not feasible; not easily done or put to use; impracticable.

in·feçt′, *v.t.*; infected, *pt.*, *pp.*; infecting, *ppr.* [OFr. *infecter*; L. *infectus*, pp. of *inficere*, to put or dip into, to tinge, stain; *in*, in, and *facere*, to do, to make.]

1. to contaminate with a disease-producing organism or matter.

2. to cause to become diseased by bringing into contact with such an organism or matter.

3. to affect or imbue with one's feelings or beliefs; especially, to affect in a harmful or undesirable way; to corrupt.

4. in law, to contaminate with illegality.

Syn.—defile, pollute, poison, vitiate, corrupt.

in·feçt′, *a.* infected. [Obs.]

in·feç′tẽr, *n.* same as *infector*.

in·feçt′i·ble, *a.* that can be infected. [Rare.]

in·feç′tion, *n.* [LL. *infectio* (*-onis*), a dyeing, from L. *infectus*, pp. of *inficere*, to dip in, tinge, infect.]

1. an infecting; specifically, (a) the act of causing to become diseased; (b) the act of affecting with one's feelings or beliefs.

2. the fact or state of being infected.

3. something resulting from an infecting; specifically, (a) a disease resulting from the presence of certain microorganisms or matter in the body; (b) a feeling, belief, influence, etc. transmitted from one person to another.

4. anything that infects.

5. in law, contamination by illegality, as in cases of contraband goods.

in·feç′tious (-shus), *a.* 1. likely to cause infection; containing disease-producing organisms or matter.

2. designating a disease caused by infection: see *infectious disease*.

3. tending to spread or to affect others; catching; as, an *infectious* laugh.

4. infected with disease. [Obs.]

5. in law, contaminating with illegality; exposing to seizure and forfeiture.

in·feç′tious diṣ·ēaṣe′, any disease caused by the presence in the body of bacteria, protozoa, viruses, or other parasites: it may or may not be contagious, i.e., transmitted directly from person to person.

in·feç′tious·ly, *adv.* in an infectious manner.

in·feç′tious·ness, *n.* the quality of being infectious.

in·feç′tive, *a.* [L., *infectivus*, for dyeing, from *infectus*, pp. of *inficere*, to dye, infect.] likely to cause infection; infectious.

in·feç′tŏr, *n.* one who or that which infects.

in·fē′çund (*or* in-fek′und), *a.* [ME. *infecunde*; L. *infecundus.*] not fecund; not fertile; barren.

in·fe·çun′di·ty, *n.* [L. *infecunditas*, from *infecundus*, unfruitful; *in-* priv., and *fecundus*, fruitful.] the quality or state of being infecund.

in·fe·çun′dous, *a.* sterile; not producing offspring. [Obs.]

in·fee′ble, *v.t.* to enfeeble. [Obs.]

in·feft′ment, *n.* in Scots law, the act of giving symbolic possession of inheritable property.

in·fē·lic′i·tous, *a.* not felicitous; specifically, (a) unfortunate; unhappy; (b) not appropriate; unsuitable.

in·fē·lic′i·ty, *n.* [L. *infelicitas.*]
1. the quality or condition of being infelicitous.
2. *pl.* **in·fē·lic′i·tieṣ,** something infelicitous; an unsuitable or inappropriate remark, action, etc.

in·fē·lō′ni·ous, *a.* not felonious.

in·felt′, *a.* inwardly and deeply felt; affecting the emotions.

in·feo·dā′tion (-fū-), *n.* same as *infeudation.*

in·feoff′ (-fef′), *v.t.* to enfeoff. [Obs.]

in·feoff′ment, in·feof′ment, *n.* enfeoffment. [Obs.]

in·fẽr′, *v.t.*; inferred, *pt., pp.*; inferring, *ppr.* [L. *inferre*, to bring or carry in, to infer; *in*, in, and *ferre*, to bring, carry.]
1. originally, to bring on; to induce.
2. to conclude or decide from something known or assumed; to derive by reasoning; to draw as a conclusion.
3. to lead to as a conclusion; to indicate; to imply: generally regarded as a loose usage.

in·fẽr′, *v.i.* to draw inferences.

in·fẽr′à·ble, *a.* that can be inferred: written also *inferrible.*

in′fẽr·ence, *n.* [LL. *inferentia*, an inference, from L. *inferre*, to bring in, to infer.]
1. the act of inferring.
Unjust and mistaken in the method of *inference.* —Glanvill.
2. something inferred; a deduction; logical conclusion.
Syn.—conclusion, deduction.—*Conclusion* signifies the final logical result in a process of reasoning. *Deduction* signifies the bringing or drawing of one thing from another. A *conclusion* is full and decisive; an *inference* is partial and indecisive; a *conclusion* ends all further reasoning.

in·fẽr·en′tiăl (-shăl), *a.* based on or having to do with inference.

in·fẽr·en′tiăl·ly, *adv.* in an inferential manner.

in·fē′ri·ae, *n.pl.* [L., from *inferi*, those inhabiting the infernal regions, the dead, from *inferus*, below.] sacrifices offered by the ancient Romans to the souls of deceased heroes or friends.

in·fē′ri·ŏr, *a.* [L. *inferior*, lower, inferior, comp. of *inferus*, low, below.]
1. lower in space; placed lower down.
2. low or lower in order, status, rank, etc.; subordinate.
3. lower in quality or value than (with *to*).
4. poor in quality; below average; mediocre.
5. in anatomy, located below or directed downward: opposed to *superior.*
6. in botany, growing below another part or organ: used especially with reference to the position of the ovary when it seems to lie below the calyx.
7. in astronomy, (a) situated or occurring between the earth and the sun; (b) below the celestial pole.
8. in printing, placed below the type line, as 2 in NO_2.
inferior valve; in zoology, the valve of an adherent bivalve by which it is attached to other substances.

INFERIOR OVARY

in·fē′ri·ŏr, *n.* an inferior person or thing.
A person gets more by obliging his *inferior* than by disdaining him. —South.

in·fē·ri·or′i·ty, *n.* [LL. *inferioritas*, from L. *inferior*, lower, inferior.] the state, quality, or condition of being inferior.

in·fē·ri·or′i·ty çom′plex, 1. in psychology, a neurotic condition resulting from various feelings of inferiority, such as derive from physical inadequacy or situations of early childhood, and often manifested in excessive aggressiveness, a domineering attitude, etc.: so used by Adler.
2. popularly, any feeling of inferiority, inadequacy, etc. whether or not a neurotic condition exists.

in·fē′ri·ŏr·ly, *adv.* in an inferior manner, or on the inferior part.

in·fẽr′năl, *a.* [ME. *infernal*; OFr. *enfernal*; LL. *infernalis*, pertaining to the lower regions, from *infernus*, underground, lower, infernal, from *inferus*, below.]
1. (a) of the ancient mythological world of the dead; (b) of hell.
2. hellish; diabolical; fiendish; inhuman.
3. hateful; abominable; outrageous. [Colloq.]
infernal machine; any hidden or disguised device designed to explode or to cause injury or destruction.
infernal stone; formerly, lunar caustic; also, caustic potash.
Syn.—hellish, fiendish, devilish, malicious, diabolical.

in·fẽr′năl, *n.* an inhabitant of hell, or of the lower regions.

in·fẽr′năl·ly, *adv.* in an infernal manner; diabolically; wickedly.

in·fẽr′nō, *n.* [It., hell, from L. *infernus*, below, infernal.]
1. hell; the infernal regions.
2. any place suggesting hell, usually characterized by great heat or flames.
3. [I—] that section of Dante's *Divine Comedy* which describes hell and the sufferings of the damned.

in′fe·rō-, [from L. *inferus*, below.] a combining form meaning *low, below, underneath*; as, *infero*lateral, *infero*median.

in″fe·rō·an·tē′ri·ŏr, *a.* [*infero-*, and L. *anterior*, toward the front.] situated below and in front.

in′fe·rō·branch, *n.* one of the *Inferobranchiata.*

In″fe·rō·bran′chi·à, *n.pl.* same as *Inferobranchiata.*

in″fe·rō·bran′chi·ăn, *n.* an inferobranch.

In″fe·rō·bran·chi·ā′tà, *n.pl.* [*infero-*, and L. *branchiæ*, gills.] an order of nudibranchiate gastropods, which have their branchiae arranged in the form of two long series of leaflets on the two sides of the body, under the advanced border of the mantle.

in″fe·rō·bran′chi·āte, *a.* pertaining to or characteristic of the *Inferobranchiata.*

in″fe·rō·lat′ẽr·ăl, *a.* [*infero-*, and L. *latus* (*-eris*), side.] situated below and to one side.

in″fe·rō·mē′di·ăn, *a.* [*infero-*, and L. *medianus*, situated in the middle, from *medius*, middle.] situated in the middle of the underside.

in″fe·rō·pos·tē′ri·ŏr, *a.* [*infero-*, and L. *posterior*, behind, comp. of *posterus*, next, following.] situated below and behind.

in·fẽr′rẽr, *n.* a person who infers.

in·fẽr′ri·ble, *a.* inferable.

in·fẽr′tile, *a.* [LL. *infertilis*; L. *in-* priv., and *fertilis*, fertile.]
1. not fertile; not fruitful or productive; barren; as, an *infertile* soil.
2. not fertilized, as an egg.

in·fẽr′tile·ly, *adv.* in an unproductive manner.

in·fẽr·til′i·ty, *n.* the quality or state of being infertile; unfruitfulness; unproductiveness; barrenness; as, the *infertility* of land.

in·fest′, *v.t.*; infested, *pt., pp.*; infesting, *ppr.* [OFr. *infester*; L. *infestare*, to attack, disturb, trouble, from *infestus*, hostile.] to overrun or inhabit in large numbers, usually so as to be harmful or bothersome; to swarm in or about.

in·fest′, *a.* hostile. [Obs.]

in·fes·tā′tion, *n.* the act of infesting or state of being infested.

in·fest′ẽr, *n.* one who or that which infests.

in·fest′ẽred, *a.* rankling; inveterate. [Obs.]

in·fest′ive, *a.* having no mirth; cheerless; forlorn. [Rare.]

in·fes·tiv′i·ty, *n.* want of festivity, or of cheerfulness and mirth. [Rare.]

in·fes′tū·ous, *a.* mischievous. [Obs.]

in·feū·dā′tion, *n.* [LL. *infeudatio* (*-onis*), from *infeudare*, to put one in possession in fee; L. *in*, in, and LL. *feudum*, a feud, fee, from O.H.G. *fihu*, cattle.]
1. in feudal law, the act of putting one in possession of an estate in fee; enfeoffment.
2. the granting of tithes to laymen.

in·fib·ū·lā′tion, *n.* [L. *infibulare*, to fasten with a clasp or buckle; *in*, in, and *fibula*, a clasp, buckle.]
1. the act of clasping or confining with or as with a buckle or padlock.
2. the attachment of a ring, clasp, buckle, or the like, to the organs of generation so as to prevent copulation.

in′fi·del, *a.* [L. *infidelis*, unfaithful (LL., unbelieving); *in-* priv., and *fidelis*, faithful.]
1. (a) not believing in religion; (b) not believing in a certain religion or the prevailing religion, especially Christianity; heathen; pagan.
2. of infidels or infidelity.

in′fi·del, *n.* 1. a person who does not believe in a certain religion or the prevailing religion; a non-Christian, non-Moslem, etc.
2. a person who does not believe in any religion.
3. a person who does not accept some particular belief.
Syn.—unbeliever, freethinker, deist, atheist, skeptic.—A *freethinker* rejects the tenets and traditions of formal religion as incompatible with reason. An *unbeliever* is one who does not accept any religious belief. A *deist* believes in one God and a divine providence, but rejects revelation. An *atheist* denies the being of God. A *skeptic* is one whose faith in the reliability of evidence is weakened or destroyed, so that he doubts religious doctrines.

in·fi·del′i·ty, *n.*; *pl.* **in·fi·del′i·tieṣ,** [Fr. *infidélité*; L. *infidelitas*, faithlessness, infidelity, from *infidelis*, unfaithful; *in-* priv., and *fidelis*, faithful.]
1. lack of faith, trust, or loyalty.
2. lack of belief in all religion or in any one religion, especially Christianity.
3. unfaithfulness, particularly in married persons; a violation of the marriage covenant by adultery.
4. an unfaithful or disloyal act; treachery; deceit.

in′field, *n.* 1. (a) the diamond of the baseball field; the space ninety feet square within the base lines; (b) the infielders collectively.
2. the land of a farm nearest the farmhouse; hence, land kept continually under crop.

in·field′, *v.t.* to enclose, as a piece of land. [Rare.]

in′field″ẽr, *n.* in baseball, a player whose position is in the infield; shortstop, first baseman, second baseman, or third baseman: the pitcher and the catcher are considered infielders when fielding the ball: distinguished from *outfielder.*

in·fīle′, *v.t.* to place in a file; to arrange in a file or rank. [Obs.]

in′fill, *v.t.* to fill in.

in′fill·ing, *n.* filling; that which fills in.

in·film′, *v.t.* to cover with or as with a film.

in·fil′tẽr, *v.t.* and *v.i.*; infiltered, *pt., pp.*; infiltering, *ppr.* to filter or sift in.

in·fil′trāte (*or* in′fil-), *v.t.* and *v.i.*; infiltrated, *pt., pp.*; infiltrating, *ppr.* 1. to pass, or cause (a fluid) to pass, through small gaps or openings; to filter.
2. to pass through, as in filtering; specifically, in military usage, to pass, or cause (individual troops) to pass, through weak places in the enemy's lines in order to attack the enemy's flanks or rear.

in·fil′trāte, *n.* something that infiltrates.

in·fil·trā′tion, *n.* 1. the act or process of infiltrating; also, the state of being infiltrated.
2. that which infiltrates.
3. in pathology, the entrance into the tissue spaces or into the tissue elements of some abnormal substance or of a normal substance in excess.

in·fil′trà·tive, *a.* pertaining to infiltration.

in′fi·nite, *a.* [ME. *infinite*; L. *infinitus*, boundless, unlimited; *in-* priv., and *finitus*, pp. of *finire*, to limit, bound.]
1. without limits; unbounded; boundless; not circumscribed; extending beyond measure or comprehension; endless; immeasurable.
2. indefinitely large; immense; inexhaustible; vast; exceedingly great in excellence, degree, capacity, and the like.
Infinite riches in a little room.—Marlowe.
3. in mathematics, of a greater value (*positively infinite*) or a lesser value (*negatively infinite*) than any assigned quantity.
4. in music, capable of being repeated to infinity: said of a canon.
infinite decimal; a decimal which is interminate, or which may be carried to infinity: thus, if the diameter of a circle be 1, the circumference is 3.14159265 . . . , carried to infinity.
infinite series; a series the terms of which go on increasing or diminishing without coming to an end.
Syn.–unlimited, boundless, illimitable, immeasurable, interminable, eternal, countless, unbounded.

in′fi·nite, *n.* 1. anything infinite; infinity.

2. in mathematics, an infinite quantity.
the Infinite (*Being*); God.

in'fi·nite·ly, *adv.* 1. without bounds or limits; as, an *infinitely* large number.
2. extremely; greatly; to a great extent or degree.

in'fi·nite·ness, *n.* the state of being infinite; immensity; greatness; infinity.

in″fin·i·tes'i·măl, *a.* [L. *infinitus*, infinite.]
1. in mathematics, continually diminishing and approaching zero as its limit: said of a variable.
2. infinitely small; too small to be measured.

in″fin·i·tes'i·măl, *n.* an infinitesimal quantity.

in″fin·i·tes'i·măl·ly, *adv.* by infinitesimals; in infinitely small quantities.

in·fin·i·tī'văl, *a.* in grammar, pertaining to the infinitive.

in·fin'i·tive, *a.* [LL. *infinitivus*, unlimited, undefined, from L. *infinitus*, infinite.]
1. of or connected with an infinitive.
2. not defined or limited.

in·fin'i·tive, *n.* the simple, uninflected form of the verb, expressing existence or action without reference to person, number, or tense: in English, it is preceded by *to*, as *to go, to think*, or by another verb form, as ***can he go, make us think***.

in·fin'i·tive·ly, *adv.* in grammar, in the manner of an infinitive.

in·fi·nï'tō, *a.* [It.] in music, perpetual, as a canon whose end leads back to the beginning.

in·fin'i·tūde, *n.* [L. *infinitus*, infinite.]
1. infinity; infiniteness; the quality or state of being without limits.
2. immensity; greatness; vastness.
3. an infinite quantity, number, or extent.

in·fin'i·tū·ple, *a.* multiplied an infinite number of times. [Rare.]

in·fin'i·ty, *n.*; *pl.* **in·fin'i·tieș,** [L. *infinitas*, boundlessness, endlessness, from *infinitus*, infinite, boundless.]
1. the quality of being infinite.
2. anything infinite; endless or unlimited space, time, distance, quantity, etc.
3. an indefinitely large number or amount.
4. in geometry, a point or space infinitely distant from the point or space being considered.
5. in mathematics, an infinite quantity, indicated by ∞.
6. in photography, a distance so great that rays of light originating there may be considered as parallel.
to infinity; without limit or end.

in·firm', *a.* [OFr. *infirm*; L. *infirmus*, weak, not strong; *in-* priv., and *firmus*, strong.]
1. not firm or sound physically; weak; feeble; as, an *infirm* body, an *infirm* constitution.
2. not firm in mind; irresolute; unstable; vacillating; as, *infirm* of purpose.
3. not solid, firm, sound, or stable; frail; shaky, as a structure. [Rare.]
4. not secure or valid; as, an *infirm* title to property.
Syn.—decrepit, weak, debilitated, feeble, vacillating, wavering.

in·firm', *v.t.* to weaken. [Rare.]

in·fir·măr'i·ăn, *n.* one who helps in an infirmary or has charge of it; especially, one who has charge of an infirmary in a monastery.

in·fir'mȧ·ry, *n.*; *pl.* **in·fir'mȧ·rieș,** [OFr. *enfermerie*; LL. *infirmarium*, a hospital or infirmary, from L. *infirmus*, weak, infirm.] a hospital or place where the sick and injured are lodged and nursed; especially, the building or room in a school, etc. that serves as a hospital or dispensary.

in·firm'ȧ·tive, *a.* weakening; annulling, or tending to make void. [Obs.]

in·firm'ȧ·tō·ry, *n.* an infirmary. [Obs.]

in·fir'mi·ty, *n.* [ME. *infirmite*; OFr. *enfermete*; L. *infirmitas*, weakness, infirmity, from *infirmus*, weak, infirm.]
1. the quality or state of being infirm; especially, an unsound or unhealthy state of the body; weakness; feebleness.
2. *pl.* **in·fir'mi·tieș,** an instance of weakness; specifically, (a) a physical weakness or defect; frailty or ailment, as from old age; (b) a moral weakness; defect.
A friend should bear his friend's *infirmities*. —Shak.
Syn.—feebleness, debility, imperfection, failing, foible, weakness.

in·firm'ly, *adv.* in an infirm manner.

in·firm'ness, *n.* weakness; feebleness; unsoundness.

in·fix', *v.t.*; infixed (-fixt'), *pt., pp.*; infixing, *ppr.* [OFr. *infixer*; L. *infixus*, pp. of *infigere*, to fix, to thrust or drive in; *in*, in, and *figere*, to fix, fasten.]
1. to fasten or set firmly in or on; especially, to fix by piercing or thrusting in; as, to *infix* a sting, spear, or dart.
2. to implant, instill, or teach, as principles, thoughts, or instructions.
3. in grammar, to insert as an infix.

in'fix, *n.* in linguistics, an element consisting of one or more sounds or syllables placed within the body of a word to modify its meaning: it corresponds in function to a suffix or prefix. Example: Arabic *-ta-* in *iq-ta-riba*, to cause oneself to come near (from *qariba*, to come near).

in flȧ·gran'tē de·liç'tō, [L.] in the very act of committing the offense; red-handed.

in·flāme', *v.t.*; inflamed, *pt., pp.*; inflaming, *ppr.* [ME. *enflawmen*; OFr. *enflammer*; L. *inflammare*, to set on fire, to kindle; *in*, in, and *flamma*, a flame.]
1. to set on fire; to kindle; to cause to burn with a flame.
2. to arouse passion, desire, or violence in; to excite intensely, especially with anger; to excite to violent action; as, to *inflame* the populace.
3. to increase the intensity of (passion, desire, violence, etc.).
4. in medicine, to set up inflammation in; as, to *inflame* the eyes.
5. to increase; to augment. [Obs.]
Syn.—anger, arouse, kindle, excite, incense, provoke, irritate.

in·flāme', *v.i.* 1. to become roused, excited, stimulated, etc.
2. to catch fire.
3. to become hot, feverish, swollen, red, sore, etc.

in·flāmed', *a.* 1. set on fire; enkindled; heated; provoked; exasperated.
2. in heraldry, blazoned or decorated with flames; as, a bend *inflamed*.

in·flām'ēr, *n.* the person or thing that inflames.

in·flam·mȧ·bil'i·ty, *n.* the quality or condition of being inflammable; specifically, (a) a tendency to burn readily or the degree of this tendency; (b) excitability.

in·flam'mȧ·ble, *a.* 1. easily set on fire; that will burn readily or quickly; combustible.
2. easily angered or excited; irascible.
inflammable air; formerly, in chemistry, hydrogen.

in·flam'mȧ·ble, *n.* anything inflammable.

in·flam'mȧ·ble·ness, *n.* inflammability.

in·flam'mȧ·bly, *adv.* in an inflammable manner; so as to be easily inflamed.

in·flam·mā'tion, *n.* [Fr. *inflammation*; L. *inflammatio* (*-onis*), a kindling, setting on fire, from *inflammare*, to set on fire, inflame.]
1. the act of inflaming or the state of being inflamed.
2. violent excitement; heat; animosity; turbulence.
3. in medicine, a diseased condition of some part of the body, resulting from injury, infection, irritation, etc. and characterized by redness, pain, heat, and swelling.

in·flam'mȧ·tive, *a.* inflammatory.

in·flam'mȧ·tō·ry, *a.* [L. *inflammare*, to inflame.]
1. rousing or likely to rouse excitement, anger, violence, rioting, etc., as a speech.
2. in medicine, of, caused by, or characterized by inflammation.

in·flāt'ȧ·ble, *a.* that can be inflated.

in·flāte', *v.t.*; inflated, *pt., pp.*; inflating, *ppr.* [L. *inflatus*, pp. of *inflare*, to blow into, inflate; *in*, in, and *flare*, to blow.]
1. to blow full or distend by injecting air or gas; to expand; as, to *inflate* a bladder, to *inflate* the lungs.
2. to raise in spirits; to make proud or elated.
3. to increase or raise beyond normal or valid proportions.
4. to increase the amount of (currency in circulation).
Opposed to *deflate*.

in·flāte', *v.i.* to distend; to swell out; to become inflated; opposed to *deflate*.

in·flāte', *a.* inflated. [Rare.]

in·flāt'ed, *a.* 1. swollen or distended with gas or air; puffed out.
2. turgid; pompous; bombastic; high-flown.
3. increased or raised beyond normal or valid proportions.
4. in botany, hollow and distended, as a perianth or pericarp.

in·flāt'ēr, *n.* one who or that which inflates.

in·flāt'ing·ly, *adv.* in a manner tending to inflate.

in·flā'tion, *n.* [L. *inflatio* (*-onis*), from *inflare*, to blow into, inflate.]
1. the act of inflating or the condition of being inflated.
2. an increase in the amount of currency in circulation, resulting in a relatively sharp and sudden fall in its value and rise in prices: it may be caused by an increase in the volume of paper money issued or of gold mined, or a relative increase in expenditures, as when the supply of goods fails to meet the demand.
Opposed to *deflation*.

in·flā'tion·ăr·y, *a.* of, causing, or characterized by inflation.

in·flā'tion·ist, *n.* a person who favors inflation; especially, an advocate of an increased issue of paper money.

in·flā'tŏr, *n.* an inflater.

in·flā'tus, *n.* [L., from *inflatus*, pp. of *inflare*, to blow into, to inflate.] a blowing or breathing into; hence, inspiration. [Rare.]

in·fleçt', *v.t.*; inflected, *pt., pp.*; inflecting, *ppr.* [L. *inflectere*, to bend, inflect; *in*, in, and *flectere*, to bend.]
1. to bend; to turn from a direct line or course, usually inward.
2. to vary or change the tone or pitch of (the voice); to modulate.
3. to change the form of (a word) by inflection, as in conjugating or declining.

in·fleçt'ed, *a.* 1. bent or turned from a direct line or course.
2. in biology, bent inward or downward; inflexed.
3. in grammar, changed in form and function by inflection.

in·fleç'tion, *n.* [L. *inflexio* (*-onis*), a bending, swaying, from *inflexus*, pp. of *inflectere*, to bend, inflect.]
1. the act of turning from a direct line, or the condition of being so turned.
2. a turn, bend, or curve.
3. modulation; any change in the pitch or tone of the voice.
4. (a) the change of form by which some words indicate certain grammatical relationships, as number, case, gender, tense, etc.; (b) an inflected form; (c) an inflectional element, as those used in English to form the plural and possessive case of nouns (ship*s*, ship'*s*) and the past tense and third person singular, present indicative, of verbs (he shipp*ed*, ship*s*).
5. a change of a curve or arc from convex to concave or the reverse.
6. in optics, diffraction. [Obs.]
point of inflection; in geometry, the point at which a curve changes from convex to concave or the reverse.

in·fleç'tion·ăl, *a.* of, having, or showing grammatical inflection.

in·fleç'tion·ăl lan'guăġe, a language in which inflection is the principal grammatical device; specifically, a language in which the subject-object relation is indicated by inflection: Greek and Latin are inflectional languages, whereas English is syntactically analytical.

in·fleç'tion·less, *a.* without inflection.

in·fleçt'ive, *a.* 1. having the power of bending; tending to bend or curve.
2. in grammar, inflectional.

in·flesh', *v.t.* same as *enflesh*.

in·flex', *v.t.*; inflexed (-flext'), *pt., pp.*; inflexing, *ppr.* [L. *inflexus*, pp. of *inflectere*, to turn or bend, inflect.] to bend; to curve; to flex. [Rare.]

in·flexed', *a.* 1. turned; bent; bent inward.
2. in botany and zoology, abruptly turned inward; bent toward the axis.

in·flex·i·bil'i·ty, *n.* the quality or condition of being inflexible; unyielding stiffness; obstinacy.

in·flex'i·ble, *a.* [L. *inflexibilis*, that cannot be bent; *in-* priv., and *flexibilis*, that can be bent, flexible, from *flectere*, to bend.]
1. unbending; rigid; that cannot be bent or curved.
2. firm in mind or purpose; not to be prevailed on; stubborn; unyielding; unshakeable.
3. not to be changed or altered; fixed.

in·flex'i·ble·ness, *n.* inflexibility.

in·flex'i·bly, *adv.* in an inflexible manner.

in·flex'ion (-flek'shun), *n.* inflection: chiefly British spelling.

in·flex'ive, *a.* inflective. [Rare.]

in·flex'ūre, *n.* an inflection; a bend. [Obs.]

in·fliçt', *v.t.*; inflicted, *pt., pp.*; inflicting, *ppr.* [L. *inflictus*, pp. of *infligere*, to strike or beat

against, to strike on; *in*, on, against, and *fligere*, to strike.]
 1. to give or cause (pain, wounds, blows, etc.) by or as by striking; to cause to be borne.
 2. to impose (a punishment, disagreeable task, etc.).

in·flict′ẽr, *n.* one who inflicts.

in·flic′tion, *n.* [LL. *inflictio (-onis)*, from L. *inflictus*, pp. of *infligere*, to strike on or against, to inflict.]
 1. an inflicting.
 2. that which is inflicted, as pain or punishment.

in·flict′ive, *a.* of or characterized by infliction.

in·flō·res′cence, *n.* [LL. *inflorescens (-entis)*, ppr. of *inflorescere*, to begin to blossom; L. *in*, in, and *florescere*, incept. of *florere*, to blossom.]
 1. a flowering; the unfolding of blossoms.
 2. the arrangement of flowers on a stem or axis.
 3. a flower cluster on a common axis.
 4. flowers collectively.
 5. a single flower.

in·flō·res′cent, *a.* [LL. *inflorescens*; see *inflorensc**ence*.] in flower; flowering.

in·flōw′, *v.i.*; inflowed, *pt., pp.*; inflowing, *ppr.* to flow from without toward a center or interior: opposed to *outflow*.

in′flōw, *n.* 1. that which flows in.
 2. the act of flowing in or into.

in·flow′ẽr·ing, *n.* the process of extracting the aroma of flowers for use in the making of perfumes.

in′flū·ence, *n.* [ME. *influence*; OFr. *influence*; LL. *influentia*, a flowing in, from L. *influens (-entis)*, ppr. of *influere*, to flow in; *in*, in, and *fluere*, to flow.]
 1. an influx. [Obs.]
 2. originally, the supposed flowing of an ethereal fluid or power from the stars, thought to affect the characters and actions of people.
 3. (a) the power of persons or things to affect others, seen only in its effects; (b) the action or effect of such power.
 4. the power of a person or group to produce effects without the exertion of physical force or authority, based on wealth, social position, ability, etc.
 5. a person or thing that has influence.
 6. in physics, induction.
 Syn.—power, control, sway, authority, weight.

in′flū·ence, *v.t.*; influenced, *pt., pp.*; influencing, *ppr.* to exercise or have influence on; to modify or affect in some way; to act on; to bias; to sway; as, the sun *influences* the tides; to *influence* a person by fears or hopes.

in′flū·en·cẽr, *n.* one who or that which influences.

in·flū·en′cive, *a.* having influencing qualities or properties. [Rare.]

in′flū·ent, *a.* [OFr. *influent*, influential, lit., flowing in, from L. *influens (-entis)*, ppr. of *influere*, to flow in.]
 1. flowing in.
 2. having influence. [Obs.]

in′flū·ent, *n.* anything flowing in, as a tributary.

in·flū·en′tiăl (-shăl), *a.* 1. exerting influence; possessing influence.
 2. having great influence; powerful; effective.
 Syn.—potent, powerful, efficacious, forcible, persuasive, controlling, guiding, authoritative, leading.

in·flū·en′tiăl·ly, *adv.* in an influential manner; so as to incline, move, or direct.

in·flū·en′zȧ, *n.* [It. *influenza*, influenza, lit., an influence, so called because formerly attributed by astrologers to the influence of the stars, from LL. *influentia*, an influence, lit., a flowing in, from L. *influens (-entis)*, ppr. of *influere*, to flow in.] an acute, contagious, infectious disease, caused by any of several viruses and characterized by inflammation of the respiratory tract, fever, muscular pain, and, often, intestinal disorders: also called *grippe*, *flu*.

in·flū·en′zăl, *a.* of influenza.

in′flux, *n.* [L. *influxus*, a flowing in, properly pp. of *influere*, to flow in; *in*, in, and *fluere*, to flow.]
 1. (a) a flowing in; an inpouring; inflow, as of a liquid, gas, etc.; (b) a continual coming in of persons or things; as, an *influx* of customers.
 2. the point where a river joins another body of water.
 3. influence; power. [Obs.]

in·flux′iŏn (-fluk′shun), *n.* influx. [Rare.]

in·flux′ious (-fluk′shus), *a.* influential. [Obs.]

in·flux′ive, *a.* having influence. [Rare.]

in·flux′ive·ly, *adv.* by influxion. [Rare.]

in·fōld′, *v.t.*; infolded, *pt., pp.*; infolding, *ppr.* 1. to wrap up or enwrap; to enclose.
 2. to clasp with the arms; to embrace.
 Also spelled *enfold*.

in·fōld′ment, *n.* the act of infolding; also, the state of being infolded.

in·fō′li·āte, *v.t.* to cover or overspread with leaves. [Rare.]

in·fọrm′, *v.t.*; informed, *pt., pp.*; informing, *ppr.* [ME. *informen*; OFr. *enformer*; L. *informare*, to shape, fashion, represent, instruct; *in*, in, and *formare*, to form, from *forma*, form, shape.]
 1. (a) to give form or character to; to be the formative principle of; (b) to give, imbue, or inspire with some specific quality or character; to animate.
 2. to form or shape (the mind); to teach. [Rare.]
 3. to give knowledge of something to; to tell; to acquaint with a fact, etc.
 Syn.—acquaint, apprise, instruct, notify, tell, teach, enlighten.

in·fọrm′, *v.i.* 1. to take shape; to become manifest. [Obs.]
 2. to give information, especially information laying blame or accusation upon another.

in·fọrm′, *a.* without regular form; shapeless; formless.

in·fọrm′ăl, *a.* [L. *in-* priv., and *forma*, form.]
 1. not formal; specifically, (a) not according to prescribed or fixed customs, rules, ceremonies, etc.; (b) casual, easy, unceremonious, or relaxed; (c) designed for use or wear on everyday occasions; (d) not requiring formal dress; (e) colloquial.
 2. deranged in mind. [Obs.]

in·fọr·mal′i·ty, *n.* 1. the condition or quality of being informal; lack of customary formality.
 2. *pl.* **in·fọr·mal′i·tieṣ,** an informal act.

in·fọrm′ăl·ly, *adv.* in an informal manner; without the usual forms.

in·fọrm′ănt, *n.* [L. *informans (-antis)*, ppr. of *informare*, to inform.]
 1. one who gives information.
 2. one who offers an accusation against a person; an informer.
 3. a native speaker who repeats the forms, correct sounds, etc. of his language for the benefit of linguists, teachers, translators, etc.
 Syn.—informer.—An *informer* is one who, for selfish ends, volunteers accusations with a view to having others punished; an *informant* is one who simply acquaints us with something we had not known before.

in·fọr·mā′tion, *n.* [OFr. *information*; L. *informatio (-onis)*, a representation, an outline, sketch, from *informare*, to give form to, to represent, inform.]
 1. an informing or being informed; especially, a telling or being told of something.
 2. something told; news; intelligence; word.
 3. knowledge acquired in any manner; facts; data; learning; lore.
 4. a person or agency answering questions as a service to others.
 5. in law, an accusation of criminal offense, not by indictment of a grand jury, but by a public officer, such as a prosecutor.
 Syn.—intelligence, notice, advice, counsel, instruction, news.

in·fọr·mā′tiŏn·ăl, *a.* of or giving information.

in·fọrm′ȧ·tive, *a.* 1. having power to animate.
 2. giving information; instructive.

in·fọrm′ȧ·tō·ry, *a.* informative.

in·fọrmed′ (-fọrmd′), *a.* 1. having much information, knowledge, or education.
 2. ill-formed; misshapen. [Obs.]

in·fọrm′ẽr, *n.* 1. one who animates. [Obs.]
 2. one who makes an accusation against, or gives evidence of the guilt of, another.
 3. one who informs; an informant.
 common informer; one who makes a business of giving information of violations of law, for the purpose of obtaining a portion of the fine imposed.

in·fọr′mi·dȧ·ble, *a.* not formidable. [Rare.]

in·fọrm′i·ty, *n.* [LL. *informitas*, unshapeliness; L. *informis*, unshapely; *in-* priv., and *forma*, shape.] lack of regular form; shapelessness. [Obs.]

in·fọrm′ous, *a.* of no regular form or figure; shapeless. [Obs.]

in·fọr′tū·nāte, *a.* unfortunate. [Obs.]

in·fọr′tū·nāte·ly, *adv.* unfortunately. [Obs.]

in·fọr′tūne, *n.* [OFr. *infortune*; L. *infortunium*, misfortune, punishment, *in-* priv., and *fortuna*, chance, fortune.]
 1. misfortune. [Obs.]
 2. in astrology, any one of the planets, Saturn, Mars, or Mercury, believed to be of evil influence.

in·fọr′tūned, *a.* unfortunate. [Obs.]

in·found′, *v.t.* to infuse. [Obs.]

in′frȧ, *adv.* and *prep.* [L. *infra*, adv. and prep., on the under side, below, underneath, contr. of *infera*, abl. f. of *inferus*, below, beneath.] below, beneath: used especially in Latin phrases.

in′frȧ-, [from L. *infra*, adv. *and* prep., below, underneath.] a prefix meaning *below, beneath*, as in *infrared*, *infracostal*.

in″frȧ-ax′il·lȧ·ry, *a.* [*infra-*, and L. *axilla*, axil.]
 1. in botany, below the axil.
 2. in zoology, below the axilla.

in·frȧ·bran′chi·ăl, *a.* [*infra-*, and L. *branchiæ*, gills.] situated beneath the gills.

in·frȧ·buc′căl, *a.* [*infra-*, and L. *bucca*, the cheek, mouth.] below the buccal mass of a mollusk; as, an *infrabuccal* nerve.

in·frȧ·cos′tăl, *a.* [from *infra-*, and L. *costa*, a rib; and *-al*.] situated beneath the ribs.

in·fract′, *a.* unbroken. [Obs.]

in·fract′, *v.t.*; infracted, *pt., pp.*; infracting, *ppr.* [L. *infractus*, pp. of *infringere*, to break off, break, bruise.] to break or violate (a law, pledge, etc.).

in·fract′ed, *a.* in zoology, bent inward; geniculate.

in·fract′i·ble, *a.* breakable. [Rare.]

in·frac′tion, *n.* [L. *infractio (-onis)*, a breaking to pieces, from *infractus*, pp. of *infringere*, to break off, break; *in*, in, and *frangere*, to break.] the act of breaking; breach; violation; nonobservance; as, an *infraction* of a treaty, compact, agreement, or law.

in·fract′ŏr, *n.* one who violates an agreement, law, etc.

in′frȧ dig·ni·tā′tem, [L.] beneath (one's) dignity.

in·frā′grănt, *a.* not fragrant.

in·frȧ·hȳ′oid, *a.* [*infra-*, and Gr. *hyoeidēs*, hyoid.] beneath the hyoid.

in·frȧ·lā′bi·ăl, *a.* [*infra-*, and L. *labia*, a lip.] beneath the lower lip; as, *infralabial* scales.

in·frȧ·lap·sā′ri·ăn, *a.* pertaining to the infralapsarians, or to their doctrine.

in·frȧ·lap·sā′ri·ăn, *n.* any of a group of Calvinists who held that God's plan of salvation for some people followed and was a consequence of the fall of man from grace: opposed to *supralapsarian*.

in″frȧ·lap·sā′ri·ăn·iṣm, *n.* the doctrine of the infralapsarians.

in·frȧ·mär′gi·năl, *a.* [*infra-*, and L. *margo (-inis)*, border, margin.]
 1. below the outer edge or margin, as of the convolutions of the brain.
 2. in entomology, posterior to a marginal cell.

in·frȧ·max′il·lȧ·ry, *a.* [*infra-*, and L. *maxilla*, jaw.] in anatomy, situated under the jaw; belonging to the lower jaw.

in·frȧ·mē′di·ăn, *a.* [*infra-*, and L. *medius*, middle.] designating those areas of the ocean bottom ranging in depth from three hundred to six hundred feet.

in·frȧ·mun′dāne, *a.* [*infra-*, and L. *mundus*, the world.] lying or being beneath the world.

in·fran′chiṣe, *v.t.* same as *enfranchise*.

in·fran′chiṣe·ment, *n.* same as *enfranchisement*.

in·fran·gi·bil′i·ty, *n.* the condition of being infrangible.

in·fran′gi·ble, *a.* [Fr. *infrangible*; L. *in-* priv., and *frangere*, to break.]
 1. that cannot be broken or separated into parts.
 2. that cannot be violated or infringed; as, an *infrangible* vow.

in·fran′gi·ble·ness, *n.* infrangibility.

in·frȧ·oc′ū·lăr, *a.* [*infra-*, and L. *oculus*, eye.] in zoology, located beneath the eyes: said of the antennae of certain insects.

in·frȧ·ō′răl, *a.* [*infra-*, and L. *os*, *oris*, the mouth.] in zoology, located beneath the mouth.

in·frȧ·or′bit·ăl, *a.* [*infra-*, and L. *orbita*, orbit.] in anatomy, located beneath the orbit of the eye.

in·frȧ·pōṣe′, *v.t.* to put below or beneath.

in·frȧ·pō·si′tion (-zish′un), *n.* [*infra-*, and L. *positio (-onis)*, position.] a position underneath.

in·frȧ·red′, *a.* [*infra-*, and *red*.] designating or of those invisible rays just beyond the red of the visible spectrum: their waves are longer than those of the spectrum colors but shorter than radio waves, and have a penetrating, heating effect.

in·frȧ·scap'ū·lăr, *a.* [*infra-*, and L. *scapula*, the shoulder blade.] in anatomy, situated beneath the shoulder blade; subscapular.

in·frȧ·spī'năl, *a.* same as *infraspinous*.

in·frȧ·spī'nāte, *a.* same as *infraspinous*.

in·frȧ·spī'nous, *a.* [*infra-*, and L. *spina*, the spine.] in anatomy, located under the spine, especially that of the scapula; as, the *infraspinous* fossa of the shoulder blade.

in''frȧ·stȧ·pē'di·ăl, *a.* [*infra-*, and LL. *stapes*, stirrup.] of or pertaining to the columella of the ear.

in''frȧ·stȧ·pē'di·ăl, *n.* an infrastapedial bone.

in·frȧ·stẽr'năl, *a.* [*infra-*, and Gr. *sternon*, the breast.] beneath the sternum, or breastbone.

in·frȧ·stip'ū·lăr, *a.* [*infra-*, and L. *stipula*, stalk.] in botany, growing beneath the stipules.

in'frȧ·struc''ture, *n.* [*infra-* and *structure.*] a substructure or underlying foundation; especially, the basic economic, social, or military facilities and installations of a community, state, etc.

in·frȧ·tem'pō·răl, *a.* [*infra-*, and L. *tempora*, the temples.] in anatomy, below the temporal bone.

in·frȧ·ter·ri·tō'ri·ăl, *a.* [*infra-*, and LL. *territorialis*, territorial, from L. *territorium*, territory.] within the boundaries of a state or territory.

in·frȧ·troch'lē·ăr, *a.* [*infra-*, and L. *trochlea*, a pulley.] in anatomy, lying beneath a trochlea; as, the *infratrochlear* nerve.

in·frē'quence (-kwens), *n.* same as *infrequency*.

in·frē'quen·cy, *n.* [L. *infrequentia*, a small number, scantiness, from *infrequens* (*-entis*), rare, infrequent.]

1. uncommonness; rareness; the state or fact of being infrequent.

2. the state of being unfrequented. [Obs.]

in·frē'quent, *a.* [L. *infrequens* (*-entis*), rare, uncommon, unusual; *in-* priv., and *frequens* (*-entis*), frequent, repeated.] not frequent; rare; uncommon; seldom happening or occurring.

in·frē'quent·ly, *adv.* not frequently.

in·frig'i·dāte, *v.t.* to make cold. [Rare.]

in·frig·i·dā'tion, *n.* the act of making cold. [Rare.]

in·fringe', *v.t.*; infringed, *pt.*, *pp.*; infringing, *ppr.* [L. *infringere*, to break off, break, impair, violate; *in*, in, and *frangere*, to break.]

1. to break; to violate; to transgress; to neglect to obey; as, to *infringe* a law.

2. to destroy or hinder; as, to *infringe* efficacy. [Obs.]

in·fringe', *v.i.* to break in; encroach or trespass (*on* or *upon* the rights, patents, etc. of others).

Syn.—violate, transgress, encroach, infract, intrude, invade, trespass.

in·fringe'ment, *n.* an infringing; violation or encroachment.

in·frin'ġẽr, *n.* one who infringes; a violator.

in·fruc'tū·ōse, *a.* same as *infructuous*.

in·fruc'tū·ous, *a.* [L. *infructuosus*; *in-* priv., and *fructuosus*, fruitful.] not productive; not fruitful.

in·frụ'găl, *a.* not frugal; prodigal.

in'fū·lȧ, *n.*; *pl.* **in'fū·lae,** [L., a band, fillet.]

1. among the ancient Romans, a woolen band, generally red and white, worn on the forehead by priests and vestal virgins as a sign of their calling, by emperors and the higher magistrates on solemn occasions, and by those seeking protection or sanctuary.

2. in the early Christian church, the head covering of a priest; now a pendent ornament at the back of a miter.

in'fū·māte, *v.t.*; infumated, *pt.*, *pp.*; infumating, *ppr.* [L. *infumatus*, pp. of *infumare*, to smoke; *in*, in, on, and *fumare*, to smoke; from *fumus*, smoke.] to cure or dry by smoking. [Rare.]

in'fū·māte, *a.* in entomology, having a brownish-black color as if from infumating.

in'fū·mā·ted, *a.* same as *infumate*.

in·fū·mā'tion, *n.* the process of infumating; the act of drying in smoke. [Rare.]

in·fūmed', *a.* dried in smoke.

in·fun·dib'ū·lăr, *a.* 1. having the shape of a funnel.

2. of or having an infundibulum.

In·fun·dib·ū·lā'tȧ, *n.pl.* [L. *infundibulum*, a funnel.] in zoology, an order or group of polyzoans having infundibulate cell mouths.

in·fun·dib'ū·lāte, *a.* same as *infundibular*.

in·fun·dib'ū·li·fọrm, *a.* [L. *infundibulum*, a funnel, and *forma*, form.] having the shape of a funnel.

in·fun·dib'ū·lum, *n.* [L., a funnel, from *infundere*, to pour into; *in*, in, and *fundere*, to pour.] in anatomy and zoology, a funnel-shaped organ or passage; specifically, (a) the extension of the third ventricle of the brain to the pituitary body; (b) the bronchiole endings in the lungs; (c) the siphon of a cephalopod; (d) the gastric cavity of a ctenophore; (e) the oviduct of a bird.

in·fū'nẽr·ăl, *v.t.* to bury with funeral ceremonies. [Obs.]

in·fũr·cā'tion, *n.* [L. *in*, in, and *furca*, a fork.] a forked divergence or expansion.

in·fū'ri·āte, *a.* [ML. *infuriatus*, pp. of *infuriare*, to enrage; L. *in*, in, and *furiare*, to enrage, from *furia*, rage, anger.] enraged; furious; very angry.

in·fū'ri·āte, *v.t.*; infuriated, *pt.*, *pp.*; infuriating, *ppr.* to make furious or very angry; to enrage.

in·fū·ri·ā'tion, *n.* an infuriating or being infuriated.

in·fus'cāte, *a.* darkened or tinged with a brownish color, as an insect's wing.

in·fus'cāte, *v.t.*; infuscated, *pt.*, *pp.*; infuscating, *ppr.* [L. *infuscatus*, pp. of *infuscare*, to darken, to obscure; *in*, in, on, and *fuscare*, to make dark, from *fuscus*, dark.] to darken; to make dusky. [Obs.]

in·fus'cā·ted, *a.* same as *infuscate*.

in·fus·cā'tion, *n.* the act of darkening or blackening. [Rare.]

in·fūṣe', *v.t.*; infused (-fūzd), *pt.*, *pp.*; infusing, *ppr.* [ME. *enfusen*, from L. *infusus*, pp. of *infundere*, to pour in; *in*, in, and *fundere*, to pour.]

1. to pour (a liquid) in, into, or upon.

2. to put (qualities, etc.) in, as by pouring; to instill; impart.

3. to fill; pervade; imbue; inspire.

4. to steep or soak so as to extract certain qualities; as, tea is *infused* in hot water.

5. to diffuse. [Obs.]

in·fūṣe', *n.* infusion. [Obs.]

in·fūṣ'ẽr, *n.* one who or that which infuses.

in·fū·ṣi·bil'i·ty, *n.* the quality of being infusible.

in·fū'ṣi·ble, *a.* [L. *infusus*, pp. of *infundere*, to infuse.] capable of being infused; as, good principles are *infusible* into the minds of youth.

in·fū'ṣi·ble, *a.* [L. *in-* priv., and *fusus*, pp. of *fundere*, to pour in.] not fusible; that cannot be fused or melted.

in·fū'ṣi·ble·ness, *n.* infusibliity.

in·fū'ṣion (-zhun), *n.* [L. *infusio* (*-onis*), a pouring in, from *infusus*, pp. of *infundere*, to pour in, infuse.]

1. the act or process of infusing.

2. something infused; tincture; admixture.

3. the liquid extract that results when a substance is infused in water.

in·fū'ṣion·iṣm, *n.* the doctrine that the human soul enters the body by divine infusion at conception or birth: opposed to *creationism* and *traducianism*.

in·fū'sive, *a.* having the quality or power of infusion.

In·fū·sō'ri·ȧ, *n.pl.* [from L. *infusus*, pp. of *infundere*, to pour in, infuse: so called from their occurrence in infusions exposed to the air.]

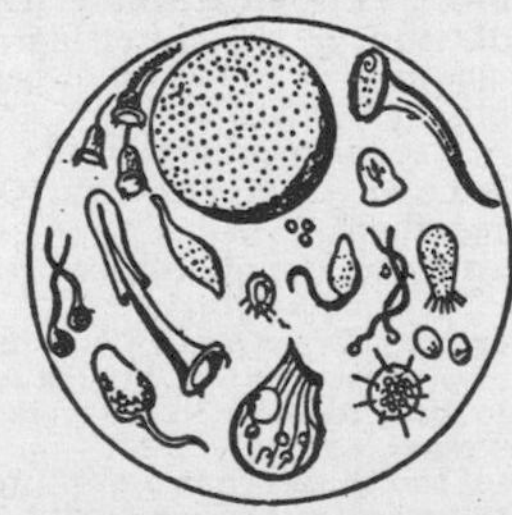

MAGNIFIED DROP OF WATER, SHOWING INFUSORIA, ETC.

1. formerly, a large group consisting of most of the microscopic organisms found in decayed organic matter and stagnant water.

2. a class of very small one-celled animals (*Protozoa*) characterized by cilia which permit free movement, found especially in exposed bodies of water.

in·fū·sō'ri·ăl, *a.* pertaining to the *Infusoria*; composed of or containing *Infusoria*.

infusorial earth; a loose, slightly coherent earth formed of the skeletons of diatoms, a type of algae, and used as an absorbent for nitroglycerin in dynamite: also called *kieselguhr*.

in·fū·sō'ri·ăn, *n.* any member of the *Infusoria*.

in·fū·sō'ri·ăn, *a.* of the infusorial class.

in·fū·sō'ri·fọrm, *a.* [L. *infusus*, pp. of *infundere*, to pour in, and *forma*, form.] resembling an infusorian in shape: said of certain larvae.

in·fū'sō·ry, *a.* infusorial.

in·fū'sō·ry, *n.*; *pl.* **in·fū'sō·rieṣ,** an individual infusorian.

in fū·tū'rō, [L.] in the future.

-ing, a suffix of various origins and meanings: (a) [ME.; AS.] used primarily to form nouns, meaning *related to*, *made of*, *descended from*, as in farth*ing*, athel*ing*: also used to form diminutives; (b) [ME.- *ing*, *-yng*, orig. *-end*, *-and*, *-ind*, from AS. *-ende*, suffix of ppr. of verbs.] used to form the present participle, as in hear*ing*, notic*ing*; (c) [ME. *-ing*, *-yng*; AS. *-ung*.] added to verbs or, sometimes, nouns, to form verbal nouns meaning: (1) *the act* or *an instance of* (a specified verb), as in talk*ing*, digg*ing*; (2) *something produced by the action of* (a specified verb), as in a paint*ing*; (3) *something that does the action of* (a specified verb), as in a cover*ing* for her head; (4) *material used for* (a specified thing), as in blanket*ing*, carpet*ing*.

ing, *n.* [ME. *ing*; AS. *ing*, a meadow.] a pasture or meadow. [Brit. Dial.]

in'găn, in'gun, *n.* an onion. [Dial.]

in·gan·nā'tion, *n.* cheat; fraud. [Obs.]

in'gāte, *n.* 1. entrance; passage in. [Brit. Dial.]

2. in founding, the opening through which metal is poured into a mold.

in·gath'ẽr, *v.t.* and *v.i.* to gather in; to harvest.

in·gath'ẽr·ing, *n.* the gathering in of the fruits of the earth; harvest; as, the feast of *ingathering*.

in·gel'ȧ·ble, *a.* [L. *in-* priv., and *gelare*, to freeze.] that cannot be congealed.

in·ġem'i·nāte, *a.* [L. *ingeminatus*, pp. of *ingeminare*, to redouble, repeat; *in*, in, to, and *geminare*, to double.] redoubled; repeated. [Rare.]

in·ġem'i·nāte, *v.t.*; ingeminated, *pt.*, *pp.*; ingeminating, *ppr.* to stress or make more forceful by repeating; to reiterate.

in·ġem·i·nā'tion, *n.* repetition; an ingeminating.

in·ġen'dẽr, *v.t.* and *v.i.* to engender. [Obs.]

in·ġen·ẽr·ȧ·bil'i·ty, *n.* incapacity of being engendered. [Obs.]

in·ġen'ẽr·ȧ·ble, *a.* [L. *in-* priv., and *generare*, to generate.] that cannot be engendered or produced. [Rare.]

in·ġen'ẽr·ȧ·bly, *adv.* not in a generable manner. [Rare.]

in·ġen'ẽr·āte, *a.* [L. *ingeneratus*, pp. of *ingenerare*, to generate within; *in*, in, and *generare*, to generate.] inborn; innate; inbred; as, *ingenerate* powers of body.

in·ġen'ẽr·āte, *v.t.*; ingenerated, *pt.*, *pp.*; ingenerating, *ppr.* to generate or produce within.

in·ġen'ẽr·āte, *a.* [L. *in-*, not, and *generatus*.] not generated or produced, but originating and existing in itself.

in·ġen·ẽr·ā'tion, *n.* the act of generating within. [Rare.]

in·ġē'ni·āte, *v.t.* and *v.i.* to originate, plan, devise, etc. [Obs.]

in'ġē·nie, *n.* ingeny. [Obs.]

in·ġē·ni·os'i·ty, *n.* the quality of being cunning or skillful. [Rare.]

in·ġēn'ious, *a.* [L. *ingeniosus*, of good capacity, gifted with genius, ingenious, from *ingenium*, innate or natural quality, inclination, ability; *in*, in, and *gignere*, to produce.]

1. originally, having genius; having great mental ability.

2. clever, resourceful, original, and inventive.

3. cleverly or originally made or done; characterized by originality, inventiveness, and skill.

Syn.—inventive, talented, witty, skillful, clever, resourceful.

in·ġēn'ious·ly, *adv.* in an ingenious manner.

in·ġēn'ious·ness, *n.* the quality of being ingenious; ingenuity; as, the *ingeniousness* of an author.

in·ġen'it, in·ġen'ite, *a.* [L. *ingenitus*, pp. of *ingignere*, to implant; *in*, in, and *gignere*, to produce.] innate; inborn; inbred. [Obs.]

in·gé·nue′ (an-zhi-nü′; Fr. añ-zhā-nü′), *n.* [Fr., f. of *ingénu*; L. *ingenuus*, ingenuous.]
1. an innocent, inexperienced, unworldly young woman.
2. in the theater, (a) the role of such a character; (b) an actress playing such a role.

in·ġe·nū′i·ty, *n.* [L. *ingenuitas*, the condition of a freeborn man, a mode of thinking worthy of a freeman, from *ingenuus*, native, freeborn; *in*, in, and *gignere*, to produce.]
1. the quality of being ingenious; cleverness, originality, skill, etc.
2. the quality of being ingenuous. [Rare.]

in·ġen′ū·ous, *a.* [L. *ingenuus*, native, inborn, freeborn, noble, frank, from *ingignere*, to ingenerate; *in*, in, and *gignere*, to produce.]
1. originally, of honorable birth, nature, or character; noble.
2. frank; open; candid; straightforward.
3. simple; artless; innocent; naive; without guile.
4. noble; generous; high-minded. [Archaic.]
Syn.—open, frank, artless.—One who is *open* speaks out at once what is uppermost in his mind; one who is *frank* does so from a natural boldness or dislike of self-restraint; one who is *ingenuous* is actuated by candor and love of truth, which makes him willing to confess his faults and speak his mind without reserve.

in·ġen′ū·ous·ly, *adv.* in an ingenuous manner.

in·ġen′ū·ous·ness, *n.* the state or quality of being ingenuous.

in′ġē·ny, *n.* wit; ingenuity. [Obs.]

in·ġẽr′mi·nāte, *v.t.*, ingerminated, *pt.*, *pp.*; ingerminating, *ppr.* to germinate. [Rare.]

in·ġest′, *v.t.*; ingested, *pt.*, *pp.*; ingesting, *ppr.* [L. *ingestus*, pp. of *ingerere*, to carry, throw on, put into; *in*, into, and *gerere*, to carry, bear.] to take or put (food, drugs, etc.) into the body for digestion.

in·ġes′tȧ, *n.pl.* [L., neut. pl. of *ingestus*, pp. of *ingerere*, to carry or put in, to ingest.] things taken into the body through the stomach: the opposite of *egesta*.

in·ġes′tion (-chun), *n.* [LL. *ingestio* (*-onis*), an uttering, from L. *ingestus*, pp. of *ingerere*, to carry or pour in, to ingest.] the act or process of ingesting.

in·ġes′tive, *a.* serving or tending to ingest: the opposite of *egestive*.

iñ·ghäl′lȧ, *n.* [S. African.] in zoology, the South African rietbok, *Eleotragus arundinaceus*.

Ing′hăm·īte, *n.* in church history, a person who embraced the doctrine and practices inaugurated by Benjamin Ingham, who in the eighteenth century founded a sect with a creed partaking of Methodism and Moravianism.

in·ġirt′, *v.t.* to engirt. [Obs.]

iñ′gle, *n.* [Scot.; Gael. *aingeal*, fire.] 1. a fire or blaze, especially on a hearth.
2. a fireplace.

iñ′gle, *v.t.* to wheedle; to coax. [Obs.]

iñ′gle·nook, *n.* a corner by a fireplace; a chimney corner. [Chiefly Brit.]

iñ′gle·sīde, *n.* a fireside.

in·glō′bāte, *a.* [L. *in*, in, and *globus*, a circle, sphere.] formed or shaped into a globe: said of nebulous matter collected into globular form by the force of gravity.

in·glōbe′, *v.t.* to put into globular form; to fix firmly, as within a globe. [Obs.]

in·glō′ri·ous, *a.* 1. without glory; not famous; little-known; obscure.
2. not giving, receiving, or deserving glory; shameful; disgraceful; as, he charged his troops with *inglorious* flight.

in·glō′ri·ous·ly, *adv.* in an inglorious manner; dishonorably; with shame.

in·glō′ri·ous·ness, *n.* the state of being inglorious or without celebrity.

in·glü′vi·ăl, *a.* in zoology, relating to the ingluvies.

in·glü′vi·ēş, *n.* [L., a maw, crop, prob. from *in*, in, and *glutire*, to swallow.] in zoology, an enlargement of a digestive tube, as the craw or crop of a bird or the paunch of a ruminant.

in·glü′vin, *n.* [L. *ingluvies*, maw, crop, and *-in*.] in medicine, a peptic preparation from the inner coating of a fowl's gizzard, used as a remedy for dyspepsia.

in·glü′vi·ous, *a.* given to excessive eating. [Obs.]

in′gō·ing, *a.* going in; entering.

in·gorge′, *v.t.* and *v.i.* same as *engorge*.

iñ′got, *n.* [ME. *ingot*, lit., that which is poured in, a mold for molten metal, from AS. *in*, in, and *geotan*, to pour.]
1. a mass of metal cast into a bar or other convenient shape.
2. a mold for casting metal into a bar. [Obs.]

iñ′got ī′ron (-ũrn), decarbonized pig iron; Bessemer steel.

iñ′got mōld, a mold for casting ingots.

in·grāce′, *v.t.* to ingratiate. [Obs.]

in·grā′cious (-shus), *a.* ungracious. [Obs.]

in·grȧft′, *v.t.* same as *engraft*.

in·grȧf·tā′tion, *n.* same as *ingraftment*.

in·grȧft′ẽr, *n.* a person who ingrafts.

in·grȧft′ment, *n.* 1. the act of ingrafting.
2. the thing ingrafted.

in′grāin, *a.* 1. dyed in the yarn before weaving and fulling; dyed before manufacture; thoroughly dyed.
2. dyed with grain (kermes). [Obs.]
ingrain carpet; a carpet made of ingrain material, either worsted or cotton, and woven in either two or three webs so that the pattern appears on both sides.

in·grāin′, *v.t.*; ingrained, *pt.*, *pp.*; ingraining, *ppr.* 1. to dye in the grain; to dye in the fiber before manufacture.
2. to work into the natural texture; to impregnate the whole matter or substance; to imbue the entire being; as, stubbornness seems to be *ingrained* in the man.

in′grāin, *n.* yarn, carpeting, etc. dyed before manufacture.

in·grāined′, *a.* 1. worked into the grain or fiber; deeply infused or imbued; firmly established; as, *ingrained* principles.
2. inveterate; thoroughgoing; as, an *ingrained* liar.

in·gram·mat′i·cişm, *n.* [L. *in-* priv., and *grammatica*, grammar.] a form or expression not grammatically correct. [Rare.]

in·grap′ple, *v.t.* and *v.i.* to grapple. [Obs.]

in′grāte, *a.* [OFr. *ingrat*; L. *ingratus*, unpleasant, disagreeable, ungrateful; *in-* priv., and *gratus*, grateful, pleasing.] ungrateful; unthankful. [Obs.]

in′grāte, *n.* an ungrateful person.

in·grāte′ful, *a.* 1. ungrateful; unthankful.
2. displeasing to the senses; as, *ingrateful* food, an *ingrateful* odor. [Obs.]

in·grāte′fụl·ly, *adv.* ungratefully.

in·grāte′fụl·ness, *n.* ungratefulness.

in′grāte·ly, *adv.* in the manner of an ingrate. [Obs.]

in·grā′ti·āte (-shi-), *v.t.*; ingratiated, *pt.*, *pp.*; ingratiating, *ppr.* [prob. via It. *ingratiare* (now *ingraziare*), from L. phrase *in gratiam*, for the favor of, from *in*, in, and *gratia*, favor, agreeableness.] to bring (oneself) into another's favor or good graces.

in·grā″ti·ā′tion, *n.* an ingratiating.

in·grā′ti·ȧ·tō·ry, *a.* ingratiating or serving to ingratiate.

in·grat′i·tūde, *n.* [LL. *ingratitudo* (*-inis*), from L. *ingratus*, ungrateful; *in-* priv., and *gratus*, grateful.] lack of gratitude; ungratefulness.
Ingratitude is abhorred both by God and man. —L'Estrange.

in·grāve′, *v.t.* to engrave. [Rare.]

in·grāve′, *v.t.* to bury. [Obs.]

in·grȧ·ves′cent, *a.* [L. *ingravescens* (*-entis*), *ppr.* of *ingravescere*, to grow heavier; *in-*, intens., and *gravescere*, to grow heavy, from *gravis*, heavy.] in pathology, increasing in severity; as, *ingravescent* apoplexy.

in·grav′i·dāte, *v.t.* to impregnate. [Obs.]

in·grav·i·dā′tion, *n.* the act of ingravidating or impregnating, or the state of being pregnant or impregnated. [Obs.]

in·greāt′, *v.t.* to make great. [Obs.]

in·grē′di·ence, *n.* 1. ingrediency. [Obs.]
2. an ingredient. [Obs.]

in·grē′di·en·cy, *n.* the quality or condition of being an ingredient. [Obs.]

in·grē′di·ent, *n.* [Fr. *ingrédient*, an ingredient, from L. *ingrediens* (*-entis*), ppr. of *ingredi*, to step or go into, to enter in, to engage in; *in*, into, and *gradi*, to go.]
1. any of the things that a mixture is made of; as, the *ingredients* of ice cream.
2. a component part, or constituent, of anything.
Syn.—element, component, constituent.

in·grē′di·ent, *a.* forming an ingredient; constituent.

in′gress, *n.* [ME. *ingress*, from L. *ingressus*, pp. of *ingredi*, to step or go into, to enter in; *in*, into, and *gradi*, to go.]
1. the act of entering.
2. the right or permission to enter.
3. a place or means of entering; entrance.
4. in astronomy, (a) the entrance of the moon into the shadow of the earth in eclipses; (b) the sun's entrance into a sign.

in·gress′, *v.t.* and *v.i.* to enter. [Rare.]

in·gres′sion (-gresh′un), *n.* [L. *ingressio* (*-onis*), a going into, entering, from *ingressus*, pp. of *ingredi*, to go into, to enter.] the act of entering; entrance.

in·griēve′, *v.t.* to engrieve. [Obs.]

in·grōss′, *v.t.* to engross. [Obs.]

in′-gröup, *n.* any group of people regarded from the point of view of any of its members as contrasted to all outside groups (outgroups).

in′grōw·ing, *a.* growing within, inward, or into; especially, growing into the flesh; as, an *ingrowing* hair.

in′grōwn, *a.* 1. grown within, inward, or into; especially, grown into the flesh; as, an *ingrown* toenail.
2. inborn; native; innate.

in′grōwth, *n.* a growing inward; also, that which grows inward.

iñ′guen (-gwen), *n.* [L.] the groin.

iñ′gui·năl (-gwi-), *a.* [L. *inguinalis*, from *inguen* (*-inis*), the groin.] of or near the groin; as, the *inguinal* glands.

iñ′gui·nō- a combining form meaning *inguinal* or *inguinal and*: also, before a vowel, *inguin-*.

in·gulf′, *v.t.* same as *engulf*.

in·gulf′ment, *n.* same as *engulfment*.

in·gũr′ġi·tāte, *v.t.*; ingurgitated, *pt.*, *pp.*; ingurgitating, *ppr.* [L. *ingurgitatus*, pp. of *ingurgitare*, to pour in like a flood, to gormandize; *in*, in, and *gurges* (*-itis*), an abyss, gulf.]
1. to swallow greedily or in great quantity.
2. to engulf.

in·gũr′ġi·tāte, *v.i.* to swill or gorge.

in·gũr·ġi·tā′tion, *n.* [LL. *ingurgitatio* (*-onis*), from L. *ingurgitare*, to gormandize.]
1. an ingurgitating or being ingurgitated.
2. that which is ingurgitated.

in·gust′ȧ·ble, *a.* [L. *ingustabilis*; *in-* priv., and *gustabilis*, tastable, from *gustare*, to taste.] not perceptible to taste. [Obs.]

Iñg·win′i·ȧn, *a.* [from AS. *Ingeine*, lit., friend of *Ing*.]
1. designating or of a group of Low German peoples whose tutelary deity was *Ing* and who inhabited the Jutland Peninsula and adjacent regions during the Dark Ages: the Angles, Saxons, Jutes, and Frisians were Ingwinian.
2. designating or of the group of closely associated Low German dialects spoken by these peoples.

Iñg·win′i·ȧn, *n.* the Ingwinian language, regarded as the immediate ancestor of Anglo-Saxon and Old Frisian: also called *Anglo-Frisian*.

in·hab′ile, *a.* [L. *inhabilis*, unmanageable, unwieldy; *in-* priv., and *habilis*, manageable, fit, proper, from *habere*, to have.]
1. not apt or fit; unfit; not convenient; as, *inhabile* matter. [Obs.]
2. unskilled; unready; unqualified: used of persons. [Obs.]

in·hȧ·bil′i·ty, *n.* unaptness; unfitness; want of skill. [Obs.]

in·hab′it, *v.t.*; inhabited, *pt.*, *pp.*; inhabiting, *ppr.* [ME. *enhabiten*; OFr. *enhabiter*; L. *inhabitare*, to dwell in, inhabit; *in*, in, and *habitare*, to dwell.] to live or dwell in; to occupy as a place of settled residence; as, wild beasts *inhabit* the forest; men *inhabit* cities and houses.
Syn.—dwell, occupy, sojourn, stay, remain, abide, reside.

in·hab′it, *v.i.* to dwell; to live; to abide. [Archaic.]

in·hab·it·ȧ·bil′i·ty, *n.* the fact or quality of being inhabitable, or habitable.

in·hab·it·ȧ·bil′i·ty, *n.* the fact or quality of being inhabitable, or not habitable. [Rare.]

in·hab′it·ȧ·ble, *a.* [LL. *inhabitabilis*, inhabitable, from L. *inhabitare*, to inhabit.] habitable; capable of being inhabited, or of affording habitation.

in·hab′it·ȧ·ble, *a.* not habitable. [Rare.]

in·hab′it·ănce, *n.* inhabitancy. [Obs.]

in·hab′it·ăn·cy, *n.*; *pl.* **in·hab′it·ăn·cieş,** 1. residence; the act of inhabiting or the condition of being inhabited; occupancy.
2. place of residence; home; dwelling.

in·hab′it·ănt, *n.* [OFr. *inhabitant*, an inhabitant, from L. *inhabitans* (*-antis*), ppr. of *inhabitare*, to dwell within, to inhabit.] a person or animal that inhabits some specified region, house, etc.; a permanent resident.

in·hab·i·tā′tion, *n.* [ME. *inhabitacioun*; Anglo-Fr. *enhabitacion*; LL. *inhabitatio* (*-onis*), a dwelling, from L. *inhabitare*, to dwell within, to inhabit.]

1. an inhabiting or being inhabited.
2. abode; place of dwelling. [Obs.]
3. population; whole mass of inhabitants. [Obs.]

in·hab′i·tā″tive, *a.* pertaining to inhabitation.
in·hab′i·tā″tive·ness, *n.* inhabitiveness.
in·hab′it·ed, *a.* uninhabited. [Obs.]
in·hab′it·ed, *a.* having inhabitants; lived in; populated; as, a densely *inhabited* county.
in·hab′it·ẽr, *n.* an inhabitant. [Archaic.]
in·hab′i·tive·ness, *n.* in phrenology, a desire or natural inclination to reside permanently in a place or abode; love of country or home.
in·hab′it·ress, *n.* a female inhabitant. [Rare.]
in·hāl′ănt, *a.* [L. *inhalans* (*-antis*), ppr. of *inhalare*, to breathe in, inhale.] used in inhalation; inhaling; as, the *inhalant* end of a duct.
in·hāl′ănt, *n.* a medicine or other substance to be inhaled as a vapor.
in·hȧ·lā′tion, *n.* 1. the act of inhaling.
2. that which is inhaled; specifically, in pharmacy, a preparation in the form of a vapor intended to be inhaled.
in′hȧ·lā·tŏr, *n.* 1. an apparatus for administering medicinal vapors in inhalation.
2. same as *respirator* (sense 2).
in·hāle′, *v.t.*; inhaled, *pt.*, *pp.*; inhaling, *ppr.* [L. *inhalare*, to breathe in, inhale; *in*, in, and *halare*, to breathe.] to draw into the lungs; to breathe in; as, to *inhale* air: opposed to *exhale*.

Martin was walking forth to *inhale* the fresh breeze of the evening. —Arbuthnot.

in·hāle′, *v.i.* to breathe a substance into the lungs; especially, to breathe in tobacco smoke.
in·hāl′ent, *a.* inhalant.
in·hāl′ẽr, *n.* 1. a person who inhales.
2. same as *respirator* (sense 1).
3. same as *inhalator* (sense 1).
in·hȧnce′, *v.t.* to enhance. [Obs.]
in·hȧnce′ment, *n.* enhancement. [Obs.]
in·här·mon′iç, *a.* not harmonic; out of harmony; discordant.
in·här·mon′iç·ăl, *a.* inharmonic.
in·här·mō′ni·ous, *a.* 1. not harmonious; unmusical; discordant.
2. disagreeing; conflicting; not in accord.
in·här·mō′ni·ous·ly, *adv.* without harmony; discordantly.
in·här·mō′ni·ous·ness, *n.* the quality or state of being inharmonious; discord.
in·här′mō·ny, *n.* lack of harmony; discord.
in′hau̇l, *n.* an inhauler.
in′hau̇l·ẽr, *n.* among seamen, a rope employed to haul in a sail.
in·hēarse′, *v.t.*; inhearsed, *pt.*, *pp.*; inhearsing, *ppr.* to put or place in a hearse. [Rare.]
in·hēre′, *v.i.*; inhered, *pt.*, *pp.*; inhering, *ppr.* [L. *inhærere*, to stick in, to adhere, or cleave to; *in*, in, and *hærere*, to stick.] to exist or be fixed in; to be an inseparable part of something; to be a member, adjunct, or quality of something; to be inherent or innate.
in·hēr′ence, *n.* the state or fact of inhering or of being inherent; specifically, in philosophy, the relation of an attribute to its subject.
in·hēr′en·cy, *n.*; *pl.* **in·hēr′en·cieș**, 1. inherence.
2. something inherent.
in·hēr′ent, *a.* [L. *inhærens* (*-entis*), *ppr.* of *inhærere*, to stick in or to, to inhere.] existing in someone or something as a natural and inseparable quality, characteristic, or right; innate; basic; inborn; as, the *inherent* right of men to life, liberty, and the pursuit of happiness.

A most *inherent* baseness. —Shak.

Syn.—inbred, inborn, innate, natural, inseparable, indwelling.
in·hēr′ent·ly, *adv.* by virtue of its inherent qualities; basically.
in·her′it, *v.t.*; inherited, *pt.*, *pp.*; inheriting, *ppr.* [ME. *inheriten*, *enheriten*; OFr. *inheriter*, *enheriter*, to inherit, from LL. *inhereditare*, to appoint as heir, to inherit; L. *in*, in, and *heres* (*-edis*), an heir.]
1. to transfer property to (an heir). [Obs.]
2. to receive (property) by the laws of inheritance.
3. to have (certain characteristics) by heredity.
in·her′it, *v.i.* to receive an inheritance; to come into possession, as an heir or successor; to become an heir.

Thou shalt not *inherit* in our father's house. —Jud. xi. 2.

in·her″it·ȧ·bil′i·ty, *n.* the quality or state of being inheritable.
in·her′it·ȧ·ble, *a.* [OFr. *inheritable*, *enheritable*, from *inheriter*, LL. *inhereditare*, to inherit.]
1. capable of being inherited; transmissible or descendible from the ancestor to the heir by course of law; as, an *inheritable* estate.
2. capable of being transmitted from the parent to the child; as, *inheritable* qualities or infirmities.
3. capable of taking by inheritance; having the rights of an heir.
in·her′it·ȧ·bly, *adv.* by inheritance; so as to be inheritable.
in·her′it·ȧnce, *n.* [OFr. *enheritance*, an inheriting, from *enheriter*, LL. *inhereditare*, to inherit.]
1. the action of inheriting.
2. something inherited or to be inherited; legacy; bequest.
3. ownership by virtue of birthright; right to inherit.
4. any blessing or possession coming as a gift.
5. any characteristic passed on by heredity.
inheritance tax; a tax on inherited property.
in·her′it·ŏr, *n.* an heir; one who inherits or may inherit.
in·her′it·ress, *n.* an heiress.
in·her′it·rix, *n.* an inheritress.
in·hē′șion (-zhun), *n.* [LL. *inhæsio* (*-onis*), a clinging or fixing to, from L. *inhæsus*, pp. of *inhærere*, to stick in, inhere; *in*, in, and *hærere*, to stick.] inherence.
in·hī·ā′tion, *n.* a gaping after; eager desire. [Obs.]
in·hib′it, *v.t.*; inhibited, *pt.*, *pp.*; inhibiting, *ppr.* [L. *inhibitus*, pp. of *inhibere*, to hold back, restrain, curb; *in*, in, on, and *habere*, to have, to hold.]
1. to prohibit; to forbid; especially, to forbid (a priest, etc.) to perform church functions.
2. to suppress; withhold; check.
in·hib′i·tẽr, *n.* an inhibitor.
in·hi·bi′tion (-bish′un), *n.* [L. *inhibitio* (*-onis*), a restraining, a holding back, from *inhibere*, to hold back, to restrain.]
1. an inhibiting or being inhibited.
2. anything that inhibits; especially, a mental or psychological process that restrains or suppresses an action, emotion, or thought.
in·hib′i·tive, *a.* inhibitory.
in·hib′i·tŏr, *n.* a person or thing that inhibits; especially, any substance that slows or prevents a chemical or organic reaction.
in·hib′i·tō·ry, *a.* of, or having the nature of, inhibition; inhibiting.
inhibitory nerves; nerves the stimulation of which inhibits or lessens the activity of an organ.
in·hōld′, *v.t.* to contain in itself. [Obs.]
in·hōld′er, *n.* that which holds or contains. [Obs.]
in·hoop′, *v.t.* to confine or enclose in or as in a hoop. [Obs.]
in·hos′pi·tȧ·ble, *a.* 1. not hospitable; not offering hospitality to visitors or guests.
2. not offering protection or refuge; barren; forbidding: said of a country, region, etc.
in·hos′pi·tȧ·ble·ness, *n.* the quality of being inhospitable.
in·hos′pi·tȧ·bly, *adv.* in an inhospitable manner.
in·hos·pi·tal′i·ty, *n.* lack of hospitality; inhospitable treatment.
in·hū′măn, *a.* not human; not having the characteristics considered normal to human beings; especially, unfeeling, hard-hearted, cruel, barbarous, etc.
in·hū·māne′, *a.* [*in-* (not) and *humane*; also older sp. for *inhuman*.] not humane; unmoved by the suffering of others; cruel, brutal, unkind, etc.
Syn.—cruel, savage, barbarous, unfeeling, pitiless, ruthless.
in·hū·man′i·ty, *n.* [L. *inhumanitas* (*-atis*), inhuman conduct, savageness, incivility, from *inhumanus*, barbarous, inhuman.]
1. the quality or state of being inhuman; barbarity; cruelty.
2. *pl.* **in·hū·man′i·tieș**, an inhuman act or remark.
Syn.—unkindness, cruelty, barbarity, brutality.
in·hū′măn·ly, *adv.* in an inhuman manner.
in·hū′māte, *v.t.* to inhume. [Rare.]
in·hū·mā′tion, *n.* 1. the act of burying; interment.
2. in old chemistry, a method of distilling substances by burying the vessel containing them in warm earth.
in·hūme′, *v.t.*; inhumed (-hūmd), *pt.*, *pp.*; inhuming, *ppr.* [L. *inhumare*, to bury in the earth, to inter; *in*, in, and *humus*, earth, ground.]
1. to bury; to inter, as a dead body.
2. in old chemistry, to distill by inhumation.
-ī′nī, [masc. pl. of L. *-inus*.] a suffix used to form Latinized names of some groups in zoology; as, Acanthur*ini*.
in′i·ȧ, *n.* [S. Am. native name.] a dolphin found in the fresh waters of South America.
in′i·ăl, *a.* in anatomy, relating to the inion.
in·im·aġ′in·ȧ·ble, *a.* unimaginable; inconceivable. [Obs.]
in·im′iç·ăl, *a.* [LL. *inimicalis*, hostile, unfriendly, from L. *inimicus*, hostile, an enemy; *in-* priv., and *amicus*, a friend.]
1. unfriendly; like an enemy; hostile.
2. adverse; hurtful; repugnant; as, acts *inimical* to peace.
Syn.—adverse, unfriendly, harmful, contrary, hostile, opposed, repugnant.
in·im·i·çal′i·ty, *n.* unfriendliness.
in·im′iç·ăl·ly, *adv.* in an unfriendly manner.
in·im·i·ci′tious (-sish′us), *a.* not friendly. [Obs.]
in·im′i·çous, *a.* inimical. [Obs.]
in·im″i·tȧ·bil′i·ty, *n.* the quality or state of being inimitable.
in·im′i·tȧ·ble, *a.* [L. *inimitabilis*, not to be imitated; *in-* priv., and *imitabilis*, imitable, from *imitare*, to imitate.] not to be imitated or copied; surpassing imitation.
in·im′i·tȧ·ble·ness, *n.* inimitability.
in·im′i·tȧ·bly, *adv.* so as to be inimitable.
in′i·on, *n.* [Gr. *inion*, the back of the head, from *is*, *inos*, a sinew, muscle, lit., strength.] the bulging part at the rear of the human skull.
in·iq′ui·tous (-ik′wi-), *a.* showing iniquity; unjust; wicked.
Syn.—wicked, nefarious.
in·iq′ui·tous·ly, *adv.* unjustly; wickedly.
in·iq′ui·ty, *n.* [ME. *iniquite*; OFr. *iniquité*; L. *iniquitas* (*-atis*), unevenness, inequality, injustice, from *iniquus*, unequal; *in-* priv., and *æquus*, level, equal.]
1. lack of justice or righteousness; wickedness; sin.
2. *pl.* **in·iq′ui·tieș**, a wicked, unjust, or unrighteous act.
in·ī′quous, *a.* unjust. [Obs.]
in·ir″ri·tȧ·bil′i·ty, *n.* the quality of being irritable.
in·ir′ri·tȧ·ble, *a.* not irritable; that cannot be irritated: said especially of muscles.
in·ir′ri·tā·tive, *a.* not accompanied with excitement; as, an *inirritative* fever.
in·isle′ (-īle′), *v.t.* to enisle.
in·i′tiăl (-ish′ăl), *a.* [L. *initialis*, pertaining to the beginning, initial, from *initium*, a beginning, from *inire*, to go into, to enter upon, begin; *in*, into, in, and *ire*, to go.]
1. having to do with, indicating, or occurring at the beginning; as, the *initial* symptoms of a disease.
2. designating the first letter or syllable of a word.
initial tension; the strain upon any part of a structure or mechanism which is inherent in the structure itself and not external: also called *initial stress*.
in·i′tiăl, *v.t.*; initialed *or* initialled, *pt.*, *pp.*; initialing *or* initialling, *ppr.* to designate by using an initial or initials; to place one's initials upon.
in·i′tiăl, *n.* a letter beginning a word; specifically, (a) an extra-large capital letter at the start of a printed paragraph, chapter, etc.; (b) the first letter of a name.
in·i′tiăl·ly, *adv.* at first; at the beginning.
In·i′tiăl Teach′ing Al′phȧ·bet, an alphabet of 44 characters, with a single sound for each character, devised by Sir James Pitman (1901–), of England, for teaching beginners to read English.
in·i′ti·āte (-ish′i-), *v.t.*; initiated, *pt.*, *pp.*; initiating, *ppr.* [from L. *initiatus*, pp. of *initiare*, to enter upon, initiate, from *initium*, a beginning.]
1. to bring into practice or use; to introduce by first doing or using.
2. to teach the fundamentals of some subject to; to help (someone) to begin doing something.
3. to admit as a member into a fraternity, club, etc., especially through use of secret ceremony or rites.
Syn.—begin, commence, start, install, induct, inaugurate.
in·i′ti·āte, *v.i.* to do the first act; to perform the first rite.
in·i′ti·āte, *a.* 1. initiated.
2. beginning; commenced; in the first stage.
initiate tenant by courtesy; in law, a tenant

who becomes so by the birth of a child, but whose estate is not consummated till the death of the wife.

in·i′ti·āte (-i′shi-), *n.* one who has recently been, or is about to be, initiated.

in·i·ti·ā′tion, *n.* [Fr. *initiation*; L. *initiatio* (-*onis*), an initiation, a taking part in sacred rites, from *initiare*, to initiate.]
1. an initiating or being initiated.
2. the ceremonies or rites by which a person is initiated into a fraternity, etc.

in·i′ti·ȧ·tive, *a.* of, or having the nature of, initiation; introductory; initial.

in·i′ti·ȧ·tive, *n.* 1. the action of taking the first step or move; responsibility for beginning or originating.
2. the characteristic of originating new ideas or methods; ability to think and act without being urged; enterprise.
3. (a) the right of a legislature to introduce new legislation on some specified matter; (b) the right of a group of citizens to introduce a matter for legislation either to the legislature or directly to the voters; (c) the procedure by which such matters are introduced, usually a petition signed by a specified percentage of the voters.

in·i′ti·ā·tŏr, *n.* [LL. *initiator*, from *initiare*, to begin (L., to initiate).] one who or that which initiates.

in·i′ti·ȧ·tō·ry, *a.* 1. of or pertaining to or suitable for a beginning or introduction; introductory; initial; as, an *initiatory* step.
2. initiating or serving to initiate; used in an initiation; as, *initiatory* ceremonies.
Two *initiatory* rites of the same general import cannot exist together.—J. M. Mason.

in·i′ti·ȧ·tō·ry, *n.* an introductory rite. [Rare.]

in·i′ti·ā·trix, *n.* [LL. f. of *initiator*, a beginner, initiator.] a woman who initiates. [Rare.]

in·i′tion (-ish′un), *n.* a beginning.

in·jeçt′, *v.t.*; injected, *pt.*, *pp.*; injecting, *ppr.* [Fr. *injecter*, from L. *injectus*, pp. of *injicere*, to throw, cast, or put in; *in*, in, and *jacere*, to throw.]
1. to force or drive (a fluid) into some passage or cavity; especially, to introduce or force (a liquid) into some part of the body by means of a syringe, hypodermic needle, etc.
2. to fill (a cavity, etc.) by injection.
3. to introduce or throw in a remark, etc.; to interject.
4. to cast or throw (*on*). [Obs.]

in·jeç′tion, *n.* [L. *injectio* (-*onis*), a throwing or casting into, a laying on, from *injectus*, pp. of *injicere*, to throw or cast into, to inject.]
1. an injecting.
2. something injected; especially, a liquid injected into the body.
3. congestion.

in·jeç′tion çock, the cock in a steam engine by which cold water is admitted into a condenser.

in·jeç′tion en′ġine, a steam engine in which the steam is condensed by a jet of cold water injected into the condenser.

in·jeç′tion pīpe, a pipe through which water is injected into the condenser of a steam engine, to condense the steam.

in·jeç′tion valve, the valve in a steam engine through which cold water is admitted into the condenser.

in·jeç′tion wa̤′tēr, the water injected into the condenser of a steam engine to condense the steam.

in·jeçt′ŏr, *n.* [from L. *injectus*, pp. of *injicere*, to inject.] one who or that which injects; especially, a device for injecting water into a steam boiler.

in·jel′ly, *v.t.* to bury in jelly. [Rare.]

in·join′, *v.t.* to enjoin. [Obs.]

in·joint′, *v.t.* to unite; joint. [Obs.]

in·jū·çun′di·ty, *n.* unpleasantness; disagreeableness. [Obs.]

in·jū·di′ciȧl (-dish′ȧl), *a.* not according to the forms of law. [Rare.]

in·jū·di′cious, *a.* 1. not judicious; showing poor judgment; lacking discretion; unwise; as, an *injudicious* person.
2. not according to sound judgment or discretion; unwise; as, an *injudicious* measure.
Syn.—unwise, indiscreet, hasty, imprudent, rash, undiscerning, ill-advised.

in·jū·di′cious·ly, *adv.* in an injudicious manner; unwisely.

in·jū·di′cious·ness, *n.* the quality of being injudicious.

in·junç′tion, *n.* [LL. *injunctio* (-*onis*), a command, order, from L. *injunctus*, pp. of *injungere*, to command, order, enjoin, lit., to join or fasten into; *in*, into, and *jungere*, to join.]
1. an enjoining; a bidding; a command.
2. something enjoined; a command; an order.
3. a legal order from a court prohibiting a person or group from carrying out a given action, or ordering a given action to be done.
Syn.—command, order, precept, behest, mandate.

in′jūre, *v.t.*; injured, *pt.*, *pp.*; injuring, *ppr.* [Fr. *injurier*; L. *injuriari*, to injure, from *injuria*, an injury, wrong; *in-* priv., and *jus*, *juris*, right, law.]
1. to do physical harm or damage to; to hurt.
2. to wrong or offend deeply; to be unjust to.
Syn.—damage, impair, deteriorate, hurt, harm, spoil, abuse, wrong.

in′jūr·ēr, *n.* one who or that which injures.

in·jū′ri·ȧ, *n.*; *pl.* **in·jū′ri·ae,** [L.] in law, a legal wrong; an act or omission of which the law takes cognizance as a wrong.

in·jū′ri·ous, *a.* [Fr. *injurieux*; L. *injuriosus*, harmful, unjust, injurious, from *injuria*, a wrong, injury.]
1. injuring or likely to cause injury; of a harmful character; hurtful; detrimental.
2. insolent; insulting; slanderous or libelous.
Injurious duke, that threat'st where is no cause. —Shak.
Syn.—hurtful, deleterious, prejudicial, noxious, detrimental, baneful, pernicious, mischievous, damaging.

in·jū′ri·ous·ly, *adv.* in an injurious manner; wrongfully; hurtfully; mischievously.

in·jū′ri·ous·ness, *n.* the quality of being injurious; injury.

in′jụ·ry, *n.*; *pl.* **in′jụ·rieṣ,** [ME. *injurie*; OFr. *injure*; L. *injuria*, wrong, an injury, an unjust act, from *injuriosus*, acting unjustly; *in-* priv., and *jus*, *juris*, right, justice.]
1. physical harm or damage to a person, property, etc.
2. unjust treatment; violation of rights; offense.
3. an injurious act.
4. insult. [Obs.]
Syn.—damage, hurt, harm, mischief, detriment, wrong, impairment.—*Damage* is that injury to a thing which occasions loss to a person or a diminution of value to a thing; *hurt* implies a wound inflicted physically or emotionally that destroys the soundness or integrity of things; *harm* suggests the causing of pain or distress; *mischief* suggests a troublesome injury, that may simply produce inconvenience or annoyance.

in·just′, *a.* unjust. [Obs.]

in·jus′tice, *n.* [OFr. *injustice*; L. *injustitia*, injustice, from *injustus*, not just; *in-* priv., and *justus*, just.]
1. the quality of being unjust or unfair; lack of justice; wrong.
2. an unjust act; an injury.
Syn.—injury, unfairness, grievance, wrong, iniquity.

iñk, *n.* [ME. *inke*, *ynke*; OFr. *enque*; LL. *encaustum*; Gr. *enkauston*, a purple or red ink, from *enkaustos*, burnt in, from *enkaiein*, to burn in; *en*, in, and *kaiein*, to burn.]
1. a colored liquid used for writing, drawing, etc.
2. a sticky, colored paste used in printing; printer's ink.
3. a dark, liquid secretion squirted out by cuttlefish, etc. to cloud the water for protection.
China ink; see *India ink*.
indelible ink; an ink that makes a mark which cannot easily be erased or removed: called also *marking ink*, *permanent ink*.
invisible ink; a colorless ink that cannot be seen on paper until it is treated with heat, vapor, or a chemical reagent: also called *sympathetic ink*.
lithographic ink; an ink used for writing on stone or for transferring autographically from paper to stone. It is composed of wax, dry white soap, tallow or lard, shellac, mastic, and lampblack.
permanent ink; same as *indelible ink*.
sympathetic ink; same as *invisible ink*.

iñk, *v.t.*; inked (inkt), *pt.*, *pp.*; inking, *ppr.* 1. to cover with ink; to spread ink on.
2. to mark or color with ink.

iñk, *n.* [etym. unknown.] the socket of a mill spindle.

iñk bag, the bladder-shaped sac in cuttlefish, etc., containing a black, viscid fluid resembling ink which, in case of danger, the animals eject in order to make the surrounding water opaque and thus conceal themselves: called also *ink gland*, *ink sac*.

iñk′ber″ry, *n.*; *pl.* **iñk′ber″rieṣ,** 1. an evergreen holly growing in eastern North America.
2. the pokeweed.
3. the dark-purple or black fruit of either of these plants.

iñk′ēr, *n.* a person or thing that inks; specifically, in printnig, a roller for spreading ink on type.

iñk′fish, *n.* a cuttlefish or squid.

iñk foun′tain (-tin), an inking trough.

iñk′hǫrn, *n.* a small vessel formerly used to hold ink, made of horn or other material.

iñk′hǫrn, *a.* affectedly learned; pedantic.

iñk′hǫrn·iṣm, *n.* an affected, pedantic, or bombastic expression. [Obs.]

iñk′i·ness, *n.* 1. the condition of being covered with ink.
2. blackness; darkness.

iñk′ing rōll′ēr, in printing, a roller with an elastic covering made of glue, molasses, etc., used to supply the form with ink.

iñk′ing trough (trǫf), a trough from which an inking roller receives its supply of ink: also called *ink fountain*.

iñ′kle, *n.* [prob. from obs. D. *inckel* (D. *enkel*), single (with reference to the narrow width).]
1. a kind of braided linen tape.
2. the thread or yarn from which this is made.

iñ′kle, *v.t.* to have a hint of; to guess. [Brit. Dial.]

iñ′kling, *n.* [from ME. *inclen*, to give an inkling of.]
1. a hint; a suggestion; a slight indication.
2. a vague idea or notion; a suspicion.

iñk mush′rọom, a mushroom, *Coprinus atramentarius*, that yields a fluid resembling ink.

in′kneed (-nēd), *a.* knock-kneed.

in·knit′ (-nit′), *v.t.*; inknitted, *pt.*, *pp.*; inknitting, *ppr.* to knit up; to draw together. [Obs.]

in·knot′ (-not′), *v.t.*; inknotted, *pt.*, *pp.*; inknotting, *ppr.* to bind, as with a knot. [Rare.]

iñk nut, the fruit of several species of *Terminalia*, as *Terminalia bellerica*, *Terminalia chebula*, etc., used in making black ink and dye.

iñk plant, 1. a shrub of New Zealand, *Coriaria thymifolia*: the juice of the fruit forms a red ink.
2. a related shrub, *Coriaria myrtifolia*, of Europe: its leaves yield a black dyestuff.

iñk pow′dēr, a powder which when dissolved will make ink.

iñk′rọot, *n.* the marsh rosemary or sea lavender, *Statice limonium*.

iñk′stand, *n.* 1. an inkwell.
2. a receptacle to contain ink, pens, and other materials used in writing.

iñk′stōne, *n.* a stone slab on which ink is mixed.

iñk′well, *n.* a container for holding ink, usually set in a desk, inkstand, etc.

iñk′wood, *n.* a tropical tree of the soapberry family, having dark wood and growing in Florida and the West Indies.

iñk wrīt′ēr, an instrument which makes a record in ink, used in telegraphy.

iñk′y, *a.*; *comp.* inkier; *superl.* inkiest, 1. resembling ink; black; dark.
2. colored, marked, covered, or smeared with ink.

in·lāce′, *v.t.* see *enlace*.

in·lag′ȧ·ry, *n.* [AS. *in*, in, and *lagu*, law.] in old English law, the restitution of an outlawed person to the protection of the law. [Obs.]

in·lȧ·gā′tion, *n.* inlagary. [Obs.]

in·lāid′, *a.* [pp. of *inlay*.]
1. set in a surface so as to form a decoration, usually level with the surface.
2. decorated with material set in the surface.

in′lănd, *n.* the interior of a country or region; inland areas.

in′lănd, *a.* 1. interior; confined to a country; remote from the sea or ocean; as, an *inland* town or lake.
2. carried on within a country; domestic; not foreign; as, *inland* trade or transportation; *inland* navigation.

in′lănd, *adv.* into or toward the interior; away from the coast or border.

in′lănd·ēr, *n.* one who lives in the interior of a country, or at a distance from the sea.

in·la̤w′, *v.t.* [ME. *inlawen*; AS. *inlagian*.] to restore the benefits and protection of the law to (an outlaw): opposed to *outlaw*.

in'-law, *n.* [contr. from *mother-in-law*, etc.] a relative by marriage. [Colloq.]

in·lāy', *v.t.*; inlaid, *pt.*, *pp.*; inlaying, *ppr.* 1. to set (pieces of wood, gold, etc.) in a surface so as to form a decoration, usually level with the surface.

2. to decorate with pieces of wood, gold, etc. set in the surface.

in'lāy, *n.*; *pl.* **in'lāys,** 1. inlaid decoration or material.

2. a filling for a tooth, consisting of a solid mass of metal, porcelain, etc., made to fit into a cavity and then cemented in.

in'lāy·ẽr, *n.* the person or thing that inlays.

in·lāy'ing, *n.* the art or operation of making inlays.

in·league' (-lēg'), *v.t.* to enleague. [Obs.]

in·lēa guẽr (-gẽr), *v.t.* and *v.i.* to beleaguer. [Obs.]

in·let', *v.t.*; inlet, *pt.*, *pp.*; inletting, *ppr.* to inlay or insert.

in'let, *n.* 1. a passage or opening by which an enclosed place may be entered; place of ingress; entrance.

Doors and windows, *inlets* of men and of light, I couple together. —Wotton.

2. a small bay or narrow strip of water extending into a body of land from a sea, lake, etc.; a creek.

3. a narrow strip of water between islands.

4. any material or substance let in, inserted, or inlaid.

in'lī·ẽr, *n.* a portion of an older rock formation completely surrounded by another younger formation that rests upon it: opposed to *outlier*.

in·līght'en (-līt'), *v.t.* see *enlighten*.

in·list', *v.t.* and *v.i.* to enlist. [Obs.]

in·list'ment, *n.* enlistment. [Obs.]

in·līve', *v.t.* to enlive. [Obs.]

in·lock', *v.t.* to enlock. [Obs.]

in lō'çō, [L.] in the place; in the right or specified place.

in lō'çō pȧ·ren'tis, [L.] in the place of a parent: said of a person acting temporarily with parental authority.

in'look, *n.* introspection.

in·lū'mine, *v.t.* to illumine. [Obs.]

in'ly, *a.* [ME. *inliche*; AS. *inlice.*] internal; interior; secret. [Obs.]

in'ly, *adv.* internally; deep within; in the heart. [Poetic.]

in'māte, *n.* 1. a person living with others in the same building; an occupant.

2. a person lodged with others, and often confined, in an institution, asylum, etc.

3. an inhabitant.

in'māte, *a.* admitted as a dweller; resident. [Rare.]

in'māte·cy, *n.* the state of being an inmate. [Obs.]

in'mēats, *n.pl.* 1. the entrails. [Obs. or Dial.]

2. the inner parts of an animal used for food, as the liver, kidneys, heart, etc. [Obs. or Dial.]

in mē'di·as rēs, [L.] into the midst of things; in the middle of the action rather than at the beginning, as in commencing an epic.

in me·mō'ri·am, [L.] in memory (of): put on tombstones, in obituary notices, etc.

in·mesh', *v.t.* to enmesh.

in'-mī'grȧnt, *n.* an in-migrant person or animal.

in'-mī'grȧnt, *a.* coming in from another region of the same country; as, *in-migrant* workers.

in'-mī'grāte, *v.i.*; in-migrated, *pt.*, *pp.*; in-migrating, *ppr.* to come in from another region of the same country.

in'-mī·grā'tion, *n.* an in-migrating.

in'mōst, *a.* 1. located farthest within; deepest in from the edge or outside; innermost.

2. most intimate or secret; as, *inmost* thoughts.

inn, *n.* [ME. *inn*, AS. *inn*, a house, chamber, inn, from *in*, *inn*, in, within.]

1. originally, any dwelling or lodging.

2. (a) an establishment or building providing food, drink, bedrooms, etc. for travelers; a hotel, especially one in the country or along a highway; (b) a restaurant or tavern: now usually only in the names of such places.

3. formerly, a house providing board and lodging for students; as, an *Inn of Court*.

Inn of Court; (a) one of the four London legal societies having the exclusive right to admit persons to practice at the bar; (b) one of the four groups of buildings (*Inner Temple*, *Middle Temple*, *Lincoln's Inn*, and *Gray's Inn*) belonging to these societies.

Inns of Chancery; in London, colleges in which young students formerly began their law studies. These are now occupied chiefly by attorneys, solicitors, etc.

inn, *v.i.* to take up lodging; to lodge at an inn.

inn, *v.t.* to house; to lodge at an inn.

in'nărds, *n. pl.* (altered from *inwards*.)

1. the internal organs of the body; viscera; entrails. [Dial.]

2. the inner parts of anything. [Dial.]

in'nāte (*or* -nāt'), *a.* [L. *innatus*, innate, properly pp. of *innasci*, to be born in, to originate in; *in*, in, and *nasci*, to be born.]

1. inborn; native; natural; not acquired; as, *innate* affection.

2. derived from the constitution of the mind, as contrasted with what is derived from experience; intuitive.

3. in botany, (a) growing upon anything by one end, as an anther which is joined by its base to the apex of a filament; (b) originating within the substance of the plant.

innate ideas; in philosophy, ideas supposed to be inborn and to belong to the mind from birth, as the idea of God or of immortality.

Syn.—inborn, inherent, native, inbred.

in·nāte', *v.t.* to make innate; to produce within something. [Obs.]

in'nāte·ly (*or* -nāt'), *adv.* naturally; natively; in an innate manner.

in'nāte·ness, *n.* the quality of being innate.

in·nā'tive, *a.* native or natural. [Rare.]

in·nav'i·gȧ·ble, *a.* [L. *innavigabilis*; *in-* priv., and *navigabilis*, navigable, from *navigare*, to navigate.] unnavigable; impassable by ships or vessels.

in·nav'i·gȧ·bly, *adv.* so as to be innavigable.

inne (in), *adv.* and *prep.* in. [Obs.]

in'nẽr, *a.* [ME. *inner*; AS. *innera*, inner, comp. of *inne*, within, in.]

1. interior; farther inward; as, an *inner* chamber; the *inner* court of a temple.

2. interior; internal; not outward; of the mind or spirit; as, to refresh the *inner* man.

3. more intimate or secret; as, *inner* emotions.

Inner House; the chambers in which the first and second divisions of the Court of Session hold their sittings in Edinburgh, Scotland; also, the divisions themselves.

inner jib; see under *jib*.

inner part or *voice*; in music, a part between the highest and lowest, as the contralto or tenor.

in'nẽr, *n.* 1. the inside.

2. the circle of a target next to the bull's-eye, or center.

3. a shot that hits this.

in'nẽr cĩr'çle, a small group of people who control or influence customs, thoughts, etc.

in'nẽr cit'y, the sections of a large city in or near its center, especially when crowded or blighted.

In'nẽr Līght (līt), in Quaker doctrine, a guiding influence resulting from the presence of God in the soul of the individual: also *Inner Word*.

in'nẽr·ly, *adv.* inwardly; internally. [Obs.]

in'nẽr man, 1. originally, one's spiritual being; mind or soul.

2. humorously, one's stomach or palate.

in'nẽr·mōst, *a.* furthest inward; most remote from the outside; inmost.

in'nẽr·mōst·ly, *adv.* in the innermost part.

in'nẽr·spring, *a.* made with coil springs inside; as, an *innerspring* cushion.

innerspring mattress; a mattress made with built-in coil springs for continued resilience.

In'nẽr Tem'ple, an Inn of Court.

in·nẽr'vāte, *v.t.*; innervated, *pt.*, *pp.*; innervating, *ppr.* [L. *in*, in, and *nervus*, nerve.]

1. to supply (a part of the body) with nerves.

2. to stimulate to movement or action.

in·nẽr·vā'tion, *n.* [L. *in*, in, and *nervus*, nerve.]

1. the arrangement or disposition of nerves in the animal body or any of its parts.

2. the sending out of necessary nerve impulses to some part of the body.

in·nẽrve', *v.t.*; innerved, *pt.*, *pp.*; innerving, *ppr.* to innervate.

inn'hōld·ẽr, *n.* a person who keeps an inn; an innkeeper.

in'ning, *n.* [ME. *inninge*; AS. *innung*, a putting or getting in, gerund of *innian*, to get in, put in.]

1. (a) a taking in, enclosing, or reclaiming, as of wasteland; (b) [*pl.*] lands reclaimed, as from the sea.

2. in baseball and [*often pl.*] cricket, (a) the period of play in which a team has a turn at bat, completed in baseball by three outs; (b) a numbered round of play in which both teams have a turn at bat: a baseball game normally consists of nine innings.

3. [*often pl.*] the time a person or political party is in power; period of or opportunity for action, expression, etc.; as, the election gave him his *inning*.

in·nī'ten·cy, *n.* [L. *innitens* (*-entis*), ppr. of *inniti*, to lean or rest upon.] a resting upon; pressure. [Obs.]

inn'keep·ẽr, *n.* the proprietor of an inn; an innholder; a taverner.

in'nō·cence, *n.* [OFr. *innocence*; L. *innocentia*, harmlessness, integrity, from *innocens* (*-entis*), harmless, innocent.]

1. the quality or state of being innocent; specifically, (a) freedom from sin, evil, or guilt; (b) freedom from knowledge of evil; (c) freedom from guile or cunning; simplicity; (d) silliness; foolishness; (e) incapability of harming, injuring, or corrupting.

2. an innocent person.

3. the bluet, a meadow plant with bluish or white flowers, common in the United States.

Syn.—innocuousness, harmlessness, inoffensiveness, guilelessness, guiltlessness, simplicity, purity, sinlessness.

in'nō·cen·cy, *n.* 1. the quality or condition of being innocent; innocence.

2. *pl.* **in'nō·cen·cies,** an instance or act of innocence.

in'nō·cent, *a.* [OFr. *innocent*; L. *innocens* (*-entis*), innocent, harmless; *in-* priv., and *nocens* (*-entis*), ppr. of *nocere*, to do wrong to.]

1. free from sin, evil, or guilt; specifically, (a) doing or thinking nothing morally wrong; pure; (b) not guilty of a specific crime or offense; guiltless; (c) free from evil or harmful effect or cause; that cannot harm, injure, or corrupt; (d) not malignant; benign; as, an *innocent* tumor.

2. (a) knowing no evil; (b) without guile or cunning; artless; simple; (c) foolish; ignorant.

Syn.—blameless, pure, undefiled, faultless, guiltless, innocuous, immaculate, sinless, spotless, virtuous.

in'nō·cent, *n.* 1. one free from guilt or sin; an innocent person.

2. a simple person; a natural; an idiot; a simpleton.

3. [*pl.*] bluets.

Innocents' Day; see *Childermas*.

in'nō·cent·ly, *adv.* in an innocent manner; harmlessly; guilelessly.

in·nō·çū'i·ty, *n.* the state or quality of being innocuous; innocuousness.

in·noç'ū·ous, *a.* [L. *innocuus*, harmless; *in-* priv., and *nocere*, to harm, injure.] harmless; producing no ill effect; innocent.

Syn.—harmless, inoffensive, innoxious.

in·noç'ū·ous·ly, *adv.* in an innocuous manner; without harm; without injurious effects.

in·noç'ū·ous·ness, *n.* the state or quality of being innocuous; harmlessness.

in'nō·dāte, *v.t.* to bind up or fasten, as in a knot. [Obs.]

in·nom'i·nȧ·ble, *a.* not to be named. [Rare.]

in·nom'i·nāte, *a.* [LL. *innominatus*, unnamed; L. *in-* priv., and *nominatus*, pp. of *nominare*, to name.]

1. not named; anonymous.

2. having no specific name.

innominate bone; either of the two bones to which the posterior limbs are attached and which form the pelvic basin; the innominatum.

innominate contracts; in Roman law, unclassified contracts.

in·nom·i·nā'tum, *n.*; *pl.* **in·nom·i·nā'tȧ,** [neut. of LL. *innominatus*, unnamed, innominate.] the innominate bone.

in'nō·vāte, *v.t.*; innovated, *pt.*, *pp.*; innovating, *ppr.* [L. *innovatus*, pp. of *innovare*, to renew; *in*, in, and *novare*, to alter, to make new, from *novus*, new.]

1. to change or alter by introducing something new; to remodel. [Obs.]

2. to bring in as something new; to introduce as a novelty. [Rare.]

in'nō·vāte, *v.i.* to introduce novelties; to make changes in anything established; to bring in innovations.

in·nō·vā'tion, *n.* [LL. *innovatio* (*-onis*), from L. *innovatus*, pp. of *innovare*, to renew, to innovate.]

1. the act of innovating or effecting a change in the established order; introduction of something new.

2. the change made by innovating; any custom, manner, etc. newly introduced.

3. in bryology, a new shoot or a new annual growth upon an old stem.

4. in Scots law, the renewal of an obligation to pay.

in·nō·vā′tion·ăl, *a.* of or characterized by innovation.

in·nō·vā′tion·ist, *n.* one who advocates innovations; a believer in changes for experiment.

in′nō·vā·tive, *a.* having a tendency to innovate.

in′nō·vā·tŏr, *n.* one who introduces novelties, or who makes changes by introducing something new.

in·nox′ious (-nok′shus), *a.* [L. *innoxius*, harmless; *in-* priv., and *noxius*, harmful.]

1. free from noxious qualities; innocent; harmless; as, an *innoxious* drug.

2. free from crime; pure; innocent. [Obs.]

in·nox′ious·ly, *adv.* in an innoxious manner.

in·nox′ious·ness, *n.* harmlessness.

in′nū·āte, *v.t.* to insinuate. [Obs.]

in·nū′bi·lous, *a.* free from clouds. [Obs.]

in·nū·en′dō, *n.*; *pl.* **in·nū·en′dōes,** [L., abl. of gerund of *innuere*, to nod to, to intimate, hint.]

1. in law, that part of a complaint in an action for libel or slander which explains the expressions alleged to be libelous or slanderous: such material is usually introduced in a legal document by the Latin formula *innuendo*, meaning "that is to say."

2. an indirect remark, gesture, or reference, usually implying something derogatory; hint; insinuation.

In′nū·it, In′ū·it, *n.* [Eskimo, lit., the people.] an Eskimo of America.

in·nū″mĕr·ȧ·bil′i·ty, *n.* state of being innumerable.

in·nū′mĕr·ȧ·ble, *a.* [OFr. *innumerable*; L. *innumerabilis*, countless, without number; *in-* priv., and *numerabilis*, that can be numbered, from *numerare*, to number.] not to be counted; too many to be enumerated or numbered; of a very great number.

in·nū′mĕr·ȧ·ble·ness, *n.* innumerability.

in·nū′mĕr·ȧ·bly, *adv.* so as to be innumerable; in very great numbers.

in·nū′mĕr·āte, *a.* [*in-*, and *numerate.*] lacking the knowledge to deal with scientific, especially mathematical, concepts. [Chiefly Brit.]

in·nū′mĕr·ous, *a.* [L. *innumerus*; *in-* priv., and *numerus*, number.] too many to be counted or numbered; innumerable. [Poetic.]

in·nū·tri′tion (-trish′un), *n.* lack of nutrition; failure of nourishment.

in·nū·tri′tious (-trish′us), *a.* not nutritious; not supplying nourishment; not nourishing.

in·ō·bē′di·ence, *n.* disobedience. [Obs.]

in·ō·bē′di·ent, *a.* disobedient. [Obs.]

in·ō·bē′di·ent·ly, *adv.* disobediently. [Obs.]

in·ob·sẹrv′ȧ·ble, *a.* that cannot be seen, perceived, or observed.

in·ob·sẹrv′ănce, *n.* 1. lack of attention; disregard.

2. failure to observe a custom, rule, etc.

in·ob·sẹrv′ăn·cy, *n.* the habit of not observing.

in·ob·sẹrv′ănt, *a.* [LL. *inobservans* (*-antis*), not observant, inattentive; L. *in-* priv., and *observans* (*-antis*), ppr. of *observare*, to observe.] showing inobservance.

in·ob·sẹrv′ănt·ly, *adv.* in an inobservant manner.

in·ob·sẹr·vā′tion, *n.* neglect or lack of observation. [Rare.]

in·ob·trū′sive, *a.* not obtrusive.

in·ob·trū′sive·ly, *adv.* unobtrusively.

in·ob·trū′sive·ness, *n.* the quality of being inobtrusive.

In·ō·cär′pus, *n.* [Gr. *is*, *inos*, a fiber, nerve, and *karpos*, fruit.] a genus of the bean family, including the *Inocarpus edulis*, or Otaheite chestnut, whose seeds are edible and also produce a red dye.

in·oc·cū·pā′tion, *n.* lack of occupation.

In·ō·cer′ȧ·mus, *n.* [Gr. *is*, *inos*, a fiber, sinew, muscle, and *keramos*, a tile, shell.] in paleontology, a genus of bivalvular mollusks whose fossils are found in Cretaceous rocks.

in·oc″ū·lȧ·bil′i·ty, *n.* the state of being inoculable.

in·oc′ū·lȧ·ble, *a.* 1. that can be inoculated.

2. that can be communicated by inoculation.

3. that may be used in inoculation.

in·oc′ū·lănt, *n.* an inoculum.

in·oc′ū·lăr, *a.* [L. *in*, in, and *oculus*, eye.] in entomology, inserted in the inner margin of the compound eye: said of the antennae of certain insects, as the *Cerambycidæ*.

in·oc′ū·lāte, *v.t.*; inoculated, *pt.*, *pp.*; inoculating, *ppr.* [L. *inoculatus*, pp. of *inoculare*, to engraft an eye or bud from one plant to another, to inoculate; *in*, in, and *oculus*, an eye, bud.]

1. originally, (a) to insert (a bud or shoot of one plant) into the stem or trunk of another; (b) to insert a bud or shoot of one plant into (the stem or trunk of another).

2. (a) to inject a serum, vaccine, etc. into, especially in order to prevent, cure, or experiment with disease, usually so as to make immune; (b) to inject (a disease virus, etc.) into by inoculation.

3. to put or implant bacteria, etc. into (soil, a culture medium, etc.).

4. to introduce ideas, etc. into the mind of; to imbue; infect.

in·oc′ū·lāte, *v.i.* 1. to propagate by budding.

2. to impart a disease by inoculation.

in·oc·ū·lā′tion, *n.* [L. *inoculatio* (*-onis*), an engrafting, inoculation, from *inoculatus*, pp. of *inoculare*, to engraft, inoculate.] an inoculating; especially, (a) the injection of a disease virus into the body, usually to cause a mild form of the disease and build up immunity to it; (b) the putting of bacteria, serum, etc. into soil, a culture medium, etc.

in·oc′ū·lā·tive, *a.* of or characterized by inoculation.

in·oc′ū·lā·tŏr, *n.* [L. *inoculator*, an engrafter, from *inoculare*, to engraft, inoculate.] a person or thing that inoculates; one who propagates plants or diseases by inoculation.

in·oc′ū·lum, *n.* material used in making an inoculation, as bacteria, viruses, spores, etc.: also *inoculant.*

in·ō′di·āte, *v.t.* to make hateful. [Obs.]

in·ō′dŏr·āte, *a.* having no odor. [Obs.]

in·ō′dŏr·ous, *a.* [L. *inodorus*; *in-* priv., and *odor*, a smell.] having no smell; odorless.

in·ō′dŏr·ous·ness, *n.* the condition or quality of being inodorous.

in·of·fen′sive, *a.* 1. giving no offense or provocation; causing no uneasiness or disturbance; as, an *inoffensive* sight.

2. harmless; doing no injury or mischief.

Thy *inoffensive* satires never bite.—Dryden.

in·of·fen′sive·ly, *adv.* in an inoffensive manner.

in·of·fen′sive·ness, *n.* the quality of being inoffensive.

in·of·fi′ciăl (-fish′ăl), *a.* not official. [Rare.]

in·of·fi′cious, *a.* [LL. *inofficiosus*, regardless of duty, harmful; L. *in-* priv., and *officiosus*, obliging, dutiful, from *officium*, duty.]

1. without office or function; inoperative.

2. disobliging. [Obs.]

3. in law, showing neglect of or opposition to moral duty.

in·of·fi′cious·ly, *adv.* not officiously.

in′ō·gen, *n.* [Gr. *is*, *inos*, a fiber, nerve, and *-genēs*, producing.] a hypothetical substance believed to occur in muscular tissue and to undergo decomposition during contraction.

in·ō·gen′iç, *a.* pertaining to inogen.

in·op′ĕr·ȧ·ble, *a.* not operable; specifically, (a) not practicable; (b) in surgery, not suitable to be operated on; as, an *inoperable* cancer.

in·op′ĕr·ȧ·tive, *a.* not operative; not active; having no operation; producing no effect; as, laws rendered *inoperative* by neglect.

in·ō·pẽr′cū·lăr, *a.* same as *inoperculate.*

in·ō·pẽr′cū·lāte, *a.* [L. *in-* priv., and *operculatus*, covered, from *operculum*, a cover, lid.]

1. in botany, without an operculum or lid.

2. in zoology, having no operculum, as a snail.

in·ō·pẽr′cū·lā·ted, *a.* inoperculate.

in·ō·pīn′ȧ·ble, *a.* unthinkable. [Obs.]

in·op′i·nāte, *a.* not expected. [Rare.]

in·op·pŏr·tūne′, *a.* [L. *inopportunus*, unsuitable, inconvenient; *in-* priv., and *opportunus*, suitable.] not opportune; inconvenient; unseasonable; as, an *inopportune* statement.

in·op·pŏr·tūne′ly, *adv.* unseasonably; at an inconvenient time.

in·op·pŏr·tūne′ness, *n.* the quality of being inopportune.

in·op·pŏr·tū′ni·ty, *n.* unseasonableness; inopportuneness.

in·op·press′ive, *a.* not oppressive; not burdensome. [Rare.]

in·op′ū·lent, *a.* not opulent; not wealthy; not affluent or rich.

in·ọr′di·nȧ·cy, *n.* 1. the quality or condition of being inordinate.

2. *pl.* **in·ọr′di·nȧ·cies,** an inordinate act or practice.

in·ọr′di·nāte, *a.* [L. *inordinatus*, not arranged, out of order; *in-* priv., and *ordinatus*, pp. of *ordinare*, to arrange, put in order, from *ordo* (*-inis*), order.]

1. disordered; not regulated.

2. without restraint or moderation; excessive; immoderate.

inordinate proportion; in mathematics, a proportion in which the order of the terms is irregular.

Syn.—excessive, immoderate, undue, intemperate, overmuch.

in·ọr′di·nāte·ly, *adv.* irregularly; excessively; immoderately.

in·ọr′di·nāte·ness, *n.* inordinacy.

in·ọr·di·nā′tion, *n.* irregularity; inordinateness. [Obs.]

in·ọr·gan′iç, *a.* not organic; specifically, (a) designating or composed of matter that is not animal or vegetable; not characterized by vital processes; not having the organized structure of living things; (b) not like an organism in structure; without design, relation, and co-ordination of parts; (c) designating or of any chemical compound not classified as organic: most inorganic compounds do not contain carbon and are derived from mineral sources; (d) designating or of the branch of chemistry dealing with these compounds.

in·ọr·gan′iç·ăl, *a.* inorganic.

in·ọr·gan′iç·ăl·ly, *adv.* so as to be inorganic.

in·ọr·gan′i·ty, *n.* the quality or state of being without organs. [Obs.]

in·ọr′găn·ī·zȧ·ble, *a.* not organizable.

in·ọr″găn·i·zā′tion, *n.* the state of being unorganized; absence of organization.

in·ọr′găn·ized, *a.* not having organic structure.

in·ọr·thog′rȧ·phy, *n.* incorrect spelling. [Obs.]

in·os′cū·lāte, *v.t.* and *v.i.*; inosculated, *pt.*, *pp.*; inosculating, *ppr.* [L. *in*, in, on, and *osculum*, dim. of *os*, mouth.]

1. (a) to join together by openings at the ends: said of arteries, ducts, etc.; (b) to intertwine: said of vines, etc.

2. to join, blend, or unite in an intimate manner.

in·os·cū·lā′tion, *n.* an inosculating or being inosculated.

in·os′iç, *a.* [Gr. *is*, *inos*, strength, force, nerve, and *-ic.*] in chemistry, pertaining to inositol.

inosic acid; an amorphous nucleotide, $C_{10}H_{13}N_4O_8P$, present in muscle.

in·ō·sin′iç, *a.* inosic.

in′ō·sīte, *n.* inositol.

in·ō′si·tōl, *n.* a crystalline alcohol, $C_6H_6(OH)_6$, existing in several isomeric forms and found in both plant and animal tissues: one of the B complex vitamins, sometimes erroneously called *muscle sugar.*

in·ox′i·dī·zȧ·ble, *a.* that cannot be oxidized.

in·ox′i·dīze, *v.t.*; inoxidized, *pt.*, *pp.*; inoxidizing, *ppr.* to prevent oxidation in.

in′pȧ·rab″ō·lȧ, *n.* an inscribed parabola.

in′pā·tient (-shent), *n.* one who receives such medical or surgical treatment in a hospital as necessitates his residence there over a period of time: opposed to *outpatient.*

in pa·tri·mō′ni·ō, [L.] in Roman law, subject to certain property rights.

in′pāy·ment, *n.* a payment (to someone or toward something); also, the act of paying in.

in′pen·sion·ẽr (-shun-), *n.* a resident of a charitable institution who receives a pension.

in pẽr·pet′ū·um, [L.] in perpetuity; forever.

in pẽr·sō′nam, [L.] in law, designating an action or judgment against a person rather than against property (*in rem*).

in pet′tō, [It.] 1. literally, in the breast; in the heart.

2. secretly; not revealed: said of cardinals appointed by the Pope but not named in consistory.

in′phāṣe, *a.* having the same phase or timing: in electricity, applied to that component or portion of a current wave which is in phase with the voltage wave, that is, which has the same frequency and arrives at its maximum and minimum values at the same instant as the voltage wave; as, the *inphase* component.

in plāce, in the original, natural, or desired position; specifically, in geology, said of a fossil, rock, or type of soil.

in plā′nō, in geometry, lying or occurring in a particular or specified plane.

in′pol″y·gon, *n.* an inscribed polygon.

in pos′sē, [L. *in*, in, and *posse*, to be able.] in possibility; only potentially; possible but not actual.

in′pōur, *n.* an inrush, as of water; a rushing in.

in′pōur, *v.t.* and *v.i.* to pour in.

in prō′pri·ȧ pẽr·sō′nȧ, [L.] in one's own person.

in′put, *n.* 1. anything that is put in.
2. in electricity, the power or energy received or used in a machine.

in·quar·tā′tion, *n.* quartation.

in′quest, *n.* [ME. *enquest*; OFr. *enqueste*; L. *inquisita*, something inquired or sought for, an inquest, properly f. of *inquisitus*, pp. of *inquirere*, to inquire into, inquire.]
1. in law, a judicial inquiry, especially one held before a jury, as a coroner's investigation of a death.
2. the jury or group, holding such an inquiry, particularly a coroner's jury, assembled to inquire into the cause of a sudden death.
3. the verdict of such an inquiry.
4. inquiry; search. [Rare.]
inquest of office; an inquiry made by the sheriff, coroner, or escheator, concerning any matter that entitles the crown or the state to the possession of lands, tenements, goods, or chattels: it is made by a jury of no determinate number.

in·quī′et, *v.t.* to disturb; to trouble. [Obs.]

in·quī′et, *a.* [ME. *inquyet*; Early Fr.; L. *inquietus*.] not quiet; uneasy; disturbed.

in·quī·e·tā′tion, *n.* disturbance. [Obs.]

in·quī′et·ness, *n.* inquietude. [Obs.]

in·quī′e·tūde, *n.* [Fr. *inquiétude*; LL. *inquietudo*, uneasiness, from L. *inquietus*, restless, unquiet; *in-* priv., and *quietus*, quiet.] a disturbed state; restlessness; uneasiness, either of body or mind; disquietude.

in′qui·line, *n.* [L. *inquilinus*, an alien, one living in a place not his own, from *incola*, an inhabitant, from *incolere*, to inhabit; *in*, in, and *colere*, to dwell.] an animal that lives in an abode properly belonging to another, as any of certain insects that live in galls made by the true gall insects.

in′qui·line, *a.* like an inquiline in character.

in′qui·nāte, *v.t.* to defile; to pollute; to contaminate. [Obs.]

in·qui·nā′tion, *n.* the act of defiling, or the state of being defiled; pollution; corruption. [Obs.]

in·quīr′ȧ·ble, *a.* capable of being inquired into; subject to inquisition or inquest.

in·quīr′ănce, en·quīr′ănce, *n.* inquiry. [Obs.]

in·qui·rā′tion, *n.* inquiry. [Dial.]

in·quīre′, *v.i.*; inquired, *pt.*, *pp.*; inquiring, *ppr.* [L. *inquirere*, to seek after, search for, inquire; *in*, into, and *quærere*, to seek.]
1. to ask a question or questions; to seek for truth or information by asking questions.
We will call the damsel and *inquire*.
—Gen. xxiv. 57.
2. to seek for truth by investigation or examination (usually with *into*).
Also spelled *enquire*.
to inquire after; to pay respects by asking about the health of (someone).
to inquire for; (a) to ask to see (someone); (b) to try to get by asking.
Syn.—ask, question, seek, interrogate.

in·quīre′, *v.t.* to ask about; to seek knowledge of by asking; as, he *inquired* the way: also spelled *enquire*.

in·quīr′ent, *a.* making inquiry. [Obs.]

in·quīr′ēr, *n.* one who inquires; one who searches or examines; an investigator.

in·quīr′ing, *a.* given to inquiry; disposed to investigate causes; as, an *inquiring* mind.

in·quīr′ing·ly, *adv.* by way of inquiry.

in·quīr′y (*or* in′qui-ry), *n.*; *pl.* **in·quīr′ies**,
1. the act of inquiring; a seeking for information by asking questions; interrogation.
2. search for truth, information, or knowledge; an investigation; examination into facts or principles.
3. a question; a query.
Also *enquiry*.
writ of inquiry; a writ addressed to a sheriff commanding him that by a jury of twelve men he inquire what damages the plaintiff has sustained, and return the findings into court.
Syn.—interrogation, question, asking, investigation, search, examination, research, scrutiny, exploration.

in·quiș′i·ble, *a.* admitting of judicial inquiry. [Obs.]

in·qui·și′tion (-zish′un), *n.* [L. *inquisitio* (*-onis*), a seeking or searching for, an inquiring into, from *inquisitus*, pp. of *inquirere*, to seek for, inquire into.]
1. inquiry; examination; investigation; the act of inquiring.
2. in law, an inquest.
3. [I–] in the Roman Catholic Church, (a) a search for and punishment of nonbelievers or heretics; (b) the general tribunal established in the 13th century for the discovery and suppression of heresy and the punishment of heretics: also called the *Holy Office*; (c) the activities of this tribunal.
4. any strict or arbitrary suppression or punishment of those believed to be dangerous to the ruling powers.

in·qui·și′tion, *v.t.* to inquire into; to investigate.

in·qui·și′tion·ăl, *a.* 1. of, characterized by, or pertaining to inquisition; inquisitorial.
2. [I–] relating to the Inquisition.

in·qui·și′tion·ā·ry, *a.* inquisitional. [Rare.]

in·qui·și′tion·ist, *n.* an inquisitor.

in·quiș′i·tive, *a.* [OFr. *inquisitif*, inquisitive, from L. *inquisitus*, pp. of *inquirere*, to inquire into, to inquire.]
1. asking more questions than is necessary or proper; prying; unnecessarily curious.
The whole neighborhood grew *inquisitive* after my name and character.—Addison.
2. inclined to seek knowledge by discussion, investigation, observation, questioning, etc.; eager to learn; given to research.
A young, *inquisitive*, and sprightly genius.
—Watts.
Syn.—curious, prying.

in·quiș′i·tive, *n.* a person who is inquisitive.

in·quiș′i·tive·ly, *adv.* in an inquisitive manner.

in·quiș′i·tive·ness, *n.* the quality or state of being inquisitive, especially in a prying or impertinent way.

in·quiș′i·tŏr, *n.* [L. *inquisitor*, a searcher, examiner, a police agent, from *inquisitus*, pp. of *inquirere*, to search for, inquire.]
1. one who inquires; particularly, one whose official duty it is to inquire and examine, or to make an inquisition; investigator.
2. [I–] an official of the Inquisition.
3. an inquisitive or curious person. [Obs.]

in·quiș·i·tō′ri·ăl, *a.* 1. pertaining to, or having the nature of, an inquisitor or an inquisition; making strict or searching inquiry; as, *inquisitorial* power.
2. inquisitive; unnecessarily or unpleasantly curious.

in·quiș·i·tō′ri·ăl·ly, *adv.* in an inquisitorial manner.

in·quiș·i·tō′ri·ous, *a.* making strict inquiry. [Obs.]

in·quiș·i·tū′ri·ent, *a.* given to inquisition, or making strict inquiry; inquisitorial. [Obs.]

in·rac′i·nāte, *v.t.*; inracinated, *pt.*, *pp.*; inracinating, *ppr.* [Fr. *inraciner*, from L. *in*, in, and OFr. *racine*, a root.] to root; to implant. [Rare.]

in·rāil′, *v.t.* to rail in. [Obs.]

in rē, [L.] in the matter (of); concerning.

in·reg′is·tēr, *v.t.* to enregister. [Obs.]

in rem, [L., against the thing.] in law, designating an action or judgment against property, as distinguished from one against a person (*in personam*).

in′rō, *n.* [Japan. from Chinese *yin*, a seal, and *lūng*, basket.] a small set of lacquered receptacles forming a flattened cylinder, formerly worn at the girdle by the Japanese, and used to hold perfumes, medicines, etc.

in′rōad, *n.* [*in-* (in), and *road* (in obs. sense of "riding").]
1. a sudden invasion or raid.
2. [*usually in pl.*] any injurious or wasting encroachment; as, these long hours will make *inroads* on your health.
Syn.—invasion, irruption, raid, incursion.

in·rōad′, *v.t.* and *v.i.* to make inroad into; to invade. [Rare.]

in·rōll′, *v.t.* to enroll. [Obs.]

in′rush, *n.* a rushing in; inflow; influx.

in·rush′, *v.i.* to rush in. [Obs.]

in sae′çū·lȧ sae·çū·lō′rum (sek′u-lȧ sek-ū-lō′rum), [L., into ages of ages.] for ever and ever; for all eternity.

in·sāfe′ty, *n.* lack of safety. [Obs.]

in·sal′i·vāte, *v.t.*; insalivated, *pt.*, *pp.*; insalivating, *ppr.* to mix with the saliva, as food in chewing.

in·sal·i·vā′tion, *n.* the mixture of food with saliva during mastication.

in·sȧ·lū′bri·ous, *a.* not salubrious; not healthful; unwholesome; as, an *insalubrious* air or climate.

in·sȧ·lū′bri·ty, *n.* lack of salubrity; unhealthfulness; unwholesomeness; as, the *insalubrity* of air.

in·sal′ū·tā·ry, *a.* [LL. *insalutaris*, not salutary; L. *in-* priv., and *salutaris*, healthful, salutary.]
1. not salutary; not favorable to health. [Obs.]
2. not having a good effect; producing evil.

in·san·ȧ·bil′i·ty, *n.* state of being incurable. [Obs.]

in·san′ȧ·ble, *a.* [L. *insanabilis*; *in-* priv., and *sanabilis*, curable, from *sanus*, sound.] incurable; that cannot be healed. [Obs.]

in·san′ȧ·ble·ness, *n.* insanability. [Obs.]

in·san′ȧ·bly, *adv.* incurably. [Obs.]

in·sāne′, *a.* [L. *insanus*, unsound in mind, mad, insane; *in-* priv., and *sanus*, sound.]
1. unsound in mind; mentally ill or deranged.
2. for insane persons; as, an *insane* hospital.
3. making mad; causing madness; as, the *insane* root. [Obs.]
4. very foolish, impractical, extravagant, etc.; senseless.
the insane; insane people.

in·sāne′ly, *adv.* madly; foolishly; without reason.

in·sāne′ness, *n.* insanity; madness.

in·sā′ni·āte, *v.t.* to madden. [Obs.]

in·sā′nie (-ni), *n.* madness. [Obs.]

in·san′i·tā·ry, *a.* unhealthy; likely to cause disease.

in·san·i·tā′tion, *n.* lack of sanitation; unhealthfulness.

in·san′i·ty, *n.* [L. *insanitas* (*-atis*), unsoundness, unhealthiness, insanity, from *insanus*, unsound, insane.]
1. the state of being insane; mental illness or derangement, usually excluding amentia; madness: not a scientific term.
2. in law, such mental unsoundness as frees a person from criminal responsibility, or such as renders a person incapable of making a valid contract, conveyance, or will, or of conducting his own affairs. It usually implies a need for hospitalization.
3. great folly; extreme senselessness.
Syn.—lunacy, madness, derangement, alienation, aberration, mania, delirium, frenzy, monomania, dementia, paranoia.—*Insanity* is the generic term for mental disease in one who formerly had mental health; *lunacy* is specifically used to denote periodical insanity; *madness*, *derangement*, *aberration*, *alienation* are popular terms for *insanity*; *deririum*, *mania*, and *frenzy* denote excited states of the disease; *dementia* denotes the loss of mental stability; *monomania* is insanity upon a single subject; *paranoia* is dementia with delusions.

in·sā′pō·ry, *a.* [L. *in-* priv., and *sapor*, taste, flavor, from *sapere*, to taste.] without taste; lacking flavor. [Rare.]

in·sā·tiȧ·bil′i·ty (-shȧ-) *n.* [LL. *insatiabilitas*, from L. *insatiabilis*, insatiable.] greediness that cannot be satisfied or appeased.

in·sā′tiȧ·ble, *a.* [L. *insatiabilis*, that cannot be satisfied; *in-* priv., and *satiare*, to satiate, satisfy.] incapable of being satisfied or appeased; very greedy; as, an *insatiable* appetite or desire.
Syn.—voracious, unappeasable, ravenous, rapacious, greedy.

in·sā′tiȧ·ble·ness, *n.* insatiability.

in·sā′tiȧ·bly, *adv.* 1. in an insatiable manner.
2. to an insatiable degree.

in·sā′ti·āte (-shi-), *a.* [LL. *insatiatus*, not satisfied; L. *in-* priv., and *satiatus*, pp. of *satiare*, to satiate, satisfy.] insatiable.

in·sā′ti·āte·ly, *adv.* insatiably.

in·sā′ti·āte·ness, *n.* insatiability.

in·sȧ·tī′e·ty, *n.* [L. *insatietas*; *in-* priv., and *satietas*, satiety.] insatiableness.

in·sat·is·fac′tion, *n.* lack of satisfaction. [Obs.]

in·sat′ū·rȧ·ble, *a.* not to be saturated, filled, or glutted.

in′science (-shens), *n.* ignorance; lack of knowledge. [Obs.]

in′scient (-shent), *a.* without knowledge. [Obs.]

in′scient, *a.* [L. *in*, in, and *sciens* (*-entis*), ppr. of *scire*, to know.] possessed of insight; discerning. [Rare.]

in·sçonce′, *v.t.* to ensconce. [Obs.]

in·sçrīb′ȧ·ble, *a.* that may be inscribed.

in·sçrīb′ȧ·ble·ness, *n.* state of being inscribable.

in·sçrībe′, *v.t.*; inscribed, *pt.*, *pp.*; inscribing, *ppr.* [L. *inscribere*, to write in, to write upon; *in*, in, on, and *scribere*, to write.]
1. to mark or engrave (words, symbols, etc.) on some surface.
2. to mark or engrave (a surface) with words, symbols, etc.
3. to add the name of (someone) to a list; enroll.
4. to dedicate (a book, song, etc.) briefly and informally.

5. to fix or impress deeply or lastingly in the mind, memory, etc.
6. in geometry, to draw (a figure) inside another figure so that their boundaries touch at as many points as possible.

in·sçrībed′, *a.* in entomology, marked or figured as though by written characters.

in·sçrīb′ẽr, *n.* one who inscribes.

in·sçrip′tion, *n.* [L. *inscriptio* (*-onis*), an inscription, title, lit., a writing upon, from *inscriptus*, pp. of *inscribere*, to write upon.]
1. the act of inscribing.
2. something written or engraved; any character, word, or sentence written or engraved on a solid substance, especially in raised or incised letters; as, *inscriptions* on monuments, coins, pillars, etc.
3. a brief or informal dedication in a book, etc. to a friend or patron.
4. words or letters in a straight line across a medal or coin, as distinguished from a *legend*, which is usually curved.
5. lettering on an engraving or etching.
6. an entry upon a list, register, etc.; as, the *inscription* on a document.
7. in civil law, the agreement of a plaintiff or accuser to assume a penalty if the defendant is not convicted.

in·sçrip′tion·ăl, *a.* inscriptive.

in·sçrip′tive, *a.* of, or of the nature of, an inscription.

in·sçrōll′, *v.t.* to write or record on a scroll.

in·sçrū·tȧ·bil′i·ty, *n.* 1. the quality or state of being inscrutable.
2. *pl.* **in·sçrū·tȧ·bil′i·tieṣ**, something inscrutable.

in·sçrū′tȧ·ble, *a.* [LL. *inscrutabilis*, inscrutable; L. *in-* priv., and *scrutari*, to search carefully, examine.] not capable of being searched into and understood by inquiry or study; incapable of being discovered, comprehended, or accounted for; incomprehensible; unfathomable; completely obscure or mysterious.

in·sçrū′tȧ·ble·ness, *n.* inscrutability.

in·sçrū′tȧ·bly, *adv.* in an inscrutable manner; so as to be inscrutable.

in·sçulp′, *v.t.* to engrave; to carve. [Obs.]

in·sçulp′tion, *n.* inscription. [Obs.]

in·sçulp′tūre, *n.* an engraving; sculpture.

in·sçulp′tūred, *a.* engraved.

in·sēam′, *v.t.*; inseamed, *pt.*, *pp.*; inseaming, *ppr.* to impress or mark with a seam or cicatrix.

in·search′ (-sẽrch′), *v.t.* and *v.i.* to ensearch. [Obs.]

in·seç′ȧ·ble, *a.* [L. *insecabilis*; *in-* priv., and *secabilis*, able to be cut, from *secare*, to cut.] that cannot be divided by a cutting instrument; indivisible. [Rare.]

in′seçt, *n.* [L. *insectum*, an insect, properly neut. of *insectus*, pp. of *insecare*, to cut into; *in*, into, and *secare*, to cut, divide; so called because the bodies of some insects seem to be cut or divided into segments.]

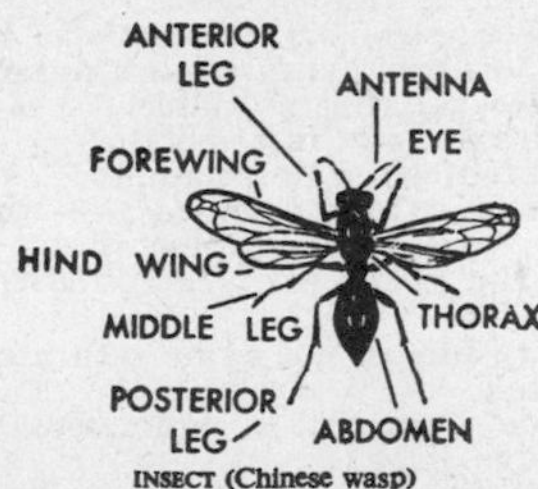

INSECT (Chinese wasp)

1. a member of a class of small invertebrate animals of the division *Arthropoda*, distinguished from the other classes of the division by the fact that the three divisions of the body—the head, thorax, and abdomen—are always distinct from one another. There are always three pairs of legs in the adult, and these are all borne upon the thorax; respiration is effected by means of air tubes or tracheae, and in most insects two pairs of membranous wings are developed from the back of the second and third segments of the thorax. The integument is more or less hardened by the deposition of chitin in it. The head is composed of several segments amalgamated together, and carries a pair of jointed feelers or antennae, a pair of eyes, usually compound, and the appendages of the mouth. The thorax is composed of three segments, also amalgamated. Beetles, bees, flies, wasps, mosquitoes, etc. are insects.
2. popularly, any of a group of small animals, usually wingless, including spiders, centipedes, wood lice, ticks, mites, etc.
3. a small, unimportant, contemptible person.

In·seç′tȧ, *n.pl.* [L., pl. of *insectum*, an insect.] a class of *Arthropoda* generally restricted to the *Hexapoda*, or six-legged insects.

in·seç·tā′ri·um, *n.*; *pl.* **in·seç·tā′ri·ȧ**, [Mod. L.]
1. a place where insects are raised, especially for study.
2. a collection of living insects kept in such a place.

in′seç·tȧ·ry, *n.*; *pl.* **in′seç·tȧ·rieṣ**, an insectarium.

in·seç·tā′tŏr, *n.* one who rails, or slanders; a railer. [Obs.]

in·seçt′ed, *a.* divided into segments like an insect. [Rare.]

in·seç·ti·cī′dăl, *a.* [L. *insectum*, an insect, and *cædere*, to kill.] possessing properties destructive to insects, as an insect powder.

in·seç′ti·cīde, *n.* any substance or preparation used to kill insects.

in·seç′ti·fūġe, *n.* any preparation that will drive away insects.

in·seç′tile, *a.* 1. of, or having the nature of, insects.
2. consisting of insects.

in·seç′tion, *n.* a cutting in; incision.

in·seç·tī′văl, *a.* of or like an insect.

In·seç·tiv′ō·rȧ, *n.pl.* [L. *insectum*, an insect, and *vorare*, to devour.]
1. an order of mammals that feed principally on insects, having the molar teeth set with sharp, conical cusps. They are usually of small size, and many of them live underground, hibernating for some months. The shrew, hedgehog, and mole are members of this order.
2. a group of bats that feed upon insects.

in·seç′ti·vōre, *n.* any animal or plant that feeds on insects; especially, a member of the *Insectivora*.

in·seç·tiv′ō·rous, *a.* 1. feeding or subsisting chiefly on insects.
2. of the *Insectivora*.

in·seç·tol′ō·ġẽr, *n.* a student of insectology.

in·seç·tol′ō·ġy, *n.* [Fr. *insectologie*.] the study of insects, especially of their economic effects in agriculture and industry.

in′seçt pow′dẽr, a powder used in destroying insects; particularly, a powder made from the dried flowers of certain species of plants belonging to the genus *Pyrethrum*.

in·sē·çūre′, *a.* not secure; specifically, (a) not safe from danger; unprotected; (b) feeling more anxiety than seems warranted; (c) not firm or dependable; unreliable.

in·sē·çūre′ly, *adv.* without security or safety; in an insecure manner.

in·sē·çūre′ness, *n.* the state of being insecure.

in·sē·çū′ri·ty, *n.* [ML. *insecuritas*.]
1. the quality or state of being insecure.
2. *pl.* **in·sē·çū′ri·tieṣ**, something insecure.

in·sē·çū′tion, *n.* pursuit. [Obs.]

in·sem′i·nāte, *v.t.*; inseminated, *pt.*, *pp.*; inseminating, *ppr.* [from L. *inseminatus*, pp. of *inseminare*, to sow in; *in-*, in, and *seminare*, to sow, from *semen*, seed.] to sow seeds in; especially, to impregnate by sexual intercourse or by artificially injecting semen.

in·sem·i·nā′tion, *n.* an inseminating or being inseminated.

in·sen′sāte, *a.* [LL. *insensatus*; *in-*, not, and *sensatus*, gifted with sense, from *sensus*, sense.]
1. lacking sensation; not feeling or incapable of feeling sensation; inanimate.
2. without sense or reason; foolish; stupid.
3. lacking sensibility; without regard or feeling; cold; hardened.

in·sen′sāte·ly, *adv.* in an insensate manner.

in·sen′sāte·ness, *n.* the state of being insensate.

in·sense′, *v.t.*; insensed, *pt.*, *pp.*; insensing, *ppr.* to cause to perceive or understand. [Brit. Dial.]

in·sen·si·bil′i·ty, *n.* the quality or condition of being insensible.

Syn.—apathy, immobility, indifference, stoicism, stupidity, unfeelingness.

in·sen′si·ble, *a.* [LL. *insensibilis*, that cannot be felt, unable to feel; L. *in-* priv., and *sensibilis*, perceptible by the senses, from *sensus*, sense, perception.]
1. so small, slight, or gradual as to be virtually imperceptible; that cannot be felt or perceived; as, the motion of the earth is *insensible* to the eye.
2. lacking the power of feeling or perceiving with the senses.
3. not recognizing or realizing; unaware; void of feeling; indifferent; as, to be *insensible* to the sufferings of our fellow men.
4. having lost sensation; unconscious.
5. void of sense or meaning; as, *insensible* words. [Obs.]

Syn.—dull, hard, impassive, indifferent, unfeeling, senseless.

in·sen′si·ble·ness, *n.* inability to perceive; lack of sensibility.

in·sen′si·bly, *adv.* by degrees so slight as to be virtually imperceptible; in a manner not to be felt or perceived by the senses.

The hills rise *insensibly*. —Addison.

in·sen′si·tive, *a.* lacking sensitiveness; incapable of being impressed or influenced; insensate.

in·sen′sū·ous (-shū-), *a.* free from sensuousness; not appealing to the senses. [Rare.]

in·sen′ti·ent (-shi-ent), *a.* not having life, consciousness, or perception.

in·sep·ȧ·rȧ·bil′i·ty, *n.* [LL. *inseparabilitas*, from L. *inseparabilis*, inseparable.] the quality or state of being inseparable, or incapable of disjunction.

in·sep′ȧ·rȧ·ble, *a.* [L. *inseparabilis*; *in-* priv., and *separabilis*, separable, from *separare*, to separate.] that cannot be separated or disjoined; not to be parted; not separable.

in·sep′ȧ·rȧ·ble·ness, *n.* inseparability.

in·sep′ȧ·rȧ·bleṣ, *n.pl.* inseparable persons or things.

in·sep′ȧ·rȧ·bly, *adv.* in a manner that prevents separation; so as to be inseparable; with indissoluble union.

in·sep′ȧ·rāte, *a.* not separate.

in·sep′ȧ·rāte·ly, *adv.* so as not to be separated.

in·sẽrt′, *v.t.*; inserted, *pt.*, *pp.*; inserting, *ppr.* [L. *insertus*, pp. of *inserere*, to put or thrust in, to introduce, to insert; *in*, into, and *serere*, to join.] to put or fit (something) into something else; to set in or among; as, to *insert* an advertisement in a paper.

in′sẽrt, *n.* anything inserted or for insertion; especially, an extra leaf or section inserted in a newspaper, etc.

in·sẽrt′ed, *a.* in botany, joined by natural growth; as, the stamens are *inserted* in or upon the calyx.

in·sẽrt′ing, *n.* 1. a setting in.
2. anything set in or to be set in, as lace, etc. in a garment.

in·sẽr′tion, *n.* [LL. *insertio* (*-onis*), a putting or thrusting in, from L. *insertus*, pp. of *inserere*, to put or thrust in, to insert.]
1. the act of setting or placing in or among other things, or the state of being thus set; as, the *insertion* of passages in writings.
2. something inserted; especially, (a) an additional passage in a manuscript; (b) a band of lace or embroidery set in a fabric for purposes of ornament; (c) an advertisement in a newspaper.
3. in biology, (a) the point of attachment of one part to another, as of a muscle to the part that it moves; (b) the manner of attachment of parts to each other.

epigynous insertion; an insertion on the summit of the ovary.

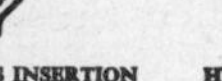

EPIGYNOUS INSERTION HYPOGYNOUS INSERTION

hypogynous insertion; an insertion beneath the ovary.

perigynous insertion; an insertion upon the calyx surrounding the ovary.

PERIGYNOUS INSERTION

in·sẽrve′, *v.t.* to be of use to. [Obs.]

in·sẽrv′i·ent, *a.* conducive. [Obs.]

in·ses′sion (-sesh′un), *n.* [LL. *insessio* (*-onis*), a sitting on, from L. *insessus*, pp. of *insidere*,

 fāte, fär, fȧst, fạll, finăl, cãre, at; mēte, prẹy, hẽr, met; pīne, marïne, bïrd, pin; nōte, mōve, fọr, atŏm, not; mọọn, book;

to sit upon; *in*, on, upon, and *sedere*, to sit.]

1. the act of seating oneself; specifically, the act of sitting in a bath. [Obs.]

2. a sitz bath. [Obs.]

in·ses′sŏr, *n.* one who sits in or on. [Rare.]

In·ses·sō′rēṣ, *n.pl.* in former classifications, an order of birds comprising those having feet adapted for perching, including most of the songbirds.

in·ses·sō′ri·ăl, *a.* perching: said of certain birds whose feet are formed for grasping.

in·set′, *v.t.*; inset, *pt., pp.*; insetting, *ppr.* [ME. *insetten*; AS. *insettan*, to set in, to appoint; *in*, in, and *settan*, to set.] to put into something; to insert.

in′set, *n.* something set in; insert; especially, a smaller picture or map set within the border of a larger one.

in·sev′ēr·ȧ·ble, *a.* that cannot be severed.

in·shād′ed, *a.* marked with different shades. [Obs.]

in′shāve, *n.* in mechanics, an edge tool or plane for smoothing concave surfaces, especially of barrels, casks, etc.

in·shēathe′, *v.t.*; insheathed, *pt., pp.*; insheathing, *ppr.* to enclose in a sheath or as in a sheath; as, to *insheathe* a sword: spelled also *ensheathe.*

in·shell′, *v.t.* to hide in a shell. [Rare.]

in·ship′, *v.t.* to ship; to embark. [Obs.]

in′shōre, *adv.* 1. in toward the shore.

2. near the shore.

inshore of; nearer than (something else) to the shore.

in·shrīne′, *v.t.* same as *enshrine.*

in′sīde′, *n.* 1. the part lying within; the inner side, surface, or part; interior.

2. the part of a sidewalk or path lying farthest from the road.

3. [*pl.*] the internal organs of the body, as the stomach and intestines. [Colloq.]

patent inside or *patent outside*; a newspaper sheet printed on one side only and furnished to publishers in country towns, who print upon the other side such matter as pertains to their respective localities.

in′sīde′, *a.* 1. lying on or in the inside; internal.

2. of or suited for the inside.

3. working or used indoors; indoor.

4. known only to insiders; secret or private; as, the *inside* story.

inside calipers; in mechanics, calipers adapted to the taking of inside measurements, as the diameter of a hollow cylinder.

inside finish; in architecture, joiner work done to complete a building.

inside job; a criminal act, as a theft or burglary, ascribed to a person employed by the victim or to one in whom confidence is placed and who would normally be considered above suspicion. [Colloq.]

inside track; (a) the inner, shorter way around a race track; hence, (b) a favorable position or advantage.

in′sīde′, *adv.* 1. on or in the inside of; within.

2. indoors.

inside of; in less than (a specified time); within the space of. [Colloq.]

inside out; with the inside where the outside should be; showing the inside; reversed.

in·sīde′, *prep.* inside of; in; within; as, he went *inside* the house for safety; the letter is *inside* the book.

in·sid′i·āte, *v.t.* to lie in ambush for. [Obs.]

in·sid′i·ā·tŏr, *n.* one who lies in ambush. [Obs.]

in·sid′i·ous, *a.* [Fr. *insidieux*; L. *insidiosus*, deceitful, sly, treacherous, lit., lying in wait, from *insidiæ*, an ambush, plot, from *insidere*, to sit in or upon, to lie in wait for; *in*, in, and *sedere*, to sit.]

1. characterized by treachery or slyness; crafty; wily.

2. operating in a slow or not easily apparent manner; more dangerous than seems evident; as, an *insidious* disease.

Syn.—artful, crafty, cunning, deceitful, intriguing, tricky, wily, guileful, foxy, designing, deceptive.

in·sid′i·ous·ly, *adv.* in an insidious manner; deceitfully; treacherously; with malicious artifice or stratagem.

in·sid′i·ous·ness, *n.* the quality of being insidious; deceitfulness; treachery.

in′sight (-sīt), *n.* 1. the ability to see and understand clearly the inner nature of things.

2. a clear understanding of the inner nature of some specific thing.

Syn.—discernment, inspection, introspection, acumen, perspicacity, shrewdness, keenness, penetration, cleverness.

in·sig′ni·ȧ, *n.pl.*; *sing.* **in·sig′nē** or, now sometimes, **in·sig′ni·ȧ,** [L. *insigne*, pl. *insignia*, a sign, decoration, badge of honor, neut. of *insignis*, distinguished by a mark, striking, eminent; *in*, in, and *signum*, a mark, sign.]

1. badges, emblems, or other distinguishing marks of office or honor; as, the *insignia* of an order of knighthood.

2. marks, signs, or visible impressions by which anything is known or distinguished.

in·sig·nif′i·cănce, *n.* 1. the quality or state of being insignificant; lack of significance or meaning; as, the *insignificance* of words or phrases.

2. unimportance; lack of force or effect; triviality.

in·sig·nif′i·căn·cy, *n.* 1. insignificance.

2. *pl.* **in·sig·nif′i·căn·cieṣ,** an insignificant person or thing.

in·sig·nif′i·cănt, *a.* 1. not significant; void of signification; meaningless; as, *insignificant* words.

2. having no weight or effect; unimportant; trivial; as, *insignificant* rites.

3. small; unimposing; mean; contemptible; as, an *insignificant fellow.*

Syn.—immaterial, inconsiderate, trivial, unimportant, small, irrelevant, paltry.

in·sig·nif′i·cănt·ly, *adv.* in an insignificant manner; without meaning; without importance or effect.

in·sig·nif′i·cȧ·tive, *a.* [LL. *insignificativus*; L. *in-* priv., and *significativus*, significative, from L. *significatus*, pp. of *significare*, to mean, signify.] not expressing by external signs; not significative. [Obs.]

in·sim′ū·lāte, *v.t.* to accuse. [Obs.]

in·sin·cēre′, *a.* [L. *insincerus*, not pure, adulterated; *in-* priv., and *sincerus*, pure, real, genuine.]

1. not sincere; dissembling; hypocritical; false; deceitful.

To be always polite, you must be sometimes
insincere. —Charles Reade.

2. imperfect; unsound. [Obs.]

Syn.—disingenuous, dissembling, false, deceptive.

in·sin·cēre′ly, *adv.* without sincerity; hypocritically.

in·sin·cer′i·ty, *n.* 1. the quality of being insincere.

2. *pl.* **in·sin·cer′i·tieṣ,** an insincere action, remark, etc.

In condemnation of the fashionable *insincerities* of his day. —A. Dobson.

in·sin′ew, *v.t.* to strengthen; to give vigor to. [Obs.]

in·sin′ū·ănt, *a.* insinuating. [Rare.]

in·sin′ū·āte, *v.t.*; insinuated, *pt., pp.*; insinuating, *ppr.* [L. *insinuatus*, pp. of *insinuare*, to introduce by windings and turnings, to insinuate, to work one's way into; *in*, in, and *sinus*, a curved surface, a fold, a bay, a bosom.]

1. to introduce gently, as by a devious course or narrow passage; as, water *insinuates* itself into the crevices of rocks.

2. to push or worm into favor; to introduce by slow, gentle, or artful means.

He *insinuated* himself into the very good
grace of the Duke of Buckingham.
—Clarendon.

3. to hint or suggest (something) indirectly; to imply.

And all the fictions bards pursue,
Do but *insinuate* what's true. —Swift.

4. to instill; to infuse gently; to introduce artfully.

All the arts of rhetoric, besides order and clearness, are for nothing else but to *insinuate* wrong ideas. —Locke.

Syn.—hint, intimate, suggest.

in·sin′ū·āte, *v.i.* 1. to creep in; to wind in; to flow in; to enter gently, slowly, or imperceptibly, as into crevices. [Obs.]

2. to gain on the affections by gentle or artful means, or by imperceptible degrees; to ingratiate oneself. [Obs.]

in·sin′ū·ā·ting, *a.* creeping or winding in; flowing in; tending to enter sinuously; insensibly winning favor and confidence.

His sly, polite, *insinuating* style.—Pope.

in·sin′ū·ā·ting·ly, *adv.* by insinuation; in an insinuating manner.

in·sin·ū·ā′tion, *n.* [L. *insinuatio (-onis)*, an insinuation, from *insinuare*, to insinuate.]

1. the act of insinuating; a creeping or winding in; a flowing in.

2. the act of gaining favor or affection by gentle or artful means.

3. the art or power of pleasing or gaining affection.

He had a natural *insinuation* and address, which made him acceptable in the best company. —Clarendon.

4. that which is insinuated; a hint; a suggestion or intimation by distant allusion; as, slander may be conveyed by *insinuations.*

Syn.—innuendo, implication.

in·sin′ū·ā·tive, *a.* 1. insinuating or tending to insinuate.

2. using or containing an insinuation; subtly suggestive.

in·sin′ū·ā·tŏr, *n.* one who insinuates.

in·sin′ū·ā·tō·ry, *a.* of an insinuating nature.

in·sip′id, *a.* [Fr. *insipide*; LL. *insipidus*, tasteless; L. *in-* priv., and *sapidus*, savory, from *sapere*, to taste.]

1. tasteless; without flavor; vapid; flat in taste; as, *insipid* liquor, *insipid* fruit.

2. wanting spirit, life, or animation; lacking in the power of exciting emotion; flat; dull; heavy; as, an *insipid* composition.

His wife a faded beauty of the baths,
Insipid as the queen upon a card.
—Tennyson.

Syn.—tasteless, vapid, uninteresting, characterless, flavorless, flat, lifeless, stale.

in·si·pid′i·ty, *n.* [Fr. *insipidité.*]

1. an insipid quality or state.

2. *pl.* **in·si·pid′i·tieṣ,** something insipid.

in·sip′id·ly, *adv.* without taste; without spirit or life.

in·sip′id·ness, *n.* the state or quality of being insipid.

in·sip′i·ence, *n.* [OFr. *insipience*; L. *insipientia*, lack of wisdom, from *insipiens (-entis)*, unwise, foolish; *in-* priv., and *sapiens (-entis)*, wise.] lack of wisdom; folly; foolishness; lack of understanding.

in·sip′i·ent, *a.* [L. *insipiens (-entis)*; *in-* priv., and *sapiens (-entis)*, wise.] unwise; stupid.

in·sip′i·ent, *n.* an unwise person. [Obs.]

in·sist′, *v.i.*; insisted, *pt., pp.*; insisting, *ppr.* [Fr. *insister*; L. *insistere*, to stand or tread upon, to pursue or follow diligently, persist; *in*, in, on, and *sistere*, to stand, to cause to stand.] to take and maintain a stand; to make a firm demand (often with *on* or *upon*); as, he *insists on* the rights of the minorities.

in·sist′, *v.t.* to demand strongly; as, I *insist* that you come.

Syn.—persist, demand, maintain, contend, urge, require.

in·sist′ence, *n.* 1. the quality of being insistent.

2. the act or an instance of insisting.

in·sist′en·cy, *n.*; *pl.* **in·sist′en·cieṣ,** insistence.

in·sist′ent, *a.* [L. *insistens (-entis)*, ppr. of *insistere*, to stand upon, to insist.]

1. standing or resting on something; as, an *insistent* wall. [Rare.]

2. urgent; pressing; persistent.

3. standing out conspicuously; compelling the attention; as, an *insistent* rhythm.

4. in zoology, said of the hind toe of a bird when inserted so that it bends downward and merely touches the ground: the correlative of *incumbent.*

in·sist′ent·ly, *adv.* with insistence.

in·sis′tūre, *n.* persistence; fixedness. [Obs.]

in·si′ti·en·cy (-sish′i-), *n.* freedom from thirst. [Obs.]

in·si′tion (-sish′un), *n.* [L. *insitio (-onis)*, an engrafting, from *insitus*, pp. of *inserere*, to engraft, implant; *in*, in, and *serere*, to sow.] the insertion of a scion in a stock; engraftment. [Obs.]

in sī′tū, [L. *in*, in, and *situ*, abl. of *situs*, position, site.] in position; in its original place.

in·snāre′, *v.t.* same as *ensnare.*

in·snār′ēr, *n.* same as *ensnarer.*

in·snärl′, *v.t.* same as *ensnarl.*

in·sō·brī′ē·ty, *n.* lack of sobriety; intemperance, especially in drinking; drunkenness.

in·sō·ciȧ·bil′i·ty (-shiȧ-), *n.* the quality of being not sociable; the lack of sociability. [Rare.]

in·sō′ciȧ·ble (-shiȧ-), *a.* 1. not sociable; not given to conversation; unsociable; taciturn. [Rare.]

2. that cannot be joined or connected. [Obs.]

in·sō′ciȧ·bly, *adv.* not sociably. [Rare.]

in·sō′ci·āte (-shi-), *a.* unconnected; alone; without an associate. [Obs.]

in·sō·fär′, *adv.* to the degree that (with *as*); as, *insofar as* I can say now, I shall come: often *in so far.*

in′sō·lāte, *v.t.*; insolated, *pt., pp.*; insolating, *ppr.* [L. *insolatus*, pp. of *insolare*, to expose to the sun; *in*, in, and *sol* (*solis*), sun.] to put out in the sun for drying, bleaching, etc.

in·sō·lā′tion, *n.* [L. *insolatio* (*-onis*), from *insolare*, to expose to the sun, to insolate.]
1. an insolating.
2. the treatment of disease by exposure to the sun's rays.
3. sunstroke.
4. in meteorology, (a) the radiation from the sun received by a surface, especially the earth's surface; (b) the rate of such radiation per unit of surface.

in′sōle, *n.* 1. the inside sole of a shoe.
2. an extra, removable inside sole put in for comfort or waterproofing.

in′sō·lence, *n.* [ME.; OFr.; L. *insolentia*, from *insolens*.]
1. the quality of being insolent; impudence; arrogance.
2. insolent behavior, action, or speech.
3. the quality of being unusual. [Obs.]
Syn.—impudence, arrogance, boldness, insult, sauciness, disrespectfulness, impertinence.

in′sō·len·cy, *n.* insolence. [Rare.]

in′sō·lent, *a.* [OFr. *insolent*; L. *insolens* (*-entis*), contrary to custom, excessive, haughty; *in-* priv., and *solens* (*-entis*), ppr. of *solere*, to be accustomed.]
1. showing haughty disregard of others; overbearing; domineering; as, an *insolent* master. [Obs.]
2. disrespectful of custom or established authority; impertinent; impudent; insulting; as, *insolent* words or behavior.
3. unwonted; unusual. [Obs.]
Syn.—saucy, impertinent, impudent, rude, arrogant, overbearing.

in′sō·lent·ly, *adv.* in an insolent manner; rudely; saucily.

in·sō·lid′i·ty, *n.* lack of solidity; weakness. [Obs.]

in·sol·ū·bil′i·ty, *n.* [LL. *insolubilitas*, from L. *insolubilis*, that cannot be loosed, insoluble.]
1. the quality of not being soluble or dissolvable, particularly in a fluid; as, the *insolubility* of carbon.
2. inexplicability, as of a line of conduct or of a mathematical problem.

in·sol′ū·ble, *a.* [OFr. *insoluble*; L. *insolubilis*, that cannot be loosed; *in-* priv., and *solvere*, to loosen.]
1. that cannot be dissolved, particularly by a liquid; as, a substance is *insoluble* in water when its parts will not separate and unite with that fluid.
2. that cannot be solved or explained; not to be resolved; as, an *insoluble* doubt or difficulty.
3. that cannot be separated into parts or loosened; hence, of great strength. [Rare.]

in·sol′ū·ble·ness, *n.* insolubility.

in·solv′ȧ·ble, *a.* that cannot be solved.

in·sol′ven·cy, *n.*; *pl.* **in·sol′ven·cieṣ,** the fact or condition of being insolvent; bankruptcy.

in·sol′vent, *a.* [L. *in-* priv., and *solvens* (*-entis*), *ppr.* of *solvere*, to loosen, dissolve, pay.]
1. not solvent; unable to pay debts; bankrupt.
2. not enough to pay all debts; as, an *insolvent* inheritance.
3. of insolvents or insolvency.
insolvent law; see *bankrupt law* under *bankrupt*.
Syn.—bankrupt, ruined, penniless, beggared.

in·sol′vent, *n.* an insolvent person.

in·som′ni·ȧ, *n.* [L., from *insomnis*, sleepless; *in-* priv., and *somnus*, sleep.] prolonged or abnormal inability to sleep.

in·som′ni·aç, *n.* a person who has insomnia.

in·som′ni·ous, *a.* [L. *insomniosus*, from *insomnia*, sleeplessness, insomnia.] having insomnia.

in·som′nō·lence, *n.* insomnia. [Rare.]

in′sō·much′, *adv.* 1. to such a degree or extent; so (usually with *as* or *that*); as, he worked very fast, *insomuch that* he was through in an hour.
2. inasmuch (with *as*).

in·sō·nō′rous, *a.* unmelodious. [Rare.]

in·sooth′, *adv.* in truth; truly. [Archaic.]

in·sou′ci·ȧnce (*or Fr. pron.* an-sö-syoṅs′), *n.* [Fr., from *insouciant*, careless.] gay heedlessness; lighthearted unconcern.

in·sou′ci·ȧnt (*or Fr. pron.* an-sö-syoṅ′), *a.* [Fr., gay, careless; *in-* priv., and *souciant*, ppr. of *soucier*, to regard, to care, from *souci*, care.] gay and unconcerned; carefree; indifferent.

in·sōul′, *v.t.* to ensoul.

in′span, *v.t.* and *v.i.*; inspanned, *pt., pp.*; inspanning, *ppr.* [D. *inspannen*, to yoke or harness; *in*, in, and *spannen*, to fasten, join, tie.] in South Africa, to harness horses, mules, or oxen to a wagon, etc.

in·speçt′, *v.t.*; inspected, *pt., pp.*; inspecting, *ppr.* [L. *inspectare*, to look at, observe, freq. of *inspicere*, to look into, examine; *in*, in, at, and *specere*, to look at, behold.]
1. to look at carefully; to examine critically.
2. to examine or review officially; as, the captain will *inspect* Company B.

in·speçt′, *n.* close examination. [Obs.]

in·speç′tion, *n.* [OFr. *inspection*; L. *inspectio* (*-onis*), a looking into, inspection, from *inspectus*, pp. of *inspicere*, to look into, inspect.]
1. careful investigation; critical examination.
2. official examination or review; as, the *inspection* of pork; the *inspection* of troops.
trial by inspection; in old English law, the trial of a case by a judge alone, without jury.

in·speçt′ive, *a.* inspecting; admitting of inspection or subject to inspection.

in·speçt′ŏr, *n.* [L. *inspector*, one who inspects or views, from *inspectus*, pp. of *inspicere*, to view, inspect.
1. a person who inspects; an official examiner; an overseer; as, an *inspector* of health, an *inspector* of the press.
2. an officer on a police force, ranking next below a superintendent.

in·speçt′ŏr·ăl, *a.* of an inspector.

in·speçt′ŏr·āte, *n.* 1. the position or duties of an inspector.
2. inspectors collectively.
3. the district supervised by an inspector.

in·speçt′ŏr ġen′ẽr·ăl, an officer having general charge of a system of inspection; as, the *inspector general* of the United States Army.

in·speç·tō′ri·ăl, *a.* relating to an inspector or to his duties.

in·speçt′ŏr·ship, *n.* the position or tenure of an inspector.

in·spẽrse′, *v.t.* to sprinkle upon. [Obs.]

in·spẽr′sion, *n.* the act of sprinkling on. [Obs.]

in·spex′i·mus, *n.* [L., we have inspected, 1st pers. pl. perf. ind. act. of *inspicere*, to examine, inspect.] in England, the first word of ancient charters, confirming a grant made by a former king; hence, a royal grant.

in·sphēre′, *v.t.* same as *ensphere*.

in·spīr′ȧ·ble, *a.* that can be inspired.

in·spi·rā′tion, *n.* [OFr. *inspiration*; LL. *inspiratio* (*-onis*), inspiration, from L. *inspiratus*, pp. of *inspirare*, to blow or breathe into or upon, to inspire.]
1. a breathing in; a drawing of air into the lungs; inhaling: opposed to *expiration*.
2. an inspiring or being inspired mentally or emotionally.
3. an inspiring influence; any stimulus to creative thought or action.
4. an inspired idea, action, etc.
5. a prompting of something written or said; suggestion.
6. in theology, a divine influence upon human beings resulting in writing, as of the Scriptures, or in action, as of a saint.
plenary inspiration; in theology, inspiration that is perfect in the utterance of the inspired word.
verbal inspiration; in theology, inspiration that attaches to the very words used in voicing the inspired message.

in·spi·rā′tion·ăl, *a.* 1. of or giving inspiration; inspiring.
2. produced, influenced, or stimulated by inspiration; inspired.

in·spi·rā′tion·ist, *n.* one who believes in inspiration, especially of the Holy Scriptures.

in′spi·rā·tŏr, *n.* [LL. *inspirator*, one who inspires, from L. *inspiratus*, pp. of *inspirare*, to blow into or upon, to inspire.] in a steam engine, a kind of injector in which the water is first raised by a jet of steam and then injected into the boiler under pressure.

in·spīr′ȧ·tō·ry, *a.* of, for, or characterized by inspiration or inhalation.

in·spīre′, *v.t.*, inspired, *pt., pp.*; inspiring, *ppr.* [ME. *inspiren*; OFr. *inspirer*; L. *inspirare*, to blow into or upon, to breathe into; *in*, in, on, and *spirare*, to breathe.]
1. originally, (a) to breathe or blow upon or into; (b) to infuse (life, etc. *into*) by breathing.
2. to draw (air) into the lungs; to inhale: opposed to *expire*.
3. to have an animating effect upon; to influence, stimulate, or impel; especially, to stimulate or impel to some creative or effective effort.
4. to cause, guide, communicate, or motivate by divine influence; as, God *inspired* the Scriptures.
5. to arouse or produce (a thought or feeling); as, kindness *inspires* love.
6. to affect with a specified feeling or thought; as, it *inspired* us with fear.
7. to occasion, cause, or produce.
8. to prompt, or cause to be written or said, by influence, without acknowledgment of the real authorship.
Syn.—animate, cheer, enliven, exhilarate, encourage, incite.

in·spīre′, *v.i.* 1. to inhale.
2. to give inspiration.

in·spīred′, *a.* 1. breathed in; inhaled; infused.
2. informed or directed by supernatural influence.
3. produced under inspiration; as, the *inspired* writings.

in·spīr′ẽr, *n.* he who inspires; any agent of inspiration.

in·spīr′ing, *a.* infusing spirit or courage; animating.

in·spir′it, *v.t.*; inspirited, *pt., pp.*; inspiriting, *ppr.* to infuse or excite spirit in; to enliven; to animate; to give new life to; to encourage; to invigorate.

in·spis′sȧnt, *a.* [L. *in*, in, to, and *spissans* (*-antis*), ppr. of *spissare*, to thicken.] tending to thicken; as, the *inspissant* agency of evaporation upon sugar water.

in·spis′sȧnt, *n.* anything that produces an inspissant effect, as evaporation.

in·spis′sāte, *v.t.* and *v.i.* inspissated, *pt., pp.*; inspissating, *ppr.* [LL. *inspissatus*, thick; L. *in*, in, and *spissatus*, pp. of *spissare*, to thicken, from *spissus*, thick.] to thicken by evaporation, etc.; to condense.

in·spis′sāte, *a.* thick; thickened by evaporation. [Obs.]

in·spis·sā′tion, *n.* the act or operation of rendering a liquid substance thicker by evaporation, etc.

in·stȧ·bil′i·ty, *n.*; *pl.* **in·stȧ·bil′i·tieṣ,** [L. *instabilitas* (*-atis*), lack of stability, from *instabilis*, unsteady, unstable; *in-* priv., and *stabilis*, steady, stable.]
1. lack of stability; lack of firmness in purpose; inconstancy; fickleness; mutability of opinion or conduct; as, *instability* is the characteristic of weak minds.
2. changeableness; mutability; as, the *instability* of laws, plans, or measures.

in·stā′ble, *a.* 1. inconstant; prone to change or recede from a purpose; mutable; unstable.
2. not steady or fixed; changeable.

in·stā′ble·ness, *n.* unstableness; mutability; instability.

in·stall′, *v.t.*; installed, *pt., pp.*; installing, *ppr.* [Fr. *installer*; LL. *installare*, to put in a place or seat; L. *in*, in, and LL. *stallum*, from O.H.G. *stal*, a place, seat, stall.]
1. to place (a person) in an office, rank, etc., with formality or ceremony.
2. to establish in a place or condition; to settle; as, we *installed* ourselves in the balcony.
3. to fix in position for use; as, we *installed* new light fixtures.

in·stăl·lā′tion, *n.* [Fr. *installation*; LL. *installatio* (*-onis*), from *installare*, to put in a place or seat, to install.]
1. an installing or being installed.
2. a complete mechanical apparatus fixed in position for use; as, a heating *installation*.

in·stall′ment, in·stal′ment, *n.* [earlier *estallment*, from *estall*, to arrange payments for, from OFr. *estaler*, to stop, fix, from *estal*, a halt, place, from O.H.G. *stal*, a place, seat, stall.]
1. any of the parts of a debt or other sum of money to be paid at regular times over a specified period.
2. any of several parts appearing at intervals; as, the story was published in *installments*.

in·stall′ment, in·stal′ment, *n.* an installing or being installed; installation.

in·stall′ment plan, a credit system by which debts, as for purchased articles, are paid in installments.

in·stamp′, *v.t.* to enstamp. [Obs.]

in′stănce, *n.* [OFr. *instance*; LL. *instantia*, an objection, instance, from L. *instantia*, a standing upon or near, a being present, from *instans*

(-*antis*), ppr. of *instare*, to stand upon, press upon; *in*, in, on, and *stare*, to stand.]
1. originally, an urgent plea; persistent solicitation.
2. a request; suggestion; instigation; as, his case was reviewed by the dean at the *instance* of the student council.
3. an example; case; illustration.
4. a step in proceeding; occasion; as, in the first *instance*.
5. a motive; cause. [Obs.]
6. in law, a process or proceeding in a court; suit.
causes of instance; in law, such causes as proceed at the request or solicitation of some party.
court of first instance; the first court which tries a case.
for instance; for example; by way of illustration.
instance court; in English law, a branch of the court of admiralty distinct from the prize court.
Syn.—request, prompting, persuasion, example, solicitation, case, illustration, exemplification, occurrence, point.

in'stănce, *v.t.*; instanced (-stănst), *pt., pp.*; instancing, *ppr.* 1. to show by an instance; to exemplify; as, the game was exciting, as was *instanced* by the score.
2. to give as an example; to cite.

in'stănce, *v.i.* to give or offer an example or case. [Rare.]

in'stăn·cy, *n.* the quality or condition of being instant; specifically, (a) urgency; pressure; insistence; (b) [Rare.] imminence; immediateness; (c) [Rare.] instantaneousness.

in'stănt, *a.* [OFr. *instant*, from L. *instans* (-*antis*), pressing, urgent, ppr. of *instare*, to stand upon or near, to press; *in*, in, upon, and *stare*, to stand.]
1. urgent; pressing.
2. of the current month; as, yours of the 13th *instant* received.
3. soon to happen; imminent.
4. without delay; immediate; as, I demand *instant* obedience.

in'stănt, *n.* 1. a point or very short space of time; a moment.
2. a particular moment.
on the instant; without delay; immediately.
the instant; as soon as.

in'stănt, *adv.* without delay; instantly. [Poet.]

in''stăn·tȧ·nē'i·ty, *n.* the quality or state of being instantaneous.

in·stăn·tā'nē·ous, *a.* 1. done, made, or happening in an instant.
2. done or made without delay; immediate; as, an *instantaneous* response.
instantaneous axis of rotation; in dynamics, the line, in a body having both rotary and translatory motion, which for the instant is stationary.
instantaneous center of rotation; in dynamics, the point, in a plane figure having both rotary and translatory motion, which for the instant is stationary.

in·stăn·tā'nē·ous·ly, *adv.* in an instant; immediately; without any perceptible lapse of time.

in·stăn·tā'nē·ous·ness, *n.* the quality of being instantaneous.

in·stan'tẽr, *adv.* [L., earnestly, pressingly, from *instans* (-*antis*), urgent, pressing, instant.] immediately; without delay; as, the party was compelled to plead *instanter*.

in'stănt·ly, *adv.* 1. in an instant; without delay; immediately.
2. urgently; pressingly. [Archaic.]

in'stănt·ly, *conj.* as soon as; the instant that; as, I came *instantly* I saw the need.

in'stănt re'play, the showing over again of an action, as of a play in a sports contest, often in slow motion, immediately after it has been recorded on videotape.

in'stär, *n.* [L., a shape, form.] any of the various forms of an insect or other arthropod between stages of molting.

in·stär', *v.t.*; instarred, *pt., pp.*; instarring, *ppr.* 1. to set as a star; to make a star of.
2. to stud or adorn with or as with stars.

in·stāte', *v.t.*; instated, *pt., pp.*; instating, *ppr.* 1. to set or place; to establish, as in a rank, position, or condition; as, to *instate* a person in greatness or in favor.
2. to invest; to endow. [Obs.]
3. to confer (with *on* or *upon*). [Obs.]

in·stau·rā'tion, *n.* [L. *instauratio* (-*onis*), a renewing, repetition, from *instauratus*, pp. of *instaurare*, to renew, repeat.] renewal; repair; re-establishment; the restoration of a thing to its former state, after decay, lapse, or dilapidation.

in'stau·rā·tŏr, *n.* one who renovates or restores to a former condition.

in·stead' (-sted'), *adv.* in place of the person or thing mentioned; as an alternative or substitute; as, since we had no sugar, we used honey *instead*.
instead of; in place of; rather than.

in·steep', *v.t.* to steep or soak; to drench; to imbrue. [Rare.]

in'step, *n.* 1. the upper surface of the arch of the foot, between the ankle and the toes.
2. the part of a shoe or stocking that covers this surface.
3. the front surface of the hind leg of a horse, between the hock and the pastern joint.

in'sti·gāte, *v.t.*; instigated, *pt., pp.*; instigating, *ppr.* [L. *instigatus*, pp. of *instigare*, to prick or goad on, to stimulate.]
1. to urge on, spur on, or incite to some action or course of action; as, Mephistopheles *instigated* Faust to sin.
2. to cause by inciting; to foment; as, they *instigated* a rebellion.
Syn.—provoke, incite, tempt, impel, encourage, stimulate, induce, egg on.

in'sti·gā·ting·ly, *adv.* incitingly; so as to instigate.

in·sti·gā'tion, *n.* [L. *instigatio* (-*onis*), from *instigare*, to goad, to instigate.] an instigating; incitement.

in'sti·gā·tive, *a.* instigating or tending to instigate.

in'sti·gā·tŏr, *n.* one who or that which instigates.

in·still', in·stil', *v.t.*; instilled, *pt., pp.*; instilling, *ppr.* [Fr. *instiller*; L. *instillare*, to pour in by drops, to instill; *in*, in, and *stillare*, to drop, from *stilla*, a drop.]
1. to infuse by drops.
2. to put (a notion, principle, feeling, etc.) *in* or *into* little by little; to impart gradually; as, to *instill* good principles *into* the mind.
Syn.—implant, inculcate, infuse, insinuate.

in·stil·lā'tion, *n.* [L. *instillatio* (-*onis*), from *instillare*, to pour in by drops, to instill.]
1. an instilling.
2. anything instilled.

in·stil'lȧ·tō·ry, *a.* relating to instillation. [Rare.]

in·still'ẽr, *n.* one who or that which instills.

in·still'ment, in·stil'ment, *n.* 1. the act of instilling.
2. anything instilled.

in·stim'ū·lāte, *v.t.* to stimulate; to incite. [Obs.]

in·stim·ū·lā'tion, *n.* the act of stimulating, inciting, or urging forward. [Obs.]

in'stinct, *n.* [L. *instinctus*, instigation, impulse, properly pp. of *instinguere*, to impel, instigate; *in-* in, and *stinguere*, to prick.]
1. (an) inborn tendency to behave in a way characteristic of a species; natural, unacquired mode of response to stimuli; as, suckling is an *instinct* in mammals.
2. a natural or acquired tendency, aptitude, or talent; bent; knack; gift; as, she has an *instinct* for doing the right thing.

in·stinct', *a.* filled or charged (*with*); as, the speech was *instinct with* emotion.

in·stinct', *v.t.* to implant as an instinct. [Obs.]

in·stinc'tion, *n.* instinct. [Obs.]

in·stinc'tive, *a.* 1. of, or having the nature of, instinct.
2. caused, prompted, or done by instinct.
Syn.—natural, voluntary, spontaneous, intuitive, impulsive, inborn, automatic.

in·stinc'tive·ly, *adv.* by force of instinct; without reasoning, instruction, or experience; by natural impulse.

in·stinc·tiv'i·ty, *n.* disposition to instinctive action. [Rare.]

in·stinc'tū·ăl, *a.* having to do with instinct.

in·stip'ū·lāte, *a.* same as *exstipulate*.

in'sti·tŏr, *n.* [L., a broker, agent, huckster, from *institus*, pp. of *insistere*, to stand or tread upon, pursue, follow; *in*, in, on, and *sistere*, to stand.] in civil law, a person in charge of the business of another.

in·sti·tō'ri·ăl, *a.* pertaining to an institor, or to his office and duties.

in'sti·tūte, *a.* instituted; settled. [Obs.]

in'sti·tūte, *v.t.*; instituted, *pt., pp.*; instituting, *ppr.* [L. *institutus*, pp. of *instituere*, to set up, erect, construct; *in*, in, on, and *statuere*, to cause to stand, set up, place.]
1. to set up; establish; found; introduce.
2. to start; initiate; as, the city council *instituted* an investigation.
3. to appoint to or install in an office, position, benefice, etc.

in'sti·tūte, *n.* [L. *institutum*, an arrangement, plan, intention.] something instituted; specifically, (a) an established principle, law, custom, or usage; (b) [*pl.*] a summary or digest of established principles, especially in law; (c) an organization for the promotion of art, science, education, etc.; (d) the building in which such an organization is housed; (e) a type of school for higher education in technical subjects: it may be part of a university; (f) an institution for advanced study, research, and instruction in a restricted field, organized in connection with a university; (g) a short teaching program established for a special group concerned with some special field of work.
Syn.—establishment, training school, training college, academy, seminary.

in·sti·tū'tion, *n.* [L. *institutio* (-*onis*), a disposition, arrangement, establishment.]
1. an instituting or being instituted; establishment.
2. an established law, custom, practice, system, etc.
3. an organization having a social, educational, or religious purpose, as a school, church, hospital, reformatory, etc.
4. the building housing such an organization.
5. a familiar person or thing. [Colloq.]
6. in ecclesiastical usage, (a) the establishment of a sacrament by Jesus; (b) the establishment of a clergyman in a benefice.
7. in law, a collection of established principles or fundamental rules.
8. a system of the elements or rules of any art or science. [Obs.]
9. education; instruction. [Obs.]

in·sti·tū'tion·ăl, *a.* 1. of, or having the nature of, an institution.
2. organized so as to function in social, charitable, and educational activities; as, *institutional* religion.
3. in advertising, intended primarily to gain prestige and good will rather than to increase immediate sales.

in·sti·tū'tion·ăl·ism, *n.* a belief in and support of the usefulness or sanctity of established institutions.

in·sti·tū'tion·ăl·īze, *v.t.* 1. to make into or consider as an institution.
2. to make institutional.
3. to put (a person) into an institution. [Colloq.]

in·sti·tū'tion·ā·ry, *a.* 1. of legal institutes.
2. of clerical institution.
3. of institutions; institutional.

in'sti·tū·tive, *a.* 1. instituting or tending to institute; of institution.
2. sanctioned by law, custom, or usage; established.

in'sti·tū·tive·ly, *adv.* according to the laws or customs of an institution.

in'sti·tū·tŏr, *n.* [L., a founder, establisher, from *institutus*, pp. of *instituere*, to set up, erect, institute.]
1. one who institutes or establishes; a founder; organizer.
2. an instructor; one who educates; as, an *institutor* of youth. [Obs.]
3. in the Episcopal Church, a presbyter appointed by the bishop to institute a rector or assistant minister in a parish church.

in·stop', *v.t.* to stop; to close; to fasten. [Obs.]

in·stōre', *v.t.* (a) to restore; (b) to establish; (c) to supply. [Obs.]

in·strat'i·fied, *a.* stratified within something else; interstratified.

in·struct', *v.t.*; instructed, *pt., pp.*; instructing, *ppr.* [L. *instructus*, pp. of *instruere*, to pile upon, put in order, erect, prepare, teach, instruct; *in*, in, upon, and *struere*, to pile up, arrange, build.]
1. to communicate knowledge to; to teach; educate.
2. to give the facts of the matter to; to inform; as, a judge *instructs* the jury.
3. to give directions or orders to; as, the officer *instructed* the sentry to shoot.
Syn.—direct, educate, teach, train, inform.

in·struct', *a.* instructed; trained. [Obs.]

in·struct'i·ble, *a.* that can be instructed. [Rare.]

in·struc'tion, *n.* [LL. *instructio* (-*onis*), instruction; L. *instructio* (*-onis*), a constructing, erecting.]

1. an instructing; education.

2. knowledge, information, etc. given or taught; any teaching; lesson.

3. [*pl.*] directions; orders.

in·strug′tion·ăl, *a.* of or for instruction; educational.

in·strug′ive, *a.* conveying knowledge; serving to instruct or inform.

in·strug′ive·ly, *adv.* so as to afford instruction.

in·strug′ive·ness, *n.* power of instructing.

in·strug′tŏr, *n.* [LL., from L. *instructor*, one who prepares.]

1. a person who instructs; a teacher.

2. a college teacher ranking below an assistant professor.

in·strug′tŏr·ship, *n.* the position of an instructor.

in·strug′tress, *n.* a woman instructor.

in′strụ·ment, *n.* [L. *instrumentum*, a tool or tools, implement, stock in trade, furniture, dress, from *instruere*, to furnish, equip; *in*, in, and *struere*, to pile up, arrange.]

1. (a) a thing by means of which something is done; means; (b) a person used by another to bring something about.

2. a tool or implement, especially one used for delicate work or for scientific or artistic purposes.

3. any of various devices producing musical sound, as a piano, violin, oboe, etc.

4. in law, a formal document, as a deed, contract, etc.

instrument flying; the navigation of an aircraft completely by the use of instruments.

instrument panel (or *board*); a panel or board with instruments, gauges, etc. mounted on it, as in an automobile or airplane.

in·strụ·men′tăl, *a.* [ME.; OFr.; ML. *instrumentalis*.]

1. serving as a means; helpful.

2. of or performed with an instrument or tool.

3. of, performed on, or written for a musical instrument or instruments.

4. in grammar, designating or of a case showing means or agency: the instrumental case is found in Anglo-Saxon, Sanskrit, Slavonic, etc.

in·strụ·men′tăl·ism, *n.* in philosophy, the pragmatic doctrine that ideas are plans for action which serve as instruments for adjusting the organism to its environment.

in·strụ·men′tăl·ist, *n.* 1. one who performs upon a musical instrument.

2. a person who believes in instrumentalism.

in″strụ·men·tal′i·ty, *n.*; *pl.* **in″strụ·men·tal′i·ties,** the condition, quality, or fact of being instrumental, or serving as a means; agency; means; as, the *instrumentality* of the law.

in·strụ·men′tăl·ly, *adv.* 1. by way or means of an instrument; in the nature of an instrument, as means to an end.

2. with musical instruments.

in·strụ·men′tăl·ness, *n.* usefulness, as of means to an end; instrumentality. [Obs.]

in·strụ·men·tā′tion, *n.* 1. the arrangement of music for a combined number of instruments; also, the art or manner of playing on an instrument; execution; as, his *instrumentation* was defective.

2. the use of, or work with, scientific instruments.

in′strụ·men·tist, *n.* same as *instrumentalist*.

in·stȳle′, *v.t.* to call; to denominate. [Obs.]

in·suav′i·ty (-swav′), *n.* lack of suavity or pleasing qualities. [Rare.]

in·sub·jeç′tion, *n.* state of disobedience; not subject to authority.

in·sub·mis′sion, (-mish′un), *n.* lack of submission; disobedience. [Rare.]

in·sub·ọr′di·nāte, *a.* not submitting to authority; disobedient.

in·sub·ọr′di·nāte, *n.* an insubordinate person.

in·sub·ọr·di·nā′tion, *n.* the condition or fact of being insubordinate; disobedience.

in·sub·stan′tiăl, *a.* not substantial; specifically, (a) unreal; imaginary; (b) not solid or firm; weak or flimsy.

in·sub·stan·ti·al′i·ty (-shi-al′), *n.* the quality or state of being insubstantial.

in·suç·çā′tion, *n.* [L. *insucatus*, pp. of *insucare*, *insuccare*, to soak in; *in*, in, and *sucus*, *succus*, juice.] the act of soaking or moistening; maceration. [Obs.]

in·suç·cess′, *n.* lack of success.

in·sūe′, *v.i.* to ensue. [Obs.]

in′suē·tūde (-swē-), *n.* [L. *insuetudo*, from *insuetus*, unaccustomed to.] the state of being out of use; unusualness. [Rare.]

in·suf′fẽr·ȧ·ble, *a.* intolerable; that cannot be borne or endured; as, *insufferable* pain.

Syn.—intolerable, unpermissible, unallowable, unendurable, unbearable.

in·suf′fẽr·ȧ·bly, *adv.* 1. in an insufferable manner.

2. to an insufferable degree.

in·suf·fi′cience (-fish′ens), *n.* insufficiency. [Rare.]

in·suf·fi′cien·cy, *n.* 1. lack of sufficiency; deficiency; inadequacy; incapacity.

2. failure of an organ or tissue to perform its normal function: said especially of a heart valve or muscle.

in·suf·fi′cient, *a.* [LL. *insufficiens* (*-entis*); *in-* priv., and *sufficiens* (*-entis*), sufficient.]

1. not sufficient; inadequate to any need, use, or purpose.

2. lacking in strength, power, ability, or skill; incapable; unfit; as, a person *insufficient* to discharge the duties of his office.

in·suf·fi′cient·ly, *adv.* in an insufficient manner; inadequately.

in·suf′flāte, *v.t.*; insufflated, *pt.*, *pp.*; insufflating, *ppr.* [from L. *insufflatus*, pp. of *insufflare*, to blow or breathe into; L. *in*, in, and *sufflare*, to blow from below; *sub*, under, and *flare*, to blow.]

1. to blow or breathe into or on.

2. to breathe on (baptismal waters or a person being baptized).

3. in medicine, (a) to blow (a powder, vapor, air, etc.) into a cavity of the body, especially the lungs; (b) to blow such a substance into (the lungs, etc.).

in·suf·flā′tion, *n.* an insufflating or being insufflated.

in′suf·flā·tŏr, *n.* an instrument for blowing something, as powder, gas, vapor, or water, into a cavity, opening, or organ of the body; an injector used for forcing air into a furnace.

in·sūit·ȧ·bil′i·ty, *n.* lack of suitability. [Obs.]

in·sūit′ȧ·ble, *a.* unsuitable. [Obs.]

in′sū·lȧ, *n.*; *pl.* **in·sū·lae,** [L., an island.]

1. in anatomy, a group of radiating cerebral convolutions lying beneath the frontal, parietal, and temporal lobes: also called *island of Reil*.

2. in Roman archaeology, a consolidated block of buildings surrounded by four streets, as found in the excavations of Pompeii.

in′sū·lăr, *a.* [L. *insularis*, from *insula*, an island.]

1. of, or having the form of, an island.

2. living or situated on an island.

3. like an island; detached; insulated.

4. of, like, or characteristic of islanders.

5. of narrow views; illiberal; prejudiced; as, his ideas of government are *insular*.

6. in medicine, characterizing isolated patches; also, of the islands of Langerhans or other islands of tissue.

in′sū·lăr, *n.* one who resides on an island.

in·sū·lar′i·ty, *n.* 1. the state of being an island.

2. the state of living on an island.

3. narrowness; lack of liberality in opinion; prejudice.

in′sū·lăr·ly, *adv.* in an insular manner.

in′sū·lȧ·ry, *a.* insular. [Obs.]

in′sū·lāte, *v.t.*; insulated, *pt.*, *pp.*; insulating, *ppr.* [from L. *insulatus*, made like an island, pp. of *insulare*, to make like an island, from L. *insula*, an island.]

1. to set apart; detach from the rest; isolate.

2. to separate or cover with a nonconducting material in order to prevent the passage or leakage of electricity, heat, or sound.

3. to make an island of.

in′sū·lāte, *a.* situated alone.

in′sū·lā·ted, *a.* 1. standing by itself; isolated; as, an *insulated* house or column.

2. placed, by means of nonconductors, so that electricity or heat is prevented from passing.

3. in astronomy, so far separated that gravitational force may be regarded as nil.

insulated wire; wire covered with some insulating substance, as silk, paraffined cotton, etc.

in·sū·lā′tion, *n.* 1. an insulating or being insulated.

2. material of a nonconducting character used for insulating.

in′sū·lā·tŏr, *n.* anything that insulates; especially, a device, usually of glass or porcelain, for insulating and supporting electric wires.

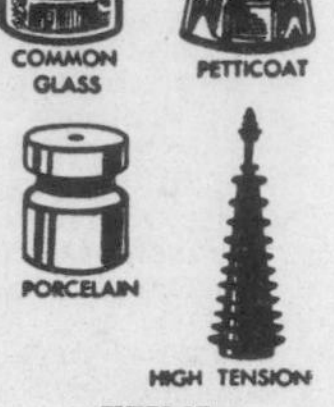

TYPES OF INSULATOR

in′sū·lin, *n.* [L. *insula*, island; and *in*: after the islands of Langerhans, in the pancreas.]

1. a secretion of the islands of Langerhans, in the pancreas, which helps the body use sugar and other carbohydrates.

2. a product extracted from the pancreas of sheep or oxen and used hypodermically in the treatment of diabetes mellitus: a trade-mark (*Insulin*).

in′sū·lin shock, an abnormal condition caused by an overdose or excess secretion of insulin, resulting in a sudden reduction in the sugar content of the blood: it is characterized by tremors, cold sweat, convulsions, and coma.

in′sū·līze, *v.t.*; insulized, *pt.*, *pp.*; insulizing, *ppr.* to treat with insulin.

in·sulse′, *a.* [L. *insulsus*, unsalted, insipid; *in-* priv., and *salsus*, pp. of *salere*, to salt.] dull; insipid. [Rare.]

in·sul′si·ty, *n.* the quality of being insulse. [Rare.]

in′sult, *n.* [LL. *insultus*, an insult, lit., a leaping upon, from L. *insultus*, pp. of *insilire*, to leap upon, to insult; *in*, in, on, and *salire*, to leap.]

1. originally, an attack; onset.

2. any gross abuse offered to another, either by words or actions; any act or speech meant to hurt the feelings or self-respect of another.

The ruthless sneer that *insult* adds to grief. —Savage.

Syn.—abuse, affront, contempt, indignity, insolence, outrage.

in·sult′, *v.t.*; insulted, *pt.*, *pp.*; insulting, *ppr.* 1. to attack or leap on. [Obs.]

2. to treat with gross abuse, insolence, or contempt, by words or actions; to subject to an insult.

in·sult′, *v.i.* 1. to spring; to leap. [Obs.]

2. to behave insolently. [Archaic.]

in·sult′ȧ·ble, *a.* capable of being insulted; easily offended. [Rare.]

in·sult′ănce, *n.* insolence; offense. [Obs.]

in·sult′ănt, *a.* [L. *insultans* (*-antis*), ppr. of *insultare*, to leap upon, insult.] tending to insult. [Rare.]

in·sul·tā′tion, *n.* 1. the act of insulting or offending. [Obs.]

2. insolent triumph or exultation. [Obs.]

in·sult′ẽr, *n.* one who insults or affronts.

in·sult′ing, *a.* characterized by insolence or insult; of an offending nature; derogatory; abusive.

Syn.—contemptuous, impertinent, insolent, rude.

in·sult′ing·ly, *adv.* in an insulting manner; with insolent contempt.

in·sult′ment, *n.* the act of insulting. [Obs.]

in·sūme′, *v.t.* [L. *insumere*; *in*, in, and *sumere*, to take.] to take in. [Obs.]

in·sū″pẽr·ȧ·bil′i·ty, *n.* the quality or state of being insuperable.

in·sū′pẽr·ȧ·ble, *a.* [L. *insuperabilis*; *in-* priv., and *superabilis*, that may be surmounted, from *superare*, to overcome, surpass.] that cannot be overcome or surmounted; insurmountable.

in·sū′pẽr·ȧ·ble·ness, *n.* the quality of being insuperable or insurmountable.

in·sū′pẽr·ȧ·bly, *adv.* 1. in an insuperable manner.

2. to an insuperable degree.

in·sup·pōrt′ȧ·ble, *a.* [LL. *insupportabilis*; L. *in-* priv., and *supportare*, to carry on, convey.] that cannot be borne or endured; insufferable; intolerable.

Syn.—unbearable, intolerable, insufferable, unendurable.

in·sup·pōrt′ȧ·ble·ness, *n.* the quality of being insupportable.

in·sup·pōrt′ȧ·bly, *adv.* 1. in an insupportable manner.

2. to an insupportable degree.

in·sup·pōṣ′ȧ·ble, *a.* inconceivable; not supposable.

in·sup·press′i·ble, *a.* that cannot be suppressed or concealed.

in·sup·press′i·bly, *adv.* in a manner that cannot be suppressed; so as to be insuppressible.

in·sup·press'ive, *a.* not suppressible. [Rare.]

in·sūr·ȧ·bil'i·ty, (-shūr-), *n.* the quality or condition of being insurable.

in·sūr'ȧ·ble, *a.* that can be insured against loss or damage.

insurable interest; a right to or equity in a given property sufficient to legalize insurance thereon.

in·sūr'ănce, *n.* 1. an insuring or being insured against loss; a system of protection against loss in which a number of individuals agree to pay certain sums for a guarantee that they will be compensated for any specified loss by fire, accident, death, etc.

2. a contract whereby, in return for a fixed payment (*premium*), the insurer guarantees the insured that a certain sum will be paid for a specified loss: usually called *insurance policy*.

3. the fixed payment made by the insured; premium.

4. the amount for which life, property, etc. is insured.

5. the business of insuring against loss.

6. a pledge, as of betrothal. [Obs.]

accident insurance; see *accident insurance*.

endowment insurance; see *endowment policy*.

fire insurance; see *fire insurance*.

fraternal insurance; life insurance based upon a co-operative plan, provided by a fraternal order.

insurance agent; a representative of an insurance company, authorized to transact certain business, as soliciting risks, issuing policies, etc.

life insurance; see *life insurance*.

old-line insurance company; an insurance company in which the reserve and the premium rate are fixed and cannot be raised during the life of the contract, as opposed to assessment or variable premium companies.

social insurance; see under *social*, a.

in·sūr'ăn·cẽr, *n.* an underwriter. [Obs.]

in·sūr'ănt, *n.* one who is insured.

in·sūre', *v.t.*; insured, *pt.*, *pp.*; insuring, *ppr.* [ME. *insuren, ensuren*; OFr. *enseurer*, to assure, *en*, in, and *seur*, sure.]

1. to make sure or secure; to guarantee; as, to *insure* the safety of one's family.

2. to get as a certainty; to secure; as, your degree will *insure* you a job.

3. to make safe; to guard against injury, damage, etc.; to protect; as, care *insures* one against error.

4. to assure against loss; to contract to be paid or to pay money in the case of loss of (life, property, etc.); to take out or issue insurance on (something or someone).

Also spelled *ensure*.

in·sūre', *v.i.* to underwrite; to give or take out insurance: also spelled *ensure*.

in·sūred', *n.* one whose life, property, etc. is insured against loss.

in·sūr'ẽr, *n.* one who insures; the person or company that contracts to pay the losses of another for a premium; an underwriter.

in·sŭr'ġence, *n.* a rising in revolt; an uprising; an insurrection.

in·sŭr'ġen·cy, *n.* 1. the quality, state, or fact of being insurgent.

2. insurgence.

in·sŭr'ġent, *a.* [L. *insurgens* (*-entis*), ppr. of *insurgere*, to rise up, rise up against; *in*, in, upon, and *surgere*, to rise.] rising in opposition to governmental or political authority; insubordinate; as, *insurgent* provinces.

in·sŭr'ġent, *n.* an insurgent person.

in·sŭr·mount·ȧ·bil'i·ty, *n.* the quality or state of being insurmountable; insurmountableness.

in·sŭr·mount'ȧ·ble, *a.* insuperable; that cannot be surmounted or overcome; as, an *insurmountable* difficulty.

in·sŭr·mount'ȧ·ble·ness, *n.* insurmountability.

in·sŭr·mount'ȧ·bly, *adv.* 1. in an unsurmountable manner.

2. to an insurmountable degree.

in·sŭr·reçt', *v.i.* to rise up in insurrection. [Colloq.]

in·sŭr·reç'tion, *n.* [L. *insurrectus*, pp. of *insurgere*, to rise up, rise up against; *in*, in, upon, and *surgere*, to rise.] a rising against governmental or political authority; rebellion; revolt.

It is found that this city of old time hath made *insurrection* against kings.
—Ezra iv. 19.

Syn.—sedition, revolt, rebellion.—*Sedition* is the raising of commotion in a state without aiming at open violence against the laws; *insurrection* is a rising up of individuals to prevent the execution of law, by force of arms; *revolt* is a casting off of the authority of a government with a view to put it down by force; *rebellion* is organized, armed, open resistance to the authority or government in power.

in·sŭr·reç'tion·ăl, *a.* pertaining to or like insurrection.

in·sŭr·reç'tion·ā·ry, *a.* pertaining or suitable to insurrection; engaged in insurrection.

in·sŭr·reç'tion·ā·ry, *n.*; *pl.* **in·sŭr·reç'tion·ā·rieṣ,** an insurgent; a rebel.

in·sŭr·reç'tion·ist, *n.* one who favors or takes part in insurrection; an insurgent.

in·sus·cep·ti·bil'i·ty, *n.* lack of susceptibility; the fact, quality, or state of being insusceptible.

in·sus·cep'ti·ble, *a.* not susceptible; not easily capable of being moved, affected, or impressed.

in·sus·cep'ti·bly, *adv.* not susceptibly.

in'swept, *a.* tapering at the front: said of an automobile frame.

in·taçt', *a.* [L. *intactus*, untouched, uninjured; *in-* priv., and *tactus*, pp. of *tangere*, to touch.] untouched; undamaged; remaining complete; sound; unimpaired.

in·taç'ti·ble, in·taç'tȧ·ble, *a.* not perceptible to the touch. [Obs.]

in·tagl'iā·ted (-tal'yā-), *a.* engraved or stamped in, especially as an intaglio.

in·tagl'iō (-tal'yō), *n.*; *pl.* **in·tagl'iōṣ, in·tagl'i** (-yē), [It., from *intagliare*, to cut in, engrave.]

1. a design or figure carved or engraved below the surface.

2. a gem or stone ornamented with such a design or figure: opposed to *cameo*.

3. the art or process of making such designs or figures: usually in phrase *in intaglio*.

4. a die cut to produce a design in relief.

in·tagl'iō, *v.t.* 1. to engrave a design on.

2. to cut (a design) in a surface.

in·tāil', *v.t.* to entail. [Obs.]

in'tāke, *n.* 1. a taking in.

2. what is taken in; as, a small pipe has little *intake*.

3. the influx point of a tube or pipe; as, the *intake* of a sewer.

4. a narrowing; an abrupt lessening in breadth.

5. in mechanics, the amount of energy taken in.

6. in mining, an air shaft.

in·tam'i·nā·ted, *a.* [L. *intaminatus*, unsullied, undefiled.] not contaminated. [Obs.]

in·tan·ġi·bil'i·ty, *n.* 1. the quality of being intangible.

2. *pl.* **in·tan·ġi·bil'i·tieṣ,** something intangible.

in·tan'ġi·ble, *a.* 1. that cannot be touched; not perceptible to the touch.

A corporation is an artificial, invisible, *intangible* being. —Marshall.

2. that cannot be easily defined, formulated, or grasped; vague.

in·tan'ġi·ble, *n.* something intangible, as good will or a similar asset.

in·tan'ġi·ble·ness, *n.* intangibility.

in·tan'ġi·bly, *adv.* in an intangible manner; vaguely; impalpably.

in·tär'si·ȧ, *n.* [It. *intarsio*, from *intarsiare*, to inlay, incrust, from *in-*, in, and Ar. *tarṣi*, incrustation.] a surface decoration made by inlaying small pieces of wood in patterns; mosaic woodwork.

in·tāst'ȧ·ble, *a.* tasteless. [Rare.]

in'tē·ġẽr, *n.* [L. *integer*, untouched, whole, entire; *in-* priv., and *tangere*, to touch.]

1. anything complete in itself; entity; whole.

2. a whole number (e.g., 5, 10, 748, etc.): distinguished from *fraction*.

complex integer; the sum of a real and an imaginary integer.

in'tē·ġẽr vī'tae, [L., lit., unblemished in life.] blameless; upright: from Horace, *Odes*, I.

in″tē·grȧ·bil'i·ty, *n.* the quality of being integrable.

in'tē·grȧ·ble, *a.* in mathematics, capable of being integrated, as a function or equation.

in'tē·grăl, *a.* [LL. *integralis*, from L. *integer*, untouched, whole, entire.]

1. whole; entire; lacking nothing; complete as an entity.

2. making part of a whole, or necessary to make a whole.

3. in mathematics, (a) of or having to do with an integer or integers; not fractional; (b) of or relating to integrals or integration.

in'tē·grăl, *n.* 1. a whole; an entire thing.

2. in mathematics, the function or sum of any proposed differential quantity: denoted by the symbol $\int$.

elliptic integral; an integral which expresses the length of an elliptical arc.

in'tē·grăl çal'çū·lus, see under *calculus*.

in·tē·gral'i·ty, *n.* the quality or state of being integral; wholeness.

in'tē·grăl·ly, *adv.* wholly; completely.

in'tē·grand, *n.* [L. *integrandus*, gerundive of *integrare*.] in mathematics, the function or equation to be integrated.

in'tē·grănt, *a.* [L. *integrans* (*-antis*), ppr. of *integrare*, to make whole, renew.] making part of a whole; integral.

in'tē·grāte, *v.t.*; integrated, *pt.*, *pp.*; integrating, *ppr.* [L. *integratus*, pp. of *integrare*, to make whole, renew, from *integer*, untouched, whole, entire.]

1. to make whole or complete by adding or bringing together parts.

2. to put or bring (parts) together into a whole; to unify.

3. to give or indicate the whole, sum, or total of.

4. (a) to remove the legal and social barriers imposing segregation upon (racial groups) so as to permit free and equal association; (b) to abolish segregation in; desegregate (a school, neighborhood, etc.).

5. in mathematics, (a) to calculate the integral or integrals of (a function, equation, etc.); (b) to perform the process of integration upon.

integrated circuit; an electronic circuit containing many interconnected amplifying devices and circuit elements formed on a single body, or chip, of semiconductor material.

in'tē·grāte, *v.i.* to unite or become whole.

in·tē·grā'tion, *n.* 1. an integrating or being integrated.

2. in mathematics, the process of finding the quantity or function of which a given quantity or function is the derivative or differential: opposed to *differentiation*.

3. in psychoanalysis, the organization of various traits or tendencies into one harmonious personality.

in'tē·grā·tive, *a.* 1. of integration.

2. integrating.

in'tē·grā·tŏr, *n.* one who or that which integrates; specifically, an instrument for calculating integrals.

in″tē·gri·pal'li·āte, *a.* see *integropalliate*.

in·teg'ri·ty, *n.* [L. *integritas*, wholeness, soundness, from *integer*, untouched, whole, entire.]

1. the quality or state of being complete; wholeness; entireness; unbroken state.

2. the entire, unimpaired state or quality of anything; perfect condition; soundness.

3. the quality or state of being of sound moral principle; uprightness, honesty, and sincerity.

in″tē·grō·pal'li·āte, *a.* in conchology, having the pallial line integral or unbroken by notches.

in·teg·ū·mā'tion, *n.* integumentation. [Obs.]

in·teg'ū·ment, *n.* [L. *integumentum*, a covering, from *integere*, to cover; *in*, in, upon, and *tegere*, to cover.] an outer covering, as of the body or of a plant; skin, shell, hide, husk, rind, etc.

in·teg·ū·men'tȧ·ry, *a.* belonging to, like, or composed of an integument.

in·teg″ū·men·tā'tion, *n.* the operation of covering with integuments; also, the condition of being so covered, or the covering itself.

in'tel·leçt, *n.* [L. *intellectus*, a perceiving, understanding, from *intellegere*, *intelligere*, to perceive, understand; *inter*, between, among, and *legere*, to gather, pick, choose.]

1. the ability to reason, perceive, or understand; ability to perceive relations, differences, etc.: distinguished from *will*, *feeling*.

2. great mental ability; high intelligence.

3. (a) a mind or intelligence, especially a superior one; (b) a person of intelligence; (c) minds or intelligent persons, collectively.

in·tel·leç'tion, *n.* [L. *intellectio* (*-onis*), from *intellegere*, *intelligere*, to perceive, understand.]

1. the process of using the intellect; thinking; cognition.

2. an act of the intellect; a thought or perception.

in·tel·leç'tive, *a.* 1. having power to understand.

2. produced by the understanding.

3. capable of being perceived by the understanding, not by the senses. [Obs.]

in·tel·leç′tive·ly, *adv.* in an intellective manner.

in·tel·leç′tū·ăl, *a.* [L. *intellectualis*, pertaining to the understanding, from *intellectus*, perception, understanding, intellect.]

1. of or done by the intellect.
2. appealing to the intellect.
3. requiring or using intelligence.
4. having or showing a high degree of intelligence; having superior mental powers.

in·tel·leç′tū·ăl, *n.* 1. a person with intellectual interests or tastes.

2. a person who does intellectual work.
3. a member of the intelligentsia.
4. the intellect or understanding. [Obs.]

in·tel·leç′tū·ăl·işm, *n.* 1. intellectuality.

2. in philosophy, the theory that all knowledge is derived from the intellect without aid from the senses.

in·tel·leç′tū·ăl·ist, *n.* 1. one who tends to overemphasize intellectual pursuits.

2. in philosophy, a believer in intellectualism.

in·tel·leç·tū·al′i·ty, *n.* [LL. *intellectualitas*, from *intellectualis*, pertaining to the understanding, from L. *intellectus*, perception.]

1. intellectual ability or nature.
2. the quality of being intellectual.

in·tel·leç′tū·ăl·īze, *v.t.*; intellectualized, *pt.*, *pp.*; intellectualizing, *ppr.* to attribute intellectual characteristics to; to endow with an intellect or intellectual significance.

in·tel·leç′tū·ăl·īze, *v.i.* to reason; to think.

in·tel·leç′tū·ăl·ly, *adv.* 1. in an intellectual manner.

2. as concerns the intellect.

in·tel′li·ġence, *n.* [OFr. *intelligence*; L. *intelligentia*, perception, discernment, from *intelligens* (*-entis*), ppr. of *intelligere*, to perceive, understand.]

1. (a) the ability to learn or understand from experience; ability to acquire and retain knowledge; mental ability; (b) the ability to respond quickly and successfully to a new situation; use of the faculty of reason in solving problems, directing conduct, etc. effectively; (c) in psychology, measured success in using these abilities to perform certain tasks.

2. news; tidings; information.

3. the gathering of secret information, as for military or police purposes.

4. the persons or agency employed at this; secret service.

5. intelligence personified; an intelligent spirit or being.

6. familiar terms of acquaintance; intercourse. [Obs.]

He lived rather in a fair *intelligence* than any friendship with the favorites.
—Clarendon.

intelligence department (or *bureau*); a division of a government gathering information for the use of a country's navy and army in military operations, or for the guidance of a state department or foreign office in its formation of foreign policy.

intelligence office; (a) an intelligence department; (b) [Obs.] an employment office or agency for domestic help.

intelligence quotient; a number indicating level of intelligence, obtained by multiplying the mental age by 100 and dividing by the chronological age: abbreviated *IQ*, *I. Q.*

intelligence test; a standardized series of problems progressively graded in difficulty, intended to test an individual's intelligence.

in·tel′li·ġen·cẽr, *n.* 1. one who sends or conveys intelligence; one who gives notice of private or distant transactions; especially, a spy or secret agent.

2. formerly, a newsletter or newspaper.

in·tel′li·ġent, *a.* [L. *intelligens* (*-entis*), ppr. of *intellegere*, to perceive, understand; *inter*, between, and *legere*, to gather, choose.]

1. knowing; understanding; well informed; sensible; having intelligence; skilled.

2. having or showing a high intelligence; quick to learn.

3. having knowledge, understanding, or or awareness (*of* something).

4. giving information. [Obs.]

in·tel·li·ġen′tiăl (-shăl), *a.* 1. of, like, or having to do with intelligence or intellect.

2. conveying intelligence or information; as, *intelligential* channels.

in·tel·li·ġen′ti·ā·ry (-shi-), *n.* an intelligencer. [Obs.]

in·tel′li·ġent·ly, *adv.* in an intelligent manner.

in·tel·li·ġent′si·ȧ, *n.* collectively, the people regarded as, or regarding themselves as, the intellectual or learned class.

in·tel″li·ġi·bil′i·ty, *n.* 1. the quality or state of being intelligible; capability of being understood.

2. *pl.* **in·tel″li·ġi·bil′i·ties,** something intelligible.

in·tel′li·ġi·ble, *a.* [L. *intelligibilis*, *intellegibilis*, from *intellegere*, to perceive, understand.]

1. that may be understood or comprehended; clear; comprehensible; as, an *intelligible* account.

2. in philosophy, understandable by the intellect only; conceptual.

in·tel′li·ġi·ble·ness, *n.* intelligibility.

in·tel′li·ġi·bly, *adv.* in a manner to be understood; clearly; plainly; as, to write or speak *intelligibly.*

in·tem′ẽr·āte, in·tem′ẽr·ā·ted, *a.* [L. *intemeratus*, undefiled.] pure; undefiled; unpolluted.

in·tem′ẽr·āte·ness, *n.* the state of being unpolluted.

in·tem′pẽr·ȧ·ment, *n.* a distempered condition; as, the *intemperament* of an ulcerated part. [Obs.]

in·tem′pẽr·ănce, *n.* [L. *intemperantia*, from *intemperans* (*-antis*), without self-restraint, extravagant, intemperate.]

1. lack of moderation or restraint; excess in any kind of action or indulgence; as, *intemperance* in study or in labor, in eating or drinking, or in any other gratification.

2. excessive indulgence in alcoholic liquors.

Should a foreign army land on our shores, to levy such a tax upon us as *intemperance* levies, no mortal power could resist the swelling tide of indignation that would overwhelm it.
—L. Beecher.

in·tem′pẽr·ăn·cy, *n.* intemperance. [Obs.]

in·tem′pẽr·ănt, *a.* intemperate. [Obs.]

in·tem′pẽr·ănt, *n.* a drunkard. [Obs.]

in·tem′pẽr·āte, *a.* [L. *intemperatus*; *in-* priv., and *temperatus*, tempered, moderate, pp. of *temperare*, to combine in due proportion, qualify, from *tempus*, a portion or period of time.]

1. not temperate; specifically, (a) not moderate; excessive; going to extremes; (b) severe or violent; inclement; as, an *intemperate* wind.

2. addicted to an excessive use of alcoholic liquors.

in·tem′pẽr·āte, *v.t.* to disorder. [Obs.]

in·tem′pẽr·āte·ly, *adv.* with excessive indulgence of appetite or passion; immoderately; excessively.

in·tem′pẽr·āte·ness, *n.* 1. lack of moderation; excessive indulgence; as, the *intemperateness* of appetite or passion.

2. immoderate degree of any quality in the weather, as in cold, heat, or storms.

in·tem′pẽr·ȧ·tūre, *n.* excess. [Obs.]

in·tem·pes′tive, *a.* [L. *intempestivus*; *in-* priv., and *tempestivus*, timely, seasonable.] untimely. [Obs.]

in·tem·pes′tive·ly, *adv.* unseasonably. [Obs.]

in·tem·pes·tiv′i·ty, *n.* untimeliness. [Obs.]

in·ten′ȧ·ble, *a.* that cannot be held or maintained; that is not defensible; as, an *intenable* opinion; an *intenable* fortress. [Obs.]

in·tend′, *v.t.*; intended, *pt.*, *pp.*; intending, *ppr.* [L. *intendere*, to stretch out, aim at; *in*, in, at, and *tendere*, to stretch.]

1. to have in mind as something to be accomplished; to be intent upon; to mean; to purpose; to contemplate: often followed by an infinitive or a clause introduced by *that*; as, I *intend* to go; they *intend that* she shall remain.

2. to mean (something) to be or be used for; to design; destine; as, the cake was *intended* for the party.

3. to mean or take to mean; to signify.

4. in law, to construe or interpret legally.

5. to stretch; to strain; to extend; to distend. [Obs].

6. to regard; to fix the mind on; to attend; to take care of. [Obs.]

7. to feign; to pretend. [Obs.]

8. to bend; to direct; as, they *intend* their thoughts homeward. [Archaic.]

9. to make intense; to intensify. [Obs.]

Syn.—contemplate, design, plan, purpose.

in·tend′, *v.i.* to have a purpose or intention.

in·tend′ănce, *n.* [Fr., from *intendant.*]

1. superintendence; supervision.
2. intendancy.
3. an administrative department, as in France.
4. an intendant's official quarters.

in·tend′ăn·cy, *n.*; *pl.* **in·tend′ăn·cieș,** 1. the position or duties of an intendant.

2. intendants collectively.

3. in South America, the district supervised by an intendant.

in·tend′ănt, *n.* [Fr., from L. *intendens* (*-entis*), ppr. of *intendere*, to stretch out, aim at, exert oneself, intend.] one who has the charge, oversight, direction, or management of some public business; a superintendent: used as a title of public officers in some countries, as the supervisors of any of certain districts in South America.

in·tend′ed, *a.* 1. designed; purposed; planned; intentional; as, the insult was *intended.*

2. prospective; future; as, an *intended* wife.

3. stretched; made intense. [Obs.]

in·tend′ed, *n.* the person to whom one is engaged to be married: with a possessive pronoun; as, she is my *intended.* [Colloq.]

in·tend′ed·ly, *adv.* with purpose or intention; by design; intentionally. [Rare.]

in·tend′ẽr, *n.* one who intends.

in·tend′i·ment, *n.* attention; understanding. [Obs.]

in·tend′ment, *n.* [OFr. *entendement*; LL. *intendimentum*, attention, purpose, understanding, from L. *intendere*, to intend.]

1. intention; design; purpose. [Archaic.]

2. in law, the meaning (of a word, etc.) as used in law; legal meaning.

3. intelligence; understanding. [Obs.]

in·ten′ẽr·āte, *v.t.* [L. *in*, in, and *tener*, soft, tender.] to make tender; to soften. [Rare.]

in·ten′ẽr·āte, *a.* made tender; tender; soft; intenerated. [Rare.]

in·ten·ẽr·ā′tion, *n.* the act of intenerating or making soft or tender. [Rare.]

in·ten′sāte, *v.t.* to make intense or more intense. [Rare.]

in·ten·sā′tion, *n.* the act of intensating. [Rare.]

in·ten′sȧ·tive, *a.* intensifying. [Rare.]

in·tense′, *a.* [L. *intensus*, pp. of *intendere*, to stretch, intend.]

1. occurring or existing in a high degree; very strong; violent, excessive, or vivid; as, an *intense* light.

2. strained to the utmost; strenuous; earnest; fervent; zealous; as, *intense* thought.

3. having or showing strong emotion, firm purpose, great seriousness, etc.; as, an *intense* person.

4. characterized by much action, emotion, etc.

5. in photography, dense or opaque.

in·tense′ly, *adv.* 1. to an extreme degree; extremely; as, weather *intensely* cold.

2. in an intense manner; with strong feeling; earnestly.

in·tense′ness, *n.* the state of being intense; intensity.

in·ten″si·fi·cā′tion, *n.* the act of intensifying or the state of being intensified.

in·ten′si·fī·ẽr, *n.* 1. one who or that which intensifies.

2. in photography, any solution used to increase the printing density of a negative.

3. in physics, an apparatus for intensifying the pressure upon a mass of confined fluid.

in·ten′si·fȳ, *v.t.*; intensified, *pt.*, *pp.*; intensifying, *ppr.* [L. *intensus*, intense, and *-ficare*, from *facere*, to make.]

1. to make intense or more intense; to increase; to strengthen.

2. in photography, to make (a film, etc.) dense or opaque by treating with an intensifier.

in·ten′si·fȳ, *v.i.* to become intense or more intense; to act with increased vigor or force.

in·ten′sion, *n.* [L. *intensio* (*-onis*), from *intensus*, pp. of *intendere*, to stretch out, intend.]

1. a straining, stretching, or bending; also, the state of being strained; as, the *intension* of a musical string. [Rare.]

2. intentness; determination.

3. intensification.

4. the quality of being intense; intensity; extreme degree.

5. in logic, all the qualities or properties which a term or concept signifies; connotation: opposed to *extension.*

in·ten′si·ty, *n.*; *pl.* **in·ten′si·tieș,** 1. the quality of being intense; specifically, (a) extreme degree of anything; (b) great energy or vehemence of emotion, thought, or activity.

2. in photography, the density or opaqueness of an image.

3. in physics, the amount of force or energy of heat, light, sound, electric current, etc. per unit area, volume, charge, etc.

4. in psychology, the relative strength of a stimulus or sensation.

Syn.—tension, force, strain, concentration, attention, eagerness, ardor, energy.

in·ten′sive, *a.* [Fr. *intensif*, from L. *intensus*; see *intend.*]

1. increasing or causing to increase in degree or amount.

2. of or characterized by intensity; thorough, profound, and intense; not broad or extensive; concentrated or exhaustive.

3. of or characterized by logical intension.

4. in agriculture, designating a system of farming which aims at the increase of crop yield per unit area.

5. in grammar, giving force or emphasis; emphasizing; as, *oneself* is frequently *intensive.*

in·ten′sive, *n.* 1. that which intensifies.

2. in grammar, an intensive word, prefix, etc.

in·ten′sive·ly, *adv.* by increase of degree; in a manner to give force.

in·ten′sive·ness, *n.* the condition or quality of being intensive.

in·tent′, *a.* [L. *intensus*, pp. of *intendere*, to stretch, intend.]

1. firmly directed or fixed; earnest; intense; as, an *intent* look.

2. (a) having the mind or attention firmly directed or fixed; engrossed; as, he was *intent* on his studies; (b) strongly resolved; as, he was *intent* on going.

in·tent′, *n.* 1. an intending.

2. something intended; specifically, (a) a purpose; object; (b) [Obs.] meaning.

to all intents and purposes; in almost every respect; practically; virtually.

in·ten·tā′tion, *n.* a threatening. [Obs.]

in·ten′tion, *n.* [L. *intentio* (*-onis*), a stretching out, exertion, purpose, from *intendere*, to stretch out, intend.]

1. a stretching or bending of the mind, as toward an object; hence, fixedness of attention; intentness; earnestness. [Archaic.]

> *Intention* is manifest when the mind, with great earnestness, and of choice, fixes its view on any idea, considers it on every side, and will not be called off by the ordinary solicitation of other ideas. —Locke.

2. the fixed direction of the mind to a particular object; a determination to do a specified thing or to act in a particular manner; as, it is my *intention* to proceed to Paris.

3. (a) anything intended; ultimate end or purpose; as, what is your *intention?* (b) [*pl.*] purpose in regard to marriage.

4. meaning or intent. [Archaic or Rare.]

5. in logic, the general concept of a thing.

6. in surgery, the manner or process by which a wound heals: the three degrees (*first, second,* and *third intention*) are distinguished by the relative amounts and types of granulation that occur.

7. the state of being strained. [Obs.]

first intention; in logic, a first or general concept, as of an object as a whole.

second intention; in logic, a conception gained by generalizing from the first conception.

in·ten′tion·ăl, *a.* 1. having to do with intention or purpose. [Rare.]

2. intended; designed; done with design or purpose; as, the act was *intentional*, not accidental.

Syn.—purposed, designed, deliberate, intended, contemplated, premeditated, studied.

in·ten·tion·al′i·ty, *n.* the quality of being intentional; aim; design.

in·ten′tion·ăl·ly, *adv.* by design; purposely; not casually.

in·ten′tioned (-shund), *a.* having (specified) plans or intentions; as, a generously *intentioned* person: used often in hyphenated compounds, as ill-*intentioned.*

in·ten′tive, *a.* attentive; having the mind closely applied. [Obs.]

in·ten′tive·ly, *adv.* closely; with close application. [Obs.]

in·ten′tive·ness, *n.* closeness of attention or application of mind. [Obs.]

in·tent′ly, *adv.* in an intent manner; with close attention or application; with eagerness or earnestness; as, to have the eyes *intently* fixed.

in·tent′ness, *n.* the state of being intent; close application.

in′tẽr-, [ME. *enter-*, *inter-*; OFr. *entre-*, *inter-*; L. *inter-*, from *inter*, prep. between, among, during; *in*, in, within, and *-ter*, a comp. suffix.]

1. a prefix meaning *between, among,* as in *inter*flow, *inter*change.

2. a prefix meaning *with* or *on each other* (or *one another*), *together, mutual, reciprocal, mutually, reciprocally,* as in *inter*act.

in·tẽr′, *v.t.*; interred, *pt., pp.*; interring, *ppr.* [OFr. *enterrer*; LL. *interrare*, to put in the earth; L. *in*, in, and *terra*, earth.] to place in the earth or in a tomb, as a dead body; to bury.

in·tẽr·act′, *v.i.* to act mutually; to perform reciprocal acts.

in·tẽr·act′, *n.* 1. intermediate employment or time.

2. an entr'acte.

in·tẽr·ac′tion, *n.* 1. intermediate action.

2. action on each other; reciprocal action or effect.

in·tẽr·ac′tive, *a.* interacting.

in·tẽr·ad′di·tive, *n.* something interpolated, as a word or phrase in a sentence. [Rare.]

in·tẽr·ā′ġen·cy, *n.* an intervening or intermediate agency.

in·tẽr·ā′ġent, *n.* an intermediate agent.

in′tẽr ā′li·ȧ, [L.] among other things.

in′tẽr ā′li·ōs, [L.] among other persons.

in′tẽr·ạll, *n.* an entrail. [Obs.]

in″tẽr·al·vē′ō·lăr, *a.* [L. *inter*, between, and *alveolus*, a small cavity or hollow.]

1. in anatomy, lying between cells or cavities, especially of the lungs.

2. in zoology, between the alveoli; as, the *interalveolar* muscles of a sea urchin.

in·tẽr·am·bū·lā′crăl, *a.* relating to the interambulacra.

in·tẽr·am·bū·lā′crum, *n.*; *pl.* **in·tẽr·am·bū·lā′crȧ,** [*inter-*, and L. *ambulacrum*, an alley or covered way.] in zoology, a zone between two ambulacra in echinoderms.

in″tẽr-Ȧ·mer′i·căn, *a.* between or among nations of North, South, and Central America.

in·tẽr·am′ni·ăn, *a.* [LL. *interamnus*; *inter*, between, and *amnis*, river.] situated between rivers.

in·tẽr·an′i·māte, *v.t.* to animate mutually. [Obs.]

in·tẽr·är·bō·rā′tion, *n.* the interlacing or mingling of the branches of trees. [Obs.]

in″tẽr·är·tiç′ū·lăr, *a.* in anatomy, being between the joints, or articulating parts of bones.

in″tẽr·ȧ·tom′iç, *a.* in physics and chemistry, acting between atoms.

in·tẽr·ạu′liç, *a.* [L. *inter*, between, and *aula*, a hall.] existing or carried on between sovereigns or courts. [Rare.]

in″tẽr ạu·riç′ū·lăr, *a.* in anatomy, situated between the auricles.

in·tẽr·ax′ăl, *a.* relating to an interaxis.

in·tẽr·ax′il·lā·ry, *a.* in botany, between the axils of leaves.

in·tẽr·ax′is, *n.*; *pl.* **in·tẽr·ax′ēs,** [L. *inter*, between, and *axis*, axis.] in architecture, the space between axes.

in″tẽr·bas·tā′tion, *n.* quilting. [Obs.]

in·tẽr·bed′ded, *a.* in geology, interstratified; interleaved.

in′tẽr·bŏr·ough (-ō), *a.* between or among boroughs.

in·tẽr·brā′chi·ăl, *a.* [L. *inter*, between, and *bracchium*, or *brachium*, arm.] in zoology, situated between brachia, as in the starfish.

in′tẽr·brāin, *n.* in anatomy, the diencephalon.

in·tẽr·brañ′chi·ăl, *a.* in zoology, situated between the branchiae or gills, as in fishes.

in·tẽr·breed′, *v.t.* to cross different varieties of (animals or plants) in breeding.

in·tẽr·breed′, *v.i.* to breed with each other: said of different varieties of animals or plants.

in·tẽr′cȧ·lăr, *a.* intercalary. [Obs.]

in·tẽr′cȧ·lăr·y, *a.* [L. *intercalarius*, *intercalaris*, that is inserted, from *intercalare*, to intercalate.]

1. added to the calendar: said of a day, month, etc. added as in leap year to make the calendar correspond to the solar year.

2. having such a day, month, etc. added: said of a year.

3. interpolated; added or inserted; introduced; as, *intercalary* lines.

in·tẽr′cȧ·lāte, *v.t.*; intercalated, *pt., pp.*; intercalating, *ppr.* [L. *intercalatus*, pp. of *intercalare*, to insert; *inter*, between, and *calare*, to call, proclaim.]

1. to add (a day, month, etc.) to the calendar.

2. to interpolate or insert.

3. in geology, to insert, as a layer of rock between two other layers.

in·tẽr·çȧ·lā′tion, *n.* 1. an intercalating; interpolation.

2. something intercalated.

in″tẽr·çȧ·rot′iç, in″tẽr·çȧ·rot′id, *a.* in anatomy, between the outer and inner carotid arteries.

in·tẽr·çär′păl, *a.* in anatomy, situated between the bones of the wrist.

in·tẽr·çav′ẽrn·ous, *a.* in anatomy, relating to or connected with the cavernous sinuses of the brain.

in·tẽr·cēde′, *v.i.*; interceded, *pt., pp.*; interceding, *ppr.* [L. *intercedere*, to go or come between, interpose; *inter*, between, and *cedere*, to go.]

1. to pass between; to intervene. [Obs.]

> He supposes that a vast period *interceded* between that origination and the age in which he lived. —Hale.

2. to mediate; to interpose; to intervene between contending parties with a view to reconciling them.

3. to plead or make a request in favor of another or others.

4. in ancient Rome, to interpose a veto: said of a tribune or other magistrate.

Syn.—interpose, mediate, interfere, intermeddle.

in·tẽr·cēd′ence, *n.* the act of mediating, interposing, or interceding. [Rare.]

in·tẽr·cēd′ent, *a.* [L. *intercedens* (*-entis*), ppr. of *intercedere*, to go or come between.] passing between; mediating; pleading for. [Rare.]

in·tẽr·cēd′ent·ly, *adv.* in an intercedent manner. [Rare.]

in·tẽr·cēd′ẽr, *n.* one who intercedes or interposes between parties to effect a reconciliation; a mediator; an intercessor.

in·tẽr·cel′lū·lăr, *a.* lying between or among cells.

a a. INTERCELLULAR SPACES

in·tẽr·cen′trăl, *a.* 1. between or connecting centers.

2. pertaining to an intercentrum.

intercentral nerves; in physiology, nerves that convey impulses from nerve center to nerve center, as distinguished from nerves that transmit impulses between surface points and nerve centers.

in·tẽr·cen′trum, *n.*; *pl.* **in·tẽr·cen′trȧ,** [L. *inter*, between, and *centrum*, center.] in anatomy, a centrum intervening between vertebrae, as in the spine of a fossil batrachian.

in′tẽr·cept, *n.* in geometry, the part of a line, plane, etc. intercepted.

in·tẽr·cept′, *v.t.*; intercepted, *pt., pp.*; intercepting, *ppr.* [L. *interceptus*, pp. of *intercipere*, to take between, interrupt; *inter*, between, and *capere*, to take.]

1. to seize or stop on the way, before arrival at the intended place; to stop or interrupt the course of; to cut off.

2. to stop, hinder, or prevent; as, he *intercepted* the escape of the thief.

3. to cut off communication with, sight of, etc.

4. in mathematics, to cut off, mark off, or bound between two points, lines, or planes.

in·tẽr·cept′ẽr, *n.* one who or that which intercepts; an interceptor.

in·tẽr·cep′tion, *n.* the act of intercepting or the fact of being intercepted.

in·tẽr·cep′tive, *a.* intercepting or tending to intercept.

in·tẽr·cep′tŏr, *n.* a person or thing that intercepts; especially, a fast-climbing military airplane used in fighting off surprise attacks.

in·tẽr·ces′sion (-sesh′un), *n.* [L. *intercessio*, from *intercedere*, to come or go between, intercede.] the act of interceding; mediation between conflicting parties with a view to reconciliation; prayer or pleading in behalf of another or others, or sometimes against another.

> Your *intercession* now is needless grown;
> Retire, and let me speak with her alone.
> —Dryden.

in·tẽr·ces′sion·ăl, *a.* containing, characterized by, or pertaining to intercession or entreaty.

in·tẽr·ces′sion·āte, *v.t.* to implore. [Obs.]

in·tẽr·ces′sŏr, *n.* 1. a mediator; one who intercedes; one who pleads in behalf of another.

2. a bishop who, during a vacancy of the see, administers the bishopric till a successor is elected.

in″tẽr·ces·sō′ri·ăl, *a.* pertaining to an intercessor.

in·tẽr·ces′sō·ry, *a.* of or serving as intercession; interceding.

in·tẽr·chāin′, *v.t.*; interchained, *pt.*, *pp.*; interchaining, *ppr.* to chain; to link together. [Obs.]

in′tẽr·chānġe, *n.* 1. an interchanging; mutual giving in exchange; barter; as, the *interchange* of commodities between New York and Havana.

2. alternate succession; as, the *interchange* of light and darkness.

3. any of the places on a freeway where traffic can enter or depart, usually by means of a cloverleaf.

in·tẽr·chānġe′, *v.t.*; interchanged, *pt.*, *pp.*; interchanging, *ppr.* [ME. *enterchangen*; OFr. *entrechangier*; *entre-*, between, and *changier*, *changer*, to change.]

1. to give and take mutually; to exchange; as, they *interchanged* presents.

2. to change by putting each of two things in the place of the other; as, to *interchange* places.

3. to cause alternation or a following in succession; as, he *interchanged* work with play.

in·tẽr·chānġe′, *v.i.* to make an interchange; to change in a reciprocal manner.

in·tẽr·chānġe·ȧ·bil′i·ty, *n.* the quality or state of being interchangeable.

in·tẽr·chānġe′ȧ·ble, *a.* 1. that can be interchanged; that can be given and taken mutually; especially, that can be put or used in place of each other.

2. following each other in alternate succession; as, the four *interchangeable* seasons.

in·tẽr·chānġe′ȧ·ble·ness, *n.* interchangeability.

in·tẽr·chānġe′ȧ·bly, *adv.* so as to be interchangeable; alternately; by reciprocation.

in·tẽr·chānġe′ment, *n.* exchange; mutual transfer. [Obs.]

in·tẽr·chap′tẽr, *n.* an interpolated chapter.

in·tẽr′ci·dence, *n.* a happening in between. [Obs.]

in·tẽr′ci·dent, *a.* [L. *intercidens* (*-entis*), ppr. of *intercidere*, to fall between; *inter*, between, and *cadere*, to fall.] falling or coming between. [Obs.]

in·tẽr·cip′i·ent, *a.* [L. *intercipiens* (*-entis*), *ppr.* of *intercipere*, to take between, intercept.] intercepting; seizing by the way; stopping. [Obs.]

in·tẽr·cip′i·ent, *n.* one who or that which intercepts or stops. [Obs.]

in·tẽr·ci′ṣion (-sizh′un), *n.* [LL. *intercisio* (*-onis*), a cutting through; L. *inter*, between, and *cædere*, to cut.] interruption by cutting off. [Obs.]

in·tẽr·cit′i·zen·ship, *n.* the right secured to the citizens of different states to enjoy mutual civic rights and privileges.

in′tẽr·ċlȧss′, *a.* between or among classes; as, *interclass* debates.

in·tẽr·ċlav′i·ċle, *n.* in anatomy and zoology, a membrane bone lying between and sometimes uniting the clavicles of certain animals, as the frog, the turtle, and the duckbill.

in″tẽr·ċlȧ·viç′ū·lăr, *a.* in zoology, situated between the clavicles; relating to the interclavicle.

in·tẽr·ċlōṣe′, *v.t.* to shut in; to surround. [Obs.]

in·tẽr·ċloud′, *v.t.* to surround with clouds; to obscure. [Rare.]

in·tẽr·ċlūde′, *v.t.* [L. *intercludere*; *inter*, between, and *claudere*, to shut, close.] to shut from a place or course by something intervening; to intercept; to cut off; to interrupt. [Obs.]

in·tẽr·ċlū′ṣion, *n.* [L. *interclusio* (*-onis*), from *intercludere*, to shut off, shut in.] an obstruction by shutting off. [Obs.]

in″tẽr·ċŏl·lē′ġi·āte, *a.* between or among colleges and universities; as, an *intercollegiate* oratorical contest; *intercollegiate* football.

in·tẽr·ċol′line, *a.* [L. *inter*, between, and *collis*, a hill.] between hills, especially between the hills formed by the erupted matter of volcanoes. [Rare.]

in″tẽr·ċō·lō′ni·ăl, *a.* between or among colonies; having to do with the mutual relations of colonies; as, *intercolonial* commerce.

in″tẽr·ċō·lō′ni·ăl·ly, *adv.* as between colonies.

in·tẽr·ċō·lum′năr, *a.* between columns; as, an *intercolumnar* statue.

in″tẽr·ċō·lum·ni·ā′tion, *n.* [L. *intercolumnium*; *inter*, between, and *columna*, a column.]

1. the space between two columns, measured from their axes.

2. in architecture, the art or method of placing columns with reference to their spacing. Vitruvius enumerates five varieties of intercolumniation, and assigns to them definite proportions expressed in measures of the inferior diameter of the column; as the pycnostyle, of one diameter and a half; the systyle, of two diameters; the diastyle, of three diameters; the areostyle, of four or sometimes five diameters; and the eustyle, of two and a quarter diameters.

in′tẽr·ċom, *n.* an intercommunication system, as between the pilot and the bombardier in an airplane. [Slang.]

in·tẽr·ċom′bat, *n.* a fight. [Obs.]

in·tẽr·ċŏm′ing, *a.* coming between. [Obs.]

in·tẽr·ċom′mŏn, *v.i.* 1. to have mutual dealings; to associate. [Obs.]

2. in English law, to graze cattle in a common pasture; to use a common with others, or to possess or enjoy the right of feeding in common.

> Common because of vicinage is where the inhabitants of two townships contiguous to each other have usually *intercommoned* with one another. —Blackstone.

in·tẽr·ċom′mŏn·āġe, *n.* mutual commonage.

in·tẽr·ċom′mŏn·ẽr, *n.* one privileged to intercommon.

in″tẽr·ċŏm·mūne′, *v.i.* to hold mutual communication. [Obs.]

in″tẽr·ċŏm·mū′ni·ċȧ·ble, *a.* that may be mutually communicated.

in″tẽr·ċŏm·mū′ni·ċāte, *v.t.* and *v.i.*; intercommunicated, *pt.*, *pp.*; intercommunicating, *ppr.* to communicate mutually; to hold mutual communication.

in″tẽr·ċŏm·mū·ni·ċā′tion, *n.* reciprocal communication.

in″tẽr·ċŏm·mūn′iŏn, *n.* mutual communion, as among religious groups.

in″tẽr·ċŏm·mū′ni·ty, *n.* the quality of being common to two or more; a sharing of something in common.

in″tẽr·ċŏm·par′i·sŏn, *n.* mutual or common comparison.

in·tẽr·ċon′dy·lăr, *a.* intercondyloid.

in·tẽr·ċon′dy·loid, *a.* in anatomy, lying between condyles.

in″tẽr·ċŏn·neçt′, *v.t.* and *v.i.* to connect or be connected with each other or one another.

in″tẽr·ċŏn·neç′tion, *n.* mutual union.

in·tẽr·ċon·ti·nen′tăl, *a.* between or among continents.

in″tẽr·ċŏn·vẽrt′i·ble, *a.* mutually exchangeable.

in·tẽr·ċos′tăl, *a.* [L. *inter*, between, and *costa*, a rib.] placed or lying between the ribs; as, an *intercostal* muscle, artery, or vein.

in′tẽr·ċōurse, *n.* [ME. *entercourse*; OFr. *entrecors*, *intercours*; L. *intercursus*, a running between, intervention, from *intercurrere*, to run between; *inter*, between, and *currere*, to run.]

1. connection by reciprocal action or dealings, as between persons or nations; interchange of thought, feeling, products, services, etc.; communication; commerce; association; communion; as, to have much *intercourse* together.

2. the sexual joining of two individuals; coitus; copulation: usually *sexual intercourse*.

Syn.—correspondence, dealing, intercommunication, intimacy, connection, commerce.

in·tẽr·ċrop′, *v.t.* and *v.i.*; intercropped, *pt.*, *pp.*; intercropping, *ppr.* [*inter-* and *crop*.] to cultivate (land) by planting different crops in alternate rows.

in′tẽr·ċrop, *n.* any of the crops grown in intercropping.

in·tẽr·ċross′, *v.i.* and *v.t.*; intercrossed (-krost), *pt.*, *pp.*; intercrossing, *ppr.* 1. to cross (one another).

2. to interbreed.

in′tẽr·ċross, *n.* 1. an interbreeding.

2. the hybrid resulting from this.

in·tẽr·ċrū′răl, *a.* lying between the crura.

in·tẽr·ċul′tūr·ăl, *a.* 1. between or among different cultures or ethnic groups.

2. in agriculture, (a) designating the cultivation of one crop between the rows of another; (b) relating to cultivation by stirring the soil lying between individual plants, as in the cultivation of corn with a hoe or with a cultivator.

in·tẽr·ċũr′, *v.i.* to intervene; to come in the meantime. [Obs.]

in·tẽr·ċur′rence, *n.* an intervening occurrence.

in·tẽr·ċur′rent, *a.* [L. *intercurrens* (*-entis*), ppr. of *intercurrere*, to run between; *inter*, between, and *currere*, to run.]

1. running between; intervening.

2. in medicine, designating a disease which starts up during the course of another disease and modifies it.

in·tẽr·ċur′rent, *n.* something happening between; an intervention. [Obs.]

in·tẽr·ċū·tā′nē·ous, *a.* being within or under the skin.

in′tẽr·dēal, *n.* mutual dealing; traffic. [Obs.]

in″tẽr·dē·nom·i·nā′tion·ăl, *a.* between, among, shared by, or involving different religious denominations.

in·tẽr·den′tăl, *a.* 1. between the teeth, as of an animal or a toothed wheel.

2. pronounced with the tip of the tongue between the teeth, as certain consonants.

in·tẽr·den′til, *n.* in architecture, the space between two dentils.

in″tẽr·dē·pärt·men′tăl, *a.* between or among departments.

in″tẽr·dē·pend′ence, *n.* mutual dependence.

in″tẽr·dē·pend′en·cy, *n.* mutual dependence.

in″tẽr·dē·pend′ent, *a.* mutually dependent.

in·tẽr·diçt′, *v.t.*; interdicted, *pt.*, *pp.*; interdicting, *ppr.* [L. *interdictus*, pp. of *interdicere*, to speak between, to forbid, prohibit; *inter*, between, and *dicere*, to speak, say.]

1. to forbid; to prohibit with authority; as, our intercourse with foreign nations was *interdicted*.

2. to restrain from doing or using something.

3. in the Roman Catholic Church, to exclude (a person, parish, etc.) from certain church offices, sacraments, or privileges.

in′tẽr·diçt, *n.* [L. *interdictum*, a prohibition.]

1. prohibition; a prohibiting order or decree.

2. in the Roman Catholic Church, an interdicting of a person, parish, etc.

3. in Scots law, an injunction.

in·tẽr·diç′tion, *n.* 1. the act of interdicting or the state of being interdicted.

2. a judicial order of a restraining nature placed on a person of unsound mind in order to preserve his legal rights.

in·tẽr·diç′tive, *a.* same as *interdictory*.

in·tẽr·diç′tō·ry, *a.* serving to prohibit.

in·tẽr·diġ′i·tăl, *a.* between the digits, as the web or membrane between the toes.

in·tẽr·diġ′i·tāte, *v.t.* and *v.i.* to interlock; to interweave.

in·tẽr·diġ·i·tā′tion, *n.* the condition of being interdigitated or the process of interdigitating.

in′tẽr·dōme, *n.* a space between two shells of a domelike structure.

in·tẽr·ē·pim′ẽr·ăl, *a.* situated between epimera.

in′tẽr·ess, *v.t.* and *n.* interest. [Obs.]

in′tẽr·est, *n.* [ME. *interest*; OFr. *interest*, interest, concern, prejudice, from L. *interest*, it concerns, it is to the advantage, 3rd pers. sing. of *interesse*, to be between.]

1. a right or claim to something.

2. a share or participation in something.

3. anything in which one participates or has a share.

4. [*often pl.*] profit; welfare; benefit.

5. a group of people having a common concern in some industry, occupation, cause, etc.; as, the steel *interest*.

6. social or political influence.

7. (a) a feeling of intentness, concern, or curiosity about something; (b) the power of causing this feeling; (c) something causing this feeling.

8. importance; consequence; as, a matter of little *interest*.

9. (a) money paid for the use of money; (b) the rate of such payment, expressed as a percentage per unit of time.

10. an increase or addition over what is owed; as, he repaid her kindness with *interest*.

in′tẽr·est, *v.t.* 1. to involve the interest, or concern, of; to have an effect upon.

2. to cause to have an interest, or share, in; as, can I *interest* you in joining our club?

3. to excite the attention or curiosity of.

in′tẽr·est·ed, *a.* 1. having an interest or share; concerned.

2. influenced by personal interest; biased or prejudiced.

3. feeling or showing interest, or curiosity.

in′tẽr·est·ed·ly, *adv.* in an interested manner.

in′tẽr·est·ed·ness, *n.* the condition of being interested.

in′tẽr·est·ing, *a.* engaging the attention or curiosity; of interest; as, an *interesting* story.

in′tẽr·est·ing·ly, *adv.* in an interesting manner.

in′tẽr·est·ing·ness, *n.* the quality of being interesting.

in′tẽr·fāce, *n.* 1. a surface that lies between two parts of matter or space and forms their common boundary.
2. a point or means of interaction between two systems, disciplines, groups, etc.

in′tẽr·fāce, *v.t.* and *v.i.;* interfaced, *pt. pp.;* interfacing, *ppr.* 1. to sew material between the outer fabric and the facing of (a collar, lapel, etc.) so as to give body or prevent stretching.
2. to interact with another system, discipline, group, etc.

in·tẽr·fā′ciăl (-shăl), *a.* included between two faces of a crystal or crystal form; as, an *interfacial* angle is formed by the meeting of two planes.

in″tẽr·fas·ciç′ū·lăr, *a.* in anatomy and botany, located between fascicles.

in·tẽr·fem′ō·răl, *a.* in anatomy, between the femora; as, the *interfemoral* membrane of a bat.

in·tẽr·fen·es·trā′tion, *n.* in architecture, the process or art of arranging windows with special regard to the spaces between them.

in·tẽr·fēr′ănt, *n.* one of the parties in a suit for interference in the Patent Office of the United States.

in·tẽr·fēre′, *v.i.*; interfered, *pt., pp.*; interfering, *ppr.* [ME. *enterferen*; OFr. *entreferir*, to exchange blows; L. *inter*, between, among, and *ferire*, to strike.]
1. to come in or between for some purpose; to intervene.
2. to intermeddle; to enter without invitation or right into the concerns of others.
3. to clash; to come in collision; to be in opposition; as, the claims of two nations may *interfere*.
4. in farriery, to strike the hoof or shoe of one hoof against the fetlock of the opposite leg.
5. in physics, to act reciprocally upon each other so as to modify the effect of each by augmenting, diminishing, or nullifying it: said of waves of light, heat, sound, etc.
6. in patent law, to claim priority for an invention, as when several applications for its patent are pending.
7. in football, to act defensively in guarding the player who has the ball; also, to hinder illegally the player who is about to catch a pass.
8. in radio, to create interference in reception.

in·tẽr·fēr′ence, *n.* 1. an interfering.
2. in physics, the mutual action of waves of any kind, as of water, sound, heat, or light, upon each other, by which the vibrations and their effects are reinforced or neutralized.
3. in football, (a) the act of the players who obstruct opposing tacklers in order to clear the way for the ball carrier; (b) the act of unlawfully obstructing a player catching a pass.
4. in psychology, a blocking, usually temporary, of the memory, during which more or less familiar things cannot be recalled; temporary forgetfulness.
5. in radio, the distortion of the sounds reproduced by a radio receiver due to static, unwanted signals, etc.

in″tẽr·fē·ren′tiăl, *a.* in physics, pertaining to results obtained by interference.

in·tẽr·fēr′ẽr, *n.* one who or that which interferes.

in″tẽr·fẽr·om′e·tẽr, *n.* an instrument for measuring wave lengths of light and for analyzing small parts of a spectrum by means of the interference phenomena of light.

in·tẽr·flōw′, *v.i.* to flow in or between. [Rare.]

in·tẽr′flu·ent, in·tẽr′flu·ous, *a.* flowing between or among.

in·tẽr·fōld′, *v.t.* and *v.i.* to fold together or inside each other.

in·tẽr·fōld′ed, *a.* folded or clasped together.
With hands *interfolded.* —Longfellow.

in·tẽr·fō·li·ā′ceous, *a.* [L. *inter*, between and *folium*, a leaf.] in botany, being between opposite leaves, but placed alternately with them; as, *interfoliaceous* flowers or peduncles.

in·tẽr·fō′li·āte, *v.t.* same as *interleave.*

in·tẽr·fūṣe′, *v.t.*; interfused, *pt., pp.*; interfusing, *ppr.* [L. *interfusus*, pp. of *interfundere*, to pour between, among; *inter*, between, among, and *fundere*, to pour.]
1. to combine by mixing, blending, or fusing together.
2. to cause to pass into or through a substance; infuse.
3. to spread itself through; pervade; as, prejudice *interfused* his remarks.

in·tẽr·fūṣe′, *v.i.* to fuse; to blend.

in·tẽr·fū′ṣion, *n.* the act of interfusing or the state of being interfused.

in·tẽr·glā′ciăl (-shăl), *a.* in geology, formed or occurring between two periods of glacial action.

in·tẽr·glob′ū·lăr, *a.* in anatomy, lying between globules, as the minute spaces in certain tissues.

in·tẽr·grā·dā′tion, *n.* an intergrading.

in′tẽr·grāde, *n.* an intermediate form in a graded series.

in·tẽr·grāde′, *v.i.*: intergraded, *pt., pp.*; intergrading, *ppr.* to pass into another form or kind by a series of intermediate grades.

in·tẽr·grāve′, *v.t.*; intergraved, *pt., pp.*; intergraving, *ppr.* to grave or mark between; also, to engrave or carve in every other space.

in·tẽr·hē′măl, in·tẽr·hae′măl, *a.* in anatomy, situated between the hemal processes or spines.

in·tẽr·hē′măl, in·tẽr·hae′măl, *n.* an interhemal bone or spine.

in·tẽr·hȳ′ăl, *a.* relating to the space in the hyoid arch.

in·tẽr·hȳ′ăl, *n.* a bone or cartilage situated within the hyoid arch.

in′tẽr·im, *n.* [L., in the meantime, meanwhile.]
1. an intermediate period; intervening time; as, in the *interim.*
2. [I–] in history, any of the three provisional arrangements of Emperor Charles V of Germany in an attempt to establish a truce or interval of peace between the Protestant and the Roman Catholic parties in the sixteenth century.

in′tẽr·im, *a.* for or during an interim; temporary; provisional; as, an *interim* council.

in·tē′ri·ŏr, *a.* [L. *interior*, inner, comp., from *inter*, between, within.]
1. internal; being within: opposed to *exterior*; as, the *interior* surface of a hollow ball; the *interior* parts of the earth.
Aiming, belike, at your *interior* hatred,
That in your outward action shows itself.
—Shak.
2. inland; at some distance from the coast; as, the *interior* parts of a country.
3. of the internal, or domestic, affairs of a country: opposed to *foreign.*
4. of the inner nature of a person or thing; private, secret, etc.
interior decoration; the art or profession of decorating or furnishing the interiors of rooms, houses, etc.; also, such decorating or furnishing.
interior planets; in astronomy, the planets between the earth's orbit and the sun.

in·tē′ri·ŏr, *n.* 1. the internal part of a thing; the inside.
2. the inside of a room or building.
3. the inner nature of a person or thing.
4. the inland part of a country or region.
5. the internal, or domestic, affairs of a country; as, the United States Department of the *Interior.*
6. [I–] the Department of the Interior.

in·tē′ri·ŏr deç·ō·rā′tion, 1. the decorating and furnishing of the interior of a room, house, etc.
2. the art or business of decorating and furnishing such interiors.

in·tē·ri·or′i·ty, *n.* 1. the condition or state of being interior or inside.
2. inner nature or character.

in·tē′ri·ŏr·ly, *adv.* 1. in, or with respect to, the interior; internally; inwardly; on the inside.
2. in, or with respect to, the inner nature of a person or thing.

in·tẽr·jā′cence, in·tẽr·jā′cen·cy, *n.* a lying or being between; intervention; as, the *interjacency* of the Mississippi between Illinois and Iowa.

in·tẽr·jā′cent, *a.* [L. *interjacens* (-*entis*), ppr. of *interjacere*, to lie between; *inter*, between, and *jacere*, to lie.] lying or being between; intervening; as, *interjacent* islands.

in·tẽr·jaç′ū·lāte, *v.t.* to interject an ejaculation.

in·tẽr·jan′gle, *v.i.*; interjangled, *pt., pp.*; interjangling, *ppr.* to jangle together.

in·tẽr·jeçt′, *v.t.*; interjected, *pt., pp.*; interjecting, *ppr.* [L. *interjectus*, pp. of *interjicere*, *interjacere*, to throw between; *inter*, between, and *jacere*, to throw.] to throw in between; to interrupt with; to insert; as, to *interject* a remark.

in·tẽr·jeçt′, *v.i.* to interpose; to come between. [Obs.]

in·tẽr·jeç′tion, *n.* [L. *interjectio* (-*onis*), a throwing or placing between, interjection, from *interjicere*, to interject.]
1. an interjecting.
2. something interjected; an exclamation.
3. in grammar, an exclamation thrown in without grammatical connection (e.g., *ah! lo! pshaw! good-by!*).

in·tẽr·jeç′tion·ăl, *a.* 1. of, or having the nature of, an interjection.
2. interjected.
3. containing an interjection.

in·tẽr·jeç′tion·ăl·ly, *adv.* in an interjectional manner; as an interjection.

in·tẽr·jeç′tion·ā·ry, *a.* same as *interjectional.*

in·tẽr·jeçt′ŏr, *n.* a person or thing that interjects.

in·tẽr·jeç′tō·ry, *a.* same as *interjectional.*

in·tẽr·join′, *v.t.* to join mutually; to unite. [Obs.]

in′tẽr·joist, *n.* 1. the space or interval between two joists.
2. a heavy middle joist or crossbeam.

in·tẽr·junç′tion, *n.* a mutual joining together. [Rare.]

in·tẽr·knit′ (-nit′), *v.t.* and *v.i.*; interknitted or interknit, *pt., pp.*; interknitting, *ppr.* to knit together; to join closely.

in·tẽr·knōw′ (-nō′), *v.t.* to know mutually. [Obs.]

in·tẽr·knowl′edge (-nol′lej), *n.* mutual knowledge. [Obs.]

in·tẽr·lāce′, *v.t.* and *v.i.*; interlaced (-lāst), *pt., pp.*; interlacing, *ppr.* 1. to unite by intercrossing; to pass over and under each other; to weave together; intertwine.
2. to connect intricately.
interlacing arches; in architecture, arches so joined that they seem to be interwoven.

INTERLACING ARCHES

in·tẽr·lāce′ment, *n.* 1. an interlacing or being interlaced.
2. that which is interlaced in arrangement or structure.

in·tẽr·lam′el·lăr, *a.* in anatomy, placed between lamellae.

in·tẽr·lam′i·nāte, *v.t.*; interlaminated, *pt., pp.*; interlaminating, *ppr.* 1. to put between laminae.
2. to place in alternate laminae.

in·tẽr·lam·i·nā′tion, *n.* the condition of being interlaminated; also, an interlaminated formation.

in′tẽr·lapse, *n.* the lapse of time between two events.

in·tẽr·lärd′, *v.t.*; interlarded, *pt., pp.*; interlarding, *ppr.* 1. to put strips or pieces of fat, bacon, etc. in with (meat to be cooked).
2. to intersperse; to diversify; as, the professor *interlarded* his lecture with quotations.
3. to be intermixed in: said of things.

in·tẽr·lāy′, *v.t.*; interlaid, *pt., pp.*; interlaying, *ppr.* 1. to lay or put between or among.
2. to ornament with something laid or put between.

in′tẽr·lēaf, *n.*; *pl.* **in′tẽr·lēaveṣ,** 1. a leaf, usually blank, bound between the other leaves of a book, for notes, etc.
2. what is written or printed on such a leaf.

in·tẽr·lēave′, *v.t.*; interleaved, *pt., pp.*; interleaving, *ppr.* to insert a leaf in; to insert a blank leaf or leaves in or between, as in a book.

in·tẽr·lēaved′, *a.* 1. inserted between leaves, or having blank leaves inserted between other leaves.
2. in geology, interbedded.

in·tẽr·lī′bel, *v.t.* to libel reciprocally.

in·tẽr·līne′, *v.t.*; interlined, *pt., pp.*; interlining, *ppr.* 1. to write or print between the line of (a text, document, etc.).
2. to insert between the lines; as, he *interlined* notes on the pages.

in′tẽr·līne, *v.t.*; interlined, *pt., pp.*; interlining, *ppr.* to put an inner lining between the outer material and the ordinary lining of (a garment).

in·tẽr·lin′ē·ăl, *a.* 1. interlinear.
2. arranged in alternate lines.

in·tẽr·lin′ē·ăr, *a.* [LL. *interlinearis*; L. *inter*, between, and *linea*, a line.]

1. placed between lines previously written or printed.

2. having the same text in different languages printed in alternate lines; as, an *interlinear* Bible.

in·tẽr·lin′ē·ăr·ly, *adv.* in an interlinear manner; by interlineation.

in·tẽr·lin′ē·ā·ry, *n.* a book having insertions between the lines. [Rare.]

in·tẽr·lin′ē·ā·ry, *a.* interlinear.

in·tẽr·lin′ē·āte, *v.t.* [from ML. *interlineatus*, pp.] to interline (insert between lines). [Rare.]

in·tẽr·lin·ē·ā′tion, *n.* 1. the act of inserting words or lines between written or printed lines.

2. the word, passage, or line inserted between written or printed lines.

in·tẽr·lin′ing, *n.* 1. an inner lining put between the outer material and the ordinary lining of a garment.

2. any fabric used as an interlining.

in·tẽr·link′, *v.t.*; interlinked (-linkt), *pt., pp.*; interlinking, *ppr.* to connect by links; to join together by a link.

in′tẽr·link, *n.* an intermediate link.

in·tẽr·lō′bāte, *a.* in geology, located between or adjacent to mounds of glacial deposit.

in·tẽr·lob′ū·lăr, *a.* in anatomy, lying between lobes or lobules, as in a gland.

in″tẽr·lō·cā′tion, *n.* a placing between; interposition.

in·tẽr·lock′, *v.t.* and *v.i.* 1. to lock together; to join with one another.

2. to connect or be connected so that neither part can be operated independently.

interlocking directorates; boards of directors having some members in common, so that the corporations concerned are more or less under the same control.

interlocking signals; railroad signals interlocked with each other so that when one has been lowered the others cannot be changed until the train has passed.

in′tẽr·lock, *n.* the condition of being interlocked.

in″tẽr·lō·cū′tion, *n.* [L. *interlocutio* (*-onis*), from *interloqui*, to speak between, interrupt; *inter*, between, and *loqui*, to speak.]

1. talk between two or more people; dialogue; conference; interchange of speech.

2. in law, an intermediate act or decree before a final decision; an intermediate argument. [Rare.]

in·tẽr·loc′ū·tŏr, *n.* 1. one who takes part in a conversation or dialogue.

2. in Scots law, a judgment or sentence of a court.

3. an entertainer in a minstrel show who asks questions of the end men.

in·tẽr·loc′ū·tō·ry, *a.* 1. consisting of dialogue; having the nature of dialogue; occurring in dialogue.

2. interjected; as, *interlocutory* wit.

3. in law, intermediate; not final or definitive; pronounced during the course of a suit, pending final decision; as, an *interlocutory* divorce decree.

in·tẽr·loc′ū·tō·ry, *n.* a discussion or conversation. [Obs.]

in·tẽr·loc′ū·tress, in·tẽr·loc′ū·trice, *n.* a woman or girl interlocutor.

in·tẽr·lōpe′, *v.i.*; interloped (-lōpt′), *pt., pp.*; interloping, *ppr.* 1. originally, to intrude on another's trading rights or privileges.

2. to intrude or meddle where one has no business or right.

in′tẽr·lō·pẽr, *n.* [prob. from D. *enterlooper*, a coasting vessel, smuggler; Fr. *entre*, between, and D. *loopen*, to run.]

1. (a) originally, an unauthorized trading vessel in areas assigned to monopolies or chartered companies; (b) any unauthorized trader.

2. one who interlopes; an intruder.

in·tẽr·lū′cāte, *v.t.* to let light through by cutting away branches of trees. [Obs.]

in″tẽr·lū·cā′tion, *n.* the act of interlucating. [Obs.]

in·tẽr·lū′cent, *a.* [L. *interlucens* (*-entis*), ppr. of *interlucere*, to shine between; *inter*, between, and *lucere*, to shine, from *lux*, light.] shining between.

in′tẽr·lūde, *n.* [OFr. *entrelude*; LL. *interludium*; L. *inter*, between, and *ludus*, play.]

1. a short entertainment performed between the acts of a play, or between a play and an afterpiece.

2. a short instrumental piece of music played between the stanzas of a song or hymn, between the acts of a drama, etc.

3. a type of short humorous play, usually with two characters, formerly presented between the parts of miracle plays or moralities, at entertainments, etc.

4. a short play, either farcical or moralistic in tone, as presented in the hall of a Tudor noble before an aristocratic audience by professional players: the typical interlude, as written by John Heywood and others, draws its plot from French farce, the morality play, or the Latin school play: regarded as the earliest form of modern English drama.

5. anything that fills time between two events; as, *interludes* of waiting between trains.

in′tẽr·lū·dẽr, *n.* a performer in an interlude. [Obs.]

in·tẽr·lū′en·cy, *n.* [L. *interluens* (*-entis*), ppr. of *interluere*, to flow between; *inter*, between, and *luere*, to wash.] a flowing between. [Rare.]

in·tẽr·lū′năr, in·tẽr·lū′nȧ·ry, *a.* [L. *inter*, between, and *luna*, moon.] of the time when the moon, at or near its conjunction with the sun, is invisible; between the old moon and the new moon.

in″tẽr·man·dib′ū·lăr, *a.* situated between the mandibles or rami of the lower jaw.

in·tẽr·mar′riage (-rij), *n.* 1. marriage between persons of different families, nations, tribes, etc.

2. marriage between closely related persons.

in·tẽr·mar′ry, *v.i.*; intermarried, *pt., pp.*; intermarrying, *ppr.* 1. to become connected by marriage: said of different families, ranks, tribes, or the like.

2. to marry: said of closely related persons.

in″tẽr·max·il′lȧ, *n.*; *pl.* **in″tẽr·max·il′lae,** the anterior part of the upper jawbone; the premaxilla.

in·tẽr·max′il·lā·ry, *a.* situated between the upper jawbones.

in·tẽr·max′il·lā·ry, *n.* same as *intermaxilla*.

in′tẽr·mēan, *n.* an interact; something done in the meantime. [Obs.]

in·tẽr·med′dle, *v.i.*; intermeddled, *pt., pp.*; intermeddling, *ppr.* to meddle in the affairs of others.

in·tẽr·med′dle, *v.t.* to mix together; to cause to mingle. [Obs.]

in·tẽr·med′dlẽr, *n.* one who meddles or intrudes into business in which he has no right.

in·tẽr·med′dle·sōme, *a.* tending to intermeddle; meddlesome.

in·tẽr·med′dle·sōme·ness, *n.* the quality of being intermeddlesome.

in·tẽr·med′dling, *n.* officious interposition.

in·tẽr·mēde′, *n.* [Fr., from L. *inter*, between, and *medius*, middle.] an interlude. [Obs.]

in·tẽr·mē′di·ȧ·cy, *n.* the state of being intermediate; interposition; intervention.

in·tẽr·mē′di·ae, *n.pl.* [f. pl. of L. *intermedius*, intermedial.] the middle pair of quill feathers in the tail of a bird.

in·tẽr·mē′di·ăl, *a.* [L. *intermedius*; *inter*, between, and *medius*, middle.] lying between; intervening. [Now Rare.]

in·tẽr·mē′di·ā·ry, *a.* 1. acting between two persons; acting as mediator.

2. being or happening between; intermediate.

in·tẽr·mē′di·ā·ry, *n.*; *pl.* **in·tẽr·mē′di·ā·ries,** 1. a go-between; a mediator.

2. a medium; a means; an agency.

3. an intermediate form, phase, etc.

in·tẽr·mē′di·āte, *a.* [LL. *intermediatus*, pp. of *intermediare*, to come between, from L. *intermedius*, that is between; *inter*, between, and *medius*, middle.] being or happening between; in the middle; between two extremes; intervening; interposed.

Syn.—intervening, included, interposed, comprised, middle, moderate, interjacent.

in·tẽr·mē′di·āte, *n.* 1. anything intermediate.

2. an intermediary.

in·tẽr·mē′di·āte, *v.i.*; intermediated, *pt., pp.*; intermediating, *ppr.* to act as an intermediary; to mediate.

in·tẽr·mē′di·āte·ly, *adv.* by way of intervention.

in·tẽr·mē·di·ā′tion, *n.* intervention; an act of intermediating.

in·tẽr·mē′di·ā·tŏr, *n.* one who mediates.

in·tẽr·mē′di·ous, *a.* intermediate. [Obs.]

in·tẽr·mē′di·um, *n.*; *pl.* **in·tẽr·mē′di·ȧ,** [L. *intermedium*, neut. of *intermedius*, that is between; *inter*, between, and *medius*, middle.]

1. intermediate space. [Rare.]

2. an intervening agent.

3. in anatomy, a median carpal or tarsal bone.

in·tẽr·mell′, *v.t.* and *v.i.* [OFr. *entremeller*, *entremesler*, to intermix.] to intermix or intermeddle. [Obs.]

in·tẽr·mem′brăl, *a.* in anatomy, designating relations between the members or limbs; as, *intermembral* similarities.

in·tẽr′ment, *n.* [ME. *enterment*; OFr. *enterrement*; LL. *interramentum*, burial, from, *interrare*, to put in the earth; L. *in*, in, and *terra*, earth.] the act of depositing a dead body in the earth; burial.

in·tẽr·men′tion, *v.t.* to mention among other things; to include. [Obs.]

in·tẽr·meṣ·en·ter′iç, *a.* in biology, between the layers of the mesentery or between mesenteries; as, *intermesenteric* spaces.

in·tẽr·met·ȧ·çär′păl, *a.* in anatomy, situated between bones of the metacarpus.

in·tẽr·met·ȧ·tär′săl, *a.* in anatomy, situated between bones of the metatarsus.

in·tẽr·mew′ (-mū′), *v.i.* [*inter-*, and OFr. *muer*, from L. *mutare*, to change.] in falconry, to shed the feathers while confined.

in·tẽr·mez′zō (-met′sō), *n.*; *pl.* **in·tẽr·mez′zoṣ, in·tẽr·mez′zi** (-met′si), [It., from L. *intermedius* intermediate.]

1. a short, light dramatic, musical, or ballet entertainment between the acts of a play or opera.

2. in music, (a) a short movement connecting the main parts of a composition; (b) any of certain short instrumental pieces similar to this.

in·tẽr·mī·grā′tion, *n.* reciprocal migration; removal from one country to another by men or tribes which take the place each of the other.

in·tẽr′mi·nȧ·ble, *a.* [ME. *intermynable*; OFr.; LL. *interminabilis.*] boundless; endless or apparently endless; admitting or seeming to admit no limit; as, *interminable* space or duration; *interminable* sufferings.

in·tẽr′mi·nȧ·ble·ness, *n.* the state of being interminable.

in·tẽr′mi·nȧ·bly, *adv.* without end.

in·tẽr′mi·nāte, *a.* [L. *interminatus*; *in-* priv., and *terminatus*, pp. of *terminare*, to bound.] unbounded; unlimited; endless; as, *interminate* sleep.

in·tẽr′mi·nāte, *v.t.* to menace. [Obs.]

in·tẽr′mi·nā·ted, *a.* without end. [Obs.]

in″tẽr·mi·nā′tion, *n.* [L. *interminatus*, pp. of *interminari*, to threaten; *inter*, between, and *minari*, to threaten.] a menace or threat. [Obs.]

in·tẽr·mīne′, *v.t.* to cut through or across with mines.

in·tẽr·min′gle, *v.t.* and *v.i.*; intermingled, *pt., pp.*; intermingling, *ppr.* to mingle or mix together; to blend.

in′tẽr·mīṣe, *n.* interference; interruption; intervention. [Obs.]

in·tẽr·mis′sion (-mish′un), *n.* [L. *intermissio* (*-onis*), a breaking off, interruption, from *intermissus*, pp. of *intermittere*, to interrupt, discontinue; *inter*, between, and *mittere*, to send.]

1. an intermitting or being intermitted; interruption.

2. an interval of time between periods of activity; as, *intermissions* between acts of a play.

Syn.—interlude, interruption, recess, cessation.

in·tẽr·mis′sive, *a.* of, or having the nature of, an intermission; not continual.

in·tẽr·mit′, *v.t.*; intermitted, *pt., pp.*; intermitting, *ppr.* [L. *intermittere*, to interrupt, discontinue; *inter*, between, and *mittere*, to send.] to cause to cease for a time; to make intermittent; to interrupt; to suspend.

Syn.—abate, suspend, discontinue.

in·tẽr·mit′, *v.i.* to cease for a time; to be intermittent; to go away at intervals, as a fever.

in·tẽr·mit′tence, *n.* the state or fact of being intermittent.

in·tẽr·mit′ten·cy, *n.* intermittence.

in·tẽr·mit′tent, *n.* a disease which entirely subsides or ceases at certain intervals, as in fever and ague.

in·tẽr·mit′tent, *a.* stopping and starting again at intervals; pausing from time to time; periodic.

intermittent current; an electric current interrupted at intervals but always flowing in the same direction.

intermittent fever; a fever characterized by periodic intervals when the body temperature returns to normal.

intermittent gearing; in machinery, a device

which receives and imparts motion intermittently.

intermittent spark; an electrical spark which occurs at intervals.

in·tẽr·mit′tent·ly, in·tẽr·mit′ting·ly, *adv.* with intermissions; at intervals.

in·tẽr·mit′tẽr, *n.* a person or thing that intermits.

in·tẽr·mix′, *v.t.* and *v.i.*; intermixed (-mixt′), *pt., pp.*; intermixing, *ppr.* to mix together, to blend; to intermingle.

in·tẽr·mix′ed·ly, *adv.* in a mixed or intermingled way.

in·tẽr·mix′tūre, *n.* 1. an intermixing or being intermixed.

2. a mixture.

3. an added ingredient; admixture.

in″tẽr·mō·bil′i·ty, *n.* the quality of being capable of moving among each other.

in″tẽr·mō·leç′ū·lăr, *a.* designating or relating to the spaces or areas existing between the molecules of a substance.

in·tẽr·mon′tāne, *a.* [L. *inter*, between, and *mons, montis*, a mountain.] between or among mountains; as, *intermontane* soil.

in·tẽr·mun′dāne, *a.* [L. *inter*, between, and *mundus*, world.] being between worlds, or between orb and orb.

in·tẽr·mun′di·ăn, *a.* intermundane. [Rare.]

in·tẽr·mū′răl, *a.* [L. *intermuralis*; *inter*, between, and *murus*, wall.] between walls.

in·tẽr·mūre′, *v.t.* to surround with walls; to wall in. [Obs.]

in·tẽr·mus′çū·lăr, *a.* between the muscles.

in·tẽr·mū·tā′tion, *n.* [LL. *intermutare*, to interchange; L. *inter*, between, and *mutare*, to change.] interchange; mutual or reciprocal change.

in·tẽr·mū′tū·ăl, *a.* mutual.

in·tẽr·mū′tū·ăl·ly, *adv.* mutually.

in·tẽrn′, in·tẽrne′, *a.* [Fr. *interne*; L. *internus*, inward, internal.] internal. [Archaic.]

in′tẽrn, *n.* [Fr. *interne*, from L. *internus*, inward, internal.] a doctor serving as an assistant resident in a hospital generally just after his graduation from medical school: also spelled *interne*.

in′tẽrn, *v.i.* to be, or act as, an intern.

in·tẽrn′, *v.t.*; interned, *pt., pp.*; interning, *ppr.* 1. to detain and confine within a country or a definite area; as, countries often *intern* aliens in time of war.

2. to detain (ships) in port.

in·tẽr′năl, *a.* [ML. *internalis*, from L. *internus*, within, inward, from *inter*, between, from *in*, in, within.]

1. of or on the inside; inward; inner; interior: opposed to *external*.

2. having to do with or belonging to the inner nature of a thing; intrinsic; as, *internal* evidence.

3. having to do with or belonging to the inner nature of man; subjective.

4. domestic; as, *internal* wars, *internal* revenue: opposed to *foreign*.

5. to be taken or applied inside the body; as, *internal* remedies.

6. in anatomy, situated toward the inside of the body or closer to its center.

internal angle; any angle included between the sides within a rectilinear figure; also, any of the four angles formed between two parallel lines by a line intersecting these lines.

internal ear; that part of the ear in the temporal bone, consisting of the labyrinth and semicircular canals.

internal gear; in machinery, a wheel whose cogs are on the internal perimeter.

internal medicine; the branch of medicine that deals with the diagnosis and treatment of diseases of the internal organs.

internal revenue; governmental income from taxes on income, profits, amusements, luxuries, etc.

internal work; see under *work*.

in·tẽr′năl, *n.* 1. [*pl.*] the internal organs of the body; entrails.

2. inner, intrinsic, or essential quality or attribute.

in·tẽr′năl-çŏm·bus′tion (-bus′chun), *a.* designating or of an engine, used in airplanes, automobiles, etc., in which the power is produced by the explosion of a fuel-and-air mixture within the cylinder or cylinders.

in·tẽr·nal′i·ty, *n.* the quality or state of being internal; interiority; inwardness.

in·tẽr′năl·ly, *adv.* 1. with respect to or as concerns the inside or interior of anything; in or on the inside.

2. inwardly; subjectively or intrinsically.

3. inside the body; as, apply the medicine *internally*.

in·tẽr·nā′ṣăl, *a.* in anatomy, situated between the nasal passages.

in·tẽr·na′tion·ăl (-nash′un-), *a.* 1. between or among nations; as, an *international* treaty.

2. concerned with the relations between nations; as, an *international* court.

international candle; a unit of measure of the intensity of light, equal to the light given off by the flame of a sperm candle 7/8 inch in diameter burning at the rate of 7.776 grams per hour.

international code; in nautical usage, a common system of maritime signaling by means of flags, now adopted by commercial nations generally, in order to facilitate communication between vessels at sea or between vessels at sea and stations on shore.

international copyright; see under *copyright*.

international date line; an imaginary line drawn north and south through the Pacific Ocean, largely along the 180th meridian: it is the line at which, by international agreement, each calendar day begins at midnight, so that when it is Sunday just west of the line, it is Saturday just east of it.

international law; the system of rules generally observed and regarded as binding in the relations between states.

International News Service; a large, privately owned agency for gathering and distributing news among member newspapers.

International Phonetic Alphabet; a phonetic alphabet sponsored by the International Phonetic Association, a society founded in 1886 for the advancement of the study of phonetics: this alphabet, used in one form or other by most phoneticians and linguists, consists of letters to symbolize the position of the articulating organs, and thus has the same symbol for the same sound irrespective of the language, or period in the development of a language, in which the sound occurs: abbreviated IPA (no period).

private international law; international law which deals with the private relations and rights of persons of different nationalities.

in·tẽr·na′tion·ăl, *n.* 1. a person having connections with two different countries, as a resident, alien, etc.

2. [I–] any of several international socialist organizations.

Iṇ·ter·na·tion·āle (*or Fr.* aṅ-ter-nȧ-syō-nȧl′), *n.* a revolutionary socialist hymn written in 1871 by Eugène Pottier, with music by Adolphe Degeyter.

in·tẽr·na′tion·ăl·iṣm, *n.* 1. the principle of international co-operation for the common good.

2. international character, quality, etc.

in·tẽr·na′tion·ăl·ist, *n.* 1. a person who believes in internationalism.

2. a specialist in international law and relations.

in·tẽr·na·tion·al′i·ty, *n.* the quality or state of being international.

in·tẽr·na·tion·ăl·i·zā′tion, *n.* an internationalizing or being internationalized.

in·tẽr·na′tion·ăl·īze, *v.t.*; internationalized, *pt., pp.*; internationalizing, *ppr.* to make international; to bring under international control.

in·tẽr·na′tion·ăl·ly, *adv.* in an international manner; so as to affect the mutual relations or interests of nations; from an international point of view.

in′tẽrne, *n.* same as *intern*.

in·tẽr·nē′ciȧ·ry (-shȧ-), *a.* internecine. [Rare.]

in·tẽr·nec′i·năl, *a.* internecine. [Rare.]

in·tẽr·nē′cine, *a.* [L. *internecinus*, for *internecivus*, deadly, murderous, from *internecare*, to kill, destroy; *inter*, between, and *necare*, to kill.]

1. deadly; destructive; characterized by great slaughter.

2. deadly to both sides; mutually destructive.

in·tẽr·nē′cion, *n.* [L. *internecare*, to kill, slaughter.] mutual slaughter or destruction. [Rare.]

in·tẽr·nē′cive, *a.* internecine. [Rare.]

in·tẽr·nee′, *n.* one who is interned.

in·tẽr·neū′răl, *a.* in anatomy, situated between the neural arches or spines.

in·tẽr·neū′răl, *n.* an interneural bone or spine.

in·tẽr′nist, *n.* a doctor who specializes in internal medicine.

in·tẽr′ni·ty, *n.* [L. *internus*, inner, internal.] the state of being internal. [Obs.]

in·tẽrn′ment, *n.* an interning or being interned.

in·tẽr·nō′dăl, *a.* 1. intervening between nodes or joints.

2. in botany, of or pertaining to an internode.

in′tẽr·nōde, *n.* [L. *internodium*; *inter*, between, and *nodus*, a knot, joint.]

1. in botany, the space between two successive nodes, or points of the stem from which the leaves arise.

a. NODES OR JOINTS b. INTERNODES

2. in anatomy and zoology, a part between two nodes; especially, a segment of nerve fiber.

in·tẽr·nō′di·ăl, *a.* internodal. [Rare.]

in·tẽr·nō′di·um, *n.* in anatomy and zoology, an internode.

in·tẽr·nō·mē′di·ăn, *a.* [L. *internus*, inward, internal, and *medianus*, middle.] in entomology, situated between the median and internal vein.

in′tẽr nōs, [L.] between ourselves.

in′tẽrn·ship, *n.* 1. the position of an intern.

2. the period of service as an intern.

in·tẽr·nun′ciăl (-shăl), *a.* 1. of or belonging to an internuncio or his office.

2. in physiology, pertaining to, resembling, or possessing the function of the nervous system as communicating between different parts of the body.

in·tẽr·nun′ci·ō (-shi-), *n.*; *pl.* **in·tẽr·nun′ci·ōṣ,** [It. *internuncio*; L. *internuncius*, *internuntius*, a messenger between two parties; *inter*, between, and *nuncius*, *nuntius*, a messenger.]

1. a messenger between two parties; envoy.

2. an envoy of the Pope, ranking below a nuncio.

in·tẽr·nun′ci·ō·ship, *n.* the rank or office of an internuncio.

in·tẽr·nun′ci·us, *n.* same as *internuncio*.

in·tẽr·ō·cē·an′iç (-shi-), *a.* between oceans; uniting oceans; as, an *interoceanic* railroad or canal.

in″tẽr·ō·cep′tive, *a.* of or arising from an interoceptor.

in″tẽr·ō·cep′tŏr, *n.* [Mod. L.; cf. *internal* and *receptor*.] a specialized cell or end organ that responds to and transmits stimuli from the internal organs, muscles, blood vessels, and the ear labyrinth.

in·tẽr·oç′ū·lăr, *a.* between the eyes, as the antennae of some insects.

in″tẽr·ō·pẽr′çle, *n.* same as *interoperculum*.

in″tẽr·ō·pẽr′çū·lăr, *a.* pertaining to an interoperculum.

in″tẽr·ō·pẽr′çū·lăr, *n.* same as *interoperculum*.

in″tẽr·ō·pẽr′çū·lum, *n.*; *pl.* **in″tẽr·ō·pẽr′çū·lȧ,** [L. *inter*, between, and *operculum*, a cover, lid.] one of the four bones forming the gill cover of fishes: it lies behind the angle of the jaw, below the preoperculum.

in·tẽr·op′tiç, *a.* [L. *inter*, between, and Gr. *optikos*, optic.] situated between the optic lobes.

in·tẽr·ọr′bit·ăl, *a.* situated between the orbits of the eyes.

in·tẽr·os′çū·lănt, *a.* [L. *inter*, between, and *osculans* (*-antis*), ppr. of *osculari*, to kiss.] connecting two objects or classes, as a species connecting two genera.

in·tẽr·os′çū·lāte, *v.i.*; interosculated, *pt., pp.*; interosculating, *ppr.* 1. to intermix; to intermingle.

2. in biology, to have some common characteristics: said of species.

in·tẽr·os·çū·lā′tion, *n.* an interosculating.

in·tẽr·os′sē·ăl, *a.* interosseous.

in·tẽr·os′sē·ous, *a.* [L. *inter*, between, and *os*, *ossis*, a bone.] situated between bones; as, an *interosseous* ligament.

in·tẽr·pāle′, *v.t.* to place pales between; to divide by means of pales.

in″tẽr·pȧ·rī′e·tăl, *a.* situated between the parietal bones.

in″tẽr·pȧ·rī′e·tăl, *n.* an interparietal bone or cartilage.

in′tẽr·pąuṣe, *n.* a stop or pause between; a temporary cessation. [Rare.]

in·tẽr·pēal′, *v.t.* to peal between.

in″tẽr·pē·dun′çū·lăr, *a.* in anatomy, situated between the cerebral or cerebellar peduncles.

in·tẽr·pel′, *v.t.* [L. *interpellare*, to interrupt.] to interfere with; to intercede with; to break in upon. [Obs.]

in·tẽr·pel′lănt, *a.* interpellating.
in·tẽr·pel′lănt, *n.* one who interpellates.
in·tẽr·pel′lāte, *v.t.*; interpellated, *pt., pp.*; interpellating, *ppr.* [L. *interpellatus*, pp. of *interpellare*, to interrupt in speaking; *inter*, between, and *pellere*, to drive, urge.] to ask (a person) formally for an explanation of his action or policy: a form of political challenge to governmental ministers, executives, etc. in legislative bodies of certain countries.
in″tẽr·pel·lā′tion, *n.* an interpellating; a formal calling to account of a minister, etc. by a legislative body.
in·tẽr·pen′ē·trāte, *v.t.*; interpenetrated, *pt., pp.*; interpenetrating, *ppr.* to penetrate thoroughly; to pervade; permeate.
in·tẽr·pen′ē·trāte, *v.i.* 1. to penetrate each other.
2. to penetrate between parts, etc.
in·tẽr·pen·ē·trā′tion, *n.* 1. the act of interpenetrating; the act of penetrating between or within bodies; thorough or mutual penetration.
2. in architecture, a design of continuous moldings.
in·tẽr·pen′ē·trā·tive, *a.* penetrating or tending to penetrate between or within other bodies; mutually penetrative.
in·tẽr·pet′i·ō·lăr, *a.* situated between petioles.
in″tẽr·phȧ·lan′ġē·ăl, *a.* in anatomy, situated between two successive phalanges of a finger or toe.
in′tẽr·phōne, *n.* a telephone system for communication between the members of the crew of an airplane, tank, etc.
in′tẽr·pi·las″tẽr, *n.* in architecture, the interval between two pilasters.
in·tẽr·plāce′, *v.t.* to place between or among. [Obs.]
in·tẽr·plan′e·tăr·y, *a.* 1. between planets; in the planetary region.
2. within the solar system but outside the atmosphere of any planet or the sun.
in′tẽr·plāy, *n.* action, effect, or influence on each other or one another; interaction.
in·tẽr·plāy′, *v.i.* to exert influence reciprocally.
in·tẽr·plēad′, *v.i.* in law, to go to trial with each other in order to settle a dispute in which a third party is concerned; to initiate an interpleader.
in·tẽr·plēad′ẽr, *n.* a legal proceeding by which a person sued by two others having the same claim against him may compel them to go to trial with each other to determine what settlement should be made.
in·tẽr·point′, *v.t.* to point; to distinguish by stops or marks; to punctuate.
in·tẽr′pō·lȧ·ble, *a.* capable of being interpolated or inserted; suitable for interpolation.
in·tẽr′pō·lăr·y, *a.* pertaining to interpolation.
in·tẽr′pō·lāte, *v.t.*; interpolated, *pt., pp.*; interpolating, *ppr.* [L. *interpolatus*, pp. of *interpolare*, to polish, dress up, corrupt, from *interpolis*, altered by furbishing, repaired; *inter*, between, and *polire*, to polish.]
1. to carry on with intermissions; to interrupt or discontinue for a time. [Obs.]
2. to alter, enlarge, or corrupt (a book, manuscript, etc.) by putting in new words, subject matter, etc.
3. to insert between or among others.
4. in mathematics, to supply (intermediate terms) in a series of terms.
in·tẽr′pō·lāte, *v.i.* to make interpolations.
in·tẽr·pō·lā′tion, *n.* [L. *interpolatio* (*-onis*), an alteration, furbishing, from *interpolare*, to alter, interpolate.]
1. the act of interpolating or the state of being interpolated.
2. that which is interpolated.
3. in mathematics and physics, the operation of finding terms between any two consecutive terms of a series, which shall conform to the law of the series.
4. in surgery, the transfer of tissue in a plastic operation.
in·tẽr′pō·lā·tŏr, *n.* [LL.] one who interpolates.
in·tẽr·pōne′, *v.t.* [L. *interponere*; *inter*, between, and *ponere*, to set, place.] to set or insert between; to interpose. [Rare.]
in·tẽr·pō′nent, *n.* one who or that which interpones, or interposes. [Rare.]
in·tẽr·pŏr′tăl, *a.* occurring or carried on between ports, especially ports of the same country; as, *interportal* trade.
in·tẽr·pōṣ′ăl, *n.* the act of interposing; interposition.
in·tẽr·pōṣe′, *v.t.*; interposed, *pt., pp.*; interposing, *ppr.* [OFr. *interposer*; L. *interponere*; *inter*, between, and *ponere*, to place.]
1. to place or put between; to insert.
2. to introduce by way of intervention; to put forward as interference.
3. to introduce (a remark, opinion, etc.) into a conversation, debate, etc.; to put in as an interruption.
in·tẽr·pōṣe′, *v.i.* 1. to be or step in between; to mediate.
2. to interrupt.
3. to intervene; to stand or come between.
Syn.—intermeddle, interfere, intercede, mediate meddle, intervene.
in′tẽr·pōṣe, *n.* interposition.
in·tẽr·pōṣ′ẽr, *n.* one who or that which interposes; a mediator or agent between parties.
in·tẽr·pō·ṣi′tion, *n.* [L. *interpositio* (*-onis*), from *interponere*, to place or set between.]
1. a being, placing, or coming between; mediation; intervention.
2. that which is interposed.
in·tẽr·pō′ṣūre (-zhŭr), *n.* interposition. [Obs.]
in·tẽr′pret, *v.t.*; interpreted, *pt., pp.*; interpreting, *ppr.* [ME. *interpreten*; OFr. *interpreter*; L. *interpretari*, to explain, expound, from *interpres* (*-etis*), an agent between two parties, a broker, negotiator, interpreter.]
1. to explain the meaning of; to make understandable, as by translating; to elucidate.
2. to have or show one's own understanding of the meaning of; to construe; as, he *interpreted* the silence as contempt.
3. to bring out the meaning of, especially to give one's own conception of, in performing, criticizing, or producing a work of art; as, the theatrical company *interpreted* Shakespeare's *Julius Caesar* in the light of modern political conflicts.
Syn.—expound, explain, translate, decipher, construe, unravel, unfold, solve, elucidate.
in·tẽr′pret, *v.i.* to act as an interpreter; to make an interpretation.
in·tẽr′pret·ȧ·ble, *a.* that can be interpreted or explained.
in·tẽr′prē·tȧ·ment, *n.* interpretation. [Obs.]
in·tẽr·prē·tā′tion, *n.* [L. *interpretatio* (*-onis*), an explanation, from *interpretari*, to explain, interpret.]
1. an interpreting.
2. the result of this; explanation; meaning; translation; exposition.
3. the expression of a person's conception of a work of art, subject, etc. through acting, playing, writing, criticizing, etc.; as, the pianist's *interpretation* of the sonata.
Syn.—construction, explanation, version, elucidation, translation, rendition, solution, exposition.
in·tẽr′prē·tā·tive, *a.* 1. designed or used to explain; explaining; explanatory.
2. according to interpretation; constructive; inferential.
in·tẽr′prē·tā·tive·ly, *adv.* so as to interpret, or give ground for interpretation; in an interpretative manner.
in·tẽr′pret·ẽr, *n.* [OFr. *interpreteur*; LL. *interpretator*, from L. *interpretari*, to explain, expound.] a person who interprets; specifically, a person whose work is translating a foreign language orally, as in a conversation between people speaking different languages.
in·tẽr′pre·tive, *a.* interpretative.
in·tẽr·pū′biç, *a.* in anatomy, situated between the pubic bones.
in·tẽr·punç′tion, *n.* [L. *interpunctio* (*-onis*), from *interpungere*, to place points between words; *inter*, between, and *pungere*, to point.] the placing of points between sentences or parts of a sentence; punctuation.
in·tẽr·rā′ciăl (-shăl), *a.* 1. between, among, or involving different races.
2. of or for persons of different races.
in·tẽr·rā′di·ăl, *a.* [L. *inter*, between, and *radius*, a ray.] situated between the radii or rays.
in·tẽr·rā′di·ăl, *n.* a part situated between rays.
in·tẽr·rā′di·ăl·ly, *adv.* between rays.
in·tẽr·rā′di·um, *n.*; *pl.* **in·tẽr·rā′di·ȧ,** an area or zone between rays.
in·tẽr·rā′di·us, *n.*; *pl.* **in·tẽr·rā′di·ī,** in zoology, an interradial part.
in·tẽr·rā′măl, *a.* [L. *inter*, between, and *ramus*, a branch.] in zoology, between the rami, or branches, of the lower jaw.
in·tẽr·ram′i·çorn, *n.* [L. *inter*, between, and *ramus*, a branch, and *cornu*, a horn.] a horny part of the bill between the rami of the lower mandible of some birds.
in·tẽr·rē′găl, *a.* among kings.
in·tẽr·rē′ġen·cy, *n.* an interregnum. [Obs.]
in·tẽr·rē′ġent, *n.* one who governs during an interregnum; an interrex. [Obs.]
in·tẽr·rē′ġēṣ, *n.* plural of *interrex*.
in·tẽr·reg′num, *n.*; *pl.* **in·tẽr·reg′numṣ, in·tẽr·reg′nȧ,** [L. *interregnum*; *inter*, between, and *regnum*, reign, rule.]
1. an interval between two successive reigns, when the country has no sovereign.
2. a suspension of governmental or administrative functions; a period without the usual ruler, governor, etc.
3. any break in a series or in a continuity; a pause or interval.
in′tẽr·reign (-rān), *n.* [Fr. *interrègne*, from L. *interregnum*, an interregnum.] an interregnum. [Now Rare.]
in″tẽr·rē·lāte′, *v.t.* to cause to become mutually related.
in″tẽr·rē·lāt′ed, *a.* having a close connection with each other or one another; mutually related.
in″tẽr·rē·lā′tion, *n.* the state or fact of being interrelated; mutual relationship.
in·tẽr·rē′năl, *a.* [L. *inter*, between, and *renalis*, from *renes*, the kidneys.] between the kidneys.
in·tẽr·rē′năl, *n.* an interrenal body, an organ of certain fishes.
in·tẽr′rẽr, *n.* one who inters, or buries.
in′tẽr·rex, *n.*; *pl.* **in·tẽr·rē′ġēṣ,** [L., from *inter*, between, and *rex*, *regis*, a king.] a person who acts as the ruler during an interregnum.
in·ter′rō·gāte, *v.t.*; interrogated, *pt., pp.*; interrogating, *ppr.* [L. *interrogatus*, pp. of *interrogare*, to question, ask; *inter*, between, and *rogare*, to ask.] to ask questions of formally; to examine by questioning; as, he *interrogated* the witness.
Syn.—ask, examine, inquire of, question, interview.
in·ter′rō·gāte, *v.i.* to ask questions.
in·ter′rō·gāte, *n.* a question; an interrogation. [Obs.]
in·ter″rō·gā·tee′, *n.* one who is interrogated.
in·ter·rō·gā′tion, *n.* 1. the act of questioning; examination by questions.
2. a question; an inquiry.
3. an interrogation mark.
in·tẽr·rō·gā′tion märk (or **point**), a mark of punctuation (?) used to indicate that the sentence preceding it is a direct question, and also to show doubt, uncertainty, etc.: also called *question mark*.
in·tẽr·rog′ȧ·tive, *a.* [L. *interrogativus*, from *interrogare*, to question, ask, interrogate.]
1. asking, or having the form of, a question; as, an *interrogative* phrase or sentence; an *interrogative* sign.
2. used in asking a question.
in·tẽr·rog′ȧ·tive, *n.* an interrogative word, construction, or element (e.g., what? where?).
in·tẽr·rog′ȧ·tive·ly, *adv.* in the form of a question; in an interrogative manner.
in·ter′rō·gā·tŏr, *n.* one who interrogates or asks questions.
in·tẽr·rog′ȧ·tō·ri·ly, *adv.* in an interrogative manner.
in·tẽr·rog′ȧ·tō·ry, *a.* [LL. *interrogatorius*, consisting of questions, from L. *interrogare*, to question, ask.] containing a question; expressing a question; as, an *interrogatory* sentence.
in·tẽr·rog′ȧ·tō·ry, *n.*; *pl.* **in·tẽr·rog′ȧ·tō·rieṣ,** an interrogating; a formal question or set of questions; specifically, in law, a question asked in writing.
in·tẽr·rupt′, *v.t.*; interrupted, *pt., pp.*; interrupting, *ppr.* [L. *interruptus*, pp. of *interrumpere*, to break apart, break off; *inter*, between, and *rumpere*, to break.]
1. to break into or in upon (a discussion, train of thought, etc.); also, to break in upon (a person) while he is speaking, singing, etc.; to hinder; to stop temporarily.

Do not *interrupt* me in my course.
—Shak.

2. to make a break in the continuity of; to get in the way of; to cut off; obstruct.
in·tẽr·rupt′, *v.i.* to break in upon an action, talk, etc.; to make an interruption.
in·tẽr·rupt′, *a.* irregular; interrupted. [Obs.]
in·tẽr·rupt′ed, *a.* 1. broken by interruptions or discontinuity; not continuous.
2. in botany, asymmetrical; irregular.
in·tẽr·rupt′ed·ly, *adv.* with breaks or interruptions.
in·tẽr·rupt′ed sçrew, a device for closing the breech of certain guns in which the breech and the block have alternate threads and slots that permit the block to be locked or released by giving it a partial turn.
in·tẽr·rupt′ẽr, *n.* 1. one who or that which interrupts.

2. in electricity, any device for interrupting, or opening and closing, a circuit.

in·tẽr·rup′tion, *n.* [L. *interruptio* (*-onis*), an interrupting, from *interruptus*, pp. of *interrumpere*, to break off, interrupt.]

1. an interrupting or being interrupted.

2. anything that interrupts; obstruction or hindrance caused by a breaking in upon any course, current, progress, or motion; stoppage; as, the author met with many *interruptions* in the execution of his work.

3. cessation; intermission; the interval during which something is interrupted.

Amidst the *interruptions* of his sorrow. —Addison.

in·tẽr·rupt′ive, *a.* tending to interrupt.

in·tẽr·rupt′ive·ly, *adv.* by interruption.

in·tẽr·sçap′ū·lăr, *a.* [L. *inter*, between, and *scapulæ*, the shoulder blades.]

1. situated between the shoulder blades.

2. in zoology, pertaining to the part between the scapulae, or shoulder blades; as, an *interscapular* feather.

in·tẽr·sçap′ū·lăr, *n.* in zoology, an interscapular feather.

in·tẽr·sçap′ū·lum, *n.*; *pl.* **in·tẽr·sçap′ū·lȧ,** in ornithology, the part of the back between the scapulae.

in·tẽr·sçhō·las′tiç, *a.* [*inter-* and *scholastic.*] of any activity that is carried on between or among schools; as, an *interscholastic* spelling match.

in·tẽr·sçhō·las′tiç, *n.* an interscholastic contest.

in·tẽr·sçrībe′, *v.t.* to write between; to interline. [Obs.]

in′tẽr sē′, [L.] between (or among) themselves.

in·tẽr·sē′çȧnt, *a.* dividing into parts; crossing. [Rare.]

in·tẽr·seçt′, *v.t.*; intersected, *pt.*, *pp.*; intersecting, *ppr.* [L. *intersectus*, pp. of *intersecare*, to cut between, cut off; *inter*, between, and *secare*, to cut.] to cut across; to divide into two parts by passing through or across; as, the ecliptic *intersects* the equator.

in·tẽr·seçt′, *v.i.* to meet and cross each other; to cut into each other; as, the point where two lines *intersect*.

in·tẽr·seç′tion, *n.* [L. *intersectio.*]

1. an intersecting.

2. a place of intersecting; specifically, (a) the point or line where two lines or surfaces meet or cross; (b) the place where two streets cross.

in·tẽr·seç′tion·ăl, *a.* relating to or formed by an intersection or intersections.

in″tẽr·seg·men′tăl, *a.* in zoology, located between or uniting segments.

in·tẽr·sep′tăl, *a.* situated between septa or between pairs of septa.

in·tẽr·sẽrt′, *v.t.* [L. *intersertus*, pp. of *interserere*, to place between; *inter*, between, and *serere*, to join, weave.] to insert; to set or put in between other things. [Obs.]

in·tẽr·sẽr′tion, *n.* the act of interserting; anything interserted. [Obs.]

in·tẽr·set′, *v.t.* to set or put between. [Rare.]

in·tẽr·shock′, *v.t.* to strike mutually. [Rare.]

in″tẽr·sī·dē′rē·ăl, *a.* situated between or among the stars; interstellar.

in·tẽr·sō′ciăl (-shăl), *a.* relating to social intercourse or association; having mutual relations or social intercourse.

in·tẽr·som′ni·ous, *a.* [L. *inter*, between, and *somnus*, sleep.] occurring in an interval of wakefulness. [Rare.]

in′tẽr·spāce, *n.* an intervening space.

in·tẽr·spāce′, *v.t.*; interspaced, *pt.*, *pp.*; interspacing, *ppr.* 1. to make spaces between.

2. to fill spaces between.

in·tẽr·spē·cif′iç, *a.* between species.

in′tẽr·speech, *n.* a colloquy. [Obs.]

in·tẽr·spẽrse′, *v.t.*; interspersed (-sperst′), *pt.*, *pp.*; interspersing, *ppr.* [L. *interspersus*, pp. of *interspergere*, to scatter between; *inter*, between, and *spargere*, to scatter.]

1. to scatter here and there among other things; as, to *intersperse* shrubs among trees.

2. to decorate or diversify by scattering or disposing various objects here and there.

in·tẽr·spẽr′sion, *n.* the act of interspersing, scattering, or placing here and there.

in·tẽr·spiç′ū·lăr, *a.* between or among spicules.

in·tẽr·spī′năl, *a.* in anatomy, lying between the processes of the spine, as muscles, nerves, etc.

in″tẽr·spi·nā′lis, *n.*; *pl.* **in″tẽr·spi·nā′lēs,** one of several muscles connecting the spinous processes of the contiguous vertebrae.

in·tẽr·spī′nous, *a.* interspinal.

in″tẽr·spi·rā′tion, *n.* a breathing space. [Obs.]

in″tẽr·stȧ·pē′di·ăl, *a.* between the stapes and the mediostapedial, as a columnlike part of the ear.

in″tẽr·stȧ·pē′di·ăl, *n.* an interstapedial part.

in′tẽr·stāte, *a.* between or among states of a federal government; as, *interstate* commerce.

In′tẽr·stāte Çom′mẽrce Çŏm·mis′sion, a United States Federal commission created in 1887 to regulate the commerce between the States: it has eleven members, appointed by the President.

in·tẽr·stel′lăr, *a.* [L. *inter*, between, and *stella*, star.] between or among the stars; as, *interstellar* space.

in·tẽr·stel′lȧ·ry, *a.* interstellar.

in·tẽr·stẽr′năl, *a.* 1. in anatomy, situated between the sternal segments.

2. in zoology, situated between the sternites of an arthropodal animal.

in·tẽr′stice, *n.*; *pl.* **in·tẽr′sti·ceṣ,** [Fr. *interstice*, from L. *interstitium*, a space between; *inter*, between, and *sistere*, to set, from *stare*, to stand.]

1. a space which intervenes between one thing and another; especially, a narrow or small space between things close together or between the component parts of a body; a chink; a crevice or cranny.

2. an interval of time; specifically, an interval which canon law in the Roman Catholic Church requires between promotions from lower to higher degrees of orders.

in·tẽr′sticed (-stist), *a.* having interstices or spaces between; situated at intervals.

in·tẽr·stinç′tive, *a.* distinguishing. [Obs.]

in·tẽr·sti′tiăl (-stish′ăl), *a.* [L. *interstitium*, a space between, and *-al.*]

1. of, forming, or occurring in interstices.

2. in anatomy, situated between the cellular components of an organ or structure.

in·tẽr·sti′tion, *n.* a period of time; an interval. [Obs.]

in·tẽr·strat″i·fi·çā′tion, *n.* in geology, the state of being stratified between other strata; also, that which is so stratified.

in·tẽr·strat′i·fīed, *a.* stratified among or between other strata.

in·tẽr·strat′i·fȳ, *v.t.*; interstratified, *pt.*, *pp.*; interstratifying, *ppr.* in geology, to cause to occupy a position among or between other strata.

in·tẽr·strat′i·fȳ, *v.i.* to assume a position between or among other strata.

in′tẽr·strēam, *a.* between streams; as, an *interstream* range of hills.

in·tẽr·tạlk′ (-tạk′), *v.i.* to exchange conversation; to converse. [Rare.]

in·tẽr·tañ′gle, *v.t.* to intertwist; to entangle.

in·tẽr·tär′săl, *a.* situated or occurring between the tarsal bones.

in·tẽr·tẽr′găl, *a.* [L. *inter*, between, and *tergum*, back.] situated between the terga or tergites of an arthropod.

in·tẽr·tex′, *v.t.* [L. *intertexere*, to interweave.] to interweave; to intertwine. [Obs.]

in·tẽr·tex′tūre, *n.* 1. the act of interweaving, or the state of things interwoven.

2. that which is interwoven.

in·tẽr·tīd′ăl, *a.* living between high-water mark and low-water mark, as the limpet.

in′tẽr·tīe, *n.* a short piece of timber used to bind upright posts together.

in·tẽr·tis′sūed (-tish′ūd), *a.* interwoven.

in·tẽr·traf′fiç, *n.* traffic between two or more persons or places; mutual trade. [Obs.]

in″tẽr·tran·spiç′ū·ous, *a.* transpicuous within or between. [Rare.]

in·tẽr·trans·vẽr·sā′lis, *n.*; *pl.* **in·tẽr·trans·vẽr·sā′lēṣ,** [L. *inter*, between, and *transversus*, transverse.] in anatomy, any of a number of short bundles of muscular fibers extending between the transverse processes of contiguous vertebrae.

in″tẽr·trans·vẽrse′, *a.* in anatomy, connecting the transverse processes of contiguous vertebrae.

in·tẽr·trīb′ăl, *a.* between or among tribes.

in·tẽr·trī′gō, *n.* [L. *intertrigo*; *inter*, between, and *terere*, to rub.] in pathology, an eruption of the skin produced by friction of adjacent parts.

in·tẽr·trō·çhan·ter′iç, *a.* in anatomy, situated between the trochanters.

in·tẽr·trop′iç·ăl, *a.* within or between the tropics (of Cancer and Capricorn).

in·tẽr·tū′bū·lăr, *a.* lying between tubes; as, the *intertubular* cells.

in·tẽr·twīne′, *v.t.* and *v.i.*; intertwined, *pt.*, *pp.*; intertwining, *ppr.* to twine together; to intertwist; as, the strands of a rope are *intertwined*.

in′tẽr·twīne, *n.* an intertwining or being intertwined.

in·tẽr·twīn′ing·ly, *adv.* by intertwining or being intertwined.

in·tẽr·twist′, *v.t.* and *v.i.*; intertwisted, *pt.*, *pp.*; intertwisting, *ppr.* to twist one with another; to twist together.

in·tẽr·twist′ing·ly, *adv.* by intertwisting or being intertwisted.

in·tẽr·uñ′gū·lăr, *a.* located between ungulae.

in·tẽr·un′gū·lāte, *a.* interungular.

in·tẽr·ūr′băn, *a.* [L. *inter*, between, and *urbs*, city.] between cities or towns; as, an *interurban* railway.

in·tẽr·ūr′băn, *n.* 1. an interurban railway, trolley route, etc.

2. an interurban train, railway car, trolley car, etc.

in′tẽr·văl, *n.* [L. *intervallum*, a space between, pause, lit., space between two palisades, or walls; *inter*, between, and *vallum*, a palisade, wall.]

1. a space between things; a void space intervening between any two objects; as, an *interval* between two houses or walls.

2. a period of time between any two points or events, or between the return of like conditions; as, the *interval* between two wars; an *interval* in fever.

3. in music, the difference in pitch between two tones.

4. the extent of difference between two qualities, conditions, etc.

5. an intervale.

at intervals; (a) once in a while; (b) here and there.

augmented interval; in music, an interval lengthened by a semitone.

Syn.—interim, gap, intermission, cessation.

in′tẽr·vāle, *n.* [a blending of *interval* and *vale.*] a tract of low ground between hills or along the banks of rivers: also called *interval*.

in·tẽr·val′liç, *a.* of or pertaining to an interval.

in·tẽr·val′lum, *n.* an interval. [Obs.]

in·tẽr·vā′ry, *v.i.* to alter; to vary.

in·tẽr·vẹined′, *a.* intersected with or as with veins.

in·tẽr·vēne′, *v.i.*; intervened, *pt.*, *pp.*; intervening, *ppr.* [L. *intervenire*, to come between; *inter*, between, and *venire*, to come.]

1. to come, lie, or be between; as, hills *intervene* between two valleys.

2. to come or happen between two points of time or events.

3. to come or be in between as something unnecessary or irrelevant.

4. to come between as an influencing force; to come in to modify, settle, or hinder some action, argument, etc.

5. in law, to come in as a third party to a suit, for the protection of one's own interests.

in·tẽr·vēne′, *v.t.* to divide; to come between. [Rare.]

in·tẽr·vēn′ẽr, *n.* one who intervenes.

in·tẽr·vēn′ience (-yens), *n.* the act of coming between; interposition; intervention. [Rare.]

in·tẽr·vēn′ien·cy, *n.* intervenience. [Rare.]

in·tẽr·vēn′ient, *a.* [L. *interveniens*, ppr.] intervening.

in·tẽr·vēn′ient, *n.* an intervening person or thing.

in·tẽr·vē′ni·um, *n.* [L. *intervenium*, the space between veins; *inter*, between, and *vena*, a vein.] in botany, the space or area occupied by parenchyma between the veins of leaves.

in·tẽr·vent′, *v.t.* [L. *interventus*, pp. of *intervenire*, to come between; *inter*, between, and *venire*, to come.] to obstruct or thwart. [Obs.]

in·tẽr·ven′tion, *n.* [L. *interventio* (*-onis*), from *intervenire*, to come between; *inter*, between, and *venire*, to come.]

1. a state of coming or being between; interposition; as, light is not interrupted by the *intervention* of a transparent body.

2. interposition; mediation; any interference in the affairs of others; especially, interference of one state in the affairs of another.

3. in law, the act by which a third party interposes and becomes a party to a suit pending between other parties.

in·tẽr·ven′tion·ist, *n.* one who advocates or practices intervention, especially in international affairs.

in·tẽr·ven′tion·ist, *a.* 1. of intervention or interventionists.

2. favoring or practicing intervention.

in·tẽr·ven′tŏr, *n.* [L. *interventor*, one who comes in, a visitor (LL., an intercessor), from *interventus*, pp. of *intervenire*, to come between.]

1. a mediator.

2. formerly, a person designated by a church to reconcile parties and unite them in the choice of officers.

in″tẽr·ven·triç′ū·lăr, *a.* situated between the ventricles.

in·tẽr·ven′ūe, *n.* interposition. [Obs.]

in·tẽr·ven′ū·lăr, *a.* [L. *inter*, between, and *vena*, a vein.] lying between the veins of an insect's wing.

in·tẽr·vẽrt′, *v.t.* [L. *intervertere*, to turn aside.] to turn to another course or to another use.

in·tẽr·vẽr′tē·brăl, *a.* being between the vertebrae.

in·tẽr·vẽr′tē·brăl·ly, *adv.* in an intervertebral position.

in′tẽr·view (-vū), *n.* [OFr. *entrevue*, from *entrevoir*, to meet, visit; *entre*, from L. *inter*, between, and *voir*, from L. *videre*, to see.]

1. a meeting of people face to face to confer about something; as, an *interview* between an employer and an applicant for a job.

2. a meeting between a reporter and a person whose activities, views, etc. are to be the subject of a published article.

3. a journalistic article giving such information.

in′tẽr·view, *v.t.* to hold an interview with.

in′tẽr·view·ẽr, *n.* one who interviews.

in′tẽr·view·ing, *n.* the act or practice of holding interviews.

in·tẽr·viș′i·ble, *a.* in surveying, designating stations that are mutually visible, or that can be seen from one another.

in·tẽr·viș′it, *v.i.* to interchange visits. [Rare.]

in·tẽr·vī′tăl, *a.* [L. *inter*, between, and *vita*, life.] between two lives.

in″tẽr·vō·căl′iç, *a.* [L. *inter*, between, and *vocalis*, a vowel.] in phonetics, situated between two vowels.

in″tẽr·vō·lū′tion, *n.* the state of being intervolved.

in·tẽr·volve′, *v.t.* and *v.i.*; intervolved, *pt.*, *pp.*; intervolving, *ppr.* [L. *inter*, between, and *volvere*, to roll.]

1. to wind or roll up together; to coil up.

2. to involve or be involved with one another.

in·tẽr·wēave′, *v.t.* and *v.i.*; interwove, *pt.*; interwoven, *pp.*; interweaving, *ppr.* 1. to weave together; to intermix or unite in texture or construction; as, threads of silk and cotton *interwoven*.

2. to intermingle; to connect or blend together as though woven; as, to *interweave* truth with falsehood.

in·tẽr·wish′, *v.t.* to wish mutually to each other. [Obs.]

in·tẽr·wŏrk′ing, *n.* the act of working together.

in·tẽr·wōve′, *v.* past tense of *interweave*.

in·tẽr·wōv′en, *v.* past participle of *interweave*.

in·tẽr·wrēathe′ (-rēth′), *v.t.* and *v.i.* to weave into a wreath.

in·tes′tȧ·ble, *a.* [L. *intestabilis*, disqualified from witnessing or making a will; *in-* priv., and *testabilis*, from *testari*, to be a witness, make one's will.] not capable of making a will; legally unqualified or disqualified to make a testament.

in·tes′tȧ·cy, *n.* the fact or state of dying intestate.

in·tes′tāte, *a.* [ME.; OFr. *intestat*; L. *intestatus*; *in-* priv., and *testatus*, pp. of *testari*, to make a will.]

1. not having made a valid will; as, when a man dies *intestate*, his estate is committed for settlement to administrators.

2. not devised; not disposed of by will; as, an *intestate* estate.

in·tes′tāte, *n.* a person who has died intestate.

in·tes′ti·năl, *a.* of or in the intestines.

intestinal canal; the part of the alimentary canal between the stomach and the anus.

intestinal fortitude; courage and perseverance; grit; pluck: a euphemism for *guts*, in the same sense.

in·tes′tin·ăl·ly, *adv.* in, through, or by the intestines.

in·tes′tine, *a.* [L. *intestinus*, inward, internal (neut. pl., *intestina*, entrails), from *intus*, within, from *in*, in.]

1. internal; inward. [Obs.]

2. internal with regard to a state or country; domestic; not foreign; as, *intestine* feuds; *intestine* war; *intestine* enemies.

3. depending upon the subjective character of a being or thing.

in·tes′tine, *n.* [L. *intestinum*, a gut, an intestine, properly neut. sing. of *intestinus*, inward, internal, from *intus*, within.] [*usually pl.*] the lower part of the alimentary canal, extending from the stomach to the anus and consisting of a convoluted upper part (*small intestine*) and a lower part of greater diameter (*large intestine*); bowel(s): food passes from the stomach into the intestines for further digestion.

INTESTINES

a, stomach; *b*, duodenum; *c*, jejunum; *d*, ileum; *e*, caecum and ascending colon; *f*, transverse colon; *g*, descending colon; *h*, rectum; *i*, appendix; *j*, pancreas; *k*, gall bladder; *l*, liver; *m*, esophagus

in′text, *n.* [L. *intextus*, pp. of *intexere*, to interweave.] the text or contents of a book. [Obs.]

in·tex′tine, *n.* [L. *int*us, within, and *ext*er, on the outside, and *-ine*.] in botany, that membrane of the pollen grain which is situated next to the extine, or outermost membrane.

in·tex′tūred, *a.* inwrought; woven in.

in·thrąll′, in·thrąl′, *v.t.*; inthralled, *pt.*, *pp.*; inthralling, *ppr.* to enthrall.

in·thrąll′ment, in·thrąl′ment, *n.* same as *enthrallment*.

in·thrōne′, *v.t.*; inthroned, *pt.*, *pp.*; inthroning, *ppr.* to enthrone.

in·thrọng′, *v.i.* to crowd or throng together. [Rare.]

in·thrōn·i·zā′tion, *n.* same as *enthronization*.

in·thrōn′ize, *v.t.* to enthrone.

in·tīce′, *v.t.* to entice. [Obs.]

in′ti·mȧ, *n.*; *pl.* **in′ti·mae,** [Mod. L., from L. *intimus*, inmost, superl. of *intus*, within.]

1. the innermost layer of the walls of an artery, vein, or lymphatic.

2. the lining membrane of an insect's trachea.

in′ti·mȧ·cy, *n.*; *pl.* **in′ti·mȧ·cieș,** 1. the state or fact of being intimate; intimate association; familiarity.

2. an intimate act; especially, illicit sexual intercourse: a euphemism.

in′ti·mȧte, *a.* [L. *intimus*, inmost, superl. of *intus*, within.]

1. inmost; essential; most inward; internal; as, *intimate* impulse.

2. most private or personal; as, one's *intimate* feelings.

3. closely acquainted or associated; very familiar; as, an *intimate* friend.

4. (a) resulting from careful study or investigation; (b) very close.

5. having illicit sexual relations: a euphemism.

in′ti·mȧte, *n.* an intimate friend or companion.

in′ti·māte, *v.t.*; intimated, *pt.*, *pp.*; intimating, *ppr.* [L. *intimatus*, pp. of *intimare*, to bring or press into, announce, from *intimus*, inmost, innermost, superl. of *intus*, within.]

1. to hint; to suggest obscurely, indirectly, or not very plainly; to give slight notice of.

2. to announce; to make known formally.

in′ti·mȧte·ly, *adv.* in an intimate manner.

in·ti·mā′tion, *n.* [L. *intimatio* (*-onis*), from *intimare*, to announce.]

1. the act of intimating.

2. proclamation; a formal notice or announcement.

3. a hint; an obscure or indirect suggestion or notice; as, he left us without any previous *intimation* of his intention.

in·tim′i·dāte, *v.t.*; intimidated, *pt.*, *pp.*; intimidating, *ppr.* [LL. *intimidatus*, pp. of *intimidare*, to make afraid; L. *in*, in, and *timidus*, afraid, fearful.]

1. to make timid; to make afraid; overawe.

2. to force or deter with threats or violence; to cow.

in·tim·i·dā′tion, *n.* an intimidating or being intimidated.

in·tim′i·dā·tŏr, *n.* one who intimidates.

in·tim′i·dȧ·tō·ry, *a.* causing or tending to cause intimidation.

in·tinç′tion, *n.* [LL. *intinctio* (*-onis*), a dipping in, baptizing, from L. *intingere*, to dip in; *in*, in, and *tingere*, to tinge, dye.]

1. a method or practice of administering both elements of the Eucharist at the same time, by dipping the bread or wafer into the wine before passing it.

2. the act or process of dyeing. [Obs.]

in′tine, *n.* [L. *intus*, within, and *-ine*.] a thin, transparent membrane forming the innermost layer of the coat of a pollen grain.

in·tīre′, *a.* entire. [Obs.]

in·tīre′ly, *adv.* entirely. [Obs.]

in·tī′tle, *v.t.*; intitled, *pt.*, *pp.*; intitling, *ppr.* to entitle.

in·tit′ūle, *v.t.*; intituled, *pt.*, *pp.*; intituling, *ppr.* [Fr. *intituler*; LL. *intitulare*, to entitle; L. *in*, in, on, and *titulus*, title.] to give a name or title to (a legislative act, etc.).

in′tö, *prep.* [ME. *into*; AS. *in tō*, in to; *in*, in, and *tō*, to.]

1. from the outside to the inside of; toward and within; as, *into* a house.

2. advancing or continuing to the midst of (a period of time); as, they danced far *into* the night.

3. to the form, substance, or condition of; as, turned *into* a swan, divided *into* parts.

4. in mathematics, (a) [Rare.] (multiplied) by; times; as, 7 (multiplied) *into* 3 is 21; (b) *used as an indication of division*; as, 3 *into* 21 is 7.

in·tol″ẽr·ȧ·bil′i·ty, *n.* the state or quality of being intolerable.

in·tol′ẽr·ȧ·ble, *a.* [OFr. *intolerable*; L. *intolerabilis*, that cannot be borne; *in-* priv., and *tolerabilis*, tolerable, from *tolerare*, to bear, endure.] not tolerable; unbearable; too severe, painful, cruel, etc. to be endured.

in·tol′ẽr·ȧ·ble·ness, *n.* intolerability.

in·tol′ẽr·ȧ·bly, *adv.* in an intolerable manner; so as to be intolerable; unbearably.

in·tol′ẽr·ănce, *n.* 1. lack of tolerance, especially in matters of religion; bigotry.

2. inability to endure; as, an *intolerance* for sulfa drugs.

in·tol′ẽr·ăn·cy, *n.* same as *intolerance*.

in·tol′ẽr·ănt, *a.* [L. *intolerans* (*-antis*); *in-* priv., and *tolerans* (*-antis*), ppr. of *tolerare*, to bear, endure.] not tolerant; unwilling to tolerate others' opinions, religious beliefs, etc.; bigoted; illiberal.

in·tol′ẽr·ănt, *n.* one who is intolerant.

in·tol′ẽr·ănt·ly, *adv.* in an intolerant manner.

in·tol′ẽr·ā·ted, *a.* not endured; not tolerated.

in·tol′ẽr·ā·ting, *a.* intolerant. [Rare.]

in·tol·ẽr·ā′tion, *n.* intolerance.

in·tömb′ (-töm′), *v.t.* to entomb.

in·tömb′ment, *n.* entombment.

in·tō′nä·çō, *n.* [It., roughcast, plaster, from *intonacare*, to coat with plaster; *in*, on, and *tonica*, from L. *tunica*, a robe, tunic.] the final or ground coat of plaster in fresco painting.

in′tō·nāte, *v.t.*; intonated, *pt.*, *pp.*; intonating, *ppr.* [from ML. *intonatus*, pp. of *intonare*; see *intone*.]

1. to intone.

2. in phonetics, to voice. [Rare.]

in′tō·nāte, *v.i.* [L. *intonatus*, pp. of *intonare*, to thunder, resound; *in*, in, and *tonare*, to thunder.] to thunder. [Obs.]

in·tō·nā′tion, *n.* [from *intonate* and *-ion*.]

1. an intoning.

2. the manner of producing or uttering tones with regard to rise and fall in pitch.

3. the manner of applying final pitch to a spoken sentence or phrase; as, he spoke the words with a rising *intonation*.

4. (a) the opening phrase of a Gregorian chant; (b) the reciting of this by a priest or a few choristers.

in·tō·nā′tion, *n.* thunder. [Obs.]

in·tōne′, *v.t.*; intoned, *pt.*, *pp.*; intoning, *ppr.* [ML. *intonare*; L. *in*, in, and *tonus*, a sound.]

1. to utter or recite in a singing tone or in prolonged monotones; to chant.

2. to give a particular intonation to.

3. to sing the opening phrase of (a chant, canticle, etc.).

in·tōne′, *v.i.* 1. to speak or recite in a singing tone or in prolonged monotones; to chant.

2. to utter a long, drawn-out sound; as, dogs *intone* to the moon.

in·tọr′sion, *n.* [Fr.; L. *intortio*, from *intortus*.] an intorting, as in plant stems.

in·tọrt′, *v.t.*; intorted, *pt.*, *pp.*; intorting, *ppr.* [from L. *intortus*, pp. of *intorquere*, to twist; *in*, in, and *torquere*, to twist.] to twist inward; to curl or twine.

in·tọr′tion, *n.* same as *intorsion*.

in tō′tō, [L.] wholly; entirely.

in·tox′i·çănt, *n.* [from ML. *intoxicans*, ppr. of *intoxicare*.] something that intoxicates; specifically, (a) a drug that intoxicates; (b) alcoholic liquor.

in·tox′i·çănt, *a.* intoxicating.

in·tox′i·çāte, *v.t.*; intoxicated, *pt.*, *pp.*; intoxicating, *ppr.* [ML. *intoxicatus*, pp. of *intoxi-*

care, to poison, drug; L. *in*, in, and *toxicum*, poison.]

1. to inebriate; to make drunk.

2. to excite the spirits to a kind of delirium; to elate to enthusiasm, frenzy, or madness; as, *intoxicated* with zeal.

3. in medicine, to poison or have a poisonous effect on.

in·tox′i·çāte, *a.* intoxicated. [Archaic.]

in·tox′i·çā·ted·ness, *n.* the state of intoxication.

in·tox′i·çā·ting, *a.* having qualities or properties which produce intoxication; as, *intoxicating* liquors.

in·tox·i·çā′tion, *n.* 1. an intoxicating or becoming intoxicated; specifically, (a) a making or becoming drunk; (b) in medicine, a poisoning or becoming poisoned.

2. great excitement; rapture; frenzy.

in′trȧ-, [L., from *intra*, within, inside.] a combining form meaning *within*, *inside of*, as in *intra*mural, *intra*venous.

in·trȧ·çap′sū·lăr, *a.* in biology, contained within a capsule.

in·trȧ·çär′di·aç, *a.* [*intra-*, and Gr. *kardia*, heart.] in anatomy, within the heart.

in·trȧ·çär′pel·lā·ry, *a.* in botany, within the carpel.

in·trȧ·cel′lū·lăr, *a.* situated or occurring within a cell.

in·trȧ·çol′iç, *a.* existing within the colon.

in″trȧ·çol·lē′ġi·āte, *a.* done or carried on within one college or university.

in·trȧ·çrā′ni·ăl, *a.* [*intra-*, and L. *cranium*, the skull.] situated inside the skull.

in·traçt·ȧ·bil′i·ty, *n.* the state or quality of being intractable.

in·traçt′ȧ·ble, *a.* [L. *intractabilis*, not to be handled, unmanageable; *in-* priv., and *tractabilis*, from *tractare*, to handle, manage.] not tractable; specifically, (a) hard to manage; unruly or stubborn; (b) hard to work, manipulate, cure, treat, etc.

Syn.—obstinate, stubborn, ungovernable, unmanageable, untoward.

in·traçt′ȧ·ble·ness, *n.* intractability.

in·traçt′ȧ·bly, *adv.* in an intractable manner.

in·traçt′ile, *a.* not capable of extension; not tractile.

in·trȧ·cyst′iç, *a.* occurring or locked within a cyst.

in·trä′dȧ, *n.* [It. *intrata*, an entrance.] in music, a prelude.

in·trā′dōs, *n.* [Fr., from L. *intra*, within, and *dorsum*, the back.] the inside curve or surface of an arch or vault.

in·trȧ·fō·li·ā′ceous, *a.* [*intra-*, and L. *folium*, leaf.] in botany, growing on the inside or in front of a leaf; as, *intrafoliaceous* stipules.

in·trȧ·lob′ū·lăr, *a.* located in a lobule.

in·trȧ·mär′ġin·ăl, *a.* within the margin.

in·trȧ·mẽr·çū′ri·ăl, *a.* situated within the orbit of the planet Mercury.

in·trȧ·mō·leç′ū·lăr, *a.* acting, existing, or taking place within a molecule or molecules.

in·trȧ·mun′dāne, *a.* [*intra-*, and L. *mundus*, world.] situated or occurring within the material world.

in·trȧ·mū′răl, *a.* [*intra-*, and L. *murus*, wall.]

1. within the walls or limits of a city, college, etc.; as, *intramural* athletics.

2. in anatomy, etc., within the substance of the walls of an organ.

in·trȧ·mus′çū·lăr, *a.* located or injected within the substance of a muscle.

in·tran·quil′li·ty, *n.* unquietness; inquietude.

in·trans·çā′lent, *a.* [L. *in-* priv., and *trans*, across, through, and *calescens* (*-entis*), ppr. of *calescere*, to grow hot.] impervious to heat.

in·trans·gress′i·ble, *a.* not transgressible.

in·tran′sient (-shent), *a.* not passing to another. [Rare.]

in̊·trän̊·ṣi·geäṅce′ (aṅ-trän̊-zē-zhäṅs′), *n.* [Fr.] intransigence.

in̊·trän̊·ṣi·geäṅt′ (aṅ-trän̊-zē-zhäṅ′), *n.* [Fr., from Sp. *intransigente*, from L. *in-* priv., and *transigens*, pp. of *transigere*, to come to a settlement.] an intransigent.

in̊·trän̊·ṣi·geäṅt′, *a.* intransigent.

in·tran′si·gence, in·tran′si·gen·cy, *n.* quality, state, or instance of being intransigent.

in·tran′si·gent, *a.* [Fr. *intransigeant*, from Sp. (los) *intransigentes*, the intransigents.] refusing to compromise, come to an agreement, or be reconciled; uncompromising.

in·tran′si·gent, *n.* a person who is intransigent, especially in politics.

in·trans′i·gent·ist, *n.* same as *intransigent*.

in·tran′si·tive, *a.* [LL. *intransitivus*, not transitive; L. *in-* priv., and *transitivus*, passing over, from *transire*, to go or pass over; *trans*, across, and *ire*, to go.] in grammar, not transitive; not used with an object to complete its meaning: said of certain verbs; as, I walk; I run; I sleep. It is also applied in a wider sense to verbs that are used without an expressed object though they may be really transitive in meaning; as, *build* in the sentence, "they *build* without stopping;" or *intoxicate* in "this liquor *intoxicates*."

in·tran′si·tive, *n.* an intransitive verb or construction.

in·tran′si·tive·ly, *adv.* without an object following; in the manner of an intransitive verb.

in tran′si·tū, [L., from *in*, in, and *transitu*, abl. of *transitus*, passage.] in transit; while being conveyed.

in·trans·mis′si·ble, *a.* not transmissible.

in·trans·mū·tȧ·bil′i·ty, *n.* the quality of being intransmutable.

in·trans·mū′tȧ·ble, *a.* not transmutable.

in′trănt, *n.* [from L. *intrans*, ppr. of *intrare*, to enter.] a person who enters a public office, holy orders, membership in a club, etc.

in′trănt, *a.* entering.

in·trȧ·nū′çlē·ăr, *a.* within the nucleus, as of an atom, cell, etc.

in·trȧ·oç′ū·lăr, *a.* [*intra-*, and L. *oculus*, eye.] situated in the eye.

in·trap′, *v.t.* to entrap. [Obs.]

in·trȧ·pȧ·rī′e·tăl, *a.* [*intra-*, and L. *paries* (*-etis*), a wall.]

1. located or occurring within walls; private; as, an *intraparietal* hanging. [Rare.]

2. within the parietal lobe of a brain.

in·trȧ·pet′i·ō·lăr, *a.* [*intra-*, and L. *petiolus*, a little stalk.] in botany, (a) denoting a pair of stipules at the base of a petiole united by those margins which are next to the petiole, and thus seeming to form a single stipule between the petiole and the stem or branch; (b) situated within a petiole.

in′trȧ·stāte′, *a.* within a state; especially, within a State of the United States.

in″trȧ·tel·lū′riç, *a.* [*intra-* and *telluric*.]

1. formed, located, or occurring deep inside the earth: used especially to refer to the minerals of igneous rocks before eruption.

2. designating or of the period when rocks crystallize, before eruption.

in·trȧ·ter·ri·tō′ri·ăl, *a.* situated within a territory.

in″trȧ·thō·rac′iç, *a.* situated within the thorax.

in·trȧ·trop′iç·ăl, *a.* situated within the tropics.

in·trȧ·ū′tẽr·ine, *a.* within the uterus.

intrauterine (*contraceptive*) *device*; any of various devices, as a coil or loop of plastic, for insertion in the uterus as a contraceptive.

in·trȧ·valv′ū·lăr, *a.* located between valves.

in·trav·ȧ·sā′tion, *n.* [*intra-* and *extravasation*.] the entry of a foreign substance into a blood or lymph vessel.

in·trȧ·vē′nous, *a.* [*intra-* and *venous*.] in, into, or within a vein or veins; as, an *intravenous* injection.

in″tra·ven·triç′ū·lăr, *a.* within ventricles.

in·treaṣ′ūre (-trezh′ūr), *v.t.* to lay up, as in a treasury. [Obs.]

in·trēat′, *v.t.* and *v.i.* to entreat.

in·trēat′ȧ·ble, *a.* inexorable. [Obs.]

in·trench′, *v.t.* 1. to dig or cut a trench in.

2. to surround or fortify with a trench or trenches: also spelled *entrench*.

3. to establish securely: also spelled *entrench*.

in·trench′, *v.i.* to encroach (with *upon*): also spelled *entrench*.

in·trench′ănt, *a.* not to be divided or cut. [Obs.]

in·trench′ing tọọl, any of various small tools, as a spade or pickax, carried by a combat soldier, for digging foxholes, etc.

in·trench′ment, *n.* 1. the act or process of intrenching or the condition of being intrenched.

2. in fortification, a defensive work consisting usually of a trench and a parapet.

3. any defense or protection.

4. invasion; infringement. [Obs.]

Also spelled *entrenchment*.

in·trep′id, *a.* [L. *intrepidus*; *in-* priv., and *trepidus*, alarmed, anxious, shaken.] not trembling or shaking with fear; hence, fearless; bold; brave; undaunted; as, an *intrepid* soldier.

in·trē·pid′i·ty, *n.* the quality of being intrepid; fearlessness; fearless bravery in danger.

in·trep′id·ly, *adv.* without trembling or shrinking from danger; fearlessly; daringly; resolutely.

in′tri·çȧ·ble, *a.* entangling. [Obs.]

in′tri·çȧ·cy, *n.* 1. the quality or state of being intricate; complexity.

2. *pl.* **in′tri·çȧ·cieṣ**, something intricate; involved matter, proceeding, etc.; complication.

Syn.—complication, complexity, involution, perplexity.

in′tri·çāte, *a.* hard to follow or understand because entangled, involved, complicated, or perplexing; as, *intricate* plots, accounts, etc.

Syn.—complex, complicated.—A thing is *complex* when it is made up of many interrelated parts; it is *complicated* when those parts are so many or so arranged as to make it difficult to understand their relationship; it is *intricate* when it has numerous windings and confused involutions which are difficult to follow.

in′tri·çāte, *v.t.* [L. *intricatus*, pp. of *intricare*, to entangle, perplex, embarrass; *in*, in, and *tricæ*, vexations, perplexities.] to perplex; to entangle. [Now Rare.]

in′tri·çāte·ly, *adv.* with perplexity or intricacy.

in′tri·çāte·ness, *n.* the state of being involved; complication.

in·tri·çā′tion, *n.* entanglement. [Obs.]

in′tri·gănt (*or Fr.* aṅ-trē-gäṅ′), *n.*; *pl.* **in′tri·gănts** (*or Fr.* -gäṅ′), [Fr.] a man given to or involved in intrigue.

in·tri·gante′ (*or Fr.* aṅ-trē-gäṅt′), *n.*; *pl.* **in·tri·gantes′** (*or Fr.* -gäṅt′), [Fr., f. of *intrigant*.] a woman given to or involved in intrigue.

in·trïgue′ (-trēg′), *v.i.*; intrigued, *pt.*, *pp.*; intriguing, *ppr.* [Fr. *intriguer*; OFr. *intriquer*, from L. *intricare*, to entangle, perplex, embarrass.]

1. to form a plot or scheme secretly and underhandedly; as, the courtier *intrigues* with the minister.

2. to carry on a secret love affair.

in·trïgue′, *v.t.* 1. to perplex. [Rare.]

2. to bring on or get by secret or underhanded plotting.

3. to excite the interest or curiosity of; to fascinate; as, the puzzle *intrigued* her.

in·trïgue′ (-trēg *or* in′trēg), *n.* 1. an intriguing; secret or underhanded plotting.

2. a secret or underhanded plot or scheme; machination.

3. a secret love affair.

4. intricacy; complication. [Obs.]

in·trïgu′ẽr (-trēg′), *n.* one who intrigues.

in·trïgu′ẽr·y, *n.* intriguing arts.

in·trïgu′ing·ly, *adv.* after the manner of an intrigue.

in·trin′siç, *a.* [Fr. *intrinsèque*; ML. *intrinsicus*, from L. *intrinsecus*, on the inside, inwardly; *intra*, within, and *secus*, otherwise, beside.]

1. belonging to the real nature of a thing; not dependent on external circumstances; essential; inherent.

2. in anatomy, located within, or exclusively of, a part.

Opposed to *extrinsic*.

intrinsic energy; the energy or force latent in any mechanism or form of matter; actual present power.

Syn.—real, genuine, native, inward, internal, true.

in·trin′siç, *n.* something genuine. [Obs.]

in·trin′siç·ăl, *a.* intrinsic; inherent.

in·trin·si·çal′i·ty, *n.* the quality of being intrinsic.

in·trin′siç·ăl·ly, *adv.* naturally; essentially; inherently.

A lie is a thing absolutely and *intrinsically* evil. —South.

in·trin′siç·ăl·ness, *n.* intrinsicality.

in·trin′si·çāte, *a.* intricate. [Obs.]

in′trō-, [L., from *intro*, inwardly, on the inside.] a combining form meaning *into*, *within*, *inward*, as in *intro*vert, *intro*spective.

in·trō·ces′sion (-sesh′un), *n.* a depression, or sinking of parts inward. [Rare.]

in·trō·dūce′, *v.t.*; introduced (-dūst), *pt.*, *pp.*; introducing, *ppr.* [L. *introducere*, to lead or bring in; *intro*, within, in, and *ducere*, to lead.]

1. to lead or bring into a given place or position; to conduct in.

2. to bring (a person) into society or a group.

3. to put in or within; to insert; as, he *introduced* an electric wire into the conduit.

4. to bring in or add as a new feature; to bring or put into some action, composition, etc.; as, he *introduced* some humor into his play.

5. to bring into use, knowledge, or fashion; to give currency to; to institute; as, the war *introduced* many new words.
6. to offer (a new product) for sale.
7. (a) to bring to and make known to; to make acquainted with; to present to; as, please *introduce* me to your friend; (b) to give knowledge or experience of; as, they *introduced* him to city life.
8. to bring forward; to bring to notice formally; as, *introduce* a bill into Congress.
9. to start; open; begin; as, he *introduced* his speech with a joke.
Syn.—preface, present, usher in.

in·trō·dūce′ment, *n.* introduction. [Obs.]

in·trō·dū′cẽr, *n.* one who or that which introduces.

in·trō·duçt′, *v.t.* to introduce. [Obs.]

in·trō·duç′tion, *n.* [L. *introductio* (*-onis*), a leading or bringing in, introduction, from *introducere,* to lead or bring in, introduce.]
1. an introducing or being introduced.
2. anything introduced, or brought into use, knowledge, or fashion.
3. anything that introduces, or prepares the way for; specifically, (a) the preliminary section of a book, speech, etc., usually explaining or defining the subject matter; preface or foreword, often by someone other than the author; (b) an opening section of a musical composition; (c) a preliminary guide or text.
4. the formal presentation of one person to another, to an audience, to society, etc.
Syn.—induction, importation, presentation, insertion, commencement, preliminary, preface, initiative, preamble, prelude.

in·trō·duç′tive, *a.* same as *introductory.*

in·trō·duç′tive·ly, *adv.* same as *introductorily.*

in·trō·duç′tŏr, *n.* an introducer. [Obs.]

in·trō·duç′tō·ri·ly, *adv.* in an introductory manner; as an introduction.

in·trō·duç′tō·ry, *a.* [LL. *introductorius,* from L. *introductus,* pp. of *introducere,* to introduce.] serving to introduce; used as an introduction; prefatory; preliminary; as, *introductory* remarks.

in·trō·duç′tress, *n.* a woman who introduces.

in·trō·fleç′tion, *n.* [*intro-,* and L. *flexio* (*-onis*), a bending, from *flectere,* to bend.] the condition of being introflexed.

in·trō·flexed′ (-flekst′), *a.* flexed or bent inward.

in·trō-flex′iŏn (-flek′shun), *n.* same as *introflection.*

in·trō·gres′sion (-gresh′un), *n.* [L. *introgressus,* pp. of *introgredi,* to go in; *intro,* within, and *gradi,* to go.] entrance.

in·trō′it, *n.* [L. *introitus,* a going in, entrance, from *introire*; *intro,* within, and *ire,* to go.]
1. in the Anglican Church, a psalm or hymn sung or played at the opening of the Communion service.
2. [I-] in the Roman Catholic Church, the first variable part of the Mass, consisting of a psalm verse and an antiphon followed by the *Gloria Patri.*

in·trō·jeç′tion, *n.* [*intro-* and pro*jection.*] in psychiatry, the incorporating of external events into the psyche and reacting to them as though they were internal, as when a person suffers the same pains as another, without physical cause: opposed to *projection.*

in·trō·mis′sion (-mish′un), *n.* 1. an intromitting or being intromitted.
2. in Scots law, an intermeddling with the effects of another.

in·trō·mit′, *v.t.*; intromitted, *pt., pp.*; intromitting, *ppr.* [L. *intromittere,* to send in; *intro,* within, and *mittere,* to send.]
1. to cause to enter; to put in; to insert.
2. to allow to enter; to let in; to admit; as, glass in the window *intromits* light.

in·trō·mit′, *v.i.* in Scots law, to intermeddle with the effects of another.

in·trō·mit′tent, *a.* [L. *intromittens* (*-entis*), ppr. of *intromittere,* to send in.] that intromits or can intromit; as, an *intromittent* instrument, an *intromittent* organ.

in·trō·mit′tẽr, *n.* one who or that which intromits.

in·trō·pres′sion (-presh′un), *n.* internal pressure. [Rare.]

in″trō·rē·cep′tion, *n.* the act of admitting into or within.

in·trorse′, *a.* [L. *introrsus, introrsum,* toward the inside, contr. of *introversus*; *intro,* within, and *versus,* turned.] in botany, facing inward, or toward the center.

in·trō·speçt′, *v.t.* [L. *introspectare,* freq. of *introspicere,* to look within; *intro,* within, and *spicere,* to look.] to look into (one's own mind, feelings, reactions, etc.). [Rare.]

in·trō·speçt′, *v.i.* to look into one's own mind, etc.; to practice introspection.

intrō·speç′tion, *n.* a looking into one's own mind, feelings, reactions, etc.; observation and analysis of oneself.

in·trō·speç′tion·ist, *n.* one who practices introspection.

in·trō·speç′tive, *a.* of, based on, inclined toward, or characterized by introspection.

in·trō·sūme′, *v.t.* [*intro-,* and L. *sumere,* to take.] to suck in; to absorb. [Obs.]

in″trō·sus·cep′tion, *n.* [*intro-,* and L. *susceptio* (*-onis*), from *suscipere,* to take up or in.] same as *intussusception.*

in·trō·vēn′ient (-yent), *a.* [L. *introveniens* (*-entis*), ppr. of *introvenire,* to come in, enter; *intro,* within, and *venire* to come.] coming in or between; entering. [Rare.]

in·trō·vẽr′sion, *n.* [Mod. L. *introversio* (after *introvert*), from *intro-,* and L. *versus,* pp. of *vertere,* to turn.]
1. an introverting or being introverted.
2. in psychology, a tendency to direct one's interest upon oneself rather than upon external objects or events.

in·trō·vẽr′sive, *a.* of or tending to introversion.

in·trō·vẽrt′, *v.t.*; introverted, *pt., pp.*; introverting, *ppr.* [from *intro-,* and L. *vertere,* to turn.]
1. to direct (one's interest, mind, or attention) upon oneself; to introspect.
2. to bend (something) inward.
3. in zoology, etc., to draw (a tubular organ or part) inward upon itself.

in·trō·vẽrt′, *v.i.* to engage in or occupy oneself with introversion; to become introverted.

in′trō·vẽrt, *n.* 1. a thing that is or can be introverted.
2. in psychology, a person characterized by introversion: opposed to *extrovert.*

in′trō·vẽrt, *a.* of or characterized by introversion.

in·trō·vẽr′tive, *a.* same as *introversive.*

in·trụde′, *v.t.*; intruded, *pt., pp.*; intruding, *ppr.* [L. *intrudere,* to thrust in; *in,* in, and *trudere,* to thrust, push.]
1. to push or force (something) in or upon.
2. to force (oneself) upon others without being asked or welcomed.
3. in geology, to force (melted rock) into another stratum: usually in the passive.

in·trụde′, *v.i.* to intrude oneself.

in·trụd′ẽr, *n.* one who intrudes; one who thrusts himself in, or enters where he has no right or is not welcome.

They were all strangers and *intruders.*
—Locke.

in·trụd′ress, *n.* a woman who intrudes.

in·truñk′, *v.t.* to enclose as in a trunk or case. [Obs.]

in·trụse′, *a.* [L. *intrusus,* pp. of *intrudere,* to thrust in.] in botany, growing inward.

in·trụ′ṣion, *n.* [ME. *intrucioun*; OFr.; ML. *intrusio* (*-onis*), a thrusting in, from L. *intrudere*; *in,* in, and *trudere,* to thrust, push.]
1. the act of thrusting in, or of entering into a place or state without invitation, right, or welcome.

Why this *intrusion?*
Were not my orders that I should be private?
—Addison.

2. in geology, the penetrating of one rock, while in a melted state, into the cavities of other rocks; also, intrusive rock.
3. in law, an unlawful entry into lands and tenements void of a possessor by a person who has no right to the same; hence, the illegal entering or taking of another's property.

in·trụ′ṣion·ăl, *a.* pertaining to intrusion.

in·trụ′ṣion·ist, *n.* 1. one who intrudes.
2. formerly, in Scotland, one who favored the settlement of a pastor in a church or congregation contrary to the will of the people or without their consent.

in·trụ′sive, *a.* [from L. *intrusus,* pp. of *intrudere*; and *-ive.*]
1. intruding or tending to intrude.
2. in geology, (a) forced into another stratum while in a molten state: said of rock; (b) formed of such rock.

in·trụ′sive·ly, *adv.* in an intrusive manner.

in·trụ′sive·ness, *n.* the quality of being intrusive.

in·trust′, *v.t.* to entrust.

in′tū·bāte, *v.t.*; intubated, *pt., pp.*; intubating, *ppr.* to treat by intubation.

in·tū·bā′tion, *n.* [from *in-,* in, and *tube,* and *-ation.*] the insertion of a tube into an orifice or hollow organ, as into the larynx to permit air to enter in severe cases of diphtheria.

in′tū·it, *v.t.* and *v.i.* [L. *intuitus,* pp. of *intueri,* to look on, consider; *in,* in, on, and *tueri,* to look.] to know or learn by intuition.

in·tū·i′tion (-ish′un), *n.* [LL. *intuitio* (*-onis*), a regarding, looking at, from L. *intueri,* to consider, look on.]
1. the immediate knowing or learning of something without the conscious use of reasoning; instantaneous apprehension.
2. something known or learned in this way.
3. a looking on; a sight or view; hence, a regard to; an aim. [Obs.]
Syn.—instinct, apprehension, recognition, insight.

in·tū·i′tion·ăl, *a.* of, having the nature of, or resulting from intuition.

in·tū·i′tion·ăl·iṣm, *n.* the philosophical doctrine that absolute truth or any given truth can be perceived by intuition: also called *intuitionism.*

in·tū·i′tion·ăl·ist, *n.* one who believes in intuitionalism.

in·tū·i′tion·iṣm, *n.* 1. intuitionalism.
2. the doctrine that the reality of perceived objects is known by intuition.
3. in ethics, the doctrine that moral principles are acquired by intuition; intuitivism.

in·tū·i′tion·ist, *n.* one who believes in intuitionism.

in·tū′i·tive, *a.* [LL. *intuitivus,* from L. *intueri,* to look on, consider; *in,* in, on, and *tueri,* to look at, regard.]
1. knowing, learning, acting, or characterized by intuition.
2. that is or can be perceived by intuition; as, an *intuitive* truth.
3. seeing clearly; as, an *intuitive* view. [Obs.]

in·tū′i·tive·ly, *adv.* in an intuitive manner; by intuition.

in·tū′i·tiv·iṣm, *n.* in ethics, intuitionism.

in·tū·mesce′, *v.i.*; intumesced (-mest′), *pt.; pp.*; intumescing, *ppr.* [L. *intumescere,* to swell up; *in,* in, on, and *tumescere,* incept. of *tumere,* to swell.] to swell; to enlarge or expand with or as with heat.

in·tū·mes′cence, *n.* 1. an intumescing or being intumesced.
2. a swollen or enlarged organ or part, as a tumor; swelling.

in·tū·mes′cent, *a.* intumescing; swelling; swollen.

in·tū′mū·lā·ted, *a.* [LL. *intumulatus,* pp. of *intumulare,* to bury; L. *in-* priv., and *tumulus,* a tomb.] buried; entombed. [Obs.]

in·tūne′, *v.t.* to intone. [Obs.]

in·tũr′bid·āte, *v.t.*; inturbidated, *pt., pp.*; inturbidating, *ppr.* [L. *in,* in, and *turbidus,* full of confusion, muddy, thick.] to render turbid, dark, or confused. [Rare.]

in·tũr·ġes′cence, *n.* a swelling; the act of swelling or state of being swollen.

in′tũrn, *n.* a bending or turning inward, especially of the toes.

in′tūse, *n.* a bruise. [Obs.]

in″tus·sus·cept′, *v.t.* [from L. *intus,* within, and *susceptus,* pp. of *suscipere,* to take up.] to receive within itself or into another part; specifically, to telescope (one section of the intestines) into another; to invaginate; introvert.

in″tus·sus·cep′tion, *n.* [from L. *intus,* within, and *susceptio,* a taking up, from pp. of *suscipere,* to take up, from *sub-,* under, and *capere,* to take.]
1. an intussuscepting or being intussuscepted.
2. the process of taking in food or other foreign matter and converting it into tissue.

in″tus·sus·cep′tive, *a.* of, characterized by, or caused by intussusception.

in·twīne′, *v.t.* and *v.i.* to entwine.

in·twist′, *v.t.* to entwist.

in·ū·en′dō, *n.* same as *innuendo.*

In′ū·lȧ, *n.* [Mod.L., from L. *inula,* elecampane.] a genus of perennial herbs of the group *Compositæ,* natives of the temperate regions of Europe, Asia, and Africa. They have yellow flowers with large heads.

in′ū·lāse, *n.* [from *inulin* and *-ase.*] an enzyme that converts inulin into levulose.

in′u·lin, *n.* [from Mod. L. *Inula*; see *Inula,* and *-in.*] a white polysaccharide found in the roots of many plants, which yields levulose when hydrolyzed.

in′ū·loid, *n.* a substance similar to inulin found

in the unripe buds of several plants of the group *Compositæ*.

in·um′brāte, *v.t.* [L. *inumbratus*, pp. of *inumbrare*, to cast a shadow upon; *in*, in, on, and *umbra*, a shadow.] to obscure; to shade. [Obs.]

in·unc̄′ted, *a.* anointed. [Rare.]

in·unc̄′tion, *n.* [L. *inunctio*.]
 1. an anointing or being anointed.
 2. the rubbing of ointment, etc. into the skin.
 3. an ointment, liniment, etc.

in·unc̄·tū·os′i·ty, *n.* absence of greasiness or oiliness. [Rare.]

in·un′dănt, *a.* overflowing.

in′un·dāte, *v.t.*; inundated, *pt.*, *pp.*; inundating, *ppr.* [L. *inundatus*, pp. of *inundare*, to overflow; *in*, in, on, and *undare*, to move in waves, to flood, from *unda*, a wave.]
 1. to overflow; to deluge; to spread over with a flood; as, the lowlands along the Mississippi are *inundated* almost every spring.
 2. to fill with an overflowing abundance or superfluity; as, he was *inundated* with letters.

in·un·dā′tion, *n.* [L. *inundatio* (*-onis*), from *inundare*, to overflow, inundate.]
 1. the act of inundating or the state of being inundated; an overflow of water or other fluid; a flood; a rising and spreading of water over low grounds; as, Holland has frequently suffered by *inundations* of the sea.
 2. an overspreading of any kind; an overflowing or superfluous abundance; as, an *inundation* of poor literature.

in′un·dā·tŏr, *n.* something that inundates.

in·un′dȧ·tō·ry, *a.* of, characterized by, or like an inundation.

in·un·dēr·stand′ing, *a.* not understanding. [Obs.]

in·ūr·bāne′, *a.* [L. *inurbanus*; *in-* priv., and *urbanus*, civil, polite, from *urbs*, a city.] not urbane; crude; impolite; discourteous; unpolished.

in·ūr·bāne′ly, *adv.* without urbanity.

in·ūr·bāne′ness, *n.* inurbanity.

in·ūr·ban′i·ty, *n.* incivility; rude, unpolished manners or deportment; lack of courteousness.

in·ūre′, *v.t.*; inured, *pt.*, *pp.*; inuring, *ppr.* [*in-*, and ME. *ure*; OFr. *eure*, *ovre*; L. *opera*, work.]
 1. to habituate; to accustom; to cause to become used to (something difficult, painful, etc.).

> We may *inure* ourselves by custom to bear the extremities of weather without injury.
> —Addison.

 2. to establish in use. [Obs.]

in·ūre′, *v.i.* to come into use; to take or have effect; to serve to the use or benefit of; as, a gift of land *inures* to the heirs of the grantee, or it *inures* to their benefit.

in·ūre′ment, *n.* an inuring or being inured.

in·ūrn′, *v.t.*; inurned, *pt.*, *pp.*; inurning, *ppr.* to put (ashes of the dead) in an urn; hence, to bury; to inter; to entomb.

in·ū′ṣi·tāte, *a.* [L. *inusitatus*, unused, uncommon.] unused or uncommon. [Rare.]

in·ū·ṣi·tā′tion, *n.* lack of use. [Rare.]

in·ust′, *a.* burnt in. [Obs.]

in·us′tion (-chun), *n.* the act of burning in; a branding; the act of marking by burning. [Obs.]

in·ū′tile, *a.* unprofitable; useless.

in·ū·til′i·ty, *n.* [L. *inutilitas*, uselessness, from *inutilis*, useless; *in-* priv., and *utilis*, useful.]
 1. uselessness; the quality of being unprofitable; unprofitableness; as, the *inutility* of vain speculations and visionary projects.
 2. *pl.* **in·ū·til′i·tieṣ,** a useless person or thing.

in·ut′tēr·ȧ·ble, *a.* unutterable.

in vac̨′ū·ō, [L.] in a vacuum, or empty space.

in·vāde′, *v.t.*; invaded, *pt.*, *pp.*; invading, *ppr.* [L. *invadere*, to come or go in; *in*, in, and *vadere*, to come or go.]
 1. to go into; to enter. [Obs.]
 2. to enter, as an army, with hostile intentions; to enter, as an enemy, with a view to conquest or plunder; to attack; as, the French armies *invaded* Holland in 1795.
 3. to crowd into; throng; as, the children *invaded* the kitchen.
 4. to intrude upon; infringe; violate; as, he *invaded* my privacy.
 5. to enter and spread through with harmful effects; as, disease *invades* tissue.

in·vāde′, *v.i.* to make an invasion.

in·vād′ēr, *n.* one who or that which invades.

in·vaġ′i·nāte, *v.t.*; invaginated, *pt.*, *pp.*; invaginating, *ppr.* [L. *in*, in, and *vagina*, a sheath.]
 1. to place or receive into a sheath.
 2. to intussuscept.

in·vaġ′i·nāte, *v.i.* to become invaginated.

in·vaġ′i·nāte, in·vaġ′i·nā·ted, *a.* sheathed; received as into a sheath.

in·vaġ·i·nā′tion, *n.* 1. an invaginating or being invaginated.
 2. an invaginated part.

in·vȧ·les′cence, *n.* [L. *invalescere*, to become strong.] strength; health. [Obs.]

in·val·ē·tū′di·nā·ry, *a.* lacking health. [Obs.]

in·val′id, *a.* [L. *invalidus*, not strong, weak; *in-* priv., and *validus*, strong, from *valere*, to be strong.]
 1. not valid; weak; of no force, weight, or cogency.
 2. in law, having no force, effect, or efficacy; void; null; as, an *invalid* contract or agreement.

in′vȧ·lid, *a.* [Fr. *invalide*, from L. *invalidus*.]
 1. not well; weak and sickly; infirm.
 2. of or for invalids; as, an *invalid* home.

in′vȧ·lid, *n.* a person who is weak and infirm; especially, one who is chronically ill or disabled; a person who is wounded, maimed, or otherwise disabled for active service, as a soldier or seaman.

in′vȧ·lid, *v.t.*; invalided, *pt.*, *pp.*; invaliding, *ppr.* 1. to make invalid; to disable or weaken.
 2. to put (a soldier, sailor, etc.) on a sick list or dismiss from active service because of injury or illness.

in′vȧ·lid, *v.i.* 1. to become an invalid.
 2. to retire from the army, navy, etc. because of ill health.

in·val′i·dāte, *v.t.*; invalidated, *pt.*, *pp.*; invalidating, *ppr.* to make invalid; to weaken or lessen the force of; to destroy the strength or validity of; to render of no legal force or effect; as, to *invalidate* an agreement or a contract.

in·val·i·dā′tion, *n.* an invalidating or being invalidated.

in′vȧ·lid·iṣm, *n.* the condition of being an invalid; chronic ill health or disability.

in·vȧ·lid′i·ty, *n.* lack of validity.

in·val′id·ly, *adv.* without validity.

in·val′id·ness, *n.* invalidity.

in·val′ŏr·ous, *a.* without valor; cowardly; timid.

in·val′ū·ȧ·ble, *a.* precious; priceless; so valuable that its worth cannot be estimated; inestimable.

in·val′ū·ȧ·bly, *adv.* so as to be invaluable.

in·val′ūed, *a.* inestimable; invaluable. [Rare.]

in·vär′, *n.* [from *invariable*.] a steel alloy containing 36 per cent nickel, used in the manufacture of precision instruments because of its low coefficient of expansion: a trade-mark (*Invar*).

in·vā″ri·ȧ·bil′i·ty, *n.* the quality of being invariable; immutability.

in·vā′ri·ȧ·ble, *a.* constant; immutable; unalterable; unchangeable; that does not vary; always uniform.

in·vā′ri·ȧ·ble, *n.* in mathematics, an invariant; a constant.

in·vā′ri·ȧ·ble·ness, *n.* constancy of state, condition, or quality; immutability; unchangeableness.

in·vā′ri·ȧ·bly, *adv.* constantly; uniformly; without alteration or change; as, we are bound to pursue *invariably* the path of duty.

in·vā′ri·ănce, *n.* in mathematics, the property of remaining invariable after the process of linear transformation.

in·vā′ri·ănt, *a.* not varying; constant.

in·vā′ri·ănt, *n.* in mathematics, a function of the coefficients of a quantic, such that if the quantic is subjected to the process of linear transformation, the corresponding function of the new coefficients is equivalent to the original function multiplied by some power of the modulus of transformation.

in·vā′ried, *a.* unvaried. [Rare.]

in·vā′ṣion (-zhun), *n.* [Fr.; LL. *invasio* (*-onis*), from L. *invadere*, to go in; *in*, in, and *vadere*, to go or come.]
 1. a hostile entrance into the possessions of another; especially, the entrance of an attacking army into a country.
 2. an attack on the rights of another; infringement or violation.
 3. attack of a disease or anything pernicious; as, the *invasion* of a plague.
 4. the act of invading, encroaching, or trespassing.
 Syn.—incursion, irruption, inroad.

in·vā′sive, *a.* [Fr.; LL. *invasivus*, from L. *invasus*, pp. of *invadere*, to invade.] of, like, or having the nature of, invasion.

in·veck′ée (-ā), *a.* [etym. doubtful.] in heraldry, double-arched: said of a line or the edge of an ordinary bent into curves.

A CHIEF INVECKÉE

in·vec̨′ted, *a.* [L. *invectus*, pp. of *invehere*, to bring in, to penetrate.] in heraldry, having all the points turning inward to the ordinary, with the small semicircles outward to the field.

in·vec̨′tive, *a.* [ME. *invectiff*; Late OFr. *invectif*; L. *invectivus*, scolding, abusive, from *invectus*, pp. of *invehere*, to bring in, attack, scold; *in*, in, to, and *vehere*, to carry.] inveighing; using, inclined to use, or characterized by invective.

A PALE INVECTED

in·vec̨′tive, *n.* 1. a violent verbal attack; strong denunciation; vituperation.
 2. [*often in pl.*] an abusive word; as, a volley of *invectives*.

in·vec̨′tive·ly, *adv.* in an invective manner.

in·veigh′ (-vā′), *v.i.*; inveighed, *pt.*, *pp.*; inveighing, *ppr.* [L. *invehere*, to bring in, to attack with words, scold; *in*, in, to, and *vehere*, to carry.] to make a violent verbal attack; to make strong denunciations; to utter invective; to rail: usually with *against*; as, men *inveigh against* the follies of fashion.

in·veigh′ēr (-vā′), *n.* one who inveighs.

in·vēi′gle (-vē′ *or* -vā′), *v.t.*; inveigled, *pt.*, *pp.*; inveigling, *ppr.* [prob. a corruption of OFr. *aveugler*, to blind, delude, from LL. *aboculus*, blind; L. *ab*, from, and *oculus*, eye.] to lead on with deception; to wheedle; to entice or trick into doing something, going somewhere, etc.

in·vēi′gle·ment, *n.* an inveigling or being inveigled.

in·vēi′glēr, *n.* one who inveigles.

in·veil′, *v.t.*; inveiled, *pt.*, *pp.*; inveiling, *ppr.* to cover or conceal, as with a veil.

> Her eyes *inveiled* with sorrow's clouds.
> —W. Browne.

in·vend·i·bil′i·ty, *n.* the state or quality of being invendible.

in·vend′i·ble, *a.* not vendible; unsaleable.

in·ven′ŏm, *v.t.* to envenom. [Obs.]

in·vent′, *v.t.*; invented, *pt.*, *pp.*; inventing, *ppr.* [ME. *inventen*; OFr. *inventer*, from L. *inventus*, pp. of *invenire*, to come upon, meet with, discover; *in*, in, to, and *venire*, to come.]
 1. to think up; to devise or fabricate in the mind; as, try to *invent* an alibi.
 2. to think out or produce (a new device, process, etc.); to originate, as by experiment; to devise for the first time; as, Edison *invented* the phonograph.
 3. to find; to come upon; discover. [Archaic.]
 Syn.—devise, discover, fabricate, feign.

in·vent′ēr, *n.* same as *inventor*.

in·vent′fụl, *a.* full of invention. [Rare.]

in·vent′i·ble, *a.* that can be invented.

in·vent′i·ble·ness, *n.* the state of being inventible.

in·ven′tion, *n.* [L. *inventio* (*-onis*), a discovery, invention, from *inventus*, pp. of *invenire*, to come upon, discover.]
 1. an inventing or being invented.
 2. the power of inventing; ingenuity.
 3. something invented; specifically, (a) something thought up or mentally fabricated; falsehood; (b) something originated by experiment, etc.; a new device or contrivance.
 4. in music, a short piano composition developing a single theme in two-part counterpoint; especially, any of a group of these by Bach.

in·ven′tion·ăl, *a.* of or like an invention.

in·ven′tious (-shus), *a.* inventive. [Obs.]

in·vent′ive, *a.* 1. of or pertaining to invention.
 2. skilled or resourceful in inventing; as, an *inventive* genius.
 3. indicating an ability to invent; as, *inventive* powers.

in·vent′ive·ly, *adv.* by the power of invention.

in·vent′ive·ness, *n.* the quality of being inventive.

in·vent′ŏr, *n.* [L. *inventor*, a discoverer, inventor, from *invenire*, to find, discover.] a person who invents; especially, one who makes or introduces a new contrivance, device, etc.: also spelled *inventer*.

in·ven·tō′ri·ăl, *a.* of, or having the nature of, an inventory.

in·ven·tō'ri·ăl·ly, *adv.* in the manner of an inventory.

in'ven·tō·ry, *n.*; *pl.* **in'ven·tō·ries,** [LL. *inventorium*, a list, inventory, from L. *inventus*, pp. of *invenire*, to come upon, discover.]

1. an itemized list or catalogue of goods, property, etc.; especially, such a list of the stock of a business, taken annually.

2. the store of goods, etc., which are or may be so listed; stock.

to take inventory; (a) to make an inventory of stock on hand; (b) to make an appraisal, as of one's skills, personal characteristics, etc.

in'ven·tō·ry, *v.t.*; inventoried, *pt., pp.*; inventorying, *ppr.* 1. to make an inventory of; to make a list, catalogue, or schedule of; as, to *inventory* a stock of books.

2. to place on an inventory.

in·vent'ress, *n.* a woman who invents.

in·vē·rac'i·ty, *n.*; *pl.* **in·vē·rac'i·ties,** falsehood; lack of veracity.

in·ver''i·si·mil'i·tūde, *n.* lack of verisimilitude; improbability.

In·vër·ness', *n.* [often i–], (a) a kind of overcoat with a long, removable, sleeveless cape; (b) the cape: also *Inverness cape*.

in·vërse' (*or* in'vërs), *a.* [L. *inversus*, pp. of *invertere*, to turn about; *in*, in, to, toward, and *vertere*, to turn.]

1. inverted; reversed in order or relation; directly opposite.

2. in mathematics, opposite in nature and effect: said of any two operations which, when both are performed in succession upon a quantity, leave the quantity with its original value; as, addition is *inverse* to subtraction.

inverse or *reciprocal proportion*; an equality between a direct ratio and a reciprocal ratio; thus, $4 : 2 :: \frac{1}{3} : \frac{1}{6}$, or $4 : 2 :: 3 : 6$, *inversely*.

inverse or *reciprocal ratio*; the ratio of the reciprocals of two quantities.

in·vërse', *n.* any inverse thing; direct opposite; as, love is the *inverse* of hate.

in·vërse', *v.t.*; inversed, *pt., pp.*; inversing, *ppr.* to invert; to reverse.

in·vërse'ly, *adv.* in an inverse order or manner.

in·vër'sion, *n.* [L. *inversio* (*-onis*); from *invertere*, to turn about.]

1. an inverting or being inverted.

2. something inverted; reversal.

3. in chemistry, a chemical change in which an optically active substance is converted into another substance having no effect, or the opposite rotatory effects, on the plane of polarization; as, sucrose yields dextrose and levulose by *inversion*.

4. in grammar and rhetoric, a reversal of the normal order of words in a sentence.

5. in mathematics, (a) the process of using an opposite rule or method; (b) an interchange of the terms of a ratio.

6. in medicine and pathology, introversion.

7. in music, the reversal of the position of the tones in an interval chord, etc., as by raising the lower tone by an octave, etc.

8. in phonetics, a position of the tongue in which the tip is turned upward and backward.

9. in psychiatry, homosexuality.

10. in geology, the apparent reversion of the regular order of succession of layers of strata.

in·vër'sive, *a.* showing or causing inversion.

in·vërt', *v.t.*; inverted, *pt., pp.*; inverting, *ppr.* [L. *invertere*, to turn about; *in*, in, to, toward, and *vertere*, to turn.]

1. to turn upside down.

2. to change to the direct opposite; to reverse the order, position, direction, etc. of.

3. to subject to inversion (in various senses).

in·vërt', *v.i.* to be subjected to chemical inversion.

in'vërt, *a.* in chemistry, inverted; as, *invert* sugar.

in'vërt, *n.* 1. an inverted person or thing.

2. in masonry, an inverted arch.

3. in psychiatry, a homosexual.

in·vër'tāse, *n.* [*invert*, and *-ase*.] an enzyme, present in certain plants and in the small intestine of animals, which changes sucrose into dextrose and levulose.

in·vër'tē·brăl, *a.* invertebrate. [Rare.]

In·vër·tē·brā'tȧ, *n.pl.* [L. *in-* priv., and *vertebratus*, vertebrate, from *vertebra*, a joint, especially of the spine.] one of the two great divisions of the animal kingdom (the other being the *Vertebrata*), including all animals having no backbone, or spinal column.

in·vër'tē·brāte, in·vër'tē·brā·ted, *a.* 1. not vertebrate; having no backbone, or spinal column.

2. of invertebrates.

3. having no moral backbone; lacking courage, resolution, etc.

in·vër'tē·brāte, *n.* any animal without a backbone, or spinal column: the classification includes all animals except fishes, amphibians, reptiles, birds, and mammals.

in·vërt'ed, *a.* turned to a contrary direction; changed in order; inverse; reversed; specifically, (a) in heraldry, turned toward the middle of the field; (b) in geology, lying apparently in inverse order, as beds and strata which have been upheaved and folded back on each other by the intrusion of igneous rocks.

inverted arch; an arch put in place with its crown downward, used in building sewers, foundations, etc.

inverted commas; quotation marks. [Brit.]

in·vërt'ed·ly, *adv.* in a reversed order.

in·vërt'ër, *n.* in electricity, a device for transforming direct current into alternating current.

in·vërt'i·ble, *a.* [L. *in*, in, on, and *vertere*, to turn.] that can be inverted or subjected to inversion.

in'vërt sug'ăr (shug'), a mixture of dextrose and levulose in approximately equal proportions, found in fruits and produced artificially by the inversion of sucrose.

in·vest', *v.t.*; invested, *pt., pp.*; investing, *ppr.* [L. *investire*, to clothe, cover; *in*, in, and *vestire*, to clothe, from *vestis*, clothing.]

1. to clothe; array; adorn. [Rare.]

2. (a) to cover, surround, or envelop like, or as if with, a garment; as, fog *invests* the city; (b) to endue.

3. to install in office with ceremony.

4. to furnish with power, privilege, or authority.

5. (a) to vest or settle (a power or right) in a person, legislative body, etc.; (b) to put on; to don. [Rare.]

6. to put (money) into business, real estate, stocks, bonds, etc., for the purpose of obtaining an income or profit.

7. in military usage, to hem in or besiege (a town, port, enemy salient, etc.).

in·vest', *v.i.* to invest money; to make an investment; as, to *invest* in railway shares.

in·vest'ient (-yent), *a.* covering. [Obs.]

in·ves'ti·gȧ·ble, *a.* that can be investigated.

in·ves'ti·gāte, *v.t.*; investigated, *pt., pp.*; investigating, *ppr.* [L. *investigatus*, pp. of *investigare*, to trace out, search into; *in*, in, and *vestigare*, to track, from *vestigium*, a track, foot-track.] to search into; to inquire into systematically; to examine in detail with care and accuracy; as, to *investigate* the powers and forces of nature; to *investigate* the conduct of an agent.

in·ves'ti·gāte, *v.i.* to make an investigation.

in·ves·ti·gā'tion, *n.* an investigating; careful search; detailed examination; systematic inquiry; as, the *investigations* of the scientist; the *investigations* of a district attorney.

Syn.—examination, inquiry, inquisition, research, search, scrutiny.

in·ves'ti·gā·tive, *a.* 1. of, or having the character of, investigation.

2. inclined to investigation.

in·ves'ti·gā·tŏr, *n.* one who investigates.

in·ves'ti·gȧ·tō·ry, *a.* investigative.

in·ves'ti·tive, *a.* [from L. *investitus*, pp. of *investire*, to invest; and *-ive*.]

1. that invests or can invest authority, etc.

2. of such investing.

in·ves'ti·tūre, *n.* [ME.; ML. *investitura*, from L. *investire*, to clothe, cover; *in*, in, and *vestire*, to clothe, from *vestis*, clothing.]

1. a formal investing with an office, power, authority, etc.

2. anything that clothes or covers; vesture.

3. in feudal law, the livery of seizin: a ceremonial conveyence of land.

in·vest'ment, *n.* 1. the act of investing; specifically, (a) the act of surrounding, blocking up, or besieging by an armed force; (b) the laying out of money in the purchase of some kind of property; (c) investiture.

2. the property in which one invests or may invest; also, the capital invested.

3. that which invests or clothes; dress.

in·vest'ment fund, a trust or corporation that invests in securities the funds obtained from the sale of its own shares and distributes a return to its shareholders from the income on the securities.

in·vest'ŏr, *n.* one who invests.

in·ves'tūre, *n.* investment; investiture. [Obs.]

in·ves'tūre, *v.t.* to invest; to clothe. [Obs.]

in·vet'ër·ȧ·cy, *n.* 1. the state or quality of being inveterate.

2. *pl.* **in·vet'ër·ȧ·cies,** an enmity or prejudice of long standing.

in·vet'ër·āte, *a.* [L. *inveteratus*, pp. of *inveterare*, to make or become old, from *in-*, in, and *vetus*, old.]

1. deep-rooted; firmly established over a long period; of long standing; as, an *inveterate* disease, an *inveterate* abuse.

2. settled in a habit, practice, prejudice, etc.; habitual.

3. violent; obstinate; as, *inveterate* malice. [Now Rare.]

4. old; long-established. [Archaic.]

Syn.—confirmed, established, deep-rooted.

in·vet'ër·āte, *v.t.* to make inveterate. [Archaic.]

in·vet'ër·āte·ly, *adv.* in an inveterate manner.

in·vet'ër·āte·ness, *n.* inveteracy.

in·vet·ër·ā'tion, *n.* the act of making inveterate. [Rare.]

in·vexed' (-vekst'), *a.* [LL. *invexus*, equivalent to L. *convexus*, arched, vaulted.] in heraldry, arched or inarched.

CHIEF INVEXED

in·vict', *a.* unconquered; indomitable. [Obs.]

in·vid'i·ous, *a.* [L. *invidiosus*, from *invidia*, envy, ill will, from *invidere*, to look askance at.]

1. envious. [Obs.]

2. likely to incur ill will or hatred, or to provoke envy; giving offense, especially, by discriminating unfairly; as, *invidious* comparisons.

3. enviable; desirable. [Obs.]

Syn.—envious, hateful, odious.

in·vid'i·ous·ly, *adv.* in an invidious manner.

in·vid'i·ous·ness, *n.* the quality of being invidious.

in·vig'i·lănce, in·vig'i·lăn·cy, *n.* lack of vigilance. [Rare.]

in·vig'i·lāte, *v.i.*; invigilated, *pt., pp.*; invigilating, *ppr.* [L. *invigilatus*, pp. of *invigilare*, to watch diligently.]

1. to watch diligently.

2. to keep watch over students during a written examination. [Chiefly Brit.]

in·vig'i·lā·tŏr, *n.* a person who invigilates. [Chiefly Brit.]

in·vig'ŏr, *v.t.* to invigorate. [Rare.]

in·vig'ŏr·ănt, *n.* a thing that invigorates.

in·vig'ŏr·āte, *v.t.*; invigorated, *pt., pp.*; invigorating, *ppr.* [L. *in*, in, and *vigor*, strength, courage.] to give vigor to; to strengthen; to animate; to give life and energy to.

in·vig·ŏr·ā'tion, *n.* the act of invigorating or state of being invigorated.

in·vig'ŏr·ā·tive, *a.* invigorating or tending to invigorate.

in·vig'ŏr·ā·tŏr, *n.* a person or thing that invigorates.

in·vīle', *v.t.* [LL. *invilare*; L. *in*, in, and *vilis*, vile, worthless.] to make vile. [Obs.]

in·vil'lāged, *a.* turned into a village. [Obs.]

in·vin·ci·bil'i·ty, *n.* the quality or state of being invincible.

in·vin'ci·ble, *a.* [L. *invincibilis*; *in-* priv., and *vincibilis*, conquerable, from *vincere*, to conquer, defeat.] not to be conquered or subdued; that cannot be overcome; unconquerable; insuperable; as, an *invincible* army.

in·vin'ci·ble·ness, *n.* same as *invincibility*.

in·vin'ci·bly, *adv.* in an invincible manner; so as to be invincible.

in vī'nō ver'i·tăs, [L.] in wine (there is) truth.

in·vī''ō·lȧ·bil'i·ty, *n.* the quality or state of being inviolable.

in·vī'ō·lȧ·ble, *a.* [L. *inviolabilis*, imperishable, indestructible; *in-* priv., and *violabilis*, from *violare*, to treat with violence, dishonor.]

1. not to be violated; not to be injured, broken, polluted, or treated with irreverence; as, an agreement or promise should be considered *inviolable*.

2. that cannot be violated; indestructible; as, the *inviolable* heavens.

in·vī'ō·lȧ·ble·ness, *n.* same as *inviolability*.

in·vī'ō·lȧ·bly, *adv.* so as to remain inviolate.

in·vī'ō·lȧ·cy, *n.* the quality of being inviolate.

in·vī'ō·lāte, *a.* [L. *inviolatus*; *in-* priv., and *violatus*, pp. of *violare*, to treat with violence, injure.]

1. not violated; kept sacred or unbroken; unprofaned.

2. inviolable. [Rare.]

in·vī'ō·lā·ted, *a.* same as *inviolate*.

in·vī'ō·lāte·ly, *adv.* in an inviolate manner; so as to be inviolate.

in·vī′ō·lāte·ness, *n.* the quality of being inviolate.

in′vi·ous, *a.* [L. *invius*; *in-* priv., and *via*, way, road.] impassable; untrodden. [Obs.]

in′vi·ous·ness, *n.* state of being invious. [Obs.]

in·vir′ile, *a.* [L. *in-* priv., and *virilis*, belonging to man, from *vir*, a man.] lacking in virility.

in·vi·ril′i·ty, *n.* lack of virility.

in·vis′çāte, *v.t.* to make sticky.

in·vis′cẽr·āte, *v.t.* to root or implant deeply. [Obs.]

in·viş·i·bil′i·ty, *n.* the quality or state of being invisible.

in·viş′i·ble, *a.* [L. *invisibilis*; *in-* priv., and *visibilis*, visible, from *videre*, to see.]
1. not visible; that cannot be seen.
2. out of sight; not apparent.
3. too small or too faint to be seen; imperceptible; indistinct.
4. kept hidden; as, *invisible* assets.
invisible green; a shade of green so dark as scarcely to be distinguishable from black.
invisible ink; see *invisible ink*, under *ink*.

In·viş′i·ble, *n.* 1. [i–] an invisible thing or being.
2. a Rosicrucian. [Obs.]
3. a heretic of the sixteenth century, who denied the visibility of the church.
the Invisible; (a) God; (b) the unseen world.

in·viş′i·ble·ness, *n.* invisibility.

in·viş′i·bly, *adv.* in an invisible manner; so as to be invisible.

in·vi′şion, *n.* lack of vision or the power of seeing. [Obs.]

in·vi·tā′tion, *n.* [L. *invitatio* (*-onis*), from *invitare*, to invite, ask.]
1. the act of inviting; solicitation to do something or to come somewhere; the requesting of a person's company, as to visit or to dine.
2. a written, printed, or spoken message requesting one's presence.
3. temptation; enticement; attraction.

in·vī′tȧ·tō·ry, *a.* pertaining to or containing an invitation.

in·vī′tȧ·tō·ry, *n.*; *pl.* **in·vī′tȧ·tō·rieş,** [LL. *invitatorius*, inviting, from L. *invitator*, one who invites, from *invitare*, to invite.] a form of invitation used in worship to call to prayer or praise.

in·vīte′, *v.t.*; invited, *pt.*, *pp.*; inviting, *ppr.* [Fr. *inviter*, from L. *invitare*, to ask, treat as a guest, entertain.]
1. to ask (a person) courteously to do some act or to come to some place; to request the company of; as, to *invite* friends to a wedding.
2. to make a request for; as, the speaker *invited* questions.
3. to allure; to attract; to tempt.
4. to give or offer favorable chance or opening for; to tend to bring on; as, such talk *invites* scandal.

in·vīte′, *v.i.* to extend invitation.

in′vīte, *n.* an invitation. [Slang.]

in·vīte′ment, *n.* invitation. [Obs.]

in·vīt′ẽr, *n.* one who invites.

in·vi′ti·āte (-vish′i-), *a.* not vitiated; pure; undefiled. [Rare.]

in·vīt′ing, *a.* alluring; enticing; attractive; as, an *inviting* spot.

in·vīt′ing·ly, *adv.* in an inviting manner.

in·vīt′ing·ness, *n.* the quality of being inviting.

in″vit·ri·fī′ȧ·ble, *a.* that cannot be vitrified.

in′vō·çāte, *v.t.* and *v.i.*; invocated, *pt.*, *pp.*; invocating, *ppr.* [from L. *invocatus*, pp. of *invocare*; *in-*, in, on, and *vocare*, to call.] to speak or ask in invocation. [Rare.]

in·vō·çā′tion, *n.* 1. the act of calling on God, a saint, the Muses, etc. for blessing, help, inspiration, protection, etc.
2. (a) a formal prayer used in invoking, as at the beginning of a church service; (b) a formal plea for aid from a Muse, god, etc., at the beginning of an epic or similar poem.
3. (a) a conjuring of evil spirits; (b) an incantation used in conjuring.
4. in law, a formal request from the bench for the papers or evidence pertaining to a case other than that under trial.

in·voç′ȧ·tō·ry, *a.* of, having the nature of, or used in invocation.

in′voice, *n.* [earlier *invoyes*, pl.; Fr. *envois*, pl. of *envoi*, a sending, conveyance, from *envoyer*, to send.]
1. an itemized list of goods shipped to a buyer, stating quantities, prices, shipping charges, etc.
2. a shipment of invoiced goods.

in′voice, *v.t.*; invoiced (-voist), *pt.*, *pp.*; invoicing, *ppr.* to make a written account or invoice of, as goods or property with their prices; to list in an invoice.

in·vōke′, *v.t.*; invoked (-vōkt′), *pt.*, *pp.*; invoking, *ppr.* [L. *invocare*, to call upon; *in*, in, on, and *vocare*, to call.]
1. to call on (God, a saint, the Muses, etc.) for blessing, help, inspiration, protection, etc.
2. to summon (evil spirits) by incantation; to conjure.
3. to ask solemnly for; to beg for; to implore; entreat.

in·vol′ū·cel, *n.* [Mod. L. *involucellum*, dim. from L. *involucrum*.] a secondary involucre; a ring of small leaves, or bracts, at the base of each flower of a cluster.

in·vō·lū′cel·lāte, *n.* having involucels.

in·vō·lū′çrăl, *a.* of or like an involucre.

in·vō·lū′çrāte, in·vō·lū′çrā·ted, *a.* having an involucre.

in·vō·lū′çre (-kẽr), *n.* [L. *involucrum*, a wrapper, case, envelope, from *involvere*, to roll up, wrap up; *in*, in, and *volvere*, to roll.]
1. in anatomy, a membranous covering or envelope.
2. in botany, a ring of small leaves, or bracts, at the base of a flower, flower cluster, or fruit: involucres often resemble calyxes and are found in all composite plants.

INVOLUCRE OF HEMLOCK PLANT

in·vō·lū′çred (-kẽrd), *a.* having an involucre; involucrate.

in·vō·lū′çrum, *n.*; *pl.* **in·vō·lū′çrȧ,** an involucre.

in·vol·un·tăr′i·ly, *adv.* not by choice; not spontaneously; in an involuntary manner.

in·vol′un·tăr·i·ness, *n.* the state or quality of being involuntary.

in·vol′un·tăr·y, *a.* [LL. *involuntarius*; L. *in-* priv., and *voluntarius*, willing, from *voluntas*, will, choice, from the root of *velle*, to will.] not voluntary; specifically, (a) not done of one's own free will; not done by choice; (b) unintentional; accidental; (c) not consciously controlled; automatic; as, digestion is *involuntary*.

in′vō·lūte, in′vō·lū·ted, *a.* [L. *involutus*, pp. of *involvere*, to roll up, wrap up; *in*, in, and *volvere*, to roll.]
1. intricate; involved.
2. rolled up or curled in a spiral; having the whorls wound closely around the axis; as, *involute* shells.
3. in botany, rolled inward at the edges; as, *involute* leaves.

in′vō·lūte, *n.* 1. anything intricate or involved. [Rare.]
2. in geometry, the curve traced by the end of a taut string when it is wound upon or unwound from a fixed curve on the same plane with it: correlative to *evolute*.

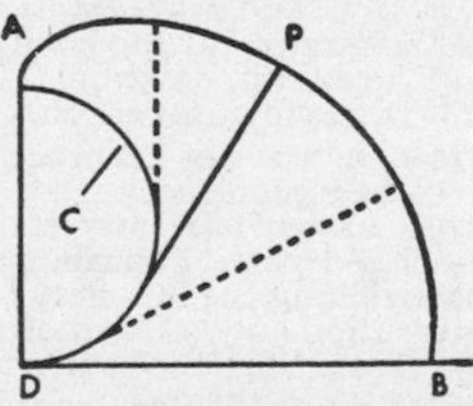

INVOLUTE
AB, involute made by point P of string unrolled from curve C

in·vō·lū′tion, *n.* [LL. *involutio* (*-onis*), a rolling up, from L. *involutus*, pp. of *involvere*, to roll up.]
1. an involving or being involved; entanglement.
2. anything that is involved; complication; intricacy.
3. in anatomy, a part formed by rolling or curling inward.
4. in biology, a retrograde or degenerative change.
5. in grammar, an involved construction, especially one created by a clause separating a subject from the predicate.
6. in mathematics, the raising of a quantity to any given power.
7. in medicine, (a) the return of an organ to its normal size after distention; as, the *involution* of the womb after childbirth; (b) a decline in the normal functions of the body or an organ; especially, the changes occurring at the menopause.

in·vō·lū′tion·ăl, *a.* of or resulting from involution.

in·vō·lū′tion·ăr·y, *a.* of or characterized by involution.

in·volve′, *v.t.*; involved, *pt.*, *pp.*; involving, *ppr.* [L. *involvere*, to roll up, wrap up; *in*, in, and *volvere*, to roll.]
1. to roll up; to wrap; enfold; envelop; as, fog *involved* the shoreline.
2. to wind spirally; to coil up; as, the serpent *involved* its body.
3. to make intricate or tangled; to complicate.
4. to entangle in trouble, difficulty, danger, etc.; to implicate.
5. to roll up within itself; to include; as, the procession *involved* thousands as it moved toward the Bastille.
6. to bring into connection; to require; as, expansion in business *involves* expenditure.
7. to occupy the attention of; as, he was *involved* in working out a solution to the problem.
8. in mathematics, to raise (a quantity) to a given power.
Syn.—embarrass, entangle, include, implicate, imply.

in·volved′, *a.* not easily understood; intricate; complicated.

in·volv′ed·ness, *n.* the state or quality of being involved.

in·volve′ment, *n.* 1. an involving or being involved.
2. anything that is involved; a complicated state of affairs.

in·vul′găr, *v.t.* to make vulgar. [Obs.]

in·vul′găr, *a.* not vulgar. [Obs.]

in·vul″nẽr·ȧ·bil′i·ty, *n.* the quality or state of being invulnerable, or secure from injury.

in·vul′nẽr·ȧ·ble, *a.* [L. *invulnerabilis*; *in-* priv., and *vulnerare*, to wound, from *vulnus* (*-eris*), a wound.]
1. that cannot be wounded or injured.
2. unassailable, as an argument; able to reply to all arguments; proof against attack.

in·vul′nẽr·ȧ·ble·ness, *n.* invulnerability.

in·vul′nẽr·ȧ·bly, *adv.* in an invulnerable manner; so as to be invulnerable.

in·vul′nẽr·āte, *a.* uninjured. [Obs.]

in·wąll′, *v.t.*; inwalled, *pt.*, *pp.*; inwalling, *ppr.* to enclose or fortify with or as with a wall.

in′wąll, *n.* an inner wall, as the lining wall of a blast furnace.

in′wărd, *a.* [ME. *inward*; AS. *inneweard*; *inne*, in, and *-weard*, -ward.]
1. situated within; being on the inside; internal; as, the *inward* organs of the body.
2. of or belonging to the inner nature of a person; mental or spiritual.
3. directed toward the inside; ingoing; as, the *inward* pull of a centrifuge.
4. of the inside or inner part, as of the body.
5. inland; as, *inward* Asia.
6. inherent; intrinsic.
7. domestic. [Archaic.]
8. (a) intimate; familiar; (b) private; secret. [Obs.]

in′wărd, *n.* 1. the inside; inward part.
2. [*pl.*] the entrails.
3. [*pl.*] imported articles, or dues on these. [Brit.]
4. an intimate friend. [Obs.]

in′wărd, in′wărdş, *adv.* 1. toward the inside, interior, or center.
2. into the mind, thoughts, or soul.
3. internally. [Obs.]

in′wărd·ly, *adv.* 1. in the inner part; on the inside; internally.
2. in the mind or spirit; privately; secretly.
3. toward the center; inward.
4. familiarly; intimately. [Archaic.]

in′wărd·ness, *n.* 1. the inner nature, essence, or meaning.
2. the quality or state of being inward; spirituality.
3. depth of thought or feeling; sincerity.

in′wărdş, *adv.* see *inward*.

in·wēave′, *v.t.*; inwove, *pt.*; inwoven, *pp.*; inweaving, *ppr.* to weave in; to interweave.

in·wheel′ (-hwēl′), *v.t.* to enwheel. [Obs.]

in·wīnd′, *v.t.* to wind in; to wind about; to entwine.

in′wit, *n.* mind; understanding; conscience. [Obs.]

in·with′, *prep.* within. [Obs.]

in·wŏrk′, *v.t.*; inworked (-wŏrkt), *pt., pp.*; inworking, *ppr.* to work in or into.

in·wōrn′, *a.* worn or wrought in or into. [Rare.]

in·wōve′, *v.* past tense of *inweave.*

in·wōv′en, *v.,* past participle of *inweave.*

in·wrap′ (-rap′), *v.t.*; inwrapped (-rapt), *pt., pp.*; inwrapping, *ppr.* to enwrap.

in·wrēathe′ (-rēth′), *v.t.*; inwreathed, *pt., pp.* inwreathing, *ppr.* to enwreathe.

in·wrought′ (-rąt′), *a.* 1. worked into a fabric: said of a pattern, etc.; inwoven; interwoven.
2. having a decoration worked in.
3. closely blended with other things.

ī′ō, *interj.* [L. *io*; Gr. *iō.*] a cry of pleasure or triumph.

Ī′ō, *n.* [L.; Gr. *Iō.*]
1. in Greek mythology, a maiden loved by Zeus and changed into a heifer by jealous Hera, or, in some tales, by Zeus, to protect her: she was watched by hundred-eyed Argus and was driven to Egypt, where she regained her natural form.
2. the innermost moon of Jupiter.

Io, in chemistry, ionium.

iod-, see *iodo-.*

ī·ō″dȧ·moe′bȧ, *n.* in zoology, a genus of amoebae parasitic in the human intestine.

ī′o·dāte, *n.* [*iod-,* and *-ate.*] any salt of iodic acid.

ī′ō·dāte, *v.t.*; iodated, *pt., pp.*; iodating, *ppr.* to treat with iodine.

ī·ō·dā′tion, *n.* an iodating or being iodated.

ī·od′iç, *a.* 1. of or containing iodine.
2. caused by iodine; as, *iodic* poisoning.
3. designating or of a chemical compound in which iodine has a valence of five; specifically, designating or of an oxygen acid of iodine, HIO_3, also called *hydrogen iodate.*

ī′ō·dide, *n.* [*iod-,* and *-ide.*] a compound of iodine with another element, as in sodium iodide, NaI, or with a radical, as in methyl iodide, CH_3I.

ī′ō·din, *n.* iodine.

ī′ō·dīne (*or* -din), *n.* [Fr. *iode,* iodine, from Gr. *iōdēs,* violetlike (from *ion,* a violet, and *eidos,* form); and *-ine.*]
1. a nonmetallic chemical element belonging to the halogen family and consisting of grayish-black crystals that volatilize into a violet-colored vapor: used as an antiseptic, in the manufacture of dyes, in photography, etc.: symbol, I; atomic weight, 126.92; atomic number, 53.
2. tincture of iodine, used as an antiseptic. [Colloq.]
iodine green; a green pigment derived from coal tar.
iodine scarlet; red mercuric iodide used as a pigment.

ī′ō·diṣm, *n.* a diseased condition caused by iodine or its compounds used in excess; iodine poisoning.

ī′ō·dīze, *v.t.*; iodized, *pt., pp.*; iodizing, *ppr.* to treat (a wound, photographic plate, etc.) with iodine or an iodide.

ī′ō·dīzed sąlt, common table salt to which a small amount of sodium iodide or potassium iodide has been added.

ī′ō·dī·zẽr, *n.* one who or that which iodizes.

ī·ō′dō- (*or* ī′ō-dō-), [from Mod.L. *iodum,* iodine.] a combining form meaning *iodine* or *a compound of iodine,* as in *iodo*form: also, before a vowel, *iod-.*

ī·od′ō·form, *n.* [*iodo-,* and *form*yl.] a yellowish, crystalline compound of iodine, CHI_3, used as an antiseptic in surgical dressings.

ī″ō·dō·hȳ′driç, *a.* same as *hydriodic.*

ī″ō·dō·met′riç, *a.* [*iodo-,* and Gr. *metron,* a measure.] of or relating to iodometry.

ī·ō·dom′e·try, *n.* quantitative determination of iodine, or of substances that will react with it or liberate it, by volumetric analytical methods.

ī·ō′dous, *a.* 1. of or containing iodine.
2. designating or of a chemical compound in which iodine has a valence of less than five.
3. designating or of a hypothetical acid, HIO_2, in which iodine has a valence of three: sodium hypoiodite, NaIO, is a salt of this acid.

ī·od′y·rīte, *n.* [*iod-,* and Gr. argyros, silver, and *-ite.*] a yellowish mineral iodide of silver, AgI, found in thin, hexagonal plates.

ī′ō·līte, *n.* [Gr. *ion,* a violet, and *lithos,* stone.] a bluish or violet, crystalline mineral, a silicate of aluminum, iron, and magnesium; cordierite: it is used as a gem.

Ī′ō moth, a large American moth with an eyelike spot on each hind wing.

ī′ŏn, *n.* [Gr. *ion,* ppr. of *ienai,* to go.] an electrically charged atom or group of atoms, the electrical charge of which results when a neutral atom or group of atoms loses or gains one or more electrons: the loss of electrons results in a positively charged ion (*cation*), the gain of electrons in a negatively charged ion (*anion*): such loss or gain occurs during chemical reactions in which electrons are transferred from one atom to another, by the action on matter of X rays, ultraviolet light, and certain other forms of radiant energy, or by the impact of alpha and beta particles, protons, deuterons, etc. on atoms and molecules.

-ion, [from Fr. or L.; Fr. *-ion*; L. *-io,* nom., *-ionis,* genit.] a noun-forming suffix meaning *a ——ing, a being ——ed,* or *the result of ——ing,* as in fus*ion,* translat*ion,* conscript*ion,* correct*ion.*

Ī·ō′ni·ăn, *a.* 1. of Ionia, an ancient district of Asia Minor, its people, or their culture.
2. of an ancient Greek people who settled in eastern Greece and Ionia.
3. in music, (a) designating or of one of the ancient Greek modes; (b) designating or of the six medieval church modes, corresponding to the modern major diatonic scale.

Ī·ō′ni·ăn, *n.* an Ionian Greek.

Ī·on′iç, *a.* 1. of Ionia or its people; Ionian.
2. designating or of a branch of the ancient Greek language, including that of Attica.
3. designating or of a Greek style of architecture characterized by ornamental scrolls on the capitals.
4. of the Ionic of Greek and Latin prosody.
Ionic order; one of the three Greek orders of architecture, distinguished by the volute of its capital. The shaft, including the base, which is half a diameter, and the capital to the bottom of the volute, is about 9 diameters high, and usually fluted in 24 flutes.

IONIC ORDER

Ī·on′iç, *n.* 1. in Greek and Latin prosody, (a) either of two feet consisting of four syllables, the first two long and the second two short (¯ ¯ ˘ ˘) (*greater Ionic*) or the first two short and the second two long (˘ ˘ ¯ ¯) (*smaller* or *lesser Ionic*); (b) verse or meter of such feet.

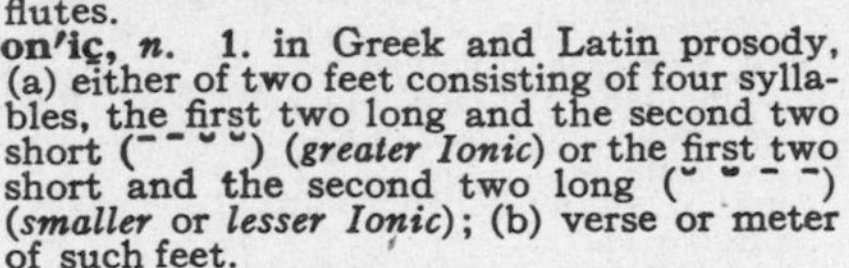

2. in printing, a kind of heavy-faced type that is easy to read.
This line is set in Ionic.
3. the Ionic dialect.

Ī·on′iç, *a.* of, or being in the form of, an ion or ions.

ī·ō′ni·um, *n.* [*ion,* and uran*ium.*] a radioactive isotope of thorium, resulting from the disintegration of uranium: symbol, Io; atomic weight, 230; atomic number, 90.

ī″on·i·zā′tion, *n.* the act or process of ionizing; state of being ionized.

ī″on·i·zā′tion chām′bẽr, any of various devices, as a closed vessel containing a suitable gas, for determining the intensity of X rays or the disintegration rate of a radioactive material, by measuring the current flow between electrodes in the gas.

ī′on·īze, *v.t.* and *v.i.*; ionized, *pt., pp.*; ionizing, *ppr.* to change or be changed into ions; to dissociate into ions, as a salt dissolved in water, or become electrically charged, as a gas under the influence of radiation.

ī·on′ō·ġen, *n.* a substance that can be ionized or that produces ions.

ī′o·nōne, *n.* [Gr. *ion,* violet; and *-one.*] a colorless liquid, $C_{13}H_{20}O$, made from citral and acetone and used in perfume manufacture for its violetlike odor.

ī·on′ō·sphēre, *n.* [*iono-,* and *-sphere.*] the outer part of the earth's atmosphere, extending far beyond the stratosphere and consisting of a series of constantly changing layers of heavily ionized molecules.

ī·ō′tȧ, *n.* [Gr.] 1. the ninth letter of the Greek alphabet, corresponding to English *I, i.*
2. a very small quantity; a jot.
iota subscript; in Greek grammar, iota when silent written beneath *α, η,* or *ω,* with which it forms a diphthong, as ᾳ, ῳ.

ī·ō′tȧ·ciṣm, *n.* [LL. *iotacismus*; Gr. *iōtakismos,* too much use of iota, from *iōta,* iota.]
1. excessive use of *i* (Gr. *iota*).
2. a tendency to give the sound of this letter to other vowels.

I O U, 1. I owe you.
2. a paper bearing these letters, acknowledging a specified debt and signed by the debtor.

-i·ous, [*-i-,* thematic vowel, and *-ous.*] a suffix used to form adjectives corresponding to nouns ending in *-ion,* as in rebell*ious,* relig*ious,* or to form analogous adjectives meaning *having, characterized by,* as in fur*ious,* anx*ious.*

Ī′ō·wăn, *n.* a native or inhabitant of Iowa.

Ī′ō·wăn, *a.* of Iowa.

ip′ē·çaç, *n.* [contr. from *ipecacuanha.*]
1. a tropical South American creeping plant of the madder family, with small, drooping flowers.
2. the dried roots of this plant.
3. a preparation from the dried roots, used in the treatment of laryngitis, bronchitis, and chronic diarrhea.

ip·ē·çaç·ū·an′hȧ (-an′ȧ), *n.* [Port., from Tupi *ipe-kaa-guéne,* small emetic plant.] ipecac.

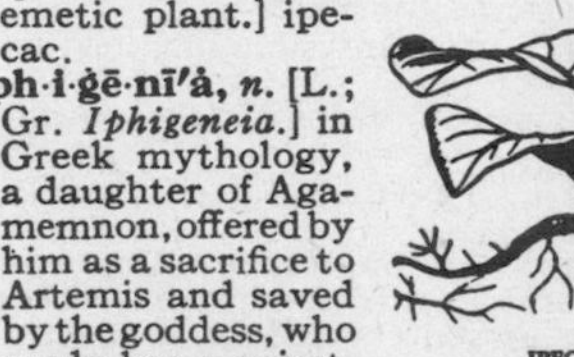
IPECACUANHA (*Cephaelis ipecacuanha*)

Iph·i·ġē·nī′ȧ, *n.* [L.; Gr. *Iphigeneia.*] in Greek mythology, a daughter of Agamemnon, offered by him as a sacrifice to Artemis and saved by the goddess, who made her a priestess: subject of tragedies by Euripides and Goethe.

Ip·ō·moe′ȧ, *n.* [Gr. *ips, ipos,* a worm, and *homoios,* like.] any of a group of twining or creeping plants, including the morning-glory, with trumpet-shaped flowers.

ip′sē dix′it, [L., he himself has said (it).], an arbitrary or dogmatic statement.

ip·sis′si·mȧ vẽr′bȧ, [L.] the very words.

ip′sō faç′tō, [L.] by the fact (or act) itself; by that very fact.

ip′sō jū′rē, [L.] by the law itself.

ir-, (a) in- (not); (b) in- (in). Used before *r.*

Ir, in chemistry, iridium.

IRA, I.R.A., [*i*ndividual *r*etirement *a*ccount.] a personal retirement plan for a worker whereby a limited amount of annual earnings may be invested, as in mutual funds or a savings account, with the invested money and its earnings being tax-free until a specified retirement age is reached.

ī′rȧ·çund, *a.* [L. *iracundus,* from *ira,* anger, wrath.] angry; irritable; passionate.

ī·rä′de, *n.* [Turk.] formerly, a decree issued by the Sultan of Turkey.

Ī·rä′ni, *a.* Iranian.

Ī·rā′ni·ăn, *a.* of Iran, its people, their language, or culture.

Ī·rā′ni·ăn, *n.* 1. one of the people of Iran; a Persian.
2. a branch of the Indo-European family of languages that includes languages now spoken in the Iranian Plateau and a small area of the Caucasus: among the extant languages of the group are Persian, Kurdish, and Pushtu.

I·ran′iç, *a.* and *n.* Iranian (language).

Ī·rä′qi (-ki), *n.* 1. a native of Iraq.
2. the dialect of Arabic spoken by the Iraqis.

Ī·rä′qi, *a.* of Iraq, its people, their language, or culture.

ī·ras·ci·bil′i·ty, *n.* the fact or quality of being irascible.

ī·ras′ci·ble, *a.* [LL. *irascibilis,* from L. *irasci,* to be angry, from *ira,* anger.] easily provoked or inflamed to anger or wrath; irritable; as, an *irascible* temper.
Syn.—angry, fiery, hasty, choleric.

ī·ras′ci·ble·ness, *n.* irascibility.

ī·ras′ci·bly, *adv.* in an irascible manner.

ī·rāte′, *a.* [L. *iratus,* from *irasci,* to be angry, from *ira,* anger.] angry; incensed; wrathful.

īre, *n.* [OFr. *ire,* from L. *ira,* anger, wrath.] anger; wrath; keen resentment.
Syn.—fury, rage, resentment.

īre′fụl, *a.* full of ire; angry; furious with anger.

īre′fụl·ly, *adv.* in an angry manner.

īre′fụl·ness, *n.* the state or quality of being ireful.

ī′rē·närçh, *n.* [LL. *irenarcha, irenarches*; Gr. *eirēnarchēs*; *eirēnē,* peace, and *archein,* to govern, rule.] an officer of the Eastern Roman Empire whose duties were those of a justice of the peace.

Ī·rē′nē, *n.* [L. *Irene*; Gr. *Eirēnē*, lit., peace.] in Greek mythology, the goddess of peace, daughter of Zeus and Themis: identified by the Romans with Pax.

ī·ren′iç, ī·ren′iç·ăl, *a.* pacific; promoting or desirous of peace.

ī·ren′i·çon, *n.*; *pl.* **ī·ren′i·çȧ,** [Gr. *eirēnikon*, neut. of *eirēnikos*, of or for peace, from *eirēnē*, peace.]

1. a proposition, plan, or arrangement designed for peace, especially in the church.

2. [*pl.*] in the Orthodox Eastern Church, a petition for peace with which the liturgy begins.

ī·ren′içs, *n.pl.* [*construed as sing.*] the doctrine or practice of promoting peace among Christian churches in relation to theological differences.

ī′ri·ăn, *a.* relating to the iris of the eye.

Ī′ri·cism, *n.* an Irishism. [Rare.]

ir′id-, see *irido-*.

Ī·ri·dā′cē·ae, *n.pl.* [Gr. *iris* (*-idos*), a rainbow.] a family of endogenous plants, usually with equitant leaves, including the crocus, gladiolus, and iris: also called *Irideæ*.

ir·i·dā′ceous, *a.* of or pertaining to the family *Iridaceæ*.

ī′ri·dăl, *a.* [Gr. *iris* (*-idos*), a rainbow.] pertaining to or resembling the rainbow or the iris.

ir·i·deç′tō·my, *n.*; *pl.* **ir·i·deç′tō·mieṣ,** [Gr. *iris* (*-idos*), the iris, rainbow, and *ektomē*, a cutting out; *ek*, out, and *temnein*, to cut.] a surgical removal of part of the iris of the eye.

ir″i·dē·rē′mi·ȧ, *n.* [Gr. *iris* (*-idos*), the iris, and *erēmia*, solitude, desolation.] partial or total absence of the iris.

ī′ri·dēṣ, *n.* alternative plural of *iris*.

ir·i·des′cence, *n.* the quality or fact of being iridescent.

ir·i·des′cent, *a.* [Gr. *iris* (*-idos*), a rainbow, and *-escent*.] having or showing an interplay of colors like the rainbow; prismatic.

ī·rid′i·ăn, *a.* pertaining to the iris of the eye.

ī·rid′iç, *a.* relating to the iris of the eye.

ī·rid′iç, *a.* 1. of or containing iridium.

2. designating or of a chemical compound in which iridium has a valence of four.

ī·rid′i·ous, ir′id·ous, *a.* of or containing iridium having a valence of three.

ī·rid′i·sçōpe, *n.* a device for viewing the interior of the eye: spelled also *iridioscope*.

ī·rid′i·um, *n.* [from Gr. *iris* (*-idos*), a rainbow: so called because of the changing color of some of its salts.] a white, heavy, brittle, metallic chemical element found in platinum ores: alloys of iridium are used for pen points, contact points in telegraphy, and bearings of watches and scientific instruments: symbol, Ir; atomic weight, 193.1; atomic number, 77.

ir′i·dīze, *v.t.*; iridized, *pt.*, *pp.*; iridizing, *ppr.* 1. to cause to become iridescent, as glass.

2. to apply iridium to, as the point of a pen.

ir′id·ō-, [from Gr. *iris*, *iridos*, iris.] a combining form meaning *the iris* (of the eye): also, before a vowel, *irid-*, as in *irid*ectomy.

ir·i·doṣ′mine, ir·i·doṣ′mi·um, *n.* osmiridium.

Ī′ris, *n.* [L.; Gr. *Iris*; see *iridescent*.] in Greek mythology, the goddess of the rainbow: in the *Iliad*, she is the messenger of the gods.

ī′ris, *n.*; *pl.* **ī′ris·eṣ, ī′ri·dēṣ,** [L. *iris*; Gr. *iris*, rainbow.]

1. a rainbow.

2. a rainbowlike show or play of colors.

3. the round, pigmented membrane surrounding the pupil of the eye, having muscles that adjust the size of the pupil to regulate the amount of light entering the eye.

4. any of a large group of plants with sword-shaped leaves and a conspicuous flower composed of three petals and three drooping sepals of widely varying color: also called *flag*.

YELLOW IRIS (*Iris pseudacorus*)

5. the flower of this plant: also called *flag*.

6. the inmost circle of color in an ocellus of a butterfly's wing.

ī′ris·ȧ·ted, *a.* iridescent; irised.

ī·ri·sā′tion, *n.* the act or process of making iridescent; iridescence.

ī′ri·sçōpe, *n.* a plate of polished black glass that exhibits iridescent colors when the breath is blown on it through a tube.

ī′ris dī′ȧ·phragm (-fram), a device consisting of thin, overlapping metal plates that can be adjusted to form an aperture of varying size for camera lenses, etc.

ī′rised (-rist), *a.* having colors like those of the rainbow.

Ī′rish, *n.* [ME. *Irish, Irysh*; AS. *Irisc*, from *Iras*, the Irish, from Ir. *Eire, Erin*, Ireland.]

1. the Goidelic, Celtic language spoken by some of the Irish; Erse.

2. the English dialect of Ireland.

3. temper; chiefly in *to get one's Irish up*, to arouse one's temper. [Colloq.]

the Irish; the Irish people.

Ī′rish, *a.* of Ireland, its people, their language, or culture.

Irish elk; a species of huge elk or deer, long extinct, remains of which are found under the peat bogs of Ireland: it stood over six feet in height, and had palmated antlers with a spread of from twelve to fifteen feet.

Irish moss; carrageen, a seaweed dried and bleached for use as a medicine, a thickening agent in food, etc.

Irish potato; the common white potato: so called because extensively cultivated in Ireland.

Irish Republican Army; a secret organization founded to work for Irish independence from England: it continued to exist after the establishment of the Irish Free State, which declared it illegal in 1936.

Irish setter; any of a breed of setter with a coat of long, silky, reddish-brown hair.

Irish stew; a stew of vegetables and meat cut into small pieces.

Irish terrier; any of a breed of small, lean, active dog with a wiry, reddish-brown coat.

Irish wolfhound; any of a breed of very large, heavy, powerful dog with a hard, rough coat, formerly used in hunting wolves.

Ī′rish·iṣm, *n.* an Irish idiom, custom, etc.

Ī′rish·măn, *n.*; *pl.* **Ī′rish·men,** 1. a native or inhabitant of Ireland, especially a man.

2. a person of Irish ancestry, especially a man.

Ī′rish·wom·ăn (-woom-), *n.*; *pl.* **Ī′rish·wom·en** (-wim-), 1. a woman who is a native or inhabitant of Ireland.

2. a woman of Irish ancestry.

ī·rī′tis, *n.* inflammation of the iris of the eye.

ĩrk, *v.t.* [ME. *irken*, to loathe, be weary of; prob. from northern and north Midland adj. *irk, yrk*, weary, troubled, bored.] to make tired; to disgust; annoy; trouble; vex; bore.

ĩrk′sŏme, *a.* wearisome; tedious; tiresome; giving uneasiness; troublesome by long continuance or repetition; as, *irksome* hours.

ĩrk′sŏme·ly, *adv.* in an irksome manner.

ĩrk′sŏme·ness, *n.* tediousness; wearisomeness.

ī′ron (ī′ũrn), *n.* [ME. *iron, iren*; AS. *iren, isen, isern*, iron.]

1. a metallic chemical element, white, malleable, and ductile, the most common and most useful of all the metals: symbol, Fe; atomic weight, 55.85; atomic number, 26.

2. (a) any tool, implement, device, apparatus, etc. made of iron; (b) such a device with a flat, smooth undersurface, used, when heated, for pressing clothes or cloth.

3. [*pl.*] iron shackles or chains.

4. firm strength; power.

5. a shooting iron; small firearm. [Slang.]

6. in golf, a club having a metal head.

7. in medicine, a tonic or other preparation containing iron.

bar iron; wrought iron in bars.

gray iron; cast iron containing graphite.

in irons; (a) bound with fetters; imprisoned; (b) in nautical usage, failing to come about or fill away: said of a sailing vessel.

magnetic iron; magnetite.

malleable iron; wrought iron.

meteoric iron; iron, usually alloyed with nickel and cobalt, found in meteorites.

pig iron; crude iron cast in pigs, or oblong masses.

Russia iron; a hard, glossy variety of sheet iron which does not rust readily.

specular iron; crystalline hematite.

to have irons in the fire; to have or be engaged in activities, enterprises, etc.

to strike while the iron is hot; to be prompt in taking advantage of circumstances.

white iron; a whitish crystalline variety of cast iron.

wrought iron; a soft, ductile, tough, malleable iron containing some slag and a very low percentage of carbon: it cannot be tempered or easily fused.

ī′ron, *a.* 1. of or consisting of iron.

2. like iron; strong, firm, or unyielding; as, an *iron* temperament.

3. cruel; merciless.

Iron Age; (a) a period of civilization (c. 1000 B.C.–100 A.D.) characterized by the introduction and development of iron tools and weapons: it followed the Bronze Age; (b) [i–] in classical mythology, the last and worst age of the world, characterized by wickedness, selfishness, and degeneracy.

iron clay; clay mixed with iron ore.

Iron Cross; a silver-edged Maltese cross of iron, award by Germany for conspicuous service in warfare: instituted in 1813.

Iron Crown; an antique crown of gold set with jewels, made originally for the Lombard kings, which was supposed to confer the right of sovereignty over all Italy on the wearer. It enclosed an iron circlet claimed to be forged from one of the nails used in the Crucifixion of Jesus.

IRON CROWN OF LOMBARDY

iron curtain; a term popularized by Winston Churchill in a speech (1946) to connote secrecy and censorship forming a Soviet-made barrier around the Soviet Union and some other countries regarded as in its sphere.

iron froth; a spongy variety of the mineral hematite.

iron gray; a gray like that of freshly broken cast iron.

Iron Guard; a Romanian fascist organization active before World War II.

iron hand; firm, rigorous, severe control.

iron hat; a headpiece of metal worn by soldiers during the twelfth to the seventeenth centuries.

iron horse; (a) a locomotive; (b) a bicycle or tricycle. [Colloq.]

iron liquor; acetate of iron, used as a mordant by dyers.

iron lung; a large metal respirator which encloses all of the body but the head, used for maintaining artificial respiration in a person who has difficulty in breathing as a result of infantile paralysis, gas poisoning, etc.

iron mold; a brownish stain made on cloth by iron rust or ink.

iron pyrites; a gold-colored ore of iron; fool's gold.

iron sand; granular iron ore.

iron scale; the scale formed on the surface of white-hot iron by oxidation.

iron shrub; St. Martin's herb.

iron tree; any of a number of hardwood trees, as *Ixora ferra*.

ī′ron (ī′ũrn), *v.t.* 1. to furnish or cover with iron.

2. to put (a prisoner) in irons.

3. to press (clothes or cloth) flat with a hot iron.

to iron out; to smooth out; eliminate.

ī′ron, *v.i.* to iron clothes or cloth.

ī′ron·bärk, *n.* any of various eucalyptus trees of Australia, having hard, durable wood, as the *Eucalyptus resinifera*: also *ironbark tree*.

ī′ron·bound, *a.* 1. bound with iron.

2. edged with rocks or cliffs; rugged; as, an *ironbound* coast.

3. unyielding; unalterable; as, *ironbound* laws.

ī′ron-çāsed (-kāst), *a.* encased in iron; ironclad.

ī′ron·çlad, *a.* 1. clad in iron; covered or protected with iron.

2. difficult to change or break; as, an *ironclad* lease.

ī′ron·çlad, *n.* a vessel sheathed with a defensive covering of iron or steel plates; an armored warship: nineteenth-century term.

ī′ron·ẽr, *n.* a person or thing that irons.

ī′ron-fist′ed, *a.* closefisted; penurious.

ī′ron-found′ẽr, one who makes iron castings.

ī′ron-found′ry, the place where iron castings are made.

ī′ron glȧnce, a crystallized variety of hematite.

ī′ron-grāy, *a.* of a gray hue approaching the color of freshly broken cast iron.

ī′ron·hand′ed, *a.* firm and rigorous; strict and severe; as, an *ironhanded* king.

ī′ron·headṣ, *n.* a plant, the *Centaurea nigra*, having purple flowers resembling iron balls.

ī′ron-heärt′ed, *a.* cruel; merciless; pitiless.

ī·ron′iç, *a.* ironical.

ī·ron′iç·ăl, *a.* [from L. *ironicus*; Gr. *eirōnikos*, from *eirōneia*, dissimulation, irony.]

1. meaning the contrary of what is expressed.

2. using, or given to the use of, irony.
3. having the quality of irony; directly opposite to what is or might be expected.

ī·ron′iç·ăl·ly, *adv.* in an ironical manner.

ī′ron·ing (ī′ŭrn-), *n.* 1. a smoothing with an iron.
2. the articles ironed or to be ironed.

ī′ron·ing bōard, a cloth-covered board upon which clothes are ironed.

ī′ron·ish, *a.* like iron; as, an *ironish* taste. [Rare.]

ī′ron·man, *n.* 1. a maker of or dealer in iron.
2. a spinning mule.
3. a machine for cutting coal. [Brit. Dial.]

ī′ron·mȧs″tēr, *n.* one who manufactures or deals in iron.

ī′ron·mŏn″gẽr, *n.* a dealer in articles made of iron and other metals; a hardware dealer. [Brit.]

ī′ron·mŏn″gẽr·y, *n.* 1. articles made of iron; hardware. [Brit.]
2. an ironmonger's shop. [Brit.]
3. an ironmonger's business. [Brit.]

ī′ron-sick, *a.* having the bolts and nails so much corroded or eaten with rust as to become leaky: said of a wooden ship. [Obs.]

ī′ron·side, *n.* 1. a courageous, resolute man.
2. [I–] Oliver Cromwell: also *Ironsides.*

ī′ron-sīd″ed, *a.* having sides of iron or of the firmness of iron; also, rough; unfeeling.

I′ron·sides, *n.pl.* 1. [*construed as sing.*] Oliver Cromwell.
2. (a) the regiment led by Oliver Cromwell in the English Civil War; (b) the whole army of Oliver Cromwell.
3. [i–] [*construed as sing.*] an ironclad.

ī′ron·smith, *n.* 1. a worker in iron; a blacksmith.
2. a bird having a note like the sounds made by a smith; as, the *Megalæma faber* of the island of Hainan.

ī′ron·stōne, *n.* an ore of iron, containing clay.
ironstone china; a kind of hard, white pottery.

ī′ron·wāre, *n.* hardware; ware made of iron.

ī′ron·weed, *n.* [so named from its hard stem.] a plant of the aster family, with clusters of red, purple, or white tubular flowers.

ī′ron·wood, *n.* any of many trees having very hard, heavy wood, as some species of trees of the genus *Sideroxylon*; also, the wood.

ī′ron·wŏrk, *n.* the parts of a building, vessel, carriage, etc. which consist of iron; anything made of iron.

ī′ron·wŏrk·ẽr, *n.* 1. a person who makes iron or articles of iron.
2. a worker who builds the framework of steel bridges, etc.

ī′ron·wŏrks, *n. pl.* [*also construed as sing.*] an establishment where iron is manufactured, wrought, or cast into ironwork.

ī′ron·wŏrt, *n.* 1. a plant of the genus *Sideritis.*
2. one of the hemp nettles, *Galeopsis tetrahit* or *Galeopsis ladanum.*

ī′ron·y (ī′ŭrn-), *a.* 1. made or consisting of iron; of the nature of iron; as, *irony* chains, *irony* particles.
2. resembling iron; hard.

ī′rŏn·y, *n.*; *pl.* **ī′rŏn·ieṣ,** [Fr. *ironie*; L. *ironia*; Gr. *eirōneia*, dissimulation, irony, from *eirōn*, a dissembler in speech, from *eirein*, to speak.]
1. a method of humorous or sarcastic expression in which the intended meaning of the words used is the direct opposite of their usual sense; as, the speaker was using *irony* when he said that the stupid plan was "very clever."
2. an instance of this.
3. a combination of circumstances or a result that is the opposite of what might be expected or considered appropriate; as, it was an *irony* of fate that the fireboat burned and sank.
4. the feigning of ignorance in argument: more frequently *Socratic irony* (after Socrates, who uses this device in Plato's *Dialogues*).

Ir·ō·quoi′ăn (-kwoi′), *a.* of an important linguistic family of North American Indians, including speakers of Huron (Wyandot), Seneca, Mohawk, Tuscarora, Oneida, Onondaga, and Cherokee.

Ir·ō·quoi′ăn, *n.* 1. a member of an Iroquoian tribe.
2. the Iroquoian languages collectively.

Ir′ō·quois (-kwoi, -kwoiz), *n.* [from native Indian name.] a member of a confederation of Iroquoian Indian tribes that lived in western and northern New York.

Ir′ō·quois, *a.* pertaining to the Iroquois or their tribes.

ī′rous, *a.* angry. [Obs.]

irpe, *n.* [origin doubtful.] a smirk of the face; a twisting of the body. [Obs.]

ir·rā′di·ănce, *n.* an irradiating; radiance.

ir·rā′di·ăn·cy, *n.* the fact or quality of being irradiant.

ir·rā′di·ănt, *a.* emitting rays of light; shining brightly.

ir·rā′di·āte, *v.t.*; irradiated, *pt., pp.*; irradiating, *ppr.* [L. *irradiatus*, pp. of *irradiare*, to beam upon, illumine; *in*, in, on, and *radiare*, to beam.]
1. to illuminate; to brighten; to make splendid; to adorn with luster.
2. to enlighten intellectually; to illuminate; as, to *irradiate* the mind.
3. to heat with radiant energy.
4. to diffuse; to radiate; to spread; to give out.
5. in medicine, to treat with or expose to, X rays, ultraviolet rays, radium, or some other form of radiant energy.

ir·rā′di āte, *v.i.* 1. to emit rays; to shine.
2. to become radiant.

ir·rā′di·āte, *a.* irradiated.

ir·rā′di·āt·ed, *a.* 1. in heraldry, shown with rays; having or surrounded with rays, as of light.
2. in medicine, treated with rays or by irradiation.

ir·rā·di·ā′tion, *n.* 1. an irradiating or being irradiated.
2. something irradiated; specifically, (a) a ray of light, etc.; (b) intellectual enlightenment.
3. in optics, an apparent enlargement of the area of a highly luminous body or of a white body on a dark background.
4. in medicine, treatment by some form of rays, as X rays or ultraviolet rays.
5. in physiology, the scattering of a nerve impulse past the usual course of conduction.

ir·rā′di·ā·tive, *a.* having the power to irradiate.

ir·rad′i·çāte, *v.t.* [L. *in*, in, and *radicare*, to take root, from *radix* (*-icis*), a root.] to root deeply. [Rare.]

ir·ra′tion·ăl (-rash′un-ăl), *a.* [L. *irrationalis*; *in-* priv., and *rationalis*, reasonable, from *ratio* (*-onis*), the process of thinking, reason.]
1. not rational; lacking reason or understanding; as, brutes are *irrational* animals.
2. not according to reason; contrary to reason; absurd; senseless; as, to act in an *irrational* manner.
3. in mathematics, not being expressible by either an integer or a quotient of an integer, as the square root of two; surd.
4. in Greek and Latin prosody, (a) designating a syllable which is long when it should be short according to the normal meter; (b) a foot with such a syllable.

ir·ra′tion·ăl·iṣm, *n.* irrational thought, belief, or action.

ir·ra·tion·al′i·ty, *n.* 1. the quality or state of being irrational.
2. *pl.* **ir·ra·tion·al′i·tieṣ,** an instance of this.

ir·ra′tion·ăl·ly, *adv.* without reason; in a manner contrary to reason; absurdly.

ir·ra′tion·ăl·ness, *n.* irrationality.

ir·rē·but′tȧ·ble, *a.* not to be rebutted.

ir·rē·cep′tive, *a.* having no inclination to receive; not receptive.

ir·rē·çlaim·ȧ·bil′i·ty, *n.* the quality or state of being irreclaimable.

ir·rē·çlaim′ȧ·ble, *a.* that cannot be reclaimed.

ir·rē·çlaim′ȧ·bly, *adv.* so as to be irreclaimable.

ir·reç·ŏg·ni′tion (-nish′un), *n.* absence of recognition.

ir·reç′ŏg·nī·zȧ·ble, *a.* unrecognizable.

ir·reç·ŏn·cīl·ȧ·bil′i·ty, *n.* impossibility of being reconciled.

ir·reç·ŏn·cīl′ȧ·ble, *a.* that cannot be reconciled; not capable of being made to agree or be consistent; conflicting; incompatible; as, *irreconcilable* absurdities.

ir·reç·ŏn·cīl′ȧ·ble, *n.* 1. a person who is irreconcilable and refuses to make any compromise.
2. [*pl.*] ideas, beliefs, etc. that cannot be brought into agreement with each other.

ir·reç·ŏn·cīl′ȧ·ble·ness, *n.* the quality of being irreconcilable; incompatibility.

ir·reç·ŏn·cīl′ȧ·bly, *adv.* in an irreconcilable manner.

ir·reç′ŏn·cīle, *v.t.* to prevent from being reconciled. [Obs.]

ir·reç′ŏn·cīle·ment, *n.* absence of reconciliation; disagreement.

ir·reç·ŏn·cil·i·ā′tion, *n.* absence of reconciliation.

ir·rē·çord′ȧ·ble, *a.* that cannot be recorded.

ir·rē·çŏv′ẽr·ȧ·ble, *a.* that cannot be recovered, regained, or remedied; as, an *irrecoverable* loss.

ir·rē·çŏv′ẽr·ȧ·ble·ness, *n.* the state of being irrecoverable.

ir·rē·çŏv′ẽr·ȧ·bly, *adv.* beyond recovery.

ir·rē·çū′pẽr·ȧ·ble, *a.* [LL. *irrecuperabilis*, irrecoverable; L. *in-* priv., and *recuperare*, to recover, recuperate.] irrecoverable. [Obs.]

ir·rē·çū′pẽr·ȧ·bly, *adv.* irrecoverably. [Obs.]

ir·rē·çūred′, *a.* not curable. [Obs.]

ir·rē·çū′ṣȧ·ble, *a.* [LL. *irrecusabilis*; L. *in-* priv., and LL. *recusabilis*, that should be rejected, from L. *recusare*, to refuse.] that cannot be refused or rejected.

ir·rē·çū′ṣȧ·bly, *adv.* in an irrecusable manner.

ir·rē·deem·ȧ·bil′i·ty, *n.* irredeemableness.

ir·rē·deem′ȧ·ble, *a.* 1. that cannot be brought back.
2. that cannot be converted into coin, as certain kinds of paper money.
3. that cannot be changed; hopeless.
4. that cannot be reformed; beyond redemption.

ir·rē·deem′ȧ·ble·ness, *n.* the quality or fact of being nonredeemable.

ir·rē·deem′ȧ·bly, *adv.* in an irredeemable manner; so as to be irredeemable.

ir·rē·den′tȧ, *a.* [It.] unredeemed: said of a region or regions populated chiefly by the natives of a specified country which formerly held it and seeks to recover it (especially *Italia irredenta*).

Ir·rē·den′tiṣm, *n.* the program or policy of the Irredentists, a political party of Italy formed in 1878 for the purpose of joining to that country adjacent regions populated largely by Italians but ruled by other governments.

Ir·rē·den′tist, *n.* [It. *irredentista*, from *irredento*, unredeemed, from L. *in-* priv., and *redemptus*, pp. of *redimere*, to redeem.]
1. any member of the Italian political party advocating Irredentism.
2. any person who advocates a similar policy with regard to territory formerly a part of his country.

ir·rē·dū·ci·bil′i·ty, *n.* the quality of being irreducible.

ir·rē·dū′ci·ble, *a.* 1. that cannot be reduced; that cannot be brought to a desired state or changed to a different state.
2. in mathematics, not capable of reduction to a simpler form.

ir·rē·dū′ci·ble·ness, *n.* the quality of being irreducible.

ir·rē·dū′ci·bly, *adv.* in an irreducible manner; so as to be irreducible.

ir·rē·fleç′tion, *n.* absence of reflection.

ir·rē·fleçt′ive, *a.* lacking the quality of reflection.

ir·rē·form′ȧ·ble, *a.* that cannot be reformed; beyond the possibility of reformation.

ir·ref″rȧ·gȧ·bil′i·ty, *n.* the quality of being irrefragable.

ir·ref′rȧ·gȧ·ble, *a.* not refragable; incapable of being refuted; unanswerable; incontestable; undeniable; as an *irrefragable* argument, *irrefragable* evidence.

ir·ref′rȧ·gȧ·ble·ness, *n.* irrefragability.

ir·ref′rȧ·gȧ·bly, *adv.* in an irrefragable manner.

ir·rē·fran·ġi·bil′i·ty, *n.* the quality of being irrefrangible.

ir·rē·fran′ġi·ble, *a.* 1. in optics, not capable of being refracted.
2. that cannot be broken or violated; inviolable.

ir·rē·fran′ġi·ble·ness, *n.* irrefrangibility.

ir·ref″ū·tȧ·bil′i·ty, *n.* the state or quality of being irrefutable.

ir·ref′ū·tȧ·ble, *a.* [LL. *irrefutabilis*; L. *in-* priv., and *refutare*, to refute.] that cannot be refuted; incapable of being disproved.

ir·ref′ū·tȧ·ble·ness, *n.* the state or quality of being irrefutable.

ir·ref′ū·tȧ·bly, *adv.* in an irrefutable manner; so as to be irrefutable.

ir·rē·gärd′less, *a.* and *adv.* regardless: a substandard or humorous redundancy.

ir·rē·ġen′ẽr·ȧ·cy, *n.* unregeneracy. [Rare.]

ir·rē·ġen·ẽr·ā′tion, *n.* an unregenerate state. [Obs.]

ir·reg′ū·lăr, *a.* [LL. *irregularis*, not regular; L. *in-* priv., and *regularis*, pertaining to rules, from *regula*, a rule.] not regular; specifically, (a) not according to common form or rules; (b) not according to established principles or customs; deviating from usage; as, the *irregular* proceedings of a legislative body; (c) not even in occurrence or succession; as, an *irregular* pulse; (d) not according to the rules of art; immethodical; as, *irregular* verse; (e) not in conformity with legal or moral requirements; lawless; disorderly; as, *irregular* conduct or propensities; (f) not straight or even; as, an *irregular* line or course; (g) not uniform; as, *irregular* motion; (h) in grammar, deviating from the common form of inflections; as, an *irregular* verb; (i) in botany, not having the parts of the same size or form or arranged with symmetry; as, the petals of a labiate flower are *irregular*; (j) in military usage, not belonging to the regularly established army.

Syn.—immethodical, unsystematic, anomalous, erratic, devious, eccentric, crooked, unsettled, variable, changeable, mutable, desultory, disorderly, wild, immoderate, intemperate, inordinate, vicious.

ir·reg′ū·lăr, *n.* 1. a person or thing that is irregular.

2. [*usually in pl.*] a soldier who belongs to an irregular military force.

ir·reg′ū·lăr·ist, *n.* one who is irregular. [Obs.]

ir·reg·ū·lar′i·ty, *n.* 1. the quality or state of being irregular; deviation from a straight line or from any common or established rule; deviation from method or order; as, the *irregularity* of proceedings.

2. *pl.* **ir·reg·ū·lar′i·tieṣ,** that which is irregular.

ir·reg′ū·lăr·ly, *adv.* in an irregular manner; without rule, method, or order.

ir·reg′ū·lāte, *v.t.* to make irregular; to disorder. [Obs.]

ir·reg′ū·lous, *a.* licentious; lawless; irregular. [Obs.]

ir·rē·jeçt′ȧ·ble, *a.* that cannot be rejected. [Obs.]

ir·rē·laps′ȧ·ble, *a.* not relapsable; incapable of falling back; permanent. [Obs.]

ir′rē·lāte, *a.* not related. [Rare.]

ir·rē·lā′tion, *n.* the condition of being unrelated; lack of relation.

ir·rel′ȧ·tive, *a.* 1. not relative; unrelated.

2. irrelevant.

3. in music, having no tones in common; as, *irrelative* chords.

ir·rel′ȧ·tive·ly, *adv.* in an irrelative manner.

ir·rel′ē·vănce, *n.* 1. inapplicability; the quality or state of being irrelevant; as, the *irrelevance* of an argument or of testimony to a case in question.

2. something irrelevant.

ir·rel′ē·văn·cy, *n.*; *pl.* **ir·rel′ē·văn·cieṣ,** same as *irrelevance.*

ir·rel′ē·vănt, *a.* not relevant; not applicable or pertinent; not relating to the subject.

ir·rel′ē·vănt·ly, *adv.* in an irrelevant manner.

ir·rē·liēv′ȧ·ble, *a.* not admitting relief.

ir·rē·lig′iŏn (-ŏn), *n.* [from Fr. or L.; Fr. *irrêligion*; L. *irreligio.*] lack of, or indifference or hostility to, religion; state of being irreligious.

ir·rē·lig′iŏn·ist, *n.* one who is irreligious.

ir·rē·lig′ious (-us), *a.* [LL. *irreligiosus*; L. *in-* priv., and *religiosus*, religious, from *religio* (*-onis*), religion.]

1. not religious; indifferent or hostile to religion.

2. not in accord with religious principles; impious; profane; wicked; as, *irreligious* conduct.

ir·rē·lig′ious·ly, *adv.* in an irreligious manner.

ir·rē·lig′ious·ness, *n.* lack of religious principles or practices; ungodliness.

ir·rem′ē·ȧ·ble, *a.* admitting no return; as, an *irremeable* way.

ir·rē·mē′di·ȧ·ble, *a.* [L. *irremediabilis*, incurable; *in-* priv., and *remediabilis*, curable, from *remedium*, a cure.]

1. not to be remedied; that cannot be cured; as, an *irremediable* disease or evil.

2. not to be corrected or redressed; as, *irremediable* error or mischief.

ir·rē·mē′di·ȧ·ble·ness, *n.* the state of being irremediable.

ir·rē·mē′di·ȧ·bly, *adv.* in a manner or degree that prevents remedy, cure, or correction.

ir·rē·mis′si·ble, *a.* [LL. *irremissibilis*; L. *in-* priv., and LL. *remissibilis*, pardonable, from L. *remittere*, to pardon.] not to be pardoned; that cannot be forgiven or remitted.

ir·rē·mis′si·ble·ness, *n.* the quality of being irremissible.

ir·rē·mis′si·bly, *adv.* so as not to be pardoned.

ir·rē·mis′sion (-mish′un), *n.* the act of refusing or delaying to remit or pardon; the act of withholding remission or pardon.

ir·rē·mis′sive, *a.* not remitting. [Rare.]

ir·rē·mit′tȧ·ble, *a.* irremissible; unpardonable.

ir·rē·möv·ȧ·bil′i·ty, *n.* the quality or state of being irremovable.

ir·rē·möv′ȧ·ble, *a.* that cannot be removed.

ir·rē·möv′ȧ·bly, *adv.* so as to be irremovable.

ir·rē·möv′ăl, *n.* absence of removal. [Rare.]

ir·rē·mū′nẽr·ȧ·ble, *a.* that cannot be remunerated.

ir·rē·nowned′, *a.* not renowned. [Obs.]

ir·rep″ȧ·rȧ·bil′i·ty, *n.* the quality or state of being irreparable.

ir·rep′ȧ·rȧ·ble, *a.* [L. *in-* priv., and *reparabilis*, that can be repaired or regained.]

1. that cannot be repaired or mended; as, an *irreparable* breach.

2. that cannot be recovered or regained; as, an *irreparable* loss.

ir·rep′ȧ·rȧ·ble·ness, *n.* the state of being irreparable.

ir·rep′ȧ·rȧ·bly, *adv.* in a manner or degree that prevents recovery or repair; so as to be irreparable.

ir·rē·pēal·ȧ·bil′i·ty, *n.* the quality or state of being irrepealable.

ir·rē·pēal′ȧ·ble, *a.* that cannot be legally repealed or annulled.

ir·rē·pēal′ȧ·ble·ness, *n.* irrepealability.

ir·rē·pēal′ȧ·bly, *adv.* in an irrepealable manner.

ir·rē·pent′ănce, *n.* want of repentance; impenitence.

ir·rē·plāce′ȧ·ble, *a.* that cannot be replaced.

ir·rē·plev′i·ȧ·ble, ir·rē·plev′i·ṣȧ·ble, *a.* that cannot be replevied.

ir·rep·rē·hen′si·ble, *a.* not reprehensible; not to be blamed or censured; free from fault.

ir·rep·rē·hen′si·ble·ness, *n.* the quality or state of being irreprehensible.

ir·rep·rē·hen′si·bly, *adv.* in a manner not to incur blame; without blame.

ir·rep·rē·ṣent′ȧ·ble, *a.* that cannot be represented.

ir·rē·press·i·bil′i·ty, *n.* the quality or state of being irrepressible.

ir·rē·press′i·ble, *a.* that cannot be repressed or restrained.

Syn.—unrepressible, ungovernable, uncontrollable, insuppressible, free, unconfined, excitable.

ir·rē·press′i·bly, *adv.* in an irrepressible manner.

ir·rē·prōach′ȧ·ble, *a.* not reproachable; above reproach; blameless; faultless.

ir·rē·prōach′ȧ·ble·ness, *n.* the quality or state of being irreproachable.

ir·rē·prōach′ȧ·bly, *adv.* in a manner not to deserve reproach; blamelessly; as, conduct *irreproachably* upright.

ir·rē·pröv′ȧ·ble, *a.* that cannot be justly reproved; blameless; upright. [Rare.]

ir·rē·pröv′ȧ·ble·ness, *n.* the quality or state of being irreprovable.

ir·rē·pröv′ȧ·bly, *adv.* so as not to be liable to reproof or blame.

ir·rep·ti′tious (-tish′us), *a.* [L. *irreptus*, pp. of *irrepere*, to creep in.] secretly introduced; surreptitious. [Rare.]

ir·rep′ū·tȧ·ble, *a.* not reputable; disreputable. [Obs.]

ir·rē·ṣil′i·ent, *a.* [L. *in-* priv., and *resiliens* (*-entis*), ppr. of *resilire*, to spring back.] not resilient; inelastic.

ir·rē·ṣist′ănce, *n.* forbearance to resist; nonresistance; submission.

ir·rē·ṣist·i·bil′i·ty, *n.* the state or quality of being irresistible; power or force beyond resistance or opposition.

ir·rē·ṣist′i·ble, *a.* that cannot be successfully resisted or opposed; superior to opposition; overpowering.

ir·rē·ṣist′i·ble·ness, *n.* irresistibility.

ir·rē·ṣist′i·bly, *adv.* with a power that cannot be successfully resisted or opposed.

ir·rē·ṣist′less, *a.* that cannot be resisted. [Obs.]

ir·reṣ′ō·lū·ble, *a.* 1. that cannot be resolved; insoluble.

2. that cannot be relieved.

ir·reṣ′ō·lū·ble·ness, *n.* the quality of being irresoluble.

ir·reṣ′ō·lūte, *a.* not resolute; not firm or constant in purpose, decision, or opinion; not decided; not determined; wavering; given to doubt.

ir·reṣ′ō·lūte·ly, *adv.* in an irresolute manner; without decision.

ir·reṣ′ō·lūte·ness, *n.* lack of firm determination or purpose; vacillation.

ir·reṣ·ō·lū′tion, *n.* lack of resolution; indecision; vacillation.

ir·rē·ṣolv·ȧ·bil′i·ty, *n.* the state or quality of not being resolvable.

ir·rē·ṣolv′ȧ·ble, *a.* 1. that cannot be resolved into elements or parts.

2. that cannot be solved.

ir·rē·ṣolv′ȧ·ble·ness, *n.* irresolvability.

ir·rē·ṣolv′ed·ly, *adv.* without decision.

ir·rē·speç′tive, *a.* not having regard for persons or consequences. [Rare.]

> According to this doctrine, it must be resolved wholly into the absolute, *irrespective* will of God. —Bacon.

irrespective of; regardless of; independent of.

ir·rē·speç′tive·ly, *adv.* without regard to persons or circumstances.

ir·res′pi·rȧ·ble, *a.* unfit for respiration; not suitable to be breathed; as, *irrespirable* air.

ir·rē·spon·si·bil′i·ty, *n.* lack of responsibility; the fact or state of being irresponsible.

ir·rē·spon′si·ble, *a.* 1. not responsible; not liable or able to answer for consequences; not answerable.

2. lacking a sense of responsibility; not to be relied upon or trusted.

Syn.—unbound, not answerable, excusable, lawless, arbitrary, unreliable.

ir·rē·spon′si·ble, *n.* an irresponsible person.

ir·rē·spon′si·bly, *adv.* in an irresponsible manner; so as not to be responsible.

ir·rē·spon′sive, *a.* unable or disinclined to respond; not responsive.

ir·rē·sus′ci·tȧ·ble, *a.* [L. *in-* priv., and *resuscitare*, to revive.] not capable of being revived.

ir·rē·sus′ci·tȧ·bly, *adv.* so as not to be resuscitable.

ir·rē·ten′tion, *n.* lack of retention.

ir·rē·ten′tive, *a.* not retentive or apt to retain.

ir·rē·trāce′ȧ·ble, *a.* that cannot be retraced.

ir·rē·traçt′ile, *a.* without power of retraction.

ir·rē·triēv·ȧ·bil′i·ty, *n.* the state or quality of being irretrievable.

ir·rē·triēv′ȧ·ble, *a.* that cannot be retrieved, restored, recovered, or repaired; irrecoverable; irreparable; as, an *irretrievable* loss.

ir·rē·triēv′ȧ·ble·ness, *n.* the state of being irretrievable.

ir·rē·triēv′ȧ·bly, *adv.* so as to be irretrievable; irreparably; irrecoverably.

ir·rē·tũrn′ȧ·ble, *a.* that cannot be returned. [Obs.]

ir·rē·vēal′ȧ·ble, *a.* that cannot be revealed.

ir·rē·vēal′ȧ·bly, *adv.* so as not to be revealable.

ir·rev′ẽr·ence, *n.* [L. *irreverentia*, irreverence, from *irreverens* (*-entis*), irreverent.]

1. lack of reverence or of veneration; want of a due regard for authority; disrespect.

2. an act or statement showing this.

3. the condition of not being treated with reverence.

ir·rev′ẽr·end, *a.* not reverend.

ir·rev′ẽr·ent, *a.* [L. *irreverens* (*-entis*), irreverent; *in-* priv., and *reverens* (*-entis*), ppr. of *revereri*, to stand in awe of.] lacking in reverence; not reverent; showing disrespect.

ir·rev′ẽr·ent·ly, *adv.* without reverence.

ir·rē·vẽrs·i·bil′i·ty, *n.* the state or quality of being irreversible.

ir·rē·vẽrs′i·ble, *a.* incapable of being reversed; specifically, (a) that cannot be recalled, repealed, or annulled; as, an *irreversible* decree or sentence; (b) that cannot be turned inside out, run backward, etc.

ir·rē·vẽrs′i·ble·ness, *n.* irreversibility.

ir·rē·vẽrs′i·bly, *adv.* in an irreversible manner.

ir·rev″ō·çȧ·bil′i·ty, *n.* the state or quality of being irrevocable.

ir·rev′ō·çȧ·ble, *a.* [L. *irrevocabilis*; *in-* priv., and *revocabilis*, revocable, from *revocare*, to call back.] incapable of being recalled, undone, altered, or revoked; that cannot be reversed, repealed, or annulled; as, an *irrevocable* decree, sentence, edict, or doom.

ir·rev′ō·çȧ·ble·ness, *n.* irrevocability.

ir·rev′ō·çȧ·bly, *adv.* beyond recall; in an irrevocable manner.

ir·rev′ō·lū·ble, *a.* that has no finite cycle of revolution. [Rare.]

ir·rhē·tor′iç·ăl (-rē-), *a.* not rhetorical; unpersuasive. [Rare.]

ir′ri·gȧ·ble, *a.* that can be irrigated; as, an *irrigable* region.

ir′ri·gāte, *v.t.*; irrigated, *pt.*, *pp.*; irrigating, *ppr.* [L. *irrigatus*, pp. of *irrigare*, to bring water to or upon; *in*, in, to, upon, and *rigare*, to water, moisten.]

1. to water; to wet; to moisten; to refresh by or as by watering.

2. to supply (land) with water by means of artificial ditches or channels.

3. in medicine, to cleanse or flush (a cavity or canal) with water or other fluid.

ir·ri·gā′tion, *n.* [L. *irrigatio* (*-onis*), from *irrigare*, to irrigate.]

1. an irrigating or being irrigated.
2. in agriculture, the operation of causing water to flow through lands for nourishing plants.
3. in medicine, the cleansing of a body cavity, tooth socket, suppurating surface, etc. by directing a stream of water or antiseptic fluid into or against it.

ir·ri·gā′tion·ăl, *a.* of irrigation.

ir′ri·gā·tive, *a.* irrigating.

ir′ri·gā·tŏr, *n.* a person or thing that irrigates.

ir·rig′ū·ous, *a.* 1. watered; watery; moist.
2. irrigating.

ir·ris′i·ble, *a.* ridiculous. [Obs.]

ir·ri′ṣion, *n.* derision. [Rare.]

ir″ri·tȧ·bil′i·ty, *n.*; *pl.* **ir″ri·tȧ·bil′i·tieṣ,** [L. *irritabilitas* (*-atis*), from *irritabilis*, irritable.]
1. the quality or state of being easily irritated, annoyed, or provoked to anger; impatience; fretfulness; as, *irritability* of temper.
2. in physiology, the property of living matter to react when stimulated.
3. in medicine, an excessive responsiveness of an organ or part to a mild stimulation.
4. in botany, that quality in certain plants by which they exhibit motion on the application of stimuli.

ir′ri·tȧ·ble, *a.* [L. *irritabilis*, from *irritare*, to irritate.]
1. easily annoyed or provoked to anger; impatient; fretful; as, an *irritable* temper.
2. in physiology, susceptible to irritation; able to respond when stimulated.
3. in medicine, excessively sensitive to the influence of irritants or stimuli.

ir′ri·tȧ·ble·ness, *n.* irritability.

ir′ri·tȧ·bly, *adv.* in an irritable manner.

ir′ri·tăn·cy, *n.* the state or quality of being irritating; irritation.

ir′ri·tăn·cy, *n.* in Scots law, the state of being irritant or of no force, or of being null and void.

ir′ri·tănt, *n.* 1. anything that excites or irritates.
2. in physiology and medicine, any chemical, mechanical, or electrical agent which causes irritation.

ir′ri·tănt, *a.* [L. *irritans* (*-antis*), ppr. of *irritare*, to irritate.] irritating; causing irritation or inflammation.

ir′ri·tănt, *a.* [LL. *irritans* (*-antis*), ppr. of *irritare*, to make void; from L. *irritus*, void, invalid.] in Scots law, rendering null and void; as, an *irritant* clause.

ir′ri·tāte, *v.t.*; irritated, *pt.*, *pp.*; irritating, *ppr.* [L. *irritatus*, pp. of *irritare*, to excite, stimulate, irritate.]
1. in medicine, to cause to be inflamed or sore; as, to *irritate* a wounded part by a coarse bandage.
2. to excite to impatience or anger; to provoke; to tease; to exasperate; as, he was *irritated* by her questions.
3. to increase action or violence in; to heighten excitement in. [Obs.]
4. in physiology, to excite (an organ, muscle, etc.) to a characteristic action or function by a stimulus.

ir′ri·tāte, *v.t.* in Scots law, to render null and void.

ir′ri·tāte, *a.* excited; irritated. [Obs.]

ir·ri·tā′tion, *n.* 1. the act or process of irritating.
2. the fact or condition of being irritated.
3. something that irritates.
4. in medicine, an excessive response to stimulation in an organ or part.

ir′ri·tā·tive, *a.* 1. serving to excite or irritate; causing irritation.
2. accompanied with or produced by irritation; as, an *irritative* fever.

ir′ri·tȧ·tō·ry, *a.* exciting; producing irritation. [Rare.]

ir′rō·rāte, *v.t.* to moisten with dew. [Obs.]

ir′rō·rāte, *a.* in zoology, marked with small dewlike spots, as the wings of some butterflies.

ir·rō·rā′tion, *n.* the act of bedewing; also, the state of being moistened with dew. [Obs.]

ir·rō·tā′tion·ăl, *a.* in physics, without rotation: said of the movement of a liquid.

ir·rụ′briç·ăl, *a.* opposed to the rubric; nonrubrical.

ir′rụ·gāte, *v.t.* [L. *irrugatus*, pp. of *irrugare*; *in*, in, on, and *rugare*, to wrinkle.] to render rugose; to wrinkle. [Obs.]

ir·rupt′, *v.t.* and *v.i.* to break in(to); burst in.

ir·rup′tion, *n.* [L. *irruptio* (*-onis*), from *irrumpere*, to break in, burst in; *in*, in, and *rumpere*, to break, burst.]
1. a bursting in; a breaking or sudden violent rushing into.
2. a swift invasion or incursion; a sudden, violent inroad or entrance of invaders; as, the *irruption* of the belligerents into Africa.
Syn.—incursion, inroad, raid, foray.

ir·rup′tive, *a.* 1. bursting or rushing in or upon; tending to sudden, violent invasion.
2. in geology, intrusive.

Īr′ving·īte, *n.* one of a religious denomination named after Edward Irving (1792–1834), a Scotch minister and promulgator of doctrines relative to the organization of the Christian church and the strict observance of ritualistic practices.

īs-, see *iso-*.

iṣ, *v.i.* [AS. *is*. It represents Goth. *ist*, L. *est*, Gr. *esti*, and Sans. *asti*, is.] the third person singular, present indicative, of *be*.
as is; as it now is; without change from its present condition.

Ī′ṣăaç, *n.* [LL. *Isaacus*; Heb. *yitsḥāq*, lit., laughter.] in the Bible, one of the patriarchs, son of Abraham and Sarah, and father of Jacob and Esau: Gen. xxi. 3.

Iṣ′ȧ·bel, Iṣ′ȧ·belle, *n.* [Fr. *Isabelle*, a woman's name: said to be so called from *Isabella* of Austria, who vowed she would not change her linen until Ostend was taken.] a brownish-yellow color.

iṣ′ȧ·bel·īte, *n.* [*Isabelle*, a woman's name, and *-ite*.] a variety of angelfish.

iṣ·ȧ·bel′lȧ moth, an American moth, *Pyrrharctia isabella*.

iṣ·ȧ·bel′lȧ wood, in botany, an American tree of the genus *Persea*; the red bay.

iṣ·ȧ·bel′line, *a.* of the color of Isabel.

ī·sab·nor′măl, *n.* same as *isoabnormal*.

īs·ȧ·çous′tiç, *a.* [*is-*, and *acoustic*.] of or having to do with equal intensity of sound.

ī·sȧ·del′phous, *a.* [*is-*, and Gr. *adelphos*, a brother.] in botany, designating or of a diadelphous flower in which the separate bundles of stamens are equal in number.

ī·sȧ·gō′ġē, *n.* [Gr. *eisagōgē*, an introduction, from *eisagein*, to lead in, introduce.] an introduction, as to a book, a branch of study, the works of an author, etc.

ī·sȧ·goġ′iç, ī·sȧ·goġ′iç·ăl, *a.* [L. *isagogicus*; Gr. *eisagogikos*, introductory, from *eisagōgē*, an introduction, from *eisagein*, to lead in; *eis*, in, and *agein*, to lead.] introductory.

ī·sȧ·goġ′iċs, *n.pl.* [*construed as sing.*] [*isagog*ic, and *-ics*.] introductory study; especially, the study of the literary history of the Bible, considered as introductory to the study of Bible interpretation.

ī′sȧ·gon, *n.* [Gr. *isos*, equal, and *gōnia*, an angle.] in geometry, a figure whose angles are equal. [Rare.]

Ī·ṣā′iăh (-zā′ȧ), *n.* [Heb. *yĕsha ʻyah*, lit., God is salvation.]
1. a Hebrew prophet of the eighth century B.C.
2. a book of the Old Testament containing his teachings.

Ī·ṣāi′ăs, *n.* [L.] Isaiah: form used in the Douay Bible.

ī·san′drous, *a.* [*is-*, and Gr. *anēr*, *andros*, a man, male.] in botany, designating a flower having similar stamens and of the same number as the divisions of the corolla.

ī·san′thēr·ous, *a.* [*is-*, and Gr. *antherōs*, flowery, from *anthos*, a flower.] in botany, designating a flower with equal anthers. [Rare.]

ī·san′thous, *a.* [*is-*, and Gr. *anthos*, a flower.] in botany, designating a plant with regular flowers.

īs·ap·os·tol′iç, *a.* [*is-*, and Gr. *apostolikos*, apostolic, from *apostolos*, one sent away, a messenger.] equal to, or contemporary with, the apostles: said of bishops consecrated by the apostles and of others in the early church distinguished for their faith.

ī·sat′iç, ī·sȧ·tin′iç, *a.* derived from or relating to isatin; as, *isatic* acid.

ī′sȧ·tīde, ī′sȧ·tīd (*or* -tid), *n.* a substance obtained by reducing isatin.

ī′sȧ·tin, *n.* [*isat*is and *-in*.] a compound, $C_8H_5NO_2$, obtained by oxidizing indigo: it forms hyacinth-red or reddish-orange crystals of a brilliant luster and is used in making dyes: written also *isatine*.

Ī′sȧ·tis, *n.* [L. *isatis*; Gr. *isatis*, a kind of plant, used in healing wounds, woad.] in botany, a genus of herbs of the order *Cruciferæ*; *Isatis tinctoria* or dyer's woad is cultivated as a dye plant.

Is·car′i·ŏt, *n.* [L. *Iscariota*; Gr. *Iskariōtēs*; Heb. *īsh-qĕrīyōth*, man of Kerioth (town in Palestine).]
1. in the Bible, the surname of the disciple Judas, who betrayed Jesus: Luke xxii. 3.
2. a traitor.

is·çhē′mi·ȧ, is·çhae′mi·ȧ, *n.* [Mod. L., from Gr. *ischaimos*, quenching blood; *ischein*, to hold, and *haima*, blood.] in pathology, a suppression of the flow of blood in an organ or tissue; local anemia.

is·çhē′miç, *a.* relating to or having ischemia, or local anemia.

is′çhi·ȧ, *n.*, plural of *ischium*.

is·çhi·ad′iç, *a.* same as *ischiatic*.

is′çhi·ăl, *a.* [Gr. *ischion*, the hip joint.] ischiatic.

is·çhi·al′ġi·ȧ, *n.* same as *sciatica*.

is·çhi·at′iç, *a.* [Gr. *ischion*, the hip, hip joint, and *-atic*.] pertaining to the ischium or hip; ischiadic; ischial.
ischiatic callosity; one of the small areas of hairless bright-colored skin on the hips and buttocks of certain species of monkeys.

is·çhi·drō′sis, *n.* suppression of sweat or perspiration.

is′çhi·ō-, [from Gr. *ischion*, hip, hip joint.] a combining form used in anatomy, medicine, etc. to denote *relation to the ischium* or *the hip*.

is″çhi·ō·çap′sū·lăr, *a.* [*ischio-*, and L. *capsula*, a capsule, case.] in anatomy, relating to the ischium and the capsular ligament of the hip joint.

is″çhi·ō·çē′rīte, *n.* [*ischio-*, and Gr. *keras*, horn, and *-ite*.] in zoology, the third segment in a developed antenna of a crustacean.

is·çhi·op′ō·dīte, *n.* [*ischio-*, and Gr. *pous*, *podos*, foot.] in zoology, the third segment in a developed endopodite of a crustacean.

is″çhi·ō·reç′tăl, *a.* in anatomy, between or connecting the ischium and the rectum.

is′çhi·um, *n.*; *pl.* **is′çhi·ȧ,** [Gr. *ischion*, the hip, hip joint.]
1. in anatomy, the posterior and inferior part of the pelvic arch in vertebrates; the lowermost of the three portions forming the innominate bone; the lowermost part of the hipbone, on which the body rests when sitting.
2. in zoology, same as *ischiopodite*.

is·çhū·ret′iç, *a.* efficacious in the treatment of ischuria.

is·çhū·ret′iç, *n.* a medicine for the relief of ischuria; a diuretic.

is·çhū′ri·ȧ, is′çhū·ry, *n.* [LL. *ischuria*; Gr. *ischouria*, retention of urine, from *ischourein*; *ischein*, to hold, and *ouron*, urine.] a stoppage or suppression of urine.

-iṣe, same as *-ize*.

ī·sen·ẽr′ġiç, *a.* [*is-*, and Gr. *energeia*, action, energy.] in physics, relating to or having equal energy.

ī·sen·trop′iç, *a.* [*is-*, and Gr. *entropē*, a turning about; *en*, in, and *trepein*, to turn.] in physics, equal in entropy.
isentropic lines; the connecting lines between points of equal entropy.

ī·seth·i·on′iç, *a.* [*is-* and *ethionic*.] designating or of the sulfonic acid $C_2H_6O_4S$.

I·seult′, *n.* [Fr.] see *Isolde*.

-ish, [ME. *-ish*, *-issh*, *-isch*; AS. *-isc*.] a suffix meaning: (a) *of* or *belonging to* (a specified nation or people), as in Span*ish*, Ir*ish*; (b) *like* or *characteristic of*, as in devil*ish*, boy*ish*; (c) *tending to*, *verging on*, as in book*ish*, knav*ish*; (d) *somewhat*, *rather*, as in tall*ish*, blu*ish*; (e) [Colloq.] *approximately*, *about*, as in thirty-*ish*.

-ish, [ME. *-ishen*, *-ischen*, *-issen*; OFr. *-iss-*, *-is-*, the ending of some parts of verbs, as ppr. of *finir*, to finish, from L. *-escere*, *-iscere*, an ending of incept. verbs.] a verb suffix appearing in verbs of French origin or verbs similarly formed; as, furn*ish*, fin*ish*, pun*ish*.

Ish′mā·el, *n.* [LL. *Ismaël*; Heb. *yishmāʻēl*, lit., God hears.]
1. in the Bible, the son of Abraham and Hagar: at Sarah's insistence, he and his mother were made outcasts: Gen. xvi. 12.
2. an outcast.

Ish′mā·el·īte, *n.* 1. a descendant of Ishmael.
2. one at war with society; an outcast.
3. an Arab: the Arabs claim to be descended from Ishmael.

Ish″mā·el·ī′tish, *a.* like Ishmael; partaking of the nature of an Ishmaelite.

ish·piñ′gō, *n.* [prob. from native name.] a South American tree of the genus *Nectandra*: called also *Santa Fé cinnamon*.

Ish′tär, *n.* the Babylonian and Assyrian goddess of love and fertility.

Ī′si·aç, *a.* [L. *Isiacus*; Gr. *Isiakos*, from *Isis*, Isis.] relating to the female deity Isis.

ī′si·çle, *n.* an icicle. [Obs.]

Is·i·dō′ri·ăn, *a.* relating to St. Isidore, archbishop of Seville during the seventh century.

ī′sin·glȧss, *n.* [prob. altered from M.D. *huizenblas*, lit., sturgeon bladder; *huizen*, a sturgeon, and *blas*, a bladder.]

1. a form of gelatin prepared from the internal membranes of fish bladders: it is used as a clarifying agent and adhesive.

2. mica, especially when it occurs in thin sheets.

Ī′sis, *n.* [L., from Gr. *Isis*, the goddess Isis.] one of the chief deities of the ancient Egyptian religion. She was regarded as the sister or sister-wife of Osiris and the mother of Horus. She was worshiped by the Egyptians as the being who had first civilized them and as the goddess of fertility, and was represented with a cow's horns and the sun's disk as a crown.

ISIS

Is′lȧm, *n.* [Ar. *islām*, obedience to the will of God, submission, the orthodox faith.]

1. the monotheistic Moslem religion, of which Mohammed was the prophet.

2. Moslems collectively.

3. all the lands in which the Moslem religion predominates.

Is·lȧm′iç, *a.* of Islam; Moslem.

Is′lăm·iṣm, *n.* the religion, doctrines, customs, etc. of Islam.

Is′lăm·īte, *n.* a Moslem.

Is·lăm·it′iç, *a.* pertaining to Islam; Moslem.

Is′lăm·ize, *v.i.* and *v.t.*; Islamized, *pt., pp.*; Islamizing, *ppr.* to bring into or be in conformity with Islam.

īs′lănd (ī′), *n.* [ME. *iland, yland*; AS. *igland, iglond, iland*; *ig*, island, and *land*, land. The *s* was inserted in the sixteenth century because of confusion with *isle*.]

1. a tract of land not as large as a continent, surrounded by water, whether of the sea, a river, or a lake.

2. anything resembling an island in position or isolation, as a safety zone.

3. in anatomy, a tissue or cluster of cells differing from surrounding tissue in size, structure, formation, staining properties, etc.

īs′lănd, *v.t.*; islanded, *pt., pp.*; islanding, *ppr.* 1. to cause to become or appear like an island or islands; to isolate by surrounding, as with water.

2. to dot with or as with islands.

īs′lănd·ẽr, *n.* a native or inhabitant of an island.

īs′lănd hop′ping, in World War II, the advancement of a military force by seizing consecutive islands as bases.

īs′lăndṣ (or **īs′lets**) **ŏf Lăñ′gẽr·häns,** [after Paul *Langerhans* (1847–1888), G. histologist.] irregular groups of cells in the pancreas that produce the hormone insulin: their degeneration is believed to be a cause of diabetes mellitus.

Īs′lăndṣ ŏf the Bless′ed, in Greek and Roman mythology, the islands of bliss in the Western Ocean, where heroes went after death.

īs′lănd ū′ni·vẽrse, any of the large number of galaxies of stars like the one containing the earth.

īs′lănd·y (ī′), *a.* 1. relating to islands or to an island.

2. having islands; abounding in islands; as, an *islandy* sea.

is′lāy, *n.* an evergreen shrub, *Prunus ilicifolia*, which bears a small plum.

īsle (īl), *n.* aisle. [Obs.]

īsle, *n.* [ME. *ile, yle, isle*; OFr. *ile, isle*, from L. *insula*, an island.] an island or islet.

īsle, *v.i.*; isled, *pt., pp.*; isling, *ppr.* to live on an isle.

īsle, *v.t.* to island.

īs′let (ī′), *n.* [OFr. *islet*, dim. of *isle*, an island, from L. *insula*, an island.]

1. a little island.

2. anything resembling a little island, as a mark on the wing of an insect or on a leaf or flower.

-iṣm, [L. *-ismus*; Gr. *-ismos*.] a noun-forming suffix meaning: (a) *the act, practice*, or *result of*, as in terror*ism*; (b) *the condition of being*, as in barbar*ism*, pauper*ism*; (c) *action, conduct*, or *qualities characteristic of*, as in scoundrel*ism*, patriot*ism*, American*ism*; (d), *the doctrine, theory*, or *principle of*, as in atom*ism*, social*ism*; (e) *devotion to*, as in national*ism*; (f) *an instance, example*, or *peculiarity of*, as in Gallic*ism*, wittic*ism*; (g) *an abnormal condition caused by*, as in alcohol*ism*.

iṣm, *n.* [from its common use as a suffix in words signifying doctrine or theory, etc.] a doctrine, system, theory, etc. whose name ends in *-ism*: generally used contemptuously; as, away with your *isms* and ologies.

Is·mā·il′i·ăn, Is·mā·ē′li·ăn, *n.* a member of a sect of the Shiite branch of Moslems which maintains that the office of imam should have gone to the descendant of the deceased Ismail, and not to his younger brother Moussa, to whom their father Jafar willed it at his death in 765 A.D.: written also *Ismaelite*.

iṣ′n't, is not.

ī′sō-, [from Gr. *isos*, equal.] a combining form meaning *equality, identity, similarity*, as in *iso*dactylous, *iso*dulcite, *iso*cyanic, *iso*gnathous: also, before a vowel, *is-*

ī″sō·ăb·nor′măl, *n.* [*iso-*, and L. *abnormis*, deviating from a rule.] in meteorology, a line on a map passing through those points of the earth's surface where the variation of temperature from the normal for a certain period is the same: written also *isabnormal*.

ī″sō·ăg·glū·ti·nā′tion, *n.* [*iso-*, and *agglutination*.] the clumping of the red blood cells of an individual by the blood serum of another member of the same species.

ī″sō·ăg·glū′ti·nin, *n.* [*iso-*, and *agglutinin*.] a substance in the blood that is capable of clumping the red cells of other members of the same species.

ī′sō·bär, *n.* [*iso-* and Gr. *baros*, weight.]

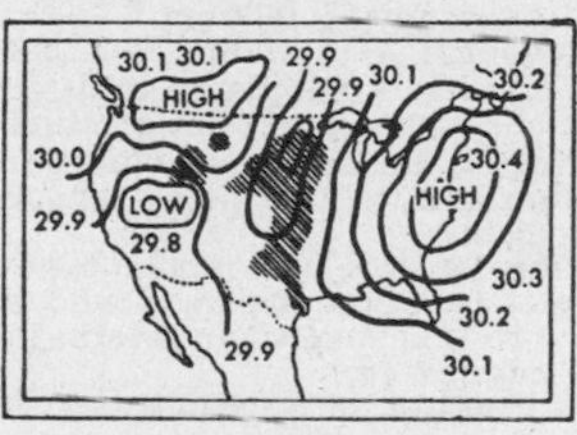

ISOBARS

1. in physical geography, a line drawn on a map to connect those places on the surface of the globe having equal barometric pressure over a given period or at a given time: written also *isobare*.

2. any of two or more forms of an atom having the same atomic weight (or mass number) but different atomic numbers and representing different chemical elements: distinguished from *isotope*.

ī·sō·bar′iç, *a.* 1. of or having isobars.

2. having or showing equal barometric pressure.

ī·sō·bar′iç ī′sō·tōpe, any of two or more forms of radioactive atoms having the same atomic weight (or mass number) and the same atomic number and representing different chemical elements because of differences in the nature of their radioactive disintegration: such isotopes are produced artificially.

ī′sō·bär·iṣm, *n.* equality or similarity of weight or pressure.

ī·sō·bar·ō·met′riç, *a.* [*iso-*, and Gr. *baros*, weight, and *metron*, a measure.] same as *isobaric*.

ī·sō·bath′y·thẽrm, *n.* [*iso-*, and Gr. *bathys*, deep, and *thermē*, heat.] in physical geography, a line on a map connecting points on the surface of the earth beneath which the temperature is constant at a given depth.

ī·sō·bath·y·thẽr′miç, *a.* pertaining to an isobathytherm.

ī′sō·bront, *n.* [*iso-*, and Gr. *brontē*, thunder.] a line on a map passing through those points on the surface of the earth at which the first peal of thunder of a thunderstorm is heard at the same time.

ī·sō·ceph′ȧ·liṣm, *n.* [*iso-*, and Gr. *kephalē*, head.] the designing of bas-reliefs in such a manner as to keep the heads of human figures at the same distance from the ground, regardless of size or position.

ī·sō·cẽr′căl, *a.* [*iso-*, and Gr. *kerkos*, tail.] in ichthyology, having the caudal vertebrae extended in a stright line, not bent upward, and the caudal fin equally developed above and below.

ī′sō·cẽr·cy, *n.* the state of having the caudal vertebrae isocercal.

ī′sō·chaṣm, *n.* [*iso-*, and Gr. *chasma*, a gap, gulf.] in physical geography, a line on a map passing through those points on the earth's surface at which the frequency of the occurrence of auroral displays is the same.

ī·sō·chaṣ′miç, *a.* designating or of an isochasm.

ī′sō·cheīm, *n.* [from *iso-*, and Gr. *cheima*, winter.] a line on a map connecting points on the earth's surface that have the same mean winter temperature: also written *isochime*.

ī·sō·cheī′măl, *a.* 1. of or having isocheims.

2. having or showing the same mean winter temperature.

Also written *isochimal*.

ī·sō·cheī′mē·năl, *a.* isocheimal.

ī·sō·cheī′mē·năl, *n.* an isocheim.

ī′sō·chor, ī′sō·chore, *n.* [*iso-*, and Gr. *chōra*, space, room, country.] a line on a thermodynamic graph representing the parallel variations in pressure and temperature of a constant volume of gas.

ī·sō·chor′iç, *a.* pertaining to an isochor.

ī·sō·chrō·mat′iç, *a.* [*iso-*, and Gr. *chrōma* (*-atos*), color.]

1. in optics, having the same color: said of lines or curves in figures formed by interfering light waves from biaxial crystals.

2. in photography, same as *orthochromatic*.

ī·soch′rō·năl, ī·sō·chron′iç, *a.* [*iso-*, and Gr. *chronos*, time.]

1. equal in length of time.

2. occurring at equal intervals of time.

ī·soch′rō·niṣm, *n.* the quality, condition, or fact of being isochronal.

ī·soch′rō·nīze, *v.t.*; isochronized, *pt., pp.*; isochronizing, *ppr.* to make isochronal.

ī·soch′rō·non, *n.* [Gr. *isochronon*, properly neut. of *isochronos*, equal in time; *isos*, equal, and *chronos*, time.] a clock designed to keep perfectly accurate time.

ī·soch′rō·nous, *a.* same as *isochronal*.

ī·soch′rō·ous, *a.* [Gr. *isochroos*, like-colored; *isos*, equal, and *chroa*, color.] in botany, being of equal color throughout.

ī·sō·clī′năl, *a.* 1. of equal inclination or dip.

2. connecting or showing points on the earth's surface having equal magnetic inclination or dip; as, *isoclinal* lines on a map.

3. in geology, dipping in the same direction: said of strata.

ī·sō·clī′năl, *n.* an isoclinal line.

ī′sō·clīne, *n.* [*iso-*, and Gr. *klinein*, to slope, incline.] in geology, any fold of stratified rocks in which the two parts are parallel or have the same angle of dip, as in certain mountain rocks.

ī·sō·clin′iç, *a.* same as *isoclinal*.

ī·soç′rȧ·cy, *n.* [Gr. *isokratia*.] a system of government in which everybody has equal political power.

ī·sō·cry̆′măl, *a.* pertaining to or having the nature of an isocryme.

ī′sō·crȳme, *n.* [*iso-*, and Gr. *krymos*, cold.] in physical geography, a line on a map connecting points having the same mean temperature during the coldest months of the year.

ī·sō·cry̆m′iç, *a.* same as *isocrymal*.

ī·sō·cy·an′iç, *a.* [*iso-* and *cyanic*.] pertaining to isocyanic acid.

isocyanic acid; a volatile, colorless, unisolated liquid compound isomeric with cyanic acid.

ī·sō·cy̆′ȧ·nide, *n.* same as *carbamine*.

ī·sō·cy̆′ȧ·nin, *n.* isocyanine.

ī·sō·cy̆′ȧ·nīne, *n.* [*iso-* and *cyanine*.] any of a group of quinoline dyes used in sensitizing photographic plates and films.

ī·sō·cy·ȧ·nū′riç, *a.* fulminuric.

ī·sō·daç′tyl·ous, *a.* [*iso-*, and Gr. *daktylos*, a digit.] in zoology, having all the toes alike, especially in length.

ī·sō·dī·ȧ·bat′iç, *a.* [*iso-*, and Gr. *diabatikos*, able to pass through, from *diabainein*, to pass through.] in physics, designating isothermal curves representing variations in the pressure and density of a body, the quantity of heat received or given out being constant.

ī·sō·dī·ȧ·met′riç, *a.* [*iso-*, and Gr. *diametros*, diameter.]

1. in crystallography, having equal development in the directions of the lateral axes.

2. in botany, uniform in diameter: said of cells or organs.

ī·sod′i·çon, *n.*; *pl.* **ī·sod′i·çȧ,** [L. Gr. *eisodikon*, neut. of *eisodikos*, pertaining to the entrance, from Gr. *eisodos*, entrance; *eis*, into, and *hodos*, way.] in the Greek church, a brief anthem sung during the entrance and passage of an officiating priest through the church to the chancel.

ī″sō·dī·mor′phiç, *a.* see *isodimorphous.*

ī″sō·dī·mor′phişm, *n.* [*iso-*, and Gr. *dimorphos*, two-formed; *dis*, twice, and *morphē*, form.] a similarity of crystalline form between the two forms of two dimorphous substances.

ī″sō·dī·mor′phous, *a.* of or possessing the characteristics of isodimorphism.

ī·sod′ō·mon, ī·sod′ō·mum, *n.* [Gr. *isodomon*, properly neut. of *isodomos*, built alike; *isos*, equal, and *demein*, to build.] in Grecian architecture, a construction in which the blocks are of equal thickness and length.

ISODOMON

ī′sō·dont, *a.* [*is-*, and Gr. *odous*, *odontos*, a tooth.] in zoology, having all the teeth alike or of the same class.

ī·sō·dul′cīte, *n.* [*iso-* and *dulcite.*] a crystalline compound resembling sugar.

ī″sō·dȳ·nam′iç, *a.* [*iso-*, and Gr. *dynamis*, power, force.]
1. of or having equal force.
2. connecting or showing points on the earth's surface having equal magnetic intensity; as, *isodynamic* lines on a map.

ī″sō·dȳ·nam′iç, *n.* an isodynamic line.

ī″sō·dȳ·nam′i·çăl, *a.* isodynamic.

ī·sō·dȳ′nȧ·mous, *a.* [Gr. *isodynamos*; *isos*, equal, and *dynamis*, power.] having equal force; of equal size.

ī″sō·ē·leç′triç, *a.* having equal electric potential.

Ī·sō·ē·tā′cē·ae, *n.pl.* [L. *isoetes*, a houseleek, from Gr. *isoetēs*, an evergreen plant, lit. equal in years; *isos*, equal, and *etos*, a year, and *-aceæ*]. a family of vascular cryptogamous aquatic plants, comprising a single genus, *Isoetes*, the quillwort.

ī·sō·ē·tā′ceous, *a.* belonging or pertaining to the family *Isoetaceæ.*

Ī·sō·ē′tē·ae, *n.pl.* same as *Isoetaceæ.*

Ī·sō′ē·tēş, *n.* the only known genus of *Isoetaceæ.*

i″sō·gȧ·mēte′, *n.* a gamete not differentiated sexually or otherwise from another that it unites with: opposed to *heterogamete.*

ī·sog′ȧ·mous, *a.* characterized by isogamy.

ī·sog′ȧ·my, *n.* [*iso-*, and Gr. *gamos*, marriage.] in botany, reproduction by the union of two isogametes.

ī·sog′e·nous, *a.* [*iso-* and *-genous.*] in biology, of the same origin.

ī·sog′e·ny, *n.* [*iso-* and *-geny.*] in biology, the condition of being isogenous; identity of origin.

ī·sō·gē′ō·thẽrm, *n.* [*iso-*, and Gr. *gē*, earth, and *thermē*, heat.] in physical geography, an imaginary line or surface under the earth's surface passing through points having the same mean temperature.

ī·sō·gē·ō·thẽr′măl, *a.* relating to or having the characteristics of an isogeotherm.

ī·sō·gē·ō·thẽr′miç, *a.* isogeothermal.

ī′sō·glŏss, *n.* [*iso-*, and Gr. *glossa*, tongue, speech.] in linguistics, an imaginary line of demarcation between regions differing in some feature of pronunciation, syntax, etc.

ī·sog′nȧ·thous, *a.* [*iso-*, and Gr. *gnathos*, jaw.] in odontology, having the teeth in both the upper and the lower jaw alike.

ī′sō·gon, *n.* [*iso-* and *-gon.*] a polygon with all angles equal.

ī·sog′ō·năl, *a.* equiangular.

ī·sō·gon′iç, *a.* [Gr. *isogōnios*, having equal angles; *isos*, equal, and *gōnia*, an angle.]
1. of or having equal angles.
2. connecting or showing points on the earth's surface having the same magnetic declination; as, *isogonic* lines on a map.

ī·sō·gon′iç, *n.* an isogonic line.

ī·sō·gon′iç, *a.* in biology, pertaining to isogonism.

ī·sō·gō′ni·ō·stat, *n.* [Gr. *isogōnios*, having equal angles, and *statos*, verbal adj. of *histanai*, to stand.] a device for regulating the motion of prisms, as in a spectroscope.

ī·sog′ō·nişm, *n.* [*iso-*, and Gr. *gonos*, an offspring.] in biology, the production of like reproductive parts from dissimilar stocks, as in certain hydroids.

ī′sō·grȧph, *n.* a drawing instrument which serves as a protractor and square: it consists of two short, straight edges of metal, joined at the top by a circular plate marked with angular degrees.

ī·sō·grȧph′iç, *a.* pertaining to isography.

ī·sog′rȧ·phy, *n.* [*iso-*, and Gr. *graphein*, to write.] the imitation of another's handwriting. [Rare.]

ī·sog′y·nous, *a.* [*iso-*, and Gr. *gynē*, a female.] in botany, having the pistils or the parts of a compound ovary agreeing in number with the sepals.

ī·sō·hal′sīne, *n.* [*iso-*, and Gr. *hals*, salt, and *-ine.*] in physical geography, an imaginary line passing through those points in the ocean at which the salinity of the water is equal.

ī·sō·hȳ′e·tăl, ī·sō·hȳ′e·tōse, *a.* [*iso-*, and Gr. *hyetos*, rain.] designating or of a line on a map connecting those places on the surface of the globe where the quantity of rain which falls annually is the same.

ī·sō·hȳ′e·tăl, ī·sō·hȳ′e·tōse, *n.* an isohyetal line.

ī′sō·lȧ·ble (*or* is′ō-), *a.* [*isolate* and *-able.*] that can be isolated; specifically, in chemistry, capable of being obtained pure, or uncombined with any other substance.

ī′sō·lāte (*or* is′ō-), *v.t.*; isolated, *pt.*, *pp.*; isolating, *ppr.* [It. *isolato*, pp. of *isolare*, to isolate, from *isola*, L. *insula*, an island.]
1. to set apart from others; to place alone.
2. in bacteriology, to grow a pure culture of (a specific bacterium).
3. in chemistry, to separate (an element or compound) in pure form from substances with which it is combined or mixed.
4. in medicine, to place (a patient with a contagious disease) apart from others to prevent the spread of infection.

ī′sō·lā·ted, *a.* 1. standing detached from others of a like kind; placed by itself.
2. in chemistry, pure; not combined.

ī·sō·lā′tion, *n.* an isolating or being isolated.

ī·sō·lā′tion·işm, *n.* the policy advocated by isolationists.

ī·sō·lā′tion·ist, *n.* a person who believes in or advocates isolation; a person who wants his country to take no part in international alliances, leagues, etc.

ī·sō·lā′tion·ist, *a.* of isolationists or isolationism.

ī′sō·lā·tŏr, *n.* a person or thing that isolates.

I·sōlde′, *n.* [G.; OFr. *Isolt*, *Iseul*; OHG. *Isold*; prob. from *is*, ice and *waltan*, to rule.] in medieval legend, (a) the Irish princess married to King Mark of Cornwall and beloved by Tristram; (b) the daughter of the king of Brittany, married to Tristram. Also *Iseult.*

ī·sol′ō·gous, *a.* [*iso-*, and Gr. *logos*, proportion, and *-ous.*]
1. designating or of any of two or more chemical compounds of similar structure but consisting of different atoms of the same valence and usually of the same periodic group.
2. designating or of a series formed by such compounds.

ī′sō·logue (-log), *n.* an isologous compound.

ī″sō·mag·net′iç, *a.* 1. of equality of magnetic force.
2. connecting or showing points on the earth's surface having the same magnetic intensity; as, *isomagnetic* lines on a map.

ī″sō·mag·net′iç, *n.* an isomagnetic line.

ī·sō·mas′ti·gāte, *a.* [*iso-*, and Gr. *mastix* (*-igos*), a whip.] in biology, having the flagella alike, especially as to size and form.

ī′sō·mẽr, *n.* [Gr. *isomerēs*, having equal parts; *isos*, equal, and *meros*, part.] any of two or more chemical compounds having the same constituent elements in the same proportion by weight but differing in physical or chemical properties because of differences in the structure of their molecules.

ī′sō·mēre, *n.* [Gr. *isomerēs*, having equal parts.] in zoology, some part, as a limb or the segment of a limb, having a homologous part in some other animal.

ī·sō·mer′iç, ī·sō·mer′iç·ăl, *a.* [*isomer*ous and *-ic.*]
1. in chemistry, having the same percentage composition, but showing different properties.
2. in zoology, relating to an isomere.

ī·sō·mer′iç·ăl·ly, *adv.* in an isomeric manner.

ī·som′ẽr·ide, *n.* same as *isomer.*

ī·som′ẽr·işm, *n.* [*isomer*ous and *-ism.*] in chemistry, the state or relation of isomers.

ī·sō·mer·ō·mor′phişm, *n.* [*iso-*, and Gr. *meros*, part, and *morphē*, form.] in crystallography, isomorphism between isomeric substances.

ī·som′ẽr·ous, *a.* [Gr. *isomerēs*, having equal parts; *isos*, equal, and *meros*, part.]
1. having the same number of parts, markings, etc.
2. in botany, having the same number of parts in each whorl: opposed to *heteromerous.*
3. isomeric.

ī·sō·met′riç, ī·sō·met′riç·ăl, *a.* [Gr. *isometros*, of equal measure; *isos*, equal, and *metron*, measure.]
1. of, indicating, or having equality of measure.
2. designating a crystalline form that has three equal axes at right angles to one another.
3. designating or of exercises in isometrics.

ī·sō·met′riç, *n.* 1. *pl.* a method of physical exercise in which one set of muscles is briefly tensed in opposition to another set of muscles or in opposition to a solid surface.
2. in thermodynamics, a line indicating changes of pressure or temperature at constant volume.

ī·sō·met′riç prō·jeç′tion, a method of drawing figures and maps so that three dimensions are shown not in perspective but in their actual measurements.

ī·sō·met′rō·grȧph, *n.* [*iso-*, and Gr. *metron*, a measure, and *graphein*, to write.] a contrivance for drawing equidistant parallel lines.

ī″sō·mē·trō′pi·ȧ, *n.* [Mod. L., from *iso-*, and Gr. *metron*, measure, and *-opia.*] the condition of being equal in refraction: said of the two eyes.

ī·som′e·try, *n.* [*iso-* and *-metry.*]
1. equality of measure.
2. in geography, equality of height above sea level.

ī′sō·morph, *n.* [*iso-*, and Gr. *morphē*, form.] a substance or organism isomorphic with another or others.

ī·sō·mor′phiç, *a.* 1. showing isomorphism; isomorphous.
2. having the same or a similar appearance or form.

ī·sō·mor′phişm, *n.* 1. an identity or close similarity of crystalline form, as (a) between substances of similar composition or atomic proportions, as arsenic acid and phosphorous acid, each containing five equivalents of oxygen; (b) sometimes, between compounds of unlike composition or atomic proportions, as the metal arsenic and oxide of iron, the rhombohedral angle of the former being 85°41′, of the latter 86°4′.
2. in biology, a similarity in the appearance or structure of organisms of different species or races.

ī·sō·mor′phous, *a.* [*iso-*, and Gr. *morphē*, form.] having isomorphism; isomorphic.

ī″sō·my·ā′ri·ăn, *a.* [*iso-*, and Gr. *mys*, *myos*, muscle, and *-arian.*] in conchology, having the two adductor muscles alike, or nearly alike, in size and form.

-i·sŏn, [OFr. *-ison*, *-eson*, *-eison*, *-aison*; L. *-atio*, *-ationis.*] a formative suffix seen in nouns derived from Old French, corresponding to *-ation*, as in compar*ison.*

Ī·sō·nan′drȧ, *n.* [*iso-*, and Gr. *anēr*, *andros*, a man, male.] a genus of East Indian trees including a species from which gutta-percha is obtained.

ī″sō·nē·phel′iç, *a.* [*iso-*, and Gr. *nephelē*, a cloud.] in physical geography, designating a line on a map connecting points having the same percentage of cloudiness during a stated period.

ī·sō·niç′ō·tine, *n.* a crystalline compound isomeric with nicotine.

ī·sō·niç·ō·tin′iç, *a.* pertaining to isonicotine.

ī·sō·nom′iç, *a.* equal in law, right, or privilege.

ī·son′ō·my, *n.* [Gr. *isonomia*, equality of rights; *isos*, equal, and *nomos*, distribution, custom, law.] equality of laws, rights, or privileges.

ī·sop′ȧ·thy, *n.* [*iso-*, and Gr. *pathos*, suffering, disease.] (a) the theory that diseases are cured by the products of the diseases themselves, as smallpox by homeopathic doses of variolus matter; (b) the notion that a diseased organ is cured by eating the same organ of a healthy animal.

ī·sō·per·i·met′riç·ăl, *a.* [*iso-*, and Gr. *peri*, around, and *metron*, a measure.] in geometry, having equal boundaries; as, *isoperimetrical* figures.

ī″sō·per·im′e·try, *n.* in geometry, the science dealing with isoperimetrical figures.

ī·sō·pet′ȧ·lous, *a.* [*iso-*, and Gr. *petalon*, a leaf, petal.] in botany, having all the petals alike.

ī″sō·pī·es′tiç, *a.* [*iso-*, and Gr. *piezein*, to press, and *-ic.*] indicating equal pressure.

ī″sō·pī·es′tiç, *n.* an isobar.

ī′sō·pleth, *n.* [from Gr. *isoplēthēs*, equal in number or quantity, from *isos*, equal and *plethos*, number, quantity.]

1. a graph plotting the occurrence or frequency of a phenomenon in meteorology, etc. as a function of two variables, time and space.

2. the line connecting points on a graph that have equal or corresponding values with regard to certain variables.

Ī·sō·pleū′rȧ, *n.pl.* [Gr. *isopleuros*, having equal sides; *isos*, equal, and *pleura*, side.] a subdivision of gastropods comprising those which are bilaterally symmetrical.

ī′sō·pod, *a.* pertaining to the *Isopoda*.

ī′sō·pod, *n.* a crustacean of the order *Isopoda*.

Ī·sop′ō·dȧ, *n.pl.* [*iso-*, and Gr. *pous*, *podos*, a foot.] an order of crustaceans with a flat, oval body and seven pairs of legs of similar size and form, each pair attached to a segment of the thorax.

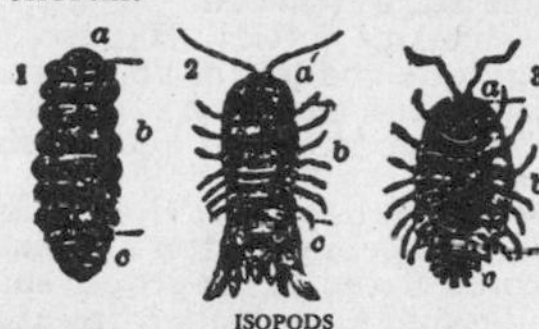

ISOPODS
1. *Bopyrus squillarum*, sedentary section
2. *Cymodocealamarcki*, natatory section
3. *Oniscus asellus*, cursorial section, *a*, head; *b*, thorax; *c*, abdomen

ī·sop′ō·dăn, *a.* and *n.* isopod.

ī·sō·pod′i·form, *a.* formed like an isopod.

ī·sop′ō·dous, *a.* same as *isopod*.

ī·sō·pog′ō·nous, *a.* [*iso-*, and Gr. *pōgōn*, beard.] in zoology, having equal webs: said of feathers.

ī·sō·pol′i·ty, *n.* [Gr. *isopoliteia*, from *isopolites*, a citizen with equal civil rights; *isos*, equal, and *polites*, a citizen.] equality or reciprocity of civil and political rights as secured to the citizens of different states.

ī′sō·prēne, *n.* [apparently arbitrarily coined by C. G. Williams.] a colorless, volatile liquid, C_5H_8, prepared by the dry distillation of raw rubber or synthetically: when heated with sodium it polymerizes to form a substance closely resembling natural rubber.

ī·sō·prō′pyl, *n.* the univalent propyl radical $(CH_3)_2CH$, an isomer of the univalent propyl radical, C_3H_7.

ī·sō·pyç′nic, *a.* [*iso-*, and Gr. *pyknos*, dense, solid.] in physics, relating to or exhibiting equality of density, as in a body at different points; as, an *isopycnic* line.

ī·sō·pyç′nic, *n.* an isopycnic surface or line.

ī′sō·pȳre, *n.* [*iso-*, and Gr. *pyr*, fire.] a kind of opal containing iron or other impurities.

ī·sor′cin, *n.* [*iso-* and *orcin*.] in chemistry, a crystalline compound produced by artificial means, metameric with orcin: also called *cresorcinol*, *cresorcin*.

ī·sor·rop′iç, *a.* [*iso-*, and Gr. *rhopē*, downward inclination.] in mathematics, designating a line connecting points in a plane for which the value of a function remains constant.

ī·sos′ce·lēs, *a.* [L. *isosceles*; Gr. *isoskelēs*, with equal legs; *isos*, equal, and *skelos*, a leg.] having two equal legs or sides; as, an *isosceles* triangle.

ISOSCELES TRIANGLE

ī·sō·seīs′măl, *a.* [*iso-*, and Gr. *seismos*, a shaking, an earthquake.]

1. of equal intensity of earthquake shock.

2. connecting or showing points of such intensity on the earth's surface; as, *isoseismal* lines on a map.

ī·sō·seīs′măl, *n.* an isoseismal line.

ī·sō·seīs′miç, *a.* same as *isoseismal*.

Ī·sō·spon′dy·lī, *n.pl.* [*iso-*, and Gr. *spondylos*, vertebra.] a large order of fishes including those having all the vertebrae essentially similar, embracing most malacopterygian fishes, such as the salmon, the herring, etc.

ī·sō·spon′dy·lous, *a.* of or pertaining to the *Isospondyli*.

ī′sō·spōre, *n.* [*iso-*, and Gr. *sporos*, seed.]

1. a zygospore.

2. a plant which produces only one kind of spore.

ī·sō·spōr′iç, *a.* same as *homosporous*.

ī·sos′tȧ·sy, *n.* [*iso-*, and Gr. *stasis*, a standing still.]

1. the state or quality of being isostatic.

2. in geology, universal equilibrium in the earth's crust, the maintenance of which is supposedly due to gravitational yielding of rocks beneath the earth's surface.

ī·sō·stat′iç, *a.* [*iso-* and *static*.]

1. denoting a condition in which there is equal pressure on every side.

2. in hydrostatic equilibrium.

ī·sō·stem′ō·nous, *a.* [*iso-*, and Gr. *stēmōn*, thread.] in botany, having as many stamens as divisions of the perianth.

ī·sō·stem′ō·ny, *n.* the condition of being isostemonous.

ī″sō·sul·fō·cȳ′ȧ·nāte, *n.* in chemistry, a salt resulting from the action of isosulfocyanic acid on certain bases.

ī″sō·sul·fō·cȳ·an′iç, *a.* designating a colorless acid isomeric with the sulfacid HSCN.

ī·sot′e·ly, *n.* [Gr. *isoteleia*, equality of taxation, from *isotelēs*, paying alike; *isos*, equal, and *telos*, tax.] civil equality granted certain aliens of ancient Athens, who were given some of the privileges and immunities of citizens.

ī·soth′ẽr·ăl, *a.* [*iso-*, and Gr. *theros*, summer.]

1. having or showing the same mean summer temperature

2. of or having isotheres.

ī·soth′ẽr·ăl, *n.* an isothere.

ī′sō·thēre, *n.* a line passing through places having the same mean summer temperature.

ī′sō·thẽrm, *n.* [*iso-*, and Gr. *thermē*, heat.]

1. a line on a map connecting points on the earth's surface having the same mean temperature or the same temperature at a given time.

2. a line representing changes of volume or pressure at constant temperature.

ī·sō·thẽr′măl, *n.* an isotherm.

ī·sō·thẽr′măl, *a.* [*iso-* and *thermal*.]

1. of or indicating equality of temperature.

2. of or indicating changes of volume or pressure at constant temperature; as, an *isothermal* line.

3. of an isotherm or isotherms.

isothermal region; see *stratosphere*.

isothermal zones; spaces on opposite sides of the equator having the same mean temperature or bounded by corresponding isothermal lines.

ī·sō·thẽr′mō·bath, *n.* [*iso-*, and Gr. *thermē*, heat, and *bathos*, depth.] in physical geography, an imaginary line connecting such points of equal temperature as are included within a fixed vertical section of the ocean.

ī·sō·thẽr·mō·bath′iç, *a.* pertaining to an isothermobath.

ī″sō·thẽr·ŏm′brōse, *a.* [*iso-*, and Gr. *theros*, summer, and *ombros*, rain.] designating a line on a map connecting places on the surface of the earth where the same quantity of rain falls during the summer.

ī·sō·ton′iç, *a.* [Gr. *isotonos*, having equal accent or tone; *isos*, equal, and *tonos*, accent, tone.]

1. in music, having equal tones.

2. having equal tension.

3. having the same osmotic pressure; especially, designating or of a salt solution having the same osmotic pressure as blood, so that it will not destroy the red blood corpuscles when injected into the blood stream.

ī″sō·tō·nic′i·ty, *n.* the property of being isotonic.

ī′sō·tōpe, *n.* [*iso-*, and Gr. *topos*, place.] any of two or more forms of an element having the same or very closely related properties and the same atomic number but different atomic weights (or mass numbers); as, U 235, U 238, and U 239, are three *isotopes* of uranium: distinguished from *isobar*.

ī·sō·top′iç, *a.* of or relating to isotopes.

ī·sot′ō·py, *n.* the state or relation of isotopes.

ī·sō·trī·mor′phiṣm, *n.* [*iso-*, and Gr. *tris*, thrice, and *morphe*, form, and *-ism*.] in crystallography, a similarity of crystalline form between the members of two trimorphous groups.

ī″sō·trī·mor′phous, *a.* characterized by isotrimorphism.

ī·sō·trop′iç, *a.* [*iso-*, and Gr. *tropē*, a turning, from *trepein*, to turn.] in physics, having the same properties, as elasticity, conductivity, etc., in like degree in all directions.

ī·sot′rō·piṣm, *n.* same as *isotropy*.

ī·sot′rō·pous, *a.* same as *isotropic*.

ī·sot′rō·py, *n.* the state or quality of being isotropic.

ī′sō·tȳpe, *n.* [Gr. *isotypos*, shaped alike; *isos*, equal, and *typos*, impression, form, type.] in zoogeography and phytogeography, an organism represented by a species, genus, or family in different parts of the world.

ī·sō·ū′riç, *a.* [*iso-* and *uric*.] pertaining to an odorless, tasteless compound isomeric with uric acid.

ī·sō·zō′oid, *n.* [*iso-*, and Gr. *zōon*, an animal, and *eidos*, form.] a zooid resembling its parent.

is′pȧ·ghụl, (-gụl), *n.* [E. Ind.] an East Indian species of plantain, *Plantago ispaghula*, bearing seeds used in the preparation of a native drink.

Ī′-spȳ, *n.* hide-and-seek, a children's game.

Iṣ′rā·el, *n.* 1. in the Bible, Jacob: so named after wrestling with the angel: Gen. xxxii. 28.

2. the Jewish people: so named because regarded as descendants of Jacob.

Iṣ·rā′el·i, *a.* of Israel (the modern republic) or its people.

Iṣ·rā′el·i, *n.* a native or inhabitant of Israel (the modern republic).

Iṣ′rā·el·īte, *n.* [LL. *Israēlita*; Gr. *Israēlitēs*, a descendant of Israel, from *Israēl*; Heb. *Yisrāēl*, Israel, Jacob, lit., champion of God; *sārāh*, to fight, and *el*, God.]

1. any of the people of ancient Israel or their descendants; a Jew.

2. any member of a group regarded by others or itself as chosen by God. [Rare.]

Iṣ′rā·el·īte, *a.* of ancient Israel or the Israelites; Jewish.

Iṣ″rā·el·it′iç, *a.* pertaining to Israel; Jewish.

Iṣ″rā·el·ī′tish, *a.* Israelitic.

is′sei′ (-sā′), *n.*; *pl.* **is′sei′, is′seiṣ′,** [Japan., lit., first generation.] [*also* I–] a Japanese who emigrated to the United States after the Oriental exclusion proclamation of 1907 and is thus ineligible by law to become an American citizen: distinguished from *nisei*, *kibei*.

is′sū·ȧ·ble (ish′ū-), *a.* 1. that may be issued or can issue.

2. that can be raised as an issue at law.

is′sū·ȧ·bly, *adv.* in an issuable manner.

is′sū·ănce, *n.* the act of issuing; an issue.

is′sū·ănt, *a.* 1. issuing.

2. in heraldry, denoting an animal of which only the upper part is visible.

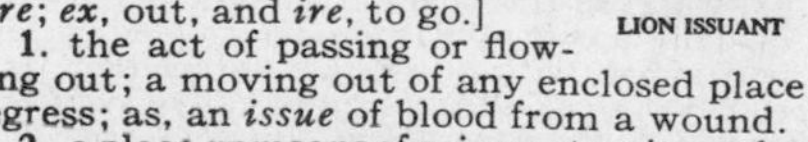

LION ISSUANT

is′sūe (ish′ū), *n.* [ME. *issue*, *issu*, *isshue*; OFr. *issue*, *eissue*, a going out, outlet, from *issu*, pp. of *issir*, *eisser*, to go out, from L. *exire*; *ex*, out, and *ire*, to go.]

1. the act of passing or flowing out; a moving out of any enclosed place; egress; as, an *issue* of blood from a wound.

2. a place or means of going out; exit; outlet.

3. event; consequence; end or ultimate result; as, the *issue* was favorable.

4. a child or children; offspring; as, the man died without *issue*.

5. produce of the earth or profits of land; as, the *issues*, rents, etc. of an estate.

6. a point, matter, or question to be disputed or decided.

7. a sending or giving out; a putting forth.

8. the thing or set of things issued; the entire amount put forth and circulated at one time; as, the January *issue* of a magazine, an *issue* of bonds.

9. in medicine, (a) a discharge of blood, pus, etc.; (b) an incision or artificial ulcer made so that pus may be discharged.

at issue; opposing; disagreeing; in contention.

to join issue; (a) to enter into conflict, argument, etc. with another or each other; (b) to join in submitting an issue for decision at law.

to take issue; to disagree; to differ.

is′sūe, *v.i.*; issued, *pt.*, *pp.*; issuing, *ppr.* 1. to pass or flow out; to run out; to proceed, as from a source; as, blood *issues* from wounds; light *issues* from the sun.

2. to be descended; to be born.

3. to be derived; to result, as from a cause.

4. to end (*in*); to result, as in an effect or consequence.

5. to come as revenue; to accrue.

6. to be published; to be put forth and circulated.

7. in legal pleadings, to come to a point in fact or law on which the parties join and rest the decision of the cause.

is′sūe, *v.t.* 1. to send out; to put into circulation; as, to *issue* money from a treasury or notes from a bank.

2. to send out; to deliver from authority; as, to *issue* a writ.

3. to deliver for use; as, to *issue* provisions from a store.

is′sū·ẽr, *n.* one who issues or emits.

-ist, [L. *-ista*, *-istes*; Gr. *-istēs*, from verbs ending in *-izein*.] a noun suffix meaning *one who* *practices or is occupied with*, or *a believer in*, as in evangel*ist*, pian*ist*, abolition*ist*, theor*ist*.

is't, a contraction of *is it*. [Archaic and Dial.]

isth'mi·ăn (is' *or* isth'), *a.* 1. pertaining to an isthmus.

2. [I–] pertaining to the Isthmus of Panama.

3. [I–] pertaining to the Isthmus of Corinth.

Isthmian games; one of the four great festivals of ancient Greece: so called because celebrated on the Isthmus of Corinth.

isth'mi·ăn, *n.* a native or inhabitant of an isthmus.

isth'mi·āte, *a.* in zoology, having a narrow part between two broader parts.

isth'mus (is' *or* isth'), *n.* [L. *isthmus*; Gr. *isthmos*, a neck, narrow passage, an isthmus.]

1. a neck or narrow strip of land by which two larger bodies of land are connected, or by which a peninsula is united to the mainland; as, the *isthmus* of Panama connects North and South America.

2. in anatomy, (a) a narrow strip of tissue connecting two larger parts of an organ; as, the *isthmus* of the thyroid or prostate; (b) a narrow passage between two larger cavities; as, the *isthmus* of the Fallopian tubes.

the Isthmus; (a) the Isthmus of Panama; (b) the Isthmus of Suez.

-is'tiç, [from *-ist*, and *-ic*.] a suffix forming adjectives corresponding to nouns ending in *-ism* and *-ist*; as, lingu*istic*, eulog*istic*, euphu*istic*.

-is'tiç·ăl, same as *-istic*.

is'tle, (ist'li), *n.* [Mex.] a species of strong, coarse fiber furnished by one of several tropical American plants, especially by *Bromelia sylvestris* and *Agave rigida*: called also *pita*, *silk grass*, and *Tampico fiber*.

Is'tri·ăn, *a.* of Istria, a peninsula in northeastern Italy.

Is'tri·ăn, *n.* a native or inhabitant of Istria.

it, *pron.* [ME. *it*, *hit*; AS. *hit*, neut. of *he*, he.] the neuter singular form of the third person pronoun, corresponding to the masculine and feminine forms *he* and *she* and having the plural forms *they*, *their*, *them*: it is used (a) to represent anything regarded as having no sex and in situations where sex is not specified; as, water is transparent when *it* is pure; the bird has a tuft of feathers on *its* head; (b) impersonally, with no definite antecedent; as, *it* snows; (c) as the grammatical subject of a clause of which the actual subject is the clause or phrase following; as, *it* is well known that wood is combustible; (d) to intensify the meaning of an intransitive verb; as, to rough *it*; to go *it*; (e) as the antecedent to a relative pronoun from which it is separated by a predicate; as, *it* is your car that we want; (f) as a term of reference to something indefinite but understood, as the state of affairs; as, *it's* all right, I didn't hurt myself.

it, *n.* in the game of "tag," etc., the player who must do some specific thing, as trying to touch or find another.

ī'tȧ·cism, *n.* the pronunciation of the Greek letter *eta* like the *e* in *be*: see also *etacism*.

ī'tȧ·cist, *n.* one who prefers itacism to etacism.

it·ȧ·çol'ū·mīte, *n.* [from *Itacolumi*, a mountain in Brazil, and *-ite*.] a laminated talcose sandstone, in connection with which the diamond is sometimes found: also called *flexible sandstone*.

it·ȧ·çon'iç, *a.* [from *aconitic*, by a transposition of the letters.] pertaining to an acid, $C_5H_6O_4$, obtained from various organic substances.

it'ȧ·kȧ wood, the wood of a leguminous tree of British Guiana.

It'ȧ·lȧ, *n.* [properly f. of L. *Italus*, Italian.] an early Latin version of the Scriptures.

Ī·täl'iȧ ir·re·den'tȧ, an Italian-speaking district under foreign rule: see *irredenta*.

I·tal'iăn, *a.* [L. *Italus*, Italian.] pertaining to Italy, its people, their language, or culture.

I·tal'iăn, *n.* a native of Italy; also, the language of Italy or the Italians.

Italian juice; a kind of licorice.

I·tal'iăn·āte, *v.t.* to Italianize.

I·tal'iăn·āte, *a.* Italianized.

I·tal'iăn·işm, *n.* 1. an Italian expression, manner, or custom.

2. Italian spirit, quality, etc.

3. fondness for Italian customs, ideas, etc.

I·tal·iăn·i·zā'tion, *n.* an Italianizing or being Italianized.

I·tal'iăn·īze, *v.t.* and *v.i.*; Italianized, *pt.*, *pp.*; Italianizing, *ppr.* to make or become Italian in form, character, etc.

I·tal'iăn son'net, a Petrarchan sonnet.

I·tal'iç, *a.* [L. *Italicus*, Italian, from *Italia*, Italy.]

1. of ancient Italy, its people, etc.

2. designating or of the subfamily of the Indo-European languages that includes Latin, the Italian dialects contemporary with Old Latin, and the languages descended from Latin, as Italian, French, Spanish, Portuguese, Romanian, etc.

i·tal'iç, *a.* [so called because first used in an Italian edition of Virgil, printed in Venice in 1501.] designating a type in which the letters slant upward to the right, used to give emphasis to words, to indicate foreign words and phrases, etc.: *this is italic type*.

i·tal'iç, *n.* in printing, a style of type with inclined letters.

I·tal'i·cism, *n.* 1. same as *Italianism*.

2. [i–] in printing, the use of italics.

i·tal'i·cīze, *v.t.*; italicized, *pt.*, *pp.*; italicizing, *ppr.* to print in italic characters; also, in copy for the printer, to underscore with a single line to indicate what is to be printed in italics.

I·tal'i·ot, I·tal'i·ōte, *a.* [Gr. *Italiōtēs*, from *Italia*, Italy.] pertaining to the Greek residents of Italy.

I·tal'i·ot, I·tal'i·ōte, *n.* a Greek resident of Italy.

ī'tȧ päլm (päm), *n.* in botany, a tall palm, *Mauritia flexuosa*, growing in the Amazon and Orinoco regions.

itch, *n.* 1. a contagious skin disease appearing in small, watery pustules, accompanied by intense irritation of the skin, and caused by the presence within the epidermis of a species of mite, *Sarcoptes scabiei*; scabies (with *the*.)

2. the irritation in the skin occasioned by this disease.

3. a constant restless desire; as, an *itch* for praise; an *itch* for scribbling.

4. any irritating sensation of the skin that causes a desire to scratch the affected part.

baker's itch; see under *baker*.

barber's itch; see under *barber*.

bricklayer's itch; a form of eczema caused by the action of lime on the epidermis.

itch, *v.i.*; itched (icht), *pt.*, *pp.*; itching; *ppr.* [ME. *icchen*, *iken*, *giken*; AS. *giccan*, to itch.]

1. to feel an unpleasant irritation of the skin, with the desire to scratch the part.

2. to have a constant desire or restless inclination; as, to *itch* after honors.

an itching palm; an avaricious disposition; an inordinate love of money.

itch'i·ness, *n.* the state or quality of being itchy.

itch'less, *a.* free from the itch or its sensation.

itch mīte, a microscopic articulated insect, *Sarcoptes scabiei*, of the class *Arachnida*, which produces the itch in man.

itch'y, *a.* itching; like, feeling, or causing an itch.

-ite, [L. *-itus*, *-ita*, *-itum*, pp. ending of verbs of 2nd, 3rd, and 4th conjugations.] a suffix of some adjectives, of nouns from such adjectives, and of some verbs derived from Latin; as, exquis*ite*, opposi*te*, un*ite*, requis*ite*.

-īte, [Fr. *-ite*; L. *-ita*, *-ites*; Gr. *-itēs*, f. *-itis*.] a noun-forming suffix meaning: (a) *a native, inhabitant*, or *citizen of*, as in Brooklyn*ite*; (b) an *adherent of, believer in*, as in Buchman*ite*; (c) *a commercially manufactured product*, as in luc*ite*, dynam*ite*, vulcan*ite*; (d) *a fossil*, as in ammon*ite*; (e) *a part of a body* or *bodily organ*, as in som*ite*; (f) *a salt* or *ester of an acid whose name ends in -ous*, as in nitr*ite*, sulf*ite*; (g) *a* (specified) *mineral* or *rock*, as in anthrac*ite*, dolom*ite*.

ī'tem, *adv.* [L. *item*, also.] also: a word used before each article in a series being enumerated.

ī'tem, *n.* 1. originally, a hint; an innuendo.

2. an article; a separate particular in an account; as, the account consists of many *items*.

3. a short paragraph or bit of information in a newspaper or other periodical; as, an *item* about a fire.

ī'tem, *v.t.* to make a note or memorandum of.

ī'tem·īze, *v.t.*; itemized, *pt.*, *pp.*; itemizing, *ppr.* to state in items; to set down or describe by particulars; as, I will *itemize* the bill.

ī'tem vē'tō, the power of the governors of some States to veto a section of an appropriation bill, without vetoing the bill as a whole.

ī'tẽr, *n.* [L., a going, way, from *ire*, to go.] a passage; specifically, in anatomy, a passage or duct, especially the tubular cavity between the third and fourth ventricles of the brain; the aqueduct of Sylvius.

it'ẽr·ȧ·ble, *a.* capable of being repeated.

it'ẽr·ănce, *n.* iteration; repetition.

it'ẽr·ănt, *a.* [L. *iterans* (*-antis*), ppr. of *iterare*, to do a thing a second time, to repeat, from *iterum*, again.] repeating; as, an *iterant* echo.

it'ẽr·āte, *v.t.*; iterated, *pt.*, *pp.*; iterating, *ppr.* [L. *iteratus*, pp. of *iterare*, to repeat, from *iterum*, again.] to repeat; to utter or do a second time; as, to *iterate* advice or admonition.

it'ẽr·āte·ly, *adv.* by means of repetition or iteration.

it·ẽr·ā·tion, *n.* [L. *iteratio* (*-onis*), from *iterare*, to repeat.]

1. repetition; recital or performance a second time.

2. something iterated.

it'ẽr·ȧ·tive, *a.* [Fr. *iteratif*, from L. *iteratus*.]

1. characterized by iteration.

2. in grammar, frequentative.

it'ẽr·ȧ·tive·ly, *adv.* in an iterative manner.

Ith'ȧ·çăn, *a.* relating to the island of Ithaca.

Ith·ȧ·cen'si·ăn, *a.* Ithacan.

Ī'thunn, Ī'thun, *n.* [ON. *Ithunn*.] in Norse mythology, the goddess of youth and spring, wife of Bragi and guardian of the golden apples that the gods ate to keep their youth: also *Idun*.

I·thū'ri·el, *n.* [Heb. *yithūrī'ēl*, lit., superiority of God.] an angel in Milton's *Paradise Lost*, who restored Satan to his proper shape.

I·thū'ri·el's spēar, [so called from *Ithuriel's spear*, in Milton's *Paradise Lost*, which caused everything it touched to assume its proper shape.] a liliaceous plant of northern California, *Brodiæa laxa*.

ith·y·phal'liç, *a.* [L. *ithyphallicus*; Gr. *ithyphallikos*, from *ithyphallos*, a phallus; *ithys*, straight, erect, and *phallos*, a phallus.]

1. of the phallus carried in the rites of Bacchus.

2. lewd; obscene; lascivious.

3. in the meter of the Bacchic hymn.

ith·y·phal'liç, *n.* an ithyphallic poem, written in lines of three trochees.

ī·tin'ẽr·ȧ·cy, *n.* same as *itinerancy*.

ī·tin'ẽr·ăn·cy, *n.* 1. (a) an itinerating; a traveling from place to place; (b) the state of being itinerant.

2. a group of itinerant preachers or judges.

3. official work requiring constant travel from place to place or frequent change of residence, as preaching or presiding over courts in a circuit.

ī·tin'ẽr·ănt, *a.* [LL. *itinerans* (*-antis*), ppr. of *itinerari*, to travel, go on a journey.] traveling from place to place; wandering; not settled; as, an *itinerant* preacher.

ī·tin'ẽr·ănt, *n.* one who travels from place to place, particularly a preacher; one who is unsettled.

ī·tin'ẽr·ănt·ly, *adv.* in an unsettled or wandering manner.

ī·tin'ẽr·ȧ·ry, *n.*; *pl.* **ī·tin'ẽr·ȧ·rieş**, [LL. *itinerarium*, an account of a journey, a roadbook, neut. of *itinerarius*, pertaining to a journey.]

1. a route.

2. a record of a journey.

3. a guidebook; roadbook.

4. a plan or outline of a journey or route.

ī·tin'ẽr·ȧ·ry, *a.* of traveling, journeys, routes, or roads.

ī·tin'ẽr·āte, *v.i.*; itinerated, *pt.*, *pp.*; itinerating, *ppr.* [LL. *itineratus*, pp. of *itinerari*, to go on a journey, travel, from L. *iter*, a going, journey.] to travel from place to place, especially for the purpose of preaching, lecturing, etc.; to wander without a settled dwelling.

ī·tin·ẽr·ā'tion, *n.* 1. an itinerating.

2. a circuit; a tour.

-ī'tion, [L. *-itio* (*-onis*), from *-i-*, thematic vowel, and *-tio* (*-onis*).] a noun-forming suffix corresponding to *-ation*, as in sed*ition*, fru*ition*, erud*ition*, requis*ition*.

-ī'tious (-ish'us), [L. *-icius*, *-itius*.] a suffix meaning *of*, *having the nature of*, *characterized by*, used to form adjectives corresponding to nouns ending in *-ition*, as in nutr*itious*, sed*itious*.

-ī'tis, [L. *-itis*; Gr. *-itis*, originally an adj. suffix, signifying of the nature of, used to modify *nosos*, disease (later understood, but omitted).] a noun-forming suffix meaning *inflammatory disease* or *inflammation of* (a specified part or organ), as in bronch*itis*, arthr*itis*, enter*itis*.

it'll a contraction of (a) it will; (b) it shall.

-i·tōl', [*-ite*, and *-ol*.] a suffix used in forming the names of certain alcohols with more than one hydroxyl group, as in mann*itol*.

its, *pron.* [Early Mod. Eng. analogical formation, from *it* and *'s*; written *it's* until early 19th c.; the ME. and AS. form was *his.*] that or those belonging to it.

its, *possessive pronominal, a.* of, belonging to, or done by it.

it's, a contraction of (a) it is; (b) it has.

it·self', *pron.* a form of the third person singular, neuter pronoun, used: (a) as an intensive; as, the picture frame *itself* is a work of art; (b) as a reflexive; as, the dog scratched *itself.*

it'tri·ȧ, *n.* same as *yttria.*

it'tri·um, *n.* same as *yttrium.*

it'ty-bit'ty, *a.* [baby talk alteration, from *little bit.*] very small; tiny: a facetious imitation of child's talk. Also **it'sy-bit'sy.**

-i·ty, [Fr. *-ité*; L. *-itas,* acc. *-itatem,* formed from *-i-* and *-tas.*] a suffix meaning *state, character, condition,* as in frugal*ity,* nobil*ity.*

it'zi·bū, *n.* a former Japanese coin: spelled also *itzeboo, itzebu,* and *itchebu.*

Ī·ū'lus, *n.* [L. *iulus*; Gr. *ioulos,* down, a catkin, centipede.] a genus of *Myriapoda,* order *Chilognatha* or *Diplopoda,* a semicylindrical worm, with moniliform antennae and two articulated palpi. The common gallyworm, *Iulus terrestris,* is the type of the genus.

Ī've, a contraction of I have.

-ive, [L. *-ivus, -iva,* f., *-ivum,* neut.] a suffix meaning: (a) *related to, belonging to, of the nature* or *quality of,* as in collect*ive,* act*ive,* correct*ive*; (b) *tending to, given to,* as in creat*ive,* destruct*ive.*

ī'vied (-vid), *a.* covered or overgrown with ivy.

ī'vō·ry, *n.*; *pl.* **ī'vō·ries,** [ME. *ivory, ivorie*; L. *ebur, eboris,* ivory.]

1. the white substance forming the tusks of elephants, walruses, etc.: it is a hard, solid, fine-grained form of dentine.

2. (a) any form of dentine; (b) any substance like ivory in appearance, use, etc.

3. the color of ivory; creamy white.

4. a tusk of an elephant, walrus, etc.

5. [*pl.*] things made of, resembling, or suggesting ivory; specifically, (a) piano keys; (b) teeth; (c) dice; (d) billiard balls. [Slang.]

ī'vō·ry, *a.* 1. consisting of ivory; made of ivory; as, an *ivory* comb.

2. creamy-white, like ivory.

ī'vō·ry·bill, *n.* a large woodpecker, *Campophilus principalis,* found in the Gulf States and characterized by its hard, white bill, resembling ivory.

ī'vō·ry black, a fine black pigment prepared from burnt ivory.

ī'vō·ry gull, a small white gull, *Larus eburneus,* of the arctic regions.

ī'vō·ry nut, the nut of a species of tropical palm tree, *Phytelephas macrocarpa,* often as large as a hen's egg, resembling ivory and often used in making buttons, ornaments, etc.: called also *vegetable ivory.*

ī'vō·ry pälm (päm), the tree that produces the ivory nut.

ī'vō·ry shell, a univalve shell of a species of *Eburna.*

ī'vō·ry tow'ẽr, figuratively, a place of mental withdrawal from reality and action: used as a symbol of escapist tendencies.

ī'vō·ry·tȳpe, *n.* in photography, a picture having the appearance of being made in natural colors upon ivory: the effect is produced by superimposing a light print, tinted on the back and made translucent by varnishing, on a stronger print.

ī"vō·ry-white', *a.* creamy-white.

ī'vy, *n.*; *pl.* **ī'vieṣ,** [ME. *ivi*; AS. *ifig, ifegn.*]

1. a variety of climbing vine, *Hedera helix,* with a woody stem and evergreen leaves, grown as ornamentation on buildings, walls, etc.: also *English ivy.*

2. any of various similar climbing plants; as, poison *ivy.*

American ivy; the Virginia creeper.

English ivy; the common European ivy, *Hedera helix.*

German ivy; a creeping South African plant, *Senecio mikanioides.*

Japanese ivy; a woody vine of China and Japan, *Ampelopsis tricuspidata,* bearing three-lobed leaves: also called *Boston ivy.*

Kenilworth ivy; a European trailing plant of the figwort family, *Linaria cymbalaria,* having ivylike leaves.

Mexican ivy; a tropical climbing plant, *Cobæa scandens,* having large, purple flowers.

West Indian ivy; a climbing plant, *Marcgravia umbellata.*

ī'vy bīnd'weed, the black bindweed, *Polygonum convolvulus.*

ī'vy bush, 1. the mountain laurel or calico bush, *Kalmia latifolia.* [Dial.]

2. in England, a branch of the common ivy hung over a door as a sign. [Obs.]

Ī'vy League, [many of the buildings are traditionally ivy-covered.] a group of colleges in the northeastern United States forming a league for intercollegiate sports: often used to describe the fashions, standards, attitudes, etc. associated with their students.

ī'vy-man"tled, *a.* covered with ivy.

ī'vy owl, the brown or tawny owl of Europe, *Syrnium aluco.*

ī'vy tod, an ivy plant or bush.

ī'vy tree, a New Zealand evergreen tree, *Panax colensoi.*

ī'vy vīne, 1. an American woody vine of the grape family, with heart-shaped leaves.

2. the Virginia creeper.

i·wis', y·wis', *adv.* [ME. *iwis, iwisse*; AS. *gewis, gewisse.*] certainly; assuredly. [Archaic.]

Ix'i·ȧ, *n.* [Gr. *ixos,* birdlime: so called because of the viscid nature of some of the species.] an extensive genus of South African plants of the order *Iridaceæ,* having narrow, sword-shaped leaves, slender, simple or branched stems, and spikes of large, showy flowers.

Ix·ī'ŏn, *n.* [L.; Gr. *Ixiōn.*] in Greek legend, a Thessalian king and father of the Centaurs, who was bound to a constantly revolving wheel in Hades because he sought the love of Hera.

Ix·ō'dēṣ, *n.* [Gr. *ixōdēs,* like birdlime; *ixos* birdlime, and *eidos,* form.] a genus of parasitic insects including several species of tick.

ix·ō'di·ăn, *n.* any of the *Ixodes.*

Ix·ō'rȧ, *n.* [from *Iswara,* a Hind. divinity to whom flowers are offered, from Sans. *icvara,* master, lord.] an extensive genus of rubiaceous tropical shrubs and small trees.

ix'tlē, ix'tlĭ, *n.* same as *istle.*

I'yär, *n.* [Heb.] the eighth month of the Jewish year.

iz'ăr, *n.* 1. a garment worn by Mohammedans.

2. [I–] a star in the constellation Boötes.

iz'ărd, *n.* [Fr. *isard.*] a kind of chamois.

-ī·zā'tion, a compound suffix forming nouns from verbs ending in *-ize,* as in real*ization.*

-īze, [Fr. *-ise*; LL. *-izare,* from Gr. *-izein.*] a suffix forming verbs, meaning (a) *to cause to be* or *become, make conform with* or *resemble, make,* as in democrat*ize,* American*ize,* steril*ize*; (b) *to become, become like,* as in crystall*ize*; (c) *to subject to, treat with, combine with,* as in oxid*ize,* galvan*ize*; (d) *to engage in, act in a specified way,* as in theor*ize,* soliloqu*ize.* Sometimes spelled *-ise.*

Iz'ē·dĭ, *n.* a member of a sect in Mesopotamia and neighboring regions, who are said to worship the devil: also written *Yezdi, Yezidi.*

Iz'ē·diṣm, *n.* the doctrine or belief of the Izedis.

iz'zărd, *n.* same as *izard.*

iz'zărd, *n.* [earlier *ezed, ezod*; OFr. *ezed*; Pr. *izedo,* from Gr. *zēta.*] the letter Z. [Archaic or Dial.]

J

J, j (jā), *n.* 1. the tenth letter of the English alphabet: formerly a variant of I, i, in the seventeenth century it became established as a consonant only, as in *Julius,* originally spelled *Iulius.*

2. the sound of J or j.

3. a type or impression for J or j.

4. *a symbol for* the tenth in a sequence or group.

J, j, *a.* 1. of J or j.

2. tenth in a sequence or group.

J, *n.* an object shaped like J.

J, *a.* shaped like J.

J, in physics, joule.

jä (yä), *adv.* [G.] yes.

jä'ăl gōat, [Heb. *yā'ēl,* wild goat.] an Ethiopian wild goat or ibex, *Capra jaala*: sometimes called *beden.*

jab, *v.t.* and *v.i.*; jabbed, *pt., pp.*; jabbing, *ppr.* [var. of *job* (to poke, stab); ME. *jobben,* to peck.]

1. to poke or thrust, as with a sharp instrument.

2. to punch with short, straight blows.

jab, *n.* a quick punch; a thrust; a poke; a stab.

jab'bẽr, *v.t.* and *v.i.*; jabbered, *pt., pp.*; jabbering, *ppr.* [prob. echoic.] to pronounce or utter indistinctly or rapidly; to chatter; to gibber.

jab'bẽr, *n.* rapid talk with indistinct utterance of words; gibberish.

jab'bẽr·ẽr, *n.* one who talks rapidly, indistinctly, or unintelligibly.

jab'bẽr·ing·ly, *adv.* in a confused or jabbering manner.

jab'i·rū, *n.* [Sp. *jabirú,* from Tupi *jabirú.*] a large wading bird of the stork family, found in Africa and tropical America; the wood ibis.

jab·ō·ran'di, *n.* [Port., from Tupi.] the dried leaves of a South American plant, from which a poisonous drug is obtained.

jab'ō·rīne, *n.* [*jaborandi,* and *-ine.*] one of the alkaloids obtained from jaborandi leaves, similar in properties to atropine.

jȧ·bōt' (zhȧ·bō'), *n.* [Fr.] 1. a kind of ruffle or frill used as an ornament for the front of a woman's bodice.

2. formerly, a ruffle on a man's shirt front.

jȧ·cal' (hä·käl'), *n.*; *pl.* **jȧ·ca'leṣ,** in Mexico and the southwestern United States, a rude hut built of logs and daubed with mud.

jaç'ȧ·mär, *n.* [S. Am.] a brilliant tropical American bird resembling the kingfisher, having a long, slender bill.

ja·çȧ·nȧ' (zhä·sȧ·nä'), *n.* [Port., from Tupi *jaçanam, jassanam.*] a bird of South America and India, with long toes that enable it to walk on the leaves of water plants.

LONG-TAILED JACANA (*Parra sinensis*)

Jaç·ȧ·ran'dȧ, *n.* [Braz.]

1. a genus of bignoniaceous trees, including the rosewood.

2. [j–] a tree of this genus; also, certain trees of other genera resembling the rosewood.

jaç'ȧ·rẹ, *n.* [Port. *jacaré,* from Braz. name.] a Brazilian alligator having a ridge from eye to eye, fleshy eyelids, the cervical distinct from the dorsal scutes, and small webs on the feet.

jaç'chus, *n.* [L. *Jacchus*; Gr. *Iakchos,* a name of Bacchus.] a kind of marmoset.

jac'cō·net, *n.* same as *jaconet.*

jā'cent, *a.* [L. *jacens* (*-entis*), ppr. of *jacere,* to lie.] lying at length; recumbent; prone. [Rare.]

jā'cinth, *n.* [ME. *jacinte, jacinct;* OFr. *iacinte, iacinct;* L. *hyacinthus,* a hyacinth.]
1. a reddish-orange precious stone, a variety of zircon; a hyacinth.
2. a reddish-orange color.

jac·i·tä'rȧ päl̤m, (päm), [S.Am. *jacitara,* and Eng. *palm.*] a South American palm with hooked spines at the ends of the leaves, valued for its fiber; the *Desmoncus macroacanthus.*

jack, *n.* [ME. *Jacke, Jake;* OFr. *Jaque, Jaques;* LL. *Jacobus;* Gr. *Iakōbos,* from Heb. *ya'aqōb,* Jacob, lit., seizing by the heel, a supplanter. From the nickname being used for a servant or boy who made himself generally useful, it is applied to lifting instruments.]
1. [*often* J–] originally, a common fellow or boy assistant.
2. [*often* J–] a man or boy; a fellow.
3. [*often* J–] a sailor; a jack-tar.
4. a lumberjack.
5. [*sometimes* J–] a worker at odd jobs; a jack-of-all-trades.
6. a bootjack.
7. a device for turning a roast; a kitchen jack.
8. any of various machines used to lift, hoist, or move something heavy a short distance; as, a *jack*screw, hydraulic *jack,* automobile *jack,* etc.
9. a male donkey; a jackass.
10. a jack rabbit.
11. a jackdaw.
12. a male salmon.
13. money. [Slang.]
14. in games, (a) a playing card with a page boy's picture on it; a knave; (b) a small ball used as the center mark in bowling; (c) one of the small metal pieces or stones used in playing jackstones.

LIFTING JACK

15. in hunting, (a) a torch or light used to attract game or fish at night; (b) the container holding the lighting fuel.
16. in navigation, a small flag flown on a ship's bow as a signal or to show nationality; a union jack.
17. in electricity, a plug-in receptacle used to make electric contact.
18. a drinking vessel holding less than a pint. [Brit. Dial.]
19. any of several fishes, especially the pike, the pike perch, and the Californian rockfish.
20. in textile manufacturing, a creel; in cotton spinning, a machine which twists the strand as it leaves the carding machine.
builders' jack; a seat or brace used to support a workman while repairing a building.
every man jack; every man; everyone.
hydraulic jack; a lifting jack in which the power is obtained by the action of a force pump upon a liquid confined in a cylinder.
Jack Ketch; [after a famous public executioner in England, ?–1686.] an official hangman; a public executioner. [Brit.]

jack, *v.t.* 1. to raise by means of a jack.
2. to hunt or fish for with a jack lamp.
to jack up; (a) to raise by means of a jack; (b) [Colloq.] to raise (prices, salaries, etc.); (c) [Colloq.] to reproach for misbehavior or neglect; to encourage to duty.

jack, *v.i.* to hunt or fish with a jack lamp.

jack, *a.* male: of some animals; as, *jack* rabbit.

jack, *n.* [ME. *jakke;* OFr. *jaque;* Sp. *jaco;* prob. from Ar. *shakk.*]
1. a sleeveless coat, usually of leather, worn by a medieval foot soldier.
2. a drinking mug of leather.

jack, *n.* [Port. *jaca;* Malay *chakka.*]
1. an East Indian tree like the breadfruit.
2. its large, heavy fruit, which has tasteless pulp and edible seeds.
3. its wood.

jack, *n.* a Jacqueminot rose. [Colloq.]

jack-, [see *jack* (a man, boy, etc.).] a combining form meaning: (a) *male,* as in *jack*ass, *jack*daw; (b) *large* or *strong,* as in *jack*boot, *jack*knife; (c) *boy, fellow:* used in hyphenated compounds, as *jack-in-the-box.*

Jack Ad'ămṣ, a simple fellow. [Brit. Dial.]

'ack'-ȧ-dan'dy, *n.* a little, foppish, impertinent fellow.

·k'a̤l, *n.* [Turk. *chagāl;* Per. *shagāl,* a jackal.]
1. a yellowish-gray, meat-eating wild dog of Asia and northern Africa, smaller than the wolf: it runs in packs and hunts its prey at night.

JACKAL
(*Canis aureus*)

2. a person who does low or dishonest work for another: from the notion that the jackal hunts game for the lion and eats the leavings.
3. a person who cheats or swindles in a mean, underhanded way.

jack'ȧ·nāpes, *n.* [earlier *Jack a Napes,* as if *Jack of Naples;* refashioning of *Jack Napes,* nickname of William de la Pole, Duke of Suffolk (d. 1450), whose badge was a clog and a chain like a tame ape's.]
1. formerly, a monkey.
2. a conceited, insolent, presumptuous fellow.
3. a pert, monkeylike, mischievous child.

jack'ass, *n.* 1. a male donkey.
2. a stupid or foolish person; a nitwit.

jack'bo͝ot, *n.* a heavy, sturdy boot that reaches above the knee: also written *jack boot.*

jack'da̤w, *n.* a European black bird like the crow, but smaller.

jack'et, *n.* [OFr. *jaquette,* dim. of *jaque,* a coat of mail, a jack.]
1. a short coat, usually with sleeves.
2. an outer coating or covering, such as the removable paper cover of a book, the metal covering of a bullet, the insulating casing on a pipe or boiler, the skin of a potato, etc.

Jack Frost, frost or cold weather personified.

Jack Ho̤rn'ẽr pīe, a container shaped like a large pie, from which favors, trinkets, etc. are pulled at a party.

jack-in-ȧ-box, *n.; pl.* **jack-in-ȧ-box'eṣ,** 1. a tropical tree having pulpy fruit which rattles when dry.
2. a jack-in-the-box.

jack-in-the-box, *n.; pl.* **jack-in-the-box'eṣ,** a toy consisting of a box from which a grotesque little figure on a spring jumps up when the lid is lifted.

jack-in-the-green, *n.; pl.* **jack-in-the-greenṣ,** a chimney sweep dressed up in leaves for a May Day procession. [Brit.]

jack-in-the-pul'pit, *n.; pl.* **jack-in-the-pul'pits,** an American plant of the lily family, with a flower spike partly arched over by a hoodlike covering.

jack'knīfe (-nīf), *n.; pl.* **jack'knīveṣ,** 1. a large pocketknife.
2. a dive in which the diver keeps his legs straight and touches his feet with his hands just before plunging into the water.

jack'knīfe, *v.t.* to cut or stab with a jackknife.

jack'knīfe, *v.i.* to bend at the middle, as in a dive.

jack lan'tẽrn, a torch for hunting at night; also, a Jack-o'-lantern.

jack-of-a̤ll-trādeṣ, *n.; pl.* **jacks-of-a̤ll-trādeṣ,** [*often* J–] a person who can do many kinds of work acceptably; a handy man.

jack'-o'-lan'tẽrn, *n.; pl.* **jack'-o'-lan'tẽrnṣ,** [abbrev. of *Jack of* (*or with*) *the lantern.*]
1. a shifting, elusive light seen over marshes at night; a will-o'-the-wisp.
2. a hollow pumpkin, real or artificial, cut to look like a face and used as a lantern.

jack pīne, the gray pine, *Pinus banksiana,* of the northern United States and Canada.

jack'pot, *n.* [*jack,* the playing card, and *pot.*]
1. cumulative stakes in a poker game, which can be played for only when some player has a pair of jacks or better with which to open.
2. any cumulative stakes, as in a bingo game or a slot machine.
3. the highest stakes that can be won in any enterprise. [Colloq.]
Also written *jack pot.*
to hit the jackpot; (a) to win the jackpot; (b) to attain the highest success. [Slang.]

jack rab'bit, any of several species of large hares, of the genus *Lepus,* with long ears and strong hind legs, found on the western prairies of North America.

jack raft'ẽr, any short rafter used in the construction of a roof, as in a hip roof.

jacks, *n.pl.* [*construed as sing.*] the game of jackstones.

jack sal'mŏn (sam'), a fresh-water fish of the genus *Stizostedium;* a wall-eyed perch.

jack'sa̤w, *n.* the merganser: so called from its sharply serrated bill. [Brit. Dial.]

jack'sc̣rew, *n.* a lifting jack operated by the turning of a screw.

jack'shaft, *n.* in mechanics, a shaft receiving its motion from the main shaft; a countershaft.

jack'slāve, *n.* an inferior or menial servant. [Obs.]

jack'smith, *n.* a smith who makes kitchen jacks. [Obs.]

jack'snīpe, *n.; pl.* **jack'snīpes** or **jack'snīpe,** in zoology, any of several snipes; specifically, (a) the common American snipe, *Gallinago wilsoni;* (b) the pectoral sandpiper, *Tringa maculata;* (c) the English snipe, *Gallinago gallinula;* (d) the dunlin, *Tringa alpina.*

Jack·sō'ni·ȧ, *n.* [after George *Jackson,* an English botanist.] a genus of Australian shrubs of the order *Leguminosæ,* the chief characteristic of which is the absence of leaves, their places being taken by spinelike branches.

Jack·sō'ni·ăn, *a.* in United States history and politics, pertaining to Andrew Jackson, the seventh president of the United States, or to his administration, policies, etc.

Jack'sŏn'ṣ bro͞om, in botany, the Australian dogwood, *Jacksonia scoparia.*

jack staff, the staff on the bowsprit or forepart of a vessel on which the union jack or other flag is flown.

jack'stāy, *n.* 1. a rope or staff along a ship's yard, to which the sail is fastened.
2. a rope or rod that runs up and down a ship's mast, on which the yard moves.

jack'stōne, *n.* [for dial. *checkstone,* from *check, chuck,* pebble.]
1. one of several stones or metal pieces used in playing the game of jackstones, usually having six arms, each at right angles to four others.
2. [*pl. construed as sing.*] a child's game of tossing, catching, or picking up jackstones, played in various ways: often shortened to *jacks.*

jack'stra̤w, *n.* 1. a figure or effigy of a man, made of straw; hence, a man without any substance or means.
2. one of the straws, or strips of metal, etc., used in playing jackstraws.
3. [*pl. construed as sing.*] a game in which straws, strips of wood, metal, ivory, or the like are dropped in a jumbled pile, from which the players must remove each one singly without moving or touching any other.

jack-tär, *n.* [*often* J–] a sailor.

jack tim'bẽr, in architecture, a timber in a bay which, being intercepted by some other piece, is shorter than the rest.

jack tow'el, a coarse towel hanging from a roller for general use.

jack tree, same as *jack* (tree).

jack'wood, *n.* the wood of the jack tree, used in carpentry and in cabinetwork.

jack'y, *n.; pl.* **jack'ieṣ,** [dim. of *Jack.*] a sailor.

jack'y, *n.* English gin. [Brit. Slang.]

jack yärd, a spar extended above the gaff in order to allow greater spread to a topsail.

Jā'c̣ŏb, *n.* [LL. *Jacobus;* Gr. *Iakōbos;* Heb. *Ya'aqob,* Jacob, lit., one who seizes by the heel, a supplanter.] in the Bible, a son of Isaac and father of the founders of the twelve tribes of Israel: also called *Israel:* Gen. xxv.–l.

jăc̣·ō·bae'ȧ, *n.* in botany, the ragwort of Europe, *Senecio jacobaea.*

jăc̣·ō·bae'ȧ lil'y, a bulbous Mexican amaryllis, *Sprekelia formosissima,* which has a single large blossom, resembling a deep-red lily.

Jaç·ō·bē'ăn, *a.* [Mod. L. and LL. *Jacobaeus,* from *Jacobus;* Latinized form of the name of James I.]
1. of James I of England.
2. of the period in England when he was king (1603–1625); as, *Jacobean* literature, architecture, etc.

Jaç·ō·bē'ăn, *n.* a poet, diplomat, etc. of this period.

Jȧ·c̣ō'bi·ăn, *n.* [after K. G. J. Jacobi (1804–

1851), German mathematician.] a determinant composed of the first derivatives of *n* functions of *n* variables.

Jaç'ō·bin, *n.* [OFr. *Jacobin*, from LL. *Jacobinus*, from *Jacobus*, Jacob, James.]
1. a French Dominican friar: so called because the Dominicans were established in a convent at the Church of St. Jacques (St. James of Compostella) in Paris.
2. any member of a society of revolutionary democrats in France during the Revolution of 1789: so called because their meetings were held in the Jacobin friars' convent.
3. a political radical.
4. [j–] a kind of pigeon with hoodlike neck feathers resembling a Dominican cowl.

Jaç'ō·bin, *a.* same as *Jacobinic.*

Jac·ō·bin'iç, Jaç·ō·bin'iç·ăl, *a.* of, pertaining to, or resembling the Jacobins of France; holding radical democratic principles.

Jaç·ō·bin'iç·ăl·ly, *adv.* in a manner resembling that of the Jacobins.

Jaç'ō·bin·işm, *n.* 1. the political doctrines of the Jacobins.
2. political radicalism.

Jaç'ō·bin·īze, *v.t.*; Jacobinized, *pt., pp.*; Jacobinizing, *ppr.* to make Jacobinic.

Jaç'ō·bīte, *n.* [LL. *Jacobus*; Gr. *Iakōbos*, Jacob, James.]
1. a partisan or adherent of James II, king of England, after he abdicated the throne, or of his descendants.
2. one of a sect of Christians in Syria and Mesopotamia: so named from Jacob Baradzi, their leader, in the sixth century.

Jaç'ō·bīte, *a.* pertaining to the Jacobites.

Jaç·ō·bit'iç, *a.* relating to Jacobitism.

Jaç·ō·bit'iç·ăl, *a.* belonging to the Jacobites.

Jaç·ō·bit'iç·ăl·ly, *adv.* after the spirit or manner of the Jacobites.

Jaç'ō·bit·işm, *n.* the principles of the partisans of James II.

Jā'çŏb'ş-lad'dẽr, *n.* a garden herb, *Polemonium cæruleum*, whose leaves and blue blossoms are arranged in a ladderlike formation.

Jā'çŏb'ş lad'dẽr, 1. in the Bible, the ladder from earth to heaven that Jacob saw in a dream: Gen. xxviii. 12.
2. a ladder made of rope, wire, etc., used on ships.

Jā'çŏb'ş staff, 1. a pilgrim's staff.
2. a staff concealing a dagger. [Obs.]
3. a cross staff; a kind of astrolabe.
4. the single staff used by surveyors to support a compass.

jȧ·çō'bus, *n.* a gold coin of England in the reign of James I, of the value of about six dollars.

jaç'ō·net, *n.* [from *Jagannath*, India, where it was manufactured.]
1. a soft, white, lightweight cotton textile, used for children's clothing.
2. cotton cloth glazed on one side and dyed. Also spelled *jacconet, jacconot.*

Jăç·quärd' (-kärd'), *a.* of or invented by Jos. Marie Jacquard (1752–1834) of Lyons, France.

Jăç·quärd' lọọm, a loom for weaving patterns into fabrics: it has an endless belt of cards with holes in them arranged to produce the desired pattern.

Jăç·quärd (wēave), a figured weave produced by a Jacquard loom.

Jȧcque'mi·nōt (-nō; *Fr. pron.* zhȧk-mē-nō'), *n.* [after J. F. *Jacqueminot* (1787–1865), Fr. general.] a deep-red, hybrid perennial rose.

Jȧcque·rie' (zhȧk-rē'), *n.* [Fr., from *Jacques Bonhomme*, name applied to a peasant by the nobles.]
1. a French peasants' revolt of 1358.
2. [often j–] any peasants' revolt.

jaç'tăn·cy, *n.* boastfulness; vainglory.

jaç·tā'tion, *n.* [L. *jactatio* (*-onis*), a throwing, vaunting, boasting, from *jactare*, to shake, agitate, boast.]
1. in medicine, jactitation.
2. the act of bragging.

jaç·ti·tā'tion, *n.* [LL. *jactitatio* (*-onis*), from L. *jactitare*, to bring forward in public, utter, freq. of *jactare*, to throw, shake, discuss.]
1. bragging.
2. in law, a false boast or false statement that causes harm to another person.
3. in medicine, a restless tossing or twitching of the body, a muscle, etc.
jactitation of marriage; in English law, a false claim of being married to another.

jaç'ū·lāte, *v.t.* to dart; to hurl; to launch. [Rare.]

jaç·ū·lā'tion, *n.* the act of darting, throwing, or launching, as missile weapons. [Rare.]

jaç'ū·lā·tŏr, *n.* 1. the archerfish, *Toxotes jaculator.*
2. one who hurls or darts. [Rare.]

jaç'ū·lȧ·tō·ry, *a.* darting or throwing out suddenly, or suddenly thrown out; ejaculatory.

jad, *v.t.* to cut a pit or hole, as in coal or stone, in order to blast or wedge off a mass. [Brit. Dial.]

jāde, *n.* [Fr. *jade*; Sp. *jade*, jade, from *piedra de yjada*, stone of the side: so called because the stone was supposed to cure pain in the side.]
1. a hard ornamental stone, either jadeite (true jade) or nephrite, usually green or white.
2. the green color of this stone.

jāde, *a.* 1. made of jade.
2. green like jade.

jāde, *n.* [ME.; perh. from ON. *jalda*, a mare.]
1. a horse, especially a worn-out, worthless one.
2. a loose or disreputable woman.
3. any woman: a playful or ironic usage.

jāde, *v.t.* and *v.i.*; jaded, *pt., pp.*; jading, *ppr.* to make or become tired, weary, or worn-out.

jād'ed, *a.* 1. tired; worn-out; wearied.
2. dulled or satiated, as from overuse.

jāde'ite, *n.* a complex silicate, hard, tough, and translucent, usually green or white; true jade.

jād'ẽr·y, *n.* the behavior of a jade.

jād'ish, *a.* 1. tired, mean, or worn-out: applied to a horse.
2. unchaste: applied to a woman.

jae'gẽr (yā'), *n.* 1. a jäger.
2. (*also* jā'gẽr), a robber bird of the gull family, which forces other weaker birds to leave or give up their prey: also spelled *jäger.*

Jā'el, *a.* [Heb. *yā'el*, lit., mountain goat.] in the Bible, the woman who killed Sisera by hammering a spike through his head while he slept: Jud. iv. 17–22.

jag, *n.* [ME. *jagge*, projecting point; prob., from dial. var., from AS. *sceacga.*]
1. a notch or pointed tear, as in cloth.
2. a sharp, toothlike projection or similar indentation.

jag, *v.t.*; jagged (jagd), *pt., pp.*; jagging, *ppr.* [ME. *jaggen, joggen*, from the noun.]
1. to cut jags in; to notch; to pink (cloth, etc.).
2. to cut unevenly; to tear raggedly.

jag, *n.* [prob. special use of *jag* (a notch) with sense "load of scrub wood."]
1. a small load or amount, as of wood, hay, etc. [Colloq.]
2. an intoxicated condition due to alcoholic liquor or drugs. [Slang.]
3. a drunken celebration; spree. [Slang.]

jag, *v.t.* to carry, as a load of hay. [Colloq.]

Jag'ȧn·näth (jug'ȧ-nät), *n.* [Hind. *Jagannāth*; Sans. *Jagannatha*, lit., ruler of men and beasts; *jagat*, all that moves, and *natha*, ruler, protector.] lord of the earth: a title given to one of the incarnations of Vishnu: see *Juggernaut.*

ja'gȧt (jug'ȧt), *n.* [Sans. living.] in Hinduism, animate beings.

Jag''ȧ·taī', *n.* a dialect of Turkish spoken in southern Turkestan and parts of the southwestern Asiatic U.S.S.R.

jag bōlt, a bolt barbed to resist withdrawal.

jä'ger (yā'gẽr), *n.* [G., huntsman, from *jagen*, to hunt.]
1. a hunter.
2. [often J–] a rifleman in the old Austrian and German armies.
3. (*also* jā'gẽr), a jaeger.
Also spelled *yager.*

jag'ged, *a.* having sharp projecting points or notches; ragged.

jag'ged·ly, *adv.* in a jagged manner; so as to be jagged.

jag'ged·ness, *n.* the state of being jagged; unevenness.

jag'gẽr, *n.* one who or that which jags.

jag'gẽr, *n.* one who carries a jag or wallet; a peddler. [Scot.]

jag'gẽr·y, *n.* [Anglo-Ind.; Hind. *jagri*, from Sans. *sarkarā*, sugar.] a dark, crude sugar, specifically that made from the sap of East Indian palm trees.

jag'ging ī'ron (-ũrn), a wheel with a notched or jagged edge for decorating pastry, etc.

jag'gy, *a.* set with teeth; denticulated; jagged.

jä·ghīr', jä·ghīre', *n.* [Per. *jāgīr.*] in India, the revenues of a district of land, or the product thereof, assigned by the government to an individual, commonly for the support of some public establishment, particularly of a military nature: also spelled *jagir.*

jä'ghīr·där, *n.* a person holding a jaghir: also spelled *jagirdar.*

jä'guä pälm (hä'gwä päm), [from native name.] a large Brazilian palm, the woody spathes of which harden when dry and are used as baskets, etc. by the natives.

jag'uär (jag'wär *or* jag'ū-är), *n.*; *pl.* **jag'uärş** or **jag'uär,** [Port., from Tupi.] a wild animal of the cat family, yellowish with black spots, found in Central and South America: it is like the leopard, but larger.

jä·guȧ·ron'di, (-gwȧ-), *n.* [native name.] a South American carnivorous animal, *Felis jaguarondi*, resembling a very large brown cat.

Jäh, *n.* same as *Jehovah.*

Jäh'vęh (*or* yä'), *n.* Jehovah: also spelled *Jahve.*

Jäh'vist, *n.* same as *Jehovist.*

Jäh·vis'tiç, *a.* same as *Jehovistic.*

jaī-ȧ·laī' (hī-ȧ-lī'), *n.* [Sp., from Basque *jai*, celebration, and *alai*, merry.] a game like handball, played with a basketlike racket fastened to the arm: it is popular in Latin America.

jāil, *n.* [ME. *jaile, gaile, gayhol*; OFr. *jaiole, jaole, gaole*, a cage, prison; LL. *gabiola*, dim. of *gabia*, a cage, prob. from L. *cavea*, a cage, coop.] a building for the confinement of people who have broken the law or are awaiting trial; prison, especially for those convicted of minor offenses: also, British, *gaol.*
jail liberties or *limits*; formerly, the district to which a prisoner for debt who had given bond was restricted.

jāil, *v.t.*; jailed, *pt., pp.*; jailing, *ppr.* to put or keep in jail; to imprison: also, British, *gaol.*

jāil'bīrd, *n.* 1. a person sentenced to jail; a prisoner. [Colloq.]
2. a person often put in jail; a habitual law breaker. [Colloq.]

jāil dē·liv'ẽr·y, 1. in English law, the trial of all persons detained in a prison.
2. the forcible escape of prisoners from a jail.

jāil'ẽr, jāil'ŏr, *n.* a person in charge of a jail or of prisoners.

jāil fē'vẽr, typhus fever, frequent in unsanitary jails.

Jaīn, Jaī'nȧ, *n.* [Hind. *Jaina*, from *jina*, victorious.] a believer in Jainism.

Jaīn, Jaī'nȧ, *a.* of the Jains or Jainism.

Jaīn'işm, *n.* a Hindu religious creed resembling Buddhism, founded about 500 B.C.: it teaches reverence of wise and good men and respect for animals.

jak, *n.* same as *jack tree.*

jāke, *a.* just right; satisfactory. [Slang.]

jākes, *n.* a privy. [Archaic or Dial.]

jak'ō, *n.* the gray African parrot, *Psittacus erithacus.*

jal'ăp, *n.* [Fr., from Sp. *jalapa*, from *Jalapa*, a city in Mexico from which it is imported.] the root of the climbing plant *Ipomæa purga*, or the plant itself; also, a medicinal preparation of purgative properties, derived from the root.

JALAP
(*Ipomæa purga*)

false jalap; the root of the *Mirabilis jalapa*, the four-o'clock.

jȧ·lap'iç, *a.* pertaining to jalap.

jal'ȧ·pin, *n.* [*jalap* and *-in.*] a resin which is the purgative principle of the roots and tubers of jalap.

jȧ·lop'y, *n.*; *pl.* **jȧ·lop'ieş,** an old, worn automobile or airplane: also spelled *jallopy.* [Slang.]

jȧ·lou·şie' (zhȧ-), *n.* [Fr., jealousy, envy, a latticed window.] a window shade of horizontal slats that slope and overlap, used to keep out sun while letting in light and air; a kind of Venetian blind.

jȧ·lou·ṣied′, *a.* having jalousies.

jam, *n.* [prob. from *jam*, to press, squeeze; compare Ar. *jāmid*, ice, jelly, from *jamada*, to thicken, freeze.] a food made by cooking fruit with sugar to a thick mixture: distinguished from *preserve, jelly.*

jam, *n.* [Per. and Hind. *jāmah*, raiment, robe.] a kind of frock for children. [Brit.]

jam, *v.t.*; jammed, *pt., pp.*; jamming, *ppr.* [formerly *jamb*, as if squeezed between *jambs* or from *cham, champ*, to chew, tread heavily.]

1. to press; to crowd; to wedge or squeeze into or through a tight space.
2. to bruise; crush.
3. to push; shove; crowd.
4. to fill or block (a passageway, etc.) by crowding or squeezing into it.
5. to cause to become wedged so that it cannot move; as, the door was *jammed.*
6. in radio, to make (broadcasts or signals) unintelligible by sending out others on the same wave length.

jam, *v.i.* 1. (a) to become wedged or stuck fast; (b) to become unworkable through such jamming of parts.
2. to push against one another in a confined space.
3. in jazz, to improvise. [Slang.]

jam, *n.* a jamming or being jammed; as, a traffic *jam.*

jam′ȧ·där (jum′), *n.* same as *jemidar.*

Jȧ·māi′cȧ ġin′ġēr, the white ginger grown in the West Indies: the drug prepared from it is a common stimulant and antispasmodic.

Jȧ·māi′căn, *a.* pertaining to Jamaica, its people, or culture.

Jȧ·māi′căn, *n.* an inhabitant of Jamaica.

Jȧ·māi′cȧ rōṣe, any of several tropical American shrubs of the order *Melastomaceæ*, as *Blakea trinervis.*

jamb, jambe (jam), *n.* [ME. *jambe, jamne*; OFr. *jambe*, a leg, shank, pier, side post of a door, from LL. *gamba*, a hoof.]

1. in architecture, a side or vertical piece of any opening in a wall, such as a door, window, or chimney.
2. a jambeau.

jamb, *v.t.* to jam. [Obs.]

jam′beau (-bō), *n.*; *pl.* **jam′beaux** (-bōz), [OFr. *jambe*, leg.] a piece of armor for the legs.

jam·bee′, *n.* a kind of walking stick. [Obs.]

jam·bō·lä′nȧ, *n.* [E. Ind.] a tropical, fruit-bearing tree of the genus *Eugenia*; also, a medicine derived from its seeds or bark.

jam′bōne, *n.* in euchre, a variation in the play of lone hands by which the cards must be exposed, face up, on the table, and so played, the player to the left having the privilege of calling the first card to be played. Five tricks score eight points; a euchre of a jambone scores two points.

jam′bọọ, *n.* same as *jambu.*

jam′bọọl, *n.* same as *jambolana.*

jam·bō·ran′di, *n.* same as *jaborandi.*

jam·bō·ree′, *n.* 1. a hilarious party; a noisy revel. [Colloq.]
2. a large, especially international, assembly of boy scouts.
3. in euchre, a variation by which the player holding the five highest trumps may show them and score sixteen points without playing out the hand.

Jam′bŏs, Jam·bō′sȧ, *n.* a branch of the genus *Eugenia*, including the Java plum and rose apple.

jam·bō′sȧ, *n.* the rose apple.

jam·bō′sïne, *n.* a crystalline alkaloid. $C_{10}H_{15}O_3N$, obtained from the root of jambosa.

jamb shȧft, a slender column near or a part of the jamb of a door or window.

jam′bù, *n.* [E. Ind.] an East Indian shrub, *Eugenia jambos*; the rose apple tree.

jam′bụl, *n.* same as *jambolana.*

jäm·dä′nï, *n.* [Hind. *jāmdānī*, a flowered muslin fabric; *jāma*, a garment, robe, and *dānī*, bountiful, liberal.] an East Indian cloth with a flowered pattern woven in the loom.

Jāmeṣ, *n.* [Fr., from LL. *Jacobus*; Gr. *Iakōbos*; Heb. *ya'aqob*, Jacob, lit., seizing by the heel, a supplanter.] in the Bible, (a) a Christian apostle, Zebedee's son: called *the Greater*; (b) a Christian apostle, Alphaeus' son: sometimes called *the Less*; (c) a brother of Jesus: Gal. i. 19; (d) one of the books of the New Testament.

jāme′sŏn·īte, *n.* [named after Prof. *Jameson*, of Edinburgh (1773–1854).] a steel-gray ore of antimony and lead.

Jāmeṣ′town weed, same as *Jimson weed.*

jam nut, same as *check nut.*

jam′pan, *n.* [E. Ind.] in the East Indies, a sedan chair supported between two bamboo poles, and borne by four men.

jam′rō·ṣāde, *n.* [from the E. Ind. name, *jambos*, the rose apple, influenced by L. *rosa*, rose.] the fruit of the jambu; the rose apple.

jam ses′sion (sesh′un), a meeting of jazz musicians at which they play popular music with much spontaneous interpolation and improvisation. [Slang.]

Jam·shïd′, Jam·shyd′ (-shïd′), *n.* [Per.] in Persian mythology, the king of the peris: because he boasted that he was immortal, he had to live as a human being on earth, where he became a famous ruler.

jan′ȧ·pȧ, jan′ȧ·pum, *n.* Bengal hemp.

jan′cȧ tree, [W. Ind. *janca*, and E. *tree.*] an evergreen tree of the West Indies.

Jāne, *n.* 1. a bang of hair worn over the forehead.
2. a girl or woman: used derogatorily. [Slang.]

jāne, *n.* [ME. *jane*, from LL. *Janua*; L. *Genua*, Genoa.]
1. a coin of Genoa.
2. a twilled cotton cloth.

jan·gä′dȧ, *n.* [Sp. and Port.] a South American form of catamaran.

jañ′gle, *v.i.*; jangled, *pt., pp.*; jangling, *ppr.* [ME. *janglen, jangelen*; OFr. *jangler, gangler*, to jangle, prattle, wrangle.]
1. to quarrel; to altercate; to bicker; to wrangle.
2. to make a harsh, discordant sound, as a bell out of tune.

jañ′gle, *v.t.* 1. to utter in a harsh, inharmonious manner.
2. to cause to make a harsh sound.

jañ′gle, *n.* 1. noisy talk.
2. a harsh sound; discordant ringing.
3. bickering; quarrel.

jañ′glēr, *n.* a noisy fellow; a babbler.

jañ′glēr·ess, *n.* a woman who jangles. [Obs.]

jañ′glēr·y, *n.* chatter; jangling. [Obs.]

jañ′gling, *n.* babble; wrangling; discord.

jañ′gly, *a.* discordant; inharmonious.

Jan′is·sȧr·y, *n.* [often j–] a Janizary.

jan′i·tŏr, *n.* [L., a doorkeeper, from *janua*, door.]
1. a doorkeeper; a porter.
2. the caretaker of a building, apartment house, etc.

jan′i·tress, *n.* a woman janitor.

jan′i·trix, *n.* a woman janitor.

Jan·i·zȧr′i·ăn, *a.* [often j–] pertaining to the Janizaries.

Jan′i·zȧr·y, *n.*; *pl.* **Jan′i·zȧr·ieṣ,** [OFr. *jannissaire*, from Turk. *yeñicheri*, lit., new troops or soldiers.] [often j–] formerly, a soldier of the Turkish foot guards, a body of infantry who finally became rebellious and, rising in arms against the sultan, were attacked, defeated, and destroyed in Constantinople, in June, 1826; hence, any soldier in the Turkish army.

jañ′kēr, *n.* a pole mounted on two wheels, used in Scotland for transporting logs of wood.

jann, *n. sing.* and *pl.* [Per. *jān*, soul, spirit.] a demon of the lowest order in the Mohammedan mythology; also, the jinn collectively.

Jan′sen·iṣm, *n.* the doctrine of the Jansenists.

Jan′sen·ist, *n.* a follower of Cornelius Jansen (1585–1638), a Roman Catholic bishop of Ypres, in Flanders, who denied free will and believed in irresistible grace and limited atonement.

Jan′sen·ist, Jan·sen·is′tiç, *a.* of Jansen or Jansenism.

Jan′thi·nȧ, *n.* a genus of gastropods, the *Ianthina.*

jan′ti·ly, *adv.* same as *jauntily.*

jan′ti·ness, *n.* same as *jauntiness.*

jan′ty, *a.* same as *jaunty.*

Jan′ū·ȧr·y, *n.* [L. *Januarius* (supply *mensis*, month), the month of Janus, from *Janus*; Janus, to whom the month of January was sacred.] the first month of the year, containing thirty-one days.

Jā′nus, *n.* [L.] in Roman mythology, the god who was guardian of portals and patron of beginnings and endings: he is shown as having two faces, one in front, the other at the back of his head, symbolizing his powers. His temple, at Rome, was never closed except in a time of universal peace.

Jā′nus-fāced (-fāst), *a.* having two faces; two-faced; deceitful.

Jā′nus-head″ed (-hed″), *a.* double-headed.

Jap, *n.* and *a.* Japanese: a shortened form often expressing contempt, hostility, etc.

jȧ·pan′, *n.* 1. a hard lacquer or varnish giving a glossy finish: it was originally from Japan.
2. a liquid mixture used as a paint drier.
3. objects decorated and lacquered in the Japanese style.
4. any of various black varnishes.
5. a japanned black cane. [Obs.]

jȧ·pan′, *v.t.*; japanned, *pt., pp.*; japanning, *ppr.* to cover with or as with japan.

Jȧ·pan′, *a.* [Chinese *Jih-pun*, lit., sunrise; *jih*, sun, and *pun*, origin.] of or pertaining to Japan; Japanese.

Japan allspice; a Japanese shrub, *Chimonanthus fragrans.*

Japan black; a jet-black varnish or lacquer, usually made of asphaltum, linseed oil, and turpentine: called also *japan, japan lacquer*, and *Brunswick black.*

Japan clover; a plant of the bean family, *Lespedeza striata*, introduced into southern United States from Japan or China, and of much value for fodder.

Japan current; a warm current in the Pacific, flowing east of Formosa and northeast past Japan.

Jap·ȧ·nēṣe′, *n.* 1. *pl.* **Jap·ȧ·nēṣe,** a native of Japan.
2. the language of the inhabitants of Japan.

Jap·ȧ·nēṣe′, *a.* pertaining to Japan or its inhabitants, language, culture, etc.

Jap·ȧ·nēṣe′ bee′tle, a green-and-brown beetle, originally from Japan, which eats leaves, fruits, and grasses, and is damaging to crops.

Jap·ȧ·nesque′ (-nesk′), *a.* in the Japanese manner.

jȧ·panned′, *a.* varnished with or as with japan.

jȧ·pan′nēr, *n.* 1. one who japans.
2. a shoeblack. [Rare.]

jȧ·pan′ning, *n.* the art of varnishing with japan.

Jȧ·pan′nish, *a.* characteristic of the Japanese or their work. [Rare.]

jāpe, *v.i.*; japed, *pt., pp.*; japing, *ppr.* [ME. *japen*; OFr. *japer*, to jest.]
1. to jest.
2. to play tricks.

jāpe, *v.t.* 1. to make fun of; to mock.
2. to play tricks on; to fool.

jāpe, *n.* a jest; a joke; also, a trick.

jāp′ēr, *n.* one who japes.

jāp′ēr·y, *n.*; *pl.* **jāp′ēr·ieṣ,** 1. a japing; joking; trickery. [Archaic.]
2. ribaldry. [Archaic.]

Jā′pheth, *n.* [L.; Gr. *Iapheth*; Heb. *yepheth*, lit., enlargement.] in the Bible, the youngest of Noah's three sons: Gen. v. 32.

Jȧ·phet′iç, *a.* 1. pertaining to or descended from Japheth.
2. formerly, in linguistics, Indo-European: distinguished from *Hamitic* and *Semitic.*

Jā′phet·īte, *n.* any of Japheth's descendants.

jȧ·pon′i·cȧ, *n.* [from Japan.] any of various plants originally native to Japan; especially, (a) *Camellia japonica*; (b) *Pyrus japonica.*

Jap′ō·niṣm, *n.* [Fr. *Japon*, Japan; and *-ism.*] any characteristic of the Japanese; a Japanese idiom, principle of art, mannerism, etc.

Jā′quēṣ, *n.* a character in Shakespeare's *As You Like It*, a cynically philosophic nobleman who is one of the attendants of the exiled duke.

jä′quï·mä (hä′kē-), *n.* [Sp. *jáquima.*] the headstall of a bridle or halter.

jär, *n.* [ME. *char*; AS. *cyrr*, a turn.] a turn or turning: now used only in the phrases *on a jar, on the jar*, that is, ajar, or partially open.

jär, *v.i.*; jarred (järd), *pt., pp.*; jarring, *ppr.* [compare ME. *charken*, to creak; AS. *ceorian*, to murmur.]
1. to produce a harsh or grating sound; to strike or sound discordantly; to be discordant; as, a *jarring* noise.
2. to clash; to act in opposition; to conflict; to quarrel.
3. to have or receive a short quivering, shaking, or jolting motion, as from a sudden impact.
4. to have a harsh, irritating effect (*on* one).

jär, *v.t.* 1. to make vibrate or shake by sudden impact.
2. to cause to give a harsh, grating sound or discord.

3. to jolt or shock.

jär, *n.* 1. a vibration due to a sudden impact.
2. a jolt or shock.
3. a harsh sound; discord.
4. clash of interest or opinions; conflict; discord; debate.
5. in well drilling, a device which, on the upstroke, lifts the drill with a sudden jerk in order to loosen it if caught.

jär, *n.* [OFr. *jare*; Sp. *jarra*, a jar, pitcher, from Per. *jarrah*, a jar, earthen water vessel.]
1. a vessel with a large, cylindrical body and broad mouth, made of earthenware, stone, or glass.
2. the quantity held by a jar; as, a *jar* of oil.

jär·ȧ·rä′çȧ (zhär-), *n.* [from native name.] a species of snake of Brazil, of a dusky, brownish color, variegated with red and black spots: it is very poisonous.

jär′ble, *v.t.* to bemire. [Brit. Dial.]

järde, *n.* [Fr.] a callous tumor on the leg of a horse, below the bend of the ham on the outside.

jär·di·nière′ (*Fr.* zhär-dē-nyâr′), *n.* [Fr., a flower stand, a woman gardener.] an ornamental holder for plants or flowers, as (a) a decorative vessel to hold a common flowerpot; (b) a jar or vase to hold flowers for table decoration; (c) a stand for flowerpots.

jär′dŏn, *n.* a jarde.

jär′flȳ, *n.* a cicada.

jär′gle, *v.i.* to emit a harsh or shrill sound. [Obs.]

jär′gŏn, *n.* [OFr. *jargon, gergon*, gibberish.]
1. confused, unintelligible talk or language; gabble; gibberish.
2. the dialect resulting from the mixture of languages; as, the Chinook *jargon*.
3. a language or dialect that is incomprehensible, outlandish, etc. to one.
4. the specialized vocabulary and idioms of those in the same work, way of life, etc., as journalism or social work: somewhat derogatory term, implying unintelligibility.
5. speech or writing full of long, unfamiliar, or roundabout words or phrases.

jär′gŏn, *v.i.* jargoned, *pt., pp.*; jargoning, *ppr.* [Fr. *jargonner*, from *jargon*, gibberish.] to talk gibberish or jargon; to gabble.

jär′gŏn, *n.* [Fr. *jargon*; It. *giargone*, a sort of yellow diamond; perhaps from Per. *zargūn*, gold-colored; *zar*, gold, and *gūn*, color.] a colorless or smoky variety of zircon.

jär·gō·nelle′, jär·gō·nel′, *n.* [Fr. dim. of *jargon*, the mineral.] an early harvest pear.

jär·gon′iç, *a.* pertaining to the mineral jargon.

jär′gŏn·ist, *n.* one who uses jargon.

jär′gŏn·īze, *v.i.*; jargonized, *pt., pp.*; jargonizing, *ppr.* to talk or write in jargon.

jär′gŏn·īze, *v.t.* to express in jargon; to make jargon of.

jär′goon, *n.* same as *jargon* (zircon).

järl (yärl), *n.* [Scand.] an ancient Scandinavian nobleman, chief, or leader.

jȧ·rool′, *n.* [E. Ind.] a valuable timber tree found in tropical Asia.

jȧ·rō′sīte, *n.* [named from Barranco *Jaroso*, in Spain.] a yellowish hydrous sulfate of potassium and iron.

jär′ō·vize (yär′), *v.t.*; jarovized, *pt., pp.*; jarovizing, *ppr.* [Russ. *yar'*, spring grain.] to bring about early maturing of (a plant) by retarding the germination of the seed, as through exposure to low temperature and darkness for a time; to vernalize: also spelled *yarovize*.

jär′-owl, *n.* the goatsucker.

jär′räh, *n.* [Australian.] a tree, *Eucalyptus marginata*, of Australia, having a close-grained, heavy, red wood; also, the wood of the tree, resembling mahogany.

jär′ring·ly, *adv.* in a jarring or discordant manner.

jär′vey, jär′vy, *n.*; *pl.* **jär′veyṣ**, a hackney coach, or one who drives a hackney coach. [Brit. Colloq.]

jā′sey, *n.* a wig, made of or like Jersey yarn. [Brit. Colloq.]

jas′mine, jas′min (*or* jaz′), *n.* [Fr. *jasmin*; Ar. *yāsmīn*; Per. *yāsmīn*, jasmine.]
1. any species of the genus *Jasminum*, of the olive family, with fragrant flowers of yellow, red, or white. The common white jasmine, *Jasminum officinale*, is a climbing shrub, growing, on supports, 15 to 20 feet high: also called *jessamine*.
2. any of various other plants similar to the true jasmine; as, the Cape *jasmine*, the yellow or false *jasmine*, etc.

American jasmine; the *Ipomœa* or *Quamoclit coccinea*, the so-called red morning-glory of the southern United States.

COMMON WHITE JASMINE

Cape jasmine; the *Gardenia jasminoides*, a Chinese shrub, having white or cream-colored flowers.

false jasmine; the yellow jasmine.

French jasmine; the *Calotropis procera*, a shrub from which madar fiber is obtained.

red jasmine; the *Plumeria rubra*, the frangipani.

yellow jasmine; the *Gelsemium sempervirens*, a shrub having showy, fragrant, yellow flowers.

jas′mine tree, the red jasmine.

Jas′mi·num, *n.* a genus of the family *Oleaceæ*, whose species are cultivated for their flowers or fragrant oils.

Jā′sŏn, *n.* [L. *Iāson*; Gr. *Iāson*, lit., healer.] in Greek legend, a prince who led the Argonauts and, with Medea's help, got the Golden Fleece in spite of the fire-breathing bulls and the dragon guarding it.

jas′pȧ·çhāte, *n.* agate jasper. [Obs.]

jas·pé′ (zhȧs-pā′), *a.* [Fr.] in ceramics, streaked and mottled in imitation of jasper.

jas′pẽr, *n.* [ME. *jasper, jaspr*; OFr. *jaspre, jaspe*, L. *iaspis*, Gr. *iaspis*, a green-colored precious stone.]
1. an opaque variety of quartz, of red, yellow, or brown. When the colors are in stripes or bands, it is called *banded* or *striped jasper*; when it has layers of chalcedony, it is called *agate jasper*.
2. in the Bible, probably a green ornamental stone.

jas′pẽr·ā·ted, *a.* mixed with jasper, containing particles of jasper; as, *jasperated* agate.

jas′pẽr·īze, *v.t.*; jasperized, *pt., pp.*; jasperizing, *ppr.* to cause to become or become like jasper; as, to *jasperize* wood.

jas′pẽr ō′păl, a kind of opal containing yellow iron oxide, which gives the appearance of yellow jasper.

jas′pẽr wãre, a white porcelain bisque or variety of terra-cotta invented and used by Josiah Wedgwood, particularly for cameo effects.

jas′pẽr·y, *a.* having the qualities of jasper.

jas·pid′ē·ăn, jas·pid′ē·ous, *a.* like jasper; consisting of or containing jasper.

jas′pi·līte, *n.* a siliceous jaspoid rock.

jas′poid, *a.* [Gr. *iaspis*, jasper, and *eidos*, form.] resembling jasper.

jasp·ō′nyx, *n.* [L. *iasponyx*; Gr. *iasponyx*, *iaspis*, jasper, and *onyx*, onyx.] a jasper having layers of contrasting colors like an onyx.

Jät, *n.* [Hind.] a member of a large race or caste in India, living largely in the Punjab district.

jat·ȧ·man′si, *n.* the East Indian true spikenard, *Nardostachys jatamansi*.

Jat″ē·ō·rhī′zȧ, *n.* [Gr. *iatēr* or *iatros*, a physician, and *rhiza*, a root.] a genus of climbing plants of Africa containing *Jateorhiza calumba* which yields columbo.

Jat′rō·phȧ, *n.* [Gr. *iatros, iatēr*, a physician, and *trophē*, nourishment, food.] a genus of woody plants of the family *Euphorbiaceæ*, found in the tropical parts of America.

jȧ·troph′iç, *a.* of or resembling the seeds of species of the genus *Jatropha*.

jąunce, *v.t.* and *v.i.* to jounce. [Obs.]

jąun′dice, *n.* [ME. *jaundys, jandis*; OFr. *jaunisse*, jaundice, yellows, from *jaune*, yellow.]
1. a diseased condition characterized by suppression and alteration of the liver functions, yellowness of the eyes, skin, and urine, clayeyness of the discharges from the intestines, distress of the stomach, loss of appetite, and general languor and lassitude.
2. a soured state of mind, caused by jealousy, envy, etc., in which judgment is distorted.

jąun′dice, *v.t.*; jaundiced (-dist), *pt., pp.*; jaundicing, *ppr.* 1. to affect with jaundice.
2. to affect with prejudice or envy.

jąun′dice ber′ry, jąun′dice tree, the barberry.

jąunt, *v.i.*; jaunted, *pt., pp.*; jaunting, *ppr.* [compare Scot. *jaunder*, to ramble.]
1. to take a short trip for pleasure.
2. to ride about in a jaunting car.
3. to jounce. [Obs.]

jąunt, *v.t.* to shake; to jolt. [Obs.]

jąunt, *n.* an excursion; a short trip for pleasure.

jąun′ti·ly, *adv.* in a jaunty manner.

jąun′ti·ness, *n.* the quality or state of being jaunty.

jąun′ting çär, a light, topless, two-wheeled cart used in Ireland, with seats on both sides, arranged back to back.

jąun′ty, *a.*; *comp.* jauntier; *superl.* jauntiest, [from Fr. *gentil*, genteel.]
1. gay and easy in manner; airy; sprightly; perky; as, he walked along with quite a *jaunty* air.
2. stylish; chic.

Jä′vȧ, *n.* 1. any of a breed of chickens with black or mottled black plumage.
2. a kind of coffee grown in Java and the islands near it.
3. [often j–] any coffee. [Slang.]

Java cotton; kapok.

Java man; a type of primitive man known from fossil remains found in Java in 1891: formerly called *Pithecanthropus* (*erectus*).

Java sparrow; the *Padda oryzivora*, a Javanese finch, common as a cage bird.

Jav·ȧ·nēṣe′, *a.* pertaining to the island of Java, its inhabitants, their language, or culture.

Jav·ȧ·nēṣe′, *n.* 1. *pl.* **Jav·ȧ·nēṣe′**, a native of Java, especially a member of a group of tribes occupying the main part of Java.
2. the Indonesian language of these tribes.
3. a group of Malayo-Polynesian languages spoken in Java, Bali, and near-by islands.

jav′el, *n.* a low fellow; a vagabond. [Obs.]

jave′lin, *n.* [OFr. *javelin*, masc., *javeline*, f.; akin to Sp. *jabalina*; Arm. *gavlin, gavlod*, a javelin, from *gavl*, the fork of a tree.]
1. a light spear for throwing, having the shaft of wood and pointed with steel.
2. a pointed wooden shaft, about 8½ feet long, thrown for distance in a contest.

jave′lin, *v.t.* to strike or wound with or as with a javelin.

jave·lin·eer′, *n.* [OFr.] a soldier whose weapons are javelins.

Jȧ·vel′ (*or* **Jȧ·velle′**) **wạter** (zhȧ-), a solution of sodium hypochlorite, NaOCl, in water, used as a bleaching agent or disinfectant.

jąw, *n.* [a modification of *chaw*, or *chew*, under the influence of Fr. *joue*, jaw.]
1. either of the two parts or structures that hold the teeth and constitute the framework of the mouth; also, a bone, or the bones collectively, constituting the skeleton of such a part: the lower jaw is called the mandible, the upper the maxilla.
2. any mouth part, as in an invertebrate, similar in function or position to the jaw of a vertebrate.
3. anything resembling a jaw in form or use; specifically, (a) either of two mechanical parts that open and close to grasp or crush something, as in a monkey wrench or vise; (b) the hollowed inner end of a boom or gaff reaching partway around a mast.
4. [*pl.*] the entrance of (a canyon, valley, etc.).
5. talk; especially, offensive or abusive talk. [Slang.]

jąw, *v.t.*; jawed, *pt., pp.*; jawing, *ppr.* to scold or reprove. [Slang.]

jąw, *v.i.* to talk. [Slang.]

jąw bit, in railroads, a bar which connects the two car truck pedestals.

jąw′bōne, *n.* a bone of a jaw, particularly either of the two bones of the lower jaw.

jąw′bōne, *v.t.* and *v.i.*; jawboned, *pt., pp.*; jawboning, *ppr.* to attempt to persuade by using one's high office or position to apply pressure, as the President might in proposing price and wage controls to business and labor.

jąw′break″ẽr, *n.* a word not easily pronounced; also, a piece of hard candy. [Slang.]

jąwed, *a.* having jaws: usually in compounds; as, square-*jawed*.

jaw′fall″en, *a.* crestfallen; discouraged. [Rare.]

jaw′foot, *n.* same as *maxilliped.*

jaw′ing, *n.* a scolding. [Colloq.]

jaw′less, *a.* having no jaws.

jaw rōpe, the rope with which the jaws of a gaff are fastened to the mast.

jaw tooth, a tooth in the back part of the jaw; a molar.

jaw′y, *a.* relating to the jaws.

jāy, *n.* [ME. *jay*; OFr. *jay, gay, gai,* a jay, from *gai,* gay: so called from its gay plumage.]
1. a bird of the family *Corvidæ,* having the tail wedge-shaped and rather long, and the feathers of the forehead erectile. The European jay, *Garrulus glandarius,* has, to some extent, the faculty of imitating the voice of other birds. The American jay, or bluejay, *Cyanocitta cristata,* is a bird of very brilliant plumage, ornamented with a crest of light blue or purple feathers.
2. a stupid, foolish, or talkative person. [Slang.]
3. a loud or gaudy woman. [Obs.]

jāy′hawk″ẽr, *n.* 1. a tarantula or spider, especially one of the genus *Mygale.*
2. a member of one of the bands of abolitionist guerillas who roved through Kansas and neighboring states during the Civil War. [Slang.]
3. [J–] a native or inhabitant of the state of Kansas. [Colloq.]

jāy′walk (wạk), *v.i.* [*jay,* stupid person, and *walk.*] to walk in or across a street without regard to traffic rules and signals.

jāy′walk′ẽr, *n.* one who jaywalks.

jazz, *n.* [from Creole patois *jass,* sexual term applied to the Congo dances (New Orleans).]
1. a kind of music, originally improvised but now also arranged, characterized by syncopation, rubato, heavily accented 4/4 time, dissonances, melodic variations, and unusual tonal effects on the saxophone, clarinet, trumpet, trombone, etc.: it originated among New Orleans Negro musicians.
2. any popular dance music.
3. a quality reminiscent of jazz music; lively spirit. [Slang.]

jazz, *a.* of, in, or like jazz.

jazz, *v.t.* to play or arrange as jazz.

jazz′i·ly, *adv.* in a jazzy manner.

jazz′y, *a.* 1. characterized by the qualities of jazz music.
2. lively. [Slang.]

jeal′ous (jel′), *a.* [ME. *jelous, gelous*; OFr. *jalous,* from LL. *zelosus,* full of zeal, from L. *zelus*; Gr. *zēlos,* zeal, emulation.]
1. suspicious; apprehensive of rivalry; as, her husband was *jealous* of the other man.
2. resulting from such a feeling; as, a *jealous* rage.
3. demanding exclusive loyalty; as, the Lord is a *jealous* God.
4. resentfully envious.
5. careful in protecting; watchful; solicitous; as, *jealous* of one's reputation.
6. doubtful. [Obs.]
Syn.—envious, covetous, invidious, suspicious.

jeal′ous·ly, *adv.* in a jealous manner.

jeal′ous·y, *n.*; *pl.* **jeal′ous·ieṣ,** [ME. *jelousie, gelousy*; OFr. *gelosie, jalousie,* from *gelos,* jealous.]
1. the state or quality of being jealous.
2. an instance of this.

jēan (jēn *or* jān), *n.* [LL. *Janua*; L. *Genua,* Genoa.]
1. strong, twilled cotton cloth for overalls.
2. [*pl.*] trousers or overalls of this material.

jed′ding ax, a cavel; an ax for trimming stone.

jee, *n., v.t.* and *v.i.* gee.

jeep, *n.* [orig. military slang from sound made by droll little animal (Eugene the Jeep) with extraordinary powers, in comic strip by E. C. Segar (1894–1938); supposedly suggested by *G. P., General Purpose Car.*] 1. a small, rugged automotive vehicle with a ¼-ton capacity and a four-wheel drive, capable of carrying four men or three men and a machine gun: first used by U. S. armed forces in World War II: also called *peep.*
2. a similar vehicle for civilian use.
3. in many military units, a larger vehicle with a ¾-ton capacity, used as a reconnaissance and command car: distinguished from *peep.*

jeer, *v.t.* and *v.i.*; jeered, *pt., pp.*; jeering, *ppr.* [perh. altered form of *cheer.*] to make fun of (a person or thing) in a rude, sarcastic manner; to mock; to taunt; to scoff (at).

jeer, *n.* railing language; a scoff; a taunt; a biting jest; a gibe; mockery; derision; ridicule with scorn.

jeer′ẽr, *n.* a scoffer; a railer; a scorner; a mocker.

jeer′ing·ly, *adv.* in a jeering manner; derisively.

jeerṣ, *n.pl.* [perh. altered form of *gears.*] the tackle by which the lower yards of a sailing vessel are hoisted or lowered.

Jef′fẽr·sō′ni·à, *n.* [after Thomas *Jefferson.*] a genus of herbaceous plants of the family *Berberidaceæ.*

Jef′fẽr·sō′ni·ăn, *a.* 1. of or characteristic of Thomas Jefferson.
2. of or like his ideas and principles; democratic.

Jef·fẽr·sō′ni·ăn, *n.* a follower of Thomas Jefferson; a believer in Jefferson's democratic ideas.

Jef·fẽr·sō′ni·ăn·iṣm, *n.* the practices which characterized the administration (1801–1809) of President Jefferson; the principles of Thomas Jefferson as diplomat and statesman.

jef′fẽr·sŏn·īte, *n.* [after Thomas *Jefferson.*] a variety of augite containing zinc, of a dark olive-green color passing into brown.

jeg, *n.* a jig or templet.

jē·häd′, *n.* same as *jihad.*

Jē·hosh′à·phat, *n.* [Heb. *yehoshaphat,* lit., God has judged.] in the Bible, a king of Judah in the 9th century B.C., noted for his righteousness: 2 Chron. xvii. ff.

Jē·hō′vȧh, *n.* [modern transliteration of the Heb. sacred name for God, the so-called tetragrammaton, YHWH; the vowels appear through arbitrary transference of the vowel points of *adōnāi,* my Lord.] God; (the) Lord.

Jē·hō′vȧh′ṣ Wit′nes·seṣ, a Christian sect founded by Charles T. Russell (1852–1916) and led after 1916 by Joseph F. ("Judge") Rutherford (1869–1942): its members are opposed to war and refuse to accept the authority of any government in matters of religious conscience: formerly called *International Bible Students Association* or *Russellites.*

Jē·hō′viç, *a.* of Jehovah.

Jē·hō′vist, *n.* 1. a person holding the opinion that the correct transliteration of the Hebrew sacred name for God is *Jehovah.*
2. the author of those parts of the Old Testament in which *Jehovah* (*Yahweh*) is used as the name of God; a Yahwist.

Jē·hō·vis′tiç, *a.* 1. pertaining to a Jehovist, or his views.
2. using the word *Jehovah* (*Yahweh*) as the name for God: distinguished from *Elohistic.*

Jē′hū, *n.* [Heb.] 1. in the Bible, a king of Israel in the 9th century B.C., described as a furious charioteer: 2 Kings ix. 6 and 20.
2. [j–] a fast, reckless driver or coachman: humorous term.

jē·jū′năl, *a.* relating to the jejunum.

jē·jūne′, *a.* [L. *jejunus,* empty, dry, barren.]
1. not nourishing; barren.
2. not satisfying; not interesting; dull and flat; as, a *jejune* story.

jē·jū·neç′tō·my, *n.* [*jejunum,* and *-ectomy.*] the surgical removal of all or part of the jejunum.

jē·jūne′ly, *adv.* in a jejune, barren manner.

jē·jū′ni·ty, *n.* quality or state of being jejune.

jē·jū′num, *n.* [L. *jejunus,* empty, dry, barren.] the portion of the intestines between the duodenum and the ileum: so named because thought to be empty after death.

Je′kyll, Dr., a doctor in Robert Louis Stevenson's story *Dr. Jekyll and Mr. Hyde,* who discovers drugs that enable him to change back and forth between his own pleasant personality and a vicious, brutal one named Mr. Hyde.

jel′ẽr·ang, *n.* a large squirrel of Java and Asia; the Java squirrel.

jell, *v.i.* and *v.t.* [from *jelly.*]
1. to become or cause to become jelly. [Colloq.]
2. to take or cause to take definite form; to crystallize; as, our plans haven't *jelled* yet. [Colloq.]

jell, *n.* jelly. [Colloq.]

jel′lied, *a.* 1. changed into jelly.
2. served in or with jelly.
3. coated with jelly.

jel′li·fȳ, *v.t.* and *v.i.*; jellified, *pt.*; *pp.*; jellifying, *ppr.* to change into jelly.

jel′ly, *n.*; *pl.* **jel′lieṣ,** [formerly *gelly,* from ME. *gely, gelé*; OFr. *gelée,* a frost, jelly, properly f. pp. of *geler,* from L. *gelare,* to freeze.]
1. a soft, resilient, partially transparent, semisolid, gelatinous food resulting from the cooling of fruit juice boiled with sugar, or of meat juice cooked down.
2. any substance like this; gelatinous substance.
jelly bag; a bag for straining jelly.
jelly plant; an Australian seaweed used for making jelly.
jelly powder; an explosive compound of collodion and nitroglycerin which has the appearance of jelly.

jel′ly, *v.t.*; jellied, *pt., pp.*; jellying, *ppr.* 1. to make into jelly.
2. to put jelly on.

jel′ly, *v.i.* to become jelly.

jel′ly·bēan, *n.* a small, gelatinous candy shaped like a bean.

jel′ly·fish, *n.*; *pl.* **jel′ly·fish, jel′ly·fish·eṣ,** 1. any of a number of related sea animals with a body made up largely of jellylike substance and shaped like an umbrella; medusa: it has long, hanging tentacles with stinging hairs on them.
2. a weak-willed person. [Colloq.]

jel′ly·rōll, *n.* a thin sheet of sponge cake spread with jelly and rolled so as to form layers.

jem′à·där, *n.* [Hind., from Per. *jemā'at,* body of men, and *dar,* one who holds.] formerly, a native officer in the army of India, second in rank in a sepoy company.

Jem′lȧh gōat, the thar.

jem′mi·ness, *n.* spruceness. [Obs. except Dial.]

jem′my, *a.* spruce. [Obs. except Dial.]

jem′my, *n.*; *pl.* **jem′mieṣ,** [from dim. of *James*; compare *jack,* a mechanical device.]
1. a short, stout crowbar used by housebreakers for opening doors; a jimmy.
2. a baked sheep's head. [Brit. Slang.]
3. a sort of riding boot. [Obs.]

jem′my, *v.t.*; jemmied, *pt., pp.*; jemmying, *ppr.* to jimmy.

jē nē sāis quoi (zhẽ nē sākwä′), [Fr.] I know not what; hence, a thing hard to describe or express.

jē′nīte, *n.* same as *yenite.*

Jeñ′kinṣ, *n.* one who toadies to prominent people. [Colloq.]

jen′net, *n.* [OFr. *genette*; Sp. *jinete,* a nag, originally a mounted soldier, Ar. *Zenāta,* a tribe of Barbary.]
1. any of a breed of small Spanish horses.
2. a female donkey.

jen′net·ing, *n.* [Fr. *Jeannet, Jem,* John: so named for being ripe on St. John's day, June 24.] a species of early apple.

jen′ny, *n.*; *pl.* **jen′nieṣ,** 1. a spinning machine with a number of spindles; a spinning jenny.
2. the female of some animals; as, a *jenny* wren.

jen′ny wren (ren), a plant, *Geranium robertianum*; the American herb Robert.

jeof′āil (jef′āl), *n.* [Fr. *j'ai failli,* I have failed.] formerly, in law, an oversight in pleading or other proceeding; also, the acknowledgment of a mistake.

jeop′ärd (jep′), *v.t.* to hazard; to put in danger; to jeopardize.

jeop′ärd·ẽr, *n.* one who puts in jeopardy.

jeop′ärd·īze, *v.t.*; jeopardized, *pt., pp.*; jeopardizing, *ppr.* to expose to loss, damage, or failure of; to put in jeopardy; to endanger.

jeop′ärd·ous, *a.* exposed to danger; perilous; hazardous.

jeop′ärd·ous·ly, *adv.* in a jeopardous manner.

jeop′ärd·y, *n.*; *pl.* **jeop′ärd·ieṣ,** [ME. *jepardie, jeopardie*; OFr. *jeu parti,* lit., a divided game, a game in which the chances are even; LL. *jocus partitus,* an even chance, an alternative; L. *jocus,* a joke, play, game, and *partire,* to divide.]
1. risk; danger; peril.
2. in criminal law, exposure to conviction; situation of an accused person when being tried.

jeop′ärd·y, *v.t.* same as *jeopardize.*

Jeph′thȧh, *n.* [Heb.] in the Bible, the judge who killed his only daughter because he had vowed that if he won in battle he would sacrifice to God whatever he first met coming from his house on his return, and this turned out to be his daughter: Judg. xi. 30–40.

jē·quir′i·ty, *n.* [Fr. *jéquirity,* from Tupi-Guarani.]
1. the poisonous, red and black seed of the Indian licorice plant, used for beads, as a weight, and in medicine.
2. the plant it grows on.
Also *jequirity bean.*

jẽr·bō′à, *n.* [Ar. *yarbū,* an oblique, descending muscle: so called in allusion to the strong muscles of its hind legs.] a small, leaping rodent of northern Africa and Asia, with long hind legs.

JERBOA
(15 in. long, including tail)

jerboa kangaroo; a small marsupial of Australia; the bettong.
jerboa mouse; a kangaroo rat.

jer·eed′, *n.* [Ar. *jerīd, jarīd,* rod, shaft, javelin.]
1. a blunted javelin used by Turks, Arabs, etc. in warlike games.
2. a mock battle with such javelins.
Also spelled *jerid, jerreed, jerrid.*

jer·ē·mī′ad, jer·ē·mī′ade, *n.* [Fr. *jérémiade,* from *Jérémie,* Jeremiah.] a lamentation or tale of woe: in allusion to the *Lamentations of Jeremiah* in the Bible.

Jer·ē·mī′ȧh, *n.* 1. in the Bible, a Hebrew prophet of the 6th and 7th centuries B.C.
2. a book of the Old Testament containing his prophecies.

Jer·ē·mī′ăs, *n.* Jeremiah: form used in the Douay Bible.

jĕr′fal″çŏn (-fa̤″kn *or* -fal″kŏn), *n.* same as *gerfalcon.*

jer·īd′, *n.* same as *jereed.*

jĕrk, *n.* [from Sp. *charqui,* dried meat.] jerked meat, especially beef.

jĕrk, *v.t.*; jerked, *pt., pp.*; jerking, *ppr.* to preserve (meat) by slicing it into strips and drying these in the sun or over a fire.

jĕrk, *v.t.*; jerked, *pt., pp.*; jerking, *ppr.* [etym. uncertain.]
1. to pull at, twist, push, thrust, or throw with a sudden, sharp movement.
2. to utter in quick, sharp ejaculations or gasps (with *out*).

jĕrk, *v.i.* 1. to move with a jerk or in jerks.
2. to twitch.

jĕrk, *n.* 1. a sharp, abrupt movement; a quick pull, twist, push, etc.
2. a sudden muscular contraction caused by a reflex action.
3. a person regarded as stupid, dull, eccentric, etc. [Slang.]

jĕrk, jĕrque, *v.t.* [It. *cercare* (*pron.* cher-kä′re), to search.] to search (a vessel) for unentered goods. [Brit. Dial.]

jĕrked beef, beef cut into long strips and dried in the sun.

jĕrk′ĕr, jĕr′quĕr, (-kĕr), *n.* a customs officer who searches vessels for unentered goods. [Brit. Dial.]

jĕrk′ĕr, *n.* one who or that which jerks.

jĕrk′i·ly, *adv.* in a jerky manner; with abrupt starts and stops.

jĕr′kin, *n.* [perh. from OFr. *Joire, Jour,* familiar form of George, and *-kin,* dim. suffix.]
1. a short, close-fitting coat or jacket, often sleeveless, worn in the 16th and 17th centuries.
2. a short, sleeveless vest worn by women and girls.
3. a kind of hawk, the male of the gerfalcon.

jĕrk′i·ness, *n.* the quality of moving jerkily.

jĕrk′ing·ly, *adv.* in a jerking manner; with or by jerks.

jĕr′kin-head (-hed), *n.* the end of a roof formed into a shape intermediate between a gable and a hip: the gable rises about halfway to the ridge, so as to have a truncated shape, and the roof is hipped or inclined backward from this level.

JERKINHEAD ROOF

jĕrk′wa̤·tĕr, *n.* [*jerk,* v., to pull, and *water.*] a train on an early branch railroad.

jĕrk′wa̤·tĕr, *a.* small, unimportant, etc.; as, a *jerkwater* town. [Colloq.]

jĕrk′y, *a.*; *comp.* jerkier; *superl.* jerkiest. 1. characterized by jerks; making sudden starts and stops.
2. making convulsive or spasmodic movements.

jĕrk′y, *n.* [from Sp. *charqui,* dried meat.] jerked beef.

jĕr·mo̤on′ăl, *n.* a species of snow partridge found in the Himalayas.

Jĕr·ō·bō′ăm, *n.* [Heb. *yārobh'ām,* lit., prob., the people increases.] in the Bible, (a) the first king of the northern kingdom, Israel, after the death of Solomon, and the division into the kingdoms of Israel and Judah: 1 Kings xi. 26–xiv. 20; (b) a rich king of Israel: 2 Kings xiv. 23–29.

Jē·ron′y·mīte, *n.* same as *Hieronymite.*

jer·ō·pig′i·ȧ, *n.* same as *geropigia.*

jĕr′quĕr (-kĕr), *n.* see *jerker* (customs officer).

jĕr·reed′, jĕr·rid′, *n.* same as *jereed.*

Jer′ry, *n.*; *pl.* **Jer′ries,** [from *German.*] a German, especially a German soldier. [Chiefly Brit. Slang.]

jer′ry-build″ĕr (-bild″), *n.* one who builds cheap, unsubstantial buildings of inferior materials.

jer′ry-built, *a.* [originated in Liverpool, England, c. 1860; prob. from name *Jerry,* reinforced by nautical term *jury.*] built hurriedly and of inferior materials; flimsy.

Jĕr′ṣey, *n.* any of a breed of small, reddish-brown dairy cattle, originally from Jersey, one of the Channel islands: its milk has a high butterfat content.

jĕr′ṣey, *n.*; *pl.* **jĕr′ṣeyṣ,** [from *Jersey,* the Channel island.]
1. a soft, elastic, knitted cloth of wool, cotton, silk, or rayon.
2. a close-fitting pull-on sweater or shirt worn by athletes, sailors, etc.
3. any close-fitting, knitted upper garment.

Jĕr′ṣey cen′ta̤u·ry, a perennial Mediterranean herb, *Centaurea aspera,* having purple flower heads resembling the thistle.

Jĕr′ṣey çrēam (krēm), a light reddish yellow having a high brilliance and low saturation point.

Jĕr′ṣey çud′weed, the common European everlasting of the genus *Gnaphalium.*

Jĕr′ṣey līght′ning (-līt), applejack. [Slang.]

Jĕr·ū′sȧ·lem är′ti·chōke, [altered from It. *girasole,* sunflower, from L. *girare,* to turn, and *sol,* sun.]
1. a kind of sunflower with coarse hairy leaves, small yellow flowers, and potatolike tubers used as a vegetable.
2. a tuber of this plant.

Jĕr·ū′sȧ·lem cher·ry, a plant, or its fruit, a bright-red berry, belonging to the family *Solanaceæ.*

Jĕr·ū′sȧ·lem ōak, a common aromatic weed of the goosefoot family.

Jĕr·ū′sȧ·lem pō′ny, an ass.

jĕr′vine, jĕr′vin, *n.* [Sp. *jerva,* the poison of the *Veratrum,* and *-ine.*] a weakly poisonous alkaloid obtained from the root of *Veratrum album,* or white hellebore.

jess, *n.* [ME. *ges*; OFr. *gies, ges, gets,* pl.; see *jet* (a gush): so called from its use in letting a hawk fly.] a strap for fastening around a falcon's leg, with a ring at one end for attaching a leash.

jess, *v.t.* to fasten a jess on.

jes′sȧ·mine, jes′sȧ·min, *n.* same as *jasmine.*

jes′sănt, *a.* [corruption of *issuant.*] in heraldry, shooting forth; issuing.

jes′sănt-de-līs′ (-lē′), *n.* in heraldry, the head of a leopard having a fleur-de-lis passing through it.

JESSANT-DE-LIS

Jes′sē, *n.* [L.; Gr. *Iessai*; Heb. *yīshay*; meaning uncertain.] in the Bible, the father of David: 1 Sam. xvi.
Jesse window; in architecture, a window depicting the genealogical descent of Jesus from Jesse, either painted on the glass or carved on the mullions.

jessed (jest), *a.* in heraldry, having jesses on, as a hawk.

jest, *n.* [ME. *geste, jeste*; OFr. *geste,* an exploit, tale of exploits; L. *gesta,* neut. pl. pp. of *gerere,* to perform, carry out.]
1. a mocking or bantering remark; a jibe; a taunt.
2. a joke; a witticism.
3. a joking; fun; ridicule.
4. something to be laughed at or joked about.
5. (a) a notable deed; (b) a story of exploits; (c) an unfounded tale. [Obs.]

jest, *v.i.* 1. to jeer; to mock; to banter.
2. to be playful in speech and actions; to joke.

jest′book, *n.* a book made up of jokes and humorous anecdotes.

jest′ĕr, *n.* a person given to jesting, sportive talk, and merry pranks; a joker; especially, a professional fool employed by a ruler in the Middle Ages to amuse him with antics, tricks, and jokes.

jest′fu̦l, *a.* given to jesting; full of jokes.

jest′ing, *a.* joking; talking for diversion or merriment.

jest′ing, *n.* a joking; the act of jesting or of making a jest.

jest′ing·ly, *adv.* in a jesting manner.

jest′ing·stock, *n.* a laughingstock: a butt for ridicule. [Rare.]

Jē′ṣū, *n.* Jesus. [Poetic.]

Jeṣ′ū·āte, *n.* [It. *Gesuato,* from *Gesu,* Jesus.] a member of a religious order founded by Colombini in 1367 and abolished by Pope Clement IX in 1668.

Jeṣ′ū·it, *n.* [Fr. *Jésuite,* from L. *Iesus* or *Jesus,* Jesus, and *-ite.*]
1. a member of the Society of Jesus, a Roman Catholic religious order founded by Ignatius Loyola in 1534.
2. [j–] a crafty schemer; a cunning dissembler; a casuist: hostile term.
Jesuit bark; Peruvian bark; the bark of certain species of *Cinchona.*
Jesuit nut; the water chestnut.
Jesuits' powder; powdered cinchona bark. [Obs.]
Jesuits' tea; maté; Mexican tea.

Jeṣ·ū·it′iç, Jeṣ·ū·it′iç·ăl, *a.* 1. pertaining to the Jesuits or their principles, practices, etc.
2. [j–] cunning; deceitful: hostile term.

jeṣ·ū·it′iç·ăl·ly, *adv.* craftily.

Jeṣ′ū·it·iṣm, *n.* 1. the teachings, principles, and practices of the Jesuits.
2. [j–] cunning; deceit; hypocrisy: hostile term, as used by anti-Jesuits.

Jeṣ″ū·it·oç′rȧ·cy, *n.* Jesuitical government; also, the entire body of Jesuits, as in a country.

Jeṣ′ū·it·ry, *n.* Jesuitism.

Jē′ṣus, *n.* [L. *Iesus*; Gr. *Iēsous*; from Heb. *yēshū'a,* contr. of *yehōshu'a,* help of Jehovah; *yāh,* Jehovah, and *hōshīa,* to help.]
1. the founder of the Christian religion: 4? B.C.–29? A.D. (the birth date is the result of later revision of the calendar): often *Jesus Christ, Jesus of Nazareth.*
2. the author of *Ecclesiasticus,* one of the books of the Apocrypha.
the Society of Jesus; see *Jesuit.*

jet, *n.* [ME. *jet, jette, get*; OFr. *get, giet, ject,* a throw, spurt, from L. *jactus,* a throw, cast, properly pp. of *jacere,* to throw.]
1. a stream of water or other liquid suddenly emitted, as from a spout; a gush.
2. a similar stream of gas.
3. a spout or nozzle for emitting a stream of water or gas.
4. a jet-propelled airplane.

jet, *v.t.* and *v.i.*; jetted, *pt., pp.*; jetting, *ppr.* [Fr. *jeter*; LL. *jectare*; L. *jactare,* to throw, from *jacere,* to throw.] to spout, gush, or shoot out in a stream, as liquid or gas.

jet, *a.* jet-propelled.

jet, *n.* [ME. *jet, geete*; OFr. *jaiet*; L. *gagates*; Gr. *gagatēs,* jet, from *Gagas,* a town and river of Lycia in Asia Minor.]
1. a variety of lignite, of a very compact texture and velvet-black color, susceptible of a good polish and glossy in its fracture: used in jewelry when polished.
2. a deep, glossy black.

jet, *a.* made of jet; black, like jet.

jet′-black′, *a.* very glossy black, like jet.

jet d'eau′ (zhā dō′); *pl.* **jets d'eau′** (zhā), [Fr. a jet of water.] a stream of spouting water, as in a fountain.

Jeth′rō, *n.* [Heb. *yitherō.*] in the Bible, the father of Moses' wife: Ex. xviii.

jet′līn·ĕr, *n.* [*jet,* and *liner.*] a commercial jet aircraft for carrying passengers.

jet′ŏn, *n.* see *jetton.*

jet′pōrt, *n.* [*jet,* and air*port.*] an airport with long runways, for use by jet airplanes.

jet′-prō·pelled′, *a.* driven by jet propulsion.

jet prō·pul′sion, a method of propelling airplanes, boats, and bombs by causing gases to be emitted under pressure through a vent at the rear.

JET-PROPELLED PLANE

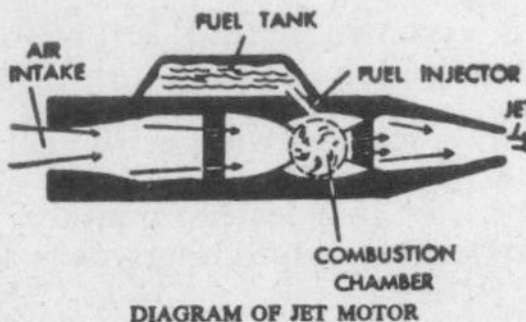

DIAGRAM OF JET MOTOR

jet'sam, jet'som, *n.* [OFr. *getaison, gettaison,* a throwing, jetsam, from L. *jactatio* (*-onis*), a throwing, from *jactare,* to throw, hurl.]
 1. that part of the cargo thrown overboard to lighten a ship in danger: distinguished from *flotsam.*
 2. such discarded cargo washed ashore.
 3. discarded things.

jet'tẽr, *n.* [ME. *jettour, jectour;* OFr. *jettour, jetteur,* from L. *jactator,* a boaster.] a spruce fellow; one who struts or swaggers. [Obs.]

jet'ti·sŏn, *n.* [OFr. *getaison, gettaison,* a throwing, jetsam, from L. *jactatio,* a throwing, from *jactare,* to throw, hurl.]
 1. a throwing overboard of goods to lighten a ship, airplane, etc. in an emergency.
 2. jetsam.

jet'ti·sŏn, *v.t.* 1. to throw (goods) overboard.
 2. to throw (something) away as useless or a burden.

jet'tŏn, *n.* [Fr. *jeton,* a throw, counter, from *jeter,* to throw, cast.] a small metal counter used in some games of cards.

jet'ty, *n.; pl.* **jet'ties,** [OFr. *jetée, jettee, getee,* a cast, jetty, jutty, from *jetter, jeter,* to throw.]
 1. a kind of wall built out into the water to restrain currents, protect a harbor or the end of a pier, etc.
 2. a landing pier.
 3. a projecting portion of a building, especially a portion that projects so as to overhang the wall below, as in the upper stories of a frame house. [Obs.]

jet'ty, *v.t.* jettied, *pt., pp.;* jettying, *ppr.* to furnish with a jetty; as, to *jetty* the mouth of a river.

jet'ty, *v.i.* to jut; to extend out or over. [Obs.]

jet'ty, *a.* very black, like jet.

jet'ty·head (-hed), *n.* the projecting part of a jetty or wharf. [Brit.]

jeu (zhũ), *n.; pl.* **jeux** (zhũ), [Fr.] a game; diversion.

jeu de mōts' (zhũ de mō'), [Fr.] a play on words; a pun.

jeu d'es·prit' (zhũ de-sprē'), [Fr., lit., a play of spirit.] a witticism; a play of wit; a clever turn of phrase.

jeune fille (zhũn fē'y), [Fr.] a young girl.

jeu·nesse' do·rée' (zhũ-nes' do-rā'), [Fr., lit., gilded youth.] the rich, fashionable youth of a community; specifically, in France, the fashionable set of the reactionary party in 1794.

Jew (jü), *n.* [ME. *Jew, Giw;* OFr. *jeu, geu;* L. *Judæus;* Gr. *Ioudaios,* a Jew, an inhabitant of Judea, from *Ioudaia,* Judea, from Heb. *yehūdhāh,* Judah.]
 1. a person descended, or regarded as descended, from the ancient Hebrews of Biblical times.
 2. a person whose religion is Judaism.

Jew, *a.* Jewish: in this sense used vulgarly, as by anti-Semites.

jew, *v.t.* to get the better of in bargaining, as by sharp practices, or haggle with in order to get a lower price or a better bargain (usually with *down*): vulgar and offensive expression, in allusion to methods attributed to Jewish merchants by anti-Semites. [Colloq.]
 Jew's frankincense; a resin obtained from the plant *Styrax officinale.*
 Jew's pitch; bitumen of Judea; asphalt.

Jew'-bāit"ẽr, *n.* a person who abuses or persecutes Jews.

Jew'-bāit"ing, *n.* persecution of Jews, as a manifestation of anti-Semitism.

jew'bush, *n.* a West Indian plant, *Pedilanthus tithymaloides,* having drastic emetic qualities.

Jew çrōw, the hooded crow; the chough. [Brit. Dial.]

jew'el, *n.* [ME. *jewel, jouel, jowel;* OFr. *jouel, joel;* hyp. ML. *jocale,* from L. *jocus,* a trifle, joke.]
 1. a valuable ornament, often set with gems.
 2. a precious stone; a gem.
 3. any person or thing very dear to one.
 4. a small gem or gemlike object used as one of the bearings in a watch.

jew'el, *v.t.;* jeweled *or* jewelled, *pt., pp.;* jeweling *or* jewelling, *ppr.* to decorate or set with jewels.

jew'el block, in nautical usage, either of two small blocks suspended from the ends of a yardarm to lead the studdingsail halyards through.

jew'el çāse (or **box**), a case or box to keep jewels in.

jew'el·ẽr, jew'el·lẽr, *n.* [ME. *jueler;* OFr. *joieleor,* from *joel, jouel,* a jewel.] one who makes, deals in, or repairs jewels, watches, etc.

jew'el·house, *n.* the place in the Tower of London where the royal ornaments are deposited. [Brit.]

jew'el·līke, *a.* brilliant as a jewel.

jew'el·ry, jew'el·lẽr·y, *n.* jewels collectively.

jew'el·weed, *n.* any of a number of related plants bearing yellow or orange-yellow flowers with three sepals and a spur, and seed pods that curl at the touch when ripe; touch-me-not; snapweed.

Jew'ess, *n.* a Jewish woman or girl: often a patronizing or contemptuous term.

jew'fish, *n.; pl.* **jew'fish·eș, jew'fish,** any of several fishes, including *Promicrops guasa* and *Megalops atlanticus,* the tarpon, of the Atlantic coast, and the black sea bass of the California coast.

jew'ing, *n.* the wattle at the base of the beak of certain pigeons and other birds.

Jew'ish, *a.* of, characteristic of, or relating to the Jews.

Jew'ish, *n.* popularly, Yiddish.

Jew'ish çal'en·dăr, a calendar used by the Jews in calculating Jewish history, holidays, etc., based on the lunar month and reckoned from 3761 B.C., the traditional date of the Creation.

Months of the Jewish Calendar
1. *Tishri* (30 days)
2. *Cheshvan* (29 or 30 days)
3. *Kislev* (29 or 30 days)
4. *Tebet* (29 days)
5. *Shebat* (30 days)
6. *Adar* (29 or 30 days)
7. *Nisan* (30 days)
8. *Iyar* (29 days)
9. *Sivan* (30 days)
10. *Tammuz* (29 days)
11. *Ab* (30 days)
12. *Elul* (29 days)

N.B. About once every three years (seven times in each nineteen years) an extra month, *Veadar* (29 days), falls between *Adar* and *Nisan,* as the Jewish year has only 354 days. The first month, *Tishri,* begins in late September or early October. Alternative names of the months are: for *Tishri, Ethanim;* for *Cheshvan, Marcheshvam* or *Bul;* for *Nisan, Abib;* for *Iyar, Zif;* for *Veadar, Adar Sheni.*

Jew'ish dāy, the period from sunset to sunset.

Jew'ish hol'i·dāyș, the holidays of the Jewish religion, including:
 1. *Rosh Hashana,* New Year (*Tishri* 1, 2)
 2. *Yom Kippur,* Day of Atonement (*Tishri* 10)
 3. *Sukkoth,* Feast of Tabernacles (*Tishri* 15–22)
 4. *Simchath Torah,* Rejoicing in the Law (*Tishri* 23)
 5. *Hanukkah,* Feast of the Dedication, Festival of Lights (*Kislev* 25–*Tebet* 2)
 6. *Purim,* Feast of Lots (*Adar* 14)
 7. *Pesach,* the Passover (*Nisan* 15–22)
 8. *Lag b'Omer,* 33d day from the 2d of Passover (*Iyar* 18)
 9. *Shabuoth,* Feast of Weeks, Pentecost (*Sivan* 6, 7)
 10. *Tishah b'Ab,* a day of fasting (*Ab* 9), in commemoration of the destruction of the Temple.

Jew'ish·ly, *adv.* after the custom of the Jews.

Jew'ish·ness, *n.* the state of being Jewish.

Jew'ry, *n.* [OFr. *juerie,* from *Jeu,* a Jew.]
 1. a district inhabited only or mainly by Jews; ghetto.
 2. the Jewish people; Jews collectively.

Jew'ș'-ap"ple, *n.* same as *eggplant.*

Jew'ș'-ēar, *n.* an edible fungus, *Hirneola auricula-judæ.*

jew'ș'-härp, jewș''-härp, *n.* 1. an instrument of music usually made of iron and played by placing against the slightly sepa-

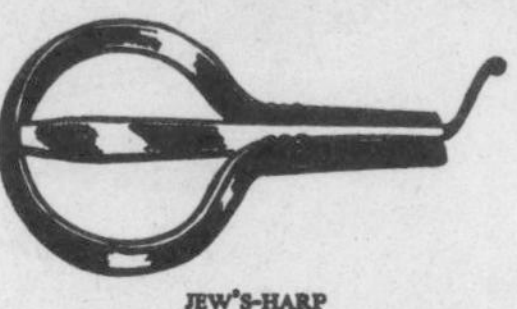
JEW'S-HARP

rated front teeth its two parallel jaws, between which a steel tongue is made to vibrate by plucking a projecting bent piece with the finger: it produces twanging tones.
 2. in nautical usage, a kind of fastening by which a cable is attached to the anchor ring.

Jewș' mal'lōw, a plant, a species of *Corchorus.*

Jewș''-stōne, Jew'stōne, *n.* the club-shaped spine of a fossil echinus.

Jewș''-thorn, *n.* same as *Christ's-thorn.*

Jez'e·bel, *n.* [from *Jezebel,* the wife of Ahab (1 Kings xvi. 31).] any woman regarded as shameless, wicked, etc.

jhä'răl, *n.* [native name.] the thar, a wild mountain goat of India, *Capra jemlaica.*

jhīl, jheel, *n.* [Hind.] in India, a pool or lagoon left after an inundation and covered or surrounded with a rank growth of plants.

jib, *n.* [prob. from *gibbet.*] the projecting arm of a crane; boom of a derrick.

jib, *v.i.* and *v.t.;* jibbed, *pt., pp.;* jibbing, *ppr.* [var. of former *gibe.*] in nautical usage, to jibe; to shift: also spelled *jibb.*

jib, *n.* [prob. from *jib,* to shift, because the sail is easily jibbed.] the foremost sail of a ship, being a large, triangular staysail extended from the outer end of the jib boom toward the foretopmasthead.
 inner jib; the after of two jibs which take the place of one large jib on a boom: distinguished from the *outer jib,* which is the forward jib of the two.
 the cut of one's jib; one's personal appearance or way of dressing. [Colloq.]

jib, *v.i.;* jibbed, *pt., pp.;* jibbing, *ppr.* [ME. *regibben,* to kick back; OFr. *regiber,* to wince, kick; prob. of Scand. origin.]
 1. to stop and refuse to go forward; to balk.
 2. to move backward or sideways instead of ahead.
 3. to start or shy (*at* something).

jib, *n.* [prob. from *jib, v.i.*]
 1. a jibbing, or balking, etc.
 2. an animal that jibs, or balks, as a horse.

jib'bẽr, *n.* one who jibs; a horse that jibs.

jib boom, a spar run out from the extremity of the bowsprit of a ship, serving as a continuation of it: beyond it is sometimes extended the flying-jib boom.

jib dōor, *n.* a door which stands flush with the wall, without dressing or moldings.

jībe, *v.i.;* jibed, *pt., pp.;* jibing, *ppr.* [from D. *gijpen,* to shift over (of sails).]
 1. to shift from one side of a ship to the other: said of a fore-and-aft sail or its boom when the course is changed in a following or quartering wind.
 2. to change the course of a ship so that the sails shift thus; to change tack without going about.
 3. to be in harmony, agreement, or accord; as, our views don't *jibe.* [Colloq.]

jībe, *v.t.* in nautical usage, to cause to jibe.

jībe, *n.* 1. a shift of sail or boom from one side of a ship to another.
 2. a change of course brought about by jibing.

jībe, *v.i.* and *v.t.;* jibed, *pt., pp.;* jibing, *ppr.* [var. of *gibe.*] to jeer; to scoff (at).

jībe, *n.* a jeer; a taunt.

jib'head (-hed), *n.* in nautical usage, a piece of iron fastened to the end of a shortened jib.

jib'head·ed, *a.* 1. cut like a jib; triangular: said of fore-and-aft sails.
 2. rigged with sails (especially the mainsail) so cut.

jib'-head"ẽr, *n.* a topsail that has the shape of a jib.

jib top'sāil (*or* -sl), a small jib set between the mast and the boom, flying from the extremity of the flying-jib boom.

jiff, *n.* a jiffy. [Colloq.]

jif'fy, *n.*; *pl.* **jif'fies,** [early 18th-c. slang.] a very short time; an instant; as, I will be there in a *jiffy*.

jig, *n.* [OFr. *gigue, gige*, a fiddle, a kind of dance; M.H.G. *gige*, a fiddle.]
1. a fast, gay, springy sort of dance, usually in triple time.
2. the music for such a dance.
3. any of several kinds of fishhook, sometimes arranged in sets, having a spoonlike part that twirls in trolling so as to attract fish.
4. any of several mechanical devices operated in a jerky manner, as a sieve for separating ores, a pounding machine, or a drill.
5. a device, often with metal surfaces, used as a guide for a tool or as a template.
6. a sportive trick or practical joke. [Brit. Dial.]
the jig is up; that ends it; all chances for a successful completion are gone: said of enterprises involving risk or danger.

jig, *v.i.* and *v.t.*; jigged, *pt. pp.*; jigging, *ppr.*
1. to dance or perform (a jig or in jig style).
2. to move jerkily and quickly up and down or to and fro.
3. to use a jig (on) in working or fishing.
4. to deceive; to delude; to cheat; to defraud. [Obs.]

jig'-drill"ing, *n.* drilling by the use of a jig, so as to secure accuracy of dimension or of position.

jig'-fil"ing, *n.* filing by the use of a jig, so as to secure exactness of dimension.

jig'gẽr, *n.* 1. a person who jigs.
2. a small cup or glass used to measure liquor, containing usually $1^1/_2$ fluid ounces.
3. the quantity of liquor in a jigger.
4. any thing, device, or contraption whose name does not occur to one; gadget.
5. in billiards, a support or bridge for the cue.
6. in fishing, a jig, or kind of hook.
7. in golf, a short club with an iron head and narrow face, used for approach shots: it is like a midiron.
8. in mechanics, any of several devices with a jerky motion in operation.
9. in mining, a jig, or kind of sieve.
10. in nautical usage, (a) a small tackle; (b) a small sail; (c) a small boat with such a sail; (d) a jigger mast.
11. in printing, a compositor's guide mark.
12. in radio, an oscillation transformer.
13. in agriculture, the person who shakes down the grain into sacks during bagging.

jig'gẽr, *n.* [altered from *chigoe.*]
1. a small tropical flea.
2. a mite larva or tick that burrows into the skin.

jig'gẽr mȧst, the aftmost mast of a four-masted ship; also, the small stern mast of a yawl.

jig'ging, *n.* in mining, the process of separating ore with a jigger.

jig'ging mȧ· chine', 1. a machine for separating ore by jigging.
2. a machine having a tool for cutting or for boring, the action of which is controlled by a jig.

jig'gish, *a.* 1. of, pertaining to, resembling, or suitable to a jig.
2. frolicsome; playful.

jig'gle, *v.t.* and *v.i.*; jiggled, *pt., pp.*; jiggling, *ppr.* [dim. or freq. of *jig*, v.] to move in a succession of quick, slight jerks; to rock lightly.

jig'gle, *n.* a jiggling movement.

jig'-jog, *n.* a jolting motion; a jog; a push.

jig pin, a pin used by miners to hold the turnbeams and prevent them from turning.

jig'saw, *n.* [*jig*, v., and *saw*, n.] a saw with a narrow blade set in a frame, used with a vertical motion for cutting along wavy or irregular lines, as in scroll work: also *jig saw.*

jig'saw puz'zle, a toy consisting of irregularly cut pieces of pasteboard, wood, etc. which when correctly fitted together form a picture, etc.

ji·hȧd', *n.* [Ar., a contest, war.]
1. a Moslem holy war; campaign against unbelievers or enemies of Islam.
2. a campaign for or against an idea, etc.; crusade.
Also spelled *jehad.*

Jill, *n.* [often j–] a young woman; also, a sweetheart.

jill'flirt, *n.* a light, wanton woman.

jilt, *n.* one who rejects a lover capriciously or wantonly.

jilt, *v.t.*; jilted, *pt., pp.*; jilting, *ppr.* to reject or cast off (a previously accepted lover or sweetheart); to trick in love; as, to *jilt* a lover.

jilt, *v.i.* to play the jilt; to practice deception in love.

jim'çrack, *n.* same as *gimcrack.*

Jim'-Crōw', *a.* discriminating against or segregating Negroes; as, *Jim-Crow* laws, schools, etc.

Jim Çrōw, [name of an early Negro minstrel song.]
1. discrimination against or segregation of Negroes: the current sense. [Colloq.]
2. a Negro: hostile term, now seldom used in this sense. [Slang.]
3. a planing machine having a reversible cutting tool.

jim'-çrōw', *a.* Jim-Crow. [Colloq.]

jim'-çrōw', *n.* 1. Jim Crow (sense 1).
2. in machinery, a strong iron frame with a screw for holding and straightening or bending iron rails or bars.

jim'-çrōw', *v.t.* to subject to Jim-Crow practices.

jim'jams, *n.pl.* [arbitrary echoic formation.]
1. delirium tremens. [Slang.]
2. a nervous feeling: also called *the jitters.* [Slang.]

jim'my, *n.*; *pl.* **jim'mies,** [dim. of *James.*] a burglar's tool used to break open doors and windows; a small crowbar: also *jemmy.*

jim'my, *v.t.*; jimmied, *pt., pp.*; jimmying, *ppr.* to use a jimmy on; to pry open with a jimmy or similar tool: also *jemmy.*

jimp, *a.* neat; handsome; slender in form. [North Eng. and Scot.]

jim'sŏn weed, Jim'sŏn weed, [altered from *Jamestown weed*, from *Jamestown*, Virginia.] a poisonous weed, *Datura stramonium*, the thorn apple.

jin, *n.* same as *jinn.*

jiñ'gal, *n.* [Hind. *jangāl*, a large musket, a swivel.] a large musket mounted as a swivel gun, formerly used in warfare in central Asia.

jiñ'gle, *v.i.*; jingled, *pt., pp.*; jingling, *ppr.* [ME. *gingelen, ginglen*, to jingle, akin to *chink.*]
1. to make a succession of light, ringing sounds, as small bells or bits of metal striking together; to tinkle.
2. to have obvious easy rhythm, simple repetitions of sound, etc., as some poetry and music.

jiñ'gle, *v.t.* to cause to jingle.

> The bells she *jingled*, and the whistle blew.
> —Pope.

jiñ'gle, *n.* 1. a jingling sound, as of little bells or pieces of metal.
2. a verse that jingles; jingling arrangement of words or syllables.
3. anything that makes a jingling sound, as a little bell or rattle.
4. a two-wheeled, covered cart used in the south of Ireland.
Syn.—rhyme, chime, tinkle, clink.

jiñ'glẽr, *n.* one who or that which jingles.

jiñ'gle shell, a bivalve shell; the gold shell.

jiñ'gling, *n.* a sharp, fine, tinkling sound, as of little bells.

jiñ'gly, *adj.* of or like a jingle; jingling.

jiñ'gō, *n.*; *pl.* **jiñ'gōes,** a person who boasts of his patriotism and favors an aggressive, threatening, warlike foreign policy; chauvinist: originally one of those who maintained that Great Britain should actively support the Turks in the Turko-Russian war of 1877–78: from the words of a song then popular:

> We don't want to fight, but, by *jingo*, if we do,
> We've got the ships, we've got the men, we've got the money, too.

by jingo! a meaningless exclamation used to indicate strong assertion, surprise, etc.

jiñ'gō, *a.* of jingoes; jingoistic; as, a *jingo* policy; *jingo* bluster.

jiñ'gō·ism, *n.* the principles and policy of jingoes.

jiñ·gō·is'tiç, *a.* of jingoes or jingoism.

jiñk, *v.i.* [Scot., from name of 17th-c. dance, *Hey-Jinks.*]
1. to move nimbly; to dodge. [Scot.]
2. to take all the tricks in some card games.

jiñk, *v.t.* to elude by moving nimbly; to dodge; to cheat. [Scot.]

jiñk, *n.* 1. a quick illusory turn; the act of eluding another. [Scot.]
2. [*pl.*] lively pranks; boisterous fun; horseplay: in full, usually, *high jinks.*

jinn, *n.* 1. plural of *jinni.*
2. *pl. jinns*, popularly, a jinni.

jin·ni', *n.*; *pl.* **jinn,** [Ar., pl. *jinn.*] in Moslem legend, a supernatural being that can take human or animal form and influence human affairs: also *jennee, genie.*

jin'ny rōad, in mining, an inclined railroad which loaded cars descend by their own weight, causing empty cars to ascend. [Brit.]

jin·rik'i·shȧ (-rik'shȧ), *n.* [Japan., from *jin*, a man, *riki*, power, and *sha*, carriage.] a small, two-wheeled oriental carriage with a hood, pulled by one or two men: also spelled *jinricksha, jinriksha, jinrickshaw.*

JINRIKISHA

jiñx, *n.* [perhaps from L. *iynx*, Gr. *iynx*, the wryneck, a bird used in incantations and charms.] a person or thing supposed to cause bad luck; hoodoo. [Slang.]

jiñx, *v.t.*; jinxed, *pt., pp.*; jinxing, *ppr.* to cause bad luck to. [Slang.]

jï·pi·jä'pä (hē-pi-hä'pä), *n.* a Central and South American plant whose leaves are extensively used in the manufacture of panama hats; also, a panama hat made from these leaves: after a town of this name in Ecuador.

jit'ney, *n.*; *pl.* **jit'neys,** [c. 1915; early prevalence of sense 3 suggests origin in Fr. automotive slang; perhaps from Fr. *jeter*, to throw.]
1. a five-cent coin; a nickel. [Slang.]
2. a bus or car that carries passengers for a small fare, originally five cents. [Slang.]
3. a small, cheap automobile. [Brit.]

jit'tẽr, *v.i.* [perhaps echoic.]
1. to be nervous; to have the jitters; fidget. [Slang.]
2. to jitterbug. [Slang.]
the jitters; a nervous feeling; fidgets. [Slang.]

jit'tẽr·bug, *n.* 1. one who dances to jazz music in a fast, acrobatic manner. [Slang.]
2. a devotee of jazz music, who listens to such music with obvious appreciation, often expressed in extravagant gestures and shouts. [Slang.]

jit'tẽr·bug, *v.i.*; jitterbugged, *pt., pp.*; jitterbugging, *ppr.* to dance in the manner of a jitterbug. [Slang.]

jit'tẽr·y, *a.* having the jitters; in a state of intense nervousness. [Slang.]

jiu·jit'su (jụ-), *n.* same as *jujitsu.*

jiu·jut'su (-jit' *or* -jụ'), *n.* same as *jujitsu.*

jīve, *n.* [perhaps a coinage, after *jibe.*]
1. in jazz, talking or joking while playing.
2. the jargon of jazz musicians and jazz devotees.
3. loosely, jazz.
[Slang in all senses.]

jō, jōe, *n.*; *pl.* **jōes,** a sweetheart. [Scot.]

Jō'ab, *n.* in the Bible, the commander of David's army.

job, *n.* [ME. *jobbe*, a portion, lump; orig., mouthful, from Celt. *gob, gop*, the mouth.]
1. a piece of work; a definite piece of work, as in one's trade, or done by agreement for pay.
2. anything one has to do; task; chore; duty.
3. the thing or material being worked on.
4. a thing done supposedly in the public interest but actually for private gain; dishonest piece of official business.
5. a position of employment; situation; work.
6. a criminal act or deed, as a theft, etc. [Colloq.]
7. any happening, affair, etc. [Colloq.]
by the job; at a stated price for a certain piece of work.
odd jobs; miscellaneous pieces of work.
on the job; (a) [Colloq.] while working at one's job; (b) [Slang.] attentive to one's task or duty.

job, *a.* hired or done by the job.

job, *v.i.*; jobbed, *pt., pp.*; jobbing, *ppr.* 1. to do odd jobs.
2. to act as a jobber or broker.
3. to do public or official business dishonestly for private gain.

job, *v.t.* 1. to buy (goods) in quantity from importers or manufacturers and sell to dealers; to handle as middleman.
2. to let or sublet (work, contracts, etc.).
3. to transact (public business) dishonestly for private gain.
4. to hire or let for hire, as a horse or carriage.

job, *n., v.t.* and *v.i.*; jobbed, *pt., pp.*; jobbing, *ppr.* [ME. *jobben*, to peck.] jab.

Jōb, *n.* in the Bible, (a) a man who endured much suffering and trouble but did not lose his faith in God; (b) a book of the Old Testament telling of him.
Job's comforter; a person who, while pretending to sympathize with one, really adds to one's afflictions by administering rebukes: see Job iv–vi.

job ac′tion, a joint refusal by a group of employees to perform all or part of their duties in an attempt to force the granting of certain demands; especially, such an action by a group forbidden by law to strike.

job ȧ·nal′y·sis, a study of a specific job, as in industry, with respect to operations and hazards involved, qualifications required of the worker, etc.

jō·bā′tion, *n.* a scolding; a long, tedious reproof. [Colloq.]

job′bẽr, *n.* 1. a person who jobs; one who buys goods in quantity from manufacturers or importers and sells them to dealers.
2. a person who works by the job; also, one who does piecework or hack work.
3. a person who does public or official business dishonestly for his own gain.
4. a person who deals in stock-exchange securities: distinguished from *broker*. [Brit.]

job′bẽr·y, *n.* the act or practice of carrying on public or official business dishonestly for private gain.

job′bing, *a.* pertaining to jobbery.

job′hōld·ẽr, *n.* a person who has a steady job; specifically, a government employee.

job′less, *a.* 1. without a job; unemployed.
2. having to do with the unemployed.

job lot, a miscellaneous assortment of goods, sold as a lot, usually to a retail merchant.

job print′ẽr, a printer who does various kinds of printing such as letterheads, circulars, posters, etc.

Jōb's′-tēars′, *n.* 1. a variety of grass, *Coix lacryma-jobi*, with hard, droplike, gray or whitish seeds.
2. its seeds, used as a cereal in the Orient, or as beads.

Jō·ças′tȧ, *n.* in Greek legend, the woman who unwittingly married her own son, Oedipus: she killed herself when she found out.

jock, *n.* 1. a jockey. [Colloq.]
2. a jockstrap. [Colloq.]

jock·ette′ (-et′), *n.* a woman jockey (sense 1.) [Colloq.]

jock′ey, *n.*; *pl.* **jock′eys,** [from *Jocky, Jockie*, the northern Eng. and Scot. pronunciation of *Jacky*, dim. of *Jack*, a name applied to boy servants, grooms, etc.]
1. one whose job is to ride a horse in a race.
2. a dealer in horses; one whose business is buying and selling horses for gain. [Dial.]
3. a cheat; one who deceives or takes undue advantage in trade.
4. same as *jockey pulley*.

jock′ey, *v.t.* and *v.i.*; jockeyed, *pt.*, *pp.*; jockeying, *ppr.* 1. to ride (a horse) in a race.
2. to cheat; to trick; to deceive in trade.
3. to maneuver for position or advantage.

jock′ey club, a club or association of persons interested in horse racing, etc.

jock′ey pul′ley, a small wheel which revolves on the rim of a larger grooved wheel, used to prevent a rope or hawser from slipping out of the groove.

jock′ey wheel (-hwēl), same as *jockey pulley*.

jock′ō, *n.* [Fr., earlier *engeco*, from *ncheko*, the native name in W. Africa.]
1. a chimpanzee.
2. any monkey.

jock′strap, *n.* [*jock*, male genital organs, from *Jock*, Scot. form of *Jack*; and *strap*.] an elastic belt with a groin pouch, worn for support by male athletes: also called *athletic supporter*.

jō·çōse′, *a.* [L. *jocosus*, from *jocus*, a joke, jest.]
1. given to jokes and jesting; merry; waggish.
2. containing a joke; of the nature of a joke; sportive; merry; as, a *jocose* or comical air.
Syn.—facetious, jocular, merry, humorous, waggish, witty, comical, droll.

jō·çōse′ly, *adv.* in a jocose manner; in jest; for sport or game; waggishly.

jō·çōse′ness, *n.* the quality of being jocose; waggery; merriment.

jō·ços′i·ty, *n.* 1. the quality or state of being jocose.
2. *pl.* **jō·ços′i·ties,** a jocose act or saying; a joke.

joç′ū·lăr, *a.* [L. *jocilaris*, from *jocus*, a joke, jest.]
1. jocose; waggish; merry; given to jesting; joking; humorous; full of fun.
2. said as a joke.

joç·ū·lar′i·ty, *n.* 1. the quality or state of being jocular.
2. *pl.* **joç·ū·lar′i·ties,** a jocular action or remark.

joç′ū·lăr·ly, *adv.* in jest; for sport or mirth.

joç′ū·lā·tŏr, *n.* [L., from *joculari*, to joke, jest, from *jocus*, a joke, jest.] a professional jester; also, a minstrel. [Obs.]

joç′ū·lā·tō·ry, *a.* droll. [Obs.]

joç′und (*or* jō′kund), *a.* [ME.; OFr. *jocond*; LL. *jocundus*; L. *jucundus*, pleasant, agreeable, orig., helpful, from *juvare*, to help.] merry; gay; cheerful; genial; sportive.
Syn.—gay, lighthearted, lively, merry, vivacious, mirthful, sprightly, sportive, cheerful.

jō·çun′di·ty, *n.* 1. the state of being jocund or merry; gaiety.
2. *pl.* **jō·çun′di·ties,** a jocund action or remark.

joç′und·ly, *adv.* in a jocund manner; merrily; gaily.

joç′und·ness, *n.* same as *jocundity*.

jō′del (yō′), *v.* and *n.* same as *yodel*.

jodh′pụrs (jod′), *n. pl.* riding breeches made loose and full above the knees and close-fitting below them: after *Jodhpur*, a former native state of the province of Rajputana, in northwestern India.

jōe, *n.* 1. a fourpenny piece: so named after Joseph Hume, M. P. [Brit. Slang.]
2. [J–] same as *Joe Miller*.

jōe, *n.* [abbrev. of *Johannes*.] a coin.

Jō′el, *n.* in the Bible, the book in the Old Testament containing the preachings of the Hebrew prophet Joel, probably of the fifth century B.C.

Jōe Mil′lẽr, [after *Joe* or *Joseph Miller*, an English comic actor, whose name was attached to a jest book published in 1739, the year after his death.] an old jest; a stale joke; also, a jest book.

jōe-pȳe′ weed, [perhaps from the name of an Indian doctor said to have used the plant as medicine.] any of three kinds of eupatorium, a tall plant of the composite family, with clusters of pink or purplish flowers.

jō′ey, *n.* [Australian native name, *joè*.]
1. a young kangaroo.
2. any young animal.

jō′ey, *n.* [dim. of *Joe*, an abbrev. of *Joseph*.] a coin; a joe. [Brit. Slang.]

jog, *v.t.*; jogged, *pt.*, *pp.*; jogging, *ppr.* [ME. *joggen*, from W. *gogi*, to shake, agitate.]
1. to push or shake with the elbow or hand; to push so as to give notice or excite attention; to nudge.
Sudden I *jogged* Ulysses. —Pope.
2. to remind; to shake up or revive (a person's memory).
3. to cause to jog or move slowly; as, to *jog* a horse.

jog, *v.i.* to move by jogs or small shocks, like those of a slow trot; to walk or travel idly, heavily, or slowly: usually followed by *along* or *on*.
Thus they *jog on*, still tricking, never thriving. —Dryden.

jog, *n.* 1. a push; a slight shake; a nudge; a shake or push intended to give notice or awaken attention.
2. a slow, steady, jolting motion or trot: also *jog trot*.

jog, *n.*. [var. of *jag*.] a projecting or notched part, especially one at right angles, in a surface or line; as, a *jog* in the wall.

jog′gẽr, *n.* one who or that which jogs.

jog′gle, *v.t.* and *v.i.*; joggled, *pt.*, *pp.*; joggling, *ppr.* [freq. of *jog*.] to shake or jolt slightly.

jog′gle, *n.* a joggling.

jog′gle, *n.* [perhaps from *jog*, a projection.]
1. a joint made between two surfaces of wood, stone, etc. by cutting a notch in one and making a projection in the other to fit into it.
2. a notch or projection for such a joint.
3. a jog; a jolt.

jog′gle, *v.t.*; joggled, *pt.*, *pp.*; joggling, *ppr.* to fasten or join by joggles.

jog′gle bēam, a built beam the parts of which are united by teeth fitting into notches.

jog′gle piēce, the upright member in the middle of a truss; a king post.

jog′gle pōst, 1. a post having shoulders to receive the feet of struts.
2. a post built of pieces of timber held together by joggles.

jog′gle·wŏrk, *n.* in masonry, work in which the courses are secured by joggling.

jog trot, 1. a slow, steady trot.
2. a routine, monotonous, or leisurely way of doing something.

jog′-trot, *a.* easygoing; monotonous; humdrum.

Jō·han′nē·ăn, *a.* [LL. *Johannes*, *Joannes*, John.] of or pertaining to the apostle John, or the book of the New Testament written by him: written also *Johannine*.

jō·han′nēs, jō·an′nēs, *n.* [LL. *Johannes*, *Joannes*, John.] a Portuguese gold coin of the eighteenth and early nineteenth centuries, worth a little less than nine dollars.

Jō·han′nine, *a.* Johannean.

jō·han′nīte, *n.* [LL. *Johannes*, John.]
1. a mineral of an emerald or apple green color, a hydrous sulfate of the protoxide of uranium.
2. [J–] a member of the Knights Hospitalers of St. John of Jerusalem. [Obs.]

John (jon), *n.* in the Bible, (a) a Christian apostle, credited with having written the Gospel of Saint John, the three Epistles of John, and the book of Revelation: called *the Evangelist* and *the Divine*; (b) the fourth book of the New Testament; (c) any of the three Epistles of John; (d) John the Baptist.

john, *n.* a toilet. [Slang.]

John′ȧ·drēams, *n.* a dreamy, idle fellow.

John′-ap·ple, *n.* same as *applejohn*.

John Bär′ley·çorn, a personification of corn liquor, malt liquor, etc.

John Bụll, England, or an Englishman, personified.

John Crōw, in Jamaica, the turkey buzzard.

John Dōe, a fictitious name used in legal papers, etc. for that of a person who is not known.

John Dō′ry, *pl.* **John Dō′rys,** [*John*, and *dory*, the fish.] an edible salt-water fish with a yellow-ringed black spot on each side of its flat body: also spelled *John Doree*.

John Han′çock, a person's signature: so called because John Hancock's signature on the Declaration of Independence is bold and legible. [Colloq.]

John′i·ăn, *n.* a member or graduate of St. John's College, Cambridge, England.

John′nie, John′ny, *n.*; *pl.* **John′nies,** 1. any man or boy. [Slang.]
2. a fop; a dandy. [Slang.]
3. a Confederate: so called by the Union soldiers during the Civil War.
4. a kind of penguin, *Pygoscelis tæniata*.
5. a cottoid fish, *Oligocottus maculosus*.

john′ny, *n.*; *pl.* **john′nies,** [origin unknown.] a short muslin gown with short sleeves and a back opening that is closed with ties, worn as by hospital patients.

john′ny·çāke, *n.* [altered from *Shawnee-cake*, a kind of bread made by Shawnee Indians.] a kind of corn bread baked on a griddle.

John′ny-jump′-up, *n.* 1. any early spring violet, as the bird's-foot violet, *Viola pedata*.
2. the wild pansy.
Also *Johnny jumper*.

John′ny-on-the-spot′, *a.* ready and at hand whenever needed. [Colloq.]

John′ny-on-the-spot′, *n.* a person who is Johnny-on-the-spot. [Colloq.]

John′ny Rạw, a beginner; a novice. [Slang.]

John′ny vẽrde, a serranoid fish of California, *Paralabrax nebulifer*.

John Pạw, a serranoid fish, *Epinephelus drummondhayi*, found along the coast of the Gulf of Mexico.

John·sŏn·ēse′, *n.* 1. the literary style of Samuel Johnson.
2. a literary style more or less like Johnson's, heavy, pompous, erudite, etc.: generally a derogatory term.

John′sŏn grȧss, a kind of grass, *Sorghum halepense*, highly prized for fodder: called also *Arabian* or *evergreen millet*, *Cuba grass*, and *Means grass*: named after William *Johnson*, who introduced it into Alabama from South Carolina about 1840.

John·sō′ni·ăn, *a.* 1. of or like Samuel Johnson or his writings.
2. full of Johnsonese.

John·sō′ni·ăn, *n.* 1. an imitator or admirer of Johnson.

2. a person who makes a special study of Johnson and his work.

John·sō′ni·ăn·ism, *n.* a word, idiom, or habit peculiar to Samuel Johnson, or a style resembling his.

John′sŏn·ism, *n.* Johnsonianism.

John′sŏn noișe, [after J. B. *Johnson*, 20th-century American physicist.] thermal background noise in a radio receiver.

John's′-wŏrt, *n.* same as *St.-John's-wort*.

John the Bap′tist, in the Bible, the forerunner and baptizer of Jesus: he was killed by Herod: Matt. iii.

John tö·whit′, a species of greenlet, *Vireo altiloquus*.

joie dē vi′vre (zhwȧ dē vē′vr), [Fr.] joy of living; zestful enjoyment of life.

join, *v.t.*; joined, *pt., pp.*; joining, *ppr.* [ME. *joynen, joignen*; OFr. *joindre, juindre*, from L. *jungere*, to yoke, bind together.]

1. to connect or bring together; to fasten; to couple; to combine.

2. to make into one; to unite.

What therefore God hath *joined* together,
let not man put asunder.—Matt. xix. 6.

3. to enter into association with; to become connected with; as, to *join* a society; to *join* an army.

And *joins* the sacred senate of the skies.
—Pope.

4. to go to and combine with; as, the path *joins* the highway.

5. to enter into the company of; to accompany; as, *join* me in a walk, *join* us soon.

6. to go to and take one's proper place in; as, a soldier must *join* his regiment when his leave is over.

7. to adjoin. [Colloq.]

8. in geometry, to connect with a straight line or curve.

Syn.—combine, append, unite, connect, attach, couple.

to join battle; to start fighting or competing.

join, *v.i.* 1. to be contiguous, close, or in contact; to come together; to meet.

2. to unite; to league; to confederate; to enter into association.

3. to participate (*in* a conversation, singing, etc.).

The rougher voices of the men *joined in* the
song. —William Morris.

4. to meet in hostile encounter; to join battle. [Obs.]

join, *n.* 1. a joining or being joined.

2. a place of joining; as, a seam in a coat is a *join*.

join′ănt, *a.* [OFr. *joignant*, ppr. of *joindre*, to join.]

1. adjoining. [Obs.]

2. in heraldry, conjoined.

join′dẽr, *n.* [Fr. *joindre*, a use of inf. as n.]

1. a joining; act of meeting or coming together.

2. in law, (a) a joining of causes; (b) a joining of parties as co-plaintiffs or co-defendants; (c) a uniting on facts or procedure; (d) an accepting of an issue offered.

join′ẽr, *n.* [ME. *joinour*; OFr. *joignour*, from *joindre*.]

1. a person or thing that joins.

2. a carpenter, especially one who finishes interior woodwork, as doors, molding, stairs, etc.

3. a person given to joining various organizations. [Colloq.]

join′ẽr·y, *n.* 1. the art or occupation of a joiner.

2. the things made by a joiner.

join′hand, *n.* writing in which letters are joined in words; cursive writing. [Obs.]

joint, *n.* [ME.; OFr. *joint, joinct*; LL. *juncta*, a joining, joint, connection, from L. *junctus*, pp. of *jungere*, to yoke, join.]

1. the place or part where two parts or things are joined or united.

A scaly gauntlet now with *joints* of steel,
Must glove this hand. —Shak.

2. the way in which two things are joined at such a part.

3. one of the parts or sections of a jointed whole.

4. a large cut of meat with the bone still in it, as for a roast.

5. in anatomy, (a) a place or part where two bones or corresponding structures are joined, usually so that they can move; (b) the way in which they are joined.

6. in botany, a point where a branch or leaf grows out of the stem.

7. in geology a fissure in a rock mass, without displacement of strata.

8. a saloon, cheap restuarant, etc. [Slang.]

9. any house, building, etc. [Slang.]

10. in architecture, the surface of contact between two bodies that are held firmly together by means of cement, mortar, etc., or by a superincumbent weight; as, the *joint* between two stones.

out of joint; dislocated, as when the head of a bone is displaced from its socket; hence, figuratively, confused; disordered.

joint, *a.* 1. shared by two or more; held jointly; as, *joint* property.

2. united in action, relation, or interest; acting together; sharing with someone else; as, a *joint* heir; *joint* debtors.

3. united, combined; especially, joined as to time; concurrent; as, *joint* force; *joint* efforts; *joint* vigor.

joint and several; united in obligation, debt, etc., in such a manner that individually or collectively all are chargeable.

joint tenancy; in law, a tenure of estate by unity of interest, title, time, and possession.

joint tenant; in law, one who holds an estate by joint tenancy.

joint, *v.t.*; jointed, *pt., pp.*; jointing, *ppr.* 1. to fasten together by a joint or joints.

2. to give a joint or joints to.

3. to cut (meat) into joints; to separate at the joints.

joint, *v.i.* to unite, as by joints or parts fitting into each other; as, stones cut so as to *joint* into each other.

joint ac̦·count′, a bank account in the name of two or more persons, each of whom may withdraw funds.

joint chāir, in railroading, the chair at the joining of two rail ends.

joint c̦lāy, a clay which when dried breaks up into angular blocks.

joint c̦ŏm·mit′tee, a committee with members from both houses of a legislative body, or from two or more organizations.

joint c̦oup′ling (kup′), a form of universal joint for coupling sections of shafting.

joint′ed, *a.* provided with joints; formed with knots or nodes; as, a *jointed* stem.

joint′ed·ly, *adv.* by joints.

joint′ẽr, *n.* 1. a person or machine that joints.

2. a long plane used in dressing boards.

3. a triangular device with an edge, fastened to a plow beam.

4. a bent iron bar for holding stones together.

joint fīr, 1. any plant of the natural order *Gnetaceæ*.

2. any coniferous plant of the family *Taxaceæ*.

joint grȧss, 1. a grass, *Paspalum distichum*, growing in the southern United States.

2. any one of several species of the genus *Equisetum*.

3. the yellow bedstraw or goose grass, *Galium verum*.

joint hinġe, same as *strap hinge*.

joint′ing, *n.* the act or process of making a joint; also, a joint thus made.

joint′ing plāne, a plane with a long stock used to dress the edges of boards or staves which are to be accurately fitted together.

joint′ing rụle, a straight rule about six feet long, used by bricklayers in marking with white paint along each joint of the brickwork.

joint′less, *a.* having no joint; rigid; stiff.

joint′ly, *adv.* in a joint manner; together.

joint oil, same as *Synovia*.

joint ōwn′ẽr·ship, ownership of property in common with two or more persons.

joint reș·ō·lū′tion, a résolution passed by both houses of a bicameral legislature: it has the force of an act if signed by the chief executive or passed over his veto.

joint′ress, *n.* a woman who has a jointure.

joint rē·tŭrn′, a single income tax return filed by a married couple, combining their individual incomes.

joint snāke, same as *glass snake*.

joint splīce, a reinforced splice for securing firmly two parts of anything.

joint stock, stock or capital held in the form of a common fund.

joint′-stock′ c̦ŏm′pȧ·ny, a business firm with a joint stock, owned by the stockholders in shares which each may sell or transfer independently.

joint stoọl, *n.* 1. a stool made with jointed parts; a folding stool.

2. a block holding up the ends of parts which belong in apposition, as railway rails.

join′tūre, *n.* [OFr. *jointure, joincture*, from L. *junctura*, a joining, from *jungere*, to join.]

1. in law, (a) an arrangement by which a husband settles property on his wife for her use after his death; (b) the property thus settled; widow's portion; (c) [Obs.] the holding of property jointly.

2. a joining; junction. [Obs.]

join′tūre, *v.t.*; jointured, *pt., pp.*; jointuring, *ppr.* to settle a jointure upon.

join′tūre·less, *a.* having no jointure.

join′tūr·ess, *n.* a jointress.

joint′weed, *n.* 1. a plant, *Polygonella articulata*, of the buckwheat family, with threadlike leaves, jointed stems, and clusters of small, white flowers.

2. a species of the genus *Equisetum*.

3. the mare's-tail, *Hippuris vulgaris*.

joint wīre, a tubular wire used for the joints of watchcases, lockets, etc.

joint′wŏrm, *n.* any of the larvae of various small flies, which produce gall-like swellings in the joints of grain stems.

joint′y, *a.* full of joints.

joist, *n.* [ME. *giste, gyste*, a joist, beam; OFr. *giste*, a bed, couch, beam, from *gesir*, to lie, from L. *jacere*, to lie.] any of the parallel timbers that hold up the planks of a floor or the laths of a ceiling.

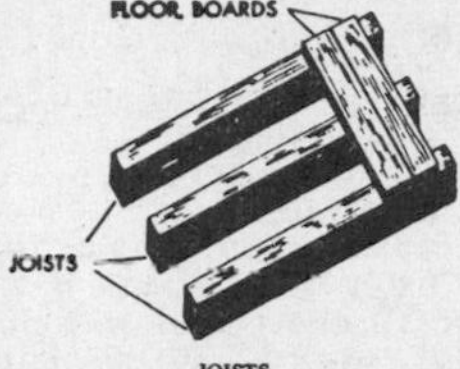

JOISTS

joist, *v.t.*; joisted, *pt., pp.*; joisting, *ppr.* to fit or furnish with joists.

jōke, *n.* [L. *jocus*, a joke, jest.]

1. anything said or done to arouse laughter; funny anecdote; witty, amusing remark; amusing trick played on someone.

2. something not meant to be taken seriously; thing done or said in fun.

Inclose whole downs in walls, 'tis all a *joke*!
—Pope.

3. a person or thing to be laughed at, not to be taken seriously.

in joke; in jest; for the sake of raising a laugh; not in earnest.

no joke; a serious matter.

jōke, *v.i.*; joked (jōkt), *pt., pp.*; joking, *ppr.* 1. to make jokes; to say or do things meant to amuse.

2. to say something not meant to be taken seriously.

jōke, *v.t.* to make fun of; to make (a person) the object of jokes or teasing.

jōk′ẽr, *n.* 1. a person who jokes.

2. a hidden or cunningly worded provision put into a law, legal document, etc. to make it different from what it seems to be.

3. any hidden, unsuspected difficulty.

4. an extra playing card, used in some games to represent the highest trump or any card the holder desires.

jōk′ing·ly, *adv.* in a joking manner.

jōk′ish, *a.* jocular. [Rare.]

jōle, *n.* and *v.* same as *jowl*.

jol′li·ẽr, *n.* a person who jollies others. [Colloq.]

jol·li·fi·c̦ā′tion, *n.* a scene or occasion of merriment; noisy festivity; merrymaking. [Colloq.]

jol′li·fȳ, *v.t.* and *v.i.*; jollified, *pt., pp.*; jollifying, *ppr.* to make or be jolly or merry. [Colloq.]

jol′li·ly, *adv.* in a jolly manner.

jol′li·ment, *n.* mirth; merriment. [Obs.]

jol′li·ness, *n.* the quality or state of being jolly.

jol′li·ty, *n.* [OFr. *jolite*, from *joli*, jolly.]

1. the quality or state of being jolly; fun; noisy mirth; gaiety; merriment; festivity.

All now was turned to *jollity* and game.
—Milton.

2. *pl.* **jol′li·tieș,** a jolly occasion; a festive gathering. [Brit.]

Syn.—festivity, gaiety, frolic, hilarity, joviality, merriment, mirth.

jol′lŏp, *n.* the wattle of a fowl.

jol′ly, *a.*; *comp.* jollier; *superl.* jolliest. [OFr. *jolif, joli*, gay, joyful, merry, prob. from Ice. *jol*, the feast of Christmas.]

1. merry; gay; lively; full of high spirits and mirth; jovial; as, a *jolly* crew.

2. expressing mirth or inspiring it; exciting mirth and gaiety; characterized by mirth; as, a *jolly* trip.

3. enjoyable; pleasant. [Colloq.]

4. of fine appearance; handsome. [Obs.]

5. brave; courageous. [Obs.]
Syn.—gay, mirthful, jovial, lively, merry, sportive, sprightly.
jol′ly, *adv.* exceedingly; very; as, *jolly* good. [Brit. Colloq.]
jol′ly, *v.t.* and *v.i.*; jollied, *pt., pp.*; jollying, *ppr.* 1. to try to make (a person) feel good or agreeable by coaxing, flattering, joking, etc. (often with *along*). [Colloq.]
2. to make fun of (someone). [Colloq.]
jol′ly, *n.* a British marine. [Brit. Slang.]
jol′ly-bōat, *n.* [prob. from D. *jolle*, or Dan. *jolle*, a yawl.] a ship's small boat: also *jolly boat, jolly.*
jol′ly·head (-hed), *n.* a state of jollity. [Obs.]
Jol′ly Rog′ēr, [*jolly*, and *Roger*, pirate flag, from the proper name *Roger*.] a black flag with white skull and crossbones, emblem of piracy.
jol′ly·tāil, *n.* a Tasmanian fish of the genus *Galaxias.*
jōlt, *v.t.*; jolted, *pt., pp.*; jolting, *ppr.* [earlier *jot*, v., influenced by *jowl*.] to shake with sudden jerks, as a vehicle running on a rough surface.
Jolted and commended in a stagecoach. —Tatler.
jōlt, *v.i.* to move along in a bumpy, jerky manner.
jōlt, *n.* 1. a sudden jerk, bump, or shake, as from a blow.
2. a shock or surprise; as, the news gave us all a *jolt.*
jōlt′ēr, *n.* one who or that which jolts.
jōlt′ēr·head (-hed), *n.* same as *jolthead.*
jōlt′head (-hed), *n.* a dunce; a blockhead.
jōlt′ing·ly, *adv.* in a jolting manner.
jōlt′y, *a.* jolting; bumpy.
Jō′nȧh, *n.* 1. in the Bible, a Hebrew prophet: thrown overboard in a storm sent because he had disobeyed God, he was swallowed by a big fish, but three days later was cast up on the shore unharmed.
2. a book of the Old Testament telling Jonah's story.
3. any person said to bring bad luck just by being present: from the fact that Jonah brought bad luck to the sailors.
Jō′nȧh çrab, a crab, *Cancer borealis*, found along the Atlantic coast of the United States.
Jō′nȧs, *n.* Jonah: form used in the Douay Bible.
Jon′ȧ·thăn, *n.* 1. in the Bible, Saul's oldest son, a close friend of David: 1 Sam. xviii–xx.
2. a late fall variety of apple.
jond′lȧ, *n.* [E. Ind.] the Indian millet.
joṅ′glēur, *n.* [OFr. *jongleur*, a juggler.]
1. in France and England during the Middle Ages, a strolling minstrel who sang songs, usually of his own composition.
2. a juggler; a mountebank. [Rare.]
jon′quil, *n.* [Fr. *jonquille*, from L. *juncus*, a rush.]
1. a plant of the genus *Narcissus*, chiefly *Narcissus jonquilla*, resembling a daffodil, with small, fragrant, yellow or white flowers and long, slender leaves. *Narcissus odorus* is the sweet-scented jonquil.
2. its bulb or flower.
3. a light-yellow color.

JONQUIL (*Narcissus jonquilla*)

jon′quille, *n.* same as *jonquil.*
jọok, *v.i.* same as *jouk.*
jō′răm, *n.* same as *jorum.*
jọr′dăn, *n.* [ME. *jurdan*, from name *Jordan, Jourdain.*]
1. a large-necked pot or vessel formerly used by alchemists. [Obs.]
2. a chamber pot. [Obs. or Dial.]
Jọr′dăn äl′mŏnd, a variety of large Spanish almond much used in confections.
jọr′dăn·īte, *n.* [named after Dr. *Jordan*, of Prussia.] an orthorhombic mineral, occurring in fine crystals in the dolomite of the Binnenthal, Switzerland. It is a sulfide of arsenic and lead.
jọr·nä′dä (họr-), *n.* [Sp., a journey.]
1. a day's travel.
2. in the southwestern United States and Mexico, a long stretch of desert land.
jō′rum, *n.* a large bowl or vessel for drinking; also, the quantity of liquor contained in such a vessel.
Jō′ṣeph, *n.* in the Bible, (a) one of Jacob's sons, who was sold into slavery in Egypt by his jealous brothers but became a high official there: Gen. xxxvii, xxxix–xli; (b) the husband of Mary, mother of Jesus: Matt. i. 18–25.
jō′ṣeph, *n.* [prob. from *Joseph's* "coat of many colors" (Gen. xxxvii. 3).] a riding coat or habit for women, with buttons down to the skirts, in use in the eighteenth century.
Jō′ṣeph of Ar″i·mȧ·thē′ȧ, in the Bible, a wealthy disciple who provided a tomb for Jesus' body: Matt. xxvii. 57–60.
Jō′ṣeph's-çōat, *n.* a variety of border plants, *Amarantus tricolor.*
Jō′ṣeph's-flow″ēr, *n.* the goat's-beard, *Tragopogon pratensis*, a composite plant of Europe.
josh, *v.t.* and *v.i.* [said to merge *joke* and *bosh.*] to ridicule in a good-humored way; to tease jokingly; to banter. [Slang.]
Josh′ū·ȧ, *n.* 1. in the Bible, Moses' successor, and leader of the Israelites into the Promised Land.
2. a book of the Old Testament telling about him.
Josh′ū·ȧ tree, a tree, *Yucca brevifolia*, found in some desert altitudes of the southwestern United States.
Jō·sī′ȧh, *n.* in the Bible, a king of Judah in the 7th century B.C.: 2 Kings xxii, xxiii.
joss, *n.* [Pid. Eng.; var. of Port. *deos*, L. *deus*, God.] a figure of a Chinese god; a Chinese idol.
jos′sȧ, *interj.* a word of command to horses, probably equivalent to *whoa*, or *stand still.* [Obs.]
joss house, a Chinese temple.
joss stick, a small reed covered with a paste made of the dust of fragrant woods, burned by the Chinese as incense.
jos′tle (-l), *v.t.*; jostled, *pt., pp.*; jostling, *ppr.* [freq. from ME. *justen*; OFr. *juster, joster*, to come together, tilt.] to run against and shake; to crowd against so as to make unsteady; to elbow; to hustle.
jos′tle, *v.i.* to hustle; to shove about, as in a crowd; to be shoved about.
jos′tle, *n.* a pushing against; crowding; a rough bump or shove.
jos′tle·ment, *n.* the act of jostling or crowding against.
Jos′ū·ē, *n.* Joshua: form used in the Douay Bible.
jot, *n.* [LL. *iota*; Gr. *iōta*, *i*, the smallest letter in the Greek alphabet, something small.] an iota; a very small or trifling amount.
One *jot* or one tittle shall in no wise pass from the law. —Matt. v. 18.
jot, *v.t.*; jotted, *pt., pp.*; jotting, *ppr.* to set down quickly, as in hasty writing; to make a memorandum or brief note of: usually with *down.*
jot′tēr, *n.* 1. one who jots down notes or memoranda.
2. the book in which notes or memoranda are made.
jot′ting, *n.* a memorandum; a brief note.
Jō′tunn, Jō′tun (yō′), *n.* [ON. *jōtunn.*] in Norse mythology, a giant.
Jö′tunn (yoo′), *n.* same as *Jotunn.*
Jō′tunn·heim, Jō′tun·heim (yō′tun-hām), *n.* [ON. *jötunheimar*, n. pl.] in Norse mythology, the home of the giants, at the northwestern edge of the world: also *Jotunnheimr, Jötunnheim.*
jöu′bärb, *n.* [Fr. *joubarbe*, from L. *Jovis barba*, Jupiter's beard.] the houseleek.
jöugṣ, *n.pl.* [OFr. *joug*, from L. *jugum*, a yoke.] an instrument of punishment formerly used in Scotland, consisting of an iron collar fastened to a wall or tree by an iron chain.
jöu′i·sänce, jöu′is·sănce, *n.* [Fr.] jollity; merriment. [Obs.]
jöuk, *v.i.* to perch; to roost. [Obs.]
jöuk, jọok, *v.i.* to bend or incline the body forward with a quick motion in order to avoid a blow or injury; to dodge; to duck. [Scot.]
joule (*or* jūl), *n.* [named after J. P. *Joule*, English physicist.] a unit of electrical energy or work which is equivalent to the work done in raising the potential of one coulomb of electricity one volt, or in maintaining for one second a current of one ampere against a resistance of one ohm; a volt-coulomb. One joule is equivalent to 10,000,000 ergs or .73732 foot-pound.
Joule's equivalent; see *mechanical equivalent of heat* under *equivalent.*
joule′mē″tēr, *n.* a meter in which the joule is employed as the unit of energy.
jounce, *v.t.* and *v.i.*; jounced, *pt., pp.*; jouncing, *ppr.* to jolt; to shake, especially by rough riding.
jounce, *n.* a jolt; a shake.
jou̇r′năl, *a.* daily; quotidian; diurnal. [Obs.]
jou̇r′năl, *n.* [OFr. *journal, jornal, jurnal*, daily, a journal, from L. *diurnalis*, daily, from *dies*, day.]
1. a daily record of happenings.
2. a diary.
3. a record of the transactions of a legislature, committee, club, etc.
4. a ship's logbook.
5. a daily newspaper.
6. any newspaper or periodical; a magazine.
7. in bookkeeping, (a) a daybook; (b) a book of original entry, used, in the double-entry system, for recording all transactions with an indication of the special accounts to which they belong.
8. in mechanics, the part of a rotatory axle or shaft that turns in a bearing.
9. a day's work; a journey. [Obs.]
jou̇r′năl, *v.t.*; journaled *or* journalled, *pt., pp.*; journaling *or* journalling, *ppr.* to adjust or insert, as a shaft, in a journal box or bearing.
jou̇r′năl beăr′ing, the support of an axle or shaft.
jou̇r′năl box, in mechanics, (a) a bearing for a journal; (b) a casing or housing for a journal.
jou̇r·năl·ēṣe′, *n.* a style of writing and diction characteristic of many newspapers, magazines, etc.; facile style, with hackneyed expressions and effects.
jou̇r′năl·iṣm, *n.* 1. the keeping of a journal. [Rare.]
2. the work of gathering news for, writing for, editing, or directing the publication of a newspaper or other periodical.
3. journalistic writing.
4. newspapers and magazines collectively.
jou̇r′năl·ist, *n.* 1. the writer of a journal, or diary.
2. one whose occupation is journalism; an editor, correspondent, critic, or reporter of a newspaper; a newspaperman.
jou̇r·năl·is′tiç, *a.* of or characteristic of journals, journalism, or journalists; as, *journalistic* literature.
jou̇r·năl·is′tiç·ăl·ly, *adv.* 1. in a journalistic manner.
2. from the standpoint of journalism.
jou̇r′năl·īze, *v.t.*; journalized, *pt., pp.*; journalizing, *ppr.* to enter in a journal or diary; to set down a daily account of (events, transactions, etc.).
jou̇r′năl·īze, *v.i.* to enter records in a journal; to contribute to or aid in conducting a journal.
jou̇r′ney, *n.*; *pl.* **jou̇r′neyṣ,** [ME. *journee, jorney*; OFr. *journee, jornee*; hyp. LL. *diurnata*, a day's journey, day's work, from L. *diurnus*, daily.]
1. a day's work or travel. [Obs.]
2. travel from one place to another; passage; trip; as, a *journey* from London to Paris.
3. figuratively, passage through life.
Syn.—tour, excursion, pilgrimage, travel, trip, voyage.—*Journey* suggests the idea of a somewhat prolonged traveling directly from one place to another. A *tour* suggests a roundabout course from place to place, usually for pleasure. An *excursion* is always for pleasure, health, etc. A *pilgrimage* implies travel to a place hallowed by religious affections, or by sentimental associations.
jou̇r′ney, *v.i.*; journeyed, *pt., pp.*; journeying, *ppr.* to travel from place to place; to go on a trip.
Abram *journeyed*, going on still toward the south. —Gen. xii. 9.
jou̇r′ney-bāt″ed, *a.* fatigued or worn out with a journey. [Obs.]
jou̇r′ney·ēr, *n.* one who journeys.
jou̇r′ney·măn, *n.*; *pl.* **jou̇r′ney·men,** 1. originally, a man hired to work by the day.
2. formerly, a mechanic or workman who had served his apprenticeship and thus qualified himself to work at his trade.
3. now, a worker who has learned his trade.
jou̇r′ney·wŏrk, *n.* 1. work done by the day. [Obs.]
2. work done by a journeyman.
joust (just *or* joust), *n.* [ME. *jouste, juste*; OFr. *jouste*, from *jouster*, to joust.]
1. a combat or mock combat with lances, between two knights on horseback.
2. [*pl.*] a tournament.
Also *just.*
joust, *v.i.* [ME. *justen, justien*; OFr. *juster, joster, jouster*; LL. *juxtare*, to approach, tilt,

from L. *juxta*, close to.] to engage in a joust: also *just*.

joust'ẽr, *n.* one who jousts, as in a tournament: also *juster*.

Jōve, *n.* [L. *Jovis*, genit. of *Jupiter*, Jupiter.]
1. the chief of the Roman gods; Jupiter. [Poetic.]
2. the planet Jupiter. [Poetic.]
3. in alchemy, the metal tin. [Obs.]
by Jove; an exclamation expressing astonishment, emphasis, etc.

Jōve's'-fruit, *n.* an American shrub, *Benzoin melissæfolium*, a species of wild allspice.

Jōve's nuts, acorns. [Brit. Dial.]

jō'vi·ăl, *a.* 1. pertaining to Jove, the god or the planet.
2. under the influence of Jupiter, the planet. [Obs.]
3. gay; merry; joyous; jolly; characterized by gaiety; as, a *jovial* disposition.
4. [J–] in alchemy, pertaining to the metal tin. [Obs.]

jō'vi·ăl·ist, *n.* one who lives a jovial life. [Obs.]

jō·vi·al'i·ty, *n.* 1. the state or quality of being jovial; merriment; festivity.
2. *pl.* **jō·vi·al'i·ties**, a jovial act or remark.

jō'vi·ăl·īze, *v.t.*; jovialized, *pt.*, *pp.*; jovializing, *ppr.* to cause to be jovial or gay.

jō'vi·ăl·ly, *adv.* in a jovial manner; merrily; gaily.

jō'vi·ăl·ness, *n.* joviality; gaiety.

jō'vi·ăl·ty, *n.* joviality. [Rare.]

Jō'vi·ăn, *a.* 1. of or like Jove (the god Jupiter); majestic.
2. of the planet Jupiter.

Jō·vi·cen'triç, *a.* [L. *Jovis*, genit. of *Jupiter*, or *Juppiter*, Jupiter, and *centrum*, center.] in astronomy, having relation to Jupiter as a center.

jō'vi·lābe, *n.* [L. *Jovis*, of Jupiter, and *-labe*, as in *astrolabe*.] an instrument for determining the positions of the satellites of the planet Jupiter.

Jō·vin'iăn·ist, *n.* a follower of Jovinian, a monk of the fourth century, who denied the perpetual virginity of Mary and denounced asceticism.

Jō'vīte, *n.* a high explosive, made up of nitro compounds and sodium nitrate: a trade-mark (*Jonite*).

jowl (*or* jōl), *n.* [ME. *chaul*, *chavel*; AS. *ceafl*, jaw, cheek.]
1. a jawbone or jaw, especially the lower jaw with the chin and cheeks.
2. the cheek.

jowl (*or* jōl), *n.* [ME. *chol*, *cholle*; AS. *ceolc*, throat.]
1. the fleshy, hanging part under the lower jaw.
2. (a) the dewlap of cattle; (b) the wattle of fowl.
3. the head and adjacent parts of a fish.

jōwl, jōll, *v.t.* to strike, as with the head; to butt. [Obs.]

jōwl, *v.i.* to scold; to jaw. [Obs.]

jōwl'ẽr, *n.* a dog with heavy jaws, as a beagle, hound, or other hunting dog. [Scot. and Brit. Dial.]

jow'tẽr, *n.* one who sells fish about the country on horseback. [Brit. Dial.]

joy, *n.* [ME. *joye*, *joie*; OFr. *joie*, *joye*, joy, pleasure, from LL. *gaudia*, f., joy, a jewel, from L. *gaudium*, joy.]
1. a very glad feeling; happiness; great pleasure; delight.
2. the cause of joy or happiness.
3. the expression of this feeling.
Syn.—delight, gladness, rapture, ecstasy, happiness, exultation.

joy, *v.i.*; joyed, *pt.*, *pp.*; joying, *ppr.* to rejoice; to be glad; to be full of joy.

I will *joy* in the God of my salvation.
—Hab. iii. 18.

joy, *v.t.* 1. to give joy to; to congratulate. [Obs.]
2. to gladden; to make joyful.
3. to enjoy; to have or possess with pleasure, or have pleasure in the possession of. [Archaic.]

joy'ănce, *n.* joy; rejoicing. [Archaic.]

joy'ăn·cy, *n.* joyance. [Rare.]

joy'ful, *a.* 1. full of joy.
2. feeling, expressing, or causing joy; glad; happy.

joy'ful·ly, *adv.* in a joyful manner; with joy; gladly.

joy'ful·ness, *n.* the state of being joyful; gladness; joy.

joy'less, *a.* 1. lacking or without joy; unhappy; sad.
2. giving no joy or pleasure.

joy'less·ly, *adv.* in a joyless manner; without joy.

joy'less·ness, *n.* the state of being joyless.

joy'ous, *a.* [OFr. *joyous*, from *joie*, joy.]
1. glad; gay; merry; joyful.
2. giving or inspiring joy.

joy'ous·ly, *adv.* in a joyous manner; with joy or gladness.

joy'ous·ness, *n.* the state of being joyous.

joy'-pop', *v.i.*; joy-popped, *pt.*, *pp.*; joy-popping, *ppr.* to inject a narcotic drug under the skin, especially in small quantities and infrequently. [Slang.]

joy'-pop'pẽr, *n.* one who joy-pops. [Slang.]

joy'-rīde, *v.i.* to take a joy ride. [Colloq.]

joy rīde, an automobile ride merely for pleasure, often with reckless speed, rowdy behavior, etc. [Colloq.]

joy·rīd'ẽr, *n.* one who takes a joy ride. [Colloq.]

joy'sōme, *a.* causing joy or gladness. [Rare.]

joy stick, the control stick of an airplane. [Slang.]

jū'bȧ, *n.*; *pl.* **jū'bae**, [L., a mane.]
1. an animal's mane.
2. in botany, a loose panicle, like that of many grasses. [Rare.]

jū'bȧ, *n.* [perh. from Bantu; perh. back-formation from *jubilee*.] a Southern Negro dance, characterized by a lively rhythm marked by clapping the hands.

Jū'băl, *n.* in the Bible, one of Cain's descendants, a musician or inventor of musical instruments: Gen. iv. 19–21.

Jū'bȧ's-brush, Jū'bȧ's-bush, *n.* an American plant, *Iresine paniculata*, of the amaranth family.

jū'bāte, *a.* [L. *jubatus*, from *juba*, a mane.] having a mane; fringed with long hair like a mane.

jub'bȧh, *n.* [Ar.] a long outer garment worn by both men and women in some Moslem countries.

jū'bē, *n.* [Fr., from imperative of L. *jubere*, to bid, command: so called from a prayer that begins *Jube*, spoken from this gallery.] a loft or gallery over the rood screen in a church.

jū'bi·lănce, *n.* a jubilant feeling; a rejoicing.

jū'bi·lănt, *a.* [L. *jubilans* (*-antis*), ppr. of *jubilare*, to shout for joy.] joyful and triumphant; elated.

While the bright pomp ascended *jubilant*.
—Milton.

Syn.—joyous, triumphant, exultant.

jū'bi·lănt·ly, *adv.* in a jubilant manner.

Jū·bi·lä'tē, *n.* [L., imper., of *jubilare*, to shout for joy, rejoice.]
1. the third Sunday after Easter: so called because the Introit for the day begins with the words of the 66th Psalm, *Jubilate Deo.*
2. in the Bible, the 100th Psalm (99th in the Vulgate and Douay versions).

jū'bi·lāte, *v.i.*; jubilated, *pt.*, *ppr.*; jubilating, *ppr.* [L. *jubilatus*, pp. of *jubilare*, to shout for joy, from *jubilum*, a wild cry.] to rejoice; to exult.

jū·bi·lā'tion, *n.* 1. a jubilating; a rejoicing.
2. a happy celebration, as of victory.

jū'bi·lee, *n.* [ME. *jubilee*; OFr. *jubile*; LL. *jubilæus*; Gr. *iōbēlaios*, from Heb. *yōbēl*, the blast of a trumpet, the sabbatical year which was announced by the blast of a trumpet.]
1. in Jewish history, a year-long celebration held every fifty years in which all bondmen were freed, mortgaged lands were restored to the original owners, and land was left fallow: Lev. xxv. 8–17.
2. a fiftieth or twenty-fifth anniversary, or a celebration of this.
3. a time or occasion of rejoicing.
4. jubilation; a rejoicing.
5. in the Roman Catholic Church, a feast first instituted in the year 1300 by Boniface VIII, who proposed that it should be celebrated at the beginning of each succeeding century. The period was afterward reduced to fifty, and later to twenty-five years. The jubilee is a year of plenary indulgence in which remission of punishment for sin may be obtained by those who comply with certain conditions and perform certain acts.

jū·çun'di·ty, *n.* pleasantness. [Obs.]

Jū·dae'ăn, *a.* and *n.* same as *Judean.*

Jū'dȧh, *n.* in the Bible, (a) one of Jacob's sons; (b) the tribe descended from him, strongest of the twelve tribes of Israel.

Jū'dȧh·īte, *n.* a member of the tribe of Judah; a member of the kingdom of Judah; a Jew.

Jū·dā'iç, *a.* [L. *Judaicus*; Gr. *Ioudaikos*, from *Ioudaia*, Judea.]
1. of Judah.
2. of the Jews, their culture, etc.; Jewish.
3. of Judaism.

Jū·dā'iç·ăl, *a.* Judaic.

Jū·dā'iç·ăl·ly, *adv.* in a Judaic manner.

Jū'dā·ism, *n.* [LL. *Judaismus*; Gr. *Ioudaismos*, Judaism, from *Ioudaizein*, to Judaize.]
1. the Jewish religion.
2. conformity to the Jewish rites, ceremonies, customs, rules, etc.

Jū'dā·ist, *n.* an adherent of Judaism.

Jū·dā·is'tiç, *a.* relating to Judaism.

Jū·dā·is'tiç·ăl·ly, *adv.* in a Judaistic manner.

Jū·dā·i·zā'tion, *n.* the act of Judaizing; a conforming to the Jewish customs, beliefs, etc.

Jū'dā·īze, *v.i.*; Judaized, *pt.*, *pp.*; Judaizing, *ppr.* [LL. *Judaizare*; Gr. *Ioudaizein*, to live or act like Jews, from *Ioudaios*, a Jew.] to conform to the religious doctrines, customs, etc. of the Jews.

Jū'dā·īze, *v.t.* to bring into conformity with Judaism.

Jū'dā·i·zẽr, *n.* 1. one who conforms to Judaism.
2. in the early church, a Jew who accepted Christianity but adhered to the Mosaic law.

Jū'dăs, *n.* [LL. *Judas*; Gr. *Ioudas*, from Heb. *yehūdah*, Judah.]
1. Judas Iscariot, the apostle who betrayed Jesus for pay: Matt. xxvi. 14, 48.
2. a treacherous person; one who betrays under the semblance of friendship.
3. Jude, the apostle.
4. a brother of Jesus and James: Mark vi. 3, Matt. xiii. 55.
5. same as *Judas hole.*

Jū'dăs-çol"ŏred, *a.* red: applied to hair, from the notion that Judas had red hair.

There's treachery in that *Judas-colored* beard.
—Dryden.

Jū'dăs hōle, a small trap or peephole in a door.

Jū'dăs līght (līt), an imitation of a paschal candle, made of wood.

Jū'dăs tree, [so called because Judas is said to have hanged himself on a tree of this kind.]
1. a leguminous tree, *Cercis siliquastrum*, of Europe, bearing rose-colored flowers.
2. the redbud of America, *Cercis canadensis*.
3. the elder, *Sambucus nigra.*

jud'çock, jud'dŏck, *n.* see *jacksnipe.*

Jūde, *n.* 1. in the Bible, a Christian apostle and saint: also called *Judas* (not Iscariot): John xiv. 22, Luke vi. 13–16.
2. a book of the New Testament, the Epistle of Jude.
3. its author, perhaps the Judas called Jesus' brother.

Jū·dē'ăn, Jū·dae'ăn, *a.* [L. *Judæus*; Gr. *Ioudaios*, a Jew, of or pertaining to Judea, from *Ioudaia*, Judea.]
1. of Judea or its people.
2. Jewish.

Jū·dē'an, Jū·dae'ăn, *n.* 1. a native or inhabitant of Judea.
2. a Jew.

judġe, *n.* [OFr. *juge*, from L. *judex* (*-icis*), a judge, one who declares the law; *jus*, the law, and *dicere*, to say, declare.]
1. an elected or appointed public official invested with authority to hear and decide civil and criminal cases in a court of law.
2. one who has skill, science, or experience sufficient to decide upon the merits, value, or quality of anything; a connoisseur; a critic; as, a good *judge* of music, a poor *judge* of books.
3. a person appointed to determine the winner, settle a controversy, etc.
4. in Jewish history, a ruler or governor of the ancient Israelites before the time of the kings.
Syn.—umpire, arbitrator, referee.

judġe, *v.t.* and *v.i.*; judged, *pt.*, *pp.*; judging, *ppr.* [ME. *juggen*; OFr. *juger*, from L. *judicare*, to judge, declare the law, from *judex* (*-icis*), a judge.]
1. to hear and pass judgment on (persons or cases) in a court of law.
2. to determine the winner of (a contest); to settle (a controversy).
3. to decree.
4. to form an idea or opinion about (any matter).
5. to criticize or censure.
6. to think or suppose.

If ye have *judged* me to be faithful to the Lord.
—Acts xvi. 15.

7. in Jewish history, to rule or govern.

judġe ad'vō·çāte, *pl.* **judġe ad'vō·çātes**, a military legal officer; especially, an officer designated to act as prosecutor at a court-martial.

Judge Lynch, the personification of lynch law.

judge'-māde, *a.* made by judges or by their decisions taken as precedent.

judg'ẽr, *n.* one who judges.

Judg'es, *n. pl.* [*construed as sing.*] a book of the Old Testament telling the history of the Jews from the death of Joshua to the birth of Samuel.

judge'ship, *n.* the position, functions, or term of office of a judge.

judg·mat'iç, *a.* [from *judge* and *-matic* as in *dogmatic.*] discerning; judicious. [Colloq.]

judg'ment, *n.* [ME. *jugement*; OFr. *jugement*; LL. *judicamentum*, a judgment, from L. *judicare*, to judge.]

1. the act of judging; the act or process of the mind in comparing its ideas to find their agreement or disagreement, and to ascertain truth; the process of examining facts and arguments to ascertain propriety and justice; the process of examining the relations between one proposition and another.

2. the ability to come to opinions of things; the power to compare ideas and ascertain the relations of terms and propositions; understanding; good sense; as, a man of sound *judgment*.

3. a legal decision; an order or sentence given by a judge or law court.

4. a debt resulting from a court order.

5. opinion; notion; as, in my *judgment*, the case is hopeless.

6. criticism or censure.

7. a misfortune looked on as a punishment from God.

8. in the Bible, justice; right.

9. [J–] in theology, (a) God's final sentence as judge of all things; (b) the time of this: often called *the Last Judgment.*

Also spelled *judgement.*

arrest of judgment; see under *arrest.*

Syn.—discernment, discrimination, penetration, sagacity, decision.

judg'ment dāy, Judg'ment Dāy, in theology, the last day, or the day when final judgment will be pronounced by God on all people; the end of the world.

judg'ment debt (det), in law, a debt secured to the creditor by a judge's order and in respect of which he can at any time attach the debtor's goods and chattels.

judg'ment hall, the hall where courts are held.

judg'ment sēat, 1. the seat or bench on which judges sit in court.

2. a court of law; a tribunal.

jū'di·cȧ·ble, *a.* 1. that can be judged.

2. liable to be judged.

jū'di·cȧ·tive, *a.* having power to judge; judging; judicial.

jū'di·cȧ·tō·ry, *a.* dispensing justice; pertaining to judicial jurisdiction and administration.

jū'di·cȧ·tō·ry, *n.*; *pl.* **jū'di·cȧ·tō·ries,** 1. a court of law; a tribunal.

2. the system of administration of justice; law courts collectively.

jū'di·cȧ·tūre, *n.* [Fr. *judicature*; ML. *judicatura*, from L. *judicare*, to judge.]

1. the administering of justice.

2. the position, functions, or legal power of a judge.

3. the extent of legal power of a judge or court of law; jurisdiction.

4. a court of law.

5. judges or courts of law collectively.

jū·di'ciăl (-dish'ăl), *a.* 1. of judges, law courts, or their functions.

2. allowed, enforced, or set by order of a judge or law court.

3. administering justice.

4. like or befitting a judge.

5. fair; unbiased; carefully considering the facts, arguments, etc., and reasoning to a decision.

6. in astrology, giving judgments regarding the supposed influence of the planets, stars, etc. on future events.

7. judicious. [Obs.]

jū·di'ciăl·ly, *adv.* in a judicial manner; after a judicial form.

jū·di'ci·ar·y (-dish'i-er-i, -dish'ẽr-i), *a.* [L. *judiciarius*, pertaining to a court of justice, from *judicium*, judgment, a court of justice, from *judex* (*-icis*), a judge.] pertaining to judges, law courts, or their functions.

jū·di'ci·ar·y, *n.*; *pl.* **jū·di'ci·ar·ies,** 1. that branch of government which is concerned with the administration of justice; system of law courts.

2. judges collectively.

jū·di'cious (-dish'us), *a.* [LL. *judiciosus*, prudent, judicious, from L. *judicium*, judgment.]

1. according to sound judgment; possessing sound judgment; wise; as, a *judicious* magistrate, a *judicious* historian.

2. judicial. [Obs.]

Syn.—wise, sagacious, expedient, sensible, prudent, discreet, well-judged, well-advised, politic, discerning, thoughtful.

jū·di'cious·ly, *adv.* in a judicious manner; wisely.

jū·di'cious·ness, *n.* the quality of being judicious.

Jū'dith, *n.* [L.; Gr. *Ioudith*; Heb. *yehūdhīth*, woman of Judah, lit., praised (by the Lord).]

1. a book of the Apocrypha and the Douay Bible.

2. the Jewish woman told about in this book, who saved her people by killing the Assyrian general Holofernes.

jū'dō, *n.* [Japan., from *jū*, soft, and *dō*, art.] a form of jujitsu developed as a sport and as a means of self-defense without the use of weapons.

jug, *n.* [perhaps connected with *Jug* or *Judge*, familiar nicknames of *Judith*, and equivalent to *Joan* or *Jenny.*]

1. a container for liquids, usually of earthenware, glass, or metal, with a swelling body, a narrow mouth, and a handle.

2. a jail or prison. [Slang.]

jug, *v.t.*; jugged, *pt.*, *pp.*; jugging, *ppr.* 1. to pour into a jug; also, to heat in a jug.

2. to shut up or imprison. [Slang.]

jug, *n.* [echoic.] a sound meant to imitate a nightingale's note.

jug, *v.t.*; jugged, *pt.*, *pp.*; jugging, *ppr.* to utter a sound resembling this word, as certain birds do, especially the nightingale.

jug, *v.i.* to come close together, as birds in nestling.

jū'găl, *a.* [L. *jugalis*, pertaining to a yoke, matrimonial, from *jugum*, a yoke.]

1. pertaining to the cheekbone or to the region of the cheekbone.

2. having reference to a yoke, or to marriage. [Obs.]

jū'găl, *n.* in anatomy, the malar, or cheekbone.

jū·gā'tȧ, *n.pl.* two heads represented together on a coin or medal.

jū'gāte, *a.* [L. *jugatus*, pp. of *jugare*, to yoke, connect, from *jugum*, a yoke.]

1. in botany, coupled together, as the pairs of leaflets in compound leaves.

2. in biology, paired.

3. in numismatics, joined or overlapping, as two heads on a coin.

jū'gā·ted, *a.* same as *jugate.*

juge, *n.* and *v.* judge. [Obs.]

juge'ment, *n.* judgment. [Obs.]

jū'ge·rum, *n.*; *pl.* **jū'ge·rȧ,** [L.] in Roman land measurement, a piece of land two hundred and forty feet in length by one hundred and twenty feet in breadth.

jug'gẽr, *n.* [E. Ind.] an East Indian falcon, *Falco jugger*: written also *juggur* and *lugger.*

Jug'gẽr·naut, *n.* [Sans. *Jagannātha*, lit., lord of the world.]

1. an incarnation of the Hindu god Vishnu, whose idol, it is said, so excited his worshipers when it was hauled along on a large car during religious rites that they threw themselves under the wheels and were crushed: also *Jagannath.*

2. [*often* j–] anything that exacts blind devotion or terrible sacrifice.

3. [*often* j–] any terrible, irresistible force.

jug'gle, *v.t.*; juggled, *pt.*, *pp.*; juggling, *ppr.* [ME. *juglen, jogelen*; OFr. *jogler*, to juggle, play false, from L. *joculari*, to jest, joke, from *joculus*, dim. of *jocus*, a joke, jest.]

1. to perform skillful tricks of sleight of hand with (balls, knives, etc.).

2. to manipulate or practice trickery on (a thing or a person) so as to deceive or cheat; as, the cashier *juggled* the figures to show a profit.

jug'gle, *v.i.* to toss up a number of balls, knives, etc. and keep them continuously in the air.

jug'gle, *n.* 1. an act of juggling.

2. a clever trick or deception.

jug'gle, *n.* [cf. *joggle, n.*] a square-ended block of timber cut to a certain length.

jug'glẽr, *n.* one who juggles; also, a cheat; a deceiver; a trickish fellow.

jug'glẽr·ess, *n.* a woman who juggles.

jug'glẽr·y, *n.*; *pl.* **jug'glẽr·ies,** 1. the art or act of juggling; sleight of hand.

2. trickery; deception.

jug'gling, *n.* 1. the art or practice of one who juggles.

2. trickery; deceit.

jug'gling·ly, *adv.* in a deceptive manner.

juggs, *n.pl.* same as *jougs.*

Jū·glan·dā'cē·ae, *n.pl.* [L. *juglans* (*-andis*), a walnut, walnut tree, and *-aceæ.*] the walnut family of exogenous plants found chiefly in North America. They are trees with alternate pinnate stipulate leaves, and unisexual flowers.

jū·glan·dā'ceous, *a.* of or pertaining to the *Juglandaceæ.*

jug'lan·din, jug'lan·dine, *n.* [L. *juglans* (*-andis*), a walnut, walnut tree, and *-in, -ine.*] in chemistry, (a) a compound derived from the juice of walnut shells, used medicinally as an alterative and also as a hair dye; (b) an alkaloid found in the leaves of *Juglans regia.*

Jū'glāns, *n.* [L., a walnut, walnut tree.] in botany, a genus of trees in which are included the true European walnut and the black walnut and butternut of America.

jū'glōne, *n.* [L. *juglans*, the walnut, and *-one.*] a crystalline substance, $C_{10}H_6O_3$, obtained from the walnut: called also *nucin.*

Jū'gō·släv', Jū'gō-Släv' (yū'), *n.* same as *Yugoslav.*

Jū'gō·släv'i·ăn, *a.* and *n.* same as *Yugoslavian.*

Jū'gō·släv'iç, *a.* same as *Yugoslavic.*

jū'gū·lȧ, *n.* pl. of *jugulum.*

jug'ū·lăr, *a.* [L. *jugulum*, the collarbone, the neck, throat, dim. of *jugum*, a yoke.]

1. in anatomy, of the neck or throat.

2. of the jugular vein or the jugulum of a bird.

3. in zoology, of or having ventral fins in front of the pectoral, under the throat.

jugular artery; in anatomy, one of the trunk arteries of the neck.

jugular vein; in anatomy, one of the trunk veins of the neck.

jug'ū·lăr, *n.* 1. a jugular vein.

2. a member of the group *Jugulares.*

Jū·gū·lā'rēs, *n.pl.* [L. *jugularis*, jugular, from *jugulum*, the collarbone, neck, throat.] a division of fishes whose ventral fins are placed anterior to the pectoral.

jū'gū·lāte, *v.t.* 1. to cut the throat of or strangle.

2. in medicine, to halt (a disease) by severe measures.

jū·gū·lā'tion, *n.* [LL. *jugulatio* (*-onis*), from *jugulare*, to cut the throat of, kill, from *jugulum*, the throat.] the act of jugulating.

jū'gū·lum, *n.*; *pl.* **jū'gū·lȧ,** [L.] in ornithology, the lower section of the throat; also, an analogous part in an invertebrate.

jū'gum, *n.*; *pl.* **jū'gȧ,** [L., a yoke, crossbeam, ridge.]

1. in botany, one of the ridges on the carpels of umbelliferous plants; also, paired leaflets in a compound leaf.

2. in zoology, a backward-extending lobe near the inner marginal base of the anterior wing of an insect.

jūice (jūs), *n.* [ME. *juis, juce, jus*; OFr. *jus*, from L. *jus*, broth, soup, juice.]

1. the liquid part of a fruit or vegetable.

2. a liquid in or from animal tissue; as, gastric *juice*, meat *juice.*

3. the essence of anything.

4. electricity. [Slang.]

5. gasoline, oil, or any other liquid that supplies power. [Slang.]

jūice, *v.t.*; juiced, *pt.*, *pp.*; juicing, *ppr.* 1. to moisten. [Rare.]

2. to extract juice from. [Colloq.]

jūice'less, *a.* without moisture; not juicy.

jūic'ẽr, *n.* a device or appliance for extracting juice from fruit.

jūi'ci·ly, *adv.* in a juicy manner.

jūi'ci·ness, *n.* the state or quality of being juicy.

jūi'cy, *a.*; *comp.* juicier; *superl.* juiciest, 1. full of juice; moist; succulent.

2. full of interest, as a joke or story; piquant; lively; racy; spicy.

jū·jit'sū, *n.* [Japan. *jū-jutsu*, lit., soft art; *jū*, soft, pliant, and *jutsu*, art.] a Japanese system of wrestling in which the strength and weight of an opponent are used against him by means of anatomical knowledge and the principle of leverage: also called *jiujitsu, jiujutsu, jujutsu.*

jū'jū, *n.* [W. Afr.; perhaps from Fr. *joujou*, a toy.]

1. a magic charm or fetish used by some West African tribes.
2. its magic.
3. a taboo connected with its use.

jụ'jụbe, *n.* [Fr., from L. *zizyphum*; Gr. *zizyphon*, from Per. *zīzafūn, zayzafun, zizfun*, the jujube tree.]
1. the edible, datelike fruit of any of a number of trees and shrubs of the genus *Zizyphus*, growing in warm climates.
2. a tree or shrub bearing this fruit.
3. a jelly made from this fruit.
4. a lozenge of gelatinous candy flavored with or like this fruit.

jụ·jụt'sụ (*or* -jit'), *n.* same as *jujitsu*.

jụke box, [Negro Gullah *jook-house*, roadhouse; orig., house of prostitution.] a phonograph that plays a selected record automatically when a coin is inserted: used in some restaurants, saloons, etc. [Colloq.]

Jụkes, the (jụks), the fictitious name of a New York family whose case history over several generations, compiled by nineteenth-century sociologists, shows an abnormally high incidence of poverty, disease, criminality, etc.: a similar study was made of a New Jersey family (fictitious name, *the Kallikaks*).

jụ·lā'ceous, *a.* [L. *julus*, a catkin, and *-aceous.*] in botany, like a catkin in character or appearance; bearing catkins; amentaceous.

jụ'lep, *n.* [Fr. *julep*; Sp. *julepe*; Ar. *jūlāb*; Per. *jūlāb, gūlāb*, julep, rose water; *gūl*, rose, and *āb*, water.]
1. a cool drink containing aromatic herbs.
2. a cold drink made of whisky or brandy flavored with sugar and fresh mint: also *mint julep*.
3. a mixture of water with sirup or sugar for administering medicine.

Jụl'iăn, *a.* [L. *Julianus*, from *Julius*, Julius.] of or pertaining to Julius Caesar.
Julian calendar; the calendar as regulated by Julius Caesar, giving every fourth year 366 days, the other years having 365 days each: the months were the same as in the Gregorian or New Style calendar now used.
Julian epoch; the epoch of the commencement of the Julian calendar, which began in 46 B.C.
Julian period; a period consisting of 7,980 Julian years. The number 7,980 is formed by the multiplication of the three numbers 28, 19, and 15; that is, of the cycle of the sun, the cycle of the moon, and the cycle of the indiction.
Julian year; the year, as regulated by Julius Caesar, which continued to be used in England until 1752, when the Gregorian, or New Style, year was adopted.

Jụl'iăn·ist, *n.* one of a section of the early Coptic church, who held the body of Christ to be incorruptible: so called from Julian of Halicarnassus, their leader.

jụ·li·enne' (-en'), *n.* [named after *Julien*, a French caterer of Boston.] a clear soup containing vegetables cut into strips or bits.

jụ·li·enne', *a.* in cooking, cut into strips: said of vegetables.

Jụ'li·et, *n.* [Fr. *Juliette*, dim. from L. *Julia*.] the heroine of Shakespeare's tragedy *Romeo and Juliet*.

Jụ'li·et çap, a girl's small cap, worn usually on the back of the head.

jụ'li·fọrm, *a.* [L. *julus*, a catkin, and *forma*, form.] in botany, shaped like a julus. [Rare.]

jụ'lus, *n.*; *pl.* **jụ'lī,** [L. *julus*, from Gr. *ioulos*, down, a catkin, centipede.] in botany, a catkin or ament.

Jụ·ly̆', *n.*; *pl.* **Jụ·līeṣ',** [Anglo-Fr. *Julie*; L. *Julius*, from *mensis Julius*, the month of Julius (Caesar).] the seventh month of the Gregorian year, during which the sun enters the sign Leo: it has thirty-one days.

Jụ·ly̆'flow"ẽr, *n.* the gillyflower.

jụ'märt, *n.* [Fr.] the fabled offspring of a bull and a mare.

jum'ble, *n.* [prob. OFr. *jumel, gemel* (Fr. *jumeau*), twin.] a kind of cooky shaped like a ring: also spelled *jumbal*.

jum'ble, *v.t.*; jumbled, *pt., pp.*; jumbling, *ppr.* [freq. from *jump*.]
1. to mix in a confused mass: often followed by *together* or *up*; as, to *jumble together* passages of Scripture.
2. to confuse mentally.

jum'ble, *v.i.* to meet, mix, or unite in a confused manner.

jum'ble, *n.* 1. a confused mixture, mass, or collection.
2. a muddle.

jum'ble bēad, a seed of the wild licorice, used in India for stringing as a bead.

jum'ble·ment, *n.* confused mixture.

jum'blẽr, *n.* one who mixes things in confusion.

jum'bling·ly, *adv.* in a confused manner.

jum'bō, *n.*; *pl.* **jum'bōṣ,** [so called from *Jumbo*, the famous elephant exhibited by P.T. Barnum; prob. from *mumbo jumbo*.] a large, clumsy person, animal, or thing; an unusually large thing of its kind.

jum'bō, *a.* very large; larger than usual of its kind: sometimes used as a trade classification of size, as of olives.

jum'buk, *n.* in Australia, a sheep: so called by the aborigines and bushmen.

jụme, *n.* [S. Am.] a South American plant which is unusually rich in carbonate of soda.

jụ'ment, *n.* [Fr.] a beast of burden. [Obs.]

jump, *v.i.*; jumped (jumt), *pt., pp.*; jumping, *ppr.* [perh. It. loan word (16th c.), from orig. Gmc. source.]
1. to move oneself suddenly from the ground, etc. by using the leg muscles; to leap; spring.
2. to be moved with a jerk; to bob; bounce.
3. to start in sudden surprise.
4. to pass suddenly from one thing or topic to another.
5. to rise suddenly; as, prices have *jumped*.
6. in checkers, to move a piece over an opponent's piece, thus capturing it.
7. to agree; to tally; to coincide.
to jump at; (a) to reach (a conclusion) hastily, without careful consideration; (b) to accept hastily and eagerly.
to jump off; to start an attack. [Military Slang.]
to jump on; to scold; censure. [Slang.]

jump, *v.t.* 1. to leap over; as, to *jump* a hurdle.
2. to cause to leap; as, to *jump* a horse over a fence.
3. (a) to leap upon; spring aboard; (b) to leap from (a moving train, etc.).
4. to cause (prices, etc.) to rise.
5. to attack suddenly. [Slang.]
6. to leave suddenly; to flee; as, he *jumped* town. [Slang.]
7. in bridge, to raise (a partner's bid) or, in contract, to make an unnecessarily high bid in (a partner's suit).
8. in checkers, to capture (an opponent's piece).
9. in journalism, to continue (a story) on another page.
10. to break in continuity of action, as a motion-picture image, because of faulty alignment of the film.
11. in blacksmithing, to unite by a butt weld.
12. to bore or drill with a jumper.
13. to skip over; to neglect; as, to *jump* pages in reading.
14. to jeopardize; to hazard. [Obs.]
to jump a claim; to seize mining rights or land claimed by someone else.
to jump one's bail; to abscond while under bail, thereby forfeiting one's bail bonds.
to jump the gun; (a) to begin a race before the signal has been given; hence, (b) to begin anything before the proper time. [Slang.]
to jump the track; to go suddenly off the rails.

jump, *n.* 1. the act of jumping; a leap; a spring; a bound.
2. the distance covered by a leap; hence, an omission; a passing over.
3. a thing to be jumped over.
4. a sudden transition.
5. a sudden rise, as in prices.
6. a sudden, nervous start or jerk; a twitch.
7. [*pl.*] chorea; also, delirium tremens (usually with *the*).
8. in athletics, a contest in jumping; as, the high *jump*, the broad *jump*.
9. in checkers, a move by which an opponent's piece is captured.
10. in journalism, a line telling on what page a story is continued.
11. in geology, a dislocation of a stratum or vein.
12. in construction, an abrupt rise in a level course of brickwork or masonry to accommodate the work to the inequality of the ground.
13. a risk; a venture; a hazard. [Obs.]
Our fortune lies upon this *jump*.—Shak.
from the jump; from the beginning.
on the jump; busily moving about; very busy. [Colloq.]
to get (or *have*) *the jump on*; to get (or have) an earlier start than and thus have an advantage over. [Slang.]

jump, *n.* [prob. from Fr. *jupe*, a long skirt.]
1. a kind of under bodice formerly worn by women.
2. a short, loose coat worn by men. [Brit. Dial.]

jump, *a.* exact; matched. [Obs.]

jump, *adv.* exactly; as, *jump* at the dead of night. [Obs.]

jump ball, in basketball, a ball tossed by the referee between two opposing players, as in beginning or resuming play.

jump bid, in bridge, a bid that is higher than is necessary to increase the previous bid.

jump'ẽr, *n.* 1. one who or that which jumps.
2. a kind of sled which consists of a box placed on runners.
3. a spring which controls the motion of the star wheel of a watch; also, a pawl to prevent reverse motion of a ratchet wheel.
4. a short wire to close a break in, or cut out part of, a circuit.
5. a man or boy who delivers packages from a delivery truck.
6. in mining, a boring tool that is operated with an up-and-down jumping motion.
7. one of a sect of fanatics among the Calvinistic Methodists and others in Wales: from their violent agitations and motions during the time of divine worship.
8. one who attempts to seize a land or mining claim already held by another.

jump'ẽr, *n.* [from earlier dial. *jump*, short coat.]
1. a loose jacket or blouse, worn by workmen and sailors to protect clothing.
2. a sleeveless dress for wearing over a blouse or sweater.
3. a hooded fur jacket.
4. [*pl.*] rompers.

jum'pẽr stāy, in navigation, an additional stay for holding a yard or boom more securely in heavy weather.

jump'i·ly, *adv.* in a jumpy manner.

jump'i·ness, *n.* the quality or state of being jumpy.

jump'ing, *n.* the act of leaping or springing.
jumping bean; the seed of any of several related Mexican plants, which is caused to jump and roll about by the movements of a moth larva inside it.
jumping deer; same as *mule deer*.
jumping hare; a South African rodent with very long tail and hind legs.
jumping jack; a child's toy consisting of a little jointed figure made to jump or dance about by pulling a string or pushing an attached stick.
jumping louse; a plant louse of the family *Psyllidæ*.
jumping mouse; same as *deer mouse*.
jumping mullet; a food fish, *Mugil albula*.
jumping rat; (a) a jumping mouse; (b) any rodent of the family *Dipodidæ*.
jumping seed; same as *jumping bean*.
jumping shrew; a shrewlike insectivore of the genus *Macroscelides*.
jumping spider; a spider which does not spin a web but captures its prey by leaping upon it.

jump'ing-off' plāce, 1. any isolated or remote place regarded as the outmost limit of civilization or of the civilized world.
2. the extreme limits of one's ability to cope with a situation; as, they had reached the *jumping-off place* in their marriage.

jump joint, a butt joint; a joint made without lapping.

jump sēat, a small folding seat, as one behind the front seat of a limousine, taxi, etc.

jump shot, in basketball, a shot made by a player while in the air during a jump.

jump spärk, a spark produced by the jumping of an electric current across a space between permanently fixed poles, as in the ignition system of some engines.

jump sūit, 1. a coverall worn by paratroops, garage mechanics, etc.
2. a woman's lounging outfit somewhat like this, usually tight-fitting.

jump weld, a butt weld.

jump'y, *a.*; *comp.* jumpier; *superl.* jumpiest,
1. moving in jumps, jerks, or abrupt variations.
2. easily made nervous; apprehensive.

Jun̄·çā'cē·ae, *n.pl.* [L. *juncus*, a rush, and *-aceæ*.] in botany, a family of monocotyledonous plants, the rush family.

jun̄·çā'ceous, *a.* of or pertaining to the *Juncaceæ*.

juñ'çāte, *n.* junket. [Obs.]

jun'cīte, *n.* [L. *juncus*, a rush, and *-ite*.] in geology, a striated, grooved, and tapering, rushlike fragment of a fossil leaf occurring in the Devonian formation.

Juñ'çō, *n.* [prob. from Sp. *junco*, a rush; L. *juncus*, a rush.]
1. in zoology, a North American genus of the finch family; the snowbirds.
2. [j–] *pl.* **juñ'çōẹ,** any bird belonging to this genus.

juñ'çous, *a.* [L. *juncosus*, full of rushes, from *juncus*, a rush.] of or pertaining to the order *Juncaceæ*.

juñç'tion, *n.* [L. *junctio* (*-onis*), from *jungere*, to join.]
1. the act of joining or the state of being joined; union; combination.
2. the place or point of union or meeting; specifically, the crossing place of two or more highways or railroads.

juñç'tion plāte, a piece of boiler plate used for uniting two plates which make a butt joint.

juñç'tūre, *n.* [L. *junctura*, from *jungere*, to join.]
1. a joining or being joined.
2. the line or point at which two bodies are joined; a joint; an articulation.
3. a point of time; specifically, a point rendered critical or important by a concurrence of circumstances; a crisis.
4. a state of affairs.

Juñ'çus, *n.* [L., a rush.] the type genus of the *Juncaceæ*, or rush family.

Jụne, *n.* [L. *Junius* (supply *mensis*, month), June, from *Junius*, a Roman family name.] the sixth month of the year, having thirty days, in which the sun enters the sign Cancer.

jụ'nēat·ing, *n.* same as *jenneting*.

Jụne bee'tle, 1. a large, brown beetle of the cockchafer group, found in the northern U.S.: so called because it begins to fly about June 1.
2. the figeater, a large, green beetle of the southern United States.

Jụne'ber″ry, *n.*; *pl.* **Jụne'ber″rieṣ,** a small North American tree, *Amelanchier canadensis*, which bears a berry of pleasant flavor; also, its fruit or berry: called also *shadbush* and *serviceberry*.

Jụne bug, a June beetle.

Jụne grȧss, the blue grass of Kentucky, *Poa pratensis*.

Juñ·gẽr·man'ni·ȧ, *n.* [named after *Jungermann*, a German botanist.] a formerly accepted genus of the family *Jungermanniaceæ*.

Juñ·gẽr·man·ni·ā'cē·ae, *n.pl.* [*Jungermannia* and *-aceæ*.] a family of leafy liverworts; the scale mosses.

juñ·gẽr·man·ni·ā'ceous, *a.* of or pertaining to the family *Jungermanniaceæ*.

juñ'gle, *n.* [Hind. *jangal*, desert, forest, jungle, from Sans. *jangala*, dry, desert.]
1. land covered with a dense growth of trees, tall vegetation, vines, etc., typically in tropical regions.
2. any thick, tangled growth.
3. a hoboes' camp. [Slang.]

juñ'gle beār, the sloth bear of India.

juñ'gle çock, same as *jungle fowl*.

juñ'gle fē'vẽr, a malarial fever prevalent in the jungle districts of India and Africa: called also *hill fever*.

juñ'gle fowl, 1. any of several species of wild fowl of the genus *Gallus*, found in India and Malaysia: the red Indian species is regarded as the ancestor of the present-day domestic fowl.
2. an Australian wild fowl, as *Megapodius tumulus*.

juñ'gly, *a.* 1. covered with jungle.
2. of or like a jungle.

jụn'iŏr, *a.* [L., contr. of *juvenior*, compar. of *juvenis*, young.]
1. the younger: written *Jr.* after the name of a son who bears the same name as his father: opposed to *senior*.
2. of more recent position or lower status; as, a *junior* partner, a *junior* lien.
3. of later date.
4. made up of younger members.
5. relating to a third-year student or class in a high school or college.

jụn'iŏr, *n.* 1. a person younger than another.
The fools, my *juniors* by a year.—Swift.
2. a person of lower standing or rank.
3. one in the junior year of his high-school or college course.

jụn'iŏr çol'leġe, a college in which but a two-years' course in regular college work is given.

jụn'iŏr hīgh sçhool, a school intermediate between elementary school and senior high school: it usually has the seventh, eighth, and ninth grades.

jụn·ior'i·ty (-yor'), *n.* the quality or state of being junior, as in age or rank.

Jụn'iŏr Lēague (lēg), any one of a group of associated organizations, the members of which are young women of leisure and the upper social class organized to engage in volunteer welfare work.

Jụn'iŏr Lēa'guẽr, a member of a Junior League.

jụn'iŏr vär'si·ty, a team, usually of lowerclassmen, that represents a university, college, or school in a secondary level of competition, especially in an athletic sport.

jụ'ni·pẽr, *n.* [L. *juniperus*, juniper, properly youth-producing; *juvenis*, young, and *parere*, to produce.]
1. a coniferous shrub or tree of the genus *Juniperus*, closely allied to the cedar, with berrylike cones that yield an oil which is used medicinally, in flavoring gin, and for other purposes.
2. any of several similar trees that bear cones.

JUNIPER
(*Juniperus communis*)

jụ'ni·pẽr·in, *n.* a black or yellow resinous extract of juniper berries.

Jụ·nip'e·rus, *n.* [L., juniper.] a genus of evergreen trees and shrubs.

jụ'ni·pẽr wŏrm, the larva of a moth, *Phalonia rutilana*, which lives upon juniper leaves.

juñk, *n.* [ME. *jonke*; OFr. *jonc*, a rush; Port. *junco*, junk, a rush; L. *juncus*, a rush: so called from rushes being used to weave ropes.]
1. old cable or rope used for making oakum, mats, etc.
2. old metal, paper, glass, and other refuse.
3. a piece or chunk.
4. useless stuff; trash; rubbish. [Colloq.]
5. salt beef: so called from its resembling old ropes' ends in hardness and toughness.
6. the mass of cellular tissue in the head of a sperm whale, containing oil and spermaceti.
7. a narcotic drug; especially, heroin. [Slang.]

juñk, *v.t.* to throw away as worthless; to discard; scrap. [Colloq.]

juñk, *n.* [Sp. and Port. *junco*, from Malay *dgong*.] a flat-bottomed ship with battened sails, used in China and Japan.

CHINESE JUNK

juñk bot'tle, a thick strong bottle, usually made of stout green glass.

juñk dēal'ẽr, the proprietor of a junk shop.

Jụñ'kẽr, jụñ'kẽr (yun'), *n.* [G., from MHG. *junc herre*, young nobleman; OHG. *jung*, young, and *herro*, lord.]
1. a member of the privileged, land-owning class in Germany; a Prussian aristocrat.
2. a German military officer, especially one who is autocratic, illiberal, etc.

Jụñ'kẽr, jụñ'kẽr, *a.* of or like the Junkers.

Jụñ'kẽr·iṣm, *n.* the policy of the aristocratic party in Prussia.

juñ'ket, *n.* [formerly also *juncate*, from It. *giuncata*, a sweetmeat, cream cheese, from L. *juncus*, a rush: so called because brought to market on rushes.]
1. curds with cream.
2. milk sweetened, flavored, and thickened into curd with rennet.
3. a feast; a picnic.
4. an excursion for pleasure.
5. an excursion paid for out of public funds.

juñ'ket, *v.i.*; junketed, *pt., pp.*; junketing, *ppr.* to go on a junket or excursion, especially one paid for out of public funds.

juñ'ket, *v.t.* to entertain, as on a junket.

juñ'ket·ing, *n.* a festivity; a picnic.

juñk fọọd, any of various snack foods processed as with chemical additives and of low nutritional value.

junk'ie, junk'y, *n.*; *pl.* **junk'ies,** [from *junk*, *n.* 7.] a narcotics addict, especially one addicted to heroin. [Slang.]

juñk jew'el·ry, inexpensive costume jewelry. [Colloq.]

juñk māil, advertisements, solicitations, etc. mailed indiscriminately in large quantities.

juñk'man, *n.*; *pl.* **juñk'men,** a dealer in old metal, glass, paper, rags, etc.

juñk ring, in steam engines, a ring fitting into a groove round a piston to keep it steam-tight.

juñk shop, a shop where junk, such as old metal, bottles, rags, etc., is bought and sold.

juñk vat, in tanning, a tank or vat for containing the spent tan liquor.

juñk'yärd, *n.* a place where old metal, paper, etc. is kept, sorted, and sold.

Jụ'nō, *n.* [L.] 1. in Roman mythology, the goddess of marriage, queen of the gods, wife of Jupiter, and the second highest divinity: identified with the Greek Hera.
2. in astronomy, one of the small planets or asteroids which revolve round the sun between the orbits of Mars and Jupiter.
3. *pl.* **Jụ'nōṣ,** a stately, regal woman.

Jụ·nō·esque' (-esk'), *a.* stately and regal like Juno.

Jụ·nō'ni·ăn, *a.* pertaining to, or having the characteristics of, Juno.

JUNO

jun'tȧ, *n.* [Sp., from L. *juncta*, f. of *junctus*, pp. of *jungere*, to join.]
1. an assembly or council, particularly a Spanish or Latin-American legislative or administrative body.
2. a group of political intriguers; especially, such a group of military men who gain power by means of a coup d'etat: also **jun'tō,** *pl.* **jun'tōṣ**

jụ'pȧ·ti pälm (päm), [*jupati*, S. Am. name.] a Brazilian palm, *Raphia tædigera*, having enormous leaves and leaf stalks.

jụpe, *n.* same as *jupon*.

Jụ'pi·tẽr, *n.* [L. *Juppiter* or *Jupiter*, from Old L. *Jovis*, Jove, and *pater*, father.]
1. in Roman mythology, the god ruling over all other gods and all people: identified with the Greek Zeus.
2. the largest planet in the solar system and the fifth in distance from the sun: diameter, 87,000 mi.; period of revolution, 11.86 yrs.; symbol, ♃.

Jụ'pi·tẽr Plụ'vi·us, [L., lit., Jupiter who brings rain; *pluvius*, rainy, from *pleure*, to rain.] Jupiter regarded as the giver of rain.

Jụ'pi·tẽr'ṣ-bēard, *n.*
1. an evergreen plant, *Anthyllis barba-jovis*.
2. the houseleek.
3. a European perennial herb, *Centranthus ruber*.

JUPITER

jụ·pon', jụp·pon', *n.* [OFr. *jupon*, from *jupe*; Sp. *juba*; Ar. *jubbah*, *aljubbah*, a garment so called.]
1. a tight-fitting garment without sleeves,

formerly worn over or under armor and descending just below the hips: also *gipon.*
2. a petticoat.
Jụ'rả, *n.* the Jurassic period or rocks.
jụ'rả, *n.* [L.] plural of *jus,* law.
jụ'răl, *a.* [L. *jus, juris,* right, law, and *-al.*]
1. of law; legal.
2. pertaining to rights and duties.
jụ"rả·men·tä'dō, *n.* a Filipino Moslem who takes a solemn oath before a priest that he will die killing Christians.
jụ·rả·men'tum, *n.* [L.] an oath.
jụ'rănt, *n.* [L. *jurans,* ppr. of *jurare,* to swear.] one who is under oath.
jụ'rănt, *a.* in law, taking oath; swearing.
Jụ·ras'siç, *a.* designating or of the second period of the Mesozoic Era, immediately following the Triassic and preceding the Cretaceous, characterized by the dominance of dinosaurs and the appearance of flying reptiles and birds.
the Jurassic; the Jurassic Period or its rocks.
jụ'rat, *n.* [Fr. *jurat,* from LL. *juratus,* lit., one sworn, from L. *juratus,* pp. of *jurare,* to swear.]
1. a person legally sworn. [Obs. except Historical.]
2. a municipal officer or magistrate in certain French towns and the Channel Islands.
3. in law, a statement added to an affidavit, telling when and before whom (also, in British usage, where) the affidavit was made.
jụ'rả·tō·ry, *a.* [LL. *juratorius,* from L. *jurator,* a sworn witness, from *jurare,* to swear.] of or comprising an oath; as, *juratory* caution.
jụ'rē di·vī'nō, [L.] by divine law.
jụ'rē hū·mā'nō, [L.] by human law.
jụ'rel, *n.* [Sp.] a food fish of the genus *Caranx,* found in warm seas, having typically narrow bodies and widely forked tails.
jụ·rid'iç, *a.* juridical.
jụ·rid'iç·ăl, *a.* [L. *juridicus,* from *jus, juris,* law, and *dicare,* to point out, declare.]
1. acting in the distribution of justice; pertaining to a judge.
2. of judicial proceedings, jurisprudence, or law.
juridical days; those days on which courts are in session.
jụ·rid'iç·ăl·ly, *adv.* according to forms of law; with legal authority.
jụ·ris·çon'sult, *n.* [L. *jurisconsultus; jus, juris,* law, and *consultus,* pp. of *consulere,* to consult.] a man learned in the law; a counselor-at-law; one versed in civil law; a jurist.
jụ·ris·diç'tion, *n.* [L. *jurisdictio (-onis), juris dictio,* administration of the law; *jus, juris,* right, law, and *dictio (-onis),* from *dicere,* to speak, declare.]
1. the legal power or authority to hear and decide cases; the power of executing the laws and administering justice.
2. the power or right of exercising authority.
3. the limit within which power may be exercised.
4. the territorial range of authority.
5. a law court or system of law courts.
jụ·ris·diç'tion·ăl, *a.* pertaining to jurisdiction.
jụ·ris·diç'tive, *a.* having jurisdiction.
jụ·ris·prụ'dence, *n.* [L. *jurisprudentia; jus, juris,* right, law, and *prudentia,* a foreseeing, knowledge, skill.]
1. the science or philosophy of law.
2. a system of laws.
3. a part or division of law.
medical jurisprudence; forensic medicine.
jụ·ris·prụ'dent, *n.* a student of jurisprudence.
jụ·ris·prụ'dent, *a.* skilled in the law.
jụ·ris·prụ·den'tiăl, *a.* pertaining to jurisprudence.
jụ'rist, *n.* [Fr. *juriste;* LL. *jurista,* from L. *jus, juris,* right, law.] a man who professes the science of law; one versed in the law; a scholar or writer in the field of law.
jụ·ris'tiç, jụ·ris'tiç·ăl, *a.* pertaining to a jurist or jurisprudence; juridical; legal.
jụ·ris'ti·çăl·ly, *adv.* in a juristic manner.
jụ'rŏr, *n.* [ME. *jurour;* OFr. *jureur, jureor,* from L. *jurator,* a swearer, one who takes an oath, from *jurare,* to swear.]
1. one who serves on a jury; a juryman.
2. one of a group of persons selected to award prizes, etc. in a competition or contest.
jụ'ry, *n.; pl.* **jụ'rieș,** [OFr. *jurée,* an oath, judicial inquest, from LL. *jurata,* a jury, a sworn body of men, properly f. pp. of L. *jurare,* to swear, to take an oath, from *jus, juris,* law.]
1. in a law, a number of qualified persons, selected in the manner prescribed by law, empaneled and sworn to inquire into the facts in a law case, and to give a decision on the evidence given them in the case.
2. a body of persons, often experts, selected to award prizes, etc. in a competition or contest.
grand jury; a jury of from 12 to 23 citizens that investigates accusations against persons charged with crime and indicts them for trial before a petit jury if there is sufficient evidence.
jury of matrons; a jury of women chosen to determine whether or not a woman is pregnant.
petit (or *petty*) *jury;* a jury consisting usually of twelve persons selected to weigh evidence and try issues of a trial in court: distinguished from *grand jury.*
special jury; a jury called for a particular purpose, as a jury of a certain class or trade called to determine a question relating to their occupation or profession.
jụ'ry, *a.* [perh. from OFr. *ajurie,* relief, from L. *adjutare,* to help.] for temporary or makeshift use on a ship; as, a *jury* mast.
jụ'ry box, the place in a court where the jury sits.
jụ'ry·măn, *n.; pl.* **jụ'ry·men,** one who is empaneled on a jury, or who serves as a juror.
jụ'ry-rigged (-rigd), *a.* rigged for temporary use on a ship.
jụs (zụ), *n.* [Fr.] juice; gravy; as, *au jus,* with gravy.
jụs, *n.; pl.* **jụ'rả,** [L.] 1. (a or the) law.
2. a legal principle, right, or power.
jụs çả·nō'ni·çum, [L.] canon law.
jụs ci·vī'li, [L.] civil law.
jụs di·vī'num, [L.] divine law.
jụs ġen'ti·um (-shi-), [L., law of nations.]
1. ancient Roman law for aliens.
2. international law.
jụs nả·tū'rae, [L.] law of nature; natural law.
jus'sive, *a.* [from L. *jussus,* a command; and *-ive.*] in grammar, expressing a command.
juș'sive, *n.* in grammar, a jussive word, form, or mood.
just, *a.* [OFr. *juste;* L. *justus,* lawful, rightful, proper, from *jus,* right, law.]
1. upright; honest; having principles of rectitude; righteous; as, a *just* man.
2. equitable; impartial; fair; as, a *just* decision.
3. exact; accurate; precise; neither too much nor too little; neither more nor less; as, a *just* description.
4. correct; true.
5. deserved; merited; as, a *just* rebuke.
6. legally right; lawful; rightful.
7. right; proper.
8. well-founded; as, a *just* suspicion.
Syn.—exact, honest, impartial, precise, proper, upright.
just, *adv.* 1. exactly; precisely; as, *just* one o'clock.
2. almost exactly.
3. only; no more than; as, *just* a simple soul.
4. by a very little; barely; as, he *just* missed the train.
5. a very short time ago; as, she has *just* left.
6. quite; really; as, it's *just* beautiful. [Colloq.]
just, *n.* and *v.i.* same as *joust.*
juste'au·çorps (zhust'ō-kọr), *n.* [Fr., close to the body.] a close-fitting coat.
just'ẽr, *n.* same as *jouster.*
just'ice, *n.* [O.Fr., from L. *justitia,* justice, from *justus,* lawful, rightful, just, from *jus,* law, right.]
1. the quality of being righteous; honesty.
2. impartiality; fair representation of facts.
3. the quality of being correct or right; as, he proved the *justice* of his claim.
4. vindictive retribution; merited reward or punishment; as, *justice* overtook the criminal.
5. sound reason; rightfulness; validity.
6. the use of authority and power to uphold what is right, just, or lawful.
7. the administration of law; procedure of a law court.
8. a judge.
9. a justice of the peace.
justice of the peace; a magistrate having the power to try minor cases, perform marriages, etc. within a specified district.
to bring to justice; to cause (a wrongdoer) to be tried in court and duly punished.
to do justice to; (a) to treat fitly or fairly; (b) to treat with due appreciation; to enjoy properly.
to do oneself justice; (a) to do something in a manner worthy of one's abilities; (b) to be fair to oneself.
Syn.—equity, law, impartiality, fairness, right, reasonableness, propriety, uprightness.
jus'tice, *v.t.* to administer justice. [Obs.]
jus'tice·ả·ble, *a.* justiciable. [Obs.]
jus'tice·hood, *n.* justiceship. [Rare.]
jus'tice·ment, *n.* judicial procedure. [Obs.]
jus'ti·cẽr, *n.* an administrator of justice. [Obs.]
jus'tice·ship, *n.* the position, functions, or term of office of a justice.
jus·ti'ci·ả·ble (-tish'i-), *a.* 1. liable for trial in court.
2. subject to court jurisdiction.
jus·ti'ci·ăr (-tish'i-), *n.* same as *justiciary.*
jus·ti'ci·ā·ry, *n.; pl.* **jus·ti'ci·ā·ries,** 1. an administrator of justice, especially the judge of a superior court.
2. in English history, the chief political and judicial officer under the Norman and early Plantagenet kings.
3. the jurisdiction of a justiciary.
jus·ti'ci·ā·ry, *a.* relating to the administration of justice or the office of a judge.
jus'ti·çō, jus ti·çōat, *n.* same as *justeaucorps.*
jus·ti·fī·ả·bil'i·ty, *n.* the quality or state of being justifiable.
jus'ti·fī·ả·ble, *a.* that can be justified, vindicated, or defended.
jus'ti·fī·ả·ble hom'i·cīde, the killing of a person when the act is absolutely necessary to prevent the commission of some other serious crime; the killing of a person in self-defense, etc.
jus'ti·fī·ả·ble·ness, *n.* the quality of being justifiable.
jus'ti·fī·ả·bly, *adv.* in a justifiable manner.
jus"ti·fi·cā'tion, *n.* 1. the act of justifying or the state of being justified.
2. a fact that justifies or vindicates.
3. in law, (a) the showing of a sufficient reason in court why a defendant did what he is called to answer; (b) proof of qualification as bailor or surety, as by showing ownership of enough property.
4. in theology, remission of sin, and absolution from guilt and punishment.
5. in printing, the adjustment of type by proper spacing.
justification by faith; in theology, the act by which a sinner is freed through faith from the penalty of his sin and is accepted by God as righteous or worthy of being saved.
jus'tif·i·çả·tive, *a.* justifying; vindicatory.
jus'ti·fi·çā·tŏr, *n.* one who justifies; a justifier.
jus·tif'i·çả·tō·ry, *a.* vindicatory; defensory.
jus'ti·fī·ẽr, *n.* 1. one who justifies; one who vindicates, supports, or defends.
2. one who or that which justifies lines of type, as an automatic attachment to a typesetting machine.
jus'ti·fȳ, *v.t.;* justified, *pt., pp.;* justifying, *ppr.* [ME. *justifien;* OFr. *justifier;* LL. *justificare,* to act justly toward, to justify; L. *justus,* just, and *-ficare,* from *facere,* to do, make.]
1. to prove or show to be just, or conformable to law, right, justice, propriety, or duty; to defend or maintain; to vindicate as right.
2. to declare free from guilt or blame; to absolve; to clear.
3. in theology, to pardon and clear from guilt; to treat as just; to pardon.
4. to supply good or lawful grounds for; to warrant.
5. in printing, to adjust (type) in lines by proper use of spaces.
Syn.—excuse, defend, warrant, maintain, vindicate.
jus'ti·fȳ, *v.i.* 1. in printing, to agree; to fit; to conform exactly; to form an even surface or true line with something else, as type.
2. in law, (a) to show an adequate reason for something done; (b) to prove qualified as surety.
Jus·tin'i·ăn, *a.* of or pertaining to the code of laws (*Justinian Code*) arranged by the Byzantine emperor Justinian (527–565 A.D.).
jus'tle (-l), *n., v.t.* and *v.i.* jostle.
just'ly, *adv.* 1. in a just manner.
2. rightly.
3. deservedly.

just'ness, *n.* 1. accuracy; exactness; conformity to truth; as, the *justness* of a description.
2. the quality of being just; justice; reasonableness; equity.

jut, *v.i.*; jutted, *pt., pp.*; jutting, *ppr.* [var. of *jet.*] to extend forward; to project; to protrude; to stick out; as, the *jutting* part of a building.

jut, *n.* a part that juts; a projection.

jüte, *n.* [Hind. *jūt*; Sans. *juṭa*, matted hair, *jaṭa*, matted hair, fibrous roots.]

JUTE
(*Corchorus capsularis*)

1. a fibrous substance resembling hemp, obtained from the East Indian plants, *Corchorus olitorius* and *Corchorus capsularis*. It is used for making burlap, sacks, mats, rope, etc.
2. either of the two East Indian plants from which this fiber is obtained.
American jute; a fiber resembling the jute of East India but obtained from the velvetleaf, *Abutilon avicennæ*.

jüte, *a.* of jute.

Jüte, *n.* a member of any of several Germanic tribes that originally lived in Jutland and who accompanied the Angles and Saxons in their invasion of England in the fifth century.

Jūt'ish, *a.* of the Jutes.

Jut'länd·ẽr, *n.* a native or inhabitant of Jutland.

Jut'länd·ish, *a.* belonging to or like Jutland or the Jutlanders.

jut'ting·ly, *adv.* projectingly.

jut'ty, *n.*; *pl.* **jut'ties,** [prob. a form of *jetty.*] a projection of a building, wall, etc.; also, a pier or mole; a jetty. [Obs.]

jut'ty, *v.t.* and *v.i.* to project; to overhang. [Obs.]

Jü·tūr'na, *n.* [L.] in Roman mythology, the presiding deity of a spring near the temple of Vesta; a water nymph.

Jü·vā'vi·ăn, *a.* [Fr.; ML. *Juvavia, Juvavum* Salzburg.] in geology, that which specifies the second highest portion of the Trias of the Alps.

jü've·năl, *n.* a youth. [Obs.]

jü·ve·nes'cence, *n.* a growing young or youthful.

jü·ve·nes'cent, *a.* becoming young.

jü've·nile, *a.* [L. *juvenilis*, from *juvenis*, young.]
1. young; youthful; immature.
2. pertaining to, characteristic of, or suited for children or young persons; as. *juvenile* sports.
Syn.—youthful, young, infantine, boyish, girlish, early, immature, adolescent, pubescent.

jü've·nile, *n.* 1. a young person; a child.
2. an actor who takes youthful roles.
3. a book for children.

jū've·nile çourt, a law court that tries the cases involving children under a fixed age.

jü've·nile·ness, *n.* juvenility. [Rare.]

jü·ve·nil'i·å, *n.pl.* [L., neut. pl. of *juvenilis*, juvenile.] writings, paintings, etc. done in childhood or youth.

jü·ve·nil'i·ty, *n.*; *pl.* **jü·ve·nil'i·ties,** 1. the quality or state of being juvenile.
2. a childish action, manner, or characteristic.
3. juveniles collectively.

jü'vi·å, *n.* the tree on which brazil nuts grow, *Bertholletia excelsa*.

jux'tå-, [from L. *juxta*, near, beside.] a combining form meaning *near, beside, close by*, as in *juxta*position.

jux'tå·pōṣe, *v.t.*; juxtaposed, *pt., pp.*; juxtaposing, *ppr.* to place side by side.

jux·tå·poṣ'it, *v.t.* to juxtapose. [Rare.]

jux"tå·pō·ṣi'tion, *n.* 1. a placing or being placed side by side or close together.
2. the position of being side by side or close together.

K

K, k (kā), *n.*; *pl.* **K's, k's, Ks, ks** (kāz), 1. the eleventh letter of the English alphabet: from the Greek *kappa*, a borrowing from the Phoenician.
2. the sound of K or k: when used as the first letter of a word and followed by *n*, it is usually not pronounced (e.g., *knee, knife*).
3. a type or impression for K or k.
4. *a symbol for* the eleventh in a sequence or group (or the tenth if J is omitted).

K, k (kā), *a.* 1. of K or k.
2. eleventh in a sequence or group (or tenth if J is omitted).

K (kā), *n.* 1. an object shaped like K.
2. a Roman numeral for 250: with a superior bar ($\bar{K}$), 250,000.
3. in assaying, *the symbol for* carat.
4. *kalium* [Mod. L.], in chemistry, *the symbol for* potassium.
5. in mathematics, *a symbol for* constant.
6. in meteorology, *a symbol for* cumulus.

K (kā), *a.* shaped like K.

kä, *n.* [Egypt.] in ancient Egyptian religion, the soul, regarded as dwelling in a person's body or in an image and continuing after death.

Käa'bå, Çäa'bå (kä'), *n.* [Ar. *ka'bah*, a square building, from *ka'b*, a cube.] the sacred Moslem shrine at Mecca, toward which believers turn when praying: it contains a black stone supposedly given to Abraham by the angel Gabriel.

käa'må, *n.* same as *caama*.

kab, *n.* same as *cab* (measure).

kab'å·lå, kab'bå·lå, *n.* same as *cabala*.

kå·bas'söu, *n.* same as *cabasou*.

kå·bob', *n.* and *v.t.* same as *cabob*.

kå·bo̤ok', *n.* in Ceylon, a building stone which becomes very hard after being quarried.

Kä·bü'ki, *n.* [Japan., from *kabu*, music and dancing, and *ki*, spirit.] [also k-] a form of Japanese drama dating from the 17th century: it is based on popular themes, with male and female roles performed exclusively by men, chiefly in formalized pantomime, dance, and song.

Kå·byle', *n.* [Fr., from Ar. *qabā'il*, pl. of *qabīlah.*]
1. a member of the Algerian or Tunisian Berber tribes.
2. the Berber language of the Kabyles.

käd'dish, *n.* [Aramaic *qaddīsh*, holy.] in Judaism, a hymn in praise of God, recited as a mourners' prayer.

kä'di (*or* kā'), *n.* same as *cadi*.

kä·di·les'kẽr, *n.* same as *cadilesker*.

Kaf'fir, *n.* [from Ar. *kāfir*, infidel, from *kafara*, to be skeptical about religion.]
1. a South African Bantu.
2. the language of the Kaffirs.
3. a Kafir.

kaf'fir, *n.* [from *Kaffir.*] any of a group of grain sorghums grown in dry regions for grain and fodder: also *kaffir corn*.

kä'fi·lå, *n.* same as *caffila*.

Kaf'ir, *n.* [Ar. *kāfir*, an unbeliever, infidel.]
1. a member of an Indo-Iranian people of Kafiristan.
2. a Kaffir.

Kaf'ir, *a.* relating to the Kafirs, their language or customs: written also *Caffer, Caffre, Kaffer, Kaffre.*

kaf'ir, *n.* same as *kaffir*.

Kaf'ir bo̤om, a leguminous tree of South Africa, of the genus *Erythrina*.

Kaf'ir bread (bred), the pith from the stem of a tree in South Africa, used for food; also, the tree itself, *Encephalartos caffer*.

kaf'tå, *n.* [Ar.] the leaves of a celastraceous shrub, *Catha edulis*, of Arabia, used in making a beverage.

kaf'tăn, *n.* same as *caftan*.

kä'gō, *n.* [Japan.] in Japan, a chair made of basketwork and slung from a pole to be borne by two men in carrying a traveler.

kä'gü, *n.* [native name.] a wading bird of New Caledonia distinguished by its long, erectile nuchal crest.

kä'hau, *n.* [native name, so called from its cry.] the proboscis monkey, *Nasalis larvatus*, of Borneo, characterized by its very long nose.

kä"hi·kä·te̤'å, *n.* [Maori name.] a tall coniferous tree of New Zealand, *Podocarpus dacrydioides*, bearing edible fruit.

kaī ap'ple, same as *kei apple*.

Kähn test, [after R. L. *Kahn* (1887-), Am. immunologist, who developed it.] a modified form of the Wassermann test for the diagnosis of syphilis.

kaī'ak, *n.* a kayak.

kāil, *n.* same as *kale*.

kāil'yärd, *n.* [Scot.] a kaleyard: applied to fiction by J. M. Barrie and others (the *kailyard school*) treating Scottish life and using much Scottish dialect.

kāi·må·kam', *n.* [Turk. *kāīmakām*, from Ar. *qāim-makām*, one standing in the place of another.] in Turkey, an officer having the rank of lieutenant colonel in the army, or of lieutenant governor in the civil service.

kāin, *n.* in Scotland, a duty paid in kind by a tenant to his landlord, as poultry, eggs, butter, etc.: also spelled *cain*.

kā'i·nīte, *n.* [Gr. *kainos*, new, recent, and *-ite.*] a mineral, $MgSO_4·MgCl_2·K_2SO_4·6H_2O$, much used in fertilizers as a source of potassium.

Kaī·nō·zō'iç, *a.* same as *Cenozoic*.

kaī'rīne, kaī'rin, *n.* [prob. from Gr. *kairos*, the right opportunity.] in pharmacy, $C_{10}H_{13}NO$, an artificial crystalline alkaloid obtained from quinoline.

kaī'rō·line, kaī'rō·lin, *n.* [Gr. *kairos*, and *-ine.*] in pharmacy, $C_{10}H_{13}NO$, an artificial liquid alkaloid obtained from quinoline.

kaī'ṣẽr, *n.* [ME. *kaiser, cayser*, from AS. *casere*, from L. *Cæsar*, family name of first Roman emperors.] emperor: the title [K-] of (a) the rulers of the Holy Roman Empire, 962–1806; (b) the rulers of Austria, 1804–1918; (c) the rulers of Germany, 1871–1918.

kä'kå, *n.* [Maori.] a parrot of New Zealand, *Nestor meridionalis*, having an olive-brown body with markings of various other colors.

kä·kä·pō′, *n.* [Maori; *kaka,* parrot, and *po,* night.] the owl parrot or night kaka, *Strigops habroptilus,* a small parrot having a green body with brown and yellow markings: called also *night parrot, ground parrot,* the latter because it occupies a hole in the ground during the day.

käk·ȧ·räl′i, *n.* [native name.] a large tree common in British Guiana, *Lecythis ollaria,* the wood of which is very durable in salt water.

kä·kẹ·mō′nō, *n.* [Japan.; *kake,* to hang, and *mono,* thing.] a Japanese hanging or scroll made of silk or paper with an inscription or picture on it and a roller at the bottom.

kä′kï, *n.*; *pl.* **kä′kïṣ,** [Japan.]
1. the Japanese persimmon, or date plum, *Diospyros kaki,* an Asiatic tree of the ebony family.
2. its edible fruit.

kak·is·toç′rȧ·cy, *n.*; *pl.* **kak·is·toç′rȧ·cieṣ,** [Gr. *kakistos,* superl. of *kakos,* bad, and *-kratia,* from *kratein,* to rule.] government by the worst men in the state: opposed to *aristocracy.*

kak′ō·dyl, kak′ō·dyle, *n.* same as *cacodyl.*

kȧ·kox′ēne, kȧ·kox′ïne, *n.* same as *cacoxene.*

kä·lä-ä·zär′, *n.* [Hind. *kālāāzār,* lit., black disease.] an infectious disease caused by a protozoan parasite and characterized by an enlarged spleen and liver, irregular fever, anemia, etc.: also called *black fever, visceral leishmaniasis.*

kä′lan, *n.* [native name.] a fur-bearing mammal, *Enhydris marina,* of the North Pacific coast, closely related to the otter and much valued for the quality of its fur: called also *sea otter.*

kä·lȧ·sïe′, *n.* a monkey, *Semnopithecus rubicundus,* of Borneo, characterized by a tuft of long hair on its head.

kāle, kāil, *n.* [Scot. *kale, kail,* var. of *cole.*]
1. a hardy, nonheading cabbage with loose, spreading, curled leaves; cole or colewort.
2. (a) any cabbage or greens; (b) a broth made of cabbage or other greens. [Scot.]
3. money; especially, paper money. [Slang.]

kȧ·leeġe′, *n.* [E. Ind. *kalij.*] any of several species of crested pheasants of India: spelled also *kalij, caliage.*

kȧ·leī′dō·phon, kȧ·leī′dō·phōne, *n.* [Gr. *kalos,* beautiful, and *eidos,* form, and *phōnē,* sound.] an instrument for illustrating the phenomena of sound waves.

kȧ·leī′dō·sçōpe, *n.* [Gr. *kalos,* beautiful, and *eidos,* form, and *skopein,* to view.]
1. an optical instrument which, by an arrangement of reflecting surfaces and loose bits of colored glass, exhibits various symmetrical patterns as the device is rotated: invented by Sir David Brewster in 1815.
2. anything that constantly changes, as in color and pattern.

kȧ·leī·dō·sçop′iç, *a.* 1. of a kaleidoscope.
2. resembling the figures in a kaleidoscope; going through varied changes in form.

kȧ·leī·dō·sçop′iç·ăl, *a.* kaleidoscopic.

kȧ·leī·dō·sçop′iç·ăl·ly, *adv.* in a kaleidoscopic manner.

kal′en·dăr, *n.* and *v.t.* same as *calendar.*

kal·en·dăr′i·ăl, *a.* same as *calendarial.*

kal′en·dẽr, *n.* and *v.t.* same as *calender.*

kal′endṣ, *n.pl.* same as *calends.*

kāle tŭr′nip, a kind of cabbage, *Brassica oleracea,* developing into a turnip form just above the ground; a turnip cabbage; kohlrabi.

Kä·lē·vä′lä, *n.* [Finn.; *kaleva,* heroic, and *-la,* abode, hence, lit., land of heroes.] a Finnish epic poem in unrhymed trochaic verse, compiled by Elias Lönnrot from the oral transmission of folklore and mythology and first published in 1835.

kāle′yärd, *n.* a kitchen garden; especially, a cabbage garden. [Scot.]

kal′i (*or* kā′li), *n.* [Ar. *qalīy,* alkali.] the glasswort; saltwort: when burned it yields soda ash.

kä′lï, *n.* [Per. *kālī,* a large carpet.] among the Persians, a very large ruglike carpet with long nap, placed in the middle of a room.

kā′lif, *n.* same as *caliph.*

kā′li·fôrm, *a.* [Ar. *qalīy,* alkali, and L. *forma,* form.] having the form of saltwort. [Rare.]

kȧ·liġ′e·nous, *a.* [Gr. *kali,* alkali, and *-genēs,* producing.] having the property of forming an alkali when oxidized; as, potassium and sodium are *kaligenous* metals.

kal′i·nïte, *n.* [G. *kali,* potash, **-n-,** and **-ite.**] in mineralogy, native alum.

kā′liph, *n.* same as *caliph.*

kā′li·um, *n.* [Mod. L.] potassium: the source of its symbol K.

Kal′kï, *n.* [Sans.] the tenth and last incarnation of Vishnu.

Kal′li·kaks, the, see *Jukes, the.*

Kal′mi·ȧ, *n.* [after Peter *Kalm* (1715–1779), Swedish botanist.] a genus of evergreen shrubs of the heath family, native to North America, chiefly the Appalachian region: it has clusters of white, rose, or purple flowers: various species are called *calico bush, laurel, mountain laurel.*

Kal′muck, *n.* [Turk. *kalmuk,* lit., that part (of the tribe) remaining (at home), orig. pp. of *kalmak,* to remain.]
1. a member of a group of Mongol peoples living chiefly in the Kalmuck Autonomous Soviet Socialist Republic and northern Sinkiang.
2. the Altaic, western Mongolic language of the Kalmucks.

Kal′myk (-mik), *n.* same as *Kalmuck.*

kä′long, *n.* [Jav. *kaloṅ.*] a large, long-muzzled, fruit-eating bat of Malaysia and near-by regions.

kȧ·loy′ẽr, *n.* same as *caloyer.*

Kal′pȧ, *n.* [Sans.] in Hindu cosmogony, a period of time equal to **4,320,000,000** solar years; one day and night of Brahma.

kal′pak, *n.* same as *calpak.*

kal′pis, *n.* [Gr. *kalpis,* a pitcher, urn.] a kind of vase or pitcher with three handles, used in ancient Greece.

kal′sō·mīne, *n.* and *v.t.* same as *calcimine.*

Kä′mȧ, *n.* [Sans. *kāma,* love, the god of love.] in Hindu mythology, the god of love.

kȧ·mä′lȧ, *n.* [Sans.]
1. a powder obtained from an East Indian tree, used as the base of an orange-red dye for silk and wool.
2. the tree.

kam′as, kam′ass, *n.* same as *camass.*

kȧ·mas′si, *n.* [S. African.] a small tree, *Gonioma kamassi,* of the dogbane family; also, its yellow wood, used in woodwork.

kam·bä′lȧ, *n.* [E. Ind.] a tree, *Sonneratia apetala,* growing in India and belonging to the myrtle family; also, its hard red wood.

Kam·chat′kăn, *n.* a native of Kamchatka, a peninsula in northeastern Siberia.

kāme, *n.* [north Brit. dial. var. of *comb, coomb.*] a ridge formed by stratified glacial drift; a low mound or hill composed of sand, gravel, etc.

kä·me·räd′ (rät′), *n.* [G.] comrade: a German soldier's cry of surrender.

kä′mï, *n.* [Japan.] a Japanese title belonging primarily to the celestial gods who formed the first mythological dynasty, then extended to the terrestrial gods of the second dynasty, and then to the long line of spiritual princes who are still represented by the mikado.

kä·mi·kä′zē, *n.* [Japan., lit., divine wind, from *kami,* (Shinto) god or goddess, and *kaze,* the wind.]
1. a suicide attack by a Japanese airplane pilot in World War II.
2. the airplane or pilot in such an attack.

kamp·tū′li·çon, *n.* [Gr. *kamptos,* flexible, and *oulos,* thick, close-pressed.] a warm, soft, and elastic kind of floor cloth, composed of india rubber, gutta-percha, and ground cork.

kam·seen′, kam′sin, *n.* same as *khamsin.*

Kȧ·nä′kȧ, *n.* [Hawaiian, a man.] a Hawaiian; also, any South Sea islander: written also *Kanacha, Kanaker,* and *Kanak.*

Kä·nȧ·rēṣe′, *a.* of Kanara (a region in India), its people, or their language.

Kä·nȧ·rēṣe′, *n.*; *pl.* **Kä·nȧ·rēṣe′,** 1. any of a group of Dravidian people living chiefly in Kanara.
2. their language, a dialect belonging to the Dravidian family of languages.
Also spelled *Canarese.*

kȧ·nä′ri, *n.* [Javanese.] a tree of the East Indies, *Canarium commune,* known as the Java almond, the seeds of which yield the valuable kanari oil, used as an illuminant.

kan′chil, *n.* [E. Ind.] a small, agile deer of Java and adjacent islands; specifically, the *Tragulus pygmæus.*

kand, *n.* same as *cand.*

Kan·dē′li·ȧ, *n.* [from *kandel,* the Malabar name.] a genus of trees of East India whose bark yields a reddish dye.

kañ·gȧ·rọọ′, *n.*; *pl.* **kañ·gȧ·rọọṣ′, kañ·gȧ·rọọ′,** [prob. from former native Australian name in Queensland.] any of a group of leaping, plant-eating mammals native to Australia and neighboring islands, with short forelegs, strong, large hind legs, and a long, thick tail: the female has a pouch, or marsupium, in front, in which she carries her young.

KANGAROO (*Macropus giganteus*)

kañ·gȧ·rọọ′ap′ple, the yellow edible fruit of the solanaceous plant, *Solanum aviculare,* of Tasmania and Australia; also, the plant itself.

kañ·gȧ·rọọ′ bee′tle, a beetle with large hind legs, of the genus *Sagra.*

kañ·gȧ·rọọ′ çlō′ṣūre, a parliamentary plan adopted by a chairman to shorten or end a debate or discussion by limiting consideration of the subject to only a few of its leading features. [Brit.]

kañ·gȧ·rọọ′ çōurt, [said to be so named because its justice progresses by leaps and bounds.] an unauthorized, irregular court, usually disregarding normal legal procedure, as an irregular court in a frontier region or a mock court set up by prison inmates. [Colloq.]

kañ·gȧ·rọọ′ẽr, *n.* a kangaroo hunter.

kañ·gȧ·rọọ′ grȧss, a perennial forage grass of Australia.

kañ·gȧ·rọọ′ hãre, a small, Australian, harelike kangaroo.

kañ·gȧ·rọọ′ hound, a kind of greyhound used for hunting kangaroos in Australia.

kañ·gȧ·rọọ′ mouse, a mouse of North America resembling the kangaroo in its manner of leaping; the jumping mouse.

kañ·gȧ·rọọ′ rat, 1. a small Australian kangaroo somewhat resembling a rat.
2. a rodent living in the desert regions of the United States and Mexico.

kañ·gȧ·rọọ′ thorn, a prickly plant, *Acacia armata,* of Australia, used for making hedges.

kañ·gȧ·rọọ′ vīne, a climbing plant of Australia, *Cissus baudiniana*: called also *kangaroo grape.*

Kan′săn, *a.* of Kansas.

Kan′săn, *n.* a native or inhabitant of Kansas.

kän·tär′, *n.* [Ar. *qintār,* from L. *quintarius,* containing five, from *quintus,* five.] an Egyptian weight equal to 99.05 pounds: it corresponds to the hundredweight.

Kant′i·ăn, *a.* relating to the German philosopher Immanuel Kant (1724–1804), or to his works and doctrines; resembling or conforming to the philosophy of Kant.

Kant′i·ăn, *n.* a follower or disciple of Kant or Kantianism.

Kant′i·ăn·iṣm, *n.* the philosophy of Kant, who held that the content of knowledge comes a posteriori from sense of perception, but that its form is determined by a priori categories of the mind: he also declared that God, freedom, and immortality cannot be denied and must necessarily be presupposed, although they cannot be proved.

Kant′iṣm, *n.* Kantianism.

Kant′ist, *n.* a disciple or follower of Kant.

kä·ō·li·ang′, *n.* [Chin., lit., tall grain.] any of a group of grain-bearing sorghums of eastern Asia: some are now grown in the United States.

kā′ō·lin, kā′ō·line, *n.* [Chinese *kaoling,* high ridge, the name of a hill where it is found.] a fine white clay used in making porcelain, as a filler in textiles, paper, rubber, etc., and in medicine.

kā′ō·lin·īte, *n.* in mineralogy, hydrous aluminum silicate, the main constituent of kaolin.

kā·ō·lin·i·zā′tion, *n.* the process of kaolinizing.

kā′ō·lin·īze, *v.t.*; kaolinized, *pt., pp.*; kaolinizing, *ppr.* to change into kaolin, as feldspar.

Kä·pel′le, *n.*; *pl.* **Kä·pel′len,** [G.] a chapel; also, in music, the choir or orchestra, or both combined; any musical establishment, especially orchestral.

Kä·pell′meis″tẽr, *n.*; *pl.* **Kä·pell′meis″tẽr,**

[G. *kapelle*, chapel, and *meister*, master.] in music, the conductor of a choir or orchestra.

käph, *n.* [Heb.] the eleventh letter of the Hebrew alphabet, corresponding to English *K*, *k*.

kā′pok, *n.* [Malay *kapoq*.] the silky fibers around the seeds of the tropical silk-cotton tree (*kapok tree*), used for stuffing pillows, mattresses, etc.: also called *Java cotton*.

kap′pȧ, *n.* [Gr.] the tenth letter of the Greek alphabet, corresponding to English *K*, *k*: it often appears as *c* in English words derived from Greek, as in *center*, *cosmetic*.

kȧ·put′, *a.* [via soldiers' slang from G. *kaput*, lost, spoiled, done for.] ruined, destroyed, defeated, etc. [Colloq.]

kar′ȧ·gan, *n.* a small fox, *Vulpes karagan*, of Siberia: written also *karagane*.

Kā′rȧ·iṣm, *n.* the teachings and beliefs of the Karaites.

Kā′rȧ·īte, *n.* [Heb. *karaīm*, readers, from *kara*, to read.] one of a sect of Jews who adhere to scriptural as contrasted with rabbinical teaching, denying the authority of the Talmud as binding.

Kä·rä-Käl·päk′, *n.* 1. a member of a Turkic people living in the Uzbek Soviet Socialist Republic.

2. the language of this people.

kar′ȧ·kul, *n.* [from *Kara Kul*, lit., black lake, lake in Bokhara.]

1. a sheep of central Asia.

2. the loosely curled, usually black fur made from the fleece of its newborn lambs.

Also spelled *caracul*, *karakule*.

kar′ăt, *n.* same as *carat*.

kȧ·rā′tȧs, *n.* [S. Am.] 1. a plant of the West Indies and South America, *Nidularium karatas*, of the pineapple family, yielding a valuable fiber: called also *silk grass*.

2. [K–] a genus of tropical American plants of the family *Bromeliaceæ*, several species of which are cultivated for ornament.

kȧ·rä′tē, *n.* [Japan., lit., open hand, from *kara*, empty, and *te*, hand.] a Japanese system of self-defense characterized chiefly by chopping blows delivered with the side of the open hand.

kȧ·rat′tō, *n.* same as *keratto*.

Kȧ·rē′li·ăn, *a.* of Karelia, its people, etc.

Kȧ·rē′li·ăn, *n.* 1. a member of a branch of the Finnish people living in Karelia and eastern Finland.

2. the Finnish dialect of the Karelians.

kar′i·tē, *n.* same as *shea tree*.

kär′mȧ, *n.* [Sans. a deed, act.] 1. in Buddhism and Hinduism, the totality of a person's actions in one of the successive states of his existence, thought of as determining his fate in the next.

2. loosely, fate; destiny.

Kär·mā′thi·ăn, *n.* one of a heretical Mohammedan sect founded in the ninth century by Karmat, who regarded the Koran as merely allegorical and rejected all revelation, fasting, and prayer.

kȧ·rọọ′, **kăr·rọọ′**, *n.*; *pl.* **kȧ·rọọṣ′**, [Hottentot; perh. from *karusa*, dry, hard.] in South Africa, a dry tableland.

kȧ·ross′, *n.* [S. African.] among the natives of South Africa, a rude ruglike cloak made of animal skins: written also *carosse*.

kär′phō·līte, *n.* [Gr. *karphos*, dry stalk, straw, and *lithos*, stone.] in mineralogy, a yellow fibrous mineral, a hydrated silicate of alumina and manganese: written also *carpholite*.

kȧr·rọọ′, *n.* see *karoo*.

kär′sten·īte, *n.* same as *anhydrite*.

kar·y·as′tẽr, *n.* [Gr. *karyon*, a nut, and *astēr*, a star.] a starlike group of filaments in a nucleus at a certain stage of karyokinesis.

kar′y·ō-, [from Gr. *karyon*, a nut.] a combining form used in biology to denote a nucleus, as in *karyo*lymph, *karyo*plasm.

kar″y·ō·ki·nē′sis, *n.* [*karyo-*, and Gr. *kinēsis*, movement, change.] in embryology, a series of complicated nuclear changes taking place before the division of a cell.

kar″y·ō·ki·net′iç, *a.* in embryology, of the nature of or relating to karyokinesis.

kar′y·ō·lymph, *n.* [*karyo-*, and L. *lympha*, water.] the more liquid portion of a nucleus, surrounding and holding the denser parts.

kar·y·om′i·tōme, *n.* [*karyo-*, and Gr. *tomē*, a cutting, from *temnein*, to cut.] in biology, the reticular structure in a nucleus.

kar′y·ō·plaṣm, *n.* [*karyo-*, and Gr. *plasma*, anything formed, from *plassein*, to form, mold.] nuclear protoplasm: distinguished from *cytoplasm*.

kar′y·ō·sōme, *n.* [*karyo-* and *-some*, body.] in biology, (a) an aggregation of chromatin in a resting nucleus; (b) chromosome; (c) the nucleus of a cell.

kar·y·ō′tin, *n.* [*karyo-* and chroma*tin*.] same as *chromatin*.

Käṣ′bäh, *n.* the native quarter of Algiers: also spelled *Casbah*.

kä′shȧ, *n.* [Russ., partly via Yid.] cracked buckwheat, wheat, etc. cooked into a mushlike consistency and served with meat, in soup, etc.

kä′shẽr, *a.*, *n.*, and *v.t.* same as *kosher*.

Kash·mïr′i, *n.* 1. the Indic, Indo-European language of the Kashmirians.

2. *pl.* **Kash·mïr′i**, a Kashmirian.

Kash·mïr′i·ăn, *a.* of Kashmir, its people, their language, or culture.

Kash·mïr′i·ăn, *n.* a native or inhabitant of Kashmir.

kas′sū, *n.* [E. Ind.] an astringent substance extracted from the betel nut.

kat, *n.* in ancient Egypt, the principal unit of weight, equivalent to about 150 grains.

kat′ȧ-, cata-: also, before a vowel, *kat-*.

kȧ·tab′ȧ·sis, *n.*; *pl.* **kȧ·tab′ȧ·sēṣ**, [Gr., from *katabainein*, to go down; *kata-*, down, and *bainein*, to go.]

1. literally, a going down.

2. [K–] the retreat to the sea made by the Greek mercenaries who followed Cyrus against Artaxerxes, as described by Xenophon in the *Anabasis*.

3. any similar retreat.

kat·ȧ·bol′iç, *a.* same as *catabolic*.

kȧ·tab′ō·liṣm, *n.* same as *catabolism*.

kat′ȧ·stāte, *n.* same as *catastate*.

kat·ȧ·tō′ni·ȧ, *n.* same as *catatonia*.

kat″ē·leç·trot′ō·nus, *n.* same as *catelectrotonus*.

kath′ē·tăl, *a.* same as *cathetal*.

kath·ē·tom′e·tẽr, *n.* same as *cathetometer*.

kath′ō·dăl, *a.* same as *cathodal*.

kath′ōde, *n.* same as *cathode*.

kat′i·ŏn, *n.* same as *cation*.

ka′ti·pō, *n.* [native name.] a venomous spider of New Zealand.

kat·ti·mun′dọọ, *n.* same as *cattimandoo*.

kā′ty·did, *n.* any of several large, green, tree insects resembling and related to the grasshopper: so called from the shrill sound made by the males.

kä′ụ·ri, *n.* [Maori]. 1. a tall pine tree of New Zealand: also called *kauri pine*.

2. its wood.

3. a resin (*kauri resin*, *kauri gum*) from this tree, used in varnish.

kä′vä, *n.* [Maori *kawa*, lit., bitter.]

1. a plant of Polynesia, *Macropiper latifolium*, having a root which yields an intoxicating beverage.

2. the beverage itself.

kä·vä·kä′vä, *n.* kava.

kȧ·vass′, *n.* same as *cavass*.

kąw, *v.i.* same as *caw*.

kȧ·wä′kȧ, *n.* [Maori.] a timber tree of New Zealand.

kąwn, *n.* same as *khan*.

kāy, *n.* see *cay*.

Kāy, Sir, in Arthurian legend, one of the knights of the Round Table, the boastful, rude, malicious seneschal and foster brother of King Arthur.

kaȳ′ak, *n.* [Esk.] 1. an Eskimo canoe made of skins, especially sealskins, stretched over a frame of wood so as to cover it completely except for an opening in the middle for the paddler.

2. any similar canoe.

Also spelled *kaiak*, *kyack*.

kaȳ′ak·ẽr, *n.* one who uses a kayak.

kāy′ō′, *v.t.*; kayoed (-ōd′), *pt.*, *pp.*; kayoeing, *ppr.* [from *k*nock *o*ut.] in boxing, to knock out. [Slang.]

kāy′ō′, *n.* in boxing, a knockout. [Slang.]

kȧ·zọọ′, *n.* [arbitrary or echoic.] a toy musical instrument consisting of a small tube containing a membrane or piece of paper that vibrates and produces a buzzing sound when one hums into the tube.

kẹ′ä, *n.* [Maori.] a large, green, mountain parrot of New Zealand, which kills sheep by tearing at their backs to eat the fat there.

keb, *n.* a tick or sheep louse. [Scot.]

ke·bäb′, *n.* [Ar. *kabāb*.]

1. [*often pl.*] a dish consisting of small pieces of marinated meat stuck on a skewer, often alternated with pieces of onion, tomato, etc., and broiled or roasted.

2. a piece of such meat.

keb′buck, **keb′bŏck**, *n.* [Gael. *ceapag*, a cheese, wheel.] a cheese. [Scot. and Irish Dial.]

keb′lȧh, *n.* see *kiblah*.

keck, *v.i.* [echoic.] 1. to retch or heave, as if about to vomit.

2. to feel or show great disgust.

keck, *n.* a retching or heaving of the stomach.

keç′kle, *v.t.*; keckled, *pt.* *pp.*; keckling, *ppr.* in nautical usage, to treat or cover, as a chain, cable, or the like, with a substance or covering so as to prevent wear.

keç′kle, *v.i.* to cackle. [Scot.]

keç′kling, *n.* in nautical usage, material used for wrapping ropes or cables.

keç′klish, *a.* sick at the stomach; having a desire to vomit. [Rare.]

keck′sy, *n.* same as *kex*.

ked′dăh, *n.* [Hind. *khedā*.] an elephant trap: also spelled *khedah*.

kedġe, *n.* [prob. form of *cadge*, variant of *catch*, in the sense "that which catches."] a light anchor, used especially in warping a ship or freeing it when ashore: also *kedge anchor*.

kedġe, *v.t.*; kedged, *pt.*, *pp.*; kedging, *ppr.* [compare Sw. dial. *keka*, to tug, drag oneself slowly forward.] to warp or pull (a ship) along by means of a rope fastened to an anchor dropped at some distance.

kedġe, *v.i.* 1. to move a ship by kedging.

2. to move by being kedged.

kedġe, *a.* [ME. *kydge*, *kygge*; Ice. *kykr*, contr. of *kvikr*, quick.] brisk; lively. [Scot.]

kedġ′ẽr, *n.* [from *kedge*.] a small anchor used in a river. [Obs.]

kedġ′ẽr, *n.* a fisherman; one who deals in or peddles fish. [Brit. Dial.]

ked′lock, *n.* charlock. [Brit. Dial.]

kee, *n.* plural of *cow*. [Brit. Dial.]

keech, *n.* a mass or lump, as of fat rolled together. [Obs.]

keek, *v.i.* to peep; to spy. [Scot. and Brit. Dial.]

keel, *n.* [Ice. *kjölr*, a keel of a ship.]

1. the principal timber or steel piece in a ship, extending from stem to stern at the bottom and supporting the whole frame.

2. a ship. [Poet.]

3. anything resembling a ship's keel.

4. (a) in botany, the lower pair of petals of a papilionaceous flower; (b) in zoology, a ridgelike process.

5. in aeronautics, the assembly of beams, girders, etc. at the bottom of a rigid or semirigid airship to prevent sagging or buckling.

false keel; a strong, thick piece of timber bolted to the bottom of the keel for protection and increased steadiness.

on an even keel; (a) in an upright, level position, without dipping to either side; (b) with an even, smooth, steady motion.

keel, *v.t.* 1. to furnish with a keel.

2. to turn (a ship) over on its side; to turn up the keel of.

keel, *v.i.* to turn up the keel.

to keel over; (a) to turn over; to turn upside down; to upset; capsize; (b) to fall over suddenly, as in a faint. [Colloq.]

keel, *n.* [ME. *kele*, from M.D. *kiel* or MLG. *kēl*.]

1. a flat-bottomed ship; especially, a low, flat-bottomed coal barge or lighter, used on the Tyne.

2. a barge load of coal.

3. a British unit of weight for coal, equal to 21.2 long tons.

keel, *v.t.* [ME. *kelen*; AS. *celan*, to cool, from *col*, cool.] to cool (a hot liquid) by stirring, skimming, etc. [Obs. or Dial.]

keel, *n.* [prob. from Ir. or Gael. *cīl*, ruddle.] a red stain used for marking lumber, etc.; ruddle.

keel′ăġe, *n.* duty paid for a ship entering a port; also, the right to demand such a duty.

keel′bōat, *n.* a boat without sails, decked over, and built with a keel: used for transporting freight on rivers and canals.

keeled, *a.* 1. in botany, carinated; having a longitudinal prominence on the back; as, a *keeled* leaf, calyx, or nectary.

2. in zoology, having a ridge along the

keel′ẽr, *n.* a keelman. [Obs.]

keel′ẽr, *n.* a shallow tub.

keel′fat, *n.* [AS. *celan*, to cool, and *fæt*, a vat.] a vessel in which liquor is set for cooling.

keel′haul, *v.t.*; keelhauled, *pt.*, *pp.*; keelhauling, *ppr.* 1. to haul (a person) through the water under the keel of a ship from one side to the other: a punishment formerly inflicted in various navies for certain offenses.

2. to scold or rebuke harshly.

keel′ing, *n.* [ME. *keling*; compare Ice. *keila*, Sw. *kolja*, a cod.] a kind of small cod from which stockfish is made. [Scot. and Brit. Dial.]

kee'li·vīne, *n.* a pencil made of either red or black lead: called also *keelyvine pen.* [Scot. and Brit. Dial.]

keel'măn, *n.* a worker on a keel, or barge; a keeler.

keel piēce, one of the pieces composing a keel.

keel'rāke, *v.t.* same as *keelhaul.*

keel'sŏn, *n.* [from Sw. *kölsvin*; Norw. *kjölsvill,* keelson; *kjöl,* keel, and *svill,* sill.] a longitudinal beam or set of timbers or metal plates fastened over and along a ship's keel to add structural strength: also *kelson.*

cross keelson; a strong timber laid transverse to the keelson to give support to heavy machinery, as engines, boilers, etc.

keel'vat, *n.* same as *keelfat.*

keen, *a.*; *comp.* keener; *superl.* keenest. [ME. *kene*; AS. *cene, cyne,* bold, wise, clever, from *cunnan,* to be able.]

1. having a sharp edge or point; that can cut well; as, a *keen* knife, a *keen* edge.

2. sharp; cutting; piercing; as, *keen* appetite, *keen* wind.

3. very sensitive; very perceptive; penetrating; acute; as, *keen* eyes, a *keen* intelligence.

4. sharp-witted; mentally acute; shrewd.

5. eager; enthusiastic; much interested.

6. intense; strong; vivid; pungent.

7. good; excellent: a generalized term of approval. [Slang.]

8. bitter; piercing; acrimonious; as, *keen* satire or sarcasm.

keen, *v.t.* to sharpen. [Obs.]

keen, *n.* [Ir. *caoine,* a wail for the dead.] a piercing lamentation made over a corpse; a dirge. [Irish.]

keen, *v.i.* and *v.t.* to lament or wail for (the dead). [Irish.]

keen'ly, *adv.* in a keen manner.

keen'ness, *n.* the state or quality of being keen.

Syn.—eagerness, earnestness, asperity, acumen, sharpness.

keep, *v.t.*; kept, *pt., pp.*; keeping, *ppr.* [ME. *kepen, kipen*; AS. *cepan,* to keep, observe, await.]

1. to observe or pay regard to; specifically, (a) to observe with due or prescribed acts, ceremonies, etc.; to celebrate or solemnize; as, they *kept* the Sabbath; (b) to fulfill (a promise, etc.); (c) [Archaic.] to show observance by regularly attending (church, etc.).

2. to take care of, or have and take care of; specifically, (a) to protect; guard; defend; (b) to look after; watch over; tend; (c) to raise (livestock); (d) to maintain in good order or condition; to preserve; (e) to supply with food, shelter, etc.; to provide for; support; (f) to supply with food or lodging for pay; as, she *keeps* boarders; (g) to have or maintain in one's service or for one's use; as, they *keep* servants; (h) to set down regularly in writing; to maintain (a continuous written report or record); as, he *keeps* an account of sales in the store; (i) to make regular entries in; to maintain a continuous record of transactions, accounts, or happenings in; as, businessmen *keep* books, she *keeps* a diary; (j) to carry on; conduct; manage.

3. to maintain, or cause to stay or continue, in a specified condition, position, etc.; as, *keep* your engine running.

4. to have or hold; specifically, (a) to have or hold for future use or for a long time; (b) to have usually in stock for sale.

5. to have or hold and not let go; specifically, (a) to hold in custody; to prevent from escaping; (b) to prevent from leaving; detain; (c) to hold back; restrain; as, the rain *kept* us from going out; (d) to withhold; (e) to conceal; not tell (a secret, etc.); (f) to continue to have or hold; not lose or give up; (g) to stay in or at; not leave (a path, course, or place).

to keep a stiff upper lip; to put on a bold front; to refuse to be discouraged under difficulties.

to keep back; (a) to conceal; as, I will *keep* nothing *back,* but will tell all I know; (b) to hold back, to restrain; as, *to keep back* the encroachment of a flood.

to keep company; see under *company.*

to keep down; (a) to prevent from rising or becoming too eager; to subject to discipline; (b) in the fine arts, to modify a prominence or a too intense coloring, so that an important but less prominent feature may receive due attention.

to keep house; see under *house.*

to keep one's hand in; to retain one's skill or dexterity by regular practice.

to keep one's own counsel; see under *counsel.*

to keep open house; see under *house.*

to keep the peace; in law, to prevent breaches of the law and of good order.

to keep to oneself; to treat (information, etc.) as confidential; not tell.

to keep under; to keep in a subordinate state or position; to treat oppressively.

to keep up; (a) to maintain in good order or condition; (b) to prevent from going down or lower; (c) to continue; not stop or end.

keep, *v.i.* 1. to remain in a specified condition, position, etc.; as, to *keep* at a distance.

2. to continue; to go on; to persevere (often with *on*); as, he *keeps* moving; *keep on* talking.

3. to hold oneself back; to refrain (usually with *from*); as, she can't *keep from* telling us.

4. to stay in good condition; to last; to endure; not to perish or be impaired; as, apples that *keep* well.

5. to lodge; to dwell; to reside for a time. [Colloq.]

Knock at study, where, they say, he *keeps.*
—Shak.

6. to be in session; as, school does not *keep* today. [Colloq.]

7. to take care; to be alert; to watch. [Obs.]

to keep in with; to remain on good terms with. [Colloq.]

to keep on; to go forward; to proceed; to continue.

to keep to; to adhere strictly; not to neglect or deviate from; as, *to keep to* a rule; *to keep to* one's word or promise.

to keep to oneself; to avoid the company of others.

to keep up; (a) to maintain the pace; not lag behind; (b) to remain informed about (with *on* or *with*); (c) to remain in good order or condition.

keep, *n.* 1. originally, care, charge, or custody.

2. (a) the strongest, innermost part or central tower of a medieval castle; donjon; (b) a stronghold; fort; castle.

3. a keeping or being kept. [Rare.]

4. what is needed to keep a person or animal; food and shelter; support; livelihood.

5. that which is kept. [Obs.]

for keeps; (a) with the agreement that the winner will keep what he wins; (b) permanently; for good. [Colloq.]

keep'ēr, *n.* a person or thing that keeps; specifically, (a) a guard, as of prisoners, animals, etc.; (b) a guardian or protector; (c) a custodian; caretaker; (d) [Brit.] a gamekeeper; (e) any of several devices for keeping something in place; a lock nut, clasp, etc.; (f) something that keeps, or lasts (well or poorly); (g) one who owns or carries on some business.

keeper of a magnet; an armature of soft iron connecting the poles of a magnet when not in use to prevent diminution of magnetism.

keeper of the forest; in English law, an officer whose duty was to look after the forests.

Keeper of the Great Seal; in England, a high officer of state in charge of the Great Seal, an office now administered by the Lord Chancellor.

Keeper of the King's Conscience; in England, the Lord Chancellor in his ecclesiastical capacity.

Keeper of the Privy Seal; in England, an officer who passes upon all documents prior to their being stamped with the Great Seal.

keep'ēr·ship, *n.* the office of a keeper.

keep'ing, *n.* 1. observance (of a rule, holiday, promise, etc.).

2. care; custody; charge.

3. maintenance or means of maintenance; keep.

4. the condition in which something is kept.

5. retention.

6. reservation for future use; preservation.

7. agreement; conformity; as, in *keeping* with his character.

keep'ing rọọm, a common parlor in which a family generally lives; living room. [Dial.]

keep'sāke, *n.* anything kept, or given to be kept, for the sake of, or in memory of, the giver; a token of friendship.

keesh, *n.* same as *kish.*

kees'họnd (-họnt), *n.*; *pl.* **kees'họnd″en** (-họnt″n), [D., from *Kees* de Gyselaer, 18th-c. D. patriot, and *hond,* a dog.] any of a breed of small dog with a thick, gray-and-black coat of long, straight hair, small, pointed ears, and a tail that curls over the back.

keeve, *n.* [AS. *cyfe,* a tub or vat.] any of various kinds of tubs, as a brewer's mash tub.

keeve, *v.t.*; keeved, *pt., pp.*; keeving, *ppr.* 1. to set in a keeve for fermentation.

2. to tip up, as a cart. [Brit. Dial.]

Kee·wä'tin, *a.* in geology, designating or of the older of two series of rocks of the Archean system.

the Keewatin; the Keewatin series of rocks.

kef, *n.* [colloq. form of Ar. *kaif,* well-being.]

1. a drowsy, dreamy condition, produced by smoking narcotics.

2. Indian hemp or other narcotic smoked to produce this.

kef'fē·kil, *n.* kiefekil. [Obs.]

kef'fi·ẹh, *n.* [Ar.] a kind of kerchief worn as a headdress by some of the tribes on the Asiatic deserts, particularly the Bedouins.

ke'fīr, *n.* [Russ., from a Caucasian word.] a sour, slightly alcoholic drink fermented from cow's milk.

keg, *n.* [Ice. *kaggi*; Sw. and Norw. *kagge,* a keg, a heap.]

1. a small cask or barrel, usually one holding less than ten gallons.

2. a unit of weight for nails, equal to 100 pounds.

keg'lēr, *n.* [G., from *kegel,* (nine) pin, (ten) pin.] a bowler; one engaged in the sport of bowling. [Colloq].

Keī ap'ple, [S. African *kei* or *kai,* and E. *apple.*] a South African shrub, *Dovyalis caffra,* used for hedges and bearing an edible fruit: written also *Kai apple.*

keīl'hau·īte, *n.* [named after Prof. *Keilhau* of Norway.] a Norwegian mineral related in form to titanite, containing iron, yttrium, and aluminum.

kēir, *n.* [Ice. *ker,* a tub.] a kier.

keī't'lō·ȧ, *n.* [Bantu *kgetlwa, khetlwa.*] a large, black rhinoceros of southern Africa having nearly equal posterior and anterior horns.

kel'ep, *n.* [native name in Guatemala.] a Central American stinging ant that feeds on insects.

kē'lis, *n.* [Gr. *kēlē,* a tumor.] in pathology, localized scleroderma.

kelk, *v.t.* to beat soundly. [Rare.]

kelk, *n.* [prob. from Gael. and Ir. *clach,* a stone.] a blow; also, a large stone. [Brit. Dial.]

kell, *n.* kale. [Obs.]

kell, *n.* [ME. *calle, kalle*; OFr. *cale,* a kind of cap.] one of various membranes or substances resembling network, as a caul, a chrysalis, etc. [Dial.]

kē'loid, *n.* [Fr. *kéloïde, chéloïde,* from Gr. *chēlē,* crab's claw; and *-oid.*] a fibrous tumor arising from connective tissue of the skin, generally an excessive growth of scar tissue: also spelled *cheloid.*

kē'loid, *a.* of or relating to a keloid.

kē·lō·tō'mi·ȧ, kē·lot'ō·my, *n.* same as *celotomy.*

kelp, *n.* [ME. *culp, culpe.*]

1. any of various large, coarse, brown seaweeds; specifically, *Macrocystis pyrifera,* a large seaweed of the Pacific coast.

2. ashes of seaweed, formerly used in the manufacture of carbonate of soda, now in the production of iodine.

kelp çrab, a spider crab having the color of the seaweeds among which it lives.

kelp'fish, *n.* any of several fishes living among seaweeds, especially the food fish *Heterostichus rostratus.*

kel'pie, kel'py, *n.*; *pl.* **kel'pieṣ,** in Gaelic folklore, a water spirit, supposed to take the form of a horse and drown people or warn them that they will be drowned.

kelp pig'eŏn, a sea bird of the antarctic islands related to the plovers and characterized by white plumage and a sheathed bill.

kelp salm'ŏn (sam'), the rock bass of the American Pacific coast.

kelp'wŏrt, *n.* a kind of glasswort; a seaweed yielding kelp.

kel'py, *n.* same as *kelpie.*

kel'sŏn, *n.* same as *keelson.*

Kelt, *n.* same as *Celt.*

kelt, *n.* in Scotland, a salmon after spawning.

kelt, *n.* a rough, black woolen cloth. [Scot. and Brit. Dial.]

kel'tēr, *n.* see *kilter.*

Kelt'iç, *a.* and *n.* same as *Celtic.*

Kel'vin sçāle, [after Baron *Kelvin.*] in physics, a scale of temperature measured in degrees centigrade from absolute zero, −273.15°C.

kem'ē·lin, *n.* a tub: written also *kimnel.* [Obs.]

kemp, *n.* [ME. *kempe, campe,* rough, shaggy.] the coarse hairs mingled with the fur of some animals.

ken, *v.t.*; kenned, *pt., pp.*; kenning, *ppr.* [ME.

kennen; Ice. *kenna*, to know; AS. *cennan*, caus. of *cunnan*, to know.]
  1. to know. [Scot.]
  2. to see; to look at; to descry. [Archaic.]
  3. to recognize. [Archaic or Dial.]

ken, *v.i.* to know (*of* or *about*). [Scot.]

ken, *n.* 1. range of vision or sight. [Rare.]
  2. mental perception or recognition; range of knowledge.

ken, *n.* [perh. abbrev. of *kennel*.] a lodge for low or disreputable characters; as, a sporting *ken*. [Brit. Slang.]

ke·naf′, *n.* [Per., akin to *kanab*, hemp.]
  1. a tropical Asiatic plant, *Hibiscus cannabinus*, of the mallow family, grown for its fiber, which is similar to jute.
  2. this fiber.

kench, *n.* a box or receptacle for curing fish or green hides by salting.

Ken′dȧl green, 1. a coarse, green woolen cloth, originally woven and dyed at Kendal, Westmorland, England.
  2. its color.
  Also *Kendal*.

ken′dō, *n.* [Japan.] stylized swordplay in which bamboo swords are used: a Japanese sport.

Ken·nē′dy·ȧ, *n.* [named after Lewis *Kennedy*, an English gardener.] a genus of leguminous Australian plants cultivated for their showy flowers.

ken′nel, *n.* [ME. *kenel, kenell*; LL. *canile*, a house for a dog, kennel, from L. *canis*, a dog.]
  1. a house for dogs; a doghouse.
  2. [*often pl.*] a place where dogs are bred or kept.
  3. a pack of dogs.
  4. the hole of a fox or other beast; a haunt. [Obs.]

ken′nel, *v.i.*; kenneled *or* kennelled, *pt., pp.*; kenneling *or* kennelling, *ppr.* to lodge or take shelter in a kennel.

ken′nel, *v.t.* to keep or confine in a kennel.

ken′nel, *n.* [ME. *canel*; OFr. *canel, chanel*, a channel.] the gutter of a street; a little canal or channel.

ken′nel çoal, cannel coal. [Obs.]

Ken′nel·ly-Heav′i·sīde lāy′ẽr, [named for A. E. *Kennelly*, American electrical engineer, and O. *Heaviside*, British physicist.] a highly ionized layer of the upper atmosphere, variously estimated as being from 60 to 70 miles above the earth's surface and believed to reflect radio waves so that they travel parallel to the earth's surface: also *Heaviside layer*.

ken′ning, *n.* [ME.] 1. (a) knowledge or recognition; (b) a small or recognizable quantity. [Scot.]
  2. in early Germanic poetry, a metaphorical name for something (e.g., *sea-stead* for *ship*): in Anglo-Saxon most kennings are compounds; they are called *true kennings* when neither element is a true name for the object, *half-kennings* when one element is.

Ken′ny meth′ŏd (*or* **trēat′ment**), [after Elizabeth *Kenny* (1884?–1952), Australian nurse who developed it.] a method of treating poliomyelitis by relaxing and stimulating the affected muscles with hot applications, etc., and then bringing the muscles back into use by moving them and helping the patient to learn again how to co-ordinate them.

kē′nō, *n.* [Fr. *quine*, five winners, from L. *quini*, five each, from *quinque*, five.] a game of chance similar to lotto, played with numbered balls and cards.

kē·nō′sis, *n.* [Gr. *kenōsis*, an emptying, from *kenos*, empty; compare Phil. ii. 6, 7.] in theology, Jesus' humbling Himself by taking on the form of man.

kē·not′iç, *a.* relating to kenosis.

ken′speç·kle, *a.* recognizable by distinguishing marks; conspicuously marked. [Scot. and Brit. Dial.]

kent, *n.* a pole; especially, a vaulting pole. [Scot.]

kent, *v.t.* and *v.i.* to punt or propel, as a boat. [Scot.]

Kent bū′gle, the key bugle: probably named after a duke of Kent.

Kent′ish, *a.* of Kent, England, or its people.

Kent′ish, *n.* the dialect of Kent, England, especially in its Anglo-Saxon and Middle English stages of development.

ken′tle, *n.* a quintal. [Obs.]

kent′ledġe, *n.* pig iron for permanent ballast in a ship.

ken′trō·līte, *n.* [Gr. *kentron*, a point, center, and *lithos*, stone.] a lead manganese silicate, occurring in sharp-pointed crystals.

Ken·tuck′i·ăn, *a.* of Kentucky.

Ken·tuck′i·ăn, *n.* a native or inhabitant of Kentucky.

Ken·tuck′y çof′fee tree, a large North American tree with brown, curved pods containing seeds sometimes used as a substitute for coffee.

Ken·tuck′y çolo′nel (kẽr′nl), an unofficial honorary title commonly conferred in Kentucky.

Ken·tuck′y Dẽr′by, an annual horse race run at Churchill Downs in Louisville, Kentucky.

Kē′ŏgh plan (-ō), [named after E. J. *Keogh*, 20th-century U.S. congressman.] a retirement plan for self-employed persons and certain groups of employees, similar to an IRA: see *IRA*.

keph′ȧ·lin, *n.* [Gr. *kephalē*, and *-in*.] a substance found in brain tissue, containing nitrogen and phosphorus.

keph′ïr, *n.* [Caucasian.] a kind of kumiss, or fermented milk, used as a food by the inhabitants of the northern Caucasus.

kep′i, *n.* [Fr.] a kind of cap with a circular, flat top and a stiff, horizontal visor, worn by French soldiers.

kept, *v.* past tense and past participle of *keep*.

kē·rä′nȧ, *n.* [Per.] in music, a Persian trumpet.

kē·rär′ġy·rīte, *n.* same as *cerargyrite*.

ker′ȧ·sin, *n.* same as *cerasin*.

ker′ȧ·sine, *a.* same as *cerasine*.

ker′ăt-, see *kerato-*.

ker′ȧ·tin, *n.* [*kerat-* and *-in*.] an albuminous substance forming the principal matter of hair, nails, horn, etc.

ke·rat′i·nous, *a.* of, or having the nature of, keratin; horny.

ker·ȧ·tī′tis, *n.* [*kerat-* and *-itis*.] inflammation of the cornea.

ker′ȧ·tō-, [from Gr. *keras, keratos*, horn.] a combining form meaning: (a) *horn, hornlike, horny tissue*, as in *kerato*genous; (b) *the cornea*, as in *kerato*tomy. Also, before a vowel, *kerat-*.

ker·ȧ·toġ′e·nous, *a.* [*kerato-* and *-genous*.] causing the growth of horn or horny tissue.

ker′ȧ·toid, *a.* [Gr. *keratoeidēs*.] hornlike; horny.

ker′ȧ·tō·plas″ty, *n.*; *pl.* **ker′ȧ·tō·plas″tieș,** [*kerato-* and *-plasty*.] the surgical operation of grafting a new cornea or piece of corneal tissue onto an eye.

Ker·ȧ·tō′șȧ, *n.* same as *Ceratospongiæ*.

ker′ȧ·tōse, *n.* same as *ceratose*.

ker′ȧ·tōse, *n.* [*kerat-* and *-ose*.] a horny substance in the skeleton of some sponges and other invertebrates; keratode.

ker′ȧ·tōse, *a.* of or like keratose.

ker·ȧ·tō′sis, *n.* [Mod. L., from *kerat-* and *-osis*.]

ker·ȧt·ot′ō·my, *n.* [*kerato-* and *-tomy*.] surgical incision of the cornea.

ker·at′tō, *n.* a West Indian plant, *Agave keratto*, or the fiber obtained from it.

kē·rau′lō·phon, *n.* [Gr. *keras*, a horn, and *aulos*, a flute, pipe, and *phōnē*, voice, sound.] an organ stop giving a light, smooth, reedy tone.

kē·rau′nō·grȧph, *n.* [Gr. *keraunos*, a thunderbolt, and *graphein*, to write, register.] a mark or impression made by lightning.

kẽrb, *n.* curb (of a pavement): British spelling.

kẽrb′stōne, *n.* curbstone: British spelling.

kẽr′chẽr, *n.* a kerchief. [Obs.]

kẽr′chẽred, *a.* kerchiefed. [Obs.]

kẽr′chief (-chif), *n.* [ME. *kerchef, curcheff, courchef, coverchief*; OFr. *covrechef, couvrechef*, a kerchief; *covrir*, to cover, and *chef, chief*, head.]
  1. a piece of cloth, usually square, worn over the head or around the neck.
  2. a handkerchief.

ker′chiefed, ker′chieft, *a.* wearing a kerchief; covered with a kerchief.

kẽrf, *n.* [ME. *kerf, kyrf*; AS. *cyrf*, a cutting, from *ceorfan*, to cut.]
  1. a cutting or cut; especially, a cut or notch made by an ax, a saw, or other instrument; the notch or slit made in wood by cutting.
  2. a strip, piece, or quantity cut off.

kẽrfed (kẽrft), *a.* having cuts or slits; as, a *kerfed* beam.

kẽr′mēș, *n.* [Ar. and Per. *qirmiz*, kermes, crimson; from Sans. *krimija*, produced by a worm; *krimi*, a worm, and the root of *jan*, to produce.]
  1. a red dye made from the dried bodies of the females of the scale insect *Coccus ilicis*, found in Mediterranean regions: spelled also *chermes*.
  2. [K–] a genus of *Coccinæ*, or scale insects.
  3. an oak tree on which the insect *Coccus ilicis* feeds; the kermes oak.

kẽr′mē·ṣīte, *n.* [*kermes* and *-ite*.] a very hard, cherry-red mineral containing antimony and sulfur (Sb_2S_2O), crystallizing in the monoclinic system.

kẽr′mēș min′ẽr·ăl, an orange-red amorphous trisulfide of antimony.

kẽr′mis, kẽr′mess, kïr′mess, *n.* [D. and Flem. *kermis, kerkmis*; M.D. *kermisse, kerckmiss*, a church festival, lit., church mass.]
  1. an annual outdoor festival held in the Netherlands, Belgium, etc., characterized by feasting, dancing, clownish processions, and other forms of amusement.
  2. in the United States, a somewhat similar fair or entertainment held indoors, usually for charity.

kẽrn, *n.* [Fr. *carne*, projecting angle, hinge, from dial. form of OFr. *charne*, a hinge, corner, edge, from L. *cardo, cardinis*, a hinge.] that part of the face of a letter of type which projects beyond the body.

kẽrn, *v.t.* to make (type) with a kern; to put a kern on (type).

kẽrn, kẽrne, *n.* [ME. *kerne*; Ir. *ceatharnach*, a soldier.]
  1. a medieval foot soldier of Ireland and the Scottish Highlands armed with light weapons. [Archaic.]
  2. an Irish peasant.
  3. an idle person or vagabond. [Obs.]

kẽrn, *n.* [var. of *corn*.] a kernel. [Obs.]

kẽrn, *v.i.*; kerned, *pt., pp.*; kerning, *ppr.* [ME. *kernen, kurnen, curnen*, to form corns, sow with corn, from *corn*, corn.]
  1. to harden, as corn in ripening. [Dial.]
  2. to take the form of corns; to granulate. [Dial.]

kẽrned, *a.* in printing, having a part projecting beyond the body: said of type, especially the letters *f* and *j*.

kẽr′nel, *n.* [ME. *kirnel, kyrnel*; AS. *cyrnel*, a little corn or grain, dim. of *corn*, a corn.]
  1. a grain or seed, as of corn, wheat, etc.
  2. the inner, softer part of a nut, fruit stone, etc.
  3. the central part of anything; a small mass around which other matter is concreted; a nucleus.
  4. a hard concretion in the flesh. [Dial.]
  5. the central, most important part of anything; the essence; as, the *kernel* of an argument.

kẽr′nel, *v.i.*; kerneled *or* kernelled, *pt., pp.*; kerneling *or* kernelling, *ppr.* to harden or ripen into kernels, as the seeds of plants.

kẽr′nel, *v.t.* to enclose as a kernel.

kẽr′neled, *a.* having a kernel.

kẽr′nel·ly, *a.* full of kernels; resembling kernels.

kẽr′nel sen′tence, in generative grammar, a simple declarative sentence in the active voice from which both simpler and more complicated English sentences may be derived.

kẽrn′īte, *n.* [from *Kern* County, California, where it is mined, and *-ite*.] a monoclinic mineral, $Na_2B_4O_7 \cdot 4H_2O$, an important ore of boron.

ker′ō·ġen, *n.* [from Gr. *kēros*, wax, and *-gen*.] solid bituminous material in some shales, which yields petroleum when heated.

ker′ō·sēne, *n.* [Gr. *kēros*, wax, and *-ene*.] a thin, volatile oil distilled from petroleum and other hydrocarbons and extensively used in lamps, stoves, engines, etc.: called also *coal oil*.

Ker′ri·ȧ, *n.* [named after John B. *Ker*, an English botanist.] a genus of plants of the rose family, native to Japan and cultivated throughout the world; the *Kerria japonica* is the only known species.

Ker′ry, *n.*; *pl.* **Ker′rieș,** any of a breed of small, black dairy cattle: so called because originally from County Kerry in southwestern Ireland.

kẽr′șey, *n.*; *pl.* **kẽr′șeyș,** [so called from *Kersey*, a village in Suffolk, England, once a seat of wool manufacture.] a kind of coarse, lightweight woolen cloth, usually ribbed and with a cotton warp.

kẽr′șey·mēre, *n.* [altered after *kersey*, from *cassimere*.] cassimere, a fine, twilled woolen cloth.

ke·ryg′mȧ, *n.* [Gr., a proclamation, from *kēryssein*, to proclaim, from *kēryx*, a herald.] in theology, (a) preaching of the Gospel; (b) emphasis on the essence of the Gospel, as in preaching, catechesis, etc.

kē′șăr, *n.* kaiser. [Obs.]

keș′lŏp, *n.* the dried fourth stomach of a calf; rennet: called also *keeslip*. [Brit. Dial.]

kest, *v.* obsolete past tense of *cast*.

kes'trel, *n.* [OFr. *quercerelle, cercerelle, cresserelle,* a kestrel, from L. *querquedula,* a kind of teal.] a small European falcon that can hover in the air against the wind; windhover.

KESTREL (*Falco tinnunculus*)

ket, *n.* carrion; filth of any kind. [Brit. Dial.]

ket-, see *keto-*.

ketch, *n.* [Fr. *caiche, caique;* Turk. *qāiq, qaïq,* a boat, skiff.] a fore-and-aft rigged sailing vessel with a mainmast toward the bow and a relatively tall mizzenmast, forward of the rudder post, toward the stern: distinguished from *yawl.*

ketch'up, *n.* [Malay *kēchap,* taste, from Chin. *ke-tsiap.*] a sauce for meat, fish, etc., especially a thick sauce (*tomato ketchup*) made of tomatoes flavored with onion, salt, sugar, and spice: also *catsup, catchup.*

kē'tēne, kē'ten, *n.* [*ket-* and *-ene.*]
1. a colorless gas, $H_2C{:}CO$, with a penetrating odor: it combines with water to form acetic acid.
2. any of a series of related organic compounds of which ketene is the simplest.

kē'tin, kē'tine, *n.* in chemistry, an unstable organic oily base, $C_6H_8O_2$, with an aromatic odor, obtained by the reduction of certain compounds of the ketones.

kē'tō-, a combining form meaning *ketone, of ketones,* as in *keto*genesis: also, before a vowel, *ket-*.

kē·tō·ġen'e·sis, *n.* the formation of ketones, such as acetone, in the body.

kē·tō·ġen'iç, *a.* convertible into ketones.

kē'tōle, *n.* [*ket*one and ind*ole.*] in chemistry, one of a series of nitrogenous substances related to indole.

kē'tōne, *n.* [an arbitrary variation of *acetone.*] an organic chemical compound containing the divalent carbonyl group, CO, in combination with two hydrocarbon radicals: when these radicals are alike, the ketone is called *simple,* when unlike, *mixed.*

kē'tōne bod'y, any of three related substances, including acetone, important in human metabolism: also called *acetone body.*

kē·ton'iç, *a.* of or related to a ketone.

kē·tō·nū'ri·ȧ, *n.* [Mod. L.] the presence of ketone bodies in the urine.

kē·tō'sis, *n.* a condition characterized by overformation in the body of ketones, occurring as a complication of diabetes mellitus, etc.

ket'tle, *n.* [ME. *ketel, kettyl;* AS. *cetel, cytel,* from L. *catillus,* dim. of *catinus,* a deep vessel, bowl, pot.]
1. a vessel of iron or other metal, of various shapes, with or without a cover, used for heating and boiling water or other liquids.
2. in geology, any cavity or depression resembling a kettle, as (a) a deep rounded-out hole at the bottom of a river; (b) a cavity in solid rock made through erosion or other causes: also *kettle hole.*
3. a teakettle.
4. a kettledrum.
a kettle of fish; a difficult or embarrassing situation.

ket'tle·drum, *n.* a drum consisting of a hollow hemisphere of brass or copper, covered with a parchment top that can be tightened or loosened to change the pitch; a timpano.

KETTLEDRUM

ket'tle·drum"mẽr, *n.* one who plays the kettledrum.

ket'tle hōle, in geology, a kettle.

Kē·tū'pȧ, *n.* [Javanese.] a genus of fish-eating owls of India, characterized by large ear tufts and including three species, among which is the Indian fish owl, *Ketupa ceylonensis.*

Keu'pẽr (koi'), *n.* [G.] in geology, a division of the Triassic in Europe, especially in Germany, where rock salt and gypsum formations are found.

kev'el, *n.* [ME. *keuil, kyuil;* ONorm.Fr. *keville;* L. *clavicula,* small key, dim. of *clavis,* key.] a cleat or peg for fastening the heavy lines of a ship.

kex, *n.* [ME. *kex, kix;* W. *cecys,* pl., dry stalks, hemlock.]
1. a hollow stalk. [Brit. Dial.]
2. a husk no longer useful, as the larval covering of an insect. [Obs.]

kēy, *n.; pl.* **kēyṣ,** [ME. *keye, keie, kay;* AS. *cæg, cæge,* a key.]
1. an instrument, usually of metal, for moving the bolt of a lock and thus locking or unlocking something.
2. any of several instruments or mechanical devices somewhat resembling or suggesting this in form or use; specifically, (a) a device to turn a bolt, etc.; as, a skate *key,* a watch *key;* (b) a pin, bolt, wedge, cotter, or similar device put into a hole or space to lock or hold parts together; (c) something that completes or holds together the parts of another thing, as the keystone of an arch or that part of the first coat of plaster which passes between the laths and forms a secure base for later coats; (d) any of a set of levers, or the disks, buttons, etc. connected to them, pressed down in operating a piano, accordion, clarinet, typewriter, linotype, etc.; (e) a device for opening or closing an electric circuit; (f) a small metal piece for fastening a wheel, pulley, etc. to a shaft.
3. something regarded as like a key in opening or closing a way, revealing or concealing, etc.; specifically, (a) a place so located as to give access to or control of a region; as, Vicksburg was the *key* to the lower Mississippi; (b) a thing that explains or solves something else, as a book of answers, the explanations on a map, the code to a system of pronunciation, etc.; (c) a controlling or essential person or thing.
4. tone of voice; pitch.
5. tone or style of thought or expression; as, he wrote and spoke in a cheerful *key.*
6. in botany, a key fruit.
7. in music, (a) [Obs.] the keynote of a scale; (b) a system of related notes or tones based on and named after a certain note (*keynote, tonic*) and forming a given scale; tonality; (c) the main tonality of a composition.
analytical key; in biology, an arrangement of groups, orders, families, etc., with their characteristics, in such a way as to facilitate the placing of an individual.

kēy, *v.t.;* keyed, *pt., pp.;* keying, *ppr.* 1. to bind or fasten with a key; to tighten.
2. to furnish with a key; specifically, (a) to put the keystone in (an arch); (b) to provide with an explanatory key.
3. to regulate the tone or pitch of.
4. to bring into harmony, as in style of expression.
to key up; (a) to raise the key of; (b) to bring into a state of nervous tension, as in anticipation.

kēy, *a.* controlling; essential; important; as, he has a *key* position in the department.

kēy, *n.; pl.* **kēyṣ,** [Sp. *cayo;* Taino *cayo,* small island.] a reef or low island.

kēy, *n.* a quay. [Rare.]

key, *n.* [from Sp. pron. of 1st syllable of *kilogramo,* kilogram.] a kilogram (of marijuana or a narcotic drug). [Slang.]

kēy'āġe, *n.* money paid for the use of a key, or quay.

kēy bed, a groove or slot cut in metal into which a key is inserted, as in a shaft carrying a pulley, to prevent slipping or turning of the shaft in the pulley.

kēy'bōard, *n.* 1. the row or rows of keys of a piano, typewriter, linotype, etc.
2. a musical instrument with a keyboard; especially, an electronic piano, synthesizer, etc. as employed in a rock or jazz group.

kēy'bōard, *v.t.* and *v.i.* to set (type) using a keyboard typesetting machine.

kēy bōlt, a bolt held in place by a key inserted in a hole near the end of the bolt.

kēy bū'gle, a kind of bugle having six keys and a compass of about two octaves.

KEY BUGLE

kēy çlub, a private night club, restaurant, or café, to which each member has his own key.

kēyed, *a.* 1. having keys; as, a *keyed* instrument.
2. fastened or reinforced with a key or keystone.
3. pitched in a specific key.
4. adjusted so as to conform.

kēy fruit, a dry, winged fruit, as of the maple, ash, or sycamore, containing the seed or seeds; samara.

kēy'hōle, *n.* 1. a hole or opening in a door or lock into which a key is inserted.
2. in carpentry, a hole or slot in timbers designed for joining with a key or wedge.

kēy'hōle lim'pet, a limpet with a hole at the apex of its shell; any of the *Fissurellidæ.*

kēy'hōle saw, a handsaw with a stiff, narrow blade used in following sharp curves.

kēy'hōle ūr'chin, any of several species of sea urchins with holes in their disks resembling keyholes.

kēy'nōte, *n.* 1. the lowest fundamental tone of a musical scale, or key.
2. the basic fact or thought in a discourse or discussion; as, the *keynote* of the address.

kēy'nōte, *v.t.;* keynoted, *pt., pp.;* keynoting, *ppr.* to give the keynote of (a political platform, etc.).

kēy'nōt·ẽr, *n.* a person who delivers a keynote speech, as at a political convention.

kēy'nōte speech, a speech, as at the convention of a political party, that sets forth the main line of policy.

key punch, a machine, operated from a keyboard, that records data by punching holes in cards that can then be fed into machines for sorting, accounting, etc.

kēy ring, a metal ring for holding keys.

kēy sēat, a key bed.

kēy sig'nȧ·tūre, in music, one or more sharps or flats placed after the clef at the beginning of a staff to indicate the key.

kēy'stōne, *n.* 1. the stone on the top or middle of an arch or vault, which, being wider at the top than at the bottom, enters like a wedge and binds the work: it is sometimes projected outward and ornamented.
2. that one of a number of associated parts or things that supports or holds together the others; the main part or principle.
3. the first drawing in chromolithography.

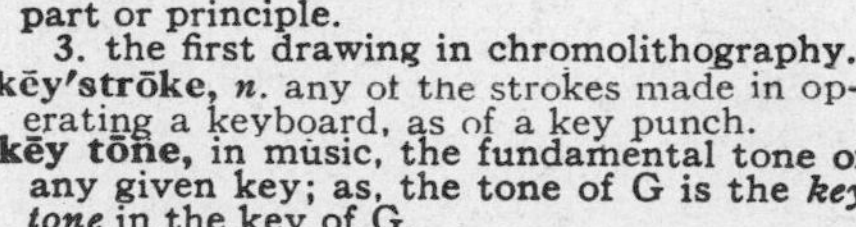

KEYSTONE

kēy'strōke, *n.* any of the strokes made in operating a keyboard, as of a key punch.

kēy tōne, in music, the fundamental tone of any given key; as, the tone of G is the *key tone* in the key of G.

kēy'wāy, *n.* 1. a groove or slot cut in a shaft, hub, etc. to hold the key.
2. the slot for the key in a lock operated by a flat key.

KGB, K.G.B., [Russ. *Komitet Gosudarstvennoye Bezopastnosti,* Committee of State Security.] the security police, or intelligence agency, of the Soviet Union, formed in 1954.

khäir tree (kär), [E. Ind.] an East Indian leguminous tree, *Acacia catechu,* producing catechu.

khä'ki (kä' *or* ka'), *a.* [E. Ind. *khākī,* dusty, dust-colored, from *khāk,* dust, earth.]
1. dull yellowish-brown.
2. made of khaki cloth.

khä'ki, *n.; pl.* **khä'kiṣ,** 1. a dull yellowish brown.
2. strong, twilled wool or, especially, cotton cloth of this color, used for military uniforms.
3. [*often pl.*] a khaki uniform or uniforms.

khä'lif (kā'), *n.* same as *caliph.*

khȧm'sin, khȧm'seen (kȧm'), *n.* [Ar. *khamsīn,* from *khamsūn,* fifty, fiftieth.] a very warm and dry south wind blowing over Egypt from the Sahara region for about fifty days in the spring season (from late March until early May).

khän (kän), *n.* [Turki *khān,* a prince; of Tatar origin.]
1. a title given to Genghis Khan and his successors, who ruled over Turkish, Tatar, and Mongol tribes and dominated most of Asia during the Middle Ages.
2. a title given to various dignitaries in Central Asia, Iran, Afghanistan, etc.

khän (kän), *n.* [Turk. *khān;* Per. *khāna,* a house, dwelling.] in Turkey and other Eastern countries, an inn or caravansary.

khän'āte (kän'), *n.* 1. the dominion or jurisdiction of a khan.
2. the position or tenure of a khan.

khän'sȧ·mäh (kän'), *n.* [Hind. *khānsāmān.*] in India, a steward or butler.

khä′nu̇m, *n.* [Turk. *khānim*, f. of *khān*, lord.] a woman of high rank in Oriental countries.

khäph, *n.* [Heb.] a variant of the eleventh letter (*kaph*) of the Hebrew alphabet, corresponding to Scottish *ch*, as in *loch*.

Khä′yȧ (kä′), *n.* [from native name in Senegambia.] a genus of hard, mahoganylike trees growing in tropical Africa: its wood is used in cabinetwork.

khed′ȧh (ked′), *n.* same as *keddah*.

khe·dīve′ (ke-), *n.* [Turk. *khidīv*, from Per. *khidīw*, *khadīw*, lord, great prince, king.] the title of the Turkish viceroys of Egypt, from 1867 to 1914.

kheth, *n.* the eighth letter of the Hebrew alphabet, a velar fricative corresponding to the Scottish *ch*, as in *loch*.

khid′mut·gär (kid′), *n.* [Hind. *khidmatgār*, a servant, butler; *khidmah*, attendance, service, and *-gār*, suffix denoting agent.] in India, a male waiter; a table servant.

Khmer (k′mer), *n.* [from the Khmer name.]
 1. one of a native people of Cambodia: they had a highly developed civilization in the Middle Ages.
 2. their language.

Khond (kond), *n.* [from the native Dravidian name.] a member of a group of Dravidian tribes of east central India.

khut′bȧh, *n.* [Ar. *khutba*, *khotba*, an address.] a Moslem formal address and prayer delivered at the beginning of the midday service in a mosque every Friday.

kï·ȧ·bo͞o′çȧ wood, [E. Ind. *kiabooca*, and E. *wood*.] same as *Amboina wood*: spelled also *kyabuka wood*.

kib′bē, kib′bēh, *n.* [Ar. *kubbah*.] a Near Eastern dish of finely ground lamb mixed with wheat and pine nuts and baked or eaten raw.

kib′ble, *n.* a hoisting bucket in a well or mine: written also *kibbal*. [Brit.]

kib·bu̇tz′, *n.*; *pl.* **kib″bu̇t·zïm′,** [Mod. Heb.] an Israeli collective settlement, especially a collective farm.

kībe, *n.* [W. *cibi*, a chilblain.] a chap or crack in the flesh caused by cold; an ulcerated chilblain, especially on the heels.

kībed, *a.* chapped; cracked with cold; affected with chilblains; as, *kibed* heels.

kï′bei (-bā), *n.*; *pl.* **kï′bei, kï′beis,** [Japan.] [also K–] a native American citizen born of immigrant Japanese parents but educated largely in Japan: distinguished from *issei*, *nisei*.

ki·bit′kȧ, *n.* [Russ.] 1. a Russian vehicle, consisting of a frame of wood rounded at top, covered with felt, and placed on wheels, serving as a portable shelter.
 2. among the Kirghiz, a round-topped tent.

kib′itz, *v.i.* to act as a kibitzer. [Colloq.]

kib′itz·ẽr, *n.* [Yid., from colloq. G. *kiebitzen*, to look on (at cards), from *kiebitz*, orig., plover, meddlesome onlooker.] anyone who meddles in the affairs of another and offers his advice without invitation; specifically, an onlooker at a card game who volunteers advice. [Colloq.]

kib′läh, *n.* [Ar. *qibla*, opposite, the south, from *qabala*, to be opposite.] the direction toward the Kaaba in the great mosque at Mecca, toward which the Moslem turns when he prays.

kī′bosh, *n.* [earlier also *kyebosh*, *kybosh*, prob. from Yid.] nonsense: now usually in *put the kibosh on*, to put an end to; squelch; veto. [Slang.]

kick, *v.i.*; kicked, *pt.*, *pp.*; kicking, *ppr.* [ME. *kiken*; perh. from or akin to ON. *kika*, to bend at the knee, *kikna*, to bend from the knees.]
 1. to thrust out the foot or feet with violence, as in resistance or anger; also, to strike out with the foot or feet, as in swimming, soccer, etc.
 2. to recoil, as a firearm on being discharged.
 3. to offer objection; to express dissatisfaction; as, the employees *kicked* at the requirement. [Colloq.]
 to kick around (or *about*); (a) to move from place to place; (b) to go about unnoticed or neglected. [Colloq.]
 to kick back; to recoil suddenly and in an unexpected way. [Colloq.]
 to kick off (or *in*); to die. [Slang.]
 to kick out; in football, to make a kick out of bounds.
 to kick over; to begin to operate, as an internal-combustion engine.
 to kick over the traces; to resist control; to manifest insubordination.

kick, *v.t.* 1. to strike or shove suddenly with the foot or feet.
 2. to drive or move (a ball, etc.) by striking with the foot.
 3. to spring back against suddenly, as a gun when fired.
 4. to make or force (one's way, etc.) by kicking.
 5. to score (a goal or point in football) by kicking.
 to kick around (or *about*); (a) to treat roughly; (b) to think about or discuss. [Colloq.]
 to kick back; (a) to give back (stolen goods); (b) to give back (part of money received as pay, commission, etc.), often as a result of coercion or a previous understanding. [Slang.]
 to kick in; to pay (one's share). [Slang.]
 to kick out; to get rid of; to eject; dismiss. [Colloq.]
 to kick up; (a) to raise by kicking; (b) [Slang.] to make or cause (trouble, confusion, etc.).

kick, *n.* 1. a blow with the foot or feet; also, a striking with the foot.
 2. a sudden recoil, as of a gun when fired.
 3. an objection; complaint. [Colloq.]
 4. (a) a stimulating or intoxicating effect, especially of alcoholic liquor; (b) pleasurable excitement; thrill. [Colloq.]
 5. in football, (a) a kicking of the ball; (b) the kicked ball; (c) the distance that it travels; (d) one's turn at kicking.
 6. a projection upon a mold to form a depression in the thing molded; also, the depression itself; as, the *kick* in the bottom of a bottle reduces its capacity.
 7. the part of the blade of a pocketknife that acts as a stop in closing.

kick′ȧ·ble, *a.* that can be or ought to be kicked.

Kick′ȧ·po͞o, *n.*; *pl.* **Kick′ȧ·po͞os,** 1. any member of a tribe of American Indians once occupying a region along the Illinois River; a branch of the Algonquian Indians.
 2. their Algonquian language.

kick′back, *n.* 1. a sharp, violent reaction. [Colloq.]
 2. (a) a giving back of stolen goods; (b) a giving back of part of money received as payment, commission, etc., often as a result of coercion or a previous understanding; (c) the money so returned. [Slang.]

kick′ẽr, *n.* one who or that which kicks.

kick′off, *n.* in football, the act of putting the ball in play by a place kick.

kick′shaw, kick′shaws, *n.* [properly *kickshaws*, a corruption of Fr. *quelque chose*, something.]
 1. a fancy food or dish; delicacy; tidbit.
 2. a trinket; trifle; gewgaw.

kick′up, *n.* 1. a row or commotion. [Colloq.]
 2. a river steamer with a propelling wheel at the stern. [Slang.]
 3. a bird of the genus *Seiurus*, named from its manner of jerking its tail.

kick′y, *a.*; *comp.* kickier; *superl.* kickiest, 1. fashionable; stylish. [Slang.]
 2. stimulating; exciting. [Slang.]

kid, *n.* [ME. *kid*, *kide*, *kydde*; Ice. *kidh*; compare Dan. and Sw. *kid*, O.H.G. *kizzi*, *chitzi*.]
 1. a young goat or, occasionally, antelope.
 2. its flesh used as a food.
 3. a young roe deer.
 4. the leather made from the skin of a young goat, or an imitation of it made of various other skins.
 5. [*pl.*] gloves or shoes made of the skin of a young goat, or of an imitation of it.
 6. (a) a child; (b) any young person. [Colloq.]
 7. a hoax. [Slang.]

kid, *a.* 1. made of the leather called kid; as, a *kid* glove.
 2. younger; as, my *kid* sister. [Colloq.]

kid, *v.t.* and *v.i.*; kidded, *pt.*, *pp.*; kidding, *ppr.* 1. to give birth to (a kid or kids): said of goats or antelopes.
 2. (a) to try to make (a person) believe what is not true; to deceive; fool; delude; hoax; (b) to tease or ridicule playfully with jokes, banter, misleading talk, etc. [Slang.]

kid, *n.* [W. *cidys*, fagots.] a bundle of heath and furze. [Brit. Dial.]

kid, *v.t.* to make into a bundle, as fagots, etc. [Brit. Dial.]

kid, *n.* [perh. var. of *kit* (tub).] a small wooden tub in which rations were formerly served to sailors.

kid′dẽr, *n.* a person who kids, or deceives, teases, etc. [Slang.]

Kid′dẽr·min·stẽr, *n.* a two-ply carpet, originally made at Kidderminster, England.

kid′di·ẽr, kid′dẽr, *n.* a huckster. [Brit. Dial.]

kid′dle, *n.* [OFr. *quidel*, a kiddle; Arm. *kidel*, a net at the mouth of a stream.] a kind of weir in a river, for catching fish.

kid′dy, kid′die, *n.*; *pl.* **kid′dies,** [dim. of *kid*.] a child. [Colloq.]

kid glŏves, soft, smooth gloves made of kidskin.
 to handle with kid gloves; to handle or treat with care, tact, etc. [Colloq.]

kid′nap, *v.t.*; kidnaped *or* kidnapped (-napt), *pt.*, *pp.*; kidnaping *or* kidnapping, *ppr.* [*kid*, a child, and *nap*, a variant of *nab*, to snatch.]
 1. to steal (a child).
 2. to seize and hold or carry off (a person) against his will, by force or fraud, often for ransom.

kid′nap·ẽr, kid′nap·pẽr, *n.* one who kidnaps.

kid′nap·ing, kid′nap·ping, *n.* the act of forcibly abducting a human being.

kid′ney (-ni), *n.* [ME. *kidenei*, from *kiden-*, perh. genit. pl. of *kid* (young goat), and *ei*, *ey*, an egg.]
 1. in anatomy, one of two bean-shaped glands, situated on either side of the lumbar vertebrae, surrounded with fatty tissue. They are of a reddish-brown color, and secrete the urine. Each kidney consists of a cortical or outer part, and a medullary or central portion. The gland is essentially composed of numerous minute tubes, which are straight in the outer and convoluted in the central part. The tubes are lined with cells, and the cells separate water and waste products of metabolism from the blood brought to the kidney and excrete them as urine through the ureter into the bladder.

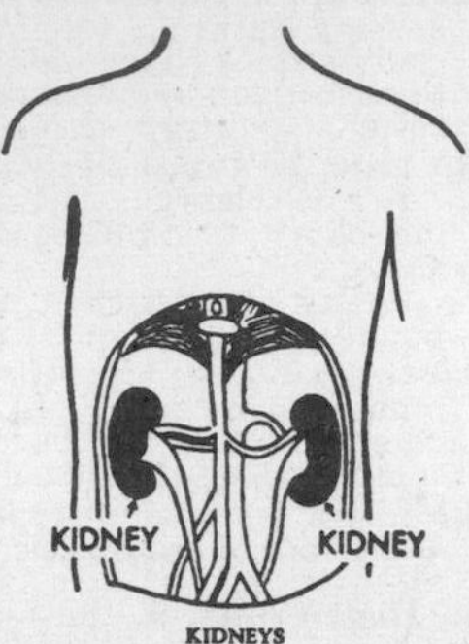

KIDNEYS

 2. character; disposition; temperament; also, class; kind; sort.
  There are millions in the world of this man's *kidney*. –L'Estrange.
 3. an animal's kidneys, used as food.
 4. anything resembling a kidney in shape.
 5. a waiter. [Obs.]

kid′ney bēan, 1. a bean shaped like a kidney.
 2. the scarlet runner, a tropical American bean.

kid′ney çot′tŏn, a species of cotton, *Gossypium brasiliense*: so called from the shape of its seed groups.

kid′ney liñk, a link used in harness to connect the pole chain with the horse's collar.

kid′ney ōre, in mineralogy, a kind of iron ore which occurs in reniform masses.

kid′ney-shāped (-shāpt), *a.* having the form of a kidney.

KIDNEY-SHAPED LEAF

kid′ney stōne, a hard, mineral deposit (*renal calculus*) formed in the kidney from phosphates, urates, etc.

kid′ney vetch, a leguminous plant, *Anthyllis vulneraria*, once used as a remedy in disorders of the kidneys.

kid′ney·wŏrt, *n.* 1. the *Cotyledon umbilicus*: called also *navelwort*.
 2. the star saxifrage.

kid′skin, *n.* leather from the skin of young goats, used for gloves, shoes, etc.

kï′ḙ·kï·ḙ, *n.* [Maori.] a New Zealand plant, *Freycinetia banksii*, of the screw pine family.

kiē·bä′sȧ, *n.*; *pl.* **kiē·bä′sï** or **kiē·bä′sȧs,** [Pol.] a type of smoked Polish sausage, flavored with garlic, etc.

kiēr, *n.* [prob. from ON. *ker*, tub.] a large vat to hold cloth for bleaching, boiling, etc.

kiē′sel·gu̇hr, *n.* [G., from *kiesel*, flint, flintstone, and *guhr*, an earthy sediment deposited in water.] diatomite.

kiē′sẽr·īte, *n.* [named after D. G. *Kieser*, German scientist.] hydrous magnesium sulfate, $MgSO_4 \cdot H_2O$.

kiēve, *n.* same as *keeve*.

kīke, *n.* [perh. extension of -(*s*)*ky* or -(*s*)*ki* ending of names of some Eastern European Jews.] a Jew: vulgar, offensive term of hostility and contempt, as used by anti-Semites. [Slang.]

ki·ku̇′el oil, [E. Ind. *kikuek*, and E. *oil*.] a vegetable fat from the seeds of an Oriental tree, *Salvadora persica*.

kil-, kill-, [Celt., from L. *cella*, a cell.] a common element in Celtic names of places, signifying *cell, church, churchyard, burying place*; as, *Kil*kenny, *Kil*bride, etc.

kil'dẽr·kin, *n.* [ME. *kylderkin*; altered from M.D. *kinderkin*, quarter tun.] a small barrel; also, an old English liquid measure equal to 18 gallons: written also *kinderkin*.

kil'ẽrg, *n.* [Gr. *chilioi*, a thousand, and *ergon*, work.] in physics, a unit of work equal to one thousand ergs.

kill, *n.* [D. *kil*, a channel; Ice. *kill*; Norw. *kil*, a channel, inlet.] a channel or a stream: used chiefly in composition of place names; as, Schuyl*kill*, Cats*kill*, etc.

kill, *v.t.*; killed, *pt., pp.*; killing, *ppr.* [ME. *killen, kyllen, cullen*, to strike, cut, from Ice. *kolla*, to hit on the head, injure, from *kollr*, head.]
1. to cause the death of; to put to death; to slay.
2. (a) to destroy the vital or active qualities of; (b) to destroy; to put an end to; to ruin.
3. to prevent the passage of (legislation); to defeat or veto.
4. to spend (time) on matters of little or no importance.
5. to cause (an engine, etc.) to stop.
6. to prevent publication of; as, the editor *killed* the story.
7. to spoil the effect of; to destroy by contrast: said of colors, etc.
8. to overcome, as with laughter or embarrassment. [Colloq.]
9. in printing, to mark as not to be used; to score out; to cancel.
10. in tennis, to return (the ball) with such force that it cannot be played back; to smash.

kill, *v.i.* 1. to destroy life.
2. to be killed; as, these plants *kill* easily.

kill, *n.* a killing; also, the animal or animals killed; as, the hunters made a good *kill*.

kil'läs, *n.* [Corn.] in mining, clay slate.

kill'dee, *n.*; *pl.* **kill'dees** or **kill'dee,** same as *killdeer*.

kill'deer, *n.*; *pl.* **kill'deers** or **kill'deer,** [echoic of its cry.] a small North American wading bird, *Ægialitis vocifera*, of the plover family.

kill'ẽr, *n.* 1. a person, animal, or thing that kills; especially, one that kills habitually.
2. a killer whale.

kill'ẽr whāle (hwāl), a fierce dolphin that hunts in large packs and preys on large fish, seals, and whales.

kil·lesse', *n.* a coulisse.

kil'lick, *n.* [New England dial.] a small anchor; often, an anchor weighted with a stone, or a stone used for an anchor: also *killock*.

kil'li·fish, *n.*; *pl.* **kil'li·fish·es** or **kil'li·fish,** [D. *kil*, channel, and E. *fish*.] any one of several small striped fish living in brackish or fresh water, mostly of the genus *Fundulus*.

kil'li·grew, *n.* [Corn.] a crow with red feet and beak.

kil"li·ki·nick', *n.* same as *kinnikinick*.

kill'ing, *a.* 1. causing, or able to cause, death; destructive; deadly.
2. exhausting; fatiguing.
3. very attractive. [Colloq.]
4. very funny; very comical. [Colloq.]

kill'ing, *n.* 1. slaughter; murder.
2. a sudden great profit or success. [Colloq.]

kill'ing·ly, *adv.* in a killing manner.

kil'li·nite, *n.* a mineral, a variety of spodumene.

kill'-joy, *n.* one who destroys or lessens other people's enjoyment.

kil'lŏck, *n.* same as *killick*.

kil'lōw, *n.* graphite. [Obs.]

kiln (kil, kiln), *n.* [ME. *kylne, kulne*; AS. *cyln, cylene*, a kiln, drying house, from L. *culina*, a kitchen.] a furnace or oven which may be heated for the purpose of hardening, burning, or drying anything; as, a *kiln* for baking or hardening earthenware or porcelain; a *kiln* for drying grain, meal, or lumber.

kiln, *v.t.* to dry, burn, or bake in a kiln.

kiln'-drȳ, *v.t.*; kiln-dried, *pt., pp.*; kiln-drying, *ppr.* to dry in a kiln; as, to *kiln-dry* meal or grain.

kiln'hōle, *n.* the opening of a drying oven or kiln.

kil'ō-, [Fr., from Gr. *chilioi*, thousand.] a combining form used in the metric system, meaning *one thousand*, as in *kilo*gram, *kilo*dyne.

kï'lō, *n.*; *pl.* **kï'lōs,** a kilogram; also, a kilometer.

kil'ō·çal·ō·rie, *n.* the amount of heat needed to raise the temperature of one kilogram of water one degree centigrade; 1,000 calories; a great calorie.

kil'ō·cȳ·çle, *n.* 1. 1,000 cycles.
2. former name for *kilohertz*.

kil'ō·dȳne, *n.* [*kilo-*, and Gr. *dynamis*, power.] in physics, a unit of force equivalent to one thousand dynes.

kil'ō·gram, kil'ō·gramme, *n.* [Fr. *kilogramme*; *kilo-*, and Gr. *gramma*, a weight.] a unit of weight and mass, equivalent to 1,000 grams, or 2.2046 pounds.

kil'ō·gram·mē'tẽr, *n.* a unit of energy or work, being the amount needed to raise one kilogram one meter: it is equal to 7.2334 foot-pounds.

kil'ō·hẽrtz", *n.*; *pl.* **kil'ō·hẽrtz",** [*kilo-* and *hertz*.] a unit of frequency, equal to one thousand hertz.

kil'ō·li·tẽr, kil'ō·li·tre (-tẽr), *n.* [Fr. *kilolitre*; *kilo-*, and Gr. *litra*, a pound.] a unit of capacity, equal to 1,000 liters, or one cubic meter (264.17 gallons, or 1.308 cubic yards).

kil'ō·mē·tẽr, kil'ō·mē·tre, *n.* [Fr. *kilomètre*; *kilo-*, and Gr. *metron*, a measure.] a linear unit of measure equivalent to 1,000 meters, or about five-eighths of a mile.

kil·ō·met'riç, *a.* 1. of a kilometer.
2. marking, or measured in, kilometers.

kil'ō·stēre, *n.* [Fr. *kilostère*; *kilo-*, and Gr. *stereos*, solid.] a cubic measure equivalent to 1,000 cubic meters.

kil'ō·wätt, *n.* [*kilo-* and *watt*.] a unit of electrical power equivalent to 1,000 watts.

kil'ō·wätt-hour (-our), *n.* a unit of electrical energy or work, equal to that done by one kilowatt acting for one hour.

kilt, *n.* [ME. (northern) *kilte*; prob. from ON. hyp. *kilta* (cf. ON. *kilting*, a skirt).] a short, pleated skirt reaching to the knees, worn by men of the Scottish Highlands.

KILT

kilt, *v.t.* 1. to tuck up (skirts); to fasten up (often with *up*). [Scot.]
2. to pleat.

kilt, *v.* obsolete or dialectal past participle of *kill*.

kilt'ed, *a.* 1. dressed in a kilt.
2. made after the manner of a kilt as to pleating, tucking, etc.; as, a *kilted* costume.

kil'tẽr, *n.* orderly arrangement; proper disposition; good condition: now always preceded by *in* or *out of*: spelled also *kelter*.

kilt'ing, *n.* [*kilt, v.*, and *-ing*.] flat pleats, each folded so as to half cover the one before it.

kim'bō, *a.* set akimbo. [Obs.]

Kim·mē'ri·ăn, *n.* and *a.* same as *Cimmerian*.

kim'nel, *n.* a large tub for general household use. [Obs.]

ki·mō'nō, *n.*; *pl.* **ki·mō'nōs,** [Japan.] 1. a loose outer garment with short, wide sleeves and a sash, worn by both men and women in Japan.
2. a woman's loose dressing gown like this.

Kim'ri, Kim'ry, *n.pl.* same as *Cymry*.

-kin, [ME. *-kin*, prob. from D. *-ken*, a dim. suffix.] a diminutive suffix attached to nouns, as in lamb*kin*, cat*kin*.

kin, *n.* [ME. *kin, kyn, kun*; AS. *cynn, cyn*, kin, kind.]
1. relatives; family; kinsfolk; kindred.
2. family relationship; connection by birth or, sometimes, by marriage.
near of kin; closely related.
of kin; related.

kin, *a.* of the same nature; kindred; related.

kin·aes·thē'si·ȧ (-es-), *n.* same as *kinesthesia*.

kin·aes·thē'sis, *n.* same as *kinesthesia*.

kin·aes·thet'iç, *a.* same as *kinesthetic*.

kin'çob, *n.* [Anglo-Ind., from Hind. *kimkhāb*.] a kind of silk or silk and cotton fabric brocaded with silver or gold, made in India: spelled also *kinkhab*.

kīnd, *n.* [ME. *kinde, kynde, kunde*; AS. *cynd*, natural, inborn, native.]
1. (a) origin; (b) nature; (c) manner; way. [Rare or Archaic.]
2. a natural group or division; race; as, the rodent *kind*.
3. sort; variety; class.
after one's (or *its*) *kind*; in agreement with one's (or its) nature; with one's (or its) natural group. [Archaic.]
in kind; (a) in goods or produce instead of money; (b) with something like that received; in the same way.
kind of; somewhat; rather; almost. [Colloq.]
of a kind; (a) of the same kind; alike; (b) of poor quality; makeshift; mediocre; as, entertainment *of a kind*.

kīnd, *a.* [ME. *kinde, kynde, kunde*; AS. *gecynde, cynde*, natural, inborn, native.]
1. sympathetic, friendly, gentle, tenderhearted, generous, etc.
2. cordial; as, *kind* regards.
3. (a) natural; native; (b) rightful; (c) wellborn. [Obs.]
Syn.—tender, affectionate, well-disposed, courteous.

kin'dẽr·gär"ten, *n.* [G., lit., garden of children; *kinder*, genit. pl. of *kind*, a child, and *garten*, garden.] a school or class for young children, usually four to six years old, that develops basic skills and social behavior by games, exercises, toys, simple handicraft, etc.

kin'dẽr·gärt"nẽr, kin'dẽr·gär"ten·ẽr, *n.* 1. a kindergarten teacher.
2. a child who attends kindergarten.

kīnd'heärt·ed, *a.* having or showing much kindness of nature; sympathetic; generous.

kīnd'heärt·ed·ness, *n.* the quality of being kindhearted.

kin'dle, *v.t.*; kindled, *pt., pp.*; kindling, *ppr.* [ME. *kindlen, kyndlen*, to set on fire, from ON. *kynda*, to set on fire.]
1. to set on fire; to ignite.
2. to light (a fire).
3. to arouse or excite (interest, feelings, etc.).
4. to cause to light up; to make bright.

kin'dle, *v.i.* 1. to catch fire; to start burning.
2. to become aroused or excited.
3. to light up; to become bright; as, her eyes *kindled* with joy.

kin'dlẽr, *n.* one who or that which kindles or sets on fire.

kīnd'less, *a.* 1. lacking kindness. [Poet.]
2. lacking natural feeling; unnatural. [Obs.]

kīnd'li·ness, *n.* 1. the state or quality of being kindly; benignity.
2. a kindly act.

kin'dling, *n.* 1. bits of wood or other easily lighted material for starting a fire.
2. the act of one who kindles.

kīnd'ly, *a.*; *comp.* kindlier; *superl.* kindliest, [ME. *cyndelich*; AS. *cyndelic*, natural, from *cynde*; see *kind*.]
1. kind; gracious; benign; benevolent.
2. agreeable; pleasant; genial; as, a *kindly* climate.
3. natural; native; innate. [Archaic.]

kīnd'ly, *adv.* 1. in a kind, gracious manner.
2. agreeably; favorably.
3. please; as, *kindly* shut the door.
4. naturally: now only in *take kindly to*. [Obs.]
to take kindly to; to be naturally attracted to.

kīnd'ness, *n.* [ME. *kyndeness*.]
1. the state, quality, or habit of being kind.
2. kind act or treatment.
3. kind feeling; affection; good will. [Rare.]

kin'dred, *n.* [with intrusive *-d-*, from ME. *kinrede, kinreden*, from AS. *cynn*, kin, and *-ræden*, state, condition.]
1. relationship by birth or, sometimes, by marriage; family relationship; kinship.
2. relatives or family; kin; kinsfolk.
3. resemblance in qualities; likeness.
Syn.—relationship, affinity, consanguinity.

kin'dred, *a.* 1. related by birth or common origin.
2. of like nature or qualities; similar; as, they are *kindred* spirits.

kīne, *n.* [archaic double pl. of *cow*, from AS. *cy*, pl. of *cu*, and -(*e*)*n*.] cows; cattle. [Archaic or Dial.]

kin·ē·mat'iç, *a.* 1. of motion in the abstract.
2. of kinematics.
kinematic curve; in mechanics, any curve described by a point in a piece of a machine in motion, as distinguished from a mathematical curve.

kin·ē·mat'iç·ăl, *a.* kinematic.

kin·ē·mat'içs, *n.pl.* [*construed as sing.*] [Gr. *kinēma* (-*atos*), movement, from *kinein*, to move.] that branch of mechanics which treats of motion in the abstract, without reference to the force or mass.

kin·ē·mat'ō·grȧph, *n.* same as *cinematograph*.

kīne'pox, *n.* same as *cowpox*.

kin'ē·sçōpe, *n.* [*kine*to- and *-scope*.] a form of cathode-ray receiving tube used in television: it has a luminescent screen at one end, on which the images are reproduced: a trademark (*Kinescope*).

kin·ē·si·at'riçs, *n.* [Gr. *kinesis*, motion, and *iatrikos*, pertaining to medicine, from *iatros*, a physician.] in medicine, muscular exercise as a remedy for disease: also called *kinesipathy.*

kin·ē·si·ol′ō·ġy, *n.* [Gr. *kinēsis*, motion, from *kinein*, to move, and *-logy.*] the science or study of human muscular movements, especially as applied in physical education.

kin·ē·sod′iç, *a.* [Gr. *kinēsis*, movement, and *hodos*, way.] conveying impulses of motion: particularly relating to the nerves of the spinal cord.

kin″es·thē′si·ȧ, *n.* [Gr. *kinein*, to move, and *aisthēsis*, perception.] the sensation of position, movement, tension, etc. of parts of the body, perceived through nerve end organs in muscles, tendons, and joints: also spelled *kinaesthesia.*

kin′es·thē′sis, *n.* same as *kinesthesia.*

kin″es·thet′iç, *a.* relating to kinesthesia.

-ki·net′iç, a combining form indicating motion.

ki·net′iç, *a.* [Gr. *kinētikos*, putting in motion, from *kinētos*, verbal adj. of *kinein*, to move.] in physics, having to do with motion; producing motion or arising from motion.

ki·net′iç en′ẽr·ġy, that energy of a body which results from its motion: it is equal to $\frac{1}{2}mv^2$, where *m* is mass and *v* is velocity: opposed to *potential energy.*

ki·net′içs, *n.pl.* [*construed as sing.*] the science that deals with the motion of masses in relation to the forces acting on them.

ki·net′iç thē′ō·ry, the theory that the minute particles of all matter are in constant motion and that the temperature of a substance is dependent on the velocity of this motion, increased motion being accompanied by increased temperature: according to the kinetic theory of gases, the elasticity, diffusion, pressure, and other physical properties of a gas are due to the rapid motion in straight lines of its molecules, to their impacts against each other and the walls of the container, to weak cohesive forces between molecules, etc.

ki·net′ō-, [from Gr. *kinētos*, movable, from *kinein*, to move.] a combining form meaning *moving, motion,* as in *kinetograph.*

ki·nē·tō·ġen′e·sis, *n.* [Gr. *kinētos*, verbal adj. of *kinein*, to move, and *genesis*, birth.] in biology, the genesis of organic structures by kinetic operations; the doctrine that animal structures are produced by movements of the animal.

ki·nē′tō·grȧph, *n.* [Gr. *kinētos*, verbal adj. of *kinein*, to move, and *graphein*, to write.] a motion-picture camera.

ki·nē′tō·phōne, *n.* [Gr. *kinētos*, verbal adj. of *kinein*, to move, and *phōnē*, sound.] an invention of Edison, consisting of synchronizing apparatus combined with the phonograph and projecting kinetoscope, so arranged and operated as to reproduce simultaneously sound and motion previously recorded and photographed.

ki·nē′tō·sçōpe, *n.* [Gr. *kinētos*, verbal adj. of *kinein*, to move, and *skopein*, to view.]

1. an instrument for illustrating various combinations of kinematic curves.

2. a machine for producing a picture with moving figures.

kin′fōlk (-fōk), *n.pl.* kinsfolk. [Dial.]

king, *n.* [ME. *kyng(e)*; AS. *cyng*, a contr. of *cyning.*]

1. a male ruler of a nation or state usually called a kingdom; a male sovereign, limited or absolute; monarch.

2. a man who is supreme or highly successful in some field; as, an oil *king.*

3. something supreme in its class.

4. in card games, a playing card with a conventionalized picture of a king on it.

5. in checkers, a piece that has moved across the board to the opponent's base and been crowned, so that it can move both forward and backward.

6. in chess, the chief piece, which can move one square in any direction: the game is ended when either player's king is checkmated.

king, *v.t.* to place on a throne; to make a king of; to elevate to a kingdom. [Rare.]

king, *a.* chief (in size, importance, etc.): often in combination.

king ap′ple, a large winter apple with red stripes.

King Är′thūr, a real or legendary king of Britain: see *Arthur.*

king′bïrd, *n.* in zoology, any of several flycatchers of the *Tyrannidæ*, common in the United States: also called *bee bird* or *bee martin.*

king bïrd of par′ȧ·dīse, one of the several birds of paradise; the *Cincinnurus regius.*

king′bōlt, *n.* in a wagon, carriage, etc., the vertical bolt that connects the hind part of the running gear with the front axle and serves as a pivot when the vehicle turns.

king çärd, in whist, the highest card that has not been played.

King Chärleş span′iel (-yel), a small English spaniel with long, silky fur, usually black and tan, and drooping ears: so called because made fashionable by Charles II.

king çō′brȧ, a large, poisonous snake native to India.

King Çōle, a legendary king of England, the subject of a nursery rhyme.

king çoñch, a large univalve shell of the West Indies.

King Cot′tŏn, the personification of the staple crop of the southern United States.

king çrab, 1. the horseshoe crab, *Limulus polyphemus*, of the Atlantic Ocean.

2. the *Maia squinado*, or thornback crab.

KING CRAB (*Limulus polyphemus*)

king′crȧft, *n.* the craft of kings; the art of governing as a monarch.

king çrōw, a species of shrike, *Dicrurus macrocercus.*

king′çup, *n.* 1. the buttercup, *Ranunculus bulbosus*, a species of crowfoot.

2. the marsh marigold.

king dev′il, in botany, a hawkweed of the composite family, a pest to farmers, introduced from Europe; the *Hieracium prœaltum.*

king′dŏm, *n.* [ME. *kingdom, kyngdom*, AS. *cyningdom*; *cyning*, king, and *dom*, jurisdiction.]

1. a government or country headed by a king or queen; a monarchy.

2. a realm; domain; as, the *kingdom* of poetry.

3. one of the three great divisions into which all natural objects have been classified (the animal, vegetable, and mineral kingdoms).

4. the position, rank, or power of a king. [Archaic.]

5. the spiritual realm of God.

kingdom come; [from "thy kingdom come," in the Lord's Prayer] the next world; the hereafter; heaven.

king′dŏmed, *a.* having the authority and dignity of a king; furnished with a kingdom.

king duck, an eider duck, *Somateria spectabilis*, of the arctic regions.

king ēa′gle, the imperial eagle, *Aquila heliaca*, of Asia and southern Europe.

king fẽrn, the royal fern, *Osmunda regalis*, common in swamps and wet woods.

king′fish, *n.* 1. *pl.* **king′fish** *or* **king′fish·eş,** any of several large food fishes found along the Atlantic or Pacific coast, including the California whiting, the opah, and the pintado.

2. the acknowledged head or dictator of some group, lawmaking body, place, etc. [Colloq.]

king′fish″ẽr, *n.* [orig. (ME.) *king's fisher*; cf. Fr. *martin-pêcheur.*] any of a large family of birds, usually bright-colored and having a large, crested head, a large, strong beak, and a short tail: many kingfishers eat fish.

SPOTTED KINGFISHER (*Ceryle guttata*)

king hāke, a fish, *Phycis regius.*

king′hood, *n.* state of being a king.

king′hunt″ẽr, *n.* a bird of the kingfisher kind without aquatic habits.

King Họrn, the hero of an English metrical romance of the same name (c. 1225), and of various other romances in English, Scottish, and French.

King Jāmeş Vẽr′şion, the Authorized Version of the Bible, a revised English translation published in 1611 with the authorization of King James I.

King Lēar, 1. a famous tragedy by Shakespeare (1606?).

2. the main character of this play, a legendary British king who divides his kingdom between his two older daughters, Goneril and Regan, and disinherits his youngest, Cordelia. Goneril and Regan prove wicked and ungrateful, driving Lear insane by their mistreatment; when Cordelia tries to rescue him she is caught and hanged, and Lear dies of grief.

king′less, *a.* having no king.

king′let, *n.* [*king* and dim. *-let.*]

1. a petty, unimportant king, as of a small country.

2. any of several small greenish songbirds with bright-colored crowns, including the golden-crested wren, *Regulus cristatus.*

king′li·hood, *n.* kingliness; royal dignity.

king′li·ness, *n.* the quality or state of being kingly.

king′ling, *n.* a little king; a kinglet.

king′ly, *a.*; *comp.* kinglier; *superl.* kingliest,

1. belonging to a king; suitable to a king; as, a *kingly* coach.

2. royal; sovereign; monarchial; as, a *kingly* government.

3. noble; august; splendid; becoming a king; as, *kingly* magnificence.

Syn.—regal, royal, imperial, sovereign, splendid, monarchical, powerful.

king′ly, *adv.* with an air of royalty; with a superior dignity. [Archaic.]

king′māk″ẽr, *n.* one who wields powerful influence in the enthronement of a king: in English history, said of Richard Neville, Earl of Warwick (1428–1471).

king mul′let, *Upeneus maculatus*, a goatfish of the West Indies.

king′nut, *n.* the shellbark hickory; also, its fruit.

king′-of-ärmş′, *n.* in England, any of the three chief officers of the Heralds' College: in order of rank, they are Garter, Clarenceux, and Norroy. Others with this title in Great Britain are Bath King-of-Arms, Lyon King-of-Arms of Scotland, and Ulster King-of-Arms of Ireland: also *king of arms.*

king of bēasts, the lion.

king of the for′est, the oak.

king ọr′tō·lăn, the marsh hen, *Rallus elegans.*

king pen′guin, the great penguin, *Aptenodytes pennanti*; also, other species of *Aptenodytes.*

king′pin, *n.* 1. a kingbolt.

2. the pin at the apex (or the one in the center) in bowling, tenpins, etc.

3. the main or essential person or thing. [Colloq.]

king plant, in botany, a cultivated orchid from Java, the *Anæctochilus setaceus*, characterized by yellow lines on its purplish-brown leaves.

king pōst, in carpentry, a beam in the frame of a roof, rising from the tie beam to the ridge.

king rāil, the marsh hen, *Rallus elegans.*

king rod, in architecture, an iron rod used as a king post.

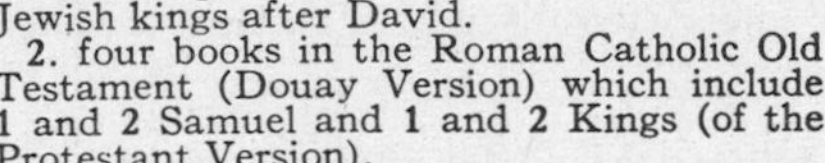

KING POST

Kinġs, *n.pl.* 1. the two books (1 Kings, 2 Kings) in the Old Testament which give the history of the reigns of the Jewish kings after David.

2. four books in the Roman Catholic Old Testament (Douay Version) which include 1 and 2 Samuel and 1 and 2 Kings (of the Protestant Version).

king salm′ŏn (sam′ŏn), the quinnat salmon, (*Oncorrhynchus quinnat*) of the Columbia and other rivers of the Pacific slope, the most valuable species of the genus: also called *quinnat.*

King′ş (or **Queen′ş**) **Bench,** [so called because the sovereign used to sit there on a raised bench.] a former court of record and the highest court of common law in England; King's Bench Division of the High Court of Justice.

King′ş (or **Queen′ş**) **Çoun′sel,** a senior member of the bar in England, appointed to his honorary office by the Crown on the Lord Chancellor's nomination.

king′ş çush′iŏn (-un), a seat made by two persons, each clasping one of his own wrists and then with the free hand clasping the free wrist of the other; a lady chair. [Brit. Dial.]

king′ş (or **queen′ş**) **Eñg′lish,** standard (especially British) English; accepted English usage in speech or writing: so called from the notion of royal sanction.

king′ş (or **queen′ş**) **ev′i·dence,** in English law, state's evidence.

king′ş ē′vil, scrofula: so called from the old notion that a king's touch could cure it.

king′ship, *n.* 1. the position, rank, dignity, or dominion of a king.

2. the rule of a king; monarchical government.

3. majesty: a title sometimes used (with *his*) in referring to a king.

king'-sīze, *a.* of greater than normal size; as, a *king-size* cigarette. [Colloq.]

king'-sīzed, *a.* king-size. [Colloq.]

king snāke, in zoology, a large, harmless, spotted snake of the southern United States, which kills and eats rodents and other snakes; genus *Lampropeltis.*

king's ran'sŏm, a large sum of money.

king's (or **queen's**) **schol'ăr,** in England, a scholar supported by a royal fund or one in a royally endowed school.

king's-spēar, *n.* in botany, *Asphodeline lutea*, the white asphodel, a liliaceous plant.

king'stŏn, *n.* the angel fish, *Squatina angelus.*

king's yel'lōw, yellow orpiment, a pigment.

king tō'dy, in zoology, a small tropical fly-catching bird with a broad fan-shaped red crest bordered with black.

king truss, in carpentry, a truss having a king post for strength and support.

king tȳ'rănt, same as *kingbird.*

king vul'tūre, in zoology, the *Sarcoramphus papa*, of the intertropical regions of America, belonging to the family *Cathartidæ*: named from its dominance over other vultures in seizing carrion.

king'wood, *n.* a Brazilian wood used much in cabinetwork on account of its streakings of violet tints; a species of *Dalbergia* of the family *Leguminosæ*: called also *violet wood.*

kī'nin, *n.* [from *kin*etic, and *-in.*] a short-lived relatively simple peptide produced in blood and other fluids to fulfill immediate hormonal needs.

kiñk, *n.* [prob. from D. or Sw. *kink*, twist or curl in a rope.]

1. a short twist, curl, or bend in a thread, rope, hair, wire, etc.

2. a painful muscle spasm or cramp in the neck, back, etc.; a crick.

3. (a) a mental twist; a queer notion; whim; crochet; eccentricity; (b) a quirk; peculiarity.

kiñk, *v.i.*; kinked (kiñkt), *pt., pp.*; kinking, *ppr.* to form kinks; as, the yarn *kinks.*

kiñk, *v.t.* to form a kink or kinks in; as, to *kink* a rope by twisting and releasing.

kiñk, *n.* a fit of coughing; a convulsive fit of laughter. [Brit. Dial.]

kiñ'kȧ·jöu, *n.* [Fr. *quincajou*; Sp. *quincajú*; Port. *kinkaju*, from native Brazilian (Tupi) name.] a flesh-eating mammal of Central and South America, somewhat like a raccoon, with soft, yellowish-brown fur, large eyes, and a long prehensile tail: it lives in trees and moves about at night.

KINKAJOU
(about 3 ft. long including tail)

kiñk'çough (-kǫf), *n.* the whooping cough. [Brit. Dial.]

kiñk'hōst, kiñk'haust, *n.* same as *kink cough.*

kiñk'i·ness, *n.* the state or quality of being kinky.

kiñk'y, *a.*; *comp.* kinkier; *superl.* kinkiest, 1. kinked; having kinks; tightly curled; as, *kinky* hair.

2. figuratively, whimsical; given to eccentric notions; full of crotchets. [Colloq.]

kin"ni·ki·nick', kin"ni·ki·niç', *n.* [Am. Ind., lit., a mixture.]

1. the dried bark or leaves of plants, as sumac, willow, etc., formerly used for smoking by American Indians.

2. a species of cornel, *Cornus amomum*, whose bark was used by American Indians for smoking; also, the astringent leaves of the bearberry, *Arctostaphylos uva-ursi.*

kī'nō, *n.* [from W. Africa (Mandingo) native name.] a dark-red or reddish-brown gum obtained from certain tropical trees, used chiefly in tanning and as an astringent in medicine: also *kino gum.*

ki'nōne, *n.* same as *quinone.*

kins'fōlk (-fōk), *n.* relations; kindred; kin; persons of the same family.

kin'ship, *n.* 1. family relationship.

2. relationship; close connection.

kins'măn, *n.*; *pl.* **kins'men,** a man of the same race or family; a relative; one related by blood; loosely, one related by marriage.

kins'măn·ship, *n.* family relationship.

kins'wom"ăn (-woom"), *n.*; *pl.* **kins'wom"en** (-wim"), a female relative.

kint'ledge, *n.* same as *kentledge.*

ki·osk', *n.* [Fr. *kiosque*, from Turk. *kiūshk*, pavilion, from Per. *kūshk*, palace.]

1. in Turkey and Persia, a summerhouse or pavilion of open construction.

2. (*also pron.* kī'osk), a somewhat similar small structure open at one or more sides, used as a newsstand, bandstand, covering for the entrance to a subway, etc.

KIOSK (sense 2)

kī'ō·tōme, *n.* [Gr. *kiōn*, and *-tome.*] in surgery, a special knife designed particularly for dividing rectal and renal adhesions or for excising the uvula.

Kī'ō·wăn, *a.* of or pertaining to the Kioways or their language.

Kī'ō·wāys, *n.pl.*; *sing.* **Kī'ō·wāy,** in ethnology, a tribe of American Plains Indians: their descendants live in Oklahoma.

kip, kipp, *n.* [G. *kippe.*]

1. in gymnastics, the feat of elevating the body above or over parallel or horizontal bars, particularly when swinging free of the floor, support being maintained by the hands or arms: a forward and upward swing of the legs bends the body at the hips, the upward kick providing the impulse necessary to carry the body over or above the bar or bars.

2. a tilt, as of the nose. [Scot.]

3. a hill, particularly one having a pointed peak. [Scot.]

4. any sharp, projecting point. [Scot.]

kip, *n.* in Australia, a small bit of wood used in playing the game of two-up.

kip, *n.* [similar to Dan. *kippe*, a hovel or low inn.] a place in which to sleep; an inn; a bed in a lodging house. [Slang.]

kip, *n.* [earlier kippe; prob. from D. *kip, kijp* (in sense 2).]

1. the untanned hide of a calf, lamb, or other young or small animal.

2. a set of such hides.

kīpe, *n.* [AS. *cȳpe*, a basket.] a kind of basket made of osier, for catching fish. [Brit. Dial.]

kip'pẽr, *n.* [ME. *kypre*; AS. *cypera.*]

1. a male salmon or sea trout during or shortly after the spawning season: at this time, the male salmon grows a hook of cartilage (dialectally called a *kip*) on its lower jaw, used in fighting.

2. a kippered herring, salmon, etc.

kip'pẽr, *v.t.*; kippered, *pt., pp.*; kippering, *ppr.* to cure (herring, salmon, etc.) by cleaning, salting, and drying or smoking.

kip'pẽr, *a.* 1. gay; chipper; saucy; full of spirit. [Brit. Dial.]

2. in zoology, having a drooping or hooked lower jaw, as that of a male salmon after spawning.

Kir·ghiz' (-gēz'), *n.* [native name: said to be after a legendary chief of the same name.]

1. *pl.* **Kir·ghiz', Kir·ghiz'es,** a member of a Mongolian people in west central Asia.

2. their Turko-Tatar language.

kip'skin, *n.* same as *kip* (untanned hide).

kĩrk, *n.* [ME. *kirke*; AS. *cyrc, cyric*, a church.] a church. [Scot. and Brit Dial.]

the Kirk; the (Presbyterian) Church of Scotland: so used in England.

kĩrk'măn, *n.*; *pl.* **kĩrk'men,** 1. a member or adherent of the (Presbyterian) Church of Scotland.

2. a church member or clergyman. [Scot.]

kĩrk'yärd, *n.* a churchyard. [Scot.]

Kir'lĭ·ăn phō·tog'rȧ·phy, [after S. *Kirlian*, its Soviet developer in 1939.] a method of capturing on a photographic plate an image of what is purported to be an aura of energy that emanates from animals and plants and that undergoes changes in accordance with physiological or emotional changes.

kĩr'mess, *n.* same as *kermis.*

kĩrn, *n.* [perh. var. of *churn.*] in Scotland, (a) a feast to celebrate the end of the harvest; harvest home; (b) the last sheaf of the harvest.

kĩrsch, *n.* same as *kirschwasser.*

kĩrsch'was"sẽr (-väs"), *n.* [G., from *kirsche*, cherry, and *wasser*, water.] an alcoholic drink distilled from the fermented juice of black cherries.

kĩr'tle, *n.* [ME. *kirtel, kyrtel*; AS. *cyrtel*, a kirtle.]

1. a man's tunic or coat. [Archaic.]

2. a woman's dress or skirt. [Archaic.]

kĩr'tled, *a.* wearing a kirtle.

ki·rum'bō, *n.* [Malagasy.] a crested bird of Madagascar belonging to the *Leptosomidæ*, the only representative of its family.

kish, *n.* [G. *kies*, gravel, pyrites.] a substance resembling graphite, consisting of carbon and manganese, found in some iron-smelting furnaces.

kis'kȧ·tom, *n.* the hickory nut.

Kis'lev, Kis'lew (-lef), *n.* [Heb.] the third month of the Jewish year.

kis'māt, *n.* same as *kismet.*

kis'met, *n.* [Turk. *qismet*; Ar. *qismah*, from *qasama*, to divide.] doom; appointed lot; fate; predetermined fortune.

kiss, *v.t.* and *v.i.*; kissed (kist), *pt., pp.*; kissing, *ppr.* [ME. *kissen, kyssen*; AS. *cyssan*, to kiss, from *coss*, a kiss.]

1. to caress with the lips; to touch or press with the lips; to give a kiss to (a person, a thing, or one another).

2. to touch lightly or gently.

When the sweet wind did gently *kiss* the trees. —Shak.

to kiss hands; to perform a courtesy to a superior by kissing the hand.

to kiss the dust; to fall in combat.

to kiss the rod; to accept punishment submissively.

kiss, *n.* [ME. *kiss, kyss, cuss*, from AS. *coss*, a kiss.]

1. a touch or caress with the lips, often with some pressure and suction, as an act of affection, desire, greeting, etc.

2. (a) any of various candies; (b) a baked confection of egg white and powdered sugar.

3. a light, gentle touch or slight contact, as of billiard balls in motion.

kiss of death; an action or quality, often seemingly helpful, which is actually harmful or ruinous.

kiss of peace; in the early Christian church, a kiss as a token of love and confidence, a manifestation of peace or the absence of any ill will: still used in certain churches.

kiss'ẽr, *n.* 1. one who kisses.

2. the mouth or lips. [Slang.]

kiss'ing bug, any of various poisonous, blood-sucking insects that bite the face, lips, etc.

kiss'ing çŏm'fit, a perfumed confection to sweeten the breath. [Obs.]

kiss'ing çrust, the edge of crust that hangs from a loaf and touches another while baking.

kiss'-mē, *n.* the *Viola tricolor*, or wild pansy.

kist, *n.* [ME. *kist, kiste*; ON. *kista*; L. *cista*, a chest.] a chest, box, or locker, as for holding money. [Chiefly Scot. and Brit. Dial.]

kist, *n.* same as *cist.*

kist, *n.* [E. Ind.] in the East Indies, a stated payment, as for rent, taxes, etc.

kist'văen, *n.* same as *cist* (tomb).

kit, *n.* [D. *kit*, a beaker; M.D. *kitte*, a beaker, a large drinking vessel made of staves and hoops.]

1. a small wooden tub, used in packing various commodities; as, a *kit* of fish, butter, etc.

2. (a) a soldier's equipment, exclusive of arms: now called *pack*; (b) personal equipment, especially as packed for travel; (c) a set of tools or implements; (d) equipment for some particular activity, sport, etc.

3. a box, bag, or other container for carrying such equipment or tools.

4. a set; lot; collection. [Colloq.]

the whole kit and caboodle; the whole lot; everybody or everything. [Colloq.]

kit, *n.* [abbrev. of *kitten.*] a kitten.

kit, *n.* [AS. *cytere*, a gittern.] a small violin. [Rare.]

Kit'-çat, *a.* 1. designating a club in London, to which Addison and Steele belonged; so called from Christopher (Kit) Cat, a pastry cook, who served the club with mutton pies.

2. [k–] designating portraits a little less than half-length in size: so called because such portraits of members were placed in the rooms of the Kit-cat Club.

Kit'-çat, *n.* a portrait resembling in size those of the members of the Kit-cat Club.

kitch'en, *n.* [ME. *kitchen, kichen, kechen, cochine*; AS. *cycen, cycene*, from L. *coquina*, a kitchen, cooking room, from *coquere*, to cook.]

1. a room or place for the preparation and cooking of food.

2. the cooking department; cuisine.

3. a portable outfit for cooking; as, an army field *kitchen*.

kitch'en, *v.t.* to feed or supply with food from a kitchen. [Obs.]

kitch'en·ẽr, *n.* 1. one who works in or has charge of a kitchen, especially in a monastery.

2. a range or cookstove. [Brit.]

kitch·en·ette', kitch·en·et', *n.* a small kitchen, or an alcove or corner of a room arranged as a kitchen, as in some apartments.

kitch'en gär'den, a garden for raising vegetables and, sometimes, fruit, usually for the table.

kitch'en·māid, *n.* a domestic worker who helps the cook.

kitch'en mid'den, [Dan. *kjokkenmödding*.] a heap of refuse, shells, bones, etc. such as often marks the location of a prehistoric settlement: also *midden*.

kitch'en pō·lïce', 1. soldiers detailed to assist the cooks in an army kitchen.

2. this duty.

Abbreviated *KP, K.P.*

kitch'en·wāre, *n.* kitchen utensils; pots, pans, etc.

kīte, *n.* [ME. *kite, kete*; AS. *cyta*, a kite (bird).]

1. a bird of the hawk family, *Milvinæ*, a subfamily of *Falconidæ*, characterized by a gliding motion when flying, and having a forked tail and long, pointed wings.

2. a greedy, grasping person; a sharper; a rogue.

3. [*pl.*] the highest sails of a ship, used in a light breeze.

4. a light frame, usually of wood, covered with paper or cloth constructed for flying in the air at the end of a string.

KITE (*Milvus ictinus*)

5. in business, negotiable paper of no value, floated for the purpose of raising money or sustaining credit temporarily.

kīte, *v.i.*; kited, *pt., pp.*; kiting, *ppr.* 1. to fly like a kite; to move lightly and rapidly; to soar or glide. [Colloq.]

2. in business, to get money or credit by using bad checks, etc.

kīte, *v.t.* in business, to issue (a bad check, etc.) as a kite.

kīte fąl'cọn (fą'), a falcon resembling a kite, of the genus *Avicida* or *Baza*.

kīte'flī·ẽr, *n.* in business, one who issues bad checks, worthless paper, etc. [Colloq.]

kīte'flȳ·ing, *n.* 1. the act of flying a kite.

2. the act of transacting business by kiting.

kith, *n.* [ME. *kith, kyth, cuth*; AS. *cyth, cythth*, from *cuth*, known, pp. of *cunnan*, to know.] acquaintances or relations: now only in *kith and kin*. [Archaic.]

kith and kin; one's friends, acquaintances, and kinsfolk: now often restricted to mean only kinsfolk.

kith'ȧ·rȧ, *n.* same as *cithara*.

kithe, *v.t.* and *v.i.* [AS. *cythan*, to make known.] to recognize or to be recognized. [Obs.]

kīt'ish, *a.* resembling a kite.

kit'ling, *n.* [Ice. *ketlinger*, a kitten.]

1. a whelp; a cub. [Obs.]

2. a kitten. [Scot. and Brit. Dial.]

kit'mut·gär, *n.* same as *khidmutgar*.

kitsch (kich), *n.* [G., gaudy trash, from dial. *kitschen*, to smear.] art, writing, etc. of a pretentious, but shallow kind, calculated to have popular appeal.

kit'ten, *n.* [dim. from *cat*.] a young cat: occasionally applied to the young of other small animals.

kit'ten, *v.t.* and *v.i.*; kittened, *pt., pp.*; kittening, *ppr.* to give birth to (kittens).

kit'ten·ish, *a.* like a kitten in disposition or action; frolicsome: often, playfully coy.

kit'tie, *n.* same as *kitty*.

kit'ti·wāke, *n.*; *pl.* **kit'ti·wākes** or **kit'ti·wāke,** [so called from its cry.] a three-toed sea gull, *Rissa tridactyla*, of the *Laridæ* family, found along the coasts of the North Atlantic and Arctic Oceans.

kit'tle, *v.t.*; kittled, *pt., pp.*; kittling, *ppr.* [ME. *kitelin*; AS. *citelian*, to tickle.]

1. to tickle. [Scot.]

2. to puzzle. [Scot.]

kit'tle, *a.* ticklish; skittish; hard to deal with; troublesome. [Scot.]

kit'tlish, *a.* ticklish; difficult to manage. [Scot.]

kit·tụl', *n.* [Singhalese.] a fiber from the *Caryota urens*, an Asiatic palm: spelled also *kittool*.

kit'ty, *n.*; *pl.* **kit'tieṣ,** 1. a kitten.

2. a pet name for a cat of any age.

kit'ty, *n.*; *pl.* **kit'tieṣ,** [prob. from *kit* (tub).]

1. the stakes or pool in a poker game.

2. money pooled by card players, etc. for some particular purpose, as to pay for the cards.

3. in certain card games, an extra hand or part of a hand, dealt to the table, etc.

kit'ty, *n.* a kittiwake.

kit'ty·sol, *n.* [Port. *quitasol*, an umbrella; *quitar*, to remit, hinder, and *sol*, sun.] a parasol made of bamboo and paper; specifically, a Chinese umbrella or parasol.

kï'vȧ, *n.* [Hopi.] in a Pueblo Indian dwelling, a large room used for religious and other purposes.

kīve, *n.* same as *keeve*.

kiv'ẽr, *v.t.* and *n.* cover. [Obs.]

Kï·wä'ni·ăn, *n.* a person who belongs to a Kiwanis Club.

Kï·wä'ni·ăn, *a.* of Kiwanis Clubs or Kiwanians.

Kï·wä'nis, *n.* [from Am. Ind. *keewanis*, to make (oneself) known.] an international group of clubs of business and professional men.

kï'wi, *n.*; *pl.* **kï'wiṣ,** [Maori: echoic of its cry.]

1. any of a genus, *Apteryx*, of tailless New Zealand birds, with undeveloped wings, hairlike feathers, and a long, slender bill: it feeds chiefly on insects and worms.

2. [K–], the brown, oval, hairy, egg-sized fruit of a subtropical vine, *Actinidia chinensis*, with a sweet, green pulp having a strawberry-like flavor.

Klä'măth, *n.* one of the Indians living on the reservation at Lake Klamath, California.

Klan, *n.* 1. the Ku Klux Klan.

2. any of its chapters.

klȧng, *n.* [G.] in music, a tone made by a combination of the fundamental with its overtones.

klȧng·fär'be, *n.* timbre.

Klanṣ'măn, *n.*; *pl.* **Klanṣ'men,** a member of the Ku Klux Klan.

klätch, klätsch, *n.* [G. *klatsch*, gossip.] an informal gathering, as for conversation or gossip. [Colloq.]

klax'ŏn, *n.* [arbitrary coinage.] a kind of electric horn with a loud, shrill sound: a trademark (*Klaxon*).

klē̆a'gle, *n.* [perh. from *klan*, and *eagle*.] an official in the Ku Klux Klan.

Klebṣ-Löff'ler bȧ·cil'lus (-lef'lẽr), [after Edwin *Klebs* (1834–1913) and Friedrich *Löffler* (1853–1915), G. bacteriologists who identified it.] the bacillus that causes diphtheria.

kleene'bok, *n.* [D., from *kleen*, little, and *bok*, buck.] a small antelope (*Cephalophus pygmæus*) of South Africa: called also *royal antelope*.

kleen'ex, *n.* a small piece of soft, absorbent paper tissue, used as a handkerchief, to clean the face of cosmetics, etc.: a trade-mark (*Kleenex*).

klēig līght (klēg līt), same as *klieg light*.

klepht, *n.* [Mod. Gr. *klephtēs*, robber; Gr. *kleptēs*, thief.]

1. a member of the Greek patriot bands who held out in the mountains after the Turkish conquest of Greece.

2. a brigand.

klep·tō·mā'ni·ȧ, *n.* [Mod. L., from Gr. *kleptēs*, thief; and *mania*.] an abnormal, persistent impulse or tendency to steal.

klep·tō·mā'ni·aç, *n.* a person who has kleptomania.

klick'et, *n.* [OFr. *cliquet*, the latch of a door.] in fortification, a small gate for passage through a palisade. [Rare.]

kliēg līght (klēg līt), [for *Kliegl light*, after the brothers A. and J. *Kliegl*, the inventors.] a very bright, hot arc light used to light motion-picture sets: also spelled *kleig*.

Klīne test, [after Benjamin S. *Kline*, Am. pathologist by whom it was developed.] a modified form of the Kahn test for the diagnosis of syphilis.

Kling'ṣor, *n.* [G.] in Wagner's *Parsifal*, a magician who is the main enemy of the Knights of the Holy Grail and tries to seduce them into sin.

kliñk'stōne, *n.* same as *clinkstone*.

klī·nom'e·tẽr, *n.* same as *clinometer*.

klī'nō·stat, *n.* same as *clinostat*.

klip, *n.* [S. African D.] in South Africa, a steep rock or cliff.

klip'das, *n.* [D. *klipdas*; *klip*, a cliff, and *das*, a badger.] a small ungulate mammal, *Hyrax capensis*, bearing some resemblance to a rabbit.

klip'spring"ẽr, *n.*; *pl.* **klip'spring"ẽrṣ** or **klip'spring"ẽr,** [S. Afr. D., from *klip*, a cliff, and *springer*, springer.] a small, agile mountain antelope, *Oreotragus saltatrix*, of southern and eastern Africa, somewhat resembling the chamois.

kloof, *n.* [D.] in South Africa, a gulch, gorge, or ravine.

klȳs'trŏn, *n.* [Gr. *klys-* (as in *clyster*); and *electron*.] an electron tube, used in television, etc., for converting a stream of electrons into ultra high-frequency waves which it transmits as a pencillike radio beam.

knab (nab), *v.t.* to nab. [Obs.]

knab'ble (nab'), *v.i.* to nibble. [Obs.]

knack (nak), *n.* [ME. *knakke*; D. *knak*; G. *knack*; W. *cnec*, a knock, crack, snap.]

1. a snap; a crack. [Obs.]

2. a trick or device; also, a clever expedient or way of doing something.

3. ability to do something easily; dexterity; adroitness.

4. a knickknack; a trinket; a trifle. [Rare.]

knack, *v.i.* 1. to crack; to make a sharp, abrupt noise. [Obs.]

2. to speak in an affected manner. [Brit. Dial.]

knack'ȧ·wāy, *n.* [altered from *anaqua*, the Sp. Am. name.] a tree, *Ehretia elliptica*, of Texas and Mexico, having hard close-grained wood and bearing edible fruit.

knack'ẽr, *n.* [Early Mod. Eng., harness maker.]

1. in England, a person who buys and slaughters worn-out horses and sells their flesh as dog's meat, etc.

2. a person who buys and wrecks old houses, etc. and sells their materials.

knack'ẽr, *n.* one of the pieces held between the fingers for making a clacking, as in some classes of music; a bone; a clacker.

knack'ish, *a.* trickish. [Obs.]

knack'ish·ness, *n.* artifice; trickishness. [Obs.]

knack'-kneed, *a.* knock-kneed. [Obs.]

knäck'wŭrst (näk'), *n.* [G., from *knacken*, to crack, to split, and *wurst*, sausage.] a thick, highly seasoned sausage.

knack'y, *a.* having special aptitude.

knag (nag), *n.* [ME. *knagg*; L.G. *knagge*, a knob, thick piece; Dan. *knage*, a knot in wood.]

1. a knot in wood or a protuberant knot; a wart; hence, a peg for hanging things on. [Now Rare.]

2. a prong of a deer's horns. [Obs.]

3. a rugged hilltop. [Brit. Dial.]

knag'ged, *a.* knotted. [Rare.]

knag'gi·ness, *n.* the state of being knaggy, or knotty.

knag'gy, *a.* knotty; full of knots; rough.

knap (nap), *n.* [ME. *knap*, from AS. *cnæp*, *cnæpp*, top, knob, button.] a mound or rise of ground; a summit. [Chiefly Dial.]

knap, *v.t.* and *v.i.*; knapped (napt), *pt., pp.*; knapping, *ppr.* [MScot.; of echoic origin.]

1. to knock, rap, or snap. [Dial.]

2. to break or shape (stones or flints) by a quick, hard blow. [Dial.]

3. to bite sharply; to snap; to nibble. [Dial.]

knap, *n.* a short, sharp blow. [Dial.]

knap'bot"tle, *n.* a plant, *Silene inflata*; the bladder campion.

knap'pẽr, *n.* one who uses a knapping hammer.

knap'ping, *n.* breaking stones for macadamizing.

knap'ping ham'mẽr, a hammer for breaking stones.

knap'pish, *a.* snappish. [Obs.]

knap'ple, *v.i.* to nibble. [Obs.]

knap'sack, *n.* [D. *knapzak*, from *knappen*, to snap, eat, and *zak*, sack.] a case of leather or canvas for carrying equipment or supplies on the back: used by soldiers, travelers, etc.

knap'weed, *n.* a plant, *Centaurea nigra*, having knoblike heads of light-purple flowers: called also *knobweed, bullweed*.

knär (när), *n.* [ME. *knarre*; prob. from M.L.G. or M.D.] a knot in wood; especially, a bark-covered protuberance on a tree trunk or root.

knärl, *n.* a gnarl. [Obs.]

knärled, *a.* knotted; gnarled. [Obs.]

knärred, *a.* having knars, or knots; gnarled; knotty.

knär′ry, *a.* knotty. [Obs.]

knāve (nāv), *n.* [ME. *knave, cnave;* AS. *cnafa,* a boy.]
1. a boy; a male child. [Obs.]
2. (a) a serving boy or male servant; (b) a man of humble birth or status. [Archaic.]
3. a false, deceitful person; a tricky rascal; a rogue.
4. a playing card with a page's picture on it; a jack.
knave bairn; a male child. [Obs.]
Syn.—rascal, rogue, scoundrel, villain.

knāv′ẽr·y, *n.* 1. dishonesty; petty villainy; fraud.
2. mischievous tricks or practices. [Obs.]

knāv′ish, *a.* like or characteristic of a knave; especially, dishonest; fraudulent.
Syn.—dishonest, fraudulent, villainous.

knāv′ish·ly, *adv.* in a knavish manner.

knāv′ish·ness, *n.* the quality of being knavish; dishonesty.

knạw (nạ), *v.t.* to gnaw. [Obs.]

knạw′el, *n.* [compare G. *knauel, knäuel,* a clue, ball of thread.] a plant, *Scleranthus annuus,* of the pink family, growing in gravelly soil, with awl-shaped leaves and small, greenish flowers.

knēad (nēd), *v.t.;* kneaded, *pt., pp.;* kneading, *ppr.* [ME. *kneden;* AS. *cnedan,* to knead.]
1. to work and press into a plastic mass, usually with the hands: said of dough, clay, etc.
2. to treat by working and pressing as if kneading dough; to massage.
3. to make by kneading.

knēad′ȧ·ble, *a.* that can be kneaded.

knēad′ẽr, *n.* a person who kneads, or a machine for kneading.

knēad′ing·ly, *adv.* in the manner of working and mixing.

knēad′ing trough (trọf), a trough or vessel in which dough is worked and mixed.

kneb′el·īte (*or* neb′), *n.* [named after Major von *Knebel.*] a brittle silicate of manganese and iron.

knee (nē), *n.* [ME. *kne, knee, know, cneowe;* AS. *cneow,* knee.]
1. (a) the joint between the thigh and the lower part of the human leg; (b) the front part of the leg about this joint.
2. a joint regarded as corresponding or similar to the human knee, as in the hind limb of a vertebrate, in the forelimb of a hoofed, four-footed animal (*carpal joint*), or the tarsal joint of a bird.
3. anything resembling or suggesting a knee, especially a bent knee, as a bent piece of wood used as a brace.
4. the part of a stocking, trouser leg, etc. covering the knee.
5. the upward projection of the base of a tree root, as in the cypress.
6. reverence signified by a bending of the knee.
housemaid's knee; see under *housemaid.*
to bend the knee to; (a) to pray to; (b) to show submission to or great respect for.
to bring to one's knees; to force to submit or give in.

knee, *v.t.;* kneed, *pt., pp.;* kneeing, *ppr.* 1. to hit or touch with the knee.
2. in carpentry, to fasten with a knee or knees (sense 3).

knee ac̦′tion, a type of suspension for the front wheels of automobiles which permits their independent vertical movement.

knee breech′es (brich′), breeches reaching to the knees or just below them.

knee′brush, *n.* 1. the bunch of hair on the knee of an animal, as an antelope.
2. the bunch of fine hairs or bristles on the leg of a bee to which pollen clings.

knee′c̦ap, *n.* 1. the patella, a movable bone at the front of the human knee; kneepan.
2. a protective covering or padding for the knee.

knee′-c̦rook″ing, *a.* obsequious.

kneed, *a.* 1. having knees: used in hyphenated compounds, as weak-*kneed.*
2. in botany, geniculated; bent like a knee.

knee′-deep, *a.* 1. rising to the knees; as, water *knee-deep.*
2. sunk to the knees; as, wading *knee-deep* in water.

knee′-hīgh (-hī), *a.* so high or tall as to reach to the knees.

knee′hōle (nē′hōl), *n.* a space for the knees under a table or desk: also used attributively; as, a *kneehole* desk.
kneehole desk; a desk having a kneehole in the center.

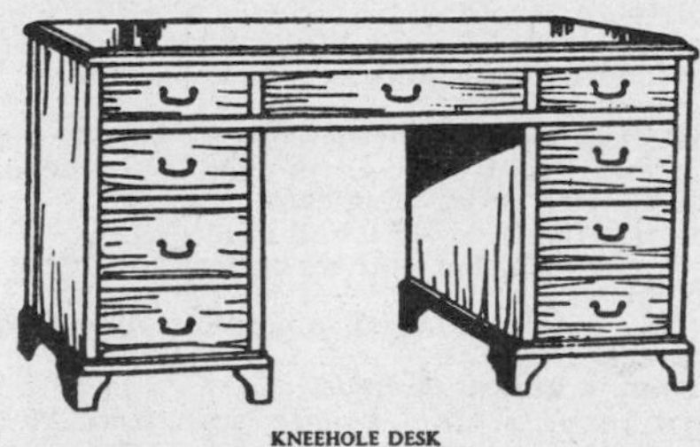

KNEEHOLE DESK

knee′hol″ly, *n.* butcher's-broom, a plant of the genus *Ruscus.*

knee′-jẽrk, *a.* [from *knee jerk.*] designating, characterized by, or reacting with an automatic, predictable response; as, a *knee-jerk* bigot. [Colloq.]

knee jẽrk, same as *patellar reflex.*

knee joint, 1. the joint which connects the thigh and leg bones; the joint of the knee.
2. in machinery, a toggle joint.

knee′-joint″ed, *a.* in botany, kneed; geniculated.

kneel (nēl), *v.i.;* knelt *or* kneeled, *pt., pp.;* kneeling, *ppr.* [ME. *knelen, cneolien,* to kneel, from AS. *cneow,* knee.] to bend or rest on one's knee or knees.

kneel′ẽr, *n.* 1. one who kneels, as in worship.
2. a bench, pad, etc. used for kneeling.

kneel′ing·ly, *adv.* in a kneeling position.

knee′pad, *n.* a protective pad worn around the knee, as by basketball players.

knee′pan, *n.* the kneecap; patella.

knee′piēce, *n.* 1. a piece of armor to protect the knee.
2. a piece of wood shaped like a knee, as in a rafter.

knee′-sprung, *a.* having the knees bent forward as a result of a shortening of the flexor tendons: said of a horse.

knee tim′bẽr, timber suitable for making knees, either by natural growth or by bending.

knell (nel), *n.* [ME. *knel, knul;* AS. *cnyll,* a loud noise, from *cnyllan,* to beat noisily.]
1. the sound of a bell, especially of a bell rung slowly, as at a funeral.
2. an omen of death, extinction, failure, etc.
3. a mournful sound.

knell, *v.i.;* knelled, *pt., pp.;* knelling, *ppr.* 1. to ring in a slow, solemn way; toll.
2. to sound ominously or mournfully.

knell, *v.t.* [ME. *knellen, knyllen;* AS. *cnyllan,* to knock, to beat noisily.]
1. to call by the sounding of a bell.
2. to ring or toll (a bell). [Obs.]

knelt, *v.* alternative past tense and past participle of *kneel.*

knew (nū), *v.* past tense of *know.*

Knick′ẽr·bock·ẽr (nik′), *n.* [from Diedrich *Knickerbocker,* fictitious D. author of Washington Irving's *History of New York* (1809).]
1. a descendant of the early Dutch settlers of New York.
2. any New Yorker.
3. [k–] [*pl.*] short, loose trousers gathered in at or just below the knees; knickers, as those worn by Dutch settlers of New York.

knick′ẽrṣ, *n.pl.* 1. knickerbockers.
2. a bloomerlike undergarment worn by women or girls. [Chiefly Brit.]
3. panties. [Brit.]

knick′knack (nik′nak), *n.* [a reduplication of *knack,* a trick, toy.] a trifle or toy; any small article more ornamental than useful: also spelled *nicknack.*

knick′knack·ȧ·tō·ry, *n.* a house or room for a collection of knickknacks; also, the collection itself.

knick′knack·ẽr·y, *n.* articles classified as knickknacks.

knīfe (nīf), *n.; pl.* **knīveṣ,** [ME. *knif, knyf;* AS. *cnif,* a knife.]
1. an instrument for cutting, having one or more sharp-edged blades, often pointed, and set in a handle.
2. a cutting part of an instrument or machine.
3. a sword. [Obs.]
under the knife; undergoing surgery. [Colloq.]
war to the knife; unceasing strife; combat to end in death; mortal conflict.

knīfe, *v.t.;* knifed (nīft), *pt., pp.;* knifing, *ppr.*
1. to stab with or as with a knife.
2. to use underhand methods in order to hurt, defeat, or betray. [Colloq.]

knīfe bär, the bar holding the blades in a harvester.

knīfe′bōard, *n.* a board on which knives are cleaned.

knīfe′-edġe, *n.* 1. the edge of a knife.
2. any very sharp edge.
3. a metal wedge whose fine edge serves as the fulcrum for a scale beam, pendulum, etc.
knife-edge file; a file having one sharp edge.

knīfe grȧss, a plant, *Scleria latifolia,* of tropical America, with very sharp-edged leaves.

knīfe switch, an electrical switch in which the hinged, knifelike contact blade is pressed down between the contact clips.

knīght (nīt), *n.* [ME. *knight, kniht, cniht;* AS. *cniht,* a boy, youth, attendant.]
1. in the Middle Ages, (a) a military servant of the king or other feudal superior; a tenant holding land on condition that he serve his superior as a mounted man-at-arms; (b) later, a man, usually one of high birth, who after serving as page and squire was formally raised to honorable military rank by the king or other qualified lord and pledged to chivalrous conduct.
2. in Great Britain, a man who for some achievement or service to his country is given honorary nonhereditary rank next below a baronet, entitling him to use *Sir* before his given name.
3. an ancient Roman, Athenian, etc. whose status is regarded as equivalent to that of a knight.
4. a member of any order or society that officially calls its members *knights.*
5. (a) a lady's devoted champion or attendant; (b) a devoted follower of some cause, person, etc. [Poetic.]
6. in chess, a piece shaped like a horse's head: in a single move it is advanced one square, whether occupied or unoccupied, in any vertical or horizontal direction, and then one square diagonally, coming to rest on a different color from that on which it started.
7. a youth; a young man. [Obs.]
knight of industry; a person who lives by cheating, trickery, and theft. [Obs.]
knight of the post; a person who had been dubbed at the whipping post; a person who could be hired to give false testimony; an acknowledged rascal.
Knights of Columbus; an international fraternal and benevolent society of Roman Catholic men, founded in 1882.
Knights of Labor; an organization of workers, founded in 1869 and dissolved about 1900.
Knights of Malta; see *Hospitaler.*
Knights of Pythias; a secret fraternal order founded in Washington, D. C., in 1864.
Knights of the Round Table; a legendary order of knights said to have been established by Arthur, a legendary king of Britain, and to have gathered at a round table as signifying equality of rank.

knīght, *v.t.;* knighted, *pt., pp.;* knighting, *ppr.* to make (a man) a knight.

knīght′āġe, *n.* knights collectively, or a body of knights, of a country or district.

knīght bach′e·lŏr, *pl.* **knīghts bach′e·lŏrṣ,** a member of the oldest and lowest class of British knights.

knīght ban′nẽr·et, *pl.* **knīghts ban′nẽr·ets,** see *banneret,* sense 2.

knīght-er′rănt, *n.; pl.* **knīghts-er′rănt,** 1. a medieval knight wandering in search of adventures, especially those in which to redress wrongs or show his prowess.
2. a chivalrous or quixotic person.

knīght-er′rănt·ry, *n.; pl.* **knīght-er′rănt·rieṣ,** the behavior, character, or action of a knight-errant; quixotic behavior or act.

knīght′head (-hed), *n.* in shipbuilding, either of two pieces of timber rising on either side of the bowsprit, to secure its inner end; also, either of two strong frames of timber which enclose and support the ends of the windlass.

knīght′hood, *n.* 1. the rank or status of a knight.
2. the profession or vocation of a knight.

3. knightliness.
4. knights collectively.
Order of Knighthood; an organized body of knights, belonging to one of two classes: either associations or fraternities, possessing property and rights of their own as independent bodies, or honorary associations established by sovereigns within their respective dominions. To the former class belonged the three military and religious orders founded during the Crusades: Templars, Hospitalers, and Teutonic Knights. The other class, consisting of titular orders, includes most of the existing European orders. The orders have insignia, which generally include a badge or jewel, a collar, a colored ribbon, and a star.

INSIGNIA OF THE ORDER OF ST. PATRICK

Knīght'i·ȧ, *n.* [named after Thomas A. *Knight*, an English horticulturist.] a genus of plants, belonging to the order *Proteaceæ*, of Australia and adjacent regions: only three species are known, the wood of one, the *Knightia excelsa* of New Zealand, being used in ornamental work and cabinetmaking (called *rewa-rewa*, *New Zealand oak*).
knīght'less, *a.* unbecoming a knight. [Obs.]
knīght'li·ness, *n.* the quality of being like a knight; chivalry.
knīght'ly, *a.*; *comp.* knightlier; *superl.* knightliest, 1. of, characteristic of, like, or befitting a knight; chilavrous, brave, etc.
2. consisting of knights.
knīght'ly, *adv.* in a knightly manner. [Archaic.]
knīght sẽrv'ice, in English feudal law, a tenure of lands held by knights on condition that they perform military service.
knīghts'wŏrt, *n.* a plant of Great Britain having leaves like the blade of a sword.
Knīght Tem'plăr, 1. *pl.* **Knīghts Tem'plărs**, a member of a military and religious order established among the Crusaders early in the twelfth century to protect pilgrims to the Holy Land: it was suppressed in 1312.
2. *pl.* **Knīghts Tem'plăr**, a member of a certain order of Masons.
Knip·hō'fi·ȧ (nip-), *n.* [named after Prof. J. H. *Kniphof*, of Erfurt, Germany.] a genus of South African plants called torch lilies, characterized by their showy spiked flowers.
knit (nit), *v.t.*; knitted *or* knit, *pt.*, *pp.*; knitting, *ppr.* [ME. *knitten*, *knutten*; AS. *cnyttan*, to knit, from *cnotta*, a knot.]
1. to make (cloth or a piece of clothing) by looping together yarn or thread by means of special needles.
2. to form into cloth in this way instead of by weaving.
3. to fasten together closely and firmly; to unite.
4. to draw (the brows) together; to contract in wrinkles.
5. to tie or fasten in or with a knot. [Archaic and Dial.]
knit, *v.i.* 1. to make cloth or a piece of clothing by looping together yarn or thread.
2. to unite closely; to grow together, as a broken bone.
3. to become drawn together in wrinkles; as, his brows *knit* in thought.
knit, *n.* 1. a knitting or style of knitting; texture.
2. the kind of stitch used in knitting; as a ribbed *knit*.
3. in mining, a small piece of galena, or lead ore. [Brit. Dial.]
knit'back, *n.* common comfrey, *Symphytum officinale*: so named because of its healing properties.
knitch, *n.* a fagot or burden of wood. [Brit. Dial.]
knitch'et, *n.* a knitch. [Obs.]
knit'stẽr, *n.* a woman who knits. [Obs.]
knit'tẽr, *n.* one who or that which knits.
knit'ting, *n.* 1. the action of one who or that which knits.
2. knitted work.
knit'ting çāse, a case to hold knitting needles.
knit'ting mȧ·chine', a machine for knitting.
knit'ting nee'dle, an eyeless, usually long, needle of metal, bone, etc., with a blunt point at one or both ends, used in pairs, etc. in knitting by hand.
knit'ting shēath, an instrument with a small perforation to receive the end of the needle in knitting; a knitting case.
knit'tle (nit'), *n.* [*knit* and dim. *-le*.]
1. a string that gathers or draws together a purse.
2. a small line used in ships to sling hammocks, etc.
knīveş, *n.* plural of *knife*.
knob (nob), *n.* [ME. *knobbe*; prob. from M.H. G. *knobbe*, a knot, knob, bud.]
1. a hard protuberance; a hard swelling or rising.
2. a handle, usually round, of a door, drawer, etc.
3. a rounded hill or mountain; a knoll.
4. in architecture, a boss; a rounded ornament at the intersection of the ribs of a groined arch.
knob, *v.i.* to develop into knobs.
knob, *v.t.* to produce or to form a knob or knobs on.
knobbed, *a.* supplied with a knob or knobs; ending in a knob; as, *knobbed* antennae.
knob'bẽr, *n.* a male deer in its second year. [Brit.]
knob'bi·ness, *n.* the quality of having knobs, or of being full of protuberances.
knob'bing, *n.* the act of knocking off the knobs from a block of stone in quarrying.
knob'ble, *v.t.*; knobbled, *pt.*, *pp.*; knobbling, *ppr.* [freq. of *knob*.] to free from knobs, as in stonecutting.
knob'blẽr, *n.* a knobber.
knob'by, *a.*; *comp.* knobbier; *superl.* knobbiest,
1. like a knob.
2. covered with knobs.
knob'ker"rie, *n.* [S. Afr. D.] a stick with a round head on one end, used by some South African tribes as a striking or throwing weapon: also spelled *knobkerry*.
knob'stick, *n.* 1. a knobkerrie.
2. a person who refuses to join a trade union or who withdraws from one; a scab. [Brit.]
knock (nok), *v.i.*; knocked (nokt), *pt.*, *pp.*; knocking, *ppr.* [ME. *knokken*; AS. *cnucian*, to knock, beat.]
1. to strike or beat with something thick or heavy, or with the fist; especially, to rap on a door.
2. to bump; to collide; to clash.
3. in machinery, to strike, as one part of a machine against another, producing a metallic sound, as a piston hitting against a cylinder wall; also, to explode with a knocking sound, as fuel when burning improperly.
4. to criticize captiously; to oppose; to find fault. [Colloq.]
5. in gin rummy, to end a deal by exposing one's hand and showing a surplus of not more than ten points in unmatched cards.
to knock about (or *around*); to go from one place; to saunter about without definite aim. [Colloq.]
to knock off; to quit; to cease working.
to knock under; to yield; to submit; to acknowledge to be conquered.
knock, *v.t.* 1. to strike; to hit.
2. to hit so as to cause to fall (with *down* or *off*).
3. to make by hitting or striking; as, he *knocked* a hole in the screen.
4. to find fault with; to criticize adversely. [Colloq.]
to knock about (or *around*); to treat roughly. [Colloq.]
to knock down; (a) to strike down; to fell; (b) to disconnect the parts of machinery or furniture for convenience in shipping; (c) to indicate the sale of (an article) at an auction, as by a blow of the auctioneer's hammer.
to knock off; (a) [Colloq.] to deduct; (b) [Colloq.] to do; to accomplish; (c) [Slang.] to kill, overcome, etc.
to knock on the head; to kill by a blow or by blows.
to knock out; (a) to force out by a blow or blows; (b) in boxing, to defeat (an opponent) by knocking him to the ground so that he cannot rise within a specified time; (c) to make unconscious or exhausted; (d) to defeat; (e) [Colloq.] to do; to make.
to knock out of the box; in baseball, to make so many hits against (an opposing pitcher) as to cause his removal.
to knock together; to make or compose hastily or crudely.
to knock up; (a) [Brit. Colloq.] to tire out; to exhaust; (b) [Slang.] to make pregnant.
knock, *n.* 1. a blow; a stroke with something thick or heavy.
2. a sharp or resounding blow; a rap, as on a door.
3. a thumping or rattling noise in an internal-combustion engine, etc., as because of faulty combustion.
4. an adverse criticism. [Colloq.]
knock'ȧ·bout, *n.* 1. a small, one-masted yacht with a mainsail, a jib, and a centerboard or keel, but no bowsprit.
2. in Australia, a man employed for doing odd jobs.
knock'ȧ·bout, *a.* 1. rough; noisy; boisterous.
2. made or suitable for knocking about or rough use.
knock'down, *a.* 1. so severe as to knock down; overwhelming.
2. made so as to be easily taken apart; as, a *knockdown* table.
knock'down, *n.* 1. a knocking down; a felling.
2. a blow, stroke, etc. that knocks one down.
3. an introduction (to a person). [Slang.]
knocked down (nokt), in commerce, not assembled: said of furniture, etc.
knock'ẽr, *n.* 1. one who or that which knocks.
2. an instrument or kind of hammer, fastened by a hinge to a door to be used in knocking for admittance.
3. a person who captiously criticizes; a faultfinder. [Colloq.]
knock'ing, *n.* the act or sound of one who or that which knocks; a beating; a rap.
knock'ingş, *n.pl.* 1. in mining, the larger pieces of ore before being crushed.
2. the chips of stone knocked off by a stonemason.
knock'-knee (-nē), *n.* 1. a condition in which the legs bend inward so that the knees knock together or touch each other in walking: opposed to *bowleg*.
2. [*pl.*] such knees.
knock'-kneed, *a.* affected by knock-knee: opposed to *bowlegged*.
knock'out, *a.* causing prostration; disabling; as, a *knockout* blow.
knock'out, *n.* 1. a knocking out or being knocked out.
2. a blow that knocks out; a blow that causes a boxer to fall and fail to resume the fight before the referee has counted ten.
3. a person or thing that is very attractive or striking. [Slang.]
knockout drops; a drug put into a drink to cause the drinker to become stupefied or unconscious. [Slang.]
knock'stōne, *n.* a heavy, flat stone or metal plate on which ore is broken into small pieces for smelting.
knōll (nōl), *v.t.* and *v.i.*; knolled, *pt.*, *pp.*; knolling, *ppr.* [AS. *cnyllan*, to beat or strike.] to knell. [Archaic and Brit. Dial.]
knōll, *n.* a knell. [Archaic and Brit. Dial.]
knōll, *n.* [ME. *knol*; AS. *cnol*, *cnoll*, a top, summit; compare W. *cnol*, dim. of Gael. *cnoc*, a hill, knoll.] the top or crown of a hill; a hillock or mound.
knop (nop), *n.* [ME. *knop*, *knoppe*; compare D. *knop*, a knob, bud.]
1. a knob; a tufted top; a bud; a bunch; a button.
2. a knoblike architectural ornament.
knop'pẽr, *n.* [G. *knopper*, a gallnut.] a kind of gall formed by the puncture of insects on the unripe acorns of various oaks, used in tanning and dyeing.
knop'weed, *n.* same as *knapweed*.
knosp, *n.* [G. *knospe*, a bud.] in architecture, a knop.
knot (not), *n.* [ME. *knotte*; AS. *cnotta*, a knot.]
1. a lump or knob in a thread, cord, etc., formed by passing one free end through a loop and drawing it tight, or by a tangle drawn tight.
2. a fastening made by intertwining or tying together pieces of string, cord, rope, etc.
3. an ornamental bow of ribbon or twist of braid; cockade; epaulet.
4. a small group or cluster.
5. something that ties or fastens closely or intricately; a bond of union; especially, the bond of marriage.

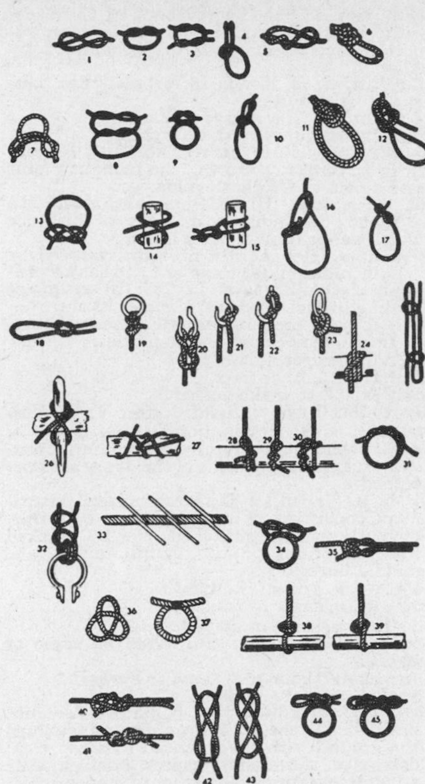

KNOTS

1. figure-of-eight knot; 2. overhand knot; 3. thief knot; 4. half hitch; 5. stevedore's knot; 6. loop knot; 7. harness hitch; 8. reef knot; 9. granny knot; 10. bowline knot; 11. bowline on a bight; 12. bowline with a bight; 13. prolonge knot; 14. clove hitch; 15. round turn and two half hitches; 16. running bowline; 17. slide knot; 18. slipknot; 19. fisherman's bend; 20. cat's-paw; 21. single Blackwall hitch; 22. double Blackwall hitch; 23. studding-sail tack bend; 24. magnus hitch; 25. sheepshank; 26. half hitch over pin; 27. rolling hitch; 28. studding-sail halyard bend; 29. timber hitch; 30. timber hitch and a half hitch; 31. surgeon's knot; 32. anchor knot; 33. long splice; 34. surgeon's knot; 35. sheet bend; 36. trefoil knot; 37. throat seizing; 38. outside clinch; 39. inside clinch; 40. double sheet bend; 41. Englishman's tie; 42. single carrick bend; 43. double carrick bend; 44. single bowknot; 45. double bowknot

6. a problem; difficulty; entanglement.

7. a knotlike part; a node or lump; as, a *knot* sometimes forms in a tense muscle; specifically, (a) a hard lump on a tree where a branch grows out; (b) a cross section of such a lump, appearing as cross-grained in a board or log; (c) a joint on a plant stem where leaves grow out; (d) a fungous disease of trees, in which abnormal protuberances appear.

8. in nautical usage, (a) a division of the log line, by which a ship's rate of speed is measured; (b) a unit of speed of one nautical mile (6,080.27 feet) an hour; as, the ship can easily make a speed of 10 *knots*; (c) loosely, a nautical mile.

9. any figure the lines of which frequently intersect each other, as in embroidery, etc.

Syn.—bond, connection, tie, snarl, tangle, bunch, collection, perplexity.

knot, *v.t.*; knotted, *pt., pp.*; knotting, *ppr.* 1. to tie in a knot or knots; to form a knot or knots in.

2. to entangle; to tie or unite closely or intricately.

3. to make (fringe) by tying knots.

knot, *v.i.* 1. to form a knot or knots; to become entangled.

2. to knit knots for fringe.

knot, *n.* [rare ME. *knotte*; also (17th c.) *gnat*; perh. analogical sp., after preceding *knot*, for partly assimilated *gn-*.] a small, red-breasted sandpiper that breeds in arctic regions and then migrates.

knot'ber"ry, *n.* a plant of the genus *Rubus*, having knotted stems.

knot'grȧss, *n.* 1. any of several species of plants with jointed or knotty stems; specifically, *Polygonum aviculare*, of the buckwheat family: called also *knotweed, goose grass, doorweed*.

2. oat grass or any of various similar grasses with bent stems.

knot'hōle, *n.* a hole in a board, etc. where a knot has fallen out.

knot'less, *a.* free from knots; without knots.

knot'ted, *a.* 1. tied or fastened in with a knot or knots.

2. full of knots; having knots.

3. having intersecting figures; tangled; intricate.

4. puzzling; knotty.

knotted pillar; in architecture, a pillar of the Romanesque style carved in such a way as to appear knotted in the middle.

KNOTTED PILLAR

knot'tẽr, *n.* 1. a person or thing that ties knots.

2. a remover of knots.

knot'ti·ness, *n.* 1. the quality of having many knots or swellings.

2. difficulty of solution; intricacy.

knot'ting, *n.* fringe made of knotted threads.

knot'ty, *a.*; *comp.* knottier; *superl.* knottiest. 1. full of knots; having many knots; as, *knotty* timber.

2. hard; rugged.

3. difficult to solve or explain; intricate; perplexing; as, a *knotty* question or point.

knot'weed, *n.* 1. same as *knotgrass*.

2. same as *knapweed*.

knot'wŏrt, *n.* any of various plants of the genus *Illecebrum*.

knout (nout), *n.* [Fr. *knout*; Russ. *knut*, a whip scourge; compare Ice. *knutr*, a knot.] a leather whip formerly used in Russia to flog criminals.

knout, *v.t.*; knouted, *pt., pp.*; knouting, *ppr.* to flog with a knout.

knōw (nō), *v.t.*; knew, *pt.*; known, *pp.*; knowing, *ppr.* [ME. *knowen, knawen*; AS. *cnawan*, to know; akin to L. *gnoscere, noscere*, Gr. *gignōskein*, to know, Sans. root *jnā*, to know.]

1. to perceive with certainty; to understand clearly; to be sure of or well informed about; as, we *know* the facts.

2. to be aware or cognizant of; to have perceived or learned; as, he *knew* that we were home.

3. to have a firm mental grasp of; to have securely in the memory; as, the actor *knows* his lines.

4. to be acquainted or familiar with.

5. to have understanding of or skill in as a result of study or experience; as, she *knows* music.

6. to recognize by recollection, remembrance, representation, or description; as, I'd *know* that face anywhere.

7. to recognize as distinct; to distinguish; as, it's not always easy to *know* right from wrong.

8. in Biblical and legal usage, to have sexual intercourse with.

to be in the know; to have confidential information. [Colloq.]

to know the ropes; to be acquainted with all the details of any business or procedure. [Colloq.]

to know what's what; to know all about anything; to be proof against trickery. [Colloq.]

knōw (nō), *v.i.* [ME. *knowen, knawen*; AS. *cnawan*, to know.]

1. to have clear and certain perception; to have knowledge.

> If any man will do his will, he shall *know* of the doctrine, whether it be of God, or whether I speak of myself.
> —John vii. 17.

2. to be informed, sure, or aware.

3. to take cognizance; to examine.

knōw'ȧ·ble, *a.* that can be known; that can be discovered, understood, or ascertained.

knōw'ȧ·ble·ness, *n.* the quality of being knowable.

knōw'-ạll, *n.* a know-it-all. [Colloq.]

knōw'ẽr, *n.* one who knows.

knōw'-how, *n.* knowledge of how to do something; technical skill. [Colloq.]

knōw'ing, *a.* 1. having knowledge or information; well-informed; well-instructed; as, a *knowing* man.

2. shrewd; cunning; worldly-wise.

3. implying shrewd understanding or possession of secret or inside information; as, a *knowing* look.

4. deliberate; intentional.

Syn.—astute, discerning, sharp, acute, sagacious, penetrating, proficient, intelligent, experienced, accomplished.

knōw'ing, *n.* knowledge; means of obtaining knowledge.

knōw'ing·ly, *adv.* 1. in a knowing manner.

2. with knowledge; designedly; as, he would not *knowingly* offend.

knōw'ing·ness, *n.* the quality of having knowledge or of being shrewd or artful.

knōw'-it-ạll, *a.* pretending or claiming to know much about almost everything. [Colloq.]

knōw'-it-ạll, *n.* a know-it-all person. [Colloq.]

knowl'edġe (nol'ej), *n.* [ME. *knowlege, knowleche*, knowledge; *knowen*, to know, and *-leche, -leke*, from Ice. *-leikr, -leiki*, a suffix used in forming abstract nouns.]

1. a clear and certain perception of something; the act, fact, or state of knowing; understanding.

2. learning; all that has been perceived or grasped by the mind.

> Ignorance is the curse of God,
> *Knowledge* the wing wherewith we fly to heaven. —Shak.

3. practical experience; skill; as, a *knowledge* of seamanship.

4. acquaintance or familiarity (with a fact, place, etc.).

5. cognizance; recognition.

6. information; the body of facts accumulated by mankind.

7. acquaintance with facts; range of awareness, or understanding.

8. sexual intercourse: generally preceded by *carnal*. [Archaic.]

Syn.—learning, skill, erudition, understanding, information, lore.

to (the best of) one's knowledge; as far as one knows; within the range of one's information.

knowl'edġe, *v.t.* to acknowledge. [Obs.]

knowl'edġe·ȧ·ble, *a.* having or showing knowledge or intelligence. [Colloq.]

Knōwl·tō'ni·ȧ (nōl-), *n.* [named after Thomas *Knowlton*, an English botanist.] a genus of herbaceous plants belonging to the order *Ranunculaceæ*, native to the Cape of Good Hope.

knōwn, *v.* past participle of *know*.

knōw'-nŏth"ing, *n.* 1. an ignorant person; an ignoramus.

2. an agnostic.

3. [K- N-] a member of the American party: see *American party* under *American*.

Knōw'-Nŏth·ing·iṣm, *n.* the principles and doctrines of the Know-Nothing, or American, party.

knōwn quän'ti·ty, an algebraic quantity whose value is given: usually represented by *a*, *b*, etc.

knub (nub), *n.* [var. of *knob*.]

1. a knob. [Dial.]

2. the husklike envelope of a silk cocoon.

knub, *v.t.* to beat; to strike with the knuckles. [Obs.]

knuç'kle (nuk''l), *n.* [ME. *knokel, knokil*; compare G. *knöchel*; D. *knokkel*, a joint, knuckle.]

1. (a) a joint of the finger; especially, any of the joints connecting the fingers to the rest of the hand; (b) the rounded knob formed by the bones at such a joint.

2. the knee or hock joint and near-by parts of a pig or other animal, used as food.

3. the joint of a plant. [Obs.]

4. in mechanics, (a) the part or parts of a hinge carrying the hinge pin; (b) a part of an automatic car coupler.

5. [*pl.*] a knuckle-duster.

6. something resembling a knuckle.

7. in shipbuilding, an angular fitting of timbers rather than a continuously curved one.

knuç'kle, *v.i.*; knuckled, *pt., pp.*; knuckling, *ppr.* to rest the knuckles on the ground in shooting a marble (often with *down*).

to knuckle down; (a) to work energetically; to apply oneself seriously; (b) to yield to, as an opponent; to give up in a contest: also *to knuckle under*.

knuç'kle, *v.t.* to strike, press, or touch with the knuckles.

knuç'kle ball, in baseball, a slow ball pitched with the two middle fingers tucked under and pressing against the top of the ball.

knuç'kle·bōne, *n.* 1. any bone of a human knuckle.

2. (a) an animal's limb bone with a rounded knob at the joint end; (b) the knob.

3. [*pl.*] an old game played with the knucklebones of sheep.

knuç'kled, *a.* jointed. [Obs.]

knuç'kle-dust"ẽr, *n.* linked metal rings or a

metal bar with holes for the fingers, worn for rough fighting: now usually *brass knuckles*.

knuç'kle·head, *n.* a stupid person. [Colloq.]

knuç'kle joint, 1. any articulation, or point of movement, between two bones forming a knuckle.

2. a hinged joint formed by a projection between two others.

knūr, knūrr, *n.* [compare O.D. *knorre*; G. *knorren*, a lump, knot.] a knot, as on the trunk or branch of a tree.

knūrl, *n.* [as if dim. of *knur*; prob. phonetic var. of *gnarl*.]

1. a knot, knob, nodule, etc.

2. a ridge or any of a series of small beads or ridges on a metal surface, as on the edge of a coin or nut.

3. a short, thickset person. [Scot.]

knūrl, *v.t.* to make knurls on; to mill.

knūrled, *a.* full of knots; gnarled.

knūrl·y, *a.*; *comp.* knurlier; *superl.* knurliest; full of knots, or knurls, as wood; gnarled.

knūr'ry, *a.* full of knots. [Obs.]

KO (kā'ō), *v.t.*; KO'd, *pt.*, *pp.*; KO'ing, *ppr.* in boxing, to knock out: also *kayo*, *K.O.*, *k.o.* [Slang.]

KO (kā'ō), *n.*; *pl.* **KO'ṣ** (kā'ōz), in boxing, a knockout: also *kayo*, *K.O.*, *k.o.* [Slang.]

kō'ȧ, *n.* [Hawaiian.] a leguminous Hawaiian tree, *Acacia koa*, its wavy-grained wood being used for cabinetwork and its bark for tanning.

kō·ä'lȧ, *n.* [native name] a tree-dwelling marsupial animal, *Phascolarctos cinereus*, of Australia, somewhat resembling a bear: it is about two feet long and has thick, gray fur and large, tufted ears.

KOALA (24 in. long)

kob, *n.* [African.] any of several species of African antelope belonging to the genus *Kobus*.

kō'bȧ, *n.* a kob.

kō'bạlt, *n.* same as *cobalt*.

kō'bel·līte, *n.* [named after Franz von Kobell, a German mineralogist.] a dark-gray sulfide containing antimony, bismuth, and lead.

kō'bold, *n.* [G., from M.H.G. *kobolt*, fairy.] in German folklore, (a) a helpful or mischievous sprite in households; a brownie; (b) a gnome in mines and other underground places.

Kō'çhi·ȧ, *n.* [named after W. D. J. *Koch*, a German botanist.] a genus of plants belonging to the goosefoot family.

kō'dak, *n.* [arbitrary formation.] a small, portable camera for taking photographs on a roll of film: a trade-mark (*Kodak*).

kō'dak, *v.t.* and *v.i.*; kodaked, *pt.*, *pp.*; kodaking, *ppr.* to photograph by means of a kodak; figuratively, to portray or depict briefly.

kō'di·ak beār, a large bear found on Kodiak Island, Alaska: it can attain a weight of 1,500 pounds.

kō'el, *n.* [Prakrit *koelo*, from Sans. *kokila*, a cuckoo.] any of various cuckoos found in the East Indies, India, and Australia.

Koel·reu·tē'ri·ȧ (kel-), *n.* [named after Joseph G. *Kölreuter*, a German naturalist.] a genus of small Chinese trees of the soapberry family, having showy flowers.

koff, *n.* [D. *kof.*] a small, two-masted Dutch vessel, used for fishing.

koft'gä·ri, *n.* [Hind. *koftgari*; *kofta*, pounded, and *-garī*, doing, making.] ornamental metalwork of steel inlaid with gold, made in India.

Kō·hel'eth, *n.* [Heb. *qōheleth*.]

1. in the Bible, the book of Ecclesiastes.

2. Solomon: so called in this book.

Kōh'-i-noor, Kōh'-i-nūr, Kōh'i·nọọr, *n.* [Per. *kōh-i-nūr*, lit., mountain of light.] a famous diamond of India, belonging to the British crown, weighing over 100 carats.

kōhl, *n.* [Ar. *al-koh'l*; *al-*, the, and *koh'l*, a fine powder of antimony.] an antimonial powder for darkening the eyelids: used in certain Eastern countries.

kōhl·rä'bi, *n.* [G.] a kind of cabbage with an edible, bulbous stem that looks somewhat like a turnip: called also *kale turnip*.

koi·nḗ', Koi·nḗ', *n.* [Gr.] the language used throughout the Greek world, from Syria to Gaul, during the Hellenistic and Roman periods: its spoken form consisted of colloquial Attic, supplemented by numerous Ionic words and some borrowings from other dialects: the New Testament is written in the koine.

kŏk'-sa·gyz' (-gēz'), *n.* [Russ., from Turk. *kŏk*, a root, and East Turk. *sagīz*, rubber, gum.] a Russian plant of the dandelion family, from roots of which rubber can be made.

kō'lȧ, *n.* 1. the kola nut.

2. the tree that it grows on.

3. an extract or stimulant made from kola nuts.

Also spelled *cola*.

kō'lȧ nut, the brown, bitter nut of either of two tropical trees: it contains some caffeine and theobromine and is used in making certain soft drinks.

Kō·lā'ri·ăn, *n.* an aboriginal linguistic stock of India.

kōl·bäs'ī, kōl·bäs'sï, *n.* same as *kielbasa*.

kō·lin'sky, *n.* [Russ. *kolinski*, from *Kola*, a district in northern Russia.]

1. Asiatic mink, *Mustela siberica*; or, especially among furriers, any Asiatic mink.

2. the golden-brown fur of such a mink.

kōl·khōz', *n.* [Russ. *kollektivnoe*, collective, and *khozaīstvo*, household, farm.] a collective farm in the Soviet Union: also spelled *kolhoz*, *kolkhos*.

Kōl Nid're, [Heb. *kōl nidhrē*, lit., all our vows (opening words of the prayer).]

1. the prayer of atonement recited in Jewish synagogues at the opening of the Yom Kippur eve services.

2. the traditional music to which this is sung.

kō·mec'e·ras, *n.* [Gr. *komē*, hair, and *keras*, horn.] a horn formed of highly compacted hairs and shed annually, as in the pronghorn of America: also written *komoceras*.

Kom'in·tērn, *n.* [G.] same as *Comintern*.

Kō·mō'dō drag'ŏn, [from *Komodo* island, Indonesia.] a giant, flesh-eating lizard, *Varanus komodoensis*, of the jungles of southeastern Asia: it is the largest living lizard, reaching a length of 9 feet.

kō'mŏn·dọr, *n.* [Hung.] any of a breed of large, powerful dog with a shaggy, white coat, originally used in Hungary to guard herds.

kō·ni·ol'ō·gy, *n.* [Gr. *konia*, dust, and *-logia*, from *legein*, to speak.] the science dealing with germs and particles of dust floating in the air.

kō'nīte, *n.* same as *conite*.

kọọ·chäh'bee, *n.* [Am. Ind.] a food collected from salt lakes by Indians in the western part of the United States, consisting of the larvae of certain dipterous insects.

kọọ'dọọ, *n.* same as *kudu*.

kọọk, *n.* [prob. contracted from *cuckoo*.] a person regarded as silly, eccentric, etc. [Slang.]

kọọk'ȧ·būr·rȧ, *n.* [from native name in Australia.] a large kingfisher of Australia and New Guinea: also called *laughing jackass*.

kọọk'y, kọọk'iē, *a.*; *comp.* kookier; *superl.* kookiest; of or characteristic of a kook; silly, eccentric, crazy, etc. [Slang.]

kọọ·lō·kam'bȧ, *n.* [native name.] an anthropoid ape of equatorial Africa.

kọọn'ti, *n.* same as *coontie*.

kọọ'rȧ·jọng, *n.* same as *kurrajong*.

kọọr'bash, *n.* [Ar. *kurbāj*, from Turk. *qirbāch*, a whip, scourge.] a whip made of heavy rawhide, used in Africa.

Kọọrd, *n.* same as *Kurd*.

Kọọrd'ish, *a.* same as *Kurdish*.

Kọọ'te·nāy, Kọọ'te·nāi (-nā), *n.* 1. *pl.* **Kọọ'te·nāy, Kọọ'te·nāi,** a small group of Indian tribes living in Montana, Idaho, and British Columbia.

2. their language.

Also spelled *Kutenai*, *Kutenay*.

kop, *n.* [S. Afr. D., from D. *kop*, a head.] in South Africa, a mountain or hill.

kō'peck, kō'pek, *n.* [Russ. *kopeika*, from *kopye*, a lance.] a small Russian coin of bronze or copper (originally silver), equal to $^{1}/_{100}$ ruble: also spelled *copeck*.

kōph, *n.* [Heb. *qoph*.] the nineteenth letter of the Hebrew alphabet corresponding to English *K*, *k*: also spelled *qoph*.

kop'je (-i), *n.* [S. Afr. D.] a hill or hillock; a hill with a steep side and a flat top.

kōr, *n.* [Heb. *kōr*, lit., round vessel.] an old Hebrew measure of capacity; a homer.

Kō·rän' (*or* kō-ran'), *n.* [Ar. *qurān*, *qorān* (written with article *al-*, the), book, reading, from *qarā*, to read.] the sacred book of the Moslems, written in Arabic: its contents are reported revelations made to Mohammed by Allah.

Kō·rē'ăn, *a.* of Korea, its people, their language, or culture.

Kō·rē'ăn, *n.* 1. a native of Korea.

2. the language of the Koreans.

kō·ru'nä, *n.*; *pl.* **kō·ru'ny, kō·run',** [Czech, from L. *corona*, a crown.] the monetary unit and a coin of Czechoslovakia.

kōs, *n.*; *pl.* **kōs,** [Hind., from Sans. *krósa*, lit., a shout.] in India, a measure of distance which varies from 1.5 to 3 miles.

kō'shēr, *a.* [Heb. *kāshēr*, fit, right, proper.]

1. in Judaism, (a) clean or fit to eat according to the dietary laws: Lev. xi; (b) serving or dealing in such food; as, a *kosher* kitchen.

2. loosely, prepared according to traditional Jewish recipes; as, *kosher* pickles.

3. fit; proper. [Slang.]

kō'shēr, *n.* kosher food.

kosh'ēr, *v.t.* to make kosher.

Kos·te·letz'ky·ȧ, *n.* [named after V. F. *Kosteletzky*, a Bohemian botanist.] a genus of herbs of the mallow family, resembling *Hibiscus*, except that the cells of the ovary are one-seeded.

kō'tō, *n.* [Japan.] a Japanese musical instrument consisting of an oblong box with thirteen silk strings stretched over it, plucked with plectrums on the thumb, index, and middle fingers.

kō'tow', *n.* and *v.i.* kowtow.

kot'wạl, *n.* same as *cutwal*.

köu'lȧn, *n.* same as *dziggetai*.

köu'mis, köu'miss, köu'myss, *n.* same as *kumiss*.

kour·bash' (koor-), *n.* same as *kurbash*.

köus'sō, *n.* same as *cusso*.

kow'tow' (*or* kō'tow'), *n.* [Chin. *k'o-t'ou*, lit., knock head.] the act of kneeling and touching the ground with the forehead to show great deference, submissive respect, homage, etc.: a Chinese form of salutation to a superior.

kow'tow', *v.i.* 1. to make a kowtow.

2. to show great deference, submissive respect, etc. (*to* a person).

Kr, in chemistry, krypton.

krä, *n.* [E. Ind.] an ape with a long tail, native of India and Sumatra, *Macacus cynomolgus*.

kräal, *n.* [S. Afr. D., a village pen, enclosure, from Port. *curral*, a pen for cattle.]

1. a village of South African natives, surrounded by a stockade for protection.

2. a fenced enclosure for cattle or sheep in South Africa; a pen.

3. a corral for elephants. [Ceylon.]

kräal, *v.t.* to shut up in a kraal.

kraft (*or* kräft), *n.* [G., strength.] strong wrapping paper, usually brown, made from sulfate pulp: also *kraft paper*.

kraīt, *n.* [Hind. *karait*.] a cobralike poisonous snake, *Bungarus cæruleus*, of India.

krä'ken (*or* krā'), *n.* [Norw.] a legendary sea monster of northern seas.

krȧ·kō'wi·ȧk, *n.* [from Krakow, Cracow, a city in Poland.] a spirited Polish dance.

krā'mȧ, *n.* [Gr. *krama*, a mixture, from *kra*, the root of *kerannynai*, to mix.] in the Eastern Church, a mixture of water amd wine used in the Eucharist.

Krȧ·mē'ri·ȧ, *n.* [named after J. G. H. and W. H. *Kramer*, German botanists.] a genus of bushy, many-stemmed shrubs of South America, belonging to the family *Polygalaceæ*, among which is the *Krameria triandra*, which yields the rhatany used in medicine.

krȧ·mer'iç, *a.* [see preceding entry.] pertaining to or derived from rhatany.

krameric acid; in chemistry, an astringent compound crystalline substance derived from the root of *Krameria triandra*.

krang, *n.* [D. *kreng*, a carcass.] the body of a whale stripped of its blubber: spelled also *kreng*.

krang'ing hook, in whaling, a hook used for holding the blubber until it is cut loose.

krȧntz, *n.* [S. Afr. D., from D. *krans*, a garland, cornice.] in South Africa, a precipitous elevation; a high, steep cliff.

K ra'tion (rash'un *or* rā'shun), a United States Army ration consisting of a small can of meat or cheese, hard crackers, powdered beverage, confection, and a few cigarettes, compactly boxed.

krau·rō'sis, *n.* [Gr. *krauros*, dry, brittle, and *-osis*.] in pathology, a disease marked by a dry and shriveled condition of the skin or mucous membrane.

krau'ṣen, *v.t.* [G., to curl.] in brewing, to add

strong, fermenting wort to beer in order to condition it.

krau′sen, *n.* fermenting wort.

krem′lin, *n.* [Fr. *kremlin,* from Russ. *kreml′,* a citadel, fortress.] in Russia, the citadel of a town or city.

the Kremlin; (a) the citadel of Moscow, which houses the government offices of the Soviet Union; hence, (b) the government of the Soviet Union.

kremș, *n.* same as *white lead.*

kreng, *n.* same as *krang.*

kren′nẽr·īte, *n.* [named after Prof. J. A. *Krenner,* of Budapest.] in mineralogy, a telluride of silver and gold.

kreut′zẽr, kreu′zẽr (kroit′sẽr), *n.* [G. *kreuzer,* from *kreuz,* a cross; so called because the figure on the coin was a cross.] a former copper coin of Austria and Germany, of the value of about one half of a cent.

Krieg, *n.* [G.] war.

krieg′spiel, *n.* [G., from *krieg,* war, and *spiel,* a game.] a game for teaching or practicing military tactics by the use of small figures representing troops, tanks, etc. moved about on a large map or representation of the terrain.

Kriem′hild (*or G.* -hilt), *n.* [G.; M.H.G. *Kriemhilt.*] in the *Nibelungenlied,* the wife of Siegfried: after he was killed at her brother's command, she married Etzel (Atilla), king of the Huns, and with his help avenged the murder.

krill, *n.*; *pl.* **krill,** [Norw. *kril,* young fry (of fish).] a small, shrimplike crustacean, especially genus *Euphausia,* the main food of baleen whales.

krim′mẽr, *n.* [G. *krimmer,* from *Krim,* Crimea.] the fur or pelt of the young lamb found in the Crimea: this fur is gray, short, and somewhat curled, and resembles astrakhan: also spelled *crimmer.*

kris, *n.* same as *creese.*

Krish′nȧ, *n.* [Sans. Kṛṣṇa.] an important Hindu god, an incarnation of Vishnu, second god of the Hindu trinity.

KRISHNA

Krish′nȧ·ism, *n.* the worship or cult of Krishna.

Kriss Krin′gle, [G. *Christkindel;Christ,* Christ, and *kindel,* dim. of *kind,* child.] Santa Claus.

krī′tärch·y, *n.* [Gr. *kritēs,* a judge, and *archē,* rule.] government by judges, as by the judges of Israel. [Rare.]

krō′nȧ, *n.*; *pl.* **krō′nor,** [Sw., from L. *corona,* crown.] the monetary unit and a silver coin of Sweden: also called *crown.*

krō′ne, *n.*; *pl.* **krō′nen,** [G., from L. *corona,* crown.]

1. a former German gold coin.

2. the former monetary unit or a silver coin of Austria.

Also called *crown.*

krō′ne, *n.*; *pl.* **krō′ner,** [Dan., from L. *corona,* crown.] the monetary unit and a silver coin of Denmark or Norway: also called *crown.*

Kroo, *n.* [African.] one of a tribe of Negroes on the western coast of Africa, especially skilled as seamen: spelled also *Kru.*

Kroo′măn, *n.*; *pl.* **Kroo′men,** a Kroo: also spelled *Kruman.*

kroon, *n.*; *pl.* **kroons, kroon′i,** [Estonian *kron;* see *krona.*] formerly, the monetary unit of Estonia, equivalent to the krona of Sweden.

krū′gīte, *n.* [named after *Krug* von Nidda, a mining director of Germany.] in mineralogy, a sulfide of potassium, calcium, and magnesium, akin to polyhalite.

krul′lẽr, *n.* same as *cruller.*

krumm′horn, *n.* [G., from *krumm,* crooked, and *horn,* horn.] in music, an obsolete wind instrument, curved in form; also, a reed stop of an organ.

Krupp gun, see under *gun.*

krȳ′ō·līte, *n.* same as *cryolite.*

krȳ·om′e·tẽr, *n.* same as *cryometer.*

kryp′ton, *n.* [Mod. L., from Gr. *krypton,* properly neut. of *kryptos,* hidden, from *kryptein,* to hide.] a rare chemical element, an inert gas present in very small quantities in air: symbol, Kr; atomic weight, 83.7; atomic number, 36.

kșär (zär), *n.* czar. [Obs.]

Kshat′ri·yȧ, *n.* [Sans. *kṣatriya,* from *kṣatra,* rule.] among the Hindus, a member of the military caste, second of the four great castes.

kū′chen (-khun), *n.* [G., cake.] a kind of German coffeecake, made of yeast dough covered with sugar and spices, and often containing raisins, nuts, etc.

kū′dos, *n.* [Gr. *kydos,* glory, fame.] fame; honor; glory; renown; prestige; credit, as for an achievement. [Colloq.]

kụ′dụ, *n.*; *pl.* **kụ′dụș** or **kụ′dụ,** [Hottentot.] a large, grayish-brown African antelope with white markings: also spelled *koodoo.*

Kū′fiç, *a.* [from *Kufa* (Ar. *al-Kūfah*) town on the Euphrates, south of Babylon; and *-ic.*] designating or of an early Arabic alphabet used in a region south of Babylon: also spelled *Cufic.*

kụ·kang′, *n.* [Javanese.] in zoology, *Nycticebus coucang,* a lemur of the East Indies.

Kū′-Klux, Kū′klux, *n.* [from Gr. *kyklos,* a circle.]

1. the Ku Klux Klan.

2. a member of the Ku Klux Klan.

Kū Klux Klan, [for *Ku-Klux Clan:* sp. altered for alliteration.]

1. a secret society of white men founded in the Southern States after the Civil War to reestablish and maintain white supremacy.

2. a secret society organized in Atlanta, Georgia, in 1915 as "the Invisible Empire, Knights of the Ku Klux Klan": it is anti-Negro, anti-Semitic, anti-Catholic, etc., and uses terrorist methods.

Kū Klux Klan′nẽr, a member of the Ku Klux Klan.

kụ·läk′, *n.* [Russ., lit., fist, hence, tightwad, from Estonian.] a well-to-do farmer in Russia who profited from the labor of poorer peasants: the kulaks as a class opposed Soviet policies, especially the collectivization of the land.

kụ′lan, *n.* [Per.] the dziggetai.

Kụl·tụr′, *n.* [G.] civilization; social organization; especially, the highly systematized social organization of Hohenzollern or Nazi Germany: now usually ironic in application with reference to chauvinism, militarism, terrorism, etc.

Kụl·tụr′kämpf, *n.* [G.; *kultur* (see *Kultur*), and *kampf,* a battle.] the struggle between the Roman Catholic Church and the German government from 1873 to 1887, mainly over the government's efforts to control education, civil marriage, church appointments, etc.

kụ′miss, *n.* [G., Russ. *kumis,* from Tatar *kumiz.*]

1. mare's or camel's milk fermented (or distilled) and used as a drink by Tatar nomads of Asia.

2. a similar drink made from cow's milk, used in certain special diets.

Also spelled *koumis, koumiss, koumyss.*

küm′mel (kim′l; *G.* kụm′el), *n.* [G.] a liqueur flavored with caraway seeds, anise, cumin, etc.

kum′mẽr·bund, *n.* same as *cummerbund.*

kum′quät, *n.* [from dial. pronun. of Chin. *chin-chü,* lit., golden orange.]

1. an orange-colored, oval fruit about the size of a small plum, with a sour pulp and a sweet rind, used in preserves and confections.

2. the tree that it grows on.

Also spelled *cumquat.*

KUMQUAT

Kun′dry, *n.* [G.] in Wagner's *Parsifal,* a woman doomed to eternal punishment because she had laughed at Jesus carrying the Cross.

kung fu, [from Chin.] a Chinese system of self-defense, like karate but emphasizing circular rather than linear movements.

kunz′īte (koonts′), [after George F. *Kunz* (1856–1932), Am. expert in gems; and *-ite.*] a transparent variety of spodumene, occurring in lilac crystals and used as a gem.

Kuō′min·tang′ (kwō′; *Chin.* gwō′min′däng′), *n.* [Chinese, *kuo,* nationalist, *min,* people's, and *tang,* party.] nationalist political party of China, organized and formed chiefly by Sun Yat-sen in 1911 and afterward controlled and led by Chiang Kai-shek.

kur′bash, *n.* [Turk. *qirbāch.*] a leather whip formerly used in Turkey, Egypt, etc. for punishing offenders.

kur′bash, *v.t.* to flog with a kurbash.

Kūrd, *n.* [Turk. and Ar.] any of a nomadic Moslem people living chiefly in Kurdistan and the southern Caucasus.

Kūr′dish, *a.* of the Kurds, their language, culture, etc.

Kūrd′ish, *n.* the Iranian language of the Kurds.

Kūr′di·stan, *n.* any of various rugs made by Kurds, especially in Iran.

Kụ·ril′i·ăn, *a.* relating to the Kurile Islands, a chain of islands in the North Pacific.

Kụ·ril′i·ăn, *n.* a native of the Kurile Islands.

Kụ·rō·shī′wō, *n.* [Japan., from *kuro,* black, and *shiwo,* tide.] the Japan current.

kūr′rȧ·jong, *n.* [from native name in Australia.] any of several Australian trees and shrubs of the mallow family, which yield fibers used by the natives for weaving nets, mats, etc.: also *koorajong, currajong,* etc.

Kush, *n.* same as *Cush.*

Kush·it′iç, *a.* and *n. Cushitic.*

kus′kus, *n.* same as *cuscus.*

kutch, *n.* same as *cutch.*

kutch′ẽr·ry, *n.* same as *cutcherry.*

Kụ′te·nāi, Kụ′te·nāy, *n.* same as *Kootenay.*

kväss, kväs (*or* kvas), *n.* [Russ. *kvas.*] a Russian fermented drink like sour beer, made from rye, barley, rye bread, etc.: also spelled *quass.*

kvetch, *v.i.*; kvetched, *pl., pp.*; kvetching, *ppr.* [from Yid. *kvechen,* from G. *quetschen,* to pinch, squeeze.]

1. to be urgent or insistent; press; strain. [Slang.]

2. to complain in a nagging or whining way. [Slang.]

kwä′zō·kụ, *n.* the Japanese nobility.

kȳ′ack, *n.* in the western United States, a packsack swung on either side of a packsaddle.

kȳ′ak, *n.* same as *kayak.*

kȳ′ȧ·nīte, *n.* same as *cyanite.*

kȳ′ăn·ize, *v.t.*; kyanized, *pt., pp.*; kyanizing, *ppr.* [named after J. H. *Kyan* (1774–1850), the Ir. inventor of the process.] to make (wood) resistant to decay by treatment with a solution of corrosive sublimate.

kȳ′ȧ·nol, *n.* [Gr. *kyanos,* blue, and *-ol.*] in chemistry, same as *aniline.*

kȳ·an′ō·phyl, *n.* same as *cyanophyl.*

kye, *n.pl.* kine. [Obs.]

kȳke, *v.i.* to keek. [Obs.]

kȳ′lōe, *n.*; *pl.* **kȳ′lōeș,** [Gael.] one of the Hebridean or Scottish-Highland cattle.

kȳ′mō·grȧph, *n.* [from Gr. *kyma,* a wave; and *-graph.*] an apparatus consisting of a rotating drum for recording wavelike motions, variations, or modulations, such as muscular contractions, the pulse, etc.: also *cymograph.*

kȳ·mō·graph′iç, *a.* of or recorded by a kymograph.

Kym′riç, *a.* and *n.* Cymric; Welsh.

Kym′ry, Kym′ri, *n.*; *pl.* **Kym′ry** or **Kym′ri, Kym′rieș,** Cymry; the Welsh.

kȳ′phos, *n.* [Gr. *kyphos,* a hump, hunch.] the hump in the spine of a humpback.

kȳ·phō′sis, *n.* [Mod. L.; Gr. *kyphōsis,* from *kyphos,* humpbacked.] abnormal curvature of the spine resulting in a hump; humpback.

kȳ·phot′iç, *a.* of or having kyphosis.

Kyr′i·ē e·lẹ′i·sŏn, [LL.; Gr. *Kyrie eleēson,* Lord, have mercy (upon us).]

1. a brief prayer of the Orthodox Eastern Church.

2. (a) a part of the Roman Catholic service after the introit in the Mass; (b) the music for this.

3. a response in the Anglican service of Holy Communion.

kyr·i·ō·log′iç, kyr·i·ō·log′iç·ăl, *a.* same as *curiologic.*

kȳthe, *v.t.* and *v.i.* same as *kithe.*

L

L, l (el), *n.*; *pl.* **L's, l's, Ls, ls,** (elz), 1. the twelfth letter of the English alphabet: from the Greek *lambda*, a borrowing from the Phoenician.
 2. the sound of L or l.
 3. a type or impression for L or l.
 4. *a symbol for* the twelfth (or the eleventh if J is omitted) in a sequence or group.

L, l (el), *a.* 1. of L or l.
 2. twelfth (or eleventh if J is omitted) in a sequence or group.

L (el), *n.* 1. an object shaped like L; especially, an extension of a house or building that gives the whole a shape resembling L.
 2. a Roman numeral for 50: with a superior bar (L̄), 50,000.
 3. in geodesy, *the symbol for* longitude.
 4. in physics, *the symbol for* latent heat.

L (el), *a.* shaped like L.

L (el), *n.* [for *el*, short for *elevated*.] in certain American cities, an elevated railroad: also spelled *el*.

L-, liaison: followed by a number to designate a specific model of United States Army airplane designed for reconnaissance and liaison work.

lä, *n.* in music, a syllable representing the sixth tone of the diatonic scale.

lä, *interj.* oh! look!: an exclamation of surprise or emphasis. [Dial. or Archaic.]

La, in chemistry, lanthanum.

läa′gẽr, lä′gẽr, *n.* [S. Afr. D., from D. *leger*, a camp.] in South Africa, a temporary camp surrounded by wagons and impedimenta as a defense.

läa′gẽr, lä′gẽr, *v.t.* to arrange or distribute so as to form a defensive enclosure, or laager.

läa′gẽr, lä′gẽr, *v.i.* to camp in a laager.

lab, *n.* a laboratory. [Colloq.]

Lab′ȧ·dist, *n.* a follower of Jean de Labadie (1610–1674), French mystic who founded a Protestant sect.

lab′ȧ·rum, *n.*; *pl.* **lab′ȧ·rȧ,** [LL.; Gr. *labaron*.] the royal cavalry standard carried before the Roman emperors in war, especially that first carried by Constantine, the first emperor to adopt Christianity: it usually bore the first two letters (XP) of the Greek *Khristos* (Christ).

LABARUM

lab′dȧ·num, *n.* [ML.; L. *ladanum*, *ledanum*; Gr. *ladanon*, *lēdanon*, from *lēdon*, mastic; Ar. *lādan*; Per. *lādan*.] a dark resin obtained from certain varieties of the rockrose: also *ladanum*.

lab·ē·fac′tion, *n.* [L. *labefactus*, pp. of *labefacere*, to cause to totter or fall.] a weakening or loosening; a falling; decay; downfall; ruin: also written *labefactation*.

lab′ē·fȳ, *v.t.*; labefied, *pt.*, *pp.*; labefying, *ppr.* to weaken or impair. [Rare.]

lā′bel, *n.* [ME. *label*; OFr. *label*, a rag, strip, tatter, from O.H.G. *lappa*, a rag, shred.]
 1. a narrow band of cloth, etc.; fillet.
 2. a narrow strip of ribbon attached to a document to hold the seal.
 3. a card, strip of paper, etc. marked and attached to an object to indicate its nature, contents, ownership, destination, etc.
 4. a descriptive word or phrase applied to a person, group, theory, etc. as a convenient generalized classification.
 5. in architecture, a projecting molding over a door, window, etc.
 6. in heraldry, a horizontal bar with several dependent points on the coat of arms of an eldest son.

LABEL (sense 6)

 7. any paper annexed to a will by way of addition, as a codicil. [Obs.]
 8. a long, thin, brass rule, with a small sight at one end, and a center hole at the other, commonly used with a tangent line on the edge of a circumferentor, to take altitudes. [Obs.]

lā′bel, *v.t.*; labeled *or* labelled, *pt.*, *pp.*; labeling *or* labelling, *ppr.* 1. to affix a label to; to mark with a label.
 2. to classify; to designate.

lā′bel·ẽr, lā′bel·lẽr, *n.* one who labels.

lȧ·bel′lum, *n.*; *pl.* **lȧ·bel′lȧ,** [L., dim. of *labrum*, a lip.]
 1. in botany, the lowest of the three petals forming the corolla of an orchid, usually larger than the other two petals, and often spurred.
 2. in zoology, (a) a subsidiary labrum; (b) a swollen termination of the proboscis, of certain dipterous insects.

lā′bi·ȧ, *n.* plural of *labium*.

lā′bi·ăl, *a.* [LL. *labialis*, pertaining to the lips, from L. *labium*, the lip.]
 1. pertaining to the labia, or lips.
 2. in phonetics, formed mainly with the lips; as, a *labial* articulation. Thus *b*, *p*, and *m* are *labial* articulations.
 3. in zoology, pertaining to the liplike organ of an insect.
 4. in music, designating tones produced by a liplike structure, as in the organ pipe.
 5. in anatomy, relating to or associated with the lip or lips; as, a *labial* vein, artery, or gland.

lā′bi·ăl, *n.* 1. a labial sound, as, *b*, *f*, *m*, *p*, *v*.
 2. in music, an organ pipe with a liplike structure for producing sound.
 3. in zoology, an appendage upon or closely associated with the mouth; as, the *labials* of a snake, a fish, etc.

lā′bi·ăl·iṣm, *n.* 1. the tendency to labialize sounds; especially, a speech defect characterized by this.
 2. the quality of being labial.

lā″bi·ăl·i·zā′tion, *n.* a labializing or being labialized.

lā′bi·ăl·īze, *v.t.*; labialized, *pt.*, *pp.*; labializing, *ppr.* in phonetics, (a) to pronounce (a sound or sounds) by using the lips, sometimes excessively; (b) to round (a vowel).

lā′bi·ăl·ly, *adv.* in a labial manner.

lā′bi·ȧ mȧ·jō′rȧ, [L., lit., greater lips.] the outer folds of skin on either side of the vulva.

lā′bi·ȧ mi·nō′rȧ, [L., lit., lesser lips.] the folds of mucous membrane within the labia majora.

Lā·bi·ā′tae, *n.pl.* [L. *labium*, the lip, and *-atæ*.] the mint family, including herbaceous aromatic plants with square stems, opposite simple leaves, and two-lipped corollas, and with the ovary four-parted.

lā′bi·āte, *a.* [Mod. L. *labiatus*, from L. *labium*, lip.]
 1. formed or functioning like a lip.
 2. having a lip or lips; lipped.
 3. in botany, having the calyx or corolla so divided that one part overlaps the other like a lip.

LABIATE COROLLA

lā′bi·āte, *n.* one of the *Labiatæ*.

lā′bi·ā·ted, *a.* labiate.

lā·bi·ā·ti·flō′rous, *a.* in botany, having labiate flowers.

lab·i·dom′e·tẽr, *n.* [Gr. *labis* (*-idos*), forceps, and *metron*, a measure.] in obstetrics, a graduated instrument for ascertaining the diameter of the head of a fetus.

lā′bile, *a.* [L. *labilis*, liable to slip, from *labi*, to slip, fall.]
 1. liable to err, fall, or lapse.
 2. liable to change; unstable; as, certain chemical compounds are *labile*.
 3. in electrotherapy, passing over or gliding across: said of the application of an electric current by passing an electrode over the diseased part.

lȧ·bil′i·ty, *n.* the condition or quality of being labile.

lā′bi·ō-, [from L. *labium*, lip.] a combining form meaning *the lips, the lips and*, as in *labiodental*.

lā″bi·ō·den′tăl, *a.* [*labio-* and *dental*.] in phonetics, formed by placing the lower lip against the upper teeth and forcing the breath through them: said of *f* and *v*.

lā″bi·ō·den′tăl, *n.* a labiodental sound.

lā″bi·ō·nā′ṣăl, *a.* [*labio-* and *nasal*.] in phonetics, formed with the lips but having nasal resonance: said of *m*.

lā″bi·ō·nā′ṣăl, *n.* a labionasal sound.

lā′bi·ōse, *a.* in botany, of the nature or appearance of a labiate.

lā″bi·ō·vē′lăr, *a.* [*labio-* and *velar*.] in phonetics, formed by rounding and half closing the lips and placing the back of the tongue against or near the velum, or soft palate: said of *w*.

lā″bi·ō·vē′lăr, *n.* a labiovelar sound.

lā′bis, *n.* [L.Gr. *labis*, a spoon; Gr. *labis*, a handle, holder, forceps, from *lambanein*, to take.] in the Orthodox Eastern Church, a spoonlike implement for administering the Eucharist where the bread and wine are served together.

lā′bi·um, *n.*; *pl.* **lā′bi·ȧ,** [L., a lip.] a lip or liplike organ; especially, (a) [*pl.*] the outer folds of skin (*labia majora*) or the inner folds of mucous membrane (*labia minora*) of the vulva; (b) the lower, liplike part of the corolla of of certain flowers; (c) the lower lip of an insect.

lab′lab, *n.* in the East Indies, the Egyptian bean, *Dolichos lablab*.

lā′bŏr, *n.* [ME. *labour*; OFr. *labor*; L. *labor*, labor, exertion, hardship, pain.]
 1. physical or mental exertion; work; toil.
 2. a specific task; piece of work.
 3. (a) all wage-earning workers: distinguished from *capital* or *management*; (b) all manual workers whose work is characterized largely by physical exertion: distinguished from *white-collar* or *professional workers*.
 4. the work accomplished or the part played in society by all workers.
 5. in medicine, the process of childbirth; parturition; especially, the muscular contractions of giving birth.
 Syn.—drudgery, exertion, effort, pains, painstaking, task, toil, travail, undertaking, work.

lā′bŏr, *v.i.*; labored, *pt.*, *pp.*; laboring, *ppr.* [ME. *labouren*; OFr. *laborer*; L. *laborare*, to labor, strive, toil, from *labor*, toil, exertion, labor.]
 1. to work; to toil.
 Six days shalt thou *labor*, and do all thy work. —Ex. xx. 9.
 2. to exert oneself to get or do something; to work hard; to strive; to take pains.
 3. (a) to move irregularly with little progress; as, the old car *labored* up the hill; (b) to pitch and roll heavily, as a ship in a turbulent sea.
 4. to be in travail; to suffer the pangs of childbirth.
 to labor under; to be afflicted with; to be burdened or distressed with; as, *to labor under* a mistaken notion.

lā′bŏr, *v.t.* 1. to cause to labor. [Obs.]
 2. to work at; to till; to cultivate. [Rare.]
 The most excellent lands are lying fallow, or only *labored* by children. —Tooke.
 3. to spend too much time and effort on; to

develop in too great detail; as, to *labor* a point or argument.

4. to form or fabricate with exertion; as, to *labor* arms for Troy. [Archaic.]

5. to beat; to belabor. [Obs.]

Lā′bŏr and Sō′ciăl·ist In·tẽr·na′tion·ăl, an association formed in Hamburg in 1923 by a merging of the Second International and the Vienna International.

lab′ō·rȧ·tō·ry, *n.*; *pl.* **lab′ō·rȧ·tō·rieṣ,** [LL. *laboratorium*, a workshop or place to labor, from L. *laborare*, to labor.]

1. a room or building for scientific experimentation or research.

2. a place for preparing chemicals, drugs, etc.

lab′ō·rȧ·tō·ry, *a.* of or performed in, or as in, a laboratory.

Lā′bŏr Dāy, in most States of the United States, the first Monday in September, set aside as a legal holiday in honor of labor.

lā′bŏred, *a.* made or done with great effort; not effortless and natural; as, a *labored* style.

lā′bŏred·ly, *adv.* in a labored manner.

lā′bŏr·ẽr, *n.* [ME. *laborer, labourer*; OFr. *laboreor, laborier*; LL. *laborator, laborarius*, a laborer, from L. *laborare*, to labor, from *labor*, labor, toil.] a person who labors; especially, a wage-earning worker, skilled or semiskilled, whose work is characterized largely by physical exertion.

lā′bŏr·ing, *a.* 1. working as a laborer; as, a *laboring* man.

2. undergoing suffering or painful experience; struggling under difficulties, etc.

lā·bŏr-in·ten′sive, *a.* requiring a large labor force and a relatively small investment in capital goods; as, a *labor-intensive* industry.

lȧ·bō′ri·ous, *a.* [L. *laboriosus*, from *labor*, labor.]

1. industrious; hard-working; diligent in work or service; assiduous; as, a *laborious* mechanic.

2. requiring labor; toilsome; tiresome; not easy; as, *laborious* duties or services.

Syn.—assiduous, diligent, painstaking, indefatigable, arduous, burdensome, toilsome, wearisome, industrious, hard-working, active, difficult, tedious.

lȧ·bō′ri·ous·ly, *adv.* with labor, toil, or difficulty.

lȧ·bō′ri·ous·ness, *n.* 1. the quality of being laborious, or attended with toil; toilsomeness; difficulty.

2. diligence; assiduity.

lā′bŏr·īte, *n.* 1. a member or supporter of a labor party.

2. [L—] a member or supporter of the British Labor Party.

lā′bŏr·less, *a.* not laborious; not requiring labor; without labor.

lā′bŏr of lŏve, [after 1 Thess. i. 3.] work that one enjoys doing.

lā′bor om′ni·ȧ vin′cit, [L.] labor conquers all.

lā′bŏr pär′ty, 1. a political party organized to protect and further the rights of workers, or professing to do so.

2. [L— P—] such a party in Great Britain: British spelling, *Labour Party.*

lā′bŏr-sāv″ing, *a.* saving labor; lessening the amount of work required: as, *labor-saving* devices.

lā′bŏr·sŏme, *a.* 1. made with great labor and diligence; also, industrious; hard-working.

2. given to rolling and pitching in a storm: said of ships. [Obs.]

lā′bŏr ūn′iŏn (-yun), an association of workers to promote and protect the welfare, interests, and rights of its members, primarily by collective bargaining.

lā′bŏur, *n.*, *v.t.* and *v.i.* labor: British spelling.

lā′brȧ, *n.* pl. of *labrum.*

Lab′rȧ·dọr Cŭr′rent, an icy arctic current flowing southward past Labrador and Newfoundland.

Lab′rȧ·dọr duck, an extinct species of sea duck, *Camptorhynchus labradorius.*

lab′rȧ·dọr·īte, *n.* [after *Labrador*, where excellent specimens have been found.] a variety of feldspar showing a play of colors: also called *Labrador spar.*

Lab′rȧ·dọr tēa, either of two species of evergreen shrub, *Ledum palustre* and *Ledum latifolium*, the leaves of which have been used for tea.

lā′bret, *n.* [L. *labrum*, lip.] an ornament of wood, bone, etc. worn (by some primitive tribes) in a hole pierced through the lip.

Lab′ri·dae, *n.* [L. *labrum*, lip.] a family of sea fishes related to the sea perches, including the wrasses and parrot fishes: the *Labrus* is the type genus.

lab′roid, *a.* of, pertaining to, or resembling the *Labridæ.*

lab′roid, *n.* a fish of the family *Labridæ.*

lā′brōse, *a.* [L. *labrosus*, from *labrum*, lip.] having thick lips.

lā′brum, *n.*; *pl.* **lā′brȧ,** [L., a lip, edge, margin.] a lip or liplike edge; especially, in zoology, (a) the upper or front lip of insects and other arthropods; (b) the outer edge of a univalve shell.

Lā′brus, *n.* [L. *labrum*, lip: so called from the thick, fleshy lips.] a genus of fishes typical of the *Labridæ.*

lȧ·bŭr′num, *n.* [L.] any of a genus of small trees and shrubs of the pea family, with three-part leaves and drooping clusters of yellow flowers.

lab′y·rinth, *n.* [L. *labyrinthus*: Gr. *labyrinthos*, a labyrinth, from *laura, labra*, an alley, lane.]

1. an intricate structure or enclosure containing a series of winding passages hard to follow without losing one's way; a maze.

2. [L—] in Greek legend, such a structure built by Daedalus for King Minos of Crete, to house the Minotaur.

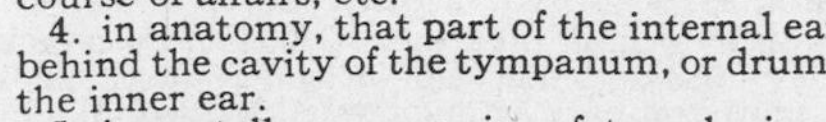

LABYRINTH

3. a complicated, perplexing arrangement, course of affairs, etc.

4. in anatomy, that part of the internal ear behind the cavity of the tympanum, or drum; the inner ear.

5. in metallurgy, a series of troughs in a stamping mill, through which water passes for washing pulverized ore.

6. in architecture, a design in the tiling of a floor.

Syn.—maze.

lab·y·rin′thăl, *a.* same as *labyrinthine.*

lab·y·rin′thi·ăn, *a.* same as *labyrinthine.*

lab·y·rin′thi·branch, *n.* [Gr. *labyrinthos*, a labyrinth, and *branchia*, gills.] one of the order of *Labyrinthici.*

lab·y·rin′thiç, *a.* same as *labyrinthine.*

lab·y·rin′thiç·ăl, *a.* labyrinthic.

Lab·y·rin′thi·cī, *n.pl.* an order of fishes furnished with a labyrinthine gill chamber whereby they retain water sufficient to allow them to live in the air.

lab·y·rin′thi·fọrm, *a.* [L. *labyrinthus*, a labyrinth, and *forma*, form.] having the form of a labyrinth; intricate.

lab·y·rin′thine, *a.* 1. of or constituting a labyrinth.

2. like a labyrinth; intricate; complicated; puzzling.

Lab·y·rin′thō·don, *n.* [Gr. *labyrinthos*, a labyrinth, and *odous, odontos*, tooth.] a genus of gigantic fossil amphibians, having a peculiar labyrinthine structure of teeth.

lab·y·rin′thō·dont, *a.* having the characteristics of the *Labyrinthodonta*, especially in the structure of the teeth.

lab·y·rin′thō·dont, *n.* a member of the *Labyrinthodonta.*

Lab·y·rin·thō·don′tȧ, *n.pl.* [Gr. *labyrinthos*, a labyrinth, and *odous, odontos*, tooth.] an order of fossil amphibia of Paleozoic times, of which *Labyrinthodon* is a typical genus.

laç, lakh, *n.* [Hind. *lākh*; Sans. *lākshā*, a hundred thousand.] in India, the sum of 100,000, especially in counting money; as, a *lac* of rupees (written Rs. 1,00,000); also, a large, indefinite quantity.

laç, *n.* [Hind. *lākh*; Sans. *lākshā*.] a resinous substance deposited upon certain trees in southern Asia by a variety of scale insect. While still attached to twigs and dried, it is called *stick-lac*; when dissolved out and separated from the twigs it is called *seed-lac*, and when strained through a cloth and dried it constitutes *shell-lac*, or the *shellac* of commerce. Lac is used extensively in making varnishes, lacquers, sealing wax, dyes, etc.

laç′cāte, *a.* in botany, appearing as if having been varnished or lacquered: said of leaves.

laç′cin, *n.* [*lac* and *-in.*] a substance derived from lac, brittle, yellow, and translucent.

laç′cō·lite, *n.* same as *laccolith.*

laç′cō·lith, *n.* [from Gr. *lakkos*, a cistern; and *-lith.*] an irregular formation of igneous rock intruded between the layers of sedimentary rock so as to cause them to bulge upward.

laç·cō·lith′iç, *a.* relating to or having the form of a laccolith.

laç dȳe, dye extracted from stick-lac, resembling cochineal in color.

lāce, *n.* [ME. *las*; OFr. *las, laqs*, a snare, string, cord; L. *laqueus*, a noose, snare, trap.]

1. a string, ribbon, etc. used to draw together and fasten the parts of a shoe, corset, etc. by being drawn through eyelets or over hooks.

2. a fine netting or openwork fabric of linen, cotton, silk, etc., woven in ornamental designs.

3. a snare; a gin. [Obs.]

4. a dash of some alcoholic liquor added to coffee or other beverage.

5. gold or silver braid used as trimming for uniforms, fancy dress costumes, etc.

lāce, *v.t.*; laced (lāst), *pt., pp.*; lacing, *ppr.* 1. to draw the ends of (a garment, shoe, etc.) together and fasten with a lace.

2. to compress the waist of by lacing a corset, etc. (often with *up*).

3. to weave together; to intertwine.

4. to decorate with lace.

5. to streak, as with color.

6. to thrash; to whip.

7. to add a dash of alcoholic liquor to (a beverage).

to lace into; (a) to attack physically; assail; (b) to attack verbally; criticize sharply; scold. [Colloq.]

lāce, *v.i.* to be fastened with a lace; as, the boot *laces* in front.

lāce′bärk, *n.* a West Indian shrub, *Lagetta lintearia*, having a lacelike inner bark.

lāced, *a.* fastened with a lace or string; also, ornamented with lace.

laced mutton; a prostitute. [Obs. Slang.]

Lac″e·dae·mō′ni·ăn, *a.* and *n.* [L. *Lacedæmonius*; Gr. *Lakedaimonios*, Lacedaemonian, from *Lakedaimōn*, Sparta, Lacedaemon, Laconia.] Spartan.

lāce fẽrn, an American fern, *Cheilanthes gracillima.*

lāce′lēaf, *n.* same as *latticeleaf.*

lāce liz′ărd, a large water lizard, *Varanus giganteus*, of Australia.

lāce′măn, *n.*; *pl.* **lāce′men,** a man who deals in lace.

lāce pā′pẽr, paper cut or stamped out in figures resembling those of lace.

lāce′pïece, *n.* in shipbuilding, the piece supporting the beak.

lāce pil′lōw, a pillow or cushion held in the lap or on the knees and used for holding the work and material in making lace by hand.

lac′ẽr·ȧ·ble, *a.* that can be lacerated.

lac′ẽr·āte, *v.t.*; lacerated, *pt., pp.*; lacerating, *ppr.* [L. *laceratus*, pp. of *lacerare*, to tear, lacerate, from *lacer*, mangled, lacerated.]

1. to tear; to rend; to mangle (something soft, as flesh).

2. to wound or hurt (one's feelings, etc.); to distress.

lac′ẽr·āte, lac′ẽr·ā·ted, *a.* 1. mangled; torn.

2. in botany and zoology, having the edge variously cut into irregular segments; as, a *lacerate* leaf or organ.

lac·ẽr·ā′tion, *n.* [L. *laceratio (-onis)*, from *lacerare*, to tear, mangle.]

1. a lacerating.

2. the result of lacerating; a jagged tear or wound.

lac′ẽr·ȧ·tive, *a.* tearing; having the power to tear.

lȧ·cẽrt′, *n.* a muscle. [Obs.]

Lȧ·cẽr′tȧ, *n.* [L. *lacertus* or *lacerta*, a lizard.]

1. in zoology, a large genus of lizards, slender of form, with a long, slender tail and nonimbricated scales.

2. in astronomy, the Lizard, a small northern constellation.

lȧ·cẽr′ti·ăn (-shi-ăn), *a.* and *n.* same as *lacertilian.*

Lac·ẽr·til′i·ȧ, *n.pl.* [L. *lacerta*, a lizard.] a division of reptiles, including the lizards proper, the slowworms, monitors, iguanas, chameleons, and geckos.

lac·ẽr·til′i·ăn, *a.* of, pertaining to, or having the characteristics of the *Lacertilia.*

lac·ẽr·til′i·ăn, *n.* one of the *Lacertilia.*

lȧ·cẽr′ti·loid, *a.* [L. *lacerta*, a lizard, and Gr. *eidos*, form.] lizardlike.

lȧ·cẽr′tine, *a.* same as *lacertian* and *lacertiloid.*

lāce′wing, *n.* a neuropterous insect with four delicate, gauzy wings, of the family *Hemerobiidæ*, and especially of the genus *Chrysopa.*

lāce′wŏrk, *n.* 1. lace.

2. any openwork decoration like lace.

lach′eṣ, *n.* [OFr. *lachesse*, negligence, laxness,

from *lache*, lax, negligent.] negligence; inexcusable delay; specifically, in law, failure to do the required thing at the proper time (e.g. inexcusable delay in forwarding a claim).

Lach'ē·sis, *n.* [L., from Gr. *lachesis*, lit., lot, fate, from *lanchanein*, to obtain by lot or fate, to happen.] in Greek and Roman mythology, that one of the three Fates who measured out the span of mortal life.

lach'ry·măl, *a.* [ML. *lacrimalis, lachrymalis*, from L. *lacrima*, a tear.] of, for, or producing tears: also spelled *lacrimal*.

lach'ry·măl, *n.* 1. any of a number of small vases found in ancient Roman sepulchers, popularly supposed to have been a receptacle for the tears of mourners; a lachrymatory.

2. [*pl.*] the lachrymal glands, which produce tears.

Also spelled *lacrimal*.

lach·ry·mā'tion, *n.* the act of shedding tears; weeping.

lach'ry·mā·tŏr, *n.* [from L. *lacrima*, a tear; and *-ator*.] a substance that irritates the eyes and produces tears, as tear gas: also spelled *lacrimator*.

lach'ry·mȧ·tō"ry, *n.*; *pl.* **lach'ry·mȧ·tō"ries,** [ML. *lacrimatorium*, from *lacrima*, a tear.] a lachrymal vase: also spelled *lacrimatory*.

lach'ry·mȧ·tō"ry, *a.* of, causing, or producing tears: also spelled *lacrimatory*.

lach'ry·mi·form", *a.* shaped like a tear.

lach'ry·mōse, *a.* [L. *lacrimosus*, from *lacrima*, a tear.]

1. inclined to shed many tears; mournful.

2. causing to cry and shed tears; sad.

Also spelled *lacrimose*.

lāc'i·ly, *adv.* in a lacy manner or pattern.

lāc'i·ness, *n.* a lacy quality or state.

lāc'ing, *n.* 1. the act of one who laces.

2. a thrashing.

3. a cord used in drawing tight or fastening; laces in general; specifically, (a) in bookbinding, the cords which pass through holes pierced in the boards of the book, binding them to the back; (b) in nautical usage, the cord or rope used to fasten two parts of a sail or awning together or to bind them to yard, boom, or gaff; (c) in machinery, a thong or narrow strip of leather by which belts are joined; a belt lace.

4. gold or silver braid used to trim a uniform, etc.

5. in bridge building, a system of braces which connect the bars of a truss, without crossing each other.

6. in ornithology, a border of a feather, which differs in color from the web: also, the resultant coloration of the plumage, considered collectively.

7. in mathematics, a complex of three or more bands so arranged that they cannot be separated without breaking, although no two are interlinked.

lȧ·cin'i·ȧ, *n.*; *pl.* **lȧ·cin'i·ae,** [L., the lappet or hem of a garment.]

1. in botany, one of the straps or tags forming the fringe on the outer portion of the blade of the petals of certain flowers; also, one of the incisions making this fringe.

2. in entomology, the blade or apex of the maxilla of an insect.

lȧ·cin'i·āte, lȧ·cin'i·āt·ed, *a.* [L. *lacinia*, a hem.]

1. adorned with fringes; fringed.

2. cut deeply into narrow, jagged segments: said of leaves, petals, bracts, etc.

lȧ·cin'i·form, *a.* [L. *lacinia*, a hem, and *forma*, form.] resembling fringe.

lac·i·nī'ō·lȧ, *n.*; *pl.* **lac·i·nī'ō·lae,** [dim. of *lacinia*.] a minute lacinia.

lȧ·cin'i·ō·lāte, *a.* [*laciniola* and *-ate*.] same as *lacinulate*.

lȧ·cin'i·ōse, *a.* same as *laciniate*.

lȧ·cin'ū·lȧ, *n.*; *pl.* **lȧ·cin'ū·lae,** [dim. from L. *lacinia*, a flap, hem.] in botany, (a) a minute lacinia; (b) the abruptly inflexed acumen or point of each of the petals of an umbelliferous flower.

lȧ·cin'ū·lāte, *a.* in botany, (a) having minute laciniae; (b) having lacinulae, as the petals of umbelliferous flowers.

lack, *n.* [ME. *lak, lac*, defect, want; compare D. *lak*, a stain; Ice. *lakr*, lacking, defective.]

1. the fact or condition of not having enough; shortage; deficiency.

2. the fact or condition of not having any; complete absence.

3. the thing that is lacking or needed.

4. absence; the state of being away. [Obs.]

5. blame; rebuke; censure. [Obs.]

6. a fault; an offense; a blemish, especially a moral blemish; a defect in character. [Obs.]

to supply the lack; to provide with whatever is needed.

lack, *v.i.*; lacked (lakt), *pt., pp.*; lacking, *ppr.* [ME. *lakken*, to lack, blame; compare D. *laken*, to blame, O.D. *læcken*, to fail.]

1. (a) to be short (with *of* or *in*); (b) to be in need.

The young lions do *lack* and suffer hunger.
—Ps. xxxiv. 10.

2. to be wanting or missing; to be deficient.

Peradventure there shall *lack* five of the fifty righteous. —Gen. xviii. 28.

lack, *v.t.* 1. to be deficient in or entirely without.

If any of you *lack* wisdom, let him ask of God. —James i. 5.

2. to want; to need.

3. to blame; to reproach; to detract. [Obs.]

4. to suffer the absence or deprivation of; to miss. [Obs.]

lack, *v.t.* in nautical usage, to pierce the hull of (a ship) with shot. [Rare.]

lack, *interj.* an exclamation of sorrow or regret; alas!: usually preceded by *good*. [Obs.]

lack·ȧ·dāi'si·căl, *a.* showing lack of interest or spirit; languid; listless.

lack·ȧ·dāi'si·căl·ly, *adv.* in a lackadaisical manner.

lack'ȧ·dāi·sy, *a.* same as *lackadaisical*.

lack'ȧ·dāi·sy, *interj.* same as *lackaday*.

lack'ȧ·dāy, *interj.* an exclamation of sorrow or regret. [Archaic.]

lack'ẽr, *n.* one who lacks.

lack'ẽr, *n.* and *v.t.* lacquer. [Obs.]

lack'ey, *n.*; *pl.* **lack'eys,** [OFr. *laquay*, a lackey, also a soldier; Sp. *lacayo*, a lackey, footman; compare Ar. *luka*, worthless, servile, Pr. *lacai*, a gormand.]

1. a male servant of low rank, usually in some sort of livery or uniform.

2. a follower who has no will of his own; a toady.

lack'ey, *v.t.*; lackeyed, *pt., pp.*; lackeying, *ppr.* to attend as or as if a lackey; to attend servilely.

lack'ey, *v.i.* to act as lackey; to pay servile attendance.

lack'ey cat'ẽr·pil·lăr, the larva of a lackey moth.

lack'ey moth, a common European moth of the genus *Clisiocampa*, especially *Clisiocampa neustria*: so called because the forewings, which are striped, are supposed to resemble a lackey's livery.

lack'lus"tẽr, lack'lus"tre (-tẽr), *a.* lacking brightness; dull; as, *lackluster* eyes.

lack'lus"tẽr, lack'lus"tre, *n.* absence of brightness; dullness. [Rare.]

lac'moid, *n.* [*lacmus* and *-oid*.] a violet-blue dye.

lac'mus, *n.* [D. *lakmoes*, lacmus; *lak*, lac, and *moes*, pulp.] same as *litmus*.

Lȧ·cō'ni·ăn, *a.* [L. *Laconia*, Laconia, Sparta, from *Laco* (*-onis*); Gr. *Lakōn*, a Spartan.] of or pertaining to Laconia in ancient Greece, or to its inhabitants; Spartan; Lacedaemonian.

Lȧ·cō'ni·ăn, *n.* a native or inhabitant of Laconia; a Spartan; a Lacedaemonian.

Lȧ·con'ic, *a.* [L. *Laconicus*; Gr. *Lakōnikos*, pertaining to Laconia, Laconian, from *Lakōn*, an inhabitant of Laconia, a Laconian or Spartan.]

1. same as *Laconian*. [Rare.]

2. [l–] short; brief; pithy; sententious; expressing much in few words, after the manner of the Laconians; as, a *laconic* phrase.

Syn.—concise, pithy, short, brief, curt, epigrammatic, terse.

lȧ·con'ic, *n.* 1. laconism; a brief, pithy mode of expression. [Rare.]

2. a brief, pithy expression; a laconism: used chiefly in the plural; as, he spoke in *laconics*.

3. a laconic person.

lȧ·con'i·cȧ, *n.* pl. of *laconicum*.

lȧ·con'i·căl·ly, *adv.* in a laconic manner; briefly; concisely.

lȧ·con'i·cism, *n.* same as *laconism*.

lȧ·con'i·cum, *n.*; *pl.* **lȧ·con'i·cȧ,** [L.] in ancient Rome, a vapor bath; a chamber either in a bathing establishment or separate, heated by hot air.

lac'ō·nism, *n.* [Gr. *Lakōnismos*, the imitation of the Lacedaemonians or Spartans in manners, dress, etc., from *Lakōnizein*, to imitate the Lacedaemonians, to speak laconically, to laconize.]

1. brevity of speech or expression.

2. a laconic speech or expression.

lac'ō·nīze, *v.t.* and *v.i.*; laconized, *pt., pp.*; laconizing, *ppr.* to imitate the Laconians in their thrift, frugality, austerity of life, or pithiness of expression.

Lac"ō·sō·mat'i·dae, *n.pl.* a family of moths.

lac'quẽr (-kẽr), *n.* [Fr. *lacre*, from *laca*, gum lac, from Per. *lak*, lac.]

1. a clear varnish consisting of shellac or gum resins dissolved in alcohol and other quick-drying solvents, with or without nitrocellulose: pigments may be added to lacquers to form lacquer enamels.

2. a resinous varnish obtained from certain trees in China and Japan, used to give a hard, smooth, highly polished finish to wood.

3. a decorative article or articles made of wood and coated with this lacquer.

Formerly, also spelled *lacker*.

lac'quẽr, *v.t.* to varnish; to coat with lacquer; to decorate with lacquer: formerly, also spelled *lacker*.

lac'quẽr·ẽr, *n.* one who lacquers; a lacquer maker.

lac'quẽr·ing, *n.* the act of putting on lacquer; also, the covering of lacquer or varnish put on.

lac'quẽr red, a yellowish-red color, often used in lacquer work.

lac'quẽr tree, a tree, *Rhus vernicifera*, of the cashew family.

lac'quey (-key), *n.*, *v.t.* and *v.i.* lackey. [Obs.]

lac'ri·măl, *a.* and *n.* same as *lachrymal*.

lä"cri·män'dō, *a.* [It.] in music, plaintive; lamenting: a direction to the performer.

lac'ri·mā·tŏr, *n.* same as *lachrymator*.

lac'ri·mȧ·tō"ry, *a.* and *n.*; *pl.* **lac'ri·mȧ·tō"ries,** same as *lachrymatory*.

lac'ri·mōse, *a.* same as *lachrymose*.

lä·cri·mō'sō, *a.* same as *lagrimoso*.

lȧ·croix'ite (lȧ-krwäz'īte), *n.* [named after Antoine *Lacroix*, a French mineralogist.] a basic, hydrous fluophosphate of aluminum, calcium, manganese, and sodium: it is found in yellowish-green crystals.

lȧ·crosse' (-kros'), *n.* [Fr. *la crosse*; *la*, the, and *crosse*, a crutch, hockey stick, cross.] a game of ball, originated by the North American Indians, in which two teams of ten men each, using long-handled, webbed rackets, try to advance the ball across the field into the opponents' goal. It is a favorite field sport in Canada, and is also played in England and the United States.

LACROSSE PLAYER

lȧ·crosse' stick, the racket used in playing the game of lacrosse.

lac'ry·măl, *a.* and *n.* same as *lachrymal*.

lac'ry·măr·y, *a.* and *n.* same as *lachrymatory*.

lac'ry·mȧ·tō·ry, *n.* and *a.* same as *lachrymatory*.

lac'ry·mōse, *a.* same as *lachrymose*.

lact-, same as *lacto-*.

lac'tam, *n.* [*lact*one and *am*ino.] any of a group of organic cyclic compounds containing the –NH–CO– group in the ring, formed by the elimination of water from the amino and carboxyl groups; an inner anhydride of an amino acid.

lac·tam'ide, *n.* [*lac*tic and *amide*.] a colorless, crystalline substance, $C_3H_7NO_2$.

lac'tănt, *a.* [L. *lactans* (*-antis*), ppr. of *lactare*, to contain milk, to give suck, from *lac, lactis*, milk.] suckling; giving suck. [Rare.]

lac'tȧ·rēne, lac'tȧ·rine, *n.* a preparation of casein or milk curds, used in calico printing to set the colors.

lac'tȧ·ry, *a.* of or for milk.

lac'tȧ·ry, *n.*; *pl.* **lac'tȧ·ries,** a dairy.

lac'tāse, *n.* [*lact-* and dias*tase*.] an enzyme, present in certain yeasts and in the intestines of animals, which splits lactose into glucose and galactose.

lac'tāte, *v.i.*; lactated, *pt., pp.*; lactating, *ppr.* [L. *lactatus*, pp. of *lactare*, to contain milk, to give suck, from *lac, lactis*, milk.]

1. to secrete milk.

2. to suckle young.

lac'tāte, *v.t.* to convert into milk; to make milklike. [Rare.]

lac'tāte, *n.* [L. *lac, lactis*, milk, and *-ate*.] a salt or ester of lactic acid.

lac·tā'tion, *n.* 1. the secretion of milk by a mammary gland.

2. the period during which milk is secreted.
3. the suckling of young.

laç′tē·ăl, *a.* [L. *lacteus*, milky, from *lac*, *lactis*, milk.]
1. of or like milk; milky.
2. containing or carrying chyle, the milky fluid that is a product of digestion.

laç′tē·ăl, *n.* any of the lymphatic vessels that take up chyle from the small intestine and carry it to the thoracic duct.

laç′tē·ăl·ly, *adv.* milkily.

laç′tē·ăn, *a.* [L. *lacteus*, milky, and *-an*.] lacteal.

laç′tē·ous, *a.* [L. *lacteus*, from *lac*, *lactis*, milk.]
1. milky; resembling milk.
2. lacteal; conveying chyle; as, a *lacteous* vessel.

laç·tes′cence, *n.* 1. the act or process of becoming milky.
2. milkiness.
3. the flow of a milky fluid or sap from certain plants when they are gashed or wounded.

laç·tes′cen·cy, *n.* same as *lactescence*.

laç·tes′cent, *a.* [L. *lactescens* (*-entis*), ppr. of *lactescere*, to turn into milk, incept. of *lactare*, to be milky, from *lac*, *lactis*, milk.]
1. becoming milky.
2. milky.
3. producing milk or a juice resembling milk, as the milkweed.

laç′ti-, [from L. *lac*, *lactis*, milk.] a combining form meaning *milk* or *like milk*, as in *lacti*florous.

laç′tiç, *a.* [L. *lac*, *lactis*, milk, and *-ic*.]
1. of the nature of, pertaining to, or obtained from milk.
2. designating or of a clear, sirupy acid, $CH_3CHOHCOOH$, formed by the fermentation of lactose when milk sours, or produced from sucrose and some other carbohydrates by the action of certain microorganisms.

laç′tīde, *n.* [L. *lac*, *lactis*, milk, and *-ide*.] a substance, $C_6H_8O_4$, which is one of the products of the dry distillation of lactic acid.

laç·tif′ẽr·ous, *a.* [LL. *lactifer*, from L. *lac*, *lactis*, milk, and *ferre*, to bear.]
1. yielding or conveying milk; as, a *lactiferous* duct.
2. producing a milky juice, as a plant.

laç·tif′iç, laç·tif′iç·ăl, *a.* [*lacti-*, and L. *facere*, to make.] producing milk.

laç·ti·flō′rous, *a.* bearing flowers of milk-white color.

laç·tif′ū·găl, *a.* serving or tending to check the secretion of milk; having the properties and powers of a lactifuge.

laç′ti·fūġe, *n.* [*lacti-*, and L. *fugare*, to put to flight, from *fugere*, to flee.] a substance which checks the secretion of milk.

laç·tim′ide, laç·tim′id, *n.* [*lactic* and *imid*, or *amide*.] a white crystalline substance obtained by heating lactamic and hydrochloric acids together.

laç′tō-, [from L. *lac*, *lactis*, milk.] a combining form meaning: (a) *milk*, as in *lacto*scope; (b) in chemistry, *lactic* or *lactate*, as in *lact*one: also, before a vowel, *lact-*.

laç″tō·al·bū′min, *n.* [*lacto-*, and L. *albumen*, whiteness, from *albus*, white.] the albumin found in milk.

laç·tō·bȧ·cil′lus, *n.* [Mod. L.; *lacto-* and *bacillus*.] any of a group of bacteria that ferment milk, carbohydrates, etc. to produce lactic acid.

laç″tō·bū″ty·rom′ē·tẽr, *n.* [*lacto-*, and L. *butyrum*, butter, and *metrum*, a measure.] a device for ascertaining the percentage of butter in a given quantity of milk.

laç′tō·cēle, *n.* [*lacto-*, and Gr. *kēlē*, a tumor.] a tumor containing milk or a fluid resembling it: also called *galactocele*.

laç″tō·den·sim′ē·tẽr, *n.* [*lacto-*, and L. *densus*, thick, dense, and *metrum*, a measure.] a hydrometer so constructed as to show the density of milk.

laç·tō·flā′vin, *n.* riboflavin; vitamin B_2.

laç·tom′ē·tẽr, *n.* [*lacto-*, and Gr. *metron*, a measure.] an instrument for determining the specific gravity, and hence the richness, of milk: called also *galactometer*.

laç′tōne, *n.* [L. *lac*, *lactis*, milk, and *-one*.]
1. any of a group of organic compounds formed by the elimination of a molecule of water from the —OH and —COOH groups of a molecule of a hydroxy acid.
2. a colorless, volatile liquid possessing an aromatic odor and produced, along with lactide, by the dry distillation of lactic acid. [Obs.]

laç·tō·prō′tē·id, *n.* same as *lactoprotein*.

laç·tō·prō′tē·in, *n.* [*lacto-*, and Gr. *prōtos*, first, and *-in*.] any of the proteins found in milk.

laç′tō·sçōpe, *n.* [*lacto-* and *-scope*.] an instrument for determining the opacity of milk, so that its cream content may be estimated.

laç′tōse, *n.* [L. *lac*, *lactis*, milk, and *-ose*.] a white, crystalline sugar, $C_{12}H_{22}O_{11}$, found in milk and obtained by evaporation of the whey and the subsequent crystallization of the sugar: it is used in food and medicine.

laç·tō·sū′ri·ȧ, *n.* [*lacto-*, and Gr. *ouron*, urine.] the presence of lactose, or milk sugar, in the urine.

Laç·tū′çȧ, *n.* [L., lettuce.] a genus of liguliflorous herbs of the aster family, to which the lettuce, *Lactuca sativa*, belongs.

laç·tū·cãr′i·um, *n.* [L. *lactuca*, lettuce.] the inspissated juice of a species of lettuce (*Lactuca virosa*), sometimes used as a mild narcotic and sedative.

laç·tū′ciç, *a.* of, pertaining to, or derived from lettuce.
lactucic acid; an acid obtained from the strong-scented lettuce, *Lactuca virosa*.

laç·tū′cin, *n.* [L. *lactuca*, lettuce, and *-in*, *-ine*.] one of the essential ingredients of lactucarium, a bitter, crystalline substance with a neutral reaction.

laç·tū′çōne, *n.* [L. *lactuca*, lettuce, and *-one*.] in chemistry, a tasteless substance, white and crystalline, obtained from lactucarium.

laç′tyl, *n.* [*lactic* and *-yl*.] in chemistry, a lactic acid anhydride.

lȧ·çū′nȧ, *n.*; *pl.* **lȧ·çū′nȧṣ, lȧ·çū′nae,** [L., a ditch, hole, cavity, pool, from *lacus*, a hollow, tank, lake.]
1. space where something has been omitted or has come out; a gap; a hiatus.
2. a small opening; a small pit or depression.
3. in botany, one of the small hollows or pits on the upper surface of a lichen's thallus.
4. in anatomy, (a) one of a multitude of follicles in the mucous membranes, as in those of the urethra; (b) any of the very small cavities in bone that are filled with bone cells.
5. in zoology, one of the spaces left among the tissues of the lower animals and serving in place of vessels for the circulation of the fluids of the body.

lȧ·çū′năr, lȧ·çū′năl, *a.* pertaining to or having lacunae.

lȧ·çū′năr, *n.*; *pl.* **lȧ·çū′nărṣ** or **laç·ū·nā′ri·ȧ,** [L., a panel ceiling, from *lacuna*, a hollow pit.] in architecture, a ceiling made up of sunken panels.

laç′ū·năr·y, *a.* pertaining to a lacuna; lacunar.

lȧ·çūne′, *n.* [Fr., from L. *lacuna*, a hollow.] a lacuna. [Rare.]

lȧ·çū′nōse, *a.* [L. *lacunosus*, full of holes, from *lacuna*, a hollow, cavity.] furrowed or pitted; abounding in cavities or lacunae; as, a *lacunose* leaf; a *lacunose* elytra of a beetle.

laç″ū·nō″sō·rū′gōse, *a.* in botany, having deep irregular pits or furrows, as a peach stone.

lȧ·çū′nū·lōse, *a.* having minute lacunae.

lȧ·çus′tri·ăn, *a.* same as *lacustrine*.

lȧ·çus′tri·ăn, *n.* a lake dweller.

lȧ·çus′trine, lȧ·çus′trăl, *a.* [L. *lacus*, a lake.]
1. of or pertaining to a lake.
2. found on or in a lake.
lacustrine dwelling; same as *lake dwelling*.

laç′wŏrk, *n.* Japanese lacquer.

lā′cy, *a.*; *comp.* lacier; *superl.* laciest, 1. of lace.
2. like lace; having a delicate open pattern. Also spelled *lacey*.

lad, *n.* [ME. *ladde*, of Celtic origin; compare Ir. *lath*, a youth, AS. *leod*, a man.]
1. a boy; a young man.
2. a man of any age: familiar term.
3. a male lover or sweetheart. [Scot.]
4. a male servant. [Obs.]

lad′ȧ·num, *n.* same as *labdanum*.

lad′dẽr, *n.* [ME. *laddere*; AS. *hlæder*, *hlædder*, a ladder.]
1. a frame of wood, metal, or rope, consisting of two parallel sidepieces, connected by rounds or rungs inserted in them at suitable distances and thus forming steps by which persons may climb up or down.
2. anything by which a person ascends or rises; means of ascending.

Lowliness is young ambition's *ladder*.
—Shak.

lad′dẽr-back chāir, a chair with a back consisting of two upright posts connected by horizontal slats.

lad′dẽr bee′tle, a beetle, *Chrysomela scalaris*, very common in America. It lives and feeds upon leaves, and has silvery-white forewings striped with green.

lad′dẽr shell, a sea mollusk of the genus *Scalaria*: so called because of the conspicuous transverse ribs, which are thought to resemble the rounds of a ladder; a wentletrap.

lad′dẽr stitch, an embroidery stitch with parallel crossbars in a ladderlike design.

lad′die, *n.* a lad. [Chiefly Scot.]

lāde, *v.t.* and *v.i.*; laded, *pt.*; laden *or* laded, *pp.*; lading, *ppr.* [ME. *laden*; AS. *hladan*, to heap, pile on, load, draw.]
1. to load; to put on or in, as a burden or freight; as, to *lade* a ship with cotton.
2. to dip or draw out, as a fluid, with a ladle or dipper; to bail; to ladle; as, to *lade* water out of a tub.
3. to admit (water), as a leaky ship. [Obs.]

lāde, *n.* [ME. *lode*; AS. *lad*, a way, course, path.]
1. the mouth of a river. [Obs.]
2. a watercourse; a millrace. [Scot.]

lä′-dē-dä′, *a.*, *n.*, *interj.* same as *la-di-da*.

lāde′măn, *n.* [ME. *lodeman*; AS. *ladman*, a leader, guide; *lad*, way, path, course, and *man*, man.] a servant employed by a miller to return to the owners their quantities of meal when ground. [Scot.]

lād′en, *v.* alternative past participle of *lade*.

lād′en, *a.* 1. loaded.
2. burdened; afflicted; as, *laden* with pain.

lād′en, *v.t.* and *v.i.* to lade.

lä′-di-dä′, *a.* [imitation of affected speech.] characterized by affectation; foppish. [Slang.]

lä′-di-dä′, *n.* an affected, foppish person. [Slang.]

lä′-di-dä′, *interj.* an exclamation of derision at affectation, foppishness, etc.

lā′died, *a.* ladylike. [Obs.]

lā′di·fȳ, *v.t.* to render ladylike; to make a lady of; to give the title or style of lady to.

Lȧ·dĭn′, *n.* [Rhaeto-Romanic *ladin*; L. *Latinus*, Latin.]
1. a dialect of the Rhaeto-Romanic language used in the southeastern part of Switzerland, the upper part of the Tyrol, and northern Italy.
2. a native of these regions who speaks this dialect.

lād′ing, *n.* [ME. *lading*; AS. *hladung*, a drawing, loading, from *hladan*, to load, draw.]
1. the act of loading.
2. that which constitutes a load or cargo; freight; as, the *lading* of a ship.

Lȧ·dī′nō, *n.*; *pl.* **Lȧ·dī′nōṣ,** [Sp., from L. *Latinus*, Latin.]
1. the mixed Spanish and Hebrew dialect spoken by Sephardic Jews in Turkey and some other countries.
2. in Spanish America, a mestizo; a person of mixed blood.

lad′kin, *n.* a little lad; a youth. [Rare.]

lā′dle, *n.* [ME. *ladel*; AS. *hlædel*, a ladle, from *hladan*, to draw water, to lade.]
1. a cuplike spoon with a long handle, used for lading or dipping.
2. the receptacle of a mill wheel, which receives the water which moves it.
3. in gunnery, (a) an instrument for drawing the charge of a cannon; (b) a ring provided with one or more handles for carrying shot.
4. in founding, an iron vessel, often with two handles, in which liquid metal is carried from the furnace to the mold.

lā′dle, *v.t.* and *v.i.*; ladled, *pt.*, *pp.*; ladling, *ppr.*
1. to lift or dip out with or as with a ladle; as, to *ladle* out soup.
2. to lift out and carry in a ladle.

lā′dle·ful, *n.*; *pl.* **lā′dle·fulṣ,** the quantity contained in a ladle.

lā′dle·wood, *n.* a small South African tree, *Cassine colpoon*, with very hard, beautifully veined wood which is valuable for carving and in cabinetwork; also, this wood.

lȧ·drōne′, *n.* [Sp. *ladrón*, from L. *latro* (*-onis*), a mercenary soldier, a servant, a freebooter, a robber.] a bandit; a robber; a thief: a term used with reference to Spanish-speaking regions.

lȧ·drōn′iṣm, *n.* in the Philippines, organized banditry.

lā′dy, *n.*; *pl.* **lā′dieṣ,** [ME. *lavedi*, *levedy*; AS. *hlæfdige*, a lady, mistress, from *hlaf*, loaf, and *-dige*, from base of *dæge*, (bread) kneader.]
1. a woman who has the rights, rule, or authority of a lord.
2. any woman: used in polite reference or [*pl.*] in addressing a group of women.
3. a woman loved by a man; sweetheart.

4. a woman of good breeding or some social position: the correlative to *gentleman.*
5. a wife; a spouse.
6. mistress; the woman who presides or has authority over a household, estate, or family: now obsolete except in the phrase *the lady of the house.*
7. [L–] the Virgin Mary (usually with *Our*).
8. [L–] in the British Empire, the title of respect given to a marchioness, countess, viscountess, or baroness, to the daughter of a duke, marquis, or earl, or to the wife of a baronet, knight, or holder of a courtesy title of *Lord.*
9. the calcareous apparatus in a lobster's stomach in which its food is pulverized.
lady in waiting; a lady of rank who is a member of the royal household and in attendance on a queen or princess.
Lady of the Lake; in Arthurian legend, Vivian, mistress of Merlin: she lived in a castle surrounded by a lake.
lady of the manor; a lady who is the head of a manor or the wife of the lord of the manor.
leading lady; the actress who plays the leading female role in a theatrical performance.

Lā′dy ạl′tăr, the altar of a Lady chapel.

lā′dy bee′tle, same as *ladybug.*

lā′dy·bird, *n.* same as *ladybug.*

Lā′dy Boun′ti·fụl, (a) a wealthy, charitable lady in Farquhar's comedy *The Beaux' Stratagem* (1707); hence, (b) any charitable woman.

lā′dy·bug, *n.* any of the beetles of the family *Coccinellidæ* and order *Coleoptera*, typically small and roundish, with a spotted back often brightly colored. Both adults and larvae are very useful because they feed on insect pests and their eggs. Also called *ladybird, ladyclock, lady beetle,* and *ladyfly.*

Lā′dy chap′el, in Roman Catholic churches, a chapel dedicated to the Virgin Mary. It is usually behind the high altar at the eastern end of the church.

lā′dy·çlock, *n.* same as *ladybug.*

lā′dy çourt, the court of a lady of the manor.

lā′dy çrab, an edible crab of the United States, found in great numbers on the Atlantic coast.

Lā′dy Dāy, Annunciation Day, a church festival celebrated on March 25.

lā′dy fērn, a species of polypodiaceous fern, the *Asplenium filix-fæmina*, widely distributed. It has bipinnate or tripinnate fronds of delicate texture and a plumy structure.

lā′dy·fiṅ″gẽr, *n.* a cooky made of spongecake dough and shaped somewhat like a finger: also *lady's-finger.*

lā′dy·fish, *n.* 1. a brilliant, silvery-colored fish, *Albula vulpes*, abundant in the warmer waters of both the Atlantic and Pacific.
2. a brilliant labroid fish, *Harpe rufa*, common along the West Indian and Florida coasts.
3. the saury, *Scomberesox saurus*: so called in Florida.

lā′dy·flȳ, *n.* same as *ladybird.*

lā′dy·hood, *n.* the state or condition of being a lady; the character, personality, quality, rank, etc. of a lady.

lā′dy-kill″ẽr, *n.* a man who is supposed to have great powers of fascination over women. [Slang.]

lā′dy·kin, *n.* a little lady: used as a term of endearment.

lā′dy·līke, *a.* 1. like a lady in any respect; genteel; well-bred; refined; delicate.
2. characteristic of or suitable for a lady.
3. affected; effeminate.
Spruce *ladylike* preachers. —Jer. Taylor.

lā′dy·līke·ness, *n.* the condition or quality of being ladylike.

lā′dy·lŏve, *n.* a sweetheart.

Lā′dy Măss, a Mass in honor of the Virgin Mary.

lā′dy′ṣ-bed′strạw, *n.* an herb, *Galium verum.*

lā′dy′ṣ-bow′ẽr, *n.* the only British species of virgin's-bower, or clematis, *Clematis vitalba.*

lā′dy′ṣ çloth, a smooth, heavy woolen cloth resembling broadcloth but of lighter weight.

lā′dy′ṣ-çōmb (-kōm), *n.* same as *Venus's-comb.*

lā′dy′ṣ-çush′iŏn (-un), *n.* a plant, *Saxifraga hypnoides.*

lā′dy′ṣ-ēar′drops, *n.* the fuchsia.

lā′dy′ṣ-fiṅ″gẽr, *n.* 1. a variety of apple.
2. a variety of potato.
3. the kidney vetch, *Anthyllis vulneraria.*
4. one of the gills attached to the base of a lobster's leg.
5. a ladyfinger.

lā′dy′ṣ-glŏve′, *n.* the purple foxglove, *Digitalis purpurea.*

lā′dy′ṣ gown, in Scots law, a gift sometimes made by a purchaser to a seller's wife on her renouncing her life interest in the real estate sold.

lā′dy′ṣ-hāir′, *n.* the quaking grass, *Briza media.*

lā′dy·ship, *n.* 1. the position or rank of a lady.
2. [often L–] the form used in speaking to or of a woman having the title of *Lady*: always preceded by *your* or *her.*

lā′dy′ṣ māid, a woman servant who attends a lady, especially one who assists her at her toilette.

lā′dy′ṣ (or **lā′dieṣ′**) **man,** a man very fond of the company of women and very attentive and gallant to them.

lā′dy′ṣ-man′tle, *n.* *Alchemilla vulgaris*, an herb.

lā′dy′ṣ-sēal′, *n.* a plant, *Tamus communis*: also called *black bryony.*

lā′dy′ṣ-slip′pẽr, lā′dy-slip′pẽr, *n.* 1. any orchid of the genus *Cypripedium*: so called because the flowers resemble a slipper.
2. the garden balsam, *Impatiens balsamina.*

lā′dy′ṣ-smock′, lā′dy-smock′, *n.* a cruciferous plant, *Cardamine pratensis*: also called *cuckooflower.*

lā′dy′ṣ-thim′ble, *n.* the harebell, *Campanula rotundifolia.*

lā′dy′ṣ-thumb′ (-thum), *n.* the common persicaria, *Polygonum persicaria*: it is an annual weed with oblong spikes of reddish flowers and tapering leaves with a dark spot in the center.

lā′dy′ṣ-tress′eṣ, lā′dy′ṣ-trā′ceṣ, *n.* any orchid of the genus *Spiranthes*: so called because the spikes of white, spirally-arranged flowers resemble braided hair.

laem′mẽr·geȳ·ẽr, *n.* same as *lammergeier.*

lae·mod′i·pod, *a.* pertaining to or having the characteristics of the *Læmodipoda.*

lae·mod′i·pod, *n.* one of the *Læmodipoda.*

Lae·mō·dip′ō·dȧ, *n.pl.* [Gr. *laimos*, the throat, and *dipous* (*-podos*), two-footed; *dis*, double, and *pous, podos*, foot.] an order of marine sessile-eyed crustaceans which have the anterior pair of feet attached to the cephalic segment. The females have a kind of pouch under the second and third segments, in which the ova are carried. The whale louse, *Cyamus*, and *Caprella* are examples.

lae″mō·pȧ·ral′y·sis, *n.* [Gr. *laimos*, the throat, and *paralysis*, paralysis.] paralysis of the esophagus: also spelled *lemoparalysis.*

lae·ō·trop′iç, lae·ot′rō·pous, *a.* [Gr. *laios*, left, and *tropos*, a turning.] sinistral; turned or turning to the left: opposed to *dexiotropic* and *dexiotropous.*

Lā·ẽr′tēs, *n.* [L.; Gr. *Laertēs.*]
1. in Greek legend, the father of Odysseus.
2. in Shakespeare's *Hamlet*, the brother of Ophelia.

Lae·tā′rē, *n.* the fourth Sunday in Lent: so called because the ancient Christian church began its service on that day with *Lætare, sterilis*, or *Lætare, Jerusalem*, Rejoice, barren one, or Rejoice, Jerusalem.

lā′e·trile, *n.* [*lae*vorotatory glycosidic ni*trile.*] any of several organic compounds obtained from various related plant substances, as apricot kernels and almond seeds, and claimed to be effective in a program of treating many types of cancer.

laev′i·gāte, *a.* same as *levigate.*

lae′vō-, same as *levo-.*

laev·ō·glū′çōse, *n.* same as *levoglucose.*

lae·vō·gȳ′rāte, *a.* same as *levogyrate.*

lae·vō·rō′tȧ·tō·ry, *a.* same as *levorotatory.*

laev′ū·lōse, *n.* same as *levulose.*

lä″fȧ·yette′, *n.* 1. a sciaenoid fish, *Liostomus xanthurus*, of the northern part of the United States.
2. the dollarfish, *Stromateus triacanthus*: also called *butter-fish* and *harvest fish.*

Laf′fẽr Curve, [after A. *Laffer* (1940?—), U.S. economist.] [*also* L- c-] a graph illustrating a theory that increasing tax rates beyond a certain point reduces revenues by discouraging production and investment.

laft, laf′te, *v.* obsolete past tense of *leave.*

lag, *a.* [Celtic origin, compare W. *llag*, slack, sluggish, Gael. and Ir. *lag*, weak, feeble.]
1. coming after or behind; slow; sluggish; tardy. [Obs.]
2. last; long delayed; as, the *lag* end.
3. of the poorest quality, as if made last, and hence of refuse. [Obs.]

lag, *v.i.*; lagged, *pt., pp.*; lagging, *ppr.* [prob. specialized form of *lack*, v.t., with variant final consonant.]
1. to fall behind; to move slowly; loiter; linger.
2. in billiards, to strike the cue ball with the cue so that it rebounds from the end rail and returns toward the head rail: done to decide the order of play, the winner being the player whose stroke brings the ball nearest to the head rail.
3. in marbles, to toss one's shooting marble, or taw, toward a line marked on the ground (*lag line*) in order to decide the order of play.

lag, *n.* 1. a falling behind or being retarded in motion, development, etc.
2. the amount of such falling behind.
3. in billiards and marbles, a lagging.
4. in electricity, the delay in the phase of current peak behind the corresponding voltage peak in an alternating-current circuit.
5. in physiology, the time interval between a stimulus and the response.

lag, *n.* [prob. from Anglo-N.]
1. a barrel stave.
2. any of the narrow strips of insulating material used for covering boilers, cylinders, etc.

lag, *v.t.*; lagged, *pt., pp.*; lagging, *ppr.* to cover with lags.

lag, *v.t.*; lagged, *pt., pp.*; lagging, *ppr.* [perh. from prec. *lag* via thieves' slang.]
1. to send to penal servitude or transport as a criminal. [Slang.]
2. to arrest. [Slang.]

lag, *n.* 1. a person transported or sentenced to penal servitude; a convict.
2. a term of transportation or penal servitude.

lag′ăn, *n.* [ML. and OFr. *lagan.*] in maritime law, goods cast overboard, as in a storm, but with a buoy attached to identify the owner: also *ligan, lagend.*

lȧ·gär′tō, *n.* [Sp.] an alligator. [Obs.]

lag bōlt, a bolt with a square head.

Läg b′Ō′mẽr, [Heb. *lag b'ōmer*, 33d (day) of the omer (the count of 49 days from the second day of Passover to the first day of Shabuoth).] a Jewish holiday.

lȧ·gē′nȧ, *n.*; *pl.* **lȧ·gē′nae,** [L. *lagena, lagæna, lagona*; Gr. *lagēnos, lagynos*, a flagon, a flask.] the saccular extremity of the cochlea in birds and reptiles.

Lag·ē·nā′ri·ȧ, *n.* [L. *lagena*, a bottle.] a genus of plants of the family *Cucurbitaceæ*. There is only one species, *Lagenaria vulgaris*, the bottle gourd.

lag′end, *n.* same as *lagan.*

lȧ·gē′ni·fọrm, *a.* [L. *lagena*, a flask, and *forma*, form.] in botany and zoology, flask-shaped; of the form of a Florentine vase.

lä′gẽr, *n.* same as *laager.*

lä′gẽr beer, [G. *lagerbier*, lit., store beer; *lager*, storehouse, a place for storing things, and *bier*, beer.] a beer, originally made in Germany, which is aged for several months after it has been brewed: also *lager.*

Lā·gẽr·stroe′mi·ȧ, *n.* [named after Magnus von *Lagerström*, a Swedish merchant.] a genus of polypetalous, lythraceous trees and shrubs. They are native to tropical Asia, Africa, Australia, and Madagascar. Some species, as the crape myrtle or Indian lilac, are cultivated on account of their beauty.

lag′gärd, *a.* slow; sluggish; backward.

lag′gärd, *n.* one who lags; a loiterer.

lag′gẽr, *n.* a person or thing that lags.

lag′ging, *n.* 1. the strips of wood or other nonconducting material with which a boiler, cylinder, wall, etc. is covered.
2. the act of covering with lags.
3. an open frame woodwork to support an arch while it is being built.
4. a lining of strips of wood, used to support the roof of a mine.

lag′ging·ly, *adv.* loiteringly; tardily.

la·gniappe′, la·gnappe′ (lan-yap′) *n.* [etym. doubtful.] a small gift or present added to a purchase by a tradesman as a favor to customers. [Dial.]

lag′o-, [from Gr. *lagōs, lagos*, a hare.] a combining form used in zoology, anatomy, etc. to signify *a hare* or *harelike*, as in *lagostoma, lagomys.*

lag′ō·mọrph, *n.* one of the *Lagomorpha.*

Lag·ō·mọr′phȧ, *n.pl.* [*lago-*, and Gr. *morphē*, form, shape.] an order of rodent mammals characterized by two pairs of upper incisors, one behind the other, as the hares, rabbits, pikas, etc.: also called *Duplicidentata*.

là·goon′, *n.* [It. and Sp. *laguna*, from L. *lacuna*, a ditch, pool, from *lacus*, lake.]
1. a shallow lake or pond, especially one connected with a larger body of water.
2. an area of shallow salt water separated from the sea by sand dunes: also spelled *lagune*.
3. the area of water surrounded by an atoll, or circular coral reef.

là·goon′ is′land (ī′), **là·goon′ reef**, an atoll.

lag·oph·thal′mi·à, lag·oph·thal′mus, *n.* [*lago-*, and Gr. *ophthalmos*, the eye.] the continued abnormal retraction of the upper eyelid which prevents its covering the eyeball during sleep: so called from the supposition that this is the natural condition of the eye of the hare when asleep.

lag·oph·thal′miç, *a.* pertaining to or affected with lagophthalmia.

là·gō′pous, *a.* [Gr. *lagōpous*, harefooted.] in botany, hare-footed; having a covering of soft, long hairs and so resembling the foot of a hare.

là·gos′tō·mà, *n.* [*lago-*, and Gr. *stoma*, mouth.] harelip.

là·got′iç, *a.* [*lago-*, and Gr. *ous*, *ōtos*, the ear.] having ears like a rabbit.

lä·grï·mō′sō, *a.* [It., from L. *lacrimosus*, tearful, mournful, from *lacrima*, a tear.] in music, denoting or indicating passages to be rendered in a mournful or plaintive manner: also written *lacrimoso*.

Läg′ting, Läg′thing (-ting), *n.* [Norw. *lagthing*, *lagting*; *lag*, company, society, law, and *thing*, *ting*, parliament.] the upper house of the Norwegian parliament, or Storting.

là·gūne′, *n.* same as *lagoon*.

lā′iç, *a.* [LL. *laicus*; Gr. *laïkos*, of or belonging to the people, from *laos*, the people.] of the laity, in distinction from the clergy; secular; lay.

lā′iç, *n.* a layman.

lā′i·çăl, *a.* laic.

lā·iç·al′i·ty, *n.* the state or quality of being laic.

lā′iç·ăl·ly, *adv.* in a laic manner.

lā″i·ci·zā′tion, *n.* the act of laicizing; removal from clerical rank or power.

lā′i·cīze, *v.t.*; laicized, *pt.*, *pp.*; laicizing, *ppr.* to render lay or laic (nonclerical); to open (an office or position) to laymen; to deprive of clerical rank or power.

lāid, *v.* past tense and past participle of *lay*.
laid up; (a) stored away; (b) dismantled and out of use, as a ship; (c) [Colloq.] so ill or injured as to be confined or disabled.

lāid′ly, *a.* unsightly; extremely ugly. [Scot.]

lāid pā′pẽr, paper which is watermarked with parallel lines from the wires on which the pulp was laid in the process of manufacture: opposed to *wove paper*.

lāin, *v.* past participle of *lie* (to recline).

lāin′ẽr, lāin′ēre, *n.* a leather thong or strap. [Obs.]

lāir, *n.* [ME. *leir*; AS. *leger*, a bed, couch, place of rest, from *licgan*, to lie.]
1. a bed or resting place, especially of a wild animal; a den.
2. a pasture; a field; the ground. [Obs.]
3. a litter, as of rabbits. [Obs.]
4. in Scotland, a portion of a burying ground affording space sufficient for one or more graves.

lāir, *v.i.* to go to, rest in, or have a lair.

lāir, *v.t.* 1. to place in or provide with a lair.
2. to serve as a lair for.

lāird, *n.* a landowner, especially a wealthy one. [Scot.]

lāird′ship, *n.* the estate of a laird; the rank of a laird. [Scot.]

lāis·sez-fāire′ (les-ā-fâr′), *a.* of or based on laissez faire.

lāis′sez fāire′, lāis′ser fāire′ (les′ā fâr′), [Fr. let (people) do (as they please).] noninterference; letting people do as they please; especially, noninterference in matters of economics and business; letting the owners of industry and business fix the rules of competition, the conditions of labor, etc. as they please, without governmental regulation or control.

lā′i·ty, *n.*; *pl.* **lā′i·ties**, [LL. *laicus*; Gr. *laïkos*, belonging to the people, from *laos*, the people.]
1. the people, as distinguished from the clergy; the body of the people not in orders; laymen collectively.
2. people outside of any profession, as distinguished from those belonging to it.
3. the state of a layman.

Lā′ius (-yus), *n.* in Greek legend, a king of Thebes and the father of Oedipus.

lāke, *n.* [see *lac* (resin).]
1. a dark-red pigment prepared from cochineal.
2. its color.
3. an insoluble coloring compound precipitated from a solution of a dye by adding a metallic salt, which acts as a mordant: used in the application of certain dyes to cloth.

lāke, *v.i.*; laked, *pt.*, *pp.*; laking, *ppr.* to play; to sport. [Brit. Dial.]

lāke, *n.* a kind of fine, white linen, used chiefly for shirts. [Obs.]

lāke, *n.* [ME. *lake*, *lak*; AS. *lacu*, a lake, pool; L. *lacus*, a hollow, a basin, tub, pool, lake.]
1. an inland body of water, usually fresh water, formed by glaciers, river drainage, etc., larger than a pool or pond.
2. a pool of oil or other liquid.
3. a place where a river widens out greatly.

lāke dwell′ẽr, one who lives in a lake dwelling.

lāke dwell′ing, a dwelling built on small islands in lakes, or on platforms supported by piles rising above the surface of a lake; especially, such a dwelling erected in prehistoric times.

lāke fē′vẽr, malaria. [Dial.]

lāke flȳ, 1. a dayfly, *Ephemera simulans*, which swarms on the Great Lakes in the latter part of the summer.
2. a midge of the genus *Chironomus*.

lāke her′ring, a variety of the cisco, *Coregonus artedii*.

Lāke′land ter′ri·ẽr, [after the *Lake District* of England, where originally bred.] any of a breed of small, sturdy terrier with a square build and a hard wiry coat.

lāke′let, *n.* a small lake.

Lāke pō′ets, the English poets Wordsworth, Coleridge, and Southey, who lived in the Lake District.

Lāke sçhool, the Lake poets.

lāke shad, any of several inferior food fishes, as suckers, found in the Great Lakes.

lāke stûr′geŏn, a food fish, *Acipenser fulvescens*, of the Great Lakes and Mississippi River.

lāke trout, any of several varieties of trout and salmon found in lakes; especially, the namaycush of the northern United States, Canada, and Alaska.

lāke′weed, *n.* the common smartweed or water pepper, *Polygonum hydropiper*.

lāke whit′ing, the whitefish.

lakh (lak), *n.* a lac (one hundred thousand).

lāk′in, *n.* a plaything; a toy. [Obs.]

lā′kin, *n.* ladykin. [Obs.]

lāk′y, *a.* of, pertaining to, or like a lake.

lāk′y, *a.* of the color of the pigment lake; specifically, in medicine, designating blood in which the red corpuscles have been partially destroyed.

Lā·lique′ (-lēk′) **glȧss**, see under *glass*.

Lal′lăn, *a.* [dial. for *lowland*.] of, pertaining to, or belonging to the Lowlands of Scotland. [Scot.]

Lal′lăn, *n.* the dialect of the Lowlands of Scotland.

lal·lā′tion, *n.* [Fr., from L. *lallare*, to sing a lullaby.] an imperfect pronunciation of the letter *r*, which makes it sound like *l*.

lä′lō, *n.* [African.] same as *baobab*.

là·lop′à·thy, *n.* [Gr. *lalein*, to talk, and *pathos*, suffering.] any defect of the organs of speech or disturbance of the function of language.

lam, *v.t.*; lammed, *pt.*, *pp.*; lamming, *ppr.* [Ice. *lemja*, to beat.] to beat; to thrash; to flog. [Slang.]

lam, *n.* hurried flight, usually to escape punishment for a crime. [Slang.]
on the lam; in headlong flight. [Slang.]
to take it on the lam; to make a getaway; to escape. [Slang.]

lam, *v.i.*; lammed, *pt.*, *pp.*; lamming, *ppr.* to flee; to escape. [Slang.]

lā′mȧ, *n.* in zoology, same as *llama*.

lä′mȧ, *n.* [Tibetan *blama*, a chief, high priest.] a priest or monk belonging to that variety of Buddhism which is known as Lamaism, and prevails in Tibet, Mongolia, and the extreme western part of China. There are several grades of lamas, both male and female, of whom the *Dalai Lama* and the *Teshu Lama* are regarded as supreme pontiffs.
Grand Lama; the Dalai Lama.

là·mā′iç, *a.* pertaining to or made up of lamas.

Lä′mȧ·işm, *n.* the religious system of the lamas, a variety of Buddhism characterized by elaborate ritual and strong hierarchal organization. The highest object of worship is Buddha, who is regarded as the founder of the religion, and the first in rank among the saints.

Lä′mȧ·ist, Lä′mȧ·īte, *n.* one who believes in Lamaism.

Lä·mȧ·is′tiç, *a.* of or pertaining to Lamaism; lamaic.

là·man′tin, *n.* same as *manatee*.

Là·märck′i·ăn, *a.* of or pertaining to Lamarck, the French naturalist, or to Lamarckism.

Là·märck′i·ăn, *n.* an adherent of Lamarckism.

Là·märck′i·ăn·işm, *n.* same as *Lamarckism*.

Là·märck′işm, *n.* in biology, the theory of organic evolution propounded by Lamarck, a distinguished French naturalist, early in the nineteenth century: it states that acquired characteristics can be inherited.

lä′mȧ·ser·y, *n.*; *pl.* **lä′mȧ·ser·ieş**, [Tibetan *blama*, a chief, lama, and Per. *sarāī*, an inn.] a monastery of lamas.

Là·mäze′, *n.* [after F. *Lamaze*, 20th-century Fr. physician who developed it.] a training program in natural childbirth, emphasizing breathing control and relaxation and the role of the father to help bring these about.

lamb (lam), *n.* [ME. *lamb*; AS. *lamb*, *lomb*, lamb.]
1. a young sheep.
2. the flesh of a young sheep, used for food.
3. lambskin.
4. a gentle or innocent person, particularly a child.
5. a person easily tricked or outwitted, as an inexperienced speculator.
the Lamb or *the Lamb of God*; in Scripture, Jesus Christ, who was typified by the paschal lamb.

Behold *the Lamb of God*, which taketh away the sin of the world. —John i. 29.

lamb, *v.i.*; lambed (lamd), *pt.*, *pp.*; lambing, *ppr.* to bring forth young: said of a ewe.

lamb′āle, *n.* a former feast at the time of shearing lambs. [Brit.]

lam·bast′, *v.t.* to lambaste. [Dial.]

lam·bāste′, *v.t.*; lambasted, *pt.*, *pp.*; lambasting, *ppr.* 1. to beat or thrash severely. [Slang.]
2. to scold or denounce severely. [Slang.]

lamb′dȧ (lam′dȧ), *n.* [Gr. *lambda*, lambda.]
1. the eleventh letter of the Greek alphabet, corresponding to the English *L*, *l*.
2. in craniology, the junction of the sagittal and lambdoid sutures.

lamb′dȧ·cişm, *n.* [LL. *lambdacismus*; Gr. *lambdakismos*, a lambdacism, from *lambdakizein*, to pronounce *l* imperfectly, from *lambda*, lambda, the letter *l*.]
1. a too frequent repetition of the letter *l* in speaking or writing, as in Martial's line: *Sol et luna luce lucent alba, leni, lactea.*
2. a faulty pronunciation of *ll*, as when the tongue is pressed against the palate and produces a sound similar to *lli* in *million*.
3. an imperfect pronunciation of the letter *r*, which is made to sound like *l*; lallation.

lamb′doid, lamb·doid′ăl, *a.* [Gr. *lambda*, the letter Λ, lambda, and *eidos*, form.] resembling in shape the Greek capital letter lambda: specifically applied, in craniology, to the suture between the occipital and parietal bones.

lam′ben·cy, *n.* 1. the fact, state, or quality of being lambent.
2. *pl.* **lam′ben·cieş**, that which is lambent.

lam′bent, *a.* [L. *lambens* (*-entis*), ppr. of *lambere*, to lick, lap.]
1. licking. [Rare.]
2. playing lightly over a surface without burning it; flickering: said of a flame, etc.
3. giving off a soft radiance.
4. playing lightly and gracefully over a subject: said of wit, humor, etc.

lam′bẽrt, *n.* [after Johann Heinrich *Lambert* (1728–1777), G. physicist, astronomer, and mathematician.] the centimeter-gram-second unit of brightness, equal to the brightness of a perfectly diffusing surface that radiates or reflects light at the rate of one lumen per square centimeter.

Lam′beth Pal′āce, the official London residence of the archbishops of Canterbury since 1197.

lamb′kill (lam′), *n.* the sheep laurel, *Kalmia angustifolia*: so called because its leaves are supposed to be poisonous to sheep.

lamb′kin, *n.* a small lamb: sometimes applied to a child or young person as a term of affection.

lamb′līke, *a.* like, or having qualities attributed to, a lamb; gentle; humble; meek; mild; innocent; unassuming; as, a *lamblike* temper.

lam′boys, *n.pl.* [OFr. *lambeau*, a shred, flap.] in armor, the imitation in steel of the plaited skirts or bases worn over the thighs. They were worn especially in Germany in the earlier part of the sixteenth century.

LAMBOYS
1. time of Henry VIII; 2. from a German suit, early sixteenth century

lam′bre·quin (-kin), *n.* [Fr., the coverings or trappings of a helmet, a mantel, scallop.]
1. in medieval armor, a sort of scarf worn over the helmet, as an ornament or for protection from heat or wetness.
2. a piece of cloth, leather, lace, etc. forming a sort of curtain for the upper part of an opening, as a doorway, window, or arch, or an ornamental drapery of a mantel, etc.
3. in heraldry, the mantling.
4. in decorative art, imitation of a lambrequin design, as in certain Chinese vases which display a solid color above and an edge of jagged or ornamented outline below.

lamb′skin (lam′), *n.* 1. the skin of a lamb, especially one dressed with the fleece on and sometimes colored.
2. leather or parchment made from the skin of a lamb from which the fleece has been removed.
3. woolen cloth made to resemble the dressed skin of a lamb.

lamb′skin·net, *n.* same as *lansquenet* (card game).

lamb′s′-let″tuce (-is), *n.* same as *corn salad.*

lamb′s′-quar″tẽrs (-kwąr″), *n.* a European weed, *Atriplex patula*; also, an American weed, the white goosefoot.

lamb′s wool, 1. wool obtained from lambs.
2. a cloth made from the wool of lambs.
3. ale mixed with sugar, nutmeg, and the pulp of roasted apples.

la·mé′ (lȧ-mā′), *n.* [Fr., *lamé*, laminated, from *lame*, a plate or sheet of metal; metallic thread, especially gold or silver thread.] a fabric made of metal threads, especially of gold or silver, sometimes interwoven with silk, wool, or cotton: it is a heavy material, usually lustrous and rich, and often figured.

lāme, *n.* [Fr., from L. *lamina*, *lamna*, a thin piece of metal or wood.]
1. a thin plate, usually of metal.
2. [*pl.*] the thin, overlapping metal plates in a piece of armor.

lāme, *a.*; *comp.* lamer; *superl.* lamest, [ME. *lame*; AS. *lama*, lame.]
1. crippled; disabled; especially, having an injured leg or foot; unable to use a limb or limbs properly; limping; halting; as, a *lame* man.
2. unsound from a defect or injury; crippled; stiff and very painful; as, a *lame* back or arm.
3. poor; ineffectual; imperfect; not satisfactory or convincing; hobbling; lacking in smoothness; as, a *lame* excuse.
lame duck; (a) anything or anyone that is disabled, inefficient, ineffectual, or helpless; (b) a speculator who is unable to fulfill his obligations, especially a defaulter on the stock exchange; (c) a member of a legislative body, especially (formerly) of Congress, whose term extends beyond the time of the election at which he was not re-elected.
Lame Duck Amendment; the twentieth Amendment to the Constitution of the United States, which abolished the short Congressional session, *Lame Duck Session* (after October 15, 1933), by requiring each Congress to meet not less than once a year, beginning January 3.
Lame Duck Session; formerly, the session of Congress immediately following the November elections which included members of Congress who had failed to be re-elected: abolished by the *Lame Duck Amendment.*
Syn.—weak, faltering, hobbling, hesitating, ineffective, impotent, crippled, halt, defective, imperfect.

lāme, *v.t.*; lamed, *pt.*, *pp.*; laming, *ppr.* to make lame; to cripple or disable; to make imperfect and unsound; as, to *lame* an arm or a leg.

lāme, *v.i.* to become lame.

lä′medh, lä′med, *n.* [Heb., lit., a whip, or club.] the twelfth letter of the Hebrew alphabet, corresponding to English *L, l.*

lam′el, *n.* same as *lamella.*

lȧ·mel′lȧ, *n.*; *pl.* **lȧ·mel′lae**, [L., a small or thin plate, from *lamina*, a thin piece of metal or wood.]
1. a thin plate, leaf, layer, or scale, as of bone or animal tissue; specifically, in zoology, one of the thin plates or scales which compose certain shells, or of which the gills of certain mollusks, as the oyster, are composed.
2. in botany, (a) any of the gills forming the hymenium of an agaric; (b) any of the foliaceous erect scales on the corolla of many plants.

lam′el·lăr, *a.* having, resembling, or composed of thin plates, layers, or scales; arranged in thin plates or scales; lamellate.

lȧ·mel′lăr·ly, *adv.* in thin plates or scales.

lam′el·lăr-stel′lāte, *a.* in mineralogy, formed of lamellae arranged in the form of a star.

lam′el·lāte, lam′el·lā·ted, *a.* formed in or covered with thin plates or scales; consisting of, resembling, or furnished with lamellae or little plates.

lȧ·mel′li-, [from L. *lamella*, a small or thin plate.] a combining form meaning *of, like,* or *consisting of a lamella* or *lamellae*, as in *lamelli*form, *lamelli*branch.

lȧ·mel′li·brañch, *a.* having lamellate gills; of, pertaining to, or having the characteristics of the *Lamellibranchia.*

lȧ·mel′li·brañch, *n.* any of the *Lamellibranchia.*

Lȧ·mel″li·brañ′chi·ȧ, Lȧ·mel″li·brañ″chi·ā′tȧ, *n.pl.* [*lamelli-*, and L. *branchiæ*, gills.] a class of *Mollusca*, including all the true or common bivalve mollusks, as oysters, clams, etc. They have no distinct head or cephalic eyes. The valves of the shell articulate over the back, and are opened by an elastic ligament and closed by one or two adductor muscles. They have two pairs of lamellated gills. Also called *Acephala, Bivalvia, Conchifera, Cormopoda,* and *Pelecypoda.*

lȧ·mel″li·brañ′chi·āte, *a.* and *n.* same as *lamellibranch.*

lȧ·mel′li·cọrn, *n.* any of the *lamellicornia.*

lȧ·mel′li·cọrn, lȧ·mel″li·cọr′nāte, *a.* [*lamelli-*, and L. *cornu*, horn.]
1. ending in flattened plates: said of the antennae of some beetles.
2. having such antennae; of or pertaining to the *Lamellicornia.*

Lȧ·mel″li·cọr′nēs, *n.pl.* same as *Lamellicornia.*

Lȧ·mel″li·cọr′ni·ȧ, *n.pl.* [*lamelli-*, and L. *cornu*, horn.] a suborder of *Coleoptera* (beetles) in which the antennae are inserted into a deep cavity under the lateral margin of the head. The antennae are short, and the last three joints are platelike and arranged somewhat like the teeth of a comb. This large suborder includes the dung beetles, stag beetles, cockchafers, etc.

lam″el·lif′ẽr·ous, *a.* [*lamelli-*, and L. *ferre*, to bear.] having lamellae or a structure composed of thin layers; having a foliated structure.

lȧ·mel′li·fọrm, *a.* [*lamelli-*, and L. *forma*, form.] having the form of a lamella; platelike or scalelike.

lȧ·mel′li·ped, *a.* [*lamelli-*, and L. *pes, pedis*, foot.] having a flattened foot in the shape of a lamella, as some mollusks.

lȧ·mel′li·ped, *n.* a mollusk having a lamelliform foot.

lȧ·mel·li·ros′tẽr, *n.* a lamellirostral bird.

lȧ·mel·li·ros′trăl, *a.* of or pertaining to the *Lamellirostres.*

lȧ·mel·li·ros′trăl, *n.* any of the *Lamellirostres.*

Lȧ·mel″li·ros′trēs, *n.pl.* [*lamelli-*, and L. *rostrum*, a beak.] a family of water birds, as ducks, geese, and swans, characterized by having the beak flattened and covered with a soft skin. The margins of the tongue and beak are furnished with numerous lamellae or dental plates, arranged in a regular series.

lȧ·mel′lōse, *a.* lamellate; having or covered with lamellae.

lāme′ly, *adv.* in a lame manner; imperfectly.

lāme′ness, *n.* the state of being lame; imperfection; weakness.

lȧ·ment′, *v.i.*; lamented, *pt.*, *pp.*; lamenting, *ppr.* [Fr. *lamenter*; L. *lamentari*, to mourn, lament, from *lamentum*, a mourning, wailing.] to mourn; to grieve; to weep or wail; to express or feel deep sorrow.

Jeremiah *lamented* for Josiah.
—2 Chron. xxxv. 25.

lȧ·ment′, *v.t.* 1. to feel or express deep sorrow for; to bewail; to mourn or grieve for; to bemoan; to deplore.
2. to regret deeply.
Syn.—bemoan, bewail, complain, grieve, deplore, mourn, regret.

lȧ·ment′, *n.* [L. *lamentum*, a mourning, wailing.]
1. an outward expression of grief or sorrow; lamentation; a weeping.
2. a literary or musical composition, as a dirge, elegy, or mournful ballad, about some loss or calamity.

lam′en·tȧ·ble, *a.* [L. *lamentabilis*, from *lamentari*, to mourn, lament.]
1. to be lamented; grievous; deplorable; distressing.
2. mournful; expressing grief or sorrow; as, a *lamentable* speech.
3. miserable; pitiful; low; wretched; of poor quality; as, a *lamentable* piece of acting.

lam′en·tȧ·ble·ness, *n.* the state or quality of being lamentable.

lam′en·tȧ·bly, *adv.* in a lamentable manner; so as to be lamentable.

lam′en·tā′tion, *n.* [OFr. *lamentation*; L. *lamentatio* (*-onis*), a weeping, lamenting, from *lamentari*, to weep, lament.]
1. outward expression of sorrow; cries of grief; the act of wailing.
2. [L–] [*pl.*] the Lamentations of Jeremiah, a book of the Old Testament attributed to Jeremiah.
3. [*pl.*] in the Roman Catholic Church, the music to which are sung parts of the Lamentations of Jeremiah, used in the Tenebrae.

lȧ·ment′ed, *a.* bewailed; mourned for: usually said of someone dead.

lȧ·ment′ẽr, *n.* one who mourns, or cries out with sorrow.

lȧ·ment′ing, *n.* a mourning; lamentation.

lȧ·ment′ing·ly, *adv.* in a lamenting manner; with lamentation.

lȧ·met′tȧ, *n.* [It., dim. of *lama*, a plate of metal, from L. *lamina*, a thin piece of metal, wood, marble, etc.] gold, silver, or brass wire or foil.

lā′mi·ȧ, *n.* [L. *lamia*; Gr. *lamia*, a female demon.]
1. in Greek and Roman mythology, one of a class of man-devouring monsters, represented with a woman's head and breasts and a serpent's body, supposed to lure children in order to suck their blood.
2. a vampire; a female demon; a sorceress.
3. [L–] a genus of longicorn beetles belonging to the family *Cerambycidæ*, the male having antennae four times as long as the body.

lā·mi·ā′ceous, *a.* [from Mod. L. *Lamium*, genus of herbs, from L. *lamium*, dead nettle.] of the mint family of plants, mainly aromatic herbs and shrubs, including mint, rosemary, and bergamot.

lam′i·nȧ, *n.*; *pl.* **lam′i·nae, lam′i·nȧs**, [L. *lamina*, a thin plate of metal, wood, or marble.]
1. a thin plate, flake, or scale; a layer or coat lying over another, as of metal, animal tissue, etc.
2. in anatomy, a bone, or part of a bone, resembling a thin plate, such as the cribriform plate of the ethmoid bone.
3. in botany, (a) the border, or the upper broad or spreading part of the petal in a polypetalous corolla; (b) the part of a leaf which is flat and expanded; the blade, as distinguished from the stem.
4. in ornithology, one of the thin flat scales or plates in the feather.
5. in geology, the thinnest distinct layer or sheet into which a stratified rock can be divided.
lamina cribrosa; in anatomy, the sievelike plate of the bone which forms the roof of the nasal depressions or fossae and part of the floor of the anterior hollow of the skull; also, a horizontal, platelike bone from which the labyrinth is suspended on either side with the vertical plate of the ethmoid bone in the center: it contains numerous openings for the passage of the olfactory nerves and articulates with the ethmoidal notch of the frontal bone.

lam″i·nȧ·bil′i·ty, *n.* the state of being laminable.

lam′i·nȧ·ble, *a.* capable of being formed or pressed into a lamina or separated into laminae.

lam′i·năl, lam′i·năr, *a.* arranged in or composed of thin plates or layers; laminate.

Lam″i·nā′ri·ȧ, *n.* [L. *lamina*, a thin plate.] a

family of dark-spored seaweeds, belonging to the order *Laminariaceæ*.

Lam″i·nā″ri·ā′cē·ae, *n.pl.* [*Laminaria* and *-aceæ*.] one of the orders into which the *Algæ* are divided.

lam·i·nā·ri·ā′ceous, *a.* [from Mod. L. *Laminaria*, family of brown algae, and *-aceous*.] of a family of brown algae containing many giant kelps and seaweeds.

lam″i·năr′i·ăn, *a.* of or pertaining to the family *Laminaria*; specifically, noting that belt or zone of marine life which extends from low-water mark to a depth of from **40** to **90** feet, where the *Laminariaceæ* are found.

lam′i·nȧ·rīte, *n.* [*Laminaria* and *-ite.*] a broad-leaved fossil alga, found in the upper secondary and tertiary formations.

lam′i·năr·y, *a.* laminar.

lam′i·nāte, *v.t.*; laminated, *pt.*, *pp.*; laminating, *ppr.* [LL. *laminatus*, pp. of *laminare*, to flatten into a thin plate, from L. *lamina*, a thin plate.]

1. to form or press into a thin sheet or layer.
2. to separate into thin sheets or layers.
3. to cover with thin layers.
4. to make by building up in layers, as plywood.

lam′i·nāte, *v.i.* to become divided or separated into laminae or thin layers.

lam′i·nāte, lam′i·nā·ted, *a.* plated; consisting of or arranged in thin plates, scales, or layers.

lam·i·nā′tion, *n.* 1. the act of laminating or the state of being laminated.

2. a laminated structure; something built up in layers.

3. a lamina; a thin layer; a ply.

lam″i·nif′ēr·ous, *a.* [L. *lamina*, a thin plate, and *ferre*, to bear.] having a structure consisting of laminae, or layers.

lȧ·min′i·fọrm, *a.* [L. *lamina*, a thin plate, and *forma*, form.] having the form of a lamina; laminar.

lam″i·ni·plan′tăr, *a.* [L. *lamina*, a thin plate, and *planta*, sole.] in ornithology, having laminate tarsi; having two lateral laminae which meet in a sharp ridge and cover the back of the tarsus, as in most singing birds except the larks.

lam″i·nī′tis, *n.* inflammation of the laminae, especially in the interstitial tissue of a horse's foot; the founder.

lam′i·nōse, *a.* laminate.

lam′i·nous, *a.* laminate.

lām′ish, *a.* somewhat lame.

lamm, *v.t.* to lam. [Obs.]

Lam′măs, *n.* [ME. *lammasse*; AS. *hlammæsse*, for *hlafmæsse*, lit., loaf mass, bread feast; *hlaf*, loaf, and *mæsse*, mass, festival.]

1. formerly, in England, the festival of the wheat harvest or loaf mass, held on the first day of August, when bread baked from the first crop of wheat was consecrated at Mass.

2. in Great Britain, the first of August, which is quarter day in Scotland, and in England half-quarter day or cross-quarters: also called *Lammas day*.

3. in the Roman Catholic Church, a festival which falls on the first day of August and commemorates the imprisonment and miraculous deliverance of the Apostle Peter.

Lam′măs dāy, same as *Lammas*, sense 2.

Lam′măs land, formerly, cultivated land under the control of individual owners until harvest, or Lammastide, when it was thrown open for common pasturage until sowing time.

Lam′măs·tīde, *n.* the time or season of Lammas.

lam′mēr·geī·ēr, laem′mēr·geī·ēr (lam′), *n.* [G. *lämmergeier*; *lämmer*, pl. of *lamm*, a lamb, and *geier*, a vulture.] a bird of prey, *Gypaëtos barbatus*, family *Vulturidæ*, living in the Swiss and German Alps, as well as the higher mountains of Asia and Africa: it is the largest European bird of prey, measuring about four feet from beak to tail, and having a wing expansion of about ten feet: written also *lammergeir*, *lemmergeyer*, *laemmergeyer*: also called *bearded vulture*.

lam′my, lam′mie, *n.* a thick, warm, quilted jumper worn as an outer garment by sailors in severe weather. [Rare.]

lamp, *n.* a thin plate or lamina. [Obs.]

lamp, *n.* [ME. *lampe*; OFr. *lampe*; L. *lampas* (*-adis*); Gr. *lampas* (*-ados*), a lamp, torch, light, from *lampein*, to shine.]

1. a container with a wick for burning oil, alcohol, etc. to produce light or heat: the wick is often enclosed in a glass tube, or chimney, to protect the flame.

2. any device for producing light or therapeutic rays, as a gas jet, electric light, or sun-ray lamp.

3. a source of knowledge or wisdom.

4. the sun, moon, a star, etc. [Rare or Poetic.]

5. [*pl.*] the eyes. [Slang.]

aphlogistic lamp; a lamp in which a coil of platinum wire is kept in continued ignition by incandescence without flame.

Argand lamp; see under *Argand*.

Döbereiner's lamp; a hydrogen lamp for producing an instantaneous flame by throwing a jet of hydrogen gas upon platinum sponge: invented in **1824** by J. W. Döbereiner, German chemist.

flameless lamp; same as *aphlogistic lamp*.

Fresnel lamp; an oil lamp surrounded by a hollow cylindrical lens (*Fresnel lens*), which projects a beam of light that can be seen for several miles: used in lighthouses.

safety lamp; (a) a miner's lamp in which a protective enclosure, as of wire gauze, surrounds the flame; (b) any lamp constructed to avoid explosion, fire, etc.

student, *student's*, or *study lamp*; a reading lamp in which the direction of the light rays can be adjusted.

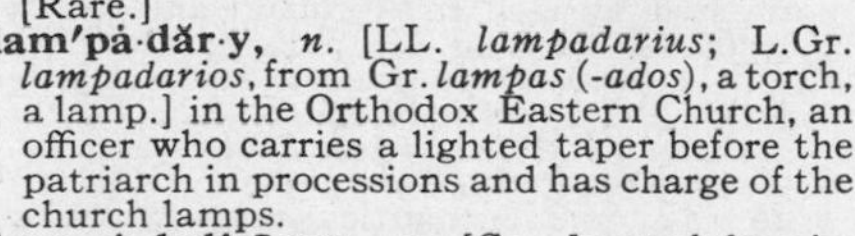

SAFETY LAMP

lamp, *v.t.* 1. to supply light to; to illuminate.

2. to look at. [Slang.]

lamp, *v.i.* to shine. [Rare.]

lam′pad, *n.* a lamp, torch, or candlestick. [Rare.]

lam′pȧ·dăr·y, *n.* [LL. *lampadarius*; L.Gr. *lampadarios*, from Gr. *lampas* (*-ados*), a torch, a lamp.] in the Orthodox Eastern Church, an officer who carries a lighted taper before the patriarch in processions and has charge of the church lamps.

lam·pȧ·ded′rō·my, *n.* [Gr. *lampadēdromia*; *lampas* (*-ados*), a torch, lamp, and *dromos*, race.] in ancient Greece, a torch race in honor of Prometheus, in one form of which each contestant carried a lighted torch, the victor being the one who reached the goal first, with his torch unextinguished.

lam pad′ē·phōre, *n.* [Gr. *lampadēphoros*, a torchbearer; *lampas* (*-ados*), a torch, lamp, and *pherein*, to carry.] in ancient Greece, one who ran as a contestant in a lampadedromy.

lam·pad·ē·phō′ri·ȧ, *n.* [Gr. *lampadēphoria*, the carrying of torches; from *lampas* (*-ados*), a torch, and *pherein*, to carry.] a lampadedromy.

lam·pad′ō·man·cy, *n.* [Gr. *lampas* (*-ados*), a lamp, and *manteia*, divination.] an ancient method of divination by means of the flame of a lamp or torch.

lam·pȧ·doph′ō·ros, lam′pȧ·dist, *n.* same as *lampadephore*.

lam′pȧ·drōme, *n.* same as *lampadedromy*.

lam′păs, *n.* [OFr., from *lampas*, the throat.] an inflammatory swelling of the fleshy lining of the roof of the mouth of a horse: also called *lampers*.

lam′păs, *n.* [Fr.] an ornamentally designed cloth; especially, a silk cloth like damask.

lamp′black, *n.* a fine soot consisting of particles of carbon, formed by the incomplete combustion of oil, pitch, or resinous substances: it is used in the manufacture of paints and inks.

lamp bŭrn′ēr, that part of a lamp within which the wick burns.

lamp chim′ney, a funnel of glass or other material used to enclose the flame of a lamp.

lam′pēr eel, 1. a lamprey.

2. the muttonfish or eelpout, *Zoarces anguillaris*.

lam′pērn, *n.* the river lamprey, *Petromyzon fluviatilis*.

lam′pērș, *n.* same as *lampas* (the disease).

lamp′flȳ, *n.* a firefly.

lamp′-hour (-our), *n.* in electricity, the amount of energy necessary to keep one light burning one hour.

lamp′ing, *a.* shining; bright; brilliant; sparkling.

lam′pi·ŏn, *n.* [Fr.; It. *lampione*, from *lampa*, a lamp; L. *lampas*, a lamp.] a small oil lamp, usually with a colored glass chimney, for decorative outdoor illumination.

lamp jack, a hood or covering placed over a lamp chimney or vent to protect the light from wind and rain.

lamp′less, *a.* having no lamp or light; hence, figuratively, lacking perception; not mentally bright.

lamp′light (-līt), *n.* light given off by a lamp.

lamp′light″ēr, *n.* 1. a person whose work is lighting and extinguishing gas street lamps.

2. a roll of paper, wood splinter, etc. used to light lamps.

3. the calico bass.

lam·pọon′, *n.* [Fr. *lampon*, from *lampons*, let us drink (refrain in a drinking song), from *lamper*, to drink.] a piece of strongly satirical writing, usually attacking or ridiculing someone.

Syn.—satire, invective, parody.

lam·pọon′, *v.t.*; lampooned, *pt.*, *pp.*; lampooning, *ppr.* to attack or ridicule by means of a lampoon.

lam·pọon′ēr, *n.* a lampoonist.

lam·pọon′ēr·y, *n.* 1. the writing of lampoons.

2. the satirical quality of lampoons.

lam·pọon′ist, *n.* a writer of lampoons.

lamp′pōst, *n.* a pillar or similar support for a street lamp.

lam′prel, *n.* a young lamprey. [Obs.]

lam′prey, *n.*; *pl.* **lam′preyș,** [ME. *lampreie*; OFr. *lamproie*; LL. *lampreda*, *lampetra*, a lamprey, lit., lickrock, said to be so called from their habit of clinging to rocks with their mouths; L. *lambere*, to lick, and *petra*, a rock.] any of a group of eellike water animals with a funnel-shaped, jawless, sucking mouth: also called *lamper eel*.

lam′prŏn, *n.* the lampern. [Obs.]

lam′prō·phȳre, *n.* [Gr. *lampros*, bright, and *porphyreos*, purple.] a fine-grained, dark-colored kind of rock occurring in dikes in strata of the Paleozoic Age.

lam″prō·phȳr′iç, *a.* of the nature of, composed of, or pertaining to lamprophyre.

Lamp′sȧ·nȧ, *n.* same as *Lapsana*.

lamp shell, a mollusk of the class *Brachiopoda*.

lamp′wick, *n.* 1. the wick of a lamp.

2. a cultivated evergreen shrub, *Phlomis lychnitis*, of the mint family, native to the southern part of Europe: so called because its leaves are said to have been used as lampwicks.

lam′py·rid, *a.* and *n.* same as *lampyrine*.

Lam·pyr′i·dae, *n.pl.* a family of coleopterous insects of the section *Malacodermi*.

lam′py·rīne (*or* rin), *a.* of or pertaining to the *Lampyridæ*.

lam′py·rīne, *n.* any of the *Lampyridæ*.

Lam′py·ris, *n.* [L. *lampyris*; Gr. *lampyris*, or *lampouris*, a glowworm, from *lampouros*, bright-tailed, having a shining tail; *lampein*, to shine, and *ouron*, tail.] the type genus of the *Lampyridæ*, including the common firefly, glowworm, etc.

lä′nȧ, *n.* a tough, close-grained wood obtained from *Genipa americana*, a South American and West Indian tree of the order *Rubiaceæ*. Genipap, the fruit, yields a pigment (called *lana dye*).

lä·nä′i, *n.* [Haw.] in Hawaii, a porch.

lan′ărk·īte, *n.* [after *Lanarkshire*, Scotland, where it is found in quantities.] a greenish-white mineral formed principally of lead sulfate (Pb_2SO_5).

lā′nāte, lā′nā·ted, *a.* [L. *lanatus*, woolly, from *lana*, wool.] woolly; covered with a hairy substance; as, a *lanated* leaf or stem.

Laṅ′çăs·tēr, *n.* the ruling family of England (1399–1461): founded by Henry IV.

Laṅ·çăs·tē′ri·ăn, *a.* relating to the monitorial educational system introduced into some English primary schools at the end of the eighteenth century by Joseph Lancaster: it included teaching by advanced pupils.

Laṅ·cas′tri·ăn, *a.* 1. of the English royal house of Lancaster.

2. from Lancaster or Lancashire.

Laṅ·cas′tri·ăn, *n.* 1. a member or follower of the house of Lancaster, especially in the Wars of the Roses.

2. a native or inhabitant of Lancaster or Lancashire.

lȧnce, *n.* [ME. *launce*; OFr. *lance*; L. *lancea*, a light spear, lance.]

1. a thrusting weapon consisting of a long wooden shaft with a sharp-pointed head of steel or other metal.
2. a soldier armed with a lance; a lancer.
3. any sharp instrument resembling a lance, as a fish spear.
4. a lancet used by surgeons.
5. an iron rod used to hold a founding core in place when a shell is being cast in the mold.

6. the rammer used with muzzle-loading guns. [Obs.]
7. a small paper case filled with a combustible colored substance, used to mark out the outlines of figures in large pyrotechnical displays.
8. a spear with which a whale is killed, after being harpooned.
to break a lance; see under *break*.
lànce, *v.t.*; lanced, *pt.*, *pp.*; lancing, *ppr.* 1. to attack or pierce with a lance, or with a sharp-pointed instrument.
2. to pierce or cut; to open with a lancet; as, to *lance* a vein or an abscess.
3. to throw in the manner of a lance; to hurl. [Rare.]
lànce, *n.* a launce.
lànce buck'et, a rest for the butt of a lance, attached to a cavalryman's stirrup leather.
lànce çor'pō·răl, [after obs. *lance-pesade*; OFr. *lance-pessade*; It. *lancia spezzata*, lit., broken lance.] in the British Army, a private acting temporarily as a corporal, without the extra pay.
lànce'fish, *n.* the English sand lance, a long, slender sea fish of the genus *Ammodytes*.
lànce'gāy, *n.* a kind of slender spear or javelin, tipped with iron. [Obs.]
lànce'-knīght (-nīt), *n.* a mercenary foot soldier; a lansquenet. [Obs.]
lànce'let, *n.* any of a group of small, fishlike sea animals of the genus *Amphioxus* (or *Branchiostoma*), closely related to the vertebrates.
Lån'ce·lot, *n.* [Fr.] in Arthurian legend, the bravest and most celebrated of the Knights of the Round Table: he was Guinevere's lover.
lànce'ly, *a.* suitable to a lance. [Obs.]
lan'cē·ō·lăr, *a.* lanceolate.
lan'cē·ō·lāte, lan'cē·ō·lā·ted, *a.* [L. *lanceola*, dim. of *lancea*, a lance.] shaped like a lance; narrow and gradually tapering toward the outer extremity; as, a *lanceolate* leaf.
lànce·pe·sāde', *n.* [Fr. *lancepessade*, a lance corporal; It. *lancia spezzata*, a broken lance or demilance.] a lance corporal. [Obs.]
lån'cēr, *n.* [Fr. *lancier*.] a soldier, especially a cavalry soldier, armed with a lance.

LANCEOLATE LEAF

lån'cērs, *n.pl.* [*construed as sing.*] [from *lancer*.]
1. a form of nineteenth-century square dance, or quadrille.
2. music for this.
Also spelled *lanciers*.
lànce ser'geănt (sär'), in the British Army, a corporal acting temporarily as a sergeant, without the extra pay.
lànce snāke, same as *fer-de-lance*.
lån'cet, *n.* [ME. *launcet*; OFr. *lancete*, dim. of *lance*, a lance.]
1. a surgical instrument, sharp-pointed and two-edged, used in operations, as in opening tumors, abscesses, etc.
2. in architecture, a lancet window or lancet arch.
lån'cet ärch, a narrow, sharply-pointed arch.
lån·cet·ed, *a.* having lancet arches or windows.
lån'cet fish, 1. a fish of the family *Teuthididæ* or *Acanthuridæ*: also called *barberfish*, *doctorfish*, and *surgeonfish*.
2. a large, voracious fish, of the *Alepidosauridæ*, having large teeth shaped like lances. It is found in deep seas.
lån'cet win'dōw, a high and narrow window pointed like a lancet and without tracery. Lancet windows are a marked characteristic of the early English style of Gothic architecture. They are often double or triple, and sometimes five are placed together.

LANCET WINDOW

lànce'wood, *n.* 1. a tough, elastic wood used for lance shafts, fishing rods, etc.
2. any of various tropical American trees yielding this wood.
lànch, *v.* and *n.* launch. [Dial.]
lån'ciērș, *n.pl.* [*construed as sing.*] lancers.
lan·cif'ēr·ous, *a.* [L. *lancea*, a lance, and *ferre*, to bear.] bearing a lance.
lan'ci·form, *a.* [L. *lancea*, a lance, and *forma*, form.] having the form of a lance.
lan'ci·nāte, *v.t.*; lancinated, *pt.*, *pp.*; lancinating, *ppr.* [L. *lancinatus*, pp. of *lancinare*, to tear.] to tear; to lacerate; especially figuratively, as, he was *lancinated* with pain.
lan·ci·nā'tion, *n.* a tearing; laceration; a piercing pain.
land, *n.* [ME. *land*; AS. *land*, land.]
1. the solid part of the earth's surface: distinguished from *sea*.
2. a specific part of the earth's surface; as, the *land* of the Seminoles.
3. (a) a country, region, etc.; (b) the inhabitants of such an area; a nation's people.
4. ground or soil in terms of its quality, location, etc.; as, rich *land*, high *land*.
5. ground considered as property; estate; as, *land* is a good investment.
6. [*pl.*] specific holdings in land.
7. rural regions as distinguished from urban regions; as, let us go back to the *land*.
8. that part of a grooved surface which is not indented, as any of the ridges between the grooves in the bore of a rifle.
9. the Lord: a euphemism, as in the phrase *for land's sake*!
10. in economics, natural resources.
Bad Lands; tracts of land in the western part of the United States, particularly in South Dakota, consisting of horizontal strata void of vegetation and broken by erosion into fantastic superficial forms. The name *mauvaises terres*, bad lands, originated with the French Jesuit explorers.
land ho; a cry used by sailors to signal the sight of land.
land (or *house*) *of bondage*; in Biblical history, Egypt; hence, any place of oppression or persecution.
Land of Nod; (a) in the Bible, the country to which Cain journeyed after slaying Abel: Gen. iv. 16; (b) sleep.
Land of Promise; (a) in the Bible, Canaan, promised by God to Abraham and his descendants: Gen. xv. 18, xvii. 8; hence, (b) [l- p-] a place where one expects to improve his lot. Also *Promised Land*.
Land of the Midnight Sun; Norway.
Land of the Rising Sun; Japan.
to make land; in nautical usage, to see or reach the shore.
to set the land; to see by the compass how the shore bears from the ship.
to shut in the land; to lose sight of the land by the intervention of a point or promontory.
land, *v.t.*; landed, *pt.*, *pp.*; landing, *ppr.* [ME. *landen*; AS. *lendan*, to land, from *land*, land.]
1. to put, or cause to go, on shore from a ship.
2. to bring into; as, this train will *land* you in Denver tomorrow morning.
3. to cause to enter or become confined in a particular place; as, this fight *landed* them both in jail.
4. to set (an aircraft) down on land or water.
5. to draw successfully onto land or into a boat; to catch; as, he *lands* the fish which she hooks.
6. to get, win, or secure; as, he *landed* a job. [Colloq.]
7. to deliver (a blow). [Colloq.]
land, *v.i.* 1. to leave a ship and go on shore; to disembark.
2. to come to a port or to shore: said of a ship.
3. to arrive at a specified place; to end up.
4. to alight or come to rest, as after a flight, jump, or fall.
-land, a combining form meaning; (a) *a kind* or *quality of land*, as in grass*land*, high*land*; (b) *a particular territory* or *country*, as in Eng*land*; (c) figuratively, *a place having a* (specified) *character* or *quality*, as in cloud*land*.
land ā'ġent, a real-estate agent.
lan'dåm·măn, *n.* [G., from *land*, land, country, and *ammann*, for *amtmann*, bailiff, magistrate.] a chief magistrate in some of the Swiss cantons.
lan'dau, *n.* [from *Landau*, German town where made.]
1. a four-wheeled covered carriage with the top in two sections, either of which can be lowered independently.
2. a former style of automobile with a somewhat similar top.
lan·dau·let', lan·dau·lette', *n.* 1. a small landau or one with only one seat.
2. same as *landau*, n. 2.
land bank, a bank that finances transactions in real estate.
land'blink, *n.* in the arctic regions, a peculiar atmospheric brightness noted on approaching snow-covered land: it is yellower than *iceblink*.
land bōat, a vehicle with wheels designed to be propelled by means of sails.
land breeze, a current of air blowing from the land toward the sea.
land chāin, a surveyor's chain.
land çrab, a crustacean whose habits are terrestrial, as distinguished from one whose habits are aquatic; particularly, one of the species of *Gecarcinus*.
land çroç'ō·dīle, a monitor lizard or sand monitor, *Psammosaurus arenarius*.
land'-damn (-dam), *v.t.* to make a hell on earth for (a person): the word occurs in Shakespeare's *Winter's Tale* and is so construed by some authorities.
lånd'drōst, *n.* [D., from *land*, land, and *drost*, an officer, magistrate.] in South Africa, a local official who acts as a chief magistrate.
lande, *n.* [Fr.] a heath; a heathy or sandy plain; specifically applied, in the plural, to extensive areas in France stretching from the mouth of the Garonne along the Bay of Biscay and inward toward Bordeaux.
land'ed, *a.* 1. having an estate in land; as, a *landed* gentleman.
2. consisting of real estate or land; as, *landed* security, *landed* property.
land'ēr, *n.* 1. one who lands or makes a landing.
2. one who lands or sets on land; especially, in mining, the one who works at the mouth of the pit to receive the kibble or bucket in which ore is brought to the surface.
land'fall, *n.* [*land* and *fall* (a happening).]
1. a sighting of land from a ship at sea.
2. the land sighted.
3. a landing by ship or airplane.
land fish, any one out of his natural element, as a fish would be out of water; any one acting contrary to his usual character.
land'flood (-flud), *n.* an inundation.
land fōrce, a military force serving on land, as distinguished from a naval force.
land'-grab"bēr, *n.* a person who gets possession of land unfairly or fraudulently.
land grant, a grant of land by the government, as for roads, railroads, or agricultural and industrial colleges.
land-grant, *a.* designating any of a number of colleges and universities originally given federal land on condition that they offer instruction in agriculture and the mechanical arts: they are now supported by the individual States with supplementary funds from the Federal government.
land'grāve, *n.* [G. *landgraf*; *land*, land, and *graf*, a count.]
1. in medieval Germany, a count having jurisdiction over a specified territory.
2. later, the title of any of certain German princes.
land·grā'vi·āte, *n.* the territory held by a landgrave, or his office, jurisdiction, or authority.
land'grȧ·vīne, *n.* the wife of a landgrave; also, any woman equal in rank to a landgrave.
land'hōld·ēr, *n.* a holder, owner, or proprietor of land.
land'hōld·ing, *a.* owning or occupying land.
land'hōld·ing, *n.* the act of owning or occupying land.
land īce, a field or floe of ice stretching along the land which lies between two headlands.
land'ing, *n.* [ME. *londyng*; AS. *lending*, a landing, verbal n. of *lendan*, to go on shore, land.]
1. the act of coming to shore or of going or putting ashore.
2. the place where a ship is unloaded or loaded.
3. a platform at the end of a flight of stairs.
4. the act of alighting, or coming to the ground, as after a flight, jump, or fall.
land'ing, *a.* of or pertaining to the act of settling down or coming to rest.
landing speed; the minimum speed at which an airplane will maintain horizontal flight and remain under control; the speed at which an airplane must fly in order to land safely.
land'ing chär'ġeș, charges to be paid on goods landed; also, fees for landing goods.
land'ing fiēld, a field provided with a smooth surface to enable airplanes to land and take off easily.
land'ing ġēar, the undercarriage of an aircraft, including wheels, pontoons, etc., for support on land or water.
land'ing net, a small, baglike net used by anglers for taking a hooked fish from the water.

land'ing plāce, a place for the landing of persons or goods from a vessel, or for alighting or resting.

land'ing stāġe, a platform or float attached to a wharf, for the landing of goods or passengers from vessels.

land'ing sũr·vey'ŏr, in Great Britain, an officer of the customs who appoints and superintends the landing waiters.

land'ing wāit'ẽr, a coastwaiter.

land'lā·dy, *n.*; *pl.* **land'lā·dieş,** 1. a woman who leases land, houses, etc. to others.
2. the mistress of an inn, a boardinghouse, or a rooming house.

land'lēap''ẽr, *n.* a landloper. [Obs.]

land leech, a terrestrial leech of the genus *Hæmodipsa*. It is found in great numbers in Ceylon, especially in the rainy season, is about an inch long and very slender, and is a great pest to man and beast.

Länd'ler (lent'lẽr), *n.* [G., from dial. *Landl*, upper Austria, dim. from *land*, land.]
1. an Austrian country dance in slow rhythm and triple time.
2. music for this.

land'less, *a.* [AS. *landleas*; *land*, land, and *-leás*, -less.] destitute of land; having no property in land.

land'locked (-lokt), *a.* 1. encompassed or nearly encompassed by land, as a bay or a country.
2. inhabiting landlocked waters; shut off from the sea: applied especially to fishes which naturally seek the sea after spawning; as, the *landlocked* salmon.

land'lō''pẽr, *n.* [D. *landlooper*; *land*, land, and *loopen*, to run.] a person who wanders about the country; a vagabond.

land'lō''ping, *a.* wandering about; vagrant; vagabond.

land'lọrd, *n.* [ME. *londelorde*; AS. *landhlaford*; *land*, land, and *hlaford*, lord.]
1. originally, the lord of a manor or of land; hence, a man who leases land, houses, etc. to others.
2. a man who keeps a rooming house, inn, etc.

land'lọrd·işm, *n.* the principles and practices of landlords collectively; especially, the economic system under which land is privately owned and rented to tenants.

land'lọrd·ry, *n.* the state of a landlord; also, landlords as a class.

land'lŏup''ẽr, *n.* same as *landloper*.

land'lub''bẽr, *n.* a landsman; one who is awkward or inexperienced on a ship; a raw seaman: used by sailors in ridicule or contempt.

land'măn, *n.*; *pl.* **land'men,** a man who lives, works, or serves on land: opposed to *seaman*.

land'märk, *n.* [AS. *landmearc*; *land*, land, and *mearc*, mark.]
1. a mark to designate the boundary of land; any mark or fixed object, as a marked tree, a stone, a ditch, or a heap of stones, by which the limits of a farm, a town, or other portion of territory may be known and preserved.
2. any prominent object marking a locality, oftentimes one of historical interest; any elevated object on land that serves as a guide.
3. an event considered as a high point or turning point of a period.

land meaş'ūre (mezh'ūr), 1. a system of square measure for finding the area of a piece of land.
2. any unit of measurement in such a system, as an acre, hectare, etc.

land mīne, an explosive charge hidden under the surface of the ground and discharged by the pressure of troops or vehicles upon it.

land of'fice, a government office that handles and records the sales and transfers of public lands.

land'-of·fice busi'ness (biz'nes), [with reference to Western U.S. land offices in the 19th c.] a booming business. [Colloq.]

Lan·dol'phi·ȧ, *n.* [after Capt. *Landolph* of the French navy.] a genus of climbing shrubs of the family *Apocynaceæ*.

land'ōwn''ẽr, *n.* one who owns land or real estate.

land'ōwn''ẽr·ship, *n.* the state of being an owner or proprietor of land.

land'ōwn''ing, *a.* of or pertaining to landowners; possessing land; as, the *landowning* interests.

land'ōwn''ing, *n.* the owning of land.

land pat'ent, a legal document granting ownership of a piece of public land.

land pīke, 1. the sauger, *Stizostedion canadense*.
2. an American batrachian having a naked skin, limbs, and a tail, as a menopome, hellbender, or axolotl.

land plas'tẽr, rock gypsum used as a fertilizer after being ground to a powder.

land'-poor', *a.* owning land, often much land, but poor or lacking ready money because of high taxes, etc.

land pow'ẽr, 1. military strength on land.
2. a nation having great military strength on land.

land rāil, 1. the European corn crake, *Crex pratensis*.
2. an Australian rail, *Hypotænidia philippensis*.

land'reeve, *n.* a subordinate officer on an extensive estate, who acts as an assistant to the steward.

Land'sat, *n.* [*land* and *sat*ellite.] any of a system of United States satellites for gathering and transmitting data about the earth's natural resources, topography, etc.

land'sçāpe, *n.* [17th-c. art borrowing from D. *landschap*; *land*, land, and *-schap*, -ship.]
1. a picture representing a section of natural, inland scenery, as of prairie, woodland, mountains, etc.
2. the branch of painting, photography, etc. dealing with such pictures.
3. an expanse of natural scenery seen by the eye in one view.

land'sçāpe, *v.t.* to improve by landscape gardening.

land'sçāpe, *v.i.* to engage in landscape gardening.

land'sçāpe är'çhi·teçt, a person skilled in landscape architecture.

land'sçāpe är'çhi·teç·tūre, the art of changing the natural scenery of a place so as to produce the most attractive or desirable effect.

land'sçāpe gär'den·ẽr, a person skilled in landscape gardening.

land'sçāpe gär'den·ing, the art or work of placing or arranging lawns, trees, bushes, etc. on a plot of ground to make it more attractive.

land'sçāp·ist, *n.* one who paints landscapes.

land sçrip, a certificate entitling the holder to the possession of a certain piece or pieces of the public land in the United States.

land shärk, 1. one who defrauds sailors on shore.
2. a speculator in land; a land-grabber.

land sīde, the flat side of a plow which is away from the furrow and presses against the unplowed land.

land'skip, *n.* landscape. [Obs.]

land'slāt·ẽr, *n.* a land crustacean; a sow bug.

land'slīde, *n.* 1. the sliding of a mass of loosened rocks or earth down a hillside or slope.
2. the mass of loosened material sliding down.
3. an overwhelming majority of votes for one candidate or party in an election.
4. any overwhelming victory.

land'slip, *n.* a landslide (senses 1 and 2). [Chiefly Brit.]

landş'măn, *n.*, *pl.* **landş'men,** 1. one who lives on the land: opposed to *seaman*.
2. in nautical usage, a new, inexperienced sailor.
3. a fellow countryman. [Rare.]

land snāil, any one of several species of snails that live on land.

land'spout, *n.* a variety of waterspout that occurs over land during a tornado.

land stā'tion, a radio transmitting station situated on land, established for communication with stations on airplanes, ships, etc.

land stew'ărd, one who is in charge of a landed estate.

Länds'ting, Länds'thing (läns'ting), *n.* [Dan., from *land* (poss. *lands*), land, and *thing*, parliament.] the upper house of the parliament or Rigsdag of the constitutional monarchy of Denmark, the lower house being known as the Folketing.

Länd'stụrm (länt'shtụrm), *n.* [G., lit., landstorm; orig. Swiss G., after Fr. *levée en masse*.]
1. in Germany and, later, other countries, a general levy in time of war of men under sixty not already in the armed services or in the reserve, generally made only in a great emergency or for home defense.
2. the force so called out or subject to such levy.

Länd'täg (länt'täkh), *n.* [G., lit., land diet or day; *land*, land, and *tag*, day, diet.] formerly, the legislative assembly of a German state, especially of Prussia.

land tax, a tax assessed on land and buildings.

land tọr'toise (-tis), any tortoise that exists almost entirely on land: also called *land turtle*.

land tũr'tle, a land tortoise.

land ũr'chin, a hedgehog.

land'wāit''ẽr, *n.* same as *coastwaiter*.

land'wărd, land'wărdş, *adv.* toward the land.

land'wărd, *a.* 1. lying or facing toward the land, or toward the interior, or away from the seacoast.
2. situated in or forming part of the country, as opposed to the town; rural. [Scot.]

land wär'rănt, in the United States, a security or title authorizing a person to take possession of a tract of public land.

Länd'wehr (länt'vār), *n.* [G., from *land*, country, and *wehr*, defense, from *wehren*, to defend, ward off.] in Germany and, later, in other countries, the military reserve of trained men.

land'whin (-hwin), *n.* in botany, the restharrow, *Ononis arvensis*.

land wind, a wind blowing seaward from the land.

lāne, *n.* [ME. *lane*, *lone*; AS. *lane*, a lane.]
1. a narrow way between hedges, walls, buildings, etc.; a narrow country road or city street.
2. any narrow way, as an opening in a crowd of people.
3. a path or course designated, for reasons of safety, for ships, aircraft, automobiles, etc.
4. a path or course marked off for each contestant in a race, etc.
5. in basketball, an area 12 feet wide extending from the free-throw line to just below the basket.
6. in bowling, same as *alley* (sense 6 a and b).

lāne, *a.* lone. [Scot.]

läng'lauf, *n.* [G.; *lang*, long, and *lauf*, a course, from *laufen*, to run.] in skiing, a cross-country run.

lang'läuf·er (läng'loi-fẽr), *n.* [G.; see *langlauf*.] in skiing, a participant in a cross-country run.

lañ'grāġe, lañ'gridge, *n.* [perh. for earlier *langrel*, after *cartridge*.] a type of irregularly shaped shot formerly used in naval battles to damage the enemy's rigging and sails.

lañ'grel, *n.* same as *langrage*.

Langş·dọrf'fi·ȧ, *n.* [Named after G. H. von *Langsdorff*, a German traveler and scientist.] a genus of herbs of the order *Balanophoreæ*, having only one species, *Langsdorffia hypogæa*, native to the tropics of South America.

lang''sȳne', *adv.* long ago; long since. [Scot.]

lang''sȳne', *n.* [Scot., from *lang*, long, and *syne*, since.] the past; the days of long ago: also written *lang syne*. [Scot.]

A friend, in short, of the happy *langsyne*.
—Lord Lytton.

lañ'guāġe (-gwāj), *n.* [ME. *langage*; OFr. *langage*; L. *lingua*, a tongue, language, lit., the tongue.]
1. (a) the expression or communication of thoughts and feelings by means of vocal sounds, and combinations of such sounds, to which meaning is attributed; human speech; (b) the ability to express or communicate by this means; (c) the vocal sounds so used, or the written symbols for them.
2. any means of expressing or communicating, as gestures, signs, animal sounds, etc.
3. all the vocal sounds, words, and the ways of combining them common to a particular nation, tribe, or other group; as, the English *language*.
4. (a) the particular form or manner of selecting and combining words characteristic of a person, group, etc.; form, style, or kind of expression in words; as, the *language* of poetry; (b) the particular words and phrases of a profession, group, etc.; as, the *language* of the army.
5. the study of language in general or of some particular language or languages; linguistics.

Syn.—speech, tongue, idiom, dialect.—*Speech* is the *language* of articulate sounds; *idiom* denotes the forms of construction peculiar to a *language*; *dialects* are varieties of expression which spring up in different parts of a country, or in different professions, etc.

lañ'guāġe, *v.t.*; languaged, *pt.*, *pp.*; languaging, *ppr.* to express in language; to put into words. [Archaic.]

lañ′guāġed, *a.* 1. having a language.
2. skilled in language or learned in several languages.

lañ′guāġe·less, *a.* without speech; without language.

langued (langd), *a.* [Fr. *langue,* a tongue.] in heraldry, having a tongue: applied to beasts and birds when bearing a tongue of a different tincture from themselves.

läñgue d′ọç (läñg dọk), a group of French dialects spoken in southern France in the Middle Ages and surviving in the Provençal language: from its word for *yes* being *oc,* a form of the Latin *hoc,* this.

läñgue d′ọ·ïl′ (dọ-ēl′), a group of French dialects spoken in most of central and northern France in the Middle Ages: from its word for *yes* being *oïl.* It is the Old French from which modern French is derived.

lȧn·guen′tẹ (-gwen′), *adv.* [It.] in music, in a languishing manner: a direction to the performer.

lañ·gues′cent, *a.* growing languid or tired. [Rare.]

lañ′guet (-gwet), *n.* [Fr., dim. of *langue;* L. *lingua,* tongue.] anything in the shape of a tongue; specifically, (a) on the hilt of a sword, a small hinged piece of metal, which overlaps the scabbard; (b) in zoology, one of the series of small tonguelike processes along the median line of the pharyngeal cavity or branchial sac of an ascidian; (c) in entomology, same as *languette,* sense 2(a); (d) in music, same as *languette,* sense 3.

lañ′guette (-gwet), *n.* [Fr., dim. of *langue,* tongue.]
1. a kind of hood, much worn by women in the seventeenth century.
2. in zoology, (a) the tonguelet or ligula of an insect; (b) the organ of a mollusk which secretes the byssus.
3. in music, (a) a key of a wind instrument; (b) the slip or tongue of a reed in a harmonium or reed organ.

lañ′guid (-gwid), *a.* [L. *languidus,* from *languere,* to be faint or listless.]
1. flagging; drooping; feeble; weak; indisposed to exertion; as, the body is *languid* after excessive action, which exhausts its powers.
2. slow; sluggish; as, *languid* motion.
3. dull; spiritless; without animation.
And fire their *languid* souls with Cato's virtue. —Addison.
Syn.—drooping, dull, exhausted, faint, weak.

lañ′guid·ly, *adv.* in a languid manner; weakly; slowly; listlessly.

lañ′guid·ness, *n.* the state or condition of being languid; slowness; listlessness; languor.

lañ′guish, *v.i.*; languished, *pt., pp.*; languishing, *ppr.* [ME. *languishen;* OFr. *languir;* L. *languescere,* to grow weak, incept. of *languere,* to be faint or weary, to languish.]
1. to lose vigor or vitality; to fail in health; become weak; droop.
2. to live under unfavorable or dispiriting conditions; to continue in a state of suffering; as, he *languished* in poverty many years.
3. to become slack or dull; to lose intensity.
4. to suffer with longing; to pine.
5. to put on an air of sentimental tenderness or wistful melancholy.

lañ′guish, *v.t.* to cause to droop or pine. [Obs.]

lañ′guish, *n.* the act of languishing; also, a soft and tender look or appearance.

lañ′guish·ẽr, *n.* one who languishes or pines.

lañ′guish·ing, *a.* 1. becoming or being feeble; losing strength; pining; withering; fading.
2. tender; sentimental; wistfully amorous.

lañ′guish·ing·ly, *adv.* in a languishing manner.

lañ′guish·ment, *n.* 1. a languishing.
2. the state of being weak or drooping.
3. a languishing look, expression, or feeling.

lañ′guŏr (-gẽr *or* -gwẽr), *n.* [ME. *langour;* OFr. *langueur;* L. *languor,* faintness, feebleness, from *languore,* to be faint or weary.]
1. a lack of vigor or vitality; weakness.
2. a lack of interest or spirit; listlessness; indifference.
3. tenderness of mood or feeling.
4. a lack of or lull in activity; sluggishness; dullness.
5. heaviness; oppressiveness; stillness: used with reference to the atmosphere.
Syn.—feebleness, lethargy, faintness, weariness, dullness, heaviness, lassitude, listlessness.

lañ′guŏr, *v.i.* to languish. [Obs.]

lañ′guŏr·ous, *a.* characterized by or suggesting languor; inducing or tending to induce languor; seductive; as, *languorous* eyes.

lȧn·gŭr′, *n.* see *entellus.*

lan′i-, [from L. *lana,* wool.] a combining form meaning *wool.*

lan′iȧrd (-yẽrd), *n.* same as *lanyard.*

lā″ni·ar′i·fọrm, *a.* [L. *laniare,* to tear, rend, and *forma,* shape.] shaped like the laniaries or canine teeth of the *Carnivora.*

lā′ni·ăr·y, *n.* a canine tooth.

lā′ni·ăr·y, *a.* [L. *laniarius,* pertaining to a butcher, from *lanius,* a butcher, from *laniare,* to tear, rend.] lacerating or tearing: applied especially to the canine teeth, when fully developed.

lā′ni·āte, *v.t.* [L. *laniatus,* pp. of *laniare,* to tear, rend.] to tear in pieces. [Rare.]

lān′i·ẽr, *n.* same as *lanner.*

lȧ·nif′ẽr·ous, *a.* [L. *lanifer; lana,* wool, and *ferre,* to bear.] bearing or producing wool or fine hairs resembling wool; fleecy.

lȧ·nig′ẽr·ous, *a.* [L. *laniger; lana,* wool, and *gerere,* to produce.] laniferous.

Lȧ·nī′i·dae, *n.pl.* [*lanius* and *-idæ.*] a family of insessorial or perching birds, in which the bill is abruptly hooked at the end; the shrikes. They are insectivorous, but some prey on small birds and mammals.

Lā″ni·ī′nae, *n.pl.* [*lanius* and *-inæ.*] a subfamily of the *Laniidæ,* having the bill short and the terminal hook or tooth very prominent.

lā′ni·oid, *a.* of or pertaining to the *Laniidæ.*

lan′i·tal, *n.* [It. *lana,* wool, and *Italia,* Italy.] a synthetic wool fabric made from casein.

Lā′ni·us, *n.* [L. *lanius,* a butcher.] the typical genus of the *Laniidæ;* the shrikes, or butcherbirds.

lañk, *a.*; *comp.* lanker; *superl.* lankest, [ME. *lank;* AS. *hlanc,* lank, slim, flexible.]
1. slim; lean; long and slender; as, his *lank* figure.
2. loose or lax and easily yielding to pressure; not distended; not stiff or firm by distention; not plump; as, a *lank* purse.
3. straight, flat, and long; as, *lank* hair.
4. languid; drooping. [Obs.]

lañk, *v.t.* and *v.i.* to make or become lank or lean. [Obs.]

lañk′i·ly, *adv.* in a lanky form.

lañk′i·ness, *n.* a lanky quality or state.

lañk′ly, *adv.* in a lank manner.

lañk′ness, *n.* the state or quality of being lank; leanness.

lañk′y, *a.*; *comp.* lankier; *superl.* lankiest, awkwardly tall and lean or long and slender.

lan′nẽr, *n.* [OFr. *lanier,* a kind of falcon or hawk, from L. *laniarius,* of or pertaining to a butcher, from *lanius,* a butcher.] a species of falcon or hawk, *Falco laniarius,* especially the female of the species, found in the south and east of Europe.

lan′nẽr·et, *n.* [dim. of *lanner.*] the male of the lanner: it is smaller than the female.

lan′ō·lin, *n.* [L. *lana,* wool, and *oleum,* oil.] a fatty substance obtained from wool and used as a base for ointments, cosmetics, etc.

lan′ō·line, *n.* lanolin.

lā′nōse, *a.* [L. *lanosus,* from *lana,* wool.] resembling wool; woolly.

lan′sȧ, lan′seh, *n.* [E. Ind.] the fruit of *Lansium domesticum.*

lanș′downe (-doun), *n.* a finely woven silk and wool dress fabric.

Lan′si·um, *n.* [*lansa* or *lanseh,* the E. Ind. name.] a genus of trees belonging to the family *Meliaceæ,* the most important species of which is *Lansium domesticum,* native to India, the large yellowish fruit of which is highly esteemed, and eaten either fresh or prepared in various ways.

lans′que·net (-ke-), *n.* [Fr., from G. *landsknecht,* a foot soldier; *land,* land, and *knecht,* a boy, servant.]
1. a German mercenary foot soldier of the sixteenth and seventeeth centuries.
2. a game of cards of German origin: also called *lambskinnet.*

lant, *n.* [AS. *hland,* urine.] urine, especially when stale, used as a detergent in scouring wool. [Rare.]

lant, *n.* same as *lanterloo.*

lant, *n.* the sand eel.

Lan·tā′nȧ, *n.* [Mod. L., viburnum.]
1. a genus of shrubby plants belonging to the family *Verbenaceæ,* growing in tropical and subtropical America.
2. [l—]any plant belonging to this genus.

lan′tẽr·lọọ, *n.* a game at cards, now called *loo,* sometimes *lant.* [Obs.]

lan′tẽrn, *n.* [ME. *lanterne;* Fr. *lanterne;* L. *lanterna;* Gr. *lamptēr,* a lantern, a light, a stand or grate for lighting, from *lampein,* to shine.]
1. a transparent case enclosing a light and protecting it from wind and rain, sometimes portable and sometimes fixed.

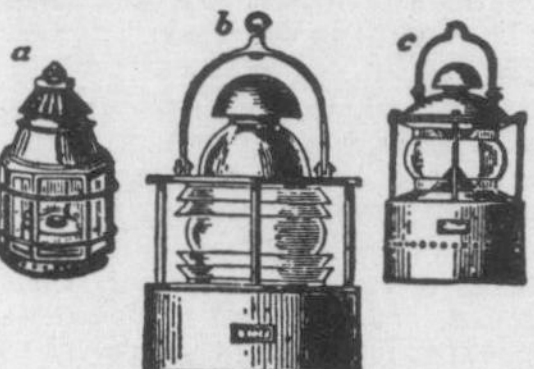

SHIP'S LANTERNS
a, octagon; *b,* masthead; *c,* signal

2. in architecture, an open structure on the roof of a building or in the upper part of a tower or the like, to admit light and air.
3. the upper part of a lighthouse, where the light is shown.
4. in machinery, same as *lantern wheel.*
5. in founding, a short core with holes bored in it, used in making hollow castings.
6. a magic lantern.
Chinese lantern; a lantern made of thin paper, usually variously colored, much used in illuminations.
dark lantern; a lantern with a single opening, which may be closed so as to conceal the light.
lantern of Aristotle or *Aristotle's lantern;* the oral skeleton and soft parts of the sea urchin, the most highly complex dentary structure to be found in the *Echinoidea.* It has twenty important parts, including five teeth, five alveoli, five rotulae, and five radii.
magic lantern; see under *magic.*

lan′tẽrn, *v.t.*; lanterned, *pt., pp.*; lanterning, *ppr.* 1. to furnish or equip with a lantern or light; as, to *lantern* a lighthouse.
2. to kill by hanging to a lamppost, as was done during the French Revolution.

lan′tẽrn car′ri·ẽr, same as *lantern fly.*

lan′tẽrn fish, the smooth sole. [Brit. Dial.]

lan′tẽrn flȳ, any of a group of large, brightly colored South American insects having a long head with a hollow part formerly supposed to give off light.

LANTERN FLY
(Fulgora lanternaria)

lan′tẽrn jack, the ignis fatuus.

lan′tẽrn jaw, [from resemblance to the early lantern with long sides of thin, concave horn.]
1. a projecting lower jaw.
2. [*pl.*] long, thin jaws that give the face a lean appearance.

lan′tẽrn-jawed″, *a.* having lantern jaws or a long, thin visage.

lan′tẽrn pin′iŏn (-yun), see *lantern wheel.*

lan′tẽrn shell, the translucent shell of any bivalve of the genus *Anatina.*

lan′tẽrn slīde, a photographic slide for projection, as, originally, by a magic lantern.

lan′tẽrn wheel (hwēl), an old type of gearwheel consisting of two circular discs connected by projecting bars.

LANTERN WHEEL

lan′thȧ·nīte, *n.* [*lanthanum* and *-ite.*] in mineralogy, a rare basic carbonate of lanthanum, $La_2(CO_3)_3 \cdot 9H_2O$, found in white, grayish-white, or pink, tabular crystals.

lan′thȧ·num, *n.* [Gr. *lanthanein,* to be concealed.] a silvery, lustrous metallic chemical element of the rare-earth group: symbol, La; atomic weight, 138.92; atomic number, 57.

lan′thō·pīne, *n.* [Gr. *lanthanein,* to be concealed, and *opion,* poppy juice.] a white crystalline alkaloid, $C_{20}H_{25}NO_4$, found in opium.

lant′hōrn, *n.* [altered from *lantern* after *horn,* material once used for the sides.] a lantern. [Archaic.]

lȧ·nū′ġi·nous, lȧ·nū′ġi·nōse, *a.* [L. *lanuginosus,* from *lanugo (-inis),* down, from *lana,* wool.] downy; covered with down, or fine, soft hair.

lȧ·nū′gō, *n.* [L., down, from *lana,* wool.] in

anatomy, the coat of delicate, downy hairs with which the human fetus is covered.

lan'yärd, lan'iärd, *n.* [ME. *lanyer*; Fr. *lanière*; OFr. *lasniere*, from *lasne*, noose; altered after *yard* (spar).]

1. a short rope or cord used on board ship for holding or fastening something.

2. a cord used by sailors to hang a knife around their necks.

3. a cord with an attached hood, used in firing certain types of cannon.

Lā·oc'o·ön (lā-ok'ō-on), *n.* [L., from Gr. *Laokoōn*, Laocoön.]

1. in Greek legend, a priest of Troy who, with his two sons, was destroyed by two huge sea serpents after he had warned the Trojans against the wooden horse.

2. a famous sculpture in the Vatican, representing Laocoön and his sons in the coils of the serpents.

THE GROUP OF THE LAOCOÖN

lā·od·i·cē'ăn, *a.* 1. of or pertaining to Laodicea, an ancient city of Phrygia Major, or to its inhabitants.

2. like the early Christians of Laodicea; lukewarm in religion.

Lā·od·i·cē'ăn, *n.* [L. *Laodicea*; Gr. *Laodikei*, Laodicea.]

1. a native or inhabitant of Laodicea.

2. one who resembles the early Christians of Laodicea; a lukewarm, unenthusiastic Christian.

Lā·om'ē·don, *n.* in Greek legend, father of Priam and founder of Troy.

lap, *n.* [ME. *lappe*; AS. *læppa*, the edge or flap of a garment, a fold.]

1. the loose lower part of a garment, which may be doubled or folded over; a skirt of a coat or gown.

2. the front part of the skirt when held up to form a hollow place in which things can be carried.

3. (a) the front part from the waist to the knees of a person in a sitting position; (b) the part of the clothing covering this.

4. anything hollow like a lap; as, the *lap* of a green valley.

5. that in which a person or thing rests or is cared for, sheltered, or coddled.

6. a part extending over another part; an overlapping part.

7. (a) such extension; overlapping; (b) amount or place of this.

8. a turn or loop, as of a rope around a post.

9. a revolving disk for cutting and polishing glass, gems, etc.

10. one complete circuit of a race track, in a race consisting of more than one.

11. a lapping.

in the lap of luxury; surrounded by luxury.

in the lap of the gods; beyond human control or power.

lap, *v.t.*; lapped, *pt.*, *pp.*; lapping, *ppr.* [ME. *lappen*.]

1. to fold (*over* or *on*).

2. to wrap; to enfold.

3. to hold in or as in the lap; to envelop; as, he was *lapped* in luxury.

4. to place partly upon something else; as, you must *lap* the second board over the first.

5. to lie partly upon; as, the second board *laps* the first.

6. to cut or polish with a lap, as glass or gems.

7. to get a lap ahead of (an opponent) in a race.

lap, *v.i.* 1. to be folded; as, rough edges must *lap* under.

2. to lie partly upon something or upon one another; to overlap.

3. to project beyond something in space, or extend beyond something in time (with *over*).

lap, *v.i.* and *v.t.*; lapped, *pt.*, *pp.*; lapping, *ppr.* [ME. *lappen*; AS. *lapian*, to lick, lap.]

1. to take up (liquid) with the tongue in the manner of a dog.

2. to move or strike gently with a light, splashing sound such as a dog makes in lapping: said of waves, etc.

Waters *lapping* on the crag.—Tennyson.

to lap up; (a) to take up (liquid or liquid food) by lapping; (b) [Colloq.] to eat or drink greedily; hence, to take in eagerly.

lap, *n.* 1. a lapping.

2. the sound of lapping.

3. something that is, or is intended to be, lapped up.

Lap''ā·ġē'ri·ȧ, *n.* [after Josephine de *la Pagerie*, the Empress Josephine.] a genus of Chilean plants of the lily family.

lap'ȧ·rō-, [from Gr. *lapara*, the flank.] a combining form meaning *the flank, the abdominal wall*, as in *laparo*tomy: also, before a vowel, *lapar-*.

lap'ȧ·rō·cēle, *n.* [Gr. *lapara*, the loins, and *kēlē*, tumor.] a lumbar hernia.

lap'ȧ·rō·sçōpe'', *n.* [*laparo-* and *-scope.*] an instrument introduced surgically into the abdomen for examining the pelvic organs: used in diagnosis, female sterilization, etc.

lap''ȧ·rō·sçop'iç, *a.* pertaining to or obtained by laparoscopy.

lap·ȧ·ros'çō·py, *n.* examination of the pelvic organs by means of a laparoscope.

lap·a·rot'ō·my, *n.* [Gr. *lapara*, the loins, and *tomē*, a cutting.] a surgical incision into the cavity of the abdomen.

lap'bōard, *n.* a flat board, usually shaped so as to fit the body while held on the lap, used by tailors, cobblers, etc., in place of a table.

lap dis·ṣolve', in motion pictures, a dissolving view in which a new scene is blended in with a scene being faded out, as by lapping two exposures on one film.

lap dog, any pet dog small enough to be held in the lap.

la·pel', *n.* that part of a coat, jacket, etc. which is made to lap or fold over on the chest, forming a continuation of the collar.

la·pelled', *a.* furnished with lapels.

LAPELS

lap'ful, *n.* as much as the lap can contain.

lap'i·cīde, *n.* a stonecutter.

lap''i·dā'ri·ăn, *a.* same as *lapidary*.

lap'i·dȧ·rist, *n.* an expert in precious stones and in the art of cutting them.

lap'i·dãr·y, *n.*; *pl.* **lap'i·dãr·ieṣ,** [L. *lapidarius*, of or belonging to stones, from *lapis* (*-idis*), a stone.]

1. a workman who cuts, polishes, and engraves precious stones.

2. an expert in precious stones; a collector of or dealer in gems.

lap'i·dãr·y, *a.* 1. of or pertaining to a stone or stones.

2. of or pertaining to the art of cutting and engraving precious stones.

3. inscribed upon stone; of or pertaining to inscriptions on stone; monumental; as, *lapidary* lettering.

lap'i·dāte, *v.t.*; lapidated, *pt.*, *pp.*; lapidating, *ppr.* [from L. *lapidatus*, pp. of *lapidare*, to stone, from *lapis*, a stone.]

1. to throw stones at.

2. to stone to death.

lap·i·dā'tion, *n.* [L. *lapidatio* (*-onis*), from *lapidare*, to stone.] a lapidating.

lȧ·pid'ē·ous, *a.* stony; of the nature of stone; as, *lapideous* matter.

lap·i·des'cent, *a.* [L. *lapidescens* (*-entis*), ppr. of *lapidescere*, to become stone, from *lapis* (*-idis*), a stone.]

1. turning to stone. [Obs.]

2. petrifying. [Obs.]

lap''i·dif'iç, lap''i·dif'i·çăl, *a.* [L. *lapis* (-idis), a stone, and *facere*, to make.] forming or converting into stone.

lȧ·pid''i·fi·çā'tion, *n.* petrifaction; a lapidifying or being lapidified.

lȧ·pid'i·fȳ, *v.t.*; lapidified, *pt.*, *pp.*; lapidifying, *ppr.* [L. *lapis* (*-idis*), a stone, and *facere*, to make.] to form into stone; to petrify.

lȧ·pid'i·fȳ, *v.i.* to turn into stone; to become stone; to petrify.

lap'i·dist, *n.* a connoisseur of gems or lapidary work; a lapidary. [Rare.]

lȧ·pil'li·form, *a.* [L. *lapillus*, a small stone, and *forma*, form.] formed like small stones.

lȧ·pil'lus, *n.*; *pl.* **lȧ·pil'lī,** [L., dim. of *lapis* (*-idis*), a stone.]

1. a small, glassy igneous rock ejected from a volcano, varying in size from that of a pea to that of a walnut.

2. in anatomy, an otolith.

lap'in, *n.* [Fr. *lapin*, a rabbit.] rabbit fur, generally dyed in imitation of more valuable skins.

lā'pis, *n.*; *pl.* **lap'i·dēṣ,** [L., a stone.] a stone: used chiefly in Latin phrases.

lapis causticus; caustic potash.

lapis infernalis; fused nitrate of silver; lunar caustic.

lapis lazuli; (a) an azure-blue, opaque, semiprecious stone, a mixture of various minerals; (b) its color.

lapis ollaris; soapstone, potstone, or talc; a hydrated silicate of magnesia.

Lap'ith, *n.*; *pl.* **Lap'i·thae, Lap'iths,** one of the Lapithae.

Lap'i·thae, *n.pl.* [L., from Gr. *Lapithai*, the Lapithae.] In Greek mythology, a race of warriors, who inhabited Thessaly, and were said to be descended from Lapithes, a son of Apollo.

lap'-joint, *v.t.* to join by a lap joint.

lap joint, a joint in which the edge of one of the component parts overlaps the other.

lap'-joint''ed, *a.* having lap joints.

Lap'land·ẽr, *n.* a Lapp.

Lap'land·ish, *a.* pertaining to Lapland or the Laplanders.

lap'ling, *n.* one who indulges in ease and sensual delights. [Obs.]

Lapp, *n.* [Sw. *Lapp*, a Lapp.]

1. a member of a people living in Lapland, having short stature, short, broad heads, high cheekbones, flat noses, and other Mongoloid characteristics: before 1900 they were completely nomadic.

2. their Finno-Ugric language.

lap·pā'ceous, *a.* [L. *lappaceus*, from *lappa*, a bur.] in botany, of, pertaining to, or resembling a bur.

lap'pẽr, *n.* a person or animal that laps liquids or food.

lap'pẽr, *n.* one who laps, wraps, folds, or uses a lap.

lap'pet, *n.* [dim. of *lap* (a fold).]

1. a small, loose flap or fold of a garment.

2. any fleshy or membranous part hanging loosely or in a fold, as the dewlap of a cow, the lobe of the ear, etc.

3. any of certain bombycid moths, as *Lasiocampa quercifolia* or *Lasiocampa ilicifolia*.

lap'pet, *v.t.* to provide with a lappet.

lap'pet moth, same as *lappet*, sense 3.

Lap'piç, *a.* same as *Lappish*.

lap'ping, *n.* 1. the act of wrapping or folding.

2. that which is lapped; a flap or pendant.

3. a kind of blanket or wrapper used on a calico printing machine.

4. the act or process of forming a lap joint or of placing the edge of one material above that of another.

5. in textile manufacturing, the act or process of forming a fleecy fibrous material for a carding machine.

Lap'pish, *a.* of or pertaining to Lapland or the Lapps.

Lap·pō'ni·ăn, *a.* same as *Lappish*.

lap rōbe, a heavy blanket, fur covering, etc. laid over the lap and knees for warmth when riding in an automobile, watching outdoor sports, etc.

laps'ȧ·ble, *a.* capable of lapsing, falling, or relapsing; liable to lapse: also spelled *lapsible*.

Lap'sȧ·nȧ, *n.* [L. *lapsana*; Gr. *lapsanē*, the charlock, or nipplewort.] a genus of European plants of the order *Compositæ*, including the species *Lapsana communis*, the nipplewort.

lapse, *n.* [L. *lapsus*, a falling, pp. of *labi*, to slip, fall.]

1. a slip of the tongue, pen, or memory; a small error; a fault.

2. a falling away from a moral standard; a moral slip.

3. a falling or slipping into a lower condition.

4. a falling into ruin.

5. a gliding or passing away, as of time or of anything continuously flowing.

6. in law, (a) the termination or forfeiture

of a right or privilege through disuse or through failure to meet stated obligations within a stated time; (b) the failure of a bequest to take effect because of the death of the person who was intended to receive it.

lapse, *v.i.*; lapsed (lapst), *pt., pp.*; lapsing, *ppr.* [L. *lapsare*, to slip, stumble, freq. of *labi*, to slip, fall.]

1. to slip or fall; especially, to slip into a specified state; as, he *lapsed* into unconsciousness.

2. to slip or deviate from virtue; to fall back into former unregenerate ways.

3. to pass away; to elapse.

4. to become forfeit or void because of the holder's failure to pay his premium at the stipulated time: said of an insurance policy.

5. in law, to pass to another proprietor by reason of negligence or death.

lapse, *v.t.* 1. to let slip. [Obs.]

2. to surprise in a fault; to apprehend; to overtake. [Obs.]

lapse rāte, the rate of decrease of atmospheric temperature with increase of altitude.

Lap′sī, *n.pl.* [L., masc. pl. of *lapsus*, pp. of *labi*, to fall.] among the early Christians, those who renounced their faith when persecuted.

laps′i·ble, *a.* same as *lapsable.*

lap′sīd″ed, *a.* same as *lopsided.*

lap′stōne, *n.* a stone on which shoemakers beat leather, held on the knees.

lap′strāke, lap′strēak, *a.* constructed of boards overlapping one another at the edges; clinker-built: said of a boat.

lap′strāke, lap′strēak, *n.* a clinker-built boat.

lap′sus, *n.* [L.] a slip; an error; a lapse.

lap′sus lin̄′guae (-gwē), [L.] a slip of the tongue.

lap′sus mē·mō′ri·ae, [L.] a slip of the memory.

Lȧ·pū′tȧ, *n.* in Swift's *Gulliver's Travels*, a flying island inhabited by impractical, visionary philosophers, who do various absurd things.

Lȧ·pū′tăn, *a.* pertaining to Laputa in Swift's *Gulliver's Travels*; hence, chimerical; ridiculous.

lap′wing, *n.* [ME. *lapwing*, for *lapwink*; AS. *hleapewince*, the lapwing; *hleapan*, to leap, and *wince*, probably from *wincan*, to totter.] any of a genus of Old World crested birds belonging to the family *Charadriidæ* (plovers), noted for its irregular, wavering flight, and characterized by having a hind toe, and nasal grooves along two-thirds of the beak: also called *pewit*.

LAPWING
(*Vanellus cristatus*)

lap′wŏrk, *n.* metalwork in which one part laps over another.

laq′uay (lak′ē), *n.* a lackey. [Obs.]

laq′uē·ăr, *n.*; *pl.* **laq′uē·ăr′i·ȧ**, [L.] in architecture, a ceiling divided into sunken compartments with beams or spaces between.

laq′uē·ăr·y, *a.* [L. *laqueus*, a noose.] using a noose in combat. [Obs.]

lär, *n.* singular of *lares.*

lȧ·rā′ri·um, *n.*; *pl.* **lȧ·rā′ri·ȧ**, [L.] in ancient Rome, the shrine of the lares, or household gods.

lär′bōard, *n.* [ME. *laddebord*, the larboard, lit., prob. the lading side; AS. *hlcdan*, to lade, and *bord*, side.] the left-hand side of a ship when facing toward the bow: *port* and *left-rudder* have been substituted for *larboard* to avoid possible confusion in sound with *starboard.*

lär′bōard, *a.* and *adv.* situated on or relating to the left-hand side of a ship; port; as, the *larboard* anchor; *port* and *left-rudder* have been substituted for *larboard* to avoid possible confusion in sound with *starboard.*

lär′ce·nēr, lär′ce·nist, *n.* one guilty of larceny.

lär′ce·nous, *a.* 1. of, or having the quality of, larceny.

2. guilty of larceny.

lär′ce·ny, *n.*; *pl.* **lär′ce·nieș**, [OFr. *larrecin*; L. *latrocinium*, robbery, from *latrocinari*, to rob, plunder, from *latro* (*-onis*), a freebooter, mercenary soldier, hired servant, robber.] in law, theft; the act of taking and carrying away the goods or personal property of another without his consent and with the intention of depriving him of it.

grand larceny; in law, (a) theft in which the property stolen has a value equaling or exceeding a certain amount fixed by law: the amount varies from State to State but is usually between $25 and $50: distinguished from *petit* (or *petty*) *larceny*; (b) in some States, the theft of property of any value directly from the person of the victim, but without the use of force.

petit (or *petty*) *larceny*; theft involving a sum smaller than that which constitutes grand larceny.

lärch, *n.* [OFr. *larege, larice*; L. *larix* (*-icis*); Gr. *larix* (*-ikos*), the larch.]

1. any tree of the genus *Larix*, as *Larix americana*, the black larch, or tamarack, of North America, a conifer whose deciduous needles are borne in clusters or fascicles upon drooping branches. *Larix europæa*, the European larch, has bark that is used medicinally. *Larix occidentalis* is the western larch of Washington and Oregon.

2. the wood of any of these trees.

lärch′en, *a.* of or relating to the larch.

lärd, *n.* [ME. *larde*; OFr. *lard*, bacon, pig's fat, the blubber of whales, from L. *lardum*, the fat of bacon.]

1. the fat of hogs, after being melted and separated from the flesh; especially, the inner abdominal fat.

2. bacon; the flesh of hogs. [Obs.]

leaf lard; lard rendered from the internal layers or leaves of fat surrounding a hog's kidneys, etc.; also, the leaves before rendering.

lärd, *v.t.* [Fr. *larder*, from *lard*, bacon.]

1. to stuff (meat or poultry) with bacon or pork before cooking; to place strips of pork or bacon in.

2. to mix with something by way of improvement; to garnish; to enrich.

3. to grease; to baste; to cover with lard or other fat.

4. to fatten; to enrich. [Obs.]

lär·dā′cē·in, *n.* [*lardaceous* and *-in.*] an albuminoid product occurring in certain tissues affected with amyloid degeneration, as in infiltrations of the pancreas, spleen, liver, etc.

lär·dā′ceous, *a.* of the nature of lard or lardacein.

lärd′ēr, *n.* [ME. *larder*; OFr. *lardier*, a larder, a tub for bacon; LL. *lardarium*, a room for meats, from L. *lardum*, the fat of bacon, lard.]

1. a room where meat and other articles of food are kept; a pantry.

2. a household's supply of food; provisions.

lärd′ēr bee′tle, the bacon beetle.

lärd′ēr·ēr, *n.* one who has charge of a larder.

lärd′ēr·y, *n.* a larder. [Obs.]

lärd oil, an oil derived from lard used as a lubricant and lighting fluid

lär′dŏn, lär·dọon′, *n.* [Fr. *lardon*, from *lard*, bacon, pig's fat.] a strip of bacon or pork used in larding.

lärd′ry, *n.* a larder. [Obs.]

lärd′y, *a.*; *comp.* lardier; *superl.* lardiest. 1. covered with or containing lard.

2. like lard.

lär′ēș, *n.pl.*; *sing.* **lär**, [L., pl. of *lar*, household spirit.] in ancient Rome, guardian spirits; especially, the deified spirits of ancestors, who watched over and protected the households of their descendants.

lär′ēș and pē·nā′tēș, 1. the household gods of the ancient Romans.

2. the treasured belongings of a family or household.

lär″gä·men′tẹ, *adv.* [It., from *largo*, large.] in music, with a broad, slow, full movement.

lär·găn′dō, *a.* and *adv.* [It.] in music, gradually slower and louder: a direction to the performer.

lärġe, *a.* [OFr. *large*; L. *largus*, abundant, copious, plentiful, large.]

1. of more than the average size, extent, range, dimensions, bulk, capacity, quantity, number, etc., relative to other things of the same kind.

2. big; great; specifically, (a) taking up much space; bulky; (b) enclosing much space; spacious; as, a *large* office; (c) of great extent or amount; as, a *large* sum of money.

3. operating on a big scale; as, a *large* manufacturer.

4. embracing many objects; far-reaching; many-sided; comprehensive; as, he has *large* views on the subject.

5. in nautical usage, blowing in a favorable direction: said of the wind.

6. free; unrestrained; licentious; boisterous. [Obs.]

7. free; unencumbered. [Obs.]

8. lavish; prodigal. [Archaic or Rare.]

lärġe, *n.* 1. liberty: now only in *at large.*

2. in music, a note equal to four breves. [Obs.]

at large; (a) without restraint or confinement; not in jail; (b) diffusely; fully; to a full extent; (c) in general; taken altogether; (d) not confined to a particular district; for an entire State; as, a congressman *at large.*

Syn.—big, great, bulky, huge, extensive, wide, spacious, colossal, gigantic, grand, immense, massive, vast, capacious, comprehensive, ample, abundant, plentiful, populous, copious, diffuse, liberal.

lärġe, *adv.* 1. in a large way; so as to be large; as, do not write so *large.*

2. in nautical usage, with a favorable wind.

3. freely; fully. [Obs.]

lärġe′-ā′çred (-kẽrd), *a.* having much land.

lärġe′-hand′ed, *a.* 1. having large hands.

2. rapacious; grasping; greedy.

3. generous; liberal; freehanded.

lärġe′heärt′ed, *a.* having a large heart or liberal disposition; generous; liberal; magnanimous.

lärġe″heärt′ed·ness, *n.* the quality of being largehearted; liberality.

lärġe in·tes′tine, the relatively large part of the intestines between the small intestine and the anus, including the caecum, colon, and rectum.

lärġe′ly, *adv.* 1. much; in great amounts.

2. for the most part; mainly.

lärġe′-mīnd′ed, *a.* liberal in one's views; tolerant; broad-minded.

lärġe′mouth, *n.* any of a variety of fresh-water black bass with a large mouth.

lärġe′ness, *n.* the quality or condition of being large; greatness; amplitude; extensiveness; comprehensiveness.

lärġe′-sçāle′, *a.* 1. drawn to a large scale: said of a map, etc.

2. of wide scope; over a large area; extensive; as, *large-scale* business operations.

lär′ġess, *n.* [OFr. *largesse*, a bounty, from L. *largiri*, to give bountifully, from *largus*, abundant, large.] a present; a gift or donation generously given; also, generous giving.

lär′ġesse, *n.* same as *largess.*

lär′get, *n.* a piece of iron cut to a size for rolling into a sheet.

lär·ghet′tō, *a.* and *adv.* [It., somewhat slow, from *largo*, large, bulky; L. *largus*, large.] in music, relatively slow, but faster than largo: a direction to the performer.

lär·ghet′tō, *n.*; *pl.* **lär·ghet′tōș**, a larghetto movement or passage.

lär·ġif′i·căl, *a.* benevolent; generous; liberal. [Obs.]

lär·ġif′lū·ous, *a.* flowing copiously. [Obs.]

lär·ġil′ō·quent (-kwent), *a.* grandiloquent. [Obs.]

lär′ġish, *a.* somewhat large.

lär·ġi′tion, *n.* the giving of a largess or gift. [Obs.]

lär′gō, *a.* and *adv.* [It., large, slow, from L. *largus*, large.] in music, slow and stately: a direction to the performer.

lär′gō, *n.*; *pl.* **lär′gōș**, a largo movement or passage.

lar′i·ăt, *n.* [Sp. *la reata*; *la*, the, and *reata*, a rope.]

1. a rope used for tethering, grazing horses, etc.

2. a lasso.

lar′i·ăt, *v.t.*; lariated, *pt., pp.*; lariating, *ppr.* to fasten with a lariat; to catch with a lariat.

Lar′i·dae, *n.pl.* [LL. *larus*; Gr. *laros*, a ravenous sea bird, and *-idæ.*] a family of aquatic birds; the gull family.

lar′ine, *a.* 1. of or pertaining to the *Laridæ*, or gull family.

2. of or like a gull.

Lar′ix, *n.* [L. *larix*, the larch.] a genus of coniferous trees with deciduous leaves; the larches.

lärk, *n.* [ME. *larke*; AS. *laferce, lauerce*, a lark.]

1. a small songbird of the family *Alaudidæ*, the species being mostly migratory birds of Europe, Asia, and Africa; especially, the skylark of Europe, *Alauda arvensis*, which rises high in the air and sings with a very clear note.

SKYLARK
(*Alauda arvensis*)

2. any of a number of similar birds, as the wagtail, pipit, and meadow lark.

lärk, *v.i.* to catch larks.

lärk, *v.i.* [S. Eng. alteration (after *lark*, bird) of northern dial. *lake*; ME. *laike*, to play, from ON. *leika*.] to make sport; to sport; to frolic. [Colloq.]

lärk, *v.t.* 1. to make fun of; to tease. [Colloq.]
2. to hurdle (a fence, etc.), especially on horseback.

lärk, *n.* a frolic or spree; a merry prank.

lärk bun′ting, a bird of the family *Fringillidæ* inhabiting the western plains of the United States.

lärk′ẽr, *n.* a catcher of larks.

lärk′ẽr, *n.* one who frolics.

lärk finch, same as *lark sparrow*.

lärk′līke, *a.* resembling a lark.

lärk spar′rōw, a fringilloid bird, *Chondestes grammacus*, of the Mississippi Valley and the western United States; the lark finch.

lärk′spūr, *n.* any of a group of plants with green, feathery leaves and spurred flowers of blue or, occasionally, white or pink; delphinium.

lärme, *n.* [Fr., a tear, from L. *lacrima*, a tear.] a design resembling a teardrop: used in lace patterns and in heraldry.

lär′mi·ẽr, *n.* [Fr., from *larme*, a tear or drop.]
1. the flat, jutting part of a cornice; the eaves of a house.
2. the lacrymal sinus in deer and antelope; the tearpit.

lar′oid, *a.* [Gr. *laros*, a sea bird, and *eidos*, form.] like or resembling a bird of the gull family *Laridæ*.

lar′ri·găn, *n.* [prob. of Canad. origin.] a high moccasin made of oiled leather, worn by lumbermen and trappers.

lar′ri·kin, *n.* [said to have been first used for *larking*, by James Dalton, a police sergeant in Melbourne, Australia, of Irish birth.] a boisterous, rude person; a rowdy; a hoodlum.

lar′ri·kin, *a.* rough and disorderly.

lar′ri·kin·iṣm, *n.* the practices of a larrikin; rowdyism; extreme rudeness.

lar′rup, *v.t.*; larruped (-rupt), *pt., pp.*; larruping, *ppr.* [East Anglian dial.; compare D. *larpen*, to thresh; *larp*, a whip.] to thrash or beat. [Colloq.]

lär′ry, *n.* same as *lorry*.

lar′um, *n.* [for *alarum*.] an alarm; a noise giving notice of danger.

lär′vȧ, *n.*; *pl.* **lär′vae,** [L. *larva*, a ghost, specter.]
1. an insect in the earliest stage of development, after it is hatched and before it is changed into a pupa; a caterpillar, maggot, or grub.
2. the early form of any animal that changes structurally when it becomes an adult; as, the tadpole is the *larva* of the frog.

lär′văl, *a.* 1. belonging to or like a larva or larvae.
2. in the form of a larva.

Lär·vā′li·ȧ, *n.pl.* [L. *larvalis*, pertaining to a ghost, from *larva*, ghost.] a class of tunicates that retain certain larval features through life.

lär·vãr′i·um, *n.*; *pl.* **lär·vãr′i·ȧ, lär·vãr′i·umṣ,** a shelter for larvae, as the web of the caterpillar; also, a box or case for the rearing of insects.

lär′vāte, lär′vā·ted, *a.* [L. *larva*, a ghost, specter.] masked; clothed as with a mask; obscure; difficult to find.

lärve, *n.* a larva. [Rare.]

lär′vi-, [from L. *larva*, a ghost, specter, mask.] a combining form meaning *larva*, as in *larvigerous*.

lär′vi·fọrm, *a.* [*larvi-*, and L. *forma*, form.] having the form or condition of a larva.

lär·vig′ẽr·ous, *a.* [*larvi-*, and L. *gerere*, to produce.] bearing the larval skin in the pupa state: said of the pupa of dipterous insects.

lär·vip′ȧ·rous, *a.* [*larvi-*, and L. *parere*, to bring forth.] producing the living larva, instead of an egg: said of some insects.

lär·viv′ō·rous, *a.* [*larvi-*, and L. *vorare*, to devour.] living on the larvae of insects; as, *larvivorous* birds.

lȧ·ryng′-, see *laryngo-*.

lȧ·ryn′găl, *a.* produced in the larynx.

lȧ·ryn′ġē·ăl, *a.* 1. of, in, or near the larynx.
2. used for treating the larynx.

lȧ·ryn′ġē·ăn, *a.* same as *laryngeal*.

lar·yn·ġeç′tō·my, *n.* [*laryng-*, and Gr. *ektomē*, a cutting out; *ek*, out, and *tomē*, a cutting, from *temnein*, to cut.] the operation of cutting away a part of the larynx.

lar·yn·ġiṣ′mus, *n.* [Gr. *laryngismos*, a croaking, from *laryngizein*, to shout, croak, from *larynx*, the larynx.] a spasmodic action of the glottal muscles, causing involuntary closing of the glottis.

lar·yn·ġit′iç, *a.* of or having laryngitis.

lar·yn·ġī′tis, *n.* [Gr. *larynx*, *laryngos*, the larynx, and *-itis*.] an inflammation of the larynx characterized by a sore throat, hoarseness, and, often, a temporary loss of voice.

lȧ·ryn′gō-, [from Gr. *larynx*, *laryngos*, larynx.] a combining form meaning: (a) *the larynx*, as in *laryngo*scope; (b) *laryngeal and*, as in *laryngo*pharyngeal. Also, before a vowel, *laryng-*.

lȧ·ryn″gō·loġ′i·căl, *a.* pertaining to laryngology.

lar·yn·gol′ō·ġist, *n.* an expert in laryngology.

lar·yn·gol′ō·ġy, *n.* [*laryngo-*, and Gr. *-logia*, from *legein*, to speak.] that branch of medicine which has to do with the study and treatment of the larynx and adjacent parts.

lȧ·ryn″gō·phȧ·ryn′ġē·ăl, *a.* of both the larynx and the pharynx.

lar·yn·goph′ō·ny, *n.* [*laryngo-*, and Gr. *phōnē*, voice.] the sound heard through the stethoscope when placed over the larynx while the patient is speaking.

lȧ·ryn′gō·sçōpe, *n.* [*laryngo-*, and Gr. *skopein* to view.] an instrument for examining the larynx by means of mirrors attached to a rod.

lȧ·ryn·gō·sçop′iç, *a.* of or pertaining to the examination of the larynx by means of the laryngoscope.

lar·yn·gos′çō·pist, *n.* an expert in the use of the laryngoscope.

lar·yn·gos′çō·py, *n.* the science or practice of making examinations with the laryngoscope.

lar·yn·got′ō·my, *n.* [*laryngo-*, and Gr. *tomē*, a cutting, from *temnein*, to cut.] the surgical operation of cutting into the larynx; especially, the making of an incision into the larynx for assisting respiration when obstructed, or for removing foreign bodies.

lȧ·ryn·gō·trā′çhē·ăl, *a.* [*laryngo-*, and Gr. *tracheia*, the trachea.] of or pertaining to both the larynx and the trachea.

lȧ·ryn″gō·trā·çhē·ot′ō·my, *n.* [*laryngo-*, and Gr. *tracheia*, the trachea, and *tomē*, a cutting.] the surgical operation performed to relieve obstructed breathing by cutting into the larynx and the upper part of the trachea.

lar′ynx, *n.*; *pl.* **lȧ·ryn′ġēṣ, lar′ynx·eṣ,** [Gr. *larynx*, *laryngos*, the larynx.]

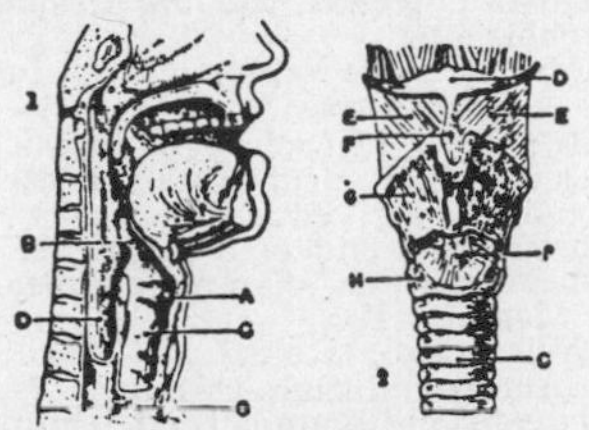

LARYNX
1. internal view; 2. external view

1. the upper part of the human windpipe, or trachea, a cartilaginous and muscular structure, containing the vocal cords and serving as the organ of voice: it is connected with the pharynx by means of the glottis which is covered by a lid called the epiglottis, preventing solid substances from entering the trachea. Fig. 1. above shows, A, the larynx internally, B being the epiglottis, CC the trachea, and D the esophagus or gullet. In fig. 2, C is the trachea, D the hyoid bone, EE the thyrohyoid membrane, F the thyrohyoid ligament, G the thyroid cartilage, H the cricoid cartilage, P the cricothyroid ligament.
2. a similar structure in other animals.

lȧ·ṣä′gnȧ (-nyȧ), *n.* [It. (pl. *lasagne*), the noodle, from L. *lasanum*, a pot, from Gr. *lasanon*, pot with feet.] a dish of wide, flat noodles baked in layers with cheese, tomato sauce, and ground meat: also *lasagne*.

las′căr, *n.* [Hind. *lashkar*, an army camp; *lashkarī*, belonging to the army, a soldier, from Per. *lashkar*, the army.] in the East Indies, a native sailor; also, a low-ranking native artilleryman in the British army.

las·civ′i·ous, *a.* [L. *lascivus*, wanton, from *laxus*, loose, open.]
1. characterized by or expressing lust or lewdness; wanton.
2. tending to excite lustful desires.

las·civ′i·ous·ly, *adv.* wantonly; lewdly.

las·civ′i·ous·ness, *n.* 1. wantonness; lustfulness.
2. tendency to excite lust.

lā′ṣẽr, *n.* [*l*ight *a*mplification by *s*timulated *e*mission of *r*adiation.] a device, containing a crystal, gas, or other suitable substance, in which atoms, when stimulated by focused light waves, amplify and concentrate these waves, then emit them in a narrow, very intense beam.

Las·ẽr·pi′ti·um (-pish′i-), *n.* [L. *laserpicium*, laserwort.] a genus of umbelliferous perennial herbs native to the Old World, having medicinal roots.

lā′sẽr·wŏrt, *n.* the plant *Laserpitium latifolium*, or any other plant of the same genus.

lash, *n.* [ME. *lassche*.]
1. any thong, cord, or the like for flogging; a whip, especially the flexible striking part as distinguished from the handle.
2. a stroke with a whip or anything pliant and tough.
3. an expression or retort that censures, rebukes, or ridicules.
4. an eyelash.

lash, *v.t.*; lashed (lasht), *pt., pp.*; lashing, *ppr.*
1. to strike with a lash or anything pliant; to whip or scourge; to beat.
2. to fling quickly; to switch energetically or angrily; as, the cat *lashed* her tail.
3. to strike with great force; to dash against; as, the waves *lashed* the white cliffs.
4. to attack violently in words; to censure, rebuke, or ridicule.
5. to incite by appealing to the emotions; as, he *lashed* the crowd into a frenzy of anger.

lash, *v.i.* 1. to move quickly or violently; to switch; as, the lion's tail *lashed* back and forth.
2. to make strokes with or as with a whip (with *at*); as, he *lashed at* everything that came near.
to lash out; (a) to strike out violently; (b) to speak angrily or bitterly; to rebuke violently.

lash, *v.t.* [OFr. *lachier*, *lacier*, to lace.] to fasten or tie with a rope, etc.

lash′ẽr, *n.* 1. one who lashes.
2. a lashing; a cord used as a fastening.

lash′ẽr, *n.* sluggish water above a dam; hence, a dam or weir. [Brit. Dial.]

lash′ing, *n.* a piece of rope for binding or making fast one thing to another; also, the act of fastening such a rope.

lash′ing, *n.* 1. the act of a person or thing that lashes; specifically, (a) a whipping; (b) a strong rebuke; as, he got a tongue *lashing*.
2. [*pl.*] abundance; profusion; as, *lashings* of drink. [Ir. or Scot.]

lask, *v.i.* to sail with a quartering wind, or with a wind about 45° abaft the beam. [Rare.]

lask, *n.* diarrhea; flux. [Obs.]

las′ket, *n.* [compare Sw. *laska*, to stitch, Dan. *laske*, to join, *lask*, a scarf; perh. from L. *laxus*, loose.] a loop or lashing for a sail.

L′-as·păr·ȧ·ġin′āse, *n.* (el′-), [*l*evorotatory, and *asparagin*, and *-ase*.] an enzyme that destroys asparagin, an amino acid apparently needed as a nutrient by leukemic cells: used experimentally in treating leukemia.

lass, *n.* [ME. *lasse*; of Celtic origin.]
1. a young woman; a girl.
2. a sweetheart.
3. a girl servant; a maid. [Scot.]

Läs′să fē′vẽr, [after *Lassa*, village in eastern Nigeria where first detected.] an acute virus disease endemic to western Africa, characterized by high fever and inflammation of various body organs and parts.

las′sie, *n.* a young girl; also, a sweetheart. [Scot.]

las′si·tūde, *n.* [L. *lassitudo* (*-inis*), from *lassus*, faint, weary.] a state or feeling of being tired or weak; weariness; languor.

lass′lọrn, *a.* forsaken by a lass or sweetheart.

las′sō, *n.*; *pl.* **las′sōṣ, las′sōeṣ,** [Port. *laço*; L. *laqueus*, a noose, snare, trap.] a rope or leather line, with a running noose, used for catching wild horses, etc.

las′sō, *v.t.*; lassoed, *pt., pp.*; lassoing, *ppr.* to catch or take by using a lasso.

las′sō cell, a thread cell or stinging cell of certain coelenterates from which a long thread may be cast to sting or capture prey.

lȧst, *n.* [AS. *hlæst*, a load, from *hladan*, to load.]
1. a certain weight or measure, generally estimated at 4,000 pounds, but varying for different articles and in different places.
2. a ship's cargo.

lȧst, *n.* [ME. *last*, *lest*; AS. *last*, *læst*, a footstep, track, *læst*, a boot, *læste*, a last.]

1. a mold or form of the human foot, made of wood, on which shoes are built or repaired.

2. a particular form or shape of shoe.

to stick to one's last; to do one's own work; to attend to one's own business.

låst, *v.t.* to fit to or shape with a last.

låst, *a.* [alternative superl. of *late.*] [ME. *last, latst*, contr. of *latest*, superl. of *late*, from AS. *læt*, slow, late.]

1. (a) coming after or following all others in order of place or time; furthest from the first or beginning; latest; hindmost; closing; final; as, the *last* hour of the day, the *last* page of a book; (b) only remaining.

2. most recent; next before the present; as, *last* week.

3. utmost; greatest: usually in the phrase *of the last importance*.

4. coming after all others in importance; lowest; least; as, the *last* prize.

5. most unlikely; furthest from what is expected; as, the *last* man to do such a thing.

6. newest; as, the *last* thing in topcoats.

7. conclusive; authoritative; as, the *last* word in scientific research.

Syn.—latest, final, ultimate.

låst, *adv.* [alternative superl. of *late.*] 1. following all else in time or place; at the end; as, news told *last*.

2. at the time or occasion next before the present; as, I saw him *last* in the depot.

3. in conclusion; finally.

låst, *n.* 1. the conclusion; end; as, he remained a cynic to the *last*.

2. someone or something which comes last; as, this is the *last* of the apples.

at last; finally; at the end of a long time.

to see the last of; to see for the last time; to never see again.

låst, *v.i.*; lasted, *pt.*, *pp.*; lasting, *ppr.* [ME. *lasten*; AS. *læstan*, to accomplish, follow, perform, endure, lit., to follow closely in track, from *last*, a track, footprint.]

1. to continue in time; to endure; to remain in existence or operation; as, the services *lasted* an hour.

2. to continue unimpaired; to wear well; as, select for winter the best apples to *last*.

3. to hold out; to continue unconsumed, unspent, etc.; as, the ship had water on board to *last* a week.

låst, *n.* endurance; stamina.

låst′åġe, *n.* [ME. *last*; AS. *hlæst*, a load.]

1. the lading of a ship; ballast. [Obs.]

2. space to stow goods.

3. a duty on goods sold by the last.

låst′-ditch′ (-dich′), *a.* made, done, used, etc. in a final, often desperate act, as of resistance.

låst′ẽr, *n.* one who or that which shapes parts of boots or shoes on a last.

las′tex, *n.* a fine, round rubber thread wound with cotton, rayon, silk, etc. and woven into cloth or knitted into other fabrics: a trademark (*Lastex*).

låst hur·räh′, a final attempt or appearance, as in politics.

låst′ing, *n.* 1. a strong twilled fabric used for shoe uppers, covering buttons, etc.

2. endurance; durability; permanence.

låst′ing, *a.* continuing in time; enduring; durable; permanent; as, a *lasting* peace.

låst′ing·ly, *adv.* durably; with continuance.

låst′ing·ness, *n.* durability; the quality or state of lasting.

Låst Judġ′ment, 1. in theology, the final judgment of mankind by God or Jesus, at the end of the world.

2. the time of this.

låst′ly, *adv.* in the last place, in conclusion; at last; finally.

låst of′fic·eṣ, final rites and prayers for a dead person.

låst quar′tẽr, 1. the period when the moon's apparent shape is changing from half-moon to new moon.

2. the moon's apparent shape at the beginning of this period.

låst rītes, 1. final rites and prayers for a dead person.

2. sacraments administered to a dying person.

låst sleep, death.

låst straw, [from the last straw that broke the back of the overburdened camel in the fable.] the last of a sequence of annoyances or troubles that results in a breakdown, defeat, etc.

låst wŏrd, 1. the final word or speech, regarded as settling the argument.

2. something regarded as incapable of improvement.

3. the very latest style, model, development, etc. [Colloq.]

lät, *n.*; *pl.* **läts, lä′tū,** [Lett. *lats*, pl. *lati*, from *Latvia*.] former monetary unit of Latvia.

låt, *v.t.* and *v.i.* to let. [Obs.]

lät, *n.* [Hind.] an isolated column, common in Indian architecture, used for inscriptions, to bear a statue, or as a flagstaff.

Lat″å·kī′å, *n.* a fine variety of Turkish smoking tobacco: so named from Latakia, a seaport in Syria, near which it is produced.

Lå·tā′ni·å, *n.* [*Latania*, the native name of a species in the Isle of Bourbon.] a genus of fan palms, native to the Mascarene Islands.

latch, *n.* [ME. *lacche*, from *lacchen*, to fasten, latch.]

1. a fastening for a door or gate, especially one capable of being worked from either side by means of a lever and consisting of a bar that falls into a notch in a piece attached to the doorjamb or gatepost: sometimes said of a spring lock on a door.

2. a fastening for a window, etc.

3. a lasket. [Rare.]

on the latch; fastened by the latch but not bolted.

latch, *v.t.* and *v.i.* to fasten or close with a latch.

latch′et, *n.* [ME. *lachet*; OFr. *lacet*, dim. of *laz*, a string, lace.] a strap or lace used to fasten on a sandal. [Archaic.]

latch′ing, *n.* a lasket.

latch′kēy, *n.* a key for drawing back or unfastening the latch of a door, especially of an outer door, from the outside.

latch′string, *n.* a string fastened to the bar of a latch and passed through a hole in the door, used to lift up the latch from the outside.

lāte, *a.*; *comp.* later *or* latter; *superl.* latest *or* last, [ME. *lat*; AS. *læt*, slow, tardy, late.]

1. coming after the usual, proper, or expected time; slow; tardy; long delayed; as, a *late* spring, a *late* crop.

2. happening, being, continuing, etc. far on in the day, night, year, etc.; as, the *late* afternoon, a *late* party.

3. happening, being, continuing, etc. toward the end; far advanced in a period, development, etc.; as, the *late* Middle Ages.

4. existing not long ago but now dead or gone out of office; as, the *late* president; the *late* archbishop.

5. not long past; happening not long ago; recent; as, *late* years.

lāte, *adv.*; *comp.* later; *superl.* latest *or* last. 1. after the usual, proper, or expected time; tardily; as, he arrived *late*.

2. toward the end of a given period, development, etc.; as, mammals appeared *late* in the Mesozoic Era.

3. not long ago; lately.

And round them throng
With leaps and bounds the *late* imprisoned young. —Pope.

4. at or until an advanced time of the night, day, week, year, etc.; as, to stay up *late* at night.

of late; in time not long past, or near the present; recently; as, the practice is *of late* uncommon.

lāt′ed, *a.* belated. [Poetic.]

lå·teen′ *a.* [Fr. *latine*, f. of *latin*, Latin (for *voile latine*, Latin sail), from L. *Latinus*, Latin.]

LATEEN SAILS

1. of or relating to a triangular sail, extended by a long yard and slung about one quarter the distance from the lower end, which is brought down at the tack, while the other end is elevated at an angle of about 45°: used formerly by Portuguese explorers and now on Mediterranean vessels.

2. having such a sail.

lå·teen′, *n.* a vessel having a lateen sail.

lå·teen′-rigged, *a.* having a lateen sail.

Lāte Greek, the Greek language of the period after classical Greek: term applied chiefly to the written language seen in patristic writings and texts from the early Byzantine Empire, from 200–300 A. D. to about 600 A. D.

Lāte Lat′in, the Latin language of the period after classical Latin, seen chiefly in late Western Roman Empire and patristic writings from 200–300 A. D. to about 600 A. D.

lāte′ly, *adv.* not long ago; recently; during a recent period.

lā′ten·cy, *n.* the quality or condition of being latent.

lāte′ness, *n.* the quality or condition of being late, or of coming after the usual time.

lā′tent, *a.* [L. *latens* (*-entis*), ppr. of *latere*, to lie hidden or concealed, to lurk.]

1. lying hidden and undeveloped within a person or thing, as a quality or power; as yet concealed; unrevealed.

2. in biology, dormant but capable of normal development under the best conditions: said of buds, spores, cocoons, etc.

3. in law, not appearing on the face of a thing; hidden; as, a *latent* ambiguity.

latent ambiguity; doubt as to the meaning of a legal instrument, arising not from the document itself, but from extrinsic causes; as, a legacy to James Jones of Tor becomes ambiguous when it is discovered that there are two men of that name in Tor. Doubt caused by the wording of the instrument itself, and obvious upon reading it, is *patent ambiguity*.

latent heat; additional heat required to change the state of a substance from solid to liquid at its melting point, or from liquid to gas at its boiling point, after the temperature of the substance has reached either of these points.

latent period; (a) the time during which a disease exists in the system before its symptoms become manifest; (b) the interval between a stimulus and its response.

lā′tent·ly, *adv.* in a latent manner.

lāt′ẽr, *adv.* [comp. of *late.*] hereafter; afterward; at a later time; as, I will tell you *later*.

later on; subsequently.

lāt′ẽr, *a.* alternative comp. of *late*.

lat′e·rå, *n.* plural of *latus*.

lat′ẽr·ad, *adv.* [L. *latus* (*-eris*), the side, and *ad*, to, toward.] in anatomy, toward a side.

lat′ẽr·ăl, *a.* [L. *lateralis*, from *latus* (*-eris*), a side.]

1. of, at, from, or toward the side; sideways; as, *lateral* movement.

2. descended from a brother or sister of a person; as, the *lateral* branch of a family.

3. in phonetics, formed in such a manner that the breath can escape along the side or sides of the tongue, as English *l*.

lateral line; in fishes, a longitudinal line consisting of a row of tubes along each side of the body and generally marked by a difference in structure or color of the skin.

lat′ẽr·ăl, *n.* 1. anything located, done, etc. to the side; a lateral part, growth, branch, etc.

2. in football, a lateral pass.

3. in mining, a drift off to the side of and parallel to a main drift.

4. in phonetics, a lateral sound.

lat·ẽr·al′i·ty, *n.* the quality of having distinct sides. [Rare.]

lat′ẽr·ăl·ly, *adv.* in a lateral manner; especially, (a) in a lateral direction; sideways; (b) from a lateral branch (of a family, etc.).

lat′ẽr·ăl påss, in football, a short pass parallel to the goal line or in a slightly backward direction: distinguished from *forward pass*.

Lat′ẽr·ăn, *n.* 1. the church of St. John Lateran, the cathedral church of the Pope as bishop of Rome.

2. the palace adjoining this church: it is now a museum.

Lat′ẽr·ăn, *a.* of the Lateran church or palace; specifically, designating or of certain Catholic general councils held there in 1123, 1139, 1179, 1215, and 1512–1517.

lat′ẽr·i-, [from L. *latus* (*-eris*), side.] a combining form meaning *on the side*, or *toward the side*, as in *laterigrade*, *laterifolious*.

lat′ẽr·i·grāde″, *a.* [*lateri-*, and L. *gradi*, to step.] progressing sidewise, as certain crabs.

lat′ẽr·i·grāde, *n.* an animal that progresses

sidewise, especially one of a family of spiders that run sidewise and backward.

lat′ẽr·īte, *n.* [L. *later* (*-eris*), a brick, tile.] a red, porous deposit containing large amounts of aluminum and ferric hydroxides, formed by the decomposition of certain rocks.

lat″ẽr·it′iç, *a.* of or pertaining to laterite.

lat″ẽr·i′tious (-shus), *a.* same as *latericeous.*

Lā′tēṣ, *n.* [Gr. *latos*, a fish of the Nile.] a genus of fishes found in the Nile, the Ganges, etc., belonging to the perch family, used as food.

lȧ·tes′cence, *n.* the quality or condition of becoming latent, or obscure.

lȧ·tes′cent, *a.* [L. *latescens* (*-entis*), ppr. of *latescere*, to lie hidden, incept. of *latere*, to lurk, lie hidden.] becoming latent, or hidden; withdrawing into obscurity.

lāt′est, *adv.* and *a.* alternative superl. of *late,*
 1. most recent; newest.
 2. last. [Archaic and Poetic.]
 at the latest; no later than (the time specified).
 the latest; the most recent thing, development, etc.

lāte′wāke, *n.* likewake. [Obs.]

lāte′wȧrd, *a.* and *adv.* late; backward. [Obs.]

lā′tex, *n.*; *pl.* **la′tex·eṣ, lat′i·cēṣ,** [L. *latex*, *laticis*, a fluid, liquid; Gr. *latax*, a drop, wine lees.] a milky liquid in certain plants and trees, as the rubber tree, milkweed, and poppy: the basis of various commercial products, notably rubber.

lȧth, *n.* [ME. *laththe*; AS. *lætt*, a narrow strip of wood, lath.]
 1. any of the thin, narrow strips of wood used in building lattices or nailed to the rafters, studs, etc. of a building, as a groundwork for tiles, plaster, or other covering.
 2. light sheet metal with holes (or wire cloth) designed for similar uses.
 3. lathing.
 4. the bow portion of a crossbow. [Obs.]

lȧth, *v.t.* to cover or line with laths.

lȧth brick, a long brick used in malt-drying kilns.

lāthe, *n.* granary; a barn. [Obs.]

lāthe, *n.* [AS. *læth*, *leth*, a district.] in Anglo-Saxon England, a district or division of a county: now used only of the five divisions of the county of Kent.

lāthe, *n.* [ME., turning lathe, supporting stand; prob. from MD. *lade* in the same senses.]

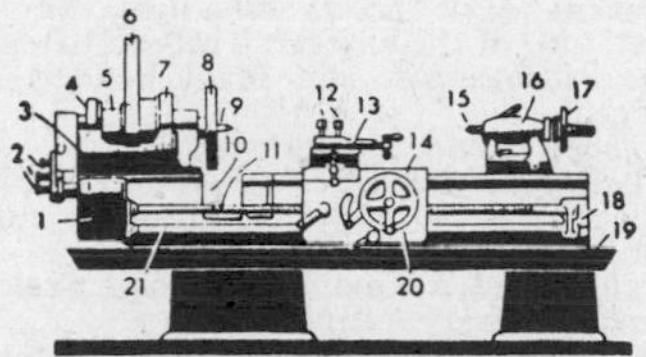

DIAGRAM OF ENGINEER'S LATHE

(1) change-speed box; (2) studs carrying change gears; (3) headstock; (4) guards; (5) pulley; (6) driving belt; (7) guard; (8) faceplate; (9) center; (10) gap; (11) lead screw; (12) clamps for securing turning tool; (13) cross slide; (14) saddle; (15) center; (16) loose headstock; (17) wheel for adjusting center; (18) bed; (19) tray for catching turnings; (20) apron holding control levers; (21) shaft giving automatic feeds

 1. a machine for shaping an article of wood, metal, etc. by holding and turning it rapidly against the edge of a cutting tool.
 2. a variety of potter's wheel.

lāthe, *v.t.*; lathed, *pt.*, *pp.*; lathing, *ppr.* to shape on a lathe.

lāthe, *n.* that part of a loom in which the reed is fixed, and by the movements of which the weft threads are laid parallel to each other in the process of weaving; a lay; a batten.

lath′ẽr, *n.* [AS. *leathor*, niter, lather.]
 1. foam or froth made by soap moistened with water.
 2. foam or froth from profuse sweat, as that on a race horse.

lath′ẽr, *v.t.*; lathered, *pt.*, *pp.*; lathering, *ppr.* [AS. *lethrian*, to smear, lather, anoint, from *leāthor*, lather.]
 1. to spread over with lather.
 2. to flog soundly. [Colloq.]

lath′ẽr, *v.i.* to form or become covered with lather.

lāthe′reeve, lȧth′reeve, *n.* the reeve of a lathe, or county district.

lath′ẽr·y, *a.* made of, covered with, or capable of forming lather.

lȧth′ing, *n.* 1. a covering or lining of laths for walls, etc.
 2. the act of covering with laths.

lȧth nāil, a small nail used in lathing.

lȧth pot, a closed lobster trap made of laths.

lȧth′wŏrk, *n.* lathing.

lȧth′y, *a.*; *comp.* lathier; *superl.* lathiest, like a lath; thin as a lath; long and slender.

lath′y·riṣm, *n.* a diseased condition caused by eating the seeds of a plant of the genus *Lathyrus*, of the bean family.

lat′i-, [from L. *latus*, broad.] a combining form meaning *wide, broad*; as in *lati*foliate, *lati*pennate.

Lā′tiăn, *a.* of or relating to Latium, one of the countries of early Italy; Latin.

lȧ·tib′ū·līze, *v.i.* [L. *latibulum*, a hiding place.] to retire into a den, burrow, or cavity, and lie dormant in winter; to hibernate. [Rare.]

lȧ·tib′ū·lum, *n.*; *pl.* **lȧ·tib′ū·lȧ,** [L., from *latere*, to lurk.] a secret place of hiding; a lair or den. [Rare.]

lat′i·cēṣ, *n.* alternative plural of *latex.*

lat″i·cif′ẽr·ous, *a.* [L. *latex* (*-icis*), a liquid, and *ferre*, to bear.] bearing, producing, or secreting latex.

lat′i·çlāve, *n.* [L. *laticlavus*; *latus*, broad, and *clavus*, a stripe.] a distinctive badge worn by Roman senators consisting of two broad stripes of purple on the front of the tunic.

lat″i·ços′tāte, *a.* [*lati-*, and L. *costatus*, ribbed, from *costa*, a rib.] broad-ribbed.

lat″i·den′tāte, *a.* [*lati-*, and L. *dentatus*, toothed, from *dens*, *dentis*, a tooth.] broad-toothed.

lat″i·fō′li·āte, lat″i·fō′li·ous, *a.* broad-leaved.

lat″i·fun′di·um, *n.*; *pl.* **lat″i·fun′di·ȧ,** [L., from *latus*, broad, and *fundus*, estate.] a large landed estate, as in ancient Rome.

lä′tï·gō, *n.* [Sp. *látigo*, a thong.] a strap with which a saddle girth is adjusted.

lat′i·mẽr, *n.* one having a knowledge of Latin; hence, an interpreter. [Obs.]

Lat′in, *a.* [ME. *Latin*, *Latyn*; OFr. *latin*; L. *Latinus*, Latin, of or pertaining to Latium, from *Latium*, a country in Italy.]
 1. of ancient Latium or its people.
 2. of ancient Rome or its people.
 3. of or in the language of ancient Latium and ancient Rome.
 4. designating or of the languages derived from Latin, the peoples who speak them, their countries, cultures, etc.
 5. of the Roman Catholic Church, especially as distinguished from the Orthodox Eastern Church.

Lat′in, *n.* 1. the Italic language of ancient Latium and ancient Rome.
 2. a native or inhabitant of ancient Latium or ancient Rome; a Roman.
 3. a member of one of the modern peoples whose language is derived from the Latin of the ancient Romans, as the Spanish, Italians, Portuguese, etc.
 4. in Turkey, a person of foreign ancestry belonging to the Roman Catholic Church.
 5. a member of the Roman Catholic Church: especially so used by Eastern Christians.
 6. an exercise in schools consisting of translating another language into Latin. [Obs.]

Lat′in, *v.t.* to express in Latin. [Obs.]

Lat′in, *v.i.* to use Latin. [Obs.]

Lat′in À·mer′i·çȧ, the countries in North America, South America, Central America, and the West Indies where Spanish, Portuguese, and French are spoken; all of the Western Hemisphere excluding the United States and its possessions, Canada, and the British possessions.

Lat′in-À·mer′i·çăn, *a.* of Latin America, its people, or their culture.

Lat′in À·mer′i·çăn, a native or inhabitant of a Latin-American country.

Lat′in·āte, *a.* of or derived from Latin.

Lat′in Chũrch, that part of the Catholic Church which adheres to the Latin Rite; the Roman Catholic Church.

Lat′in çross, a plain, right-angle cross whose lowest limb is longer than any of the other three.

Lat′in·ẽr, *n.* one skilled in Latin; an interpreter. [Rare.]

Lȧ·tin′iç, *a.* of Latin.

Lat′in·iṣm, *n.* a form of expression characteristic of Latin; an idiom or expression of Latin used in another language.

Lat′in·ist, *n.* one skilled in Latin.

Lat″in·is′tiç, *a.* resembling the Latin idiom.

Lȧ·tin′i·tas·tẽr, *n.* one who has a fragmentary or superficial knowledge of Latin. [Rare.]

Lȧ·tin′i·ty, *n.* [L. *latinitas* (*-atis*), from *Latinus*, Latin, and *-aster*.] the manner of speaking or writing Latin; the use of Latin.

Lat″in·i·zā′tïon, *n.* a Latinizing or being Latinized.

Lat′in·īze, *v.t.*, Latinized, *pt.*, *pp.*; Latinizing, *ppr.* [LL. *latinizare*, to translate into Latin, from L. *Latinus*, Latin.]
 1. to translate into Latin.
 2. to give Latin form or characteristics to.
 3. to transliterate into the Latin alphabet; to Romanize.
 4. to make conform to the rites, practices, etc. of the Roman Catholic Church.

Lat′in·īze, *v.i.* to use Latin expressions, forms, etc.

Lat′in·ly, *adv.* in good Latin style. [Obs.]

Lat′in Quar′tẽr, [transl. of Fr. *Quartier Latin.*] a section of Paris, south of the Seine, where many artists and students live.

Lat′in Rīte, 1. the Latin liturgies used in the Latin Church.
 2. the Latin Church.

lā′tion, *n.* conveyance; motion. [Obs.]

lat·i·pen′nāte, lat·i·pen′nine, *a.* [*lati-*, and L. *pennatus*, winged, from *penna*, a wing.] having broad wings.

lat·i·ros′trăl, lat·i·ros′trous, *a.* having a broad beak, as a bird.

Lat·i·ros′trēṣ, *n.pl.* [*lati-*, and L. *rostrum*, a beak.] a group of singing birds having wide bills.

lat·i·sep′tāte, *a.* [*lati-*, and L. *sæptum*, *septum*, a partition.] in botany, having a broad partition, as some cruciferous fruits.

lāt′ish, *a.* and *adv.* somewhat late.

lat·i·stẽr′năl, *a.* [*lati-*, and Gr. *sternon*, the breast, chest.] in zoology, having a broad sternum.

lat′i·tăn·cy, *n.* the state of lying concealed; the state of lurking. [Rare.]

lat′i·tănt, *a.* lurking; concealed. [Rare.]

lat′i·tat, *n.* [L., he lurks, 3rd pers. sing. pres. ind. of *latitare*, to lurk, freq. of *latere*, to hide, lurk.] in Old English law, a writ by which a person was summoned in the King's Bench to answer charges: so called because these writs were sanctioned by the false supposition that the person was hiding.

lat·i·tā′tion, *n.* a lying in concealment. [Rare.]

lat′i·tūde, *n.* [OFr. *latitude*; L. *latitudo* (*-inis*), breadth, width, extent, latitude.]
 1. breadth; extent from side to side. [Rare.]
 2. extent; scope; range of applicability.
 3. freedom from narrow restrictions; allowed freedom of opinion, conduct, or action.
 4. a region considered with reference to its distance north or south of the equator; as, in this *latitude* we rarely see the northern lights.

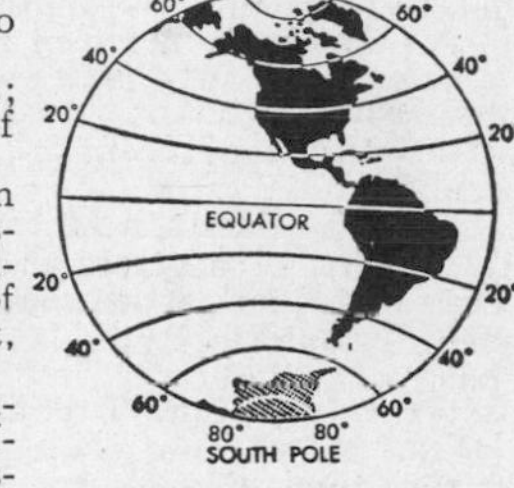

PARALLELS SHOWING LATITUDE

 5. in astronomy, the angular distance of a heavenly body from the plane in which the earth moves around the sun.
 6. in geography, the angular distance of any place on the globe, north or south of the equator, measured in degrees.

lat·i·tū′di·năl, *a.* pertaining to latitude.

lat″i·tū″di·nãr′i·ăn, *n.* [L. *latitudo* (*-inis*), breadth.]
 1. one who is moderate or liberal in his notions, or not restrained by precise settled limits in opinion; one who indulges freedom in thinking; one who, in religion, cares little about particular creeds and forms.
 2. any of a group of Anglican churchmen of the seventeenth century who favored freedom of belief and was not opposed to varying forms of worship or doctrine.

lat″i·tū″di·nãr′i·ăn, *a.* liberal in one's views; permitting free thought, especially in religious matters; very tolerant of the differing opinions of others; as, *latitudinarian* opinions or doctrines.

lat″i·tū″di·nār′i·ăn·iṣm, *n.* [*latitudinarian,* and *-ism.*] broadness and tolerance, especially in religion; liberal interpretation of doctrines, creeds, etc.

lat·i·tū′di·nous, *a.* having extent or latitude.

lat′on, lat′oun, *n.* latten. [Obs.]

Lȧ·tō′nȧ, *n.* [L.] in Roman mythology, the mother of Apollo and Diana: identified with the Greek Leto.

lā′trănt, *a.* barking. [Obs.]

lā′trāte, *v.i.* to bark as a dog. [Obs.]

lȧ·trā′tion, *n.* a barking. [Obs.]

lȧ·treu′tiç·ăl, *a.* [Gr. *latreuein,* to serve, to work for hire, from *latris,* a hired servant.] of or relating to latria. [Rare.]

lȧ·trī′ȧ, *n.* [LL. *latria;* Gr. *latreia,* service, worship, from *latreuein,* to work for hire, to serve, worship, from *latris,* a hired servant.] in the Roman Catholic Church, the highest kind of worship, due to God alone: distinguished from *dulia,* the inferior worship paid to saints.

lȧ·trīne′, *n.* [L. *latrina,* a bath, privy, contr. of *lavatrina,* a bath, from *lavare,* to wash.] a toilet, or privy, for the use of a large number of people, as one used in a camp, barracks, etc.

lȧ·trōbe′, *n.* [named after its inventor, I. *Latrobe,* of Baltimore.] a stove placed in a fireplace and used to heat both by radiation and hot air: known also as the *Baltimore heater.*

Lat·rō·cin′i·um, *n.* [L., the military service of a mercenary, from *latro* (*-onis*), a hired servant, a robber.] a council of the early Christian church held at Ephesus in **449 A.D.**: so called because of the violent and turbulent character of its proceedings.

-lat·ry, [Gr. *-latreia,* from *latreia.*] a combining form meaning ***worship of*** or ***excessive devotion to,*** as in ido*latry.*

lat′ten, *n.* [ME. *laton, latoun;* OFr. *laton, laiton;* prob. from M.H.G. *latte,* thin plate, lath.]

1. brass or a brasslike alloy hammered into thin sheets, formerly used for making church vessels.

2. any metal, expecially tin, in thin sheets.

black latten; plates of milled brass.

roll latten; sheet brass polished on both sides.

white latten; an alloy of copper, zinc, and tin in thin sheets.

lat′tẽr, *a.* [alternative comp. of *late.*] [ME. *later, lætter,* comp. of *lat;* AS. *læt,* late.]

1. (a) later; more recent; (b) nearer the end or close; as, in the *latter* part of the year.

2. mentioned the last of two: opposed to *former:* often used absolutely (with *the*).

> The difference between reason and revelation—and in what sense *the latter* is superior. —Watts.

lat′tẽr-dāy, *a.* of recent or present time; modern.

Lat′tẽr-dāy Sāint, a Mormon.

lat′tẽr·kin, *n.* a glazing tool, used particularly on leaden latticework.

lat′tẽr·ly, *adv.* lately; of late; in time not long past.

lat′tẽr·mȧth, *n.* the latter mowing; aftermath. [Dial.]

lat′tẽr·mōst, *a.* last in succession; farthest toward the rear.

lat′tice (-tis), *n.* [OFr. *lattis,* a lattice, from *latte;* AS. *lætt,* a lath.]

1. an openwork structure of wood, metal, etc. made by crossing laths, rods, or bars, and forming a network used as a screen, support, etc.; as, the *lattice* of a window.

2. a window, door, gate, etc. screened by such a structure.

3. something resembling or suggesting such a network, as, in heraldry, a bearing of crossbars, vertical and horizontal.

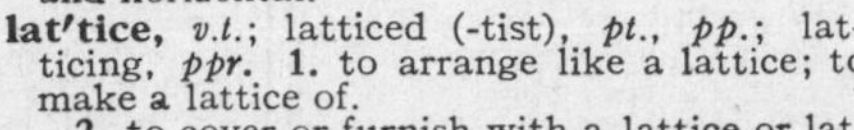

LATTICE-WINDOW

lat′tice, *v.t.;* latticed (-tist), *pt., pp.;* latticing, *ppr.* 1. to arrange like a lattice; to make a lattice of.

2. to cover or furnish with a lattice or latticework.

lat′tice·lēaf, *n.* a plant, *Ouvirandra fenestralis,*

LATTICELEAF (*Ouvirandra fenestralis*)

with leaves like latticework, found in Madagascar and belonging to the pondweed family.

lat′tice-win′dōw, *n.* a window enclosed by or covered with a lattice.

lat′tice·wŏrk, *n.* 1. a lattice.

2. lattices collectively; trelliswork.

3. embroidery in imitation of a lattice.

LATTICEWORK

lat′ti·cing, *n.* 1. making or placing a lattice or latticework.

2. a lattice or latticework, as a series of cross-timbers or cross-irons placed as braces to the regular supports of a bridge.

lät″tï·cï′ni·ō (-chï′), *n.* [It., from L. *lacticinium,* milk food, from *lac, lactis,* milk.] a milky-white Italian glass worked into decorative designs.

lä′tụ, *n.* alternative plural of *lat.*

lā′tus, *n.; pl.* **lat′e·rȧ,** [L.] a side.

latus rectum; the parameter of a conic section.

latus transversum; in geometry, the transverse axis of a conic section.

Lat′vi·ăn, *a.* 1. of Latvia or its people; Lettish.

2. of the group of Baltic dialects spoken in Latvia.

Lat′vi·ăn, *n.* 1. a native or inhabitant of Latvia.

2. the Lettish language: with Lithuanian and Old Prussian it represents the Baltic branch of the Indo-European family of languages.

lau′băn·ïte, *n.* a hydrous silicate of calcium and aluminum, snow-white in color.

laud, *n.* [L. *laus, laudis,* praise, commendation, glory, fame, esteem.]

1. praise; commendation.

2. any song or hymn of praise.

3. [pl.] (a) [often L–] an early morning church service that includes the singing of psalms of praise to God; (b) [L–] in the Roman Catholic Church, the service of dawn which constitutes the second (or, when said together with matins, the first) of the canonical hours.

laud, *v.t.* [ME. *lauden;* L. *laudare,* to praise, from *laus, laudis,* praise, glory.] to praise; to extol.

laud·ȧ·bil′i·ty, *n.* the quality of being laudable; praiseworthiness; commendability.

laud′ȧ·ble, *a.* [L. *laudabilis,* from *laudare,* to praise.]

1. worthy of being lauded; praiseworthy; commendable; as, *laudable* motives, *laudable* actions.

2. in medicine, such as indicates an improving condition; healthy; salubrious; normal; as, *laudable* pus. [Obs.]

laud′ȧ·ble·ness, *n.* the quality of deserving praise; praiseworthiness.

laud′ȧ·bly, *adv.* in a manner deserving praise.

lau′dȧ·nïne, *n.* an alkaloid derived from opium.

lau′dȧ·num, *n.* [L. *ladanum,* labdanum.]

1. formerly, any of various preparations containing opium.

2. tincture of opium; a solution of opium in alcohol.

3. labdanum. [Obs.]

lau·dā′tion, *n.* [L. *laudatio* (*-onis*), from *laudare,* to praise.] a lauding or being lauded; praise; commendation.

laud′ȧ·tive, *n.* a panegyric. [Obs.]

laud′ȧ·tive, *a.* eulogistic; laudatory.

laud′ȧ·tō·ry, *a.* containing or expressing praise; tending to praise; eulogistic.

laud′ȧ·tō·ry, *n.* that which contains praise; a eulogy. [Obs.]

laud′ẽr, *n.* one who praises.

läugh (läf *or* laf), *v.i.;* laughed (läft *or* laft), *pt., pp.;* laughing, *ppr.* [ME. *laughen;* AS. *hlehhan, hlihhan,* to laugh; of imitative origin.]

1. to make the sounds and exhibit the movements of the features and body characteristic in the expression of mirth, joy, ridicule, etc.

2. to feel or suggest joyousness; to be gay; to appear gay, cheerful, pleasant, lively, or brilliant.

> Then *laughs* the childish year with flowerets crowned. —Dryden.

to laugh at; (a) to be amused by; (b) to make fun of; ridicule; deride; (c) to be indifferent to or contemptuous of; disregard.

to laugh in one's sleeve; to laugh to oneself and secretly, especially while outwardly serious.

to laugh out of (or *on*) *the other* (or *wrong*) *side of the mouth;* to change from joy to sorrow, from amusement to annoyance, etc.

läugh, *v.t.* 1. to ridicule or deride. [Obs.]

2. to produce an effect upon by laughter; as, to *laugh* one out of a plan.

3. to utter laughingly; to express with laughter.

to laugh away; to get rid of (something unpleasant or embarrassing) by laughter.

to laugh down; to silence or suppress by laughing.

to laugh off; to scorn, avoid, or reject by laughter or ridicule.

läugh, *n.* 1. the act or sound of laughing; an expression of mirth, satisfaction, or derision.

2. anything that provokes or is fit to provoke laughter.

to have the last laugh; to win after apparent defeat and discomfiture.

läugh′ȧ·ble, *a.* capable of exciting laughter; amusing or ridiculous; as, a *laughable* story.

läugh′ȧ·ble·ness, *n.* the quality of being laughable.

läugh′ȧ·bly, *adv.* in a manner to excite laughter.

läugh′ẽr, *n.* 1. one who laughs or is fond of merriment.

> The *laughers* are much the majority. —Pope.

2. one of a breed of pigeons: so called from their cry.

läugh′ing, *a.* 1. that laughs; expressing or uttering laughter.

2. causing laughter; as, a *laughing* matter.

laughing bird; *Gecinus viridis,* the green woodpecker. [Brit. Dial.]

laughing falcon; a South American hawk of the genus *Herpetotheres.*

laughing gas; see under *gas,* n.

laughing goose; in zoology, the whitefronted goose, *Anser albifrons.*

laughing gull; *Larus atricilla,* the black-headed gull of the eastern United States; also, *Xema ridibundus,* the black-headed European gull.

laughing hyena; the spotted hyena.

laughing jackass; *Dacelo gigas,* an Australian kingfisher with a harsh, cackling cry suggestive of loud laughter; kookaburra.

laughing owl; a New Zealand owl, *Sceloglaux albifacies,* nearly extinct.

läugh′ing·ly, *adv.* in a merry way; with laughter.

läugh′ing·stock, *n.* an object of ridicule; a butt.

läugh′tẽr, *n.* [ME. *laughter, lauhter;* AS. *hleahtor,* laughter, from *hlehhan,* to laugh.]

1. the action of laughing or the sound resulting.

2. a matter for or cause of laughter.

Syn.—merriment, glee, derision, ridicule, cachinnation, contempt.

läugh′tẽr·less, *a.* without laughter.

läugh′wŏr″thy, *a.* deserving to be laughed at.

lau′mont·ïte, *n.* an efflorescent hydrous silicate of aluminum and calcium: so called from Laumont, its discoverer.

launce, *n.* a balance. [Obs.]

launce, *n.* [ME. *launce, lance,* lance.] any of a small group of sea fishes with a pointed snout and a long, slender body, found in American coastal waters: also *lance, lant, sand launce, sand eel.*

launce′gāy, *n.* a lancegay. [Obs.]

launch, *v.t.;* launched, *pt., pp.;* launching, *ppr.* [ME. *lanchen, launchen;* OFr. *lanchier, lancier,* to throw, hurl as a lance, from *lance;* L. *lancea,* a lance.]

1. to hurl, discharge, or send off (a weapon, blow, etc.).

2. to send forth with some force; as, the catapult *launched* the plane into the air.

3. to cause (a newly built vessel) to slide from the land into the water; to set afloat.

fāte, fär, fȧst, fạll, finăl, cãre, at; mēte, prey, hẽr, met; pīne, marïne, bīrd, pin; nōte, mōve, fọr, atŏm, not; mọọn, book;

4. to set in operation; to start; as, the army *launched* an attack.

5. to start (a person) on some course or career.

6. to pierce or cut with or as with a lance; to lance. [Obs.]

launch, *v.i.* 1. to put to sea (often with *out* or *forth*).

2. to start on some new course, career, or enterprise.

3. to throw oneself (*into*) with vigor; to rush; plunge; as, she *launched into* a seething rebuke.

to launch out; (a) to put to sea; (b) to begin something new; (c) to be reckless in action or thought.

launch, *n.* 1. the act of launching. [Brit. Dial.]

2. the sliding or movement of a ship from the land into the water on ways prepared for the purpose.

3. a trap for eels. [Brit. Dial.]

4. a stab; a cut. [Obs.]

launch, *n.* [Sp. or Port. *lancha*; prob. from Malay *lanca*, three-masted boat, from *lancār*, speedy, quick.]

1. the largest boat carried by a warship.

2. a large, open motorboat.

launch pad, the platform from which a rocket, guided missile, etc. is launched: also *launching pad.*

launch win′dōw, the period of time during which conditions are favorable for launching a spacecraft on a particular mission.

laund, *n.* a lawn; a glade. [Obs.]

laun′dēr, *n.* [ME. *launder*, from *lavander*, a washerwoman: see *laundry*.]

1. a washerwoman. [Obs.]

2. a water trough, especially one used in mining to receive the powdered ore and wash the dirt from it.

laun′dēr, *v.t.* 1. to wash (clothes, etc.); to wash and iron.

2. to wet; also, to cover with a thin coating, as a metal. [Obs.]

laun′dēr, *v.i.* 1. to withstand washing; as, this fabric *launders* well.

2. to do laundry.

laun′dēr·ēr, *n.* one who carries on the business of washing clothes.

laun′dress, *n.* a washerwoman; a woman whose employment is to wash clothes, iron, etc.

laun′dress, *v.i.* to serve as laundress. [Obs.]

laun′dry, *n.*; *pl.* **laun′dries,** [ME. *lavendrie*, from *lavander*, a washerwoman, from OFr. *lavandier*; LL. *lavandarius*, masc., *lavandaria*, f., a washer, from L. *lavandus*, gerundive of *lavare*, to wash.]

1. a laundering.

2. a place where clothes are laundered.

3. clothes, etc. ready for, at, or returned from such a place.

laun′dry·măn, *n.*; *pl.* **laun′dry·men,** a man who works in or for a laundry, especially one who collects and delivers clothes, etc. for laundering service.

laun′dry·wom″ăn (-woom″), *n.*; *pl.* **laun′dry·wom″en** (-wim″), a laundress.

lau′rȧ, *n.* [Gr. *laura*, an alley, lane, a narrow passage between houses.] formerly, and especially in the Levant, a collection of cells or hermitages where the monks did not live in community, but were governed by the same superior.

Lau·rā′cē·ae, *n.pl.* [L. *laurus*, the laurel, and *-aceæ*.] a family of apetalous aromatic trees and shrubs, including the laurel, avocado, nutmeg, cinnamon, cassia, and sassafras.

lau·rā′ceous, *a.* of or pertaining to the family *Lauraceæ*.

lau′rē·āte, *a.* [L. *laureatus*, from *laurea*, the laurel tree, from *laurus*, laurel.]

1. woven of sprigs of laurel: said of a crown or wreath.

2. crowned with a laurel wreath as a mark of honor or distinction.

3. worthy of honor; distinguished; preeminent, especially among poets.

lau′rē·āte, *n.* 1. a person crowned with laurel.

2. a poet laureate.

3. a student crowned with laurel, when receiving a degree in rhetoric and poetry.

lau′rē·āte, *v.t.*; laureated, *pt.*, *pp.*; laureating, *ppr.* 1. to honor or confer distinction upon by crowning with laurel.

2. to appoint to the poet laureateship.

lau′rē·āte·ship, *n.* 1. the position of poet laureate.

2. the time during which a poet holds this position.

lau·rē·ā′tion, *n.* the act of conferring a degree in a university together with a wreath of laurel.

lau′rel, *n.* [ME. *loral*, *laurer*; OFr. *laurier*; L. *laurus*, the bay tree, laurel.]

LAUREL (*Laurus nobilis*)

1. any shrub or tree of the genus *Laurus*, especially the sweet bay, *Laurus nobilis*, a native of the north of Africa and south of Europe, and widely cultivated in the United States. It has large, glossy, aromatic leaves, greenish-yellow flowers, and black berries. In ancient times, heroes and scholars were crowned with wreaths made of its leaves. Also called *bay tree*.

2. any of various similar shrubs, as *Prunus laurocerasus*, the cherry laurel, *Daphne laureola*, the spurge laurel, *Kalmia latifolia*, the mountain laurel, and *Rhododendron maximum*, the great laurel, or rosebay.

3. a crown or wreath of laurel, as a mark of honor, fame, or distinction.

4. [*pl.*] (a) fame; honor; glory; (b) victory.

5. a gold coin of the reign of James I, struck in 1619: so called from the head of the king being crowned with laurel.

to look to one's laurels; to beware of having one's achievements or record surpassed.

to rest on one's laurels; to be satisfied with what one has already achieved or accomplished.

lau′rel, *v.t.*; laureled *or* laurelled, *pt.*, *pp.*; laureling *or* laurelling, *ppr.* 1. to crown with laurel.

2. to honor.

lau′reled (-reld), *a.* crowned or decorated with laurel or with a laurel wreath; laureate.

lau′rel wa̤′tēr, a sedative narcotic water distilled from cherry laurel leaves.

Lau·ren′tiăn (-shăn), *a.* 1. relating to or adjacent to the St. Lawrence River; as, the *Laurentian* hills.

2. of or pertaining to Lorenzo de' Medici or to the library in Florence founded by Pope Clement VII and named in honor of Lorenzo.

3. relating to the Laurentian.

Lau·ren′tiăn, *n.* the younger of two series of crystalline rocks of the Archaean epoch, found in eastern Canada.

lau′riç, *a.* [L. *laurus*, laurel.] of or derived from *Laurus nobilis*, the laurel or bay.

lauric acid; $C_{12}H_{24}O_2$, a compound obtained from several sources, particularly from the laurel.

lau·rif′ēr·ous, *a.* [L. *laurus*, laurel, and *ferre*, to bear.] producing or bringing laurel.

lau′rin, *n.* [L. *laurus*, laurel, and *-in*.] a fatty, acrid, crystalline substance contained in the berries of the laurel.

lau′ri·nōl, *n.* [*laurin* and *-ol*.] camphor.

lau′ri·ŏn·īte, *n.* [so called from *Laurion*, Greece, where it is found.] a prismatic hydroxychloride of lead found in lead slags in the vicinity of Laurion, Greece.

lau′rīte, *n.* [from *Laura*, a woman's name.] a crystalline sulfide of ruthenium and osmium found in platinum mines in Borneo and also in Oregon.

lau′rōne, *n.* a crystalline derivative of lauric acid.

Lau′rus, *n.* [L., the laurel or bay tree.] a genus of the *Lauraceae*, which includes the bay tree.

lau′rus·tine, *n.* [Mod. L. *laurustinus*, from L. *laurus*, *laurel*, and *tinus*, the laurustine.] a tall evergreen shrub grown in the Mediterranean regions of Europe for its fragrant, white or pinkish flowers.

laus Dē′ō, [L.] praise (be) to God.

Lau′wine, *n.* same as *Lawine*.

lä′vȧ, *n.* [It. *lava*, a stream, lava, from *lavare*; L. *lavare*, to wash.]

1. a mass or stream of melted minerals or stony matter which bursts or is thrown from the mouth or sides of a volcano.

2. the same matter when cool and hardened.

lȧ·vā′bō, *n.*; *pl.* **lȧ·vā′bōes,** [L., lit., I shall wash, 1st pers. sing. fut. ind. act. of *lavare*, to wash.] [sometimes L–] in the Roman Catholic Church, (a) the ritual of washing the celebrant's hands after the offertory, accompanied by the repetition of verses 6–12 of Psalm 25 (26 in the Authorized and Revised Versions), beginning with *lavabo*: a similar ritual is used in some Episcopal churches; (b) these verses; (c) the washbowl or basin used; (d) in monasteries, the room containing this; (e) the small towel for drying the celebrant's hands.

lav′ăġe, *n.* [L. *lavare*, to wash.] a washing; specifically, in medicine, the washing out of the stomach or intestinal tract.

lä′vä-lä′vä, *n.* [Samoan.] a calico loincloth or waistcloth worn by Samoans and other South Sea islanders.

lav·ȧ·liēre′, lav·ȧ·liēr′ (-lēr′), *n.* [from Duchesse de *La Vallière* (1644–1710), mistress of Louis XIV.] an ornament hanging from a chain, worn around the neck.

la·val·lière′ (lav-ȧ-lēr′, lȧ-vȧ-lyâr′), *n.* [Fr.] a lavaliere.

Lȧ·van′dū·lȧ, *n.* [LL. *lavandula*, *lavendula*, lavender; It. *lavanda*, lavender, from L. *lavare*, to wash.] a genus of perennial shrubs and plants of which lavender, *Lavandula vera*, is the type.

lav′ȧ·ret, *n.* [Fr.] a species of whitefish found in Europe.

lȧ·vat′iç, *a.* resembling or composed of lava.

la·vā′tion, *n.* [L. *lavatio*, from *lavare*, to wash.]

1. a washing.

2. water for washing.

lav′ȧ·tō·ry, *n.*; *pl.* **lav′ȧ·tō·ries,** [LL. *lavatorium*, a place for bathing, from *lavator*, a clothes washer, from L. *lavare*, to wash.]

1. a bowl or basin for washing the face and hands.

2. a room equipped with such a basin or basins: now often a euphemism for *toilet*.

3. in ecclesiastical usage, the ritual washing of the celebrant's hands at the offertory: cf. *lavabo*.

4. a wash or lotion or a diseased part. [Obs.]

lav′ȧ·tō·ry, *a.* of or pertaining to washing.

lāve, *v.t.* and *v.i.*; laved, *pt.*, *pp.*; laving, *ppr.* [ME. *laven*; OFr. *laver*; L. *lavare*, to bathe, wash.]

1. to wash; to bathe. [Poetic.]

2. to flow along or against. [Poetic.]

lāve, *v.t.*; laved, *pt.*, *pp.*; laving, *ppr.* [ME. *laven*; AS. *lafian*.] to dip or pour with or as with a ladle.

lāve, *v.i.* to droop; to be pendent. [Obs.]

lāve, *n.* [ME. *lave*, *lafe*; AS. *laf*, the remainder.] the remainder; what is left over. [Scot.]

lāve′ment, *n.* [Fr.] 1. a washing or bathing.

2. a clyster.

lav′en·dēr, *n.* [ME.; Anglo-Fr. *lavendre*: ML. *livendula*, *lavendula*; perh. from L. *livere*, to be bluish, or *lividus*, blue.]

1. any of a group of fragrant European plants of the mint family (genus *Lavandula*), having spikes of pale-purplish flowers and yielding an aromatic oil (*oil of lavender*).

2. the dried flowers, leaves, and stalks of this plant, used to fill sachets and to perfume clothes, linens, etc.

3. a pale purple, the color of the flowers of this plant.

LAVENDER (*Lavendula spica*)

lav′en·dēr, *a.* pale-purple.

lav′en·dēr, *v.t.* to perfume with lavender.

lav′en·dēr çot′tŏn, a small shrub with wiry twigs covered with a hoary pubescence: called also *ground cypress*.

lav′en·dēr thrift, the marsh rosemary or sea lavender.

lav′en·dēr wa̤′tēr, a perfume or toilet water containing oil of lavender.

lā′vēr, *n.* [ME. *laver*, *lavour*; OFr. *lavor*, *lavur*; LL. *lavatorium*; a place for bathing, from L. *lavare*, to wash.]

1. a vessel for washing; a large basin; in Scripture, a basin placed in the court of the Jewish tabernacle, where officiating priests washed their hands and feet. [Archaic.]

2. that which cleanses or laves spiritually; especially, the water of baptism or the font containing this.

lāv′ēr, *n.* one who washes or laves. [Obs.]

lā′vēr, *n.* [L., a water plant.] the fronds or leaves of certain marine plants, or the same prepared as food.

lav′ēr·ock, *n.* the lark. [Archaic or Scot.]

lä′viç, *a.* resembling lava; lavatic.

lav′ish, *a.* [ME. *lavage*, from *laven*; AS. *lafian*, to pour out, sprinkle water.]

1. prodigal; very generous or liberal in giving or spending, often extravagantly so.
2. unrestrained; excessive; more than enough; very abundant.

lav'ish, *v.t.*; lavished (-isht), *pt.*, *pp.*; lavishing, *ppr.* 1. to give or spend with profusion; as, to *lavish* praise.
2. to waste; to squander; as, to *lavish* money on vices.

lav'ish·ẽr, *n.* a person who lavishes.

lav'ish·ly, *adv.* in a lavish manner.

lav'ish·ment, *n.* the act of expending lavishly. [Rare.]

lav'ish·ness, *n.* profusion; prodigality.

là·vol'tà, là·volt', *n.* [It. *la volta*, the turn.] an old dance somewhat resembling a waltz. [Obs.]

là·vol'te·tēre, *n.* one who dances the lavolta. [Obs.]

lav'rock, *n.* a laverock. [Obs.]

lav'rō·vīte, *n.* pyroxene of a greenish color, due to the presence in it of vanadium.

la̤w, la̤ws, *interj.* [a corruption of *Lord*; or same as *la!*] an exclamation expressing astonishment.

la̤w, la̤we, *a.* low. [Obs.]

la̤w, *n.* a hill or mound. [Scot.]

la̤w, *n.* [ME. *lawe, laghe*; AS. *lagu*, law, that which is laid or fixed, from *licgan*, to lie.]
1. all the rules of conduct established and enforced by the authority, legislation, or custom of a given community or other group; as, a basic tenet of English *law*.
2. any one of such rules.
3. the condition existing when obedience to such rules is general; as, they have established *law* and order.
4. the branch of knowledge dealing with such rules; jurisprudence.
5. the system of courts in which such rules are referred to in defending one's rights, securing justice, etc.; as, they had to resort to *law* to settle the matter.
6. all such rules having to do with a particular sphere of human activity; as, business *law*.
7. in England, common law, as distinguished from equity.
8. the profession of lawyers, judges, etc. (often with *the*).
9. knowledge of the law (sense 1); as, his *law* is sound.
10. (a) a sequence of events in nature or in human activities that has been observed to occur with unvarying uniformity under the same conditions: often *law of nature*; (b) the formulation in words of such a sequence; as, the *law* of gravitation, the *law* of diminishing returns.
11. any rule or principle expected to be observed; as, the *laws* of health, a *law* of grammar.
12. inherent tendency; instinct; as, the *law* of self-preservation.
13. in ecclesiastical usage, (a) a divine commandment; (b) all divine commandments collectively.
14. in mathematics, a general principle to which all applicable cases must conform; as, the *laws* of exponents.
15. in sports, an allowance in distance or time, as in a race; handicap. [Chiefly Brit.]

Syn.- act, canon, code, command, commandment, common law, decree, edict, enactment, formula, injunction, mandate, order, ordinance, principle, regulation, rule, statute. —*Law* is the general term signifying a rule laid down or established, whether by custom or as the expression of the will of a person or power able to enforce its demands. *Law* implies a penalty or inconvenience for disobedience, and also generality of application as distinguished from a special *command*. A *rule* is a regular established method of procedure or action; as, office *rules*. A *code* is an entire system of rules or laws. A *command, commandment*, or *mandate* is a specific act of authority; as, a parent's *command*; the *mandate* of a court. *Common law* is the entire body of rules of conduct established by long usage and the decisions of law courts. A *decree* or an *edict* is a law or decision given by a sovereign power; as, an *edict* of Caesar; a *decree* of the court. An *act, enactment*, or *statute* is a specific law enacted by the lawmaking body of a state, while an *ordinance* is usually a municipal regulation. These are *law* only if they do not conflict with the organic *law* or constitution. *Injunction* is specifically applied to an order of a court of equity. A *formula* is a conventional form or a set *rule*.

Bode's law; in astronomy, the law that the relative distances of the planets from the sun are indicated approximately by the series 4, 7, 10, 16, 28, etc.; a series formed by adding 4 to each term of the series 0, 3, 6, 12, 24, etc. Neptune is an exception.

Boyle's law; in physics, the law of compressibility of gases, viz.: the temperature remaining the same, the volume of a given quantity of a gas is inversely proportional to the pressure which it bears.

Charles's law; in physics, the law that all gases have the same coefficient of expansion; i. e., the volume or the pressure of all gases varies directly as the change in temperature.

civil law; (a) Roman law, especially the part that applied to Roman citizens; (b) the body of law having to do with private rights: it developed from Roman law.

commercial law, or *law merchant*; the rules observed by merchants and other business men in their dealings with each other, now part of the common law recognized and enforced by the courts.

common law; the unwritten law of a country based on custom, usage, and the decisions of law courts, as contrasted with *statute law*: it is now largely codified by legislative definition.

Kepler's laws; three important laws of planetary motion: (a) the orbits of the planets about the sun are ellipses, of each of which the sun occupies one focus; (b) the area described by the radius vector of a planet is the same for equal periods of time; (c) the squares of the periods of revolution about the sun of the several planets are in the proportion of the cubes of their mean solar distances.

law French; the Anglo-French formerly used in legal proceedings in England.

law language; the language used in legal documents.

law Latin; a corrupt form of Latin used in legal documents and in medieval statutes.

law merchant; commercial law.

law of diminishing return; the law that an increase of labor or capital applied beyond a certain point, as in the cultivation of land, causes a less than proportionate increase in production.

law of nations; international law.

law of nature; (a) a physical law; (b) that portion of morality which supplies the more important and universal rules for the governance of the outward acts of mankind.

law of the Medes and Persians; unchangeable law.

laws of honor; see under *honor*.

laws of motion; in physics, the laws relating to bodies in motion: sometimes called *Newton's laws*: (a) every body continues in its state of rest or of uniform motion in a straight line, except as it is compelled by force to change that state; (b) change of motion takes place in the direction of the straight line in which an applied force acts and is directly proportional to the amount of that force; (c) every action has an equal and contrary reaction; i.e., the mutual actions of two bodies on each other are always forces equal in amount and opposite in direction.

Lenz's law; in electricity, the law that induced currents are always such as, by their direction or action, to oppose the inducing cause.

Mariotte's law; same as *Boyle's law*.

maritime or *marine law*; the system of law which relates to marine affairs generally, including navigation, ships, seamen, and the transportation of persons and property by sea.

martial law; the military rules and regulations by which the civil authority is superseded in time of war or during public emergencies: established and enforced by the officer in charge in accordance with military law and the usages of war.

military law; the system of rules and regulations which govern a nation's military forces: not to be confused with *martial law*, which controls all persons within its jurisdiction, civilians as well as soldiers.

moral law; (a) that system of rules of human action which has its origin in a general sense of the members of any community of what is right and wrong, and which derives its authority from the general disapprobation of acts contrary to its principles; (b) the decalogue and moral maxims of the Mosaic law.

municipal law; a system of rules of human action established by the governmental power of a state.

Ohm's law; a law, formulated by G. S. Ohm, which states that the intensity of a constant electrical current in a circuit is directly proportional to the electromotive force and inversely proportional to the resistance.

Roman law; same as *civil law*, (a).

statute law; law established by a legislative body.

sumptuary laws; laws restricting or regulating extravagance in food, dress, etc. on religious or moral grounds.

the Law; (a) the Mosaic code, or the part of the Old Testament containing it; (b) the Old Testament; (c) [l–] [Colloq.] a policeman, or the police.

to go to law; to take a problem or dispute to a law court for settlement.

to lay down the law; (a) to give explicit orders in an authoritative manner; (b) to give a scolding (*to*).

to read law; to study to become a lawyer.

to take the law into one's own hands; to punish a criminal or defend one's rights without regular legal procedure.

wager of law; a legal procedure formerly used in England, in which the defendant gave security that he would, on a certain day, make his law; that is, make oath that he owed nothing to the plaintiff, and would produce eleven of his neighbors as compurgators, who should swear that they believed in their consciences that he had sworn the truth.

la̤w'-à·bīd″ing, *a.* observant of the law; obeying the law; as, *law-abiding* citizens.

la̤w bīnd'ing, the style of light-brown leather binding commonly used on law books: called also *law calf*.

la̤w'book, *n.* a book containing laws or discussing laws; especially, such a book used as a textbook for students of law.

la̤w'brea̤k″ẽr, *n.* one who violates the law.

la̤w'brea̤k·ing, *n.* violation of the law.

la̤w'brea̤k·ing, *a.* violating the law.

la̤w bũr'rōws, in Scots law, a writ or document in the name of the sovereign, commanding a person to give security against offering violence to another.

la̤w ça̤lf (kȧf), same as *law binding*.

la̤w çōurt, a court for the administration of justice under the law; a judicial tribunal.

la̤w dāy, 1. a day of open court. [Obs.]
2. a leet or sheriff's court. [Obs.]
3. the last day upon which a debt secured by a mortgage could be paid and the debtor be secure from forfeiture.

la̤w'fu̇l, *a.* 1. agreeable to law; conformable to law; allowed by law; legitimate; as, a *lawful* act.
2. recognized by law; rightful; as, the *lawful* owner of lands.

la̤w'fu̇l·ly, *adv.* in a lawful manner; legally; without violating law.

la̤w'fu̇l·ness, *n.* the quality of being conformable to law; legality.

la̤w'giv″ẽr, *n.* a person who draws up, introduces, or enacts a code of laws for a nation or people; a lawmaker; legislator.

la̤w'giv″ing, *a.* making or enacting laws.

Lä·wï'ne (-vē'), *n.*; *pl.* **Lä·wï'nen** (-vē'), [G.] an avalanche.

la̤w'ing, *n.* 1. expeditation; the act of cutting off the claws and balls of the forefeet of mastiffs, to prevent them from running after deer. [Obs.]
2. litigation. [Colloq.]
3. a tavern bill. [Scot.]

la̤w'less, *a.* 1. without law; not regulated by the authority of law; as, a *lawless* city.
2. contrary to law; illegal; unauthorized; as, *lawless* practices.
3. not obeying the law; unruly; disorderly.

la̤w'less·ly, *adv.* in a manner contrary to law.

la̤w'less·ness, *n.* the quality or state of being unrestrained by law; disorder.

la̤w'māk″ẽr, *n.* a person who makes or helps to make laws; especially, a member of a legislature; a legislator.

la̤w'māk″ing, *n.* the making of laws; legislation.

la̤w'māk″ing, *a.* making laws; legislative.

la̤w'mŏñ″gẽr, *n.* an unethical lawyer; a pettifogger.

la̤wn, *n.* [ME. *launde*; OFr. *lande*, a heath; of Celtic origin; compare W. *llan*, a lawn.]
1. land covered with grass kept closely mown, especially in front of or around a house.
2. an open space in a forest; a glade. [Archaic.]

lạwn, *n.* [prob. from *Laon*, a town in France.] a thin, fine linen or cotton used for handkerchiefs, blouses, curtains, etc.

lạwn, *a.* made of lawn.

lạwn mōw'ẽr, a hand-propelled or power-driven machine for cutting grass on lawns.

lạwn ten'nis, a kind of tennis usually played out of doors on a smooth surface, as on a lawn: see *tennis*.

lạwn'y, *a.* resembling a lawn.

lạwn'y, *a.* made of or resembling lawn (cloth).

lạw'ren·cīte, *n.* [named after J. *Lawrence* Smith, an American mineralogist.] a native ferrous chloride sometimes found in meteorites.

lạw·ren'ci·um, *n.* [named after E. O. *Lawrence*, an American physicist.] a radioactive chemical element produced by bombarding californium with boron nuclei; symbol, Lr; atomic weight, 256(?); atomic number, 103.

Lạw·sō'ni·ȧ, *n.* [named after Dr. John *Lawson*, Scot. botanist.] a genus of Eastern shrubs containing only one species, the henna plant, *Lawsonia inermis*, bearing white flowers: henna is obtained from the leaves.

lạw'sūit, *n.* a suit in law or in equity; case presented before a civil court for decision.

lạw'yẽr, *n.* [from *law* and *-yer, -ier*.]

1. a person who has been trained in the law, especially one whose profession is advising others in matters of law or representing them in lawsuits.

2. in zoology, (a) the black-necked stilt; (b) the burbot; (c) the bowfin.

3. the thorny stem of a bramble or brier. [Brit. Dial.]

lạw'yẽr·līke, lạw'yẽr·ly, *a.* like or appropriate to a lawyer.

lax, *a.*; *comp.* laxer; *superl.* laxest. [L. *laxus*, slack, loose, open.]

1. (a) loose; emptying easily: said of the bowels; (b) having lax bowels.

2. slack; of a loose texture; not rigid or tight.

3. not strict or exact; careless; as, *lax* morals.

4. in botany, loose; open: said of a flower cluster.

5. in phonetics, pronounced with the jaw and tongue relatively relaxed: said of certain vowels, as *e* in *met*, *i* in *hill*.

lax, *n.* a lax vowel.

lax·ā'tion, *n.* the act of loosening or slackening; also, the state of being loosened or slakened.

lax'ȧ·tive, *a.* [Fr. *laxatif*; L. *laxativus*, mitigating, loosening, from *laxare*, to loosen, from *laxus*, loose.] tending to make lax; specifically, making the bowels loose and relieving constipation.

lax'ȧ·tive, *n.* a laxative medicine; mild cathartic.

lax'ȧ·tive·ness, *n.* the quality of relaxing.

lax·ā'tŏr, *n.*; *pl.* **lax·ȧ·tō'rēs,** [from L. *laxatus*, pp. of *laxare*, to loosen.] in anatomy, a part, especially a muscle, which relaxes.

lax·i·flō'rous, *a.* [L. *laxus*, loose, and *flos*, *floris*, a flower.] in botany, having the flowers loose or scattered.

lax'i·ty, *n.* [Fr. *laxité*; L. *laxitas* (-*atis*), looseness, from *laxus*, loose, slack.] looseness; the quality or condition of being lax.

lax'ly, *adv.* loosely; without exactness.

lax'ness, *n.* looseness; softness; laxity.

lāy, *v.* past tense of *lie*.

lāy, *v.t.*; laid, *pt.*, *pp.*; laying, *ppr.* [ME. *leyen*, *leien*; AS. *lecgan*, to cause to lie, to lay, from *licgan*, to lie.]

1. to cause to come down or fall with force; to knock down, as from an erect position; as, he *laid* his opponent low with one punch.

2. to cause to lie; to place or put so as to be in a resting or recumbent position; to deposit (with *on* or *in*); as, *lay* the pencil *on* the table.

3. (a) to put down in the correct position for a specific purpose, as bricks, carpeting, etc.; (b) to cause to be situated in a particular place or condition; as, the scene is *laid* in France.

4. to place; put; set; of something abstract, as, he *lays* great emphasis on accuracy.

5. to produce and deposit (an egg or eggs): said of a bird, etc.

6. (a) to cause to subside or settle; as, *lay* the dust; (b) to allay, suppress, overcome, or appease; as, this *laid* the ghost; his doubts were *laid*.

7. to press or smooth down; as, she *laid* the nap of the cloth.

8. to bet (a specified sum, etc.).

9. to impose (a tax, penalty, etc.).

10. to work out; devise; as, *lay* your plans carefully.

11. to prepare (a table) for a meal; to set with silverware, plates, etc.

12. to advance, present, or assert; as, he *laid* claim to the property.

13. to attribute; ascribe; charge; impute; as, the murder was *laid* to Jones.

14. (a) to form (the strands of a rope) by twisting yarn; (b) to form (a rope) by arranging and twisting the strands.

15. to have sexual intercourse with. [Slang.]

to lay a course; (a) in nautical usage, to proceed in a certain direction without tacking; (b) to make plans to do something.

to lay aside; (a) to put to one side; to lay out of the way; (b) to save; to lay away.

to lay away; (a) to place aside for keeping; (b) to discard; to lay aside; (c) to set (merchandise) aside for future delivery; (d) to bury (usually in the passive).

to lay before; to present for consideration.

to lay by; to lay away.

to lay down; (a) to resign, as an office; (b) to deposit, as a pledge; (c) to offer, assert, or declare, as a principle or a command; (d) to preserve, to lay by, as salt meats or provisions; (e) to draft, as a plan or diagram; (f) to sacrifice or give up (one's life); (g) to bet; wager.

to lay (fast) by the heels; (a) to put in chains or fetters; to imprison; (b) to deprive of freedom of movement.

to lay in; (a) to get and lay aside; to store; (b) to put in; to enter; as, *to lay in* a claim.

to lay it on; (a) to exaggerate; (b) to flatter; to give effusive compliments. [Colloq.]

to lay off; (a) to put off or aside, as a burden; (b) to turn, as the body of a boat or vessel from any point; (c) to discharge or dismiss temporarily, as employees; (d) to draw on paper, as a chart; (e) to transfer (the plans of a ship) from the paper to the full size on the floor of the molding loft; (f) to mark off the boundaries of; (g) [Slang.] to cease.

to lay on; (a) to apply with force, as blows; (b) to spread on.

to lay oneself open; to expose oneself to attack, blame, etc.

to lay oneself out; to try very hard. [Colloq.]

to lay open; to open; to make bare; to expose; to reveal; to make an opening in.

to lay out; (a) to expend; as, *to lay out* money; (b) to plan; to arrange after a plan; as, *to lay out* a garden; (c) to dress in graveclothes and place in a suitable posture; as, *to lay out* a corpse; (d) to exert; as, *to lay out* one's strength; (e) [Slang.] to knock down or disable; (f) to spread out (clothes, equipment, etc.) ready for wear, inspection, etc.

to lay to; (a) to apply with vigor; (b) to attack; (c) to impute; to charge with; (d) to check the motion of (a ship) and cause her to become stationary.

to lay up; (a) to store for future use; (b) to confine to a bed or room; (c) to dismantle and put out of use, as a ship.

to lay waste; to devastate, make desolate, or ravage.

lāy, *v.i.* 1. to produce and give forth eggs, as hens.

2. in nautical usage, to go to a station or to assume a position; as, to *lay* aft; to *lay* aloft.

3. to put up a wager; to make a bet.

4. to lie; recline: substandard usage.

5. to apply oneself with energy; as, the sailors *lay* to their oars.

to lay about one; (a) to deliver blows on all sides; (b) to act energetically.

to lay for; to be waiting to assault or capture. [Colloq.]

to lay in for; to make overtures for; to engage or secure the possession of. [Obs.]

to lay into; (a) to attack and hit repeatedly; to beat; (b) to attack with words; to scold. [Slang.]

to lay out; to purpose; to intend; as, he *lays out* to make a journey.

to lay over; to stop a while in a place before continuing a journey.

lāy, *n.* 1. the way or position in which something is situated or arranged; as, the *lay* of the land.

2. a share in the profits of some enterprise, especially of a whaling expedition.

3. the direction or amount of twist of the strand of a rope, cable, etc.

4. that which lies or is laid; specifically, a row; a stratum; a layer; one rank in a series reckoned upward; as, a *lay* of wood. [Obs.]

5. a bet; a wager. [Obs.]

6. a scheme; a plan; as, what's your *lay*? [Slang.]

7. station; rank. [Obs.]

8. a certain quantity of thread or yarn.

9. in a loom, the lathe or batten.

lāy, *a.* [OFr. *lai*; LL. *laicus*, the laity; Gr. *laikos*, from *laos*, the people.]

1. pertaining to the laity, or ordinary people, as distinguished from the clergy.

2. not belonging to or connected with a given profession; nonprofessional; as, a *lay* opinion as to the law.

lay analyst; a psychoanalyst who is not a medical doctor.

lay baptism; baptism administered by one of the laity.

lay brother; (a) one received under religious vows into a monastery, but not in holy orders: lay brothers are generally employed in manual labor; (b) a layman.

lay clerk; a layman who leads the responses, etc. in a church service.

lāy, *n.* a lea; meadow. [Obs.]

lāy, *n.* 1. faith; religious creed. [Obs.]

2. a vow; pledge. [Obs.]

3. a law. [Obs.]

lāy, *n.* [ME. *laye*, *lai*; OFr. *lai*, *lais*, a song; prob. of Celtic origin.]

1. a short poem, especially a narrative poem, for singing: originally applied to a short narrative poem for performance by a minstrel and with a story drawn from Arthurian or Breton tradition.

2. a song or melody. [Archaic or Poetic.]

lāy dāy, 1. any of the days allowed to a person chartering a vessel, in which to load or unload the cargo without payment of extra charge.

2. any of the days that a ship is delayed in port.

lāy'ẽr, *n.* 1. one who or that which lays.

2. that which is laid on any surface; a stratum; a bed; a thickness or fold spread over another; as, a *layer* of clay or sand.

3. a shoot or twig of a plant, not detached from the stock, bent down and partly covered with earth so that it may take root.

4. an oyster bed made artificially.

lāy'ẽr, *v.t.* and *v.i.* to grow (plants) by layering.

lāy'ẽr·ȧġe, *n.* the growing of plants by layering.

lāy'ẽr çāke, a cake baked in two or more layers, which are placed one on the other, usually with icing, etc. in between.

lāy'ẽr·ing, *n.* a method of growing plants and shrubs by bending a shoot or twig and covering it with earth until it has rooted.

LAYER

lāy'ẽr-out', *n.* one who expends money.

lāy·ette' (-et'), *n.* [Fr.] an entire outfit prepared for a newborn baby, as the bedding, clothing, etc.

lāy fig'ūre, 1. an artist's jointed model of the human body. It can be placed in any position or attitude, and serves, when clothed, as a model for drapery, etc.

2. any person acting as a mere figurehead for another.

LAY FIGURE

lāy'ing, *n.* 1. the first coat on laths of plasterer's two-coat work.

2. the act or period of laying eggs; also, the eggs laid for a single incubation.

lāy'măn, *n.*, *pl.* **lāy'men,** 1. one not a clergyman; one of the laity; also, one who is not a member of a given profession, in distinction from one who is.

2. a figure used by painters; a lay figure. [Obs.]

lāy'nẽr, *n.* a lannier; a whiplash. [Obs.]

lāy'off, *n.* 1. a putting out of work or being put out of work, especially temporarily.

2. the period of such unemployment.

lāy of the land, 1. the way the land is situated; arrangement of the terrain.

2. the existing state or disposition of affairs. Also *lie of the land*.

lāy'out, *n.* 1. the act of laying something out.

2. the manner in which anything is laid out; arrangement; specifically, the plan or

make-up of a newspaper, book, page, advertisement, etc.
3. the thing laid out.
4. an outfit or set, as of tools.

lāy′ō·vẽr, *n.* a stopping for a while in some place during a journey.

lāy rāce, a shuttle race.

lāy′stall, *n.* a heap of dung, or a place where dung is laid. [Brit.]

lāy′up, *n.* in basketball, a leaping, one-handed shot made from a position very close to the basket, usually off the backboard.

lā′zăr, *n.* [ME. *lazar, lazer*; OFr. *lazar*; LL. *lazarus*, a leper, from L. *Lazarus*; Gr. *Lazaros*, Lazarus, the beggar spoken of in the parable, Luke xvi. 19–31, from Heb. *El'āzār*, lit., he whom God helps.] an impoverished beggar infected with a pestilential disease; especially, a leper. [Rare.]

laz·à·ret′, laz·à·rette′, *n.* [Fr. *lazaret*, from It.] same as *lazaretto*.

laz·à·ret′tō, *n.*; *pl.* **laz·à·ret′tōs,** [It.; Venetian *lazareto, nazareto*, from Venetian church of Santa Madonna di *Nazaret*, used as a plague hospital during the 15th c.; initial *l*- by analogy with *lazzaro*, leper.]
1. a public hospital for poor people having contagious diseases, especially for lepers.
2. a building or ship used as a quarantine station.
3. in certain ships, a space between decks, used for storing provisions.

lā′zăr house, a lazaretto.

Laz′à·rist, Laz′à·rīte, *n.* a member of an order of missionaries in the Roman Catholic Church, established in 1624.

lā′zăr·līke, *a.* full of sores; leprous.

Laz′à·rus, *n.* 1. in the Bible, (a) the brother of Mary and Martha, raised from the dead by Jesus: John xi; (b) the diseased beggar in Jesus' parable of the rich man and the beggar: Luke xvi. 19–31.
2. [often l–] any horribly diseased beggar, especially a leper.

lāze, *v.i.*; lazed, *pt., pp.*; lazing, *ppr.* [back-formation from *lazy*.] to be lazy or idle; to loaf.

lāze, *v.t.* to spend (time, etc.) in idleness (often with *away*).

lā′zi·ly, *adv.* in a lazy manner; sluggishly.

lā′zi·ness, *n.* the state or quality of being lazy; indisposition to action or exertion; indolence.

laz′ū·lī, *n.* lapis lazuli.

laz′ū·lī finch, a bird of brilliant blue coloring, *Passerina amæna*, common to western North America.

laz′ū·līte, *n.* [from ML. *lazulum*, azure; and *-ite*.] a glassy, azure-blue mineral, hydrous aluminum phosphate, with varying amounts of iron and magnesium.

lā′zy, *a.*; *comp.* lazier; *superl.* laziest, [Early Mod. Eng.; prob. from M.L.G. or M.D.]
1. disinclined to action or exertion; slothful; indolent; averse to labor.
2. slow; moving slowly or sluggishly; as, a *lazy* stream.
3. tending to cause laziness; as, a *lazy* day.

lā′zy·bōnes, *n.* one who is lazy. [Colloq.]

Lā′zy Sū′sǎn, a large revolving tray for food.

lā′zy tongs, a mechanical device in the form of extensible tongs by which objects at a distance may be grasped.

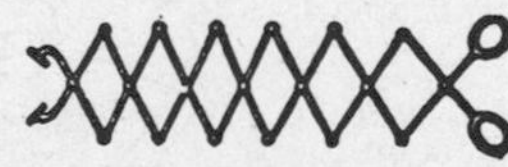

LAZY TONGS

laz·zà·rō′ne, *n.*; *pl.* **laz·zà·rō′ni,** [It., from *lazzaro*, leper.] any of a class of homeless beggars formerly common on the streets of Naples.

L bär (or **bēam**), a steel bar or beam made in the shape of an L.

LCD, [*l*iquid *c*rystal *d*isplay.] a device for alphanumeric displays, as on digital watches, using a liquid with certain characteristics of crystals that is sealed between two pieces of glass and polarizers and activated by an external light source.

-le, [ME. *-le, -el*; AS. *-ol, -ul*, or *-el*.] an old suffix meaning: (a) *small*, as in icic*le*; (b) *a person that does* (something specified), as in bead*le*; (c) *a thing used for doing* (something specified), as in gird*le*, hand*le*.

-le, [ME. *adj.* suffix *-el*, from AS. *-ol*.] an old suffix meaning *having a tendency toward*, as in britt*le*, fick*le*.

-le, [ME. v. suffix *-len*; AS. *-lian*.] an old suffix used with a frequentative force, as in babb*le*.

-le, [ME. n. suffix *-el*, from OFr. *-el, -aille*, or *-eille*.] an old suffix of various meanings, as in bott*le*, mant*le*.

lēa, *a.* untilled; fallow, as land. [Brit.]

lēa, *n.* a scythe. [Brit. Dial.]

lēa, *n.* [ME. *ley, lay*; AS. *leah*, a meadow, pasture, lea.] a meadow, grassy field, or pasture; grassland. [Chiefly Poet.]

lēa, *n.* [perhaps taken as sing. from *leas*, from OFr. *lesse, laisse*, leash.]
1. a measure of yarn varying from 80 to 300 yards, according to the kind of yarn (usually 80 yards for wool, 120 yards for silk and cotton, 300 yards for linen).
2. one of the alternating sets of warp threads in a loom.

lēach, *n.* same as *leech* (edge of a sail).

lēach, *v.t.*; leached (lēcht), *pt., pp.*; leaching, *ppr.* [AS. *leccan*, to wet, moisten.]
1. to cause (a liquid) to filter down through some material.
2. to subject to the washing action of a filtering liquid; as, wood ashes are *leached* to extract lye.
3. to extract (a soluble substance) from some material by causing water to filter down through the material; as, lye is *leached* from wood ashes.

lēach, *v.i.* 1. to lose soluble matter as a result of the filtering through of water; as, ashes *leach*.
2. to dissolve and be washed away.

lēach, *n.* 1. a leaching.
2. a sievelike container used in leaching.
3. the substance through which a liquid is leached

lēach′y, *a.* incapable of retaining water; porous; as, a *leachy* soil.

lead (led), *n.* [ME. *leed*; AS. *lead*, lead.]
1. a heavy, soft, malleable, bluish-gray metallic chemical element used for piping and in numerous alloys and compounds: symbol, Pb; atomic weight, 207.21; atomic number, 82.
2. a plummet of lead, used for sounding depths at sea: it is attached to a line and tossed over the side of the ship.
3. [*usually in pl.*] a thin strip of type metal or brass, used to separate lines in printing.
4. a small cylinder of graphite in a lead pencil.
5. white lead.
6. [*pl.*] sheets of lead used as a roof covering; also, a roof thus covered. [Brit.]
7. [*usually in pl.*] any of the strips of lead used to hold the individual panes in ornamental windows.
8. a cauldron. [Dial.]
9. bullets.

lead (led), *a.* made of or containing lead.

lead (led), *v.t.*; leaded, *pt., pp.*; leading, *ppr.*
1. to fit, cover, or weight with lead or leads.
2. in printing, to insert metal strips between (lines of type) in order to increase the space between them.
3. to glaze (pottery) with a glaze made primarily of lead.

lead (led), *v.i.* to become filled or covered with lead, as a rifle groove.

lēad (lēd), *v.t.*; led, *pt., pp.*; leading, *ppr.* [ME. *leden*; AS. *lædan*, to lead, from *lidhan*, to go, glide on.]
1. to guide by holding the hand, pulling a rope, etc.; as, to *lead* a child.
2. (a) to guide or conduct by showing the way; to direct; as, the Israelites were *led* by a pillar of cloud by day; (b) to guide the course or direction of (water, rope, etc.).
3. to conduct, as a chief or commander; to direct and govern; as, a general *leads* his troops to battle; the orchestra was *led* by an old man.
4. to precede; to introduce by going first.
5. to hold the first place in rank or dignity among; as, she *leads* the class.
6. to show the method of attaining an object; to direct, as in an investigation; as, self-examination may *lead* us to a knowledge of ourselves.
7. to begin; to open; specifically, in card playing, to commence a round or trick with; as, he *leads* hearts; he *led* the ace of trumps.
8. to draw; to entice; to allure; as, the love of pleasure *leads* men into vices.
9. to induce; to prevail on; to influence.
10. to pass; to spend; as, to *lead* a life of gaiety, or a solitary life.
11. to cause to pass; to cause to spend; to cause to endure.

You remember the life he *led* his wife and daughter. —Dickens.

12. in hunting, to aim a rifle, etc. just ahead of (a moving target).

to lead astray; to lead from the right path; to seduce.

to lead on; (a) to conduct further; (b) to encourage to continue; to lure.

to lead one a chase (or *dance*); to cause a person trouble by luring him into a vain pursuit.

Syn.—conduct, guide, precede, induce, commence, inaugurate, convey, persuade, direct, influence.

lēad, *v.i.* 1. to show the way by going before or along; to act as guide; to guide; conduct.
2. to submit to being led; to be tractable.
3. to be or form a way; to tend in a certain direction; to go (with *to, from, under*, etc.).
4. to bring as a result (with *to*); as, one thing *led* to another.
5. to be first, chief, or head; to act as leader.
6. to begin.
7. in boxing, to strike a first blow or one designed to test an opponent's defense; as, never *lead* with your right.
8. in card games, to play, or have the right to play, the first card of a hand or round.

to lead off or *out*; to begin.

to lead up to; to prepare the way for.

lēad, *n.* 1. the part of director or leader; leadership; as, in community projects he always took the *lead*.
2. example; as, we will follow your *lead*.
3. first or front place; precedence; as, he took the *lead* at the first turn.
4. the extent of distance ahead or precedence; as, we now hold a safe *lead*.
5. anything that leads or serves as a clue.
6. in boxing, a leading, or the blow used.
7. in card games, act or right of playing first, as in a hand, or the card or suit played.
8. in electricity, (a) a wire carrying current from one point to another in a circuit; (b) a wire or cable carrying current to or from a piece of apparatus.
9. in the theater, (a) the principal role, or a leading role, in a play or other production; (b) the actor or actress who plays such a role.
10. in journalism, the opening paragraph of a news story, containing all the essential facts of the story.
11. in mining, a stratum of ore in an old river bed; lode.
12. in nautical usage, the course of a rope.

Syn.—priority, precedence, pre-eminence, initiative, guidance, control.

lēad, *a.* acting as leader; as, the *lead* horse.

lead ac′e·tāte (led), a poisonous, colorless, crystalline compound, $Pb(C_2H_3O_2)_2 \cdot 3H_2O$, used as a mordant in dyeing, and in making varnishes; sugar of lead.

lead är′sen·āte, a very poisonous, colorless, crystalline compound, $Pb_3(AsO_4)_2$, used as an insecticide.

lead′ed (led′), *a.* 1. fitted or provided with lead.
2. separated by leads, as lines in printing.

lead′en, *a.* 1. made of lead.
2. figuratively, having one or more of the qualities of lead; blue-gray, heavy, gloomy, hard to move or lift, dull, or sluggish; as, a *leaden* sky; a *leaden* weight, face, gait, etc.

lēad′ẽr, *n.* [ME. *leder*; AS. *lædere*, a leader, from *lædan*, to lead.]
1. a person or thing that leads; directing, commanding, or guiding head, as of a group or activity.
2. a horse harnessed before all others in the same hitch or as one of the two horses in the foremost span.
3. a pipe for carrying water, etc.
4. a tendon.
5. a featured article of trade, especially one offered at an attractively low price.
6. in fishing, a short piece of catgut, etc., often used to attach the hook, lure, etc. to the fishline proper.
7. in journalism, one of the main editorials or articles, as in a newspaper.
8. in music, (a) a conductor, especially the conductor of a dance band; (b) the main performer in an instrumental or vocal section, generally given the solo passages.
9. in nautical usage, a wooden block or metal piece with holes in it for leading lines to their proper places.
10. [*pl.*] in printing, dots, dashes, etc. in a line, used to direct the eye across the page, as in a table of contents.

lēad′ẽr·ship, *n.* 1. the position or guidance of a leader.
2. the ability to lead.

lead′hill·ite (led′), *n.* in mineralogy, a sulfate and carbonate of lead, found at Leadhills, Scotland.

lēad′in, *n.* the wire leading from the aerial to a radio receiver or transmitter.

lēad′-in, *a.* leading in; as, a *lead-in* wire or cable for a radio.

lead′ing (led′), *n* 1. work made of lead, as a roof, or as the cames in certain windows.
2. a covering or being covered with lead.
3. strips or sheets of lead, collectively.

lēad′ing, *n.* the action of one that leads; guidance; direction; leadership.

lēad′ing, *a.* 1. guiding; conducting; preceding; drawing; alluring.
2. chief; principal; capital; most influential; as, a *leading* motive.
3. showing the way by going first; constituting a precedent.
4. playing the lead in a play, motion picture, etc
leading article; a principal editorial or article in a newspaper.
leading case; in law, a reported case which is considered to determine the law upon the points in question.
leading edge; (a) in aeronautics, the foremost part of a wing or propeller blade: also called *entering edge*; (b) in nautical usage, that edge of the sail which first encounters the wind.
leading light; (a) a light used to guide ships into and out of a harbor; (b) [Slang.] one of the most important members of a club, community, etc.
leading question; a question so worded as to suggest the answer desired.
leading strings; (a) strings or straps used to guide and support a young child learning to walk; (b) guidance; especially, excessive guidance or control.
leading tone; in music, the seventh tone of a scale, a half tone below the tonic.

lead līne (led), in nautical usage, a line used in taking soundings, having marks at intervals for noting depths

lead mill (led), 1. a grinding wheel of lead used in gem cutting.
2. a mill in which white lead is ground.

lead ō′ch̤ēr (-kẽr), same as *massicot.*

lēad′ǫff, *n.* a beginning; especially, in certain sports, the first blow, play, or turn.

lēad′-ǫff, *a.* that leads off, or begins.

lead pen′cil (led), a pencil consisting of a slender stick of graphite encased in wood, etc.; common pencil.

lead plant, a small leguminous shrub, *Amorpha canescens*, found in the western United States.

lead poi′ṣŏn·ing (led), an acute or chronic poisoning caused by the absorption of lead or any of its salts into the body: it may result in anemia, constipation, colic, paralysis, etc.

lēad sçrew (skrụ), in a lathe, the screw which gives longitudinal motion to the slide rest.

leadṣ′măn, *n.*; *pl.* **leadṣ′men,** in nautical usage, the sailor who takes soundings by heaving the lead.

lead tet·rȧ·eth′yl (led), a heavy, colorless, poisonous compound of lead, $Pb(C_2H_5)_4$, added to gasoline to increase power and prevent engine knock: also *tetraethyl lead.*

lēad tīme, in manufacturing, the period of time required from the decision to make a product to the beginning of actual production.

lead tree, 1. a leguminous tree, *Leucæne glauca*, of the American tropics.
2. the treelike crystallization of lead obtained by hanging zinc in a lead acetate solution.

lead′wŏrt, *n.* a herbaceous plant, *Plumbago europæa*, or any other plant of the same genus.

lead′y, *a.* resembling lead; leaden.

lēaf, *n.*; *pl.* **lēaveṣ** (lēvz), [ME. *leef*; AS. *leaf*, a leaf.]
1. any of the flat, thin, expanded organs, usually green, growing from the stem or twig of a plant: it usually consists of a broad blade, a petiole, or stalk, and stipules.
2. in popular usage, (a) the blade of a leaf; (b) a petal; as, a tulip *leaf.*
3. leaves collectively; as, a consignment of choice tobacco *leaf.*
4. a sheet of paper, especially as part of a book, with a page on each side.
5. (a) a very thin sheet of metal; lamina; (b) such sheets collectively; as, a frame covered with gold *leaf.*
6. (a) a hinged section of a table top, forming an extension when raised into place; (b) a board inserted into a table top to increase its surface.
7. a flat, hinged or movable part of a folding door, shutter, etc.
8. one of a number of metal strips laid one upon another to make a leaf spring.
in leaf; having leaves grown; with foliage.
to take a leaf from one's book; to follow one's example.
to turn over a new leaf; to make a new start.

lēaf, *v.i.*; leafed (lēft), *pt., pp.*; leafing, *ppr.* to put forth or bear leaves; to leave (often with *out*); to produce leaves.

lēaf, *v.t.* to turn the pages of (a book, etc.) as in looking through it quickly (often with *through*).

lēaf′ăġe, *n.* foliage.

lēaf bee′tle, any beetle of the *Chrysomelidæ*, as the common potato beetle, which feeds on potato leaves.

lēaf blīght (blīt), a disease due to parasitic fungi, affecting chiefly the leaves of trees.

lēaf bridġe, a drawbridge having a leaf or platform on each side, which rises and falls.

lēaf bud, a plant bud producing a leaf rather than a flower.

lēaf but′tēr·flȳ, any butterfly that in appearance and color resembles a leaf, as those of the genus *Kallima* of Asia.

lēaf çrump′lēr, a moth having larvae that crumple leaves together to make nests; especially, a member of the genus *Phycis.*

lēaf′çup, *n.* a coarse weed of North America belonging to the genus *Polymnia.*

lēaf çut′tēr, a wild bee, especially one of the genus *Megachile*, that cuts out small portions of leaves to line its nest.

lēaf fat, the fat that lies in leaves or layers within the body of an animal; especially, fat built up in layers around the kidneys of a pig.

lēaf flēa, a kind of psyllid or plant louse.

lēaf frog, a tree frog of the genus *Phyllomedusa.*

lēaf green, chlorophyll.

lēaf hop′pēr, an insect that leaps from one plant to another, sucking the juices and causing destruction.

lēaf′i·ness, *n.* the state of being leafy.

lēaf in′seçt, an insect of the family *Phasmidæ*, whose wings, etc. are leaf-shaped.

lēaf lärd, lard made from leaf fat.

lēaf′less, *a.* having no leaves; as, a *leafless* tree.

lēaf′less·ness, *n.* absence or lack of leaves.

lēaf′let, *n.* 1. one of the divisions of a compound leaf.
2. a small or young leaf.
3. a separate sheet of printed matter, often folded but not stitched; folder; as, propaganda *leaflets.*

lēaf louse, an aphid; a plant louse.

lēaf met′ăl, metal, as silver or gold, prepared for use in thin sheets.

lēaf mīn′ēr, an insect larva that feeds between the two surfaces of a leaf.

lēaf mōld, soil composed of decayed leaves.

lēaf′-nōṣe, *n.* a leaf-nosed bat.

lēaf′-nōṣed, *a.* having the snout provided with leaflike appendages, as certain bats.

lēaf notch′ēr, a beetle of Florida, *Artipus floridanus*, which cuts into the edges of orange leaves.

lēaf rōll′ēr, an insect larva that rolls up leaves to make its nest.

lēaf sīght (sīt), a sight for a gun, hinged so as to be lifted vertically.

lēaf spring, a spring built up of curved strips of metal.

lēaf stąlk (stąk), *n.* a supporting stem by which a leaf is attached to a twig or larger branch; petiole.

lēaf valve, a flap valve; a hinged valve.

lēaf wäsp, a sawfly.

lēaf′y, *a.*; *comp.* leafier; *superl.* leafiest. 1. of, covered with, consisting of, or like a leaf or leaves.
2. having many leaves.
3. having broad leaves; as, lettuce and spinach are *leafy* vegetables.

lēague (lēg), *n.* [ME. *lege*; OFr. *legue*; LL. *lega, leuca*, a Gallic mile; of Celtic origin.] a measure of distance varying in different times and countries: in English-speaking countries it is usually about 3 statute miles or 3 nautical miles.

lēague, *n.* [ME. *lege*; OFr. *ligue*; LL. *liga, lega*, an alliance or league, from L. *ligare*, to bind.]
1. a compact made by nations, groups, or individuals for promoting common interests, assuring mutual protection, etc.
2. an association or alliance of individuals, groups, or nations, formed by such a covenant.
in league; associated for a common purpose; allied.
the League; the League of Nations.

lēague, *v.i.*; leagued (lēgd), *pt., pp.*; leaguing, *ppr.* to unite or join in a league; to confederate.

lēague, *v.t.* to cause to unite for a common purpose.

Lēague of Nā′tionṣ, an association of nations, established January 10, 1920, by the Versailles treaty, to promote international co-operation and peace: it was dissolved in April, 1946, and was succeeded by the United Nations after World War II.

lēa′guēr (-gẽr), *n.* one who joins in a league.

lēa′guēr, *n.* [D. *leger*, a bed, couch, camp.]
1. a siege.
2. a besieging army.
3. the camp of such an army.
[Archaic in all senses.]

lēa′guēr, *v.t.* to besiege. [Archaic.]

lēa′guēr·ēr, *n.* a besieger. [Obs.]

Lē′ăh, *n.* in the Bible, the elder daughter of Laban, given in marriage to Jacob after Jacob had served Laban seven years believing he would receive Rachel, the younger daughter: Gen. xxix. 13–30.

lēak, *v.i.* [ME. *leken*, from ON. *leka*, to drip.]
1. to let a fluid substance out or in accidentally; as, the ship *leaks.*
2. to enter or escape accidentally from an object or container (often with *in* or *out*).
3. to become known little by little by accident, carelessness, or treachery; as, the truth *leaked* out.

lēak, *v.t.* to permit (water, air, etc.) to pass accidentally in or out; to allow to leak.

lēak, *n.* 1. an accidental hole, crack, or crevice that lets something out or in.
2. any means of escape for something that ought not to be let out, lost, etc.
3. the fact of leaking; leakage.
4. (a) a loss of electrical charge through faulty insulation; (b) the point where this occurs.

lēak′ăġe, *n.* 1. a leaking in or out; a leak.
2. something that leaks in or out.
3. the quantity of fluid, electricity, light, etc. that leaks in or out.
4. in commerce, an allowance of a certain rate per cent for the leaking of casks, etc.

lēak′ăġe çŏn·duçt′ŏr, a conductor arranged to dispose of leakage in electric circuits, usually a heavy, grounded wire.

lēak′i·ness, *n.* a leaky condition, quality, or state.

lēak′y, *a.*; *comp.* leakier; *superl.* leakiest. 1. allowing the accidental entrance or escape of a fluid, light, etc.; having one or more leaks; as, a *leaky* camera, cask, etc.
2. apt to disclose secrets; tattling. [Colloq.]

lēal, *a.* [north Brit. dial. form of *loyal*, from OFr. *leal*; from L. *legalis*, legal.] faithful; true; loyal. [Archaic or Scot.]
land of the leal; heaven. [Scot.]

lēa′lănd, *n.* fallow land.

lēam, *n.* and *v.* gleam. [Obs.]

lēan, *v.i.*; leaned *or* leant (lent), *pt., pp.*; leaning, *ppr.* [ME. *lenen*; AS. *hlinian*, to lean.]
1. to deviate or move from a perpendicular line; to incline; as, the column *leans* to the north.
2. to incline in sentiment, conduct, or opinions (with *to* or *toward*).
3. to rely; to depend for advice, encouragement, etc. (with *upon* or *on*).
4. to bend or incline so as to rest on something; as, to *lean* on the arm of another.
Syn.—incline, rest, support, tend, bend, depend, hang, repose, confide, slope.

lēan, *v.t.* [ME. *lenen*; AS. *hlænan*, to cause to lean.]
1. to cause to bend from an upright position; as, the storm *leaned* the telephone poles over.
2. to place (something) so that it rests against something else; as, *lean* the ladder against the house.

lēan, *n.* a bend or deviation from the upright; incline; slant.

lēan, *v.t.* to conceal. [Obs.]

lēan, *a.*; *comp.* leaner; *superl.* leanest, [ME. *lene*; AS. *hlæne*, meager, lean.]
1. with little flesh or fat; thin; spare: opposed to *fat.*
2. containing little or no fat: said of meat.
3. lacking in richness, profit, productiveness, etc.; meager.

4. in printing, formerly, unprofitable; requiring extra time or labor without extra compensation; as, *lean* work.

Syn.—meager, lank, emaciated, shriveled, thin, skinny, scanty, slender.

lēan, *n.* 1. meat containing little or no fat.

2. in printing, formerly, unprofitable work or copy.

Lē·an′dẽr, *n.* in Greek legend, the lover of Hero: see *Hero*.

lēan′-fāced (-fāst), *a.* having a thin face; specifically, in printing, designating a type that has little breadth in proportion to height.

lēan′ing, *n.* 1. the act of a person or thing that leans.

2. penchant; predilection; tendency; inclination.

lēan′ly, *adv.* without fat; meagerly.

lēan′ness, *n.* the quality or state of being lean.

leant (lent), *v.* alternative past tense and past participle of *lean*.

lēan′-tö″, *n.*; *pl.* **lēan′-tōs″,** 1. a roof with a single slope, its upper edge abutting a wall or building.

2. a shed with a one-slope roof, the upper end of the rafters resting against an external support, such as trees or the wall of a building.

3. a structure, as the wing of a building, whose roof is a lean-to.

lēan′-tö″, *a.* constructed as or like a lean-to.

lēan′-wit″ted, *a.* having scanty wit or shrewdness.

lēan′y, *a.* lean. [Obs.]

lēap, *v.i.*; leaped (lĕpt) *or* leapt (lept, lēpt), *pt.*, *pp.*; leaping, *ppr.* [ME. *lepen*; AS. *hleápan*, to leap.]

1. to move oneself suddenly from the ground, etc. by using one's leg muscles; to spring; to jump; to vault; as, a man *leaps* over a fence or *leaps* upon a horse.

2. to move suddenly, as if by jumping; to bound; as, one's blood *leaps*.

lēap, *v.t.* 1. to pass over by leaping; to spring or bound from one side of to the other; as, to *leap* a wall.

2. to cause or force to vault or jump; as, to *leap* a horse over a wall.

3. to cover; to copulate with: said of the male of certain animals.

lēap, *n.* [ME. *leep*; AS. *hlyp*, a leap, from *hleápan*, to leap.]

1. a jump; a spring; a bound; the act of leaping.

2. the distance covered in a jump.

3. a place that is, or is to be, leaped over or from.

4. a sudden transition.

5. the act of the male of animals in copulating with the female.

6. in music, the passing from one note to another at a distance of two or more diatonic intervals.

7. in mining, a fault.

lēap, *n.* a wicker fish snare. [Obs.]

lēap′ẽr, *n.* 1. one who or that which leaps; specifically, a salmon.

2. a hook used to untwist old rope.

lēap′frog, *n.* a leaping game, in which one player stoops down and another leaps over him by placing his hands on the shoulders of the former.

lēap′ful, *n.* a basketful. [Obs.]

lēap′ing house, a brothel. [Obs.]

lēap′ing·ly, *adv.* by leaps.

leapt (lept, lēpt), *v.* alternative past tense and past participle of *leap*.

lēap yēar, a year of 366 days, occurring every fourth year: the additional day, given to February, makes up for the time lost annually when the approximate 365 1/4-day cycle is computed as 365 days: a leap year is a year whose number is exactly divisible by four, or, in the case of century years, by 400.

Lēar, *n.* King Lear.

lēar, *n.* lore. [Obs.]

lēar, *v.t.* and *v.i.* to teach; also, to learn. [Obs.]

lẽarn, *v.t.*; learned *or* learnt, *pt.*, *pp.*; learning, *ppr.* [ME. *lernen, leornen*; AS. *leornian*, to learn.]

1. to gain knowledge of (a subject); to acquire information concerning, as by instruction, study, observation, experience, etc.; to acquire skill in (anything); as, to *learn* the news, or a lesson; to *learn* instrumental music.

2. to come to know; as, I *learned* that he had been sick.

3. to come to know how; as, we are *learning* to swim.

4. to fix in mind; to memorize.

5. to acquire as a habit or attitude; as, you have *learned* humility.

6. to teach: formerly a standard usage, now substandard.

lẽarn, *v.i.* 1. to gain or receive knowledge, instruction, or skill; as, he *learns* easily.

2. to be informed; to hear (*of*).

lẽarn′ȧ·ble, *a.* capable of being learned.

lẽarn′ed, *a.* 1. (a) having or showing much learning; well-informed; erudite; (b) having or showing much learning in some special field; as, a *learned* doctor.

2. of scholarship and study; as, a *learned* society.

3. characterized by, resulting from, or requiring study and learning.

lẽarn′ed·ly, *adv.* with learning or erudition.

lẽarn′ed·ness, *n.* the condition of being learned.

lẽarn′ẽr, *n.* [ME. *lernere*; AS. *leornere*, from *leornian*, to learn.] one who is learning; a pupil.

lẽarn′ing, *n.* [ME. *lernyng*; AS. *leornung*, the act of learning, verbal n. of *leornian*, to learn.]

1. the act of gaining knowledge or skill.

2. acquired knowledge or skill; especially, much knowledge in a special subject; erudition; as, a judge of great *learning* in the law.

lẽarnt, *v.* alternative past tense and past participle of *learn*.

lēas′ȧ·ble, *a.* capable of being leased.

lēase (lēs), *n.* [OFr. *lais, lays, lees*, a thing left by will, a lease, from *laisier*, to let go, to lease.]

1. a contract by which one party (landlord, or lessor) gives to another (tenant, or lessee) the use and possession of lands, buildings, etc. for a specified time and for fixed payments.

2. the document in which this contract is written.

3. the period of time for which such a contract is in force; as, during his *lease* the property was well kept up.

new lease on life; a chance to live better or more happily because of a recovery of health, position, money, etc.

lēase, *v.t.*; leased, *pt.*, *pp.*; leasing, *ppr.* [OFr. *laisier, leisseir*, to lease, let out; L. *laxare*, to loosen, relax, from *laxus*, loose.]

1. to let; to give by a lease; as, A *leased* to B his land in Dale.

2. to get by a lease; to take a lease on; as, B *leased* the land from A.

lēașe, *v.i.* to glean; to gather what harvesters have left. [Dial.]

lēase′hōld, *n.* 1. a holding by lease.

2. lands, buildings, etc. held by lease.

lēase′hōld, *a.* held by lease; as, a *leasehold* tenement.

lēase′hōld·ẽr, *n.* a tenant who holds a lease; a lessee.

lēaș′ẽr, *n.* a gleaner. [Dial.]

lēas′ẽr, *n.* a liar. [Obs.]

lēash, *n.* [ME. *leesshe, lese, lees*; OFr. *lesse*; LL. *laxa*, a loose cord, a thong, snare, properly f. of L. *laxus*, loose.]

1. a cord, strap, etc. by which a dog or other animal is held in check.

2. in hunting, a set of three; a brace and a half; tierce; three creatures of any kind, especially hounds, foxes, bucks, and hares.

3. in the harness of a loom, a thread or wire holding a loop through which a warp thread passes and is lifted and guided in weaving.

to hold in leash; to control; to curb; restrain. *to strain at the leash*; to be eager to do as one pleases without restraint; to be impatient to have freedom.

lēash, *v.t.*; leashed (lēsht), *pt.*, *pp.*; leashing; *ppr.* to bind with a leash; to attach a leash to; to check or hold by or as by a leash.

lēaș′ing, *n.* [ME. *leesing*; AS. *leásung*, the act of lying, verbal n. of *leásian*, to tell a lie, from *leás*, false.] falsehood; lies; lying. [Obs.]

lēa′sōw, *n.* a pasture. [Obs.]

lēast, *a.* [ME. *leste, lest*; AS. *læst*, least, contr. of *læsast*, superl. of *læs*, less.]

1. smallest in size, degree, extent, importance, etc.; slightest; as, the *least* insect; the *least* mercy.

2. smallest or youngest; as, her *least* child is sick. [Dial.]

least squares; in mathematics, a method of finding the probable error in assuming a mean of a number of varying observations of a phenomenon; the rule being that the most probable result is the one which makes the sum of the squares of the errors the least possible.

lēast, *a.* alt.superl. of *little*.

lēast, *adv.* in the smallest or lowest degree.

lēast, *adv.* [superl. of *little*.] in the smallest degree.

lēast, *n.* the smallest in size, amount, importance, etc.

at (the) least; (a) at the very lowest figure, amount, etc.; with no less; (b) at any rate; in any event.

not in the least; not at all; not in the smallest degree.

lēast çom′mŏn dē·nom′i·nā·tŏr, the least common multiple of the denominators of a number of fractions.

lēast çom′mŏn mul′ti·ple, the lowest number that exactly contains each of two or more given numbers; as, the *least common multiple* of 4, 5, and 10 is 20.

lēast′wāyș, *adv.* [from phr. *at the least ways.*] leastwise. [Chiefly Dial.]

lēast′wīșe, *adv.* at least; anyway. [Colloq.]

lēat, *n.* [AS. *lædan*, to lead.] an artificial trench to conduct water, as to a mill; a flume. [Brit.]

leath′ẽr (leth′), *n.* [ME. *lether*; AS. *lether*, leather.]

1. a material consisting of animal skin prepared for use by removing the hair and tanning.

2. any of various articles or parts made of this material.

3. dressed hides in general.

4. skin: in an ironical sense.

leath′ẽr, *a.* of or made of leather; as, *leather* belting.

leath′ẽr, *v.t.*; leathered, *pt.*, *pp.*; leathering, *ppr.* 1. to cover or furnish with leather.

2. to beat, as with a thong of leather. [Colloq.]

leath′ẽr·back, *n.* a nonedible tropical sea turtle, *Dermochelys coriacea*, covered with a tough, dark-brown, leathery upper shell spotted with yellow: it is the largest of the turtle family, weighing up to 1,500 pounds.

leath′ẽr·bōard″, *n.* a composition of paper, leather scraps, etc., used to imitate sole leather.

leath′ẽr çärp, a carp having few or no scales.

leath′ẽr·çōat, *n.* anything having a tough skin or rind; especially, an apple, the golden russet.

leath·ẽr·ette′, leath·ẽr·et′ (-et′), *n.* imitation leather made of paper or cloth.

leath′ẽr·flow″ẽr, *n.* a vine, *Clematis viorna*, having purple blossoms of a leathery texture.

leath′ẽr·head (-hed), *n.* 1. the friar bird.

2. a blockhead; a dull-witted fellow.

leath′ẽr·i·ness, *n.* the quality or condition of being leathery.

leath′ẽr·ing, *n.* 1. a flogging. [Colloq.]

2. a covering of leather.

leath′ẽr jack′et, 1. the hickory eucalyptus or any of various similar trees.

2. any of various fishes, as (a) the triggerfish (genus *Balistes*) of the Atlantic; (b) an allied fish (genus *Monacanthus*) of Australian waters; (c) *Oligoplites saurus*, a fish of tropical seas.

leath′ẽr·lēaf″, *n.* a small evergreen shrub, *Cassandra calyculata*, with leathery leaves.

leath′ẽr-mouthed (-moutht), *a.* having the mouth without teeth and of a leathery smoothness and toughness.

leath′ẽrn, *a.* [ME. and AS. *letheren*.]

1. made of or consisting of leather.

2. like leather.

leath′ẽr·neck, *n.* a United States marine. [Slang.]

leath′ẽr·oid, *n.* a leatherlike material made of vegetable fibers chemically treated.

leath′ẽr plant, in New Zealand, any plant of the genus *Celmisia*.

leath′ẽr·sīde, *n.* a minnow, *Cheonda copei*.

leath′ẽr·wood, *n.* a small shrub, *Dirca palustris*, of North America, having a tough, leathery bark and tough, flexible roots; moosewood.

leath′ẽr·y, *a.* resembling leather in appearance or texture; tough and flexible.

leave (lēv), *v.t.*; left, *pt.*, *pp.*; leaving, ppr. [ME. *leeven, leven*; AS. *læfan*, to leave, from *laf*, a heritage, something left or remaining.]

1. to cause or allow to remain; not take away; as, the pickers *left* much fruit on the trees.

2. to make, place, deposit, etc., and cause to remain behind one; as, the invaders *left* a trail of destruction.

3. to have remaining after one; as, the deceased *leaves* a widow and two children.

4. to bequeath; as, she *left* her fortune to charity.

5. to commit; to entrust (with *to* or *up to*); as, he *leaves* such decisions up to me.

6. to allow to remain unremoved or unchanged; as, ten minus two *leaves* eight.
7. to reject; as, here is my proposal—take it or *leave* it.
8. to go away from.
9. to go away from and let remain in a certain condition; as, I *left* him alone in the building.
10. to give up; to abandon; forsake.
11. to stop living in, working for, or belonging to.
12. to let; as, *leave* us go now. [Slang.]
13. to allow; to permit; as, I *leave* you to decide. [Dial.]
to leave in; in bridge, to let the declared suit of (one's partner) stand by refusing to bid further.
to leave off; to stop doing, using, or wearing.
to leave one alone; not to bother or disturb one.
to leave out; (a) to omit; (b) to fail to consider; ignore.

lēave, *v.i.* 1. to cease; to desist: usually with *off*; as, where did I *leave off?*
2. to go; to depart; as, he *leaves* at ten.

lēave, *v.i.*; leaved, *pt., pp.*; leaving, *ppr.* to leaf; to put forth, or bear, leaves.

lēave, *n.* [ME. *leve, leef*; AS. *leáf*, permission, license.]
1. permission.
2. permission to be absent from duty or work; especially, in military usage, such permission given to officers in any of the armed services or to enlisted personnel in the navy.
3. the period for which such permission is granted.
by your leave; with your permission.
on leave; absent from duty with permission.
to beg leave; to ask permission.
to take leave of; to say good-by to.
to take one's leave; to go away; to depart.
Syn.—liberty, permission, license.

lēave, *v.t.* to raise; to levy. [Obs.]

lēaved, *a.* 1. in leaf.
2. having (a specified number or kind of) leaves: usually in hyphenated compounds, as narrow-*leaved*.

leav′en (lev′n), *n.* [ME. *levain, levein*; OFr. *levain*; LL. *levamen*, leaven; L. *levamen*, an alleviation, mitigation, solace, from *levare*, to make light, relieve, lift up, raise.]
1. sour dough, which, mixed with other dough or paste, produces fermentation in it and makes it light; hence, any substance causing fermentation, as yeast.
2. anything that makes a general change in a mass; tempering quality or thing; as, the *leaven* of discontent.

leav′en, *v.t.*; leavened, *pt., pp.*; leavening, *ppr.*
1. to produce fermentation in by means of yeast or other ferment; to make (dough) rise.
2. to spread through, causing a gradual change.

leav′en·ing, *n.* 1. a causing to ferment by leaven.
2. leaven; that which leavens.

leav′en·ous, *a.* containing leaven. [Obs.]

lēave of ab′sence, a leave (*n.* 2).

lēav′ẽr, *n.* one who leaves or relinquishes.

lēaveṣ, *n.* pl. of *leaf*.

lēave′-tāk″ing, *n.* the act of taking leave, or saying good-by.

lēav′i·ness, *n.* leafiness. [Obs.]

lēav′ing, *n.* 1. [*usually in pl.*] a thing left; leftover; remnant.
2. [*pl.*] refuse; offal.

lēav′y, *a. comp.* leavier; *superl.* leaviest, leafy. [Poetic.]

leb′ăn, *n.* [Ar. *leban*.] artificially soured milk used as food or drink by Arabs: also written *leben, lebban*.

Leb·ȧ·nēṣe′, *a.* of Lebanon or its people.

Leb·ȧ·nēṣe′, *n.*; *pl.* **Leb·ȧ·nēṣe′,** a native or inhabitant of Lebanon.

Lẹb′ens·raum, *n.* [G., living space, space in which to live and grow.] territory for political and economic expansion: term of German imperialism.

le·çä′mȧ, *n.* the hartebeest.

leçȧ′·nō·man″cy, *n.* [Gr. *lekanomanteia*; *lekanē*, a dish, pan, and *manteia*, divination.] divination by examining the water in a basin.

Leç·ȧ·nō′rȧ, *n.* [Gr. *lekanē*, a dish; so called from the form of the shields.] a genus of lichens of the order *Parmeliaceæ*, resembling *Lecidea*, but having the border formed from the thallus: several of the species furnish dyes.

leç·ȧ·nō′riç, *a.* [*Lecanora* and *-ic*.] in chemistry, derived from lichens of the genus *Lecanora*; as *lecanoric* acid.

lē′chee, *n.* [S. African.] an antelope of South Africa.

lech′ẽr, *n.* [ME. *letchour*; OFr. *lecheor, lecheur*, a glutton, a lewd man, from *lecher*, to lick, to indulge in lust.] a man given to lewdness or to excessive sexual indulgence.

lech′ẽr, *v.i.* to practise lewdness. [Obs.]

lech′ẽr·ẽr, *n.* one given to lechery.

lech′ẽr·ous, *a.* [ME. *lecherous*, from OFr. *lecherie*, lewdness, lechery.]
1. addicted to lewdness; unrestrained in sexual indulgence; lustful; lewd; as, a *lecherous* man.
2. provoking lust; as, a *lecherous* novel.

lech′ẽr·ous·ly, *adv.* lustfully; lewdly.

lech′ẽr·ous·ness, *n.* the state or quality of being lecherous.

lech′ẽr·y, *n.* [OFr. *lecherie, lescherie*, from *lecher*, to lick, to indulge in lust.] lewdness; unrestrained, excessive indulgence of sexual desires; gross sensuality.

lec′i·thin, *n.* [Gr. *lekithos*, the yolk of an egg, and *-in*.] a nitrogenous, fatty substance found in nerve tissue, blood, milk, egg yolk, and some vegetables: it is used in medicine, foods, etc.

leç′tẽrn, *n.* [ME. *lectorn, letteron*; OFr. *lettrin*; LL. *lectrinum, lectrum*, a pulpit, a reading desk, from Gr. *lektron*, a couch, bed, a support for books.] a reading desk in some churches; specifically, a desk from which a part of the Scripture is read in a church service.

LECTERN

leç′tion, *n.* [L. *lectio (-onis)*, a gathering, selecting, reading, from *lectus*, pp. of *legere*, to gather, select, read.]
1. a reading, as found in a particular text.
2. a part of the Scriptures read in a church service.

leç′tion·ăr·y, *n.*; *pl.* **leç′tion·ăr·ieṣ,** [ML. *lectionarium*, from L. *lectio*.] a sequence or list of lections to be read in church services during the year.

leç·ti·stẽr′ni·um, *n.*; *pl.* **leç·ti·stẽr′ni·ȧ,** [L., from *lectus*, couch, and *sternere*, to spread.] among the ancient Greeks and Romans, a feast and sacrifice at which images of the gods were placed on couches at the table.

leç′tŏr, *n.* [L., a reader, from *lectus*, pp. of *legere*, to read.]
1. a person designated to read parts of the Bible in church services; specifically, in the Roman Catholic Church, a member of one of the minor orders leading to the priesthood.
2. a foreign lecturer in a German, Swiss, or Scandinavian university.

leç′tress, *n.* a woman reader.

leç′tū·ăl, *a.* [LL. *lectualis*, pertaining to a bed, from L. *lectus*, bed.] relating to extended confinement in bed.

leç′tūre, *n.* [LL. *lectura*, a reading, lecture, properly f. of L. *lecturus*, fut. p. of *legere*, to read.]
1. (a) an informative talk given before a class, audience, etc., and usually prepared beforehand; (b) the text of such a talk.
2. a reading; the act or practice of reading. [Obs.]
3. a lengthy scolding; a formal reproof.

leç′tūre, *v.i.*; lectured, *pt., pp.*; lecturing, *ppr.* to read or deliver a lecture.

leç′tūre, *v.t.* 1. to instruct by discourses.
2. to speak to dogmatically or authoritatively; to reprove; as, to *lecture* one for his faults.
3. to influence by a lecture or reprimand; as, *lecture* him into the notion.

leç′tūr·ẽr, *n.* a person who gives lectures, especially by profession or in connection with teaching duties, as at a college or university: sometimes used as an academic title for one who teaches at a college or university but does not have the rank or tenure of a regular faculty member.

leç′tūre·ship, *n.* the position or rank of a lecturer.

leç′tūrn, *n.* same as *lectern*.

Lec′y·this, *n.* [LL. *lecythus*; Gr. *lēkythos*, an oil flask; so named from the shape of the seed vessels.] a genus of large tropical trees of the order *Myrtaceæ*.

lec′y·thus, *n.*; *pl.* **lec′y·thī,** [LL., from Gr. *lēkythos*, an oil vase.] in Grecian archaeology, a tall narrow-necked earthenware vase for oil or perfume.

led, *v.* past tense and past participle of *lead* (to guide).

led, *a.* under control; as, a *led* farm, that is, one not occupied by the owner or lessee.
led captain; a henchman; an obsequious follower. [Obs.]
led horse; a spare horse; a pack horse.

Lē′dȧ, *n.* in Greek mythology, a Spartan queen, wife of Tyndareus: she was the mother of Clytemnestra (by Tyndareus) and (by Zeus, who visited her in the form of a swan) of Helen of Troy and Castor and Pollux.

led′dy, *n.* lady. [Dial.]

led′en, led′den, *n.* language; voice. [Obs.]

ledġe (lej), *n.* [from the same root as AS. *licgan*, to lie; of Scand. origin, compare Sw. *lagg*, Ice. *lögg*, the rim of a cask.]
1. a shelf or shelflike projection.
2. (a) a projecting ridge of rocks; (b) such a ridge beneath the water near the shore.
3. in architecture, a horizontal rectangular molding.
4. in mining, a layer of ore-bearing rock; a vein.
5. in a ship, a part of the deck frame.
6. a bar for a gate. [Brit. Dial.]

ledġed (lejd), *a.* having or resembling a ledge.

ledġe′ment, *n.* same as *ledgment*.

ledġ′ẽr, *n.* [compare D. *legger*, a layer, daybook, from O.D. *leggen*, to lie, from same root as AS. *licgan*, to lie.]
1. in bookkeeping, the book of final entry in which a record of debits, credits, and all money transactions is kept.
2. a slab, beam, or the like made to lie stationary, as, (a) in a scaffolding, a horizontal timber supporting the putlogs; (b) a slab of stone placed horizontally upon a tomb or grave; (c) the wall under a lode.
3. in fishing, ledger bait.
4. a resident ambassador or agent. [Obs.]

ledġ′ẽr, *a.* that lies or remains where it is placed; stationary: now only in a few expressions.

ledġ′ẽr bāit, fishing bait hooked to a floating line fastened to the bank of a stream, etc.

ledġ′ẽr blade, in a machine for shearing cloth, the fixed blade against which the moving blades work.

ledġ′ẽr bōard, a board forming the topmost rail of a fence, balustrade, or the like.

ledġ′ẽr līne, see *added line*.

ledġ′ẽr pā′pẽr, writing paper for use in ledgers.

ledġ′ẽr taç′kle, fishing tackle arranged so that the bait lies on the bottom of the water.

ledġ′ment, *n.* 1. a horizontal course of moldings.
2. the development, on a plane, of a curved surface, showing the dimensions of the different sides.

ledġ′y, *a.* having many ledges.

Lē′dum, *n.* [Gr. *lēdon*, ladanum.] a genus of small white-flowered shrubs, having fragrant leaves and commonly known as Labrador tea. *Ledum palustre*, or wild rosemary, furnishes an essential oil called *Ledum oil*.

lee, *v.i.* to lie; to tell lies. [Scot. and Dial.]

lee, *n.* [ME. *lee, le*; AS. *hleo, hleow*, a shelter, protection.]
1. a calm or sheltered place; a place defended from the wind; hence, shelter; protection.
2. in nautical usage, the side or part of a ship, etc. farthest from the side from which the wind blows; the side or part away from the wind.
under the lee; in nautical usage, on that

side, or in a position, sheltered from the wind; as, *under the lee* of a ship or a breakwater.

lee, *a.* 1. of or relating to the side or quarter sheltered from the wind.

2. of or in the direction toward which the wind is blowing: opposed to *weather*.

3. in geology, of or relating to the side (of glaciated rocks) facing in the direction that the glacier moved.

lee shore; the shore on the lee side of a ship.

lee tide; a tide running in the direction in which the wind blows.

lee′bōard, *n.* a large, flat board or piece of metal let down into the water on the lee side of a sailboat to lessen its drift to that side.

leech, *n.* [Early Mod. Eng. phonetic sp. of ME. *lich*; akin to ON. *lik*, a leech line.] the free or outside edge of a sail: distinguished from *luff*.

leech, *n.* [ME. *leeche*; AS. *læce*, a physician, prob. from *lac*, medicine.] formerly, a physician; a doctor.

leech, *v.t.* formerly, to heal.

leech, *n.* [ME. *leche*; AS. *læce*, a leech, from *læce*, a physician.]

1. a bloodsucking worm of the genus *Hirudo* or allied genera, living in water or wet earth and used in medicine, especially in former times, to bleed patients.

2. one who clings to another to get some gain out of him; a parasite.

3. in medicine, a suction apparatus for drawing blood.

leech, *v.t.* to bleed with a leech.

leech′crȧft, *n.* the art of healing. [Archaic.]

leech′ēat″ẽr, *n.* a plover of Egypt, the crocodile bird.

lee′chee, *n.* same as *litchi*.

leech līne, a rope for hauling a sail to its yard.

leech rōpe, the part of the boltrope that has the leech of a sail attached to it.

leef, *adv.* lief. [Obs.]

lee gāuġe, a position on the lee side: said of a ship with reference to another.

leek, *n.* [ME. *lek, lik*; AS. *leac*, a leek.] a plant, *Allium porrum*, with a bulbous cylindrical root and long, broad, succulent leaves, allied to and resembling the onion: it is the national emblem of Wales.

wild leek; an American plant, *Allium tricoccum*.

LEEK

lee′lāne, *adv.* all alone. [Scot.]

leem, *v.* and *n.* same as *leam*.

leer, *a.* empty; riderless, as a horse. [Obs.]

leer, *n.* [ME. *lere*; AS. *hleor*, the cheek, face.]

1. the cheek; the face; hence, the complexion. [Obs.]

2. a sly, sidelong look showing ill will, lustfulness, malicious triumph, etc.

leer, *v.i.*; leered, *pt., pp.*; leering, *ppr.* to look with a leer.

leer, *v.t.* to allure; to entice with a leer.

leer, *n.* an oven for annealing glass.

leer, *v.t.* to learn. [Obs.]

leer, *n.* braid; tape. [Obs.]

leer′ing·ly, *adv.* with a leer.

leer′y, lēar′y, *a.* 1. knowing. [Colloq.]

2. wary; suspicious. [Colloq.]

leeṣ, *n.pl.* [pl. of *lee* (obs. in sing.); ME. and OFr. *lie*; ML. *lia*.] dregs; grounds; sediment, as of wine.

leeṣe, *v.t.* to lose. [Obs.]

leeṣe, *v.t.* to hurt. [Obs.]

leet, *n.* [AS. *læth*, a territorial division.] in England, formerly, a manorial court or its jurisdiction; also, the day on which such a court was held.

leet, *v.* obsolete past tense of *let*.

leet, *n.* [Ice. *leiti*, a share, a part.] a list, as of persons eligible to an office. [Chiefly Scot.]

leet, *n.* a leat; a flume. [Obs.]

leet′mȧn, *n.*; *pl.* **leet′men,** a man subject to the jurisdiction of a court leet. [Obs.]

lee·wăn′, *n.* same as *lewan*.

lee′wȧrd (*or in nautical usage,* lū′ẽrd), *a.* in the direction toward which the wind blows; of the lee part or side: opposed to *windward*.

lee′wȧrd, *n.* the lee part or side.

lee′wȧrd, *adv.* toward the lee.

lee′wȧrd·ly, *a.* apt to fall off to leeward.

lee′wāy, *n.* 1. the leeward drift of a ship or aircraft from the true course.

2. (a) margin of time, money, etc.; (b) room for freedom of action. [Colloq.]

lēfe, *n.* one loved; a friend. [Obs.]

left, *v.* past tense and past participle of *leave* (to go away).

to get left; (a) to be left behind; (b) to be outdone or frustrated. [Slang.]

left, *a.* [ME. *left, lift*; AS. *lyft, left*, weak, worthless.]

1. (a) of or designating that side of one's body which is toward the west when one faces north, usually the side of the less-used hand; (b) of or designating the corresponding side of anything; (c) closer to the left side of a person directly before and facing the thing mentioned or understood; as, the top *left* drawer of a desk.

2. of the political left; liberal or radical. Opposed to *right*.

left, *n.* 1. (a) all or part of the left side; (b) what is on the left side.

2. in boxing, (a) the left hand; (b) a blow delivered with the left hand.

3. [*often* L—] in politics, a liberal or radical position, party, or group (often with *the*): so called from the position of the seats occupied in some European legislatures.

left, *adv.* on or toward the left hand or side.

left fiēld, in baseball, the left-hand part of the outfield (as viewed from home plate).

left′-hand, *a.* 1. being on or directed toward the left.

2. of, for, or with the left hand.

left′-hand′ed, *a.* 1. using the left hand more skillfully than, and in preference to, the right.

2. done with the left hand.

3. clumsy; awkward.

4. insincere; dubious; as, a *left-handed* compliment.

5. morganatic: from the former custom in which the groom gave the left hand to the bride in the ceremony of such marriages.

6. made for use with the left hand.

7. turning from right to left; worked by counterclockwise motion.

left′-hand′ed, *adv.* with the left hand; as, he writes *left-handed*.

left″-hand′ed·ness, left″-hand′i·ness, *n.* the quality or state of being left-handed.

left′iṣm, *n.* in politics, liberal or radical ideas or actions.

left′ist, *n.* in politics, a person whose political position is liberal or radical; a member of the left.

left′ist, *a.* in politics, liberal or radical.

left′-ọff, *a.* cast aside.

left′ō·vẽr, *n.* something left over, as from a meal.

left′ō·vẽr, *a.* remaining unused, uneaten, etc.

left′wȧrd, *a.* and *adv.* on or toward the left.

left′-wing, *a.* of the left wing; leftist.

left wing, in politics, the more liberal or radical section of a party, group, etc.

left-wing′ẽr, *n.* in politics, a member of the left wing.

left′y, *n.*; *pl.* **left′ieṣ,** a left-handed person: often used as a nickname. [Slang.]

leg, *n.* [ME. *leg*, pl. *legges*; Ice. *leggr*, a leg, hollow bone.]

1. one of the limbs of man or of an animal, used in supporting the body, and in walking and running; specifically, that part of the limb from the knee to the foot, but in a more general sense, the whole limb, including the thigh, the leg, and the foot.

2. the part of a garment covering the leg.

3. anything that resembles a leg in shape or use; specifically, (a) a bar or pole used as a support or prop; (b) one of the supports of a piece of furniture; (c) one of the branches of a forked or jointed object.

4. one of the stages of a journey or other course.

5. in bridge, the first game of a rubber, for either side.

6. in cricket, that part of the field which lies to the left and back of the batsman.

7. in mathematics, either of the sides of a triangle other than its base or, in a right-angled triangle, its hypotenuse.

8. a blackleg. [Brit. Slang.]

9. the distance traversed by a ship on one tack.

10. the water leg of a steam boiler, a downward projection which often surrounds part of the furnace.

11. the case of a grain elevator bucket belt.

on one's last legs; about to die, collapse, fall, etc. [Colloq.]

to give a leg up; to help to mount or advance. [Colloq.]

to have legs; in nautical usage, to have momentum or speed. [Slang.]

to make a leg; to bow: from the practice of drawing the right leg backward.

to pull one's leg; to make fun of or fool a person by playing on his credulity. [Colloq.]

to shake a leg; (a) to hurry; (b) to dance. [Slang.]

to stretch one's legs; to walk, especially after sitting a long time.

leg, *v.i.*; legged, *pt., pp.*; legging, *ppr.* 1. to bow. [Obs.]

2. to run or walk: usually with *it*; as, to *leg it*. [Colloq.]

leg′ȧ·cy, *n.*; *pl.* **leg′ȧ·cieṣ,** [OFr. *legacie*; L. *legatum*, a bequest, legacy, from *legatus*, pp. of *legare*, to bequeath.]

1. a bequest; property or money given by last will or testament; hence, anything handed down from, or as from, a predecessor or ancestor; as, a *legacy* of power.

2. a commission. [Obs.]

legacy duty; a tax on inheritances.

leg′ȧ·cy hunt′ẽr, one who flatters and courts for legacies.

lē′găl, *a.* [Fr. *légal*; L. *legalis*, legal, from *lex, legis*, law.]

1. of, based upon, or authorized by law.

2. in conformity with the positive rules of law; permitted by law; as, a *legal* act.

3. that can be enforced in a court of law; as, *legal* rights: distinguished from *equitable*.

4. of or applicable to lawyers; as, *legal* ethics.

5. in terms of the law; as, a *legal* offense.

6. in theology, (a) of the Mosaic law; (b) of the doctrine of salvation by good works rather than free grace.

lē′găl çap, a kind of writing paper, varying in size from $8^1/_2$ by 14 inches to 13 by 16 inches, with the fold at the top, made for use by lawyers.

lē′găl·iṣm, *n.* 1. strict, often too strict and literal, adherence to law.

2. in theology, the doctrine of salvation by good works.

lē′găl·ist, *n.* 1. one who practices legalism.

2. one who is skilled in law.

lē·găl·is′tiç, *a.* of or characterized by legalism.

lē·gal′i·ty, *n.*; *pl.* **lē·gal′i·tieṣ,** [Fr. *légalité*; LL. *legalitas*, lawfulness, from L. *legalis* legal.]

1. quality, condition, or instance of being legal or lawful; conformity with the law.

2. the spirit or a characteristic of the legal profession.

lē″găl·i·zā′tion, *n.* a legalizing or being legalized.

lē′găl·īze, *v.t.*; legalized, *pt., pp.*; legalizing, *ppr.* 1. to make legal or lawful; to render conformable to law; to authorize; to sanction; to give the authority of law to.

2. to apply (the Scriptures) in accordance with theological legalism.

lē′găl·ly, *adv.* lawfully; according to law; in a legal manner.

lē′găl rē·ṣẽrve′, the sum of money that a bank is required by law to have for covering deposits.

lē′găl sep·ȧ·rā′tion, in law, a separation of husband and wife so that they do not live together but are not divorced: also called *judicial separation*.

lē′găl ten′dẽr, all money that must be accepted for goods purchased, and also for the discharge of just debts: treasury notes are legal tender to unlimited amounts, silver coins up to $10, and pennies up to 25c.

leg′ȧ·tăr·y, *n.* [L. *legatarius*, from *legatum*, a legacy.] a legatee.

leg′ăte, *n.* [Fr. *légat*; L. *legatus*, a legate, deputy, properly pp. of *legare*, to appoint, choose, to send as an ambassador, from *lex, legis*, law.]

1. an ambassador or envoy.

2. the Pope's ambassador to a foreign prince or state; a cardinal or bishop sent as the Pope's representative or commissioner to a sovereign power.

3. in ancient Rome, (a) an assistant to a general or governor of a province; (b) after 31 B.C., the governor of a province.

leg·ȧ·tee′, *n.* [L. *legatus*, pp. of *legare*, to bequeath.] one to whom a legacy is bequeathed.

leg′ăte·ship, *n.* the office, authority, or tenure of a legate.

leg′ȧ·tine, *a.* 1. pertaining to a legate; as, *legatine* power.

2. made by or proceeding from a legate; as, a *legatine* constitution.

lē·gā′tion, *n.* [Fr. *légation*; L. *legatio* (*-onis*), an embassy, from *legatus*, pp. of *legare*, to send as ambassador.]

1. (a) the act of sending a legate on a mission; (b) the mission on which he is sent.
2. a legate and his staff collectively, representing their government in a foreign country and ranking just below an embassy.
3. the building or buildings housing such a legation.
4. the position or authority of such a legation.

lẹ·gä′tō, *a.* and *adv.* [It. pp. of *legare*; L. *ligare*, to tie, bind.] in music, in a close, smooth, gliding manner: a direction to the performer: opposed to *staccato*.

lẹ·gä′tō, *n.* a legato style or passage.

lē·gā′tŏr, *n.* [L., from *legatus*, pp. of *legare*, to bequeath.] a testator.

leg′ȧ·tūre, *n.* legateship. [Obs.]

leg bāil, escape from custody. [Old Slang.]
to give leg bail; to elude arrest or imprisonment by flight. [Old Slang.]

leġ′end, *n.* [OFr. *legende*, LL. *legenda*, a story, legend, neut. pl. of L. *legendus*, gerundive of *legere*, to read.]
1. (a) a story of the life of a saint; (b) a collection of such stories. [Obs.]
2. a story of some wonderful event, handed down for generations among a people and popularly believed to have a historical basis, although not verifiable: distinguished from *myth*.
3. all such stories belonging to a particular group of people; as, a name famous in Irish *legend*.
4. an inscription on a coin, coat of arms, etc.
5. a title, brief description, or key accompanying an illustration or map.

leġ′end, *v.t.* to tell or narrate as a legend. [Rare.]

lē·ġen′dȧ, *n.pl.* [LL., neut. pl. of L. *legendus*, gerundive of *legere*, to read.] in ecclesiastical usage, things which are to be read, as distinct from *credenda*, things which are to be believed.

leġ′end·ăr·y, *a.* of, based on, or presented in a legend or legends; traditional.

leġ′end·ăr·y, *n.* a collection of saints' lives.

leġ′end·ry, *n.* legends collectively.

leġ′ẽr, *n.* and *a.* a ledger.

leġ′ẽr, *a.* [OFr. *legier*, from L. *levis*, light.] fine; light; slender. [Obs.]

leġ″ẽr·dē·māin′, *n.* [Fr., light of hand; *léger*, from L. *levis*, light, *de*, from L. *de*, of, from, and *main*, from L. *manus*, hand.]
1. sleight of hand, a deceptive performance which depends on dexterity of hand; tricks of a stage magician.
2. trickery of any sort; deceit.

leġ″ẽr·dē·māin′ist, *n.* one skilled in legerdemain; a prestidigitator.

lē·ġer′i·ty, *n.* lightness; nimbleness. [Obs.]

le′ġēs̩, *n.* plural of *lex*.

legge (leg), *v.t.* to alleviate; to allay. [Obs.]

leg′ged (*or* legd), *a.* having (a specified number or kind of) legs: used in composition; as, a two-*legged* animal.

leġ·ġiä′drō, leġ·ġiẹ′rō, *a.* and *adv.* [It.] in music, in a light, gay style: a direction to the performer.

leg′ging, *n.* [*usually in pl.*] a covering of canvas, leather, etc. for protecting the leg below the knee.

leg′gy, *a.* having long (and awkward) legs; as, a *leggy* colt.

leg′hǫrn (*or* leg′ẽrn), *n.* 1. a fine plaiting made from a certain kind of wheat straw, used in making hats, etc.: so named because chiefly exported from Leghorn, Italy.
2. a hat or bonnet of such plaiting.
3. [*usually* L–] any of a breed of small chicken originally developed in the Mediterranean region.

leġ·i·bil′i·ty, *n.* the quality or state of being legible.

leġ′i·ble, *a.* [LL. *legibilis*, from L. *legere*, to read.]
1. (a) that can be read or deciphered; (b) that can be read or deciphered easily.
2. that may be discovered or understood by visible marks or indications.

leġ′i·ble·ness, *n.* the quality or state of being legible.

leġ′i·bly, *adv.* in a legible way; so as to be legible.

lē·ġif′iç, *a.* [L. *lex*, *legis*, law, and *facere*, to make.] of or pertaining to legislating. [Rare.]

lē′ġiŏn (-jun), *n.* [OFr. *legiun*; L. *legio* (*-onis*), a legion, from *legere*, to choose, select.]
1. in ancient Rome, a military body consisting of from three to six thousand foot soldiers besides from three to seven hundred cavalry. Each legion of six thousand was divided into ten cohorts of three maniples each, and each maniple into two centuries.
2. a large group of soldiers; an army.
3. a great number; a host; a multitude; as, his honors are *legion*.
4. in zoology, a subdivision of a class higher in rank than an order.
American Legion; an organization of American veterans of World War I or II, formed in 1919.
Foreign Legion; a military corps composed of persons not citizens of the country that they serve; especially, such a French force based in North Africa.
Legion of Honor; an order instituted in 1802 in France by Napoleon Bonaparte, as a reward of merit, both civil and military.
Legion of Merit; a United States military decoration given to officers, enlisted men, and soldiers of allies for extraordinary fidelity and essential service.

lē′ġiŏn·ăr″y, *a.* [L. *legionarius*, of or pertaining to a legion, from *legio* (*-onis*), a legion.]
1. relating to or consisting of a legion or legions; as, a *legionary* force.
2. containing a great number; as, a *legionary* body of errors.

lē′ġiŏn·ăr″y, *n.*; *pl.* **lē′ġiŏn·ăr″ies̩,** a member of a legion.

lē″ġiŏn·nāire′, *n.* [Fr. *légionnaire*.] one who belongs to a legion; specifically, [L–] one who is a member of the American Legion.

leġ′is·lāte, *v.i.*; legislated, *pt.*, *pp.*; legislating, *ppr.* to make or enact a law or laws.

leġ′is·lāte, *v.t.* to effect or affect by legislation; as, to *legislate* an office into being.

leġ·is·lā′tion, *n.* [L. *legis latio* (*-onis*); *lex*, *legis*, law, and *latio* (*-onis*), a bringing, proposing, from *latus*, pp. of *ferre*, to bring.] the act of passing a law or laws; enacting of laws; also, the laws enacted.

leġ′is·lā·tive, *a.* 1. giving or enacting laws.
2. capable of enacting laws.
3. pertaining to the enacting of laws; suitable to laws; as, the *legislative* style.
4. brought about or enforced by legislation.

leġ′is·lā·tive, *n.* the lawmaking branch of a government; legislature.

leġ′is·lā·tive·ly, *adv.* by legislation.

leġ′is·lā·tŏr, *n.* [L. *legis lator*, or *legum lator*, a lawgiver; *legis*, genit. sing., *legum*, genit. pl. of *lex*, law, and *lator*, a mover or proposer of a law, from *latus*, pp. of *ferre*, to bring.] a lawgiver; one who makes laws, or is a member of a legislature.

leġ″is·lȧ·tō′ri·ăl, *a.* 1. of or relating to a legislator, a legislature, or legislation.
2. having legislative power; lawmaking.

leġ′is·lā·tŏr·ship, *n.* the office of a legislator.

leġ′is·lā″tress, leġ″is·lā′trix, *n.* a woman who makes laws.

leġ′is·lā·tūre, *n.* [L. *lex*, *legis*, law, and LL. *latura*, a bringing, carrying, from L. *latus*, pp. of *ferre*, to bring, bear.]
1. a body of persons given the responsibility and power to make laws for a country or state; specifically, the lawmaking body of a State, corresponding to the Congress of the United States.
2. legislative power. [Rare.]

lē′ġist, *n.* [OFr. *legiste*; LL. *legista*, one skilled in the law, from *lex*, *legis*, law.] a person versed in the laws; a lawyer.

lē·ġit′, *n.* the legitimate theater, drama, stage, etc. [Slang.]

lē·ġit′, *a.* legitimate. [Slang.]

leġ′i·tim, *n.* same as *legitime*.

lē·ġit′i·mȧ·cy, *n.* the quality or state of being legitimate.

lē·ġit′i·măte, *a.* [LL. *legitimatus*, pp. of *legitimare*, to make lawful, from L. *legitimus*, lawful, from *lex*, *legis*, law.]
1. conceived or born of parents legally married to each other.
2. sanctioned by law or custom; lawful; allowed; as, a *legitimate* claim.
3. ruling by the rights of heredity; as, a *legitimate* king.
4. reasonable; logically correct; as, a *legitimate* inference.
5. in the theater, (a) formerly, of recognized literary merit; in conformity with certain literary standards; as, the *legitimate* drama; (b) designating or of stage plays, as distinguished from motion pictures, burlesque, vaudeville, etc.

lē·ġit′i·māte, *v.t.*; legitimated, *pt.*, *pp.*; legitimating, *ppr.* [LL. *legitimatus*, pp. of *legitimare*, to make lawful, from L. *legitimus*, lawful, from *lex*, *legis*, law.]
1. to make or declare legitimate.
2. to justify or authorize.

lē·ġit′i·măte·ly, *adv.* in a legitimate manner; so as to be legitimate.

lē·ġit′i·măte·ness, *n.* the state or quality of being legitimate.

lē·ġit·i·mā′tion, *n.* a legitimating or being legitimated.

lē·ġit′i·mȧ·tist, *n.* same as *legitimist*.

lē·ġit′i·mȧ·tīze, *v.t.*; legitimatized, *pt.*, *pp.*; legitimatizing, *ppr.* to legitimate.

leġ′i·time, *n.* [Fr. *légitime*; L. *legitimus*, fixed or allowed by law, legitimate, from *lex*, *legis*, law.] in civil law, that portion of a man's estate of which he cannot disinherit his children.

lē·ġit′i·mis̩m, *n.* the principles of a legitimist.

lē·ġit′i·mist, *n.* [Fr. *légitimiste*, from L. *legitimus*, legitimate, from *lex*, *legis*, law.]
1. one who upholds legitimate authority or, especially, the claims to monarchy based on the rights of heredity.
2. [L–] in France, an adherent of the elder branch of the Bourbon family, descendants of Louis XIV.
3. [L–] in Spain, a Carlist.

lē·ġit·i·mi·zā′tion, *n.* legitimation.

lē·ġit′i·mīze, *v.t.*; legitimized, *pt.*, *pp.*; legitimizing, *ppr.* to legitimate.

leg′less, *a.* without legs.

leg′let, *n.* an ornamental leg band.

leg-of-mut′tŏn, *a.* shaped somewhat like a leg of mutton; much larger at one end than at the other: said of a sleeve, sail, etc.

Lē·gree′, Sī′mŏn, in Harriet Beecher Stowe's *Uncle Tom's Cabin*, a man typifying the cruel, brutal, ruthless slave dealer; hence, one who is tyrannical and cruel; a hard taskmaster.

lē·guän′ (-gwän), *n.* [Braz. *leguana*.] an iguana or other large lizard.

leg″ū·lē′iăn, *a.* [L. *leguleius*, a pettifogging lawyer.] pettifogging.

leg″ū·lē′iăn, *n.* a pettifogger.

leg′ūme (*or* lē·gūm′), *n.* [Fr. *légume*; L. *legumen*, pulse, any leguminous plant, lit., anything that may be gathered, from *legere*, to gather.]
1. any of a large group of plants of the pea family, characterized by true pods enclosing seeds: because of their ability to store up nitrates, legumes are often plowed under to fertilize the soil.
2. the fruit of any plant of the pea family, often used as food; pod.
3. the seed of such a plant, contained in the pod.

lē·gū′men, *n.* same as *legume*.

lē·gū′min, *n.* [*legumen* and *-in*.] a caseinlike globulin found in legumes.

Lē·gū·mi·nō′sae, *n.pl.* [L. *legumen* (*-inis*), any leguminous plant.] one of the largest and most important families of plants, including about seven thousand species, dispersed throughout the world.

lē·gū′mi·nōse, *a.* leguminous.

lē·gū′mi·nous, *a.* [L. *legumen* (*-inis*), any leguminous plant.]
1. of, having the nature of, or bearing a legume or legumes.
2. of the group of plants bearing legumes, or pods, to which peas and beans belong.

leg wŏrk, walking; especially, much walking or traveling as the necessary, but routine, part of a job, as of a newspaper reporter, etc. [Colloq.]

lẹ·hụ′ä, *n.* 1. a tropical tree of the myrtle family, with clusters of bright-red flowers and hard wood: it grows in Hawaii and other Pacific islands.
2. its wood.
3. its flower.

lẹ′ī (*or* lā), *n.*; *pl.* **lẹ′īs̩** (*or* lāz), [Haw.] in Hawaii, a garland or wreath of flowers and leaves, generally worn about the neck.

lẹi (lā), *n.* plural of *leu*.

Leices′tẽr (les′tẽr), *n.* any of a breed of long-wooled sheep originally developed in Leicestershire, England.

Leī·ō·phyl′lum, *n.* [Gr. *leios*, smooth, and *phyllon*, leaf.] a genus of the *Ericaceæ*, of which *Leiophyllum buxifolium*, the sand myrtle, is the only known species.

Leī·ot′ri·chăn, *a.* relating to the Leiotrichi.

Leī·ot′ri·chī, *n.pl.* [Gr. *leios*, smooth, and *thrix*, *trichos*, hair.] smooth-haired people; a division of mankind characterized by smoothness of the hair, the other division being *Ulotrichi*, crisp or woolly-haired people.

leī·ot′ri·chous, *a.* of or belonging to the Leiotrichi; having smooth hair.

leī·pō′ȧ, *n.* [from Gr. *leipein*, to leave, and *ōa*, pl. of *ōon*, an egg.] the native pheasant of Australia, which does not sit on its eggs, but builds mounds of sand and weeds in which the eggs are hatched by the heat produced by decomposition of the weeds: called also *mound bird*.

leī·pō·thym′iç, *a.* same as *lipothymic*.

leish·man·ī′ȧ·sis, *n.* [Mod. L., from *Leishmania*, name of the parasitic genus; after Gen. Sir William Boog *Leishman* (1865–1926), Brit. army surgeon.] any of various diseases caused by a variety of protozoan parasite; especially, kala-azar.

lēis′tẽr, *n.* [ON. *ljoster*, from *ljosta*, to strike.] a spear, generally three-pronged and barbed, for taking fish.

lēis′tẽr, *v.t.* to spear (fish) with a leister.

lēi′ṣūr·ȧ·ble (-zhūr-), *a.* leisure; leisurely.

lēi′ṣūr·ȧ·bly, *adv.* at leisure.

lēi′ṣūre (lē′zhūr *or* lezh′ūr), *n.* [ME. *leiser*, *leyser*; OFr. *leisir*, leisure, permission, from L. *licere*, to be permitted.]

1. freedom from occupation or business; idle time; time free from employment, during which a person may indulge in rest, recreation, etc.

2. time at one's disposal; convenience.

at leisure; (a) having free or spare time; (b) with no hurry; (c) not occupied or engaged.

at one's leisure; when one has time or opportunity; when it is convenient for one.

lēi′ṣūre, *a.* 1. free and unoccupied; spare; as, *leisure* time.

2. having much leisure; not working for a living; as, the *leisure* class.

lēi′ṣūred, *a.* 1. having much leisure.

2. without haste; leisurely.

lēi′ṣūre·li·ness, *n.* the quality of being leisurely; freedom from haste.

lēi′ṣūre·ly, *a.* characterized by or having leisure; without haste; deliberate; slow; as, we made a *leisurely* inspection of the old ruin.

lēi′ṣūre·ly, *adv.* in an unhurried manner.

leīt′mō·tīf″, leīt′mō·tīv″, *n.* [G., lit., leading motive.] in music, a distinguishing theme or melodic phrase representing and recurring with a given character, situation, or emotion in an opera: first developed by Richard Wagner.

lem′ăn, *n.* [ME. *lemman*, *lefman*, from *lef*, *leve*, dear, and *man*.] a sweetheart or lover (man or woman); especially, a mistress. [Archaic.]

lēme, *n.* a gleam. [Obs.]

lem′mȧ, *n.*; *pl.* **lem′mȧṣ, lem′mȧ·tȧ,** [L., a theme, subject; Gr. *lēmma*, anything received, an assumption, from *lambanein*, to take, assume.]

1. in mathematics, etc., a secondary proposition demonstrated or assumed for the purpose of being used in the demonstration of some other proposition.

2. in logic, formerly, a premise, especially a hypothetical major premise.

3. a theme; a subject or thesis.

4. a membrane; a sheath, as that of the germinal vesicle: also used in combination; as, sarco*lemma*.

lem′ming, *n.*; *pl.* **lem′mingṣ** or **lemming,** [Norw.] any of various small arctic rodents resembling mice but having short tails and fur-covered feet. The common or European lemming is very prolific, and vast hordes periodically migrate from the mountains to the sea, destroying vegetation in their path.

COMMON LEMMING (*Lemmus lemmus*)

Lem′nȧ, *n.* [Gr. *lemna*, a water plant.] a genus of aquatic plants of the *Lemnaceæ* or duckweed tribe. They consist of small floating fronds, almost destitute of vascular tissue. The very minute flowers are produced from the edge of the frond. They are known by the common name of *duckmeat* or *duckweed*.

Lem·nā′cē·ae, *n.pl.* a family of monocotyledons, of which *Lemna* is the typical genus.

Lem′ni·ăn, *a.* [L. *Lemnius*; Gr. *Lēmnios*, Lemnian, from *Lēmnos*, the isle of Lemnos.] of or relating to the isle of Lemnos, in Greece.

Lemnian earth; sphragide or cimolite, a kind of stringent, medicinal earth, of a fatty consistence and yellowish color; a kind of clay used as fuller's earth.

Lemnian reddle; a deep-red ocher of firm consistence, found with Lemnian earth.

lem·nis′çāte, *n.* [L. *lemniscatus*, adorned with pendent ribbons, from *lemniscus*, a ribbon.] in geometry, the name of a curve in the form of the figure 8, forming the locus of the base of a perpendicular drawn from the center to the tangent to an equilateral hyperbola.

lem·nis′çus, *n.*; *pl.* **lem·nis′cī,** [L., a ribbon adorning a victor's wreath; Gr. *lēmniskos*, a fillet or band.]

1. a various-colored woolen fillet or ribbon pendent at the back part of the head, from diadems, crowns, etc., and likewise attached to prizes as a mark of additional honor.

ANCIENT LEMNISCUS

2. one of the minute ribbon-shaped appendages of the generative pores of some entozoans.

3. a band of longitudinal nerve fibers at the base of the brain in the pons and crura: called also *fillet*.

lem′ŏn, *n.* [Fr. *limon*; Sp. *limón*; Ar. *laimon*.]

1. a small, egg-shaped, edible citrus fruit with a pale-yellow rind and a juicy, sour pulp, rich in vitamin C.

2. the small, spiny, semitropical evergreen tree (*Citrus limon*) that it grows on.

3. something or someone undesirable or inadequate. [Slang.]

lem′ŏn, *a.* 1. of the pale-yellow color of lemon rind.

2. made with or from lemons.

3. having a flavor more or less like that of lemons.

lem·ŏn·āde′, *n.* [Fr. *limonade*.] a drink made of water, lemon juice, and sugar.

lem′ŏn but′tẽr, 1. a spread made of butter flavored with lemon.

2. a sauce of melted butter, lemon juice, and seasoning, used on fish, vegetables, etc.: also called *lemon butter sauce*.

lem′ŏn drop, a small, hard, lemon-flavored candy.

lem′ŏn gràss, a fragrant East Indian grass, *Andropogon schænanthus*, and other allied species which yield a fragrant oil, used in perfumery.

lem′ŏn jụice, the juice of the lemon. It is somewhat opaque and extremely sour, owing its acidity to citric and malic acids.

lem′ŏn squäsh, a drink of lemon juice, sugar, and soda water. [Brit.]

lem′ŏn vẽr·bē′nȧ, a Chilean shrub, *Aloysia triphylla*, having leaves with an odor like that of a lemon.

lem·pī′rȧ, *n.* [Am. Sp., after *Lempira*, native chief who resisted the Spaniards.] the monetary unit of Honduras.

lē′mūr, *n.* [L. *lemur*, found only in pl. *lemures*, ghosts, specters; so called from its nocturnal habits.] any of a family of small, nocturnal, quadrumanous mammals, closely allied to monkeys, with large eyes, a pointed muzzle, and soft, woolly fur. They inhabit Madagascar and the East Indian islands.

RED LEMUR (*Lemur ruber*)

lem′ū·rēṣ, *n.pl.* [L.] in Roman mythology, the night-walking spirits of the dead.

Lē·mū′ri·ȧ, *n.* [Mod. L.: so called from Haeckel's idea that it was the original home of lemuroid primates.] a hypothetical continent thought by some to have existed long ago, now supposedly covered by the Indian Ocean.

lem′ū·rid, *a.* and *n.* same as *lemuroid*.

lem′ū·rine, lē·mū′ri·dous, *a.* lemuroid.

lem′ū·roid, *a.* relating to or resembling lemurs; of or relating to the *Lemuroidea*.

lem′ū·roid, *n.* one of the *Lemuroidea*.

Lem·ū·roi′dē·ȧ, *n.pl.* a suborder of primates akin to monkeys, including the lemurs, or *Prosimæ*.

Lē·naī′ȧ, *n.pl.* [Gr. *Lēnaia*, from *lēnaios*, belonging to the wine press, from *lēnos*, the wine press.] one of a series of festivals in honor of Dionysus, celebrated at Athens in January.

Len′ȧ·pē, *n.*; *pl.* **Len′ȧ·pē,** [short for *Lenilenape*, lit., real man.]

1. a member of the Delaware Indians.

2. their Algonquian language.

Also *Leni-Lenape*, *Lenni-Lenape*.

Len′ȧ·pē, *a.* of the Lenape or their language.

lend, *v.t.*; lent, *pt.*, *pp.*; lending, *ppr.* [ME. *lenen*; AS. *lænan*, to lend, from *lan*, *læn*, a loan.]

1. to grant to another for temporary use, on the express or implied condition that the thing shall be returned, or its equivalent in kind; as, to *lend* a book, or sum of money: opposed to *borrow*.

2. to let out (money) at interest.

3. to afford; to grant; to furnish; as, to *lend* assistance; to *lend* an ear to a discourse.

to lend itself (or *oneself*) *to*; to be adapted to, useful for, or open to.

lend, *v.i.* to grant a loan; to make a business of lending.

lend′ȧ·ble, *a.* that can be lent.

lend′ẽr, *n.* [ME. *lendare*, *lenere*; AS. *lænere*, a lender, from *lænan*, to lend.]

1. one who lends.

2. one who makes a trade of putting money to interest; a moneylender.

lend′ing, *n.* the act of lending; also, a loan.

lend′ing lī′brȧ·ry, a library from which books may be borrowed, usually for a fee.

lend′-lēase′, *n.* in World War II, material aid in the form of airplanes, munitions, tools, food, etc., granted to foreign countries whose defense was deemed vital to the defense of the United States, under the provisions of the Lend-Lease Act of March 11, 1941.

lend′-lēase′, *v.t.*; lend-leased, *pt.*, *pp.*; lend-leasing, *ppr.* to grant (material aid) to a foreign country in accordance with the Lend-Lease Act.

lend′-lēase′, *a.* operating under or pertaining to the system of lend-lease.

lē′nē, *n.* the mark for smooth breathing.

length, *n.* [ME. *lengthe*; AS. *lengthu*, length, from *lang*, long.]

1. the measure of how long a thing is; measurement of anything from end to end; the greatest of the two or three dimensions of anything: opposed to *width* or *breadth*.

2. extent in space; distance anything extends.

3. extent in time; duration.

4. a long stretch or extent.

5. the quality, state, or fact of being long: opposed to *shortness*.

6. a piece of a certain or standardized length; as, a *length* of stovepipe.

7. a unit of measure consisting of the length of an object or animal competing in a race; as, his boat won by two *lengths*.

8. in phonetics, (a) the duration of the pronunciation of a vowel; as, the *i* in *bride* has greater *length* than the *i* in *bright*; (b) popularly, the quality of a vowel.

9. in prosody, syllabic quantity.

at full length; stretched out; completely extended.

at length; (a) after a long time; finally; (b) in or to the whole extent; in full.

to go to any length; to do whatever is necessary; to scruple at nothing.

to keep at arm's length; to act coldly toward.

length′en, *v.t.*; lengthened, *pt.*, *pp.*; lengthening, *ppr.* 1. to extend in length; to make longer; to elongate; as, to *lengthen* a line.

2. to draw out or extend in time; to protract; to continue in duration; as, to *lengthen* life.

3. to draw out in pronunciation; as, to *lengthen* a sound or a syllable.

length′en, *v.i.* to become longer; to extend in length; as, the days *lengthen* with spring.

length′ful, *a.* of great length. [Rare.]

length′i·ly, *adv.* in a lengthy manner.

length′i·ness, *n.* the quality of being lengthy.

length′wāyṣ, *adv.* and *a.* same as *lengthwise*.

length′wīṣe, *adv.* and *a.* in the direction of the length.

length′y, *a.*; *comp.* lengthier; *superl.* lengthiest. 1. having length; long; especially, too long; so long as to be tiresome: said of speeches, writings, etc.

2. tall: of a person. [Colloq.]

lē′ni·ence, *n.* same as *leniency*.

 fāte, fär, fȧst, fạll, finăl, cāre, at; mēte, prey, hẽr, met; pīne, marīne, bīrd, pin; nōte, mōve, for, atŏm, not; moon, book;

lē′ni·en·cy, *n.* 1. the quality or condition of being lenient.
2. *pl.* **lē′ni·en·cies,** a lenient act.

lē′ni·ent, *a.* [L. *leniens* (*-entis*), ppr. of *lenire*, to soften, alleviate, from *lenis*, soft, mild.]
1. softening; assuasive; relaxing; emollient. [Archaic.]
2. indulgent; merciful; not severe or harsh; mild; as, a *lenient* disposition.

lē′ni·ent, *n.* in medicine, an emollient; a lenitive. [Obs.]

lē′ni·ent·ly, *adv.* in a lenient way.

len′i·fȳ, *v.t.* to assuage; to mitigate. [Rare.]

Len-i-Len′ȧ·pē, *n. sing.* and *pl.* Lenape.

Len′in·iṣm, *n.* the political theories of Vladimir Ilyich Lenin (1870–1924), especially the methods and tactics which he taught and carried through during and after the October Revolution in Russia. These practical policies are founded upon Marxism and dialectic materialism. The central point of Lenin's theories was the dictatorship of the proletariat, springing from the hegemony of the working class. The New Economic Policy, better known as Nep, instituted under his guidance, was, he taught, a step forward toward a Socialist Russia.

Len′in·ist, *n.* one who believes in Lenin's policies and tactics; a follower of Leninism: also used attributively; as, *Leninist* ideas; *Leninist* dialectics.

Len′in·ite, *n.* and *a.* same as *Leninist.*

lē′nis, *n.*; *pl.* **lē′nēṣ,** [L., gentle, smooth, soft, mild.] a weakly articulated speech sound, especially a stop: opposed to *fortis.*

lē′nis, *a.* in phonetics, weakly articulated; as, a *lenis* stop.

len′i·tive, *a.* [L. *lenitus*, pp. of *lenire*, to soften, assuage.]
1. assuasive; emollient; palliative.
2. formerly, acting as a mild laxative.

len′i·tive, *n.* 1. a medicine or application for easing pain.
2. a palliative; anything that soothes.

len′i·tive·ness, *n.* quality or state of being lenitive.

len′i·ty, *n.* [OFr. *lenite*; L. *lenitas* (*-atis*), smoothness, softness, from *lenis*, smooth, soft, mild.]
1. the quality or condition of being lenient; mildness; gentleness; mercifulness.
2. *pl.* **len′i·tieṣ,** a lenient act.

Len-ni-Len′ȧ·pē, *n. sing.* and *pl.* Lenape.

lē′nō, *n.* [Fr. *linon*, from *lin*, flax.]
1. a type of weave in which the warp yarns are paired and twisted.
2. a soft, light fabric of this weave.

lē·noc′i·nȧnt, *a.* inciting to lewdness. [Obs.]

lenṣ, *n.* [L. *lens*, a lentil, which resembles a double-convex lens.]
1. a piece of glass, or other transparent substance, with two curved surfaces, or one plane and one curved, regularly bringing together or spreading rays of light passing through it: a lens or combination of lenses is used in optical instruments to form an image: for kinds of lenses, see illustrations following *concave* and *convex.*

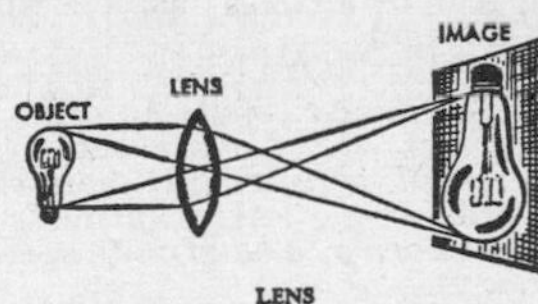

2. a combination of two or more such pieces.
3. in anatomy, a transparent, biconvex body situated between the iris and the vitreous humor of the eye: its function is to focus upon the retina light rays entering the pupil.

lenṣ çap, a cover fitting into or over the end of the tube in which a lens is mounted.

lenṣ cell, a cell whose function is believed to be light sensitivity: it is found in the epidermis of leaves and other organs.

lenṣ hōld′ẽr, a support for a lens, used in adjusting an object to the focus.

lenṣ hood, in photography, a lens screen.

lenṣ′less, *a.* not provided with a lens.

lenṣ′less çam′ẽr·ȧ, a camera with a minute aperture and no lens; a pinhole camera.

lenṣ′-mount, *n.* in photography, a tube, usually of metal, which supports the lens.

lenṣ sçreen, in photography, a hood which shields the lens from stray light; a lens hood.

lenṣ stär, a starlike figure made in the crystalline lens by its radiating fibers.

Lent, *n.* [ME. *lenten*; AS. *lencten*, the spring, from *lang*, long: so called from the lengthening of the days in the spring.]
1. the period of forty weekdays from Ash Wednesday to Easter, observed in Christian churches by fasting and penitence to commemorate Jesus' fasting in the wilderness.
2. in the Middle Ages, the period from Martinmas (November 11) to Christmas: in full, *St. Martin's Lent.*

lent, *v.* past tense and past participle of *lend.*

-lent, [L. *-lentus*, -ful.] a suffix meaning *full of, characterized by,* as in viru*lent*, fraudu*lent*, pesti*lent*.

lęn″tä·men′tę, *adv.* [It.] in music, slowly: a direction to the performer.

lęn·tän′dō, *a.* [It., ppr. of *lentare*, to make slow, from *lento*, L. *lentus*, slow, sluggish.] in music, rallentando; gradually becoming slower: a direction to the performer.

Lent′en, *n.* Lent. [Obs.]

Lent′en, lent′en, *a.* 1. of, connected with, or suitable for Lent.
2. meager; cheerless; as, *Lenten* fare.

Lent′en·tīde″, *n.* the Lenten season.

Len·tib″ū·lā″ri·ā′cē·ae, *n.pl.* [L. *lens, lentis*, a lentil, and *tubulus*, a small pipe.] a small order of aquatic or subaquatic herbs; the bladderworts.

len′ti·cel, *n.* [Fr. *lenticelle*, dim. of *lenticule*, lens-shaped, from L. *lens, lentis*, lentil.]
1. in botany, a lenticular cluster of cells in the periderm of plants, functioning as a breathing pore.
2. a lenticular gland.

len·ti·cel′lāte, *a.* having lenticels.

len·tiç′ū·lȧ, *n.*; *pl.* **len·tiç′ū·lae,** [L. *lenticula*, a lentil, a vessel shaped like a lentil, a freckle, from *lens, lentis*, a lentil.]
1. in medicine, a freckle.
2. in optics, a small-sized lens.
3. in botany, a lenticel.

len·tiç′ū·lăr, *a.* [L. *lenticularis*, from *lenticula*, a lentil.]
1. shaped like a lentil or double-convex lens.
2. of a lens.
3. of the lens of the eye.
4. in motion pictures, lenticulated.

len·tiç′ū·lăr·ly, *adv.* in a lenticular manner.

len·tiç′ū·lāt·ed, *a.* 1. lenticular.
2. in motion pictures, designating a film having microscopic lenses embossed on its base side and used with a special color filter to produce pictures in natural color.

len′ti·fọrm, *a.* [L. *lens, lentis*, a lentil, and *forma*, form.] lenticular.

len·tiġ′i·nous, *a.* [LL. *lentiginosus*, freckled, from L. *lentigo* (*-inis*), a freckly eruption, from *lens, lentis*, a lentil.] speckled with dots like freckles; freckly.

len·tī′gō, *n.* a freckle; also, a freckly condition of the skin.

len′til, *n.* [ME. *lentil*; OFr. *lentille*; L. *lenticula*, dim. of *lens, lentis*, a lentil.]
1. an annual plant, *Lens esculenta*, belonging to the pea family, with small, edible seeds shaped like double-convex lenses.
2. the seed of this plant.

len′tisk, len·tis′çus, *n.* [ME. *lentiske*; L. *lentiscus*, or *lentiscum*, the mastic tree.] the mastic tree.

len·tis′si·mō, *adv.* and *a.* [It., superl. of *lento*, slow.] in music, very slow: a direction to the performer.

len′tō, *a.* and *adv.* [It.] in music, slow: a direction to the performer.

len′toid, *a.* lens-shaped.

len′tŏr, len′tŏur, *n.* 1. tenacity; viscosity. [Rare.]
2. slowness; delay; sluggishness. [Rare.]

len′tous, *a.* viscid; viscous; tenacious. [Obs.]

l'en·voi′, l'en·voy′ (len- *or Fr. pron.* lon̈-vwä′), *n.* [OFr., lit., the sending; *le*, the, and *envoi*, a sending.]
1. originally, a dedication or postscript to a poem, essay, or book, directing it to a specific person's attention.
2. a concluding stanza added to a ballade and some other forms, customarily a direct address to a prince, princess, lord, lady, etc. Also *envoy.*

Lē′ō, *n.* [L., a lion, the constellation Leo.]
1. a constellation between Cancer and Virgo, supposedly outlining a lion: it contains the bright star Regulus.
2. the fifth sign of the zodiac, entered by the sun about July 22.
Leo Minor; a constellation smaller than Leo, between it and the Great Bear.

lē′ŏn, *n.* a lion. [Obs.]

lē′ŏnced (-ŏnst), *a.* in heraldry, same as *lionced.*

Lē″ō·nēṣe′ (*or* -nēs′), *a.* [Sp. *Leonés*, from *Leon*, Leon.] pertaining to Leon, a province in Spain.

Lē″ō·nēṣe′, *n. sing.* and *pl.* a person or persons born or living in Leon.

Lē′ō·nid, *n.*; *pl.* **Lē′ō·nidṣ, Lē·on′i·dēṣ,** any of a shower of meteors observed in the month of November each year: so called because they seem to radiate from the constellation Leo.

lē′ō·nīne, *a.* [OFr. *leonin*; L. *leoninus*, like a lion, from *leo* (*-onis*), a lion.]
1. belonging to, characteristic of, or resembling a lion; as, *leonine* fierceness or rapacity.
2. consisting of hexameters or of hexameters and pentameters in which the final syllable rhymes with one in the middle of the line.

lē′ō·nīne·ly, *adv.* in the manner of a lion.

lē·on·tī′ȧ·sis, *n.* [Gr., from *leōn* (*-ontos*), a lion, and *-iasis.*] a variety of leprosy in which the face resembles that of a lion.

Lē·on′tō·don, *n.* [Gr. *leōn* (*-ontos*), a lion, and *odous, odontos*, tooth.] a genus of the *Compositæ. Leontodon autumnale* is the fall dandelion.

Lē·on·tō·pō′di·um, *n.* [Gr. *leōn* (*-ontos*), a lion, and *pous, podos*, foot.] a genus of the *Compositæ*, including the edelweiss.

leop′ărd (lep′), *n.* [ME. *lepard, lepart, leopard*; OFr. *leopard*; L. *leopardus*; Gr. *leopardos* or *leontopardos*, the leopard; *leōn* (*-ontos*), a lion, and *pardos*, a pard, panther.]
1. a large, ferocious animal of the cat family, usually having a tawny coat spotted with black, found in Africa and southern Asia: also called *panther.*

LEOPARD (*Felis pardus*)

2. the jaguar, or American leopard.
3. in heraldry, a lion represented in side view, with one foreleg raised and the head facing to the front.

leop′ărd çat, a small spotted cat of Asia, Africa, and the East Indies; also, the ocelot of America.

leop′ar·dé (-ăr-dā), *a.* [Fr.] in heraldry, passant gardant.

leop′ărd·ess, *n.* a female leopard.

leop′ărd flow′ẽr, the blackberry lily.

leop′ărd frog, the common frog (*Rana pipiens*) of America.

leop′ărd mär′mot, a gopher or spermophile.

leop′ărd moth, a common spotted moth, *Zeuzera pyrina*, of Europe.

leop′ărd·wood, *n.* the spotted wood of *Brosimum aubletii*, a tropical tree: called also *snakewood* and *letterwood.*

lē′ō·tärd, *n.* [after *Léotard*, 19th-c. French aerial performer.] a one-piece, sleeveless, tight-fitting garment, worn by acrobats, dancers, etc.

lep, *v.* obsolete past tense of *leap.*

lep′ȧ·doid, *n.* [Gr. *lepas* (*-ados*), a limpet, and *eidos*, form.] a goose barnacle.

lep′ăl, *n.* [L. *lepis*; Gr. *lepis*, a scale.] a sterile stamen transformed into a scale.

Lē′pas, *n.* [L. *lepas* (*-adis*); Gr. *lepas* (*-ados*), a limpet, from *lepas*, a bare rock.] a genus of cirripeds of which the barnacle, *Lepas anatifera*, is an example.

lep′ẽr, *n.* [ME. *lepre*; OFr. *liepre*; L. *lepra* or *lepræ*; Gr. *lepra*, leprosy, from *lepros*, rough, scaly; *lepos*, a scale, from *lepein*, to peel or bark.] a person having leprosy.

lep′ẽred, (-ẽrd), *a.* stricken with leprosy.

lep′ẽr·ous, *a.* same as *leprous.*

lep′id, *a.* pleasant; jocose. [Rare.]

lep′id-, same as *lepido-.*

lep′i·dīne, *n.* [*Lepid*ium and *-ine.*] an oily compound, $C_{10}H_9N$, obtained by distilling cinchonine.

Lē·pid′i·um, *n.* [L. *lepidium*, from Gr. *lepidion*, a plant, prob. pepperwort, dim. of *lepis* (*-idos*), a scale: so called from the form of the little pouches.] a genus of plants of the mustard family; the peppergrasses.

lep′i·dō-, [from Gr. *lepis* (*-idos*), a scale, husk.] a combining form used in botany, zoology, etc., to signify *scaly*, as in *lepido*dendron, *lepi-dosiren*.

lep″i·dō·den′droid, *a.* [*lepido-*, and Gr. *dendron*, a tree, and *eidos*, form.] pertaining to lepidodendrons.

lep″i·dō·den′drŏn, *n.* [*lepido-*, and Gr. *dendron*, a tree.] a fossil tree of the genus *Lepidodendron*, occurring in the coal formations: so named from the scaly appearance of the stem, produced by the separation of the leaf stalks.

lep″i·dō·gan′oid, *n.* [*lepido-*, and Gr. *ganos*, brightness, and *eidos*, form.] one of a family of extinct ganoid fishes with scales.

lē·pid′ō·līte, *n.* [*lepido-*, and Gr. *lithos*, stone.] a variety of mica of a lilac or rose-violet color: it usually occurs in masses consisting of small scales.

lep″i·dō·mē·lāne′, *n.* [*lepido-*, and Gr. *melas* (*-anos*), black.] a scaly black iron-potash mica.

lep·i·dop′tēr, *n.* one of the *Lepidoptera*.

Lep·i·dop′tēr·ȧ, *n.pl.* [*lepido-*, and Gr. *pteron*, a wing.] an order of insects, including the butterflies and moths, characterized by two pairs of broad, membranous wings covered with very fine scales, often brightly colored.

lep·i·dop′tēr·ăl, *a.* lepidopterous.

lep·i·dop′tēr·ăn, *n.* a lepidopterous insect.

lep·i·dop′tēr·ăn, *a.* lepidopterous.

lep·i·dop′tēr·ist, *n.* a student of the *Lepidoptera*.

lep·i·dop′tēr·on, *n.*; *pl.* **lep·i·dop′tēr·ȧ**, a lepidopterous insect.

lep·i·dop′tēr·ous, *a.* of or belonging to the order of *Lepidoptera*.

lep″i·dō·sī′ren, *n.* [*lepido-*, and L. *siren*; Gr. *seirēn*, a siren.] an eel-shaped fish with both gills and lungs, found in South America.

lep′i·dōte, lep′i·dō·ted, *a.* [Gr. *lepidōtos*, covered with scales, from *lepidoun*, to make scaly, from *lepis* (*-idos*), a scale.] in botany, with a coat of scurfy scales.

Lē·pis′mȧ, *n.* [Gr. *lepisma*, peel, anything peeled off, from *lepizein*, to husk, peel, from *lepis* (*-idos*), a husk, scale.] a genus of insects with a long, flat body covered with scales; the bristletails.

lē·pis′moid, *a.* [Gr. *lepisma*, peel, and *eidos*, appearance.] relating to the *Lepisma*.

lep′ō·cȳte, lē·poc′y·tȧ, *n.* [Gr. *lepos*, a husk, scale, and *kytos*, a hollow.] a protozoan with a cell membrane.

lep′ō·rid, *n.*; *pl.* **le·por′i·dae**, [ML. *Leporidae*, name of the family, from *lepus*, *leporis*, a hare.] any of a family of animals consisting of the hares and rabbits.

lep′ō·rid, *a.* of this family.

lep′ō·ride, *n.* [from L. *lepus*, *leporis*, hare.] a cross between a European hare and European rabbit; Belgian hare.

lep′ō·rīne (*or*-rin), *a.* [L. *leporinus*, from *lepus* (*-oris*), a hare.] pertaining to or having the qualities of the hare.

lep′rȧ, *n.* [L., from Gr. *lepra*, leprosy.] leprosy.

lep′re·chaun, *n.* [Ir. *lupracān*; old Ir. *luchorpan*, from *lu*, little, and *corpān*, dim. of *corp*, body, from L. *corpus*, body.] in Irish folklore, a fairy in the form of a little old man who can reveal hidden treasure to anyone who catches him.

lep·rō·sār′i·um, *n.* [Mod. L., from *leprosy* and *sanitarium*.] a hospital or colony for lepers.

lep′rōse, *a.* in botany, scaly; scurfy.

lep·ros′i·ty, *n.* the condition of being leprous. [Obs.]

lep′rō·sy, *n.* [OFr. *leprosie*; prob. from ML. *leprosus*.] a chronic infectious disease that attacks the skin, tissues, or nerves: it is characterized by nodules, ulcers, white scaly scabs, deformities, and wasting of body parts, and is apparently communicated only after long and close contact.

lep′rous, *a.* [OFr. *leprous*, *lepros*; LL. *leprosus*, from L. *lepra*; Gr. *lepra*, leprosy.]
1. of, like, or infected with leprosy.
2. covered with scales; leprose.

lep′rous·ly, *adv.* in a leprous manner.

lep′rous·ness, *n.* the state of being leprous.

lep′ry, *n.* leprosy. [Obs.]

-lep′sy, -lep′si·ȧ, [Mod.L. *-lepsia*; Gr. *-lēpsia*.] combining forms meaning *a fit*, *attack*, as in cata*lepsy*.

Lep·tan′drȧ, *n.* [Gr. *leptos*, fine, delicate, and *aner*, *andros*, man, male.] the rhizome of *Veronica virginica*.

lep·tan′drin, *n.* [*Leptandra* and *-in*.] a glucoside derived from Leptandra, used as a cathartic.

lep′ti·fọrm, *a.* [Gr. *leptos*, fine, delicate, and L. *forma*, form.] shaped like a leptus.

lep′tō-, [from Gr. *leptos*, thin, fine, small.] a combining form meaning *thin*, *fine*, *narrow*, as in *lepto*cephaly, *lepto*meninx.

lep″tō·çär′di·ăn, *a.* of or like the *Leptocardii*.

Lep·tō·çär′di·ī, *n.pl.* [*Lepto-*, and Gr. *kardia*, heart.] a group of *Vertebrata* without a skull, brain, heart, limbs, and jaws. The blood is colorless and the mouth longitudinal, and the notochord takes the place of a backbone. There are about six known species, including *Amphioxus*.

lep″tō·cē·phal′iç, *a.* characterized by leptocephaly.

lep·tō·ceph′ȧ·ly, *n.* [*lepto-*, and Gr. *kephalē*, head.] extreme narrowness of the skull.

lep·tō·daç′tyl, *a.* same as *leptodactylous*.

lep·tō·daç′tyl, *n.* a leptodactylous animal.

lep″tō·daç′ty·lous, *a.* having slender toes, as some birds.

lep′tōme, *n.* [Gr. *leptos*, fine, thin, slender.] the fibrous portion or phloem of a fibrovascular bundle.

lep″tō·mē·nin′ġēş, *n.pl.* [*lepto-*, and Gr. *mēninx*, *mēningos*, a membrane.] in anatomy, the arachnoid and the pia mater.

lep·tō·men·in·ġī′tis, *n.* inflammation of the leptomeninx.

lep·tō·mē′ninx, *n.*; *pl.* **lep″tō·mē·nin′ġēş**, [*lepto-*, and Gr. *mēninx*, *mēningos*, a membrane.] the pia mater or the arachnoid.

lep′ton, *n.*; *pl.* **lep′tȧ**, [Gr. *lepton*, a small coin, properly neut. of *leptos*, thin, fine, small.]
1. an ancient Greek coin of small value.
2. a modern Greek bronze coin, worth about $^1/_{100}$ of a drachma.

lep′tō·rhīne (-rīn *or* -rin), *a.* [*lepto-*, and Gr. *rhis*, *rhinos*, nose.] with narrow nasal bones.

Lep·tō·spēr′mum, *n.* [*lepto-*, and Gr. *sperma*, seed.] a genus of the *Myrtaceæ*, having about twenty-five species, mostly Australian.

lep″tō·spō·ran′ġi·āte, *a.* [*lepto-*, and Gr. *spora*, a seed, and *angeion*, a vessel.] having sporangia that are each developed from a single cell of the epidermis, as in most ferns.

Lep·tos′trȧ·çȧ, *n.pl.* [*lepto-*, and Gr. *ostrakon*, a shell.] an order of bivalve crustaceans including the genus *Nebalia*.

Lep′tō·thrix, *n.* [*lepto-*, and Gr. *thrix*, hair.] a bacterium in which the slender, hairlike cells continue joined end to end after fission.

lep′tus, *n.* [Gr. *leptos*, thin, fine, slender, delicate.] a larva having six legs, as in the harvest mites.

lep′ty·nīte, *n.* [Gr. *leptynein*, to make thin, from *leptos*, thin, slender, and *-ite*.] granulite.

Lē′pus, *n.* [L., a hare.] a southern constellation supposedly outlining a hare.

lēre, *n.* learning; lesson. [Obs.]

lēre, *v.t.* and *v.i.* to learn; to teach. [Obs.]

lēr′ed, *a.* learned. [Obs.]

Lēr·nae′ȧ, *n.* [L., f. of *Lernæus*; Gr. *Lernaios*, Lernaean, from *Lerna* or *Lernē*, Lerne, a district in Argolis; so called in reference to the Lernaean hydra.] a genus of suctorial crustaceans that are parasitic on fishes; the typical genus of the fish lice family.

lēr·nae′ăn, *n.* a member of the *Lernæa*.

lēr·nae′oid, *a.* resembling the lernaeans.

ler′ŏt, *n.* [Fr.] the garden dormouse.

lērp, *n.* [Australian.] a sweet secretion of a kind of plant louse found on certain eucalyptus leaves.

les, *n.* a leash. [Obs.]

Leş′bi·ăn, *a.* [L. *Lesbius*; Gr. *Lesbios*, from *Lesbos*, the isle of Lesbos.]
1. of ancient Lesbos, an island in the Aegean sea now called Mytilene.
2. (a) homosexual: only of women, from the homosexuality attributed to Sappho and her followers in Lesbos; (b) [Rare.] erotic.

Leş′bi·ăn, *n.* 1. a native or inhabitant of Lesbos.
2. a homosexual woman.

Leş′bi·ăn·işm, *n.* the sexual practices of Lesbians; homosexuality between women.

Leş′bi·ăn lŏve, same as *Lesbianism*.

lēşe maj′es·ty, [Fr. *lèse-majesté*; LL. *læsa majestas*, high treason; L. *læsa*, f. of *læsus*, pp. of *lædere*, to hurt, injure, and *majestas*, majesty.] treason; any offense against the sovereign of a state.

lē′şion, *n.* [Fr. *lésion*; L. *læsio* (*-onis*), a hurt, injury, from *læsus*, pp. of *lædere*, to harm, injure.]
1. a hurt, wound, or injury.
2. in medicine, an injury or other alteration of any organ or tissue resulting in impairment or loss of function.
3. in civil law, an injury sustained by one who fails to receive a just equivalent for what he has given in a contract.

Les″pe·dē′zȧ, *n.* in botany, a genus of shrubby plants: *Lespedeza striata* is used for forage.

less, *a.*, [alt. comp. of *little*,] [ME. *lesse*, *lasse*, AS. *læssa*, smaller, inferior, less.] smaller; inferior; not so large, so much, or so great; as, *less* in size or value.

less, *adv.*, [comp. of *little*,] [ME. *lesse*, *les*; AS. *læs*, less.] not so much; in a smaller or lower degree.

less, *n.* a smaller amount.

less, *prep.* with the deduction of; minus; as, total income *less* earned income.

-less, [ME. *-les*, *-leas*; AS. *-leás*, from *leás*, free, loose.] a suffix meaning *without*, *lacking*, *not capable of being*, as in love*less*, law*less*, daunt*less*.

les·see′, *n.* [OFr. *lessé*, pp. of *lesser*, to let, from L. *laxare*, to loosen.] the person to whom a lease is given, or who takes an estate by lease; a tenant.

less′en, *v.t.*; lessened, *pt.*, *pp.*; lessening, *ppr.*
1. to make less; to diminish; to reduce in bulk, size, quantity, number, or degree; to make smaller.
2. to degrade; to belittle; to depreciate; to minimize.

less′en, *v.i.* to become less; to shrink; to contract in bulk, quantity, number, or amount; to be diminished; as, the apparent magnitude of objects *lessens* as we recede from them.

less′en·ēr, *n.* one who or that which makes less.

less′ēr, *a.* less; smaller; minor; as, the *lesser* prophets.

less′ēr, *adv.* less. [Obs.]

Less′ēr Beãr, the constellation Ursa Minor.

les′seş, *n.pl.* the dung of the wild boar, bear, wolf, etc. [Obs.]

les′sŏn, *n.* [ME. *lessoun*; OFr. *leçon*, a lesson, from L. *lectio* (*-onis*), a reading, from *lectus*, pp. of *legere*, to read.]
1. something to be learned; specifically, (a) an exercise or assignment that a student is to prepare or learn within a given time; unit of instruction; (b) the instruction given during one class or instruction period; (c) something that needs to be learned (or the event through which it is learned) for the sake of one's safety, well-being, etc.; as, breaking through thin ice has taught many a skater a *lesson*; (d) [*pl.*] course of instruction; as, music *lessons*.
2. a portion of the Bible read in a church service.
3. a lecture; reproof; rebuke.
4. a musical composition written as an exercise for an instrument; exercise; étude.

les′sŏn, *v.t.*; lessoned, *pt.*, *pp.*; lessoning, *ppr.*
1. to teach; to instruct.
2. to rebuke; to reprove.

les′sŏr, *n.* [OFr., from *lesser*, to lease.] one who leases; the person who lets to a tenant or gives a lease; a landlord.

lest, *conj.* [ME. *leste*, *les the*, lest; AS. *thy læs the*, lit., by the less that.]
1. that . . . not; in order that . . . not; as, take care *lest* you stumble; that is, take care *that* you stumble *not*.
2. that; for fear that: with expressions indicating fear or anxiety; as, she worried *lest* he should forget.

lest, *a.* least; last. [Obs.]

-let, [OFr. *-let*, masc., *-lette*, f., dim.; *-el*, from L. *-ellus*, and *-et*.] a noun suffix, generally meaning *small*, as in ring*let*, ham*let*: used in some words (e.g., ank*let*, arm*let*) meaning *small object worn as a band on* (a specified part of the body).

let, *v.t.*; letted, *pt.*, *pp.*; letting, *ppr.* [ME. *letten*; AS. *lettan*, lit., to make late.] to hinder; to obstruct; to prevent. [Archaic.]

let, *n.* 1. a hindrance; obstacle; impediment; delay: used commonly only in the legal phrase, *without let or hindrance*.
2. in tennis, etc., an interference with the course of the ball in some way specified in the rules, making it necessary to play the point over again.

let, *v.t.*; let *or obs.* letted, *pt.*, *pp.*; letting, *ppr.* [ME. *leten*, *laten*; AS. *lætan*, to let, allow, permit.]
1. to leave; forsake; abandon: now only in phrases *let alone*, *let be*.
2. (a) to give temporary use of (a house, room, etc.) to a tenant in return for rent; to rent; hire out; (b) to give out (work); to assign (a contract).
3. to allow or cause to escape; to cause to flow or come out, as by shedding, emitting, etc.; as, to *let* blood.
4. to allow to pass, come, or go.
5. to allow; to permit: (a) followed by an infinitive, often without *to*; as, will you *let* me

smoke?; (b) with the following verb understood; as, don't *let* me down.

6. to cause: usually with *know* or *hear*; as, *let* me hear from you.

7. to suppose; assume; regard as.

When used in commands or suggestions with a noun or pronoun as object, *let* serves as an auxiliary; as, *let* us give generously.

to let down; (a) to lower; to permit to descend; (b) to soften the temper of, as steel; (c) to disillusion or disappoint.

to let drive at; to strike a powerful blow at.

to let in; (a) to admit; (b) to inlay or insert, as a piece into a place prepared.

to let out; (a) to allow to flow, run, etc. away; to release; (b) to give forth; to emit; (c) to lease or rent out; (d) to reveal (a secret, etc.); (e) to make a garment larger by reducing (the seams, hem, etc.); (f) [Colloq.] to dismiss, as school.

let, *v.i.* to be leased or rented; as, the flats *let* quickly.

to let on; (a) to tell; to divulge; as, never *let on*; (b) to pretend; to feign. [Colloq.]

to let up; (a) to abate; to cease; as, the rain will soon *let up*; (b) to slacken; to relax. [Colloq.]

letch, *n.* a leach; a leach tub.

letch, *v.t.* and *v.i.* same as *leach*.

letch, *n.* passion; ardent desire. [Obs. or Brit. Dial.]

let′down, *n.* 1. a slowing up, relaxing, or slackening, as after great excitement, effort, etc.

2. a disappointment or disillusionment. [Colloq.]

lete, *v.t.* to let or leave. [Obs.]

lē′thăl, *a.* [L. *letalis* or *lethalis*, from *letum* or *lethum*, death.]

1. deadly; mortal; fatal.

2. of or suggestive of death.

lē′thăl chām′bẽr, 1. a room where persons may be painlessly executed by gases.

2. a similar room for killing dogs and cats.

lē·thal′i·ty, *n.* mortality; deadliness. [Rare.]

lē·thär′gic, lē·thär′gi·căl, *a.* [L. *lethargicus*; Gr. *lēthargikos*, drowsy, slothful, from *lēthargos*, forgetful, from *lēthē*, forgetfulness.] relating to, like, or causing lethargy; also, having lethargy; drowsy; dull; apathetic.

lē·thär′gic·ăl·ly, *adv.* in a lethargic manner.

lē·thär′gic·ăl·ness, lē·thär′gic·ness, *n.* the quality or condition of being lethargic.

leth′ăr·gize, *v.t.*; lethargized, *pt.*, *pp.*; lethargizing, *ppr.* to cause to be lethargic.

leth′ăr·gy, *n.* [ME. *letharge*; OFr. *letharge*; LL. *lethargia*; Gr. *lēthargia*, sleepiness, from *lēthargos*, forgetful; *lēthē*, forgetfulness, and *algos*, pain.]

1. (a) an abnormal drowsiness; great lack of energy; inertness; (b) a prolonged and unnatural sleep.

2. total indifference; apathy.

leth′ăr·gy, *v.t.* to lethargize. [Obs.]

Lē′thē, *n.* [L., from Gr. *lēthē*, forgetfulness, oblivion.]

1. in Greek and Roman mythology, one of the rivers of Hades, whose waters caused those who drank of them to forget all their former life.

2. oblivion; forgetfulness.

3. death. [Obs.]

Lē·thē′ăn, *a.* [L. *Lethæus*; Gr. *Lēthaios*, from *lēthē*, oblivion.] of or like the waters of Lethe; also, inducing forgetfulness.

Lē′thē′d, *a.* Lethean; as if caused by Lethe. [Obs.]

lē′thē·ŏn, *n.* ethyl ether, used as an anesthetic. [Obs.]

lē′thē·ŏn·ize, *v.t.* to anesthetize with letheon. [Obs.]

lē·thif′ẽr·ous, *a.* deadly; mortal; bringing death or destruction.

lē′thy, *a.* lethean. [Obs.]

Lē′tō, *n.* in Greek mythology, the mother of Apollo and Artemis: identified by the Romans with Latona.

let′off, *n.* a releasing device, especially that in a loom for letting off the warp from the beam.

let's, let us.

Lett, *n.* a member of a people who live in Latvia and adjacent Baltic regions; also, their Baltic language; Lettish.

let′ted, *v.* 1. obsolete past tense and past participle of *let* (to allow).

2. alternative past tense and past participle of *let* (to hinder).

let′ten, *a.* in law, leased; demised.

let′tẽr, *n.* one who lets.

let′tẽr, *n.* [ME. *lettre*, *letre*; OFr. *lettre*; L. *littera*, a letter of the alphabet, in pl. a letter, epistle.]

1. a mark or character used as the representative of a speech sound: in English many words contain letters that are no longer pronounced.

2. in printing, a type or impression of a character of the alphabet; also, a style of type face; as, a Gothic *letter*.

3. a written or printed personal or business message, usually sent by mail in an envelope.

4. the first letter of the name of a school or college, awarded and worn for superior activity in sports, etc.

5. the exact or literal meaning; as, the *letter* of the law.

6. [*pl.*] learning; erudition; literature; as, a man of *letters*; the field of *letters*.

7. an official document granting certain rights or powers; as, *letters* patent, *letter* of attorney.

letter of advice; a letter notifying the receiver of a special fact, as that a bill of exchange has been drawn on him or that a consignment of goods has been sent to him.

letter of credit; a letter from a bank asking that the holder of the letter be allowed to draw specified sums of money from other banks or agencies, to be charged to the account of the writer of the letter.

letters (or *letter*) *of credence*; a formal document which a country's diplomatic representative carries as his credentials to a foreign government.

letters (or *letter*) *of marque*; (a) originally, a governmental document authorizing an individual to make reprisals on the subjects or citizens of an enemy nation for injuries done him by enemy troops; (b) later, a governmental document authorizing an individual to arm a ship and capture the merchant ships and property of an enemy nation: also *letters* (or *letter*) *of marque and reprisal*.

letters patent; a document issued by a government to a person, authorizing him to perform some act or to enjoy some privilege, such as exclusive right to an invention: so called because the document is not sealed but open.

letters testamentary; in law, a document granted after probate of a will by the probate court or some officer who has authority, directing the person named as executor in the will to act in that capacity.

let′tẽr, *v.t.* 1. to make hand-printed letters on; to mark with letters; as, the poster was artistically *lettered*.

2. to set down in hand-printed letters; as, on the blank page he *lettered* his name.

let′tẽr, *v.i.* to make hand-printed letters; as, she learned to *letter* in art school.

let′tẽr box, a box to hold mail being sent or delivered; mailbox.

let′tẽr căr′ri·ẽr, one who collects and delivers mail; a postman.

let′tẽred, *a.* 1. literate; able to read and write.

2. very well educated; learned.

3. bearing an inscription or letters.

let′tẽr·ẽr, *n.* one who letters.

let′tẽr found′ẽr, a type founder.

let′tẽr·gram, *n.* a telegram of more than ordinary length, which is sent at special rates: also called *day letter* or *night letter*.

let′tẽr·head (-hed), *n.* 1. the name, address, etc. of a person or firm printed as a heading on a sheet of letter paper.

2. a sheet of letter paper with such a heading printed on it.

let′tẽr·ing, *n.* 1. the act of impressing or marking with letters, especially by hand-printing, drawing, or painting.

2. the letters impressed or marked; an inscription.

let′tẽr·less, *a.* illiterate; unlettered.

let′tẽrn, *n.* same as *lectern*.

let′tẽr-pẽr″fect, *a.* 1. correct in all its letters, or in every respect.

2. knowing one's lines, part, or lesson perfectly: said of an actor, etc.

let′tẽr·press, *n.* print; text; printed letters and words, as distinguished from illustrations.

let′tẽr·press, *a.* printed from type in contrast to matter printed from plates, etc.; as, *letterpress* printing.

let′tẽr press, a press used to make copies of letters.

let′tẽr·wood, *n.* same as *leopardwood*.

let′tẽr wrīt′ẽr, 1. one who writes letters.

2. a book giving forms and instructions for writing various kinds of letters.

Let′tiç, *a.* 1. designating or of a branch of the Baltic languages, including Lettish and Lithuanian.

2. Lettish.

Let′tiç, *n.* the Lettic language.

Let′tish, *a.* relating to the Letts or their language.

Let′tish, *n.* the Baltic language of the Letts.

let′tre dē çà·chet′ (let′r dē kà-shā′), [Fr.] a sealed letter; especially, a letter containing a royal warrant for the imprisonment without trial of a specified person, common in France before the Revolution.

let′trure, *n.* literature. [Obs.]

lett′sŏm·īte, *n.* same as *cyanotrichite*.

let′tuce (-is), *n.* [ME. *letuce*; L. *lactuca*, lettuce, from *lac*, *lactis*, milk; so called from its milky juice.]

1. any of several species of *Lactuca*, especially *Lactuca sativa*.

2. the crisp, green leaves of such a plant, much used for salads.

3. paper money. [Slang.]

let′tuce bīrd, the American goldfinch.

let′ū·ȧ·ry, *n.* a lectuary. [Obs.]

let′up, *n.* 1. cessation; stop; pause; as, there was no *letup* to the pain. [Colloq.]

2. a slackening; a lessening. [Colloq.]

leu (lā), *n.*; *pl.* **lei** (lē), [Romanian, lit., lion.] the monetary unit and a silver coin of Romania: also *ley*.

leuç-, same as *leuco-*.

Leu·çȧ·den′drŏn, *n.* [*leuc-*, and Gr. *dendron*, tree.] a South African genus of shrubs and trees. *Leucadendron argenteum*, which has silky, silvery leaves, is the silver tree or witteboom of the Cape of Good Hope.

leū·çan′i·līne, *n.* [*leuc-*, and Ar. *an-nīl*, *al-nīl*, the indigo plant.] a white, crystalline coal-tar derivative yielding rosaniline when oxidized.

leū·cē′mi·ȧ, leū·cae′mi·ȧ, *n.* same as *leukemia*.

leū′ciç, *a.* relating to or derived from leucine.

leū′cīne, leū′cin, *n.* [Gr. *leukos*, white, and *-ine*.] an amino acid, $C_6H_{13}NO_2$, produced by the hydrolysis of proteins by pancreatic enzymes during digestion and by the putrefaction of nitrogenous organic matter.

leū′cīte, *n.* [Gr. *leukos*, white, and *-ite*.]

1. a white or gray mineral, $KAl(SiO_3)_2$, found in igneous rocks.

2. in botany, same as *leucoplast*.

leū·cit′iç, *a.* of or like leucite.

leū′ci·toid, *n.* [Gr. *leukos*, white, and *eidos*, form.] a trapezohedron: named from the crystalline form of leucite.

leū′çō-, [from Gr. *leukos*, white.] a combining form meaning *white* or *colorless*, as in leucocyte, *leuc*emia: also, before a vowel, *leuc-*: words beginning with *leuc-* or *leuco-* are now often spelled *leuk-*, *leuko-*.

leū′çō·blast, *n.* [*leuco-*, and Gr. *blastos*, a bud, germ.] the germ cell of a leucocyte.

leū′çō·çyte, *n.* [*leuco-*, and Gr. *kytos*, hollow.] any of the small, colorless cells in the blood, lymph, and tissues, which move like amoebae and destroy organisms that cause disease; white blood corpuscle.

leū″çō·çy·thē′mi·ȧ, leū″çō·çy·thae′mi·ȧ, *n.* same as *leukemia*.

leū·çō·çyt′iç, *a.* 1. of leucocytes.

2. having an excess of leucocytes.

leū·çō·çy·tō·gen′e·sis, *n.* [*leuco-*, and Gr. *kytos*, a hollow, and *genesis*, generation.] the origin and growth of leucocytes.

leū″çō·çy·tō′sis, *n.* [*leuco-*, and Gr. *kytos*, a hollow, and *-osis*.] an increase in the number of leucocytes in the blood: it is a normal occurrence in digestion and during pregnancy but a pathological condition in infections, anemia, and certain fevers.

leū·çō·çy·tot′iç, *a.* of or having leucocytosis.

leū·çō·dẽr′mi·ȧ, leū·çō·dẽr′mȧ, *n.* [*leuco-*, and Gr. *derma*, skin.] a congenital deficiency of pigment in the skin, resulting in abnormal white patches.

leū·çō′mȧ, *n.* [Gr. *leukōma*, anything whitened, a white spot in the eye, from *leukoun*, to whiten, from *leukos*, white.] a whitish cloudiness of the cornea, caused by ulceration.

leū·çō′mȧ·ine, *n.* [*leuco-*, and *-maine*, as in pto*maine*.] any of a large group of basic substances present in the body as normal products of protein metabolism.

leū″çō·me·lan′iç, *a.* same as *leucomelanous*.

leū·çō·mel′ȧ·nous, *a.* having a light complexion and dark hair (and, sometimes, dark eyes).

Leū·çō·nos′toç, *n.* [*leuco-*, and G. *nostoch*, nostoc.] a genus of bacteria characterized by the production of gelatinous masses.

leū′çō·phāne, *n.* [L.Gr. *leukophanēs*, of white

or bright appearance; Gr. *leukos*, white, and *-phanēs*, from *phainesthai*, to appear.] a greenish-yellow mineral, a fluosilicate of calcium, sodium, and beryllium.

leū·cō·phleg′mȧ·cy, *n.* [Gr. *leukophlegmatia*, the dropsy; *leukos*, white, and *phlegma*, phlegm.] a tendency to a dropsical condition. [Obs.]

leū″cō·phleg·mat′iç, *a.* characterized by leucophlegmacy. [Obs.]

leū″cō·phyl′lous, *a.* having white foliage.

leū′cō·plast, leū·cō·plas′tid, *n.* [*leuco-*, and Gr. *plastos*, formed, verbal adj. of *plassein*, to form, mold.] a colorless granule forming a nucleus in the protoplasm of certain vegetable cells for the accumulation of starch.

leū·çop′y·rīte, *n.* a metal, almost silver-white in color, consisting mostly of arsenic and iron.

leū·çor·rhē′ȧ, leū·çor·rhoe′ȧ, *n.* [*leuco-*, and Gr. *rhoia*, a flowing, from *rhein*, to flow.] the whites; a whitish mucous discharge from the vagina and uterus, usually resulting from chronic infection.

leū′cō·ryx, *n.* [*leuco-*, and Gr. *oryx*, a kind of gazelle.] a large North African species of antelope.

leū′cō·sçōpe, *n.* [*leuco-*, and Gr. *skopein*, to view.] an instrument used to test the ability of the eye to distinguish variations in color or intensity of light.

leū·cō′sis, *n.* [Gr. *leukōsis*, whiteness, from *lekoun*, to make white, from *leukos*, white.]
 1. albinism; an abnormal whitening of the skin.
 2. the development of a leucoma.

leū′cō·sphēre, *n.* [*leuco-*, and Gr. *sphaira*, a sphere.] the inner portion of a solar corona. [Rare.]

leū·cō·tū′riç, *a.* pertaining to or designating a white compound obtained from uric acid; as, *leucoturic* acid.

leū′cous, *a.* [Gr. *leukos*, bright, white.] albinistic; abnormally white, as an albino.

leū·cox′ēne, *n.* [*leuco-*, and Gr. *xenos*, a stranger.] a white substance resulting from the decomposition of titanic iron.

leuk-, leuko-, see *leuco-*.

leū·kē′mi·ȧ, leū·kae′mi·ȧ, *n.* a disease of the blood-forming tissues, characterized by an abnormal and persistent increase in the number of leucocytes and the amount of bone marrow, with enlargement of the spleen and lymph glands.

leū·kop′ȧ·thy, *n.* same as *albinism*.

leū·kō·pē′ni·ȧ, *n.* [Mod. L., from *leuco-*, and Gr. *penia*, poverty.] a decrease in the number of leucocytes in the blood.

leū·kō·pē′niç, *a.* of or having leukopenia.

lev (lef), *n.*; *pl.* **le′vȧ,** [Bulg., lit., lion.] the monetary unit and a copper coin of Bulgaria.

Lē·vant′, *n.* [Fr., from LL. *levans* (*-antis*), the east, sunrise, from L. *levans* (*-antis*), ppr. of *levare*, to raise.]
 1. the regions on the eastern Mediterranean and the Aegean, from Greece to Egypt, including Syria, Lebanon, and Palestine.
 2. [l–] a levanter, an easterly wind.
 3. [l–] fine morocco leather.

lē·vant′, *v.i.* [Sp. *levantar*, to raise, lift up, to start, from L. *levare*, to raise.] to decamp; to run away; to abscond.

Lē·vant′ dol′lăr, an Austrian monetary unit used only in trade.

lē·vant′ẽr, *n.* [Fr. *Levant*, the East, the Orient, the Levant.]
 1. a strong easterly wind in the Mediterranean.
 2. [L–] a Levantine.

lē·vant′ẽr, *n.* one who runs away or decamps.

Lē·van′tine, *a.* of, relating to, or from the Levant.

Lē·van′tine, *n.* [from Fr. *Levant*, the Levant.]
 1. one born or living in the Levant.
 2. a ship of the Levant.
 3. [l–] a strong, twilled, black silk cloth.

Lē·vant′ mō·roç′çō, a fine morocco leather with a large, irregular grain, used especially in bookbinding.

lē·vā′rī fā′ci·as (-shi-), [L., lit., cause to be levied.] in law, a writ of execution: now superseded by the writ of *elegit*.

lē·vā′tion, *n.* elevation. [Obs.]

lē·vā′tŏr, *n.*; *pl.* **lev·ȧ·tō′rēș,** [L., a raiser, lifter, from *levatus*, pp. of *levare*, to raise.]
 1. in anatomy, a muscle that serves to raise some part, as the lip or the eyelid.
 2. a surgical instrument used to raise depressed fragments of bone in a skull fracture.

lēve, *v.t.* to believe. [Obs.]

lēve, *v.i.* to leave. [Obs.]

lēve, *v.i.* to live. [Obs.]

lēve, *n.* leave; permission. [Obs.]

lev′ee, *n.* [Fr. *lever*, arising, a morning reception, from *lever*; L. *levare*, to rise.]
 1. a morning reception held by a sovereign or person of high rank when rising from bed.
 2. a reception held by the President or other high official.
 3. a court assembly held in the early afternoon, attended only by men. [Brit.]
 4. the act or time of rising. [Obs.]

lev′ee, *v.t.* to attend the levees of. [Obs.]

lev′ee, *n.* [Fr. *levée*, a raising, embankment.]
 1. a bank along a river to prevent inundation; as, the *levees* along the Mississippi.
 2. a landing place along the bank of a river; a quay.

lev′ee, *v.t.*; leveed, *pt.*, *pp.*; leveeing, *ppr.* to embank or provide with a levee or levees; as, to *levee* a river.

lev′el, *n.* [ME. *level*, *livel*; OFr. *livel*; L. *libella*, a level, dim. of *libra*, a balance, level.]
 1. an instrument for determining whether a surface is on an even horizontal plane or for adjusting a surface to such a plane: it has a glass tube partly filled with ether or alcohol so as to leave an air bubble that moves to the exact center of the tube when the instrument is on an even horizontal plane.

LEVEL (*n.* 1)

 2. a measuring of differences in height, or altitude, with such an instrument.
 3. a horizontal plane or line; especially, such a plane taken as a basis for the measurement of elevation; as, sea *level*.
 4. a relatively flat and even area of land or other surface; horizontal area.
 5. the same horizontal plane; as, the tops of the pictures should be on a *level*.
 6. height; altitude; as, water boils more quickly at this *level*.
 7. usual or normal position or height; as, water seeks its *level*.
 8. position or elevation considered as one of the planes in a scale of values; as, few can rise to the *level* of a great man.
 9. a horizontal walk or passageway, as between tiers of seats.
 10. the line of aim or direction, as of a gun.
 11. a more or less horizontal passage or drift of a mine.

lev′el, *a.* 1. even; flat; not having one part higher than another; parallel with the free surface of a liquid at rest; as, a *level* surface.
 2. horizontal; not ascending or descending; as, a *level* floor; a *level* road.
 3. even with, of the same height as, or on the same line or plane with something else; as, *level* with his ability.
 4. equal in rank or degree; as, *level* in value.
 5. even; uniform; unchanging; as, a *level* voice; a *level* hue.
 6. equally advanced in development.
 7. even with the top of the container; not heaping; as, a *level* teaspoonful.
 8. not having or showing sudden differences or inequalities; well balanced; equable.
 9. direct; straightforward; undeviating; as, a *level* story. [Rare.]

lev′el, *adv.* in a level or horizontal line; evenly; directly; steadily; as, aim it *level*.

lev′el, *v.t.*; leveled *or* levelled, *pt.*, *pp.*; leveling *or* levelling, *ppr.* 1. to make level; specifically, (a) to make perfectly horizontal by means of a level; (b) to make even; to give a flat, horizontal surface to (often with *off*); (c) to equalize in height, importance, rank, quality, etc. (often with *down* or *up*); (d) to make even in tone, color, pitch, etc.
 2. to knock to the ground; to demolish; to lay low; as, the storm *leveled* everything in its path.
 3. to raise (a gun, etc.) to a level position for firing.
 4. to aim.
 5. in surveying, to determine the differences in altitude in (a plot of ground).

lev′el, *v.i.* 1. to aim a gun or other weapon (with *at*).
 2. to select some person or thing as a target or goal.
 3. to bring people or things to an equal rank, condition, etc. (usually with *down* or *up*).
 4. to be aimed; to accord; to suit. [Rare.]
 5. to guess; to conjecture. [Obs.]

lev′el çross′ing, a place where a road crosses one or more railroads on the same level.

lev′el·ẽr, *n.* 1. a person or thing that levels.
 2. a person who wishes to abolish social inequalities.
 3. [L–] a member of a party that arose in the army of the Long Parliament (c. 1647) and advocated the leveling of all ranks and establishment of a more democratic government: also spelled *leveller*.

lev′el·head′ed (-hed′), *a.* possessing good judgment and an even temper; sensible.

lev′el·head′ed·ly, *adv.* in a levelheaded manner.

lev′el·head′ed·ness, *n.* good judgment.

lev′el·ing, *n.* 1. the reduction of uneven surfaces to a level or plane.
 2. in surveying, the art or practice of finding a horizontal line, or of ascertaining the different elevations of objects on the surface of the earth.

lev′el·ing in′strụ·ment, a surveying instrument consisting of a telescope with a spirit level connected.

lev′el·ing pōle, lev′el·ing rod, same as *leveling staff*.

lev′el·ing stȧff, a graduated pole used in conjunction with a leveling instrument to determine the difference in elevation between two points.

lev′el·ișm, *n.* advocacy of the abolition of social ranks. [Rare.]

lev′el·ly, *adv.* evenly; sanely.

lev′el·ness, *n.* level state or quality.

lev′en, *n.* a lawn. [Scot.]

lev′ẽr (*or* lē′vẽr), *n.* [ME. *lever*, *levour*; OFr. *leveor*, a lifter, lever; L. *levator*, a lifter, from *levatus*, pp. of *levare*, to raise up, lift.]
 1. a bar or other rigid structure, turning on a support called the fulcrum, and used to overcome a certain resistance or weight at one point by means of a power applied at another point. Levers are divided into three classes: first, when the fulcrum is between the resistance and the power, as in a crowbar or scissors; second, when the resistance is between the power and the fulcrum, as in nutcrackers or a wheelbarrow; third, when the power is between the resistance and the fulcrum, as in sugar tongs or the forearm. Fig. 1 represents a lever of the first class; fig. 2, one of the second class; fig. 3, one of the third class. In each, A is the power, W the resistance, and C the fulcrum.

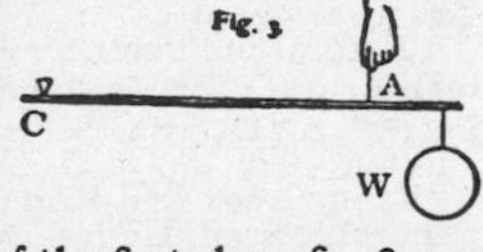

 2. (a) in a steam engine, a bar controlling the steam valves; (b) in firearms, a rod used to open and close a breech-loading gun; (c) in dentistry, formerly, a turnkey; (d) in surgery, an arm of an obstetrical forceps.
 3. any bar used as a pry.
 compound lever; a system of two or more simple levers acting upon one another.
 universal lever; a device securing rotary motion by the reciprocating action of a lever.

lev′ẽr, *v.t.* 1. to move, lift, etc. with or as with a lever.
 2. to use as a lever.

lev′ẽr, *v.i.* to use a lever.

lev′ẽr, *a.* comparative of *lief*. [Obs.]

lev′ẽr·ȧge, *n.* 1. the action of a lever.
 2. the mechanical power resulting from this.
 3. increased means of accomplishing some purpose.

lev′ẽr·et, *n.* [OFr. *levret*, dim. of *levre*; L. *lepus* (*-oris*), a hare.] a hare in the first year of its age.

lev′et, *n.* a blast of a trumpet as a morning call; reveille. [Obs.]

Lē′vī, *n.* [Heb. *lēwī*, lit., joining.] in the Bible, the third son of Jacob and Leah: Gen. xxix. 34.

lev'i·a·ble, *a.* 1. that may be levied upon; taxable; assessable.
2. that can be levied.

lē·vī'a·thăn, *n.* [LL. *leviathan*; Heb. *livyāthān*, the leviathan.]
1. a large and powerful aquatic animal described in Job xli., and mentioned in other passages of Scripture: variously thought of as a whale or a reptile.
2. anything huge of its kind.
3. [L—] a political treatise by Thomas Hobbes (1651), upholding the supreme authority of the sovereign.

lev'i·ẽr, *n.* one who levies.

lev'i·gȧ·ble, *a.* susceptible of levigation.

lev'i·gāte, *a.* made smooth; polished.

lev'i·gāte, *v.t.*; levigated, *pt., pp.*; levigating, *ppr.* [L. *levigatus*, pp. of *levigare*, to make smooth, polish, from *levis*, smooth.]
1. to rub or grind to a fine, impalpable powder, as by rubbing a moist substance between hard, flat surfaces.
2. to make a smooth paste of; to mix thoroughly.

lev·i·gā'tion, *n.* [L. *levigatio* (*-onis*), a smoothing, from *levigatus*, pp. of *levigare*, to make smooth.] a levigating or being levigated.

lev'in, *n.* [ME. *levene*.] lightning. [Archaic.]

lev'in·ẽr, *n.* a fleet hound. [Obs.]

lē'vīr, *n.* [L.] a brother of a husband under the custom of the levirate.

lev'i·rāte, *n.* [L. *levir*, a husband's brother, brother-in-law.] a custom prescribed by the Mosaic code, by which a dead man's brother was obligated to marry the widow if there were no sons. Deut. xxv. 5–10.

lev'i·rāte, lev·i·rat'iç·ăl, *a.* of or relating to the levirate.

lev·i·rā'tion, *n.* leviratical marriage.

Lev·i·ros'trēş, *n.pl.* [L. *levis*, light, and *rostrum*, beak.] a former division of supposedly related birds, including the parrots, toucans, hornbills, etc.

lē'vīş, *n.pl.* [after *Levi* Strauss, the Am. maker.] overalls; especially, bibless overalls, worn by cowboys, reinforced at the seams, etc. with small copper rivets: a trade-mark (*Levis*).

Lē·vis'ti·çum, *n.* [L. *ligusticum*, lovage.] a genus of the *Umbelliferæ*, having only one known species, the garden lovage.

lev'i·tāte, *v.t.*; levitated, *pt., pp.*; levitating, *ppr.* [L. *levitas* (*-atis*), lightness, buoyancy, from *levis*, light.] to make light or buoyant so as to cause to rise and float in the air. [Rare.]

lev'i·tāte, *v.i.* to rise and float in the air because of, or as if because of, lightness and buoyancy.

lev·i·tā'tion, *n.* 1. a levitating or being levitated.
2. the illusion of raising and keeping a heavy body in the air with little or no physical support.

Lē'vīte, *n.* [LL. *Levites*, *Levita*; Gr. *Levites*, a Levite, from Heb. *Levi*, Levi.]
1. in the Bible, one of the tribe or family of Levi, chosen to assist the Jewish priests.
2. in the early Christian church, a deacon
3. a clergyman; a priest. [Obs.]

Lē·vit'iç·ăl, *a.* 1. belonging to the Levites, or descendants of Levi; as, the *Levitical* law.
2. priestly. [Rare.]
3. of Leviticus or its laws.

Lē·vit'iç·ăl·ly, *adv.* after the manner of Levites.

Lē·vit'i·çus, *n.* [LL., pertaining to the Levites, from *Levites*, *Levita*, a Levite.] the third book of the Old Testament, containing the laws and regulations which relate to the priests and Levites, or the body of the ceremonial law.

lev'i·ty, *n.* [L. *levitas* (*-atis*), lightness, gaiety, levity, from *levis*, light.]
1. lightness of weight; buoyancy. [Rare.]
2. a hypothetical force contrary to gravity, formerly believed to be inherent in certain bodies; also, a tendency to rise by the action of such force.
3. lightness of temper or conduct; lack of seriousness; disposition to trifle; frivolity.
4. fickleness, instability.

lē'vō-, [from L. *lævus*, left.] a combining form meaning: (a) *on* or *to the left*, as in *levo*gyrate; (b) *levorotatory*.
Also spelled *laevo-*.

lē·vō·duç'tion, *n.* [*levo-*, and L. *ductio*, a leading.] motion toward the left, as of an eye.

lē·vō·glū'çōse, *n.* [*levo-*, and Gr. *glykys*, sweet.] levulose.

lē·vō·ġȳ'rāte, *a.* [*levo-*, and L. *gyratus*, pp. of *gyrare*, to turn round in a circle.] turning toward the left, or counterclockwise; levorotatory.

lē·vō·ġȳ'rous, *a.* levogyrate.

lē·vō·rō·tā'tion, *n.* [*levo-*, and L. *rotatus*, pp. of *rotare*, to turn.] rotation to the left; counterclockwise rotation: usually said of the plane of polarization of light.

lē·vō·rō'tȧ·tō·ry, *a.* 1. turning or circling to the left, in a counterclockwise direction.
2. that turns the plane of polarized light to the left, or in a counterclockwise direction: said of certain crystals, etc.

lev'ū·lin, *n.* [*levul*ose and *-in*.] a starchlike carbohydrate, $C_6H_{10}O_5$, derived from various tubers, yielding levulose upon decomposition.

lev·ū·lin'iç, *a.* of or derived from levulin.
levulinic acid; an acid derived from levulin, levulose, and the like; acetyl propionic acid.

lev·ū·lō'săn, *n.* an unfermentable derivative of levulose.

lev'ū·lōse, *n.* [L. *lævus*, left.] a levorotatory sugar. It is an isomer of dextrose and occurs with it in fruits, honey, invert sugar, and other substances, usually as a sirup; fructose: called also *fruit sugar*.

lev'y, *n.*; *pl.* **lev'ieş,** [ME. *levy*, *levey*; OFr. *levee*, a raising, a raising of troops, of taxes, etc., from LL. *levata*, something raised, a tax, properly f. of L. *levatus*, pp. of *levare*, to raise.]
1. the act of imposing and collecting a tax or other payment.
2. anything collected by a levy, as money for taxes.
3. the compulsory enlistment of personnel, as for military service.
4. a group so enlisted.
levy in mass; the act of levying for military service all the able-bodied men in a country.

lev'y, *v.t.*; levied, *pt., pp.*; levying, *ppr.* 1. to impose (a tax, tribute, fine, etc.).
2. to enlist (troops) for military service, usually by force.
3. to wage (war).
4. in law, to seize (property) under a writ of execution.
to levy a fine; to commence and carry on a suit for assuring the title to lands or tenements.

lev'y, *v.i.* to seize property in making a levy; to make a levy: usually with *on*; as, to *levy on* goods and chattels.

lev'y, *n.* [abbrev. of *eleven-penny bit*, or *elevenpence*.]
1. a small Spanish silver coin, a real, or eighth of a dollar, formerly current in the eastern United States. [Obs.]
2. a bit; the sum of twelve and a half cents. [Rare.]

lev'yn·īte, *n.* [named after A. *Lévy*, a French mineralogist.] a hydrous silicate of calcium and aluminum.

lew (lū), *a.* tepid; lukewarm; weak. [Obs.]

lē'wän', *n.* [Ar.] a kind of reception room in some Oriental houses, usually having its floor raised above the court upon which it opens, and furnished with rugs and divans.

lewd (lūd), *a.* [ME. *lewde*; AS. *læwed*, unlearned, ignorant.]
1. lustful; libidinous; licentious; indecent; unchaste.
2. exhibiting or proceeding from lust.
3. vile; wicked; base; vicious. [Obs.]
4. ignorant; unlearned. [Obs.]

lewd'ly, *adv.* in a lewd manner.

lewd'ness, *n.* the state or quality of being lewd.

lewd'stẽr, *n.* one who is lewd. [Obs.]

lew'is, lew'is·sŏn, *n.* [perh. from the name *Lewis*.]
1. an instrument of iron used in raising large stones by dovetailing one of its ends into an opening in the stone.
2. a variety of shears.

lew'is hōle, a hole into which a lewis is to be fitted.

lew'is·īte, *n.* an arsenical compound, $ClCH=CHAsCl_2$, used as a blistering poison gas.

Lew'is mȧ·chïne' gun, [after the Am. inventor, Col. I. N. *Lewis* (1858–1931) of the U. S. Army.] an air-cooled, automatic firearm having a circular cartridge drum and designed to be held and fired by one man: also *Lewis gun*, *Lewis automatic rifle*.

lew'is·sŏn, *n.* a lewis.

lex, *n.*; *pl.* **lē'ġēş,** [L.] law.

lex'i·çăl, *a.* 1. of or relating to the vocabulary of a language, as distinct from its grammar.
2. pertaining to a lexicon or lexicography.

lex'i·çăl·ly, *adv.* as regards words or vocabulary.

lex″i·çog'rȧ·phẽr, *n.* [L.Gr. *lexikographos*, one who writes a lexicon; Gr. *lexikon*, a lexicon, and *graphein*, to write.] a person who writes or compiles a dictionary.

lex″i·çō·graph'iç, lex″i·çō·graph'i·çăl, *a.* pertaining to the writing or compilation of a dictionary.

lex″i·çō·graph'i·çăl·ly, *adv.* in a lexicographic manner.

lex·i·çog'rȧ·phist, *n.* a lexicographer. [Rare.]

lex″i·çog'rȧ·phy, *n.* [Gr. *lexikon*, a lexicon, and *graphein*, to write.] the act, process, art, or work of writing or compiling a dictionary or dictionaries.

lex·i·çol'ō·ġist, *n.* one skilled in lexicology.

lex·i·çol'ō·ġy, *n.* [Gr. *lexikon*, a lexicon, and *-logia*, from *legein*, to speak.] that science which treats of words, their derivation, meaning, form, and application.

lex'i·çŏn, *n.* [LL. *lexicon*; Gr. *lexikon*, a lexicon, properly neut. of *lexikos*, of or belonging to words, from *lexis*, a saying, phrase, word, from *legein*, to say, speak.]
1. a dictionary, especially of an ancient language.
2. a special vocabulary, as of an author, science, etc.
3. in linguistics, the total stock of morphemes in a language.

lex'i·çŏn·ist, *n.* a writer of a lexicon. [Rare.]

lex·i·graph'iç, *a.* relating to lexigraphy.

lex·ig'rȧ·phy, *n.* [Gr. *lexis*, a word, and *-graphia*, from *graphein*, to write.] the art or practice of defining words. [Rare.]

lex·i·phan'iç, *a.* [Gr. *lexiphanēs*, a phrasemonger; *lexis*, a phrase, word, and *phainein*, to show.] relating to lexiphanicism; bombastic; turgid; inflated.

lex·i·phan'i·ciṣm, *n.* the habit of using an inflated, pompous style in speaking or writing.

lex·i·phär'miç, *a.* antidotal. [Obs.]

lex lō'cī, [L.] the law of the place.

lex non sçrip'tȧ, [L., lit., unwritten law.] common law.

lex sçrip'tȧ, [L., lit., written law.] statute law.

lex ta·li·ō'nis, [L.] the law of retaliation.

ley, *n.* a leu.

ley, *v.t.* to wager; to bet. [Obs.]

lēy (lī), *n.* lye. [Obs.]

lēy, *n.* a lea. [Obs.]

ley, *n.* [Sp., lit., law, from L. *lex*, *legis*, law.] assay percentage; yield; quantity.

Ley'den jär (or **vī'ăl**), [from *Leiden*, Netherlands city where it was invented.] a glass jar coated inside and outside with tin foil to within a third of the top, and usually having a metallic knob at the top connected with the inside coating: it is used as a condenser for static electricity.

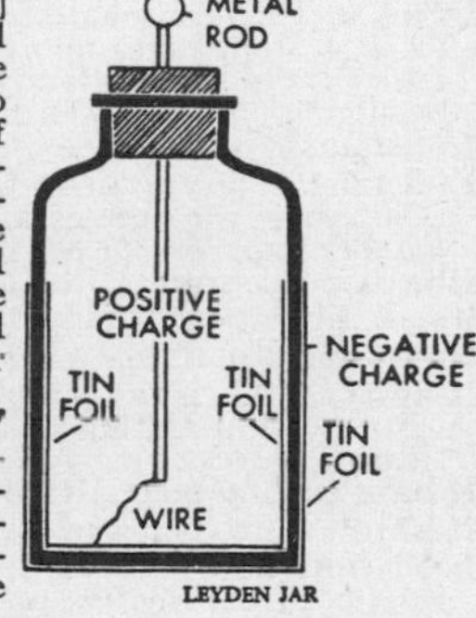

LEYDEN JAR

Ley'dig's cell (lī'diks), [named after Franz von *Leydig*, a Ger. anatomist.] an interstitial cell of the testis.

Ley'dig's cyl'in·dẽrş, bundles of muscular fibers which are separated from each other by walls of protoplasm.

Ley'dig's duct, same as *Wolffian duct*.

ley pew'tẽr, pewter, having a high percentage of lead.

lēy'şẽr, *n.* leisure. [Obs.]

lēze maj'es·ty, same as *lese majesty*.

lhẽrz'īte, *n.* [*lherz*, from Lake *Lherz*, and Gr. *lithos*, stone.] a crystalline rock containing pyroxene, chrysolite, diallage, and picotite, occurring around Lake Lherz in the French Pyrenees.

lī, *n.* [arbitrary modification of *la*.] in music, a syllable representing the tone intermediate between la and ti of the diatonic scale.

lī, *n.* [Chinese.] 1. a Chinese measure of distance, equal to about 1,900 feet.
2. a Chinese measure of weight, equal to $^1/_{1000}$ tael, or about .6 grain.

Li, in chemistry, lithium.

lī·ȧ·bil'i·ty, *n.*; *pl.* **lī·ȧ·bil'i·tieş,** 1. the state of being liable.
2. anything for which a person is liable.
3. [*usually in pl.*] a debt; as, accounts pay-

able, surplus, losses, and capital stock are *liabilities* of a corporation: opposed to *asset*.
4. something that works to one's disadvantage.

lī'ȧ·ble, *a.* [from Fr. *lier*; L. *ligare*, to bind.]
1. legally bound, as to make good any loss or damage that occurs in a transaction; answerable; responsible.
2. likely to have, suffer from, etc.; exposed to or subject to; as, he is *liable* to heart attacks.
3. (a) subject to the possibility of; disagreeably likely: used with the infinitive; (b) [Colloq.] likely; as, I am *liable* to be there.
Syn.—apt, likely.—*Apt* indicates a characteristic tendency; as, a chipped cup is *apt* to break. *Likely* indicates a probability or an eventuality that can reasonably be expected; as, so cold it is *likely* to snow. *Liable* indicates the possibility of an undesirable event; as, he is *liable* to be killed playing with firearms.

lī'ȧ·ble·ness, *n.* the quality or state of being liable.

lī·ăi·ṣŏn' (*or* -zon'), *n.* [Fr., a binding, a union, from L. *ligatio* (*-onis*), a binding, from *ligatus*, pp. of *ligare*, to bind.]
1. a linking up or connecting of the parts of a whole, intended to bring about proper coordination of activities; especially, intercommunication between units of a military force.
2. an illicit love affair.
3. in the French language, the linking of words by pronouncing the final consonant, usually silent, as if it were the initial consonant of a succeeding word when such a word begins with a vowel or mute *h*, as in *les hommes*. In such cases, *s* and *x* take the sound of *z*, *d* of *t*, and *g* of *k*.
4. in cookery, a thickening, as of eggs, used to combine the components of a dish.
liaison officer; a staff officer whose function is to insure proper co-ordination between parts of an army, allied armies, etc. involved in a military operation.

lī·ä'nȧ, lī·äne', *n.* [Fr. *liane*, a tropical creeper from *lier*, to bind.] any luxuriantly growing, woody, tropical vine that roots in the ground and climbs, as around tree trunks.

lī'ăr, *n.* [ME. *leigher, leghere*; AS. *leogere*, a liar, from *leogan*, to lie.] a person who tells lies; one who declares to another as a fact what he knows to be untrue, with the intention to deceive him.

liärd (lyär), *n.* [Fr., from OFr. *liar, liard*, a small coin.] a former coin of France valued at 1/4 sou.

Lī'ăs, *n.* [Fr. *liais*, a hard freestone; Arm. *liach, leach*, a stone.] an important series of bluish rocks, the oldest strata of the Jurassic system, occurring principally in England.

Lī·as'siç, *a.* of or relating to the Lias.

Lī·ā'tris, *n.* [etym. unknown.] a genus of the *Compositæ*: the species are commonly called *button snakeroot, blazing star*.

lib, *v.t.* to castrate. [Brit. Dial.]

lib, *n.* liberation. [Colloq.]

lib'ȧ·ment, *n.* a libation. [Obs.]

lī'bănt, *a.* [L. *libans* (*-antis*), ppr. of *libare*, to taste, to sip.] tasting or touching delicately. [Rare.]

lī·bāte', *v.t.* to pour. [Rare.]

lī·bāte', *v.i.* to perform a libation. [Rare.]

lī·bā'tion, *n.* [Fr. *libation*; L. *libatio* (*-onis*), a libation, from *libatus*, pp. of *libare*, to taste, pour out.]
1. the act of pouring out wine or oil upon the ground or on a victim for sacrifice in honor of a god.
2. the liquid poured out.
3. an alcoholic drink: used humorously.

lī'bȧ·tō·ry, *a.* of or relating to libation.

lib'bărd, *n.* a leopard. [Obs.]

lī·bec'ciō (-bet'chō), *n.* [It., from L. *Libs*; Gr. *Lips*, the southwest wind.] the southwest wind.

lī'bel, *n.* [OFr. *libel, libeau*, masc., *libele, libelle*, f.; L. *libellus*, a little book, tablet, note, writing, lampoon, dim. of *liber*, a book.]
1. any written or printed statement, or any sign, picture, or effigy, not made in the public interest, tending to expose a person to public ridicule or contempt or to injure his reputation in any way: cf. *slander*.
2. the act of publishing such a thing.
3. anything that gives an unflattering or damaging picture of the subject with which it is dealing.
4. in admiralty and ecclesiastical law, the plaintiff's written statement of the wrongs he has suffered.
5 a lampoon. [Obs.]

lī'bel, *v.t.*; libeled *or* libelled, *pt., pp.*; libeling *or* libelling, *ppr.* 1. to publish or make a libel against.
2. to give an unflattering or damaging picture of; to say or print unfavorable or false things about.
3. in admiralty and ecclesiastical law, to bring suit against by presenting a written statement of grievances.

lī'bel, *v.i.* to spread defamation: with *against*. [Obs.]

lī'bel·ănt, lī'bel·lănt, *n.* [Fr., properly ppr. of *libeller*, to draw up a legal demand, to libel.] a person who sues by filing a libel in an admiralty or ecclesiastical court.

lī·bel·ee', lī·bel·lee', *n.* the party defendant in an admiralty suit.

lī'bel·ẽr, lī'bel·lẽr, *n.* one who libels.

lī'bel·ist, lī'bel·list, *n.* a libeler.

lī·bel'lū·lid, *n.* [L. *libellulus*, a very small book, dim. of *libellus*, a little book: so called from its resemblance to a book when flying.] a dragonfly.

lī'bel·ous, lī'bel·lous, *a.* 1. of the nature of a libel; involving a libel.
2. given to writing and publishing libels; slanderous; vilifying; defamatory.

lī'bel·ous·ly, *adv.* in a libelous manner.

lī'bẽr, *n.* [L., the inner bark of a tree, a book: so called because bark was used to write upon.]
1. in botany, the inner, newly-formed bark of an exogen, characterized by the presence of long, fibrous cells.
2. a book; especially, a book of public records, as of mortgages or deeds.

lib'ẽr·ăl, *a.* [ME. *liberal*; OFr. *liberal*; L. *liberalis*, of or pertaining to a freeman, befitting a freeman, noble, liberal.]
1. originally, suitable for a freeman; not restricted: now obsolete except in *the liberal arts, liberal education*, etc.
2. free to give or bestow; generous; giving largely; as, a *liberal* donor.
3. ample; large; abundant; as, a *liberal* donation.
4. free; not literal or strict; as, a *liberal* interpretation of the Constitution.
5. not narrow or bigoted; broad-minded.
6. of democratic or republican forms of government, as distinguished from monarchies, aristocracies, etc.
7. favoring reform or progress, as in religion, education, etc.; specifically, favoring political reforms tending toward democracy and personal freedom for the individual; progressive: now sometimes distinguished from *progressive*, as connoting somewhat more conservatism.
8. [L-] designating or of a political party upholding liberal principles, especially such a party in England that developed from a coalition of the Whigs and Radicals in the first half of the nineteenth century.
9. excessively free or indecorous in behavior; licentious. [Obs.]
10. not mean; not low in birth or mind.
liberal arts; the subjects of an academic college course, including literature, philosophy, languages, history, etc., as distinguished from professional or technical subjects; primarily cultural studies: sometimes referred to as *arts* (e.g., Bachelor of *Arts*, as distinguished from Bachelor of *Science*).
liberal education; a general extensive education, not necessarily preparing the student for any specific profession.

lib'ẽr·ăl, *n.* 1. one who advocates greater freedom of thought or action; one who has liberal principles.
2. [L-] a member of a Liberal political party, as in Great Britain, Canada, etc.

lib'ẽr·ăl·iṣm, *n.* 1. the quality or state of being liberal, especially in politics or religion.
2. liberal principles and ideals.

lib'ẽr·ăl·ist, *a.* liberalistic.

lib'ẽr·ăl·ist, *n.* a liberal.

lib"ẽr·ăl·is'tiç, *a.* of or exhibiting liberalism.

lib"ẽr·al'i·ty, *n.*; *pl.* **lib"ẽr·al'i·tieṣ**, [OFr. *liberalite*; L. *liberalitas* (*-atis*), a way of thinking or acting befitting a freeman; nobleness, generosity, liberality.]
1. munificence; the quality of being liberal.
2. a particular act of generosity.
3. absence of narrowness or prejudice in thinking; impartiality; broad-mindedness.

lib"ẽr·ăl·i·zā'tion, *n.* a liberalizing or being liberalized.

lib'ẽr·ăl·īze, *v.t.*; liberalized, *pt., pp.*; liberalizing, *ppr.* to make or become liberal.

lib'ẽr·ăl·īz"ẽr, *n.* one who or that which liberalizes or makes liberal.

lib'ẽr·ăl·ly, *adv.* in a liberal manner.

lib'ẽr·āte, *v.t.*; liberated, *pt., pp.*; liberating, *ppr.* [L. *liberatus*, pp. of *liberare*, to set free, release, from *liber*, free.]
1. to free; to release from restraint or bondage; to set at liberty.
2. in chemistry, to free from combination in a compound.
3. to appropriate or steal from an enemy or an occupied country; to loot. [Military Slang.]

lib·ẽr·ā'tion, *n.* [L. *liberatio* (*-onis*), from *liberatus*, pp. of *liberare*, to set free, liberate.]
1. the act of liberating or the state of being liberated.
2. the securing of equal social and economic rights; as, the women's *liberation* movement.

lib·ẽr·ā'tion·ist, *n.* one who believes in or practices liberation.

lib'ẽr·ā·tŏr, *n.* [L., from *liberatus*, pp. of *liberare*, to liberate.] one who liberates; especially, one who frees his country from an enemy or tyranny.

lib'ẽr·ȧ·tō·ry, *a.* tending to set free. [Rare.]

Lī·bē'ri·ăn, *a.* of Liberia, its people, or their culture.

Lī·bē'ri·ăn, *n.* a native or inhabitant of Liberia.

lib"ẽr·ō·mō'tŏr, *a.* [L. *liberare*, to liberate, and *motor*, a mover.] in physiology, liberating motor energy.

lib·ẽr·târ'i·ăn, *a.* pertaining to the doctrines of libertarians.

lib·ẽr·târ'i·ăn, *n.* 1. one who holds to free will.
2. one who advocates full civil liberties for the individual.

lib·ẽr·târ'i·ăn·iṣm, *n.* the principles or doctrines of libertarians.

li·ber·té' é·ga·li·té' fra·ter·ni·té' (lē-ber-tā' ā-gȧ-lē-tā' frȧ-ter-nē-tā'), [Fr.] liberty, equality, fraternity: the motto of the French Revolution of 1789.

li·bẽr·ti·cīd'ăl, *a.* tending to destroy liberty.

li·bẽr'ti·cīde, *n.* [L. *libertas* (*-atis*), liberty, and *cædere*, to kill.]
1. destruction of liberty.
2. a destroyer of liberty.

li·bẽr'ti·cīde, *a.* destroying liberty.

lib'ẽr·tin·ăġe, *n.* libertinism; license.

lib'ẽr·tīne, *n.* [L. *libertinus*, of or belonging to the condition of a freedman, a freedman, from *libertus*, a freedman, from *liber*, free.]
1. among the Romans, a freedman, or the child of a freedman.
2. one who indulges his desires without restraint; a rake; a debauchee.
3. [L-] a member of a pantheistic sect of the sixteenth century in Holland, who maintained that nothing is sinful but to those who think it sinful, and that perfect innocence is to live without doubt.
4. a member of a political party in Geneva, Switzerland, that opposed the reforms of Calvin.
5. a free-thinker; sceptic. [Rare.]

lib'ẽr·tīne, *a.* licentious; dissolute; morally unrestrained.

lib'ẽr·tin·iṣm, *n.* 1. the state of a freedman. [Rare.]
2. the behavior of a libertine; licentiousness.

lib'ẽr·ty, *n.* [OFr. *liberte*; L. *libertas* (*-atis*), freedom, from *liber*, free.]
1. freedom or release from slavery, imprisonment, captivity, or any other form of arbitrary control.
2. the sum of rights and exemptions possessed in common by the people of a community, state, etc.
3. a particular right, franchise, or exemption from compulsion; as, he has the *liberty* of coming with us.
4. [*usually pl.*] unnecessary or excessive freedom or familiarity.
5. a place or area in which certain privileges or immunities prevail.
6. the limits within which a certain amount of freedom may be exercised; as, you may have the *liberty* of the third floor.
7. (a) permission given to a sailor to go ashore; (b) the period of forty-eight hours or less for which such permission is given.
8. in philosophy, freedom to choose; absence of the control of necessity.
9. a curvature in a horse's bit to allow room for the tongue.
at liberty; free from occupation, constraint, restraint, or use.
civil liberties; see under *civil*.

Liberty Bell; see under *bell*.

Liberty bond; a U. S. government bond issued to help finance the costs of World War I.

liberty cap; a soft, close-fitting, visorless cap, adopted by the French Revolutionists as a symbol of liberty.

Liberty loan; the first issue of Liberty bonds made during World War I.

liberty of the press; same as *freedom of the press*.

to take liberties; to be too free or familiar in action or speech.

li·beth′en·īte, *n.* an olive-green mineral, first found at Libethen, in Hungary, consisting of basic copper phosphate.

li·bid′i·năl, *a.* of the libido.

li-bid′i-nist, *n.* a lecher. [Obs.]

li·bid′i·nīze, *v.t.*; libidinized, *pt., pp.*; libidinizing, *ppr.* [from L. *libido*, pleasure, and *-ize.*] to regard or treat as an area or source of sexual gratification; as, the skin as a *libidinized* organ.

li·bid′i·nous, *a.* [Fr. *libidineux*; L. *libidinosus*, *lubidinosus*, full of desire or passion, licentious, from *libido*, or *lubido* (*-inis*), desire, pleasure, inclination, passion, wantonness, from *libet* or *lubet*, it pleases.] lustful; lewd; lascivious.

li·bid′i·nous·ly, *adv.* lustfully.

li·bid′i·nous·ness, *n.* the state or quality of being lustful.

li·bī′dō, *n.* 1. the sexual urge or instinct.

2. in psychoanalysis, psychic energy generally; driving force behind all human action.

Lī′brȧ, *n.* [L., a balance, a Roman pound.]

1. the seventh sign of the zodiac, which the sun enters at the autumnal equinox about September 23.

2. a constellation of the southern heavens between Virgo and Scorpio supposedly resembling a pair of scales in shape.

lī′brȧ, *n.*; *pl.* **lī′brae,** [L.] 1. pound: the Brittish symbol for the monetary unit is derived from the first letter of this word.

2. an ancient Roman unit of weight, equal to about 12 ounces.

3. [Sp.] a former gold coin of Peru.

lī·brâr′i·ăn, *n.* [L. *librarius*, adj., pertaining to books; n., a transcriber of books, a keeper of books, from *liber*, a book.]

1. one who has charge of a library or collection of books.

2. a person trained in library science and working in a library.

lī·brâr′i·ăn·ship, *n.* the office of a librarian.

lī′brâr·y, *n.* [OFr. *librarie*, a bookcase, a bookseller's shop, library; L. *libraria*, a bookseller's shop (also, LL., a library), from *librarius*, belonging to books, from *liber*, a book.]

1. a room or building where a collection of books, etc. is kept for reading or reference.

2. (a) a public or private institution in charge of the care and circulation of such a collection; (b) a commercial establishment that rents books.

3. a collection of books, especially a large, systematically arranged collection for reading or reference.

4. a set or series of books issued in the same format by a publishing house.

circulating library; a library from which books may be borrowed, sometimes for a small daily fee.

Library of Congress; the large public library in Washington, D. C., established in 1800 and rebuilt in 1815.

lī′brāte, *v.i.*; librated, *pt., pp.*; librating, *ppr.* [L. *libratus*, pp. of *librare*, to weigh, balance, from *libra*, a balance.]

1. to move back and forth slowly like the beam of a balance before it comes to rest; to oscillate.

2. to poise; to hover; to remain balanced.

lī′brāte, *v.t.* to balance. [Obs.]

lī·brā′tion, *n.* [Fr., from L. *libratio* (*-onis*), a balancing, from *libratus*, pp. of *librare*.]

1. the act of balancing or oscillating; the state of being balanced.

2. in astronomy, an oscillatory motion, either actual or apparent, of a heavenly body to either side of its mean position.

libration of the moon; an apparent oscillating of the moon by which certain parts of it alternately appear and disappear. The moon always turns nearly the same face to the earth; but, by the libration in longitude, the parts near the eastern and western borders alternately appear and disappear; by the libration in latitude, the parts about the poles alternately appear and disappear; by the diurnal, or parallactic libration, more of the upper limb is brought into view at rising and setting.

lī′brȧ·tō·ry, *a.* balancing; poising or oscillating.

li·bret′tist, *n.* the composer of a libretto or librettos.

li·bret′tō, *n.*; *pl.* **li·bret′tōs, li·bret′ti,** [It., dim. of *libro*, a book, from L. *liber*, a book.] the words of an opera, oratorio, or other long choral composition; also, a book containing them.

lī′brī, *n.* plural of *liber*.

lī′bri·form, *a.* [L. *liber*, the inner bark of a tree, and *forma*, form.] like the liber in form or substance.

Lib′y·ăn, *n.* [L. *Libys*, or *Libycus*; Gr. *Libys*, Libyan, from *Libyē*, Libya.]

1. a native or inhabitant of Libya.

2. a group of Berber languages of the Hamitic group, spoken especially in ancient Libya: they are known from inscriptions found chiefly in Numidia but also in scattered localities from Sinai to the Canary Islands.

Lib′y·ăn, *a.* of Libya or its people.

līce, *n.* plural of *louse*.

lī′cens·ȧ·ble, *a.* capable of being licensed.

lī′cense, lī′cence, *n.* [OFr. *licence*; L. *licentia*, freedom, liberty, license, from *licens* (*-entis*), ppr. of *licere*, to be permitted.]

1. a formal permission to do something; especially, authorization by law to do some specified thing; as, *license* to marry, practice medicine, hunt, etc.

2. a document indicating that such permission has been granted.

3. (a) freedom to deviate from strict conduct, rule, or practice, generally permitted by common consent; as, poetic *license*; (b) an instance of such deviation.

4. excessive, undisciplined freedom, constituting an abuse of liberty.

lī′cense, lī′cence, *n. v.t.*; licensed (-senst), *pt., pp.*; licensing, *ppr.* [Fr. *licencier*; LL. *licentiare*, to license, from L. *licentia*, license.] to permit by grant of authority; to remove legal restraint by a grant of permission.

lī′censed, lī′cenced (-senst), *a.* permitted by license.

licensed victualer; one having a license to sell alcoholic liquor.

lī·cen·see′, lī·cen·cee′, *n.* the holder of a license.

lī′cense plāte, a numbered or lettered metal tag displayed on a motor vehicle, indicating that a license to drive it has been obtained.

lī′cens·ẽr, lī′cenc·ẽr, *n.* a person with authority to grant licenses.

lī′cens·ŏr, *n.* in law, a licenser.

lī′cen·sure (-shūr), *n.* a licensing.

lī·cen′ti·āte (-shi-) *n.* [LL. *licentiatus*, pp. of *licentiare*, to license.]

1. one who has a license to practice a specified profession.

2. in certain European universities, a degree between the baccalaureate and the doctorate.

lī·cen′tious, *a.* [L. *licentiosus*, wanton, unrestrained, using license, from *licentia*, license.]

1. disregarding accepted rules and standards; indulging freedom to excess; unrestrained by law; loose. [Rare.]

2. morally unrestrained; wanton; lascivious.

Syn.—voluptuous, dissolute, debauched, profligate, unbridled.

lī·cen′tious·ly, *adv.* in a licentious way.

lī·cen′tious·ness, *n.* a licentious state or quality.

lī′cet, [L.] it is allowed; it is legal.

lich, *a.* like; equal. [Obs.]

lich, *n.* a dead body; a corpse. [Scot. and Brit. Dial.]

lī′chee, *n.* same as *litchi*.

lī′chen, *n.* [L. *lichen*; Gr. *leichēn*, a tree moss, a lichenlike eruption on the skin, scurvy, prob. from *leichein*, to lick.]

1. one of a group of cellular cryptogamic plants without a stem or leaves and consisting of algae and fungi growing in close association. They appear in patches on rocks and tree trunks. They include the Iceland moss and reindeer moss, but are distinct from the true mosses, *Musci*.

2. any of various eruptive skin diseases.

LICHEN
reindeer moss (*Cladonia rangiferina*)

lī·chen·ā′ceous, *a.* of or like a lichen.

lī′chened, *a.* covered or coated with lichens.

lī·chen′iç, *a.* of, like, or derived from lichens; as, *lichenic* acid.

lichenic acid; fumaric acid, derived from Iceland moss.

lī·chen·iç′ō·lous, *a.* [L. *lichen*, a lichen, and *colere*, to inhabit.] inhabiting a lichen as a parasite.

lī·chen′i·form, *a.* [L. *lichen*, a lichen, and *forma*, form.] formed like a lichen.

lī′chen·in, *n.* a carbohydrate having the same empirical formula as starch $(C_6H_{10}O_5)_n$, obtained from Iceland moss and other lichens.

lī′chen·ism, *n.* the symbiotic condition between algae and fungi producing lichens.

lī″chen·ō·graph′iç, lī″chen·ō·graph′iç·ăl, *a.* pertaining to lichenography.

lī·chen·og′rȧ·phist, *n.* one who describes the lichens.

lī·chen·og′rȧ·phy, *n.* [Gr. *leichēn*, a lichen, and *graphein*, to write.] the science that describes and classifies lichens.

lī′chen·oid, *a.* [Gr. *leichēn*, a lichen, and *eidos*, form.] like a lichen or lichens.

lī·chen·ol′ō·gist, *n.* an expert in lichenology.

lī·chen·ol′ō·gy, *n.* [Gr. *leichēn*, a lichen, and *-logia*, from *legein*, to speak.] the systematic study of lichens.

lī′chen·ōse, *a.* lichenous.

lī′chen·ous, *a.* of, like, or covered with lichens.

lich fowl, [AS. *lic*, a body, and *fugol*, fowl.] the European goatsucker.

lich gāte, [AS. *lic*, a body, and *geat*, a gate.] a churchyard gate, with a roof under which a coffin can be set while awaiting the arrival of the clergyman.

lī′chī, *n.* same as *litchi*.

lich owl, [AS. *lic*, a body, corpse, and *ule*, an owl.] a screech owl, superstitiously supposed to forebode death.

licht, *n., a., v.t.* and *v.i.* light. [Scot.]

lich′wāle, *n.* a plant, the gromwell. [Obs.]

lich′wāy, *n.* [AS. *lic*, a corpse, and *weg*, way.] the path used in carrying a corpse to burial.

lich′wŏrt, *n.* [AS. *lic*, a body, and *wyrt*, a plant.] a plant, the wall pellitory. [Obs.]

lic′it, *a.* [L. *licitus*, lawful, permitted, properly pp. of *licere*, to be permitted.] lawful.

lic″i·tā′tion, *n.* [L. *licitatio* (*-onis*), a bidding at sales, from *licitatus*, pp. of *licitari*, to bid, offer a price.] the act of offering at auction; especially, in law, such a sale of jointly owned property, from which the proceeds are divided among the owners. [Rare.]

lic′it·ly, *adv.* lawfully.

lic′it·ness, *n.* lawfulness.

lick, *v.t.*; licked (likt), *pt., pp.*; licking, *ppr.* [ME. *licken*; AS. *liccian*, to lick.]

1. to pass or draw the tongue over; as, a dog *licks* a wound.

2. to bring into a certain condition by passing the tongue over; as, the child *licked* his fingers clean.

3. to pass lightly over like a tongue; as, the flames are licking the ends of the logs.

4. (a) to whip; to thrash; (b) to overcome (a person or thing); to vanquish. [Colloq.]

to lick into shape; to bring into shape by gradual treatment. [Colloq.]

to lick up; to consume by or as by licking or lapping.

lick, *v.i.* 1. to move lightly and quickly, as a flame; as, the waves *licked* about her feet.

2. to be victor; as, he *licked*. [Colloq.]

lick, *n.* 1. the act of licking with the tongue.

2. a small quantity.

3. a deposit of natural salt cropping out at the surface of the earth, where animals come to lick the salt.

4. (a) a sharp blow; (b) a short, rapid burst of activity, often careless, as in cleaning up, etc.; a spurt of energy; (c) a fast pace; a clip; a spurt of speed. [Colloq.]

5. a phrase of jazz music, especially an interpolated ornamentation. [Slang.]

6. [*often in pl.*] chance; turn; as, I'll get my *licks* in later. [Slang.]

lick′ẽr, *n.* one who or that which licks.

lick′ẽr-in,′ *n.* a drum in a carding machine, which conveys the fibers from the feed rolls to the main carding cylinder.

lick′ẽr·ish, lick′ẽr·ous, *a.* 1. tempting the appetite; appetizing. [Obs.]

2. eager; greedy to swallow; eager to taste or enjoy; having a keen relish.

3. lecherous; sensual; lewd; lustful.

Also spelled *liquorish*.

lick′ẽr·ous·ness, *n.* keen desire; sensuality. [Obs.]

lick′et·y-split′, lick′et·y-çut′, *adv.* recklessly; headlong; rapidly; at great speed. [Slang.]

lick′ing, *n.* 1. the act of a person or thing that licks.

2. a whipping; a thrashing. [Colloq.]

lick′pen″ny, *n.* a greedy miser. [Obs.]

lick′-spig″ŏt, *n.* a tapster. [Obs.]

lick′spit″tle, lick′spit, *n.* a servile flatterer or parasite; a toady.

liç′ō·rice, *n.* [OFr. *licorice*; LL. *liquiritia*, altered from L. *glycyrrhiza*; Gr. *glycyrrhiza*, licorice; *glykys*, sweet, and *rhiza*, root.]

1. a European plant of the pea family, with spikes of blue flowers and short, flat pods.

2. the dried root of this plant or the black extract made from it, used in medicine.

3. candy flavored with or as with this extract.

4. any of various plants having sweet roots, as (a) *Abrus precatorius*, or Indian licorice; (b) *Galium lanceolatum* or *Galium circæzans*, wild licorice.

Also spelled *liquorice*.

LICORICE PLANT (*Glycyrrhiza glabra*)

liç′tŏr, *n.* [L., from *ligare*, to bind, in allusion to the bundles of bound rods which he bore.] a minor officer among the Romans, who bore an ax and fasces as ensigns of his office. The duty of a lictor was to attend the chief magistrates when they appeared in public, to clear the way, and cause due respect to be paid to them, and also to apprehend and punish criminals.

lid, *n.* [ME. *lid*; AS. *hlid*, a lid, cover, from *hlidan*, to cover, conceal.]

1. a movable cover, hinged or unattached, as for a box, trunk, pot, etc.; a top.

2. an eyelid.

3. a book cover. [Dial.]

4. a curb or restraint; as, the police put the *lid* on vice. [Colloq.]

5. a cap, hat, etc. [Slang.]

6. in botany, the top portion of a pyxis; also, an operculum.

7. a roof timber supported by an upright in a coal mine.

8. a small package of marijuana, usually about an ounce. [Slang.]

lī′där, *n.* [*li*ght, and ra*dar*.] a meteorological instrument using transmitted and reflected laser light for detecting atmospheric particles, as pollutants, and determining their elevation, concentration, etc.

lid′ded, *a.* 1. covered with or as with a lid.

2. having (a specified kind of) eyelids: usually in hyphenated compounds, as heavy-*lidded*.

lid′less, *a.* 1. having no lid.

2. without eyelids.

3. watchful; not sleeping. [Poetic.]

lī′dō·cāine, *n.* [diethylaminoacetoxy*lid*ide, and *-o-*, and *cocaine*.] a synthetic crystalline compound, $C_{14}H_{22}N_2O$, used especially in the form of its hydrochloride as a local anesthetic and to control irregularity in the heartbeat.

līe, *v.i.*; lied (līd), *pt.*, *pp.*; lying, *ppr.* [ME. *lien*, *lyen*; AS. *leógan*, to lie, tell a falsehood.]

1. to utter falsehood with an intention to deceive; also, to utter falsehoods habitually.

2. to cause an incorrect impression; to present a misleading appearance; to deceive one; as, figures frequently *lie*.

to lie in one's throat; to tell a great or outrageous lie.

to lie out of; to get out of (trouble, etc.) by lying.

līe, *v.t.* to bring, put, accomplish, etc. by lying; as, he *lied* himself into office.

līe, *n.* 1. a false statement or action, especially one made with intent to deceive.

2. anything that gives or is meant to give a false impression.

3. the charge of lying.

to give the lie to; (a) to charge with telling a lie; (b) to prove to be false; to belie.

līe, *v.i.*; lay, *pt.*; lain, *pp.*; lying, *ppr.* [ME. *lien*, *lyen*; AS. *licgan*, to lie.]

1. to be in a horizontal position, or nearly so; to rest on some supporting surface: said of inanimate things.

2. to be or place oneself in a horizontal or nearly horizontal position; as, to *lie* down upon a couch.

3. to be situated; as, Ireland *lies* west of England.

4. to sojourn; to lodge; to sleep. [Archaic.]

5. to be or remain in a specified condition; as, to *lie* fallow; to *lie* open; to *lie* hid; to *lie* at the mercy of a creditor.

6. to extend; stretch; as, the road *lies* straight across the prairie.

7. to be; exist; be found; as, the remedy *lies* within yourself.

8. to be buried or entombed.

9. to be sustainable in law; to be capable of being maintained or admitted; as, an action *lies* against the tenant for waste.

to lie along; to lean over with a side wind, as a ship.

to lie along the land; to keep a course nearly parallel to the land.

to lie at one's heart; to be an object of affection, desire, etc.

to lie by; (a) to remain near; to be deposited or remaining with; as, he has the manuscript *lying by* him; (b) to rest; to intermit labor; as, we *lay by* during the heat of the day.

to lie down on the job; to put forth less than one's best efforts. [Colloq.]

to lie hard or *heavy upon*; to press; to oppress; to burden.

to lie in; to be in childbed.

to lie in wait; to wait for in concealment; to lie in ambush; to watch for an opportunity to attack or seize.

to lie on or *upon*; (a) to be a matter of obligation or duty to; as, it *lies on* the plaintiff to maintain his action; (b) to depend on.

to lie over; (a) to remain unpaid after the time when payment is due, as a note in a bank; (b) to stay and wait until some future time.

to lie to; to be stationary with the head to the wind, as a ship.

to lie to one's work; to exert all one's strength or powers in the performance of one's work.

to lie with; (a) [Archaic.] to lodge or sleep with; (b) [Archaic.] to have sexual intercourse with; (c) to belong to.

līe, *n.* 1. the way in which something is situated or arranged; the lay; as, the *lie* of the land.

2. a haunt, lair, or place frequented by an animal.

3. on a railroad, a side track; a siding.

4. in golf, the relative situation of a ball with reference to the advantage it offers the player; as, a good *lie*.

Liēb′çhen (lēp′), *n.* [G.] sweetheart or darling.

liē′ben·ẽr·īte, *n.* a kind of pinite.

liē′bẽr·kụhn, *n.* [named after J. N. *Lieberkühn*, its inventor.] an annular concave reflector around the object glass of a microscope to focus light on the field.

liē·bẽr·kụh′ni·ăn, *a.* [after Johann Nathanael *Lieberkühn* (1711–1756), a scientist of Berlin.] designating or of certain glands, crypts, or follicles of the small intestine.

Liēb′frau·milçh (lēp′frow-milk), *n.* [G.] a Rhine wine of Hesse.

Liē′big çŏn·dens′ẽr, in chemistry, a condenser made of two tubes, one within the other with space between permitting the circulation of fluids.

liēd (lēt), *n.*; *pl.* **liē′dẽr,** [G.] a German lyric or song.

Liē′dẽr·kränz (-kränts), *n.* [G., from *lieder*, pl. *of lied*, a song, lay, and *kranz*, a garland, wreath.]

1. a group of songs.

2. a men's singing society.

3. a soft cheese having a strong odor and flavor: a trade-mark.

līe dē·tec̦t′ŏr, equipment for recording changes in blood pressure, pulse beat, respiratory rate, etc. and increased perspiration: popular designation for it as used during questioning of criminal suspects, etc. for such signs of emotional stress as might indicate that the subject is lying.

liēf, *a.* [ME. *leef*; AS. *leóf*, dear, beloved.]

1. dear; beloved. [Obs.]

2. willing; inclined. [Obs.]

liēf, *n.* a darling; a loved one. [Obs.]

liēf, *adv.* gladly; willingly: only in *would* (or *had*) *as lief*, etc. [Rare.]

liēġe, *a.* [OFr. *lige*, *liege*, liege, free; LL. *ligius*, *legius*, unlimited, complete, liege; M.H.G. *ledic*, *ledec*, free, unhindered.]

1. sovereign; bound by feudal laws to protection and justice, and having the right to loyal service; as, a *liege* lord.

2. bound by feudal tenure to be faithful and loyal to a superior, as a vassal to his lord; as, a *liege*man.

3. loyal; faithful.

liēġe, *n.* in feudal law, (a) a vassal; a liegeman; (b) a lord or sovereign.

liēġe′dŏm, *n.* the rank, position, or domain of a liege.

liēġe lọrd, a feudal lord.

liēġe′măn, *n.*; *pl.* **liēġe′men,** 1. a vassal.

2. a loyal follower; a devoted adherent.

Also *liege man*.

liēġe pous′tie, [OFr. *liege poustee*, free sovereignty; *liege*, free, and *poustie*, from L. *potestas*, power.] in Scots law, that state of health which gives a person full power to dispose of his heritable property.

lie′ġẽr, *n.* a resident ambassador. [Obs.]

lī′en, *v.* obsolete past participle of *lie* (to be in a horizontal position).

lī′en (*or* lēn), *n.* [Fr. *lien*; L. *ligamen*, a band, from *ligare*, to bind, tie.] in law, a claim on the property of another as security against the payment of a just debt.

lī′en, *n.*; *pl.* **lī′en·eṣ,** [L.] the spleen.

lī·ē′năl, *a.* splenic; relating to the spleen.

lī·eñ′çū·lus, *n.*; *pl.* **lī·eñ′çū·lī,** [a dim. from L. *lien*, the spleen.] a small body consisting of splenic tissue found near the spleen.

lī′en·ŏr (*or* lēn′ŏr), *n.* one who holds a lien.

lī·en·ter′iç, *a.* [Gr. *leienteria*, the passing of one's food without digesting; *leios*, smooth, and *enteron*, intestine.] pertaining to or having lientery.

lī′en·ter·y, *n.* diarrhea in which the food is discharged partially or wholly undigested.

lī′ẽr, *n.* one who lies down; one who rests or remains; as, a *lier* in wait or in ambush.

lī·ẽrne′, *n.* [Fr., from *lier*; L. *ligare*, to bind.] in architecture, a short rib used in Gothic vaulting to connect the bosses and intersections of the main ribs.

lieū (*or* lū), *n.* [Fr., from L. *locus*, place.] place; stead: now used only in a phrase, *in lieu of*, instead of.

lieū·ten′ăn·cy (*or* lū), *n.*; *pl.* **lieū·ten′ăn·cieṣ,**

1. the rank, commission, status, or authority of a lieutenant.

2. the territory within a lieutenant's jurisdiction.

3. the collective body of lieutenants. [Obs.]

lieū·ten′ănt, *n.* [ME. *levetenant*; OFr. *lieutenant*; LL. *locum tenens* (*-entis*), one holding the place of another; L. *locum*, acc. of *locus*, place, and *tenens* (*-entis*), ppr. of *tenere*, to hold.]

1. an officer, civil or military, who occupies the place of a superior in his absence or who acts under his orders, as (a) in an army, a commissioned officer next in rank below a captain; (b) in the United States and British navies, a commissioned officer next in rank below a lieutenant commander. In Great Britain the word is generally pronounced *leften′ant*.

2. anyone empowered to act for or represent another; a deputy.

lieū·ten′ănt çolo′nel (kẽr′), a military officer next in rank below a colonel.

lieū·ten′ănt çŏm·mănd′ẽr, a naval officer next in rank below a commander.

lieū·ten′ănt ġen′ẽr·ăl, a military officer next in rank below a general.

lieū·ten′ănt gŏv′ẽrn·ŏr, 1. an elected official of a State performing the duties of a governor in case of his absence, illness, disability, or death.

2. in certain countries, an official substituting for the governor general of a province or district.

lieū·ten′ănt jụn′iŏr grāde, a naval officer ranking below a lieutenant and above an ensign.

lieū·ten′ănt·ry, *n.* lieutenancy. [Obs.]

lieū·ten′ănt·ship, *n.* lieutenancy.

līfe, *n.*; *pl.* **līveṣ,** [ME. *lif*; AS. *lif*, life.]

1. that property of plants and animals which makes it possible for them to take in food, get energy from it, grow, adapt themselves to their surroundings, and reproduce their kind: it is the quality that distinguishes a living animal or plant from inorganic matter or a dead organism.

2. the state of possessing this property; as, we tried to bring the drowned child back to *life*.

3. a living being, especially a human being; as, the cyclone took a heavy toll of *lives*.

4. living things collectively, often of a specified kind; as, plant *life*.

5. the time a person or thing is alive, or a

specific portion of such time; as, Shakespeare's *life* in London.

6. one's manner of living; as, his was a *life* of poverty.

7. the activities of a given time or in a given setting, and the people who take part in them; as, military *life*.

8. lives considered together as belonging to a certain class or type; as, low *life*.

9. (a) an individual's animate existence; (b) an account of this; a biography.

10. the existence of the soul; as, the eternal *life*.

11. something essential to the continued existence of something else; as, freedom of speech is the *life* of democracy.

12. the source of vigor or liveliness; as, she was the *life* of the party.

13. vigor; liveliness; animation; vivacity.

14. the period of flourishing, usefulness, etc.; period during which anything lasts; as, most fashions have a short *life*.

15. in the fine arts, (a) a lifelike quality or appearance; (b) representation from living models; as, a class in *life*.

16. a person as dear as one's existence; as, my *life*! my own!

17. a life insurance policy; also, a person as a subject for insurance. [Slang.]

18. another chance, as in the phrase *to get a life*. [Colloq.]

for life; (a) for the duration of one's life; (b) in order to save one's life.

to bring to life; (a) to bring to consciousness; (b) to make lively; to animate.

to come to life; (a) to recover consciousness; (b) to become lively or animated.

to take life; to kill.

to take one's own life; to commit suicide.

true to life; corresponding to what happens or exists in real life; true to reality.

līfe ar′rōw, an arrow shot from a gun to carry a line to a vessel needing help.

līfe as·sūr′ănce (-shūr′), same as *life insurance*.

līfe belt, a life preserver in the form of a belt, worn around a person's chest.

līfe′blood″ (-blud″), *n.* 1. the blood necessary to life; vital blood.

2. the vital part or animating influence of anything.

līfe′bōat″, *n.* 1. a strong, seaworthy boat kept in readiness on the shore for use in rescuing people in danger of drowning: it is

LIFEBOAT

usually built with air chambers, etc. for more buoyancy.

2. one of the small boats carried by a ship for use in case the ship has to be abandoned.

life buoy (boi *or* bo̤o̤′i), same as *life preserver*, sense 1.

life çȧst, a cast or mold taken from a living model.

life çlȧss, a group of art students who paint or draw from living models.

līfe cȳ′çle, the series of changes in form undergone by an organism in development from its earliest stage to the recurrence of the same stage in the next generation.

līfe′drop, *n.* a drop of lifeblood. [Rare.]

līfe es·tāte′, an estate limited to the duration of someone's life.

līfe ev·ēr·lȧst′ing, a plant of the genus *Gnaphalium*; cudweed.

līfe ex·peçt′ăn·cy, the average number of years that an individual of a given age may expect to live.

līfe′fụl, *a.* full of life; giving life.

līfe′-giv·ēr, *n.* a life-giving person or thing.

līfe′-giv″ing, *a.* giving life or spirit; having power to give life; inspiriting; invigorating.

līfe′guärd, *n.* an expert swimmer employed at bathing beaches, pools, etc. to prevent drownings.

Līfe Guärdṣ, two regiments of British cavalry which act as a bodyguard for the king and queen.

līfe his′tō·ry, 1. the history of the changes undergone by an organism in development from the egg, spore, etc. to its death as an adult.

2. one series of such changes.

līfe′hōld, *n.* life land.

līfe in·sūr′ănce (-shūr′), insurance in which a stipulated sum is paid to the beneficiary or beneficiaries at the death of the insured, or to the insured when he reaches a specified age: also *life assurance*.

līfe in′tēr·est, an interest (in property) held only during the life of a person: it cannot be passed on by him to another or others at his death.

līfe land, land held on a lease during the term of a life or lives.

līfe′less, *a.* [ME. *lifles*; AS. *lifleas*; *lif*, life, and *-leas*, -less.]

1. dead; without life; inanimate; as, *lifeless* matter; a *lifeless* body.

2. having no power, force, vigor, or spirit; dull.

līfe′less·ly, *adv.* in a lifeless manner.

līfe′less·ness, *n.* lifeless quality or state.

līfe′līke, *a.* 1. resembling actual life; as, this writer gives a *lifelike* picture of early America.

2. closely resembling a real person or thing; as, a *lifelike* portrait.

līfe līne, 1. a rope shot to a ship in distress near the shore in order that connection may be established between it and the shore.

2. any rope fastened where it may be clutched by persons in danger of being swept away and drowned.

3. the rope by means of which a diver is raised and lowered, used by him for signaling.

4. a line in the palm of the hand, curving about the base of the thumb, supposed (in palmistry) to reveal facts about the person's life.

5. a commercial, especially maritime, route of great importance: the route from England to India via the Suez Canal is often called the *life line* of the British Empire.

6. a route that is the only one over which supplies can be transported to a certain place.

līfe′long, *a.* enduring or uninterrupted throughout one's life.

līfe net, a strong net used by firemen, etc. to catch people jumping from a height, as to escape from a burning building.

līfe of Rī′ley, a life of ease and pleasure. [Slang.]

līfe plant, an evergreen of the genus *Bryophyllum*, having leaves which develop buds, roots, and new plants when laid on moist ground.

līfe prē·ṣērv′ēr, 1. a device for saving a per-

RING

JACKET

TYPES OF LIFE PRESERVER

son from drowning by keeping his body afloat: it is usually a ring or sleeveless jacket of canvas-covered cork.

2. a walking stick loaded with lead, carried for self-defense.

līf′ēr, *n.* a person sentenced to imprisonment for life. [Slang.]

līfe′sāv·ēr, *n.* 1. a person or thing that saves people from drowning.

2. a lifeguard.

3. a person or thing that is essential to one's work, welfare, etc. [Colloq.]

līfe′sāv″ing, *a.* saving, or intended to save, human life: as, a *lifesaving* device.

Lifesaving Service; in the United States, an organization under the Coast Guard, which maintains a series of lifesaving stations along the coasts.

līfe′sāv″ing, *n.* the saving of human life, especially through the prevention of drowning.

līfe′-sīze″, *a.* of the size of the person or thing represented: said of a picture, sculpture, etc.

līfe′-sīzed, *a.* same as *life-size*.

līfe′sŏme, *a.* lively; gay; vivacious.

līfe stȳle, the consistent, integrated way of life of an individual as typified by his manner, attitudes, possessions, etc.

līfe tā′ble, same as *mortality table*.

līfe′tīme, *n.* the time during which the life of an individual lasts.

līfe′tīme, *a.* lasting for such a period; as, a *lifetime* job.

līfe′wŏrk, *n.* the work to which a person devotes his life; most important work of one's life.

lift, *n.* [AS. *lyft*, the air, sky.] the sky; the heavens; the atmosphere. [Scot.]

lift, *v.t.*; lifted, *pt.*, *pp.*; lifting, *ppr.* [ME. *liften*, *lyften*, from Ice. *lypta*, to lift, to raise in the air, from *lopt*, the air.]

1. to move or raise to a higher position; to elevate; as, to *lift* a load.

2. to raise in estimation, dignity, rank, spirits, etc.; to elevate to a higher state, level, or degree; to exalt; as, his merits *lifted* him into notice.

3. to hold up; to support high in the air; as, the mountain *lifts* its snow-capped peaks toward the sky.

4. to pick up and set; as, to *lift* a baby down from its high chair.

5. to cancel (a mortgage) by paying it off.

6. to change (a person's face) by means of a surgical operation intended, ordinarily, to remove wrinkles and give a more youthful appearance.

7. to plagiarize; as, he *lifted* a passage from Milton. [Colloq.]

8. in agriculture, to loosen and remove (seedlings) from a seed bed in preparation for transplanting.

9. in golf, (a) to hit (a ball) unusually high by means of an upward stroke; (b) to pick (a ball) up in one's hand, as from an unplayable position.

10. to steal. [Slang.]

lift, *v.i.* 1. to try to raise; to exert the strength for the purpose of raising or bearing.

2. to rise or appear to rise and disappear in the air; to be dispelled; as, a fog *lifts*; the gloom *lifted*.

3. to become raised or elevated; to go up.

4. to flutter or shake, as a sail of a ship when it is close to the wind.

lift, *n.* 1. a lifting, raising, or rising; upward movement.

2. the amount lifted at one time.

3. (a) a rise; a degree of elevation; as, the *lift* of a lock in canals; (b) a swell or rise in the ground.

4. in nautical usage, a rope from the masthead to the extremity of a yard, used to support the yard and raise the end.

5. the means by which anything lifts or is lifted, as (a) [Brit.] an elevator; (b) a hoisting apparatus; (c) a machine for exercising the muscles; (d) a handle.

6. (a) the distance through which something is lifted; (b) the extent of rise or elevation.

7. lifting power or influence.

8. elevation of spirits or mood.

9. elevated position or carriage; as, the proud *lift* of her head.

10. a ride in the direction in which one is going.

11. help of any kind.

12. in horology, that period of the oscillation of a balance which gives the impulse.

13. in shoemaking, a thickness of leather in a heel.

14. a lift gate.

15. in aeronautics, the upward pull resulting from the force of the air against an airfoil passing through it.

lift′ȧ·ble, *a.* capable of being lifted.

lift bridġe, a form of bridge in which a movable part may be lifted.

lift′-drag′ rā′tiō (-shō), in aeronautics, the ratio of the lift of a body to its drag.

lift′ēr, *n.* one who or that which lifts or raises;

(a) [Slang.] a thief; as, a cattle *lifter*; (b) a device used to lift stove lids. (c) an apparatus for lifting goods or persons; a lift; (d) in founding, a tool for dressing the mold; also, a device to hold the sand together in lifting the cope; (e) in the steam engine, the arm on a lifting rod that raises the puppet valve; (f) a bucket wheel used to lift paper pulp.

lift gāte, a gate that must be raised to be opened.

lift'ing sāil, a sail tending to raise a ship's bow out of the water, as the jib.

lift'ing set, a set or series of pumps used to lift water from a mine, by a series of lifts.

lift'off, lift'-off, *n.* the launching of a rocket or spacecraft.

lift pump, a suction pump that raises a column of liquid to the level of a spout out of which the liquid runs of its own accord: opposed to *force pump.*

lift tent'ẽr, a windmill governor to control the speed of the vanes, or to regulate the space between millstones driven by the windmill.

lift wall, a cross wall in a lock of a canal.

lig, *v.i.* to lie (recline). [Now Dial.]

lig'ȧ·ment, *n.* [Fr. *ligament*; L. *ligamentum*, a band, bandage, from *ligare*, to tie, bind.]

1. anything that ties or unites one thing or part to another; a bond; a tie.

2. in anatomy, a band of tough tissue serving to connect one bone to another, or to hold an organ in position: it is a white, solid, inelastic, tendinous substance, softer than cartilage, but harder than membrane.

3. in a bivalve shell, the elastic cuticular band uniting the valves at the hinges.

lig"ȧ·men'tăl, lig"ȧ·men'tous, *a.* composing a ligament or having the nature of a ligament; as, a *ligamentous* membrane.

lig'ȧ·men·tȧ·ry, *a.* same as *ligamental.*

lī'găn, *n.* same as *lagan.*

lī'gāte, *v.t.*; ligated, *pt., pp.*; ligating, *ppr.* [L. *ligatus*, pp. of *ligare*, to bind, tie.] to tie or bind with a ligature, as a bleeding artery.

lī·gā'tion, *n.* [L. *ligatio (-onis)*, a binding, from *ligatus*, pp. of *ligare*, to bind.] the act of binding or state of being bound; also, a thing that binds; a tie; a bond; a ligature.

lī·gā'tŏr, *n.* a surgical instrument used in ligation.

lig'ȧ·tūre, *n.* [Fr., from LL. *ligatura*, a band, from L. *ligare*, to bind.]

1. anything that binds; a bandage, tie, bond, etc.

2. the act of binding or tying together; as, a strict *ligature* of the parts.

3. in music, a curved line connecting notes to be sung or played as one phrase; a slur; also, the notes so connected.

4. in printing, a double character, or a type consisting of two or more letters or characters united, as *fl, fi, ff, ffi*, æ, œ; also, the character employed to indicate connection of letters.

5. in surgery, a cord or thread for tying the blood vessels.

6. impotence supposed to be caused by magic. [Obs.]

lig'ȧ·tūre, *v.t.* ligatured, *pt., pp.*; ligaturing, *ppr.* to ligate.

lī'ġeănce, *n.* 1. allegiance. [Archaic.]

2. in law, the power or territory of a ruler.

lig'ge, lig'e, *v.i.* to recline; to lie. [Obs.]

lig'gẽr, *n.* 1. a horizontal scaffold beam. [Brit. Dial.]

2. a plank pathway across a ditch. [Brit. Dial.]

3. a coverlet. [Brit. Dial.]

4. a fishline with a float, used in fishing for pike. [Brit. Dial.]

light (lit), *n.* [ME. *liht*; AS. *leoht*, light, from the Teut. root *luh*, to be light.]

1. (a) that which makes it possible to see: opposed to *darkness*; form of radiant energy that acts upon the retina of the eye, optic nerve, etc., making sight possible: this energy is transmitted at a velocity of about 186,000 miles per second by wavelike or vibrational motion; (b) a form of radiant energy similar to this, but not acting on the normal retina, as ultraviolet and infrared radiation.

2. the rate of flow of light radiation with respect to the sense of sight: it is measured in *lumens.*

3. the sensation that light stimulates in the organs of sight.

4. anything that emits, or is a source of, light, as a lamp, candle, taper, lighthouse, star, etc.; specifically, in fireworks, a piece giving a brilliant flame; as, a Bengal *light.*

5. a place that admits light; a window or windowpane; as, a broken *light* in the sash.

6. the physical conditions constituting day; daylight; dawn; as, rise with the *light.*

7. position or circumstances in which any matter is regarded or seen; as, that puts matters in a different *light.*

8. brightness; illumination: usually with reference to a particular case.

9. a thing by means of which something can be started burning; as, a *light* for a cigarette.

10. knowledge; enlightenment; mental illumination; as, early writings shed *light* on our past.

11. public knowledge or view; as, every day new facts are brought to *light.*

12. facial expression showing a mental or emotional state; as, a *light* of recognition came into his eyes.

13. a person whose brilliant record makes him an example for others; an outstanding figure; as, a shining *light.*

14. in the fine arts, (a) the quality suggestive of light; (b) the part of a picture upon which light is represented as falling.

15. in law, the right to have the access of the sun's rays to one's windows free from any obstruction on the part of one's neighbors.

according to one's lights; as one's opinions, information, or abilities may direct.

to bring to light; to reveal; to disclose.

to come to light; to be revealed or disclosed.

Syn.—luminosity, radiance, beam, gleam, phosphorescence, scintillation, coruscation, flash, brightness, brilliancy, effulgence, splendor, blaze, candle, lamp, lantern, explanation, instruction, illumination, understanding, interpretation.

light, *a.* [ME. *light, liht*; AS. *leoht, liht*, light, bright; from Teut. root *luh* in verbs signifying to be light.]

1. bright; clear; not dark or obscure; as, the morning is *light*; the apartment is *light.*

2. in colors, white or whitish; pale; fair; as, a *light* brown, a *light* complexion.

light, *adv.* palely; as, the ribbon is *light* blue.

light, *v.t.*; lighted *or* lit, *pt., pp.*; lighting, *ppr.* [ME. *lighten, lichten*; AS. *lyhtan, lihtan*, to shine, to make light, from *leoht*, bright, light.]

1. to kindle; to inflame; to set fire to; as, to *light* a bonfire.

2. to cause to give off light; as, she *lit* the lamp.

3. to give light to; furnish with light; as, lamps *light* the streets.

4. to brighten; animate: often with *up.*

5. to show the way by or as by giving light; as, the beacon *lighted* the planes safely to the airport.

light, *v.i.* 1. to ignite; to kindle; to catch fire; as, his cigar would not *light.*

2. to grow luminous or bright; to be lighted; to brighten: usually with *up*; as, the clouds *light up* at sunrise.

light, *a.* [ME. *lighte*; AS. *leoht, liht*, light.]

1. having little weight; not heavy; as, a feather is *light.*

2. not burdensome; easy to bear; as, a *light* tax.

3. slight; trifling; not important; as, a *light* conversation.

4. having little weight for its size; of low specific gravity.

5. less than usual or normal in amount, extent, intensity, force, etc.; specifically, (a) falling or striking with little force or impact; as, a *light* blow; (b) of less than the usual quantity or density; as, a *light* vote, a *light* rain; (c) not thick, coarse, or massive; delicate and graceful in structure; as, *light* tracery, *light* architecture; (d) not violent or intense; mild; as, a *light* wind; (e) soft, muted, or muffled; as, a *light* sound; (f) not prolonged or intense; as, *light* applause.

6. free from a burden of pain, care, or trouble; cheerful; gay; as, *light* of heart.

7. having a feeling of lightness; dizzy; giddy; as, *light* in the head.

8. not of the usual or defined weight; clipped; as, *light* coin.

9. easy to do; not difficult; as, *light* work.

10. flighty; frivolous; fickle; capricious.

11. loose in morals; wanton.

12. of an amusing or nonserious nature; as, *light* entertainment, *light* reading.

13. containing little alcohol; as, *light* wine.

14. characterized by qualities suggestive of little weight; not dense, hard, full, etc.; specifically, (a) not as full as usual; moderate; as, a *light* meal; (b) easy to digest; (c) well leavened; soft and spongy; as, a *light* cake; (d) loose in consistency; easily crumbled; porous; as, *light* sand.

15. moving with ease and nimbleness; as, she is *light* on her feet.

16. carrying little weight; as, we shall travel *light.*

17. unstressed or slightly stressed: said of a syllable in phonetics, prosody, etc.

18. having light weapons, armor, equipment, etc.; as, a *light* tank.

19. sickly; feeble. [Brit. Dial.]

to make light of; to treat as of little consequence; to pay little or no attention to.

Syn.—buoyant, volatile, easy, active, unencumbered, empty, scanty, slight, gentle, delicate, unsteady, capricious, vain, frivolous, characterless, thoughtless, inadequate, unsubstantial, gay, bright, lively.

light, *adv.* lightly.

light, *v.i.*; lighted *or* lit, *pt., pp.*; lighting, *ppr.* [ME. *lihten*; AS. *lihtan, lyhtan*, to dismount, to alight, originally to relieve of the rider's burden, to make light, from *leoht, liht*, light.]

1. to come by chance; to happen: with *on* or *upon*; as, to *light upon* a treasure.

2. to descend, as from a horse or carriage; to alight. [Rare.]

He *lighted* down from his chariot.
—2 Kings v. 21.

3. to come to rest after traveling through the air; as, the bee *lights* on this flower and that.

4. to fall or strike suddenly, as a blow.

to light into; (a) to attack; (b) to scold; to berate. [Slang.]

to light out; to hurry away; to abscond. [Slang.]

light, *v.t.* [ME. *lighten, lychten*; AS. *lihtan*, to make light, from *leoht*, light.]

1. to lighten. [Obs.]

2. to deliver, as in childbirth. [Brit. Dial.]

light'ȧ·ble, *a.* capable of being lighted.

light'-ärmed', *a.* armed with light weapons.

light ball, in military usage, a flare fired from a mortar to furnish light for one's own operations or to reveal the enemy's operations.

light'bōat, *n.* a lightship.

light box, a lightroom.

light'-cen'tū·ry, *n.* the distance which light travels in a century.

light dūes, dues or tolls charged upon shipping for lighthouse maintenance.

light'en, *v.t.*; lightened, *pt., pp.*; lightening, *ppr.* [ME. *lightnen, lightenen*, to become light.]

1. to make light; to illuminate; as, to *lighten* an apartment.

2. to cause to flash in or as in lightening (with *out* or *forth*).

3. to cause to become lighter in color.

4. to shed knowledge or spiritual light on; to enlighten.

light'en, *v.i.* 1. to give off flashes of lightening.

2. to become more light; to grow less dark or gloomy; to clear; as, the sky *lightens.*

3. to shine brightly; to flash.

light'en, *v.t.* 1. to make lighter; to reduce in weight; to make less heavy; as, to *lighten* a burden.

2. to make less severe, harsh, troublesome, etc.; to alleviate.

3. to cheer; to exhilarate; to gladden.

light'en, *v.i.* 1. to grow lighter or less heavy.

2. to light; to alight; to descend. [Obs.]

light'en·ing, *n.* 1. lightning. [Obs.]

2. fulguration.

3. a becoming light or bright.

light'ẽr, *n.* [D. *lighter*, from *ligt*, light.] a large, open, flat-bottomed barge, used in unloading and loading ships wherever shallow water prevents these from coming into shore.

light'ẽr, *v.t.* and *v.i.* to transport (goods) by means of a lighter; as, to *lighter* coal to a ship.

light'ẽr, *n.* one who or that which lights; as, a cigarette *lighter*, etc.

light'ẽr·āġe, *n.* 1. conveyance by a lighter (barge).

2. the act of loading or unloading a cargo by a lighter.

3. the cost of transportation, etc. by a lighter.

light'ẽr·măn, *n.*; *pl.* **light'ẽr·men,** a manager of or an employee on a lighter.

light'ẽr stȧff, a lever controlling the adjustment of the bridgetree of a grain mill.

light'ẽr-than-āir', *a.* of less weight than the air displaced: said of aircraft.

light'fāce, *n.* type having light, thin lines: opposite of *blackface* or *boldface.*

light'fāce, *a.* having light, thin lines.

light fil'tẽr, a color screen.

light′-fin′gẽred, *a.* 1. skillful at stealing, especially by picking pockets; thievish.
2. having a light touch, as in piano playing.

light′-foot, *a.* light-footed. [Poetic.]

light′-foot′ed, *a.* stepping lightly and gracefully; nimble of foot.

light′-hand′ed, *a.* 1. light of touch.
2. carrying little in one's hands.
3. short-handed; lacking the regular number of hands or assistants, as a ship, factory, etc.

light′head (-hed), *n.* a lightheaded person.

light′head′ed, *a.* 1. delirious.
2. dizzy; giddy.
3. frivolous; thoughtless.

light″head′ed·ness, *n.* the state of being lightheaded.

light′heärt′ed, *a.* free from grief or anxiety; gay; cheeful; merry.

light″heärt′ed·ly, *adv.* with a light heart.

light″heärt′ed·ness, *n.* the state of being free from care or grief; cheerfulness.

light heav′y·weight (hev′i-wāt), a boxer or wrestler who weighs between 161 and 175 pounds.

light′-heeled′, *a.* lively in walking or running; brisk; swift.

light horse, light-armed cavalry.

light′-horse″măn, *n.*; *pl.* **light′-horse″men,** a light-armed cavalryman.

light′house, *n.* a tower or other lofty structure with a powerful light at the top, erected at some place important or dangerous to navigation to serve as a guide or warning to ships at night.

light house′keep·ing, housekeeping confined to light housework.

light′hous″es, *n.pl.* green amaranth plants.

light in′făn·try, infantry carrying light weapons and equipment.

light′ing, *n.* [ME. *lihtinge*; AS. *lihtung*, verbal n. of *lihtan, leóhtan*, to make light, illuminate.]
1. a giving light or being lighted; illumination; ignition.
2. the distribution of light and shade in a painting.
3. in the theater, (a) the art, practice, or manner of using and arranging lights on the stage; (b) the stage lights collectively.
4. same as *annealing*.

light′keep″ẽr, *n.* one whose duty is to care for the light of a lighthouse or lightship.

light′less, *a.* [AS. *leohtleas*, without light; *leoht*, light, and *-leas*, -less.] dark; having no light.

light′ly, *adv.* [ME. *lightly, lihtliche*; AS. *leohtlice*, lightly, from *leohtlic*, light, *leoht*, light, and *-lic*, -ly.]
1. with little weight; not heavily or severely; as, to walk *lightly*, to punish *lightly*.
2. with lightness or levity; gaily; cheerfully.
3. with little or no reason.
4. easily; readily; without difficulty. [Archaic.]
5. nimbly; with agility; quickly.
6. wantonly; shamelessly.
7. gently.
8. to a small degree or amount; as, to spend *lightly*.
9. with indifference or neglect.
10. usually. [Obs.]

light′măn, *n.* 1. a lightkeeper.
2. a linkman. [Obs.]

light′-mīnd′ed, *a.* inconsiderate; flighty; thoughtless.

light′-mīnd′ed·ness, *n.* the state or quality of being light-minded.

light′ness, *n.* 1. the state, quality, or intensity of lighting; brightness.
2. the state of being nearer to white than to black; paleness; whitishness.

light′ness, *n.* 1. the state of being light, not heavy.
2. mildness, nimbleness, delicacy, cheerfulness, lack of seriousness, etc.

light′ning, *n.* [from *lighten*, to illuminate.] a discharge of atmospheric electricity, accompanied by a vivid flash of light; also, the flash thus caused. It is caused by the discharge of electricity from one cloud to another, sometimes from a cloud to the earth.

light′ning, *n.* a lightening in weight. [Obs.]

light′ning ar·rest′ẽr, a device that protects radio or electrical equipment from lightning by causing the discharge to be grounded.

light′ning bug (or **bee′tle**), a firefly.

light′ning rod, a pointed metal rod placed high on a building, etc. and grounded at the lower end to act as a conductor and divert lightning from the structure.

light′-ō′-lŏve′, *n.* 1. an old dance tune.
2. a loose, wanton, or light woman.

light op′ẽr·ȧ, a musical play with humorous situations, some spoken dialogue, and a story that ends happily; an operetta.

light pen, a penlike electronic device which detects information displayed on a computer-controlled cathode-ray tube and permits response to or manipulation of such retrieved data by simply pointing to it.

light quăn′tum, a unit of radiant energy equal to the quantum; photon.

light′room, *n.* 1. a room beside the magazine of a warship, having windows through which light can be supplied to the magazine without danger of an explosion.
2. the room in a lighthouse containing the lamp.

lights, *n.pl.* [so called from their being lighter in weight than the rest of the body.] the lungs of animals, as sheep, hogs, cattle, etc., used as food.

light′ship, *n.* a ship moored in a place dangerous to navigation and bearing a bright light at the masthead to warn pilots away from the spot.

LIGHTSHIP

light′sŏme, *a.* 1. luminous; not obscure.
2. well-lighted; bright.

light′sŏme, *a.* 1. nimble, buoyant, graceful, or lively.
2. lighthearted; cheerful; gay.
3. frivolous.

light′sŏme·ly, *adv.* in a lightsome way; nimbly.

light′sŏme·ness, *n.* the quality or condition of being lightsome (nimble).

lights out, a signal, as in a military camp, etc., to extinguish lights at bedtime.

light′-struck, *a.* in photography, accidentally exposed to light; fogged by exposure to light.

light′weight (-wāt), *a.* 1. of less than a certain fixed weight; specifically, in boxing and wrestling, between a featherweight and a welterweight; between 127 and 135 pounds.
2. light in weight.

light′weight, *n.* 1. a lightweight boxer or wrestler.
2. one below normal weight.
3. a person of low mentality or little importance. [Colloq.]

light whis′ky, a light-colored, mild whisky aged in new or used casks for not less than four years.

light′wood, *n.* 1. wood, especially southern pine, which burns readily and makes a bright light.
2. in Australia, a species of acacia; blackwood.

light′y, *a.* illuminated; bright. [Obs.]

light′-yēar, *n.* a unit of astronomical distance, equal to the distance that light travels in one year, approximately 6,000,000,000,000 miles.

lign-, see *ligni-*.

lign·al′ōes (līn-al′ōz), *n.* [ME. *lign aloes*; OFr.; L. *lignum aloes*, wood of aloe.]
1. the resinous wood of the aloes tree, burnt for its pleasant aroma.
2. aloes, the drug.

ligne (lēn′y′), *n.* [Fr., line.] a French measure equal to 0.0888 of an inch.

lig′nē·ous, *a.* [L. *ligneus*, from *lignum*, wood.] of, consisting of, or resembling wood; woody.

lig·nes′cent, *a.* partly woody.

lig′ni-, [from L. *lignum*, wood.] a combining form meaning *wood*, as in *lignify*: also *ligno-*, or, before a vowel, *lign-*.

lig·nif′ẽr·ous, *a.* [L. *lignifer*; *lignum*, wood, and *ferre*, to produce.] yielding wood.

lig″ni·fi·cā′tion, *n.* the process of becoming wood.

lig′ni·form, *a.* [L. *lignum*, wood, and *forma*, form.] like wood; resembling wood.

lig′ni·fȳ, *v.i.*; lignified, *pt., pp.*; lignifying, *ppr.* [L. *lignum*, wood, and *facere*, to make.] to convert into or to become wood by the depositing of lignin in the cell walls.

lig′ni·fȳ, *v.t.* to make into wood.

lig′nin, *n.* [L. *lignum*, wood, and *-in*.] an organic substance closely allied to cellulose and forming the essential part of woody fiber.

lig·ni·pẽr′dous, *a.* [L. *lignum*, wood, and *perdere*, to destroy.] causing destruction to wood, as certain insects.

lig′nīte, *n.* [L. *lignum*, wood, and *-ite*.] a soft, brownish-black coal in which the texture of the original wood can still be seen: it is denser and contains more carbon than peat: also called *brown coal*.

lig·nit′iç, *a.* containing lignite; resembling lignite; relating to lignite.

lig·ni·tif′ẽr·ous, *a.* bearing lignite.

lig·niv′ō·rous, *a.* [L. *lignum*, wood, and *vorare*, to devour.] eating wood, as certain insect larvae.

lig′nō-, see *ligni-*.

lig·nō·cel′lū·lōse, *n.* [*ligno-*, and *cellulose*.] any of several combinations of lignin and cellulose: it forms the essential part of woody tissue.

lig·nō·cer′iç, *a.* [L. *lignum*, wood, and *cera*, wax, and *-ic*.] of or derived from the tar of wood.
lignoceric acid; a white, fatty crystalline substance derived from beech and other woods by distillation.

lig′nōne, *n.* [L. *lignum*, wood, and *-one*.] a form of lignin.

lig′nōse, *a.* [L. *lignosus*, woody, from *lignum*, wood.] ligneous. [Rare.]

lig′nōse, *n.* 1. lignin.
2. a nitroglycerin wood fiber explosive.

lig′nous, *a.* ligneous. [Rare.]

lig′num, *n.* [L.] woody tissue. [Obs.]

lig′num rhō′di·um, [L. *lignum*, wood, and Gr. *rhodon*, a rose.] rosewood.

lig′num vī′tae, [L. *lignum*, wood, and *vitæ*, genit. of *vita*, life.]
1. a tree, *Guaiacum officinale*, of tropical America, having a hard, solid, heavy greenish-brown wood, leathery leaves, and small purple flowers.
2. any of several similar trees, as *Acacia falcata* and *Eucalyptus polyanthema* of New South Wales, *Vitex lignum vitæ* of Queensland, and *Sarcomphalus laurinus* of Jamaica, the bastard lignum vitae.
3. the wood of these trees.

lig′rō·in, lig′rō·ine, *n.* an inflammable distillate of petroleum, used as a solvent and illuminant.

lig′ū·lȧ, *n.*; *pl.* **lig′ū·lae, lig′ū·lȧs,** [L. *ligula* or *lingula*, dim. of *lingua*, tongue.]
1. in botany, same as *ligule*.
2. in zoology, (a) the distal portion of an insect's labium, usually divided into the glossa and paraglossae. In some insects, as the bee, it serves as a proboscis; (b) a linguiform lobe of the lateral appendages of certain annelids.
3. in anatomy, a border of white nervous matter in the covering of the fourth cerebral ventricle.

lig′ū·lăr, *a.* of, like, or consisting of ligulae or ligules.

lig′ū·lāte, lig′ū·lā·ted, *a.* [L. *ligula*, a tongue, strap, and *-ate*.]
1. shaped like a tongue or strap; strap-shaped.
2. of or having a ligula or ligule.

lig′ūle, *n.* [L. *ligula* or *lingula*, a small tongue, tongue of a shoe, a strap.]
1. a strap-shaped corolla in certain flowers of the *Compositæ*.
2. a thin membrane at the base of the lamina of a grass leaf, at the point where the blade meets the leafstalk, as that of millet grass, *Milium multiflorum*, shown in the figure.
3. an outgrowth on the inner side of certain petals, as in *Silene*.

L. LIGULE

Lig″ū·li·flō′rae, *n.pl.* [L. *ligula*, a small tongue, a strap, and *flos, floris*, a flower.] in the *Compositæ*, a group of plants having ligulate florets, including lettuce, dandelion, hawkweed, chicory, etc.

lig″ū·li·flō′rous, *a.* 1. producing ligulate florets.
2. of or pertaining to the *Liguliflorae*.

li·gū′li·form, *a.* [L. *ligula*, a small tongue, strap, and *forma*, form.] flat and straplike; ligulate.

lig′ū·loid, *a.* resembling a strap, tongue, or ligula.

Li·guō′rist (-gwō′), *n.* one who follows the theological theories of St. Alfonso Maria da

Liguori (1696–1787); a Redemptorist: called also *Liguorian.*

lig'ūre, *n.* [LL. *ligurius*; L.Gr. *ligyrion.*] in the Bible, a precious stone, being one of the twelve in the breastplate of the Jewish high priest: it is believed by some to be the yellow jacinth: Ex. xxviii. 19.

Li·gū'ri·ăn, *a.* [L. *Liguria*, Liguria, from *Ligus* or *Ligur (-uris)*, a Ligurian.]
 1. belonging to Liguria, an ancient country located near Genoa.
 2. of the modern department of Liguria, its people, etc.
 3. of the dialect of Italian spoken in Liguria.

Li·gū'ri·ăn, *n.* 1. one of an ancient race inhabiting Liguria, conquered by the Romans.
 2. a native or inhabitant of the department of Liguria.
 3. the Ligurian dialect of Italian.

Li·gus'ti·çum, *n.* [L., a plant native to Liguria, from *Ligusticus*, Ligurian, from *Ligus* or *Ligur*, a Ligurian.] a genus of the *Umbelliferæ*, characterized by the presence of oil tubes in the fruit.

li·gus'trin, *n.* [*ligustrum* and *-in.*] a bitter substance derived from *Ligustrum vulgare*, the privet.

Li·gus'trum, *n.* [L., the privet.] a genus of the *Oleaceæ*, including the common privet.

līk'ȧ·ble, *a.* having qualities that inspire liking; worthy of being liked; attractive, pleasant, genial, etc.: also spelled *likeable.*

līke, *n.* [ME. *like, lyke*; AS. *lic*, the body.] body; person; form; also, a corpse. [Obs.]

līke, *a.* [ME. *like, lyke*; AS. *gelic*, like, lit., having the same body; *ge-*, together, and *lic*, body.]
 1. similar; having the same or nearly the same qualities, characteristics, etc.; equal; as, a cup of sugar and a *like* amount of flour.
 2. alike. [Rare.]
 3. probable; likely; as, he is *like* to die. [Dial.]

līke, *adv.* 1. in the same or a similar way; in the manner of; equally; as, he works *like* mad.
 2. likely; probably; as, *like* as not, he is already there. [Colloq.]
 3. as one may say; somewhat; as, he seemed friendly *like.* [Dial.]

līke, *prep.* 1. similar to; somewhat resembling; as, she is *like* a bird.
 2. in a manner characteristic of; similarly to; as, she sings *like* a bird.
 3. in accord with the nature of; characteristic of; as, it was not *like* him to forget her birthday.
 4. in the mood for; desirous of; as, I feel *like* sleeping.
 5. indicative or prophetic of; as, it looks *like* a clear day tomorrow.
 Like was originally an adjective in senses 1, 3, 4, 5, and an adverb in sense 2, and is still considered so by conservative grammarians.
 like anything (or *blazes, crazy, the devil, mad,* etc.); with furious energy, speed, etc. [Colloq. or Slang.]
 nothing like; not at all like; completely different from.
 something like; almost like; about.

līke, *conj.* 1. as; as, it was just *like* you said. [Colloq.]
 2. as if; as, it looks *like* he is signaling to us. [Colloq.]

līke, *n.* a person or thing resembling or equal to another; as, where can you find his *like?*
 and the like; and others of the same kind.
 the like (or *likes*) *of*; any person or thing like. [Colloq.]

līke, *v.i.*; liked (likt), *pt., pp.*; liking, *ppr.* to come near (*to* doing something): in this use the verb is equal to the adverb *almost.* [Dial.]

līke, *v.t.* to compare; to liken. [Obs.]

līke, *v.t.*; liked (līkt), *pt., pp.*; liking, *ppr.* [ME. *liken, lyken*; AS. *lician, lican*, to like, to please, prob. from *lic*, form, body.]
 1. to be pleased with; to approve; to have a liking for; to enjoy; as, he *likes* books.
 2. to wish; as, I should *like* to go there.

līke, *v.i.* 1. to please; to be agreeable to: with the dative; as, it *likes* me not. [Obs.]
 2. to be pleased; to choose; as, do as you *like.*
 3. to thrive. [Obs.]

līke, *n.pl.* preferences, tastes, or affections; as, *likes* and dislikes.

-līke, a suffix from the adjective *like*, used with nouns (a) to form adjectives meaning *like, characteristic of, suitable for*, as in war*like*, man*like*; (b) to form adverbs meaning *in the manner of.* Words formed with *-like* are usually written as one word, but are hyphenated if three l's fall together (e.g., *ball-like*).

līke'ȧ·ble, *a.* same as *likable.*

līke'hood, *n.* likelihood. [Rare.]

līke'li·hood, *n.* 1. probability; likeliness.
 2. something that is likely to happen; a probability.
 3. likeness; resemblance. [Obs.]

līke'li·ness, *n.* the state or quality of being likely; likelihood; suitableness; resemblance.

līke'ly, *a.*; *comp.* likelier; *superl.* likeliest, [ME. *likli*; AS. *geliclic*, from *gelic*, like.]
 1. having the appearance of truth; credible; probable; as, a *likely* story.
 2. seeming as if it would happen or make happen; reasonably to be expected; apparently destined; as, it is *likely* to leave at any minute.
 3. such as will probably be satisfactory or rewarding; suitable; as, a *likely* place to find deer.
 4. promising; as, a *likely* lad.
 5. such as may be liked; pleasing; agreeable; good-looking; as, a *likely* lass. [Chiefly Dial.]
 6. similar. [Obs.]

līke'ly, *adv.* probably.

līke'-mīnd'ed, *a.* having a like disposition; having similar purposes, motives, and desires.

līk'en, *v.t.*; likened, *pt., pp.*; likening, *ppr.* to compare; to represent as like, or similar.

līke'ness, *n.* [ME. *liknesse*; AS. *gelicnes*, resemblance, likeness, from *gelic*, like.]
 1. the state or quality of being like; resemblance; similitude; similarity.
 2. (the same) form; shape; semblance; as, Jupiter appeared in the *likeness* of a swan.
 3. that which resembles something else; a copy; a portrait; a representation.

lik'ẽr·ous, *a.* lickerous. [Obs.]

līke'wāke, *n.* a wake or watch with a corpse. [Obs.]

līke'wīṣe, *adv.* 1. in the same manner.
 2. also; moreover; too.

lī'kin', *n.* [Chinese, from *li*, the thousandth part of a tael, and *kin*, money.] in China, a provincial tax on merchandise in transit, collected at various barriers.

līk'ing, *n.* 1. fondness; affection.
 2. inclination; desire; pleasure; predilection; as, not to my *liking.*
 3. bodily health or appearance. [Obs.]
 on liking; on approval; on trial. [Dial.]

līk'ing, *a.* good-looking; pleasing. [Obs.]

lī'lăç, *a.* of a pale-purple color.

lī'lăç, *n.* [Sp., from Ar. *lūlāk*; Per. *lilaj* or *lilanj*, the lilac, the indigo plant, from *nīlah*, or *nīl*, the indigo plant, from Sans. *nīla*, dark-blue indigo.]
 1. any of a group of hardy shrubs or trees of the genus *Syringa* with large clusters of tiny, fragrant flowers ranging in color from white, through many shades of lavender, to deep crimson.
 2. the flower or flower cluster of this plant.
 3. the pale-purple color often characteristic of this flower.

lil'ȧ·cine, *n.* [*lilac* and *-ine.*] syringin.

Lil·i·ā'cē·ae, *n.pl.* [from L. *lilium*, a lily, and *-aceæ.*] a family of endogens, including many flowers and several vegetable species, as the true lilies, tulips, hyacinths, aloes, onions, leeks, etc.

lil·i·ā'ceous, *a.* [LL. *liliaceus*, pertaining to the lily, from L. *lilium*, a lily.]
 1. of, characteristic of, or like a lily.
 2. of or characteristic of the *Liliaceæ.*

lil'i·ăl, *a.* resembling lilies. [Obs.]

lil'ied, *a.* 1. having many lilies; decorated or covered with lilies.
 2. like a lily; fair.

lil'i·fọrm, *a.* [L. *lilium*, lily, and *forma*, form.] shaped like a lily.

Lil'ith, *n.* [Heb. *līlīth*; Assyr.-Bab. *lilītu*, lit., of the night.]
 1. in early Semitic folklore, a female demon or vampire believed to live in ruins and other desolate places.
 2. in medieval Jewish folklore, the first wife of Adam, before the creation of Eve.
 3. in medieval folklore, a witch believed to menace little children.

Lil'i·um, *n.* [L., a lily.] a genus of the *Liliaceæ* including the true lilies.

lill, *v.i.* to loll. [Obs.]

lill, *n.* 1. one of the holes of a wind instrument. [Scot.]
 2. a little pin.

lil''li·bul·lē'rō, *n.* 1. part of the refrain of a political song popular during the revolution of 1688 in England, ridiculing the Irish Catholics.
 2. this song.

Lil'li·put, *n.* in Swift's *Gulliver's Travels*, a land inhabited by tiny people about six inches tall.

Lil·li·pū'tiăn, *a.* 1. of or relating to Lilliput or to its people.
 2. tiny; very small; dwarfed; diminutive.

Lil·li·pū'tiăn, *n.* 1. an inhabitant of Lilliput.
 2. a person of very small size; a dwarf.

lil'ly-pil'ly, *n.* a large hardwood tree, *Eugenia smithii*, of Australia, having white flowers that are borne in terminal panicles: its bark is rich in tannin.

lilt, *v.t.* and *v.i.*; lilted, *pt., pp.*; lilting, *ppr.* [compare Norw. *lilla, lirla*, to sing in a high tone.] to speak, sing, or play with animation, gaiety, and a light, graceful rhythmic movement or swing.

lilt, *n.* 1. a gay song or tune with a light, swingy, and graceful rhythm.
 2. a light, swingy, and graceful rhythm or movement.

lil'y, *a.* resembling a lily, as in whiteness, delicacy, purity, etc.

lil'y, *n.*; *pl.* **lil'ieṣ,** [ME. *lilie*; AS. *lilie* or *lilige*; L. *lilium*; Gr. *leirion*, a lily.]

 1. any plant of the genus *Lilium*, grown from a bulb and having scaly bulbs, tall slender stems, alternate or somewhat whorled leaves, and erect or drooping trumpet-shaped flowers, white or colored.
 2. the flower or the bulb of any of these plants.
 3. any of various other plants whose flowers resemble lilies, as the calla lily, water lily, pond lily, etc.
 4. the flower of any of these plants.

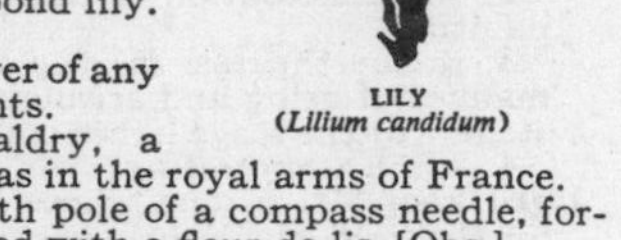

LILY (*Lilium candidum*)

 5. in heraldry, a fleur-de-lis, as in the royal arms of France.
 6. the north pole of a compass needle, formerly marked with a fleur-de-lis. [Obs.]

lil'y bee'tle, a small beetle, *Crioceris merdigera*, that infests the white lily.

lil'y daf'fō·dil, a daffodil.

lil'y en'çri·nīte, an encrinite or stone lily.

lil'y·hand''ed, *a.* having white, delicate hands.

lil'y hȳ'ȧ·cinth, a bulbous perennial of the genus *Scilla*, having blue flowers.

lil'y ī'ron (-ūrn), a harpoon with a barbed removable head; also, the head.

lil'y-liv''ẽred, *a.* white-livered; cowardly.

lil'y of the val'ley, *pl.* **lil'ieṣ of the val'ley,** a plant of the genus *Convallaria*, having two ovate lanceolate leaves and a raceme of small, pure white, very fragrant, bell-shaped flowers.

LILY OF THE VALLEY (*Convallaria majalis*)

lil'y pad, one of the large, flat, floating leaves of the water lily.

lil'y-whīte' (-hwīt'), *a.* white as a lily.

lil'y·wŏrt, *n.* any plant of the *Liliaceæ.*

Lī'mȧ bärk, the bark of a species of *Cinchona.*

Lī'mȧ bēan, [after *Lima*, Peru: from being native to tropical America.]
 1. a common variety of bean plant with creamy flowers and broad pods.
 2. the broad, flat, nutritious bean of this plant.

lī·mā'ceous, *a.* [L. *limax (-acis)*, a snail, slug.] of or like a slug; limacine.

lī·mac'i·fọrm, *a.* [L. *limax (-acis)*, a slug, and *forma*, form.] shaped like a slug.

Lī''mȧ·çī'nȧ, *n.* [L. *limax (-acis)*, a snail, slug, and *-ina.*]
 1. a genus of pteropods of the polar seas.
 2. [l–] a member of this genus.

lim'ȧ·cīne, *a.* [from L. *limax (-acis)*, a slug; and *-ine.*] of or like slugs or shell-less snails.

li·ma·çon' (lī-mȧ-soṅ'), *n.* [Fr., a snail, from L. *limax (-acis)*, a snail.] a unicursal curve of the fourth order investigated and named by Pascal.

lī·măn', *n.* [Russ.] a marsh at a river's mouth.

lī·mā'tion, *n.* [L. *limatus*, pp. of *limare*, to file, from *lima*, a file.] the act of filing or polishing. [Rare.]

lī′mȧ·tūre, *n.* [L. *limatura*, from *limare*, to file, from *lima*, a file.] filing; also, filings. [Rare.]

Lī′mȧ wood, same as *brazilwood*.

Lī′max, *n.* [L., a snail, slug.] a genus of naked gastropods; the slugs.

limb (lim), *n.* [with unhistoric -*b*, from ME. *lim*; AS. *lim*, a member of the body, a limb.]
1. an arm, leg, or wing.
2. a large branch of a tree.
3. any projecting part like an arm or leg or forming an outgrowth or extension from a larger body.
4. a person or thing regarded as a branch, part, agent, or representative; as, a policeman is a *limb* of the law.
5. a young scamp; an imp; a naughty child.
6. the part of a bow on either side of the handle or grip.
out on a limb; in a precarious or vulnerable position or situation. [Colloq.]

limb, *v.t.*; limbed, *pt.*, *pp.*; limbing, *ppr.* 1. to remove the limbs from; to dismember; as, to *limb* a chicken.
2. to put limbs on. [Rare.]

limb, *n.* [Fr. *limbe*; L. *limbus*, border, hem, edge.]
1. in astronomy, the border or outermost edge of a heavenly body.
2. the graduated edge of a quadrant.
3. in botany, (a) the border or upper spreading part of a monopetalous corolla, of a sepal, or of a petal; (b) a leaf blade or lamina.

lim′bat, *n.* in the island of Cyprus, a cool northwest wind.

lim′bāte, *a.* [LL. *limbatus*, edged, bordered, from L. *limbus*, edge, border.] bordered, as a flower when one color is surrounded by an edging of another.

lim·bā′tion, *n.* in zoology, a border.

lim′beç, lim′beck, *n.* an alembic; a still. [Obs.]

lim′beç, lim′beck, *v.t.* to strain or pass through a still. [Obs.]

limbed (limd), *a.* having (a specified number or kind of) limbs: usually in hyphenated compounds, as crooked-*limbed*.

lim′bẽr, *a.* [compare Ice. *limpa*, weakness.]
1. easily bent; flexible; pliant; not stiff; as, *limber* joints.
2. able to bend the body easily; supple; lithe.
Syn.—supple, pliable, pliant, flexible, limp, lithe.

lim′bẽr, *v.t.* to make pliable or limber.

lim′bẽr, *v.i.* to make oneself limber; as, the dancers were *limbering* up.

lim′bẽr, *n.* [prob. from Ice. *limar*, limbs, boughs, pl. of *lim*, foliage, from *limr*, a branch, limb.]
1. the two-wheeled, detachable front part of a gun carriage, usually supporting an ammunition chest.

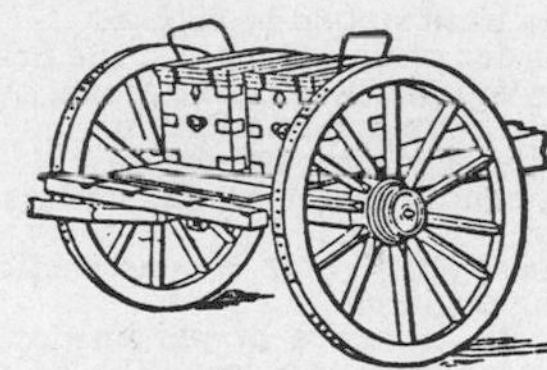

LIMBER OF GUN CARRIAGE

2. [*pl.*] shafts; thills. [Brit. Dial.]

lim′bẽr, *v.t.*; limbered, *pt.*, *pp.*; limbering, *ppr.* to attach the limber to (a gun carriage).

lim′bẽr, *v.i.* to attach the limber to a gun carriage, as in preparing to move off (often with *up*).

lim′bẽr bōard, a plank cover to keep the limbers of a vessel from becoming filled with dirt.

lim′bẽr box, a limber chest.

lim′bẽr chāin, a chain in a ship's limbers used to keep them clean: called also *limber clearer*.

lim′bẽr chest, the chest for ammunition on a limber.

lim′bẽr·ness, *n.* limber quality or state.

lim′bẽrs̹, *n. pl.* [prob. from Fr. *lumière*, a hole, aperture, lit., light.] in nautical usage, holes or channels made near a ship's keel or keelson to drain water into the pump well.

lim′bẽr strāke, the breadth of planking nearest to the keelson in a ship's hull.

lim′biç, *a.* of or constituting a limbus.

limb′less, *a.* lacking limbs.

lim′bō, *n.* [L. *limbo*, in phrase *in limbo*, in or on the border.]
1. in some Christian theologies, a region bordering on hell, the abode for the souls of good men who lived before the coming of Christ and the souls of unbaptized infants.
2. a prison or imprisonment.
3. a place or condition of neglect or oblivion to which unwanted things or persons are relegated.

lim′bous, *a.* bordered; having edges partly overlapping, as a suture.

Lim′bũrg·ẽr (or **Lim′bũrg**) **chees̹e,** see under *cheese*.

lim′bus, *n.* [L., edge, border.]
1. same as *limbo*.
2. in biology, a margin; a distinct edging or border.

līme, *v.t.*; limed, *pt.*, *pp.*; liming, *ppr.* [ME. *limen*; AS. *limian*, to smear with lime, from *lim*, lime.]
1. to apply lime to; to treat with lime; specifically, (a) to manure with lime; (b) to soak hides in limewater to loosen the hair; (c) to sprinkle with lime as a disinfectant; (d) to put lime into, to kill the fish; as, to *lime* a pond.
2. to smear with birdlime.
3. to catch with or as with birdlime.
4. to cement.

līme, *n.* [ME. *lim*; AS. *lim*.]
1. birdlime. [Rare.]
2. a white substance, calcium oxide, CaO, obtained by the action of heat on limestone, shells, and other material containing calcium carbonate, and used in making mortar and cement and in neutralizing acid soil: also called *quicklime, burnt lime, caustic lime.*

līme, *n.* [Fr.; Sp. *lima*; Ar. *limah*; Per. *līmūn*, lemon, citron.]
1. a small, lemon-shaped, greenish-yellow fruit with a juicy, sour pulp, rich in vitamin C.
2. the small, thorny, semitropical tree that it grows on, originally native to southern Asia but now widely cultivated.

līme, *a.* 1. made with or of limes.
2. having a flavor like that of limes.

līme, *n.* [from earlier *line*, from ME. *lind*, from AS. *lind*, linden.] the linden tree.

līme′āde, *n.* [*lime* and -*ade*.] a drink of lime juice, sugar, and water.

līme bũrn′ẽr, one who burns limestone to make lime.

Līme′house, *n.* a district in the East End of London, on the Thames, inhabited largely by sailors and dock workers.

līme jụ̈ice, the juice of the lime.

līme′kiln (*or* -kil), *n.* a kiln or furnace in which lime is made by burning limestone, shells, etc.

līme′līght (-līt), *n.* 1. a brilliant light created by the oxidation of lime and formerly used in theaters to throw an intense beam of light upon a particular part of the stage, a certain actor, etc.
2. the part of a stage where a limelight or spotlight is cast.
3. a prominent or conspicuous position before the public.

lī′men, *n.* [L. *limen*, *liminis*, threshold.] in psychology and physiology, the least degree of stimulation that produces a response: also called *threshold*.

līme pit, a limestone quarry; also, a limekiln.

lim′ẽr·ick, *n.* a nonsense poem, consisting of five anapestic lines, of which the first, second, and fifth are of three feet, and rhyme, while the third and fourth lines are of two feet, and rhyme: probably so called from the use in an Irish refrain of Limerick, a county and city in Ireland: the form was popularized by Edward Lear.

lī′mēs̹, *n.*; *pl.* **lim′i·tēs̹,** [L., a boundary, limit.]
1. originally, a Roman frontier fortification; as, the *Limes* Germanicus protected the southern German provinces.
2. [L–] a series of German defenses built to oppose the French Maginot line: also called *Siegfried line*.

līme′stōne, *n.* rock composed entirely or chiefly of carbonate of calcium, from which building stones, lime, etc. are made. When containing sand or silica, it is called *siliceous*; containing clay, it is *argillaceous*; and containing carbonate of magnesium, it is *dolomitic.* When crystallized by heat and pressure it becomes marble.

līme sul′fũr, a mixture made by boiling together sulfur, water, and lime: used as an insecticide and fungicide, especially in the form of a spray.

līme tree, 1. the linden or basswood tree.
2. the sour or black gum tree of the southern United States; tupelo.

līme twig, 1. a twig smeared with birdlime to snare birds.
2. any kind of snare.

līme′-twig, *v.t.*; lime-twigged, *pt.*, *pp.*; lime-twigging, *ppr.* to entangle; to snare. [Rare.]

līme′wash, *v.t.* to whitewash.

līme′wạ″tẽr, *n.* a saturated solution of lime in water, used to neutralize acids.

līm′ey, *n.* [from the *lime* juice formerly served to the crew on British ships to prevent scurvy.]
1. an English soldier or sailor. [Slang.]
2. any Englishman. [Slang.]
A generally patronizing or contemptuous term.

Lī·miç′ō·lae, *n.pl.* [L. *limus*, mud, slime, and *colere*, to inhabit.]
1. a group of wading birds, including most of those whose broods are able to run about as soon as hatched, as snipes, plovers, sandpipers, curlews, etc.
2. a group of aquatic worms having well-developed looped canals.

lī·miç′ō·līne, *a.* living on the shore; specifically, of or belonging to the *Limicolæ*.

lī·miç′ō·lous, *a.* living in mud.

lim′i·năl, *a.* [L. *limen* (-*inis*), the threshold.] of or at the limen or threshold; of the first stage.

līm′i·ness, *n.* the condition of being limy.

līm′ing, *n.* limewater, used in bleaching.

lim′it, *n.* [ME. *limite*, *lymyte*; OFr. *limite*; L. *limes* (-*itis*), a boundary line, limit, cross path between two fields, a border.]
1. the point, line, or edge where something ends or must end; the boundary or border beyond which something ceases to be or to be possible.
2. [*pl.*] bounds; boundary lines.
3. the greatest number or amount allowed; as, they soon caught the *limit* for one day of trout fishing.
4. anything having bounds; a period; a space; region; as, divided into five *limits*. [Archaic.]
5. in mathematics, that point at which the independent variable of a function moves through infinity; a determinate quantity or point to which a variable continuously approaches, and may come nearer than any given difference, but with which it can never coincide.
6. in poker, etc., the maximum amount by which a bet may be raised at one time.
7. a limb. [Obs.]
the limit; any person or thing regarded as almost or completely unbearable, remarkable, etc. [Colloq.]

lim′it, *v.t.*; limited, *pt.*, *pp.*; limiting, *ppr.* [ME. *limiten*; OFr. *limiter*; L. *limitare*, to bound, limit, define, from *limes* (-*itis*), a boundary, limit.] to bound; to set bounds to; to confine within bounds; to restrict; to restrain.

lim′it, *v.i.* to exercise any function, as begging, within a definite district; as, a *limiting* friar. [Obs.]

lim′it·ȧ·ble, *a.* that can be limited.

lim·i·tā′nē·ous, *a.* pertaining to bounds. [Obs.]

lim·i·tãr′i·ăn, *a.* having a tendency to limit.

lim·i·tãr′i·ăn, *n.* in theology, one who maintains that only a limited segment of mankind is to be saved.

lim′i·tãr·y, *a.* [L. *limitaris*, on the border, from *limes* (-*itis*), border, limit.]
1. limiting; marking or constituting a limit.
2. limited; kept within limits.

lim′i·tãr·y, *n.* 1. a limit or boundary; a boundary region. [Obs.]
2. a limiter, or begging friar. [Obs.]

lim′i·tāte, *a.* [L. *limitatus*, pp. of *limitare*, to bound, limit.] having a distinct boundary line.

lim·i·tā′tion, *n.* [L. *limitatio* (-*onis*), a bounding, limiting, from *limitatus*, pp. of *limitare*, to limit, bound, from *limes* (-*itis*), a limit.]
1. the act of restricting; the state of being restricted.
2. something that limits, as some lack in a person's make-up which restricts the scope of his activity or accomplishment; a qualification; a restriction.
3. in law, a period of time, fixed by statute, during which legal action can be brought, as for the settlement of a claim.

4. the district in which a limiter, or friar, was allowed to beg. [Obs.]

lim′i·tā·tive, *a.* limiting; restrictive.

lim′it·ed, *a.* 1. restricted; bounded; kept within fixed limits; narrow.

2. accommodating a restricted number of passengers or making a restricted number of stops, and often charging extra fare: said of a train, bus, etc.

3. exercising governmental powers under constitutional restrictions; not having absolute power; as, a *limited* monarch.

4. restricting the liability of each partner or shareholder to the amount of his actual investment in the business; as, a *limited* company.

lim′it·ed, *n.* a limited train, bus, etc.

lim′it·ed ē·di′tion, a special, finely bound edition of a book, of which only a predetermined number of copies are printed.

lim′it·ed·ly, *adv.* with limitation.

lim′it·ed·ness, *n.* the state of being limited.

lim′it·ẽr, *n.* 1. one who or that which limits or confines.

2. a friar licensed to beg within certain bounds, or whose duty was limited to a certain district. [Obs.]

lim′i·tēs̨, *n.* plural of *limes.*

lim′it·ing, *a.* in grammar, designating or of any of a class of adjectives that limit or restrict the words modified (e.g., *several, these, four,* etc.).

lim′i·tive, *a.* designed to limit. [Rare.]

lim′it·less, *a.* having no limits; unbounded, infinite.

lī·miv′ō·rous, *a.* [L. *limus,* mud, and *vorare,* to devour.] in zoology, eating mud for the organic matter contained in it.

lim′mȧ, *n.* [LL., from Gr. *leimma,* a remnant, remainder, from *leipein,* to leave.]

1. a semitone in Pythagorean music.

2. a time period in the rhythm of verse, equal to a mora, but having no corresponding syllable in the words; a pause.

lim′mẽr, *n.* a manrope beside a ladder. [Obs.]

lim′mẽr, *n.* a scoundrel; a jade. [Scot.]

limn (lim), *v.t.*; limned, *pt., pp.*; limning, *ppr.* [ME. *limnen,* contr. of *luminen,* for *enluminen*; OFr. *enluminer*; L. *illuminare,* to make light.]

1. to draw or paint; portray; delineate.

2. to illuminate, as manuscripts. [Obs.]

3. to portray in words; to describe.

limn, *v.i.* to paint, especially in water colors. [Obs.]

Lim′nae·ȧ, *n.* [Gr. *limnaios,* marshy, of or from a marsh, from *limnē,* a stagnant lake, a marsh.] a genus of pond snails common in inland waters.

lim′nẽr, *n.* [OFr. *enlumineur*; LL. *illuminator,* an illuminator, limner.]

1. an illuminator of books or parchments. [Archaic.]

2. one who paints or draws.

lim′ni·ad, *n.* [Gr. *limnē,* a pool, lake.] a water nymph; a Naiad. [Rare.]

limn′ing, *n.* the act or art of drawing or painting.

lim·nol′ō·ġy, *n.* [Gr. *limnē,* marsh, and *-ology.*] the scientific study of the biological, chemical, geographical, and physical features of fresh waters, especially lakes and ponds.

lim·noph′i·lous, *a.* [Gr. *limnē,* a pool, and *philos,* loving.] living in fresh-water ponds or marshes.

Lī·mōġes′ (-mōzh′), *n.* a fine chinaware o porcelain made in Limoges, France.

Lim′ō·nēne, *n.* [from Mod. L. *limonum* lemon; and *-ene.*] any of three isomeric terpenes, $C_{10}H_{16}$, present in many plant products such as lemon peel, orange oil, pine needles, peppermint, etc.

lī·mō′ni·ad, *n.* same as *limniad.*

lim′ō·nin, *n.* [Fr. *limon,* lemon, and *-in.*] a bitter, crystallizable matter found in the seeds of oranges, lemons, etc.

lī′mō·nīte, *n.* [Gr. *leimon,* meadow, and *-ite.*] an iron ore, $H_6Fe_4O_9$, found in earthy, concretionary, and fibrous forms. Its brownish-yellow streak distinguishes it from hematite.

lī·mō·nit′iç, *a.* of or like limonite.

lī′mōse, *a.* of or growing in mud. [Rare.]

lim·ōu·ṡine′, *n.* [Fr., lit., a hood: from the costume worn in *Limousin,* France.]

1. an automobile with a closed compartment seating three or more passengers: the top is extended forward over the driver's seat, which is open at the sides.

2. any large, luxurious sedan, usually with back and front seats separated by a glass partition.

limp, *v.i.*; limped (limpt), *pt., pp.*; limping, *ppr.* [from AS. *limpan,* to occur, to befall, to walk lamely.]

1. to walk with or as with a lame or partially disabled leg.

2. to move unevenly, jerkily, or laboriously.

limp, *n.* the act of limping; a halt or lameness in walking.

limp, *a.* 1. lacking or having lost starch or stiffness; wilted; flexible.

2. lacking firmness, energy, or vigor.

limp, *n.* a wooden or iron scraper to scrape ore from a sieve.

limp′ẽr, *n.* one who limps.

lim′pet, *n.* [ME. *lempet,* a limpet, from AS. *lempedu,* a lamprey.]

1. a marine gastropod having an open, conical shell not perforated at the apex: usually found adhering to intertidal rocks by means of its thick, fleshy foot.

2. any of various gastropods having a shell like that of the true limpets.

lim′pid, *a.* [Fr. *limpide*; L. *limpidus,* clear, bright.] characterized by clearness; clear; transparent; as, a *limpid* stream.

Syn.—transparent, lucid clear, crystal.

lim·pid′i·ty, *n.* [Fr. *limpidité*; LL. *limpiditas* (*-atis*), from L. *limpidus,* limpid.] the state of being limpid; limpidness.

lim′pid·ly, *adv.* in a limpid manner.

lim′pid·ness, *n.* the state or quality of being limpid; transparency; clearness.

lim′pin, *n.* a limpet. [Obs.]

limp′ing·ly, *adv.* in a limping or halting manner; lamely.

limp′kin, *n.* a courlan, *Aramus vociferus,* a bird found in the West Indies and Florida.

limp′ly, *adv.* in a limp manner.

limp′ness, *n.* the quality or condition of being limp.

limp′sy, *a.* limp; flabby; flimsy. [Dial.]

lī′mụ, *n.* [Hawaiian.] seaweed.

lim′ū·loid, *n.* a limuloid crab.

lim′ū·loid, *a.* pertaining to or characteristic of the genus *Limulus.*

Lim′ū·lus, *n.* [L. *limulus,* somewhat askance, dim. of *limus,* sidelong, askance.]

1. the genus of the king crabs, or horseshoe crabs.

2. [l–] a king crab.

līm′y, *a.*; *comp.* limier; *superl.* limiest, containing, resembling, or covered with lime; having the qualities of lime.

lin, *v.i.* to cease; to desist. [Dial.]

lin, linn, *n.* the linden.

lin, linn, *n.* [Gael. *linne,* a pool, pond.] a pool or collection of water, particularly one above or below a fall of water.

lin, linn, *n.* [AS. *hlynn,* a torrent.]

1. a cataract or waterfall.

2. a steep ravine.

lin′aç, *n.* [*lin*ear, and *ac*celerator.] in nuclear physics, a device that accelerates charged particles in a straight line at periodic intervals as they pass between metal tubes along the flight path.

Lī·nā′cē·ae, *n.pl.* same as *Lineæ.*

lī·nā′ceous, *a.* pertaining or belonging to the *Linaceæ.*

līn′āġe, līne′āġe, *n.* 1. in printing and advertising, the space occupied in a single column by a given number of lines of type, using agate type as a standard of measurement.

2. payment based on the number of lines produced by a writer.

3. the number of written or printed lines on a page.

4. alignment.

lī·nä′lō·ȧ, *n.* [Sp. *lináloe,* aloe.] the wood of a species of myrrh found in Mexico, from which an oil is derived for use in perfumery.

lin·al′o·ōl (lin-al′ō-ōl), *n.* [from *linaloa,* and *-ol.*] a terpene alcohol, $C_{10}H_{17}OH$, present in several essential oils.

lin′ȧ·ment, *n.* [L. *linamentum,* linen stuff, from *linum,* flax.] in surgery, lint; a tent for a wound. [Obs.]

Li·nā′ri·ȧ, *n.* [L. *linum,* flax, and *-aria.*] a genus of herbs of the family *Scrophularineæ,* comprising about 130 species.

lī′nȧ·rīte, *n.* [from *Linares,* a town in Spain, and *-ite.*] a sky-blue, hydrous sulfate of lead and copper, crystallizing in the monoclinic system.

linch, *n.* [ME. *lynch*; AS. *hlinc,* a ridge of land.] a ledge, projection, cliff, terrace, ridge, or bank; a pathway on a steep bank. [Brit. Dial.]

linch hoop, a ring on the spindle of a carriage axle, held in place by the linchpin.

linch′pin, *n.* [AS. *lynis,* the axletree, and *pinn,* pin.] a pin at the end of an axletree to prevent the wheel of a vehicle from sliding off.

Lin′cōln (-kun), *n.* a breed of sheep having long wool: originally from Lincoln, England.

Lin′çōln green, a bright-green cloth originally made in Lincoln, England: associated especially with Sherwood Forest.

Lin′cōln's Inn, an incorporated law society of London, which, with the Inner and Middle Temples and Gray's Inn, has the sole right to admit law students to the English bar.

linç′tus, *n.* same as *lincture.*

lind, *n.* the linden. [Obs.]

lin′dāne, *n.* [named after T. van der *Linden,* Du. chemist who first isolated the isomer, and *-ane.*] an isomeric form of benzene hexachloride, $C_6H_6Cl_6$, widely used as an insecticide.

lin′den, *n.* [ME. *linden*; AS. *linden,* of the linden, from *lind,* the lind, linden.] any of a group of trees with dense, heart-shaped leaves and fragrant, yellowish flowers, widely cultivated throughout the North Temperate Zone: the American variety is also called *basswood.*

lin′dō, *n.* [Sp., Port., and It. *lindo,* beautiful, fine, elegant.] a bright-colored tanager of the genus *Euphonia.*

līne, *n.* [ME. *lin*; AS. *lin,* linen, flax, from L. *linum,* flax.]

1. linen. [Obs.]

2. the long and fine fiber of flax. [Obs.]

line, *v.t.*; lined, *pt., pp.*; lining, *ppr.* [ME. *linen,* to cover on the inside, prob. lit., to cover with linen, from *line*; AS. *lin,* linen.]

1. to cover on the inside; as, to *line* a garment with fur; to *line* a box with tin.

2. to put in the inside of; to stuff; as, to *line* a purse with money.

3. to be used as a lining in; as, canvas *lined* the trunk.

līne, *n.* [ME. *line,* merging AS. *line,* a cord, with OFr. *ligne* (both from L. *linea,* lit., linen thread, n. use of fem. of *lineus,* of flax, from *linum,* flax).]

1. (a) a cord, rope, wire, or string; (b) a long, fine, strong cord with a hook or hooks, used in fishing; (c) a cord, steel tape, etc. used in measuring or leveling; (d) [*often pl.*] a rein, especially when long.

2. (a) a wire or wires connecting stations in a telephone or telegraph system; (b) the whole system of such wires; (c) effective contact between stations; as, hold the *line,* please.

3. any wire, pipe, system of pipes or wires, etc. conducting fluid, electricity, etc.

4. a very thin threadlike mark; specifically, (a) a long, thin mark made by a pencil, pen, chalk, etc.; (b) a similar mark cut in a hard surface; (c) a thin crease in the palm or on the face.

5. a mark made on the ground in certain sports; specifically, (a) one of the straight, narrow marks dividing a football field, tennis court, etc.; (b) a mark indicating a starting point or a limit not to be crossed.

6. a border or boundary; as, the State *line.*

7. a division between conditions, qualities, classes, etc.; limit; demarcation.

8. outline; contour; lineament.

9. [*pl.*] conditions or circumstances of life; one's fate.

10. [*usually pl.*] a plan of construction; plan of making or doing.

11. a row or series of persons or things, especially when more or less alike, as in shape, size, etc.; specifically, (a) a row of written or printed characters extending across or part way across a page; (b) a straight row of persons waiting in turn to buy something, enter a room, etc.

12. agreement; conformity; harmony; as, he brought the troublemakers into *line.*

13. a connected series of persons or things following each other in time or place; succession; as, a *line* of Democratic presidents.

14. lineage.

15. (a) a transportation system or service consisting of regular trips by buses, ships, etc. between two or more points; (b) a company operating such a system; (c) one branch or division of such a system; as, the main *line* of a railroad; (d) a single track of a railroad.

16. the course or direction anything moving takes; path; as, the *line* of fire.

17. a course of conduct, action, explanation, etc.; as, the *line* of an argument.

18. a person's trade or occupation, or the things he deals in; as, his *line* is leather goods.

19. a stock of goods of a particular type

considered with reference to quality, quantity, variety, etc.
20. the field of one's special knowledge, interest, or ability; as, debating was right in his *line*.
21. a short letter, note, or card; as, drop me a *line* when you get to Portland.
22. (a) a single metrical unit consisting of a specified number of feet; verse of poetry; (b) a verse which in its form is typical of a poet or style; as, Marlowe's mighty *line*.
23. [*pl.*] all the speeches in a play; especially, all the speeches of any one character in a play.
24. 1/12 of an inch.
25. in bridge, the horizontal line dividing trick scores from honor scores; as, a game is based only on the score below the *line*.
26. in football, (a) the players arranged in a row even with the ball at the start of each play, or those directly opposite them; centers, guards, tackles, ends; (b) the line of scrimmage.
27. in geography, an imaginary circle or arc used for convenience of division; as, the date *line*.
28. in mathematics, (a) the path of a moving point, thought of as having length but not breadth, whether straight or curved; (b) such a path when considered perfectly straight.
29. in military usage, (a) a formation of ships, troops, etc. in which elements are abreast of each other: distinguished from *column* in which elements are one behind the other; (b) the area or position in closest contact with the enemy during combat; (c) the troops in this area; (d) those troops that do the actual fighting on the ground; combatant troops: sometimes distinguished from *staff*; (e) the officers in immediate command of fighting ships.
30. in music, any of the long parallel marks forming the staff.
all along the line; (a) everywhere; (b) at every turn of events.
hard lines; misfortune; bad luck. [Slang.]
in line; (a) in a straight row; in alignment; (b) in harmony or agreement; (c) in readiness; prepared.
in line of duty; in the performance of authorized or prescribed duty: a military term used with reference to sickness, injury, or death of someone resulting from no fault or neglect of his.
on a line; in the same plane; level.
out of line; (a) not in a straight line; not in alignment; (b) not in agreement or conformity.
to bring into line; to bring or cause to come into a straight row or into conformity; to bring into alignment.
to come into line; (a) to become part of a straight row; to become straight; (b) [Colloq.] to correspond; agree; harmonize; (c) [Colloq.] to behave properly.
to draw the (or *a*) *line*; to set a limit.
to get a line on; to find out about. [Colloq.]
to hit the line; (a) in football, to try to carry the ball through the opposing line; (b) to try boldly or firmly to do something.
to hold the line; to stand firm; not permit a breakthrough or retreat: often used figuratively.
to read between the lines; to discover a hidden meaning or purpose in something written, said, or done.
to toe the line; to do exactly what has been commanded.

līne, *v.t.* [Fr. *ligner*; L. *lineare*, to fasten to a straight line (LL., also, to draw lines upon), from *linea*, a line.]
1. to draw lines upon; to mark with lines or threadlike strokes; as, to *line* a writing tablet.
2. to arrange, as a body of soldiers, so that they form an even line: usually with *up*.
3. to form a line along; as, great elms *line* the streets.
4. to place objects along the edge of: as, to *line* the walk with flowers.
to line bees; to track wild bees to their nests by following their line of flight.
to line out; in baseball, to get (a hit) by batting the ball in a straight, nearly horizontal line.
to line up; (a) to bring into a line; (b) to organize effectively, secure a pledge of support from, etc.

līne, *v.i.* to form a line: usually with *up*.
to line out; in baseball, to be put out by batting a liner straight to a fielder.
to line up; (a) to form a line; (b) to take a position (*against* a competitor or rival).

Lin'ē·ae, *n.pl.* [L. *linum*, flax, and *-eæ*.] an order of exogens, the flax family, characterized by regular flowers with imbricate glandular sepals. It comprises 15 genera and about 235 species, which are widely distributed.

lin'ē·ăge, *n.* [ME. *linage*; OFr. *lignage*, descent, lineage, from *ligne*; L. *linea*, a line.]
1. descent in a line from an ancestor.
2. ancestry; family.

līne'ăge, *n.* same as *linage.*

lin'ē·ăl, *a.* [L. *linealis*, from *linea*, line.]
1. composed of lines; delineated; as, *lineal* designs.
2. in a direct line from an ancestor; hereditary: opposed to *collateral*; as, *lineal* descent.
3. in the direction of a line; pertaining to a line; linear; as, *lineal* measure: in this sense usually *linear*.

lin·ē·al'i·ty, *n.* the state of being lineal.

lin'ē·ăl·ly, *adv.* in a direct line; in a lineal manner.

lin'ē·ȧ·ment, *n.* [L. *lineamentum*, line, feature, lineament, from *lineare*, to fashion to a straight line, from *linea*, a line.]
1. [*usually in pl.*] any of the features of the face, especially with regard to its outline.
2. [*usually in pl.*] a distinctive feature or characteristic.

lin'ē·ăr, *a.* [L. *linearis*, pertaining to or consisting of lines, linear, from *linea*, a line.]
1. of a line or lines.
2. made of or using lines; as, *linear* design.
3. having length only; extended in a line.
4. in botany, narrow and uniform in width, as the leaves of certain willows.
linear differential equation; an equation of the first degree formed by equating to zero an expression understood to be a linear function of the dependent variable and its derivatives.
linear equation; an algebraic equation whose variable quantity or quantities are in the first power only. Example: $a + b - 5 = 0$.
linear measure; (a) measurement of length, as distinguished from volume, weight, etc.; (b) a system of measuring length; especially, the system in which 12 inches = 1 foot, 3 feet = 1 yard, 5½ yards = 1 rod, 40 rods = 1 furlong, and 8 furlongs (1,760 yards or 5,280 feet) = 1 mile.
linear perspective; perspective which regards only the positions, magnitudes, and forms of the objects delineated: distinguished from *aerial perspective* (which see under *perspective*).
linear problem; a problem that may be solved geometrically by the intersection of two right lines, or algebraically by an equation of the first degree.
linear programming; in mathematics, a procedure for minimizing or maximizing a linear function of many variables, subject to a finite number of linear restrictions on these variables.
linear transformation; in algebra, a change of variables in which a function of the first degree takes the place of each variable changed.

lin'ē·ăr·ȧ·cūte', *a.* [L. *linearis*, linear, and *acutus*, acute.] in botany, acuminate.

Lin'ē·ăr B, a Minoan pictographic script inscribed on clay tablets discovered on Crete, found to be an archaic form of Greek.

lin"ē·ăr-en'sāte, *a.* [L. *linearis*, linear, and *ensis*, sword.] in botany, having the form of a long, narrow sword.

lin·ē·ar'i·ty, *n.* the state of being linear.

lin'ē·ăr·ly, *adv.* in a linear manner; with lines.

lin'ē·ă·ry, *a.* linear. [Obs.]

lin'ē·āte, *a.* [L. *lineatus*, pp. of *lineare*, to fashion to a straight line, from *linea*, a line.] marked with lines; streaked; as, a *lineate* leaf.

lin'ē·ā·ted, *a.* lineate.

lin·ē·ā'tion, *n.* [L. *lineatio*, from *lineatus*, pp. of *lineare*, to fashion to a line.]
1. (a) a marking with lines; (b) a system or series of lines.
2. a dividing into lines.

lin'ē·ȧ·tūre, *n.* anything that has outline. [Obs.]

līne'back"ẽr, *n.* in football, any of the players stationed directly behind the line in a defensive formation.

līne'-breed, *v.t.* to use line breeding among.

līne breed'ing, the producing of desired characteristics in animals by inbreeding through several successive generations.

līne çonçh, a large gastropod, *Fasciolaria distans*, of Florida and the West Indies, marked by several black revolving lines.

līne en·grāv'ing, in art, (a) the process of engraving designs on metal by incised lines; (b) a plate engraved by such a process; (c) a print produced from such a plate.

līne'măn, *n.*; *pl.* **līne'men**, 1. a man who carries a surveying line, tape, or chain.
2. a man whose work is setting up and repairing telephone wires or other lines conducting electricity.
3. a man whose work is inspecting railroad tracks.
4. in football, one of the players in the line; center, tackle, guard, or end: distinguished from a *back*.

lin'en, *n.* [ME. *linen*, *lynen*; AS. *linen*, made of flax, linen, from *lin*, flax.]
1. yarn, thread, or cloth made of flax.
2. articles made of linen, as tablecloths and sheets.
3. similar articles made of cotton or other cloth like linen, as shirts, underwear, etc.
4. fine stationery originally manufactured from linen rags.

lin'en, *a.* 1. made of flax fiber; as, *linen* thread.
2. made of linen.
3. resembling linen cloth; white; pale. [Rare.]

lin'en çloș'et, a closet for sheets, towels, table linen, etc.

lin'en drā'pẽr, one who deals in linen or goods made from linen.

lin'en·ẽr, *n.* a linen draper. [Obs.]

lin'en pat'tẽrn, a linen scroll.

lin'en sçrōll, in architecture, an ornament employed to fill panels: so called from its resemblance to the convolutions of a folded napkin: also called *linen fold.*

LINEN SCROLL

līne of bat'tle, troops or ships in a position ready to fight.

līne of dē·fense', any natural or artificial barrier that can be employed for defense against invasion or attack.

līne of dip, in geology, the line of greatest inclination of a stratum to the horizon.

līne of fīre, 1. the course of a bullet, shell, etc. that has been, or is to be, fired.
2. a position open to attack of any kind.

līne of fọrce, a line in a field of electrical or magnetic force that shows the direction taken by the force at any point.

līne of märch, the direction in which a body of troops marches.

līne of sīght, 1. an imaginary straight line joining the center of the eye of the observer with the object viewed: also *line of vision.*
2. in radio and television, the straight path from a transmitting antenna to the horizon, representing the normal range of high-frequency wave propagation.

lin'ē·ō·lāte, *a.* [LL. *lineola*, dim. of L. *linea*, a line, and *-ate*.] in zoology and botany, marked with minute, usually parallel, lines.

lin'ē·ō·lā·ted, *a.* lineolate.

lin"ē·ō·lin'ē·ăr, *a.* [L. *linea*, a line, and *linearis*, linear.] in mathematics, designating a function which is linear with respect to each of two different variables or sets of variables.

līn'ẽr, *n.* 1. one who lines; a person or thing that traces lines or stripes.
2. same as *ship of the line* under *ship*.
3. (a) a vessel belonging to a steamship line, which makes voyages to and from certain ports, usually on scheduled time; (b) a passenger airplane in similarly regular service.
4. in baseball, a batted ball that travels in a nearly straight horizontal line. [Colloq.]

līn'ẽr, *n.* 1. a person who makes or attaches linings.
2. a lining or something which suggests a lining; as, a helmet *liner*.
3. in machinery, a thin piece inserted between parts to adjust them; a packing piece.

līneș'măn, *n.*; *pl.* **līneș'men**, 1. a lineman.
2. in football, an official who measures and records the gains or losses in ground and determines where the ball goes out of bounds.
3. in tennis, an official who watches one or more lines on the court and reports faults involving his line or lines.

līne'-up, līne'up, *n.* an arrangement of persons or things in or as in a line; specifically, (a) a group of suspected criminals lined up for inspection and identification by the police; (b) in football, baseball, etc., the list of a team's players arranged according to the positions they play, their order at bat, etc.

līne'y, *a.* same as *liny.*

ling, *n.* [ME. *lenge, leenge,* from AS. *lang,* long.]
1. a gadoid food fish, *Molva vulgaris,* inhabiting the seas of northern Europe and Greenland.
2. any of various other fishes, as the burbot.

ling, *n.* [ME.; ON. *lyng.*] common heather, *Calluna vulgaris.*

-ling, [ME. *-ling, -lyng;* AS. *-ling,* a suffix used with a diminutive force.] a suffix used with nouns to give generally a diminutive or depreciative force; as, gos*ling,* duck*ling,* hire*ling.*

-ling, [ME. *-linge, -linges;* AS. *-ling, -lang;* now usually replaced by *-long* in directional senses.] a suffix used to form adverbs meaning *direction, extent,* or *condition,* as in dark*ling.*

lin̄'gȧ, *n.* same as *lingam.*

lin̄'găm, *n.* [Sans.] in Hinduism, the phallic symbol worshiped as representative of the god Siva or of the productive power of nature.

ling'bĩrd, *n.* the meadow pipit, *Anthus pretensis.* [Brit. Dial.]

lin̄'gel, lin̄'gle, *n.* a shoe latchet or other leather thong. [Obs.]

lin'ġence, *n.* a tincture. [Obs.]

lin̄'gẽr, *v.i.;* lingered, *pt., pp.;* lingering, *ppr.* [ME. *lengen,* to tarry; AS. *lengan,* to prolong, put off, from *lang,* long.]
1. to continue to stay, especially through reluctance to leave; as, he *lingered* before the fire.
2. to continue to live or exist although very close to death or the end.
3. to be unnecessarily slow in doing something; to delay; loiter.
Syn.—tarry, loiter, lag, hesitate, saunter, delay.

lin̄'gẽr, *v.t.* to spend (time) lingeringly.

lin̄'gẽr·ẽr, *n.* one who lingers.

lin″ġe·rīe' (län'zhē-rē *or* lan″zhē-rē'), *n.* [Fr., from *linger,* a dealer in linen, from *linge,* L. *linum,* flax, linen.]
1. formerly, articles made of linen.
2. women's underwear of linen, silk, rayon, etc.

lin̄'gẽr·ing, *a.* 1. delaying; loitering.
2. drawing out in time; remaining long, protracted; as, a *lingering* disease.

lin̄'gẽr·ing·ly, *adv.* in a lingering manner; with delay; slowly; tediously.

lin̄'get, *n.* same as *lingot.*

ling'iṣm, *n.* [named after Peter H. *Ling,* a Swedish physician.] a Swedish gymnastic treatment for disease. [Rare.]

lin̄'gō, *n.; pl.* **lin̄'gōeṣ,** [L. *lingua,* tongue, language.] language; especially, a dialect, jargon, or special vocabulary that one is not familiar with; as, the *lingo* of medical men: a humorous or disparaging term.

lin̄'gŏt, *n.* [Fr. *l'ingot,* lit., the ingot.]
1. a mass of metal cast in a mold; an ingot.
2. a mold in which an ingot is cast.

-lings, same as *-ling* (adverbial suffix).

ling'thọrn, *n.* a starfish found in European waters, *Luidia fragilissima.*

lin̄'guȧ (-gwȧ), *n.; pl.* **lin̄'guae,** [L.] the tongue; also, the central lobe of the ligula of insects which has the functions of a tongue.
lingua franca; (a) a hybrid language of Italian, Spanish, French, Greek, Arabic, and Turkish elements, spoken in certain Mediterranean ports; (b) any hybrid language used for communication between different peoples, as pidgin English; (c) any mixture of dialects similarly used; as, the East Anglian *lingua franca.*

lin̄·guā'cious (-gwā'), *a.* talkative; loquacious. [Obs.]

lin̄·guȧ·den'tăl, *a.* and *n.* [L. *lingua,* tongue, and *dens, dentis,* tooth.] same as *dentilingual.*

lin̄'guăl, *a.* [L. *lingua,* the tongue.]
1. pertaining to the tongue; as, the *lingual* nerves.
2. pronounced chiefly by means of the tongue; as, a *lingual* consonant.
lingual ribbon; in zoology, the radula or odontophore.

lin̄'guăl, *n.* a sound, or a letter representing it, pronounced chiefly by means of the tongue, as *t* or *d.*

lin̄·gual'i·ty, *n.* the condition or quality of being lingual.

lin̄'guăl·ly, *adv.* in a lingual manner.

Lin̄·guat·ū·lī'dȧ, *n.pl.* [L. *linguatus,* tongued, from *lingua,* a tongue.] an order of parasitic vermiform arachnidans, found in the young state in the internal organs of various animals.

lin̄·gui·den'tăl, *a.* and *n.* same as *dentilingual.*

lin̄'gui·fọrm, *a.* [L. *lingua,* tongue, and *forma,* form.] having the form or shape of the tongue.

lin̄'guist, *n.* [L. *lingua,* the tongue.]
1. a person skilled in languages; polyglot.
2. a specialist in linguistics.

lin̄·guis'tiç, *a.* relating to language or linguistics.

lin̄·guis'ti·căl, *a.* linguistic.

lin̄·guis'ti·căl·ly, *adv.* with respect to language or linguistics.

lin̄·guis'tiç fọrm, any speech unit having meaning; base, word, phrase, affix, etc.

lin̄·guis'tiçs, *n.pl.* [*construed as sing.*] 1. the science of language, including phonology, morphology, syntax, and semantics: often *general linguistics:* usually subdivided into *descriptive, historical, comparative,* and *geographical linguistics.*
2. the study of the structure, development, etc. of a particular language and of its relationship to other languages; as, English *linguistics.*

lin̄·guis'tiç stock, 1. a parent language and all the languages and dialects derived from it.
2. all the native speakers of any of these languages or dialects.

lin̄'gū·lȧ, *n.; pl.* **lin̄'gū·lae,** [L., dim of *lingua,* tongue.]
1. in anatomy, a process or part shaped like a tongue.
2. in zoology, any brachiopod of the genus *Lingula* or family *Lingulidæ.*

lin̄'gū·lāte, *a.* [L. *lingulatus,* from *lingula,* dim. of *lingua,* tongue.] shaped like a tongue.

lin'i·ment, *n.* [Fr., from LL. *linimentum,* a soft ointment, from L. *linere,* to smear.] an oily, medicated liquid preparation intended for application to the skin, in cases of muscular affections, bruises, etc.

lī'nin, *n.* [L. *linum,* flax, and *-in.*]
1. the achromatic substance constituting the netlike structure that connects the granules of chromatin in the nucleus of a cell.
2. a white, bitter cathartic obtained from a variety of flax.

līn'ing, *n.* 1. the act of covering the inner surface of something.
2. the material used or suitable for this purpose.
3. the contents of something.
The *lining* of his coffers. —Shak.

lin̄k, *n.* a torch, especially one made of tow and pitch.

lin̄k, *n.* [ME. *linke,* from Anglo-N.]
1. any of the series of rings or loops making up a chain or chain armor.
2. (a) a section of something resembling a chain; as, a *link* of sausage; (b) a point or stage in a series of circumstances; as, a weak *link* in the evidence.
3. a cuff link.
4. anything serving to connect or tie; as, a *link* with the past.
5. one length in a surveyor's chain, equal to 7.92 inches.
6. in mechanics, a short connecting rod for transmitting power or motion.

lin̄k, *v.t.;* linked (lin̄kt), *pt., pp.;* linking, *ppr.* to unite or connect by or as if by a link or links; to unite by something intervening; to couple; to join.
Link towns to towns with avenues of oak. —Pope.

lin̄k, *v.i.* to be or become connected; to join.

lin̄k'āġe, *n.* 1. a linking or being linked.
2. a series or system of links; especially, a series of connecting rods for transmitting power or motion.
3. in biology, the tendence of some genes to remain together and act as a unit (*linkage group*) in inheritance, generally in the same chromosome, without segregation throughout maturation.
4. in electricity, the product of a magnetic flux by the number of turns in the coil surrounding it.

lin̄k block, in a steam engine, the movable sliding or die block in a slot link, to which the valve rod is connected.

lin̄k'boy, *n.* in the days before street lighting, a boy or man hired to carry a torch to light the way for people at night: also *linkman.*

lin̄k'ing vẽrb, a verb that functions chiefly as a connection between a subject and a predicate complement (e.g., *be, appear, seem, become,* etc.).

lin̄k'măn, *n.; pl.* **lin̄k'men,** a linkboy.

lin̄k mō'tion, motion communicated by links: applied especially to a system of gearing for working the valves of locomotive, marine, and similar engines by a slotted bar linked with the eccentric rods.

lin̄ks, *n.pl.* [AS. *hlinc,* hill, ridge.]
1. the crooks or windings of a river; also, the grounds lying along such windings; as, the *links* of the Forth. [Scot.]
2. a stretch of flat or slightly undulating ground on the seashore, often in part sandy and covered with bent grass, furze, etc. [Scot.]
3. the grounds laid out for playing golf; a golf course.

Link trāin'ẽr, [after Edward A. *Link* (1904–), Am. inventor.] an apparatus for training student airplane pilots under simulated conditions of flight: it consists of a hooded cockpit containing the necessary instruments, and is pneumatically operated on a grounded turntable.

lin̄k'wŏrk, *n.* 1. the system of rods, levers, and links connected with an engine slide valve.
2. anything made by joining together links, as a chain.

linn, *n.* see *lin.*

Lin·nae'ȧ, *n.* [after *Linnaeus,* a celebrated Swedish botanist.] a genus of plants of the family *Caprifoliaceæ,* containing but one species, *Linnæa borealis,* the twinflower.

Lin·nae'ăn, Lin·nē'ăn, *a.* of Linnaeus, the Swedish botanist; especially, designating or of his system of classifying plants and animals by using a double name, the first word naming the genus, and the second the species.

lin·nae'īte, *n.* [*linnæus* and *-ite.*] a sulfide of cobalt, Co_3S_4, crystallizing in the isometric system. It is of a pale steel-gray color.

lin'net, *n.* [OFr. *linette,* a linnet, from *lin,* flax; so called from its feeding on the seed of flax.] one of several species of singing birds of the family *Fringillidæ,* especially *Linota cannabina,* found in Europe, Asia, and Africa. In autumn and winter the plumage is brown; in the breeding season, the breast and head of both sexes become a crimson-red. It is popularly known, according to its sex and the season of the year, as the *red linnet, gray linnet,* or *brown linnet.*

lin″ō·lē'iç, *a.* [L. *linum,* flax, and *oleum,* oil, and *-ic.*] designating or of an unsaturated fatty acid, $C_{18}H_{32}O_2$, found as a glyceryl ester in linseed oil and other drying oils.

li·nō'lē·in, *n.* [*linoleic* and *-in.*] the glyceride of linoleic acid.

li·nō'lē·um, *n.* [L. *linum,* flax, and *oleum,* oil.]
1. linseed oil hardened by oxidizing.
2. a hard, smooth, washable floor covering made of a mixture of ground cork and oxidized linseed oil spread over a burlap or canvas backing.

līn'ō·tȳpe, *n.* [from *line of type.*] a typesetting machine that casts an entire line of type in one bar: it is operated from a keyboard like that of a typewriter: a trade-mark (*Linotype*).

līn'ō·tȳpe, *v.t.* and *v.i.;* linotyped, *pt., pp.;* linotyping, *ppr.* to set (matter) with a linotype.

līn'ō·tȳp·ẽr, *n.* a person who operates a linotype.

līn'ō·tȳp·ist, *n.* a linotyper.

li·nox'in, li·nox'yn, *n.* [*lin*oleic and *oxy*gen and *-in.*] a substance obtained in a resinous state from linseed oil through a process of oxidation.

lin'sang, *n.* [E. Ind.] an animal allied to the civet, found in Australia and the East Indies; *Prionodon gracilis* is the common linsang.

lin'seed, *n.* [ME. *linseede, linsede;* AS. *linsæd; lin,* flax, and *sæd,* seed.] the seed of flax.

lin'seed çāke, the solid mass or cake that remains when oil is extracted from flaxseed: called also *oil cake.*

lin'seed mēal, linseed cake pulverized.

lin'seed oil, oil obtained from flaxseed by pressure: it is used, because of its drying qualities, in making oil paints, printer's ink, etc.

lin'ṣey, *n.* linsey-woolsey.

lin'ṣey-wool'ṣey, *a.* [ME. *lynsy wolsye,* from *linsel,* linen, and *wolsye,* wool.] made of linen and wool; hence, of different and unsuitable parts; ill-sorted.

lin'ṣey-wool'ṣey, *n.; pl.* **lin'ṣey-wool'ṣeyṣ,** 1. stuff made of linen and wool or cotton and wool.
2. jargon; gibberish. [Obs.]

lin'stock, lint'stock, *n.* [D. *lontstok, lont,* a match used for firing a cannon, and *stok,* a stick.] a long pointed staff with a crotch or fork at one end to hold a lighted match, used in firing cannon.

lint, *n.* [ME. *lynete;* L. *linteum,* linen cloth, from *linum,* flax.]

1. scraped and softened linen formerly used as a dressing for wounds.
2. bits of thread, ravelings, or fluff from cloth or yarn.
3. the fiber surrounding the seed of unginned cotton.

lin'tel, *n.* [ME. *lintel, lyntell;* OFr. *lintel;* LL. *lintellus,* the headpiece of a door or window, the lintel, from L. *limes (-itis),* a border, boundary, limit.] in architecture, a horizontal piece of timber or stone over a door, window, or other opening, to support the superincumbent weight.

lin'tēr, *n.* 1. a machine for removing the short fibers which remain stuck to cotton seeds after ginning.
2. [*pl.*] these fibers, used in making cotton batting.

lin'tie (-ti), *n.* the linnet. [Scot.]

lint'seed, *n.* linseed.

lint'stock, *n.* see *linstock.*

lint'white, *n.* [AS. *linetwige,* a linnet, from *lin,* flax.] the European linnet.

lint'y, *a.; comp.* lintier; *superl.* lintiest, of, like, or covered with lint.

Li'num, *n.* [L., flax, hemp.] a genus of herbs of the order *Lineæ,* including *Linum usitatissimum,* the common flax plant.

lin'wood, *n.* the American linden tree.

līn'y, *a.; comp.* linier; *superl.* liniest, 1. like a line; thin.
2. marked with, or full of, lines or streaks: also spelled *liney.*

lī"ō·my·ō'mȧ, *n.* [Gr. *leios,* smooth, and *mys,* a muscle, and *-oma.*] a tumor composed of unstriated or smooth muscular tissue.

lī'ŏn, *n.* [ME. *lion, lioun;* OFr. *lion;* L. *leo, leonis;* Gr. *leōn, leontos,* a lion.]
1. a large, powerful mammal of the cat family, found in Africa and southwest Asia, with a tawny coat, a tufted tail, and, in the adult male, a shaggy mane: in folklore and fable the lion is considered king of the beasts; it is also the symbol of Great Britain.
2. a person of great courage or strength.
3. a person who arouses great interest and is invited to many social affairs; celebrity.
4. [L–] (a) the constellation Leo; (b) the fifth sign of the zodiac.
lion's share; the whole or an unreasonably large share of anything.
to put one's head into the lion's mouth; to put oneself into a position of great danger.

lī'ŏn ȧnt, the ant lion.

lī'ŏnced, lē'ŏnced (-ŏnst), *a.* in heraldry, adorned with lions' heads, as a cross the ends of which terminate in lions' heads.

lī'ŏn·cel, lī'ŏn·celle, *n.* [OFr. *lioncel,* dim. of *lion,* a lion.] in heraldry, a young lion used as a bearing in a coat of arms.

lī'ō·nel, *n.* [OFr. *lionel,* dim. of **lion,** a lion.]
1. a lion's whelp; a young lion.
2. in heraldry, a lioncel.

lī'ŏn·ess, *n.* [OFr. *lionnesse,* f. of **lion,** a lion.] a female lion.

lī'on·et, *n.* a young or small lion.

lī'ŏn·heärt, *n.* one who has great courage.

lī'ŏn·heärt·ed, *a.* having great courage; brave and magnanimous.

lī'ŏn·iṣm, *n.* the treating of a person as a celebrity.

lī"ŏn·i·zā'tion, *n.* a lionizing or being lionized.

lī'ŏn·īze, *v.t.;* lionized, *pt., pp.;* lionizing, *ppr.*
1. to treat as a celebrity.
2. to visit the interesting sights of (a place). [Now Rare.]

lī'ŏn·īze, *v.i.* to visit the objects of interest or curiosity of a place. [Rare.]

lī'ŏn·līke, *a.* like a lion in strength or courage.

lī'ŏn liz'ărd, a lizard, the basilisk.

lī'ŏn·ly, *a.* like a lion; fierce. [Rare.]

lī'ŏn mŏñ'key, a South American long-maned tamarin.

lī'ŏn's-ēar, *n.* 1. any labiate plant of the genus *Leonotis.*
2. any one of various composite plants of South America, of the genera *Culcitium* and *Espeletia.*

lī'ŏn's-foot, *n.* 1. either of two composite plants, *Prenanthes alba* or *Prenanthes serpentaria,* of the United States.
2. the lady's-mantle, *Alchemilla vulgaris;* also, the edelweiss, *Leontopodium alpinum.*

lī'ŏn·ship, *n.* the state of being a lion.

lī'ŏn's-lēaf, *n.* a plant of the genus *Leontice;* especially, *Leontice leontopetalum* of Europe.

lī'ŏn's-mouth, *n.* the snapdragon, *Antirrhinum majus.*

lī'ŏn's-tāil, *n.* any labiate plant of the genus *Leonurus,* as *Leonurus cardiaca,* the motherwort.

lī'ŏn's-tooth, *n.; pl.* **lī'ŏn's-teeth,** a composite plant of the genus *Leontodon;* the dandelion.

lī'ŏn's-tūr"nip, *n.* the tuberous root of the lion's-leaf.

lī·ot'ri·chous, leī·ot'ri·chous, *a.* [Gr. *leios,* smooth, and *thrix, trichos,* hair.] in anthropology, having smooth hair.

lip, *n.* [ME. *lip, lyp;* AS. *lippa, lippe,* lip.]
1. either of the two fleshy folds, normally pink or reddish in color, forming the edges of the mouth in man and many animals. In man the lips are important in speech; hence, the lips, by a figure, denote the mouth, or all the organs of speech, and sometimes speech itself.
2. anything resembling a lip; the edge or border of anything; specifically, (a) the edge of a wound; (b) the projecting rim of a pitcher, cup, etc.
3. in botany, (a) either of the two opposite divisions of a labiate corolla; (b) the lower petal of an orchid.
4. in zoology, any part or organ resembling a lip.
5. the cutting edge of any of certain tools.
6. abusive or impertinent talk. [Slang.]
7. the mouthpiece of a wind instrument.
8. the position of the lips in playing a wind instrument.
to bite one's lip; to keep back one's anger, annoyance, etc.
to hang on the lips of; to listen to with close attention.
to keep a stiff upper lip; to fail to become frightened or discouraged under difficulties. [Colloq.]
to smack one's lips; to express great satisfaction in anticipating or remembering something pleasant.

lip, *v.t.;* lipped (lipt), *pt., pp.;* lipping, *ppr.* 1. to touch with the lips; specifically, (a) to kiss; (b) to place the lips in the proper position for playing (a wind instrument).
2. to speak. [Rare.]
3. to clip; to trim. [Obs.]
4. in golf, to hit the ball just to the edge of (the cup).

lip, *v.i.* to shape one's lips to the mouthpiece of a wind instrument.

lip, *a.* 1. merely spoken or superficial; not genuine, sincere, or heartfelt; as, *lip* service.
2. formed with a lip or the lips; labial; as, a *lip* consonant.

lip-, see *lipo-.*

lī·pae'mi·ȧ, *n.* [Gr. *lipos,* fat, and *haima,* blood.] the presence of fat globules in the blood.

Lī·päns', *n.pl.; sing.* **Lī·pän',** a tribe of North American Indians originally inhabiting the region of the Rio Grande, Texas.

li·pär'i·ăn, *n.* any of the gypsy moths.

Lip'ȧ·ris, *n.* [Gr. *liparos,* oily, shining, greasy, from *lipos,* fat.]
1. in botany, a genus of orchids, both terrestrial and epiphytic, comprising about 120 species, found in warm regions.
2. a genus of fishes; the suckers or sea snails.

lip'ȧ·rīte, *n.* [named after the *Lipari* Islands in the Mediterranean.] rhyolite.

lip'ȧ·rō·cēle, *n.* [Gr. *liparos,* oily, and *kēlē,* a tumor.] same as *lipoma.*

lip'ȧ·roid, *a.* [from Gr. *liparos,* oily, from *lipos,* fat; and *-oid.*] fatty; like fat.

lip'āse (*or* lī'pās), *n.* [Gr. *lipos,* fat.] an enzyme found in the pancreas, liver, stomach, and other organs of digestion: it changes fats into fatty acids and glycerin.

lip cŏm'fŏrt, consolation given by utterance of words only.

lip cŏm'fŏrt·ēr, one who consoles with empty words.

lip dē·vō'tion, prayers uttered by the lips without feeling.

lip fērn, a fern of the genus *Cheilanthes,* having a liplike indusium.

lip'-good, *a.* good in assertion only.

li·phae'mi·ȧ, *n.* [Gr. *lipein,* or *leipein,* to leave, and *haima,* blood.] an impoverished condition of the blood; deficiency of blood: also spelled *leiphaemia.*

lip head, a head of a bolt projecting on one side only.

lip'hook, *n.* 1. in angling, the upper one of a number of hooks attached to a line, which is passed through the lips of a fish used as live bait.
2. a sort of grapnel used for towing a dead whale.

lip'id, lip'īde, *n.* any of a group of organic compounds consisting of the fats and other substances of similar properties: they are insoluble in water, soluble in fat solvents and alcohol, and greasy to the touch: also *lipoid.*

lip·id'iç, *a.* relating to or containing a lipide or lipides.

lip lā'bŏr, action of the lips without feeling; words without sentiment.

lip lañ'guȧġe, oral or articulate language, as distinguished from that of signs or the fingers.

lip'less, *a.* having no lips.

lip'let, *n.* a little lip.

lip'ō-, [from Gr. *lipos,* fat.] a combining form meaning *of* or *like fat, fatty,* as in *lipolysis:* also, before a vowel, *lip-.*

lip'ō-, [from Gr. *leipein,* pres., *lipein,* aor., to leave, lack, be wanting.] a combining form meaning *lacking, without,* as in *Lipobranchia.*

Lip·ō·brā'chi·ȧ, *n.pl.* [*lipo-* (without), and L. *brachium,* arm.] a group of echinoderms having no arms, as the holothurians.

lip·ō·brā'çhi·āte, *a.* without arms or rays; specifically, pertaining to the *Lipobrachia.*

Lip·ō·brañ'çhi·ȧ, *n.pl.* [*lipo-,* and Gr. *branchia,* gills.] a division of arachnidan arthropods comprising the weasel spiders, false scorpions harvestmen, and mites.

lip·ō·brañ'çhi·āte, *a.* pertaining to the *Lipobranchia.*

Lip·ō·ceph'ȧ·lȧ, *n.pl.* the *Lamellibranchia,* or bivalve mollusks.

lip·ō·ceph'ȧ·lous, *a.* pertaining to the *Lipocephala;* headless: said of bivalve mollusks.

lip'ō·çhrōme, *n.* [Gr. *lipos,* fat, and *chroma,* pigment.] any of a special group of pigments found in animal fat or fat solvents; specifically, the coloring factors in butter, fat, egg yolk, etc.

lip"ō·fī·brō'mȧ, *n.* [Gr. *lipos,* fat, and L. *fibra,* fiber, and *-oma.*] a lipoma, or fatty tumor, containing fibrous tissue.

lip"ō·gas·trō'sis, *n.* [*lipo-,* and Gr. *gaster, gastros,* stomach, and *-osis.*] absence of a stomach; in sponges, absence of the paragaster.

lip"ō·gas·trot'iç, *a.* without a stomach; in sponges, characterized by lipogastrosis.

lip·ō·ġen'e·sis, *n.* [Gr. *lipos,* fat, and *genesis,* generation.] the formation of fat.

li·poġ'e·nous, *a.* generating or tending to generate fat.

lip'ō·gram, *n.* [*lipo-,* and Gr. *gramma,* a letter.] a writing that omits or dispenses with all words containing a particular letter of the alphabet, as the Odyssey of Tryphiodorus, in which there was no *a* in Book I., no *b* in Book II., etc.

lip"ō·gram·mat'iç, *a.* [Gr. *lipogrammatos,* or *leipogrammatos,* having a letter omitted; *leipein, lipein,* to leave, omit, and gramma, a letter.] of or pertaining to lipograms; of the nature of a lipogram; as, *lipogrammatic* writings.

lip·ō·gram'mȧ·tiṣm, *n.* the art or practice of writing lipograms.

lip·ō·gram'mȧ·tist, *n.* a writer of lipograms.

lip'oid, *n.* [Gr. *lipos,* fat, and *eidos,* form.] same as *lipide.*

lip'oid, *a.* fatty; resembling fat.

li·pol'y·sis, *n.* [Mod. L.; *lipo-,* and *-lysis.*] the decomposition of fat, as during digestion.

lip·ō·lyt'iç, *a.* [from *lipolysis.*] that can decompose fats.

li·pō'mȧ, *n.* [Gr. *lipos,* fat, and *-oma.*] a fatty tumor.

li·pō·mȧ·tō'sis, *n.* [*lipoma (t-),* and *-osis.*] in pathology, a general deposition of fat; obesity; fatty degeneration.

li·pom'ȧ·tous, *a.* of the nature of a lipoma.

lip"ō·myx·ō'mȧ, *n.; pl.* **lip"ō·myx·ō'mȧ·tȧ,** [Gr. *lipos,* fat, and *myxa,* phlegm, mucus, and *-oma.*] in pathology, a myxoma combined with fatty tissue.

lip'ō·pod, *a.* pertaining to the *Lipopoda.*

lip'ō·pod, *n.* any of the *Lipopoda.*

Li·pop'ō·dȧ, *n.pl.* [*lipo-,* and Gr. *pous, podos,* foot.] a division of rotifers having no footlike appendages, including the three orders, *Ploima, Bdelligrada,* and *Rhizota.*

lip·ō·prō'tēin, *n.* any of a group of proteins combined with a lipid, found in blood plasma, egg yolk, brain tissue, etc.

Lī·pos'tō·mȧ, *n.pl.* same as *Lipostomata.*

Lī·pō·stō'mȧ·tȧ, *n.pl.* [*lipo-,* and Gr. *stoma (-atos),* mouth.] a group of corticate protozoans having no mouth; the sporozoans.

lip·ō·stom'ȧ·tous, *a.* pertaining to the *Lipostomata;* mouthless.

lip·ō·stō·mō'sis, *n.* absence of a mouth; in sponges, absence of an osculum.

lip·ō·stō·mot′iç, *a.* lacking a mouth; in sponges, lacking an osculum.

lī·pos′tō·mous, *a.* lipostomatous.

lī·pos′tō·my, *n.* [*lipo-*, and Gr. *stoma*, mouth.] imperfect development of the mouth.

lī·pō·thym′i·ȧ, *n.* same as *lipothymy.*

lī·pō·thym′iç, *a.* lipothymous.

lī·poth′y·mous, *a.* [Gr. *lipothymos*, fainting; *leipein*, *lipein*, to leave, and *thymos*, soul, life.] given to swooning; fainting.

lī·poth′y·my, *n.* in pathology, faintness; syncope.

lip′ō·tȳpe, *n.* [*lipo-*, and Gr. *typos*, an impression, type.] a type of animal life the absence of which is characteristic of a particular district or region.

Lip·ō·typh′lȧ, *n.pl.* [*lipo-*, and Gr. *typhlos*, blind.] a division of *Insectivora* lacking a caecum.

lip·ō·typ′iç, *a.* [*lipo-*, and Gr. *typos*, impression, type.] pertaining to a lipotype.

lī·pox′e·nous, *a.* [*lipo-*, and Gr. *xenos*, host, and *-ous.*] designating certain parasitic fungi which desert their host and complete their development from the reserve previously taken from it.

lī·pox′e·ny, *n.* in botany, the abandoning of its host by a parasitic plant.

lipped (lipt), *a.* 1. having a lip or lips: often in compounds, as tight-*lipped.*

2. having a spoutlike projection in the rim: said of a pitcher, cup, etc.

3. in botany and zoology, labiate.

lip′pẽr, *n.* a thin, oblong-shaped piece of blubber for wiping up refuse from the deck of a whaler.

lip′pẽr, *n.* [North Eng. and Scot.; prob. from base of *lap* (of waves).]

1. a gentle ruffling movement of the surface of the sea.

2. light spray caused by this.

Lip′pi·ȧ, *n.* [named after Augustus *Lippi*, a French physician and traveler.] a genus of mainly tropical American shrubs of the vervain family, including *Lippia citriodora*, the lemon verbena.

lip′pi·tūde, *n.* [L. *lippitudo*, from *lippus*, bleareyed.] soreness of the eyes; blearedness.

Lip·pi·zän′ẽr, Lip·iz·zän′er (lip-it-sän′ẽr), *n.* [after *Lippiza*, the imperial Austrian stud farm, near Trieste.] any of a breed of gray to white horses used especially in certain horse exhibitions.

lip′py, *a.* saucy; impudent. [Slang.]

lip′-rēad, *v.t.* and *v.i.* to recognize (a speaker's words) by watching the movements of his lips.

lip rēad′ẽr, a person skilled in lip reading.

lip rēad′ing, the art of recognizing a speaker's words by watching the movements of his lips: it is often taught to the deaf.

lip salve (sav), 1. a salve or ointment for the lips.

2. figuratively, flattering speech. [Obs.]

lip sẽrv′ice, insincere expression of affection, respect, loyalty, etc.

lip′stick, *n.* 1. rouge compressed into stick form, used to color the lips.

2. a similar stick of colorless pomade for softening and protecting the lips.

lip′-syn̄ç′, *v.t.* and *v.i.*; lip-synced, *pt.*, *pp.*; lip-syncing, *ppr.* [from *lip synch*ronization.] to synchronize lip movements with (recorded speaking or singing).

lip′-syn̄ç′, *n.* the act or process of lip-syncing.

lip wiṣ′dŏm, wisdom in talk or words but not in action or experience; theory dissociated from practice.

lip wŏrk, 1. same as *lip labor.*

2. the act of kissing: used humorously.

liq′uȧ·ble (-wȧ-), *a.* capable of being liquefied or melted.

lī′quāte, *v.i.* to melt; to liquefy; to become dissolved. [Obs.]

lī′quāte, *v.t.*; liquated, *pt.*, *pp.*; liquating, *ppr.* to melt; to liquefy; specifically, in metallurgy, to heat (a metal, etc.) in order to separate a fusible substance from one less fusible.

lī·quā′tion, *n.* [LL. *liquatio* (*-onis*), a melting.]

1. the act or operation of liquating or melting.

2. the condition of being melted.

3. in metallurgy, the process of separating, by means of heat, an easily fusible metal from one less fusible.

liq·uē·fā′cient, *n.* [L. *liquefaciens* (*-entis*), *ppr.* of *liquefacere*, to melt, dissolve.]

1. that which liquefies or tends to liquefy.

2. in medicine, an agent that promotes the liquefying processes.

liq·uē·faç′tiȯn, *n.* [LL. *liquefactio* (*-onis*), a melting.]

1. a liquefying or being liquefied.

2. the conversion of a gas or vapor into a liquid by cold or pressure; as, the *liquefaction* of air.

liq·uē·faç′tive, *a.* pertaining to or causing liquefaction.

liq′uē·fī·ȧ·ble, *a.* capable of being liquefied.

liq′uē·fī·ẽr, *n.* an apparatus for liquefying gases.

liq′uē·fȳ, *v.t.* and *v.i.*; liquefied, *pt.*, *pp.*; liquefying, *ppr.* [L. *liquefieri*, to become liquid, pass. of *liquefacere*, to make liquid, melt, dissolve; *liquere*, to be fluid, or liquid, and *facere*, to make.] to change into a liquid.

li·ques′cence, li·ques′cen·cy, *n.* the condition or quality of being liquescent.

li·ques′cent, *a.* [L. *liquescens* (*-entis*), ppr. of *liquescere*, to become liquid.] melting; becoming liquid.

li·queur′ (-kẽr′), *n.* [Fr.] any of certain strong, sweet, sirupy alcoholic liquors, variously flavored.

li·queur′, *v.t.*; liqueured, *pt.*, *pp.*; liqueuring, *ppr.* to treat or mix with liqueur, as wine.

liq′uid, *n.* 1. a substance that, unlike a solid, flows readily but, unlike a gas, does not tend to expand indefinitely.

2. in grammar, a nonfrictional and vowellike consonant; a letter with a smooth, flowing sound; as, *l*, *m*, *n*, *r*.

Burnett's liquid; a solution of chloride of zinc used as a preservative, disinfectant, and antiseptic.

liq′uid, *a.* [L. *liquidus*, liquid, fluid, from *liquere*, to be fluid or liquid.]

1. fluid; flowing, or capable of flowing; not fixed or solid.

2. clear; transparent; limpid.

The deep *liquid* blue of the sky.
—Butterworth.

3. flowing smoothly or easily; sounding agreeable or smooth to the ear; not harsh; as, *liquid* melody.

4. readily convertible into cash.

5. nonfrictional and vowellike: term sometimes used in nonscientific context to describe certain consonants, especially *l* and *r*.

6. watery; suggestive of liquid; as, a *liquid* look.

liquid air; air brought to a liquid state by being subjected to great pressure and then cooled by its own expansion to a temperature below the boiling point of its constituents, nitrogen and oxygen: it is used as a refrigerant.

liquid assets; in banking, coin, bank notes, and securities which can be instantly converted into cash.

liquid crystal; a liquid that has certain characteristics of crystals, as interference colors and double refraction.

liquid debt; in Scots law, a debt, the amount of which is ascertained and constituted against the debtor, either by a written obligation or by the decree of a court.

liquid fire; an inflammable chemical composition which can be shot in a jet for a considerable distance: used in war against tanks and fortified positions.

liquid measure; (a) the measurement of liquids; (b) a system of measuring liquids; especially, the system in which

4 gills	=	1 pint
2 pints	=	1 quart
4 quarts	=	1 gallon
31 ½ gallons	=	1 barrel
2 barrels	=	1 hogshead.

Liq′uid·am″bãr, *n.* [L. *liquidus*, liquid, and LL. *ambar*, amber.]

1. a genus of trees of the witch-hazel family, consisting of two species. *Liquidambar orientale* of Asia Minor yields a balsam known as liquid storax. The other species, *Liquidambar styraciflua*, is found in Mexico and the United States, and is known as the sweet gum.

2. [l–] a tree of this genus.

3. [l–] the balsamic juice of these trees, used in medicine.

liq′uid·am″bẽr, *n.* same as *liquidambar*, sense 2.

liq′ui·dāte, *v.t.*; liquidated, *pt.*, *pp.*; liquidating *ppr.* [LL. *liquidatus*, pp. of *liquidare*, to make liquid or clear, from L. *liquidus*, liquid.]

1. to settle by agreement or legal process the amount of (indebtedness, damages, etc.).

2. to clear up the affairs of (a bankrupt business firm that is closing, etc.); to settle the accounts of, by apportioning assets and debts.

3. to pay (a debt).

4. to convert into cash.

5. to dispose of; to get rid of, as by killing.

6. to make plain or clear. [Rare.]

7. to cause to become liquid. [Obs.]

liquidated damages; in law, a certain fixed and ascertained sum, in contradistinction to a penalty which is both uncertain and unascertained.

liq′ui·dāte, *v.i.* to liquidate one's debts.

liq·ui·dā′tion, *n.* liquidating or being liquidated.

to go into liquidation; to close one's business by gathering in assets and settling all debts.

liq′ui·dā·tŏr, *n.* one who liquidates, especially one legally in charge of liquidating a company, estate, etc.

li·quid′i·ty, *n.* [LL. *liquiditas* (*-atis*), from L. *liquidus*, fluid, liquid.]

1. the state or quality of being liquid.

2. the quality of being smooth, flowing, and agreeable: said of sound, music, and the like.

liq′uid·īze, *v.t.*; liquidized, *pt.*, *pp.*; liquidizing, *ppr.* to cause to become liquid. [Rare.]

liq′uid·ly, *adv.* in a liquid or flowing manner.

liq′uid·ness, *n.* the state or quality of being liquid; fluency.

liq′uŏr (lik′ẽr), *n.* [ME. *licour*, *lycour*; OFr. *licor*; L. *liquor*, fluidity, a liquor, from *liquere*, to be liquid or fluid.]

1. any liquid or juice; as, meat *liquor*.

2. an alcoholic drink, especially one made by distilling, as whisky or rum, as distinguished from such beverages as wine or beer, that have undergone fermentation.

3. in pharmacy, any aqueous solution that does not contain sugar and does not hold gaseous or volatile matter in solution.

liquor amnii; the fluid contained in the amniotic sac.

liquor sanguinis; the blood plasma.

liq′uŏr, *v.t.* 1. to give alcoholic liquor to (usually with *up*). [Slang.]

2. to oil; to grease.

liq′uŏr, *v.i.* to drink alcoholic liquor, especially in large quantities (usually with *up*). [Slang.]

liq′uŏr·ice, *n.* same as *licorice.*

liq′uŏr·ish, *a.* 1. same as *lickerish.*

2. fond of liquor.

liq′uŏr·ous, *a.* lickerous. [Obs.]

liq′uŏr thiēf, a tube put through the bunghole of a cask to draw out liquor; a sampling tube.

lī′rȧ, *n.*; *pl.* **lī′re, lī′rȧṣ,** [It., from L. *libra*, a balance, pound.] the monetary unit of Italy, San Marino, Turkey, and Vatican City.

li·rel′lȧ, *n.* [dim., from L. *lira*, a furrow.] in botany, a linear shield with a channel along the middle, characteristic of some lichens.

li·rel′lāte, *a.* having the character of or resembling a lirella.

li·rel′li·form, *a.* lirellate.

Lir″i·ō·den′drŏn, *n.* [Gr. *leirion*, a lily, and *dendron*, tree.]

1. a genus of North American trees of the magnolia family, including *Liriodendron tulipifera*, the tulip tree.

2. [l–] a tree of this genus.

lir′i·pīpe, *n.* [ML. *liripipium*; perh. altered from LL. *cleri ephippium*, from Gr. *ephippion*, saddlecloth.] in early academic costume, a long tail to a hood.

lir′i·po͝op, *n.* [OFr. *liripipion*; LL. *liripipium*, perh. altered from *cleri ephippium*, lit., caparison of a cleric.]

1. a liripipe.

2. a degree of learning worthy the wearer of a liripipe; acuteness; smartness; a smart trick. [Obs.]

3. a silly person. [Obs.]

lī·roç′ō·nīte, *n.* [Gr. *leiros*, pale, and *konia* or *konis*, dust, powder.] a crystalline hydrated arsenate of copper, azure or blue-green in color.

Liṣ′bŏn, *n.* 1. a white or light-colored wine, produced in the province of Estremadura, Portugal: so called from being shipped at Lisbon.

2. a kind of soft sugar. [Obs.]

lis′keärd·īte, *n.* [from *Liskeard*, in Cornwall, England, where it is found.] a hydrous arsenate of aluminum and iron occurring in thin, fibrous crusts.

līsle (līl), *n.* [from *lisle*, earlier spelling of *Lille*, France.]

1. a fine, hard, extra-strong cotton thread: in full, *lisle thread.*

2. a fabric, stockings, gloves, etc. knit or woven of lisle.

līsle, *a.* made of lisle.

lisp, *v.i.*; lisped (lispt), *pt., pp.*; lisping, *ppr.* [ME. *lispen, lipsen*, from AS. *wlisp, wlips*, a stammering, lisping.]

1. to pronounce the sibilant letters *s* and *z* imperfectly, giving them the sound of *th* or *th*.

2. to speak imperfectly or like a child; to utter in a hesitating way.

I *lisp'd* in numbers, for the numbers came. —Pope.

lisp, *v.t.* 1. to pronounce with a lisp or in an imperfect or childlike way.

2. to speak in a timid, secret, or confidential manner; as, to *lisp* treachery.

lisp, *n.* 1. the habit or act of lisping.

2. the sound of lisping, or a sound like this.

lis pen'dens, [L.] literally, a pending suit: with reference to the legal doctrine that a court acquires jurisdiction over property involved in a suit.

lisp'ēr, *n.* one who lisps.

lisp'ing·ly, *adv.* in a lisping manner; with a lisp.

liss, *v.t.* to free, as from care or pain; to ease; to abate. [Obs.]

liss, *n.* abatement; relief; ease; happiness. [Obs.]

lis'sen, *n.* a cleft. [Brit. Dial.]

Lis·sen·ceph'ȧ·lȧ, *n.pl.* [Gr. *lissos*, smooth, and *enkephalos*, brain.] a group of mammalia having smooth cerebral hemispheres which have few folds, the cerebellum and part of the olfactory nerves being exposed: it includes the *Chiroptera, Insectivora, Rodentia*, and *Edentata*.

lis·sen·ceph'ȧ·lous, *a.* 1. having a smooth brain.

2. of or pertaining to the *Lissencephala*.

lis'sŏme, lis'sŏm, *a.* [altered from *lithesome*.]

1. limber; supple; flexible.

2. nimble; agile.

lis'sŏme·ness, *n.* the state of being lissome or lithesome; flexibility; agility; lightness.

lis·sō·trich'i·ăn, *a.* lissotrichous.

lis·sot'ri·chous, *a.* [Gr. *lissos*, smooth, and *thrix, trichos*, hair.] having smooth hair; liotrichous.

list, *v.i.*; listed, *pt., pp.*; listing, *ppr.* [ME. *listen, lysten*; AS. *lystan*, to please, from *lust*, pleasure, desire.]

1. to wish; to choose; to prefer. [Archaic.]

The wind bloweth where it *listeth*. —John iii. 8.

2. to be pleasing (*to* someone). [Archaic.]

list, *n.* [ME. *list, lyst*; AS. *lust*, desire, pleasure.] wish; choice; desire; inclination; also, lust. [Obs.]

list, *v.t.* and *v.i.* to tilt to one side, as a ship.

list, *n.* an inclination or a careening to one side; as, the ship has a *list* to port.

list, *v.t.* [ME. *listen, lesten*; AS. *hlystan*, to listen, harken, from *hlyst*, hearing.] to harken to; to hear; to listen to. [Archaic.]

list, *v.i.* to harken; to attend; to listen. [Archaic.]

list, *n.* [OFr. *liste*, a roll, list, border, band, from M.H.G. *liste*, a border, strip, edge.] a series of names, words, numbers, etc. set forth in order, usually in writing; a roll or catalogue; a schedule; a record; a register.

civil list; see under *civil*.

free list; see under *free*.

list, *v.i.* 1. to enlist in the armed forces. [Rare.]

2. to plow with a lister.

list, *v.t.* to enclose.

list, *n.* [ME. *list, liste*; AS. *list*, a list or border of cloth.]

1. a narrow strip of cloth; especially, the selvage cut from a wide piece of goods.

2. a limit or boundary.

3. in architecture, a small square molding; a fillet: also called *listel*.

4. (a) the first thin coat of tin applied in tinning iron plates; (b) a selvage of wire or tin formed on the under edge of tin plates.

5. in ropemaking, a woolen flap held in the hands, through which the yarn goes.

6. in carpentry, (a) the upper rail of a railing; (b) a narrow strip of wood, as one cut from the edge of a plank.

7. a stripe of color.

8. the lobe of the ear; the ear itself. [Obs.]

9. a ridge of earth between two furrows.

list, *v.t.* 1. to edge with a strip or strips of cloth.

2. to arrange in stripes or bands.

3. (a) to set forth (a series of names, words, etc.) in order; (b) to enter in a list, directory, catalogue, etc.; as, no such name is *listed* here.

4. (a) to plow (ground) with a lister; (b) to plant (corn) with a lister having a seed drill attached to it.

5. in carpentry, to reduce in breadth, as a board, by cutting off the sapwood from the edge.

list'el, *n.* in architecture, a fillet; a list.

lis'ten (lis'n), *v.i.*; listened, *pt., pp.*; listening, *ppr.* [ME. *listnen, lustnen, listen*; AS. *hlystan*, to listen, to list, from *hlyst*, hearing.]

1. to make a conscious effort to hear; to attend closely, so as to hear.

2. to give heed; take advice; as, to *listen* to warning.

to listen in; to be a listener to a telephone conversation of others, a radio program, etc.

lis'ten, *v.t.* to hear; to attend to. [Archaic.]

lis'ten, *n.* a listening.

lis'ten·ēr, *n.* one who listens.

lis'ten·ing pōst, 1. in military usage, an advanced, concealed position near the enemy's lines, for detecting the enemy's movements by listening.

2. any position for securing information unobserved.

list'ēr, *n.* one who makes a list or roll.

lis'ter, *n.* same as *leister*.

list'ēr, *n.* [so called in reference to the ridges and furrows formed, from AS. *list*, a border of cloth; O.H.G. *lista*, a border.] a double-moldboard plow which heaps the earth on both sides of the furrow: it is sometimes combined with a drill that plants seed in the same operation.

Lis'te·rȧ, *n.* [named after Martin *Lister*, an English physician and naturalist.] a genus of small orchids, native to Europe, northern Asia, and North America.

Lis·tē'ri·ăn, *a.* of or pertaining to Sir Joseph Lister, an English physician, or to his antiseptic method of surgery.

Lis'tēr·ism, *n.* [after Sir Joseph *Lister*.] the general principles and practice of antisepsis and aseptic surgery.

Lis'tēr·īze, *v.t.*; Listerized, *pt., pp.*; Listerizing, *ppr.* to treat (wounds) by the antiseptic method introduced by Sir Joseph Lister.

list'fụl, *a.* attentive. [Archaic.]

list'ing, *n.* 1. the act of making a list.

2. the fact of being listed, as in a directory.

3. the selvage of cloth; list.

list'ing plow, same as third *lister*.

list'less, *a.* 1. indifferent to or taking no pleasure in what is going on about one, as a result of illness, weariness, dejection, etc.; languid; spiritless.

2. characterized by inactivity and languor; as, a *listless* attitude.

list'less·ly, *adv.* in a listless manner.

list'less·ness, *n.* the state of being listless; indifference to what is going on.

list'ly, *a.* quick of hearing. [Brit. Dial.]

list'ly, *adv.* easily; distinctly. [Brit. Dial.]

list prīce, price shown in a list or catalogue: dealers usually receive a discount from it.

lists, *n.pl.* [ME. *listes*, specialized use of *liste*, border, hedging, boundary.]

1. in the Middle Ages, a high fence of stakes enclosing the area in which a tournament was held.

2. this area itself or the tournament held there.

3. in modern usage, an arena or place of combat.

to enter the lists; to enter a contest or struggle.

list'wŏrk, *n.* rough embroidery work in which list is sewed upon a garment, edge to edge or overlapping.

lit, *v.* alternative past tense and past participle of *light* (to illuminate), and *light* (to alight).

lit, *n.* [Lith., from *Litva*, Lithuanians.] formerly, the monetary unit and a silver coin of Lithuania, valued at about 10 cents: replaced by the ruble.

lit'ȧ·ny, *n.*; *pl.* **lit'ȧ·nies,** [OFr. *letanie*; LL. *litania*; Gr. *litaneia*, an entreating prayer, from *litainein*, to pray, entreat, from *litesthai, lissesthai*, to pray, beg, from *litē*, a prayer.]

1. a form of prayer in which the clergy and the congregation take part alternately, with recitation and response.

2. [L–] a special form of service of this kind in the Book of Common Prayer (with *the*).

Lesser Litany; (a) the petitions, *Lord, have mercy upon us; Christ, have mercy upon us; Lord, have mercy upon us*, sometimes repeated three times, as at the beginning of the Mass or Eucharist; (b) an abbreviated form of the litany in which some of the invocations and responses are omitted: used in the Protestant Episcopal church.

lit'ȧ·ny desk, in the Anglican church, a portable desk placed in the center of the choir or the chancel, facing the Communion table, and at which the minister kneels to recite the litany.

lit'ȧ·ny stọọl, same as *litany desk*.

Lī'tchī (-chē), *n.* [Chinese, *lichi*.]

1. a genus of Chinese evergreen trees of the soapberry family, containing but one species, *Litchi chinensis*, which is cultivated in warm climates for its fruit.

2. [l–] a tree belonging to this genus.

3. [l–] the fruit of this tree (*litchi nut*) eaten dried or preserved: it consists of a single seed surrounded by a sweet, edible, raisinlike pulp, enclosed in a rough, brown, papery shell.

Also spelled *lichee*.

lī'tchī nut, the fruit of the litchi tree.

-līte, [L. *-lithus*, from Gr. *lithos*, a stone.] a suffix used chiefly in names of minerals and rocks, meaning *stone*, as in chryso*lite*, cryo*lite*.

līte, *a.* and *n.* little. [Obs.]

lī'tēr, lī'tre (-tēr), *n.* [Fr. *litre*, from Gr. *litra*, a pound.] the basic unit of capacity in the metric system, equal to 1 cubic decimeter, or 61.025 cubic inches (1.0567 liquid quarts or .906 dry quarts): it is the volume of a kilogram of distilled water at 4°C.

lit'ēr·ȧ·cy, *n.* the condition of being literate.

lit'ēr·ăl, *a.* [OFr. *literal*; LL. *litteralis, literalis*, belonging to letters, literal, from L. *littera* or *litera*, a letter.]

1. of, involving, or expressed by a letter or letters of the alphabet; as, a *literal* grade.

2. following or representing the exact words of the original; word-for-word; as, a *literal* translation.

3. (a) based on the actual words in their ordinary meaning; not figurative or symbolical; as, the *literal* meaning of a passage; (b) giving the actual denotation of the word: said of the senses of words; (c) giving the original or earlier meaning of a word; etymological; as, the *literal* meaning of *ponder* is *weigh*.

4. habitually interpreting statements or words according to their actual denotation; prosaic; matter-of-fact; as, a *literal* mind.

5. real; not going beyond the actual facts; accurate; unvarnished; as, the *literal* truth.

6. virtual: used as an intensive. [Colloq.]

literal contract; in law, a contract the entire evidence of which is in writing.

literal equation; in mathematics, an equation in which letters are used to represent the known quantities.

lit'ēr·ăl, *n.* literal meaning. [Obs.]

lit'ēr·ăl·ism, *n.* 1. the tendency or disposition to take words, statements, etc. in their literal sense.

2. in the fine arts, thoroughgoing realism.

lit'ēr·ăl·ist, *n.* 1. one who adheres to the letter or literal sense; one given to literalism.

2. in the fine arts, one who represents realistically.

lit·ēr·ăl·ist'iç, *a.* of, based on, or favoring literalism.

lit·ēr·al'i·ty, *n.* 1. the quality of being literal.

2. *pl.* **lit·ēr·al'i·ties,** literal meaning or interpretation.

lit''ēr·ăl·ī·zā'tion, *n.* the act of literalizing.

lit'ēr·ăl·īze, *v.t.*; literalized, *pt., pp.*; literalizing, *ppr.* 1. to render literal, as a translation.

2. to interpret or put in practice according to the strict meaning of the words.

lit'ēr·ăl·ī·zēr, *n.* one who literalizes, or interprets literally.

lit'ēr·ăl·ly, *adv.* 1. according to the strict meaning of the words; not figuratively; as, a man and his wife cannot be *literally* one flesh.

2. with close adherence to words; word by word; as, to quote a writer *literally*.

3. virtually: used as an intensive, in a sense opposite to sense 1, as, he *literally* flew into the room: regarded by many as an erroneous usage. [Colloq.]

lit'ēr·ăl-mīnd'ed, *a.* unimaginative; prosaic.

lit'ēr·ăl·ness, *n.* the state or quality of being literal.

lit'ēr·ăr·i·ness, *n.* a literary quality.

lit'ēr·ăr·y, *a.* [L. *litterarius, literarius*, of or belonging to letters, from *littera, litera*, a letter.]

1. of, having the nature of, or dealing with literature.

2. appropriate to literature; as, he has a *literary* style.

3. (a) skilled in learning and literature; (b) making literature a profession.

literary agent; a person whose profession it is to sell the manuscripts of authors to publishers, usually on a commission basis.

literary property; property consisting in written or printed composition; also, the exclusive legal right to publish such compositions.

lit′ẽr·āte, *a.* [L. *litteratus*, or *literatus*, lettered, learned, from *littera* or *litera*, a letter, pl. learning.]

1. educated; especially, able to read and write: opposed to *illiterate*.

2. having or showing extensive knowledge, experience, or culture.

3. of or skilled in literature.

lit′ẽr·āte, *n.* 1. a literary person.

2. in the Church of England, a candidate for holy orders who does not have a university degree.

lit·ē·rā′tī (*or* -rä′ti), *n.pl.* [see *literatus*.] men of letters; scholarly or learned people.

lit·ē·rā′tim, *adv.* [LL., from L. *littera* or *litera*, letter.] letter for letter.

lit·ēr·ā′tion, *n.* the act or process of representing by letters.

lit′ẽr·ā·tōr, *n.* 1. a petty schoolmaster; a dabbler in learning. [Obs.]

2. a literary man; a man of literary culture; a man of letters.

lit′ẽr·ȧ·tūre, *n.* [OFr. *literature*; L. *litteratura*, or *literatura*, a writing, grammar, philology, learning, from *littera* or *litera*, a letter, pl. learning.]

1. the profession of an author; production of writings, especially of imaginative prose, verse, etc.

2. (a) all writings in prose or verse, especially those of an imaginative or critical character, without regard to their excellence: often distinguished from scientific writing, news reporting, etc.; (b) all the writings of a particular time, country, region, etc.; as, American *literature*; (c) all of such writings considered as having permanent value, excellence of form, great emotional effect, etc.; (d) all the writings dealing with a particular subject.

3. all the compositions for a specific musical instrument or ensemble.

4. printed matter of any kind, as advertising, campaign leaflets, etc. [Colloq.]

5. learning; acquaintance with letters or books. [Rare.]

lit′ẽr·ȧ·tūred, *a.* learned; literate. [Obs.]

lit·ē·rā′tus, *n.*; *pl.* **lit·ē·rā′tī,** [L., learned, from *littera*, *litera*, a letter, pl. learning.] a man of letters or learning; a savant: used chiefly in the plural.

-lith, [L. *-lithus*, from Gr. *lithos*, a stone.] a combining form meaning *stone*, as in eo*lith*, mono*lith*.

lith-, see *litho-*.

lith, *n.* a joint of the human body; a member; a limb; a division. [Obs.]

li·thae′mi·ȧ, *n.* see *lithemia*.

li·thae′miç, *a.* see *lithemic*.

lith′ȧ·gogue (-gog), *n.* [*lith-*, and Gr. *agōgos*, a leading, guiding, from *agein*, to lead.] in medicine, any agent tending to expel calculi from the bladder.

lith′ȧ·gogue, *a.* in medicine, having the power of expelling calculi from the bladder or kidneys.

lith′ȧ·nōde, *n.* [*lith-* and *anode*.] a hard peroxide of lead used in storage batteries.

lith·an′thrax, *n.* [*lith-*, and Gr. *anthrax*, coal.] mineral coal, as distinguished from *xylanthrax*, or charcoal. [Obs.]

lith′ärġe, *n.* [OFr. *litarge*; L. *lithargyrus*; Gr. *lithargyros*, the spume or foam of silver; *lithos*, stone, and *argyros*, silver.] the yellow or reddish protoxide of lead partially fused. It is much used in the manufacture of glass, enamel, varnishes, paints, and insecticides.

lith′āte, *n.* [*lith*ic and *-ate*.] a salt of uric acid. [Obs.]

līthe, *a.* [ME. *lithe*, *lythe*; AS. *lithe*, soft, pliant, gentle.]

1. easily bent; pliant; flexible; limber; as, a *lithe* acrobat.

2. mild; agreeable; gentle; calm. [Obs.]

lithe, *v.t.* to soften; to mitigate. [Obs.]

līthe, *v.t.* to listen to; to give ear to. [Obs.]

līthe, *v.i.* to listen; to give ear. [Obs.]

līthe′ly, *adv.* in a lithe manner.

li·thē′mi·ȧ, li·thae′mi·ȧ, *n.* [*lith-*, and Gr. *haima*, blood.] in pathology, a diseased condition of the blood, due to the presence of an excess of uric acid.

li·thē′miç, li·thaē′miç, *a.* of or having lithemia.

līthe′ness, *n.* flexibility; limberness; the condition or quality of being lithe.

lī′thẽr, *a.* bad; corrupt; wicked. [Obs.]

lī′thẽr, *a.* pliant; flexible. [Archiac.]

lī′thẽr·ly, *a.* wicked; mischievous; idle; lazy. [Obs.]

lī′thẽr·ly, *adv.* wickedly; badly; mischievously. [Obs.]

lī′thẽr·ness, *n.* laziness; wickedness. [Obs.]

lī′thẽr·ness, *n.* the condition or quality of being lither; flexibility. [Obs.]

līthe′sōme, *a.* pliant; limber; nimble; lissome.

līthe′sōme·ness, *n.* the condition of being lithesome.

lith′i·ȧ, *n.* [Gr. *lithos*, a stone.] an oxide of lithium of a white color. It dissolves slowly in water, forming a hydrate of lithium.

lith′i·ȧ, *a.* containing a compound of lithium; as, *lithia* water.

li·thī′ȧ·sis, *n.* [Gr. *lithiasis*, from *lithos*, a stone.] in pathology, the formation of calculi, or mineral concretions, in the body.

lith′i·āte, *n.* same as *lithate*.

lith′i·ȧ wa′tẽr, a mineral water containing lithium salts, used as a diuretic and in the treatment of rheumatism and lithiasis.

lith′iç, *a.* [Gr. *lithikos*, of or pertaining to stone, from *lithos*, a stone.]

1. of stone; as, *lithic* ornaments.

2. pertaining to stone in the bladder; uric. *lithic acid*; see *uric acid* under *uric*.

lith′iç, *a.* of the element lithium.

lith′iç, *n.* a medicine used in treating stone in the bladder.

-lith′iç, a combining form meaning *of a* (specified) *stage in the use of stone*, as in neo*lithic*.

lith″i·fi·cā′tion, *n.* [Gr. *lithos*, a stone, and L. *facere*, to make.] the conversion or consolidation of loose mineral or sand particles into stone.

lith·i·oph′i·līte, *n.* [Gr. *lithos*, a stone, and *philos*, loving, and *-ite*.] in mineralogy, a vitreous phosphate of lithium and manganese. It is a variety of triphylite.

lith′is·tid, *a.* pertaining to the *Lithistida*.

lith′is·tid, *n.* a sponge of the division *Lithistida*.

Li·this′ti·dȧ, *n.pl.* [Gr. *lithizein*, to look like a stone, from *lithos*, stone.] a division of siliceous sponges. They have a corallike skeleton, are generally cuplike, lamellar lip-shape, cylindrical, or occasionally brushlike with a stalk and roots.

li·this′ti·dăn, *a.* pertaining to the *Lithistida*.

li·this′ti·dăn, *n.* a sponge of the division *Lithistida*.

lith′i·um, *n.* [Gr. *lithos*, a stone.] a silver-white monatomic element of the alkali group of metals. Lithium is the lightest known metal, its specific gravity being 0.5936. It forms salts analogous to those of potassium and sodium. Symbol, Li; atomic weight, 6.940; atomic number, 3.

lith′i·um çär′bŏn·āte, a white, powdery salt, Li_2CO_3, used in the manufacture of glass, ceramics, dyes, etc. and in psychiatry to treat manic-depressive disorders.

lith′ō-, lith-, [from Gr. *lithos*, a stone.] a combining form meaning *stone*, *rock*, *calculus*, as in *litho*sphere, *litho*graph.

lith′ō·çärp, *n.* [*litho-*, and Gr. *karpos*, fruit.] fossil fruit; a fruit petrified; a carpolite.

lith″ō·çhrō·mat′iç, *a.* pertaining to lithochromatics.

lith″ō·çhrō·mat′içs, *n.* [*litho-*, and Gr. *chrōma*, color.] the art of painting in oil upon stone, and of taking impressions from it on canvas.

lith ō·çhrō″mȧ·tō·graph′iç, *a.* same as *chromolithographic*.

lith ō·çhrō′miç, *a.* lithochromatic.

lith″ō·çhrō′miçs, *n.* same as *lithochromatics*.

lith′ō·çlast, *n.* [*litho-*, and Gr. *klān*, to break in pieces.] in surgery, a powerful forcepslike instrument used in crushing stony concretions in the bladder.

lith″ō·çlas′tiç, *a.* pertaining to the crushing of calculi in the bladder.

lith′ō·cyst, *n.* [*litho-*, and Gr. *kystis*, a bladder, cyst.] in zoology, one of the sense organs or marginal bodies of the *Lucernarida* or steganophthalmate *Medusæ*.

lith″ō·dī·al′y·sis, *n.* [*litho-*, and Gr. *dialysis*, a breaking up, destroying, from *dialyein*, to part asunder, break up.] in pathology, (a) the solution of stony concretions in the bladder; (b) the operation of breaking a vesical calculus, previous to its removal.

lith′ō·dōme, *n.* [Gr. *lithodomos*, a mason; *lithos*, stone, and *domos*, house.] any of several species of mollusks which make holes in rocks, shells, etc., in which they live; one of the genus *Lithodomus*.

li·thod′ō·mous, *a.* of or pertaining to the genus *Lithodomus*.

Li·thod′ō·mus, *n.* 1. a genus of bivalve mollusks of the family *Mytilidæ*. They bore holes in rocks, shells, etc., in which they live. Called also *Lithotomus* and *Lithophagus*.

2. [l–] a mollusk of the genus *Lithodomus*.

lith″ō·fraç′tēur, *n.* [Fr., from Gr. *lithos*, stone, and L. *fractus*, pp. of *frangere*, to break.] a highly explosive compound composed of nitroglycerin, infusorial silica and sand, carbon, and sulfur. It is principally used in blasting.

lith″ō·ġen′e·sy, *n.* [*litho-*, and Gr. *genesis*, birth, generation.] the doctrine or science of the origin of minerals composing the earth, and of the causes which have produced their form and disposition.

li·thoġ′e·nous, *a.* [Gr. *lithos*, stone, and *-genēs*, producing.] having the power of forming stone, as the polyps which make coral.

lith′ō·glyph, *n.* [Gr. *lithoglyphos*, carving stone; *lithos*, stone, and *glyphein*, to carve.] an engraving or carving on a precious stone; also, an engraved stone.

li·thog′ly·phẽr, *n.* one who engraves gems. [Obs.]

lith″ō·glyph′iç, *a.* relating to the art of engraving gems.

lith″ō·glyp′tiç, *a.* pertaining to the art of engraving precious stones.

lith″ō·glyp′tiçs, *n.* the art of cutting or engraving precious stones.

lith′ō·gråph, *n.* [*litho-*, and Gr. *graphein*, to write.] a print made by the process of lithography.

lith′ō·gråph, *v.i.*; lithographed, *pt.*, *pp.*; lithographing, *ppr.* to make prints by the process of lithography.

lith′ō·gråph, *v.t.* to reproduce (a picture, writing, etc.) by the process of lithography.

li·thog′rȧ·phẽr, *n.* a person who makes lithographs.

lith″ō·graph′iç, *a.* of or pertaining to lithography or lithographs; done by lithography; printed from stone; used in lithography; as, *lithographic* engravings, a *lithographic* press.

lith″ō·graph′iç·ăl, *a.* lithographic.

lith″ō·graph′iç·ăl·ly, *adv.* by lithography.

li·thog′rȧ·phy, *n.* [*litho-*, and Gr. *graphein*, to write.] the art or process of printing from a flat stone or metal plate by a method based on the repulsion between grease and water: the design is put on the surface with a greasy material, and then water and printing ink are successively applied; the greasy parts, which repel water, absorb the ink but the wet parts do not.

lith′oid, *a.* [Gr. *lithos*, stone, and *eidos*, form.] resembling a stone; of a stony nature or structure.

li·thoid′ăl, *a.* lithoid.

lith′ō·lābe, *n.* [Gr. *lithos*, stone, and *labein*, to seize.] in surgery, an instrument for grasping a stone in the bladder, and keeping it fixed while it is being crushed.

lith″ō·lȧ·pax′y, *n.* [*litho-*, and Gr. *lapaxis*, removal.] in surgery, an operation for crushing a stone in the bladder, and removing the fragments by irrigation.

li·thol′ȧ·trous, *a.* practicing or pertaining to litholatry; as, *litholatrous* persons or rites.

li·thol′ȧ·try, *n.* [*litho-*, and Gr. *latreia*, worship.] the worship of stones of particular shapes.

lith″ō·loġ′iç, *a.* of or pertaining to lithology, or the science of stones; pertaining to the character of a rock, as derived from the nature and mode of aggregation of its mineral contents.

lith″ō·loġ′iç·ăl, *a.* lithologic.

lith″ō·loġ′iç·ăl·ly, *adv.* in a lithological manner; according to lithology.

li·thol′ō·ġist, *n.* a person versed in lithology.

li·thol′ō·ġy, *n.* [Gr. *lithos*, stone, and *-logia*, from *legein*, to speak.]

1. the science which treats of the mineral constituents and stratigraphical arrangement of rocks.

2. in medicine, the science of the nature and treatment of calculi.

li·thol′y·sis, *n.* lithodialysis.

lith′ō·märġe, *n.* [*litho-*, and L. *marga*, marl.] a compact clay of a fine, smooth texture, and very sectile.

lith″on·thryp′tiç, *a.* same as *lithotritic*.

lith″ō·pae′di·on, lith″ō·pē′di·on, *n.* same as *lithopaedium*.

lith″ō·pae′di·um, *n.* [*litho-*, and Gr. *paidion*, dim. of *pais*, *paidos*, a child.] in pathology, a retained fetus that has become calcified.

li·thoph′a·gous, *a.* [*litho-*, and Gr. *phagein*, to eat.]
1. eating or swallowing stones or gravel, as the ostrich.
2. burrowing into stones; lithodomous.

lith′ō·phāne, *n.* [*litho-*, and Gr. *-phanēs*, from *phainesthai*, to appear.] a style of ornamentation adapted for lamps, decorative windows, and other transparencies, produced by impressing thin sheets of porcelain, when in a soft state, into figures, which become visible when viewed by transmitted light.

lith′ō·phōne, *n.* [*litho-*, and Gr. *phōnē*, sound, voice.] an instrument by which the presence of calculi in the bladder is detected by sound. [Obs.]

lith″ō·phō·tog′ra·phy, *n.* same as *photolithography.*

lith′ō·phyl, lith′ō·phyll, *n.* [*litho-*, and Gr. *phyllon*, a leaf.] a fossil leaf or impression of a leaf; a stone containing such a leaf or impression.

lith″ō·phȳ′sa, *n.*; *pl.* **lith″ō·phȳ′sae,** [*litho-*, and Gr. *physa*, bellows.] a concentrically chambered cavity found in some volcanic rocks.

lith′ō·phȳse, *n.* same as *lithophysa.*

lith′ō·phȳte, *n.* [*litho-*, and Gr. *phyton*, a *plant*.]
1. a plantlike organism, as a coral, that is stony in structure.
2. a plant that grows on rock or stone.

lith″ō·phyt′iç, *a.* same as *lithophytous.*

lith″ō·phȳ′tous, *a.* pertaining to or consisting of lithophytes.

lith′o·pōne, *n.* [from *litho-*, and (?) L. *ponere*, to put: from being put on stone as paint.] a white pigment made by mixing barium sulfate with zinc sulfide, used in paints, linoleum, etc.

lith′ō·print, *v.t.* and *v.i.* to lithograph.

lith′ō·print, *n.* a lithographed book.

Li·thō′si·a, *n.* [from Gr. *lithos*, a rock, stone.] a genus of bombycid moths, of the family *Lithosiidæ.*

li·thō′si·ăn, *n.* a lithosiid.

li·thō′si·id, *a.* of or pertaining to the *Lithosiidæ.*

li·thō′sid, *n.* a moth of the family *Lithosiidæ*; a footman moth.

Lith″ō·si′i·dae, *n.pl.* a family of bombycid moths including about 100 genera; the footmen moths.

lith″ō·spẽr′mous, *a.* [*litho-*, and Gr. *sperma*, seed.] in botany, having seeds which are hard and stonelike.

Lith″ō·spẽr′mum, *n.* [L. *lithospermon*; Gr. *lithospermon*, gromwell; *lithos*, stone, and *sperma*, seed; so called from its hard seeds.] a genus of plants of the borage family, including about forty species, native to eastern Africa and North and South America. The roots of *Lithospermum tinctorium* contain a reddish substance used as a dye.

lith′ō·sphēre, *n.* [*litho-*, and Gr. *sphaira*, a sphere.] the earth's crust or solid part: distinguished from *atmosphere* and *hydrosphere.*

lith′ō·tint, *n.* [*litho-* and *tint.*]
1. a former method of producing pictures with a tinted effect from lithographic stones.
2. a picture so produced.

lith′ō·tōme, *n.* [Gr. *lithotomos*, cutting stones; *lithos*, stone, and *temnein*, to cut.]
1. a stone so formed by nature as to appear to have been cut artificially.
2. in surgery, a cystotome.

lith″ō·tom′iç, lith″ō·tom′iç·ăl, *a.* pertaining to or performed by lithotomy.

li·thot′ō·mist, *n.* one who performs lithotomy; one skilled in lithotomy.

li·thot′ō·mīze, *v.t.*; lithotomized, *pt.*, *pp.*; lithotomizing, *ppr.* to perform lithotomy on.

li·thot′ō·my, *n.* [LL. *lithotomia*; Gr. *lithotomia*, a cutting of stones, from *lithotomos*; *lithos*, stone, and *temnein*, to cut.] in surgery, the surgical removal of a calculus, or mineral concretion, by cutting into the bladder.

lith″ō·trip′sy, *n.* same as *lithotrity.*

lith″ō·trip′tiç, *a.* same as *lithotritic.*

lith″ō·trip′tist, *n.* same as *lithotritist.*

lith′ō·trip·tŏr, *n.* same as *lithotrite.*

lith′ō·trīte, *n.* [*litho-*, and L. *tritus*, pp. of *terere*, to rub, grind.] an instrument for crushing a vesical calculus: written also *lithotritor.*

lith″ō·trit′iç, *a.* of or pertaining to lithotrity; destroying or tending to destroy stone in the bladder.

li·thot′ri·tist, *n.* one who performs lithotrity.

lith′ō·trī·tŏr, *n.* a lithotrite.

li·thot′ri·ty, *n.* [*litho-*, and L. *tritus*, pp. of *terere*, to rub, grind.] the process of crushing a calculus in the bladder into very small pieces so that it can be eliminated in the urine.

lith′ō·tȳpe, *n.* [*litho-*, and Gr. *typos*, impression, type.] a kind of stereotype plate produced by lithotypy.

lith′ō·tȳpe, *v.t.*; lithotyped, *pt.*, *pp.*; lithotyping, *ppr.* to prepare for printing by lithotypy.

lith″ō·typ′iç, *a.* pertaining to or printed by lithotypy.

lith′ō·typ″y, *n.* a process of stereotyping by pressing the types into a soft mold, or matrix, the resulting hollows being filled with a mixture of gum shellac, fine sand, tar, and linseed oil in a heated state, which is later solidified.

li·thox′yle, *n.* [*litho-*, and Gr. *xylon*, wood.] petrified wood.

li·thox′yl·īte, *n.* lithoxyle.

Lith″ụ·ā′ni·ăn, *a.* of or pertaining to Lithuania, or to its people or language.

Lith″ụ·ā′ni·ăn, *n.* a native or inhabitant of Lithuania; also, the Baltic language of Lithuania.

lith″ū·rē′sis, *n.* [*lith-*, and Gr. *ourēsis*, from *ourein*, to urinate.] in pathology, the voiding of small calculi with the urine.

li·thū′ri·a, *n.* [*litho-*, and Gr. *ouron*, urine.] in pathology, a condition marked by excess of uric acid or its salts in the urine.

līth′y, *a.* easily bent; pliable. [Dial.]

līth′y tree, a shrub, *Viburnum lantana*, the European wayfaring tree.

lit′i·ga·ble, *a.* capable of being litigated, or contested in law.

lit′i·gănt, *a.* [L. *litigans* (*-antis*), ppr. of *litigare*, to litigate.] disposed to litigate; contending in law; engaged in a lawsuit; as, the parties *litigant.*

lit′i·gănt, *n.* a person engaged in a lawsuit.

lit′i·gāte, *v.t.*; litigated, *pt.*, *pp.*; litigating, *ppr.* [L. *litigatus*, pp. of *litigare*, to dispute, carry on a suit; *lis*, *litis*, a dispute, quarrel, and *agere*, to drive, carry on.] to contest in a lawsuit.

lit′i·gāte, *v.i.* to carry on a suit by judicial process.

lit·i·gā′tion, *n.* [LL. *litigatio* (*-onis*), a dispute.] the act or process of litigating or carrying on a suit in a court of law or equity; also, a lawsuit.

lit′i·gā·tŏr, *n.* [L.] one who litigates.

li·ti″ġi·os′i·ty, *n.* [from L. *litigiosus*, quarrelsome, contentious.] the character or quality of being litigious.

li·ti′ġious, *a.* [L. *litigiosus*, quarrelsome, contentious.]
1. given to carrying on lawsuits; quarrelsome.
2. disputable at law.
3. of lawsuits.

li·ti′ġious·ly, *adv.* in a litigious or contentious manner.

li·ti′ġious·ness, *n.* the condition or quality of being litigious; a disposition to engage in or carry on lawsuits.

lī″tis·çon·tes·tā′tion, *n.* [LL. *litis contestatio* (*-onis*); L. *lis*, *litis*, strife, lawsuit, and *contestatio*, an attesting by witnesses.] in Scots law, the appearance of parties in court to contest their rights.

lit′mus, *n.* [ON. *litmose*, lichen used in dyeing, from *litr*, color, and *mosi*, moss.] a purple coloring matter obtained from various lichens and used as an acid-base indicator in chemical analysis: it turns blue in bases and red in acids.

lit′mus pā′pẽr, absorbent paper treated with litmus and used as an acid-base indicator.

lit′ō·răl, *a.* same as *littoral.*

lī′tō·tēs, *n.* [Gr. *litotēs*, simplicity, from *litos*, smooth, plain, from *lis*, smooth.] in rhetoric, a figure in which an affirmative is expressed by a negation of the contrary. Thus "a citizen of no mean city" means "one of an illustrious or important city."

lī′tre, *n.* same as *liter.*

lit′ten, *a.* lighted. [Poet.]

lit′tẽr, *n.* [ME. *liter*, *litere*; OFr. *litiere*; LL. *lectaria*, a litter, from L. *lectus*, a couch.]
1. a framework having long horizontal shafts near the bottom and enclosing a couch on which a person can be carried.
2. a stretcher for carrying the sick or wounded.
3. straw, hay, leaves, etc. used as bedding for animals, as a protective covering for plants, as scratch material for fowl, etc.
4. the young borne at one time by a dog, cat, or other animal which normally produces several young at birth.
5. things lying about in disorder; rubbish.
6. untidiness; disorder.
7. in forestry, the surface layer of the forest floor, in which the leaves are slightly decomposed.

lit′tẽr, *v.t.*; littered, *pt.*, *pp.*; littering, *ppr.*
1. to supply with a bed, covering, etc. of straw, hay, etc.
2. to bring forth (a number of young) at one time: said of certain animals.
3. to make untidy (often with *up*); as, he *littered* (*up*) the floor with peanut hulls.
4. to scatter about in a careless manner; as, he *littered* peanut hulls over the floor.

lit′tẽr, *v.i.* 1. to be supplied with litter for bedding; to sleep in litter; as, he *littered* in the straw.
2. to give birth to a number of young at one time: said of certain animals.

lit″tẽr·a·teūr′, *n.* [Fr.] a literary man; one engaged in literary work; a man of letters: also written *littérateur.*

lit′tẽr·y, *a.* 1. consisting of litter; covered or encumbered with litter.
2. serving as or serviceable for litter, or bedding.

lit′tle, *a.*; *comp.* littler *or* less *or* lesser; *superl.* littlest *or* least, [ME. *litel*, *lutel*; AS. *lytel*, *litel*, a lengthened form of *lyt*, little.]
1. small in size; not big, large, or great.
2. small in amount, number, or degree; not much.
3. short in duration or distance; brief; not long.
4. small in importance or power; as, the rights of the *little* man.
5. small in force, intensity, etc.; weak.
6. trivial; trifling.
7. lacking in breadth of vision; narrow-minded; illiberal; as, a *little* mind.
8. young: of children or animals.

Little is sometimes used with implications of pleasing or endearing qualities; as, bless your *little* heart.

Little Bear; the constellation Ursa Minor.

Little Corporal; Napoleon Bonaparte.

Little Dipper; a group of stars in the constellation Ursa Minor (the Little Bear), supposed to outline a dipper.

little finger; the finger farthest from the thumb; smallest finger.

Little Fox; Vulpecula, a small northern constellation

little hours; in the Roman Catholic Church, the offices of prime, tierce, sext, and nones.

Little John; in English Legend, a famous member of Robin Hood's band.

little office; in the Roman Catholic Church, an office similar to but shorter than the breviary; especially, such an office in honor of the Virgin Mary.

little ones; small children.

little people; the fairies.

little Russian; same as *Ukranian.*

little slam; in bridge, the winning of all but one trick.

little theater; (a) a theater of a small community, college, or art group, usually noncommercial and amateur, that produces experimental or low-cost drama; (b) experimental drama, or drama of limited audience appeal, as produced by such theaters.

lit′tle, *n.* 1. a small amount, degree, etc.; as, *little* will be done about it.
2. a short time or distance.

in little; on a small scale; in miniature.

little by little; by slow degrees; gradually; by small amounts.

not a little; considerably; as, he was *not a little* surprised.

to make little of; to consider or treat as not very important; to depreciate; to pay little attention to.

to think little of; (a) to consider as not very important or valuable; (b) to have no hesitancy about.

lit′tle, *adv.*; *comp.* less; *superl.* least, 1. in a little or small degree or quantity; not much; slightly; as, he worries *little.*
2. not in the least; as, he *little* suspects the plot.

lit′tle-ēase, *n.* the stocks, pillory, or other similar uncomfortable punishment, or an uncomfortable part of a prison. [Obs.]

lit′tle·neck″, *n.* [after *Little Neck*, Long Island.] the young of the quahog, a round, thick-shelled clam, usually eaten raw: also *littleneck clam.*

lit′tle·ness, *n.* the state or quality of being little, in any sense.

lit′tle·wŏrth, *a.* of little worth or value; worthless. [Archaic or Scot.]

lit′lish, *a.* rather little.

lit′tō·răl, *a.* [L. *littoralis, litoralis*, from *littus, litus*, seashore, coast.] of or pertaining to a shore, as of the sea or a great lake; inhabiting the shore.

littoral zone; the interval or zone on a seacoast between high- and low-water mark.

lit′tō·răl, *n.* the shore; the region on the shore of the sea or a large lake.

Lit″tō·rī′nȧ, *n.* [L. *littus, littoris*, the seashore, and *-ina.*] a genus of pectinibranchiate mollusks, found on the seashores in nearly all parts of the world. They feed on seaweed and have a thick turbinated shell, of which the aperture presents a small angle, and is without a ridge. The common periwinkle is a specimen of this genus. Also spelled *Litorina.*

lit·tō·rī′noid, *a.* of or pertaining to the genus *Littorina.*

lit′tress, *n.* a smooth kind of cartridge paper used in making cards.

lit′ū·ī, *n.* pl. of *lituus.*

lit′ū·i·fọrm, *a.* [L. *lituus*, an augur's staff, trumpet, and *forma*, form.] curved like a lituus.

lit′ū·īte, *n.* [L. *lituus*, an augur's staff, trumpet, and *-ite.*] a fossil cephalopodous mollusk belonging to the genus *Lituites.*

lit′ū·rāte, *a.* [LL. *lituratus*, pp. of *liturare*, to rub out, erase, from L. *litura*, a blot, blur.]

1. in botany, having spots or rays which seem formed by the abrasion of the surface.

2. in entomology, marked with liturae or indefinite spots which grow paler at their edge.

li·tûr′giç, *a.* liturgical.

li·tûr′giç·ăl, *a.* pertaining to liturgies or to public prayer and worship.

li·tûr′giç·ăl·ly, *adv.* in a liturgical manner.

li·tûr′giçs, *n. pl.* [*construed as sing.*] the science of public worship; the study of liturgies.

li·tûr·gi·ol′ō·gist, *n.* one who studies or is versed in liturgiology.

li·tûr·gi·ol′ō·gy, *n.* the science or system of liturgies, and of their symbolic meanings.

lit′ûr·gist, *n.* 1. one who upholds or adheres strictly to a liturgy.

2. a specialist in the study of liturgies.

lit′ûr·gy, *n.*; *pl.* **lit′ûr·gieṣ,** [OFr. *liturgie*; LL. *liturgia*; Gr. *leitourgia*, public service; *leitos*, public, and *ergon*, work.]

1. prescribed forms or ritual for public worship in any of various Christian churches.

2. the Eucharistic service: called *Divine Liturgy* in the Orthodox Eastern Church and *Mass* in the Roman Catholic Church.

3. in ancient Athens, a form of personal service which the wealthier citizens were obliged to discharge to the state at their own expense, when called upon. Such services sometimes consisted of the defrayal of the expenses of festivals, dramatic performances, equipment of ships in case of war, etc.

lit′ū·us, *n.*; *pl.* **lit′ū·ī,** [L.] 1. in ancient Rome, (a) a crooked staff frequently represented in works of art as borne by the augurs in their divinations; (b) a trumpet having a mouth which curved suddenly upward, used by priests and cavalry.

2. in mathematics, a spiral, of which the characteristic property is that the squares of any two radii vectores are reciprocally proportional to the angles which they respectively make with a certain line given in position, and which is an asymptote to the spiral.

liv′ȧ·ble, *a.* 1. fit or pleasant to live in; habitable: said of a house, room, etc.

2. that can be lived through; endurable: said of life or of a specified sort of existence.

3. agreeable to live with (often followed by *with*): said of a person.

Also spelled *liveable.*

live (liv), *v.i.*; lived, *pt., pp.*; living, *ppr.* [ME. *liven, livien*; AS. *lifian, libban*, to live.]

1. to be alive; to have life.

2. (a) to remain alive; (b) to last; endure.

3. (a) to pass life in a specified manner; as, they *lived* wretchedly; (b) to regulate or conduct one's life; to govern one's way of life; as, the Spartans *lived* by a rigorous discipline.

4. to enjoy a full and varied life.

5. to maintain life; to support oneself; as, she *lives* on twenty dollars a week.

6. to feed; to subsist; to have as one's usual food; as, bats *live* on insects and fruit.

7. to make one's dwelling; to reside.

8. to remain in the memory of man; as, their evil deeds *live* after them.

9. to remain afloat under trying conditions: said of a ship.

to live and let live; to do as one pleases and let other people do the same; to be tolerant.

to live high; to live in luxury.

to live in; in domestic service, to sleep at one's place of work.

to live out; in domestic service, to sleep away from one's place of work.

to live through; to experience and survive; to endure.

to live up to; (a) to live or act in accordance with (one's ideals, reputation, etc.); (b) to fulfill (something expected).

to live well; (a) to live in luxury; (b) to lead a virtuous life.

to live with; (a) to dwell or to be a lodger with; (b) to cohabit with.

Syn.—dwell, exist, reside, subsist, continue, endure.

live, *v.t.* 1. to practice or carry out in one's life; as, he *lives* his faith.

2. to spend; pass; as, she *lived* a useful life.

to live down; to live in such a way as to wipe out the memory or shame of (some fault, misdeed, etc.).

to live out; to live until the end of; to last through.

līve, *a.* [short for *alive.*]

1. having life; not dead.

2. of the living state or living beings.

3. energetic; wide-awake; as, the company needs a *live* executive.

4. of immediate or present interest; as, a *live* campaign issue.

5. still burning or glowing; as, a *live* spark.

6. not burned; unstruck; as, a *live* match.

7. unexploded; as, a *live* shell.

8. unused; unexpended; as, *live* steam.

9. bright; vivid; as, a *live* color.

10. carrying electrical current; as, a *live* wire.

11. in the native state; not quarried or mined; as, *live* rocks.

12. stirring or swarming with living beings.

13. fresh; pure: said of the air.

14. in mechanics, imparting motion or power.

15. in printing, set up ready to be printed.

live axle; a driving axle.

live bait; living fish bait, as minnows.

live center; the center in the revolving spindle of a lathe or other machine on which work is turned.

live circuit; a circuit through which an electric current is passing.

live feathers; feathers plucked from the living bird, and therefore stronger and more elastic.

live gang; same as *live saw.*

live load; any moving load, not constant in its application, which a bridge or other structure carries in addition to its own weight.

live oak (a) a wide-spreading, evergreen oak native to the southeastern United States; (b) the hard wood of this tree, used in shipbuilding and other construction.

live ring; a series of wheels or rollers upon a circular track, used as a movable base for swing bridges, turntables, and the like.

live saw; a gang saw mill so arranged as to cut through and through the logs without previous slabbing.

live shell; in gunnery, a shell loaded and fused ready for firing; also, a shell which has not exploded after having been fired.

live steam; steam fresh from the boiler: distinguished from *exhaust steam.*

live trap; a trap in which animals can be captured alive.

live wire; (a) a wire charged with electricity; (b) [Colloq.] a person who is alert and energetic.

līve, *n.* life. [Obs.]

live′ȧ·ble, *a.* livable.

līved, *a.* having life; existing: used in combination; as, long-*lived*, short-*lived.*

live′-fọr·ev″ēr, *n.* an evergreen rock-garden plant, *Sedum telephium*, which derives its name from its drought-resisting powers.

līve′li·hood, *n.* liveliness. [Obs.]

līve′li·hood, *n.* [ME. *livelode, liflode*, course of life, support, maintenance; AS. *lif*, life, and *lad*, road, way.] means of maintaining life; support of life; maintenance; subsistence.

līve′li·ly, *adv.* in a lively manner.

līve′li·ness, *n.* 1. the quality or state of being lively or animated; sprightliness; vivacity; animation; spirit; as, the *liveliness* of youth.

2. an appearance of life, animation, or spirit; as, the *liveliness* of the eye or countenance in a portrait.

3. briskness; activity; effervescence, as of liquors.

Syn.—gaiety, animation, vivacity.

live′lọng, *a.* 1. whole; long in passing; tedious.

How could she sit the *livelong* day,
Yet never ask us once to play? —Swift.

2. lasting; durable. [Obs.]

live′lọng, *n.* same as *live-forever.*

līve′ly, *a.*; *comp.* livelier; *superl.* liveliest, 1. lifelike. [Rare.]

2. full of life; active; vigorous.

3. full of spirit; exciting; animated; as, a *lively* session of the council.

4. showing or inspiring liveliness; gay; cheerful.

5. moving quickly and lightly, as a dance.

6. brisk; as, a *lively* breeze.

7. vivid; keen; intense; as, *lively* colors.

8. bounding back with, or having, great resilience; as, a *lively* ball.

līve′ly, *adv.* 1. briskly; vigorously; in a lively manner.

2. in a lifelike manner. [Obs.]

lī′ven, *v.t.* and *v.i.* to make or become lively or gay; to cheer (often with *up*).

liv′ēr, *n.* 1. one who lives; one who has life.

2. one who resides; a resident; a dweller; as, a *liver* in Chicago.

3. one who lives (in a specified manner); as, an evil *liver*; a fast *liver*; a loose *liver* (that is, a person of evil, fast, or loose habits).

liv′ēr, *n.* [ME. *liver*; AS. *lifer*, liver.]

1. the largest glandular organ in vertebrate animals, located in the upper part of the abdomen: it secretes bile, has an important function in carbohydrate, fat, and protein metabolism, and contains a substance essential to the normal production of red blood cells.

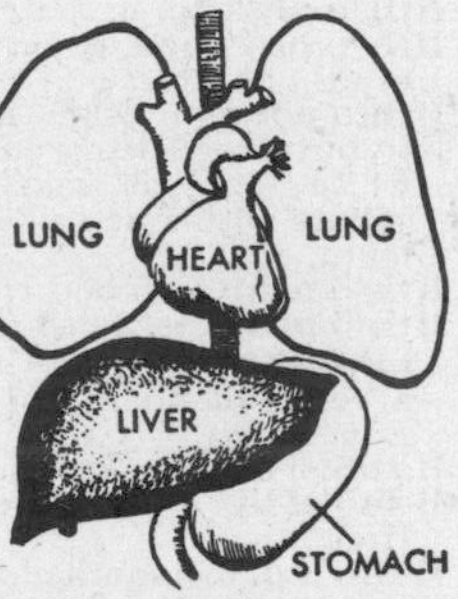

2. the flesh of this organ in cattle, fowl, etc., used as food.

3. a similar organ or tissue in invertebrate animals.

4. the liver thought of as the seat of emotion or desire.

floating liver; a displaced and movable liver.

liver extract; a substance obtained from the livers of mammals: it is nonprotein, nitrogenous, and water-soluble and is used in treating pernicious anemia.

liver of antimony; a sulfuret of antimony and potassium.

liver of sulfur; fused sulfuret of potassium: so called from its liver color.

liv′ēr, *n.* a bird, the glossy ibis.

liv′ēr çŏl′ŏr, a reddish-brown or dull brown mingled with a little yellow.

liv′ēr-çŏl″ŏred, *a.* of the color of the liver; reddish-brown.

liv′ēr çŏm·plāint′, a disorder of the liver.

liv′ēred, *a.* having a liver: used in combination; as, white-*livered.*

liv′ēr flūke, a trematoid worm, *Distoma hepatica.*

liv′ēr-grōwn, *a.* having an abnormally large liver. [Obs.]

liv′ēr·ied, *a.* wearing a livery, as a servant.

liv′ēr·ing, *n.* a kind of pudding or sausage made of liver. [Obs.]

liv′ēr·ish, *a.* 1. having a disordered liver; bilious. [Colloq.]

2. having or displaying a sour disposition; peevish; cross. [Colloq.]

liv′ēr lēaf, a stemless plant, *Anemone hepatica*, having three-lobed leaves and bearing early spring flowers on hairy scapes.

liv′ēr lil′y, in the eastern United States, the blue flag or iris.

liv′ēr rot, in veterinary medicine, a disease attacking sheep and other animals.

liv′ēr shärk, same as *basking shark.*

liv′ēr spot, a yellowish-brown spot or patch on the skin, especially one caused by faulty functioning of the liver.

liv′ēr stōne, a variety of barite.

liv′ēr·wŏrt, *n.* [so called from having liver-shaped parts.]

1. any of a group of green, red, purple, or yellow-brown plants, undifferentiated as to stems and leaves: they somewhat resemble

the mosses, together with which they constitute the bryophytes.

2. a hepatica.

liv′ẽr-wūrst, *n.* a sausage containing ground liver, or other ingredients having the taste of liver.

liv′ẽr·y, *n.*; *pl.* **liv′ẽr·ieṣ,** [ME. *liverey, liveree,* a gift of clothes made by a master to his servant, properly a thing delivered; OFr. *liveree;* LL. *liberata,* properly f. pp. of *liberare,* to give up, deliver; L. *liberare,* to free.]

1. an identifying uniform such as was formerly worn by feudal retainers or is now worn by servants or those in some particular group, trade, etc.

2. the people wearing such uniforms.

3. characteristic dress or appearance.

4. the keeping and feeding of horses for a fixed charge.

5. the keeping of horses, vehicles, or both, for hire.

6. a livery stable.

7. in law, the legal delivery of property, especially landed property, into the hands of the new owner.

livery company; any of the London city companies that grew out of earlier trade guilds, characterized by a distinctive dress.

livery of seizin; the putting of a person in corporal possession of a freehold by performing some ceremony before witnesses which clearly places the party in possession.

liv′ẽr·y, *v.t.* to clothe in or as in livery.

liv′ẽr·y·măn, *n.*; *pl.* **liv′ẽr·y·men,** 1. formerly, a liveried retainer or servant.

2. a member of any of the London city companies.

3. a person who owns or works in a livery stable.

liv′ẽr·y stā′ble, a stable where horses and vehicles can be had for hire, or where horses are kept and fed for a fixed charge.

līveṣ, *n.* pl. of *life.*

līve′stock, *n.* domestic animals kept for use on a farm or raised for sale and profit.

Liv′i·ăn, *n.* Livonian (the language).

liv′id, *a.* [L. *lividus,* from *livere,* to be black and blue.]

1. discolored by a bruise; black-and-blue: said of the flesh.

2. grayish-blue; lead-colored; as, *livid* with rage.

li·vid′i·ty, *n.* the state or quality of being livid.

liv′id·ness, *n.* same as *lividity.*

liv′ing, *n.* 1. the state of existing; the power of continuing life.

2. means of subsistence; livelihood.

Thus earn'd a scanty *living* for himself.
—Tennyson.

3. the benefice of a clergyman; an ecclesiastical charge which a minister receives.

4. manner of life; as, high *living;* a low standard of *living.*

the living; those that are still alive.

liv′ing, *a.* 1. alive; having life; not dead.

2. full of vigor; in active operation or use; as, a *living* institution.

3. of persons alive; as, within *living* memory.

4. gushing forth; flowing; as, a *living* stream.

5. still spoken as a native tongue: said of a language.

6. true; lifelike; exact: now mainly in the phrase *the living image.*

7. (a) of life or the sustaining of life; as, *living* conditions; (b) enough to maintain a reasonable standard of existence; as, a *living* wage.

living death; a life of unrelieved misery.

living picture; a tableau vivant.

living room; a room (in a home) furnished with sofas, chairs, etc., used as for conversation, reading, or entertaining guests, etc.: also called *parlor, sitting room.*

living rock (or *stone*); rock or stone in its original state or place.

living wage; a wage sufficient to enable a person to maintain himself and his family in reasonable comfort.

living will; a document, legal in some States, directing that all measures to support life be ended if the signer should be dying of an incurable condition.

liv′ing·ly, *adv.* in a living state.

liv′ing·ness, *n.* the state of living; animation; the quality of being energetic, vigorous, or alive.

Li·vō′ni·ăn, *a.* of or pertaining to Livonia, a former Russian province adjoining the Baltic.

Li·vō′ni·ăn, *n.* 1. a native or inhabitant of Livonia.

2. the High Lettish Baltic dialect spoken by some Livonians.

lī′vŏr, *n.* [L. *livor,* lividness, envy, from *livere,* to be livid or envious.]

1. malignity; envious hatred. [Obs.]

2. in medicine, lividity of a corpse.

lī′vre (-vẽr), *n.* [Fr., from L. *libra,* a Roman pound.] a former French money of account and a silver coin, originally equivalent in value to a pound of silver: it was gradually reduced in value and was replaced by the franc.

lix·iv′i·ăl, *a.* [L. *lixivius,* made into lye, from *lix,* ashes, lye.]

1. obtained by lixiviation; impregnated with alkaline salts, extracted from wood ashes.

2. of the color of lye; resembling lye.

3. having the qualities of alkaline salts from wood ashes.

lixivial salts; salts obtained by passing water through wood ashes.

lix·iv′i·āte, *v.t.*; lixiviated, *pt., pp.*; lixiviating, *ppr.* to form into lye; to impregnate with salts from wood ashes; to leach.

lix·iv·i·ā′tion, *n.* the operation or process of extracting alkaline salts from ashes by pouring water on them; leaching.

lix·iv′i·ous, *a.* lixivial. [Rare.]

lix·iv′i·um, *n.* [L. *lixivium, lixivia,* lye, from *lix,* ashes, lye.]

1. lye; water impregnated with alkaline salts from wood ashes.

2. any solution which has been leached out.

liz′ărd, *n.* [OFr. *lezard, lesard,* from L. *lacertus, lacerta,* a lizard.]

1. any of a large group of reptiles with a long slender body and tail, a scaly skin, and four legs, sometimes merely vestigial: most species live in hot, dry regions, as the gecko, horned lizard, chameleon, and iguana.

2. loosely, any of various similar reptiles, as the salamanders.

3. in nautical usage, a piece of rope having a thimble or block spliced into one or both of its ends, used as a leader.

liz′ărd fish, 1. any of a group of brightly colored, tropical sea fishes with a slender body, lizardlike head, and large mouth.

2. in Australia, the saury.

liz′ărd stōne, a variety of serpentine marble found near Lizard Point in Cornwall, England.

liz′ărd-tāil, liz′ărd′ṣ-tāil, *n.* a perennial marsh herb of the genus *Saururus,* having white flowers blooming on a wandlike terminal spike.

llä′mȧ (lä′mȧ), *n.* [Peruv.]

1. any of a group of South American animals related to the camel but smaller and without humps: it is used as a beast of burden and as a source of wool, meat, and milk.

2. cloth made from the woolly hair of this animal.

LLAMA

Llan·deī′lō group, (lan-), [so called from *Llandeilo,* Wales.] a series of fossiliferous strata of the Lower Silurian in England.

llȧ·ne′rō (lȧ-), *n.* [Sp., from *llano,* a plain, level.] an inhabitant of the llanos.

llä′nō (lä′nō *or Sp.* lyä′nọ), *n.*; *pl.* **llä′nōṣ,** [Sp., a plain, level.] an extensive, treeless plain; especially, a great level tract of grassy land in the northern part of South America.

Lloyd′ṣ (loidz), *n.* [from *Lloyd's* coffeehouse, the meeting place of the original association.] an association of insurance underwriters in London formed in the early 18th century to subscribe marine insurance policies and to publish shipping news: it now handles many kinds of insurance.

Lloyd's Register; an annual list issued by Lloyd's, giving the rating of the seagoing vessels of all nations.

lō, *interj.* [ME. *lo, loo;* AS. *la,* an interj.] look; see; behold; observe: used to attract attention to some object of sight or subject of discourse: now mainly in *lo and behold.*

lō′ȧ, *n.* a parasitic, nematode worm of Africa, *Silaria oculi,* which infests the eye.

lōach, *n.* [Fr. *loche.*] a small fish of the genus *Cobitis* and allied genera, inhabiting small, clear streams of Europe and Asia.

lōad, *n.* [ME. *lode, loode,* a burden, way, a carrying, from AS. *lad,* a way, carrying, carriage.]

1. something carried or to be carried at one time or in one trip; burden.

2. a measure of weight or quantity, varying with the type of conveyance; as, a *load* of wood.

3. something carried with difficulty; specifically, (a) a heavy burden or weight; (b) a great mental or spiritual burden; as, that's a *load* off my mind.

4. the weight borne up by a structure.

5. a single charge, as of powder and bullets, for a firearm.

6. [*often in pl.*] a great amount or quantity; as, she has *loads* of friends. [Colloq.]

7. the amount of time or work that an employee, especially a teacher, has contracted to carry; as, thirty hours a week is a heavy teaching *load.*

8. in electricity, the amount of current supplied by a dynamo or other source of electric power.

9. in mechanics, the amount of work performed by an engine, etc.; specifically, the external resistance offered to an engine by the machine that it is operating.

Syn.—weight, lading, cargo, oppression, incubus, drag, burden.

lōad, *v.t.*; loaded, *pt., pp.*; loading, *ppr.* 1. to put something to be carried into or upon; especially, to fill or cover with as much as can be carried; as, they *loaded* the boxcars with wheat.

2. to put into or upon a carrier; as, they *loaded* the wheat into the boxcars.

3. to weigh down with or as with a heavy load; to burden; to oppress.

4. to supply in large quantities; to give much of something to; as, they *loaded* him with honors.

5. to put a charge of ammunition into (a firearm, etc.).

6. to put a roll of film or a plate into (a camera).

7. to add weight to, especially so as to make one end or one side heavier; as, he *loaded* the dice.

8. to add a foreign substance to; to adulterate; to doctor; as, they *loaded* the wine.

lōad, *v.i.* 1. to put a charge of ammunition into a firearm.

2. to receive a charge of ammunition; as, these mortars *load* at the muzzle.

lōad dis·plāce′ment, the displacement of a completely loaded ship.

lōad′ed, *a.* 1. carrying a load.

2. having a charge of ammunition in it.

3. weighted; specifically, weighted on certain sides so as to fall with the desired sides up: said of fraudulent dice.

4. intoxicated. [Slang.]

5. well supplied with money. [Slang.]

lōad′ẽr, *n.* one who or that which loads; specifically, (a) a loading device for a shell or cartridge; (b) a hay loader.

lōad faç′tŏr, in electricity, the ratio of average load to greatest load.

lōad′ing, *a.* made so as to be loaded; charging: used in hyphenated compounds; as, a breech-*loading* gun.

lōad′ing, *n.* 1. the act of putting a load on or into.

2. a cargo; a burden; anything that makes part of a load.

3. that which is added to a substance in order to give it weight or body.

lōad′ing çoil, a coil placed in an electric circuit to increase its inductance.

lōad līne, the line on a vessel showing the depth to which it sinks when fully loaded.

lōadṣ′măn, *n.* a lodesman. [Obs.]

lōad′stär, *n.* same as *lodestar.*

lōad′stōne, *n.* [*load, lode,* and *stone.*]

1. a strongly magnetic variety of the mineral magnetite.

2. something that attracts as with magnetic force.

Also spelled *lodestone.*

lōaf (lōf), *n.*; *pl.* **lōaveṣ,** [ME. *lof, loof;* AS. *hlaf,* bread, a loaf of bread.]

1. a portion of bread baked in one piece, commonly in a standardized size convenient for table use.

2. a fairly large cake baked in one piece: also called *loaf cake:* opposed to *layer cake.*

3. any mass of food shaped somewhat like a loaf of bread and baked; as, a salmon *loaf.*

4. a piece of loaf sugar, usually shaped like a cone.

loaf sugar; sugar that has been refined and molded into small loaves, usually in the form of a cone.

lōaf, *v.i.*; loafed (lōft), *pt., pp.*; loafing, *ppr.* [prob. back-formation from *loafer.*]
1. to loiter or lounge about doing nothing; to idle.
2. to work in a lazy way, accomplishing little; as, he *loafs* on the job.

lōaf, *v.t.* to spend (time) idly: often with *away*; as, to *loaf away* one's time.

lōaf, *n.* the act of loafing.

lōaf'ẽr, *n.* [18th-c. Western New England dial., "one who owns but does not actively work his own farm;" prob. from Hudson Valley D.; akin to G. *laufen*, to run.]
1. a person who loafs; lounger; idler.
2. a moccasinlike sport shoe for informal wear.

lōam, *n.* [AS. *lām*, loam.]
1. a rich soil composed of clay, sand, and some organic matter.
2. a mixture of clay, sand, and straw used in making foundry molds, plastering, etc.
3. popularly, any rich, dark soil.

lōam, *v.t.*; loamed, *pt., pp.*; loaming, *ppr.* to fill or cover with loam.

lōam mōld, a mold made of loam for castings of iron or brass.

lōam'y, *a.*; *comp.* loamier; *superl.* loamiest, consisting of loam; having the nature of or resembling loam.

lōan, *n.* [ME. *lone, lane*; AS. *lān, læn*, a loan, grant, fief.]
1. the act of lending; a lending.
2. that which is lent; anything furnished for temporary use to a person at his request, on the condition that it shall be returned, or its equivalent in kind, with or without a compensation for its use; especially, a sum of money lent, often for a specified period and repayable with interest.
3. a grant or gift from a superior. [Obs.]

lōan, *v.t.* and *v.i.*; loaned, *pt., pp.*; loaning, *ppr.* to lend.

lōan'ȧ·ble, *a.* that may be loaned or is available for being loaned; as, *loanable* funds.

lōan çŏl·leç'tion, a collection of pictures, curios, etc. lent for temporary public exhibition.

lōan'ing, lōan'in, *n.* [Scot.] a space between cultivated fields through which cattle are driven, and which sometimes serves as a milking place for cows; a lane. [Chiefly Scot. and Brit. Dial.]

lōan'mŏṅ″gẽr, *n.* one who negotiates loans.

lōan of'fice, 1. an office where loans are made.
2. a pawnshop.
3. a public office for receiving subscriptions to government loans, as formerly established in some States by the Revolutionary Continental government.

lōan shärk, a person who lends money at exorbitant or illegal rates of interest. [Colloq.]

lōan sō·cī'e·ty, a group of people who pay various sums into a fund which is then used as a source of loans to them and, sometimes, to others.

lōan wŏrd, a word of one language adopted into another and naturalized. English examples: *kindergarten* (from German), *depot* (from French).

lōath, lōth, *a.* [ME. *loth, lath*; AS. *lāth*, causing evil, hostile, odious.]
1. hateful; odious. [Obs.]
2. unwilling; reluctant; averse: usually followed by an infinitive; as, *loath* to leave one's friends.
nothing loath; not reluctant(ly); willing(ly).

lōathe, *v.t.*; loathed, *pt., pp.*; loathing, *ppr.* [ME. *lothen*; AS. *lāthian*, to be evil, hateful, from *lāth*, hateful.]
1. to feel disgust at; to have an extreme aversion for; as, to *loathe* food or drink.
2. to hate; to dislike greatly; to abhor.

Ye shall *loathe* yourselves in your own sight.
—Ezek. xx. 43.

Syn.—hate, abhor, detest, abominate.

lōathe, *v.i.* 1. to be odious or hateful; to cause disgust. [Obs.]
2. to feel disgust. [Obs.]

lōath'ẽr, *n.* one who loathes or abhors.

lōath'ful, *a.* loathsome. [Rare.]

lōath'ing, *n.* extreme disgust; abhorrence.

lōath'ing·ly, *adv.* with extreme disgust or abhorrence.

lōath'li·ness, *n.* the quality of being loathly; loathsomeness. [Obs.]

lōath'ly, *a.* loathsome; disgusting. [Rare.]

Changed to a lazar's vile and *loathly* ward.
—J. Baillie.

lōath'ly (also, formerly, lōth'li), *adv.* 1. with loathness; unwillingly; reluctantly. [Rare.]
2. in a loathsome manner; filthily. [Rare.]

lōath'ness, *n.* the state of being loath; unwillingness; reluctance; as, *loathness* to speak.

lōath'sŏme, *a.* such as to cause loathing; exciting disgust or abhorrence; disgusting; odious; detestable; as, the most *loathsome* disease.

lōath'sŏme·ly, *adv.* in a loathsome manner.

lōath'sŏme·ness, *n.* the state or quality of being loathsome.

lōaveṣ, *n.* plural of *loaf.*

lob, *n.* [ME. *lobbe, lob-*, lit., "heavy, hanging, thick."]
1. a big, slow, clumsy person. [Dial.]
2. in cricket, a slow underhand throw.
3. in tennis, a stroke in which the ball is sent high into the air, usually with the intention of dropping it into the back of the opponent's court.
4. something thick and heavy; a lump. [Chiefly Dial.]
5. the pollack. [Brit.]

lob, *v.t.*; lobbed, *pt., pp.*; lobbing, *ppr.*
1. to allow to droop; to hang languidly. [Obs.]
2. to throw or toss, as a ball, with slow, deliberate aim and in a high curve.

lob, *v.i.* 1. to move heavily and clumsily (often with *along*).
2. to lob a ball.

lō'bär, *a.* of a lobe or lobes; as, *lobar* pneumonia.

lō'bāte, lō'bā·ted, *a.* 1. furnished or provided with a lobe or lobes; lobed; as, a *lobate* foot; a *lobate* fin.
2. formed or shaped like a lobe or lobes.

LOBATE FOOT OF GREBE

lō'bāte·ly, *adv.* in such a manner as to form lobes.

lō·bā'tion, *n.* 1. lobate formation; a being lobed.
2. a lobe.

lob'bẽr *n.* a person or thing that lobs.

lob'bish, *a.* like a lob; clownish; stupid. [Obs.]

lob'by, *n.*; *pl.* **lob'bieṣ,** [LL. *lobia, laubia*, a portico, gallery, from O.H.G. *louba, loupa*, an arbor, from *loub*, a leaf.]
1. a hall, vestibule, or corridor serving for a waiting room, etc., as in an apartment house, hotel, theater, etc.
2. a large hall adjacent to the assembly room of a legislative or deliberative body and open to the public.
3. a group of lobbyists representing the same special interest; as, a cotton *lobby.*
4. in a ship, an apartment under the quarter-deck, immediately in front of the captain's cabin. [Obs.]
5. a place in which cattle are confined near the farmyard, formed by hedges, trees, and other fencing.

lob'by, *v.i.*; lobbied, *pt., pp.*; lobbying, *ppr.* to act as a lobbyist.

lob'by, *v.t.* to get or try to get legislators to vote for (a measure) by acting as a lobbyist (often with *through*).

lob'by·iṣm, *n.* the practice of lobbying.

lob'by·ist, *n.* [*lobby*, and *-ist.*] a person who tries to get legislators to introduce or vote for measures favorable to a special interest that he represents.

lob'by mem'bẽr, a lobbyist.

lob'cock, *n.* a sluggish, stupid, inactive person; a lob. [Now Dial.]

lōbe, *n.* [Gr. *lobos*, the lobe of the lower part of the ear or liver.]
1. a projection or protuberance of rounded or globular form; specifically, in anatomy, (a) a rounded part or division of an organ, separated by fissures, as in the liver, lungs, brain, etc.; (b) the fleshy lower end of the human ear.
2. in botany, any projection or division, especially a rounded one, of a leaf, fruit, or other organ of a plant.
3. in zoology, a flap or projection that is imperfectly connected with other parts, as on the toes of certain birds, as the coot.
4. in machinery, the projecting or more prominent part of a cam wheel.

lō·beç'tō·my, *n.* [from *lobe*, and *-ectomy.*] the surgical removal of a lobe, as of the brain, etc.

lōbed (lōbd), *a.* having lobes, or divisions, that extend less than halfway from the margin to the middle of the base: said of leaves.

lōbe'foot, *n.* a bird having lobate feet, as the grebe.

lōbe'foot″ed, *a.* lobiped.

lōbe'let, *n.* a lobule; a small lobe.

Lō·bē'li·ȧ, *n.* [named after Matthias de *Lobel*, Fl. physician and botanist to James I.]
1. a very extensive genus of herbs with long clusters of blue, red, or white flowers. The best-known species are *Lobelia inflata*, or Indian tobacco, which is cultivated in North America and employed in medicine as an emetic, expectorant, etc., and *Lobelia cardinalis* or the cardinal flower, known for its vivid red flowers.
2. [l-] any plant of this genus.

lō·bē″li·ā'ceous, *a.* of, pertaining to, or resembling the family of plants of which *Lobelia* is the typical genus.

lō'be·lin, lō'be·līne, *n.* [*lobel*ia and *-in(e).*] a poisonous liquid alkaloid procured from *Lobelia inflata*, resembling nicotine: it is used medicinally as an acronarcotic and emetic.

lō'bi·ped, *a.* [*lobe*, and L. *pes, pedis*, a foot.] having lobate feet.

lō'bi·ped, *n.* a lobefoot.

lob'lol·ly, *n.*; *pl.* **lob'lol·lieṣ,** [16th-c.; prob. from *lob*, heavy, thick, and dial. *lolly*, broth, soup.]
1. a thick gruel. [Obs.]
2. a mudhole; muddy puddle. [Colloq.]
3. (a) any of various thick-barked pines of the southern United States; (b) the wood of any of these trees: also *loblolly pine.*
4. a loutish, uncouth, or foolish person. [Obs.]

lob'lol·ly bāy, *Gordonia lasianthus*, an elegant ornamental evergreen tree of the southern United States.

lob'lol·ly boy, the attendant of a ship's doctor. [Obs.]

lob'lol·ly pīne, a large tree, *Pinus tæda*, found growing in the southern United States.

lob'lol·ly tree, one of several trees of the West Indies, especially *Cupania glabra.*

lō'bō, *n.* [Sp., a wolf, from L. *lupus*, a wolf.] the large, gray timber wolf of the western United States.

Lō·bō'sȧ, *n.* [from Gr. *lobos*, a lobe.] an order of *Rhizopoda*, of a shapeless character and having pseudopodia of a thick and irregular form, as in the amoeba.

lō·bot'ō·my, *n.* [*lobe* and *-tomy.*] a surgical operation in which a lobe of the brain, especially the frontal lobe of the cerebrum, is cut into or across, as in the treatment of certain psychoses.

lob'sçourse, *n.* same as *lobscouse.*

lob'sçouse, *n.* [*lob* in basic sense of "heavy, thick" and dial. *scouse*, stew.] a sailor's stew of meat, vegetables, and ship's biscuit.

lob'sīd″ed, *a.* same as *lopsided.*

lobṣ'pound, *n.* a prison. [Obs.]

lob'stẽr, *n.* [ME. *lopstere, loppester*; AS. *loppestre, lopustre*, a lobster; prob. altered from L. *locusta*, a marine shellfish.]
1. any of a genus, *Homarus*, of edible sea crustaceans, with compound eyes, long antennae, and five pairs of legs, the first pair of which are modified into large, powerful pincers: lobsters are greenish or dark gray in color when alive, but turn bright red when boiled. The common lobster, *Homarus vulgaris*, is found in great abundance on many of the European shores, while *Homarus americanus* is common to the Atlantic coast of North America.
2. the flesh of this animal used as food.
3. the sea crawfish, or spiny lobster, *Palinurus vulgaris.*
4. a British soldier: probably so called originally because of his stiff cuirass, later because of his red coat. [Brit. Slang.]
5. an awkward, troublesome, or gullible person. [Slang.]

lob'stẽr çat'ẽr·pil·lăr, the larva of the European bombycid, or lobster moth.

lob'stẽr louse, a parasite found on the gills of the European lobster.

lob'stẽr·măn, *n.*; *pl.* **lob'stẽr·men,** a man whose work is catching lobsters.

lob'stẽr moth, the bombycid moth of Europe: so called from the larvae, which have legs whose third and fourth segments are very long.

lob'stẽr pot, a basketlike trap for lobsters.

lob'stẽr-tāil, *n.* a piece of armor made of steel plates which overlap.

lob'stẽr-tāiled, *a.* resembling the abdomen or tail of a lobster: especially applied to armor composed of overlapping plates.

lob'stẽr thẽr'mi·dọr, a dish consisting of lobster flesh, mushrooms, etc. in a sauce, served in half of a lobster shell.

lob'stick, *n.* in Canada, a tree denuded of the lower branches, and having the top ones trained to point the way in several directions.

lob'ū·lăr, *a.* pertaining to or resembling a lobule or lobules.

lob'ū·lāte, lob'ū·lā·ted, *a.* consisting of or divided into lobules.

lob'ūle, *n.* [compare Fr. *lobule*, dim. of *lobe*, a lobe.]
 1. a small lobe.
 2. a subdivision of a lobe.

lob·ū·lette', *n.* [dim. of *lobule*.] a minute lobule or part of a lobule.

lob'wŏrm, *n.* same as *lugworm*.

lō'çăl, *a.* [Fr. *local*; LL. *localis*, pertaining or belonging to a place, from L. *locus*, place.]
 1. relating to place.
 2. of, characteristic of, or confined to a particular place; as, items of *local* interest.
 3. restricted; narrow; confined; as, *local* outlook.
 4. of or for a particular part or specific area of the body.
 5. making all stops along its run; as, a *local* train.
 6. in mathematics, related to or concerning a locus.
 local action; in law, an action which must be brought in the particular county or jurisdiction where the cause arises.
 local attraction; (a) in magnetism, any attraction near the compass causing the needle to deviate; (b) in astronomy, deviations from the direction of gravity, caused by attraction due to irregularities in the density or form of the earth's crust.
 local battery; a battery that supplies the power for recording instruments in a telegraph office as distinguished from the battery supplying a current for the line.
 local circuit; in telegraphy, the circuit of a local battery.
 local color; customs and other features characteristic of a certain region or time, introduced into a novel, play, etc. to supply realism.
 local government; (a) government of the affairs of a town, district, etc. by the people living there; (b) the people chosen to administer this government.
 local option; the right of determing by a vote of the residents whether something, especially the sale of intoxicating liquors, shall be permitted, restricted, or forbidden in their locality.
 local preacher; a layman in the Methodist church licensed to preach within a certain district.
 local time; the time of a place according to its particular meridian.
 local value; in arithmetic, the value attached to the place of a digit.

lō'çăl, *n.* 1. a local train, bus, etc.
 2. a newspaper item relating to a particular community and having interest only to the residents of it.
 3. a chapter or branch of a larger organization, especially of a labor union.
 4. in telegraphy, a local-circuit battery or the circuit itself.

lō·çăle', *n.* [Fr. *local*, a locality.]
 1. a place, spot, or site; specifically, a location considered with reference to the events and circumstances surrounding it.
 2. anything limited to a certain locality.

lō'çăl·ișm, *n.* 1. the state or condition of being local; the influence that a particular place or locality exerts.
 2. affection for a particular place.
 3. the narrowness or limitation of thought or feeling growing out of such affection: provincialism.
 4. a way of speaking or acting that is peculiar to a certain locality; a local custom.
 5. a word, meaning, expression, pronunciation, etc. peculiar to one locality.

lō·çal'i·ty, *n.*; *pl.* **lō·çal'i·tieș,** [LL. *localitas*, from *localis*, belonging to a place, from L. *locus*, a place.]
 1. the state or condition of existing in a place or in a certain portion of space; position with regard to surrounding objects, landmarks, etc.; as, a sense of *locality*.
 2. a district; neighborhood; situation; place; particularly, geographical place or situation.
 3. limitation to a county, district, or place; as, *locality* of trial.
 4. in phrenology, the faculty which enables one to remember the relative positions of places.

lō'çăl·ī·zā·ble, *a.* capable of being localized or given a definite place.

lō''çăl·i·zā'tion, *n.* 1. the act of localizing or the state of being localized.
 2. in psychology, the reference of sensation to a certain part of the body where it originates.

lō'çăl·īze, *v.t.*; localized, *pt.*, *pp.*; localizing, *ppr.* 1. to make local; to limit or confine to a particular place, area, or locality.
 2. to determine the specific local origin of, as a tradition.

lō'çăl·ly, *adv.* 1. in a local way; with respect to place; in place; as, to be *locally* distant.
 2. within a given area or areas; as, the tornado did much damage *locally*.

lō'çāte (*or* lō-kāt'), *v.t.*; located, *pt.*, *pp.*; locating, *ppr.* [L. *locatus*, pp. of *locare*, to place, from *locus*, a place.]
 1. to fix or establish in a particular spot or position; to place; to settle; as, to *locate* oneself upon a certain street.
 2. to select, survey, and settle the bounds of, as a particular tract of land; to designate and determine the site of; as, to *locate* a church or a school.
 3. to discover the position of after a search; as, he *located* the seat of the trouble.
 4. to show the position of; as, *locate* Guam for me on this map.
 5. to assign to a particular place, function, occupation, etc.

lō'çāte, *v.i.* to settle; as, they *located* in Iowa. [Colloq.]

lō·çā'tion, *n.* 1. a locating or being located.
 2. situation; position in space; place where a factory, house, etc. is; as, the *location* of the city is favorable for commerce.
 3. that which is located; an area marked off or designated for a specific purpose.
 4. an outdoor set, away from the studio, where scenes for a motion picture are photographed.
 5. in civil law, a leasing on rent.
 contract of location; a contract for personal services or for the use of a chattel for determined hire.

loç'à·tive, *a.* 1. in grammar, designating or of a case expressing place where, or in which, as in Latin, Greek, Sanskrit, etc.
 2. serving to indicate or locate the position of something.

loç'à·tive, *n.* 1. the locative case.
 2. a word in the locative case.

lō'çā·tŏr, *n.* one who locates land for settlement.

lō·cel'lāte, *a.* divided into compartments or locelli.

lō·cel'lus, *n.*; *pl.* **lō·cel'lī,** [L., dim. of *loculus*, a little place.] a small loculus, or secondary cell.

loçh, *n.* [Gael. *loch*, a lake.]
 1. a lake. [Scot.]
 2. a bay or arm of the sea, especially when narrow and nearly surrounded by land. [Scot.]

loçh, *n.* same as *lambative*.

Loçh·ä'bēr ax, a weapon of war formerly used by the Scottish Highlanders.

loçh'āġe, *n.* [Gr. *lochagos*, from *lochos*, a body of men, and *agein*, to lead.] in ancient Greece, an officer who commanded a company.

lōche, *n.* same as *loach*.

lō'çhi·à (*or* lok'i-à), *n.pl.* [Gr. *lochia*, neut. pl. of *lochios*, pertaining to childbirth, from *lochos*, a lying-in, childbirth.] the discharge from the vagina for several weeks after childbirth.

lō'çhi·ăl, *a.* pertaining to lochia.

Loçh·in·vär', *n.* the hero of a ballad in Scott's *Marmion*, who boldly rides off with his sweetheart just as she is about to be married to another.

lō'cī, *n.* plural of *locus*.

lock, *n.* [ME. *lokke*; AS. *loc*; basic sense "a bend, twist."]
 1. a tuft of hair; a tress; a ringlet.
 A *lock* of hair will draw more than a cable rope. —Grew.
 2. [*pl.*] the hair of the head. [Poetic.]
 3. a tuft of cotton, wool, etc.
 4. a small quantity of hay, straw, etc.; a handful. [Dial.]

lock, *n.* [ME. *lokke*; AS. *loc*, a bolt, bar, fastening.]
 1. a mechanical device furnished with a spring and bolt, for fastening a door, strongbox, etc. by means of a key or combination.
 2. anything that fastens something else and prevents it from opening, turning, etc.
 3. a locking together; jam.
 4. an enclosed part of a canal, waterway, etc. equipped with gates so that the level of the water can be changed to raise or lower boats from one level to another.

CANAL LOCK

 5. the mechanism of a firearm used to explode the ammunition charge.
 6. in engineering, an airtight room opening into a compartment where the air is under compression.
 7. in wrestling, any of several holds; as, an arm *lock*.
 8. in sheet-metal working, a joint made when two lapped edges are folded over.
 9. in plastering, the projection of the plaster behind the laths, by means of which it is held in place.
 combination lock; see under *combination*.
 lock, stock, and barrel; completely. [Colloq.]
 under lock and key; locked up; safely put away.

lock, *v.t.*; locked (lokt), *pt.*, *pp.*; locking, *ppr.* [ME. *lokken*, *louken*; AS. *lucan*, to shut, close, fasten.]
 1. to fasten by means of a lock; as, to *lock* a door; to *lock* a trunk.
 2. to jam together so as to make immovable; as, the gears are *locked*.
 3. to shut (*up*, *in*, or *out*); to confine with, or as with, a lock, or in an enclosed place; as, to be *locked* in a prison; to *lock* money up in a box.
 4. to close fast; to press together closely; to seal; as, the frost *locks* up our rivers.
 5. to join or unite firmly, as by intertwining or infolding; as, to *lock* arms.
 6. to embrace closely; as, to *lock* one in the arms.
 7. to equip (a canal, etc.) with a lock or locks.
 8. to move or pass (a ship) through a lock.
 to lock away; to store or safeguard in a locked box, container, etc.
 to lock out; (a) to shut out by or as by locking the door against; (b) to keep (workers) from a place of employment in an attempt to make them accept the employer's terms.
 to lock up; (a) to fasten the doors of (a house, etc.) by means of locks; (b) to enclose or store in a locked container; (c) to put in jail.
 to lock up a form; in printing, to fix the types or pages in a mental frame so as to prepare them for the press.

lock, *v.i.* 1. to become locked.
 2. to be capable of being locked.
 3. to intertwine or interlock; to link together.
 4. to close tightly and firmly; as, his jaws *locked*.
 5. to jam, as gears.
 6. in fencing, to engage.

lock'āġe, *n.* 1. materials for locks in a canal; works which form a lock on a canal.
 2. the act of moving a ship from one water level to another by means of a lock.
 3. the construction or operation of locks in a canal, etc.
 4. toll paid for passing the locks of a canal.
 5. elevation or amount of elevation and descent made by the locks of a canal.

lock bāy, the water held by a lock.

lock chām'bēr, the space surrounded by the walls and gates of a canal lock.

lock'ēr, *n.* 1. one who or that which locks.
 2. a chest, closet, compartment, drawer, etc., usually of metal, which can be fastened with a lock, especially such a container for individual use.
 3. a chest or compartment in a ship's cabin to store things in.

4. in ecclesiastical usage, a recess or niche near the altar intended as a depository for water, oil, etc.

chain locker; the locker that holds the chain cables of a ship.

Davy Jones's locker; see under *Davy Jones*.

not a shot in the locker; not a cent in the pocket.

lock'ẽr rọọm, a room equipped with lockers, especially one used as a place for changing and storing one's clothes, as in a gymnasium, club, etc.

lock'et, *n.* [ME. *loket*; OFr. *locquet, loquet*, dim. of *loc*, a latch, lock.]

1. a small, hinged case of gold, silver, or other metal, for holding a picture, lock of hair, etc.: it is usually worn suspended from a necklace.

2. a small lock; a catch or spring to fasten a necklace or other ornament. [Obs.]

3. that part of a sword scabbard where the hook is attached.

lock gāte, a gate used to open and close a canal or river lock.

lock'hōle, *n.* 1. a keyhole. [Obs.]

2. the recess into which the lock of a gunstock fits.

lock hos'pi·tăl, a hospital for the treatment of venereal diseases. [Brit.]

Lock'i·ăn, *a.* of or pertaining to John Locke (1632–1704), an English philosopher.

Lock'i·ăn, *n.* a follower of John Locke.

lock'ing pal'let, a detent tooth in the escapement of chronometers and watches which engages the scape-wheel teeth in succession.

lock'ing plāte, 1. a rub iron.

2. a nut lock.

3. in a clock, the notched wheel that regulates the number of strokes.

lock'jạw, *n.* [short for earlier *locked jaw*.] a form of the disease tetanus, in which the jaws become firmly closed because of spasmodic muscular contraction.

lock'less, *a.* without a lock.

lock'măn, *n.* 1. in Scotland, a public executioner. [Obs.]

2. in the Isle of Man, a coroner's summoner.

lock'nut, *n.* a lock nut.

lock nut, 1. a thin nut screwed down hard on an ordinary nut to prevent the latter from working loose.

2. a specially designed nut that locks itself when screwed down tight.

lock'out, *n.* the refusal by an employer to allow his employees to come in to work unless they agree to his terms.

lock plāte, the plate to which the lock of a gun is fastened.

lock rāil, the rail of a door to which the lock is fastened.

lock'răm, *n.* [Fr. *locrenan*, a kind of unbleached linen, from *Locrenan*, in Brittany, the place where it was made.]

1. a sort of coarse linen.

2. nonsense; gibberish. [Brit. Dial.]

lock'smith, *n.* one whose work is making or repairing locks and keys.

lock step, a method of marching in such close file that the corresponding legs of the marchers must keep step precisely.

lock stitch, a stitch, as by a sewing machine, in which two threads are interlocked at short intervals.

lock'up, *n.* 1. a locking up.

2. a being locked up, as in a jail.

3. a jail.

lock'y, *a.* having locks or tufts.

lō'cō, *n.* [Sp. *loco*, mad, insane.]

1. same as *locoweed*.

2. loco disease.

lō'cō, *v.t.*; locoed, *pt., pp.*; locoing, *ppr.* 1. to poison with locoweed; to affect with the loco disease.

2. to craze. [Slang.]

lō'cō, *a.* crazy; demented. [Slang.]

lō'cō-, [from L. *locus*, a place.] a combining form, meaning: (a) *from place to place*, as in *locomotive*; (b) *a particular place*, as in *locodescriptive*.

lō'cō ci·tā'tō, [L.] in the place cited or quoted: used in footnotes to refer to a previously cited passage.

lō''cō·dē·sçrip'tive, *a.* [*loco-*, and *descriptive*.] describing a particular place or places.

lō'cō dis·ēaṣe', *n.* a chronic nervous disease of horses, cattle, and sheep, caused by locoweed poisoning.

lō·çō·fō'çō, *n.*; *pl.* **lō·çō·fō'çōṣ,** [a term coined in 1834 on the model of *locomotive* (which was interpreted to mean *self-moving*), and applied to a cigar with a self-lighting composition at the end of it; from L. *locus*, place, and It. *fuoco*, fire; LL. *focus*, fire, from L. *focus*, hearth.]

1. a friction match; also, a kind of self-lighting cigar. [Obs.]

2. (a) [L–] a faction of the Democratic party (c. 1835), called the Equal Rights party; (b) a member of this faction.

3. formerly, any Democrat.

lō''cō·mō'bile, *a.* moving by its own power; self-propelling. [Rare.]

lō·çō·mō'tion, *n.* [*loco-*, and *motion*.]

1. the act of moving from place to place.

2. the power of moving from place to place; as, most animals possess *locomotion*; plants have life, but not *locomotion*.

lō·çō·mō'tive, *a.* [*loco-*, and LL. *motivus*, moving.]

1. of locomotion.

2. moving or capable of moving from one place to another; not stationary.

3. of engines that move under their own power; as, *locomotive* design.

lō·çō·mō'tive, *n.* an engine that can move about by its own power; especially, an electric, steam, or diesel engine on wheels, designed to push or pull a railroad train.

compound locomotive; a locomotive constructed on the principle of the compound steam engine.

consolidation locomotive; a locomotive used in freight traffic, having four pairs of driving wheels.

mogul locomotive; a freight engine having three pairs of connected driving wheels and a swinging two-wheeled truck in front.

lō''çō·mō'tive en'ġine, same as *locomotive*.

lō·çō·mō'tive·ness, lō''çō·mō·tiv'i·ty, *n.* the quality of being locomotive.

lō·çō·mō'tŏr, *n.* [*loco-*, and L. *motor*, a mover, from *movere*, to move.] one who or that which has power of locomotion.

lō·çō·mō'tŏr, *a.* of locomotion.

locomotor ataxia; a chronic disease of the nervous system, usually caused by syphilis: it is characterized at first by intense pain, and later by disturbances of sensation, loss of reflexes and of muscular co-ordination, functional disorders of organs, etc.

lō'çō·plant, *n.* same as *locoweed*.

lō'çō·weed, *n.* any of a number of plants of the pea family, with dense clusters of small flowers resembling sweet peas: it grows on western prairies and causes loco disease in sheep, horses, or cattle that have eaten it.

loç'ū·lȧ·ment, *n.* in botany, same as *loculus*.

loç'ū·lăr, *a.* [LL. *locularis*, contained in boxes or cells, from L. *loculus*, a cell, box.] in botany and zoology, of, having the nature of, or consisting of cells, or loculi: used most frequently in combination, as tri*locular*.

loç'ū·lāte, loç'ū·lāt·ed, *a.* same as *locular*.

loç'ūle, *n.* a loculus, or cell.

loç''ū·li·cī'dăl, *a.* [L. *loculus*, a compartment, and *cædere*, to cut.] in botany, cutting into or through the loculus.

loç'ū·lōse, loç'ū·lous, *a.* [L. *loculosus*, full of small compartments, from *loculus*, a small compartment, dim. of *locus*, a place.] divided internally into loculi, or cells. [Rare.]

loç'ū·lus, *n.*; *pl.* **loç'ū·lī,** [L., a small compartment, box, dim. of *locus*, a place.]

1. a small space or place; a little chamber or cell; specifically, any small cavity, cell, or chamber in plant or animal tissue.

LOCULICIDAL DEHISCENCE
v, valves; *d*, dissepiments; *c*, axis

2. in ancient tombs, a recess or small chamber for the reception of an urn or body.

lō'çum tē'nenṣ, [L., holding the place; *locum*, accus. of *locus*, place, and *tenens*, ppr. of *tenere*, to hold.] one who assumes the place of another temporarily; a temporary substitute, as for a doctor or clergyman. [Chiefly Brit.]

lō'çus, *n.*; *pl.* **lō'cī,** [L. *locus*, place.]

1. a place; a locality.

2. in mathematics, (a) any system of points, lines, etc. which satisfies one or more given conditions; (b) a line, plane, etc. every point of which satisfies a given condition and which contains no point that does not satisfy this condition.

lō'çus çlas'si·çus, *pl.* **lō'cī çlas'si·cī,** [L.] a passage generally recognized as authoritative or illustrative of its subject and hence often cited.

lō'çus in quō, [L.] the place in which.

lō'çust, *n.* [ME. and OFr. *locuste*; L. *locusta*, a locust.]

LOCUST (*Pachytylus migratorius*)

1. any of various large winged insects, related to the grasshoppers and crickets: certain locusts travel in large swarms destroying nearly all vegetation in their path.

2. a cicada or harvest fly.

3. a tree, *Robinia pseudacacia*, common throughout the eastern United States, belonging to the pulse family and having delicate pinnate leaves, thorny branches, and dense clusters of white, heavily-scented flowers: also called *black locust*. Its wood is very serviceable for posts, turnery, etc.

4. the yellowish, exceedingly hard and durable wood of this tree.

5. any tree the pods of which resemble those of the *Robinia pseudacacia*, especially the carob tree.

6. the honey locust.

bristly locust; the *Robinia hispida* of the southern United States, cultivated for its rose-pink blossoms: also called *rose acacia*.

clammy locust; a leguminous shrub, *Robinia viscosa*, resembling the bristly locust and found in the same region.

lō·çus'tȧ, *n.* a small spike or elongated cluster of flowers in grasses.

lō'çust bēan, the fruit of the carob tree.

lō'çust bee'tle, a beetle, *Cyllene robiniæ*, the larvae of which bore into the locust tree.

lō'çust bīrd, the rose-colored starling, *Pastor roseus*, of Asia. It feeds upon locusts.

lō''çus·tel'lē, *n.* [from L. *locusta*, a locust; so called because its note resembles that of the locust.] the European grasshopper warbler.

lō·çus'tid, *n.* a green grasshopper or katydid, of the locust family.

Lō·çus'ti·dae, *n.pl.* a family of orthopterous insects, having much-compressed bodies, long threadlike antennae, and four jointed tarsi: the best-known species are the green grasshoppers, katydids, and crickets.

lō'çust·ing, *a.* swarming and devastating after the manner of locusts. [Rare.]

lō'çust shrimp, same as *squilla*.

lō·çū'tion, *n.* [L. *locutio (-onis)*, a speaking, from *loqui*, to speak.]

1. a word, phrase, or expression.

2. a particular style of speech.

loc'ū·tō·ry, *n.* [ML. *locutorium*, a room for conversation, from *locutor*, a speaker, from *loqui*, to speak.] a place where conversation is permitted; specifically, an apartment in a monastery or convent where the inmates may meet friends.

lōde, *n.* [ME. *lode, lod*; AS. *lad*, a way, path, a carrying, from *lithan*, to go, to travel.]

1. a path; a course. [Brit. Dial.]

2. a reach of water; a watercourse; a ditch. [Brit. Dial.]

3. in mining, (a) a vein containing metallic ore and filling a well-defined fissure in the rock; (b) any deposit of ore separated from the adjoining rock.

lōde'măn·ȧġe, *n.* pilotage; skill of a pilot. [Obs.]

lōdeṣ'măn, *n.* a pilot. [Obs.]

lōde'stär, lōad'stär, *n.* [ME. *lodesterre*; *lode*, from AS. *lad*, a way, course, and *sterre*, from AS. *steorra*, a star.]

1. a star by which one directs his course; especially, the North Star.

2. a guiding ideal; a model for imitation.

lōde'stōne, *n.* same as *loadstone*.

lodġe, *n.* [ME. *logge, loge*, hut, mason's workshop; OFr. *loge*, a lodge, hut; LL. *lobia, laubia*, a gallery, covered way; O.H.G. *lauba, loupa*, an arbor, from *loub*, a leaf.]

1. (a) the hut or tent of an American Indian; (b) those who live in it.

2. a temporary habitation; a cabin erected for temporary occupancy. [Now Dial.]

3. a small house, especially one for a servant, or one for use during a special season; as, a caretaker's *lodge*, a hunting *lodge*.

4. the den of a wild animal, especially of a beaver.

5. (a) the place where members of a local chapter of an association, especially of a secret fraternal organization, hold their meetings; (b) the local chapter itself; (c) a meeting of such a chapter.

6. in mining, the place at the shaft where the ore is dumped before hoisting; also, a sump.

7. a group of objects contiguously placed. [Obs.]

lodġe, *v.t.*; lodged, *pt.*, *pp.*; lodging, *ppr.* [ME. *loggen, logen*; OFr. *loger*, from *loge*, a lodge, hut.]

1. to furnish with a temporary habitation; to house.

2. to rent rooms to; to take as a paying guest.

3. to set, lay, or deposit for keeping or preservation, for a longer or shorter time; as, the men *lodged* their arms in the arsenal.

4. to fix; to settle in the heart, mind, or memory; to contain for keeping.

I can give no reason
More than a *lodged* hate. —Shak.

5. to put or send into a place or position by shooting, thrusting, etc.; to place; to plant; to infix.

He *lodged* an arrow in a tender breast. —Addison.

6. in hunting, to harbor; to cover; to drive to shelter; as, to *lodge* a deer.

7. to beat down (growing crops), as rain.

8. to bring (an accusation, complaint, etc.) before legal authorities.

9. to confer (powers) upon (with *in*).

Syn.—entertain, harbor, shelter.

lodġe, *v.i.* 1. to reside; to dwell; to rest in a place.

And *lodge* such daring souls in little men? —Pope.

2. to rest or dwell for a time, as for a night, a week, or a month.

3. to live (*with* another or *in* his home) as a paying guest.

4. to fall down and become entangled, as grain.

5. to come to rest or be placed and remain firmly fixed (with *in*); as, the bullet *lodged* in the tree trunk.

lodġed, *a.* in heraldry, at rest and lying on the ground, as a buck, hart, hind, etc.

A BUCK LODGED

lodġ'ẽr, *n.* one who or that which lodges; especially, one who lives in a rented room or rooms in the house of another.

lodġ'ing, *n.* 1. a place of rest for a night, or of residence for a time; quarters.

2. [*pl.*] a room or rooms rented in the house of another.

3. place of residence; harbor; cover.

The *lodging* of delight. —Spenser.

lodġ'ing house, a house in which lodgings are let; a rooming house.

lodġ'ment, lodġe'ment, *n.* 1. the act of lodging, or the state of being lodged.

2. an accumulation or collection of something deposited or remaining at rest, often in the nature of an obstruction; a deposit; as, the *lodgment* of mud in a tank.

3. a lodging place.

4. in military science, the occupation of a position, as in a siege, by the besieging party, and the formation of an intrenchment thereon to maintain it against recapture.

lod'i·cūle, *n.* [L. *lodicula*, dim. of *lodix* (*-icis*), a coverlet.] in botany, one of the scales which occur at the base of the fruit of grasses.

Lod″ō·ic'ē·ȧ, *n.* [named after *Laodice*, daughter of Priam, king of Troy.] in botany, a genus of fan palms found in the Seychelles Islands. *Lodoicea sechellarum*, the double cocoanut, is the only species.

loel'ling·īte, *n.* [so called from *Lölling*, in Austria, and *-ite*.] in mineralogy, a light-colored arsenide of iron, $FeAs_2$, which crystallizes in the orthorhombic system.

loe·mog'rȧ·phy, *n.* same as *loimography*.

lō'ess (lō'is), *n.* [G. *löss, loess*.] a fine-grained, yellowish-brown, extremely fertile loam deposited by the wind.

loffe, *v.i.* to laugh. [Obs.]

loft, *n.* [ME. *lofte*; Late AS. *loft*, from ON. *loft*, air, heaven, upper room.]

1. (a) an attic or atticlike space, usually not partitioned off into rooms, immediately below the roof of a house, barn, etc.; (b) any of the upper stories of a warehouse or factory.

2. a gallery or raised apartment within a larger apartment, as in a church, hall, etc.; as, an organ *loft*; a hay *loft*.

3. in golf, (a) the slope given to the face of a club to aid in knocking the ball in a high curve; (b) a stroke that knocks the ball in a high curve.

loft, *v.t.*; lofted, *pt.*, *pp.*; lofting, *ppr.* 1. to store in a loft.

2. to provide with a loft.

3. in golf, (a) to strike (a ball) in such a way as to knock it in a high curve; (b) to hold (a club) so that the face slants back.

loft, *v.i.* in golf, to knock a ball in a high curve.

loft, *a.* proud; lofty. [Obs.]

loft'ẽr, *n.* a golf club with a sloping face to aid in lofting the ball: also called *lofting iron*.

loft'i·ly, *adv.* in a lofty manner.

loft'i·ness, *n.* the state or quality of being lofty.

loft'ing ī'ron (-ũrn), same as *lofter*.

lofts'măn, *n.*; *pl.* **lofts'men,** in shipbuilding, one who lays out the figure of a ship to full scale on the floor of a mold loft.

loft'y, *a.*; *comp.* loftier; *superl.* loftiest. 1. elevated; very high; towering.

2. elevated in character, quality, or condition; sublime; exalted; eminent; dignified.

3. proud; haughty; arrogant.

Syn.—high, exalted, stately, sublime, proud, arrogant.

log, *n.* [ME. *logge*; prob. from M. Scand. dial.]

1. a section of the trunk of a felled tree, either in its natural state or cut up for use in building, as firewood, etc.

2. [so called because originally it was a quadrant of wood.] a device for measuring the speed of a ship: an old form is a piece of board forming the quadrant of a circle of about six inches radius, balanced by a small plate of lead nailed on the circular part, so as to lie perpendicularly in the water, with about two-thirds immersed under the surface. One end of a line, called the log line, is fastened to the log, while the other is wound round a reel at the stern of the ship. When the log is thrown out, it unwinds the line from the reel as the ship moves forward, and the length of line unwound in a given time gives the rate of the ship's sailing. This is calculated by knots made on the line at certain distances, while the time is measured by a sandglass of a certain number of seconds. The length between the knots is so proportioned to the time of the glass that the number of knots unwound while the glass runs down shows the number of miles the ship is sailing per hour. An improved form of the log is a piece of mechanism towed astern of the ship, the distance traversed being indicated on a dial.

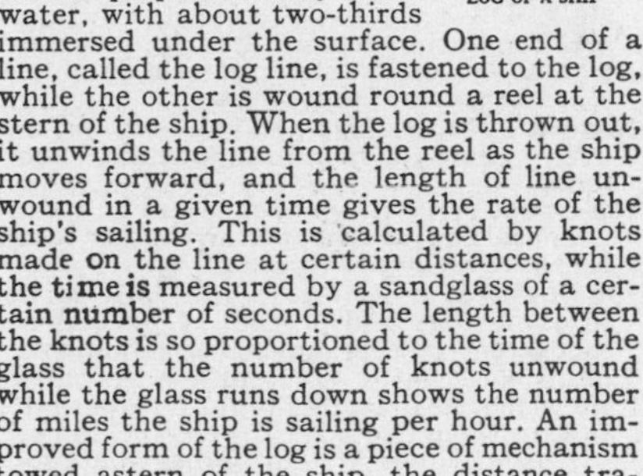

LOG OF A SHIP

3. a daily record of a ship's speed and progress; a logbook: in it are usually entered the ship's position and any notable incidents of the voyage.

4. (a) a record of the operating history of an aircraft or of its engines; (b) a record of a pilot's flying time, experience, etc.

5. any record of progress, as on a journey, in an experiment, etc.

log, *a.* made of a log or logs.

log, *v.t.*; logged, *pt.*, *pp.*; logging, *ppr.* 1. to saw (trees) into logs.

2. to cut down the trees of (a region).

3. to enter in a ship's log.

4. to sail (a specified distance) as indicated by a log.

log, *v.i.* to cut down trees and transport the logs to a sawmill.

log, *v.t.* and *v.i.* to move to and fro; to rock. [Brit. Dial.]

log-, same as *logo-*.

log, *n.* [Heb. *lōgh*.] a Hebrew measure of liquids equivalent to about a pint.

log'ăn, *n.* same as *loggan*.

lō'găn·ber·ry, *n.*; *pl.* **lō'găn″ber″ries,** [after Judge J. H. *Logan*, of California, who developed it in 1881.]

1. a hybrid bramble developed from the blackberry and the red raspberry and extensively grown for its fruit.

2. the highly acid, purplish-red fruit of this shrub.

Lō·gā'ni·ȧ, *n.* [named after James *Logan*, an Irish botanist.] in botany, the typical genus of the *Loganiaceæ*.

Lō·gan·i·ā'cē·ae (*or* -gā-ni-), *n.pl.* [*Logania* and *-aceæ*.] a family of tropical exogens, consisting of trees, shrubs, and herbaceous plants.

lō·gan·i·ā'ceous, *a.* of or pertaining to the *Loganiaceæ*.

log·ȧ·oed'iç, *a.* [LL. *logaœdicus*; L.Gr. *logaoidikos*, from Gr. *logos*, speech, prose, and *aoidē*, song.] having a meter of combined dactyls and trochees or anapests and iambics.

log·ȧ·oed'iç, *n.* a logaoedic verse.

log'ȧ·rithm, *n.* [Gr. *logos*, word, proportion, ratio, and *arithmos*, number.] the exponent of the power to which it is necessary to raise a fixed number (the *base*) to produce the given number (the *antilogarithm*). The logarithm of N to the base a is thus expressed, $\log_a N$. By taking different values of N in each system, different values of x will be found in each system, and such numbers being registered will form tables of logarithms. In the common system of logarithms, the logarithm of 100 is 2, because 10 raised to the second power = 100; similarly, the logarithm of 1,000 = 3, of 10,000 = 4, and so on. When the logarithms form a series in arithmetical progression, the corresponding natural numbers form a series in geometrical progression, thus—

Logarithms..	0	1	2	3	4	5
Natural numbers....	1	10	100	1,000	10,000	100,000

The logarithms of numbers between 1 and 10 consist of decimals; of numbers between 10 and 100, they consist of the integer 1 and a decimal; of numbers between 100 and 1000, of the integer 2 and a decimal, and so on. The integral part of a logarithm is called the index or characteristic, and it is always less by 1 than the number of integer places in the corresponding natural number: thus the index of the logarithm of 3 is 0, of 30 is 1, of 300 is 2, and so on. The decimal part of a logarithm is called the mantissa. Logarithms are of great service in shortening and facilitating the arithmetical operations of multiplication and division. They were invented by Lord Napier of Scotland in 1614, and improved by Henry Briggs, professor of geometry at Oxford, in 1624.

arithmetical complement of a logarithm; the difference between the given logarithm and 10.

binary logarithms; see under *binary*.

Briggsian or *common logarithms*; logarithms having 10 for a base: named after Henry Briggs, who invented them.

decimal logarithms; Briggsian logarithms.

Gaussian logarithms; tables of logarithms compiled by Karl F. Gauss to simplify the process of finding the logarithm of the sum or difference of two numbers from the logarithms of the numbers.

hyperbolic logarithms; see under *hyperbolic*.

log″ȧ·rith·met'iç, *a.* logarithmic. [Rare.]

log″ȧ·rith·met'i·căl, *a.* logarithmic. [Rare.]

log″ȧ·rith·met'i·căl·ly, *adv.* logarithmically.

log″ȧ·rith'miç, *a.* of a logarithm or logarithms.

logarithmic curve; same as *logistic curve* under *logistic*.

logarithmic spiral; a curve line somewhat analogous to the common logarithmic curve. It intersects all its radiants at the same angle, and the tangent of this angle is the modulus of the system of logarithms which the particular spiral represents.

log″ȧ·rith'mi·căl, *a.* same as *logarithmic*.

log″ȧ·rith'mi·căl·ly, *adv.* by the use or aid of logarithms.

log″ȧ·rith'mō·teçh″ny, *n.* [E. *logarithm*, and Gr. *technē*, art.] the art of calculating logarithms.

log'book, *n.* a log (senses 3 and 4).

log chip, a flat piece of wood attached to a line and reel and thrown into the water to measure a ship's rate of speed.

log'çock, *n.* the North American pileated woodpecker.

lōge (lōzh), *n.* [Fr.] 1. a lodge. [Obs.]

2. a box at a theater, opera house, etc.

log'fish, *n.* the barrel fish or rudder fish.

log frāme, a gang saw for sawing timber into planks.

log'găn, *n.* a rocking stone; a large stone so balanced as to be easily made to rock to and fro.

log'găt, *n.* logget. [Obs.]

logged (logd), *a.* water-logged; rendered or heavy, as by being saturated with water.

log'gẽr, *n.* 1. a person whose work is logging; lumberjack.

2. a machine for loading logs on flatcars.

log'gẽr·head (-hed), *n.* 1. a blockhead; a dunce: a dolt.

2. a spherical mass of iron, with a long handle, used to heat tar, etc.

3. a species of marine turtle, *Thalassochelys caouana* or *caretta*, found in the warmer parts of the Atlantic, near America: the name is also given to *Thalassochelys olivacea*, a turtle found in the Indian Ocean.

4. a shrike, *Lanius ludovicianus*, found in the southern part of the United States.

5. a timberhead in a whaleboat around which a turn of the harpoon line is taken.

6. the flycatcher: a West Indian name.

at loggerheads; engaged in a dispute; at variance.

to fall or *go to loggerheads*; to come to blows.

log′gẽr·head″ed, *a.* dull; stupid; doltish.

log′gẽr·hēat, *n.* same as *loggerhead*, sense 2.

log′get, *n.* 1. a small log. [Obs.]

2. [*pl.*] an English game, played by fixing a stake in the ground and pitching small pieces of wood at it, the nearest thrower winning. [Obs.]

loġ′ġiȧ (lod′jȧ), *n.* [It.] an arcaded or roofed gallery built into or projecting from the side of a building, particularly one overlooking an open court.

LOGGIA

log′ging, *n.* the occupation of cutting down trees, cutting them into logs, and transporting them to the sawmill.

log glȧss, a small hourglass used in heaving the log to obtain the rate of sailing.

log′i·ȧ, *n. pl.*; *sing.* **log′i·on,** [Gr., pl., sayings, from *logos*, word.] maxims attributed to a religious leader; especially, [L–], sayings attributed to Jesus but not recorded in the Gospels.

-loġ′iç, same as *-logical*.

loġ′iç, *n.* [L. *logica*; Gr. *logikē*, logic, f. of *logikos*, pertaining to speech, reason, from *logos*, speech, reason.]

1. the science of correct reasoning; the science which deals with the criteria of valid thought.

2. a book dealing with this science.

3. correct reasoning; valid induction or deduction; as, *logic* shows us a better course.

4. way of reasoning, whether correct or incorrect; as, at this point our *logic* was at fault.

5. the system of principles underlying any art or science.

6. necessary connection or outcome, as through the working of cause and effect; as, the *logic* of events.

loġ′i·căl, *a.* 1. of or used in the science of logic.

2. according to the principles of logic, or correct reasoning.

3. necessary or to be expected because of what has gone before; that follows as reasonable.

4. using or accustomed to use correct reasoning.

-loġ′i·căl, [Gr. *-logikos*, from *logikos*, pertaining to speech, from *logos*, speech.] a suffix used to form adjectives corresponding to nouns ending in *-logy*, as in bio*logical*, patho*logical*.

loġ·i·cal′i·ty, *n.* the quality of being logical; logicalness.

loġ′iç·ăl·ly, *adv.* according to the rules of logic; as, to argue *logically*.

loġ′iç·ăl·ness, *n.* the quality of being logical.

loġ′i·căl poș′i·tiv·ișm, a movement in philosophy concerned with the unification of the sciences, especially by an analysis of the language of science and the consequent development of a vocabulary applicable to all sciences: also called *logical empiricism*.

lō·ġi′ciăn, *n.* a person skilled in logic.

Each fierce *logician* still expelling Locke.
—Pope.

log′i·ŏn, *n.* singular of *logia*.

lō·ġis′tiç, *a.* [from *logistics*.] of logistics.

lō·ġis′tiç, *a.* [Gr. *logistikos*, skilled in calculating, from *logistēs*, a calculator, from *logizesthai*, to compute, from *logos*, calculation.] of calculation.

logistic line or *curve*; a curve whose ordinates are in arithmetical progression, while its abscissas are in geometrical progression: called also *logarithmic curve*.

lō·ġis′tiç, *n.* the art of calculation; common arithmetic. [Rare.]

lō·ġis′tiç·ăl, *a.* same as *logistic*.

lō·ġis′tiçs, *n.* [*construed as sing.*], [Fr. *logistique*, from *loger*, to quarter.] the branch of military science having to do with moving, supplying, and quartering troops.

log līne, a graduated line attached to a log chip.

log′ō-, [from Greek *logos*, word, speech, ratio, proportion.] a combining form meaning *word, speech, discourse*, as in *logo*grapher, *logo*metric, etc.

log·ō·daed′ȧ·ly (-ded′), *n.* [Gr. *logodaidalia*, from *logodaidalos*; *logos*, word, speech, and *daidalos*, cunningly wrought.] a playing with words, as by passing from one meaning of them to another. [Rare.]

log′ō·gram, *n.* [Gr. *logos*, word, and *gramma*, letter, sign.] a phonogram or sign which represents a word, as **$** for *dollar*.

log·ō·gram·mat′iç, *a.* of or using logograms.

log′ō·grȧph, *n.* a logogram.

lō·gog′rȧ·phẽr, *n.* 1. one who is skilled in logography.

2. a historian or chronicler.

log·ō·graph′iç, *a.* pertaining to logography.

log·ō·graph′iç·ăl, *a.* logographic.

lō·gog′rȧ·phy, *n.* [Gr. *logographia*, from *logographos*, a writer of speeches, a historian, secretary; *logos*, word, speech, and *graphein*, to write.]

1. the use of logotypes in printing.

2. a method of reporting speeches in longhand. It requires a number of reporters acting at once, each of whom in succession takes down a few words.

log′ō·griph, *n.* [*logo-*, and Gr. *griphos*, a fishing basket, riddle.]

1. an anagram.

2. a kind of word puzzle in which it is required to discover a certain word by combining the letters of various given words.

lō·gom′ȧ·chist, *n.* one who contends about words.

lō·gom′ȧ·chy, *n.*; *pl.* **lō·gom′ȧ·chieș,** [Gr. *logomachia*, from *logomachos*, a fighter about words; *logos*, a word, and *machē*, a fight, battle.]

1. contention in words merely, or a contention about words; a war of words.

2. the game of anagrams.

lō·gom′ē·tẽr, *n.* [*logo-*, and Gr. *metron*, measure.] a scale for measuring chemical equivalents.

log·ō·met′riç, *a.* used to measure or ascertain chemical equivalents; pertaining to a logometer; as, a *logometric* scale.

log·ŏr·rhē′ȧ, *n.* [Gr. *logos*, word, and *roia*, flow.] in psychology and psychiatry, excessive and incoherent talking; abnormal volubility.

Log′os, *n.* [L. *logos*; Gr. *logos*, a word; the word by which the inward thought is expressed, the inward thought itself, from *legein*, to speak.]

1. [sometimes l–] in Greek philosophy, reason, thought of as constituting the controlling principle of the universe and as being manifested by speech.

2. in Christian theology, the Word of God; Jesus as the second person of the Trinity. John 1.

log′ō·thēte, *n.* [L.Gr. *logothetēs*, one who audits accounts; Gr. *logos*, word, account, and *thetos*, verbal adj. of *tithenai*, to place.] any of various officers of the Byzantine Empire; as, (a) the public treasurer; (b) the head of any administrative department; also, a chancellor, especially in Sicily.

log′ō·tȳpe, *n.* [*logo-*, and Gr. *typos*, an impression, type.] in typography, two or more letters, often making up a short word, cast in one piece but not united as in a ligature.

log pẽrch, a fresh-water American fish, *Percina caprodes*, the largest of the darter fishes: called also *hogfish* and *rockfish*.

log reel, a reel on which the log line is wound.

log′rōll, *v.i.*: logrolled, *pt.*, *pp.*; logrolling, *ppr.* to take part in logrolling.

log′rōll, *v.t.* to get passage of (a bill) by logrolling.

log′rōll·ẽr, *n.* 1. one who engages in logrolling in the political sense.

2. a mechanical device for loading logs on the carriage of a saw.

log′rōll·ing, *n.* 1. the act of rolling logs, as when a group of neighbors help to clear off land by rolling logs into some spot for burning, etc.

2. (a) a giving of help, praise, etc. in return for help, praise, etc.; (b) in politics, mutual aid among politicians, as by reciprocal voting for each other's bills.

3. the sport of birling.

log rụle, a mathematical table used to estimate the amount of lumber in board feet that can be sawed from a log of given size.

log slāte, in navigation, a slate on which is recorded the events of each day, to be afterward condensed and transferred to the ship's logbook.

-logue (-log), [Fr.; L. *-logus*; Gr. *-logos*, from *logos*, a word, speech, etc.] a combining form meaning *a* (specified kind of) *speaking* or *writing*, as in mono*logue*: also *-log*.

log′wood, *n.* 1. a tree, *Hæmatoxylon campechianum*, of Central America and the West Indies.

2. the hard, brownish-red wood of this tree, which is much used in dyeing.

LOGWOOD (*Hæmatoxylon campechianum*)

-lō′ġy, [Gr. *-logia*, from *legein*, to speak.] a combining form meaning: (a) *a* (specified kind of) *speaking*, as in eu*logy*; (b) *science, doctrine, theory of*, as in geo*logy*, theo*logy*.

lō′gy, *a.*; *comp.* logier; *superl.* logiest, [D. *log*, heavy, unwieldy.] dull or sluggish, as from overeating. [Colloq.]

Lō′hen·grin (lō′en-), *n.* in German legend, a knight of the Holy Grail, son of Parsifal: title character of an opera (1850) by Richard Wagner.

lō′hock, *n.* a lincture: also called *loch, lohoch*.

loi′miç, *a.* [Gr. *loimikos*, from *loimos*, a plague.] pertaining to contagious diseases; pestilential.

loi·mog′rȧ·phy, *n.* [Gr. *loimos*, plague, and *graphein*, to write.] a treatise on contagious epidemic diseases.

loi·mol′ō·ġy, *n.* [Gr. *loimos*, a plague, and *-logia*, from *legein*, to speak.] the science of epidemic diseases.

loin, *n.* [ME. *loine*; OFr. *logne, longe*, from L. *lumbus*, loin.]

1. [*usually in pl.*] the lower part of the back on either side of the backbone between the hipbones and the ribs.

2. the front part of the hindquarters of beef, lamb, mutton, veal, etc. with the flank removed.

3. [*pl.*] the hips and the lower abdomen regarded as a part of the body to be clothed or as the region of strength and procreative power.

to gird up one's loins; to get ready to do something difficult or strenuous.

loin′clọth, *n.* a cloth worn about the loins, as by some tribes in warm climates.

loir (lwär), *n.* [Fr.] a species of dormouse, *Myoxus glis*.

loi′tẽr, *v.i.*; loitered, *pt.*, *pp.*; loitering, *ppr.* [ME. *loitren*; M.D. *loteren*, to linger, loiter.]

1. to spend time idly (often with *about*); to linger; dawdle.

2. to walk or move slowly and indolently, with frequent stops and pauses; as, he *loitered* on the way.

loi′tẽr, *v.t.* to consume in trifles; to waste carelessly: used with *away*; as, he *loitered away* most of his leisure.

Syn.—linger, delay, tarry.

loi′tẽr·ẽr, *n.* a lingerer; one who delays, or is slow in motion; an idler; one who is sluggish or dilatory.

loi′tẽr·ing·ly, *adv.* in a loitering manner.

lō·kä′ō, *n.* [Chinese.] a green vegetable pigment; Chinese green indigo.

lōke, *n.* [AS. *loca*, a bar, bolt, an enclosure.] a private lane or road; a gateway; a hatch. [Brit. Dial.]

Lō′ki, *n.* [ON.] in Norse mythology, the god who constantly created discord and mischief: he caused the death of Balder.

Lō·lī′gō, *n.* [L., a cuttlefish.] a genus of cephalopods with lidless eyes, the fourth pair of arms hectocotylized, and a horny gladius.

Lō′li·um, *n.* [L., darnel, cockle, tares.] a genus of grasses containing a few species common in many parts of the Northern Hemisphere, two of the best-known being rye grass and darnel.

loll, *v.i.*; lolled, *pt.*, *pp.*; lolling, *ppr.* [ME. and M.D. *lollen*.]

1. to lean idly; to lie at ease; to lounge about in a relaxed or lazy manner.

Void of care, he *lolls* supine in state.
—Dryden.

2. to hang in a relaxed manner; to droop; as, their heads *lolled* forward in their sleep.

3. to hang extended from the mouth, as the tongue of an ox or a dog when heated with labor or exertion.

loll, *v.t.* to let hang loosely, as the tongue.

loll, *n.* the act of lolling.

lol·lȧ·pȧ·lọo′zȧ, lol·lȧ·pȧ·lọo′șȧ, *n.* something very striking or excellent. [Slang.]

Lol′lărd, *n.* [M.D. *lollaerd*, one who mumbles prayers or hymns, from *lollen*, to sing softly, to hum.] a member of a group of political and religious reformers of fourteenth- and fifteenth-century England, followers of John Wycliffe, whose doctrines anticipated many points in the later Protestant Reformation.

Lol'lărd·ism, *n.* same as *Lollardry.*

Lol'lărd·ry, Lol'lărd·y, *n.* the principles or tenets of the Lollards.

loll'ẽr, *n.* 1. one who lolls; a loafer.
2. [L–] a Lollard. [Obs.]

loll'ing·ly, *adv.* in a lolling manner.

lol'li·pop, lol'ly·pop, *n.* [child's word.] a piece of hard candy attached to the end of a small stick, etc.: also called *sucker.*

lol'lŏp, *v.i.* to move heavily; to lounge. [Brit. Dial.]

lol'ly, *n.* slush ice formed by the grinding together of ice floes.

lol'ly·gag, *v.i.*; lollygagged, *pt., pp.*; lollygagging, *ppr.* to waste time in trifling or aimless activity; fool around. [Colloq.]

lō'mȧ, *n.*; *pl.* **lō'mȧ·tȧ,** [L.Gr. *lōma* (-*atos*), hem fringe.] in ornithology, a membranous lobe; a flap, as on the toe of a bird.

lō'mȧ·tine, *a.* same as *lomatinous.*

lō·mat'i·nous, *a.* having lomata.

Lom'bȧrd, *n.* [OFr. *Lombard*; LL. *Lombardus,* a Lombard, from *Longobardus,* lit., long-beard, perh. from O.H.G. *lang,* long, and *bart,* beard.]
1. a native or inhabitant of Lombardy in Italy.
2. a member of a Germanic tribe that settled in the Po Valley.
3. [*also* l–] a banker or moneylender: so called because of the famous moneylenders of Lombardy.
4. [*also* l–] an institution for lending money.

Lom'bȧrd, *a.* of or pertaining to Lombardy or the Lombards.
Lombard Street; a street in London where many banks and financial houses are located; hence, the financial market or financiers of London.

lom'bȧrd, *n.* a kind of cannon formerly used.

Lom·bär'diç, *a.* 1. pertaining to the Lombards or Lombardy.
2. of the medieval architecture of northern Italy.
3. of the Renaissance painters in Lombardy.

Lom'bȧr·dy pop'lȧr, a tall, slender variety of the black poplar tree, with upward-curving branches.

Lom·brō'şi·ăn Sçhōol, a school of criminologists adhering to the theories and methods of Cesare Lombroso, an Italian criminologist, who regarded the criminal as a distinct and atavistic type of person.

lō'ment, *n.* the seed pod of the indehiscent legumes, which separates at the constrictions between the seeds when ripe.

LOMENT

lō·men·tā'ceous, *a.* 1. resembling a loment.
2. having loments.

lō·men'tum, *n.* same as *loment.*

lom'ō·nīte, *n.* same as *laumontite.*

lomp'ish, *a.* lumpish. [Obs.]

lond, *n.* land. [Obs.]

Lŏn'dŏn broil, a boneless cut of beef, as of the flank, that is marinated, then broiled, and served in thin slices cut usually on a diagonal.

Lon'dŏn·ẽr, *n.* a native or inhabitant of London.

Lŏn·dŏn·ēşe', *a.* pertaining to London.

Lŏn·dŏn·ēşe', *n.* the English language as spoken by Londoners; especially, cockney speech.

Lŏn'dŏn·īze, *v.t.* to make like London or the people of London.

Lŏn'dŏn prīde, 1. a hardy perennial herbaceous plant, *Saxifraga umbrosa,* which is native to Ireland and is cultivated in English gardens.
2. sweet William. [Brit. Dial.]

Lŏn'dŏn rock'et, a European plant, *Sisymbrium irio,* first appearing in London on the ruins of the fire of 1666.

Lŏn'dŏn tuft, sweet William.

lōne, *n.* a lane. [Brit. Dial.]

lōne, *a.* [from *alone.*]
1. by oneself; alone; solitary.
2. lonesome.
3. unmarried or widowed: a humorous usage.
4. (a) standing apart from others of its kind; isolated; (b) unfrequented.

lōne hand, 1. in card games, a hand played without help from a partner.
2. a person who operates alone.

lōne'li·ness, *n.* a lonely state or quality.

lōne'ly, *a.*; *comp.* lonelier; *superl.* loneliest, [*lone,* and *-ly.*]
1. alone; solitary.
2. (a) standing apart from others of its kind; isolated; (b) unfrequented.
3. unhappy at being alone; longing for friends, company, etc.
4. giving such a feeling.
Syn.—solitary, lone, lonesome, retired, unfrequented, sequestered, secluded.

lōne'ness, *n.* solitude; seclusion.

lōne'sōme, *a.* 1. solitary; unfrequented; desolate.
2. having or causing a lonely feeling.

lōne'sōme·ly, *adv.* in a lonesome manner.

lōne'sōme·ness, *n.* the state of being lonesome.

Lōne Stär Stāte, the nickname for Texas.

lōne wolf (wụlf), a person who by choice plays a solitary role in his ventures.

lọng, *a.*; *comp.* longer; *superl.* longest, [AS. *lang, long,* long.]
1. measuring much from end to end in space or time; not short or brief.
2. measured from end to end; as, the *long* dimension.
3. of a specified extent in length; as, the parade was a mile *long.*
4. of greater than usual or standard length, quantity, etc.; as, a *long* dozen, a *long* game.
5. containing many items or members: said of a series, list, etc.
6. overextended in length.
7. tedious; slow.
8. extending to what is distant in space or time; far-reaching; as, he took a *long* view of the matter.
9. large; big; as, a bet at the *long* odds of 100 to 1; he's taking a *long* chance.
10. having an abundance of (with *of* or *on*); as, he was *long on* excuses.
11. in finance, holding a large supply of a commodity or stock in anticipation of a scarcity and rise in price.
12. in phonetics, (a) held for a relatively long time: said of a pronounced vowel or consonant; (b) popularly, having the quality determined by its relative back position as compared with other vowel variants: said of a vowel.
13. in prosody, (a) requiring a relatively long time to pronounce: said of syllables in quantitative verse; (b) stressed: said of syllables in accentual verse.
in the long run; ultimately; eventually; in the final result.
long ballot; a ballot having the names of candidates to be voted upon, arranged either alphabetically under the offices to be filled or in columns having party symbols at the top.
long clam; the common clam, *Mya arenaria,* of Canada and the United States.
long dozen; thirteen.
long home; the grave.
long measure; same as *linear measure* under *linear.*
long meter; see under *meter.*
long price; the full price at retail.
Syn.—protracted, produced, far-reaching, dilatory, lengthy, tedious, prolix, extensive, diffuse.

lọng, *n.* 1. formerly, a musical note equal to two breves or four semibreves.
2. a long vowel, consonant, or syllable.
3. in finance, a person who buys or is on the long side of the market.
as (or *so*) *long as*; (a) during the time that; (b) seeing that; since; (c) provided that.
before long; soon.
the long and the short of; the whole story of in a few words; the gist or point of.

lọng, *adv.* [ME. *longe*; AS. *lange,* from *lang,* long.]
1. to a great extent in space: now used only in combination with participial adjectives; as, a *long*-extended line.
2. for a long time.
3. at a much earlier or a much later time than the time indicated; remotely; as, it happened *long* ago.
4. through the whole extent or duration; from the beginning to the end.

lọng, *adv.* [abbrev. from *along.*] by means of; by the fault of; owing to. [Archaic or Dial.]
Mistress, all this coil is *long* of you.—Shak.

lọng, *v.i.*; longed, (lọngd), *pt., pp.*; longing, *ppr.* [ME. *longen, longien*; AS. *langien,* to lengthen, stretch out the mind after, crave, from *lang,* long.] to desire greatly; to wish earnestly; to have a strong craving or yearning: followed by *for, after,* or an infinitive.

lọng, *v.i.* [ME. *longen,* from *long,* aphetic form of AS. *gelang,* dependent on.]
1. to be fitting or appropriate. [Archaic and Poet.]
2. to belong. [Obs.]

loñ'găn, *n.* [Chinese *lung-yen,* dragon's eye.]
1. an East Indian evergreen tree, *Nephelium longanum,* bearing an edible fruit.
2. the fruit itself, which is exported in a dried state.

loñ·gȧ·nim'i·ty, *n.* [LL. *longanimitas*; L. *longus,* long, and *animus,* mind.] forbearance; patient endurance of injuries.

loñ·gan'i·mous, *a.* forbearing. [Rare.]

lọng'bēak, *n.* a bird, the dowitcher.

lọng'bēard, *n.* 1. same as *long moss.*
2. a graybeard, a stoneware drinking mug.
3. a man having a long beard.

lọng'bōat, *n.* the largest boat carried on a merchant sailing ship.

lọng'bōw, *n.* a bow drawn by hand and shooting a long, feathered arrow; especially, a bow of considerable size used in Europe during the Middle Ages: distinguished from crossbow.
to draw (or *pull*) *the longbow*; to exaggerate in telling something.

lọng'çloth, *n.* a fine quality of soft cotton cloth.

lọng'-dis'tănce, *a.* to or from a distant place; connecting distant places; as, *long-distance* telephone calls.

lọng dis'tănce, 1. the exchange or operator giving long-distance connections.
2. in athletics, any distance over a mile.

lọng'-dis'tănce, *v.t.* to lay out (a telephone line, etc.) for long-distance calls.

lọng di·vi'şion, the process of dividing a number by another number containing, ordinarily, two or more figures and of putting the steps down in full.

lọng'-drạwn', *a.* continuing for a long or very long time; prolonged.

lŏnġe, lunġe, *n.* [Fr., back-formation from *allonge,* extension, from *allonger,* from LL. *elongare,* to prolong.]
1. a long rope fastened at one end to a horse's head and held at the other end by the trainer, who causes the horse to move around in a circle.
2. the use of the longe in training horses.

lŏnġe, lunġe, *v.t.*; longed, lunged, *pt., pp.*; longing, lunging, *ppr.* to put (a horse) through his paces, using a longe.

lŏnġe, *n.* the lake trout.

lọng'ẽr, *n.* one who longs for anything.

loñ'gẽr, *n.* in nautical usage, any of a number of casks stored next to the keelson. [Rare.]

lon'ġe·rŏn (*Fr.pron.* lōñ-zhe-rōñ'), *n.* [Fr.] a main structural part of the framework of an airplane fuselage which runs lengthwise across several supporting points.

lon·ġē'văl, *a.* long-lived.

lon·ġev'i·ty, *n.* [LL. *longævitas,* from L. *longævus,* of great age, aged; *longus,* long, and *ævum,* age.] long life; great span of life.

lon·ġē'vous, *a.* [L. *longævus,* of great age, aged.] living a long time; of great age. [Rare.]

lọng'-fāced' (-fāst), *a.* 1. having a long face.
2. glum; disconsolate.

lọng green, paper money. [Slang.]

lọng'hand, *n.* ordinary handwriting, in which the words are written out in full: distinguished from *shorthand.*

lọng'head (-hed), *n.* 1. a head with a cephalic index of less than 80.
2. a person having such a head; a dolichocephalic person.

lọng head, much foresight; shrewdness; good sense.

lọng'-head''ed, lọng'head''ed, *a.* 1. shrewd; farseeing; discerning.
2. having a longhead; dolichocephalic.

lọng''-head'ed·ness, lọng''head'ed·ness, *n.* 1. the condition or quality of being shrewd or discerning.
2. dolichocephaly.

lọng'họrn, *n.* 1. any of a breed of long-horned cattle formerly raised in great numbers in the southwestern United States: also *Texas longhorn.*
2. any animal with long horns.
3. an insect with long antennae.

lọng'-họrned, *a.* 1. having long horns; as, the *long-horned* breed of cattle.
2. having long antennae, as certain insects.

lọng house, a communal home or council hall among the Iroquois and other Indian tribes.

lọng hun'dred·weight (-wāt), the British hundredweight, equal to 112 pounds.

lon′gi-, [L., from *longus*, long.] a combining form meaning *long*, as in *longi*pennate.

lon″gi·cau′dāte, *a.* [*longi-*, and L. *cauda*, tail.] long-tailed.

lon′gi·corn, *a.* [*longi-*, and L. *cornu*, horn.] having long antennae, as the *Longicornia*.

lon′gi·corn, *n.* one of the *Longicornia*.

Lon·gi·cor′ni·ȧ, *n.pl.* [*longi-*, and L. *cornu*, horn.] a group of tetramerous beetles having long antennae, which, in the males of some of the species, are several times longer than their bodies. The larvae bore into wood, often attacking the roots of plants.

lon·gi·lat′ẽr·ăl, *a.* [*longi-*, and L. *latus*(*-eris*), *side*.] long-sided.

lon·gil′ō·quence (-kwens), *n.* [*longi-*, and L. *loquentia*, a talking.] long-windedness.

lon·gim′ȧ·nous, *a.* [*longi-*, and L. *manus*, *hand*.] having long hands.

lon·gim′e·try, *n.* [*longi-*, and Gr. *metron*, a measure.] the measuring of distances or lengths.

long′ing, *n.* an eager or strong desire; a craving or yearning.

long′ing, *a.* feeling or showing a yearning.

long′ing·ly, *adv.* with eager wishes or desire.

lon·gin′qui·ty, *n.* [L. *longinquitas*, from *longinquus*, remote, extensive, from *longus*, long.] great distance; remoteness. [Rare.]

lon′gi·palp, *n.* [*longi-*, and Fr. *palpe*, a feeler.] one of the *Longipalpi*, a division of beetles having extended maxillary palpi.

Lon″gi·pen·nā′tae, *n.pl.* same as *Longipennes*.

lon·gi·pen′nāte, *a.* having long wings.

Lon″gi·pen′nēṣ, *n.pl.* [*longi-*, and L. *penna*, a wing.] a family of aquatic birds, including the gulls, characterized by well-developed wings and a pointed and, sometimes, hooked bill.

lon·gi·pen′nine, *a.* of or pertaining to the *Longipennes*; longipennate.

lon·gi·ros′tẽr, *n.* [*longi-*, and L. *rostrum*, a beak.] one of the *Longirostres*.

lon·gi·ros′trăl, *a.* of or pertaining to the *Longirostres*.

Lon·gi·ros′trēṣ, *n.pl.* [*longi-*, and L. *rostrum*, beak.] a group of wading birds characterized by having long, slender, soft bills used in feeding in mud and marshy soil. This group comprises the snipes, sandpipers, curlews, avoset, etc.

a b c

LONGIROSTERS
a, black-tailed godwit; b, stilt plover; c, glossy ibis

long′ish, *a.* somewhat long.

lon′gi·tūde, *n.* [Fr. *longitude*; L. *longitudo* (*-inis*), length, from *longus*, long.]

1. length: now used humorously.

2. angular distance east or west on the earth's surface, measured by the angle (expressed in degrees up to 180° in either direction) which the meridian passing through a particular place makes with a standard or prime meridian, usually the one passing through Greenwich, England, or by the difference in time between the two meridians.

NORTH POLE
20° 0° 20° 40° 60° 80° 100° 120° 140° 160°
SOUTH POLE

MERIDIANS SHOWING LONGITUDE

3. in astronomy, the arc of the ecliptic measured eastward from the vernal equinox to the point where the ecliptic is intersected by the great circle through the star, planet, etc. and the poles of the ecliptic: also called *celestial longitude*.

lon·gi·tū′di·năl, *n.* a railway sleeper laid parallel with the rails.

lon·gi·tū′di·năl, *a.* 1. pertaining to longitude; as, *longitudinal* distance.

2. running lengthwise; placed lengthwise: opposed to *transverse*.

3. of or in length.

lon·gi·tū′di·năl·ly, *adv.* in the direction of length.

long jump, a track and field event that is a jump for distance rather than height, made either from a stationary position or with a running start: the official name in the Olympic games. Also called *broad jump*.

long′lēaf, long′-lēaf, *n.* Georgia pine: also *longleaf pine*, *longleaf yellow pine*.

long′-lēaved (pitch) pīne, a longleaf.

long′legs, *n.* a daddy-longlegs.

long′-līved′, *a.* having or tending to have a long life span or existence; living long; lasting long.

long′ly, *adv.* 1. with longing desire. [Obs.]

2. for a long time. [Obs.]

long moss, an American epiphytic plant, *Tillandsia usneoides*, which grows in large, hanging tufts on tree trunks and branches in the southern United States.

long′ness, *n.* length. [Rare.]

long′nōṣe, *n.* the garfish.

Lon·gō·bär′dī, *n.pl.* [LL., pl. of *Longobardus*.] the Lombards.

Long Pär′liȧ·ment, the English Parliament that met in 1640, was expelled by Cromwell in 1653, reconvened in 1659, and was dissolved in 1660.

long pig, human flesh or a human body as food for cannibals: from the Maori and Polynesian term.

long prim′ẽr, a size of type between small pica and bourgeois, 10 point.

This line is set in long primer.

long pũr′pleṣ, the early orchis, *Orchis mascula*, a plant bearing purple flowers. [Brit. Dial.]

long′-rānġe′, *a.* 1. designed to shoot over a great distance; as, *long-range* guns.

2. taking the future into consideration; as, *long-range* plans.

long′shanks, *n.* a bird, the stilt.

long′shōre, *a.* [from *alongshore*.] employed, existing, occurring, or working along a shore or water front.

long′shōre, *adv.* along the shore.

long′shōre″măn, *n.*; *pl.* **long′shōre″men,** [*longshore* and *man*.] a person who works on a water front loading and unloading ships.

long shot, 1. in betting, a choice that has only a slight chance of winning and, hence, carries great odds. [Colloq.]

2. in motion pictures, a scene photographed with the camera at some distance from the action.

not by a long shot; absolutely not; not at all. [Colloq.]

long′-sīght′ed (-sīt′), *a.* farsighted.

long′-sīght′ed·ness, *n.* the state of being long-sighted.

long′sōme, *a.* tiresome; tedious. [Dial.]

long′sōme·ness, *n.* tedium; monotony. [Dial.]

long′spun, *a.* spun or extended to a great length.

long′spũr, *n.* any of a group of birds related to the sparrows and finches and distinguished by their long hind claws: they breed in the arctic regions and winter over a wide expanse of the United States.

long′-stand″ing, *a.* having continued for a long time.

long stop, in cricket, formerly, one of the fielders standing behind the wicketkeeper to stop passed balls.

long′-suf′fẽr·ănce, *n.* long-suffering. [Archaic.]

long′-suf′fẽr·ing, *a.* bearing injuries, insults, trouble, etc. for a long time; patient; not easily provoked.

long′-suf′fẽr·ing, *n.* long and patient endurance of injuries, insults, trouble, etc.

long suit, 1. in card games, the suit in which a player holds the most cards.

2. something at which one excels.

long′tāil, *n.* an animal, especially, a dog, having an uncut tail.

long tŏn, a unit of weight, equal to 2,240 pounds avoirdupois.

long′-tongue (-tung), *n.* 1. a person who gossips. [Dial.]

2. a bird, the wryneck. [Brit. Dial.]

long′-tongued′, *a.* 1. having a long tongue.

2. tattling; gossipy; loquacious.

lon′gū·līte, *n.* [L. *longulus*, dim. of *longus*, long, and *-ite*.] a crystallite having a needle-shaped form.

long′-wāist′ed, *a.* 1. having a long waist.

2. long from the armpits to the waist or narrowest part, as a dress.

long′-wāve, *a.* of, by, or for long waves.

long wāve, a radio wave 600 meters or more in length: frequencies of long waves are lower than 500 kilocycles.

long′wāyṣ, *adv.* lengthwise.

long′-wind′ed, *a.* 1. capable of considerable exertion without getting out of breath.

2. (a) speaking or writing at great, often tiresome length; (b) tiresomely long: said of a speech, writing, etc.

long′-wind′ed·ness, *n.* length; tediousness.

long′wīṣe, *adv.* in the direction of length; lengthwise.

loo, lū, *n.* [abbrev. of *lanterloo*, from Fr. *lanturelu*, the name of the game.]

1. a card game played for a pool made up of stakes and forfeits.

2. a stake or forfeit in the game.

loo, *v.t.* to cause to pay a forfeit at loo.

loob, *n.* [Corn.] the sludge that comes from washing tin ore.

loo′bi·ly, *a.* like a looby. [Obs.]

loo′by, *n.*; *pl.* **loo′bieṣ,** [ME. *loby*, *lobie*, prob. from W. *llob*, a dull, unwieldy fellow.] an awkward fellow; a lout; a lubber.

loof, *v.i.* same as *luff*.

loo′făh, *n.* [Ar. *lūfah*.] the fibrous substance of the pod of a tropical gourd, used as a sponge in bathing, etc.

loo′ie, loo′ey, *n.* [short for *lieutenant*.] a lieutenant. [Military Slang.]

look, *v.i.*; looked (lookt), *pt.*, *pp.*; looking, *ppr.* [ME. *loken*, *lokien*; AS. *locian*, to look.]

1. to make use of the sense of sight; to see.

2. (a) to direct one's eyes in order to see; (b) to direct one's attention mentally upon something.

3. to try to see or find something; to search.

4. to appear; to seem.

5. to be facing or turned in a specified direction.

6. to expect (followed by an infinitive).

7. to take heed or care; to watch; to mind. [Archaic.]

Look that you bind them fast. —Shak.

it looks like; (a) it seems that there will be; (b) [Colloq.] it seems as if.

to look about; to look on all sides or in different directions.

to look about one; to be on the watch; to be vigilant; to be circumspect or guarded.

to look after; (a) to attend; to take care of; (b) [Obs.] to expect; to be in a state of expectation; (c) to seek; to search for.

to look alive; to be alert; to act or move quickly: usually in the imperative. [Colloq.]

to look back; to recall the past; to recollect.

to look down on (or *upon*); (a) to regard as an inferior; (b) to regard with contempt; to despise.

to look for; (a) to expect; to anticipate; (b) to seek or search for.

to look forward to; to anticipate, especially eagerly.

to look in (*on*); to pay a brief visit (to).

to look into; to inspect closely; to observe narrowly; to examine carefully.

to look on; (a) to regard; to esteem; to consider; to view; (b) to be an observer or spectator.

Her friends would *look on* her the worse. —Prior.

to look out; to be on the watch; to be careful.

to look over; to examine; to inspect.

to look through; (a) to see through; to see or understand perfectly; (b) to take a view of the contents of; to examine.

to look to; (a) to watch; to take care of; (b) to resort to with confidence or expectation of receiving something; to rely upon; (c) to look forward to; to expect.

to look up; to get better; to improve. [Colloq.]

to look up and down; to search everywhere.

to look up to; to regard with great respect; to admire.

look, *v.t.* 1. to direct one's eyes on; as, he couldn't *look* us in the face.

2. to seek. [Obs.]

3. to bring to a certain condition by looking. [Rare.]

And *look* the world to law.—Dryden.

4. to express or manifest by a look.

Soft eyes *looked* love to eyes that spake again. —Byron.

5. to appear as having attained (some age); as, she scarcely *looks* her years.

to look daggers; to look with anger; to glare.

to look oneself; to seem in normal health, spirits, etc.

to look out; to search for and discover; to choose; to select; as, *look out* associates of good reputation. [Brit.]

to look up; (a) to search for in a book of reference, etc.; (b) [Colloq.] to pay a visit to; to call on.

to look up and down; to examine with an appraising eye; to scrutinize.

look, *n.* 1. cast of countenance; expression of the face; aspect.
2. the act of looking or seeing; as, every *look* filled him with anguish.
3. [*pl.*] (a) appearance; as, I don't like the *looks* of things; (b) personal appearance, especially of a pleasing nature; as, she has *looks* and youth.
Syn.—sight, glance, aspect, appearance, air, mien, manner.

look, *interj.* 1. see!
2. pay attention!

look'down, *n.* the moonfish.

look'ēr, *n.* 1. one who looks.
2. a handsome person; especially, a pretty woman. [Slang.]

look''ēr-on', *n.*; *pl.* **look''ērs-on',** an observer; a spectator.

look'-in'', *n.* 1. a hasty glance.
2. a brief visit.

look'ing, *n.* 1. the act of regarding or seeking.
2. appearance. [Obs.]

look'ing glȧss, a (glass) mirror.

look'out, *n.* 1. a careful looking or watching for any person or thing.
2. (a) a place for keeping watch, usually one at a height affording an extensive view; (b) in nautical usage, a crow's nest.
3. a person detailed to watch.
4. outlook; prospect.
5. concern; worry; as, that is none of my *lookout.* [Colloq.]

look'-see', *n.* a quick look; a brief inspection. [Slang.]

loom, *n.* 1. a bird, the loon.
2. a guillemot.

loom, *n.* [ME. *lome*; AS. *geloma,* a tool, implement.]
1. a frame or machine for weaving thread or yard into cloth.
2. the art of weaving.
3. the shaft of an oar.

loom, *v.i.*; loomed, *pt., pp.*; looming, *ppr.* [earlier *lome, loam*; prob. from a L. G. or Scand. source via nautical language.] to appear, take shape, or come in sight indistinctly as through a mist, especially in a large, portentous, or threatening form (often with *up*); as, the peak *loomed up* before us; also used figuratively, as, the specter of revolution *loomed* ahead.

loom, *n.* a looming appearance, as of land or a ship in the fog.

loo'-mȧsk, *n.* a partial mask for the face. [Obs.]

loom cōmb (kōm), the reed of a loom.

loom gāle, a gentle gale of wind. [Obs.]

loom'ing, *n.* the indistinct and magnified appearance of objects seen under certain atmospheric conditions.

loon, *n.* [perh. from D. *loen,* a stupid fellow.]
1. a clumsy, stupid person; a lout; a dolt.
2. a boy. [Scot.]
3. a servant or other person of low rank. [Archaic.]
4. a rogue; a scamp. [Archaic.]

loon, *n.* [earlier *loom,* from ON. *lomr.*] any of a group of fish-eating, diving birds somewhat like ducks but with a pointed bill and a weird cry, found mainly in subarctic regions: also called *loom, great northern diver, embergoose.*

loon'ghee (-gē), *n.* [E. Ind. *lūngi.*] same as *lungi.*

loon'y, *a.*; *comp.* loonier; *superl.* looniest, [from *lunatic.*] crazy; demented: also spelled *luny.* [Slang.]

loon'y, *n.*; *pl.* **loon'ies,** a loony person: also spelled *luny.* [Slang.]

loop, *n.* [ME. *loupe*; OFr. *loup,* a narrow window, prob. from D. *luip,* an ambush, a peeping place, from *luipen,* to peep, lurk.] a small, narrow opening; a loophole. [Archaic.]

loop, *n.* [compare Ir. and Gael. *lub,* a loop, fold, thong.]
1. the more or less circular figure formed by a line, thread, wire, etc. that crosses itself.
2. anything having or forming this figure; as, a written *l* can be described as a lengthened *loop.*
3. a sharp bend, as in a mountain road, which almost comes back upon itself.
4. a ring-shaped fastening or ornament; as, staples, eyelets, and various sewing stitches are *loops.*
5. in aeronautics, a movement in which an airplane describes a closed curve or circle in the vertical plane: it is an *inside loop* when the top of the airplane is toward the center of the circle, and an *outside loop* when it faces away from the center.
6. in electricity, a complete circuit.
7. in physics, the part of a vibrating string, air column, etc. between the nodes; antinode.
the Loop; the main business, shopping, and theater district in downtown Chicago: so called because the elevated railway makes a loop around this area.

loop, *v.t.* 1. to make a loop or loops in or of.
2. to wrap around one or more times; as, *loop* the wire around that post.
3. to fasten with a loop or loops; as, she *looped* back the draperies from the window.
4. in electricity, to join (conductors) so as to complete a circuit.
to loop the loop; to make a vertical loop in the air, as in an airplane or roller coaster.

loop, *v.i.* 1. to form into a loop or loops.
2. to progress as a measuring worm does by alternately straightening the body and drawing it up into a loop.
3. in aeronautics, to perform a loop or loops.

loop, *n.* the part of a row or block of cast iron, melted off for the forge or hammer.

looped (lōpt), *a.* 1. full of holes. [Obs.]
2. fashioned into a loop or loops.

loop'ēr, *n.* 1. the larva of a geometrid moth; a measuring worm.
2. a kind of needle or bodkin used in making loops in yarn, etc.
3. a device (on a sewing machine) for making loops.

loop'hōle, *n.* 1. a small opening in the wall of a fort, etc. for looking or shooting through.
2. a hole or aperture that gives a passage.
3. a means of escaping or evading something unpleasant.

loop'hōled, *a.* full of holes or openings for escape.

loop'ie, *a.* sly; underhanded; tricky; deceitful. [Scot.]

loop'ing, *n.* [compare D. *loopen,* to run.] in metallurgy, the running together of an ore into a mass, when the ore is only heated for calcination.

loop'ing snāil, any snail of the genus *Truncatella.*

loop knot (-not), a knot so tied that there is a loop beyond the knot: see *knot,* illus.

loop'līght (-līt), *n.* a loophole through which light is admitted.

loop stitch, a sewing stitch that forms connecting loops.

loord, *a.* and *n.* lourd. [Obs.]

loose, *a.*; *comp.* looser; *superl.* loosest, [ME. *los, lous,* from Anglo-N.]
1. not confined or restrained; free; unbound.
2. not put up in a container; as, *loose* salt.
3. readily available; not put away under lock and key; as, *loose* cash.
4. not firmly fastened down or in; as, the leg of this table is *loose.*
5. not tight; giving enough room; as, *loose* clothing.
6. not compact or compactly constructed; as, a *loose* frame, *loose* soil.
7. not restrained; irresponsible; as, *loose* talk.
8. not precise or close; inexact; as, a *loose* translation.
9. sexually immoral; lewd.
10. moving freely or excessively; as, *loose* bowels.
at loose ends; confused; without order; poorly managed.
Syn.—vague, lax, dissolute, licentious, slack, unrestrained, unconnected, untied.

loose, *adv.* loosely; in a loose manner.
to break loose; (a) to free oneself by force; (b) to shake off restraint.
to cast loose; to untie or unfasten; to become or set free.
to cut loose; (a) to break or cut from a connecting tie; to make or become unfastened; (b) to become free; to escape; (c) [Colloq.] to have fun in a free, unrestrained manner.
to let loose (*with*); to set free or give out; release.
to set (or *turn*) *loose*; to make free; to release.

loose, *v.t.*; loosed (lōst), *pt., pp.*; loosing, *ppr.* 1. to make loose; specifically, (a) to set free; to unbind; (b) to make less light; (c) to make less compact; (d) to free from restraint; to make less rigid; to relax; (e) to free from an obligation or responsibility; to absolve.
2. to let fly; to release; as, he *loosed* the arrow into the air.
Syn.—untie, unfasten, let go.

loose, *v.i.* to loose something or become loose.

loose, *n.* 1. freedom from restraint; liberty.
2. the act of letting fly; discharge, as of an arrow.
on the loose; (a) not confined or bound; free; (b) [Colloq.] having fun in a free, unrestrained manner.

loose'box, *n.* a box or stall in a stable or barn in which a horse, cow, or other animal may be housed without being tied; a box stall.

loose'-joint'ed, *a.* 1. having loose joints.
2. limber; moving freely and flexibly.

loose'-lēaf, *a.* having or designed to have leaves which can easily be removed or inserted; as, a *loose-leaf* notebook.

loose'ly, *adv.* in a loose manner; wantonly; negligently.

loos'en, *v.t.*; loosened, *pt., pp.*; loosening, *ppr.* 1. to free from tightness, tension, firmness, or fixedness; as, to *loosen* a knot; to *loosen* a rock in the earth; to *loosen* the earth about the roots of a tree.
2. to free from restraint; to set free.

loos'en, *v.i.* to become loose; to become less tight, firm, or compact.

loos'en·ēr, *n.* one who or that which loosens.

loose'ness, *n.* 1. the state or quality of being loose; as, the *looseness* of a cord; the *looseness* of the skin.
2. laxity; instability; habitual deviation from strict rules; as, *looseness* of life.

loose sen'tence, a sentence in which the grammatical form and essential meaning are complete before the end: distinguished from *periodic sentence.*

loose'strīfe, *n.* [a trans. of Gr. *lysimachia, lysimachion,* loosestrife.]
1. any of various plants of the genus *Lysimachia,* with leafy stems and loose spikes of white, rose, or yellow flowers.
2. a variety of this plant with whorls of yellow flowers on fringed petioles.
3. any of a number of related plants of the genus *Lythrum,* with whorled leaves and spikes of purple flowers: also *purple loosestrife.*
false loosestrife; a plant of the genus *Ludwigia.*
tufted loosestrife; a plant of the genus *Lysimachia,* especially *Lysimachia thyrsiflora.*

loose'-tŏngued' (-tungd'), *a.* talking too much; careless or irresponsible in speech.

loot, *n.* [Hind. *lūt,* from Sans. *lunt,* to rob.] goods stolen or taken by force, as from a captured enemy city in wartime or by a corrupt official; plunder; spoils.

loot, *v.t.* and *v.i.*; looted, *pt., pp.*; looting, *ppr.* to plunder; to ransack and carry off booty from, as a fallen city.

loot, *v.i.* to engage in plundering.

loot'ēr, *n.* one who loots; a plunderer.

loo'vēr, *n.* same as *louver.*

lop, *v.t.*; lopped (lopt), *pt., pp.*; lopping, *ppr.* [ME. *loppen.*]
1. to trim (a tree, etc.) by cutting off branches, twigs, or stems.
2. to remove by or as by cutting off (usually with *off*).

lop, *n.* 1. the act of lopping.
2. something lopped off.

lop, *n.* a flea. [Brit. Dial.]

lop, *v.i.*; lopped, *pt., pp.*; lopping, *ppr.* to hang down loosely, as the ears of a rabbit.

lop, *v.t.* to cause to hang down loosely.

lōpe, *v.* obsolete past tense of *leap.*

lōpe, *n.* a long, swinging stride.

lōpe, *v.i.*; loped (lōpt), *pt., pp.*; loping, *ppr.* [ME. *lopen*; ON. *hlaupa,* to leap, run.] to move with a long, swinging stride; as, he *lopes* like a horse.

lōpe, *v.t.* to cause to lope.

lop'eared (-ērd), *a.* having ears which hang down or droop.

lōp'ēr, *n.* 1. one who or that which lopes, as a loping horse.
2. in the old process of ropemaking, a swivel hook used for laying the strands.

Lō'pez root, [after Juan *Lopez* Pinheiro, the discoverer of an East Indian species.] in botany, the root of the prickly climber, *Toddalia aculeata,* used for medicinal purposes in India.

Lō·phī'i·dae, *n.pl.* [Gr. *lophos,* a crest, and *-idæ.*] a family of fishes of froglike appearance typified by the genus *Lophius.*

lō'phīne (*or* -fin), *n.* [Gr. *lophos,* a crest of feathers, and *-ine.*] in chemistry, a crystalline compound, $C_{21}H_{16}N_2$, derived from amarine by distillation.

Lō·phī'ō·don, *n.* [Gr. *lophion,* dim. of *lophos,* summit, crest, and *odous, odontos,* tooth.]
1. the type genus of the family *Lophiodon-*

tidæ, consisting of fossil animals allied to the rhinoceros and tapir.

2. [l–] any animal of this genus.

lō′phi·ō·dont, *a.* in zoology, relating to or characteristic of the genus *Lophiodon* or the family *Lophiodontidæ*.

lō′phi·ō·dont, *n.* one of the *Lophiodontidæ*.

Lō″phi·ō·don′ti·dae, *n.pl.* a family of fossil quadrupeds allied to the rhinoceros and tapir, and ranging in size from that of a hare to that of an ox.

Lō·phī′ō·mys, *n.* [Gr. *lophia*, a mane, and *mys*, a mouse.] in zoology, a rodent of the northeastern part of Africa, the only species of the family *Lophiomyidæ*, remarkable for the peculiar formation of the skull.

Lō′phi·us, *n.* [Gr. *lophos*, a crest.] a genus of voracious fishes of the family *Lophiidæ*, having a head of considerable width furnished with long tendrils and an enormous mouth. *Lophius piscatorius*, the best-known species, is known as the angler.

lō′phō-, [from Gr. *lophos*, ridge, crest, tuft of hair.] a combining form used in zoology, anatomy, etc. meaning *ridge, crest*, as in *Lopho*branchii, *Lopho*comi.

loph′ō·brañch, *a.* having tufted gills, as the *Lophobranchii*.

loph′ō·brañch, *n.* one of the *Lophobranchii*.

lō″phō·brañ′chi·āte, *a.* relating to or characteristic of the *Lophobranchii*; lophobranch.

Lō″phō·brañ′chi·ī, *n.pl.* [*lopho-*, and Gr. *branchia*, gills.] a family of teleostean fishes in which the gills are arranged in small round tufts: it includes the pipefishes.

lō′phō·dont, *a.* [*lopho-*, and Gr. *odous*, *odontos*, tooth.] in zoology, having the molar teeth crested or ridged, as elephants.

lō′phō·phōre, *n.* [*lopho-*, and Gr. *-phoros*, from *pherein*, to bear.] in zoology, the oral disk of the *Polyzoa*, bearing a circlet of ciliated tentacles.

Lō·phop′ō·dȧ, *n.pl.* same as *Phylactolæmata*.

lō·phos′tē·on, *n.*; *pl.* **lō·phos′tē·ȧ,** [Gr. *lophos*, a crest, and *osteon*, a bone.] the central element of the breastbone in birds.

lop′pȧrd, *n.* a tree with the top lopped off; a pollard. [Rare.]

lop′pẽr, *n.* one who lops.

lop′pẽr, *v.i.*; loppered, *pt.*, *pp.*; loppering, *ppr.* to turn sour and coagulate from standing too long, as milk. [Dial.]

lop′ping, *n.* a cutting off, as of branches; also, that which is cut off.

lop′py, *a.* hanging down; pendulous.

lop′seed, *n.* a perennial herb, *Phryma leptostachya*, of the vervain family, having small purple flowers which, in fruit, lop or bend back close against the axis.

lop′sīd′ed, *a.* noticeably heavier, bigger, or lower on one side; not symmetrical.

lō·quā′cious, *a.* [L. *loquax* (*-acis*), talkative, from *loqui*, to speak.] talkative; given to continual talking.

Loquacious, brawling, ever in the wrong. —Dryden.

Syn.—garrulous, talkative.

lō·quā′cious·ly, *adv.* in a loquacious manner.

lō·quā′cious·ness, *n.* loquacity.

lō·quac′i·ty, *n.* [L. *loquacitas*, talkativeness, from *loquax* (*-acis*), talkative, from *loqui*, to speak.] talkativeness; the habit or practice of talking continually or excessively; garrulity.

lō′quät, *n.* [Chinese *lukwat*; *luh*, a rush, and *kiuh*, an orange.]

1. a small evergreen tree of the rose family, native to China and Japan.

2. the small, yellow, edible, plumlike fruit of this tree.

lō′quence, *n.* [L. *loquentia*, from *loqui*, to speak.] eloquence; discourse. [Rare.]

lō′qui·tŭr, [L.] he (or she) speaks.

lō′răl, *a.* [from L. *lorum*, a thong.] of or pertaining to the lore, or lorum.

lō′răl, *n.* one of certain plates at the side of the head, as in some snakes.

Lọr′an, lọr′an, *n.* [from *Long Range Navigation*.] a system by which a ship or aircraft can determine its position by radar and radio signals sent from known stations.

lō′ranth, *n.* any plant of the mistletoe family.

Lō·ran·thā′cē·ae, *n.pl.* [L.Gr. *lōron*, *lōros*, a thong, and Gr. *anthos*, a flower.] in botany, an order of apetalous plants of the mistletoe family, parasitic on trees, with fleshy leaves and hermaphrodite or unisexual flowers.

lō′rāte, *a.* [L. *loratus*, bound with thongs, from *lorum*, a thong.] in botany, ligulate; strap-shaped.

lọr′chȧ, *n.* [Port.] a light Chinese vessel, with the hull of European model, but rigged as a junk.

lọrd, *n.* [ME. *lord*, *loverd*, *laferd*; AS. *hlaford*, a master of a household, a lord.]

1. a person having great power and authority; ruler; master.

2. the owner and head of a feudal estate.

3. a husband: now humorous.

4. [L–] (a) God (with *the* except in direct address); (b) Jesus Christ (often with *Our*).

5. in Great Britain, (a) a nobleman holding the rank of baron, viscount, earl, or marquis; member of the House of Lords; (b) a man who by courtesy or because of his office is given the title of Lord, as a bishop, the son of a duke, or a lord mayor.

6. [L–] [*pl.*] the House of Lords in the British Parliament (usually with *the*).

7. [L–] in Great Britain, the title of a lord, variously used: as Earl of Leicester, John Doe would be called *Lord* Leicester; as a baron, John, *Lord* Doe; as the son of a marquis or duke, *Lord* John Doe.

House of Lords; one of the houses of the British parliament, consisting of the nobility and high-ranking clergy.

Lord Chief Justice; the highest judicial officer of England.

Lord (*High*) *Chancellor*; the highest officer of state of Great Britain, Keeper of the Great Seal, privy councilor, presiding officer of the House of Lords, etc.

Lord Justice Clerk; the judge who takes second rank in the Supreme Court of Scotland.

Lord Justice General or *Lord President*; the judge highest in rank of the Supreme Court of Scotland.

Lord Lieutenant; (a) formerly, in Ireland, the representative of British royalty in that country; (b) [l–l–] in an English county, one deputed by the sovereign, originally to manage its military concerns, now to appoint its justices of the peace, etc.

Lord Mayor; the title of the mayor of London and of the mayor of any of several other English cities.

Lord of hosts; Jehovah; God.

Lord of Misrule; one formerly chosen to direct the sports and revels of an English family during Christmas holidays.

lords spiritual; the archbishops and bishops of the Anglican church who have seats in the House of Lords.

lords temporal; those members of the British House of Lords who are not clergy.

the Lord's Day; Sunday.

the Lord's Prayer; the model prayer taught by Jesus to his disciples: Matt. vi. 9-13.

the Lord's Supper; (a) the Last Supper; final supper of Jesus with his disciples before the Crucifixion; (b) Holy Communion; Eucharist: so called because it commemorates the Last Supper.

the Lord's table; the altar or table upon which the elements of the sacrament are laid; also, the sacrament itself.

lọrd, *v.t.* 1. to invest with the dignity and privileges of a lord.

2. to rule or preside over.

lọrd, *v.i.*; lorded, *pt.*, *pp.*; lording, *ppr.* to domineer; to rule with arbitrary or despotic sway: sometimes followed by *over*, and sometimes by *it*, in the manner of a transitive verb; as, I see them *lording it* in London streets.

They *lorded over* them whom they now serve. —Milton.

lọrd′ing, *n.* 1. a petty or minor lord; lordling: usually contemptuous.

2. a lord. [Archaic.]

3. [*pl.*] gentlemen; lords: a term of address. [Archaic.]

lọrd′kin, *n.* a small or young lord.

lọrd′līke, *a.* 1. becoming a lord.

2. haughty; proud; insolent.

[Obs. in both senses.]

lọrd′li·ness, *n.* 1. dignity; high station.

2. pride; haughtiness.

lọrd′ling, *n.* a petty or minor lord: usually contemptuous.

lọrd′ly, *a.*; *comp.* lordlier; *superl.* lordliest. 1. pertaining to a lord; noble; aristocratic.

Lordly sins require *lordly* estates to support them. —South.

2. like a lord; proud; haughty; imperious; insolent.

lọrd′ly, *adv.* in a manner becoming a lord; proudly; imperiously; despotically.

lọrd·ol′ȧ·try, *n.* [*lord*, and Gr. *latreia*, worship.] lord-worship; reverence for the aristocracy.

lọr·dō′sis, *n.* [Gr. *lordōsis*, a bending, from *lordos*, bent back.] in pathology, any irregular curvature of the bones; especially, a curvature of the spine forward, producing a hollow in the back.

lọr·dot′iç, *a.* resembling or pertaining to lordosis; suffering from lordosis.

lọrdṣ′-ănd-lā′dieṣ, *n.* in botany, the European wake-robin, *Arum maculatum*.

lọrd′ship, *n.* [AS. *hlafordscipe*, lordship, power; *hlaford*, lord, and *-scipe*, -ship.]

1. the state or quality of being a lord; hence, a title of honor used in speaking to or of a lord in Great Britain, with the exception of a duke, who has the title of *grace*.

2. dominion; power; authority.

3. seigniory; domain; the territory of a lord over which he holds jurisdiction; a manor.

lōre, *n.* [ME. *lore*, *lare*; AS. *lar*, teaching, learning.]

1. (a) a teaching or being taught; instruction; (b) something taught. [Archaic.]

2. knowledge or learning; specifically, all the knowledge of a particular group or having to do with a particular subject, especially that of a traditional nature.

lōre, *n.* [Fr. *lore*; L. *lorum*, a thong.]

1. in ornithology, the space between the bill and the eye.

2. a part in reptiles and fishes on the side of the head between the nostril and the eye.

3. a corneous angular growth in the mouth of insects which enables them to push forward or retract the trophi.

lōr′ē·ăl, *a.* and *n.* same as *loral*.

Lọr′e·leī, *n.* [G.] in German legend, a siren whose singing on a rock in the Rhine lured sailors to shipwreck on the reefs: also *Lurlei*.

Lō·ret·tīne′, *n.* one of an order of nuns founded early in the nineteenth century in Kentucky, and devoted to the education of girls, especially destitute orphans. They are also called *Sisters of Loretto*.

lọr·gnette′ (-nyet′), *n.* [Fr., from *lorgner*, to spy, peep, quiz.]

1. a pair of eyeglasses attached to a handle.

2. an opera glass similarly mounted.

lọr·gnoñ′ (-nyōñ′), *n.* 1. a single or double eyeglass, as a monocle or pince-nez.

2. a lorgnette.

lō′ri, *n.* same as *loris*.

lō·rī′cȧ, *n.*; *pl.* **lō·rī′cae,** [L., from *lorum*, a thong.]

1. a cuirass or corselet of leather, metal, or horn, worn by a Roman legionary.

2. in zoology, a protective covering or coat, as in rotifers or infusorians.

3. in old chemistry, a luting used to protect chemists' vessels from the action of fire.

Lor·i·çā′tȧ, *n.pl.* [L. *loricatus*, pp. of *loricare*, to clothe in mail, from *lorica*, a coat of mail.]

1. a suborder of the genus *Edentata*, having a bony, scaly covering resembling armor: it includes the armadillos.

2. a family of reptiles including the crocodiles, alligators, etc.; the *Crocodilia*.

lor′i·çāte, *v.t.*; loricated, *pt.*, *pp.*; loricating, *ppr.* [L. *loricatus*, pp. of *loricare*, to clothe in mail, from *lorica*, a coat of mail.] to plate over; to cover with any protective coating or crust.

lor′i·çāte, *a.* covered over with or consisting of a lorica; enclosed in a hard shell or case.

lor′i·çāte, *n.* one of the *Loricata*.

lor′i·çāt·ed, *a.* loricate.

Lor·i·çā′tī, *n.pl.* same as *Loricata*.

lor·i·çā′tion, *n.* 1. the act or operation of covering anything with a lorica or crust for defense.

2. a defensive covering of scales or plates.

lor′i·keet, *n.* [*lory* and parra*keet*.] any one of numerous species of small parrots or lories of the *Trichoglossus*, *Loriculus*, and allied genera. They are native to Australia, New Guinea, and the East Indies.

lor′i·mẽr, lor′i·nẽr, *n.* a maker of bits, spurs, and metal mountings for bridles and saddles; hence, a saddler. [Obs.]

lō′ri·ot, *n.* [Fr.] the golden oriole, *Oriolus galbula*, of Europe.

lō′ris, *n.*; *pl.* **lō′ris,** [D. *læris*, a clown, booby.] either of two small, slow-moving species of lemur, which inhabit Ceylon and Java. They are quadrumanous mammals, closely related to the monkeys.

lọrn, *a.* [ME. *lorn*, *loren*; AS. *loren*, pp. of *leósan*, to lose.]

1. lost, ruined, or undone. [Obs.]

2. forsaken; forlorn, bereft, or desolate. [Archaic.]

lor′ry, lor′rie, *n.*; *pl.* **lor′ries,** 1. a cart used in coal mines.
2. a kind of railway baggage truck.
3. a transport wagon with a long, very low platform and four small wheels.
4. a motor truck. [Brit.]

lō′rum, *n.* same as *lore* (in zoology).

lō′ry, *n.*; *pl.* **lo′ries,** [Malay *lūrī*, a lory.] any of a subordinate genus of birds of the parrot

LORY
(*Lorius domicellus*)

family, usually of a red color, inhabiting southeastern Asia, Oceania, and the Malay Archipelago.

lōs′à·ble, *a.* capable of being lost.

lōse, *v.t.*; lost, *pt.*, *pp.*; losing, *ppr.* [ME. *losien*; AS. *losian*, to lose.]
1. to bring to ruin or destruction.
2. to become unable to find; to mislay; as, he *lost* his keys.
3. to have taken from one by negligence, accident, death, removal, separation, etc.; to suffer the loss of; to be deprived of.
4. to fail to keep (a state of mind or body, one's position, etc.); as, he *loses* his temper easily.
5. (a) to fail to see, hear, or understand; as, she did not *lose* a word of his lecture; (b) to fail to keep in sight, mind, or existence.
6. to fail to have, get, take advantage of, etc.; to miss; as, he *lost* a good opportunity.
7. to fail to win or gain; as, we *lost* the game.
8. to cause the loss of; as, his negligence *lost* him his job.
9. to wander from and not be able to find (one's way, the right track, etc.).
10. to spend unprofitably or uselessly; to waste; squander; as, we can't afford to *lose* any time.
11. to outdistance in a race.
12. to engross or preoccupy: usually in the passive; as, he was *lost* in reverie.
to lose oneself; (a) to lose one's way; to go astray; to become bewildered; (b) to become absorbed.
to lose sight of; to fail to see; hence, figuratively, to overlook; to forget; to fail to see the significance of; as, he *lost sight of* the fact that his cause was unpopular.
Syn.—miss, drop, mislay, forfeit.

lōse, *v.i.* 1. to undergo or suffer loss.
2. to be defeated in a contest, etc.

lōs′el, *a.* [ME. *losel*, *lorel*, from *loren*, pp. of *lesen*; AS. *leósan*, to lose.] worthless; wasteful. [Archaic or Dial.]

lōs′el, *n.* a worthless fellow; a scamp. [Archaic or Dial.]

los′en·gēr, *n.* [ME., from OFr. *losengeor*, a flatterer, from *losenge*, flattery.] a flatterer. [Obs.]

los′en·gēr·ye, *n.* flattery. [Obs.]

lōs′ēr, *n.* 1. a person or thing that loses.
2. a person who reacts to loss or defeat in a specified way; as, a bad *loser*.

lōs′ing, *a.* 1. that incurs or results in loss; as, a *losing* game or business.
2. that loses: as, a *losing team*.

lōs′ing·ly, *adv.* in a manner to incur loss.

loss, *n.* [ME. *los*; AS. *los*, from *leósan*, to lose.]
1. a losing or being lost.
2. an instance of this.
3. the damage, trouble, disadvantage, deprivation, etc. caused by losing something.
4. the person, thing, or amount lost.
5. in electricity, any reduction of voltage, current, or power between parts of a circuit or between different circuits, due to resistance of the elements.
6. in insurance, death, injury, damage, etc. that is the basis for a valid claim for indemnity under the terms of the policy.
7. in military usage, (a) the losing of soldiers in battle by death, injury, or capture; (b) [*pl.*] soldiers lost in this way.
to be at a loss; to be puzzled; to be in a state of uncertainty.
to be at a loss to; to be unable to; to be uncertain how to.
Syn.—privation, deprivation, forfeiture, detriment, injury, damage, disadvantage.

loss lēad′ēr, any article that a store sells cheaply or below cost in order to attract customers.

loss rā′tiō (-shō), the ratio between the losses incurred and the premiums earned by an insurance company during a specified time.

lost, *a.* [pt. and pp. of *lose*.]
1. ruined; destroyed.
2. not to be found; missing.
3. no longer held or possessed; parted with.
4. no longer seen, heard, or known; as, a person *lost* in a crowd.
5. not gained or won; attended with defeat.
6. having wandered from the way.
7. bewildered; perplexed.
8. not spent profitably or usefully; wasted.
9. spent away from one's place of work, as because of illness; as, he made up all his *lost* time.
lost in; absorbed in; engrossed in.
lost on; without effect on; failing to influence.
lost to; (a) no longer in the possession or enjoyment of; (b) no longer available to; (c) having no sense of (shame, right, etc.); insensible to.

lost cause, an undertaking or movement that has failed or is certain to fail.

lost mō′tion, the difference in the rate of motion of driving and driven parts of a machine, due to faulty fittings, etc.

lost trībes, the ten tribes making up the kingdom of Israel that were carried off into Assyrian captivity about 722 B.C.: 2 Kings xvii. 6.

Lot, *n.* in the Bible, Abraham's nephew, who, warned by two angels, fled from the doomed city of Sodom: his wife, who glanced back to behold the destruction, was turned into a pillar of salt: Gen. xix. 1–26.

lot, *n.* [ME. *lot*; AS. *hlot*, lot, share.]
1. an object used in deciding a matter by chance, a number of these being placed in a container and then drawn or cast out at random one by one.
2. the use of such an object or objects in determining a matter; as, ten men were chosen by *lot*.
3. the decision or choice arrived at by this means, regarded as the verdict of chance.
4. what a person receives as the result of such a decision; share.
5. one's portion in life; fortune; as, her *lot* was not a happy one.
6. a plot of ground; specifically, (a) subdivision of a block in a town or city; (b) a parcel of land in a cemetery.
7. a number of persons or things regarded as a group.
8. [*often pl.*] a great number or amount; as, we saw a *lot* of wild ducks. [Colloq.]
9. sort (of person); as, he's a bad *lot*. [Colloq.]
10. in motion pictures, a studio with the surrounding area belonging to it.
the lot; the whole of a quantity or number. [Colloq.]
to cast in one's lot with; see under *cast*.
to draw (or *cast*) *lots*; to decide an issue by using lots.

lot, *v.t.*; lotted, *pt.*, *pp.*; lotting, *ppr.* 1. to divide into lots.
2. to allot. [Rare.]

lot, *v.i.* to cast or draw lots.

lō′tà, *n.* [E. Ind.] a small globular vessel of polished brass used in India to draw and hold water: also written *lotah*, *loto*.

lōte, *v.i.* to lie hidden; to lurk. [Obs.]

lōte, *n.* same as *lotus*.

lōth, *a.* same as *loath*.

Lō·thār′i·ō, *n.* [from *Lothario*, a character in Rowe's play, *The Fair Penitent*.] a libertine; a roué; a gay seducer of women.

lō′tion, *n.* [L. *lotio* (*-onis*), from *lotus*, *lavatus*, pp. of *lavare*, to wash, bathe.]
1. a washing; particularly, a washing of the skin. [Obs.]
2. a liquid preparation for washing some part of the body.
3. in pharmacy, a preparation applied to the skin to stimulate action, to relieve pain, and the like.

lō′tō, *n.* same as *lotto*.

Lō·toph′à·gī, *n.pl.* [L., from Gr. *Lōtophagoi*, lotus-eaters; *lōtos*, lotus, and *phagein*, to eat.] a legendary people, visited by Ulysses, who lived upon the fruit of the lotus plant and consequently became indolent, dreamy, and forgetful.

lō′tōs, *n.* same as *lotus*.

lot′tēr·y, *n.*; *pl.* **lot′tēr·ies,** [Fr. *loterie*, lottery, from *lot*, lot.]
1. allotment or distribution of anything by fate or chance; a procedure or scheme for the distribution of prizes by lot; the drawing of lots.
2. specifically, a scheme for the distribution of prizes by chance, in which a number of tickets are sold, one or more of which draw prizes.

lot′tō, *n.* [It. *lotto*, lot, lottery.] a parlor game of chance having the essential features of a lottery, being played with numbered cards and disks.

lō′tus, *n.* [L., from Gr. *lōtos*.]
1. in Greek legend, (a) the fruit eaten by the Lotophagi, which was supposed to induce a dreamy languor and forgetfulness; (b) the plant bearing this fruit.
2. any of several tropical water lilies of the genus *Nymphæa*, especially the blue African lotus, a similar species from India, and the white lotus of Egypt.
3. a representation of any of these plants in ancient, especially Egyptian, sculpture and architecture.
4. [L–] a genus of shrubs and herbs of the pea family, with irregular, pinnate leaves and pealike flowers of yellow, purple, or white.
Also spelled *lotos*.
East Indian lotus, *Indian lotus*; a water lily, *Nymphaea stellata*, of the East Indies.
European lotus; a species of lotus tree, *Diospyrus lotus*, bearing a fruit resembling the plum.

LOTUS

lō′tus-ber″ry, *n.* the edible fruit of a tree of the West Indies, *Byrsonima coriacea*; also, the tree itself.

lō′tus-ēat″ēr, *n.* one of the Lotophagi; hence, an indolent dreamer.

lō′tus pō·si′tion, in yoga, an erect sitting posture with the legs crossed and with each foot, sole upturned, resting on the upper thigh of the opposite leg.

lō′tus tree, any one of the many trees supposed to have furnished the food of the Lotophagi.

loud, *a.*; *comp.* louder; *superl.* loudest, [ME. *loud*, *lud*; AS. *hlud*, loud.]
1. striking with force on the organs of hearing; of great intensity; strongly audible: said of sound.
2. making a sound or sounds of great intensity; as, a *loud* bell.
3. noisy.
4. clamorous; emphatic; insistent; as, *loud* denials.
5. too vivid; showy; flashy; as, a *loud* pattern in clothes. [Colloq.]
6. unrefined; vulgar. [Colloq.]
Syn.—clamorous, noisy, vociferous, resounding, blatant, ostentatious.

loud, *adv.* in a loud manner; loudly.

loud′en, *v.t.* and *v.i.* to make or become loud or louder.

loud′ish, *a.* somewhat loud.

loud′ly, *adv.* in a loud manner.

loud′mouthed, *a.* having a noisy, offensive manner of speaking; blatant.

loud′ness, *n.* the state or quality of being loud.

loud′-spēak′ēr, *n.* in radio and communications, a device for converting audio-frequency electric currents into sound waves and for amplifying this sound to the desired volume.

loud′-voiced (-voist), *a.* having a loud and clamorous voice.

lough (lokh), *n.* [Gael. and Ir. *loch*, a lake, lough.] a lake, or arm of the sea; a loch.

lough (lof), *v.* obsolete past tense of *laugh*.

lōu′is d′ōr′ (lō′i), [Fr., louis of gold.]
1. a gold coin of France, first struck in 1640, in the reign of Louis XIII, and superseded in 1795.
2. a later French gold coin worth 20 francs.

Lōu·i″si·an′à Pūr′chāse, the territory purchased by the U.S. from France in 1803, at a cost of $15,000,000: it covered a vast sweep of country, extending westward from the Mississippi to the Rockies, and northward from the Gulf of Mexico to Canada: at the time of the purchase, Napoleon was First Consul in France, and Thomas Jefferson was president of the U. S.

Lö̤u'is Quȧ·tọrze' (lö'i kȧ-tọrz'), designating or of a style of massive baroque architecture and furniture prevalent in France in the reign of Louis XIV.

Lö̤u'is Quinze (kańz), designating or of the style of furniture, architecture, etc. of the time of Louis XV of France, characterized by rococo treatment with emphasis on curved lines and highly decorative forms based on shells, flowers, etc.

Lö̤u'is Seize (sez), designating or of the style of furniture, architecture, etc. of the time of Louis XVI of France, characterized by a return to straight lines, symmetry, and classic ornamental details.

Lö̤u'is Treize (trez), designating or of the style of furniture, architecture, etc. of the time of Louis XIII of France, characterized by Renaissance forms, rich inlays, deep moldings, etc.

loun, lound, *a.* same as *lown.*

lounġe, *v.i.*; lounged, *pt., pp.*; lounging, *ppr.* [ME. *lungis*; OFr. *longis*, a drowsy, awkward fellow, from L. *longus*, long.]

1. to move idly about; to spend time lazily; to act in a lazy, listless manner.

2. to recline at ease; to loll.

lounġe, *v.t.* to spend by lounging; as, they *lounged* the summer away.

lounġe, *n.* 1. an act or time of lounging.

2. a lounging gait or stroll.

3. a room, as in a hotel, equipped with comfortable furniture for lounging.

4. a couch or sofa, especially a backless one with a headrest at one end.

lounġ'ẽr, *n.* an idler; one who loiters away his time.

lö̤up (lö), *n.* [Fr., a mask, from *loup*, wolf.] a mask or half-mask worn by masqueraders.

lö̤up, *n.* see *loop.*

lö̤up'-cer·vier' (lö'sär-viā'), *n.* [Fr., lynx, from *loup*, wolf. and L. *cervus*, a deer.] the Canada lynx.

lö̤up-gȧr·öu' (lö-gȧr-ö'), *n.*; *pl.* **lö̤ups-gȧr·öus'** (lö-gȧr-ö'), [Fr.; *loup*, wolf, and *garou*, werewolf.] a werewolf.

lour, *v.i.* and *n.* lower (scowl).

lö̤urd, *a.* [OFr. *lourd*, heavy.] dull; sluggish. [Obs.]

lö̤urd, *n.* a stupid, loutish person. [Obs.]

lou'ry, *a.* same as *lowery.*

louse, *n.*; *pl.* **līce,** [ME. *lous*; AS. *lus*, a louse.]

1. any of several small, flat, wingless parasitic insects, with either biting or sucking mouth parts, that infest the hair or skin of man and other warm-blooded animals.

2. any of various other small insects, arachnids, and crustaceans, parasitic on plants or animals.

3. a person regarded as mean, contemptible, etc. [Slang.]

louse, *v.t.* to rid of lice; to delouse. [Rare.]

to louse up; to botch; to bungle; spoil; ruin. [Slang.]

louse'ber″ry, *n.* the spindle tree.

louse bũr, the cocklebur.

louse flȳ, a pupiparous dipterous parasite infesting animals.

louse'wõrt, *n.* a plant of the genus *Pedicularis*, having soft, hairy, fernlike leaves and spiked clusters of reddish and yellowish flowers; wood betony: so named because sheep were supposed to become infested with vermin by feeding on it.

lous'i·ly, *adv.* in a mean, paltry manner; scurvily.

lous'i·ness, *n.* the state of being lousy.

lous'y, *a.*; *comp.* lousier; *superl.* lousiest, 1. infested with lice.

2. dirty, disgusting, or contemptible. [Slang.]

3. poor; inferior: a generalized epithet of disapproval or condemnation. [Slang.]

4. well supplied or oversupplied (*with*). [Slang.]

lout, *v.i.*; louted, *pt., pp.*; louting, *ppr.* [ME. *louten*; AS. *lutan*, to bend, stoop.] to bend; to bow; to stoop. [Archaic and Dial.]

lout, *n.* [prob. from or connected with ME. *lowt*, a rag.] a stupid awkward fellow; a bumpkin; a boor.

lout, *v.t.* to treat as a lout; to make a fool of. [Obs.]

lout'ish, *a.* like or characteristic of a lout; clumsy and stupid; boorish.

lout'ish·ly, *adv.* in a loutish manner.

lout'ish·ness, *n.* the quality of being loutish.

lö̤u'vẽr, lö̤u'vre (-vẽr), *n.* [OFr. *lover*, *luver*, from O.H.G. *louba*, upper story, gallery.]

1. in medieval architecture, an open turret or lantern on the roof of a building.

2. (a) a window or opening in a turret, etc. furnished with louver boards; (b) a louver board.

3. any ventilating slit, as in the side of an automobile hood.

LOUVER

lö̤u'vẽr bōard, any of a series of sloping slats set in a window or other opening to provide air and light but to shed rainwater outward: also *louver boarding.*

lö̤u'vẽred, *a.* having a louver or resembling a louver in construction.

lö̤u'vẽr·wõrk, *n.* work in which slats are used.

Lö̤u'vre, *n.* an ancient royal palace in Paris, converted into a museum in the eighteenth century: it contains many of the world's great art treasures.

lŏv·ȧ·bil'i·ty, *n.* the quality of being lovable.

lŏv'ȧ·ble, *a.* worthy of love; endearing; possessing qualities that attract love: also spelled *loveable.*

lŏv'ȧ·bly, *adv.* in a lovable manner; so as to be lovable: also spelled *loveably.*

lŏv'ȧġe, *n.* [ME. *loveache*; OFr. *luvesche*, *levesche*; L. *levisticum*, *ligusticum*, lovage, a plant native to Liguria, from neut. of *Ligusticus*, pertaining to Liguria.] a European herb, *Levisticum officinale*, known as Italian lovage or garden lovage; also, a related plant, *Ligusticum scoticum*, the Scotch lovage: both were formerly cultivated for use as a home medicine.

lŏve (luv), *n.* [ME. *love*, *luve*; AS. *lufu*, *lufe*, love.]

1. a strong affection for or attachment or devotion to a person or persons.

2. a strong liking for or interest in something; as, her *love* of acting.

3. a strong, usually passionate, affection for a person of the opposite sex.

4. the person who is the object of such an affection; a sweetheart; a lover.

5. sexual passion or its gratification.

6. [L–] (a) Cupid, or Eros, as the god of love; (b) [Rare.] Venus.

7. in tennis, a score of zero.

8. in theology, (a) God's benevolent concern for mankind; (b) man's devout attachment to God; (c) the feeling of benevolence and brotherhood that people should have for each other.

for love; as a favor or for pleasure; without payment.

for the love of; for the sake of; with loving regard for.

in love; enamored with or loving another.

labor of love; any work done or task performed with eager willingness, either from fondness for the work itself or from the regard one has for the person or cause for whom it is done.

love game; a tennis game in which one side does not score.

no love lost between; no liking or affection existing between.

to fall in love; to begin to love; to feel a strong, usually passionate, affection.

to make love to; to court; to woo; to embrace or kiss as lovers do.

lŏve, *v.t.*; loved, *pt., pp.*; loving, *ppr.* 1. to feel love for.

2. to show love for by embracing, fondling, kissing, etc.

3. to delight in; to take pleasure in; as, she *loves* good music.

lŏve, *v.i.* to be in love; to feel the emotion of love.

lŏve'ȧ·ble, *a.* same as *lovable.*

lŏve af·fâir', an amorous or romantic relationship or episode between two people not married to each other.

lŏve ap'ple, [cf. Fr. *pomme d'amour*; orig. probably folk etym. for earlier It. *pomi dei Mori*, lit., apples of the Moors.] the tomato: former name.

lŏve bēads, a long strand of colorful beads worn by both men and women as a symbol of the counterculture.

lŏve'bĩrd, *n.* any of various small birds of the parrot family, originally from Africa or South America, often kept as cage birds: so called because mates appear to be greatly attached to each other.

SWINDERN'S LOVEBIRD
(*Psittacula swinderniana*)

lŏve chärm, a charm by which love was supposed to be excited; a philter.

lŏve chīld, an offspring of illicit love.

lŏve därt, a slender, conical, calcareous style or rod found in some snails in a gland of the generative organs.

lŏve drink, same as *love potion.*

lŏve fēast, 1. among the early Christians, a meal eaten together as a symbol of affection and brotherhood.

2. in certain modern religious denominations, a feast or gathering imitating this.

3. any feast or gathering characterized by friendliness and good feeling.

lŏve'flow″ẽr, *n.* any of various flowers of the genus *Agapanthus*; the African lily.

lŏve'fụl, *a.* full of love. [Rare.]

lŏve god, Cupid; Eros.

lŏve grȧss, any of the grasses of the genus *Eragrostis.*

lŏve'-in-ȧ-mist', *n.* a fennel flower, *Nigella damascena.*

West Indian love-in-a-mist; a passion flower, *Passiflora fœtida.*

lŏve'-in-ȧ-puz'zle, *n.* same as *love-in-a-mist.*

lŏve'-in-ī'dle·ness, *n.* the wild pansy; heartsease.

lŏve knot (not), a knot, usually a bow of ribbon, tied, given, or worn as a token of love; a true-lover's knot.

lŏve'lȧss, *n.* a sweetheart.

lŏve'less, *a.* without love; specifically, (a) feeling no love; (b) receiving no love; unloved.

lŏve let'tẽr, a letter professing love.

lŏve'-līes-bleed'ing, *n.* a species of amaranth, especially *Amarantus caudatus*, with drooping spikes of small, red flowers.

lŏve līfe, that part of one's life having to do with amorous or sexual relationships. [Colloq.]

lŏve'li·ly, *adv.* in a lovely manner; in a manner to excite love.

lŏve'li·ness, *n.* the quality of being lovely or lovable.

lŏve'lock, *n.* a curl or long lock of hair worn by men of fashion in the reigns of Elizabeth I and James I; a curl or lock of hair hanging by itself or so as to appear prominently.

lŏve'lọrn, *a.* forsaken by one's love; pining or suffering from love.

lŏve'ly, *a.*; *comp.* lovelier; *superl.* loveliest, having those qualities that inspire love, affection, or admiration; specifically, (a) beautiful; exquisite; (b) morally or spiritually attractive; gracious; (c) [Colloq.] highly enjoyable; as, a *lovely* party.

lŏve'ly, *adv.* lovingly. [Obs.]

lŏve'-māk″ing, *n.* the act of making love; wooing or embracing, fondling, kissing, etc.

lŏve match, a marriage in which love is the controlling or only consideration.

lŏve par'ȧ·keet, a lovebird.

lŏve pō'tion, a drink intended to arouse love for a certain person in the drinker.

lŏv'ẽr, *n.* a person who loves; specifically, (a) a sweetheart; (b) [*pl.*] a man and a woman in love with each other; (c) a paramour: now usually applied only to a man; (d) a person who greatly enjoys some (specified) thing; as, a *lover* of good music.

lŏv′ẽr·ly, *adv.* and *a.* like, or in the manner of, a lover.

lŏv′ẽr·wīse, *adv.* in a loverlike manner.

lŏve scēne, a demonstrative exhibition of mutual love; such a scene as given in a picture, play, novel, etc.

lŏve sēat, a double chair or small sofa seating two persons.

lŏve set, in tennis, a set in which the loser wins no games.

lŏve′sick, *a.* 1. languishing with love; as, a *lovesick* maid.
2. expressive of languishing love; as, a *lovesick* sigh.

lŏve′sick·ness, *n.* the state or quality of being lovesick.

lŏve′sŏme, *a.* 1. charming; lovable. [Archaic or Dial.]
2. loving; affectionate. [Archaic or Dial.]

lŏve sūit, courtship.

lŏve tap, a light blow or tap used as a caress.

lŏve tō′ken, anything given as a token of love.

lŏve tree, the Judas tree, *Cercis siliquastrum.*

lŏv′ing, *a.* [ppr. of *love.*]
1. feeling love; devoted.
2. expressing love; as, a *loving* act.

lŏv′ing çup, a large drinking cup of silver, etc., with two or more large handles by which it was formerly passed from guest to guest at banquets: now often given as a prize in sporting events, etc.

lŏv′ing-kīnd′ness, *n.* tender regard; loving care.

lŏv′ing·ly, *adv.* in a loving manner; with love; affectionately.

lŏv′ing·ness, *n.* affection; kind regard.

lōw, *v.i.*; lowed, *pt., pp.*; lowing, *ppr.* [ME. *lowen*; AS. *hlowan*, to bellow, low.] to moo; to utter the soft hollow sound or bellow characteristic of cattle.

lōw, *v.t.* to express by lowing.

lōw, *n.* the characteristic sound of a cow; a moo; a soft bellow.

lōw, *n.* a mound; a hill. [Obs.]

lōw, *n.* a blaze; a fire. [Scot. and Brit. Dial.]

lōw, *v.i.* to blaze; to flame. [Scot. and Brit. Dial.]

lōw, *v.t.* to make low; to lower. [Obs.]

lōw, *a.*; *comp.* lower; *superl.* lowest, [ME. lowe; AS. *lah.*]
1. of little height or elevation; not high or tall.
2. depressed below the surrounding surface or normal elevation; as, water stood in the *low* places.
3. of little depth; shallow; as, the river is *low.*
4. of little quantity, degree, intensity, value, etc.; as, a *low* cost, *low* pressure.
5. of less than normal height, elevation, depth, quantity, degree, etc.
6. near the horizon; as, the sun was *low.*
7. near the equator; as, a *low* latitude.
8. cut so as to expose the neck or part of the shoulders, chest, or back; décolleté; as, a dress with a *low* neckline.
9. (a) prostrate or dead; as, he was laid *low*; (b) in hiding or obscurity; as, I must stay *low* until the trial is over.
10. deep; as, a *low* bow.
11. lacking energy; enfeebled; weak.
12. depressed in spirits; melancholy.
13. not of high rank; humble; plebeian; as, his *low* origin did not hamper him.
14. vulgar; coarse; debased; undignified.
15. poor; slight; unfavorable; as, she has a *low* opinion of him.
16. not rich or nourishing; simple; plain; as, a *low* diet.
17. not advanced in evolution, development, complexity, etc.; inferior; as, a *low* form of plant life.
18. relatively recent; as, a manuscript of a *low* date.
19. designating the gear ratio of a motor vehicle, etc. producing the lowest speed and the greatest power.
20. (a) not well supplied with; short of (with *on*); as, to be *low on* ammunition; (b) [Colloq.] not having any or much money; short of ready cash.
21. of little intensity; not loud: said of a sound.
22. designating or producing tones made by relatively slow vibrations; deep in pitch.
23. in the Anglican Church, relating to the Low Church or its doctrines.
24. in phonetics, pronounced with the tongue depressed in the mouth: said of certain vowels, such as the *a* in *calm.*
low area; in meteorology, an area or region in which the barometric pressure is low compared with the surrounding regions.
Low Church; that party of the Anglican Church which attaches little importance to ritual, sacraments, etc., and holds to a more evangelical doctrine than the High Church.
low comedy; comedy that gets its effect mainly from action and situation, as burlesque, farce, slapstick, and horseplay, rather than from witty dialogue and characterization; broadly humorous comedy.
Low Countries; the Netherlands, Belgium, and Luxemburg.
low latitude; near or not very distant from the equator, such latitudes being expressed by low numbers.
low life; humble or obscure life.
Low Mass; a Mass said without music and with less ceremonialism than High Mass: it is conducted by one priest with, usually, only one server, or altar boy.
low relief; bas-relief.
Low Sunday; the first Sunday after Easter.
low tide; (a) the lowest level reached by the ebbing tide; (b) the time when this point is reached; (c) the lowest point reached by something.
low visibility; a low degree of visibility due to atmospheric conditions making it difficult or impossible to see objects at a distance.
low water; (a) water at its lowest level, as in a stream; (b) low tide.
low wine; a weak spirit produced by the first distillation of fermented liquors.

lōw, *adv.* 1. in, to, or toward a low position, direction, etc.; as, hit them *low.*
2. in a low manner.
3. quietly; softly; as, talk *low* so as not to disturb the others.
4. with a deep pitch.
5. in a low rank or humble position.
6. cheaply; as, sell high and buy *low.*
7. so as to be near the horizon or near the equator.
to lay low; (a) to cause to fall by hitting; (b) to overcome or kill.
to lie low; to keep oneself hidden or inconspicuous.

lōw, *n.* something low; specifically, (a) that gear of a motor vehicle, etc. producing the lowest speed and the greatest power; (b) [Colloq.] a low level of accomplishment; as, her performance represents a new *low* in acting; (c) in certain card games, the lowest trump; (d) in certain sports, games, etc., the lowest score or number, or the person or team having this; (e) in meteorology, a low-pressure area.

lōw′ăn, *n.* the leipoa of Australia.

lōw′bell, *n.* 1. a bell used in a kind of fowling in the night, in which the birds are wakened by the bell, and blinded by a light, so as to be easily taken.
2. a bell for a cow's or sheep's neck.

lōw′bell, *v.t.* to frighten with or as with a lowbell; also, to capture by using a lowbell. [Obs.]

lōw′bọrn, *a.* born into a low, or humble, rank or position.

lōw′boy, *n.* a chest of drawers mounted on short legs to about the height of a table: distinguished from *highboy.*

lōw′bred, *a.* 1. of inferior stock; poorly born.
2. ill-mannered; vulgar; crude; coarse.

lōw′-brow, *n.* a person lacking or considered to lack highly cultivated and intellectual tastes: usually a term of contempt or of false humility. [Slang.]

lōw′-brow, *a.* of or for a low-brow. [Slang.]

Lōw′-Chŭrch′, *a.* of or like that party of the Anglican Church which stresses simplicity in religious observance; evangelical: opposed to *High-Church.*

Lōw′-Chŭrch′măn, *n.* a member of the Low-Church party, opposing excessive ritualism and rejecting apostolic succession as an essential of a valid ministry.

lōw′-cọst′, *a.* available at a low cost.

lōw′-çoun″try, *a.* of the Low Countries.

lōw′-down′, *a.* mean; base; degraded; vulgar. [Colloq.]

lōw′-down, *n.* the pertinent facts; especially, secret information (with *the*).

low′ẽr, *v.i.*; lowered, *pt., pp.*; lowering, *ppr.* [ME. *lowren, luren*, to frown.]
1. to appear dark or gloomy; to be clouded.
2. to frown; to look sullen; to scowl.

low′ẽr, *n.* a frowning or threatening look.

lōw′ẽr, *v.t.* [from *lower*, comp. of *low.*]
1. to let or put down; as, he *lowered* the window.
2. to reduce in height, amount, value, etc.; as, he will *lower* his prices.
3. to weaken or lessen; as, a cold had *lowered* his resistance.
4. to cause to be less respected; as, such acts *lowered* him in our eyes.
5. to reduce (a sound) in volume or in pitch.

lōw′ẽr, *v.i.* to sink; to fall; to become lower.

lōw′ẽr bound, in mathematics, a number that is less than or equal to any number in a set.

lōw′ẽr cāse, [from their being kept in the lower of two cases of type.] small-letter type used in printing as distinguished from capital letters (*upper case*).

lōw′ẽr-çāse′, *a.* in printing, designating, of, or in small letters, as distinguished from capital (*upper-case*) letters.

lōw′ẽr-çāse, *v.t.*; lower-cased, *pt., pp.*; lower-casing, *ppr.* to set up in, or change to, small letters.

lōw′ẽr çlȧss, the social class below the middle class; working class, or proletariat.

lōw′ẽr·çlȧss′măn, *n.*; *pl.* **lōw′ẽr·çlȧss′men,** a student in either of the first two years of a four-year course in a school or college; a freshman or sophomore.

Lōw′ẽr House, [*sometimes* l– h–] the popular and, usually, larger and more representative branch of a legislature having two branches, as the House of Representatives of the United States Congress.

low′ẽr·ing, *a.* [ppr. of *lower* (to scowl).]
1. scowling, frowning darkly.
2. dark, as if about to rain; overcast.

low′ẽr·ing·ly, *adv.* in a lowering manner.

lōw′ẽr·mōst, *a.* lowest.

lōw′ẽr Si·lūr′i·ăn, in geology, the Ordovician.

lōw′ẽr wŏrld, 1. the supposed abode of the dead; hell; Hades; Sheol.
2. the earth.

low′ẽr·y, *a.* gloomy; cloudy; lowering.

lōw′est çom′mŏn mul′ti·ple, the lowest number exactly divisible by each of two or more numbers.

Lōwes′toft (lōs′), *n.* a variety of chinaware made in Lowestoft, England.

lōw′-frē′quen·cy, *a.* in electricity, designating or of an alternating current or oscillation with a relatively low frequency, now usually less than 10,000 cycles per second.

Lōw Ġẽr′măn, 1. (a) the German dialects spoken in the northern lowlands of Germany, the Netherlands, etc.; (b) Plattdeutsch.
2. that branch of the Germanic subfamily of the Indo-European family of languages which includes English, Frisian, Dutch, Flemish, Old Saxon, Plattdeutsch, etc.: distinguished from *High German.*

lōw′-grāde′, *a.* of inferior quality.

lōw′ing, *n.* the low or bellow of cattle.

lōw′ish, *a.* rather low.

lōw′-kēy′, *a.* of low intensity, tone, etc.; subdued or restrained.

lōw′-kēyed′, *a.* same as *low-key.*

lōw′lȧnd, *a.* pertaining to a low country or to the Lowlands of Scotland; as, *Lowland* Scottish, *lowland* animals.

lōw′lȧnd, *n.* land which is low with respect to the neighboring country.
the Lowlands; the eastern and southern districts of Scotland: distinguished from *the Highlands.*

lōw′lȧnd·ẽr, *n.* 1. one who was born or who lives in a lowland.
2. [L–] a native or inhabitant of the Lowlands.

Lōw Lat′in, the Latin language from 200–300 A.D. to the time when Latin disappeared as a vernacular distinct from the various Romance languages.

lōw′-līfe, *n.* a mean, contemptible person. [Slang.]

lōw′li·hood, lōw′li·head (-hed), *n.* the state of being humble. [Obs.]

lōw′li·ness, *n.* the state or condition of being lowly.

lōw′-līved, *a.* having mean and vulgar characteristics; contemptible.

lōw′ly, *a.*; *comp.* lowlier; *superl.* lowliest, 1. of or suited to a low position or rank.
2. humble; meek.
3. low.

lōw′ly, *adv.* 1. humbly; meekly; modestly.
2. meanly; in a low condition, position, etc.; without dignity.

lōw'-mīnd'ed, *a.* having or showing a coarse, vulgar mind.

lown, loun, *a.* serene; calm; tranquil. [Scot.]

lōw'-necked' (-nekt'), *a.* décolleté; having a low neckline, as a gown.

lōw'ness, *n.* the state or quality of being low.

lōw'-pitched' (-picht'), *a.* 1. having a low tone or a low range of tone; as, a *low-pitched* voice.

2. having little pitch, or slope: said of a roof.

lōw'-pres'sūre (-presh'ūr), *a.* having or using relatively low pressure, as of steam.

lōw prō'fīle, an unobtrusive, barely noticeable presence, or hidden, inconspicuous activity.

lōw'-rīse', *a.* designating or of a building, especially an apartment house, having only a few stories.

low'ry, *n.*; *pl.* **low'ries,** a kind of open boxcar.

lōw'-spir'it·ed, *a.* depressed; dejected.

lōw'-spir'it·ed·ness, *n.* a state of low spirits.

lōw'-stud'ded, *a.* having low studs.

lōw'-ten'sion, *a.* in electricity, having, or carrying a current of, low potential.

lōw'-test', *a.* having a high boiling-point range: said of gasoline.

lox, *n.* [via Yid. from G. *lachs*, salmon.] a variety of salty smoked salmon.

lox'ō-, [from Gr. *loxos*, slanting.] a combining form used in medicine, anatomy, zoology, etc. to signify *slanting, oblique*; as, *loxo*dont, *loxo*tomy.

lox·ō·cȳ·ē'sis, *n.* [*loxo-*, and Gr. *kyēsis*, pregnancy.] displacement of the uterus during pregnancy.

lox'ō·dont, *a.* [*loxo-*, and Gr. *odous, odontos*, tooth.] having teeth with shallow and open intervals between the crests, as certain elephants.

lox'ō·dont, *n.* a loxodont elephant.

lox·ō·drom'iç, *a.* [*loxo-*, and Gr. *dromos*, a running.] pertaining to oblique sailing by the rhumb; as, *loxodromic* tables.

loxodromic curve or *spiral*; a line, as on a map or chart, that cuts across every meridian at the same angle and is oblique to the equator; a rhumb line.

lox·ō·drom'içs, *n.* the art or practice of oblique sailing.

lox·od'rō·my, *n.* loxodromics.

lox·ot'iç, *a.* in medicine, askew; distorted.

lox·ot'ō·my, *n.* [*loxo-*, and Gr. *tomē*, a cutting.] amputation in oblique section.

loy, *n.* in Ireland, a kind of spade.

loy'ăl, *a.* [Fr. *loyal*; OFr. *loial, leial*, from L. *legalis*, pertaining to law, from *lex, legis*, law.]

1. faithful to the constituted authority of one's country.

2. faithful to those persons, ideals, etc. that one stands under an obligation to defend or support.

3. relating to or indicating loyalty.

loy'ăl·ist, *n.* 1. a person who is loyal; especially, one who supports the established government of his country during times of revolt.

2. [*often* L–] in the American Revolution, a colonist who was loyal to the British government.

3. [L–] in the Spanish Civil War, one who remained loyal to the elected government of the Republic in opposition to the insurrection led by Franco.

loy'ăl·ly, *adv.* in a loyal manner.

loy'ăl·ness, *n.* fidelity; loyalty.

loy'ăl·ty, *n.*; *pl.* **loy'ăl·ties,** the state or quality of being loyal; faithfulness or faithful adherence to a person, government, cause, duty, etc.

lōz'el, *n.* and *a.* same as *losel*.

loz'enġe, *n.* [OFr. *losenge*; prob. from Pr. *lausa*, stone slab.]

1. a figure with four equal sides, having two acute and two obtuse angles; a rhomb; a diamond.

2. something having the shape of a lozenge, as (a) in heraldry, an escutcheon used by widows and spinsters; also, a diamond-shaped bearing; (b) a cough drop, candy, etc., originally a rhomb, but now variously shaped.

loz'enġe çōach, a coach adorned with the lozenge-shaped escutcheon of a widow. [Obs.]

loz'enġed, *a.* rhomb-shaped; divided into lozenges.

loz'enġe mōld'ing, a molding having lozenged ornaments.

LOZENGE MOLDING

loz'enġe-shāped (-shāpt), *a.* rhomb-shaped; also, square and set cornerwise.

loz'en·ġy, *a.* in heraldry, divided by transverse diagonal lines into equal lozenges or squares of different tinctures.

LOZENGY ESCUTCHEON

LSD, [*lysergic acid diethylamide*.] a chemical compound extracted from ergot alkaloids, used in the study of schizophrenia and other mental disorders and as a psychedelic drug: it produces hallucinations, delusions, etc. resembling those occurring in a psychotic state.

Lu, in chemistry, lutetium.

lū·au' (-ou'), *n.* [Haw.] a Hawaiian feast, usually with entertainment.

lub'bẽr, *n.* [ME. *lobre, lobur*, from *lobbe*; see 1st *lob*.] a heavy, clumsy fellow; a lout; especially, an awkward, unskilled seaman.

lubber's hole; the hole between the head of a lower mast and the edge of the top, through which sailors may mount without climbing outside the rim by the futtock shrouds.

lub'bẽr, *a.* big and clumsy.

lub'bẽr grass'hop·pẽr, an awkward, lubberly locust, *Romalea microptera*.

lub'bẽr līne, the line in the case of a compass indicating the bow of the ship.

lub'bẽr·li·ness, *n.* a lubberly quality.

lub'bẽr·ly, *a.* bulky and heavy; clumsy.

lub'bẽr·ly, *adv.* clumsily; awkwardly.

lūbe (*or* lüb), *n.* [short for *lubricating oil*.]

1. a lubricating oil for machinery: also *lube oil*.

2. a lubrication. [Colloq.]

lū'briç, lū'briç·ăl, *a.* lubricous. [Rare.]

lū'bri·çănt, *a.* [L. *lubricans (-antis)*, ppr. of *lubricare*, to make smooth.] reducing friction by providing a smooth film as a covering over parts that move against each other; lubricating.

lū'bri·çănt, *n.* any substance used for lessening friction, as oil or grease.

lū'bri·çāte, *v.t.*; lubricated, *pt., pp.*; lubricating, *ppr.* [L. *lubricatus*, pp. of *lubricare*, to make smooth or slippery, from *lubricus*, smooth.]

1. to make slippery or smooth.

2. to apply a lubricant to (machinery, etc.) in order to reduce friction in operation.

lū'bri·çāte, *v.i.* to serve as a lubricant.

lū·bri·çā'tion, *n.* a lubricating or being lubricated.

lū'bri·çā·tive, *a.* lubricating or able to lubricate.

lū'bri·çā·tŏr, *n.* one who or that which lubricates; a device for oiling machinery.

lū·bric'i·ty, *n.*; *pl.* **lū·bric'i·ties,** [LL. *lubricitas*, from L. *lubricus*, smooth, slippery.]

1. smoothness of surface; slipperiness; aptness to facilitate the motion of bodies in contact by diminishing friction.

2. instability; trickiness; as, the *lubricity* of fortune.

3. lasciviousness; lewdness; lechery.

lū'bri·çous, *a.* [L. *lubricus*.] having or characterized by lubricity.

lū·çărne', *n.* [Fr., from L. *lucerna*, a lamp.] a vertical window set in a sloping roof. [Archaic.]

Luç·chēse' (*or* -kēs'), *n. sing.* and *pl.* [It., from *Lucca*, Lucca.] a citizen of Lucca, in Italy, or the citizens of Lucca collectively.

lūce, *n.* [OFr. *lus, luz*, a luce, from LL. *lucius*, a kind of fish.] a pike, especially one full grown.

lū'cen·cy, *n.* the quality or state of being lucent.

lū'cent, *a.* [L. *lucens (-entis)*, ppr. of *lucere*, to shine.]

1. shining; bright.

2. translucent.

lū·cẽrn', *n.* same as *lucerne*.

lū·cẽrn', *n.* a lynx; also, its fur. [Obs.]

lū·cẽrn', *n.* a lamp. [Obs.]

lū·cẽr'năl, *a.* [L. *lucerna*, a lamp.] of or like a lamp.

Lū·cẽr·nā'ri·ȧ, *n.* [L. *lucerna*, a lamp.] a genus of hydrozoans of the order *Lucernariadæ*. The body is somewhat bell-shaped and the tentacles are arranged in eight tufts. They affix themselves by a slender peduncle to seaweeds, etc. and are phosphorescent.

lū·cẽr·nā'ri·ăn, *a.* of or resembling the *Lucernaria*.

lū·cẽr·nā'ri·ăn, *n.* one of the *Lucernaria*.

Lū·cẽr·năr'i·dȧ, *n.pl.* a subclass of hydrozoans equivalent in extent to the *Discophora*.

lū·cẽrne', *n.* [Fr.] alfalfa, *Medicago sativa*, a cloverlike forage plant: the common name in Australia and New Zealand.

lū'cēs, *n.* alternative plural of *lux*.

lū'cid, *a.* [L. *lucidus*, light, clear, from *lucere*, to shine.]

1. shining; bright; resplendent; as, the *lucid* orbs of heaven. [Poet.]

2. clear; transparent; as, a *lucid* stream.

3. sane; mentally sound.

4. (a) clear; distinct; presenting a clear view; easily understood; as, a *lucid* order or arrangement; (b) clearheaded; rational; as, a *lucid* thinker.

5. in astronomy, visible to the naked eye: said of a star.

lū'ci·dȧ, *n.*; *pl.* **lū'ci·dae,** the brightest star in a constellation.

lū·cid'i·ty, *n.* the state or quality of being lucid.

lū'cid·ly, *adv.* clearly; in a lucid manner.

lū'cid·ness, *n.* lucidity.

Lū'ci·fẽr, *n.* [L. *lucifer*, light-bringing; *lux, lucis*, light, and *ferre*, to bear.]

1. the planet Venus, when it is the morning star. [Poet.]

2. Satan, especially as the leader of the revolt of the angels before his fall.

And when he falls, he falls like *Lucifer*,
Never to hope again. —Shak.

3. [l–] an early type of friction match.

Lū·ci·fē'ri·ăn, *a.* pertaining to Lucifer; satanic.

lū·cif'ẽr·in, *n.* a substance in the blood of fireflies, some sea mollusks, etc. that combines with an enzyme in their bodies to produce light.

lū·cif'ẽr·ous, *a.* [L. *lucifer*, light-bringing, and *-ous*.] giving light; affording light or means of insight.

lū·cif'ẽr·ous·ly, *adv.* in a luciferous manner.

lū·cif'iç, *a.* [LL. *lucificus*, light-making; L. *lux, lucis*, light, and *facere*, to make.] producing light.

lū'ci·fọrm, *a.* [L. *lux, lucis*, light, and *forma*, form.] having the form of light; resembling light.

Lū·cif'ri·ăn, *a.* same as *Luciferian*.

lū·cif'ū·gous, *a.* [L. *lux, lucis*, light, and *fugere*, to flee.] avoiding light: said of nocturnal animals, as bats, owls, and certain insects.

lū'ci·gen, *n.* [L. *lux, lucis*, light, and the root *gen*, to produce.] a lamp which burns oil and hot air mixed, producing a very bright light.

lū'cīte, *n.* [L. *lux, lucis*, light; and *-ite*.] a crystal-clear synthetic resin, plastic under heat: it is used for airplane windshields, store fronts, light panels, etc.: a trade-mark (*Lucite*).

luck, *n.* [ME. *luk, lukke*; compare D. *luk, geluk*.]

1. the seemingly chance happening of events which affect one; fortune; lot; fate.

2. good fortune; success, prosperity, advantage, etc.

3. an object believed to bring good luck.

down on one's luck; in misfortune; unlucky.

in luck; fortunate; lucky.

out of luck; unfortunate; unlucky.

to crowd (or *push*) *one's luck*; to take superfluous risks in an already favorable situation.

to try one's luck; to try to do something without being sure of one's ability or of the outcome.

worse luck; unfortunately; unhappily.

luck, *v.i.* to be lucky enough to come (*into, on, through*, etc.). [Colloq.]

to luck out; to have things turn out favorably for one; be lucky. [Colloq.]

luck'i·ly, *adv.* fortunately; by or with good luck; with a favorable issue; as, *luckily*, we escaped injury.

luck'i·ness, *n.* 1. the state of being fortunate; as, the *luckiness* of a man, or of an event.

2. good fortune; a favorable issue or event; luck.

luck'less, *a.* unfortunate; meeting with ill success; as, a *luckless* gamester.

luck'less·ly, *adv.* unfortunately; unsuccessfully.

luck'less·ness, *n.* unluckiness.

luck pen'ny, in Scotland, a small sum given back to the payer by one who receives money under a contract or bargain.

luck'y, *a.*; *comp.* luckier; *superl.* luckiest,

1. having good luck; fortunate.

2. happening or resulting fortunately; as, a *lucky* change.

3. bringing or believed to bring good luck; as, a *lucky* coin.

Syn.—fortunate, prosperous, successful.

luck'y bag, a catchall in which are placed all

small articles heedlessly left on deck on a war vessel.

luck'y prōach, a fish; the father-lasher. [Scot.]

lū·crà·tive, *a.* [L. *lucrativus,* profitable, from *lucrari,* to gain.]
 1. gainful; profitable; producing wealth or profit; as, a *lucrative* business.
 2. grasping; greedy for profit. [Obs.]

lū'crà·tive·ly, *adv.* profitably.

lū'çre (-kẽr), *n.* [OFr. *lucre,* from L. *lucrum,* gain.] riches; money: now chiefly in a humorously derogatory sense, as in *filthy lucre.*

lū'çre, *v.t.* to gain money or wealth. [Obs.]

Lū·çrē'tiăn, *a.* relating to Titus Lucretius Carus (96?–55 B.C.), the Roman poet and philosopher.

lū·crif'ẽr·ous, *a.* gainful; profitable. [Obs.]

lū·crif'iç, *a.* producing profit; gainful. [Obs.]

lū'çū·brāte, *v.t.* to elaborate or perfect by laborious effort, as by candlelight.

lū'çū·brāte, *v.i.*; lucubrated, *pt., pp.*; lucubrating, *ppr.* [L. *lucubratus,* pp. of *lucubrare,* to work by candlelight, from *lux, lucis,* light.]
 1. to study by candlelight or a lamp; to study, work, or write laboriously, especially late at night.
 2. to write in a scholarly manner.

lū·çū·brā'tion, *n.* 1. a lucubrating; laborious work, study, or writing, especially that done late at night.
 2. something produced by such work, study, or writing; especially, a learned or carefully elaborated production.
 3. [*often in pl.*] any literary composition: humorous usage suggesting pedantry.

lū'çū·brā"tŏr, *n.* one who lucubrates.

lū'çū·brā·tō"ry, *a.* [L. *lucubratorius,* working by candlelight, from *lucubrare,* to work by candlelight.] pertaining to night studies; composed by night or by candlelight.

lū'çūle, *n.* [dim. from L. *lux, lucis,* light.] in astronomy, a bright spot on the surface of the sun.

lū'çū·lent, *a.* [L. *luculentus,* full of light, bright, from *lux, lucis,* light.]
 1. lucid; clear; transparent; as, *luculent* rivers.
 2. clear; evident; luminous.

lū'çū·lent·ly, *adv.* in a lucid manner.

Lū·çū'li·à, *n.* in botany, a genus of shrubs or small trees of the madder family, bearing handsome cymes of fragrant tubular pink flowers.

Lū·çul'lăn, *a.* of or like Lucullus, Roman consul of the first century B.C., or the extravagant banquets given by him; rich and luxurious.

Lū·çul·lē'ăn, Lū·çul'li·ăn, *a.* Lucullan.

lū·çul'līte, *n.* [from *Lucullus,* a Roman consul, and *-ite.*] in mineralogy, a variety of black limestone, often polished for ornamental purposes.

Lū·çū'mà, *n.* [from native Peruv. name.] a genus of tall evergreen tropical trees of the *Sapodilla* family, bearing a sweet and edible fruit.

Lud'dīte, *n.* one of a body of English workmen who from 1811 to 1816 endeavored to prevent the introduction of labor-saving machinery by burning factories and destroying machines: said to be named after Ned Lud, an imbecile who broke two improved stocking frames.

lū'di·çrous, *a.* [L. *ludicrus,* sportive, from *ludere,* to play.]
 1. causing laughter because absurd or ridiculous; laughably absurd.
 2. sportive; jocular. [Obs.]

lū'di·çrous·ly, *adv.* in a ludicrous manner.

lū'di·crous·ness, *n.* the quality of being ludicrous.

lū"di·fi·çā'tion, *n.* [L. *ludificatio* (*-onis*), from *ludificare,* to make sport of.] act of deriding. [Rare.]

Lud·wig'i·à, *n.* in botany, a genus of plants of the evening primrose family: named after the German botanist C. G. Ludwig; false loosestrife.

lū'ēș, *n.* [L.] 1. pestilence; plague; an infectious or contagious disease. [Obs.]
 2. syphilis: formerly also called *lues venerea.*

lū·et'iç, *a.* and *n.* syphilitic.

luff, *n.* [ME. *lof, loof,* a leeboard; prob. from O.D.]
 1. in navigation, the weather gauge or part of a vessel toward the wind. [Rare.]
 2. the sailing of a ship close to the wind.
 3. [from indicating a luff by its shaking.] the forward edge of a fore-and-aft sail.
 4. [orig., from location of leeboard.] the broadest part of a ship's bow: also called *loof.*
 5. a luff tackle.

luff, *v.i.*; luffed, *pt., pp.*; luffing, *ppr.* 1. to turn the bow of a ship toward the wind; to sail near or nearer the wind.
 2. to cause a sail to shake by turning too close to the wind.

Luf'fà, *n.* [Ar. *lūfa,* the name of one of the species.] in botany, a genus of dicotyledonous plants of the gourd family, some species of which bear a fruit in which the seeds are enclosed in a strong fibrous network, which when dry is detached and may be used in place of a sponge for bathing.

luf'fẽr, *n.* same as *louver.*

luff taç'kle, large tackle composed of a double and single block, movable at pleasure.

Luft' wäf·fe (-väf-), *n.* [G.] the Nazi air force in World War II.

lug, *v.t.*; lugged, *pt., pp.*; lugging, *ppr.* [ME. *luggen*; prob. from ON.; cf. Sw. *lugga,* to pull, lit., pull by the hair, from *lugg,* the forelock.]
 1. to haul; to drag; to pull with force, as something heavy and moved with difficulty.
 2. to introduce (a topic, story, etc.) without good reason into a conversation, discourse, etc.
 to lug out; to draw, as a sword. [Archaic.]

lug, *n.* [Sw. *lugg,* the forelock.]
 1. an ear. [Scot.]
 2. anything projecting or hanging like the ear or its lobe, as a block for keeping a slide in place.
 3. anything fitted for taking hold of or for fastening, as the ear of a kettle or of a compositor's rule.
 4. the act of lugging.
 5. money exacted for political purposes: chiefly in *to put the lug on,* to exact a contribution from. [Slang.]
 6. a stupid fellow. [Slang.]
 7. a heavy nut used with a bolt to secure a wheel to an axle.
 8. a shallow box in which fruit, as cherries, grapes, etc., is packed and shipped by growers.

lug, *n.* same as *lugsail.*

lug, *n.* same as *lugworm.*

lug, *n.* 1. a linear measure of sixteen and one-half feet; a pole. [Obs.]
 2. a pliable twig used in thatching. [Brit. Dial.]

lug, *v.i.* to drag; to move heavily.

Lū·gän'dä, *n.* a dialect used in Baganda, the Bantu.

lug bōlt, in metalwork, a bolt with a head in the form of a strap or flat iron bar.

lug chāir, a wing chair. [Brit.]

lū'gẽr, *n.* [G.] a German semiautomatic pistol: a trademark (*Luger*).

lug fore'sail, in nautical usage, a foresail without a boom.

lug'gāge, *n.* [from *lug* (to haul), and *-age.*]
 1. anything cumbersome and heavy, to be carried or moved by hand.
 2. suitcases, valises, trunks, etc.; baggage.
 3. reddish brown or tan.

lug'gāge, *a.* reddish-brown or reddish-tan.

lug'gar (-gẽr), *n.* any of several large Asiatic falcons.

lug'gẽr, *n.* a small vessel equipped with a lugsail or lugsails.

LUGGER

lug'gẽr, *n.* same as *jugger.*

lug'sāil, *n.* a four-cornered sail without boom, or lower yard: it is attached to an upper yard that hangs obliquely on the mast.

lū·gū'bri·ous, *a.* [L. *lugubris,* from *lugere,* to mourn.] mournful; very sad; dismal; doleful: usually implying ridiculously excessive grief; as, a *lugubrious* look.

lū·gū'bri·ous·ly, *adv.* in a lugubrious manner.

lū·gū'bri·ous·ness, *n.* the state or quality of being lugubrious.

lug'wŏrm, *n.* a large marine worm with a double row of tufted gills on the back, living in sandy beaches and used by fishermen for bait: also called *lobworm.*

Lū'i·ăn, Lū'ish, *n.* and *a.* same as *Luwian.*

lūke, *a.* [ME. *luke, lewke,* an extension of *lew,* warm; compare AS. *wlæc,* tepid.] moderately warm; not hot; tepid. [Dial.]

Lūke, *n.* in the Bible, (a) one of the four Evangelists, a physician and companion of the Apostle Paul and the reputed author of the third book of the New Testament and the Acts of the Apostles: he was probably a Gentile: also *Saint Luke*; (b) the third book of the New Testament, telling the story of Jesus' life.

lūke'wạrm, *a.* 1. moderately warm; tepid; as, *lukewarm* water.
 2. not ardent; not zealous; cool; indifferent; as, *lukewarm* obedience, *lukewarm* patriots.

lūke'wạrm·ly, *adv.* with moderate warmth; with indifference.

lūke'wạrm·ness, *n.* a mild or moderate heat; indifference; want of zeal or ardor.

lull, *v.t.*; lulled, *pt., pp.*; lulling, *ppr.* [ME. *lullen, lollen*; compare O.D. *lullen,* to sing to sleep, to hum.]
 1. to calm or soothe by gentle sound or motion or both: chiefly in *lull to sleep.*
 2. to bring (a person) into a specified condition by soothing and reassuring him.
 3. to make less intense; mitigate; allay.

lull, *v.i.* to subside; to become calm; as, the wind *lulls.*

lull, *n.* 1. power or quality of soothing. [Rare.]
 2. a short period of quiet or of comparative calm.

lull'à·bȳ, *n.*; *pl.* **lull'à·bīeș,** [from *lull,* v., and *by!*]
 1. a song to quiet children or to lull them to sleep; a cradlesong.
 2. music for this.
 3. good night or good-by; a farewell [Obs.]

lull'à·bȳ, *v.t.*; lullabied, *pt., pp.*; lullabying, *ppr.* to lull with or as with a lullaby.

lull'ẽr, *n.* one who lulls; one who fondles.

lull'i·lo̤o, *v.t.* and *v.i.* [imitative.] to welcome with a joyful song; to sing a joyful welcome.

lull'ing·ly, *adv.* in a manner that is soothing.

lū'lū, *n.* any person or thing outstanding for some quality, as a beautiful girl, a difficult course, etc. [Slang.]

lum, *n.* [W. *llumon,* a chimney, from *llum,* that shoots up or projects.] a chimney. [Brit. Dial.]

lum, *n.* a deep pool; a pond. [Dial.]

lū'mà·chelle, lū'mà·chel, *n.* [It. *lumachella,* lumachelle, from *lumachella,* dim. of *lumaca,* a snail, from L. *limax,* a snail.] in mineralogy, a kind of limestone displaying a variety of colors on account of the fossil shells contained in it: also called *fire marble.*

lum·bag'i·nous, *a.* pertaining to lumbago.

lum·bā'gō, *n.* [LL., from L. *lumbus,* loin.] a backache, especially in the loins and small of the back; rheumatic pain in the joints of the lumbar region.

lum'băl, *a.* lumbar. [Obs.]

lum'băr, *a.* [L. *lumbus,* loin.] pertaining to or near the loins.
 lumbar region; in anatomy, the region around the lumbar vertebrae; the region of the small of the back.
 lumbar vertebrae; in anatomy, those vertebrae lying immediately anterior to or above the sacrum, to which no movable ribs are attached.

lum'băr, *n.* a lumbar nerve, artery, vertebra, etc.

lum'bẽr, *n.* [prob. the contents of a *lumber* room, from *lombard*-room, the room where the *Lombard* banker stored his unredeemed pledges.]
 1. miscellaneous discarded household articles, furniture, etc. stored away or taking up room.
 2. timber sawed or split for use, as beams, joists, boards, planks, staves, hoops, and the like; specifically, boards.

lum'bẽr, *v.t.*; lumbered, *pt., pp.*; lumbering, *ppr.*
 1. to fill or obstruct with useless articles or rubbish; to clutter.
 2. to remove (timber) from an area; to cut down (trees).

lum'bẽr, *v.i.* to cut down timber and saw it into lumber.

lum′bẽr, *v.i.* [ME. *lomeren*, from ON.]
1. to move heavily, clumsily, and noisily.
2. to rumble.

lum′bẽr, *n.* a rumbling sound.

lum′bẽr·ẽr, *n.* one employed in getting lumber from the forest.

lum′bẽr·ing, *a.* 1. moving heavily, clumsily, or noisily.
2. rumbling.

lum′bẽr·ing, *n.* the act or employment of cutting trees and preparing lumber for market.

lum′bẽr·jack, *n.* [*lumber*, and *jack* (man, boy, etc.).]
1. a man whose work is cutting down timber and preparing it for the sawmill.
2. a short, straight coat or jacket of leather, wool, etc., originally made to resemble those worn by lumberjacks.

lum′bẽr kiln (kil), a room in which lumber is dried or seasoned by means of artificial heat.

lum′bẽr·măn, *n.*; *pl.* **lum′bẽr·men,** 1. a lumberjack (sense 1).
2. a man who buys or sells lumber; a person employed in the lumber business.

lum′bẽr rōōm, a room used for storing lumber, or useless things.

lum′bẽr wag′ŏn, 1. a heavy wagon with a box, built without springs and used by farmers in their heavy work about the farm.
2. a wagon used to haul lumber.

lum′bẽr·yärd, *n.* a place where lumber is kept for sale.

lum′bō-, [from L. *lumbus*, loin.] a combining form meaning *loin* or *lumbar*: also *lumb-*.

lum·bō·dor′săl, *a.* [L. *lumbus*, loin, and *dorsum*, the back.] in anatomy, relating to or denoting parts in the region of the loins and back.

lum·bō·sā′crăl, *a.* [L. *lumbus*, loin, and LL *sacrum*.] in anatomy, relating to or denoting parts in the region of the loins and sacrum.

lum′bric·ăl, *a.* designating or of the lumbricales.

lum·bri·cā′lis, *n.*; *pl.* **lum·bri·cā′lēs,** [Mod. L., from L. *lumbricus*, intestinal worm, earthworm: from the shape of the muscles.] any of four small muscles in the palm of the hand and in the sole of the foot.

lum·bric′i·form, *a.* [L. *lumbricus*, a worm, and *forma*, form.] resembling a worm in shape.

lum′bri·coid, *a.* [L. *lumbricus*, a worm, and Gr. *eidos*, form.]
1. resembling an earthworm.
2. designating a particular variety of roundworm.

lum′bri·coid, *n.* a parasitic roundworm that infests the human intestine.

lū′men, *n.*; *pl.* **lū′mi·nȧ, lū′mens,** [L. *lumen*, light.]
1. a unit of measure for the flow of light, equal to the amount of flow through a unit solid angle from a uniform point source of one international candle.
2. in anatomy, the passage within a tubular organ.
3. in botany, the internal space of a cell.

lū′men-hour′, *n.* a lumen of light acting for one hour.

lū′min·ăl, *a.* of or pertaining to a lumen.

lū′min·ăl, *n.* phenobarbital, a sedative and hypnotic: a trade-mark (*Luminal*).

lū′mi·nănce, *n.* 1. the state or the quality of being luminant.
2. luminous intensity, expressed in candles per unit projected area for the luminous surface, measured as in square meters.

lū′mi·nănt, *a.* emitting light; luminous.

lū′mi·năr·ist, *n.* in art, one skilled in the effects of light or of lights and shadows.

lū′mi·năr″y, *n.*; *pl.* **lu′mi·năr″ies,** [OFr. *luminarie*; LL. *luminare*, a lamp, a light; L. *luminare*, a window, from *lumen*, a light.]
1. any body that gives light, but chiefly applied to the sun and moon.
2. one who sheds light on some subject or enlightens mankind; a famous intellectual; as, the great *luminaries* of Europe.
3. any well-known person.

lū′mi·nāte, *v.t.* [LL. *luminatus*, pp. of *luminare*, to shine, from L. *lumen*, a light.] to illuminate.

lū·mi·nā′tion, *n.* same as *illumination*.

lū′mine, *v.t.* to illumine. [Obs.]

lū·mi·nesce′, *v.i.*; luminesced, *pt.*, *pp.*; luminescing, *ppr.* [back-formation from *luminescent*.] to be or become luminescent.

lū·mi·nes′cence, *n.* [from L. *lumen*, a light; and *-escence*.] any giving off of light caused by the absorption of radiant or corpuscular energy and not by incandescence; any cold light.

lū·mi·nes′cent, *a.* [from L. *lumen*, a light, and *-escent*.] of, exhibiting, or capable of exhibiting luminescence.

lū·mi·nif′ẽr·ous, *a.* [from L. *lumen*, a light; and *-ferous*.]
1. producing light; yielding light.
2. allowing or facilitating the passage of light.

lū·mi·nos′i·ty, *n.* [from L. *luminosus*, full of light, bright; and *-ity*.]
1. the quality or condition of being luminous.
2. *pl.* **lū·mi·nos′i·ties,** something luminous.

lū′mi·nous, *a.* [ME. *luminose*; L. *luminosus*, from *lumen*, a light.]
1. giving off light; bright.
2. flooded with light.
3. clear; readily understood.
4. intellectually brilliant.
Syn.—lucid.—A thing is *lucid* when pervaded by light; it is *luminous* when it sends forth light to surrounding objects..

lū′mi·nous en′ẽr·ġy, light.

lū′mi·nous flux, the rate of flow of light radiation.

lū′mi·nous·ly, *adv.* in a luminous manner.

lū′mi·nous·ness, *n.* the state or quality of being luminous.

lū′mi·nous pāint, a paint made with a phosphorescent substance which, after exposure to a strong light, is luminous in the dark for a period of time.

lum′mŏx, *n.* a clumsy or stupid person. [Colloq.]

lump, *n.* [ME. *lompe*, *lumpe*; prob. from Anglo-N. or M.L.G.]
1. an indefinitely shaped mass of something, usually small enough to be taken up in the hand.
2. a small cube, especially of sugar.
3. a swelling.
4. aggregate; collection.
5. a dull, clodlike person.
6. soft coal in pieces ranging from the size of a goose egg to several times as large.
7. a protuberance at the breech end of the barrel of a gun to receive the nipple.
in the lump; in the mass or aggregate; all together.

lump, *a.* forming or formed into a lump or lumps; as, *lump* sugar.

lump, *v.t.*; lumped, (lumpt), *pt.*, *pp.*; lumping, *ppr.* 1. to put together in a lump or lumps.
2. to put together; to treat or deal with in a mass; to include in one group.
3. to make lumps in.

lump, *v.i.* 1. to become lumpy.
2. to move heavily and laboriously (usually with *along*).

lump, *v.t.* [Early Mod. Eng., to look sour.] to put up with (something disagreeable); as, if you don't like it, you can *lump* it. [Colloq.]

lump′en, *a.* [from G. *lumpen-*, trashy, from *lump*, a rascal, scoundrel, lit., rag, from M.H.G. *lumpe*.] designating or of persons or groups regarded as belonging to a low or contemptible segment of their class or kind because of their unproductiveness, shiftlessness, alienation, degeneration, etc.

lump′en, *n.* a person or group that is lumpen.

lump′ẽr, *n.* 1. a laborer who helps to load and unload ships; a stevedore.
2. a militiaman. [Brit. Slang.]
3. one who lumps or throws together.

lump′fish, *n.*; *pl.* **lump′fish, lump′fish·es,** [so called from its bulkiness.] a plump, clumsily shaped fish, *Cyclopterus lumpus*, found on both sides of the North Atlantic, with a thick, greenish skin studded with bony tubercles, or knobs: its pelvic fins unite to form a sucker.

lump′i·ly, *adv.* so as to form lumps.

lump′i·ness, *n.* the quality or state of being lumpy.

lump′ing, *a.* bulky; heavy; ponderous.

lump′ish, *a.* like a lump; heavy; gross; bulky; dull; inactive.

lump′ish·ly, *adv.* heavily; with dullness or stupidity.

lump′ish·ness, *n.* heaviness; dullness; stupidity.

lump′suck·ẽr, *n.* same as *lumpfish*.

lump sum, a gross, or total, sum paid at one time.

lump′y, *a.*; *comp.* lumpier; *superl.* lumpiest,
1. full of lumps or small, compact masses.
2. covered with lumps; having an uneven surface.
3. rough: said of water.
4. like a lump; clumsy; dull; lumpish.

lump′y jąw, same as *actinomycosis*.

Lū′nȧ, *n.* [L. *luna*, the moon.]
1. in Roman mythology, the goddess presiding over the moon and the months; hence, by personification, the moon.
2. [l–] in alchemy, silver.
luna cornea; in old chemistry, fused chloride of silver: so called from its hornlike appearance.

lū′nȧ·cy, *n.*; *pl.* **lū′nȧ·cies,** [*luna*tic and *-cy*.]
1. (a) originally, intermittent insanity, formerly supposed to change in intensity with the phases of the moon; (b) mental unsoundness; insanity.
2. great folly; utter foolishness.

Lū′nȧ moth, a large North American moth, *Tropaea luna*, characterized by pastel-green wings, each having a luniform spot bordered by rings of light yellow, blue, and black. The wings, the hind pair of which end in elongated tails, are also tipped anteriorly with purple, the remaining margins showing a delicate yellow.

lū′năr, *a.* [L. *lunaris*, pertaining to the moon, from *luna*, moon.]
1. pertaining to the moon; as, *lunar* observations.
2. measured by the revolutions of the moon; as, *lunar* days.
3. resembling the moon; specifically, (a) pale; pallid; (b) round or crescent-shaped.
4. under the influence of the moon. [Obs.]
5. of or containing silver.
lunar caustic; fused silver nitrate, used in medicine for cauterizing.
lunar cycle; see *Metonic cycle* under *cycle*.
lunar day; the time between two successive transits of the moon on a given meridian.
lunar distance; the angular distance of the moon from the sun, or from a fixed star or planet lying nearly in the line of its path, by means of which the longitude of a ship at sea is found.
lunar month; the interval from one new moon to the next, equal to about 29 1/2 days; the time in which the moon completes one full revolution about the earth.
lunar tables; in astronomy, tables showing the motions of the moon, from which the true place of the moon at any given time may be found; in navigation, logarithmic tables for correcting the apparent distance of the moon from the sun, or from a fixed star, on account of refraction and parallax.
lunar year; the period of twelve lunar months, or about 354 1/3 days.

lū′năr, *n.* 1. in anatomy, the lunare.
2. in navigation, same as *lunar distance*.

lū·nā′rē, *n.*; *pl.* **lū·nā′ri·ȧ,** [neut. of L. *lunaris*, pertaining to the moon.] a carpal bone, the middle of the upper row.

Lū·nā′ri·ȧ, *n.* [L. *lunaris*, pertaining to the moon.] a genus of biennial and perennial cruciferous herbs: so called from the broad, silvery dissepiments of the pod resembling a full moon.

lū·nā′ri·ăn, *n.* 1. a supposed inhabitant of the moon.
2. one who makes a study of the moon.

lū′nȧ·ry, *a.* lunar. [Obs.]

lū′nȧ·ry, *n.* moonwort or honesty; also, the fern *Botrychium lunaria*.

lū′nāte, lū′nā·ted, *a.* [L. *luna*, moon, and *-ate*.] formed like a half-moon; crescent-shaped.

lū′nȧ·tiç, *a.* [ME. *lunatik*; OFr.; LL. *lunaticus*, mad, moonstruck, from L. *luna*, moon.]
1. suffering from lunacy; mad; insane; as, a *lunatic* person.
2. indicating or exhibiting lunacy.
3. of or for insane persons.
4. utterly foolish.

lū′nȧ·tiç, *n.* an insane person.
Syn.—madman, maniac, monomaniac.

lū·nat′i·căl, *a.* same as *lunatic*.

lū′nȧ·tiç ȧ·sy′lum, a hospital for the mentally ill: term no longer in good usage.

lū′nȧ·tiç fringe, the minority considered foolishly extremist, fanatical, etc. in any political, social, religious, or other movement.

lū·nā′tion, *n.* [LL. *lunatio* (-*onis*), the revolution of the moon, from L. *luna*, moon.] the period of a synodic revolution of the moon, or the time from one new moon to the following, equal to about 29 1/2 days; lunar month.

lū·nā′tum, *n.*; *pl.* **lū·nā′tȧ,** [L., neut. of *lunatus*, crescent-shaped.] the lunare.

lunch, *n.* [a variant of *lump*.]
1. a lump or slice, as of food. [Obs.]
2. a light repast taken between breakfast and dinner; a luncheon.
3. the food prepared for such a meal; as, the children took their *lunches* to school.

lunch, *v.i.*; lunched (luncht), *pt., pp.*; lunching, *ppr.* to eat lunch.

lunch, *v.t.* to provide lunch for.

lunch'eŏn, *n.* 1. a lump or piece of bread. [Obs.]
 2. a lunch; especially, a formal lunch.

lunch'eŏn, *v.i.* to take luncheon.

lunch″eŏn·ette', *n.* a light lunch or meal; also, a place where such lunches or snacks are sold and eaten, usually in connection with soda fountain service.

lunch'rōōm, *n.* an eating place specializing in quick, light meals; a place to eat a lunch of any sort.

lūne, *n.* [Fr. *lune*; L. *luna*, moon.]
 1. anything in the shape of a half-moon.
 2. in geometry, a figure in the form of a crescent, bounded by two arcs of circles intersecting at its extremities.

lūne, *n.* [var. of *loyn*; OFr. *loigne*.] a leash for a hawk.

Lū·nel', *n.* [named after *Lunel* in France.] a kind of muscatel wine.

lūneṣ, *n.pl.* fits of lunacy.

lū·nette', *n.* [Fr. *lunette*, dim. of *lune*, the moon.]
 1. in military science, a projecting fieldwork consisting of two faces and two flanks.
 2. in farriery, the front half of a horseshoe.
 3. a kind of watch crystal which is more than ordinarily flattened in the center; a concavo-convex lens for spectacles.
 4. a piece of felt to cover the eye of a vicious horse.
 5. in architecture, (a) a crescent-shaped opening in a vaulted roof to admit light; (b) a semicircular space, often containing a windowpane or a mural, above a door or window.
 6. in the Roman Catholic Church, a crescent-shaped crystal fitted to cover the Host for solemn exposition.
 7. in artillery, an iron loop or ring at the end of the stock of a gun carriage.
 8. a crescent or half-moon. [Obs.]
 9. the crescent-shaped aperture at the base of a guillotine into which the victim's neck is placed.
 10. a small, glass-bottomed, open frame carried by divers.
 11. in glassmaking, the hole that connects the melting furnace with the arch.
 12. in the game of Polish checkers, a position assumed by two pieces of the same color, permitting the opponent to place himself either behind or between them.
 Formerly also *lunet*.

LUNETTES

lung, *n.* [ME. *lunge, longe*; AS. *lungen* (pl. *lungena*), lung.]
 1. either of the two spongelike respiratory organs in the thorax of vertebrates, that oxygenate the blood and remove carbon dioxide from it. In man they are situated one on each side of the chest, and separated from each other by the heart and larger blood vessels. Each is enclosed in its own serous membrane, called the pleura, with its base resting on the diaphragm.

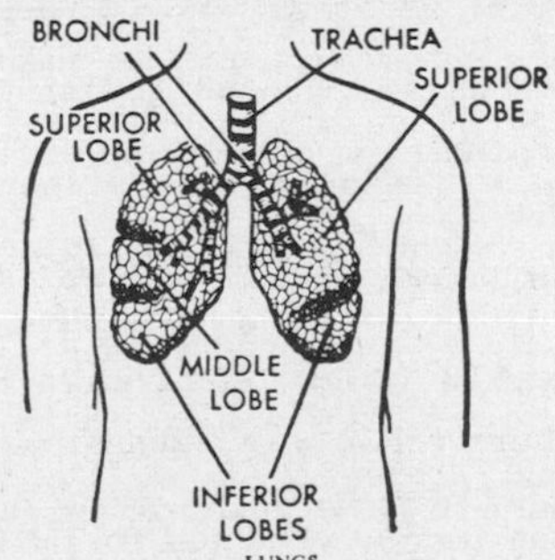

LUNGS

 2. any analogous organ in invertebrates.
 3. [*pl.*] a servant who blew the fire of an alchemist. [Obs.]
 at the top of one's lungs; in one's loudest voice.

lunġe, *n.* [short for *allonge*; Fr. *allonge*, lit., a lengthening, from *allonger*, to lengthen, thrust, from *a-* (L. *ad*), to, and *long* (L. *longus*), long.]
 1. a sudden thrust with a sword or other weapon.
 2. a sudden plunge forward.

lunġe, *v.i.*; lunged, *pt., pp.*; lunging, *ppr.* 1. to make a lunge.
 2. to move with a lunge.

lunġe, *v.t.* 1. to cause to lunge.
 2. in horsemanship, to train or exercise, as a horse, by causing him to go rapidly around a circle at the end of a long halter.

lunġe, *n.* and *v.t.*; lunged, *pt., pp.*; lunging, *ppr.* same as *longe*.

lunged, *a.* having lungs: used especially in hyphenated compounds, as strong-*lunged*.

luñ'gee, *n.* same as *lungi*.

lunġ'ẽr, *n.* that which lunges or drives forcefully in any direction.

lung'ẽr, *n.* one affected with any disease of the lungs; particularly, one with tuberculosis of the lungs. [Slang.]

lung fē'vẽr, pneumonia.

lung'fish, *n.*; *pl.* **lung'fish, lung'fish·eṣ,** a fish having both lungs and gills; a dipnoan: also called *mudfish*.

lung'-grōwn, *a.* having lungs that adhere to the pleura.

luñ'gï, *n.* [Hind. and Per. *lungī*.] in India, (a) a long cloth used for loincloths, scarves, turbans, etc.; (b) a loincloth. Also spelled *lungee*.

lung'ie, *n.* the guillemot. [Brit.]

lun'ġis, *n.* a lingerer; a dull, drowsy fellow. [Obs.]

lung'less, *a.* without lungs.

luñ'gōōr, *n.* [E. Ind.] a monkey, *Semnopithecus schistaceus*, of India, having a long tail and a bearded face.

lung'-sick, *a.* having a form of pleuropneumonia chiefly affecting oxen in South Africa.

lung'wŏrm, *n.* any parasitic nematoid worm which infests the lungs of animals.

lung'wŏrt, *n.* 1. a boraginaceous plant of the genus *Pulmonaria*, a common garden flower, having red and purple tubular blossoms, and leaves speckled like human lungs.
 2. a lichen, *Sticta pulmonaria*, growing abundantly on trunks of trees in moist alpine countries.
 bullock's or *cow's lungwort*; the common mullen, *Verbascum thapsus*.
 French or *golden lungwort*; a European wall hawkweed, *Hieracium murorum*.
 sea lungwort; *Metensia maritima*, a plant found on the American seacoast.
 tree lungwort; same as *lungwort*, sense 2.

lū'ni-, [from L. *luna*, the moon.] a combining form meaning: (a) *moon*, as in *luni*tidal; (b) *of the moon and*, as in *luni*solar.]

lū·ni·çũr'rent, *a.* [*luni-* and *current*.] having currents which depend on the phases of the moon.

lū'ni·fọrm, *a.* [*luni-*, and L. *forma*, form.] having the shape of the moon, particularly the crescent.

lū·ni·sō'lăr, *a.* [*luni-* and *solar*.] involving the mutual relationship or combined attraction of the moon and sun; as, *lunisolar* tides.
 lunisolar precession; in astronomy, that part of the annual precession of the equinoxes which depends upon the joint influence of the sun and moon.
 lunisolar year; a period of time consisting of 532 common years, found by multiplying the cycle of the sun by that of the moon, at the end of which time the new and full moon and the eclipses occur on the same days of the year, month, and week as they did at the end of the preceding cycle.

lū'ni·stice, *n.* [*luni-*, and L. *status*, a standing, from *stare*, to stand.] the farthest point of the moon's northing and southing in its monthly revolution.

lū·ni·tīd'ăl, *a.* [*luni-* and *tidal*.] pertaining to the movements in the tides which are caused by the attraction of the moon alone.
 lunitidal interval; the interval by which the lunar high tide lags behind the transit of the moon.

luñk'head (-hed), *n.* [prob. echoic alteration of *lump-* after *hunk-*, etc.] a stupid person. [Colloq.]

lunt, *n.* [D. *lont*, a match, earlier lamp wick.]
 1. (a) a slow-burning match; (b) a torch. [Scot.]
 2. smoke [Scot.]

lunt, *v.t.* and *v.i.* to kindle or smoke. [Scot.]

lū'nū·lȧ, *n.*; *pl.* **lū'nū·lae,** [L. *lunuta*, dim. of *luna*, the moon.]
 1. a lunule.
 2. in geometry, a lune.

lū'nū·lăr, *a.* [L. *lunula*, a crescent.] of, or having the nature of, a lunule; crescent-shaped.

lū'nū·lāte, lū'nū·lā·ted, *a.* [L. *lunula*, a crescent, and *-ate*.]
 1. crescent-shaped.
 2. having crescent-shaped markings.

lū'nūle, *n.* [L. *lunula*, dim. of *luna*, a moon.]
 1. anything in the shape of a half-moon or small crescent.
 2. in anatomy, any structure or marking in the shape of a crescent, as the whitish half-moon at the base of a fingernail.
 3. in zoology, any crescent-shaped part or marking, as on the shell of a mollusk or the wing of a moth.

lū'nū·let, *n.* [dim. of *lunule*.] in zoology, any small, crescent-shaped mark, especially on the wing of an insect.

lū'nū·līte, *n.* [L. *lunula*, a little moon, and *-ite*.] a small fossil coral, especially one which is circular or crescent-shaped.

lū'ny, *a.*; *comp.* lunier; *superl.* luniest, same as *loony*.

lū'ny, *n.*; *pl.* **lū'nieṣ,** same as *loony*.

Lū'pẽr·çăl, *n.* Lupercalia. [Rare.]

Lū'pẽr·çăl, *a.* pertaining to the Lupercalia. [Rare.]

Lū·pẽr·çā'li·ȧ, *n.pl.* [L., from *Lupercalis*, of Lupercus, from *Lupercus*, from *lupus*, a wolf.] an ancient Roman festival with fertility rites, held on February 15 in honor of Lupercus, a pastoral god sometimes identified with Faunus.

Lū·pẽr·çā'li·ăn, *a.* of or connected with the Lupercalia.

lū″pin·as'tẽr, *n.* [L. *lupinus*, a lupine, and *aster*, a star.] a species of clover found in Siberia, *Trifolium lupinaster*: called also *bastard lupine*.

lū'pine, *n.* [ME. *lupyne*; L. *lupinus*, a lupine.]
 1. a leguminous plant of the genus *Lupinus*, with long spikes of white, rose, yellow, or blue flowers and pods containing white, beanlike seeds.
 2. the seed of this plant, used in some parts of Europe as food.
 bastard lupine; same as *lupinaster*.

lū'pīne, *a.* [L. *lupinus*, belonging to a wolf, from *lupus*, a wolf.]
 1. like a wolf; ravenous; fierce.
 2. of or pertaining to the group of animals including the wolves, dogs, etc.
 3. related to the wolf.

lū'pin·in, *n.* [*Lupinus*, and *-in*.] a bitter substance extracted from the leaves of the white lupine, *Lupinus albus*.

Lū·pī'nus, *n.* [L. *lupinus*, a lupine.] a genus of leguminous plants, many species of which are cultivated for their white, rose, yellow, or blue flowers.

lū'pū·lin, *n.* [*lupul*us, and *-in*, *-ine*.] a resinous powder obtained from the strobiles of hops, used in medicine as a sedative.

lū″pū·lin'iç, *a.* of, pertaining to, or obtained from hops.

lū'pū·lus, *n.* [dim. from L. *lupus*, the hop, apparently identical with *lupus*, a wolf.] the common hop plant.

Lū'pus, *n.* [L., a wolf.] in astronomy, a constellation supposedly outlining a wolf, situated south of Scorpio.

lū'pus, *n.* [L., a wolf: from eating into the substance.] any of various skin diseases; especially, a chronic tuberculous disease of the skin or mucous membrane, characterized by the formation of reddish-brown nodules.

lũrch, *n.* [Fr. *lourche*, name of a game like backgammon; prob. from OFr. *lourche*, deceived, duped.]
 1. in cribbage, the condition of a player who fails to score a specified number of points in losing to his opponent.
 2. a game lost in this way.
 to leave in the lurch; to leave in a difficult situation or in embarrassment; to leave (a person) in a forlorn state or without help.

lũrch, *v.i.* [earlier *lee-lurch*, from *lee-larch*, from *lee-latch*, a falling to leeward of one's course.] to roll, pitch, or sway suddenly to one side.

lũrch, *n.* a lurching movement; a sudden rolling, pitching, etc.

lũrch, *v.i.*; lurched (lũrcht), *pt., pp.*; lurching, *ppr.* [var. of *lurk*.]
 1. to withdraw to one side or to a private

place; to lie in ambush or in secret; to lie close; to lurk. [Obs.]

Fond of prowling and *lurching* out at night after their own sinful pleasures. —Kingsley.

2. to cheat; to trick; to rob. [Archaic.]

I am fain to shuffle, to hedge, and to *lurch*. —Shak.

lũrch, *v.t.* 1. to prevent (a person) from getting his share of something by getting ahead of him. [Archaic.]

2. to cheat; to trick; to rob. [Archaic.]

lũrch, *n.* a lurching or lurking. [Obs.]

lũrch'ẽr, *n.* 1. one who lies in wait or lurks.

2. a thief; a poacher.

3. a crossbred dog that lies in wait for game, and is often used by poachers. [Brit.]

lũrch'ẽr, *n.* a glutton; a gormandizer. [Obs.]

lũrch'līne, *n.* in catching birds with a net, the line by which the net is drawn over the birds.

lũr'dăn, lũr'dāne, *n.* [OFr. *lourdin*, from *lourd*, heavy, dull, stupid.] a lazy, dull person. [Archaic or Dial.]

lũr'dăn, lũr'dāne, *a.* lazy and dull. [Archaic or Dial.]

lūre, *n.* [OFr. *loerre, leurre*, from M.H.G. *luoder*, bait, decoy.]

1. a device consisting of a bunch of feathers on the end of a long cord, often baited with food: it is used in falconry to recall the hawk.

2. any enticement; that which invites by the prospect of advantage or pleasure; as, the *lure* of the stage.

3. in heraldry, the representation of a lure in falconry.

4. a bait, especially an artificial one, used in fishing.

lūre, *v.t.*; lured, *pt., pp.*; luring, *ppr.* [ME. *luren*; OFr. *leurrer*, to lure, from *leurre*, a decoy, lure.]

1. to recall (a falcon) with a lure.

2. to entice; to attract; to tempt (often with *on*).

lūre, *v.i.* to call hawks.

lũrg, *n.* [etym. unknown.] the marine worm of European and American coasts, *Nephthys cæca*.

lū'rid, *a.* [L. *luridus*, pale-yellow, ghastly.]

1. ghastly pale; gloomy; dismal. [Rare.]

2. glowing through a haze, as flames enveloped by smoke.

3. (a) vivid in a harsh or shocking way; startling; sensational; (b) characterized by violent passion or crime; as, a *lurid* tale.

lũrk, *v.i.*; lurked (lũrkt), *pt., pp.*; lurking, *ppr.* [ME. *lurken, lorken*; prob. from Sw. *lurka*, to lurk.]

1. to lie hidden, ready to spring out, attack, etc.; to lie in wait.

2. to lie concealed or unperceived; as, no selfish motive *lurks* in his heart.

3. to move furtively; to keep out of sight.

lũrk'ẽr, *n.* one who lurks or keeps out of sight.

Lūr'leī, *n.* same as *Lorelei*.

lur'ry, *n.*; *pl.* **lur'ries,** a confused, inarticulate sound or utterance. [Archaic.]

lur'ry, *n.* same as *lorry*.

lus'cious, [ME. *lucius*, thought to be var. of *licious*, aphetic form of *delicious*; prob. influenced by *lush*.]

1. sweet and very toothsome; very sweet; delicious; highly gratifying to taste or smell.

And raisins keep their *luscious* native taste. —Dryden.

2. pleasing; delighting any of the senses; enticing.

He will bait him in with the *luscious* proposal of some gainful purchase. —South.

3. oversweet; nauseating.

4. lascivious; wanton. [Obs.]

lus'cious·ly, *adv.* in a luscious manner.

lus'cious·ness, *n.* the quality of being luscious.

lush, *n.* [prob. shortened from (*City of*) *Lushington*, name of actors club at the Harp Tavern in London, dissolved 1895.]

1. alcoholic liquor. [Slang.]

2. a drunken person. [Slang.]

lush, *v.t.* and *v.i.*; lushed (lusht), *pt., pp.*; lushing, *ppr.* to drink (liquor). [Slang.]

lush, *n.* same as *losh*.

lush, *a.* [ME. *lusch*, echoic var. of *lassch*, soft, flaccid; OFr. *lasche*, lax, loose, from *laschier*, to loosen.]

1. full of juice; succulent.

How *lush* and lusty the grass looks; how green! —Shak.

2. of luxuriant growth; as, *lush* vegetation.

3. characterized by a rich growth of vegetation; as, *lush* fields.

4. characterized by rich and extravagant ornamentation, invention, etc. often tending to excess; as, *lush* writing. [Colloq.]

lush'bũrg, *n.* an old counterfeit of the English penny, made at Luxemburg. [Obs.]

Lū'si·ad, *n.* [Port. *Lusiadas*, Portuguese, from L. *Lusitania*, a province of Hispania.] a celebrated Portuguese epic poem written by Camões on the establishment of the Portuguese government in India.

Lū''si·tā'ni·ăn, *n.* an inhabitant of Lusitania.

Lū''si·tā'ni·ăn, *a.* pertaining to the region formerly called Lusitania, now almost identical with Portugal.

lusk, *a.* lazy; slothful. [Obs.]

lusk, *n.* a lazy fellow; a lubber. [Obs.]

lusk, *v.i.* to be idle or unemployed. [Obs.]

lusk'ish, *a.* inclined to be lazy. [Obs.]

lusk'ish·ly, *adv.* lazily. [Obs.]

lusk'ish·ness, *n.* tendency toward indolence; laziness. [Obs.]

lū·sō'ri·ous, *a.* used in play; sportive. [Obs.]

lū'sō·ry, *a.* used in play; playful.

lust, *n.* [ME. *luste*; AS. *lust*, lust, desire, pleasure.]

1. overmastering desire; eagerness to possess or enjoy; as, a *lust* for power.

2. a desire to gratify the senses; bodily appetite.

3. (a) sexual desire; (b) excessive sexual desire, especially as seeking unrestrained gratification.

4. vigor; active power. [Obs.]

5. desire; wish; inclination. [Obs.]

6. pleasure. [Obs.]

lust, *v.i.*; lusted, *pt., pp.*; lusting, *ppr.* [ME. *lusten, lysten*; AS. *lystan*, from *lust*, desire, pleasure.]

1. to feel an intense desire, especially sexual desire; to long: often with *after* or *for*; as, to *lust after* gold.

Lust not *after* her beauty in thy heart. —Prov. vi. 25.

2. to list; to like. [Obs.]

lust'ẽr, *n.* one actuated by lust or strong desire.

lus'tẽr, lus'tre (-tẽr), *n.* same as *lustrum*.

lus'tẽr, lus'tre, *n.* [Fr. *lustre*; It. *lustro*, from *lustrare*; L. *lustrare*, to light, illumine.]

1. gloss; sheen; as, the *luster* of silk.

2. brightness; splendor; brilliancy; as, the *luster* of the stars.

3. brilliant beauty or fame; renown; distinction.

4. one of the glass pendants on a chandelier.

5. a chandelier ornamented with drops or pendants of cut glass.

6. a substance used for polishing.

7. a glossy fabric made of cotton and wool; a kind of poplin.

8. a metallic, sometimes iridescent, appearance given to pottery by a glaze.

9. in mineralogy, a variation in the nature of the reflecting surface of minerals. In this sense it designates, first, the kind or quality of the light reflected; second, the degree of intensity. The principal kinds of luster are: metallic, adamantine, vitreous, resinous, pearly, silky, and greasy.

cantharid luster; a luster which exhibits the green and blue iridescence of the Spanish fly.

lus'tẽr, *v.t.*; lustered, *pt., pp.*; lustering, *ppr.*

1. to make lustrous or shining. [Rare.]

2. to give a lustrous finish or gloss to; as, to *luster* furs.

Also spelled *lustre*.

lus'tẽr·less, lus'tre·less, *a.* without luster.

lus'tẽr·wāre, lus'tre·wāre, *n.* highly glazed earthenware decorated by the application of metallic oxides to the glaze.

lust'fụl, *a.* 1. having lascivious desires; libidinous; lewd.

2. characterized by lust; exciting lust.

Thence his *lustful* orgies he enlarged. —Milton.

3. vigorous; robust; stout; lusty. [Archaic.]

lust'fụl·ly, *adv.* in a lustful manner.

lust'fụl·ness, *n.* the state of being lustful.

lus'tick, *a.* lusty; vigorous; jovial. [Obs.]

lus'ti·head (-hed), *n.* lustihood. [Archaic.]

lus'ti·hood, *n.* lustiness. [Archaic.]

lus'ti·ly, *adv.* in a lusty manner; vigorously.

lus'ti·ness, *n.* the quality or state of being lusty; vigor; robustness.

lust'less, *a.* listless; languid; indifferent. [Obs.]

lus'trȧ, *n.* alternative plural of *lustrum*.

lus'trăl, *a.* [L. *lustralis*, from *lustrum*, a purificatory sacrifice.]

1. used in, pertaining to, or connected with ceremonial purification.

2. pertaining to a lustrum, or five-year period.

lus'trāte, *v.t.*; lustrated, *pt., pp.*; lustrating, *ppr.* [L. *lustratus*, pp. of *lustrare*, to purify by means of a propitiatory sacrifice, from *lustrum*, a purificatory sacrifice.] to make clear or pure; to purify by means of certain ceremonies.

lus·trā'tion, *n.* 1. the act of lustrating or making pure; a ceremonial cleansing.

And holy water for *lustration* bring. —Dryden.

2. an ancient sacrifice or ceremony by which cities, fields, armies, or people, defiled by crimes, were purified.

lus'trȧ·tive, *a.* of lustration; purifying.

lus'tre (-tẽr), *n., v.t.* and *v.i.*; lustred, *pt., pp.*; lustring, *ppr.* same as *luster*.

lus'tri·căl, *a.* [L. *lustricus*, of or belonging to purification, from *lustrum*, a purificatory sacrifice.] same as *lustral*.

lus'tring, *n.* [Fr. *lustrine*; It. *lustrino*, a shining silk tinsel, from *lustro*, luster.] a kind of glossy silk cloth: also *lutestring*.

lus'trous, *a.* having luster; bright; shining; luminous.

lus'trous·ly, *adv.* in a lustrous manner; brilliantly; luminously.

lus'trum, *n.*; *pl.* **lus'trums, lus'trȧ,** [L. *lustrum*, a purificatory sacrifice, a space of five years.]

1. in ancient Rome, a purification of the whole Roman people, performed by means of certain ceremonies at the end of every five years, after the census.

2. a five-year period.

lust'y, *a.*; *comp.* lustier; *superl.* lustiest, [from *lust*.]

1. full of or characterized by youthful spirit, vigor, etc.; stout; vigorous; robust; healthy; lively.

2. bulky; large; of great size. [Obs.]

3. beautiful; handsome; pleasing. [Obs.]

4. impudent. [Obs.]

5. lustful. [Obs.]

lū'sus nȧ·tū'rae, [L.] a sport or freak of nature; a monstrosity.

lūt'ȧ·nist, *n.* [LL. *lutanista*, from *lutana*, a lute.] a person who plays on the lute; a composer for the lute: also spelled *lutenist*.

lū·tā'ri·ous, *a.* pertaining to or living in mud. [Obs.]

lū·tā'tion, *n.* [L. *lutatio* (*-onis*), from *lutare*, to daub with mud, from *lutum*, mud.] the act or method of sealing with lute (clayey cement).

lūte, *n.* [ME. *lute*; Sp. *laúd*, a lute; Ar. *al'ūd*, a lute.] an old stringed instrument related to the guitar, with a body shaped like half of a pear and six to thirteen strings stretched along the fretted neck, which is often bent to form a sharp angle.

LUTE

lūte, *v.t.*; luted, *pt., pp.*; luting, *ppr.* to play on or as on a lute.

lūte, *v.i.* 1. to play the lute.

2. to sound sweetly, like a lute: chiefly a poetical use.

lūte, *n.* [OFr. *lut*; L. *lutum*, mud, clay, anything that is washed down, from *luere*, to wash.]

1. a clayey cement used for making the joints of pipes airtight and as a sealing agent generally.

2. a packing ring of rubber, placed between the lid and the lip of a jar, so as to make it airtight.

3. a straight-edged tool used to strike off the surplus clay from a brick mold.

lūte, *v.t.*; luted, *pt., pp.*; luting, *ppr.* to seal with lute.

lūte'-backed (-bakt), *a.* having a curved spine.

lū·tē'ci·um (-shi-), *n.* lutetium: the former spelling.

lū'tē·in, *n.* [L. *luteus*, golden-yellow, and *-in*.] a yellow pigment obtained from the corpus luteum.

lūt'ē·nist, *n.* same as *lutanist*.

lū'tē·ō-, [from L. *luteus*, golden-yellow, from *lutum*, weed used in dyeing yellow.] a combining form meaning *yellow* or *yellowish*, as in *luteo*lin.

lū'tē·ō·lin, *n.* [Fr. *lutéoline*, from Mod. L. (*Reseda*) *luteola*, lit., yellowish (reseda); L. *luteolus*, yellowish, dim of *luteus*, yellow.] a yellow crystalline compound, $C_{15}H_{10}O_6$, used for dyeing cloth.

lū·tē′ō·lous, *a.* [L. *luteolus*, yellowish, dim. of *luteus*, golden-yellow.] yellowish; slightly luteous; fulvous.

lū′tē·ous, *a.* [L. *luteus*, golden-yellow, from *lutum*, a weed used in dyeing yellow.] orange-yellow or reddish-yellow.

lū′tē·ous, *a.* [L. *luteus*, muddy, from *lutum*, mud, clay.] muddy; of a clayey color. [Rare.]

lūt′ẽr, *n.* a lutist; a lute player.

lū·tes′cent, *a.* [L. *luteus*, yellow, and *-escent.*] yellowish in color; luteous.

lūte′string, *n.* [altered from *lustring.*] same as *lustring.*

lūte′string, *n.* 1. the string of a lute.
2. a noctuid moth having wings marked with lines resembling the strings of a lute.

lū·tē′ti·um (-shi-) *n.* [Mod. L., from L. *Lutetia*, city in Gaul (now Paris).] a metallic chemical element of the rare-earth group: symbol, Lu; atomic weight, 174.99; atomic number, 71: formerly spelled *lutecium.*

Lū′thẽr·ăn, *a.* 1. of Martin Luther.
2. of the Protestant denomination founded by Luther, or of its doctrines, etc.

Lū′thẽr·ăn, *n.* a disciple or follower of Luther; one who adheres to the doctrines of Luther; a member of the Lutheran church.

Lū′thẽr·ăn·iṣm, *n.* the doctrines taught by Luther, or the doctrines of the Lutheran church.

Lū′thẽr·iṣm, *n.* 1. same as *Lutheranism.*
2. a characteristic of Luther.

Lū′thẽr·ist, *n.* one who studies the life and works of Luther.

lū′thẽrn, *n.* [perh. altered from *lucarne.*] same as *dormer window.*

lū′ti·dine (*or* -dēn), *n.* [a transposition of *toluidine.*] in chemistry, an organic base, isomeric with toluidine, obtained from bone oil.

lūt′ing, *n.* lute (cement).

lūt′ist, *n.* 1. one who plays on a lute.
2. a maker of lutes.

lū′tōse, *a.* [L. *lutosus*, from *lutum*, mud.] muddy; miry; covered with clay.

lū′trin, *n.* same as *lectern.*

lū′tū·lence, *n.* the state of being lutulent or muddy. [Obs.]

lū′tū·lent, *a.* [L. *lutulentus*, from *lutum*, mud.] muddy; turbid; thick. [Obs.]

Lū′vi·ăn, *n.* and *a.* same as *Luwian.*

Lū′wi·ăn (lū′i-ăn), *n.* [from the native name.] an extinct Anatolic language of the Indo-Hittite language family, recorded in scanty inscriptions discovered in Asia Minor: it is now regarded as closely related to cuneiform and hieroglyphic Hittite: also *Luian, Luvian, Luish*, etc.

Lū′wi·ăn, *a.* of Luwian: also *Luian, Luvian, Luish*, etc.

lux, *n.*; *pl.* **lux′eṣ, lū′cēṣ**, [L., light.] a unit of illumination, equal to one lumen per square meter or the illumination of a surface uniformly one meter distant from a point source of one international candle.

lux, *v.t.* to luxate; to dislocate. [Obs.]

lux′āte, *a.* luxated; dislocated. [Obs.]

lux′āte, *v.t.*; luxated, *pt.*, *pp.*; luxating, *ppr.* [L. *luxatus*, pp. of *luxare*, to dislocate, from *luxus*, dislocated, from Gr. *loxos*, slanting.] to put (a joint) out of position; to put out of joint; to dislocate.

lux·ā′tion, *n.* [LL. *luxatio* (*-onis*), a dislocation.] a luxating or being luxated.

lüxe (*or* luks), *n.* [Fr.; L. *luxus*, luxury.] special quality; richness; elegance: usually in *de luxe.*

lux′ive, *a.* voluptuous. [Obs.]

lux·ul′li·ăn·īte, *n.* [from *Luxullian*, in Cornwall, England, where it is found.] a granitoid rock, composed of schist in patches, a flesh-colored orthoclase, and quartz.

lux·ū′ri·ănce (lugz- *or* luks-), *n.* the quality or condition of being luxuriant; strong, vigorous growth; exuberance.

lux·ū′ri·ăn·cy, *n.* luxuriance.

lux·ū′ri·ănt, *a.* [L. *luxurians* (*-antis*), ppr. of *luxuriare*, to be rank, luxuriant, from *luxuria*, luxury.]
1. very productive; fertile; as, *luxuriant* soil. [Rare.]
2. growing with vigor and in great abundance; lush; teeming.
3. characterized by rich and extravagant ornamentation, invention, etc., often tending to excess; as, a *luxuriant* imagination.

lux·ū′ri·ănt·ly, *adv.* in a luxuriant manner or degree.

lux·ū′ri·āte, *v.i.*; luxuriated, *pt.*, *pp.*; luxuriating, *ppr.* [L. *luxuriatus*, pp. of *luxuriare*, to be rank, luxuriant, from *luxuria*, luxury.]
1. to grow with vigor and in great abundance.
2. to live in great luxury.
3. to take great pleasure; to revel (with *in*).

lux·ū·ri·ā′tion, *n.* a luxuriating.

lux·ū·rī′e·ty, *n.* luxuriance. [Obs.]

lux·ū′ri·ous, *a.* [L. *luxuriosus*, from *luxuria*, luxury.]
1. fond of or indulging in luxury.
2. constituting or contributing to luxury; splendid, rich, confortable, etc.
3. lustful; libidinous. [Obs.]
4. luxuriant; exuberant. [Rare.]

lux·ū′ri·ous·ly, *adv.* in a luxurious manner; deliciously; voluptuously.

lux·ū′ri·ous·ness, *n.* the state or quality of being luxurious.

lux′ụ·rist (luk′shụ-), *n.* one given to luxury. [Obs.]

lux′ụ·ry (luk′shụ-), *n.*; *pl.* **lux′ụ·rieṣ**, [ME. and OFr. *luxurie*; L. *luxuria*, rankness, riotous living, extravagance, from *luxus*, extravagance, luxury.]
1. the use and enjoyment of the best and most costly things that offer the most physical comfort and satisfaction.

Riches expose a man to pride and *luxury.*
—Spectator.

2. anything contributing to such enjoyment, usually something considered unnecessary to life and health.
3. (a) the unusual intellectual or emotional pleasure derived from some specified thing; as, she can't do without the *luxury* of tears; (b) something producing this pleasure.
4. lust; lewd desire. [Obs.]
5. luxuriance; exuberance of growth. [Obs.]

Syn.—voluptuousness, epicurism, gratification, delight, enjoyment.

luz, *n.* [Heb.] an unidentified bone in the human body which the rabbinical writers affirmed to be indestructible.

Lū′zū·lȧ, *n.* [Old It. *luzziola, lucciola*, a glowworm.] a genus of plants of the family *Juncaceæ*: they are like rushes, but always perennial with more grasslike foliage, fringed with long white hairs.

-ly, [ME. *-ly, -lich, -liche*; AS. *-lic.*] a suffix used in forming adjectives from nouns, and meaning: (a) *like, characteristic of, suitable to*, as in woman*ly*, earth*ly*, god*ly*; (b) *happening* (*once*) *every* (specified period of time), as in hour*ly*, month*ly*.

-ly, [ME. *-ly, -lich, -liche*; AS. *-lice*, from *-lic.*] a suffix used in forming adverbs from adjectives, and meaning: (a) *in* (a specified) *manner, to* (a specified) *extent* or *direction, in* or *at* (a specified) *time* or *place*, as in harsh*ly*, outward*ly*, hour*ly*; (b) *in* (the specified) *order of sequence*; as in second*ly*, third*ly*.

lȳ′ăm, *n.* a leash. [Obs.]

lȳ′căn·thrōpe, *n.* [Gr. *lykanthrōpos*, a wolf-man; *lykos*, a wolf, and *anthrōpos*, man.]
1. a man fabled to have been transformed into a wolf; a werewolf.
2. a person affected with lycanthropy; one who imagines himself to be a wolf.

lȳ·căn·thrō′pi·ȧ, *n.* same as *lycanthropy.*

lȳ·căn·throp′iç, *a.* of or pertaining to lycanthropy.

lȳ·çan′thrō·pist, *n.* same as *lycanthrope.*

lȳ·çan′thrō·pous, *a.* lycanthropic.

lȳ·çan′thrō·py, *n.* [Gr. *lykanthrōpia*, madness in which one imagines oneself a wolf, from *lykanthrōpos*, a wolf-man, lycanthrope.]
1. in folklore, the belief that one can transform oneself or another into a wolf by the use of magic.
2. a form of mental disorder in which the patient supposes himself to be a wolf.

Lȳ·çā′ŏn, *n.* in Greek mythology, a king of Arcadia who was turned into a wolf by Zeus because he tested the divinity of the disguised god by offering him human flesh as food.

ly·cée′ (lē-sā′), *n.* [Fr.] in France, a school for higher education preparatory to a course at a university; a public secondary school.

lȳ·cē′um (*or* lī′si-) *n.* [L. *lyceum*; Gr. *Lykeion*, the Lyceum, so called from the neighboring temple of *Apollōn Lykeios*, Apollo the wolf-slayer, prob. from *lykeios*, pertaining to a wolf, from *lykos*, a wolf.]
1. a lecture hall.
2. in France, a lycée.
3. [L–] a gymnasium or public palestra with covered walks in the eastern suburb of Athens, in which Aristotle taught philosophy.
4. an organization providing public lectures, concerts, etc.

lyçh, lȳçhe (līk), *a.* like. [Obs.]

ly′chee (lē′chē), *n.* same as *litchi.*

lych gāte, same as *lich gate.*

Lyçh′nis, *n.* [L. *lychnis*; Gr. *lychnis*, a bright scarlet flower.]
1. a genus of herbs, belonging to the family *Caryophyllaceæ*, with red, pink, or white flowers.
2. [l–] a plant of the genus *Lychnis.*

lyçh′nō·sçōpe, *n.* [Gr. *lychnos*, a lamp, and *skopein*, to view.] in architecture, a small narrow window in the chancel of a medieval church, supposedly constructed so that lepers and anchorets from the outside could see the altar lights.

Lyc′i·ăn (lish′), *a.* of Lycia, an ancient country is Asia Minor, its people, or their language.

Lyc′i·ăn, *n.* 1. a native or inhabitant of Lycia.
2. the language of the Lycians, probably akin to cuneiform Hittite.

Lyc′i·um, *n.* [Gr. *lykion*, a kind of thorny shrub from Lycia.] a genus of mainly South American plants of the nightshade family.

Lȳ·çō·pẽr′don, *n.* [Gr. *lykos*, wolf, and *perdesthai*, to break wind.] a genus of fungi that grow in the shape of balls which burst and discharge their spores in the form of a fine dust: also called *puffball. Lycoperdon gemmatum*, the common puffball, acts as a styptic. Most species are edible.

lȳ·çō·pẽr′don nuts, a subterranean fungi of the genus *Elaphomyces*, belonging to the truffle family.

Lȳ·çō·pẽr′si·çum, *n.* [Gr. *lykos*, a wolf, and *persikos*, a peach.] a genus of plants of the nightshade family, native to South America, including *Lycopersicum esculentum*, the tomato.

lȳ′çō·pod, *n.* any plant of the genus *Lycopodium*, or family *Lycopodiaceæ.*

lȳ′çō·pōde, *n.* vegetable brimstone, a highly inflammable powder contained in the spore cases of species of *Lycopodium*, especially *Lycopodium clavatum* and *Lycopodium selago.*

Lȳ·çō·pō·di·ā′cē·ae, *n.pl.* [*lycopodium* and *-aceæ.*] a family of erect or creeping, flowerless, evergreen plants with scalelike leaves: also called *club moss. Lycopodium* is the typical genus.

lȳ·çō·pō·di·ā′ceous, *a.* belonging to, or having the nature of, the *Lycopodiaceæ.*

lȳ·çop′ō·dīte, *n.* a fossil club moss of the genus *Lycopodium.*

Lȳ·çō·pō′di·um, *n.* [Gr. *lykos*, a wolf, and *pous, podos*, a foot.] a genus of cryptogamous plants of the family *Lycopodiaceæ*, including *Lycopodium dendroideum*, the ground pine, and *Lycopodium clavatum*, the common club moss.

lȳ·çō·pō′di·um pow′dẽr, same as *lycopode.*

Lȳ′çō·pus, *n.* [LL., from Gr. *lykos*, wolf, and *pous*, foot; so named from the appearance of the leaves.] a genus of labiate plants found in the temperate regions of both hemispheres. *Lycopus virginicus*, the bugleweed, is a common North American species.

lȳ·çot′rō·păl, *a.* [Gr. *lykos*, a hook, and *tropos*, a turning.] in botany, bent or turned downward like a horseshoe, as an orthotropal ovule.

lȳ·çot′rō·pous, *a.* lycotropal.

lydd′īte, *n.* [from *Lydd*, England, and *-ite.*] a highly explosive compound containing picric acid.

lyddite shell; a shell in which lyddite is used as the explosive.

Lyd′i·ăn, *a.* [L. *Lydius*, from *Lydia*; Gr. *Lydia*, Lydia.]
1. of Lydia, an ancient country in Asia Minor, its people, or their language.
2. (a) soft; gentle; effeminate; (b) voluptuous; sensual.

Lyd′i·ăn, *a.* 1. a native or inhabitant of Lydia.
2. their language, probably Anatolic.

Lydian stone; a type of black stone formerly used to test the purity of gold and silver; touchstone.

lȳe, *n.* [ME. *ley*; AS. *leāh*, lye.]
1. (a) originally, a strong, alkaline solution obtained by leaching wood ashes; (b) now, any strongly alkaline substance. Lye is used in cleaning and in making soap.
2. any substance obtained by leaching.

Lȳ·en·ceph′ȧ·lȧ, *n.pl.* [Gr. *lyein*, to loose, and *enkephalos*, the brain.] a primary division of mammals, according to Owen, characterized by the fact that the cerebral hemispheres are without folds, and leave the cerebellum, the olfactory lobes, and part of the optic lobes uncovered.

lȳ·en·ceph′ȧ·lous, *a.* pertaining to the *Lyencephala.*

Lȳ·ġae'i·dae, *n.pl.* [*lygæus* and *-idæ.*] a family of insects having the tarsi three-jointed and antennae four-jointed.

Lȳ·ġae'us, *n.* [Gr. *lygaios*, dark, shadowy, from *lygē*, twilight.] the typical genus of the *Lygæidæ.*

Lȳ·gō'di·um, *n.* [Gr. *lygōdēs*, like a willow twig, from *lygos*, a willow twig, and *eidos*, form.] a small genus of climbing or twining ferns, with opposite divisions stalked and variously lobed, and with ovoid spore cases. Most species are tropical; the climbing fern, *Lygodium palmatum*, is the only species in North America.

lȳ'ing, *a.* telling falsehoods; not truthful.

Syn.—mendacious, false, untrue, untruthful.

lȳ'ing, *n.* the practice of telling lies.

lȳ'ing, *v.* present participle of *lie* (to recline).

lȳ'ing-in', *n.* confinement in childbirth.

lȳ'ing-in', *a.* of or for childbirth; as, a *lying-in* hospital.

lȳ'ing·ly, *adv.* falsely; mendaciously.

lȳme grȧss, any of several species of the genus *Elymus*, a coarse perennial grass.

Lȳ·mex'y·lon, *n.* [Gr. *lymē*, destruction, and *xylon*, wood.] a genus of serricorn beetles, closely allied to *Elateridæ* and *Buprestidæ.* The larvae are very destructive to oak trees, especially those of the *Lymexylon navale.*

lymph (limf), *n.* [L. *lympha*, from Gr. *nymphē*, a nymph.]

1. a spring of clear water. [Poet. or Obs.]

2. a clear, yellowish, alkaline fluid found in the lymphatic vessels of the body: it resembles blood plasma but contains only colorless corpuscles.

3. any of various colorless liquids similar to this; especially, the clear liquid given off from inflamed body tissue.

lymph-, see *lympho-.*

lym'phad, *n.* [from Gael. *longfhada*, a galley.] an ancient ship with one mast, frequently borne as a charge in the heraldry of Scotland.

LYMPHAD

lym·phad"ē·nī'tis, *n.* [*lymph-*, and Gr. *adēn*, a gland, and *-itis.*] inflammation of the lymph glands.

lym·phad'ē·noid, *a.* [*lymph-*, and Gr. *adēn*, a gland, and *eidos*, form.] pertaining to or resembling a lymphatic gland.

lym·phȧ·dē·nō'mȧ, *n.* [*lymph-*, and Gr. *adēn*, a gland, and *-oma.*] same as *lymphoma.*

lym·phan'ġi·ăl, *a.* [*lymph-*, and Gr. *angeion*, a vessel.] relating to the lymphatic vessels.

lym·phan·ġi·eç'tȧ·sis, *n.* [*lymph-*, and Gr. *angeion*, a vessel, and *ektasis*, extension, dilation.] persistent and pronounced dilatation of the lymphatic vessels.

lym·phan"ġi·eç·tat'iç, *a.* pertaining to lymphangiectasis.

lym·phan"ġi·ī'tis, *n.* same as *lymphangitis.*

lym·phan'ġi·ō-, a combining form meaning *lymphangial*: also, before a vowel, *lymphangi-.*

lym·phan·ġi·ō'mȧ, *n.* [*lymph-*, and Gr. *angeion*, a vessel, and *-oma.*] a localized tumorous dilatation of the lymphatic vessels.

lym·phan·ġī'tis, *n.* inflammation of the lymphatic vessels.

lym·pnat'iç, *a.* [from *lymph*, after L. *lymphaticus*, frenzied, panic-stricken; transl. of Gr. *nympholēptos*, caught by nymphs.]

1. of, containing, or conveying lymph.

2. of, or caused by improper functioning of, the lymph glands.

3. sluggish; without energy: a sluggish condition was formerly thought to be due to too much lymph in the body.

lym·phat'iç, *n.* a vessel that contains or conveys lymph.

lym·phat'iç gland, a lymph gland.

lym'phȧ·tō-, a combining form meaning *lymphatic*, as in *lymphato*lysis.

lym·phȧ·tol'y·sis, *n.* [*lymphato-* and *-lysis.*] the destruction of lymphatic tissue.

lymph cell, a lymphocyte.

lymph chan'nel, any duct or vessel conveying lymph.

lymph duçt, a lymphatic.

lymph gland, any of the many glandlike structures lying in groups along the course of the lymphatic vessels and producing lymphocytes: also *lymph node.*

lym'phō-, a combining form meaning *of lymph* or *the lymphatics*, as in *lympho*cyte: also, before a vowel, *lymph-.*

lym'phō·cȳte, *n.* [*lymph-*, and Gr. *kytos*, a cell.] a variety of colorless corpuscle formed in the tissue of the lymph glands and passed from the lymph into the blood.

lym"phō·cȳ·tō'sis, *n.* a condition characterized by an abnormal increase in the number of lymphocytes in the blood.

lymph'oid, *a.* [*lymph-*, and Gr. *eidos*, form.] of or like lymph or the tissue of the lymph glands.

lym·phō'mȧ, *n.* [*lymph-*, and Gr. *-oma.*] a tumor made up of lymphadenoid tissue; by extension, certain hyperplastic formations not properly tumors.

lym·phor·rhē'ȧ, *n.* [*lympho-*, and Gr. *rhein*, to flow.] lymph flowing from a ruptured lymphatic vessel.

lym·phos'tȧ·sis, *n.* [*lympho-*, and Gr. *stasis*, a standing, from *histanai*, to stand.] a cessation in the flow of lymph.

lym·phot'ō·my, *n.* [*lymph-*, and Gr. *tomē*, a cutting, from *temnein*, to cut.] the anatomy of the lymphatic system.

lymph'y, *a.* containing or resembling lymph. [Rare.]

lyn·cē'ăn, *a.* [Gr. *lynkeios*, from *lynx*, a lynx.] of or like a lynx; especially, having the keenness of sight attributed to the lynx.

lynch, *v.t.*; lynched (lincht), *pt.*, *pp.*; lynching, *ppr.* [from *lynch law.*] to kill (an accused person) by mob action and without lawful trial, as by hanging, usually in defiance of local authority.

Judge Lynch; lynch law personified.

lynch'ẽr, *n.* one who lynches or participates in a lynching.

lynch'ing, *n.* the act of lynching; mob violence.

lynch la̤w, [formerly *Lynch's law*; perh. after Col. Charles *Lynch* (1736–1796), Virginia magistrate who during the Revolution harassed and illegally punished Loyalists; or perh. after Capt. William *Lynch* (1742–1820), justice of Pittsylvania county court in Virginia, who because of the unsettled conditions during the Revolution assumed for the county courts jurisdiction over criminal offenses normally tried at the court in Williamsburg.] the practice of killing by lynching.

lynx, *n.*; *pl.* **lynx'eṣ** or **lynx,** [L. *lynx*; Gr. *lynx*, a lynx, a wildcat.]

1. any of a group of wildcats found throughout the northern hemisphere and characterized by a ruff on each side of the face, long legs, a short tail, long, tufted ears, and keen vision: the North American species are the *Canada lynx* and the *Bay lynx*, or *bobcat.*

LYNX (3 ft. long)

2. the long, silky, tawny fur of the lynx, sometimes dyed black.

3. [L–] a northern constellation lying between Auriga and Ursa Major.

lynx'-eȳed, *a.* having acute sight.

lȳ·ŏn·nāiṣe' (-nāz'), *a.* [Fr., f. of *Lyonnais*, pertaining to Lyons, from *Lyon*, Lyons.] prepared with finely sliced onions; especially, designating potatoes prepared with fried onions.

Lȳ·on·nesse' (-nes'), *n.* [OFr. *Leonois*, orig. *Lothian*, former division of Scotland.] in Arthurian legend, a region in southwest England, apparently near Cornwall, supposed to have sunk beneath the sea.

Lȳ·ō·pō'mȧ·tȧ, *n.pl.* [Gr. *lyein*, to loose, and *pōma (-atos)*, a lid, cover.] a family of inarticulate brachiopods.

Lȳ'rȧ, *n.* [L., from Gr. *lyra*, a lyre.]

1. a northern constellation containing a white star of the first magnitude, called Alpha Lyra.

2. [l–] the central part of the arch of the brain: so named from the resemblance to a harp.

Lȳ'rȧ·id, *n.* a meteor moving from that part of the heavens in which Lyra is situated.

lȳ'rāte, lȳ'rā·ted, *a.* [L. *lyra*, a lyre, and *-ate.*]

1. designating leaves that are shaped like a lyre.

LYRATE LEAF

2. in zoology, lyre-shaped, as the tail of a bird.

lȳre *n.* [L. *lyra*; Gr. *lyra*, a lyre, lute.]

1. a small stringed instrument of the harp family, used by the ancient Greeks to accompany singers and reciters.

2. [L-] in astronomy, same as *Lyra.*

lȳre bat, a small bat, *Lyroderma lyra*, of India and Ceylon.

lȳre'bīrd, *n.* an Australian songbird, *Menura superba* or *Menura alberti*, the male of which has sixteen tailfeathers arranged when spread in the shape of a lyre: also called *lyre pheasant, lyretail.*

VARIOUS FORMS OF EGYPTIAN, ASSYRIAN, AND GREEK LYRES

lȳre'măn, *n.*; *pl.* **lȳre'mănṣ,** a large cicada or harvest fly.

lȳre tûr'tle, a large sea turtle: also called *leatherback.*

lyr'iç, *a.* [L. *lyricus*; Gr. *lyrikos*, of or pertaining to a lyre, from *lyra*, a lyre.]

1. of a lyre.

2. suitable for singing, as to the accompaniment of a lyre; songlike; specifically, designating poetry or a poem expressing the poet's personal emotion or sentiment rather than telling of external events: sonnets, elegies, odes, hymns, etc. are lyric poems.

3. writing or having written lyric poetry.

4. in music, (a) characterized by a relatively high compass and a light, flexible quality; as, a voice of *lyric* quality; (b) having such a voice; as, a *lyric* tenor. Opposed to *dramatic.*

lyr'iç, *n.* 1. a lyric poem.

2. [*usually pl.*] the words of a song, as distinguished from the music.

lyr'iç·ăl, *a.* 1. lyric.

2. expressing feelings of enthusiasm, etc. in strong, emotional language; as, he became *lyrical* in his account of the performance.

lyr'iç·ăl·ly, *adv.* in a lyrical manner.

lyr'i·ciṣm, *n.* 1. lyric quality, style, or character; as, Shelly's *lyricism.*

2. emotional and poetic expression of enthusiasm, etc.

lyr'i·cist, *n.* a writer of lyrics, especially lyrics for popular songs.

lyr'i·çō-, [from L. *lyricus.*] a combining form meaning *lyric and.*

lȳ'rie, *n.* a small European fish whose body is armed with eight rows of bony plates and spines projecting from its nose: also called *pogge.*

lȳ·rif'ẽr·ous, *a.* [L. *lyra*, a lyre, and *ferre*, to bear.] in ichthyology, having the scapular arch shaped like a lyre: said of certain fishes.

lȳr'i·fo̤rm, *a.* shaped like a lyre.

lȳr'iṣm *n.* [Fr. *lyrisme*; Gr. *lyrismos.*]

1. the act of playing on a lyre.

2. (lir'izm), lyricism.

lȳr'ist, *n.* [Gr. *lyristēs*, from *lyrizein*, to play on a lyre.]

1. a player on a lyre.

2. (lir'ist), a lyric poet.

-lȳṣe, same as *-lyze.*

lȳ'si-, [Gr. *lysi-*, from *lysis.*] a combining form meaning *freeing, relieving, loosening, dissolving*, as in *lysi*meter: also, before a vowel, *lys-.*

lȳ"si·ġē·net'iç, *a.* same as *lysigenous.*

lys·i·gen'iç, *a.* lysigenous.

lȳ·siġ'ē·nous, *a.* [Gr. *lysis*, a setting free, and *genesis*, origin.] in botany, made by the breaking down of adjoining cells, as certain intercellular spaces.

Lȳ·si·mā'çhi·ȧ, *n.* [Gr. *lysimachion*, a medicinal herb, loosestrife; *lyein*, to loose, and *machē*, strife, battle.] a genus of herbs of the primrose family, having many species with variously colored flowers; the loosestrifes.

lȳ·sim′ē·tẽr, *n.* [Gr. *lysis*, a loosening, and *metron*, a measure.] a device for determining the solubility of substances.

lȳ′sin, *n.* [from Gr. *lysis* and *-in*.]
 1. any antibody dissolving bacteria, blood corpuscles, etc.
 2. lysine.

lȳ′sine, *n.* an amino acid, $C_6H_{14}N_2O_2$, obtained synthetically or by the hydrolysis of certain proteins in digestion.

-lȳ′sis, [from Gr. *lysis*, a loosening.] a combining form meaning *a dissolution, destruction, dissolving*, as in electro*lysis*, para*lysis*.

lȳ′sis, *n.* [Gr. *lysis*, a loosing, from *lyein*, to loose.]
 1. the gradual and successful ending of a disease.
 2. the process of cell destruction through the action of specific lysins.

lȳ′sōl, *n.* [Gr. *lysis*, a loosing, and L. *oleum*, oil.] a brown liquid antiseptic and disinfectant, which is a saponified product of coal tar and soluble in water: a trade-mark (*Lysol*).

lys′sȧ, *n.* same as *hydrophobia*.

lys·sō·phō′bi·ȧ, *n.* [Gr. *lyssa*, madness, and *phobos*, fear.] an abnormal fear of becoming insane.

-lȳte, [from Gr. *lytos*.] a combining form meaning *a substance subjected to a process of decomposition* (indicated by the corresponding noun in *-lysis*), as in hydro*lyte*.

-lȳte, same as *-lite*.

lȳ·tē′ri·ăn, *a.* [Gr. *lytērios*, loosing, releasing, from *lytēr*, a deliverer, from *lyein*, to loose.] in medicine, ending or indicating the end, or lysis, of a disease.

Lyth·rā′cē·ae, *n.pl.* [*Lythrum* and *-aceæ*.] a family of herbs, shrubs, or trees, the loosestrife family, having a free calyx bearing deciduous petals.

lyth·rā′ceous, *a.* pertaining to the *Lythraceæ*.

Lyth′rum, *n.* [Gr. *lythron*, *lythros*, gore: so called from the purple color of the flowers.] a genus of plants belonging to the family *Lythraceæ*.

lyt′iç, *a.* 1. of a lysin.
 2. of or causing lysis.

-lyt′iç, [Gr. *-lytikos*, from *lytikos*, able to loose.]
 1. a suffix used to form adjectives corresponding to nouns ending in *-lysis*, as in cata*lytic*, hydro*lytic*.
 2. in biochemistry, a suffix meaning *undergoing hydrolysis by enzymes*.

lyt′tȧ, *n.*; *pl.* **lyt′tae,** [L. *lytta*, a worm said to grow under the tongues of dogs and to cause madness; from Gr. *lytta*, *lyssa*, madness.] in dogs and certain other carnivorous mammals, a cartilaginous vermiform strip extending lengthwise along the lower side of the tongue.

-lȳze, [Fr. *-lyser*, from nouns ending in *-lysis* and *-er*, inf. ending.] a combining form used to form verbs corresponding to nouns ending in *-lysis*, as in para*lyze*, electro*lyze*: also spelled *-lyse*.

M

M, m (em), *n.*; *pl.* **M's, Ms, m's, ms** (emz),
 1. the thirteenth letter of the English alphabet, from the Greek *mu*, derived ultimately from the Phoenician.
 2. the sound for M or m.
 3. a type or impression for M or m.
 4. *a symbol for* the thirteenth in a sequence or group (or the twelfth if J is omitted).
 5. in printing, an em.

M, m (em), *a.* 1. of M or m.
 2. thirteenth (or twelfth if J is omitted) in a sequence or group.

M (em), *n.* 1. an object shaped like M.
 2. a Roman numeral for 1,000: with a superior bar ($\overline{M}$), 1,000,000.
 3. in chemistry, *the symbol for* an element in electrolysis.
 4. in electricity, *the symbol for* mutual inductance (in henrys).
 5. in logic, *the symbol for* the middle term of a syllogism.

M, *a.* shaped like M.

m-, in chemistry, meta-.

mä, *n.* mama; mother. [Colloq.]

mä, *conj.* [It.] in music, but, as in the phrase "allegro, *ma* non troppo" (fast, *but* not too much so).

Ma, in chemistry, masurium.

ma′am (mam *or* mäm), *n.* madam: used in direct address. [Colloq.]

mää′rȧ shell, a shell, *Turbo margaritaceus*, found in the South Pacific.

Mab, *n.* Queen Mab.

mab, *v.i.* to dress negligently. [Obs.]

mab, *n.* a slattern. [Obs.]

Mā′bȧ, *n.* [native Tonga name.] a genus of trees and shrubs belonging to the ebony family. *Maba buxifolia* is the East Indian satinwood.

mab′ble, *v.t.* to wrap. [Obs.]

mä·bō′lō, *n.* [Tag.] a tropical tree, *Diospyros discolor*, of the ebony family; also, its edible fruit.

Mac-, [from Gael. *mac*, son.] a prefix meaning *son of*, used in Scottish and Irish family names: also *Mc-*, *Mc*, *M'*: in alphabetizing, all these forms are sometimes placed together.

mȧ·çä′bẽr, *a.* macabre.

mȧ·çä′bre (-br *or* -bẽr), *a.* [OFr. (*danse*) *Macabré*, (dance) of death.] gruesome; grim and horrible; ghastly.

mȧ·çā′çō, *n.* [Port. *macaco*, from Braz. (Tupi) *macaca*.]
 1. any of several African and Asiatic lemurs; especially, the black lemur.
 2. [from African (Congo) native name.] a macaque.

mȧ·çā′çō wŏrm, the larva of a fly, *Dermatobia noxialis*, of South America and Mexico, which is parasitic on men and animals.

Mȧ·çā′çus, *n.* [from native (Tupi) name.] a genus of monkeys in the Orient, having short tails and heavy eyebrows.

măç·ad′ăm, *n.* [after John L. *Macadam* (1756–1836), Scottish engineer who invented the process.] broken stone for spreading upon a roadway; also, the roadway so made.

măç·ad″ăm·i·zā′tion, *n.* the process of making a roadway of broken stone.

măc·ăd′ăm·īze, *v.t.*; macadamized, *pt.*, *pp.*; macadamizing, *ppr.* 1. to make (a road) by rolling successive layers of small broken stones (*macadam*) on a dry earth roadbed, often with tar or asphalt for binding.
 2. to repair or cover (a road) by this process.

mȧ·çäque′ (-käk′), *n.* [Fr.] a monkey of the genus *Macacus*.

maç′ȧ·riṣm, *n.* joy in another's happiness. [Rare.]

maç′ȧ·rīze, *v.t.* [Gr. *makarizein*, to bless, call happy, from *makar*, happy, blessed.] to pronounce happy or blessed. [Rare.]

maç·ȧ·rō′ni, *n.*; *pl.* **maç·ȧ·rō′niṣ, maç·ȧ·rō′nieṣ,** [It. *maccaroni*, macaroni, originally a mixture of flour, cheese, and butter.]
 1. long, thin, hollow tubes made of dried flour paste, to be cooked and used as food.
 2. an 18th-century English dandy who affected foreign mannerisms and fashions.
 3. a droll medley, as in poetry.
 Also spelled *maccaroni*.

maç·ȧ·rō′ni·ăn, *a.* macaronic.

maç·ȧ·ron′iç, *a.* [Fr. *macaronique* or It. *maccaronico*, from *maccaroni*.]
 1. involving or characterized by a mixture of languages; especially, designating or of burlesque verse in which real or coined words from two or more languages are mixed or vernacular words of a modern language or languages are given Latin case endings and mixed with Latin words and hybrid forms.
 2. having the nature of a medley; mixed; jumbled. [Obs.]
 Also spelled *maccaronic*.

maç·ȧ·ron′iç, *n.* 1. [*usually in pl.*] macaronic verse.
 2. a jumble; medley. [Obs.]
 Also spelled *maccaronic*.

maç·ȧ·ron′iç·ăl, *a.* macaronic.

maç·ȧ·rọọn′, *n.* [Fr. *macaron*, macaroni, a bun or cake, from It. *maccaroni*, macaroni.] a small, sweet cooky made chiefly of egg white, crushed almonds or coconut, and sugar.

Mȧ·cärt′ney, *n.* a species of pheasant, *Euplocamus ignitus*, introduced into Europe from China by Lord Macartney, 18th-century English diplomat.

mȧ·çaw′, *n.* [from *macao*, native Braz. name.] any of a group of large, bright-colored, harsh-voiced parrots of Central and South America.

RED-AND-BLUE MACAW (*Ara macao*)

mȧ·çaw′ bush, a large prickly weed of the West Indies, *Solanum mammosum*.

mȧ·çaw′ tree, an American palm, *Acrocomia sclerocarpa*: called also *macaw palm* and *grugru*.

Maç·beth′, *n.* 1. a famous tragedy by Shakespeare (1606?).
 2. the main character of this play, who, urged by his ruthlessly ambitious wife, murders his king, Duncan, and becomes king himself, but is finally killed by the patriot Macduff.

Maç·çȧ·bē′ăn, *a.* pertaining to the Maccabees or to Judas Maccabeus, their leader of a successful second-century (B.C.) revolt against the Syrians.

Maç′çȧ·bees, *n.pl.* 1. the name of a heroic Jewish family (including Judas Maccabeus), which rescued Judea from the tyranny of Antiochus Epiphanes and made it independent for about a century.
 2. two Apocryphal books of the Old Testament that give an account of the revolt of the Maccabees.

maç·çȧ·rō′ni, *n.* macaroni (all senses).

maç·çȧ·ron′iç, *a.* macaronic.

maç′çou·bȧ, maç′ou·bȧ, *n.* a fine dark snuff made from tobacco originally grown at Macouba, in the island of Martinique, usually rose-scented: spelled also *maccoboy*, *maccaboy*.

māce, *n.* [OFr. *mace*, *mache*, a club, from an assumed L. *matea*, which appears only in the dim. *mateola*, a mallet.]

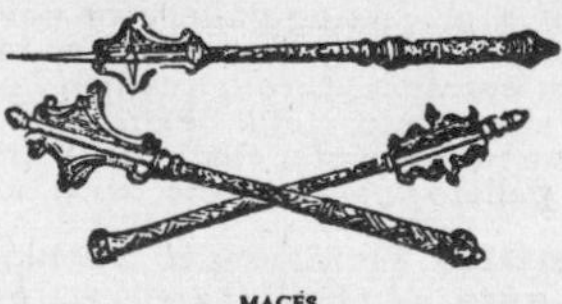

MACES

 1. a heavy, armor-breaking club with a metal head, often spiked, used in the Middle Ages.
 2. any similar weapon.

3. a staff used as a symbol of authority by certain officials.

4. a person who carries a mace.

5. a light, flat-headed stick formerly used in billiards instead of a cue, for certain shots.

māce, *n.* [ME. *mace*; OFr. *macis*, mace; L. *macir*; Gr. *maker*, an East Indian spice.] a spice, usually ground, made from the dried outer covering of the nutmeg.

māce āle, ale spiced with mace.

māce′-beȧr″ēr, *n.* a person who carries a mace in ceremonial processions.

ma·cé·doine′ (mȧ-sā-dwon′), *n.* [Fr., orig., a kind of parsley.]

1. a mixture of vegetables or fruits served as a salad, cocktail, etc., often in jelly.

2. a medley.

Mac·ē·dō′ni·ăn, *a.* [L. *Macedonius*; Gr. *Makedonios*, of or pertaining to Macedonia, from *Makedōn*, a Macedonian.] of or pertaining to Macedonia, its people, or languages.

Mac·ē·dō′ni·ăn, *n.* 1. a native or inhabitant of Macedonia.

2. the ancient Indo-European language of the Macedonians, akin either to Greek or to Illyrian.

Mac·ē·dō′ni·ăn, *n.* a follower of Macedonius, a bishop of Constantinople about the fourth century, who denied the divinity of the Holy Ghost.

Mac·ē·dō′ni·ăn·iṣm, *n.* the doctrine held by the followers of Macedonius.

māc′ēr, *n.* one who bears the mace; specifically, in Scotland, an officer of the court.

mac′ēr·āte, *v.t.*; macerated, *pt., pp.*; macerating, *ppr.* [L. *maceratus*, pp. of *macerare*, to make soft or tender, to weaken, to harass.]

1. (a) to soften by soaking in liquid for some time; (b) to separate the parts of by soaking; specifically, to soften (food) in the digestive system.

2. to cause to waste away or grow thin.

3. to torment.

mac′ēr·āte, *v.i.* to undergo maceration; to waste away; to grow thin.

mac·ēr·ā′tion, *n.* the operation of macerating.

mac′ēr·ā·tŏr, *n.* a person who macerates; also, a tool or machine for macerating: also spelled *macerater*.

Măçh, *n.* same as *Mach number*.

mȧ·çhaī′rō·dont, *n.* [Gr. *machaira*, a sword, saber, and *odous*, *odontos*, tooth.] an animal belonging to the genus *Machairodus*.

mȧ·çhaī′rō·dont, *a.* pertaining to a machairodont; having long, sharp teeth.

Mȧ·çhaī′rō·dus, *n.* [Gr. *machaira*, a sword, saber, and *odous*, a tooth.] a genus of catlike mammals now extinct, named for their unusually long and strong upper canine teeth: it included the saber-toothed tiger.

mä·çhe′te (*or* mȧ-shet′), *n.* [Sp.] 1. a cutlass-shaped knife used in Cuba, the Philippines, and Spanish America: it is used either as a weapon or a cutting tool.

2. a fish, *Elops affinis*.

Maçh″i·ȧ·vel′li·ăn, *a.* pertaining to Niccolo Machiavelli (1469–1527), Florentine statesman, or denoting the political principles of craftiness and duplicity advocated by him: also written *Machiavelian*, *Macchiavelian*, *Macchiavellian*.

Maçh″i·ȧ·vel′li·ăn, *n.* one who adopts the principles and methods of Machiavelli.

Maçh″i·ȧ·vel′li·ăn·iṣm, Maçh″i·ȧ·vel′iṣm, *n.* the principles and methods of Machiavelli; political cunning and duplicity, intended to favor arbitrary power.

mȧ·chiç′ō·lāte, *v.t.*; machicolated, *pt., pp.*; machicolating, *ppr.* [ML. *machicolatus*, from Pr. *machacol*, balcony, from *macar*, to beat, and *col*, neck.] to put machicolations in (a parapet, etc.).

mȧ·chiç′ō·lā·ted, *a.* having machicolations, as castles.

mȧ·chiç·ō·lā′tion, *n.* 1. an opening in the floor of a projecting gallery or parapet, between the supports or corbels, or in the roof over an entrance, through which hot liquids, heavy stones, etc. could be dropped or hurled by the defenders of a castle or fortress.

2. a gallery, parapet, etc. with such openings.

mȧ·çhin′ăl, *a.* pertaining to machines. [Obs.]

maçh′i·nāte, *v.i.*; machinated, *pt., pp.*; machinating, *ppr.* [L. *machinatus*, pp. of *machinari*, to devise, plan, plot.] to plot; to form a scheme artfully, especially with evil intent.

maçh′i·nāte, *v.t.* to plan, especially with evil intent.

maçh·i·nā′tion, *n.* 1. the act of machinating; a scheming. [Rare.]

2. [*usually in pl.*] a plot or intrigue, especially one with evil intent.

maçh′i·nā·tŏr, *n.* one who schemes or plots with evil intent.

mȧ·çhine′, *n.* [Fr. *machine*; L. *machina*; Gr. *mēchanē*, a machine, engine, device.]

1. a structure or built-up fabric of any kind; specifically, the human or animal frame. [Rare or Archaic.]

2. (a) a vehicle, as, formerly, a carriage, cart, etc.; (b) a vehicle operated mechanically; specifically, an automobile.

3. a structure consisting of a framework and various fixed and moving parts, for doing some kind of work; mechanism; as, a sewing *machine*.

4. a person or organization regarded as acting like a machine, without thought or will.

5. (a) the members of a political party or group who control policy and confer patronage; (b) the party organization generally.

6. a device or apparatus, as in the ancient theater, for producing stage effects: see *deus ex machina*.

7. a literary device for dramatic presentation, as a supernatural agent or agency introduced into a poem.

8. in mechanics, a device that transmits, or changes the application of, energy; the lever, wheel, and screw are called *simple machines*.

mȧ·çhine′, *a.* 1. of a machine or machines.

2. made or done by machinery.

3. standardized; stereotyped.

mȧ·çhine′, *v.t.*; machined, *pt., pp.*; machining, *ppr.* to make, shape, etc. by machinery.

mȧ·çhine′, *v.i.* to be used on machinery; also, to serve as the effective agency, or machine, in a dramatic plot.

mȧ·çhine′ bōlt, an iron bolt with a head of various forms, threaded only at the lower end and having a nut to fit it, as a stove bolt or a coupling bolt.

mȧ·çhine′-gun, *v.t.*; machine-gunned, *pt., pp.*; machine-gunning, *ppr.* to fire at with, or hit by fire from, a machine gun.

mȧ·çhine′ gun, see under *gun*.

mȧ·çhine′-māde, *a.* made by or as by machinery, not by hand.

mȧ·çhin′ēr, *n.* in England, a horse that draws or assists in drawing a public coach. [Archaic.]

mȧ·çhin′ēr·y, *n.*; *pl.* **mȧ·çhin′ēr·ieṣ,** 1. the component parts of a complex machine.

2. machines collectively.

3. any combination of persons or things, the harmonious workings of which result in a desired end; as, the *machinery* of government.

4. the supernatural agencies employed in a classical drama or epic poem, by means of which the plot is carried out and the conclusion effected; as, the *machinery* of the Iliad.

mȧ·çhine′ sçrew, a machine bolt.

mȧ·çhine′ shop, a workshop, factory, or part of a factory in which machinery is made, altered, or repaired.

mȧ·çhine′ tool, an automatic or semiautomatic power-driven tool, as an electric lathe, drill, or planer: machine tools are used in making machines or machine parts.

mȧ·çhine′-tool, *a.* of, for, or by a machine tool.

mȧ·çhine′ wŏrk, work done by machinery, as distinguished from work done by hand; also, the product of machinery.

mȧ·çhin′ist, *n.* 1. a person who makes or repairs machinery.

2. a worker skilled in using machine tools.

3. a worker who operates a machine.

mä·chiṣ′mō, *n.* [Sp., from *macho*, strong man, and *-ismo*, -ism.] strong or assertive masculinity, characterized by virility, courage, aggressiveness, etc.

Măçh num′bēr, [named after Ernst *Mach*, Austrian physicist.] [also m-] a number representing the ratio of the speed of an object to the speed of sound in the surrounding medium, as air, through which the object is moving.

mä′chō, *n.*; *pl.* **mä′chōṣ,** [Sp., from Port., ultimately from L. *masculus*, masculine.] a strong, virile man.

mä′chō, *a.* masculine, virile, courageous, etc.

mȧ·çhrēe′, *n.* [Ir. *mo*, my, and *croidhe*, heart.] literally, my heart: Anglo-Irish term of endearment; as, Mother *machree*.

-mȧ·çhy, [from Gr. *machē*, a battle.] a combining form meaning *struggle*, *contest of*, as in giganto*machy*.

mac′i·len·cy, *n.* leanness. [Rare.]

mac′i·lent, *a.* [L. *macilentus*, from *macies*, leanness.] lean; thin. [Rare.]

maç′in·tosh, *n.* same as *mackintosh*.

mack′ēr·el, *n.* a pander or pimp. [Obs.]

mack′ēr·el, *n.* [OFr. *makerel*, *maquerel*; LL. *macarellus*, mackerel.]

1. an edible fish of the North Atlantic, genus *Scomber*, 12–18 inches long, with a greenish, blue-striped back and a silvery belly.

MACKEREL (*Scomber scombrus*)

2. any of various other related fishes.

mack′ēr·el bīrd, the English wryneck: so called because it makes its appearance about the time the mackerel season begins.

mack′ēr·el çock, a kind of petrel or puffin, *Puffinus puffinus*, a precursor of the arrival of schools of mackerel off the Irish coast. [Ir. Dial.]

mack′ēr·el gāle, a (strong) breeze that ruffles the water so as to favor the catching of mackerel.

mack′ēr·el gull, any of several species of gull, including the tern, kittiwake, etc., which feed upon the mackerel.

mack′ēr·el midġe, the young of some species of *Motella* or *Onos*, once regarded as a distinct species of fish: common around the British coasts.

mack′ēr·el pīke, any fish of the *Scomberesocidæ*, or saury family, characterized by long thin jaws.

mack′ēr·el plow, a tool used for creasing the sides of lean mackerel to give them the appearance of being fat: also called *fatting knife*.

mack′ēr·el sçad, a small fish of the Atlantic Ocean allied to the mackerel, silvery above and lead-colored below, the operculum being marked with a black spot.

mack′ēr·el sçāleṣ, a variety of mackerel sky having cloudlets whose angular forms suggest the scales of a mackerel.

mack′ēr·el sçout, the mackerel guide.

mack′ēr·el shärk, the porbeagle, which resembles the mackerel in having a forked tail.

mack′ēr·el skȳ, a sky covered with rows of small, fleecy clouds, suggesting the streaks on a mackerel's back.

mack′i·naw, *n.* 1. a Mackinaw blanket.

2. a Mackinaw coat.

3. a Mackinaw boat.

Mack′i·naw blaṅk′et, a thick woolen blanket, often woven in bars of bright colors, much used by Indians, lumbermen, etc. in the American Northwest.

Mack′i·naw bōat, a rowboat or sailboat with a flat bottom, sharp bow, and square or pointed stern, used on and around the upper Great Lakes.

Mack′i·naw çōat, a short, double-breasted coat made of heavy woolen cloth, often plaid.

Mack′i·naw trout, the namaycush, *Salvelinus namaycush*, of the Great Lakes.

mack′in·tosh, *n.* [from Charles *Macintosh* (1766–1843), the Scot. inventor.]

1. a waterproof outer coat; raincoat.

2. the fabric used for this, made waterproof by cementing layers of cloth with rubber.

maç′kle, *n.* [OFr. *macle*, from L. *macula*, a spot, stain.] among printers, a blur or blurred sheet: also spelled *macule*.

maç′kle, *v.t.* and *v.i.* to blur in printing.

maç′le (mak′l), *n.* [ML. *mascula*, mesh of a net, from L. *macula*, a spot or stain.]

1. a twin crystal, as of a diamond.

2. a dark spot in certain minerals.

maç′led (-ld), *a.* having a double structure; also, spotted.

Mȧ·çlū′rē·ȧ, *n.* [after William *Maclure*, Am. geologist.] a genus of large, fossil, spiral operculated shells, characteristic of the lower Silurian.

macr-, see *macro-*.

mac·rȧ·mé′(mak-rȧ-mā′), *n.* [Turk. *maqramah*, napkin, towel.] an ornamental trimming or lace of coarsely knotted thread: also *macramé lace*.

maç·ran′drous, *a.* [*macr-*, and Gr. *anēr*, *andros*, a man, male.] in botany, characterized by very tall male plants: said of certain algae.

maç′rō-, maçr-, [from Gr. *makros*, long.] a combining form meaning *long* (*in extent* or *duration*), *large*, *enlarged* or *elongated* (in a specified part), as in *macro*cosm: opposed to *micro-*.

mac″rō·bī·ō′sis, *n.* [*macro-*, and Gr. *bios*, life.] longevity.

mac″rō·bī·ot′ic, *a.* long-lived.

mac″rō·bī·ot′ics, *n.* [Gr. *makrobiotos* or *makrobios*, having a long life; *makros*, long, and *bios*, life.] in physiology, the study of longevity.

mac″rō·cē·phal′iç, *a.* same as *macrocephalous*.

mac·rō·ceph′ȧ·lous, *a.* [*macro-*, and Gr. *kephalē*, head.]

1. having an unusually large head or cranial capacity.

2. in botany, having the embryonic cotyledons massive in comparison with other parts of the embryo.

mac·rō·ceph′ȧ·ly, *n.* a condition marked by abnormally large size of the head: exemplified in a certain type of idiot: opposed to *microcephaly*.

mac·rō·çhem′is·try, *n.* that branch of chemistry which deals with substances and compounds that can be tested by the naked eye, as opposed to *microchemistry*.

Mac·rō·chī′rēs, *n.pl.* [*macro-*, and Gr. *cheir*, hand.] a group of long-winged birds, of which the swifts and humming birds are types: so called from the length of the terminals of their wings.

mac·rō·coc′cus, *n.*; *pl.* **mac·rō·coc′cī,** [*macro-*, and Gr. *kokkos*, a berry.] any very large coccus or bacillus.

mac″rō·cō·nid′i·um, *n.* [*macro-*, and *conidium*, dim. from L. *conus*, a cone.] in botany, any very large conidium.

mac′rō·cosm, *n.* [*macro-*, and Gr. *kosmos*, world.] the great world, the universe, or the visible system of worlds: opposed to *microcosm*.

mac·rō·cos′miç, *a.* relating to the macrocosm.

mac′rō·cyst, *n.* a large or enlarged cyst; especially, in botany, a large reproductive cyst in certain fungi.

Mac·rō·cys′tis, *n.* [*macro-*, and Gr. *kystis*, a bladder.] a genus of marine plants, belonging to the order *Algæ*; specifically, *Macrocystis pyrifera*, remarkable for the great length it attains and for its being borne up by many air vessels at the bases of the leaves.

mac′rō·cȳte, *n.* [*macro-* and *-cyte*.] an abnormally large red blood corpuscle occurring especially in pernicious anemia.

mac″rō·dī·ag′ō·năl, *n.* [*macro-*, and Gr. *diagōnios*, diagonal.] the longer of the diagonals of a rhombic prism.

mac′rō·dōme, *n.* [*macro-*, and Gr. *domos*, house, dome.] in crystallography, a dome or rooflike prism with its planes parallel to the macrodiagonal of an orthorhombic crystal.

mac′rō·dont, *a.* [*macro-*, and Gr. *odous*, *odontos*, a tooth.] in zoology, large-toothed.

mac′rō·dont, *n.* a large-toothed animal.

mac″rō·gȧ·mēte′, *n.* [*macro-* and *gamete*.] the larger of two conjugating cells or spores, usually considered to be female.

mac·rō·glos′si·ȧ, *n.* [*macro-*, and Gr. *glossa*, tongue.] in pathology, a swelling or enlargement of the tongue.

mac·rog·nath′iç, *a.* [*macro-*, and Gr. *gnathos*, jaw.] having very long jaws, as some prehistoric skulls.

mac″rō·gō·nid′i·um, *n.* [*macro-*, and *gonidium*, from Gr. *gonē*, that which generates.] in botany, a comparatively large-sized gonidium.

mac′rō·gràph, *n.* [*macro-*, and Gr. *graphein*, to write.] a drawing or photograph of an object as seen with little or no magnification.

mȧ·crog′rȧ·phy, *n.* 1. examination of an object with the naked eye instead of with a microscope: opposed to *micrography*.

2. large handwriting, often a sign of nervous disorder.

Mac·rō·lep·i·dop′tēr·ȧ, *n.pl.* [*macro-*, and Gr. *lepis* (*-idos*), a scale, and *pteron*, a wing.] the larger insects of the *Lepidoptera*, as some of the moths and butterflies: distinguished from the smaller forms, called *Microlepidoptera*.

mȧ·crol′ō·ġy, *n.* [*macro-*, and Gr. *legein*, to speak.] long and tedious talk; prolonged discourse without ideas; superfluity of words; redundancy.

mac′rō·mēre, *n.* [*macro-*, and Gr. *meros*, part, portion.] one of the larger cells or blastomeres into which a telolecithal ovum is divided: distinguished from *micromere*.

mac″rō·mē·rit′iç, *a.* in geology, having or being composed of grains large enough to be visible to the naked eye: contrasted with *micromeritic*.

mȧ·crom′e·tēr, *n.* [*macro-*, and Gr. *metron*, a measure.] an instrument for measuring inaccessible heights or objects by means of two reflectors on a common sextant.

mā′crŏn, *n.* [Gr. *makron*, neut. of *makros*, long.] a horizontal line placed over a vowel to show that it has a long sound, as in *lāme*, *tēam*, etc.

mac·rō·nū′clē·us, *n.* [*macro-*, and L. *nucleus*, a kernel, dim. of *nux*, a nut.] the larger of two nuclei, as distinguished from the smaller, or *micronucleus*.

mac·rō·pet′ăl·ous, *a.* [*macro-*, and Gr. *petalon*, a leaf.] with long or large petals, as in some species of *Ranunculus*.

mac·rō·phō·tog′rȧ·phy, *n.* [*macro-* and *photography*.] the method in photography by which enlarged copies of pictures are obtained.

mȧ·croph′yl·lous, *a.* [*macro-*, and Gr. *phyllon*, a leaf.] in botany, having large leaves.

mac·rō·phys′iḉs, *n.* [*macro-* and *physics*.] the branch of physics concerned with masses large enough to be examined separately and directly.

mac·rō·pin′ȧ·çoid, *n.* [*macro-*, and Gr. *pinax* (*-ākos*), a board, tablet, and *eidos*, form.] in crystallography, a plane of an orthorhombic crystal parallel to its vertical and macrodiagonal axes.

mac′rō·pod, *n.* [Gr. *makropous* (*-odos*); *makros*, long, and *pous*, *podos*, foot.] a long-legged animal; specifically, one of a family of crabs called *spider crabs*.

mac′rō·pod, *a.* having long legs and large feet; large-footed.

mȧ·crop′ō·dăl, *a.* macropod.

mȧ·crop′ō·dous, *a.* [*macro-*, and Gr. *pous*, *podos*, foot.] in botany, having a long stem or footstalk; as, a *macropodous* leaf; having an elongated radicle, as in a dicotyledonous embryo.

mȧ·crop′tēr·ăn, *n.* [Gr. *makropteros*; *makros*, long, and *pteron*, a wing.] having long or large wings or pectoral fins: said of birds or of flying fishes.

Mȧ·crop′te·rēs, *n.pl.* [*macro-*, and Gr. *pteron*, wing.] in zoology, a division of birds characterized by long wings.

mȧ·crop′tēr·ous, *a.* having wings of great length; longipennate.

Mac′rō·pus, *n.* [*macro-*, and Gr. *pous*, *podos*, foot.] a genus of marsupial mammals, the type of the family *Macropodidæ*; the kangaroos. They have elongated hind limbs with four toes, forefeet with five toes, and a well-developed tail.

mac·rō·scop′iç, mac·rō·scop′iç·ăl, *a.* visible to the naked eye: opposed to *microscopic*.

mac·rō·sep′tum, *n.* [*macro-*, and L. *septum*, a partition.] one of the large, fertile septa of an actinozoan.

mac·rō·sī′phon, *n.* [*macro-*, and Gr. *siphōn*, a siphon.] the large, tubular siphon of certain cephalopods, as of the orthoceratite.

mac″rō·sī·phon′ū·lȧ, *n.* [*macro-*, and Gr. *siphōn*, a siphon, and dim. *-ula*.] the larval stage of certain cephalopods at which the macrosiphon first appears.

mac·ros·mat′iç, *a.* [*macr-*, and Gr. *osmē*, smell.] with organs of smell well developed, as in mammals.

mac″rō·sō·mā′ti·ȧ (-shi-ȧ), *n.* largeness of body.

mac·rō·som′ȧ·tous, *a.* [*macro-*, and Gr. *sōma* (*-atos*), body.] having a very large body.

mac·rō·sō′mīte, *n.* [*macro-*, and Gr. *sōma*, body.] a very large primary segment in the development of an animal, as in the embryonic divisions of insects.

mac·rō·spō·ran′ġi·um, *n.*; *pl.* **mac·rō·spō·ran′ġi·ȧ,** [*macro-*, and Gr. *spora*, seed, and *angeion*, a vessel.] a megasporangium.

mac′rō·spōre, *n.* [*macro-*, and Gr. *spora*, seed.]

1. a large spore.

2. a magaspore.

mac·rō·spō′rō·phyl, mac·rō·spō′rō·phyll, *n.* [*macro-*, and Gr. *spora*, seed, and *phyllon*, a leaf.] in botany, a leaf or frond on which the macrosporangium is developed.

Mac·rō·stach′y·ȧ, *n.* [*macro-*, and Gr. *stachys*, stachys, lit., a spike of grain.] in botany, a genus of plants now extinct whose fossil remains are found in the rocks of the Carboniferous Period.

mac·rō·stom′ȧ·tous, *a.* [*macro-*, and Gr. *stoma* (*-atos*), mouth.] large-mouthed.

mac′rō·stȳle, *a.* [*macro-*, and Gr. *stylos*, a pillar.] in botany, with a long style.

mac′rō·tōne, *n.* same as *macron*.

mȧ·crō′tous, *a.* [*macr-*, and Gr. *ous*, *ōtos*, ear.] in zoology, long-eared or large-eared.

mȧ·crot′y·pous, *a.* [*macro-*, and Gr. *typos*, form, image.] in mineralogy, having a long shape.

Mȧ·crōu′rȧ, *n.pl.* same as *Macrura*.

mȧ·crōu′rous, *a.* same as *macrurous*.

mac·rō·zō′ō·spōre, *n.* [*macro-*, and Gr. *zōon*, an animal, and *spora*, a seed.]

1. in botany, a relatively large zoospore with vibrating cilia.

2. in zoology, a large ciliate zoospore.

Mȧ·crū′rȧ, *n.pl.* [*macr-*, and Gr. *oura*, tail.] a family of stalk-eyed decapod crustaceans, including the lobster, prawn, and shrimp: so called from their large abdomens and long tails.

mȧ·crū′răl, *a.* of or belonging to the *Macrura*.

mȧ·crū′răn, *a.* macrural.

mȧ·crū′răn, *n.* any one of the *Macrura*.

mȧ·crū′roid, *a.* of or resembling the family *Macrura*.

mȧ·crū′rous, *a.* relating to the *Macrura*; characterized by a long tail.

mac·tā′tion, *n.* [LL. *mactatio* (*-onis*), from L. *mactare*, to offer for sacrifice, kill, slaughter.] the killing of anything to be offered as a sacrifice.

Mac′trȧ, *n.* [Gr. *maktra*, a kneading trough.] a genus of lamellibranchiate mollusks, the type of the family *Mactridæ*.

mac·trā′ceous, *a.* same as *mactroid*.

mac′troid, *a.* related to or resembling the genus *Mactra*.

mac′troid, *n.* any mollusk of the genus *Mactra*.

mac′ū·lȧ, *n.*; *pl.* **mac′ū·lae,** [L., a spot, stain.]

1. a spot, as on the skin, or on the surface of the sun or the moon.

2. in zoology, a blotch; a colored spot of rather large size.

macula lutea; in anatomy, the yellow spot on the retina.

mac′ū·lăr, *a.* marked with or constituting spots or stains; characterized by maculae.

mac′ū·lāte, *v.t.*; maculated, *pt.*, *pp.*; maculating, *ppr.* [L. *maculatus*, pp. of *maculare*, to spot, speckle, from *macula*, a spot, stain.] to spot; to stain; to defile.

mac′ū·lāte, *a.* spotted; marked with maculae; hence, defiled.

mac′ū·lā·ted, *a.* maculate.

mac·ū·lā′tion, *n.* 1. a spotting.

2. a spot; stain; blemish.

3. the pattern of spots on an animal or plant.

mac′ū·lȧ·tō·ry, *a.* causing a spot or blemish; defiling.

mac′ū·lȧ·tūre, *n.* soiled paper; also, paper which has been spoiled. [Obs.]

mac′ūle, *n.* a macula or mackle.

mac′ūle, *v.t.* and *v.i.*; maculed, *pt.*, *pp.*; maculing, *ppr.* to mackle; to blur.

mac′ū·lōse, *a.* [L. *maculosus*, from *macula*, a spot, stain.] covered with spots; defiled.

mad, *a.*; *comp.* madder; *superl.* maddest, [ME. *made*, *maad*, mad; AS. *gemæd*, *gemad*, mad, senseless, foolish.]

1. mentally ill; insane; crazy.

2. frenzied; wildly excited; frantic; as, *mad* with fear.

3. showing or resulting from lack of reason; foolish and rash; senseless; unwise.

4. blindly and foolishly enthusiastic or fond; infatuated; as, she's *mad* about him.

5. wildly gay; hilarious.

6. having rabies; as, a *mad* dog.

7. angry; enraged; furious (often with *at*). [Colloq.]

like mad; in the manner of an insane person; in a reckless or furious manner.

mad as a hatter (or *March hare*); completely crazy.

to have a mad on; to be angry. [Colloq.]

to run mad; to act madly through excitement.

to run mad after; to seek after as a result of mad infatuation; as, the world *runs mad after* money.

Syn.—crazy, delirious, distracted, frantic, frenzied, insane, raging, rabid, angry.

mad, *v.t.* and *v.i.*; madded, *pt.*, *pp.*; madding, *ppr.* to madden. [Rare.]

mad, *n.* [ME. *mathe*; AS. *mathu*, *matha*, a worm, maggot.] an earthworm; also, a grubworm; a maggot.

Mad·ȧ·gas′căn, *a.* of Madagascar or its people.

Mad·ȧ·gas′căn, *n.* a native or inhabitant of Madagascar.

mad′ăm, *n.*; *pl.* **mad′ăms**; for sense 1, usually **mes·dämes′** (mā-däm′), [Fr. *madame*, originally *ma dame*, from L. *mea domina*, my lady; *mea*, f. of *meus*, my, and *domina*, lady, mistress.]

1. a woman; lady: a polite title used in speaking to or of a woman: often *ma'am*.

2. the mistress of a household.

3. a woman in charge of a brothel.

mad'äme (*or Fr.* mȧ-dȧm'), *n.*; *pl.* **mes-dämes'** (mā-däm'), [Fr.] a married woman: French title equivalent to *Mrs.*: generally used of all foreign married women, in American and British usage.

mad·ȧ·pol'lăm, *n.* a cotton cloth of good quality first made in Madapollam, India.

mad ap'ple, the eggplant.

mad·ȧ·rō'sis, *n.* [Gr. *madarōsis*, from *madaros*, bald.] the loss of hair through disease; in particular, the loss of the eyelashes.

mad'brāin, *a.* ungoverned; hotheaded; prodigal.

mad'brāin, *n.* one who is hotheaded or ungoverned; a madcap.

mad'brāined, *a.* madbrain.

mad'çap, *n.* a reckless, impulsive person, especially a girl.

mad'çap, *a.* 1. having a disposition for wild sports; taking great pleasure in dangerous or ridiculous amusements.

2. wild; dangerous; extravagant.

mad'den, *v.t.*; maddened, *pt., pp.*; maddening, *ppr.* to make mad; to make insane, angry, or wildly excited.

Syn.—infuriate, enrage, exasperate, inflame, craze.

mad'den, *v.i.* to become mad; to become angry or insane; to act as if mad.

They rave, recite, and *madden* round the land. —Pope.

mad'dẽr, *n.* [AS. *mædere, mæddre*, madder.]

1. any of a number of plants of the genus *Rubia* that yield medicines and dyes; especially, *Rubia tinctorum*, a vine with small, yellow flowers and berries.

2. (a) the red root of this plant; (b) a red dye made from this: the term is also applied to a synthetic coal-tar dye, alizarim.

3. bright red; crimson.

Indian madder; the *Rubia cordifolia* of the East Indies, used as a dye: called also *munjeet*.

MADDER PLANT (*Rubia tinctorum*)

mad'dẽr, *a.* comparative of *mad*.

mad'dẽr·wŏrt, *n.* any plant of the madder family.

mad'ding, *a.* 1. raving; frenzied; as, "the *madding* crowd." [Rare.]

2. maddening; making mad. [Rare.]

mad'ding·ly, *adv.* in a madding manner. [Rare.]

mad'dish, *a.* slightly mad.

māde, *v.* past tense and past participle of *make*.

māde, *a.* [pp. of *make*.]

1. constructed; shaped; formed; as, a well-*made* play.

2. produced artificially; not natural; as, *made* ground.

3. invented; contrived; as, a *made* word.

4. specially prepared; as, a *made* dish.

5. sure of success or fortune; successful; as, a *made* man.

mad·ē·faç'tion, *n.* [L. *madefactus*, pp. of *madefacere*, to make wet, moisten; *madere*, to be wet, and *facere*, to make].

1. the act of making wet. [Rare.]

2. the state of being wet. [Rare.]

mad'ē·fȳ, *v.t.*; madefied, *pt., pp.*; madefying, *ppr.* [L. *madere*, to be wet, and *facere*, to make.] to make wet or moist; to moisten. [Obs.]

mȧ·dēi'rȧ (*or*-dā'), *n.* a strong white wine made on the island of Madeira.

Mȧ·dēi'rȧ nut, the English walnut.

Mȧ·dēi'rȧ vīne, a climbing vine, *Boussingaultia baselloides*, native to the Andes.

Mȧ·dēi'rȧ wood, the true mahogany, *Swietenia mahogoni*, of Florida and farther south; also, a tree of the West Indies, *Lysiloma latisiliqua*, which furnishes a wood prized for interior woodwork.

mȧ·de·moi·ṣelle' (măd-mwȧ-zel' *or* mad"e-mō-zel'), *n.*; *pl.* **mes·de·moi·ṣelles'** (mād-mwȧ-zel'), [Fr., from *ma*, my, and *demoiselle*, damsel.]

1. an unmarried woman or girl: French title equivalent to *Miss*.

2. in zoology, *Bairdiella chrysura*, a food fish of the Atlantic off the southern United States coast, known as *silver perch*.

māde'-tö-or'dẽr, *a.* 1. made to conform to the customer's specifications or measurements; custom-made: opposed to *ready-made*.

2. perfectly suitable or conformable.

māde'-up', *a.* 1. put together; arranged; as, a *made-up* page of type.

2. invented; fabricated; false; as, a *made-up* story.

3. with cosmetics applied.

madġe, *n.* in zoology, (a) a species of bird of the genus *Pica*; a magpie, *Pica rustica*; (b) the barn owl, *Strix flammea*.

mad'-head"ed (-hed"), *a.* hot-brained; rash.

mad'house, *n.* 1. a place of confinement for the mentally ill; insane asylum.

2. any place of turmoil, noise, and confusion.

Mā'di·ȧ, *n.* [from *madi*, the Chilean name.] a genus of South American plants of which one species, *Madia sativa*, is cultivated for the edible oil yielded from its seeds.

mad'id, *a.* [L. *madidus*.] wet; moist. [Rare.]

Mad'i·sŏn Av'e·nūe, [named after a street in New York City, regarded as the center of the American advertising industry.] the American advertising industry, its practices, influence, etc.

mad·is·tē'ri·um, *n.* [Gr. *madistērion*.] a surgical instrument used for pulling out hairs.

mad'joun, *n.* same as *majun*.

mad'ly, *adv.* in a mad manner; without reason or understanding; rashly; wildly; foolishly.

mad'măn, *n.*; *pl.* **mad'men**, a demented person; a lunatic; a maniac.

mad'ness, *n.* 1. dementia; insanity; lunacy.

2. great anger; fury.

3. great folly.

4. wild excitement or enthusiasm.

5. rabies.

Syn.—insanity, craziness, lunacy, mania, rage, frenzy, monomania, distractedness.

mȧ·don'nȧ, *n.* [It., my lady.]

1. a former Italian style of address equivalent to *madam*.

2. [M–] the Virgin Mary; "Our Lady"; also, a picture or statue of the Virgin; as, Raphael painted many *Madonnas*.

mȧ'dō·quȧ (-kwȧ), *n.* [Ethiopian.] a very tiny antelope of Ethiopia, *Neotragus saltianus*.

mȧ·drȧgue' (-drăg'), *n.* [Fr.] a kind of huge net used for catching tunny in the Mediterranean.

ma'drȧs (*or* mȧ-drȧs'), *n.* [from *Madras*, India.]

1. a fine, firm cotton cloth, usually striped, used for shirts, dresses, etc.

2. a durable silk cloth, usually striped.

3. a figured cotton or rayon cloth in leno weave, used for draperies.

4. a large, bright-colored kerchief of silk or cotton.

ma'drȧs, *a.* made of madras.

mäd'rẹ·pẽrl, *n.* same as *mother-of-pearl*.

Mad·rē·pō'rȧ, *n.* [Fr. *madrépore*; It. *madrepora*, coral, lit., mother-stone; *madre*, from L. *mater*, mother, and Gr. *pōros*, a soft stone.] in zoology, a genus of reef-building animals typical of the *Madreporidæ*; the madrepores.

Mad"rē·pō·rā'cē·ȧ, *n.pl.* a suborder of the *Madreporaria*.

mad"rē·pō·rā'cē·ăn, *a.* of the *Madreporaracea*.

mad·rē·pō'răl, *a.* relating to the *Madrepora*.

Mad"rē·pō·rā'ri·ȧ, *n.pl.* [*Madrepora*, and *-aria*.] in zoology, an extensive group of coral-making animals, including the *Madreporidæ*, *Astræidæ*, and allied families.

mad"rē·pō·rā'ri·ăn, *n.* one of the *Madreporaria*.

mad"rē·pō·rā'ri·ăn, *a.* of the *Madreporaria*.

mad'rē·pōre, *n.* any of a group of corals, usually branching, which form coral reefs and islands in tropical seas.

mad·rē·pō'ri·ăn, *a.* relating to a madrepore or to the *Madrepora*.

mad·rē·pō'riç, *a.* madreporian.

madreporic plate; in zoology, a disclike perforated plate in the body of an echinoderm.

Mad·rē·pō'ri·dae, *n.pl.* the madrepore family, of which the typical genus is *Madrepora*.

mad·rē·pō'ri·fọrm, *a.* in zoology, formed like a madrepore.

mad'rē·pō·rīte, *n.* [*Madrepora* and *-ite*.]

1. fossil coral, or limestone composed of fossil coral.

2. the plate from the body of an echinoderm.

mȧ·driẽr', *n.* [Fr.] in military engineering, a plank used for supporting the earth in a mine, moat, or ditch.

mad'ri·găl, *n.* [It. *madrigale*.]

1. a short poem, usually a love poem, which can be set to music.

2. a contrapuntal song with parts for several voices, sung without accompaniment, popular in the fifteenth, sixteenth, and seventeenth centuries.

3. loosely, any song, especially a part song.

mad'ri·găl·ẽr, *n.* a madrigalist.

mad'ri·găl·ist, *n.* a composer of madrigals.

ma·dri·lène' (-len'), *n.* [Fr. (*consommé*) *Madrilène*, Madrid (consommé), from Sp. *Madrileño*, of Madrid.] a highly seasoned consommé made with tomatoes.

Mad·ri·lē'ni·ăn, *n.* [Sp. *Madrileño*, from *Madrid*.] a native or inhabitant of Madrid, Spain.

Mad·ri·lē'ni·ăn, *a.* of Madrid or its people.

mȧ·drō'ña (mȧ-drō'nyȧ), *n.* [from *madroño*, the Sp. name.] an evergreen tree or shrub, *Arbutus menziesii*, of California, having edible berries called *madroña apples*: written also *madroño* and *madrone*.

mad'stōne, *n.* a small porous stone supposed to absorb the venom from the bite of a snake and to cure hydrophobia: also called *snake-stone*.

Mȧ·dū'rȧ foot, [from Madura, in southern India.] in medicine, mycetoma.

mȧ·dụ'rō, *a.* [Sp., *mature*, from L. *maturus*.] dark and strong: said of cigars.

mad'wom"ăn (-woom"), *n.*; *pl.* **mad'wom"en** (-wim"), a demented or insane woman.

mad'wŏrt, *n.* [so named because supposed remedy for rabies.] any of a group of plants or shrubs of the mustard family, with grayish leaves and small, pale flowers; alyssum.

Mae·an·drī'nȧ, *n.* [L. *mæander*, a winding, and *-ina*.] in zoology, a typical genus of the *Mæandrinidæ*, a family of madreporian animals, which build massive coral, such as brain coral and the like: spelled also *Meandrina*.

BRAIN CORAL (*Mæandrina cerebriformis*)

Mae·an·drin'i·dae, *n.pl.* [*Mæandrina* and *-idæ*.] in zoology, a family including the builders of corallum or massive coral, having on the surface rows of formations resembling the convolutions of the brain, and other winding forms.

Mae·cē'năs, *n.* [from Gaius Cilnius *Mæcenas*, Roman statesman and patron of literature.] any wealthy and generous patron, especially of literature or art.

māel'strŏm, *n.* [Early Mod. D., from *malen*, to grind, whirl round, and *stroom*, a stream; first applied by 16th-century Dutch geographers.]

1. [M–] a famous and dangerous whirlpool off the west coast of Norway.

2. any large or violent whirlpool.

3. a violently confused, turbulent, or dangerously agitated state of mind, emotions, affairs, etc.

mae'nad, *n.*; *pl.* **mae'nadṣ, maen'ȧ·dēṣ** (-men'), [L. *mænas*; Gr. *mainas* (*-ados*), raving, frantic; as noun, a madwoman, maenad, from *mainesthai*, to rave.] in Greek and Roman mythology, a priestess of Bacchus; a female celebrant at the feasts of Bacchus; a bacchante; a frantic or frenzied woman: also spelled *menad*.

mae·nad'iç, *a.* of, like, or characteristic of a maenad.

mä·es·tō'sō, *a.* and *adv.* [It.] in music, with majesty or dignity: a direction to the performer.

mä·es'trō, *n.*; *pl.* **mä·es'trōṣ, mä·es'trī**, [It.] a master in any art; especially, a great composer, conductor, or teacher of music.

Māe West, a variety of inflated life preserver worn around the chest by airmen and sailors: from Mae West, stage and screen actress.

Mä'fi·ȧ, Mäf'fi·ȧ, *n.* [It. *maffia*.]

1. in Sicily, (a) [m–] an attitude of popular hostility to law and government; (b) any of the groups of brigands characterized by this attitude.

2. a secret society of criminals thought to exist in the United States and other countries, engaging in blackmail, illicit trade in narcotics, etc.

mä·fi·ō'sō, *n.* [It.] a member of the Mafia.

mȧ·fur'rȧ tree, [from *mafurra*, native name,

and E. *tree*.] in botany, a large tree, *Trichilia emetica*, of the family *Meliaceæ*, native to East Africa and Madagascar, its seeds yielding a hard oil used in the manufacture of soap and candles.

mag·ȧ·zïne′, *n.* [OFr. *magazin*; It. *magazzino*; Ar. *makhāzin*, pl. of *makhzan*, a storehouse, granary.]

1. a place of storage, as a warehouse, storehouse, or military supply depot.

2. a space in which explosives are stored, as a building or room in a fort, or a section of a warship.

3. a supply chamber, as the space in a rifle or pistol from which the cartridges are fed, the space in a camera from which the plates or rolls of film are fed, or the part of a stove in which the fuel is stored.

4. the things kept in a magazine, as munitions or supplies.

5. [from the idea of "storehouse of information."] a publication, usually paper-backed and sometimes illustrated, that appears at regular intervals and contains stories, articles, etc. by various writers and, usually, advertisements.

mag·ȧ·zïne′, *v.t.*; magazined, *pt.*, *pp.*; magazining, *ppr.* to store or place in a magazine for safety or for future use; as, to *magazine* ammunition.

mag·ȧ·zïne′ gun, a gun containing a receptacle for a number of cartridges automatically moved into position for discharging.

mag·ȧ·zïne′ stōve, a stove having a receptacle for supplying it with fuel by an automatic feed, as in a base burner.

mag·ȧ·zïn′ēr, *n.* one who writes for a magazine.

Mag′dȧ·lēne, Mag′dȧ·len, *n.* [LL., from *Magdala*, town on the Sea of Galilee.]

1. [*also* mag-dȧ-lē′ni), Mary Magdalene (preceded by *the*): Luke viii. 2 (identified with the repentant woman in Luke vii. 37).

2. [m–] (a) a reformed and repentant prostitute; (b) a reformatory for prostitutes.

Mag·dȧ·lē′ni·ăn, *a.* [Fr. *magdalenien*, after *La Madeleine*, in west central France, where many of the artifacts were found.] designating or of a late period of the Old Stone Age, characterized by cave art and tools of polished stone and bone.

mag·dā′lē·on, *n.* [OFr. *magdaleon*, from Gr. *magdalia*, a crumb of bread.] in medicine, a cylindrical roll of plaster, salve, or any medicinal substance. [Obs.]

māġe, *n.* a magician; a wizard. [Archaic.]

Mag·el·lan′iç, *a.* relating to Ferdinand Magellan, the Portuguese navigator.

Magellanic cloud; (a) either of two large, cloudlike phenomena containing star clusters, in the Milky Way in the southern hemisphere; (b) a dark area in the Milky Way, near the Southern Cross.

mȧ·ġen′tȧ, *n.* [from *Magenta*, in Italy: so called because the dye was discovered about the time (1859) of the battle fought there.] fuchsin, a coal-tar dyestuff producing a purplish-red color; also, the color itself.

mȧ·ġen′tȧ, *a.* purplish-red.

magged (magd), *a.* among sailors, worn-out; and inefficient: said of a rope.

mag′gŏt, *n.* [ME. *magotte*; prob. from earlier *mathek*, flesh worm.]

1. a wormlike insect larva, as the legless larva of the housefly: maggots are usually found in filth and decaying matter.

2. an odd notion; a whim.

mag′gŏt·i·ness, *n.* the state of being maggoty.

mag′gŏt·y, *a.* 1. full of maggots.

2. full of whims; capricious; whimsical.

Mā′ġī, *n.pl.*; *sing.* **Mā′gus**, [O.Pers. *magu*, member of a priestly caste, magician.]

1. the priestly caste in ancient Media and Persia, supposedly having occult powers.

2. in the Bible, the three wise men from the East who came bearing gifts to the infant Jesus: Matt. ii. 1–13.

Mā′ġi·ăn, *a.* 1. of the Magi.

2. [m–] magical. [Rare.]

Mā′ġi·ăn, *n.* 1. one of the Magi.

2. an adherent of the Magi.

3. [m–] a magician; wizard.

Mā′ġi·ăn·iṣm, *n.* the philosophy or doctrines of the Magi.

maġ′iç, *n.* [L. *magice*, from Gr. *magikē* (supply *technē*, art), the magic art, sorcery, from *magikos*, of the Magi, from *magoi*, the Magi or priests of the Medes and Persians skilled in sorcery.]

1. the pretended art of producing effects or controlling events by charms, spells, and rituals supposed to govern certain natural or supernatural forces; sorcery; witchcraft.

2. any mysterious, seemingly inexplicable, or extraordinary power or influence; as, the *magic* of love.

3. the art of producing baffling effects or illusions by sleight of hand, concealed apparatus, etc.

celestial magic; a form of magic which attributes to spirits a kind of dominion over the planets, and to the planets an influence over men.

natural magic; the art of employing the powers of nature to produce effects apparently supernatural.

maġ′iç, *a.* [L. *magicus*; Gr. *magikos*, of magic, properly, of the Magi.]

1. pertaining to magic; used in magic; having the power of magic; as, a *magic* wand, *magic* art.

2. producing extraordinary results, as if by magic or supernatural means.

magic lantern; an optical instrument with an arrangement of lenses and a light for projecting on a screen a magnified image of a picture on a small slide or card.

magic square; a square figure, formed by a series of numbers in arithmetical progression, so arranged in parallel ranks, that the sum of each row or line, taken perpendicularly, horizontally, or diagonally, is constant. Analogous magic squares may be formed by taking numbers in geometrical progression, etc.

maġ′iç·ăl, *a.* magic (especially in sense 2): used predicatively as well as attributively, whereas *magic* tends to be attributive only.

maġ′iç·ăl·ly, *adv.* by the arts of magic; according to the rules or rites of magic; as if by magic.

mȧ·ġi′ciăn (-jish′ăn), *n.* [OFr. *magicien*, from L. *magice*; Gr. *magike*, magic.] an expert in magic; specifically, (a) a sorcerer; wizard; (b) a performer who produces baffling effects or illusions by sleight of hand, concealed apparatus, etc.

mȧ·gilp′, mȧ·gilph′, *n.* a gelatinous compound of linseed oil and mastic varnish, used by artists as a vehicle for colors: also spelled *megilp*, *megilph*.

Mä·gi·nōt′ līne (-zhē-nō′) [after André *Maginot* (1877–1932), Fr. minister of war.] a system of heavily fortified pillboxes, tank traps, etc. on the eastern frontier of France, built before World War II: though considered impregnable, it failed to prevent invasion by the Nazi armies.

mȧ·ġis′tēr, *n.* [L., a master, head, teacher.] master; head: a title of the Middle Ages, accorded for literary or scientific distinction: used now only in the form of the university degree, *magister artium*, master of arts.

maġ·is·tē′ri·ăl, *a.* [LL. *magisterius*, from L. *magister*, master.]

1. pertaining to a magistrate; suitable or fitting to a master; authoritative.

2. proud; lofty; arrogant; imperious; domineering.

> Pretenses go a great way with men that take fair words and *magisterial* looks for current payment. —L'Estrange.

3. in old chemistry, pertaining to magistery.

maġ·is·tē·ri·al′i·ty, *n.* the state or quality of being magisterial; magisterialness.

maġ·is·tē′ri·ăl·ly, *adv.* with the air of a master; arrogantly; authoritatively.

maġ·is·tē′ri·ăl·ness, *n.* the character of a master; haughtiness; imperiousness; peremptoriness.

maġ′is·ter·y, *n.* [L. *magisterium*, the position or office of a master or chief director, from *magister*, a master.] in old chemistry, a precipitate; a fine substance deposited by precipitation: usually applied to particular kinds of precipitates, as that of bismuth, sulfur, etc.

maġ′is·trȧ·cy, *n.*; *pl.* **maġ′is·trȧ·cieṣ**, 1. the position, office, function, or term of a magistrate.

2. magistrates collectively.

3. the district under a magistrate; a magistrate's jurisdiction.

maġ′is·trăl, *a.* [L. *magistralis*, from *magister*, master.]

1. of the nature of a magistrate or master; magesterial; authoritative or imperious.

2. in pharmacy, prepared especially; not kept on hand: opposed to *officinal*.

3. in medicine, having great efficacy. [Obs.]

4. guiding; main; as, a *magistral* line in fortification.

maġ′is·trăl, *n.* 1. in medicine, a sovereign remedy. [Obs.]

2. in military fortification, the main or magistral line, which establishes the location of other parts of the fortification.

3. copper pyrites in a pulverized form employed in the amalgamation of silver ores.

maġ·is·tral′i·ty, *n.* despotic authority in opinion; dictatorialness. [Obs.]

maġ′is·trăl·ly, *adv.* authoritatively; with imperiousness.

maġ′is·trāte, *n.* [L. *magistratus*, the office of a master, chief, or director, from *magister*, a master.]

1. a civil officer empowered to administer and enforce the law: the President of the United States is sometimes called the *first* (or *chief*) *magistrate*.

2. a minor official with certain limited judicial and executive powers, as a justice of the peace or judge of a police court.

maġ·is·trat′iç, maġ·is·trat′iç·ăl, *a.* having the authority of a magistrate; of or pertaining to a magistrate. [Obs.]

maġ′is·trā·tūre, *n.* magistracy.

mag′mȧ, *n.*; *pl.* **mag′mȧṣ, mag′mȧ·tȧ**, [Gr. *magma*, anything kneaded, from *massein*, to knead.]

1. a thin paste composed of crude mixed mineral or organic matter.

2. in geology, molten rock deep in the earth, from which igneous rock is formed.

3. in pharmacy, a suspension of precipitated matter in a watery substance.

mag·mat′iç, *a.* of, like, or produced by magma.

Mag′nȧ Çhär′tȧ, Mag′nȧ Çär′tȧ, [ML., lit., great charter.]

1. the great charter that King John of England was forced by the English barons to grant at Runnymede, June 15, 1215: it guaranteed certain civil and political liberties to the English people.

2. any basic constitution that guarantees civil and political liberties.

mag′nȧ çum lau̇′dē, [L.] with great praise: phrase used to signify graduation with high honors from a university or college.

mag·nȧ·nim′i·ty, *n.* [L. *magnanimitas*, greatness of soul, from *magnanimus*; *magnus*, great, and *animus*, mind, soul.]

1. the quality or state of being magnanimous.

2. *pl.* **mag·nȧ·nim′i·tieṣ**, a magnanimous act.

Syn.—generosity, high-mindedness, chivalrousness.

mag·nan′i·mous, *a.* [L. *magnanimus*; *magnus*, great, and *animus*, mind, soul.]

1. noble in mind; elevated in soul or in sentiment; rising above pettiness or meanness; generous in overlooking injury or insult.

2. dictated by magnanimity; exhibiting nobleness of soul; liberal and honorable; not selfish.

> There is an indissoluble union between a *magnanimous* policy and the solid rewards of public prosperity and felicity. —Washington.

Syn.—noble, high-minded, exalted, high-souled, great-souled, lofty, honorable.

mag·nan′i·mous·ly, *adv.* in a magnanimous manner; with greatness of mind; with dignity and elevation of sentiment.

mag′nāte, *n.* [LL. *magnas*, pl. *magnates*, a great man, nobleman, from L. *magnus*, great.]

1. a very important or influential person in any field of activity, especially in a large business.

2. formerly, in Hungary and Poland, a member of the upper branch of the Diet.

mag″nē·çrys·tal′liç, *a.* [*magnet* and *crystallic*.] relating to the action of a magnet upon a crystallized object.

mag′nēṣ, *n.* a magnet. [Obs.]

mag·nē′ṣiȧ (-shȧ *or* -zhȧ), *n.* [LL. *magnesia*, a mineral said to be brought from Magnesia (district in Thessaly), from *Magnesius*, pertaining to Magnesia.]

1. magnesium oxide, MgO, a white, tasteless powder, used as a mild laxative and antacid, and as an insulating substance, in firebrick, etc.

2. hydrated magnesium carbonate, also used as a laxative: also called *magnesia alba*.

mag·nē′ṣiăn, *a.* pertaining to magnesia or

partaking of its qualities; containing magnesia; resembling magnesia.

magnesian limestone; same as *dolomite*.

mag·nē′siç, *a.* [*magnes*ium and *-ic.*] pertaining to or containing magnesium.

mag·nē″si·ō·fer′rīte, *n.* [*magnes*ium and L. *ferrum*, iron, and *-ite.*] a ferromagnesic oxide of the spinel group: also called *magnoferrite*.

mag′nē·sīte, *n.* [*magnes*ium and *-ite.*] magnesium carbonate found uncombined, crystalline, granular, or compact in form.

mag·nē′si·um (-shi- *or* -zhi-), *n.* [Mod. L., from *magnesia.*] a light, silver-white metallic chemical element, malleable and ductile: used in making several alloys and, because it burns with a hot, white light, in photographic flash bulbs, incendiary bombs, etc.: symbol, Mg; atomic weight, 24.32; atomic number, 12.

magnesium sulfate; in chemistry, a hydrated sulfate, $MgSO_4 \cdot 7H_2O$: also called *Epsom salts*.

mag′net, *n.* [ME. *magnete*; OFr. *magnete*; L. *magnes* (*-etis*), from Gr. *Magnēs, Magnētis lithos*, magnet, lit., stone of Magnesia, from *Magnesia* (district in Thessaly).]

1. any piece of iron, steel, or, originally, magnetite (*loadstone*) that has the property of attracting iron or steel, etc.: this property may be naturally present or artificially induced, as by passing an electric current through a coil of wire wrapped around the metal.

2. a person or thing that attracts.

compound magnet; a magnet consisting of a number of single magnets united, with similar poles arranged adjacently.

deflecting magnet; a magnet useful for deflecting the needle of a galvanometer.

permanent magnet; a steel magnet which retains indefinitely the magnetism imparted to it: distinguished from a *temporary magnet*.

temporary magnet; a magnet of soft iron, which loses its magnetism when the magnetizing cause ceases to act, as in an electromagnet.

mag·net′iç, *n.* 1. any metal which may receive the properties of the loadstone.

2. a magnet. [Obs.]

mag·net′iç, *a.* [*magnet* and *-ic.*]

1. having the properties of a magnet; as, *magnetic* iron.

2. of, producing, caused by, or operated by magnetism.

3. of the earth's magnetism; as, the *magnetic* meridian.

4. that can be magnetized.

5. powerfully attractive: said of a person, personality, etc.

6. mesmeric.

magnetic amplitude; see under *amplitude*.

magnetic axis; the straight line joining the two poles of a magnet: if the magnet is freely suspended, the magnetic axis will parallel the lines of magnetic force.

magnetic battery; same as *compound magnet* under *magnet*.

magnetic circuit; the entire course of a magnetic line of force.

magnetic compass; an instrument for indicating geographical directions by the action of the earth's magnetic field on a bar magnet (*magnetic needle*) suspended so as to swing freely on a pivot.

magnetic compensator; a device for neutralizing or eliminating the effect of the iron in a ship upon the needle of its compass: also called *compensating magnet*.

magnetic course; an airplane's course reckoned from the magnetic north.

magnetic creeping; the slow process of magnetization under a magnetizing influence, due to the resistance of a previous condition.

magnetic curves; curves representing magnetic lines of force as seen when iron filings are placed upon a sheet of paper in proximity to a magnet.

MAGNETIC CURVES

magnetic density; the intensity or strength of magnetism indicated by the number of magnetic lines of force in a given cross-sectional area at right angles to the lines of force.

magnetic elements of a place; (a) the intensity of terrestrial magnetic attraction; (b) the degree of the needle's inclination; (c) the degree of the needle's declination.

magnetic equator; see under *equator*.

magnetic field; the space around a magnet in which its magnetic force is appreciable.

magnetic fluid; a hypothetical fluid formerly assumed to exist for the purpose of treating and explaining the phenomena of magnetism.

magnetic flux; the total flow of magnetism or magnetic lines of force through a magnetic circuit.

magnetic force; the force with which a magnet attracts (or repels) a piece of iron or steel.

magnetic induction; the power of a magnet to induce magnetism in a piece of iron, steel, etc. brought into its magnetic field.

magnetic intensity; same as *magnetic force*.

magnetic meridian; that circle of the celestial sphere which passes through the zenith and the Magnetic Poles.

magnetic mine; a naval mine designed to explode when the metal hull of a ship passing near it deflects a magnetic needle, closing an electric circuit and thus detonating the charge.

magnetic moment; the force exerted by one pole of a magnet, multiplied by the distance between the poles.

magnetic needle; a slender strip of magnetized steel which, when mounted so as to swing freely on a pivot, will point along the line of the magnetic meridian toward the Magnetic Poles, approximately north and south: it is the essential part of a magnetic compass.

magnetic north; the direction toward which a magnetic needle points: in most places it is not true north.

magnetic pickup; a pickup, often used in electric phonographs, in which the varying movements of the needle produce corresponding variations in electrical output to the amplifier through an arrangement of a magnet and coils: distinguished from *crystal pickup*.

magnetic pole; (a) either pole of a magnet, where the magnetic lines of force seem to be concentrated; (b) [M– P–] either point on the earth's surface toward which the needle of a magnetic compass points: the North and South Magnetic Poles do not precisely coincide with the geographical poles.

magnetic pyrites; a magnetic iron sulfide: also called *pyrrhotine*.

magnetic recording; the recording of electrical signals by means of changes in areas of magnetization on a tape, wire, or disk: used for recording sound, video material, digital computer data, etc.

magnetic storm; sudden and violent disturbances or changes in the magnetic force of the earth, probably resulting from solar activity.

magnetic tape; a thin plastic ribbon coated with a suspension of ferromagnetic iron oxide particles, used as a storage medium for magnetic recording.

magnetic telegraph; a telegraph which is operated by a magnet; the electromagnetic telegraph.

mag·net′iç·ăl, *a.* magnetic.

mag·net′iç·ăl·ly, *adv.* in a magnetic manner.

mag·net′iç·ăl·ness, *n.* the quality of being magnetic. [Obs.]

mag·nē·ti′ciăn, *n.* a magnetist.

mag·net′içs, *n.pl.* [*construed as sing.*] the branch of physics dealing with magnets and magnetic phenomena.

mag·net·if′ẽr·ous, *a.* [L. *magnes* (*-etis*), a magnet, and *ferre*, to bear.] producing or conducting magnetism.

mag′net·ism, *n.* 1. the property, quality, or condition of being magnetic; as, a loadstone has *magnetism*.

2. the force to which this is due.

3. the branch of physics dealing with magnets and magnetic phenomena; magnetics.

4. power to attract; personal charm or allure.

5. mesmerism.

animal magnetism; mesmerism.

terrestrial magnetism; the magnetism or magnetic properties of the earth, the effect of which is seen in the behavior of magnetized needles, telegraphic instruments, etc.

mag′net·ist, *n.* one proficient in magnetism; a magnetician.

mag′net·īte, *n.* an important iron ore, a black iron oxide, Fe_3O_4, occurring either in massive form or in isometric crystals: called also *loadstone, magnetic iron ore*, when magnetic.

mag·net·it′iç, *a.* pertaining to, characteristic of, or containing magnetite.

mag′net·ī·zȧ·ble, *a.* susceptible to magnetic influence; that can be magnetized; magnetic.

mag″net·i·zā′tion, *n.* the act of magnetizing; the condition of being magnetized.

mag′net·īze, *v.t.*; magnetized, *pt., pp.*; magnetizing, *ppr.* [*magnet* and *-ize.*]

1. to give magnetic properties to (steel, iron, etc.); to make into a magnet; as, to *magnetize* a needle.

2. to attract or influence, as if by a magnet; to captivate.

3. to mesmerize. [Rare.]

mag′net·īze, *v.i.* to acquire magnetic properties; to become magnetic.

mag′net·īz·ẽr, *n.* one who or that which magnetizes or induces magnetism.

mag·nē′tō, *n.*; *pl.* **mag·nē′tōṣ,** a dynamo in which one or more permanent magnets produce the magnetic field; especially, a small machine of this sort connected with and run by an internal-combustion engine, used to generate the electric current providing a spark for the ignition: in full, *magnetoelectric machine*: also *magnetogenerator*.

mag·nē′tō-, [from L. *magnes* (*-etis*), a magnet.] a combining form meaning: (a) *magnetism, magnetic force*, as in *magneto*electric; (b) *magnetoelectric*.

mag·nē″tō·çhem′is·try, *n.* [*magneto-* and *chemistry.*] that branch of chemistry dealing with the relationship between chemical phenomena and magnetic force.

mag·nē″tō·dȳ′nȧ·mō, *n.* a dynamo with permanent field magnets.

mag·nē″tō·ē·leç′triç, mag·nē″tō·ē·leç′triç·ăl, *a.* of or characterized by electricity produced by magnets.

magnetoelectric machine; a machine in which electromagnets are replaced by permanent magnets.

mag·nē″tō·ē·leç·triç′i·ty, *n.* 1. electricity produced by the relative movement of electric conductors and magnets.

2. the science dealing with this.

mag·nē″tō·ġen′ẽr·ā·tōr, *n.* a magneto.

mag·nē′tō·gram, *n.* [*magneto-*, and Gr. *gramma*, a writing.] a record showing variations in the earth's magnetic field as recorded by a magnetograph or other indicator.

mag·nē′tō·graph, *n.* [*magneto-*, and Gr. *graphein*, to write.] an automatic instrument for recording magnetic variations of the earth or of a magnetic field.

mag·nē·tom′e·tẽr, *n.* [*magneto-*, and Gr. *metron*, a measure.]

1. an instrument to measure the force and the variations in the force of magnetism.

2. an instrument for magnetically detecting concealed metallic weapons on the person or in the luggage of airline passengers.

mag·nē″tō·met′riç, *a.* of or pertaining to magnetometry.

mag·nē·tom′e·try, *n.* [*magneto-*, and Gr. *-metria*, from *metron*, a measure.] the science of measuring the intensity of a magnetic force and of observing the phenomena of a magnetic field.

mag·nē″tō·mō′tive, *a.* designating or of a force that gives rise to magnetic flux.

mag·nē″tō·mō′tōr, *n.* [*magneto-*, and LL. *motor*, from L. *movere*, to move.] a voltaic series of two or more large plates producing electricity of low tension. [Rare.]

mag′nē·tōn, *n.* in physics, the unit by which magnetic moment is measured.

mag·nē″tō·op′tiç, *a.* of or pertaining to magnetooptics.

mag·nē″tō·op′tiçs, *n.* the branch of physics dealing with the modifications that light undergoes in passing through a magnetic field.

mag′nē·tron, *n.* [*magnet* and *electron.*] a vacuum tube in which the flow of ions from the heated cathode to the anode is controlled by a magnetic field externally applied and perpendicular to the electric field by which they are propelled: used to produce very short radio waves.

mag′net schọọl, a public school which offers innovative courses, specialized training, etc. in order to attract students from a broad urban area and thereby help to bring about desegregation.

mag′ni- [from L. *magnus*, great.] a combining form meaning *great, big, large*, as in *magni*ficent, *magni*loquence; also, in zoology, *long*.

mag′ni·fī·ȧ·ble, *a.* that can be magnified.

mag·nif′iç, mag·nif′i·çăl, *a.* 1. magnificent.

2. imposing in size, dignity, etc.

3. (a) pompous; (b) grandiloquent.
4. eulogistic.
[Archaic in all senses.]

mag·nif'i·çăl·ly, *adv.* in a magnific manner. [Archaic.]

Mag·nif'i·çat, *n.* [L.] 1. (a) the hymn of the Virgin Mary in Luke i. 46–55, beginning *Magnificat anima mea Dominum,* "My soul doth magnify the Lord"; (b) any musical setting for this.
2. [m–] any song, poem, or hymn of praise.

mag·nif'i·çāte, *v.t.* to magnify. [Obs.]

mag"ni·fi·çā'tion, *n.* 1. a magnifying or being magnified.
2. the power of magnifying.
3. a magnified image, model, or representation.

mag·nif'i·cence, *n.* the condition or quality of being magnificent; grandeur; richness and splendor, as of furnishings, color, dress, etc.

mag·nif'i·cent, *a.* [LL. *magnificens* (*-entis*), doing great things; L. *magnus,* great, and *faciens* (*-entis*), ppr. of *facere,* to do.]
1. splendid; stately; imposingly beautiful; grand; rich or sumptuous, as in construction, decoration, etc.
2. exalted: said of ideas, etc., and also of some former rulers, as, Lorenzo the *Magnificent.*
Syn.—glorious, splendid, grand, gorgeous, superb, princely, stately.

mag·nif'i·cent·ly, *adv.* in a magnificent manner.

mag·nif'i·çō, *n.* [It., from L. *magnificus,* noble, great.]
1. a grandee of ancient Venice.
2. a person who is lordly or who affects lordliness.

mag'ni·fī·ẽr, *n.* 1. one who or that which magnifies.
2. a lens or a combination of lenses for magnifying.

mag'ni·fȳ, *v.t.*; magnified, *pt., pp.*; magnifying, *ppr.* [ME. *magnifien*; OFr. *magnifier*; L. *magnificare*; *magnus,* great, and *facere,* to make.]
1. to make greater in size, status, or importance; to enlarge. [Rare.]
2. to cause (a person or thing) to seem greater, more important, etc. than is really so; to exaggerate; as, she *magnified* her sufferings in telling about them.
3. to cause to seem larger than is really so; to increase the apparent size of (an object), especially by means of a lens or lenses.
4. to glorify; to praise; to extol. [Archaic.]

mag'ni·fȳ, *v.i.* to have the power of increasing the apparent size of any object; as, telescopes and microscopes *magnify.*

mag'ni·fȳ·ing glȧss, a lens or combination of lenses that increases the apparent size of an object seen through it.

mag·nil'ō·quence, *n.* a lofty manner of speaking; tumid, pompous words or style; magniloquent quality.

mag·nil'ō·quent, *a.* [L. *magnus,* great, and *loquens* (*-entis*), ppr. of *loqui,* to speak.]
1. lofty, pompous, or grandiose in speech or style of expression.
2. boastful; bombastic; talking big.

mag·nil'ō·quent·ly, *adv.* in a magniloquent manner.

mag'ni·tūde, *n.* [L. *magnitudo,* greatness, bulk, size, from *magnus,* great.]
1. (a) greatness, specifically of size, of extent, or of importance or influence; (b) [Obs.] greatness of character.
2. (a) size or measurable quantity; as, the *magnitude* of a velocity; (b) importance or influence.
3. in astronomy, (a) any of the classes into which fixed stars are arranged according to degree of brightness with reference to the polestar as the standard: the brightest stars are of the first magnitude; stars just visible to the unaided eye are of the sixth magnitude; (b) a number expressing brightness.
4. in mathematics, a number given to a quantity for purposes of comparison with other quantities of the same class.
apparent magnitude; magnitude as conceived by the visual angle, varying inversely with the distance from the eye.
of the first magnitude; of the greatest importance.
Syn.—size, extension, bulk, volume, greatness, bigness, extent, measure, largeness.

Mag·nō'li·ȧ, *n.* [after Pierre *Magnol* (1638–1715), French botanist.]
1. a genus of subtropical trees and shrubs of the family *Magnoliaceæ,* with large, fragrant flowers of white, pink, or purple.
2. [m–] any plant or flower of this genus.

Mag·nō·li·ā'cē·ae, *n.pl.* a large family of trees and shrubs, of which the genus *Magnolia* is typical.

mag·nō·li·ā'ceous, *a.* related to or resembling the *Magnoliaceæ.*

mag'num, *n.* [L. *magnum,* neut. of *magnus,* great.]
1. a bottle holding two quarts, or the amount such a bottle holds.
2. in anatomy, a bone of the distal row, the largest of the human carpus.

mag'num ō'pus, [L.] 1. a great work, especially of art or literature; a masterpiece.
2. a person's greatest work or undertaking.

Mag'nus ef·feçt', [after H. G. *Magnus* (1802–1870), G. scientist.] the sideways thrust on a rotating cylinder with its axis perpendicular to an air current, used to propel rotor ships, etc.

mag'nus hitch, [L. *magnus,* large.] a kind of knot: see *knot,* illus.

mag'ŏt, *n.* [Fr. *magot,* the Barbary ape.]
1. a small, grotesque figure, as of ivory.
2. in zoology, the Barbary ape.

mag'pīe, *n.* [ME. *magot pie*; *magot,* from Fr. *margot,* a magpie, a familiar form of *Marguerite,* and *pie,* from Fr. *pie,* L. *pica,* a woodpecker.]
1. any of a number of birds of the crow family, related to the jays and characterized by black-and-white coloring, a long, tapering tail, and a habit of noisy chattering.
2. a person who chatters.
3. a person who collects odds and ends.

mag'pīe mọth, a black-and-white moth belonging to the family *Geometridæ.*

mag'pīe shrīke, 1. a South American bird, *Cissopis leverianus.*
2. any of several Australian shrikes.

mȧ·guä'ri (-gwä'), *n.* [S. Am.] a stork of South America, *Euxenura galeata.*

mag'uey (-wā), *n.* [Sp.] any of a number of related fleshy-leaved or fiber-yielding plants of the southwestern United States, Mexico, and Central America; an agave or related plant; especially, the century plant; American aloe.

Mā'gus, *n.*; *pl.* **Mā'ġī,** [L., from Gr. *magos,* one of a Medean tribe, an enchanter.]
1. one of the Magi (in either sense).
2. [m–] a magician, sorcerer, or ancient astrologer; especially, Simon Magus (Acts viii. 9–24).

Mag'yär, *n.* [Hung.] 1. a member of the people constituting the main ethnic group in Hungary.
2. their Ugrian language; Hungarian.

Mag'yär, *a.* of the Magyars, their language, or culture.

Mȧ·hä·bhä'rȧ·tȧ, *n.* [Sans. *mahābhārata,* lit., the great story.] one of the two great epics of India, written in Sanskrit about 200 B.C.: it combines stories and poems with history and mythology: also *Mahabharatam.*

mä'hȧ·leb, *n.* [*mahleb,* Ar. name.] a European species of cherry, *Prunus mahaleb*: its fruit is used for making a violet dye and a fermented liqueur like kirschwasser.

mȧ·hä'rä'jȧ, mȧ·hä'rä'jȧh (*or Eng.* mä-hä-rä'jȧ), *n.* [Sans., *mahārāja*; *maha,* great, and *rājā,* a king.] in India, a sovereign prince, especially the prince of any of the chief native states: a title higher than *rajah.*

mȧ·hä·rä'ni, mȧ·hä·rä'nee, *n.* [Hind. *mahārānī*; *maha,* great, and *rānī,* queen.]
1. the wife of a maharajah.
2. a sovereign queen or princess of this rank in her own right.

mȧ·hä·ri'shï, *n.* [Hindi *mahārishi,* from *mahā,* great, and *ṛshi,* sage.] a Hindu teacher of mysticism and transcendental meditation.

mȧ·hät'mȧ, *n.* [Sans. *mahātman,* from *maha,* great, and *ātman,* soul.] in theosophy and esoteric Buddhism, one of a class of wise and holy persons, supposed to have unusual powers: Mohandas Gandhi was often called *the Mahatma.*

Mäh'dï, *n.* [Ar. *mahdīy,* a guide, leader, spiritual director.] a leader and prophet expected by Moslems to appear on earth before the world ends; Moslem Messiah: the title has been assumed by various leaders, especially Mohammed Ahmed, who led a revolt in the Egyptian Sudan in 1883.

Mäh'di·ăn, *n.* one who believes in Mahdi.

Mäh'dịsm, Mäh'di·ịsm, *n.* the belief and advocacy of the doctrine that Mahdi will yet appear as a leader of the faithful.

Mäh'dist, *n.* 1. a believer in Mahdism.
2. a follower of a person calling himself the Mahdi.

Mȧ·hẽr'ni·ȧ, *n.* [a transposition of *Hermannia,* from Paul *Hermann,* a Dutch botanist.] a genus of herbaceous or shrubby plants of South Africa, belonging to the family *Sterculiaceæ,* including *Mahernia verticillata,* which has fragrant, yellow, bell-like flowers.

Mȧ·hï'çăn, *n.* [Am. Ind. (Algonquian), lit., a wolf.]
1. a confederacy or tribe of Algonquian Indians that lived chiefly in the upper Hudson Valley.
2. an Indian belonging to this confederacy.
3. Mohegan.
Also *Mohican.*

Mȧ·hï'çăn, *a.* of the Mahican tribe or confederacy: also *Mohican.*

mäh'-jŏngg', mäh'jŏng', *n.* a Chinese game, played, usually by four persons, with 136 or 144 pieces resembling dominoes, marked in suits and called *tiles*: the object is to build combinations or sets by drawing, discarding, and exchanging these.

mähl'stick, *n.* same as *maulstick.*

mȧ·hōe', *n.* [native name.]
1. any of several tropical trees having a strong, fibrous, inner bark; specifically, *Hibiscus tiliaceus,* having an inner bark used for making twine and cordage.
2. the inner bark of the mahoe.

mȧ·hog'ȧ·ny, *n.* [from *mahogoni,* S. Am. name.]
1. (a) the hard wood of a tropical American tree, much used for furniture: it varies in color from reddish brown to yellow; (b) the tree.
2. (a) any of various woods of similar properties and color; as, Philippine *mahogany*; (b) a tree from which such wood is obtained.
3. reddish brown.
bastard mahogany; any of several trees whose wood resembles mahogany, especially the Jamaican tree, *Matayba apetala,* of the family *Sapindaceæ,* and several species of eucalyptus in Australia.

MAHOGANY (*Swietenia mahogani*)

mȧ·hog'ȧ·ny, *a.* 1. made of mahogany.
2. reddish-brown.

mȧ·hō'li, *n.* [native name.] a lemur of Africa, *Galago maholi.*

Mȧ·hom'et·ăn, *a.* and *n.* same as *Mohammedan.*

Mȧ·hom'et·ăn·ịsm, *n.* same as *Mohammedanism.*

Mȧ·hom'et·ist, *n.* Mohammedan. [Obs.]

Mȧ·hom'et·ry, *n.* Mohammedanism. [Obs.]

Mȧ·hō'ni·ȧ, *n.* [named after Bernard *McMahon.*] a grape, *Mahonia aquifolium,* that grows in Oregon: also called *holly berberis.*

Mä'hō·rï, *n.* same as *Maori.*

Mä'hound, Mä'houn, *n.* [OFr. *Mahon, Mahum*; Ar. *Muhammad,* Mohammed.]
1. Mohammed. [Archaic.]
2. Satan: from a confused association of Mahomet as a false prophet. [Scot.]

mȧ·hout', *n.* [E. Ind.] in India and the East Indies, one who cares for and drives an elephant.

Mȧh·rȧt'tȧ, *n.* same as *Maratha.*

Mȧh·rȧt'ti, Mȧh·rȧt'i, *n.* same as *Marathi.*

mäh'wȧ, *n.* [E. Ind.] an East Indian tree, *Bassia latifolia,* valued for its timber and for its oil, which is used for making soap and as a food.

mäh'zŏr (mäkh'zẽr), *n.*; *pl.* **mäh'zŏrṣ** *or Heb.* **mäh·zō'rim,** [Heb., cycle.] the Jewish prayer book that contains the liturgy for festivals and holy days: distinguished from *siddur.*

Mā'i·ȧ, *n.* [Gr. *maia,* a large kind of crab.]
1. a genus of spider crabs typical of the family *Maiidæ.*
2. a silkworm moth, *Bombyx mori.*

Mā'i·ȧ, *n.* [L.; Gr. *Maia.*]
1. in Greek mythology, the eldest and loveliest of the Pleiades, mother of Hermes by Zeus.
2. in Roman mythology, an earth goddess, sometimes identified with the Greek Maia: the month of May was named in her honor.

mā'iăn (-yăn), *a.* and *n.* same as *maioid.*

māid, *n.* [shortened from *maiden*; compare AS. *mægeth, mægth,* a maid.]
1. (a) a young unmarried woman or girl; (b) a virgin.
2. a girl or woman servant: often in compounds, as bar*maid*, house*maid*, etc.
3. a man who has never had sexual intercourse. [Obs.]
4. any of various fishes; specifically, (a) a female skate; (b) the thornback ray; (c) the twait shad.
5. an unmarried woman; a spinster: now *old maid*.
maid of honor; (a) an unmarried woman acting as chief attendant to the bride at a wedding; (b) an unmarried woman, usually of noble birth, attending a queen or princess.

mai·dan′, *n.* [Per.] an open grassy area in or near a town, used for military parades, racing, etc.: also spelled *meidan*.

māid′en, *n.* [ME. *maiden, mayden*; AS. *mægden, mæden,* a maiden, from *mægeth,* a maid, from *magu,* a son, servant.]
1. (a) a girl or young unmarried woman; (b) a virgin.
2. [M–] an instrument resembling the guillotine, formerly used in Scotland for beheading criminals.
3. a race horse that has never won a race.
4. in cricket, an over in which no runs are scored: in full, *maiden over*.

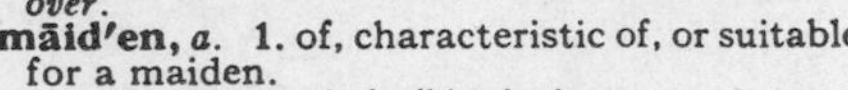
MAIDEN

māid′en, *a.* 1. of, characteristic of, or suitable for a maiden.
2. (a) unmarried; (b) virgin.
3. inexperienced; untried; unused; new; fresh.
4. first or earliest; as, a *maiden* speech, a *maiden* voyage.
5. (a) never having won a race; as, a *maiden* horse; (b) for such horses; as, a *maiden* race.
maiden name; the surname of a woman before her marriage.
maiden over; a maiden (sense 4).
maiden stakes; in horse racing, stakes to be contended for by horses which have never won a race.

māid′en, *v.i.* to speak and act demurely or modestly. [Obs.]

māid′en·hāir, *n.* a species of fern of the genus *Adiantum*, having dark-colored slender stems and delicate fronds.

māid′en·hair tree, same as *ginko*.

māid′en·head, *n.* [ME. *maydenhede, meidenhed,* var. of *maidenhood*.]
1. maidenhood; virginity. [Archaic.]
2. newness; freshness. [Obs.]
3. the hymen.

māid′en·hood, *n.* the state or time of being a maiden.

māid′en·līke, *a.* like a maid; modest.

māid′en·li·ness, *n.* the quality of being maidenly.

māid′en·ly, *a.* 1. of a maiden or maidenhood.
2. like, characteristic of, or suitable for a maiden; modest, gentle, etc.

māid′en·ly, *adv.* in a maidenly manner.

māid′en·ship, *n.* maidenhood. [Obs.]

māid′hood, *n.* maidenhood.

māid in wāit′ing, *pl.* **māids in wāit′ing,** an unmarried woman, usually of noble birth, attending a queen or princess.

Māid Mar′i·ăn, 1. a character in old May Day games and morris dances, variously a May queen, a boy dressed as a girl, or a buffoon.
2. Robin Hood's sweetheart.

māid of the mead′ōw, a European plant, *Spiræa ulmaria,* of the rose family: called also *English meadowsweet*.

māid′sērv″ănt, *n.* a girl or woman servant.

mā·ieū′tiç, *a.* [Gr. *maieutikos,* pertaining to midwifery, from *maieuesthai,* to act as a midwife, from *maia,* a midwife.] designating or of the Socratic method of helping a person to bring forth and become aware of his latent ideas or memories.

mā·ieū′tiç·ăl, *a.* maieutic.

māi′gre (-gēr), *a.* [Fr. *maigre,* lean, spare; as a noun, lean meat, food other than meat.] fleshless; hence, suitable for eating on fast days; pertaining to a fast day.
maigre day; in the Roman Catholic Church, a day on which the use of meat as a food is forbidden.

māi′gre, *n.* a European food fish, *Sciæna aquila*.

māi′hem, *n.* same as *mayhem*.

Mā′ii·dae, *n.pl.* [*maia* and *-idæ*.] a family of decapod crustaceans with short tails, of which the genus *Maia* is typical.

mäi·kong′, *n.* [Guiana.] a wild dog, *Canis cancrivorus,* found in South America.

māil, *n.* [ME. *maile, male, maille*; OFr. *maile, maille,* a link, mesh; from L. *macula,* a spot, mesh of a net.]
1. one of the parts of a coat of mail, as a scale or link. [Obs.]
2. a flexible body of armor made of small, overlapping metal rings, loops of chain, or scales.
3. any defensive armor.
4. in zoology, the hard, bony, or chitinous covering of some animals, as the shell of a turtle or of a lobster.

CHAIN MAIL RING MAIL

māil, *v.t.*; mailed, *pt., pp.*; mailing, *ppr.* to cover or protect with or as with mail.

māil, *n.* [ME. *male*; OFr. *male, maile,* from LL. *mala,* a wallet; O.H.G. *malaha, malha,* a wallet.]
1. (a) [Obs. except Scot.] a bag or piece of baggage; (b) [Archaic.] a bag or packet of letters, etc. to be transported by post.
2. (a) letters, papers, packages, etc. handled, transported, and delivered by the post office; (b) letters, papers, etc. received by, or for, a person; as, my *mail* is full of bills.
3. a person or, especially, boat, train, etc. that transports letters, packages, etc.
4. the system of collection, transportation, and delivery of letters, packages, etc.; a postal system.
5. the collection or delivery of letters, packages, etc. at a certain time; as, the morning *mail* is late.

māil, *v.t.* to send by mail; to post; to turn over to the postal department for transmission.

māil, *a.* of mail; carrying, or used in the handling of, mail.

māil′ȧ·ble, *a.* that can be sent by mail.

māil′bag, *n.* a bag for carrying mail.

māil′bōat, *n.* a boat that transports mail: also *mail boat*.

māil′box, *n.* 1. a box or compartment into which mail is put when delivered, as at one's home.
2. a box, as on a street corner, into which mail is put for collection.
Also *mail box*.

māil çär, a railroad car equipped for handling mail.

māil′-cheeked′ (-chēkt′), *a.* having the sides of the head and jaws covered and protected by a hard plate, as in some fishes.

māil′çlad, *a.* covered with or as with a coat of mail.

māil çrāne, a crane for holding mailbags in position to be taken up by the mailcatchers of passing railroad trains.

māiled, *a.* 1. covered with or clad in mail or a maillike outer layer, as of scales.
2. spotted; speckled. [Obs.]

māiled fist, the use or threat of force, as between nations.

māil′ẽr, *n.* 1. a person who mails or addresses letters, etc.
2. a mailing machine.
3. an envelope or container in which something is to be mailed.
4. an advertising leaflet for mailing out.

māil′gram, *n.* a telegram delivered by the postal service with the regular mail: a trademark (*Mailgram*).

māil′ing mȧ·çhïne′, a machine for stamping or addressing letters, cards, etc.

māil′ing tūbe, a pasteboard cylinder in which printed matter or fragile objects are inserted for mailing.

mail·lōt′ (mī-yō′), *n.* [Fr., dim. from *maille,* knitted material, lit., mail.]
1. a swimming suit; especially, a one-piece swimming suit.
2. a garment like this, worn by gymnasts, etc.

māil′man, *n.*; *pl.* **māil′men,** a man whose work is carrying or delivering mail; a postman.

māil ọr′dẽr, an order for goods to be sent by mail.

māil′-ọr″dẽr, *a.* pertaining to a mail order.

māil′-ọr″dẽr house, a concern whose business consists of filling mail orders.

māil′plāne, *n.* an airplane that transports mail: also *mail plane*.

māil pouch, a strong mailbag fitted with a secure fastening and lock, used for carrying letters and valuables.

māil sack, a mailbag.

māil′shell, *n.* a gastropod mollusk with a chitinous dorsal shell consisting of eight movable plates: called also *chiton*.

māim, *v.t.*; maimed, *pt., pp.*; maiming, *ppr.* [ME. *maime, maine*; OFr. *mahaigner,* to maim; prob. of Celtic origin.]
1. to deprive of the use of a limb, so as to make a person less able to defend himself.
2. to deprive of a necessary part; to cripple; to mutilate; to disable.

māim, *n.* [ME. *maim, mayheym*; OFr. *mahaing, mehain,* a bodily defect through injury.]
1. an injury causing the loss or crippling of some necessary part of the body; mutilation; disablement. [Obs.]
2. injury; mischief; mayhem. [Obs.]
3. essential defect. [Obs.]

māim′ed·ly, *adv.* in a maimed manner.

māimed′ness, *n.* a state of being maimed.

Maī·mon·i·dē′ăn, *a.* relating to the rabbi Moses Maimonides of Spain, or to his philosophy of reform in Judaism.

māin, *a.* [ME. *mayn,* from Ice. *meginn, megn,* strong, mighty, influenced by OFr. *maine, magne,* great, chief, from L.*magnus,* great.]
1. originally, strong; powerful.
2. chief in size, extent, importance, etc.; principal; leading.
3. designating a broad expanse of land, sea, or space.
4. of, near, or connected with the mainmast or mainsail.
5. remarkable; considerable. [Brit. Dial.]
6. very essential, important, high in rank, etc. [Obs.]
by main force (or *strength*); by sheer or utter force (or strength).
main keel; the principal keel in a ship, as distinguished from the false keel.
Main Street; (a) the principal street in many towns and cities in the United States; (b) the typical inhabitants of a small town or rural community; (c) as an attribute, of any place, person, or thing that exhibits provincialism and narrow-mindedness; as, he has a *Main Street* attitude toward his sister's conduct.

māin, *n.* [AS. *mægen,* strength, power, force.]
1. strength; force; power: now only in the phrase *with might and main*.
2. the principal or most important part or point: usually in the phrase *in the main,* mostly, chiefly.
3. a principal pipe, conduit, or line in a distributing system for water, gas, electricity, etc.
4. a railroad trunk line.
5. the high, or open, sea; ocean. [Poet.]
6. in nautical usage, (a) mainmast; (b) mainsail.
7. the mainland. [Archaic.]
8. any broad expanse. [Obs.]
forcing main; in hydraulics, a pipe for receiving and conveying water under pressure.
hydraulic main; see under *hydraulic*.
with might and main; vigorously; with the use of all one's physical strength; strenuously.

māin, *n.* [prob. from *main, a.,* as in *main chance*.]
1. in dice playing, (a) a number called by a player before he throws; (b) a throw or match; (c) a stake played for.
2. a match at cockfighting.

māin, *adv.* very; exceedingly. [Dial.]

māin bēam, 1. the working beam in a steam engine.
2. in a ship, the beam forward of the main hatch, being the transverse measure of the ship.

māin bọom, the boom on which a fore-and-aft sail is extended.

māin brāce, 1. in mechanics, the brace sustaining the greater part of the strain.
2. in a ship, the brace sustaining the mainyard.

māin cen′tẽr, in a steam engine, the shaft of the working beam or of a similar lever.

māin çlause, in a complex sentence, a clause that can function syntactically as a complete sentence by itself; independent clause: distingusihed from *subordinate* (or *dependent*) clause. Example: *She will visit us* if she can.

māin çou′ple (kup′), the main truss of a roof.

māin çōurse, the mainsail of a square-rigged vessel.

māin deck, the principal deck of a vessel; specifically, (a) in a warship, the topmost deck, from stem to stern; (b) in a merchantman, the part of the upper deck between the forecastle and the poop.

māin drag, the principal street of a city or town. [Slang.]

māin′frāme, *n.* the central processing unit of a computer.

māin′lănd, *n.* the continent; the principal land, as opposed to an island or peninsula.

māin′līne, *n.* the principal road, course, etc.

māin′līne, *v.t.*; mainlined, *pt., pp.*; mainlining, *ppr.* to inject (a narcotic drug) directly into a large vein. [Slang.]

māin′ly, *adv.* 1. chiefly; principally.

2. (a) strongly; (b) very much. [Archaic.]

māin′măst, *n.* the principal mast of a vessel: in a schooner, brig, bark, etc., the mast second from the bow; in a ketch or yawl, the mast nearer the bow.

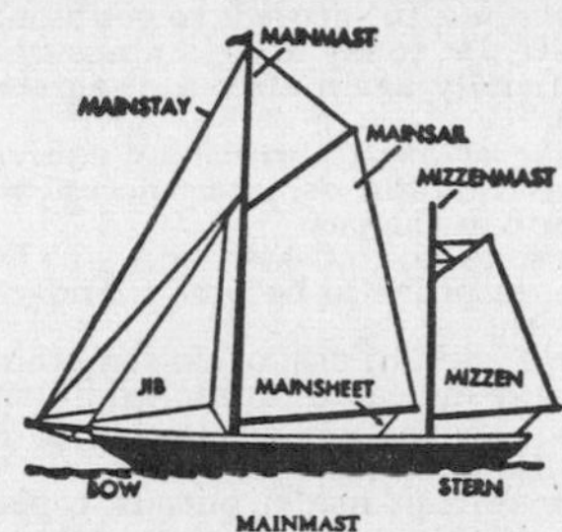

MAINMAST

māin′ŏur, māin′ŏr, *n.* [ME. *mainoure, meinoure*; OFr. *maineuvre, manovre*, work of the hand; *main*, hand, and *œuvre*, work.] in old English law, any stolen property found in the thief's possession upon his arrest.

to be taken with the mainour; to be taken in the very act of stealing or with the thing stolen.

māin′pẽr·nŏr, *n.* [OFr. *mainpernour, mainpreneur*, from *mainprendre*, to take surety.] in law, formerly, a surety for a prisoner's appearance in court at a fixed day.

māin′prīṣe, māin′prīze, *n.* [OFr. *mainprise, meinprise*, surety, bail, from *mainprendre*; *main*, hand, and *prendre*, to take.] in law, formerly, a writ directed to the sheriff, commanding him to take sureties or mainpernors for the prisoner's appearance, and to let him go at large.

māin′prīṣe, māin′prīze, *v.t.* to suffer (a prisoner) to go at large on his finding sureties or mainpernors for his appearance at a day.

māinṣ, *n.* the lands attached to a home. [Scot. and Brit. Dial.]

māin′sāil (*or* -sl), *n.* the principal sail in a ship: the mainsail of a square-rigged vessel is extended by a yard attached to the mainmast, and that of a fore-and-aft rig by the main boom.

māin′sheet, *n.* the sheet or rope that extends and fastens the mainsail.

māin′spring, *n.* 1. the principal spring in a clock, watch, or other mechanism; the driving spring, by the steady uncoiling of which the mechanism is kept going.

2. the chief motive, incentive, or impelling cause; as, profit is the *mainspring* of business.

māin′stāy, *n.* 1. in a ship, the cable that runs forward from the mainmast of a vessel, serving to support or stay it.

2. the principal means of support.

māin stem, same as *main drag*. [Slang.]

māin·tāin′, *v.t.*; maintained, *pt., pp.*; maintaining, *ppr.* [ME. *mainteinen*; OFr. *maintenir*, to keep, maintain, from L. *manu tenere*, to hold in hand; *manu*, abl. of *manus*, hand, and *tenere*, to hold.]

1. to keep or keep up; to continue in or with; to carry on.

2. (a) to keep in existence or continuance; as, food *maintains* life; (b) to keep in a certain condition or position, especially of efficiency, good repair, etc.; to preserve; as, the state *maintains* the roads.

3. to keep or hold (a place, position, etc.) against attack; to defend.

4. to uphold or defend, as by argument; to declare to be true; to affirm; as, he *maintains* his contentions.

5. to support by aid, influence, protection, etc.

6. to support by providing means of existence; to bear the expenses of; as, he can't *maintain* his family.

māin·tāin′, *v.i.* 1. to affirm a position; to assert.

2. to preserve one's bearing.

māin·tāin′ȧ·ble, *a.* that may be maintained, supported, preserved, or sustained.

māin·tāin′ẽr, *n.* one who supports, preserves, sustains, or vindicates.

māin·tāin′ŏr, *n.* in law, one who aids others with money, or maintains them in a suit in which he has no interest.

māin′te·nănce, *n.* [OFr. *maintenance*, from *maintenir*, to maintain.]

1. a maintaining or being maintained; upkeep, support, defense, etc.

2. means of support or sustenance; livelihood; as, her job provided a mere *maintenance*.

3. in common law, support or assistance that a person is legally bound to give to another or others.

4. in criminal law, the act of interfering unlawfully in a suit between others by helping either party, as by giving money, etc., to carry it on.

cap of maintenance; see under *cap*.

māin′te·nănce of mem′bẽr·ship, in some union contracts, a provision by which all employees who are already members of the union, and all who join during the time covered by the contract, must remain members and pay dues or be discharged by the employer.

māin′top, *n.* a platform at the head of the lower section of the mainmast.

māin′top·gal′lănt (*or* mān′tȧ-gal′ănt), *n.* the mast, sail, or yard above a ship's maintopmast.

māin·top′măst, *n.* the section of the mainmast above the maintop.

māin·top′sāil (*or* -top′sl), *n.* the sail above the mainsail on the mainmast.

māin′-trav·eled, māin′-trav·elled, *a.* much traveled on: said of roads, etc.

māin yärd, the yard on which the mainsail is extended, supported by the mainmast.

māi′oid, *a.* [Gr. *maia*, a large kind of crab, and *eidos*, form.] characteristic of or relating to the genus *Maia* or to the family *Maiidæ*.

māi′oid, *n.* one of the *Maiidæ*.

māir, *a.* more. [Scot.]

mai·son′ de san·té′ (mā-zôn′ dē sän-tā′), [Fr., lit., house of health.] a hospital or sanitarium.

māist *a.* most. [Scot.]

māis′tẽr, *n.* master. [Obs.]

māis′tresse, *n.* mistress. [Obs.]

maî′tre d'hô·tel′ (me′tr dō-tel′), [Fr., lit., master of the house.]

1. a butler or steward; major-domo.

2. a hotel manager.

3. a headwaiter.

4. (with) a sauce of melted butter, parsley, and lemon juice or vinegar.

māize, *n.* [Sp. *maiz*; W. Ind. *mahiz, mahis*, the native name of the plant.]

1. a plant, *Zea mays*, the native corn of America, much cultivated for food; Indian corn; also, its ears of kernels or the kernels themselves.

2. its color (when ripe); yellow.

māize, *a.* yellow.

māize′bird, *n.* a red-winged blackbird, named from its fondness for corn: also called *maize thief*.

māize smut, a species of smut or parasitic fungus that attacks maize.

māize yel′lōw, the name of a light yellow color corresponding to that of the ripe grains of yellow corn.

MAIZE (*Zea mays*)

mȧ·jes′tiç, *a.* having or characterized by majesty; stately; noble; august.

mȧ·jes′tiç·ăl, *a.* majestic.

mȧ·jes′tiç·ăl·ly, *adv.* with dignity; with grandeur; with a lofty air or appearance.

mȧ·jes′tiç·ăl·ness, *n.* the state or quality of being majestic.

mȧ·jes′tiç·ness, *n.* majesticalness. [Rare.]

maj′es·ty, *n.*; *pl.* **maj′es·tieṣ,** [OFr. *majestet*; L. *majestas* (-*atis*), greatness, grandeur, from *majus*, neut. of *major*, comp. of *magnus*, great.]

1. loftiness of appearance; dignity; grandeur; stateliness; nobility.

2. (a) the dignity or power of a sovereign; (b) sovereign power; as, the *majesty* of the law; (c) a sovereign.

3. [M-] a title used in speaking to or of a sovereign, preceded by *His, Her*, or *Your*.

4. in heraldry, the condition of an eagle, crowned, and holding a scepter.

AN EAGLE IN HER MAJESTY

mȧ·jol′i·çȧ, *n.* [It. *majolica*, from the earlier name of *Majorca*, whence the first specimens came.] a kind of enameled decorative pottery first made in Italy in the fifteenth century and imitated in modern times.

mā′jŏr, *a.* [L., comp. of *magnus*, great.]

1. (a) greater in size, amount, number, or extent; (b) greater in importance or rank. Opposed to *minor*.

2. of full legal age.

3. constituting the majority: said of a part, etc.

4. in education, designating a field of study in which a student specializes and receives his degree.

5. in logic, broader; more inclusive.

6. in music, (a) designating an interval higher than the minor by a half tone; (b) designating a tone distant by a major interval from another tone; (c) characterized by major intervals, scales, or tones; as, the *major* mode or key; (d) based on the scale pattern of the major mode: see *major scale*.

major axis; see *transverse axis* under *axis*.

major offense; in law, an offense including or implying a less offense, as robbery by housebreaking.

major sixth; a sixth consisting of two tones separated in pitch by four and one-half intervals or steps.

major third; in music, a third consisting of two tones separated in pitch by two intervals or steps.

mā′jŏr, *n.* [Fr. *major*, from L. *major*, an elder, adult (LL., also, a chief officer), properly comp. of *magnus*, great.]

1. a superior in some class or group.

2. in military affairs, an officer next in rank above a captain and below a lieutenant colonel.

3. in education, the special branch of learning which is selected by a candidate for a degree; also, a person specializing in a (specified) subject; as, he's a biology *major*.

4. in law, a person having arrived at his majority (full legal age).

5. in logic, a major term or premise.

6. in music, a major interval, key, mode, etc.

mā′jŏr, *v.i.*; majored, *pt., pp.*; majoring, *ppr.* to follow a course of study with a certain subject or branch of subjects as a major: used with *in*; as, he *majored in* chemistry.

mȧ·jō·rät′ (mȧ-zō-rä′), *n.* [Fr. *majorat*; LL. *majoratus*, pp. of *majorare*, to make greater, increase, from L. *major*, greater.]

1. in some continental countries of Europe, the right of succession to property according to age.

2. formerly, in France, property attaching to a title and descending with it.

mā·jŏr·ā′tion, *n.* increase; enlargement. [Obs.]

Mȧ·jor′căn, *a.* relating to Majorca.

Mȧ·jor′căn, *n.* a native or inhabitant of Majorca.

mā·jŏr-dō′mō, *n.*; *pl.* **mā·jŏr-dō′mōṣ,** [Sp. *mayordomo*; ML. *major domus*, from L. *major*, greater, an elder, and *domus*, genit. of *domus*, house.]

1. a man in charge of a great, royal, or noble household; chief steward.

2. a steward or butler: humorous usage.

mā′jŏr ġen′ẽr·ăl, *pl.* **mā′jŏr ġen′ẽr·alṣ,** a military officer next in rank below a lieutenant general and above a brigadier general.

Mā′jŏr·ist, *n.* a follower of and a believer in the doctrines of a German theologian, Georg Major (1502–1574), who taught that good works were a necessary result of Christian faith and were therefore essential to salvation.

mȧ·jor·i·tār′i·ăn, *a.* [*majority* and *-arian.*] of or decided by the majority.

mȧ·jor·i·tār′i·ăn, *n.* an advocate of majoritarian rule.

mȧ·jor′i·ty, *n.*; *pl.* **mȧ·jor′i·tieṣ,** [ML. *majoritas*, from L. *major*, greater, comp. of *magnus*, great.]

1. the greater part or larger number; more

than half; as, a *majority* of votes in Congress: opposed to *minority*.

2. the excess of the larger number of votes cast for one candidate, bill, etc. over all the rest of the votes: if candidate A gets 100 votes, candidate B, 200, and candidate C, 350, C has a majority of 50.

3. the group, party, or faction with the larger number of votes.

4. the full legal age, at which one is legally no longer a minor; as, he reached his *majority* at the age of 21.

5. the military rank or position of a major.

6. the state, quality, or fact of being greater; superiority. [Obs.]

7. ancestors; ancestry. [Obs.]

to join the (great) majority; to die.

mā′jŏr-lēague′ (-lēg′), *a.* of, in, or suitable to a major league or leagues.

mā′jŏr lēagues, the two main leagues of professional baseball clubs in the United States, the National League and the American League.

mā′jŏr prem′ise (-is), the premise (in a syllogism) that contains the major term.

mā′jŏr scāle, one of the two standard diatonic musical scales, consisting of eight tones with half steps instead of whole steps after the third and seventh tones: distinguished from *minor scale*.

mā′jŏr·ship, *n.* the position or rank of a major.

mā′jŏr sūit, in bridge, spades or hearts: so called from their higher value in scoring.

mā′jŏr tērm, the predicate of the conclusion of a syllogism.

maj·oūn′, *n.* same as *majun*.

maj·ūn, *n.* [Turk. *ma'jūn*, paste, putty, a kind of taffy.] in the East Indies, a confection compounded from Indian hemp and other narcotic plants, mixed with sugar or honey.

mȧ·jus′çū·lȧ, *n.*; *pl.* **mȧ·jus′çū·lae**, [L. *majuscula*.] a majuscule.

mȧ·jus′çū·lăr, *a.* 1. of, or having the nature of, a majuscule.

2. written in majuscules.

mȧ·jus′çūle, *n.* [Fr.; L. *majuscula*, fem. of *majusculus*, somewhat larger, dim. from *major*.]

1. a large letter, capital or uncial, as in medieval manuscripts.

2. writing in which such letters are used.

mȧ·jus′çūle, *a.* majuscular.

māk′ȧ·ble, *a.* such as may be made; capable of being devised or manufactured.

Mȧ·kȧs′săr oil, an oil originally obtained from Macassar, probably derived from the sandalwood tree: it was much used in hair dressing: now the term is applied to a substitute consisting of coconut oil, olive oil, or castor oil, highly perfumed.

māke, *v.t.*; made, *pt.*, *pp.*; making, *ppr.* [ME. *maken*, *makien*; AS. *macian*, to make; compare AS. *genæc*, fit, suitable.]

1. to bring into being; specifically, (a) to form by shaping or putting parts or ingredients together, physically or mentally; to build, construct, fabricate, fashion, create, compose, devise, formulate, etc.; (b) to cause; bring about; produce; as, what *made* this sudden change?

2. to bring into a specified condition; specifically, (a) to cause to be or become; as, they *made* him president; (b) to cause to seem; as, this portrait *makes* her an old woman. Sometimes used reflexively; as, *make* yourself comfortable.

3. to prepare for use; to arrange; as, *make* the beds.

4. (a) to amount to; to add up to; to form as a total; as, four quarts *make* a gallon; (b) to count as; to constitute; as, this *made* the tenth and last of his novels.

5. to turn out to be; to have, or prove to have, the essential qualities of; as, he will *make* a good doctor.

6. to set up; to establish; as, we *made* a rule that only members might attend.

7. (a) to get or acquire, as by one's behavior; as, he *made* many friends; (b) to get by earning, etc.; as, we all want to *make* money.

8. to cause the success of; as, this lucky venture *made* him.

9. to understand or regard as the meaning (*of*); as, what do you *make of* his queer actions?

10. to estimate to be; to regard as; as, I *make* the distance about 500 miles.

11. (a) to do or perform (the action indicated by the object); to execute; accomplish; as, she *made* a quick movement; (b) to engage in; to carry on; as, *make* war.

12. to deliver (a speech) or utter (remarks, etc.).

13. to cause or force to: followed by an infinitive without *to*; as, *make* the machine work, *make* him behave.

14. (a) to arrive at; to reach; as, the ship *made* port; (b) to arrive at in time; as, he *made* the train; (c) to arrive at and do business in; as, the salesman *made* six towns on this trip.

15. (a) to go; travel; traverse; as, they *made* the distance in five hours; (b) to go or travel at (a specified speed); as, my car can *make* 90 miles an hour.

16. to succeed in getting membership in, a position on, the status of, recognition in, etc.; as, he *made* the team, she *made* the headlines. [Colloq.]

17. to succeed in becoming the lover of. [Slang.]

18. in card playing, (a) to win (tricks); (b) to take a trick with (a card); (c) to name (the trump or a bid); (d) to shuffle (the cards).

19. in electricity, to close (a circuit); to effect (a contact).

20. in games, to score; to get as a score.

21. in law, (a) to perform, execute, or sign (a will or other legal instrument); (b) to do (what one has bound himself to do). To *make oath* is to swear in the legally prescribed form; to *make default* is to fail in a prescribed or accepted duty.

to make a clean sweep; to sweep every obstruction away; to leave nothing to hinder; to win all the events, prizes, offices, etc. possible.

to make a fool (or *ass*, etc.) *of*; to cause to seem a fool (or ass, etc.).

to make a hit; to prove successful; to please greatly. [Colloq.]

to make a meal on (or *of*); to eat as a meal.

to make believe; to endeavor to induce belief by pretending; to simulate.

to make heavy weather; in nautical usage, to pitch and roll, as in rough water.

to make it; to do or achieve a certain thing. [Colloq.]

to make little of; (a) to depreciate; (b) to accomplish without difficulty.

to make much of; to value highly or enjoy greatly; also, to give earnest attention to.

to make no difference; to be a matter of little importance.

to make no doubt; to be without doubt.

to make no matter; to be without importance.

to make one's mark; to rise to distinction.

to make or break; to cause the success or failure of.

to make out; (a) to see with some difficulty; to descry; (b) to understand; (c) to write out; (d) to fill out (a blank form, etc.); (e) to show or prove to be; (f) to try to show, affirm, or imply to be.

to make over; (a) to change; to renovate; (b) to transfer the ownership of by or as by signing a legal document.

to make sail; in navigation, to put on more sail; also, to hoist sail for departure from a port.

to make shift; to devise some expedient in an emergency.

to make suit to; to seek favor in courtship.

to make the feathers fly; to engage in furious conflict, creating commotion, as of birds fighting: applied to verbal as well as to physical conflict.

to make things hum; to create great activity in any business; to keep everything moving at a rapid rate. [Colloq.]

to make up; (a) to put together; compose; compound; (b) to form; constitute; (c) to invent; create; (d) to complete by providing what is lacking; (e) to arrange; (f) to settle (an argument or differences) in a friendly manner; (g) to put on the required costume, cosmetics, etc. for a role in a play; also, to put cosmetics on; (h) to resolve to decide (one's mind); (i) to select and arrange type, illustrations, etc. for (a book, magazine, page, etc.); (j) in education, to take again (an examination or course that one has failed) or to take (an examination that one has missed).

to make water; (a) in a ship, to spring a leak; to admit water into the hull; (b) to discharge urine.

to make way; to go ahead.

to make words; to be loquacious; to engage in wordy discussion.

māke, *v.i.* 1. to start (to do something); as, she *made* to go.

2. (a) to go; proceed; as, he *made* for the door; (b) to tend, extend, or point (*to*, *toward*, etc.).

3. to behave in a specified manner: with a following adjective; as, *make* bold, *make* merry, etc.

4. to cause something to be in a specified condition; as, *make* ready, *make* fast, etc.

5. to increase in depth or volume; to rise or accumulate, as tide, snow, water in a ship, etc.

6. to mature: said of hay, etc.

to make after; to chase or follow.

to make against; to be unfavorable to; to tend to injure.

to make as if (or *as though*); to behave as if.

to make at; to approach with violent intent.

to make away with; see under *away*.

to make for; (a) to head for; go toward; (b) to charge at; attack; (c) to tend toward; help effect.

to make like; to imitate; impersonate. [Slang.]

to make off; to go away; run away.

to make off with; to steal.

to make out; to succeed; to get along.

to make up; to lay aside animosity and become friendly again after a disagreement or quarrel.

to make up for; to furnish an equivalent or compensation for; as, later success *makes up for* failure in the past.

to make up to; to flatter, or try to be agreeable to, in order to become friendly or intimate with.

to make with; to use, or do something with, in the way indicated or implied. [Slang.]

māke, *n.* 1. the act or process of making; especially, manufacture.

2. the amount made; output, especially of manufacture.

3. the way in which something is made; style; build.

4. type, sort, or brand: with reference to the maker or the place, time, etc. of making; as, an automobile of English *make*.

5. disposition; character; nature; as, a man of this *make*.

6. in bridge, the declaration.

7. in electricity, the closing of a circuit by making contact.

on the make; (a) [Colloq.] trying to succeed financially, socially, etc.: usually derogatory, implying pushing behavior and neglect of other values; (b) [Slang.] trying to get a lover.

māke, *n.* [ME.; AS. *gemaca* and cognate ON. *maki*.]

1. an equal; a peer. [Obs. or Brit. Dial.]

2. a mate, companion, consort, or spouse. [Obs. or Brit. Dial.]

māke ănd breāk, in electricity, a device by which a circuit may be made and broken at regular intervals, usually acting automatically by means of an electromagnet and a spring.

māke′bāte, *n.* one who excites contentions and quarrels. [Obs.]

māke′-bē·liēve″, *n.* 1. pretense; feigning.

2. a pretender.

māke′-bē·liēve″, *a.* pretended; unreal; feigned.

māke′fȧst, *n.* a buoy, post, pile, etc. to which a boat is fastened.

māke′gāme, *n.* one who is made an object of ridicule.

māke′less, *a.* without a mate. [Obs.]

māke′-pēace, *n.* a peacemaker.

māk′ẽr, *n.* 1. a person or thing that makes (in various senses).

2. [M–] God.

3. a poet. [Archaic.]

4. in law, the signer of a promissory note.

māke′-read″y (-red″), *n.* in printing, the operation of leveling a type form by the use of overlays and underlays to obtain a clean impression; also, the sheet or sheets used.

māke′shift, *n.* a thing that will do for a while as a substitute; a temporary expedient.

māke′shift, *a.* that will do for a while as a substitute.

māke′-up, *n.* 1. the way in which something is put together; composition; construction.

2. nature; disposition; constitution; as, he has a stolid *make-up*.

3. (a) the way in which an actor is costumed, painted, etc. for a role; (b) the costumes, cosmetics, etc. used.

4. (a) cosmetics generally; rouge, lipstick, mascara, etc.; (b) the way in which these are applied or worn.

5. the arrangement of type, illustrations, etc. in a book, newspaper, page, etc.
6. a special test taken by a student to make up for a test that he has missed or failed to pass. [Colloq.]

māke′-up, *a.* of or for making up.

māke′weight (-wāt), *n.* 1. that which is put into a scale to complete the required weight.
2. an unimportant person or thing added to make up some lack.

māke′-wŏrk, *a.* designating a job, project, assignment, etc. that serves no useful purpose other than to give an otherwise idle or unemployed person something to do.

mä′ki, *n.* [Malagasy.] an animal of the genus *Lemur*; specifically, the ring-tailed lemur, *Lemur catta.*

RINGED-TAILED MAKI (*Lemur catta*)

mä″ki·mō′nō, *n.* [Japan.] a Japanese art scroll which is intended to be held in the hands while being examined.

māk′ing, *n.* 1. the act of one that makes or the process of being made; formation, construction, creation, production, composition, manufacture, development, performance, etc.
2. the cause or means of success or advancement; as, this experience will be the *making* of him.
3. (a) something made; (b) the quantity made at one time; (c) [*pl.*] earnings; profits.
4. (a) [*often pl.*] the material or qualities needed for the making or development of something; as, he has the *making(s)* of a good doctor; (b) [*pl.*] [Colloq.] tobacco and paper for making cigarettes.
5. a poem. [Obs.]

māk′ing ī′ron (-ūrn), a chisel-shaped tool with a fluted face used to finish the calking in the seams of a wooden ship.

māk′ing-up, *n.* 1. the act of becoming friendly after estrangement.
2. the reducing of spirits to a standard of strength, usually called proof.

mal-, [Fr. *mal-*; L. *male-*, from *male*, adv., badly, from *malus*, bad.] a prefix meaning *bad* or *badly, wrong, ill,* as in *mal*feasance, *mal*adroit: also, *male-*, as in *male*diction, *male*ficient.

mā′lȧ, *n.pl.*; *sing.* **mā′lum,** evils.
mala in se; evils in themselves; in law, offenses against common law without respect to statute.
mala prohibita; in law, offenses differing from *mala in se* in that they are prohibited by statute.

mal′ăc-, see *malaco-*.

mal·ȧ·çȧ·tūne′, *n.* same as *melocoton.*

Mȧ·laç′çȧ çane, [from the city of *Malacca.*] a lightweight walking stick of rattan, often mottled brown.

mȧ·lā′ceous, *a.* [from L. *malum*, an apple; and *-aceous.*] of the apple family of plants and trees.

Mal′ȧ·çhī, *n.* [Heb. *malākhī*, lit., my messenger.]
1. a Hebrew prophet of the fifth century B.C.: the last of the minor prophets.
2. a book of the Old Testament attributed to him.

mal′ȧ·çhīte, *n.* [Gr. *malachē*, mallow, and *-ite*: so called from its resembling the color of the leaf of the mallow.] native basic copper carbonate, $CuCO_3 \cdot Cu(OH)_2$, a mineral occurring in green mammillary masses, consisting of concentric layers having a fibrous structure. It takes a high polish, and is used for making ornamental articles.

mal′ȧ·çhīte green, 1. malachite, or its color.
2. an aniline dyestuff producing a brilliant green, or the color thus produced.

mȧ·lā′ci·ȧ, *n.* [Gr. *malakos*, soft.] in medicine, a morbid softening of tissue.

mal′ȧ·çō-, [from Gr. *malakos*, soft.] a combining form meaning: (a) *soft*, as in *malaco*pterygian; (b) *mollusks*, as in *malaco*logy: also, before a vowel, *malac-*.

Mal″ȧ·çob·del′lȧ, *n.* [*malaco-*, and Gr. *bdella*, a leech.] a genus of leechlike worms found in bivalve mollusks.

mal′ȧ·çō·dērm, *n.* [*malaco-*, and Gr. *derma* (*-atos*), skin.]
1. in zoology, a beetle with a soft body.
2. one of a division of animals with soft coverings.

mal″ȧ·çō·dēr′mȧ·tous, *a.* in zoology, having a soft, flexible covering.

Mal″ȧ·çō·dēr′mī, *n.pl.* a section of the *Coleoptera*, composed of beetles having soft, flexible bodies.

mal′ȧ·çoid, *a.* [Gr. *malakos*, soft, and *eidos*, form.] in biology, having a soft body; soft in texture: said of both animals and plants.

mal′ȧ·çō·līte, *n.* [Gr. *malachē*, mallow, and *lithos*, stone: so called from its color.] a variety of pyroxene.

mal·ȧ·çol′ō·ġist, *n.* one who is a student of or specialist in malacology.

mal·ȧ·çol′ō·ġy, *n.* [*malaco-*, and *-logy.*] the branch of zoology dealing with mollusks.

Mal·ȧ·çop′ō·dȧ, *n.pl.* [*malaco-*, and Gr. *pous*, *podos*, foot.] in zoology, a class of air-breathing arthropods of a single genus, *Peripatus*, having flexible bodies with many pairs of short legs and a pair of prominent antennae.

mal·ȧ·çop′ō·dous, *a.* having the characteristics of the *Malacopoda.*

mal·ȧ·çop′tēr·ous, *a.* [*malaco-*, and Gr. *pteron*, a wing.] of or pertaining to the *Malacopterygii.*

mal·ȧ·çop·tēr·yġ′i·ăn, *n.* one of the order of the *Malacopterygii.*

mal·ȧ·çop·tēr·yġ′i·ăn, *a.* soft-finned; having the characteristics of the *Malacopterygii.*

Mal·ȧ·çop·tēr·yġ′i·ī, *n.pl.* [*malaco-*, and Gr. *pterygion*, dim. of *pteryx*, a wing, fin.] a group of fishes characterized chiefly by their soft or spineless fins.

mal·ȧ·çop·tēr·yġ′i·ous, *a.* see *malacopterygian.*

mal·ȧ·çō′sis, *n.* [Gr. *malakos*, soft, and *-osis.*] in pathology, a softening of tissue, as of the brain or of an artery; malacia.

mal·ȧ·ços′tē·on, *n.* [*malac-*, and Gr. *osteon*, bone.] in pathology, softening and weakening of osseous tissue; malacia of the bones.

mal·ȧ·ços′tō·mous, *a.* having soft jaws without teeth, as a fish.

Mal·ȧ·ços′trȧ·çȧ, *n.pl.* [Gr. *malakostrakos*, soft-shelled; *malakos*, soft, and *ostrakon*, a shell.] one of the principal divisions of crustaceans, embracing crabs, shrimps, lobsters, etc.

mal·ȧ·ços′trȧ·çăn, *n.* a crustacean belonging to the division *Malacostraca.*

mal·ȧ·ços′trȧ·çăn, *a.* of or pertaining to the malacostracans.

mal·ȧ·ços·trȧ·çol′ō·ġy, *n.* [*malac-*, and Gr. *ostrakon*, shell, and *-logia*, from *legein*, to speak.] the systematic study of *Crustacea.*

mal·ȧ·ços′trȧ·çous, *a.* belonging to or characteristic of the *Malacostraca.*

mal·ȧ·çō·toon′, *n.* same as *melocoton.*

Mal″ȧ·çō·zō′ȧ, *n.pl.* [*malaco-*, and Gr. *zōon* (pl. *zōa*), an animal.] a group of soft-bodied animals, including mollusks, brachiopods, and polyzoans.

mal″ȧ·çō·zō′iç, *a.* relating to the *Malacozoa.*

mal·ȧ·dapt′ed, *a.* not suited or properly adapted (to a function, situation, etc.)

mal·ad·dress′, *n.* bad, awkward, or ungracious manner of address; tactless behavior.

mal·ad·just′ed, *a.* poorly adjusted.

mal·ad·just′ment, *n.* poor adjustment, especially to the environment.

mal·ad·min′is·tēr, *v.t.* to administer badly; to conduct without efficiency or honesty.

mal·ad·min·is·trā′tion, *n.* [*mal-* and *administration.*] bad management of public affairs; vicious or defective conduct in administration or the performance of official duties.

mal·ȧ·droit′, *a.* [Fr., from *mal*, bad, and *adroit*, skillful, adroit.] lacking adroitness; clumsy; awkward; bungling: opposed to *adroit.*

mal·ȧ·droit′ly, *adv.* in an awkward manner.

mal·ȧ·droit′ness, *n.* awkwardness; clumsiness.

mal′ȧ·dy, *n.*; *pl.* **mal′ȧ·dieș,** [ME. *maladye*; OFr. *maladie*, sickness, disease, from L. *male habitus*, out of condition; *male*, badly, and *habitus*, held, pp. of *habere*, to hold.]
1. any sickness or disease; an illness.
The *maladies* of the body may prove medicines to the mind. —Buckminster.
2. moral defect or corruption.

Mal′ȧ·gȧ, *n.* 1. a species of white wine, originally from Malaga, in Spain.
2. a white grape from which Malaga is made.

Mal·ȧ·gas′y, *a.* of or pertaining to Madagascar or the language of the Madagascans.

Mal·ȧ·gas′y, *n.*; *pl.* **Mal·ȧ·gas′y** or **Mal·ȧ·gas′ieș,** a Madagascan; the Madagascans; also, the language of the Madagascans.

mal·ȧ·guẹ′ñȧ (-gān′yȧ), *n.* [Sp. *malagueña*, orig. fem. of *malagueño*, of Málaga (seaport in Spain).] any of several Spanish folk tunes or dances, especially one like the fandango.

mȧ·lāiṣe′, *n.* [Fr., uneasiness, discomfort.] a vague feeling of physical discomfort or uneasiness, as before an illness.

mȧ·lam′bō, *n.* [Port.] the aromatic bark of a shrub in South America, used in medicine and in making perfumery.

mä′lȧ·mūte, *n.* [from native name.] a large, strong Alaskan dog with a thick coat of gray or black-and-white fur: also spelled *malemute, malemiut.*

mal′ăn·dērș, mal′lăn·dērș, *n.pl.* [Fr. *malandre*, from L. *malandria*, blisters or pustules on the neck, especially of horses.] a disease in horses, consisting of ulcerous chaps on the inside of the forelegs: compare *sallenders.*

mal′ȧ·pērt, *a.* [OFr. *malapert*, over-ready, impudent; *mal*, badly, and *apert*, open, adroit.] saucy; impertinent; without respect or decency; bold; forward. [Archaic.]

mal′ȧ·pērt, *n.* a saucy, impudent person. [Archaic.]

mal′ȧ·pērt·ly, *adv.* saucily; with impudence. [Archaic.]

mal′ȧ·pērt·ness, *n.* sauciness; impudent pertness or forwardness. [Archaic.]

mal′ȧ·prop·ișm, *n.* [after Mrs. *Malaprop* in Sheridan's play *The Rivals.*]
1. ridiculous misuse of words, especially through confusion caused by resemblance in sound.
2. an instance of this (e.g., *progeny* for *prodigy*).

mal″ap·rō·pōs′ (-pō′), *adv.* [Fr. *mal à propos*; *mal*, bad, ill, and *à*, to, and *propos*, purpose.] in an inopportune or inappropriate manner; unseasonably; unsuitably.

mal″ap·rō·pōs′, *a.* at an awkward or improper time or place; inopportune; inappropriate.

Mal·ap·te·rū′rus, *n.* [Gr. *malakos*, soft, and *pteron*, wing, fin, and *oura*, tail.] a genus of African catfishes characterized by an adipose dorsal fin near the tail and an electric apparatus connected with the tail: also called *electric catfish.*

mā′lăr, *a.* [L. *mala*, the cheek.] of the cheek, the cheekbone, or the side of the head.

mā′lăr, *n.* the cheekbone.

mȧ·lăr′i·ȧ, *n.* [Fr. *malaria*, from It. *mal'aria*, lit., bad air.]
1. unwholesome or poisonous air, as from marshy ground; miasma.
2. [from the former notion that it was caused by the bad air of swamps.] an infectious disease, generally intermittent and recurrent, caused by any of various protozoa that are parasitic in the red blood corpuscles and are transmitted to man by the bite of an infected anopheles mosquito: it is characterized by severe chills and fever.

mȧ·lăr′i·ăl, *a.* 1. of, having the nature of, or caused by malaria.
2. having malaria.

mȧ·lăr′i·ăn, *a.* malarial.

mȧ·lăr′i·ous, *a.* malarial.

mȧ·lär′kēy, mȧ·lär′ky, *n.* insincere or meaningless talk; nonsense; buncombe. [Slang.]

mal·as·sim·i·lā′tion, *n.* [*mal-*, and *assimilation.*] in pathology, imperfect or incomplete assimilation or nutrition; faulty digestion, conversion, and appropriation of nutriment.

mal′āte, *n.* [*mal*ic and *-ate.*] a salt or ester of malic acid.

mal·ȧ·thī′on, *n.* [from *mal*ic acid, and *thion*ic.] an organic phosphate, $C_{10}H_{19}O_6S_2P$, of relatively low toxicity for mammals, used as an insecticide.

mal′ax·āte, *v.t.* [L. *malaxatus*, pp. of *malaxare*, to soften.] to soften; to knead to softness.

mal·ax·ā′tion, *n.* the act of moistening and softening; the forming of ingredients into a mass for pills or plasters.

mal′ax·ā·tŏr, *n.* a mixing machine, as a grinder in brickmaking.

Mȧ·lax′is, *n.* a genus of small terrestrial orchids of the family *Orchidaceae*: also called *Microstylis.*

Mā′lāy, Mȧ·lāy′, *n.* [Malay *malāyu.*] 1. a member of a large group of brown-skinned, short, black-haired peoples living in the Malay Peninsula, the Malay Archipelago, and near-by islands.
2. their Indonesian language, widely used in the Far East as a trade language.
3. one of an oriental breed of game fowls.

Mā′lāy, Mȧ·lāy′, *a.* of the Malays, their country, language, culture, etc.
malay apple; in botany, a tree, *Eugenia mal-*

accensis, or its applelike fruit. The tree is found in the Pacific islands, where it is cultivated for the fruit.

Mal·ȧ·yä′lȧm, *n.* a Dravidian language spoken on the Malabar Coast, southeastern India.

Mȧ·lāy′ăn, *n.* and *a.* Malay.

Mȧ·lāy′ō-, a combining form meaning *Malay*, *Malay and*.

Mȧ·lāy′ō-Pol·y·nē′siăn, *a.* Austronesian.

Mȧ·lāy′siăn, *a.* of Malaysia, its peoples, or their culture.

Mȧ·lāy′siăn, *n.* a native of Malaysia.

mal′brouk, *n.* [Fr.] an ape of the genus *Cercocebus*.

Mal′chus, *n.* a short two-edged sword, such as medieval artists represented as being in the hand of St. Peter when he cut off the ear of Malchus.

mal″con·fọr·mā′tion, *n.* [*mal-* and *conformation*.] ill form; disproportion of parts.

mal′cŏn·tent, *n.* a discontented, dissatisfied, or rebellious person; especially, a discontented subject of government.

mal′cŏn·tent, *a.* [*mal-* and *content*.] discontented with the laws or the administration of government; uneasy; dissatisfied; rebellious.

mal·cŏn·tent′ed, *a.* malcontent.

mal·cŏn·tent′ed·ly, *adv.* in a discontented manner.

mal·cŏn·tent′ed·ness, *n.* the state or quality of being malcontent.

māl dē mer, [Fr.] seasickness.

māl dů pays (pā-ē′), [Fr.] homesickness.

male-, see *mal-*.

māle, *a.* [OFr. *male*, *masle*, from L. *masculus*, male, from *mas*, *maris*, a male, a man.]

1. designating or of the sex that fertilizes the ovum and begets offspring: opposed to *female*.
2. of, characteristic of, or suitable for members of this sex; masculine; virile.
3. strong; vigorous.
4. consisting of men or boys.
5. in botany, (a) designating or of fertilizing bodies, organs, or parts; as, *male* gametes; (b) designating plants with such organs; having stamens but no pistil.
6. in mechanics, designating or having a part shaped to fit into a corresponding hollow part (called *female*): said of a gauge, etc.

male coffee berry; in botany, a berry of the coffee tree, spheroid in shape and resembling a pea; a peaberry.

male fern; in botany, a species of *Aspidium* used in medicine for the extermination of tapeworm.

male rhyme; same as *masculine rhyme*.

māle, *n.* a male person, animal, or plant.

mȧ·lē′āte, *n.* [*male*ic and *-ate*.] a salt of maleic acid.

mal·ē·dī′cen·cy, *n.* [L. *maledicentia*; *male*, badly, and *dicens* (*-entis*), ppr. of *dicere*, to speak.] the practice of evil-speaking; reproachful language. [Obs.]

mal·ē·dī′cent, *a.* speaking reproachfully; slanderous. [Rare.]

mal′ē·dict, *a.* accursed. [Archaic.]

mal·ē·dic′tion, *n.* [OFr. *malediction*; L. *maledictio* (*-onis*), evil-speaking (LL., also, the act of cursing); *male*, badly, and *dicere*, to speak.]

1. invocation of evil; a cursing; curse or imprecation: opposed to *benediction*.
2. a speaking of evil about someone; slander.

mal·ē·dic′tō·ry, *a.* of, having the nature of, or expressing a malediction.

mal·ē·fac′tion, *n.* a criminal deed; a crime; an offense against the laws.

mal′ē·fac·tŏr, *n.* [L. *malefactor*, from *malefacere*, to do evil or harm; *male*, evil, and *facere*, to do.]

1. one who commits a crime; one guilty of violating the laws in such a manner as to subject him to public prosecution and punishment, particularly to capital punishment; a criminal.
2. one who does evil by injuring another: opposed to *benefactor*.

Syn.—evildoer, culprit, convict, criminal.

mal′ē·fac·tress, *n.* a woman malefactor.

mȧ·lef′ic, *a.* harmful; evil.

mal′ē·fice, *n.* an evil deed; also, black magic. [Obs.]

mȧ·lef′i·cence, *n.* evil; mischief; harm.

mȧ·lef′i·cent, *a.* [L. *male*, evil, and *faciens* (in comp. *-ficiens*), ppr. of *facere*, to do.] doing evil or mischief; causing injury, especially to others; harmful; hurtful: opposed to *beneficent*.

mal·ē·fi′ciăl (-fish′ăl), *a.* maleficent. [Rare.]

mal·ē·fi′ci·āte (-fish′i-āt), *v.t.* [LL. *maleficiatus*, pp. of *maleficiare*, from L. *maleficium*, an evil deed, enchantment.] to bewitch. [Obs.]

mal·ē·fi·ci·ā′tion, *n.* a bewitching. [Obs.]

mȧ·lē′ic, *a.* [from Fr. *maléique*, from L. *malum*, apple.] designating or of a white, crystalline acid, $C_4H_4O_4$, an isomer of fumaric acid, used as a dye, etc.

mȧ·lel′lȧ, *n.*; *pl.* **mȧ·lel′lae,** [dim. from L. *mala*, jaw, cheek.] a toothed appendage of the outer stipes, or second joint, of the second pair of jaws in certain insects, as myriapods.

mä′le·mūte, mä′le·miūt, *n.* a malamute.

mȧl′en·gine, *n.* [OFr. *malengin*, from L. *malus*, evil, and *ingenium*, contrivance.] guile; deceit. [Obs.]

mȧl·en·ten·dů′ (mȧl-äṅ-täṅ-dü′), *a.* [Fr.] misunderstood; poorly conceived.

mȧl·en·ten·dů′, *n.* a misunderstanding.

mal′ē·ō, *n.* [native name.] a mound bird of Celebes, *Megacephalon maleo*, related to the brush turkey.

Mal·ē·shēr′bi·ȧ, *n.* [named after Lamoignon de *Malesherbes* (1721–1794), French statesman.] a genus of erect undershrubs found in South America, some species of which bear showy yellow flowers; the type and sole genus of the family *Malesherbiaceæ*.

Mal·ē·shēr·bi·ā′cē·ae, *n.pl.* [*Malesherbia* and *-aceæ*.] a family of plants whose seeds divide into two seed lobes, closely allied to the *Passifloraceæ*, and consisting of the single genus *Malesherbia*.

male′tōlt, male′tōte, *n.* [OFr. *maletolte*; LL. *mala tolta*; L. *malus*, bad, and *tollere*, to raise.] an exorbitant or unjust tax. [Obs.]

mȧ·lev′ō·lence, *n.* [L. *malevolentia*, from *malevolens*, wishing ill; *male*, ill, badly, and *volens* (*-entis*), ppr. of *velle*, to wish.] the quality of being malevolent; ill will; personal hatred.

mȧ·lev′ō·lent, *a.* 1. having an evil disposition toward another or others; wishing evil to others; ill-disposed or disposed to injure others; as, a *malevolent* heart rejoices in the misfortunes of others.

2. unfavorable; unpropitious; bringing calamity. [Obs.]

Syn.—malicious, malignant, spiteful.

mȧ·lev′ō·lent·ly, *adv.* in a malevolent manner.

mȧ·lev′ō·lous, *a.* malevolent. [Obs.]

mal″ex·ē·cū′tion, *n.* [*mal-* and *execution*.] evil or wrong execution; bad administration.

mal·fēa′ṣănce, *n.* [Fr. *malfaisance*, evil-doing, wrongdoing, from *malfaisant*; *mal*, evil, and *faisant*, ppr. of *faire*, L. *facere*, to do.] wrongdoing or misconduct, especially in handling public affairs; as, an official who takes graft or otherwise violates his trust is guilty of *malfeasance*.

mal·fēa′ṣănt, *a.* and *n.* [Fr. *malfaisant*.] criminal.

mal·fọr·mā′tion, *n.* [*mal-* and *formation*.] ill or wrong formation; irregular or anomalous formation or structure of parts.

mal·fọrmed′, *a.* having a faulty form; lacking congruity; misshapen.

mal·fung′tion, *v.i.* to fail to function as it should.

mal·fung′tion, *n.* the act or an instance of malfunctioning.

mal·gré luí′ (mal-grā lwē′), [Fr.] in spite of oneself.

mal′ic ac′id, [Fr. *malique*, from L. *malum*, from Gr. *mēlon*, apple.] a colorless, crystallizable acid, $C_4H_6O_5$, occurring in apples and some other fruits.

mal′ice, *n.* [OFr. *malice*, from L. *malitia*, bad quality, badness, roguery, from *malus*, bad.]

1. active ill will; desire to harm others or do mischief; spite.
2. in law, evil intent; state of mind shown by intention to do, or intentional doing of, something unlawful.

malice aforethought (or *prepense*); a deliberate intention and plan to do something unlawful, as murder.

Syn.—rancor, spite, grudge, pique, malevolence, malignity, hatred.

mal′ice, *v.t.* to regard with extreme ill will. [Obs.]

mȧ·li′cious (-lish′us), *a.* [ME. *malicious*; OFr. *malicios*, from L. *malitiosus*, full of wickedness, crafty, from *malitia*, badness, malice.]

1. harboring ill will or enmity; spiteful; malevolent; malignant.
2. proceeding from extreme hatred or ill will; dictated by malice; as, a *malicious* report.

malicious prosecution; a wanton prosecution, by regular process, without probable cause.

Syn.—malevolent, malignant, spiteful.

mȧ·li′cious·ly, *adv.* in a malicious manner; with extreme enmity or ill will.

mȧ·li′cious·ness, *n.* the quality of being malicious; extreme enmity; malignity.

mȧ·lign′ (-līn′), *a.* [L. *malignus*, of an evil nature, from *maligenus*, ill-born; *male*, ill, badly, and the base of *genus*, birth, kind.]

1. malevolent; malicious.
2. evil; baleful; as, a *malign* influence.
3. very harmful; malignant.

mȧ·lign′, *v.t.*; maligned, *pt.*, *pp.*; maligning, *ppr.* [OFr. *malignier*, *maliner*, to pervert, deceive.] to speak evil of; to defame; slander.

mȧ·lign′, *v.i.* to entertain malice. [Obs.]

mȧ·lig′năn·cy, mȧ·lig′nănce, *n.* the quality or condition of being malignant.

The *malignancy* of my fate might distemper yours. —Shak.

mȧ·lig′nănt, *a.* [L. *malignans* (*-antis*), ppr. of *malignare*, *malignari*, to do or make maliciously, from *malignus*, of an evil nature.]

1. having an evil influence; malign.
2. wishing evil; very malevolent or malicious.
3. very harmful.
4. very dangerous or virulent; causing or likely to cause death; not benign; as, a cancer is a *malignant* tumor.
5. malcontent; rebellious; disaffected. [Obs.]

malignant pustule; the initial lesion of anthrax.

mȧ·lig′nănt, *n.* a malcontent: term applied by supporters of Parliament to followers of Charles I, and by Puritans to their opponents. [Obs.]

mȧ·lig′nănt·ly, *adv.* in a malignant manner.

mȧ·lign′ēr (-līn′), *n.* one who maligns.

mȧ·lig′ni·fy̆, *v.t.* to render malign. [Rare.]

mȧ·lig′ni·ty, *n.* [L. *malignitas*, ill will, malice, from *malignus*, malign.]

1. persistent, intense ill will or desire to harm others; great malice.
2. the quality of being very harmful or dangerous; malignancy.
3. *pl.* **mȧ·lig′ni·tieṣ,** a malignant act, event, or feeling.

Syn.—animosity, malevolence, rancor, spite.

mȧ·lign′ly (-līn′), *adv.* in a malign manner; unpropitiously; perniciously.

mä·li·hi′nï, *n.* [Haw.] a newcomer to Hawaii.

mȧ·līnes′ (-lēn′), *n.* [Fr., from *Malines* (Mechlin), Belgium.

1. Mechlin (lace).
2. a thin, somewhat stiff, silk net used in dressmaking, etc.

Also spelled *maline*.

mȧ·lin′gēr, *v.i.*; malingered, *pt.*, *pp.*; malingering, *ppr.* [Fr. *malingre*, diseased, sickly, from *mal*, badly, ill, and OFr. *haingre*, *heingre*, thin, emaciated.] to feign illness in order to avoid duty; to shirk.

mȧ·lin′gēr·ēr, *n.* one who feigns illness in order to avoid duty.

mȧ·lin′gēr·y, *n.* spirit or practices of a malingerer.

mal′i·ṣŏn, *n.* [OFr. *malison*, *maldeceon*; L. *maledictio* (*-onis*), evil-speaking.] malediction; curse. [Archaic.]

mal′kin (*or* mą′), *n.* [ME. *malkyn*, *malkyne*, dim. of *Malde*, Maud, itself dim. of *Matilda*.]

1. a slovenly or lewd woman. [Obs. or Dial.]
2. a mop. [Obs. or Dial.]
3. a scarecrow. [Obs. or Dial.]
4. a hare. [Chiefly Scot.]
5. a cat.

Also *maukin*, *mawkin*.

mąll, *n.* [var. of *maul*, mallet.]

1. originally, (a) a large heavy mallet, used in the game of pall-mall; (b) the game itself; (c) a lane or alley where the game was played.
2. a shaded walk or public promenade.
3. (a) a street for pedestrians only, with shops on each side, and often with decorative plantings, benches, etc.; (b) a completely enclosed, air-conditioned shopping center like this.

mąll, *n.* and *v.t.* maul.

mal′lăn·dēr̤s, *n.pl.* same as *malanders*.

mal′lărd, *n.* [OFr. *malard*, *malart*, from *male*, a male, and *-ard*, *-art*.]

1. (a) the male, or drake, of the common wild duck; (b) [Obs.] any drake.
2. the common wild duck (male or female), *Anas boscas*, from which the domestic duck is descended: the male has a green or bluish-

black head and a band of white around the neck.

mal″lē·ȧ·bil′i·ty, *n.* the quality or condition of being malleable.

mal′lē·ȧ·ble, *a.* [Fr. *malléable*, from LL. *malleare*, to beat with a hammer, from L. *malleus*, a hammer.]

1. that can be hammered, pounded, or pressed into various shapes without breaking or returning to its original shape: said of metals.

2. yielding; amenable; adaptable.

mal′lē·ȧ·ble ī′ron (ī′ũrn), 1. cast iron made from a kind of pig iron by a special process of long heating at a high temperature: it is especially strong and malleable: also *malleable pig iron*.

2. wrought or forged iron.

mal′lē·ȧ·ble·īze, *v.t.* to make malleable.

mal′lē·ȧ·ble·ness, *n.* malleability.

mal′lē·ăl, *a.* pertaining to the malleus.

mal′lē·āte, *v.t.*; malleated, *pt., pp.*; malleating, *ppr.* to hammer; to draw into a plate or leaf by beating.

mal·lē·ā′tion, *n.* the act of beating into a plate or leaf, as a metal.

mal′lē·chō, *n.* mischief. [Obs.]

mal′lee, *n.* [Australian.] any one of several small species of eucalyptus growing in Australia, notably *Eucalyptus dumosa*; also, the scrubby thicket formed by the plants.

mal′lee bīrd, a mound bird of Australia, *Leipoa ocellata*.

mal·lē′i·fọrm, *a.* [L. *malleus*, a hammer, and *forma*, form.] having the form of a hammer.

mal′lē·in, *n.* a culture of the glanders baccillus: used to diagnose the disease.

mal′lē·muck, *n.* [D. *mallemok*, from *mal*, foolish, and *mok*, a gull.] any one of several species of large ocean birds, as the petrel or albatross; especially, the *Fulmarus glacialis*: also written *mallemock*, *mallemoke*.

mal′len·dẽrṣ, *n.pl.* same as *malanders*.

mal·lē′ō·lăr, *a.* in anatomy, pertaining to the malleolus or the malleoli.

mal·lē′ō·lus, *n.*; *pl.* **mal·lē′ō·lī,** [L. *malleolus*, dim. of *malleus*, a hammer.] a rounded bony protuberance on each side of the ankle joint.

mal′let, *n.* [OFr. *mallet*, *maillet*, dim. of *mal*, *mail*, a hammer.]

1. a kind of hammer, usually with a heavy wooden head and a short handle, for driving a chisel, etc.

2. (a) a long-handled hammer with a cylindrical wooden head, used in playing croquet; (b) a similar but lighter instrument used in playing polo.

mal′lē·us, *n.*; *pl.* **mal′lē·ī,** [L. *malleus*, a hammer.]

1. in anatomy, the largest and outermost of the three small bones of the middle ear, shaped somewhat like a hammer: also called *hammer*.

2. in zoology, a hammer-shaped body forming part of the masticatory apparatus in some microscopic forms, as *Chætonotus*.

3. [M–] a genus of irregular and inequivalve mollusks, including the hammer shells.

Mal·loph′ȧ·gȧ, *n.pl.* [Gr. *mallos*, a lock of wool, and *phagein*, to eat.] a large group of wingless insects that live as parasites on birds: called also *bird lice*.

mal·loph′ȧ·găn, *a.* same as *mallophagous*.

mal·loph′ȧ·găn, *n.* an insect of the group *Mallophaga*.

mal·loph′ȧ·gous, *a.* 1. devouring feathers, fur, etc.

2. relating to the *Mallophaga*.

mal′lōw, *n.* [ME. *malowe*, *malue*; AS. *malwe*, *mealwe*, from L. *malva*, mallow.]

1. any of a family of plants, including the hollyhock, cotton, marsh mallow, and okra, typically with large, showy flowers and a sticky juice in their stems, leaves, and roots.

2. any of a certain genus of plants in this family; especially, the wild mallow, a plant with purplish, pink, or white flowers and hairy leaves and stems.

Indian mallow; see under *Indian*.

mallow rose; (a) any of several mallows with large pink or white flowers; (b) the flower itself: also called *rose mallow*.

mal′lōw·wŏrt, *n.* any plant of the mallow family.

mal′lum, mal′lus, *n.* [LL., of Teut. origin, compare O.H.G. *mahal*, assembly; AS. *mæl*, time, mark.] under old English law, a kind of court or council.

mälm (mäm), *n.* [ME. *malm*; AS. *mealm*, sand.] a kind of calcareous soil suitable for making brick: called also *malmstone* and *malm rock*; also, the brick made from the soil; malmbrick. [Brit. Dial.]

mal′mag, *n.* [native name.] a nocturnal lemur of Madagascar.

mälm′brick, *n.* brick made from malm, a kind of light-colored calcareous earth found in the southern part of England. [Brit. Dial.]

mal·mi·gnatte′ (-nyat′), *n.* [It. *malmignatta*.] a black, red-spotted spider, *Latrodectus malmignattus*, of southern Europe, reputed to be very poisonous.

mälm′ṣey (mäm′zi), *n.* [ME. *malvesie*, *malweysy*; OFr. *malvesie*, *malvoisie*, from It. *malvasia*, a kind of wine, from *Malvasia*, a city on the southeast coast of Laconia, Greece.]

1. a strong, full-flavored, sweet white wine.

2. the grape from which this is made.

mal·nū·tri′tion, *n.* [*mal-* and *nutrition*.] faulty or inadequate nutrition; undernourishment resulting from insufficient food, improper diet, etc.

mal·ob·ṣẽr·vā′tion, *n.* [*mal-* and *observation*.] faulty or defective observation.

mal·oç·çlū′ṣion, *n.* improper occlusion of the upper teeth with the lower.

mal·ō′dŏr, *n.* [*mal-* and *odor*.] an offensive odor; a bad smell.

mal·ō′dŏr·ous, *a.* having a bad smell; of bad odor.

mal·ō′dŏr·ous·ness, *n.* the quality of having a bad smell.

mal′ō·nāte, *n.* [*malon*ic and *-ate*.] a salt of malonic acid.

mȧ·lō′niç, *a.* of or produced by the oxidation of malic acid.

malonic acid; a colorless, crystalline, dibasic acid, $C_3H_4O_4$, derived from malic acid by oxidation.

mal′ō·nyl, *n.* [*malon*ic and *-yl*.] a radical contained in the compounds of malonic acid.

mä′loo, *n.* a plant of the genus *Bauhinia*.

Mal′ō·pē, *n.* [L. *malope*, a mallow.]

1. a genus of malvaceous herbs of the Mediterranean region cultivated for their handsome flowers.

2. [m–] a plant of the genus *Malope*.

mal′pais, *n.* [Fr. *mal pays*; *mal*, from L. *malus*, bad, and *pays*, from L. *pagus*, country.] rough, cooled and hardened lava.

Mal·pigh′i·ȧ (-pig′), *n.* [after Marcello *Malpighi*, 17th-c. Italian scientist.] a genus of shrubs of the family *Malpighiaceæ* of tropical America.

Mal·pigh″i·ā′cē·ae, *n.pl.* [*Malpighia* and *-aceæ*.] a family of tropical plants, with leaves set oppositely and red or yellow flowers having a pentamerous calyx and three carpels.

mal·pigh″i·ā′ceous, *a.* of or related to the *Malpighiaceæ*.

Mal·pigh′i·ăn, *a.* of, related to, discovered by, or associated with Marcello Malpighi, the scientist.

Mal·pigh′i·ăn bod′y (or **çor′pus·cle**), 1. any nodule of lymphatic tissue in the spleen.

2. any of a number of small masses of blood vessels (*Malpighian tufts*) in the kidney, enclosed by a capsule that is an enlargement of the end of a tubule through which urine passes.

Mal·pigh′i·ăn lāy′ẽr, the soft, lowest layer of the epidermis from which the other layers are derived.

Mal·pigh′i·ăn tūbeṣ (or **ves′selṣ**), a group of small, tubular glands that open into the hind part of the alimentary canal in most insects.

Mal·pigh′i·ăn tuft, see *Malpighian body*.

mal·pō·ṣi′tion (-zish′un), *n.* a faulty, abnormal, or wrong position, especially of the fetus in the uterus.

mal·praç′tice, *n.* [*mal-* and *practice*.]

1. injurious or unprofessional treatment or culpable neglect of a patient by a physician or surgeon.

2. misconduct or improper practice in any professional or official position.

3. in general, wrongdoing; criminal practice; illegal or immoral conduct.

malt, *n.* [ME. *malt*; AS. *mealt*, malt.]

1. barley or other grain steeped in water till it germinates, and then dried in a kiln. It is used in brewing and in the distillation of certain alcoholic liquors.

2. such liquor; beer, ale, etc.

malt, *a.* made with malt.

malt, *v.t.* 1. to change (barley, etc.) into malt or something maltlike.

2. to treat or prepare (milk, etc.) with malt or malt extract.

malt, *v.i.* 1. to be changed into malt or something maltlike.

2. to change barley, etc. into malt; to germinate grain artificially in order to change the starch into a sugar.

Mal′tȧ fē′vẽr, [so named because prevalent in Malta and other Mediterranean areas.] undulant fever: also called *Mediterranean fever*.

malt′āse, *n.* [*malt* and *-ase*.] an enzyme, occurring in animals, plants, bacteria, etc., that changes maltose into dextrose.

malt dust, the refuse from the grain in malting.

malt′ed milk, 1. a powdered preparation of dried milk and malted cereals.

2. a drink made by mixing this with ice cream, whole milk, and flavoring.

Mal·tēṣe′, *a.* [*Malta* and *-ese*.]

1. relating to the island of Malta or to its people, their language, etc.

2. of the medieval Knights of Malta.

Mal·tēṣe′, *n.* 1. *pl.* **Mal·tēṣe′,** a native or inhabitant of Malta.

2. the language spoken in Malta, a mixture of Arabic and Italian.

3. a Knight of Malta.

4. a Maltese cat or dog.

Mal·tēṣe′ çat, a variety of domestic cat with bluish-gray fur.

Mal·tēṣe′ çross, [so called from its use as an emblem by the medieval Knights of Malta.] a cross whose arms look like arrowheads pointing inward: see illustration with *cross*.

Mal·tēṣe′ dog, a variety of small spaniel with long, silky, white hair, originated in Malta.

malt ex′traçt, an extract of malt evaporated to a sirup and used in medicine as a remedy for debility.

malt flōor, a floor for drying malt.

mal′thȧ, *n.* [L., from Gr. *maltha*, *malthē*, a mixture of wax and pitch for calking ships.] a kind of mineral pitch, a black, semisolid bitumen.

malt hŏrse, a horse employed in grinding malt; hence, a dull fellow. [Obs.]

malt′house, *n.* a building used for malting.

Mal·thū′ṣi·ăn, *a.* relating to the English writer, Thomas R. Malthus (1766–1834), or to his doctrines and theories.

Mal·thū′ṣi·ăn, *n.* a disciple or follower of Malthus.

Mal·thū′ṣi·ăn·iṣm, *n.* the doctrine of Malthus that the increase in population is greater than the increase in the means of subsistence, and that unless birth is controlled, poverty and war must serve as a natural restriction of the increase.

malt′in, *n.* maltine.

malt′īne, *n.* [*malt* and *-ine*.] a former medicinal preparation from malt.

malt′ing, *n.* the act or process of making malt.

malt kiln (kil), a structure for drying malt to retard or stop fermentation.

malt liq′uŏr (lik′ẽr), beer, ale, or other fermented liquor made with malt or barley.

mält′-mad, *a.* made mad or intoxicated by drinking; drunken.

malt′măn, *n.*; *pl.* **malt′men,** a maltster.

mält mȧs′tẽr, a chief maltmaker.

mal·ton′iç, *a.* produced from maltose; as, *maltonic* acid.

malt′ōse, *n.* [*malt* and *-ose*.] a white, crystalline, dextrorotatory sugar, $C_{12}H_{22}O_{11}$, obtained by the action of the diastase of malt on starch; malt sugar.

mal·trēat′, *v.t.*; maltreated, *pt., pp.*; maltreating, *ppr.* [*mal-* and *treat*.] to treat ill; to abuse; to treat roughly, rudely, unkindly, brutally, etc.

mal·trēat′ment, *n.* mistreatment; ill usage; abuse.

malt′stẽr, *n.* [*malt* and *-ster*.] a maker of or dealer in malt; a maltman.

malt suġ′ăr (shoog′), maltose.

malt′wŏrm, *n.* a tippler.

malt′y, *a.*; *comp.* maltier; *superl.* maltiest,

1. of, like, or containing malt.

2. fond of malt liquor.

3. drunk. [Slang.]

mal·ū·lel′lȧ, *n.*; *pl.* **mal·ū·lel′lae,** [a double dim. from L. *mala*, jaw.] an appendage to the edge of the second pair of jaws of a myriapod.

mā′lum, *n.*; *pl.* **mā′lȧ,** [L.] an evil.

Mal′vȧ, *n.* [L. *malva*, mallow.] a genus of plants typical of the family *Malvaceæ*, or mallow family.

Mal·vā′cē·ae, *n.pl.* [*malva* and *-aceæ*.] the mallow family of plants, characterized chiefly by having the stamens monadelphous and the anthers unicellular. Well-known plants of this order are the cotton plant, *Gossypium herbaceum*, and the hollyhock, *Althea rosea*.

mal·vā′ceous, *a.* of or relating to the genus *Malva*, or the mallow family.

Mal·vā′lēs, *n.pl.* [L. *malva*, mallow.] an order of plants embracing *Malvaceæ* and other families.

mal·vȧ·sï′ȧ, *n.* [It., from *Malvasia*, a town of Lacedaemonia.]
 1. the grape from which malmsey is made.
 2. malmsey.

mal·vȧ·sï′ăn, *a.* of malvasia.

mal·vēr·sā′tion, *n.* [Fr. *malversation*, evil conduct, from L. *male*, badly, and *versatio* (*-onis*), a turning, from *versari*, to turn, occupy oneself.] improper behavior; fraudulent tricks; corruption, fraud, or extortion in public office or other position of trust.

mal′vē·șie, *n.* malvoisie. [Obs.]

mal′voi·șie, *n.* [Fr.] malmsey (wine or grape). [Archaic.]

mam, *n.* mamma. [Colloq.]

mä′mȧ (*or* mȧ-mä′), *n.* mamma; mother.

Mam′ȧ·lūke, *n.* same as *Mameluke*.

mäm′bȧ, *n.* [Zulu *im-amba*.] any of several poisonous snakes of southern Africa, related to the cobras but not hooded; especially, a common green or black snake of this sort.

mäm′bō, *n.* [Sp.Am.; musicians' slang term equivalent to "riff".]
 1. a rhythmic musical form of Cuban Negro origin, in 4/4 syncopated time and with a heavy accent on the second and fourth beats of every measure.
 2. an American ballroom dance to music of this sort.

mäm′bō, *v.i.* to dance the mambo.

mam′ē·lŏn, *n.* [Fr., nipple, breast, small conical hill, from L. *mamma*, breast.] a rounded elevation of land; a hummock; a knoll.

mam·ē·lū′çō, *n.* [Port., from Ar. *mamlūk*, a slave.] a person having an Indian mother and a white father. [S. Am.]

Mam′ē·lūke, *n.* [Ar. *mamlūk*, a purchased slave, a captive, from *malaka*, to possess.]
 1. a member of a military force, originally made up of slaves, that seized power in Egypt in about 1250, ruled there until 1517, and remained powerful until destroyed in 1811 by Mehamet Ali.
 2. [m-] in Moslem countries, a slave: sometimes figurative.

mä·mēy′, *n.* a mammee.

mȧ·mil′lȧ, *n.* same as *mammilla*.

Mam·il·lā′ri·ȧ, *n.* [L. *mamilla*, breast, and *-aria*; so called from the protuberances on the stem.] a genus of small round cactuses growing in the western United States and Mexico, cultivated for their showy flowers.

mam′il·lā·ry, *a.* same as *mammillary*.

mäm′mȧ (*or* mȧ-mä′), *n.* [like L. *mamma*, mother, Sans. *mā*, Gr. *mammē*, from baby talk; sp. prob. affected by association with L. *mamma*, breast.] mother: a child's word, corresponding to *papa* for *father*: also *mama*, *ma*, *mam*, *mom*, *maw*, etc.

mam′mȧ, *n.*; *pl.* **mam′mae,** [L. *mamma*; Gr. *mammē*, the breast, pap.] a glandular secretory organ in all mammals (but usually rudimentary and functionless in the male), whose function is secreting milk; an udder.

mam′măl, *n.*; *pl.* **mam′măls,** [LL. *mammalis*, of the breast, from L. *mamma*, the breast, pap.] any of a group of vertebrates the females of which have milk-secreting glands for feeding their offspring.

Mam·mā′li·ȧ, *n.pl.* [neut. pl. from LL. *mammalis*, of the breast, from L. *mamma*, breast, pap.] in zoology, mammals as a class.

mam·mā′li·ăn, *a.* pertaining to the *Mammalia*.

mam·mā′li·ăn, *n.* a mammal.

mam·mȧ·lif′ēr·ous, *a.* [*mammalia*, and L. *ferre*, to produce.] in geology, bearing evidences of mammalian life: said of stratified rocks.

mam·mȧ·log′iç·ăl, *a.* related to mammalogy.

mam·mal′ō·gist, *n.* an expert in mammalogy.

mam·mal′ō·gy *n.* [L. *mamma*, the breast, pap, and Gr. *-logia*, from *legein*, to speak.] the branch of zoology dealing with mammals.

mam′mȧ·ry, *a.* designating or of the milk-secreting glands; as, the *mammary* veins.

mam·mee′, *n.* [native name.]
 1. any of three tropical American trees with large, edible, yellow or brown fruit; marmalade tree (*Calocarpum sapota*), mammee apple tree, or sapodilla.
 2. the fruit of these trees, which is covered with a thick, tough rind.
 Also spelled *mamey*.

mäm·mee′sȧ·pō′tȧ, see *mammee* (sense 1).

mam·mel·lière′ (-lyăr′), *n.* [Fr., from *mamelle*, the breast, from L. *mamilla*, dim. of *mamma*, the breast.] in medieval armor, (a) a kind of plate fastened to the breast of a full coat of mail to serve as an attachment for a chain carrying a sword, war hammer, etc.; (b) one of two steel plates worn for the protection of the breast: also written *mamelière*.

MAMMELLIÈRES

mam′mēr, *v.i.* to hesitate. [Obs.]

mam′mēr·ing, *n.* hesitation; confusion. [Obs.]

mam′met, *n.* same as *maumet*.

mam′mi·chug, *n.* same as *mummychog*.

mam′mie, *n.* same as *mammy*.

mam′mi·fēr, *n.* [L. *mamma*, the breast, and *ferre*, to bear.] an animal which has breasts for nourishing its young; a mammal. [Obs.]

mam·mif′ēr·ous, *a.* having mammae, or breasts.

mam′mi·fọrm, *a.* [L. *mamma*, breast, and *forma*, form.] having the form of mammae, or breasts.

mam·mil′lȧ, *n.*; *pl.* **mam·mil′lae,** [L. *mamilla* or *mammilla*, dim. of *mamma*, the breast.] the prominence through which the milk is extracted from the breast; the nipple.

mam′mil·lā·ry, *a.* [L. *mammilla*, *mamilla*, the breast, nipple, dim. of *mamma*, the breast.]
 1. of or like a nipple: applied to two small protuberances found under the fore ventricles of the brain, and to a process of the temporal bone.
 2. in mineralogy, composed of convex concretions.
 3. in botany, resembling a nipple, as in the genus *Mamillaria* of the cactus family.

mam′mil·lāte, *a.* in biology, (a) having mammillae, or nipples; (b) having the form of a mammilla.

mam′mil·lā·ted, *a.* having small nipples, or protuberances like nipples.

mam·mil′li·fọrm, *a.* [L. *mammilla*, nipple, and *forma*, form.] formed like a nipple.

mam′mil·loid, *a.* [L. *mammilla*, nipple, and Gr. *eidos*, form.] resembling a nipple or teat.

mam·mī′tis, *n.* inflammation of the breast.

mam′mŏck, *n.* [Gael. *mam*, a round hill, and *-ock*, dim. suffix.] a shapeless piece; a fragment; a shred; a scrap. [Archaic or Dial.]

mam′mŏck, *v.t.* to tear or break into fragments or shreds.

mam·mog′rȧ·phy, *n.* [from *mamma* (secretory organ), and *-o-*, and *-graphy*.] an X-ray technique for the detection of breast tumors before they can be seen or felt.

mam′mŏn, *n.* [LL. *Mammon*; Gr. *Mammōnas*; Syr. *māmōnā*, riches.]
 1. [*usually* M-] the false god of riches and avarice.
 2. riches regarded as an object of worship and greedy pursuit; wealth as an evil, more or less personified.

 Ye cannot serve God and *mammon*.
 —Matt. vi. 24.

mam′mŏn·ish, *a.* greedily intent on getting money.

mam′mŏn·ișm, *n.* worship of mammon; devotion to the greedy pursuit of riches.

mam′mŏn·ist, *n.* a person devoted to the greedy acquisition of wealth.

mam′mŏn·īte, *n.* a worshiper of mammon; a mammonist.

mam′mŏn·īze, *v.t.*; mammonized, *pt.*, *pp.*; mammonizing, *ppr.* to make mammonish.

Mam·mon·tē′us, *n.* the genus to which the woolly mammoth of Siberia belonged.

mam·mōse′, *a.* [L. *mammosus*, full-breasted, from *mamma*, a breast.] in botany, shaped like the breast; mammiform.

mam′mŏth, *n.* [Russ. *Mammot'*.] a huge extinct elephant with a hairy skin and long tusks curving upward: remains have been found in North America, Europe, and Asia.

mam′mŏth, *a.* large; of gigantic size.

mam′mŏth çlō′vēr, one of the common red clovers, *Trifolium pratense*, cultivated as a yearly forage crop.

mam′mō·thrept, *n.* [Gr. *mammothreptos*; *mamma*, a grandmother, and *threptos*, verbal adj. of *trephein*, to nourish, rear.] literally, a child reared by its grandmother; hence, a spoiled child. [Obs.]

mam′mŏth tree, the redwood tree; the giant sequoia.

mam′mū·lȧ, *n.* [L., dim. of *mamma*, the breast.] in zoology, a very small, somewhat conical protuberance, as the spinneret of a spider.

mam′my, *n.*; *pl.* **mam′mies,** 1. mother; mamma: a child's word.
 2. a Negro foster mother or nurse of white children: so used especially in the southern States.

mä′mō, *n.* a Hawaiian bird, *Drepanis pacifica*, now extinct. Its black and yellow feathers were used for the cloaks of the native chiefs.

man, *n.*; *pl.* **men,** [AS. *man*, *mon*; akin to Goth. *manna*; perhaps from the root *man*, to think.]
 1. a human being; a person, whether male or female.
 2. the human race; mankind: used without *the* or *a*.
 3. (a) an adult male human being; (b) sometimes, a boy.
 4. (a) an adult male servant, follower, attendant, or subordinate; (b) a male employee; workman; as, the employer talked to the *men*; (c) [*usually in pl.*] a soldier, sailor, etc.; especially, one of the rank and file; as, officers and *men*; (d) [Archaic.] a vassal.
 5. (a) a husband; as, they are *man* and wife; (b) a lover.
 6. a person with qualities conventionally regarded as manly, such as strength, courage, etc.
 7. manly qualities; virility.
 8. a player on a team.
 9. one of the pieces used in chess, checkers, etc.
 10. in nautical usage, a ship: used in compounds, as *man*-of-war, merchant*man*.
 Man is also used as a term of address.
 as a (or *one*) *man*; in unison; unanimously.
 man about town; a man who spends much time in fashionable restaurants, clubs, bars, and places of amusement.
 man and boy; first as a boy and then as a man; from boyhood.
 man in the street; the average man; the ordinary person.
 Man of Destiny; Napoleon I: self-applied term.
 Man of Galilee; Jesus.
 man of God; (a) a holy man; saint, hermit, etc.; (b) a clergyman, minister, priest, rabbi, etc.
 Man of Sorrows; Jesus: cf. Isaiah liii. 3.
 man of the world; a man familiar with and tolerant of various sorts of people and their ways; sophisticate.
 man on horseback; a military man with such influence and power over the people as to threaten the current regime or administration.
 to a man; with no one as an exception; every one.
 to be one's own man; to have control of one's own actions; to be free from the dictates of another.

man, *v.t.*; manned, *pt.*, *pp.*; manning, *ppr.* 1. to furnish with men for work, defense, etc.; as, they *manned* the ship.
 2. to take assigned places in, on, or at for work or defense; as, *man* the guns!
 3. to strengthen; to brace; fortify; nerve; as, he *manned* himself for the ordeal.
 4. in falconry, to tame or accustom (a hawk) to the presence of man.
 to man the yards; to send a number of men upon the yards of a ship to reef or furl the sails; also, to range men in a standing position along the tops of the yards as a salute.

man, *interj.* an exclamation of pleasure, surprise, etc. [Slang.]

man, *a.* male.

-man, a combining form meaning *man* or *person*; specifically, (a) *a member of a* (specified) *nation*, as in French*man*; (b) *a person engaged in a* (specified) *kind of work*, as in laundry*man*; (c) *a person operating a* (specified) *device*, as in motor*man*.

mä′nä, *n.* [native Polynesian term.] the impersonal supernatural force to which certain primitive peoples attribute good fortune, magical powers, etc.

man′ȧ·çle, *n.* [OFr. *manicle*; LL. *manicula*, a handcuff, dim. of L. *manus*, hand.] [*usually in pl.*] an instrument of iron for fastening the hands; handcuff; shackle; hence, any restraint.

man'ȧ·çle, *v.t.*; manacled, *pt.*, *pp.*; manacling, *ppr.* 1. to put handcuffs on; to fetter.
2. to confine; to restrain; to hamper.

man'ȧġe, *v.t.*; managed, *pt.*, *pp.*; managing, *ppr.* [It. *maneggiare*, from L. *manus*, hand.]
1. originally, to train (a horse) in his paces; to cause to do the exercises of the manège.
2. (a) to handle; to wield (a weapon, instrument, etc.); (b) to control, guide, or work (a vehicle, boat, etc.).
3. to have charge of; to direct; conduct; administer; as, she *manages* the household.
4. to handle or use (money, supplies, etc.) carefully. [Rare.]
5. to get (a person) to do what one wishes, especially by skill, tact, flattery, etc.; to make docile or submissive to control.
6. to bring about by contriving; to contrive; to succeed in accomplishing: often used ironically; as, I *managed* to make a mess of it.

man'ȧġe, *v.i.* 1. to direct or conduct affairs; to carry on concerns or business.
Leave them to *manage* for thee.—Dryden.
2. to contrive to get along; to succeed.
Syn.—administer, conduct, control, direct, regulate, wield.

man'ȧġe, *n.* [OFr. *manège*; It. *maneggio*, the handling or training of a horse, from *maneggiare*, to handle, manage, from *mano*; L. *manus*, hand.]
1. the training of a horse; manège. [Obs.]
2. management. [Obs.]

man"ȧġe·ȧ·bil'i·ty, *n.* the quality or condition of being manageable.

man'ȧġe·ȧ·ble, *a.* that can be managed; controllable, tractable, contrivable, etc.

man'ȧġe·ȧ·ble·ness, *n.* the quality of being manageable; tractableness.

man'ȧġe·ȧ·bly, *adv.* in a manageable manner.

man'ȧġed cũr'ren·cy, currency whose buying power is arbitrarily stabilized, as by varying the gold value of the basic monetary unit, to control price fluctuations.

man'ȧġe·less, *a.* that cannot be managed. [Rare.]

man'ȧġe·ment, *n.* 1. (a) the act, art, or manner of managing, or handling, controlling, directing, etc.; (b) a being managed.
2. skillful managing; careful, tactful treatment.
3. skill in managing; executive ability.
4. (a) the person or persons managing a business, institution, etc.; as, labor and *management* failed to agree on wages; (b) such persons collectively, regarded as a distinct social group with special interests, characteristic economic views, etc.
Syn.—treatment, conduct, administration, government, address, skill, superintendence, control, handling.

man'ȧ·ġẽr, *n.* 1. one who has the conduct or direction of anything; as, the *manager* of a railroad; the *manager* of a lottery.
A skilful *manager* of the rabble.—South.
2. one who conducts affairs with economy and frugality; a good economist.
A prince of great aspiring thoughts; in the main, a *manager* of his treasure.
—Temple.
3. one who is skilled in contriving, planning, or intriguing so as to accomplish his purpose.
Syn.—director, leader, overseer, boss, supervisor.

man'ȧ·ġẽr·ess, *n.* a woman manager. [Chiefly Brit.]

man·ȧ·ġē'ri·ăl, *a.* relating to or characteristic of management or a manager.

man'ȧ·ġẽr·ship, *n.* the authority, rank, and duties of a manager.

man'ȧġe·ry, *n.* the act of managing. [Obs.]

măn'ȧ·ġing, *a.* 1. conducting; regulating; directing; governing; as, a *managing* editor; a *managing* director.
2. careful; economical; skillful in management.

man'ȧ·kin, *n.* 1. any of various small birds of Central and South America, mostly brightly colored.
2. a manikin.

ma·ña'na (mä·nyä'nȧ), *n.* [Sp.] tomorrow.

ma·ña'na (mä·nyä'nȧ), *adv.* 1. tomorrow.
2. at some indefinite time in the future.

Mȧ·nas'seh, *n.* [Heb. *mĕnaṣṣeh*, lit., causing to forget.] in the Bible, (a) the eldest son of Joseph; (b) one of the twelve tribes of Israel, said to be descended from him; (c) a king of Judah in the 7th century B.C.: 2 Kings xxi. 1–18.

man'-at-ärmṣ', *n.*; *pl.* **men'-at-ärmṣ',** a fully equipped or heavy-armed cavalryman of former times, especially of the Middle Ages; hence, any soldier.

man·ȧ·tee', *n.* [Sp. *manatí*, from Carib name.] any of several large, plant-eating aquatic mammals living in shallow tropical waters near the coasts of North and South America and West Africa, having flippers and a broad, flat, rounded tail; sea cow.

MANATEE
(*Manatus americanus*)

mȧ·nā'tion, *n.* [L. *manatio* (*-onis*), from *manare*, to flow.] the act of issuing or flowing out. [Obs.]

man'ȧ·toid, *a.* pertaining to or resembling the manatee.

Man'ȧ·tus, *n.* a genus of aquatic mammals, including the manatees.

mȧ·nav'el, *v.t.* and *v.i.* in nautical slang, to steal small articles, especially food; to pilfer.

mȧ·nav'el·inṣ, *n.pl.* in nautical slang, odds and ends; leftovers; scraps.

man'bōte, *n.* [AS. *man*, man, and *bot*, amends, recompense.] in Anglo-Saxon law, compensation for the killing of a vassal paid in money to the lord of the person slain.

màn·çan'dō, *a.* and *adv.* in music, gradually growing softer; calando; diminuendo: a direction to the performer.

manche, manch, *n.* [Fr., from L. *manica*, a long sleeve, from *manus*, hand.]

MANCHE OF MANCH
Fig. 1. manche as a heraldic bearing
Fig. 2. sleeve of the period of Henry III

1. an old-fashioned sleeve with long, hanging ends. [Obs.]
2. in heraldry, a bearing representing such a sleeve.

man'chet, *n.* [from OFr. *paindemaine* (L. *panis dominicus*), lit., lord's bread.]
1. white bread made of the finest wheat flower.
2. a roll or small loaf of such bread.
[Archaic in both senses.]

man·chette', *n.* [Fr., dim. of *manche*, a sleeve.] an ornamental cuff on a garment.

man'-chīld, *n.*; *pl.* **man'-chil·dren,** a male child; a boy.

man·chi·neel', *n.* [Fr. *mancenille*, *manzanille*; Sp. *manzanillo*, from *manzana*, an apple, from L. *Matiana mala*, a kind of apple, from *Matius*, the name of a Roman gens and of the author of a manual on cookery.]
1. a tropical American tree with poisonous, yellowish-green, applelike fruit and milky juice.
2. its wood.
bastard manchineel; a West Indian tree, *Cameraria latifolia*, having poisonous qualities similar to true manchineel.

MANCHINEEL
(*Hippomane mancinella*)

Man·chụ', Man·chọọ', *n.* [Manchu, lit., pure.]
1. a member of a Mongolian people of Manchuria: the Manchus conquered China in 1643–1644 and set up a dynasty that ruled until 1912.
2. the Tungus language of the Manchus.

Man·chụ', Man·chọọ', *a.* relating to the Manchus, their language, or their country.

Man·chụ'ri·ăn, *a.* of Manchuria, China, or its people.

Man·chụ'ri·ăn, *n.* a native or inhabitant of Manchuria, China.

man'ci·pāte, *v.t.* [L. *mancipatus*, pp. of *mancipare*, to make over, or deliver up as property by a formal act of purchase, transfer, from *manceps* (*-ipis*), a buyer.] to enslave; to bind; to restrict. [Obs.]

man·ci·pā'tion, *n.* slavery; involuntary servitude. [Obs.]

man'ci·ple, *n.* [ME. *manciple*, from *mancipe*, a steward, servant, from L. *manceps* (*-ipis*), a purchaser.] a steward; a purveyor, especially of an English college, monastery, etc.

Man·çū'ni·ăn, *n.* [ML. *Mancunium*, Manchester.] a native or inhabitant of Manchester, England.

Man·çū'ni·ăn, *a.* of Manchester, England.

mañ'çus, *n.* [AS.] the Anglo-Saxon mark, coined in both gold and silver, equal to 30 pence.

-man'cy, [Gr. *manteia*, divination, from *mantis*, a prophet.] a combining form meaning *divination*, as in necro*mancy*, chiro*mancy*.

Man·dae'ăn, *a.* and *n.* Mandean.

man·dā'mus, *n.* [L., we command.] in law, a writ, or written order, requiring that a specified thing be done, issued by a higher court to a lower one, or to a corporation, city, official, etc.: originally, in England, it was a writ of royal prerogative.

man·dā'mus, *v.t.* to serve with a command by such a writ. [Colloq.]

Man'dan, *n.*; *pl.* **Man'dan, Man'danṣ,** 1. a member of a tribe of Siouan Indians who lived in the Missouri River Valley.
2. their language.

Man'dan, *a.* of or developed by the Mandan; as, *Mandan* corn.

man'dănt, *n.* a mandator.

man'dȧ·rin, *n.* [Port. *mandarim*, a mandarin, from Malay *mantrī*, a minister of state, from Hind. *mantrī*; Sans. *mantrin*, a councilor, minister of state, from *mantra*, counsel.]
1. a high official of China under the Empire: the nine classes of mandarin were distinguished from one another by a certain kind of jeweled button worn on the cap.
2. [M-] the dialect of Chinese spoken by officials and the educated classes; the official or main dialect of Chinese.
3. (a) a small, sweet orange with a loose rind; a tangerine; (b) the tree that it grows on; (c) any of several related trees.
4. a deep-orange dye.
5. (a) a long, brocaded Chinese coat with loose sleeves, worn by mandarins; (b) a woman's evening coat like this: also *mandarin coat*.

man'dȧ·rin·āte, *n.* 1. the office held by a mandarin; the jurisdiction or district of a mandarin.
2. the mandarins collectively.

man'dȧ·rin duck, a bright-colored, crested Asiatic duck.

man·dȧ·rin'iç, *a.* pertaining or appropriate to a mandarin.

man'dȧ·rin·iṣm, *n.* mandarinic government, character, or spirit.

man·dat' (moṅ-dä'), *n.* 1. in French law, a mandate or injunction.
2. in French history, a kind of currency similar to a promissory note, issued in 1796 by the revolutionary government.

man'dȧ·tā·ry, *n.*; *pl.* **man'dȧ·tā·rieṣ,** [LL. *mandatarius*, one to whom a charge is given, from L. *mandatum*, a command, charge.]
1. a person to whom a mandate has been given. [Rare.]
2. a country to which a mandate has been given.
Also *mandatory*.

man'dāte, *n.* [L. *mandatum*, a charge, command, commission, neut. of *mandatus*, pp. of *mandare*, to command, commission; lit., to put into one's hand; *manus*, hand, and *dare*, to give.]
1. an authoritative order or command, especially a written one.
2. (a) formerly, a commission from the League of Nations to a country (called the *mandatary*) to administer some region, colony, etc.; (b) the area so administered.
3. the wishes of constituents expressed to a representative, legislature, etc. as an order, or regarded as an order.
4. in law, (a) an order from a higher court or official to a lower one: a *mandate on remission* is a mandate from an appellate court to the lower court, communicating its decision in a case appealed; (b) in canon law, a papal rescript, especially one having to do with preferment to a benefice; (c) in English law, a bailment of personal property with no con-

sideration; (d) in Roman law, a commission or contract by which a person undertakes to do something for another, without recompense but with indemnity against loss; (e) any contract of agency.

man′dāte, *v.t.*; mandated, *pt.*; *pp.*; mandating, *ppr.* to assign (a territory, etc.) to a certain government in order that it may be controlled by this government; also, to administer under a mandate; to supervise; to control.

man·dā′tŏr, *n.* [L. *mandator*, from *mandare*, to charge, command.] a director; one giving a mandate.

man′dȧ·tō·ry, *a.* 1. of, having the nature of, or containing a mandate.

2. authoritatively commanded or required; obligatory.

3. having received a mandate over some territory; being a mandatary.

man′dȧ·tō·ry, *n.* same as *mandatary*.

Man·dē′ăn, *n.* [from Mandean *mandayyā*, lit., having knowledge.]

1. a member of an ancient Gnostic sect (*Christians of St. John*), still extant in southern Iraq.

2. the Eastern Aramaic dialect used in Mandean writings: it was spoken along the Euphrates from the 7th to the 9th centuries A.D.

Also spelled *Mandaean*.

Man·dē′an, *a.* 1. of the Mandeans, their doctrines, etc.

2. of Mandean.

Also spelled *Mandaean*.

man′del·āte, *n.* [*mandelic* and *-ate*.] a salt of mandelic acid.

man·del′iç ac′id, a colorless, crystalline hydroxy acid, $C_6H_5CH(OH)CO_2H$.

man′del·stōne, *n.* same as *amygdaloid*.

man′dẽr, *v.i.* same as *maunder*.

man′dẽr·il, *n.* a mandrel. [Obs.]

man′di·ble, *n.* [LL. *mandibula*, f., *mandibulum*, neut., a jaw, from L. *mandere*, to chew.] the jaw, especially the lower jaw, or any part corresponding to this; specifically, (a) either part of a bird's beak; (b) either of the pair of outermost, biting jaws of an insect or other arthropod.

man·dib′ū·lȧ, *n.* [LL.] the mandible.

man·dib′ū·lăr, *a.* [L. *mandibula*, jaw.] of or like a mandible.

man·dib′ū·lăr, *n.* the mandible; lower jaw bone.

Man·dib·ū·lā′tȧ, *n.pl.* [from L. *mandibula*, a jaw.] in old classifications, a large group of insects having jaws for chewing.

man·dib′ū·lāte, *a.* 1. provided with mandibles, as many insects.

2. adapted for chewing.

man·dib′ū·lāte, *n.* a mandibulate insect.

man·dib′ū·lāt·ed, *a.* mandibulate.

man·dib′ū·li·fŏrm, *a.* [LL. *mandibula*, a jaw, and L. *forma*, form.] formed like a mandible or mandibles; specifically, designating the jaws of an insect when hard, horny, and coincident.

man·dib″ū·lō·hȳ′oid, *a.* related to or situated between the hyoid bone and the mandibula.

man′dil, *n.* a turban.

man·dil′ion (-yun), *n.* [OFr. *mandillon*.] a soldier's coat; a loose garment worn as an overcoat by men servants.

Man·diñ′gȧ, *n.* and *a.* Mandingo.

Man·diñ′găn, *a.* of the Mandingos or their language.

Man·diñ′găn, *n.* Mandingo.

Man·diñ′gō, *n.*; *pl.* **Man·diñ′gōṣ, Man·diñ′gōeṣ,** [from the native name.]

1. one of a group of Negroes inhabiting the region of the Niger River.

2. the language spoken by the Mandingos.

Man·diñ′gō, *a.* of the Mandingos or their language.

man·dō′lȧ, man·dō′rȧ, *n.* [It.] a mandolin of large size and low tone.

man′dō·lin, man′dō·line, *n.* [Fr., from It. *mandolino*, dim. of *mandola*, *mandora*, from L. *pandura*, a kind of lute.] a musical instrument with eight, ten, or twelve metal strings, usually paired, stretched over a deep, rounded sound box: it is played with a plectrum, which is moved rapidly back and forth to give a tremolo effect.

man′dōre, *n.* same as *mandola*.

man′dọr·lȧ, *n.* [It.] in fine arts, anything in the shape of an almond, as a panel.

Man·drag′ō·rȧ, *n.* [L. *mandragoras*, from Gr. *mandragoras*, the mandrake.] a genus of herbaceous plants of the nightshade family, to which the mandrake belongs; also [m–], the mandrake.

man′drāke, *n.* [corruption of *mandragora*.]

1. a poisonous plant of the nightshade family, genus *Mandragora*, found in the Mediterranean regions: it has a short stem, purple or white flowers, and a thick root, often forked, used in medicine for its narcotic and emetic properties.

2. the root, formerly thought to resemble the human shape.

3. the May apple.

man′drel, man′dril, *n.* [a corruption of Fr. *mandrin*, a blow, mandrel.]

1. a tight-fitting metal spindle or bar, often cone-shaped, inserted into something to hold it while it is being machined or turned on a lathe, etc.

2. a metal rod or bar used as a core around which metal, glass, etc. is cast, molded, or shaped, as in forging, or wire is wound.

3. a form that metalwork is pressed against in spinning.

man′drel lāthe, a lathe used for spinning hollow ware.

man′drel press, in machinery, a press that forces mandrels into holes prepared for them.

man′dri·ärçh, *n.* [It. *mandriarcha*, from late Gr. *mandriarchēs*, *mandra*, a fold, as a monastery, and Gr. *archein*, to rule.] a founder or ruler of an order as of monks.

man′drill, *n.* [*man* and *drill* (baboon).] a large, fierce, strong baboon of western Africa: the male has blue and scarlet patches on the face and rump.

man′dū·çȧ·ble, *a.* that can be chewed; fit to be eaten.

man′dū·çāte, *v.t.* [L. *manducatus*, pp. of *manducare*, to chew, a form of *mandere*, to chew.] to chew; masticate. [Rare.]

man·dū·çā′tion, *n.* the act of chewing or eating.

man′dū·çȧ·tō·ry, *a.* pertaining to or employed in chewing.

man·dū′çus, *n.* [L., a glutton, chewer, from *mandere*, to chew.] a comical mask having the appearance of a face distorted, as by chewing.

man′dy·ȧs, *n.* [Gr. *mandyas*, *mandya*, a woolen cloak.] a long, flowing wrap, fastened at the neck, worn by monks and church dignitaries.]

māne, *n.* [ME. *mane*, *mayne*; AS. *manu*, mane.]

1. the long hair growing from the top or sides of the neck of certain animals, as the horse, bison, lion, etc.

2. long, thick human hair.

man′-ēat″ẽr, *n.* 1. a cannibal.

2. an animal that eats, likes to eat, or is thought to eat, human flesh; specifically, (a) a certain shark of tropical waters; (b) a lion, tiger, etc. with a taste for human flesh.

māned, *a.* having a mane.

ma·nège′, mȧ·neġe′ (ma-nezh′, mȧ-nāzh′), *n.* [Fr.] 1. the art of riding and training horses; horsemanship.

2. the paces and exercises of a trained horse.

3. a school for training horses and teaching riders; a riding academy.

mā′nĕh (-nē), *n.* [Heb.] a Hebrew weight, the mina.

māne′less, *a.* without a mane.

man′-en′ġine, *n.* a crude form of elevator, used in some deep mines, consisting of stationary and movable platforms. By stepping from one to the other at proper intervals, a man may be lowered or raised.

man′e·quin (-kin), *n.* same as *manikin*.

mā′nēṣ, Mā′nēṣ, *n.pl.* [L.] 1. in ancient Roman religion, the souls of the dead, especially of dead ancestors, regarded as gods.

2. [*construed as sing. or pl.*] the soul or shade of some dead person.

māne′sheet, *n.* a hood devised to cover a horse's mane.

Mȧ·net′ti, *n.* [named after an Italian botanist, Saverio *Manetti* (1723–1784).] in horticulture, kind of rose with a dwarf stock much used in budding.

mȧ·neū′vẽr, *v.t.* and *v.i.*; maneuvered, *pt.*, *pp.*; maneuvering, *ppr.* 1. to perform or cause to perform a maneuver or maneuvers.

2. to manage or plan skillfully or shrewdly; to manipulate or scheme.

3. to move, get, put, make, compel, etc. (a person or thing) by some stratagem or scheme; as, he *maneuvered* his way to victory; she *maneuvered* herself out of an embarrassing position.

Also spelled *manoeuvre*.

mȧ·neū′vẽr, *n.* [Fr. *manœuvre*; from *main*, L. *manus*, the hand, and *œuvre*, L. *opera*, work.]

1. a planned and controlled tactical or strategic movement of troops, warships, etc.

2. [*pl.*] large-scale practice movements and exercises of troops, warships, etc. under conditions resembling those of combat.

3. any movement or procedure intended as a skillful or shrewd step toward some objective; stratagem; artifice; scheme; as, the child tried various *maneuvers* to get his own way.

Also spelled *manoeuvre*.

mȧ·neū·vẽr·ȧ·bil′i·ty, *n.* the quality or state of being maneuverable.

mȧ·neū′vẽr·ȧ·ble, *a.* that can be maneuvered.

man Frī′dāy, 1. in Defoe's *Robinson Crusoe*, the hero's devoted servant: so named because rescued from cannibals on a Friday.

2. a loyal and devoted or servile follower or servant.

man′fụl, *a.* having the spirit of a man; bold, brave, courageous, noble, honorable, etc.

man′fụl·ly, *adv.* boldly; courageously; honorably.

man′fụl·ness, *n.* boldness; courageousness; resolution.

mañ′gȧ·bey, *n.* [from *Mangabey*, in Madagascar.] any of several species of African monkeys of the genus *Cercocebus*, having the tail longer than the body.

mañ′găn, *n.* same as *mangonel*.

mañ′gȧ·nāte, *n.* [*manganic* and *-ate*.] a salt of manganic acid; as, potassium *manganate*, K_2MnO_4.

mañ·gȧ·nēse′, *n.* [Fr. *manganèse*; It. *manganese*; by metathesis from ML. *magnesia*.] a grayish-white metallic chemical element, usually hard and brittle, which rusts like iron but is not magnetic: it is used in the manufacture of alloys of iron, aluminum, and copper: symbol, Mn; atomic weight, 54.93; atomic number, 25.

manganese bronze; a compound of zinc, copper, and a small percentage of manganese.

manganese spar; rhodonite.

manganese steel; a hard, malleable and ductile steel containing 12 to 14 per cent of manganese.

mañ·gȧ·nē′siăn, *a.* pertaining to manganese; consisting of manganese or partaking of its qualities.

mañ·gȧ·nē′sious (-shus), *a.* manganous.

mañ·gȧ·net′iç, *a.* same as *manganiferous*.

mañ·gan′iç, *a.* [*manganese* and *-ic*.]

1. designating or of chemical compounds in which manganese has a higher valence than in the corresponding manganous compounds.

2. designating or of an acid, H_2MnO_4, existing only as salts, the manganates.

mañ·gȧ·nif′ẽr·ous, *a.* [*maganese*, and L. *ferre*, to bear.] bearing manganese: said of ores.

mañ′gȧ·nin, *n.* [*manganese* and *-in*.] an alloy consisting mainly of copper with some manganese and nickel: it is used in electrical heating elements, rheostats, etc.

mañ′gȧ·nīte, *n.* 1. hydrous manganese trioxide, $Mn_2O_3{\cdot}H_2O$, a steel-gray or black, crystalline mineral with a metallic luster.

2. any of a series of salts that may be considered as derivatives of manganous acid, the hydroxide of tetravalent manganese.

mañ·gā′ni·um, *n.* manganese. [Rare.]

mañ·gan′ō·sīte, *n.* a mineral protoxide of manganese.

mañ′gȧ·nous, *a.* [*manganese* and *-ous*.] designating or of chemical compounds in which manganese has a lower valence than in corresponding manganic compounds.

mānġe, *n.* [OFr. *mangeue*, *mangue*, itch, eating, from L. *manducare*, to chew.] any of various skin diseases of domestic animals, and occasionally of man, especially one caused by a parasitic mite and characterized by a loss of hair.

mañ′gel-wŭr″zel, *n.* [G., corrupted from *mangoldwurzel*, beet root; *mangold*, beet, and *wurzel*, a root.] in botany, a large, coarse beet, *Beta vulgaris*, cultivated and used as food for cattle.

mān′ġẽr, *n.* [OFr. *mangeoire*, *mangeure*, from *mangier*; L. *manducare*, to eat, from *mandere*, to chew.]

1. a trough or box in which fodder is laid for cattle; a place in which horses and cattle are fed.

2. in ships, a space across the deck, within the hawse holes, separated from the after part of the deck, to prevent the water which enters the hawse holes from running over the deck.

mān′ġẽr bōard, the bulkhead on a ship's deck

that separates the manger from the rest of the deck.

Man·ġif'e·rȧ, *n.* [from *mango*, and L. *ferre*, to bear.] a genus of Asiatic trees of the cashew family, of which the mango is a type.

mān'ġi·ly, *adv.* in a mangy manner.

mān'ġi·ness, *n.* the quality or condition of being mangy.

man̄'gle, *v.t.*; mangled, *pt.*, *pp.*; mangling, *ppr.* [Anglo-Fr. *mangler*, *mahangler*, freq. of OFr. *mehaigner*, to maim.]

1. to mutilate or disfigure by repeatedly and roughly cutting, tearing, hacking, or crushing; to lacerate and bruise badly; as, the body was *mangled* beyond recognition.

2. to spoil; botch; mar; garble; as, the text was *mangled*.

Syn.—tear, mutilate, lacerate.

man̄'gle, *n.* [D. *mangel*, a mangle; LL. *mangonum*, *mango* (*-onis*), from Gr. *mangonon*, a war engine for throwing stones.] a machine for pressing and smoothing cloth, especially sheets and other flat pieces, between rollers.

man̄'gle, *v.t.*; mangled, *pt.*, *pp.*; mangling, *ppr.* to press in a mangle.

man̄'glẽr, *n.* one who uses a mangle.

man̄'glẽr, *n.* a person or thing that mangles, or mutilates.

man̄'gle rack, a mechanical device for changing circular motion into reciprocating motion in a straight line, first put into common use in the mangle.

man̄'gō, *n.*; *pl.* **man̄'gōeṣ, man̄'gōṣ,** [Malay *mañgga*, the mango.]

1. a yellow-red, oblong tropical fruit, *Mangifera indica*, with a thick rind, somewhat acid and juicy pulp, and a hard stone: it is eaten when ripe, or preserved or pickled when unripe.

2. the tree that it grows on.

3. pickled muskmelon or cucumber.

man̄'gō bird, the yellow oriole, *Oriolus kundoo*, found in India.

man̄'gōld-wûr"zel, *n.* same as *mangel-wurzel*.

man̄'gō·nel, *n.* [OFr. *mangonel*, from LL. *mangonellus*, a mangonel.] a military apparatus formerly used for throwing stones, etc.

man̄'go·steen, *n.* [Malay *mangustan*.] a tree, *Garcinia mangostana*, of the tropics; also, its fruit.

wild mangosteen; a closely-branched tree, *Disopyros embryopteris*, of the East Indies.

man̄'gō tree, the tree, *Mangifera indica*, bearing the mango.

man'grōve, *n.* [from Port. *mangue* or Sp. *mangle*, from the W. Ind. name.] any of a group of tropical trees or shrubs growing in swampy ground along river banks, with branches that spread and send down roots, thus forming more trunks and causing a thick growth.

man'grōve snap'pẽr, a fish, *Lutjanus griseus*: called also *bastard snapper*.

man̄gue, *n.* [Fr., from native name.] a carnivorous animal of Africa related to the civets; the *Crossarchus obscurus*.

mān'ġy, *a.*; *comp.* mangier; *superl.* mangiest.

1. having, infected with, resembling, or caused by the mange.

2. shabby and filthy; sordid; squalid.

3. mean and low; despicable.

man'han"dle, *v.t.*; manhandled, *pt.*, *pp.*; manhandling, *ppr.* 1. to move or do by human strength only, without machines. [Rare.]

2. to handle roughly.

Man·hat'tăn, *n.* 1. any member of a tribe of Algonquian Indians who lived on Manhattan Island.

2. a cocktail made of whisky and vermouth, usually with a dash of bitters and a maraschino cherry.

Man·hat"tăn·i·zā'tion, *n.* a Manhattanizing or being Manhattanized.

Man·hat'tăn·ïze, *v.t.*; Manhattanized, *pt.*, *pp.*; Manhattanizing, *ppr.* [after *Manhattan*, island forming part of New York City.] to alter the architectural appearance of (a city) by the construction of skyscrapers and high-rise buildings.

man'hōle, *n.* a hole through which a man can get into a drain, subway, or parts of machinery, to inspect or repair it.

man'hood, *n.* 1. the state or time of being a man (human being or, especially, adult male human being).

2. manly character or qualities; virility; courage, resolution, etc.

3. men collectively.

man'-hour' (-our'), *n.* a unit of work, equal to that done by one man in one hour.

man'hunt, *n.* a hunt or search for a man or men, especially for a fugitive.

man'hunt'ẽr, *n.* one who leads, or takes part in, a manhunt; a detective; an investigator.

mā'ni·ȧ, *n.* [L., from Gr. *mania*, madness, from *mainesthai*, to rage.]

1. wild or violent insanity; specifically, the manic phase of manic-depressive psychosis, characterized generally by abnormal excitability, exaggerated feelings of well-being, flight of ideas, excessive activity, etc.

2. an excessive, persistent enthusiasm, liking, craving, or interest; obsession; craze; as, a *mania* for collecting stamps.

-mā'ni·ȧ, a combining form meaning, (a) *a* (specified) *type of mental disorder* or *manic state*, as in klepto*mania*; (b) *an excessive, persistent enthusiasm, craving,* or *liking for, obsession with,* or *craze for* (a specified thing), as in biblio*mania*.

Syn.—madness, insanity, craze, delirium.

man'i·ȧ·ble, *a.* [Fr., from *manier*, to handle, manage.] that can be handled; tractable.

mā'ni·aç, *a.* [L. *mania*; Gr. *mania*, madness.] mad; raving with madness; raging with disordered intellect.

mā'ni·aç, *n.* a madman; lunatic.

-mā'ni·aç, a combining form used to form adjectives and nouns (referring to persons) from corresponding nouns ending in *-mania*, as in klepto*maniac*.

mȧ·nī'ȧ·căl, *a.* of, having, or showing mania; wildly insane; raving.

mȧ·nī'ȧ·căl·ly, *adv.* with madness; in a maniacal manner.

man'iç, *a.* in psychiatry, (a) having or characterized by mania; (b) of or like mania.

man'i·cāte, *a.* [L. *manicatus*, sleeved, from *manica*, a long sleeve, from *manus*, a hand.] in botany, covered with impubescence so interwoven as to form a kind of mat separable from the surface.

man'iç-dē·pres'sive, *a.* designating, of, or having a psychosis characterized by alternating periods of mania and melancholia, or mental depression.

man'iç-dē·pres'sive, *n.* a person who has manic-depressive psychosis.

Man·i·chae'ăn, Man·i·chē'ăn, *a.* relating to Manichaeus or to the Manichaeans.

Man·i·chae'ăn, Man·i·chē'ăn, *n.* a believer in the teachings of Manichaeus.

Man·i·chae'ăn·iṣm, Man·i·chē'ăn·iṣm, *n.* Manichaeism.

Man'i·chae·iṣm, Man'i·chē·iṣm, *n.* a religious philosophy taught from the third century to the seventh century A.D. by the Persian Manes, or Manichaeus, and his followers, combining Zoroastrian, Gnomic Christian, and pagan elements, and based on the doctrine of the two contending principles of good (light, God, the soul) and evil (darkness, Satan, the body).

Man'i·chee, *n.* a Manichaean.

Man'i·chē·ist, *n.* a Manichaean.

man·i·cot'tï, *n.* [It., lit., muffs, pl. of *manicotto*.] pasta, in the form of long, broad tubes, usually boiled, stuffed with cheese, and baked with a tomato sauce.

man'i·cūre, *n.* [L. *manus*, hand, and *cura*, care.]

1. one who is employed to care for the hands, particularly the nails. [Rare.]

2. the care of the hands; especially, trimming, polishing, etc. of the fingernails.

man'i·cūre, *v.t.* and *v.i.*; manicured, *pt.*, *pp.*; manicuring, *ppr.* to take care of (the hands and fingernails); to do the work of a manicurist for (a person or persons).

man'i·cūr"ist, *n.* one who is employed to perform a manicure of the hands or to clean and polish the fingernails.

mā'nid, *n.* one of the *Manidæ*, or anteaters.

man'i·fest, *a.* [L. *manifestus*, evident, clear, plain; lit., struck by the hand; *manus*, hand, and *fendere* (used in combination), to strike.] plain; open; clearly visible to the eye or obvious to the understanding; apparent; not obscure or difficult to be seen or understood.

Thus *manifest* to sight the god appeared.
—Dryden.

manifest eyestrain; eye muscle defects which are at once discovered by diffusion tests.

Syn.—clear, plain, obvious, evident.

man'i·fest, *n.* 1. (a) an itemized list of a ship's cargo, telling the place of lading, destination, etc., to be shown to customs officials; (b) a waybill of lading.

2. perishable goods, as livestock, carried by fast freight.

3. (a) a manifestation; (b) a manifesto. [Obs.]

man'i·fest, *v.t.*; manifested, *pt.*, *pp.*; manifesting, *ppr.* [L. *manifestare*, to make plain, from *manifestus*, clear, plain, evident.]

1. to make clear or evident; to show plainly; reveal; evince.

2. to prove; to be evidence of.

3. (a) to enter in a ship's manifest; (b) to show the manifest of (cargo).

man'i·fest, *v.i.* to appear to the senses; to show itself.

Syn.—reveal, show, exhibit, display, declare, discover.

man·i·fest'ȧ·ble, *a.* that can be made evident.

man·i·fes'tănt, *n.* a person who takes part in a manifestation, or public demonstration.

man·i·fes·tā'tion, *n.* 1. a manifesting or being manifested.

2. something that manifests; as, his silence was a *manifestation* of cowardice.

3. a public demonstration, as by a government, party, etc., for political effect.

Man'i·fest Des'ti·ny, the nineteenth-century doctrine that it is the destiny of the Anglo-Saxon nations, especially of the United States, to dominate the entire Western hemisphere.

man'i·fest·ly, *adv.* clearly; evidently; plainly; in a manner to be clearly seen or understood.

man'i·fest·ness, *n.* clearness to the sight or mind; obviousness.

man·i·fes'tō, *n.*; *pl.* **man·i·fes'tōeṣ,** [It. *manifesto*, an edict, as adj. evident, from L. *manifestus*, clear, plain, evident.] a public declaration of motives and intentions by a government or by a person or group regarded as having some public importance.

man·i·fes'tō, *v.t.* and *v.i.* to issue a manifesto; to affect by a manifesto. [Rare.]

man'i·fōld, *a.* [ME. *manifold*, *manyfold*; AS. *manigfeald*; *manig*, many, and *-feald*, -fold.]

1. having many and various forms, features, parts, etc.; as, *manifold* wisdom.

2. of many sorts; many and varied; multifarious: used with a plural noun; as, *manifold* duties.

3. being such in many and various ways or for many reasons; as, a *manifold* villain.

4. comprising, consisting of, or operating several units or parts of one kind: said of certain devices.

man'i·fōld, *n.* 1. what is manifold.

2. any of many copies made by manifolding.

3. a pipe or tube with at least one inlet and two or more outlets, for connecting one pipe with others, as between the engine and carburetor in an automobile.

man'i·fōld, *adv.* with many repetitions; in many ways; over and over. [Obs.]

man'i·fōld, *v.t.*; manifolded, *pt.*, *pp.*; manifolding, *ppr.* 1. to make manifold; to multiply.

2. to make more than one copy of; as, she will *manifold* the letter with carbon paper.

man'i·fōld·ẽr, *n.* a person or thing that manifolds; specifically, a machine for making copies of documents, etc.

man'i·fōld·ly, *adv.* in a manifold manner; in many ways. [Rare.]

man'i·fōld·ness, *n.* 1. multiplicity.

2. in mathematics, (a) the quality of magnitude in general; (b) the number of different prime factors of a number.

Man'i·hot, *n.* [Mod. L.; Fr., from Braz. (Tupi) *mandioca*.]

1. a genus of tropical American plants found mainly in Brazil, including the cassava, or manioc, from which tapioca is obtained, and others that yield a kind of rubber.

2. [m—] any plant of this genus.

man'i·kin, *n.* [D. *manneken*, a little man; *man*, man, and dim. suffix *-ken*.]

1. a little man; a dwarf.

2. an anatomical model of the human body, usually with movable and detachable parts, used in medical schools, etc.

3. a mannequin.

Mȧ·nil'ȧ, mȧ·nil'ȧ, *n.* 1. Manila hemp.

2. Manila paper.

3. Manila rope.

4. a kind of cigar made in Manila, the capital of the Philippines.

Sometimes spelled *Manilla*.

Manila hemp; a strong fiber from the leafstalk of a Philippine tree related to the banana; abacá: it is used for making rope, paper, etc.

Manila paper; a strong, brownish wrapping paper, originally made of Manila hemp, now of various fibers.

Manila rope; strong rope made of Manila hemp.

Ma·nil′la, *n.* same as *Manila.*
ma·nil′la, *n.* [from Fr. and Sp.; Fr. *manille;* Sp. *malilla (carta),* from *malillo,* dim. of *malo,* bad (L. *malus*).] in ombre, quadrille, and some other card games, the second-highest trump: also *manille.*
ma·nil′la, *n.* [Sp., from LL. *monilia,* a bracelet, from L. *manus,* hand.] a metal ring or bracelet worn on the arm or wrist and used as a medium of exchange by certain African tribes: also *manilio.*
ma·nille′, *n.* same as *manilla* (trump).
man′i·nōse, *n.* [Am. Ind. *mananosay.*] a long, soft-shelled clam of the shores of Virginia and Maryland: also called *mannynose* and *manninose.*
man′i·oc (*or* mā′ni-), *n.* [Fr., from Braz. (Tupi) *mandioca.*]
1. a cassava, a tropical plant with edible starchy roots.
2. the starch from these roots, used in making bread and tapioca.
Also *mandioc, mandioca.*
man′i·ple, *n.* [ME.; OFr.; L. *manipulus,* a handful, a bundle, a number of soldiers belonging to the same standard, a company, from *manus,* hand, and the root of *plere,* to fill.]
1. a subdivision of the ancient Roman legion; one third of a cohort, consisting of either 60 or 120 common soldiers.
2. a silk band worn hanging over the left forearm as a Eucharistic vestment.
ma·nip′ū·lăr, *a.* 1. of a maniple (in the ancient Roman army).
2. of manipulation.
ma·nip′ū·lăr, *n.* a soldier of a maniple.
ma·nip′ū·lāte, *v.t.*; manipulated, *pt., pp.*; manipulating, *ppr.* [back-formation from *manipulation.*]
1. to work or operate with or as with the hand or hands; to handle or use, especially with skill; as, the pilot of an airplane must *manipulate* various controls.
2. to manage or control artfully or by shrewd use of influence, especially in an unfair or fraudulent way; as, the political boss *manipulated* the voting.
3. to change or falsify (figures, accounts, etc.) for one's own purposes or profit; to juggle; to rig; specifically, to cause (prices of stocks, etc.) to fall or rise, as by wash sales.
ma·nip′ū·lāte, *v.i.* to use the hands, as in scientific experiments, artistic processes, mechanical operations, or the like; as, he *manipulates* neatly or successfully.
ma·nip·ū·lā′tion, *n.* [Fr.; as if from L. (hyp.) *manipulatio,* from pp. of (hyp.) *manipulare,* from *manipulus;* see *maniple.*]
1. a handling or being handled; especially, skillful handling or operation.
2. artful management or control, as by shrewd use of influence, especially in an unfair or fraudulent way.
3. change or falsification (of figures, prices, etc.) for one's own purposes or profit.
ma·nip′ū·lā·tive, *a.* pertaining to or performed by manipulation.
ma·nip′ū·lā·tŏr, *n.* 1. one who or that which manipulates.
2. a mechanical device that is operated by remote control, as for handling radioactive materials.
ma·nip′ū·lā·tō·ry, *a.* same as *manipulative.*
Mā′nis, *n.* [from L. *manes,* shades or ghosts:

MANIS

so called because of the nocturnal habits of the animals.]
1. a genus of edentate mammals, covered with large, hard, triangular scales with sharp edges which overlap each other: they inhabit the warmest parts of Asia and Africa, and feed on ants.
2. [m-] any animal of this genus: also called *scaly lizard, scaly anteater,* and *pangolin.*
man′it, *n.* [from *man* and *unit.*] a standard unit expressing the amount of work that may be done or produced by a man in one minute: used in time study and production scales.
man′i·tō, *n.* [Am. Ind. (Massachusetts) *manitto,* he is a god.] in Algonquian Indian religion, a spirit or force underlying the world and life, understood as a nature spirit of both good and evil influence: also *manitou, manitu.*
Man·i·tō′băn, *a.* of Manitoba.
Man·i·tō′băn, *n.* a native or inhabitant of Manitoba.
man′i·toū, man′i·tū, *n.* same as *manito.*
man′i·trunk, *n.* [L. *manus,* hand, and *truncus,* trunk.] the prothorax of an insect.
man·kīnd′ (*also, and for 2 and 3 always,* man′kīnd), *n.* 1. the human race; man taken collectively; all human beings.
The proper study of *mankind* is man. —Pope.
2. the males of the human race, as distinguished from the females; the male sex.
3. human feelings; humanity. [Obs.]
man′kīnd, *a.* 1. resembling man, not woman, in form or nature; unwomanly; coarse: often applied by the older poets to woman in a bad sense. [Obs.]
2. of virile power; ferocious. [Obs.]
Manks, *n.* and *a.* same as *manx.*
man′less, *a.* 1. without men; not manned, as a boat.
2. without manliness; inhuman. [Obs.]
man′less·ly, *adv.* in an unmanly or inhuman manner. [Obs.]
man′līke, *a.* 1. like or characteristic of a man or men.
2. fit for a man; masculine.
man′li·ness, *n.* the quality or state of being manly; virility.
man′ling, *n.* a little man. [Obs.]
man′ly, *a.*; *comp.* manlier; *superl.* manliest, 1. having the qualities generally regarded as those that a man should have; virile; strong, resolute, honorable, etc.
2. fit for a man; masculine; as, *manly* sports.
man′ly, *adv.* in a manly way.
man′-māde′, *a.* made by man; artificial.
man′na, *n.* [AS. *manna;* L. *manna;* Gr. *manna;* Heb. *mān.*]
1. in the Bible, a substance miraculously furnished as food for the Israelites in their journey through the wilderness.
And the house of Israel called the name thereof *Manna;* and it was like coriander seed, white; and the taste of it was like wafers made with honey.—Ex. xvi. 31.
2. anything thought of as like this; any needed sustenance that seems miraculously supplied.
3. in medicine, a sweet, gummy juice obtained from certain European ash trees, used as a laxative; especially that taken by incision from the *Fraxinus ornus,* of southern Europe.
Madagascar manna; same as *dulcitol.*
man′na croup, 1. same as *semolina.*
2. the prepared seeds of manna grass, *Glyceria fluitans.*
Mann Act (man), [after James Robert *Mann* (1856–1922), U. S. Congressman.] an act of Congress (June, 1910) prohibiting the interstate transportation of women for immoral purposes (*white slavery*).
man′na grass, a grass, *Glyceria fluitans,* having sweet seeds; by extension, any plant of the genus *Glyceria.*
man′na gum, a tall evergreen tree, *Eucalyptus viminalis,* of Australia, which bears a small fruit resembling manna.
man′ne·quin (-kin), *n.* [Fr., from D. *manneken.*]
1. a model of the human body, used by tailors, window dressers, artists, etc.
2. a woman whose work is exhibiting new clothes in stores, etc. by wearing them.
man′nēr, *n.* [OFr. *manere, maniere,* habitual, accustomed, skillful, from L. *manus,* hand.]
1. the way in which anything is done or happens; the way of performing or effecting anything; mode of action; method; style; form; fashion.
2. (a) a way of acting; personal behavior or bearing; as, his *manner* showed his anger; (b) distinguished bearing or behavior; as, she has *manner.*
Air and *manner* are more expressive than words. —Richardson.
3. a usual way of acting; customary behavior; habit; as, it is his *manner* to be sarcastic.
4. [*pl.*] (a) ways of social life; prevailing social conditions or customs; as, a comedy of *manners;* (b) ways of social behavior; deportment, especially with reference to polite conventions; as, good *manners,* bad *manners;* (c) polite ways of social behavior; deportment conforming with polite conventions; as, the child really has *manners.*
5. (a) characteristic style or method in art, music, literature, etc.; (b) mannerism.
6. (a) kind; sort; as, what *manner* of man is he?; (b) kinds; sorts; as, all *manner* of things. [Archaic or Literary.]
by all manner of means; of course; surely.
by no manner of means; in no way, definitely not.
in a manner; in a certain degree, measure, or sense; to a certain extent; as, it is *in a manner* done already.
to the manner born; (a) accustomed to something, as wealth, social advantages, or the like, from birth; (b) naturally fitted for a certain thing.
Syn.—form, method, custom, habit, fashion, air, look, mien, aspect, appearance.
Män′ner·chor (men′ẽr-kōr), *n.* [G., from *männer,* pl. of *mann,* man, and *chor,* a chorus.] a German men's choral group or singing society.
man′nẽred, *a.* 1. having manners of a specified sort; as, ill-*mannered,* well-*mannered.*
2. marked by mannerism; affected; as, a *mannered* literary style.
man′nẽr·ism, *n.* 1. excessive use of some distinctive, often affected, manner or style in art, literature, speech, or behavior.
2. a peculiarity of manner in behavior, speech, etc.
man′nẽr·ist, *n.* a person characterized by mannerism; especially, an artist or writer whose work shows a persistent or excessive adherence to some style or method.
man′nẽr·less, *a.* lacking good manners; impolite; unmannerly.
man′nẽr·li·ness, *n.* the quality or state of being mannerly.
man′nẽr·ly, *a.* having or showing good manners; polite; well-behaved.
man′nẽr·ly, *adv.* politely; respectfully; without rudeness.
Männ′heīm gōld, a variety of brass made as an imitation of gold: first made at Mannheim, Germany.
man′nīde, *n.* [*mannite* and anhy*dride.*] an anhydride of a mannitol: formula, $C_6H_{10}O_4$.
man·nif′ẽr·ous, *a.* [L. *manna,* manna, and *ferre,* to bear.]
1. bearing manna.
2. causing the production of manna; as, *manniferous* insects.
man′ni·kin, *n.* same as *manikin.*
man′ni·nōse, *n.* same as *maninose.*
man′nish, *a.* 1. having the nature of man; human. [Obs.]
2. characteristic of, imitating, or resembling a man, as distinguished from a woman; hence, as applied to a woman, masculine; unwomanly.
man′nish·ly, *adv.* in the manner of a man.
man′nish·ness, *n.* the state or quality of being mannish.
man′ni·tan, *n.* [*mannite* and *an*hydride.] a sirup, $C_6H_{12}O_5$, with a slightly sweetish taste, obtained by heating mannite to 200° Fahr., or by boiling it with concentrated hydrochloric acid.
man′nīte, *n.* [*manna* and *-ite.*] same as *mannitol.*
man·nit′ic, *a.* [*mannite* and *-ic.*] of or obtained from mannitol.
man′ni·tol, *n.* [*mannite* and alco*hol.*] a colorless, crystalline alcohol, $C_6H_8(OH)_6$, occurring in various plants and animals, as the flowering ash, sponges, etc.
man′ni·tōse, *n.* same as *mannose.*
man′nōse, *n.* [*mannitol* and *-ose.*] a sugar, $C_6H_{12}O_6$, formed by the oxidation of mannitol.
man′ny·nōse, *n.* same as *maninose.*
ma·noeu′vre (-nū′vẽr), *n., v.i.* and *v.t.*; manoeuvred, *pt., pp.*; manoeuvring, *ppr.* maneuver.
man-ŏf-wãr′, *n.*; *pl.* **men-ŏf-wãr′,** an armed naval vessel; a warship.
man-of-war bird; see under *bird.*
man-of-war hawk; the frigate bird.
man-of-war's man; a seaman belonging to a ship of war.
ma·nom′e·tẽr, *n.* [Fr. *manomètre,* from Gr. *manos,* rare, and Fr. *-mètre,* -meter.]

1. an instrument, usually a U-shaped tube, for measuring the pressure of gases or vapors.
2. an instrument for measuring blood pressure by measuring the pressure of compressed air necessary to equalize the tension in the blood vessels.

man·ō·met′riç, *a.* of or made by the manometer; as, *manometric* measurements.
manometric flames; flames as modified by the impulses of a series of sound waves and shown by means of reflections from a rotating mirror.

man′ŏr, *n.* [OFr. *manoir*, a manor house, mansion, from *manoir, maneir*, to dwell, from L. *manere*, to remain.]
1. in England, (a) in feudal times, the district over which a lord held authority, subject to the jurisdiction of his court; land belonging to a lord and partly divided among his peasants in return for rent of some kind, or land reserved by him for his own use; (b) more recently, a landed estate, usually with a main residence, the owner of which still holds some feudal rights over the land.
2. in the United States during colonial times, a district granted as a manor and leased to tenants at a set rental.
3. (a) a mansion; (b) the main residence on an estate; (c) a lord's mansion with its land. [Obs.]

man′ŏr house, the house of the lord of a manor.

mȧ·nō′ri·ăl, *a.* of, like, or constituting a manor.

man′ō·sçōpe, *n.* manometer. [Rare.]

man′pow″ẽr, *n.* 1. power furnished by human physical strength.
2. the normal rate at which a man is able to work, equal to 1/10 horsepower.
3. the collective strength, ability to work, or availability for work of the people in any given area, nation, etc.
Also *man power*.

mäṅ″qué′ (-kā′), *a.* [Fr., from pp. of *manquer*, to fail, be lacking.] that has failed or falls short of the goal; defective: placed after the noun it modifies, as poet *manqué*.

man′quell′ẽr, *n.* [AS. *mancwellere*; *mann*, man, and *cwellere*, a killer.] a murderer; a manslayer. [Obs.]

man′red, man′rent, *n.* vassalage. [Obs.]

man′ro͝ot, *n.* a species of morning-glory, *Ipomœa leptophylla*, having a large root.

man′rōpe, *n.* in a ship, a rope serving as a handrail to a gangway, ladder, etc.

man′särd, *n.* [after François *Mansard* (1598–1666), Fr. architect.]
1. a roof with two slopes on each of the four sides, the lower steeper than the upper: also *mansard roof*.
2. a garret; an attic; the story under such a roof.

MANSARD ROOF

manse, *n.* [OFr. *manse*; ML. *mansum, mansa*, a dwelling, from L. *mansus*, pp. of *manere*, to remain, dwell.]
1. a parsonage; a residence of a minister, especially a Scottish Presbyterian minister.
2. (a) a mansion; (b) enough land to support a family. [Obs.]

man′sẽrv″ănt, *n.*; *pl.* **men′sẽrv″ănts,** a male servant: also *man servant*.

man′sion, *n.* [L. *mansio (-onis)*, a staying, abiding, an abode, from *manere*, to remain.]
1. formerly, a manor house.
2. a large, imposing house; a stately residence.
3. a stay; sojourn. [Obs.]
4. [Archaic.] (a) a dwelling place; (b) [*usually pl.*] [Chiefly Brit.] an apartment house.
5. in astrology, (a) a house; (b) one of the 28 parts of the moon's course occupied on successive days.

man′sion, *v.i.* to dwell; to reside. [Obs.]

man′sion·ăr·y, *a.* resident; residentiary; as, *mansionary* canons. [Rare.]

man′sion house, the house in which one resides; an inhabited house. [Obs.]
The Mansion house; the official residence of the lord mayor of London.

man′sion·ry, *n.* mansions collectively. [Obs.]

man′-sīzed″, *a.* of a size fit for a man; large; big. [Colloq.]

man′slaugh″tẽr (-slą″), *n.* 1. the killing of a human being by another.
2. in law, the unlawful killing of a human being without malice, express or implied. This may be voluntary, upon a sudden heat or excitement of anger, or involuntary, but in the commission of some unlawful act.

man′slāy″ẽr, *n.* one who commits homicide or manslaughter.

man′stēal″ẽr, *n.* one who steals or kidnaps men.

man′stēal″ing, *n.* the act of stealing a human being.

man′-stop″ping, *a.* designating a pistol or rifle bullet which, because of its especially great force on impact, will stop a man's advance.

man′suē·tūde (-swē-), *n.* [L. *mansuetudo*, from *mansuetus*, tame, gentle.] tameness; mildness; gentleness.

man′sweăr, *v.i.* to commit perjury. [Obs.]

man′tȧ, *n.* [Sp. *manta*, a blanket.]
1. coarse cotton cloth used for cheap shawls, capes, etc. in Latin America.
2. a shawl, cape, etc. made of this.
3. a kind of horse blanket or cloth for covering a pack-animal's load.
4. a mantelet. [Obs.]
5. in zoology, a very large ray; a devilfish: also *manta ray*.

Mant·cho͞o′, *a.* and *n.* same as *Manchu*.

man′teau (-tō; *Fr.* mäṅ-tō′), *n.*; *pl.* **man′teauş** (-tōz), Fr. **mäṅ·teaux′** (-tō′), [Fr., from OFr. *mantel*; see *mantle*.]
1. (a) woman's cloak or mantle; (b) any mantle.
2. a mantua, or woman's loose gown. [Obs.]

man′tel (-tl), *n.* [see *mantle*.]
1. the facing of stone, marble, etc. about a fireplace, including a projecting shelf or slab above it.
2. the shelf or slab.

man′tel·et (*or* mant′let), *n.* [OFr., dim. of *mantel*; see *mantle*.]
1. a short mantle, cape, or cloak.
2. a movable or stationary protective shelter or screen; especially, (a) a movable roof or screen formerly used in war to protect besiegers from the enemy; (b) a bulletproof shield or screen, as about a gun to protect the gun crew; (c) a bulletproof enclosure for observation in target shooting. Also (for 2) *mantlet*.

man·tel·let′tȧ, *n.* [It.] in the Roman Catholic Church, a sleeveless vestment worn by cardinals, bishops, etc.

man′tel·piēce, *n.* a mantel (sense 2).

man′tel·shelf, *n.* same as *mantelpiece*.

man′tel·tree, *n.* 1. a beam, stone, or arch above the opening of a fireplace, supporting the masonry above.
2. a mantelpiece. [Archaic.]

man′tiç, *a.* [Gr. *mantikos*, from *mantis*, a seer, prophet.] relating to prophecy or soothsaying, or to one practicing divination; prophetic.

-man′tiç, [from Gr. *mantikos*; see *mantic*.] a combining form used to form adjectives corresponding to nouns ending in *-mancy*, as in necro*mantic*.

man·ti·chō′rȧ, *n.* same as *manticore*.

man·ti·çō′rȧ, *n.* same as *mantocire*.

man′ti·çore, *n.* [L. *mantichora*; Gr. *mantichōras, martichōras*, a fabulous Indian beast; from Per. *mardkhora*, man-eater; *mard*, man, and *khaur*, eater.] in mythology, a monster with the head of a man, the body of a tiger or lion, and the feet and tail of a scorpion or of a dragon.

man·til′lȧ, *n.* [Sp.] 1. a woman's head covering, which falls down upon the shoulders and may be used as a veil: worn in Spain, Mexico, etc.
2. a short mantle, cape, or cloak.

MANTILLA

Man′tis, *n.* [Gr. *mantis*, a prophet, seer; also, a kind of locust or grasshopper.]
1. a genus of orthopterous insects that hold their forelegs folded as if praying, and feed on other insects.
2. [m-] *pl.* **man′tis·eş, man′tēş,** any insect of this genus: often *praying mantis*.

man′tis çrab, a squilla.

man·tis′pid, *n.* [Gr. *mantis*, a grasshopper, and *ōps, ōpos*, face.] an insect of the genus *Mantispa*, and kindred genera of neuropterous insects.

man·tis′sȧ, *n.* [L. *mantissa*, an addition, a makeweight.] in mathematics, the decimal part of a logarithm: so called because added to the integral part, or *characteristic*. Thus, in the logarithm of 900=2.95424 the *characteristic* is 2, and the *mantissa* is .95424.

man′tis shrimp, a squilla.

man′tle, *n.* [ME. *mantel*, from AS. *mentel* and OFr. *mantel*; both from L. *mantellum, mantelum*, a cloak, mantle, napkin, prob. from *manus*, hand, and *tela*, a web.]
1. a kind of cloak or loose, sleeveless garment to be worn over other garments.
2. anything that cloaks, covers, envelops, or conceals; as, the *mantle* of charity.
3. a small hood or cap, usually cylindrical, of a meshwork substance, such as a thorium or cerium compound, which when placed over a flame becomes white-hot and gives off light.
4. the outer covering of a wall.
5. the outer wall and casing of a blast furnace, above the hearth.
6. a covering of clay put over a wax model so as to form a mold when the wax is melted out.
7. a mantel.
8. in anatomy, the cortex of the cerebrum.
9. in geology, the soil, sand, and other loose material covering the solid bedrock of the earth.
10. in zoology, (a) the membranous flap or folds of the body wall of a mollusk or similar organism, containing glands that secrete a shell-forming fluid; (b) the soft outer body; wall of a tunicate or barnacle; (c) the back and folded wings of a bird.
11. in heraldry, same as *mantling*.
12. a closed waterway leading to a water wheel.

man′tle, *v.t.*; mantled, *pt., pp.*; mantling, *ppr.*
1. to cover with a mantle.
2. to conceal; to cloak; to cover; to disguise.

man′tle, *v.i.* 1. to be or become covered, as a surface with scum or froth.
2. to form a covering; to spread like a mantle, as a blush over the face.
3. to blush or flush; as, her cheeks *mantled* at the praise.
4. in falconry, (a) to spread first one wing, then the other, over the outstretched legs: said of a perched hawk; (b) to spread out: said of the wings.

man′tlet, *n.* same as *mantelet* (sense 2).

man′tling, *n.* in heraldry, the representation of a mantle, or the drapery of a coat of arms.

man′tō, *n.* a mantle or cloak.

man′toid, *a.* [*mant*is and *-oid*.] of or pertaining to the family *Mantidæ*.

man′toid, *n.* a mantis; an individual of the family *Mantidæ*.

man·tol′ō·ġist, *n.* one who practices divination; a soothsayer. [Rare.]

man·tol′ō·ġy, *n.* [Gr. *mantis*, a prophet, and *-logia*, from *legein*, to speak.] the act or practice of divination or of prophesying. [Rare.]

man′trȧ, *n.* [Sans.] 1. an invocation used by the Hindus in worship in the form either of a brief petition or of the repetition of a sacred word.
2. a hymn of praise contained in the Vedas.

man′trap, *n.* a device formerly employed to entrap trespassers on private grounds.

man′tū·ȧ, *n.* [a corruption of Fr. *manteau*, a mantle, cape.]
1. a kind of loose gown or cloak formerly worn by ladies; a manteau. [Obs.]
2. a superior kind of silk formerly made at Mantua, Italy. [Obs.]

man′tū·ȧ-māk″ẽr, *n.* one who makes gowns for women; a dressmaker.

Man′tū·ăn, *a.* pertaining to Mantua, a city in northern Italy.

Man′tū·ăn, *n.* a native or inhabitant of Mantua.
the Mantuan; Virgil.

Mȧ′nū, *n.* [Sans.] in Hindu mythology, an all-wise creature, issuing from Brahma, one of fourteen such said to be the progenitors of the human race. Manu is reputed to have codified the laws which are still observed by the Hindus.

man′ū·ăl, *a.* [ME. and OFr. *manuel*; L. *manualis*, pertaining to the hand, from *manus*, the hand.]
1. of a hand or the hands; made, done, worked, or used by the hands.

2. of the nature of a manual, or handbook.
3. in law, in actual possession.
manual alphabet; hand language, used by deaf-mutes, in which the letters of the alphabet are represented by certain positions and motions of the fingers and hands.
manual exercise; the exercise employed in teaching soldiers the use of arms.
manual method; the system of deaf-mute instruction which makes use of the manual alphabet, as distinguished from the *oral method*.
manual training; training in woodwork, sewing, metalworking, and similar arts and crafts, as in a school.

man'ū·ăl, *n.* 1. a handy book for use as a guide, reference, etc.; a handbook.
2. in the Middle Ages, the service book of the Roman Catholic Church.
3. in an organ or similar musical instrument, a keyboard, or a key to be played by the hands; as, a three-*manual* organ.
4. an exercise prescribed for the drill of recruits or soldiers, to perfect them in the handling of a weapon, especially a rifle: also *manual of arms*.

man'ū·ăl·ist, *n.* one who performs labor with his hands; a workman; a craftsman. [Rare.]

man·ū·al'i·tĕr, *adv.* in organ music, manually: a direction to the performer to play with the manuals and not with the pedals.

man'ū·ăl·ly, *adv.* 1. with the hand or hands; by hand.
2. as regards work with the hands.

man'ū·ā·ry, *a.* [L. *manuarius*, of the hand, from *manus*, the hand.] manual. [Obs.]

man'ū·ā·ry, *n.* 1. manual labor. [Obs.]
2. a manual laborer. [Obs.]

mȧ·nū'bri·ăl, *a.* of or resembling a manubrium; shaped like a handle.

mȧ·nū'bri·um, *n.*; *pl.* **mȧ·nū'bri·ȧ, mȧ·nū'bri·ums,** [L. *manubrium*, a handle, haft, hilt, from *manus*, hand.]
1. a part or process thought to resemble a handle in shape; especially, the presternum, or the uppermost of the three bony segments composing the sternum.
2. the pendent axial part of a medusa or jellyfish: also called *hypostoma*.
3. in botany, a cylinderlike cell projecting from the inner face of a shield in the wall of the antheridium of certain algae.

man·ū·çap'tŏr, *n.* [LL. *manucaptor*; L. *manus*, hand, and *captor*, a taker, from *capere*, to take.] in old law, a bondsman; one who guarantees the appearance of another in court.

man'ū·çōde, *n.* [Malay *manuk-dewata*; lit., the bird of the gods.] a bird of the genus *Manucodia* of Australia and New Guinea, related to the bird of paradise and distinguished for its loud and clear notes.

man·ū·duç'tion, *n.* guidance by the hand; direction; introduction.

man·ū·duç'tŏr, *n.* [LL. *manuductor*, from *manuducere*, to lead by the hand.] in the Middle Ages, a choir director.

man·ū·duç'tō·ry, *a.* leading by the hand; serving as a conductor or leader.

man·ū·faç'tō·ry, *n.*; *pl.* **man·ū·faç'tō·rieṣ,** [L. *manus*, hand, and LL. *factorium*, a place where something is made, from L. *factus*, pp. of *facere*, to make.]
1. a place where goods are manufactured; a factory.
2. the act of manufacturing. [Obs.]

man·ū·faç'tō·ry, *a.* relating to or employed in manufacturing. [Obs.]

man·ū·faç'tūr·ăl, *a.* pertaining or relating to manufactures.

man·ū·faç'tūre, *n.* [Fr.; ML. *manufactura*, a making by hand; L. *manu*, abl. of *manus*, hand, and LL. *factura*, a making, from L. *factus*, pp. of *facere*, to make.]
1. the making of goods and articles by hand or, especially, by machinery, often on a large scale and with division of labor.
2. anything so made; manufactured product.
3. the making of something in any way, especially when regarded as merely mechanical.
Syn.—production, fabrication, composition, construction, manipulation, molding.

man·ū·faç'tūre, *v.t.*; manufactured, *pt.*, *pp.*; manufacturing, *ppr.* 1. to make by hand or, especially, by machinery, often on a large scale and with division of labor.
2. to work (wool, steel, etc.) into usable form.
3. to produce (art, literature, etc.) in a way regarded as mechanical.
4. to make up (excuses, evidence, etc.); to invent; fabricate; concoct.

man·ū·faç'tūre, *v.i.* to be occupied in manufacturing.

man·ū·faç'tūr·ĕr, *n.* one who is in the business of manufacturing; especially, a factory owner.

man·ū·faç'tūr·ing, *a.* 1. employed in making goods; as, a *manufacturing* company.
2. relating to manufacture; as, *manufacturing* interests.

mȧ'nù·kȧ, *n.* [Maori.] a shrub of the myrtle family, *Leptospermum scoparium*, very useful to the natives of New Zealand. From its twigs brooms are manufactured, and the leaves form a cheap substitute for tea.

mȧ'nŭl, *n.* a small wildcat of Asia, with black and white markings.

man'ū·mīṣe, *v.t.* to manumit. [Obs.]

man·ū·mis'sion (-mish'un), *n.* [L. *manumissio* (*-onis*), from *manumittere*, to let go from the hand, to set free.] a freeing or being freed from slavery; liberation; emancipation.

man·ū·mit', *v.t.*; manumitted, *pt.*, *pp.*; manumitting, *ppr.* [L. *manumittere*, to let go from the hand, set at liberty, free; *manu*, abl. of *manus*, hand, and *mittere*, to send.] to release from slavery; to liberate from personal bondage or servitude; to free, as a slave.

man·ū·mō'tive, *a.* [L. *manu*, abl. of *manus*, hand, and LL. *motivus*, moving, from L. *movere*, to move.] movable by hand.

mȧ·nūr'ȧ·ble, *a.* that can be manured.

mȧ·nūr'āġe, *n.* cultivation of land. [Obs.]

mȧ·nūr'ănce, *n.* cultivation of land. [Obs.]

mȧ·nūre', *v.t.*; manured, *pt.*, *pp.*; manuring, *ppr.* [ME. *menuren*; OFr. *manœvrer*, *manovrer*, to work with the hand, cultivate.]
1. to cultivate by manual labor; to till. [Obs.]
2. to put manure on or into; to fertilize (soil).

mȧ·nūre', *n.* any substance put on or into soil in order to fertilize it, as animal excrement, guano, compost, etc.

mȧ·nūre'ment, *n.* cultivation; improvement. [Obs.]

mȧ·nūr'ĕr, *n.* one who manures land.

mȧ·nū'ri·ăl, *a.* pertaining to manures.

mȧ·nūr'ing, *n.* a dressing or spread of manure on land; the act of fertilizing land with manure.

mā'nus, *n.*; *pl.* **mā'nus,** [L., the hand, hence, power.]
1. the terminal part of the forelimb of a vertebrate, as the hand of a person or the forefoot of a four-legged animal.
2. in Roman law, the authority of a husband over his wife.

man'ū·sçript, *a.* [L. *manu scriptus*, written by hand; *manu*, abl. of *manus*, a hand, and *scriptus*, pp. of *scribere*, to write.] written by hand or with a typewriter, not printed.

man'ū·sçript, *n.* [LL. *manuscriptum*, from L. *manu scriptus*, written by hand.]
1. a book or document written by hand, especially before the invention of printing.
2. a written or typewritten document or paper, especially an author's copy of his work, as submitted to an editor or publisher.

man'ū·sçript·ăl, *a.* of the nature of manuscript. [Rare.]

man·ū·ten'en·cy, *n.* maintenance. [Obs.]

man'wărd, *a.* and *adv.* toward man; in relation to man.

man'wărdṣ, *adv.* manward.

man'wāy, *n.* a passageway large enough to permit one man to pass through at a time.

man'wīṣe, *adv.* as a man would do; like a man.

Manx, *a.* [for *Mansk*, from ON. *manskr*, from *Man-*, inflectional base of *Mon*, Isle of Man.] of the Isle of Man, its people, or their language.

Manx, *n.* the Gaelic language spoken on the Isle of Man, now almost extinct.
the Manx; the people of the Isle of Man.

manx cat, Manx cat, a variety of domestic cat with a rudimentary tail.

Manx'măn, *n.*; *pl.* **Manx'men,** a native or inhabitant of the Isle of Man.

man'y, *n.* a retinue of servants; a household. [Obs.]

man'y (men'y), *a.*; *comp.* more; *superl.* most, [ME. *many*, *mani*, *moni*; AS. *manig*, *monig*, *mænig*, many.]
1. numerous; consisting of some large, indefinite number (of persons or things).

Thou shalt be a father of *many* nations.
—Gen. xvii. 4.

2. relatively numerous (preceded by *as*, *too*, etc.).
many a (or *an*, *another*) followed by a singular noun or pronoun is equivalent to *many* followed by the corresponding plural (e.g., many a man has tried).
to be one too many for; to defeat; to overwhelm.

man'y, *n.* a large number (of persons or things).

O thou fond *many*. —Shak.

a good many; [*construed as pl.*] a relatively large number (of persons or things).
a great many; [*construed as pl.*] an extremely large number (of persons or things).
the many; (a) the majority of people; (b) the people; the multitude; the masses.

man'y, *pron.* many persons or things.

man'y·ber''ry (men'), *n.* the hackberry; any tree of the genus *Celtis*, characterized by its small fruit and its leaves which resemble those of the elm.

man'-yēar', *n.* a unit of measurement used in production, being the work of one man for one year.

man'y-head''ed (men'i-hed''ed) **bēast, man'y-head''ed mon'stĕr,** the populace; *belua multorum capitum* (monster of many heads), an epithet Horace applied to the people of Rome.

man'y·plīeṣ, *n.* [from *many* and *ply*.] the third stomach of a ruminant; omasum: so called from the many plies, or folds, of its lining membrane.

man'y·root, *n.* in botany, a plant of the *Acanthus* family, *Ruellia tuberosa*, found in the southern United States and in tropical America, its many tuberous roots being used in medicine for their emetic properties: called also *spiritleaf* and *spiritweed*.

man'y-sīd''ed, *a.* 1. having many sides or faces.
2. having many possibilities, qualities, interests, or accomplishments; as, a *many-sided* woman.

man'y-sīd''ed·ness, *n.* the state of being many-sided.

man'y·where (-hwār), *adv.* in many places. [Rare.]

man'y·wīṣe, man'y·wāyṣ, *adv.* in various ways; in a versatile manner.

man·zȧ·nil'lȧ, *n.* [Sp.] a pale dry sherry.

man·zȧ·ni'tȧ, *n.* [Sp., dim. of *manzana*, an apple.] any of several evergreen shrubs or small trees of the western United States; bearberry.

Mä'ō·ri (*or* mou'ri), *n.* [from Maori; said to mean "native, of the usual kind."]
1. *pl.* **Mä'ō·riṣ,** a member of a brown-skinned people native to New Zealand, of Polynesian origin.
2. their Polynesian language.

Mä'ō·ri, *a.* of the Maoris, their language, etc.

mao tai, mao tai, (mou'tī') *n.* [after *Mao-t'ai*, town in southwestern China.] a strong, colorless, Chinese liquor distilled from grain.

map, *n.* [OFr. *mappe*, a map, in *mappemonde*; ML. *mappa mundi*, map of the world; L. *mappa*, a napkin, signal cloth, map, and *mundus*, world.]
1. a drawing or other representation of the surface of the earth, or of any part of it, drawn on paper or other material, exhibiting the lines of latitude and longitude, and the positions of countries, cities, mountains, rivers, etc.; as, a *map* of Europe, a *map* of Illinois.
2. a similar representation of part of the sky, showing the relative position of the stars, planets, etc.
3. any maplike delineation or representation.
4. the face. [Slang.]
to put on the map; to make well known. [Colloq.]

map, *v.t.*; mapped (mapt), *pt. pp.*; mapping, *ppr.* 1. to make a map or maps of; to represent or chart on or as on a map.
2. to arrange or plan in detail (often with *out*); as, he *mapped out* his working time.
3. to survey or explore for the purpose of making a map.

mä'pä·ū, *n.* a New Zealand tree, *Myrsine urvellei* whose wood is used for fuel.

mā'ple, *n.* [ME. *mapil*, from AS. *mapel* (*treow*), maple (tree).]
1. any of a large genus, *Acer*, of trees with dry, two-winged fruits and opposite leaves, grown for wood, sap, or shade.
2. the hard close-grained, light-colored

wood of such a tree, used for furniture, flooring, etc.

3. the reddish-yellow or yellowish color of the finished wood.

4. the flavor of maple sirup or of the sugar made from this.

mā'ple, *a.* 1. of or made of maple.

2. flavored with maple.

SUGAR MAPLE
(*Acer saccharinum*)

mā'ple bōr'ẽr, in zoology, any one of several insects whose larvae bore under the bark of the maple: specifically, the *Ægeria acerni* and the *Glycobius speciosus*, whose larvae are destructive to the sugar-maple tree.

mā'ple mō·lȧs'seṣ, maple sirup.

mā'ple sçāle, in entomology, any one of a great number of scale insects affecting maple trees.

mā'ple sir'up, sirup made by boiling down the sap of a certain variety of maple.

mā'ple suġ'ãr (shụg'), sugar made by boiling down maple sirup.

mā'ple wŏrm, in zoology, a moth larva that injures or destroys leaves of the maple.

mä'quï (-kē), *n.* [Sp., from native name.] an ornamental evergreen shrub of the linden family in Chile, whose tough bark is used for making strings for native musical instruments, and its berries for making wine; the *Aristotelia maqui*.

mȧ·quis' (-kē'), *n.* [Fr., from It. *macchia*, a thicket, from L. *macula*, a spot.]

1. a zone of shrubby plants, chiefly evergreens, growing in the area around the Mediterranean, known as a hiding place for fugitives, guerrilla fighters, etc.

2. [*often* M-] *pl.* **mä·quis'** (-kē'), a French guerrilla fighter against the Nazis in World War II; a member of the military branch of the French underground movement (French Forces of the Interior).

mär, *v.t.*; marred, *pt.*, *pp.*; marring, *ppr.* [ME. *marren*, *merren*, from AS. *merran* in *amerran*, *amyrran*, to dissipate, hinder, obstruct.] to injure or damage so as to make imperfect, less attractive, etc.; to spoil; to impair; to disfigure.

Syn.—botch, hurt, deform, injure.

mär, *n.* 1. something that mars; an injury; a blemish; a disfigurement.

2. a lake. [Brit. Dial.]

mä'rȧ, *n.* [S. Am.] a large guinea pig of Patagonia, *Dolichotis patachonica*, resembling a hare; the cavy of Patagonia.

mar'ȧ·bōu, *n.* [Fr.; Port. *marabute*; Ar. *murābiṭ*, hermit.]

1. any of several large storks, especially one of a kind found in Africa.

2. the adjutant, a bird of India.

3. soft feathers from the wing coverts and tail of the marabou, used in millinery.

4. a delicate, white raw silk that can be dyed even though the natural gum has not been taken out.

5. the offspring of a griffe and a mulatto; a person five-eighths Negro. [Dial.]

mar'ȧ·bout, *n.* [Fr.; Port. *marabuto*; Ar. *murābit*, hermit.]

1. a Moslem hermit or holy man, especially among the Berbers and Moors.

2. the tomb or shrine of such a man.

3. marabou.

mȧ·rä'çȧ, *n.* [Port. *maracá*, from the Braz. native name.] a percussion instrument consisting of a dried gourd or a gourd-shaped rattle with loose pebbles in it.

mar'ȧ·çan, *n.* [*Maracana*, Braz. name.] a species of parrot in Brazil; a macaw.

mar'ȧ·çock, *n.* same as *maypop*.

mar·ȧ·nath'ȧ, *n.* [Gr. *maranatha*, from Aramaic *māran atha*, the Lord cometh.] an invocation to the Lord. sometimes regarded as forming, with the preceding anathema (in 1 Cor. xvi. 22.), an intensified curse or malediction.

Mȧ·ran'tȧ, *n.* [named after B. *Maranti*, a Venetian physician and botanist.] in botany, a genus of herbaceous plants of tropical America belonging to the ginger family, characterized by tuberous rootstocks, the *Maranta arundinacea* furnishing much of the arrowroot of commerce.

mȧ·ran'tiç, *a.* relating to marasmus.

mȧ·ras'çȧ, *n.* [It. *marasca*, *amarasca*, a black, hard, sour cherry, from *amaro*, L. *amarus*, bitter.] a wild cherry from which maraschino is made: the fruit is small, black, and bitter.

mar·as·çhi'nō, *n.* [It., from *marasca*, a kind of cherry.] a strong, sweet liqueur or cordial distilled from the fermented juice of the marasca and flavored with its crushed pits; also, other cordials made in a similar way.

mar·as·çhi'nō cher'rieṣ, cherries in a sirup flavored with maraschino.

mȧ·raṣ'miç, *a.* of or having marasmus.

Mȧ·ras'mi·us, *n.* [from Gr. *marasmos*, a wasting, withering.] an extensive genus of fungi having a leathery umbrellalike top that folds up in dry weather and expands in moist weather. The edible fairy-ring mushroom is included in this genus.

mȧ·raṣ'mus, *n.* [Gr. *marasmos*, a wasting away, from *marainein*, to put out, quench, cause to waste away.] atrophy; a wasting of the flesh without fever or apparent disease; a condition of progressive emaciation, especially in children, because of malnutrition.

Mȧ·rä'thȧ (-tȧ), *n.* [Marathi *Marāṭhā* (Hind. *Marhaṭā*); Sans. *Mahārāṣṭra*, lit., great country.] a member of a people of Bombay state, in south central India; also *Mahratta*.

Mȧ·rä'thi (-ti), *n.* the Indic language of the Marathas: also *Mahratti*.

mar'ȧ·thon, *n.* 1. a foot race of 26 miles, 385 yards, run over an open course: so called in allusion to the story of the Greek runner who went from Marathon to Athens to tell of the victory over the Persians (490 B.C.), and then dropped dead.

2. any long-distance or endurance contest; as, a dance *marathon*.

Mȧ·rat'ti·ȧ, *n.* [named after J. F. *Maratti*, It. botanist.] a genus of tropical ferns with large, coarse, branched fronds.

mȧ·raud', *v.i.*; marauded, *pt.*, *pp.*; marauding, *ppr.* [Fr. *marauder*, from *maraud*, a vagabond.] to rove in search of plunder; to make an excursion for booty; to plunder.

mȧ·raud', *v.t.* to raid; to plunder; to pillage.

mȧ·raud', *n.* an excursion in search of plunder; a raid; a foray.

mȧ·raud'ẽr, *n.* a rover in search of booty or plunder; a plunderer; a freebooter.

mar·ȧ·ve'di, *n.* [Sp., from Ar. *Murābiṭīn*, the steadfast, the name of a Moorish dynasty at Córdoba (1086–1147).]

1. a gold coin used by the Moors in Spain in the eleventh and twelfth centuries.

2. an obsolete Spanish copper coin.

mär'ble, *n.* [OFr. *marble*, *marbre*, from L. *marmor*, marble; Gr. *marmaros*, a white, glistening stone, from *marmairein*, to shine.]

1. a hard, crystalline or granular, metamorphic limestone, white or variously colored and sometimes streaked or mottled, which can take a high polish: it is much used in building and sculpture.

2. a piece or slab of this stone, used as a monument, inscribed record, etc.

3. anything resembling marble in hardness, smoothness, coldness, coloration, etc.

4. a little ball of stone, glass, or clay, used in games.

5. [*pl.*] (a) [*construed as sing.*] a children's game in which a marble is propelled by the thumb to hit other marbles, usually to drive them out of a marked circle; (b) a group of sculptures in marble.

6. a marbled pattern; marbling.

7. [*pl.*] brains; good sense; as, to lose one's *marbles*. [Slang.]

Arundelian marbles; see under *Arundelian*.

to go for all the marbles; to take a great risk in the hope of a great gain. [Slang.]

mär'ble, *a.* 1. made or consisting of marble; as, a *marble* pillar.

2. like marble in some way; hard, cold, smooth, white, etc., or streaked, mottled, etc.

mär'ble, *v.t.*; marbled, *pt.*, *pp.*; marbling, *ppr.* to variegate in color; to cloud; to stain or vein (paper, book edges, etc.) like marble.

mär'ble çāke, a cake made of light and dark batter mixed to give a streaked, marblelike appearance.

mär'bled (-bld), *a.* diversified in color; veined like marble; having markings resembling marble.

mär'ble-edġed, *a.* having the edges marbled, as a book.

mär'ble·head (-hed), *n.* a petrel, *Fulmarus glacialis*.

mär'ble·īze, *v.t.*; marbleized, *pt.*, *pp.*; marbleizing, *ppr.* to give an appearance of marble to, as by staining, painting, or fusing.

mär'blẽr, *n.* 1. a worker in marble. [Obs.]

2. one who gives a marbled appearance to, as by painting, staining, etc.

mär'ble·wood, *n.* a tree, *Diospyros kurzii*, of the East Indies, valued for its hard, mottled wood.

mär'bling, *n.* 1. the art or practice of variegating in color, in imitation of marble.

2. any marking resembling that of veined marble; as, the *marbling* of meat produced by the fat and lean being intermixed.

3. in bookbinding, the decoration of paper, book edges, etc. in marblelike patterns.

mär'bly, *a.* resembling marble in structure or in appearance; cold, hard, smooth, etc.

märç, *n.* [Fr., from L. *emarcus*, a wine of middling quality.]

1. refuse of grapes, seeds, fruits, etc. after pressing.

2. a brandy distilled from this.

3. any insoluble matter left after treating a substance with a solvent.

märç, *n.* a mark (weight or coin). [Obs.]

mär·çän'dō, *a.* [It., ppr. of *marcare*, to mark.] same as *marcato*.

mär'çan·tant, *n.* a merchant. [Obs.]

mär'çȧ·sīte, *n.* [Fr. *marcassite*, prob. of Ar. origin.]

1. formerly, crystallized iron pyrites, used in the eighteenth century for ornaments.

2. a piece of this, especially as an ornament.

3. iron disulfide, FeS_2, a mineral resembling iron pyrites.

mär·çȧ·sit'iç, mär·çȧ·sit'iç·ăl, *a.* pertaining to marcasite; of the nature of marcasite.

mär·çaṣ'sin, *n.* [Fr.] in armorial bearings, a young wild boar.

mär·çä'tō, *a.* [It., pp. of *marcare*, to mark.] in music, emphatic; accented.

mär·cel', *n.* [after M. *Marcel*, 19th-c. Fr. hairdresser.] a series of even waves or tiers put in the hair: also *marcel wave*.

mär·cel', *v.t.*; marcelled, *pt.*, *pp.*; marcelling, *ppr.* to put such waves in (hair).

mär'cel·ine, *n.* [Fr., from L. *marcere*, to be weak or thin.] a thin fabric of silk used for lining women's garments.

mär·cel' wāve, same as *marcel*.

mär·ces'cent, *a.* [L. *marcescens* (-*entis*), ppr. of *marcescere*, to wither, decay, incept. of *marcere*, to wither.] in botany, withering but not falling off.

mär·ces'cent, *n.* a plant with marcescent parts.

mär·ces'ci·ble, *a.* liable to wither. [Obs.]

Märch, *n.* [ME. *March*, *Marche*, *Marz*; OFr. *march*, *mars*, from L. *Martius* (supply *mensis*, month), the month of Mars, from *Mars*, the god of war.] the third month of the year, having 31 days. In this month occurs the vernal equinox (March 21).

märch, *n.* [Fr. *marche*, a frontier; O.H.G. *marcha*; AS. *mearc*, a mark, boundary.]

1. a frontier or boundary of a territory; a border; especially applied to the boundaries or confines of political divisions.

2. a borderland, especially one disputed between countries.

the Marches; the borderlands between England and Scotland, or between England and Wales.

märch, *v.i.*; marched, *pt.*, *pp.*; marching, *ppr.* [ME. *marchen*, *marken*; AS. *mearcian*, from *mearc*, a mark, boundary.] to border; to be contiguous. [Rare.]

märch, *n.* [Fr. *marche*, from *marcher*, to march.]

1. the process or exercise of marching or moving from place to place in an orderly manner, as of soldiers.

2. a regular forward movement; a steady advance; progress; as, the *march* of events.

3. a regular, steady step or pace.

4. a long, tiring walk.

5. the distance covered in a period of marching; as, a *march* of ten miles.

6. a kind of music suited to the action of marching.

on the march; marching.

to make a march; in euchre, to take every trick of a hand.

to steal a march on; to get an advantage over without being perceived.

märch, *v.i.* [ME. *marchen*; OFr. *marcher*, to walk, move on, tread, prob. from L. *marcus*, a hammer, from the regular beating of the ground with the feet.]
1. to walk with regular, steady steps of equal length, usually in a group or military formation.
2. to go or advance steadily; to progress or proceed regularly.
3. to walk in a grave, deliberate, or stately manner.

märch, *v.t.* 1. to cause to move in military order; to cause to move in a body; to cause to move in regular procession.
2. to cause to go anywhere at one's command and under one's guidance; as, the policeman *marched* his prisoner to the station.

Mär′chen (mär′khen), *n.*; *pl.* **Mär′chen,** [G.] a story; a tale; especially, a fairy tale or folk tale.

märch′ẽr, *n.* one who marches, or walks with regular, steady steps.

märch′ẽr, *n.* 1. a person who lives in a march, or borderland.
2. the lord or officer who governed or defended the marches or borders of a territory.

mär·çhe′sä, *n.*; *pl.* **mär·çhe′ṣe,** [It.] the wife or widow of a marchese; an Italian marchioness.

mär·çhe′ṣe, *n.*; *pl.* **mär·çhe′ṣi,** [It.] an Italian nobleman ranking just above a count and just below a prince; a marquis.

Mär·chesh′vǎn (-khesh′), *n.* [Heb.] Cheshvan.

mär′chet, *n.* [LL. *marcheta*, a fee of a mark.] in old English and Scottish law, a fee or fine paid to his lord by a tenant upon the marriage of a daughter.

March hãre, a hare in breeding time, proverbially regarded as an example of madness.

märch′ing, *n.* military movement; passage of troops.
marching order; in military usage, equipment for marching: called *heavy marching order* when the equipment is for continued service, as in a campaign, and *light marching order* when only a temporary march is required, as in drill or in a reconnaissance.
marching orders; orders to march, go, or leave.

märch′ing mŏn′ey, additional money allotted to a soldier while marching.

mär′çhion·ess (-shun-), *n.* [LL. *marcionissa*, f. of *marchio* (*-onis*), a prefect of the marches, from O.H.G. *marcha*, a boundary, march.]
1. the wife or widow of a marquis.
2. a lady whose rank in her own right equals that of a marquis.

märch′land, *n.* [*march* (border) and *land*.] borderland.

March′-mad, *a.* excited; rash; without self-control. [Obs.]

märch′mǎn, *n.*; *pl.* **märch′men,** a borderer. [Obs.]

märch′pāne, *n.* [OFr. *marcepain*; It. *marzapane*, prob. from L. *marza*, frumenty, and *panis*, bread.] a kind of sweet bread or biscuit made of almonds, egg white, and sugar: also *marzipan*.

march wạrd, one who acts as warden of the marches.

Mär′ciǎn, *a.* Martian. [Obs.]

mär′cid, *a.* [L. *marcidus*, withered, from *marcere*, to wither.]
1. pining; wasted away; lean; withered. [Obs.]
2. causing emaciation.

mär·cid′i·ty, *n.* the condition or quality of being withered or emaciated. [Rare.]

Mär′cion·īte (-shun-), *n.* a follower of Marcion, a Gnostic of the second century, who adopted the Oriental idea of the two conflicting principles, and imagined that between them there existed a third power, neither wholly good nor evil.

Mär·cō·brun′nẽr, *n.* a German wine: named from the fountain Markbrunnen, near which it is made.

mär·con′i·gram, *n.* [*marconi* and *-gram*.] a message sent by the Marconi system of wireless telegraphy; a radiogram: formerly so called.

Mär·cō′ni sys′tem, same as *wireless telegraphy*.

mär′çŏr, mär′çŏur, *n.* [L. *marcor*, from *marcere*, to wither.] the state of withering or wasting; leanness; waste of flesh. [Rare.]

Mär·cō′ṣiǎn (-zhǎn), *n.* a follower of Marcus, a Gnostic of the second century.

Mär′dï gräs (grä), [Fr., lit., fat Tuesday, from *Mardi*, Tuesday, and *gras*, fat; so called from the French custom of parading a fat ox during the celebration of this day.] the day before the beginning of Lent; Shrove Tuesday: celebrated in some places by an elaborate parade and carnival.

Mär′duk, *n.* [Bab.] the chief god of the ancient Babylonian religion, originally a local sun god.

mãre, *n.* [ME. *mare*, *mere*; AS. *mere*, *myre*, f. of *mearh*, a horse.] a female horse, mule, donkey, burro, etc.

mãre, *n.* [ME. *mare*, *mere*; AS. *mara*, an incubus.] the spirit or goblin formerly believed to produce nightmares. [Obs.]

mā′rē, *n.*; *pl.* **mā′ri·ȧ,** [L., sea.]
1. a sea.
2. a dark area on the moon's surface, formerly supposed to be a sea.

Ma′ré·chal Niel (mä′rā-shäl nyel), [Fr.] a yellow fragrant rose of large size: also *Marshal Niel*.

mā′rē çlau′sum, [L., a closed sea.] a closed sea; a sea or a part of the sea within the jurisdiction of a single country or nation and not open to all others.

mär′eis (-is), *n.* a marish. [Obs.]

mā′rē lī′bẽr·um, [L., free sea.] a sea open to all nations.

mȧ·rem′mȧ, *n.*; *pl.* **mȧ·rem′mē,** [It., from L. *maritimus*, maritime.] low, unhealthy, but fertile marshy land near the sea, especially in Italy.

mā′rē nos′trum, [L.] our sea: Roman name for the Mediterranean.

märe′schǎl (mär′shǎl), *n.* [OFr.] a marshal. [Obs.]

mãre′ṣ′-nest, *n.* something of great interest or importance announced as discovered, but which has no real existence; a hoax or delusion; earlier called *horse-nest*.

mãre′ṣ′-tāil, *n.* 1. long, narrow formations of cirrus cloud somewhat like a horse's tail in shape, supposed to be a sign of bad weather.
2. a water plant with tiny flowers and narrow, hairlike leaves growing in thick whorls around the slender, erect stems.
3. the horsetail, a plant with jointed, hollow stems.

mär′gȧ·rāte, *n.* [*margar*ic and *-ate*.] a compound of margaric acid with a base.

mär′gȧ·ret grunt, same as *margate fish*.

mär·gar′iç, *a.* [Fr. *margarique*, from Gr. *margaron*, a pearl: so called from the pearly luster of its crystals.] designating a white, crystalline fatty acid, $C_{16}H_{33}CO_2H$, obtained from lichens or synthetically.

mär′gȧ·rin, *n.* [Fr. *margarine*, from *margarique*, margaric.]
1. a fatty compound found in certain animal and vegetable oils, consisting of a mixture of stearin and palmitin.
2. the glyceride of margaric acid.
3. margarine.

mär′gȧ·rine (*or* -rēn), *n.* [Fr., orig., a mistaken use of the chemical term, from the belief that margaric acid was contained in all fats and oils.] a blend of refined, edible vegetable oil or meat fat or both, churned with cultured skim milk to the consistency of butter and generally fortified with a minimum of 9,000 U.S.P. units of vitamin A per pound: it is used like butter.

mär·gȧ·rī′tȧ, *n.* [L.Gr. *margaritēs*, a crumb of sacramental bread, from Gr. *margaritēs*, a pearl.] in the Orthodox Eastern Church, (a) a vessel used in administering the sacrament; (b) a small piece of bread placed in the wine to symbolize the union of the blood and the body of Jesus.

mär″gȧ·ri·tā′ceous, *a.* relating to pearl or mother-of-pearl.

mär′gȧ·rīte, *n.* [L. *margarita*; Gr. *margaritēs*, a pearl.]
1. a pearl. [Obs.]
2. a hydrated silicate of calcium and aluminum, found as scales with a pearly luster.
3. tiny, round crystals forming a beadlike design in glassy igneous rocks.

mär″gȧ·ri·tif′ẽr·ous, *a.* [L. *margarita*, a pearl, and *ferre*, to bear.] bearing, producing, or furnishing pearls.

mär·gar′ō·dīte, *n.* [Gr. *margarōdēs*, pearllike, and *-ite*.] a hydrous mica resembling muscovite in crystallization and physical character and having a pearly luster.

mär′gȧ·ron, mär′gȧ·rōne, *n.* [*margar*ic and *-on*, *-one*.] a fatty substance, crystallizing in pearly scales, produced by the distillation of a mixture of margaric acid and lime.

mär′gȧ·rous, *a.* same as *margaric*.

mär′gȧ·ry·īze, *v.t.*; margaryized, *pt.*, *pp.*; margaryizing, *ppr.* [so called from the inventor of the process, J. J. Lloyd *Margary*.] to make (wood) durable by treating it with copper sulphate in solution.

mär′ġāte fish, a fish, *Hæmulon gibbosum*, of the West Indies and the Gulf of Mexico: also called *maggot fish*, *margaret grunt*, *market fish*.

mär′ġāy, *n.* [Braz.] a wild cat of Central and South America, the *Felis margay* or *Felis tigrina*, spotted with black and having a long tail: also called *long-tailed cat*.

märġe, *n.* [Fr., from L. *margo* (*-inis*), margin.] a margin, border, or edge. [Archaic or Poet.]

mär′ġent, *a.* marginal. [Archaic.]

mär′ġent, *n.* [from *margin*, with unhistoric *-t*.]
1. a margin. [Archaic.]
2. marginal comment in a book. [Archaic.]

mär′ġent, *v.t.* to note or enter on the margin. [Obs.]

mär′ġin, *n.* [L. *margo* (*-inis*), edge, border, margin.]
1. a border; edge; brink; verge; as, the *margin* of a lake.
2. the edge of the leaf or page of a book left blank.
3. a limit.
4. an amount of money, supplies, etc. reserved or allowed beyond what is needed; an extra amount for contingencies or emergencies; as, we allow a *margin* of **$35** a month in our budget.
5. provision for increase, addition, or advance.
6. in business, (a) the difference between the cost and the selling price of merchandise, stocks, etc.; (b) money or collateral deposited with a broker to insure him against loss on contracts which he undertakes for the actual buyer or seller of stocks, etc.; (c) speculation in which the broker advances part of the money, with reservations to protect him against loss, and the buyer deposits the rest, taking the profit and loss on fluctuations in value; (d) a customer's equity if his account is closed at the prevailing prices.
7. in economics, (a) the minimum return, below which activities are not profitable enough to be continued; (b) the difference between selling price and cost of production.
8. in psychology, the fringe of consciousness.
margin of a course; in roofing, the part of a course, or row, of slates left exposed to the weather.
Syn.—brink, brim, rim, border, verge, edge.

mär′ġin, *v.t.*; margined, *pt.*, *pp.*; margining, *ppr.* [L. *marginare*, to furnish with a border, from *margo* (*-inis*), edge, border, margin.]
1. to provide with a margin; to be a margin to; to border.
2. to enter, place, or summarize in the margin of a page or sheet.
3. in business, (a) to deposit a margin upon; (b) to hold by depositing or adding to a margin upon.

mär′ġin·ǎl, *a.* 1. pertaining to a margin.
2. written or printed in the margin; as, a *marginal* note.
3. at, on, or close to the margin.
4. in economics, designating land capable of providing an economic return at existing prices but so low in productivity that it tends to remain unused until better land is very scarce.
5. in botany, having a line or nerve running parallel to the edge of a leaf but some distance from it.

mär·ġi·nā′li·ȧ, *n.pl.* [from L. *margo* (*-inis*), a margin.] notes written on the margins of books.

mär′ġin·ǎl·ly, *adv.* in the margin, as of a book.

mär′ġin·ǎl ū·til′i·ty, in economics, the minimum degree of utility, below which activity is not profitable enough to be continued.

mär′ġin·āte, *v.t.*; marginated, *pt.*, *pp.*; marginating, *ppr.* to provide with a margin.

mär′ġin·āte, mär′ġin·ā·ted, *a.* having a distinct margin.

mär·ġin·ā′tion, *n.* a marginating or being marginated.

mär′ġined, *a.* 1. possessing a margin.
2. in zoology, having a distinct colored border.

Mär·ġi·nel′lȧ, *n.* [dim. from L. *margo* (*-inis*), edge, margin.] the typical genus of *Marginellidæ*.

Mär·ġi·nel′li·dae, *n.pl.* [*Marginella* and *-idæ*.] a family of *Gastropoda*, small snails found in warm seas, having a simple siphon, a polished, oval shell, more or less spiral, a few rough teeth on the edge, and plicate columella.

mär′ġin·i·cī″dǎl, *a.* [L. *margo* (*-inis*), edge, border, and *cædere*, to cut.] in botany, being dehiscent along the external line of union of the carpels only.

mär·gō′sȧ, *n.* [E. Ind.] a large tree, *Melia azadirachta*, of India. Its bark is used in making a tonic; an oil is made from its seed, and gum is taken from its trunk.

mär′grāve, *n.* [Fr. *margrave*; M.H.G. *marcgrave*; *mark*, march, border, and *graf*, a count, earl.]
 1. originally, a military governor of a march, or border province, in Germany.
 2. the hereditary title of certain princes of the Holy Roman Empire or Germany.

mär·grā′vi·āte, mär′grȧ·vāte, *n.* the territory or jurisdiction of a margrave.

mär′grȧ·vïne, *n.* the wife of a margrave.

mär′gue·rïte (-ge-), *n.* 1. a daisy with a yellow center and white petals; oxeye daisy or common garden daisy.
 2. any of several chrysanthemums with a single flower.

Mär″ġy·ri·çär′pus, *n.* [Gr. *margaritēs*, a pearl, and *karpos*, fruit.] a genus of South American rosaceous plants.

mä·rï·ä′chï, *n.*; *pl.* **mä·rï·ä′chïș**, [Mex. Sp.]
 1. a member of a strolling band of musicians in Mexico.
 2. such a band.
 3. their music.

mȧ·rï·äge′ dē çōn·ve·näṅce′ (äzh′), [Fr.] a marriage of convenience; marriage entered into from calculated self-interest or expediency.

mȧ·rï′ȧ·līte, *n.* [after *Marie* Rose, wife of the German mineralogist G. von Rath.] in mineralogy, a highly siliceous scapolite, crystallizing in the tetragonal system.

Mā̃r′i·ăn, *a.* 1. of the Virgin Mary.
 2. of Queen Mary of England.
 3. of Mary, Queen of Scots.

Mā̃r′i·ăn, *n.* 1. a worshiper or devotee of the Virgin Mary.
 2. a follower or defender of Mary, Queen of Scots.

Mā̃r·i·anne′, *n.* a personification of the French Republic, as on coins.

mȧ·riç′ō·lous, *a.* [L. *mare*, the sea, and *colere*, to dwell.] in zoology, sea-dwelling; marine.

mar′i·çul·tūre, *n.* [from L. *mare*, sea, and *culture*.] saltwater aquiculture.

mar′i·gōld, *n.* [*Mary* (prob. the Virgin Mary), and *gold*.]
 1. any of several plants of the composite family, with red, yellow, or orange flowers.
 2. the flower of any of these plants.

mar′i·grȧph, *n.* [L. *mare*, the sea, and Gr. *graphein*, to write.] an automatic tide gauge for making a continuous record of the height of the tide.

mä·rï·juä′nä, mä·rï·huä′nä (-hwä′), *n.* [Am. Sp.] 1. the hemp plant.
 2. its dried leaves and flowers, smoked, especially in the form of cigarettes, for the psychological and euphoric effects.

mar·i·kï′nȧ, *n.* [from native name.] a small, South American monkey with fine, silky hair of a golden-yellow color and a mane about the neck: also called *silky tamarin*.

mȧ·rim′bȧ, *n.* [from Afr. (Bantu) *marimba*, *malimba*, pl. of *limba*, a kind of musical instrument.] a musical instrument somewhat like a xylophone, consisting of a series of hard wooden bars, usually with resonators beneath, played by being struck with small hammers.

MARIMBA

mar·i·mon′dȧ, *n.* [Sp.] a spider monkey, *Ateles belzebuth*, of Central and South America.

mȧ·rï′nȧ, *n.* [It. and Sp., seacoast, from L. *marinus*, marine.] a small harbor or boat basin providing dockage, supplies, and services for small pleasure craft.

mar·i·nāde′, *n.* [Fr., from Sp. *marinada*, from *marinar*, to pickle in brine, from *marino*, from L. *marinus*, marine.]
 1. vinegar, wine, or a mixture of both, usually spiced, in which meats and fish are pickled.
 2. meat or fish pickled in this.

mar·i·nāde′, *v.t.*; marinaded, *pt., pp.*; marinading, *ppr.* to marinate.

mä·rï·nä′rȧ, *a.* [from It. *marinare*, to pickle.] designating or of a tomato sauce seasoned with garlic and spices and served with pasta, seafood, etc.

mar′i·nāte, *v.t.*; marinated, *pt., pp.*; marinating, *ppr.* 1. to soak (meat or fish) in marinade; to steep in brine.
 2. to let (salad ingredients, etc.) stand in French dressing for a time before serving; to steep in oil and vinegar.

mȧ·rïne′, *a.* [OFr. *marin*, from L. *marinus*, of or belonging to the sea, from *mare*, the sea.]
 1. of the sea or ocean; inhabiting, found in, or formed by the sea.
 2. (a) of navigation on the sea; nautical; (b) of naval affairs; naval; (c) of shipping by sea; maritime.
 3. used, or to be used, at sea; as, a *marine* engine.
 4. trained for service at sea, etc., as certain troops.
 5. of such troops; of the marines.
 marine barometer; see under *barometer*.
 marine belt; in international law, a strip of sea extending three miles from the coast over which the nation whose territory it borders has complete jurisdiction.
 Marine Corps; a branch of the United States armed forces, established by the Continental Congress in 1775, equipped and trained for land, sea and aerial combat: the Commandant of the Marine Corps is responsible to the Secretary of the Navy.
 marine engine; any steam engine built specially for propelling a ship.
 marine glue; see under *glue*.
 marine insurance; insurance against loss at sea.
 marine railway; a railway extending into the water used to pull vessels onto the shore for repair or transporting them to another body of water.
 marine store; a junk shop where nautical appliances are kept for sale.

mȧ·rïne′, *n.* 1. one of a class of troops trained for service at sea, etc.; specifically, [*often* M-] a member of the Marine Corps.
 2. naval or merchant ships collectively; the seagoing ships of a nation; a fleet; as, the merchant *marine*.
 3. in some countries, the department of government in charge of naval affairs.
 4. a picture of a ship or sea scene.
 merchant marine; see under *merchant*.

mar′i·nēr, *n.* [ME. *mariner*; OFr. *marinier*, from *marin*, of the sea, from L. *mare*, the sea.] a seaman or sailor.
 mariner's compass; see under *compass*.

mar′i·nēr·ship, *n.* seamanship. [Obs.]

mar·i·nō·rä′mȧ, *n.* [L. *marinus*, of or pertaining to the sea, and Gr. *horama*, a view, from *horān*, to see.] a panoramic representation of views of the sea.

Mā·ri·ol′ȧ·tēr, *n.* one who worships the Virgin Mary: opprobrious term.

Mā·ri·ol′ȧ·try, *n.* [Gr. *Maria*, Mary, and *latreia*, worship.] worship of the Virgin Mary, regarded as carried to an idolatrous extreme: opprobrious term.

mar″i·ō·nette′, *n.* [Fr., from *mariolette*, dim. of *mariole*, a name formerly given to little figures of the Virgin Mary.]
 1. a puppet or little jointed doll made to look like a person or animal and moved by strings or wires, often on a miniature stage.
 2. the buffle-headed duck. [Brit. Dial.]

mä·ri·pō′sȧ lil′y (or **tū′lip**), 1. any of a group of plants of the lily family, found in the western United States and Mexico, with tuliplike flowers of white, red, yellow, or violet.
 2. the flower of any of these plants.

mar′ish, *n.* [OFr. *mareis*; LL. *mariscus*, a marsh, from L.G. *marsch*, a marsh.] low ground, wet or covered with water and coarse grass; a marsh. [Archaic, Poetic, or Dial.]

mar′ish, *a.* marshy. [Archaic, Poetic, or Dial.]

Mā′rist, *a.* 1. of or dedicated to the Virgin Mary.
 2. of the Society of Mary (*Marist Fathers*), a congregation of missionary priests founded in 1824, or the Little Brothers of Mary (*Marist Brothers of the Schools*), an institute of teaching brothers founded in 1817.

Mā′rist, *n.* a member of a Marist society.

mar′i·tăl, *a.* [L. *maritalis*, pertaining to a husband, from *maritus*, a husband.]
 1. of or pertaining to a husband.
 2. of marriage; matrimonial; connubial.

mȧ·rit′i·măl, *a.* maritime. [Obs.]

mar′i·tïme, *a.* [L. *maritimus*, from *mare*, the sea.]
 1. on, near, or living near the sea; as, *maritime* provinces, a *maritime* people.
 2. of the sea in relation to navigation, shipping, etc.; as, *maritime* law.
 3. characteristic of sailors; nautical.
 Syn.—naval, nautical, oceanic, marine.

mär′jō·răm, *n.* [ME. *marjoran*; OFr. *majorane*, from LL. *majorana*, prob. ultimately from L. *amaracus*, *amaracum*; Gr. *amarakos*, *amarakon*, marjoram.] a plant of any species of the genus *Origanum* of the mint family; especially, the sweet marjoram, *Marjorana hortensis*, used extensively as a flavoring in cookery.

Märk, *n.* the second book of the New Testament, telling the story of Jesus' life, reputedly written by the Evangelist Mark.

märk, *n.* [ME. *mark*, *merk*; AS. *mearc*, a mark, sign.]
 1. a visible trace or impression on a surface, as a line, dot, spot, stain, scratch, blemish, mar, bruise, dent, etc.; a distinctive feature produced by drawing, coloring, stamping, etc.
 2. a sign, symbol, or indication; specifically, (a) a printed or written sign or stroke; as, punctuation *marks*; (b) a brand, label, seal, or tag put on an article to show the owner, maker, etc.; as, a trade-*mark*; (c) a sign or indication of some quality, character, etc.; as, politeness and consideration for others are *marks* of a good upbringing; (d) a letter or figure used in schools, etc. to show quality of work or behavior; a grade; a rating; as, a *mark* of B in history; (e) a cross or other sign made on a document as a substitute for a signature by a person unable to write.
 3. a standard of quality, proficiency, propriety, etc.; as, this novel doesn't come up to the *mark*.
 4. importance; distinction; eminence; as, a man of *mark*.
 5. impression; influence; as, good teachers leave their *mark* on their students.
 6. a visible object of known position, serving as a guide or point of reference; as, the tower was a *mark* for fliers.
 7. a line, dot, notch, etc. used to indicate position, as on a graduated scale.
 8. (a) an object aimed at; a target; (b) an object desired or worked for; an end; goal.
 9. an observing; a taking notice; heed.
 10. (a) a boundary, border, or borderland; a march; (b) among Germanic peoples in earlier times, land held or worked in common by a community. [Archaic.]
 11. in nautical usage, (a) one of the knots, bits of leather, or colored cloth placed at intervals on a sounding line to indicate depths in fathoms; (b) the Plimsoll mark.
 12. in sports, (a) the starting line of a race; (b) the jack in the game of bowls.
 beside the mark; (a) not striking the point aimed at; (b) not to the point; irrelevant.
 save the mark!; an exclamation of humorous astonishment, irony, contempt, etc.
 to hit the mark; (a) to achieve one's aim; to be successful in one's attempt; (b) to be accurate; to be right.
 to make one's mark; to achieve success or fame.
 to miss the mark; (a) to fail in achieving one's aim; to be unsuccessful in one's attempt; (b) to be inaccurate.
 wide of the mark; (a) not striking the point aimed at; (b) not to the point; irrelevant.
 Syn.—sign, note, brand, token, badge, scar, guide, limit, line.

märk, *v.t.*; marked, *pt., pp.*; marking, *ppr.* [ME. *marken*, *merken*; AS. *mearcian*, from *mearc*, a mark, sign.]
 1. to put or make a mark or marks on.
 2. to identify or designate by or as by a mark or marks; as, his abilities *marked* him for success.
 3. to trace, make, or produce by or as by marks; to draw, write, etc.
 4. to show or indicate by a mark or marks.
 5. to show plainly; to make clear or perceptible; as, her smile *marked* her happiness.
 6. to distinguish; to set off; characterize; as, great scientific discoveries *marked* the nineteenth century.
 7. to observe; to note; to pay attention to; to take notice of; to heed; as, *mark* my words.
 8. to give a grade or grades to; to rate; as, the teacher *marked* the examination papers.
 9. to put price tags on (merchandise).
 10. to keep (score, etc.); to record.
 to mark down; (a) to make a note of; to write down; to record; (b) to mark for sale at a reduced price.
 to mark off (or *out*); to mark the limits of; to demarcate.

to mark out for; to select for or note as selected for.

to mark time; (a) to keep time while at a halt by lifting the feet alternately as if marching; (b) to suspend progress for a time, as while awaiting developments; (c) to perform the motions of action without really getting anything done.

to mark up; (a) to cover with marks; (b) to mark for sale at an increased price; (c) to add overhead and profit to the cost of in order to arrive at the selling price.

Syn.—brand, impress, imprint, print, stamp, spot, label.

märk, *v.i.* 1. to make a mark or marks.

2. to observe; to take note.

3. in games, to keep score.

märk, *n.* [ME. *marke*; AS. *marc.*]

1. an old European unit of weight for gold and silver, equal to about eight ounces.

2. a coin or money of account, originally equivalent in value to about eight ounces of silver; specifically, (a) an obsolete Scottish silver coin worth 13 shillings, 4 pence; (b) a silver coin and the gold monetary unit of the old German empire: also, the monetary unit of East Germany.

3. a markka.

4. a Deutschemark.

märk'down, *n.* 1. a marking for sale at a reduced price.

2. the amount of reduction in price.

märked (märkt), *a.* 1. having a mark or marks; as, *marked* cards.

2. singled out to be watched or looked for as an object of suspicion, hostility, etc.; as, a *marked* man.

3. noticeable; obvious; appreciable; distinct; conspicuous; as, a *marked* change in behavior.

märk'ed·ly, *adv.* conspicuously; in a marked manner.

märk'ẽr, *n.* a person or thing that marks; specifically, (a) a person who keeps score in a game; (b) a device for keeping score; (c) a device for marking lines, as on a tennis court; (d) a bookmark; (e) a memorial tablet or gravestone; (f) a milestone or similar sign.

mär'ket, *n.* [AS. *market*, from L. *mercatus*, trade, market place, from *mercatus*, pp. of *mercari*, to trade, from *merx*, *mercis*, wares, merchandise.]

1. (a) a gathering of people for buying and selling things, especially provisions or livestock; (b) the people gathered; (c) the time of such a gathering.

2. an open space or a building where goods are shown for sale, usually with stalls or booths for the various dealers: also *market place.*

3. a store or shop for the sale of provisions; as, a meat *market.*

4. a region in which goods can be bought and sold; place where there is a demand for goods; as, the Latin-American *market.*

5. (a) buying and selling; trade in goods, stocks, etc.; as, an active *market*; (b) trade in a specified commodity; as, the wheat *market*; (c) a place where such trade is carried on; (d) the group of people associated in such trade.

6. opportunity to sell, or demand (for goods or services); as, industry has a good *market* for its products during boom times.

7. opportunity to buy, or supply (of goods or services); as, industry has a good labor *market* during a depression.

8. market price or market value.

at the market; at the price prevailing when the customer's order (for stocks, etc.) is executed.

buyer's market; a state of trade favorable to the buyer (relatively heavy supply and low prices).

curb market; see under *curb.*

in the market; for sale; purchasable.

market basket; a basket for carrying articles to and from a market.

market bleach; a bleach used to prepare white goods for the trade.

market cross; a cross set up where a market is to be held.

market garden; a garden producing vegetables for the market.

market hunter; one who hunts wild game for a living.

market keeper; one who owns or runs a market or a stall at a market.

market letter; a bulletin by a broker or trader giving market notes and advice.

market order; an order to buy goods, stock, etc. at the prevailing price.

market place; see *market*, sense 2.

market price; the price for which something sells in a given market; the prevailing price.

market research; the study of the demands or needs of consumers in relation to particular goods or services.

market town; a town in which public markets are held at specified times and places.

market value; in economics, the price a thing can be expected to bring in a given market; the average value of a commodity.

seller's market; a state of trade favorable to the seller (relatively heavy demand and high prices).

to be in the market for; to be seeking to buy.

to be on the market; to be offered for sale.

to put on the market; to offer for sale.

mär'ket, *v.i.*; marketed, *pt.*, *pp.*; marketing, *ppr.* 1. to deal in market; to buy or sell.

2. to buy provisions or goods.

mär'ket, *v.t.* 1. to send or take to market.

2. to offer for sale.

3. to sell.

mär″ket·ȧ·bil'i·ty, *n.* the quality or condition of being marketable.

mär'ket·ȧ·ble, *a.* 1. that can be sold; fit for sale.

2. of buying or selling; as, *marketable* value.

mär'ket·ȧ·ble·ness, *n.* marketability.

mär'ket·ẽr, *n.* one who goes to a market, either for selling or buying.

mär'ket·ing, *n.* 1. the act or business of buying or selling in the market.

2. the commodities bought or sold in the market.

märk'hor, märk'hoor, *n.* [E. Ind.] a large goat, *Capra megaceros*, of northern India, with enormous flat, twisted horns: called also *serpent eater.*

märk'ing, *n.* 1. the act of making a mark or marks.

2. the mark or marks characteristic of anything.

3. the particular arrangement, color, size, shape, etc. of characteristic marks; as, the *markings* of a leopard or of a zebra.

märk'ing ink, indelible ink used for marking clothes, etc.

märk'ing ī'ron (-ūrn), an iron for marking.

märk'ing nut, the nut of *Semecarpus anacardium*, whose juice is made into an indelible ink for marking linen: also called *Malacca bean* and *Oriental cashew nut.*

märk'kȧ, *n.*; *pl.* **märk'kää** (-kä), [Finn.] the monetary unit and a coin of Finland.

märks'măn, *n.*; *pl.* **märks'men,** 1. a person who shoots, especially one who shoots well.

2. in the United States Army, (a) the lowest of the three ratings of proficiency of a rifleman; (b) a soldier with this rating.

märks'măn·ship, *n.* skill in hitting a mark; the condition of being a marksman.

märk'up, *n.* 1. a marking for sale at an increased price.

2. the amount of increase in price.

3. the amount added to the cost to cover overhead and profit in arriving at the selling price.

märl, *n.* [OFr. *marle*, *merle*; LL. *margila*, dim. of L. *marga*, marl.]

1. a crumbly soil consisting mainly of clay, sand, and calcium carbonate, used as a fertilizer and in making cement or bricks.

2. any soft, crumbly stratum.

3. earth. [Poet.]

märl, *v.t.*; marled, *pt.*, *pp.*; marling, *ppr.* to overspread or manure with marl.

märl, *v.t.* [D. *marlen*, to fasten with marline.] in nautical usage, to wind or twist a small line or rope around (another).

märl, *n.* in angling, certain fibers from the feathers of a peacock used in making artificial flies.

mär·lā'ceous (-shus), *a.* of or resembling marl.

märl'ber″ry, *n.* in botany, a tropical tree, *Ardisia paniculata*, of the family *Myrsinaceæ*, found in Florida, bearing clusters of dark berries and valued for its rich brown wood: called also *cherry.*

mär'li, *n.* [Fr.] in ceramics, the rim of a flat dish projecting nearly parallel with the bottom.

mär'lin, *n.* [from *marlinespike*, referring to its shape.]

1. any of several large, slender deep-sea fishes related to the sailfish and spearfish.

2. a spearfish.

mär'line, *n.* [D. *marlijn*, marline; *marren*, to tie, and *lijn*, a line.] a small cord composed of two strands loosely twisted and either tarred or white, used for winding round ropes and cables to prevent their being frayed by the blocks, etc.

mär'line, *v.t.*; marlined, *pt.*, *pp.*; marlining, *ppr.* to wind marline round (a rope); to marl.

mär'line·spīke, *n.* 1. an iron tool tapering to a point, used to separate the strands of a rope in splicing: written also *marlinspike* and *marlingspike.*

2. a bird with a tail resembling a marlinespike; a kind of gull.

märl'īte, *n.* a variety of marl that resists the action of the air.

mär·lit'iç, *a.* having the qualities of marlite.

märl'pit, *n.* a pit where marl is dug.

märl'stōne, *n.* in geology, a kind of clayey limestone containing iron, found in the Lias group of England.

märl'y, *a.* 1. consisting of or resembling marl.

2. abounding with marl.

marly clay; a kind of clay used for fertilizing and for making bricks of a pale color.

mär'mȧ·lāde, *n.* [OFr. *marmelade*; Port. *marmelada*, marmalade, originally a confection of quinces, from *marmelo*, a quince, from L. *melimelum*, a quince, from Gr. *melimēlon*, a sweet apple, from *meli*, honey, and *mēlon*, apple.] the pulp of fruit preserved with sugar; especially, a jamlike preserve of orange rinds boiled with sugar.

mär'mȧ·lāde tree, a tree, *Lucuma mammosa*, of tropical America belonging to the family *Sapotaceæ* and characterized chiefly by its plumlike fruit, which is used for preserving: also called *mammee sapota.*

mär·mȧ·rō'sis, *n.* [Gr. *marmaros*, marble, and *-osis.*] in geology, the change which takes place when limestone becomes marble.

mär'mȧ·tīte, *n.* [from *Marmato*, in Colombia, S. Am., where it is found.] a black mineral consisting of the sulfurets of zinc and iron; a variety of sphalerite.

mär'mō·līte, *n.* [Gr. *marmaros*, marble, and *lithos*, stone.] a foliated serpentine, of a pearly-gray, bluish, or greenish color, cleaving into thin, brittle laminae.

mär·mō·rā'ceous, *a.* pertaining to or like marble.

mär'mō·rāte, *a.* [L. *marmoratus*, pp. of *marmorare*, to cover with marble, from *marmor*, marble.]

1. variegated like marble; also, covered with marble.

2. in botany, veined so as to resemble marble.

mär·mō·rā'tion, *n.* a covering or encrusting with marble, or as with marble.

mär·mō·rā'tum, *n.* [L., neut. of *marmoratus*, pp. of *marmorare*, to overlay with marble.] in architecture, a cement formed of pounded marble and lime well beaten and mixed.

marmoratum opus; in architecture, a finish for plasterwork made by adding plaster of Paris to lime or marble dust: also called *hard finish.*

mär·mō'rē·ăl, *a.* [L. *marmoreus*, pertaining to marble, from *marmor*, marble.]

1. of marble.

2. like marble; cold, white, smooth, hard, etc.

mär·mō'rē·ăl·ly, *adv.* in imitation of marble.

mär·mō'rē·ăn, *a.* marmoreal.

mär·mor·tin'tō, *n.* [It. *marmore*, marble, and *tinto*, tint.] in eighteenth century Italian decorative art, tinting with marble dust on ceilings and walls previously covered with adhesive material.

mär'mōse, *n.* [Fr.] an animal resembling the opossum, but smaller and pouchless; any species of *Didelphys* of South America.

MARMOSE
(*Didelphys murina*)

mär'mō·ṣet, *n.* [OFr. *marmouset*, grotesque figure.] in zoology, any one of several species of South American midoid monkeys, having bright-colored woolly hair and a nonprehensile tail: called also *squirrel monkey.*

mär′mŏt, *n.* [Fr. *marmotte*; prob. from L. *mus montanus,* a mountain mouse.]

1. a quadruped of the genus *Arctomys,* allied to the murines. It is about the size of the rabbit, and inhabits the higher region of the Alps and Pyrenees. The woodchuck, *Arctomys monax,* represents the genus in North America.

2. a related genus, *Spermophilus,* including the gopher, ground squirrel, prairie dog, etc.

3. any member of the genus *Hyrax,* as the *Hyrax capensis* of South Africa.

mär′mŏt squir′rel (skwir′), the pouched marmot; the gopher.

mär′mō·zet, *n.* a marmoset.

Mar′ō·nist, *n.* an admirer or student of the Roman poet Virgil, surnamed Maro. [Rare.]

Mar′ō·nīte, *n.* in church history, one of a body of Arabic-speaking Christians, who reside on Mount Lebanon and in Syria. They take their name from Maron, a Syrian bishop of about the sixth century.

mȧ·roon′, *n.* [Fr. *marron,* abbrev. from Sp. *cimarron,* wild, unruly, from *cima,* mountain top.]

1. (a) originally, a fugitive Negro slave living upon a West Indian island or in Dutch Guiana; (b) a descendant of such slaves.

2. a marooned person. [Rare.]

mȧ·roon′, *v.t.*; marooned, *pt., pp.*; marooning, *ppr.* 1. to put ashore in a desolate place, as a desert island; as, to *maroon* a criminal.

2. to leave abandoned, isolated, or helpless.

mȧ·roon′, *v.i.* 1. in the southern part of the United States, to camp out in a wild or secluded place as a recreation.

2. to loiter or loaf.

marooning party; a social party spending a season of recreation in a secluded place, as among the mountains or on an unfrequented shore.

mȧ·roon′, *n.* [Fr. *marron,* chestnut, chestnut color.]

1. a shade of dark brownish red.

2. a coal-tar dyestuff obtained in the manufacture of magenta.

3. a kind of bomb made of a paper box filled with gunpowder, used in fireworks to imitate the report of a cannon.

4. an Italian chestnut: called also *marron.*

mȧ·roon′, *a.* of a dark brownish-red color.

mȧ·roon′ēr, *n.* 1. a runaway slave.

2. one of a marooning party.

mȧ·rotte′ (-rot′), *n.* [Fr.] a fool's bauble.

mär′plot, *n.* one who, by his officious interference, mars or defeats a plan.

märque (märk), *n.* [OFr. *marque,* a boundary, a seizure of goods, from O.H.G. *marcha,* a boundary, march.] reprisal: obsolete except in *letters of marque.*

mär·quee′ (-kē′), *n.* [Fr. *marquise,* a marchioness, a tent of a marchioness.]

1. a large field tent; any large tent or temporary structure for a special gathering.

2. a rooflike structure or awning projecting over an entrance, as to a theater.

mär′quess (-kwis), *n.* a marquis.

mär″quet·e·riē′ (-ket-), *n.* same as *marquetry.*

mär′quet·ry (-ket-), *n.*; *pl.* **mär′quet·ries,** [Fr. *marqueterie,* from *marqueter,* to spot, inlay, from *marque,* a mark, spot.] inlaid work; work inlaid with different pieces of variously colored fine wood, shells, ivory, and the like.

mär′quis (-kwis), *n.* [OFr. *markis,* from ML. *marchensis,* a prefect of a frontier town, from O.H.G. *marcha,* a frontier, march.] a title of honor in some European countries, below that of duke and above that of count or earl.

mär′quis·ăl, *a.* relating to a marquis or his office.

mär′quis·āte, *n.* the seigniory, dignity, or rank of a marquis; also, the estate or territory of a marquis.

mär′quis·dŏm, *n.* a marquisate. [Obs.]

mär·quiṣe′ (-kēz′), *n.* [Fr., f. of *marquis,* a marquis.]

1. (a) the wife or widow of a marquis; (b) a lady whose rank in her own right equals that of a marquis. Not used of a British lady of this rank, who is called *marchioness.*

2. a marquee.

3. (a) a ring with jewels set in the shape of a pointed oval; (b) a jewel or ring setting of this shape.

mär·qui·ṣette′ (-ki-zet′), *n.* [diminutive of *marquise,* Fr. for awning or settee.] a sheer fabric of cotton, silk, rayon, or nylon, used for curtains, dresses, etc.

mär′quis·ship, *n.* marquisate. [Obs.]

mar′răm, *n.* [Norw. *marhalm,* grass wrack, lit., sea halm, from Ice. *marr,* the sea, and *halmr,* straw.] in botany, a kind of coarse grass, *Ammophila arundinacea,* growing on sandy beaches of northern shores: also called *beach grass.*

mȧr·rä′nō, *n.* [Sp., lit., swine (expression of contempt).] in the Spanish Inquisition, a Jew or Moor who professed to accept Christianity in order to escape persecution.

mär′rēr, *n.* one who or that which mars.

mar′ri·ȧ·ble, *a.* marriageable. [Rare.]

mar′riaġe (-rij), *n.* [OFr. *mariage,* from LL. *maritaticum,* marriage, from L. *maritus,* husband.]

1. the state of being married; relation between husband and wife; married life; wedlock; matrimony.

2. the act of marrying; wedding.

3. the rite or form used in marrying.

4. any close or intimate union.

5. in pinochle, etc., the king and queen of a suit.

marriage brokage; the act of negotiating a marriage for another or others, or the fee paid for such negotiation.

marriage contract; (a) a promissory engagement to marry; (b) a formal and legal contract specifying conditions as to property rights of the contracting parties.

marriage portion; a dowry.

marriage settlement; in law, a disposal of property preliminary to, or as a consideration for, marriage.

civil marriage; see under *civil.*

common-law marriage; a marriage by mutual agreement of the parties without formal ceremony, and provable by their subsequent conduct, such as living together as man and wife, acknowledging their relation before others, etc.

morganatic marriage; marriage between a man of high rank and a woman of lower rank, contracted with the agreement that neither the wife nor any offspring of the marriage shall ever inherit the rank, title, or property of the husband.

Syn.—matrimony, wedding, wedlock, nuptials.—*Marriage* is the act which unites the two parties, and *matrimony* the state into which they enter.

mar·riaġe·ȧ·bil′i·ty, *n.* the state of being marriageable.

mar′riaġe·ȧ·ble, *a.* of an age suitable for marriage; fit to be married.

mar′riaġe·ȧ·ble·ness, *n.* fitness for the married state.

mar′ried, *a.* 1. united in wedlock; wedded.

2. having a husband or wife.

3. of marriage or married people; connubial; conjugal.

4. closely or intimately joined.

mar′ri·ēr, *n.* one who marries.

mar′ron (*or Fr.* mȧ-rōṅ′), *n.* [Fr.; It. *marrone,*; chestnut.]

1. a large, sweet European chestnut, often used in confectionery.

2. the color of its shell.

3. a paper shell used to make an explosive noise.

4. *pl.* **mar′ronṣ,** chestnuts preserved in vanilla sirup.

mar·rons′ glȧ·cés′ (mȧ-rōṅ′ glȧ-sā′), marrons in sirup or glazed with sugar; candied chestnuts.

mȧr·roon′, *n.* and *a.* same as *maroon.*

mar′rot, *n.* [etym. doubtful.] any one of several northern sea birds allied to the auks, as the guillemot, the puffin, and the razor-billed auk: also written *marrott* and *morrot.*

mar′rōw, *n.* [ME. *marow, merow*; AS. *mearg, mearh,* marrow.]

1. the soft, vascular, fatty tissue contained in the cavities of most bones.

2. the essence; the best part.

3. vitality.

4. in a plant or fruit, the inner part. [British.]

vegetable marrow; a variety of garden squash, *Cucurbita pepo,* having a close-grained flesh.

mar′rōw, *v.t.*; marrowed, *pt., pp.*; marrowing, *ppr.* to fill with marrow or with fat; to glut.

mar′rōw, *v.t.* to associate with. [Scot.]

mar′rōw·bōne, *n.* 1. a bone containing marrow, or boiled for its marrow.

2. [*pl.*] (a) the bones of the knees: humorous usage; (b) crossbones.

mar′rōw·fat, *n.* a kind of rich pea which matures late.

mar′rōw·ish, *a.* of the nature of marrow.

mar′rōw·less, *a.* having no marrow.

mar′rōw squäsh, one of the varieties of squashes, a fine-grained type similar to vegetable marrow.

mar′rōw·y, *a.* full of marrow; pithy.

Mar·rū′bi·um, *n.* [L. *marrubium,* hoarhound.] a genus of bitter aromatic perennial herbs of the mint family, of which common hoarhound is the best-known species. These herbs are often used medicinally.

mar′ry, *v.t.*; married, *pt., pp.*; marrying, *ppr.* [ME. *maryen, marien*; OFr. *marier,* from L. *maritare,* to wed, marry, from *maritus,* husband.]

1. to unite in wedlock; to join as husband and wife.

2. to join (a man) to a woman as her husband, or (a woman) to a man as his wife.

3. to take for husband or wife; as, a man *marries* a woman.

4. to give in marriage (often with *off*): said of a parent or guardian.

5. to unite intimately or by some close bond of connection.

Married to immortal verse. —Milton.

6. in nautical usage, to splice, as two ropes, in such a manner that the ends will pass freely through a block.

mar′ry, *v.i.* 1. to take a husband or a wife.

2. to enter into a close or intimate relationship.

mar′ry, *interj.* [euphemistic respelling of (the Virgin) *Mary.*] indeed; forsooth: an exclamation of surprise, anger, etc. [Archaic or Dial.]

Märṣ, *n.* 1. in Roman mythology, the god of war, identified with the Greek Ares.

MARS

2. war.

3. a planet of the solar system, fourth in distance from the sun, notable for its red light: diameter, c. 4,230 mi.; diurnal rotation, 24 hrs., 37 min.; year, 686.9 days; symbol, ♂.

4. in alchemy, iron.

5. in heraldry, a name for the color gules, or red, in the coats of sovereign princes.

Mars brown; a bright brown tinged with yellow.

Mars colors; the first colors in the spectrum and most of their compounds, as red, orange, yellow, and brown.

Märs, Märse, *n.* Master: approximate phonetic spelling of the word as used by Negroes during slavery.

Mar·sä′lȧ, *n.* a light, sweet wine made originally in the region about Marsala, a city of Sicily.

Märṣ·dē′ni·ȧ, *n.* [named after William *Marsden* of England, an Oriental scholar.] a genus of plants of the milkweed family, mostly twining and bearing fragrant flowers: one species furnishes a blue dyestuff and another a valuable fiber.

Mär·seil·lāiṣ′, Mär·seil·lāiṣe′ (-se-lāz′ *or Fr.* -se-yez′), *a.* [Fr.] relating to Marseilles, France.

Mär·seil·lāiṣ′, Mär·seil·lāiṣe′, *n.* 1. a native or an inhabitant of Marseilles, France.

2. the national anthem of France, composed by Rouget de Lisle in 1792 during the French Revolution.

mär·ṣeilleṣ′ (-sālz′), *n.* a thick, strong, figured or striped cotton cloth with a raised weave, somewhat resembling piqué, used for bedspreads, etc.: it was originally made in Marseilles.

märsh, *n.* [ME. *mersh, mersch*; AS. *mersc, mærsc,* a marsh, wet ground, from *mere,* a lake.] a tract of low land, usually very wet and miry and overgrown with coarse grass, or with detached clumps of sedge; a fen: written also *marish*.

mär′shăl, *n.* [ME. *marshal, marschal*; OFr. *mareschal, marescal*; LL. *marescalcus, mariscalus*, from O.H.G. *marahscalh*, a groom, master of horse, marshal, lit., horse servant; *marah*, horse, and *scalh*, a servant.

1. originally, a groom or, later, a master of the horse in a medieval royal household.

2. a high official of a royal household or court, as in medieval times, in charge of military affairs, ceremonies, etc.

3. a military commander; specifically, (a) a field marshal; (b) in various foreign armies, a general officer of the highest rank; (c) in the British armed forces, a commander of a specified branch; as, an air *marshal*.

4. an official in charge of ceremonies, processions, rank and order, etc.; as, the *marshal* of a parade arranges the order of march.

5. in the United States, an officer of various kinds; specifically, (a) a Federal officer appointed to a judicial district to carry out court orders and perform functions like those of a sheriff; (b) a minor officer of the law in some cities; (c) the head of the police or fire department in some cities.

mär′shăl, *v.t.*; marshaled, *pt., pp.*; marshaling, *ppr.* 1. to dispose in order; to arrange in a suitable manner; as, to *marshal* an army; to *marshal* troops.

2. (a) to direct as a marshal; to manage; (b) to lead or guide ceremoniously.

3. in heraldry, (a) to combine (coats of arms) on a single shield; (b) to associate (accessories) about a shield so as to form a complete escutcheon.

mär′shăl·cy, *n.* the position, rank, or authority of a marshal.

mär′shăl·ẽr, *n.* one who marshals.

mär′shăl·ing, *n.* 1. the act of arranging in due order.

2. in heraldry, an arrangement in a shield which exhibits the alliances of a family.

Mär′shăl·sēa, *n.* in England, a prison in Southwark for debtors, etc., abolished in 1842.

Court of Marshalsea; a court formerly held before the steward and marshal of the king's house to administer justice between the king's domestic servants: abolished in 1849.

mär′shăl·ship, *n.* the office of a marshal.

märsh bee′tle, the common cattail, *Typha latifolia*: also called *marsh pestle* and *marish beetle*.

märsh black′bīrd, the American red-winged blackbird, *Agelæus phœniceus*; also, the European red-winged thrush, *Turdus iliacus*.

märsh cin̄que′foil (sin̄k′), a plant, *Comarum palustre*: also called *marsh fivefinger*.

märsh çress, a plant, *Roripa palustris*: also called *marsh watercress*.

märsh el′dẽr, in botany, (a) the *Viburnum opulus*, or snowball tree, cultivated for ornament; (b) *Iva frutescens*, a maritime species of composite plants of the *Helianthoidea* group.

märsh fẽrn, a shield fern, *Aspidium thelypteris*, growing in marshes: also called *lady fern*.

märsh fīve′fin̄·gẽr, marsh cinquefoil.

märsh′flow″ẽr, *n.* any plant of the genus *Limnanthemum*.

märsh gas, methane, CH_4, a colorless, odorless, inflammable gas occurring as a product of decomposition in marshes.

märsh gráss, any grass growing only in marshy places; specifically, a grass of the genus *Spartina*.

märsh har′ri·ẽr, a bird of prey belonging to the genus *Circus*, a large European bird frequenting marshes: also called *moor buzzard, moor hawk*, and *marsh hawk*.

märsh hạwk, 1. a hawk, *Circus hudsonius*, related to the marsh harrier and found in both Europe and America: also called *American harrier*.

2. same as *marsh harrier*.

märsh hen, any one of several birds of the family *Rallidæ*, as the American gallinule or the coot; a mud hen.

märsh′i·ness, *n.* the state or quality of being marshy.

märsh′mal″lōw, *n.* [AS. *merscmealwe*; *merse*, marsh, and *mealwe*, mallow.]

1. originally, a confection made from the root of the marsh mallow.

2. a soft, spongy candy made of sugar, starch, corn sirup, and gelatin, coated with powdered sugar.

märsh mal′low, a plant of the mallow family, with large, pink flowers, growing in marshes: the root is used in medicine and confectionery.

märsh mar′i·gōld, a plant, *Caltha palustris*, of the crowfoot family, growing in swamps and bearing bright yellow flowers; a cowslip.

märsh pen′ny·wỏrt, an umbelliferous plant of European species, *Hydrocotyle vulgaris*: also called *water pennywort*.

märsh pes′tle (pes′l), same as *marsh beetle*.

märsh plŏv′ẽr, in zoology, (a) the *Tringa maculata*, or pectoral sandpiper; (b) loosely, in the United States, a snipe.

märsh quāil, the meadow lark, *Sturnella magna*.

märsh rob′in, the *Pipilo erythrophthalmus*, or towhee bunting; the chewink.

märsh rōṣe′mā̃r·y, a plant of the leadwort family whose strongly astringent root is used in medicine.

märsh sam′phīre, a leafless plant, *Salicornia herbacea*, of the goosefoot family, growing in salt marshes; one of the glassworts.

märsh St.-John's-wỏrt, a species of St.-John's-wort growing in marshy places, *Elodes virginica*.

märsh′wỏrt, *n.* in botany, (a) the creeping cranberry; (b) a European umbelliferous plant.

märsh wren, any one of several wrens that live and breed exclusively in salt marshes, fastening their nests to the stems of marsh plants.

märsh′y, *a.*; *comp.* marshier; *superl.* marshiest, 1. of, consisting of, or containing a marsh or marshes.

2. like a marsh; soft and wet; boggy; swampy.

3. growing in marshes.

Mär·sil′ē·ȧ, *n.* [named after Aloysius *Marsili*, an Italian botanist.] a typical genus of the *Marsileaceæ*, a family of fernlike cryptogamous plants floating upon the surface of water in shallow places and bearing four-petaled leaves.

mär′si·pō·bran̄ch, *n.* any one of the class of *Marsipobranchii*.

mär″si·pō·bran̄′çhi·āte, *a.* relating to the *Marsipobranchii*; having pouched gills.

Mär″si·pō·bran̄′çhi·ī, *n.pl.* [Gr. *marsipos* or *marsupos*, a pouch, bag, and *branchia*, gills.] in zoology, a class or division of vertebrates including the lampreys and hags, characterized by the absence of ribs, limbs, and jaws, and by having pouched instead of ciliated gills.

mär·sọọn′, *n.* [alteration of OFr. *marsouin*, from O.H.G. *meriswin*, lit., sea hog.] the white whale, *Beluga leucas*: so called in Canada.

mär·sū′pi·ăl, *a.* [L. *marsupium*, a pouch, bag.]

1. of or like a marsupium, or pouch.

2. of a group of lower mammals that lack a placenta and have an external abdominal pouch containing the teats: the prematurely born offspring is placed within the pouch by the mother immediately after birth to complete its development.

marsupial frog; a frog of South America, *Nototrema marsupiatum*, having a pouch for nourishing its young.

mär·sū′pi·ăl, *n.* one of the *Marsupialia*.

Mär·sū·pi·ā′li·ȧ, *n.pl.* [L. *marsupium*, a pouch, bag.] an order of marsupial animals, including the kangaroo and opossum: also called *Marsupiata*.

mär·sū·pi·ā′li·ăn, *a.* and *n.* same as *marsupial*.

mär·sū′pi·ăn, *a.* and *n.* same as *marsupial*.

mär·sū′pi·āte, *a.* marsupial.

mär′sū·pīte, *n.* [L. *marsupium*, a pouch, bag, and *-ite*.] in paleontology, a species of fossil crinoid having a purselike form, the remains of a genus of free-floating crinoids found in the Chalk formation.

mär·sū′pi·um, *n.*; *pl.* **mär·sū′pi·ȧ,** [L., from Gr. *marsipion*, dim. of *marsipos, marsupos*, a pouch, bag.]

1. a fold of skin on the abdomen of the female of certain lower mammals (*marsupials*), forming a pouch in which the young are carried and complete their development, feeding from the mammary glands which it encloses.

2. a structure like this, in some crustaceans, fishes, etc.

märt, *n.* [from D. *markt.*]

1. a place of sale or traffic; a market.

2. (a) a fair; (b) buying and selling; trade; bargaining; (c) a bargain. [Obs.]

märt, *v.t.* to buy or sell. [Obs.]

märt, *n.* [Gael.] a cow or ox fattened, killed, and salted for winter provision. [Scot.]

mär′tȧ·gŏn, *n.* [Fr.] 1. a lily of Europe and Asia, *Lilium martagon*: also called *Turk's-cap lily*.

2. an American lily, *Lilium superbum*.

mär′tel, *n.* a hammer; a martel-de-fer.

mär′tel, *v.i.* to strike with or as with a hammer. [Obs.]

mär′tel-dē-fer, *n.* [OFr., hammer of iron.] in the Middle Ages, a weapon resembling a pick, with a hammer at one end, used in piercing and breaking armor: also called *horseman's hammer*.

MARTELS-DE-FER
1. horseman's hammer of about the time of Edward IV; 2. martel-de-fer, time of Henry VIII; 3. martel-de-fer, time of Edward VI; 4. martel-de-fer with hand gun, time of Queen Elizabeth I

mär′te·line, *n.* [Fr., dim. of *martel*, a hammer.] a small hammer pointed at one end, used by sculptors and workers in marble.

Mär·tel′lō tow′ẽr, [It. *martello*, a hammer (used for *mortella*, a tower, from *Mortello*, in Corsica, where such a tower was attacked by the English fleet in 1794).] a circular fort of masonry, formerly built on coasts to protect against invaders: also *martello*.

mär′ten, *n.* [Fr. *martre, marte*, from LL. *martus, marturis*, a marten; of Germanic origin; compare O.H.G. *marder*, mart; AS. *mearth*, a marten.]

1. a carnivorous animal of the genus *Mustela*, related to the weasel: several species are valued for their furs, as the American pine marten, *Mustela americana*, and the beech marten, *Mustela foina*, of Great Britain and other parts of Europe.

PINE MARTEN
(*Mustela americana*)

2. the fur of the marten or a garment made of it: also called *sable*.

3. any carnivorous marsupial of Australia belonging to the genus *Phascogale*, as the spotted marten.

mär′tenṣ·īte, *n.* [after A. *Martens*, G. metallurgist.] a very hard, brittle, solid solution of iron and carbon or the carbide of iron, Fe_3C, produced when hot steel is suddenly chilled by cold water.

mär′text, *n.* a stupid, blundering preacher.

Mär′thȧ, *n.* in the Bible, sister of Lazarus and Mary, and a friend of Jesus: she was rebuked by Jesus for doing housework while he talked with Mary: Luke x. 40; hence, a woman who does the housework and looks after practical affairs.

mär′tiăl (-shăl), *a.* [L. *martialis*, pertaining to Mars or war, from *Mars, Martis*, god of war.]

1. pertaining to war; suited to war; as, *martial* equipage; *martial* music; a *martial* appearance.

2. warlike; given to war; as, a *martial* nation or people.

3. suited to battle; as, a *martial* array.

4. belonging to an army and navy or to military life: opposed to *civil*; as, *martial* law; *martial* discipline.

5. of or like iron. [Archaic.]

6. [M–] in astrology, under the dire influence of Mars.

martial art; any of various systems of self-defense originating in the Orient, such as karate, also engaged in as a sport.

martial law; see under *law*.

mär′tiăl·iṣm, *n.* warlike qualities; bellicosity.

mär′tiăl·ist, *n.* a warrior; a fighter.

mär′tiăl·īze, *v.t.*; martialized, *pt., pp.*; martializing, *ppr.* to make martial, or warlike.

mär′tiăl·ly, *adv.* in a martial manner.

mär′tiăl·ness, *n.* the quality of being warlike.

Mär′tiăn, *a.* [L. *Martius*, pertaining to *Mars*, from *Martis*, god of war.] relating to Mars, the god of war, or to the planet Mars.

Mär′tiăn, *n.* a hypothetical inhabitant of the planet Mars.

mär′tin, *n.* [Fr. *martin*, from proper name *Martin*.]

1. a bird, *Hirundo urbica*, of the swallow family, which often forms its nest in buildings: also called *martinet* and *martlet*.

HOUSE MARTIN (*Hirundo urbica*)

2. a bird of the genus *Progne*, as the *Progne purpurea* or *subis*, of America, the purple martin.

mär·ti·net′, *n.* [after *Martinet*, 17th-c. Fr. general.]

1. a very strict military disciplinarian.

2. any very strict disciplinarian or stickler for rigid regulations.

mär′ti·net, *n.* [Fr.] formerly, one of the small lines fastened to the leech of a sail, to bring it close to the yard when the sail is furled.

mär′ti·net, *n.* martin. [Obs.]

mär′tin·gāle, mär′tin·gal, *n.* [Fr.; Pr. *martengalo, martegalo*.]

1. the forked strap of a horse's harness passing from the noseband to the girth between the forelegs, to keep the horse from rearing or throwing back its head.

2. (a) a lower stay for the jib boom or flying jib boom of a sailing vessel, to bear the strain of the head stays; (b) a short spar extending straight down from the end of the bowsprit: also called *dolphin striker*.

3. any system of trying to make up one's losses in previous bets by doubling or otherwise increasing the amount bet.

mär·tï′nï, Mär·tï′nï·, *n.* [from *Martini* and Rossi, firm that makes vermouth.] a cocktail made from gin and dry vermouth, usually served with an olive or a twist of lemon peel.

Mär′tin·ist, *n.* 1. in ecclesiastical history, one of a school of religionists founded a short time before the French Revolution by the Chevalier St. Martin.

2. one of the authors of secretly printed pamphlets attacking prelacy in England in the sixteenth century: so called from the pseudonym of the reputed publisher of the pamphlets, Martin Marprelate.

Mär′tin·măs, *n.* St. Martin's day, a church festival held on November 11.

mär′tīte, *n.* [L. *Mars, Martis*, the god of war (LL., a name for iron), and *-ite*.] in mineralogy, a ferric oxide of iron, Fe_2O_3, isomeric with hematite, occurring in isometric crystals.

Mär′tle·mas, *n.* Martinmas. [Obs.]

märt′let, *n.* [Fr. *martelet*, from *martinet*, dim. of *martin*.]

1. in heraldry, a bird without feet or beak. It is added to the family arms by the fourth of the junior branches of a family, as its mark of cadency.

2. same as *martin*.

MARTLET

Mär·tyn′i·ȧ, *n.* [Mod.L., after John *Martyn* (1699–1768), professor of botany at Cambridge.] in botany, a genus of herbaceous American plants found in the tropics and as far north as Illinois, characterized by clammy, pubescent leaves of heavy odor, large, violet, gamopetalous flowers, and fruit with a long-beaked capsule.

mär′tyr (-tūr), *n.* [ME. *martir*; AS.; LL.; Gr. *martyr, martys*, a witness.]

1. a person who chooses to suffer or die rather than give up his faith or his principles; a person tortured or killed because of his beliefs.

2. a person who suffers great pain or misery for a long time.

mär′tyr, *v.t.*; martyred (-tūrd), *pt., pp.*; martyring, *ppr.* 1. to put to death or torture for adherence to a belief.

2. to torture; to make suffer greatly; persecute.

mär′tyr·dŏm, *n.* [AS. *martyrdom*; *martyr*, a martyr, and *dom*, condition.]

1. the state of being a martyr.

2. the death or sufferings of a martyr.

3. severe, long-continued suffering; torment; torture.

mär′tyr·ess, *n.* a woman martyr. [Rare.]

mär″tyr·i·zā′tion, *n.* a martyrizing or being martyrized.

mär′tyr·īze, *v.t.*; martyrized, *pt., pp.*; martyrizing, *ppr.* to make a martyr of.

mär′tyr·īze, *v.i.* to be or become a martyr.

mär′tyr·ly, *adv.* like a martyr. [Rare.]

mär′tyr·ō·lōġe, *n.* a register of martyrs. [Obs.]

mär″tyr·ō·loġ′i·căl, *a.* registering or registered in a catalogue of martyrs.

mär·tyr·ol′ō·ġist, *n.* a student or writer of martyrology.

mär·tyr·ol′ō·ġy, *n.*; *pl.* **mär·tyr·ol′ō·ġies,** [ML. *martyrologium*; L.Gr. *martyrologion*; Gr. *martyr*, a witness, and *logos*, an account, from *legein*, to speak.]

1. a list of martyrs.

2. a historical account of religious martyrs, especially Christian martyrs.

3. such accounts collectively.

4. the branch of ecclesiastical history dealing with the lives of martyrs.

mär′tyr·y, *n.*; *pl.* **mär′tyr·ies,** a shrine built in memory of a martyr.

mär′vel, *n.* [ME. *marveyle, mervaile*; OFr. *merveille*, a wonder, from L. *mirabilia*, wonderful things, neut. pl. of *mirabilis*, wonderful, from *mirari*, to wonder at, admire.]

1. a wonderful or astonishing thing; a prodigy or miracle.

2. astonishment. [Archaic.]

Syn.—miracle, prodigy, wonder.

mär′vel, *v.i.*; marveled *or* marvelled, *pt., pp.*; marveling *or* marvelling, *ppr.* to become full of wonder; to to be greatly surprised.

mär′vel, *v.t.* to wonder at or about (followed by a clause).

mär′vel-ŏf-Pe·rū′, *n.* the four-o'clock (a plant).

mär′vel·ous, mär′vel·lous, *a.* [OFr. *merveillos*, wonderful, from *merveille*, a wonder.]

1. causing wonder; surprising, astonishing, or extraordinary.

2. so extraordinary as to be improbable, incredible, or miraculous.

3. fine; splendid: a generalized term of approval. [Colloq.]

Syn.—wonderful, surprising, extraordinary.

mär′vel·ous·ly, *adv.* wonderfully; strangely; in a manner to excite wonder or surprise.

mär′vel·ous·ness, *n.* wonderfulness; strangeness.

mär′vẽr, *n.* [alteration of Fr. *marbre*, marble.] in glassmaking, a table or slab of polished iron upon which hot glass from the blowpipe is placed to give it form.

Märx′i·ăn, *a.* and *n.* same as *Marxist*.

Märx′i·ăn·iṣm, *n.* same as *Marxism*.

Märx′iṣm, *n.* the system of thought developed by Karl Marx, his co-worker Friedrich Engels, and their followers.

Märx′ist, *a.* 1. of Karl Marx.

2. of, characteristic of, or in accord with Marxism.

Märx′ist, *n.* a follower of Karl Marx; a believer or expert in Marxism.

Mãr′y, *n.*; *pl.* **Mãr′yṣ, Mãr′ieṣ,** 1. in the Bible, (a) the mother of Jesus: Matt. i. 18–25: often referred to as the (*Blessed*) *Virgin Mary*, *Saint Mary*; (b) the sister of Martha and Lazarus: Luke x. 38–42; (c) Mary Magdalene.

2. in pidgin English, a woman.

mãr′y·bud, *n.* in botany, the flower of the marigold. [Obs.]

Mãr′y Jāneṣ, low-heeled slippers, usually of patent leather with a strap across the instep, worn by little girls: a trade-mark.

Mãr′y Mag′dȧ·lēne, in the Bible, a woman out of whom Jesus cast seven devils: Luke viii. 2: usually identified with the repentant woman whom Jesus forgave: Luke vii. 37 ff.

Mãr′y·măss, *n.* a festival of the Virgin Mary; also, the day of the festival; specifically, Annunciation day, March 25.

Mãr·y·ŏl′ȧ·try, *n.* same as *Mariolatry*.

mãr′y·sōle, *n.* a pleuronectoid fish of British waters: also called *smear dab* and *sand fluke*. [Brit. Dial.]

mär′zi·pan, *n.* same as *marchpane*.

-măs, a combining form for *Mass*, meaning *a* (specified) *festival* or *celebration*, as in *Christmas*.

mas·căgn′ine (mas-kan′yin), *n.* [after P. *Mascagni*, who discovered it.] in mineralogy, native sulfate of ammonia, found in volcanic districts.

mas′çȧ·lonġe, *n.* same as *muskellunge*.

mas·çȧ′rȧ, *n.* [Sp. *máscara*, a mask.] a cosmetic preparation, usually black, dark-blue, or dark-brown, for coloring the eyelashes and eyebrows.

mas·çȧ′ra, *v.t.*; mascaraed, *pt., pp.*; mascaraing, *ppr.* to put mascara on.

mas′çle, *n.* [OFr. *mascle, macle*, from L. *macula*, a spot.]

1. any of many small, diamond-shaped steel plates, linked together to make up a kind of armor used in the 13th century.

2. in heraldry, a diamond-shaped figure with a diamond-shaped opening: also called *lozenge voided*.

MASCLE

mas′çled (-kld), *a.* having or showing mascles.

mascled armor; armor such as that worn by Norman soldiers, composed of small lozenge-shaped metallic plates fastened on a leather or quilted undercoat.

mas′çot, *n.* [Fr. *mascotte*, from Pr. *mascot*, dim. of *masco*, sorcerer, lit., a mask.] any person, animal, or thing supposed to bring good luck by being present.

mas′çū·lāte, *v.t.* to make masculine. [Rare.]

MASCLED ARMOR

mas′çū·line, *a.* [ME. and OFr. *masculin*; [L. *masculinus*, masculine, from *masculus*, male, dim. form of *mas*, a male.]

1. male; of men or boys.

2. having qualities regarded as characteristic of men and boys, as strength, vigor, etc.; manly; virile.

3. suitable for or characteristic of a man.

4. mannish: said of women.

5. in grammar, designating or of the gender of words denoting or referring to males or things originally regarded as male.

mas′çū·line, *n.* 1. (a) that which is male; (b) a man or boy.

2. (a) the masculine gender; (b) a word or form in this gender.

mas′çū·line·ly, *adv.* in a masculine manner.

mas′çū·line·ness, *n.* same as *masculinity*.

mas′çū·line rhyme, a rhyme of only a single stressed syllable; single rhyme (e.g., *enjoy, destroy*): distinguished from *feminine rhyme*.

mas·çū·lin′i·ty, *n.* the quality or state of being masculine.

mas′çū·lin·īze, *v.t.*; masculinized, *pt., pp.*; masculinizing, *ppr.* to make masculine; especially, to produce male characteristics in (a female).

mā′ṣẽr, *n.* [*m*icrowave *a*mplification by *s*timulated *e*mission of *r*adiation.] a device, operating at microwave, infrared, etc. frequencies, in which atoms in a crystal or a gas are concentrated, raised to a higher energy level by excitation, then emitted in a very narrow beam when the excited atoms return to their original energy level.

mash, *n.* [ME. *masche, maske*; AS. *masc-*, in *mascwyrt*, mashwort; akin to G. *meisch, meische*, mash.]

1. crushed or ground malt or meal soaked in hot water for making wort, used in brewing beer.

2. a mixture of bran, meal, etc. in warm water, for feeding horses, cattle, etc.

3. any soft mixture or mass.

4. trouble; a muddle.

mash, *v.t.*; mashed (masht), *pt., pp.*; mashing, *ppr.* [ME. *maschen*, to mash, from the n.]

1. to mix (crushed malt, etc.) in hot water for making wort.

2. to change into a soft or uniform mass by beating, crushing, etc.

3. to try to attract the amorous attention of; to flirt with or ogle. [Earlier Slang.]

mash, *v.i.* to flirt or ogle. [Earlier Slang.]

mash, *n.* a marsh. [Dial.]

mash çool′ẽr, a trough or bin where mash is cooled by stirring.

mash'ẽr, *n.* a person or thing that mashes; specifically, (a) a device for mashing vegetables, fruit, etc.; (b) [Slang.] a man who annoys women not acquainted with him, by attempting familiarities.

mash'ie, mash'y, *n.*; *pl.* **mash'ieṣ,** an iron-headed golf club of medium loft, for making shots of medium length: now usually called *number 5 iron.*

mash'ie nib'lick, an iron-headed golf club with slightly more loft than a mashie but less than a niblick, for making approach shots: now usually called *number 7 iron.*

măsh'rū (mush'), *n.* [East Ind.] a cotton and silk fabric worn by Moslems at prayer, pure silk being prohibited.

mash tub, in brewing, a large tub or vat in which ground malt is steeped: called also *mashing tub.*

mash'y, *a.*; *comp.* mashier; *superl.* mashiest, produced by crushing and mixing; resembling or containing mash.

mas'jid (mus'), *n.* [Ar., a place of worship.] a mosque; a Moslem place of worship: also spelled *musjid.*

mȧsk, *n.* [Fr. *masque*, a mask, visor, from Ar. *maskharah*, a buffoon.]

1. a covering for the face or part of the face, to conceal or disguise the identity.

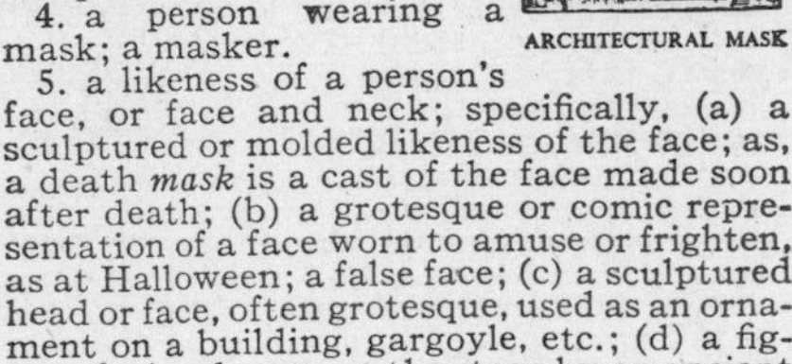

ARCHITECTURAL MASK

2. anything that conceals or disguises; as, a *mask* of snow on the ground.

3. a party, carnival, etc. where masks are worn; a masquerade: often spelled *masque.*

4. a person wearing a mask; a masker.

5. a likeness of a person's face, or face and neck; specifically, (a) a sculptured or molded likeness of the face; as, a death *mask* is a cast of the face made soon after death; (b) a grotesque or comic representation of a face worn to amuse or frighten, as at Halloween; a false face; (c) a sculptured head or face, often grotesque, used as an ornament on a building, gargoyle, etc.; (d) a figure of a head worn on the stage by an ancient Greek or Roman actor to identify a character and amplify the voice.

6. a protective covering for the face or head, as a wire screen, metal shield, or respirator (*gas mask*).

7. the face or head of a fox, dog, etc.

8. something serving to conceal artillery, military operations, etc. from observation; a piece of camouflage.

9. an opaque border used to cover unwanted parts of a photograph or to alter its shape.

10. a masque (senses 2 and 3).

11. in zoology, a masklike formation about the head, as the enlarged lower lip of a dragonfly larva.

the man in the iron mask; a noted prisoner of state during the reign of Louis XIV, who wore a black mask which was never removed in the presence of any one, and whose identity has never been definitely established.

mȧsk, *v.t.*; masked (mȧskt), *pt.*, *pp.*; masking, *ppr.* [Fr. *masquer*, from *masque*, a mask.]

1. to conceal or cover with or as with a mask.

2. to conceal or disguise.

Masking the business from the common eye. —Shak.

mȧsk, *v.i.* to put on a mask; to wear a disguise, as for taking part in a masquerade.

Syn.—hide, screen, cloak, disguise, conceal, cover.

mas'kȧ·longe, *n.* same as *muskellunge.*

mas'kȧ·nonge, *n.* same as *muskellunge.*

mȧsk crab, a European crab, *Corystes cassivelaunus*, characterized by markings resembling a human face.

mȧsked (mȧskt), *a.* 1. wearing a mask.

2. concealed; disguised; camouflaged.

3. in botany, masklike; personate.

4. in zoology, having masklike markings, as some pupae.

masked ball; a ball at which masks and fancy costumes are worn.

masked pig; a domesticated hog of Japan, *Sus pliciceps*, characterized by long, hanging ears and a deeply furrowed face.

mȧsk'ẽr, *n.* one who masks or wears a mask: also spelled *masquer.*

mȧsk'ẽr, *v.t.* to confuse. [Obs.]

mȧsk'ẽr·y, *n.* the disguise of a masker [Obs.]

mȧsk'flow"ẽr, *n.* a plant of the genus *Alonsoa*, of which there are several species, native to tropical America. The flowers are generally of a brilliant red, and very showy.

mȧsk'ing tāpe, an adhesive tape for covering and protecting margins, etc., as during painting.

mas'ki·nonġe, *n.* same as *muskellunge.*

mȧsk'oid, *n.* [*mask* and *-oid.*] a masklike face carved in stone or wood.

maṣ'lin, *n.* [ME. *maslin, mastlyng*, from AS. *mæstling, mæsling*, a kind of brass.] brass; also, a dish or vessel of brass. [Obs.]

maṣ'lin, *n.* mixed grain, as rye and wheat. [Dial.]

maṣ'ŏch·iṣm (*now often* mas'), *n.* [after Leopold von Sacher-*Masoch* (1835–1895), Austrian writer in whose stories it is described.]

1. the getting of sexual pleasure from being dominated, mistreated, or hurt physically or otherwise by one's partner.

2. the getting of pleasure from being dominated, mistreated, or hurt in some way.

maṣ'ŏch·ist, *n.* a person characterized by masochism.

maṣ·ŏch·is'tiç, *a.* of or characterized by masochism.

maṣ·ŏch·is'tiç·al·ly, *adv.* in a masochistic manner.

mā'sŏn, *n.* [ME. *mason, masoun*; OFr. *maçon, masson*; LL. *macio, maco*, a mason.]

1. a person whose work is building with stone, brick, etc.

2. a stonecutter.

3. [M–] a Freemason.

mā'sŏn, *v.t.* to build of or reinforce with masonry.

mā'sŏn bee, a hymenopterous insect of the genera *Osmia* and *Chalicodoma*, a solitary bee that builds its nest of clay, sand, mud, etc.

Mā'sŏn-Dix'ŏn Līne, the boundary between Pennsylvania and Maryland, surveyed by Charles Mason and Jeremiah Dixon from 1763 to 1767: regarded as the line of demarcation between the North and the South: also *Mason and Dixon's line.*

Mȧ·son'iç, mȧ·son'iç, *a.* of Masons (Freemasons) or Masonry (Freemasonry).

mā'sŏn·īte, *n.* [after W. H. *Mason* (1877–), Am. engineer.] a kind of fiberboard made from pressed wood fibers, used as building material, insulation, etc.: a trade-mark (*Masonite*).

Mā'son jär, a glass jar with a screw top of metal or glass, for home canning or preserving: patented in 1857 by John L. Mason of New York.

mā'sŏn moth, a moth that makes its cocoon from mud, building it underground.

mā'sŏn·ry, *n.*; *pl.* **mā'sŏn·rieṣ,** [ME. *masonerie.*]

1. the craft or business of a mason.

2. the work done by a mason.

3. that which is built of the materials used by masons, as stone, tiles, brick, etc.; brickwork or stonework; as, the *masonry* in that building is of the best.

4. [*usually* M–] Freemasonry; specifically, (a) the principles of the Society of Freemasons; (b) Freemasons collectively.

dry masonry; masonry in which no mortar is used.

mā'sŏn spī'dẽr, a trap-door spider.

mā'sŏn wäsp, a solitary wasp which constructs hard mud nests for its young.

mȧ·so͝o'lȧ bōat, mȧ·sụ'lȧ bōat, [Anglo-Ind.] a large East Indian boat used on the coast of Madras, for conveying passengers and goods between ships and the shore. They stand high out of the water, the planks being fastened together by coconut fibers. They are rowed sometimes with as many as sixteen oars.

Mȧ·sō'rȧ, Mȧ·sō'rāh, *n.* [Mod. Heb. *māsōrāh*, tradition; Heb. *māsōreth.*]

1. all the accumulated Jewish tradition concerning the correct Hebrew text of the Old Testament.

2. the marginal notes of Old Testament scripts embodying this tradition, compiled in the tenth century A.D.

Mas'ō·rēte, *n.* [from Heb. *māsōreth.*] any of the tenth-century Jewish scribes who compiled the Masora.

Mas·ō·ret'iç, *a.* relating or belonging to the Masora or the Masoretes.

Mas·ō·ret'iç·ăl, *a.* same as *Masoretic.*

Mas'ō·rīte, *n.* same as *Masorete.*

mȧsque (mȧsk), *n.* 1. a masquerade; a masked ball.

2. a form of dramatic entertainment popular among the aristocracy in England during the 16th and 17th centuries, usually based on a mythical or allegorical theme, and with the dialogue subordinated to lavish costumes, scenery, music, dancing, etc.: originally it contained no dialogue.

3. a dramatic composition written for such an entertainment, usually in verse.

Also spelled *mask.*

mas·quẽr·āde', *n.* [altered (after *masque*) from Fr. *mascarade*, from Sp. *mȧscarada*, a masquerade, from *mascara*, a mask.]

1. a ball or party at which masks and fancy costumes are worn.

2. a costume for such a ball or party.

3. (a) a disguise or false show; (b) a living or acting under false pretenses.

mas·quẽr·āde', *v.i.*; masqueraded, *pt.*, *pp.*; masquerading, *ppr.* 1. to take part in a masquerade.

2. to assume a disguise as to manners or actions so as to appear other than what one really is; to go about disguised; as, he *masquerades* as a philanthropist and scholar.

mas·quẽr·āde', *v.t.* to cover with a mask or disguise.

mas·quẽr·ād'ẽr, *n.* a person wearing a mask; one disguised; one who masquerades.

mass, *n.* [ME. *masse*; OFr. *masse*, from L. *massa*, that which adheres together like dough, a lump; from Gr. *maza*, a barley cake.]

1. a quantity of matter forming a body of indefinite shape and size, usually of relatively large size; a lump.

2. a large quantity or number; as, a *mass* of bruises.

3. bulk; size; magnitude.

4. the main or larger part; majority.

5. in mining, a mineral deposit of irregular shape: distinguished from *bed, vein.*

6. in pharmacy, the paste or plastic combination of drugs from which pills are made.

7. in physics, the quantity of matter in a body as measured in its relation to inertia: mass is determined for a given body by dividing the weight of the body by the acceleration due to gravity.

blue mass; see under *blue.*

in mass; in a position or condition in which they occupy the least possible space while retaining military order: formerly used, as of a battalion.

in the mass; collectively; as a whole.

the masses; the common people; the working people; lower classes in the social order: opposed to *the classes.*

Syn.—bulk, heap, lump, aggregate, substance, total, sum, whole.

mass, *a.* 1. of a large number of things; large-scale; as, *mass* production.

2. of, characteristic of, or for the masses; as, *mass* education.

mass, *v.t.* and *v.i.* to gather or assemble into a mass.

Mass, mass, *n.* [ME. *masse, messe*; AS. *mæsse*, a mass, church festival; LL. *missa*, dismissal, properly f. pp. of L. *mittere*, to send. The word came from *ite, missa est* (supply *ecclesia*, church), "go, the congregation is dismissed," the proclamation used at the end of the service.]

1. the celebration or service of the Eucharist, a sacrament of the Roman Catholic Church, consisting of a series of prayers and ceremonies: the term is also used in some High Anglican churches. *High Mass* is celebrated with incense and music, the priest being assisted by a deacon and subdeacon; *Low Mass* is celebrated by one priest, without music and with little ceremony.

2. a musical setting for certain parts of this service.

mas'sȧ·çre (-kẽr); *n.* [Fr.; OFr. *maçacre, macecle*, butchery.]

1. the indiscriminate, merciless killing of a number of human beings or, sometimes, animals; wholesale slaughter.

2. an overwhelming defeat, as in sports. [Slang].

mas'sȧ·çre, *v.t.*; massacred (-ẽrd), *pt.*, *pp.*; massacring, *ppr.* 1. to kill (many people or animals) indiscriminately and mercilessly; to slaughter wholesale.

2. to defeat overwhelmingly. [Slang.]

mas'sȧ·çrẽr, *n.* one who massacres.

mȧs·säġe' (-säzh'), *n.* [Fr., from *masser*, to massage, from Port. *amassar*, to knead, from *massa*, a lump; L. *massa*, a lump.] a rubbing, kneading, etc. of part of the body, usually with the hands, as to stimulate circulation and make muscles or joints supple.

mȧs·säġe, *v.t.*; massaged, *pt.*, *pp.*; massaging, *ppr.* to give a massage to.
mȧs·säġ'ẽr (-säzh'), *n.* one who massages.
mȧs·säġ'ist, *n.* same as *massager.*
mas·sȧ·sa̤u'gȧ, *n.* [Am. Ind.] a variety of small rattlesnake found in dry regions of the southern United States.
Mass bell, same as *Sanctus bell.*
Mass book, same as *missal.*
Mass çärd, a printed card stating that a Mass will be offered, as for a deceased person, sent by the donor, as to the bereaved.
Mass'-dāy, *n.* a day on which High Mass is celebrated. [Archaic.]
mass dē·fect', in physics, the amount by which the mass of the nucleus of an atom is less than the sum of the masses of the particles of which the nucleus is constituted.
mas·sé' (mas-sā'), *n.* [Fr., from *masser*, to make a massé shot, from *masse*, a cue.] in billiards, a shot made with the cue held in a vertical or nearly vertical position.
mas·sé' shot, same as *massé.*
mas·sē'tẽr, *n.* [Mod. L.; Gr. *masētēr*, a chewer, from *masasthai*, to chew.] either of a pair of large muscles in the angle of the lower jaw which raise the jaw in chewing, etc.
mas·sē·ter'iç, *a.* in anatomy, relating to the masseter.
mȧs·sēur', *n.* [Fr., from *masser*, to knead.] a man whose work is massaging.
mȧs·sēuṣe', *n.* a woman whose work is massaging.
mas'si·çot, *n.* [Fr.] a yellow oxide of lead, PbO, produced by heating lead in air to just above the melting point, used as a pigment and in the production of red lead.
mȧs'sïf, *n.* [Fr., bulky, massive, from *masse*, a mass.]
1. the dominant, central mass of a mountain ridge, more or less defined by lengthwise or crosswise valleys.
2. a diastrophic block of the earth's crust that is isolated by boundary faults and has shifted as a whole.
mass'i·ness, *n.* the state of being massy.
mas'sive, *a.* [Fr. *massif*, from *masse*, L. *massa*, a lump, mass.]
1. forming or consisting of a large mass; large and heavy; big and solid; bulky; ponderous.
2. solid, not hollow or plated: said of articles made of gold or silver.
3. large and imposing or impressive; of considerable magnitude.
4. in geology, (a) homogeneous in structure, without stratification, foliation, etc.; as, *massive* rock formations; (b) occurring in thick beds, without minor joints and lamination: said of some stratified rocks.
5. in mineralogy, irregular in form, though occasionally crystalline in internal structure.
Syn.—bulky, heavy, ponderous, weighty, large.
mass'ive·ly, *adv.* in a mass; heavily.
mass'ive·ness, *n.* the quality of being massive.
mass mē'di·ȧ, those means of communication that reach and influence large numbers of peoples, especially newspapers, popular magazines, radio, and television.
mass meet'ing, a large public meeting to hear speakers, discuss public affairs, demonstrate public approval or disapproval, etc.
mass num'bẽr, in atomic and nuclear physics, the whole number by which the fundamental unit of mass, 1.6603×10^{-24} gram (almost the mass of a proton, the nucleus of a hydrogen atom), is multiplied to find the approximate mass of the nucleus of an atom: it is equal to the sum of the numbers of protons and neutrons in the nucleus and is always at least twice as great as the atomic number, except in the case of hydrogen and a certain rare isotope of helium.
Mas'sō·rēte, Mas'sō·rīte, *n.* same as *Masorete.*
mas·sō·ther'ȧ·py, *n.* [from *massage* and *therapy.*] the treatment of disease by massage.
Mass priēst, a Roman Catholic priest; a hostile term.
mass prō·duç'tion, the production or manufacture of goods in large quantities, especially by machinery and division of labor.
mass speç'trō·graph, an instrument for sorting and analyzing streams of ionized particles by passing these through deflecting fields, typically designed to focus particles of equal mass on a fluorescent screen or photographic plate: used to detect various particles, to determine the relative abundance of isotopes in an element, etc.: also called *mass spectrometer.*

mas'sū·lȧ, *n.*; *pl.* **mas'sū·lae,** [L. *massula*, dim. of *massa*, a lump, mass.] in botany, (a) in ferns, a mucilaginous mass of spherical shape enclosing a mass of microspores; (b) in flowering plants, a little group of adherent pollen grains produced by the same mother cell.
mass'y, *a.*; *comp.* massier; *superl.* massiest, having much mass; heavy; large; weighty. [Archaic or Poet.]
mast-, same as *masto-.*
mȧst, *n.* [ME. *mast*; AS. *mæst*, the stem of a tree, bough, mast.]
1. a tall spar, sometimes in sections, rising vertically from the keel or deck of a vessel and used to support the sails, yards, etc.: modern masts are often hollow structures made of wooden strips, tubular steel, extruded aluminum, etc.
2. a specified section of this; as, the topmast.
3. any vertical pole, as in a crane or derrick.
4. the foremast.
5. [M-] in the United States Navy, a summary session held by an officer to impose discipline and hear complaints.
at the mast; in the United States Navy, at the mainmast on the spar deck, the place of meeting for interview between officers and men.
before the mast; (a) in the sailors' quarters on a ship, forward of the foremast, as distinguished from the officers' quarters aft; (b) as a common sailor; as an unlicensed seaman.
mȧst, *v.t.*; masted, *pt.*, *pp.*; masting, *ppr.* to attach a mast or masts to, as a ship; as, the ship is properly *masted.*
mȧst, *n.* [ME. *mast*; AS. *mæst*, food, mast, beechnuts.] beechnuts, acorns, chestnuts, etc., especially as food for hogs.
mȧst, *v.t.* to furnish with mast as food; as, to *mast* swine in the fall. [Obs.]
mas'tȧ·bȧ, mas'tȧ·băh, *n.* [Ar. *mastabah.*] an oblong structure with a flat roof and sloping sides, built over the opening of a mummy chamber or burial pit in ancient Egypt and used as a tomb or mortuary chapel.

MASTABA

mas'tax, *n.* [Gr. *mastax*, the mouth, jaws, from *masasthai*, to chew.] the pharyngeal bulb containing the food-crushing apparatus of a rotifer.
mȧst çōat, in a ship, a kind of conical roof of canvas fitted around the foot of a mast to prevent water from entering between the mast and the deck.
mas·teç'tō·my, *n.* [*mast-* and *-ectomy.*] the surgical removal of a breast.
mȧst'ed, *a.* furnished with a mast or masts.
mȧs'tẽr, *n.* [ME. *maister*, *meister*; OFr. *maistre*, master, from L. *magister*, master, chief, head, from root of *magnus*, great.]
1. a man who rules others or has control, authority, or power over something; specifically, (a) a man who is head of a household or institution; (b) an employer; (c) an owner of an animal or slave; (d) the captain of a merchant ship; (e) a victor; as, he proved to be the *master* of the other runners in the race; (f) [Chiefly Brit.] a male schoolteacher or tutor; (g) a person whose teachings in religion, philosophy, etc. one follows or professes to follow; (h) [M-] Jesus Christ (with *our*, *the*, etc.)
2. something regarded as having control, power, etc.; as, love is his *master.*
3. a person very skilled and able in some work, profession, science, etc.; expert; specifically, (a) a skilled workman or craftsman qualified to follow his trade independently; (b) an artist regarded as great.
4. a work by such an artist; as, this painting is an old *master.*
5. [M-] a title variously applied to (a) originally, a man of high rank; (b) later, any man or youth: now superseded by the variant *Mister*, usually written *Mr.*; (c) a boy regarded as too young to be addressed as *Mr.*; (d) a man who heads some institution, group, activity, or place; as, *Master* of the Foxhounds; (e) in Scotland, the heir apparent of a viscount or baron; (f) a person holding a certain degree from a college or university, denoting completion of a prescribed course of graduate study in some field and ranking above that of *Bachelor* and below that of *Doctor*; as, *Master* of Arts.
6. a metal matrix or mold made from the original recording and used to produce phonograph records in quantity.
7. in law, any of several court officers appointed to assist the judge by hearing evidence, reporting on certain matters, etc.; as, a *master* in chancery.
Little Masters; a group of German artists in the sixteenth and seventeenth centuries, distinguished for the excellence of their little illustrative engravings on both wood and copper.
master in chancery; in England, an assistant of the lord chancellor, chosen from among the barristers to sit in chancery or at the rolls; in the United States, an officer in a court of equity whose duty it is to inquire into and to report on matters of fact referred to him, and to perform any duties required of him by the court under whose authority he serves.
master of the horse; the third great officer in the British court, having the management of the royal stables, etc. In solemn cavalcades he rides next to the sovereign.
Master of the Rolls; in England, an officer who has charge of the rolls and patents that pass the great seal, and of the records of the court of chancery.
to be master of oneself; to have complete self-control, especially in respect to passions, impulses, and motives.
to be one's own master; to be untrammeled; to be subject only to one's own wishes and desires, with freedom to act.
Syn.—chief, director, head, manager, boss, proprietor, owner, superintendent.
mȧs'tẽr, *a.* 1. being master.
2. of a master.
3. chief; principal; main; controlling; specifically, designating a mechanism or contrivance that controls others or sets a standard or norm; as, a *master* switch, a *master* test sheet.
mȧs'tẽr, *v.t.*; mastered, *pt.*, *pp.*; mastering, *ppr.* 1. to become master of; to conquer; to overpower; to subdue; to bring under control.

Evil customs must be *mastered* by degrees. —Calamy.

2. to rule or govern as master.
3. to become an expert at; as, to *master* a science.
4. to possess. [Obs.]
Syn.—conquer, overcome, acquire, attain, learn.
mȧs'tẽr-at-ärmṣ', *n.*; *pl.* **mȧs'tẽrṣ-at-ärmṣ',** a naval petty officer responsible for keeping order, maintaining discipline, taking charge of prisoners, etc. on a warship: the rating no longer exists in the United States Navy.
mȧs'tẽr build'ẽr (bild'), 1. a person skilled in, or in charge of, building; especially, an architect: often figurative.
2. a building contractor.
mȧs'tẽr·dŏm, *n.* mastery.
mȧs'tẽr·fu̇l, *a.* 1. having or showing the skill of a master; expert.
2. fond of acting the part of a master; imperious; arbitrary.
mȧs'tẽr·fu̇l·ly, *adv.* in the manner of a master.
mȧs'tẽr hand, 1. an expert.
2. great ability or skill.
mȧs'tẽr·hood, *n.* the position of master.
mȧs'tẽr joint, in geology, the most important among many joints in a mass of rock.
mȧs'tẽr kēy, a key for opening more than one of a set of locks; a passkey; hence, figuratively, a general clue to lead out of many difficulties.
mȧs'tẽr·less, *a.* 1. without a master or owner.
2. ungoverned; unsubdued.
mȧs'tẽr·less·ness, *n.* lack of a master.
mȧs'tẽr·li·ness, *n.* the quality or state of being masterly.
mȧs'tẽr·ly, *a.* 1. formed or executed with superior skill; suitable to a master; most excellent; skillful; as, a *masterly* design; a *masterly* performance; a *masterly* stroke of policy.
2. imperious. [Obs.]
Syn.—finished, artistic, consummate, skillful, dexterous, expert.
mȧs'tẽr·ly, *adv.* with the skill of a master.
mȧs'tẽr mā'sŏn, 1. a skilled mason; expert worker in brick or stone.
2. [M- M-] a Freemason of the third degree.

mas′tẽr mē·chan′iç, a skilled mechanic, especially one serving as foreman.

mas′tẽr·mīnd, *n.* a person of great intelligence, especially one with the ability to plan or direct a group project.

mas′tẽr·mīnd, *v.t.* to be the mastermind of (a project, etc.).

Mas′tẽr of Ärts, 1. a degree given by a college or university to a person who has completed a prescribed course of graduate study in the humanities, social sciences, etc.: it ranks above the degree of *Bachelor* and below that of *Doctor*.
 2. a person who has this degree.

mas′tẽr of cer′ē·mō·nieṣ, 1. a person who supervises a ceremony.
 2. a person who presides over an entertainment, as on a radio broadcast or in a night club, introducing the speakers or performers, filling in the intervals with jokes, etc.

Mas′tẽr of Sci′ence, 1. a degree given by a college or university to a person who has completed a prescribed course of graduate study in science rather than the humanities: it ranks above the degree of *Bachelor* and below that of *Doctor*.
 2. a person who has this degree.

mas′tẽr·ous, *a.* masterly. [Obs.]

mas′tẽr·piēce, *n.* 1. a great work of art or craftmanship; chef-d'oeuvre; anything done or made with superior or extraordinary skill.
 2. the greatest work made or done by a person or group.

mas′tẽr ser′ġeănt (sär′), a noncommissioned officer of the highest rank in the United States armed forces: since 1948 any personnel with the occupational designation of *first sergeant* hold the rank of *master sergeant*.

mas′tẽr·ship, *n.* 1. the state of being a master; dominion; rule; supreme power.
 2. the position, duties, or term of office of a master, especially a schoolmaster.
 3. masterly ability; expert skill or knowledge.
 4. the status or degree of a master (in a trade, university, etc.).
 5. chief work; masterpiece. [Obs.]
 6. a title of respect. [Obs.]

mas′tẽr sin′ew, a main sinew; especially, a sinew that surrounds the hock of a horse, and corresponds to the tendon of Achilles in man.

mas′tẽr·sing″ẽrṣ, *n.pl.* same as *Meistersinger*.

mas′tẽr strōke, a capital or masterly performance, action, move, or achievement.

mas′tẽr tap, a standard tap of a screw, not used except for reference in measurement.

mas′tẽr touch (tuch), a touch that represents the master.

mas′tẽr·wŏrk, *n.* a masterpiece.

mas′tẽr wŏrk′măn, 1. an expert workman, craftsman, or artist.
 2. in some trades, a foreman or overseer.

mas′tẽr·wŏrt, *n.* in botany, an umbelliferous herb: in Europe, *Peucedanum* (formerly *Imperatoria*) *ostruthium*); in the United States, *Heracleum lanatum*, the cow parsnip.

mas′tẽr·y, *n.*; *pl.* **mas′tẽr·ieṣ**, [ME. and OFr. *maistrie*, from *maistre*, a master.]
 1. mastership; dominion; power of governing or commanding.
 2. superiority or victory in competition or war; the upper hand.
 3. a struggle for advantage. [Obs.]
 4. a masterpiece. [Obs.]
 5. masterly ability; expert knowledge; eminent skill or power.
 6. the act of mastering (an art, science, etc.).
 Syn.—ascendancy, dominion, dominance, control.

mast′fụl, *a.* abounding with mast.

mast′head (-hed), *n.* 1. the top part of a ship's mast, especially of the lower mast.
 2. a sailor stationed in a crow's-nest near the masthead as a lookout.
 3. that part of a newspaper or magazine stating the publishers, owners, and editors, the location of the business, advertising, and editorial offices, etc.

mast′head, *v.t.* 1. to send (a sailor) to the masthead to remain there for a certain time as a punishment.
 2. to elevate to or carry at a masthead; as, to *masthead* the colors.

mast hoop, in a ship, a hoop for attaching a sail to a mast.

mast′house, *n.* in shipbuilding, a spacious structure in which masts are made and which is provided with appliances for stepping and unstepping masts: also called *masting house*.

mas′tiç, mas′tiçh, *n.* [ME. *mastik*; OFr. *mastic*; L. *mastiche*, from Gr. *mastichē*, mastic, from *mastizein*, to chew: so called because it was used in the East for chewing.]
 1. a yellowish resin exuding from a small Mediterranean evergreen tree, *Pistacia lentiscus*, obtained by making transverse incisions in the bark, from which it issues in drops: it is used as an astringent and in making varnish, chewing gum, incense, etc. Barbary mastic is obtained from the *Pistacia atlantica*, which grows in the north of Africa and the Levant.
 2. the tree from which the resin is obtained: often *mastic tree*.
 3. a liquor flavored with mastic.
 4. any of various quick-drying, pasty cements used for cementing tiles to a wall, etc.
 Peruvian mastic; the California pepper tree, *Schinus molle*, a shrub having red berries whose flavor resembles pepper.
 West Indian mastic; a large tree, *Bursera gummifera*, of the myrrh family.

mas′ti·ça·ble, *a.* capable of being masticated.

mas′ti·çāte, *v.t.*; masticated, *pt.*, *pp.*; masticating, *ppr.* [LL. *masticatus*, pp. of *masticare*, to chew, originally, to chew mastic, from *mastiche*, mastic.]
 1. to chew; to grind with the teeth and prepare for swallowing and digestion; as, to *masticate* food.
 2. to crush, cut, knead, or grind (rubber, etc.) to a pulp.

mas·ti·çā′tion, *n.* a masticating or being masticated.

mas′ti·çā·tŏr, *n.* a person or thing that masticates; specifically, (a) a person or animal that chews; (b) an organ for chewing; (c) a machine for crushing, grinding, or cutting something into small pieces.

mas′ti·ça·tō·ry, *a.* of or for mastication; specifically, adapted for chewing.

mas′ti·ça·tō·ry, *n.*; *pl.* **mas′ti·ça·tō·rieṣ**, any substance to be chewed to increase the saliva flow.

mas′tiçh, *n.* same as *mastic*.

mas′tiç hẽrb (ẽrb), *Thymus mastichina*, a plant which grows in Spain. It is a low, shrubby plant, and has a strong agreeable smell like mastic.

mas′ti·cin, *n.* a substance which remains after dissolving mastic in alcohol.

mas′ti·çot, *n.* massicot. [Obs.]

mas′tiff, *n.* [ME. *mastyf*, *mestif*; OFr. *mastin*, a mastiff, *mestif*, a mongrel, mixed breed, from L. *mixtus*, mixed, pp. of *miscere*, to mix.] any of a breed of large, powerful, smooth-coated dog with hanging lips and drooping ears, formerly used for hunting and as watchdogs.

MASTIFF
(30 in. high at shoulder)

mas′tiff bat, an Asiatic and South African bat of the genus *Molossus*: so called from its head resembling that of a mastiff: also called *bulldog bat*.

mas·tiġ′i·um, *n.*; *pl.* **mas·tiġ′i·ȧ**, [Gr. *mastix* (*-igos*), a whip.] in zoology, an organ occurring in a few species of caterpillars, from which whiplike processes are extended to keep parasites away.

mas″ti·gō·brañ′çhi·ȧ, *n.* [Gr. *mastix* (*-igos*), a whip, and *branchia*, gills.] in zoology, a flabellum or gill brush of certain crustaceans.

mas·ti·goph′ō·rous, mas″ti·gō·phor′iç, *a.* [Gr. *mastigophoros*, bearing a whip; *mastix* (*-igos*), a whip, and *-phoros*, from *pherein*, to bear.] provided with whiplike cilia, as the *Flagellata*.

mas′ti·gō·pod, *n.* any of the *Mastigopoda*.

Mas·ti·gop′ō·dȧ, *n.pl.* [Gr. *mastix* (*-igos*), a whip, and *pous*, *podos*, a foot.] a group of *Protozoa* with whiplike appendages or cilia.

mas′ti·gūre, *n.* [Gr. *mastix* (*-igos*), a whip, and *oura*, a tail.] an Asiatic or African lizard characterized by spiny scales in bands upon the tail.

mas·tī′tis, *n.* [Gr. *mastos*, a breast, and *-itis*.] inflammation of the breast, or mammary gland.

mast′less, *a.* 1. having no mast, as a vessel.
 2. bearing no mast; as, a *mastless* oak or beech.

mast′lin, *n.* same as *maslin*.

mas′tō-, mast-, [from Gr. *mastos*, breast.] a combining form used in medicine, anatomy, zoology, etc., and meaning *of* or *like a breast*, or *mammary gland*, as in *masto*don.

mas′tō·don, *n.* [Gr. *mastos*, breast, and *odous*, *odontos*, tooth: so called from the nipplelike processes on the molar teeth.] any of various large, extinct animals resembling the elephant but larger, and differing from it and the mammoth mainly in the structure of the molars.

MASTODON RESTORED
1. molar tooth; 2. skull of mastodon of Micoene period

Mas″tō·don·sau′rus, *n.* [*mastodon*, and Gr. *sauros*, a lizard.] a genus of extinct amphibians belonging to the *Labyrinthodonta*.

mas′tō·dont, mas·tō·don′tiç, *a.* of, relating to, or like a mastodon; as, *mastodont* dentition, *mastodontic* proportions.

mas′tō·dont, *n.* a mastodontic animal.

mas·tō·dyn′i·ȧ, *n.* [*mast-*, and Gr. *odynē*, pain.] a painful affection of the mammary gland.

mas′toid, mas·toid′ăl, *a.* [Gr. *mastos*, breast, and *eidos*, form.]
 1. shaped like a breast or nipple.
 2. designating, of, or near a projection of the temporal bone behind the ear.

mas′toid, *n.* 1. the mastoid projection, or process.
 2. mastoiditis. [Colloq.]

mas·toid·eç′tō·my, *n.* the surgical removal of part or all of a mastoid.

mas·toid·ī′tis, *n.* an inflammation of the mastoid.

mas·tol′ō·ġy, *n.* mammalogy.

mas·tor·rhā′ġi·ȧ, *n.* [*masto-*, and Gr. *rhagia*, from *rhēgnynai*, to break.] mammary hemorrhage.

mas′tress, *n.* mistress. [Obs.]

mas′tũr·bāte, *v.i.*; masturbated, *pt.*, *pp.*; masturbating, *ppr.* to engage in masturbation.

mas·tũr·bā′tion, *n.* [L. *masturbatus*, pp. of *masturbari*, to practice masturbation.] genital self-excitation, usually by manipulation; auto-erotism: also called *self-abuse*, *onanism*.

mast′y, *a.* yielding abundance of mast. [Obs.]

ma·sü′lȧ bōat, a masoola boat.

ma·sụ′ri·um, *n.* [Mod. L., from *Masuria*, where first found.] a name given to chemical element 43, supposedly discovered in columbite, gadolinite, etc., in 1925: symbol, Ma: cf. *technetium*.

mat, *n.* [ME. *matte*; AS. *meatt*, from L. *matta*, a mat.]
 1. a flat, coarse fabric made of woven or plaited hemp, straw, rope, rushes, etc., often used as a floor covering.
 2. a piece of this, or any more or less similar flat article, often corrugated or roughened, put down near a door, etc., for people to wipe their shoes on; a door mat.
 3. a flat piece of cloth, woven straw, or other material, put under a vase, dish, etc., or used as an ornament, as on a table.
 4. a thickly padded floor covering, especially one used in a gymnasium for tumbling, wrestling, etc.
 5. anything densely interwoven or felted, or growing in a thick tangle; as, a *mat* of hair.
 6. in nautical usage, (a) a thick web of rope yarn, used to protect rigging from wear; (b) a web or pad used as a bumper or to plug large leaks in a hull.
 7. in lacemaking, the more closely worked part as distinguished from the open part.

 fāte, fär, fȧst, fạll, finăl, cãre, at; mēte, prẹy, hẽr, met; pīne, marīne, bīrd, pin; nōte, mōve, fọr, atŏm, not; mọọn, book;

mat, *v.t.*; matted, *pt., pp.*; matting, *ppr.* 1. to cover with or as with a mat or mats.

2. to interweave felt, or tangle together into a thick mass.

mat, *v.i.* to be interwoven, felted, or tangled together into a thick mass.

mat, *a.* [Fr., from OFr. *mat,* overcome, defeated, exhausted, from Ar. *māt.*] not glossy or shiny; lusterless; dull: said of a surface, finish, or color.

mat, *n.* [Fr.] 1. a dull surface or finish, often roughened: also spelled *matte.*

2. a border, as of dull gilt or white cardboard, put around a picture, either as the frame or, usually, between the picture and the frame.

3. in printing, a matrix.

mat, *v.t.*; matted, *pt., pp.*; matting, *ppr.* to produce a dull surface or finish on (metal, glass, etc.).

Mat·à·bē′lē, *n.*; *pl.* **Mat·à·bē′lē, Mat·à·bē′lēş,** a member of a Zulu tribe driven out of the Transvaal by the Boers in 1837.

mat·à·ҫhīn′, *n.* [Sp., a buffoon, a grotesque dance.] an old dance with swords and bucklers.

mat′à·cō, *n.* [S. Am.] a South American three-banded armadillo: written also *matico.*

mat′à·dōr, *n.* [Sp., a murderer, slayer, from *matar,* to kill, from L. *mactare,* to sacrifice, immolate.]

1. a bullfighter whose specialty is killing the bull with a sword thrust at the end of a bullfight after performing a series of formalized actions with a cape to anger and tire the animal.

2. in card playing, (a) any one of the four jacks or knaves, the highest trumps in skat; (b) any one of the highest three trumps in ombre, solo, or quadrille; (c) a game played with dominoes, in such a manner that the sum of the spots of any two adjacent ends is always seven; also, the 1 : 6, 2 : 5, 3 : 4, or double blank in that game.

mat·à·gasse′, *n.* [Fr., a shrike.] the great shrike or butcherbird of Europe. [Obs.]

mä′tä·i, *n.* [native name.] a New Zealand conifer, *Podocarpus spicata*: also called *red pine* and *black pine.*

mä·tà·mä′tà, *n.* [S. Am.] *Chelys fimbriata,* a species of turtle of tropical America characterized by leaflike processes on the axial appendages.

mà·tan′zà, *n.* [Sp., slaughter, from *matar,* to kill.] a slaughterhouse, especially for the securing of tallow and hides. [Dial.]

match, *n.* [ME. *macche*; OFr. *mesche, meische,* a wick of a candle, match, from L. *myxus,* a wick of a candle; Gr. *myxa,* nozzle of a lamp.]

1. originally, a wick or cord prepared to burn at a uniform rate, used for firing guns or explosives.

2. a slender piece of wood, cardboard, waxed cord, etc. tipped with a composition that catches fire by friction, sometimes only on a specially prepared surface.

3. a slip of paper, splinter of wood, etc. dipped in sulfur so that it can be ignited with a spark, for lighting candles, lamps, etc. [Obs.]

match, *n.* [ME. *matche, macche,* from AS. *gemæcca, gemaca,* a companion, comrade.]

1. a person, group, or thing equal to another in strength or other quality; one able to cope with another.

> Government makes an innocent man of the lowest ranks a *match* for the mightiest of his fellow subjects. —Addison.

2. (a) a counterpart or facsimile; (b) either of two corresponding things or persons; one of a pair.

3. two or more persons or things that go together in appearance, size, or other quality; pair; as, her purse and shoes were a good *match.*

4. a contest or game involving two or more contestants.

5. (a) an agreement to marry or mate; (b) a marriage or mating; as, she made a good *match.*

> Love doth seldom suffer itself to be confined by other *matches* than those of its own making. —Boyle.

6. a person regarded as a suitable or possible mate.

> She inherited a fair fortune of her own, and was looked upon as the richest *match* in the west. —Clarendon.

Syn.—equal, mate, companion, tally, equality, pair.

match, *v.t.*; matched (macht), *pt., pp.*; matching, *ppr.* 1. to join in marriage; to mate.

> A senator of Rome, while Rome survived, Would not have *matched* his daughter with a king. —Addison.

2. (a) formerly, to meet as an antagonist; hence, (b) to compete with successfully.

3. to put in opposition (*with*); to pit (*against*).

4. to be equal, similar, suitable, or corresponding to in some way; as, his looks *match* his character.

5. to make, show, produce, or get a competitor, counterpart, or equivalent to; as, I want to *match* this cloth.

6. to suit or fit (one thing) to another.

7. to fit (things) together; to make similar or corresponding.

8. to compare.

9. (a) to flip or reveal (coins) as a form of gambling or to decide something contested, the winner being determined by the combination of faces thus exposed; (b) to match coins with (another person), usually betting that the same faces will be exposed.

Syn.—equal, compare, oppose, pit, adapt, suit, mate.

match, *v.i.* 1. to be united in marriage; to mate.

> Let tigers *match* with hinds, and wolves with sheep. —Dryden.

2. to suit; to correspond; to be equal, similar, suitable, or corresponding in some way; to tally; as, this piece of cloth does not *match* with the other.

match′à·ble, *a.* equal, similar, suitable, or corresponding in some way.

match′à·ble·ness, *n.* the quality of being matchable.

match′bōard, *n.* any of a number of identical thin boards with a tongue formed along one edge and a groove cut along the other so that the tongue of one can be fitted into the groove of the next, as in making floors or ceilings.

match′box, *n.* a small box for holding matches.

match′clọth, *n.* a kind of coarse cloth formerly used in making matchcoats, probably in imitation of skins sewed together.

match′cōat, *n.* a kind of mantle made of skins sewed together, formerly worn by North American Indians; later, a coat made of matchcloth.

matched (macht), *a.* [pp. of *match.*] having a tongue formed along one edge and a groove cut along the other, as some boards.

match′ẽr, *n.* one who matches; also, a machine for matching.

match′ing mà·ҫhīne′, a machine for making matchboards.

match′less, *a.* 1. having no equal; as, *matchless* impudence.

2. unmatchable. [Obs.]

Syn.—incomparable, peerless, inimitable.

match′less·ly, *adv.* in a manner or degree not to be equaled.

match′less·ness, *n.* the state or quality of being without an equal.

match′lock, *n.* 1. an old type of gunlock in which the charge of powder was ignited by a slow match (of wicking or cord).

2. a musket with such a gunlock.

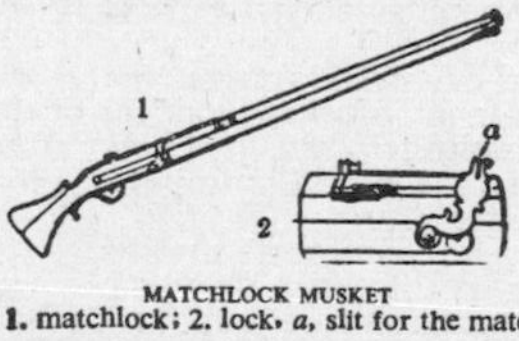

MATCHLOCK MUSKET
1. matchlock; 2. lock; *a,* slit for the match

match′māk″ẽr, *n.* one who makes matches (for burning).

match′māk″ẽr, *n.* 1. a person who arranges a marriage or marriages for others, or tries to do so by scheming.

2. a person who arranges wrestling matches, prize fights, etc.

match′māk″ing, *n.* the work or business of making matches (for burning).

match′māk″ing, *n.* 1. the act or practice of arranging or trying to arrange marriages.

2. the arranging of wrestling matches, prize fights, etc.

match′māk″ing, *a.* of matchmaking or matchmakers (in any sense).

match′märk, *n.* a mark put on machine parts to distinguish them as an aid in assembling.

match′märk, *v.t.* to put matchmarks on.

match plāne, either of the two planes used to groove or tongue the edges of matchboards.

match plāte, a board or plate used to hold both halves of a pattern on a molding machine.

match plāy, 1. play in a match, as in tennis, etc.

2. in golf, a form of competitive play in which the score is calculated by counting holes won rather than strokes taken: distinguished from *medal play.*

match point, the final point needed to win the match, as in tennis.

match wheel (hwēl), in machinery, a gear wheel that meshes properly with another, having the same pitch as the other; also, one of two meshing wheels of equal size.

match′wood, *n.* 1. wood for making matches.

2. very small pieces; splinters.

māte, *n.* [ME.; prob. from M.L.G. *mate,* a companion, from *gemate,* from *ge-,* together, and *mat,* meat, food.]

1. a companion, comrade, or fellow worker: often used in compounds, as class*mate,* and, among sailors, British workingmen, etc., as a familiar form of address.

2. one of a pair, especially of a matched pair.

3. (a) a husband or wife; spouse; (b) the male or female of animals paired for propagation.

4. an equal; a fit associate. [Archaic.]

5. in nautical usage, (a) an officer of a merchant ship, ranking below the captain; (b) an assistant.

6. in the United States Navy, any of various petty officers; as, a boatswain's *mate.*

māte, *v.t.* and *v.i.*; mated, *pt., pp.*; mating, *ppr.* 1. to join as a pair; to couple.

2. to join as mates; to couple in marriage or sexual union.

māte, *n.* and *interj.* checkmate.

māte, *v.t.*; mated, *pt., pp.*; mating, *ppr.* 1. to checkmate.

2. to enervate; to subdue; to crush. [Obs.]

ma′té, ma′te (mä′tā *or* mat′ā), *n.* [Sp., from Peruv. *mati,* calabash: so called in allusion to the gourd or calabash in which it is steeped.]

1. a species of South American holly, *Ilex paraguayensis,* from the leaves of which an infusion resembling tea is made and used as a beverage by the people of South America.

2. the leaves of this plant.

3. the tea made from the leaves of this plant.

Also called *yerba, Jesuits' tea,* and *Paraguay tea.*

ma·te·las·sé′ (mȧt-lä-sā′), *a.* [Fr., pp. of *matelasser,* to cover with a mattress, from *matelas,* a mattress.] having a surface that appears as if quilted: said of fabrics, usually silks, with depressed markings and raised designs.

ma·te·las·sé′, *n.* a matelassé fabric.

mate′less, *a.* having no mate.

mat′e·lōte, *n.* [Fr., from *matelot,* sailor.] stewed fish in a sauce of wine, oil, onions, mushrooms, etc.

mat′e·lotte, *n.* same as *matelote.*

mā′tẽr (*or* mä′tẽr), *n.* [L., mother.]

1. mother: often preceded by *the.* [Chiefly Brit. Colloq.]

2. in anatomy, either of two membranes (*pia mater* and *dura mater*) forming, with the arachnoid, a covering for the brain and spinal cord.

mā′tẽr dō·lō·rō′sȧ, [L.] sorrowful mother: a name given to the Virgin Mary.

mā″tẽr·fȧ·mil′i·as, *n.* [L., mother of a family.] the mother of a family; the woman head of a household: distinguished from *paterfamilias.*

mȧ·tē′ri·ăl, *a.* [LL. *materialis,* of or pertaining to matter, from L. *materia,* matter.]

1. of matter; of substance; relating to or consisting of what occupies space; physical; as, a *material* object, *material* forces.

2. (a) of the body or bodily needs, satisfactions, etc.; corporeal, sensual, or sensuous; as, *material* pleasures; (b) of or fond of comfort, pleasure, wealth, etc. rather than spiritual values; worldly; as, *material* success.

3. important, essential, or pertinent (*to* the matter under discussion).

> In the account of simple ideas, I shall set down only such as are most *material to* our present purpose. —Locke.

4. in law, important enough to affect the outcome of a case, the validity of a legal instrument, etc.

5. in philosophy, of the matter of reasoning, as distinguished from the formal element.

material cause; see under *cause.*

material evidence; in law, evidence that

proves or disproves an important view of the cause in dispute.

material fallacy; in logic, a fallacy growing out of the matter of the premises while the syllogism conforms to all the rules of the science.

mȧ·tē′ri·ăl, *n.* 1. what a thing is, or may be, made of; elements, parts, or constituents; as, raw *material*.

2. ideas, notes, observations, sketches, etc. that may be worked up or elaborated; data.

3. cloth or other fabric.

4. [*pl.*] tools, implements, articles, etc. needed to make or do something; as, writing *materials*.

mȧ·tē′ri·ăl, *v.t.* to materialize. [Obs.]

mȧ·tē′ri·ăl·ism, *n.* 1. in philosophy, (a) the doctrine that matter is the only reality and that everything in the world, including thought, will, and feeling, can be explained only in the terms of matter: opposed to *idealism*; (b) the doctrine that comfort, pleasure, and wealth are the only or highest goals or values.

2. the tendency to be more concerned with material than with spiritual goals or values.

3. matter; material substances in the aggregate. [Obs.]

mȧ·tē′ri·ăl·ist, *n.* 1. one who believes in materialism (sense 1).

2. one who is characterized by materialism (sense 2).

mȧ·tē′ri·ăl·ist, *a.* of materialism or materialists (esp. in sense 1).

mȧ·tē″ri·ăl·is′tiç, *a.* 1. of materialism or materialists (esp. in sense 2).

2. characterized by materialism: concerned with worldly goals.

mȧ·tē″ri·ăl·is′tiç·ăl, *a.* materialistic.

mȧ·tē″ri·ăl·is′tiç·ăl·ly, *adv.* 1. in a materialist or materialistic manner.

2. from the viewpoint of materialism.

mȧ·tē·ri·al′i·ty, *n.* 1. the state or quality of being material, or physical.

2. matter; substance.

3. *pl.* **mȧ·tē·ri·al′i·tieș,** something material; body.

mȧ·tē″ri·ăl·i·zā′tion, *n.* a materializing or being materialized.

mȧ·tē′ri·ăl·īze, *v.t.*; materialized, *pt., pp.*; materializing, *ppr.* 1. to give material form or characteristics to; represent in material form.

2. to make (a spirit, etc.) appear in bodily form.

3. to make materialistic.

mȧ·tē′ri·ăl·īze, *v.i.* 1. to appear in the flesh: said of a spirit, etc.

2. to become fact; to be realized; to turn out as promised: said of plans, etc.

mȧ·tē′ri·ăl·ly, *adv.* 1. with regard to material objects, interests, etc.; physically.

2. with regard to the matter, substance, or content, and not the form.

An ill intention may spoil an act *materially* good. —South.

3. in an important manner or degree; essentially; substantially; as, it *materially* concerns us to know the real motives of our actions.

mȧ·tē′ri·ăl·ness, *n.* the state of being material; importance.

mȧ·tē′ri·ȧ med′i·cȧ, [L., medical matter; *materia*, matter, material, and *medica*, f. of *medicus*, medical.] in medicine, (a) the drugs and other substances from which medicines are made; (b) a branch of the science treating of such substances, their uses, etc.

mȧ·tē′ri·āte, *a.* consisting of matter; material. [Obs.]

mȧ·tē·ri·ā′tion, *n.* the act of forming matter. [Obs.]

mȧ·tē·ri·el′, ma·té·ri·el′ (mȧ-tēr-i-el′; *Fr.* mȧ-tā-ryel′), *n.* [Fr.]

1. materials and tools necessary to any work, enterprise, etc.; specifically, weapons, equipment, supplies, etc. of armed forces: distinguished from *personnel*.

2. nonexpendable weapons, equipment, etc. of armed forces: distinguished from *supplies*.

mȧ·tē′ri·ous, *a.* material. [Obs.]

mȧ·tẽr′năl, *a.* [Fr. *maternel*, from L. *maternus*, from *mater*, mother.]

1. of, like, or characteristic of a mother or motherhood; motherly; as, *maternal* love, *maternal* tenderness.

2. derived, received, or inherited from a mother.

3. on the mother's side of the family; as, *maternal* grandparents.

mȧ·tẽr′năl·īze, *v.t.* to make maternal.

mȧ·tẽr′năl·ly, *adv.* in a maternal manner.

mȧ·tẽr′ni·ty, *n.*; *pl.* **mȧ·tẽr′ni·tieș,** [LL. *maternitas*, from L. *maternus*, pertaining to a mother, from *mater*, mother.]

1. the state of being a mother; motherhood.

2. the character or qualities of a mother; motherliness.

mȧ·tẽr′ni·ty, *a.* for prospective mothers; for pregnant women; as, a *maternity* dress.

mȧ·tẽr′ni·ty hos′pi·tăl, a hospital for women giving birth and for the care of newborn babies; a lying-in hospital.

māte′y, *a.* [*mate* (companion) and *-y*.] friendly; companionable; chummy. [Brit. Colloq.]

māte′y, *n.* a companion; chum. [Brit. Colloq.]

mat′fel·ŏn, *n.* [ME. *matfelon*; OFr. *matefelon*, knapweed.] the knapweed. [Brit. Dial.]

mȧth, *n.* [AS. *mæth*, a mowing, from *mawan*, to mow.] a mowing. [Obs.]

math, *n.* mathematics. [Colloq.]

math·ē·mat′iç, *a.* mathematical. [Rare.]

math·ē·mat′iç, *n.* mathematics. [Rare.]

math·ē·mat′iç·ăl, *a.* [from L. *mathematicus*; Gr. *mathēmatikos*, from *mathēma*, what is learned, from *manthanein*, to learn; and *-al*.]

1. of, having the nature of, or concerned with mathematics.

2. rigorously exact, precise, accurate, etc.

math·ē·mat′iç·ăl log′iç, a modern type of formal logic using special symbols that can be handled according to exact principles: also called *symbolic logic*.

math·ē·mat′iç·ăl·ly, *adv.* 1. by or according to mathematics.

2. with mathematical certainty; rigorously exact; demonstrably.

math″ē·mȧ·ti′ciăn (-tish′ăn), *n.* an expert or specialist in mathematics.

math·ē·mat′içs, *n.pl.* [*construed as sing.*] [see *mathematical* and *-ics*.] the group of sciences (including arithmetic, geometry, algebra, calculus, etc.) dealing with quantities, magnitudes, and forms, and their relationships, attributes, etc., by the use of numbers and symbols.

math′ē·meg, *n.* [prob. Am. Ind.] a fish of the genus *Amiurus* inhabiting the basin of the Saskatchewan.

math′eș, *n.* [a corruption of Gr. *anthemis*, equivalent to *anthos*, a flower.] the mayweed, *Maruta cotula*.

mȧ·thē′sis, *n.* [Gr. *mathēsis*, from *manthanein*, *mathein*, to learn.] learning; particularly, mathematics. [Rare.]

Math′ū·rin, *n.* same as *Trinitarian*, sense 2.

mat′i·cō, *n.* same as *mataco*.

mȧ·tī′çō, *n.* [Sp.] in botany, a variety of pepper plant found in Peru, used in medicine as an astringent.

mȧt′ie, *n.* [origin doubtful.] a fat herring in which the roe is small. [Chiefly Scot.]

mȧ·tin′ (mä-tañ′), *n.* a large kind of dog, allied to the Danish dog, but now scarcely seen except in France, where it is supposed to have been introduced from the north.

mat′in, *n.* [Early ME. *matyn*; OFr. *matin*, from L. *matutinus*, of the morning, from *Matuta*, goddess of dawn.]

1. [*pl.*] [*sometimes* M-] (a) in the Roman Catholic Church, the first of the seven canonical hours in the breviary, properly recited at midnight, but often at daybreak, and followed by lauds; (b) in the Anglican Church, the order for, or the service of, public morning prayer: often spelled *mattins* in British usage.

2. a morning song, especially of birds. [Poet.]

mat′in, *a.* [Fr. *matin*, from L. *matutinus*, of the morning, from *Matuta*, goddess of dawn.]

1. pertaining to the morning; used in the morning; as, a *matin* trumpet.

2. of matins.

mat′in·ăl, *a.* 1. of or at matins.

2. of or in the morning.

mat·i·nēe′, mat·i·née′ (-nā′), *n.* [Fr. *matinée*, from *matin*, morning.] a reception or entertainment held in the daytime; especially, a performance, as of a play, held in the afternoon.

mat·i·nēe′ ī′dŏl, an actor whose looks and manner make him popular with women theater goers.

māt′ing, *n.* a pairing or matching.

māt′ing, *a.* of or for mating; as, the *mating* season.

mat′răss, *n.* [Fr. *matras*, from *matras*, kind of arrow, from Gaulish *mataris*, javelin.]

1. a glass container with a rounded body and a long neck, formerly used in distilling, etc.

2. a slender, hard glass tube used in blowpipe analysis.

Also spelled *mattrass*.

mā′tri-, [from L. *mater*, *matris*, a mother.] a combining form meaning *mother*, as in *matriarch*.

mā′tri·ärçh, *n.* [*matri-* and *-arch* as in *patriarch*.] a mother who rules her family or tribe; specifically, in sociology, a woman holding a position analogous to that of a patriarch.

mā·tri·är′çhăl, *a.* 1. of, or having the nature of, a matriarch or matriarchy.

2. fit for a matriarch.

mā′tri·ärçh·āte, *n.* 1. a family, tribe, etc. ruled by a matriarch.

2. a matriarchal government or system.

mā·tri·är′çhiç, *a.* of, or having the nature of, a matriarchy; matriarchal.

mā′tri·ärçh·y, *n.*; *pl.* **mā′tri·ärçh·ieș,** 1. a form of social organization in which the mother is recognized as the head of the family or tribe, descent and kinship being traced through the mother instead of the father.

2. government by women.

Mat·ri·çā′ri·ȧ, *n.* [L. *matrix* (*-icis*), the womb; so called from formerly being used in uterine complaints.] a large genus of herbs of the family *Compositæ* containing many species abounding in the Old World and parts of the United States.

mā′trice, *n.* same as *matrix*.

māt′ri·cēș, *n.* alternative pl. of *matrix*.

mā·tri·cīd′ăl, *a.* of, like, or having the nature of, a matricide or a matricide.

mā′tri·cīde, *n.* [L. *matricidium*, from *mater*, mother, and *cædere*, to slay.] the killing or murder of a mother by her child.

mā′tri·cīde, *n.* [L. *matricida*, *mater*, mother, and *caedere*, to kill.] one who kills or murders his own mother.

mat·ri·clī′nous, *a.* [L. *mater*, mother, and Gr. *klinein*, to bend.] in biology, pertaining to or having hereditary characteristics derived from the mother.

mȧ·triç′ū·lȧ, *n.* [LL., dim. of *matrix*, a public register, source, origin, the womb, from L. *matrix*, a female animal kept for breeding.] a register, roll, or list of persons belonging to a society, order, etc. [Obs.]

mȧ·triç′ū·lănt, *n.* a candidate for registration or matriculation.

mȧ·triç′ū·lāte, *v.t.* and *v.i.*; matriculated, *pt.*, *pp.*; matriculating, *ppr.* [LL. *matriculatus*, pp. of *matriculare*, to register, enroll, from *matricula*, dim. of *matrix*, a public register.] to enroll, especially as a student or candidate for a degree in a college or university.

mȧ·triç′ū·lāte, *a.* admitted and enrolled.

mȧ·triç′ū·lāte, *n.* one who has been matriculated.

mȧ·triç·ū·lā′tion, *n.* a matriculating or being matriculated.

mȧ·triç′ū·lā·tŏr, *n.* a matriculant.

mā·tri·lin′ē·ăl (*or* mat-ri-), *a.* [*matri-* and *lineal*.] designating or of descent, kinship, or derivation through the mother instead of the father.

mā·tri·lin′ē·ăr, *a.* same as *matrilineal*.

mat·ri·mō′ni·ăl, *a.* [LL. *matrimonialis*, from L. *matrimonium*, marriage.]

1. pertaining to matrimony; marital; connubial; nuptial; hymeneal; as, *matrimonial* rights or duties.

2. derived from marriage.

mat·ri·mō′ni·ăl·ly, *adv.* 1. according to the customs or laws of marriage.

2. by or as regards matrimony.

mat·ri·mō′ni·ous, *a.* matrimonial. [Rare.]

mat′ri·mō·ny, *n.*; *pl.* **mat′ri·mō·nieș,** [ME. and OFr. *matrimoine*; L. *matrimonium*, from *mater*, *matris*, a mother.]

1. the act of marrying; the rite or sacrament of marriage.

2. the state of being husband and wife.

3. married life.

4. (a) a card game with any number of players; (b) a combination of the king and queen of trump, as in this game.

mat′ri·mō·ny vīne, the boxthorn, *Lycium halimifolium*, a shrub having purple flowers and red berries.

mā′trix (*or* mat′), *n.*; *pl.* **mā′tri·cēș** (*or* mat′ri-), **mā′trix·eș** (*or* mat′), [LL. *matrix*, the womb, source, origin, a public register; L. *matrix*, a female animal kept for breeding, from *mater*, mother.]

1. originally, the womb; the uterus.

2. that within which, or within and from which, something originates, takes form, or develops; specifically, (a) the rock in which a gem, mineral, fossil, etc. is enclosed or embedded; also, the impression left in such rock when the embedded object is removed; (b) a die or mold for casting or shaping; (c) a metal plate, usually of copper, for molding the face

of a type; (d) a papier-mâché, plaster, or similar impression of type, etc., from which a plate can be made for printing, as in stereotypy: also *mat*.

3. (a) the substance between the cells of animal or plant tissue; (b) the formative cells from which a nail, tooth, etc. grows.

4. in mathematics, any rectangular arrangement of symbols. Thus:

$$\begin{matrix} a_1 & b_1 & c_1 & d_1 \\ a_2 & b_2 & c_2 & d_2 \\ a_3 & b_3 & c_3 & d_3 \end{matrix}$$

is a rectangular matrix consisting of four columns and three lines or rows.

mā′trŏn, *n.* [Fr. *matrone*, from L. *matrona*, a married woman, matron, from *mater*, mother.]

1. a married woman; a wife or widow, especially one who has had children or is not very young.

2. a woman superintendent or manager of the domestic arrangements of a hospital, prison, or other institution.

3. a woman attendant or guard in charge of women or children, as in an institution.

mā′trŏn·āġe (*or* mat′run-), *n.* 1. matrons collectively.

2. the state of being a matron.

3. matronly care or supervision.

mā′trŏn·ăl, *a.* [L. *matronalis*, from *matrona*, a married woman.] pertaining to a matron; suitable to an elderly lady or to a married woman; grave; motherly.

mā′trŏn·hood, *n.* the state of a matron.

mā′trŏn·īze, *v.t.*; matronized, *pt., pp.*; matronizing, *ppr.* 1. to make matronly.

2. to chaperon; to have charge of, in the place of a mother.

mā′trŏn·līke, *a.* having the manners of an elderly woman; grave; sedate; becoming a matron.

mā′trŏn·li·ness, *n.* the quality or state of being matronly.

mā′trŏn·ly, *a.* of, characteristic of, like, or suitable for a matron; dignified, sedate, staid, etc.

mā′trŏn·ly, *adv.* in a matronly manner.

mā′trŏn of hon′ŏr (on′), a married woman acting as chief attendant to the bride at a wedding.

mat·rō·nym′iç, *n.* and *a.* metronymic.

mȧ·tross′, *n.* [D. *matroos*, a sailor, from Fr. *matelot*, a sailor, seaman.] formerly, in a train of artillery, an assistant whose duty was to aid the gunners in loading, firing, and swabbing the guns.

mat rush, a bulrush, *Scirpus lacustris*, used in making floor mats in Europe.

mat′sụ, *n.* [from Japan. *matsŭ*, a pine.] a pine, *Pinus massoniana*, of Japan and China, which furnishes a tough wood much used in Japan for interior woodwork, the roots being used in making lampblack: also called *Japanese pine* and *Masson's pine*.

mat·tȧ·ges′, mat·tȧ·gess′, mat·tȧ·gesse′, *n.* same as *matagasse*.

mat′tȧ·mōre, *n.* [Fr. *matamore*, from Ar. *metmur*, a ditch, cavern, cave.] in the Orient, a subterranean storehouse. [Rare.]

matte (mat), *n.* [Fr., from dial. *mate*, a lump.] an impure mixture of sulfides that is produced in smelting the sulfide ores of copper, nickel, lead, etc.

matte (mat), *n.* a mat (dull finish).

mat′ted, *a.* [G. *matt*, dull, dim.] having a lusterless surface.

matted glass; in ornamental work, glass with figures set on a lusterless ground.

mat′ted, *a.* 1. closely tangled together in a dense mass; as, *matted* hair.

2. covered with a dense growth.

3. covered with or enclosed in matting or mats.

mat′tẽr, *n.* [ME. *matter*, *mater*; OFr. *matiere*, *matere*, from L. *materia*, matter, stuff of which anything is composed.]

1. what a thing is made of; constituent substance or material.

2. what all (material) things are made of; whatever occupies space and is perceptible to the senses in some way: in modern physics, matter and energy are regarded as equivalents, mutually convertible according to Einstein's formula, $E=mc^2$ (i.e., energy equals mass multiplied by the square of the velocity of light); in dualistic thinking, matter is regarded as the opposite of mind, spirit, etc.

3. any specified sort of substance; as, coloring *matter*.

4. material of thought or expression; what is spoken or written, regarded as distinct from how it is spoken or written; content, as distinguished from manner, style, or form.

5. an amount or quantity, usually indefinite; as, a *matter* of a few days.

6. (a) something that is the subject of discussion, concern, action, etc.; thing or affair; as, a *matter* of course, a *matter* of fact, business *matters*; (b) cause, occasion, or grounds; as, no laughing *matter*.

7. (a) an important affair; thing of some moment or significance; (b) importance; moment; significance; as, it's of no *matter*.

8. a disagreeable state of affairs; trouble; difficulty (with *the*); as, what's *the matter?*

9. documents, letters, etc. sent, or to be sent, by mail; mail; as, second-class *matter*.

10. pus.

11. in philosophy, that which has yet to take on form; undifferentiated substance of reality or experience.

12. in printing, (a) material set up, or to be set up, in type; copy; (b) type set up.

as a matter of fact; in fact; in actuality; really.

dead matter; in printing, type in form that has been printed from and is of no further use; matter ready for distribution or destruction: opposed to *live matter*.

for that matter; in regard to that; as far as that is concerned: also *for the matter of that*.

live matter; in printing, type in form that has not yet been printed from or that is to be used again; matter not to be distributed or destroyed: opposed to *dead matter*.

matter of course; a thing to be expected as a natural or logical occurrence in the course of events.

matter of opinion; something about which there can be more than one opinion; a debatable question.

matter of record; in law, any matter that has been duly recorded by an authorized officer and which may be proved by the record.

no matter; (a) it is of no importance; (b) regardless of.

mat′tẽr, *v.i.*; mattered, *pt., pp.*; mattering, *ppr.* 1. to be of importance or consequence; to import; to signify: used with *it, this, that,* or *what*.

> *It matters* little to me what school of theology rises or falls, so only that Christ may rise in all his Father's glory.
> —H. W. Beecher.

2. to form and discharge pus; to collect, as matter in an abscess.

> Each slight sore *mattereth*. —Sidney.

mat′tẽr, *v.t.* to regard as weighty or important; to care for. [Obs.]

mat′tẽr·less, *a.* 1. devoid of matter; as, *matterless* spirits, a *matterless* speech.

2. without importance.

mat′tẽr-of-çourse′, *a.* 1. coming as a natural or logical occurrence in the course of events; to be expected; routine.

2. taking things as a matter of course.

mat′tẽr-of-façt′, *a.* sticking strictly to facts; literal, unimaginative, practical, prosaic, etc.

mat′tẽr·y, *a.* 1. purulent; generating pus; as, a *mattery* cough.

2. important; full of substance.

Mat′thew (math′ū), *n.* [ultimately from Heb. *mattithyāh*, lit., gift of God.] in the Bible (a) one of the four Evangelists, a customs collector who was a believer in Jesus and was chosen as one of the twelve apostles: also *Saint Matthew*; (b) the first book of the New Testament: ascribed to Matthew.

Mat·thī′ăs (mȧ-thī′ăs) *n.* in the Bible, one of the apostles, chosen by lot to replace Judas Iscariot.

Măt·thī′ō·lȧ, *n.* [after P. A. *Mattioli*, an Italian physician.] in botany, a genus of herbs and shrubs having petals arranged like the arms of a cross and bearing large purple or white flowers. Of the numerous species found in the Old World, many are cultivated under the name of stock or stock gillyflower.

mat′ting, *n.* 1. a fabric of rushes, flags, grass, straw, etc., used in packing various articles, and for covering the floors of houses.

2. the act of interweaving materials so as to make a mat; the process of becoming entangled or matted.

3. material for mats; matwork.

4. an ornamental border, as a picture mat.

5. in nautical usage, a web or pad made of strands of old rope, or of spun yarn, beaten flat and interwoven, used to protect rigging from wear.

mat′ting, *n.* [G. *matt*, dull.]

1. a surface without luster, especially on metal; a dull surface.

2. the act or process of producing a dull or lusterless surface on metal, etc.

mat′tinṣ, *n.pl.* matins: Anglican spelling.

mat′tŏck, *n.* [ME. *mattocke*, *mattoke*; AS. *mattuc*, *mattoc*.] a tool for loosening the soil, digging up and cutting roots, etc.: it is like a pickax but has a flat, adz-shaped blade on one or both sides.

> 'Tis you must dig with *mattock* and with spade. —Shak.

mat′toid, *n.* [L. *mattus*, intoxicated.] a person of unbalanced mind verging on insanity. [Rare.]

mat′trăss, *n.* a matrass.

mat′tress, *n.* [ME. *mattress*; OFr. *materas*, from LL. *matratum*, from Ar. *matrah*, a mattress, foundation, place where anything is thrown.]

1. a casing of strong cloth or other fabric filled with cotton, hair, foam rubber, etc., often quilted or tufted at intervals, and used on or as a bed: some mattresses (called *innerspring mattresses*) are made with wire springs inside.

2. a mass or mat of interwoven brushwood, poles, etc. used to protect an embankment or dike from erosion, etc.

mat′ū·rănt, *n.* [L. *maturans* (*-antis*), ppr. of *maturare*, to ripen.] in pharmacy, a medicine, or application to an inflamed part, which promotes suppuration. [Obs.]

mat′ū·rāte, *v.t.*; maturated, *pt., pp.*; maturating, *ppr.* [L. *maturatus*, pp. of *maturare*, to ripen, bring to maturity, from *maturus*, ripe, of full age.]

1. to promote suppuration of, as of a boil or an abscess.

2. to ripen; to bring to maturity.

mat′ū·rāte, *v.i.* 1. to suppurate; to discharge pus.

2. to ripen; to mature.

mat·ū·rā′tion, *n.* 1. the formation or discharge of pus; suppuration.

2. a ripening or maturing.

3. in biology, the final stages in the development of gametes in which the normal number of chromosomes is reduced by half.

mȧ·tūr′ȧ·tive, *a.* 1. ripening; conducing to ripeness.

2. conducing to suppuration, or to the formation of matter in an abscess.

mȧ·tūre′, *a.* [L. *maturus*, ripe, of full age.]

1. full-grown, as plants or animals; ripe, as fruits; fully developed, as a person, a mind, etc.

2. fully or highly developed, perfected, worked out, considered, etc.; as, a *mature* scheme.

3. of a state of full development; as, a person of *mature* age.

4. due; payable: said of a note, bond, etc.

5. in geology, having reached maximum development and accentuation of form, or maximum vigor and efficiency of action: said of streams adjusted to their surroundings, topography resulting from erosion, etc.

Syn.—ripe, complete, perfect, ready.

mȧ·tūre′, *v.t.*; matured, *pt., pp.*; maturing, *ppr.* [Fr. *maturer*; L. *maturare*, to ripen, make ripe, from *maturus*, ripe, of full age.]

1. to bring to full growth or development; to cause to ripen.

2. to develop or work out fully.

mȧ·tūre′, *v.i.* 1. to advance toward ripeness; to become fully grown or developed; to ripen; as the judgment *matures* with age and experience.

2. to become due; as, a note *matures* on a certain date.

mȧ·tūre′ly, *adv.* in a mature manner.

mȧ·tūre′ness, *n.* maturity.

mȧ·tūr′ẽr, *n.* one who brings to maturity.

mat·ū·res′cent, *a.* [L. *maturescens* (*-entis*), ppr. of *maturescere*, to become ripe, ripen, incept. of *maturare*, to ripen, from *maturus*, mature.] approaching maturity.

mȧ·tūr′ing, *a.* ripening; being in or coming to maturity; as, *maturing* apples, *maturing* notes or accounts.

mȧ·tū′ri·ty, *n.* [L. *maturitas*, from *maturus*, ripe, of full age.]

1. the state or quality of being mature; specifically, (a) a being full-grown, ripe, or fully developed; (b) a being perfect, complete, or ready.

2. (a) a becoming due; (b) the time at which a note, etc. becomes due.

3. *pl.* **mȧ·tū′ri·tieṣ,** a mature act, trait, etc.

mȧ·tū′ti·năl, *a.* [L. *matutinalis*, from *matutinus*, belonging to the morning, from *Matuta*, the goddess of morning.] pertaining to or occurring in the morning.

mat′weed, *n.* in botany, one of several species

of seaside grass, among which are the *Lygeum spartum*, or hooded matweed of the Mediterranean, and the *Ammophila arundinacea* of Holland, which is used in binding the dikes: also called *sea matweed, halm,* and *marram*.
small matweed; a tufted grass, *Nardus stricta*.
māt'y, *n.*; *pl.* **māt'ies,** in India, a native house servant or servant of all work.
mätz'ōs, *n.pl.* matzoth.
mätz'ōth, *n.pl.* [Heb. *matstsōth*, pl. of *matstsāh*, unleavened.] flat, thin pieces of unleavened bread, eaten at the feast of the Passover by the Jews.
mau·cā'çō, *n.* same as *macaco*.
maud, *n.* [perhaps from proper name *Maud*.]
1. a gray striped plaid, worn by shepherds in southern Scotland.
2. a shawl, wrap, or rug made of such plaid.
mau'dle, *v.t.* to put in a maudlin condition. [Obs.]
maud'lin, *a.* [Fr. *maudlin*, a corruption of *Magdalen* (Mary Magdalene), who is represented by painters with eyes red and swollen from weeping.]
1. foolishly and tearfully or weakly sentimental.
2. tearfully sentimental from too much drink.
maud'lin, *n.* [ME. *Maudelein*; OFr. *Magdeleine*, Magdalen.] a plant of the genus *Achillea*; a species of yarrow: called also *sweet maudlin*; also, a species of tansy, *Tanacetum balsamita*.
maud'lin·ism, *n.* the state or condition of being maudlin.
maud'lin·wŏrt, *n.* in botany, *Chrysanthemum leucanthemum*.
mau'gre (-gẽr), *prep.* [OFr. *maugre, malgre*, ill will, from L. *malus*, bad, evil, and *gratum*, a pleasant thing.] in spite of; in opposition to; notwithstanding: also written *mauger*. [Archaic.]
This, *mauger* all the world, will I keep safe.
—Shak.
mau'gre, *v.t.* to withstand in a defiant manner. [Obs.]
mau'kin, *a.* and *n.* same as *malkin*. [Scot.]
maul, *n.* [another spelling of *mall*, from L. *malleus*, a hammer, maul.]
1. a very heavy hammer or mallet, often of wood, for driving stakes, wedges, etc.
2. (a) a mace; (b) a wooden club. [Archaic.]
maul and wedges; the implements required by a wood chopper or rail splitter in splitting logs: used sometimes colloquially to express the whole of a man's earthly possessions.
maul, *v.t.*; mauled, *pt., pp.*; mauling, *ppr.* [LL. *malleare*, to beat with a hammer, from L. *malleus*, a hammer.]
1. to injure by beating or tearing; to bruise or lacerate.
2. to handle roughly or clumsily; to manhandle; to paw.
3. to split (rails, stumps, etc.) with a maul and wedge.
Also *mall*.
maul'ẽr, *n.* 1. a person or thing that mauls.
2. a boxer or wrestler. [Slang.]
maul'ing, *n.* a heavy beating. [Colloq.]
maul ōak, in botany, a live oak of California.
maul'stick, *n.* a long, light stick used by painters as a rest for steadying the brush hand while at work: also *mahlstick*.
mau'met, mam'met, maw'met, *n.* [ME. *maumet*, an idol; OFr. *mahumet*, an idol, from *Mahomet*, Mohammed.]
1. an idol: from the notion that the Moslems worshiped Mohammed as a god. [Obs.]
2. (a) a doll or puppet; (b) a guy. [Brit. Dial.]
mau'met·ry, *n.* worship of images; idolatry. [Archaic.]
maun, *v.i.* must. [Scot.]
maund, *v.i.* to beg. [Obs.]
maund, *n.* a hand basket or hamper. [Scot.]
maund, *n.* [Hind. *man*, a measure of weight.] a unit of weight used in India, Turkey, Iran, etc., varying from somewhat less than 20 to somewhat more than 160 pounds avoirdupois.
maun'dẽr, *v.i.* [Early Mod. Eng. *mander, maunder*, to grumble; prob. freq. of obs. *maund*, to beg.]
1. to mutter; to grumble. [Obs.]
2. to move or act in a dreamy, vague, aimless way.
3. to talk in an incoherent, rambling way; to drivel.
maun'dẽr, *n.* a beggar. [Obs.]
maun'dẽr·ẽr, *n.* a grumbler. [Obs.]
maun'dy, *n.* [ME. *maundee*; OFr. *mandé*, from L. *mandatum*, a command, neut. of *mandatus*, pp. of *mansare*, to command.]
1. the ceremony of washing the feet of the poor on Maundy Thursday.
2. [M-] the service or office read during the ceremony of foot washing.
3. [M-] the sacrament. [Obs.]
4. alms annually distributed in England on Maundy Thursday.
maundy money, maundy coins; money distributed by or by order of the sovereign in England to the poor at the service on Maundy Thursday.
Maunday Thursday; the Thursday of Passion Week; the day before Good Friday.
Mau·ran'di·à, *n.* [after Dr. *Maurandy*, of Cartagena, Spain.] a genus of Mexican climbing plants, including *Lithospermum*.
Mau·resque' (-resk'), *a.* and *n.* same as *Moresque*.
Mau'rist, *n.* [after St. *Maur*.] one of a class of Benedictine monks in France in the seventeenth century.
Mau·ri'tià (-rish'yà), *n.* [after Prince *Maurice* of Nassau.] a genus of tall fan palms of South America.
Mau·ri'tius weed (-rish'us), a species of lichen, *Rocella fuciformis*, found in Mauritius and in the Canary and Cape Verde islands.
Mau'sẽr, *n.* [after P. P. *Mauser* (1838–1914), G. inventor.] [*sometimes* m-] a high-powered repeating magazine rifle or pistol: a trademark.
mau·sō·lē'ăn, *a.* of, or having the nature of, a mausoleum.
mau·sō·lē'um, *n.*; *pl.* **mau·sō·lē'ums, mau·sō·lē'à,** [L., from Gr. *Mausōleion*, the tomb of Mausolus.]
1. [M-] the tomb of Mausolus, king of Caria, erected by his queen at Halicarnassus about 350 B.C., and splendidly decorated with sculpture: among the ancients one of the seven wonders of the world.
2. any tomb of more than ordinary splendor, especially a tomb designed for the members of a great or royal family: humorously applied to any large building or room regarded as like such a tomb.
mau'thẽr, *n.* a foolish young girl; an awkward young woman. [Brit. Dial.]
mau·vāise' honte (mō-vāz' ǫnt), [Fr.] bashfulness; false modesty.
mauve (mōv), *n.* [Fr., mallow, from L. *malva*, mallow: so called from the resemblance of the color to that of the mallow.]
1. a purple dye and pigment obtained from a coal-tar dyestuff produced by oxidizing aniline.
2. any of several shades of delicate purple.
mauve (mōv), *a.* having the color of mauve.
mauve'ine, mauve'in (mōv'), *n.* in chemistry, the base of the aniline dye mauve, ($C_{27}H_{24}N_4$): also called *aniline purple, mauve, mauvine*.
mā'ven, mā'vin, *n.* [Yid., from Late Heb. *mēvin*.] an expert or connoisseur, often especially a self-proclaimed one.
mav'ẽr·ick, *n.* [so called from Samuel *Maverick*, a Texas cattle owner who did not brand his cattle. The herd stampeded and mixed with the neighboring cattle, and in rounding them up all unbranded cattle were claimed as *Maverick's*.]
1. an unbranded animal, especially a lost calf, formerly the legitimate property of the first person who branded it.
2. a person not labeled as belonging to any one party, faction, etc., who acts independently. [Colloq.]
mā'vis, *n.* [ME. *mavis*; OFr. *mauvis*, a throstle.] the throstle or European song thrush, *Turdus musicus*.
maw, *n.* [ME. *maw, maghe*; AS. *maga*, maw, stomach.]
1. (a) originally, the stomach or its cavity; (b) the stomach of an animal; specifically, the fourth stomach of a cud-chewing animal.
2. the craw or crop of a bird.
3. the air bladder of a fish.
4. the throat, gullet, jaws, or oral cavity (of some voracious animals).
maw, *n.* ma; mother; mamma. [Dial.]
maw, *n.* an early game of cards.
mawk, *n.* [ME. *mawk*; Ice. *madhkr*, a maggot.] a maggot. [Scot. and Brit. Dial.]
maw'kin, *n.* a malkin. [Obs.]
mawk'ish, *a.* [from *mawk*, a maggot and *-ish*.]
1. nauseating; sickening; having a sickly, insipid flavor.
2. sentimental in a weak, sickly, insipid way.
So sweetly *mawkish*, and so smoothly dull.
—Pope.
mawk'ish·ly, *adv.* in a mawkish way.
mawk'ish·ness, *n.* the quality of being mawkish.
mawk'y, *a.* maggoty; mawkish. [Brit. Dial.]
maw'mish, *a.* mawkish; nauseous. [Obs.]
maw'wŏrm, *n.* in zoology, any worm or larva that infests the stomach.
max'i, *n.*; pl. **max'is,** [from *maxi-*.] a very long, usually ankle-length, skirt, dress, coat, etc. [Colloq.]
max'i-, [*maxi*mum.] a combining form meaning *maximum, very large, very long*, as in *maxicoat*: used freely to form nonce word compounds, often hyphenated, meaning "of greater scope, extent, etc. than usual", as in *maxi-power*.
max·il'là, *n.*; *pl.* **max·il'lae,** [L., dim. of *mala*; a jaw, jawbone.]
1. in vertebrates, a jaw or jawbone, especially the upper jaw, as distinguished from the mandible.
MAXILLAE
2. in most arthropods, as insects, crabs, etc., either of a pair of accessory jaws or appendages just behind the mandibles.
max'il·lăr, *a.* and *n.* same as *maxillary*.
Max·il·lā'ri·à, *n.* a genus of orchids with parts of the flowers resembling maxillae.
max'il·lăr·y, *a.* [L. *maxillaris*, from *maxilla*, jawbone, jaw.] pertaining to the jaw or jawbone, especially the upper one; relating to a maxilla or to the maxillae.
max'il·lăr·y, *n.*; *pl.* **max'il·lăr·ies,** a maxilla; a maxillary bone.
maxillary process; in anatomy, the bony plate descending from the upper border projection of the inferior turbinated bone.
max·il·lif'ẽr·ous, *a.* [L. *maxilla*, jawbone, and *ferre*, to bear.] in zoology, having maxillae.
max·il'li·form, *a.* [L. *maxilla*, jawbone, and *forma*, form.] in the form of a jawbone or of a maxilla.
max·il'li·ped, *n.* [L. *maxilla*, jawbone, and *pes, pedis*, foot.] in zoology, one of the footlike appendages situated just back of the maxillae in a crustacean and functioning as both a masticatory and a locomotive organ.
max·il'lō-, [from L. *maxilla*, jawbone, jaw.] a combining form meaning *of the maxilla and*, as in *maxillo*palatine, *maxillo*turbinal.
max·il''lō·man·dib'ū·lăr, *a.* relating to both the maxilla and mandible.
max·il·lō·pal'à·tīne, *a.* relating to both the maxilla and the palate or the palatine region.
max·il·lō·pal'à·tīne, *n.* an inward projection of the superior maxillary in birds.
max·il·lō·tūr'bi·năl, *a.* relating to the maxillary and the turbinal parts of the skull.
max'im, *n.* [Fr. *maxime*, from L. *maxima*, a maxim, abbrev. from *maxima propositio*, the greatest or chief premise, f. of *maximus*, greatest, superl. of *magnus*, great.]
1. a concisely expressed principle or rule of conduct, or a statement of a general truth; a precept.
2. in music, the longest note formerly used, equal to two longs, or four breves; a large.
Syn.—precept, rule, law, adage, apothegm, byword, aphorism, proverb, saw, saying.
max'i·mà, *n.* alternative plural of *maximum*.
Max·i·mal'ist, *n.* 1. a member of the left wing of the (former) Russian Social Revolutionaries.
2. a Bolshevik (sense 1).
Opposed to *Minimalist*.
Max'im gun, a single-barreled, water-cooled machine gun in which the recoil of one shot is used to fire the next one: invented by H. S. Maxim.
Max·i·mil·i·ā'nà, *n.* [after *Maximilian* Alexander Philipp, Prince of Neuwied.] a small genus of South American palms, topped by a tuft of large leaves.
max'im·īte, *n.* [after Hudson *Maxim* (1853–1927), the inventor.] a high explosive made with picric acid, formerly much used as the bursting charge for armor-piercing projectiles.
max''i·mi·zā'tion, *n.* the act or process of reaching or producing a maximum.
max'i·mīze, *v.t.*; maximized, *pt., pp.*; maximizing, *ppr.* to increase to the highest limit; to bring to a maximum.
max'i·mum, *n.*; *pl.* **max'i·mums, max'i·mà,** [L., neut. of *maximus*, greatest, superl. of *magnus*, great.]

1. the greatest quantity, number, or degree possible or permissible.
2. the highest degree or point (of a varying quantity, as temperature) reached or recorded; the upper limit of variation.
3. in astronomy, (a) the moment of greatest brilliance of a variable star; (b) the star's magnitude at this moment.
Opposed to *minimum*.
maxima and minima; in mathematics and physics, values of a function at the moment of its ceasing to increase and beginning to decrease, and at the moment of its ceasing to decrease and beginning to increase.

max'i·mum, *a.* 1. greatest or highest possible, permissible, or reached.
2. of, marking, or setting a maximum or maximums.
Opposed to *minimum*.

mà·xi'xe (mà-shē'shā *or* mak-sēks'), *n.* a dance of Brazilian origin in polka time, somewhat resembling the two-step in action and rhythm.

max'well, *n.* [after James C. *Maxwell* (1831–1879), Scot. physicist.] the C.G.S. and international unit of magnetic flux, equal to the flux through one square centimeter normal to a magnetic field with an intensity of one gauss.

māy, *v.*; might, *pt.*; mayest *or* mayst, *archaic 2d pers. sing.*; no other forms now in use, [ME. *may, mai, mey*.] an auxiliary preceding an (expressed or implied) infinitive (without *to*) and expressing: (a) originally, ability or power: now generally replaced by *can*; (b) possibility or likelihood; as, it *may* rain; (c) permission or chance; as, you *may* go; (d) contingency, as in clauses of purpose, result, concession, or condition; as, he is telling us so that we *may* be forewarned; (e) wish, hope, or prayer: used in exclamations and apostrophes; as, *may* he go!

Māy, *n.* [OFr. *mai*, from L. *Maius* (supply *mensis*, month), from *Maia*, goddess of increase or growth.]
1. the fifth month of the year, having 31 days.
2. (a) springtime; (b) the springtime of life; youth; prime.
3. [m–] the English hawthorn: also *may bush*.
4. the festivities of May Day.

Māy, *v.i.* to gather flowers in the spring.

māy, *n.* a virgin; a maiden. [Archaic or Poetic.]

Mä'yȧ, *n.* [from native name.]
1. a member of a race of Indians who formerly lived in southeastern Mexico and Central America and are still found in Yucatan, British Honduras, and northern Guatemala: the Mayas had a highly developed civilization when discovered by Europeans early in the sixteenth century.
2. (a) their Mayan language; (b) one of the two branches of the Mayan family of languages.

Mä'yȧ, *n.* [Sans. *māyā*.]
1. the Hindu goddess Devi, or Sakti, consort of Siva.
2. in Hindu philosophy, illusion, often personified as a woman.

Mā·yaç'ȧ, *n.* [from native name.] a genus of inconspicuous mosslike plants typical of the order *Mayacaceæ*, found in both North and South America.

Mä'yăn, *a.* 1. designating or of a Central American Indian linguistic family including the language of the Mayas and consisting of twenty-seven languages divided into two branches, the Maya and the Huastek.
2. Maya.

Mä'yăn, *n.* 1. a Mayan Indian.
2. the Mayan linguistic family.

Māy ap'ple, 1. a North American plant with shield-shaped leaves and a single large, white, cuplike flower.
2. its edible, yellow, lemon-shaped fruit.

MAY APPLE (*Podophyllum peltatum*)

māy'bē, *adv.* it may be that; it is possible that; as, *maybe* it will turn out favorably.

māy'bē, *a.* barely possible; doubtful; in the realm of possibility. [Rare.]

māy'bē, *n.* that which may come to pass; a possibility; a contingency.

Māy bee'tle, 1. the June bug, a scarabaeid beetle, *Lachnosterna fusca*; also, other species of this genus: called also *dor bug*.
2. the May bug, *Melolontha vulgaris*: also called *cockchafer*. [Brit.]

Māy'bïrd, *n.* any of several birds; specifically, (a) in the United States, the bobolink, or reedbird; (b) in England, the whimbrel, or curlew.

Māy blob, the marsh marigold and the lady's-smock, or cuckooflower. [Brit. Dial.]

Māy'blo̤om, *n.* the hawthorn or its blossoms.

Māy blos'sŏm, the lily of the valley, *Convallaria majalis*.

Māy bug, same as *May beetle*, sense 2.

māy bush, a plant of the genus *Cratægus*; the may or hawthorn.

māy'çock, *n.* the black-bellied plover of the United States and Europe, *Charadrius squatarola*.

Māy çũr'lew, the small curlew or whimbrel, *Numenius phæopus*: also called *Mayfowl*. [Brit. Dial.]

Māy Dāy, May 1: as a traditional spring festival, often celebrated by dancing, crowning a May queen, etc.; as a more recent international labor holiday (of American origin), observed in many countries by parades, demonstrations, etc.

Māy'dāy, *n.* [from Fr. *m'aidez*, help me.] the international radiotelephonic signal for help, used by ships and aircraft in distress.

Māy'-dew, *n.* the dew of May, which is said to whiten linen, and to have other special properties.

Māy Dūke, a variety of cherry.

may'est, *v.* archaic second person singular of *may*: used with *thou*.

Māy'fâir, *n.* [after an annual fair held there (prior to 1708) in May.] a fashionable residential district of the West End, London.

māy'fish, *n.* a small American fish of the genus *Fundulus*; a black-striped minnow.

Māy'flow"ẽr, *n.* 1. any of various plants that flower in May or early spring; especially, (a) in the United States, the trailing arbutus, any of several anemones, etc.; (b) in England, the hawthorn, cowslip, marsh marigold, etc.
2. the ship on which the Pilgrims came to America (1620).

Māy fly, 1. the dayfly, a delicate, slender insect with large forewings and small hind wings.
2. an angler's artificial fly made to resemble this insect.

māy'hap, *adv.* [from *it may hap(pen)*.] perhaps; maybe; perchance. [Archaic.]

māy"hap'pen, *adv.* mayhap. [Archaic.]

Māy haw, a hawthorn, *Cratægus æstivalis*, of the southern United States, having a juicy fruit that ripens in May, used for making jelly and preserves.

māy'hem, *n.* [earlier spelling of *maim*.] in law, the offense of maiming a person; the act of intentionally mutilating a person's body of injuring it so as to deprive him of a limb or any organ of the body that he needs to defend or take care of himself: also spelled *maihem*.

Māy'ing, *n.* the gathering of flowers on May Day; participation in the festivities of May Day.

māy'n't, may not.

māy'ō, *n.* same as *mayonnaise*. [Colloq.]

māy·ŏn·nāișe', *n.* [Fr.]
1. a creamy salad dressing or sauce made of salad oil, yolks of eggs, vinegar, lemon juice, etc. beaten together to a thick consistency.
2. a dish of meat or fish made with this.

māy'ŏr (*or* mār), *n.* [OFr. *maire*; LL. *major*, a prefect, chief, from L. *major*, comp. of *magnus*, great.] the chief administrative officer of a city, town, or other municipality. In the larger cities of the United States, the duties of a mayor are altogether executive; in smaller municipalities, the mayor sometimes performs judicial functions, especially as judge of offenses committed against the ordinances of the city.

māy'ŏr·ăl, *a.* relating to a mayor or his office and duties.

māy'ŏr·ăl·ty, *n.*; *pl.* **māy'ŏr·ăl·ties,** the office or term of office of a mayor.

māy'ŏr·ess, *n.* the wife of a mayor.

māy'ŏr·ship, *n.* the office or dignity of a mayor.

Māy'pōle, *n.* a high pole wreathed with flowers and garlands around which merrymakers dance on May Day.

māy'pop, *n.* the passion flower, *Passiflora incarnata*, growing in the southern United States; also, its edible fruit, which is yellow when ripe and of the size of a small apple.

Māy queen, a girl or a young woman crowned with flowers and honored by merrymakers as queen on May Day.

māyst, *v.* archaic second person singular of *may*: used with *thou*.

Māy'thorn, *n.* the hawthorn.

Māy'tīde, *n.* the month of May.

Māy'tīme, *n.* the month of May.

māy tree, the hawthorn. [Brit.]

māy'weed, *n.* a bad-smelling weed of the composite family, growing along roadsides, with white rays and yellow disk flowers, and leaves thrice pinnately divided, having an acrid taste; the *Maruta cotula* of the *Compositæ*, closely related to camomile: also called *dog's camomile, stinking camomile*.

Māy wīne, [after the month of May, when the woodruff blossoms.] white wine flavored with woodruff and slices of pineapple and orange.

Māy'wŏrt, *n.* a species of *Galium*, or bedstraw, that blooms in May: also called *crosswort, mugweed*.

Maz'ȧ·gan, *n.* [named from *Mazagan*, a town in Morocco.] a small early bean, *Vicia faba*, grown in America.

mȧ·zä'mȧ, mȧ·zä'mę, *n.* [Mex. *mazame*, the pronghorn.]
1. the mountain goat, *Haplocerus montanus*, of the Rocky Mountains.
2. the pampas deer.

maz'ärd, *n.* 1. the jaw, face, skull, or head. [Obs.]
2. a mazer. [Obs.]
3. a black cherry.

maz'ärd, *v.t.* to knock on the head. [Obs.]

Maz'ȧ·rin Bī'ble, the first Bible printed from movable type, issued from the press of Gutenberg about 1450: so called from the copy found in the library of Cardinal Jules Mazarin.

maz·ȧ·rïne', *n.* 1. mazarine blue.
2. a particular way of dressing fowls.
3. a small dish set in a large one. [Obs.]
4. a mazarine-blue gown.

maz·ȧ·rïne', *a.* pertaining to Cardinal Mazarin, prime minister to Louis XIV of France.
mazarine blue; a deep, rich blue.

Maz'dȧ, *n.* [after Avestan *mazda*: chosen because it suggested the light-giving firmament.]
1. a trade-mark for electric light bulbs conforming to certain standards.
2. [m–] a bulb bearing this trade-mark.

Maz'dȧ·ișm, Maz'dē·ișm, *n.* [from Avestan *mazda* and *-ism*.] Zoroastrianism.

Maz'dē·ăn, *a.* Zoroastrian.

māze, *v.t.*; mazed, *pt., pp.*; mazing, *ppr.* [ME. *masen*; compare Norw. *masa*, to pore over a thing; Sw. dial. *masa*, to be lazy; Ice. *masa*, to talk idly, prattle.]
1. to stupefy; to daze. [Archaic.]
2. to bewilder; to confound. [Archaic.]

māze, *v.i.* to be bewildered. [Obs.]

māze, *n.* 1. confusion of thought; perplexity; uncertainty.
2. a confusing, intricate network of winding pathways; a labyrinth.

mā'zẽr, *n.* [ME. *maser*; OFr. *masere*, maple wood.] a large drinking bowl or goblet, originally of a hard wood, probably maple, later of metal: also *mazard*.

mā'zẽr tree, the common maple of Europe.

mā'zi·ly, *adv.* in a mazy manner.

mā'zi·ness, *n.* the quality or state of being mazy.

maz·ō·log'iç·ăl, *a.* pertaining to mazology. [Obs.]

mȧ·zol'ō·ġist, *n.* one versed in mazology. [Obs.]

mȧ·zol'ō·ġy, *n.* [Gr. *mazos*, breast, and *-logia*, from *legein*, to speak.] that branch of zoology dealing with mammiferous animals. [Obs.]

mȧ·zũr'kȧ, *n.* [Pol. *mazurka*, from *Mazur*, a native of Mazovia, Poland.]
1. a polish dance resembling the polka, having two sliding steps in place of one.
2. music for this, generally in 3/4 or 3/8 time.
Also written *mazourka*.

mā'zy, *a.*; *comp.* mazier; *superl.* maziest. like a maze; intricately winding; bewildering.

maz'zärd, *n.* [earlier *mazer*: apparently from the hardness and knotty appearance of the wood.] a small, sweet wild cherry, used as a rootstock for cultivated varieties.

mäz'zel·tōv, *interj.* [Yid., from Heb. *mazal*, luck, and *tov*, good.] good luck: an expression of congratulation: also *mazzel tov*.

Mc-, Mc- (mak *or* mȧk), see *Mac-*.

Mç·Çoy', the (rēal), [said to be from advertisements of prize fights stating that a celebrated boxer named *McCoy* would participate, not an inferior boxer of the same name.] the genuine person or thing; the real thing, not a substitute. [Slang.]

Mç'In·tosh (mak'), *n.* [after John *McIntosh*,

Ontario who discovered and cultivated it (1796).] a late-maturing variety of red apple: also *McIntosh Red.*

M′-dāy, *n.* [*m*obilization *day.*] the day on which the War Department orders active mobilization for war.

mē, *pron.* [AS. *me* acc. and dat.; G. *mich* acc., *mir* dat.; Goth. *mis*; L. *me* acc.; Gr. *eme* acc.; Sans. acc. *mām, mā,* me.] the objective case of *I*, the pronoun of the first person: also used colloquially as a predicate complement with a linking verb (e.g., that's *me*).

mēach, *v.i.* same as *miche.*

mēa′çock, *a.* cowardly. [Obs.]

mēa′çock, *n.* a cowardly fellow. [Obs.]

mē′ȧ çul′pȧ, [L.] (by) my fault; I am to blame.

mēad, *n.* [AS. *medu, meodu, medo*; compare D. *mede,* Ice. *mjöthr,* Dan. *miöd,* Sw. *mjöd,* W. *medd,* Ir. *meadh,* mead; Gr. *methy,* wine; Slav. *med,* Russ. *med, meda,* Sans. *mādhu,* honey.]

1. an alcoholic liquor made of fermented honey, malt, spices, and water to which yeast has been added.

2. formerly, a soft drink made with a sirup of sarsaparilla and carbonated water.

mēad, *n.* a meadow. [Poet.]

mead′ōw (med′), *n.* [AS. *mædwe,* a meadow, oblique case of *mæd,* a mead.]

1. a tract of grassland, especially one producing grass suitable for hay.

2. low, level grassland near a stream, lake, etc.

3. the ground where fish feed.

mead′ōw beaū′ty, an herb of the genus *Rhexia*; deer grass.

mead′ōw bīrd, a bobolink.

mead′ōw fox′tāil, a forage grass resembling timothy, but with shorter, softer heads.

mead′ōw grȧss, any of various grasses grown on meadows.

mead′ōw hāy, any of various sedges cut for hay.

mead′ōw hen, any of various American birds, as the bittern, the coot, and the clapper rail.

mead′ō·wiñk, *n.* a bobolink.

mead′ōw lärk, *pl.* **mead′ōw lärks** or **mead′ōw lärk,** any of a number of related North American songbirds, including the *southern meadow lark,* which is brownish or grayish above with black markings on a yellow breast, and the *eastern meadow lark* and *western meadow lark,* both of which have a yellow breast and are about as large as the robin.

mead′ōw mouse, a rodent of the genus *Arvicola,* the field vole of Europe.

mead′ōw mus′sel, the ribbed mussel, *Modiola plicatula,* found in quantities in salt marshes.

mead′ōw ōre, in mineralogy, conchoidal bog iron ore.

mead′ōw pärs′nip, a plant of the genus *Thaspium*; also, in England, the cow parsnip.

mead′ōw piñk, any of various wild flowers; specifically, (a) the maiden pink, *Dianthus deltoides*; (b) the ragged robin, *Lychnis flos-cuculi*; (c) the wild pink, *Dianthus armeria.*

mead′ōw pip′it, a bird, the titlark.

mead′ōw rụe, any of a group of plants of the crowfoot family, with leaves like those of rue.

mead′ōw saf′frŏn, a bulbous plant, *Colchicum autumnale.*

mead′ōw sāġe, a plant, *Salvia pratensis.*

mead′ōw sax′i·frāġe, 1. a plant of the parsley family, resembling saxifrage.

2. any of numerous related herbs.

3. any plant of the genus *Seseli.*

mead′ōw·sweet, *n.* 1. any of a group of plants of the rose family; especially, a shrub with thick clusters of small, fragrant flowers of white or pink.

2. any plant of a related group.

mead′ōw·wŏrt, *n.* a variety of meadowsweet.

mead′ōw·y, *a.* 1. resembling a meadow.

2. full of meadows.

mēa′gẽr, mēa′gre (-gẽr), *a.* [OFr. *megre, maigre, magre,* from L. *macer,* lean, thin, meager.]

1. emaciated; thin; lean.

2. lacking richness, fertility, strength, etc.; deficient in quantity or poor in quality; mean; poor; insignificant; small; scanty.

3. in mineralogy, dry and harsh to the touch.

4. fit for Lent; Lenten.

Syn.—thin, lean, lank, scanty, barren, dry, tame, starved.

mēa′gẽr, mēa′gre, *v.t.* to make lean. [Obs.]

mēa′gẽr, *n.* same as *maigre.*

mēa′gẽr·ly, *adv.* in meager manner; poorly; thinly.

mēa′gẽr·ness, *n.* the state or quality of being meager; poorness.

mēak, *n.* [compare AS. *mece,* a sword.] a hook with a long handle. [Brit. Dial.]

mēal, *n.* [AS. *mæl,* time, portion, repast; compare D. and Dan. *maal,* G. *mahl,* Ice. *mal,* a part, repast, measure, time.]

1. a portion of food taken at one time; a repast.

2. any of the times, especially the customary times, for eating; breakfast, lunch, dinner, etc.

-mēal, [ME. *-mele*; AS. *-mælum,* from *mæl,* measure, time, and adv. dat. *-um*; basic sense "measure (taken at a time)."] a suffix used to form adverbs meaning *amount done* or *used at one time*: obsolete except in piece*meal.*

mēal, *n.* [ME. *mele,* AS. *melu.*]

1. any edible grain, or the edible part of any grain, coarsely ground and unbolted; as, corn *meal.*

2. any substance similarly ground or powdered.

mēal, *v.t.*; mealed, *pt., pp.*; mealing, *ppr.* 1. to sprinkle with meal, or to mix meal with.

2. to grind, as meal.

mēal bee′tle, the adult of the meal worm.

mēal ber′ry, the bearberry.

mēal′ieṣ, *n.pl.*; *sing.* **mēal′ie, mēal′y,** [from S. Afr. D. *milje,* from Port. *milho,* millet, in *milho grande,* etc., maize.] in South Africa, (a) maize; Indian corn; (b) [*sing.*] an ear of maize.

mēal′i·ness, *n.* the quality or state of being mealy; softness or smoothness to the touch.

mēal mọth, a lepidopterous insect, *Asopia farinalis,* the larvae of which feed upon meal.

mēal tick′et, 1. a ticket, card, etc. entitling the owner or bearer to a specified value in meals at the restaurant where it was bought.

2. a person, job, etc. depended on as a means of livelihood. [Slang.]

mēal′tīme, *n.* the usual period when meals are eaten.

mēal wŏrm, the wormlike larva of any of various beetles, which infests granaries and bakeries, destroying flour, meal, etc.

mēal′y, *a.*; *comp.* mealier; *superl.* mealiest, 1. like meal; powdery, dry, soft, etc.

2. of or containing meal.

3. sprinkled or covered with meal.

4. spotty or flecked: said of color, etc.

5. pale; floury in color.

6. mealy-mouthed.

mēal′y, *n.* alternative singular of *mealies.*

mēal′y·bug, *n.* any bug of a family, *Pseudococcidae,* of destructive, homopterous insects, having a soft body protected by a white, flourlike or cottony wax secretion.

mēal′y-mouthed, *a.* not outspoken or blunt; not willing to state the facts in simple, direct words; euphemistic and insincere.

mēal′y-mouth″ed·ness, *n.* the quality or state of being mealy-mouthed.

mēan, *a.*; *comp.* meaner; *superl.* meanest, [AS. *mæne,* wicked; D. *gemeen,* vulgar, common; Ice. *meinn,* bad, mean; M.H.G. *mein,* false.]

1. low in quality or grade; poor; inferior.

2. low in social status or rank; of humble origin or antecedents.

3. low in dignity; unimposing.

4. of slight value, importance, or consequence; paltry.

5. poor in appearance; shabby; as, a *mean* appearance.

6. ignoble; base; small-minded; petty.

7. stingy; miserly; penurious.

8. bad-tempered; vicious; unmanageable: said of a horse, etc.

9. (a) pettily or contemptibly selfish, bad-tempered, disagreeable, malicious, etc.; (b) humiliated or ashamed; (c) in poor health; not well; ill; indisposed. [Colloq.]

10. (a) hard to cope with; difficult; as, he throws a *mean* curve; (b) skillful; expert. [Slang.]

Syn.—abject, base, beggarly, contemptible, degenerate, degraded, despicable, disgraceful, dishonorable, groveling, ignoble, menial, paltry, servile, shameful, slavish, sordid, spiritless, vile, vulgar, wretched.

mēan, *a.* [OFr. *meien*; L. *medianus,* occupying a middle position, from *medius,* middle.]

1. occupying a middle position as to place, time, quantity, quality, kind, value, degree, etc.; middle; intermediate; halfway between extremes.

Of middle age and a *mean* stature.
—Sir P. Sidney.

2. intermediate in any kind of superiority or excellence; medium; average; middling.

Accordingly to the fittest style of lofty, *mean,* or lowly. —Milton.

3. in mathematics, designating a quantity having an intermediate value between others.

mean distance; the arithmetical mean of the greatest and least distances in the orbit of a planet from the sun, equal to half the major axis of the orbit.

mean latitude; middle latitude.

mean line; in crystallography, a bisectrix.

mean moon; a hypothetical moon supposed to pass through its orbit with a uniform motion throughout: used in computations.

mean noon; the time when the mean sun would reach the meridian.

mean place; in logic, a place which partly agrees with, and partly differs from, the character of the things to be proved.

mean position; in fencing, a position of the wrist intermediate between pronation and supination, in which the thumb is above the fingers.

mean proportional; the square root of the product of two numbers; also, the second of any three quantities in continued proportion.

mean solar time; mean time.

mean sun; in astronomy, a hypothetical sun used in time reckoning because of the variable motion of the real sun. It is assumed to move uniformly around the celestial equator so as to be on the meridian each day at mean noon.

mean time; time computed by the mean sun or by a perfect clock moving at a uniform rate, such as would be if all the days of the year were of a uniform length: distinguished from *apparent time,* as measured by the sun, and *sidereal time,* as measured by the stars: also *mean solar time.*

mēan, *n.* 1. that which is intermediate or has a value intermediate between two extremes; the middle rate, degree, or point of place.

2. absence or avoidance of extremes or excess; moderation.

3. in mathematics, (a) a quantity with a value intermediate between the values of two or more other quantities; especially, the average (also called the *arithmetical mean*), obtained by dividing the sum of two or more quantities by the number of these quantities; (b) the second or third term of a four-term proportion; (c) the square root of the product of two given numbers: called the *geometric mean.*

4. in music, an intermediate voice or part, as tenor or alto. [Obs.]

5. intervening time; interval of time; interim; meantime. [Obs.]

6. a go-between; an agent; a mediator. [Obs.]

7. in logic, the middle term in a syllogism.

See also *means.*

quadratic mean; the square root of the arithmetical mean of the squares of the given quantities.

mēan, *v.t.*; meant (ment), *pt., pp.*; meaning, *ppr.* [ME. *menen*; AS. *mænan,* to mean, intend, purpose.]

1. to have in mind, view, or contemplation; to intend; to purpose; to design.

Ye thought evil against me, but God *meant* it unto good. —Gen. i. 20.

2. to intend to express, signify, or indicate; as, just what do you *mean?*

3. to signify; to denote; convey; import; as, the German word "*ja*" *means* "yes."

4. to effect; to bring about; as, money *means* happiness.

Syn.—intend, purpose, design, contemplate, signify, denote, indicate, suggest, propose.

mēan, *v.i.* 1. to have thought or ideas; to think; to imagine. [Obs.]

2. to have a purpose or intention in mind; to be minded or disposed: now chiefly in *mean well,* to have good intentions.

3. to have a (specified) degree of importance, effect, or influence; as, money *means* little to me.

mē·an′dẽr, *n.* [L. *mæander*; Gr. *maiandros,* a winding stream or canal, from *Maiandros,* the Meander, a river in Phrygia noted for its winding course.]

MEANDER

1. [*often in pl.*] a winding course; a winding or turning in a passage; a convolution.

While lingering rivers in *meanders* glide.
—Blackmore.

2. a style of ornamental design in which the lines interlace: it has often been used in decorating vases, and is also sometimes employed in architecture.
3. an aimless wandering; a rambling.

mē·an′dẽr, *v.i.*; meandered, *pt., pp.*; meandering, *ppr.* 1. to wind or turn in a course or passage; to be intricate.
2. to wander aimlessly or idly; to ramble.

mē·an′dẽr, *v.t.* to make or traverse by meandering; to wind, turn, or flow round.

mē·an′dri·ăn, *a.* winding; having many turns. [Obs.]

mē·an′dri·çăl·ly, *adv.* in a meandering manner.

Mē·an·drī′nȧ, *n.* same as *Mæandrina.*

mē·an′drous, *a.* winding; flexuous.

mē·an′dry, *a.* meandrous. [Obs.]

mēan′ing, *a.* 1. that has significance; significant; suggestive; as, a *meaning* look.
2. intending; having purpose.

mēan′ing, *n.* 1. that which exists in the mind, view, or contemplation as a settled aim or purpose; that which is meant or intended to be done; intent; purpose; aim; object. [Archaic.]
2. that which is intended to be, or in fact is, conveyed, denoted, signified, or understood by acts or language; the sense, signification, or import of words; significance; force.

Old events have modern *meanings.* —Lowell.

3. sense; understanding; knowledge. [Obs.]
Syn.—import, intention, design, intent, purport, sense, signification.

mēan′ing·ful, *a.* full of meaning; having significance.

mēan′ing·less, *a.* having no meaning; without significance; senseless.

mēan′ing·ly, *adv.* in a meaning manner; significantly.

mēan′ly, *adv.* moderately. [Obs.]

mēan′ly, *adv.* in a mean manner or degree; contemptibly; ungenerously; disrespectfully; also, humbly; in a lowly manner.

mēan′ness, *n.* 1. the state or quality of being mean in any sense.
2. a mean or contemptible act.
Syn.—sordidness, lowness, scantiness, closeness, miserliness, penuriousness, stinginess.

mēanș, *n.pl.* [from *mean,* n.]
1. [*construed as sing. or pl.*] that by which something is done or obtained; agency; as, this is a *means* to an end.
2. resources; property; riches; as, her *means* are adequate.
by all means; (a) without fail; (b) of course; certainly.
by any means; in any way possible; at all; somehow.
by means of; by using; with the aid of; through.
by no (*manner of*) *means*; not at all; in no way; certainly not.
means to an end; a method of getting or accomplishing what one wants.

mēan′-spir″it·ed, *a.* having a mean spirit.

mēanș test, in Great Britain, the test of financial resources that an unemployed person must undergo when his unemployment insurance payments stop, to find out whether he is eligible to get further payments from other funds.

meant (ment), *v.* past tense and past participle of *mean.*

mēan′tīme, *n.* the interval between one specified period and another: also *meanwhile.*

mēan′tīme, *adv.* 1. during the interval; in the interval between one specified period and another.
2. at the same time.
Also *meanwhile.*

mēan′whīle (-hwīl), *n.* and *adv.* same as *meantime.*

mēar, *n.* a boundary. [Dial.]

mēase (*or* mēz), *n.* a measure of herrings, 500 in number. [Brit. Dial.]

mēa′șle (-zl), *n.* 1. an excrescence on a tree. [Obs.]
2. [*usually in pl.*] the larva of a tapeworm, especially of *Tænia solium,* which produces measles in swine.

mēa′șled, *a.* infected or spotted with measles (larval tapeworms).

mēa′șled·ness, *n.* the condition of being measled.

mēa′șleș, *n.pl.* [ME. *meseles*; D. *mazelen*; M.D. *maseren,* measles, lit., little spots.]
1. [*construed as sing.*] (a) an acute, infectious, communicable virus disease, characterized by a skin eruption, high fever, and nasal catarrh, and occurring most frequently in children; (b) any of various similar but milder diseases; especially, German measles.
2. (a) [*construed as sing.*] a disease of hogs and cattle, due to the presence in the body of *Cysticercus cellulosæ* and larvae of other tapeworms; (b) these larvae.
3. a disease of trees characterized by a blighted appearance of the leaves.
black measles; a serious form of measles in which the eruption is hemorrhagic.
German measles; see under *German.*

mēa′șly, *a.* 1. infected with measles (the disease).
2. containing larval tapeworms: said of meat.
3. contemptibly slight, worthless, or skimpy. [Colloq.]

meaș″ūr·ȧ·bil′i·ty ((mezh″), *n.* the state or quality of being measurable.

meaș′ūr·ȧ·ble, *a.* [OFr. *mesurable*; L. *mensurabilis,* from *mensurare,* to measure.]
1. capable of being measured; susceptible of mensuration or computation.
2. moderate; temperate; slight; limited; as, *measurable* chastisement. [Obs.]

meaș′ūr·ȧ·ble·ness, *n.* the quality of being measurable.

meaș′ūr·ȧ·bly, *adv.* 1. in a measurable manner; to a measurable degree or extent; noticeably; perceptibly.
2. moderately; in a limited degree. [Obs.]

meaș′ūre (mezh′), *n.* [OFr. *mesure*; L. *mensura,* a measuring, measurement, from *mensus,* pp. of *metiri,* to measure.]
1. the size, capacity, extent, volume, or quantity of anything, especially as determined by comparison with some standard or unit.
2. a standard of measurement; a definite unit of capacity or extent, fixed by law or custom, in terms of which the relative sizes and capacities of things are ascertained and expressed; as, a foot, a yard, a mile, are *measures* of length; a pint, a gallon, *measures* of capacity; a square foot, a *measure* of area; a cubic foot, a *measure* of volume, etc.
3. any standard of valuation, comparison, judgment, etc.; criterion.

Still make themselves the *measure* of mankind. —Pope.

4. the act or process of measuring; a series of measurements taken for a specified purpose; measurement.
5. a system of measurement, as, dry *measure,* board *measure.*
6. that by which anything is measured; an instrument for measuring the size or quantity of anything, or a container of standard capacity; as, a foot *measure*; a quart *measure.*
7. a definite quantity measured out or thought of as measured; that which is measured out, allotted, or assigned; as, a *measure* of meal.

Make me to know mine end, and the *measure* of my days. —Ps. xxxix. 4.

8. (a) an extent or degree not to be exceeded; as, remain within *measure*; (b) moderation; just degree or amount; reasonable limits; as, grieved beyond *measure.*
9. (certain) proportion, quantity, or degree; as, a large *measure* of patience.
10. means to an end; anything done as a preparatory step toward the end to which it is intended to lead; an act, step, or proceeding designed for the accomplishment of an object; as, wise *measures*; prudent *measures,* etc.
11. a legislative enactment, statute; law.
12. in music, (a) the notes or rests, or both, contained between two vertical lines on the staff, subdividing a part of a composition into equal groups of beats; bar; (b) musical time or rhythm.

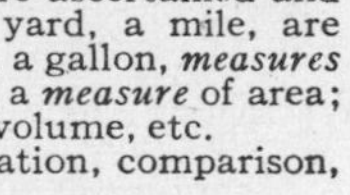

MEASURES
MEASURE (sense 12a)

13. in printing, the width of a column or page.
14. full or sufficient quantity. [Rare.]
15. in mathematics, a number contained in another number a certain number of times with no remainder; as, the greatest common *measure.*
16. in poetry, (a) the arrangement of the syllables in each line with respect to quantity or accent; rhythm; meter; as, iambic *measure*; hexameter *measure*; (b) a metrical unit; a foot of verse.
17. (a) a dance, especially a slow and stately dance such as the minuet; (b) any regulated or graceful motion, especially motion adjusted to musical time.
18. [*pl.*] in geology, a series of related beds or strata; as, coal *measures.*
19. in fencing, the distance between two fencers, as governed by the extent of reach when lunging.
above or *beyond measure*; exceedingly; excessively; to an immeasurable extent.
angular measure; the system of units used in measuring angles.
apothecaries' measure; a fluid measure having for its unit the fluid ounce.
circular measure; see under *circular.*
cubic measure; the system of units used in the measurement of volume, as of solids.
dry measure; see under *dry.*
in a measure; to some extent; somewhat.
lineal or *linear measure*; see under *linear.*
liquid measure; the measure of liquids.
long measure; see *linear measure* under *linear.*
made to measure; made to fit one's own measurements; custom-made: said of clothes.
measure of a number or *quantity*; a number or quantity contained in another a certain number of times exactly, with no remainder.
measure of capacity; dry or liquid measure.
measure of curvature; the mean curvature at any given part of a curve or surface.
measure of solidity; cubic measure.
metric measure; same as *metric system.*
out of measure; excessively; beyond reasonable bounds; disproportionately.
square measure; the system of units employed for measuring areas, the unit of which is the square of the unit of long measure.
to have hard measure; to be harshly or oppressively treated.
to take measures; to provide means; to do things to accomplish a purpose; to take action or steps.
to take one's measure; (a) to take one's measurements, as for a garment; (b) to make an estimate or judgment of one's ability, character, etc.
to tread a measure; to dance.

meaș′ūre, *v.t.*; measured, *pt., pp.*; measuring, *ppr.* [ME. *mesuren*; OFr. *mesurer*; L. *mensurare,* to measure, from *mensura,* a measure.]
1. to compute, estimate, or ascertain the extent, quantity, dimensions, or capacity of, especially by a certain rule or standard; to take the dimensions of; as, to *measure* the capacity of a ship; to *measure* a piece of land.
2. to get, take, set apart, or mark off by measuring (often with *off* or *out*).
3. (a) to serve as the measure of; as, a clock *measures* time; (b) to be adequate to express the size of.

An ell and three-quarters will not *measure* her from hip to hip. —Shak.

4. to estimate by reference to any standard; to judge of the value, extent, magnitude, or greatness of; to value; to appraise; to weigh.
5. to bring into comparison or rivalry (*against*); as, I'll *measure* my talents *against* his.
6. to pass through or over; to cover or traverse as if measuring.

We must *measure* twenty miles to-day. —Shak.

7. to adjust, proportion, or accommodate by a standard; as, *measure* your speech by your listeners' reactions.
8. to allot or distribute by measure; to mete: often with *out*; as, to *measure out* food; to *measure out* justice.
to measure one's length; to fall, lie, or be thrown down at full length.
to measure strength; to ascertain by trial which of two parties is the stronger; specifically, to engage in a contest.
to measure swords; (a) to fight with swords; (b) to duel, fight, or contend.

meaș′ūre, *v.i.* 1. to take a measurement or measurements.
2. (a) to result or turn out on being measured; as, the yield of corn *measured* well; (b) to be in extent or quantity; as, the track *measures* one mile.
3. to allow of measurement.
to measure up to; to come up to; to meet (expectations, a standard, etc.).

meaș′ūred, *a.* [pp. of *measure.*]
1. determined, ascertained, or proportioned by a standard.
2. (a) regular, steady, or uniform; (b) steady, slow, and deliberate; as, he walked with *measured* tread.

3. (a) rhythmical; (b) metrical; in verse.
4. calculated, restrained, and deliberate; careful and guarded: said of speech, etc.

meas'ūred·ly, *adv.* in a deliberate manner.

meas'ūre·less, *a.* too large to be measured; unlimited; immeasurable.

Syn.—unbounded, unlimited, immeasurable, boundless, vast, limitless.

meas'ūre·less·ness, *n.* the quality or state of being measureless.

meas'ūre·ment, *n.* 1. the act of measuring or a being measured; mensuration.
2. (a) the amount, quantity, or extent ascertained by measuring; capacity; size; area; contents; bulk; (b) [*usually in pl.*] a dimension; as, a person's *measurements* are the size of his waist, chest, hips, etc.
3. a system or way of measuring or measures.
measurement goods; light goods the transportation charges of which are calculated according to bulk, as distinguished from heavy goods, which are charged by weight.

meas'ūr·ēr, *n.* one who or that which measures; specifically, (a) one whose occupation or duty is to measure commodities in market; (b) one who measures work on a building as a basis for contractors' prices; (c) formerly, an officer in the city of London who measured woolen cloths, coals, etc: also called a *meter*; (d) an instrument for measuring; (e) a measuring worm.

meas'ūr·ing wŏrm, the caterpillar larva of any geometrid moth, which creeps in a looping manner by alternately advancing the front end of its body and bringing the rear end forward: also called *looper*.

MEASURING WORM

mēat, *n.* [AS. *mete*, meat.]
1. food; especially, solid food, as distinguished from drink: now archaic or dialectal except in *meat and drink*.
2. the flesh of animals used as food; usually, the flesh of mammals, as distinguished from fish and fowl.
3. the edible part; as, the *meat* of a nut.
4. the substance, meaning, or gist; as, the *meat* of a story.
5. a meal; especially, dinner: now obsolete except in *at meat*, *before meat*, etc.
6. one's quarry.
7. something that one especially enjoys or is skillful at; as, golf's my *meat*.

mēat, *v.t.* to feed; to give food to. [Dial.]

mē·ā'tăl, *a.* pertaining to or having the character of a meatus.

mēat'ball, *n.* 1. a small ball of ground meat, seasoned and cooked, usually with sauce, gravy, etc.
2. a stupid, awkward, or boring person. [Slang.]

mēat'ed, *a.* 1. fed; fattened. [Obs.]
2. having meat: used in composition; as, juicy-*meated*.

mēat flȳ, a flesh fly.

mēath, *n.* mead (drink). [Obs.]

mēat'i·ness, *n.* the condition or quality of being meaty.

mēat'less, *a.* 1. having no meat or food.
2. when no meat is to be eaten; as, a *meatless* day.

mēat'man, *n.*; *pl.* **mēat'men,** a man who sells meat; butcher.

mē·ȧ·tom'e·tēr, *n.* [L. *meatus*, a passage, and Gr. *metron*, a measure.] in surgery, an instrument for measuring the external orifice of the urethra.

mē·at'ō·tōme, *n.* [L. *meatus*, a passage, and Gr. *tomē*, a cutting, from *temnein*, to cut.] a surgical instrument for urethral operations.

mē·ā'tus, *n.*; *pl.* **mē·ā'tus·es, mē·ā'tus,** [L. *meatus*, a passage, from *meare*, to go, pass.] in anatomy, a natural passage or duct in the body, or its opening; as, the urethral *meatus*.

mēat'y, *a.*; *comp.* meatier; *superl.* meatiest, 1. of, or having the flavor or quality of, meat.
2. like meat.
3. (a) full of meat; (b) stout; heavy; fat.
4. full of substance; thought-provoking; pithy.

Meç'çȧ, *n.* [from *Mecca*, a city in Arabia, the birthplace of Mohammed and hence a holy city to which Moslems make pilgrimages.] [*often* m-] (a) any place visited by many people; (b) any place that one yearns to go to; (c) anything hat one greatly desires or tries to achieve.

Meç'căn, *a.* pertaining to Mecca, holy city in Arabia.

Meç'căn, *n.* an inhabitant or native of Mecca.

meçh'ȧ·meck, *n.* [N. Am. Ind.] the wild potato vine.

mē·çhan'iç, *n.* [OFr. *mecanique*; L. *mechanicus*, from Gr. *mēchanikos*, from *mēchanē*, a machine, contrivance.]
1. a worker skilled in using tools or making, operating, and repairing machines.
2. (a) an artisan; handicraftsman; (b) a low, vulgar fellow. [Archaic.]
3. mechanics. [Obs.]
4. mechanism. [Obs.]

mē·çhan'iç, *a.* 1. mechanical; as, the *mechanic* arts. [Archaic.]
2. of or involving manual labor or skill. [Archaic.]
3. performing manual labor. [Archaic.]
4. pertaining to or characteristic of a mechanic. [Obs.]
5. common; vulgar. [Obs.]
6. atomistic.

mē·çhan'i·căl, *a.* [*mechanic* and *-al.*]
1. having to do with machinery or tools.
2. produced or operated by machinery or a mechanism.
3. pertaining to, in accordance with, or using the principles and terminology of, the science of mechanics; as, a *mechanical* contrivance.
4. machinelike; automatic, as if from force of habit; lacking spontaneity, expression, intelligence, etc.; as, her acting is *mechanical*.
5. (a) of manual labor; (b) of manual laborers; of the artisan class; (c) base or vulgar. [Archaic.]
mechanical construction of a curve; a construction made by using other instruments besides ruler and compass.
mechanical drawing; a drawing made with the use of T squares, scales, compasses, etc.
mechanical effect; useful work done by a mechanical contrivance in a given time.
mechanical philosophy; any theory which seeks to account for the phenomena of the universe by the laws of physics and chemistry.
mechanical work; the work of moving a body through space, usually against the force of gravitation.

mē·çhan'i·căl, *n.* a mechanic. [Obs.]

mē·çhan'i·căl·īze, *v.t.* to make mechanical.

mē·çhan'i·căl·ly, *adv.* 1. in a mechanical manner.
2. in regard to mechanical features.
3. toward mechanics; as, he is *mechanically* inclined.

mē·çhan'i·căl·ness, *n.* the state of being mechanical.

meçh·ȧ·ni'ciăn (-nish'ăn), *n.* one skilled in the theory, design, operation, or care of machinery; a machinist; a mechanic.

mē·çhan"i·cō·çhem'iç·ăl, *a.* pertaining to or dependent on both mechanics and chemistry: used specifically of the sciences of galvanism, electricity, and magnetism, which exhibit phenomena that require for their explanation an application of the laws of mechanics and chemistry.

mē·çhan'iċs, *n.pl.* [*construed as sing.*] 1. the branch of physics that deals with motion and the phenomena of the action of forces on bodies.
2. theoretical and practical knowledge of the design, construction, operation, and care of machinery.
3. the mechanical aspect; technical part; as, the *mechanics* of writing.
analytic mechanics; the science of mechanics treated by differential and integral calculus.
animal mechanics; the branch of physiology that deals with motion and equilibrium in the animal body.
applied mechanics; the application of the principles of mechanics to practical purposes, as the construction of machines, buildings, etc.

meçh'ȧ·nişm, *n.* [LL. *mechanisma*, a contrivance, from Gr. *mēchanē*, a machine, contrivance.]
1. the parts collectively, or the arrangement of the parts, of a machine, engine, or instrument intended to apply power to a useful purpose; mechanical construction; machinery; as, the *mechanism* of a piano.
2. (a) a system whose parts work together like those of a machine; as, the *mechanism* of the universe; (b) any system or means for doing something; physical or mental process or processes, whether conscious or unconscious, by which some result is produced; machinery; as, his boasting is a defense *mechanism*.
3. the mechanical aspect; technical part.
4. the theory or doctrine that all the phenomena of the universe, particularly life, can ultimately be explained in terms of physics and chemistry, and that the difference between the organic and the inorganic is only in degree: opposed to *vitalism*.
5. action according to the laws of mechanics; mechanical action. [Rare.]

meçh'ȧ·nist, *n.* 1. a mechanician; one skilled in mechanics.
2. a believer in the theory of mechanism.

meçh·ȧ·nis'tiç, *a.* 1. pertaining to, or characteristic of the theory of, mechanism; relating to mechanists.
2. of mechanics or mechanical concepts.

meçh·ȧ·nis'ti·căl·ly, *adv.* in a mechanistic manner.

meçh"ȧ·ni·zā'tion, *n.* 1. a mechanizing or being mechanized.
2. the degree or extent of this.

meçh'ȧ·nīze, *v.t.*; mechanized, *pt.*, *pp.*; mechanizing, *ppr.* 1. to make mechanical.
2. to do or operate by machinery, not by hand.
3. to bring about the use of machinery in (an industry, etc.).
4. to equip (an army, etc.) with motor vehicles, tanks, self-propelled guns, etc., so as to increase mobility and striking power.

meçh'ȧ·nīz·ēr, *n.* 1. one who mechanizes or constructs mechanically.
2. a mechanist, sense 2.

meçh'ăn·ō·grȧph, *n.* [Gr. *mēchanē*, a machine, and *graphein*, to write.] one of a set of multiplied copies of an original, executed by means of a machine.

meçh"ăn·ō·graph'iç, *a.* 1. treating of mechanics. [Rare.]
2. pertaining to mechanography.

meçh·ăn·og'rȧ·phist, *n.* one who, by mechanical means, multiplies copies of any work of art, writing, etc.

meçh·ăn·og'rȧ·phy, *n.* [Gr. *mēchanē*, a machine, and *-graphia*, from *graphein*, to write.] the art of multiplying copies of a writing or any work of art by the use of a machine.

mech"ăn·ō·ther'ȧ·py, *n.* [from Gr. *mēchanē*, a machine; and *therapy*.] the treatment of disease by mechanical means, such as massage.

Meçh'i·tär·ist, *n.* same as *Mekhitarist*.

Meçh'lin, *n.* [from *Mechlin*, English name of Malines, city in Belgium where it is made.] a fine lace with the design clearly outlined by a thread: also *Mechlin lace*, *malines*.

Mē·chō'ȧ·căn root, see under *root*.

Meck·ē'li·ăn, *a.* pertaining to J. F. Meckel (1781–1833), a German anatomist.
Meckelian or *Meckel's cartilage*; a process from the first branchial arch, from which the internal lateral ligament of the lower jaw is formed.

mē·çom'e·tēr, *n.* [Gr. *mēkos*, length, and *metron*, a measure.] a graduated compass used for measuring length.

meç'ō·nāte, *n.* a salt of meconic acid.

mē·çon'iç, *a.* [Gr. *mēkōnikos*, of or pertaining to the poppy, from *mēkōn*, a poppy.] pertaining to or derived from the poppy.
meconic acid; a bitter, white crystalline acid, $C_7H_4O_7$, with which morphine is combined in opium.

mē·çon'i·dine, *n.* an unstable alkaloid contained in opium.

meç·ō·nid'i·um, *n.*; *pl.* **meç·ō·nid'i·ȧ,** [dim. of Gr. *mēkōn*, the poppy, the poppy seed.] the fixed reproductive medusoid, resembling a poppy capsule, of hydroids of the genus *Gonothyrea*.

meç'ō·nin, *n.* a crystalline neutral substance, $C_{10}H_{10}O_4$, existing in opium. It is white and fusible.

mē·çō'ni·oid, *a.* pertaining to or resembling meconium.

mē·çō"ni·or·rhoe'ȧ, *n.* an abnormally heavy discharge of meconium.

mē·çō'ni·um, *n.* [Gr. *mēkōnion*, the juice of

the poppy, the first feces of infants, from *mēkōn*, the poppy.]
 1. the juice of the poppy. [Obs.]
 2. the first fecal discharges of a newborn infant.

meç-ō-nol′ō-ġy, *n.* the study of, or a treatise on, opium.

meç-ō-noph′ȧ-ġiṣm, *n.* the practice of opium-eating; the opium habit.

meç-ō-noph′ȧ-ġist, *n.* [Gr. *mēkōn*, the poppy, opium, and *phagein*, to eat.] an opium eater.

Mē-çop′tēr-ȧ, *n.pl.* [Gr. *mēkos*, length, and *pteron*, a wing.] an order of neuropterous insects; the scorpion flies.

med′ăl, *n.* [OFr. *medaille*, a medal, from L. *metallum*, metal.] a piece of metal resembling a coin, stamped or inscribed with some figure, design, inscription, or device to preserve the portrait of some distinguished person, or the memory of an illustrious action or event, or as a reward for some distinguished action, merit, etc.

med′ăl, *v.t.*; medaled *or* medalled, *pt., pp.*; medaling *or* medalling, *ppr.* to present or honor with a medal.

med′ăl-et, *n.* any small medal.

med′ăl-ist, med′ăl-list, *n.* 1. one who collects medals.
 2. one who has gained a medal as the reward of merit.
 3. one who designs or engraves medals.
 4. in golf, the winner at medal play.

mē-dal′liç, *a.* 1. pertaining to a medal or to medals.
 2. shown on a medal.

mē-dal′liŏn (-yun), *n.* [Fr. *médaillon*, from *médaille*, a medal.]
 1. a large medal.
 2. an oval or circular design, portrait, relief carving, etc. resembling a medal in shape: medallions are sometimes used as a decorative form in carpets, textiles, and lace.

Med′ăl of Hon′ŏr (on′ẽr), the Congressional Medal of Honor.

med′ăl plāy, in golf, a form of competitive play in which the score is calculated by counting the total number of strokes taken to play the designated number of holes: distinguished from *match play*.

med′dle, *v.i.*; meddled, *pt., pp.*; meddling, *ppr.* [ME. *medlen*; OFr. *medler*, *mesler*, to mix, to meddle, from L. *miscere*, to mix.]
 1. to concern oneself with or take part in other people's affairs without being asked or needed; to interfere (*in* or *with*).
 2. to tamper (*with*).
 3. (a) to mix; mingle; (b) to fight; contend. [Obs.]
 Syn.—interpose, interfere, mix, intermeddle.

med′dle, *v.t.* to mix; to mingle. [Obs.]

med′dlẽr, *n.* one who meddles; one who interferes or busies himself with things in which he has no concern; an officious person; a busybody.

med′dle-sŏme, *a.* given to meddling; inclined to interpose in the affairs of others; officiously intrusive.
 Syn.—officious, obtrusive, intrusive, interfering.

med′dle-sŏme-ness, *n.* officious interposition in the affairs of others.

med′dling, *a.* officious; busy or officiously interposing in other people's affairs; as, a *meddling* neighbor.

med′dling, *n.* officious interposition.

med′dling-ly, *adv.* in a meddling manner; officiously; interferingly.

Mēde, *n.* [L. *Medus*; Gr. *Mēdos*.] a native or inhabitant of Media, an ancient kingdom of Asia.

Mē-dē′ȧ, *n.* [Gr. *Mēdeia*.] in Greek legend, a sorceress who helped Jason get the Golden Fleece and, later, when deserted by him, killed her rival and her own children, burned down her palace, and fled to Athens: the subject of several classical tragedies.

Mē-dē′ō-lȧ, *n.* [L. *Medea*, from Gr. *Mēdeia*, Medea, a sorceress.] a genus of plants of the lily family, of which the Indian cucumber root, *Medeola virginica*, is the only species.

mē′di-, same as *medio-*.

mē′di-ȧ, *n.* plural of *medium*.

mē′di-ȧ, *n.*; *pl.* **mē-di-ae,** [L., properly f. of *medius*, middle.]
 1. in anatomy, the middle coat of the wall of an artery.
 2. in phonetics, formerly, a voiced stop.

mē′di-ȧ-cy, *n.* 1. the quality or state of being mediate.
 2. mediation.

mē′di-ad, *adv.* in anatomy and zoology, toward the median plane or line.

mē-di-ae′văl, mē-di-ae′văl-iṣm, etc. see *medieval*, etc.

mē′di-ăl, *a.* [LL. *medialis*, from L. *medius*, middle.]
 1. of or in the middle; neither beginning nor ending; median.
 2. nearer the median plane or axis of a body or part: opposed to *lateral*.
 3. (a) of an average or mean; (b) average; ordinary.

mē′di-ăl, *n.* 1. (a) a medial letter; (b) a form (of a letter) used medially.
 2. in phonetics, any of various voiced stops (*b, d, g*) considered as intermediate in sound between surds (*p, t, k*) and aspirates (Sp. *b*, Ar. *dh*, G. *ch*): term now seldom used.

mē′di-ăl-ly, *adv.* in a medial position.

mē″di-ȧ-lū′nȧ, *n.* [Sp.] a fish, *Cæsiosoma californica*, the half-moon.

mē′di-ăn, *a.* [L. *medianus*, from *medius*, middle.]
 1. middle; intermediate.
 2. (a) designating the plane that divides a body or part lengthwise into symmetrical halves; (b) situated in this plane.
 3. in statistics, (a) designating the middle number in a series containing an odd number of items (e.g., 7 in the series 1, 4, 7, 16, 43); (b) designating the number midway between the two middle numbers in a series containing an even number of items (e.g., 10 in the series 3, 4, 8, 12, 46, 72). Distinguished from *average*, *mean*.

mē′di-ăn, *n.* 1. a median number, point, or line.
 2. a median artery, vein, nerve, etc.
 median line; (a) in geometry, a line drawn from any angle of a triangle to the middle point of the side subtending the angle; (b) in crystallography, same as *bisectrix*.
 median point; in geometry, the point in a triangle where the three median lines intersect.

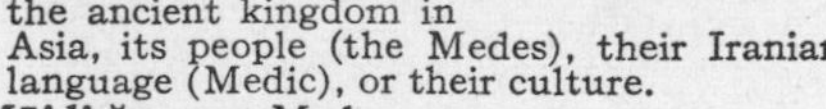

MEDIANS
BD, median of triangle ABC; HI, median of trapezoid DEFG

Mē′di-ăn, *a.* of Media, the ancient kingdom in Asia, its people (the Medes), their Iranian language (Medic), or their culture.

Mē′di-ăn, *n.* a Mede.

mē″di-ȧ-nim′iç, *a.* mediumistic.

mē′di-ănt, *n.* [It. *mediante*.] the third tone of a musical scale, halfway between the tonic and the dominant.

mē″di-as-tī′nȧ, *n.* plural of *mediastinum*.

mē″di-as-tī′năl, *a.* pertaining to the mediastinum.

mē-di-as-ti-nī′tis, *n.* inflammation of the cellular tissue of the mediastinum.

mē″di-as-tī′num, *n.*; *pl.* **mē″di-as-tī′nȧ,** [neut. of L. *mediastinus*, a helper, assistant, lit., being in the middle or midst, from *medius*, middle.]
 1. a membranous partition between two cavities of the body, especially that separating the lungs or the two pleural sacs.
 2. the space between the pleural sacs, containing the heart and other chest viscera except the lungs.

mē′di-āte, *a.* [LL. *mediatus*, pp. of *mediare*, to divide in the middle, from L. *medius*, middle.]
 1. intermediate or intervening.
 2. dependent on, acting by, or connected through some intervening agency; related indirectly: opposed to *immediate*.

mē′di-āte, *v.i.*; mediated, *pt., pp.*; mediating, *ppr.* 1. to be in an intermediate position or location.
 2. to be an intermediary or conciliator between persons or sides.

mē′di-āte, *v.t.* 1. to settle by mediation; to bring about by intervention.
 2. to be the medium for bringing about (a result), conveying (an object), communicating (information), etc.

mē′di-āte-ly, *adv.* in a mediate manner; by mediation.

mē′di-āte-ness, *n.* the state of being mediate.

mē-di-ā′tion, *n.* [OFr. *mediation*, from LL. *mediare*, to divide in the middle, from L. *medius*, middle.]
 1. a mediating; intercession or friendly intervention, usually by consent or invitation, for settling differences between persons, nations, etc.
 2. the state of being mediated.

mē′di-ā-tive, *a.* of or pertaining to a mediator or mediation; mediating.

mē″di-ȧ-ti-zā′tion, *n.* the act of mediatizing.

mē′di-ȧ-tīze, *v.t.*; mediatized, *pt., pp.*; mediatizing, *ppr.* 1. in Germany under the Holy Roman Empire, to reduce (a prince or state) from the status of an immediate vassal of the Empire to that of a mediate vassal.
 2. later, to annex a smaller state to a larger one, leaving the ruler his title and some authority.
 3. to make mediate.

mē′di-ȧ-tīze, *v.i.* to mediate.

mē′di-ā-tŏr, *n.* one who or that which mediates; one who interposes between parties at variance for the purpose of reconciling them; an intercessor.

mē″di-ȧ-tō′ri-ăl, *a.* mediating; mediatory.

mē″di-ȧ-tō′ri-ăl-ly, *adv.* in the manner of a mediator.

mē′di-ā-tŏr-ship, *n.* the office, position, or character of a mediator.

mē′di-ȧ-tō-ry, *a.* pertaining to mediation or to a mediator; mediatorial.

mē′di-ā-tress, *n.* a mediatrix.

mē-di-ā′trix, *n.* a woman mediator.

med′iç, med′ick, *n.* [L. *medica*; Gr. *mēdikē*, Median grass, a kind of clover brought from Media, prob. f. of *Mēdikos*, of Media.] a plant of the genus *Medicago*; especially, *Medicago sativa*, the lucerne or purple medic.

med′iç, *a.* medical. [Rare.]

med′iç, *n.* 1. a physician or surgeon.
 2. a medical student or intern.
 3. a member of a military medical corps, especially one who gives first aid in combat. [Colloq. in all senses.]

Mē′diç, *n.* the language of the ancient Medes.

med′i-çȧ-ble, *a.* [L. *medicabilis*, from *medicari*, to cure, heal.] that can be cured or healed.

Med-i-çā′gō, *n.* [alteration of Gr. *Mēdikē poa*, Median grass, so called because lucerne was said to have been brought from Greece during the expedition of Darius.] a genus of plants of the bean family, comprising between forty and fifty species native to the eastern hemisphere.

med′iç-ăl, *a.* [LL. *medicalis*, from L. *medicus*, healing; as n., a physician, from *mederi*, to heal.]
 1. pertaining to or employed in the science, study, or practice of medicine, or the art of healing diseases.
 2. medicinal; as, the *medical* properties of a plant. [Rare.]
 medical examiner; (a) a coroner or similar public officer; (b) a physician who examines applicants for life insurance.
 medical jurisprudence; the branch of medicine dealing with the application of medical knowledge to questions of criminal and civil law; forensic medicine.

med′iç-ăl-ly, *adv.* in a medical manner; according to the rules of medicine; for the purpose of healing.

mē-diç′ȧ-ment (*or* med′i-kȧ-), *n.* [L. *medicamentum*, a drug, remedy, from *medicari*, to heal.] anything used for curing, healing, or relieving pain; a medicine.

med″i-çȧ-men′tăl, *a.* relating to or having the qualities of medicaments. [Rare.]

med″i-çȧ-men′tăl-ly, *adv.* after the manner of healing applications. [Rare.]

Med′i-çāre″, *n.* [*medical* and *care*.] a system of government insurance for providing medical and hospital care for the aged from Federal social security funds.

med′i-ças-tẽr, *n.* a quack; a medical charlatan.

med′i-çāte, *v.t.*; medicated, *pt., pp.*; medicating, *ppr.* [L. *medicatus*, pp. of *medicari*, to heal.]
 1. to tincture or impregnate with anything medicinal.
 2. to treat with medicine.

med-i-çā′tion, *n.* 1. the act or process of medicating or treating with medicinal substances.
 2. a medicament.

med′i-çā-tive, *a.* 1. healing; medicinal.
 2. having the nature of medication.

Med-i-cē′ăn, *a.* of, characteristic of, or pertaining to the Medici, a rich, powerful Florentine family, who were patrons of art and literature.

mē-diç′i-nȧ-ble, *a.* medicinal. [Obs.]

mē-diç′i-năl, *a.* [L. *medicinalis*, pertaining to medicine, from *medicina*, medicine.]
 1. having the property of healing or relieving disease; adapted to the cure or allevia-

tion of bodily disorders; as, *medicinal* plants; *medicinal* springs.

2. pertaining to medicine; medical. [Obs.]

mē·dic′i·năl·ly, *adv.* in a medicinal manner.

med′i·cine, *n.* [L. *medicina*, medicine, the healing art, from *medicus*, a physician.]

1. the science and art of diagnosing, treating, curing, and preventing disease, relieving pain, and improving and preserving health.

2. the branch of this science and art that makes use of drugs, diet, etc., as distinguished especially from surgery and obstetrics.

3. (a) any drug or other substance used in treating disease, healing, or relieving pain; (b) [Obs.] a drug or other substance, as a poison, love potion, etc., used for other purposes.

4. among North American Indians; (a) any object, spell, rite, etc. supposed to have natural or supernatural powers as a remedy, preventive, protection, etc.; (b) magical power or rite.

5. a medicine man. [Obs.]

med′i·cine, *v.t.*; medicined, *pt.*, *pp.*; medicining, *ppr.* to administer medicine to; to treat as with medicine; to heal; to cure.

med′i·cine bag, among the North American Indians, a bag in which supposed charms were worn or carried by a medicine man; any receptacle for magic charms or remedies.

med′i·cine ball, a large, heavy, leather-covered ball, tossed from one person to another for physical exercise.

med′i·cine dance, among North American Indians, etc., a ritual dance to drive out disease or make magic.

med′i·cine man, among North American Indians, etc., a man supposed to have supernatural powers of curing disease and controlling spirits; shaman; magician.

med′i·çō, *n.* [It.] a medical man; a doctor; also, a medical student. [Colloq.]

med′i·çō-, a combining form meaning *medical* or *medical and.*

med″i·çō·chī·rŭr′ġiç·ăl, *a.* pertaining conjointly to medicine and surgery.

med″i·çō·lē′găl, *a.* pertaining to medical jurisprudence, or law as affected by medical facts.

med·i·çom′mis·sūre, *n.* [L. *medius*, middle, and *commissura*, a joining together.] in anatomy, the middle or soft commissure of the brain.

med·i·çor′nū, *n.*; *pl.* **med·i·çor′nū·ȧ,** [L. *medius*, middle, and *cornu*, horn.] in anatomy, the middle cornu of each lateral ventricle of the brain.

med′içs, *n.* the science of medicine. [Obs.]

mē·dī′ē·ty, *n.* [L. *medietas* (*-atis*), the mean, middle, from *medius*, middle.] the middle state or part; half; moiety. [Obs.]

mē·di·ē′văl, mē·di·ae′văl, *n.* one who lived in the Middle Ages.

mē·di·ē′văl, mē·di·ae′văl, *a.* [L. *medius*, middle, and *ævum*, age.] pertaining to, suggestive or characteristic of, or belonging to the Middle Ages; as, *medieval* architecture; *medieval* art.

Mē·di·ē′văl Greek, the Greek language as it was used in the Middle Ages, from about 700 A.D. to about 1500: also called *Middle Greek.*

mē·di·ē′văl·iṣm, mē·di·ae′văl·iṣm, *n.* 1. the spirit, beliefs, habits of thought, customs, etc. of the Middle Ages.

2. devotion to or acceptance of medieval beliefs, habits, customs, etc.

3. a belief, habit of thought, custom, etc. characteristic of or surviving from the Middle Ages.

mē·di·ē′văl·ist, mē·di·ae′văl·ist, *n.* 1. a specialist in the history of the Middle Ages.

2. one devoted to the customs, habits of thought, etc. of the Middle Ages.

Mē·di·ē′văl Lat′in, the Latin language as it was used throughout Europe in the Middle Ages, from about 700 A.D. to about 1500, characterized by many Latinized borrowings from other languages: also called *Middle Latin.*

mē·di·ē′văl·ly, mē·di·ae′văl·ly, *adv.* in a medieval manner; in accordance with medievalism.

mē′di·fixed (-fikst), *a.* [L. *medius*, middle, and *fixus*, fastened, fixed.] in botany, fastened by the middle, as an anther.

Med·i·nil′lȧ, *n.* [after D. J. de *Medinilla* y Pineda, a governor of the Ladrone Islands.] a large genus of shrubs of the *Melastoma* family, native to the East Indies.

mē′di·ō-, [L. *medius.*] a combining form meaning *middle*: also, before a vowel, *medi-*.

mē′di·ō·çrăl, *a.* of a middle quality; mediocre. [Obs.]

mē′di·ō·çre (-kẽr *or* mē-di-ō′kẽr), *a.* [L. *mediocris*, moderate, ordinary, from *medius*, middle.] of a middle quality; indifferent; ordinary; commonplace; as, *mediocre* intellect.

mē′di·ō·çrist, *n.* a person of middling abilities. [Rare.]

mē·di·oç′ri·ty, *n.*; *pl.* **mē·di·oç′ri·tieṣ,** [L. *mediocritas* (*-atis*), from *mediocris*, moderate, middling, from *medius*, middle.]

1. the quality or state of being mediocre.

2. mediocre ability or attainment.

3. a person of mediocre abilities or attainments.

4. moderation; temperance. [Obs.]

mē″di·ō·dor′săl, *a.* situated in the middle part of the back.

me″di·ō·stȧ·pē′di·ăl, *a.* [L. *medius*, middle, and LL. *stapes*, stirrup.] connecting the stapes with the other parts of the columella of the ear.

mē″di·ō·stȧ·pē′di·ăl, *n.* the mediostapedial part of the columella of the ear.

mē″di·ō·tär′săl, *a.* situated in the middle of the tarsus.

mē·di·seçt′, *v.t.*; medisected, *pt.*, *pp.*; medisecting, *ppr.* [L. *medius*, middle, and *sectus*, pp. of *secare*, to cut.] to cut through the middle.

mē·di·seç′tion, *n.* a medisecting or being medisected.

med′i·tāte, *v.i.*; meditated, *pt.*, *pp.*; meditating, *ppr.* [L. *meditatus*, pp. of *meditari*, to think or reflect upon, revolve in one's mind.] to dwell on anything in thought; to contemplate deeply and continuously; to ponder; to ruminate; to reflect.

med′i·tāte, *v.t.* 1. to think about; to contemplate. [Rare.]

2. to plan; to intend; to purpose.

Syn.—study, ponder, consider, ruminate, revolve, contemplate, intend.

med·i·tā′tion, *n.* [L. *meditatio* (*-onis*), a thinking over, contemplation, from *meditari*, to meditate.]

1. the act of meditating; close or continued thought; the turning or revolving of a subject in the mind; serious contemplation; mental reflection.

> Let the words of my mouth and the *meditation* of my heart be acceptable in thy sight. —Ps. xix. 14.

2. solemn reflection on sacred matters as a devotional act.

3. a short literary theme treated meditatively.

med·i·tā′tion·ist, *n.* one who writes meditations.

med′i·tā·tist, *n.* one given to meditation. [Rare.]

med′i·tā·tive, *a.* [LL. *meditativus*, from L. *meditari*, to meditate, ponder.]

1. meditating or inclined to meditate.

2. indicating meditation.

med′i·tā·tive·ly, *adv.* in a meditative manner.

med′i·tā·tive·ness, *n.* the state or quality of being meditative.

med′i·tā·tŏr, *n.* a person who meditates.

Med″i·tēr·rā′nē·ăn, *a.* [L. *mediterraneus*, midland, inland; *medius*, middle, and *terra*, land.]

1. [m—] (a) far from the coast; inland: said of land; (b) surrounded, or almost surrounded by land; landlocked: said of water.

2. of the Mediterranean Sea or near-by regions.

3. of Mediterranean peoples.

4. in ethnology, designating or of one of the three main divisions of the Caucasian, or white, race: term used to denote typically long-headed, short, olive-skinned peoples living around the Mediterranean Sea, including ancient Iberian, Ligurian, Pelasgian, and Hamitic peoples and their descendants.

5. designating or of a style of furniture made, as through the use of plastic moldings, to simulate the heavy wood, massive lines, and ornate carving of a kind of Renaissance furniture.

Med″i·tēr·rā′nē·ăn, *n.* 1. the Mediterranean Sea.

2. a person who lives in a region near this sea.

3. a member of the Mediterranean division of the Caucasian race.

Med″i·tēr·rā′nē·ăn fē′vẽr, undulant fever.

med″i·tēr·rā′nē·ous, *a.* inland; remote from the ocean or sea. [Obs.]

mē·di·thō′rax, *n.* in entomology, the mesothorax.

mē′di·um, *n.*; *pl.* **mē′di·umṣ, mē′di·ȧ,** [L. *medium*, the middle. neut. of *medius*, middle.]

1. (a) something intermediate; (b) a middle state or degree; mean.

2. an intervening thing through which a force acts or an effect is produced; as, the ether is a supposed *medium* for radio waves.

3. any means, agency, or instrumentality; as, radio is a *medium* of communication.

4. any surrounding or pervading substance in which bodies exist or move.

5. environment.

6. a sterilized nutritive substance, as agar, for cultivating bacteria, viruses, etc.

7. a person through whom communications are supposedly sent to the living from the spirits of the dead.

8. any material used for expression or delineation in art; as, this sculptor's favorite *medium* is stone.

9. a liquid mixed with pigments to give fluency.

10. a size of writing paper (19 x 24 inches) or printing paper (18 x 23 inches).

circulating medium; coin and bank notes, or paper convertible into money on demand; currency.

medium of exchange; anything used as money; currency, checks, etc.

mē′di·um, *a.* in a middle position; intermediate in quantity, quality, place, size, or degree.

mē″di·um·is′tiç, *a.* of or like a medium (sense 7).

mē′di·um-sīzed, *a.* of medium size; as, a *medium-sized* horse.

mē′di·us, *n.*; *pl.* **mē′di·ī,** [LL., from L. *medius*, middle.] the third finger of the hand; the middle finger.

Me·dji′di·e (-jē′), *n.* [Turk. *mejīdī*, from *mejīd*, glorious.]

1. in Turkey, an order of knighthood established by the sultan Abdul-Medjid in 1851.

2. [m—] a gold or silver coin of Turkey, varying in value according to the metal of which it is minted.

med′lăr, *n.* [ME. *medler*; OFr. *medler*, *mesler*; L. *mespilus*, *mespilum*; Gr. *mespilon*, *mespilē*, a medlar tree.]

1. a small tree, *Mespilus germanica*, of the rose family, growing in Europe and Asia.

2. its brown fruit, which is like a small apple and edible only after it begins to decay.

Japan medlar; the loquat.

Neapolitan or *Welsh medlar*; the azarole.

med′lăr wood, the hardwood of various trees of the genus *Myrtus* found in Mauritius.

med′le, *v.t.* to meddle. [Obs.]

med′ley, *n.*; *pl.* **med′leyṣ,** [ME. *medle*; OFr. *medlee*, a mixing, properly f. of *medle*, *mesle*, pp. of *medler*, *mesler*, to mix, from L. *miscere*, to mix.]

1. a mixture of things not usually placed together; heterogeneous assortment or collection; hodgepodge.

2. (a) a musical composition made up of passages, usually incongruous passages, from various other compositions; (b) a group of dance tunes, etc. arranged for playing as a continuous whole.

3. a melee. [Archaic.]

med′ley, *a.* 1. mingled; mixed; confused; variegated.

2. motley. [Obs.]

med′ley rāce, 1. a relay race in which each contestant must cover a different distance.

2. a swimming race in which a different stroke must be used for each length of the pool.

Mé′doc (mā′dok *or* mȧ-dok′), *n.* a red wine made in Medoc, a grape-growing district of southwestern France: also *Medoc.*

med′rē·gal, *n.* a fish, the bonito.

med′rick, *n.* the tern.

mē·dul′lȧ, *n.*; *pl.* **mē·dul′lae,** [L. *medulla*, the marrow, from *medius*, middle.]

1. in anatomy, (a) the medulla oblongata; (b) the marrow of bones; (c) the inner substance of an organ, as of the kidney, adrenal gland, etc.

2. in botany, the pith; (a) the central column of cellular matter around which the wood is formed in exogens; (b) the inner tissue of the thallus in lichens.

mē·dul′lȧ ob·lon·gä′tȧ, the widening continuation of the spinal cord forming the lowest part of the brain and containing vital nerve centers for the control of breathing, circulation, etc.

mē·dul′lăr, *a.* same as *medullary.*

med′ul·lăr·y (*or* me-dul′ȧ-ri), *a.* [LL. *medullaris*, situated in the marrow.]

1. pertaining to, consisting of, or resembling

the medulla or medulla oblongata; as, *medullary* substance.

2. in botany, pithy; filled with spongy pith.

medullary groove; in embryology, a groove in the germinal membrane of an ovum which becomes the spinal cord and brain of the developed vertebrate.

medullary ray; (a) in anatomy, extensions of the kidney tubules into the cortical substance; (b) in botany, strands of parenchymatous tissue extending from the pith and separating the vascular bundles in the stems of certain plants (dicotyledons and gymnosperms).

medullary sheath; (a) in anatomy, myelin; (b) in botany, a ring of primary xylem around the pith of some stems.

med′ul·lā·ted, *a.* having a medullary sheath; covered with a medullary substance.

med·ul·lī′tis, *n.* myelitis.

med″ul·li·zā′tion, *n.* softening of the bone in inflammation.

med′ul·lōse, *a.* having a soft spongy texture like pith.

Mē·dū′sȧ, *n.* [L. *Medusa*; Gr. *Medousa*, lit., guardian.]

1. in Greek mythology, one of the three Gorgons, a monster with snakes for hair and a gaze that turned into stone anyone who looked at her: she was slain by Perseus, who gave her head to Athena.

2. [m-] *pl.* **mē·dū′sȧs, mē·dū′sae**, in zoology, a jellyfish.

mē·dū′sȧ bud, a rudimentary free-swimming hydrozoan.

mē·dū′săn, *a.* of a medusa, or jellyfish.

mē·dū′săn, *n.* a medusa, or jellyfish.

Mē·dū′sȧ's head (hed), 1. in botany, the plant, *Euphorbia caput-medusæ*.

2. a crinoid, *Pentacrinus caput-medusæ*, still extant.

3. a basket fish.

mē·dū′si·ăn, *n.* a jellyfish.

mē·dū′si·fọrm, *a.* having the form of a medusa.

mē·dū′soid, *a.* like a medusa, or jellyfish.

mē·dū′soid, *n.* a gonophore of a hydrozoan, having the form of a medusa.

meech, *v.i.* to miche. [Now Dial.]

meed, *n.* [ME. *mede*; AS. *med*, reward, recompense.]

1. reward; recompense; that which is bestowed or rendered in consideration of merit. [Poet.]

2. merit or desert. [Obs.]

3. a bribe; also, a gift. [Obs.]

meed, *v.t.* to deserve; also, to reward. [Obs.]

meed′fụl, *a.* deserving of reward. [Obs.]

meed′fụl·ly, *adv.* according to merit. [Obs.]

meek, *a.*; *comp.* meeker; *superl.* meekest, [ME. *meek*, *meke*, from O.N. *miukr*, soft, pliant.]

1. patient and mild; not inclined to anger or resentment.

2. (a) tamely submissive; easily imposed on; (b) too submissive; spineless; spiritless.

3. gentle or kind. [Obs.]

meek, *v.t.* to make meek; to soften; to render mild. [Obs.]

meek′en, *v.t.* to make meek. [Obs.]

meek′ly, *adv.* mildly; gently; in a meek manner.

meek′ness, *n.* the state or quality of being meek.

meer, *a.* and *n.* same as *mere*.

meer′kat, *n.* 1. an ichneumonlike animal, *Cynictis penicillata*.

2. the suricate.

meer′schạum (-shạm *or* -shum), [G., lit., sea foam; *meer*, the sea, and *schaum*, foam; perhaps after Fr. (*pipe*) *d'écume de mer*, for (*pipe*) de *Kummer*, Kummer's pipe.]

1. a soft, white, claylike, heat-resistant mineral, a hydrous magnesium silicate, $H_4Mg_2Si_3O_{10}$, used for tobacco pipes, etc.; sepiolite.

2. a pipe made of this.

meet, *a.* [ME. *mete*; AS. (*ge*)*mæte*, suitable, *mæte*, moderate, from *metan*, to measure.] fit; suitable; proper; qualified; convenient; adapted; as, it is *meet* that you should go.

meet, *adv.* meetly. [Obs.]

meet, *v.t.*; met, *pt.*, *pp.*; meeting, *ppr.* [ME. *meeten*, *meten*; AS. *metan*, to meet, come together, encounter, from *mot*, or *gemot*, a coming together.]

1. to come upon; to come across; to encounter (a person).

2. to come face to face with or up to (a person or thing moving from a different direction); to confront.

3. to be present at the arrival of; as, he *met* the bus.

4. to come into contact, connection, or conjunction with; as, her hand *met* his face in a resounding slap.

5. (a) to come into the presence or company of; (b) to be introduced to; to get acquainted with; (c) to keep an appointment or engagement with.

6. (a) to encounter in or as in battle; to fight with; (b) to face; as, he *met* angry words with a laugh; (c) to refute; to deal with effectively; as, we can *meet* this objection.

7. to experience; as, their plan will *meet* disaster.

8. to come within the perception of (the eye, ear, etc.).

9. (a) to comply with; to satisfy (a demand, etc.); (b) to pay (a bill, etc.).

to meet halfway; to meet at an equal distance from where each started; hence, to make a compromise with.

meet, *v.i.* 1. to come together, as from different directions.

2. to come into contact, connection, or conjunction.

3. to become acquainted; to be introduced.

4. to be opposed in or as in battle; to fight; contend.

5. to be united.

6. to assemble.

7. (a)to agree; (b) to conflict. [Archaic.]

to meet with; (a) to experience; (b) to receive; (c) to come upon or across; to encounter.

meet, *n.* 1. a meeting, gathering, or assembling, as for a sporting event; as, a track *meet*.

2. the people who meet or assemble.

3. the place of meeting.

meet′en, *v.t.* to render meet or fit. [Rare.]

meet′ẽr, *n.* one who meets or attends a meeting.

meeth, *n.* mead. [Obs.]

meet′ing, *n.* 1. a coming together of persons or things.

2. an assembly; a gathering of people, especially to discuss or decide on matters.

3. an assembly or place of assembly for purposes of worship, as among the Friends, or Quakers.

4. a series of horse or dog races held during a period of days at a certain track.

5. a point of contact or intersection; a junction.

6. a hostile encounter; a duel.

meet′ing·ẽr, *n.* one who regularly attends the meetings of the Nonconformists. [Brit.]

meet′ing·house, *n.* a building used for public worship; a church: applied in British usage only to dissenting churches, usually disparagingly except of Friends, or Quakers.

meet′ly, *adv.* 1. fitly; suitably; properly.

2. moderately. [Obs.]

meet′ness, *n.* fitness; suitableness; propriety.

meg′ȧ-, [Gr. *mega-*, from *megas*, great, mighty.] a combining form meaning: (a) *large, great, powerful*, as in *mega*phone; (b) *a million times, a million of* (the specified unit), as in *mega*cycle. Also, before a vowel, *meg-*.

meg″ȧ·cē·phal′iç, *a.* [*mega-*, and *cephalic*.]

1. having a large head.

2. in craniometry, having a cranial capacity greater than the average.

meg·ȧ·ceph′ȧ·lous, *a.* same as *megacephalic*.

mē·gac′e·rous, *a.* [*mega-*, and Gr. *keras*, a horn.] having large horns, as the extinct Irish elk, genus *Megaceros*.

meg·ȧ·çhī′lē, *n.* [*mega-*, and Gr. *cheilos*, a lip.] a bee, the leaf cutter.

meg′ȧ·çoșm, *n.* same as *macrocosm*.

meg″ȧ·çöu·lomb′ (-lom′), *n.* [*mega-*, and *coulomb*.] in electricity, a million coulombs.

meg′ȧ·çȳ·çle, *n.* [*mega-* and *cycle*.] in physics, one million cycles.

meg′ȧ·death, *n.* one million dead persons: a unit used in computing the hypothetical victims of a nuclear explosion.

meg′ȧ·dẽrm, *n.* [*mega-*, and Gr. *derma*, skin.] any bat of the genus *Megaderma*.

Meg·ȧ·dẽr′mȧ, *n.* a genus of insectivorous bats, family *Nycteridæ*, distinguished by the extreme development of the ears and of the membranous appendages of the nose.

meg′ȧ·dont, *a.* [*mega-*, and Gr. *odous*, *odontos*, tooth.] in anatomy, having large teeth.

meg′ȧ·dȳne, *n.* [*mega-*, and Gr. *dynamis*, power.] a million dynes.

meg′ȧ·ẽrg, *n.* [*mega-*, and Gr. *ergon*, work.] a million ergs: also called *megerg* and *megalerg*.

meg′ȧ·far·ad, *n.* a million farads.

meg″ȧ·ga·mēte′ (*or* -gam′et), *n.* same as *macrogamete*.

meg′ȧ·hẽrtz″, *n.*; *pl.* **meg′ȧ·hẽrtz″**, [*mega-* and *hertz*.] one million hertz.

meg′ȧ·lẽrg, *n.* same as *megaerg*.

Meg·ȧ·lē′siăn, *a.* [L. *Megalesius*, from Gr. *Megalē*, the Great, an epithet applied to Cybele.] of or pertaining to Cybele, the mother of the gods; as, the *Megalesian* games.

meg·ȧ·leth′ō·sçōpe, *n.* [*meg-*, and Gr. *alēthēs*, true, and *skopein*, to view.] a form of stereoscope in which the photograph is considerably magnified and an increased appearance of perspective obtained.

meg′ȧ·lith, *n.* [*mega-* and *-lith*.] a huge stone, especially one used in prehistoric monuments or in the construction work of ancient peoples.

meg·ȧ·lith′iç, *a.* consisting of huge stones: applied to ancient structures and monuments constructed of large stones, such as the early Cyclopean architecture in Greece; especially, applied to a class of monuments, probably sepulchral, consisting of huge unhewn stones.

meg′ȧ·lō-, [Gr. *megalo-*, from *megas*, *megalou*, large, great.] a combining form meaning: (a) *large, great, powerful*, as in *megalo*mania; (b) *abnormal enlargement*, as in *megalo*cardia. Also, before a vowel, *megal-*.

meg″ȧ·lō·cär′di·ȧ, *n.* [*megalo-*, and Gr. *kardia*, heart.] an abnormal enlargement of the heart.

meg″ȧ·lō·çär′pous, *a.* [Gr. *megalokarpos*; *megas*, large, and *karpos*, fruit.] developing large fruit.

meg″ȧ·lō·cē·phā′li·ȧ, *n.* [*megalo-*, and Gr. *kephalē*, head.] same as *megalocephaly*.

meg″ȧ·lō·cē·phal′iç, *a.* of or having megalocephaly; megacephalic.

meg″ȧ·lō·ceph′ȧ·lous, *a.* same as *megalocephalic*.

meg″ȧ·lō·ceph′ȧ·ly, *n.* a condition in which the head is unusually large.

meg′ȧ·lō·cȳte, *n.* [*megalo-*, and Gr. *kytos*, a cavity.] an abnormally large blood corpuscle found in the blood in cases of anemia.

meg″ȧ·lō·mā′ni·ȧ, *n.* [Mod. L.; *megalo-* and *mania*.]

1. a mental disorder characterized by delusions of grandeur, wealth, power, etc.

2. a passion for, or for doing, big things.

3. a tendency to exaggerate.

meg″ȧ·lō·mā′ni·aç, *n.* a person who has megalomania.

meg″ȧ·lō·mā′ni·aç, *a.* of or having megalomania.

meg·ȧ·lon′yx, *n.* [*megalo-*, and Gr. *onyx*, a claw; so called from its enormous claw bones.] a large, slothlike edentate from the Pliocene and Pleistocene Periods of North America.

meg·ȧ·loph′ō·nous, *a.* [Gr. *megalophōnos*; *megas*, great, and *phōnē*, voice.] having an imposing sound; also, clamorous.

meg·ȧ·lop′iç, *a.* [Gr. *megalōpos*, large-eyed; *megas*, large, and *ōps*, *opos*, eye.] having large eyes; also, of, or pertaining to a megalops.

meg′ȧ·lō·pine, *a.* same as *megalopic*.

meg·ȧ·lop′ō·lis, *n.* [Gr. *megalopolis*, great city.] an extensive, heavily populated, continuously urban area, including any number of cities.

meg′ȧ·lops, *n.* [*megalo-*, and Gr. *ōps*, eye.]

1. a larval stage in the development of the crab, in which the eyes are very large, the number of appendages complete, and the abdomen comparatively long.

2. a fish, the tarpon.

meg·ȧ·lop′si·ȧ, *n.* a condition of vision in which objects appear magnified.

meg·ȧ·lop′sȳ·çhy, *n.* [Gr. *megalopsychia*, greatness of soul; *megas*, great, and *psychē*, soul.] magnanimity; largeness of soul. [Obs.]

meg′ȧ·lō·sạur, *n.* any of an extinct group of huge, flesh-eating dinosaurs of the Jurassic Period.

meg″ăl·ō·sạu′ri·ăn, *a.* of the megalosaurs.

meg″ăl·ō·sạu′ri·ăn, *n.* a megalosaur.

Meg″ȧ·lō·sạu′rus, *n.* [*megalo-*, and Gr. *sauros*, a lizard.]

1. a genus of the *Dinosauria*, of the Jurassic Period. Only one species, the megalosaur, has been referred to the genus. Its length has been estimated at between forty and fifty feet, the femur and tibia each measuring about three feet in length, giving a length of almost two yards to the hind leg. Its powerful, pointed teeth indicate its carnivorous habits.

2. [m-] a megalosaur.

mē·gam′e·tẽr, *n.* [*mega-*, and Gr. *metron*, a measure.]
1. a device for ascertaining longitude by observation of stars.
2. a micrometer. [Rare.]
3. (meg′ȧ-mē-), a million meters: also spelled *megametre.*

meg·am′pēre, *n.* [*mega-* and *ampere.*] a million amperes.

meg′ȧ·phōne, *n.* [*mega-* and *-phone.*] a large, funnel-shaped device for increasing the volume of voice sounds or other sounds, or sending them in a desired direction.

meg′ȧ·phōne, *v.t.* and *v.i.*; megaphoned, *pp.*, *pt.*; megaphoning, *ppr.* to magnify or direct (sounds) through or as through a megaphone.

Mē·gaph′y·ton, *n.* [*mega-*, and Gr. *phyton*, a plant.] a genus of extinct tree ferns having fossil stems found in the coal measures.

meg′ȧ·pod, *a.* [*mega-* and *-pod.*] having large feet.

meg′ȧ·pod, *n.* a mound bird or jungle fowl of Australia and the Malay Archipelago.

meg′ȧ·pōde, *n.* same as *megapod.*

Meg·ȧ·pō′di·us, *n.* [*mega-*, and Gr. *pous, podos*, foot.] a genus of large-footed birds resembling domestic fowl and including all the

MEGAPOD
(*Megapodius tumulus*)

mound birds except those of the genus *Leipoa.* The best-known species is the Australian jungle fowl, remarkable for erecting mounds composed of earth, stones, decayed leaves, etc., in which it deposits its eggs, leaving them to be hatched by the heat of the fermenting vegetable mass.

mē·gap′ō·lis, *n.* a metropolis. [Obs.]

Mē·gar′i·ăn, *a.* of or pertaining to Megara, a city of Megaris, in ancient Greece.
Megarian school; a school of philosophy founded by Euclid of Megara.

Mē·gar′iç, *a.* same as *Megarian.*

meg′ȧ·sçlēre, *n.* [*mega-*, and Gr. *sklēros*, hard.] a large skeletal spicule in certain sponges.

meg·ȧ·sçler′iç, *a.* of or like a megasclere.

meg·ȧ·sçlē′rous, *a.* megascleric.

meg′ȧ·sçōpe, *n.* [*mega-*, and Gr. *skopein*, to view.] a kind of magic lantern.

meg·ȧ·sçop′iç, *a.* visible to the unaided eye: opposed to *microscopic.*

meg·ȧ·sçop′iç·ăl, *a.* megascopic.

meg′ȧ·sēme, *a.* [*mega-*, and Gr. *sēma*, sign.] in anatomy, having a large orbital index.

meg′ȧ·spō·rañge, *n.* same as *macrosporangium.*

meg″ȧ·spō·ran′ġi·um, *n.*; *pl.* **meg″ȧ·spō·ran′ġi·ȧ,** [Mod. L.; *mega-*, and *sporangium.*] a sporangium, or spore case, containing only megaspores, as in some ferns; macrosporangium.

meg′ȧ·spōre, *n.* a large asexual spore produced by some seed plants and ferns, which gives rise to a female gametophyte or prothallium, as the embryo sac in a seed plant: also called *macrospore.*

meg″ȧ·spō′rō·phyll, *n.* a sporophyll producing only megasporangia.

mē·gass′, mē·gasse′, *n.* same as *bagasse.*

meg′ȧ·thēre, *n.* any one of the genus *Megatherium.*

meg·ȧ·thē′ri·ăn, *n.* a megathere.

meg·ȧ·thē′ri·ăn, *a.* pertaining to or resembling the genus *Megatherium.*

Meg″ȧ·thē·rī′i·dae, *n.pl.* [*mega-*, and Gr. *thēra*, a wild beast.] a family of extinct edentate mammals, of which the genus *Megatherium* is the type.

meg·ȧ·thē′ri·oid, *n.* one of the *Megatheriidæ.*

meg·ȧ·thē′ri·um, *n.* [*mega-*, and Gr. *thērion*, a wild beast.] any of an extinct group of very large, slothlike, plant-eating animals, classified as edentates, whose remains have been found in the Pleistocene of America.

meg·ȧ·thē′roid, *a.* resembling the *Megatheriidæ.*

meg′ȧ·tȳpe, *n.* [*mega-*, and Gr. *typos*, impression.] a picture made larger than its original photographic negative.

meg′ȧ·vōlt, *n.* [*mega-* and *volt.*] a million volts.

meg′ȧ·we̤·bẽr (-vā-), *n.* [*mega-* and *weber.*] a million webers.

meg·ȧ·zō′ō·spōre, *n.* a macrozoospore.

meg′ẽrg, *n.* a megaerg.

Mē·gil′lȧh, *n.*; *pl.* **Mē·gil′lōth,** [Heb.] any one of the five books of the Hagiographa, which are read in synagogues at certain festivals. The list comprises the Song of Songs, Ruth, Lamentations, Ecclesiastes, and Esther.

mē·gilp′, *n.* [one phonetic sp. of a form variously spelled.] a mixture of linseed oil with mastic varnish or turpentine, etc.: used in oil paints: also *magilp, megilph.*

mē·gilph′, *n.* same as *megilp.*

meg′ōhm, *n.* [*meg-* and *ohm.*] a million ohms.

mē′grim, *n.* [Fr. and OFr. *migraine*; LL. *hemigranea*; L. *hemicranium*, pain in one side of the head, a headache, from Gr. *hēmikranion*, half the skull; *hēmi-*, half and *kranion*, the skull.]
1. a severe headache, usually on only one side, with nausea; migraine.
2. a whim, fancy, or fad.
3. [*pl.*] (a) low spirits; the blues; (b) vertigo in horses and cattle: also called *blind staggers.*

Meī·bō′mi·ăn, *a.* of or named after Heinrich Meibom, a German physician (1638–1700).
Meibomian glands; sebaceous glands or follicles of the eyelids, which secrete a lubricant.

me̤in′ie, me̤in′y, *n.* [ME. *meignee, menie*, etc.; OFr. *maisniee, mesnie*, a retinue.]
1. a retinue; a band; domestics; attendants; a household. [Obs.]
2. a crowd; throng; multitude. [Scot.]

Meī′ō·cēne, meī′ō·nīte, etc. same as *Miocene*, etc.

meī·ō′sis, *n.* [Mod. L.; Gr. *meiōsis*, from *meioun*, to make smaller, from *meiōn*, less.]
1. the process of nuclear division in germ cells, in which the number of chromosomes is reduced from the diploid, or double, number found in somatic cells to the haploid, or halved, number found in gametes: also called *maturation, reduction*: distinguished from *mitosis.*
2. litotes.

meī·ot′iç, *a.* of meiosis.

Meis′tẽr·sing″ẽr (*or*-zing″), *n.*; *pl.* **Meis′tẽr·sing″ẽr,** [G., lit., master singer.] a member of one of the guilds, mainly of workingmen, organized in the chief German cities in the 14th, 15th, and 16th centuries for the purpose of cultivating music and poetry: they were successors of the minnesingers.

meī·zō·seis′măl, *a.* [Gr. *meizōn*, comp. of *megas*, great, and *seismos*, a shaking, an earthquake, from *seiein*, to shake.] pertaining to the extreme force of an earthquake.

meī·zō·seis′măl, *n.* a meizoseismal curve.
meizoseismal curve; a curve connecting points upon the earth's surface at which the destructive energy of any earthquake was greatest.

Mekh′i·tär·ist, *n.* one of a group of Armenian monks founded by Mekhitar da Pietro, for the purpose of instructing and improving the condition of his countrymen. The Venetian Republic, in 1715, granted him the island of San Lazzaro, between the Lido and Venice, where he built his convent. The Mekhitarists are devoted to literary work, especially the perfecting of Armenian, and the translation into that language of the principal productions of European literature.

Mek′kȧ, *n.* same as *Mecca.*

mel, *n.* [L.] honey, especially in the pure, clarified form used in pharmacy.

mē·laç′ō·nīte, *n.* [*mela-*, and Gr. *konis*, dust, and *-ite.*] a black, impure, earthy oxide of copper, found in Vesuvian lava, and abundantly in veins in the Lake Superior region.

mē·lā′dȧ, *n.* [Sp. *melada*, properly f. pp. of *melar*, to candy, from *miel*, L. *mel*, honey.] in sugar making, the crude undrained sugar mixed with molasses, as it comes from the vacuum pans.

mē·lae′nȧ, *n.* [Gr. *melaina* (supply *cholē*, bile), black bile, f. of *melas*, black.]
1. black vomit; a term adopted from Hippocrates to denote the vomiting of black-colored bloody matter. In yellow fever, it is a morbid secretion from the lining membrane of the stomach and small intestines mixed with blood.
2. intestinal hemorrhage.

Mel·ȧ·leū′cȧ, *n.* [Gr. *melas*, black, and *leukos*, white.] a large genus of Australian trees and shrubs of the order *Myrtaceæ.* They have yellowish, purplish, or crimson flowers, in spikes or heads. One species yields oil of cajuput.

mē′lăm, *n.* [*mel*lone and *am*monia.] a white, insoluble powder, prepared by fusing thiocyanate of ammonia.

me·lam′ed, *n.*; *pl.* **me·lăm′dim,** [Heb. *melamēdh*, from *lamēdh*, to teach.] a teacher of children in a Jewish religious school

mel′ȧ·mīne, *n.* a white crystalline substance containing three cyanamide molecules in its structure, used in making synthetic resins.

mel′ăm·pod, *n.* the black hellebore. [Obs.]

mel′ăn-, same as *melano-.*

mel·ȧ·nae′mi·ȧ, *n.* [*melan-*, and Gr. *haima*, blood.] a diseased condition of the blood characterized by the presence of black pigment.

mel·ăn·chō′li·ȧ, *n.* [LL., from Gr. *melas*, black, and *cholē*, bile.] a mental disorder characterized by excessive gloom, mistrust, and depression.

mel·ăn·chō′li·ăç, *a.* of or having melancholia.

mel·ăn·chō′li·ăç, *n.* a person who has melancholia.

mel·ăn·chō′li·ăn, *n.* a melancholic. [Obs.]

mel′ăn·chol·iç, *a.* 1. melancholy. [Now Rare.]
2. of, like, or having malancholia.

mel′ăn·chol·iç, *n.* 1. one affected with a gloomy state of mind. [Obs.]
2. a gloomy state of mind. [Obs.]

mel·ăn·chol′iç·ăl·ly, *adv.* in a melancholy manner.

mel′ăn·chol·i·ly, *adv.* in a melancholy manner.

mel′ăn·chol·i·ness, *n.* the state of being melancholy.

mel·ăn·chō′li·ous, *a.* gloomy. [Rare.]

mel′ăn·chol·ist, *n.* one affected with melancholy. [Obs.]

mel′ăn·chō·līze, *v.i.* to become gloomy. [Obs.]

mel′ăn·chō·līze, *v.t.* to make melancholy. [Obs.]

mel′ăn·chol·y, *n.*; *pl.* **mel′ăn·chol·ie̤s,** [ME. and OFr. *melancolie*; LL. *melancholia*; Gr. *melancholia*, melancholy, madness, lit., the condition of having black bile, from *melas* (*-anos*), black, and *cholē*, bile.]
1. (a) originally, black bile, one of the four chief humors, or bodily fluids, of obsolete physiology: it was thought to come from the spleen or kidneys and cause gloominess, irritability, or depression; (b) the condition of having, or the disorder supposed to result from having, too much black bile; (c) melancholia. [Obs.]
2. (a) sadness and depression of spirits; (b) a tendency to be sad, gloomy, or depressed.
3. pensiveness; sad, sober musing.
4. bad temper; irritability. [Obs.]

mel′ăn·chol·y, *a.* 1. gloomy; depressed in spirits; dejected.
2. (a) causing depression, gloom, or sadness; (b) lamentable; deplorable.
3. pensive; given to contemplation.
4. subject to melancholia; hypochondriac. [Obs.]

Mel·ȧ·nē′siăn (-shăn), *a.* [Gr. *melas* (*-anos*), black, and *nēsos*, island.] pertaining to Melanesia, its people, or their languages.

Mel·ȧ·nē′siăn, *n.* 1. a native or inhabitant of Melanesia.
2. the Austronesian languages and dialects of Melanesia.

mē·lange′ (mā-lonzh′), *n.* [Fr., from *mêler*, to mix.] a medley or mixture; a hodgepodge.

mē·lā′ni·ăn, *n.* [Gr. *melania*, blackness, from *melas* (*-anos*), black.] a gastropod having a spiral, turreted shell covered with a black epidermis.

mē·lā′ni·ăn, *a.* [Gr. *melas, melanos*, black.] black; dark-skinned.

mē·lan′iç, *a.* [Gr. *melas, melanos*, black.]
1. melanistic.
2. of, characteristic of, or having melanism or melanosis.

mē·lan′i·line, *n.* [*mela-* and *aniline.*] a crystalline derivative of aniline.

mel′ȧ·nin, *n.* [Gr. *melas, melanos*, black.] the black pigment of the eye, hair, skin, and other animal tissues.

mel′ȧ·niṣm, *n.* [Gr. *melas, melanos*, black, and *-ism.*]
1. an abnormal development of dark pigmentation in the skin, especially in the epidermis, hair, feathers, etc. of mammals and birds: opposed to *albinism.*
2. darkness of skin, hair, eyes, etc. resulting from a high degree of pigmentation.

mel·ȧ·nis′tiç, *a.* of or characterized by melanism.

mel′ȧ·nīte, *n.* [Gr. *melas, melanos,* black.] an iron-alumina variety of garnet, of a velvet black or grayish-black, occurring always in crystals of a dodecahedral form.

mel′ȧ·nō-, [from Gr. *melas, melanos,* black.] a combining form meaning *black, very dark*: also, before a vowel, *melan-*.

Mel·ȧ·noch′rō·ī, *n.pl.* [*melano-,* and Gr. *chroia,* color.] members of the Caucasian race having dark hair and a light complexion.

Mel″ȧ·nō·chrō′iç, *a.* same as *Melanochroid.*

Mel·ȧ·noch′roid, *a.* of or like the Melanochroi.

mel″ȧ·nō·chrō′īte, *n.* [*melano-,* and Gr. *chroia,* color.] a mineral consisting of a basic chromate of lead: also called *phoenicochroite.*

mel·ȧ·noch′rō·ous, *a.* melanochroic.

mel·ȧ·noç′ō·mous, *a.* [Gr. *melanokomēs*; *melas* (*-anos*), black, and *komē,* hair.] having dark hair.

Mel″ȧ·nō·den′drŏn, *n.* [*melano-,* and Gr. *dendron,* a tree.] a genus of trees belonging to the aster family of which the only species is the *Melanodendron integrifolium,* the black cabbage tree of St. Helena.

mē·lan′ō·ġen, *n.* a colorless chromogen of the urine convertible into melanin.

mel′ȧ·noid, *a.* [Gr. *melas* (*-anos*), black, and *eidos,* form.]
1. pigmented black or dark.
2. of or like melanosis.

mel·ȧ·nō′mȧ, *n.*; *pl.* **mel·ȧ·nō′mȧ·tȧ, mel·ȧ·nō′mȧş,** [Mod. L., from Gr. *melanōma,* blackness, from *melas* (*-anos*), black.] a tumor whose cells contain melanin.

mel″ȧ·nō·path′i·ȧ, mel·ȧ·nop′ȧ·thy, *n.* [*melano-,* and Gr. *pathos,* suffering.] an abnormal increase in the deposit of pigment in the skin or tissues; any disease characterized by such an increase.

Mel″ȧ·nor·rhoe′ȧ, *n.* [*melano-,* and Gr. *rhein,* to flow.] a genus of large drupaceous trees native to the East Indies.

mē·lan′ō·sçōpe, *n.* [*melano-,* and Gr. *skopein,* to view.] a device consisting of a combination of red and violet glass which transmits red light only: used to distinguish red in flames containing mixed colors.

mel′ȧ·nōse, *n.* [Gr. *melanōsis,* a turning black, from *melas* (*-anos*), black.] a fungous disease which causes the leaves of grapevines to turn brown and fall off.

mel·ȧ·nō′sis, *n.* [Gr. *melanōsis,* a becoming black, from *melas* (*-anos*), black.] the abnormal production and deposition of melanin in the body tissues.

mel·ȧ·nos′i·ty, *n.* [Gr. *melas, melanos,* black.] darkness, as of eyes, hair, and complexion.

mel″ȧ·nō·spẽr′mous, *a.* having dark seeds or spores.

mel″ȧ·nō·te′kīte, *n.* [*melano-,* and Gr. *tēkein,* to melt.] a massive black silicate of lead and iron.

mel·ȧ·not′iç, *a.* of, having, or having the nature of, melanosis; melanistic.

mel·ȧ·not′ri·chous, *a.* [*melano-,* and Gr. *thrix, trichos,* hair.] having black hair.

mē·lan′ō·type, *n.* [*melano-,* and Gr. *typos,* an impression.] a ferrotype. [Obs.]

mel′ȧ·nous, *a.* [*melan-* and *-ous.*] having dark hair and skin; brunette: opposed to *xanthous.*

mē·lan′tẽr·īte, *n.* [Gr. *melantēria,* a black metallic dye, from *melas,* black.] a green and vitreous sulfate of iron.

mel·ăn·thā′ceous, *a.* [from Mod. L. *Melanthaceæ,* name of the family.] of a family of monocotyledonous plants related to the lily but bulbless.

Mē·lan′thi·um, *n.* [Gr. *melas,* black, and *anthos,* a flower.] a genus of North American plants of the lily family. The bunchflower, *Melanthium virginicum,* is the best known species.

mel′ȧ·nūre, *n.* [*melan-,* and Gr. *oura,* tail.] the gilthead, a fish of the Mediterranean.

mel″ȧ·nū·rē′sis, *n.* same as *melanuria.*

mel·ȧ·nū′ri·ȧ, *n.* [*melan-,* and Gr. *ouron,* urine.] the discharge of darkly-stained urine.

mel·ȧ·nū′riç, *a.* 1. pertaining to or characterized by melanuria; as, *melanuric* fever.
2. pertaining to or derived from urea; as, *melanuric* acid.

mel′ȧ·phȳre, *n.* [Fr., from Gr. *melas,* black, and Fr. *porphyre,* porphyry.] an igneous porphyritic rock with a dark groundmass.

mē·laş′mȧ, *n.* [Gr. *melasma,* a black color, from *melas* (*-anos*), black.] a disease of the skin in which pigment is deposited in spots.

mē·laş′miç, *a.* pertaining to melasma.

mē·las′siç, *a.* of, pertaining to, or derived from molasses.
melassic acid; an acid which is the product of the simultaneous action of heat and alkalis on solutions of glucose.

Mē·las′tō·mȧ, *n.* [*mela-,* and Gr. *stoma,* mouth.] the typical genus of the *Melastomaceæ.*

Mel″ȧ·stō·mā′cē·ae, *n.pl.* a large family of dicotyledonous plants found in the tropics.

mel″ȧ·stō·mā′ceous, *a.* belonging or pertaining to the *Melastomaceæ.*

mel″ȧ·tō′nin, *n.* [*mela*no-, and *ton*ic, and *-in.*] a hormone produced by the pineal gland, that regulates the activity of certain glands.

Mel′bȧ tōast, [after Dame Nellie *Melba* (1861?–1931), Australian soprano.] bread sliced thin and dried by heat until brown and crisp.

Mel′chīte, *n.* [L.Gr. *Melchitēs,* from Syriac *malkāyē,* royal, from *melek,* king.] one of an eastern sect of Christians who, while adhering to the ceremonies and liturgy of the Greek church, acknowledge the papal authority.

meld, *v.t.* and *v.i.*; melded, *pt., pp.*; melding, *ppr.* [G. *melden,* to announce.] in pinochle, etc., to announce (a combination, or meld) and lay it on the table; to announce.

meld, *n.* 1. a melding.
2. a combination of cards melded or to be melded.
3. the score made by melding.

meld, *v.t.* and *v.i.* [merging of *melt* and *weld.*] to blend; merge; unite.

mel·dom′e·tẽr, *n.* [Gr. *meldein,* to melt, and *metron,* a measure.] a device consisting of a strip of platinum heated by an electric current and used to determine melting points.

Mel·ē·ā′ġẽr, *n.* [L.; Gr. *Meleagros.*] in Greek legend, one of the Argonauts, the son of Althea, queen of Calydon: he killed the Calydonian boar and, in a quarrel over its head and hide, which he had given to Atalanta, killed his maternal uncles, whereupon his mother caused his death by burning a log that she had removed from the fire at his birth because it was foretold that when it was consumed he would die.

mel·ē·ā′grīne, *a.* of or belonging to the genus *Meleagris.*

Mel·ē·ā′gris, *n.* [L. *meleagris*; Gr. *meleagris,* a guinea fowl, from *Meleagros,* the hero of the Calydonian boar hunt.] a genus of rasorial birds native to America; the turkeys.

mē·lée′, mê·lée′ (mā-lā′), *n.* [Fr., from OFr. *meslee,* a mixture, a confused mass.] a confused, general hand-to-hand fight between groups or among combatants.

mē·lē′nȧ, *n.* same as *melaena.*

Mē·lē′ti·ăn (-shăn), *n.* 1. one of the followers of Meletius, bishop of Antioch about A.D. 360.
2. one of the followers of Meletius, bishop of Lycopolis about A.D. 304.

mē·lez′i·tōse, *n.* [Fr. *mélèze,* the larch, and E. *melitose.*] an isomer of cane sugar derived from the exudations of some species of larch.

Mē′li·ȧ, *n.* [Gr. *melia,* the ash.] a small genus of trees of the family *Meliaceæ,* native to tropical Asia and Australia. *Melia azedarach,* sometimes called Persian lilac, pride-of-India, and bead tree, is native to the north of India, and much cultivated in the southern parts of the United States.

Mē·li·ā′cē·ae, *n.pl.* [Gr. *melia,* the ash, and *-aceæ.*] the mahogany family of shrubs and trees chiefly inhabiting tropical Asia and America, which possess bitter, tonic, and astringent properties.They have small paniculate flowers, and, often, pinnate leaves.

mē·li·ā′ceous, *a.* of or pertaining to the *Meliaceæ.*

Mel″i·an·thā′cē·ae, *n.pl.* [Gr. *meli,* honey, and *anthos,* a flower.] a small family of shrubs and trees, native to South Africa.

mel″i·an·thā′ceous, *a.* pertaining to the *Melianthaceæ.*

Mel·i·an′thus, *n.* the typical genus of the *Melianthaceæ.*

Mel·i·bē′ăn, Mel·i·boe′ăn, *a.* [named after *Melibœus,* an interlocutor in Virgil's first eclogue.] in prosody, responding alternately; amoebean; having the form of a dialogue.

mel′iç, *a.* [Gr. *melikos,* from *melos,* a song, melody.]
1. of song or poetry.
2. meant to be sung; lyric: applied especially to types of Greek poetry written in strophes.

Mel′i·çȧ, *n.* a genus of perennial grasses, native to temperate climates.

mel·i·cē′ris, *n.* [L. *meliceris*; Gr. *melikēris,* a tumor, from *melikēron,* a honeycomb; from *meli,* honey, and *kēros,* wax.]
1. an encysted tumor, the contents of which resembles wax or honey.
2. viscid, sirupy exudation.

mel′iç grȧss, a plant of the genus *Melica.*

mē·liç′rȧ·tō·ry, *n.* a mixture of honey, water, etc., forming a drink like mead. [Obs.]

mel′i·līte, *n.* [Gr. *meli,* honey, and *lithos,* stone.] a tetragonal mineral, occurring in yellow crystals and consisting of a silicate of iron, magnesium, aluminium, and calcium.

mel′i·lot, *n.* [OFr. *melilot*; L. *melilotos*; Gr. *melilōton, melilōtos,* a kind of clover; *meli,* honey, and *lōtos,* lotus.] a plant of the genus *Melilotus.*

mel·i·lot′iç, *a.* of, pertaining to, or obtained from melilot.
melilotic acid; a white crystalline substance found in the leaves of melilot.

Mel·i·lō′tus, *n.* a genus of leguminous plants, the sweet clovers, differing from the clovers in having racemose flowers. Two common species are the yellow melilot, *Melilotus officinalis,* and the white melilot, *Melilotus alba.*

meļ′i·nīte, *n.* [Fr.] a powerful explosive resembling lyddite, made by combining picric acid with guncotton.

mēl′iō·rȧ·ble (-yō-), *a.* that can be meliorated.

mēl′iō·rāte, *v.t.* and *v.i.*; meliorated, *pt., pp.*; meliorating, *ppr.* [LL. *melioratus,* pp. of *meliorare,* to make better, from L. *melior,* comp. of *bonus,* good.] to make or become better; to improve; to ameliorate.

mēl·iō·rā′tion, *n.* 1. a meliorating or being meliorated; improvement.
2. in linguistics, a change of meaning for the better.
Opposed to *pejoration.*

mēl′iō·rā·tive, *a.* meliorating or tending to meliorate: applied in linguistics to words whose basic meaning has been changed for the better (e.g., *marshal, knight, steward*): opposed to *pejorative.*

mēl′iō·rā·tive, *n.* a meliorative word or form: opposed to *pejorative.*

mēl′iō·rā·tŏr, *n.* one who or that which meliorates.

mēl′iō·riṣm, *n.* [L. *melior,* better, and *-ism.*]
1. the belief that the world naturally tends to get better and, especially, that it can be made better by human effort.
2. the betterment of society by improving people's health, living conditions, etc.

mēl′iō·rist, *n.* a believer in meliorism.

mēl′iō·rist, *a.* of meliorism or meliorists.

mēl·ior′i·ty, *n.* the state or quality of being better; superiority.

Mē·liph′ȧ·gȧ, *n.* a genus of the *Meliphagidæ.*

mē·liph′ȧ·găn, *a.* pertaining to the genus *Meliphaga.*

mē·liph′ȧ·găn, *n.* any bird of *Meliphaga* or allied genera; a honey eater.

Mel·i·phaġ′i·dae, *n.pl.* [Gr. *meli,* honey, and *phagein,* to eat.] a family of birds native to Australia; the honey eaters.

mel·i·phaġ′i·dăn, *n.* same as *meliphagan.*

mē·liph′ȧ·gous, *a.* feeding upon honey.

mē·lis′mȧ, *n.*; *pl.* **mē·lis′mȧ·tȧ** or **mē·lis′mȧş,** [Gr. *melisma,* a song.]
1. a melody, tune, or air; a cadence; an embellishment in music.
2. a succession of different notes sung upon a single syllable, as originally in plain song or, now especially in the ornamental phrases of Near Eastern and Asian music.

Mē·lis′sȧ, *n.* a genus of the mint family.

mē·lis′siç, *a.* [Gr. *mellissa,* a bee, honey.] of, pertaining to, or obtained from honey or beeswax.
melissic acid; a waxlike substance obtained by treating hydrate of myricyl with soda lime.

mē·lis′syl, *n.* [Gr. *melissa,* a bee, and *hylē,* matter.] a radical occurring only in combination and found in many derivatives of beeswax.

mē·lī′tis, *n.* [Gr. *mēla,* the cheeks.] inflammation of the cheek.

mel′i·tōse, *n.* [Gr. *meli, melitos,* honey.] an isomer of cane sugar, derived from some species of *Eucalyptus.*

mel·i·tū′ri·ȧ, *n.* [Gr. *meli, melitos,* honey, and *ouron,* urine.] the presence of any sugar in the urine.

mell, *n.* a mill. [Obs.]

mell, *v.t.* and *v.i.* [Fr. *meler*; OFr. *meller, mesler,* to mix.] to mix; mingle.
2. to meddle. [Obs. or Brit. Dial.]

mell, *n.* [L. *mel.*] honey. [Obs.]

mel′lāte, *n.* same as *mellitate.*
mel′lāy, *n.* same as *mêlée.*
mel′lē·ous, *a.* [L. *melleus,* from *mel, mellis,* honey.] resembling honey.
mel′liç, *a.* 1. of or resembling honey.
2. mellitic.
mel·lif′ēr·ous, *a.* [L. *mel, mellis,* honey, and *ferre,* to produce.] producing honey.
mel·lif′iç, *a.* same as *melliferous.*
mel·li·fi·çā′tion, *n.* the making or production of honey. [Obs.]
mel·lif′lū·ence, *n.* the quality of being mellifluent.
mel·lif′lū·ent, *a.* [L. *mellifluens* (*-entis*); *mel, mellis,* honey, and *fluens,* ppr. of *fluere,* to flow.] flowing as with honey; sweetly flowing; mellifluous; as, a *mellifluent* voice.
mel·lif′lū·ent·ly, *adv.* in a mellifluent manner.
mel·lif′lū·ous, *a.* flowing sweetly and smoothly; honeyed: said of words, sounds, etc.
mel·lif′lū·ous·ly, *adv.* mellifluently.
mel·liġ′ē·nous, *a.* [Gr. *meli,* honey, and *genos,* kind.] having the qualities of honey. [Rare.]
mel·lī′gō, *n.* honeydew.
mel·lil′ō·quent, *a.* [L. *mel, mellis,* honey, and *loquens,* ppr. of *loqui,* to speak.] speaking smoothly or sweetly.
mel·liph′ȧ·găn, *n.* same as *meliphagan.*
mel·liph′ȧ·gous, *a.* same as *meliphagous.*
mel′li·tāte, *n.* a salt of mellitic acid.
mel′līte, *n.* honeystone, a mineral of a honey color, found in small octahedral crystals. It consists of aluminum mellitate, and is found with brown coal.
mel·lit′iç, *a.* [*mellite* and *-ic.*] of, pertaining to, or derived from honeystone.
mellitic acid; a bitter, white, crystalline acid derived from mellite.
mel′li·tōse, *n.* [L. *mellitus,* honeyed.] same as *melitose.*
mel·liv′ō·rous, *a.* [L. *mel, mellis,* honey, and *vorare,* to devour.] eating or feeding on honey.
mel′lōne, *n.* a yellow, strongly-staining powder produced by the action of heat on certain cyanogen compounds.
mel′lon·ide, *n.* a compound of mellone with a base.
mel′lōw, *a.* [ME. *melwe,* ripe, prob. from AS. *melu,* meal.]
1. soft, sweet, and juicy because ripe: said of fruit.
2. full-flavored; matured; not acid or bitter: said of wine, etc.
3. full, rich, soft, and pure; not harsh: said of sound, light, color, weather, etc.
4. moist and rich; loamy: said of soil.
5. softened and made gentle, understanding, and sympathetic by age and experience.
6. (a) genial; jovial; (b) somewhat drunk; tipsy. [Colloq.]
7. good; excellent. [Slang.]
Syn.—ripe, rich, full-flavored, jovial, mature, soft, perfected.
mel′lōw, *v.t.* and *v.i.*; mellowed (-lōd), *pt., pp.*; mellowing, *ppr.* to make or become mellow.
mel′lōw·ly, *adv.* in a mellow manner.
mel′lōw·ness, *n.* the state or quality of being mellow.
mel′lōw·y, *a.* soft; mellow.
mell′-sup″pēr, *n.* harvest supper; the feast at harvest home. [Brit. Dial.]
mel·lū′çō, *n.* [S. Am.] a climbing plant of the goosefoot family, native to the Andes, having edible tuberous roots which resemble potatoes.
Mel·ō·çaç′tus, *n.* [LL. *melo* (*-onis*), a melon, and *cactus,* a cactus.] a genus of plants of tropical America, of the family *Cactaceæ,* characterized by a globose or conical stem, having flowers at the top on a hemispherical or cylindrical head.
mel·ō·çō·tōn′, mel·ō·çō·tōon′, *n.* [Sp. *melocoton*; LL. *melum Cydonium*; Gr. *mēlon Kydōnion*; *mēlon,* an apple, and *Kydonios,* of or pertaining to Cydonia.] a peach grafted on a quince. [Obs.]
mē·lō′dē·ŏn, *n.* [pseudo-Gr. form of *melody.*]
1. a small keyboard organ in which the tones are produced by drawing air through metal reeds by means of a bellows operated by pedals: it is much like a harmonium.
2. a kind of accordion.
mē·lō′di·ȧ, *n.* [LL., melody.] an 8-foot organ stop with wooden pipes and a flutelike tone; stopped diapason.
mē·lod′iç, *a.* [LL. *melodicus*; Gr. *melōdikos,* melodious, from *melōdia,* melody.]
1. melodious.
2. of, having the nature of, or composed of melody.
mē·lod′i·çăl·ly, *adv.* 1. in a melodic manner.
2. as regards melody.
3. by melody.
mē·lod′içs, *n. pl.* that branch of musical science which investigates the laws of melody and the pitch of tones.
mē·lō′di·ō·gràph, *n.* same as *melograph.*
mē·lō′di·ous, *a.* [OFr. *melodieus*; LL. *melodia*; Gr. *melōdia,* melody.]
1. containing or producing melody.
2. tuneful; agreeable to the ear by a sweet succession of sounds; as, a *melodious* voice.
mē·lō′di·ous·ly, *adv.* in a melodious manner.
mē·lō′di·ous·ness, *n.* the quality of being melodious.
mel′ō·dist, *n.* a composer or singer of melodies.
mel′ō·dīze, *v.t.*; melodized, *pt., pp.*; melodizing, *ppr.* 1. to make melodious; to harmonize.
2. to set to melody.
mel′ō·dīze, *v.i.* to make melody.
mel·ō·drä′mȧ, *n.* [Fr. *mélodrame,* from Gr. *melos,* a song, and *drama,* drama.]
1. originally, a sensational or romantic stage play with interspersed songs and an orchestral accompaniment.
2. now, a drama with sensational, romantic, often violent action, extravagant emotions, and, generally, a happy ending.
3. any sensational, extravagantly emotional action, utterance, etc.
4. opera. [Rare.]
mel″ō·drȧ·mat′iç, *a.* of, suitable for, or having the character of a melodrama; sensational, violent, and extravagantly emotional.
mel″ō·drȧ·mat′i·çăl·ly, *adv.* in a melodramatic manner.
mel″ō·drȧ·mat′içs, *n.pl.* melodramatic behavior.
mel·ō·dram′ȧ·tist, *n.* a writer or actor of melodramas.
mel′ō·drāme, *n.* [Fr.] melodrama.
mel′ō·dy, *n.*; *pl.* **mel′ō·dieṣ,** [ME. and OFr. *melodie*; LL. *melodia*; Gr. *melōdia,* a singing, a tune, a choral song; *melos,* a song, strain, and *ōdē,* a song.]
1. (a) an agreeable succession of sounds; sweetness of sound; music; (b) musical quality, as in the arrangement of words.

The birds chant *melody* on every bush.
—Shak.

2. in music, (a) a sequence of single tones, usually in the same key or mode, to produce a rhythmic whole; often, a tune, air, or song; (b) the element of form having to do with the arrangement of single tones in sequence: distinguished from *harmony*; (c) the leading part or voice in a harmonic composition; the air.
3. a poem composed to be sung.
Mel′ō·ē, *n.* [from Gr. *mēloun,* to probe a wound.]
1. a genus of coleopterous insects belonging to the family *Cantharidæ.*
2. [m-] an oil beetle.
mel′ō·gràph, *n.* [Gr. *melographos,* writing songs; *melos,* a song, and *graphein,* to write.] a device which records the notes played upon a musical instrument, as a piano.
mel′oid, *n.* [from Mod.L. *Meloidæ,* name of the family from *meloe,* oil beetle.] a blister beetle or other insect of the same family.
mel′oid, *a.* of blister beetles or other insects of the same family.
mel·ō·lon′thi·dăn, *n.* [Gr. *mēlolonthē,* the beetle or cockchafer.] a beetle of the genus *Melolontha,* which includes the cockchafers.
mel·ō·lon′thīne, *a.* [from Gr. *mēlolonthē,* cockchafer; and *-ine.*] of a subfamily of beetles including the cockchafers, June bugs, and rose bugs.
mel·ō·lon′thīne, *n.* any beetle of this subfamily.
mel′ŏn, *n.* [ME.; OFr. *melon*; LL. *melo* (*-onis*), for L. *melopepo*; Gr. *mēlopēpōn,* an apple-shaped melon; *mēlon,* an apple, and *pepōn,* a melon.]
1. any of several large, juicy, many-seeded fruits of certain trailing plants of the gourd family, as the watermelon, muskmelon, cantaloupe, and honeydew melon.
2. any of these plants.
3. profits, winnings, political spoils, or the like, for distribution among stockholders, etc.: chiefly in *to cut a melon,* to distribute such profits, etc. [Slang.]
4. a mass of blubber, hemispherical in shape, found on the top of the head of certain cetaceans, as the blackfish.
5. a melon shell.
mel′ŏn, *n.* same as *pademelon.*
mel′ŏn bee′tle, a small beetle, *Diabrotica vittata,* which feeds upon the leaves of the melon and similar plants.
mel′ŏn çaç′tus, any plant of the genus *Melocactus.*
mel′ō·nīte, *n.* [so called from the *Melones* mine in California, where first found.] in mineralogy, a rare nickel telluride.
mel′ŏn shell, an oval shell of the genus *Melo.*
mel″ō·pi·an′ō, *n.* [Gr. *melos,* song, and It. *piano,* piano.] a form of pianoforte having a series of small hammers set into rapid vibration by winding up a spring.
mel·ō·plas′tiç, *a.* relating to meloplasty.
mel′ō·plas·ty, *n.* [Gr. *mēla,* the cheeks, and *plassein,* to form.] in surgery, the operation of replacing, by means of transplantation of fresh tissue, the whole or part of a cheek which has been destroyed.
mel·ō·poe′iȧ (-yȧ), *n.* [LL., from Gr. *melopoiia,* the making of melodies; *melos,* a song, melody, and *poiein,* to make.] the art of composing melodies.
Mel·pom′e·nē, *n.* [Gr. *Melpomenē,* from *melpein,* to sing.]
1. in Greek mythology, the Muse of tragedy, the daughter of Zeus and Mnemosyne: generally represented as a young woman with vine leaves surrounding her head, and holding in her hand a tragic mask.
2. an asteroid revolving between the orbits of Mars and Jupiter, discovered June 24, 1852, by Professor Hind.

MELPOMENE

melt, *n.* milt. [Now Dial.]
melt, *v.t.* and *v.i.*; melted, *pt., pp.*; molten, *archaic pp.*; melting, *ppr.* [AS. *meltan, miltan,* to melt.]
1. to change from a solid to a liquid state, generally by heat.
2. to dissolve; to disintegrate.
3. to disappear or cause to disappear gradually (often with *away*).
4. to merge gradually; to blend; as, the sea seems to *melt* into the sky at the horizon.
5. to soften; to make or become gentle and tender; as, her grief *melted* our hearts.
melt, *n.* 1. a melting or being melted.
2. something melted.
3. the quantity melted at one operation or during one period.
melt′ȧ·ble, *a.* capable of being melted or fused.
melt′āġe, *n.* 1. the act of melting.
2. the thing or quantity resulting from melting.
melt′down, *n.* a situation in which a defect in the cooling system of a nuclear reactor can result in the melting of the rods of fissionable material, the sinking of the central part of the reactor containing this material, and the release of dangerous radiation.
melt′ēr, *n.* 1. one who or that which melts anything.
2. that in which anything melts; a crucible or melting pan.
melt′ing, *n.* fusion; liquefaction.
melt′ing, *a.* causing to melt or subject to melting, either literally or figuratively; as, a *melting* temperature, a *melting* mood.
melt′ing·ly, *adv.* in a melting manner.
melt′ing point, the temperature at which a specified solid is transformed into a liquid.
melt′ing pot, 1. a container in which metals or other substances are melted; a crucible.
2. a country, place, etc. in which immigrants of various nationalities and races are assimilated.
mel′tŏn, *n.* [prob. from *Melton,* in Leicestershire, England, where manufactured.] a variety of heavy woolen cloth with a smooth surface and a short nap, chiefly used in making overcoats.
Me·lun′ġeŏn, *n.* [possibly from Fr. *mélangé,* mixed.] a member of a dark-skinned people of mixed Caucasian, Negro, and Indian stock, inhabiting the Tennessee mountains.
mem, *n.* [Heb. *mēm,* lit., water.] the thirteenth letter of the Hebrew alphabet, corresponding to English *M, m.*
mem′bēr, *n.* [OFr. *membre*; L. *membrum,* a limb, part of the body, any part, portion, division.]
1. (a) a leg, arm, or other part or organ of a human or animal body; (b) a part of a plant considered with regard to structure or position rather than function.

2. (a) a distinct part or element of a whole, as of a mathematical equation, a sentence, a syllogism, a series, a building, a bridge, etc.; (b) a part or division in a system of classification; as, species are *members* of a genus.

3. a person belonging to some association, society, community, party, etc.

4. [M-] (a) a Member of Congress, in the House of Representatives; (b) a Member of Parliament, in the House of Commons.

mem′bẽred, *a.* 1. having limbs; as, a small-membered person.

2. in heraldry, having limbs which are of a tincture different from the body.

mem′bẽr·ship, *n.* 1. the state of being, or status as, a member.

2. the members of a society, or any organized body, taken collectively.

3. the number of members.

mem′brăl, *a.* pertaining to a member.

mem·brȧ·nā′ceous, *a.* same as *membranous.*

mem′brāne, *n.* [L. *membrana,* a membrane or thin skin.]

1. a thin, soft, pliable sheet or layer, especially of animal or vegetable tissue, serving as a covering or lining, as for an organ or part.

2. in zoology, the membranous transparent portion of a hemelytron.

3. a piece of skin, as parchment or vellum, prepared for being written on.

false membrane; a fibrinous deposit formed in croup and diphtheria.

Jacob's membrane; the layer of rods and cones of the retina.

membrane bone; a bone developed in a connective tissue membrane rather than in cartilage.

mem·brā′nē·ous, *a.* same as *membranous.*

mem·brȧ·nif′ẽr·ous, *a.* [L. *membrana,* membrane, and *ferre,* to bear.] having or producing membranes.

mem·brā′ni·form, *a.* [L. *membrana,* a membrane, and *forma,* form.] having the form of a membrane or of parchment.

mem·brȧ·nol′ō·ġy, *n.* [L. *membrana,* a membrane, and Gr. *logos,* description, discourse.] that part of the science of anatomy which treats of membranes.

mem′brȧ·nous (*or* mem-brā′), *a.* [Fr. *membraneux.*]

1. of, having the nature of, or like membrane.

2. characterized by the forming of a membrane: said of some diseases.

mem′brȧ·nūle, *n.* [L. *membranula,* dim. of *membrana,* a membrane.]

1. a little membrane.

2. in zoology, a minute process at the base of a wing in some dragonflies.

mē·men′tō, *n.*; *pl.* **mē·men′tōṣ, mē·men′tōeṣ,** [L., remember, 2nd pers. sing. imper. of *meminisse,* to remember.]

1. [M-] in the Roman Catholic Church, either of two prayers in the Canon of the Mass, one for the living and one for the dead, beginning "Memento."

2. anything serving as a reminder, warning, or souvenir.

mē·men′tō mō′rī, [L., remember that you must die.] any reminder of death, as a skull.

me·min′nȧ, *n.* [Singalese.] in zoology, a chevrotain of India and Ceylon.

Mem′non, *n.* 1. in Greek legend, an Ethiopian king killed by Achilles in the Trojan War and made immortal by Zeus.

2. a gigantic statue of an Egyptian king at Thebes, Egypt, said to have emitted a musical sound at sunrise.

Mem·nō′ni·ăn, *a.* relating to Memnon.

mem′ō, *n.*; *pl.* **mem′ōṣ,** a memorandum. [Colloq.]

mem′oir (-wor), *n.* [Fr. *mémoire,* a memorandum, memoir, from L. *memoria,* memory.]

1. a biography or biographical notice.

2. a report or record of a scholarly investigation or scientific study; a monograph.

3. [*pl.*] (a) a report or record of happenings that is based on the writer's personal observation and knowledge or special information; as, *memoirs* of the French Revolution; (b) an autobiography or autobiographical record; (c) a record of the transactions of a learned society.

mem′oir·iṣm, *n.* the art or act of writing memoirs.

mem′oir·ist, *n.* a writer of memoirs.

mem″ō·rȧ·bil′i·ȧ, *n.pl.*; *sing.* **mem·ō·rab′i·lē,** [L., neut. pl. of *memorabilis,* worthy to be mentioned or remembered.] things worth remembering or recording; also, the record kept of such things.

mem″ō·rȧ·bil′i·ty, *n.* the quality or condition of being memorable.

mem′ō·rȧ·ble, *a.* [L. *memorabilis,* worthy to be noticed or remembered, from *memorare,* to remind.] worthy to be remembered; noteworthy; celebrated; distinguished.

Syn.—great, striking, remarkable, conspicuous, prominent, noticeable, illustrious, extraordinary, famous, distinguished.

mem′ō·rȧ·ble·ness, *n.* the quality of being memorable.

mem′ō·rȧ·bly, *adv.* in a memorable manner.

mem·ō·ran′dum, *n.*; *pl.* **mem·ō·ran′dumṣ, mem·ō·ran′dȧ,** [L. *memorandum,* neut. of *memorandus,* to be remembered, gerundive of *memorare,* to call to remembrance, to remind.]

1. (a) a short note written to help one remember something or remind one to do something; (b) a record of events or observations, especially one for future use.

2. an informal written communication, as from one department to another in a business office.

3. in business, a statement, made by the consignor, of the goods and terms of a consignment sent with the privilege of return.

4. in diplomacy, a summary or outline of a subject under discussion, reasons for or against some action, etc.

5. in law, a short written statement of the terms of an agreement, contract, or transaction.

mem′ō·rāte, *v.t.* to commemorate. [Obs.]

mem′ō·rȧ·tive, *a.* commemorating or tending to preserve the memory of anything. [Rare.]

mē·mō′ri·a, *n.* [L. *memory.*]

1. a shrine or reliquary containing relics of a martyr.

2. a chapel or church erected in memory of a martyr or confessor.

mē·mō′ri·ăl, *a.* [OFr. *memorial;* L. *memorialis,* of or pertaining to memory, from *memoria,* memory.]

1. serving to help people remember some person or event; commemorative.

2. of memory.

mē·mō′ri·ăl, *n.* 1. anything meant to help people remember some person or event, as a statue, holiday, etc.

2. a note or hint to assist the memory; a memorandum. [Obs.]

3. a written statement of facts submitted to a person or persons in authority, as to Congress; a statement of facts accompanied with a petition.

4. memory; remembrance; that which is or may be remembered. [Obs.]

5. in diplomacy, an informal state paper, used in negotiations, and containing such documents as circulars sent to foreign agents, answers to the communications of ambassadors, and notes to foreign cabinets and ambassadors.

6. in law, a writing containing the particulars of a deed.

Mē·mō′ri·ăl Dāy, a day designated in the United States for honoring dead members of the armed forces; Decoration Day: in most States a legal holiday, falling on May 30; in Southern States, April 26, May 10, or June 3.

mē·mō′ri·ăl·ist, *n.* 1. a writer of memoirs.

2. one who draws up, signs, or presents a memorial to a legislative or other body, or to a person.

mē·mō′ri·ăl·īze, *v.t.*; memorialized, *pt., pp.*; memorializing, *ppr.* 1. to present a memorial to; to petition by memorial; as, to *memorialize* Congress.

2. to commemorate.

mē·mō′ri·ȧ teçh′ni·çȧ, [L. *memoria,* memory, and Gr. *technikos,* technical, from *technē,* art, handicraft.] technical memory; any contrivance for aiding the memory.

mē·mō′ri·ous, *a.* [LL. *memoriosus,* having a good memory, from L. *memoria,* memory.]

1. worthy of remembrance; memorable.

2. having a good memory. [Obs.]

mem′ō·rist, *n.* one who or that which commemorates, or causes to be remembered. [Obs.]

mē·mor′i·tẽr, *adv.* [L., by memory, from *memor,* mindful of, remembering.] from memory; by heart; as, to repeat a lesson *memoriter.*

mem′ō·rī·zȧ·ble, *a.* capable of being memorized.

mem″ō·ri·zā′tion, *n.* a memorizing or being memorized.

mem′ō·rīze, *v.t.*; memorized, *pt., pp.*; memorizing, *ppr.* 1. to commemorate; to cause to be remembered; to render memorable; to record. [Archaic.]

2. to commit to memory; to learn by heart.

mem′ō·rī·zẽr, *n.* one who memorizes.

mem′ō·ry, *n.*; *pl.* **mem′ō·rieṣ,** [OFr. *memorie;* L. *memoria,* the faculty of remembering, memory, from *memor,* mindful of, remembering.]

1. the power, act, or process of remembering.

2. the total of what one remembers.

3. a person, thing, happening, or act remembered.

4. the length of time over which remembering extends; as, not within the *memory* of living men has this happened.

5. commemoration or remembrance; as, in *memory* of his father.

6. fame after death; posthumous reputation; as, a man of notorious *memory.*

7. a memorial. [Obs.]

8. an act or ceremony in remembrance; a service for the dead. [Obs.]

Syn.—remembrance, recollection, reminiscence.—*Memory* denotes the power by which we reproduce past impressions; *remembrance* is an exercise of that power when things occur spontaneously to our thoughts. In *recollection* we make a distinct effort to collect again or call back what we know has been formerly in the mind. *Reminiscence* is a conscious process of recalling past occurrences, but without that distinct reference to particular things which characterizes *recollection.*

Mem′phi·ăn, *a.* 1. of ancient Memphis, Egypt.

2. Egyptian.

Mem′phīte, *a.* [L. *Memphites;* Gr. *Memphitēs,* from *Memphis,* Memphis, an ancient capital of Egypt.] of or pertaining to Memphis, a city of ancient Egypt, or to its inhabitants.

Mem′phīte, *n.* a native or inhabitant of the ancient city of Memphis.

Mem·phit′iç, *a.* Memphite.

mem′-sä″hib (-ib), *n.* [Anglo-Ind.; *mem* for Eng. *ma'am,* and Ar. *sāhib,* a master.] lady; mistress: term applied to a European woman by servants, etc. in India.

men, *n.* plural of *man.*

mē·naç′căn·ite, *n.* see *menachanite.*

mē·naç·çȧ·nit′iç, *a.* see *menachanitic.*

men′ăce, *n.* [ME. *manasce, manace;* OFr. *manace;* L. *minacia,* from *minax,* projecting, threatening, from *minari,* to threaten.]

1. a threat; a threatening; a declaration or indication of a disposition, intention, or determination to inflict punishment or other evil.

2. anything threatening harm or evil.

men′ăce, *v.t.*; menaced (-ăst), *pt., pp.*; menacing, *ppr.* [ME. *menacen;* OFr. *menacer,* to threaten, from *menace,* a threat, menace.]

1. to threaten; to express or show an intention of determination to inflict punishment, evil, or injury upon: often followed by *with;* as, to *menace* a city *with* destruction.

2. to threaten with; to express or hold out threats of.

men′ăce, *v.i.* to threaten; to be threatening.

men′ăce·ment, *n.* menace.

men′ăc·ẽr, *n.* one who menaces.

mē·nach′ăn·ite, mē·naç′căn·ite, *n.* [named from *Menachan,* in Cornwall, England, where found.] same as *ilmenite.*

mē·nach·ȧ·nit′iç, mē·naç·çȧ·nit′iç, *a.* pertaining to menachanite.

men′ȧ·cing·ly, *adv.* in a threatening manner.

mē′nad, *n.* same as *maenad.*

mé·nage′, me·nage′ (me-näzh′, mā-), *n.* [ME. *maynage;* OFr. *manaige,* etc., from L. *mansio,* a house.]

1. the occupants of a house, collectively; a household.

2. household management; housekeeping.

3. in Scotland and the north of England, a club or society of workingmen.

me·naġ′ẽr·ie, *n.* [Fr. *ménagerie,* from *ménage,* a household.]

1. a collection of wild or strange animals kept in cages or enclosures, especially for exhibition.

2. a place where such animals are kept.

men′ȧ·gogue (-gog), *n.* [Gr. *mēn,* a month, and *agōgos,* leading, from *agein,* to lead.] a medicine that promotes the menstrual flow; an emmenagogue.

Mē·naī′on, *n.*; *pl.* **Mē·naī′ȧ,** [L.Gr. *mēnaion,* from Gr. *mēn,* a month.] in the Orthodox Eastern Church, any one of the twelve volumes, one for each month, containing the offices of the church to be read in commemoration of the saints; also, a set of these volumes.

mend, *v.t.*; mended, *pt.*, *pp.*; mending, *ppr.* [ME. *menden*, to mend, from *amenden*, to amend.]

1. to repair, as something broken, rent, defaced, decayed, or the like; to restore to the original condition; to restore to a sound or prosperous state; to put into shape or order again; to patch up; as, to *mend* a road; to *mend* a chair; to *mend* a broken heart.

2. to alter for the better; to improve; to correct; to rectify; as, to *mend* one's manners.

3. to help; to advance; to further; to improve.

4. to atone for; to make amends for: now only in *least said, soonest mended.*

Syn.—improve, better, correct, amend.

mend, *v.i.* to grow better; to advance to a better state; to improve, especially in health.

mend, *n.* 1. a mending; improvement.

2. a mended place, as on a garment.

on the mend; improving, especially in health.

mend′à·ble, *a.* capable of being mended.

men·dā′cious, *a.* [L. *mendax* (*-acis*), lying, false.]

1. addicted to deception; given to lying.

2. untrue; false; as, a *mendacious* report.

men·dā′cious·ly, *adv.* in a false or mendacious manner.

men·dā′cious·ness, *n.* the quality of being mendacious.

men·dac′i·ty, *n.*; *pl.* **men·dac′i·ties**, [LL. *mendacitas* (*-atis*), falsehood, from L. *mendax* (*-acis*), lying, false.]

1. the quality or state of being mendacious.

2. a lie; a falsehood.

Men·de·le′ev's law (-efs), in chemistry, the periodic law.

men·de·lē′vi·um, *n.* [Mod. L., named after D. I. *Mendeleev* (1834–1907), Russ. chemist.] a radioactive chemical element produced by bombarding einsteinium with high-energy alpha particles in a cyclotron: symbol, Md; atomic weight, 258(?); atomic number, 101.

Men·dē′li·ăn, *a.* 1. of Gregor Mendel.

2. of, or inherited according to, the laws laid down by Gregor Johann Mendel, Austrian monk and naturalist (1822–1884).

Men·dē′li·ăn·ism, *n.* same as *Mendelism.*

Men′del·ism, *n.* the theory of heredity formulated by Gregor Mendel.

Men′del·īze, *v.i.*; Mendelized, *pt.*, *ppr.*; Mendelizing, *ppr.* to follow the Mendelian law.

Men′del's laws, the three principles of hereditary phenomena discovered and formulated by Gregor Mendel: (1) the law of independent unit characters, which states that characters, or characteristics, as height, color, etc., are inherited separately as units; (2) the law of segregation, which states that body cells and primordial germ cells contain pairs of such unit characters and that when gametes are produced, each gamete receives only one member of each such pair; (3) the law of dominance, which states that in every individual there is a pair of determining factors (see *genes*) for each unit character, one from each parent; if these factors are different (*heterozygous*), one character (the *dominant*) appears in the organism, the other (the *recessive*) being latent; the recessive character can appear in the organism only when the dominant is absent. Hence in all cross-bred generations unit characters are shown in varying combinations, each appearing in a definite proportion of the total number of offspring.

mend′ẽr, *n.* one who mends or repairs.

men′di·căn·cy, *n.* the act of begging or condition of being a beggar.

men′di·cănt, *a.* [L. *mendicans* (*-antis*), ppr. of *mendicare*, to beg, from *mendicus*, poor.]

1. of or characteristic of a beggar.

2. practicing beggary; as, a *mendicant* friar.

mendicant orders; certain monastic orders, as the Franciscans, Dominicans, Carmelites, and Augustinians, which were forbidden to acquire landed property and were required to subsist on alms.

men′di·cănt, *n.* 1. a beggar; one who begs for alms.

2. a mendicant friar.

men′di·cāte, *v.t.* and *v.i.* to beg, or practice begging. [Obs.]

men·di·cā′tion, *n.* habitual begging. [Obs.]

men·dic′i·ty, *n.* [OFr. *mendicite*; L. *mendicitas*, (*-atis*), beggary, pauperism, from *mendicus*, poor, beggarly.] same as *mendicancy.*

mend′ing, *n.* the act of repairing; also, articles that need mending, taken collectively; as, the family *mending.*

men′dip·īte, *n.* [so called from the *Mendip* hills, Somerset, England, where it is found.] a rare lead oxychloride of a white color with a tinge of yellow or red, occurring in masses, with a fibrous and sometimes radiated structure, also crystallized.

mend′ment, *n.* amendment. [Obs.]

men′dōle, *n.* [Fr.] a small Mediterranean fish: also called *cackerel.*

men′drē·gal, *n.* same as *medregal.*

men·e·ghī′nīte (-gī), *n.* [named after Prof. *Meneghini*, an Italian mineralogist.] a sulfide of antimony and lead, of a bright metallic luster and lead-gray color, occurring in fibrous masses and orthorhombic crystals.

Men·e·lā′us, *n.* in Greek legend, a king of Sparta, son of Atreus, brother of Agamemnon, and husband of Helen.

mē′nē, mē′nē, tek′el, ū·phär′sin, [Aram.] numbered, numbered, weighed, (and) divided: in the Bible, the writing on the wall, interpreted by Daniel to mean that God had weighed Belshazzar and his kingdom, found them wanting, and would destroy them. Dan. v. 25.

men′fōlk″ (fōk″), *n.pl.* men: also *menfolks.* [Dial.]

meng, *v.i.* to mingle; to mix. [Obs.]

men·hā′den, *n.* [Am. Ind.] a salt-water fish of North America, *Brevoortia tyrannus*, allied to the shad, and valued for its oil and as a fertilizer.

men′hir, *n.* [Fr.; Bret. *men*, stone, and *hir*, high, long.] in archaeology, one of a class of large monumental stones left rough and unhewn, sometimes sculptured and inscribed with writing or runes, erected probably as memorials by the prehistoric inhabitants of Brittany and northern Europe.

mē′ni·ăl, *a.* [OFr. *menial*, *mesnial*, pertaining to a household, from *meisnee*, *maisonage*, a household, from L. *mansio* (*-onis*), a house, mansion.]

1. belonging to a retinue or train of servants; serving.

2. of or fit for servants; as, *menial* tasks; hence, servile; low; mean.

mē′ni·ăl, *n.* 1. a domestic servant of humble rank; a person employed in servile work.

2. a servile, low person.

Mé·nière's′ (mā-nyârz′) **dis·ēase′**, [named after *Ménière*, a French physician.] aural vertigo; a disease which manifests itself by deafness accompanied by tinkling sensations and vertigo.

men′i·līte, *n.* [from the place where found.] a brown, impure opal, occurring in flattened, nodular concretions, at Ménilmontant, near Paris.

mē·nin′ġē·ăl, *a.* of or pertaining to the meninges.

mē·nin′ġēs, *n.pl.*; *sing.* **mē′ninx**, [Mod.L., from Gr. *mēninx*, *mēningos*, a membrane.] the three membranes that envelop the brain and the spinal cord; dura mater, arachnoid, and pia mater.

men·in·ġit′iç, *a.* of or having meningitis.

men·in·ġī′tis, *n.* [Mod.L., from Gr. *mēninx*, *mēningos*, a membrane, and *-itis.*] inflammation of the meninges, especially as the result of infection by bacteria or viruses: the three principal forms are spinal, cerebral, and cerebrospinal.

mē·niñ′gō-, mē·niñg′-, [from Gr. *mēninx*, *mēningos*, a membrane.] a combining form used in anatomy and medicine to signify connection with or relation to the meninges or other membranes.

mē·niñ′gō·cēle, *n.* [*meningo-*, and Gr. *kēlē*, a tumor.] a protrusion of the cerebral or spinal meninges, in the form of a tumor, through an opening in the skull; hernia of the brain.

mē·niñ″gō·çoç′çus, *n.*; *pl.* **mē·niñ″gō·çoç′çī**, [*meningo-*, and Gr. *kokkos*, a kernel, a berry.] the bacterium causing cerebrospinal meningitis.

me·niñ·gor·rhā′ġi·à, *n.* [*meningo-*, and Gr. *-rhagia*, from *rhēgnynai*, to break.] hemorrhage of the meninges.

mē′niñx, *n.* sing. of *meninges.*

mē·nis′căl, *a.* pertaining to or resembling a meniscus.

mē·nis′ci·form, *a.* [Gr. *mēniskos*, a crescent, and L. *forma*, form.] crescent-shaped.

mē·nis′çoid, *a.* [Gr. *mēniskos*, a crescent, and *eidos*, resemblance.] resembling a meniscus.

mē·nis′çus, *n.*; *pl.* **mē·nis′çus·es, mē·nis′cī**, [Mod.L.; Gr. *mēniskos*, a crescent, dim. of *mēnē*, the moon, from *mēn*, month.]

1. a crescent; any crescent-shaped body.

2. in optics, a lens convex on one side and concave on the other, and thicker in the middle than elsewhere.

3. in anatomy, an interarticular fibrocartilage of disklike shape, serving to adapt the articular surfaces to each other.

4. in physics, the curved upper surface of a column of liquid: as a result of capillarity it is convex when the walls of the container are dry, concave when they are wet.

A B

MENISCUS

A, convex meniscus of mercury; B, concave meniscus of water

Men″i·spẽr·mā′cē·ae, *n.pl.* [Gr. *mēnē*, the moon, and *sperma*, a seed.] the moonseed family of plants, chiefly tropical, climbing woody plants and herbs with alternate leaves and small flowers, yielding narcotic and toxic substances. *Menispermum* is the type genus.

men″i·spẽr·mā′ceous, *a.* designating or of the moonseed family of plants.

men·i·spẽr′mine, *n.* [*Menispermum* and *-ine.*] an alkaloid obtained as a white, crystalline, tasteless powder from the shell of the fruit of the *Anamirta cocculus*, formerly called *Menispermum cocculus.*

Men·i·spẽr′mum, *n.* [Gr. *mēnē*, the moon, and *sperma*, seed.] the type genus of climbing plants of the moonseed family, *Menispermaceæ.*

men′i·vẽr, *n.* miniver. [Obs.]

Men′nŏn·īte, Men′nŏn·ist, *n.* a member of an evangelical Protestant Christian sect founded in Friesland by Menno Simons during the first half of the sixteenth century and still flourishing in Europe and the United States. They reject infant baptism, believe in baptism only on profession of faith, accept the New Testament as the only rule of faith, and are opposed to the taking of oaths, military service, and the acceptance of public office. They lead lives of great simplicity, both secularly and religiously, and often live in separate communities.

men′ō-, [from Gr. *mēn*, *mēnos*, month.] a combining form used chiefly in medical or physiological terms and meaning *of* or *pertaining to the menses.*

me′nō, *adv.* [It., less.] in music, less; as, *meno* presto, less rapid.

men′ō·brañçh, men·ō·brañ′çhus, *n.* [Gr. *menein*, to remain, and *branchia*, gills.] a large tailed American amphibian of the genus *Necturus*, belonging to the salamander species, and having permanent external gills.

mē·nol′ō·ġy, men·ō·lō′ġi·um, *n.*; *pl.* **mē·nol′ō·ġies**, *or* **men·ō·lō′ġi·à**, [LL. *menologium*; L.Gr. *mēnologion*, a calendar of months; Gr. *mēn*, a month, and *logos*, an account, discourse, from *legein*, to speak.]

1. a calendar of the months, with their events.

2. a register of the saints, with brief biographies of each, arranged according to months and days, as in the Greek Church.

men′ō·pause, *n.* [*meno-*, and Gr. *pausis*, a cessation.] the permanent cessation of menstruation, normally between the ages of 45 and 50, or the period during which this occurs; female climacteric, or change of life.

Men·ō·pō′mà, *n.* [Gr. *menein*, to remain, and *pōma*, a lid; so called from the persistence of the gill openings.] a genus of amphibians including the hellbender.

men·ō′rāh, *n.* [Heb. *menōrah*, lamp stand; akin to Ar. *manārah*, lamp.] a candelabrum, as (a) one with seven branches, a traditional symbol of Judaism; (b) one with nine branches, used during the festival of Hanukkah.

men·ŏr·rhā′ġi·à, *n.* [*meno-*, and Gr. *-rhagia*, a flowing, from *rhēgnynai*, to burst forth, to flow.] excessive menstrual flow.

men·ŏr·rhē′à, *n.* menorrhagia.

men·os·tā′si·à, *n.* same as *menostasis.*

me·nos′tà·sis, *n.* [*meno-*, and Gr. *stasis*, a standing, from *histanai*, to stand.]

1. menstrual impulse without a flow of the menses.

2. the pains preceding menstruation.

men′ōw, *n.* a minnow. [Obs.]

men′sà, *n.*; *pl.* **men′sae**, [L. table.] a table or tablelike object; specifically, (a) the upper part or top of an altar; (b) in anatomy, the grinding surface of a molar.

men′săl, *a.* of or used at the table.

men′săl, *a.* [L. *mensis*, a month.] monthly.

mense, *n.* manly conduct; dignified manner; civility. [Scot. and Brit. Dial.]

mense, *v.t.* to garnish; to grace. [Scot. and Brit. Dial.]

mense′ful, *a.* discreet; judicious; prudent; becoming. [Scot. and Brit. Dial.]

mense′less, *a.* lacking discretion; unbecoming. [Scot. and Brit. Dial.]

men′sēs, *n.pl.* [L., pl. of *mensis*, month.] the periodic flow of blood from the uterus, discharged through the genital tract: it normally occurs in women about every four weeks, from puberty to menopause.

Men′she·vik, men′she·vik, *n.*; *pl.* **Men′she·viks, Men′she·vi·ki,** [Russ. (1903), from *menshe*, the smaller, less, minority.]

1. (a) originally, a member of the minority faction (*Mensheviki*) of the Social Democratic Party of Russia, who fought the more radical majority faction (*Bolsheviki*) from 1903 on; (b) after November, 1917, a member of a political group of similar views, which opposed the policies, action, and methods of the Soviet government and the Communist (Bolshevik) Party.

2. a person who has Menshevik views and traits: hostile term as applied by Communists.

Men′she·vik, men′she·vik, *a.* of or characteristic of the Mensheviks or Menshevism.

Men′she·viṣm, men′she·viṣm, *n.* the policies and practices of the Mensheviks.

Men′she·vist, men′she·vist, *n.* and *a.* same as *Menshevik.*

menṣ sā′nȧ in cor′pō·rē sā′nō, [L.] a sound mind in a sound body.

men′strụ·ăl, *a.* [L. *menstrualis*, monthly, from *mensis*, month.]

1. of the menses.
2. in astronomy, monthly.
3. of or pertaining to a menstruum.

men′strụ·ănt, *a.* [L. *menstruans* (*-antis*), ppr. of *menstruare*, to menstruate, from *menstruus*, monthly, from *mensis*, a month.] subject to menstruation.

men′strụ·āte, *v.i.*; menstruated, *pt., pp.*; menstruating, *ppr.* to have a discharge of the menses.

men·strụ·ā′tion, *n.* a discharge of the menses; also, the period of menstruating.

men′strụe, *n.* a menstruum. [Obs.]

men′strụ·ous, *a.* [L. *menstruus*, of or pertaining to a month, monthly, from *mensis*, a month.]

1. having the menses.
2. pertaining to the menses.

men′strụ·um, *n.*; *pl.* **men′strụ·umṣ, men′strụ·ȧ,** [LL., neut. of L. *menstruus*, monthly, from *mensis*, a month; prob. because the old chemists thought the moon had some influence upon the preparation of solvents.] a solvent; a liquid that dissolves a solid.

men′sū·ăl (-shū-) *a.* monthly; of or pertaining to a month.

men″sū·rȧ·bil′i·ty, *n.* the quality or state of being mensurable.

men′sū·rȧ·ble, *a.* [LL. *mensurabilis*, that can be measured, from *mensurare*, to measure, from L. *mensura*, a measuring.]

1. measurable; capable of being measured.
2. in music, having fixed rhythm and measure.

men′sū·rȧ·ble·ness, *n.* the quality or condition of being mensurable.

men′sū·răl, *a.* [LL. *mensuralis*, from L. *mensura*, a measuring.]

1. of measure.
2. in music, mensurable.

men′sū·rāte, *v.t.* to measure. [Rare.]

men·sū·rā′tion, *n.* [LL. *mensuratio* (*-onis*), a measuring, from *mensurare*, to measure, from L. *mensura*, a measure.]

1. the act, process, or art of measuring or taking the dimensions of anything.

2. the branch of mathematics that treats of methods for finding length of lines, area of surfaces, and volume of solids.

men′sū·rā·tive, *a.* for measuring.

-ment, [Fr.; L. *-mentum*.] a noun-forming suffix added to verbs, verb stems, or, rarely, adjectives, meaning: (a) *a result* or *product of the* (specified) *action*, as in improve*ment*, pave*ment*; (b) *a means, agency*, or *instrument for the* (specified) *action*, as in adorn*ment*, escape*ment*; (c) *the act, fact, process*, or *art of doing the* (specified) *act*, as in measure*ment*, move*ment*; (d) *the state, condition, fact*, or *degree of being acted upon in the* (specified) *way*, as in disappoint*ment*. Final *y* after a consonant becomes *i* before *-ment*, as in embodi*ment*.

ment, *v.* obsolete past participle of *meng*.

men·tag′rȧ, *n.* [L., from *mentum*, the chin, and Gr. *agra*, a catching, taking.] sycosis.

men′tăl, *a.* [L. *mentum*, the chin.] of or pertaining to the chin; as, the *mental* nerves.

men′tăl, *n.* a plate or scale covering the chin, as of a fish or reptile.

men′tăl, *a.* [ME.; Late OFr.; LL. *mentalis*, of or pertaining to the mind, from L. *mens*, *mentis*, mind.]

1. of or for the mind or intellect; as, *mental* powers, *mental* aids.

2. done by, or carried on in, the mind (i.e., without using written symbols); as, *mental* arithmetic.

3. diseased in mind; mentally ill; as, a *mental* patient.

4. for the mentally ill; as, a *mental* hospital.

mental age; an individual's degree of mental development measured in terms of the chronological age of the average individual of corresponding mental ability.

mental alienation; insanity.

mental arithmetic; the process or act of solving arithmetical problems without the aid of written figures.

mental blindness; a failure to recognize objects for what they are. Often used of a person who refuses to accept the facts of a situation.

mental deficiency; lack of some mental function or functions present in the normal individual; congenital subnormality of intelligence; amentia; feeble-mindedness: it ranges from idiocy to moronity.

mental healing; the treatment of diseases or disorders by mental concentration or hypnotic suggestion.

mental reservation; a qualification (of a statement) that one makes to himself but does not express.

Syn.—intellectual, metaphysical, psychical, psychological.

men·tal′i·ty, *n.*; *pl.* **men·tal′i·tieṣ,** mental power, capacity, or activity; mind.

men″tăl·ī·zā′tion, *n.* the operation of the mind; mental action.

men′tăl·īze, *v.t.* to cultivate the mind or intellect of.

men′tăl·ly, *adv.* 1. in, with, or by the mind.
2. as regards the mind.

Men′thȧ, *n.* [L. *mentha*, mint.] a genus of herbs, the mints, of which the peppermint is the best-known species, characterized by opposite leaves and small flowers forming dense axillary clusters.

men·thā′ceous, *a.* [from L. *mentha*, mint; and *-aceous*.] designating or of a group of plants of the mint family, including spearmint and peppermint.

men′thēne, *n.* [from *menth*ol and *-ene*.] a colorless, oily hydrocarbon, $C_{10}H_{18}$, derived from oil of peppermint or from menthol by dehydration.

men′thol, *n.* [L. *mentha*, mint, and *oleum*, oil.] a white, waxy, crystalline alcohol, $C_{10}H_{19}OH$, obtained from oil of peppermint and used in medicine and perfumery: also called *mint camphor* and *peppermint camphor*.

men′thō·lāt·ed, *a.* containing menthol; treated or impregnated with menthol.

men′thyl, *n.* the basic radical of menthol.

men·ti·cul′tūr·ăl, *a.* [L. *mens*, *mentis*, mind, and *cultura*, culture.] of or pertaining to culture of the mind. [Rare.]

men′tion, *n.* [ME. *mencion*; OFr. *mention*; L. *mentio* (*-onis*), a calling to mind, a cursory speaking of, mention, from *meminisse*, to have in mind.]

1. a brief, often incidental, reference (to) or statement (about); a mentioning.

2. trace; indication. [Rare.]

to make mention of; to mention.

men′tion, *v.t.*; mentioned, *pt., pp.*; mentioning, *ppr.* to refer to or speak about briefly or incidentally; to specify, as by name.

not to mention; without even mentioning.

men′tion·ȧ·ble, *a.* that may or can be mentioned; fit to be mentioned.

men·tō·hy′oid, *a.* [L. *mentum*, chin, and E. *hyoid*.] pertaining to the chin and the hyoid bone.

men″tō·meck·ē′li·ăn, *a.* [L. *mentum*, chin, and Eng. *Meckelian*.] of or pertaining to the distal portion of Meckel's cartilage, or to the chin and lower jaw.

men″tō·meck·ē′li·ăn, *n.* a cartilage or bone forming the distal extremity of the lower jaw.

men·ton·nière′ (tō-nyär′), *n.* [Fr., from *menton*, L. *mentum*, the chin.] a defense for the chin or under part of the face and throat, worn in tournaments. It was fastened to the helmet and upper part of the breastplate, and generally supplied with a small opening on one side to admit of breathing freely.

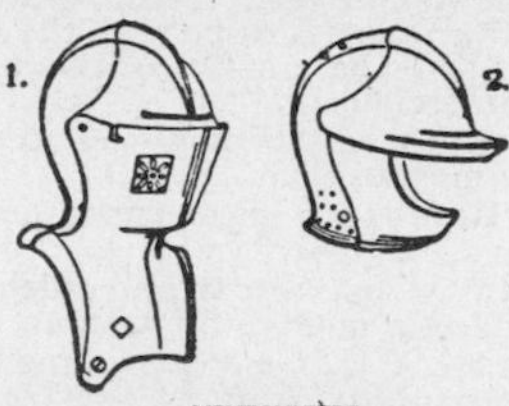

MENTONNIÈRE
1. tilting helmet with mentonnière attached; 2. the helmet without the mentonnière

men′tŏr, *n.* [from *Mentor*, the friend and counselor of Odysseus and Telemachus.] a wise and faithful counselor.

men·tō′ri·ăl, *a.* containing advice or admonition.

men′tum, *n.*; *pl.* **men′tȧ,** [L., the chin.]

1. a chin; specifically, (a) in mammals, the anterior and inferior margin of the mandible or lower jaw; (b) in insects, the postoral plate formed by the fused basal joints of the maxillae.

2. in botany, a projection in front of the flowers of some orchids, caused by the extension of the foot of the column.

men′ū (*or* mā′nū; *Fr.* mȧ-nü′), *n.*; *pl.* **men′ūṣ** (*Fr.* -nü′), [Fr., small, detailed, from L. *minutus*, pp. of *minuere*, to lessen, from *minor*, less.]

1. a detailed list of the foods served at a meal; bill of fare.

2. the foods served.

Mē·nū′rȧ, *n.* [Gr. *mēnē*, the moon, and *oura*, a tail.] a genus of birds inhabiting New South Wales, the only known species of which is the lyrebird.

mē·ow′, mē·ou′ (*or* myou), *n.* [echoic.] the characteristic vocal sound made by a cat: also *miaow, mew*, etc.

mē·ow′, mē·ou′, *v.i.* to make the vocal sound characteristic of a cat.

Mē·phis′tō, *n.* same as *Mephistopheles.*

Mē″phis·tō·phē′lē·ăn, *a.* 1. of Mephistopheles.

2. like Mephistopheles; fiendish, diabolical, crafty, malevolent, sardonic, etc.

Also spelled *Mephistophelian.*

Meph·i·stoph′e·lēṣ, *n.* [G.: of obscure origin.]

1. in medieval legend, a devil to whom Faust, or Faustus, sold his soul for riches and power: a leading character in Goethe's *Faust*, Marlowe's *Dr. Faustus*, Gounod's opera *Faust*, etc.

2. a crafty, powerful, malevolent devil; a diabolical person.

Also *Mephisto.*

mē·phit′iç, *a.* [LL. *mephiticus*, from L. *mephitis*, a pestilential exhalation.]

1. of, caused by, or pertaining to mephitis.

2. (a) offensive to the smell; foul; (b) poisonous; noxious.

mephitic air; formerly, carbon dioxide.

mē·phit′iç·ăl, *a.* mephitic.

mē·phī′tis, *n.* [L. *mephitis*, a pestilential exhalation.]

1. a foul, offensive, or noxious vapor coming out of the earth; also, any poisonous stench or bad smell.

2. [M-] a genus of mammals of which the common skunk is the best-known species.

meph′i·tiṣm, *n.* mephitic poisoning.

mē·rā′cious, *a.* strong; racy; unadulterated. [Obs.]

mẽr′çȧ·ble, *a.* merchantable. [Obs.]

mẽr′çăn·tile (*or* -tīl), *a.* [Fr.; It., from *mercante*, a merchant; L. *mercans* (*-antis*), a merchant, a trading.]

1. pertaining to or connected with merchants or trade; relating to trade and commerce, or the buying and selling of goods; commercial.

2. of mercantilism.

mercantile agency; an establishment that gathers and provides for clients information about the credit rating, financial status, etc. of individuals and firms.

mercantile paper; checks, promissory notes, bills of exchange, and other negotiable paper used in business: also called *commercial paper.*

mercantile system; same as *mercantilism.*

mẽr′çăn·til·iṣm, *n.* 1. (a) the doctrine or

policy that the economic interests of the nation as a whole are more important than those of individuals or parts of the nation, that a balance of exports over imports, with a consequent accumulation of bullion, is desirable, and that industry, agriculture, and commerce should be directed toward this objective: it arose in Europe with the decline of feudalism; (b) the practice of this policy.

2. commercialism.

mẽr′căn·til·ist, *n.* a person who advocates or practices mercantilism.

mẽr″căn·til·is′tiç, *a.* of or pertaining to mercantilism.

mẽr·cap′tăl, *n.* [*mercapt*an and *al*dehyde.] any compound of a mercaptan with an aldehyde.

mẽr·cap′tăn, *n.* [LL. *mercurius*, mercury, and L. *captans* (*-antis*), ppr. of *captare*, to take, seize.] any of a class of chemical compounds analogous to the alcohols and characterized by the substitution of sulfur for oxygen in the OH radical: also called *thiol.*

mẽr·cap′tīde, *n.* a metallic salt of a mercaptan, characterized by the substitution of a metal for the hydrogen in the SH radical.

mẽr·cap′tō, *n.* the monovalent radical SH.

Mẽr·cā′tŏr's prō·jec′tion, a method of making maps in which the earth's surface is shown as a rectangle, with the meridians as parallel straight lines spaced at equal intervals and the parallels of latitude as parallel straight lines intersecting the meridians at right angles but spaced further apart as their distance from the equator increases: areas on such maps become increasingly distorted toward the poles.

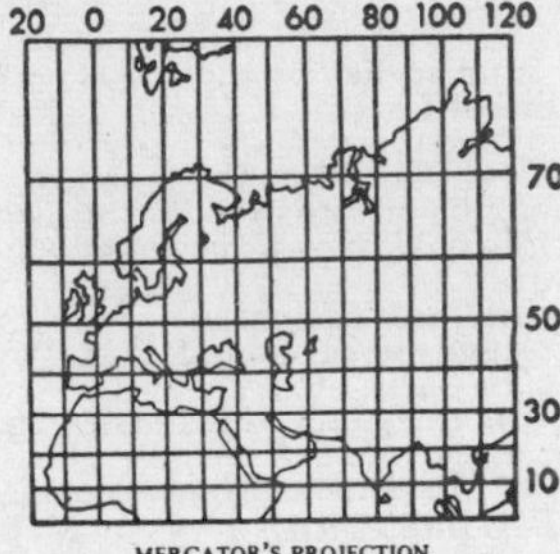

MERCATOR'S PROJECTION

mẽr′cȧ·tūre, *n.* traffic; commerce. [Obs.

mẽr·cē·nā̆r′i·ăn, *n.* a mercenary. [Obs.]

mẽr′ce·nā̆r·i·ly, *adv.* in a mercenary manner.

mẽr′ce·nā̆r·i·ness, *n.* the quality or state of being mercenary.

mẽr′ce·nā̆r·y, *a.* [L. *mercenarius, mercennarius*, hired for pay, hireling, from *merces*, pay, reward.]

1. working or done for payment only; motivated by a desire for money or other gain; venal; greedy.

2. designating a soldier serving for pay in a foreign army; hired.

mẽr′ce·nā̆r·y, *n.*; *pl.* **mẽr′ce·nā̆r·ieṣ,** 1. a professional soldier serving in a foreign army for pay.

2. a person paid for his work or services; a hireling. [Archaic.]

mẽr′cẽr, *n.* [OFr. *mercier*; LL. *merciarius*, from L. *merx, mercis*, merchandise, wares.] one who deals in textiles. [Brit.]

mẽr′cẽr·īze, *v.t.*; mercerized, *pt., pp.*; mercerizing, *ppr.* to subject (cotton thread or fabric) to the action of caustic alkali, according to a process invented by John Mercer (1791–1866) of Lancashire, England, thus giving a silky luster and greater susceptibility to dyes.

mẽr′cẽr·ship, *n.* the business of a mercer.

mẽr′cẽr·y, *n.*; *pl.* **mẽr′cẽr·ieṣ,** [OFr. *mercerie, mercierie*; LL. *merciaria*, mercer's wares, from *merciarius*, a mercer.] the commodities or goods in which a mercer deals; also, the business or shop of a mercer. [Brit.]

mẽr·chăn·dī′ṣȧ·ble, *a.* capable of being used as merchandise.

mẽr′chăn·dīṣe, *n.* [OFr. *marchandise, marchaundise*, from *marchant*, a merchant.]

1. the objects of commerce; wares; goods; commodities; whatever is usually bought or sold in trade.

2. trade; traffic; commerce. [Obs.]

mẽr′chăn·dīṣe, *v.t.* and *v.i.*; merchandised, *pt., pp.*; merchandising, *ppr.* to buy and sell; to carry on trade in (some kind of goods).

mẽr′chăn·dī·ṣẽr, *n.* a merchant.

mẽr′chăn·dīze, *n., v.t.* and *v.i.* same as *merchandise.* [Obs.]

mẽr′chăn·dī·zẽr, *n.* same as *merchandiser.*

mẽr′chănd·ry, *n.* commerce. [Obs.]

mẽr′chănt, *n.* [OFr. *marchant, marcheant*, a trader, merchant, from L. *mercans* (*-antis*), ppr. of *mercari*, to trade, buy, from *merx, mercis*, merchandise, wares.]

1. a person whose business is buying and selling goods for profit; a trader, especially one in the wholesale trade who deals with foreign countries.

2. a person who sells goods at retail; storekeeper; shopkeeper.

3. a merchantman. [Obs.]

4. a supercargo. [Obs.]

mẽr′chănt, *a.* 1. pertaining to merchants or merchandise; relating to commerce; commercial.

2. of the merchant marine.

merchant bar, merchant iron; iron in the form of bars of commercial sizes.

merchant marine; all the ships of a nation engaged in commerce on the high seas; also, their personnel.

merchant prince; a rich merchant.

merchant service; the mercantile marine; marine commerce.

merchant ship; a ship in the merchant service.

merchant tailor; a tailor who provides the materials for the clothing he makes.

mẽr′chănt, *v.i.* to trade; to buy and sell goods. [Rare.]

mẽr′chănt·ȧ·ble, *a.* marketable; that can be or is usually marketed.

mẽr′chănt·like, *a.* like a merchant.

mẽr′chănt·măn, *n.*; *pl.* **mẽr′chănt·men,** 1. a ship used in the transportation of goods, as distinguished from a ship of war.

2. a merchant. [Archaic.]

mẽr′chănt·ry, *n.* 1. merchants collectively.

2. commerce; mercantile business.

mer·cī′ (mär-), *interj.* [Fr.] thanks; thank you.

mẽr′ci·ȧ·ble, *a.* merciful. [Obs.]

Mẽr′ci·ăn (-shiun), *a.* of Mercia, a former Anglo-Saxon kingdom, its people, or their dialects.

Mẽr′ci·ăn, *n.* 1. a native or inhabitant of Mercia, a former Anglo-Saxon kingdom.

2. the Anglo-Saxon dialects of the Mercians.

3. sometimes, the Middle English dialects descended from these; Midland dialects.

mer·cī′ beau·coup′ (mär-sē′ bō-ko͞o′), [Fr.] thanks very much.

mẽr′ci·fụl, *a.* having, feeling, or exercising mercy; compassionate; tender; unwilling to punish for injuries; exhibiting mercy.

mẽr′ci·fụl·ly, *adv.* in a merciful manner.

mẽr′ci·fụl·ness, *n.* the state or quality of being merciful.

mẽr′ci·fȳ, *v.t.* to pity. [Obs.]

mẽr′ci·less, *a.* without mercy; unfeeling; pitiless; hardhearted; cruel; as a, *merciless* tyrant.

mẽr′ci·less·ly, *adv.* in a merciless manner.

mẽr′ci·less·ness, *n.* lack of mercy or pity.

mẽr″cūr·am·mō′ni·um, *n.* a basic compound of mercury and ammonia, in which part or all of the hydrogen is replaced by mercury.

mẽr′çū·rāte, *v.t.*; mercurated, *pt., pp.*; mercurating, *ppr.* to treat or combine with mercury or a compound of mercury.

mẽr·çū′ri·ăl, *a.* [L. *Mercurialis*, of or pertaining to Mercury, from *Mercurius*, the god Mercury.]

1. [M—] of Mercury (the god or planet).

2. of or containing mercury.

3. caused by the action or use of mercury.

4. having qualities attributed to the god Mercury or supposedly influenced by the planet Mercury; eloquent, clever, shrewd, thievish, etc.

5. having qualities like those of mercury; quick, quick-witted, volatile, changeable, fickle, etc.

mẽr·çū′ri·ăl, *n.* 1. a drug or preparation of mercury.

2. a person of mercurial temperament.

mẽr·çū′ri·ăl·iṣm, *n.* chronic poisoning caused by mercury or its compounds

mẽr·çū′ri·ăl·ist, *n.* one under the influence of Mercury, or one resembling Mercury in fickleness of character. [Obs.]

mẽr·çū′ri·ăl·īze, *v.t.*; mercurialized, *pt., pp.*; mercurializing, *ppr.* 1. to make mercurial.

2. to treat with mercury or a compound of mercury.

mẽr·çū′ri·ăl·ly, *adv.* in a mercurial manner.

Mẽr·cū′ri·ăn, *a.* of or pertaining to the god or planet Mercury.

mẽr·çū′riç, *a.* of or containing mercury, especially with a valence of two.

mercuric chloride; a very poisonous, white, crystalline compound $HgCl_2$, used in engraving and as an antiseptic: also called *corrosive sublimate, bichloride of mercury, mercury chloride.*

mercuric oxide; a poisonous red powder, HgO, used as a chemical reagent and in the manufacture of pigment, cosmetics, and polishing compounds.

mẽr·çu″ri·fi·çā′tion, *n.* 1. the process or operation of obtaining mercury in its liquid form from minerals.

2. the act or condition of combination with mercury.

mẽr·çū′ri·fȳ, *v.t.* 1. to obtain mercury from (an ore) by heat and condensation of the vapor.

2. to mercurialize; to mix with mercury.

mẽr·çū′rō·çhrōme, *n.* [L. *Mercurius*, Mercury, and Gr. *chroma*, color.]

1. a red, crystalline dye, $C_{20}H_8O_6Br_2Na_2Hg$.

2. an aqueous solution of this, used as an antiseptic.

A trade-mark (*Mercurochrome*).

mẽr·çū′rous, *a.* of or containing mercury, especially with a valence of one.

Mẽr′çū·ry, *n.* [L. *Mercurius*, Mercury, the god of commerce, prob. from *merx, mercis*, wares, trade.]

1. in Roman mythology, the messenger of the gods, god of commerce, manual skill, eloquence, cleverness, travel, and thievery: identified with the Greek Hermes.

2. the smallest planet in the solar system and the nearest to the sun: diameter, c. 3,000 mi.; diurnal rotation and year, 88 days; symbol, ☿.

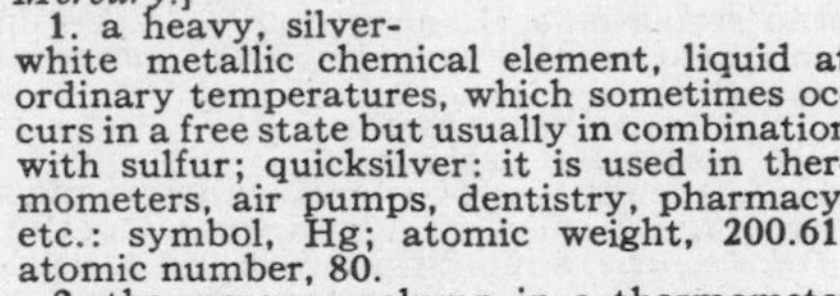
MERCURY

mẽr′çū·ry, *n.*; *pl.* **mẽr′çū·rieṣ,** [from *Mercury.*]

1. a heavy, silver-white metallic chemical element, liquid at ordinary temperatures, which sometimes occurs in a free state but usually in combination with sulfur; quicksilver: it is used in thermometers, air pumps, dentistry, pharmacy, etc.: symbol, Hg; atomic weight, 200.61; atomic number, 80.

2. the mercury column in a thermometer or barometer.

3. a messenger or guide.

4. a European plant with edible stems used like asparagus and leaves used like spinach: one variety (*dog's mercury*) is poisonous.

mercury chloride; mercuric chloride.

three-seeded mercury; any of various species of the genus *Acalypha*, allied to the genus *Mercurialis.*

mẽr′çū·ry, *v.t.* to wash with a preparation of mercury. [Obs.]

mẽr′çū·ry-vā′pŏr lamp, a glass tube or bulb in which an electric discharge passes through mercury vapor, causing it to give off a bluish-green light rich in ultraviolet and actinic rays.

Mẽr·çū′ti·ō (-shi-ō), *n.* in Shakespeare's *Romeo and Juliet*, a gay, witty, brave young nobleman, a friend of Romeo.

mẽr′cy, *n.*; *pl.* **mẽr′cieṣ,** [ME. *mercy, merci*; OFr. *merci*; LL. *merces* (*-edis*), thanks, mercy, pardon; L. *merces* (*-edis*), reward, condition, income.]

1. a refraining from harming or punishing offenders, enemies, persons in one's power, etc.; kindness in excess of what may be expected or demanded by fairness; forbearance and compassion.

2. a disposition to forgive, pity, or be kind.

3. the power to forgive or be kind; clemency; as, throw yourself on his *mercy.*

4. kind or compassionate treatment; relief of suffering.

5. a fortunate thing; a thing to be grateful for; a blessing; as, it's a *mercy* he's still alive.

at the mercy of; completely in the power of.

mẽr′cy, *interj.* a mild exclamation expressing surprise, annoyance, emphasis, etc.

Sisters of Mercy; members of various religious congregations of women founded for the purpose of nursing the sick, giving aid to the poor, and similar works of charity and mercy.

mẽr′cy kill′ing, euthanasia.

mẽr′cy sēat, 1. in ancient Jewish ritual, the gold covering on the Ark of the Covenant, which was sprinkled once a year with the blood of sacrificial animals and regarded as the resting place of God: Ex. xxv. 17.
 2. the throne of God or Christ.

mẽrd, *n.* dung. [Obs.]

mẽr·div′ō·rous, *a.* scatophagous; dung-eating, as some insects.

mēre, *a.*; *superl.* merest, [L. *merus,* unmixed.]
 1. nothing more or other than; only (as said to be); as, he's a *mere* boy.
 2. unmixed; pure; unqualified; absolute. [Obs.]
 This is *mere* falsehood. —Shak.

me′rẹ, *n.* same as *meri.*

mēre, *n.* [AS. *mere,* a lake, a pool, the sea.]
 1. (a) the sea; (b) an arm of the sea.
 2. a lake or pond.
 3. a marsh.
 [Archaic, Poetic, or Brit. Dial. in all senses.]

mēre, *n.* [ME. *meer, mere*; AS. *gemære,* a boundary, limit.] a boundary. [Archaic or Brit. Dial.]

mēre, *v.t.* and *v.i.* to divide; to limit; to set bounds. [Obs.]

mēre, *n.* a mare. [Obs.]

-mēre, [from Gr. *meros,* a part.] a combining form meaning *part,* as in blasto*mere.*

mēre′ly, *adv.* 1. no more than; only; solely; simply; for this and no other purpose.
 2. entirely; purely. [Obs.]

me·reñ′chy·mȧ, *n.* [Gr. *meros,* part, and *parenchyma,* anything poured in beside.] in botany, tissue with ellipsoidal or spheroidal cells.

mēreṣ′măn, *n.* an officer who locates boundaries. [Archaic or Brit. Dial.]

mēre′stōne, *n.* a stone that marks a boundary. [Archaic or Brit. Dial.]

mer·ē·tri′cious, *a.* [L. *meretricius,* from *meretrix,* a prostitute.]
 1. originally, of, like, or characteristic of a prostitute.
 2. alluring by false, showy charms; speciously attractive; fleshy; tawdry.

mer·ē·tri′cious·ly, *adv.* in a meretricious manner.

mer·ē·tri′cious·ness, *n.* the quality or state of being meretricious; false allurement.

mẽr·gan′sẽr, *n.*; *pl.* **mẽr·gan′sẽrṣ** or **mẽr·gan′sẽr,** [Mod. L., from L. *mergus,* diver (bird), and *anser,* goose.] any of several large, fish-eating, diving ducks with a long, slender, toothed beak hooked at the tip and, usually, a crested head: also called *goosander.*

mẽrġe, *v.t.* and *v.i.*; merged, *pt., pp.*; merging, *ppr.* [L. *mergere,* to dive, dip, immerse, sink into.] to lose or cause to lose identity by being absorbed, swallowed up, or combined; to unite indistinguishably.

mẽr′ġence, *n.* a merging or being merged.

mẽr′ġẽr, *n.* 1. a merging; specifically, (a) the combination of several companies, corporations, etc. in one, as by issuing stock of the controlling corporation to replace the greater part of that of the others; (b) the absorption of one estate, interest, obligation, contract, etc. in another, or of a lesser offense in a greater.
 2. a person or thing that merges.

me′ri, *n.* a Maori war club.

mer′i·çȧrp, *n.* [Gr. *meros,* part, and *karpos,* fruit.] either of the two halves, or carpels, of the seed of an umbelliferous plant.

mer′ide, *n.* same as *meris.*

mē·rid′i·ăn, *n.* [L. *meridianus,* pertaining to midday, or to the south, from *meridies,* midday, the south; *medius,* middle, and *dies,* day.]
 1. the highest apparent point reached by a heavenly body in its course.
 2. (a) the highest point of power, prosperity, splendor, etc.; zenith; apex; culmination; (b) the middle period of one's life, regarded as the highest point of health, vigor, etc.; prime.

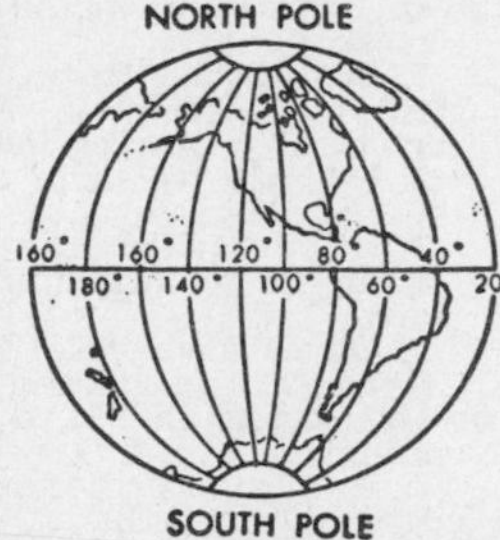

MERIDIANS

 3. noon. [Obs.]
 4. in astronomy, an imaginary great circle of the celestial sphere passing through the poles of the heavens and the zenith and nadir of any given point, and cutting the equator at right angles.
 5. in geography, (a) a great circle of the earth passing through the geographical poles and any given point on the earth's surface; (b) the half of such a circle between the poles; (c) any of the lines of longitude running north and south on a globe or map, representing such a circle or half circle.
 6. (a) a place or situation with its own distinctive character; (b) distinctive character.
 7. a graduated ring of brass, in which a globe is suspended and revolves.
 first meridian; see *prime meridian* under *prime.*
 magnetic meridian; a great circle, parallel with the direction of the magnetic needle, and passing through its poles.
 principal meridian; a carefully located meridian from which secondary or guide meridians may be constructed.

mē·rid′i·ăn, *a.* 1. of or at noon or, especially, of the position or power of the sun at noon.
 2. of or passing through the highest point in the daily course of any heavenly body.
 3. of or along a meridian.
 4. of or at the highest point of prosperity, splendor, power, etc.
 5. southern. [Rare.]

mē·rid′i·ăn cĩr′çle, a transit instrument with a graduated circle fastened at right angles to the horizontal axis and turning with it.

mē·rid′i·ō·năl, *a.* 1. southern; southerly.
 2. of or characteristic of the south or people living in the south (of Europe, especially France).
 3. of or like a meridian.
 meridional parts; the distance from the equator to any given latitude shown on a Mercator's projection as expressed in minutes of the equator.

mē·rid′i·ō·năl, *n.* [*often* M–] an inhabitant of the south (of Europe, especially France).

mē·rid″i·ō·nal′i·ty, *n.* 1. the state of being in the meridian.
 2. position in the south; aspect toward the south.

mē·rid′i·ō·năl·ly, *adv.* 1. north and south.
 2. in the direction of the poles (of a magnet).

mer·i·hed′riç, *a.* [Gr. *meros,* part, and *hedra,* side.] pertaining to less than the full number of sides of a polyhedron, taken in some regular system.

mē·ringue′ (-rang′), *n.* [Fr.]
 1. egg whites beaten stiff and mixed with sugar, often browned in the oven and used as a covering for pies, cakes, etc.
 2. a small cake made of this, often filled with fruit, etc.
 meringue glacée; a dessert made of ice cream and meringue.

me·rï′nō, *n.*; *pl.* **me·rï′nōṣ,** [Sp., roving from pasture to pasture, from *merino,* an inspector of sheepwalks, a shepherd, a royal judge, from ML. *majorinus,* the head of a village, a steward, from L. *major,* greater.]
 1. one of a hardy breed of sheep with long, fine, silky wool, originally from Spain.
 2. the wool.
 3. a fine, soft yarn made from this wool, used to make stockings, underwear, etc.
 4. a soft, thin woolen cloth made of this wool or of something like it.

me·rï′nō, *a.* designating or of merino.

mē′ris, *n.*; *pl.* **mē′ri·dēṣ,** [Gr. *meris* (*-idos*), a part, portion.] in biology, a colony of cells that may remain isolated, or may form zooids, or demes, by gemmation.

mer·is·mat′iç, *a.* [Gr. *merisma* (*-atos*), a part, from *merizein,* to divide, from *meros,* a part.] in biology, dividing by the growth of internal partitions.

mer″is·mo·pē′di·ȧ, *n.* in biology, a tesselated group of cocci or other bacteria, usually found in a multiple of four.

mer′i·spōre, *n.* [Gr. *meris,* a part, division, and *spora,* a seed.] in botany, a single spore or segment of a spore group.

mer′i·stem, *n.* [Gr. *meristos,* divisible, from *merizein,* to divide.] undifferentiated formative tissue, consisting of cells actively growing and dividing, as at the apex of young stems, leaves, and roots.

mer″i·stē·mat′iç, *a.* pertaining to or consisting of meristem.

mer″i·stē·mat′iç·ăl·ly, *adv.* after the manner of meristem.

mer·is″tō·ġē·net′ic, *a.* [Gr. *meristos,* divisible, from *merizein,* to divide, and *genesis,* generation.] developed or produced by meristem.

mer′it, *n.* [OFr. *merite*; L. *meritum,* that which one deserves, desert, from *meritus,* pp. of *merere, mereri,* to deserve, to be worthy of.]
 1. [*sometimes pl.*] the state, fact, or quality of deserving well or, sometimes, ill; desert.
 2. worth; value; excellence.
 3. something deserving reward, praise, or gratitude.
 4. a reward or honor given for praiseworthy qualities or conduct; a mark, badge, etc. awarded for excellence.
 5. [*pl.*] actual qualities or facts, good or bad; as, decide the question on its *merits.*
 Syn.—goodness, worth, worthiness, desert, excellence.

mer′it, *v.t.*; merited, *pt., pp.*; meriting, *ppr.* [OFr. *mériter*; L. *meritare,* intens. of *merere,* to earn, acquire, deserve.]
 1. to deserve; to earn by service or performance; to have a right to claim.
 Those best can bear reproof who *merit* praise. —Pope.
 2. to reward. [Obs.]

mer′it, *v.i.* to be benefited or to profit by anything; to acquire desert. [Obs.]

mer′it·ȧ·ble, *a.* deserving a reward. [Obs.]

mer′it·ed, *a.* deserved.

mer′it·ed·ly, *adv.* according to merit or desert; deservedly.

mer′i·thăl, *n.* in botany, same as *internode.*

mer′it·mŏn″ġẽr, *n.* one who depends on good works for salvation.

mer·i·tō′ri·ous, *a.* [L. *meritorius,* that brings in money, from *meritus,* pp. of *merere, mereri,* to earn, gain, deserve.]
 1. deserving reward or notice; worthy of fame, happiness, or praise.
 2. hireling; earning money. [Obs.]

mer·i·tō′ri·ous·ly, *adv.* in a meritorious manner.

mer·i·tō′ri·ous·ness, *n.* the state or quality of being meritorious.

mer′i·tō·ry, *a.* deserving reward; meritorious. [Obs.]

mer′it sys′tem, a system of hiring and promoting people to civil service positions on the basis of merit as determined by competitive examinations.

merk (märk), *n.* [Scot., from AS. *marc,* weight.] an old coin of Scotland; a mark or marc.

mẽr′kin, *n.* a cannon mop. [Obs.]

mẽrl, mẽrle, *n.* [OFr. *merle*; L. *merula,* a blackbird.] the European blackbird. [Archaic or Poetic.]

mẽr′lin, *n.* [OFr. *emerillon, esmerillon,* dim. of *esmeril,* merlin, from O.H.G. *smirl,* merlin.]
 1. a species of small falcon, *Falco æsalon,* of Europe.
 2. a related and similar American bird, the pigeon-hawk.

MERLIN
(*Falco æsolon*)

Mẽr′lin, *n.* in medieval legend, a magician and seer, helper of King Arthur.

mẽr′ling, *n.* a fish, the European whiting. [Obs.]

mẽr′lŏn, *n.* [Fr.] the solid part of a battlement or parapet that lies between two embrasures.

mẽr′lūce, *n.* [Fr. *merluche, merlus,* a hake.] the European hake, *Merlucius vulgaris.*

mẽr′māid, *n.* [AS. *mere,* a lake, sea, and *mægd,* a maid.]
 1. a legendary sea creature with the head and trunk of a beautiful woman and the tail of a fish.
 2. a girl or woman who swims well.

mẽr′māid′ṣ-glŏve, *n.* a kind of sponge, *Halichondria oculata,* the branches of which resemble the fingers of a glove.

mẽr′māid′ṣ-head (-hed), *n.* a sea urchin that resembles a head or skull.

mẽr′māid′ṣ-pũrse, *n.* the horny egg case of a shark, ray, or skate.

mẽr′māid weed, an aquatic weed, *Proserpinaca pectinacea,* with leaves resembling the teeth of a comb.

mẽr′măn, *n.*; *pl.* **mẽr′men,** 1. a legendary

sea creature with the head and trunk of a man and the tail of a fish.

2. a man or boy who swims well.

mer'ō-, [from Gr. *meros*, part.] a combining form meaning *part*, as in *mero*blast, *mero*some, *Mero*stomata.

mer'ō·blast, *n.* [*mero-*, and Gr. *blastos*, a germ.] an ovum composed partly of germinal matter: opposed to *holoblast*.

mer·ō·blas'tiç, *a.* designating or of ova that undergo only partial segmentation.

mē'rō·cēle, *n.* [Gr. *mēros*, thigh, and *kēlē*, a tumor.] hernia occurring through a canal of the thigh; femoral hernia.

mer'ō·cȳte, *n.* [*mero-*, and Gr. *kytos*, a hollow vessel.] a nucleus of an unsegmented ovum; the nucleus of a yolk or cell.

mer·ō·gas'trū·lȧ, *n.* [*mero-* and *gastrula*.] a gastrula originating in and developed from a meroblastic ovum.

mer·ō·ġen'e·sis, *n.* [*mero-*, and Gr. *genesis*, generation.] in biology, a process of segmentation by which similar parts unite to form a complex aggregate individual.

mer·ō·hē'drăl, *a.* same as *hemihedral*.

mer·ō·hēd'riṣm, *n.* same as *hemihedrism*.

mer·ō·is'tiç, *a.* [*mero-*, and Gr. *ōon*, an egg, and *-istic*.] having vitelligenous cells as well as ova in the ovary: said of certain insects.

mē·rol'ō·ġy, *n.* [Gr. *meros*, part, and *-logia*, from *legein*, to speak.] the branch of anatomy dealing with the structure of tissues; histology.

mer·ō·mọr'phiç, *a.* [*mero-*, and Gr. *morphē*, form.] in the theory of functions, having the character of a rational fraction.

Mē·rop'i·dae, *n.pl.* [L., from Gr. *merops*, the bee eater.] a family of birds native to the Old World; the bee eaters, of which *Merops* is the type genus.

mē·rop'i·dăn, *n.* a bird belonging to the family of bee eaters, *Meropidæ*.

mē·rop'i·dăn, *a.* of or pertaining to the *Meropidæ*.

mē·rop'ō·dīte, *n.* [Gr. *mēros*, thigh, and *pous*, *podos*, foot, and *-ite*.] the fourth joint in the developed appendage of a crustacean.

mē·rop·ō·dit'iç, *a.* of or resembling a meropodite.

Mē'rops, *n.* [L., from Gr. *merops*, a bird, the bee eater.] a genus of birds resembling the swallow; the bee eaters; the typical genus of the *Meropidæ*.

MEROPIDAN (*Merops apiaster*)

mer·ọr″găn·i·zā'tion, *n.* [*mero-* and *organization*.] a partial or imperfect organization. [Rare.]

mē'ros, *n.* [Gr. *mēros*, thigh.] in anatomy, the thigh.

mer'ō·sōme, *n.* [*mero-*, and Gr. *sōma*, body.] one of the segments of a vertebrate or an articulate animal.

Mer·ō·stō'mȧ·tȧ, *n.pl.* [*mero-*, and Gr. *stōma* (*-atos*), mouth.] an order of *Crustaceæ*, including forms often of gigantic size, in which the mouth is furnished with mandibles and maxillae, the ends of which become walking or swimming feet and organs of prehension.

mer'ō·stōme, *n.* any of the *Merostomata*.

-mēr·ous, [from Gr. *meros*, a part.] a suffix that means *having* (a specified number or kind of) *parts*, *partite*, as in tri*merous* (often written *3-merous*).

Mer·ō·vin'ġi·ăn, *a.* [from LL. *Merovingi*, the descendants of *Merovæus*, a legendary king of the Franks.] designating or of the Frankish line of kings who reigned in Gaul (ancient France) from c. 500 to 752 A.D.: the line was founded by Clovis I.

Mer·ō·vin'ġi·ăn, *n.* a king of the Merovingian line.

mer″ō·zō'īte, *n.* [from *mero-*, and *sporozoa*, and *-ite*.] any of a form of spore produced in the asexual stage in the reproduction of certain protozoa, as the malaria parasite.

mer'ri·ly, *adv.* in a merry manner; with gaiety and laughter; jovially.

Mer'ri·maç, *n.* the first armored warship, a United States frigate equipped by the Confederates with iron armor and used to harass Union shipping until engaged in battle (March 9, 1862) at Hampton Roads by the Monitor, a Union ironclad: Confederate name *Virginia*.

mer'ri·māke, *n.* and *v.i.* same as *merrymake*.

mer'ri·ment, *n.* 1. the act or state of being merry; mirth; gaiety with laughter or noise; hilarity; frolic.

2. something that amuses or entertains. [Obs.]

3. a farce; a short comedy or play. [Obs.]

mer'ri·ness, *n.* the quality or state of being merry; mirth; gaiety; festivity.

mer'ry, *a.*; *comp.* merrier; *superl.* merriest, [ME. *merie*, *myrie*; AS. *merige*, *myrge*, pleasant.]

1. full of fun and laughter; lively and cheerful; gay; mirthful.

2. festive; as, the *merry* month of May.

3. (a) pleasant; (b) amusing; (c) facetious. [Archaic.]

merry dancers; see under *dancers*.

merry men; retainers or followers. [Archaic.]

to make merry; to be full of laughter and gaiety; to be hilarious or festive.

Syn.—cheerful, gay, joyous, lively, mirthful, sportive, sprightly, vivacious.

mer'ry, *n.* the English wild cherry, *Prunus avium*.

mer″ry-an'drew, *n.* [*merry* and *Andrew*, given name: said to be after *Andrew* Boorde, reputed author of jest books in the time of Henry VIII.] a buffoon; a clown.

mer'ry-gō-round″, *n.* 1. a circular, revolving platform with wooden animals and seats on it, used at carnivals, amusement parks, etc.: it is turned by machinery, usually to music; a carrousel.

2. a whirl; a swift round, as of social life or business affairs.

mer'ry·māke, *v.i.*; merrymade, *pt.*, *pp.*; merrymaking, *ppr.* to make merry; to have fun. [Rare.]

mer'ry·māke, *n.* a merrymaking. [Archaic.]

mer'ry·māk″ẽr, *n.* a person taking part in merrymaking.

mer'ry·māk″ing, *a.* producing mirth; promoting good humor; gay and festive.

mer'ry·māk″ing, *n.* 1. a making merry, laughing, and having fun; conviviality; festivity.

2. a cheerful festival or entertainment.

mer'ry·meet″ing, *n.* a merrymaking.

mer'ry·thọught (-thọt), *n.* [from the supposed granting of a wish to the person winning the wishbone contest.] the wishbone.

mer'ry·wing, *n.* a duck, the goldeneye. [Dial.]

mẽrse, *v.t.*; mersed, *pt.*, *pp.*; mersing, *ppr.* [L. *mersare*, freq. of *mergere*, to dip.] to dip or plunge under a liquid; to immerse. [Rare.]

mẽr'sion, *n.* [L. *mersio* (*-onis*), a dipping, from *mergere*, to dip.] the act of sinking or plunging under a liquid; immersion. [Obs.]

Mẽr·ten'si·ȧ, *n.* [after F. C. *Mertens*, a German botanist.] a genus of plants, the lungworts, of the borage family, distinguished mainly by having smooth leaves and blue flowers.

mẽr·thī'ō·lāte, *n.* [from sodium ethyl-*mercuri-thio*salicyl*ate*.] a red or colorless liquid (sodium ethyl-mercuri-thiosalicylate), used as a antiseptic and germicide: it contains over 49 per cent of mercury in organic combination: a trade-mark (*Merthiolate*).

Mē·rụ'li·us, *n.* [L. *merula*, a blackbird.] a genus of fungi, some of the species of which are black.

mē'rus, *n.* same as *meros*.

Mer·vẹ·illeụ̈ṣe' (-yēz'), *n.* [Fr., f. of *merveilleux* marvelous.] a fashionably dressed woman in the time of the French Directory, when an attempt was made in France to revive the styles of the ancient Greeks and Romans.

mer'y·ciṣm, *n.* [Gr. *mērykismos*, from *mērykizein*, to chew the cud.] the regurgitation of food from the stomach; human rumination.

mes-, same as *meso-*.

mẹ'sȧ, *n.* [Sp. *mesa*, from L. *mensa*, a table.] a small, high plateau or flat tableland with steep sides and, often, a layer of rock covering it.

mes·aç'ō·nāte, *n.* a salt of mesaconic acid.

mes·ȧ·çon'iç, *a.* [*mes-* and *aconic*.] relating to or derived from aconic acid.

mes'ad, mes'i·ad, *adv.* [Gr. *mesos*, middle, and L. *ad*, to, toward.] toward the median plane of an organism.

mes'āil, *n.* [OFr. *mézail*.] the vizor of a helmet, especially of a helmet or headpiece made in two sections.

mes'ăl, mes'i·ăn, *a.* [Gr. *mesos*, middle, and *-al*.] of, relating to, or situated on or toward the meson, or median plane.

mé·sal'li·ance (mā-zal'-i-äns), *n.* [Fr.] a marriage with a person of lower social status.

mes'ăl·ly, mes'i·ăl·ly, *adv.* toward the mesial plane; mesad.

mes·ȧ·moe'boid, *n.* [*mes-*, and Gr. *amoibē*, change, and *eidos*, form.] an amoeboid cell developed in the mesoderm.

mes·ȧ·rā'iç, *a.* [Gr. *mesaraion*, mesentery; *mesos*, middle, and *araia*, the flank, belly.] of or pertaining to the mesentery; mesenteric. [Rare.]

mes·ăr·te·rī'tis, *n.* [*mes-*, and Gr. *artēria*, artery, and *-itis*.] inflammation of the middle part of the arterial wall.

mes″ȧ·ti·cē·phal'iç, mes″ȧ·ti·ceph'ȧ·lous, *a.* [Gr. *mesatos*, midmost, and *kephalē*, head.] neither long-headed nor broad-headed; having a medium ratio of length to breadth of cranium.

mes″ȧ·ti·pel'viç, *a.* [Gr. *mesatos*, midmost, and L. *pelvis*, a basin, laver.] having the pelvic opening neither broad and shallow nor narrow and deep; having a medium ratio of breadth to depth of pelvic opening.

mes·çal', *n.* [Sp. *mezcal*.]

1. a colorless alcoholic liquor made from pulque or the fermented juice of an agave.

2. a pulque agave or other plant from which this liquor is made.

3. a small, spineless cactus with rounded stems, whose buttonlike tops (*mescal buttons*) contain a narcotic and are chewed by the Indians for their stimulating effect.

mes'çȧ·līne, *n.* a white, crystalline alkaloid, $C_{11}H_{17}O_3N$, obtained from mescal buttons: it has narcotic properties and causes color hallucinations and convulsions: also *mezcaline*.

meṣ·dȧmes' (mā-dȧm'), *n.* plural of *madame* or *madam*.

me·seemṣ', *v. impers.*; meseemed, *pt.* it seems to me: also *meseemeth*. [Archaic.]

mē'ṣel, *n.* a leper. [Obs.]

mē'ṣel·ry, *n.* leprosy. [Obs.]

Mē·sem·bry·an'thē·mum, *n.* [Gr. *mesēmbria*, midday, the south, and *anthemon*, a flower.] a genus of plants native to South Africa, of the fig-marigold family, having the stems woody below, with thick opposite fleshy leaves and white, yellow, or rose-colored flowers growing in axillary or terminal clusters. The flowers bloom at midday, hence the name.

mes″en·cē·phal'iç, *a.* relating to the mesencephalon.

mes·en·ceph'ȧ·lon, *n.* [*mes-*, and Gr. *enkephalos*, the brain.] the middle part of the brain; the midbrain.

mes'eñ·çhȳme, mes·eñ'çhy·mȧ, *n.* [*mes-*, and Gr. *enchyma*, an infusion.] in embryology, that part of the mesoderm from which arise the connective tissues, cartilage, bone, blood, heart, and lymphatic vessels.

mē·sen'nȧ, mū·sen'nȧ, *n.* [African.] a leguminous tree of Africa, *Albizzia anthelmintica*; also, the bark of this tree, which furnishes a vermifuge.

mes·en·ter'iç, mes·en·tē'ri·ăl, *a.* of or pertaining to the mesentery; as, *mesenteric* glands or arteries.

mes·en·tē·rit'iç, *a.* of or pertaining to mesenteritis.

mes·en·tẽr·ī'tis, *n.* [Gr. *mesenteron*, mesentery, and *-itis*.] in pathology, inflammation of the mesentery.

mes·en'tẽr·on, *n.*; *pl.* **mes·en'tẽr·ȧ**, [Mod. L.; *mes-*, and *enteron*, intestine.] the middle part of the body cavity of an embryo, from which the alimentary canal, liver, pancreas, etc. develop: it is lined with endoderm.

mes'en·ter·y, *n.*; *pl.* **mes'en·ter·ieṣ**, [Gr. *mesenterion*, mesentery; *mesos*, middle, and *enteron*, intestine.] a supporting membrane or membranes enfolding some internal organ and attaching it to either the body wall or another organ; especially, a part of the peritoneum enfolding most of the small intestine and attaching it to the rear wall of the abdominal cavity.

mes·eth'moid, *a.* [*mes-* and *ethmoid*.] pertaining to the middle of the ethmoid.

mes·eth'moid, *n.* the mesethmoid bone.

mesh, *n.* [ME. *maske*; AS. *masc*, *max*, *mæscre*, a mesh, net.]

1. any of the open spaces of a net, screen, sieve, etc.: a 50-mesh screen is one with 50 such open spaces per linear inch.

2. [*pl.*] the threads, cords, etc. forming these openings.

3. a net or network.

4. anything that entangles, snares, or entraps.

5. the engagement of the teeth of gears.

in mesh; in gear; interlocked.

mesh, *v.t.* and *v.i.* 1. to entangle or become entangled.

2. to engage or become engaged: said of gears or gear teeth.

mesh, *a.* made of mesh; with an open weave, as some stockings.

Mē'shaçh, *n.* [Heb. *mēshakh.*] in the Bible, one of the three captives who came out of the blazing furnace miraculously unharmed: Dan. iii.

meshed (mesht) *a.* 1. made with meshes; having a meshy structure; representing meshes.
2. caught in a mesh or net.

mesh knot (not), a sheet bend.

mesh stick, a stick used to form the mesh in making nets.

mesh'wŏrk, *n.* meshes; network.

mesh'y, *a.* formed like network; reticulated.

mes'i·ad, *adv.* same as *mesad.*

mes'i·ăl, *a.* of, in, toward, or along the middle; middle; median; especially, designating or of a median plane or line.
mesial plane; in anatomy, the vertical plane dividing an animal into right and left halves: also called *meson.*

mes'i·ăl·ly, *adv.* in a mesial position; in or toward the middle.

mes'i·tine spär, [Gr. *mesitēs*, a mediator, and E. *spar.*] a yellowish mineral compound of iron and magnesium carbonate, $2MgCO_3 \cdot FeCO_3$.

mes'i·tīte, *n.* same as *mesitine spar.*

mes'i·tyl, *n.* [*mesit*ite and *-yl.*] a hypothetical organic radical, C_3H_5.

mē·sit'y·lēne, *n.* [*mesityl* and *-ene.*] a colorless, aromatic hydrocarbon, $C_6H_3(CH_3)_3$, found in coal tar or made by distillation of a mixture of sulfuric acid and acetone.

meş'lin, *n.* and *a.* same as *maslin.*

meş·mer'iç, meş·mer'iç·ăl, *a.* relating to or produced by mesmerism.

meş·mer'iç·ăl·ly, *adv.* in a mesmeric manner; hypnotically.

meş'mēr·işm (*or* mes'), *n.* [from F. *Mesmer* (1734–1815), G. physician.] hypnotism.

meş'mēr·ist, *n.* one who practises mesmerism; a hypnotist.

meş"mēr·i·zā'tion, *n.* the act of mesmerizing; the state of being under mesmeric influence.

meş'mēr·īze, *v.t.*; mesmerized, *pt., pp.*; mesmerizing, *ppr.* to hypnotize.

meş'mēr·ī·zēr, *n.* one who practises mesmerism.

mēsn'ăl·ty (mēn'), *n.* [legal Fr. *mesnalte, menalte.*] in law, the estate or condition of a mesne lord.

mēsne (mēn), *a.* [OFr. *mesne*, from L. *medianus*, middle.] in law, middle; intervening; intermediate: *mesne* profits are profits accruing between the illegal ejection of a tenant and his reinstatement in possession of the property.

mēsne lọrd (mēn), a feudal lord holding land from a superior.

mes'ō-, [from Gr. *mesos*, middle.] a combining form meaning: (a) *in the middle, intermediate*, as in *meso*carp; (b) in anatomy, *a mesentery*, as in *meso*gastrium; also, *a middle connective part.* Also, before a vowel, *mes-.*

mes·ō·ā'ri·um, *n.* [*mes-*, and Gr. *ōarion*, dim. of *ōon*, an egg.] the mesentery of the ovarium.

mes'ō·blast, *n.* [*meso-* and *-blast.*] the middle germ layer of an embryo; the mesoderm.

mes·ō·blas'tiç, *a.* pertaining to the mesoblast.

mes·ō·brañ'çhi·ăl, *a.* [*meso-* and *branchial.*] in zoology, relating to or designating that part of a crab's carapace which overlies the middle branchial region.

mes·ō·broñ'çhi·um, *n.*; *pl.* **mes·ō·broñ'çhi·ȧ**, one of the bronchial tubes joining the trachea with the lungs.

mes·ō·cae'çăl, *a.* relating to the mesocaecum.

mes·ō·cae'çum, *n.* [*meso-* and *caecum.*] the mesentery connecting the caecum with the wall of the body.

mes·ō·çär'di·um, *n.* [*meso-*, and Gr. *kardia*, heart.] in embryology, the serous membrane connecting the heart with the intestine and the wall of the body.

mes'ō·çärp, *n.* [*meso-* and *-carp.*] in botany, the middle coat of a pericarp.

Mes·ō·çär·pā'cē·ae, *n.pl.* [*meso-*, and Gr. *karpos*, fruit, and *-aceæ.*] a family of fresh-water algae with unbranched filaments, of the class *Conjugatæ.*

mes·ō·çär·pā'ceous, *a.* relating to or of the nature of the *Mesocarpaceæ.*

mes·ō·cē·phal'iç, *a.* [*meso-* and *cephalic.*]
1. having a medium cranial capacity.
2. having a head form intermediate between brachycephalic and dolichocephalic; having a cephalic index of from 76 to 81: category used in some systems of cranial measurement.
3. of the mesocephalon.

mes·ō·ceph'ȧ·lon, *n.* [Mod. L.; *meso-* and *cephalon* (from Gr. *kephalē*), a head.] the pons Varolii, an organ connecting the cerebrum, cerebellum, and medulla oblongata.

mes·ō·ceph'ȧ·lous, *a.* mesocephalic.

mes'ō·coele (-sēl), *n.* mesocoelia.

mes·ō·coe'li·ȧ, *n.* [*meso-*, and Gr. *koilia*, a hollow, ventricle.] the cavity in the midbrain; the aqueduct of Sylvius.

mes·ō·çol'iç, *a.* relating to the mesocolon.

mes·ō·çō'lŏn, *n.* [Gr. *mesokolon, mesokōlon*, the part of the mesentery next to the colon; *mesos*, middle, and *kolon*, colon.] in anatomy, that part of the mesentery to which the colon is attached.

mes·ō·çor'ȧ·çoid, *n.* [*meso-* and *coracoid.*] in certain fishes, a process originating from the middle of the coracoid.

mes·ō·çrat'iç, *a.* [*meso-*, and Gr. *kratein*, to rule.] in geology, containing light and dark mineral constituents in almost equal proportions, the dark slightly exceeding the light.

mes"ō·çū·nē'i·fọrm, mes·ō·çū'ni·fọrm, *n.* [*meso-*, and L. *cuneus*, a wedge, and *forma*, form.] a bone of the tarsus.

mes'ōde, *n.* [Gr. *mesōdos*, a mesode; *mesos*, middle, and *ōdē*, a song, ode.] in ancient prosody, the part of a choral ode between the strophe and the antistrophe.

mes'ō·dērm, *n.* [*meso-* and *-derm.*] the middle germ layer of an embryo, from which the muscular, vascular, and connective tissues develop; the mesoblast.

mes·ō·dēr'măl, *a.* of or derived from the mesoderm.

mes·ō·dēr'miç, *a.* having the characteristics of a mesoderm; mesodermal.

mes'ō·dont, *a.* [*meso-*, and Gr. *odous, odontos*, a tooth.]
1. in anthropology, having teeth of normal size; showing a medium dental index.
2. in zoology, having the characteristics of the *Mesodonta*, a class of extinct animals.

mes·ō·gas'tēr, *n.* [*meso-*, and Gr. *gaster*, belly.] in anatomy, the mesogastrium.

mes·ō·gas'triç, *a.* 1. of the mesogastrium.
2. in zoology, of or pertaining to the middle of the gastric lobe of the dorsal shell or crust.

mes·ō·gas'tri·um, *n.* [Mod. L., from *meso-*, and Gr. *gastēr*, belly.]
1. either mesentery of the stomach of an embryo.
2. in the human body, the middle and front part of the abdomen; the umbilical region.

mes·ō·gloe'ȧ, *n.* [*meso-*, and Gr. *gloia*, glue.]
1. in zoology, the mesoderm in sponges and other coelenterates.
2. [M-] a genus of seaweeds of a gelatinous character.

mes·ō·gloe'ăl, *a.* relating to mesogloea; of a gelatinous or viscous character.

mes·og·nath'iç, *a.* see *mesognathous.*

mē·sog'nȧ·thous, *a.* [*meso-* and *-gnathous.*]
1. having medium-sized, slightly projecting jaws.
2. having a gnathic index of from 98 to 103.

mē·sog'nȧ·thy, *n.* the quality or state of having jaws moderately projecting or of having a medium facial angle.

mes·ō·hē'pär, *n.* [*meso-*, and Gr. *hēpar*, the liver.] in anatomy, the peritoneal fold connecting the liver with the dorsal wall.

Mes·ō·hip'pus, *n.* [*meso-*, and Gr. *hippos*, a horse.] in paleontology, a genus of horses of small size, having three toes on each foot, founded upon fossils found in the early Miocene of North America.

mes'ō·lābe, *n.* [L. *mesolabium*; Gr. *mesolabon, mesolabos*; *mesos*, middle, and *lambanein*, to take.] an instrument employed by the ancients for finding two mean proportionals between two given lines, which were required in the problem of the duplication of the cube.

mes'ōle, *n.* same as *thomsonite.*

mes'ō·līte, *n.* [*meso-* and *-lite.*] a zeolite mineral containing lime and soda, occurring in slender crystals and delicate, radiated concretions.

mē·sol'ō·ġy, *n.* the science of the effects of environment on organisms.

mes·ō·mē'tri·um, *n.* same as *mesometry.*

mes·om'e·try, *n.* in anatomy, the mesentery of the uterus.

mes·ō·mor'phiç, *a.* 1. [*meso-* and *-morphic.*] of a state intermediate between the liquid and the crystalline.
2. [*meso*derm and *-morphic.*] designating or of the muscular or athletic physical type, characterized by predominance of the structures developed from the mesodermal layer of the embryo (i.e., muscle, bone, and connective tissue): distinguished from *ectomorphic, endomorphic.*

mes"ō·mȳ·ō'di·ăn, *a.* [*meso-*, and Gr. *mys, myos*, a muscle, and *ōdē*, a song.] having the intrinsic muscles attaching the upper bronchial half rings to the larynx, as in songbirds.

mes'on, *n.* see *mesial plane* under *mesial.*

mes'on, *n.* [Gr. *mesōn*, genit. pl. of *mesē*, middle note.] in music, loosely, a tetrachord.

mes'on, *n.* [*meso*tron.] a mesotron.

mes·ō·nā'şăl, *a.* [*meso-*, and L. *nasus*, the nose.] relating to the middle of the nose or of the nasal region.

mes·ō·neph'riç, *a.* relating to the mesonephron.

mes·ō·neph'ron, *n.* same as *mesonephros.*

mes·ō·neph'ros, *n.* [Mod. L.; *meso-*, and Gr. *nephros*, a kidney.] the excretory organ serving as the kidney of a vertebrate embryo: it is a long tube lying between the pronephros and metanephros, and, in the human male, develops into the epididymis and vas deferens: also called *Wolffian body.*

mes·ō·nō'tăl, *a.* of, pertaining to, or situated on the mesonotum.

mes·ō·nō'tum, *n.* [*meso-*, and Gr. *nōtos*, the back.] in zoology, the middle of the dorsal part of the mesothorax of an insect.

mes·ō·phloe'um, *n.* [*meso-*, and Gr. *phloios*, bark.] in botany, the bark of a young exogen while it is green, as in the first year's growth of a scion or branch.

mes'ō·phragm (-fram), *n.* [*meso-*, and Gr. *phragma*, a partition, fence.]
1. in an insect, an internal partition on the dorsal side between the metathorax and the mesothorax for the attachment of muscles.
2. in a crustacean, an intersternal apodeme.

mes·ō·phrag'măl, *a.* of or pertaining to the mesophragm.

mes'ō·phyll, mes'ō·phyl, *n.* the soft tissue (*green parenchyma*) lying between the upper and lower surfaces of a leaf.

mes·ō·phyl'lum, *n.* same as *mesophyl.*

mes'ō·phȳte, *n.* [*meso-* and *-phyte.*] any plant adapted to grow under medium conditions of moisture.

mes·ō·phyt'iç, *a.* of, or having the nature of, a mesophyte.

mes'ō·plast, *n.* [*meso-* and *-plast.*] in biology, the nucleus of a cell.

mes·ō·pleu'răl, *a.* in entomology, relating to the mesopleuron or to the lateral part of the mesothorax.

mes·ō·pleu'ron, *n.*; *pl.* **mes·ō·pleu'rȧ**, [*meso-*, and Gr. *pleuron*, a rib.] in entomology, the pleuron of the mesothorax of an insect.

mes·ō·pō'di·ăl, *a.* [*meso-*, and Gr. *pous, podos*, a foot.] relating to a mesopodium or to the mesopodialia.

mes·ō·pō'di·ăl, *n.* one of the mesopodial bones.

mes·ō·pō·di·ā'li·ȧ, *n.pl.* collectively, the bones of the wrist or of the ankle.

mes·ō·pō'di·um, *n.*; *pl.* **mes·ō·pō'di·ȧ**, [*meso-*, and Gr. *pous, podos*, a foot.] the middle part of the foot of a mollusk.

Mes"ō·pō·tā'mi·ăn, *a.* [Gr. *Mesopotamia*, Mesoptamia; *mesos*, middle, and *potamos*, river.] designating, belonging to, or situated in Mesopotamia, an ancient country lying between the rivers Euphrates and Tigris, or related to its people or their culture.

Mes"ō·pō·tā'mi·ăn, *n.* a native of Mesopotamia.

mē·sop·tē·ryġ'i·ăl, *a.* relating to a mesopterygium or to mesopterygia.

mē·sop·tē·ryġ'i·um, *n.*; *pl.* **mē·sop·tē·ryġ'i·ȧ**, [*meso-*, and Gr. *pterygion*, a fin.] in anatomy, the middle cartilage at the base of a fish's fin.

mē·sor'çhi·um, *n.* [*meso-*, and Gr. *orchis*, a testicle.] in embryology, the peritoneal membrane supporting the testis and connecting it with the dorsal wall.

mes·ō·reç'tăl, *a.* pertaining to the mesorectum.

mes·ō·reç'tum, *n.* [*meso-* and *rectum.*] the rectal mesentery.

mes'ō·rhīne (-rīn), *a.* [*meso-*, and Gr. *rhis, rhinos*, nose.] in anatomy, having a nose of medium width.

Mes·ō·şau'ri·ȧ, *n.pl.* see *Mosasauria.*

mes·ō·sçap'ū·lȧ, *n.*; *pl.* **mes·ō·sçap'ū·lae**, [*meso-* and *scapula.*] in anatomy, the ridgelike process of the scapula.

mes·ō·sçap'ū·lăr, *a.* relating to the mesoscapula.

mes"ō·sçū·tel'lum, *n.*; *pl.* **mes"ō·sçū·tel'lȧ**, [*meso-*, and dim. of L. *scutum*, a shield.] the scutelliform part of the mesothorax of an insect.

mes·ō·sçū'tum, *n.*; *pl.* **mes·ō·sçū'tȧ**, [*meso-*, and L. *scutum*, a shield.] the shieldlike dorsal covering of the mesothorax of an insect.

mes'ō·sēme, *a.* [*meso-*, and Gr. *sēma*, a sign,

mark.] in craniometry, having medium-sized orbits of the eyes.

mes·ō·sid′ẽr·īte, *n.* [*meso-*, and Gr. *sidēritēs*, iron.] a variety of meteorite containing iron embedded in silicates.

mes·ō·sō′mȧ, *n.*; *pl.* **mes·ō·sō′mȧ·tȧ,** [*meso-*, and Gr. *sōma*, body.] in a bivalve mollusk, the middle part of the body; the part to which the foot is attached.

mes″ō·sō·mat′iç, *a.* pertaining to a mesosoma.

mes′ō·sōme, *n.* same as *mesoma*.

mes′ō·sphēre, *n.* [*meso-*, and *sphere*.] an atmospheric zone above the stratosphere, extending between about 15 to 50 miles above the earth's surface.

mes′ō·spōre, *n.* [*meso-*, and Gr. *sporos*, seed.] in botany, the middle part of the coat of a spore which has three layers.

mes·ō·stẽr′năl, *a.* relating to the mesosternum.

mes·ō·stẽr′num, *n.* [*meso-*, and Gr. *sternon*, the breast, chest.]

1. in anatomy, the middle part, or segment, of the sternum.

2. in entomology, the ventral part of the mesothorax.

mes·ō·stē′thi·um, *n.*; *pl.* **mes·ō·stē′thi·ȧ,** [*meso-*, and Gr. *stēthion*, dim. of *stēthos*, the breast.] the part of the surface of an insect's body between the middle and the hind leg.

mes·ō·tär′sus, *n.* [*meso-* and *tarsus*.] the tarsus of the middle pair of legs of a hexapod.

mes·ō·thē·li·ō′mȧ, *n.* [*mesothelium* and *-oma*.] a tumor of the mesothelium, malignant when caused by the inhalation of asbestos particles.

mes·ō·thē′li·um, *n.* [*meso-* and epi*thelium*.]

1. epithelium of mesodermal origin.

2. a layer of mesodermal cells lining the serous cavities.

mes′ō·thẽrm, *n.* [*meso-* and Gr. *thermē*, heat.] a plant that lives and thrives in a temperature of moderate degree.

mes″ō·thō·rac′iç, *a.* pertaining to or situated on the mesothorax of an insect.

mes·ō·thō′rax, *n.* [*meso-* and Gr. *thorax*, a breastplate.] in entomology, the middle segment of the three segments of the thorax.

mes·ō·thō′ri·um, *n.* [*meso-* and *thorium*.]

1. a radioactive isotope of radium, formed from thorium: also *mesothorium 1*.

2. a radioactive isotope of actinium, formed from this isotope: also *mesothorium 2*.

Symbol, Ms-Th, MsTh.

me·sot′rō·çhȧ, *n.pl.* [*meso-*, and Gr. *trocha*, anything round.] the larvae of a kind of marine worm, characterized by a band or bands of cilia around the middle part of the body.

me·sot′rō·çhăl, *a.* relating to mesotrocha.

mes′ō·tron, *n.* [*meso-* and elec*tron*.] an unstable particle about 200 times the mass of the electron, formed by the disintegration of cosmic rays: also called *heavy electron*.

mes′ō·tȳpe, *n.* [*meso-*, and Gr. *typhos*, an impression, type.] in mineralogy, formerly, any of several zeolite minerals, including mesolite, scolecite, natrolite, etc.

mes·ō·vā′ri·um, *n.* [*meso-* and *ovarium*.] in anatomy, the fold of the peritoneum which supports the ovary and connects it with the wall of the body.

mes·ox′ȧ·lāte, *n.* a salt of mesoxalic acid.

mes·ox·al′iç, *a.* [*mes-* and *oxalic*.] designating an acid, $C_3H_2O_5$, which is easily separated into oxalic acid and carbonic acid.

Mes·ō·zō′ȧ, *n.pl.* [*meso-*, and Gr. *zōē*, life.] a division of animals intermediate between *Protozoa* and *Metazoa*.

Mes·ō·zō′iç, *a.* [*meso-*, and *zo*, and *-ic*.] designating or of the geological era after the Paleozoic and before the Cenozoic, comprising the Triassic, Jurassic, and Cretaceous periods.

the Mesozoic; the Mesozoic Era or its rocks.

mes·quīte′, mes·quīt′ (-kēt′), *n.* [Sp. *mezquite*, from Nahuatl *mizquit*.]

1. a spiny tree or shrub of the pea family, growing in the southwestern United States and in Mexico and other parts of Latin America: its sugary, beanlike pods are eaten by cattle: also *honey mesquite*.

2. a similar related plant with edible, spiral pods; screwbean: also *screw-pod mesquite*.

mes·quite′ bēan, the pod of the mesquite.

mes·quite′ grȧss, a rich pasture grass, genus *Prosopis*, growing in western Texas among mesquite trees: also called *buffalo grass* and *grama grass*.

mess, *n.* [ME. and OFr. *mes*, a dish, a course at table, properly pp. of *mettre*, to place; L. *mittere*, to send.]

1. a portion or quantity of food for a meal or dish.

2. a portion of soft or semiliquid food, as porridge.

3. unappetizing food; a disagreeable concoction.

4. a group of people who regularly have their meals together, as in the army or navy.

5. (a) the meal eaten by such a group; (b) the place where it is eaten.

6. a disorderly or confused collection or mass of things; a jumble; a hodgepodge.

7. a state of embarrassment, trouble, or difficulty; a muddle; as, he got himself into a *mess*.

8. a disorderly, untidy, or dirty state of things.

mess hall; a room or building where a group, as of soldiers or sailors, regularly have their meals.

mess jacket; a man's close-fitting, waist-length jacket, usually white, for semiformal wear in warm weather.

mess kit; the compactly arranged metal plates and eating utensils carried by a soldier or camper for use in the field: also called *mess gear*.

mess orderly; the soldier who carries the meals from the army kitchen.

mess tin; a tin cooking vessel used by soldiers.

mess, *v.t.*; messed, *pt.*, *pp.*; messing, *ppr.* 1. to supply meals to.

2. to make a mess of; specifically, (a) to make dirty, soiled, or untidy; (b) to bundle; muddle; botch. Often with *up*.

3. to serve or divide (food). [Obs. or Dial.]

mess, *v.i.* 1. to eat as one of a mess (sense 4).

2. to make a mess.

3. to putter or meddle.

to mess around; to be busy in a desultory way, without getting anything done; to putter around.

mes′săġe, *n.* [ME.; OFr.; LL. *missaticum*, a message, from L. *mittere*, to send.]

1. any communication, written or oral, sent between persons.

2. a formal, official communication, written or oral: as, the President's *message* to Congress.

3. the errand or function of a messenger.

4. an inspired or important communication, as of a prophet, poet, or philosopher.

to get the message; to get the implications of a hint, insinuation, etc. [Colloq.]

mes′săġe, *v.t.* to declare or to deliver, as a message. [Rare.]

mes′săġe stick, in Australia, a stick upon which the native cuts or carves a message to be sent, as to a distant tribe.

Mes·sā′li·ăn, *n.* same as *Euchite*.

mes·sȧ·līne′, *n.* [Fr.] a thin, soft, lustrous twilled silk cloth.

mes·sei·gnēurș′ (-en-yẽrz′), *n.* plural of *monseigneur*.

mes′sen·ġẽr, *n.* [ME. *messager*; OFr. *messagier*, a messenger, from *message*, a message.]

1. (a) one who carries a message or goes on an errand; (b) one whose work is delivering telegrams, official dispatches, etc.

2. a harbinger; a forerunner; one who or that which foreshows. [Archaic.]

3. in navigation, a hawser or small cable about sixty fathoms long, wound round the capstan, and having its two ends lashed together: formerly used in heaving up the anchor.

4. in English law, a person appointed by a court to perform certain duties pertaining to the custody of property in cases of bankruptcy.

mes′sen·ġẽr bīrd, the secretary bird.

mes′set, *n.* a dog. [Brit. Dial.]

Mes·sī′ăh, *n.* [L. *Messias*; Gr. *Messias*; Heb. *Māshīach*, anointed, from *māshach*, to anoint.]

1. in Judaism, the promised and expected deliverer of the Jews.

2. in Christianity, Jesus, regarded as this deliverer, and hence called *the Christ*.

3. [m–] any expected savior or liberator of a people, country, etc.

Also *Messias*.

mes·sī′ăh·ship, *n.* 1. the fact or state of being a messiah.

2. the work or function of a messiah.

Mes·si·an′iç, *a.* 1. of or relating to the Messiah or to his office.

2. [m–] of, like, or characteristic of a messiah.

Mes·si·dọr′, *n.* [Fr., from L. *messis*, harvest, and Gr. *dōron*, a gift.] in the French Revolutionary Calendar, the tenth month, beginning June 19 and ending July 18, adopted by the First Republic in 1793.

mes′siēurș (mes′ẽrz, mes′yẽrz, *or Fr.* mā-syų′), *n.pl.* [Fr., pl. of *monsieur*, sir.] plural of *monsieur*.

mess′i·ly, *adv.* in a messy manner.

mess′i·ness, *n.* a messy quality or state.

mess′māte, *n.* 1. a person with whom one regularly has meals, as in the army or navy.

2. an animal that feeds with others not of its kind; a commensal.

3. a stringy-bark eucalyptus tree of Australia: also called *messmate tree*.

Messrs. (mes′ẽrz), Messieurs: now used chiefly as the plural of *Mr*.

mes′suaġe (-wij), *n.* [OFr. *mesuage*, *mesnage*; LL. *mansionaticum*, a dwelling house, from L. *mansio* (-*onis*), a staying, dwelling, from *manere*, to remain.] in law, a dwelling house and adjoining land including the adjacent buildings.

mess′y, *a.*; *comp.* messier; *superl.* messiest; in, like, or characterized by a mess; untidy, disordered, dirty, etc.

mest, *a.* most. [Obs.]

mes·tee′, *n.* [altered from *mestizo*.] a mustee.

mes·tī′zȧ, *n.* a woman or girl mestizo.

mes·tī′zō, *n.*; *pl.* **mes·tī′zōș, mes·tī′zōeș,** [Sp., from L. *mixtus*, pp. of *miscere*, to mix.] a person of mixed parentage; specifically, in the western United States and in Latin American countries, the offspring of a Spaniard or Portuguese and an American Indian.

mestizo wool; a kind of wool clipped from sheep of mixed breeds in South America.

mes′tōme, *n.* [Gr. *mestōma*, fullness, from *mestos*, full.] in botany, the conductive opening in a fibrovascular structure.

Mes′ū·ȧ, *n.* [named after *Musuah*, an Arabian physician.] a genus of resinous trees and shrubs of tropical Asia of the family *Guttiferæ*, valued for the dyes and perfumes obtained from the flowers, and for its hard wood, which is used for various purposes.

met, *v.* past tense and past participle of *meet*.

met, *v.* obsolete past tense of *mete*, to measure.

met′ȧ-, [L. *meta-*; Gr. *meta-*, from prep. *meta*, in the midst of, among, between, after, according to.]

1. *changed in position* or *form*, *altered*, *transposed*, as in *meta*morphosis, *meta*thesis; equivalent to *trans-*.

2. *after*, as in *meta*physics: sometimes, as in medical terms, equivalent to *post-*.

3. *behind*, *hinder*, *at the back*, as in *meta*thorax: in anatomical terms, equivalent to *dorso-*.

4. [from supposed analogy to *metaphysics*.] beyond, higher, transcending, as in *meta*psychosis.

5. in chemistry, (a) *a polymer of*, as in *meta*ldehyde; (b) *a derivative of*, as in *meta*protein; (c) *an acid containing less water combined with the anhydride than other acids of the same nonmetallic element*, as in *meta*phosphoric; (d) *characterized by substitutions in the 1, 3 position in the benzene ring*.

Also, before a vowel, *met-*.

mē′tȧ, *n.*; *pl.* **mē′tae,** [L.] a triple and conical turning post placed at each end of the track in a Roman circus.

mē·tab′ȧ·sis, *n.* [Gr. *metabasis*, a passing over, change, from *metabainein*; *meta*, beyond, and *bainein*, to go.]

1. in rhetoric, transition; a passing from one thing to another.

2. in medicine, a change of the nature or treatment of a disease.

met·ȧ·bat′iç, *a.* [Gr. *metabatikos*, from *metabasis*, a passing over, change.] relating to a transfer or transition of energy; in physics, noting the passage of heat, as from one body to another.

me·tab′ō·lȧ, *n.* same as *metabasis*: also written *metabole*.

Me·tab′ō·lȧ, *n.pl.* [Gr. *metabolos*, changeable, *metabolē*, change; *meta*, beyond, and *ballein*, to throw.] a group of insects that undergo complete metamorphosis; that is, those which have distinct forms as larva, pupa, and imago.

met·ȧ·bō′li·ăn, *n.* an insect that undergoes complete metamorphosis.

met·ȧ·bol′iç, *a.* [Gr. *metabolos*, changeable; *metabolē*, change.]

1. in biology, relating to metamorphosis.

2. in physiology, relating to metabolism.

me·tab′ō·lism, *n.* 1. the chemical and physical processes continuously going on in living organisms and cells, comprising those by which assimilated food is built up (*anabolism*) into protoplasm and those by which protoplasm is used and broken down (*catabolism*) into simpler substances or waste matter, with the release of energy for all vital processes.

2. in entomology, metamorphosis.

3. in theology, a doctrine of some of the early fathers which regarded the Eucharist as embodying both the real and the symbolical presence.

me·tab′ō·līte, *n.* any substance produced by metabolism, as urea or carbon dioxide.

me·tab′ō·līze, *v.t.* and *v.i.*; metabolized, *pt.*, *pp.*; metabolizing, *ppr.* to change by metabolism.

met·ȧ·brañ′chi·ăl, *a.* [*meta-*, and Gr. *branchia*, gills.] in a crustacean, behind the gills; relating particularly to a lobe covering the posterior gills.

met·ȧ·çär′păl, *a.* relating to the metacarpus.

met·ȧ·çär′păl, *n.* any of the bones of the metacarpus.

met·ȧ·çär′pus, *n.*; *pl.* **met·ȧ·çär′pī, met·ȧ·çär′pus·eṣ,** [*meta-*, and Gr. *karpos*, the wrist.] in anatomy, the part of the skeleton of a vertebrate between the carpus and the phalanges; in man, the bones between the wrist and the fingers and thumb.

met·ȧ·cen′tẽr, met·ȧ·cen′tre, *n.* [Fr. *métacentre*; Gr. *meta*, beyond, and *kentron*, center.] that point in a floating body at which a vertical line drawn through its center of buoyancy when it is upright meets the vertical line drawn through its center of buoyancy when it is tipped; center of gravity of the unsubmerged part of a floating body: for stability the metacenter must be above the center of gravity.

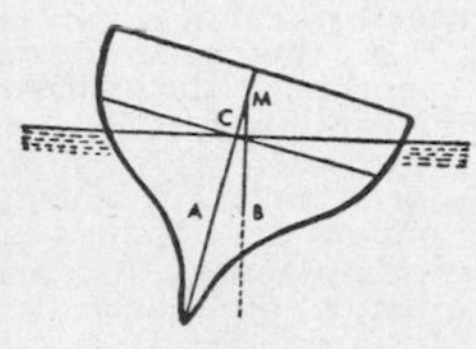

METACENTER
C, center of gravity; A, center of buoyancy of a floating body; B, center of buoyancy when body is tipped; M, metacenter at point of intersection of verticals MA and MB

met·ȧ·cen′triç, *a.* of or near the metacenter.

mē·tac′ē·tōne, *n.* [*meta-* and *acetone.*] in chemistry, a colorless liquid with the odor of peppermint, made by distilling sugar with lime.

met·ȧ·chrō′mȧ·tiṣm, *n.* [from *meta-*, and Gr. *chrōma, chrōmatos*, color; and *-ism.*] a change of color, especially as a result of a change in temperature.

mē·tach′rō·niṣm, *n.* [Gr. *metachronos*, after the time; *meta*, beyond, after, and *chronos*, time.] an error in chronology made by placing an event after its time.

met·ȧ·chrō′sis, *n.* [*meta-*, and Gr. *chrōsis*, a coloring.] the changing of color; also, the power of changing color at will through nervous action, as in certain lizards and fishes.

met·ȧ·cin′nȧ·bär·īte, *n.* [*meta-*, and *cinnabar* and *-ite.*] native grayish-black sulfide of mercury found with red cinnabar in California.

met′ȧ·ciṣm, *n.* same as *mytacism.*

met·ȧ·crē′sol, *n.* [*meta-* and *cresol.*] in chemistry, an isomeric form of cresol.

met·ȧ·crō′mi·on, *n.*; *pl.* **met·ȧ·crō′mi·ȧ,** [*meta-*, and Gr. *akrōmion, akrōmia*, the point of the shoulder blade.] in anatomy, a process projecting backward from the acromion in the scapula of certain animals, as rabbits and shrews.

met·ȧ·cy′cliç, *a.* [*meta-*, and Gr. *kyklos*, circle.] relating to or designating a permutation of the elements in a cycle.

met″ȧ·cy·ē′sis, *n.* [*meta-*, and Gr. *kyēsis*, conception.] in medicine, a form of extrauterine pregnancy.

met·ȧ·cȳ′mēne, *n.* one of three isomeric forms of cymene, a hydrocarbon derivative of benzene.

met·ȧ·dẽr·mȧ·tō′sis, *n.* [*meta-*, and Gr. *derma* (*-atos*), skin, and *-osis.*] in pathology, a cutaneous development caused by a diseased condition.

met″ȧ·dī·chlor″ō·ben′zēne, *n.* [*meta-*, *di*, two, Gr. *chlōros*, green, and *benzene.*] in chemistry, an organic compound, $C_6H_4Cl_2$, in which the two chlorine atoms are separated by one of the carbon atoms of the benzene ring.

met″ȧ·dis·çoi′dăl, *a.* [*meta-* and *discoidal.*] in anatomy, developed beyond the discoidal form, yet resembling it: said of the placenta of man and anthropoid mammals.

met″ȧ·gȧ·laç′tiç, *a.* of the metagalaxy.

met·ȧ·gal′ăx·y, *n.* in astronomy, the entire material universe; the system comprising the galaxies, nebulae, etc.

met·ȧ·gas′tẽr, *n.* the developed and differentiated primitive intestinal cavity of a vertebrate animal; the intestinal canal of all vertebrates except the *Amphioxus.*

met·ȧ·gas′trü·lȧ, *n.* [*meta-* and *gastrula.*] in biology, any gastrula which is modified or unusual.

mēt′ăġe, *n.* [AS. *metan*, to measure.] official measurement of contents or weight, as of coal; also, the price charged for its measurement.

met·ȧ·ġel′ȧ·tin, met·ȧ·ġel′ȧ·tine, *n.* [*meta-* and *gelatin.*] a preparation made from gelatin which remains liquid, formerly used in photography.

met·ȧ·ġen′e·sis, *n.* [*meta-*, and Gr. *genesis*, generation.] in biology, reproduction in which there is alternation of generations.

met″ȧ·ġē·net′iç, *a.* relating to metagenesis.

met·ȧ·ġen′iç, *a.* metagenetic.

mē·tag′nȧ·thous, *a.* [*meta-*, and Gr. *gnathos*, jaw.] having the mandibles curved so as to cross each other when the jaws are closed: said of birds, as the crossbill.

met·ag·nos′tiç, *n.* [*meta-*, and Gr. *gnōstikos*, knowing.] one who believes in and advocates metagnosticism.

met·ag·nos′ti·ciṣm, *n.* in philosophy, the doctrine that a positive knowledge of the Absolute is within the reach of human attainment, not through logical processes but through the higher religious consciousness: the opposite of *agnosticism.*

met·ȧ·gram′mȧ·tiṣm, *n.* same as *anagrammatism.*

met·ȧ·graph′iç, *a.* relating to metagraphy.

mē·tag′rȧ·phy, *n.* [Gr. *metagraphein*, to write differently, transpose; *meta*, over, and *graphein*, to write.] the act of transcribing or rewriting; specifically, translating or changing the letters of a language into corresponding letters of another language.

mē·tāi′riē, *n.* [Fr.] a piece of land cultivated by a tenant for a share of the proceeds.

met″ȧ·ki·nē′sis, *n.* [*meta-*, and Gr. *kinēsis*, movement.] in biology, the stage in cell division in which the filaments of the nuclei separate and pass toward the poles of a cell.

met′ăl (*or* -l), *n.* [OFr. *metal*; L. *metallum*; Gr. *metallon*, a mine, pit, cave, a mineral, ore.]

1. (a) any of a class of chemical elements, as iron, gold, aluminum, etc., generally characterized by ductility, malleability, luster, and conductivity of heat and electricity: these elements form bases with the hydroxyl radical and can replace the hydrogen of an acid to form a salt; (b) an alloy of such elements, as brass, bronze, etc.

2. any substance consisting of metal.

3. material; substance; stuff; hence, spirit; mettle.

4. molten cast iron.

5. molten material for making glassware or pottery.

6. broken stone, cinders, etc. used in making roads, ballasting roadbeds, etc. [Brit.]

7. in heraldry, either of the tinctures gold (*or*) and silver (*argent*).

8. in the navy, the weight of shells that the guns of a warship can shoot at one time.

9. in printing, (a) type metal; (b) composed type.

10. a mine of metallic ore. [Obs.]

heavy metal; such metals as gold, platinum, etc., having a density of more than five times that of water.

met′ăl, *a.* made of metal.

met′ăl, *v.t.*; metaled *or* metalled, *pt.*, *pp.*; metaling *or* metalling, *ppr.* to cover or supply with metal, as the bottom of a ship with copper, or the surface of a road with broken stone.

met″ăl·am·mō′ni·um, *n.* [*metal* and *ammonium.*] in chemistry, a hypothetical radical in which a metal takes the place of hydrogen in ammonium. [Obs.]

mēt·al′dē·hȳde, *n.* [*met-* and *aldehyde.*] in chemistry, a white crystalline solid isomeric with ethyl aldehyde.

met·ȧ·lep′sis, *n.* [L., from Gr. *metalēpsis*, participation, alternation, from *metalambanein*; *meta*, among, and *lambanein*, to take.] in rhetoric, the continuation of a trope in one word through a succession of meanings, or the union of two or more tropes of a different kind in one word; e.g., in one Caesar there are many Mariuses.

met·ȧ·lep′tiç, *a.* 1. pertaining to a metalepsis.

2. acting with: said of a muscle.

met·ȧ·lep′tiç·ăl, *a.* metaleptic.

met·ȧ·lep′ti·çăl·ly, *adv.* by transposition or substitution.

met′ăl·ine, *n.* [*metal* and *-ine.*] a lubricating mixture made of metallic oxides, grease, and other substances.

met′ăl·ist, met′ăl·list, *n.* 1. a worker in metals.

2. an advocate of the use of metallic instead of paper money.

met′ăl·īze, met′ăl·līze, *v.t.*; metalized *or* metallized, *pt.*, *pp.*; metalizing *or* metallizing, *ppr.*

1. to treat, cover, or impregnate with metal or a compound of metal.

2. to change into metal.

mē·tal′liç, *a.* [L. *metallicus*; Gr. *metallikos*, pertaining to mines or metal, from *metallon*, metal.]

1. of, or having the nature of, metal.

2. containing, yielding, or producing metal.

3. like, characteristic of, or suggestive of metal; as, a *metallic* sound.

metallic paper; a kind of paper prepared by a washing of lime, whiting, and size, upon which lines written with a pewter pencil are almost indelible.

metallic soap; a soaplike substance made by combining the salts of lead, aluminum, and some other metals with fatty acids: it is used in making paint, cloth, etc.

mē·tal′li·căl, *a.* metallic. [Obs.]

mē·tal′li·căl·ly, *adv.* 1. with or by means of metal; as a metal or as affected by the properties of a metal.

2. with reference to the constituent metal; as, *metallically* pure.

met·ăl·lif′ẽr·ous, *a.* [L. *metallifer*; *metallum*, metal, and *ferre*, to bear.] containing, yielding, or producing metal or ore.

mē·tal′li·fọrm, *a.* having the form of metals; like metal in structure or qualities.

met′ăl·line, *a.* 1. metallic.

2. containing metal or metallic salts.

met′ăl·line, *n.* same as *metaline.*

met′ăl·lish, *a.* metallic. [Obs.]

met′ăl·list, *n.* same as *metalist.*

met·ăl·li·zā′tion, *n.* the act or process of forming into a metal.

met′ăl·līze, *v.t.* same as *metalize.*

mē·tal′lō-, [from Gr. *metallon*, a mine, mineral, ore, metal.] a combining form meaning *metal*, as in *metallo*chrome, *metall*urgy, etc.

mē·tal′lō·chrōme, *n.* [*metallo-*, and Gr *chrōma*, color.] in electricity, a prismatic coloring given to the surface of a polished metal by the electrolysis of a salt of lead.

mē·tal′lō·graph, *n.* a print or impression produced by metallography.

met·ăl·log′rȧ·phy, *n.* [Gr. *metallon*, metal, and *-graphia*, from *graphein*, to write.]

1. the study of the structure and physical properties of metals and metallic substances, especially by the use of the microscope and X rays.

2. a method of printing resembling lithography but using metal plates instead of stones.

met′ăl·loid, *n.* [*metallo-*, and Gr. *eidos*, form.] in chemistry, (a) any nonmetal; (b) an element having some of, but not all, the properties of metals, as arsenic or silicon.

met′ăl·loid, *a.* 1. like a metal.

2. relating to a metalloid; nonmetallic.

met·ăl·loi′dăl, *a.* metalloid.

mē·tăl·lō·plas′tiç, *a.* [*metallo-*, and Gr. *plassein*, to form, mold.] pertaining to the art or process of making metal casts, as by the electrolytic process.

mē·tăl·lō·ther′ȧ·py, *n.* [*metallo-*, and Gr. *therapeia*, medical treatment.] treatment of disease by the use of metals, or especially of their salts.

met·ăl·lûr′ġiç, *a.* pertaining to metallurgy.

met·ăl·lûr′ġi·căl, *a.* metallurgic.

met′ăl·lûr·ġist, *n.* an expert in metallurgy.

met′ăl·lûr·ġy, *n.* [Mod. L. *metallurgia*; Gr. *metallourgos*, working in metals or mines; *metallon*, a metal, mine, and *ergon*, work.] the art or science of separating metals from their ores and preparing them for use, by smelting, refining, etc.

met′ăl·măn, *n.*; *pl.* **met′ăl·men,** a worker in metals.

met·ȧ·log′iç, *n.* the metaphysics of logic.

met·ȧ·log′i·căl, *a.* [*meta-* and *logical.*]

1. beyond the scope of logic; not determinable by logic.

2. relating to the metaphysics of logic.

met″ăl·ọr·gan′iç, *a.* [*metal* and *organic.*] in chemistry, designating or relating to a compound formed by the union of a metallic element with an organic radical.

met′ăl·wŏrk, *n.* 1. things made out of metal.
2. the making of such things.

met′ăl·wŏrk·ing, *n.* the act or process of making things out of metal.

met′ăl·wŏrk·ing, *a.* of, for, or engaged in metalworking.

met′ȧ·mẽr, *n.* [from *meta-*, and Gr. *meros*, a part.] any of two or more chemical compounds belonging to the same general class and having identical proportions of the same elements and the same molecular weight, but different chemical properties.

me·tam′ẽr·ăl, *a.* in zoology, metameric.

met′ȧ·mēre, *n.* [*meta-*, and Gr. *meros*, part.] in zoology, any of a longitudinal series of similar segments making up the body of a worm, crayfish, etc.; a somite.

met·ȧ·mer′iç, *a.* 1. in chemistry, relating to a metamer or metamerism.
2. in zoology, relating or pertaining to a metamere or metamerism; being a metamere; segmental.

met·ȧ·mer′i·căl·ly, *adv.* in a metameric manner; with, from, or by metamerism.

mē·tam′ẽr·iṣm, *n.* 1. in zoology, the state of being made up of metameres.
2. in chemistry, the condition of being metameric.

met″ȧ·mẽr·i·zā′tion, *n.* in zoology, arrangement into metameres.

me·tam′ẽr·y, *n.* metamerism.

met·ȧ·morph′iç, *a.* [*meta-*, and Gr. *morphē*, form.] of, characterized by, causing, or formed by metamorphism or metamorphosis.

met·ȧ·mor′phiṣm, *n.* 1. metamorphosis; change of form.
2. in geology, change in the form and structure of rocks, as by the agencies of heat, pressure, and water, causing crystallization, condensation, lamination, obliteration of fossils, etc.; as, the *metamorphism* of limestone into marble.

met·ȧ·mọr′phīze, *v.t.* same as *metamorphose*.

met″ȧ·mọr·phop′si·ȧ, *n.* [Gr. *metamorphōsis*, transformation, and *ōps*, eye.] a defective condition of the vision which gives objects a distorted appearance.

met·ȧ·mọr′phō·sçōpe, *n.* [Gr. *metamorphōsis*, transformation, and *skopein*, to view.] an optical toy in which figures of various animals as well as human figures, painted in parts on flexible strips which move at different rates on rollers and have their edges close together, produce a series of fantastic figures as they pass across the opening of the instrument.

met·ȧ·mọr′phōṣe, *v.t.* and *v.i.*; metamorphosed, *pt.*, *pp.*; metamorphosing, *ppr.* to change from one form into another; to transform; to subject to or undergo metamorphosis.

met·ȧ·mọr′phōṣe, *n.* metamorphosis. [Rare.]

met·ȧ·mọr′phōṣ·ẽr, *n.* one who or that which metamorphoses.

met·ȧ·mọr′phō·siç, *a.* of or causing metamorphosis.

met·ȧ·mọr′phō·sis, *n.*; *pl.* **met·ȧ·mọr′phō·sēṣ,** [Gr. *metamorphōsis*, a transformation, from *metamorphousthai*, to be transformed or transfigured; *meta*, over, and *morphē*, form, shape.]
1. (a) change of form, shape, structure, or substance; transformation, especially by magic or sorcery; (b) the form resulting from such change.
2. a marked or complete change of character, appearance, condition, etc.
3. in biology, a change in form, structure, or function as a result of development; specifically, (a) the physical transformation, more or less sudden, undergone by various animals during development after the embryonic state, as of the larva of an insect to the pupa and the pupa to the adult, or the tadpole to the frog; (b) the development of plant organs, originally similar in morphology, into different forms as a result of adaptation to different functions; (c) the change of form constantly going on in living cells and tissues.
4. in medicine, a morbid change of form of some tissues or parts.
5. chemical action by which a compound is caused, by the presence of a ferment or similar substance, to decompose into two or more compounds.

met·ȧ·mọr′phous, *a.* metamorphic.

met′ȧ·mọr·phy, *n.* metamorphosis. [Rare.]

met·ȧ·naụ′pli·us, *n.* the larval stage succeeding the nauplius in the development of crustaceans; also, a crustacean in that stage.

met·ȧ·neph′riç, met″ȧ·nē·phrit′iç, *a.* of or belonging to the metanephron.

met·ȧ·neph′ron, *n.* same as *metanephros*.

met·ȧ·neph′ros, *n.* [Mod. L.; *meta-*, and Gr. *nephros*, kidney.] the excretory organ lying behind the mesonephros in an embryo, which in mammals develops into the permanent kidney.

met·ȧ·nō′tum, *n.*; *pl.* **met·ȧ·nō′tȧ,** [*meta-*, and Gr. *notos*, *noton*, the back.] the dorsal surface of the metathorax of an insect.

met″an·ti·mō′nāte, *n.* a salt of metantimonic acid.

met″an·ti·mon′iç, *a.* [*met-* and *antimonic*.] of, relating to, or derived from an oxide of antimony; as, *metantimonic* acid.

met·ȧ·peç′tin, *n.* a derivative of pectin.

met·ȧ·pep′tōne, *n.* a peptone formed by the action of pepsin on albumin in an acid medium.

met′ȧ·phāṣe, *n.* [*meta-* and *phase*.] in biology, the stage in mitosis, after the prophase and before the anaphase, during which the split chromosomes are arranged along the equatorial plane of the spindle.

met′ȧ·phŏr, *n.* [L. *metaphora*; Gr. *metaphora*, a transferring to one word the sense of another, from *metapherein*; *meta*, over, and *pherein*, to bear.] a figure of speech in which one thing is likened to another, different thing by being spoken of as if it were that other; implied comparison, in which a word or phrase ordinarily and primarily used of one thing is applied to another (e.g., screaming headlines, "all the world's a stage"): distinguished from *simile*.
to mix metaphors; to use two or more inconsistent metaphors in a single expression (e.g., the storm of protest was nipped in the bud).

met·ȧ·phor′iç·ăl, met·ȧ·phor′iç, *a.* [Gr. *metaphorikos*, from *metaphora*, a metaphor.] of or relating to metaphor; comprising a metaphor or containing metaphors; figurative; not literal; as, a *metaphorical* use of words; a *metaphoric* expression.

met·ȧ·phor′i·căl·ly, *adv.* in a metaphorical manner.

met·ȧ·phor′i·căl·ness, *n.* the state or quality of being metaphoric.

met′ȧ·phŏr·ist, *n.* one who uses metaphors.

met·ȧ·phos′phāte, *n.* [*metaphosphoric* and *-ate*.] a salt of metaphosphoric acid.

met″ȧ·phos·phor′iç, *a.* [*meta-* and *phosphoric*.] of, relating to, or derived from phosphoric acid.
metaphosphoric acid; glacial phosphoric acid, HPO_3, obtained by heating orthophosphoric acid.

met′ȧ·phragm (-fram), **met·ȧ·phrag′mȧ,** *n.* [*meta-*, and Gr. *phragma*, a partition, fence.] a transverse internal septum between the abdomen and metathorax of insects.

met·ȧ·phrag′măl, *a.* pertaining to the metaphragm.

met′ȧ·phrāṣe, *n.* [Gr. *metaphrasis*, a translation or paraphrase, from *metaphrazein*; *meta-*, over, and *phrazein*, to speak.]
1. a translation; especially, a literal, word-for-word translation, as distinguished from a paraphrase.
2. a repartee.

met′ȧ·phrāṣe, *v.t.*; metaphrased, *pt.*, *pp.*; metaphrasing, *ppr.* 1. to translate, especially literally.
2. to change the wording of.

met′ȧ·phrāṣed, *a.* translated word for word.

mē·taph′rȧ·sis, *n.* same as *metaphrase*.

met′ȧ·phrast, *n.* a person who puts a piece of writing into another literary form, as prose into verse.

met·ȧ·phras′tiç, met·ȧ·phras′ti·căl, *a.* close or literal in translation.

met·ȧ·physiç, *a.* metaphysical. [Rare.]

met·ȧ·phyṣ′iç, *n.* 1. metaphysics.
2. a metaphysician. [Obs.]

met·ȧ·phyṣ′i·căl, *a.* 1. of, or having the nature of, metaphysics; of the nature of being or essential reality.
2. very abstract, abstruse, or subtle: often used derogatorily of reasoning.
3. based on abstract reasoning.
4. beyond the physical or material; incorporeal, supernatural, or transcendental.
5. fond of or skilled in metaphysics.
6. designating or of the school of early seventeenth-century English poets, including especially John Donne, George Herbert, Richard Crashaw, and Abraham Cowley, whose verse is characterized by very subtle, highly intellectualized imagery, sometimes deliberately fantastic and far-fetched: term first so used by Samuel Johnson.

met·ȧ·phyṣ′i·căl·ly, *adv.* 1. in a metaphysical manner.
2. by, or from the viewpoint of, metaphysics.

met″ȧ·phy·ṣi′ciăn (-zish′ăn), *n.* one versed in metaphysics.

met·ȧ·phyṣ′içs, *n.pl.* [*construed as sing.*] [ML. *metaphysica*, neut. pl.; Gr. *meta ta physika*, after those things relating to external nature, after physics; *meta*, after, and *physika*, physics.]
1. the branch of philosophy that deals with first principles and seeks to explain the nature of being or reality (*ontology*) and of the origin and structure of the world (*cosmology*): it is closely associated with a theory of knowledge (*epistemology*).
2. speculative philosophy in general.
3. the theory or principles (of some branch of knowledge).
4. popularly, any very subtle, perplexing, or difficult reasoning.
5. occult lore. [Archaic.]

mē·taph′y·sis, *n.* [*meta-*, and Gr. *physis*, nature.] transformation; change of nature or form.

met·ȧ·plā′si·ȧ, *n.* [Gr. *metaplasis*, transformation.] the change of one form of tissue into another, as the ossification of cartilage.

mē·tap′lȧ·sis, *n.* [Gr. *metaplasis*, transformation; *meta*, over, and *plasis*, from *plassein*, to form, mold.] in biology, the stage in which organic development is complete.

met′ȧ·plaṣm, *n.* [Gr. *metaplasmos*, a transformation; *meta*, over, beyond, and *plassein*, to form, mold.]
1. that part of the contents of a cell which consists of lifeless, nonprotoplasmic matter, as certain inclusions of fatty granules or carbohydrates.
2. a change in a word by adding, leaving out, or transposing letters or syllables.

met·ȧ·plaṣ′miç, *a.* of or characterized by metaplasm.

met′ȧ·plast, *n.* [*meta-*, and Gr. *plastos*, verbal adj. of *plassein*, to form, mold.] a word or stem exhibiting metaplasm.

met·ȧ·plas′tiç, *a.* of or due to metaplasm or to metaplasia.

met′ȧ·pleụr, *n.* [*meta-*, and Gr. *pleura*, side.] the posterior part of the epipleural fold of Amphioxus.

met·ȧ·pleụ′ron, *n.*; *pl.* **met·ȧ·pleụ′rȧ,** [*meta-*, and Gr. *pleuron*, a rib.] the pleural surface of the metathorax of an insect.

met·ap·neū′tiç, *a.* [*meta-*, and Gr. *pneustikos*, of or for breathing, from *pnein*, to breathe.] having a single open pair of spiracles for breathing at the posterior end of the body, as some insect larvae.

met′ȧ·pōde, *n.* same as *metapodium*.

met·ȧ·pō′di·ăl, *a.* pertaining to a metapodium or to the metapodialia.

met·ȧ·pō′di·ăl, *n.* one of the metapodial bones.

met·ȧ·pō·di·ā′lē, *n.*; *pl.* **met·ȧ·pō·di·ā′li·ȧ,** a metatarsal or metacarpal bone.

met·ȧ·pō′di·um, *n.*; *pl.* **met·ȧ·pō′di·ȧ,** the posterior lobe of the foot in mollusks.

met·ȧ·poph′y·sis, *n.*; *pl.* **met·ȧ·poph′y·sēṣ,** [*meta-*, and Gr. *apophysis*, a process.] one of the processes situated near the articular processes of the lumbar and dorsal vertebrae, represented by small tubercles only in man, but very largely developed in the armadillo, assisting in the support of its carapace.

met·ȧ·prō′tē·in, *n.* any of a group of substances produced by the action of acids or alkalis on proteins.

met″ȧ·psȳ·chol′ō·ġy (-sȳ-), *n.* speculation about the origin, structure, function, etc. of the mind and about the relation between the mental and the physical, regarded as supplemental to psychology.

met″ȧ·psȳ·chō′sis, *n.* action or influence between minds that occurs without any known physical medium or agency.

mē·tap·tẽr·yġ′i·ăl, *a.* pertaining to the metapterygium.

mē·tap·tẽr·yġ′i·um, *n.*; *pl.* **mē·tap·tẽr·yġ′i·ȧ,** [*meta-*, and Gr. *pterygion*, a fin.] the posterior basal cartilage in a fin.

met·ap·tō′sis, *n.* [Gr. *metaptōsis*, a change, from *metapiptein*; *meta*, over, and *piptein*, to fall.] in pathology, any change in a disease in regard to its nature or seat. [Obs.]

met·är′gon, *n.* an isotope of argon.

met″ȧ·sçū·tel′lum, *n.*; *pl.* **met″ȧ·sçū·tel′lȧ,**

[*meta-*, and LL. *scutellum*, dim. of L. *scutum*, a shield.] the scutellum of a metanotum.

met·ȧ·sçū′tum, *n.*; *pl.* **met·ȧ·sçū′tȧ,** [*meta-*, and L. *scutum*, a shield.] the scutum of a metanotum.

met·ȧ·sil′i·çāte, *n.* a bisilicate.

met″ȧ·si·lic′iç, *a.* [*meta-* and *silicic.*] derived from or containing silica.

metasilicic acid; an acid, H_2SiO_3, whose salts occur in many minerals.

met·ȧ·sō′mȧ, *n.* same as *metasome.*

met″ȧ·sō·mat′iç, *a.* of or due to metasomatosis.

met·ȧ·sō′mȧ·tism, *n.* same as *metasomatosis.*

met·ȧ·sō·mȧ·tō′sis, *n.* [*meta-*, and Gr. *sōma* (*-atos*), a body.] a chemical change in a mineral or a rock mass producing new minerals or rocks from those previously existing.

met′ȧ·sōme, *n.* [*meta-*, and Gr. *soma*, body.] the posterior portion of the body of a cephalopod: also called *metasoma.*

met·ȧ·stan′nāte, *n.* a salt of metastannic acid.

met·ȧ·stan′niç, *a.* [*meta-* and *stannic.*] of, pertaining to, or derived from an isomer of stannic acid.

mē·tas′tȧ·sis, *n.*; *pl.* **mē·tas′tȧ·sēs,** [Gr. *metastasis*, a removal, departure, from *methistanai*, to place in another way; *meta*, over, and *histanai*, to place.]

1. change of form or matter; transformation. [Rare.]

2. in biology, metabolism.

3. in medicine, the shifting of disease from one part or organ of the body to another unrelated to it, as by the transfer of pathogenic organisms or of the cells of a malignant tumor.

4. in rhetoric, an abrupt transition from one subject to another.

mē·tas′tȧ·sīze, *v.i.*; metastasized, *pt., pp.*; metastasizing, *ppr.* in medicine, to spread to some other part or parts of the body by metastasis.

met·ȧ·stat′iç, *a.* of, having the nature of, or induced by metastasis; as, a *metastatic* change.

met·ȧ·stēr′nȧl, *a.* pertaining to the metasternum.

met·ȧ·stēr′num, *n.* [*meta-*, and Gr. *sternon*, the breast.]

1. the posterior segment of the sternum; in man, the xiphoid process.

2. the ventral plate or sclerite of an insect's metathorax.

met·ȧ·sthen′iç, *a.* [*meta-*, and Gr. *sthenos*, strength.] having strong hinder parts, as a kangaroo.

met·ȧ·stig′māte, *a.* having spiracles in the posterior portion, as some larvae.

mē·tas′tō·mȧ, *n.*; *pl.* **met·ȧ·stō′mȧ·tȧ,** [*meta-*, and Gr. *stōma*, mouth.] a posterior membranous lip or appendage of the mouth of crustaceans.

met′ȧ·stōme, *n.* same as *metastoma*

met·ȧ·tär′sȧl, *a.* of the metatarsus.

met·ȧ·tär′sȧl, *n.* a metatarsal bone.

met′ȧ·tärse, *n.* the metatarsus. [Rare.]

met·ȧ·tar′sus, *n.*; *pl.* **met·ȧ·tär′sī,** [*meta-*, and Gr. *tarsos*, the flat of the foot.]

1. the part of the foot, especially the five bones, between the ankle and toes.

2. (a) the corresponding part of an animal's hind limb, between the tarsus and phalanges; (b) the bone between the tibia and the phalanges in a bird's leg.

met″ȧ·tär·tar′iç, *a.* [*meta-* and *tartaric.*] of or relating to an isomer of tartaric acid.

met·ȧ·tat′iç, met·ȧ·tat′iç·ȧl, *a.* [*meta-*, and Gr. *tatos*, verbal adj. of *teinein*, to stretch.] in physics, of or having a coincidence in the directions of stress and strain.

mē·tath′ē·sis, *n.*; *pl.* **mē·tath′ē·sēs,** [LL., from Gr. *metathesis*, transposition, a going over, from *metatithenai*, to put over, transpose; *meta*, over, and *tithenai*, to place.] transposition or interchange; specifically, (a) the transposition of letters or sounds in a word, or the result of this; as, *clasp* developed from Middle English *clapse* by *metathesis*; (b) in chemistry, the interchange of elements or radicals between compounds, as when two compounds react with each other to form two new compounds.

met·ȧ·thet′iç, met·ȧ·thet′iç·ȧl, *a.* of or by metathesis.

met″ȧ·thō·rac′iç, *a.* of or relating to the metathorax.

met·ȧ·thō′rax, *n.*; *pl.* **met·ȧ·thō′rax·es, met·ȧ·thō′rȧ·cēs,** [*meta-*, and Gr. *thōrax*, the chest.] the hindmost thoracic segment in insects.

met″ȧ·tī·tan′iç, *a.* [*meta-* and *titanic.*] of, pertaining to, or derived from titanium.

met·ȧ·tung′stāte, *n.* a salt of metatungstic acid.

met·ȧ·tung′stiç, *a.* [*meta-* and *tungstic.*] of, pertaining to, or derived from tungsten.

met·ȧ·van′ȧ·dāte, *n.* a salt of metavanadic acid.

met″ȧ·vȧ·nad′iç, *a.* [*meta-* and *vanadic.*] of, relating to, or derived from vanadium.

met·ȧ·xȳ′lem (-zī′), *n.* [*meta-* and *xylem.*] the outer part, and last to be formed, of the primary xylem, or woody tissue of a plant, consisting of thick-walled cells.

met·ȧ·xȳ′lēne (-zi′), *n.* [*meta-* and *xylene.*] a form of xylene found in light coal naphtha.

mé·ta·yage′ (mā-tā-yȧzh′), *n.* [Fr.] working land on shares; a system of land cultivation in which the owner furnishes land, tools, seed, etc. and receives a share of the produce.

mé·ta·yer′ (mā-tā-yā′), *n.* [Fr., from L. *medietarius*, one who tills the soil for half the produce, from L. *medietas*, the mean, from *medius*, middle.] a tenant under the metayage system.

Met·ȧ·zō′ȧ, *n.pl.* [*meta-*, and Gr. *zōon*, a living being.] the large zoological division made up of all animals whose bodies, originating from a single cell, are composed of many cells: distinguished from *Protozoa.*

met·ȧ·zō′ăn, *n.* one of the *Metazoa.*

met·ȧ·zō′an, *a.* of or characteristic of the *Metazoa.*

met·ȧ·zō′iç, *a.* of or like the *Metazoa.*

met·ȧ·zō′on, *n.* one of the *Metazoa*; any animal whose embryo passes through a gastrula stage.

mēte, *v.t.*; meted, *pt., pp.*; meting, *ppr.* [ME. *meten*; AS. *metan*, to measure.]

1. to allot; distribute; apportion (usually with *out*).

2. to measure. [Archaic or Poet.]

mēte, *v.i.* to measure. [Archaic.]

mēte, *n.* [AS. *gemet*, a measure, from *metan*, to measure.] measure. [Obs.]

mēte, *n.* [ME.; OFr.; L. *meta*, boundary, goal.]

1. a boundary; limit.

2. a boundary mark or line.

mēte, *v.t.* and *v.i.* to dream. [Obs.]

mēte, *n.* meat. [Obs.]

mēte, *a.* meet; fit. [Obs.]

mēte′çorn, *n.* a measure of corn given by a lord to tenants as a reward for service. [Obs.]

met·em·pir′iç, *a.* metempirical.

met·em·pir′iç, *n.* a follower of metempirical philosophy; also, metempirics.

met·em·pir′iç·ȧl, *a.* 1. of metempirics.

2. lying beyond the limits of possible experience; transcendental.

met·em·pir′i·çism, *n.* [Gr. *meta*, beyond, and *empeiria*, experience.] metempirics.

met·em·pir′i·cist, *n.* a metempiric.

met·em·pir′içs, *n.pl.* [*construed as sing.*] the study or philosophy of things regarded as beyond the knowledge obtained from experience but having some relationship to this; sometimes, transcendental philosophy.

mē·temp′sy·chōse, *v.t.*; metempsychosed, *pt., pp.*; metempsychosing, *ppr.* to translate from one body to another, as the soul.

mē·temp·sy·chō′sis, *n.*; *pl.* **mē·temp·sy·chō′sēs,** [Gr. *metempsychōsis*, from *metempsychoun*; *meta*, over, and *empsychoun*, to put a soul into; *en*, in, and *psychē*, soul, life.] transmigration; the passing of a soul after death into some other body, either human or animal.

met·emp·tō′sis, *n.* [Gr. *meta*, beyond, after, and *emptōsis*, a falling upon or in, from *empiptein*; *en*, in, and *piptein*, to fall.] the suppression of the bissextile day once in 134 years, to prevent the new moon from being indicated in the calendar a day too early: compare *proemptosis.*

met″en·ce·phal′iç, *a.* of the metencephalon.

met·en·ceph′ȧ·lon, *n.*; *pl.* **met·en·ceph′ȧ·lȧ,** [Gr. *meta*, after, and *enkephalos*, the brain.]

1. that part of the brain of an embryo from which the pons and cerebellum are derived.

2. that part of the brain consisting of the pons and cerebellum.

met·en·sō·mȧ·tō′sis, *n.* [L.Gr. *metensōmatōsis*, a putting into another body; *meta*, over, *en*, in, and *sōma* (*-atos*), body.] the transference of the elements of one body into another body and their conversion into its substance, as by assimilation.

mē′tē·ō·gram, *n.* the record or diagram made by a meteorograph.

mē′tē·ō·grȧph, *n.* a meteorograph.

mē′tē·ŏr, *n.* [ML. *meteorum*; Gr. *meteōron*, a meteor, pl. *meteōra*, things in the air, from *meteōros*, lifted up, in air; *meta*, beyond, and *aeirein*, to lift up.]

1. a meteoroid entering the atmosphere of the earth from outer space at very great speed and thus made white-hot and visible by friction with the air; a shooting star.

2. any meteoroid or meteorite.

3. in meteorology, any atmospheric phenomenon, as hail, a rainbow, etc.

mē·tē·or′iç, *a.* 1. pertaining to a meteor or meteors; having the nature of a meteor; consisting of meteors; as, *meteoric* showers.

2. atmospheric or meteorological; as, hail is a *meteoric* phenomenon.

3. transiently brilliant; flashing or swift like a meteor; as, a *meteoric* rise to fame.

meteoric showers; showers of shooting stars occurring periodically, especially in the months of August and November. The maximum brilliancy occurs every thirty-three years, and then sometimes for four years in succession there are showers of unusual magnitude.

mē·tē·or′iç·ȧl, *a.* meteoric.

mē·tē·or′iç·ȧl·ly, *adv.* 1. in a meteoric manner.

2. meteorologically.

mē′tē·ŏr·ism, *n.* abdominal distention due to gas in the intestines or in the peritoneal cavity; tympanites.

mē′tē·ŏr·īte, *n.* [*meteor* and *-ite.*] 1. a metallic or mineral mass that has fallen to the earth from outer space; a fallen meteor.

2. loosely, a meteor or meteoroid.

mē·tē·ŏr·it′iç, *a.* of a meteorite or meteorites.

mē′tē·ŏr·īze, *v.i.* to become vapor.

mē·tē·or′ō·gram, *n.* a record made by a meteorograph.

mē·tē·or′ō·grȧph, *n.* [Gr. *meteōron*, a meteor, and *graphein*, to write.] an automatic device which records simultaneously changes of various meteorological elements, as moisture, temperature, etc.

mē″tē·or·ō·graph′iç, *a.* of or relating to meteorography.

mē″tē·ŏr·og′rȧ·phy, *n.* the process of recording meteorological phenomena.

mē′tē·ŏr·oid, *n.* [Gr. *meteōron*, a meteor, and *eidos*, form.] any of the many small, solid bodies traveling through outer space, which become meteors when they enter the earth's atmosphere.

mē″tē·ŏr·oid′ȧl, *a.* pertaining to a meteoroid.

mē·tē·or′ō·līte, *n.* a meteorite.

mē″tē·ŏr·ō·log′iç, *a.* same as *meteorological.*

mē″tē·ŏr·ō·log′iç·ȧl, *a.* pertaining to the atmosphere and its phenomena; of weather or climate; relating to the science of meteorology.

meteorological elements; the facts upon which the scientific study of weather and climate is based, as the velocity and direction of the wind and clouds, the pressure, temperature, and humidity of the air, the amount of precipitation, sunshine, evaporation, etc.

meteorological table; a record or table of meteorological data: also called *meteorological register.*

mē·tē·ŏr·ō·log′iç·ȧl·ly, *adv.* 1. by or according to meteorology.

2. in meteorological respects.

mē″tē·ŏr·ol′ō·gist, *n.* one versed in meteorology.

mē″tē·ŏr·ol′ō·ġy, *n.* [Gr. *meteōron*, a meteor, and *-logia*, from *legein*, to speak.] the science which treats of the atmosphere and atmospheric phenomena; the study of weather and climate.

mē·tē·or′ō·man·cy, *n.* [Gr. *meteōron*, a meteor, and *manteia*, divination.] divination by the observation of meteors.

mē″tē·ŏr·om′e·tēr, *n.* [Gr. *meteōron*, a meteor, and *metron*, a measure.] an automatic device by which meteorographic records are transmitted to a station at a distance.

mē·tē·or′ō·sçope, *n.* [Gr. *meteōroskopion*, from *meteōroskopos*, observing the heavenly bodies; *meteōron*, a meteor, pl. heavenly bodies, and *skopein*, to view.]

1. an instrument by which the apparent path of a meteor may be measured.

2. an instrument formerly used to take the apparent magnitude and angular distances of stars.

mē·tē′ō·rous, *a.* of or like a meteor.

-mē·tēr, [from L. *metrum*, Gr. *metron*, a measure.] a suffix meaning: (a) *a device for measuring* (a specified thing), as in thermo*meter*, baro*meter*; (b) (a specified number of) *meters*, as in kilo*meter*; also, (a specified fraction of) *a meter*, as in centi*meter*; (c) *having* (a specified number of) *metrical feet*, as in penta*meter*.

mē′tẽr, *n.* [ME. *meter*, a measurer, from AS. *metan*, to measure.]
1. a person who measures; especially, an official who measures commodities.
2. an instrument or apparatus for measuring; especially, an apparatus for measuring and recording the quantity or rate of flow of gas, electricity, or water passing through it.
airspeed meter; an instrument to measure the speed of aircraft.
drift meter; an aircraft instrument to indicate the side slip of the plane through the air.
dry meter; a gas meter requiring no liquid.
wet meter; a gas meter containing a liquid and a drum which revolves, measuring the gas that passes it.

mē′tẽr, *v.t.* to measure or record with a meter or meters.

mē′tẽr, mē′tre (-tẽr), *n.* [ME. and OFr. *metre* (Fr. *mètre*); L. *metrum*; Gr. *metron*, measure.]
1. (a) rhythm in verse; measured, patterned arrangement of syllables, primarily according to stress and length; (b) the specific rhythm as determined by the prevailing foot and the number of feet in the line; as, iambic *meter*; (c) the specific rhythmic pattern of a stanza as determined by the kind and number of lines.
2. rhythm in music; especially, the division into measures, or bars, having a uniform number of beats; pattern of strong and weak beats in a measure; as, **4/4** *meter* is also called *common time*.
3. [Fr. *mètre*.] the basic unit of length in the metric system, equal to 39.37 inches: it was meant to be, and virtually is, one ten-millionth part of the distance along a meridian from the equator to the pole.
common meter; a four-line stanza having alternately four and three iambic feet.
long meter; a four-line stanza having four iambic feet to each line.
short meter; a four-line stanza having three iambic feet to the first, second, and fourth lines and four iambic feet in the third.

mē′tẽr·āġe, *n.* measurement; also, a fee for measuring.

mēte′wänd, *n.* a rod used as a measure. [Dial.]

mēte′yärd, *n.* a yardstick. [Dial.]

meth, *n.* methedrine. [Slang.]

meth·aç′ry·lāte, *n.* a salt or ester of methacrylic acid.

meth·aç′ry·lāte reş′in, any of several plastic substances formed by polymerizing esters of methacrylic acid.

meth·ȧ·çryl′iç ac′id, [from *meth*yl and *acrylic*.] a crystalline acid, $C_4H_6O_2$, obtained from camomile or made synthetically.

meth′ȧ·dōne, *n.* [from 6 di*meth*ylamino-4, 4-*d*iphenyl-3-heptan*one*, and arbitrary *-on*.] a synthetic narcotic drug used in medicine as an analgesic more potent than morphine and less rapidly habit-forming.

meth·am·phet′ȧ·mīne, *n.* [*metho-*, and *amphetamine*.] a white crystalline derivative of amphetamine, $C_{10}H_{15}N$, used in the form of its hydrochloride as a drug with a stronger stimulating action than amphetamine.

meth′āne, *n.* [*meth*yl and *-ane*.] a gaseous hydrocarbon, CH_4, of the paraffin, or methane, series. It is colorless, odorless, and inflammable and is formed by the decomposition of vegetable matter or produced artificially. It is found native in petroleum wells, in marshes as marsh gas, and in mines as firedamp. Methane is used as a fuel and for illumination.

meth′āne sē′riēş, in chemistry, a group of open-chain, saturated hydrocarbons having the general formula C_nH_{2n+2}, with methane as the first of the chain.

meth′ȧ·nōl, *n.* [*methane*, and alcoh*ol*.] a colorless, volatile, inflammable, poisonous liquid, CH_3OH, obtained by the destructive distillation of wood and used in organic synthesis, as a fuel, and in the manufacture of formaldehyde, smokeless powders, paints, etc.

meth·aq′uȧ·lōne (-ak′wȧ-), *n.* [*metho-*, and *-a-*, and *quinazolone*.] a white crystalline powder, $C_{16}H_{19}N_2O$, used in the form of its hydrochloride salt as a sedative and hypnotic.

meth′e·drīne, *n.* [*meth*amphetamine, and eph*edrine*.] methamphetamine hydroxide, $C_{10}H_{15}N{\cdot}HCl$, used in medicine like amphetamine: a trade-mark (*Methedrine*).

mē·theg′lin, *n.* [W. *meddyglyn*; *medd*, mead, and *llyn*, liquor.] an alcoholic liquor made of fermented honey and water; mead.

met·hē″mō·glō′bin, *n.* [*met-* and *hemoglobin*.] a brownish, crystalline substance derived from hemoglobin by oxidation and sometimes found in the urine and blood.

me·thē′nȧ·min, *n.* methenamine.

me·thē′nȧ·mīne, *n.* [from *methene* (from *methyl* and *-ene*) and *amine*.] hexamethylenetetramine, $(CH_2)_6N_4$, a product of the reaction of ammonia with formaldehyde, used as a diuretic, an internal antiseptic, etc.

meth′ēne, *n.* same as *methylene*.

meth′ē·nyl, *n.* [*methene* and *-yl*.] the trivalent radical CH, existing in some hydrocarbons.

meth′īde, *n.* [*methyl* and *-ide*.] a compound of an element and methyl.

mē·thiñks′, *v. impers.*; methought, *pt.* it seems to me. [Archaic.]

me·thī′ō·nāte, *n.* a salt of methionic acid.

meth·ī·on′iç, *a.* [*meth*yl and Gr. *theion*, brimstone.] of or derived from sulfur and methyl.
methionic acid; a sulfonic compound derived from methyl compounds by the action of strong sulfuric acid.

me·thī′ō·nīne, *n.* [from *meth*yl and *thion*ic and *-ine*.] an amino acid, $C_5H_{11}NO_2S$, obtained from various proteins.

meth′ō-, a combining form meaning *methyl*: also, before a vowel, *meth-*.

meth′ŏd, *n.* [Gr. *methodos*, a going after, pursuit, system; *meta*, after, and *hodos*, way.]
1. a way of doing anything; mode; procedure; process; especially, a regular, orderly, definite procedure or way of teaching, investigating, etc.
2. regularity and orderliness in action, thought, or expression; system in doing things or handling ideas.
3. regular, orderly arrangement.
the Method; a realistic style of acting originated by Stanislavsky, in which the actor strives for close personal identification with his role.
Syn.—mode, manner, order, regularity, rule, system, way.

meth′ŏd, *a.* [often M–] using the Method.

mē·thod′iç, *a.* same as *methodical*.

mē·thod′iç·ăl, *a.* [LL. *methodicus*; Gr. *methodikos*, working by rule, systematic, from *methodos*, method.] characterized by method; systematic; as, a *methodical* investigator.

mē·thod′iç·ăl·ly, *adv.* in a methodical manner.

mē·thod′iç·ăl·ness, *n.* the state or quality of being methodical.

mē·thod′içs, *n.* the science of method; methodology.

Meth′ŏd·işm, *n.* 1. [m–] methodical action; excessive adherence to systematic procedure.
2. the church system, doctrines, and worship of Methodists.

Meth′ŏd·ist, *n.* 1. [m–] one characterized by strict adherence to method; specifically, one of a sect of ancient physicians who practiced by method or theory.
2. a member of any branch of a Protestant Christian denomination that developed from the evangelistic teachings and work of John and Charles Wesley, George Whitefield, and others in the first half of the eighteenth century: so called from the methodical study and worship practiced by the founders in their "Holy Club" at Oxford University, England (1729).

Meth′ŏd·ist, *a.* pertaining to or characteristic of Methodism or Methodists.

Meth·ŏd·is′tiç, *a.* Methodist.

Meth·ŏd·is′tiç·ăl, *a.* Methodist.

Meth·ŏd·is′tiç·ăl·ly, *adv.* in a Methodistic manner.

meth″ŏd·i·zā′tion, *n.* the act of methodizing.

meth′ŏd·īze, *v.t.*; methodized, *pt., pp.*; methodizing, *ppr.* to make methodical; to systematize; to arrange in a convenient manner.

meth′ŏd·īze, *v.i.* to act according to fixed methods.

meth′ŏd·ī·zẽr, *n.* one who methodizes.

meth″ŏd·ō·loġ′iç·ăl, *a.* pertaining to methodology.

meth·ŏd·ol′ō·ġy, *n.* [Gr. *methodos*, method, and *-logia*, from *legein*, to speak.]
1. the science of method, or orderly arrangement; specifically, the branch of logic concerned with the application of the principles of reasoning to scientific and philosophical inquiry.
2. a system of methods, as in any particular science.

mē·thought′ (-thot′), *v.* past tense of *methinks*. [Archaic.]

meth·ox′yl, *n.* [*meth*yl and hydr*oxyl*.] a radical, CH_3O, an analogue of hydroxyl.

meths, *n.* methylated spirits. [Brit. Colloq.]

Mē·thū′şe·lăh, *n.* [Heb. *methūshelah*, lit., perh., man of the dart.]
1. in the Bible, one of the patriarchs, said to have lived 969 years: Gen. v. 27.
2. a very old man.

meth′yl, *n.* [Fr. *méthyle* (or G. *methyl*), backformation, from *méthylène* (or G. *methylen*).] the monovalent hydrocarbon radical CH_3, found only in combination, as in methyl alcohol.

meth′yl ac′e·tāte, a colorless, volatile, inflammable liquid, $C_3H_6O_2$, that smells like apples: it is a methyl ester of acetic acid and is used as a solvent and in flavoring extracts.

meth·yl·al′, *n.* [Fr. *méthylal*, from *méthyle*, *methyl* and *alcool*, alcohol.] a colorless, volatile, inflammable liquid, $CH_2(OCH_3)_2$, that smells like chloroform: it is produced by the incomplete oxidation of methanol and used as a solvent, anesthetic, etc.

meth′yl al′ço·hol, methanol.

meth″yl·am·īne′, *n.* a colorless gas, CH_3NH_2, having a strong ammoniacal odor, resembling ammonia in many of its reactions: it is prepared synthetically or by the distillation of wood, bone, etc.

meth′yl·āte, *n.* a derivative of methyl alcohol in which the hydrogen of the hydroxyl group is replaced by a metal.

meth′yl·āte, *v.t.*; methylated, *pt., pp.*; methylating, *ppr.* 1. to mix with methyl alcohol, often in order to make the resulting mixture undrinkable.
2. to combine with methyl.

meth′yl·āt·ed spir′it (or **spir′its**), ethyl alcohol made unfit to drink by the addition of methanol, or methyl alcohol; denatured alcohol.

meth′yl ben′zēne, toluene.

meth′yl çhlō′rīde, a gas, CH_3Cl, which when compressed becomes a sweet, colorless liquid with an etherlike smell: it is used as a refrigerant and local anesthetic.

meth′yl·ēne, *n.* [*methyl* and *-ene*.]
1. a bivalent hydrocarbon radical, CH_2, existing only in combination.
2. methanol. [Rare.]

meth′yl·ēne blūe, a bluish-green aniline dye, $C_{16}H_{18}N_3ClS{\cdot}3H_2O$, used as a bacteriological stain, an antidote in cyanide poisoning, etc.

mē·thyl′iç, *a.* of, containing, or derived from methyl; as, *methylic* alcohol.

me·thys′ti·cin, *n.* [Gr. *methystikos*, intoxicating, from *methy*, wine.] a crystalline substance derived from the roots of an East Indian pepper, *Piper methysticum*.

met′iç, *n.* in ancient Greece, a foreigner; a resident alien in a Grecian city.

mē·tiç·ū·los′i·ty, *n.* the quality or state of being meticulous.

mē·tiç′ū·lous, *a.* [Fr. *méticuleux*, from L. *meticulosus*, from *metus*, fear.] unusually or extremely careful, particularly in regard to small details or unimportant matters; fastidiously scrupulous.

mé·tier′ (mā-tyā′), *n.* [Fr.] trade; calling; profession; especially, the work that one is particularly suited for.

mé·tif′ (mā-tēf′), *n.*; *pl.* **mé·tifs′** (mā-tēfs′), **mé·tis′** (mā-tēs′), [Fr., from L. *misticius*, from *miscere*, to mix.] a person of mixed blood; especially, a person one of whose parents was French and the other North American Indian: also spelled *metiff*.

met′ō·çhē, *n.* [Gr. *metochē*, a sharing; *meta*, with, and *echein*, to have.] in architecture, the space between two dentils.

mē·toe′cious, *a.* [Gr. *meta*, beyond, and *oikos*, house.] same as *heteroecious*.

mē·toe′çişm, *n.* same as *heteroecism*.

mē′tōl, *n.* [from *me*thyl-amino-cres*ol*-sulfate.] a white, soluble powder, C_7H_9ON, used in its hydrosulfate as a photographic developer: a trade-mark (*Metol*).

Mē·ton′iç, *a.* pertaining to Meton, the Athenian astronomer.
Metonic cycle; see under *cycle*.

met′ō·nym, *n.* a word used in metonymy, as a substitute for another.

met·ō·nym′iç·ăl, met·ō·nym′iç, *a.* 1. of, or having the nature of, metonymy.
2. using or used in metonymy.

met·ō·nym′iç·ăl·ly, *adv.* by metonymy.

me·ton′y·my, *n.*; *pl.* **me·ton′y·mieş,** [LL. *metonymia*; Gr. *metōnymia*, a change of name; *meta*, after, and *onoma*, *onyma*, name.] use of the name of one thing for that of another associated with or suggested by it (e.g., "the White House has decided" for "the President has decided").

met″ō·pan·trī′tis, *n.* [Gr. *metōpon*, the forehead, and *antron*, a cave, cavity.] inflammation affecting the frontal sinuses. [Obs.]

met′ō·pē, *n.* [L. *metopa*; Gr. *metopē*, the space between the triglyphs of a frieze; *meta*, between, and *opē*, an opening, cavity.] in architecture, the space between the triglyphs of the Doric frieze, which, among the ancients, was often adorned with carved work.

met′ō·pē, *n.* [Gr. *metōpon*, the forehead.] the frontal surface.

me·top′iç, *a.* of or relating to the facies, or forehead; frontal.

met′ō·pō·man″cy, *n.* [Gr. *metōpon*, forehead, and *manteia*, divination.] fortunetelling based on a study of the human features. [Rare.]

met″ō·pō·sçop′iç, met″ō·pō·sçop′iç·ăl, *a.* derived from or relating to metoposcopy.

met·ō·pos′çō·pist, *n.* one versed in metoposcopy.

met·ō·pos′çō·py, *n.* [Gr. *metōpon*, forehead, and *skopein*, to view.] the study of physiognomy; the art of trying to judge the character of men by their features.

mē·tos′tē·on, *n.* [Gr. *meta*, after, and *osteon*, bone.] the posterior lateral piece in the sternum of birds.

mē·tral′ġi·ȧ, *n.* [Gr. *mētra*, the womb, and *algos*, pain.] in pathology, pain in the womb.

met′rȧ·zōl, *n.* [G. penta*me*thylenetet*razol*.] a drug, $C_6H_{10}N_4$, used to stimulate circulation and respiration and in the treatment of some mental illnesses: a trade-mark (*Metrazol*).

mē′tre (-tẽr), *n.* meter: chiefly British spelling.

met·reç·tō′pi·ȧ, *n.* [Gr. *mētra*, the womb, and *ektopos*, out of place.] in pathology, displacement of the womb.

mē′tri·ȧ, *n.* puerperal fever.

met′riç, *a.* [L. *metricus*; Gr. *metrikos*, pertaining to measure, from *metron*, measure.]

1. of, involving, or used in measurement.

2. [Fr. *métrique*.] (a) of the meter (unit of length); (b) designating or of the system of measurement based on the meter and the gram: see *metric system*.

3. metrical.

metric hundredweight; 50 kilograms.

metric system; a decimal system of weights and measures in which the gram (.0022046 pound), the meter (39.37 inches), and the liter (61.025 cubic inches) are the basic units of weight, length, and capacity, respectively: most names for the various other units are formed by the addition of the following prefixes:

deca- or *deka-* (ten), as, 1 decameter = 10 meters

hecto- (one hundred), as, 1 hectometer = 100 meters

kilo- (one thousand), as, 1 kilometer = 1,000 meters

deci- (one tenth), as, 1 decimeter = 1/10 meter

centi- (one hundredth), as, 1 centimeter = 1/100 meter

milli- (one thousandth), as, 1 millimeter = 1/1000 meter

Other prefixes sometimes used are *myria-* (ten thousand), *mega-* (one million), and *micro-* (one millionth).

The metric system originated in France and is now the legal standard in a number of countries, and is used in scientific measurements by nearly all civilized nations.

The following are tables of metric measures and their equivalents:

Length

1 millimeter = .03937 inch, or about 1/25 inch
1 centimeter = .3937 inch
1 decimeter = 3.937 inches
1 meter = 39.370 inches = 3.281 ft. = 1.0936 yd.
1 decameter = 10 meters = 10.94 yds.
1 hectometer = 100 meters = 109.4 yds.
1 kilometer = 1093.6 yds., or about 5/8 mile

Area

1 sq. millimeter = .00155 sq. inch
1 sq. centimeter = .155 sq. inch
1 sq. decimeter = 15.5 sq. inches
1 sq. meter = 1550 sq. inches = 10.764 sq. ft. = 1.196 sq. yd.
1 are = 100 sq. meters = 119.6 sq. yds.
1 hectare = 2.471 acres

Volume

1 cub. millimeter = .000061 cub. inch
1 cub. centimeter = .06102 cub. inch
1 cub. decimeter = 61.02 cub. inches
1 cub. meter = 61023 cub. inches = 35.31 cub. ft. = 1.308 cub. yd.

The liter (used for liquids) is the same as the cubic decimeter, and is equal to 1.0567 United States quart.

Weight

1 milligram = .01543 grain
1 gram = 15.432 grains
1 kilogram = 15432.3 grains = 2.2046 lbs. avoir.

Miscellaneous

1 gram per sq. centimeter = 2.0481 lbs. per sq. ft.
1 kilogram per sq. centim. = 14.223 lbs. per sq. in.
1 kilogram-meter = 7.233 foot-pounds

The following are tables of English measures and their metric equivalents:

Length

1 inch = 2.54 centimeters
1 foot = 30.48 centimeters
1 yard = 91.44 centimeters
1 statute mile = 160933 centimeters

Area

1 sq. inch = 6.45 sq. cm.
1 sq. foot = 929 sq. cm.
1 sq. yard = 8361 sq. cm.
1 sq. mile = 2.59×10^{10} sq. cm.

Volume

1 cub. inch = 16.39 cub. cm.
1 cub. foot = 28317 cub. cm.
1 cub. yard = 764553 cub. cm.
1 imperial gallon = 4546 cub. cm.
1 United States gallon = 3785 cub. cm.

Weight

1 grain = .0648 gram
1 oz. avoir. = 28.35 grams
1 lb. avoir. = 453.6 grams
1 short ton = $.90718 \times 10^6$ grams
1 long ton = 1.016×10^6 grams
More accurately, 1 lb. avoir. = 453.592 gm.

Velocity

1 mile per hour = 44.704 cm. per sec.
1 kilometer per hour = 27.778 cm. per sec.

Density

1 lb. per cub. foot = .0160 gm. per cub. cm.
62.4 lbs. per cub. ft. = 1 gm. per cub. cm.

Force (assuming g = 981)

Weight of 1 grain = 63.57 dynes
" 1 oz. avoir. = 2.78×10^4 dynes
" 1 lb. avoir. = 4.45×10^5 dynes
" 1 short ton = 8.899×10^8 dynes
" 1 long ton = 9.97×10^8 dynes
" 1 gram = 981 dynes
" 1 kilogram = 9.81×10^5 dynes

Work (assuming g = 981)

1 foot-pound = 1.356×10^7 ergs
1 kilogram-meter = 9.81×10^7 ergs
Work in a second by one theoretical horsepower = 7.46×10^9 ergs

Metric thread; in machinery, a type of screw thread recognized by an international congress in 1898 as standard. It is on the metric system, but otherwise similar to the American standard.

metric ton; a millier or tonneau; 1000 kilograms, equal to 2,204.62 pounds (.984 long ton or 1.023 short tons).

met′riç·ăl, *a.* 1. pertaining to or composed in meter or verse; as, *metrical* compositions.

2. of, involving, or used in measurement; metric.

met′riç·ăl·ly, *adv.* 1. in a metrical manner.

2. in metrical respects.

met′riç·ăl rō·mance′, in literature, a love story or tale of adventure told in metrical form: the term is usually applied to the narrative poetry of western Europe common during the Middle Ages.

met·ri·çā′tion, *n.* [*metric*, and *-ation*.] the process of changing over to the metric system of weights and measures.

mē·tri′ciăn, *n.* a metrist (sense 1).

met′ri·cīze, *v.t.*; metricized, *pt.*, *pp.*; metricizing, *ppr.* to change into the metric system of weights and measures.

met′riçs, *n. pl.* [*construed as sing. in senses 1 and 3.*]

1. the science or art of writing in meter.

2. metrical characteristics and details (of a poem, etc.).

3. in mathematics, the theory of measurement.

met″ri·fi·çā′tion, *n.* the writing of verse; a metrical composition.

met′ri·fȳ, *v.i.* and *v.t.*; metrified, *pt.*, *pp.*; metrifying, *ppr.* [OFr. *metrifier*; LL. *metrificare*; L. *metrum*, measure, and *facere*, to make.] to put into or write in meter; to versify.

mē′trist, *n.* [ML. *metrista*.] 1. a person who writes in meter; a writer of verse.

2. an expert or specialist in metrics (sense 1); a metrician.

mē·trī′tis, *n.* [Gr. *mētra*, the womb, and *-itis*.] in pathology, inflammation of the uterus.

Met′rō, met′rō, *n.* [short for *Metropolitan District Railway*, in London.] an underground railway, as in European cities; subway.

met′rō-, a combining form meaning *measure*, as in *metr*ology.

met′rō-, a combining form meaning *uterus*, *womb*, as in *metro*rrhagia: also, before a vowel, *metr-*.

met′rō·cēle, *n.* [Gr. *mētra*, the womb, and *kēlē*, tumor.] in pathology, uterine hernia.

met′rō·çhrōme, *n.* [Gr. *metron*, a measure, and *chrōma*, color.] a device for determining the relative strength of colors.

met′rō·gràph, *n.* [Gr. *metron*, a measure, and *graphein*, to write.] a device which records the speed of locomotives, and the time, place, and duration of all stops.

met·rō·log′iç·ăl, *a.* relating to metrology.

mē·trol′ō·ġy, *n.* [Gr. *metron*, a measure, and *-logia*, from *legein*, to speak.]

1. the science of weights and measures.

2. a book devoted to this science.

3. *pl.* **mē·trol′ō·ġieṣ,** a system of weights and measures.

met·rō·mā′ni·ȧ, *n.* [Gr. *metron*, measure, and *mania*, madness.] a mania to write verse.

met·rō·mā′ni·aç, *n.* one affected with metromania.

mē·trom′e·tẽr, *n.* [*metro-*, and Gr. *metron*, a measure.] an instrument used by physicians to ascertain the size of the uterus.

met′rō·nōme, *n.* [Gr. *metron*, measure, and *nomos*, law.] an instrument containing an inverted pendulum, set in motion by clockwork, and having a sliding weight attached to the pendulum rod, by the shifting of which the number of strokes per minute can be regulated to measure time in music.

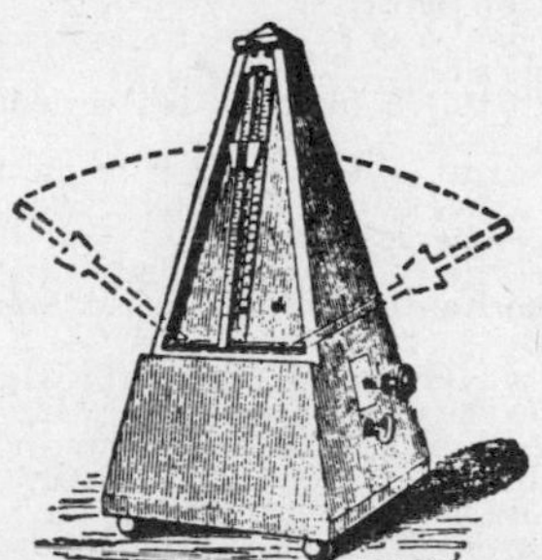

METRONOME
the dotted lines show the extent of the arc of the pendulum

met·rō·nom′iç, *a.* of or like a metronome.

mē·tron′ō·my, *n.* the measuring of time by a metronome.

mē·trō·nym′iç, *a.* [Gr. *mētēr*, mother, and *onoma*, *onyma*, name.] relating to or derived from the name of one's mother or some female ancestor.

mē·trō·nym′iç, *n.* a metronymic name.

met′rō·pōle, *n.* a metropolis. [Obs.]

mē·trop′ō·lis, *n.*; *pl.* **mē·trop′ō·lis·eṣ,** [LL., from Gr. *metropolis*; *mētēr*, mother, and *polis*, state, city.]

1. the main city, often the capital, of a country, state, or region.

2. any large city or center of population, culture, etc.

3. in ancient Greece, the mother city or state of a colony.

4. the seat, or see, of a metropolitan bishop; main diocese of an ecclesiastical province.

5. the region in which a particular species of plant or animal is found most abundantly.

met·rō·pol′i·tăn, *a.* [LL. *metropolitanus*, pertaining to a metropolis, from *metropolis*, a metropolis.]

1. of or constituting a metropolis (senses 1 and 2).

2. designating or of a metropolitan (sense 2) or metropolis (sense 4).

met·rō·pol′i·tăn, *n.* 1. a person who lives in and knows, or has the characteristic attitudes and manners of, a metropolis (senses 1 and 2).

2. (a) an archbishop having authority over the bishops of a church province; (b) in the Orthodox Eastern Church, a bishop ranking just below Patriarch.

3. in ancient Greece, a citizen of a metropolis (sense 3).

met·rō·pol′i·tăn·āte, *n.* the see presided over by a metropolitan bishop.

mē·trop′ō·līte, *n.* a metropolitan (sense 2).

met·ro·pol′i·tiç, met″rō·pō·lit′iç·ăl, *a.* pertaining to a metropolis or to a metropolitan.

mē·tror·rhā′ġi·ȧ, *n.* [*metro-*, and Gr. *rhēgnynai*, to break, burst.] in pathology, uterine hemorrhage that is not menstrual in origin.

mē′trō·scōpe, *n.* [*metro-*, and Gr. *skopein*, to view.] an instrument for examining the uterus.

mē·tros′çō·py, *n.* [*metro-*, and Gr. *skopein*, to view.] exploration of the uterus by the use of an endoscope or similar instrument.

Met″ro·sī·dē′ros, *n.* [Gr. *mētra*, the heart or pith of a tree, and *sidēros*, iron.] an extensive genus of trees and shrubs, of the order *Myrtaceæ*, native to the islands of the Pacific. *Metrosideros vera*, true ironwood, is native to Java and Amboyna. *Metrosideros robusta* is the rata of New Zealand, where it is employed in shipbuilding. The trees of this genus have thick, opposite, entire leaves and heads of showy red or white flowers.

mē′trō·tōme, *n.* [*metro-*, and Gr. *tomē*, a cutting.] an instrument for cutting the neck of the uterus through the vagina.

mē·trot′ō·my, *n.* [*metro-*, and Gr. *tomē*, a cutting.] hysterotomy; a Caesarean section.

-met′ry, [Gr. *-metria*, from *metron*, measure.] a suffix signifying *the process, art,* or *science of measuring*, as in chrono*metry*, thermo*metry*.

mette, *v.* obsolete past tense of *mete*.

met′tle, *n.* [a variant spelling of *metal*, used in a figurative sense.]

1. quality of character or temperament; especially, high quality of character; disposition; temper; spirit; ardor.

2. metal. [Obs.]

to put one on or *to one's mettle*; to incite one to do one's best.

met′tled (-tld), *a.* high-spirited; ardent; full of mettle.

met′tle·sȯme, *a.* full of spirit or mettle; possessing constitutional ardor; fiery; as, a *mettlesome* horse.

met′tle·sȯme·ly, *adv.* with high spirit.

met′tle·sȯme·ness, *n.* the state of being high-spirited.

Mē′um, *n.* [Gr. *meon*, spicknel.] a genus of plants of the order *Umbelliferæ*. *Meum athumanticum*, spicknel, which grows in the upland parts of Europe, has deeply divided leaves and white or purple flowers.

mē′um, *pron.* [L.] mine: commonly used in the phrase *meum and tuum*, mine and thine, indicating property rights.

meūte, *n.* a hawk's mew or cage.

mēve, *v.t.* and *v.i.* to move. [Obs.]

mev′y, *n.*; *pl.* **mev′ieṣ,** a mew; a gull. [Obs.]

mew, *n.* [ME. *mewe, mawe*; AS. *mæw*, a mew.] a sea gull or other gull; a sea mew, especially *Larus canus*: also *mew gull*.

mew, *n.* [OFr. *mue*, from *muer*, to change, molt.]

1. a cage, as for hawks while molting.

2. a secret place or den.

3. a place of confinement. [Obs.]

4. a mow for hay. [Brit. Dial.]

mew, *v.t.*; mewed, *pt., pp.*; mewing, *ppr.* [OFr. *muer*, to change, molt, from L. *mutare*, to change.]

1. to confine in or as in a cage; to shut up or conceal (often with *up*).

2. (a) [Archaic.] to shed or change (feathers); to molt; (b) [Obs.] to cast (horns): said of a stag.

mew, *v.i.* 1. to molt. [Archaic.]

2. to change; to put on a new appearance. [Obs.]

mew, *v.i.* [imitative.] to cry as a cat: also *meow, miaow*, etc.

mew, *n.* the characteristic cry of a cat.

mew, *n.* spicknel; baldmoney.

mewl, *v.i.*; mewled, *pt., pp.*; mewling, *ppr.* [a freq. of *mew*.]

1. to cry from uneasiness, as an infant; to whimper; to whine.

2. to mew, as a cat.

mewl, *n.* the cry of an infant.

mewl′ẽr, *n.* one who mewls.

mewṣ, *n. pl.* [*usually construed as sing.*] 1. the royal stables in London: so called because built where the king's hawks were once mewed or confined.

2. stables grouped around a court or along a lane or alley.

mẹx·çäl′, *n.* same as *mescal*.

Mex′i·çăn, *n.* 1. a native, inhabitant, or citizen of Mexico.

2. Nahuatl.

Mex′i·çăn, *a.* pertaining to Mexico, its people, their language, or their culture.

Mexican bean beetle; a species of spotted ladybug, *Epilachna corrupta*, that eats the leaves and pods of bean plants.

Mexican clover; a weed, *Richardsonia scabra*, used as a forage plant: also called *Florida clover*.

Mexican hairless; any of a breed of small dog native to Mexico, hairless except for the end of the tail and a patch on the head.

Mexican lily; a plant, *Amaryllis reginæ*, having scarlet flowers.

Mexican onyx; a form of aragonite resembling onyx, quarried in Mexico.

Mexican poppy; the prickly poppy, *Argemone mexicana*, which has yellow flowers and prickly leaves and stems.

Mexican tiger flower; a plant, *Tigridia pavonina*, with yellow or orange-spotted flowers.

Mexican War; a war between the United States and Mexico (1846–1848), settled by the Treaty of Guadalupe Hidalgo.

Mex′i·căn·īze, *v.i.* and *v.t.* to become or cause to become Mexican or like the Mexicans.

meyn′ē (men′), *n.* meinie. [Obs.]

mẹz·çäl′, *n.* same as *mescal*.

mez′cȧ·līne, *n.* mescaline.

mē·zē′rē·on, *n.* [ML.; Ar. and Per. *māzariyūn*.]

1. a small European shrub, *Daphne mezereum*, with clusters of fragrant, purplish flowers.

2. mezereum (sense 2).

mē·zē′rē·um, *n.* [Mod. L.]

1. mezereon.

2. the dried bark of mezereon, used in liniments and in the treatment of some diseases.

mez·quī′tẹ (mes-kē′), *n.* same as *mesquit*.

mez·ū′zȧh, mez·ū′zȧ, *n.*; *pl.* **mez·ū′zōth,** [Heb. *mĕzūzāh*, doorpost.] in Judaism, a piece of parchment inscribed on one side with texts from Deuteronomy (vi. 4–9 and xi. 13–21) in 22 lines and on the other side with the name of God (*Shaddai*), rolled and put into a case and attached to the doorpost of the house, as commanded in the Biblical passages.

mez′zȧ, *a.* same as *mezzo*.

mez′zȧ mȧ·jol′i·çȧ, an Italian pottery in vogue before majolica ware proper. Blue or black drawings with almost white flesh tints and blue draperies characterize the designs.

mez′zȧ·nīne, *n.* [Fr.; It. *mezzanino*, from *mezzano*, middle, from L. *medianus*.]

1. a low-ceilinged story between two main stories in a building, usually immediately above the ground floor and sometimes in the form of a balcony projecting only partly over the floor below it: also *mezzanine floor* (or *story*).

2. in some theaters, the first few rows of the balcony, separated from the others by an aisle.

3. a low window, less in height than in breadth.

mez′zō (*or* met′sō *or* med′zō), *a.* [It.] in music, medium; middle; mean; moderate.

mez′zō, *adv.* in music, moderately; somewhat.

mez″zō-rē·lie′vō, *n.*; *pl.* **mez″zō-rē·lie′vōṣ,** [It. *mezzo rilievo*; *mezzo*, from L. *medius*, middle, half, and *rilievo*, relief.] sculpture in which the figures project halfway from the background; half relief.

mez″zō-ri·liẹ′vō (med″dzō-rē-lyā′vō), *n.*; *pl.* **mez″zī-ri·liẹ′vī** (med″dzē-rē-lyā′vē), [It.] mezzo-relievo.

mez′zō-sō·prä′nō, *n.*; *pl.* **mez′zō-sō·prä′nōṣ** or **mez′zō-sō·prä′ni,** [It.] 1. a voice or part between soprano and contralto.

2. a singer with such a voice.

mez′zō-sō·prä′nō, *a.* designating or of a mezzo-soprano voice, part, or singer.

mez′zō·tint, *n.* [It. *mezzotinto*.]

1. a method of engraving on a copper or steel plate by scraping or polishing parts of a roughened surface, so that an impression of light and shade can be produced.

2. an engraving or print so produced.

mez′zō·tint, *v.t.* to engrave by the method of mezzotint.

mez′zō·tint·ẽr, *n.* a worker or engraver in mezzotint.

mez·zō·tin′tō, *n.* and *v.t.* same as *mezzotint*.

Mg, in chemistry, magnesium.

mhō (mō), *n.* [*ohm* reversed.] the unit of electrical conductance, reciprocal of the ohm.

mhōrr (mōr), *n.* same as *mohr*.

mī, *n.* [It.] in music, a syllable representing the third note of any diatonic scale, especially of the scale of C; that is, the note E.

Mī·am′i, *n.*; *pl.* **Mī·am′i, Mī·am′iṣ,** a member of a former tribe of Algonquian Indians who migrated from Wisconsin to Indiana and near-by regions: also *Miami Indian*.

mīa′mīa (mī′mī), *n.* [Austral.] an aboriginal hut.

Mi·ä′nȧ bug, [from *Miana*, a Persian town.] a tick, *Argas persicus*, found in Egypt and Persia: its bite is poisonous.

mi·aow′, mi·aou′ (-ou′), *n.* and *v.i.* meow; mew.

mī·är′ġy·rīte, *n.* [Gr. *meiōn*, less, and *argyros*, silver, and *-ite*.] a mineral sulfide of silver and antimony, iron-black, crystalline, and easily cut.

mī·ar·ō·lit′iç, *a.* [Gr. *miaros*, stained, and *lithos*, stone.] having numerous small cavities formed by the shrinkage of the magma in crystallization: said of certain granitic rocks.

mī′as, *n.* [Malay.] the orangutan.

mi·ȧsk′īte, mi·ȧsç′īte, *n.* [*Miask* and *-ite*.] a nephelite syenite found near Miask in Siberia.

mī′aṣm, *n.* same as *miasma*.

mī·aṣ′mȧ, *n.*; *pl.* **mī·aṣ′mȧṣ, mī·aṣ′mȧ·tȧ,** [Mod. L.; Gr. *miasma* (*-atos*), stain, pollution, from *miainein*, to stain, pollute.] poisonous vapor formerly supposed to arise from decomposing animal or vegetable matter, swamps, etc. and infect the air, especially at night: such vapor was once thought to cause malaria.

mī·aṣ′măl, *a.* of, producing, or caused by miasma; noxious; pestilential.

mī·aṣ·mat′iç, mī·aṣ·mat′i·çăl, *a.* same as *miasmal*.

mī·aṣ′miç, *a.* same as *miasmal*.

mī·aṣ·mol′ō·ġy, *n.* [Gr. *miasma*, stain, pollution, and *-logia*, from *legein*, to speak.] a treatise on miasma.

mi·aul′, *n.* and *v.i.* meow; mew.

mib, *n.* [altered from *marble*.]

1. a marble. [Dial.]

2. [*pl.*] the game of marbles. [Dial.]

mī′çȧ, *n.* [L. *mica*, a crumb, grain, particle; influenced by *micare*, to shine, glitter.] any of a group of minerals (complex silicates) that crystallize in thin, somewhat flexible, easily separated layers, translucent or transparent: mica is resistant to heat and electricity, and when transparent is often called *isinglass*. The varieties have received the names of biotite, lepidolite, muscovite, lepidomelane, paragonite, phlogopite, etc.

mica diorite; a rock differing from diorite by having mica in place of hornblende.

mī·çā′ceous, *a.* pertaining to or containing mica; resembling mica; laminate; sparkling.

Mī′çȧh, *n.* a book of the Old Testament, written by a Hebrew prophet of the 8th century B.C.: also, in the Douay Bible, *Micheas*.

mī′çȧ pow′dẽr, a kind of dynamite consisting of nitroglycerin and mica.

mī′çȧ schist (shist), a metamorphic rock containing a large proportion of mica, with quartz and various minor constituents, and having a slaty or schistose structure.

mīce, *n.* pl. of *mouse*.

mi·cel′la, *n.*; *pl.* **mi·cel′lae,** same as *micelle*.

mi·celle′, mi·cell′, *n.* [Mod. L. *micella*, dim., from L. *mica*, a grain, crumb, morsel.]

1. a hypothetical structural unit of an organized body.

2. the structural unit of gel-forming colloids, made up of complex molecules: it can change in size without changing chemically and may have crystalline properties.

mich, *v.i.* same as *miche*.

Mī′çhael (-kl), *n.* in the Bible, the archangel who, with an army of loyal angels, victoriously warred with the rebel angel Lucifer: Rev. xii. 7–9.

Miçh′ael·măs (-el-), *n.* [*Michael* and *mass*, a feast.] the feast of St. Michael, the archangel, celebrated on the 29th of September: in England, a quarter day.

Miçh′ael·măs dāi′ṣy, any of various asters, wild or cultivated.

miche, *v.i.* [ME. *michen, mouchen*; OFr. *muchier*, to hide, skulk.]

1. to lie hid; to skulk; to retire or shrink from view, to sneak. [Obs. or Brit. Dial.]

2. to be guilty of anything done in secret, as to carry on an illicit amour, or to pilfer secretly. [Obs. or Brit. Dial.]

Written also *meech* and *meach*.

Mī·chē′ȧs, *n.* Micah: Douay Bible form.

Mī·chē′li·ȧ, *n.* [named after *Micheli*, a Florentine botanist of the eighteenth century.] a genus of fine, lofty, Asiatic trees of the magnolia family. Several species yield useful timber as well as products used in medicine.

Mich·i·gan′dẽr (mish-) *n.* a native or inhabitant of Michigan.

Mich′i·găn·īte (mish′), *n.* same as *Michigander*.

mick, *n.* [dim. of *Michael*, taken as a typical Irish name.] an Irishman: hostile or contemptuous term. [Slang.]

mick′ey finn, Mick′ey Finn, a drink of liquor to which a powerful narcotic or purgative has been added, given to an unsuspecting person: also *mickey, Mickey*. [Slang.]

mick′le, *a., adv.,* and *n.* [ME.(Northern) *mikel*; AS. micel.] much: also *muckle*. [Archaic or Scot.]

Miç′maç, *n.*; *pl.* **Miç′maç, Miç′maçs,** [Amer. Ind., lit., allies.] a member of a tribe of Algonquian Indians in Newfoundland and the Maritime Provinces of Canada.

mī′çō, *n.* [S. Am.] a small South American monkey, *Hapale argentatus*, with hair shining and entirely white, the tail black, and the face and hands of a deep flesh color; a variety of marmoset.

Mī·çō′ni·ȧ, *n.* [named after D. *Micon*, a Spanish botanist.] a very extensive genus of trees and shrubs, native to South America.

mī′çrȧ, *n.* pl. of micron.

mī·çrȧ·çöus′tiç, *a.* [Fr. *micracoustique*.] serving to augment weak sounds.

mī·çrȧ·çöus′tiç, *n.* an instrument which augments weak sounds. [Obs.]

mī·çran′dẽr, *n.* [Gr. *mikros*, small, and *anēr, andros*, man, male.] a dwarf male plant developed from the androspores of some algae.

mī·çren·ceph′ȧ·lous, *a.* having a small brain.

mī′çri·fȳ, *v.t.*; micrified, *pt., pp.*; micrifying, *ppr.* [from *micro-* and *-fy*.] to make small or unimportant.

mī′çrō-, [Gr. *mikro-*, from *mikros*, small.] a combining form meaning: (a) *little, small, minute*; (b) *exceptionally little, abnormally small*, as in *micro*cephalic; (c) *enlarging what is small*, as in *micro*scope, *micro*phone; (d) *relation to microscopes, microscopic*, as in *micro*chemistry; (e) in the metric system, etc., *one millionth part of* (a specified unit), as in *micro*gram, *micro*farad: also, before a vowel, *micr-*.

mī″çrō·am·pēre′, *n.* [*micro-* and *ampere*.] in electricity, one millionth part of an ampere.

mī″çrō·ȧ·nal′y·sis, *n.* the chemical analysis and identification of very small quantities.

mī·çrō-au′di·phōne, *n.* [*micro-* and *audiphone*.] an instrument used for making very faint sounds audible.

mī·çrō·bar′ō·gràph, *n.* a barograph for recording very small changes in atmospheric pressure.

mī′çrōbe, *n.* [Fr., from Gr. *mikros*, small, and *bios*, life.] a very minute living thing, whether plant or animal; microorganism; especially, any of the bacteria that cause disease; germ.

mī·çrō′bi·ăl, *a.* same as *microbic*.

mī·çrō′bi·ăn, *a.* same as *microbic*.

mī·çrō′biç, *a.* of or caused by a microbe or microbes.

mī·çrō′bi·çīde, *n.* [from *microbe*, and L. *cædere*, to kill.] anything that kills microbes.

mī″çrō·bī·ol′ō·ġy, *n.* [from *micro-*, and Gr. *bios*, life, and *-logia*, from *legein*, to speak.] the branch of biology that deals with microorganisms.

mī·çrō′bi·on, *n.* same as *microbe*.

mī·çrō·cär′di·ȧ, *n.* [from *micro-*, and Gr. *kardia*, heart.] abnormal smallness of the heart.

mī″çrō·cē·phā′li·ȧ, *n.* same as *microcephaly*.

mī″çrō·cē·phal′iç, *a.* same as *microcephalous*.

mī·çrō·ceph′ȧ·lişm, *n.* the condition of being microcephalic.

mī·çrō·ceph′ȧ·lous, *a.* of or having microcephaly.

mī·çrō·ceph′ȧ·ly, *n.* [from *micro-*, and Gr. *kephalē*, head.] unnatural smallness of the head; the condition in which the head or cranial capacity is abnormally small.

mī·çrō·çhem′i·căl, *a.* of or pertaining to microchemistry.

mī·çrō·çhem′is·try, *n.* [*micro-* and *chemistry*.] the chemistry of microscopic quantities or objects.

mī″çrō·çhrō·nom′ē·tẽr, *n.* [from *micro-*, and Gr. *chronos*, time, and *metron*, a measure.] a chronoscope for registering very small periods of time, such as the time a projectile takes to pass over a short distance.

mī″çrō·çlī″mȧ·tol′ō·ġy, *n.* the study of slight differences in climate, as between adjoining terrains, due to slight differences in soil, exposure, etc.

mī′çrō·çlīne, *n.* [from *micro-*, and Gr. *klinein*, to incline.] a grayish, yellowish, greenish, or reddish mineral of the feldspar family, potassium aluminum silicate, $KAlSi_3O_8$, having a glassy luster and perfect cleavage: it occurs in igneous rocks.

mī·çrō·çoç′căl, *a.* of, pertaining to, or caused by micrococci.

Mī·çrō·çoç′çus, *n.* [from *micro-*, and Gr. *kokkos*, a kernel, berry.]

1. a genus of spherical or egg-shaped bacteria that occur in irregular masses or plates and feed on dead or living matter.

2. [m—] *pl.* **mī·çrō·çoç′çī,** any member of this genus.

mī″çrō·çōm·pūt′ẽr, *n.* [*micro-* and *computer*.] a very small computer containing a microprocessor along with supporting devices, such as a system for storing and recalling data.

mī′çrō·çoşm, *n.* [LL. *microcosmus*; L.Gr. *mikrokosmos*; *mikros*, small, and *kosmos*, world.]

1. a little world: figuratively used for man, as an epitome of the universe, or great world.

2. a community, village, etc. regarded as a miniature or epitome of the world.

mī·çrō·çoş′miç, *a.* 1. of, being, or like a microcosm.

2. designating a white, crystalline salt, sodium ammonium hydrogen phosphate, $Na(NH_4)HPO_4{\cdot}4H_2O$, used as a reagent in blowpipe analysis, in testing for metallic oxides, etc.: it was originally obtained from human urine.

mī·çrō·çoş′mi·căl, *a.* same as *microcosmic*.

mī″çrō·çoş·mog′rȧ·phy, *n.* [L.Gr. *mikrokosmos*, a little world, and *-graphia*, from *graphein*, to write.] the description of man as a microcosm.

mī″çrō·çöu·lomb′ (-lom′), *n.* [*micro-* and *coulomb*.] in electricity, one millionth of a coulomb.

mī·çrō·çrys′tăl·line, *a.* [from *micro-*, and Gr. *krystallinos*, of crystal.] having crystalline structure that can be seen only with a microscope.

mī′çrō·cyst, *n.* [from *micro-*, and Gr. *kystis*, a bladder, bag.] a resting stage, entered into by the swarm spores of certain fungi, as in *Myxomycetes*, under conditions which do not favor development.

mī′çrō·cyte, *n.* [from *micro-*, and Gr. *kytos*, a hollow, cavity.] an abnormally small red blood corpuscle, occurring especially in certain types of anemia.

mī″çrō·cȳ·thē′mi·ȧ, *n.* [from *micro-*, and Gr. *kytos*, a hollow, cavity, and *haima*, blood.] a diseased condition of the blood marked by the presence of microcytes.

mī″çrō·dē·teç′tŏr, *n.* [*micro-* and *detector*.] an instrument for detecting very small amounts of, or minute changes in, an electric current.

mī″çrō·dis·seç′tion, *n.* dissection of tissue, etc. under the microscope.

mī′çrō·dont, *a.* having very small teeth.

mī′çrō·dont, *n.* a microdont individual.

mī′çrō·dont·işm, *n.* exceptional smallness of the teeth.

mī·çrō·far′ad, *n.* [*micro-* and *farad*.] one millionth of a farad.

mī′çrō·film, *n.* 1. film on which documents, printed pages, etc. are photographed in a reduced size for convenience in storage and transportation: enlarged prints can be made from such film, or the film can be viewed directly with the help of a special optical apparatus.

2. a reproduction on microfilm.

3. loosely, a microphotograph (sense 3).

mī′çrō·film, *v.t.* and *v.i.* to photograph on microfilm.

mī′çrō·form, *n.* [from *micro-*, and L. *forma*, form.] a microscopic organism or form of organism.

mī″çrō·gȧ·mēte′, *n.* the smaller, usually the male, of a pair of conjugating gametes.

mī·çrō·ġē·ō·loġ′iç·ăl, *a.* pertaining to microgeology.

mī″çrō·ġē·ol′ō·ġy, *n.* [*micro-* and *geology*.] that branch of geology which involves the use of the microscope.

mī·çrō·glos′si·ȧ, *n.* [from *micro-*, and Gr. *glōssa*, the tongue.] in biology, exceptional smallness of the tongue.

mī″çrō·gō·nid′i·um, *n.* [*micro-* and *gonidium*.]

1. in botany, a gonidium of the smaller of two distinct sizes.

2. in zoology, a small infusorian regarded as a male sexual cell.

mī′çrō·gram, mī′çrō·gramme, *n.* [*micro-* and *gram*.] one millionth of a gram.

mī′çrō·gram, *n.* a micrograph (sense 2).

mī′çrō·gràph, *n.* [*micro-* and *-graph*.]

1. an apparatus for doing extremely small writing, drawing, or engraving.

2. a photograph or drawing of an object as seen through a microscope.

3. an apparatus by which, through the movements of a diaphragm, very slight movements can be recorded in magnified visual form and measured.

mī·çrō·graph′iç, *a.* pertaining to micrography.

mī·çrog′rȧ·phy, *n.* [*micro-* and *-graphy*.]

1. the study or description of objects too small to be discerned without the aid of a microscope.

2. the art or practice of writing in tiny characters.

mī′çrō·gro̤ove, *n.* 1. a very narrow needle groove, as in a long-playing phonograph record, allowing more matter to be recorded on a record than does the ordinary, wider groove.

2. a record having such narrow grooves.

A trade-mark (*Microgroove*).

mī·çrōhm′, *n.* [*micr-* and *ohm*.] one millionth of an ohm.

mī·çrō·lep·i·dop′tẽr, *n.* any of certain small moths.

Mī·çrō·lep·i·dop′tẽr·a, *n.pl.* [*micro-* and *Lepidoptera*.] certain of the small moths, regarded as a group.

mī′çrō·līte, *n.* [from *micro-*, and Gr. *lithos*, stone.]

1. a mineral related to pyrochlore, characterized by a brownish color and resinous luster, and occurring in very small octahedral crystals.

2. see *microlith*.

mī·çrō·lī′tẽr, *n.* [*micro-* and *liter*.] a measure of capacity of the millionth part of a liter.

mī′çrō·lith, *n.* [from *micro-*, and Gr. *lithos*, stone.] a minute isotropic needle-shaped crystal found mostly in volcanic rocks.

mī·çrō·lith′iç, *a.* [from *micro-*, and Gr. *lithos*, stone.] of, pertaining to, or consisting of small stones: opposed to *megalithic*.

mī·çrō·loġ′i·căl, mī·çrō·loġ′iç, *a.* of or pertaining to micrology.

mī·çrō·loġ′i·căl·ly, *adv.* in a micrological manner; in minute detail.

mī·çrol′ō·ġy, *n.* [Gr. *mikrologia*: see *micro-* and *-logy*.] the discussion or study of trivial matters or petty differences.

mī′çrō·mēre, *n.* [Gr. *mikromerēs*, of small parts; *mikros*, small, and *meros*, a part.] in biology, one of the smaller subdivisions of a telolecithal ovum.

Mī·çrō·mē′ri·ȧ, *n.* [from *micro-*, and Gr. *meros*, part.] a genus of plants of the family *Lamiaceæ*, comprising about sixty species, mostly of the Old World: in the United States, one representative, *Micromeria douglassii*, is known in California as *yerba buena*.

mī″çrō·mē·rit′iç, *a.* in geology, composed of grains so small as to be invisible to the naked eye: applied to rocks.

mī·çrom′ē·tẽr, *n.* [from *micro-*, and Gr. *metron*, measure.]

1. an instrument for measuring very small distances, angles, diameters, etc., used on a telescope or microscope.

2. micrometer calipers.

annular, circular, or *ring micrometer*; a micrometer for use in a telescope, consisting essentially of a thin, smooth, metal ring, adjusted with great precision in the focus of the instrument in such a way that it seems to hang in the atmosphere between the observer and the celestial dome.

double-image micrometer; a micrometer by means of which two images of an object are formed, as by a bisected lens whose halves are adjustable along the line of section.

filar micrometer; a micrometer having at the focus, as of a telescope, two parallel spider lines, one fixed and the other movable by means of a micrometer screw, by the turns of which the distance between the lines at any time is determined: used for determining the distance between two objects and the rate of their approach to or recedence from each other.

mī·crom′e·tẽr bal′ănce, a balance for delicate weighing, as of coins, adjustable by a micrometer screw.

mī·crom′e·tẽr çal′i·pẽrs (or **çal′i·pẽr**), calipers adjustable by a micrometer screw, used for measuring diameters of wires, thin leaves of metal, etc.

mī·crom′e·tẽr screw (skrụ), a finely threaded screw of definite pitch, with a head graduated to show how much the screw has been moved in or out: used in micrometers, etc. to give fine measurements, sometimes to .0001 of an inch.

MICROMETER CALIPERS
A, used for measuring inside dimensions; B, used for measuring outside dimensions

mī·crō·met′riç, mī·crō·met′riç·ăl, *a.* pertaining to or made by the micrometer.

mī·crō·met′riç·ălly, *adv.* by means of a micrometer.

mī·crom′e·try, *n.* measurement by means of micrometers.

mī·crō·mil′li·mē·tẽr, mī·crō·mil′li·mē·tre (-tẽr), *n.* [*micro-* and *millimeter.*]
1. one millionth of a millimeter; one billionth of a meter.
2. a millimicron.
3. in biology and chemistry, a micron.

mī″crō·mō′tion, *n.* one of a series of very short motions which succeed each other so quickly that the eye confuses them.

mī′cron, *n.*; *pl.* **mī′crons, mī′crȧ,** [Mod. L., from Gr. *mikron,* neut. of *mikros,* small, minute.]
1. one millionth of a meter; one thousandth of a millimeter.
2. in physical chemistry, a particle having a diameter between .01 and .0001 millimeter. Also spelled *mikron.*

Mī·crō·nē′siăn, *a.* [Gr. *mikronēsos*; *mikros,* small, and *nēsos,* island.] of or pertaining to Micronesia, its people, their language, or their culture.

Mī·crō·nē′siăn, *n.* 1. a native of Micronesia, which is inhabited by peoples of mixed Melanesian, Polynesian, and Malayan stock.
2. any of the Austronesian languages spoken in Micronesia.

mī·crō·nom′e·tẽr, *n.* same as *microchronometer.*

mī·crō·nū′clē·us, *n.*; *pl.* **mī·crō·nū′clē·ī,** [*micro-* and *nucleus.*] in biology, a small nucleus, particularly the smaller of two nuclei, as found in some infusorians: distinguished from *macronucleus.*

mī·crō·or′găn·işm, *n.* any microscopic or ultramicroscopic animal or vegetable organism; especially, any of the bacteria, protozoa, viruses, etc.; also spelled *microörganism, micro-organism.*

mī·crō·pan′tō·grȧph, *n.* [*micro-* and *pantograph.*] an instrument constructed on the general principle of the pantograph for executing extremely minute writing and engraving.

mī″crō·pȧ·thol′ō·ġy, *n.* [*micro-* and *pathology.*] that branch of pathology in which facts and conditions are revealed only by the use of the microscope, as the nature and effects of bacteria, etc.

mī·crō·peg′mȧ·tīte, *n.* [*micro-* and *pegmatite.*] a rock that shows the structure of pegmatite, or graphic granite, when examined under the microscope.

mī·crō·peg·mȧ·tit′iç, *a.* relating to or descriptive of graphic granite with microscopic markings.

mī′crō·phōne, *n.* [*micro-,* and Gr. *phōnē,* voice, sound.] a device used in radio, telephony, and sound recording, by means of which sound waves are changed to electrical impulses, permitting them to be recorded, amplified, reproduced or transmitted. The most widely used principle is the variation of electrical impedance (either resistance, capacitance, or inductance), effected by means of a diaphragm upon which sound waves are allowed to fall; the vibrations produced vary the impedance of an electrical circuit, giving the resulting oscillations the same frequency as the original sound wave with proportional amplitudes.

mī·crō·phon′iç, *a.* of, having the nature of, or like a microphone.

mī·crō·phon′içs, *n.* the science that deals with the augmenting of weak sounds.

mī·croph′ō·nous, *a.* microphonic. [Rare.]

mī·crō·phō′tō·grȧph, *n.* [*micro-* and *photograph.*]
1. a very small photograph, usually requiring enlargement to bring out the details.
2. a photograph taken through a microscope: usually *photomicrograph.*
3. an enlarged photograph printed from a microfilm.

mī″crō·phō·tog′rȧ·phy, *n.* [*micro-* and *photography.*] a photographic process by which an object is reproduced in microscopic size; the photography of microscopic objects.

mī·croph·thal′mi·ȧ, mī·croph·thal′my, *n.* [from *micro-,* and Gr. *opthalmos,* the eye.] abnormal smallness of the eye.

mī·crō·phyl′line, *a.* [from *micro-,* and Gr. *phyllon,* a leaf.] in botany, composed of or bearing very small leaves or leaflets.

mī·crō·phyl′lous, *a.* [from *micro-,* and Gr. *phyllon,* a leaf.] in botany, having small leaves.

mī·crō·phyş′içs, *n.* [*micro-* and *physics.*] that branch of physics that deals with microscopic physical phenomena.

mī·crō·phȳ′tăl, *a.* same as *microphytic.*

mī′crō·phȳte, *n.* [*micro-* and *-phyte.*] any microscopically small plant, especially one parasitic in its habits.

mī·crō·phyt′iç, *a.* of, or having the nature of, a microphyte.

mī′crō·print, *n.* a microphotograph of printed or written matter so greatly reduced that it can be read only through a magnifying device.

mī″crō·proc′es·sŏr, *n.* the controlling unit of a microcomputer, laid out on a tiny silicon chip and containing the logical elements for handling data, performing calculations, carrying out stored instructions, etc.

mī·crop′si·ȧ, mī′crop·sy, *n.* [from *micro-,* and Gr. *ōpsis,* view.] in pathology, a derangement of vision which causes objects to appear abnormally small.

mī·crop′tẽr·ous, *a.* [from *micro-,* and Gr. *pteron,* a wing, feather.] short-winged or short-finned.

mī·crō·pȳ′lăr, *a.* of, or having the nature of, a micropyle.

mī′crō·pȳle, *n.* [Fr., from Gr. *mikros,* small, and *pylē,* gate, opening.]
1. in botany, (a) a very small opening in the outer coats of an ovule, through which the pollen tube penetrates; (b) the corresponding opening in the developed seed.
2. in zoology, a very small opening in the vitelline membrane of an ovum, through which spermatozoa can enter.

mī″crō·pȳ·rom′e·tẽr, *n.* [*micro-* and *pyrometer.*] an optical instrument for determining temperature, etc. of minute bodies giving off light or heat.

mī′·crō·sclēre, *n.* [from *micro-,* and Gr. *sklēros,* hard.] in zoology, a very small sponge spicule, usually supporting a single cell.

mī′crō·scōpe, *n.* [from *micro-,* and Gr. *skopein,* to view.] an optical instrument consisting of a lens or combination of lenses, which magnifies very small objects so that their structure or texture may be examined.

compound microscope; a microscope which differs from the simple or single lens microscope in having an object lens and an eyepiece arranged to give greater magnification; the objective and eyepiece each consist of a lens or combination of lenses mounted at either end of a telescoping tube so that they can be focused by a gear.

binocular microscope; a form of compound microscope with two eyepieces permitting rays of light from an object to pass into both eyes of the observer.

oxyhydrogen microscope; a microscope in which an oxyhydrogen light is used to illuminate the object.

simple or *single microscope*; a microscope consisting of a single convex lens between the eye and the object.

solar microscope; a microscope having a reflector and a condenser connected with it, the former being employed to throw the sun's ray on the latter, by which it is condensed to illuminate the object placed in its focus.

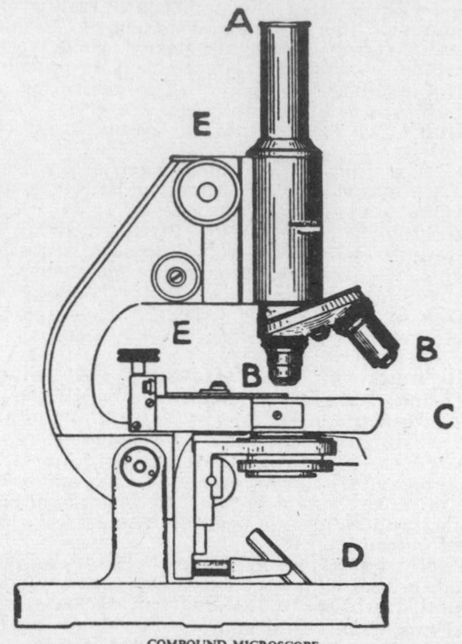

COMPOUND MICROSCOPE
A, eyepiece; B, B, objectives; C, stage; D, mirror; E, E, adjustmen heads

mī·crō·scop′iç, mī·crō·scop′iç·ăl, *a.* 1. of or pertaining to the microscope or to microscopy; for the use of a microscope; as, a microscopic mirror.
2. with or as with a microscope; made or as if made by a microscope; as, *microscopic* observations.
3. resembling or suggestive of a microscope; searching; minutely observing.
4. very small; visible only with the aid of a microscope; as, a *microscopic* insect.

mī·crō·scop′iç·ăl·ly, *adv.* 1. by using a microscope.
2. in careful detail, as if with a microscope; exactly, minutely, and searchingly.
3. so as to be microscopic; extremely; as, *microscopically* small.

mī·cros′cō·pist, *n.* one who uses, or is skilled in using, a microscope.

mī·cros′cō·py, *n.* the use of the microscope; investigation by means of a microscope.

mī·crō·seç′tion, *n.* [*micro-* and *section.*] a thin transparent slice or section, as of wood, prepared for examination by a microscope.

mī′crō·seişm, *n.* [from *micro-,* and Gr. *seismos,* a shaking.] a very weak or slight vibration of the earth's crust.

mī·crō·seiş′miç, *a.* of a microseism.

mī·crō·seiş′mō·grȧph, *n.* [from *micro-,* and Gr. *seismos,* a shaking, and *graphein,* to write.] a microseismometer.

mī″crō·seiş·mom′e·tẽr, *n.* [from *micro-,* and Gr. *seismos,* a shaking, and *metron,* measure.] an instrument for indicating the duration, intensity, and direction of microseisms.

mī·crō·sep′tum, *n.*; *pl.* **mī·crō·sep′tȧ,** [*micro-* and *septum.*] a small, imperfect septum in an anthozoan.

mī·crō·sī′phon, *n.* [from *micro-,* and Gr. *siphōn,* a tube, pipe.] the rudimentary siphon found in various cephalopods.

mī″crō·sī·phon′ū·lȧ, *n.* [from *micro-,* and Gr. *siphōn,* a tube, pipe.] the stage in the development of some cephalopods at which the microsiphon can first be seen.

mī·croş·mat′iç, *a.* [from *micr-,* and Gr. *osmē,* smell.] having the olfactory organs not well developed.

mī·crō·sō′mȧ, *n.* same as *microsome.*

mī′crō·sōme, *n.* [*micro-* and *-some* (body).] any of the minute granules in the protoplasm of an active cell.

mī·crō·speç′trō·scōpe, *n.* [*micro-* and *spectroscope.*] a spectroscope connected with a microscope for examining the spectrum of light in minute bodies.

mī″ç̣rō·spec̣·tros′c̣ō·py, *n.* the use of, or investigation by means of, a microspectroscope.

Mī·ç̣rō·spēr′mae, *n.pl.* [from *micro-*, and Gr. *sperma*, seed.] a group of monocotyledons, including the *Hydrocharideæ* and the *Orchideæ*, and named from its small seeds.

mī′ç̣rō·sphēre, *n.* [*micro-*, and *sphere.*] any of various minute globules, as an encapsulated isotope, a cell-like structure resembling a protein, etc.

mī″ç̣rō·spō·ran′ġi·um, *n.*; *pl.* **mī″ç̣rō·spō·ran′ġi·ȧ,** [*micro-* and *sporangium.*] a sporangium which contains or produces microspores, as the pollen sac of the anther in seed plants.

mī′ç̣rō·spōre, *n.* a small, asexually produced spore from which a male gametophyte develops, as a pollen grain in a seed plant.

mī·ç̣rō·spōr′iç̣, *a.* of microspores.

mī·ç̣rō·spō′rō·phyll, *n.* a sporophyll that produces microsporangia.

mī′ç̣rō·sthēne, *n.* [*micro-*, and Gr. *sthenos*, strength.] an ineducabilian.

mī·ç̣rō·sthen′iç̣, *a.* ineducabilian.

mī·ç̣rō·stom′ȧ·tous, *a.* [*micro-*, and Gr. *stōma* (-*atos*), mouth.] having a small mouth.

mī·ç̣ros′tō·mous, *a.* microstomatous.

mī·ç̣rō·stȳ′lous, *a.* [*micro-*, and Gr. *stylos*, a pillar.] having short styles and long stamens.

mī′ç̣rō·sûr″ġēr·y, *n.* surgery performed while viewing through a microscope and using minute instruments or laser beams.

mī′ç̣rō·tōme, *n.* [*micro-*, and Gr. *-tomos*, from *temnein*, to cut.] an instrument for cutting thin sections of tissue, etc. for study under the microscope.

mī·ç̣rō·tom′iç̣, *a.* of microtomy or the microtome.

mī·ç̣rot′ō·mist, *n.* one versed in microtomy.

mī·ç̣rot′ō·my, *n.* the art of preparing sections for study under the microscope, as by the use of the microtome.

mī·ç̣rō·vōlt′, *n.* [*micro-* and *volt.*] the millionth of a volt.

mī′ç̣rō·wāve, *a.* 1. designating or of that part of the electromagnetic spectrum between the far infrared and some lower frequency limit: commonly regarded as extending from 300,000 to 300 megahertz.

2. designating an oven that cooks quickly by causing microwaves to penetrate the food, generating internal heat.

mī′ç̣rō·wāve, *n.* any electromagnetic wave of microwave frequency.

mī′ç̣rō·wave, *v.t.*; microwaved, *pt.*, *pp.*; microwaving, *ppr.* to cook in a microwave oven.

mī·ç̣rō·zō′ȧ, *n.pl.* [*micro-*, and Gr. *zōon*, an animal.] animals of microscopic smallness.

mī·ç̣rō·zō′ăn, *n.* one of the microzoa.

mī·ç̣rō·zō′ăn, *a.* pertaining to the microzoa.

mī·ç̣rō·zō′oid, *n.* [*micro-* and *zooid.*] a minute free-swimming zooid, as in some flagellate *Infusoria.*

mī·ç̣rō·zō′on, *n.* one of the microzoa.

mic̣′tion, *n.* urination.

mic̣′tū·rāte, *v.i.*; micturated, *pt.*, *pp.*; micturating, *ppr.* to urinate.

mic̣·tū·ri′tion (-rish′un), *n.* [L. *micturitus*, pp. of *micturire*, to desire to make water, from *mingere*, to make water.] the act of urinating.

mid, *a.*; *superl.* midmost. [AS. *mid*, middle; compare L. *medius*, middle.]

1. middle.

2. in phonetics, pronounced with the tongue in a position approximately midway between high and low: said of certain vowels, as the *a* in *cake* or *o* in *cold.*

mid, *n.* the midst; middle. [Archaic.]

mid, ′mid, *prep.* amid. [Poet.]

mid-, a combining form meaning *middle* or *middle part of*, as in *mid*brain, *mid*-Atlantic.

mid′-āġe, *n.* middle age.

Mī′dăs, *n.* 1. in Greek legend, a king of Phrygia to whom Dionysus granted the power of turning everything that he touched into gold.

2. a genus of monkeys having long ears, including several species of marmosets, natives of South America.

Mī′dăs′ṣ-ēar, *n.* a gastropod shell, *Auricula midæ.*

mid-At·lan′tiç̣, *n.* the middle part of the Atlantic Ocean.

mid′brāin, *n.* the mesencephalon.

mid·chan′nel, *n.* the middle part of a channel.

mid·con′ti·nent, *n.* the middle part of a continent.

mid′dāy, *n.* [ME. *middai*; AS. *middæg.*] the middle part of the day; noon.

mid′dāy, *a.* of midday; as, the *midday* sun.

mid′den, *n.* [ME. *midding.*]

1. a dunghill or refuse heap. [Brit. Dial.]

2. a kitchen midden.

mid′dest, *a.* obsolete superl. of *mid.*

mid′ding, *n.* same as *midden.*

mid′dle, *a.* [ME. and AS. *middel*, middle.]

1. halfway between two given points, times, etc.; equally distant from either end, side, etc.; in the center; mean.

2. intermediate; in between; intervening.

3. in Greek grammar, designating or of a voice of the verb, passive in form, in which the subject is represented as acting reflexively.

4. [M-] in geology, designating a division of a period or a formation between those called *Upper* and *Lower.*

5. [M-] in linguistics, designating a stage in language development intermediate between those called *Old* and *Modern*; as, *Middle* English.

6. in logic, designating a term that appears in both premises of a syllogism but not in the conclusion.

7. in phonetics, medial.

mid′dle, *n.* 1. a point or part halfway between extremes; central point, part, time, etc.

2. something intermediate.

3. the middle part of the body; waist.

4. in Greek grammar, the middle voice.

5. in logic, a middle term.

mid′dle, *v.t.* and *v.i.*; middled (-dld), *pt.*, *pp.*; middling, *ppr.* 1. to put in the middle.

2. to fold (a rope, etc.) in the middle; to double.

mid′dle āġe, the time of life between youth and old age: now usually applied to the years from about 40 to about 60.

Mid′dle-Āġe′, *a.* medieval.

mid′dle-āġed′, *a.* in, of, characteristic of, or suitable for middle age.

Mid′dle Āġ′eṣ, the period of European history between ancient and modern times, c. 500 A.D.–1450 A.D.

Mid′dle A·mer′i·c̣ȧ, 1. the part of Latin America south of the United States and north of South America.

2. the American middle class, characterized generally by moderate or conservative political attitudes and conventional social values; sometimes, specifically, the middle class of Midwestern America.

Mid′dle At·lan′tiç̣ Stāteṣ, New York, New Jersey, and Pennsylvania.

mid′dle·breāk·ēr, *n.* same as *lister.*

mid′dle·brow, *n.* a person regarded as having conventional, middle-class tastes or opinions, and as being anti-intellectual or pseudo-intellectual: often a term of contempt or derision. [Colloq.]

mid′dle·brow, *a.* of a middlebrow. [Colloq.]

mid′dle·bust·ēr, *n.* same as *lister.*

mid′dle C, 1. the musical note on the first ledger line below the treble staff and the first above the bass staff.

2. the corresponding tone or key.

mid′dle-clȧss, *a.* of or characteristic of the middle class.

mid′dle clȧss, the social class between the aristocracy or very wealthy and the working class, or proletariat: owners of small businesses, professional and white-collar workers, well-to-do farmers, etc. are generally included in the middle class.

mid′dle dis′tănce, the space between the foreground and the background in a picture.

mid′dle ēar, the tympanum.

mid′dle-ēarth, *n.* the world. [Obs.]

Mid′dle Ēast, 1. the area including Iraq, Iran, Afghanistan, and, sometimes, India, Tibet, and Burma.

2. the Near East (sense 1), excluding the Balkans. [Brit.]

Mid′dle Eng′lish, the English language as written and spoken between about 1125 and about 1475: it is characterized by the loss of Anglo-Saxon inflectional endings, the emergence of a syntax based on word order, a revision of the Anglo-Saxon pronoun system, great diversity of dialectal spellings, extensive vocabulary borrowings from Latin, French, and Low German sources, and the gradual standardization of the South East Midland dialect, used in and around London, as a written language for the whole of England (c. 1375–1475).

Mid′dle Greek, Medieval Greek.

mid′dle ground, same as *middle distance.*

Mid′dle Hīgh Gēr′măn, the language of the highlands of south and central Germany as it was written and spoken between about 1100 and about 1500: in the development of German, it represents a stage analogous to that of Middle English.

Mid′dle I′rish, the Irish language as it developed in the later Middle Ages.

Mid′dle King′dŏm, 1. a kingdom of ancient Egypt, c. 2400–1580 B.C., with its capital at Heracleopolis and later at Thebes: also *Middle Empire.*

2. [transl. of Chin. *Chung kuo.*] (a) the former Chinese Empire, considered as the center of the world; (b) the eighteen provinces of China, or China proper.

Mid′dle Lat′in, Medieval Latin.

mid′dle lat′i·tūde, the latitude midway between two points in the same hemisphere.

Mid′dle Lōw Gēr′măn, the Germanic language of the northwest European lowlands, chiefly between the Rhine and the Elbe, as written and spoken between about 1100 and about 1450.

mid′dle·man, *n.*; *pl.* **mid′dle·men,** 1. a go-between; an intermediary.

2. a trader who buys commodities from the producer and sells them to the retailer or, sometimes, directly to the consumer; a broker; a jobber.

3. in Ireland, a person who rents lands from the landowner in large tracts, and lets it out in smaller portions at an increased rent.

4. in minstrelsy, the one who leads the dialogue as interlocutor, seated in the middle of the line of performers.

mid′dle·mōst, *a.* same as *midmost.*

mid′dle-of-the-rōad′, *a.* avoiding extremes, especially of the political left and right; uncommitted to either liberalism or conservatism.

mid′dle pas′sāġe, the passage across the Atlantic from West Africa to the West Indies or America: route of the former slave trade.

mid′dle pōst, same as *king post.*

mid′dlēr, *n.* one who is in an intermediate class.

mid′dle-sīzed″, *a.* of medium size.

Mid′dle Stāteṣ, those eastern States between the New England States and the South: New York, New Jersey, Pennsylvania, Delaware, and Maryland.

Mid′dle Tem′ple, one of two groups of buildings occupied by the Inns of Court in London, England: the other is the Inner Temple.

mid′dle wätch, in nautical usage, the men on watch from midnight to 4 A.M.; also, that period of time.

mid′dle·weight (-wāt), *n.* 1. one of average weight.

2. a boxer or wrestler who weighs between 148 and 160 pounds.

mid′dle·weight, *a.* of middleweights.

Mid′dle West, mid′dle west, that part of the United States between the Rocky Mountains and the Allegheny Mountains, north of the Ohio River and the southern borders of Kansas and Missouri: also *Midwest.*

mid′dling, *a.* of middle rank, state, size, or quality; medium; ordinary, mediocre.

mid′dling, *adv.* fairly; moderately; somewhat. [Colloq.]

mid′dling, *n.* 1. pork or bacon from between the ham and the shoulder.

2. [*pl.*] products of medium quality, grade, size, or price.

3. [*pl.*] particles of coarsely ground wheat mixed with bran, with a high gluten content.

mid′dling·ly, *adv.* passably; indifferently.

mid′dy, *n.*; *pl.* **mid′dieṣ,** 1. a midshipman. [Colloq.]

2. a middy blouse.

mid′dy blouse, a loose blouse having a sailor collar, worn by women and children.

mid′feath″ēr, *n.* 1. in a steam boiler, the upright water chamber in the firebox.

2. in mining, a central support in a tunnel.

mid′fiēld, *n.* the central part of the playing field in various sports, as football or soccer.

mid′fiēld·ēr, *n.* any of the players positioned in the midfield, as in soccer.

Mid′gärd, *n.* [Ice. *midhgardhr*, lit., mid-yard; *midhr*, mid, and *gardhr*, yard.] in Norse mythology, the earth regarded as midway between heaven and hell and engirdled by a huge serpent: also *Mithgärthr, Midgarth.*

midġe (mij), *n.* [AS. *mycg, mygge.*]

1. any very small gnat or gnatlike insect, as of the order *Diptera* and suborder *Nemocera.*

2. an individual otherwise normal, but of small size; a dwarf.

midġ′et, *n.* [*dim.* of *midge.*]

1. a dwarf; any abnormally small living being.

2. anything very small of its kind.

midġ'et, *a.* very small of its kind; miniature; as, a *midget* piano.

mid'-gut, *n.* the embryonic structure from which the jejunum and ileum are developed.

mid'heav"en, *n.* 1. the middle of the sky or heaven.

2. in astronomy, the meridian of any place.

Mï·dï', *n.* [Fr., south, lit. midday.] southern France.

Mid'i·ăn·īte, *n.* in the Bible, a member of a nomadic tribe of Arabs that fought the Israelites: Ex. ii. 15–22, Numb. xxxi. Judg. vi–viii.

mid'ī·ron (-ũrn), *n.* [*mid-* and *iron.*] in golf, a club with a steel or iron head and little loft, used for fairway shots of medium distance: now usually called *number 2 iron.*

mid'lănd, *n.* 1. the middle region of a country; interior.

2. [M–] the dialects of English spoken or formerly spoken in the Midlands: they are divided into eastern and western groups.

mid'lănd, *a.* 1. in or of the midland; inland.

2. [M–] of the Midlands.

the Midlands; the middle counties of England.

mid'leg, *n.* 1. the middle of the leg.

2. one of the middle, or second, pair of legs of an insect.

mid'leg, *adv.* to the middle of the leg.

Mid'-Lent, *n.* the middle of Lent; the fourth Sunday in Lent.

mid'mōst, *a.* [ME. *mydmest*; AS. *midmest.*] exactly in the middle, or nearest the middle; middlemost.

mid'mōst, *adv.* in the middle or midst.

mid'mōst, *prep.* in the middle or midst of.

mid'nīght (-nīt), *n.* 1. the middle of the night; twelve o'clock at night.

2. deep darkness.

mid'nīght, *a.* 1. relating to the middle of the night; at midnight; as, *midnight* studies.

2. like or suggestive of midnight; very dark; as, *midnight* gloom.

to burn the midnight oil; to study or work very late at night.

mid'nīght sun, the sun visible at midnight in the arctic or antarctic regions during the summer.

mid'nọọn, *n.* noon; midday. [Rare.]

Mid'rash (or -räsh), *n.*; *pl.* **Mid·rä'shim, Mid·rä'shōth,** [Heb., explanation.] any of the Jewish commentaries and explanatory notes on the Scriptures, written between the beginning of the Exile and c. 1200 A.D.

mid'rib, *n.* in botany, the central vein, or rib, of a leaf, extending from the stem to the apex.

mid'riff, *n.* [AS. *midhrif, midrif*; *mid,* middle, and *hrif,* belly.]

1. the diaphragm; partition of muscles and tendons between the chest cavity and the abdominal cavity.

2. the middle part of the body, between the abdomen and the chest.

mid'riff, *a.* designating or of a garment that bares the midriff.

mid'sēa, *n.* the open expanse of the sea.

mid'ship, *a.* being in or belonging to the middle of a ship; as, a *midship* beam.

mid'ship·măn, *n.*; *pl.* **mid'ship·men,** 1. a student in training for the rank of ensign in the United States Navy, especially at the Naval Academy at Annapolis.

2. a junior British naval officer ranking between naval cadet and sublieutenant.

3. formerly, one of a class of ship's boys assigned to British naval vessels to be trained as officers.

4. a fish of the order *Haplodoci.*

mid'ship"mīte, *n.* a midshipman: a sailors' humorous alteration.

mid'ships, *adv.* amidships.

midst, *n.* [from *middest,* in the phrase, *in the middest*; ME. *in middes,* from AS. *on middan,* amid.] the middle; the central part: now mainly in phrases.

in our (or *your, their*) *midst*; among, or in the midst of, us (or you, them).

in the midst of; (a) in the middle of; surrounded by; (b) in the course of; during.

midst, 'midst, *prep.* in the midst of; amidst; amid. [Poet.]

midst, *adv.* in the middle. [Rare.]

mid'strēam, *n.* the middle of the stream.

mid'sum"mẽr, *n.* 1. the middle of summer.

2. popularly, the time of the summer solstice, about the 21st of June.

midsummer day; a feast day, June 24; St John the Baptist's Day.

mid'sum"mẽr, *a.* of, in, or like midsummer.

mid'tẽrm, *a.* occurring in the middle of the term.

mid'tẽrm, *n.* [*often in pl.*] a midterm examination, as in a college course. [Colloq.]

mid'-Viç·tō'ri·ăn, *a.* 1. of, like, or characteristic of the middle part of Queen Victoria's reign in Great Britain (c. 1850–1890) or the culture, morals, or art of this period in Britain and the United States.

2. old-fashioned, prudish, morally strict, stuffy, etc.

mid'-Viç·tō'ri·ăn, *n.* 1. one who lived during the mid-Victorian period.

2. a person of mid-Victorian ideas, manners, attitudes, etc.

mid'wāy, *n.* [ME. *midwei*; AS. *midweg.*]

1. originally, (a) the middle of the way or distance; (b) a middle way or course.

2. that part of a fair or exposition where side shows and other amusements are located.

mid'wāy, *a.* being in the middle of the way or distance.

mid'wāy, *adv.* in the middle of the way or distance; halfway.

mid'week, *n.* 1. the middle of the week.

2. [M–] Wednesday: so called by the Friends (Quakers).

mid'week, *a.* in the middle of the week.

mid·week'ly, *a.* midweek.

mid·week'ly, *adv.* in the middle of the week.

Mid'west', *n.* the Middle West.

Mid'west', *a.* Midwestern.

Mid·west'ẽrn, *a.* of, in, or characteristic of the Middle West; Middle Western.

Mid·west'ẽrn·ẽr, *n.* a native or inhabitant of the Middle West; Middle Westerner.

mid'wīfe, *n.*; *pl.* **mid'wīves,** [ME. *midwife, mydwyfe, medewife*; AS. *mid,* with, and *wif,* wife, woman.] a woman who assists women in childbirth.

mid'wīfe, *v.i.*; midwifed (-wīft), *pt., pp.*; midwifing, *ppr.* to perform the office of midwifery.

mid'wīfe, *v.t.* to assist (a woman or offspring) in childbirth. [Now Rare.]

mid'wīfe·ry (*or* wif-), *n.* the art or practice of assisting women in childbirth; obstetrics.

mid'win'tẽr, *n.* 1. the middle of the winter.

2. popularly, the time of the winter solstice, about December 22.

mid'win'tẽr, *a.* of, in, or like midwinter.

mid'yēar", *a.* occurring in the middle of the (calendar or academic) year.

mid'yēar", *n.* [*often in pl.*] a midyear examination, as at college. [Colloq.]

miēn, *n.* [Fr. *mine*; It. *mina,* look, air, mien, from L. *minari,* to threaten.] look; air; manner; external appearance; way of carrying and conducting oneself; as, a lofty *mien.*

miff, *n.* [compare G. dial. *muff,* sullenness.] a trivial quarrel or fit of the sulks; a tiff or huff. [Colloq.]

miff, *v.t.* and *v.i.*; miffed (mift), *pt., pp.*; miffing, *ppr.* to offend or take offense. [Colloq.]

MIG, Mig, *n.* [after Artem *Mi*koyan, and Mikhail *G*urevich, its Soviet designers.] a small, fast, highly maneuverable jet military aircraft.

mig'gle, *n.* [dim. of dial. *mig,* a marble.]

1. a playing marble. [Dial.]

2. [*pl.*] the game of marbles. [Dial.]

mīght (mīt), *v.* [ME. and AS. *mihte.*]

1. past tense of *may.*

2. an auxiliary with present or future sense, generally equivalent to *may* in meaning and use, expressing especially a shade of doubt or a smaller degree of possibility (e.g., it *might* rain) or permission (e.g., *might* I go?).

mīght (mīt), *n.* [ME. *mighte, myghte*; AS. *miht, meaht,* from the root of *magan,* to be able.]

1. strength; force; power; primarily and chiefly, bodily strength or physical power; as, to work or strive with all one's *might.*

2. ability to wield force; power of control; as, the *might* of empire.

with might and main; see under *main.*

mīght'i·ly, *adv.* 1. with great power, force, or strength; vigorously; as, to strive *mightily.*

2. greatly; to a great degree; very much; as, she was *mightily* pleased.

mīght'i·ness, *n.* 1. the quality or state of being mighty; power; greatness.

How soon this *mightiness* meets misery.
—Shak.

2. a title of dignity; as, their High *Mightinesses* the States-General of Holland.

mīght'y, *a.*; *comp.* mightier; *superl.* mightiest, [AS. *mihtig, mæhtig, meahtig,* from *miht, meaht,* might.]

1. having great bodily strength or physical power; very strong or vigorous; as, a *mighty* arm.

2. very powerful in any way; having great command; as, a *mighty* potentate.

3. great; wonderful; remarkably large, extensive, etc.; as, *mighty* works, a *mighty* famine.

mīght'y, *adv.* in a great degree; very; as, *mighty* wise, *mighty* thoughtful. [Colloq.]

mign'iărd·īṣe (min'yẽrd-), *v.t.* to treat gently or delicately. [Obs.]

mi'gnon (min'yon; *Fr.* mē-nyōṅ'), *a.*; *feminine* **mi'gnonne** (min'yŏn; *Fr.* mē-nyọn'), [Fr.] small, delicately formed, and pretty; dainty.

mi·gnŏn·ette' (-et'), *n.* [Fr., dim. of *mignon.*] an annual flowering plant, *Reseda odorata,* with wedge-shaped leaves, and spikes of small, fragrant, greenish-white flowers.

mignonette pepper; pepper, coarsely ground or unground.

mī'grāine, *n.* [F., from LL. *hemicrania.,* from Gr. *hēmikrania, hēmi,* half, and *kranion,* skull.] a type of periodically returning headache, usually confined to one side of the head and accompanied by nausea, vomiting, and sensory disturbances: also called *megrim.*

mī·grāin'ous, *a.* of or pertaining to migraine.

mī'grănt, *a.* [L. *migrans* (*-antis*), ppr. of *migrare,* to migrate.] migratory; migrating.

mī'grănt, *n.* 1. a person, bird, or other animal that migrates.

2. a farm laborer who moves from place to place to harvest seasonal crops.

mī'grāte, *v.i.*; migrated, *pt., pp.*; migrating, *ppr.* [L. *migratus,* pp. of *migrare,* to move from one place to another, depart.]

1. to move from one place to another; especially, to leave one's country and settle in another.

2. to move from one region to another with the change in seasons, as many birds and some fishes.

mī·grā'tion, *n.* [L. *migratio* (*-onis*), from *migrare,* to migrate.]

1. a migrating.

2. a group of people or birds, fishes, etc. migrating together.

3. in chemistry, (a) the shifting of one or more atoms from one position in the molecule to another; (b) the movement of ions toward one electrode or the other, under the influence of electromotive force.

mī'grā·tŏr, *n.* a person or animal that migrates; specifically, a migratory bird.

mī'grā·tō·ry, *a.* 1. migrating; characterized by migration.

2. of migration.

3. roving; wandering; nomadic.

migratory locust; any one of an extensive family of insects, *Acrididæ,* allied to the grasshoppers.

migratory worker; one who travels from harvest to harvest, working until each crop is gathered or processed.

mih·räb', *n.* [Ar.] a niche, recess, or slab in a mosque to indicate the direction of Mecca.

mi·kä'dō, *n.*; *pl.* **mi·kä'dōṣ,** [Japan., lit., exalted gate; *mi,* exalted, and *kado,* gate.] [*often* M–] the emperor of Japan: title used by non-Japanese.

Mi·kā'ni·ȧ, *n.* [after J. C. *Mikan,* a Bohemian botanist.] a genus of plants comprising about 150 species of upright shrubs and twining vines, natives to the warmer parts of America.

mīke, *n.* a microphone. [Slang.]

Mik'mak, *n.* same as *Micmac.*

mī'kron, *n.* a micron.

mil, *n.* [L. *mille,* thousand.]

1. a unit of length, equal to .001 of an inch (25.4001 microns), used in measuring the diameter of wire.

2. a milliliter; a cubic centimeter.

3. a monetary unit or coin of Israel, equal to .001 of the Israeli pound.

4. in military usage, (a) a unit of angle measurement for artillery fire, equal to $^1/_{6400}$ of the circumference of a circle: in full, *artillery mil*; (b) less frequently, a unit equal to 1.018 artillery mils: in full, *infantry mil.*

circular mil; see under *circular.*

mi·lā'dy, mi·lā'di, *n.* [Fr., from Eng. *my lady.*] an English noblewoman or gentlewoman: Continental term used in speaking to or of such a woman.

mīl'āġe, *n.* mileage

Mil·ȧ·nēṣe', *a.* of or relating to Milan, Italy, or to its natives or their culture.

Mil·ȧ·nēṣe', *n. sing.* and *pl.* a native or inhabitant of Milan; the people of Milan.

milch, *a.* [ME. *milche, melche*; AS. *melc, meolce,* from *meolc,* milk.] giving milk; kept for milking; as, a *milch* cow.

mīld, *a.*; *comp.* milder; *superl.* mildest. [AS. *milde*, mild.]
1. gentle or kind in disposition, action, or effect; not severe, harsh, bitter, etc.; not extreme in any way; moderate; temperate; as, a *mild* nature.
2. having a soft, pleasant taste or flavor; not strong, sour, bitter, or sharp: said of tobacco, cheese, etc.
3. designating steel that is tough but malleable and contains only a small percentage of carbon.
Syn.—bland, easy, gentle, kind, soft, meek, mellow, sweet, tender.

mīld'en, *v.t.*; mildened, *pt.*, *pp.*; mildening, *ppr.* to render milder; to ameliorate.

mīld'en, *v.i.* to become milder, as the weather.

mil'dew, *n.* [AS. *mildeáw*, *meledeáw*, originally meaning honeydew.]
1. any fungus that attacks various plants or appears on organic matter, paper, leather, etc., especially when exposed to damp, resulting in a thin, furry, whitish coating or discoloration.
2. any such coating or discoloration; mold.
3. any plant disease caused by such a fungus.

mil'dew, *v.t.*; mildewed, *pt.*, *pp.*; mildewing, *ppr.* to affect with mildew.

mil'dew, *v.i.* to become affected with mildew.

mil'dew·y, *a.* 1. mildewed.
2. like, or having the nature of, mildew.

mīld'ly, *adv.* 1. in a mild manner.
2. to a mild extent; somewhat.
to put it mildly; to state it with restraint.

mīld'ness, *n.* the state or quality of being mild; temperateness; gentleness.

mīld'-spir''it·ed, *a.* of a mild temperament; meek.

mīld'-tem''pẽred, *a.* having a mild temper.

mīle, *n.*; *pl.* **mīleṣ,** dial. **mīle,** [AS. *mīl*; LL. *milia* a mile, from L. *milia*, *millia*, pl. of *mille*, a thousand, in *milia passuum*, a thousand paces, a mile.] a unit of linear measure, equal to 1,760 yards (5,280 feet or 1,609.35 meters), used in the United States, Great Britain, etc.: in full, *statute mile*: it is derived from an ancient Roman measure of 1,000 paces (c. 1,620 yards). The *geographical* (or *nautical*, *sea*, or *air*) *mile* is $^1/_{60}$ of one degree of the earth's equator, officially, in British Admiralty use (*Admiralty mile*), 6,080 feet (1,853.2 meters) and in the United States Coast Survey 6,080.2 feet (1,853.25 meters).

mīle'ăġe, *n.* 1. an allowance for traveling expenses at a specified amount per mile.
2. aggregate distance in miles or total number of miles traveled or covered.
3. expense or charge per mile, as for travel or the use of railroad freight cars.
4. a mileage book.
Also spelled *milage*.

mīle'ăġe book, a book of detachable coupons or tickets (*mileage tickets*), each entitling a person to transportation for a stated number of miles.

mīle'pōst, *n.* a signpost showing the distance in miles from or to a given point.

mīl'ẽr, *n.* one trained to race a mile.

mī'lēṣ glō·ri·ō'sus, [L.] a braggart soldier: the title character in Plautus' comedy.

Mī·lē'siăn, *a.* [L. *Milesius*; Gr. *Milēsios*, of or pertaining to Miletus, from *Milētos*, Miletus.] of or pertaining to the ancient city of Miletus in Asia Minor, or to its inhabitants.

Mī·lē'siăn, *n.* a native or inhabitant of Miletus.

Mī·lē'siăn (*or* -zhăn), *a.* [from *Milesius*, legendary Spanish king whose sons reputedly conquered Ireland c. 1300 B.C.; and *-an*.] Irish.

Mī·lē'siăn, *n.* 1. a legendary ancestor of the Irish.
2. an Irishman.

mīle'stōne, *n.* 1. a stone or pillar set up to show the distance in miles to or from a specified place.
2. a significant or important event in the history or career of a person, the human race, etc.

mil'foil, *n.* [L. *millefolium*, milfoil, lit., thousand leaves; *mille*, thousand, and *folium*, leaf: so called from the abundance of its leaves.] an herb of the genus *Achillea*, belonging to the aster family, growing on roadsides and in dry pastures; yarrow.

mil·i·ā'ri·ȧ, *n.* [L., f. of *miliarius*, pertaining to millet.] an acute skin disease resulting from inflammation of the sweat glands and characterized by small white or red papules or vesicles: also called *prickly heat*, *heat rash*.

mil'ĭ·ăr·y, *a.* [L. *miliarius*, from *milium*, millet.]
1. resembling millet seeds; as, a *miliary* eruption, *miliary* glands.
2. accompanied with an eruption like millet seeds; as, a *miliary* fever.

mil'ĭ·ăr·y tū·bẽr·cū·lō'sis, a form of tuberculosis in which the tubercle bacilli spread through the blood stream from a primary focus of infection to other parts of the body, where multiple tubercles are formed.

mi·lieu' (mē-lyoo'), *n.* [Fr., lit., middle.] surroundings; environment.

Mi·li'ō·lȧ, *n.* [from L. *milium*, millet.] in zoology, a genus of foraminifers typical of the family *Miliolidæ*.

Mil·i·ol'i·dae, *n.pl.* [L. *milium*, millet.] a family of imperforate foraminifers, of which *Miliola* is the typical genus.

mil·i·ol'i·fọrm, *a.* milioline.

mil'i·ō·līne, *a.* of or pertaining to the *Miliolidæ*.

mil'i·ō·līte, *a.* [*Miliola* and *-ite*.] miliolitic.

mil'i·ō·līte, *n.* a fossil foraminifer of the family *Miliolidæ*.

mil''i·ō·lit'iç, *a.* relating to or composed of miliolites.

mil'i·tăn·cy, *n.* the condition or quality of being militant; fighting spirit, attitude, or policy.

mil'i·tănt, *a.* [L. *militans* (*-antis*), ppr. of *militare*, to serve as a soldier.]
1. fighting; engaged in war; serving as a soldier.
2. of a combative or warlike character or disposition; ready and willing to fight.
church militant; see under *church*.

mil'i·tănt, *n.* a militant person.

mil'i·tănt·ly, *adv.* in a militant or warlike manner.

mil'i·tăr, *a.* military. [Obs.]

mil'i·tăr·i·ly, *adv.* 1. in a military manner.
2. from a military standpoint

mil'i·tȧ·riṣm, *n.* [Fr. *militarisme*.]
1. military spirit; ideals and attitudes of professional soldiers.
2. the glorification or prevalence of such a spirit, ideals, etc. in a nation, or the predominance of the military caste in government.
3. the policy of maintaining strong armed forces and being ready and willing to use them; aggressive preparedness.

mil'i·tȧ·rist, *n.* 1. an expert or specialist in war and military affairs.
2. one who advocates militarism or a warlike policy.

mil''i·tȧ·ris'tiç, *a.* of, characteristic of, or characterized by militarism.

mil''i·tȧ·ris'tiç·ăl·ly, *adv.* in a militaristic manner.

mil''i·tȧ·ri·zā'tion, *n.* a militarizing or being militarized.

mil'i·tȧ·rīze, *v.t.*; militarized, *pt.*, *pp.*; militarizing, *ppr.* 1. to make military; to equip and prepare for war.
2. to fill with militarism; to make warlike.

mil'i·tăr·y, *a.* [L. *militaris*, pertaining to soldiers or war, from *miles* (*-itis*), a soldier.]
1. of, characteristic of, for, fit for, or done by soldiers or the armed forces.
2. of, for, or fit for war.
3. of the army: distinguished from *naval*.
military attaché; an army officer attached to his nation's embassy or legation in a foreign country.
military feuds; the original feudal estates in England which were in the hands of military men who held them under military tenure.
military intelligence; (a) any information of military value to a nation; (b) the military department or branch whose work is getting, analyzing, and using such information.
military law; the branch of law concerned with the government and discipline of the armed forces, whether in time of war or in time of peace.
military mast; an armored, towerlike structure on a warship, containing ammunition hoists, speaking tubes, observation ports, etc.
military police; (a) troops assigned to carry on police duties for the army; (b) a civil police having a military organization, as the French gendarmerie; a constabulary.
military tenure; a tenure of land on condition of performing military service.

mil'i·tăr·y, *n.* soldiers collectively; the army (with *the*); as, *the military* took control of the government.

mil'i·tāte, *v.i.*; militated, *pt.*, *pp.*; militating, *ppr.* [L. *militatus*, pp. of *militare*, to be a soldier.]
1. originally, to serve as a soldier; to fight (*against*).
2. to be directed (*against*); to operate or work (*against* or, rarely, *for*): said of facts, evidence, actions, etc.; as, his youth *militated against* him.

mil·i·tā'tion, *n.* conflict.

mi·li'tiȧ (-lish'ȧ), *n.* [L., military service, soldiery, from *miles* (*-itis*), a soldier.]
1. (a) originally, any military force; (b) later, any army composed of citizens rather than professional soldiers, called out in time of emergency.
2. in the United States, all able-bodied male citizens between 18 and 45 years old who are not already members of the regular armed forces: members of the National Guard, Organized Reserve Corps (Army and Air), and the Naval and Marine Reserves constitute the *organized militia*; all others, the *unorganized militia*.

mi·li'tiȧ·măn, *n.*; *pl.* **mi·li'tiȧ·men,** one who belongs to the militia.

mi·li'ti·āte (-lish'i-), *v.i.* to organize for war; to raise militia. [Obs.]

mil'i·um, *n.*; *pl.* **mil'i·ȧ,** [L., millet.] a small, whitish nodule of the skin, somewhat like a millet seed, resulting from retention of the secretion of a sebaceous gland.

milk, *n.* [AS. *meoloc*, *meolc*, *milc*, milk.]
1. a white or yellowish liquid secreted by the mammary glands of female mammals for suckling their young; especially, cow's milk.
2. any liquid like this, as the juice of various plants, trees, or fruits (e.g., coconut milk), or any of various emulsions.
3. the spat of an oyster before it is discharged.
blue milk; (a) milk that has been skimmed; (b) milk rendered blue by fermentation caused by a microbe, *Bacterium cyanogenum*.
bristol milk; a drink of which the principal ingredient is sherry.
in milk; *in the milk*; milky, as wheat before the grain begins to harden, or as an oyster when it contains the spat.
milk of human kindness; natural feelings of sympathy, generosity, etc.
milk of lime; slaked lime in water: so called because it resembles milk in appearance and consistency.
milk of magnesia; a milky-white fluid, a suspension of magnesium hydroxide, $Mg(OH)_2$, in water, used as a laxative and antacid.
milk of sulfur; precipitated sulfur.
pigeon's milk; a curdy substance in the crop of pigeons, with which they feed their young by disgorging it into their mouths.
sugar of milk; same as *lactose*.
to cry over spilt milk; to feel sorry in vain about something that has happened and cannot be undone.

milk, *v.t.*; milked (milkt), *pt.*, *pp.*; milking, *ppr.* [ME. *milken*; AS. *meolcian*, from *meolc*, milk.]
1. (a) to draw or press milk from the mammary glands of (a cow, etc.); (b) to draw (milk).
2. to draw (*out*) or drain off; to extract as if by milking.
3. to drain off or extract money, ideas, strength, etc. from as if by milking; to exploit.
4. to extract juice, sap, venom, etc. from.
5. to draw out (information, etc.), as if by milking.

milk, *v.i.* 1. to draw milk.
2. to give milk; as, the cow does not *milk* easily.

milk ad'dẽr, a milk snake.

milk ab'scess, an abscess of the mammary gland during lactation.

milk'-and-wạ'tẽr, *a.* insipid; characterless; wishy-washy; as, his poems are of the *milk-and-water* species.

milk blotch, a rash on the face and scalp of infants; a form of eczema.

milk çrust, same as *milk blotch*.

milk çūre, the treatment of diseases by a diet of milk or of preparations of milk.

milk dāme, a wet nurse. [Obs.]

milk duçt, a canalicular and galactophorous duct.

milk'en, *a.* consisting of or resembling milk. [Rare.]

milk'ẽr, *n.* 1. one who or that which milks; specifically, an apparatus devised for milking cows mechanically.
2. a cow or other animal giving milk; as, she is an excellent *milker*.

milk fē'vẽr, 1. a mild fever sometimes occurring with the first secretion of milk in the breasts after childbirth: it is caused by infection.

2. a somewhat similar condition often occurring in dairy cows shortly after calving, characterized by paralysis, etc.

milk'fish, *n.*; *pl.* **milk'fish** or **milk'fish·eṣ,** a large; silvery, herringlike fish, *Chanos salmoneus*, of the Pacific Ocean.

milk glȧss, a kind of glass having a milky appearance, made from cryolite and sand: also called *cryolite glass.*

milk'i·ly, *adv.* in a milky manner.

milk'i·ness, *n.* the quality or state of being milky or having a color or consistency like milk.

milk'ing, *n.* 1. the act of a person who milks.

2. the quantity of milk obtained at one time of milking.

milk knot (not), a hard lump sometimes occurring in the breast, caused by congestion of the mammary glands.

milk leg, a condition characterized by painful swelling of the legs, caused by inflammation and clotting of the femoral veins: so called because it occurs most often during lactation after childbirth: medical name *phlegmasia alba dolens.*

milk'less, *a.* without milk.

milk'-liv″ẽred, *a.* cowardly; timorous; white-livered.

milk'māid, *n.* a woman or girl who milks cows or is employed in a dairy.

milk'man, *n.*; *pl.* **milk'men,** a man who sells or delivers milk.

milk mir'rŏr, an escutcheon (sense 2d) in cattle.

milk mō'lăr, in anatomy, a molar of the first or temporary set of teeth which is replaced by a premolar.

milk nŭrse, a wet nurse.

milk pärs'ley, an herb, *Peucedanum palustre*, of the parsley family, growing in Europe and Asia: it has an acrid milky juice.

milk pēa, a plant of the genus *Galactia.*

milk punch, a beverage made by adding brandy, whisky, or rum to milk, and flavoring with sugar and nutmeg.

milk quartz, quartz having a milk-white color.

milk shāke, a drink made of milk, flavoring, and, usually, ice cream, mixed or shaken until frothy.

milk'shed, *n.* [*milk* and *-shed*, as in *watershed.*] all the dairy farm areas supplying milk for a given city.

milk'sick, *a.* suffering from milk sickness.

milk sick'ness, a rare disease, formerly common in the western United States, caused by drinking the milk or eating the milk products or flesh of cattle that have eaten any of various poisonous weeds.

milk snāke, a small, harmless snake, gray with black-rimmed markings, related to the king snake: also called *milk adder, house snake.*

milk'sop, *n.* an unmanly man or boy; sissy.

milk sug'ăr (shug'), same as *lactose.*

milk this'tle (-sl), an esculent European plant, *Silybum marianum*, of the aster family, having the veins of its leaves of a milky whiteness.

milk thrush, same as *aphtha*, sense 2.

milk tooth, any of the temporary, first set of teeth in a young child or other mammal: also called *baby tooth.*

milk tree, either of two trees of South America, *Brosimum galactodendron* and *Tabernæmontana utilis.*

milk ves'sel, in botany, one of the tubes in which milky fluid is secreted; a lactiferous vessel.

milk vetch, an herb of the genus *Astragalus*: so called from an idea that the secretion of milk was increased in goats which fed on it.

milk'weed, *n.* any plant of the genus *Asclepias*, having a milky juice. The name is also given to various other plants which have a milky juice.

green milkweed; any plant of the genus *Acerates.*

milk'whīte' (-hwīt'), *a.* white as milk.

milk'wŏrt, *n.* a plant of the genus *Polygala*, formerly supposed to increase the flow of milk in nursing women. *Polygala vulgaris* is the common milkwort of Europe.

milk'y, *a.*; *comp.* milkier; *superl.* milkiest, 1. like milk; especially, white as milk; as, a *milky* juice; a *milky* color.

2. of, containing, or yielding milk.

3. soft; mild; timorous.

4. full of spawn; as, *milky* oysters.

Milky Way; a broad, faintly luminous band seen across the sky at night, consisting of innumerable stars and nebulae so distant as to be indistinguishable without a telescope; the Galaxy.

mill, *n.* [AS. *mylen, myln*, from LL. *molina*, a mill, properly f. of L. *molinus*, of a mill, from *mola*, a millstone, from *molere*, to grind.]

1. a building with machinery for grinding grain into flour or meal.

2. a machine for grinding grain.

3. a machine for grinding or pulverizing any solid material; as, a coffee *mill.*

4. a machine for grinding or crushing fruits or vegetables to press out the juice; as, a cider *mill.*

5. any of various machines for stamping, shaping, polishing, or dressing metal surfaces, coins, etc. or for making something by some action done again and again.

6. a building or group of buildings with machinery for manufacturing something; a factory; as, a textile *mill.*

7. a roller of hardened steel with a raised design on it, for making a die or printing plate by pressure.

8. a milling cutter.

9. a raised edge, ridged surface, etc. made by milling.

10. [from the *v.*] a fist fight; pugilistic encounter. [Slang.]

through the mill; through a hard, painful, instructive experience, training, test, etc. [Colloq.]

mill, *v.t.*; milled, *pt., pp.*; milling, *ppr.* 1. to grind, work, form, polish, etc. by, in, or as in a mill.

2. to raise and ridge the edge of (a coin), as a safeguard against wear and clipping.

3. to beat or whip (chocolate, etc.) to a froth.

4. to cause (cattle) to move around in a circle.

5. to beat with or as with the fists; to thrash. [Slang.]

mill, *v.i.* 1. to move slowly in a circle, as cattle or a confused crowd (often with *around*).

2. to fight with the fists; to box. [Slang.]

mill, *n.* [L. *mille*, a thousand.] a money of account of the United States, being the tenth part of a cent, or the thousandth part of a dollar: used in calculating but not as a coin.

mill bär, rough bar iron as drawn out by the puddlers' rolls, as distinguished from *merchant bar*, which is finished bar iron ready for sale.

mill'bōard, *n.* a heavy, flexible pasteboard used for the covers of books.

mill'çāke, *n.* the residue left after the oil has been pressed from linseed.

mill cin'dẽr, in ironworking, slag formed in the puddling furnace.

mill'dam, *n.* 1. the mound by which a watercourse is obstructed and the water raised to a sufficient height or head to turn a mill wheel.

2. a millpond.

milled, *a.* 1. ground, cut, worked, etc. by or in a mill.

2. having the edges raised and ridged or grooved, as a coin.

milled cloth; cloth that has been fulled by beating, to thicken it.

milled lead; lead rolled out into sheets by machinery.

mil″lē·fi·ō'rī glȧss, [It. *mille*, thousand; *fiori*, flower.] ornamental glasswork made by fusing together tubes of glass enamel.

mil·lē·năr'i·ăn, *a.* [LL. *millenarius*, containing a thousand, from L. *mille*, a thousand.] pertaining to or consisting of a thousand, especially a thousand years; pertaining to the millennium; chiliastic.

mil·lē·năr'i·ăn, *n.* one who believes in the coming of the millenium.

mil·lē·năr'i·ăn·iṣm, *n.* the doctrine or tenets of the millenarians.

mil'lē·năr·y, *a.* consisting of or pertaining to a thousand; lasting for a thousand years; pertaining to the millennium or millenarians.

mil'lē·năr·y, *n.*; *pl.* **mil'lē·năr·ieṣ,** [LL. *millenarius*, of or containing a thousand, from L. *mille*, a thousand.]

1. a thousand.

2. a thousand years; a millennium.

3. a thousandth anniversary.

4. a millenarian.

mil·len'ni·ăl, *a.* 1. pertaining to a millennium, or to a thousand years; as, a *millennial* period.

2. of, characteristic of, suggestive of, or fit for the millenium.

mil·len'ni·ăl·ist, *n.* a millenarian; a chiliast.

mil·len'ni·ăn·iṣm, mil·len'ni·ȧ·riṣm, *n.* millenarianism.

mil'len·nist, *n.* a millenarian. [Obs.]

mil·len'ni·um, *n.*; *pl.* **mil·len'ni·umṣ, mil·len'ni·ȧ,** [L. *mille*, a thousand, and *annus*, year.]

1. a period of a thousand years.

2. in theology, the period of a thousand years during which Satan will be bound and Christ will reign on earth (with *the*): Rev. xx. 1–5.

3. any period of great happiness, peace, prosperity, etc.; an imagined golden age.

mil'lē·pēde, mil'li·pēde, *n.* [L. *mille*, a thousand, and *pes, pedis*, a foot.]

1. a wormlike arthropod (*myriapod*) with two pairs of legs on each of most of its segments: also *millipede, milliped.*

2. a small crustacean having many legs, as a wood louse.

Mil·lep'ō·rȧ, *n.* [L. *mille*, a thousand, and *porus*, a pore.] a genus of the *Hydrocorallinæ* having numerous minute distinct cells or pores perpendicular to the surface.

mil'lē·pōre, *n.* any of the hydrozoans belonging to the genus *Millepora*: they form branching or leaflike masses of coral with many very small openings on the surface.

mil'lē·pō·rīte, *n.* a fossil millepore.

mill'ẽr, *n.* 1. a person who owns or operates a mill, especially a flour mill.

2. (a) a milling machine; (b) a tool to be used in such a machine.

3. any of various moths with wings that look dusty or powdered, suggesting a miller's clothes.

4. a fish, the eagle ray.

5. the hen harrier. [Brit. Dial.]

Mil'lẽr·iṣm, *n.* the doctrines or belief of the Millerites.

Mil'lẽr·īte, *n.* a disciple of William Miller, an American premillennialist (died 1849), who taught that the end of the world and the coming of Christ's reign on earth would be in 1843.

mil'lẽr·īte, *n.* [after W. H. *Miller*, an English mineralogist.] a sulfide of nickel, NiS, a brassy-yellow, crystalline mineral.

mill'ẽr's-dog, *n.* a variety of shark, *Galeus canis.*

mill'ẽr's-thumb (-thum), *n.* 1. a small fresh-water fish of the genus *Uranidea*, as *Uranidea gobio* of Europe, or *Uranidea richardsoni* of America.

2. a small bird, as the goldcrest or willow warbler. [Brit. Dial.]

mil·les'i·măl, *a.* [L. *millesimus*, from *mille*, a thousand.] thousandth; consisting of thousandth parts; as, *millesimal* fractions.

mil·les'i·măl, *n.* a thousandth.

mil'let, *n.* [Fr., dim. of *mil*, from L. *milium*, millet.]

1. (a) a cereal grass, *Panicum miliaceum*, whose small grain is used for food in Europe and Asia; (b) the grain.

2. any of several other similar grasses or their seed, as *Italian millet, pearl millet*, etc. Millet is used for hay in both the United States and Europe.

African millet; same as *Indian millet.*

Arabian millet or *evergreen millet*; a species of Indian millet.

East Indian, Egyptian, or *pearl millet*; *Penicillaria spicata.*

Indian millet; see under *Indian.*

Italian millet; a grass, *Setaria italica*, cultivated in America for fodder, and in the East as a cereal.

mil'let grȧss, wild millet, *Milium effusum.*

mill eȳe (ī), the eye or opening in the cases of a mill, at which the meal is let out.

mill fŭr'năce, in ironworks, a furnace in which the puddled metal is reheated before being again rolled.

mill gang, in warping, that part of the warp which is made by a descending and ascending course of the threads round the warping mill.

mill hand, a workman employed in a mill.

mill head (hed), the head of water by which a mill wheel is turned.

mil'li-, [from L. *mille*, a thousand.] a combining form meaning: (a) *one thousandth part of* (a specified unit), as in *milli*meter; (b) *one thousand*, as in *milli*fold.

mil″li·am'pēre, *n.* [*milli-* and *ampere.*] in electricity, the thousandth part of an ampere.

mil'liärd (-yärd), *n.* [Fr.] a thousand millions; a billion. [Brit.]

mil'li·āre, *n.* [Fr.] in the metric system, the thousandth part of an are, equal to 154.07 square inches.

mil'li·ăr·y, *a.* [L. *milliarius*, of or belonging to a thousand, from *mille*, a thousand.] pertaining to the ancient Roman mile of a thousand paces or five thousand Roman feet.

mil'li·ăr·y, *n.*; *pl.* **mil'li·ăr·ies,** an ancient Roman milestone.

mil'li·băr, *n.* [from *milli-*, and Gr. *baros*, weight.] a unit of measure of atmospheric pressure, equal to one thousand dynes per square centimeter.

mil'lieme' (-yem'), *n.* [Fr. *millième*, a thousandth, from MFr., from *mille*, a thousand, from L.] a unit of currency in Egypt, Sudan, and Libya, equal to 1/1000 pound.

mil'li·făr·ad, *n.* one thousandth of a farad.

mil'li·gram, mil'li·gramme, *n.* [Fr. *milligramme*; *mille*, a thousand, and *gramme*, a gram.] in the metric system, the thousandth part of a gram (.0154 of a grain).

mil'li·lam"bĕrt, *n.* [*milli-* and *lambert*.] in physics, a unit of brightness: it is equal to .001 lambert.

mil'li·lī·tĕr, mil'li·lī·tre(-tĕr), *n.* [Fr. *millilitre*; L. *mille*, a thousand, and Fr. *litre*, a liter.] in the metric system, the thousandth part of a liter (1.000027 cubic centimeters or .06102 cubic inch).

mil'li·mē·tĕr, mil'li·mē·tre(-tĕr), *n.* [Fr. *millimètre*; L. *mille*, a thousand, and Fr. *mètre*, a meter.] in the metric system, the thousandth part of a meter (.03937 inch).

mil'li·mī"çron, *n.* one thousandth of a micron, one millionth of a millimeter, or ten angstroms: a unit of length for measuring waves of light, etc.

mil"līne', *n.* [from *mil*lion and *line*.]
 1. a unit of measurement equal to a one-column agate line (of an advertisement) in one million copies of some publication.
 2. the cost per milline of an advertisement.

mil'li·nĕr, *n.* [from *Milaner*, an inhabitant of Milan, also one who imported silks and ribbons from Milan.]
 1. a person who designs, makes, trims, or sells women's hats, headdresses, etc.
 2. a dealer in ribbons, lace, gloves, etc., especially those imported from Milan. [Obs.]

mil'li·nĕr·y, *n.* 1. the business or occupation of a milliner.
 2. the articles made or sold by milliners, as hats, bonnets, ribbons, etc.

mill'ing, *n.* 1. the process or business of grinding grain into flour or meal.
 2. the grinding, cutting, working, or manufacturing of metal, cloth, etc. in a mill.
 3. the process of raising and ridging the edge of a coin, etc.
 4. the ridging thus produced; a milled edge or surface.
 5. a slow, circular motion of or as of a herd of cattle.
 6. a beating; a thrashing. [Slang.]

mill'ing çut'tĕr, a milling machine.

mill'ing mȧ·chïne', a power tool for cutting and grinding metal parts.

Mil·ling·tō'ni·ȧ, *n.* [after Thomas *Millington* (1628–1704), of Oxford.] a genus of Asiatic trees having a corky bark: *Millingtonia hortensis* is the East Indian cork tree.

mill'ing tọol, a wheel or roller which cuts or indents metal surfaces by a rotary motion.

mil'liŏn (-yun), *n.* [Late ME.; OFr.; It. *milione* (orig. *millione*) from *mille* (L. *mille*), thousand.]
 1. a thousand thousands; 1,000,000.
 2. a million (unspecified but understood) monetary units, as dollars, pounds, francs, etc.; as, he has made a *million*.
 3. an indefinite but very large number; very many.
 the million; the common people; the masses.

mil'liŏn, *a.* 1. one thousand thousand.
 2. very many.

mil·liŏn·āire', mil·liŏn·nāire', *n.* [Fr. *millionnaire*.]
 1. a person whose wealth comes to at least a million dollars, pounds, francs, etc.
 2. a very wealthy person.

mil·liŏn·āir'ess, *n.* a woman who is a millionaire, or a millionaire's wife.

mil'liŏn·ăr·y, *a.* pertaining to millions; consisting of millions; as, the *millionary* chronology of the Pundits.

mil'liŏned, *a.* numbered by millions; having millions.

mil'liŏn·fōld, *a.* and *adv.* a million times as much or as many.

mil'liŏn·iṣm, *n.* the condition of possessing millions.

mil'liŏn·ist, *n.* a millionaire. [Rare.]

mil·liŏn·nāire', *n.* same as *millionaire*.

mil'liŏnth, *a.* 1. coming last in a series of a million.
 2. designating any of the million equal parts of something.

mil'liŏnth, *n.* 1. the millionth one of a series.
 2. any of the million equal parts of something.

mil'li·pēde, mil'li·ped, *n.* same as *millepede*.

mil'li·stēre (*or* -stãr), *n.* [Fr., from L. *mille*, a thousand, and Fr. *stère*, a stere.] a liter.

mil'li·vōlt, *n.* one thousandth of a volt.

mill'măn, *n.*; *pl.* **mill'men,** a man employed at a mill.

mill pick, a tool for dressing millstones, or for giving them their corrugated or otherwise roughened surface.

mill'pond, *n.* a pond or reservoir of water formed by a milldam, from which water flows for driving a mill wheel.

mill'rāce, *n.* a current of water that turns a mill wheel; also, the channel in which it flows.

mill'rēa, mill'ree, *n.* same as *milreis*.

mill'run, *a.* just as it comes out of the mill; ordinary; average: also *run-of-the-mill*.

mill'rȳnd, *n.* the rynd of a millstone.

mill'-six"pence, *n.* a silver sixpence milled in a press.

mill'stōne, *n.* 1. either of a pair of large, flat, round stones used for grinding grain or other substances.
 2. stone used for these, usually a hard sandstone or conglomerate.
 3. a heavy burden: Matt. xviii. 6.
 4. something that grinds, pulverizes, or crushes.

mill'stōne grit, a coarse, quartzose sandstone which has been used for millstones. It constitutes one of the members of the carboniferous group underlying the true coal measures, and overlying the mountain limestone.

mill'strēam, *n.* the water flowing in a millrace.

mill'tāil, *n.* a tailrace.

mill tọoth, a molar. [Obs.]

mill wheel (hwēl), the wheel, usually a water wheel, that drives the machinery in a mill.

mill'wŏrk, *n.* 1. objects made in a mill; especially, doors, windows, etc. made in a planing mill.
 2. work done in a mill.

mill'wrīght (-rīt), *n.* 1. one who makes a business of planning and building mills or mill machinery.
 2. a worker who installs, attends, or repairs the shafting, belting, and other machinery in a mill.

mī'lō, *n.* [from Bantu *maili*.] a coarse, yellow-seeded sorghum, grown in the United States as a dry-land forage crop: popularly called *milo maize*.

mi·lord', *n.* [Fr., from Eng. *my lord*.] an English gentleman or nobleman: Continental term used in speaking to or of such a man.

mil'pȧ, *n.* [Mex. Sp., cornfield, from Nahuatl.] a small tract of arable land cleared from a forest area, cultivated until the land is exhausted, then abandoned.

milque'tōast (milk'tōst), *n.* [from Caspar *Milquetoast*, character of this sort in a comic strip by H. T. Webster (1885–1952), Am. cartoonist.] any timid, shrinking, apologetic person.

mil'rẹis, *n.*; *pl.* **mil'rẹis,** [Port., from *mil*, a thousand, and *reis*, pl. of *real*, a rei.]
 1. a former Brazilian monetary unit and silver coin, equivalent to 1,000 reis: superseded in 1942 by the *cruzeiro*.
 2. a former Portuguese monetary unit and gold coin: superseded in 1911 by the *escudo*. Also *reis*.

milt, *n.* [ME. and AS. *milte*, the spleen.] the spleen.

milt, *n.* [ME. and AS. milte.]
 1. the reproductive glands of male fishes, especially when filled with germ cells and the milky fluid containing them.
 2. such cells and fluid; fish sperm.

milt, *a.* breeding: said of male fishes.

milt, *v.t.* to fertilize (fish roe) with milt.

milt'ĕr, *n.* 1. a male fish, especially in breeding time.
 2. its milt.

Mil·tō'ni·ăn, *a.* Miltonic.

Mil·ton'iç, *a.* of, pertaining to, or resembling the English poet, John Milton (1608–1674), his poetry, or his style; hence, solemn, elevated, majestic, etc.

milt'wāste, *n.* a fern, *Asplenium ceterach*, formerly considered efficacious in diseases of the spleen.

mil'vīne, *a.* belonging to or resembling birds of the kite family.

mil'vīne, *n.* a kite; any bird related to the kite.

Mil'vus, *n.* [L. *milvus*, a kite.] a genus of falconoid birds including the kites.

mim, *a.* [echoic.] demure; primly quiet or shy. [Brit. Dial.]

mīme, *n.* [Fr. *mime*; L. *mimus*, from Gr. *mimos*, an actor, a drama.]
 1. (a) an ancient Greek or Roman farce, in which people and events were mimicked and burlesqued; (b) dialogue for this.
 2. a modern play of this kind.
 3. an actor in such a farce.
 4. a clown, jester, buffoon, or mimic.

mīme, *v.t.*; mimed, *pt.*, *pp.*; miming, *ppr.* to imitate, mimic, or act out as a mime.

mīme, *v.i.* to act as a mime; play a part with gestures and actions, but usually without words.

mim'ē·ō·grȧph", *n.* [Gr. *mimeisthai*, to imitate, and *graphein*, to write.] a machine for making copies of written or typewritten matter or drawings by means of a stencil cut on a typewriter or with a stylus: formerly a trademark (*Mimeograph*).

mim'ē·ō·grȧph", *v.t.* 1. to make copies of on a mimeograph.
 2. to make (copies) on a mimeograph.

mīm'ĕr, *n.* a mimic or buffoon.

mi·mē'sis, *n.* [Gr. *mimēsis*, imitation.] imitation; specifically, (a) in art and literature, imitation or representation, especially of speech, behavior, etc.; (b) in biology, mimicry.

mim'ē·tēne, *n.* same as *mimetite*.

mi·met'iç, *a.* [Gr. *mimētikos*, imitative, from *mimeisthai*, to imitate.]
 1. imitative; of or characterized by imitation.
 2. make-believe; mimic.
 3. of or characterized by mimicry.

mi·met'iç·ăl, *a.* mimetic.

mim'ē·tiṣm, *n.* [Gr. *mimētēs*, an imitator, and *-ite*.] mimicry.

mim'ē·tīte, *n.* a lead arsenate and chloride, $(PbCl)Pb_4(AsO_4)_3$.

mim'iç, *a.* [L. *mimicus*; Gr. *mimikos*, from *mimos*, a mime.]
 1. imitative; inclined to copy.
 2. of, or having the nature of, mimicry or imitation.
 3. make-believe; simulated; mock; as, *mimic* battles.

mim'iç, *n.* 1. one who or that which imitates or mimics; especially, an actor skilled in mimicry.
 2. an imitation; something copied.

mim'iç, *v.t.*; mimicked (-ikt), *pt.*, *pp.*; mimicking, *ppr.* 1. to imitate in speech or action, as in ridicule.
 2. to copy closely; to imitate accurately.
 3. to assume likeness to (something else) as a protection or advantage.

mim'iç·ăl, *a.* mimic. [Rare.]

mim'iç·ăl·ly, *adv.* in an imitative or aping manner.

mim'ick·ĕr, *n.* a mimic.

mim'iç·ry, *n.*; *pl.* **mim'iç·ries,** 1. the practice, art, instance, or way of mimicking.
 2. close resemblance of one organism to another or to some object in its environment, as of some insects to the leaves or twigs of plants.

Mī'mir, *n.* [ON. *Mīmir*.] in Norse mythology, a giant guarding the spring of wisdom at the root of the tree Yggdrasill.

mi·mog'rȧ·phĕr, *n.* [Gr. *mimographos*; *mimos*, a mime, and *graphein*, to write.] a writer of farces or mimes.

Mi·mō'sȧ, *n.* [from L. *mimus*, Gr. *mimos*, an imitator.]
 1. a genus of trees, shrubs, and herbs of the legume family, growing in warm regions and usually having bipinnate leaves, and heads or spikes of small white, yellow, or pink flowers: the group includes the acacia and the sensitive plant.
 2. [m–] any plant of this genus.

mi·mō'sȧ bärk, the bark of any one of several Australian acacia trees.

mim·ō·sā'ceous (-shus), *a.* of the mimosa family of plants.

mim·ō·tan'niç, *a.* [*mimosa* and *tannic*.] pertaining to a variety of tannic acid or tannin found in the plants of the mimosa family.

mim'ō·tȳpe, *n.* [Gr. *mimos*, a mimic, and *typos*, impression, type.] in zoology, a form of animal life having a strong resemblance to another form, but not closely allied to it in essential characteristics.

mimp, *n.* an affected puckering of the mouth or lips. [Scot. and Brit. Dial.]

Mim′ū·lus, *n.* [LL. *mimulus*, dim. of L. *mimus*, a mimic.] a genus of plants of the order *Scrophulariaceæ*. A number of plants of this genus now in cultivation are called *monkey flowers*.

Mī′mus, *n.* in zoology, the genus to which the mockingbirds belong.

Mi·mū′sops, *n.* [Gr. *mimō*, genit. *mimous*, an ape, and *ōps*, face: so called from the flowers' having the appearance of an ape's face.] a genus of sapotaceous, tropical hardwood trees with milky sap, bearing fragrant white flowers and yielding fleshy fruit, the seeds of which furnish an oil.

mī′nȧ, *n.*; *pl.* **mī′nae, mī′nȧs,** [L., from Gr. *mina*, a weight, a sum of money; Heb. *māneh*, a weight, portion, from *mānāh*, to divide, measure out.] a weight or denomination of money, the mina of the Old Testament being valued at 50 shekels, and the Greek or Attic mina at 100 drachmas.

mī′nȧ, mī′nȧh, *n.* a myna.

mi·nā′cious, *a.* [L. *minax* (*-acis*), full of threats.] threatening; menacing.

mi·nac′i·ty, *n.* the quality of being threatening.

Mi·naē′ȧn, *n.* [L. *Minaeus*, from *Minaei*, name of the people, and Gr. *Minaioi, Meinaioi*.] a member of the Minaean people, an ancient tribe inhabiting southwestern Arabia. Their kingdom there began about 1300 B. C. and was overthrown about 650 B. C.

Mi·naē′ȧn, *a.* pertaining to the Minaean nation or their language. Their language was a dialect similar to the later Sabaean and Himyarite dialects.

Mī·nä·häs′sä, *n.* a native of a country in northern Celebes.

Mī·nä·häs′sȧn, *a.* pertaining to the people or dialects of Minahassa.

mi·när′, *n.* [Ar. *manar*.] a tower; as, the Kutab *Minar* at Delhi in India.

min·ȧ·ret′, *n.* [Sp. *minarete*, from Ar. *manāra*, a lamp, lighthouse, minaret, from *minār*, a candlestick, lighthouse.] a high, slender tower attached to a Moslem mosque, with one or more projecting balconies, from which a muezzin, or crier, calls the people to prayer.

MINARETS

min·är′ġent, *n.* [aluminum, and L. *argentum*, silver.] an alloy used by jewelers consisting of copper, nickel, tungsten, and aluminum.

min·ȧ·tō′ri·ăl, *a.* minatory.

min·ȧ·tō′ri·ăl·ly, min′ȧ·tō·ri·ly, *adv.* in a minatory manner.

min′ȧ·tō·ry, *a.* [LL. *minatorius*, threatening.] threatening; menacing.

mi·nąul′, *n.* same as *monaul*.

mince, *v.t.*; minced, *pt.*, *pp.*; mincing, *ppr.* [ME. *mincen*; OFr. *mincier*, from LL. *minutiare*, from *minutus*, small.]

1. to cut up or chop up (meat, etc.) into very small pieces; to hash.
2. to subdivide minutely.
3. to express or do with affected elegance or daintiness.
4. to lessen the force of; to weaken, as by euphemism; as, I *minced* no words.

mince, *v.i.* 1. to speak or behave with affected elegance or daintiness.

2. to walk with short steps or in an affected, dainty manner.

mince, *n.* 1. an affectation, as of a lisp or the broad *a* in speaking, a mincing walk, etc. [Rare.]

2. mincemeat.

mince′mēat, *n.* 1. a mixture of chopped apples, spices, suet, raisins, and (now rarely) meat, used as a pie filling.

2. minced meat; meat chopped up into very small pieces. [Obs.]

to make mincemeat of; (a) to chop into small pieces; to cut to shreds; (b) to defeat or refute completely.

mince pīe, a pie with a filling of mincemeat.

min′cẽr, *n.* one who or that which minces.

min′cing, *a.* [ppr. of *mince*.]

1. affectedly elegant or dainty: of a person or his speech, manner, etc.

2. characterized by short steps or affected daintiness; as, a *mincing* walk.

min′cing·ly, *adv.* in a mincing manner; simperingly.

mīnd, *n.* [ME. *mind, mynd*; AS. *gemynd*, memory.]

1. memory; recollection or remembrance; as, this brings to *mind* another story.

2. (a) what one intends, wishes, or wills; purpose or desire; as, I have a (good) *mind* to go; (b) what one thinks; opinion.

3. (a) that which thinks, perceives, feels, wills, etc.; seat or subject of consciousness; (b) the thinking and perceiving part of consciousness; intellect or intelligence; (c) all of an individual's conscious experiences; (d) the conscious and the unconscious together as a unit; psyche.

4. the intellect in its normal state; reason; sanity; as, he has lost his *mind*.

5. a person having intelligence or regarded as an intellect; as, the great *minds* of the century.

6. way, state, or direction of thinking and feeling; as, the reactionary *mind*.

7. in philosophy, consciousness as an element in reality: contrasted with *matter*.

8. in religion, (a) a Mass in memory of a dead person: a *month's mind* is such a Mass one month after death; (b) [M–] God: in full, *Divine Mind*: so called in Christian Science.

absence of mind; inattention, usually temporary, to one's immediate surroundings; preoccupation.

meeting of minds; an agreement.

mind reader; a person who apparently guesses another's thoughts, or professes to be able to perceive them without apparent means of communication.

mind's eye; the imagination.

on one's mind; (a) occupying one's thoughts; (b) worrying one.

to bear in mind; see under *bear*.

to be in one's right mind; to be mentally well; to be sane.

to be of one mind; to have the same opinion; to agree.

to be of two minds; to be undecided or irresolute.

to be out of one's mind; (a) to be mentally ill; to be insane; (b) to be frantic (*with* worry, grief, etc.)

to call to mind; (a) to remember; (b) to be a reminder of.

to change one's mind; (a) to change one's opinion; (b) to change one's intention, purpose, or wish.

to give a person a bit, or *piece, of one's mind*; to tell a person plainly one's disapproval of him; to rebuke; to scold.

to have a (*good* or *great*) *mind to*; to have a strong inclination to; as, I *have a mind to* give up eating meat.

to have half a mind to; to be somewhat inclined to.

to have in mind; (a) to remember; (b) to think of; (c) to intend; to purpose.

to keep in mind; to remember.

to keep one's mind on; to pay attention to.

to know one's mind; to know one's real thoughts, feelings, desires, or intentions.

to lose one's mind; to become intellectually deranged; to lose the power of consecutive thought.

to make up one's mind; to resolve.

to one's mind; in one's opinion.

to pass out of mind; to be forgotten.

to put in mind; to recall attention to; to remind.

to set one's mind on; to be determined on or determinedly desirous of.

to speak one's mind; to say plainly what one thinks.

to take one's mind off; to stop one from thinking about; to turn one's attention from.

Syn.—soul, spirit, intellect, understanding, opinion, sentiment, judgment, belief, choice, inclination, desire, will, liking, purpose, impetus, memory, remembrance, recollection.

mīnd, *v.t.*; minded, *pt.*, *pp.*; minding, *ppr.*

1. to direct one's mind to; specifically, (a) to perceive; observe; notice; note; (b) to pay attention to; to heed; (c) to obey; as, the dog *minds* his master; (d) to attend to; to apply oneself to (a task, etc.); (e) to tend; to take care of; to watch over; to look after; as, *mind* the baby; (f) to be careful about; to watch out for; as, *mind* those rickety stairs.

2. (a) to care about; to feel concern about; (b) to object to; to dislike; as, I don't *mind* the cold.

3. to remember: sometimes used reflexively. [Dial.]

4. to intend; to purpose. [Dial.]

5. to remind. [Dial. or Archaic.]

never mind; do not worry; it makes no difference.

to mind your p's and q's; to be careful of your words and actions.

mīnd, *v.i.* 1. to pay attention; to give heed.

2. to be obedient.

3. to be careful; to watch out.

4. (a) to care; to feel concern; (b) to object.

mīnd′ed, *a.* 1. having a (specified kind of) mind: used in hyphenated compounds, as high-*minded*.

2. having a mind to; inclined; disposed.

mīnd′ed·ness, *n.* disposition; inclination toward anything: used in hyphenated compounds; as, absent-*mindedness*.

mīnd′ẽr, *n.* 1. one who minds; one who takes care of; as, a *minder* of horses, of a machine, or of a child.

2. one who is taken care of, as in a pauper's home. [Brit.]

mīnd′fụl, *a.* attentive; regarding with care; bearing in mind; heedful; observant.

Syn.—observant, attentive, watchful.

mīnd′fụl·ly, *adv.* in a mindful manner.

mīnd′fụl·ness, *n.* the state or quality of being mindful.

mīnd′less, *a.* 1. inattentive; heedless; forgetful; negligent; careless.

2. not endowed with mind or intellectual powers; as, *mindless* bodies.

3. stupid; unthinking; as, a *mindless* slave.

mīne, *pron.* [AS. *min*, mine, from *min*, genit. case of 1st pers. pron.] that or those belonging to me: the absolute form of *my*, used without a following noun, often after *of*, as, a friend of *mine*, that book is *mine*, *mine* are better.

mīne, *poss. pron. a.* my: formerly used before a word beginning with a vowel or *h* (e.g., *mine* eyes, *mine* honor), now used after a noun in direct address (e.g., daughter *mine*). [Mainly Archaic and Poetic.]

mīne, *n.* [ME.; Late OFr., prob. from the v.]

1. a large excavation made in the earth, from which to extract metallic ores, coal, precious stones, salt, or certain other minerals: distinguished from *quarry*.

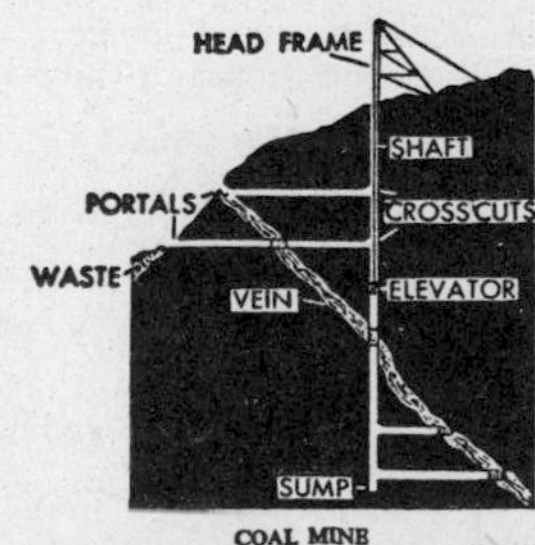

COAL MINE

2. the surface buildings, shafts, elevators, etc. of such an excavation.

3. a deposit of ore, coal, etc.

4. any great source of supply; as, a *mine* of information.

5. a kind of firework that explodes in the air and scatters a number of smaller fireworks.

6. in military science, (a) a tunnel dug under an enemy's trench, fort, etc., especially one in which an explosive is placed to destroy the enemy or its fortifications; (b) an explosive charge in a container, buried in the ground for destroying enemy objects on land, or placed in the sea for destroying enemy ships: it can be set off by direct contact, by a time fuse, or by magnetic or chemical action.

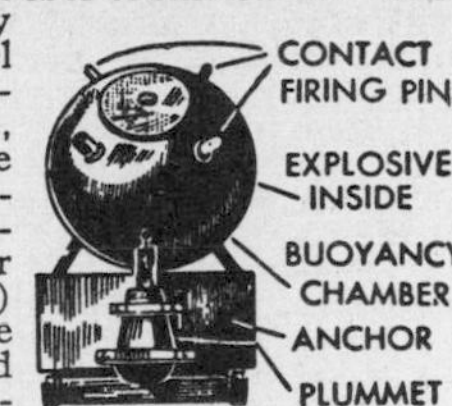

MINE (contact explosive)

7. in zoology, the burrow of an insect.

mīne, *v.i.*; mined, *pt.*, *pp.*; mining, *ppr.* [ME. *minen*; OFr. *miner.*]

1. to dig a mine; specifically, (a) to dig ores, coal, etc. from the earth; (b) to tunnel under an enemy installation.

2. to place explosive mines on land or in water.

mīne, *v.t.* 1. (a) to dig in (the earth) for ores, coal, etc.; (b) to dig (ores, coal, etc.) from the earth.

2. to dig a tunnel under (an enemy installation).

3. to destroy, or try to destroy, with an explosive mine or mines.

4. to undermine or ruin slowly by secret methods, plotting, etc.

mīne dē·tect'ŏr, an electromagnetic device for locating the position of buried explosive mines.

mīne fiēld, an area on land or in water where explosive mines have been set.

mīne'lāy"ẽr, *n.* a ship especially equipped to lay explosive mines in the water.

mīn'ẽr, *n.* [ME. and OFr. *minour.*]

1. a person whose work is digging coal, ore, etc. in a mine.

2. a soldier who digs or lays military mines.

3. in zoology, (a) one of numerous insects whose larvae make excavations in the parenchyma of leaves; (b) the honey eater of Australia.

miner's inch; same as *water-inch.*

min'ẽr·ăl (*or* min'răl), *n.* [OFr. *mineral*; LL. *minerale*, a mineral, from *minera*, a mine.]

1. an inorganic substance occurring naturally in the earth and having a consistent and distinctive set of physical properties (e.g., color, hardness, and crystalline structure) and a composition that can be expressed by a chemical formula: sometimes applied to similar substances of organic origin, as coal.

2. any naturally occurring substance that is neither vegetable nor animal.

min'ẽr·ăl, *a.* 1. of, having the nature of, consisting of, or containing a mineral or minerals.

2. impregnated with minerals; as, *mineral* water.

mineral acids; inorganic acids.

mineral blue; azurite which has been pulverized for dyeing purposes.

mineral candle; a candle made from paraffin.

mineral caoutchouc; same as *elaterite.*

mineral chameleon; same as *chameleon mineral* under *chameleon.*

mineral charcoal; see under *charcoal.*

mineral cotton; see *mineral wool* under *wool.*

mineral green; malachite.

mineral jelly; petroleum jelly.

mineral kingdom; one of the three prime divisions of nature, which includes all naturally occurring substances that are neither vegetable nor animal.

mineral lake; a substance which dyes pink.

mineral oil; any oil of mineral origin; specifically, (a) petroleum; (b) any of various colorless, tasteless oils derived from petroleum and used as a laxative.

mineral pitch; natural asphalt.

mineral purple; see *purple of Cassius* under *purple.*

mineral right; the right to minerals in a certain tract.

mineral salt; a salt derived from an inorganic acid.

mineral spring; any spring of natural mineral water.

mineral tallow; hatchettin.

mineral tar; a black, semisolid bitumen between petroleum and asphalt in consistency; maltha.

mineral water; see under *water.*

mineral wax; ozocerite.

mineral white; see *permanent white* under *permanent.*

mineral wool; see under *wool.*

min'ẽr·ăl·ist, *n.* a mineralogist. [Obs.]

min·ẽr·ăl·i·zā'tion, *n.* a mineralizing or being mineralized.

min'ẽr·ăl·īze, *v.t.*; mineralized, *pt.*, *pp.*; mineralizing, *ppr.* 1. to convert (a metal) into an ore; as, exposure to air *mineralizes* iron into iron oxide.

2. to convert (organic matter) into a mineral; to petrify.

3. to impregnate (water, etc.) with minerals.

min'ẽr·ăl·īze, *v.i.* to search for or collect minerals for study.

min'ẽr·ăl·i·zẽr, *n.* 1. an element, as arsenic, that combines chemically with a metal to form an ore.

2. a highly volatile substance that helps in the crystallization of minerals.

min·ẽr·ăl·oġ'iç·ăl, *a.* of mineralogy; as, a *mineralogical* table.

min·ẽr·ăl·oġ'iç·ăl·ly, *adv.* according to the science or principles of mineralogy.

min·ẽr·al'ō·ġist, *n.* 1. an expert or specialist in mineralogy.

2. in zoology, a carrier shell.

min·ẽr·al'ō·ġīze, *v.i.*; mineralogized, *pt.*, *pp.*; mineralogizing, *ppr.* to study mineralogy.

min·ẽr·al'ō·ġy, *n.* [from *mineral* and *-logy.*]

1. the science of minerals.

2. *pl.* **min·ẽr·al'ō·ġies,** a treatise or book on the science of minerals.

Mi·nẽr'vȧ, *n.* [L.] in Roman mythology, the goddess of wisdom, of war, and of the liberal arts: identified with the Greek Athena.

mi·ne·strō'ne, *n.* [It.; from *minestra*, soup, from *minestrare*; L. *ministrare*, to supply.] a thick vegetable soup containing vermicelli, barley, etc. in a meat broth.

mīne sweep'ẽr, 1. a ship especially equipped for destroying or removing enemy mines at sea.

2. a heavy roller attached to the front of a military tank for exploding land mines in its path.

mīne thrōw'ẽr, any of various trench mortars for throwing high-explosive shells.

mi·nette', *n.* [Fr.] a compact dike rock of dark color; mica trap.

min'ē·vẽr, *n.* same as *miniver.*

Ming, *a.* designating or of a Chinese dynasty, dating from 1368 to 1644, during which there was peace and a renaissance of the arts, especially that of porcelain making.

Ming, *n.* the Ming dynasty.

minge, *n.* a tiny fly; a midge. [Dial.]

miñ'gle (-gl), *v.t.*; mingled (-gld), *pt.*, *pp.*; mingling, *ppr.* [ME. *mengen*; AS. *mengan*, to mix.]

1. to mix up together so as to form one whole; to blend; to compound; to combine; as, to *mingle* liquors of different kinds.

2. to join in company.

Syn.—mix, compound, blend, intermingle, associate, amalgamate.

miñ'gle, *v.i.* 1. to be or become mixed, combined, blended, etc.

2. to join, unite, or take part with others.

miñ'gle, *n.* mixture. [Rare.]

miñ'gle-mañ"gle, *n.* a medley; a hotchpotch.

miñ'gle-mañ"gle, *v.t.* to mingle in disorder.

miñ'gle·ment, *n.* the act of mingling; the state of being mixed.

miñ·glẽr, *n.* one who mingles.

miñ'gling·ly, *adv.* in a mingling manner.

ming tree, [*Ming* and *tree.*] an artificial plant made in imitation of a bonsai.

min'ġy, *a.*; *comp.* mingier; *superl.* mingiest [prob. altered from *mangy*, after *stingy.*] mean and stingy. [Colloq.]

min'i-, [*mini*ature.] a combining form meaning *smaller, shorter, lesser,* etc. *than usual,* as in *minicar, miniskirt.*

min·i·ā'ceous, *a.* having the quality, more particularly the color, of minium; miniate.

min'i·āte, *a.* of or pertaining to the color of red lead; vermilion-hued.

min'i·āte, *v.t.*; miniated, *pt.*, *pp.*; miniating, *ppr.* [L. *miniatus*, pp. of *miniare*, to color with red lead.] to paint or tinge with red lead or vermilion.

min'i·ȧ·tūre (-chūr), *n.* [Fr., from It. *miniatura*, from L. *miniare*, to paint in minium.]

1. a small painting or illuminated letter, as in a medieval manuscript.

2. (a) a small painting, especially a portrait, done on ivory, vellum, etc.; (b) the art of making such paintings.

3. a copy or model on a very small scale.

in miniature; on a small scale; greatly reduced.

min'i·ȧ·tūre, *a.* on a small scale; diminutive; minute.

min'i·ȧ·tūre, *v.t.* to paint or depict upon a small scale.

min'i·ȧ·tūre çam'ẽr·ȧ, a small camera using film of 35 mm. width or less, for taking snapshots; a candid camera.

min'i·ȧ·tūr·ist, *n.* a painter of miniatures.

min'i·ȧ·tūr·īze, *v.t.*; miniaturized, *pt.*, *pp.*; miniaturizing, *ppr.* to make in a small and compact form.

min'i·bus, *n.* a small vehicle resembling an omnibus.

min'i·çam, *n.* a miniature camera.

min"i·çŏm·pūt'ẽr, *n.* a compact computer, especially one readily adapted to limited, specific functions, as the monitoring of equipment.

Min'ié (-i-ā *or* -i) **ball,** [after C. E. *Minié* (1814–1879), French inventor.] a conical leaden rifle ball hollow at the base and fitted with a plug which by the force of explosion is driven into and expands the bullet to fill the rifling in the gun barrel: used in the nineteenth century.

min'i·fȳ, *v.t.*; minified, *pt.*, *pp.*; minifying, *ppr.* [L. *minor*, less, and *-ficare*, to make.]

1. to reduce in dimensions; to make smaller; as, to *minify* a picture or a drawing.

2. to reduce in character or importance; to humiliate; as, to *minify* a hero or his deed.

min'i·kin, *n.* [M.D. *minneken*, dim. of *minne*, love.]

1. anything very small and delicate.

2. a darling or favorite. [Obs.]

3. a fine gut string for a lute. [Obs.]

min'i·kin, *a.* 1. small; diminutive. [Obs.]

2. affected or mincing.

min'im, *n.* [Fr. *minime*; L. *minimus*, least, superl. of *minor*, less.]

1. the smallest liquid measure, equal to $^1/_{60}$ fluid dram, or about a drop.

2. anything very small; a tiny portion.

3. in music, a half note.

4. in penmanship, a single downstroke, as at the end of the letter *d.*

min'im, *a.* smallest; tiniest.

min'i·mȧ, *n.* alternative plural of minimum.

min'i·măl, *a.* of or pertaining to a minimum; smallest or least possible; as, a *minimal* fraction.

Min·i·mal'ist, *n.* 1. a Menshevik (sense 1).

2. a member of the right wing of the (former) Russian Social Revolutionaries.

Opposed to *Maximalist.*

min"i·mi·zā'tion, *n.* a minimizing or being minimized.

min'i·mīze, *v.t.*; minimized, *pt.*, *pp.*; minimizing, *ppr.* 1. to reduce to a minimum.

2. to estimate or make appear to be of the least possible amount, value, or importance.

min'i·mīz·ẽr, *n.* a person who minimizes; especially, one who tries to make religious or philosophical problems appear easily explained.

min'i·mum, *n.*; *pl.* **min'i·mums, min'i·mȧ,**
1. the smallest quantity, number, or degree possible or permissible.

2. the lowest degree or point (of a varying quantity, as temperature) reached or recorded; lower limit of variation.

Opposed to *maximum.*

min'i·mum, *a.* 1. smallest possible, permissible, or reached.

2. of, marking, or setting a minimum or minimums.

Opposed to *maximum.*

min'i·mus, *n.* [L., least.] a being of the smallest size.

mīn'ing, *n.* 1. the act, process, or work of removing ores, coal, etc. from a mine.

2. the act or process of laying explosive mines.

mīn'ing, *a.* of or pertaining to mines.

mīn'ing çamp, a camp formed and occupied by miners.

min'iŏn, *n.* [Fr. *mignon*, favorite, darling.]

1. a favorite, especially one who is a servile follower: term of contempt.

2. a mistress; a paramour. [Obs.]

3. in printing, a type, in size between brevier and nonpareil, about seven-point.

This line is set in minion.

4. a small cannon used in the seventeenth century. [Obs.]

min'iŏn, *a.* delicate; pretty; dainty. [Rare.]

min'iŏn, *n.* the siftings of calcined iron ore.

min·iŏn·ette′, *n.* in printing, formerly, a size of type between minion and nonpareil.

min·iŏn·ette′, *a.* delicate; dainty. [Obs.]

min′iŏn·īze, *v.t.* to make a minion of. [Obs.]

min′iŏn·līke, min′iŏn·ly, *adv.* finely; daintily; delicately. [Obs.]

min′iŏn of the law, a policeman.

min′iŏn·ship, *n.* the state or position of being a minion. [Obs.]

min′ious (-yus), *a.* of the color of minium. [Obs.]

min′ish, *v.t.* and *v.i.* [L. *minutia,* smallness.] to lessen; to diminish. [Archaic.]

min′ish·ment, *n.* diminution. [Obs.]

min′i·skirt, *n.* [*mini-,* and *skirt.*] a very short skirt ending well above the knee.

min′is·tẽr, *n.* [ME. and OFr. *ministre;* L. *minister,* an attendant, servant (after *magister,* master).]

1. a person acting for another as his agent and carrying out his orders or designs; specifically, (a) a person appointed by the head of a government to take charge of some department of state; (b) a diplomatic officer sent to a foreign nation to represent his government, and ranking below an ambassador; (c) anyone authorized to carry out the spiritual functions of a church, conduct worship, administer the sacraments, preach, etc.; a clergyman; a pastor.

2. any person or thing thought of as serving as the agent of some power, force, etc.; as, a *minister* of evil.

Syn.—servant, delegate, official, subordinate, ecclesiastic, clergyman, parson, divine, preacher.

min′is·tẽr, *v.t.;* ministered, *pt., pp.;* ministering, *ppr.* [L. *ministrare,* to attend, serve, manage, from *minister,* a minister.]

1. to supply; to provide. [Archaic.]

2. to administer, as a sacrament.

min′is·tẽr, *v.i.* 1. to attend and serve; to perform service in any office, sacred or secular.

2. to afford supplies; to give things needful; as, to *minister* to the sick.

Syn.—serve, aid, perform, administer.

min·is·tē′ri·ăl, *a.* [Fr. *ministériel;* LL. *ministerialis.*]

1. of ministry, a minister, or ministers collectively.

2. serving as a minister, or agent; subordinate.

3. having the nature of or characteristic of the administrative functions of government; executive.

4. being a cause; instrumental.

the ministerial benches; the benches in the British House of Commons to the right of the speaker, occupied by members of the government and their supporters; by extension, the government or its supporters.

min·is·tē′ri·ăl·ist, *n.* one who supports the ministry; a supporter of the party in power.

min·is·tē′ri·ăl·ly, *adv.* in a ministerial manner or character.

min′is·tẽr plen″i·pō·ten′ti·ăr·y (-shi-ăr-y); *pl.* **min′is·tẽrs plen″i·pō·ten′ti·ăr·y,** a diplomatic representative with full authority to negotiate.

min′is·trănt, *a.* performing service as a minister; ministering.

min′is·trănt, *n.* one who ministers, or serves.

min·is·trā′tion, *n.* [L. *ministratio (-onis),* from *ministrare,* to minister.]

1. the act of serving as a minister or clergyman; performance of pastoral duties.

2. service; help.

min′is·trā·tive, *a.* serving helpfully; ministering.

min′is·tress, *n.* a woman who ministers.

min′is·try, *n.; pl.* **min′is·trieș,** [ME. *mynysterie;* L. *ministerium,* from *ministrare,* to minister.]

1. the act of ministering, or serving; ministration.

2. the office, function, or service of a minister of religion.

3. ministers collectively; the clergy.

4. (a) the department under a minister of government; (b) the term of office of such a minister; (c) such ministers collectively.

5. in certain European countries, (a) a branch of government headed by a minister; (b) its building or buildings.

min′i·um, *n.* [L.]

1. vermilion (the color).

2. red oxide of lead, Pb_3O_4: also called *red lead.*

min′i·vẽr, men′i·vẽr, *n.* [OFr. *menu ver,* lit., small fur.]

1. in medieval times, a kind of white or gray fur used for trimming garments.

2. any fine white fur; especially, the white winter fur of the ermine.

mink, *n.; pl.* **minks** or **mink,** [Late ME. *minke,* from Scand.]

1. a mammal somewhat like a large weasel, living in water part of the time and found in the cooler latitudes of the Northern Hemisphere.

2. its valuable fur, soft, thick, brown, and lustrous.

MINK (2 ft long

Min·ne·hä′hä, *n.* the Indian girl who becomes the wife of Hiawatha in Longfellow's *The Song of Hiawatha.*

min′ne·sing·ẽr, *n.* [G., from *minne,* love, and *singer,* a singer.] any of a number of German lyric poets and singers of the twelfth to the fourteenth centuries, corresponding to the minstrels or troubadours.

Min·ne·sō′tăn, *a.* of Minnesota.

Min·ne·sō′tăn, *n.* a native or inhabitant of Minnesota.

min′nōw, *n.; pl.* **min′nōwș** or **min′nōw,** [ME. *menow,* from AS. *myne,* a minnow, from *min,* small.] any one of several species of very small fresh-water fish, commonly used as bait; specifically, some species of *Phoxinus,* a small cyprinoid fish from one and a half to three inches long: also called *minny* and *minnie.*

min′ny, *n.; pl.* **min′nieș,** same as *minnow.* [Dial. or Colloq.]

mī′nō, *n.; pl.* **mī′nōș,** [Japan.] a coat made of grasses, straw, or similar material, and worn by workingmen in Japan for protection against rain.

Mi·nō′ăn, *a.* [from *Minos* and *-an.*] designating or of an advanced prehistoric culture that flourished in Crete from about 3000 to 1100 B.C.

mī′nŏr, *a.* [L., less.]

1. (a) lesser in size, amount, number, or extent; (b) lesser in importance or rank: opposed to *major.*

2. under full legal age (usually twenty-one years).

3. constituting the minority: said of a part, etc.

4. in a minor key; sad; melancholy; plaintive.

5. in education, designating a field of study in which a student specializes, but to a lesser degree than in his major.

6. in logic, narrower; less inclusive.

7. in music, (a) designating an interval higher than the corresponding major interval by a half tone; (b) designating a tone distant by a minor interval from another tone; (c) characterized by minor intervals, scales, or tones; as, the *minor* mode; (d) based on the scale pattern of the minor mode.

minor axis; see *conjugate axis* under *axis.*

minor chord; in music, a chord involving a minor third, usually between the lowest two tones.

minor key; in music, a key in the minor mode; hence, a melancholy mood.

minor mode; in music, the arrangement of tones in accordance with the intervals of the minor scale, as the basic tonal material of a composition: often associated, in the Occident, with a melancholy mood.

minor orders; the group of persons holding subordinate ecclesiastical offices.

minor premise; in logic, the premise (in a syllogism) containing the minor term.

minor scale; one of the two standard diatonic scales, consisting of eight tones, with half steps instead of whole steps (a) after the second and seventh tones in ascending and after the sixth and third tones in descending (*melodic minor scale*), or (b) after the second, fifth, and seventh tones in ascending and after the eighth, sixth, and third tones in descending (*harmonic minor scale*): distinguished from *major scale.*

minor suit; in bridge, diamonds or clubs: so called from their lower value in scoring.

minor term; in logic, the subject of the conclusion in a syllogism.

mī′nŏr, *n.* 1. in law, a person of either sex under full legal age, who is not permitted by law to enjoy full civil rights.

2. in logic, a minor term or a minor premise.

3. [M–] a Minorite; a Franciscan friar.

4. in music, a minor key, mode, interval, etc.

5. [*usually pl.*] in sports, in the United States, a minor league: usually preceded by *the;* as, *the minors* are now playing.

6. in education, a minor subject or field of study.

mī′nŏr, *v.i.;* minored, *pt., pp.;* minoring, *ppr.* to specialize to a secondary degree in some subject or field of study (with *in*); as, he will *minor in* chemistry.

mī′nŏr·āte, *v.t.* to diminish. [Rare.]

mī·nŏr·ā′tion, *n.* a lessening; diminution. [Rare.]

Mi·nọr′cȧ, *n.* any of a breed of large, long-bodied chickens with black, white, or buff feathers.

mī′nŏr·ess, *n.* 1. a female under age. [Rare.]

2. [M–] a nun under the rule of St. Francis.

Mī′nŏr·īte, *n.* [L. *minor,* less: so named because they regarded themselves as of a humbler rank than members of other orders.] a Franciscan friar.

mi·nor′i·ty, *n.; pl.* **mi·nor′i·tieș,** [Fr. *minorité,* from *mineur* (L. *minor*), less.]

1. the lesser part or smaller number; less than half of a total: opposed to *majority.*

2. a racial, religious, national, or political group smaller than and differing from the larger, controlling group of which it is a part.

3. the period or condition of being under full legal age.

mī′nŏr-lēague′ (-lēg′), *a.* of, in, or suitable to a minor league or leagues.

mī′nŏr lēague, any of the leagues of professional baseball clubs, etc. other than the major leagues.

Mī′nos, *n.* [Gr. *Minōs.*] 1. in Greek mythology, a king of Crete, son of Zeus by Europa, who after he died became one of the three judges of the dead in the lower world, with Aeacus and Rhadamanthus.

2. his grandson, for whom Daedalus built the labyrinth in Crete.

Min′ō·taur, *n.* [L. *Minotaurus;* Gr. *Minōtauros,* the Minotaur, prob. from *Minōs,* king of Crete, and *tauros,* bull.] in Greek mythology, a monster with the body of a man and the head of a bull (in some versions, with the body of a bull and head of a man), confined by Minos in a labyrinth built by Daedalus, and annually fed seven youths and seven maidens from Athens, until killed by Theseus.

MINOTAUR

min′stẽr, *n.* [ME. *mynstre, munster;* AS. *mynster,* from LL. *monasterium,* a monastery.]

1. the church of a monastery, or one to which a monastery has been attached.

2. any of various large churches or cathedrals: *-minster* occurs as an element in certain English place names, as West*minster,* Ax*minster.*

min′strel, *n.* [ME. *menestral;* OFr. *menestrel;* LL. *ministerialis,* a servant, jester, singer, from L. *minister,* a servant.]

1. any of a class of lyric poets and singers of the Middle Ages, who traveled from place to place singing and reciting, usually to the accompaniment of a harp or lute.

2. a poet; singer; musician. [Poetic.]

3. a performer in a minstrel show.

min′strel shōw, [from the Christy *Minstrels,* the first troupe organized to perform in the U. S.] a comic variety show presented by a company of performers in blackface, who sing songs, tell jokes, etc.

min′strel·sy, *n.; pl.* **min′strel·sieș,** [ME. *menestralcie.*] 1. the arts and occupation of minstrels; instrumental music and singing.

2. a company of musicians or minstrels; also, a collection of minstrel songs.

The *minstrelsy* of heaven. —Milton.

mint, *n.* [ME. *minte, mynt;* AS. *mynet, mynit,* from L. *moneta,* a place for coining money, from *Moneta*, a surname of Juno, in whose temple at Rome money was coined.]

1. a place where money is coined by authority of the government; as, the United States *mint* at Philadelphia.

2. a source of invention or manufacture; as, a *mint* of phrases; a *mint* of calumny.

3. a source of abundant supply.

mint, *a.* new or in its original condition, as if freshly minted; as, a postage stamp in *mint* condition.

mint, *v.t.* 1. to coin or stamp out (money).

2. to invent or create; to fabricate.

mint, *n.* [L. *menta, mentha*; Gr. *mintha, minthē*, mint.]

1. an aromatic plant of the genus *Mentha* whose leaves are used for flavoring and in medicine: *Mentha piperita* is used for flavoring and as a stimulant, and bergamot mint, or water mint, *Mentha aquatica*, is used by perfumers.

2. a piece of candy or chewing gum flavored with mint.

mint'ăġe, *n.* 1. the act or process of minting money.

2. the act of inventing or making.

3. money produced in a mint.

4. a fee paid to a mint for coining.

5. the stamp impressed on a coin.

mint çam'phŏr, same as *menthol*.

mint'ẽr, *n.* one who mints or stamps legal coin.

mint jū'lep, a frosted drink consisting of whisky or brandy, sugar, and mint leaves in a tall glass packed with chipped ice.

mint'măn, *n.* a coiner; one skilled in coining or in coins.

mint märk, a very small identifying mark or initial stamped on a coin, and designating usually the mint at which it was made; as *O* for New Orleans, *S* for San Francisco, etc.

mint'mȧs"tẽr, *n.* 1. the master or superintendent of a mint.

2. one who invents or fabricates. [Obs.]

mint sauce, a sauce for meat, especially lamb, consisting of chopped mint leaves, vinegar, sugar, etc.

min'ū·end, *n.* [L. *minuendus*, to be diminished, gerundive of *minuere*, to lessen, diminish.] in arithmetic, the number or quantity from which another (the *subtrahend*) is to be subtracted.

min'ū·et, *n.* [Fr. *menuet*, from *menuet*, smallish, pretty: so called from the small steps taken in the dance.]

1. a very graceful and stately slow dance, popular in fashionable circles throughout the eighteenth century.

2. the slow and stately triple measure music for such a dance.

min'um, *n.* minim. [Obs.]

mī'nus, *prep.* [L., neut. sing. of *minor*, less.]

1. less; reduced by the subtraction of; as, four *minus* two.

2. without; lacking; as, *minus* a finger. [Colloq.]

mī'nus, *a.* 1. indicating or involving subtraction; as, a *minus* sign.

2. negative; as, a *minus* quantity.

3. somewhat less than; as, a grade of A *minus*.

mī'nus, *n.* 1. a minus sign.

2. a negative quantity.

mi·nus'cū·lăr, *a.* minuscule.

mi·nus'cūle, *n.* [Fr.; L. *minusculus*, rather small, dim. of *minor*, less.]

1. a small cursive script developed from the uncial and used in medieval manuscripts: distinguished from *majuscule*.

2. a letter in this script.

3. any small, or lower-case, letter.

mi·nus'cūle, *a.* 1. of, in, like, or having the nature of, minuscules.

2. very small; tiny; minute.

mī'nus sīgn (sīn), in mathematics, a sign (−), indicating subtraction or negative quantity: opposed to *plus sign* (+).

min'u·tăr·y (min'i-), *a.* relating to a minute or to minutes; made up of minutes; occurring every minute. [Obs.]

mī·nūte' (*or* mi-), *a.* [ME; L. *minutus*, little, small, pp. of *minuere*, to lessen, diminish.]

1. very small, little, or slender; of very small bulk or size; as, a *minute* grain of sand; a *minute* filament; a *minute* blood vessel.

2. of little importance or significance; petty; as, *minute* details.

3. of, characterized by, or attentive to tiny details; exact; precise; as, *minute* observation.

min'ute (min'it), *n.* [ME. *minut*; via OFr. and ML. *minuta*, L. *minutus*, small.]

1. the sixtieth part of any of certain units; specifically, (a) $^1/_{60}$ of an hour; sixty seconds; (b) $^1/_{60}$ of a degree of an arc; sixty seconds: indicated by the symbol (′).

2. a space of time indefinitely small; a moment; an instant; as, I will be with you in a *minute*, or in a few *minutes*.

3. a specific point in time.

4. a note or memorandum; specifically, [*pl.*] an official record of what was said and done at a meeting, convention, etc.

the minute (that); just as soon as.

up to the minute; in the latest style, fashion, etc.

min'ute (-it), *a.* relating to a minute or to minutes; marking minutes; as, a *minute* gun at sea.

min'ute (-it), *v.t.*; minuted, *pt., pp.*; minuting, *ppr.* 1. to time to the minute.

2. to make a minute, or memorandum, of; to record.

min'ute book, a book of short notes or minutes of proceedings.

min'ute gun, a cannon discharged every minute as a signal of distress or mourning.

min'ute hand, the long hand that points to the minutes on a clock or watch and moves around the dial once every hour.

mī·nūte'ly, *adv.* with minuteness; in a minute manner; exactly; as, to measure the length of anything *minutely*.

min'ute·ly (min'it-), *adv.* 1. every minute.

2. often or continually.

min'ute·ly, *a.* 1. happening every minute.

2. happening very often or continually.

min'ute·man, *n.*; *pl.* **min'ute·men** (min'it-), a man ready at a minute's notice; specifically, a militiaman of the American Revolutionary period.

mī·nūte'ness, *n.* 1. extreme smallness, fineness, or slenderness; as, the *minuteness* of the filaments of cotton; the *minuteness* of details in narration.

2. attention to detail; exactness; as, the *minuteness* of observation or distinction.

min'ute steāk (min'it stāk), a small steak, often cubed, that can be cooked quickly.

min'ute wätch, a watch that distinguishes minutes of time, or on which minutes are marked.

mi·nū'ti·ȧ (-shi-), *n.*; *pl.* **mi·nū'ti·ae,** [L. *minutia*, smallness.] a triviality; a small detail: usually in the plural.

minx, *n.* 1. a pert, saucy girl.

2. a female puppy. [Obs.]

mīn'y, *a.* abounding with mines; underground.

min'yăn, *n.* in Jewish religious service, the number necessary for the conducting of public worship, no less than ten men.

Mī'ō·cēne, *a.* [Gr. *meiōn*, less, and *kainos*, recent.] designating or of the third epoch of the Tertiary Period in the Cenozoic Era, characterized by the development of large mountain ranges.

the Miocene; the Miocene Epoch or its rocks.

Mī·ō·hip'pus, *n.* [*Miocene*, and Gr. *hippos*, horse.] a genus of small fossil animals of the family *Equidæ*, found in Miocene rocks and characterized by having three separate toes on each foot.

mī'ō·nīte, *n.* a colorless, transparent mineral, crystallizing in the tetragonal system: also spelled *meionite*.

mī·ō'sis, *n.* 1. meiosis.

2. myosis.

mī·ot'iç, *a.* 1. meiotic.

2. myotic.

mī·ot'iç, *n.* a myotic.

miq'ue·let (-e-), *n.* [Sp. *miquelete.*] in Spain, a bandit soldier; a guerrilla.

mïr, *n.* emir. [Obs.]

mïr, *n.* in Russia, formerly, a village community of peasant farmers holding lands in common and regulating their own local affairs.

Mī'rȧ, *n.* [f. of L. *mirus*, wonderful.] a star, Omicron Ceti, in the constellation Cetus, remarkable for its varying brightness, increasing from the twelfth to the fourth magnitude in about six weeks.

mir'ȧ·belle, *n.* [Fr., altered from L. *myrobalanum*, fruit of a kind of palm tree; from Gr. *myrobalanan*, from *myron*, unguent, perfume, and *balanos*, acorn, date.]

1. a European variety of plum tree.

2. the sweet, small, golden fruit of this tree.

3. a brandy made from these fruits.

mi·ra'bi·le diç'tū, [L.] wonderful to tell.

Mi·rab'i·lis, *n.* [L. *mirabilis*, wonderful.] a genus of plants of the four-o'clock family.

mi·rab'i·līte, *n.* [L. *mirabilis*, wonderful, and *-ite.*] in chemistry, native sodium sulfate: popularly known as Glauber's salt.

mī'rȧ·ble, *a.* wonderful. [Obs.]

mir'ȧ·çle, *n.* [L. *miraculum*, from *mirari*, to wonder at, from *mirus*, wonderful.]

1. in theology, an event or effect that apparently contradicts known scientific laws and is hence thought to be due to supernatural causes, especially to an act of God.

2. a wonder or wonderful thing.

3. a wonderful example; as, he is a *miracle* of fortitude.

4. a miracle play.

mir'ȧ·çle man, 1. a man who professes, or is believed, to perform miracles.

2. a man who does something that supposedly could not be done. [Colloq.]

mir'ȧ·çle plāy, 1. any of a class of medieval religious dramas based on miracles worked by the saints.

2. in medieval England, a mystery play.

mi·raç'ū·līze, *v.t.* to make to appear miraculous or as if miraculous. [Rare.]

mi·raç'ū·lous, *a.* [L. *miraculum*, a wonderful thing, a miracle.]

1. supernatural; having the nature of a miracle.

2. like a miracle; wonderful; marvelous.

3. able to work miracles.

mi·raç'ū·lous·ly, *adv.* in a miraculous manner; by miracle.

Some cheats have pretended to cure diseases *miraculously*. —Porteus.

mi·raç'ū·lous·ness, *n.* the state of being miraculous.

mir·ȧ·dŏr', *n.* [Sp., from *mirar*, to behold, to view.] in architecture, a passage; a balcony or gallery commanding an extensive view.

mi·räge' (-räzh'), *n.* [Fr., from *mirer*; LL. *mirare*, to look at.] an optical illusion caused by the reflection of light through layers of air of different temperatures and densities, by which a ship, oasis in the desert, etc. appears to be very near and, often, upside down: often used figuratively of something that falsely appears to be real.

mïr'bāne, *n.* same as *Nitrobenzene*.

mī'rex, *n.* [coined from the initials of its three developers, and *-ex*, an arbitrary suffix.] an insecticide consisting of a chlorinated hydrocarbon, $C_{10}Cl_{12}$, usually mixed with a bait and used especially against a certain species of ants now found in the southern United States.

mīre, *n.* [Ice. *myrr, myri*, a bog, swamp.]

1. an area of wet, soggy ground; a bog.

2. deep mud; earth so wet and soft as to yield to the feet and to wheels; slimy soil.

mīre, *v.t.*; mired, *pt., pp.*; miring, *ppr.* 1. to cause to get stuck in mire.

2. to soil with mud or dirt.

mīre, *v.i.* to sink or stick in mud.

Mir'i·ăm, *n.* in the Bible, the sister of Moses and Aaron. Ex. xv. 20.

mi·rif'iç, mi·rif'i·çăl, *a.* [L. *mirificus*, causing wonder.] performing seemingly miraculous acts.

mīr'i·ness, *n.* the state of being miry.

mïrk, *n.* same as *murk*.

mïrk'y, *a.*; *comp.* mirkier; *superl.* mirkiest, same as *murky*.

mïr'li·tŏn, *n.* a kind of toy pipe which produces harsh musical sounds.

mī'rō, *n.* [native name.] a cone-bearing tree of Australia, *Podocarpus ferruginea*, valued for its dark ironlike wood, which is used for cabinetwork.

mir'rŏr, *n.* [ME. *mirour*; OFr. *mireor, mirour*, from LL. *mirare*, to look at; L. *mirari*, to wonder at.]

1. any polished substance that forms images by the reflection of rays of light; especially, a piece of glass coated on the reverse side with silver, etc.; a looking glass.

In the clear *mirror* of thy ruling star
I saw, alas! some dread event depend.
—Pope.

2. that which gives a true representation or description.

3. something to be imitated or emulated; model.

4. a crystal used by fortunetellers, sorcerers, etc. [Archaic.]

5. in architecture, a small oval ornament cut into deep moldings.

6. a speculum.

Claude Lorrain mirror; a convex mirror, so named because its images in their exaggerated perspective resemble pictures made by Claude Lorrain, a French artist of the seventeenth century: also called *Claude Lorrain glass*.

mir'rŏr, *v.t.*; mirrored, *pt.*, *pp.*; mirroring, *ppr.* to reflect as in a mirror; to give or show a likeness of.

mir'rŏr çärp, a kind of common carp having few scales of very large size.

mir'rŏr plāte, plate glass of such quality as to be fit for mirrors; also, a single mirror without a frame.

mir'rŏr·sçōpe, *n.* an instrument used by artists in rapid field painting or sketching.

mir'rŏr wrīt'ing, handwriting resembling the image of ordinary handwriting as seen in a mirror.

mirth, *n.* [ME. *myrthe*; AS. *mirigth, mirgth, myrth*, pleasure, joy, from *mirig, myrig*, pleasant.]

1. merriment; hilarity; noisy gaiety; jollity.

2. that which causes merriment. [Obs.]

mirth'fụl, *a.* 1. merry; jovial; festive; full of merriment.

2. exhibiting or causing mirth; as, a *mirthful* play.

mirth'fụl·ly, *adv.* in a mirthful manner.

mirth'fụl·ness, *n.* the state or quality of being mirthful.

mirth'less, *a.* without mirth or hilarity.

mirth'less·ness, *n.* absence of mirth.

MIRV, *n.*; *pl.* **MIRV's,** [*m*ultiple *i*ndependently targeted *r*eentry *v*ehicle.]

1. an intercontinental ballistic missile with several war heads, each of which can be directed to a different target or to the same target at intervals.

2. any such war head.

mīr'y, *a.* 1. full of, or having the nature of, mire; as, a *miry* road.

2. covered with mire; muddy; dirty.

mir'zä, *n.* [Per. *mīrza*, a prince.] a Persian title of honor placed after the name of a royal prince or before the name of a high official, scholar, etc.

mis-, [OFr. *mes-*, from L. *minus*, less.] a prefix meaning *less*, as in *mis*chance, *mis*prize.

mis-, [ME. *mis-, mys-*; AS. *mis-*.] a prefix meaning *wrong, bad, wrongly, badly*, as in *mis*fortune, *mis*adjust, *mis*doing.

Following is a list of words the meanings of which are either self-evident or may be found by reference to the principal element defined in the vocabulary:

misadjust
misadjustment
misadvice
misadvised
misadvisedly
misaffirm
misaimed
misallegation
misallege
misallotment
misappreciate
misarrangement
misassign
misbeseem
misbestow
misbestowal
miscensure
mischarge
mischoose
mischristen
miscite
misclaim
miscognizant
miscollocation
miscomprehend
miscomputation
miscompute
misconjecture
misconsecrate
misconsecration
misconsequence
miscopy
miscorrect
miscounsel
miscredulity
misdescribe
misdevotion
misdiet
misdisposition
misdistinguish
misdivide
misdivision
miseducate
misenter
misentry
misexplanation
misexplication
misexpound
misexpression
misfaith
misfashion
misfeature
misformation
misframe
misgotten
misguess
misimagination
misincline
misinfer
misinformer
misinstruct
misinstruction
misjoin
miskindle
mislabel
mislearn
misluck
mismake
mismark
mismeasure
mismeasurement
misnurture
misobserve
misobserver
misordination
mispaint
misperception
mispoint
mispolicy
mispractice
misproceeding
misreceive
misrecital
misrecite
misreckon
misreckoning
misrecollect
misrecollection
misregulate
misrehearse
misrelate
misrelation
misrender
misrepeat
misreport
misrepute
misseek
missend
misserve
misset
missheathed
missuggestion
missummation
misswear
mistaught
misteach
mistell
misterm
misthrive
misthrow
mistitle
mistradition
mistrain
mistranscribe
mistreatment
misturn
mistutor
miswed
misworship
misworshiper
miswrite
miswrought
misyoke
miszealous

mis-, see *miso-*.

mis·ad·ven'tūre, *n.* [OFr. *mesaventure.*] mischance; misfortune; bad luck; an unlucky accident.

homicide by misadventure; in law, accidental homicide: also called *excusable homicide*.

mis·ad·ven'tūred, *a.* unfortunate. [Obs.]

mis·ad·ven'tūr·ous, *a.* pertaining to misadventure; unfortunate.

mis·ad·vīṣe', *v.t.* to advise wrongly.

mis·af·feçt', *v.t.* to dislike. [Obs.]

mis·af·feçt'ed, *a.* ill-disposed. [Obs.]

mis·af·feç'tion, *n.* a bad or erroneous affection, or the state of being wrongly affected. [Obs.]

mis·al·lī'ănce, *n.* improper association; especially, an unsuitable marriage.

mis·al·lied', *a.* improperly allied or associated.

mis·al·lȳ', *v.t.*; misallied, *pt.*, *pp.*; misallying, *ppr.* to ally unsuitably or inappropriately.

mis·ạl'tẽr, *v.t.* to alter incorrectly, or in such a way as to make worse.

mis'an·thrōpe, *n.* [Gr. *misanthrōpos*, hating mankind; *misein*, to hate, and *anthrōpos*, man.] a hater or distruster of mankind.

mis·an·throp'iç, *a.* hating or distrusting mankind; of, having the nature of, or like a misanthrope.

mis·an·throp'i·çăl, *a.* misanthropic.

mis·an'thrō·pist, *n.* same as *misanthrope*.

mis·an'thrō·pos, *n.* a misanthrope. [Obs.]

mis·an'thrō·py, *n.* [Gr. *misanthrōpia*, from *misanthrōpos*, hating mankind.] hatred of, or dislike or distrust for, mankind; the feelings or actions of a misanthrope: opposed to *philanthropy*.

mis·ap·pli·çā'tion, *n.* a misapplying or being misapplied.

mis·ap·plȳ', *v.t.*; misapplied, *pt.*, *pp.*; misapplying, *ppr.* 1. to use badly, incorrectly, or uselessly; as, he *misapplies* his energies.

2. to apply dishonestly or illegally; as, he *misapplied* the company's money.

mis·ap·prē·hend', *v.t.* to understand wrongly; to take in a wrong sense.

mis·ap·prē·hen'sion, *n.* a mistaking or mistake; error in understanding.

mis·ap·prē·hen'sive·ly, *adv.* by or with misapprehension; mistakenly.

mis·ap·prō'pri·āte, *v.t.*; misappropriated, *pt.*, *pp.*; misappropriating, *ppr.* to appropriate to a bad, incorrect, or dishonest use; to misapply.

mis·ap·prō·pri·ā'tion, *n.* the act of misappropriating or that which is misappropriated.

mis·ar·rānġe', *v.t.* to arrange wrongly or improperly.

mis·ȧ·ven'tūre, *n.* misadventure. [Obs.]

mis·beãr', *v.t.* and *v.i.* to conduct oneself improperly; to misbehave. [Obs.]

mis·bē·çōme', *v.t.*; misbecame, *pt.*; misbecome, *pp.*; misbecoming, *ppr.* to be unbecoming to; to be unsuitable or unfit for.

mis·bē·çŏm'ing, *a.* unseemly; unsuitable; improper; indecorous.

mis·bē·çŏm'ing·ly, *adv.* in an unsuitable manner.

mis·bē·çŏm'ing·ness, *n.* unbecomingness; unsuitableness.

mis·bēde', *v.t.* to wrong. [Obs.]

mis·bē·fit'ting, *a.* not befitting. [Archaic.]

mis·bē·got'ten, mis·bē·got', *a.* wrongly or unlawfully begotten; specifically, born out of wedlock; illegitimate; bastard.

mis·bē·hāve', *v.i.*; misbehaved, *pt.*, *pp.*; misbehaving, *ppr.* to behave wrongly; to conduct oneself improperly.

mis·bē·hāve', *v.t.* to misconduct; to behave badly: used reflexively.

mis·bē·hāved', *a.* guilty of improper behavior; ill-bred; rude.

mis·bē·hāv'iŏr (-yūr), *n.* improper, rude, or uncivil behavior.

mis·bē·lief', *n.* wrong, false, or unorthodox belief or opinion, especially in religion.

mis·bē·liēve', *v.i.*; misbelieved, *pt.*, *pp.*; misbelieving, *ppr.* to believe erroneously; to hold wrong, false, or unorthodox beliefs or opinions, especially in religion.

mis·bē·liēve', *v.t.* to disbelieve. [Rare.]

mis·bē·liēv'ẽr, *n.* one who believes wrongly; one who is considered to hold a wrong, false, or unorthodox belief, especially in religion.

mis·bē·liēv'ing, *a.* believing erroneously; irreligious.

mis·brand', *v.t.* to brand or label improperly or falsely.

mis·çal'çū·lāte, *v.t.* and *v.i.*; miscalculated, *pt.*, *pp.*; miscalculating, *ppr.* to calculate incorrectly; to miscount or misjudge.

mis·çal·çū·lā'tion, *n.* incorrect calculation; error in figuring or judging.

mis·çall', *v.t.*; miscalled, *pt.*, *pp.*; miscalling, *ppr.* 1. to call by a wrong name; to name improperly.

2. to call by an evil name; to revile. [Obs. or Brit. Dial.]

mis·car'riaġe (-rij), *n.* 1. failure to reach a proper end; mismanagement.

2. failure of mail, freight, etc. to reach its destination.

3. the premature birth of a fetus, so that it does not live; abortion.

4. bad conduct; evil or improper behavior. [Obs.]

mis·car'riaġe·ȧ·ble, *a.* capable of miscarriage; liable to failure. [Rare.]

mis·çar'ry, *v.i.*; miscarried, *pt.*, *pp.*; miscarrying, *ppr.* 1. (a) to go wrong; to fail: said of a plan, project, etc.; (b) to go astray; to fail to arrive: said of mail, freight, etc.

2. (a) to give birth prematurely to a fetus, so that it does not live; (b) [Obs.] to be born prematurely.

mis·çar'ry·ing, *a.* failing of the intended effect; bringing forth prematurely.

mis·çȧst', *v.t.*; miscast, *pt.*, *pp.*; miscasting, *ppr.* 1. to cast (an actor) for a role not suited to him.

2. to cast (a play) with actors unsuited to their roles.

mis''cē·ġē·nā'tion, *n.* [L. *miscere*, to mix, and *genus*, race.] marriage or interbreeding between members of different races, especially, in the United States, between whites and Negroes.

mis''cel·lā·nãr'i·ăn, *a.* belonging to miscellanies; of miscellanies. [Rare.]

mis''cel·lā·nãr'i·ăn, *n.* a writer of miscellanies. [Rare.]

mis'cel·lāne, *a.* miscellaneous. [Obs.]

mis·cel·lā'nē·ȧ, *n.pl.* [*often construed as sing.*] a collection, as of miscellaneous matters; specifically, a collection of various literary works; a miscellany.

mis·cel·lā'nē·ous, *a.* [L. *miscellaneus*, mixed, miscellaneous, from *miscellus*, mixed, from *miscere*, to mix.]

1. mixed; consisting of several kinds; various; as, a box of *miscellaneous* candies.

2. having various qualities, abilities, etc.; many-sided.

mis·cel·lā'nē·ous·ly, *adv.* with variety or mixture.

mis·cel·lā'nē·ous·ness, *n.* the state of being mixed; composition of various kinds.

mis'cel·lā·nist, *n.* one who writes miscellanies.

mis'cel·lā·ny, *n.*; *pl.* **mis'cel·lā·nieṣ,** [L. *miscellanea*, neut. pl. of *miscellaneus*, mixed.]

1. a collection of various kinds, especially of literary works.

2. [*often pl.*] a book containing a collection of compositions on various subjects; a collection of various kinds of compositions.

mis'cel·lā·ny, *a.* miscellaneous. [Obs.]

mis·chȧnce', *n.* [OFr. *meschance, mescheance*, mischance.] bad luck; ill fortune; misfortune; mishap.

mis·chȧnce'fụl, *a.* luckless; unfortunate.

mis·çhar'aç·tẽr·ize, *v.t.* to characterize falsely or erroneously; to give a wrong character to.

mis'chief (-chif), *n.* [OFr. *meschief, meschef*, harm, mischief; *mes-* (L. *minus*, less), and *chief* (L. *caput*, head).]

1. harm; hurt; injury; damage; evil, whether intended or not, especially that done by a person.

2. a cause or source of harm, damage, or annoyance; specifically, (a) action or conduct that causes damage or trouble; (b) a person causing damage or annoyance.

3. a tendency or disposition to annoy or vex with playful tricks.

4. (a) a troublesome or annoying act; a

prank; a playful, vexing trick; (b) playful, harmless spirits; gay teasing.

Syn.—damage, harm, hurt, injury, detriment.

mis′chief, *v.t.* to hurt; to harm; to injure. [Archaic.]

mis′chief·fųl, *a.* mischievous. [Obs.]

mis′chief-māk″ēr, *n.* one who makes mischief; one who excites or instigates quarrels or hard feelings by gossiping or tale-bearing.

mis′chief-māk″ing, *n.* the act of instigating trouble.

mis′chief-māk″ing, *a.* causing harm; exciting enmity or quarrels.

mis′chiē·vous, *a.* 1. causing mischief; specifically, (a) injurious; harmful; (b) prankish; teasing; full of tricks.

2. inclined to annoy or vex with playful tricks; naughty: said especially of a child.

mis′chiē·vous·ly, *adv.* in a mischievous manner.

mis′chiē·vous·ness, *n.* the state or quality of being mischievous; disposition to do harm, or to vex or annoy.

Misch′nȧ, *n.* same as *Mishnah.*

Misch′niç, *a.* same as *Mishnic.*

mis·ci·bil′i·ty, *n.* the quality or state of being mixed.

mis′ci·ble, *a.* [Fr. *miscible*, from L. *miscere*, to mix.] that can be mixed or easily mixed; as, oil and water are not *miscible.*

mis·cī·tā′tion, *n.* a wrong citation; erroneous quotation.

mis·çŏl′ŏr, *v.t.* to color wrongly; hence, figuratively, to give a wrong impression of; as, to *miscolor* the facts in the case.

mis·çŏm′fŏrt, *n.* discomfort. [Obs.]

mis·çŏn·cēit′, *n.* misconception. [Archaic.]

mis·çŏn·cēive′, *v.t.* and *v.i.* to receive a false notion or opinion; to misjudge; to have an erroneous understanding of; as, to *misconceive* the meaning of a statement.

mis·çŏn·cēiv′ēr, *n.* one who misconceives.

mis·çŏn·cep′tion, *n.* erroneous conception; false opinion; wrong notion; misunderstanding.

mis·çŏn·çlū′şion, *n.* a false or wrong conclusion or inference.

mis·çon′duçt, *n.* 1. bad or dishonest management; specifically, malfeasance.

2. improper behavior; specifically, adultery or fornication.

mis·çŏn·duçt′, *v.t.* 1. to manage badly or dishonestly.

2. to conduct (oneself) improperly.

mis·çon′fi·dent, *a.* having a wrong confidence. [Rare.]

mis·çŏn·strū′ȧ·ble, *a.* that can be misconstrued, as a remark.

mis·çŏn·struçt′, *v.t.* 1. to construct wrongly.

2. to misconstrue, as a sentence or statement.

mis·çŏn·struç′tion, *n.* a misconstruing; incorrect interpretation; misunderstanding.

mis·çŏn·strūe′, *v.t.*; misconstrued, *pt., pp.*; misconstruing, *ppr.* to interpret erroneously; to construe wrongly; to misunderstand.

A virtuous emperor was much affected to find his actions *misconstrued.* —Addison.

mis·çon′strū·ēr, *n.* one who makes a wrong interpretation.

mis·çŏn·tent′, *a.* discontented. [Obs.]

mis·çŏn·tent′ed, *a.* discontented. [Obs.]

mis·çŏn·tent′ment, *n.* discontent. [Obs.]

mis·çŏn·tin′ū·ănce, *n.* 1. in law, an illegal continuance.

2. discontinuance. [Obs.]

mis·çount′, *v.t.* and *v.i.* to count incorrectly; to mistake in counting.

mis·çount′, *n.* an incorrect count, as of votes in an election.

mis′çrē·ănce, *n.* unbelief; false faith; adherence to a false religion. [Archaic.]

mis′çrē·ăn·cy, *n.* 1. the condition of a miscreant; wickedness. [Archaic.]

2. miscreance. [Archaic.]

mis′çrē·ănt, *a.* [OFr. *mescreant*, unbelieving; *mes-*, and *creant*, from L. *credere*, to believe.]

1. villainous; evil.

2. unbelieving; heretical; infidel. [Archaic.]

mis′çrē·ănt, *n.* 1. an evil person; a criminal; a villain.

2. an unbeliever; a heretic; an infidel. [Archaic.]

mis·çrē·āte′, *v.t.* and *v.i.* to create amiss or unnaturally.

mis·çrē·āte′, *a.* miscreated; unnaturally formed. [Archaic.]

mis·çrē·āt′ed, *a.* formed unnaturally or badly; deformed.

mis·çrē·ā′tive, *a.* tending to wrong creation. [Rare.]

mis·çrē′dent, *n.* one who believes in a false religion; a miscreant. [Obs.]

mis·çrop′, *n.* failure of a crop; a poor harvest.

mis·çūe′, *n.* 1. in billiards, pool, etc., a false stroke; the act of the cue slipping from the ball while the player is endeavoring to make a shot.

2. a mistake; an error. [Colloq.]

mis·çūe′, *v.i.* 1. to make a miscue.

2. in the theater, to miss one's cue or to answer the wrong cue.

mis·dāte′, *v.t.* to date incorrectly.

mis·dāte′, *n.* a wrong date.

mis·dēal′, *v.t.* and *v.i.*; misdealt (-delt′), *pt., pp.*; misdealing, *ppr.* to make a wrong deal in card playing; to distribute wrongly.

mis·dēal′, *n.* in card playing, an incorrect deal.

mis·deed′, *n.* an evil deed; a wicked action; a crime, sin, etc.

mis·deem′, *v.t.* to judge erroneously; to misjudge; to mistake in judging. [Obs.]

mis·dē·mēan′, *v.t.* and *v.i.* to conduct (oneself) badly; to misbehave. [Rare.]

mis·dē·mēan′ănt, *n.* 1. a person who has misbehaved.

2. in law, one guilty or convicted of a misdemeanor.

mis·dē·mēan′ŏr, mis·dē·mēan′ŏur, *n.* 1. bad behavior; evil conduct; fault; mismanagement. [Rare.]

2. in law, any minor offense, as the breaking of a municipal ordinance, for which statute provides a lesser punishment than for a felony: the penalty is usually a fine or imprisonment for a short time in a local jail, workhouse, etc.

mis·dempt′, *v.* obsolete past participle of *misdeem.*

mis·dē·pärt′, *v.t.* to distribute or divide wrongly. [Obs.]

mis·dē·rīve′, *v.t.* 1. to err in deriving; to derive improperly.

2. to divert wrongly; to misdirect. [Obs.]

mis·dīght′ (-dīt′), *a.* arrayed unsuitably. [Obs.]

mis·di·reçt′, *v.t.* to give a wrong or bad direction to; specifically, (a) to aim (a blow, etc.) badly; (b) to address (a letter) incorrectly; (c) to give incorrect instructions to.

mis·di·reç′tion, *n.* 1. the act of directing wrongly; wrong guidance or superscription.

2. in law, an error committed by a judge in charging the jury on matters of law.

mis·dö′, *v.t.*; misdid, *pt.*; misdone, *pp.*; misdoing, *ppr.* to do wrong to; to do amiss; to bungle.

mis·dö′, *v.i.* to do evil. [Obs.]

mis·dö′ēr, *n.* one who does wrong; one who commits a fault or crime.

mis·dö′ing, *n.* a wrong done; a fault or crime; an offense.

mis·doubt′ (-dout′), *v.t.* 1. to suspect of deceit or danger; to lack faith. [Archaic.]

2. to fear. [Archaic.]

mis·doubt′, *v.i.* to have doubts. [Archaic.]

mis·doubt′, *n.* suspicion of crime or danger; doubt. [Archaic.]

mis·doubt′fųl, *a.* suspicious. [Obs.]

mis·dread′ (-dred′), *n.* dread of evil. [Obs.]

miṣe, *n.* [OFr. *mise*, a putting, laying out, judgment, tax.]

1. in old English law, (a) an issue to be tried; a traverse; (b) expense; cost; tribute; tax; (c) decision by arbitration.

2. in law, the issue in a writ of right.

mis·ēaṣe′, *n.* 1. discomfort; lack of ease; distress; misery. [Archaic.]

2. poverty. [Archaic.]

mis·ēaṣed′, *a.* troubled; burdened with misery. [Obs.]

mis·ēaṣ′y, *a.* not easy or comfortable; painful. [Obs.]

mis·ē·di′tion, *n.* an inaccurate or spurious edition. [Obs.]

mis·em·ploy′, *v.t.* to employ to no purpose or to a bad purpose; to misuse; as, to *misemploy* time.

mis·em·ploy′ment, *n.* a misemploying or being misemployed.

miṣe en scène (on̄ sen′), [Fr.] 1. the staging of a play, including the setting, arrangement of the actors, etc.

2. general surroundings.

mis·en·trēat′, *v.t.* to mistreat. [Obs.]

mī′ṣēr, *n.* [L. *miser*, wretched, unfortunate, worthless.]

1. a miserable person; a wretch. [Obs.]

2. an extremely covetous person; one who for the sake of wealth makes himself miserable by the fear of poverty or diminution.

miṣ′ēr·ȧ·ble, *a.* [L. *miserabilis*, to be pitied, pitiable, from *miserari*, to pity.]

1. in a condition of misery; wretched; very unhappy.

2. causing misery, discomfort, or suffering; as, *miserable* weather.

3. bad, poor, unpleasant, inadequate, etc.: a generalized term of displeasure or disapproval.

4. pitiable.

Syn.—abject, forlorn, pitiable, wretched, worthless, despicable, disconsolate.

miṣ′ēr·ȧ·ble, *n.* a miserable person. [Obs.]

miṣ′ēr·ȧ·ble·ness, *n.* state of being miserable.

miṣ′ēr·ȧ·bly, *adv.* 1. in a miserable manner.

2. very: a general intensive. [Colloq.]

mis·ēr·ā′tion, *n.* commiseration; compassion. [Obs.]

Miṣ·e·rē′rē, *n.* [L., have mercy.]

1. the 51st Psalm of the Bible (50th in the Douay Version), beginning with *Miserere mei, Domine,* "Have mercy upon me, O God."

2. a musical setting for this; as, the *Miserere* of Bach.

3. [m–] a projecting bracket on the underside of a hinged seat in a stall of a church; also, the seat and bracket together: also called *misericord.*

miṣ′ēr·i·çord, miṣ′ēr·i·çorde, *n.* [L. *misericordia*, mercy, compassion, from *misericors*, tenderhearted.]

1. formerly, a relaxation of the strict observance of a rule or rules in a monastery.

2. a dining room in a monastery set aside for those who had received such relaxation from fasting.

3. a narrow ledge on the underside of a hinged seat in the choir of a monastic chapel: when turned up, the seat permitted one to relax while standing.

4. a slender dagger used in the Middle Ages for giving the death stroke (*coup de grâce*) to a mortally wounded knight.

mī′ṣēr·li·ness, *n.* the quality or state of being miserly.

mī′ṣēr·ly, *a.* like or characteristic of a miser; greedy and stingy.

Syn.—avaricious, niggardly, covetous, parsimonious, mean.

miṣ′ēr·y, *n.*; *pl.* **miṣ′ēr·ieṣ,** [L. *miseria*, affliction, wretchedness, from *miser*, wretched.]

1. great unhappiness; extreme pain of body or mind; wretchedness.

2. calamity; misfortune; the cause of such suffering; pain, ache, poverty, squalor, etc.

And mourn the *miseries* of human life. —Dryden.

3. a pain (in some part of the body). [Dial.]

4. covetousness. [Obs.]

mis·es·teem′, *n.* lack of esteem; disrespect; irreverence.

mis·es′ti·māte, *v.t.* to estimate incorrectly.

mis·es′ti·mȧte, *n.* an incorrect estimate.

mis·fall′, *v.t.* to befall. [Obs.]

mis·fāre′, *n.* misfortune. [Obs.]

mis·fāre′, *v.i.* to fare badly. [Obs.]

mis·fēa′ṣance, *n.* [OFr. *mesfaisance*, wrong, trespass; *mes-*, wrong, and *faisance*, ppr. of *faire*, to do.] in law, wrongdoing; specifically, the doing of a lawful act in an unlawful manner, so that there is an infringement on the rights of another or others: distinguished from *malfeasance, nonfeasance.*

mis·fēa′ṣŏr, *n.* in law, a person guilty of misfeasance.

mis·fīre′, *v.i.* 1. to fail to ignite properly or at the right time: said of an internal-combustion engine.

2. to fail to go off, or be discharged: said of a firearm.

mis·fīre′, *n.* a misfiring.

mis·fit′, *v.t.* and *v.i.* to fail to fit properly; be too large, too small, etc. for (someone or something).

mis·fit′, *n.* 1. the act or condition of misfitting.

2. anything that misfits.

3. (mis′fit), a person not suited to his position, status, etc.; a maladjusted person.

mis′fit, *a.* that does not fit.

mis·fŏrm′, *v.t.* to form incorrectly; to put in bad or improper shape.

mis·fŏr′tū·nāte, *a.* producing misfortune. [Dial.]

mis·fŏr′tūne, *n.* 1. bad luck; ill fortune; trouble; adversity.

2. an instance of this; unlucky accident; mishap; mischance.

Syn.—adversity, harm, misadventure, catastrophe, calamity.

mis·fŏr′tūne, *v.i.* to miscarry; to fail. [Obs.]

mis·fŏr′tūned, *a.* unfortunate. [Obs.]

mis·give′, *v.t.*; misgave, *pt.*; misgiven, *pp.*; misgiving, *ppr.* to create doubt, apprehension, or hesitation in: said usually of the mind, heart, conscience, etc.; as, his conscience *misgave* him.
mis·give′, *v.i.* to feel fear, doubt, suspicion, etc.
mis·giv′ing, *n.* a premonition of danger or ill fortune; a feeling of distrust, fear, doubt, apprehension, etc.
mis·gō′, *v.i.* to stray from the way; to miscarry. [Dial.]
mis·gŏv′ẽrn, *v.t.* to govern, administer, or manage badly.
mis·gŏv′ẽrn·ănce, *n.* bad government; disorder; irregularity. [Obs.]
mis·gŏv′ẽrned, *a.* rude; unrestrained.
mis·gŏv′ẽrn·ment, *n.* 1. a misgoverning; bad administration of public or private affairs.
2. irregularity; disorder; misbehavior.
mis·graff′, *v.t.* to misgraft. [Obs.]
mis·graft′, *v.t.* to graft amiss, as on the wrong stock.
mis·ground′, *v.t.* to ground, or found, erroneously.
mis·grōwth′, *n.* an abnormal growth.
mis·guīd′ănce (-gīd′), *n.* a misguiding.
mis·guīde′, *v.t.*; misguided, *pt.*, *pp.*; misguiding, *ppr.* to lead in the wrong direction; to exert an evil influence on; to mislead.
mis·guīde′, *n.* misguidance. [Obs.]
mis·guīd′ed, *a.* led into or characterized by error or misconduct; misled.
mis·guīd′ing, *a.* misleading; guiding wrongly.
mis·gȳe′, *v.t.* to misguide. [Obs.]
mis·han′dle, *v.t.* to handle badly or roughly; to abuse, maltreat, or mismanage.
mis′hap, *n.* [ME.; prob. after OFr. *mescheance*, mischance.]
1. bad luck; adversity; misfortune.
2. an instance of this; unlucky accident.
mis·hap′py, *a.* unhappy. [Obs.]
mis·hēar′, *v.t.* to hear incorrectly or poorly.
mish′mash, *n.* [redupl. of *mash*.] a mixture; a hodgepodge.
Mish′nah, Mish′nȧ, *n.*; *pl.* **Mish·nä·yōth′**, [Heb. *mishnāh*, repetition, explanation, from *shānāh*, to change, repeat.]
1. the first part of the Talmud, containing traditional oral interpretations of scriptural ordinances (*halakoth*), compiled by the rabbis about 200 A.D.
2. any of these interpretations.
3. the teachings of a rabbi.
Mish′niç, Mish·nā′iç, *a.* pertaining or relating to the Mishnah.
Mish′niç·ăl, *a.* Mishnic.
mis·im·prōve′, *v.t.* to improve to a bad purpose; to abuse. [Rare.]
mis·im·prōve′ment, *n.* misuse; misapplication. [Obs.]
mis·in·fọrm′, *v.t.* to supply with false or misleading information.
mis·in·fọrm′, *v.i.* to make false or misleading statements.
mis·in·fọrm′ănt, *n.* a person who misinforms.
mis·in·fọr·mā′tion, *n.* wrong information; false account or intelligence.
mis·in·tel′li·ġence, *n.* 1. wrong information; misinformation.
2. misunderstanding. [Obs.]
mis·in·tẽr′pret, *v.t.* to interpret erroneously; to understand or to explain incorrectly.
mis·in·tẽr·prē·tā′tion, *n.* 1. the act of interpreting erroneously.
2. an incorrect or false interpretation.
mis·in·tẽr′pret·ẽr, *n.* one who interprets erroneously.
mis·join′dẽr, *n.* in law, the introduction into a court action of parties or causes not properly belonging to that action.
mis·judge′ (-juj′), *v.t.* to judge erroneously or unjustly; to misconstrue.
mis·judġe′, *v.i.* to err in judgment; to form false opinions or notions.
mis·judġ′ment, mis·judġe′ment, *n.* a wrong or unjust judgment.
mis·kăl′, mit·căl′, *n.* [Ar. *mithqal*, a weight.] an Arabic unit of weight.
mis′ken, *v.t.* to ignore. [Scot.]
mis·ken′ning, *n.* in old law, an error in pleading. [Obs.]
mis·knōw′ (-nō′), *v.t.* to have a misconception of; to misunderstand.
mis·lāy′, *v.t.*; mislaid, *pt.*, *pp.*; mislaying, *ppr.*
1. to put in a wrong place.
2. to put in a place not recollected; to lose.
mis·lāy′ẽr, *n.* one who lays in a wrong place; one who loses by mislaying.
mis·lēad′, *v.t.*; misled, *pt.*, *pp.*; misleading, *ppr.* 1. to lead into a wrong way or path; to lead astray.
2. to guide into error (of judgment); to deceive.
3. to lead into wrongdoing.
mis·lēad′ẽr, *n.* one who misleads.
mis·lēad′ing, *a.* leading or tending to lead into error; causing to err; deceiving.
mis·lēad′ing·ly, *adv.* in such manner as to mislead.
mis′len (*or* mis′), *n.* same as *maslin*.
miṣ′le·tōe (-l-), *n.* same as *mistletoe*.
mis·līe′, *v.i.* to lie in a wrong or uncomfortable position. [Obs.]
mis·līght′, *v.t.* to mislead with its light. [Obs.]
mis·līke′, *v.t.*; misliked (-līkt′), *pt.*, *pp.*; misliking, *ppr.* 1. to displease.
2. to be displeased at; to dislike.
mis·līke′, *n.* dislike; disapprobation; aversion.
mis·līk′ẽr, *n.* one who mislikes.
mis·līk′ing, *n.* disapproval; aversion.
mis·live′, *v.i.* to live amiss. [Obs.]
mis·lodġe′ (-loj′), *v.t.* to lodge wrongly. [Obs.]
mis·man′ăġe, *v.t.* and *v.i.* to manage badly; to administer improperly; as, to *mismanage* public affairs.
mis·man′ăġe·ment, *n.* bad or improper management.
mis·man′ăġ·ẽr, *n.* one who manages badly.
mis·match′, *v.t.* to match badly or unsuitably, especially in marriage.
mis·match′, *n.* a bad match.
mis·māte′, *v.t.* and *v.i.* to mate unsuitably.
mis·mē′tẽr, mis·mē′tre, *v.t.* to give the wrong meter to, as in the composition or recitation of verse.
mis·nāme′, *v.t.* to call by the wrong name; to give an inappropriate name to.
mis·nō′mẽr, *n.* [OFr. *mesnomer*, *mesnommer*, misname; *mes-* and *nomer*, *nommer*, from L. *nominare*, to name.]
1. (a) the act of applying a wrong name or epithet to some person or thing; (b) such a name or epithet.
2. an error in naming a person or place in a legal document.
mis·nō′mẽr, *v.t.* to designate wrongly; to misname.
mis·num′bẽr, *v.t.* to number incorrectly; to attach a wrong number to.
mis′ō-, [Gr. *miso-*, from *misein*, to hate.] a combining form meaning *hated* or *hating*, as in *misogyny*; also, before a vowel, *mis-*.
mi·sog′ȧ·mist, *n.* [Gr. *misein*, to hate, and *gamos*, marriage.] one who hates marriage.
mi·sog′ȧ·my, *n.* hatred of marriage.
mi·sog′y·nist, *n.* [Gr. *misogynēs*, hating woman, a woman hater; *misein*, to hate, and *gynē*, a woman.] a person, especially a man, who hates women.
mi·sog′y·nous, *a.* hating women.
mi·sog′y·ny, *n.* [Gr. *misogynia*.] hatred of women.
mi·sol′ō·ġist, *n.* a person characterized by misology.
mi·sol′ō·ġy, *n.* [Gr. *misein*, to hate, and *-logia*, from *legein*, to speak.] aversion to discussion; hatred of argument, discussion, or reasoning.
mis·ō·nē′iṣm, *n.* [Gr. *miso-*, hating, and *neos*, new.] hatred of innovation or change.
mis′ō·thē·iṣm, *n.* [Gr. *misein*, to hate, and *theos*, God.] hatred of God or gods. [Rare.]
mis·pẽr·suāde′ (-swād′), *v.t.* to persuade amiss; to lead to a wrong notion.
mis·pẽr·suā′ṣion, *n.* a false persuasion; wrong notion or opinion.
mis·pick′el, *n.* same as *arsenopyrite*.
mis·plāce′, *v.t.*; misplaced (-plāst′), *pt.*, *pp.*; misplacing, *ppr.* 1. to put in a wrong place.
2. to bestow (one's trust, affection, etc.) on an unsuitable or undeserving object.
3. to mislay (sense 2). [Colloq.]
mis·plāce′ment, *n.* the act of misplacing; state of being misplaced.
mis·plāy′, *v.t.* and *v.i.* to play wrongly or badly, as in games or sports.
mis·plāy′, *n.* a wrong or bad play.
mis·plēad′, *v.i.* to err in pleading.
mis·plēad′ing, *n.* a mistake in pleading.
mis·print′, *v.t.* to print incorrectly.
mis·print′, *n.* a mistake in printing; a deviation from the copy.
mis·prīṣe′, *v.t.* to misprize.
mis·pri′ṣion, *n.* [OFr. *mespresion*, from pp. *mesprendre*, to take wrongly; L. *minus*, less, and *prehendere*, to take.]
1. misconduct or neglect of duty, especially by a public official.
2. a mistake. [Archaic.]
misprision of felony (or *treason*); in common law, the offense of concealing knowledge of a felony (or treason) by one who has not participated or assisted in it.
mis·prīze′, *v.t.*; misprized, *pt.*, *pp.*; misprizing, *ppr.* [OFr. *mesprisier*, from *mes-* and LL. *pretiare*, to value.] to slight or undervalue.
mis·prō·fess′, *v.t.* and *v.i.* to make a false profession (of); to make pretensions to (skill) which is not possessed.
mis·prō·nounce′, *v.t.* and *v.i.*; mispronounced (-nounst′), *pt.*, *pp.*; mispronouncing, *ppr.* to pronounce incorrectly; to give (a word) a pronunciation different from any of the accepted standard pronunciations.
mis·prō·nun·ci·ā′tion, *n.* 1. a mispronouncing or being mispronounced.
2. a mispronounced word.
mis·prō·pōr′tion, *v.t.*; misproportioned, *pt.*, *pp.*; misproportioning, *ppr.* to err in proportioning (one thing to another); to join without due proportion.
mis·quō·tā′tion, *n.* an erroneous quotation; also, the act of quoting wrongly.
mis·quōte′, *v.t.* and *v.i.*; misquoted, *pt.*, *pp.*; misquoting *ppr.* to quote erroneously; to cite incorrectly.
mis·rāte′, *v.t.* to rate erroneously; to estimate falsely.
mis·rēad′, *v.t.*; misread (-red′), *pt.*, *pp.*; misreading (-rēd′), *ppr.* to read erroneously, or so as to misunderstand.
mis·rē·mem′bẽr, *v.t.* and *v.i.* 1. to make an error in remembering.
2. to forget. [Dial.]
mis″rep·rē·ṣent′, *v.t.* to represent falsely or incorrectly; to give a false or erroneous representation of, either maliciously, ignorantly, or carelessly.
mis·rep·rē·ṣent′, *v.i.* to state a thing falsely.
mis·rep″rē·ṣen·tā′tion, *n.* 1. the act of giving a false or erroneous representation.
2. a false or incorrect account given, either from mistake, carelessness, or malice.
mis·rep·rē·ṣent′ȧ·tive, *a.* giving a wrong impression.
mis·rep·rē·ṣent′ẽr, *n.* one who gives a false or erroneous account.
mis·rule′, *n.* 1. disorder; confusion; tumult.
2. misgovernment.
mis·rule′, *v.t.* and *v.i.* to govern unwisely or badly; to misgovern.
mis·rul′y, *a.* unruly; ungovernable, turbulent. [Obs.]
miss, *n.*; *pl.* **miss′eṣ**, [contr. of *mistress*.]
1. (a) [M–] a title used in speaking to or of an unmarried woman or girl, placed before the name; as, *Miss* Smith, the *Misses* Smith; (b) a title used in speaking to an unmarried woman or girl, used without the name.
2. a young unmarried woman or girl: now usually humorous or in trade jargon; as, coats in *misses'* sizes.
miss, *v.t.*; missed (mist), *pt.*, *pp.*; missing, *ppr.* [AS. *missan*, to miss, fail to hit, escape the notice of.]
1. to fail to hit or land on (something aimed at).
2. to fail to meet, reach, attain, catch, accomplish, see, hear, perceive, etc.
3. to overlook; to let (an opportunity, etc.) go by.
4. to escape; to avoid; as, he just *missed* being struck.
5. to fail or forget to do, keep, have, be present at, etc.; as, he *missed* class yesterday.
6. to notice the absence or loss of; as, he suddenly *missed* his watch.
7. to feel or regret the absence or loss of; to want; as, he *misses* his friends.
miss, *v.i.* 1. to fail to hit something aimed at; to go wide of the mark.
2. to fail to be successful.
3. to fail to obtain, receive, etc. (with *of* or *in*). [Archaic.]
miss, *n.* a failure to hit, meet, obtain, see, etc.
a miss is as good as a mile; missing by a narrow margin is as conclusive as missing by a wide one.
Mis′sȧ, *n.*; *pl.* **Mis′sae**, [LL., a mass.] in the Roman Catholic Church, the service of the Mass.
mis′săl, *n.* [LL. *missalis*, pertaining to the Mass, from *missa*, Mass.]
1. in the Roman Catholic Church, a book containing all the prayers necessary for celebrating Mass throughout the year.
2. any book of prayers or devotions.
mis′săl, *a.* pertaining to the Mass or the Mass book.
mis·sāy′, *v.t.* and *v.i.* to say wrongly; also, to slander or vilify. [Archaic.]
mis·seem′, *v.i.* to misbecome. [Rare.]
miṣ′ṣel, *n.* 1. mistletoe. [Obs.]
2. same as *mistlethrush*.
miṣ′ṣel·dine, *n.* the mistletoe. [Obs.]

mis·sem'blănce, *n.* false resemblance.
mis·shāpe', *v.t.* to shape badly; to deform.
mis·shāp'en, *a.* badly shaped; deformed.
mis·shāp'en·ly, *adv.* in a misshapen manner.
mis·shāp'en·ness, *n.* the state of being badly shaped.
mis'sile (-sil), *a.* [L. *missilis*, from *missus*, pp. of *mittere*, to send, throw.]
1. that can be thrown, shot, or hurled, as from a gun.
2. fitted for throwing or for hurling. [Rare.]
mis'sile, *n.* a weapon or other object, as a spear, bullet, rocket, etc., designed to be thrown, fired, or launched toward a target; often, specifically, a guided missile.
mis·sil·eer', *n.* same as *missileman*.
mis'sile·măn, *n.*; *pl.* **mis'sile·men,** one who builds or launches guided missiles.
mis'sile·ry, mis'sil·ry, *n.* 1. the science of building and launching guided missiles.
2. guided missiles collectively.
miss'ing, *a.* absent; lost; lacking; specifically, absent after combat, but not definitely known to be dead or taken prisoner.
miss'ing liñk, something necessary for filling in or completing a series; specifically, a hypothetical form of animal believed to have existed in the evolutionary process intermediate between man and the anthropoid apes.
mis'sion (mish'un), *n.* [L. *missio* (*-onis*), a sending, sending away, from *missus*, pp. of *mittere*, to send.]
1. a sending out or being sent out with authority to perform a special duty; specifically, (a) the sending out of persons by a religious organization to preach, teach, or proselyte; (b) the sending out of persons to a foreign government to conduct negotiations.
2. (a) a group of persons sent by a church to spread its religion, especially in a foreign land; (b) its organization, headquarters, or place of residence.
3. a group of persons sent to a foreign government to conduct negotiations; diplomatic delegation; embassy.
4. the special duty or function on which someone is sent as a messenger or representative; errand.
5. the special task or purpose for which a person is apparently destined in life; calling; as, he considered it his *mission* to educate the ignorant.
6. any charitable or educational organization for doing welfare work for the needy of a city or district.
7. a series of special religious exercises, sermons, etc. for proselyting.
8. a district without a church of its own, served by the pastor or priest of a near-by parish.
9. [*pl.*] organized missionary work, especially for spreading Christianity.
10. in military usage, a specific combat operation assigned to an individual or unit; especially, a single combat flight by an airplane or group of airplanes.
mis'sion, *a.* of a mission or missions; specifically, of or characteristic of the early Spanish missions in the southwestern United States; specifically, designating a heavy, dark furniture with simple, square lines.
mis'sion, *v.t.* 1. to send on a mission.
2. to establish a religious mission in (a district) or among (a people).
mis'sion·ăr·y, *n.*; *pl.* **mis'sion·ăr·ies,** a person sent on a mission; specifically, a person sent out by his church to preach, teach, and proselyte in a foreign country, especially in one considered heathen.
mis'sion·ăr·y, *a.* [LL. *missionarius*, pertaining to a mission, from L. *missio* (*-onis*), a mission.] pertaining to or characteristic of missions or missionaries.
mis'sion·ẽr, *n.* a missionary; one sent on a mission; sometimes, one who conducts missionary services.
mis'sis, mis'sus, *n.* [altered from *mistress*.] a wife: used with a personal pronoun or *the*; also, the mistress of a household (with *the*). [Colloq. or Dial.]
miss'ish, *a.* characteristic of a miss; sentimental; prim; prudish.
Mis·sis·sip'pi·ăn, *a.* 1. of the Mississippi River.
2. of the State of Mississippi.
3. designating or of the first period of the Paleozoic Era in North America, characterized by the formation of coal deposits and the first appearance of reptiles.
Mis·sis·sip'pi·ăn, *n.* a native or inhabitant of Mississippi.
the Mississippian; the Mississippian Period or its rocks.
mis'sive, *a.* [LL. *missivus*, from L. *missus*, pp. of *mittere*, to send.] sent or intended to be sent. [Archaic.]
letters missive; letters of authority from a sovereign addressed to a certain person or persons.
mis'sive, *n.* 1. a letter.
2. a messenger; one sent. [Obs.]
mis·sound', *v.t.* to sound in a wrong manner; to mispronounce; as, to *missound* a letter in a word.
Mis·sour'i·ăn (mi-zoor'i-ăn), *n.* a native or inhabitant of Missouri.
Mis·sour'i·ăn, *a.* of Missouri.
mis·spēak', *v.i.* to err or mistake in speaking. [Rare.]
mis·spēak', *v.t.* to utter in a wrong manner. [Rare.]
mis·spell', *v.t.* and *v.i.*; misspelled, *pt.*, *pp.*; misspelling, *ppr.* to spell incorrectly.
mis'spell, *n.* a misspelling.
mis·spell'ing, *n.* an incorrect spelling.
mis·spend', *v.t.*; misspent, *pt.*, *pp.*; misspending, *ppr.* to spend improperly or wastefully.
mis·spend'ẽr, *n.* one who misspends.
mis·spense', *n.* a spending improperly; a wasting. [Obs.]
mis·spent', *a.* ill-spent; wasted; as, a *misspent* life.
mis·stāte', *v.t.* to state in a wrong manner or falsely; as, to *misstate* a question in debate.
mis·stāte'ment, *n.* a wrong or false statement; misrepresentation.
mis·step', *n.* 1. a wrong or awkward step.
2. a mistake in conduct; faux pas.
mis·step', *v.i.* to make a misstep.
mis'sus, *n.* missis. [Colloq. or Dial.]
mis'sy, *n.*; *pl.* **mis'sies,** miss: diminutive form, used in speaking to or of a young girl. [Colloq.]
mis'sy, *a.* like a miss; girlish.
mis'sy, *n.* same as *misy*.
mist, *v.t.* and *v.i.*; misted, *pt.*, *pp.*; misting, *ppr.* to be, become, or make misty; to dim or obscure with or as with a mist.
mist, *n.* [ME.; AS., darkness, mist.]
1. a large mass of water vapor at or just above the earth's surface and like a fog, but less dense.
2. a thin film of moisture condensed on a surface in droplets.
3. a cloud of dust, smoke, gas, etc.
4. a cloudiness or film before the eyes, dimming or blurring the vision; as, she smiled in a *mist* of tears.
5. anything that dims or obscures the understanding, memory, etc.
mis·tāk'ā·ble, *a.* that can be, or is likely to be, mistaken or misunderstood.
mis·tāke', *v.t.*; mistook, *pt.*; mistaken *or obs.* mistook, *pp.*; mistaking, *ppr.*; [Ice. *mistaka*, to take wrongly; *mis-* and *taka*, to take.]
1. to perceive or understand erroneously; to interpret or estimate incorrectly; to misunderstand or misapprehend.
'Tis to *mistake* them costs the time and pain. —Pope.
2. to recognize or identify incorrectly; to take (one thing or person) for another; to invest with the wrong personality or individuality.
3. to take by mistake. [Obs.]
mis·tāke', *v.i.* to err in opinion or judgment; to be wrong unintentionally.
mis·tāke', *n.* 1. an error in opinion, understanding, perception, interpretation, or judgment; misconception.
Infallibility is an absolute security of the understanding from all possibility of *mistake*. —Tillotson.
2. something omitted or done through ignorance or misconception.
and no mistake; surely; with certainty; positively. [Colloq.]
Syn.—blunder, error, fallacy, omission.
mis·tāk'en, *a.* 1. wrong; having an incorrect understanding, perception, interpretation, etc.: said of persons.
2. incorrect; misunderstood; erroneous: said of ideas, etc.
mis·tak'en·ly, *adv.* by mistake.
mis·tāk'ẽr, *n.* one who mistakes or misunderstands.
mis·tāk'ing, *a.* that mistakes.
mis·tāk'ing·ly, *adv.* erroneously; falsely.
mis·tem'pẽr, *v.t.* to disorder. [Obs.]
mis'tẽr, *n.* [alteration of *master*.]
1. [M–] a title used in speaking to or of a man, placed before the name or title of office and usually written *Mr.*; as, *Mr.* Stein, *Mr.* Secretary.
2. in military usage, the official title of address for (a) a warrant officer in the army; (b) a cadet in the U. S. Military Academy; (c) a naval officer below the rank of commander.
3. sir; as, what time is it, *mister*? [Colloq.]
mis'tẽr, *v.t.* to address or name by the title of *mister*; as, he *misters* everybody.
mis'tẽr, *v.t.* and *v.i.* to need. [Obs.]
mis'tẽr, *n.* 1. trade, art, or occupation. [Obs.]
2. manner; kind; sort. [Archaic or Dial.]
3. need; necessity; anything necessary. [Obs.]
mis'tẽr·y, *n.* mystery (trade). [Obs.]
mis·tetch', *n.* [ME. and OFr., *teche*, quality.] a bad habit. [Brit. Dial.]
mis·tetch', *v.t.* to teach, or lead into, bad habits. [Brit. Dial.]
mist'flow''ẽr, *n.* any of a group of tall plants with composite flowers of blue or violet; especially, an American herb, *Eupatorium coelestinum*, having violet-colored flowers.
mist'ful, *a.* clouded with mist.
mist grāy, a color of very low density, slightly reddish in hue.
mis·thiñk', *v.i.* and *v.t.* to think wrongly; to think ill of.
mis·thought' (-that'), *n.* a wrong thought.
mis'tiç, *n.* same as *mistico*.
mis'ti·çō, *n.* [Sp. *mistico*.] a small vessel used for coasting in the Mediterranean.
mis·tīde', *v.i.* 1. to befall amiss. [Obs.]
2. to experience ill fortune. [Obs.]
mist'i·fȳ, *adv.* to change to mist.
mis'ti·gris, *n.* [Fr. *mistrigri*.] in the game of poker, an extra card, as a joker, which the holder may play as any card he wishes.
mist'i·head (-hed) *n.* the state of being misty. [Obs.]
mist'i·ly, *adv.* in a misty manner; darkly; obscurely.
mis·tīme', *v.t.* 1. to time wrongly; to do or say at an inappropriate time.
2. to judge incorrectly the time of.
mist'i·ness, *n.* the state or quality of being misty; obscurity.
mis'tion (-chun), *n.* mixture. [Obs.]
mis'tle (-l), *v.i.* to mizzle. [Dial.]
mis'tle·thrush, *n.* a European thrush, *Turdus viscivorus*, which feeds on mistletoe berries: also called *misselthrush*.
mis'tle·tōe (mis'l- *or* miz'l-), *n.* [AS. *misteltan*, from *mistel*, birdlime, and *tan*, a twig.]
1. any of various parasitic evergreen plants with small yellowish-green leaves, yellowish flowers, and waxy white berries, growing on the branches of certain trees.
2. a sprig of such a plant, hung as a Christmas decoration: men are by custom privileged to kiss women standing under it.

MISTLETOE (*Viscum album*)

mis'tō·musk, *n.* [Am. Ind.] the American badger, *Taxidea americana*.
mis·took', *v.* past tense and obsolete past participle of *mistake*.
mis'trăl, *n.* [Fr., from Pr. *mistral*, lit., master wind, from *mæstre*, master.] a cold and dry north wind that blows over the Mediterranean coast of France and near-by regions.
mis·trans·lāte', *v.t.* to translate incorrectly.
mis·trans·lā'tion, *n.* an incorrect translation.
mis·tread'ing (-tred'), *n.* a treading amiss; a wayward course. [Obs.]
mis·trēat', *v.t.* to treat wrongly or badly.
mis'tress, *n.* [OFr. *maistresse*; LL. *magistressa*, f. of L. *magister*, master.]
1. a woman who rules others or has control, authority, or power over something; specifically, (a) a woman who is head of a household or institution; (b) a woman owner of an animal or slave; (c) [Chiefly Brit.] a woman schoolteacher.
2. [*sometimes* M–] something regarded as feminine that has control, power, etc.; as, England was *Mistress* of the seas.
3. a woman who has sexual intercourse with and, often, is supported by a man for a more or less extended period of time without being married to him; paramour.
4. a sweetheart. [Archaic.]
5. [M–] formerly, a title used in speaking

to or of a woman, prefixed to the name: now replaced by *Mrs.* or *Miss.*

6. a woman who is particularly skilled in something; as, she is *mistress* of arithmetic.

mis′tress, *v.i.* to be courting. [Obs.]

mis′tress·ship, *n.* female rule or dominion.

mis·trī′ăl, *n.* in law, a trial which is made void through some defect in the proceedings, or because the jury cannot reach a verdict.

mis·trist′, *v.t.* to mistrust. [Obs.]

mis·trōw′, *v.i.* and *v.t.* to doubt, distrust, or mistrust. [Obs.]

mis·trust′, *n.* lack of confidence or trust; suspicion.

mis·trust′, *v.t.* and *v.i.* 1. to have no trust or confidence in someone or something; to suspect; to doubt; to regard with suspicion.

Fate her own book *mistrusted* at the sight.
—Cowley.

2. to have a dread or apprehension of; as, to *mistrust* that an issue will be unfavorable. [Obs.]

mis·trust′ẽr, *n.* one who mistrusts.

mis·trust′fụl, *a.* suspicious; doubting; lacking trust or confidence in.

mis·trust′fụl·ly, *adv.* with suspicion or doubt.

mis·trust′fụl·ness, *n.* suspicion; doubt.

mis·trust′ing·ly, *adv.* with distrust or suspicion.

mis·trust′less, *a.* unsuspecting; unsuspicious.

mis·tūne′, *v.t.* to tune wrongly or erroneously; to put out of tune.

mis·tū′rȧ, *n.* [L., a mixing.] in medicine, a mixture.

mist′y, *a.*; *comp.* mistier; *superl.* mistiest, [ME. *misti*; AS. *mistig.*]

1. of, or having the nature of, mist.
2. characterized by or covered with mist.
3. blurred or dimmed, as by mist; obscure; vague.

mis·un·dẽr·stand′, *v.t.*; misunderstood, *pt., pp.*; misunderstanding, *ppr.* to understand incorrectly; to miscomprehend or misinterpret.

mis·un·dẽr·stand′ẽr, *n.* one who understands incorrectly.

mis·un·dẽr·stand′ing, *n.* 1. misconception; mistake as to meaning or motive; error.

2. disagreement; difference; dissension.

mis·un·dẽr·stood′, *a.* 1. incorrectly understood.

2. not properly appreciated.

mi·sụ·rä′tō, *adv.* [It.] in music, with strict regard to the measure.

mis·ūs′ȧġe, *n.* 1. incorrect usage; misapplication, as of words.

2. abuse; bad or harsh treatment.

mis·ūṣe′, *v.t.* [OFr. *mesuser*; *mes-* and *user*, to use.]

1. to treat or use improperly or incorrectly; to use for a bad purpose.
2. to abuse; to treat badly or harshly.

Syn.—abuse, misapply, pervert, ill-treat.

mis·ūse′, *n.* 1. improper use; employment to a bad purpose; incorrect use; as, the *misuse* of mercies; the *misuse* of words.

2. abuse; ill treatment. [Obs. or Rare.]

mis·ūṣe′ment, *n.* the act of misusing. [Obs.]

mis·ūṣ′ẽr, *n.* 1. in law, an unlawful use of a right, liberty, benefit, etc., or a neglect of using it in a proper manner.

2. one who misuses.

mis·val′ūe, *v.t.* to value wrongly.

mis·ween′, *v.i.* to misjudge. [Obs.]

mis·wend′, *v.i.* to go wrong. [Obs.]

mis·wŏrd′, *v.t.* to word incorrectly.

mī′sy, *n.* [L. *misy*; Gr. *misy*, a mineral, perhaps copperas.] in mineralogy, a yellow impure hydrous sulfate of iron; yellow copperas. [Obs.]

mīte, *n.* [AS. *mite*, a mite.] any of a large number of tiny arachnids, many of which live as parasites upon animals or plants, or in prepared foods, etc.

mīte, *n.* [M.D. *mijte*, a small coin, a mite.]

1. (a) a very small sum of money or contribution; (b) a coin of very small value; especially, in England, half a farthing: see Mark xii. 41–44.
2. a very small creature or object.
3. the twentieth part of a grain.

Mi·tel′lȧ, *n.* [L. *mitella*, dim. of *mitra*, a turban.] a genus of herbs of the saxifrage family, having whitish or greenish flowers, found in North America.

mī′tẽr, mī′tre (-tẽr), *n.* [OFr. *mitre*; L. *mitra*; Gr. *mitra*, a belt, fillet, headband, turban.]

1. a headdress; specifically, (a) a tall, ornamented cap with peaks in front and back, worn by the Pope, bishops, and abbots as a mark of office; (b) the official headdress of the ancient Jewish high priest; (c) in ancient Greece, a headband worn by women.

2. the office or rank of a bishop; bishopric.

MITERS
1. miter of ancient Jewish high priest; 2. miter of English bishop; 3. miter of English archbishop

3. a covering over the top of a chimney that keeps the rain out but permits the smoke to leave.

mī′tẽr, mī′tre, *v.t.* to invest with the office of bishop by placing a miter on.

mī′tẽr, mī′tre, *n.* [perh. from *miter* (headdress).]

1. in carpentry, a kind of joint formed by fitting together two pieces, each of which has been beveled to a specified angle (usually 45°), so that they form a corner (usually a right angle): also *miter joint.*
2. either of the facing surfaces of such a joint.
3. a miter square.

mī′tẽr, *v.t.*; mitered, *pt., pp.*; mitering, *ppr.* [LL. *mitrare*, from L. *mitra*, a miter.] to unite in a miter joint; to prepare for a miter.

mī′tẽr box, a frame or box with guides for a saw, used to cut strips at equal angles for a miter joint.

mī′tẽr dōve′tāil, in carpentry, a dovetail for a mitered joint in which only one line of the joint is visible.

mī′tẽr gāuġe, a gauge used by carpenters to determine the angle of a miter.

mī′tẽr joint, a joint formed by the junction of two ends beveled at equal angles, usually at angles of 45°.

a, a, MITER JOINT

mī′tẽr shell, a univalve of the genus *Mitra*, which is miter-shaped.

mī′tẽr squāre, a tool with two blades set at a 45° angle or adjustable to any angle, used to mark out angles for miter joints.

mī′tẽr wheel (hwēl), either of two gear wheels of equal diameter, each beveled at an angle of 45° and meshing together with their axes at right angles.

MITER WHEELS

mī′tẽr·wŏrt, *n.* any of a group of plants of the saxifrage family, with small, white or greenish flowers and a seed pod shaped like a bishop's miter.

mith′ẽr, *n.* mother. [Scot. and Brit. Dial.]

Mith′gär″thr, *n.* Midgard.

Mith·rā′iç, *a.* of Mithras or Mithraism.

Mith·rā′i·ciṣm, *n.* Mithraism.

Mith′rā·iṣm, *n.* the ancient Persian religion based on worship of Mithras.

Mith′rā·ist, *n.* a believer in Mithraism.

Mith·rā·is′tiç, *a.* Mithraic.

Mith′ras, Mith′rȧ, *n.* [L., from Gr. *Mithras*; Old Per. *Mitra.*] the ancient Persian god of light and truth, opponent of darkness and evil.

mith′ri·dāte, *n.* [ML. *mithridatum*; LL. *mithridatium*, from *Mithridatius*, of Mithridates VI, king of Pontus, said to have become immune to poisons by taking them in gradually increased doses.] formerly, a substance supposed to be an antidote against all poisons.

mit′i·gȧ·ble, *a.* capable of being mitigated.

mit′i·gănt, *a.* [L. *mitigans* (*-antis*), *ppr.* of *mitigare*, to mitigate.] softening; lenient; lenitive; diminishing; alleviating.

mit′i·gāte, *v.t.* and *v.i.*; mitigated, *pt., pp.*; mitigating, *ppr.* [L. *mitigatus*, pp. of *mitigare*, to make mild, soft, or tender; *mitis*, mild, soft, and *agere*, to drive, do.] to make or become milder, less severe, less rigorous, or less painful; to moderate.

We could wish that the rigor of their opinions were allayed and *mitigated.*
—Hooker.

Syn.—assuage, alleviate, abate, lessen, moderate, lighten, relieve, soften.

mit·i·gā′tion, *n.* [L. *mitigatio* (*-onis*), a soothing, calming.]

1. alleviation; abatement or diminution, as of anything painful, harsh, severe, afflictive, or calamitous; as, the *mitigation* of pain, grief, rigor, punishment, or penalty.
2. anything that mitigates.

mit′i·gā·tive, *a.* lenitive; tending to alleviate.

mit′i·gā·tive, *n.* something that mitigates, as a drug that lessens pain.

mit′i·gā·tŏr, *n.* one who or that which mitigates.

mit′i·gȧ·tō·ry, *a.* [L. *mitigatorius*, soothing.] same as *mitigative.*

mīt′ing, *n.* a little one: used in endearment or in contempt. [Obs.]

mī′tis çast′ing, [from L. *mitis*, soft.]

1. a method of making malleable iron castings from a mixture of wrought iron and aluminum.
2. a casting made in this way.

mī′tōme, *n.* [Gr. *mitos*, thread.] in biology, the more compact part of cell protoplasm.

mi·tō′sis, *n.* [Mod. L., from Gr. *mitos*, thread; and *-osis.*] in biology, the indirect, and more common, method of cell division, in which the nuclear chromatin is formed into a long thread which in turn breaks into segments (*chromosomes*) that are split lengthwise: the halves come together in two sets, each set forming the nucleus for a new cell.

mi·tot′iç, *a.* pertaining to mitosis.

mi·tot′iç·ăl·ly, *adv.* by mitosis.

Mī′trȧ, *n.* [L. and Gr. *mitra*, a turban: so called from the shape of the shell.] a genus of *Mollusca* inhabiting a small turreted shell; the miters. The shells exhibit a great variety of patterns and colors.

mi·traille′ (-trȧ′y), *n.* [Fr., from OFr. *mitaille*, coarse fragments, filings, from *mite*, a mite.] small shot, slugs, and scraps of iron formerly used in cannon as projectiles.

mi·trȧil·leur′ (-trȧ-yũr′), *n.* [Fr., from *mitrailler*, to fire grapeshot, from *mitraille*, grapeshot, from OFr. *mitre, mite*, small coin.]

1. (a) a soldier who operated a mitrailleuse; (b) a machine gunner.
2. a mitrailleuse.

mi·trȧil·leuṣe′ (-trȧ-yụz′), *n.* 1. an obsolete, breech-loading machine gun with a cluster of barrels which were fired simultaneously or in rapid succession.

2. any machine gun.

mī′trăl, *a.* [Fr., from L. *mitra*, a miter.] of or like a miter or the mitral valve.

mī′trăl valve, the valve between the left auricle and left ventricle of the heart.

mī′tre (-tẽr), *n.* same as *miter.*

mī′tre, *v.t.*; mitred, *pt. pp.*; mitring, *ppr.* to miter.

mit′ri·fọrm, *a.* [L. *mitra*, a miter, and *forma*, form.] in botany and zoology, having the form of a miter.

mits′väh, *n.*; *pl.* **mits′vōth,** same as *mitzvah.*

mitt, *n.* [abbrev. of *mitten.*] 1. a glove, often of lace or net, covering the forearm, hand, and sometimes part of the fingers.

2. a mitten.
3. a hand. [Slang.]
4. in sports, (a) a glove padded on the palm and fingers for protection and worn by baseball players in the field; (b) [*usually in pl.*] a padded mitten worn by boxers.

mit′ten, *n.* [ME. *mitaine, mytane, myten*; OFr. *mitaine, mitan*; compare Gael. and Ir. *mutan*, a muff, thick glove; Gael. *miotag*, a mitten.]

1. a glove with a thumb but no separately divided fingers.
2. a mitt (senses 1 and 4b).

to give the mitten to; to dismiss, as an unwelcome suitor. [Colloq.]

mit′ten, *v.t.*; mittened, *pt., pp.*; mittening, *ppr.*

1. to supply with mittens, as the hands.
2. to reject, as a lover. [Colloq.]

mit′tent, *a.* sending forth; emitting. [Obs.]

mit′ti·mus, *n.* [so called from the first word of the writ, L. *mittimus*, we send.]

1. in law, (a) a precept or command in writing under the hand and seal of a justice of the peace or other proper officer, directed to the keeper of a prison, requiring him to imprison an offender until delivered by due course of law; a warrant of commitment to prison; (b) a writ for removing records from one court to another.
2. dismissal, as from office.

Mit′tlẽr's green, same as *chrome green.*

mit′ty, *n.* the little petrel, *Procellaria pelagica.* [Brit. Dial.]

mī′tū, *n.* [Braz.] a South American bird of the

family *Cracidæ* and genus *Mitu* or *Mitua*, of which it is the type; the galeated curassow.
Mit'ū·ȧ, *n.* 1. a genus of insects, order *Coleoptera*.
2. a genus of birds, type of the family *Cracidæ*.
mīt'y, *a.* having or abounding in mites.
mitz'väh (mits'), *n.*; *pl.* **mitz'vōth,** in Judaism, (a) a commandment or precept, as in the Bible or from a rabbi; (b) an act fulfilling such a command or the spirit of such commands; as, an act of charity is a *mitzvah*: also spelled *mitsvah*.
mix, *v.t.*; mixed *or* mixt (mikst), *pt., pp.*; mixing, *ppr.* [ME. *mixen*; AS. *miscian*, to mix; akin to O.H.G. *miskan*, Russ. *mieshati*, W. *mysgu*, L. *miscere*, Gr. *misgein*, *mignynai*, to mix; Sans. *micra*, mixed.]
1. to unite or blend promiscuously into a mass or compound; as, to *mix* flour and salt; to *mix* wines; also, to make by putting ingredients together; as, he *mixed* a cake.
2. to join; to associate; to unite with in company.
Ephraim, he hath *mixed* himself among the people. —Hos. vii. 8.
3. to cause to join or associate.
You *mix* your sadness with some fear. —Shak.
4. to crossbreed.
Syn.—blend, compound, confuse, join, mingle, unite.
to mix up; (a) to mix thoroughly; to mingle together; (b) to confuse; to cause confusion in; also, to mistake for another (with *with*); (c) to involve or implicate (*in* some matter).
mix, *v.i.* 1. to be mixed or capable of being mixed; to be blended; to mingle; as, oil and water will not *mix* readily.
2. to associate or get along together; as, to *mix* in society.
mix, *n.* 1. a mixing or being mixed.
2. a muddle; state of confusion.
3. a prepared blend of various ingredients; mixture.
4. a beverage, usually carbonated, as soda or ginger ale, for mixing with alcoholic liquor.
mix'ȧ·ble, *a.* capable of being mixed.
mixed (mikst), *a.* 1. joined or mingled in a single mass or compound; blended.
2. made up of different or incongruous parts, elements, classes, races, etc.
3. consisting of or involving both sexes; as, a *mixed* class, *mixed* company.
4. confused; muddled.
5. in phonetics, central: said of vowels.
mixed marriage; marriage between persons of different religions or races.
mixed number; in mathematics, a number expressed by a whole number and a fraction (e.g., $2^3/_4$).
mixed voices; in music, male and female voices combined.
mix'ed·ly, *adv.* in a mixed manner; promiscuously.
mix'en, *n.* a compost heap.
mix'ẽr, *n.* 1. one who or that which mixes.
2. a kitchen apparatus, operated by hand or by an electric motor, used to mix dough, beat eggs, whip cream, etc.
3. in mechanics, a valve in which air and fuel are mixed in the proper proportions to obtain efficient combustion.
4. a person with reference to his degree of social adaptability; as, he is a good (or bad) *mixer*; also, a party or gathering for the purpose of furthering social relationships. [Colloq.]
5. in metallurgy, a tank in which molten pig iron may be stored after it has been removed from a blast furnace and before it is placed in a converter or in an open-hearth furnace.
mix'īte, *n.* [named after A. *Mixa*, a Bohemian commissioner of mines.] a mineral of a bluish green color, an arsenate of copper and bismuth, found first in Bohemia and afterward in Utah: it occurs in capillary crystals.
mix'ō-, [Gr. *mixo-*, from *mignynai*, to mix.] a combining form meaning *mixed*, as in *mixogamy*, *Mixo*dectidæ.
mix"ō·bär·bar'iç, *a.* [Gr. *mixobarbaros*, half barbarous; *mixo-*, from *mignynai*, to mix, and *barbaros*, barbarous.] not altogether barbaric; partly civilized.
Mix·ō·deç'tēş, *n.* [*mixo-*, and Gr. *dēktēs*, a biter, from *daknein*, to bite.] the typical genus of Eocene mammals of the family *Mixodectidæ*.
Mix·ō·deç'ti·dae, *n.pl.* [*Mixodectes* and *-idæ.*] a family of prosimian Eocene mammals characterized by very large incisors and simple premolars in the lower jaw.
mix·og'ȧ·mous, *a.* [*mixo-*, and Gr. *gamos*, marriage.] in ichthyology, characterized by mixogamy.
mix·og'ȧ·my, *n.* in ichthyology, the coming together of males and females in unequal numbers at spawning time, males being in excess.
mix·ō·lyd'i·ăn mōde, [Gr. *mixolydios*, half-Lydian; *mixo-*, mixed, and *Lydios*, Lydian.]
1. in ancient Greek music, one of the four principal modes.
2. in medieval music, an authentic ecclesiastical mode, the seventh in number, based on G, with D dominant and C mediant.
mixt, *v.* alternative past tense and past participle of *mix*.
Mix'teç, *n.* an Indian, one of the inhabitants of early Mexico, living in certain parts of Oaxaca and Guerrero (near the present city of Acapulco); also, the speech of these Indians, a branch of the Zapotec language.
Mix·te'çō, Mix·te'çä (mēs-), *n.* same as *Mixtec*.
mix'ti·form, *a.* [L. *mixtus*, pp. of *miscere*, to mix, and *forma*, form.] characterized by mixture in form; made of mixed materials. [Rare.]
mix·ti·lin'ē·ăl, *a.* [L. *mixtus*, mixed, and *linea*, line.] containing a mixture of lines, as straight, curved, etc.; as, a *mixtilineal* angle (i. e., an angle contained by a straight line and a curve).
mix·ti·lin'ē·ăr, *a.* mixtilineal.
mix'tion (miks'chun), *n.* [L. *mixtio* (*-onis*), a mixture, mixing.]
1. mixture; promiscuous assemblage. [Obs.]
2. a mixture of mastic, amber, etc., used as a medium or mordant for affixing gold leaf.
mix'tūre, *n.* [Late ME.; OFr.; L. *mixtura*, a mixing.]
1. the act of mixing or state of being mixed.
2. a mass or compound consisting of different ingredients blended without order.
3. something mixed, as a cloth made of differently colored thread.
4. in pharmacy, a liquid medicine which contains insoluble matter suspended in some viscid substance.
5. in chemistry, a substance containing two or more elements: distinguished from *compound* in that the constituents are not in fixed proportions and do not lose their individual characteristics.
6. in music, an organ stop, of a shrill and piercing quality, consisting of two or more ranks of pipes: called also *furniture stop*.
Syn.—compound, composition, combination.
mix'ty-max'ty, *a.* promiscuously mingled. [Scot.]
mix'-up, *n.* 1. a mingling of things or of people in disorder; a confusion; tangle.
2. a fight. [Colloq.]
miz'māze, *n.* [reduplication of *maze*.] a maze or labyrinth. [Obs.]
miz'päh, *n.* [Heb.] literally, a watchtower; the name of several places in ancient Palestine, especially applied to the heap of stones gathered in Mt. Gilead by Jacob and his brethren as a remembrance of the covenant made with Laban (Gen. xxxi. 49): in modern usage the word signifies a parting salutation, suggested by Laban's prayer—"The Lord watch between me and thee, when we are absent from one another."
miz'zen miz'en, *a.* [Late ME. *meseyn*; OFr. *misaine*; It. *mezzana*, fem. of *mezzano*, middle, from L. *medianus*, from *medius*, middle.] of the mizzenmast.
miz'zen, miz'en, *n.* 1. a fore-and-aft sail set on the mizzenmast.
2. a mizzenmast.
miz'zen·mȧst, miz'en·mȧst, *n.* the mast supporting the mizzen; the mast that stands nearest to the stern in a ship with two or three masts.
miz'zle, *v.i.* and *v.t.*; mizzled (-zld), *pt., pp.*; mizzling, *ppr.* [ME. *miselen*, freq. of *misten*, to mist.] to rain in very fine drops; to drizzle. [Obs. or Dial.]
miz'zle, *n.* fine rain; mist; drizzle. [Obs. or Dial.]
miz'zle, *v.i.* to depart suddenly; to leave unceremoniously. [Brit. Dial.]
miz'zle, *v.t.* and *v.i.* to confuse; to entangle the mind of; to become confused or entangled, as with drink. [Dial.]
miz'zly, *a.*; *comp.* mizzlier; *superl.* mizzliest; misty: said of the atmosphere.
Mn, in chemistry, manganese.
mnē·mon'iç (nē-), *a.* [Gr. *mnēmonikos*, pertaining to the memory, from *mnēmōn* (*-onis*), mindful, from *mnāsthai*, to remember.]
1. assisting or intended to assist the memory.
2. pertaining to mnemonics.
mnē·mon'iç·ăl, *a.* mnemonic.
mnē·mō·ni'ciăn (-nish'un), *n.* an expert in a system of mnemonics.
mnē·mon'içs, *n.pl.* [Gr. *mnēmonika*, mnemonics, neut. pl. of *mnēmonikos*, mnemonic.]
1. [*construed as sing.*] the science or art of improving the memory, as by the use of certain formulas.
2. formulas or other aids to help in remembering.
mnē'mō·nist, *n.* a mnemonician.
Mnē·mos'y·nē, *n.* [Gr. *mnēmosynē*, memory.] in Greek mythology, the goddess of memory and mother (by Zeus) of the Muses.
mnē'mō·teçh·ny, *n.* [Gr. *mnēmē*, memory, and *technē*, art.] mnemonics.
Mo, in chemistry, molybdenum.
-mō, in printing books, a suffix to the number designating one of the equal parts into which a sheet is divided, the size of a page varying with the size of the sheet folded; as, 12*mo*, 16*mo*.
mō'ȧ, *n.* [from native (Maori) name.] any of an extinct group of very large, flightless birds of New Zealand, related to the ostrich.
Mō'ab·īte, *n.* [Heb. *Mo'ābh*, Moab.] a native or inhabitant of Moab, an ancient kingdom east and south of the Dead Sea.
Moabite stone; a slab discovered in the country of the Moabites, dating from perhaps 900 B.C. and bearing an inscription in ancient Semitic characters.
Mō'ab·īte, *a.* of Moab or the Moabites.
Mō'ab·īt·ish, *a.* same as *Moabite*.
mōan, *n.* [ME. *mone*; prob. from base of AS. *mænen*, to complain.]
1. a complaint; lamentation. [Rare.]
2. audible expression of sorrow or suffering; grief expressed in words or cries.
Sullen *moans*, hollow groans. —Pope.
3. any sound like this.
mōan, *v.i.* 1. to grieve; to make lamentations.
Unpitied and unheard, where misery *moans*. —Thomson.
2. to utter a moan or moans; as, the sea *moans*.
mōan, *v.t.*; 1. to lament; to deplore; to bewail audibly.
Ye floods, ye woods, ye echoes, *moan*
My dear Colombo dead and gone.—Prior.
2. to distress; to afflict. [Obs.]
3. to say with a moan.
mōan'ful, *a.* sorrowful; expressing sorrow.
mōan'fu̇l·ly, *adv.* with lamentation.
mōat, *n.* [OFr. *mote*, from LL. *mota*, a mound, hill on which a castle is built, a castle, dike.]
1. a ditch or deep trench round the rampart of a castle or other fortified place, sometimes filled with water, for protection against invasion.
2. a pond; a lake. [Obs.]
mōat, *v.t.*; moated, *pt., pp.*; moating, *ppr.* to surround with a ditch for defense; as, a *moated* castle.
mob, *n.* [from L. *mobile vulgus*, the fickle crowd.]
1. a crowd or multitude of people, rude, tumultuous, and disorderly; also, any crowd.
2. a disorderly assembly.
Had every Athenian citizen been a Socrates, every Athenian assembly would still have been a *mob*. —Madison.
3. the masses; common people collectively: a contemptuous term.
4. a gang of criminals. [Slang.]
5. in Australia, a flock or herd, as of ducks, cattle, etc.
Syn.—populace, rabble, canaille.
mob, *v.t.*; mobbed, *pt., pp.*; mobbing, *ppr.* 1. to crowd around and attack.
2. to crowd around and jostle, annoy, etc., as in curiosity or anger.
mob, *v.t.* 1. to wrap in a cowl or veil so as to conceal the face, as with a cap. [Obs.]
2. to dress in an awkward manner. [Obs.]
mob'bish, *a.* like a mob; lawless and tumultuous; vulgar.
mob'by, *n.* fruit juice used in making brandy; also, the brandy after distillation.
mob'çap, *n.* [M.D. *mop*, a woman's cap.] formerly, a woman's cap or headdress, usually having broad bands to tie under the chin: also *mob*.
mō'bile (*or* -bēl), *a.* [L. *mobilis*, movable, from *movere*, to move.]
1. movable; not firm, stationary, or fixed.

2. easily moved; very fluid; not viscous, as mercury.
3. easily influenced; changeable; versatile; changing; as, a *mobile* expression.
4. in military usage, capable of being moved or transported quickly and with relative ease; as, an armored battalion is a *mobile* unit.
5. designating a form of abstract sculpture which aims to depict movement, i.e., kinetic rather than static rhythms, as by an arrangement of thin forms, rings, rods, etc. suspended in mid-air by fine wires.
mobile home; a large trailer outfitted as a home meant to be parked more or less permanently at a location.

mō'bile, *n.* 1. anything that can be moved. [Rare.]
2. a moving cause or agent. [Rare.]
3. a piece of mobile sculpture.

mob'i·lē, *n.* [L. *mobile vulgus*, the fickle crowd.] the mob; the populace. [Obs.]

mō·bil'i·ty, *n.* the state or quality of being mobile.

mō"bi·li·zā'tion, *n.* a mobilizing or being mobilized.

Mö'bi·us strip (mā'), [named after A. F. *Möbius*, Ger. mathematician.] a surface with only one side, formed by giving a half twist to a narrow, rectangular strip of paper and then pasting its two ends together.

mō'bi·līze, *v.t.*; mobilized, *pt.*, *pp.*; mobilizing, *ppr.* [Fr. *mobiliser*, from *mobile*, movable.]
1. (a) to make mobile, or movable; (b) to put into motion, circulation, or use.
2. to make (armed forces or a nation) ready for war.
3. to organize and make ready for use.

mō'bi·līze, *v.i.* to become organized and ready, as for war.

mob law, law made and administered by a mob.

mō'ble, mob'ble, *v.t.* to wrap the head in a hood. [Obs.]

mō'ble, *n.* movable property or goods. [Obs.]

mob·oc'rȧ·cy, *n.*; *pl.* **mob·oc'rȧ·cies,** [*mob* and *-cracy*, as in demo*cracy*, aristo*cracy*, etc.]
1. government or domination by a mob.
2. the mob as ruler.

mob'ō·crat, *n.* a believer in and advocate of mobocracy.

mob·ō·crat'ic, *a.* pertaining to mobocracy.

mob'stẽr, *n.* a member of a criminal mob; a gangster. [Slang.]

moc'cȧ·sin, *n.* [from Am. Ind. (Algonquian).]
1. originally, a heelless slipper, made of deerskin or other soft leather, without a stiff sole, and often ornamented on the upper side, worn by North American Indians.
2. any slipper more or less like this.
3. a poisonous water serpent, *Ancistrodon piscivorus*, of the southeastern United States; especially, the water moccasin.

moc'cȧ·sined, *a.* wearing moccasins; covered with moccasins.

moc'cȧ·sin flow'ẽr, 1. a variety of pink or yellow orchid shaped like a slipper.
2. any of several species of *Venus's-slipper*, or *Cypripedium*: variously named *lady's-slipper*, *Indian shoe*, *moccasin plant*.

mō'chȧ, *n.* 1. a choice kind of coffee, originally exported from Mocha, in Arabia.
2. any coffee. [Colloq.]
3. a soft, velvety leather made from the pelts of certain Arabian goats, and used especially for gloves.
4. [M–] any of several moths; specifically, (a) *Ephyra pendularia*, the birch mocha; (b) *Ichthyura inclusa*, the poplar mocha, or Mocha-stone moth: so named because its brown and gray markings supposedly resemble those of a moss agate.

mō'chȧ, *a.* flavored with coffee or coffee and chocolate.

Mō'chȧ stōne, dendritic agate; moss agate.

mō·chi'lȧ, *n.* [Sp.] formerly, a large flap of leather covering a saddle.

mock, *v.t.*; mocked (mokt), *pt.*, *pp.*; mocking, *ppr.* [OFr. *mocquer*, *moquer*, to mock.]
1. to imitate; to mimic; to imitate in fun or derision.
2. to deride in any way; to treat with scorn or contempt.
3. to defeat; to defy and make futile; as, the strong fortress *mocked* the invaders.
4. to lead on and disappoint; to deceive; to tantalize; as, the weather *mocked* him.
5. to simulate. [Obs.]
Syn.—mimic, imitate, ape, deride, ridicule, jeer, gibe, banter, taunt, delude, fool, tantalize, disappoint, deceive, defeat, insult.

mock, *v.i.* to use ridicule or derision; to make sport of some person or thing; to gibe or jeer: often with *at*.

mock, *n.* 1. an act or speech expressing ridicule or derision; a sneer.
2. a person or thing receiving or deserving ridicule or derision.
3. an imitation; a counterfeit.

mock, *a.* false; counterfeit; sham; imitating reality, but not real.
mock bishop's-weed; a plant of the parsley family, *Discopleura capillacea*.

mock'ȧ·ble, *a.* that can be mocked.

mock'ȧ·dō, moch'ȧ·dō, *n.* a fabric made in imitation of velvet, much used in the sixteenth and seventeenth centuries.

mock'ȧ·döur, *n.* muckender. [Obs.]

mock'bird, *n.* same as *mockingbird*.

mock'ẽr, *n.* 1. one who mocks; a scorner.
2. a deceiver; an impostor.
3. a mockingbird.

mock'ẽr·nut, *n.* a variety of hickory; also, its nut.

mock'ẽr·y, *n.*; *pl.* **mock'ẽr·ies,** 1. a mocking (in various senses).
2. a subject of laughter or ridicule.
3. vain imitation or effort; that which deceives, disappoints, or frustrates.
4. a false, derisive, or impertinent imitation; counterfeit appearance; false show.

mock'-hē·rō'ic, *a.* imitating a hero or heroic actions in a mocking way.

mock'-hē·rō'ic, *n.* a literary composition burlesquing a hero or heroic action.

mock'ing, *a.* mimicking; imitating; derisive.

mock'ing·bird, *n.* 1. a small bird, *Mimus polyglottus*, of the thrush family, *Turdidæ*, found in the southern United States. It is of an ashy-brown or gray color above, lighter below, and is characterized by its practice of imitating the calls of other birds.
2. any of various other mimicking birds, as the mock nightingale or the catbird.

MOCKINGBIRD (*Mimus polyglottus*)

mock'ing·ly, *adv.* by way of derision; in contempt.

mock'ing thrush, same as *mock thrush*.

mock'ing wren (ren), an American bird, *Thryothorus ludovicianus*, or great Carolina wren; also, any bird of the same genus.

mock'ish, *a.* spurious; bogus; mock. [Obs.]

mock or'ange (-enj), a large bushy shrub, *Philadelphus coronarius*, having fragrant creamy-white flowers that resemble orange blossoms: also called *syringa*.

mock sun, same as *parhelion*.

mock thrush, the brown thrasher, *Harporhynchus rufus*.

mock tũr'tle söup, a soup made from calf's head, veal, etc., spiced so as to taste like green turtle soup.

mock'-up, *n.* a scale model, usually a full-sized replica in wood, cardboard, canvas, etc., of a structure, apparatus, or weapon, used for instructional purposes, to test the design, or, in military use, as a dummy to draw enemy fire away from a vulnerable point.

mock vel'vet, a fabric made in imitation of velvet.

mō'cō, *n.* [Braz.] the rock cavy, *Cavia rupestris*, a South American rodent allied to the guinea pig.

mod, *n.* [from *mod*ern.] [also M–] any of the young people in England in the 1960's characterized, like the hippies of the United States, by rebellion against conventional society, the wearing of flamboyant clothes, long hair, etc.

mod, *a.* [also M–] of or characteristic of the mods.

mod·ȧ·cryl'ic, *a.* [*mod*ified and *acrylic*.] designating or of any of various manufactured fibers made from long-chain polymers: used in place of wool in fabrics, carpets, etc.

mōd'ăl, *a.* [LL. *modalis*, from L. *modus*, mode, manner.] of or indicating a mode or mood; specifically, (a) in grammar, of or expressing a mood; as, a *modal* verb; (b) in logic, expressing or characterized by modality; (c) in music, of or composed in any of the medieval church modes; (d) in philosophy, of mode, or form, as opposed to substance.

mōd'ăl, *n.* in logic, a modal proposition.

mō'dăl aux·il'iȧ·ry, an auxiliary verb used with another to indicate its mood: *may, might, must, can, would,* and *should* are modal auxiliaries.

mōd'ăl·ism, *n.* in theology, the doctrine taught by Sabellius concerning the Trinity, that the Father, the Son, and the Holy Ghost are not persons, but mere forms of manifestation of the divine nature.

mōd'ăl·ist, *n.* one who believes in or supports modalism.

mō·dal'i·ty, *n.*; *pl.* **mō·dal'i·ties,** [LL. *modalitas*, modality, from *modalis*, modal.]
1. the fact, state, or quality of being modal.
2. a special attribute, emphasis, etc. that marks certain individuals, things, groups, etc.
3. in logic, the qualification in a proposition affirming or denying possibility, impossibility, necessity, contingency, etc.

mō'dăl·ly, *adv.* in a modal manner; in a manner expressing or indicating a mode or form.

mōde, *n.* [L. *modus*, measure, manner, form.]
1. manner of existing or acting; way; method or form.
2. the prevailing style; the common usage; the current fashion, as in manners or dress.
3. in grammar, mood.
4. in logic, (a) modality or the form of a proposition with reference to its modality; (b) any of the various forms of valid syllogisms, as determined by the quantity and quality of their constituent propositions: see *syllogism*.
5. in metaphysics, the form, or way of being, of something, as apart from its substance.
6. in music, (a) any of the various forms in which the octave was arranged in classical Greek and medieval church music, according to certain fixed intervals between the tones; (b) either of the two forms of octave arrangement in modern music (*major mode* and *minor mode*).
7. in statistics, the value, number, etc. that occurs most frequently in a given series.
8. in lacemaking, (a) a portion of a pattern containing the stitch or design characteristic of a given variety of lace; (b) meshes or openwork connecting the solid portions of lace.
9. a kind of silk; alamode.

mod'el, *n.* [Fr. *modèle*; It. *modello*, dim. of *modo*, from L. *modus*, mode.]
1. anything of a particular form, shape, size, quality, construction, etc., intended or imitation; a form in miniature, in natural size, or enlarged, of something to be made in similar proportions; plan; pattern; as, the *model* of an invention, the plaster *model* of a statue.
2. (a) an imitation or copy in miniature of something already made or existing on a large scale; as, a *model* of the Cologne Cathedral. (b) an archetype; prototype. (c) a hypothetical or stylized representation, as of an atom. (d) a generalized, hypothetical description, often based on an analogy, used in analyzing or explaining something.
3. a style or design; as, last year's *model* of automobile.
4. (a) a person who poses for an artist or photographer; (b) a person, especially a woman, employed to display clothes by wearing them; a mannequin.
5. a person or thing considered as a standard of excellence to be imitated.
6. image; copy; facsimile. [Rare.]
7. a short form or abridgment. [Obs.]
Syn.—archetype, copy, pattern, sample, specimen, example, type, mold, design.

mod'el, *a.* serving as a model, pattern, or standard of excellence.

mod'el, *v.t.*; modeled *or* modelled, *pt.*, *pp.*; modeling *or* modelling, *ppr.* 1. (a) to form or plan after a model, pattern, or design; (b) to make a model of; (c) to make conform to a standard of excellence: as, he *modeled* his behavior on that of his uncle.
2. to display (a dress, etc.) by wearing.

mod'el, *v.i.* 1. to make a model or models; as, she *models* in clay.
2. to serve as a model (sense 4).
3. in painting, drawing, etc., to take on a three-dimensional appearance as a result of contrast in lighting and color.

mod'el·ẽr, mod'el·lẽr, *n.* a person who models; especially, one who models in clay, etc.

mod'el·ing, mod'el·ling, *n.* 1. the act or art of making a model, especially of making a pattern in some plastic material to be copied in stone or metal.
2. form; shape; as, the *modeling* of one's features.

3. employment as a model (sense 4).
4. in painting, drawing, etc., the indication of three dimensions by means of contrast in lighting and color.

mod′el·ing çlāy, a fine soft clay kept plastic by adding glycerin, used in making models and casts.

mod′el·ing plāne, a small plane used for planing rounded surfaces.

mod′el·ing wax, beeswax that has been prepared for modeling by being melted with a resinous substance and tinted.

mod′el·īze, *v.t.* to model. [Obs.]

mō′dem, *n.* [*mo*dulator, and *dem*odulator, a device used in radio detection.] a device that converts data to a form that can be transmitted, as by telephone, to data-processing equipment, where a similar device reconverts it.

mod′e̱·nȧ, *n.* [so called from *Modena*, Italy.] a shade of deep purple.

Mod·ē·nēṣe′, *n.* a native or inhabitant of Modena, Italy.

Mod·ē·nēṣe′, *a.* pertaining to or characteristic of Modena, Italy, or its people.

mod′ẽr·ăte, *a.* [L. *moderatus*, pp. of *moderare*, to keep within bounds, restrain, from *modus*, measure.]
1. avoiding excesses and extremes; keeping within reasonable bounds; temperate.
2. of medium quality; mediocre; as, *moderate* abilities.
3. mild; calm; gentle; not violent; as, *moderate* weather.
Syn.—limited, temperate, calm, dispassionate, sober, abstinent, sparing, steady, ordinary, medium.

mod′ẽr·ăte, *n.* a person who professes moderate views, opinions, doctrines, etc., especially in religion and politics.

mod′ẽr·āte, *v.t.*; moderated, *pt., pp.*; moderating, *ppr.* 1. to restrain; to reduce; to lessen; to allay; to repress; as, to *moderate* rage; to *moderate* heat or wind.
2. to temper; to make temperate; to qualify.
3. to decide or judge; to preside over (a meeting, etc.).
Syn.—control, soften, allay, regulate, repress, govern, temper.

mod′ẽr·āte, *v.i.* 1. to become less violent, severe, rigorous, or intense; as, the weather has *moderated*.
2. to preside at a meeting; to serve as a moderator.

mod′ẽr·ăte·ly, *adv.* in a moderate manner.

mod′ẽr·ăte·ness, *n.* the state or quality of being moderate; temperateness.

mod·ẽr·ā′tion, *n.* [L. *moderatio* (*-onis*), from *moderare*, to moderate.]
1. the act of moderating or restraining; the act of tempering, lessening, or repressing.
2. the state or quality of being moderate, or avoiding extremes; freedom from excess; temperance; restraint.
3. absence of violence; calmness.
4. the act of presiding over, regulating, or directing, as a moderator.
5. [*pl.*] at Oxford University, the first public examination for degrees.
in moderation; without excess.
Syn.—frugality, forbearance, modesty, sobriety, temperance.

mod′ẽr·ȧ·tiṣm, *n.* the quality of being moderate; the characteristic of one who practices moderation, especially in religious or political opinions or views.

mod·e·rä′tō, *a.* and *adv.* [It.] in music, with moderation in tempo: a direction to the performer.
allegro moderato; in somewhat slower time than allegro: a direction to the performer.
andante moderato; in somewhat faster time than andante: a direction to the performer.

mod′ẽr·ā·tŏr, *n.* [L., one who regulates or governs.]
1. one who or that which moderates or restrains.
2. the person who presides at a town meeting, debate, etc.
3. in the Presbyterian Church, the officer who presides over a synod or general assembly.
4. in the universities of Cambridge and Oxford, a public officer appointed to superintend the examinations for honors and degrees.

mod′ẽr·ā·tŏr lamp, a form of lamp in which the flow of oil is automatically regulated by means of a piston.

mod′ẽr·ā·tŏr·ship, *n.* the position, duties, or office of a moderator.

mod′ẽr·ā·tress, *n.* a woman moderator. [Obs.]

mod′ẽrn, *a.* [Fr. *moderne*; LL. *modernus*, of the present time, from L. *modus*, measure.]
1. of or characteristic of the present or recent times; not ancient: often used to designate certain contemporary tendencies and schools of art, music, literature, etc.; as, *modern* architecture and furniture are characterized by functionalism and lack of extraneous ornamentation.
2. up-to-date; not old-fashioned, antiquated, or obsolete.
3. [*often* M-] designating a language, or the form of a language, in current use.
4. common; trite. [Obs.]
5. of or relating to the period of history after the Middle Ages, from c.1450 A.D. to the present day.
Syn.—recent, fresh, new, novel, late.

mod′ẽrn, *n.* 1. a person living in modern times.
2. a person having modern ideas, beliefs, standards, etc.
3. in printing, a style of type face characterized by heavy down strokes contrasting with narrow cross strokes.

mod′ẽrn dȧnce, a form of dance as a performing art, variously developed in the 20th-century by Mary Wigman, Martha Graham, etc., and characterized by bodily movements and rhythms less formalized than in classical ballet.

Mod′ẽrn Eng̃′lish, the English language since about 1500.

Mod′ẽrn Greek, the Greek language as spoken and written in Greece since about 1500.

Mod′ẽrn Hē′brew, Hebrew as spoken and written after Biblical times; especially, Hebrew as the language of modern Israel.

mod′ẽrn his′tō·ry, the history of the world since the fall of Constantinople (1453).

mod′ẽrn·iṣm, *n.* **1.** (a) modern usage, practice, or thought; sympathy with modern ideas; (b) an instance of this; modern idiom, practice, or usage.
2. [M-] in Christianity, any of various movements attempting to redefine Biblical and Christian dogma and teachings in the light of modern science: condemned in the Roman Catholic Church by Pope Pius X in 1907 as a negation of faith.

mod′ẽrn·ist, *n.* 1. a person who follows or is sympathetic to modern ideas and methods.
2. [M-] a follower of Modernism.

mod·ẽrn·is′tiç, *a.* 1. of or characteristic of modernism or modernists.
2. modern: used especially to designate certain contemporary trends in art, music, etc., often in a somewhat derogatory sense.

mod·ẽrn·ist′iç·ăl·ly, *adv.* in a modernistic manner.

mō·dẽr′ni·ty, *n.* 1. the state or quality of being modern.
2. *pl.* **mō·dẽr′ni·tieṣ,** something modern.

mod·ẽrn·i·zā′tion, *n.* a modernizing or being modernized.

mod′ẽrn·īze, *v.t.*; modernized, *pt., pp.*; modernizing, *ppr.* to make modern; to adapt to modern persons or things; to cause to conform to modern ideas, style, and taste; to make characteristic of modern times.

mod′ẽrn·īze, *v.i.* to adopt modern ways; to become modern.

mod′ẽrn·ī·zẽr, *n.* one who introduces modern ideas, institutions, etc.

Mod′ẽrn Lat′in, the Latin that has come into use since the Renaissance, or about 1500, chiefly in scientific literature: it has words formed from Latin and Greek: also called *New Latin, Neo-Latin*.

mod′ẽrn·ly, *adv.* in modern times. [Rare.]

mod′ẽrn·ness, *n.* the quality or state of being modern; recentness; novelty.

mod′est, *a.* [Fr. *modeste*; L. *modestus*, moderate, unassuming, from *modus*, measure.]
1. having or showing a moderate or humble opinion of one's own value, abilities, achievements, etc.; unassuming.
2. not forward; shy or reserved; as, *modest* behavior.
3. behaving according to a standard of what is proper or decorous; decent; pure; now, especially, not displaying one's body.
4. showing or caused by moderation; not extreme or excessive; as, a *modest* request.
5. quiet and humble in appearance, style, etc.; as, a *modest* home, apartment, etc.
Syn.—reserved, unobtrusive, diffident, bashful, coy, shy, decent, becoming, chaste, virtuous.

mod′est·ly, *adv.* in a modest manner.

mod′es·ty, *n.* [Fr. *modestie*; L. *modestia*, moderation, keeping within bounds, from *modestus*, modest.] the state or quality of being modest; specifically, (a) the sense of propriety; the absence of all tendency to overestimate oneself; in a somewhat stronger sense, self-distrust; retiring disposition; unobtrusiveness; bashful reserve; (b) decorum; decency; chastity; purity; (c) moderation; freedom from exaggeration or excess.

mod′i·çum, *n.* [L., neut. of *modicus*, moderate.] a little; a small quantity; as, a *modicum* of learning.

mod·i·fī·ȧ·bil′i·ty, *n.* the quality of being liable to modification; capability of being modified.

mod′i·fī·ȧ·ble, *a.* that can be modified.

mod·i·fi·çā′tion, *n.* [L. *modificatio* (*-onis*), a measuring.]
1. a modifying or being modified; specifically, (a) a partial or slight change in form; (b) a product of such a change; as, this automobile is a *modification* of last year's model; (c) a slight reduction; moderation; (d) a qualification or limitation of meaning; (e) in biology, a change in an organism caused by its environment and not inheritable; (f) in linguistics, a change in the form of a morpheme within a construction.
2. in Scottish law, the decree of court awarding a suitable stipend to the minister of a parish.

mod′i·fi·çā·tive, *n.* that which modifies or qualifies, as a word or clause.

mod′i·fi·çā″tō·ry, *a.* tending to modify or produce change in form or condition; modifying.

mod′i·fī·ẽr, *n.* one who or that which modifies; especially, a word, phrase, or clause that limits the meaning of another word or phrase; as, adjectives and adverbs are *modifiers*.

mod′i·fȳ, *v.t.*; modified, *pt., pp.*; modifying, *ppr.* [ME. *modifien*; L. *modificare, modificari*, to limit, regulate; *modus*, measure, and *facere*, to make.]
1. to change the form or external qualities of; to vary; to give a new form to; as, to *modify* the terms of a contract.
2. to limit or reduce slightly; to moderate; as, the judge *modified* her penalty.
3. in grammar, to limit or restrict in meaning; to qualify; as, "large" *modifies* "house" in *large house*.
4. in linguistics, to change (a vowel) by umlaut.
Syn.—alter, change, qualify.

mod′i·fȳ, *v.i.* to be modified.

mō·dil′liŏn, *n.* [OFr. *modillon, modiglion*; It *modiglione*, from L. *modulus*, a model.] in architecture, a block carved into the form of an ornamental bracket, used under a projecting cornice, especially in the Corinthian order.

mō·dī′ō·lăr, *a.* pertaining to the modiolus.

mō·dī′ō·lus, *n.*; *pl.* **mō·dī′ō·lī,** [Mod. L., dim. of L. *modiolus*, a bucket on a water wheel.] the bony axis in the center of the cochlea of the ear.

mōd′ish, *a.* in the latest style; according to the mode; fashionable; as, a *modish* dress.

mōd′ish·ly, *adv.* fashionably.

mōd′ish·ness, *n.* the state of being fashionable.

mōd′ist, *n.* a follower of the mode, or fashion.

mō·diste′, *n.* [Fr., from *mode*, mode, fashion.] a woman who makes or deals in fashionable clothes, hats, etc. for women.

mō′di·us, *n.*; *pl.* **mō′di·ī,** [L., from *modus*, measure.] a Roman unit of dry measure equal to .9 peck.

Mō′doç, *n.* a member of a small tribe of North American Indians, formerly living in California.

Mō′dred, *n.* in Arthurian legend, the treacherous nephew of King Arthur: they killed each other in battle: also *Mordred*.

mod′ū·lănt, *n.* [L. *modulans* (*-antis*), ppr. of *modulari*, to modulate.] anything that modulates.

mod′ū·lăr, *a.* pertaining to a module or modulus.

mod′ū·lāte, *v.t.*; modulated, *pt., pp.*; modulating, *ppr.* [L. *modulatus*, pp. of *modulari*, to regulate, measure off, arrange, from *modulus*, measure.]
1. to regulate, adjust, or adapt.
2. to vary the pitch, intensity, etc. of (the voice).
3. to sing; to intone (a song).
4. in music, to cause to shift to another key.

5. in radio, to vary the frequency of (a radio wave, etc.), as by superimposing another, lower frequency.

mod'ū·lāte, *v.i.* 1. in music, to pass from one key into another, or from the major into the minor mode, and vice versa, by the transitional use of a chord common to both.

2. in radio, to produce modulation.

mod·ū·lā'tion, *n.* [L. *modulatio* (*-onis*), from *modulari*, to modulate.]

1. a modulating or being modulated; specifically, (a) in music, a shifting from one key to another by the transitional use of a chord common to both; (b) in radio, a variation in the frequency of a radio wave in accordance with some other impulse.

2. in linguistics, the loss of stress and weakening or shortening of the phonetic form of a word when it is used purely as an auxiliary or transitional word. Example: "I'*ve* been going" as contrasted with "I *have* friends."

3. sound modulated; melody. [Rare.]

4. in architecture, the proportion of the different parts of an order according to modules.

mod'ū·lā·tŏr, *n.* [L., from *modulari*, to modulate.] one who or that which modulates; specifically, in radio, a vacuum tube used to produce modulation.

mod'ūle, *n.* [L. *modulus*, dim. of *modus*, measure.]

1. a standard or unit of measurement; specifically, (a) in classical architecture, the diameter, or one half the diameter, of a column at the base of the shaft, used to determine the proportions of the structure; (b) any of several standardized units of measurement used in architectural planning, in the construction of building materials, etc.; as, a 4-inch *module*, a 2-foot *module*.

2. (a) any of a set of units, as tiles, wall cabinets, shelves, etc., designed to be arranged or joined in a variety of ways; (b) a detachable section, compartment, or unit with a specific purpose or function, as in a spacecraft; (c) in electronics, a compact assembly functioning as a component of a larger unit.

mod'ūle, *v.t.* to model; to shape. [Obs.]

mod'ū·lus, *n.*; *pl.* **mod'ū·lī,** [L., a measure, dim. of *modus*, measure.]

1. in mathematics, some constant multiplier, coefficient, or parameter involved in a given function of a variable quantity, by means of which the function is accommodated to a particular system or base; as, the *modulus* of an elliptic function; the *modulus* of linear transformation; the *modulus* of a congruence, etc.

2. in physics, a positive number or quantity expressing the measure of a function, force, or effect, as of elasticity, resistance, etc., especially in relation to a basic unit or to some other factor or factors.

modulus of elasticity; the measure of the elastic force of a body, expressed by the ratio of a pressure on a given unit to the accompanying compression; or an expression of the force which would be necessary to elongate a prismatic body of a transverse section equal to a given unit, or to compress it within the limits of its elasticity.

modulus of rupture; the measure of the force necessary to break a given substance.

modulus of a system of logarithms; a number by which all the logarithms in one system of notation must be multiplied to adapt them to the same number in another system.

mō'dus, *n.*; *pl.* **mō'dī,** [L., measure, mode.]

1. mode; manner; way.

2. in law, an abbreviation of *modus decimandi*, a method of tithing by composition or equivalent instead of tithes.

modus operandi; manner of operating; way or method of doing or making; procedure.

modus vivendi; literally, way of living; hence, a temporary agreement or arrangement between parties, intended to last until a final or more enduring settlement is arrived at.

mōd'y, *a.* fashionable; modish. [Obs.]

mōe, *n.* mow. [Obs.]

mōe, *v.i.* to make a wry face; to mow. [Obs.]

mōe, *a.* and *adv.* more. [Obs.]

mōe'ble, *n.* moble. [Obs.]

mō'el·lon, *n.* rubble stone mixed with mortar filled in between the facing walls of a building or between the spandrels of a bridge.

Moe'sō-Goth, Moe'sō·goth, *n.* one of a tribe of Goths who settled in Moesia (4th century A.D.).

Moe·sō-Goth'iç, Moe·sō·goth'iç, *a.* of the Moeso-Goths or their language.

Moe·sō-Goth'iç, Moe·sō·goth'iç, *n.* the language of the Moeso-Goths, as preserved in the translation of the Bible by Bishop Ulfilas (c. 350 A.D.); Gothic.

mō·fette', mōf·fette', *n.* [Fr., from It. *muffare*, to be moldy, from G. *muff*, mold.]

1. a leakage of carbon dioxide and other gases from a hole or fissure in the earth, marking the last stage in volcanic activity.

2. such a hole or fissure.

moff, *n.* [Caucasus.] a light silk fabric of Caucasian make.

mō·fus'sil, *n.* [Anglo-Ind.] in India, the rural part of a district as distinguished from the cities and residential parts; any part remote from Calcutta, Madras, or Bombay.

mog, *v.i.* to depart; to go away. [Dial.]

mog'găn, *n.* a stocking without the foot. [Scot.]

moġ·i·graph'i·ȧ, *n.* [Gr. *mogis*, with difficulty, hardly, and *graphein*, to write.] in pathology, difficulty in writing; writers' cramp.

moġ·i·lā'li·ȧ, *n.* [Gr. *mogis*, with difficulty, hardly, and *lalein*, to speak.] in pathology, difficulty in speaking, as in stammering.

Mō·gul' (*or* mō'gul), *n.* [Hind. *Mughal*, from Mongolian *Mongol*, a Mongol.]

1. a Mongol; a Mongolian; especially, any of the Mongolian conquerors of India or their descendants.

2. [m–] a powerful or important person, especially one with autocratic power.

3. [m–] a kind of steam locomotive for pulling heavy trains.

4. [m–] [*pl.*] playing cards of the best quality.

Mō·gul', *a.* relating to the Moguls or their empire.

mō'hȧ, *n.* [Fr.] a variety of millet, *Setaria italica*.

mō'hāir, *n.* [OFr. *mouhaire*, *mohere*, prob. from Ar. *mukhayyar*, a kind of goat's-hair cloth.]

1. the hair of the Angora goat.

2. cloth made of the hair of the same animal; especially, a glossy, tough, napped cloth.

3. a fabric with mohair pile on a cotton or wool backing, used in upholstery.

4. a mohair garment.

mohair glacé; a French fabric made of goat's hair and cotton.

mō'hāir, *a.* made of or upholstered with mohair.

mohair luster; a kind of dress goods similar to alpaca.

mō'hāir shell, in conchology, a species of *Voluta*, of a closely and finely reticulated texture, resembling on the surface mohair or a close web of the silkworm.

Mō·ham'med, *n.* [Ar. *Muhammed*, lit., praised.] Arabian prophet; 570–632 A.D.; founder of the Moslem religion: also *Mahomet*, *Muhammad*.

Mō·ham'med·ăn, *a.* pertaining to Mohammed or the Moslem religion.

Mō·ham'med·ăn, *n.* a follower of Mohammed; a believer in the Moslem religion: also *Muhammadan*, *Muhammedan*.

Mō·ham'med·ăn·işm, *n.* the Moslem religion, founded by Mohammed about 612 A.D.; Islam.

Mō·ham'med·ăn·īze, *v.t.* Mohammedanized, *pt.*, *pp.*; Mohammedanizing, *ppr.* to make Mohammedan.

Mō·har'răm, *n.* same as *Muharram*.

mō·hȧ·trä' (-ȧ-), *n.* [Fr., from Ar. *mokhātra*, risk.] in medieval law, a fradulent means of obtaining usury effected by conspiracy between lender and borrower, goods being sold by the lender at one price upon credit, and immediately repurchased at a lower price for cash.

Mō·hä'vē, *n.* a member of a tribe of Yuman Indians that lived around the Colorado River: also spelled *Mojave*.

Mō·hä'vē, *a.* of the Mohaves: also spelled *Mojave*.

Mō'hąwk, *n.*; *pl.* **Mō'hąwk, Mō'hąwks,** a member of a tribe of Iroquoian Indians that lived in the Mohawk Valley, New York.

Mō'hąwk, *a.* of the Mohawk.

Mō·hē'găn, *n.* 1. a member of a Mahican tribe of Algonquian Indians that lived in Connecticut, along the Thames River.

2. Mahican.

Mō·hē'găn, *a.* of the Mohegans.

Mō·hī'çăn, *n.* and *a.* same as *Mahican*.

Mō'hō, *n.* [Hawaiian.] 1. a genus of arcuate-billed birds of the Sandwich Islands, of which there are two species, *Moho nobilis* and *Moho apicalis*.

2. [m–] a bird of this genus.

Mō'hock, *n.* [var. of *Mohawk*.] any of a gang of elegant rakes and ruffians who committed outrages at night in the streets of London in the eighteenth century.

mō'hōe, *n.* same as *mahoe*.

Mō'hōle, *n.* [named after A. *Moho*rovičić, Yugoslavian geologist, and *hole*.] a proposed hole to be drilled beneath the sea through the earth's crust to the mantle.

mō·hō'li, *n.* same as *maholi*.

mōhr (mōr), *n.* [Ar.] a gazelle of West Africa, *Gazella mohr*, having graceful ringed horns.

Mōhș sçāle, [after Friedrich *Mohs* (1773–1839), G. mineralogist who devised it.] in mineralogy, a scale used to indicate relative hardness, arranged in 10 ascending degrees (1, talc; 2, gypsum; 3, calcite; 4, fluorite; 5, apatite; 6, feldspar; 7, quartz; 8, topaz; 9, sapphire; 10, diamond).

mō'hur, *n.* [Hind. and Per. *muhr*, *mohr*, a seal, a gold coin.] a former gold coin of India, equal to 15 rupees.

Mō·hur'rum, *n.* see *Muharram*.

moi'dēr, *v.t.* and *v.i.* to perplex; to moil; to toil. [Brit. Dial.]

moi'dōre, *n.* [Port. *moeda d'ouro*, lit., money or coin of gold.] a former gold coin of Portugal or Brazil.

moi'e·ty, *n.*; *pl.* **moi'e·tieș,** [ME. and OFr. *moite*; from L. *medietas*, from *medius*, middle.]

1. a half; one of two equal parts; as, a *moiety* of an estate, of goods, or of profits; the *moiety* of a jury or of a nation.

2. an indefinite share or part.

3. in anthropology, either of two primary subdivisions in some tribes.

moil, *v.t.*; moiled, *pt.*, *pp.*; moiling, *ppr.* [OFr. *moiller*, *moiler*, to wet, moisten, from L. *mollire*, to soften, from *mollis*, soft.]

1. to daub; to make dirty, as with moist matter. [Archaic or Dial.]

2. to weary; to fatigue. [Obs.]

moil, *v.i.* [perhaps from the foregoing verb, or from L. *moliri*, to toil, *moles*, a huge heavy mass.] to labor; to toil; to drudge.

moil, *n.* 1. drudgery; hard work.

2. confusion; turmoil.

3. a spot; a defilement.

moil, *n.* in mining, a tool sometimes used by miners instead of a pick, and worked like a crowbar in making accurate cuttings.

moil, *n.* a mule. [Obs.]

moi'neau (-nō), *n.* [Fr.] a small flat bastion raised in front of an intended fortification to defend it against attacks during its construction.

moire (mwär), *n.* [Fr., watered silk, from Eng. *mohair*.] a fabric, especially silk, having a watered, or wavy, pattern.

moi·ré' (mwä-rā'), *a.* [Fr.] having a watered, or wavy, pattern.

moi·ré', *n.* 1. a watered pattern pressed into cloth, etc. with engraved rollers.

2. moire.

moi·ré', *v.t.*; moiréed, *pt.*, *pp.*; moiréeing, *ppr.* to impart a watered or frosted appearance to; as, to *moiré* a textile or a sheet of tin plate.

moist, *a.* [OFr. *moiste*, from L. *mucidus*, moldy, from *mucus*, mucus.]

1. slightly wet; damp; as, a *moist* atmosphere or air.

2. suggestive of the presence of liquid; as, a *moist* sound.

3. fresh; new; lately produced. [Obs.]

moist, *v.t.* to moisten. [Obs.]

mois'ten (mois'n), *v.t.*; moistened, *pt.*, *pp.*; moistening, *ppr.* 1. to make moist.

2. to soften; to make tender; as, to *moisten* one's heart with pity. [Rare.]

mois'ten, *v.i.* to become moist.

mois'ten·ēr, *n.* one who or that which moistens.

moist'fụl, *a.* full of moisture. [Rare.]

moist'less, *a.* having no moisture. [Rare.]

moist'ness, *n.* dampness; a small degree of wetness; the state or quality of being moist.

mois'tūre, *n.* [OFr. *moisteur*, from *moiste*, moist.]

1. moistness. [Obs.]

2. water or other liquid causing a slight wetness or dampness.

mois'tūre·less, *a.* without moisture.

moist'y, *a.* drizzling; moist.

moi'thēr, *v.t.* and *v.i.* see *moider*.

Mō·jä'vē (-hä'vi), *n.* and *a.* same as *Mohave*.

mok'ȧ·dōr, *n.* moccador. [Obs.]

mōke, *n.* 1. a donkey. [Slang.]

2. a dull, stupid person. [Slang.]

mōke, *n.* a mesh, as of a net or of wickerwork; also, network; wickerwork. [Brit. Dial.]

mō′kĭ, *n.* [New Zealand.] a food fish, *Latris ciliaris*, of New Zealand.

Mō′kĭ, *n.* a Hopi Indian: also spelled *Moqui*.

mō′ky, *a.* muggy; dark; murky. [Dial.]

mōl, *n.* [G., from *molekül*, molecule.] in chemistry, a gram molecule; molecular weight (of a substance) in grams: also *mole*.

Mō′lȧ, *n.* [L., millstone.] the typical genus of fishes of the family *Molidæ*.

mō′lăl, *a.* in chemistry, relating to the mol or gram-molecular weight; specifically, designating a solution with a concentration equal to one mol of the solute in 1,000 grams of the solvent.

mō′lăr, *a.* [L. *molaris*, a mill, from *mola*, millstone.]

1. used for or capable of grinding.
2. designating or of a tooth or teeth adapted for grinding.

mō′lăr, *n.* a molar tooth: in man there are twelve molars, three on each side of each jaw, behind the bicuspids.

mō′lăr, *a.* [from L. *moles*, mass; and *-ar*.]

1. in chemistry, molal; specifically, designating a solution containing one mol of solute per liter of solvent.
2. in physics, of a body (of matter) as a whole: opposed to *molecular, atomic*.

mō′lȧ·ry, *a.* fitted for grinding or crushing food; molar.

Mō·lȧsse′, *n.* [Fr., from *mol*, soft; L. *mollis*, soft.] a formation of soft Tertiary sandstone occurring in Switzerland.

mō·lȧs′seṣ, *n.*; *pl.* **mō·lȧs′seṣ,** [from Port. *melaço*, from LL. *mellaceum*, must, from L. *mellaceus*, resembling honey, from *mel, mellis*, honey.] any of various thick, dark-colored sirups, especially that produced during the refining of sugar.

mōld, mōuld, *n.* [ME. *mold, moolde*; OFr. *molle, moule*; from L. *modulus*, a measure.]

1. a pattern, hollow form, or matrix for giving a certain shape or form to something in a plastic or molten state.
2. a frame, shaped core, etc. on or around which something is modeled.
3. a pattern after which something is formed; a model.
4. something formed or shaped in or on, or as if in or on, a mold.
5. (a) the form or shape given by a mold; (b) form or shape in general.
6. distinctive character or nature.
7. in shipbuilding, a thin, flexible piece of timber, used as a pattern by which to form the curves of the timbers and compassing pieces.
8. among goldbeaters, a number of pieces of vellum, or a like substance, laid over one another, between which the leaves of gold and silver are laid for beating.
9. in architecture, (a) a molding; (b) a group of moldings.
10. in making paper by hand, a kind of sieve for catching the pulp that forms a sheet.

mōld, mōuld, *v.t.*; molded *or* moulded, *pt., pp.*; molding *or* moulding, *ppr.* 1. to make or shape in or on, or as if in or on a mold.

2. to work into a certain form or shape; to shape.
3. to ornament by or with molding.
4. in founding, to make a mold of or from in order to make a casting.

mōld, mōuld, *n.* [ME. *moul, mowlde*, mold, mildew; sp. prob. influenced by *molde*, earth.]

1. a downy or furry growth on the surface of organic matter, caused by fungi, especially in the presence of dampness or decay.
2. any fungus producing such a growth.

mōld, mōuld, *v.t.* to cause to become moldy; as, dampness will *mold* organic substances at an ordinary temperature.

mōld, mōuld, *v.i.* to contract mold; to become moldy; to be covered or filled, wholly or partially, with mold; as, canned goods are liable to *mold*.

mōld, mōuld, *n.* [AS. *molde*, dust, ground, earth.]

1. fine soft earth, or earth easily pulverized, such as contains a large proportion of decayed and decaying organic matter; as, rich black *mold* is used in propagating plants.
2. matter of which anything is formed; composing material.

> Nature formed me of her softest *mold*. —Addison.

3. earth. [Archaic or Poet.]

mōld, mōuld, *v.t.* to cover with mold or soil; to bury.

mōld′ȧ·ble, mōuld′ȧ·ble, *a.* capable of being molded or formed.

mōld′bōard, mōuld′bōard, *n.* 1. the curved iron plate of a plow which receives the soil cut loose, and turns it over.

2. in founding, the board on which the pattern is laid for ramming: also called *follow board*.

mōld′ẽr, mōuld′ẽr, *n.* 1. one who or that which molds; specifically, in founding, one whose business it is to make molds for castings.

2. in printing, one of a set of eletrotyped plates used for making duplicate electrotypes.

mōld′ẽr, mōuld′ẽr, *v.i.*; moldered *or* mouldered, *pt., pp.*; moldering *or* mouldering, *ppr.* [from *mold*, fine earth.] to turn to dust by natural decay; to crumble; to waste away (often with *away*).

mōld′ẽr, mōuld′ẽr, *v.t.* to cause to turn to dust; to reduce to mold or soil; to cause to waste away.

> Some felt the silent stroke of *moldering* age. —Pope.

mōld′ẽr·y, mōuld′ẽr·y, *a.* having the characteristics of mold; resembling mold.

mōld fāc′ing, a layer of fine powder sprinkled over the surface of a mold to insure smoothness in the casting; a facing of pulverized charcoal, graphite, chalk, rottenstone, or the like.

mōld′i·ness, mōuld′i·ness, *n.* [from *moldy*.] the state or quality of being moldy.

mōld′ing, mōuld′ing, *n.* 1. the act or proccess of making molds or of shaping anything in or with a mold.

2. something molded.
3. (a) any of various ornamental contours given to cornices, jambs, etc.; (b) a cornice or other shaped member of wood, stone, etc., either sunk or projecting, used for ornament on a surface or angle of a structure.

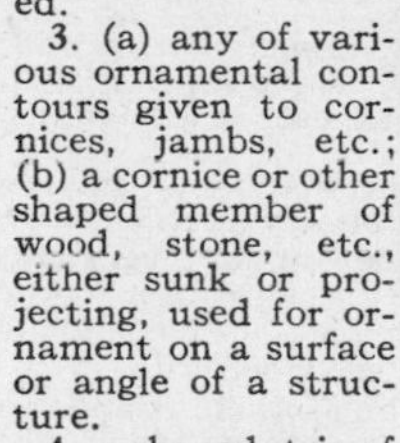

MOLDINGS
A, cyma recta; B, ovolo; C, quarter round; D, cyma reversa; E, cavetto; F, congé

4. a shaped strip of wood, etc., as around the upper part of the walls of a room, used for ornament or as a support from which to hang pictures.

mōld′ing bōard, a board on which dough is kneaded, rolled, cut, etc.

mōld′ing mȧ·chīne′, 1. in woodworking, a machine for making moldings by means of a rapidly rotating cutter provided with a bit or bits of any desired pattern.

2. in founding, a machine for making molds.

mōld′ing plāne, a plane having a bit shaped for the purpose of making moldings: also called a *match plane*.

mōld lọft, a loft or large room in which the various parts of a ship's hull are accurately constructed from the model.

mōld′wạrp, *n.* a mole; a small animal of the genus *Talpa*. [Brit. Dial.]

mōld′y, mōuld′y *a.*; *comp.* moldier; *superl.* moldiest, 1. overgrown with mold; covered with mold; as, *moldy* bread; *moldy* cheese.

2. musty or stale, as from age or decay.

mōle, *n.* [ME. and AS. *mol.*] 1. a spot, mark, or small permanent protuberance on the human body, sometimes of a dark color and hairy; especially, a pigmentary nevus.

2. a spot or stain. [Obs.]

mōle, *n.* [L. *mola*, a false conception.] a fleshy mass or swelling in the uterus, formed by a degenerated or maldeveloped ovum.

mōle, *n.* same as *mol*.

mōle, *n.* [Fr., from L. *moles*, a huge mass, a dam, a mole, a monument.]

1. a mound or massive work formed of large stones, etc. laid in the sea, extended either in a right line or an arc of a circle before a harbor which it serves to protect from the force of the waves; also, the harbor itself.
2. among the Romans, a kind of mausoleum, built like a round tower on a square base, insulated, encompassed with columns, and covered with a dome. [Rare.]

mōle, *n.* [ME. *molle*; akin to or from M.D. *mol.*]

1. a small, burrowing, insectivorous mammal of the family *Talpidæ*, characterized by a sharp snout, very small eyes, a covering of fine fur, and short, strong fore limbs with broad, fossorial feet, by means of which it burrows just beneath the surface of the ground, raising the soil into a ridge by which its movements may be traced.
2. a plow for making drains under the ground.

mōle, *v.t.*; moled (mōld), *pt., pp.*; moling, *ppr.*

1. to clear of molehills. [Brit. Dial.]
2. to burrow after the manner of a mole.

mōle′but, *n.* a short, lumplike sunfish, the *Mola rotunda*.

mōle′ċȧst, *n.* a little elevation of earth made by a mole; a molehill.

Mō′leçh, *n.* same as *moloch* (senses 1 and 2).

mōle çrick′et, an insect of the genus *Gryllotalpa*, which burrows underground and damages plants by cutting the roots. *Gryllotalpa vulgaris* is the common species of Europe, and *Gryllotalpa borealis* that of America.

MOLE CRICKET
(*Gryllotalpa vulgaris*)

mō·leç′ū·lăr, *a.* belonging to, relating to, caused by, or consisting of molecules; as, *molecular* weight, *molecular* changes.

molecular film; a film or layer (of a substance) one molecule thick: also called *monolayer*.

molecular weight; the relative average weight of a molecule of a substance, expressed by a number in a scale on which the weight of the oxygen atom is represented by 16.

mō·leç·ū·lar′i·ty, *n.* the quality of being molecular; the state of consisting of molecules.

mō·leç′ū·lăr·ly, *adv.* with respect to molecules.

mol′ē·çūle, *n.* [Fr. *molécule*; Mod. L. *molecula*, dim. from L. *moles*, a mass.]

1. the smallest particle of an element or compound that can exist in the free state and still retain the characteristics of the element or compound: the molecules of elements consist of one atom or two or more similar atoms; those of compounds consist of two or more different atoms.
2. a gram molecule.
3. a small particle.

mōle′-eyed (-īd), *a.* having very small eyes, as a mole; having defective sight.

mōle′hill, *n.* a little ridge or elevation of earth, formed by a burrowing mole; hence, proverbially, a very small hill or a trivial difficulty or impediment.

> Having leaped over such mountains, lie down before a *molehill*. —South.

mōle rat, any species of old-world rodents belonging to the genera *Spalax, Georychus*, and others, having small or rudimentary eyes and forefeet with which to burrow.

mōle shrew (shrü), a short-tailed shrew of America, of which there are several species belonging to the genus *Blarina*.

mōle′skin, *n.* 1. the soft, dark-gray skin of the mole, used as fur.

2. a strong, twilled cotton fabric with a soft nap, used for work clothes, etc.
3. [*pl.*] trousers made of this fabric.

mō·lest′, *v.t.*; molested, *pt., pp.*; molesting, *ppr.* [ME. *molesten*; OFr. *molester*, from L. *molestare*, to trouble, annoy, from *molestus*, troublesome, from *moles*, trouble, labor, distress.] to annoy, interfere with, or meddle with so as to trouble or harm, or with intent to trouble or harm.

Syn.—disturb, confuse, trouble, annoy, worry, bother.

mō·lest′, *n.* trouble; molestation. [Obs.]

mō·les·tā′tion (*or* mol-es-), *n.* a molesting or being molested.

mō·lest′ẽr, *n.* one who molests.

mō·lest′fụl, *a.* troublesome; annoying. [Rare.]

mō·les·tī′e, *n.* trouble; molestation. [Obs.]

mōle′wạrp, *n.* same as *moldwarp*.

Mol′i·dae, *n.pl.* [LL. *mola*, and *-idæ*.] a family of gymnodont fishes; the sunfishes.

mō·lim′i·nous, *a.* very important; of considerable consequence. [Obs.]

mō′line, *n.* [LL. *molinus*, pertaining to a mill, from *mola*, a mill.] same as *moline cross.*

moline cross; in heraldry, a cross resembling a mill rynd in form. Each of its arms branches off at the extremity into two curved sections.

MOLINE CROSS

Mō·lin′i·ȧ, *n.* [named after J. *Molina*, a writer on Chilean plants.] a European genus of grasses of the tribe *Festuceæ*, containing a single species.

Mō′lin·iṣm, *n.* the doctrines of the Molinists, somewhat resembling the tenets of the Arminians.

Mō′lin·ist, *n.* a follower of the doctrines of Molina, a Spanish Jesuit of the sixteenth century.

mōll, *a.* [L. *molle*, neut. of *mollis*, soft.] in music, flat; as, G *moll*; that is, G flat.

moll, *n.* 1. the mistress of a gangster, thief, or vagrant. [Slang.]

2. a prostitute. [Slang.]

mol′lȧ, mol′lȧh, *n.* same as *mullah.*

mol′le·mōke, *n.* [Sw. *mallemucke*, the storm petrel.] same as *mallemuck.*

mŏl·les′cence, *n.* a softening or tending to soften.

mŏl·les′cent, *a.* [L. *mollescens*, ppr. of *mollescere*, to soften, from *mollere*, to be soft, from *mollis*, soft.] softening or tending to soften.

mol′li·ent, *a.* [L. *molliens* (*-entis*), ppr. of *mollire*, to soften, from *mollis*, soft.] softening; assuaging; lessening; emollient.

mol′li·ent·ly, *adv.* assuagingly.

mol′li·fī·ȧ·ble, *a.* capable of being softened or assuaged.

mol″li·fi·cā′tion, *n.* a mollifying or being mollified.

mol′li·fī·ẽr, *n.* one who or that which mollifies.

mol′li·fȳ, *v.t.*; mollified, *pt.*, *pp.*; mollifying, *ppr.* [Fr. *mollifier*; LL. *mollificare*, to soften; L. *mollis*, soft, and *facere*, to make.]

1. to soften; to make less intense, severe, or violent; to reduce in harshness or asperity.

2. to soothe; to appease; to pacify; to calm or quiet.

Syn.—assuage, mitigate, ameliorate, moderate, soften.

mol·li·pī′lōse, *a.* [L. *mollis*, soft, and *pilus*, a hair.] in zoology, having a soft or fluffy coat of hair or feathers; downy; fleecy.

mŏl·li′ti·ēṣ (-lish′i-), *n.* [L., softness, from *mollis*, soft.] in pathology, softening; unnatural softening, as of an organ, gland, or tissue; as, *mollities* ossium, softening of the bones.

mol′li·tūde, *n.* softness; weakness. [Rare.]

mol′lusç, *n.* see *mollusk.*

Mŏl·lus′çȧ, *n.pl.* [L. *molluscus*, soft, from *mollis*, soft.] a large phylum of invertebrates comprising the oysters, clams, mussels, snails, slugs, squids, octopi, whelks, etc., characterized by a soft, unsegmented body enclosed, in most instances, partly or wholly in a calcareous shell of one or more pieces, and having gills, a foot, and a mantle.

mŏl·lus′căn, *n.* a mollusk; one of the *Mollusca.*

mŏl·lus′căn, *a.* pertaining to the *Mollusca.*

mŏl·lus′çoid, *a.* [*Mollusca*, and Gr. *eidos*, form.]

1. of or pertaining to the *Molluscoidea.*

2. resembling a mollusk.

mŏl·lus′çoid, *n.* one of the *Molluscoidea.*

Mol·lus·çoi′dȧ, *n.pl.* same as *Molluscoidea.*

mol·lus·çoid′ăl, *a.* molluscoid.

mol·lus·çoid′ăn, *a.* molluscoid.

Mol·lus·çoi′dē·ȧ, *n.pl.* [*Mollusca*, and Gr. *eidos*, form.] a division of animals comprising the *Bryozoa* and *Brachiopoda*, known as anthoid *Mollusca.*

mŏl·lus′çous, *a.* molluscan.

mŏl·lus′çum, *n.* [neut. of L. *molluscus*, soft.] in medicine, any of various skin diseases, as *molluscum contagiosum*, a disease marked by the formation of firm, rounded skin tubercles containing a semifluid caseous matter or solid masses made up of fat, epidermis, and peculiar capsulate bodies, usually appearing on the face.

mol′lusk, *n.* one of the *Mollusca*: also written *mollusc.*

mol′ly·cod″dle, *n.* [from *Molly*, dim. of Mary, and *coddle.*] a man or boy used to being coddled or pampered; a milksop.

mol′ly·çod″dle, *v.t.*; mollycoddled, *pt.*, *pp.*; mollycoddling, *ppr.* to pamper; to coddle.

Mol′ly Mȧ·guireṣ′ (mȧ-gwīrz′), [so called because members were sometimes disguised as women.] 1. a secret society organized in Ireland in 1843 to prevent evictions by terrorizing agents of landlords.

2. a former secret society of Irish-American miners in eastern Pennsylvania (c. 1865–1875), which opposed oppressive industrial and social conditions, sometimes with physical force.

Mō′loçh, *n.* [LL., from Gr. *Moloch*, *Molōch*, from Heb. *mōlekh.*]

1. in the Bible, a god of the ancient Phoenicians and Ammonites, to whom children were sacrificed by burning.

2. anything regarded as demanding terrible sacrifice.

3. [m-] a spiny Australian lizard, *Moloch horridus.*

mō′loid, *a.* [*Mola*, and Gr. *eidos*, form.] in zoology, pertaining to or characteristic of the *Molidæ.*

mō′loid, *n.* a sunfish.

mō·lom′pi, *n.* [native name.] the African rosewood.

mō·losse′, *n.* see *molossus.*

Mō·los′si·dae, *n.pl.* a family of bats: called *bulldog bats* from their short, stout legs and strong incisors.

mō·los′sīne, *n.* [*moluss*us and *-ine.*] a bulldog bat.

mō·los′sīne, *a.* pertaining to the *Molossidæ.*

mō·los′sus, *n.* [L., from Gr. *molossos.*] in Greek and Latin verse, a foot of three long syllables: also written *mollosse.*

Mol′ō·tọv (-tọf) **cock′tāil,** [after V.M. *Molotov* (1890–), Soviet statesman.] a bottle filled with gasoline, etc. and wrapped in a saturated rag, ignited and hurled as an antitank grenade, as by Soviet forces in World War II.

mōlt, *v.* obsolete past tense of *melt.*

mōlt, mōult, *v.i.*; molted *or* moulted, *pt.*, *pp.*; molting *or* moulting, *ppr.* [ME. *mouten*, from L. *mutare*, to change.] to shed or cast off the hair, feathers, skin, horns, etc. at certain intervals, prior to the replacement of the castoff parts by a new growth: said of certain animals, as reptiles, birds, etc.

mōlt, *v.t.* to shed and replace by molting.

mōlt, *n.* 1. the act or process of molting.

2. the parts so shed.

mōl′ten, *a.* [archaic pp. of *melt.*] 1. melted; rendered liquid by heat; as, *molten* iron.

2. made of melted metal cast in a mold; as, a *molten* image.

mōl′ten·ly, *adv.* after the manner of molten material; liquidly; as, *moltenly* ductile.

mōl′tō, *adv.* [It.] in music, much; very; as, *molto* allegro, very lively: a direction to the performer.

Mō·luç′çȧ bälm (bäm), see *moluccella.*

Mol·uç·cel′lȧ, *n.* [from the *Molucca* Islands.] a small genus of labiate plants native in the Mediterranean region, one of its two species, *Moluccella lævis*, being known as *Molucca balm*, because formerly believed to be a native of the Molucca Islands.

mō′ly, *n.* [L., from Gr. *mōly*, a fabulous herb.]

1. a mythical herb of magic powers, having black roots and white flowers, mentioned by Homer in the Odyssey as the gift of Hermes to Ulysses to shield the latter from the wiles of Circe.

2. a plant, *Allium moly*, sometimes cultivated in gardens for its large yellow flowers: also called *golden garlic.*

dwarf moly; a species of garlic, *Allium chamæmoly.*

mō·lyb′dāte, *n.* [*molybd*ic and *-ate.*] a salt of molybdic acid.

mol·yb·dē′nȧ, *n.* molybdenum. [Obs.]

mō·lyb·dē·nif′ẽr·ous, *a.* [*molybdenum*, and L. *ferre*, to bear.] having molybdenum as a component.

mō·lyb′dē·nīte, *n.* native molybdenum sulfide, MoS_2, a scaly or foliated, lead-gray mineral, the chief ore of molybdenum.

mō·lyb′dē·nous, *a.* same as *molybdous.*

mō·lyb′dē·num, *n.* [L. *molybdæna*, from Gr. *molybdaina*, galena, from *molybdos*, lead.] a lustrous, brittle, silver-white metallic chemical element, used in alloys, windings for electrical resistance furnaces, points for spark plugs, etc.: symbol, Mo; atomic weight, 95.95; atomic number, 42.

mō·lyb′diç, *a.* [*molybd*enum and *-ic.*] designating or of chemical compounds in which molybdenum has a higher valence than in the corresponding molybdous compounds.

mō·lyb′dīte, mō·lyb′din, *n.* [*molybd*enum and *-ite*, *-in.*] a yellowish trioxide of molybdenum, MoO_3: also called *molybdic ocher.*

molybdo-, [from Gr. *molybdos*, lead.] a combining form meaning *lead*, as in *molybdo*colic, *molybdo*paresis.

mō·lyb·dō·çol′iç, *n.* [*molybdo-*, and Gr. *kōlikē*, colic.] in pathology, a form of colic arising from lead poisoning; painter's colic.

mol·yb·don′ō·sus, mol·yb·dō′sis, *n.* [*molybdo-*, and Gr. *nosos*, disease.] lead poisoning.

mō·lyb·dō·par′ē·sis, *n.* [*molybdo-*, and Gr. *paresis*, palsy.] lead palsy: also called *painter's paralysis.*

mō·lyb′dous, *a.* designating or of chemical compounds in which molybdenum has a lower valence than in the corresponding molybdic compounds.

mol′y·sīte, *n.* [Gr. *molynsis*, a staining, from *molynein*, to stain, and *-ite.*] in mineralogy, a red or yellow ferric chloride, found as a thin incrustation on hardened lava.

mom, *n.* mother. [Colloq.]

mōme, *n.* [OFr. *mome*, *momme*, a masque.] a stupid fellow; a fool. [Archaic.]

mōme, *n.* [from L. *Momus.*] a captious critic. [Obs.]

mō′ment, *n.* [L. *momentum*, movement, impulse, brief space of time, importance, contr. from *movimentum*, from *movere*, to move.]

1. an indefinitely brief period of time; an instant.

2. a definite point in time or in a series of events.

3. importance; consequence; as, business of great *moment.*

4. in mechanics, (a) the tendency to cause rotation about a point or axis; (b) a measure of this tendency; (c) the product of a (specified) force, mass, volume, etc. and its perpendicular distance from its axis, fulcrum, or plane.

5. in philosophy, any of the constituent elements of a complex entity; momentum.

magnetic moment; see under *magnetic.*

moment axis of a couple; a line which in length represents the moment and direction of a couple.

moment of a couple; the moment obtained by multiplying either one of the forces of a couple by the distance between them.

moment of a force; (a) with respect to a point, the product of the force into the distance of its point from its line of action; (b) with respect to a line, the product of the perpendicular to the line (found by resolving the force into two components, one parallel and the other perpendicular to the line) into its distance from the line.

moment of inertia; of a body with respect to an axis, the summation of the products of every particle in the body times the square of the particle's distance from the axis.

moment of stability; in a body supported at a given plane joint, the moment of a couple of forces, applied in a given vertical plane to that body with its own weight added, that will transfer the center of resistance of the plane joint to the limiting position consistent with stability.

moment of truth; (a) the point in a bullfight when the matador faces the bull for the kill; (b) a critical moment or time that tests or reveals one's true self or makes one face the truth.

statical moment; the moment of equilibrium between opposite forces, as in a lever or arm balance.

the moment; the present or the immediate future.

virtual moment of a force; the product of the intensity of the force multiplied by the virtual velocity of its point of application.

mō·men′tăl, *a.* 1. lasting but a moment.

2. in mechanics, pertaining to momentum.

mō·men′tăl·ly, *adv.* for a moment. [Obs.]

mō·men·tā′nē·ous, mō′men·tā·ny, *a.* momentary. [Obs.]

mō′men·tãr·i·ly, *adv.* 1. for a short time.

2. in an instant.

3. from moment to moment.

mō′men·tãr·i·ness, *n.* the quality of being momentary.

mō′men·tãr·y, *a.* [LL. *momentarius*, from L. *momentum*, moment.]

1. continuing only a moment; lasting a very short time; as, a *momentary* pang.

2. taking place every moment. [Now Rare.]

3. likely to occur at any moment.

mō′ment·ly, *adv.* 1. from instant to instant; every moment.

2. instantly.

3. for a single instant.

mō·men′tous, *a.* [LL. *momentosus*, of a moment, from L. *momentum*, moment.] very important; weighty; of great consequence.

mō·men′tous·ly, *adv.* weightily; importantly.

mō·men′tous·ness, *n.* the state of being of great importance.

mō·men′tum, *n.*; *pl.* **mō·men′tums, mō·men′tȧ,** [L., movement, motion, change, alteration, brief space.]
1. the impetus of a moving object.
2. in mechanics, the quantity of motion of a moving object, equal to the product of its mass and its velocity.
3. a moment (sense 5).

mŏm′ish, *a.* foolish or stupid. [Obs.]

mom′my, *n.*; *pl.* **mom′mies,** mother: a child's term. [Colloq.]

Mō·mor′di·cȧ, *n.* [from L. *mordere*, to bite: so called from the seeds, which have the appearance of being bitten.] a genus of tropical climbing herbaceous plants of the family *Cucurbitaceæ*, embracing about twenty-five species, mostly of Africa, but also found in tropical Asia and in Australia.

mō′mot, *n.* same as *motmot*.

Mō·mot′i·dae, *n.pl.* [*momotus* and *-idæ*.] the motmots, a picarian family of tropical birds.

Mō·mō′tus, *n.* [from *momot* or *motmot*, so called from the bird's note.] the typical genus of the *Momotidæ*.

Mō′mus, *n.* [Gr. *mōmos*, blame, ridicule.]
1. in Greek mythology, the deity of ridicule and raillery.
2. a faultfinder.

mon, *n.* man. [Scot. and Brit. Dial.]

mon, *n.* [Japan.] in Japan, any of various family or personal crests or cognizances.

Mŏn, *n.* one of the Mon-Khmer languages.

mon-, see *mono-*.

mon·ȧ·çan′thid, *a.* [Gr. *monakanthos*, with one spine, and *-id*.] having a single row of ambulacral spines, as a starfish.

mon·ȧ·çan′thine, mon·ȧ·çan′thous, *a.* [Gr. *monakanthos*, with a single spine, and *-ine*, *-ous*.] having a single spine instead of an anterior dorsal fin, as fishes of the genus *Monacanthus*.

mon′ȧ·chăl, *a.* [L. *monachus*; Gr. *monachos*, a monk, from *monos*, alone.] pertaining to monks or a monastic life; monastic.

mon′ȧ·chism, *n.* [Fr. *monachisme*, from L. *monachus*, a monk.] monasticism; a monastic system, state, or way of life.

mon·ac′id, *a.* and *n.* same as *monoacid*.

mon·açt′, *a.* same as *monactinal*.

mon·açt′, *n.* a sponge spicule, having the shape of a rod.

mō·naç′ti·năl, mō·naç′tine, *a.* [*mon-*, and Gr. *aktis* (*-inos*), a ray.] having a single rodlike ray, as a sponge spicule.

mon′ad (*or* mō′nad), *n.* [Gr. *monas*, a unit, unity, from *monos*, alone.]
1. a unit; something simple and indivisible.
2. in biology, any simple, single-celled organism; specifically, a type of single-celled, flagellate, ameboid organism.
3. in chemistry, an atom, element, or radical with a valence of one.
4. in philosophy, an entity or elementary being thought of as a microcosm or ultimate unit.

mon′ad dēme, [*monad*, and Gr. *dēmos*, the people.] in biology, a colony of undifferentiated monads.

mon′ȧ·delph, *n.* [*mon-*, and Gr. *adelphos*, brother.] in botany, a plant with stamens united by their filaments into one set.

Mon·ȧ·del′phi·ȧ, *n.pl.* [*mon-*, and Gr. *adelphos*, brother.] a class of plants whose stamens are united into one set by their filaments, as in the mallow family.

mon·ȧ·del′phous, mon·ȧ·del′phi·ăn, *a.*
1. having the stamens united in one set or bundle by their filaments, as some plants.
2. united in this way: said of stamens.

mō·nad′iç, mō·nad′iç·ăl, *a.* [Gr. *monadikos*, from *monas* (*-ados*), a unit, unity.] having the nature or character of a monad.

mō·nad′i·form, *a.* [LL. *monas* (*-adis*), a unit, and L. *forma*, form.] in biology, having the form of a monad.

mon·ȧ·diġ′ẽr·ous, *a.* [LL. *monas* (*-adis*), a unit, and L. *gerere*, to bear.] bearing cells shaped like a monad, as in the cells lining the walls of a sponge.

mon′ȧ·dine, *a.* having the characteristics of a monad; also, relating to the flagellate infusorians as a family.

mon′ad·ism, *n.* in philosophy, the theory that the universe consists of monads.

mō·nad′nock, *n.* [from Mt. *Monadnock*, New Hampshire.] in geology, a single remnant of a former highland, which rises as an isolated rock mass above a plain.

mon·ad·ol′ō·ġy, *n.* [Gr. *monas* (*-ados*), a unit, unity, and *-logia*, from *legein*, to speak.] monadism or any similar theory.

mō·nal′, *n.* same as *monaul*.

Mō′nȧ Lï′sȧ, a famous portrait of a faintly smiling woman, by Leonardo da Vinci: also called *La Gioconda*.

mō′nȧ mŏn′key, a West African monkey of the genus *Cercopithecus*: it is characterized by a black band from eye to ear and a pair of white spots near the tail.

mō·nan′dẽr, *n.* [*mon-*, and Gr. *anēr*, *andros*, man, male.] any of the *Monandria*; a single-stamened flower.

MONANDER

Mō·nan′dri·ȧ, *n.pl.* [*mon-*, and Gr. *anēr*, *andros*, man, male.] a class of plants in the Linnean system having one stamen only.

mō·nan′dri·ăn, *a.* monandrous.

mō·nan′drous, *a.*
1. having only one husband at a time.
2. of or characterized by monandry.
3. in botany, (a) having only one stamen, as some flowers; (b) having monandrous flowers, as some plants.

mō·nan′dry, *n.* [Gr. *monandria*, the fact of having one husband; *monos*, single, and *anēr*, *andros*, man.] the state or the practice of having only one husband at a time: distinguished from *polyandry*.

mō·nan′thous, *a.* [*mon-*, and Gr. *anthos*, flower.] single-flowered; bearing only one flower: said of a plant, as the tulip.

mon′ärch, *n.* [L. *monarcha*, from Gr. *monarchēs*, a monarch, from *monarchos*, ruling alone; *monos*, alone, and *archein*, to rule.]
1. the single or sole ruler of a state.
2. the hereditary (often constitutional) head of a state; a king or emperor.
3. a person or thing that surpasses others of the same kind.
4. a species of large, migrating butterfly of North America, having reddish-brown, black-edged wings: the larvae feed on milkweed.

mō·när′chăl, *a.* pertaining to, like, suitable for, or characteristic of a monarch; sovereign; regal; imperial.

> Satan, whom now transcendent glory raised
> Above his fellows, with *monarchal* pride.
> —Milton.

mon′ärch·ess, *n.* a woman monarch. [Rare.]

mō·när′chi·ăl, *a.* same as *monarchal*.

mō·när′chi·ăn, *n.* an adherent of monarchianism.

mō·när′chi·ăn·ism, *n.* the doctrine held by several sects of the Christian Church in the second and third centuries that the Three Persons of the Trinity are manifestations of one God, single in person: opposed to *Trinitarianism*.

mō·när′chiç, *a.* same as *monarchical*.

mō·när′chiç·ăl, *a.*
1. pertaining to monarchy; resembling monarchy in character.
2. pertaining to the theory of government by a monarch.
3. adhering to or favoring a monarchy.

> It is not impossible that the political movements of our time, which seem on the surface to have a tendency to democracy, may have in reality a *monarchical* bias.
> —Disraeli.

mō·när′chiç·ăl·ly, *adv.* in the manner of a monarch; royally.

mon′ärch·ism, *n.* the principles of monarchy; also, advocacy of such principles.

mon′ärch·ist, *n.* an advocate of or supporter of the practices of monarchy.

mon′ärch·ist, *a.* monarchistic.

mō·närch·ist′iç, *a.* of monarchism or monarchists.

mon′ärch·īze, *v.i.*; monarchized, *pt.*, *pp.*; monarchizing, *ppr.* to play the king; to act the monarch.

mon′ärch·īze, *v.t.* to rule over as a monarch. [Obs.]

> As Britain-founding Brute first *monarchized* the land.
> —Drayton.

mon′ärch·i·zẽr, *n.* one who monarchizes; an advocate of monarchical rule; a monarchist.

Mō·när′chō, *n.* a nickname or epithet applied to a certain Italian, later judged insane, who believed himself to be an emperor. [Obs.]

mon′ärch·y, *n.*; *pl.* **mon′ärch·ies,** [Gr. *monarchia*, absolute rule, monarchy, from *monarchos*, a monarch.]
1. rule by only one person. [Rare.]
2. a government or state headed by a king, queen, or emperor: called *absolute* (or *despotic*) when there is no limitation on the monarch's power, *constitutional* (or *limited*) when there is such limitation.

Mō·när′dȧ, *n.* [after N. *Monardes*, 16th-c. Spanish physician and botanist.] a genus of plants of the mint family, including horsemint, wild bergamot, and bee balm, characterized by toothed leaves and large, showy, fragrant flowers.

mō·när′dȧ, *n.* any plant belonging to the genus *Monarda*.

mon·är·tiç′ū·lăr, *a.* [*mon-*, and L. *articulus*, a joint.] in medicine, of or pertaining to a single articulation or joint.

Mon′ăs, *n.* [LL. *monas*, a unit, unity.] a genus of flagellate infusorians.

mon′ăs, *n.*; *pl.* **mon′ȧ·dēs,** [LL.] a monad.

mon·ăs·tē′ri·ăl, *a.* pertaining to a monastery or monastic life; monastic.

mon·ăs·tē′ri·ăl·ly, *adv.* monastically.

mon′ăs·ter·y, *n.*; *pl.* **mon′ăs·ter·ies,** [LL. *monasterium*, from Gr. *monastērion*, from *monastēr*, a solitary, *monazein*, to be alone, from *monos*, alone, sole, single.]
1. a place of residence occupied by a group of people, especially monks, who have retired from the world under religious vows.
2. those living in such a place.

mō·nas′tiç, mō·nas′tiç·ăl, *a.* [Fr. *monastique*; LL. *monasticus*; Gr. *monastikos*, from *monos*, sole, separate.]
1. pertaining to life in a monastery; of or characteristic of monks or nuns; ascetic; as, a *monastic* life.
2. pertaining to or characteristic of monasteries.

mō·nas′tiç, *n.* one devoted to life in a monastery; a monk.

mō·nas′tiç·ăl·ly, *adv.* in a monastic manner; in the manner of monks or nuns.

mō·nas′ti·cism, *n.* monastic life; the monastic system or condition.

mon·ȧ·tom′iç, *a.* [*mon-*, and Gr. *atomos*, an atom.]
1. (a) consisting of one atom: said of a molecule; (b) having one atom in the molecule.
2. having one free valence: said of an atom or atomic group.
3. having a valence of one; monad.

mō·naul′, *n.* [Hind.] a pheasant; specifically, the impeyan or crested pheasant of India, *Lophophorus impeyanus*.

mō·nau′los, *n.*; *pl.* **mō·nau′lī,** [L. *monaulus*, from Gr. *monaulos*, a single flute; *monos*, single, and *aulos*, pipe, flute.] a Greek single-pipe musical instrument made of a reed, somewhat resembling a flageolet.

mon·au′răl, *a.* [*mon-*, and L. *auris*, ear.] relating to or having the use of only one ear.

mon·ax′i·ăl, *a.* [*mon-*, and L. *axis*, axis.]
1. having a single axis; uniaxial.
2. developing flowers on the primary axis or along a single axis.

mon·ax′on, *n.* a monaxial sponge spicule.

mon·ax·ō′ni·ăl, *a.* same as *monaxial*.

mon′ȧ·zīte, *n.* [from Gr. *monazein*, to be alone, and *-ite*.] a native phosphate of the cerium metals, of a resinous luster, and brown or brownish-red color, occurring in small isolated crystals.

Mŏn′dāy (-di), *n.* [AS. *monandæg*, moon's day; *monan*, genit. of *mona*, the moon, and *dæg*, day.] the second day of the week.
Black Monday; see under *black*.
blue Monday; see under *blue*.
Easter Monday; the day after Easter.

mōṅde, *n.* [Fr., from L. *mundus*, the world.]
1. a globe used as a symbol of royalty; a mound.
2. the world; people; especially, the world of fashionable society.

mōṅ Dieu′ (dyẽ′), [Fr.] my God: often used as an interjection.

mōne, *n.* the moon. [Obs.]

mōne, *n.* a moan; a lament. [Obs.]

mō·nē′ciăn, *a.* and *n.* same as *monoecian*.

mō·nē′cious, *a.* same as *monoecious*.

Mō·nel′ met′ăl, [after Ambrose *Monell* (d. 1921), Am. manufacturer.] an alloy of nickel, copper, iron, manganese, silicon, and carbon, very resistant to corrosion: used for screens, cooking ware, acid-resisting equipment, etc.: a trade-mark: also spelled *Monell*.

mon·em′bry·ār·y, *a.* with a single embryo.

mon″em·bry·on′iç, *a.* monembryary.

mon·em′bry·ō·ny, *n.* [*mon-*, and Gr. *embryon*, an embryo.] the condition of having a single embryo, as in an ovum or an ovule.

mō′nẽr, *n.* a nonnucleated protoplasmic body without any definite structure.

Mō·nē′rȧ, *n.pl.* [Gr. *monērēs*, single, and *ara-*

riskein, to join, fit.] a class of protozoans without definite structure and without any recognizable nucleus.

mō·nē′rȧ, *n.* alternative plural of *moneron*.

mō·nē′răl, *a.* same as *moneran*.

mō·nē′răn, *a.* relating to a moner or to the *Monera*.

mō·nē′răn, *n.* a moner.

mon′ẽr·ġiṣm, *n.* [*mon-*, and Gr. *ergon*, work.] in theology, the doctrine that regeneration is the work of the Holy Spirit alone, and that the human will, having no inclination to holiness, is incapable of assisting or co-operating.

mō·ner′iç, *a.* moneran.

mō·nē′ron, *n.*; *pl.* **mō·nē′rȧ, mō·nē′ronṣ**, a moner.

mō·nē′siȧ (-zhȧ), *n.* [origin uncertain.] in pharmacy, an extract from the bark of a Brazilian tree, *Chrysophyllum glyciphlaeum*.

mō·nē′ṣin, *n.* [*monesia* and *-in*.] an astringent, $C_{32}H_{54}O_{18}$, derived from monesia and used in medicine, isomeric and probably identical with saponin.

mō·neste′, *v.t.* to admonish. [Obs.]

mon′e·tãr·i·ly (*or* mun′), *adv.* in regard to monetary matters.

mon′e·tȧr·iṣm, *n.* a theory which holds that economic stability and growth are determined primarily by the maintenance of a steady rate of growth in the supply of money.

mon′e·tȧr·ist, *a.* designating, of, or in accord with the theory of monetarism.

mon′e·tȧr·ist, *n.* an adherent of the theory of monetarism.

mon′e·tãr·y (*or* mun′), *a.* [L. *monetarius*, pertaining to a mint, from *moneta*, a mint, money.]

1. of the coinage or currency of a country.
2. of money; pecuniary.

monetary unit; a standard unit of money current in a nation or country, as the dollar in the United States or the pound in Great Britain.

mŏn′eth, *n.* a month. [Obs.]

mon″e·ti·zā′tion, *n.* a monetizing or being monetized.

mon′e·tīze, *v.t.*; monetized, *pt.*, *pp.*; monetizing, *ppr.* [L. *moneta*, money, and *-ize*.]

1. to coin into money.
2. to legalize as money.
3. to give the nature of money to.

mŏn′ey, *n.*; *pl.* **mŏn′eyṣ** or **mŏn′ieṣ**, [OFr. *moneie*, *monnoie*, from L. *moneta*, a mint, money, from *Moneta* (from *monere*, to admonish) originally a surname of Juno, in whose temple at Rome money was coined.]

1. (a) standard pieces of gold, silver, copper, nickel, etc., stamped by government authority and used as a medium of exchange and measure of value; coin or coins: also called *hard money*; (b) any paper note issued by a government or an authorized bank and used in the same way; bank notes; bills: also called *paper money*.
2. any substance or article used as money, as bank notes, checks, etc.
3. any definite or indefinite sum of money.
4. property; possessions; wealth.
5. any form or denomination of legally current money.
6. a money of account.
7. [*pl.*] sums of money: now used chiefly in law.

conscience money; see under *conscience*.

fiat money; see under *fiat*.

for one's money; for one's choice; in one's opinion. [Colloq.]

in the money; (a) among the winners, as in a contest, race, etc.; (b) prosperous; wealthy; successful. [Slang.]

money bill; a legislative bill for raising revenue and for making appropriations of public money.

to make money; to gain profits; to become wealthy.

to put money into; to invest money in.

to put money on; to bet on.

mŏn′ey, *v.t.* 1. to furnish money to. [Obs.]

2. to dispose of for money; to turn into money. [Rare.]

mŏn′ey·bag, *n.* a bag or purse for holding money.

mŏn′ey·bagṣ, *n.pl.* 1. [*construed as sing.*] a rich person. [Colloq.]

2. wealth; riches. [Colloq.]

mŏn′ey brō′kẽr, a broker who deals in money.

mŏn′ey·chān″ġẽr, *n.* 1. a person whose business is to exchange money, usually of different countries, at a set rate.

2. a machine holding stacked coins for making change quickly.

mŏn′ey çow′ry, a small seashell, *Cypraea moneta*, used as money by natives in parts of Asia, Africa, and the islands of the South Seas.

mŏn′eyed (-id), *a.* 1. rich; wealthy; having money; as, *moneyed* men.

2. consisting of, derived from, or representing money; as, *moneyed* interests opposed the bill.

mŏn′ey·ẽr, *n.* 1. a banker or capitalist. [Obs.]

2. an authorized coiner of money. [Obs.]

mŏn′ey·grub″bẽr, *n.* a person who concentrates his energies on the acquiring of money.

mŏn′ey·lend″ẽr, *n.* a person whose business is lending money at interest.

mŏn′ey·less, *a.* without money; penniless.

mŏn′ey-māk″ẽr, *n.* 1. anyone who manufactures money; also, one who makes counterfeit money. [Obs.]

2. one who is successful at acquiring wealth; a successful business man.

3. something that produces monetary gain; a business or plan that makes money.

mŏn′ey-māk″ing, *n.* 1. the gaining of money; the acquisition of wealth.

2. the coining of money; minting.

mŏn′ey-māk″ing, *a.* 1. profitable; lucrative.

2. engaged in money-making.

mŏn′ey mär′ket, 1. the market in which money is the commodity dealt in.

2. any system for dealing with the supply of and demand for loanable funds on a short-term basis, usually for periods of from six to thirty months.

mŏn′ey of aç·count′, a monetary denomination used in keeping accounts, etc., especially one not issued as a coin (e.g., the United States mill).

mŏn′ey ọr′dẽr, an order for the payment of a specified sum of money, as one issued for a fee at one post office or bank and payable at another.

mŏn′ey sçrive′nẽr, a person who raises money for others. [Obs.]

mŏn′ey′s wŏrth, 1. something that will bring money or is worth money.

2. full value; the worth of a thing in money.

mŏn′ey·wŏrt, *n.* an evergreen trailing plant with yellow flowers and roundish leaves, belonging to the genus *Lysimachia*.

mŏng′çorn, *n.* maslin (mixed grain). [Dial.]

mŏñ′gẽr, *n.* [AS. *mangere*, a merchant, a dealer, from *mangian*, to trade, to traffic; compare Ice. *mangari*, O.D. *mangher*, *mengher*, O.H.G. *mangari*, a merchant.] a trader or dealer (in a specified commodity): used chiefly in composition, as in fish*monger*, news*monger*, iron*monger*: sometimes used figuratively and derogatorily, as in scandal*monger*. [Chiefly Brit.]

mŏñ′gẽr, *v.t.*; mongered, *pt.*, *pp.*; mongering, *ppr.* to trade or deal in: said especially of unfair or illegal methods and dealings.

Moñ′gŏl, *n.* [Mongolian *Mongol*.]

1. a native of Mongolia, Inner Mongolia, or the Buryat Mongol A.S.S.R.
2. a member of the Mongolian race.
3. any of the Mongolian languages.

Moñ′gŏl, *a.* Mongolian.

Moñ′gŏl Em′pīre, the vast thirteenth-century empire of Genghis Khan, from the Dnepr River to the Pacific.

Moñ·gō′li·ăn, *a.* 1. of Mongolia, its people, or their culture.

2. designating or of one of the three principal races of mankind, including most of the peoples of Asia, the Eskimos, North American Indians, etc., who are generally characterized by yellowish skins, straight black hair, slanting eyes, etc.

3. designating or of a subfamily of Altaic languages spoken by the Mongols, and probably related to the Turkic and Tungusic languages.

4. in medicine, having Mongolism.

Moñ·gō′li·ăn, *n.* 1. a native of Mongolia.

2. a member of the Mongolian race.

3. any of the Mongolian languages.

Moñ·gō′li·ăn id′i·ō·çy, Mongolism.

Moñ·gō′li·ăn (*or* **Moñ′gō·loid**) **id′i·ŏt**, a person having Mongolism

Moñ·gol′iç, *n.* any of the Mongolian languages.

Moñ·gol′iç, *a.* Mongolian (senses 1, 2, 3).

Moñ′gō·li·oid, *a.* Mongoloid.

Moñ′gō·liṣm, *n.* a type of congenital mental deficiency, accompanied with a flattened forehead, slanting eyes set closely together, etc.

Moñ′gō·loid, *a.* 1. of or characteristic of the natives of Mongolia.

2. of, having the nature of, or resembling the members of the Mongolian race.

Moñ′gō·loid, *n.* a member of the Mongolian race.

moñ′goose, moñ′gọọs, *n.*; *pl.* **moñ′gọọs·eṣ**, [Marathi *mangūs*.] a ferretlike, flesh-eating animal of India, known for its ability to kill rats, poisonous snakes, etc.

mŏñ′grel, *a.* [from AS. *mengan*, to mix, with dim. suffix, as in *cockerel*.] of a mixed breed, race, origin, or character; of different kinds: often used derogatively.

mŏñ′grel, *n.* 1. an animal or plant produced by the crossing of different breeds or varieties; especially, a dog of this kind.

2. anything made of incongruous parts. Often used derogatively.

mŏñ′grel·ize, *v.t.* and *v.i.* to make or become a mongrel.

′mŏngst, mŏngst, *prep.* amongst. [Poet.]

mon′ick·ẽr, *n.* a moniker.

mŏn′ied, *a.* same as *moneyed*.

mŏn′ieṣ, *n.* alternative plural of *money*.

mon′i·kẽr, *n.* [said to be from Shelta via thieves' slang.]

1. an initial or other mark of identification used by a tramp.
2. a person's name or nickname. [Slang.] Also spelled *monicker*.

mon′i·lā·ted, *a.* same as *moniliform*.

mō·nil′i·çorn, *a.* [L. *monile*, a necklace, and *cornu*, horn.] characterized by moniliform antennae.

mō·nil′i·fọrm, *a.* [L. *monile*, a necklace, and *forma*, form.] jointed at intervals so as to resemble beads on a string; specifically, in botany and zoology, consisting of, or having, a series of alternating swellings and constrictions, as some stems and roots; as, the *moniliform* root of *Pelargonium*.

MONILIFORM ROOT

mō·nil′i·oid, *a.* same as *moniliform*.

mon′i·ment, *n.* a monument. [Obs.]

Mō″nim·i·ā′cē·ae, *n.pl.* [L. *Monima*; Gr. *Monimē*, the wife of Mithridates.] a family of aromatic trees and shrubs found chiefly in the southern hemisphere, closely related to the *Lauraceæ*.

mō″nim·i·ā′ceous, *a.* belonging to the family *Monimiaceæ*.

mon′ish, *v.t.* to admonish; to warn. [Archaic.]

mon′ish·ẽr, *n.* an admonisher. [Archaic.]

mon′ish·ment, *n.* admonition. [Archaic.]

mon′iṣm, *n.* [Gr. *monos*, single, alone, and *-ism*.]

1. in philosophy, (a) the doctrine that there is only one ultimate substance or principle, whether mind (*idealism*), matter (*materialism*), or some third thing that is the basis of both; (b) the doctrine that reality is an organic whole without independent parts.

2. in biology, same as *monogenesis*.

mon′ist, *n.* a supporter, advocate, or adherent of monism.

mō·nis′tiç, *a.* pertaining to monism.

mō·nis′ti·çăl, *a.* monistic.

mō·ni′tion, *n.* [Fr., from L. *monitio* (*-onis*), from *monere*, to warn.]

1. an admonition; a warning; instruction given by way of caution; as, the *monitions* of a friend.
2. information; indication; advice. [Obs.]
3. in law, a summons or citation calling one to appear and answer in a suit, or to contempt charges.
4. an official or legal notice; specifically, a formal notice from a bishop requiring that an ecclesiastical offense be amended.

mon′i·tive, *a.* admonitory; conveying admonition. [Obs.]

mon′i·tŏr, *n.* [L., one who warns or admonishes.]

1. one who warns of faults or informs of duty; one who gives advice and instruction by way or reproof or caution. [Rare.]

You need not be a *monitor* to the king.
—Bacon.

2. in some schools, a pupil selected to help keep order, record attendance, etc.
3. something that reminds or warns.
4. any of several species of large, flesh-eating lizards of Africa, southern Asia, and Australia: so called from the notion that they warn of the presence of crocodiles.
5. formerly, an armored warship, or ironclad, with a low freeboard, low flat deck, and heavy guns fitted in one or more revolving turrets; specifically, [M–] the first ship of this kind, the Union ironclad that fought a similar Confederate ship, the Merrimac, March 9, 1862: so named by the designer, John Ericsson.

6. a mounting for a nozzle so arranged that a stream of water can be played in any direction desired, as in hydraulic mining or fire fighting.

7. in radio and television, (a) a receiver for reproducing transmission without interfering with it, used for checking on the operation of a transmitter with regard to quality, deviation from assigned bands, material transmitted, etc.; (b) a high-fidelity loudspeaker in the control room of a broadcasting studio, used for checking the quality of the transmission.

8. a device for holding tools, revolving on a pivot and thus bringing the tools into position for use.

mon′i·tŏr, *v.t.* and *v.i.* 1. to watch or check on (a person or thing) as a monitor.

2. in radio and television, to receive or check on (transmission, a transmitter, etc.) with or as with a monitor.

mon·i·tō′ri·ăl, *a.* 1. of or relating to a monitor; using a monitor or monitors.

2. monitory.

mon·i·tō′ri·ăl·ly, *adv.* in a monitorial manner.

mon′i·tŏr rọọf, a low structure, as on the roof of a railway car or the cabin of a steamboat, having windows along the sides for lighting and ventilating the room below.

mon′i·tŏr·ship, *n.* the office, function, period of service, or position of a monitor (sense 1 or 2).

mon′i·tō·ry, *a.* expressing or containing monition; admonitory; giving warning; as, a *monitory* gesture.

mon′i·tō·ry, *n.*; *pl.* **mon′i·tō·rieṣ,** 1. admonition or warning. [Obs.]

2. a monitory letter, as from a bishop.

mon′i·tress, *n.* a woman monitor.

mon′i·trix, *n.* a monitress.

mŏnk, *n.* [AS. *munec, munec*, from LL. *monachus*; L.Gr. *monachos*, one who lives alone, from *monos*, alone.]

1. originally, a man who retired from the world and lived in solitary self-denial for religious reasons.

2. a man who joins a religious order living in retirement according to a rule and under vows of poverty, obedience, and chastity.

3. in printing, a blotch or blackened spot on a page caused by an imperfect distribution of ink on the form: opposed to *friar*, a light spot. [Brit.]

4. any of several animals, as (a) any of various South American monkeys; (b) the bullfinch; (c) a white-crested domestic pigeon; (d) the monkbird.

5. a kind of fuse made of dry fungus, formerly used in firing a train of powder, as in a mine.

mŏnk bat, a bat, *Molossus nasutus*, native to South America and the West Indies: so called because the males live in colonies separated from the females.

mŏnk′bīrd, *n.* the friarbird.

mŏnk′ẽr·y, *n.*; *pl.* **mŏnk′ẽr·ieṣ,** 1. (a) the way of life, condition, behavior, etc. of monks; (b) [*pl.*] monastic practices or beliefs. Generally a term of hostility or contempt.

2. a body of monks living in a monastery; also, the monastery itself.

3. tramps collectively, or a place occupied by tramps. [Brit. Slang.]

mŏn′key, *n.*; *pl.* **mŏn′keyṣ,** [Early Mod. Eng.; prob. from M.L.G. *Moneke*, name applied in the beast epic *Reynard the Fox*; apparently associated with L.G. *monnik*, monk.]

1. any of the primates (the highest order of animals) except man and, usually, the lemurs; specifically, any of the smaller, long-tailed members of the primates, excluding the anthropoid apes.

DIANA MONKEY
(*Cercopithecus diana*)

2. the fur of some species of long-haired monkeys.

3. a person regarded as like a monkey in appearance or actions, as a mischievous or imitative child.

HOWLING MONKEY
(*Mycetes ursinus*)

4. a heavy iron weight drawn up and dropped on the head of a pile to drive it downward, used in a pile driver.

5. in shipbuilding, a kind of hammer used for driving bolts, made of a long heavy piece of iron which slides in a groove and strikes the head of a bolt.

6. in the United States $500, in Great Britain £500. [Betting Slang.]

7. a fluid compound used in soldering, made of two parts of muriatic acid to one part of zinc.

8. in glass making, a small crucible.

mŏn′key, *v.t.*; monkeyed, *pt., pp.*; monkeying, *ppr.* to ape; to imitate. [Rare.]

mŏn′key, *v.i.* to behave in a meddlesome or idle manner; to handle without permission; to play or fool (often followed by *with* or *around with*); as, don't *monkey with* that steel trap. [Colloq.]

mŏn′key block, on shipboard, (a) a small single block strapped with a swivel; (b) a block nailed on the topsail yards of some merchantmen to lead the buntlines through.

mŏn′key bōat, a small boat used in going about docks; a half decker employed on the River Thames. [Brit.]

mŏn′key bread (bred), 1. the acid, gourd-shaped fruit of the baobab tree, eaten by monkeys.

2. the tree.

mŏn′key buṣi′ness (biz′), foolish, mischievous, or deceitful tricks or behavior. [Slang.]

mŏn′key çup, any plant of the family *Nepenthaceæ*, having a pitcher-like body appearing at the apex of the prolonged tendrillike leaf stalks.

MONKEY BREAD
(*Adansonia digitata*)

mŏn′key en′ġine, the apparatus and machinery for lifting and releasing the monkey of a pile driver.

mŏn′key flow′ẽr, any one of several species of *Mimulus*, a plant of the figwort family, with spotted flowers having a corolla whose appearance suggests a gape or grimace; especially, the scarlet monkey flower.

mŏn′key gaff, in a merchant ship, a small gaff for displaying the flag.

mŏn′key grȧss, a coarse, stiff fiber obtained from the leaf stalks of a South American palm, *Attalea funifera*, used for cordage, brooms, street-sweeping brushes, etc.

mŏn′key ham′mẽr, the hammer of a drop press.

mŏn′key·ish, *a.* of, like, or characteristic of a monkey; foolish, mischievous, etc.

mŏn′key jack′et, [from the resemblance to coats worn by trained monkeys.] a short, tight jacket, as that formerly worn by sailors. [Colloq.]

mŏn′key·pot, *n.* 1. the large, woody seed vessel of any of various South American trees: so called from its urnlike shape.

2. any of these trees.

mŏn′key puz′zle, a tall Chilean pine, *Araucaria imbricata*, with branches so crowded and interwoven that it puzzles monkeys to climb it: its nuts are edible and its timber highly valued, being hard and durable.

mŏn′key rāil, a light rail raised about six inches above the quarter rail of a ship.

mŏn′key·shīne, *n.* [*usually in pl.*] a caper or antic resembling that of a monkey; a mischievous or playful trick, joke, or prank. [Slang.]

mŏn′key sūit, 1. a uniform. [Slang.]

2. a man's dress suit. [Slang.]

mŏn′key·tāil, *n.* in nautical usage, (a) a short, round lever formerly used for aiming an old type of naval gun; (b) a short piece of rope used as a hook handle to avoid injury to the hand.

mŏn′key wheel (hwēl), in nautical usage, a single tackle block; a gin block.

mŏn′key wrench (rench), a stout wrench or spanner with a movable jaw, adjustable by a screw to fit various sizes of nuts, etc.

mŏnk′fish, *n.* one of two fishes; (a) the angelfish, *Squatina angelus*, named from the resemblance of its head to the cowl of a monk; (b) the angler.

mŏnk′flow″ẽr, *n.* a terrestrial orchid of tropical America, genus *Catasetum*.

Mōn′-Khmer′ (kmer′), *a.* designating or of a group of languages spoken mainly in Indo-China, including Mon and Khmer.

mŏnk′hood, *n.* 1. character, profession, or condition of a monk.

2. monks collectively.

mŏnk′ish, *a.* like a monk or pertaining to monks; monastic: often used in hostility and contempt; as, *monkish* manners; *monkish* dress; *monkish* solitude.

mŏnk′ish·ness, *n.* the quality of being monkish.

mŏnk′ly, *a.* relating to monks; monkish. [Rare.]

mŏnk's çloth, 1. originally, a worsted cloth used for monks' garments.

2. now, a heavy cotton cloth with a basket weave, used for drapes, etc.

mŏnk sēal, a species of seal, *Monachus albiventer*, found in the Mediterranean, forming the type of the genus *Monachus*: probably the seal best known to the ancients.

mŏnks′hood, *n.* a medicinal plant, *Aconitum napellus*, of the crowfoot family; wolf's bane; aconite.

mŏnk's rhụ′bärb (rü′), a dock, *Rumex alpinus*.

mŏnk's sēam, in nautical usage, a seam made by laying the selvages of sails over each other and sewing them on both sides.

mon′ō-, [Gr. *mono-*, from *monos*, single, alone.]

1. a prefix meaning *one, alone, single*, as in *mono*clinic.

2. a prefix meaning *containing one atom* or *one group* (of a specified element), as in *mono*chloride.

3. [from *mono*molecular.] a prefix meaning *having a thickness of one molecule*, as in *mono*layer.

Also, before a vowel, *mon-*.

mō′nō, *n.* [Sp., a monkey.] a monkey, *Mycetes villosus*, native to Central America; the black howler.

mon·ō·ac′id, *a.* monoacidic.

mon·ō·ac′id, *n.* an acid having only one replaceable hydrogen atom per molecule. [Rare.]

mon″ō·ȧ·cid′iç, *a.* 1. designating a base or alcohol one molecular weight of which can react with only one equivalent weight of an acid, or that has one hydroxyl group capable of replacing one acid hydrogen atom.

2. having only one acid hydrogen atom per molecule.

mon″ō·ȧ·tom′iç, *a.* consisting of one atom: said of a molecule.

mon·ō·bā′siç, *a.* 1. in chemistry, (a) designating an acid the molecule of which contains one hydrogen atom replaceable by a metal or positive radical or capable of reacting with the hydroxyl group; (b) designating a compound in which a metal or positive radical has replaced one acid hydrogen atom.

2. in biology, based on only one species; monotypic: said of a genus.

mon·ō·blep′si·ȧ, *n.* same as *monoblepsis*.

mon·ō·blep′sis, *n.* [*mono-*, and Gr. *blepsis*, sight.] a disorder in which vision is most distinct when one eye only is used.

mon′ō·cärp, *n.* [*mono-*, and Gr. *karpos*, fruit.] a plant bearing fruit but once.

mon·ō·cär′pel·lā·ry, *a.* having a single carpel.

mon·ō·cär′piç, *a.* producing fruit but once, and then dying: said of annuals, biennials, and some trees.

mon·ō·cär′pous, *a.* [*mono-*, and Gr. *karpos*, fruit.]

1. having a gynoecium consisting of a single carpel and forming a single ovary.

2. monocarpic.

mon·ō·ceph′ȧ·lous, *a.* [*mono-*, and Gr. *kephalē*, head.] having one head only.

mon·ō·cēr′çous, *a.* [*mono-,* and Gr. *kerkos,* tail.] uniflagellate: said of infusorians.

mō·noc′ē·ros, *n.* [*mono-,* and Gr. *keras,* a horn.]
1. any real or fabulous one-horned animal; a unicorn. [Obs.]
2. [M–] the Unicorn, a constellation surrounded by Hydra, Canis Major, Orion, and Canis Minor. All the stars in it are small.

mon·ō·chā′si·ăl (-shi-), *a.* of or characterized by a monochasium or monochasia.

mon·ō·chā′si·um (-shi-), *n.*; *pl.* **mon·ō·chā′si·ȧ,** [*mono-,* and Gr. *chasis,* a chasm.] a flower cluster in which only a single branch is produced on the main axis.

Mon″ō·chlȧ·myd′ē·ae, *n.pl.* [*mono-,* and Gr. *chlamys, chlamydos,* a cloak.] a subclass of dicotyledonous plants, having a calyx without a corolla.

mon″ō·chlȧ·myd′ē·ous, *a.* having a single perianth, the corolla usually being the missing set; belonging to the *Monochlamydeæ.*

mon·ō·chlō′rīde, *n.* a chloride containing one chlorine atom per molecule.

mon′ō·chord, *n.* [ME. *monocorde,* from ML. *monochordus,* lit., single-stringed.]
1. an acoustical instrument consisting of a wooden sounding box with a single string and a movable bridge set on a graduated scale: it is used for determining musical intervals mathematically by dividing the string into separate parts whose vibrations can be measured.
2. harmony; agreement. [Rare.]

mon·ō·chrō′iç, *a.* [from Gr. *monochroos,* and *-ic.*] of one color; monochromatic.

mon·ō·chrō·mat′iç, *a.* [Gr. *monochrōmatos,* of one color; *monos,* single, and *chrōma* (*-atos*), color.]
1. of or having a single color.
2. composed of or producing light having but one wave length.
monochromatic lamp; a lamp the flame of which emits light of a single color.

mon′ō·chrōme, *n.* [*mono-,* and Gr. *chrōma,* color.]
1. a painting or other picture in a single color or in various shades of the same color.
2. the art or process of making such pictures.

mon·ō·chrō′miç, *a.* of or in a single color; painted or drawn in monochrome.

mon·ō·chrō′mi·căl, *a.* monochromic.

mon′ō·chrōm·ist, *n.* a maker of monochromes.

mon′ō·chrō·my, *n.* the art of employing a single color or its shades in painting.

mon·ō·chron′iç, *a.* [*mono-,* and Gr. *chronos,* time.] contemporaneous; in geology, deposited at or about the same time.

mon·ō·cil′i·ā·ted, *a.* [*mono-* and *cilium.*] having a single cilium.

mon′ō·çle, *n.* [LL. *monoculus,* one-eyed; Gr. *monos,* single, and L. *oculus,* eye.] an eyeglass for one eye.

mon′ō·çled, *a.* wearing a monocle.

mon·ō·clī′năl, *a.* [*mono-,* and Gr. *klinein,* to slope.]
1. having a single dip; consisting of strata dipping in one direction only.
2. of strata dipping in the same direction.

mon·ō·clī′năl, *n.* same as *monocline.*

mon′ō·clīne, *n.* [from *mono-,* and Gr. *klinein,* to incline.] in geology, a monoclinal rock fold or structure.

mon·ō·clin′iç, *a.* designating or of crystallization characterized by three axes of unequal length, two of which intersect obliquely and are perpendicular to the third.

mon·ō·clī′nous, *a.* [*mono-,* and Gr. *klinē,* bed.]
1. in botany, hermaphrodite; having both stamens and pistils in the same flower.
2. having both stamens and pistils, as some flowers.
3. in geology, monoclinal.

mon·ō·coe′li·ăn, *a.* [*mono-,* and Gr. *koilia,* a cavity.] having a single brain cavity: said of animals of the genus *Amphioxus.*

Mon·ō·çon′dy·lȧ, *n.pl.* [*mono-,* and Gr. *kondylos,* a knuckle, joint.] a group of vertebrates in which the occipital condyle is single, as in reptiles and birds; the *Sauropsida.*

mon·ō·çon′dy·lăr, *a.* monocondylian.

mon″ō·çon·dyl′i·ăn, *a.* having only one occipital condyle.

mon·ō·çot′yl, *n.* [*mono-,* and Gr. *kotylē,* a small cup.] any plant with one cotyledon.

mon·ō·çot·y·lē′dŏn, *n.* in botany, a plant having a single cotyledon, or seed leaf; specifically, any plant belonging to the *Monocotyledones.*

Mon·ō·çot·y·lē′dŏn·ēş, *n.pl.* [*mono-,* and Gr. *cotylēdōn,* a cup-shaped cavity.] that one of the two subclasses of seed plants in which the embryo has a single cotyledon and the radicle issues from a sheath and is never developed into a taproot in germination. To this class belong palms, grasses, rushes, lilies, irises, and orchids. The leaves are generally parallel-veined, the flowers usually with three organs in each whorl, and the stems endogenous.

mon·ō·çot·y·lē′dŏn·ous, *a.* having a single cotyledon; belonging to the subclass of monocotyledons.

mō·noç′rȧ·cy, *n.*; *pl.* **mō·noç′rȧ·cieş,** [L.Gr. *monokratia*; Gr. *monos,* single, alone, and *kratein,* rule.] government by one person; autocracy.

mon′ō·çrat, *n.* 1. one who governs alone.
2. a person who believes in monocracy or monarchy: term applied by Thomas Jefferson c. 1790 to pro-English Federalists in the war between England and France.

mon·ō·çrot′iç, *a.* pertaining to or exhibiting monocrotism.

mō·noç′rō·tişm, *n.* [*mono-,* and Gr. *krotos,* a beating.] the quality in a pulse wave of having a single elevation, not a dicrotic or tricrotic one.

mō·noç′ū·lăr, *a.* [LL. *monoculus,* one-eyed; Gr. *monos,* single, and L. *oculus,* eye.]
1. having one eye only; one-eyed.
2. adapted for use with one eye only; pertaining to only one eye; as, a *monocular* microscope.

mō·noç′ū·lāte, *a.* one-eyed; monocular.

mon′ō·çūle, *n.* a one-eyed crustacean.

mon′ō·çul·tūre, *n.* cultivation of a single crop or product without using the land for other purposes.

mon′ō·cy·çle, *n.* [*mono-,* and Gr. *kyklos,* a circle.] a vehicle having one wheel only.

mon·ō·cyç′liç, *a.* [*mono-,* and Gr. *kyklos,* a circle.]
1. having but one cycle.
2. in botany, in a single whorl, as the stamens or petals.

mon′ō·cyst, *n.* [*mono-,* and Gr. *kystis,* a bag.] a tumor composed of a single cyst.

mon·ō·cys′tiç, *a.* having or consisting of one cyst or sac.

mon′ō·cȳte, *n.* [*mono-* and *-cyte.*] a large, nongranular white blood cell with a relatively small, kidney-shaped nucleus.

Mon″ō·cyt·tăr′i·ȧ, *n.pl.* [*mono-,* and Gr. *kyttarion,* dim. of *kyttaros,* a hollow.] a division of radiolarians having a single central capsule.

mon″ō·cyt·tăr′i·ăn, *a.* of or pertaining to the *Monocyttaria.*

mon·ō·daç′tyl·ous, *a.* [Gr. *monodaktylos,* a finger or toe.] having a single toe, finger, claw, or chela: also *monodactyl.*

mon′ō·delph, *n.* a mammal of the *Monodelphia.*

Mon·ō·del′phi·ȧ, *n.pl.* [*mono-,* and Gr. *delphys,* womb.] a division of mammals characterized by a single uterine cavity which opens into a single vagina, and by the presence of a placenta. It includes all the *Mammalia* except the monotremes and marsupials.

mon·ō·del′phi·ăn, *n.* a monodelph.

mon·ō·del′phiç, *a.* of or like the *Monodelphia.*

mon·ō·del′phous, *a.* monodelphic.

mō·nod′iç, *a.* [Gr. *monōdikos,* from *monōdia,* a monody.] like monody; homophonous.

mō·nod′iç·ăl, *a.* monodic.

mon″ō·dī·met′riç, *a.* dimetric; tetragonal.

mon′ō·dist, *n.* one who writes or sings a monody.

mon′ō·dont, *a.* [Gr. *monodous* (*-ontos*), having one tooth.] having one tooth only.

mon′ō·drä·mȧ, *n.* [*mono-,* and Gr. *drama,* drama.] a drama acted, or written to be acted, by only one person or actor.

mon″ō·drȧ·mat′iç, *a.* like a monodrama.

mon·ō·drom′iç, *a.* [*mono-,* and Gr. *dromos,* a course, running.] in mathematics, designating a function that has but one value for the same value of a variable.

mon′ō·dy, *n.*; *pl.* **mon′ō·dieş,** [Gr. *monōdia*; *monos,* single, sole, and *ōde,* a song.]
1. in ancient Greek literature, an ode sung by a single voice, as in a tragedy; lyric solo, generally a lament or dirge.
2. a poem in which the poet mourns another's death.
3. a monotonous sound or tone, as of waves.
4. in music, (a) a style of composition in which one part, or voice, predominates, and the others serve as accompaniment; homophony, as distinguished from polyphony; (b) a composition in this style.

mon″ō·dȳ·nam′iç, *a.* [*mono-,* and Gr. *dynamis,* power.] having but one power, capacity, or talent.

mon·ō·dȳ′nȧ·mişm, *n.* the theory that all forms of activity in nature are phenomena of a single force.

Mō·noe′ci·ȧ, *n.pl.* [*mono-,* and Gr. *oikos,* house.] the twenty-first class of plants in the artificial system of Linnaeus. In this class, the stamens and pistils are in separate flowers on the same plant, as in the *Araceæ.*

mō·noe′ciăn, *a.* monoecious.

mō·noe′ciăn, *n.* any monoecious plant.

mō·noe′cious, *a.* [*mono-,* and Gr. *oikos,* house.]
1. in botany, having male and female flowers on the same individual plant.
2. in zoology, having both male and female reproductive organs in the same individual. Also spelled *monecious.*

mō·noe′cious·ly, *adv.* after the manner of a monoecian.

mō·noe′cişm, *n.* [*monoecious* and *-ism.*] the state, condition, or quality of being monoecious.

mon″ō·flȧ·ġel′lāte, *a.* [*mono-* and *flagellate.*] in zoology, having a single flagellum; as, a *monoflagellate* infusorian.

mon′ō·gam, *n.* in botany, a plant that has a solitary flower, or simple flowers with the anthers united.

Mon·ō·gā′mi·ȧ, *n.pl.* [L.Gr. *monogamos,* married but once; Gr. *monos,* single, and *gamos,* marriage.] an order of plants in the Linnean system including all plants having solitary flowers with their anthers united.

mon·ō·gā′mi·ăn, *a.* monogamous; pertaining to the *Monogamia.*

mon·ō·gam′iç, *a.* 1. in botany, having flowers distinct from each other and not collected in a head.
2. same as *monogamous.*

mō·nog′ȧ·mist, *n.* 1. one who upholds monogamy or the practice of marrying only once.
I valued myself upon being a strict *monogamist.* —Goldsmith.
2. one who has a single spouse, as opposed to *bigamist* or *polygamist.*

mō·nog′ȧ·mous, *a.* 1. practicing or advocating monogamy: opposed to *digamous.*
2. marrying only one at a time: opposed to *bigamous* or *polygamous*; as, a *monogamous* tribe.
3. in zoology, having only one mate; living in pairs; as, a *monogamous* family of birds.
4. in botany, same as *monogamic.*

mō·nog′ȧ·my, *n.* [LL. *monogamia,* married but once; from Gr. *monos,* single, and *gamos,* marriage.]
1. the practice of marrying only once, or the principle which upholds that practice; the principle that forbids a second marriage after the death of a first husband or wife: opposed to *digamy, deuterogamy.* [Rare.]
2. the practice of marrying only one person at a time: opposed to *bigamy* or *polygamy.*
3. in zoology, the habit of having only one mate; the practice of living in pairs.

mon·ō·gas′triç, *a.* [*mono-,* and Gr. *gastēr,* stomach.] having only one stomach.

mon·ō·ġen′e·sis, *n.* [*mono-,* and Gr. *genesis,* generation.]
1. the (hypothetical) descent of all living organisms from a single original organism: opposed to *polygenesis.*
2. monogenism.
3. asexual reproduction, as by budding or spore formation.
4. direct development of an ovum into an organism like the parent, without metamorphosis.

mon″ō·ġē·net′iç, *a.* 1. of, characterized by, or involving monogenesis.
2. having only one generation in the life-cycle, or no intervening asexual generation, as certain worms.
3. in geology, produced by one formative process, as a mountain range.

mon·ō·ġen′iç, *a.* 1. in zoology, reproducing in only one way.
2. developing in only one way; having a single origin.

mō·noġ′ē·nişm, *n.* [*monogeny* and *-ism.*] the doctrine that all men belong to a single race, or that all men are descended from a single pair.

mō·noġ′ē·nist, *a.* pertaining to or connected with monogenism; as, the *monogenist* hypotheses.

mō·noǵ′ē·nist, *n.* a supporter of monogenism.
According to the *monogenists* all mankind have sprung from a single pair. —Huxley.

mon″ō·ġē·nis′tiç, *a.* same as *monogenist.*

mō·noǵ′ē·nous, *a.* 1. in biology, originating by asexual reproduction, as by budding, fission, etc.
2. relating to monogenism.
3. in mathematics, having but one differential coefficient as a rule of generation: said of a function.

mō·noǵ′ē·ny, *n.* same as *monogenesis.*

mon′ō·glot, *a.* [L.Gr. *monoglōttos,* speaking but one language; Gr. *monos,* single, and *glōtta,* Attic form of *glōssa,* tongue.] knowing, speaking, writing, or written in a single language.

mon′ō·glot, *n.* a person who knows only one language.

mon″ō·gō·neū′tiç, *a.* [*mono-,* and Gr. *goneuein,* to produce, from *gonos,* offspring.] in entomology, producing only one brood annually.

Mon″ō·gō·nop′ō·rȧ, *n.pl.* [*mono-,* and Gr. *gonos,* offspring, and *poros,* passage.] a division of planarian worms characterized by a single sexual opening for both the male and female organs: it includes the families *Planariidæ* and *Geoplanidæ.*

mon″ō·gō·nop′ō·rous, *a.* having a single sexual opening; pertaining to or having the characteristics of the *Monogonopora.*

mō·nog′ō·ny, *n.* [*mono-,* and Gr. *gonos,* offspring, birth, descent.] in biology, (a) propagation by fission or gemmation; nonsexual propagation; (b) same as *monogenesis.*

mon′ō·gram, *n.* [LL. *monogramma;* Gr. *monogrammaton,* from *monos,* single, and *gramma,* a letter, from *graphein,* to write.]
1. a character or figure made up of two or more letters, often initials of a name, combined in a single design: used on writing paper, ornaments, clothing, etc.
2. a picture drawn in lines without color; a sketch. [Obs.]

mon′ō·gram·măl, *a.* same as *monogrammic.* [Rare.]

mon″ō·gram·mat′iç, *a.* in the style or manner of a monogram; pertaining to monograms.

mon·ō·gram′miç, *a.* monogrammatic.

mon′ō·gram·mous, *a.* drawn in outline; indistinct. [Obs.]

mon′ō·grȧph, *n.* [*mono-,* and Gr. *graphē,* a writing.]
1. a book, article, or paper written about a single subject; as, a *monograph* on Egyptian mummies.
2. originally, a treatise on a single genus, species, etc. of plant or animal.

mō·nog′rȧ·phēr, *n.* one who writes or composes a monograph or monographs.

mon·ō·graph′iç, *a.* 1. pertaining to or of the nature of a monograph or monogram.
2. drawn in lines without color. [Obs.]

mon·ō·graph′iç·ăl, *a.* monographic.

mon·ō·graph′iç·ăl·ly, *adv.* in the manner of a monograph; in a monograph.

mō·nog′rȧ·phist, *n.* a writer of a monograph.

mō·nog′rȧ·phy, *n.* 1. a monograph. [Rare.]
2. delineation in lines without colors; an outline sketch. [Obs.]

mon′ō·ġyn, *n.* a plant of the order *Monogynia.*

Mon·ō·ġyn′i·ȧ, *n.pl.* [*mono-,* and Gr. *gynē,* a woman.] in the Linnean system, any of the orders of plants characterized by having only one pistil or stigma, or one seed-producing organ.

mon·ō·ġyn′i·ăn, *a.* in botany, pertaining to the order *Monogynia;* having only one pistil or stigma.

mon″ō·ġy·noe′ciăl, *a.* [*mono-* and *gynœcium.*] formed of one pistil from a single flower: said of fruits.

mō·noġ′y·nous, *a.* 1. same as *monogynian.*
2. in anthropology, having only one wife.
3. in zoology, having only one female mate.

mō·noġ′y·ny, *n.* [*mono-,* and Gr. *gynē,* a woman.]
1. marriage to one wife only; the state of having only one wife at a time.
2. in botany, the state of being monogynian.

mon·ō·hem′ēr·ous, *a.* [Gr. *monohēmeros,* lasting one day; *monos,* single, and *hēmera,* day.] in medicine, existing or continuing only for a single day.

mon·ō·hȳ′drāte, *n.* a hydrate containing one gram molecular weight of water per gram molecular weight of the combining element or radical.

mon·ō·hȳ′driç, *a.* [*mono-* and *-hydric.*]
1. having one hydroxyl group; as, *monohydric* alcohol.
2. having one atom of replaceable hydrogen.

mō·noi′çous, *a.* same as *monoecious.*

mon″ō·ī·dē′iṣm, *n.* [*mono-,* and Gr. *idea,* idea, and *-ism.*] the state or condition of devotion to one idea or thought.

mon·ol′ȧ·tēr, *n.* a person who practices monolatry.

mon·ol′ȧ·try, *n.* [*mono-,* and Gr. *latreia,* worship.] the worship of one god, where several are believed to exist.

mon′ō·lāy·ēr, *n.* a layer one molecule thick.

mon′ō·lith, *n.* [Gr. *monolithos,* made of one stone; *monos,* single, and *lithos,* stone.]
1. a single large block or piece of stone, as in architecture or sculpture.
2. a monument, statue, etc. made of a single stone; as, an Egyptian obelisk is a *monolith.*

mon′ō·lith·ăl, *a.* monolithic.

mon·ō·lith′iç, *a.* 1. of the character of a monolith; formed of a single stone.
2. massively solid, single, and uniform.

mon·ō·lob′ū·lăr, *a.* [*mono-,* and Gr. *lobos,* lobe.] having but one lobe or lobule; as, a *monolobular* gland.

mon·ō·loç′ū·lăr, *a.* same as *unilocular.*

mon·ō·loġ′iç, *a.* of, having the nature of, or like a monologue.

mon·ō·loġ′i·çăl, *a.* monologic.

mō·nol′ō·ġist, *n.* a monologuist.

mon′ō·logue (-log), *n.* [Fr., from L.Gr. *monologos,* speaking alone or to oneself; *monos,* single, alone, and *legein,* to speak.]
1. a long speech by one speaker, sometimes one monopolizing the conversation.
2. a poem or other composition in which one person is represented as speaking alone.
3. a part of a play in which one character speaks alone; soliloquy.
4. a play or playlet for one actor.
5. a type of dramatic entertainment by one speaker only.
Also spelled *monolog.*

mon′ō·logu·ist (-log-), *n.* a person who delivers, or performs in, monologues.

mō·nol′ō·ġy, *n.* 1. the act or habit of indulging in monologues or of monopolizing conversation by long dissertations; a habit of soliloquizing.
2. a monologue. [Obs.]

mon·ō·mā′çhi·ȧ, *n.* monomachy.

mō·nom′ȧ·çhist, *n.* one who fights in single combat; a duelist.

mō·nom′ȧ·çhy, *n.* [Gr. *monomachia,* single combat; *monos,* single, and *machesthai,* to fight.] a duel; a single combat.

mon′ō·māne, *n.* one suffering from monomania; a monomaniac.

mon·ō·mā′ni·ȧ, *n.* [*mono-,* and Gr. *mania,* madness.]
1. an excessive interest in or enthusiasm for some one thing; a craze.
2. a mental disorder characterized by irrationality on one subject.

mon·ō·mā′ni·aç, *n.* a person having monomania.

mon·ō·mā′ni·aç, *a.* monomaniacal.

mon″ō·mȧ·nī′ȧ·çăl, *a.* 1. having or characterized by monomania.
2. pertaining to monomania; resulting from monomania.

mō·nom′ēr·ous, *a.* [*mono-* and *-merous.*]
1. in botany, having one member in each whorl: said of flowers.
2. in zoology, having only one joint, as in the tarsi of certain insects.

mon″ō·mē·tal′liç, *a.* [*mono-,* and Gr. *metallon,* metal.]
1. of, containing, or using one metal.
2. of or based on monometallism.

mon·ō·met′ăl·liṣm, *n.* 1. the use of only one metal, usually gold or silver, as the monetary standard.
2. the doctrine or policies supporting this.

mon·ō·met′ăl·list, *n.* one who believes in or advocates monometallism.

mō·nom′e·tēr, *n.* [*mono-,* and Gr. *metron,* measure.] a rhythmical series consisting of a single meter.

mon·ō·met′riç, *a.* having the axes equal or of one kind, as the cube, octahedron, and dodecahedron: applied to crystals.

mon·ō·met′ri·çăl, *a.* pertaining to or consisting of monometers; containing only one meter.

mō·nō′mi·ăl, *a.* [from *mono-,* after *binomial.*]
1. in algebra, consisting of only one term or letter.
2. in biology, consisting of only one word: said of a name.

mō·nō′mi·ăl, *n.* a monomial expression, quantity, or name.

mon″ō·mō·leç′ū·lăr, *a.* 1. of a single molecule.
2. designating or of a layer one molecule thick.

mon·ō·mor′phiç, *a.* [*mono-,* and *-morphic.*]
1. having essentially the same type of structure.
2. having only one form.

mon·ō·mor′phous, *a.* monomorphic.

Mon″ō·mȳ·ā′ri·ȧ, *n.pl.* [*mono-,* and Gr. *mys,* muscle.] an order of *Mollusca* consisting of those bivalves whose shell is closed by a single adductor muscle, as in the oyster and the pecten.

mon″ō·mȳ·ăr′i·ăn, *a.* having one adductor muscle; specifically, resembling or related to the *Monomyaria.*

mon″ō·mȳ·ăr′i·ăn, *n.* a bivalve with one adductor muscle.

mon·ō·mȳ′ȧ·ry, *a.* and *n.* same as *monomyarian.*

mon·ō·neū′răl, mon·ō·neū′riç, *a.* [*mono-,* and Gr. *neuron,* nerve.] in zoology, having only one neuron.

mon·ō·nō′mi·ăl, *a.* [*mono-,* and L. *nomen,* name.] having a name expressed in one word: used in botany and zoology.

mon·ō·nō′mi·ăl, *n.* a name of one word; a mononym: opposed to *binomial* and *polynomial.*

mon·ō·nū·clē·ō′sis, *n.* 1. the presence in the blood of an excessive number of cells having a single nucleus.
2. a disease (*infectious mononucleosis*) resulting from this, characterized by fever and enlargement of the lymph nodes.

mon′ō·nym, *n.* [Gr. *mononymos; monos,* single, and *onyma,* name.] a name expressed by a single word.

mon·ō·nym′iç, *a.* designating something, as an animal, with a single-word name.

mon·ō·öu′si·ăn, *a.* same as *monoousious.*

mon·ō·öu′si·ous, *a.* [L.Gr. *monoousios; monos,* single, and *ousia,* essence, from *einai,* to be.] in theology, having identically the same nature or essence.

mon″ō·pȧ·rē′sis, *n.* [*mono-* and *paresis.*] paresis of a single part.

mō·nop′ȧ·thy, *n.* [*mono-,* and Gr. *pathos,* suffering.] a disease affecting a single part.

mon·ō·pēr′sŏn·ăl, *a.* [*mono-,* and L. *persona,* person.] in theology, having but one person.

mon·ō·pet′ăl·ous, *a.* [*mono-,* and Gr. *petallon,* a leaf.] in botany, (a) having the petals joined together into one piece by their edges; gamopetalous; (b) having a single petal.

MONOPETALOUS FLOWER

mō·noph′ȧ·gous, *a.* [*mono-* and Gr. *phagein,* to eat.] subsisting upon only one kind of food.

mon·ō·phō′bi·ȧ, *n.* [*mono-* and *-phobia.*] an abnormal fear of being alone.

mon·ō·phon′iç, *a.* of, or having the nature of, monophony.

mō·noph′ō·ny, *n.* [*mono-* and *-phony.*]
1. music having a single melody without accompaniment or harmonizing parts: distinguished from *homophony, polyphony.*
2. monody.

mon′ŏph·thŏng, *n.* [Gr. *monophthongos,* of or with one sound; *monos,* single, and *phthongos,* sound.]
1. a single, simple vowel sound.
2. a combination of two letters representing a single vowel sound, as *ea* in *leaf;* a vowel digraph.

mon·ŏph·thŏn′găl, *a.* of, or having the nature of, a monophthong.

mon″ō·phȳ·let′iç, *a.* [Gr. *monophylos,* of one tribe; *monos,* single, and *phylē,* a tribe.]
1. of a single stock.
2. developed from a single ancestral type.

mon·o·phyl′lous, *a.* [*mono-,* and Gr. *phyllon,* a leaf.] in botany, having or formed of only one leaf.

mon·ō·phȳ′ō·dont, *n.* [Gr. *monophyēs,* of a single nature, and *odous, odontos,* tooth.] a monophyodont animal, as a sloth or an armadillo.

mon·ō·phȳ′ō·dont, *a.* having only one set of teeth; having no milk teeth.

Mō·noph′y·sīte, *n.* [L.Gr. *monophysitēs; mo-*

nos, single, and *physis*, nature.] a person who believes that Christ had but one nature, or a composite nature of both the human and the divine, a tenet held by members of the Coptic and some other churches.

Mon″ō·phy·sit′iç, *a.* of, or holding the doctrine of, the Monophysites.

Mon″ō·phy·sit′i·çăl, *a.* same as *Monophysitic.*

mon·ō·plaç′ū·lȧ, *n.* [*mono-* and *placula.*] in biology, a germ with a single layer; a placula not yet differentiated.

mon′ō·plāne, *n.* an airplane with a single supporting surface, or pair of wings.

MONOPLANE

mon′ō·plast, *n.* [*mono-*, and Gr. *plastos*, formed, molded.] in biology, a single organic element; a single plasmic cell.

mon·ō·plas′tiç, *a.* relating to or having the form or character of a monoplast.

mon·ō·plē′ġi·ȧ, *n.* [*mono-*, and Gr. *plēgē*, a stroke.] paralysis of but a single part: distinguished from *hemiplegia* and *paraplegia.*

mon·ō·ple′ġiç (*or* -plē′jik), *a.* of or having monoplegia.

Mon·op·neū′mō·nȧ, *n.pl.* [*mono-*, and Gr. *pneumōn*, lung.] a division of dipnoan fishes having only one lung, as in species of *Ceratodus*: also written *Monopneumonia.*

mon″op·neū·mō′ni·ăn, *a.* having only one lung; specifically, designating fishes of the division *Monopneumona.*

mon′ō·pōde, *a.* [Gr. *monopous* (*-podos*); *monos*, single, and *pous*, *podos*, a foot.] having only one foot.

mon′ō·pōde, *n.* 1. a creature having only one foot; specifically, one of a fabled Ethiopian race of one-legged people.
2. in botany, a monopodium.

mon·ō·pō′di·ăl, *a.* in botany, of, having the nature of, or characterized by a monopodium.

mon·ō·pod′iç, *a.* relating to or characterized by monopody.

mon·ō·pō′di·um, *n.*; *pl.* **mon·ō·pō′di·ȧ**, in botany, a single main axis that continues to extend at the apex in its original line of growth, giving off lateral branches or axes: also *monopode.*

mō·nop′ō·dy, *n.* in prosody, a measure consisting of but one foot.

mō·nop′ō·lẽr, *n.* a monopolist. [Obs.]

mō·nop′ō·liṣm, *n.* the system or existence of monopolies, or the doctrine or practice of monopolies.

mō·nop′ō·list, *n.* 1. a person who has a monopoly.
2. a person who favors or advocates monopoly.

mō·nop′ō·list, *a.* monopolistic.

mō·nop·ō·lis′tiç, *a.* 1. of monopoly, monopolies, or monopolists.
2. monopolizing; having a monopoly.

mō·nop″ō·lī·zā′tion, *n.* a monopolizing or being monopolized.

mō·nop′ō·līze, *v.t.*; monopolized, *pt.*, *pp.*; monopolizing, *ppr.* 1. to obtain, have, or exploit a monopoly of.
2. to secure and retain exclusive possession or control of; as, to *monopolize* a seat in a car.

mō·nop′ō·līz·ẽr, *n.* a monopolist.

mō·nop′ō·ly, *n.*; *pl.* **mō·nop′ō·lieṣ**, [L. *monopolium*; Gr. *monopōlion*, the right of exclusive sale, *monopōlia*, exclusive sale; *monos*, single, alone, and *pōlein*, to sell.]
1. exclusive control of a commodity or service in a given market, or control that makes possible the fixing of prices and the virtual elimination of free competition.
2. an exclusive privilege of engaging in a particular business or providing a service, granted by a ruler or by the state.
3. exclusive possession or control of something.
4. anything which is the subject of a monopoly; as, salt and precious metals were *monopolies* of the crown in Germany.
5. a combination or company that has a monopoly.

mon·ō·pol′y·logue (-log), *n.* [*mono-*, and Gr. *polylogos*, much talking; *polus*, much, and *legein*, to speak.] a dramatic performance in which one actor impersonates several characters.

mon·ō·psȳ′çhiṣm (-sī′), *n.* [*mono-*, and Gr. *psychē*, soul.] the doctrine of the existence of but one immortal soul, of which each soul is a part.

mō·nop′tẽr·ăl, *a.* of or pertaining to a monopteron.

mō·nop′tẽr·on, mō·nop′tẽr·os, *n.* [Gr. *monopteros*, with one row of pillars; *monos*, single, and *pteron*, a wing.] a circular temple of which the cella is enclosed by a cycle of columns supporting the roof.

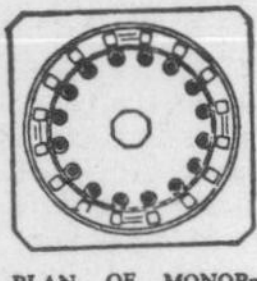

PLAN OF MONOPTERON

mon′op·tōte, *n.* [L.Gr. *monoptōtos*; Gr. *monos*, single, and *ptōsis*, case.] in grammar, a noun having only one form for all cases.

mon″ō·pȳ·rē′nous, *a.* [*mono-*, and Gr. *pyrēn*, the stone of fruit.] bearing but a single kernel or stone.

mon′ō·rāil, *n.* [*mono-* and *rail.*]
1. a single rail serving as a track for trucks or cars suspended from it or balanced on it.
2. a railway with such a track.

mon·or′çhid, *a.* [*mono-*, and Gr. *orchis*, testicle.] having but one testicle.

mon·or′çhis, *n.* one having a single testis.

mon·or′çhiṣm, *n.* the state of being a monorchis.

mon·or·gan′iç, *a.* relating to an organ or single set of organs; affecting one organ only, as a disease.

Mon·ō·rhī′nȧ (-rī′), *n.pl.* [*mono-*, and Gr. *rhis*, *rhinos*, nose.] a class of vertebrates having one nasal passage only, typified by the *Cyclostomata* or *Marsipobranchiata.*

mon·ō·rhī′năl, *a.* monorhine.

mon′ō·rhīne, *a.* of or pertaining to the *Monorhina.*

mon′ō·rhīne, *n.* one of the *Monorhina.*

mon′ō·rhȳme (-rīm), *n.* a metrical composition in which all lines end with the same rhyme: also written *monorime.*

mon·ō·saç′çhȧ·rīde, *n.* a carbohydrate not decomposable by hydrolysis; simple sugar, as glucose, fructose, etc.

mon·ō·sē′miç, *a.* [Gr. *monosēmos*; *monos*, single, and *sēma*, a sign.] in prosody, consisting of a single unit of time or one mora.

mon·ō·sep′ăl·ous, *a.* [*mono-*, and *-sepalous.*]
1. gamosepalous.
2. having only one sepal.

mon·ō·sō′di·um glū′tȧ·māte, a white crystalline powder, $C_5H_8O_4NaN$, derived from vegetable protein and used in foods as a flavor intensifier.

MONOSEPALOUS FLOWER

mon′ō·spaṣm, *n.* [*mono-*, and Gr. *spasmos*, a spasm.] spasm of a single muscle, part, or limb.

mon′ō·spẽrm, *n.* [*mono-*, and Gr. *sperma*, seed.] a plant producing but one sperm, or seed.

mon·ō·spẽr′mous, mon·ō·spẽr′măl, *a.* having only one seed.

mon·ō·spher′i·căl, *a.* [*mono-*, and Gr. *sphaira*, a sphere.] consisting of a single sphere.

mō·nos′pō·rous, *a.* [*momo-*, and Gr. *sphoros*, a seed.] having only one spore.

mō·nos′tȧ·çhous, *a.* [*mono-*, and Gr. *stachys*, an ear of corn.] having but one spike.

mon′ō·stiçh, *n.* [Gr. *monostichon*; *monos*, single, and *stichos*, a verse.]
1. a poem or epigram consisting of one metrical line.
2. one line of poetry; a verse.

mō·nos′ti·çhous, *a.* [*mono-*, and Gr. *stichos*, a line.] arranged serially on one side of an axis, as the flowers in certain grasses; uniaxial.

mon·ō·stig′mȧ·tous, *a.* [*mono-*, and Gr. *stigma* (*-atos*), a point.] having only one stigma.

mon·ō·stom′ȧ·tous, *a.* [*mono-*, and Gr. *stoma* (*-atos*), mouth.] having a single mouth: applied to animals in which the blastopore persists through life as a permanent mouth.

mon′ō·stōme, *a.* monostomous.

mō·nos′tō·mous, *a.* [*mono-* and *-stomous.*] having one mouth, stoma, or pore.

mō·nos′trō·phē, *n.* [Gr. *monostrophos*; *monos*, single, and *strophē*, a strophe.] a poem in which all the stanzas have the same metrical form.

mon·ō·stroph′iç, *a.* of or pertaining to a monostrophe.

mon·ō·stȳ′lous, *a.* [*mono-*, and Gr. *stylos*, a pillar.] in botany, having only one style.

mon″ō·syl·lab′iç, *a.* 1. having only one syllable: said of words.
2. consisting of monosyllables.
3. using, or speaking in, monosyllables.

mon″ō·syl·lab′iç·ăl·ly, *adv.* in or with monosyllables.

mon·ō·syl′lȧ·biṣm, *n.* 1. a monosyllabic character.
2. the use of monosyllables.

mon′ō·syl·lȧ·ble, *n.* [Gr. *monosyllabos*; *monos*, single, and *syllabos*, syllable.] a word consisting of a single syllable.

mon′ō·syl·lȧ·bled (-bld), *a.* merged into one syllable; expressed in monosyllables.

mon″ō·sym·met′riç, *a.* [*mono-* and *symmetric.*] in crystallography, designating a system of crystallization exhibiting but one plane of symmetry; monoclinic.

mon·ō·tes′sȧ·ron, *n.* [*mono-*, and Gr. *tessares*, four.] a narrative condensed from the statements of the four evangelists.

mon·ō·thal′ȧ·măn, *n.* an organism representing a group of the *Foraminifera*, having but one chamber: also written *monothalamian.*

Mon″ō·thȧ·lā′mi·ȧ, *n.pl.* a division of the *Foraminifera.* [Obs.]

mon·ō·thal′ȧ·miç, *a.* [*mono-*, and Gr. *thalamos*, a chamber.] designating fruit developed from one pistil only.

mon·ō·thal′ȧ·mous, *a.* [*mono-*, and Gr. *thalamos*, a chamber.] having a single chamber; unilocular.

mon·ō·thē′căl, *a.* [*mono-*, and Gr. *thēkē*, receptacle.] having one loculament, as most nuts.

mon′ō·thē·iṣm, *n.* [*mono-*, and Gr. *theos*, God.] the doctrine of or belief in the existence of only one God.

mon′ō·thē·ist, *n.* one who believes that there is but one God.

mon′ō·thē·ist, *a.* monotheistic.

mon″ō·thē·is′tiç, *a.* of or adhering to monotheism.

mon″ō·thē·is′ti·căl, *a.* monotheistic.

mon·ō·thē′li·ous, *a.* [*mono-*, and Gr. *thēlys*, female.] in zoology, polyandrous.

Mō·noth′ē·liṣm, *n.* same as *Monothelitism.*

Mō·noth′ē·līte, *n.* [L.Gr. *monothelētes*; *monos*, single, alone, and *thelein*, to will.] a supporter of the doctrine of Monothelitism; one who holds that Christ has but one will and one energy, both being divine.

Mon″ō·thē·lit′iç, *a.* of or pertaining to the Monothelites or Monothelitism.

Mō·noth′ē·lī·tiṣm, *n.* the doctrine of the Monothelites.

mon·ō·thet′iç, *a.* [*mono-*, and Gr. *thetos*, verbal adj. of *tithenai*, to put.] in philosophy, supposing or assuming a single essential element.

mon′ō·tint, *n.* a monochrome.

mō·not″ō·çăr′di·ăn, *a.* [*mono-*, and Gr. *kardia*, heart.] possessing a single auricle in the heart, as certain mollusks.

mō·not′ō·çous, *a.* [Gr. *monotokos*; *monos*, single, and *tiktein*, *tekein*, to bear.]
1. in botany, bearing fruit only once.
2. in zoology, bearing but one at a birth; laying a single egg; uniparous.

mō·not′ō·mous, *a.* [*mono-*, and Gr. *tomē*, a cutting, from *temnein*, to cut.] in mineralogy, having a cleavage distinct only in a single direction.

mon′ō·tōne, *n.* [Gr. *monotonos*; *monos*, single, and *tonos*, tone.]
1. uninterrupted repetition of the same tone; utterance of successive syllables or words without change of pitch or key.
2. monotony or sameness of tone, style, manner, color, etc.
3. a single, unchanging tone.
4. recitation, chanting, or singing in such a tone.
5. a person who sings in such a tone.

mon′ō·tōne, *v.t.* and *v.i.*; monotoned, *pt.*, *pp.*; monotoning, *ppr.* to recite in a single note without inflections or in an unvaried key.

mon′ō·tōne, *a.* monotonous.

mon·ō·ton′iç, *a.* pertaining to or uttered in a monotone; monotonous.

mon·ō·ton′iç·ăl, *a.* monotonic.

mon·ō·ton′iç·ăl·ly, *adv.* in a monotonic manner.

mō·not′ō·nist, *n.* one who keeps harping upon one subject; one who talks persistently in the same strain.

mō·not′ō·nous, *a.* [Gr. *monotonos*; *monos*, single, and *tonos*, tone.]
1. going on in the same tone without variation.
2. having little or no variation or variety.
3. tiresome because unvarying.
Syn.—changeless, unvariable, uniform, dull, humdrum, tedious, wearisome.

mō·not′ō·nous·ly, *adv.* in a monotonous manner.

mō·not′ō·nous·ness, *n.* the quality or state of being monotonous.

mō·not′ō·ny, *n.* [Gr. *monotonia*, of one and the same tone; *monos*, single, and *tonos*, tone.]
1. sameness of tone or pitch, or continuance of the same tone without variation.

2. lack of variation or variety.
3. tiresome sameness; wearisome uniformity.

Mon·ō·trē′ma̤·ta̤, *n.pl.* [*mono-*, and Gr. *trēma* (*-atos*), a hole.] the lowest order of mammals, having only one aperture for the urinary, genital, and intestinal canals. The teeth, if present, consist of four horny plates. In the order are included the duck moles and certain species of so-called prickly anteaters, and the duck-billed platypus of Australia. They lay eggs rather than producing living young.

mon·ō·trem′a̤·tous, *a.* of or pertaining to the *Monotremata*.

mon′ō·trēme, *a.* monotrematous.

mon′ō·trēme, *n.* one of the *Monotremata*.

mon′ō·trē·mous, *a.* monotrematous.

mon·ō·trich′iç, *a.* monotrichous.

mō·not′ri·chous, *a.* [from *mono-* and Gr. *thrix*, *trichos*, hair; and *-ic.*] having a single flagellum at one end, as some bacteria.

mon·ō·trī′glyph, *n.* [L. *monotriglyphus*; Gr. *monos*, single, and *triglyphos*, a triglyph.] in architecture, the intercolumniation of the Doric order which includes one triglyph and two metopes in the entablature above the space between two columns.

Mō·not′rō·cha̤, *n.pl.* [*mono-*, and Gr. *trochos*, wheel.]
1. in entomology, a division of the *Hymenoptera*, comprising those insects which have trochanters with only one joint.
2. an obsolete division of rotifers with a single, undivided, ciliated wheel.

mō·not′rō·chăl, *a.* 1. provided with a single ciliated ring, as the larvae of certain chaetopods.
2. pertaining to the *Monotrocha*; having but one trochanteric joint.

mon·ō·trō′chi·ăn, *a.* monotrochal: said of a rotifer.

mon·ō·trō′chi·ăn, *n.* a rotifer of the division *Monotrocha*. [Rare.]

mō·not′rō·chous, *a.* monotrochal.

Mō·not′rō·pa̤, *n.* [*mono-*, and Gr. *trepein*, to turn.] a genus of plants, typical of the order *Monotropeæ*. *Monotropa uniflora* is known as the Indian pipe, corpse plant, or ice plant.

Mon″ō·trō·pā′cē·ae, *n.pl.* the *Monotropeæ*.

mon″ō·trō·pā′ceous, *a.* of or pertaining to the *Monotropaceæ*.

Mon·ō·trō′pē·ae, *n.pl.* a family of leafless, exogenous, parasitic plants, of which the genus *Monotropa* is the type. The order includes nine genera and about a dozen species.

mon·ō·trop′iç, *a.* monodromic.

mon′ō·ty̆p·ăl, *a.* monotypic.

mon′ō·tȳpe, *n.* [*mono-* and *-type.*]
1. in biology, the only type of its group, as a single species constituting a genus.
2. (a) in printing, either of a pair of machines for casting and setting up type in separate characters on individual bodies: one, a casting machine, is controlled by a paper tape perforated on the other, a keyboard machine: a trade-mark (*Monotype*); (b) type produced in this way; (c) a print from a metal plate on which a picture has been made, as with printing ink; (d) the method of making such prints.

mon′ō·tȳpe, *a.* monotypic.

mon·ō·typ′iç, *a.* 1. having but one type; consisting of a single representative; as, a *monotypic* genus.
2. being or having the nature of a monotype.

mon·ō·typ′i·căl, *a.* monotypic.

mon·ō·vā′lence, *n.* the quality or state of being monovalent.

mon·ō·vā′len·cy, *n.* same as *monovalence*.

mon·ō·vā′lent, *a.* [*mono-*, and L. *valens* (*-entis*), ppr. of *valere*, to be strong.]
1. in bacteriology, capable of resisting one strain of a given species of disease-producing organism because the right antibodies or antigens are present.
2. in chemistry, (a) having a valence of one; (b) univalent.

mon·ox′īde, mō·nox′īd (*or* -id), *n.* [*mon-* and *oxide.*] in chemistry, an oxide containing but one atom of oxygen in each molecule.

mō·nox′yle, *n.* a monoxylon.

mō·nox′y·lon, *n.* [L.Gr. *monoxylon*, neut. of *monoxylos*, made of one piece of wood; *monos*, single, and *xylon*, wood.] a canoe or boat made from one piece of timber.

mō·nox′y·lous, *a.* formed of a single piece of timber.

Mŏn·rōe′ Doç′trine, the doctrine, essentially stated by President Monroe in a message to Congress (December, 1823), that the United States would regard as an unfriendly act any attempt by a European nation to interfere in the affairs of the American countries or increase its possessions on the American continents.

monṣ, *n.* [L., a mountain.] in anatomy, a prominence on the lower portion of the abdomen, covered with hair in the adult. In the male it is known as the mons pubis, and in the female, mons veneris.

Mon·sei·gnēur′, mon·sei·gnēur′ (-sen-yẽr′ *or Fr.* mọṅ-se-nyẽr′), *n.*; *pl.* **Mes·sei·gnēurṣ′, mes·sei·gnēurs′** (-en-yẽrz′ *or Fr.* mā-se-nyẽr′), [Fr., lit., my lord; *mon*, my, and *seigneur*, lord, from L. *senior*, older.]
1. a French title of honor given to persons of high birth or rank, as princes, or to important church officers, as bishops, cardinals, etc.
2. a person who has this title.

mon·siēur′ (m′syẽr′ *or Fr.* m′syẽ′), *n.*; *pl.* **mes′siēurṣ′** (-ẽrz′ *or Fr.* mā-syẽ′), [Fr., contr. of *monseigneur.*] a man; a gentleman: French title [M–], equivalent to *Mr.* or *Sir.*

Mọn·sĭ′gnor (-sēn′yẽr), *n.*; *pl.* **Mon·sĭ′gnorṣ** or It. **Mon·sĭ·gnọ′rī** (-nyọ′rē), [It., my lord.]
1. a title given to certain dignitaries of the Roman Catholic Church.
2. a person who has this title.
Also *monsignor*.

mọn·sĭ·gnọ′re (-nyọ′re), *n.*; *pl.* **mọn·sĭ·gnọr′ī** (-nyọ′rē), [It.] monsignor.

mon·sọọn′, *n.* [M.D. *monssoen*; Port. *monção*, from Ar. *mausim*, a time, a season.]
1. a seasonal wind of the Indian Ocean and southern Asia, blowing from the southwest from April to October, and from the northeast during the rest of the year.
2. the season during which this wind blows from the southwest, characterized by heavy rains.
3. any wind that reverses its direction seasonally or blows constantly between land and adjacent water.

mon·sọọn′ăl, *a.* pertaining to monsoons.

monṣ pū′bis, the fleshy, rounded elevation, covered with pubic hair, at the lower part of a man's abdomen.

mon′stẽr, *n.* [ME. and OFr. *monstre*, from L. *monstrum*, any occurrence out of the ordinary course of nature supposed to indicate the will of the gods, a marvel, a monster, from *monere*, to admonish, to warn.]
1. any plant or animal of abnormal shape or structure, as one greatly malformed or lacking some parts; a monstrosity.
2. any imaginary creature part human and part animal in form, as a centaur, or made up of the parts of two or more different animals, as a unicorn.
3. something monstrous.
4. a person so cruel, wicked, depraved, etc. as to horrify others.
5. any huge animal or thing.
6. in pathology, a malformed fetus, especially one with an excess or deficiency of limbs or parts; teratism.

mon′stẽr, *a.* of enormous or extraordinary size or numbers; huge; as, a *monster* meeting.

mon′stẽr, *v.t.* to make monstrous. [Obs.]

Mon′stẽr·a̤, *n.* a genus of araceous climbing plants, native to tropical America.

mon′stẽr·ship, *n.* the condition of being a monster.

mon′strănce, *n.* [ME. *mustraunce*, *munstraunce*; OFr., from ML. *monstrantia*, from L. *monstrare*, to show.] in the Roman Catholic Church, the transparent or glass-faced shrine in which the consecrated Host is presented for the adoration of the people, either while being carried in procession or when exposed on the altar. It is placed in a stand, generally made of precious metal and sometimes richly jeweled. Also called *ostensory*, *remonstrance*, *expositorium*, and *theotheca*.

MONSTRANCE

mon·strā′tion, *n.* a demonstration; a showing; a proof. [Obs.]

mon′stri·cīde, *n.* [L. *monstrum*, and *-cidium*, from *cædere*, to kill.] the act of slaughtering a monster.

mon·stros′i·ty, *n.* [LL. *monstrositas*, from *monstrosus*, monstrous.]
1. the state or quality of being monstrous.
2. *pl.* **mon·stros′i·tieṣ**, a monstrous thing or creature; that which is monstrous; a monstrous or unnatural production; a monster.

mon′strous, *a.* [LL. *monstrosus*, from L. *monstrum*, a portent, omen, monster.]
1. abnormally or prodigiously large; huge; enormous.
2. very unnatural or abnormal in shape, type, or character.
3. having the character or appearance of a monster.
4. horrible; hideous; shocking.
5. hideously wrong or evil; atrocious.
Syn.—prodigious, stupendous, vast, marvelous, abnormal, preposterous, atrocious, horrible.

mon′strous, *adv.* exceedingly; very much. [Colloq., Now Rare.]
Monstrous witty on the poor. —Dryden.

mon′strous·ly, *adv.* in a monstrous manner.

mon′strous·ness, *n.* the state or quality of being monstrous.

mons ven′ẽr·is, [L., lit., mount of Venus.] the fleshy, rounded elevation, covered with pubic hair, at the lower part of a woman's abdomen.

mōṅt (mōṅ), *n.* [Fr.] a mountain.

mon·täge′ (-täzh′), *n.* [Fr., a mounting, setting together, from *monter*, to mount.]
1. (a) the art or process of making a composite picture by bringing together into a single composition a number of different pictures or parts of pictures and arranging these, as by superimposing one on another, so that they form a blended whole while remaining distinct; (b) a picture so made.
2. in motion pictures, (a) the process of producing a rapid sequence of very short scenes to show a rapid succession of associated ideas or mental images, or a sequence in which images, as of objects, are shown as whirling or flashing rapidly into focus; (b) a part of a motion picture in which this is used; (c) the process of cutting and arranging the film.
3. in radio, a sequence in which voices or sounds break in on one another or blend to suggest confusion, introspection, etc.

Mon·tan′ăn, *a.* of Montana.

Mon·tan′ăn, *n.* a native or inhabitant of Montana.

mon′tāne, *a.* [Fr., from L. *montanus*, belonging to a mountain.] mountainous; of or pertaining to mountains.

Mon′ta̤·niṣm, *n.* the tenets of the Montanists.

Mon′ta̤·nist, *n.* a follower of Montanus, a Phrygian bishop and enthusiast of the second century, who claimed that the Holy Spirit, the Paraclete, dwelt in him, and employed him as an instrument for purifying and guiding men in the Christian life.

mon·ta̤·nis′tiç, *a.* pertaining to Montanus or Montanism.

mon·ta̤·nis′tiç·ăl, *a.* montanistic.

mon·tan′īte, *n.* a soft, earthy tellurate of bismuth of a yellow color, found in the state of Montana.

Mon′ta̤·nīze, *v.i.* to adhere to the opinions of Montanus.

mon′tănt, *n.* [LL. *montans* (*-antis*), rising, ppr. of *montare*, to mount, from L. *mons*, *montis*, a mountain.] in carpentry, the intermediate vertical part of a piece of framing which is tenoned with the rails. [Rare.]

mon′tănt, *a.* rising; mounting.

mon′tan wax, [from L. *montanus*, of a mountain, and *wax.*] a brown or whitish hydrocarbon wax extracted from lignite and peat, and used in making candles, polishes, phonograph records, etc.

mont-de-pié·té′ (mōṅ-de-pyā-tā′), *n.*; *pl.* **monts-de-pié·té′** (mōṅ-), [Fr.; It., *monte di pietà*, charitable bank, lit., mount of pity.] a public pawnshop, authorized and controlled by the government, for lending money to the poor at a low rate of interest.

mon′tẹ, *n.* [Sp., the stock of cards which remain after each player has received his share, from L. *mons, montis*, a mountain.] a gambling game of Spanish origin, played with a special deck of forty cards, in which the players bet against a banker on the color of cards to be turned up from the deck.

mon·tēith′, *n.* [said to be named after the inventor.]
1. a large bowl for punch, etc., usually of silver, with a brim from which glasses and ladles are hung.
2. a handkerchief having a colored ground which is variegated with white spots produced by a discharge method.

mọnte′-jụs (-zhụ), *n.* [Fr., from *monter*, to

raise, and *jus*, juice.] in a sugar refinery, a kind of force pump by which the juice from the cane mill is raised to the clarifiers on the story above.

mon'tem, *n.* [from L. *processus ad montem*, going to the hill.] formerly, a custom among the scholars at Eton school, England, of going every third year, on Whit-Tuesday, to a hillock near the Bath road, and exacting money from all passers-by, to support at Cambridge University the senior scholar of the school.

Mon·tē·neg'rin, Mon·tē·neg'rine, *a.* pertaining to Montenegro, a small European country on the Adriatic, or to its inhabitants.

Mon·tē·neg'rin, Mon·tē·neg'rine, *n.* 1. a native or inhabitant of Montenegro.

2. [m-] an ornamental outer garment worn by women.

mon·te'rō, *n.*; *pl.* **mon·te'rōs**, [Sp.]

1. a huntsman.

2. a kind of cap, properly a huntsman's cap, having a spherical crown and ear flaps.

Mon·tes·sō'ri meth'ŏd (or **sys'tem**), a system of training and teaching young children devised in 1907 by Maria Montessori, which emphasizes training of the senses and aims at self-education through guiding rather than controlling the child's activity.

Mon·te·zū'mȧ's rē·venġe', acute infectious diarrhea, especially when contracted in Mexico. [Slang.]

Mont·gol'fi·ēr (*or Fr. pron.* moṇ-gol-fyā'), *n.* a balloon filled with hot air: so called from the name of the inventors, the Montgolfier brothers, of France, who performed the first experiment with it in June, 1783.

mŏnth, *n.* [ME. *moneth*; AS. *monath, monoth*, from *mōna*, the moon.]

1. any of the main parts (in the Gregorian calendar, twelve) into which the calendar year is divided: also *calendar month*.

2. (a) the time from any day of one month to the corresponding day of the next; (b) a period of four weeks or 30 days.

3. the period of a complete revolution of the moon with reference to some fixed point (in full, *lunar month*); especially, the period from one new moon to the next (in full, *synodic month*): equivalent to 29 days, 12 hours, 44 minutes, and 2.7+seconds.

4. one twelfth of the solar year (in full, *solar month*).

a month of Sundays; a period of time of indefinite length; as, I have not seen him for *a month of Sundays*.

a month's mind; in the Roman Catholic Church, a Requiem Mass said for a person on the 30th day after death or burial.

anomalistic month; the time taken by the moon in passing from one perigee to the next, namely, 27 days, 13 hours, 18 minutes, and 37.4 seconds.

month after month; every month.

month by month; each month.

month in, month out; every month.

nodical month; see *dracontic month* under *draconic*.

sidereal month; the time taken by the moon in passing from one star to the same star again, namely, 27 days, 7 hours, 43 minutes, 11.5 seconds.

tropical month; the time taken by the moon in passing from any point of the ecliptic to the same point again, namely, 27 days, 7 hours, 43 minutes, 4.7 seconds.

mŏnth'ly, *a.* 1. continuing or lasting for a month.

2. done, happening, appearing, payable, etc. once a month, or every month; as, a *monthly* magazine.

3. of a month, or each month.

4. of the menses.

mŏnth'ly, *n.*; *pl.* **mŏnth'lies**, 1. a publication which appears regularly once a month.

2. [*pl.*] the menses.

mŏnth'ly, *adv.* once a month; every month.

mon·ti·cel'līte, *n.* [after T. *Monticelli*, an Italian chemist.] a silicate of calcium and magnesium, $CaMgSiO_4$, crystallizing in the orthorhombic system. It belongs to the chrysolite group of minerals.

Mon·ti·cel'lō (*occas.* mon-ti-chel'ō), *n.* the home of Thomas Jefferson, three miles from Charlottesville, Virginia.

mon'ti·çle, *n.* [LL. *monticulus*, dim. of L. *mons, montis*, a mountain.] a little mount; a hillock.

mon·tiç'ū·lāte, *a.* having little projections or hills.

mon'ti·çūle, *n.* [Fr.; LL. *monticulus*, dim. of *mons, montis*, mountain.]

1. a small mountain or hill.

2. a secondary cone of a volcano.

mon·tiç'ū·lous, *a.* monticulate.

mon'ti·form, *a.* [L. *mons, montis*, a mountain, and *forma*, form.] like a mountain; having the form of a mountain.

mon·tiġ'ē·nous, *a.* [LL. *montigena*; L. *mons, montis*, a mountain, and *gignere*, to be born.] produced on a mountain.

mont·mär'trīte, *n.* a soft, weather-resistant gypsum of a yellowish color, found at Montmartre, Paris.

mont·mō·ril'lō·nīte, *n.* a hydrous aluminum silicate originally found at Montmorillon, in France.

mon'ton, *n.* [Sp., from L. *mons, montis*, a mountain.] in mining, a heap of ore; a batch under process of amalgamation, varying in quantity in different mining districts.

mon'tre (-tēr), *n.* [Fr.]

1. an organ stop, the pipes of which form part of the case or are placed away from the soundboard; the open diapason of the great organ.

2. in ceramics, an opening in a kiln through which a view of the contents may be had.

mon·tross', *n.* see *matross*.

mon'tūre, *n.* 1. a saddle horse. [Obs.]

2. a setting, mounting, or frame; as, the *monture* of a diamond.

mon'ū·ment, *n.* [L. *monumentum*, from *monere*, to remind, to warn.]

1. something set up to keep alive the memory of a person or event, as a tablet, statue, pillar, building, etc.

2. a structure surviving from a former period.

3. a writing or the like serving as a memorial.

4. a work, production, etc. of enduring value or significance; as, *monuments* of learning.

5. a stone shaft or other object set in the earth to mark a boundary.

6. a tomb; sepulcher. [Obs.]

7. a statue; effigy. [Obs.]

mon'ū·ment, *v.t.* 1. to erect a monument to the memory of; as, to *monument* a noble deed.

2. to adorn with monuments.

mon·ū·men'tăl, *a.* 1. of, suitable for, or serving as a monument or monuments.

2. like a monument; massive, enduring, etc.

3. historically notable, important, or of lasting value; as, a *monumental* book.

4. great; colossal; as, *monumental* ineptitude.

5. in art, larger than life-size.

mon″ū·men·tal'i·ty, *n.* the quality or state of being monumental.

mon·ū·men″tăl·i·zā'tion, *n.* the act of making monumental; also, the condition of being monumental.

mon·ū·men'tăl·īze, *v.t.*; monumentalized, *pt., pp.*; monumentalizing, *ppr.* to make a lasting memorial or record of, as by a monument.

mon·ū·men'tăl·ly, *adv.* in a monumental manner; by way or means of monuments.

mon'y, *a.* and *n.* many. [Scot. and Brit. Dial.]

-mō'ny, [Fr. *-monie*, L. *-monia*.] a suffix used to form nouns that mean *a resulting thing, condition*, or *state*, as in patri*mony*, sancti*mony*: it is sometimes equivalent to *-ment*.

mon'zō·nīte, *n.* [from Mount *Monzoni*, in the Tyrol, where it occurs.] an igenous rock containing orthoclase and plagioclase feldspar in nearly equal amounts and, sometimes, biotite in small quantities.

mo͞o, *n.*; *pl.* **mo͞os**, [echoic.] the characteristic sound made by a cow; a lowing sound.

mo͞o, *v.i.*; mooed, *pt., pp.*; mooing, *ppr.* to make the characteristic sound of a cow; to low.

mo͞och, *v.t.* [ME. *mowchen*, dial. var. of *mychen*, to pilfer, from OFr. *muchier*, to skulk, hide.]

1. to steal; pilfer. [Slang.]

2. to get by begging or asking for, without payment, as cigarettes; to cadge [Slang.]

mo͞och, *v.i.* 1. to skulk or sneak. [Slang.]

2. to loiter, loaf, or rove about. [Slang.]

mo͞och'ēr, *n.* one who mooches; as, he is a cigarette *moocher*. [Slang.]

mo͞od, *n.* [a form of *mode*.]

1. in grammar, (a) in many languages, that aspect of verbs which has to do with the speaker's attitude toward the action or state expressed, indicating whether this is regarded as a fact (*indicative mood*), as a matter of supposal, desire, possibility, etc. (*subjunctive mood*), as a command (*imperative mood*), etc.: mood is shown by inflection, as in Latin and Greek, or by auxiliaries, as English *may, might, should*, or by both; (b) a set of forms expressing this aspect; (c) any such form. Also *mode*.

2. in logic, mode.

mo͞od, *n.* [AS. *mod*, mind, soul, courage.]

1. a particular state of mind or feeling; humor, or temper.

2. [*pl.*] fits of morose, sullen, or uncertain temper.

3. anger. [Obs.]

mo͞od'i·ly, *adv.* in a moody manner.

mo͞od'i·ness, *n.* the state or quality of being moody.

mo͞od'ish, *a.* having an inclination to be moody; subject to moods.

mo͞od'ish·ly, *adv.* in a moody manner; moodily.

mo͞od'y, *a.*; *comp.* moodier; *superl.* moodiest. 1. subject to or characterized by gloomy, sullen moods or changes of mood.

2. resulting from or indicating such a mood.

3. gloomy; sullen; depressed.

Syn.—gloomy, pensive, capricious, sullen.

mo͞o go͞o gai pan, [Chin., lit. mushroom chicken slice.] a Chinese dish consisting of slices of chicken sautéed with black mushrooms, lotus root, and assorted vegetables.

mo͞on, *n.* [AS. *mona*, the moon.]

1. the heavenly body that revolves around the earth once about every 28 days and accompanies it in its yearly revolution about the sun, reflecting the sun's light: the moon's diameter is about 2,160 miles, its mean distance from the earth is about 238,857 miles, and its mean density is 0.60.

2. this body as it appears during a particular lunar month or period of time, or at a particular time of the month: the *new moon* (the moon when in conjunction with the sun) becomes visible as a narrow crescent; the *half moon* (the moon when half of its disk is illuminated) is visible as a half circle; the *full moon* (the moon when its entire disk is illuminated) is visible as a circle; and the *old* (or *waning*) *moon* is the moon at any time after it has been full.

3. a month; especially, a lunar month.

4. moonlight.

5. anything shaped like the moon (i.e., orb or crescent).

6. any planetary satellite.

mo͞on, *v.i.* to wander or gaze idly or moodily about, as if moonstruck.

mo͞on, *v.t.* 1. to expose to the rays of the moon. [Rare.]

2. to pass (time) in mooning.

mo͞o'nack, *n.* [Am. Ind.] in the southern part of the United States, the woodchuck.

mo͞on'bēam, *n.* a ray of light from the moon.

mo͞on'-blīnd, *a.* having moon blindness.

mo͞on blīnd'ness, 1. night blindness: formerly attributed to the effects of moonlight.

2. a disease of horses, of undetermined cause, characterized by recurrent inflammation of the eyes and, eventually, blindness.

mo͞on'ċalf (-kȧf), *a.* 1. a monster; a deformed creature. [Obs.]

2. a mole, or mass of fleshy matter formed in the uterus.

3. a congenital idiot; a born fool.

mo͞on'-çul'mi·nā·ting, *a.* in astronomy, culminating at or near the same time as the moon; as, *moon-culminating* stars.

mo͞on dāi'sy, the oxeye daisy.

mo͞on dī'ăl, a dial to show the hours by the moon.

mo͞oned (*or* mo͞on'ed), *a.* 1. having the moon as a symbol; identified with the moon.

2. marked or decorated with moon-shaped signs or devices; bearing the Turkish emblem of the crescent.

3. resembling the moon; crescent-shaped.

mo͞on'ēr, *n.* one who wanders or gazes idly or moodily about, as if moonstruck.

mo͞on'et, *n.* a little moon. [Rare.]

mo͞on'eȳe (-ī), *n.* 1. an eye of a horse affected with moon blindness.

2. moon blindness.

3. an American fresh-water fish, having large eyes, belonging to the *Hyodontidæ*.

mo͞on'-eȳed (-īd), *a.* 1. moon-blind.

2. having the eyes wide open, as from fright or wonder.

mo͞on'-fāced (-fāst), *a.* having a round face, like that of the full moon.

mo͞on'fish, *n.*; *pl.* **mo͞on'fish** or **mo͞on'fish·eṣ**, 1. any of a number of sea fishes with a silvery or yellow, deep, sharply compressed body, found in the warmer coastal waters of North and South America.

2. any of various other fishes; especially, (a) the Mexican top minnow; (b) the opah.

mo͞on'flow″ẽr, *n.* 1. a night-blooming plant of the morning-glory family, with large, heart-shaped leaves and white, fragrant, trumpet-shaped flowers; also, its flower.

2. the oxeye daisy, *Chrysanthemum leucanthemum*: also called *moon daisy.*

mo͞on'ish, *a.* like the moon; changeable; fickle; capricious.

mo͞on'less, *a.* without a moon; not moonlit.

mo͞on'līght (-līt), *n.* the light afforded by the moon.

mo͞on'līght, *a.* 1. of moonlight.

2. moonlit.

3. done or occurring by moonlight, or at night.

mo͞on'līght·ing, *n.* [from the usual night hours of such jobs.] the practice of holding a second regular job in addition to one's main job.

mo͞on'lit, *a.* illuminated or lighted by the moon.

mo͞on'pōrt, *n.* [*moon,* and *-port,* as in *airport.*] an installation for launching rockets to the moon.

mo͞on'quāke, *n.* a trembling of the surface of the moon, thought to be caused by internal rock slippage or, possibly, meteorite impact.

mo͞on'rīse, *n.* the rising or time of rising of the moon above the horizon.

mo͞on'sçāpe, *n.* [*moon,* and land*scape.*] the surface of the moon or a representation of it.

mo͞on'seed, *n.* a climbing plant of the genus *Menispermum,* with crescent-shaped seeds, heart-shaped leaves, and greenish-yellow flowers.

mo͞on'set, *n.* the setting or time of setting of the moon below the horizon.

mo͞on'shee, *n.* [Anglo-Ind.] in India, a Mohammedan professor; a teacher of languages; a secretary or interpreter.

mo͞on'shīne, *n.* 1. the light of the moon.

2. foolish or empty talk, notions, plans, etc.; nonsense.

3. whisky, etc. unlawfully made or smuggled. [Colloq.]

mo͞on'shīne, *a.* 1. moonlight.

2. as unreal as moonlight; nonsensical.

3. pertaining to whisky, etc. unlawfully made or smuggled. [Colloq.]

mo͞on'shīn·ẽr, *n.* one who makes alcoholic liquor unlawfully. [Colloq.]

mo͞on'shīn·y, *a.* 1. illuminated by the moon.

I went to see them in a *moonshiny* night.
—Addison.

2. like or suggestive of moonlight.

3. unreal, unsubstantial, visionary, etc.

mo͞on'stōne, *n.* a milky-white, translucent feldspar with a pearly luster, used as a gem.

mo͞on'-striçk″en, *a.* same as *moonstruck.*

mo͞on'struck, *a.* disordered in mind or otherwise harmfully affected, supposedly by the influence of the moon; crazed; lunatic; dazed.

mo͞on'wạlk, *n.* a walking about by an astronaut on the surface of the moon.

mo͞on'wŏrt, *n.* 1. any of a group of ferns with fleshy leaves and a fruiting spike resembling a bunch of grapes.

2. the honesty, a plant with large, purple flowers and semitransparent pods.

mo͞on'y, *a.*; *comp.* moonier; *superl.* mooniest. 1. of or characteristic of the moon.

2. like the moon, especially in shape; round or crescent-shaped.

3. moonlit.

4. like moonlight.

5. mooning; listless, dreamy, or silly.

Mo͞or, *n.* [L. *Maurus*; Gr. *Mauros,* a Moor, from *mauros,* black or dark.]

1. a member of a Moslem people of mixed Arab and Berber descent living in northwestern Africa.

2. a member of a group of this people that invaded and occupied Spain in the eighth century A.D.

mo͞or, *n.* [AS. *mor,* wasteland, a moor, a fen.]

1. a tract of open wasteland, especially in the British Isles, usually covered with heather and often marshy or peaty; heath. [Brit.]

2. a tract of land on which game is preserved for the purpose of sport. [Brit.]

mo͞or, *v.t.*; moored, *pt., pp.*; mooring, *ppr.* [Early Mod. Eng.; prob. from AS.]

1. to confine or secure (a ship) in place as by cables and anchors or by chains.

2. to secure; to fix firmly.

mo͞or, *v.i.* 1. to moor a ship, etc.

2. to be held by cables or chains.

On oozy ground his galleys *moor.*
—Dryden.

mo͞or'āġe, *n.* 1. a mooring or being moored.

2. a place for mooring.

3. a charge for the use of such a place.

mo͞or'bạll, *n.* an alga, *Cladophora holsatica,* found in spongelike balls at the bottom of fresh-water lakes.

mo͞or'band, *n.* same as *moorpan.*

mo͞or bē'sŏm, heather, *Calluna vulgaris.*

mo͞or buz'zȧrd, the marsh harrier. [Brit.]

mo͞or çōal, a kind of coal easily broken, a friable lignite.

mo͞or çock, the male of the moorfowl, or red grouse. [Brit.]

mo͞or co͞ot, a gallinule.

mo͞or ē'vil, a disease of sheep and cattle. [Brit. Dial.]

mo͞or'flow″ẽr, *n.* the buck bean.

mo͞or'fowl″, *n.* the red grouse. [Brit.]

mo͞or frog, an edible frog, *Rana esculenta.* [Brit.]

mo͞or gāme, red grouse.

mo͞or gràss, a British plant of the genus *Sesleria,* the *Sesleria cærulea.* It grows on mountains in Scotland and the north of England.

mo͞or hag, very rough moorland.

mo͞or har'ri·ẽr, the marsh harrier.

mo͞or hawk, the marsh harrier.

mo͞or hen, 1. the common European gallinule, *Gallinula chloropus.* [Brit.]

2. the female of the red grouse. [Brit.]

mo͞or'ing, *n.* 1. the act of a person or thing that moors.

2. [*often in pl.*] the lines, cables, etc. by which this is done.

3. [*pl.*] a place where a ship, etc. is or can be moored; moorage.

4. [*often in pl.*] beliefs, habits, ties, etc. that make one feel secure.

mo͞or'ing block, a large cast-iron block used as an anchor to moor a ship or boat.

MOORING BLOCK

mo͞or'ing màst (or **tow'ẽr**), a mast (or tower) to which an airship is or can be moored.

mo͞or'ish, *a.* characteristic of a moor, or heath.

Mo͞or·ish, *a.* 1. of the Moors, their culture, etc.

2. in the style of the Moors: said of architecture, etc.

Moorish architecture; a style of architecture which the Moors of Spain, North Africa, etc. employed in mosques and other public edifices. Called also *Saracenic* or *Arabian architecture.* Its distinguishing features are the prevailing use of the arch of a horseshoe shape, lofty, elongated cupolas, and a profusion of elaborate surface decoration. The horseshoe arch embraces more than a semicircle, and is therefore narrower at the springing than above, as shown in the doorway here illustrated. Similar arches, pointed at the top, are also common, as well as cuspate and other forms of arches. The columns from which the arches spring are slender, sometimes in pairs, and the superincumbent masses broad and heavy. The profuse decoration of interior surfaces with richly colored arabesques and geometrical designs is another distinctive feature of this style of architecture. Mosaics of glazed tiles, such as that shown in the accompanying cut, are frequently employed to decorate walls, the star being one of the simple forms often adopted for the basis of the design. Many interesting examples of this style of architecture remain at various places in Spain, the finest of all being the Alhambra at Granada.

MOORISH DOORWAY

MOORISH WALL DECORATION

mo͞or'lănd, *n.* a waste, barren district; a moor. [Brit.]

mo͞or'pan, *n.* the hard clayey layer underlying many moors.

mo͞or'stōne, *n.* granite. [Brit. Dial.]

mo͞o'ruk, *n.* a rare and easily tamed cassowary, *Casuarius bennetti.*

mo͞or'vȧ, *n.* [E. Ind.] the plant, *Sansevieria zeylanica,* found in the East Indies; also, its hemplike fiber.

mo͞or'wŏrt, *n.* any of a group of low, evergreen shrubs growing in moors or bogs in the North Temperate Zone.

mo͞or'y, *a.* moorish; marshy; fenny; boggy.

mo͞or'y, *n.* [E. Ind.] an East Indian cloth, either brown or blue.

Mo͞ose, *n.* 1. same as *Bull Moose.*

2. a member of the Loyal Order of Moose, a secret fraternal and beneficiary society, founded in 1888 at Louisville, Kentucky.

mo͞ose, *n.*; *pl.* **mo͞ose,** [from Am. Ind. (Algonquian).]

1. the largest animal, *Alces americana,* of the deer family, native to the Northern United States and Canada: the male has huge palmate antlers. The eyes of the moose are small; the upper lip is square, hangs over the lower one, and has a deep furrow in the middle so as to appear bifid.

2. the European elk.

mo͞ose'bīrd, *n.* same as *whisky jack.*

mo͞ose elm, the slippery elm.

mo͞ose'wood, *n.* 1. the striped maple, *Acer pennsylvanicum.*

2. the shrub leatherwood, *Dirca palustris.*

mo͞ose yärd, a locality frequented by moose in winter.

mo͞ot, *n.* in shipbuilding, a ring gauge for wooden pins. [Rare.]

mo͞ot, *n.* [ME. *mote*; AS. *mot, gemot,* a meeting, assembly.]

1. an early English assembly of freemen to administer justice, decide community problems, etc.

2. a discussion or argument, especially of a hypothetical law case, as in a law school.

mo͞ot, *a.* subject to or open for discussion or debate; debatable.

mo͞ot, *v.t.*; mooted, *pt., pp.*; mooting, *ppr.* [AS. *motian,* to meet for deliberation, to treat, to discuss, to dispute, from *mot, gemot,* a meeting, an assembly.]

1. to debate; to discuss; to argue for and against.

This is the most general expression of a problem which hardly has been mentioned, much less *mooted,* in this country.
—Sir W. Hamilton.

2. to propose or bring up for discussion or debate.

3. in law, to argue or plead (a case, etc.), especially in a mock court.

mọọt, *v.i.* to argue or plead in a supposed cause. [Archaic.]

mọọt′à·ble, *a.* capable of being mooted or debated.

mọọt çāse, a case or question to be discussed, especially in a moot court by law students for practice.

mọọ′tchie wood (-chi), [Anglo-Ind.] the soft, porous white wood of *Erythrina indica*, a tree of the East Indies: used especially for toys and ornamental objects.

mọọt çourt, a mock court in which hypothetical cases are tried, as to give law students practice.

mọọt′ẽr, *n.* one who moots, debates, or discusses.

mọọt hạll, mọọt house, a town hall; a hall of debate or judgment. [Obs.]

mọọt hill, in English history, a hill where a council or moot was held.

mọọt′man, *n.*; *pl.* **mọọt′men,** in old English law, one who discussed or argued an unsettled or disputable question before any of the four societies in London which exercised the right of admitting law students to the bar.

mop, *n.* [compare W. *mop*, *mopa*, a mop; Gael. *mab*, *mob*, a tuft, tassel.]

1. a bundle of loose rags, yarns, a sponge, etc. bound to the end of a stick, as for washing floors.

2. anything resembling or suggestive of this, as a thick head of hair.

3. a market or fair where servants gather for inspection and hire. [Brit. Dial.]

mop, *v.t.*; mopped (mopt), *pt.*, *pp.*; mopping, *ppr.* to wash, rub, wipe, or remove with or as with a mop (sometimes with *up*).

to mop up; (a) [Colloq.] to finish; (b) in military usage, to clear out isolated or scattered remnants of beaten enemy forces from (a town, battle area, etc.).

mop, *n.* [M.H.G. *mupf*, *muff*, a wry face.] a wry face; a grimace.

mop, *v.i.* to grimace.

mop′bōard, *n.* a narrow board at the base of the walls of a room; a baseboard.

mōpe, *v.i.*; moped (mōpt), *pt.*, *pp.*; moping, *ppr.* [compare *mop*, a wry mouth, D. *moppen*, to pout.] to be very dull or listless; to be spiritless or gloomy.

Demoniac phrensy, *moping* melancholy.
—Milton.

mōpe, *v.t.* to make stupid or spiritless.

mōpe, *n.* 1. one who mopes or is inclined to mope.

2. [*pl.*] low spirits.

mōpe′-eyed (-īd), *a.* shortsighted; purblind.

mōp′ish, *a.* inclined to mope; spiritless; dejected.

mōp′ish·ly, *adv.* in a mopish manner.

mōp′ish·ness, *n.* dejection; dullness; gloominess.

mop′lȧh, *n.* [E. Ind.] an inhabitant of Malabar who is a believer in the Moslem religion.

mō′pōke, *n.* same as *morepork*.

mop′pet, *n.* [dim. of ME. *moppe*, rag doll.]

1. a little child or young girl: a term of affection. [Archaic or Humorous.]

2. a long-haired lap dog.

mop′stick, *n.* the handle of a mop.

mop′sy, *n.* a moppet. [Obs.]

mō·quette′ (-ket′), *n.* [Fr.] a kind of carpet or upholstery fabric with a thick, soft, napped surface.

Mō′quī (-kē), *n.* same as *Moki*.

mō′rȧ, *n.* [It., prob. from L. *mora*, delay.] a very ancient game still played in many parts of the world and very popular among the Italians and the Chinese. The object of the game, which is usually played by two persons, is to guess the number of fingers held out by the opponent in a quick movement of the hand.

mō′rȧ, *n.*; *pl.* **mō′rae, mō′rȧṣ,** [L. *mora*, delay.]

1. in civil law, inexcusable and blamable delay.

2. in prosody, the unit of metrical time, equal to the ordinary short syllable, usually indicated by a breve (˘).

mō′rȧ, *n.* [Guiana name.] a tree, *Dimorphandra* or *Mora excelsa*, of the *Leguminosæ*, valuable for its timber.

Mō·rā′cē·ae, *n.pl.* [L. *morus*, a mulberry tree, and *-aceæ*.] a family of trees or shrubs having a milky juice and apetalous flowers. Among the fifty-three genera, are the fig, the mulberry, and the Osage orange.

mō·rā′ceous, *a.* pertaining to the *Moraceæ*.

Mō·rae′à, *n.* [named after J. *Moraeus*, father-in-law of Linnaeus.] a genus of bulbous plants of the family *Iridaceæ*, native to South Africa and Australia. The flowers are brilliant and fragrant and the bulbs are edible.

mō·rāine′, *n.* [Fr. *moraine*; compare It. *mora*, a heap of stones, Prov. G. *mur*, stones broken off.] an accumulation of stones, sand, or other debris on the surface or side of glaciers or at their foot. The latter are called terminal moraines, the former lateral or medial moraines, according as they are situated at the sides or about the middle of the glacier. Medial moraines are formed by the union of the adjacent lateral moraines of two or more glaciers.

mor′ăl, *a.* [ME. *morale*; L. *moralis*, pertaining to manners or morals, from *mos*, *moris*, manner, pl. *mores*, manners, morals.]

1. relating to, dealing with, or capable of making the distinction between, right and wrong in conduct.

2. relating to, serving to teach, or in accordance with, the principles of right and wrong.

3. good or right in conduct or character; often, specifically, virtuous in sexual conduct: opposed to *immoral*.

4. based on general observation of people, etc. rather than on what is demonstrable; as, *moral* evidence.

5. designating support, etc. that involves approval and sympathy without action.

6. being virtually such because of its effect on thoughts, attitudes, etc., or because of its general results; as, a *moral* victory.

7. based on strong probability; as, a *moral* certainty.

8. moralizing. [Rare.]

moral philosophy; ethics.

moral theology; theology in its relation to ethics.

Syn.—righteous, ethical, probable, inferential, presumptive, virtuous, well-conducted.

mor′ăl, *n.* 1. the practical lesson inculcated by any story or incident; the significance or meaning, as of a fable.

2. a maxim.

3. [*pl.*] principles and practice in regard to right, wrong, and duty; ethics; general conduct or behavior, especially in sexual matters.

4. a counterpart. [Obs.]

5. a morality play. [Obs.]

mor′ăl, *v.i.* and *v.t.* to moralize. [Obs.]

mō·rāle′, *n.* [Fr.] 1. moral or mental condition as regards courage, zeal, confidence, discipline, enthusiasm, willingness to endure hardship, etc.

2. morality. [Rare.]

mor′ăl·ẽr, *n.* a moralizer. [Obs.]

mor′ăl hаz′ărd, risk (to an insurance company) arising from the possible dishonesty of the insured.

mor′ăl·iṣm, *n.* 1. moral teaching; moralizing.

2. a moral maxim.

3. belief in or practice of a system of ethics apart from religion.

mor′ăl·ist, *n.* [Fr. *moraliste*.]

1. one who teaches or writes upon ethics or morals.

2. one who lives virtuously, often without reliance on religion.

mor·ăl·is′tiç, *a.* 1. moralizing.

2. of moralism or moralists.

mō·ral′i·ty, *n.*; *pl.* **mō·ral′i·tieṣ,** [ME. *moralitee*; L. *moralitas*, from *moralis*, moral.]

1. moral quality or character; rightness or wrongness, as of an action.

2. the character of being in accord with the principles or standards of right conduct; right conduct; often, specifically, virtue in sexual conduct.

3. principles of right and wrong in conduct; ethics.

4. moral instruction or lesson.

5. a morality play.

mō·ral′i·ty plāy, any of a class of allegorical dramas of the fifteenth and sixteenth centuries, the characters of which were personifications of abstractions as Everyman, Vice, Virtue, etc.: also *morality*.

mor″ăl·i·zā′tion, *n.* 1. explanation in a moral sense.

2. the act of moralizing; a moral reflection.

mor′ăl·īze, *v.t.*; moralized, *pt.*, *pp.*; moralizing, *ppr.* [Fr. *moraliser*; LL. *moralizare*, to moralize, from L. *moralis*, pertaining to manners, moral.]

1. to apply to a moral purpose; to explain in a moral sense; to found moral reflections on.

2. to supply with a moral or practical lesson; to furnish with edifying examples.

3. to render moral or virtuous; to correct the morals of.

mor′ăl·īze, *v.i.* to think, speak, or write about matters of right and wrong; to make moral reflections.

mor′ăl·iz·ẽr, *n.* one who moralizes.

mor′ăl·ly, *adv.* 1. from a moral viewpoint; as regards morals.

2. according to moral rules; virtuously; uprightly.

3. virtually; practically; to all intents and purposes; as, *morally* certain.

mō·rass′, *n.* [D. *moeras*, a marsh, fen.] a marsh; a fen; a bog; a tract of soft, wet ground: sometimes used figuratively of a difficult, troublesome, or perplexing state of affairs.

mō·rass′y, *a.* marshy; fenny.

mō·rā′tion, *n.* tarrying; delay. [Obs.]

mor·à·tō′ri·um, *n.*; *pl.* **mor·à·tō′ri·umṣ, mor·à·tō′ri·ȧ,** [Mod.L., neut. of LL. *moratorius*, delaying, from *morari*, to delay.]

1. a legal authorization, usually by a law passed in an emergency, to delay payment of money due, as by a bank or debtor nation.

2. the effective period of such an authorization.

mor′à·tō·ry, *a.* [LL. *moratorius*: see *moratorium*.] in law, delaying; postponing; especially, designating or of a law authorizing a moratorium.

Mō·rā′vi·ăn, *a.* 1. pertaining to Moravia, its people, etc.

2. of the Moravians (religious sect).

Mō·rā′vi·ăn, *n.* 1. a native or inhabitant of Moravia.

2. the Czech dialect of Moravia.

3. a member of a Protestant sect founded in Moravia c. 1722 by disciples of John Huss: also called (*Renewed Church of the*) *United Brethren*, *Unity of the Brethren*, *Moravian Brethren*. They were expelled from Bohemia and Moravia in the beginning of the eighteenth century, but received a settlement in Saxony. They are evangelical, given to missionary effort, and where possible prefer to live in separate colonies or societies. Called in Germany *Herrnhuter*.

Mō·rā′vi·ăn·iṣm, *n.* the religious system of the Moravians, or United Brethren.

mọ·rāy′, *n.* [Port. *moreia*; L. *muraena*, kind of fish.] any of a number of eels, of the family *Murænidæ*, of warm seas, characterized by brilliant coloring and voracious behavior, found especially among coral reefs: the Mediterranean moray is valued as a food fish.

mọr′bid, *a.* [L. *morbidus*, sickly, diseased, from *morbus*, disease.]

1. of, having, or caused by disease; unhealthy; diseased.

2. resulting from or as from a diseased state of mind; especially, having or showing an unwholesome tendency to dwell on gruesome or gloomy matters.

3. gruesome; grisly; horrible; as, the *morbid* details of a story.

4. of diseased parts; pathological; as, *morbid* anatomy.

Syn.—diseased, sick, abnormal, pathological.

mọr·bi·dez′zȧ (-det′sȧ), *n.* [It.] in painting, a method of coloring by which the appearance of softness and delicacy peculiar to the living flesh is produced; also, the effect thus gained.

mọr·bid′i·ty, *n.*; *pl.* **mọr·bid′i·tieṣ,** 1. state, quality or instance of being morbid.

2. the rate of disease or proportion of diseased persons in a given locality, nation, etc.

mọr′bid·ly, *adv.* in a morbid manner.

mọr′bid·ness, *n.* the state or quality of being morbid.

mọr·bif′ẽr·ous, *a.* [LL. *morbiferus*; L. *morbus*, sickness, and *ferre*, to bear.] conveying or causing disease.

mọr·bif′iç, *a.* [L. *morbus*, disease, and *facere*, to make.] causing or leading to disease.

mọr·bif′i·çăl, *a.* morbific.

mọr·bil′lī, *n.pl.* [LL.] measles.

mọr·bil′lous, *a.* [LL. *morbilli*, measles, dim. of L. *morbus*, disease.] pertaining to the measles; having the nature of measles, or resembling the eruptions of that disease.

mọr·bōse′, *a.* morbid. [Obs.]

mọr·bos′i·ty, *n.* a state of disease. [Obs.]

mọr′bus, *n.* [L.] disease.

mọr·ceau′ (-sō′), *n.*; *pl.* **mọr·ceaux′** (-sō′), [Fr.]

1. a bit; a morsel; a fragment.

2. a short composition, passage, or excerpt, as of poetry or music.

Mor·chel'lȧ, *n.* a genus of edible fungi, having a fistular stalk and a roundish or conical pitted pileus. It includes the *Morchella esculenta,* or morel.

mor·dā'cious, *a.* [L. *mordax* (*-acis*), from *mordere,* to bite.] biting; sharp; acrid; caustic.

mor·dā'cious·ly, *adv.* in a biting manner; sarcastically; acridly.

mor·dac'i·ty, *n.* [L. *mordacitas,* from *mordax* (*-acis*), biting.] the quality of being sharp, biting, or acrid.

mor'dăn·cy, *n.* the quality of being mordant; mordacity.

mor'dănt, *a.* [ME. *mourdant,* from OFr. pp. of *mordre* (L. *mordere*), to bite.]
 1. biting, cutting, caustic, or sarcastic, as speech, wit, etc.
 2. corrosive.
 3. acting to fix colors in dyeing, etc.

mor'dănt, *n.* 1. a substance used in dyeing to fix the coloring matter, as a metallic compound that combines with the organic dye to form an insoluble colored compound, or lake, in the fiber of the fabric.
 2. an acid or other corrosive substance used in etching to bite lines, etc. into a metal surface.
 3. in gilding, any sticky substance by which the gold leaf is made to adhere.
 4. the tongue of a buckle. [Obs.]

mor'dănt, *v.t.* to treat or impregnate with a mordant.

mor'dănt·ly, *adv.* in the manner of a mordant.

Mŏr'dē·cai, *n.* in the Bible, the cousin of Esther (in the Book of Esther) who saved the Jews from the destruction planned by Haman: cf. *Purim.*

mor'dent, *n.* [G.; It. *mordente,* ppr. of *mordere* (L. *mordere*), to bite.] in music, a trill made by a rapid alternation of a principal tone with a supplementary tone a half step below it: in a *single* (or *short*) *mordent* the supplementary tone occurs once, in a *double* (or *long*) *mordent,* more than once; in an *inverted mordent,* or pralltriller, the supplementary tone is a half step above the principal tone.

MORDENTS

mor'di·căn·cy, *n.* biting quality; corrosiveness. [Obs.]

mor'di·cănt, *a.* biting; acrid. [Obs.]

mor·di·cā'tion, *n.* corrosion. [Obs.]

mor'di·cā·tive, *a.* acrid; corrosive. [Obs.]

Mor'dred, *n.* same as *Modred.*

-mōre, [from the adv. *more.*] a suffix used in comparison to intensify the comparative degree of adverbs; as, further*more,* forever*more.*

mōre, *a.*; *superl.* most, [ME.; AS. *mara,* more.; compare D. *meer,* O.H.G. *mero,* L. *major,* greater, comp. of *magnus,* great.]
 1. with singular nouns, as comparative of *much* or *some,* greater in amount, extent, degree, intensity, or the like; as, *more* land; *more* courage; *more* light. In such usages it formerly might take the indefinite or definite article before it where *greater* would now be the word used.

  Her best is bettered with a *more* delight.
   —Shak.

 2. with plural nouns, as comparative of *many,* greater in number; in greater numbers; as, *more* men.
 3. added to some former number; additional; further: used either before or after its noun.

  But Montague demands one labor *more.*
   —Addison.

mōre, *adv.*; *superl.* most, [from *more,* a., replacing earlier *mo* (AS. *ma*).]
 1. in or to a greater degree, extent, or quantity. *More* is used to modify an adjective or adverb to form the comparative degree, having the same force and effect as the ending *-er* in comparatives; as, *more* wise (*=wiser*), *more* wisely, *more* durable. It may be used before all adjectives which can be compared, and is generally used with words of more than three syllables.
 2. in addition; further; besides; again; qualified by such words as *any, no, never, once, twice.*

  Once more unto the breach, dear friends, *once more.*   —Shak.

 more and more; to an increasing degree; increasingly.
 more or less; (a) to some extent; (b) approximately.
 to be no more; to be destroyed or dead.

mōre, *n.* 1. a greater quantity, amount, or number.
 2. [*construed as pl.*] (a) a greater number (*of* persons or things); as, *more* of us are going; (b) a greater number of persons.
 3. something additional or further; as, *more* cannot be said.
 4 something of greater importance.

mōre, *v.t.* to make more. [Obs.]

mōre, *n.* [AS. *moru,* a root.] a root. [Obs.]

mōre, *n.* a moor. [Now Dial.]

mō·reen', *n.* [prob. from *moire,* and *-een,* as in *velveteen,* etc.] a stout fabric of wool or cotton, or of cotton and wool, silk, or mohair, usually having a watered finish: used for drapes, upholstery, etc.

mō·rel', *n.* [Fr. *morille*; D. *morilje.*] a small, edible mushroom, of the genus *Morchella.*

mō·rel', *n.* [Fr. *morelle,* nightshade; properly f. of OFr. *morel,* dark-colored.]

MOREL (2 in. high)

 1. any of several kinds of nightshade; especially, the black nightshade.
 2. a kind of cherry; the morello.
 3. a horse, especially of a dark color. [Obs.]

mō·relle', *n.* the nightshade, or morel.

mō·rel'lō, *n.* [It., dark-colored.] a variety of dark-red cherry, used for preserves.

mō·ren'dō, *a.* and *adv.* [It., ppr. of *morire,* to die.] in music, gradually dying away; diminuendo at the close.

mōre'ness, *n.* greatness. [Obs.]

mōre·ō'vĕr, *adv.* beyond what has been said; further; besides; also; likewise.

mōre'pŏrk, *n.* [so called from its cry.] a Tasmanian nightjar.

mō'rēs, *n.pl.*; *sing.* **mōs,** [L., customs.] folkways that are considered conducive to the welfare of society and so, through general observance, develop the force of law, often becoming part of the formal legal code.

Mō·resque' (-resk'), *a.* [Fr., from It. *moresco,* Moorish, from *Moro,* a Moor.] Moorish: said of decoration, etc.

Mō·resque', *n.* Moorish style of decoration or architecture, characterized by intricate tracery, bright colors, gilt, etc.

Mor'gāin le Fāy, Morgan le Fay.

Mor'găn, *n.* [after Justin *Morgan* (1747–1798), New Englander who owned the stallion that sired the breed.] any of a breed of strong, light trotting horses.

mor·gȧ·nat'iç, *a.* [LL. *morganatica,* a morning gift, a kind of dowry paid on the morning before or after marriage; corrupted from G. *morgengabe*; AS. *morgengifu*; *morgen,* morning, and *gifu,* gift.] designating a marriage of a man of the nobility with a woman of inferior rank, in which its is stipulated that neither she nor their children shall enjoy the rank, or inherit the possessions, of the husband.

mor·gȧ·nat'iç·ăl·ly, *adv.* in or by a morganatic marriage.

mor·gan'iç, *a.* morganatic. [Rare.]

mor'găn·īte, *n.* [after J. P. *Morgan.*] a transparent, rose-colored variety of beryl, used as a gem.

Mor'găn le Fāy, [OFr. *Morgain la fée,* lit., Morgan the fairy.] in Arthurian legend, the fairy half sister of King Arthur, usually shown as doing him harm at every opportunity; in other legends, a fairy who lives in a lake among great treasures: also *Morgain le Fay,* (*Fata*) *Morgana.*

mor'gāy, *n.* [W. *morgi,* dogfish, shark; *mor,* the sea, and *ci,* dog.] a species of shark, *Scyllium canicula*: also called the *small-spotted dogfish,* or *bounce.*

mor'gen, *n.*; *pl.* **mor'gen, mor'gens,** [from D. and G., lit., morning, hence area plowed in one morning.]
 1. a land measure formerly used in the Netherlands and its possessions, and still used in South Africa, equal to about 2 acres.
 2. a land measure formerly used in Prussia, Denmark, and Norway, equal to about 2/3 acre.

mor'glāy, *n.* a deadly weapon; a sword. [Obs.]

morgue (morg), *n.* [Fr.] 1. a place where the bodies of accident victims and unknown persons found dead are kept prior to identification and disposal.
 2. in journalism, (a) the reference library of back numbers, photographs, clippings, etc. kept by a newspaper, magazine, etc.; (b) the room in which this is kept.

Mō'ri·ăn, *n.* a Moor. [Obs.]

mor'i·bund, *a.* [L. *moribundus,* dying, from *mori,* to die.]
 1. dying.
 2. coming to an end; being terminated.

mor'i·bund, *n.* a dying person.

mō'riç, *a.* of or obtained from fustic.

mor'ice, *n.* same as *morris.*

mō·rig'ĕr·āte, *a.* obedient. [Rare.]

mō·rig·ĕr·ā'tion, *n.* obsequiousness; obedience.

mō·rig'ĕr·ous, *a.* obedient; obsequious.

mor'il, *n.* a mushroom, the morel.

mō·ril'lon, *n.* 1. same as *goldeneye.*
 2. same as *morello.*

mō'rin, *n.* [L. *morus,* mulberry, and *-in.*] a yellowish crystalline dye derived from fustic.

Mō·rin'dȧ, *n.* [L. *morus,* mulberry, and *Indicus,* Indian.] a genus of trees and shrubs belonging to the *Rubiaceæ.* Dyes are obtained from several species.

mō·rin'din, *n.* a reddish-yellow dye obtained from the bark of several species of *Morinda.*

mor'i·nel, *n.* [Fr. *morinelle,* dim. from L. *morus,* silly.] a plover, the dotterel.

Mō·riñ'gȧ, *n.* [from native name in Malabar.] a genus of trees, native to Egypt and the East Indies. The root of the horseradish tree, *Moringa pterygosperma,* has a pungent odor and an aromatic taste and is used as a stimulant. The leaves, flowers, and tender seed vessels are used in curries. The nuts are the ben nuts, from which the oil of ben is extracted.

mō'ri·on, *n.* [OFr., from Sp. *morrion,* prob. from *morra,* the crown of the head.] a type of open helmet without vizor or beaver, somewhat resembling a hat, often with a crest or comb over the top, worn in the 16th and 17th centuries.

MORION

mō'ri·on, *n.* [prob. abbrev. from L. *mormorion,* dark-brown rock crystal.] a variety of blackish, smoky quartz.

Mō·ris'cō, *a.* [Sp., from *Moro,* Moor.] Moorish.

Mō·ris'cō, *n.*; *pl.* **Mō·ris'cōs, Mō·ris'cōes,**
 1. a Moor; especially, one of the Moors of Spain.
 2. a Moorish dance: known also as *morris dance.*
 3. a dancer of the morris dance. [Obs.]
 4. Moresque architecture or ornamentation.

Mō'risk, *a.* and *n.* Morisco. [Obs.]

Mor·i·sō'ni·ăn, *n.* an adherent of the sect known as the Evangelical Union, founded by James Morison, who was expelled from the Presbyterian Church.

mō·ri·tū'rī tē sa·lū·tā'mus, [L.] we (who are) about to die salute you: Roman gladiators' shout to the emperor when they entered the arena.

mor'kin, *n.* a beast that has died by disease or accident. [Obs.]

mor'ling, mort'ling, *n.* [Fr. *mort,* death, and -ling.]
 wool plucked from a dead sheep.
 2. sheep or other animal dead by disease. [Obs.]

mor'măl, *n.* a dangerous sore; a gangrene; a canker. [Obs.]

mor'mō, *n.* a bugbear; false terror. [Obs.]

Mor'mŏn, *n.* [Gr. *mormōn,* a bugbear.]
 1. the puffins, a genus of sea birds characterized by a short, thick beak.
 2. [m–] the mandrill.

Mor'mŏn, *n.* a member of a religious body founded in the United States in 1830 by Joseph Smith, who claimed to have found an addition to the Bible, engraved on golden plates, which he translated and published under the name of the *Book of Mormon*. After the death of Joseph Smith, some members of the sect, led by Brigham Young, established themselves in Utah in 1847, the official leaders being in control of civil as well as religious affairs. The church is officially known as The Church of Jesus Christ of Latter-Day Saints.

Mor′mŏn, *a.* of or pertaining to the Mormons or their religion.

Mor′mŏn·dŏm, *n.* the country, community, or customs of the Mormons; collectively, the Mormon people.

Mor′mŏn·iṣm, *n.* the Mormon system of beliefs, practices, and government.

Mor′mŏn·īte, *a.* and *n.* same as *Mormon*.

Mor·mō′ops, *n.* a genus of bats native to tropical America.

mor·mō·răn′dō, *adv.* [It.] in a murmuring manner: a direction in music.

morn, *n.* [contr. of AS. *morgen*, morning.]

1. the first part of the day; the morning. [Poet.]

And blooming peace shall ever bless thy *morn*. —Prior.

2. morrow. [Scot.]

morne, *n.* [OFr., blunt.] a lance head that has been blunted for tilting.

mor·né′ (mor-ne′), *a.* in heraldry, designating a lion rampant, with no tongue, teeth, or claws.

morn′ing, *n.* [ME. *morwening*, *morwen*, from AS. *morgen*, morning.]

1. the first part of the day, beginning at twelve o'clock at night, or especially at dawn, and extending to noon.

2. the first or early part.

O life! how pleasant in thy *morning*! —Burns.

3. (a) the dawn; daybreak; (b) [M–] the goddess Aurora or Eos.

4. a morning dram or draught. [Scot.]

morn′ing, *a.* of, suited to, or occurring, appearing, etc. in the morning; as, *morning* dew; *morning* light; *morning* service.

morning gown; a gown worn in the morning before one is formally dressed.

morning gun; a gun fired at the time of sounding the reveille at military posts.

morning sickness; vomiting and nausea occurring in the morning during the first months of pregnancy.

morning sphinx; any hawk moth of the genus *Deilopheila*: so called because it flies in the morning.

morning star; (a) a planet, especially Venus, visible in the eastern sky before sunrise; (b) a plant with yellow flowers, native to California; (c) an ancient weapon consisting of a wooden ball, containing iron spikes, at the end of a pole, from which it was sometimes suspended by a chain: also termed a *holy-water sprinkler*.

MORNING STARS

morning watch; among seamen, the watch between four and eight o'clock in the morning.

morn′ing-glō″ry, *n.*; *pl.* **morn′ing-glō″rieṣ,**

1. a twining plant of the genus *Ipomœa*, having bright, funnel-shaped flowers of various colors.

2. any of a number of plants related to this.

morn′ing·tīde, *n.* morning. [Poet.]

morn′wărd, *adv.* toward the morn or the east. [Poet.]

Mō′rō, *n.*; *pl.* **Mō′rōṣ,** [Sp., a Moor.]

1. a member of a group of Moslem Malay tribes living in the southern Philippines.

2. their Malay language; Magindanao.

Mō′rō, *a.* of the Moros or Magindanao.

mō′rō, *n.* [L. *morus*, a mulberry tree.] a bird, *Carpodacus githagineus*.

Mō·roç′căn, *a.* of or pertaining to Morocco or its people.

Mō·roç′căn, *n.* a native or inhabitant of Morocco.

mō·roç′cō, *n.* 1. leather made, originally in Morocco, from goatskin tanned with sumac, giving a durable, flexible texture and grained surface. It is used extensively in bookbinding, upholstering, and shoemaking.

2. an imitation of true morocco; especially, a leather made of sheepskin.

Also *morocco leather*.

mō·rol′ō·ġy, *n.* [Gr. *mōrologia*, foolish talking; *mōros*, foolish, and *legein*, to speak.] foolish or nonsensical talk. [Obs.]

mō′ron, *n.* [Gr. *mōron*, neut. of *mōros*, foolish.]

1. a mentally deficient person with an intelligence quotient ranging from 50 to 75; a person mentally equal or inferior to a child between eight and twelve years old: *moron* is the highest classification of mental deficiency, above *imbecile* and *idiot*.

2. loosely, a very foolish or stupid person.

mō·ron′iç, *a.* of, characteristic of, or like a moron.

mō′ron·iṣm, *n.* same as *moronity*.

mō·ron′i·ty, *n.* the state or quality of being moronic.

mō·rō·ṣau′roid, *a.* pertaining to or resembling the genus *Morosaurus*.

mō·rō·ṣau′roid, *n.* any animal of the family *Morosauridæ*.

Mō·rō·ṣau′rus, *n.* [Gr. *mōros*, dull, stupid, and *sauros*, lizard.] an extinct genus of herbivorous animals of the order *Dinosauria*.

mō·rōse′, *a.* [L. *morosus*, peevish, fretful, fastidious.] gloomy; surly; severe; sullen and austere; as, a *morose* look; *morose* bearing.

Syn.—gloomy, sad, sullen, splenetic.

mō·rōse′ly, *adv.* in a morose manner.

mō·rōse′ness, *n.* the state or quality of being morose; sullenness.

mō·rō′sis, *n.* [Gr. *mōrōsis*, from *mōros*, foolish, stupid.] imbecility of mind; idiocy; stupidity.

mō·ros′i·ty, *n.* moroseness. [Obs.]

mō′rō·soph, *n.* a learned fool. [Obs.]

mō·rox′īte, *n.* [Gr. *moroxos*, pipe clay, and *-ite*.] a form of apatite found native in brownish or greenish-blue crystals.

-morph, [from Gr. *morphē*, form.] a combining form meaning *one having a* (specified) *form*, as in pseudo*morph*: used to form nouns generally corresponding to adjectives ending in *-morphic*, *-morphous*.

mor·phē′ȧ, *n.* [Fr. *morphée*; LL. *morphea*, a scurfy eruption.] a skin disease in which pinkish patches or bands show in firm lesions, often leaving a scarlike marking upon their disappearance.

Mor′phē·ăn, *a.* relating to Morpheus.

mor′phēme, *n.* [from Gr. *morphē*, form; and *-eme* as in *phoneme*.] in linguistics, any word or part of a word, as an affix or combining form, that conveys meaning, cannot be further divided into smaller elements conveying meaning, and usually occurs in various contexts with relatively stable meaning.

Mor′pheūs, *n.* [L., from Gr. *Morpheus*, from *morphē*, form; from the forms he causes to appear to people in their dreams.] in mythology, the god of dreams; hence, sleep.

mor′phew (-fū), *n.* a scurf on the face. [Obs.]

mor′phew, *v.t.* to cover with scurf. [Obs.]

mor′phi·ȧ, *n.* [Mod. L.] same as *morphine*.

-mor′phiç, [from Gr. *morphē*, form; and *-ic*.] a combining form meaning *having a* (specified) *form* or *shape*, as in anthropo*morphic*: also *-morphous*.

mor′phin, *n.* same as *morphine*.

mor′phīne, *n.* [G. *morphin* or Fr. *morphine* from L. *Morpheus*.] a bitter, white, crystalline alkaloid, $C_{17}H_{19}O_3N \cdot H_2O$, derived from opium and used, generally in the form of a salt, to induce sleep and relieve pain.

mor′phin·iṣm, *n.* 1. a diseased condition of the system brought about by long continued or excessive use of morphine.

2. addiction to the use of morphine.

mor″phi·ō·mā′ni·ȧ, *n.* [*morphine*, and Gr. *mania*, madness.] an abnormal craving for morphine.

Mor′phō, *n.* [Gr. *Morphō*, an epithet of Venus, from *morphē*, form.]

1. a genus of tropical butterflies including thirty species, some of which are of large size and noted for their brilliant coloring.

2. [m–] a butterfly of this genus.

mor·phoe′ȧ, *n.* same as *morphea*.

mor·phō·ġen′e·sis, *n.* morphogeny.

mor·phoġ′e·ny, *n.* [Gr. *morphē*, form, and *-geneia*, generation.] evolution as applied to structural forms.

mor·phō·loġ′iç, mor·phō·loġ′iç·ăl, *a.* pertaining to morphology or form; structural.

mor·phō·loġ′iç·ăl·ly, *adv.* according to morphology.

mor·phol′ō·ġist, *n.* one who has a knowledge of the science of morphology.

mor·phol′ō·ġy, *n.* [from Gr. *morphē*, form, and *-logy*.]

1. the branch of biology that deals with the form and structure of animals and plants, without regard to function.

2. the branch of linguistics that deals with the internal structure and forms of words: with syntax, it forms a basic division of grammar.

3. any scientific study of form and structure, as in physical geography, etc.

4. (a) form and structure, as of an organism, regarded as a whole; (b) morphological features collectively, as of a language.

mor′phon, *n.* [from Gr. *morphē*, form.] in biology, a structural unit; an individual organism: opposed to *bion*.

mor·phon′ō·my, *n.* [Gr. *morphē*, form, and *nemein*, to distribute.] the law or laws regulating morphological development.

mor·phoph′y·ly, *n.* [Gr. *morphē*, form, and *phylon*, a tribe.] the branch of phylogeny that deals with form as distinguished from function.

mor·phō′sis, *n.*; *pl.* **mor·phō′sēṣ,** [Gr. *morphōsis*, a shaping, from *morphē*, form.] the mode of formation or development of an organism or any of its parts.

mor·phot′iç, *a.* [Gr. *morphōtikos*, fit for shaping, from *morphē*, form.] in physiology, of or relating to morphosis; used in any formative process.

-mor′phous, [from Gr. *morphē*, form.] a combining form equivalent to *-morphic*, as in iso*morphous*.

mor′pi·on, *n.* [Fr., a crab louse.] the crab louse. [Obs.]

mor′rhu·ine (-ru-), *n.* [LL. *morua*, *moruta*, a cod.] a ptomaine, $C_{19}H_{27}N_3$, found in codliver oil extracted from putrefied livers.

mor′rice, *n.* and *a.* same as *morris*.

mor′ris, *a.* [earlier *morys*, Moorish.] designating or of an old folk dance formerly common in England, especially on May Day, in which fancy costumes were worn, often those associated with characters in the Robin Hood legends.

mor′ris, *n.* the morris dance.

mor′ris, *n.* an elongated fish, allied to the eels, of the genus *Leptocephalus*, having a thin, compressed body.

Mor′ris chāir, [after William *Morris*, its inventor.] a large armchair with an adjustable back and removable cushions.

mor′ris-pīke, *n.* a kind of large pike (the weapon).

mor′rō, *n.*; *pl.* **mor′rōṣ,** [Sp., any round, skull-like object.] a rounded hill, bluff, or point of land.

morro castle; a castle built on an eminence or promontory.

mor′rŏt, *n.* same as *marrot*.

mor′rōw, *n.* [ME. *morwe*, from AS. *morgen*, morning.]

1. the next day; the following day. [Archaic or Poet.]

Till this stormy night is gone,
And th' eternal *morrow* dawn.—Crashaw.

2. the time just after some particular event. [Archaic or Poet.]

3. morning. [Archaic or Poet.]

good morrow; good morning: a term of salutation.

Morṣ, *n.* [L.] in Roman mythology, death regarded as a god: identified with the Greek Thanatos.

morse, *n.* [Fr. *morse*, from Norw. *mar*, the sea, and *ros*, a horse.] the walrus.

morse, *n.* [L. *morsus*, a clasp.] a metal fastening, often jeweled, used on ecclesiastical and other garments.

Morse, *a.* [after Samuel F. B. *Morse*, the inventor.]

1. designating or of a code consisting of a system of dots, dashes, and spaces, or sounds corresponding to these, used to represent letters, numerals, etc. in telegraphy, signaling, and the like.

2. loosely, of any similar code.

Morse, *n.* the Morse code.

Morse al′phȧ·bet, the telegraphic alphabet, or code, invented by Samuel F. B. Morse. The letters of the alphabet are composed of a series of arbitrary dots and dashes, as given below:

A · —	H · · · ·	O · ·	V · · · —
B — · · ·	I · ·	P · · · · ·	W · — —
C · · ·	J — · — ·	Q · · — ·	X · — · ·
D — · ·	K — · —	R · · ·	Y · · · ·
E ·	L —	S · · ·	Z · · · ·
F · — ·	M — —	T —	
G — — ·	N — ·	U · · —	& · · · ·

The international code differs from the above in the following instances, the chief object being to avoid the space letters of the Morse code:

C — · — ·	L · — · ·	Q — — · —	Y — · — —
F · · — ·	O — — —	R · — ·	Z — — · ·
J · — — —	P · — — ·	X — · · —	

mọr′sel, *n.* [OFr. *morsel, morcel*; LL. *morsellum*, dim. from L. *morsum*, a bit, piece, from *mordere*, to bite.]

1. a bite; a mouthful; a small portion of food.

Every *morsel* to a satisfied hunger is only a new labor to a tired digestion.—South.

2. a tasty dish.

3. a small quantity of anything; a fragmentary portion; as, a *morsel* of gold; a *morsel* of comfort.

mọr′sing hộrn, a powderhorn; originally, a flask for priming.

mọr′sūre (-shūr), *n.* [L. *morsus*, pp. of *mordere*, to bite.] the act of biting. [Now Rare.]

mọrt, *n.* [perhaps from *mortal*, used as intens.] a great quantity or number. [Brit. Dial.]

mọrt, *n.* a woman or girl. [Gypsy Slang.]

mọrt, *n.* a salmon in its third year. [Brit. Dial.]

mọrt, *n.* [Fr., from L. *mors, mortis*, death.]

1. death. [Obs.]

2. in hunting, a note sounded on the horn at the death of game.

3. the skin of a sheep or lamb whose death resulted from disease. [Obs.]

mọr′tăl, *a.* [L. *mortalis*, subject to death, from *mors, mortis*, death.]

1. that must eventually die; destined to die; as, man is *mortal*.

2. of this world.

3. of death.

4. fatal; deadly; destructive to life; causing death, or certain to cause death; as, a *mortal* wound; *mortal* poison.

The fruit
Of that forbidden tree whose *mortal* taste
Brought death into the world, and all our woe. —Milton.

5. bringing death; terminating life.

Safe in the hand of one Disposing Power,
Or in the natal, or the *mortal* hour.—Pope.

6. causing death of the soul: said of sin: distinguished from *venial*.

7. to the death; as, *mortal* combat.

8. human; belonging to man, who is mortal; as, *mortal* wit or knowledge; *mortal* power.

The voice of God
To *mortal* ear is dreadful. —Milton.

9. affecting with the fear of death; dire; grievous.

The nymph grew pale, and in a *mortal* fright. —Dryden.

10. implacable; as, a *mortal* enemy.

11. (a) extreme; very great; (b) very long and tedious; (c) conceivable; possible; as, it's no *mortal* good to anyone. [Colloq.]

mọr′tăl, *n.* man; a being subject to death; a human being.

Warn poor *mortals* left behind.—Tickel.

mọr′tăl, *adv.* extremely. [Dial.]

mọr·tal′i·ty, *n.* [L. *mortalitas*, from *mortalis*, mortal.]

1. the nature of man, as having eventually to die; mortal nature.

When I saw her die,
I then did think on your *mortality*. —Carew.

2. death on a large scale, as from disease or war.

3. (a) the proportion of deaths to the population of a region, nation, etc.; death rate; (b) the proportion of deaths from a particular disease.

4. mankind; humanity as a whole.

Take these tears, *mortality's* relief.—Pope.

5. death. [Obs.]

mortality table; a statistical table, based on a sample group of the population, stating the percentage of people who live to any given age.

mọr′tăl·īze, *v.t.*; mortalized, *pt., pp.*; mortalizing, *ppr.* to make mortal.

mọr′tăl·ly, *adv.* 1. in the manner of a mortal.

2. in a manner that must cause death; fatally; as, *mortally* wounded.

3. extremely; exceedingly; intensely; very; as, *mortally* tired.

mọr′tăl·ness, *n.* the quality or state of being mortal.

mọr′tăr, *n.* [AS. *mortere*, from L. *mortarium*, a vessel or trough in which things are pounded or mixed.]

PESTLE
MORTAR
MORTAR AND PESTLE

1. a very hard bowl in which softer substances are ground or pounded to a powder with a pestle.

2. any machine in which materials are ground or pounded.

3. [Fr. *mortier*.] a short-barreled cannon with a low muzzle velocity, which throws shells in a high trajectory.

4. any of various similar devices, for shooting lifelines, flares, etc.

5. [ME. *morter*; Late OFr. *mortier*; L. *mortarium*, a mixture of sand and lime: so called from the vessel in which it was made.] a mixture of cement or lime with sand and water, used between bricks or stones in building, or as plaster.

mọr′tăr, *v.t.* to plaster or bind together with mortar.

mọr′tăr bed, the frame of wood and iron on which a mortar, or cannon, rests.

mọr′tăr·bōard, *n.* 1. a square board with a handle underneath, used by masons for holding mortar.

2. an academic cap with a square, flat, horizontal top, worn at commencements, etc. in schools and colleges.

mọr′tăr bōat, a small vessel having a relatively wide beam, for carrying a heavy mortar amidships.

mọr′tăr pïēce, a mortar. [Obs.]

mọr′tăr ves′sel, a mortar boat.

mọrt′gāġe (mọr′), *n.* [OFr. *morgage, mort gage*, lit., dead pledge; *mort*, dead, and *gage*, a pledge.]

1. the pledging of property to a creditor as security for the payment of a debt.

2. the deed by which this pledge is made.

3. the claim of the mortgagee on the property.

4. the state of being pledged; as, lands given in *mortgage*.

chattel mortgage; see under *chattel*.

mọrt′gāġe, *v.t.*; mortgaged, *pt., pp.*; mortgaging, *ppr.* 1. in law, to pledge (property) by a mortgage.

2. to put an advance claim or liability on; as, he *mortgaged* his future happiness.

Already a portion of the entire capital of the nation is *mortgaged* for the support of drunkards. —Lyman Beecher.

mọrt′gāġe deed, a deed given by way of mortgage.

mọrt·gă·ġee′, *n.* the person to whom property is mortgaged.

mọrt′gă·ġọr, mọrt′gă·ġẽr, *n.* one who mortgages property.

mọr′tice, *n.* and *v.t.*; morticed (-tist), *pt., pp.*; morticing, *ppr.* mortise.

mọr·ti′ciăn (-shun), *n.* [from L. *mors, mortis*, death; and *-ician*.] a funeral director; a professional undertaker.

mọr·tiẹr′ (-tyā′), *n.* [Fr.] a cap formerly worn by certain officials in England and in France.

mọr·tif′ẽr·ous, *a.* [L. *mortifer*; *mors, mortis*, death, and *ferre*, to bear.] bringing or producing death; deadly; fatal; destructive. [Obs.]

mọr″ti·fi·cā′tion, *n.* [LL. *mortificatio (-onis)*, a killing.]

1. the act of mortifying, or the condition of being mortified; specifically, in pathology, the death or decay of one part of the body while the rest is alive; gangrene.

It appeareth in the gangrene or *mortification* of flesh. —Bacon.

2. the act of subduing the passions and appetites by penance, abstinence, or painful severities inflicted on the body.

3. humiliation; loss of self-respect; the state of being humbled or depressed, as by disappointment or vexation; chagrin.

4. in old chemistry and metallurgy, the destruction of active qualities. [Obs.]

5. in Scots law, (a) the act of disposing of lands for religious or charitable purposes; (b) the lands disposed of for such purposes.

6. that which mortifies; the cause of chagrin, humiliation, or vexation.

Syn.—vexation, chagrin, humiliation, shame.

mọr′ti·fīed·ness, *n.* humiliation; subjection of the passions. [Rare.]

mọr′ti·fī·ẽr, *n.* one who or that which mortifies.

mọr′ti·fȳ, *v.t.*; mortified, *pt., pp.*; mortifying, *ppr.* [OFr. *mortifier*; LL. *mortificare*, to kill, destroy; L. *mors, mortis*, death, and *facere*, to make.]

1. to punish (one's body) or control (one's physical desires or passions) by self-denial, fasting, etc., as a means of religious or ascetic discipline.

2. in medicine, to cause (the tissues or a part of the body) to decay or become gangrenous.

3. to humiliate; to shame; to affect with vexation or chagrin.

The news of the fatal battle of Worchester, which exceedingly *mortified* our expectations. —Evelyn.

4. in old chemistry and metallurgy, to destroy the active powers or qualities of. [Obs.]

5. to deaden; to render insensible; to make apathetic. [Obs.]

6. in Scots law, to dispose of by mortification.

mọr′ti·fȳ, *v.i.* 1. in medicine, to decay or become gangrenous.

2. to be subdued; to die away: said of inordinate appetites, etc.

3. to practice mortification (sense 2).

This makes him give alms of all that he hath, watch, fast, and *mortify*.—Law.

mọr′ti·fȳ″ing·ly, *adv.* in a mortifying manner; so as to cause mortification.

mọr′tise, mọr′tice, *n.* [ME. *mortays*; Late OFr. *mortaise*; Ar. *murtazza*, joined, fixed in.] a notch, hole, or space cut in a piece of wood or other material to receive a corresponding projecting piece called a tenon, formed on another piece of wood, etc., in order to fix the two together at a given angle. The sides of the mortise are four planes, generally at right angles to each other and to the surface where the cavity is made. The junction of two pieces in this manner is called a *mortise joint*.

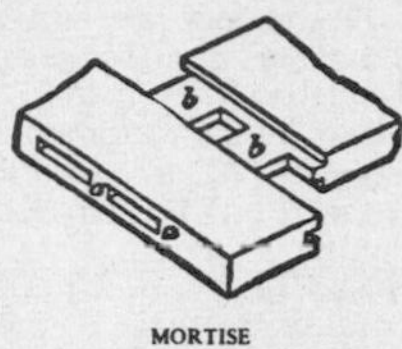

MORTISE
a a, mortise; *b b*, tenon

2. in printing, a slip or hollow constructed in such a manner that type or an engraving to be printed may be placed in it.

mọr′tise, *v.t.*; mortised (-tist), *pt., pp.*; mortising, *ppr.* 1. to cut or make a mortise in.

2. to join securely; to fasten securely, especially with a tenon and mortise; as, to *mortise* a beam into a post, or a joist into a girder.

Also spelled *mortice*.

mọr′tise lock, a lock made to fit into a mortise cut in the stile and rail of a door to receive it.

mọr′tise wheel (hwēl), a cast-iron wheel having wooden cogs set into mortises.

mọrt′māin, *n.* [OFr. *mortemain*; LL. *mortua manus*, lit., dead hand; *mortua*, f. of L. *mortuus*, pp. of *mori*, to die, and *manus*, hand.]

1. a transfer of lands or houses to a corporate body, such as a school or church, for perpetual ownership.

2. such ownership.

mọr′tress, *n.* a dish of meat of various kinds, cooked together. [Obs.]

mọr′tū·ăr·y, *n.*; *pl.* **mọr′tū·ăr·ieș,** [LL. *mortuarius*, pertaining to the dead, from *mortuus*, dead.]

1. a place where dead bodies are kept before burial or cremation, as a morgue.

2. formerly, (a) a gift left by a dying person to his parish priest; (b) a similar gift left by a priest to his superior.

mọr′tū·ăr·y, *a.* 1. of or pertaining to the burial of the dead; as, a *mortuary* chapel.

2. of or connected with death.

mor′ū·lȧ, *n.*; *pl.* **mor′ū·lae,** [dim. from L. *morum*, a mulberry.] in embryology, the solid mass of cells, somewhat like a mulberry in shape, formed by an ovum in the early stages of embryonic development.

mor′ū·lăr, *a.* of, having the nature of, or characterized by a morula.

mor·ū·lā′tion, *n.* the formation of the morula during the process of the segmentation of the egg.

mor′ū·loid, *a.* like a morula.

Mō′rus, *n.* [L. *morus*, a mulberry tree.] a genus of trees of the nettle family; the mulberries. It comprises about a dozen species found in the northern hemisphere and mountainous regions in the tropics. The leaves of some of the species are used as food for the silkworm, while other species yield an edible fruit. *Morus alba* is the white mulberry, and *Morus rubra* the common red mulberry.

Mọr′ven, *n.* a mythical kingdom, ruled by Fingal: described by Ossian in his poems.

mọr′vin, *n.* [Fr. *morve*, glanders.] in veterinary science, a filtered extract of *Bacterium mallei*, used as an injection to test for glanders.

mor'wong, *n.* in Australia, any fish of the genus *Chilodactylus.*

mōs, *n.* singular of *mores.*

mō·ṣā'iç, *n.* [ME. *musycke;* OFr. *mosaicq;* It. *mosaico, musaico,* from L.Gr. *mousaikos, mousaikon,* belonging to the Muses, artistic, from *Mousa,* a Muse.]
 1. the process of making pictures or designs by inlaying small bits of colored stone, glass, etc. in mortar.
 2. inlaid work made by this process.
 3. a picture or design so made.
 4. anything resembling this, as a number of aerial photographs pieced together to show a continuous area.
 5. in botany, any of the virus diseases that cause wrinkling or mottling of leaves.
 6. the photosensitive plate in a television camera.

mō·ṣā'iç, *a.* pertaining to or resembling mosaic; variegated like mosaic; composed of small pieces of various colors.
 mosaic gold; see under *gold.*

mō·ṣā'iç, *v.t.;* mosaicked (-ikt), *pt., pp.;* mosaicking, *ppr.* 1. to make by or as by mosaic.
 2. to decorate with mosaics.

Mō·ṣā'iç, *a.* of Moses or the writings, laws, etc. attributed to him.

mō·ṣā'i·çăl, *a.* mosaic. [Rare.]

Mō·ṣā'i·çăl, *a.* same as *Mosaic.*

mō·ṣā'i·çăl·ly, *adv.* in the manner of mosaic work.

mō·ṣā'i·cist, *n.* a person who sells, designs, or makes mosaics.

Mō·ṣā'iç law, the ancient law of the Hebrews, ascribed to Moses and contained mainly in the first five books of the Old Testament, the Pentateuch.

Mō'ṣā·ism, *n.* attachment or adherence to the Mosaic system and doctrines; the Mosaic system or the laws prescribed by Moses.

mō·san'drīte, *n.* [named after K.G. *Mosander* (1797–1858), Sw. chemist.] a mineral of a vitreous to resinous luster, found associated with various other minerals at Brevig, Norway. It is a hydrous titanic silicate of cerium, lanthanum, didymium, and calcium, with some soda and sesquioxide of iron. It occurs in monoclinic crystals.

mos'ȧ·ṣaur (*or* mō'sȧ-), *n.* a mosasaurian.

Mō·sȧ·ṣau'ri·ȧ, *n.pl.* a group of extinct marine reptiles from the Cretaceous rocks of America and Europe, typified by the genus *Mosasaurus.* Some of the species were more than fifty feet long.

mos·ȧ·ṣau'ri·ăn (*or* mō-sȧ-), *a.* pertaining to the *Mosasauria.*

mos·ȧ·ṣau'ri·ăn, *n.* one of the *Mosasauria.*

Mō·sȧ·ṣau'rus, Mō·sō·ṣau'rus, *n.* [L. *Mosa,* the river Meuse or Maas, on which the first specimen was found, and Gr. *sauros,* a lizard.] a genus of extinct marine reptiles, typical of the *Mosasauria.* The first species was discovered near Maestricht in the Netherlands.

mos'çhāte, *a.* [LL. *moschatus,* from Gr. *moschos,* musk.] having an odor like that of musk; musky.

mos·çhȧ·tel', *n.* [Fr. *moscatelle,* from LL. *muscatus,* having the odor of musk.] a plant, *Adoxa moschatellina,* of the honeysuckle family. Its leaves and greenish-white flowers smell like musk.

mos·çhif'ẽr·ous, *a.* [LL. *moschus,* musk, and L. *ferre,* to bear.] giving forth musk; producing musk.

Mō·ṣelle', *n.* a kind of white wine, made in the valley of the Moselle river, which flows through northeastern France and Germany.

mō'ṣeṣ, *n.* [W. Ind.] a boat having a flat bottom, used for carrying sugar to vessels.

Mō'ṣeṣ, *n.* 1. in the Bible, the leader who brought the Israelites out of slavery in Egypt and into the Promised Land, received the Ten Commandments from God, and gave laws to the people.
 2. a leader; lawgiver.

mō·ṣey, *v.i.* [from *vamose.*]
 1. to saunter; to dally; to proceed without haste. [Slang.]
 2. to go away; to move along. [Slang.]

mosk, *n.* same as a *mosque.*

Moṣ'lem, *n.; pl.* **Moṣ'lemṣ, Moṣ'lem,** [Ar. *moslem, muslim,* a true believer, from *salama,* to resign oneself to God.] an adherent of Islam, or follower of Mohammed: also *Muslem, Muslim.*

Moṣ'lem, *a.* of Islam or the Moslems: also *Muslem, Muslim.*

Moṣ'lem·iṣm, *n.* the religion of the Moslems; Islam; Mohammedanism.

moṣ'lingṣ, *n.pl.* the thin leather shreds removed in the process of dressing skins.

mosque (mosk), *n.* [Fr. *mosquée;* Sp. *mezquita,* from Ar. *masjid,* the place of adoration, a

MOSQUE

temple, from *sajada,* to prostrate oneself, pray.] a Moslem temple or place of religious worship.

mos·quī'tō (-kē'), *n.; pl.* **mos·quī'tōeṣ, mos·quī'tōṣ,** [Sp. and Port. *mosquito,* dim. of *mosca,* L. *musca,* a fly.] any of a large group of two-winged insects, the females of which have skin-piercing mouth parts used to extract blood from animals, including man: some varieties are carriers of certain diseases, as malaria and yellow fever.

mos·quī'tō bär, a mosquito net.

mos·quī'tō bōat, a speedy, unarmored motorboat equipped with torpedoes and small guns: now called *PT Boat.*

mos·quī'tō hạwk, 1. a dragonfly: so named because it kills mosquitoes and eats them.
 2. a nighthawk.

mos·quī'tō net, a net or curtain of gauze to keep off mosquitoes: usually placed in a window frame or over a bed.

mos·quī'tō net'ting, a gauzelike netting used for making mosquito nets.

moṣs, *n.* [AS. *mos,* a swamp.]
 1. a very small, green, bryophytic plant that grows in velvety clusters on rocks, trees, moist ground, etc.
 2. a growth of these.
 3. any of various similar plants, as some lichens.
 black moss, Florida moss, Spanish moss; see *long moss.*
 Ceylon moss; a red alga, *lichenoides,* growing in Ceylon and the East Indies, a source of agar-agar: also called *Jaffna moss.*
 Irish moss; same as *carrageen.*
 Jaffna moss; Ceylon moss.

moṣs, *v.t.;* mossed (moṣt), *pt., pp.;* mossing, *ppr.* to cover with a growth of moss.
 An oak whose boughs were *mossed* with age. —Shak.

moṣs, *n.* [AS. *mos,* a swamp.] a bog. [Chiefly Scot. and North Eng. Dial.]

moṣs ag'ăte, a variety of agate with mosslike markings.

moṣs an'i·măl, moṣs an·i·mal'çūle, a polyzoan or bryozoan.

moṣs'back, *n.* 1. an old fish, shellfish, or turtle, etc. having a growth of algae or seaweed on its back.
 2. an old-fashioned or very conservative person. [Colloq.]

moṣs bȧss, the large-mouthed black bass. [Dial.]

moṣs'ber''ry, *n.; pl.* **moṣs'ber''rieṣ,** the European cranberry, *Vaccinium oxycoccus.*

moṣs'buñk·ẽr, *n.* the menhaden fish.

moṣs çam'pi·ŏn, a plant, *Silene acaulis,* growing in mosslike tufts on high northern mountains.

moṣs'-çapped (-kapt), *a.* capped or covered with moss.

moṣs çor'ăl, a moss animal.

moṣs çrop, the cotton grass, *Eriophorum vaginatum.* [Scot.]

moṣs'-grōwn, *a.* 1. overgrown with moss.
 2. old-fashioned; antiquated.

moṣs'head (-hed), *n.* the hooded merganser. [Dial.]

moṣs'i·ness, *n.* the quality or condition of being mossy.

mōs'sō, *a.* [It., *pp.* of *muovere,* to move.] in music, rapid; fast; as, *piu mosso,* more rapid; *meno mosso,* less rapid: a direction to the performer.

moṣs piñk, a low, hardy plant, *Phlox subulata,* having pink, white, or lavender flowers.

moṣs pol'yp, a moss animal.

moṣs rōṣe, a variety of rose having a roughened, mossy stem; also, its flower.

moṣs rush, a plant, *Juncus squarrosus:* also called *goose corn.*

moṣs'troop·ẽr, *n.* 1. any of a number of bandits who infested the swampy borderland between England and Scotland in the seventeenth century: so named from the character of the country over which they ranged.
 2. any raider or marauder.

moṣs'y, *a.; comp.* mossier; *superl.* mossiest,
 1. full of or overgrown with moss or a mosslike growth.
 2. as if covered with moss.
 3. like moss.

-mōst, [AS. *-mest,* from *-ma* and *-est.*] a suffix used in forming superlatives; as, fore*most,* ut*most,* outer*most.*

mōst, *a.; comp.* more, [AS. *mæst,* most.]
 1. greatest in amount, quantity, or degree: used as the superlative of *much.*
 2. greatest in number: used as the superlative of *many.*
 3. in the greatest number of instances; as, *most* fame is fleeting.
 4. highest in rank. [Obs.]
 for the most part; generally or chiefly; in most instances.

mōst, *n.* 1. the greatest value, amount, or advantage; the utmost in extent, degree, or effect.
 A covetous man makes the *most* of what he has, and can get. —L'Estrange.
 2. [*construed as pl.*] (a) the greatest number (of persons or things); as, *most* of us are going; (b) the greatest number of persons.
 at (the) most; at the very limit; not more than.
 to make the most of; (a) to make the greatest use of; to take fullest advantage of; (b) to treat with the highest regard.

mōst, *adv.* [AS. *mæst,* properly neut. of *mæst,* adj., most.]
 1. in or to the greatest degree or extent: used with many adjectives and adverbs (regularly with those of three or more syllables) to form the superlative degree; as, *most* horrible, *most* quickly.
 2. very (often preceded by *a*); as, a *most* beautiful morning.
 3. almost; nearly. [Colloq.]

mōst'ly, *adv.* 1. for the greatest part; in the main.
 2. chiefly; principally.

mōs'tră, *n.* [It.] in music, a mark at the end of a line formerly used to indicate the first note of the next line.

mot, *n.* [OFr.] a note or brief strain on a bugle. [Archaic.]

mot (mō), *n.* [Fr.] 1. literally, a word; hence, a motto. [Obs.]
 2. a witticism; a pithy remark; a bon mot.

mot'ȧ·cil, *n.* [L. *motacilla,* a wagtail.] a bird, the wagtail.

mō·tȧ·tō'ri·ous, *a.* [LL. *motator,* a mover, from L. *movere,* to move.] constantly vibrating: said of certain flies and spiders with long vibratile legs which keep the body in almost constant motion.

Mō·taz'i·līte, *n.* a Shiite sect of Moslems founded in the eighth century.

mōte, *n.* [AS. *mot,* a mote; compare D. *mot,* dust, sweepings.] a small particle; anything proverbially small; a spot; as, *motes* seen in a ray of light.

mōte, *v.i.* [AS. *mot.*] may; might. [Archaic.]

mōt'ed, *a.* containing fine, floating dust or specks; as, *moted* air.

mō·tel', *n.* [*mo*torist and h*otel.*] a roadside hotel for motorists, usually consisting of private cabins.

mōt'ẽr, *n.* one who or that which removes motes; specifically, a contrivance in a cotton gin for removing motes or dirt.

mō·tet', *n.* [OFr. *motet,* dim. of *mot,* a word.] in music, a contrapuntal, polyphonic song of a sacred nature, generally unaccompanied.

mō·tē'tus, *n.* [LL., from *muttum,* a word.] a voice part in medieval music; a middle voice.

moth, *n.; pl.* **mothṣ** (or moths), [AS. *moththe;* G. *motte,* a moth.]
 1. any of a group of four-winged, chiefly night-flying insects related to the butterflies but generally smaller, less brightly colored, and not having the antennae clubbed.
 2. the clothes moth, a species that lays eggs in woolens, furs, etc.: the larvae eat holes in the material.

moth bạll, a small ball of naphthalene or, sometimes, camphor, the fumes of which repel moths, as from woolens, furs, etc.

moth blīght (blīt), a species of *Aleurodes,* a genus of homopterous insects related to scale insects and aphids, destructive to plants.

 fāte, fär, fȧst, fạll, fināl, cāre, at; mēte, prẹy, hẽr, met; pīne, marïne, bīrd, pin; nōte, möve, fọr, atŏm, not; mọọn, book;

mŏth′-ēat″en, *a.* 1. gnawed away in patches by moths, as cloth.
2 decayed or decrepit in appearance; worn out.
3. out-dated.

mŏth′ẽr, *n.* [ME. *moder*; AS. *modor*; compare D. *moeder*, Dan. and Sw. *moder*, G. *mutter*.]
1. a woman who has borne a child.
2. the female parent of a plant or animal.
3. that which gives birth to something, is the origin or source of something, or nurtures in the manner of a mother.
4. (a) a woman having the responsibility and authority of a mother; (b) a woman who is the head (*mother superior*) of a religious establishment.
5. an elderly woman: used as a title of affectionate respect.
6. the qualities of a mother.

mŏth′ẽr, *a.* 1. being, or being like, a mother.
2. of or characteristic of a mother; as, *mother* love.
3. derived or learned from one's mother; native; as, *mother* tongue.

mŏth′ẽr, *v.t.* mothered, *pt.*, *pp.*; mothering, *ppr.* 1. to be the mother of; to give birth to: often used figuratively.
2. to look after or care for as a mother does.
3. to acknowledge or admit that one is the mother, author, or originator of.

mŏth′ẽr, *n.* [prob., by folk etymology, from M.D. *moeder*.]
1. a stringy, gummy, slimy substance formed by bacteria in vinegar or on the surface of fermenting liquids: also called *mother of vinegar*.
2. dregs. [Obs.]

mŏth′ẽr, *v.i.* to become full of or like mother; to develop mother, as vinegar in the process of fermenting.

Mŏth′ẽr Cãr′ey's chick′en, 1. the stormy petrel.
2. any of various other petrels.

Mŏth′ẽr Cãr′ey's goose, the giant fulmar, *Ossifraga gigantea*.

mŏth′ẽr cell, in biology, a cell that reproduces by endogenous division.

mŏth′ẽr coun′try, a motherland.

mŏth′ẽred, *a.* containing mother (stringy substance); of the thickness of mother.

Mŏth′ẽr Goose, 1. the imaginary narrator of a collection of tales (c. 1697) by Charles Perrault.
2. the imaginary creator of a collection of nursery rhymes first published in London c. 1760.

mŏth′ẽr·hood, *n.* 1. the state of being a mother.
2. the quality or character of a mother.
3. mothers collectively.

mŏth′ẽr·house, *n.* in the Roman Catholic Church, 1. a convent that is the headquarters of a religious order or of any of its territorial divisions.
2. the original convent of an order.

Mŏth′ẽr Hub′bărd, 1. the subject of an old nursery rhyme.
2. a full, loose gown for women.

mŏth′ẽr·ing, *n.* the practice or custom of visiting one's parents on Mid-Lent Sunday, a former custom in the rural districts of England, probably arising from the carrying of offerings to the mother church on that day.
Mothering Sunday; the Sunday on which visits were formerly made to one's mother church or to one's parents; Mid-Lent Sunday.

mŏth′ẽr-in-law, *n.*; *pl.* **mŏth′ẽrs-in-law,** the mother of one's husband or wife.

mŏth′ẽr·land, *n.* 1. the land of one's ancestors.
2. the country of one's birth.

mŏth′ẽr·less, *a.* without a mother; having lost a mother; as, *motherless* children.

mŏth′ẽr·li·ness, *n.* the quality of being motherly.

mŏth′ẽr liq′uŏr (lik′ŏr), same as *mother water*.

mŏth′ẽr lōde, the main lode, or vein of ore, in a mine.

mŏth′ẽr·ly, *a.* 1. pertaining to a mother; as, *motherly* power or authority.
2. like or befitting a mother; tender; maternal; parental; as, *motherly* love or care.

mŏth′ẽr·ly, *adv.* in the manner of a mother.

mŏth′ẽr-nā′ked, *a.* naked as at birth.

Mŏth′ẽr of God, the Virgin Mary: title sanctioned by the Council of Ephesus (431 A.D.).

mŏth′ẽr-of-pēarl′, *n.* the hard, silvery, brilliant, internal layer of several kinds of shells, particularly oyster shells; nacre: used in the arts and in the manufacture of buttons, etc.

mŏth′ẽr-of-pēarl′, *a.* of mother-of-pearl.

mŏth′ẽr-of-thȳme′ (-tīm′), *n.* a small aromatic plant, the *Thymus serpyllum*; wild thyme.

mŏth′ẽr of vin′ē·găr, mother (stringy substance).

Mŏth′ẽr's Dāy, the second Sunday in May, a day set aside (in the United States) in honor of mothers.

mŏth′ẽr's märk, a birthmark.

mŏth′ẽr sū·pē′ri·ŏr, the woman head of a convent.

mŏth′ẽr tŏngue (tung), 1. one's native language.
2. a language in its relation to another derived from it.

mŏth′ẽr wa′tẽr, in chemical operations, liquid residue containing water, salts in solution, and impurities, remaining after crystallization.

mŏth′ẽr wit, native intelligence; common sense.

mŏth′ẽr·wŏrt, *n.* 1. an herb, *Leonurus cardiaca*, of the mint family, having small leaves, prickly, two-lipped flowers of purple, pink, etc., and a bitter taste.
2. same as *mugwort*.

mŏth′ẽr·y, *a.* like, consisting of, or containing mother, as vinegar.

moth′proof, *a.* treated with chemicals that repel moths.

moth′y, *a.*; *comp.* mothier; *superl.* mothiest, 1. infested with moths.
2. moth-eaten.

mō·tif′, *n.* [Fr.] a main element, idea, feature, etc.; specifically, in art, literature, and music, (a) a main theme or subject to be elaborated on or developed; (b) a repeated figure in a design.

mō′tile, *n.* [from L. *motus*, pp. of *movere*, to move.] in psychology, a person in whose mind ideas of action are most prominent.

mō′tile, *a.* in biology, having an inherent power of motion; exhibiting spontaneous motion.

mō·til′i·ty, *n.* the quality of being motile.

mō′tion, *n.* [L. *motio* (*-onis*), a moving.]
1. the act or process of moving; passage of a body from one place to another; movement.
2. the act of moving the body or any of its parts.
3. a meaningful movement of the hand, eyes, etc.; a gesture.
4. the ability to move.
5. an impulse; inclination; as, of one's own *motion*.
6. a proposal; a suggestion; especially, a proposal formerly made in an assembly or meeting.
7. in law, an application to a court for a ruling, order, etc.
8. in mechanics, a combination of moving parts; a mechanism.
9. in music, melodic progression, as a change from one pitch to another in a voice part.
accelerated motion; see under *accelerate*.
angular motion; see under *angular*.
center of motion; see under *center*.
compound motion; motion that is a resultant of two or more forces.
direct motion; in astronomy, motion which results in an increase of longitude.
in motion; moving; traveling or in operation.
laws of motion; see under *law*.
motion block; in machinery, a block on a crosshead, such as those in a locomotive, that rubs on the side bars.
motion plate; a connecting plate between the cylinders and the driving axle.
motion sickness; sickness characterized by nausea, vomiting, and dizziness, and caused by the motion of an aircraft, boat, etc.
motion wheel; in horology, a wheel in the motion work.
motion work; in horology, the wheels controlling the movements of the hour and minute hands.
perpetual motion; see under *perpetual*.
rectilinear motion; motion in a straight line.
to go through the motions; to do something from habit or according to formalities, but without purpose, meaning, etc.

mō′tion, *v.i.*; motioned, *pt.*, *pp.*; motioning, *ppr.* to make a significant movement or gesture with the hand, head, etc.

mō′tion, *v.t.* to give direction or invitation to by a motion or by motions; to influence by motion; as, to *motion* a person to step aside.

mō′tion·ist, *n.* one skillful in motion. [Obs.]

mō′tion·less, *a.* without or incapable of motion; being at rest.

mō′tion piç′tūre, 1. a sequence of photographs or drawings projected on a screen in such rapid succession that they create the optical illusion (because of the persistence of vision) of moving persons and objects.
2. a play or story photographed as a motion picture.
Also called *moving picture*, *cinema*, *movie*.

mō′tion-piç″tūre, *a.* pertaining to or characteristic of a motion picture.
motion-picture camera; a camera for taking motion pictures to be shown on a screen by a motion-picture projector.
motion-picture projector; a projecting machine for showing motion pictures on a screen, either photographed with a motion-picture camera or drawn by hand.

mō′tiv·āte, *v.t.*; motivated, *pt.*, *pp.*; motivating, *ppr.* to furnish with a motive or motives; to give impetus to; to incite; to impel.

mō·tiv·ā′tion, *n.* a motivating or being motivated.

mō·tiv·ā′tion·ăl rē·sēarch′, a systematic and scientific analysis of the forces influencing people so as to control the making of their decisions: applied in advertising, marketing, etc.

mō′tive, *n.* [Fr. *motif*; LL. *motivum*, a moving cause, properly neut. of *motivus*, moving.]
1. some inner drive, impulse, intention, etc. that causes a person to do something or act in a certain way; an incentive; a goal.
2. in art, literature, and music, a motif.
Syn.—inducement, incentive, spur.

mō′tive, *a.* 1. of, causing, or tending to cause motion.
2. of, or having the nature of, a motive or motives. [Rare.]

mō′tive, *v.t.*; motived, *pt.*, *pp.*; motiving, *ppr.* 1. to supply a motive for.
2. to relate (a subject) to the motif of a work of art, literature, etc. [Rare.]

-mō′tive, [from *motive*, a.] a suffix meaning *moving, of motion*, as in auto*motive*, loco*motive*.

mō′tive·less, *a.* without a motive.

mō′tive·less·ness, *n.* the state or quality of being without a motive.

mō′tive pow′ẽr, 1. any power, as steam, electricity, etc., used to impart motion; any source of mechanical energy.
2. the locomotives of a railroad, collectively.
3. an impelling force.

mō·tiv′iç, *a.* [from *motive* (*n.* 2).] of or having to do with a musical motif.

mō·tiv′i·ty, *n.* the power of producing motion.

mot juste (mō zhüst′), [Fr.] the right word; the exact, appropriate word or phrase.

mot′ley, *a.* [ME. *motteley*; prob. from OFr.]
1. of many colors or patches of color.
2. wearing many-colored garments; as, a *motley* fool.
3. having or composed of many different or clashing elements; heterogeneous; as, a *motley* group.

mot′ley, *n.* 1. cloth of mixed colors.
2. a garment of various colors, worn by a clown or jester.
3. a fool or jester. [Obs.]

mot′ley-mīnd″ed, *a.* with a mind like that of a jester; having extravagant ideas.

mot′mot, *n.* [so called from the bird's note.] any of a group of jaylike birds of tropical and subtropical America, related to the kingfishers and characterized by a long tail, a serrate bill, and plumage of green, blue, tan, and black.

mō′tō, *n.* [It., from L. *motus*, motion.] in music, movement; as, *con moto*: a direction to the performer.

mō′tō·çross, *n.* [Fr., from *motocyclette*, a motorcycle, and Eng. *cross-country*.] a race for lightweight motorcycles over a cross-country course with obstacles.

mō′tō·cȳ·çle, *n.* same as *motorcycle*.

mō′tŏr, *n.* [L., a mover, from *movere*, to move.]
1. anything that produces or imparts motion.
2. an engine; especially, an internal-combustion engine for propelling a vehicle.
3. a vehicle propelled by an engine; especially, a motorcar; an automobile.
4. in electricity, a machine for converting electrical energy into mechanical energy.
5. [*pl.*] in finance, securities issued by automobile manufacturers.

mō′tŏr, *a.* 1. producing or imparting motion.
2. of or powered by a motor or motors; as, a *motor* vehicle.

3. of, by, or for motor vehicles; as, a *motor* trip.
4. in physiology, designating or of a nerve carrying impulses from the central nervous system to a muscle producing motion.
5. in psychology, of or manifested by muscular movements; as, a tic is a *motor* neurosis.
motor area; the ascending frontal and ascending parietal convolutions of the brain.
motor drive; an electric motor and other parts of a mechanical system for operating a machine or machines.
motor generator; an apparatus consisting of one or more electric motors coupled to one or more generators, for transforming electric currents.
motor home; an automotive vehicle with a truck chassis, outfitted as a traveling home with self-contained electrical and plumbing facilities: cf. *mobile home* under *mobile*.
motor hotel; same as *motel*: also called *motor court, motor inn, motor lodge*.
motor point; in physiology, any point where if galvanic stimulation is applied it will cause contraction of a corresponding muscle.
motor pool; a group of motor vehicles kept, as at a military installation or government center, for use as needed by personnel.
motor scooter; a scooter equipped with a seat and propelled by a small internal-combustion engine.
motor ship; a ship propelled by Diesels or other internal-combustion engines.
motor truck; a motor-driven truck for hauling loads.

mō′tŏr·bīke, *n.* 1. a bicycle propelled by a motor. [Colloq.]
2. a motorcycle. [Colloq.]

mō′tŏr·bōat, *n.* a boat or launch propelled by an internal-combustion engine or other kind of motor.

mō′tŏr·bus, *n.* a passenger bus propelled by a motor, usually an internal-combustion engine.

mō′tŏr·çāde, *n.* [*motor*car and caval*cade*.] a procession of automobiles.

mō′tŏr·çär, *n.* an automobile.

mō′tŏr·cy̆·çle, *n.* [*motor* and bi*cycle*.] a two-wheeled (or, if equipped with a sidecar, three-wheeled) vehicle propelled by an internal-combustion engine and resembling a bicycle, but usually larger and heavier.

mō′tŏr·cy̆·çle, *v.i.*; motorcycled, *pt., pp.*; motorcycling, *ppr.* to ride a motorcycle.

mō′tŏr·cy̆·çlist, *n.* a person who rides a motorcycle.

mō′tŏr·drōme, *n.* a rounded track or course for automobile of motorcycle racing or testing.

mō′tŏred, *a.* having a motor or motors; especially, having (a specified number or kind of) motors: generally used in compounds, as bi-*motored*.

mō·tō′ri·ăl, *a.* same as *motor*.

mō′tŏr·ist, *n.* a person who drives an automobile or travels by automobile; especially, one who does so frequently but not as an occupation.

mō·tō′ri·um, *n.*; *pl.* **mō·tō′ri·ȧ,** [LL. *motorium*, neut. of *motorius*, moving.] in physiology, collectively, the parts of the nervous system concerned in the motions of the body: distinguished from *sensorium*.

mō″tŏr·i·zā′tion, *n.* a motorizing or being motorized.

mō′tŏr·īze, *v.t.*; motorized, *pt., pp.*; motorizing, *ppr.* 1. to equip with motor-driven vehicles (in place of horses and horse-drawn vehicles).
2. to equip (vehicles, etc.) with a motor or motors.

mō′tŏr·măn, *n.*; *pl.* **mō′tŏr·men,** 1. a person who drives an electric streetcar or electric locomotive.
2. a person who operates a motor.

mō′tŏr·neer, *n.* a motorman. [Dial.]

mō′tō·ry, *a.* same as *motor*.

motte, mott, *n.* a grove of trees growing on a prairie. [Dial.]

mot·tet′tō, *n.* same as *motet*.

mot′tle, *v.t.*; mottled, *pt., pp.*; mottling, *ppr.* [back-formation from *mottled*.] to mark with blotches, streaks, and spots of different colors or shades.

mot′tle, *n.* 1. a blotch, streak, or spot.
2. a mottled pattern or coloring, as of marble.

mot′tled, (-tld), *a.* [from *motley* and *-ed*.] marked with blotches or spots of different colors or shades of color.

mot′tō, *n.*; *pl.* **mot′tōs, mot′tōes,** [It. *motto*; Fr. *mot*, a word.]
1. a word, phrase, or sentence inscribed on something, prefixed to a literary work, etc., as expressive of or appropriate to its character.
2. a maxim adopted as a principle of behavior.

mot′tōed, *a.* having or bearing a motto.

mot′ty, *a.* having motes. [Scot.]

möu, *n.* mouth. [Scot.]

möuch, *v.t.* and *v.i.*; mouched (mōcht), *pt., pp.*; mouching, *ppr.* to mooch.

möu·çhar′ȧ·by, *n.* [Fr.] in architecture, a balcony with a parapet and machicolations, projected over a gate, originally to defend the entrance.

MOUCHARABY

möu·çhärd′ (-shär′), *n.* [Fr.] a police spy: term of contempt.

möuch′ēr, *a.* a moocher.

möu·çhoir′ (-shwär′), *n.* [Fr., from *moucher*, to wipe the nose, from L. *mucus*, the mucus of the nose.] a handkerchief.

möue (mö), *n.* [Fr.] a pouting grimace.

möu·ez′zin, *n.* see *muezzin*.

möuf′lon, *n.*; *pl.* **möuf′lons** or **möuf′lon,** [Fr. *mouflon*; It. dial. *muffolo*, for *muffione*; LL. dial. *mufro*.]
1. a wild sheep native to the mountainous regions of Corsica and Sardinia: the male has large, curving horns.
2. the wool of this sheep.
Also spelled *moufflon*.

mought (mout), *v.* obsolete past tense of *may*.

möuil·lā′tion (mö-yā′), *n.* in phonetics, the giving utterance to the sound of a mouillé.

möuil·lé′ (mö-yā′), *a.* [Fr., pp. of *mouiller*, to moisten, from L. *mollis*, soft.] in phonetics, palatalized, as Spanish *ñ* in cañon or French *ll* in *fille*.

möu·jïk′ (-zhēk′), *n.* a mushik.

möu·läge′ (-läzh′), *n.* [Fr.] 1. the science or practice of making a mold, as in plaster of Paris, of an object, footprint, etc., as in criminological identification.
2. such a mold.

mōuld, *n., v.t.* and *v.i.* mold (growth).

mōuld, *n.* mold (soil).

mōuld, *n.* and *v.t.* mold (form).

mōuld′bōard, *n.* a moldboard.

mōuld′ēr, *v.t.* and *v.i.* to molder (decay).

mōuld′ēr, *n.* a molder.

mōuld′ing, *n.* molding.

mōuld′y, *a.*; *comp.* moldier; *superl.* moldiest; moldy.

möule (mọọl), *n.* [Fr.] a mussel, especially an edible variety.

möu·lin′ (-lan′), *n.* [Fr. *moulin*, from L. *mola*, a millstone, a mill.] a nearly vertical shaft in a glacier, worn by a stream of surface water falling through a crevice in the ice.

mōult, mōult′en, etc. same as *molt, molten*, etc.

mound, *n.* [AS. *mund*, the hand, protection, defense; prob. confused with L. *mons, montis*, a mountain.]
1. a heap or bank of earth, sand, etc. built over a grave, in a fortification, etc.
2. a natural elevation like this; a small hill.
3. any heap or pile.
4. in baseball, the slightly raised area in which the pitcher must stand when pitching.
5. something that restrains, curbs, or limits. [Obs.]
Indian mounds; mounds erected by certain aboriginal tribes of North America, called Mound Builders.

mound, *v.t.*; mounded, *pt., pp.*; mounding, *ppr.* 1. to enclose or fortify with a mound.
2. to heap up in a mound.

mound, *n.* [Fr. *monde*; L. *mundus*, the world.] globe; a small, golden ball which forms part of the regalia of an emperor or king, and is the sign of sovereign authority or majesty. It is encircled with a horizontal band, from the upper edge of which springs a semicircular band, both enriched with precious stones, and is surmounted by a cross.

MOUND

mound bīrd, a bird of the genus *Megapodius*.

Mound Build′ērs, the early Indian peoples of North America who built burial mounds and fortifications and in regard to whom there has been much discussion. Some ethnologists contend that they were a race of which no other trace than their mounds has been discovered; others, that they were essentially the same as the Indians who were found here in the fifteenth century. Their mounds are found chiefly in the United States in the Middle West and the Southeast, and are very remarkable for their great size and peculiar forms.

mount, *n.* [AS. *munt*; Fr. *mont*, a mount, both from L. *mons, montis*, a hill.]
1. a high hill; a mountain: now chiefly poetical, or used for *mountain* to form a proper name; as, *Mount* Vesuvius; *Mount* Sinai.
2. in fortification, a cavalier; also, a raised fortification. [Obs.]
3. in heraldry, the representation of a mound or elevated ground covered with grass occupying the bottom or base of the shield.
4. a bank or fund of money. [Obs.]
5. in palmistry, one of the fleshy raised parts on the palm of the hand.

mount, *v.i.*; mounted, *pt., pp.*; mounting, *ppr.* [ME. *mounten*; OFr. *munter*; LL. *montare*, lit., to go up hill, from L. *mons, montis*, a mountain.]
1. to rise on high; to ascend; to climb: often with *up*.

The fire of trees and houses *mounts* on high.
—Cowley.

2. to climb up on something; especially, to get on horseback for riding.
3. to increase in amount; to rise in value; as, savings quickly *mount*.
Syn.—rise, ascend, climb, increase.

mount, *v.t.* 1. to exalt; to lift up. [Obs.]
2. to ascend; to climb; to go up; as, she *mounted* the stairs.
3. to get upon (something elevated); as, to *mount* a throne; to *mount* a stool; to *mount* a horse.
4. to put upon horseback.
5. to furnish with a horse or horses.
6. to climb on for purposes of copulation: said of the male of an animal.
7. to place on something raised (with *on*); as, he *mounted* the statue *on* a pedestal.
8. to place, fix, or fasten on or in the proper support, backing, etc. for the required purpose; specifically, (a) to fix (a jewel) in a setting; (b) to fix (a specimen) on (a slide) for microscopic study; (c) to arrange (a skeleton, dead animal, etc.) for exhibition.
9. to furnish the necessary costumes, settings, etc. for producing (a play).
10. to put on and display (an article of clothing).
11. in military and naval usage, (a) to raise or adjust (a gun) into proper position for use; (b) to be armed with (cannon); as, this ship *mounts* six cannon; (c) to post (a guard) on sentry duty; (d) to go on (guard) as a sentry.

mount, *n.* 1. the act or manner of mounting (a horse, etc.).
2. a horse, bicycle, etc. for mounting and riding.
3. the opportunity for riding a horse, etc., especially in a race.
4. the support, setting, etc. on or in which something is mounted, as the support for a cannon or microscopic slide.

mount′ȧ·ble, *a.* capable of being mounted.

moun′tain (-tin), *n.* [ME. *munteyn, monteyne, mountaigne*; OFr. *muntaine, montaigne*, from LL. *montanea, montana*; from L. *mons, montis*, a mountain.]
1. a large mass of earth and rock, rising above the common level of the surrounding land more or less abruptly, and higher than a hill.
2. [*pl.*] a chain or group of such elevations.
3. a large pile, heap, or mound; anything of so great a bulk as to suggest the size of a mountain; as, a *mountain* of refuse; a *mountain* of trouble.
4. a wine extracted from grapes which grow on mountains or high ground.
mountain damson; see *bitter damson* under *damson*.
the Mountain; the revolutionary party of the extreme Jacobins in the legislatures during the first French Revolution, prominent among whom were Robespierre, Marat, and Danton. The name was applied because they occupied the highest rows of seats in the National Assembly of 1793.

moun′tain (-tin), *a.* 1. pertaining to a mountain or mountains.

2. used in the mountains; found on mountains; growing or dwelling on a mountain; as, *mountain* air; *mountain* pines; *mountain* goats.
3. resembling a mountain; huge; vast; as, *mountain* projects.

moun'tain an'tē·lōpe, the goral.

moun'tain ash, any of various trees of the genus *Pyrus*, as *Pyrus americana* or *Pyrus sambucifolia*, of North America, or *Pyrus aucuparia*, of Europe, ornamental trees having pinnate leaves, fragrant, white flowers, and small red or orange berries.

moun'tain av'ens, a small evergreen of the family *Rosaceæ*, found on mountains and in Arctic regions.

moun'tain bälm (bäm), 1. Oswego tea, the *Monarda didyma*.
2. an evergreen, the *Eriodictyon glutinosum*.

moun'tain bāy, a small tree or shrub, *Gordonia pubescens*, having oblong, dentate leaves and white, sweet-scented flowers. It is found in the southern part of the United States.

moun'tain bēa'vẽr, the sewellel.

moun'tain blūe, blue malachite.

moun'tain çat, 1. a cougar.
2. a bobcat.

moun'tain chāin, 1. a mountain range.
2. two or more relatively adjacent mountain ranges.

moun'tain çock, the capercaillie.

moun'tain çork, a variety of asbestos, resembling cork in its texture, and floating on water.

moun'tain çrab, a land crab of the family *Gecarcinidæ*, found in warm countries.

moun'tain çran'ber·ry, a low creeping evergreen with small, dark-green, shiny leaves and dark-red berries.

moun'tain dew, 1. originally, Scotch whiskey. [Colloq.]
2. any whiskey, especially when illegally distilled, as by mountaineers. [Colloq.]

moun'tain eb'ŏn·y, the wood of an East Indian leguminous tree, *Bauhinia variegata*.

moun'tained (-tind), *a.* 1. covered with or having many mountains; as, the *mountained* earth.
2. heaped up or towering like a mountain. [Obs.]

moun·tain·eer', *n.* [OFr. *montanier, montagnier*; LL. *montanarius*, a mountaineer, from L. *mons, montis*, a mountain.]
1. an inhabitant of a mountainous region.
2. one who climbs mountains.

moun·tain·eer', *v.i.* to assume the life of a mountaineer; to make a practice of climbing mountains, as for sport.

moun'tain·ẽr, *n.* a mountaineer. [Obs.]

moun'tain·et, *n.* a small mountain. [Rare.]

moun'tain fringe, the climbing fumitory.

moun'tain gōat, a long-haired, goatlike mammal found in the mountains of the northwestern United States and western Canada: also *Rocky Mountain goat*.

moun'tain hāre, the varying hare.

moun'tain hawk, a buzzard, *Regerhinus uncinatus*, of the West Indies.

moun'tain hēath, a shrub, *Bryanthus taxifolius*, of the mountains of New England.

moun'tain hol'ly, a branching shrub, *Nemopanthes canadensis*, of the holly family, found in the northern part of the United States.

moun'tain lau'rel, 1. a small evergreen shrub with pink and white flowers and poisonous, shiny leaves, *Kalmia latifolia*, found in the eastern part of the United States; the calico bush; the ivy bush.
2. the California laurel, *Umbellularia californica*.

moun'tain leath'ẽr (leth'), a variety of asbestos, resembling leather in its texture.

moun'tain liç'ō·rice, a species of clover found in Europe, *Trifolium alpinum*: so named because its roots taste like licorice.

moun'tain lin'net, the twite. [Brit.]

moun'tain lī'ŏn, the cougar; puma.

moun'tain mag'pīe, 1. the green woodpecker.
2. the gray shrike of Europe.

moun'tain mȧ·hog'ȧ·ny, a kind of birch, *Betula lenta*.

moun'tain mēal, bergmehl.

moun'tain milk, a native calcium carbonate, which is soft and spongy.

moun'tain mint, any plant of the genus *Pycnanthemum*.

moun'tain·ous, *a.* 1. having or full of mountains; as, the *mountainous* country of the Swiss.
2. having the nature of or like a mountain; especially, large as a mountain; huge; as, a *mountainous* heap.
3. inhabiting mountains. [Obs.]

moun'tain·ous·ness, *n.* the state of being mountainous.

moun'tain plŏv'ẽr, a bird, *Ægialites montana*, found in the western part of North America.

moun'tain prīde, a Jamaican plant, *Spathelia simplex*, of the quassia family.

moun'tain quāil (kwāl), a partridge, *Oreortyx pictus*, of the western part of the United States, having two long plumes on the back of the head: also called *mountain partridge*.

moun'tain rānge, a series of connected mountains considered as a single system because of geographical proximity or common origin.

moun'tain rīce, 1. a variety of rice, *Oryza sativa*, which thrives without irrigation on dry uplands of the northern hemisphere.
2. any grass of the genus *Oryzopsis*.

moun'tain rōse, the alpine rose, *Rosa alpina*.

moun'tain sheep, any of various wild sheep found in mountain regions; especially, the bighorn of the Rocky Mountains.

moun'tain sick'ness, a feeling of weakness, nausea, etc. brought on at high altitudes by the rarefied air.

moun'tain sōap, a soft, earthy mineral, of a brownish-black color and greasy feel; rock-soap; saxonite.

moun'tain sor'rel, a perennial of the genus *Oxyria*, allied to the common sorrel.

moun'tain spar'rōw, the tree sparrow.

moun'tain spin'ăch (*or* -ij), the garden orach, *Atriplex hortensis*, cultivated as a pot herb.

Moun'tain Stan'dărd Tīme, one of the four standard times in the United States, corresponding to the mean local time of the 105th meridian west of Greenwich, England: it is seven hours behind Greenwich time and two hours behind Eastern Standard Time.

moun'tain sweet, a plant, *Ceanothus americanus*, the New Jersey tea.

moun'tain tal'lōw, hatchettin.

moun'tain tēa, the wintergreen or checker berry, *Gaultheria procumbens*.

moun'tain tō·baç'çō, a European plant, *Arnica montana*.

moun'tain witch, a variety of pigeon, *Geotrygon sylvatica*.

mount'ănce, *n.* amount; aggregate; extent. [Obs.]

mount'ănt, *n.* in photography, an adhesive substance used in mounting photographs upon cards, etc.

mount'ănt, *a.* [Fr. *montant*, ppr. of *monter*, to mount.] rising on high. [Obs.]

mount'ē·bank, *n.* [It. *montimbanco, montambanco*; *montare*, to mount, and *banco*, bench.]
1. one who mounts a bench or stage in the market or other public place, boasts of his skill in curing diseases, vends quack medicines, and attracts an audience, usually by tricks, stories, etc.; a quack.
2. any boastful and false pretender; a charlatan.

mount'ē·bank, *v.t.* to cheat by boasting and false pretenses; to gull. [Obs.]

mount'ē·bank, *v.i.* to act the part of a mountebank.

mount'ē·bank·ẽr·y, *n.* quackery; boastful and unscrupulous pretenses.

mount'ē·bank·ish, *a.* resembling a mountebank or his trickery.

mount'ē·bank·ism, *n.* same as *mountebankery*.

mount'ed, *a.* [pp. of *mount*.]
1. seated on horseback, a bicycle, etc.
2. serving on horseback; as, *mounted* police.
3. set up and ready for use; as, a *mounted* gun.
4. fixed on or in the proper backing, support, setting, etc.
5. in military usage, regularly equipped with a means of transportation, as with horses, tanks, armored vehicles, etc.
6. in heraldry, applied to a cross upon steps.

mount'e·nănce, *n.* mountance. [Obs.]

mount'ẽr, *n.* 1. one who mounts.
2. a mounted animal; a saddle horse. [Obs.]

Mount'ie, *n.* a member of the Royal Canadian Mounted Police. [Colloq.]

mount'ing, *n.* 1. the act of mounting.

There was *mounting* in hot haste.—Byron.

2. the act of preparing for use, or embellishing.
3. that by which anything is prepared for use, or set off to advantage; equipment; embellishment; something serving as a backing, support, setting, etc.; as, the *mounting* of a sword or of a diamond.

mount'ing·ly, *adv.* by rising or ascending.

mount'let, *n.* a little mountain. [Rare.]

Mount Vẽr'nŏn, *n.* the home and burial place of George Washington, on the Potomac River, in Virginia, near Washington, D. C.

mount'y, *n.* the rise of a hawk. [Obs.]

mōurn, *v.i.*; mourned, *pt., pp.*; mourning, *ppr.* [AS. *murnan, meornan*; compare O.H.G. *mornan*, Goth. *maurnan*, to grieve.]
1. to feel or express grief or sorrow; to grieve; to be sorrowful.

Man's inhumanity to man makes countless
thousands *mourn*. —Burns.

2. to grieve for someone who has died; specifically, to wear the customary habit of such grief, as black clothes; as, to *mourn* for a month.
3. to make the low, continuous sound of a dove.

mōurn, *v.t.* 1. to feel or express sorrow for (something regrettable).
2. to grieve for (someone who has died); as, to *mourn* the loss of a friend; to *mourn* a child.
3. to utter in a sorrowful manner.

The lovelorn nightingale
Nightly to thee her sad song *mourneth* well.
—Milton.

Syn.—bewail, grieve, fret, lament, deplore.

mōurn'ẽr, *n.* 1. one who mourns; specifically, one who follows a funeral in the garb of mourning, one hired to wear a mourning garb at a funeral.
2. in certain revivalist churches, a person who makes a public profession of penitence.

mōurn'ẽrș' bench, in certain revivalist churches, a front row of seats reserved for those who are to make professions of penitence.

mōurn'fụl, *a.* 1. of or characterized by mourning; intended to express sorrow; feeling, expressing, or exhibiting the appearance of grief; as, *mournful* music.

No funeral rites, nor man in *mournful*
weeds. —Shak.

2. causing sorrow; sad; calamitous; as, a *mournful* death.

mōurn'fụl·ly, *adv.* in a mournful manner.

mōurn'fụl·ness, *n.* 1. sorrow; grief.
2. appearance or expression of grief.

mōurn'ing, *a.* of or expressing mourning; grieving; lamenting; sorrowing; wearing the appearance of sorrow.

mōurn'ing, *n.* 1. the actions or feelings of sorrowing or expressing grief; lamentation; sorrow; specifically, the expression of grief at someone's death.
2. black clothes, drapery, etc., worn or displayed as the emblems or tokens of sorrow.
3. the period during which one mourns the dead.
deep mourning; the use of lusterless black garments and the cessation of social functions, amusements, etc., according to the local customs.

mōurn'ing band, a strip of black cloth or crape worn, usually around the arm, to show mourning.

mōurn'ing brīde, an ornamental garden plant, *Scabiosa atropurpurea*, usually having dark purple flowers.

mōurn'ing clōak, any of a group of butterflies having purplish-brown wings with a wide yellow border, found throughout Europe and North America.

mōurn'ing dŏve, a species of small, wild dove of the United States, the *Zenaidura carolinensis*: so called because of its cooing regarded as mournful.

mōurn'ing·ly, *adv.* in a manner expressing grief.

mōurn'ing wạr'blẽr, a ground warbler, *Geothlypis philadelphia*, having a black breast.

mōurn'ing wid'ōw, same as *mourning bride*.

mōur'ni·văl, *n.* murnival. [Archaic.]

mōurn'sŏme, *a.* mournful. [Rare.]

mouse, *n.*; *pl.* **mīce,** [ME. *mous*; AS. *mus*, pl. *mys*; compare Ice. *mus*, Dan. *muus*, D. *muis*, G. *maus*, L. *mus*, Gr. *mys*, Per. *mush*, Sans. *musha*, dim. *mushika*, mouse.]
1. any of various large groups of small rodents found throughout the world; especially, the house mouse, *Mus musculus*, inhabiting houses.
2. (a) a girl or young woman: a term of endearment; (b) a timid or spiritless person.
3. in nautical usage, (a) a knot made on a rope to keep a running eye or loop from slipping; (b) a mousing.

4. a cut of beef or of mutton below the round. [Brit. Dial.]
5. a match used in firing a mine or a gun.
6. a dark-colored, swollen bruise under the eye, as one caused by a blow; a black eye. [Slang.]
mouse, *v.i.*; moused, *pt.*, *pp.*; mousing, *ppr.* 1. to watch for or catch mice.
2. to hunt or prowl about in a sly or insidious manner.
mouse, *v.t.* 1. to tear, as a cat does a mouse. [Rare.]
2. to hunt for.
3. to fasten a small line across the upper part of (a hook) to prevent unhooking.
mouse'bird, *n.* a coly.
mouse'-col"or, *a.* like the gray color of the fur of a mouse.
mouse deer, a small ruminant resembling a deer; the kanchil.
mouse'-ear, *n.* any of various plants: so named from the shape and velvety surface of the leaves, as (a) a hawkweed, *Hieracium pilosella*; (b) any forget-me-not of the genus *Myosotis*; (c) a chickweed, as *Cerastium vulgatum*.
mouse'fish, *n.* a parti-colored fish, *Pterophryne histrio*, of the Sargasso Sea.
mouse gà·lā'gō, a small West African lemur, *Galago murinus*.
mouse'hawk, *n.* a hawk that devours mice.
mouse'hōle, *n.* a hole where mice enter or pass; a very small hole or entrance.
He can creep in at a *mousehole*.
—Stillingfleet.
mouse hunt, 1. a hunting for mice. [Rare.]
2. a mouser; one that hunts mice. [Obs.]
mouse'kin, *n.* a little or young mouse.
mous'ēr, *n.* 1. a cat, dog, etc. with reference to its ability to catch mice; as, a good (or poor) *mouser*.
2. a stealthily inquisitive or prying person.
mous'ēr·y, *n.*; *pl.* **mous'ēr·ies**, a breeding place of mice; a place abounding with mice.
mouse'tāil, *n.* any of a group of plants of the crowfoot family, with a slender spike resembling the tail of a mouse.
mouse'trap, *n.* a trap for catching mice.
mouse'trap, *v.t.* to catch, as in a trap for mice; to entrap.
mous'ey, *a.* mousy.
mous'ie, *n.* a small mouse. [Scot.]
mous'ing, *a.* 1. given to catching mice.
2. meddlesome.
mous'ing, *n.* 1. the act of catching or watching for mice.
2. in nautical usage, a shackle or lashing uniting the point and shank of a hook to prevent its spreading or unhooking.
3. the ratchet movement in a loom.
mous'ing hook, a hook provided with a mousing.
mou'sle, *v.t.* to play with roughly; to rumple. [Obs.]
möus·que·tāire' (mös-ke-tãr'), *n.* [Fr.] a musketeer; especially, [M-] any of the French royal bodyguards of the 17th and 18th centuries.
möus·que·tāire', *a.* designating any of various articles of dress somewhat resembling that of the Mousquetaires.
mousquetaire glove; a long-armed glove for women.
möusse, *n.* [Fr., foam, from L. *mulsa*, kind of mead, honey.] any of various light frozen desserts, made from whipped cream, white of egg, gelatin, etc., sweetened and flavored.
möusse·līne' (mös-lēn'), *n.* [Fr.] 1. muslin.
2. a thin glass, blown to imitate patterns in lace, used for wineglasses, etc.: also called *mousseline glass, muslin glass*.
mousseline de laine; a lightweight woolen cloth, often printed, used for dresses, etc.: also called *muslin delaine*.
mousseline de soie: a gauzelike silk or rayon cloth with a plain weave, used for blouses, etc.
möus·tàche', *n.* same as *mustache*.
Möus·tē'ri·ăn, Möus·tiē'ri·ăn, *a.* [Fr. *moustérien*: so named because remains were found at Le *Moustier*, in southern France.] in anthropology, designating or of a late paleolithic culture, believed to be that of a race of Neanderthal men.
mous'y, *a.*; *comp.* mousier; *superl.* mousiest, 1. of, characteristic of, or like a mouse, in any of various ways; quiet, timid, drab, etc.
2. infested with, full of, or smelling of mice.
möu'tan, *n.* [Chinese *meu-tang*, king of flowers.] the Chinese tree peony, *Pæonia moutan*, a shrubby plant of China.

mouth, *n.*; *pl.* **mouths**, [ME.; AS. *muth*; compare Ice. *muthr, munnr*, mouth.]
1. the opening through which an animal takes in food; specifically, the cavity, or the entire structure, in the head of any of the higher animals which contains the teeth and tongue and through which sounds are uttered.
2. (a) the mouth regarded as the organ of chewing and tasting; (b) the mouth regarded as the organ of speech.
3. a person or animal regarded as a being needing food.
4. the lips, or the part of the face surrounding the lips.
5. a wry expression of the face; a grimace.
6. anything resembling a mouth in position or use, as (a) the opening of anything hollow, as a jar, a well, a mine, a cave, etc.; (b) the opening of a firearm at the end from which the charge issues; (c) the part of a river, stream, etc. where the water empties into another body of water; (d) the opening between the lips of an organ pipe; (e) the opening in a flute across which the player blows; (f) the opening between the cheeks or jaws of a vise.
7. a principal speaker; one who utters the common opinion; an oracle. [Obs.]
8. the crossbar of the bit of a bridle, uniting the rings or the branches.
by mouth or *by word of mouth*; by speech as distinguished from writing.
down in (or *at*) *the mouth*; depressed; unhappy; discouraged. [Colloq.]
to be born with a silver spoon in one's mouth; see under *spoon*.
to give mouth to; to express in speech; to say.
to have a big mouth; to talk loudly, excessively, or impudently. [Slang.]
mouth, *v.t.* 1. to say; especially, to say in an affected or oratorical manner with much movement of the mouth; to declaim.
2. to take or put into the mouth.
3. to caress or rub with the mouth or lips.
4. to train (a horse) to become accustomed to the bit.
mouth, *v.i.* 1. to speak with a full, round, or loud, affected voice; to vociferate; to rant; as, a *mouthing* actor.
2. to kiss. [Obs.]
3. to make a grimace.
mouth'à·ble, *a.* sounding well when uttered; readily pronounced.
mouth'breed"ēr, *n.* any of a number of small fishes that carry their young in the mouth.
-mouthed, a combining form used in hyphenated compounds, meaning *having a* (specified kind of) *mouth* or (specified number of) *mouths*; as, large-*mouthed*.
mouth'ēr, *n.* one who mouths his words.
mouth'foot"ed, *a.* having certain feet altered into masticatory organs; stomatopodous.
mouth'ful, *n.*; *pl.* **mouth'fuls**, 1. as much as the mouth can hold.
2. as much as is usually taken into the mouth at one time.
3. a small amount.
4. a long word or group of words hard to pronounce. [Colloq.]
5. a pertinent, important, or correct remark: usually in *say a mouthful*. [Slang.]
mouth hon'ŏr (on'), civility expressed without sincerity.
mouth'i·ly (*or* mouth'), *adv.* in a mouthy manner.
mouth'i·ness (*or* mouth'), *n.* the quality or condition of being mouthy; talkativeness; bombast.
mouth'less, *a.* without a mouth.
mouth'-māde, *a.* expressed without sincerity.
mouth or'găn, 1. a harmonica.
2. a Panpipe.
3. in zoology, a mouth part.
mouth pärt, a part or appendage constituting an element in the mouth, as in the crustaceans.
mouth'piēce, *n.* 1. a part placed at, or forming, a mouth; as, the *mouthpiece* of a telephone, of a pipe, of a horse's bit, etc.
2. the part of a musical instrument held in or to the mouth.
3. a person, periodical, etc. serving as a spokesman for another or others.
4. a lawyer who defends criminals. [Slang.]
mouth pīpe, 1. that part of a wind instrument into which the mouthpiece is inserted.
2. an organ pipe having a lip to cut the air escaping through an aperture in a diaphragm.
mouth'y (*or* mouth'), *a.*; *comp.* mouthier; *superl.* mouthiest; loquacious; ranting.
möu'ton, *n.* [Fr., sheep.] the fur of any of certain sheep, made water-repellant and dyed to resemble any of various other furs, especially beaver.
mou·ton·née' (mö-tŏ-nā'), *a.* [Fr. *moutonnée*, f. pp. of *moutonner*, from *mouton*, sheep.] in geology, rounded like the back of a sheep, as by glacial action: said of rock formations.
möv·à·bil'i·ty, *n.* the quality or condition of being movable.
möv'à·ble, *a.* [OFr. *movable, mouvable*, from L. *movere*, to move.]
1. that can be moved from one place to another; transportable; specifically, in law, designating personal property (as distinguished from real property).
2. changing in date from one year to the next; as, *movable* holidays.
Also spelled *moveable*.
möv'à·ble, *n.* 1. something movable.
2. [*usually pl.*] in law, personal property, especially furniture.
3. in Scots law, every species of property, corporeal or incorporeal, which does not descend to the heir in heritage.
Also spelled *moveable*.
möv'à·ble·ness, *n.* same as *movability*.
möv'à·bly, *adv.* so as to be movable; in a movable manner or state.
möve, *v.t.*; moved, *pt.*, *pp.*; moving, *ppr.* [ME. *moven*; Anglo-Fr. *mover*; OFr. *movoir, mover, mouver*, from L. *movere*, to move.]
1. to change the place or position of; to push, carry, or pull from one place or position to another.
2. to set or keep in motion; to stir.
3. to cause or persuade (*to act, do, say, speak*, etc.); to prompt.
4. to arouse or stir the emotions, passions, or sympathies of; to touch the feelings of.
5. to propose or suggest; especially, to propose formally, as in a meeting.
6. to cause (the bowels) to evacuate.
7. in commerce, to dispose of (goods) by selling.
8. in such games as chess, checkers, etc., to change the position of (a piece) in the regular course of play; as, to *move* the queen's bishop.
Syn.—actuate, impel, instigate, stir, convert, influence.
möve, *v.i.* 1. to change place or posture; to stir; to pass or go in any manner or direction from one place or part of space to another.
Nor till her lay was ended could I *move*.
—Dryden.
He *moves* with manly grace. —Dryden.
2. to change residence; as, men *move* with their families from one house, town, or country to another.
3. to live or be active; to pass one's life; as, we *move* in good society.
4. to make progress; to advance.
5. to take action; to begin to act; as, to *move* in a matter of business.
6. (a) to be, or be set, in motion; (b) to operate in a certain fixed motion; to turn, revolve, etc.: said of machines.
7. to appeal; to make formal application (*for*); as, *move* for a new trial.
8. to be evacuated: said of the bowels.
9. to start leaving; to depart (often with *on*); as, let's be *moving* on. [Colloq.]
10. in chess, checkers, etc. (a) to change the position of a piece; (b) to be put in another position: said of a piece.
11. in commerce, to be disposed of by sale: said of goods.
möve, *n.* 1. the act of moving; a movement.
2. in chess and similar games, the act of changing the position of a piece or the right to so change it.
3. a proceeding; a step taken toward attaining an object; as, a disconcerting *move*.
4. a change of residence.
on the move; moving about from place to place. [Colloq.]
to get a move on; (a) to start moving; (b) to hurry; to go faster. [Slang.]
möve'à·ble, *a.* and *n.* same as *movable*.
möve'less, *a.* without motion; fixed.
möve'ment, *n.* [OFr. *movement*, from L. *movere*, to move.]
1. a moving; specifically, (a) an action of a person or group; (b) an evacuation of the bowels; also, the matter evacuated; (c) in military and naval usage, a change in the location of troops, ships, etc., as part of a maneuver.
2. a particular manner of moving.
3. a series of organized activities by people

working concertedly toward some goal: often called *the movement* by those involved in it.

4. a tendency or trend in some particular sphere of activity; as, a *movement* toward formalism in art.

5. the progress of events in a literary work; action.

6. the effect or representation of motion in painting, sculpture, etc.

7. in commerce, a change in the price of some stock or commodity.

8. in mechanics, the moving parts of a mechanism; especially, a series of connected moving parts; as, the *movement* of a clock.

9. in music, (a) tempo; (b) rhythm; (c) any of the principal divisions of a symphony, sonata, or other extended composition.

10. in prosody, rhythmic flow; cadence.

mō′vent, *a.* [L. *movens* (*-entis*), ppr. of *movere*, to move.] moving; not quiescent. [Rare.]

mō′vent, *n.* that which moves anything. [Rare.]

mōv′ẽr, *n.* 1. the person or thing that gives motion or impels to action.

2. one who or that which moves.

3. a proposer; one that offers a proposition or recommends anything for consideration or adoption; as, the *mover* of a resolution in a legislative body.

4. one who moves house furniture.

mōv′ie, *n.* [*contr.* from *moving picture.*]

1. a motion picture.

2. a motion-picture theater.

the movies; (a) motion pictures collectively; (b) the motion picture industry; (c) a showing of a motion picture; as, let's go to the *movies* tonight.

mōv′ie·gō·ẽr, *n.* a person who goes, especially often, to see motion pictures. [Colloq.]

mōv′ie house, a motion-picture theater. [Colloq.]

mōv′ing, *a.* that moves; specifically, (a) changing, or causing to change, place or position; (b) causing motion; (c) causing to act; impelling, instigating, influencing, etc.; (d) arousing or stirring the emotions or feelings; especially, arousing pathos.

mōv′ing, *n.* motive; impulse; the act of changing location or position.

mōv′ing·ly, *adv.* in a manner to excite the passions or affect sensibility.

mōv′ing·ness, *n.* the power of affecting, as the emotions.

mōv′ing piç′tūre, a motion picture; photoplay.

mōv′ing plant, a plant whose leaves have an automatic motion: also called *telegraph plant.*

mōv′ing stâir′çāse, an escalator: also called *moving stairway.*

mow, *n.* [ME. *mowe*; AS. *muga, muha*, a heap or pile of hay, a mow.]

1. a heap, mass, or pile of hay; sheaves of grain deposited in a barn.

2. the place in a barn where hay, etc. is stacked: also called *haymow, hayloft.*

mow, *v.t.* to lay (hay or sheaves of grain) in a heap or mass in a barn: often followed by *away.*

mōw, *v.t.*; mowed, *pt.*; mowing, *ppr.*; mowed or mown, *pp.* [ME. *mowen, mawen*; AS. *mawan*, to mow; compare Ice. *mugr, mugi*, a swathe; *mygja*, to mow down or destroy.]

1. to cut down with a scythe or mower, as grass or grain.

2. to cut grass or grain from; as, to *mow* a meadow.

3. to cause to fall like cut grass or grain; kill; destroy (with *down*); as, we *mowed down* the enemy.

mōw, *v.i.* 1. to cut grass or grain; to practice mowing; to use a mower or scythe.

2. to perform the business of mowing; to cut and make grass into hay; to gather the crop of grass or grain.

mow, mowe, *n.* and *v.i.* [ME. *mowe*; OFr. *moue*; M.D. *mouwe.*] grimace. [Archaic.]

mow, *v.* might; may; can. [Obs.]

mow′bũrn, *v.i.* to heat and ferment in the mow, as hay or grain when housed too green. [Obs.]

mōw′ẽr, *n.* one who or that which mows; a mowing machine.

mōw′ing, *n.* 1. the act of cutting down grass or grain.

2. the quantity of grass or grain mowed in a single specified period.

3. land from which grass is cut.

mōw′ing mȧ·çhïne′, a machine with rotating blades for mowing grass, etc.

mōwn, *a.* 1. cut with a scythe.

2. cleared of grass by mowing.

mōwn, *v.* alternative past participle of *mow* (to cut down).

mox′ȧ, *n.* [Chinese and Japan.]

1. the down of the mugwort of China; a soft substance prepared in Japan and China from the young leaves of *Artemisia moxa*, and burned on the skin as a cauterizing agent or counter irritant.

2. any substance whose gradual combustion on or near the skin is used for the relief or cure of disease.

3. a plant from which the downy substance called moxa is obtained.

mox′ie, *n.* [from *Moxie*, trademark for a soft drink.] courage, pluck, perseverance, etc.; guts. [Slang.]

moy·en âge′ (mwȧ-ye-näzh′), [Fr., lit., middle age.] the Middle Ages.

moyle, *n.* same as *moil.*

Mōz·âr′ȧb, *n.* [Sp. *Mozárabe*, from Ar. *Mostareb*, from *te'arrab*, to become an Arab.] any of a group of Spanish Christians who kept their religion in a modified form during the domination of the Moors.

Mōz·âr′ȧ·biç, *a.* of or pertaining to the Mozarabs.

mō·zet′tȧ, mōz·zet′tȧ, *n.* [It. *mozzetta*, from *mozzo*, to cut short.] a shoulder cape with a small hood attached, worn by dignitaries of the Roman Catholic Church.

Mr. (mis′tẽr), *pl.* **Messrs.** (mes′ẽrz), mister: used before the name or title of a man.

mri·dañ′gȧm, *n.* [From Sans. *mṛdanga*, clayey.] a barrel-shaped drum of India made of clay or a hollowed-out block of wood, with heads of overlapping layers of skin, each layer producing a different tone when struck.

M ro͝of (em) a kind of roof formed by the junction of two simple pitched roofs with a valley between them, so that in transverse section it resembles the letter **M**.

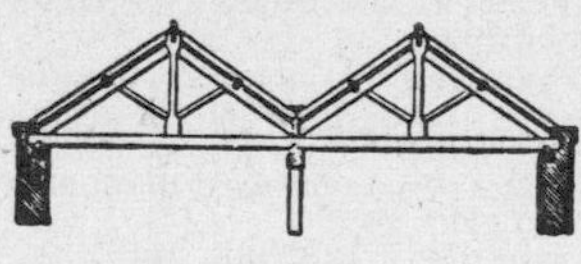

M ROOF

Mrs. (mis′iz), mistress: now used as a title before the name of a married woman.

Ms. (miz, em′es′), a title free of reference to marital status, used before the name of a woman instead of either *Miss* or *Mrs.*

m'sẽur (m'syũr′ *or Fr.* m'syẽ′), *n.* monsieur.

Ms-Th, MsTh, in chemistry, mesothorium.

mū, *n.* [Gr. *my.*] the twelfth letter of the Greek alphabet, corresponding to English M, m.

mū′ce·din, *n.* [LL. *mucedo* (*-inis*), mucus.] a nitrogenous substance obtained from the gluten of wheat, etc.: also called *mucin.* [Now Rare.]

much, *a.*; *comp.* more; *superl.* most, [ME. *moche, muche, miche*, shortened forms of *mochel, muchel*, much, great, softened from *mickle*, from AS. *mycel, micel*, much, great, many. The comp. *more* and superl. *most* are supplied from another root.]

1. many in number. [Obs.]

Edom came out against him with *much* people. —Num. xx. 20.

2. great in quantity, amount, degree, duration, etc.

Thou shalt carry *much* seed into the field, and gather but little in. —Deut. xxviii. 38.

3. of high rank. [Obs.]

much, *adv.* 1. to a great degree or extent; as, *much* more, *much* stronger, *much* heavier, *much* less, *much* smaller, *much* less distinguished, *much* finer.

A *much* afflicted, *much* enduring man. —Pope.

2. nearly; just about; almost.

All left the world *much* as they found it. —Temple.

much, *n.* 1. a great quantity; a great deal.

To whom *much* is given, of him *much* will be required. —Luke xii. 48.

2. an uncommon thing; something great or important.

It was *much* that one who was so great a lover of peace should be happy in war. —Bacon.

as much; an equal quantity: used as an adjective or noun; as, return *as much* bread as you borrowed. *Twice as much* signifies twice the quantity.

as much; in an equal degree; as, one man loves power *as much* as another loves gold.

so much; an equal quantity or a certain quantity (as a noun); to an equal degree, or to a certain degree (as an adverb).

to make much of; to treat or consider as of great importance.

mu·chä′chä, *n.* [Sp.] a girl; also, a woman servant.

mu·chä′chō, *n.* [Sp.] a boy; also, a manservant.

much′ness, *n.* the state of being much; greatness; magnitude.

much of a muchness; much the same. [Colloq.]

mū′ci-, same as *muco-.*

mū′ciç ac′id, a colorless, crystalline acid, $(CHOH)_4(CO_2H)_2$, formed by oxidizing lactose, gums, etc.

mū′cid, *a.* [L. *mucidus*, from *mucere*, to be moldy or musty.] musty; moldy; slimy.

mū·cif′ẽr·ous, *a.* same as *muciparous.*

mū·cif′iç, *a.* [*muci-*, and L. *facere*, to make.] muciparous.

mū′ci·form, *a.* [*muci-*, and L. *forma*, form.] resembling mucus in composition or appearance.

mū′ci·gen, *n.* [*mucin*, and Gr. *-genēs*, producing.] a substance secreted in the cells of the mucous membrane and related cells, which is the fundamental element of mucin.

mū·cig′e·nous, *a.* same as *muciparous.*

mū′ci·lāge, *n.* [Fr. *mucilage*; LL. *mucilago*, a musty juice, from L. *mucere*, to be musty or moldy.]

1. any of various thick, sticky substances found in certain plants.

2. any watery solution of gum, glue, etc. used as an adhesive.

mū·ci·lag′i·nous, *a.* 1. producing or secreting mucilage; as, the *mucilaginous* glands.

2. slimy; moist, soft, and viscid; of or like mucilage; as, a *mucilaginous* gum.

mū·ci·lag′i·nous·ness, *n.* sliminess; the state of being mucilaginous.

mū′cin, *n.* [L. *mucus*, mucus, and *-in.*] in biochemistry, any of various nitrogenous substances secreted by the mucous membranes.

mū·cin′ō·gen, *n.* same as *mucigen.*

mū′cin·oid, *a.* [*mucin* and *-oid.*] having the nature or appearance of mucin.

mū′cin·oid, *n.* same as *mucoid.*

mū·cip′ȧ·rous, *a.* [*muci-*, and L. *parere*, to bring forth.] secreting or producing mucus.

mū′ci·vōre, *n.* [*muci-*, and L. *vorare*, to devour.] any insect which feeds upon mucus or plant juices.

mū·civ′ō·rous, *a.* feeding on plant juices, as certain dipterous insects.

muck, *n.* [ME. *muck, mokke*; Ice. *myki*, dung.]

1. moist manure.

2. black earth containing decaying matter, used as a fertilizer.

3. something mean, vile, or filthy; dirt; filth.

4. money; wealth: used in contempt.

muck, *v.t.*; mucked (mukt), *pt., pp.*; mucking, *ppr.* 1. to fertilize with muck.

2. to dirty with or as with muck. [Colloq.]

3. in mining, etc., to remove muck from.

muck, *v.i.* to do drudgery; to work hard; to toil. [Brit. Dial.]

muck, *a.* mucky; filthy. [Rare.]

Muck′ẽr, *n.* [G. *mucker*, a hypocrite, a grumbler.] one of a religious sect of Prussia, accused of immoral practices in the early part of the nineteenth century.

muck′ẽr, *n.* 1. a stable cleaner. [Rare.]

2. a low, mean, dirty person; especially, one without honor; a cad. [Brit. Slang.]

muck′et, *n.* [etym. doubtful.] a fresh-water mussel, particularly *Actinonaias carinata*, the common species, which is much used in the manufacture of buttons.

muck fo͝rk, a fork for handling manure.

muck′hēap, muck′hill, *n.* a heap of muck.

muck′i·ness, *n.* the quality of being mucky.

muck′īte, *n.* [named after its discoverer, H. *Muck.*] in mineralogy, a resinous hydrocarbon.

muck′le (-l), *a., adv.*, and *n.* [ME. *mikel, mukel, mickel.*] much: also spelled *mickle.* [Archaic or Scot.]

muck′mid·den, *n.* a dunghill. [Scot.]

muck rāke, a rake for collecting or spreading muck.

muck′rāke, *v.i.*; muckraked, *pt., pp.*; muckraking, *ppr.* [so used in 1906 by Theodore Roosevelt in allusion to the man with the *muck rake* (in Bunyan's *Pilgrim's Progress*), who was too intent upon raking muck to consider his heavenly crown.] to search for and either charge or expose (in newspapers, etc.)

corruption by public officials, businessmen, etc.
muck′rāk″ẽr, *n.* a person, especially a newspaper reporter, who muckrakes.
muck rōlls, the pair of rolls in a rolling mill through which the iron first passes.
muck′sweat (-swet), *n.* profuse sweat.
muck′sy, *a.* mucky. [Dial.]
muck′thrift, *n.* a miserly fellow. [Rare.]
muck′wŏrm, *n.* 1. a worm or a larva that lives in muck: applied chiefly to the larvae of scaraboid beetles.
2. a miser; one who scrapes together money by mean labor and devices.
muck′y, *a.*; *comp.* muckier; *superl.* muckiest, of or like muck; especially, dirty, filthy, etc.
muck′y, *v.t.*; muckied, *pt.*, *pp.*; muckying, *ppr.* to soil; to besmirch; to make mucky. [Brit. Dial.]
mū′çō-, a combining form meaning *mucus* or *mucous membrane*; as in *muco*protein: also *muci-* or, before a vowel, *muc-*.
mū′çō·cēle, *n.* [*muco-*, and Gr. *kēlē*, a tumor.] enlargement of the lacrymal sac; also, any tumor containing mucus.
mū′çoid, *n.* [*muc*in and *-oid.*] one of a group of substances like mucin and occurringi n connective tissue, etc., but differing from it in some of its reactions.
mū′çoid, *a.* [*muco-*, and Gr. *eidos*, form.] like mucus or related to mucus.
mucoid degeneration; a gradual transformation of tissue into a liquid or semiliquid substance containing mucin.
mū′çō·nāte, *n.* a salt of muconic acid.
mū·çon′iç, *a.* designating an acid obtained from mucic acid.
muconic acid; a compound crystalline substance ($C_6H_6O_4$), obtained from mucic acid.
mū·çō·prō′tē·in, *n.* in biochemistry, any of a class of proteins combined with a carbohydrate complex.
mū·çō·pū′ru·lent, *a.* [*muco-*, and L. *purulentus*, purulent.] resembling both pus and mucus.
Mū′çŏr, *n.* [L., mold, moldiness.]
1. a genus of saprophytic mold fungi: they are extremely slender and surmounted by globular sporangia; the molds.
2. [m–] moldiness. [Rare.]
Mū·çō·rā′cē·ae, *n.pl.* a family of fungi of which *Mucor* is the typical genus. The species are found on bread, fruits, etc.
mū′çō·rine, *a.* pertaining to the genus *Mucor*.
mū·çō′sȧ, *n.*; *pl.* **mū·çō′sae,** a mucous membrane: also called *membrana mucosa*.
mū·çō′săl, *a.* pertaining to the mucous membrane.
mū·cos′i·ty, *n.* the quality or condition of being mucous.
mū·çō·sō·saç′chȧ·rine, *a.* [L. *mucosus*, slimy, and *saccharum*, sugar.] having the qualities of mucilage and sugar.
mū′çous, *a.* [L. *mucosus*, slimy, from *mucus*, mucus.]
1. of, containing, or secreting mucus.
2. like mucus or covered with or as with mucus; slimy.
mucous membrane; a mucus-secreting membrane lining body cavities and canals connecting with the external air, as the alimentary canal and respiratory tract.
mucous patches; patches of slight elevation on the mucous membrane of the mouth and anus, usually indicating syphilis.
mucous tissue; gelatinous connective tissue, as that of the umbilical cord and the vitreous humor of the eye.
mū′çous·ness, *n.* the state of being mucous; sliminess.
mū′çrō, *n.*; *pl.* **mū·çrō′nēș,** [L., a sharp point.] a short, sharp point, tip, or process projecting abruptly from certain parts and organs, as at the end of a leaf.
mū′çrō·nāte, mū′çrō·nā·ted, *a.* ending in a mucro, or sharp point; as, a *mucronate* leaf; a *mucronate* process.
mū′çrō·nāte·ly, *adv.* in a mucronate manner; with a pointed end.
mū·çrō·nā′tion, *n.* the condition of being mucronate.
mū·çron′ū·lāte, *a.* having a very small point, tip, or process.
mū′çū·lent, *a.* [L. *muculentus*, from *mucus*, mucus.]
1. slimy; moist and moderately viscous.
2. resembling mucus.
Mū·çū′nȧ, *n.* [from Braz. *mucuna*, the name of one of these plants.] a genus of leguminous plants represented by the Florida bean, *Mucuna urens*.
mū′çus, *n.* [L. *mucus*, mucus.]
1. the viscid watery secretion of the mucous membranes, that moistens and protects them.
2. a gummy substance occurring in some plants.
mū′çus·in, *n.* mucin. [Rare.]
mud, *n.* [ME., prob. from a L.G. source; cf. L.G. *mudde*, *mod*, mud, mire; compare Sw. *modd*, mud.]
1. moist, soft, sticky earth, such as is found in marshes and swamps, at the bottom of rivers and ponds, or in highways after rain.
2. defamatory remarks; libel or slander.
mud, *v.t.*; mudded, *pt.*, *pp.*; mudding, *ppr.* 1. to cover or soil with or as with mud.
2. to make turbid or foul with dirt; to stir the sediment in (liquors).
mud bȧss, a small fish, *Acantharchus pomotis*, found in the eastern United States.
mud bȧth, a bath in which mud is used, generally in connection with mineral springs.
mud bōat, mud sçow, a flatboat of strong construction for receiving and transporting mud, especially the mud of dredgings.
mud çat, in the Mississippi valley, a full-grown, edible catfish.
mud çrab, a crab of the genus *Panopæus*.
mud çracks, cracks formed in the surface layer of mud in drying, often intersecting in such a way as to form symmetrical blocks, and sometimes filled with rock material which hardens to form fossil mud cracks.
mud dab, same as *flounder* (fish).
mud daub′ẽr, a wasp which builds a nest of mud and fills its compartments with spiders, larvae of other insects, etc., to supply food for its own larvae; a mud wasp.
mud′dẽr, *n.* in horse racing, a horse that runs especially well on a wet, muddy track.
mud dev′il (-l), same as *hellbender*.
mud′di·ly, *adv.* in a muddy manner; turbidly; cloudily.
mud′di·ness, *n.* the quality or condition of being muddy.
mud dip′pẽr, same as *ruddy duck* under *ruddy*.
mud′dle, *v.t.*; muddled, *pt.*, *pp.*; muddling, *ppr.* [from *mud.*]
1. to mix up in a confused manner; to jumble; to bungle.
2. to mix or stir (a drink, etc.).
3. to make (water, etc.) turbid.
4. to confuse mentally; to befuddle, as with alcoholic liquor.
5. to confuse (the brain, mind, etc.); to befog.
mud′dle, *v.i.* to act or think in a confused way.
to muddle through; to succeed in spite of apparent blunders or confusion. [Chiefly Brit.]
mud′dle, *n.* 1. a confused or disordered condition; a mess, confusion, jumble, etc.
2. mental confusion.
mud′dle·head (-hed), *n.* a dolt.
mud′dle-head″ed (-hed″ed), *a.* stupid; blundering; confused.
mud′dlẽr, *n.* a stick for stirring mixed drinks.
mud dredġ′ẽr, a machine for dredging; a dredge.
mud drum, a drum or chamber below the main part of a boiler, in which sand and earthy matters settle.
mud′dy, *a.*; *comp.* muddier; *superl.* muddiest, 1. abounding in, covered with, or containing mud; as, a *muddy* road; *muddy* boots.
2. consisting of mud or earth; gross; impure.
3. (a) not clear; containing sediment; cloudy; as, *muddy* coffee; (b) dull; as, a *muddy* complexion.
4. cloudy in mind; confused; dull; heavy; stupid.
5. obscure in meaning; vague; confused; as, a *muddy* style of writing.
mud′dy, *v.t.* and *v.i.*; muddied, *pt.*, *pp.*; muddying, *ppr.* to make or become muddy.
mud′dy-head″ed (-hed″),*a.* having a dull understanding.
mud′dy-met″tled, *a.* dull-spirited.
mud eel, any eel; specifically, *Siren lacertina*, or a related salamander living in the mud.
mud′fish, *n.*; *pl.* **mud′fish** or **mud′fish·eș,** any of various fishes living in mud or muddy water.
mud flat, low, muddy land that is flooded at high tide and left uncovered at low tide.
mud frog, a European frog, *Pelobates fuscus*.
mud′guärd (-gärd), *n.* a cover or shield over the wheel of a bicycle, automobile, etc., to protect against mud thrown up by the wheel.
mud hen, any of various birds that live in marshes, as the coot, rail, gallinule, etc.; marsh hen.
mud′hōle, *n.* a hole or low place, as in a field or road, full of mud.
mu·dïr′, *n.* in Turkey, the governor of a city or district: also spelled *moodir*.
mud lärk, 1. one who cleans sewers. [Slang.]
2. a waif; a gamin.
3. a pipit. [Brit. Dial.]
mud lä′vȧ, mud ejected from a volcano.
mud min′nōw (-ō), any minnow of the genus *Umbra*.
mud pup′py, any of various North American salamanders that live in mud under water, especially a large variety with bushy external gills.
mud′sill, *n.* 1. the lowest timber, or sill, in the foundation of a structure, placed in or on the ground.
2. a lazy, ignorant, low person. [Dial.]
mud′sling·ẽr, *n.* a person who engages in mudslinging.
mud′sling·ing, *n.* the practice of making unscrupulous, malicious attacks against an opponent, as in a political campaign.
mud′stōne, *n.* a hardened sedimentary rock formed from clay and similar to shale, but not laminated.
mud′suck·ẽr, *n.* an aquatic bird which obtains its food from mud.
mud swäl′lōw, a bird, the cliff swallow. [Dial.]
mud tũr′tle, mud tor′toise (-tis), one of various small turtles found in inland waters of the United States.
mud vol·çā′nō, a conical hill in a volcanic region which ejects mud in large quantities, often accompanied by various gases and vapors.
mud′walled, *a.* having a wall of mud, sod, adobe, or similar material.
mud wäsp, same as *mud dauber*.
mud′weed, *n.* same as *mudwort*.
mud′wŏrt, *n.* a plant, *Limosella aquatica*, found growing in muddy places.
mu·ẽr′mō, *n.* [Chilean.] a Chilean tree, *Eucryphia cordifolia*, of the rose family.
mū·ez′zin, *n.* [Ar., from *adhana*, to proclaim, from *udhn*, an ear.] in Moslem countries, a crier in a minaret or other lofty place who calls the people to prayer at the proper hours.
muff, *n.* [D. *mof*; L.G. *muffe*, *muff*; G. *muff*, a muff, connected with O.H.G. *mouwa*, D. *mouw*, a long sleeve serving for ornament or warmth.]
1. a cover or protection for the hands in cold weather, usually cylindrical and of fur.
2. a bird, the whitethroat. [Brit. Dial.]
3. in glass blowing, glass in a circular form before flattening.
4. an end-to-end coupler for two pipes.
5. in baseball, etc., a failure to hold a ball when catching it.
6. (a) any bungling action; (b) a bungler.
muff, *v.t.* and *v.i.*; muffed, *pt.*, *pp.*; muffing, *ppr.* to do (something) badly or awkwardly; specifically, in baseball, etc. to miss (a catch) or bungle (a play).
muf·fē·tee′, *n.* a muff for the wrist. [Scot. and Brit. Dial.]
muf′fin, *n.* [prob. from OFr. *moufflet*, soft, as in *pain moufflet*, soft bread.]
1. a quick bread made with eggs and baked in a small, cup-shaped mold, usually eaten hot.
2. a similar small bread made from dough leavened with yeast.
3. a small earthen plate.
muf·fin·eer′, *n.* 1. a serving dish for keeping muffins hot.
2. a cruet for sprinkling powdered sugar or salt over muffins.
muf′fish, *a.* awkward; slow. [Colloq.]
muf′fle, *n.* 1. a muff for the hands. [Obs.]
2. a boxing glove. [Obs.]
3. a large handkerchief for protecting the throat; a muffler.
4. any cover or enclosure, particularly when used to deaden sound.
5. an oven in which pottery, etc. can be fired without being exposed directly to the flame.
6. the fleshy bare part of the upper lip and nose of ruminants and certain other mammals.
7. a pully block containing several sheaves.
muf′fle, *v.t.*; muffled, *pt.*, *pp.*; muffling, *ppr.* [compare D. *moffelen*, to conceal, pilfer.]
1. to cover from the weather by cloth, fur, or any garment; to cover closely, particularly the neck and face.
The face lies *muffled* up within the garment.
—Addison.

2. to keep (a person) from seeing or speaking by wrapping up the head.

Alas! that love, whose view is *muffled* still. —Shak.

3. to provide with a muffler or any device for deadening sound; as, to *muffle* a bell, an oar, etc.

4. to deaden (a sound), as by wrapping.

muf'fle, *v.i.* to mutter; to speak indistinctly. [Rare.]

muf'flėr, *n.* 1. a scarf, shawl, etc. worn around the throat, as for warmth.

2. any of various devices for silencing noises, as a baffle in the exhaust pipe of an internal-combustion engine.

muf'flon, *n.* same as *mouflon.*

muf'ti, *n.* [Ar., one who gives a decisive response, from *āftā*, to judge, to give a judicial decision.]

1. in Moslem countries, an interpreter or expounder of religious law.

2. plain dress worn by officers off duty; civilian dress as distinguished from uniform.

mug, *n.* [compare Ir. *mugan*, a mug, Sw. *mugg*, an earthen cup.]

1. an earthen or metal drinking cup, usually cylindrical and with a handle, formerly often ornamented with a human face.

2. as much as a mug will hold.

3. (a) the face; (b) the mouth; (c) a grimace; (d) a rough, uncouth person. [Slang.]

mug, *v.i.*; mugged, *pt.*, *pp.*; mugging, *ppr.* 1. to make grimaces; to overact to attract attention, as some actors in minor roles. [Slang.]

2. to assault a person from behind by strangling him with an arm thrown around his neck, especially with intent to rob him: also spelled *mugg.* [Slang.]

mug, *v.t.* 1. to waylay; to assault from behind: also spelled *mugg.*

2. to photograph, as a criminal for police records. [Slang.]

mū'gȧ, *n.* a silkworm, *Antheræ assama*, partially domesticated in Assam; also, its silk.

mug'găr, *n.* an East Indian crocodile, with a broad, wrinkled snout, *Crocodilus palustris*: also spelled *mugger, muggur.*

mug'gėr, *n.* 1. one who beats and robs a person from behind; a thug. [Slang.]

2. in the theater, an actor who overacts, especially by exaggerating the facial expressions. [Slang.]

mug'get, *n.* [etym. unknown.] chitterlings. [Obs.]

mug'gi·ness, *n.* the state or quality of being muggy.

mug'gins, *n.* [from personal name *Muggins*, associated with slang *mug*, simpleton, card-sharper's dupe.]

1. a variation of the game of dominoes in which the counts are made by five or some multiple of it.

2. any of various card games in which players try to match exposed cards.

3. a dupe; a fool. [Brit.]

mug'gish, *a.* muggy.

Mug·gle·tō'ni·ăn, *n.* one of a sect that arose about the middle of the seventeenth century, of which the founders were John Reeve and Ludovic Muggleton, who claimed to have the spirit of prophecy.

mug'gy, *a.*; *comp.* muggier; *superl.* muggiest. [Ice. *mugga*, mugginess, soft drizzling mist; *muggu-vethr*, muggy weather; *mygla*, to grow muggy; compare Gael. *mugach*, gloomy, cloudy.]

1. containing moisture in suspension; damp and close; warm and humid; as, *muggy* air.

2. moist; damp; moldy. [Obs.]

mug'house, *n.* an alehouse.

Mū'gil, *n.* [L., a mullet.] a genus of fishes, the mullets.

mū·gil'i·form, *a.* of the form of a mullet.

mū'gi·loid, *a.* mugiliform.

mū'gi·loid, *n.* a mugiliform fish; one of the genus *Mugil.*

mug'wet, *n.* same as *mugget.*

mug'wŏrt, *n.* an herb, *Artemisia vulgaris.*

mug'wump, *n.* [Algonquian *mugquomp*, a great man, chief.]

1. an Indian chief or leader. [Obs.]

2. a leader; in a humorous use, one who thinks himself a leader. [Rare.]

3. a Republican who refused to support the party ticket in 1884.

4. any independent, especially in politics.

mug'wump, *a.* relating to a mugwump.

mug'wump·ėr·y, mug'wump·ism, *n.* the declarations and acts of mugwumps.

Mu·ham'măd·ăn, Mu·ham'med·ăn, *a.* and *n.* same as *Mohammedan.*

Mu·har'răm, *n.* [Ar.] a religious festival observed by the Moslems, held in the first month of the Mohammedan year.

mūir, *n.* a moor or heath. [Scot.]

mū·jik' (-zhēk'), *n.* a muzhik.

mū·lat'tō, *n.*; *pl.* **mū·lat'tōes,** [Sp. *mulato*, a mulatto, of mixed breed, from *mulo*, a mule.]

1. a person one of whose parents is a Negro and the other a Caucasian, or white.

2. popularly, any person with mixed Negro and Caucasian ancestry.

mū·lat'tō, *a.* of the light-brown color of a mulatto.

mū·lat'tress, *n.* a woman mulatto.

mul'ber″ry, *n.*; *pl.* **mul'ber″ries,** [ME. *mulberie*, dissimilated var. of *murberie*; AS. *morberie*, from L. *morum*, mulberry, and AS. *berie.*]

1. the purplish-red, edible, berrylike fruit of any of a group of trees whose leaves are used as food for silkworms.

2. any tree of the genus *Morus*, which bears this fruit.

3. purplish red.

Indian mulberry; the perennial and shrubby plant, *Morinda citrifolia.*

BLACK MULBERRY (*Morus nigra*)

mul'ber″ry bĭrd, a starling, the *Pastor roseus* of the East Indies.

mul'ber″ry-fāced (-fāst), *a.* having the face blotched as though with mulberry stains.

mul'ber″ry mȧss, same as *morula.*

mulch, *n.* [ME. *molsh*, soft; akin to G. dial. *molsch*, soft.] leaves, straw, or other loose material spread on the ground around plants to prevent evaporation of water from soil, freezing of roots, etc.

mulch, *v.t.* to apply mulch to.

mulct, *n.* [L. *mulcta*, *multa*, a fine.]

1. a fine or similar penalty.

2. a fault; a blemish. [Obs.]

mulct, *v.t.*; mulcted, *pt.*, *pp.*; mulcting, *ppr.* [L. *mulctare*, from *mulcta*, *multa*, a fine.]

1. to punish (someone) by a fine; to penalize for an offense or misdemeanor by depriving of something.

2. to deprive of something, as by fraud or deceit.

3. to discipline. [Obs.]

mulc'tȧ·ry, mulc'tū·ăr·y, *a.* [L. *mulcta*, a fine.] imposing a pecuniary penalty; of the nature of a fine.

mūle, *n.* [OFr. *mule*, from L. *mulus*, a mule.]

1. the offspring of a donkey and a horse; especially, the offspring of a jackass and a mare, as distinguished from a *hinny*: mules are usually sterile.

2. a small tractor or electric engine used to tow boats along a canal.

3. a machine for drawing and spinning cotton fibers into yarn and winding the yarn on spindles.

4. a stubborn person. [Colloq.]

5. in biology, a hybrid; especially, a sterile hybrid: said especially of the offspring of a canary and some other finch.

6. a coin having the faces wrongly placed, either both alike or from different coins.

mūle, *n.* [Fr.; D. *muil*; L. *mulleus*, red or purple shoe, from *mullus*, red mullet, kind of fish.] a lounging slipper that does not cover the heel.

mūle är·mȧ·dil'lō, an armadillo of South America, having mulelike ears.

mūle deer, a long-eared deer, *Cariacus macrotis*, of the western United States.

mūle jen'ny, same as *mule*, sense 3.

mūle kill'ėr, the whip scorpion.

mūle pul'ley, a belt guide or idler between nonparallel shafts.

mūle skin'nėr, a mule driver. [Colloq.]

mū·le·teer', *n.* [Fr. *muletier*, from *mulet*, dim. from L. *mulus*, a mule.] one who drives mules.

mūle'twist, *n.* mule-spun cotton yarn.

mūle'wŏrt, *n.* any plant of the genus *Hemionitis.*

mū'ley, *a.* and *n.* same as *mulley.*

mū'ley saw, a ripsaw, with a long, stiff blade that is not stretched in a frame but is guided by clamps at either end.

mū·li·eb'ri·ty, *n.* [LL. *muliebritas*, from *muliebris*, womanly, womanish, from *mulier*, a woman.]

1. womanhood; the state of being a woman.

2. the qualities characteristic of a woman; womanliness; femininity.

Opposed to *virility.*

mū'li·ėr, *n.* [L., a woman.]

1. a woman; a wife.

2. in law, formerly, a legitimate child.

mū'li·ėr·ly, *adv.* in a legitimate manner; in wedlock. [Obs.]

mū'li·ėr·ōse, *a.* being devoted to women. [Rare.]

mū″li·ėr·os'i·ty, *n.* devotion to or fondness for women. [Rare.]

mū'li·ėr·ty, *n.* [L. *mulieritas*, womanhood, from *mulier*, a woman.] the position held by one lawfully born. [Obs.]

mūl'ish, *a.* like a mule; specifically, (a) sullen; stubborn; (b) sterile or hybrid.

mūl'ish·ly, *adv.* in a mulish manner.

mūl'ish·ness, *n.* the state or condition of being mulish.

mū·li'tȧ, *n.* the mule armadillo.

mull, *n.* [Hind. *malmal.*] a thin, soft kind of muslin.

mull, *n.* [Ice. *muli*, a snout, projecting crag.] a cape or promontory. [Scot.]

mull, *n.* a snuffbox of horn. [Scot.]

mull, *n.* dirt; rubbish. [Obs.]

mull, *v.t.*; mulled, *pt.*, *pp.*; mulling, *ppr.* [prob. from *mold-ale*, *molde-ale*, a funeral feast; *molde*, the earth, and *ale*, ale, a feast; prob. influenced by L. *mollire*, to soften.]

1. to heat, sweeten, and flavor with spices; as, to *mull* wine.

Drink new cider, *mulled* with ginger warm. —Gay.

2. to dispirit or deaden. [Obs.]

mull, *v.t.* and *v.i.* [ME. *mullen*, to grind; prob. from *mul*, dust; AS. *myl*, dust.] to cogitate or ponder (usually with *over*). [Colloq.]

mull, *v.t.* [from AS. *myl*, dust.] to grind, crumble, or pulverize. [Obs.]

mull, *n.* an inferior kind of madder.

mul″lȧ·gȧ·taw'ny, *n.* same as *mulligatawny.*

mul'lăh, mul'lȧ, *n.* [Turk., Per., and Hind. *mulla*; Ar. *mawla*, a master, sir.] a Moslem teacher or interpreter of the religious law: used as a general title of respect for a learned man: also *mollah, molla.*

mul'lăr, *n.* [OFr. *moleur*, *molleur*, a grinder, from L. *molere*, to grind.] an intaglio die used to give an impression in relief.

mul'lein (-lin), **mul'len,** *n.* [ME. *moleyn*; AS. *molegn*, mullen.] any of a group of tall plants of the figwort family, with downy leaves and spikes of variously colored flowers, the common species being *Verbascum thapsus.*

mullein foxglove; an herb, *Seymeria macrophylla*, common to the Mississippi valley, having coarse leaves and yellow flowers with a five-lobed calyx.

mull'ėr, *n.* [OFr. *moulleur*, a grinder, from *molre*, *moulre*, *mouldre*, from L. *molere*, to grind, from *mola*, a millstone.] any of various mechanical or hand devices for grinding; specifically, a sort of flat-bottomed pestle, with a rounded edge, made of stone or glass, used for grinding pigments and other substances upon a slab of similar material.

mull'ėr, *n.* a vessel in which wine, ale, or other liquor is mulled.

Mül·le'ri·an (mu·lē'ri·ăn), *a.* discovered by or named after Johannes Müller (1801–58), a German authority on physiology.

Müllerian ducts; embryonic ducts, later becoming the genital canal in the female, but practically disappearing in the male.

mul'let, *n.*; *pl.* **mul'lets** or **mul'let,** [ME. *molet*; OFr. *mulet*, dim. of *mulle*, from L. *mullus*, the red mullet.] any of a group of edible fishes found in fresh and salt waters; specifically, (a) the *gray mullet*, family *Mugilidæ*, characterized by silvery scales, a small mouth, and feeble teeth; (b) the *red mullet*, family *Mullidæ*, characterized by reddish or golden scales and two long chin barbels; surmullet.

COMMON GRAY MULLET (*Mugil capito*)

mul'let, *n.* [OFr. *molette*, *mollette*, the rowel of a spur, a dim. from L. *mola*, a millstone.]

1. in heraldry, a figure resembling the rowel of a spur, with five points in English, and six in French heraldry, used as the filial distinction of a third son.

2. [*pl.*] small pincers used for curling the hair. [Obs.]

mul′let·ry, *n.* a breeding pond for mullets.

mul′ley, *a.* [Scot. *moiley*; prob. from Celt.; orig. meaning "bald."] hornless; especially, having had the horns removed: said of cattle: also *muley*.

mul′ley, *n.* 1. a hornless cow.

2. any cow. [Brit. Dial.]

Also *muley*.

mul′lid, *a.* [L. *mullus*, the red mullet.] pertaining to the *Mullidæ*.

Mul′li·dae, *n.pl.* a family of marine fishes, closely allied to the perches (*Percidæ*); the surmullets, or red mullets.

mul′li·găn, *n.* [prob. from personal name *Mulligan, Milligan.*] a stew made of odds and ends of meat and vegetables, especially as prepared by hoboes: also *mulligan stew*. [Slang.]

mul″li·gȧ·taw′ny, *n.* [Tamil *milagu-tannir*, pepper water.] an East Indian soup of meat flavored with curry: also spelled *mullagatawny*.

mul′li·grubs, *n.* a pain in the intestines; colic; hence, ill-temper; sulkiness. [Slang.]

mul′liŏn, *n.* [prob. from OFr. *moienel*; L. *medianus*, middle.] a slender vertical dividing bar between the lights of windows, screens, etc.

WINDOWS WITH MULLIONS

mul′liŏn, *v.t.*; mullioned, *pt., pp.*; mullioning, *ppr.* to divide by or furnish with mullions.

mul′lŏck, *n.* [dim. of *mull*, dust.] in Australia, the refuse earth or rock left over in mining.

mul′mul, mull′mull, *n.* mull; muslin.

mulse, *n.* [L. *mulsum* (supply *vinum*, wine), honey wine, from *mulsus*, pp. of *mulcere*, to sweeten.] wine boiled and sweetened with honey.

mul·tañ′gū·lăr, *a.* [L. *multangulus*; *multus*, many, and *angulus*, angle.] having many angles; polygonal.

mul·tañ′gū·lăr·ly, *adv.* with many angles or corners; in a multangular manner.

mul·tañ′gū·lăr·ness, *n.* the state of being multangular.

mul·tan′i·mous, *a.* [*mult-*, and L. *animus*, mind.] exhibiting many traits of mental or moral character; many-sided. [Rare.]

mul·tär·tiç′ū·lāte, *a.* [*mult-*, and L. *articulus*, a joint.] having many joints. [Rare.]

mul·tē′i·ty, *n.* [L. *multus*, much, many.] multiplicity.

mul′ti-, mult-, [from L. *multus*, much, many.] a combining form meaning: (a) *having, consisting of*, or *affecting many*, as in *multi*colored; (b) *more than two* (or sometimes *one*), as in *multi*lateral, *multi*cylinder; (c) *many times more than*, as in *multi*millionaire.

mul·ti·ax′i·ăl, *a.* [*multi-*, and L. *axis*, an axle.] having several axes or lines of growth.

mul·ti·çam′ē·rāte, *a.* [*multi-*, and L. *camera*, a chamber.] many-celled; many-chambered.

mul·ti·çap′i·tāte, *a.* [*multi-*, and L. *capitatus*, having a head.] many-headed; multicipital.

mul·ti·çap′sū·lăr, *a.* [*multi-*, and L. *capsula*, a little box or chest.] in botany, having many capsules.

mul·ti·çar′i·nāte, *a.* [*multi-*, and L. *carina*, a keel.] having many keellike ridges.

mul·ti·çau′lin (*or* -līn), *a.* [*multi-*, and L. *caulis*, a stem.] having many stems.

mul·ti·çā′vous, *a.* [*multi-*, and L. *cavus*, a hollow.] having many holes or cavities.

mul·ti·cel′lū·lăr, *a.* [*multi-*, and L. *cellula*, a small room.] having many cells.

mul·ti·cen′trăl, *a.* [*multi-*, and L. *centrum*, center.] having many centers.

mul·ti·cip′i·tăl, *a.* [*multi-*, and L. *caput* (*-itis*), head.] in botany, having many heads.

mul′ti·çŏl·ŏr, *a.* [*multi-*, and L. *color*, color.] having many colors.

mul′ti·çŏl·ŏred, *a.* multicolor.

mul·ti·ços′tāte, *a.* [*multi-*, and L. *costa*, a rib.] having many ribs, as a shell, leaf, etc.

mul·ti·çus′pid, *a.* [*multi-*, and L. *cuspis*, a point.] having more than two points or cusps.

mul·ti·çus′pid, *n.* a tooth with more than two cusps.

mul·ti·çus′pi·dāte, *a.* multicuspid.

mul′ti·cy̆·çle, *n.* [*multi-*, and L. *cyclus*, a circle.] a velocipede having four wheels or more.

mul·ti·den′tāte, *a.* [*multi-*, and L. *dens, dentis*, a tooth.] having many teeth or toothlike processes.

mul″ti·den·tiç′ū·lāte, *a.* [*multi-*, and L. *denticulus*, dim. of *dens*, a tooth.] having many small teeth.

mul·ti·diġ′i·tāte, *a.* [*multi-*, and L. *digitus*, a finger.] having many fingers or fingerlike processes.

mul″ti·di·men′sion·ăl, *a.* in mathematics, having more than three dimensions.

mul′ti·fāced (-fāst), *a.* [*multi-*, and L. *facies*, a face.] having many faces.

mul·ti·făr′i·ous, *a.* [LL. *multifarius*, manifold, from *multus*, many.]

1. having great multiplicity, or great diversity or variety; composed of differing parts; diverse; manifold.

2. in botany and zoology, arranged in several rows. [Rare.]

3. in law, improperly joining in one bill in equity distinct and independent matters, and thereby confounding them.

mul·ti·făr′i·ous·ly, *adv.* with great multiplicity and diversity; with great variety of modes and relations.

mul·ti·făr′i·ous·ness, *n.* the state or quality of being multifarious.

mul·tif′ĕr·ous, *a.* [L. *multifer*; *multus*, many, and *ferre*, to bear.] bearing much or many. [Rare.]

mul′ti·fid, *a.* [L. *multifidus*, many-cleft; *multus*, many, and *findere*, to cleave.] having many divisions; cleft or divided into many parts; as, a *multifid* leaf or corolla.

mul·tif′i·dous, *a.* multifid.

mul·ti·flaġ′el·lāte, *a.* [*multi-* and *flagellate*.] having many flagella.

mul·ti·flō′rous, *a.* [LL. *multiflorus*; *multus*, many, and *flos, floris*, a flower.] many-flowered.

mul′ti·flūe, *a.* [*multi-* and *flue*.] possessing many flues, as a locomotive boiler.

mul′ti·foil, *a.* [*multi-*, and L. *folium*, a leaf.] having more than five foils or arcuate divisions; as, a *multifoil* arch.

mul′ti·foil, *n.* in architecture, any multifold foliation.

mul′ti·fōld, *a.* [*multi-* and *fold*.]

1. doubled or folded many times.

2. manifold.

mul′ti·fọrm, *a.* [L. *multiformis*; *multus*, many, and *forma*, form.] having many forms, shapes, or appearances.

mul′ti·fọrm, *n.* that which is multiform; that which presents a varied representation or repetition of anything.

mul·ti·fọrm′i·ty, *n.* diversity of forms; variety of shapes or appearances in the same thing.

mul·ti·fọrm′ous, *a.* multiform. [Rare.]

mul·ti·gañ′gli·ō·nāte, *a.* [*multi-*, and LL. *ganglion*, a tumor.] having many ganglia.

mul·ti·ġen′ĕr·ous, *a.* [L. *multigenerus*; *multus*, many, and *genus, generis*, kind.] having many kinds.

mul·ti·gran′ū·lāte, *a.* [*multi-*, and L. *granulum*, a grain.] consisting of or having many grains.

mul′ti·gråph, *n.* [*multi-* and *graphos*, writing.] a type of rotary printing machine used for reproducing typewritten matter: a trademark (*Multigraph*).

mul′ti·gråph, *v.t.* to reproduce with a Multigraph machine.

mul·ti·ġȳ′rāte, *a.* [*multi-* and *gyrate*.] having many gyri or convolutions.

mul·ti·jū′gāte, *a.* multijugous.

mul·ti·jū′gous, *a.* [L. *multijugus*; *multus*, many, and *jugum*, a yoke.] in botany, consisting of many pairs.

mul·ti·lam′i·nāte, *a.* [*multi-* and *laminate*.] having many laminae.

mul·ti·lat′ĕr·ăl, *a.* [*multi-*, and L. *latus*, side.]

1. having many sides.

2. participated in by more than two nations; multipartite; as, a *multilateral* treaty.

mul·ti·lat′ĕr·ăl·ly, *adv.* in a multilateral manner; specifically, by or with multilateral agreement or consent.

mul·ti·lin′ē·ăl, *a.* [*multi-*, and L. *linea*, a line.] having many lines.

mul·ti·lin′ē·ăr, *a.* multilineal.

mul·ti·lō′băr, *a.* [*multi-* and *lobar*.] multilobate.

mul·ti·lō′bāte, *a.* [*multi-* and *lobate*.] provided with many lobes.

mul′ti·lōbed, *a.* same as *multilobate*.

mul·ti·lob′ū·lăr, *a.* [*multi-*, and LL. *lobulus*, a lobule.] having many lobules.

mul·ti·loç′ū·lăr, *a.* [*multi-*, and L. *loculus*, a cell.] having many cells or compartments; as, a *multilocular* shell.

mul·ti·loç′ū·lāte, *a.* multilocular.

mul·til′ō·quence (-kwens), *n.* use of many words; talkativeness.

mul·til′ō·quent, *a.* [*multi-*, and L. *loquens* (*-entis*), ppr. of *loqui*, to speak.] speaking much; very talkative; loquacious.

mul·til′ō·quous, *a.* multiloquent.

mul·til′ō·quy (-kwy), *n.* multiloquence.

mul·ti·mil·liŏn·âire′, *n.* a person whose wealth amounts to several millions of dollars, francs, pounds, etc.

mul″ti·na′tion·ăl, *a.* [*multi-* and *national*.]

1. of or involving a number of nations.

2. designating or of a corporation with branches in a number of countries.

3. comprising persons of various nationalities.

mul″ti·na′tion·ăl, *n.* a multinational corporation.

mul·ti·nō′mi·ăl, *a.* and *n.* same as *polynomial*.

mul·ti·nū′çlē·ăr, *n.* multinucleate.

mul·ti·nū′çlē·āte, *a.* [*multi-*, and L. *nucleus*, a kernel.] having many nuclei.

mul·ti·nū′çlē·ā·ted, *a.* multinucleate.

mul·ti·nū′çlē·ō·lāte, *a.* [*multi-* and *nucleolate*.] having several nucleoli.

mul·ti·ō′vū·lāte, *a.* [*multi-* and *ovule*.] in botany, having or producing many ovules.

mul·tip′ȧ·rȧ, *n.*; *pl.* **mul·tip′ȧ·rae,** a woman who is bearing her second child or has borne two or more children.

mul·ti·par′i·ty, *n.* 1. the condition of being a multipara.

2. the production of two or more young at a birth.

mul·tip′ȧ·rous, *a.* [*multi-*, and L. *parere*, to bear.]

1. of or being a multipara.

2. in zoology, designating an animal that normally bears more than one offspring at a birth.

mul·ti·pär′tīte, *a.* [*multi-*, and L. *partitus*, divided.]

1. divided into many parts.

2. participated in by more than two nations; multilateral.

mul′ti·ped, mul′ti·pēde, *n.* an insect that has many feet. [Rare.]

mul′ti·ped, mul′ti·pēde, *a.* [L. *multipes* (*-pedis*); *multus*, many, and *pes, pedis*, a foot.] having many feet.

mul′ti·phāse, *a.* [*multi-* and *phase*.] having many phases; specifically, in electricity, polyphase.

multiphase alternating currents; several separate alternating currents which vary in phase by an established amount.

multiphase alternator; an alternator having the capacity to produce multiphase currents.

multiphase apparatus; multiphase motors, alternators, or other receptive apparatus serviceable on multiphase circuits.

multiphase induction motor; an induction motor operated by rotating magnetic fields and serviceable in connection with multiphase currents.

mul·ti·pin′nāte, *a.* [*multi-* and *pinnate*.] in botany, pinnate many times.

mul′ti·plane, *n.* an airplane with more than two sustaining surfaces, superposed or otherwise arranged.

mul′ti·ple, *a.* [LL. *multiplus*, manifold; L. *multus*, many, and *-plus*, fold.]

1. having or consisting of many parts, elements, etc.; more than one or once; manifold.

2. in electricity, designating or of a circuit having two or more conductors connected in parallel.

law of multiple proportion; in chemistry, the law that chemical elements always combine in a definite ratio or in multiples of that ratio.

multiple algebra; that branch of algebra in which units of different denominations can be multiplied together.

multiple arc; a compound electric circuit in which the separate sources, or the separate electro-receptive devices or both, are connected by one set of terminals, such as the positive, to one lead or main positive conductor, and all the negative terminals are similarly connected to another lead or main negative conductor: also called *parallel circuit*.

multiple circuit; same as *multiple arc*.

multiple factors; in genetics, a series of two or more independent genes considered to act as a single unit with a cumulative effect in the transmission of certain characteristics, such as size, pigmentation, etc.

multiple fruit; see *collective fruit* under *collective*.

multiple neuritis; neuritis affecting several nerves.

multiple point or *tangent*; see under *point*.

multiple sclerosis; a chronic disease in which there is sclerosis in various parts of the nervous system: it is characterized by muscular weakness, tremor, etc.

multiple star; see under *star*.

multiple voting; the voting of a person at a single election in all districts in which he can meet the legal qualifications, as in Great Britain before the voting reforms of 1918.

multiple windings; in electricity, independent windings arranged in a symmetrical manner upon the same armature and insulated from each other, yet carried to different segments of the commutator.

mul'ti·ple, *n.* 1. in electricity, a group of terminals so arranged that connection with the circuit can be made at any of a number of points.

2. in mathematics, a number which is a product of some specified number and another number; as, 10 is a *multiple* of 5 and 2.

common multiple; a multiple of each of two or more numbers; thus, 24 is a *common multiple* of 3 and 4.

least common multiple; the lowest number divisible by each of two or more numbers without a remainder; thus, 12 is the *least common multiple* of 3 and 4.

mul'ti·ple-choice' test, in education, an examination in which the person tested must select the correct one of a number of proposed answers for each question.

mul'ti·ple·poind''ing, *n.* in Scots law, a process by which a person holding money or other property, which is claimed by two or more persons, obtains an authoritative arrangement for the equitable division of it among the several claimants. It corresponds to interpleader in the United States and England.

mul'ti·plex, *a.* [L. *multiplex*, manifold; *multus*, many, and *plicare*, to fold.]

1. multiple; manifold.

2. designating or of a system of telegraphy or telephony in which two or more messages can be sent simultaneously in either or both directions over the same wire or on the same wave.

mul'ti·plex, *v.t.* to send (messages) by multiplex telegraphy or telephony.

mul'ti·plī·à·ble, *a.* that can be multiplied.

mul'ti·plī·à·ble·ness, *n.* the quality of being multipliable.

mul'ti·pli·cà·ble, *a.* multipliable.

mul''ti·pli·cand', *n.* [L. *multiplicandus*, to be multiplied, gerundive of *multiplicare*, to multiply.] in mathematics, the number to be multiplied by another called the multiplier.

mul'ti·pli·cāte, *a.* [L. *multiplicatus*, pp. of *multiplicare*, to multiply.] multiple.

mul''ti·pli·cā'tion, *n.* [L. *multiplicatio (-onis)*, from *multiplicare*, to multiply.]

1. a multiplying or being multiplied; specifically, in mathematics, the process of finding the number or quantity (*product*) obtained by repeating a specified number or quantity (*multiplicand*) a specified number of times (*multiplier*), indicated in arithmetic by the symbol ×: opposed to *division*.

2. in botany, an abnormal increase in parts: also called *augmentation*.

3. the supposed magic **art** of increasing gold and silver. [Obs.]

mul''ti·pli·cā'tion tā'ble, a table for memorization showing the results of multiplying each number of a series, usually 1 to 12, by each of the numbers in succession.

mul'ti·pli·cā''tive, *n.* a numeral adjective which serves to indicate how many times a thing is repeated or the number of parts of which it consists, as *single, double, triple, fourfold, fivefold*.

mul'ti·pli·cā''tive, *a.* tending to multiply; having the power to multiply or increase numbers.

mul'ti·pli·cā''tive·ly, *adv.* in such a manner as to multiply.

mul'ti·pli·cā''tŏr, *n.* [LL., a multiplier.] the number by which another number is multiplied; a multiplier. [Now Rare.]

mul·ti·pli'cious, *a.* manifold. [Obs.]

mul·ti·plic'i·ty, *n.* [LL. *multiplicitas*, from L. *multiplex*, manifold.]

1. the state of being multiplex or various; the state of being numerous.

2. many of the same kind; a great number.

mul'ti·plī·ẽr, *n.* 1. a person or thing that multiplies or increases.

2. in mathematics, the number by which another number (the *multiplicand*) is, or is to be, multiplied.

3. in physics, any device for multiplying, or intensifying, some effect.

mul'ti·plȳ, *v.t.*; multiplied, *pt.*, *pp.*; multiplying, *ppr.* [OFr. *multiplier*, from L. *multiplicare*, to multiply, increase greatly, from *multiplex*, manifold.]

1. to cause to increase in number; to make more in number by generation, reproduction, accumulation, or addition; to add to.

Impunity will *multiply* motives to disobedience. —Ames.

2. in mathematics, to add to itself (any given number) as many times as there are units in another given number; to find the product of by multiplication; thus, 7 *multiplied* by 8 produces the number 56.

3. to increase (gold or silver) by alchemy. [Obs.]

mul'ti·plȳ, *v.i.* 1. to grow or increase in number; to increase in extent; to spread.

The word of God grew and *multiplied*. —Acts xii. 24.

2. in mathematics, to perform the operation or process of multiplication.

3. to increase gold or silver by alchemy. [Obs.]

mul'ti·plȳ·ing gēar'ing, in machinery, an arrangement of cogwheels by which motion is imparted from wheels of relatively larger diameter to those of smaller, so as to increase the rate of rotation.

mul'ti·plȳ·ing lens, a lens whose curved surface is divided into a number of plain facets which give separate images.

mul'ti·plȳ·ing mà·chine', a calculating machine.

mul'ti·plȳ·ing wheel (hwēl), a wheel for increasing the number of movements in machinery.

mul·ti·pō'lăr, *a.* [*multi-*, and L. *polus*, a pole.] possessing many poles; as, a *multipolar* nerve cell, a *multipolar* dynamo.

mul·tip'ō·tent, *a.* [L. *multipotens*; *multus*, many, much, and *potens (-entis)*, powerful.] having manifold power or power to do many things.

mul·ti·preṣ'ence, *n.* the power or act of being present in more than one place at the same time; ubiquity.

mul·ti·preṣ'ent, *a.* [*multi-*, and L. *præsens (-entis)*, present.] having the quality or power of multipresence.

mul·ti·rā'di·āte, *a.* [*multi-*, and L. *radius*, a ray.] having many rays.

mul·ti·rad'i·cāte, *a.* [LL. *multiradix (-icis)*; L. *multus*, many, and *radix*, a root.] having many roots.

mul·ti·ram'i·fīed, *a.* [*multi-*, and L. *ramus*, a branch, and *facere*, to make.] having many branches.

mul·ti·rā'mōse, *a.* having many branches.

mul·ti·rā'mous, *a.* [*multi-*, and L. *ramus*, a branch.] multiramose.

mul·ti·saç'cāte, *a.* [*multi-*, and L. *saccus*, a sac.] having many sacs.

mul·tis'cient (-tish'ent), *a.* [*multi-*, and L. *sciens (-entis)*, knowing.] possessed of much knowledge.

mul'ti·seçt, *a.* [*multi-*, and L. *sectus*, pp. of *secare*, to cut.] consisting of many segments, as an insect.

mul·ti·sep'tāte, *a.* [*multi-*, and L. *septum*, an enclosure, a partition.] many-chambered, as the pith of the walnut.

mul·ti·sē'ri·ăl, *a.* [*multi-*, and L. *series*, a series.] in botany, having many horizontal rows, or parts arranged in many such rows; multifarious.

mul·ti·sē'ri·āte, *a.* multiserial.

mul·ti·sil'i·quous (-kwus), *a.* [*multi-*, and L. *siliqua*, a pod, husk.] having many pods or seed vessels.

mul·tis'ō·nous, *a.* [L. *multisonus*; *multus*, much, and *sonus*, a sound.] having or making many sounds.

mul·ti·spī'răl, *a.* [*multi-*, and L. *spira*, a spire.] in conchology, having many spiral coils or convolutions: said of an operculum.

mul'ti·stāġe, *a.* having, or operating in, more than one stage; specifically, having several propulsion systems, used and discarded in sequence: said of a rocket or missile.

mul·ti·stam'i·nāte, *a.* [*multi-*, and L. *stamen*, the warp, thread.] having many stamens.

mul·ti·strī'āte, *a.* [*multi-*, and L. *stria*, a streak.] having many streaks.

mul·ti·sul'çāte, *a.* [*multi-*, and L. *sulcus*, a furrow.] having many furrows.

mul''ti·syl·lab'iç, *a.* pertaining to or consisting of multisyllables.

mul'ti·syl·là·ble, *n.* [*multi-*, and L. *syllaba*, a syllable.] a word of more than three syllables; a polysyllable.

mul''ti·ten·taç'ū·lāte, *a.* [*multi-* and *tentaculate*.] having many tentacles.

mul·ti·tit'ū·lăr, *a.* [*multi-*, and L. *titulus*, a title.] having many titles.

mul''ti·tū·bẽr'çū·lāte, *a.* [*multi-* and *tuberculate*.] having many tubercles; as, *multituberculate* teeth.

mul''ti·tū·bẽr'çū·lā·ted, *a.* multituberculate.

mul·ti·tū'bū·lăr, *a.* [*multi-*, and L. *tubulus*, a tube.] having many tubes; as, a *multitubular* boiler.

mul'ti·tūde, *n.* [Fr. *multitude*, from L. *multitudo*, from *multus*, many, much.]

1. the quality or state of being numerous, or many.

2. a large number of persons or things, especially when gathered together or considered as a unit; host, myriad, etc.

3. the common people (preceded by *the*).

Syn.—crowd, throng, swarm.

mul·ti·tū'di·năr·y, *a.* multitudinous.

mul·ti·tū'di·nous, *a.* 1. very numerous; many.

2. consisting of many parts, elements, etc.; manifold.

3. of or like a multitude; crowded. [Rare or Poet.]

mul·ti·tū'di·nous·ly, *adv.* in a multitudinous manner.

mul·ti·tū'di·nous·ness, *n.* the quality or state of being multitudinous.

mul·tiv'à·gănt, *a.* multivagous. [Rare.]

mul·tiv'à·gous, *a.* wandering much. [Rare.]

mul·ti·vā'lence, *n.* the quality or state of being multivalent.

mul·ti·vā'lent, *a.* [*multi-*, and L. *valens (-entis)*, ppr. of *valere*, to be strong.] in chemistry, (a) having a valence of more than two; (b) polyvalent.

mul'ti·valve, *n.* [*multi-*, and L. *valva*, a door.] a mollusk that has a shell of many valves or pieces.

mul'ti·valve, *a.* having many valves; as, a *multivalve* mollusk.

mul·ti·val'vū·lăr, *a.* multivalve.

mul·ti·vẽr'sănt, *a.* [*multi-*, and L. *versans (-antis)*, ppr. of *versare*, to turn about.] protean; turning into many shapes; assuming many forms. [Rare.]

mul·ti·vẽr'si·ty, *n.*; *pl.* **mul·ti·vẽr'si·tiēs,** [*multi-*, and *university*: coined by C. Kerr, American educator.] the modern large and complex university with its many colleges, schools, extensions, etc., characteristically regarded as being impersonal, bureaucratic, etc.

mul·tiv'i·ous, *a.* having many ways or roads. [Rare.]

mul·tiv'ō·çăl, *n.* an ambiguous or equivocal term or word. [Rare.]

mul·tiv'ō·çăl, *a.* [*multi-*, and L. *vox*, *vocis*, voice.] equivocal; ambiguous: applied to a word susceptible of several meanings.

mul·ti·vol'tine, *a.* [*multi-*, and It. *volta*, a turn, winding.] in zoology, having two or more broods in a year, as some silkworms.

mul·toç'ū·lăr, *a.* [*mult-*, and L. *oculus*, an eye.] having many eyes, or more eyes than two.

mul'tum, *n.* [L. *multum*, neut. of *multus*, much.] in brewing, a compound consisting of an extract of quassia and licorice, formerly used as an adulterant.

black or *hard multum*; a preparation made from *Cocculus indicus*, which gives an intoxicating quality to beer.

mul'tum in pär'vō, [L.] much in little.

mul·tuñ'gū·lāte, *a.* [*mult-*, and L. *ungula*, a hoof.] having the hoof divided into more than two parts, as an elephant, rhinoceros, etc.

mul'tūre, *n.* [OFr. *multure*, a grinding, toll for grinding, from L. *molitura*, a grinding.] formerly, a fee paid to the owner of a mill for the privilege of having one's grain ground there, usually a percentage of the grain or of the ground flour.

mum, *a.* [imitative of a sound made with the lips closed.] silent; not speaking.

mum, *interj.* be silent!

mum's the word; say nothing; remain secretive.

mum, *n.* silence.

mum, *v.i.*; mummed, *pt., pp.*; mumming, *ppr.* [M.D. *mommen,* to mask.] to wear a mask or costume in fun; specifically, to act as a mummer at Christmas time: also spelled *mumm.*

mum, *n.* [G. *mumme,* said to be named after Christian *Mumme,* who first brewed it at Brunswick, Germany, in 1492.] a strong beer made of the malt of wheat, with the addition of a little oat and bean meal.

mum, *n.* mother. [Colloq.]

mum, *n.* chrysanthemum. [Colloq.]

mum'ble, *v.i.*; mumbled, *pt., pp.*; mumbling, *ppr.* [D. *mommelen,* Dan. *mumle,* G. *mummeln,* to mumble or mutter.]

1. to mutter; to speak with the lips partly closed, so as to render the sounds inarticulate and imperfect; to utter words in a grumbling tone.

Peace, you *mumbling* fool. —Shak.

2. to chew gently and ineffectively, as with toothless gums. [Rare.]

mum'ble, *v.t.* 1. to utter with a low inarticulate voice.

2. to chew gently; to eat with a mumbling noise. [Rare.]

mum'ble, *n.* a low, inarticulate utterance.

mum'ble·nėws (-nūz), *n.* a talebearer; a tattler. [Obs.]

mum'blēr, *n.* one who mumbles.

mum'ble·ty·peg", *n.* [from *mumble-the-peg,* from *mumble,* to bite.] a boy's game in which a jackknife must be tossed from a number of positions so that it always lands upright with the blade stuck in the ground, the loser originally having to draw a peg from the ground with his teeth.

mum'bling, *a.* indistinct; muttering; inarticulate; unintelligible.

mum'bling·ly, *adv.* in a mumbling manner.

Mum'bō Jum'bō, [orig. *mama dyambo,* in a Mandingo dialect.]

1. among certain African tribes of western Sudan, a medicine man who is supposed to protect his people from evil and terrorize the women into subjection.

2. [m– j–] an idol or fetish.

3. [m– j–] any object of fear or dread.

mum'chȧnce, *n.* 1. a silent game of hazard with cards or dice. [Obs.]

2. one who stands dumb and has not a word to say for himself; a fool. [Obs.]

mum'mēr, *n.* 1. a person who wears a mask or disguise for fun; specifically, in England, any of the masked and costumed persons who travel from house to house, as at Christmas time, acting out short pantomimes.

2. humorously, any actor.

mum'mēr·y, *n.*; *pl.* **mum'mēr·ieṣ,** [OFr. *mommerie,* from *momer,* to mum.]

1. performance by mummers.

2. any show or ceremony regarded as pretentious or hypocritical.

mum'mi·chog, *n.* see *mummychog.*

mum"mi·fi·çā'tion, *n.* a mummifying or being mummified.

mum'mi·fọrm, *a.* [*mummy,* and L. *forma,* form.] resembling a mummy: applied in entomology to the pupae of certain lepidopterous insects.

mum'mi·fȳ, *v.t.*; mummified, *pt., pp.*; mummifying, *ppr.* to make into or like a mummy.

mum'mi·fȳ, *v.i.* to shrivel up; to dry.

mum'ming, *n.* the sports of mummers.

mum'my, *n.*; *pl.* **mum'mieṣ,** [Fr. *mumie, momie*; Sp. *momia*; It. *mummia,* from Ar. *mūmiyā,* an embalmed body, a mummy, from *mum,* wax.]

1. a dead body preserved by embalming, as by the ancient Egyptians.

2. any dead body that has been naturally well preserved.

3. any thin, withered person regarded as looking like a mummy.

mum'my, *v.t.*; mummied, *pt., pp.*; mummying, *ppr.* to mummify; to embalm.

mum'my·chog, *n.* [Am. Ind. *mummachog.*] a small marine fish of the genus *Fundulus*; a killifish.

mum'my pot, a pot or vase for a small mummified animal.

mum'my whēat (hwēt), a variety of wheat, *Triticum compositum,* said to have been produced from grains found in Egyptian mummy cases.

mump, *v.t.*; mumped, *pt., pp.*; mumping, *ppr.* [D. *mompen,* to cheat, mump; a form of *mommen,* to mumble.]

1. to mutter; to mumble; to utter unintelligibly. [Dial.]

2. to chew with short, quick action; to nibble. [Dial.]

3. to cheat; to deceive; to impose upon. [Old Slang.]

mump, *v.i.* [D.] 1. to mumble; to mutter, as one in a sulk. [Dial.]

2. to chew quickly or with rapid motions; to nibble. [Dial.]

3. to chatter; to talk rapidly, like an ape. [Dial.]

4. to beg or ask for alms in a whining tone; to act as an imposter; to tell pitiful stories. [Old Slang.]

mump, *n.* [origin doubtful.] a lump; an excrescence. [Brit. Dial.]

mump'ēr, *n.* a beggar. [Dial.]

mump'ish, *a.* dull; heavy; sullen; sour.

mump'ish·ly, *adv.* dully; wearily; in a mumpish manner.

mump'ish·ness, *n.* the condition of being mumpish.

mumps, *n.pl.* [*construed as sing.*] [pl. of obs. *mump,* a grimace: probably so called from the patient's appearance.] an acute communicable disease, usually of childhood, caused by a virus and characterized by swelling of the salivary glands, especially the parotid, or, occasionally in adults, by inflammation of the testes, breasts, etc.

mump'si·mus, *n.* an error or prejudice obstinately clung to: the term is supposedly taken from the story of an illiterate priest, who, in his devotions, had for thirty years used *mumpsimus* for the proper Latin word *sumpsimus,* and who, on his mistake being pointed out to him, replied, "I will not change my old *mumpsimus* for your new *sumpsimus.*" [Archaic.]

mun, *v. aux.* must. [Dial.]

mun, *n.* the mouth. [Dial.]

munch, *v.i.* and *v.t.*; munched, *pt., pp.*; munching, *ppr.* [ME. *munchen,* to munch; imitative of the sound made by bringing the teeth together.] to chew vigorously and audibly; to eat with a crunching noise.

Mun·chau'ṣen·iṣm, *n.* [from Baron *Munchausen's* tales.] an exaggerated story or fantastic tale.

munch'ēr, *n.* one who munches.

muñ'çorn, *n.* same as *mangcorn.*

mun'dāne, *a.* [LL. *mundanus,* from L. *mundus,* the world.] belonging or pertaining to the world; worldly: distinguished from *heavenly, spiritual,* etc.

mun'dāne·ly, *adv.* in a mundane manner.

mun·dan'i·ty, *n.* worldliness.

mun·dā'tion, *n.* the act of cleansing. [Obs.]

mun'dȧ·tō·ry, *a.* cleansing; having power to cleanse. [Obs.]

mun'dȧ·tō·ry, *n.*; *pl.* **mun'dȧ·tō·rieṣ,** same as *purificator.*

mun'diç, *n.* [Cornish.] iron or arsenical pyrites.

mun·dif'i·çȧnt, *a.* [LL. *mundificans* (-*antis*), ppr. of *mundificare,* to cleanse; L. *mundus,* clean, and *facere,* to make.] healing; cleansing; having the power to cleanse.

mun·dif'i·çȧnt, *n.* a healing or cleansing ointment.

mun"di·fi·çā'tion, *n.* the act or operation of cleansing any body from dross or extraneous matter.

mun'di·fȳ, *v.t.* [LL. *mundificare*; L. *mundus,* clean, and *facere,* to make.] to cleanse.

mun·div'ȧ·gȧnt, *a.* [L. *mundus,* world, and *vagans* (-*antis*), wandering.] wandering over the world. [Rare.]

mun·duñ'gō, mun·duñ'gus, *n.* [facetious use of Sp. *mondango,* tripe.] tobacco of a dark color and disagreeable odor.

mū'nēr·āte, *v.t.* to remunerate. [Obs.]

mū·nēr·ā'tion, *n.* remuneration. [Obs.]

muñ'gȧ, *n.* [E. Ind.] see *bonnet monkey.*

muñg'çorn, *n.* same as *mangcorn.*

mun·ġeet', *n.* same as *munjeet.*

muñ'gō, *n.* [from Yorkshire dial.; prob. after personal name *Mungo.*] the waste of milled wool used with cotton, etc. to make a cheap cloth.

muñ'gō, *n.* a rubiaceous plant, *Ophiorhiza mungos,* of the East Indies. Its roots are said to cure snake bites.

muñ'gọọs, *n.* same as *mongoose.*

muñ'grel, *n.* and *a.* mongrel. [Obs.]

mū·nic'i·pȧl, *a.* [L. *municipalis,* from *municipium,* a town subject to Rome, but governed by its own laws, from *municeps,* an inhabitant of a free town, a free citizen; *munia,* official duties, functions, and *capere,* to take.]

1. (a) of or characteristic of a city, town, etc. or its local government; (b) having self-government locally.

2. of the internal, as distinguished from the international, affairs of a state or nation.

mū·nic'i·pȧl·iṣm, *n.* 1. self-government by a municipality.

2. the theory that such government should be fostered.

mū·nic'i·pȧl·ist, *n.* a supporter of municipalism.

mū·nic·i·pal'i·ty, *n.*; *pl.* **mū·nic·i·pal'i·tieṣ,** 1. a city, town, etc. having its own incorporated government.

2. the officials governing such a community.

mū·nic"i·pȧl·ī·zā'tion, *n.* a municipalizing or being municipalized.

mū·nic'i·pȧl·īze, *v.t.*; municipalized, *pt., pp.*; municipalizing, *ppr.* 1. to bring under the control or ownership of a municipality.

2. to make a municipality of.

mū·nic'i·pȧl·ly, *adv.* after the manner of a municipality; according to the principles of municipalism.

mū·ni·cip'i·um, *n.*; *pl.* **mū·ni·cip'i·ȧ,** [L.] among the ancient Romans, (a) one of certain Italian towns with a form of government which secured to the citizens the right of self-government with certain other privileges of Roman citizens; a free city; (b) later, any town under Roman rule.

mū·nif'iç, *a.* munificent. [Obs.]

mū·nif'i·çāte, *v.t.* to enrich. [Obs.]

mū·nif'i·cence, *n.* [Fr., from L. *munificentia,* bountifulness; *munus,* a gift, favor, and *facere,* to make.] the quality or state of being munificent.

mū·nif'i·cent, *a.* 1. very generous in giving; lavish.

2. characterized by great generosity; as, a *munificent* reward.

Syn.—bountiful, generous, liberal, helpful, bounteous, open-handed.

mū·nif'i·cent·ly, *adv.* liberally; generously; lavishly.

mū'ni·fȳ, *v.t.* and *v.i.* to fortify. [Obs.]

mū'ni·ment, *n.* [L. *munimentum,* a fortification, defense, protection, from *munire,* to furnish with walls, fortify.]

1. a means of protection or defense.

2. [*pl.*] in law, a writing by which claims and rights are defended or maintained, as a deed or contract.

mū·nīte', *v.t.* to fortify. [Obs.]

mū·ni'tion (-nish'un), *v.t.* to provide with munitions.

mū·ni'tion, *n.* [L. *munitio* (-*onis*), a fortifying, defending, protecting, from *munire,* to fortify.]

1. fortification. [Obs.]

2. [*pl.*] military supplies; especially, weapons and ammunition.

mū'ni·ty, *n.* freedom; security; immunity. [Obs.]

mun·jeet', *n.* see *Indian madder* under *madder.*

mun·jis'tin, *n.* [from *munjeet.*] in chemistry, a deep orange coloring matter obtained from munjeet.

mun'niŏn (-yun), *n.* a mullion.

mun'tin, mun'ting, *n.* in a door, a vertical piece between two panels; a kind of munnion. [Archaic.]

Mun·tin'ġi·ȧ, *n.* [after Abraham *Munting,* Dutch professor of botany.] a genus of tiliaceous shrubs of tropical America, bearing a cherrylike fruit with many seeds; calabur tree.

munt'jaç, munt'jack, *n.* [Javanese.] a small deer, *Cervulus muntjac,* native to the East Indies and southeastern Asia.

Muntz'ṣ met'ăl, [after the inventor, G. F. *Muntz,* of Birmingham, England.] an alloy of three parts of copper to two parts of zinc, used for sheathing ships and for other purposes: also called *yellow metal* and *patent metal.*

Mū·rae'nȧ, *n.* [L. *muræna,* a sea eel, lamprey.] a genus of fishes typical of the family *Murænidæ,* differing from common eels in having dorsal and anal fins continuous to the caudal extremity and in having no pectoral fins.

mū·rae'noid, mū·rē'noid, *a.* [L. *muræna,* a sea eel, and Gr. *eidos,* form.] of or pertaining to the *Muræna* or to the *Murænidæ.*

mū′rāġe, *n.* [Fr.] a tax formerly levied and paid for keeping the walls of a town in repair.

mū′răl, *a.* [L. *muralis,* pertaining to a wall, from *murus,* a wall.] pertaining to, resembling, situated on, or connected with a wall or walls; in or on a wall; as, *mural* plants, *mural* decorations.

MURAL CROWN

mural circle; in astronomy, a graduated circle, usually of large size, fixed permanently in the plane of the meridian, and attached firmly to a perpendicular wall: formerly used for measuring arcs of the meridian; a meridian circle.

mural crown; among the ancient Romans, a golden crown or circle of gold, indented and embattled, bestowed on the soldier who first mounted the wall of a besieged place.

mū′răl, *n.* a picture, especially a large one, painted directly on a wall (or, by extension, on a ceiling).

mū′răl·ist, *n.* a painter of murals.

mũr′dẽr, *n.* [ME. and AS. *morthor*; akin to Goth. *maurthr*; base as in L. *mors, mortis,* death.] the unlawful and malicious or premeditated killing of one human being by another; also, any killing done while committing some other felony, as rape or robbery.

murder in the first degree; murder committed premeditatedly and with malice.

murder in the second degree; murder committed without premeditation.

murder will out; (a) a murder or murderer will always be revealed; hence, (b) any secret or wrongdoing will be revealed sooner or later.

to get away with murder; to escape detection of or punishment for a blameworthy act. [Slang.]

mũr′dẽr, *v.t.*; murdered, *pt., pp.*; murdering, *ppr.* 1. to kill (a person) unlawfully and with malice.

2. to kill inhumanly or barbarously, as in warfare.

3. to spoil, mar, botch, etc., as by giving a poor performance; as, she *murdered* that song.

4. to destroy; to put an end to.

Canst thou *murder* thy breath in the middle of a word? —Shak.

Syn.—kill, slay, assassinate, destroy.

mũr′dẽr·ẽr, *n.* a person guilty of murder.

mũr′dẽr·ess, *n.* a woman guilty of murder.

mũr′dẽr·ment, *n.* murder. [Obs.]

mũr′dẽr·ous, *a.* 1. of the character of murder; cruel; heartless; as, a *murderous* act.

2. having the character of a murderer; capable or guilty of, or intending, murder; as, a *murderous* villain.

3. fit to be an instrument of murder; as, a *murderous* weapon.

mũr′dẽr·ous·ly, *adv.* in a murderous or cruel manner.

mũr′dress, *n.* a murderess.

mūre, *n.* a wall. [Obs.]

mūre, *v.t.*; mured, *pt., pp.*; muring, *ppr.* [Fr. *murer.*] to enclose in walls; to wall; to immure. [Obs.]

Mū·rē′nȧ, *n.* same as *Muræna.*

mū′ren·ġẽr, *n.* [Fr. *murager,* from *murage,* toll for repairing walls.] an overseer and repairer of town walls. [Obs.]

Mū′rex, *n.* [L. *murex,* the purple fish.] 1. a genus of gastropods, of tropical seas, having the shell covered with many spines and provided with a gland secreting a purple dye which was extensively used in ancient times.

2. [m–] *pl.* **mū′ri·cēs, mū′rex·es,** a gastropod belonging to this genus.

mū·rex′ăn, *n.* [L. *murex,* the purple fish, and *-an.*] in chemistry, a crystalline substance obtained from murexide by decomposition.

mū·rex′īde, *n.* [L. *murex,* the purple fish, and *-ide.*] a salt of purpuric acid, formerly produced from guano and formerly used extensively in red, pink, and purple dyes.

mū·rex′ō·in, *n.* [L. *murex,* the purple fish.] a red crystalline substance related to murexide.

mū′ri·āte, *n.* [L. *muria,* brine.] a salt of hydrochloric acid; especially, potassium chloride, used as a fertilizer. [Now Rare.]

mū′ri·ā·ted, *a.* containing or treated with hydrochloric acid or a chloride. [Now Rare.]

mū·ri·at′iç ac′id, hydrochloric acid: now only a commercial term.

mū′ri·çāte, *a.* [L. *muricatus,* pointed, from *murex,* the point of a rock.]

1. formed with sharp points; full of sharp points or prickles.

2. in botany, having the surface covered with sharp points or armed with prickles.

mū′ri·çā·ted, *a.* same as *muricate.*

mū′ri·çoid, *a.* [L. *murex* (*-icis*), the purple fish, and Gr. *eidos,* form.] similar to the family *Muricidæ* or to the genus *Murex.*

mū·riç′ū·lāte, *a.* [dim. from L. *muricatus,* pointed.] having small spines: said of plants.

Mū′ri·dae, *n.pl.* [L. *mus, muris,* a mouse, rat, and *-idæ.*] a large family of rodents, including rats and mice. The typical genus is *Mus.*

mū′ri·fọrm, *a.* [L. *murus,* a wall, and *forma,* form.] in botany, resembling the arrangement of bricks in the wall of a house: said of cellular tissue.

MURIFORM CELLS

mū′ri·fọrm, *a.* [L. *mus, muris,* a mouse, rat, and *forma,* form.] resembling an animal of the mouse family; murine.

mū′rīne (*or* -rin), *a.* [L. *murinus,* from *mus, muris,* a mouse.] pertaining to a mouse or to mice.

mū′rīne, *n.* a mouselike animal; a murine rodent.

mū′rin·ġẽr, *n.* same as *murenger.*

mũrk, mĩrk, *n.* [AS. *mirce, myrce,* darkness, from *mirce,* dark.] darkness; gloom.

mũrk, *a.* [AS. *mirce,* dark, gloomy.] murky.

mũrk′i·ly, *adv.* darkly; gloomily.

mũrk′i·ness, *n.* darkness; gloom.

mũrk′y, *a.*; *comp.* murkier; *superl.* murkiest, 1. dark; obscure; gloomy.

2. heavy and obscure with smoke or mist.

A *murky* storm deep lowering o'er our heads. —Addison.

mũr′lins, *n.* same as *badderlocks.*

mũr′mũr, *n.* [OFr. *murmur*; L. *murmur,* a murmur, roaring sound, muttering: an imitative word.]

1. a low, indistinct, continuous sound, as of a stream, far-off voices, etc.

2. a mumbled or muttered complaint.

3. in medicine, any abnormal sound heard by auscultation of various parts of the body; especially, such a sound in the region of the heart, resulting from lesions of the heart valves.

Syn.—undertone, whisper, mutter, grumble, complaint.

mũr′mũr, *v.i.*; murmured, *pt., pp.*; murmuring, *ppr.* [OFr. *murmurer*; L. *murmurare,* to murmur, mutter, from *murmur,* a murmur.]

1. to make a low, continuous sound, as of a swarm of bees, a stream of water, or wind in a forest; as, the *murmuring* surge.

2. to mutter; to complain; to utter complaints in a low, half-articulate voice; to utter sullen discontent: with *at* or *against*; as, *murmur* not *at* sickness; the people *murmured against* Moses.

mũr′mũr, *v.t.* to say in a murmur.

mũr′mũr·ẽr, *n.* one who murmurs; one who complains sullenly; a grumbler.

mũr′mũr·ing, *n.* the utterance of a low sound.

mũr′mũr·ing·ly, *adv.* with a murmuring sound.

mũr′mũr·ous, *a.* characterized by or giving forth murmurs; disposed to indulge in murmurs.

mũr′phy, *n.*; *pl.* **mũr′phieṣ** (-fiz), [from the Irish surname.] the Irish or white potato [Slang.]

Mũr′phy bed, [after W. L. *Murphy,* its U. S. inventor (c. 1900).] a bed that swings up or folds into a closet or cabinet when not in use.

Mũr′phy's Law, a facetious or satirical proposition stating that if there is a possibility for something to go wrong, it will go wrong.

mũrr, *n.* a catarrh. [Obs.]

mur′rȧ, *n.* in ancient Rome, an ornamental stone used in making vases, cups, and other articles.

mur′rain (-rin), *n.* [OFr. *morine*; It. *moria,* a pestilence among cattle; from L. *mori,* to die.]

1. an infectious and fatal disease of cattle.

2. a pestilence; plague. [Archaic.]

mur′rain, *a.* having murrain; infected; diseased.

Mur′rāy·ȧ, *n.* [after J. A. *Murray,* 18th-c. Sw. botanist.] a genus of rutaceous trees of tropical Asia.

Mur′rāy çod, a perchlike food fish of Australia, *Oligorus macquariensis.*

mũrre, *n.* one of various sea birds of the genus *Uria,* as the common guillemot, *Uria troile*; also, the razor-billed auk, *Alca torda.*

mũrre′let, *n.* a small North Pacific bird of the auk family, closely related to the murres.

mũr′rey, *a.* [OFr. *moree,* a dark-red color, from L. *morum,* a mulberry.] of a dark-red color.

mũr′rey, *n.* a purplish-red color; mulberry.

mũr′rey, *a.* of a purplish-red color.

mũr′rhine (-rin *or* -rīn), *a.* [L.] of an ancient Roman semiprecious stone, variously believed to be jade, fluorite, etc., used for making vases and drinking cups.

mũr′rhine glȧss, 1. glassware believed to resemble ancient Roman murrhine cups.

2. a delicate glassware having embedded pieces of colored metal, glass, etc.

mũr′ri·ŏn, *n.* a morion. [Obs.]

mũrr′nŏng″, *n.* [native name.] an Australian herb, *Microseris forsteri*; also, its root, a sweet, milky tuber.

mũr′thẽr, *n., v.t.* and *v.i.* murder. [Obs. or Dial.]

mụ·rụ′xi (-shi) **bärk,** the bark of a tropical American tree, *Byrsonima spicata*: used for tanning leather.

mụr′vȧ, *n.* [Singhalese *mūrvā.*] an Asiatic bowstring hemp, *Sansevieria roxburghiana,* cultivated in India for the leaf fibers, which are very soft and silky; also, the fiber itself.

mũr′zȧ, *n.* one of the hereditary nobility among the Tatars.

Mus, *n.* a genus of rodents typical of the *Muridæ,* including the common mouse, *Mus musculus,* and the common rat, *Mus decumanus.*

Mū′ṣȧ, *n.* [from *mauz,* the Egypt. name.] a genus of plants, including the banana and the plantain, of the family *Musaceæ.*

mū·ṣā′ceous, *a.* relating to, designating, or resembling bananalike plants of the genus *Musa* or of the family *Musaceæ.*

mū·sang′, *n.* [Malay.] a small civetlike Javanese animal, *Paradoxurus hermaphroditus.*

mū′ṣȧr, *n.* formerly, in Europe, a wandering musician who played on the musette; a Provençal ballad singer.

mū′ṣȧrd, *n.* [Fr.] a dreamer; an absent-minded person. [Obs.]

Mus′çȧ, *n.* [L., a fly.]

1. a genus of flies, including the housefly and related species.

2. in astronomy, a constellation, supposedly outlining a fly, in the southern part of the heavens near the Southern Cross.

mus′çȧ·del, *n.* same as *muscatel.*

mus′çȧ·dine, *n.* [Eng. formation based on Pr. *muscade,* f. of *muscat.*]

1. a variety of grape grown in the southern United States.

2. muscatel (wine). [Obs.]

mus′cae vo·li·tan′tēṣ, [L., flying flies.] specks that appear to float before the eyes, caused by defects or impurities in the vitrous humor of the eye.

Mus·çā′lēs, *n.pl.* [from L. *muscus,* moss.] a division of acrogenous plants, including the *Musci* and the *Hepaticæ.*

mus′çăl·lŏnġe, *n.* same as *muskallunge.*

mus′çȧr·dine, *n.* [Fr. *muscardine,* from It. *moscardino,* a musk comfit, a grape.] a disease of silkworms caused by *Botrytis bassiana,* a fungus.

mus·çar′i·fọrm, *a.* [L. *muscarium,* a fly-brush, and *forma,* form.] brush-shaped; in botany, designating a part, as a style, with a brushlike appendage.

mus′çȧ·rine, mus′çȧ·rin, *n.* [from L. *musca,* a fly.] an extremely poisonous alkaloid, $C_5H_{15}O_3N$, found in certain mushrooms, rotten fish, etc.

mus′çat, *n.* [Fr., a grape, wine, from It. *moscato,* musk, wine, from LL. *muscus,* musk.] a variety of grape with a musky flavor; also, the wine made from this grape; muscatel.

mus·çȧ·tel′, *n.* a full-bodied, strong, sweet wine made from the muscat or a similar grape and having a musky bouquet; also, the grape from which such a wine is made.

Mụsch′el·kälk (moosh′), *n.* [G. *muschel,* shell, and *kalk,* lime or chalk.] shell limestone belonging to the Triassic formation of rocks in Germany.

mus′che·tŏr, *n.* [OFr. *mouscheture,* from *mouscheter,* to spot, from *mousche,* a fly, a spot, from L. *musca,* a fly.] in heraldry, a black spot resembling the end of the ermine's tail, but without the three specks over it.

MUSCHETORS

Mus′cī, *n. pl.* [L. *muscus,* musk.] a large class of cryptogamous plants commonly called mosses; small, low plants having a distinct stem and leaves and propagating by means of spores contained in a capsule borne on the extremity of the stem.

Mus·ciç′ȧ·pȧ, *n.* [L. *musca,* a fly, and *capere,*

to take.] a genus of birds, commonly called *flycatchers.*

mus·ciç′ȧ·pine, *a.* relating to, resembling, or designating a bird of the genus *Muscicapa.*

mus′cid, *n.* an insect of the family *Muscidæ.*

mus′cid, *a.* of or pertaining to an insect of the family *Muscidæ.*

Mus′ci·dae, *n.pl.* [L. *musca,* a fly.] a large family of two-winged insects including several subfamilies.

mus′ci·fọrm, *a.* [L. *musca,* a fly, and *forma,* form.] having the form of a muscid; like a fly.

mus′ci·fọrm, *a.* [L. *muscus,* moss, and *forma,* form.] like moss in shape and structure; muscoid.

mus′cle (-l), *n.* [L. *musculus,* a muscle, a little mouse, dim. of *mus,* a mouse.]

1. a compound, fibrous, animal tissue having the property of contractility, and chemically characterized by the presence of syntonin or muscular fibrin. Striated, or striped, muscle, in which the sarcous substance is marked by minute transverse lines, includes all muscle in which contraction is voluntary and also heart muscle. Unstriated, smooth, or organic muscle includes all involuntary muscle except that of the heart, as the muscular layer of the blood vessels, intestines, etc.

2. an organ consisting of bundles of muscle fibers, having a definite location and producing motion by contraction. A muscle is divided into head, belly, and tail. The head is the part fixed on the least movable point of attachment, called its origin, and is usually tendinous; the belly is the middle fleshy part, which consists of the true muscular fibers; the tail is the tendinous portion inserted into the part to be moved.

3. strength of muscle; muscular development; as, his actions demanded considerable *muscle.*

mus′cle, *n.* same as *mussel.*

mus′cle, *v.t.*; muscled, *pt., pp.*; muscling, *ppr.* to move by applying muscular strength. [Dial.]

mus′cle, *v.i.* to make one's way by sheer strength or force (usually with *in*). [Colloq.]

mus′cle-bound, *a.* having certain muscles enlarged and deficient in elasticity, as from too much exercise.

mus′cle çũrve, a myogram representing the amount or degree of muscular contraction.

mus′cled (-ld), *a.* having muscles.

mus′cle plāte, a group of mesoblastic cells from which develop the voluntary muscles.

mus′cle sense, that sense by which muscular movement is perceived through stimuli transmitted by nerves whose ends lie in the muscles, tendons, skin, etc.

mus′cling (-ling), *n.* in a work of art, the representation of the muscles of the subject.

mus′çoid, *a.* [L. *muscus,* moss, and Gr. *eidos,* form.] mosslike; resembling moss.

mus′çoid, *n.* a mosslike plant.

mus·çol′ō·ġy, *n.* [L. *muscus,* moss, and Gr. *-logia,* from *legein,* to speak.] bryology.

mus·ços′i·ty, *n.* mossiness.

mus·çō·vȧ′dō, *n.* [Sp. *moscabado, mascobado,* unrefined, of inferior quality.] the dark raw sugar that remains after the molasses has been extracted from the juice of the sugar cane.

Mus′çō·vīte, *a.* of Muscovy, or ancient Russia; Russian.

Mus′çō·vīte, *n.* a native or inhabitant of Muscovy; a Russian.

mus′çō·vīte, *n.* [formerly called *Muscovy glass.*] the common, light-colored mica, $KH_2Al_3(SiO_4)_3$, used as an electrical insulator.

Mus′çō·vy duck, [altered from *musk duck.*] any of a group of ducks commonly domesticated in tropical America, characterized by a large crest and red wattles and by the fact that it does not quack.

Mus′çō·vy glȧss, muscovite. [Obs.]

mus′çū·lăr, *a.* [from L. *musculus,* a muscle; and *-ar.*]

1. pertaining to or consisting of muscle; as, *muscular* fiber.

2. performed by muscle; as, *muscular* motion.

3. strong; brawny; vigorous; having well-developed or prominent muscles; as, a *muscular* body.

muscular excitability; the property of a muscle by which it contracts in response to a stimulus.

muscular sense; same as *muscle sense.*

Syn.—powerful, brawny, robust, sinewy, strong, stalwart, athletic, lusty, sturdy.

mus·çū·lar′i·ty, *n.* the quality or condition of being muscular.

mus′çū·lăr·īze, *v.t.*; muscularized, *pt., pp.*; muscularizing, *ppr.* to cause to become muscular.

mus′çū·lăr·ly, *adv.* in a muscular manner.

mus·çū·lā′tion, *n.* same as *musculature.*

mus′çū·lȧ·tūre, *n.* the whole muscular system; the arrangement of the muscles of a body or of some part of the body.

mus′çū·lo-, [from L. *musculus,* a muscle.] a combining form meaning *muscle* or *the muscles*: also *muscul-.*

mus″çū·lō·çū·tā′nē·ous, *a.* [*musculo-,* and L. *cutis,* skin.] pertaining to both muscles and skin, as certain nerves.

mus″çū·lō·phren′ic, *a.* [*musculo-,* and Gr. *phrēn,* diaphragm.] pertaining to both muscles and diaphragm.

mus·cū·los′i·ty, *n.* muscular quality. [Obs.]

mus″çū·lō·spī′răl, *a.* [*musculo-,* and L. *spira,* a spire.] pertaining to muscles having a spiral direction.

mus′çū·lous, *a.* muscular. [Obs.]

mūṣe, *n.* [OFr. *musse,* a little hole or corner in which to hide things, from *musser,* to hide.]

1. an opening in a fence or thicket through which hares or other game pass: also called *muset.* [Obs.]

2. a loophole; a means of escape. [Obs.]

Mūṣe, *n.* [L. *musa*; Gr. *mousa,* a Muse, music, eloquence.]

1. in Greek mythology, any of the nine nymphs or inferior divinities, generally represented as young, beautiful, and modest virgins, who presided over the fine and liberal arts. They were the daughters of Zeus and Mnemosyne, and included Clio, the Muse of history; Euterpe, of lyric poetry; Thalia, of comedy and idyllic poetry; Melpomene, of tragedy; Terpsichore, of music and dancing; Erato, of erotic poetry; Calliope, of epic poetry and rhetoric; Urania, of astronomy; and Polyhymnia, or Polymnia, of sacred hymns and harmony.

2. [m—] the spirit regarded as inspiring a poet or other artist; source of genius or inspiration; as, his *muse* was cultivated by the classics.

3. [m—] a poet. [Rare.]

mūṣe, *v.i.*; mused, *pt., pp.*; musing, *ppr.* [OFr. *muser,* to ponder, dream; compare LL. *musare,* L. *mussare,* to murmur, mutter, be in uncertainty.]

1. to ponder; to meditate; to think closely; to study in silence.

2. to be absent in mind; to be deeply occupied in study or contemplation.

3. to gaze in thoughtful silence.

4. to wonder; to be surprised. [Obs.]

mūṣe, *v.t.* 1. to think on; to meditate on.

2. to be surprised or amazed at. [Obs.]

mūṣe, *n.* 1. deep thought; reverie; contemplation; meditation.

2. wonder; surprise. [Obs.]

mūṣe′ful, *a.* silently thoughtful; meditative.

mūṣe′fụl·ly, *adv.* meditatively.

mūṣe′less, *a.* without poetical inspiration.

mū·sen′nȧ, *n.* same as *mesenna.*

mū·ṣē·ol′ō·ġy, *n.* [Gr. *mouseion,* a museum, and *-logia,* from *legein,* to speak.] the science that deals with the preparation and arrangement of specimens and collections in museums.

mūṣ′ẽr, *n.* one who muses.

mū′ṣet, *n.* a gap in a hedge; a muse. [Obs.]

mū·ṣette′, *n.* [Fr.; dim. of OFr. *muse,* a pipe, a bagpipe, from L. *musa,* a song, Muse.]

1. a species of small, sweet-toned bagpipe formerly in use in France.

2. a melody, of a soft and sweet character, written in imitation of the bagpipe tunes; hence, a dance tune or dance in the measure of musette melodies.

mū·ṣette′ bag, in military usage, a small bag of canvas or leather for toilet articles, etc., worn suspended from a shoulder strap or strapped to the back.

mū·ṣē′um, *n.* [L., from Gr. *mouseion,* a place for the Muses or for study, a library, from *mousa,* a Muse.] a building, room, etc. for preserving and exhibiting rare, interesting, or typical specimens of works of art, science, invention, etc., or of antiquities, curiosities, or objects of natural history.

mush, *n.* [prob. a variant of *mash,* a mixture.]

1. a thick porridge made by boiling meal, especially cornmeal, in water or milk.

2. any mashed, pulpy, soft, or decayed mass.

3. maudlin sentimentality. [Colloq.]

mush, *v.t.* to cut, nick, or notch the edge of, as cloth, with a stamp or punch. [Scot.]

mush, *interj.* [perhaps altered from Fr. *marche,* imperative of *marcher,* to move forward.] in Canada and Alaska, a shout commanding sled dogs to start or to go faster.

mush, *v.i.* to travel on foot over snow, usually with a dog sled.

mush, *n.* a journey on foot over snow, usually with a dog sled.

mush′quȧsh rọọt (-kwosh), *n.* same as *musquash root.*

mush′rọọm, *n.* [OFr *mouscheron, mouseron,* a mushroom, from *mousse,* moss.]

1. any large fungus of quick growth, especially one having a pileus, or cap. The term is often used of edible varieties as distinguished from those that are poisonous (*toadstools*). The edible species of mushroom usually cultivated is the *Agaricus campestris.* Mushrooms are found in all parts of the world.

2. one who rises suddenly from a low condition or rank; hence, an upstart.

3. anything like a mushroom in shape or rapid growth.

mush′rọọm, *a.* 1. pertaining to or made of mushrooms.

2. like a mushroom in shape or suddenness of growth and lack of substantiality; ephemeral; transitory; as, *mushroom* cities; *mushroom* enterprises.

mush′rọọm, *v.i.* 1. to grow or spread rapidly.

2. to flatten out at the end so as to resemble a mushroom; as, the bullet *mushroomed* against the wall.

mush′rọọm aṅ′chŏr, an anchor with a central shank and mushroom-shaped head.

mush′rọọm cor′ăl, a coral shaped like a mushroom.

mush′rọọm spạwn, the material in which the reproductive mycelium of the mushroom is transported; also, the mycelium itself.

mush′y, *a.*; *comp.* mushier; *superl.* mushiest,

1. like mush; thick, soft, and yielding.

2. sentimental in a maudlin fashion. [Colloq.]

mū′ṣiç, *n.* [ME. *musike, musyk*; OFr. *musique*; L. *musica,* from Gr. *mousikē* (*technē,* art, understood), music, art, culture, from *mousa,* a Muse.]

1. the art and science of combining vocal or instrumental sounds or tones in varying melody, harmony, rhythm, and timbre, especially so as to form structurally complete and emotionally expressive compositions.

2. the sounds or tones so arranged, or the arrangement of these.

3. any rhythmic sequence of pleasing sounds, as of birds, water, etc.

4. (a) a musical composition; especially, the written or printed score of this; (b) such compositions collectively; as, the *music* of Brahms.

5. ability to respond to or take pleasure in music; as, he has no *music* in his soul.

6. a group of musical performers. [Rare or Obs.]

7. liveliness in speech or action; excitement. [Colloq.]

music of the spheres; an ethereal music supposed by Pythagoras and other early mathematicians to be produced by the movements of the heavenly bodies.

to face the music; see under *face.*

to set to music; to compose music for (a poem, etc.).

mū′ṣiç·ăl, *a.* 1. of or for the creation, production, or performance of music.

2. having the nature of music; melodious or harmonious.

3. fond of, sensitive to, or skilled in music.

4. set to music; accompanied by music; as, a *musical* comedy.

musical box; same as *music box.*

musical comedy; a theatrical production consisting of musical numbers, dances, and humorous or satirical skits, centered upon some slight plot and usually having elaborate costuming and staging.

musical glasses; a musical instrument consisting of a number of tuned glass goblets, played upon by rubbing with dampened fingers.

Syn.—melodious, dulcet, harmonious, concordant, tuneful, rhythmical, mellifluous.

mū′ṣiç·ăl, *n.* 1. music. [Obs.]

2. a musical comedy.

3. a musicale. [Colloq.]

mū·ṣi·çale′, *n.* [Fr.] a party or social affair featuring a musical program.

mū′sic·ăl·ly, *adv.* in a musical manner.
mū′sic·ăl·ness, *n.* the quality of being melodious or harmonious.
mū′sic book, a book containing musical compositions for the voice or for instruments.
mū′sic box, a mechanical musical instrument consisting of a case containing a bar with tuned steel teeth that are struck by pins so arranged on a revolving cylinder as to produce a certain tune or tunes.
mū′sic hall, 1. an auditorium for musical or theatrical productions.
2. a vaudeville theater. [Brit.]
mū′sic house, a business concern that deals in printed music or musical instruments.
mu·si′ciăn, *n.* one who is skilled in music; especially, a professional performer of music.
mu·si′ciăn·ly, *a.* having the qualities of a musician or of good music.
mū·si·col′ō·gist, *n.* an expert in musicology.
mū·si·col′ō·gy, *n.* the systematized study of the science, history, forms, and methods of music.
mū′sic shell, the shell of a species of gastropod, *Voluta musica*, found in the East Indies, having colored markings resembling bars of music.
mū′sic stool, a stool or seat for one who performs on a piano or similar instrument.
mus′i·mŏn, *n.* same as *mouflon*.
mūs′ing, *a.* that muses; meditative; reflective.
mūs′ing, *n.* meditation; reflection; contemplation.
mūs′ing·ly, *adv.* by musing; in a musing way.
mu·sique′ con·crète′ (mü-zēk′ kōn-kret′), [Fr., concrete (as opposed to abstract) music.] a musiclike art form composed directly on magnetic tape by the electronic manipulation, distortion, or transformation of natural sounds and noises, as of musical instruments, rain, etc.
musk, *n.* [ME.; OFr. *musc*; LL. *muscus*; Gr. *moschos*, from Ar. *mushk*, *musk*, musk, from Sans. *mushka*, a testicle.]
1. a strong-scented substance obtained from a small sac (*musk bag*) near the navel of the male musk deer, *Moschus moschiferus*, of Asia. It is a clotted, oily substance of the consistency of honey and of a reddish-brown color, and has a strong, penetrating odor. Musk is used as the base of many perfumes.
2. a similar substance secreted by various other animals, as the American muskrat.
3. the odor of any of these substances, now often created synthetically.
4. in botany, any of several varieties of plants, as the musk plant, *Mimulus moschatus*, and the musky heron's-bill, *Erodium moschatum*.
5. the musk deer.
musk, *v.t.* to perfume with musk. [Rare.]
mus′kăl·longe, *n.*; *pl.* **mus′kăl·longe,** same as *muskellonge*.
mus′kăl·lunge, *n.*; *pl.* **mus′kăl·lunge,** same as *muskellonge*.
musk bag, the sac that contains the musk of the male musk deer.
musk bēa′vẽr, the muskrat.
musk bee′tle, a large beetle of Europe, *Callichroma moschata*, which emits an odor similar to that of musk.
musk buf′fȧ·lō, the musk ox.
musk deer, 1. a small, hornless Asiatic mountain deer, that has two sharp curved tusks in the upper jaw. The male furnishes the musk of commerce.
2. a chevrotain.
musk duck, 1. the muscovy duck. 
2. an Australian duck, *Biziura lobata*, with an inflatable leathery pouch beneath the lower jaw, spikelike tail feathers, and a musklike odor during the breeding season.

MUSK DEER (*Moschus moschiferus*)

mus′keg, *n.* [from Am. Ind. (Ojibway) native name.] a kind of bog or marsh formed by the deposit of thick layers of decaying vegetable matter, mosses, etc. in a depression or hollow in the earth's surface.
mus′kel·lunge, *n.*; *pl.* **mus′kel·lunge,** [Algonquian *maskinonge*; *mas*, great, and *kinonge*, a pike (fish).] any of a group of very large pike of the Great Lakes and Mississippi Valley, valued as a game and food fish.
mus′ket, *n.* [Fr. *mousquet*, from OFr. *mousket*, *moschet*, a musket, originally a sparrow hawk (compare the names of other firearms, as *falconet*) from *mousche*, a spot resembling a fly, from L. *musca*, a fly: the bird was so called from its speckled plumage.]
1. a male sparrow hawk. [Obs.]
2. a smooth-bore, long-barreled hand firearm, used especially by infantry soldiers before the invention of the rifle. Originally it was fired with a match or matchlock; later, at successive stages of development, by the flintlock and percussion cap.
mus·ket·eer′, *n.* [Fr. *mousquetaire*.] formerly, a soldier armed with a musket.
mus·ket·oon′, *n.* [Fr. *muosqueton*, a musketoon.]
1. a short, thick musket, used prior to the introduction of breech-loading guns.
2. a soldier armed with a musketoon. [Rare.]
mus′ket·proof, *a.* capable of resisting the force of a musket ball; bulletproof.
mus′ket rest, a rest with a forked end for the support of heavy muskets: used in the sixteenth century.
mus′ket·ry, *n.* 1. (a) muskets collectively; (b) musketeers collectively.
2. the art or practice of firing muskets or other small arms.
mus′ket shot, 1. the discharge of a musket; as, the camp was alarmed by a *musket shot*.
2. the range of a musket.
musk′flow″ẽr, *n.* same as *musk plant*, sense 1.
Mus·khō′gē·ăn (-kō′), *a.* designating or of a linguistic stock of North American Indians of the southeastern United States, including the Creek, Chickasaw, Choctaw, and Seminole tribes.
mus′kie, *n.* same as *muskellunge*.
musk′i·ness, *n.* the quality or condition of being musky.
musk lor′i·keet, the Pacific or Australian lorikeet, *Glossopsittacus australis*.
musk′mal″lōw, *n.* 1. an ornamental plant, *Malva moschata*, which gives forth a faint odor of musk.
2. a tropical evergreen shrub, the abelmosk.
musk′mel″ŏn, *n.* the juicy, aromatic fruit of a trailing herb, *Cucumis melo*, oval or globular in form, and having a ribbed, netted, or gourdlike rind; also, the plant or vine. Muskmelons are cultivated in many varieties, as cantaloupes, citrons, etc.
musk or′chis, a European alpine orchid, *Herminium monorchis*, having a musky odor.
musk ox, a hollow-horned ruminant, *Ovibos moschatus*, of arctic America and Greenland. It combines some of the characteristics of the sheep and the ox. Both sexes are horned, the large horns being united at the skull, but deflected downward at each side of the head. Its hair is long, coarse, and brown, shaggy about the neck and shoulders, with yellowish wool beneath. The limbs are stout and short. It has a musklike odor, from which it derives its name. Also called *musk sheep*.
musk plant, 1. a plant, *Mimulus moschatus*, of North America, which emits a musky odor: called also *monkey flower*.
2. a grape hyacinth, *Muscari moschatum*.
3. the musky heron's-bill, *Erodium moschatum*.

MUSKRAT

musk′rat, *n.*; *pl.* **musk′rats** or **musk′rat,** 1. a common North American aquatic rodent, *Ondatra zibethica*, which resembles the beaver and yields a glossy brown fur. A gland in its groin secretes a substance having a strong musky odor. It has a long, flattened, scaly tail and partially-webbed hind feet. Called also *musquash* (the Indian name), *musk beaver*, and *ondatra*.
2. the fur of this animal.
3. the European desman.
4. the musk shrew, or Indian muskrat, *Sorex indicus*.
musk′root, *n.* in botany, the root of any of several plants having a musky odor and medicinal properties, as (a) *Ferula sumbul*, a plant of the parsley family, from Turkestan; (b) the spikenard, *Nardostachys jatamansi*.
musk rōse, a Mediterranean rose, *Rosa moschata*, with fragrant blossoms, usually white.
musk′seed, *n.* the seed of the abelmosk.
musk sheep, same as *musk ox*.
musk shrew, a muskrat of India, *Sorex indicus*, which has a strong odor of musk.
musk this′tle (-l), a kind of thistle, *Carduus nutans*, having leaves with a strong odor of musk.
musk tor′toise (-tis), a small American freshwater turtle that emits a distinct odor of musk.
musk tũr′tle, same as *musk tortoise*.
musk wēa′sel (-zl), a civet or other quadruped of the family *Viverridæ*.
musk′wood, *n.* the wood of several tropical trees, especially *Trichilia moschata*, of Jamaica.
musk′y, *a.*; *comp.* muskier; *superl.* muskiest, of, like, or smelling of musk.
Mus′lem, Mus′lim, *n.* and *a.* same as *Moslem*.
mus′lin, *n.* [Fr. *mousseline*; It. *mussolino*, from *mussolo*, muslin, from LL. *Mossula*, Ar. *Mawsil*, a city in Mesopotamia, where it was first made.]
1. a fine, thin cotton cloth of plain weave, often dyed or printed, used for wearing apparel: also called *India muslin*, etc.
2. a heavy variety of cotton cloth used for bed sheets, pillow cases, etc.
mus′lin dē·lāine′, same as *delaine*.
mus·lin·et′, *n.* a coarse cotton cloth of many varieties.
mus′lin glȧss, a variety of glassware, decorated to imitate muslin.
mus′mŏn, *n.* same as *mouflon*.
mus′nud, *n.* [Hind. *masnad*, a cushion, seat, throne.] a luxurious dais or raised seat, often richly draped, serving as a throne of state or seat of honor in India, Persia, etc.
mus′quăsh (-kwosh), *n.*; *pl.* **mus′quăsh·es** or **mus′quăsh,** [from Am. Ind. (Algonquian).] a muskrat.
mus′quăsh·root, *n.* spotted cowbane, *Cicuta maculata*, a plant whose root is poisonous.
mus′quaw, *n.* [Am. Ind.] the American black bear.
mus·quet·oon′, (-ket-), *n.* musketoon. [Obs.]
mus·qui′tō (-kē′), *n.* same as *mosquito*.
mus′rōl, *n.* [Fr. *muserolle*, from OFr. *muse*, nose.] the noseband of a horse's bridle. [Obs.]
muss, *n.* [prob. var. of *mess*.]
1. a mess; disorder. [Colloq. or Dial.]
2. a squabble; a row; a commotion. [Colloq. or Dial.]
muss, *v.t.*; mussed (must), *pt.*, *pp.*; mussing, *ppr.* to put or throw into a confused heap, as clothing, hair, etc.; to disarrange; to rumple: often with *up*. [Colloq. or Dial.]
muss, *n.* [OFr. *mousche*, the play called muss, a fly, from L. *musca*, a fly.] a scramble, as for pennies, nuts, etc. thrown out to be scrambled for and taken by those who can seize them. [Obs.]
mus·säl′, *n.* [Hind.] in India, a torch made of long strips of cotton bound tightly together and dipped in oil.
mus′sel (-sl), *n.* [ME. *muscle*, *muskle*; AS. *muxle*, from L. *musculus*, a small fish, sea mussel, a little mouse, muscle.] one of various bivalve mollusks; specifically, (a) a salt-water variety used as food; (b) a fresh-water variety whose shell is made into buttons, etc.
mus′sel dig′gẽr, the gray whale, *Rhachianectes glaucus*.
mus′sel duck, the American scaup duck.
mus·si·tā′tion, *n.* [LL. *mussitatio* (-*onis*) from L. *mussitare*, to murmur, freq. of *mussare*, to mutter.] a mumbling; specifically, in pathology, a movement of the tongue and lips, as in the act of speaking, without sound being produced.
mus′suck, *n.* [Hind. *masak*.] in India, a water bag made of the prepared skin of a goat or a sheep: also spelled *mussuk*.
Mus′sul·măn, *n.*; *pl.* **Mus′sul·măns,** [Turk. and Per. *musulmān*, a Moslem, from Ar. *muslim*, *moslim*, Moslem.] a Moslem.
Mus′sul·măn, *a.* Moslem.
Mus·sul·man′ic, *a.* pertaining to Mussulmans, or like them or their customs.
Mus′sul·măn·ish, *a.* Moslem.
Mus′sul·măn·ly, *adv.* in the manner of Mussulmans.
muss′y, *a.*; *comp.* mussier; *superl.* mussiest, rumpled; confused; disarranged. [Colloq.]
must, *v. aux.*; must, *pt.* [ME. *moste*, pt., had to; AS. *moste*, pt. of *motan*, may.] an auxiliary used with the infinitive of various verbs

(without *to*) to express: (a) *compulsion, obligation, requirement*, or *necessity*; as, I *must* pay her; (b) *probability*; as, then you *must* be my cousin; (c) *certainty* or *inevitability*; as, it *must* have rained while we were in. *Must* is sometimes used elliptically, the verb being understood; as, I *must* forth; shoot if you *must*.

must, *n.* something that must be done, had, read, seen, etc.; as, this book is a *must*.

must, *a.* that must be done, etc.; necessary; essential.

must, *n.* [L. *mustum*, new wine, neut. of *mustus*, new, fresh.]
 1. juice pressed from the grape but not yet fermented into wine.
 2. the ground pulp of potatoes, to be used for fermentation.
 3. the condition of being new, or unfermented: said of wine. [Obs.]

must, *n.* mustiness; mold.

must, *v.t.*; musted, *pt.*, *pp.*; musting, *ppr.* to make moldy and sour. [Obs.]

must, *v.i.* to grow moldy and sour; to acquire a fetid smell. [Obs.]

must, musth (must), *n.* [Hind.] 1. a frenzied state, usually associated with sexual heat, to which male elephants are subject.
 2. an elephant in this state.

must, musth, *a.* in must.

mus·tăche′, möus·tăche′, *n.* [Fr. *moustache*; It. *mostacchio, mustacchio*, a mustache, from Gr. *mystax*, the upper lip, mustache, from *mastax*, mouth, jaws.]
 1. hair on the upper lip of men; the unshaven hair of the upper lip: frequently used in the plural in reference to the two halves of the upper lip.
 2. in zoology, (a) any growth resembling a mustache; (b) a color stripe on the head of a bird.

mus·tăched′ (-tăsht′), *a.* having a mustache.

mus·tăch′i·ăl, *a.* bearing a resemblance to a mustache: applied to a bright patch on the lower mandible of a woodpecker.

mus·tăch′iō (-yō), *n.*; *pl.* **mus·tăch′iōs,** same as *mustache*.

mus·tăch′iōed, *a.* having mustachios.

mus′tang, *n.* [Sp. *mesteño*, belonging to the graziers, wild, from *mesta*, an owner of cattle.]
 1. a small, wild or half-wild horse of the southwestern plains of the United States.
 2. a United States naval officer who did not graduate from the Naval Academy but was commissioned from the ranks. [Slang.]
 mustang grape; a grape, *Vitis candicans*, having a bitter acrid taste; the cutthroat.

mus′tărd, *n.* [OFr. *moustarde*; Pr. and It. *mostarda*, mustard, from L. *mustum*, must, because it was originally made with a little must mixed in it.]
 1. a plant of the genus *Brassica*, with yellow flowers and slender pods containing round seeds. The black mustard is *Brassica nigra*; the white mustard, *Brassica alba*.
 2. a plant resembling mustard.
 3. the ground or powdered seeds of this plant, often prepared as a paste, used as a pungent seasoning for foods or as a counterirritant in medicine.
 4. the color of ground mustard, a dark yellow.

MUSTARD (*Bra·sica nigra*)

mus′tărd gas, see under *gas*.

mus′tărd oil, an intensely pungent oil obtained from mustard seed and used in making soap.

mus′tărd pā′pẽr, same as *mustard plaster*.

mus′tărd plas′tẽr, a paste made with powdered mustard, spread on a cloth and applied to the skin as a counterirritant and rubefacient.

mus′tărd pōul′tice, same as *mustard plaster*.

mus′tărd seed, 1. the seed of mustard.
 2. a fine kind of shot, dust shot, used by taxidermists and others when shooting birds, to avoid damage to the plumage.

mus′tărd shrub, a plant, *Capparis ferruginea*, of the West Indies, having an extremely pungent berry.

mus·tee′, *n.* [altered from *mestizo*.]
 1. the offspring of a white and a quadroon; an octoroon.
 2. any person of mixed ancestry.

Mus·tē′lȧ, *n.* [L. *mustela, mustella*, a weasel, from *mus*, a mouse.] a genus of animals consisting of the weasels.

mus′tē·līne, *a.* designating or of a large group of fur-bearing mammals, including the weasel, marten, polecat, mink, wolverine, etc.

mus′tē·līne, *n.* a musteline animal.

mus′tē·loid, *a.* musteline.

mus′tẽr, *v.t.*; mustered, *pt.*, *pp.*; mustering, *ppr.* [OFr. *moustrer, mostrer, monstrer*, to exhibit, to show, from L. *monstrare*, to show, from *monere*, to warn, admonish.]
 1. to collect, as troops for service, review, parade, or exercise; to review, as troops under arms, and take an account of their numbers, the condition they are in, the state of their arms, and the like.
 Gentlemen, will you go *muster* men?—Shak.
 2. to assemble; to bring together; to collect for use or exhibition.
 3. to gather, collect, or summon; with *up*; as, to *muster up* one's courage.
 to muster in (or *out*); to enlist in (or discharge from) military service.

mus′tẽr, *v.i.* to assemble; to meet in one place; specifically, to assemble as for inspection or roll call: said of troops, etc.

mus′tẽr, *n.* [ME. *moustre*; OFr. *mostre, monstre*, from LL. *monstra*, a review, show.]
 1. a gathering together or assembling, especially of troops for inspection, service, etc.
 2. the persons or things assembled; assemblage.
 Of the temporal grandees of the realm and of their wives and daughters the *muster* was great and splendid. —Macaulay.
 3. the sum or total of persons or things assembled.
 4. the roll, or list, of men in a military or naval unit: also *muster roll*.
 5. a specimen; a pattern. [Rare.]
 6. in hunting, a flock of peacocks. [Archaic.]
 to pass muster; to pass without censure through a muster, or inspection; to measure up to the required standard.

mus′tẽr mas′tẽr, formerly, one who kept an account of troops, and of their arms and accouterments.

mus′tẽr rōll, 1. a roll or register of all troops present or accounted for on muster day.
 2. a list or record of a ship's company.

musth (must), *n.* and *a.* must (frenzy).

mus′ti·ly, *adv.* in a musty manner.

mus′ti·ness, *n.* the quality of being musty; moldiness; damp foulness.

must′n′t (mus′nt), must not.

must′y, *a.*; *comp.* mustier; *superl.* mustiest, [prob. from earlier *moisty*, from *moist*.]
 1. having a stale, moldy smell or taste, as an unused room, food kept in a damp place, etc.
 2. stale or trite; antiquated; as, *musty* scholarship.
 3. dull; apathetic.
 That he may not grow *musty* and unfit for conversation. —Addison.
 Syn.—fusty, rank, moldy, stale, sour, mildewed.

mus′ty, *n.* a kind of snuff, formerly used, having a musty flavor.

mū·tȧ·bil′i·ty, *n.* [L. *mutabilitas*, from *mutabilis*, changeable, *mutare*, to change.] the state or quality of being mutable; (a) susceptibility to change in form, state, or essential qualities; (b) inconstancy, as of mind.

mū′tȧ·ble, *a.* [L. *mutabilis*, changeable, from *mutare*, to change.]
 1. subject to change; changeable; capable of alteration in form, qualities, or nature.
 2. inconstant; unsettled; unstable; susceptible of change; fickle; vacillating.
 Syn.—changeable, unstable, wavering, variable, alterable.

mū′tȧ·ble·ness, *n.* changeableness; mutability; instability.

mū′tȧ·bly, *adv.* in a mutable manner.

mū′tȧ·cism, *n.* same as *mytacism*.

mū′tăge, *n.* [Fr., from *muter*, to stop the fermentation of must, from OFr. *mut*, dumb.] a process for checking the fermentation of the must of grapes.

mū′tănt, *a.* [from L. *mutans*, ppr. of *mutare*, to mutate.] undergoing mutation, or changing.

mū′tănt, *n.* an animal or plant with inheritable characteristics that differ from those of the parents; a sport.

mū′tāte, *v.i.* and *v.t.*; mutated, *pt.*, *pp.*; mutating, *ppr.* [L. *mutatus*, pp. of *mutare*, to change.] to change; specifically, to undergo or cause to undergo mutation.

mū·tā′tion, *n.* [ME. *mutacioun*; L. *mutatio* (*-onis*), from *mutare*, to change.]
 1. the act or process of changing.
 2. change; alteration, either in form or qualities.
 The vicissitude or *mutations* in the superior globe are no fit matter for this present argument. —Bacon.
 3. in biology, (a) a sudden variation in some inheritable characteristic of an individual animal or plant, as distinguished from a variation resulting from generations of gradual change; (b) an individual resulting from such variation; a mutant.
 4. in linguistics, umlaut.
 5. the change of voice in the male at puberty.
 6. in music, the shift in position of the hand in violin playing.

mū·tā′tis mū·tan′dis, [L.] the necessary changes having been made.

mū′tȧ·tive, *a.* [ML. *mutativus*, of, tending to, or characterized by mutation.

Mū·taz′i·līte, *n.* same as *motazilite*.

mutch, *n.* [M.D. *mutse*; Late M.H.G. *mutze, mütze*; M.H.G. *almuz, armu*, from ML. *almutia*, cowl or hood.] a close-fitting linen cap worn by women and children, as in Scotland. [Scot. and Brit. Dial.]

mutch′kin, *n.* [from obs. D. *mudseken*, a measure of capacity.] a liquid measure used in Scotland, equivalent to a little less than a pint.

mūte, *v.t.* [Fr. *muter*, to stop the fermentation of must.] to cause (something, especially the must of grapes) to cease fermenting.

mūte, *a.* [L. *mutus*, dumb, silent.]
 1. silent; not speaking; uttering no sound.
 2. dumb; unable to utter articulate sound: often applied to things not sentient.
 3. in law, making no plea when arraigned: used especially in *stand mute*, to refuse to plead guilty or not guilty.
 4. not sounding when struck; not resonant or sonorous; applied to certain metals.
 5. in phonetics, (a) silent; not pronounced, as *e* in *rare*; (b) pronounced with a complete temporary stoppage of the breath, as the sounds of *p* or *k*: in this sense now generally replaced by *stopped*.
 Syn.—silent, dumb.—One is *silent* who does not speak; one is *dumb* who cannot; one is *mute* who is held back from speaking by some special cause.

mūte, *n.* 1. a person who cannot speak, or who remains silent, especially a deaf-mute; one who is dumb as a result of early deafness or of defect in the organs of speech.
 2. in law, a defendant who refuses to plead when arraigned.
 3. an actor who does not speak in the course of a play. [Now Rare.]
 4. formerly, a person employed by undertakers to stand before the door of a house in which there was a corpse, or to lead funeral processions.
 5. in certain countries of the Orient, a dumb servant, as a porter, etc.
 6. in music, a device of wood, brass, or other substance, used on different musical instruments to muffle or soften the sound. For the violin, and similar instruments, it consists of a clip which is fitted over the bridge; in the cornet and other metal wind instruments, it consists of a pear-shaped block which is inserted in the bell.
 7. in phonetics, (a) a silent letter; (b) a consonant, as *p* or *k*, formed by a complete temporary stoppage of the breath; a stop.

mūte, *v.t.*; muted, *pt.*, *pp.*; muting, *ppr.* to soften or muffle the sound of (a musical instrument, etc.), as with a mute.

mūte, *v.i.* and *v.t.* [OFr. *mutir, esmeutir, esmeltir*, to dung, mute; O.H.G. *smelzan*, to liquefy.] to eject the contents of the bowels; to void: said of birds. [Obs.]

mūte, *n.* the dung of birds. [Obs.]

mūte′ly, *adv.* silently; without uttering words or sounds.

mūte′ness, *n.* the condition of being mute; silence; forbearance from speaking.

mū′tiç, mū′ti·çous, *a.* [L. *muticus*, docked, curtailed.] in botany, pointless; blunt.

mū′ti·lāte, *v.t.*; mutilated, *pt.*, *pp.*; mutilating, *ppr.* [L. *mutilatus*, pp. of *mutilare*, to maim, mutilate, from *mutilus*, maimed.]
 1. to cut off a limb or essential part of; to mangle; to maim; to cripple; to injure; as, to *mutilate* an animal body; to *mutilate* a statue.
 2. to damage, injure, or otherwise make

imperfect, especially by removing an essential part or parts; as, the censors *mutilated* his speech.

Among the *mutilated* poets of antiquity, there is none whose fragments are so beautiful as those of Sappho.—Addison.

Syn.—mangle, garble, distort, disfigure.

mū′ti·lāte, *n.* in zoology, one of a suborder of aquatic mammals which have a fishlike form, rudimentary, paddlelike fore legs, and no hind legs. [Obs.]

mū′ti·lāte, *a.* 1. in zoology, having no hind legs, as a sirenian. [Rare.]

2. mutilated.

mū′ti·lā·ted, *a.* 1. deprived of a limb, or of an essential part.

2. partially destroyed; imperfect; damaged.

mū·ti·lā′tion, *n.* [L. *mutilatio* (*-onis*), from *mutilare*, to mutilate.]

1. the act of mutilating or the state of being mutilated.

2. the injury resulting from this.

mū′ti·lā·tive, *a.* that mutilates or tends to mutilate.

mū′ti·lā·tŏr, *n.* one who or that which mutilates.

Mū·til′la, *n.* [from L. *mutilare*, to mutilate, or a dim. from Gr. *myia*, a fly.] a genus of wasps resembling ants because of the absence of wings in the female. They are fossorial and solitary, and known also as *solitary ants*.

mū′tine, *v.i.* to mutiny. [Obs.]

mū′tine, *n.* one who mutinies. [Obs.]

mū·ti·neer′, *n.* one guilty of mutiny; especially, a person in military or naval service who rises in opposition to the authority of the officers, who openly resists the government of the army or navy, or attempts to destroy due subordination.

mū′ti·nous, *a.* 1. of, engaged in, or inclined to mutiny.

2. like or characteristic of mutiny.

Syn.—turbulent, rebellious, insubordinate.

mū′ti·nous·ly, *adv.* in a mutinous manner.

mū′ti·nous·ness, *n.* the state of being mutinous.

mū′ti·ny, *n.*; *pl.* **mū′ti·nieṣ,** [from the older *mutine*, a mutineer, from OFr. *mutin*, *meutin*, mutinous, riotous, from *meute*, a revolt, from LL. *mota*, a band or body of men raised for some expedition, from L. *movere*, *motus*, to move.]

1. forcible resistance to or revolt against constituted authority on the part of subordinates; specifically, an insurrection of soldiers or seamen against the authority of their commanders; open resistance to officers or opposition to their authority.

2. tumult; violent commotion. [Obs.]

mū′ti·ny, *v.i.*; mutinied, *pt., pp.*; mutinying, *ppr.* to rise against lawful authority, especially in military and naval service; to participate in a mutiny or mutinous conduct.

mūt′iṣm, *n.* mutage.

mūt′iṣm, *n.* the state or condition of being mute, especially, in psychiatry, as the result of psychic, rather than organic, disorders.

mū′tō·sçōpe, *n.* an apparatus for reproducing the motion of objects by means of a series of photographs.

mutt, *n.* [perh. contr. of *mutton-head*.]

1. a stupid person; a blockhead. [Slang.]

2. a mongrel dog; a cur. [Slang.]

mut′tẽr, *v.i.*; muttered, *pt., pp.*; muttering, *ppr.* [an imitative word; compare G. *muttern*, L. *muttire*, to mutter, from *mu*, the sound produced by closing the lips.]

1. to speak in a low, indistinct voice; to utter words in a low voice and with compressed lips.

The head, yet speaking, *muttered* as it fell. —Pope.

2. to grumble; to murmur.

3. to make a low, rumbling sound; to murmur.

Leaves still *muttering* as the air doth *breathe*. —Drayton.

mut′tẽr, *v.t.* to say in low, indistinct, often angry or discontented, tones.

mut′tẽr, *n.* 1. a muttering.

2. something muttered; especially, a complaint or grumble.

mut′tẽr·ẽr, *n.* one who mutters.

mut′tẽr·ing·ly, *adv.* in a muttering manner.

mut′tŏn, *n.* [Fr. *mouton*; It. *montone*, a sheep; LL. *multo*, *mutilo*, a wether, a castrated ram.]

1. the flesh of sheep used as food; especially, the flesh of grown sheep, as distinguished from lamb.

2. a sheep. [Rare.]

3. a loose woman; a prostitute: also termed *laced mutton*. [Old Slang.]

mut′tŏn·bīrd, *n.* one of various petrels of the antarctic seas, as *Œstrelata lessoni*.

mut′tŏn chop, 1. a rib of mutton for broiling or frying, having the bone cut or chopped off at the small end.

2. [*pl.*] side whiskers shaped like mutton chops (i.e., narrow at the top, and broad and rounded at the bottom), with a clean-shaven chin separating the two whiskers; burnsides.

mut′tŏn-chop, *a.* of the shape of a mutton chop.

mut′tŏn·fish, *n.* same as *eelpout*.

mut′tŏn fist, a large brawny hand. [Colloq.]

mut′tŏn-head (-hed), *n.* a stupid person; one who is uninteresting or dull. [Slang.]

mut′tŏn·mŏn″gẽr, *n.* a pimp. [Old Slang.]

mut′tŏn·y, *a.* with a flavor like mutton; resembling mutton in taste, smell, etc.

mū′tū·ăl, *a.* [Fr. *mutuel*; LL. *mutualis*, from L. *mutuus*, mutual, reciprocal, from *mutare*, to change, exchange.]

1. (a) done, felt, etc. by each of two or more for or toward the other or others; reciprocal; as, *mutual* hate; (b) of, or having the same relationship toward, each other or one another; as *mutual* enemies.

2. shared in common; joint; as, our *mutual* friend.

3. designating or of a type of insurance in which the policyholders elect their own directors, share in the profits, and agree to indemnify one another against loss.

mutual fund; a trust or corporation formed to invest, ordinarily in diversified securities, the funds which it obtains from its shareholders.

mū′tū·ăl·iṣm, *n.* 1. in biology, symbiosis with mutual advantage to both or all organisms involved.

2. in ethics, interdependence: opposed to *individualism*.

mū′tū·ăl·ist, *n.* in zoology, one of two commensals.

mū·tū·al′i·ty, *n.*; *pl.* **mū·tū·al′i·tieṣ,** 1. the state or quality of being mutual.

2. interchange of marks of affection; familiarity.

mu′tū·ăl·īze″, *v.t.* and *v.i.*; mutualized, *pt., pp.*; mutualizing, *ppr.* 1. to make or become mutual.

2. to organize or reorganize (a corporation) so that a majority of shares are held by the employees or customers.

mū′tū·ăl·ly, *adv.* 1. in a mutual manner; in the manner of giving and receiving.

The tongue and the pen *mutually* assist one another. —Holder.

2. equally; in common.

Pinch him, fairies, *mutually*. —Shak.

mū′tū·ăl sāv′ingṣ bank, a savings bank that has no capital, its depositors sharing in the profits.

mū′tū·ā·ry, *n.*; *pl.* **mū′tū·ā·rieṣ,** in law, one who borrows personal chattels to be consumed by him, return to be made to the lender in kind.

mū·tū·ā′tion, *n.* a borrowing. [Obs.]

mū′tūle, *n.* in architecture, a projecting and supporting block under the corona of the Doric cornice, in the same situation as the modillion of other orders, usually with guttae, or drops, on the underside.

MUTULE

mū′tū·um, *n.*; *pl.* **mū′tū·a,** [L. *mutuum*, a loan, neut. of *mutuus*, borrowed.] in law, a loan of chattels to be consumed by the borrower, and return made to the lender in kind.

mux, *v.t.*; muxed (muxt), *pt., pp.*; muxing, *ppr.* to botch; to spoil. [Dial.]

mux, *n.* a botch; a mess. [Dial.]

mux, *n.* filth; muck. [Brit. Dial.]

mux′y, *a.* muddy. [Brit. Dial.]

Mūz′ā·rab, *n.* same as *Mozarab*.

Mūz·ā·rab′iç, *a.* same as *Mozarabic*.

mū′zhik, *n.* [Russ. *muzhik′*.] in czarist Russia, a farmer or peasant: also spelled *muzjik*, *moujik*, *mujik*.

muzz, *v.i.* to potter; to drone along. [Brit. Dial.]

muz′zi·ness, *n.* the state or quality of being muzzy. [Colloq.]

muz′zle, *n.* [OFr. *musel*, *museau*, *muzeau*, muzzle, snout; LL. *musellus*, from *musus*, *morsus*, from L. *morsus*, bite.]

1. the projecting part of the head, including the mouth, jaws, and nose, of an animal, as of a horse; the snout.

2. the mouth of a thing; the end for entrance or discharge; especially, the front end of the barrel of a firearm.

3. a device, as of wire or straps, placed over the mouth of an animal to prevent it from biting or eating.

With golden *muzzles* all their mouths were bound. —Dryden.

4. anything that prevents free speech or discussion.

muz′zle, *v.t.*; muzzled, *pt., pp.*; muzzling, *ppr.* 1. to put a muzzle on (an animal); to fasten the mouth of to prevent biting or eating.

2. to gag; to prevent from talking or expressing an opinion; to keep under restraint; as, to *muzzle* the press.

muz′zle, *v.i.* to thrust forward the mouth or muzzle.

muz′zle bag, in nautical usage, a cap made of canvas, placed over the muzzle of a gun to keep out water.

muz′zle lash′ing, in nautical usage, a rope with which the muzzle of a gun is lashed to the upper part of a port.

muz′zle-lōad″ẽr, *n.* a gun loaded from the muzzle, as distinguished from a breechloader.

muz′zle-lōad″ing, *a.* made to receive its load at the muzzle; as, a *muzzle-loading* gun.

muz′zle ring, the metallic ring that surrounds the mouth of a cannon or other heavy gun.

muz′zle sīght, a sight near the muzzle of a gun.

muz′zle vē·loc′i·ty, the velocity of a shot at the moment when it leaves the muzzle of a firearm: expressed in feet per second.

muz′zy, *a.* confused; muddled; dazed; tipsy. [Colloq.]

mȳ, *pron.* [ME. *mi*, shortened form of *min* used before consonants; AS. *min*, of me, my, mine.] possessive form of *I*.

mȳ, *poss. pronominal a.* of, belonging to, or done by me: also used before some formal titles of address; as, *my* lord, *my* dear Mr. Brown.

mȳ, *interj.* an exclamation of surprise, dismay, etc. (often preceded by *oh*).

mȳ-, myo-.

Mȳ′a, *n.* [L., from Gr. *myax*, a sea mussel, from *mys*, a mussel.] a genus of bivalves. *Mya arenaria* is the common clam.

mȳ·ā′cē·ăn, *a.* of or pertaining to the *Myacea*, a division of bivalve mollusks.

mȳ·ā′cē·ăn, *n.* a bivalve of the division *Myacea*.

mȳ·al′gi·a, *n.* [Gr. *mys*, a muscle, and *algos*, pain.] pain in a muscle or muscles.

mȳ·al′giç, *a.* pertaining to or suffering from myalgia.

mȳ′all, *n.* any of several Australian trees of the genus *Acacia*. The wood of *Acacia homalophylla* is used in making tobacco pipes.

Mȳ·ā′ri·a, *n.pl.* same as *Myidæ*.

mȳ·ăr′i·ăn, *a.* pertaining to the *Myidæ*.

mȳ·ăr′i·ăn, *n.* a bivalve mollusk; a clam.

mȳ′ā·sis, *n.* same as *myiasis*.

mȳ·as·thē′ni·a (*or*-thē-nī′a), *n.* [Gr. *mys*, muscle, and *astheneia*, weakness.] muscular weakness.

mȳ·as·thē′ni·a grā′vis, a disease of faulty nerve conduction characterized by weakness and quick fatigue of muscles, especially of the face and neck.

mȳ·as·then′iç, *a.* pertaining to or suffering from myasthenia.

mȳ·cēle′, *n.* same as *mycelium*.

mȳ·cē′li·ăl, *a.* pertaining to or having the nature of mycelium.

mȳ·cē′li·oid, *a.* mycelial.

mȳ·cē′li·um, *n.* [Gr. *mykēs*, fungus, and *ēlos*, nail, wart.] in botany, the thallus, or vegetative part, of a fungus, made of threadlike tubes.

fibrillose mycelium; fibrous mycelium.

fibrous mycelium; mycelium in which long branching strands are formed by the union of the hyphae.

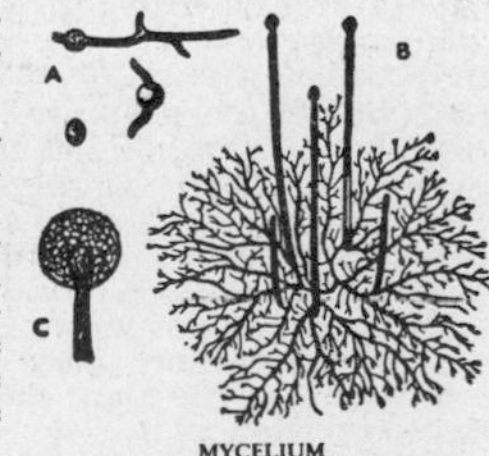

MYCELIUM
A, germination of a spore; B, mycelium; C, cross section of a spore

mȳ′cē·loid, *a.* mycelial.

Mȳ·cē·nae′ăn, *a.* 1. of Mycenae.

2. designating or of the civilization which existed in Greece, Crete, Asia Minor, etc. from 1500 to 1100 B.C.

-mȳ·cēte′, [from *-mycetes.*] a combining form meaning *one of a* (specified) *group of fungi*, as schizo*mycete*.

-mȳ·cē′tēs, [Mod. L., from Gr. *mykētes*, pl. of *mykēs*, a mushroom.] a combining form used in forming the names of large groups of fungi.

Mȳ·cē′tēs, *n.* [Gr. *mykētēs*, a bellower, from *mykāsthai*, to bellow.] a genus typical of the *Mycetinæ*, a subfamily of monkeys including the howlers.

mȳ·cē′tō-, mȳ·cēt′-, [Gr. *mykēs*, *mykētos*, fungus.] a combining form meaning *fungus*, as in *myceto*phagus, *myceto*ma.

mȳ·cē″tō·ġē·net′iç, *a.* [*myceto-*, and Gr. *-genēs*, producing.] in botany, produced by fungi.

mȳ·cē·toġ′ē·nous, *a.* mycetogenetic.

myc′ē·toid (*or* mī′cē), *a.* [*mycet-*, and Gr. *eidos*, form.] resembling a fungus.

mȳ·cē·tol′ō·ġy, *n.* same as *mycology*, sense 1.

mȳ·cē·tō′mȧ, *n.* [*mycet-* and *-oma.*] in pathology, a tumor caused by a fungus; especially, fungus foot or Madura foot, a disease endemic in India, and marked by increasing swelling of the foot, in which nodules and vesicles develop.

mȳ·cē·toph′ȧ·gous, *a.* [*myceto-*, and Gr. *phagein*, to eat.] fungivorous; eating fungi.

Mȳ·cē·tō·zō′ȧ, *n.pl.* [*myceto-*, and Gr. *zōon*, an animal.] a group of saprophytic protozoans the greater number of which are included in the *Myxomycetes*, or slime molds. They feed on decaying vegetable matter and have no mycelium.

mȳ·cē·tō·zō′ăn, *a.* of or pertaining to the *Mycetozoa.*

mȳ·cē·tō·zō′on, *n.* one of the *Mycetozoa.*

mȳ′cō-, [from Gr. *mykēs*, fungus.] a combining form meaning *fungus*, as in *myco*logy: also, before a vowel, *myc-*.

mȳ″cō·baç·tē′ri·um, *n.*; *pl.* **mȳ″cō·baç·tē′ri·ȧ**, [Mod. L.] any of a group of rod-shaped, Gram-positive bacteria, including the causative agents of tuberculosis and leprosy.

mȳ′cō·dērm, *n.* one of the *Mycoderma.*

Mȳ·cō·dēr′mȧ, *n.* [*myco-*, and Gr. *derma*, skin.]

1. a genus of protozoans remarkable for their power of converting sugar into alcohol, as an indirect effect of their metabolism. *Mycoderma vini* converts must into wine, and *Mycoderma aceti*, alcoholic fluids into vinegar.

2. [m–] an aggregation of protozoans, especially bacteria, at the surface of the liquid they inhabit, during the resting stage.

3. [m–] a fungous growth on the epiderm, forming the crust in cutaneous diseases, such as tetter.

mȳ·cō·dēr′miç, *a.* pertaining to the *Mycoderma.*

mȳ″cō·dēr·mī′tis, *n.* [*myco-*, Gr. *derma*, skin, and *-itis.*] in pathology, inflammation of a mucous membrane.

mȳ·cō·loġ′iç, *a.* mycological.

mȳ·cō·loġ′iç·ăl, *a.* of or pertaining to mycology.

mȳ·cō·loġ′iç·ăl·ly, *adv.* by or according to mycology.

mȳ·col′ō·ġist, *n.* one versed in mycology.

mȳ·col′ō·ġy, *n.* [*myco-*, and Gr. *-logia*, from *legein*, to speak.]

1. the branch of botany dealing with fungi.

2. all the fungi native to a specific region.

mȳ·cō·mel′iç, *a.* [*myco-*, and Gr. *meli*, honey.] of or relating to a complex nitrogenous compound, a member of the alloxan group.

Mȳ″cō·mȳ·cē′tēs, *n.pl.* [*myco-*, and Gr. *mykēs*, pl. *mykētes*, fungus.] one of three classes of fungi characterized by a multicellular mycelium and asexual reproduction.

mȳ″cō·mȳ·cē′tous, *a.* of or relating to the *Mycomycetes.*

mȳ·çoph′ȧ·ġist, *n.* an eater of fungi.

mȳ·çoph′ȧ·ġy, *n.* [*myco-*, and Gr. *phagein*, to eat.] the eating of or habit of eating fungi.

mȳ·cō·prō′tē·in, *n.* [*myco-* and *protein.*] the albuminous matter of bacteria.

mȳ·çor·rhī′zȧ, *n.* [*myco-*, and Gr. *rhiza*, a root.] a mycelium found in the root tubercles of certain angiosperms, especially in those of the *Leguminosæ*, supposed to assist in the nutrition of the plant and to sustain a symbiotic relation to it.

mȳ′çōse, *n.* [Gr. *mykēs*, fungus, and *-ose.*] ergot sugar or trehalose.

mȳ·çō′sis, *n.*; *pl.* **mȳ·çō′sēs**, [Gr. *mykēs*, fungus, and *-osis.*]

1. the growth of parasitic fungi in any part of the body.

2. a disease caused by such fungi.

mȳ′çō·thrix, *n.* [*myco-*, and Gr. *thrix*, hair.] the filament resulting from cell division in micrococcus, a bacterium in which the daughter cells remain in contact with the mother cell for a time.

mȳ·çot′iç, *a.* pertaining to or caused by mycosis.

mȳ·dā′lē·ine (*or* -ēn), *n.* [Gr. *mydaleos*, wet, dripping, from *mydān*, to be wet.] a poisonous ptomaine found in putrefied viscera.

mȳ′dan, *n.* maidan. [Obs.]

myd·ȧ·tox′ïne (*or* -in), *n.* [Gr. *mydān*, clammy, and *toxic.*] a poisonous ptomaine from decaying flesh.

myd′ā·us, *n.* [Gr. *mydān*, to be clammy or damp.] a genus of animals of which the teledu is a species.

mȳ′dïne (*or* -din), *n.* [Gr. *mydos*, dampness.] a nonpoisonous ptomaine from the viscera of dead bodies, and found also in cultures of the typhoid bacillus.

mȳ·drī′ȧ·sis, *n.* [Gr.] prolonged or excessive dilatation of the pupil of the eye, as the result of disease or the administration of a drug.

myd·ri·at′iç, *n.* any drug that causes mydriasis.

myd·ri·at′iç, *a.* of, pertaining to, or producing mydriasis.

mȳ′el-, same as *myelo-*.

mȳ·el·al′ġi·ȧ, *n.* [*myel-* and *-algia.*] in pathology, pain in the spinal cord.

mȳ·el·ap′ō·plex·y, *n.* [*myel-* and *apoplexy.*] in pathology, hemorrhage within the spinal cord.

mȳ″el·as·thē′ni·ȧ, *n.* [*myel-*, and Gr. *astheneia*, weakness.] in pathology, neurasthenia due to some cause which affects the spinal cord.

mȳ″e·len″cē·phal′iç, *a.* pertaining to the myelencephalon; also, myelencephalous.

mȳ″e·len·ceph′ȧ·lon, *n.* [*myel-*, and *encephalon.*] the afterbrain, or metencephalon; the posterior part of the hindbrain.

mȳ″e·len·ceph′ȧ·lous, *a.* having a brain and spinal cord.

mȳ′e·lin, mȳ′e·līne, *n.* [G., from Gr. *myelos*, marrow.] the white fatty substance forming a sheath about certain nerve fibers.

mȳ·e·lin′iç, *a.* pertaining to or of the nature of myelin.

mȳ·e·lit′iç, *a.* of, pertaining to, or suffering from myelitis.

mȳ·e·lī′tis, *n.* [*myel-* and *-itis.*] inflammation of the spinal cord or the bone marrow.

mȳ′el·ō-, [from Gr. *myelos*, marrow.] a combining form meaning *the marrow* or *the spinal cord*: also, before a vowel, *myel-*.

mȳ′e·lō·cēle, *n.* [*myelo-*, and Gr. *kēlē*, tumor.] spina bifida with protrusion of the spinal cord.

mȳ″e·lō·cer·ē·bel′lăr, *a.* pertaining to the spinal cord and the cerebellum.

mȳ′e·lō·coele, *n.* [*myelo-*, and Gr. *koilos*, a hollow.] the cavity of the spinal cord.

mȳ″e·lō·ġen′iç, *a.* [*myelo-*, and Gr. *-genēs*, producing.] produced in the bone marrow.

mȳ′e·loid, *a.* [*myelo-*, and Gr. *eidos*, form.]

1. of the spinal cord.

2. of, like, or derived from bone marrow.

mȳ·e·lō′mȧ, *n.* [*myel-* and *-oma.*]

1. any medullary tumor.

2. giant-cell sarcoma.

3. a slow-growing tumor of a tendinous sheath containing myeloplaxes.

mȳ′e·lon, *n.* [Gr. *myelon*, neut. of *myelos*, marrow.] the spinal cord.

mȳ·el′ō·năl, *a.* pertaining to or connected with the myelon.

mȳ·e·lon′iç, *a.* myelonal.

mȳ·el′ō·plax, *n.* [*myelo-*, and Gr. *plax*, anything flat or broad.] any multinuclear giant cell of the bone marrow; an osteoclast.

myġ′ȧ·lē, *n.* [L. *mygale*; Gr. *mygalē*, a field mouse.] formerly, a genus of spiders, typical of the family *Mygalidæ*. The species, which are large, with a rough hairy coat and stout hairy legs, chiefly inhabit tropical America. They reside in fissures in trees, in the crevices between stones, etc., spinning a tubular, silken dwelling. The best-known species is *Mygale avicularia.*

mȳ′iȧ·sis (-yȧ-), *n.* [LL., from Gr. *myia*, a fly.] any disease caused by maggots or flies.

Mȳ′i·dae, *n. pl.* a family of bivalves including the soft clams: also called *Myacea* and *Myaria.*

mȳ·iō′sis (-yō′), *n.* same as *myiasis.*

Mȳ′lō·don, *n.* [Gr. *mylodous* (*-ontos*), a molar tooth, a grinder; *mylē*, a mill, and *odous*, *odontos*, a tooth.]

1. an extinct genus of edentate mammals, the best-known species being *Mylodon robustus.*

SKELETON OF MYLODON

2. [m–] an edentate of this genus.

mȳ′lō·dont, *a.* of or pertaining to the mylodons.

mȳ′lō·dont, *n.* a mylodon.

mȳ·lō·hȳ′oid, *a.* [Gr. *mylē*, mill, and *hyoid.*] pertaining to the molar teeth and the hyoid or U-shaped bone at the base of the tongue.

mȳ·lō·hȳ′oid, *n.* the muscle forming the floor of the mouth.

mȳ″lō·hȳ·oi′dē·ăn, *a.* mylohyoid.

mȳ′nȧ, mȳ′nȧh, *n.* [Hind. *mainā.*] any of a group of tropical birds of southeastern Asia related to the starling; especially, such a bird of India that has the ability to mimic human speech and is often kept as a pet: also spelled *mina.*

Mȳn·heer′ (-hār′ *or* -hēr′), *n.* [D. *mijn heer*, lit., my lord.]

1. the ordinary form of address among the Dutch, equivalent to English *Mr.* or *sir.*

2. [m–] a Dutchman. [Colloq.]

mȳ′ō-, [from Gr. *mys*, *myos*, a muscle.] a combining form meaning *muscle*: used in medicine, anatomy, etc.; as, *myo*cardium: also, before a vowel, *my-*.

mȳ·ō·al′bū·mōse, *n.* a proteide from muscle juice.

mȳ·ō·at′rō·phy, *n.* [*myo-*, and Gr. *atrophia*, a wasting away.] atrophy of muscles.

mȳ′ō·blast, *n.* [*myo-*, and Gr. *blastos*, a germ.] an embryonic cell which becomes a cell of the muscle fiber.

mȳ·ō·blas′tiç, *a.* pertaining to myoblasts.

mȳ·ō·cär′di·ō·grȧph″, *n.* [*myo-* and *cardiograph.*] an instrument for recording the movements of the heart muscle.

mȳ″ō·çär·dī′tis, *n.* [*myocardium* and *-itis.*] inflammation of the myocardium; inflammation of the muscular walls of the heart.

mȳ·ō·çär′di·um, *n.* [*myo-*, and Gr. *kardia*, heart.] the muscular substance of the heart; the heart muscle.

mȳ′ō·cēle, *n.* [*myo-*, and Gr. *kēlē*, a tumor.] hernia of muscle; the protrusion of a muscle through its ruptured sheath.

mȳ·oç′lō·nus, *n.* [*myo-* and *clonus.*] clonic spasm of a muscle or of various muscles.

mȳ′ō·coele, *n.* [*myo-*, and Gr. *koilos*, a cavity.] the cavity enclosed by a myotome; the cavity of a myotome: also written *myocoelom.*

mȳ·ō·çom′mȧ, *n.*; *pl.* **mȳ·ō·çom′mȧ·tȧ**, [*myo-*, and Gr. *komma*, that which is cut off.] a sclerotome; the septum between any two myotomes.

mȳ′ō·çyte, *n.* [*myo-*, and Gr. *kytos*, a hollow cell.] a cell of the muscular tissue.

mȳ″ō·dȳ·nam′i·ȧ, *n.* [*myo-*, and Gr. *dynamis*, power.] the energy developed in muscular contraction; muscular strength.

mȳ″ō·dȳ·nam′içs, *n.* that branch of physiology treating of the principles of muscular action; the science of muscular energy or contraction.

mȳ″ō·dȳ·nȧ·mom′e·tēr, *n.* [*myo-* and *dynamometer.*] a device for testing the power of the muscles; a dynamometer.

mȳ·ō·dyn′i·ȧ, *n.* same as *myalgia.*

mȳ″ō·ep·i·thē′li·ăl, *a.* [*myo-* and *epithelial.*] pertaining to or composed of muscle and epithelium.

mȳ″ō·fī·brō′mȧ, *n.* myoma and fibroma.

Mȳ·oġ′ȧ·lē, *n.* a genus of rodents typical of the family *Myogalinæ.*

mȳ·oġ′ȧ·line, *n.* [Gr. *myogalē*, a shrewmouse.] one of the *Myogalinæ*, a subfamily of insectivorous mammals, including the desmans, musk shrews, and musk moles.

mȳ′ō·ġen, *n.* same as *myosinogen.*

mȳ″ō·ġē·net′iç, *a.* [*myo-* and *genetic.*] originating in or produced by a muscle or muscle tissue.

mȳ·ō·ġen′iç, *a.* [*myo-*, and Gr. *genos*, origin.] originating in the muscular tissue.

mȳ·ō·glob′ū·lin, *n.* [*myo-* and *globulin.*] a globulin found in the serum of muscles.

mȳ′ō·gram, *n.* [*myo-*, and Gr. *gramma*, a writing.] the record or tracing made by a myograph.

mȳ′ō·gráph, *n.* [*myo-*, and Gr. *graphein*, to write.] an apparatus for recording the effects of a muscular contraction.

mȳ·og′rá·phẽr, *n.* one who is skilled in myography.

mȳ·ō·graph′iç, *a.* pertaining to a myograph or to myography.

mȳ·ō·graph′i·çăl, *a.* myographic.

mȳ·ō·graph′i·çăl·ly, *adv.* by employing a myograph.

mȳ·ō·graph′i·ŏn, *n.* a myograph.

mȳ·og′rá·phist, *n.* a myographer.

mȳ·og′rá·phy, *n.* 1. a description of the muscles.
2. the use of the myograph.

mȳ·ō·hē′má·tin, *n.* [*myo-* and *hematin.*] a pigment supposedly occurring in muscles.

mȳ′oid, *a.* [*myo-*, and Gr. *eidos*, form.] resembling a muscle or muscular tissue.

mȳ·oi·dē′má, *n.* [*myo-*, and Gr. *oidēma*, a swelling.] edema of a muscle.

mȳ·ō·lem′má, *n.* same as *sarcolemma.*

mȳ′ō·lin, *n.* [Gr. *mys*, muscle.] the supposed material of the muscular fibrils.

mȳ·ō·loġ′iç, *a.* myological.

mȳ·ō·loġ′i·çăl, *a.* of or pertaining to myology.

mȳ·ol′ō·ġist, *n.* a person skilled or versed in myology.

mȳ·ol′ō·ġy, *n.* [*myo-*, and Gr. *-logia*, from *legein*, to speak.] the branch of anatomy dealing with the muscles.

mȳ·ō′má, *n.*; *pl.* **mȳ·ō′má·tá, mȳ·ō′más,** [*myo-* and *-oma.*] a tumor which consists of muscular tissue.

mȳ′ō·man·cy, *n.* [Gr. *mys*, mouse, and *manteia*, divination.] the foretelling of future events by movements of mice.

mȳ·om′á·tous, *a.* of, or having the nature of, a myoma.

mȳ·ō·meç′tō·my, *n.* [*myoma*, and Gr. *ektomē*, a cutting out.] surgical removal of a myoma.

mȳ′ō·mēre, *n.* [*myo-*, and Gr. *meros*, part.] a muscular segment.

mȳ′ō·morph, *n.* a member of the *Myomorpha.*

Mȳ·ō·mor′phá, *n. pl.* [Gr. *mys*, *myos*, a mouse, and *morphē*, form.] a suborder of rodents, including dormice, common mice and rats, jerboas, etc.

mȳ·ō·mot′ō·my, *n.* same as *myomectomy.*

mȳ·ō·path′iç, *a.* of or relating to myopathy.

mȳ·op′á·thy, mȳ″ō·pá·thī′á, *n.* [*myo-*, and Gr. *pathos*, suffering, disease.] any disease of a muscle.

mȳ′ōpe, *n.* [Gr. *myōps*, shortsighted, blinking; *myein*, to close, and *ōps*, eye.] a person afflicted with myopia; a nearsighted person.

mȳ′ō·phan, *n.* [*myo-*, and Gr. *-phanēs*, from *phainesthai*, to appear.] a layer of fibrillae found in the cytoplasm of certain protozoans.

mȳ′ō·phōre, *n.* [*myo-*, and Gr. *-phoros*, from *pherein*, to bear.] any process differentiated from a shell to serve for the attachment of muscles.

mȳ·ō·phyṣ′içs, *n.* [*myo-*, and Gr. *physika*, physics.] the physics of muscular phenomena.

mȳ·ō′pi·á, mȳ′ō·py, *n.* [Gr. *myōps* (*-ōpos*), shortsighted.] an abnormal eye condition in which light rays from distant objects are focused in front of the retina instead of on it, so that the objects are not seen distinctly; nearsightedness.

mȳ·op′iç, *a.* affected with or relating to myopia; nearsighted.

mȳ·ō·pō′lăr, *a.* [*myo-*, and Gr. *polos*, a pole.] relating to muscular polarity.

Mȳ·op·ō·rā′çē·ae, *n.pl.* [Gr. *myein*, to close, and *poros*, a pore.] a family of plants, distinguished from *Verbenaceæ* by the pendulous ovules and the more abundant albumen: also called *Myoporineæ.*

mȳ′ops, *n.* a myope.

mȳ·op′sis, *n.* [Gr. *myia*, a fly, and *opsis*, appearance.] a disease of the eyes in which black spots are seen passing like flies before them.

mȳ′ō·py, *n.* myopia.

mȳ′ō·sçōpe, *n.* [*myo-*, and Gr. *skopein*, to view.] an apparatus for the study of muscular contraction.

mȳ′ō·sin, *n.* [Gr. *mys*, muscle, and *-ose*, and *-in.*] a soluble protein resembling globulin, present in the tissue of the contractile muscles: its coagulation into an insoluble fibrin is believed to be the cause of rigor mortis.

mȳ·ō·sin′ō·ġen, *n.* the proteide in living muscle from which myosin is formed.

mȳ·ō′sis, *n.* [Gr. *myein*, to close, and *-osis.*] prolonged or excessive contraction of the pupil of the eye, resulting from disease or the use of a drug.

mȳ·ō·sit′iç, *a.* pertaining to myositis.

mȳ·ō·sī′tis, *n.* inflammation of the muscles; muscular rheumatism.

mȳ′ō·sōte, *n.* a myosotis.

Mȳ·ō·sō′tis, *n.* [Gr. *myosōtis*, *myos ōtis*, the mouse ear, forget-me-not; *mys*, *myos*, mouse, and *ous*, *ōtos*, ear.]
1. a genus of plants including the forget-me-not, *Myosotis palustris.*
2. [m–] any plant of this genus, having light-green leaves and white, blue, or pink flowers.

mȳ·ō·tat′iç, *a.* [*myo-*, and Gr. *tasis*, tension.] performed or induced by stretching or extending a muscle.

mȳ·ot′iç, *a.* pertaining to, having, or causing myosis.

mȳ·ot′iç, *n.* any drug causing myosis.

mȳ·ō·til′i·ty, *n.* [*myo-* and *motility.*] muscular contractility.

mȳ′ō·tōme, *n.* [*myo-*, and Gr. *tomē*, a cutting.]
1. an instrument for performing myotomy.
2. a muscular segment, or myomere.
3. a myocomma.

mȳ·ō·tom′iç, *a.* pertaining to a myotome.

mȳ·ot′ō·my, *n.* the cutting or dissection of muscular tissue or of a muscle.

mȳ·ō·tō′ni·á, *n.* myotony.

mȳ·ō·ton′iç, *a.* pertaining to myotony.

mȳ·ot′ō·ny, *n.* 1. tonic spasm of a muscle.
2. muscular tension.
3. a stretching of a muscle.

myr′i·á, [from Gr. *myrias*, the number ten thousand.] a combining form meaning: (a) *many, numerous*, as in *myria*pod; (b) in the metric system, *ten thousand*, as in *myria*meter.

myr″i·á·çan′thous, *a.* [*myri-*, and Gr. *akantha*, thorn, spine.] having numerous spines, as the rays of the genus *Myriacanthus*, and similar fishes.

myr′iá·chit (-yá-), *n.* same as *miryachit.*

myr′i·ăd, *n.* [Gr. *myrias* (*-ados*), the number ten thousand, from *myrios*, countless.]
1. ten thousand.
2. any indefinitely large number; as, *myriads* of suns.
3. a large number of persons or things.
The race was on; the souls of the racers were in it; over them bent the *myriads.*
—Lew Wallace.

myr′i·ăd, *a.* pertaining to a myriad; consisting of enormous but indefinite numbers; multitudinous; as, the *myriad* denizens of the deep.

myr′i·á·gram, *n.* [Fr. *myriagramme*; Gr. *myrioi*, ten thousand, and L.Gr. *gramma*, a small weight.] in the metric system, a measure of weight consisting of 10,000 grams, or 10 kilograms, and equal to 22.046 pounds avoirdupois.

myr′i·á·lī″tẽr, *n.* [Fr. *myrialitre*; Gr. *myrioi*, ten thousand, and *litra*, a pound.] in the metric system, a measure of capacity, of 10,000 liters, equal to 2,642 United States gallons.

myr′i·á·mē″tẽr, *n.* [Fr. *myriamètre*; Gr. *myrioi*, ten thousand, and *metron*, a measure.] in the metric system, a measure of length, consisting of 10,000 meters, equal to 6.2137 miles.

myr′i·á·nīde, *n.* a marine worm, *Myrianida pinnigera.*

myr′i·á·pod, *n.* one of the *Myriapoda*; a centipede or millepede.

myr′i·á·pod, *a.* having many legs; specifically, of or belonging to a large group of arthropods having long bodies consisting of many segments, each of which bears one or more pairs of jointed legs, as the millipedes and centipedes.

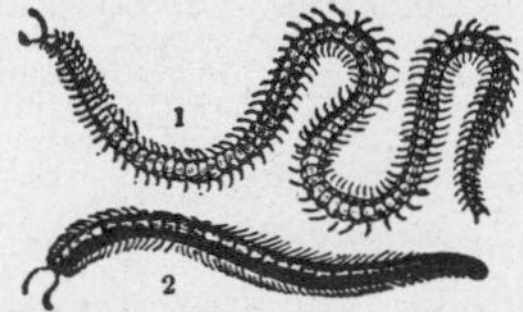

MYRIAPODS
Geophilus sefeborii, one of the *Chilopoda*; 2. *Iulus plicatus*, one of the *Chilognatha*

Myr·i·ap′ō·dá, *n.pl.* [*myria-*, and Gr. *pous*, *podos*, foot.] a group of myriapod animals formerly regarded as a class.

myr·i·ap′ō·dăn, *n.* and *a.* myriapod.

myr·i·ap′ō·dous, *a.* myriapod.

myr′i·ärçh, *n.* [Gr. *myriarchēs*, *myriarchos*; *myrioi*, ten thousand, and *archos*, a ruler.] in ancient Greece, a commander or leader of 10,000 men.

myr′i·āre, *n.* [*myri-*, and Fr. *are*, are.] in the metric system, a measure of surface, containing 10,000 ares, or 1,000,000 square meters, and equal to about 247.1 acres.

My·rī′çá, *n.* a genus of shrubs, of the order *Myricaceæ*. The berries of *Myrica cerifera*, of the Atlantic States, yield bayberry tallow.

Myr·i·çā′çē·ae, *n.pl.* an order of shrubs, the sweet-gale family, or galeworts, typifying the genus *Myrica.*

myr·i·çā′ceous, *a.* pertaining to the *Myricaceæ.*

myr′i·cin, *n.* [Gr. *myrikē*, tamarisk, and *-in.*] that portion of common beeswax which is insoluble in boiling alcohol.

myr′i·cyl, *n.* same as *melissyl.*

mȳ·rin′gá, *n.* [LL. *miringa*, a kind of membrane.] the tympanic membrane, or drum of the ear.

myr·in·ġī′tis, *n.* [*myringa* and *-itis.*] inflammation of the tympanic membrane.

myr′i·ō-, [from Gr. *myrios*, numberless, countless.] a combining form meaning *countless, numerous*: used in botany; as, *myrio*phyllous.

myr″i·ō·loġ′iç·ăl, myr″i·ō·loġ′iç, *a.* of or pertaining to a myriologue.

myr·i·ol′ō·ġist, *n.* one who sings or composes a myriologue.

myr′i·ō·logue (-log), *n.* [Fr., from modern Gr. *myriologi.*] an extempore funeral song composed and sung by women in modern Greece on the death of some person.

myr·i·oph′yl·lous, *a.* [*myrio-*, and Gr. *phyllon*, a leaf.] having very numerous leaves.

Myr″i·ō·phyl′lum, *n.* [L.Gr. *myriaphyllon*, spiked water milfoil, neut. of *myriaphyllos*; *myrios*, numberless, and *phyllon*, a leaf.] a genus of perennial aquatic herbs; the water milfoil family.

myr″i·ō·rä′má, *n.* [*myrio-*, and Gr. *horama*, a view.] a landscape picture made of a number of separate sections that can be put together in various ways so as to form distinct scenes.

myr′i·ō·sçōpe″, *n.* [*myrio-*, and Gr. *skopein*, to view.] a variety of kaleidoscope; specifically, one used in exhibiting carpets.

myr′i·ō·thē·iṣm, *n.* [*myrio-* and *theism.*] the creed of believing in numberless gods. [Rare.]

Myr″i·ō·triçh′i·á, *n.* [Mod.L., from *myrio-*, and Gr. *thrix*, *trichos*, hair.] a genus of marine algae of the order *Ectocarpales*, occurring as small, brown growths forming tufts or cushions.

myr″i·ō·triçh″i·ā′ceous, *a.* pertaining or belonging to the *Myriotrichia.*

my·ris′tāte, *n.* a salt or ester of myristic acid.

my·ris′tiç, *a.* 1. relating to or derived from the nutmeg.
2. designating an acid existing in nutmeg oil and otoba fat.

My·ris·ti·çā′çē·ae, *n.pl.* [Gr. *myristikos*, sweet-smelling, from *myron*, any sweet distillation from a plant used for perfume.] an order of fragrant tropical trees, including the genus *Myristica*. *Myristica fragrans*, native to the Malay Archipelago, is the nutmeg tree.

my·ris′ti·cin, *n.* the camphor of volatile oil of nutmeg.

my·ris′tin, *n.* myristate of glyceryl, found in nutmeg butter and other fats.

my·ris′tōne, *n.* a crystalline substance obtained by distilling calcium myristate.

myr′mē·çō-, a combining form meaning *ant*, as in *myrmecology.*

myr′mē·çōbe, *n.* [Gr. *myrmēx* (*-ēkos*), an ant, and *bios*, life.] an anteater, *Myrmecobius fasciatus*, native to Australia: it is about the size of a squirrel.

myr″mē·çō·loġ′iç·ăl, *a.* of myrmecology.

myr·mē·çol′ō·ġy, *n.* [Gr. *myrmēx* (*-ēkos*), an ant, and *-logia*, from *legein*, to speak.] the branch of entomology dealing with ants.

Myr·mē·çoph′á·gá, *n.* a genus of anteaters of South America, family *Myrmecophagidæ.*

myr·mē·çoph′á·gous, *n.* [Gr. *myrmēx* (*-ēkos*), an ant, and *phagein*, to eat.] feeding upon ants and their larvae; pertaining to the *Myrmecophaga.*

myr·mē·çoph′i·lous, *a.* [Gr. *myrmēx* (*-ēkos*), an ant, and *philos*, loving.] fond of or benefited by ants, as insects living in ant colonies, and plants in which cross-fertilization is effected by ants.

Myr·me″lē·on′i·dae, *n. pl.* [Gr. *myrmēkoleōn*, ant lion.] a family of insects belonging to the order *Neuroptera*, the ant lions.

Myr′mi·ça, *n.* the typical genus of the ant family *Myrmicinæ*.

myr′mi·cid, *n.* [Gr. *myrmēx* (-*ēkos*), an ant.] an ant belonging to the genus *Myrmica*, which includes the house ant, *Myrmica molesta*.

myr′mi·cine, *a.* of or pertaining to the *Myrmica*.

Myr′mi·don, *n.* [Gr. *Myrmidones*, the Myrmidons.]

1. any of a tribe of Thessalian warriors who, according to Greek legend, fought under Achilles, their king, in the Trojan War.

2. [m-] an unquestioning follower or subordinate who carries out orders without scruple or hesitation.

myr·mi·dō′ni·ăn, *a.* of, pertaining to, resembling, or consisting of myrmidons.

myr·mō·thē′rine, *a.* [Gr. *myrmēx*, an ant, and *thērān*, to hunt.] feeding on ants, as certain birds.

mȳ·rob′ȧ·lan, mȳ·rob′ō·lan, *n.* [L. *myrobalanum*; Gr. *myrobalanos*; *myron*, unguent, and *balanos*, a nut.] any of the dried, astringent, prunelike fruits of various tropical trees, containing tannin and used for dyeing and tanning.

mȳ·ron′iç ac′id, [Gr. *myron*, an odorous oil.] a bitter acid obtained from black mustard seed.

mȳ·rop′ō·list, *n.* one who sells unguents or perfumery. [Obs.]

mȳ′rō·sin, *n.* [*myro*nic and -*ose* and -*in*.] a nitrogenous ferment existing in mustard seed.

Mȳ·rox′y·lon, *n.* [Gr. *myron*, a sweet-smelling juice from a plant, and *xylon*, wood.] a small genus of tropical American trees, closely allied to *Myrospermum*. It contains two important species, *Myroxylon toluiferum*, from which the balsam of Tolu is obtained, and *Myroxylon pereiræ*, which yields the balsam of Peru.

MYRRH
(*Balsamodendron myrrha*)

myrrh (mũr), *n.* [L. *myrrha*, *murrha*, *murra*; Gr. *myrrha*; Ar. *murr*, myrrh, bitter.]

1. a fragrant, bitter-tasting gum resin exuded from any of several shrubs of Arabia and eastern Africa, especially from *Balsamodendron myrrha*, family *Amyridaceæ*, a spiny shrub with scanty foliage, small, green axillary flowers, and small, oval fruit. Myrrh is used in making incense, perfume, and medicine.

2. a plant of the genus *Myrrhis*.

myr′rhiç (mũr′ik), *a.* of, relating to, or derived from myrrh.

myr′rhine (mũr′in), *a.* same as *murrine*.

myrrh′ōl, *n.* [*myrrh* and -*ol*.] a volatile oil derived from myrrh.

myr·si·nā′ceous (mũr-), *a.* relating to, resembling, or belonging to the family *Myrsineæ*.

Myr′si·nē (mũr′), *n.* the typical genus of the order *Myrsineæ*.

Myr·sin′ē·ae (mũr-), *n.pl.* [Gr. *myrsinē*, myrtle.] a family of subtropical shrubs and trees closely resembling *Primulaceæ* in fructification.

Myr·tā′cē·ae (mũr-), *n.* [Gr. *myrtos*, myrtle, and -*aceæ*.] the myrtle family of shrubs and trees, an extensive family of polypetalous exogens, growing mainly in warm countries. They have simple entire leaves, often dotted with resinous pellucid glands and with an intromarginal vein, and regular, axillary, and single or spiked, corymbose or panicled white, pink, or yellow flowers, with many stamens. Some yield useful products, as guavas, cloves, pimento, and cajeput oil. Some of the largest genera are mainly Australian, as *Eucalyptus* (gum tree) and *Melaleuca*.

myr·tā′ceous (mũr-), *a.* pertaining to, resembling, or belonging to the family *Myrtaceæ*.

myr′ti·fọrm (mũr′), *a.* resembling myrtle or myrtle berries.

myr′tle (mũr′), *n.* [OFr. *mirtil*, *myrtille*, dim. of *myrte*, *murte*, from L. *myrtus*, Gr. *myrtos*, myrtle, from Per. *mŭrd*, myrtle.]

1. an evergreen shrub or tree of the genus *Myrtus*, especially *Myrtus communis*, native to southern Europe and Asia, with glossy leaves, white or pinkish flowers, and dark, fragrant berries: it was held sacred to Venus in ancient times.

2. any of various other plants; especially, the periwinkle, *Vinca minor*, and the moneywort, *Lysimachia nummularia*.

myr′tle ber′ry, the fruit of the myrtle.

myr′tle bĩrd, the golden-crowned warbler, *Dendrœca coronata*, one of the most common of the American warblers.

myr′tle wax, bayberry wax, obtained from the *Myrica cerifera*.

Myr′tus (mũr′), *n.* the typical genus of the family *Myrtaceæ*, consisting of mainly South American shrubs, having opposite dotted leaves, with white or yellowish flowers.

mȳ·self′, *pron.* [AS. *me sylf*.] a form of the first person singular pronoun, used: (a) as an intensive; as, I went *myself*; (b) as a reflexive; as, I hurt *myself*; (c) as a quasi-noun meaning "my real, true, or actual self" (e.g., I am not *myself* when I rage like that): in this construction *my* may be considered a possessive pronominal adjective and *self* a noun, and they may be separated; as, *my* own sweet *self*.

Mȳ′sis, *n.* [Gr. *mysis*, a closing of the lips or eyes, from *myein*, to close.] the opossum shrimps; a genus of crustaceans belonging to the order *Stomapoda*. They are the chief crustaceans of the Arctic Ocean, and constitute the principal food of the whalebone whale.

mys·tā′ciăl (-shăl), *a.* see *mustachial*.

mys·tȧ·gog′iç, mys·tȧ·gog′iç·ăl, *a.* of or relating to a mystagogue or the interpretation of mysteries.

mys′tȧ·gogue, *n.* [Fr., from L. *mystagogus*, from Gr. *mystagōgos*; *mystēs*, one initiated in mysteries, and *agōgos*, a leader.]

1. an interpreter of religious mysteries or one who initiates others into them.

2. a custodian of church relics exhibited to the public. [Obs.]

mys′tȧ·gō·gy, *n.* 1. the art of explaining or interpreting mysteries; the doctrines or teachings of a mystagogue.

2. in the Orthodox Eastern Church, the communion or sacraments.

mys′tax, *n.* [Gr. *mystax*, the upper lip, a mustache.] in entomology, a brushlike cluster of hairs immediately above the mouth, as in certain dipterous insects.

mys·tē′ri·ăl, *a.* mysterious. [Rare.]

mys·tē′ri·ärch, *n.* [Gr. *mystēriarchēs*; *mystērion*, mystery, and *archos*, chief.] one who presides over mysteries.

mys·tē′ri·ous, *a.* of, containing, implying, or characterized by mystery; obscure; hid from the understanding; secret; not revealed or explained; unintelligible; beyond human comprehension.

Syn.—covert, dark, cabalistic, mystic, enigmatical, obscure, occult, incomprehensible.

mys·tē′ri·ous·ly, *adv.* in a mysterious way or manner.

mys·tē′ri·ous·ness, *n.* the state, condition, or quality of being mysterious.

mys′tēr·īze, *v.t.* to express or interpret as a mystery. [Obs.]

mys′tẽr·y, *n.*; *pl.* **mys′tẽr·ieṣ,** [L. *mysterium*; Gr. *mystērion*, the secret worship of a deity, a secret thing, from *mystēs*, one initiated into the mysteries, from *myein*, to initiate into the mysteries, from *myein*, to shut the eyes.]

1. something unexplained, unknown, or kept secret; as, the *mystery* of life.

2. (a) any thing or event that remains so secret or obscure as to excite curiosity; as, a murder *mystery*; (b) a novel, story, or play involving such an event.

3. the quality of being inexplicable; obscurity or secrecy; as, an air of *mystery* surrounds this affair.

4. [*pl.*] secret rites or doctrines known only to a small, esoteric group; specifically, in ancient Greece, religious ceremonies or doctrines revealed only to the initiated.

5. [*pl.*] any of the ancient cults characterized by such ceremonies; as, the Eleusinian *mysteries*.

6. [perh. influenced by *mystery*, a craft.] a mystery play.

7. in Christianity, (a) the Mass; (b) a sacrament; especially, the Eucharist; (c) any of fifteen events in the lives of Jesus and Mary serving as a subject for meditation during the saying of the rosary.

8. in theology, any assumed truth that cannot be comprehended by the human mind but must be accepted on faith.

mystery play; any of a class of medieval dramatic representations of Biblical events, especially of the life and death of Jesus: they originated in the church liturgy but were later presented by craft guilds on improvised platforms or wagons in market places, etc.

mystery ship; in World War I, a naval warship disguised as a merchantman, used to lure enemy submarines into easy range before opening fire.

mys′tẽr·y, *n.* [ME. *misterie*, *mysterie*, a trade, craft; OFr. *mestier*, from L. *ministerium*, office, occupation.] a craft; trade. [Archaic.]

mys′tiç, *a.* [L. *mysticus*; Gr. *mystikos*, belonging to secret rites, from *mystēs*, one initiated.]

1. of mysteries, or esoteric rites or doctrines.

2. of mystics or mysticism.

3. of obscure or occult character or meaning; as, *mystic* powers.

4. beyond human comprehension; mysterious or enigmatic.

5. mystical (sense 1). [Rare.]

mys′tiç, *n.* 1. a person initiated into esoteric mysteries.

2. a believer in mysticism; specifically, one who professes to undergo mystical experiences by which he intuitively comprehends truths beyond human understanding.

mys′tiç·ăl, *a.* 1. spiritually significant or symbolic; allegorical; as, the *mystical* rose, a symbol of the Virgin Mary.

2. mystic (senses 2 and 3).

3. mysterious; enigmatic. [Rare.]

mys′tiç·ăl·ly, *adv.* mysteriously.

mys′tiç·ăl·ness, *n.* the state or quality of being mystic.

mys′ti·cēte, *a.* relating to or resembling the *Mysticeti*.

mys′ti·cēte, *n.* one of the *Mysticeti*.

Mys·ti·cē′tī, *n.pl.* a suborder of *Cetacea*; the whalebone whales.

mys′ti·cism, *n.* 1 doctrines or beliefs of mystics; specifically, the doctrine that it is possible to achieve communion with God through contemplation and love without the medium of human reason.

2. any doctrine that asserts the possibility of attaining knowledge of spiritual truths through intuition acquired by fixed meditation.

3. vague or obscure thinking or belief.

mys″ti·fi·cā′tion, *n.* the act of mystifying; also, the state or condition of being mystified; as, a cunning *mystification*.

mys′ti·fi·cā″tŏr, *n.* one who mystifies.

mys′ti·fȳ, *v.t.*; mystified, *pt.*, *pp.*; mystifying, *ppr.* 1. to puzzle or perplex; especially, to bewilder deliberately; to play on the credulity of; to hoax.

2. to involve in mystery, or obscurity; to make obscure or hard to understand.

Syn.—confuse, bamboozle, hoodwink, puzzle, confound, mislead, obfuscate.

mys·tique′ (-tēk′), *n.* [Fr., mystic.] a complex of quasi-mystical attitudes and feelings surrounding some person, institution, activity, etc.

mȳ′tȧ·cism, *n.* [LL. *mytacismus*; L.Gr. *mytakismos*, fondness for the letter μ, from Gr. *mu*, the letter μ.] abnormally frequent or incorrect use of the letter *m*, or of the sound it represents.

myth, *n.* [LL. *mythos*; Gr. *mythos*, word, speech, story, legend.]

1. a traditional story of unknown authorship, ostensibly with a historical basis, but serving usually to explain some phenomenon of nature, the origin of man, or the customs, institutions, religious rites, etc. of a people: myths usually involve the exploits of gods and heroes.

2. such stories collectively; mythology.

3. any fictitious story.

4. any imaginary person or thing spoken of as though existing.

Syn.—fable, fiction, legend, falsehood.

mythe, *n.* myth. [Obs.]

myth′iç·ăl, myth′iç, *a.* 1. of, or having the nature of, a myth or myths.

2. existing only in a myth or myths; as, a *mythical* creature.

3. imaginary or fictitious.

myth′iç·ăl·ly, *adv.* in a mythical manner.

myth′i·cīze, *v.t.*; mythicized, *pt.*, *pp.*; mythi-

cizing *ppr.* to make into, or explain as, a myth.
myth'ō-, [from Gr. *mythos*, myth.] a combining form meaning *myth*, as in *mythology*.
myth·ō·ġen'e·sis, *n.* [Gr. *mythos*, myth, and *genesis*, production.] the invention or making of myths; the rise of myths.
my·thog'rȧ·phẽr, *n.* [Gr. *mythographos*; *mythos*, a legend, myth, and *graphein*, to write.] a maker or composer of myths.
my·thol'ō·ġẽr, myth·ō·lō'ġi·ăn, *n.* a mythologist.
myth·ō·loġ'iç·ăl, myth·ō·loġ'iç, *a.* of or relating to mythology or myths.
myth·ō·loġ'iç·ăl·ly, *adv.* in a mythological manner.
my·thol'ō·ġist, *n.* 1. an expert in mythology.
2. a writer or compiler of myths.
my·thol'ō·ġize, *v.t.* to mythicize.
my·thol'ō·ġīze, *v.i.*; mythologized, *pt., pp.*; mythologizing, *ppr.* 1. to invent or construct myths.
2. to relate, explain, classify, write about, or discourse on mythology or myths.
my·thol'ō·ġī·zẽr, *n.* one who or that which mythologizes.
myth'ō·logue (-log), *n.* an explanation according to mythology; a myth. [Rare.]
my·thol'ō·ġy, *n.*; *pl.* **my·thol'ō·ġieṣ,** [LL. *mythologia*; Gr. *mythologia*, a telling of tales or legends, legendary lore; *mythos*, myth, and *-logia*, from *legein*, to speak.]
1. the science or study of myths or legends; that branch of science which investigates the meaning of myths, and the relationship between the myths of different countries or peoples.

Parts of *mythology* are religious, parts of *mythology* are historical, parts of *mythology* are poetical, but *mythology* as a whole is neither religion nor history, nor philosophy, nor poetry. It comprehends all these together under that peculiar form of expression which is natural and intelligible at a certain stage, or at certain recurring stages in the development of thought and speech, but which, after becoming traditional, becomes frequently unnatural and unintelligible. —Max Müller.

2. a book of or about myths.
3. myths collectively; especially, all the myths about a specific being, or those myths, fables, or traditions interwoven with the history, origin, deities, etc. of a specific people.
myth·ō·mā'ni·ȧ, *n.* [Mod. L., from *mytho-* and *-mania.*] in psychiatry, an abnormal tendency to lie or exaggerate.
myth·ō·poe'iç, myth·ō·pē'iç, *a.* [from Gr. *mythopoios* (from *mythos*, myth, and *poiein*, to make); and *-ic.*] of, or engaged in, the making of myths.
myth″ō·pō·et'iç, *a.* mythopoeic.
mȳ'thus, *n.* [Mod. L.] same as *myth*.
myt·i·lā'ceăn (-shăn), *a.* of or relating to the mussel family.
myt·i·lā'ceăn (-shăn), *n.* one of the mussel family.
myt·i·lā'ceous, *a.* mytilacean.
myt'i·lid, *n.* a mussel; one of the *Mytilidæ*.
Mȳ·til'i·dae, *n.pl.* the mussels; a family of conchiferous mollusks having the shell oval and equivalve, edges closely fitting, ligament internal, and the hinge edentulous. The *Mytilidæ* are mostly marine, and attached by a byssus.
myt'i·loid, *a.* belonging to, characteristic of, or resembling the *Mytilidæ*.
myt'i·loid, *n.* one of the *Mytilidæ*.
myt″i·lō·tox'in, *n.* [*Mytilus* and *toxic* and *-in.*] a poisonous alkaloid, $C_6H_{15}NO_2$, obtained from mussels.
Myt'i·lus, *n.* [L., from Gr. *mytilos*, a sea mussel.] the typical genus of the family *Mytilidæ*.
myx-, same as *myxo-*.
myx'ȧ, *n.*; *pl.* **myx'ae,** [Gr. *myxa*, nostril, beak.] in ornithology, the end of the mandible of a bird. [Rare.]
myx·ȧ·moe'bȧ, *n.* [*myx-*, and Gr. *amœbē*, change.] a myxomycete in a certain stage of development.
myx″an·gō·ī'tis, *n.* [*myx-*, and Gr. *angeion*, vessel.] in pathology, mucous inflammation of vessels.
myx·as·thē'ni·ȧ, *n.* [*myx-*, and Gr. *astheneia*, weakness.] deficiency in the secretion of mucus.
myx·e·dē'mȧ, *n.* [*myxo-*, and Gr. *oidēma*, a swelling, tumor.] a disease caused by a decreased functioning of the thyroid gland and characterized by a drying and thickening of the skin and a slowing down of physical and mental activity: also spelled *myxoedema*.
Myx·ī'nē, *n.* [Mod. L.; Gr. *myxinos*, slime fish, from *myxa*, slime, mucus.] a genus of cyclostomous fishes having one external branchial aperture on each side of the abdomen, leading by six ducts to six branchial sacs; the hags.
myx'i·noid, *a.* of or resembling the genus *Myxine* or the family *Myxinidæ*, of which it is the type.
myx'i·noid, *n.* a myxinoid fish.
myx'ō-, [from Gr. *myxa*, mucus.] a combining form meaning *slime* or *mucus*, as in *myxomycete*: also, before a vowel, *myx-*.
myx″ō·çhon·drō'mȧ, *n.* [*myxo-* and *chondroma.*] myxoma blended with chondroma.
Myx″ō·cys·tō'dē·ȧ, *n.pl.* a division of infusorians including the *Noctiluca*.
myx·ō·dẽr'mi·ȧ, *n.* [*myxo-*, and Gr. *derma*, skin.] an acute disease marked by ecchymoses, softening of the skin, and contraction of certain muscles.
myx·oe·dē'mȧ, *n.* see *myxedema*.
myx″ō·fī·brō'mȧ, *n.* myxoma blended with fibroma.
myx″ō·glī·ō'mȧ, *n.* a glioma which has undergone myxomatous degeneration.
myx'oid, *a.* [*myx-*, and Gr. *eidos*, form.] resembling mucus.
myxoid cystoma; a proliferating cyst of the ovary: so called because its inner surface resembles a mucous membrane.
myx″ō·lip·ō'mȧ, *n.* myxoma blended with lipoma.
myx·ō'mȧ, *n.*; *pl.* **myx·ō'mȧ·tȧ,** [Gr. *myxa*, mucus, and *-oma.*] a soft tumor consisting of gelatinous tissue.
cystic myxoma; a form of myxoma containing cavities.
erectile myxoma; a form of myxoma containing an excess of vessels so as to resemble an angioma.
lipomatous myxoma; a myxoma which contains a deposit of fat within the cells.
vascular myxoma; a myxoma containing many blood vessels.
myx·om'ȧ·tous, *a.* of, resembling, or pertaining to a myxoma.
myx″ō·mȳ·cēte', *n.* [*myxo-* and *-mycete.*] any of a class of primitive organisms, the slime molds, consisting of masses of naked protoplasm and having some characteristics of both plants and animals, but generally classified as plants (fungi.)
Myx″ō·mȳ·cē'tēṣ, *n.pl.* the class containing the myxomycetes.
myx″ō·mȳ·cē'tous, *a.* of or relating to the *Myxomycetes*.
myx'ō·pod, *a.* myxopodous.
myx'ō·pod, *n.* one of the *Myxopoda*.
Myx·op'ō·dȧ, *n.pl.* same as *Rhizopoda*.
myx·ō·pō'di·um, *n.*; *pl.* **myx·ō·pō'di·ȧ,** the pseudopodium of a protozoan when capable of extension and retraction.
myx·op'ō·dous, *a.* of or pertaining to the *Myxopoda*.
myx″ō·sär·çō'mȧ, *n.* [*myxo-*, and Gr. *sarkōma*, a fleshy excrescence.] a sarcoma containing mucous elements.
myx″ō·sär·çom'ȧ·tous, *a.* of, pertaining to, or affected with myxosarcoma.
Myx·ō·spŏn'ġi·ae, *n.pl.* [*myxo-*, and Gr. *spongia*, a sponge.] a division of *Spongiæ*, containing sponges in which the skeleton is absent.
myx·ō·spŏn'ġi·ăn, *a.* of or pertaining to the *Myxospongiæ*.
myx·ō·spŏn'ġi·ăn, *n.* one of the *Myxospongiæ*.
myx·ō·thē'çȧ, *n.*; *pl.* **myx·ō·thē'cae,** [*myxo-*, and Gr. *thēkē*, a case.] in ornithology, the corneous sheath at the extremity of the lower mandible of a bird.
mȳ'zont, *a.* of or relating to the *Myzontes*.
mȳ'zont, *n.* one of the *Myzontes*.
Mȳ·zon'tēṣ, *n.pl.* a division of animals, the *Marsipobranchii*.
Mȳ·zō·stom'ȧ·tȧ, Mȳ·zō·stom'i·dȧ, *n.pl.* [Gr. *myzein*, to suck, and *stoma*, mouth.] a group of minute parasitic worms infesting some species of *Crinoidea* and forming galls on the arms of its host.
mȳ·zō·stom'ȧ·tous, mȳ·zos'tō·mous, *a.* of or pertaining to the *Myzostomata*.

N

N, n (en), *n.*; *pl.* **N's, n's, Ns, ns** (enz), 1. the fourteenth letter of the English alphabet: from the Greek *nu*, a borrowing from the Phoenician.
2. the sound of N or n.
3. a type or impression for N or n.
4. *a symbol for* the fourteenth (or the thirteenth if J is omitted) in a sequence or group.
5. in printing, an en (half an em).
N, n, *a.* 1. of N or n.
2. fourteenth (or thirteenth if J is omitted) in a sequence or group.
N, (en), *n.* 1. an object shaped like N.
2. a Roman numeral for 90: with a superior bar ($\overline{N}$), 90,000.
3. in chemistry, *the symbol for* nitrogen.
N, *a.* shaped like N.
n (en), *n.* 1. in mathematics, *the symbol for* an indefinite number.
2. in physics, *the symbol for* neutron.
nä, *adv.* 1. no. [Chiefly Scot.]
2. not: usually with auxiliary verbs, as, would*na*, din*na*, etc. [Chiefly Scot.]
Also *nae*.
nä, *conj.* nor. [Chiefly Scot.]
Na, *natrium*, [L.] in chemistry, sodium.
näam'bär, *n.* [Australian.] a large, valuable Australian tree, *Melaleuca styphelioides*.
nab, *n.* [compare Ice. *nabbi*, a knob, knoll.]
1. the summit of a mountain or rock. [Scot.]
2. the hammer of a gun. [Rare.]
3. the metal catch screwed to a doorjamb to receive the bolt of a lock.
nab, *v.t.*; nabbed, *pt., pp.*; nabbing, *ppr.* [compare Dan. *nappe*, Sw. *nappa*, to catch, seize.]
1. to snatch or seize suddenly. [Colloq.]
2. to arrest or catch (someone doing something wrong). [Colloq.]
Nab'ȧ·lus, *n.* a genus of perennial herbs of the composite family, including white lettuce and many other species.
nabk, *n.* [Ar. *nabiqa, nibqa.*] a thorny plant, *Zizyphus spina-christi*, growing in northern Africa and western Asia; Christ's-thorn.
nā'bob, *n.* [Hind. *navvāb*; Ar. *nuwwāb*, pl. of *nāib*, a deputy, viceroy.]
1. a native provincial deputy or governor of the old Mogul Empire in India; a native district ruler in India.
2. a European who has become rich in India.
3. a very rich man.
nā'bob·ish, *a.* of or like a nabob.

Nā'both, *n.* [Heb. *nābhōth.*] in the Bible, the owner of a vineyard: Jezebel had him killed so that Ahab could seize the vineyard: 1 Kings xxi.

nac'ȧ·rat, *n.* [Fr. *nacarat*; Sp. and Port. *nacarado*; from Sp. *nácar*, mother-of-pearl.]
1. a pale-red color, tinged with orange.
2. fine linen or crepe dyed this color.

nȧ·celle', *n.* [Fr.; LL. *navicella*, dim. of *navis*, ship.]
1. an enclosed part in an airplane, dirigible, or other aircraft, for housing the engine, cargo, etc. or sheltering passengers.
2. the basket or car suspended from a balloon.

nack'ẽr, *n.* same as *knacker*.

nā'cre (-kẽr), *n.* [Fr.; It. *nacchera*; Ar. *naqqārah*, small kettledrum.]
1. a shellfish yielding mother-of-pearl.
2. mother-of-pearl.

na·cré' (nä-krā'), *a.* [Fr.] having or like the iridescent effect of mother-of-pearl.

nā'cred (-kẽrd), *a.* 1. covered or lined with nacre.
2. nacreous.

nā'crē·ous, *a.* 1. having an iridescent luster like mother-of-pearl.
2. producing nacre.
3. of or like nacre.

nad'dẽr, an adder. [Obs.]

Nȧ-Dēne', *n.* a family of American Indian languages, including Athapascan, Tlingit, and Haida.

nā'dīr, *n.* [OFr. *nadir*; Ar. *nazīr*, in *nazīr assamt*, nadir, lit., opposite to the zenith; *nazīr*, opposite, and *as-samt*, the zenith.]
1. that point of the celestial sphere directly opposite to the zenith; the point directly beneath the observer.
2. figuratively, the lowest point; the time of greatest depression or dejection; as, the *nadir* of human progress.
nadir basin; a basin of mercury used as a horizontal reflector in determining the nadir.
nadir of the sun; the point of the zodiac opposite to that in which the sun is.

nad'ŏr·īte, *n.* [from Djebel-*Nador*, in Algeria.] chloride of lead and antimony, having a resinous luster ($PbClSbO_2$).

nāe (nā), *a.* and *adv.* 1. no. [Scot.]
2. not. [Scot.]
Also *na*.

nae'ni·ȧ, *n.* same as *nenia*.

nāe'thing, *n.* and *adv.* nothing. [Scot.]

naēve (nēv), *n.* [L. *nævus*, a mole, birthmark, blemish.] a nevus; a blemish. [Obs.]

nae'void, *a.* same as *nevoid*.

nae'vus, *n.*; *pl.* **nae'vī,** same as *nevus*.

nag, *n.* [ME. *nagge*; M.D. *negge, negghe*, a small horse.]
1. a small saddle horse; a pony; sometimes, any horse.
2. a mediocre or poor horse.

nag, *v.t.*; nagged, *pt., pp.*; nagging, *ppr.* [compare Sw. *nagga*, to nibble, Ice. *naga*, to gnaw.] to find fault with constantly; to scold continually; to be continually pestering with complaints or faultfinding.

nag, *v.i.* to scold or find fault continually.

nag, *n.* 1. the act of nagging.
2. a person who nags, particularly a woman. [Colloq].

nā'gȧ, *n.* same as *naja*.

nȧ·gä'nȧ, *n.* [from Zulu *u(lu)-nakane*.] an infectious disease affecting horses and cattle in South Africa: it is caused by the bite of infected tsetse flies.

nä'gel·flüh, *n.* [G., from *nagel*, a nail, and *fluh*, rock.] in geology, a conglomerate of the Molasse in Switzerland, having granite pebbles studding it like nailheads, and containing terrestrial plants, fluviatile shells, and the bones of extinct land animals.

nag'gẽr, *n.* one who nags.

nag'ging, *a.* persistently annoying; faultfinding; as, a *nagging* neighbor.

nag'gy, *a.*; *comp.* naggier; *superl.* naggiest; contentious; irritable; inclined to nag or scold.

nag'gy, *n.*; *pl.* **nag'gieṣ,** a little nag.

nag·kas'săr, *n.* [Anglo-Ind.] either of two East Indian trees of the gamboge family, or the fragrant flower buds of these trees, used in making perfume and in dyeing silk orange and yellow.

nā'gọr, *n.* [African.] an antelope, *Cervicapra redunca*, of western Africa.

nag'yag·īte, *n.* [from *Nagyag*, Transylvania, where it was first found.] a rare mineral of gray color and metallic luster.

näh'lẹh, *n.* [Ar.] the date palm, *Phœnix dactylifera*.

Nä'huä (-wä), *n.* a member of the various North and Central American Indian tribes of the Nahuatl linguistic group, including the Aztecs, Toltecs, etc.

Nä·huä'tl (-wä'), *n.* a group of languages of the Uto-Aztecan family, spoken by various tribes of North and Central American Indians.

Nä·huä'tl, *a.* Nahuatlan.

Nä·huä'tlăn (-wät'lăn), *a.* of the Nahuatl group of languages.

Nä·huä'tlăn, *n.* Nahuatl.

Nā'hum, *n.* [Heb. *naḥūm*, lit., comfort.]
1. in the Bible, a Hebrew prophet of the 7th century B.C.
2. a book of the Old Testament containing his prophecies.

nāi'ad, *n.*; *pl.* **nāi'adṣ, nāi'ȧ·dēṣ,** [Gr. *Naïas* (pl. *Naïades*), a water nymph, from *naein*, to flow.]
1. in Greek and Roman mythology, a water nymph; a female deity who presides over springs and streams.
2. a girl or woman swimmer.
3. a plant of the genus *Naias* or of the family *Naiadaceæ*.
4. [N–] in zoology, (a) a species of bivalve; (b) a species of butterfly.

Nāi·ȧ·dā'cē·ae, *n.pl.* a family of spadiceous monocotyledonous aquatic plants; the pondweed family.

Nāi'ȧ·dēṣ, *n.pl.* [Gr. *Naïas* (pl. *Naïades*, water nymphs).]
1. [n–] water nymphs; naiads.
2. a family of fresh-water bivalves.
3. in botany, same as *Naiadaceæ*.

nāi'ănt, *a.* in heraldry, same as *natant*.

Nāi'as, *n.* [Gr. *Naïas*, a water nymph.] in botany, a widely distributed genus of delicate plants of the pondweed family, growing under water.

nā'id, *n.* [Gr. *Naïs*, or *Naïas* (-ados), a water nymph.] a fresh-water worm of the family *Naididæ*.

Nā·id'i·dae, *n.pl.* a family of fresh-water worms represented by the genus *Nais*.

na·if', na·ïf' (nä-ēf'), *a.* [Fr.] same as *naive*.

nā'ik, *n.* [Anglo-Ind.] in India, a sepoy corporal, ranking below a havildar, or sergeant.

nāil, *n.* [ME. *naile, nayle*; AS. *nægel*, a nail.]
1. the thin, horny plate at the ends of the fingers and toes of man, monkeys, etc.; the claw of a bird or animal.
2. a tapered piece of metal or wood, commonly pointed and having a flattened head, driven with a hammer, and used for holding pieces of wood together, as a peg, or for decoration.

A B C D E F G
NAILS
A, cut flooring; B, common wire; C, flooring; D, finishing; E, horseshoe; F, hinge (with countersunk head); G, boat

3. an old cloth measure, equal to $2^1/_4$ inches.
4. a cigarette; short for *coffin nail*. [Slang.]
on the nail; (a) immediately; (b) at the exact spot or time. [Colloq.]
to hit the nail on the head; to do or say whatever is exactly right.

nāil, *v.t.*; nailed, *pt., pp.*; nailing, *ppr.* [ME. *nailen, naylen*; AS. *næglian*, to nail, from *nægel*, a nail.]
1. to attach or fasten together or onto something else with nails.
2. to fasten as if with nails; as, he *nailed* a tent flap to the ground with a bayonet.
3. to secure, hold, or fasten shut with nails.
4. to secure; to make sure; as, he *nailed* the bargain.
5. to fix (the eyes, attention, etc.) steadily on an object.
6. to discover or expose, as a lie.
7. to catch, capture, or seize. [Colloq.]
8. to intercept and detain; as, *nail* him before he leaves. [Colloq.]
9. to stop (the vent of a cannon); to spike. [Obs.]
to nail up; (a) to fasten to a wall or at some height; (b) to fasten tightly with nails, as a door no longer used.

nāil bōne, in anatomy, either of two bones; specifically, (a) the os unguis: so called from its resemblance to the thumbnail; (b) the terminal bone of a digit.

nāil'brush, *n.* a small, stiff brush for cleaning the fingernails.

nāil çlinch'ẽr, a blacksmith's tool for clinching the point end of a nail, or what remains of it, against the hoof.

nāil'ẽr, *n.* 1. one whose occupation is making nails.
2. one who nails.

nāil'ẽr·y, *n.*; *pl.* **nāil'ẽr·ieṣ,** a place where nails are made.

nāil fīle, a small file for trimming the fingernails.

nāil'head (-hed), *n.* 1. the head of a nail.
2. in architecture, a projecting ornament resembling the head of a nail.

nāil'-head″ed, *a.* 1. having a head or part similar to a nailhead.
2. ornamented with marks or projections resembling nailheads.
nail-headed molding; a kind of molding common in Norman architecture, made up of a series of projections resembling nailheads.

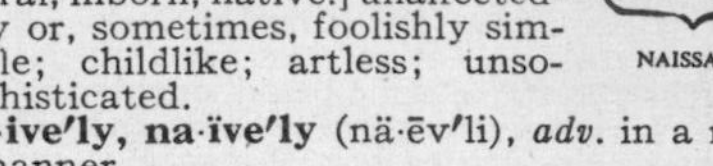
NAIL-HEADED MOLDING

nāil māk'ẽr, one who makes nails.

nāil sciṣ'ṣŏrṣ, short, pointed, curved scissors for trimming the fingernails.

nāil'set, *n.* a tool for sinking the head of a nail so that it is level with, or below, the surface of the wood: also written *nail set*.

nāil'wŏrt, *n.* 1. any plant of the genus *Paronychia*.
2. the *Draba verna*, a whitlow grass.
3. *Saxifraga tridactylites*.

nāin'sọok, *n.* [Hind. *nainsukh*, Indian muslin.] a thin, plain-woven, lightweight cotton, sometimes striped.

Nā'is *n.* 1. a genus of worms typical of the family *Naididæ*.
2. [n–] a worm of the genus *Nais*.

nāis'sănt, *a.* [Fr., from L. *nascens* (-entis), being born, ppr. of *nasci*, to be born.] in heraldry, rising or coming forth from the middle of a fesse or other ordinary.

NAISSANT

na·ive', na·ïve' (nä-ēv'), *a.* [Fr., f. of *naïf*, from L. *nativus*, natural, inborn, native.] unaffectedly or, sometimes, foolishly simple; childlike; artless; unsophisticated.

na·ive'ly, na·ïve'ly (nä-ēv'li), *adv.* in a naive manner.

na·ive·té', na·ïve·te' (nä-ēv-tā'), *n.* [Fr. *naïveté*, from LL. *nativitas*, naturalness, nativeness.]
1. the quality or state of being naive; simplicity; artlessness.
2. a naive action or remark.

na·ive'ty (nä-ēv'ti), *n.*; *pl.* **na·ive'tieṣ,** naïveté.

Nā'jȧ, *n.* [Hind. *nāg*, a snake.]
1. the typical genus of serpents of the family *Najidæ*.
2. [n–] a serpent of the genus *Naja*.

Naj'i·dae, *n.pl.* [*Naja* and *-idæ*.] a family of poisonous serpents including the cobra and the asp.

nak, *n.* [perh. from Hind. *nāk*, nose.] in botany, that part of the mango fruit which receives the pollen grains; the stigmatic point of the mango.

nā'ked, *a.* [ME. *naked*; AS. *nacod*, naked.]
1. (a) completely unclothed; bare; nude; (b) uncovered; exposed: said of parts of the body.
2. lacking clothing, means of support, etc.; destitute.
3. without protection or defense.
4. without conventional or usual covering; specifically, (a) out of its sheath; as, a *naked* sword; (b) without leaves, grass, vegetation, etc.; (c) without furnishing, decoration, etc.; as, a *naked* wall.
5. without additions, ornaments, disguises, or embellishments; plain; stark; as, the *naked* truth.
6. in law, without objective support; lacking a necessary condition; invalid; as, a *naked* contract.
7. in zoology, without hair, scales, feathers, shell, etc.
8. in botany, lacking the customary covering, as a stem or a seed.
9. in music, lacking the full complement of tones: said as of a chord of only two notes.
10. in prosody, beginning or ending a word: said of a vowel.
naked bulb; in botany, a bulb, made up of scales, as that of the lily.

naked eye; the eye unaided by any optical device.
naked flooring; in carpentry, the timberwork which supports a floor.
naked fourth; in music, the interval of a fourth without any other interval.
naked lady; a plant of the lily family, *Colchicum autumnale*: also called *meadow saffron* and *crocus*.
naked mollusk; a mollusk without a shell; a nudibranch.
naked truth; truth without concealment, evasion, or prevarication.
stark naked; absolutely naked.

nā'ked·ly, *adv.* openly; in a naked or unconcealed manner.

nā'ked·ness, *n.* 1. nudity; the condition of being open or uncovered.
2. the private parts of the body; the genitals. [Archaic.]

nā'ked·wood, *n.* either of two subtropical American trees, having firm heartwood that takes a fine polish; *Colubrina reclinata* or *Eugenia dichotoma.*

nal·ọr'phïne, *n.* [from *N-al*lylnor*morphine*.] a white crystalline powder, $C_{19}H_{21}NO_3$, a derivative of morphine used in the form of its hydrochloride to counteract the effects of narcotic overdosage and to aid in diagnosing narcotic addiction.

nal'ox·ōne, *n.* [from *N-al*lylnor*ox*ymorph*one*.] a nonaddictive, synthetic drug used to counteract the effects of narcotic overdosage.

Nä'mä, *n.* [from native name.]
1. the chief tribe of the Hottentots.
2. a Hottentot.
3. the language of the Hottentots: it belongs to the Hottentot-Bushman family and is characterized by the use of initial click sounds and three speech tones.

nām'ȧ·ble, *a.* 1. that can be named.
2. worthy of being mentioned; notable.
Also spelled *nameable.*

nam'āy·çush, *n.* [N. Am. Ind.] the lake trout, *Salvelinus namaycush*, of the Great Lakes: also called *Mackinaw trout.*

nä·mäz', *n.* [Turk.] the principal prayer of the Moslems, recited five times each day.

nam'by-pam'by, *a.* silly; affectedly pretty; weakly sentimental; insipid; vapid; as, *namby-pamby* rhymes.

nam'by-pam'by, *n.* 1. silly or weakly sentimental talk or writing.

Another of Addison's favorite companions was Ambrose Phillips, a good Whig and a middling poet, who had the honor of bringing into fashion a species of composition which has been called after his name, *Namby-Pamby.* —Macaulay.

2. *pl.* **nam'by-pam'bieṣ,** a namby-pamby person.

nāme, *n.* [ME. *name, nome*; AS. *nama.*]
1. a word or phrase by which a person, thing, or class of things is known, called, or spoken to or of; an appellation; a title.
2. a word or words expressing some quality considered characteristic or descriptive of a person or thing; an epithet; as, they called him *names.*
3. (a) fame, reputation, or character; as, a good *name*; (b) good reputation.
4. a family or clan; as, the last of my *name.*
5. reputation or appearance only, not reality; semblance; as, chief in *name* only.
6. a distinguished or noted person; as, the greatest *name* in science.
7. in logic, a designation for a concept; a term.
in the name of; (a) in appeal or reference to; (b) by the authority of; as the representative of; (c) as belonging to.
proper name; in grammar, the name of a particular person, place, or thing.
to call names; to mention in an abusive manner; to swear at.
to know only by name; to be familiar with the name of but not know personally.
to name names; to identify specific persons, especially as doing wrong.
to one's name; belonging to one; owned by one.
to take a name in vain; to use a name, especially that of the Deity, in a profane or flippant manner.
Syn.—appellation, designation, title, epithet, denomination, cognomen.

nāme, *a.* having a good reputation; well-known.

nāme, *v.t.*; named, *pt., pp.*; naming, *ppr.* 1. to give a name or title to; to entitle; to style.
2. to designate, mention, or refer to (a person or object) by name.
3. to identify by the right name; as, he *named* the State of the Union.
4. to nominate or appoint (a person) to a post, situation, or office.
5. to set or fix; to specify (a date, price, etc.).
6. to speak about; to mention.
Syn.—denominate, style, term, call, mention, specify, designate, nominate.

nāme'ȧ·ble, *a.* same as *namable.*

nāme'-çall·ing, *n.* the use of disparaging or abusive names in attacking another.

nāme dāy, 1. the day observed in honor of the saint for whom one is named.
2. day of baptism.

nāme'drop·pẽr, *n.* a person who seeks to impress others by frequently mentioning famous or important persons in a familiar way.

nāme'less, *a.* 1. not having a name.
2. left unnamed; anonymous; as, a rogue who shall be *nameless.*
3. not publicly known; obscure.
4. lacking a legal name; illegitimate.
5. that cannot be named; indescribable; as, *nameless* dread.
6. unfit for mention; as, *nameless* practices.

nāme'less·ly, *adv.* in a nameless manner.

nāme'less·ness, *n.* the state of being nameless, or without a name; the state of being undistinguished.

nāme'ly, *adv.* 1. to wit; that is to say.
2. especially; particularly. [Obs.]

nāme plāte, a plate of metal, glass, etc., bearing a person's name, such as is often placed on or near the door of a dwelling or place of business.

nām'ẽr, *n.* one who names or calls by name.

nāme'sāke, *n.* one who has the same name as another; one named after another for that other's sake.

nam'mad, *n.* see *numud.*

nan, *interj.* anan. [Obs.]

nan'dine, *n.* a carnivorous African animal, *Nandina binotata*, having a double row of black spots on its sides.

nan'dụ, nan'dōu, *n.* [S. Am.] the South American ostrich, *Rhea americana.*

nā'niṣm, *n.* [L. *nanus*; Gr. *nanos*, a dwarf, and *-ism.*] the state of being dwarfish.

nā·ni·zā'tion, *n.* the act or process of dwarfing artificially, as used on trees by Japanese.

nan·keen', nan·kīn', *n.* [from *Nankin*, a city in China, where it was first made.]
1. a buff-colored durable cotton cloth, originally from China.
2. buff (color).
3. [*pl.*] trousers made of this cloth.
nankeen porcelain; a kind of Chinese porcelain decorated in blue.

nan·keen' bīrd, the night heron of Australia.

nan·keen' hawk, the nankeen kestrel.

nan·keen' kes'trel, the Australian kestrel, *Pinnunculus cenchroides.*

nan'ny, *n.*; *pl.* **nan'nieṣ,** [from *Nan*, dim. of *Anna.*] a child's nurse. [Brit.]

nan'ny·ber″ry, *n.* the sheepberry.

nan'ny gōat, a female goat. [Colloq.]

nā'noid, *a.* [Gr. *nanos*, a dwarf, and *eidos*, form.] dwarfed; stunted.

nā·nō·sō'mi·ȧ, *n.* [Gr. *nanos*, a dwarf, and *sōma*, body.] the condition of being dwarfed.

Nan'sen bot'tle, [named after F. *Nansen*, Norw. arctic explorer.] an oceanographic instrument used to obtain water samples and temperature readings at various depths in the seas.

nan'tō·kīte, *n.* [from *Nantoco*, Chile, where it is found.] a white chloride of copper.

Nā·ō'mi, *n.* in the Bible, the mother-in-law of Ruth: Ruth i.

nā'os, *n.* [Gr. *naos*, a temple, sanctuary, lit., a dwelling, from *naein*, to dwell.]
1. a temple.
2. the inner part of a temple; a cella.

nap, *v.i.*; napped (napt), *pt., pp.*; napping, *ppr.* [ME. *nappen*; AS. *hnappian, hnæppian*, to slumber, take a nap.]
1. to have a short sleep; to be drowsy.
2. to be off one's guard.

nap, *n.* a brief, light sleep; a doze.

nap, *n.* [ME. *noppe*; AS. *hnoppa*, nap of cloth.]
1. the downy or hairy surface of cloth formed by short hairs or fibers, especially when artificially raised by brushing, etc.; pile of velvet, etc.
2. any downy surface, as on some plants.

nap, *v.t.* 1. to raise or put a nap on.
2. to smooth or trim (cloth) by shearing the nap or pile.

nap, *n.* [abbrev. of *napoleon.*] same as *napoleon*, senses 1 and 2.

nā'päl̄m, *n.* [from *na*phthenic and *palm*itic acids, whose aluminum salts are used in its manufacture.] jellied gasoline used in flamethrowers and incendiary bombs.

nāpe, *n.* [ME. *naape.*] the back of the neck.

nāpe'çrest, *n.* a plantain eater, a bird of the genus *Schizornis*, of South and West Africa.

nā'pẽr·y, *n.* [OFr. *naperie*, from *nappe*, a cloth, tablecloth.] linen for the table; linen cloth in general.

nā'phew (-fū), *n.* same as *navew.*

Naph'tȧ·lī, *n.* in the Bible, (a) a son of Jacob: Gen. xxx. 7, 8; (b) that one of the twelve tribes of Israel which was named after him: Numb. i. 15, 43.

naph'thȧ (*or* nap'), *n.* [L. *naphtha*; Gr. *naphtha*, naphtha, bitumen.]
1. an inflammable, volatile, oily liquid produced by the fractional distillation of petroleum: it is the fraction that boils at 80°–110° C. and is used as a fuel, solvent, and illuminant.
2. petroleum.
3. any of several inflammable, volatile liquids produced by the distillation of coal tar, wood, coal, and other carbonaceous materials.

naph'thȧ·lāte, *n.* a salt or ester of naphthalic acid.

naph'thȧ·lēne, *n.* [*naphtha*, and *al*cohol, and *ene.*] a white crystalline, aromatic hydrocarbon, $C_{10}H_8$, produced in the fractional distillation of coal tar: it is used in moth repellents and in the manufacture of certain dyes and other organic compounds: also *naphthalin, naphthaline.*

naph·thȧ·len'iç, *a.* obtained from or relating to naphthalene; as, *naphthalenic* acid, a yellowish crystalline derivative of naphthol.

naph·thal'iç, *a.* of, like, or obtained from naphthalene.
naphthalic acid; (a) a crystalline compound obtained from naphthalene; (b) phthalic acid.

naph·thal'i·dïne, naph·thal'i·din, *n.* same as *naphthylamine.*

naph'thȧ·lin, naph'thȧ·līne, *n.* same as *naphthalene.*

naph'thȧ·līze, *v.t.*; naphthalized, *pt., pp.*; naphthalizing, *ppr.* to mix, charge, or impregnate with naphtha.

naph'thēne, *n.* one of a series of hydrocarbons occurring in certain kinds of petroleum.

naph·thō'iç, *a.* related to or derived from naphthalene: applied to a series of acids.

naph'thōl (*or* -thol), *n.* [*naphth*alene and *-ol.*] either of two white, crystalline isomeric compounds, $C_{10}H_7OH$, derived from naphthalene and used as antiseptics and in the manufacture of dyes.

naph'thous, *a.* of or like naphtha.

naph'thyl, *n.* [*naphtha* and *-yl.*] the monatomic radical of naphthylamine.

naph″thyl·ȧ·mïne', naph·thyl·am'in, *n.* a basic crystalline compound derived from nitronaphthalene and serving as a source of several dyes.

Nȧ·piē'ri·ȧn, Nȧ·pē'ri·ȧn, *a.* of, pertaining to, or named for John Napier, the Scottish mathematician; as, *Napierian* logarithms.

Nā'piẽr'ṣ bōneṣ, a device invented by John Napier, consisting of a set of square rods of bone, ivory, or the like, numbered as in the illustration, and used in multiplication and division: also called *Napier's rods.*

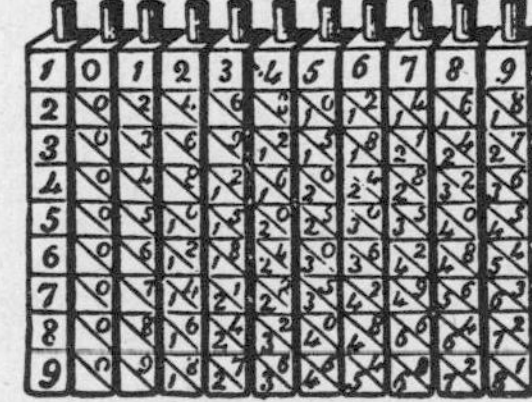

NAPIER'S BONES OR RODS

nā'pi·fọrm, *a.* [L. *napus*, a turnip, and *forma*, form.] having the shape of a turnip, large in the upper part and tapering below: said of roots.

nap'kin, *n.* [ME. *nap(p)ekyn(n)*, dim. (via M.D.), from OFr. *nap(p)e*, cloth, tablecloth, from L. *mappa*, cloth, napkin.]
1. a small piece of cloth or paper, usually square, used at table for protecting the

clothes and wiping the fingers or lips; serviette.
2. a small towel.
3. a baby's diaper. [Chiefly Brit.]
4. same as *sanitary napkin*.
5. a pocket handkerchief. [Obs. exc. Scot.]

nap'kin ring, a ring for holding a rolled-up napkin in a table setting.

nap'less, *a.* without nap; threadbare.

nȧ·pō'lē·ŏn, *n.* [Fr.] 1. a former gold coin of France, equivalent to 20 francs, with a portrait of Napoleon I (or III) on it.
2. (a) a card game; (b) a bid in this game by which a player agrees to take all five tricks. Often shortened to *nap*.
3. a kind of French pastry made of three or more layers of puff paste, usually oblong, filled with custard or cream.

Nȧ·pō·lē·on'iç, *a.* of, pertaining to, or characteristic of Napoleon I, his campaigns, period, etc.

Nȧ·pō·lē·on'iç Cōde, same as *Code Napoléon* under *code*.

Nȧ·pō'lē·ŏn·iṣm, *n.* Bonapartism.

Nȧ·pō'lē·ŏn·ist, *n.* a Bonapartist.

nappe (nap), *n.* [Fr. *nappe*, a cloth, sheet.] the whole or a continuous part of a conic surface, as of a hyperboloid of revolution.

nap'pẽr, *n.* a person who naps or is in the habit of taking naps.

nap'pẽr, *n.* an instrument or machine for putting a nap on cloth.

nap'pi·ness, *n.* the quality of having a nap.

nap'ping, *n.* a sheet of fur which becomes the nap when united to the body of a hat.

nap'py, nap'pie, *n.*; *pl.* **nap'pieṣ,** [prob. dim. of ME. *hnap*, *nap*, a bowl; AS. *hnæp(p)*.] a shallow, flat-bottomed, rounded dish with sloping sides, used for serving or cooking food.

nap'py, *a.* having or covered with nap; hairy or downy.

nap'py, *a.* [prob. from *nappy* (hairy, downy).]
1. foaming; heady; strong: said of ale.
2. slightly intoxicated.

nap'py, *n.* ale. [Scot.]

na'prȧ·path, *n.* a person who practices naprapathy.

nȧ·prap'ȧ·thy, *n.* [from Czech *naprava*, correction; and *-pathy*.] a system of treatment based on the theory that disease symptoms are due to strained or contracted ligaments and disorders of the connective tissue and can be cured by massage.

nä'pu, *n.* [native name.] the Javan deerlet, *Tragulus javanicus*.

närç, *n.* a local or federal police agent charged with enforcing the laws restricting the use of narcotics, hallucinogens, etc.: also *narco* (när'kō), *nark*. [Slang.]

när'cē·ine, *n.* [Fr. *narceine*, from Gr. *narke*, numbness, stupor; and *-ine*.] a bitter, white, crystalline alkaloid, $C_{22}H_{27}O_8N$, obtained from opium: it is a narcotic.

när'ciṣm, *n.* same as *narcissism*.

När·cis'sȧn, När·cis'sine, *a.* pertaining to or characteristic of Narcissus.

när·cis'siṣm, *n.* [G. *Narzissismus*; see *Narcissus* and *-ism*.]
1. self-love; excessive interest in one's own appearance, comfort, importance, etc.
2. in psychoanalysis, arrest at or regression to the first stage of sexual development, in which the self is an object of sexual pleasure.

när·cis'sist, *n.* one who is characterized by narcissism.

när″cis·sis'tiç, *a.* pertaining to or characteristic of narcissism or a narcissist.

När·cis'sus, *n.* [L., from Gr. *narkissos*, narcissus, so called from its narcotic properties, from *narkē*, numbness, stupor.]
1. in Greek mythology, a beautiful youth for unrequited love of whom Echo died: Nemesis in punishment caused him to pine away for love of his own reflection in a spring and changed him into the narcissus.
2. in botany, a genus of plants of several species, with smooth leaves and white, yellow, or orange flowers, including the daffodils, jonquils, etc.
3. [n–] *pl.* **när·cis'sus·eṣ, när·cis'sī,** a plant of this genus.

när'cist, *n.* same as *narcissist*.

när'cō·lep·sy, *n.* [from Gr. *narkē*, stupor; and *-lepsy*.] a condition of frequent and uncontrollable desire for sleep; paroxysmal sleep.

när·cō·lep'tiç, *a.* of or having narcolepsy.

när·çō'mȧ, *n.* [Gr. *narkē*, numbness, stupor, and *-oma*.] coma produced by narcotics.

när·cō·mā'ni·ȧ, *n.* [Mod. L., from Gr. *narkē*, stupor; and *-mania*.]
1. an abnormal craving to gain relief from pain through the use of drugs.
2. mental derangement resulting from the excessive use of alcohol.

när'çōse, *a.* [Gr. *narkē*, numbness, stupor, and *-ose*.] in a stuporous condition.

när·çō'sis, *n.* [Mod. L.; Gr. *narkōsis*, a benumbing, from *narkoun*, to benumb.] a condition of deep unconsciousness caused by a narcotic.

när·çō·syn'thē·sis, *n.* [from Gr. *narkē*, stupor; and *synthesis*.] a method of treating a neurosis by working with a patient while he is under the influence of a narcotic, as pentothal sodium.

när·çot'iç, när·çot'iç·ăl, *a.* [ME. *narcotike*; OFr. *narcotique*; Gr. *narkōtikos*, from *narkoun*, to benumb, from *narkē*, numbness, stupor.]
1. of, like, or capable of producing narcosis.
2. for treating narcotism.
3. of, by, or for narcotic addicts.

när·çot'iç, *n.* 1. any drug that induces profound sleep, lethargy, and relief of pain: it is usually an opiate.
2. a person addicted to narcotics.
3. anything that causes drowsiness, lethargy, etc.

när·çot'iç·ăl, *a.* narcotic.

när·çot'iç·ăl·ly, *adv.* in the manner of a narcotic.

när·çot'iç·ăl·ness, när·çot'iç·ness, *n.* the quality of being narcotic.

när'çō·tine, när'çō·tin, *n.* a white crystalline alkaloid extracted from opium.

när·çō·tin'iç, *a.* pertaining to narcotine.

när'çō·tiṣm, *n.* 1. the condition induced by a narcotic; narcosis.
2. a method or influence producing narcosis.
3. addiction to narcotics.

när″çō·ti·zā'tion, *n.* a narcotizing or being narcotized.

när'çō·tīze, *v.t.*; narcotized, *pt.*, *pp.*; narcotizing, *ppr.* [*narcotic* and *-ize*.] to subject to a narcotic; to stupefy; to produce narcotism in.

närd, *n.* [ME. and OFr. *narde*; L. *nardus*; Gr. *nardos*, from Per. *nard*, nard.]
1. any of several plants with heart-shaped leaves, small greenish-white flowers, and reddish berries; spikenard.
2. an ointment made from the roots of these plants.
3. a moor grass, *Nardus stricta*.
4. any of numerous species of valerian.

närd'ine, *a.* pertaining to or like nard.

när·dọọ', *n.* [Australian.] an aquatic plant, *Marsilea drummondii*, the spores and spore cases of which are made into bread by the Australian aborigines.

nāre, *n.* [L. *naris*, nostril.] a nostril. [Obs.]

nā'reṣ, *n.pl.*; *sing.* **nā'ris,** [L.] the nasal passages; especially, the nostrils.

när'ghi·lē (-gi-), *n.* [Turk. and Per. *nārgīleh*, from Per. *nargīl*, coconut tree: so called because originally made of coconut shell.] an Oriental pipe with a long, flexible tube so arranged that it draws the smoke through water in a vase or bowl and cools it; hookah: also spelled *nargile*, *nargileh*.

nā'ri·ăl, *a.* [L. *naris*, a nostril, and *-al*.] pertaining to the nares.

nar'i·çȧ, *n.* the Mexican coati.

nar'i·çorn, *n.* [L. *naris*, nostril, and *cornu*, horn.] the covering of horn over the nostrils of some birds; a rhinotheca.

nar'i·form, *a.* [L. *naris*, a nostril, and *forma*, form.] formed like a nostril.

nā'ris, *n.* sing. of *nares*.

närk, *n.* [from Gypsy *nāk*, a nose.] an informer; a stool pigeon. [Brit. Slang.]

närk, *v.i.* to act as a nark; to inform. [Brit. Slang.]

närk, *n.* same as *narc*. [Slang.]

Nar·rȧ·gan'sett, *n.*; *pl.* **Nar·rȧ·gan'sett, Nar·rȧ·gan'setts,** a member of an extinct American Indian tribe formerly living near Narragansett Bay.

när·rän'tẹ, *adv.* [It.] in music, in the style of a narrative.

nar'ras, [S. Afr. *narras*, and E. *plant*.] a bush of South Africa bearing edible fruit resembling a melon.

nar·rāte' (*or* nar'āt), *v.t.* and *v.i.*; narrated, *pt.*, *pp.*; narrating, *ppr.* [L. *narratus*, pp. of *narrare*, to relate, make known.]
1. to tell (a story) in writing or speech.
2. to give an account of (happenings, etc.).

nar·rā'tion, *n.* [L. *narratio* (*-onis*), from *narrare*, to relate, make known.]
1. the act or process of narrating; the telling of a story, or the giving of an account of happenings, etc., in writing or speech.
2. a story or account; narrative.
3. writing or speaking that narrates, as history, biography, and fiction: conventionally distinguished from *argumentation*, *description*, *exposition*.

nar'rȧ·tive, *a.* [L. *narrativus*, suitable for relation, from *narrare*, to relate, make known.]
1. of, or having the nature of, narration; in story form.
2. occupied or concerned with narration; as, a *narrative* poet.

nar'rȧ·tive, *n.* 1. a story; account; tale.
2. the art or practice of relating stories or accounts; narration.

nar'rȧ·tive·ly, *adv.* by way of narration.

nar·rā'tŏr, nar·rāt'ẽr (*now often* nar'ā·tẽr), *n.* [L., from *narratus*, pp. of *narrare*, to tell.]
1. a person who relates a story or account.
2. person who reads descriptive or narrative passages between the speeches or scenes of a play, radio show, etc.

nar'rȧ·tō·ry, *a.* giving an account of events.

nar'rōw, *a.*; *comp.* narrower; *superl.* narrowest, [ME. *narow*, *narewe*, *naru*; AS. *nearu*, narrow.]
1. of little breadth; not wide or broad; having relatively little distance from side to side; as, a *narrow* street; a *narrow* hem or border.
2. limited in meaning, size, amount, extent; as, a *narrow* space; a *narrow* compass of time.
3. limited as to means; with hardly enough to live on; as, a *narrow* fortune.
4. limited in outlook; without breadth of view or generosity; not liberal; prejudiced.
5. close; careful; minute; thorough; as, a *narrow* inspection.
6. with limited margin; with barely enough space, time, etc.; barely successful; as, a *narrow* escape.
7. covetous; not liberal or bountiful; avaricious; niggardly; as, a *narrow* heart. [Now Dial.]
8. in phonetics, tense: said of the tongue.

Syn.—close, limited, scanty, restricted, cramped.

nar'rōw, *v.i.* 1. to become less broad; to contract in breadth.
2. in horsemanship, not to take ground enough or bear out sufficiently: said of a horse.
3. in knitting, to make an article narrower by reducing the number of stitches.

nar'rōw, *v.t.* to decrease or limit (something) in width, extent, or scope; restrict; as, he *narrowed* the argument.

nar'rōw, *n.* 1. a narrow part or place; especially, a narrow part of a valley, mountain pass, road, etc.
2. [*usually pl.*] a narrow passage, as between two bodies of water; a strait.

nar'rōw·ẽr, *n.* one who or that which narrows.

nar'rōw-gāuġe' (-gāj'), *a.* 1. for or having a narrow gauge.
2. narrow-minded. [Colloq.]

nar'rōw gāuġe, 1. a width (between the rails) of less than $56^{1}/_{2}$ inches (standard gauge).
2. a railroad having such a gauge.
3. a locomotive or car for such a railroad.

nar'rōw·ing, *n.* 1. the act of one who or that which narrows or contracts.
2. the part, as of a stocking, which is narrowed.

nar'rōw·ly, *adv.* 1. with little breadth.
2. contractedly; without much extent.
3. closely; accurately; with minute scrutiny.
4. by a small distance; only just; barely; with scant margin; as, he *narrowly* escaped.

nar'row-mīnd″ed, *a.* illiberal; limited in outlook; bigoted; prejudiced.

nar'row-mīnd″ed·ness, *n.* illiberality; bigotry.

nar'rōw·ness, *n.* the state or quality of being narrow.

nar'rōw pen'nănt, a strip of long, narrow bunting flown at the masthead of a government-commissioned vessel.

nar'rōw sēaṣ, the Irish Sea and the English Channel: so called because they are arms or straits of the ocean proper.

nar'rōw·souled (-sōld), *a.* of petty, ungenerous spirit; stingy.

nar'sin·gä, *n.* a curved trumpet made of metal, used in India.

närt, art not. [Obs.]

när′thex, *n.* [L. *narthex*; Gr. *narthēx*, a tall, umbelliferous plant.]
1. (a) in ancient Christian churches, a porch at the west end for penitents and others not admitted to the church itself; (b) later, a vestibule within the church, for the same purpose.
2. any church vestibule leading to the nave.
3. [N–] a former genus of plants now classed with *Ferula*.

när′wăl, *n.* same as *narwhal*.

när′we, *a.* narrow. [Obs.]

när′whăl (-wăl *or* -hwăl), *n.* [Sw. and Dan. *narhval*, Ice. *nāhvalr*, a narwhal; *nār*, a corpse, and *hvalr*, whale: so called in allusion to its pale skin.] the *Monodon monoceros*, a cetaceous mammal found in the northern seas, averaging from 12 to 20 feet in length. It has no teeth except two canines in the upper jaw, which are sometimes developed into projecting tusks, although usually only the one on

NARWHAL
(*Monodon monoceros*)

the left side is so developed, being straight, spiral, tapering to a point, and from 6 to 10 feet in length. It is valued for its ivory and oil. From the frequency with which the male of the narwhal appears as having a single horn it has been called *sea unicorn*, *unicorn fish*, *unicorn whale*.

när′whāle (-hwāl), *n.* same as *narwhal*.

nâr′y, *a.* [altered from *ne'er a*, never a.] not any; no (with *a* or *an*); as, *nary a* doubt. [Dial. and Colloq.]

naș, has not. [Obs.]

nā′șăl, *a.* [Mod. L. *nasalis*, from L. *nasus*, a nose.]
1. of the nose.
2. produced by stopping all or part of the breath in the mouth and permitting it to pass through the nose, as the sounds of *m*, *n*, *ng*, and the French nasalized vowels.
3. characterized by such production of sounds; as, a *nasal* voice.
nasal bone; either of a pair of bones partly covering the nasal cavity and, in man, forming the bridge of the nose.
nasal fossa; either of the nasal passages or cavities.
nasal index; (a) in cephalometry, the ratio of the greatest breadth of the nose to its greatest height; (b) in craniometry, the ratio of the greatest breadth of the nasal aperture (of the skull) to its greatest height.
nasal point; the nasion.

nā′șăl, *n.* 1. a nasal sound or a letter representing such a sound.
2. in anatomy, a bone or plate of the nose.
3. [OFr. *nasal*, *nasel*, from L. *nasus*, a nose.] the protective nosepiece of a helmet.

NASAL

nā·șal′i·ty, *n.* the quality of being nasal.

nā″șăl·i·zā′tion, *n.* 1. a nasalizing or being nasalized.
2. the result of nasalizing.

nā′șăl·īze, *v.i.*; nasalized, *pt.*, *pp.*; nasalizing, *ppr.* to permit all or part of the breath to pass through the nose in pronouncing certain sounds, especially sounds not nasals; to talk through the nose.

nā′șăl·īze, *v.t.* to pronounce with a nasal sound.

nā′șăl·ly, *adv.* in a nasal manner.

nas′cence, *n.* same as *nascency*.

nas′cen·cy, *n.* [L. *nascentia*, birth, origin, from *nascens* (*-entis*), ppr. of *nasci*, to be born.] the process of being brought into being, formed, or started; birth; origin.

nas′cent, *a.* [L. *nascens* (*-entis*), ppr. of *nasci*, to be born.]
1. coming into being; being born.
2. beginning to form, start, grow, or develop: said of ideas, cultures, etc.
3. in chemistry, designating or of the state of an element just released from a compound and having unusual chemical activity because atoms of the element have not combined to form molecules; as, *nascent* chlorine.

nas′cent state (or **cŏn·di′tion**), 1. the earliest state of development.
2. in chemistry, the earliest state of an element at liberation from a compound.

nāșe′ber″ry, *n.*; *pl.* **nāșe′ber″ries,** [Sp. *níspero*, medlar, naseberry tree; L. *mespilus*, medlar.]
1. a variety of West Indian tree.
2. its edible fruit: also called *sapodilla* (*plum*).

nā·șeth′moid, *a.* belonging to both the nasal and ethmoid bones.

nā′și-, see *naso-*.

nā′și·ăl, *a.* of the nasion.

nā′și·cor′nous, *a.* [*nasi-*, and L. *cornu*, horn.] having a horn growing on the nose, as the rhinoceros.

nā′și·fōrm, *a.* [*nasi-*, and L. *forma*, form.] having the shape of a nose. [Rare.]

nā·și·lā′bi·ăl, *a.* same as *nasolabial*.

nā·și·mā′lăr, *a.* same as *nasomalar*.

nā″și·ō·al·vē′ō·lăr, *a.* pertaining to the alveolar point and the nasion.

nā″și·ō·breg·mat′ic, *a.* pertaining to the bregma and the nasion.

nā″și·ō·men′tăl, *a.* pertaining to the mentum and the nasion.

nā′și·on, *n.* [from L. *nasus*, nose.] in craniometry, the point in the skull at which the suture between the two nasal bones meets the suture between these and the frontal bone.

na·si′tis, *n.* inflammation of the nose.

nā′șō-, [from L. *nasus*, nose.] a combining form meaning: (a) *nose*, *nasal*; (b) *nasal and*, as in *naso*frontal. Also *nasi-*.

nā″șō·al·vē′ō·lăr, *a.* [*naso-*, and L. *alveolus*, a small hollow.] pertaining to the alveolar processes and the nose.

nā″șō·an·trī′tis, *n.* [*naso-*, and L. *antrum*, a cavern, cavity, and *-itis*.] inflammation of the antrum and nose.

nā·șō·buc′căl, *a.* [*naso-*, and L. *bucca*, the cheek.] connected with or pertaining to the mouth and the nose.

nā·soc′ū·lăr, *a.* [*naso-*, and L. *oculus*, eye.] pertaining to the eye and nose.

nā·șō·fron′tăl, *a.* [*naso-*, and L. *frons*, *frontis*, the forehead.] pertaining to the nasal and frontal bones.

nā·șō·lā′bi·ăl, *a.* [*naso-*, and L. *labium*, a lip.] pertaining to the nose and upper lip.

nā·șō·lach′ry·măl, *a.* [*naso-*, and L. *lacryma*, tear.] pertaining to the nose and the lachrymal apparatus.

nā·șol′ō·ġy, *n.* [*naso-*, and Gr. *-logia*, from *legein*, to speak.] the study of the structure and functions of the nose.

nā·șō·mā′lăr, *a.* [*naso-*, and L. *mala*, the cheekbone, jaw.] pertaining to the nose and the malar, or cheekbone.

nā·șō·max′il·lăr·y, *a.* [*naso-*, and L. *maxilla*, the jawbone.] pertaining to the nasal and maxillary bones.

nā·șō·pal′ȧ·tīne, nā·șō·pal′ȧ·tăl, *a.* [*naso-*, and L. *palatum*, the palate.] pertaining to or connecting the nose and palate; as, the *nasopalatine* nerve.

nā″șō·phar·yn′ġē·ăl, *a.* [*naso-*, and Gr. *pharynx*, the throat.] pertaining to the nose and the throat.

nā″șō·phar·yn·ġī′tis, *n.* inflammation of the nasopharynx.

nā·șō·phar′ynx, *n.* the part of the pharynx lying directly behind the nasal passages and above the soft palate.

nā·șō·ros′trăl, *a.* pertaining to the rostrum of the nose.

nā′șō·scōpe, *n.* an electrically lighted instrument for illuminating and inspecting the nasal cavity.

nā·șō·sep′tăl, *a.* [*naso-*, and L. *septum*, *sæptum*, an enclosure.] pertaining to the nasal septum.

nā·șō·sin·ū·ī′tis, *n.* inflammation of the accessory nasal sinuses.

nā·șō·tūr′bi·năl, *a.* [*naso-*, and L. *turbo* (*-inis*), a top, whirl.] adjacent to or connected with the nasal and turbinal bones.

Nas′sȧ, *n.* [L. *nassa*, a wicker basket: so called in allusion to the reticulation of some of the species.]
1. in zoology, a typical genus of the *Nassidæ*.
2. [n–] a gastropod of the family *Nassidæ*.

nas′sid, *n.* any of the *Nassidæ*.

Nas′si·dae, *n.pl.* [*nassa* and *-idæ*.] a family of gastropods; the dog whelks.

nas′soid, *a.* pertaining to the *Nassidæ*.

nas·sol′ō·ġy, *n.* taxidermy. [Rare.]

nas′tic, *a.* [from Gr. *nastos*, pressed close, and *-ic*.] designating, of, or exhibiting a characteristic reaction of plants by which an inequality of cellular growth or pressure on one side of the axis results in a change in the form or position of the axis.

-nas′tic, a combining form meaning *nastic by some* (specified) *means* or *in some* (specified) *direction*.

nȧs′ti·ly, *adv.* in a nasty manner.

nȧs′ti·ness, *n.* 1. the quality or condition of being nasty.
2. a nasty act, word, expression, etc.

nas·tūr′tion, *n.* same as *nasturtium*.

Nas·tūr′tium (-shum), *n.* [L., from *nasitortium*; *nasus*, nose, and *torquere*, to turn, twist; so called from the pungent odor of the plant.]
1. a genus of herbs of the family *Cruciferæ*, having pinnate leaves and yellow or white flowers, found in marshy places; the water cresses. *Nasturtium officinale* is the common water cress of springs and brooks.
2. [n–] any of several species of plants of the genus *Tropæolum*, including *Tropæolum majus*, the common nasturtium, with shield-shaped leaves and funnel-shaped red, orange, or yellow flowers: also called *Indian cress* or *lark's-heel*. The small fruits are often pickled.
3. [n–] the flower of the common nasturtium plant.

nȧs′ty, *a.*; *comp.* nastier; *superl.* nastiest, [ME. *nasty*, *nasky*, *naxty*; perh. from or akin to D. *nestig*, dirty.]
1. filthy; foul.
2. offensive in taste or smell; nauseating.
3. morally offensive; obscene.
4. very unpleasant; objectionable; as, *nasty* weather.
5. mean; malicious; ill-humored; as, a *nasty* temper.
6. very harmful or troublesome; dangerous; as, a *nasty* bruise.
Syn.—filthy, foul, dirty, unpleasant, disagreeable.

-nas′ty, a combining form used to form nouns corresponding to adjectives ending in *-nastic*.

nā′sus, *n.*; *pl.* **nā′sī,** [L., the nose.] in entomology, the clypeus.

nā′sūte, *a.* [L. *nasutus*, having a large nose, critical, from *nasus*, nose.]
1. in ornithology, having large, encased nostrils, as the petrel.
2. possessing a fine sense of smell. [Obs.]

nā′sūte, *n.* in zoology, among some species of termite, one that has a long, narrow head ending in a process resembling a nose in which a fluid, used to build and repair nest walls, is secreted.

nā·sūte′ness, *n.* keenness of scent. [Obs.]

nā·sū′ti·fōrm, *a.* [L. *nasutus*, having a large nose, and *forma*, form.] nariform; snoutlike, as a clypeus.

nat, *adv.* not. [Obs.]

nā·tȧ·bil′i·ty, *n.* [LL. *natabilis*, capable of floating.] ability to float.

nā′tăl, *a.* [L. *natalis*, from *natus*, pp. of *nasci*, to be born.]
1. pertaining to or connected with one's birth; dating from birth.
2. native. [Poet.]
3. presiding over one's nativity; as, a *natal* star. [Obs.]

nā′tăl, *a.* [L. *natis*, the rump.] pertaining to the nates, or buttocks.

nā·tȧ·li′tiăl, (-lish′ăl), **nā·tȧ·li′tious** (-lish′us), *a.* [L. *natalitius*, pertaining to the day or hour of one's birth, from *natalis*, pertaining to one's birth, natal.] pertaining to one's birthday or nativity. [Obs.]

nā·tal′i·ty, *n.* [Fr. *natalité*, from L. *natalis*, pertaining to birth.]
1. birth. [Rare.]
2. birth rate.

nȧ·tal′ō·in, *n.* [*natal* and *aloin*.] same as *aloin*.

nā′tăls, *n.pl.* a birthday celebration.

nā′tănt, *a.* [L. *natans* (*-antis*), ppr. of *natare*, to swim, freq. of *nare*, to swim.]
1. in botany, swimming or floating; especially, floating on the surface of water, as the leaf of an aquatic plant.
2. in heraldry, in a horizontal position on the field, with head toward the dexter side; as, a fish *natant*.

NATANT

nā′tănt·ly, *adv.* swimmingly; floatingly.

nā·tā′tion, *n.* [L. *natatio* (*-onis*), from *natare*, to swim.] the act or art of swimming; the act of floating on the water.

Nā·tȧ·tō′rēs, *n.* [L. *natator*, a swimmer, from *natare*, to swim.] the swimming birds.

nā·tȧ·tō′ri·ăl, *a.* same as *natatory*.

nā·tȧ·tō′ri·ous, *a.* natatory. [Rare.]

nā·tȧ·tō′ri·um, *n.*; *pl.* **nā·tȧ·tō′ri·ums, nā·tȧ·tō′ri·ȧ,** [LL. *natatorium*, a place for swimming, from *natatorius*, pertaining to a swimmer, from L. *natator*, a swimmer.] a swimming pool, especially one indoors.

nā′tȧ·tō·ry, *a.* [LL. *natatorius*, pertaining to

a swimmer or swimming, from L. *natator*, a swimmer.] of, characterized by, or adapted for swimming.

natch, *n.* [OFr. *nache, naiche*; LL. *naticæ*; from L. *nates*, the buttocks.] the rump.

Natch'ez, *n.*; *pl.* **Natch'ez**, a member of an extinct tribe of Muskhogean Indians who lived in southwestern Mississippi.

nā'tēş, *n.pl.* [L. *natis*, pl. *nates*, the buttocks, rump.]

1. in anatomy, the buttocks; also, the anterior pair of the corpora quadrigemina of the brain of man and other mammals.

2. in zoology, the umbones of a bivalve shell.

Nā'thăn, *n.* [Heb. *nāthān*, lit., gift.] in the Bible, a prophet who rebuked David for the death of Uriah: 2 Sam. xii. 1–14.

Nȧ·than'ā·el, *n.* [LL.; Gr. *Nathanaēl*; Heb. *nĕthan'ēl*, lit., gift of God.] in the Bible, one of the disciples of Jesus: John i. 45–51.

nāthe'less, *adv.* [ME. *natheles*; AS. *nathelæs*, etc.; *na*, never, *the* (for *thy*, instrumental case of def. art.), and *læs*, less.] nevertheless. [Archaic.]

nāthe'less, *prep.* notwithstanding. [Archaic.]

nath'less, *adv.* and *prep.* natheless. [Archaic.]

Nat'i·cȧ, *n.* [LL. *naticæ*, pl., the buttocks.] a genus of carnivorous sea snails typical of the family *Naticidæ*, and including some of the largest univalve shells found along the coasts of the United States.

Nȧ·tic'i·dae, *n.pl.* a family of gastropods of which *Natica* is the type genus.

nȧ·tic'i·form, *a.* [*natica*, and L. *forma*, form.] resembling *Natica* in shape.

nat'i·çoid, *a.* pertaining to the *Naticidæ*.

nā'tion, *n.* [OFr. *nacion, nation*, from L. *natic* (*-onis*), birth, a race, people, from *natus*, pp. of *nasci*, to be born.]

1. a stable, historically developed community of people with a territory, economic life, distinctive culture, and language in common.

2. the people of a territory united under a single government; a country; state.

3. (a) a people or tribe; (b) a tribe of North American Indians belonging to a confederation; as, the Six *Nations*; (c) the territory of such a tribe.

4. a great number; a multitude. [Colloq.]

5. formerly, in some European universities, one of the divisions of students in a classification according to place of birth.

Five Nations; see under *five*.

maritime nation; a nation having a seacoast and engaging in international commerce.

the nations; (a) in the Bible, the non-Jewish nations; the Gentiles; (b) [Poetic.] all the peoples of the earth.

na'tion·ăl, *a.* [Fr. *national*, from *nation*, a nation.]

1. of a nation or the nation; affecting the nation as a whole.

2. strongly devoted to one's nation or its interests; patriotic.

3. established, maintained, or owned by the federal government.

national anthem; a patriotic song of a nation; especially, a hymn officially adopted to be sung on formal occasions. The national anthem of the United States is *The Star-Spangled Banner*, according to an Act of Congress in 1931.

national bank; (a) a bank that manages and controls the finances of a nation; (b) in the United States, a bank chartered by the Federal government and under certain controls by the Federal Reserve System, of which it is a member: national banks formerly issued bank notes secured by government bonds.

National Defense Act; the Army Reorganization Act (passed June, 1916; revised in 1921) which provided for the federalization of the National Guard, a regular army, and a reserve officers' training corps.

National Economic Council; the council organized in 1919 in Germany, known as the *Reichswirtschaftsrat*, the purpose of which was to advise the government on economic and social matters: it was composed of men representing the various trades and occupations, both employers and employees. This council was reorganized in 1929, and again under Hitler.

National Education Association; a national organization representing teachers, school principals, etc., having its headquarters in Washington, D. C.

National Flag; the official flag of a nation, as the Stars and Stripes of the United States.

National Guard; (a) in French history, an armed force first organized in 1789; (b) in the United States, that part of the militia consisting of the properly organized, equipped, and trained forces of the individual States, supported in part by the Federal government: it becomes a definite component of the Army of the United States when called into active Federal service.

National Guard of the United States; those members and units of the National Guard who have been accorded Federal recognition as a component part of the Army of the United States.

national income; the total income of a nation, including all profits, rents, interest, wages, salaries, etc., during a specified period, usually a year.

National Industrial Recovery Act; an emergency act of Congress, passed June, 1933, at the time of widespread unemployment and business depression in the United States: it authorized the President to establish various measures in order to insure industrial recovery: it was declared unconstitutional by a decision of the Supreme Court.

National Labor Relations Board; an agency established to guarantee the full freedom of employees in organizing trade unions for collective bargaining.

national park; an area of scenic beauty, historical importance, etc. maintained and preserved by the national government for the enjoyment of the public.

National Party; in United States history, the Greenback Party.

National Recovery Administration; the general title covering the various agencies and officers who administered the National Industrial Recovery Act.

national salute; in the United States, a salute by the firing of as many guns as there are States in the Union.

National Socialism, National Socialist German Workers' Party; see *Nazi*.

National Weather Service; the division of the Department of Commerce that gathers and compiles data on weather conditions over the United States, on the basis of which weather forecasts are made.

na'tion·ăl, *n.* 1. a person who belongs to a certain nation by birth or naturalization.

2. loosely, a fellow citizen.

na'tion·ăl·işm, *n.* 1. (a) devotion to one's nation; patriotism; (b) excessive, narrow, or jingoist patriotism; chauvinism.

2. the doctrine that national interests, security, etc. are more important than international considerations; opposed to *internationalism*.

3. national quality or character; nationality.

4. a national idiom, trait, or custom.

5. the desire for or advocacy of national independence.

6. the policy of nationalizing all industry.

7. [N-] in Great Britain, the principles advocated by the Nationalists.

na'tion·ăl·ist, *a.* of nationalism or nationalists.

na'tion·ăl·ist, *n.* 1. a person who believes in or advocates nationalism.

2. [N-] in Great Britain, an advocator of home rule for Ireland.

na"tion·ăl·is'tiç, *a.* nationalist.

na"tion·ăl·is'ti·çăl·ly, *adv.* in a nationalistic manner.

na·tion·al'i·ty, *n.*; *pl.* **na·tion·al'i·tieş**, 1. national quality or character.

2. the condition or fact of belonging to a nation by birth or naturalization.

3. the condition or fact of being a nation.

4. a nation or national group.

na"tion·ăl·i·zā'tion, *n.* the act of making national or the state of becoming national.

na'tion·ăl·īze, *v.t.*; nationalized, *pt.*, *pp.*; nationalizing, *ppr.* 1. to make national in character.

2. to transfer ownership or control of land, resources, industries, etc. to the nation.

3. to make into a nation.

na'tion·ăl·ly, *adv.* 1. in a manner affecting the nation as a whole; throughout the nation.

2. as a nation.

nā'tion-wīde, *a.* by or through the whole nation; national.

nā'tive, *a.* [replacing ME. *natyf* (OFr. *natif*), from L. *nativus*, from *natus*, pp. of *nasci*, to be born.]

1. inborn; innate; not acquired.

2. belonging to a locality or country by birth, production, or growth; indigenous; as, a *native* Bostonian, *native* industry, *native* plants.

3. (a) related to one as the place of one's birth; as, one's *native* land; (b) belonging to one because of the place of one's birth; as, one's *native* language.

4. as found in nature; natural; not refined, adorned, or altered by man.

5. occurring in a pure state in nature; as, *native* gold.

6. of or characteristic of the inhabitants of any given region.

7. of, characteristic of, or belonging to primitive or uncivilized peoples, particularly nonwhites, living in their place of origin; as, *native* customs in Borneo.

Native American Party; see *American Party*, under *American*.

native bread; an edible Australian underground fungus, *Mylitta australis*.

native cat; in Australia, the spotted dasyure.

native hen; a bird, the Australian rail, *Tribonyx mortieri*.

native thrush; an Australian songbird, the thickhead.

native turkey; the Australian bustard, *Choriotis australis*.

Syn.—natural, natal, indigenous, endemic, aboriginal.

nā'tive, *n.* 1. a person born or thing produced in the place or country indicated.

2. (a) an original or indigenous inhabitant of a region, as distinguished from an invader, explorer, colonist, etc.; (b) an indigenous plant or animal.

3. a permanent resident, as distinguished from a temporary resident or visitor.

4. in astrology, one born under a certain sign.

5. [*pl.*] oysters raised in an artificial bed.

nā'tive-bọrn, *a.* born in a specified place or country.

nā'tive·ly, *adv.* by birth; naturally; originally.

nā'tive·ness, *n.* the state of being produced by nature.

nā'tiv·işm, *n.* 1. the practice or policy of favoring native-born citizens as distinguished from immigrants.

2. in philosophy, the theory that the human brain is capable of inborn, spontaneous thought, or innate ideas.

nā'tiv·ist, *n.* one who believes in nativism.

nā·tiv·is'tiç, *a.* pertaining to nativism.

nȧ·tiv'i·ty, *n.*; *pl.* **nȧ·tiv'i·tieş**, 1. birth.

2. the time, place, and manner of birth.

3. in astrology, a representation of the positions of the heavenly bodies at the moment of one's birth, supposed to foretell the future.

the Nativity; (a) the birth of Jesus; (b) a representation of this; (c) Christmas Day, the birthday of Jesus.

nat'ri·cīne, *a.* pertaining to a snake or snakes of the genus *Natrix*.

nā'tri·um, *n.* [Sp. *natron*; Ar. *natrūn*, *nitrūn*, native carbonate of sodium.] in chemistry, sodium: symbol, Na.

Nā'trix, *n.* a genus of colubrine snakes, that includes water snakes, garter snakes, and other similar forms.

nā'trō·līte, *n.* [*natron*, and Gr. *lithos*, stone.] a hydrous silicate of sodium and aluminum, $Na_2O \cdot Al_2O_3 \cdot 3SiO_2 \cdot 2H_2O$, generally occurring in groups of glassy, acicular crystals.

nā'trŏn, *n.* [Sp. *natron*; Ar. *natrūn*, *nitrūn*, native carbonate of sodium.] hydrated sodium carbonate, $Na_2CO_3 \cdot 10H_2O$, a mineral occurring in salt lakes or, mixed with other substances, in deposits.

nat'tẽr, *v.i.* to nag; to find fault peevishly. [Brit. and Scot. Dial.]

nat'tẽr·jack, *n.* the common toad of Europe, the back of which is marked lengthwise with a yellow line.

nattes (nats), *n.* [Fr. *natte*, a piece of matting or braiding.] an ornament used in the decoration of surfaces in the architecture of the twelfth century: so called from its resemblance to the interlaced withes of matting.

nat'ti·ly, *adv.* in a natty manner.

nat'ti·ness, *n.* the quality or condition of being natty.

nat'ty, *a.*; *comp.* nattier; *superl.* nattiest, [perh. from *neat*, *a.*] trim and smart in appearance or dress.

nat'ū·răl, *a.* [L. *naturalis*, by birth, pertaining to nature, from *natura*, birth, nature.]

1. of, forming a part of, or arising from nature; in accordance with what is found or expected in nature.

2. produced or existing in nature; real; not artificial or manufactured.

3. dealing with nature; as, a *natural* science.

4. (a) in a state provided by nature, without man-made changes; wild; uncultivated; (b) unenlightened; primitive.

5. of the physical world as distinguished from the spiritual world.

6. (a) present by virtue of nature; innate; not acquired; as, *natural* abilities; (b) having certain qualities, abilities, etc. innately; as, a *natural* comedian.

7. innately felt to be right; based on instinctive moral feeling; as, *natural* rights.

8. true to nature; realistic in appearance; lifelike; as, a *natural* likeness.

9. normal for a given person or thing; in the ordinary course of events; as, a *natural* outcome.

10. customarily expected or uncritically accepted; as, a *natural* courtesy.

11. free from affectation or restraint; at ease.

12. illegitimate; as, a *natural* child.

13. in mathematics, (a) designating or of an integer or any number referred to 1 as the base; (b) designating or of an actual number as distinguished from a logarithm; as, a *natural* sine, cosine, etc.

14. in music, (a) without flats or sharps, as the key of C major; (b) modified in pitch by the sign (♮); (c) neither sharped nor flatted.

15. native; as, one's *natural* language. [Obs.]

natural day; the day produced by the axial revolution of the earth; twenty-four hours.

natural gas; see under *gas*.

natural harmony; in music, the harmony of the triad.

natural history; (a) formerly, zoology, botany, mineralogy, geology, and other subjects dealing with the animal, vegetable, and mineral world; (b) the study of these subjects, especially of animal and plant life, in a popular, nontechnical manner.

natural law; (a) rules of conduct supposedly inherent in the relations between human beings and discoverable by reason; law based upon man's innate moral sense: contrasted with *statute law, common law*; (b) a law of nature: see *law* (sense 10); (c) the laws of nature, collectively.

natural order; in botany, a former category of classification, now called *family*.

natural person; in law, any private person as distinguished from a corporation.

natural philosophy; (a) the study of nature in general, or of the entire physical universe; (b) physics.

natural pruning; the dying and falling to the ground of the leaves and boughs of a tree when there is not sufficient light accorded for a healthy condition.

natural religion or *natural theology*; the aspect or form of religion distinguished from *revealed religion* in its exclusive apprehension and consideration of such evidences of the existence and attributes of God as are afforded in nature and natural phenomena.

natural resources; those actual and potential forms of wealth supplied by nature, as coal, oil, waterpower, arable land, etc.

natural scale; in music, a scale written without sharps or flats; the scale of C major.

natural science; (a) the systematized knowledge of nature and the physical world, including zoology, botany, chemistry, physics, geology, etc.; (b) any of these branches of knowledge. Also *science*.

natural selection; in biology, that process in nature by which individuals (of a species) best fitted for the conditions in which they are placed survive, propagate, and spread, while the less fitted die out and disappear; survival of the fittest; the preservation by their descendants of useful variations arising in animals or plants.

natural system; in botany and zoology, a classification depending upon affinities as revealed by the embryology of organisms and the structure of all their parts.

Syn.—intrinsic, regular, normal, cosmical, true, consistent, spontaneous, artless, original.

nat'ū·răl, *n.* 1. an idiot; a fool; one born without the usual powers of reason or understanding.

2. a person who is or seems to be naturally expert. [Colloq.]

3. a thing that is, or promises to be, immediately and remarkably successful. [Colloq.]

4. in music, (a) the sign (♮), used to remove the effect of a preceding sharp or flat within the measure in which it occurs: in full, *natural sign*; (b) the note so changed; (c) a white key on a piano.

5. a native; an original inhabitant. [Obs.]

6. a gift of nature; a natural quality. [Obs.]

nat'ū·răl-bọrn, *a.* 1. native; not alien; as, a *natural-born* citizen.

2. inborn; so by nature; as, a *natural-born* fool.

nat'ū·răl·iṣm, *n.* 1. action or thought based on natural desires or instincts.

2. in literature, painting, etc., (a) faithful adherence to nature; realism; specifically, the variety of realism based on the principles and methods of a group of 19th-century writers, including Émile Zola, Gustave Flaubert, and Guy de Maupassant, who believed that the writer or artist should apply scientific objectivity and precision in his observation and treatment of life, without idealizing, imposing value judgments, or avoiding what is regarded as repulsive; (b) the quality resulting from the use of such realism.

3. in philosophy, the belief that the natural world is the whole of reality and that there is no supernatural or spiritual creation, value, control, or significance: it holds that scientific laws can explain all phenomena.

4. in religion, the doctrine that religion does not depend on supernatural experience, divine revelation, etc., and that all religious truth may be derived from the natural world.

nat'ū·răl·ist, *n.* [Fr. *naturaliste.*]

1. a person who studies nature, especially by direct observation of animals and plants.

2. a person who believes in or practices naturalism in art, literature, philosophy, or religion.

nat"ū·răl·ist'iç, *a.* 1. of natural history or naturalists.

2. of or characterized by naturalism in art, literature, philosophy, or religion.

3. in accordance with, or in imitation of, nature.

nat·ū·ral'i·ty, *n.* the state of being natural.

nat"ū·răl·i·zā'tion, *n.* a naturalizing or being naturalized.

nat'ū·răl·īze, *v.t.*; naturalized, *pt., pp.*; naturalizing, *ppr.* [Fr. *naturaliser*, from *naturel*, natural.]

1. to confer upon (an alien) the rights and privileges of a native subject or citizen; to adopt into a nation or state and place in the condition of natural-born subjects.

2. to make natural or less artificial; to free from conventionality; to render easy and familiar by custom and habit; as, custom *naturalizes* labor or study.

3. to adapt (a plant or animal) to an environment not native; to make suitable; to habituate; to acclimate; as, to *naturalize* an animal or plant to a climate.

4. to adopt and make common (a custom, word, etc.) from another locality.

5. to give an explanation of (occurrences) according to natural law, rejecting supernatural influence.

nat'ū·răl·īze, *v.i.* 1. to accommodate oneself to environments and conditions; to become naturalized, or as if native.

2. to explain all phenomena according to natural law.

3. to study nature.

nat'ū·răl·ly, *adv.* 1. according to nature; by the force or impulse of nature; innately; as, we are *naturally* prone to evil.

2. in a natural manner; without affectation; with just representation; according to life.

3. according to the usual course of things; necessarily; as a matter of course; as, the effect or consequence *naturally* follows.

4. spontaneously; without art or cultivation; as, every plant must have grown *naturally* in some place.

nat'ū·răl·ness, *n.* 1. the state of being given or produced by nature; as, the *naturalness* of desire.

2. conformity to nature or to truth and reality; absence of affectation; as, the *naturalness* of one's conduct.

nā'tūre, *v.t.* to endow with natural qualities.

nā'tūre, *n.* [OFr. *nature*; L. *natura*, birth, origin, natural constitution or quality of a thing, from *nasci*, to be born.]

1. the essential character of a thing; quality or qualities that make something what it is; essence.

2. inborn character; innate disposition; inherent tendencies of a person.

3. the vital functions, forces, and activities of the organs: often euphemistic.

4. kind; sort; type; as, things of that *nature*.

5. any or all of the instincts, desires, appetites, drives, etc. of a person.

6. the sum total of all things in time and space; the entire physical universe.

7. [*sometimes* N–] the power, force, principle, etc. that seems to regulate this: often personified.

8. the primitive state of man.

9. natural scenery, including the plants and animals that are part of it.

10. in religion, the state of man unredeemed by grace.

11. birth; as, he is a Russian by *nature*. [Obs.]

by nature; naturally; inherently.

freak of nature; a monstrosity; a deformed or malformed person, animal, or thing.

ill nature; bad temper; the state of being morose, unkind, or spiteful.

in a state of nature; (a) nude; naked as one is when born; (b) uncivilized; (c) not cultivated or tamed; wild; savage; (d) unrenewed in spirit; unregenerate; at enmity with God.

of (or *in*) *the nature of*; having the essential character of; like.

to pay the debt of nature; to die.

Syn.—essence, creation, constitution, structure, disposition, truth, regularity, kind, sort, character, species, affection, naturalness.

-nā'tūred, a combining form used to form hyphenated compounds meaning *having*, or *showing a* (specified kind of) *nature, disposition*, or *temperament*, as good-*natured*.

nā'tūre·less, *a.* out of harmony with nature; unnatural.

nā'ture print'ing, a process by which objects, such as plants, mosses, ferns, lace, etc., are impressed on a metal plate so as to engrave themselves, copies or casts being then taken for printing. The object is placed between a plate of copper and one of lead, which are passed between heavy rollers, whence a perfect impression is made on the leaden plate.

nā'tūre stud'y, the study of plant and animal life by direct observation, especially in a popular, nontechnical manner.

nā'tūre wŏr'ship, 1. a form of religion in which the phenomena of nature are worshiped as gods.

2. poetic love for nature.

nā'tūr·iṣm, *n.* same as *naturalism*.

nā'tūr·ist, *n.* one who is a believer in or an advocate of naturism.

nā·tūr·ist'iç, *a.* of or pertaining to naturism.

nā'tūr·īze, *v.t.* to provide with a nature; to endow with special qualities. [Rare.]

nā·tūr·op'ȧ·thist, *n.* one who practices, or believes in, naturopathy.

nā·tūr·op'ȧ·thy, *n.* [from L. *natura*, nature; and *-pathy.*] a system of treating diseases, largely employing natural agencies, such as air, sunshine, etc., and rejecting the use of drugs and medicines.

nạu'frăġe, *n.* shipwreck. [Obs.]

nạu'fră·ġous, *a.* causing shipwreck. [Obs.]

nạught (nạt), *n.* [ME. *naught, naght, noght, naht*; AS. *nawiht*; *ne*, not, and *a*, ever, and *wiht*, a thing.]

1. nothing; as, the labor was all for *naught*.

2. in arithmetic, a cipher; zero; the figure 0.

to set at naught; to slight, disregard, or despise; as, ye have *set at naught* all my counsel.

nạught, *adv.* in no degree. [Obs.]

> To wealth or sovereign power he *naught* applied. —Fairfax.

nạught, *a.* 1. worthless; of no value or account. [Obs. or Archaic.]

> Things *naught* and things indifferent. —Hooker.

2. base; low; vile; wicked; naughty. [Obs. or Archaic.]

nạught'i·ly, *adv.* in a naughty manner.

nạught'i·ness, *n.* quality, state, or instance of being naughty.

> I know thy pride and the *naughtiness* of thy heart. —1 Sam. xvii. 28.

nạught'ly, *adv.* naughtily. [Obs.]

naught'y, *a.*; *comp.* naughtier; *superl.* naughtiest, [ME. *naugti.*]
1. not behaving properly; mischievous; disobedient: usually of children or their behavior.
2. showing lack of decorum; improper; indelicate; obscene.
3. poor; possessing little of value. [Obs.]
4. evil; wicked; corrupt. [Obs.]
5. bad; poor; worthless. [Obs.]
The other basket had very *naughty* figs.
—Jer. xxiv. 2.

nau·mā'chi·à, *n.*; *pl.* **nau·mā'chi·ăs**, **nau·mā'chi·ae** [L. *naumachia*; Gr. *naumachia*, a sea fight; *naus*, a ship, and *machē*, a fight, battle, from *machesthai*, to fight.]
1. among the ancient Romans, a mock sea fight.
2. the place where mock sea fights were exhibited.

nau'mà·chy, *n.*; *pl.* **nau'mà·chies**, a naumachia.

nau·path'i·à, *n.* [Gr. *naus*, a ship, and *pathos*, suffering.] seasickness.

nau'pli·i·form, *a.* [L. *nauplius*, a kind of shellfish, and *forma*, form.] like a nauplius in form or character.

nau'pli·oid, *a.* same as *naupliiform*.

nau'pli·us, *n.*; *pl.* **nau'pli·ī**, [L. *nauplius*, a kind of shellfish; Gr. *naus*, a ship, and *plein*, to sail.]
1. the first or larval stage in the development of certain low crustaceans, as cirripeds and entomostracans.
2. [N–] formerly and erroneously, a supposed genus containing crustaceans in this stage.

nau·rō·pom'ē·tẽr, *n.* [Gr. *naus*, a ship, and *rhopē*, inclination, a sinking, and *metron*, a measure.] a device for measuring the inclination of a ship when it heels. [Rare.]

naus'cō·py, *n.* [Gr. *naus*, a ship, and *skopein*, to view.] the art or the pretended art of sighting ships or land at great distances.

nau'se·à (-shi-à), *n.* [L. *nausea*, *nausia*; Gr. *nausia*, *nautia*, seasickness, from *naus*, a ship.]
1. sickness of the stomach, with an impulse to vomit.
2. any stomach disorder causing this feeling, as seasickness.
3. disgust; loathing.

nau'sē·ănt, *n.* a substance which produces nausea.

nau'sē·āte, *v.i.*; nauseated, *pt.*, *pp.*; nauseating, *ppr.* [L. *nauseatus*, pp. of *nauseare*, from Gr. *nausiān*, *nautiān*, to be seasick.] to feel nausea; to be inclined to vomit.

nau'sē·āte, *v.t.* 1. to affect with disgust or nausea; to make sick; as, food *nauseates* the patient.
2. to loathe; to reject with disgust; as, to *nauseate* food. [Rare.]

nau·sē·ā'tion, *n.* the act of nauseating; the condition of being nauseated.

nau'sē·à·tive, *a.* inclined to nausea. [Obs.]

nau'seous (-shus), *a.* [L. *nauseosus*, from *nausea*, seasickness.] causing nausea; specifically, (a) sickening; (b) disgusting.

nau'seous·ly, *adv.* in a nauseous manner.

nau'seous·ness, *n.* the state or quality of being nauseous.

Nau·sic'a·ä (na-sik'ā-à), *n.* in Homer's Odyssey, King Alcinoüs's daughter, who discovered the shipwrecked Ulysses and brought him to her father, from whom he received safe passage to Ithaca.

nautch (nawch), *n.* [Hind. *nāc*, a dance, prob. from Sans. *nātya*, to dance.] in the East Indies, an entertainment by professional dancers called nautch girls.

nautch girl, in India, one who performs in a nautch; a native dancing girl.
They caught them round the waists and began to haul them about as if they were *nautch girls*. —W. H. Russell.

nau'tic, *a.* same as *nautical*.

nau'tic·ăl, *a.* [L. *nauticus*; Gr. *nautikos*, from *nautēs*, a sailor, seaman, from *naus*, a ship.] pertaining to seamen, ships, or navigation; as, *nautical* skill; a *nautical* almanac.
nautical almanac; see under *almanac*.
nautical distance; distance in nautical miles measured on the arc of a rhumb line.
nautical mile; a unit of linear measure for ships and aircraft, equal to $^1/_{60}$ of a degree, or about 6,080 ft.

nau'tic·ăl·ly, *adv.* in a nautical manner.

nau'ti·form, *a.* [Gr. *naus*, a ship, and L. *forma*, form.] in the form of a vessel's hull. [Rare.]

nau'ti·līte, *n.* [L. *nautilus*, a nautilus, and *-ite*.] a fossil nautilus.

nau'ti·loid, *a.* [L. *nautilus*, a nautilus, and Gr. *eidos*, form.] resembling the nautilus in shape or character.

nau'ti·loid, *n.* a mollusk of the genus *Nautilus*.

nau'ti·lus, *n.*; *pl.* **nau'ti·lus·es** or **nau'ti·lī**, [L. *nautilus*, from Gr. *nautilos*, a sailor, a nautilus, from *naus*, a ship.]

PEARLY NAUTILUS (8 in. long)

1. [N–] a genus of tropical mollusks with many-chambered spiral shells. The chambers are separated by transverse walls, and have pearly interiors.
2. a mollusk of the genus *Nautilus*: also *pearly nautilus*.
3. the argonaut, or paper nautilus.
4. a kind of diving bell.

Nä'vä·hō, *n.*; *pl.* **Nä'vä·hōs**, **Nä'vä·hōes**, a member of a tribe of Athapascan Indians now living on reservations in Arizona, New Mexico, and Utah.

Nä'vä·jō (-hō), *n.*; *pl.* **Nä'vä·jōs**, **Nä'vä·jōes**, same as *Navaho*.

nā'văl, *a.* [L. *navalis*, pertaining to a ship or ships, from *navis*, a ship.]
1. of ships or shipping. [Obs.]
2. of, having, characteristic of, or for a navy, its ships, personnel, etc.; as, *naval* stores; a *naval* battle.
naval academy; a college for training naval officers.
naval officer; (a) an officer in the navy; (b) in a United States customhouse, an officer who assists the collector in collecting the customs on merchandise imported.
naval reserve; (a) in the United States, a kind of marine division of the various State troops kept in training for service in the navy; (b) in England, former members of the Royal Navy used as coastguardsmen and in other government employment.
naval stores; turpentine, resin, pitch, and tar.

nā'văl·ism, *n.* the policy of maintaining or increasing the naval strength.

nā'värch, *n.* [L. *navarchus*; Gr. *nauarchos*, the commander of a fleet or ship; *naus*, a ship, and *archein*, to rule.] in ancient Greece, the commander of a fleet.

nā'värch·y, *n.* knowledge of managing ships.

Nä·vär·rēse', *a.* relating to or from Navarre, a former kingdom of northern Spain and southwestern France.

Nä·vär·rēse', *n. sing.* and *pl.* a native of Navarre.

nāve, *n.* [ME. *nave*, *nafe*; AS. *nafu*, a nave.] the center of a wheel; a hub.

nāve, *n.* [OFr. *nave*, the nave of a church; L. *navis*, a ship (LL., the nave of a church).] the middle part of the body of a church, extending from the baluster, or rail, of the choir to the main entrance.

nā'vel, *n.* [ME. *navel*, *navele*; AS. *nafela*, navel.]
1. a small scar, usually in the center of the abdomen, marking the place where the umbilical cord passed out of the fetus.
2. the central point or part of anything; the middle.
3. in heraldry, the point in a shield between the middle base point and the fesse point; the nombril.
navel orange; a seedless orange having at its apex a depression like a navel, containing a small, undeveloped secondary fruit.

nā'vel gall, a bruise on the top of the chine of the back of a horse, behind the saddle.

nā'vel string, the umbilical cord.

nā'vel·wŏrt, *n.* 1. a succulent plant of the genus *Cotyledon*, resembling the houseleek.
2. either of two species of *Omphalodes*, of the borage family, the white navelwort and the blue navelwort.

nā'vew, *n.* [OFr. *naveau*, *navel*; LL. *napellus*, dim. of L. *napus*, a kind of turnip.] a plant of the mustard family, *Brassica campestris*; the wild turnip.

Nav·i·cel'là, *n.* [L. *navicula*, dim. of *navis*, a ship.]
1. in conchology, a genus of gastropods of the family *Neritidæ* having limpetlike shells with large opercula.
2. [n–] in jewelry, a small bowl-shaped piece used as a pendant, as for an earring.

nav'i·cẽrt, *n.* *navigation certificate*.] a document issued by a nation at war, declaring that a ship of a friendly or neutral nation carries no contraband and authorizing it to move through the belligerent's blockade.

Nà·vic'ū·là, *n.* [L. *navicula*, dim. of *navis*, a ship.]
1. in botany, an extensive genus of diatoms of the family *Naviculaceæ*.
2. [n–] a censer having the shape of a boat.

nà·vic'ū·lăr, *a.* [LL. *navicularis*, from L. *navicula*.]
1. pertaining to a small ship or boat.
2. shaped like a boat; cymbiform: said especially of certain bones.
3. of or relating to the genus *Navicula*.
navicular fossa; (a) a depression on the internal pterygoid process of the sphenoid bone; (b) a depression in the margin of the ear between the helix and the anthelix; (c) an expansion of the urethra in the glans penis; (d) a cavity behind the vaginal aperture.

nà·vic'ū·lăr, *n.* any of various boat-shaped bones; especially, (a) the outer bone of the first row of carpal bones in the wrist; (b) a bone on the inner side of the human foot, in front of the anklebone.

nà·vic·ū·lā'rē, *n.* a navicular.

nà·vic'ū·loid, *a.* [L. *navicula*, a small vessel, and Gr. *eidos*, form.]
1. like a navicula; boat-shaped.
2. of or resembling the genus *Navicula*.

nav·i·gà·bil'i·ty, *n.* the state or condition of being navigable; navigableness.

nav'i·gà·ble, *a.* [L. *navigabilis*, from *navigare*, to sail, navigate.]
1. wide or deep enough, or free enough from obstructions, to be traveled on by ships; as, a *navigable* river.
2. that can be steered, or directed; as, a *navigable* balloon.

nav'i·gà·ble·ness, *n.* navigability.

nav'i·gà·bly, *adv.* in a navigable manner.

nav'i·gāte, *v.i.*; navigated, *pt.*, *pp.*; navigating, *ppr.* [L. *navigatus*, pp. of *navigare*, to sail, go by sea, sail over; *navis*, a ship, and *agere*, to lead, go.]
1. to go on water in ships; to sail.
2. to steer, or direct, a ship or aircraft.

nav'i·gāte, *v.t.* 1. to travel through, on, or over (land, air, sea, etc.) in a boat or aircraft.
2. to steer, or direct (a ship or aircraft).
3. to plot the course for (a ship or aircraft).

nav·i·gā'tion, *n.* [L. *navigatio* (*-onis*), from *navigare*, to navigate.]
1. the act or practice of navigating.
2. the science or art of locating the position and plotting the course of ships and aircraft.
3. ships in general. [Poet.]
inland or *internal navigation*; the passing of boats or small vessels on rivers, lakes, or canals, in the interior of a country; conveyance by boats or vessels in the interior of a country.

nav'i·gā·tŏr, *n.* [L.] 1. one who navigates or sails; one who is skillful in the art of navigation, either of a ship or an aircraft.
2. a book on the science and art of navigation.
3. a navvy. [Brit.]

nà·vig'ẽr·ous, *a.* [L. *naviger*, ship-bearing; *navis*, a ship, and *gerere*, to bear.] capable of floating ships. [Rare.]

nav'vy, *n.*; *pl.* **nav'vies**, [abbrev. from *navigator*.] an unskilled laborer engaged in such works as the making of canals, railways, or other public works. [Brit.]

nā'vy, *n.*; *pl.* **nā'vies**, [OFr. *navie*; LL. *navia*, ships, neut. pl., from L. *navis*, a ship.]
1. a fleet of ships. [Archaic or Poet.]
2. all the ships of war belonging to a nation.
3. [*often* N–] (a) the entire sea force of a nation, including vessels, officers, men, stores, yards, etc.; (b) the governmental department in charge of this.
4. navy blue.

nā'vy bēan, the common white bean, much used in the navy.

nā′vy blūe, the dark shade of blue worn in the navy; very dark blue.

Nā′vy Cross, a decoration awarded by the United States Navy for conspicuous heroism or service in war.

Nā′vy Dāy, October 27, the anniversary of the date in 1775 when the United States Navy was founded.

nā′vy yärd, a dockyard for building and repairing naval ships, including extensive shops, storerooms, machinery, and naval material of all kinds.

nȧ·wạb′, *n.* [Hind. *navāb.*]
1. in India, a native ruler under the Mogul government.
2. [N–] in India, a title of courtesy, especially for a Moslem prince.
3. a rich Anglo-Indian who has retired; a nabob.

nāy, *adv.* [ME. *nay, ney*; Ice. *nei,* nay.]
1. no. [Archaic.]
2. not this alone, but also; intimating that something is to be added by way of amplification; as, he requested an answer; *nay,* he urged it.
to say (someone) nay; to refuse or forbid (someone).

nāy, *n.* 1. denial; refusal.
2. a negative vote or voter.
3. a negative answer.

nāy, *v.t.* and *v.i.* to refuse. [Obs.]

nȧ·yaur′, *n.* [E. Ind.] the Himalayan argali, a species of wild sheep in Tibet and northern India.

nāy′wạrd, *n.* the contrary view. [Rare.]

nāy′wŏrd, *n.* a byword; a proverbial reproach; a watchword. [Rare.]

Naz·ȧ·rēne′, *a.* [L. *Nazarenus*; Gr. *Nazarēnos,* from *Nazareth,* Nazareth.] of Nazareth or the Nazarenes.

Naz·ȧ·rēne′, *n.* 1. a native or inhabitant of Nazareth; especially, Jesus (*the Nazarene*).
2. any member of an early sect of Jewish Christians who kept the Mosaic ritual.
3. a Christian: term formerly used by Moslems, Jews, etc. [Obs.]

Naz′ȧ·rīte, *n.* [LL. *Nazarita*; Gr. *Nazaritēs,* from Heb. *nāzar,* to separate oneself, abstain.]
1. among the ancient Hebrews, a person who voluntarily assumed certain strict religious vows, such as abstaining from wine, not cutting his hair, etc.; as, Samson was a *Nazarite.*
2. a Nazarene. [Rare.]
Also spelled *Nazirite.*

Naz′ȧ·rīte·ship, *n.* the state or condition of being a Nazarite.

Naz·ȧ·rit′iç, *a.* pertaining to Nazaritism or to Nazarites.

Naz′ȧ·rī·tiṣm, *n.* the vows or practice of the Nazarites.

nāze, *n.* [compare Ice. *nös,* Sw. *näsa,* nose.] a promontory or headland.

Nä′zi (-tsi), *a.* [G., contr. of party name, *Nationalsozialistische* Deutsche Arbeiterpartei.] designating, of, or characteristic of the German fascist political party (*National Socialist German Workers' Party*), founded in 1919 and abolished in 1945: under Hitler this party seized control of Germany in 1933, systematically eliminated opposition, and put into effect its program of nationalism, racism, rearmament, aggression, etc.

Nä′zi, *n.*; *pl.* **Nä′ziṣ,** 1. a member of the Nazi party.
2. [*often* n–] a supporter or follower of the Nazi party; a fascist.

Nä′zi·fȳ (-tsi-), *v.t.*; Nazified, *pt., pp.*; Nazifying, *ppr.* to place under Nazi control or influence; to cause to be Nazi or like the Nazis: also *nazify.*

nä′zir, *n.* [Ar. *nazir,* overseer.] in India, etc., any of various officials.

Naz′i·rīte, *n.* a Nazarite.

Nä′ziṣm (-tsizm), **Nä′zi·iṣm** (-tsē-izm), *n.* the philosophy, aims, or characteristics of the Nazi Party; German fascism.

Nb, in chemistry, niobium.

Nd, in chemistry, neodymium.

nē-, same as *neo-.*

Ne, in chemistry, neon.

nēal, *v.t.*; nealed, *pt., pp.*; nealing, *ppr.* [abbrev. of *anneal.*] to temper; to anneal. [Obs.]

nēal, *v.i.* to be tempered by heat. [Obs.]

nē·ȧ·log′iç, *a.* relating to nealogy; youthful, young.

nē·al′o·ġy, *n.* [Gr. *nealēs,* young, fresh, and *-logia,* from *legein,* to speak.] the science relating to the early stages of animal development.

Nē·än′dẽr·thäl (-täl), *a.* [G., lit., Neander valley: named in honor of Joachim *Neander* (1650–1680), G. hymn writer.]
1. designating, of, or from a valley in the Rhine Province, Germany.
2. designating or of a race of early man of the paleolithic period, whose skeletal remains were first found in this valley.

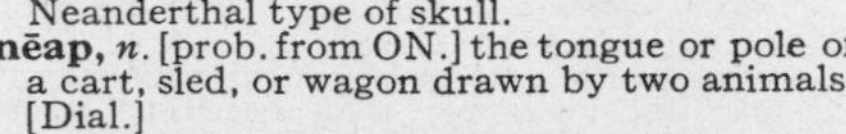
NEANDERTHAL HEAD (reconstructed)

Nē·än′dẽr·thäl·oid, *a.* pertaining to the Neanderthal type of skull.

nēap, *n.* [prob. from ON.] the tongue or pole of a cart, sled, or wagon drawn by two animals. [Dial.]

nēap, *a.* [ME. *neep*; AS. *nep,* scanty, lacking, in *nepflod,* low tide.] designating the tide occurring just after the first and third quarters of the lunar month: at these times the difference between high and low tides is smallest.

neap, *n.* neap tide.

neaped (nēpt), *a.* left aground: said specifically of a ship left aground at high tide, and unable to float again until the next high tide.

Nē·ȧ·pol′i·tăn, *a.* [L. *Neapolitanus,* of or pertaining to Naples, from *Neapolis*; Gr. *Neapolis,* Naples; *neos,* new, and *polis,* city.] belonging to Naples, in Italy.

Nē·ȧ·pol′i·tăn, *n.* an inhabitant or native of Naples.

Nē·ȧ·pol′i·tăn īce çrēam, brick ice cream containing several flavors in layers, usually chocolate, strawberry, and vanilla.

nēar, *adv.* [ME. *nere, neer*; AS. *near,* comp. of *neah,* adv., nigh.]
1. at a relatively short distance in space or time; as, summer is drawing *near.*
2. relatively close in degree; almost; as, you are *near* right: now usually *nearly.*
3. closely, intimately.
4. in a stingy manner; thriftily.

nēar, *a.*; *comp.* nearer; *superl.* nearest, 1. not far; close in distance or time; as, the time is *near.*
2. close in relationship; akin; as, a *near* relative or friend.
3. close in feelings, desires, etc.; close in friendship; intimate.
4. narrow; close in degree; as, a *near* shave.
5. next to one; on the left side: opposed to *off*; as, the *near* horse or ox in a team.
6. short; direct; as, the *nearest* way.
7. stingy; niggardly.
8. somewhat resembling; approximating; as, *near* beer.
9. close; not loose, free, or rambling; literal; as, a *near* translation.
near at hand; very close in time or space.

near, *prep.* close to or by; not far from in space, time, degree, etc.; as, *near* the shore.

nēar, *v.i.* neared, *pt., pp.*; nearing, *ppr.* to draw nigh; to approach.

nēar, *v.t.* to approach; to come nearer to; as, the ship *neared* the land.

nēar′-bȳ′, nēar′bȳ′, *a.* and *adv.* near; close at hand.

nēar bȳ, near; close at hand; close to: used adverbially or prepositionally.

Nē·ärç′tiç, *a.* [*ne-* and *arctic.*] designating the arctic and north temperate parts of North America: used in classifying some plants and animals according to geographical distribution.

Nēar East, 1. variously, the countries near or east of the eastern Mediterranean, including southwestern Asia (Turkey, Syria, Lebanon, Palestine, Trans-Jordan, Saudi Arabia, etc.) and, sometimes, the Balkans and Egypt.
2. the Balkans; especially, the lower Balkans. [British.]

nēar′-hand, *a.* close at hand; near-by. [Scot. and Brit. Dial.]

nēar′-hand, *adv.* 1. near-by. [Scot. and Brit. Dial.]
2. nearly; almost. [Scot. and Brit. Dial.]

nēar′-legged (-legd), *a.* having the feet so near each other that they touch: of horses.

nēar′ly, *adv.* 1. at no great distance; not remotely.
2. closely; as, two persons *nearly* related or allied.
3. intimately; pressingly; with a close relation to one's interest or happiness; as, it *nearly* concerns us.
4. almost; not quite; all but; as, *nearly* finished.
5. in a parsimonious or niggardly manner.

nēar miss, in military usage, a shell, aerial bomb, etc. that does not score a direct hit on the target but comes close enough to inflict some damage.

nēar′ness, *n.* the state or quality of being near.

nēar′sīght″ed (-sīt″), *a.* seeing only near objects distinctly; myopic.

nēar′sīght″ed·ness, *n.* myopia.

nēat, *n. sing.* and *pl.* [AS. *neat,* pl. *neát,* an ox, cow, cattle, prob. from *neótan, niótan,* to use.]
1. cattle of the bovine genus, collectively, as bulls, oxen, and cows.
2. an animal of the ox family; cow, steer, etc. [Obs.]

nēat, *a.* pertaining to bovine animals.

nēat, *a.*; *comp.* neater; *superl.* neatest, [Fr. *net,* f. *nete,* from L. *nitidus,* shining, elegant, smart, trim, from *nitere,* to shine.]
1. unmixed with anything; pure; undiluted: said especially of liquor drunk without a mixer or chaser.
2. free of deductions; net. [Rare.]
3. (a) trim; tidy; clean; (b) characterized by tidiness; skillful and precise; as, a *neat* worker.
4. well-proportioned; shapely.
5. cleverly or smartly phrased or done; adroit.

′nēath, nēath, *prep.* beneath. [Poet.]

nēat′hẽrd, *n.* [ME. *netherd.*] a cowherd.

nēat house, a stable for cattle.

nēat′i·fȳ, *v.t.* to cause to be neat. [Obs.]

nēat′ly, *adv.* with neatness; in a neat manner.

nēat′ness, *n.* the condition or quality of being neat.

nēat′ress, *n.* a woman who takes care of cattle. [Obs.]

nēat's foot, the foot of an ox or cow.

nēat's-foot oil, a pale, yellow, odorless oil, obtained by boiling the feet and leg bones of cattle, much used for softening leather.

nēat's tŏngue, ox tongue.

neb, *n.* [AS. *neb, nebb,* bill, beak, nose.]
1. (a) the bill, or beak, of a bird; (b) the snout of an animal.
2. the nose or mouth of a person.
3. the projecting end or point of anything; nib; tip.

Nē·bā′li·ȧ, *n.* [origin doubtful.] a genus of the lower crustaceans.

nē·bā′li·ăn, *a.* pertaining to the *Nebalia.*

nē·bā′li·ăn, *n.* a crustacean of the genus *Nebalia.*

nē·bā′li·oid, *a.* of or like the genus *Nebalia.*

Ne·bi·im′, *n.pl.* [Heb. *nebī′īm,* pl. of *nābī,* prophet.] in the Old Testament, the books of the Prophets.

neb′-neb, *n.* same as *bablah.*

Ne·bras′kăn, *a.* of Nebraska.

Ne·bras′kăn, *n.* a native or inhabitant of Nebraska.

neb′ū·lȧ, *n.*; *pl.* **neb′ū·lae, neb′ū·lȧṣ,** [L. *nebula,* a cloud, mist, vapor.]
1. any of several light, misty, cloudlike patches seen in the night sky, consisting of groups of stars too far away to be seen singly, or of masses of gaseous matter.
2. in medicine, (a) a small, cloudy opacity on the cornea; (b) a cloudiness in the urine; (c) an oily preparation used as a spray.

neb′ū·lăr, *a.* of a nebula or nebulae.
nebular hypothesis; the theory of Kant, Herschel, Laplace, and others, which supposes that the solar system once existed in the form of a nebula; that, by the effect of gravity, the matter composing the nebula became condensed toward the center; that the exterior portions, by centrifugal force, separated from the mass in the form of a ring; that thus each of the planets was separated, while the main body condensed toward the center, forming the sun; and finally, that each of the rings, by a similar process, became a planet, depositing in the meantime rings out of which its satellites were formed.

neb′ū·lā·ted, *a.* having indistinct markings; clouded.

neb·ū·lā′tion, *n.* the state of being nebulated.

neb′ūle, *n.* a cloud. [Obs.]

neb·u·lé′ (-ū-lā′), *a.* [Fr. *nebulé,* from OFr. *nebule,* a cloud.] in heraldry, made up of short curves.

neb·ū·lif′ẽr·ous, *a.* [L. *nebula,* a cloud, mist, and *ferre,* to bear.] clouded in spots; nebulous. [Rare.]

ne·bū′li·um, *n.* an unknown substance in the nebulae causing the bright green lines in the spectra.

neb″u·li·zā′tion, *n.* a nebulizing or being nebulized.

neb′ū·līze, *v.t.*; nebulized, *pt., pp.*; nebulizing, *ppr.* 1. to reduce (a liquid) to a fine spray.
2. to spray (a diseased or injured surface) with a medicated liquid.

neb′ū·lī·zẽr, *n.* an atomizer.

neb′ū·lōse, *a.* same as *nebulous.*

neb·ū·los′i·ty, *n.* 1. the quality or condition of being nebulous.
2. *pl.* **neb·ū·los′i·tieṣ,** a nebula.

neb′ū·lous, *a.* [L. *nebulosus,* from *nebula,* a cloud, mist, vapor.]
1. in astronomy, pertaining to or having the appearance of a nebula; nebular.
2. cloudy; hazy.
3. unclear; vague; indefinite.

neb′ū·lous·ly, *adv.* in a nebulous manner.

neb′ū·lous·ness, *n.* the state of being nebulous.

neb′ū·ly, *a.* same as *nebulé.*

nec·es·sā′ri·ăn, *n.* and *a.* necessitarian.

nec·es·sā′ri·ăn·iṣm, *n.* same as *necessitarianism.*

nec′es·sā·ri·ly, *adv.* 1. because of necessity; by or of necessity; as, that is not *necessarily* so.
2. as a necessary result.

nec′es·sā·ri·ness, *n.* the state of being necessary.

nec′es·sā·ry, *a.* [L. *necessarius,* unavoidable, inevitable, indispensable, needful, from *necesse,* unavoidable, necessary.]
1. that cannot be dispensed with; essential; indispensable; as, water is *necessary* to life.
2. resulting from necessity; inevitable.
3. that must be done; mandatory; not voluntary; required.
4. inherent in the situation; undeniable; unavoidable from the premises.
5. rendering some essential and intimate service. [Archiac.]

nec′es·sā·ry, *n.*; *pl.* **nec′es·sā·rieṣ,** 1. something necessary or indispensable to some purpose; as, a *necessary* of life: commonly used in the plural.
2. a privy; a water closet; toilet. [Dial.]
3. [*pl.*] in law, those things essential to maintaining an incompetent or dependent in comfort and well-being.

nē·ces·si·tā′ri·ăn, *n.* one who believes in necessitarianism: also *necessarian.*

nē·ces·si·tā′ri·ăn, *a.* of or like necessitarianism: also *necessarian.*

nē·ces·si·tā′ri·ăn·iṣm, *n.* the theory that every event is determined by causal necessity and that the action of the human will is not free, but is caused by previous actions and experiences.

nē·ces′si·tāte, *v.t.*; necessitated, *pt., pp.*; necessitating, *ppr.* [L. *necessitas* (*-atis*), necessity.]
1. to make (something) necessary or indispensable; to render unavoidable; as, sickness *necessitates* his removal.
2. to compel; to force; to oblige; to constrain: usually in passive; as, I am *necessitated* to act alone.
3. to reduce to want. [Obs.]

nē·ces·si·tā′tion, *n.* the act of making necessary; compulsion; the state of being necessary.

nē·ces′si·tous, *a.* 1. in great need; destitute; needy.
2. narrow; pinched; as, *necessitous* circumstances.

nē·ces′si·tous·ly, *adv.* in a necessitous manner.

nē·ces′si·tous·ness, *n.* extreme poverty or destitution of the means of living; pressing want.

nē·ces′si·tūde, *n.* [L. *necessitudo,* from *necesse,* inevitable, necessary.]
1. necessitousness; want; poverty.
2. close connection, alliance, or relation. [Obs.]

nē·ces′si·ty, *n.*; *pl.* **nē·ces′si·tieṣ,** [OFr. *necessite*; L. *necessitas,* unavoidableness, fate, destiny, doom, from *necesse,* unavoidable, necessary.]
1. the power of natural law that cannot be other than it is; natural causation; physical compulsion placed on man by nature; fate.
2. anything that is inevitable, etc. as a result of natural law; that which is necessary in natural sequence; as, death is a *necessity* to life.
3. the compulsion or constraint of man-made circumstances, habit, custom, law, etc.; logical or moral conditions making certain actions inevitable or obligatory.
4. what is required by this social or legal compulsion; that which is necessary in logical or moral sequence; as, a passport is a *necessity.*
5. great or imperative need; as, call me in case of *necessity.*
6. [*often in pl.*] something that cannot be done without; a necessary.
7. the state or quality of being necessary.
8. want; poverty; neediness.
doctrine of necessity; the doctrine that the will is absolutely determined by motives in all its volitions; also, fatalism, taken in a wide sense.
logical necessity; that necessity which consists in the circumstance that something cannot be conceived different from what it is.
moral necessity; necessity resulting from one's moral character.
of necessity; necessarily; inevitably.
physical necessity; that necessity which arises from the laws of the material universe. This necessity is conditional, not absolute.

neck, *n.* [ME. *necke, nekke*; AS. *hnecca,* the neck.]
1. that part of man or animal joining the head to the body, including the part of the backbone between the skull and the shoulders.
2. a narrow part between the head or end and the body or base of any object; as, the *neck* of a violin, *neck* of a goblet.
3. that part of a garment which covers, encircles, or is nearest the neck.
4. the narrowest part of any object, considered to be like a neck; specifically, (a) a narrow strip of land; (b) the narrowest part of an organ; as, the *neck* of the femur, *neck* of a tooth; (c) the narrowest or tapering part of a bottle, vase, etc.; (d) a strait or channel.
5. in geology, a column of molten rock that has hardened in the passage connecting a volcanic crater with the underground source of the lava and has been exposed later by weathering.
neck and crop; completely; entirely.
neck and neck; side by side; in a contest or election, so close together that the winner is not determined until the very end.
neck of a column; in architecture, the part that connects a capital, or head, with its body, or shaft; the part between the lowest molding of the capital and the highest molding of the shaft.
neck of a gun; the part between the muzzle moldings and the cornice ring.
neck or nothing; with determination to succeed completely or fail; at the risk of everything.
on the neck of; immediately after; following closely; on the heels of.
to break the neck of; (a) to destroy the main force of; to ruin or destroy; (b) to get more than half through.
to risk one's neck; to put one's life in danger; to do something very dangerous.
to win by a neck; (a) in horse racing, to win by the length of a horse's head and neck; (b) to win any contest by a narrow margin.

neck, *v.t.*; necked (nekt), *pt., pp.*; necking, *ppr.* 1. to kill (a fowl) by breaking its neck.
2. to kiss and caress in making love. [Slang.]

neck, *v.i.* to make love by kissing and caressing. [Slang.]

neck′band, *n.* 1. a band worn around the neck.
2. the part of a garment that encircles the neck; especially, the part to which the collar is fastened.

neck′cloth, *n.* a scarf for the neck; a neckerchief; a cravat.

necked (nekt), *a.* having a (specified kind of) neck: usually in hyphenated compounds; as, a stiff-*necked* generation.

neck′ẽr·chief (-chif), *n.* a handkerchief or scarf worn around the neck.

neck′ing, *n.* 1. in architecture, any small molding around the top of a column below the capital.
2. the act of kissing and caressing in making love. [Slang.]

neck′in·ġẽr, *n.* a neckerchief. [Dial.]

neck′lăce, *n.* [*neck* and *lace* (string).]
1. an ornament worn around the neck, usually consisting of a chain or string of gold or silver, precious stones, beads, etc.
2. in nautical usage, a strap around a lower mast to carry blocks.
3. a band for the neck. [Rare.]

neck′lăced (-lăst), *a.* having a necklace; marked as with a necklace; as, the *necklaced* snake.

neck′lăce moss, same as *beard moss.*

neck′lăce pop′lăr, the cottonwood of North America, *Populus monilifera.*

neck′lăce tree, a tree of the West Indies, *Ormosia dasycarpa,* producing seeds that are strung together for ornament.

neck′lănd, *n.* a neck, or long tract, of land. [Rare.]

neck′let, *n.* 1. a closely fitting band of fur or cloth worn around the neck.
2. a necklace.

neck′mōld, *n.* same as *neck molding.*

neck mōld′ing, in architecture, a small, convex molding surrounding a column at the junction of the shaft and capital; also, a similar member at the union of a finial with the pinnacle.

neck′piēce, *n.* 1. a decorative scarf, often of fur, worn around the neck.
2. the part of a garment closest to the neck.
3. a piece of armor for the neck.

neck′plāte, *n.* a piece of armor to protect the neck; a gorget.

neck′tīe, *n.* 1. a band, usually narrowest in the middle and widening at one or both ends, to be worn around the neck, usually under a collar and tied in a bow, knotted, or looped in front; a cravat: often *tie.*
2. a bow fastened in front of the neck.

neck′tīe pär′ty, a hanging, especially in lynching. [Slang.]

neck vẽrse, a verse of the Bible, which, when properly read by an offender, was supposed to prove him entitled to benefit of clergy and save him from the halter; hence, a shibboleth; a watchword. [Obs.]

neck′weăr, *n.* articles worn about the neck, as collars, ties, scarfs, etc.

neck′weed, *n.* 1. a common weed of America, *Veronica peregrina.*
2. hemp: a reference to the use of ropes in hanging. [Slang.]

neck′yōke, *n.* 1. a yoke with projecting ends placed around the neck and shoulders, and used in carrying a pair of buckets, etc.
2. a crossbar connecting the neck harness of horses with the tongue of a vehicle.

necr-, see *necro-.*

nē·çrae′mi·ȧ, *n.* [*necr-,* and Gr. *haima,* blood.] destruction of vital elements in the blood.

neç′rō-, [from Gr. *nekros,* dead body.] a combining form meaning *death, corpse, dead tissue,* as in *necrology*: also, before a vowel, *necr-.*

neç″rō·bi·ō′sis, *n.* [*necro-,* and Gr. *bios,* life, and *-osis.*] the process of decay and death of body cells.

neç″rō·bi·ot′iç, *a.* pertaining to necrobiosis.

neç″ro·cȳ·tō′sis, *n.* [*necro-,* and Gr. *kytos,* cell.] death and decay of cells.

neç·rō·ġen′iç, nē·çroġ′ē·nous, *a.* [*necro-,* and Gr. *gennān,* to beget, generate.] originating in dead matter.

nē·çrol′ȧ·try, *n.* [*necro-,* and Gr. *latreia,* worship.] worship of the dead; ancestor worship; excessive reverence for the dead.

neç·rō·loġ′iç·ăl, neç·rō·loġ′iç, *a.* pertaining to or giving an account of the dead, or of deaths.

nē·çrol′ō·ġist, *n.* a writer of necrologies.

nē·çrol′ō·ġy, *n.*; *pl.* **nē·çrol′ō·ġieṣ,** [*necro-,* and Gr. *-logia,* from *legein,* to speak.]
1. a list or register of people who have died in a certain time or place, as that in a newspaper.
2. a death notice; an obituary.

neç′rō·man·cẽr, *n.* 1. one who practices necromancy; one who claims to foretell the future through alleged communication with the dead.
2. a conjurer; a sorcerer; a wizard.

nec′rō·man·cy, *n.* [*necro-,* and Gr. *manteia,* divination.]
1. the art of revealing future events by means of alleged communication with the dead.
2. black magic.

neç·rō·man′tiç, *a.* pertaining to, performed by, used in, or like necromancy.

neç·rō·man′tiç, *n.* trick; conjuration. [Rare.]

neç·rō·man′tiç·ăl·ly, *adv.* by necromancy; in a magical manner.

neç·rō·neç′tō·my, *n.* [*necro-,* and Gr. *ektomē,* excision.] the surgical removal of necrotic ossicles or of any other necrotic part.

neç′rō·nīte, *n.* [Gr. *nekros,* a dead body, and

-ite.] a variety of feldspar which, when struck or broken, gives off a fetid odor like that of putrid flesh.

nē·çroph′ȧ·găn, *n.* one of the *Necrophaga*, a division of the *Coleoptera*, including beetles that feed on dead bodies.

nē·çroph′ȧ·gous, *a.* [Gr. *nekrophagos*, eating dead bodies; *nekros*, a dead body, and *phagein*, to eat.] eating or feeding on dead bodies.

neç·rō·phil′i·ȧ, *n.* necrophilism.

nē·çroph′i·liṣm, *n.* [*necro-*, and Gr. *philos*, loving.] an abnormal attraction, especially an erotic attraction, to corpses.

nē·çroph′i·lous, *a.* [*necro-*, and Gr. *philos*, loving.] fond of, or attracted to, carrion; as, *necrophilous* beetles.

neç·rō·phō′bi·ȧ, *n.* [*necro-*, and Gr. *-phobia*, from *phobos*, fear.] an abnormal fear of death or of dead bodies.

neç′rō·phōre, *n.* a burying beetle.

Nē·çroph′ō·rus, *n.* [*necro-*, and Gr. *phoros*, from *pherein*, to bear.] a genus of beetles characterized by their habit of burying the dead bodies of small animals, as mice, toads, etc., as receptacles for their larvae: also called *burying beetles*.

nē·çrop′ō·lis, *n.*; *pl.* **nē·çrop′ō·lis·eṣ, nē·çrop′ō·leis,** [Gr. *nekropolis*, a cemetery; *nekros*, a dead body, dead, and *polis*, city.] a cemetery, especially one belonging to an ancient city.

neç′rop·sy, *n.*; *pl.* **neç′rop·sieṣ,** [from *necr-*, and Gr. *opsis*, sight.] an autopsy; an examination of a dead body.

neç·rō·sçop′iç, neç·rō·sçop′iç·ăl, *a.* relating to post-mortem examinations.

nē·çros′çō·py, *n.* [*necro-*, and Gr. *-skopia*, from *skopein*, to view.] same as *necropsy*.

nē·çrōse′, *v.t.*; necrosed (crōst′), *pt., pp.*; necrosing, *ppr.* to make necrotic.

nē·çrōse′, *v.i.* to be or become necrotic.

nē·çrō′sis, *n.*; *pl.* **nē·çrō′sēṣ,** [Gr. *nekrōsis*, a killing, deadness, from *nekroun*, to make dead, mortify, from *nekros*, a dead body, dead.]

1. the death or decay of tissue in a part of the body, as a bone: it is the result of loss of blood supply, burning, and other severe injuries.

2. in botany, gradual decay of trees or plants.

nē·çro·spẽr′mi·ȧ, *n.* in pathology, the presence of a urethral discharge in which the spermatozoa are nonmotile.

nē·çrot′iç, *a.* pertaining to or affected with necrosis.

nē·çrot′ō·my, *n.*; *pl.* **nē·çrot′ō·mieṣ,** [*necro-*, and Gr. *tomē*, a cutting.]

1. the dissection of corpses.

2. the surgical removal of dead bones.

neç′tăr, *n.* [L. *nectar*; Gr. *nektar*, the drink of the gods, from base of *necros*, dead, dead body, and *-tar*, who overcomes; hence, death-overcoming: so named because the drink was held to confer immortality.]

1. in Greek mythology, the drink of the gods.

2. any very delicious beverage.

3. in botany, the sweetish liquid in many flowers, used by bees for the making of honey.

neç·tā′rē·ăl, *a.* pertaining to the nectary of a plant.

neç·tā′rē·ăn, *a.* [L. *nectareus*; Gr. *nektareos*, from *nektar*, nectar.] resembling nectar; very sweet and pleasant.

neç′tăred, *a.* containing, full of, or mingled with nectar.

neç·tā′rē·ous, *a.* 1. producing nectar.

2. resembling or pertaining to nectar; delicious; sweet.

The juice *nectareous* and the balmy dew.
—Pope.

neç·tā′rē·ous·ly, *adv.* in a nectareous manner.

neç·tā′rē·ous·ness, *n.* the quality of being nectareous.

neç·tā′ri·ăl, *a.* pertaining to, or having the nature of, the nectary of a plant.

neç′tȧ·ried, *a.* possessing a nectary.

neç·tăr·if′ẽr·ous, *a.* [L. *nectar*, nectar, and *ferre*, to bear.] producing nectar, or honey.

neç′tăr·ine, *a.* sweet as nectar.

neç·tăr·ine′, *n.* a kind of peach that has a smooth skin without down.

neç·tā′ri·um, *n.* same as *nectary*.

neç′tăr·īze, *v.t.* to sweeten. [Rare.]

neç′tăr·ous, *a.* sweet as nectar.

neç′tȧ·ry, *n.*; *pl.* **neç′tȧ·rieṣ,** [Gr. *nektar*, nectar.]

1. an organ or part (of a flower) that secretes nectar.

2. either of a pair of abdominal tubes in aphids, for sucking nectar from flowers.

neç′tō-, [from Gr. *nēktos*, swimming.] a combining form meaning *swimming*, as *nectocalyx*, *nectozooid*.

neç·tō·çal′y·cine, *a.* of or pertaining to a nectocalyx; as, *nectocalycine* canals.

neç·tō·çā′lyx, *n.*; *pl.* **neç·tō·çal′y·çēṣ,** [*necto-*, and Gr. *kalyx* (*-ikos*), a cup, calyx.] the swimming bell or disk of a medusa or jellyfish, consisting of a bell-shaped cup attached by its base to the hydrosome, and provided with a muscular lining in the interior of its cavity: the hydrosome is propelled through the water by the contractions of the nectocalyx.

neç′tō·cyst, *n.* same as *nectosac*.

neç′tō·phōre, *n.* see *nectocalyx*.

neç′tō·saç, *n.* [*necto-*, and Gr. *sakkos*, a bag, sack.] the interior of the nectocalyx of a medusa or jellyfish.

neç′tō·sōme, *n.* the part of a siphonophore used in swimming.

neç′tō·stem, *n.* [*necto-* and *stem*.] the axial line of attachment of the nectocalyces of hydrozoans.

neç·tō·zō′oid, *n.* [*necto-*, and Gr. *zōoeidēs*, like an animal; *zōon*, an animal, and *eidos*, form.] a nectocalyx considered as a zooid.

ned′dẽr, *n.* an adder. [Obs.]

ned′dy, *n.*; *pl.* **ned′dieṣ,** [dim. from *ned*, the abbreviation for *Edward*.] an ass; a donkey.

nee, née (nā), *a.* [Fr., f. of *né*, pp. of *naître*, from L. *nasci*, to be born.] born: used to introduce the maiden name of a married woman; as, Mrs. Helen Jones, *nee* Smith.

need, *n.* [ME. *need*, *nede*; AS. *nyd*, *ned*, *nied*, necessity, compulsion, want.]

1. necessity; compulsion; obligation; as, there is no *need* to worry now.

2. a lack of something useful, required, or desired; a call or demand for the presence, possession, etc. of something; as, I feel the *need* of a long rest.

3. something useful, required, or desired that is lacking; want; requirement; as, what are his daily *needs?*

4. (a) a condition in which there is a deficiency of something; a time or situation of difficulty; a condition requiring relief or supply; as, a friend in *need*; (b) a condition of poverty; state of extreme want.

if need be; if it is required; if the occasion demands.

to have need to; to be compelled or required to; must.

Syn.—exigency, emergency, strait, extremity, necessity, distress, destitution, poverty, indigence, penury.

need, *v.t.*; needed, *pt., pp.*; needing, *ppr.* [ME *neden*; AS. *nydan*, from *nyd*, need.] to have need of; to want. *Need* is often used as an auxiliary, either uninflected and followed by an infinitive without *to*, or inflected and followed by an infinitive with *to*, meaning "to be obliged, must"; as, he *need* not come, he *needs* to be careful.

need, *v.i.* 1. to be necessary: chiefly in impersonal constructions; as, it *needs* not. [Archaic.]

2. to be in need.

need, *adv.* necessarily. [Obs.]

need′-bē, *n.* a necessity. [Rare.]

need′ẽr, *n.* one who needs.

need′fụl, *a.* 1. necessary; needed; required.

2. characterized by great need or distress; needy. [Archaic.]

need′fụl·ly, *adv.* in a needful manner; necessarily.

need′fụl·ness, *n.* the state of being needful; necessity.

need′i·ly, *adv.* in a needy manner.

need′i·ness, *n.* the quality or state of being needy; want; poverty; indigence.

nee′dle, *n.* [ME. *nedle*, *nedel*; AS. *nædl*, a needle.]

1. (a) a small, slender piece of steel with a sharp point at one end and a hole for thread at the other, used for sewing by hand; (b) a similar implement with a hole for thread near the pointed end, used especially on sewing machines.

2. (a) a slender rod of steel, bone, wood, etc. with a hook at one end, used for crocheting; (b) a similar rod, usually larger and without a hook, used in knitting.

3. the short, pointed piece of metal, wood, etc. that moves in the grooves of a phonograph record and transmits vibrations.

4. (a) the magnetized pointer of a compass; (b) the indicator or pointer of a speedometer or other gauge.

5. the thin, short, pointed leaf of such trees as the pine, spruce, etc.

6. the thin rod which, when moved, opens or closes a passage in a valve and permits close adjustment.

7. the sharp, very slender metal tube at the end of a hypodermic syringe.

8. an electric needle.

9. any object roughly resembling a needle or its point in shape, as the sharp point of some crystals, a narrow, jutting, pointed rock, an obelisk, etc.

nee′dle, *v.t.*; needled, *pt., pp.*; needling, *ppr.* 1. to sew, puncture, etc. with a needle.

2. (a) to provoke into doing something; to goad; to prod; (b) to tease or heckle. [Colloq.]

3. to strengthen by adding alcohol; as, they *needled* the beer. [Slang.]

nee′dle, *v.i.* 1. to work with a needle.

2. to form needles in crystallization.

nee′dle bär, the reciprocating bar in a sewing machine that holds the needle.

nee′dle bēam, 1. a transverse beam supporting the floor of a bridge.

2. a floor support consisting of a crosspiece in a queen-post truss.

nee′dle·book, *n.* a needlecase in the form of a book.

nee′dle bug, any long, slender insect of the genus *Ranatra*.

nee′dle·çāse, *n.* a small case for holding needles.

nee′dle·fish, *n.*; *pl.* **nee′dle·fish** or **nee′dle·fish·eṣ,** 1. any of a group of long, pipelike, voracious marine fishes with a pointed snout and many sharp teeth, somewhat resembling the garfish.

2. a pipefish.

nee′dle·fụl, *n.*; *pl.* **nee′dle·fụlṣ,** the length of thread conveniently used in a needle at one time.

nee′dle fŭrze, a plant of the genus *Genista*.

nee′dle gun, an old style of rifle loaded at the breech by a cartridge containing a small quantity of detonating powder, and exploded by the rapid forward thrust of a needle or small spike.

nee′dle hōld′ẽr, in surgery, an instrument for drawing or guiding a needle.

nee′dle hook, a fishhook having no barb.

nee′dle in′strụ·ment, any of various instruments having a magnetic needle.

nee′dle lo͝om, a loom for weaving narrow fabrics, using a reciprocating needle in place of a shuttle.

nee′dle ōre, same as *aikinite*.

nee′dle point, 1. an embroidery of woolen threads upon canvas, used as a covering in upholstery.

2. needle-point lace.

nee′dle-point′, *a.* designating a kind of lace made on a pattern using a needle instead of a bobbin.

nee′dle-point″ed, *a.* having a sharp, tapering point.

nee′dle-point lāce, lace, especially that made in Venice or Brussels, in which the threads are held together by using buttonhole stitches.

nee′dlẽr, *n.* a maker or seller of needles.

nee′dle shell, a sea urchin.

nee′dle show′ẽr, a shower bath in which the water is sprayed out in fine jets.

nee′dle spär, aragonite. [Rare.]

need′less, *a.* 1. not wanted; not necessary; not requisite; as, *needless* expenses.

2. not having cause; groundless; without reason; as, *needless* fear.

need′less·ly, *adv.* without necessity.

need′less·ness, *n.* the quality of being needless.

nee′dle·stōne, *n.* natrolite, scolecite, and similiar minerals formed in acicular crystals: former name.

nee′dle tel′ē·gràph, a telegraph in which the indications are given by the deflections of a magnetic needle whose normal position is parallel to a wire through which a current of electricity can be passed.

nee′dle valve, a type of valve in which a long, cone-shaped plug instead of a disk controls the flow of fluid through the opening: used especially on high-pressure gas cylinders.

nee′dle·wom″ăn (-woom″), *n.*; *pl.* **nee′dle·wom″en** (-wim″), a woman who does needlework; especially, a seamstress.

nee′dle·wŏrk, *n.* 1. work done with a needle; embroidery; sewing.

2. the business of a seamstress.

3. an outer framework of timber and plas-

ter with which many houses were formerly constructed.

nee′dle zē′ō·līte, same as *natrolite.*

nee′dly, *a.* shaped like a needle; studded with sharp points or needles; as, a *needly* stem.

need′ment, *n.* something needed or wanted. [Rare.]

need′n′t, need not.

needș, *adv.* [ME. *needes, nedis*; AS. *nydes, nedes,* adverbial genit. of *nyd, ned,* need.] necessarily; indispensably: used with *must.*

I would have no more of these follies than *needs must.* —Scott.

need′y, *a.*; *comp.* needier; *superl.* neediest; in, or characterized by, need; not having enough to keep up an adequate standard of living; poverty-stricken; as, comfort for the *needy* poor.

neel′ghau, *n.* see *nilgau.*

neem tree, [E. Ind.] see *margosa.*

neep, *n.* a turnip. [Scot. and Brit. Dial.]

ne′er (nãr), *adv.* never. [Poetic.]

ne′er′-dö-well, *a.* worthless; good-for-nothing.

ne′er′-dö-well, *n.* a thriftless or unreliable person; one who never does anything of value.

nē ex′ē·at, same as *ne exeat regno.*

nē ex′ē·at reg′nō, [L., let him not go out of the kingdom.] in law, a writ to restrain a person from leaving the country, originally applicable to purposes of state, now an ordinary process of courts of equity, used to obtain bail or security to abide a decree.

nef, *n.* the nave of a church. [Obs.]

nē·fan′dous, *a.* [L. *nefandus,* not to be spoken.] not to be named; abominable, impious, or blasphemous in character.

nē·fā′ri·ous, *a.* [L. *nefarius,* from *nefas,* a crime, wrong; *ne,* not, and *fas,* lawful.] very wicked; abominable; atrociously sinful or villainous; detestably vile.

nē·fā′ri·ous·ly, *adv.* in a nefarious manner; abominably; atrociously.

nē·fā′ri·ous·ness, *n.* the quality of being nefarious.

nē·fȧst′, *a.* [L. *nefastus,* impious, unlawful; *ne,* not, and *fastus,* lawful.] wicked; unlawful. [Rare.]

nē·gāte′ (*or* nē′gāt), *v.t.*; negated *pt., pp.*; negating, *ppr.* [from L. *negatus,* pp. of *negare,* to deny.]

1. to deny the existence or truth of.
2. to make ineffective.

nē·gā′ted·ness, *n.* the state of being negated. [Rare.]

nē·gā′tion, *n.* [L. *negatio* (*-onis*), from *negare,* to deny; *ne,* not, and *aio,* I say.]

1. act or instance of denying; a negative answer; denial.
2. the lack or opposite of some positive character or quality, as annihilation, destruction, etc.
3. something negative; a nonentity.

neg′ȧ·tive, *a.* [L. *negativus,* from *negare,* to deny.]

1. containing, expressing, or implying a denial or refusal; saying "no": opposed to *affirmative.*
2. opposite to something considered as positive; specifically, (a) lacking in positive character or quality; lacking evidence, affirmation, etc.; having the effect of diminishing, depriving, or denying; as, a *negative* personality; (b) not demonstrating or proving the presence or existence of symptoms, bacteria, etc.
3. in logic, denying the subject or predicate of a proposition.
4. in mathematics, designating a quantity less than zero, or one to be subtracted; minus.
5. in photography, reversing the relation of light and shade of the original subject.
6. in physics, of negative electricity.

negative crystal; in crystallography, an enclosure of glass in another crystal, which assumes the form of the latter.

negative eyepiece; see under *eyepiece.*

negative quantity; see *quantity,* sense 5.

negative radical, in chemistry, any group of two or more atoms taking the place and performing the functions of a negative element in a chemical compound.

negative sign; in mathematics, the sign (−) used to indicate a negative quantity.

neg′ȧ·tive, *n.* 1. a word, term, or phrase that denies, rejects, or refuses (e.g., *no, not, by no means*).

2. a statement of denial, refusal, or rejection.
3. the point of view that denies or attacks the positive or affirmative; as, the *negative* won the debate.
4. the right of veto.
5. the plate in a voltaic battery where the lower potential is; the negative plate or pole.
6. in mathematics, a quantity less than zero, or one to be subtracted; a minus quantity.
7. in photography, an exposed and developed photographic film or plate on which light and shadow are the reverse of what they are in the positive printed from this.

double negative; repetition of the sign of negation; duplication of the negative: such usage is substandard when there is no intention of having the two negatives cancel each other.

in the negative; (a) in refusal or denial of a plan, suggestion, etc.; (b) with a denial or negative answer.

neg′ȧ·tive, *v.t.*; negatived, *pt., pp.*; negativing, *ppr.* 1. to refuse; reject; veto (a candidate, motion, or bill).

2. to deny; contradict.
3. to prove false; disprove.
4. to counteract; neutralize.

neg′ȧ·tive ē·leç·tric′i·ty, 1. electricity made by friction on resin or wax, as distinct from that made on glass.

2. electricity appearing at the pole of the plate having the lower potential in a voltaic cell.

neg′ȧ·tive·ly, *adv.* in a negative manner; specifically, (a) with or by denial or refusal; as, to answer *negatively*; (b) by means of negative reasoning; indirectly: opposed to *positively*; (c) with negative electricity; as, a body *negatively* electrified.

neg′ȧ·tive·ness, *n.* negativity.

neg′ȧ·tiv·ișm, *n.* 1. in philosophy, any system of thought opposed to positivism; a doctrine characterized not by approval and acceptance, but by doubt and question, as agnosticism or skepticism.

2. in psychology, an attitude characterized by ignoring or opposing suggestions or orders from others, most often manifested in children.

neg′ȧ·tiv·ist, *n.* a person who practices or believes in negativism.

neg′ȧ·tiv·ist, *a.* of negativism or negativists.

neg·ȧ·tiv·is′tiç, *a.* negativist.

neg·ȧ·tiv′i·ty, *n.* the quality or condition of being negative.

neg′ȧ·tō·ry, *a.* [LL. *negatorius,* from *negator,* a denier, from L. *negare,* to deny.] constituting or expressing negation; negative.

neg′ȧ·tron, *n.* [*negative* and *electron.*] in chemistry and physics, an electron. [Rare.]

neg′i·noth, *n.pl.* [Heb.] in the Bible, stringed instruments of music.

neg·leçt′, *v.t.*; neglected, *pt., pp.*; neglecting, *ppr.* [L. *neglectus,* pp. of *neglegere, negligere,* to not heed, be regardless of; *nec,* not, and *legere,* to gather.]

1. to ignore or disregard (something); as, we *neglect* modern art.
2. not to care for or attend to (something) sufficiently or properly; to slight; to treat as unimportant; as, he *neglected* his clothes.
3. to fail to carry out (an expected or required action) through carelessness or by intention; to leave undone.

Syn.—slight, overlook, omit, disregard, disesteem, despise, contemn.

neg·leçt′, *n.* [L. *neglectus,* a neglecting, from *neglegere* to neglect.]

1. a neglecting.
2. lack of sufficient or proper care; negligence; disregard.
3. the state of being neglected.

Syn.—negligence, disregard, omission, failure, default, slight, carelessness, remissness.

neg·leçt′ed·ness, *n.* state of being neglected.

neg·leçt′ēr, neg·leçt′ŏr, *n.* one who neglects.

neg·leçt′fụl, *a.* heedless; careless; inattentive; negligent (often with *of*).

neg·leçt′fụl·ly, *adv.* in a neglectful manner.

neg·leçt′fụl·ness, *n.* the quality or state of being neglectful.

neg·leç′tion, *n.* negligence. [Obs.]

neg·leçt′ive, *a.* neglectful.

né·gli·gé′ (nā-glē-zhā′), *n.* and *a.* [Fr.] negligee.

neg·li·gee′ (-zhā′), *n.* [Fr. *négligée,* f. of *négligé,* pp. of *négliger,* to neglect; L. *negligere,* to neglect.]

1. a woman's loosely fitting dressing gown, usually decorative and of a soft, flowing material.
2. any informal, careless, or incomplete attire.

neg·li·gee′, *a.* carelessly or incompletely dressed.

neg′li·ġence, *n.* [L. *negligentia,* carelessness, from *negligens* (*-entis*), careless, negligent.]

1. the quality or condition of being negligent; specifically, (a) habitual failure to do the required thing; (b) carelessness in manner or appearance; indifference.
2. an instance of such failure, carelessness, or indifference.
3. in law, failure to use a reasonable amount of care when such failure results in injury to another.

neg′li·ġent, *a.* [L. *negligens* (*-entis*), ppr. of *negligere,* to neglect.]

1. habitually failing to do the required thing; neglectful.
2. careless, lax, inattentive, or indifferent.

Syn.—thoughtless, remiss, inconsiderate.

neg′li·ġent·ly, *adv.* in a negligent manner; as, a person *negligently* dressed.

neg·li·ġi·bil′i·ty, *n.* the quality or state of being negligible.

neg′li·ġi·ble, *a.* [from L. *negligere,* to neglect; and *-ible.*] that can be neglected or disregarded because small, unimportant, etc.; trifling.

neg′li·ġi·bly, *adv.* in a negligible manner; so as to be negligible.

nē·gō·ti·ȧ·bil′i·ty (-gō-shi-), *n.* the quality or state of being negotiable.

nē·gō′ti·ȧ·ble, *a.* [LL. *negotiabilis,* from L. *negotiari,* to negotiate.] that can be negotiated; specifically, (a) transferable to a third person: said of promissory notes, checks, etc.; (b) that can be passed, crossed, surmounted, etc.

negotiable paper; any paper bearing evidence of debt and transferable by endorsement, used in commercial transactions, such as a note, a bill of exchange, a draft, etc.

nē·gō′ti·ănt, *n.* a negotiator.

nē·gō′ti·āte (-shi-), *v.i.*; negotiated, *pt., pp.*; negotiating, *ppr.* [L. *negotiatus,* pp. of *negotiari,* to carry on business, from *negotium,* business.]

1. to treat with another respecting purchase and sale; to confer with another in bargaining or trade; as, to *negotiate* with a man for the purchase of the farm.
2. to hold conference and discussion with a view to reaching agreement on a treaty, league, contract, etc.; to treat with another or others respecting peace, commerce, or any subject of common concern.

nē·gō′ti·āte, *v.t.* 1. to procure or bring about by negotiation; as, to *negotiate* a loan of money; to *negotiate* a treaty.

2. to pass in the way of business; to put into circulation; to transfer and get value for; as, to *negotiate* a bill of exchange.

The notes were not *negotiated* to them in the usual course of business or trade. —Kent.

3. to treat with dexterity and success; to overcome or surmount by skill; to cope with successfully; as, to *negotiate* an obstacle. [Colloq.]

nē·gō·ti·ā′tion, *n.* [L. *negotiatio* (*-onis*), from *negotiari,* to carry on business.]

1. a negotiating; specifically, [*often in pl.*] a conferring, discussing, or bargaining to reach agreement, as in business transactions or state matters.
2. trading; mercantile business. [Obs.]

nē·gō′ti·ā·tŏr, *n.* [L. *negotiator,* one who does business by wholesale, a banker, from *negotiari,* to carry on business.] one who negotiates.

nē·gō′ti·ȧ·tō·ry, *a.* relating to or connected with negotiation. [Rare.]

nē·gō·ti·ā′trix, *n.* [LL., f. of L. *negotiator,* one who does business.] a female negotiator.

nē·gō′tious (-shus), *a.* busy; engaged in negotiating. [Obs.]

Nē′gress, *n.* [compare Fr. *négresse,* f. of *négro,* a Negro.] [*sometimes* n–] a Negro woman or girl: often a patronizing or contemptuous term.

Nē·gril′lō, *n.*; *pl.* **Nē·gril′lōș,** [Sp., dim of *negro,* black.] an African Pygmy or Bushman.

nē·grï′tȧ, *n.* [Sp., f. of *negrito,* dim. of *negro,* black.] a black fish tinged with violet; the *Hypoplectrus chlorurus* of the West Indies.

Nē·grï′tiăn, (-grish′un), *a.* same as *Nigritian.*

Nē·grit′iç, *a.* [*sometimes* n–] of or like Negroes or Negritos.

Nē·grï′tō, *n.*; *pl.* **Nē·grï′tōș, Nē·grï′tōeș,** [Sp. *negrito,* dim. of *negro,* black, a Negro.] a member of any of various groups of dwarfish

Negroid peoples living in the East Indies, the Philippines, and Africa.

Nē′grō, *n.*; *pl.* **Nē′grōes,** [Sp. and Port. *negro*, black, a black person, from L. *niger*, black.]
1. (a) a member of the dominant black race of Africa, living chiefly in the Congo and Sudan regions; (b) a member of any of the other black races of Africa, as a Bantu, Hottentot, etc.
2. any person with some Negro ancestors. Less often *negro*.

Nē′grō, *a.* of, for, or being a Negro or Negroes.

nē′grō bat, a sooty-brown bat of the Old World; the *Vesperugo maurus*.

nē′grō bug, a very small, black hemipterous insect, *Corimelæna pulicaria*, found on various fruit plants, as the blackberry and raspberry, injuring the fruit by imparting to it a disagreeable odor and flavor.

nē′grō çorn, sorghum (the plant): so called in the West Indies.

nē′grō flȳ, a black dipterous insect, *Psila rosæ*: also called *carrot fly*.

nē′grō-head (-hed), *n.* a kind of dark-colored tobacco prepared by mixing with molasses and then pressing.

Nē′groid, *a.* [*sometimes* n–] of, like, or characteristic of the Negro or Negroes.

Nē′groid, *n.* [*sometimes* n–] a member of any dominantly Negro people.

Nē′grō·loid, *a.* Negroid.

nē′grō mŏn′key, a black monkey, *Semnopithecus maurus*, of the Javanese forests.

Nē′grō·phīle, Nē′grō·phil, *n.* [Sp. *negro*, a Negro, and Gr. *philos*, loving.] [*sometimes* n–] a person who admires, likes, or champions Negroes, their culture, etc.: often used contemptuously by Negrophobes.

Nē·groph′i·lism, *n.* the attitudes, actions, etc. of Negrophiles.

Nē·groph′i·list, *n.* a Negrophile.

Nē′grō·phōbe, *n.* [*sometimes* n–] a person who hates or fears Negroes.

Nē·grō·phō′bi·ȧ, *n.* [Sp. *negro*, Negro, and Gr. *phobos*, fear.] [*sometimes* n–] hatred or fear of Negroes.

nē′grō's-head (-hed), *n.* the ivory palm, *Phytelephas macrocarpa*: so called from the appearance of its fruit.

Nē·gun′dō, *n.* a genus of North American trees belonging to the family *Sapindaceæ* and separated from *Acer* because of its pinnated leaves and dioecious apetalous flowers. *Negundo aceroides*, also known as *Acer negundo*, is a small tree with light-green twigs and drooping clusters of small greenish flowers: also called *box elder* and *ash-leaved maple*.

nē′gus, *n.* [after Col. Francis *Negus* (d.1732), who first made it.] a beverage of hot water, wine, and lemon juice, sweetened and spiced.

Nē′gus, *n.* [Amharic.] the title of the ruler of Ethiopia.

Nē·he·mī′ȧh, *n.* [Heb. *nehemyāh*, lit., comfort of Jah (God).] in the Bible, (a) a Hebrew leader of about the fifth century B.C.; (b) a book of the Old Testament about his work.

Nē·he·mī′as, *n.* Nehemiah: form used in the Douay Bible.

nē′hi·loth, *n.* [Heb.] in the Bible, a perforated wind instrument, as a flute.

Nē·hush′tăn, *n.* [Heb. *nechushtān*, from *nechōseth*, lit., a piece of brass.] the brazen serpent set up in the wilderness by Moses. 2 Kings xviii. 4.

neigh (nā), *v.i.*; neighed, *pt.*, *pp.*; neighing, *ppr.* [ME. *neighen*, *neyen*; AS. *hnægan*, to neigh; prob. of imitative origin.] to utter the loud, characteristic cry of a horse; to whinny.

neigh, *n.* the cry of a horse; a whinnying.

neigh′bŏr (nā′), *n.* [AS. *neáhgebur*, *nēhgebur*, *neáhbur*; *neáh*, nigh, and *gebur*, a dweller.]
1. a person who lives near another.
2. a person or thing situated near another.
3. a fellow man; as, love thy *neighbor*.
4. any person: used as a term of direct address.
British spelling, *neighbour*.

neigh′bŏr, *a.* near-by; adjacent: British spelling, *neighbour*.

neigh′bŏr, *v.t.*; neighbored (-bẽrd), *pt.*, *pp.*; neighboring, *ppr.* 1. to adjoin; to border on, or be near to; as, the tenement district *neighbors* the levee.
2. to bring near or into close association with. [Rare.]
British spelling, *neighbour*.

neigh′bŏr, *v.i.* 1. to live in the vicinity, one of another; to be in the same neighborhood.
2. to be friendly; to render mutual favors or assistance; as, these families *neighbor* agreeably.
British spelling, *neighbour*.

neigh′bŏr·hood, *n.* 1. friendly relations, as of neighbors; neighborliness. [Rare.]
2. the state or quality of being neighbors.
3. a community, region, area, or territory, especially with regard to some characteristic; as, they live in an attractive *neighborhood*.
4. the people living near one another; a community.
in the neighborhood of; (a) near; close to (a place); (b) about; approximately; roughly. [Colloq.]
Syn.—vicinity, vicinage, locality, proximity.

neigh′bŏr·ing, *a.* near-by; adjacent; close together; in the same region; as, the *neighboring* inhabitants, *neighboring* countries.

neigh′bŏr·li·ness, *n.* the state or quality of being neighborly.

neigh′bŏr·ly, *a.* like, characteristic of, or appropriate to neighbors; kind, friendly, sociable, etc.

neigh′bŏr·ship, *n.* the state of being neighbors. [Rare.]

neigh′bŏur, *n.*, *a.*, *v.t.* and *v.i.* neighbor: British spelling.

nei′thẽr (*or* nī′), *a.* [AS. *nāther*, *nāthor*, *nāwther*, contr. of *nāhwæther*; *ne*, not, and *āhwæther*, *āwther*, either.] not one or the other of two; not either; as, I want *neither* book at present.

nei′thẽr, *pron.* not one or the other (of two); not either; as, of the two candidates, *neither* is eligible.

nei′thẽr, *conj.* 1. not either: the first element of the pair of correlatives *neither* . . . *nor*, implying negation of both parts of the statement; as, I can *neither* go *nor* stay.
2. nor yet; and . . . not; as, he doesn't smoke, *neither* does he drink.

nei′thẽr, *adv.* any more than the other; also (following negative expressions); as, if she won't go, I won't *neither*. [Dial. or Colloq.]

nek′tŏn, *n.* [Mod. L.; Gr. *nektōn*, neut. of *nektos*, swimming.] all the minute organisms swimming in large numbers on or near the surface of the sea.

nel′sŏn, *n.* [from personal name *Nelson*.] a hold in wrestling: see *full nelson*, *half nelson*.

Nē·lum′bi·um, *n.* same as *Nelumbo*.

Nē·lum′bō, *n.* [Mod. L., from Singhalese *nelumbu*.] 1. a genus of water lilies with blue-green leaves and flowers of white to dark red.
2. [n–] any plant belonging to this genus.

NELUMBO

nem′ȧ-, nem′ăt-, same as *nemato-*.

nem′ȧ·line, *a.* [*nema-* and *-l-* and *-ine*.] of threadlike form, fibrous.

nem′ȧ·līte, *n.* [*nema-*, and Gr. *lithos*, stone.] a fibrous brucite or native hydrate of magnesia.

Nem·ȧ·tel′mi·ȧ, *n.pl.* same as *Nemathelminthes*.

nem·ȧ·tel′minth, *n.* same as *nemathelminth*.

nem·ȧ·thē′ci·um, *n.*; *pl.* **nem·ȧ·thē′ci·ȧ,** [*nema-*, and Gr. *thēkion*, dim. of *thēkē*, a case, receptacle.] in certain red algae, a wartlike protuberance on the thallus.

nem·ȧ·thel′minth, *n.* [*nemat-* and *helminth*.] any of the *Nemathelminthes*.

Nem″ȧ·thel·min′thēs, Nem″ȧ·tel·min′thēs, *n.pl.* [*nemat-*, and Gr. *helmins* (*-inthos*), a worm.] a phylum of worms, including the roundworms, threadworms, etc.; the nematode worms.

nem′a·tō-, [from Gr. *nēma*, *nēmatos*, what is spun, thread.] a combining form meaning *thread*, *threadlike*, as in *nematocyst*: also, before a vowel, *nema-*, *nemat-*.

nem′ȧ·tō·blast, *n.* [*nemato-*, and Gr. *blastos*, a germ.] a spermatocyte.

nem″ȧ·tō·çā′lyx, *n.*; *pl.* **nem″ȧ·tō·çal′y·cēs,** [*nemato-*, and Gr. *kalyx* (*-ikos*), a calyx.] a calyx enclosing nematocysts.

Nem·ȧ·toc′e·rȧ, *n.pl.* [*nemato-*, and Gr. *keras*, horn.] the *Nemocera*.

nem′ȧ·tō·cyst, *n.* [*nemato-* and *-cyst*.] any of the stinging cells of certain hydrozoans, as the jellyfish, containing a threadlike sting.

nem″ȧ·tō·cys′tiç, *a.* of, like, or forming a nematocyst.

Nem·ȧ·tō′dȧ, *n.pl.* [see *Nematoidea*.] a group of worms of the phylum *Nemathelminthes*, with long, cylindrical, unsegmented bodies, as the hookworm, pinworm, etc.

nem′ȧ·tōde, *a.* of the *Nematoda*.

nem′ȧ·tōde, *n.* a nematode worm.

nem′ȧ·tō·gen, nem′ȧ·tō·ġēne, *n.* [*nemato-*, and Gr. *-genēs*, producing.] an embryo of certain worms, threadlike in form.

nem·ȧ·tog′nath, *n.* a fish of the order *Nematognathi*; a catfish.

Nem·ȧ·tog′nȧ·thī, *n.pl.* [*nemato-*, and Gr. *gnathos*, jaw.] an order of barbellate fishes; the catfishes.

nem′ȧ·toid, *a.* [*nemat-*, and Gr. *eidos*, form.] of the *Nematoidea*.

nem′ȧ·toid, *n.* a nematoid worm.

Nem·ȧ·toi′dē·ȧ, *n.pl.* [*nemat-*, and Gr. *eidos*, form.] same as *Nematoda*.

nem·a·toid′ē·ăn, *a.* and *n.* *nematoid*.

Nem·ȧ·toph′ō·rȧ, *n.pl.* [*nemato-*, and Gr. *phoros*, from *pherein*, to bear.] a division of the *Cœlenterata*, not including *Porifera*.

nem′ȧ·tō·phōre, *n.* [*nemato-*, and Gr. *-phoros*, from *pherein*, to bear.] a nematocalyx.

nem·ȧ·toph′ō·rous, *a.* characteristic of or pertaining to the *Nematophora*.

nem″ȧ·tō·zō′oid, *n.* [*nemato-*, and Gr. *zōoeidēs*, like an animal.] a tentacle of defense characterized as a zooid, extending from a siphonophore.

Nem′bū·tal, *n.* [*Na*(sodium) and *ethyl* and *methyl* and *butyl* and barbi*tal*.] pentobarbital sodium, used in medicine as a sedative, hypnotic, and analgesic: a trade-mark.

Nē·mē′ăn (*or* nē′mē-), *a.* [L. *Nemeus*; Gr. *Nemeos*, pertaining to Nemea, from *Nemea*, a valley in Argolis, from *nemos*, a wooded pasture.] of or pertaining to Nemea, in Argolis, Greece.

Nē·mē′ăn gāmes, an ancient Greek festival held every other year at Nemea, consisting chiefly of athletic and musical contests.

Nē·mē′ăn lī′ŏn, in Greek mythology, a fierce lion killed by Hercules in the course of his twelve labors.

nē·mẽr′tē·ăn, nē·mẽr′ti·ăn, *a.* of or belonging to the *Nemertina*.

nē·mẽr′tē·ăn, nē·mẽr′ti·ăn, *n.* any nemertean worm.

Nē·mẽr·tī′nȧ, *n.pl.* [Gr. *Nēmertēs*, the name of a Nereid, from *nēmertēs*, unerring, infallible.] a group of brightly colored marine worms living in coastal mud or sand: also called *Nemertea*, *Nemertinea*, *Nemertida*, and *Rhynchocœla*.

nē·mẽr′tine, nē·mẽr′toid, *a.* pertaining to or characteristic of the *Nemertina*.

nē·mẽr′tine, nē·mẽr′toid, *n.* any worm of the *Nemertina*.

nem·ẽr·tin′ē·ăn, *a.* and *n.* same as *nemertean*.

Nem′ē·sis, *n.* [L. *Nemesis*; Gr. *Nemesis*, from *nemein*, to distribute, deal out.]
1. in Greek mythology, the goddess of retributive justice, or vengeance.
2. [*usually* n–] *pl.* **nem′ē·sēs,** (a) just punishment; retribution; (b) one who imposes retribution.

nē′mō-, same as *nemato-*.

Nē·moc′ē·rȧ, *n.pl.* [Gr. *nēma*, a thread, and *keras*, a horn.] a group of dipterous insects, including such as have long filiform antennae, usually of more than six joints. It comprises the gnats or mosquitoes and crane flies.

nē·moc′ẽr·ăn, nē·moc′ẽr·ous, *a.* pertaining to the *Nemocera*.

Nē·moph′i·lȧ, *n.* [Gr. *nemos*, a wooded pasture, and *philos*, loving.] a genus of annual plants having diffuse brittle stems, pinnatifid leaves, and conspicuous blue or white flowers. They are common in California.

nē·moph′i·list, *n.* one who is fond of the woods.

nē·moph′i·lous, *a.* [Gr. *nemos*, a wooded pasture, and *philos*, loving.] having a love for or living in the woods.

nē·moph′i·ly, *n.* fondness for the woods or for forest scenery.

nem′ō·răl, *a.* [L. *nemoralis*, from *nemus* (*-oris*), a wood, wooded pasture.] relating to woods, groves, or wooded places. [Rare.]

nen′ū·phär, *n.* the great white water lily of Europe, or the yellow water lily.

nē′ō-, [from Gr. *neos*, new, recent, young.] a combining form meaning: (a) [*sometimes* N–] *new*, *recent*, *latest*, as in *Neo*-Catholic, *neo*classic; (b) [N–] in geology, *the chronologically* *last subdivision of a period*, as in *Neo*cene: also *ne-*.

nē·ō·ärs·phen·am′in, *n.* same as *neoarsphenamine.*

nē″ō·ärs″phen·ȧ·mīne′, *n.* a sodium compound of arsphenamine, used instead of arsphenamine because it is less toxic and more soluble: also called *Neosalvarsan.*

nē·ō·blas′tiç, *a.* [*neo-*, and Gr. *blastos*, a germ.] characteristic of a new growth.

nē·ō·bot′ȧ·ny, *n.* botany that deals with recent forms.

Nē″ō-Çath′ō·liç, *a.* 1. designating or of a group in the Anglican Church that tends toward Roman Catholic doctrine and practice.

2. in France, designating or of a group of liberal Catholics opposed to the religious supremacy of the Pope.

Nē″ō-Çath′ō·liç, *n.* a member of a Neo-Catholic group.

Nē′ō·cēne, *a.* [from *neo-*, and Gr. *kainos*, new.] designating or of the latter epoch of the Tertiary, when mammals underwent their greatest development and manlike types appeared.

the Neocene; the Neocene Epoch or its rocks.

Nē″ō-Chris·ti·an′i·ty, *n.* [*neo-*, and LL. *Christianitas*, Christianity.] Christianity adapted to rationalism.

nē·ō·çlas′siç, nē·ō·çlas′si·çăl, *a.* designating or of a revival of classic style and form in art, literature, etc., as in England from c. 1660 to c. 1740.

Nē·ō·çō′mi·ăn, *a.* [*neo-*, and Gr. *kōmē*, village.] in geology, a term applied to the lowest of the Cretaceous deposits, being the Lower Greensand and Wealden.

Nē·ō·çō′mi·ăn, *n.* the Lower Cretaceous deposits.

nē·ō·ços′miç, *a.* [*neo-*, and Gr. *kosmos*, universe.] characteristic of the universe as it now exists; also, of the history of man as long as known.

nē·oç′rȧ·cy, *n.* [*neo-*, and Gr. *-kratia*, from *kratein*, to rule.] government by new or inexperienced officials; upstart rule or supremacy. [Rare.]

nē·od′ȧ·mōde, *n.* [Gr. *neodamōdēs*; *neos*, new, and *damos*, the people, and *eidos*, form.] in ancient Sparta, a Helot newly admitted to citizenship.

Nē′ō-Där·win′i·ăn, *a.* relating to Neo-Darwinism.

Nē″ō-Där′win·işm, *n.* [*neo-* and *Darwinism.*] a biological theory which maintains that natural selection is the main factor in the evolution of animals and plants, and denies the inheritance of acquired characteristics.

nē·ō·dym′i·um, *n.* [*neo-* and di*dymium.*] a metallic chemical element of the rare-earth group: symbol, Nd; atomic weight, 144.27; atomic number, 60.

Nē·ō·ġae′ȧ, *n.* [Mod. L., from *neo-* and Gr. *gaia*, earth.] the Neotropical area of the earth, considered as one of the primary realms.

Nē·ō·ġae′ăn, *a.* of or pertaining to the Neogaea.

nē·og′ȧ·mist, *n.* [Gr. *neogamos*, one newly married.] a person recently married.

Nē′ō·ġēne, *a.* [Gr. *neogenēs*, newborn, *neos*, new, and *-genēs*, born.] Neocene. [Rare.]

nē·og′rȧ·phy, *n.* [*neo-*, and Gr. *graphein*, to write.] a novel method of writing. [Rare.]

Nē″ō-Hē·brā′iç, *n.* and *a.* Modern Hebrew.

Nē″ō-Hel′len·işm, *n.* [*neo-* and *Hellenism.*] Hellenism brought up to a modern standard; the application of ancient Greek ideals to present-day practices or arts.

nē′oid, *n.* [Gr. *neein*, to swim, and *eidos*, form.] that form of curve best adapted to the water line of a vessel, since it presents the least retardation of motion.

nē″ō·im·pres′siŏn·işm, *n.* a late nineteenth-century theory and practice of painting, based on a strict scientific application of impressionist techniques, especially pointillism.

Nē″ō-Lȧ·märck′işm, *n.* a theory of inheritance based on a modification and extension of Lamarckism, essentially maintaining the principle that acquired characters can be inherited, but admitting the importance of natural selection.

Nē″ō-Lat′in, *n.* Modern Latin.

nē′ō·lith, *n.* a neolithic implement.

nē·ō·lith′iç, *a.* [*neo-* and *-lith* and *-ic.*] designating or of the later part of the Stone Age (in the Old World), during which man developed polished stone tools and weapons, raised cattle, etc.

nē·ō·lō′ġi·ăn, *a.* relating to neology; neological.

nē·ō·lō′ġi·ăn, *n.* one who introduces new words, phrases, or interpretations; a neologist.

nē·ō·lō′ġi·ăn·işm, *n.* same as *neologism.*

nē·ō·loġ′iç·ăl, nē·ō·loġ′iç, *a.* of or characterized by neology or (a) neologism.

nē·ō·loġ′iç·ăl·ly, *adv.* in a neological manner.

nē·ol′ō·ġişm, *n.* [Fr. *néologisme.*] 1. a new word or a new meaning for an established word.

2. the use of new words or of new meanings for established words.

I learnt my complement of classic French
(Kept pure of Balzac and *neologism*).
—E. B. Browning.

3. any new doctrine or doctrines; specifically, rationalism in theology.

nē·ol′ō·ġist, *n.* 1. one who invents, or makes a practice of using, neologisms.

2. an innovator in theology; one who introduces rationalistic views or doctrines in theology.

nē·ol·ō·ġis′tiç, nē·ol·ō·ġis′tiç·ăl, *a.* of or characterized by neologism.

nē·ol″ō·ġi·zā′tion, *n.* the act of neologizing.

nē·ol′ō·ġize, *v.i.*; neologized, *pt.*, *pp.*; neologizing, *ppr.* 1. to introduce or use neologisms.

2. to introduce or adopt rationalistic views in theology; to introduce or adopt new theological doctrines.

nē·ol′ō·ġy, *n.*; *pl.* **nē·ol′ō·ġieş**, [Fr. *néologie.*] 1. neologism.

Neology, or the novelty of words and phrases, is an innovation, which, with the opulence of our present language, the English philologer is most jealous to allow. —D'Israeli.

2. rationalistic views in theology.

nē·ō·mē′ni·ȧ, *n.* [Gr. *neomēnia*; *neos*, new, and *mēn*, a month, *mēnē*, the moon.]

1. the time of new moon; the beginning of the month.

2. a heathen festival of the new moon.

3. [N—] in conchology, the typical genus of the *Neomeniidæ.*

Nē″ō·mē·nī′i·dae, *n.pl.* [*neomenia* and *-idæ.*] a division of shelled mollusks of which *Neomenia* is the typical genus.

nē′ō·morph, *n.* [*neo-*, and Gr. *morphē*, form.] in biology, a structure or organ which is the result of independent development.

nē′on, *n.* [Mod. L., from Gr. *neon*, neut. of *neos*, new.] one of the chemical elements, a rare, colorless, odorless, inert gas, discovered in the earth's atmosphere in 1898: symbol, Ne; atomic number, 10; atomic weight, 20.183.

neon lamp; a glass tube filled with neon, which ionizes and glows when an electric current is sent through it.

neon sign; a commercial display sign made up of tubes, shaped to form letters and designs: the tubes are filled with neon gas, through which an electric current is passed, causing the gas to glow with a reddish color; mercury vapors produce other colors, as blue and green.

nē·ō·nā′tăl, *a.* pertaining to the newborn.

Nē·ō·nō′mi·ăn, *n.* an upholder or adherent of Neonomianism.

Nē·ō·nō′mi·ăn, *a.* characteristic of Neonomianism or its adherents.

Nē·ō·nō′mi·ăn·işm, *n.* [*neo-*, and Gr. *nomos*, law.] the doctrine that the New Testament is a new law, superseding the old, or Mosaic, law.

nē·ō·pā′găn·işm, *n.* [*neo-*, and LL. *paganismus*, heathenism.] paganism revived.

nē·ō·phrē′ni·ȧ, *n.* [*neo-*, and Gr. *phrēn*, mind.] mental disorder occurring in early youth.

nē′ō·phȳte, *n.* [L. *neophytus*; Gr. *neophytos*, newly planted; *neos*, new, and *phytos*, verbal adj. of *phyein*, to produce, pass, *phyesthai*, to grow.]

1. a new convert or proselyte; especially, a newly baptized member of the early Christian Church.

2. a novice in a religious order; a newly ordained priest or new member of a convent.

3. a tyro; a novice; any beginner.

nē·ō·plā′şiȧ (-zhȧ), *n.* the formation of a neoplasm.

nē′ō·plaşm, *n.* [*neo-* and *-plasm.*] any abnormal formation or growth of tissue; a tumor, etc.

nē·ō·plas′tiç, *a.* of a neoplasm or neoplasty.

nē·ō·plas′ti·çişm, *n.* [*neo-* and *plastic* and *-ism.*] an early twentieth-century school of abstract painting, characterized by nonsymmetrical geometric figures.

nē′ō·plas·ty, *n.* [*neo-* and *-plasty.*] the use of plastic surgery to restore a destroyed or mutilated part of the body.

Nē″ō-plȧ·ton′iç, Nē″ō-Plȧ·ton′iç, *a.* of Neoplatonism or Neoplatonists.

Nē·ō·plā′tō·nişm, Nē·ō-Plā′tō·nişm, *n.* a school of philosophy, founded at Alexandria in the third century A.D., that tried to combine the doctrines of Plato and some other Greek philosophers with the ethical concepts common to Judaism and Christianity, and with the mysticism of the Near East.

Nē·ō·plā′tō·nist, Nē·ō·plā·tō·ni′ciăn, (-nish′un), *n.* one of the Neoplatonic school: also *Neo-Platonist, Neo-Platonician.*

nē′ō·prēne, *n.* [*neo-* and chloro*prene.*] a synthetic rubber produced by the polymerization of a chlorine derivative of acetylene: it is highly resistant to oil, heat, light, and oxidation.

nē·ō·rä′mȧ (*or* -ram′ȧ), *n.* [Attic Gr. *neos*, a temple, and *horama*, a view, from *horan*, to see.] a panorama representing the interior of a large building in which the spectator appears to be placed.

Nē″ō·sal′vär·san, *n.* neoarsphenamine: a trade-mark.

Nē″ō-Sçhō·las′ti·çişm, *n.* a philosophical system based on scholasticism but incorporating new elements, particularly emphasis on research, to make it applicable to contemporary life.

nē·os·sol′ō·ġy, *n.* [Gr. *neossos*, a young bird, and *-logia*, from *legein*, to speak.] the science of the young of birds, a branch of ornithology.

nē′ō·stȳle, *n.* [*neo-* and *style.*] a type of cyclostyle for multiple reproduction of a writing, drawing, etc.

nē′ō·stȳle, *v.t.*; neostyled, *pt.*, *pp.*; neostyling, *ppr.* to reproduce by means of a neostyle.

nē·ō-Syr′i·aç, *n.* [*neo-*, and L. *Syriacus*, from *Syria*, Syria.] a modern form of Syriac spoken in some parts of southwestern Asia.

nē·ō·ter′iç, nē·ō·ter′iç·ăl, *a.* [Gr. *neōterikos*, youthful, from *neōteros*, comp. of *neos*, young.] new; recent in origin; modern.

nē·ō·ter′iç, *n.* a modern person; one accepting new ideas and practices.

nē·ō·ter′iç·ăl·ly, *adv.* newly; lately.

nē·ot′ĕr·işm, *n.* [Gr. *neōterismos*, innovation, from *neōterizein*, to innovate.] anything new; an innovation; a neoteric word or idiom.

nē·ot′ĕr·ist, *n.* one practicing neoterism.

nē·ot′ĕr·īze, *v.i.*; neoterized, *pt.*, *pp.*; neoterizing, *ppr.* [Gr. *neōterizein*, from *neōteros*, comp. of *neos*, young, new.] to coin new words.

Nē·ō·trop′iç·ăl, Nē·ō·trop′iç, *a.* [*neo-* and *tropical.*] designating or of the region of the New World extending southward from the Tropic of Cancer.

nē″ō·vol·çan′iç, *a.* [*neo-* and *volcanic.*] characteristic of rocks erupted since the Cretaceous period.

nē″ō·yt·tĕr′bi·um, *n.* same as *ytterbium.*

nē·ō′zȧ pīne, [*neoza*, native name.] a tall pine, *Pinus gerardiana*, found in the Himalayas. It bears edible seeds, which grow in large numbers in cones five inches in diameter.

Nē·ō·zō′iç, *a.* [*neo-*, and Gr. *zōē*, life.] in geology, (a) designating or of the period including the Mesozoic and the Cenozoic; (b) Cenozoic: former name.

NEP, Nep, nep, *n.* short for New Economic Policy.

Nep·ȧ·lēşe′ (*or* -lēs′), *a.* of or pertaining to Nepal, its people, or their culture.

Nep·ȧ·lēşe′, *n.*; *pl.* **Nep·ȧ·lēşe′**, a native of Nepal.

Nē·pen·thā′cē·ae, *n.pl.* [*Nepenthes* and *-aceæ.*] a small family of climbing plants common to warmer Asia, the Indian archipelago, and Madagascar, including only the pitcher plants, genus *Nepenthes.*

nē·pen′thē, nē·pen′thēş, *n.* [L., a plant which, mingled with wine, had an exhilarating effect, from Gr. *nepenthēs*, removing sorrow; *nē-* priv., and *penthos*, sorrow, grief.]

1. a drug supposed by the ancient Greeks to cause forgetfulness of sorrow; also, the plant from which this drug was supposedly obtained.

2. anything that brings about forgetfulness of sorrow.

nē·pen′thē·ăn, *a.* of, or having the nature of, nepenthe; causing forgetfulness.

Nē·pen'thēṣ, *n.* 1. a genus of plants of the family *Nepenthaceæ* comprising the pitcher plants, having, at the ends of the leaves, large hollow pitchers, furnished with a lid, and containing limpid and slightly acid fluid, which aids in the digestion of insects.

2. [n–] a plant of this genus.

NEPENTHES (*Nepenthes distillatoria*)

Nep'ē·tȧ, *n.* [L. *nepeta*, catnip.] a large genus of spiked herbs with white or blue flowers and toothed leaves. It includes the common catnip and ground ivy.

neph'ȧ·liṣm, *n.* [Gr. *nēphelismos*, soberness, discretion, from *nēphalios*, sober, from *nēphein*, to be sober.] nonindulgence in intoxicating liquors; total abstinence; teetotalism.

neph'ȧ·list, *n.* one who believes in, advocates, or practices nephalism; a total abstainer.

neph'ē·line, *n.* same as *nephelite*.

neph'ē·lin·ite'', *n.* a dark, granular volcanic rock composed of nephelite and pyroxene.

neph'ē·līte, *n.* [from Gr. *nephelē*, a cloud; and *-ite*.] a silicate of aluminum, sodium, and potassium, found in many igneous rocks.

Nē·phē'li·um, *n.* [Gr. *nephelion*, a small cloud, dim. of *nephelē*, a cloud.] a genus of trees of Asia and Australia, with pinnate leaves and a sweet, pulpy, edible fruit.

neph'ē·loid, *a.* [Gr. *nepheloeidēs*; *nephelē*, a cloud, and *eidos*, form.] cloudy, as urine.

neph·ē·lom'ē·tēr, *n.* [Gr. *nephelē*, a cloud, and *metron*, a measure.] an apparatus for measuring the concentration of a suspension, as of bacteria or some chemical substance in solution, by comparing the brightness of light passed through it with that passed through a set of standard solutions of barium chloride.

neph'ē·lō·sçōpe, *n.* [Gr. *nephelē*, a cloud, and *skopein*, to view.] a device by which moist air is expanded to illustrate the formation of clouds.

neph'ew (nef' *or* nev'ū), *n.* [ME. *nephewe*, *nevew*; OFr. *neveu*, *nevod*, from L. *nepos* (*-otis*), a grandson, later, a nephew.]

1. (a) the son of one's brother or sister; (b) the son of one's brother-in-law or sister-in-law.

2. an illegitimate son, as of a medieval prelate: a euphemism.

3. a grandson. [Obs.]

4. a cousin. [Obs.]

neph'i·lim, *n.pl.* [Heb.] in the Bible, a race of giants.

Nē'phīte, *n.* a descendant of Nephi, mentioned in the Book of Mormon.

neph'ō-, [from Gr. *nephos*, cloud.] a combining form meaning *cloud, clouds*, as in *nephology*.

neph'ō·gram, *n.* [*nepho-* and *-gram*.] a photograph of a cloud.

neph·ō·log'iç·ăl, *a.* pertaining to nephology.

nē·phol'ō·ġy, *n.* the branch of meteorology relating to clouds.

neph'ō·sçōpe, *n.* [*nepho-* and *-scope*.] an instrument for determining the altitude of a cloud and the direction and velocity of its drift.

nephr-, same as *nephro-*.

nē·phral'ġi·ȧ, *n.* [*nephr-* and *-algia*.] pain in the kidneys.

nē·phral'ġiç, *a.* characterized by pain in the region of the kidneys.

neph·rap·os'tȧ·sis, *n.* suppurative inflammation of a kidney.

neph·reç·tā'ṣi·ȧ, *n.* [Gr. *nephros*, kidney, and *ektasis*, distention.] dilatation of a kidney.

nē·phreç'tō·my, *n.*; *pl.* **nē·phreç'tō·mieṣ**, [*nephr-* and *-ectomy*.] surgical removal of a kidney.

neph'ri·ȧ, *n.* [Gr. *nephros*, a kidney.] Bright's disease.

neph'riç, *a.* of or near the kidneys.

nē·phrid'i·ăl, *a.* of a nephridium.

nē·phrid'i·um, *n.*; *pl.* **nē·phrid'i·ȧ**, [Gr. *nephros*, a kidney.]

1. the waste-discharging organ of some invertebrates, as worms, mollusks, etc.

2. the waste-discharging organ of vertebrate embryos; the embryonic tube from which the kidney is developed.

neph'riṣm, *n.* [*nephr-*, and *-ism*.] the abnormal condition caused by chronic kidney disease.

neph'rīte, *n.* [Gr. *nephritēs*, pertaining to the kidneys, from *nephros*, a kidney.] the less valuable of the two varieties of jade, compact in structure and varying in color from white to dark green: it was formerly worn as a supposed remedy for kidney ailments.

nē·phrit'iç, *a.* [LL. *nephriticus*; Gr. *nephritikos*, from *nephritis*, nephritis.]

1. pertaining to a kidney or the kidneys; renal; as, *nephritic* disease.

2. of or having nephritis.

nephritic stone; nephrite.

nē·phrit'iç, *n.* one who has nephritis.

nē·phrit'iç·ăl, *a.* nephritic.

nē·phrī'tis, *n.* [Gr. *nephritis*, a disease of the kidneys.] an acute or chronic disease of the kidneys, characterized by inflammation, degeneration, fibrosis, etc.: certain types were formerly called *Bright's disease*.

neph'rō-, [from Gr. *nephros*, kidney.] a combining form meaning *kidney* or *nephric and*, as in *nephrotomy*: also, before a vowel, *nephr-*.

neph'rō·cēle, *n.* hernial protrusion of a kidney.

neph·rō·ġen'iç, *a.* [*nephro-*, and *-genic*.]

1. arising in the kidneys.

2. producing kidney tissue.

neph'roid, *a.* reniform; kidney-shaped.

neph'rō·lith, *n.* a renal calculus.

neph·rō·lith'iç, *a.* [*nephro-*, and Gr. *lithos*, stone.] pertaining to calculi in the kidneys.

nē·phrol'ō·ġy, *n.* [*nephro-*, and Gr. *-logia*, from *legein*, to speak.] scientific study of the kidney and its diseases.

neph'ron, *n.* [G., from Gr. *nephros*, kidney.] a single urinary tubule in the vertebrate kidney.

nē·phrop'ȧ·thy, *n.* renal disease.

neph'rō·pex·y, *n.* [*nephro-*, and Gr. *pēxis*, a fixing.] the fixation of a floating kidney.

neph·rō'sis, *n.* a degenerative disease of the kidneys, characterized by generalized edema, protein in the urine, and an increase in serum cholesterol.

neph'rō·stōme, *n.* [*nephro-*, and Gr. *stoma*, a mouth.] the ciliated opening of a nephridium.

neph'rō·tōme, *n.* [*nephro-*, and Gr. *temnein*, to cut.] a primitive segment in which the renal organs develop.

nē·phrot'ō·my, *n.*; *pl.* **nē·phrot'ō·mieṣ**, [*nephro-* and *-tomy*.] surgical incision into the kidney, as for removing a renal calculus.

Neph'thys, *n.* [Gr., from Egypt., literally, the lady of the house.] in Egyptian religion, a goddess, wife and sister of Set, who, with Isis, was concerned in the ceremonies for the dead.

nep'id, *n.* a water scorpion.

nep'id, *a.* pertaining to water scorpions.

nep·i·on'iç, *a.* next after the embryonic: said of a developmental stage.

nē plus ul'trȧ, [L., no further; literally, no or not, more beyond.]

1. the peak of achievement; the utmost perfection; that exceeding all others.

2. a block to further progress. [Now Rare.]

3. (go) no further.

nep'ō·tăl, *a.* [L. *nepos* (*-otis*), a grandson, nephew.] pertaining to a nephew.

nē·pot'iç, *a.* pertaining to nepotism.

nep'ō·tiṣm, *n.* [L. *nepos* (*-otis*), a grandson, nephew, and *-ism*: from favoritism shown to "nephews" by medieval prelates.] favoritism shown to nephews and other relations; the practice of appointing relatives to situations of emolument, in disregard of the claims of others better fitted for the offices.

nep'ō·tist, *n.* one who practices nepotism.

Nep'tūne, *n.* [L. *Neptunus*, god of the seas.]

1. in Roman mythology, the god of the sea, son of Saturn and Rhea, and brother of Jupiter and Pluto. He is generally identified with the Greek Poseidon, and is represented with a trident, a dolphin, or in a chariot drawn by sea horses, with a triton on each side.

2. the sea personified.

3. the third largest planet in the solar system and the eighth in distance from the sun: it revolves round the sun in 164.79 years, its mean distance from the sun is about 2,780,000,000 miles, and its diameter is about 33,000 miles.

NEPTUNE

Nep'tūne's-çup', *n.* *Poterion neptuni* or *Poterion amphitritiatæ*, large cup-shaped sponges.

Nep·tū'ni·ăn, *a.* 1. of the sea god Neptune.

2. of the planet Neptune.

3. [*often* n–] in geology, formerly, designating or of water-formed strata.

Neptunian theory; a theory devised by Werner (1750–1817) to account for the aspect of geological strata, which refers all rock formations to the agency of water.

nep·tū'ni·um, *n.* a chemical element produced by the irradiation of ordinary uranium atoms with neutrons: it does not occur naturally on earth: symbol, Np; atomic weight, 239; atomic number, 93.

nẽrd, *n.* [origin unknown.] a person regarded as contemptibly dull, unsophisticated, ineffective, etc. [Slang.]

Nē'rē·id, *n.*; *pl.* **Nē'rē·idṣ**, [L. *Nereis* (*-idis*); Gr. *Nēreis* (*-idos*), a sea nymph, daughter of Nereus, from *Nēreus*, a sea god, from *nēros*, wet.]

1. in Greek mythology, a sea nymph, one of the fifty daughters of Nereus and Doris. The most celebrated of them were Amphitrite, the wife of Neptune; Thetis, the mother of Achilles; Galateia, and Doto.

NEREID

2. [n–] a marine annelid, especially of the genus *Nereis*.

nē·rē'i·dous, *a.* nereidian.

Nē'rē·is, *n.* [L. *Nereis*, a Nereid.]

1. a Nereid.

2. a genus of errant marine annelids of the family *Nereidæ*, having jaws but no gills.

3. [n–] a member of this genus.

nē'rē·ite, *n.* a fossil thought to be related to the nereids.

Nē''rē·ō·cys'tis, *n.* [Gr. *Nēreus*, a sea god, and *kystis*, a bladder, bag.] a genus of seaweeds represented only by the bladder kelp, which makes floating islands on the northwest coast of America and the opposite shores of Asia.

Nē'reūs (nēr'ūs), *n.* [L.; Gr. *Nereus*.] in Greek mythology, a sea god, father of the fifty Nereids.

Nē·rī'tȧ, *n.* [L., a sea mussel; Gr. *nēritēs*, *nēreitēs*, a kind of shell.] a genus of mollusks found chiefly in tropical climates.

nē'rīte, *n.* a mollusk of the genus *Nerita*.

nē·rit'iç, *a.* relating to or found in the shallow water near a coast.

ner'i·toid, *a.* resembling the genus *Nerita*.

Nē'ri·um, *n.* a genus of shrubs including the oleander.

ne̱'rō·ăn·tī'çō, *n.* [It. *nero*, black, and *antico*, antique.] a deep black marble used in buildings in ancient Rome.

ner'ō·li, *n.* [Fr. *néroli*; It. *neroli*, *nerolo*: said to be from name of the discoverer, an Italian princess.] an oil distilled from orange flowers and used in perfumery: also *neroli oil*.

neroli camphor; a crystalline compound derived from neroli.

Nē·rō'ni·ăn, *a.* 1. of or connected with the Roman Emperor Nero or his reign (54–68 A.D.).

2. like or characteristic of Nero; cruel, depraved, despotic, etc.

nẽr'văl, *a.* neural.

nẽrv'āte, *a.* [L. *nervus*, a nerve, and *-ate*.] in botany, having nerves, or veins.

nẽr·vā'tion, *n.* [from *nerve* and *-ation*.] the arrangement of nerves, or veins, in a leaf or insect's wing; venation; neuration.

nẽrv'ȧ·tūre, *n.* same as *nervation*.

nẽrve, *n.* [ME. *nerfe*; OFr. *nerf*; L. *nervus*, a sinew, tendon, nerve.]

1. originally, a sinew or tendon: now poetic except in *to strain every nerve*.

2. any of the cordlike fibers or bundles of fibers connecting the body organs with the central nervous system (the brain and the spinal cord) and parts of the nervous system with each other, and carrying impulses to and from the brain or a nerve center.

3. emotional control; coolness in danger; courage; as, a man of *nerve*.

4. strength; energy; vigor.

5. impudent boldness; audacity; brazenness. [Colloq.]

6. in botany and zoology, a rib or vein in a leaf or insect's wing; nervure.

nerves; (a) the nervous system regarded as indicating health, courage, endurance, etc.; (b) nervousness; (c) an attack of nervousness; hysteria.

nẽrve, *v.t.*; nerved, *pt.*; *pp.*; nerving, *ppr.* to give strength or courage to; to equip with force; as, fear *nerved* his arm.

nẽrve block, a method of anesthesia by stopping the passage of impulses through a particular nerve.

nẽrve cell, a cell which with its processes forms the structural and functional unit of the nervous system; especially, a cell of the gray matter of the brain or of a ganglion; neuron.

nẽrve cen'tẽr, any group of nerve cells that function together in controlling some specific sense or bodily activity, as breathing.

nẽrved, *a.* 1. having nerves of distinctive character; as, strong-*nerved*; weak-*nerved*.

2. in biology, having nerves or nervelike structures as a part of a body or organ; as, a *nerved* leaf or wing.

nẽrve fi'bẽr, any of the threadlike elements, either dendrites or axons, making up a nerve.

nẽrve gas, any of several poisonous, odorless, colorless, and tasteless liquids that volatilize readily and are rapidly absorbed through the eyes, lungs, or skin, causing paralysis of the respiratory and central nervous systems.

nẽrve'less, *a.* (a) without strength, vigor, force, or courage; weak; inert; unnerved; (b) in biology, having no nerve or nerves.

nẽrve'less·ness, *n.* the state of being nerveless.

nẽrve'-rack"ing, nẽrve'-wrack"ing, *a.* very trying to one's patience or equanimity; causing irritation or exasperation.

nẽr·vi·mō'tion, *n.* [L. *nervus*, a nerve, and *motio* (*-onis*), motion.] in physiology, the motion excited in the nerves by stimuli and subsequently transmitted by the nerves to the muscles.

nẽr·vi·mō'tŏr, *a.* pertaining to nervimotion.

nẽr·vi·mō'tŏr, *n.* any agent capable of exciting or producing nervimotion.

nẽr·vi·mus'cū·lăr, *a.* pertaining to both nerve and muscle: also written *nervomuscular*.

nẽrv'ine (*or* -īn), *a.* [L. *nervinus*, made of sinews, from *nervus*, a sinew, tendon, nerve.] affecting, especially soothing or calming, the nerves.

nẽrv'ine, *n.* a medicine supposed to soothe or calm the nerves; nerve tonic.

nẽrv'ing, *n.* in veterinary medicine, the removal of part of a nerve trunk, as when it is chronically inflamed.

nẽr·vō·mus'cū·lăr, *a.* nervimuscular.

nẽr·vōse', *a.* in biology, same as *nerved*.

nẽr·vos'i·ty, *n.* [L. *nervositas*, from *nervosus*, full of sinews, nervous.] the state of being, or a tendency to be, abnormally nervous.

nẽrv'ous, *a.* [ME. *neruous*; L. *nervosus*.]

1. originally, strong; sinewy.

What *nervous* arms he boasts, how firm his tread,
His limbs how turn'd. —Pope.

2. vigorous in expression; animated.

3. of the nerves.

4. made up of or containing nerves.

5. characterized by or having a disordered state of the nerves.

6. characterized by or showing emotional tension, restlessness, agitation, etc.

7. fearful; apprehensive.

nervous fluid; the hypothetical fluid formerly supposed to circulate through the nerves, and regarded as the agent of sensation and motion.

nervous prostration; neurasthenia.

nervous system; all the nerve cells and nervous tissues in an organism, including, in the vertebrates, the brain, spinal cord, ganglia, nerves, and nerve centers: it co-ordinates and controls responses to stimuli and conditions behavior and consciousness.

nẽrv'ous·ly, *adv.* in a nervous manner.

nẽrv'ous·ness, *n.* the state or quality of being nervous.

nẽrv'ūle, *n.* [L. *nervulus*, dim. of *nervus*, a sinew, nerve.] a small nerve.

nẽrv'ū·lōse, *a.* in botany, nerved.

nẽrv'ūre, *n.* [Fr. *nervure*, a rib, from L. *nervus*, a sinew, tendon, nerve.]

1. in architecture, a rib.

2. in botany, the vein or nerve of a leaf.

3. in zoology, a vein or rib in an insect's wing, which helps to expand the wing and keep it tense.

nẽrv'y, *a.*; *comp.* nervier; *superl.* nerviest, 1. strong; vigorous; sinewy. [Rare.]

2. nervous; excitable; jittery. [British.]

3. full of courage; bold.

4. rudely bold; brazen; impudent. [Slang.]

nes'cience (nesh'ens), *n.* [LL. *nescientia*, from L. *nesciens* (*-entis*), ignorant.]

1. ignorance.

2. agnosticism.

nes'cient, *a.* 1. ignorant.

2. agnostic.

nesh, *a.* [AS. *hnesc*, *hnæsc*, soft, tender.]

1. soft; tender; also, succulent. [Obs.]

2. delicate; weak; liable to crumble. [Obs.]

ness, *n.* [AS. *næs*, *nes*, a headland.] a cape or headland: now chiefly in place names; as, Inver*ness*.

-ness, [ME. *-ness*, *-nisse*; AS. *-nes*(*s*), *-nis*(*s*).] a noun-forming suffix meaning: (a) *condition*, *quality*, or *state of*, as in great*ness*, sad*ness*, together*ness*; (b) *a single instance of such a condition, quality*, or *state*.

Nes'sel·rōde, *n.* [after Count K. R. *Nesselrode* (1780–1862), Russian statesman.] a mixture of preserved fruits, chopped nuts, etc., used in ice cream, pudding, or the like.

Ness"lẽr·i·zā'tion, *n.* the state of being Nesslerized.

Ness'lẽr·īze, *v.t.*; Nesslerized, *pt.*, *pp.*; Nesslerizing, *ppr.* [after Julius *Nessler* (1827–1905), German chemist.] to treat with Nessler's reagent, an aqueous solution used as a test for ammonia, consisting of 5 per cent of potassium iodide, 2.5 per cent of mercuric chloride, and 16 per cent of potassium hydrate.

Nes'sus, *n.* in Greek legend, a centaur killed by Hercules for trying to carry off his wife Deianira: a shirt that she steeped in Nessus' blood as a love charm caused the death of Hercules.

nest, *n.* [ME.; AS.; akin to G. *nest*.]

1. the structure made or the place chosen by birds for laying their eggs and sheltering their young.

2. the place used by turtles, hornets, fish, etc. for spawning or breeding.

3. a cozy or snug place to live or rest; retreat.

4. (a) a resort, haunt, or den: especially in an unfavorable sense; (b) the people who frequent such a place; as, a *nest* of criminals.

5. a brood, swarm, or colony of birds, insects, etc.

6. a set or series of similar things, each fitting within the one next larger.

7. in geology, an isolated mass of any ore or mineral within a rock.

8. in mechanics, a connected set or group of pulleys or cogwheels.

nest, *v.i.* [ME. *nesten*; AS. *nistan*, *nistian*, to build a nest, from *nest*, a nest.]

1. to build or live in a nest.

The king of birds *nested* within his leaves. —Howell.

2. to hunt for birds' nests: usually in the present participle.

nest, *v.t.* to put into or as into a nest; to build or construct a nest for; to lodge or house.

n'est-ce pas'? (nes"pä'), [Fr., lit., is it not?] isn't that so?

nest egg, 1. an artificial or real egg left in a nest to induce a hen to lay more eggs.

2. money, etc. put aside as a reserve or to establish a fund.

nest'fụl, *n.*; *pl.* **nest'fụls,** the quantity or number that will fill a nest.

nes·ti·ther'ȧ·py, *n.* treatment of disease by reducing the amount of food eaten.

nes'tle (-l), *v.i.*; nestled, *pt.*, *pp.*; nestling, *ppr.* [ME. *nestlen*, *nestelen*; AS. *nestlian*, to build a nest, from *nest*, a nest.]

1. to settle down comfortably and snugly.

2. to draw or press close for comfort or in affection.

3. to lie sheltered or partly hidden, as a house among trees.

4. to build a nest; to occupy a nest. [Obs.]

nes'tle, *v.t.* 1. to house, as in a nest.

2. to rest or press (a baby, one's head, etc.) in a snug, affectionate manner.

nes'tlẽr (-lẽr), *n.* 1. a person or thing that nestles.

2. a nestling.

nest'ling, *n.* 1. a young bird not yet ready to leave the nest

2. a baby.

3. a nest. [Obs.]

Nes'tŏr, *n.* 1. in Greek legend, a Greek chief and counselor who took part in the siege of Troy.

2. a wise old man.

3. a genus of parrots found in New Zealand. *Nestor meridionalis* is the kaka.

Nes·tō'ri·ăn, *a.* relating to Nestorius or the Nestorians.

Nes·tō'ri·ăn, *n.* an adherent of Nestorius, patriarch of Constantinople in the fifth century, who was deposed and banished as a heretic for maintaining that divinity and humanity existed as two distinct natures in Jesus and were not unified into a single personality.

Nes·tō'ri·ăn·ism, *n.* the doctrines of Nestorius or his followers.

net, *n.* [AS. *net*, *nett*, a net.]

1. a fabric made from string, cord, etc., loosely knotted or woven in an openwork pattern and used to trap or snare birds, fish, etc.

2. anything that catches or entraps; trap; snare.

3. any of various meshed fabrics used to hold, protect, or mark off something; as, a hair *net*.

4. a fine, meshed, lacelike cloth of cotton or silk.

5. a network.

6. in tennis, etc., a ball hit into the net.

7. in geometry, a figure formed of a large number of intersecting lines.

net, *a.* 1. of or like net.

2. caught in a net; netted.

net, *v.t.*; netted, *pt.*, *pp.*; netting, *ppr.* 1. to make into net or a net.

2. to make with net.

3. to trap or snare with or as with a net.

4. to protect, shelter, or enclose with or as with a net.

5. in tennis, to drive (the ball) into the net.

net, *v.i.* to make nets or network.

net, *a.* [Fr. *net*, clean, clear, pure, from L. *nitidus*, clear, shining.]

1. clear; neat; pure; unadulterated; as, *net* wines. [Rare.]

2. left over after certain deductions or allowances have been made, as for expenses, weight of containers or waste materials, nonessential considerations, etc.

net, *n.* a net amount, profit, weight, price, result, etc.

net, *v.t.* to produce or get as a net income, profit, result, etc.

neth'ẽr, *a.* [ME. *nethere*; AS. *neothera*, *neothra*, lower, from *nither*, *neothor*, adv., downward.]

1. lower or under; lying or being beneath or in a lower place; opposed to *upper*.

All my *nether* shape thus grew transformed. —Milton.

2. lying, or thought of as lying, below the earth's surface; as, the *nether* world.

Neth'ẽr·land·ẽr, *n.* a native or inhabitant of the Netherlands.

neth'ẽr·mōre, *a.* lower. [Rare.]

neth'ẽr·mōst, *a.* lowest; as, the *nethermost* abyss.

neth'ẽr·wărd, neth'ẽr·wărdṣ, *adv.* downward; in a downward course or direction.

neth'ẽr wŏrld, the world of the dead or of punishment after death; hell.

Neth'i·nim, *n.pl.* [Heb., pl. of *nāthin*, what is given or granted, from *nāthan*, to give.] among the ancient Jews, servants of the priests and Levites employed in menial services about the temple.

net'sụ·kẹ, *n.* [Japan.] a knob of wood, ivory, etc., often carved or ornamented, worn by the Japanese as a decorative article suspended from the girdle.

net'ted-vẹined', *a.* in botany, having the veins reticulated, as some leaves.

net'ting, *n.* 1. the act or process of making nets or fishing with them.

2. a piece of network; openwork fabric.

3. in nautical usage, nets of small rope formerly used on board ship for various purposes, as for holding the hammocks when on deck, or for stowing sails.

net'ting, *n.* urine. [Brit. Dial.]

net'ting knot (not), a sheet bend: see *knot*, illus.

net'tle, *n.* [ME. *nettle*, *netle*; AS. *netele*, *netle*, a nettle.]

1. a plant of the genus *Urtica*, having minute stinging hairs. *Urtica dioica* is the stinging nettle of Europe, which with *Urtica*

urens has been naturalized in America. *Urtica pilulifera* is the Roman nettle of Europe. The name nettle has also been given to any one of several plants of some other genus of the nettle family, as *Bœhmeria, Laportea*, etc.

2. any plant resembling the true nettle.

Australian nettle; a large tree, *Urtica* or *Laportea gigas*, which grows to a height of 70 feet.

false nettle; an American plant, *Bœhmeria cylindrica*.

net′tle, *v.t.*; nettled, *pt., pp.*; netling, *ppr.* 1. to sting with or as with nettles.

2. to annoy; to irritate; to vex.

I've *nettled* somebody full sore. —Fawkes.

net′tle·bīrd, *n.* the English whitethroat, which frequents nettles. [Brit. Dial.]

net′tle blīght (blīt), *n.* a parasitic fungus, *Æcidium urticæ*, found on nettles.

net′tle but′tĕr·fly, a butterfly whose larvae feed on nettles, as *Vanessa urticæ*.

net′tle cell, a nematocyst; a thread cell.

net′tle çloth, a thick cotton cloth, japanned and used for many purposes as a substitute for leather.

net′tle fē′vĕr, in medicine, urticaria.

net′tle fish, a jellyfish.

net′tlĕr, *n.* one who provokes, stings, or irritates.

net′tle rash, an allergic skin condition characterized by itching, burning, stinging, and the formation of smooth, usually red patches, or wheals; hives; urticaria.

net′tle tap, a European moth, *Simaethis fabriciana*.

net′tle thread (thred), a stinging hair of a thread cell.

net′tle tree, a tree of the genus *Celtis*, of which there are several species. They have a considerable resemblance to, and a near affinity with, the elms. Among them are the American hackberry, *Celtis occidentalis*, the European honeyberry, *Celtis australis*, and the Australian nettle tree.

net′tle·wŏrt, *n.* any plant of the nettle family.

net′tling, *n.* in ropemaking, a process of uniting two ropes end to end without making a knot or seam; also, the process of fastening together in pairs the yarns in a ropewalk, to prevent tangling.

net tŏn, a short ton.

net′ty, *a.* like a net; netted. [Rare.]

net′-vēined′, *a.* 1. in botany, netted-veined.

2. in entomology, having numerous netted nerves or veins, as in the wings of certain hemipters.

net′-winged, *a.* in entomology, having wings which are net-veined.

net′wŏrk, *n.* [*net* (knotted fabric) and *work*.]

1. any arrangement or fabric of parallel wires, threads, etc. crossed at regular intervals by others fastened to them so as to leave open spaces; netting; mesh.

2. a thing resembling this in some way; specifically, (a) a system of crossed roads, canals, etc.; (b) in radio and television, a chain of transmitting stations owned and operated as a unit.

3. the making of nets or netted fabric.

net′wŏrk, *a.* broadcast simultaneously over all or most of the stations of a network.

Neuf·châ·tel′ (nū-shȧ-tel′), *n.* [after *Neufchâtel*, town in northern France.] a soft, white cheese prepared from sweet milk with or without cream: also *Neufchâtel cheese*.

neūk, *n.* a nook; a corner. [Scot.]

neūme, neūm, *n.* [Fr. *neume*; ML. *neuma*, from Gr. *pneuma*, breath: so named from being orig. a group of notes sung to a final syllable for the duration of the breath.] in music, (a) any of a set of signs used in the Middle Ages in written church music to indicate melody, manner of performance, etc.; (b) the tone or group of tones indicated by these.

neūr-, same as *neuro-*.

neū′rad, *adv.* [Gr. *neuron*, a nerve, and L. *ad*, to, toward.] toward a neural or dorsal axis or aspect: opposed to *hemad*.

neū′răl, *a.* [*neur-* and *-al*.]

1. pertaining to a nerve or to the nerves or nervous system.

2. of or belonging to the central nervous system or to its axis.

3. on the same side with the neural axis; in vertebrates, tergal or dorsal; in invertebrates, ventral.

neural arch; the posterior rings of the vertebrae enclosing the spinal cord.

neū·ral′ġiȧ (-jȧ), *n.* [Mod. L.; *neur-* and *-algia*.]

1. a pain in a nerve or nerves; severe pain along the course of a nerve or in its area of distribution.

2. the condition characterized by such pain.

neū·ral′ġiç, *a.* of, like, or due to neuralgia.

neū·ral′ġy, *n.* neuralgia. [Chiefly Dial.]

neū·rap·ō·phyṣ′i·ăl, *a.* of or pertaining to a neurapophysis.

neū·rȧ·poph′y·sis, *n.*; *pl.* **neū·rȧ·poph′y·sēṣ,** [Gr. *neuron*, a sinew, nerve, and *apophysis*, an offshoot, a process.] in anatomy, the structure forming either side of the neural arch; also, the spinous process of a vertebra.

neū·ras·thē′ni·ȧ, *n.* [Mod. L.; from *neur-*, and Gr. *astheneia*, weakness.]

1. formerly, weakness or exhaustion of the nervous system, as from excessive expenditure of energy; nervous prostration.

2. a type of neurosis, usually the result of emotional conflicts, characterized by a wide variety of symptoms, including fatigue, depression, worry, and, often, localized pains without apparent objective causes.

neū·ras·then′iç, *a.* of or having neurasthenia.

neū·ras·then′iç, *n.* a neurasthenic person.

neū·rā′tion, *n.* [Gr. *neuron*, a sinew, nerve, and *-ation*.] nervation; nervature.

neū·rax′is, *n.* same as *axis cylinder*.

neū·reç′tō·my, *n.*; *pl.* **neū·reç′tō·mieṣ,** surgical removal of a nerve or part of a nerve.

neū·ren·ter′iç, *a.* [Gr. *neuron*, a nerve, and *enteron*, intestine.] belonging to both neuron and enteron: applied to an embryonic canal.

neū′riç, *a.* 1. neural; nervous.

2. having a nervous system.

neū′ri·dine, *n.* [Gr. *neuron*, a sinew, nerve, and *-id*, and *-ine*.] a non-poisonous ptomaine found in putrefied proteides, especially in nervous tissue.

neū·ri·lem′mȧ, *a.* [Mod. L.; altered from *neurilema*, from Gr. *neuron*, nerve, and *eilēma*, a covering.] the fine membranous sheath of a nerve fiber.

neū·ril′i·ty, *n.* [Gr. *neuron*, a sinew, nerve, and *-ile*, and *-ity*.] the power of a nerve to transmit a stimulus.

neū′rīne, neū′rīn (*or* -rin), *n.* [Gr. *neuron*, nerve, and *-ine*.]

1. a poisonous ptomaine found in putrefying proteides.

2. same as *choline*.

neū′riṣm, *n.* [Gr. *neuron*, a sinew, nerve, and *-ism*.] nerve force. [Rare.]

neū·rit′ic, *a.* of or having neuritis.

neū·rī′tis, *n.* [Mod. L.; *neur-* and *-itis*.] inflammation of a nerve or nerves, characterized by pain and muscle tenderness and accompanied by changes in sensory and motor activity in the region of the affected nerve.

neū′rō-, [from Gr. *neuron*, nerve.] a combining form meaning *of a nerve, nerves*, or *the nervous system*, as in *neuro*path: also, before a vowel, *neur-*.

neū′rō·blast, *n.* any of the embryonic cells from which the nerve cells develop.

neū·rō·cen′trăl, *a.* [*neuro-*, and Gr. *kentron*, a center.] pertaining to both the neural arch and the centrum of a vertebra; as, the *neurocentral* suture.

neū·rō·çhī′tin, *n.* [*neuro-*, and Gr. *chitōn*, tunic.] the substance forming the framework supporting nerve fibers.

neū·roc′i·ty, *n.* nerve force.

neū′rō·coele (-sēl), *n.* [*neuro-* and *-coele*.] the cavity of the cerebrospinal system consisting of the ventricles of the brain and the central canal of the spinal cord: also spelled *neurocele*.

neū′rō·çhord, *n.* [*neuro-*, and Gr. *chordē*, a gut, a string for a lyre.] in annelids, an organ lying above the ventral ganglia: also written *neurocord*.

neū′rō·çȳte, *n.* any nerve cell.

neū·rō·ep·i·dĕr′măl, *n.* [*neuro-*, and Gr. *epidermis*, the outer skin.] pertaining to or giving origin to the nervous and epidermal tissues.

neū·rog′li·ȧ, *n.* [*neuro-*, and Gr. *glia*, glue.] the connective tissue, consisting of a special type of branched cells, that binds together and supports the nerve tissue of the central nervous system.

neū·rog′rȧ·phy, *n.* [*neuro-*, and Gr. *-graphia*, from *graphein*, to write.] a treatise on the nervous system.

neū′roid, *a.* like a nerve or nerve tissue.

neū·rō·ker′a·tin, *n.* [*neuro-*, and Gr. *keras* (*-atos*), horn, and *-in*.] a form of keratin found in nerve sheaths and in the white substance of the brain.

neū·rō·log′iç·ăl, *a.* pertaining to neurology.

neū·rol′ō·ġist, *n.* an expert or specialist in neurology.

neū·rol′ō·ġy, *n.* [*neuro-* and *-logy*.] the branch of medicine dealing with the nervous system, its structure, and its diseases.

neū·rol′y·sis, *n.* [Mod. L.; *neuro-* and *-lysis*.] destruction of nerve tissue.

neū·rō′mȧ, *n.*; *pl.* **neū·rō′mȧṣ, neū·rō′mȧ·tȧ,** [Mod. L.; *neur-* and *-oma*.] a tumor derived from nervous tissue, consisting of nerve cells and fibers.

neū′rō·mȧst, *n.* [*neuro-*, and Gr. *mastos*, hillock.] an area of the epidermis having sensory functions, as in all fishes.

neū·rom′ȧ·tous, *a.* of or like a neuroma.

neū′rō·mēre, *n.* [*neuro-*, and Gr. *meros*, part.] a segment of the cerebrospinal axis.

neū″rō·mi·mē′sis, *n.* neurotic simulation of organic disease; nervous mimicry.

neū″rō·mi·met′iç, *a.* of or displaying neuromimesis.

neū·rō·mus′çū·lăr, *a.* [*neuro-*, and L. *musculus*, muscle.] intermediate in nature between nerve tissue and muscle; pertaining both to nerve and muscle; as, *neuromuscular* cells.

neū′ron, *n.* [Gr., nerve.]

1. the cerebrospinal axis; the brain and the spinal cord considered as a whole. [Rare.]

2. the structural and functional unit of the nervous system, consisting of the nerve cell body and all its processes, as the dendrites and axon.

neū′rōne, *n.* a neuron.

neū·ron′iç, *a.* of a neuron or neurons.

neū′rō·path, *n.* [from *neuropathic* (person).]

1. a person having a tendency to neurosis. [Rare.]

2. a neuropathist.

neū·rō·path′iç, *a.* pertaining to, having, or characterized by nervous disorder or disease.

neū·rō·path′iç, *n.* a neuropathic person.

neū·rop′ȧ·thist, *n.* [from *neuropathy* and *-ist*.] a doctor who specializes in nervous diseases; neurologist.

neū″rō·pȧ·thol′ō·ġy, *n.* the pathology of the nervous system and its parts; the branch of medicine dealing with diseases of the nervous system.

neū·rop′ȧ·thy, *n.* [*neuro-*, and Gr. *pathos*, suffering.] any nervous disease or disorder.

neū·rō·phyṣ·i·ol′ō·ġy, *n.* physiology of the nervous system.

neū′rō·plas·ty, *n.* plastic surgery of a nerve or of nervous tissue in general.

neū′rō·pod, *n.* [*neuro-*, and Gr. *pous, podos*, a foot.] a neuropodous animal.

neū·rō·pō′di·um, *n.* [*neuro-*, and Gr. *pous, podos*, a foot.] the ventral portion of a parapodium, as in annelids.

neū·rop′ō·dous, *a.* [*neuro-*, and Gr. *pous, podos*, a foot.] having the limbs neural, as certain invertebrates.

neū′rō·pōre, *n.* [*neuro-*, and Gr. *poros*, a pore.] an exterior opening of the neural canal, as in some embryos.

neū″rō·psy·çhī′ȧ·try (-sī-), *n.* study and treatment of nervous and psychic, or mental, disorders.

neū″rō·psy·çhō′sis (-sī-), *n.*; *pl.* **neū″rō·psy·çhō′sēṣ,** a psychosis: distinguished from *psychoneurosis*.

neū·rop′tĕr, *n.* an insect of the *Neuroptera*.

Neū·rop′tĕr·ȧ, *n.pl.* [*neuro-*, and Gr. *pteron*, a wing.] an order of insects having four membranous, transparent, naked wings, reticulated with veins or nervures. The hellgrammite and ant lion are members of the order.

neū·rop′tĕr·ăl, *a.* same as *neuropterous*.

neū·rop′tĕr·ăn, *n.* same as *neuropter*.

neū·rop′tĕr·ăn, *a.* of the neuropterous insects.

Neū·rop′tĕr·is, *n.* [*neuro-*, and Gr. *pteris*, a fern.] a genus of fossil ferns occurring abundantly in the coal strata, and, to a lesser extent, in the Permian, Trias, and Oölite: so called from the veins of its leaflets.

neū·rop′tĕr·oid, *a.* like a neuropterous insect.

neū·rop′tĕr·on, *n.* a neuropterous insect.

neū·rop′tĕr·ous, *a.* of or resembling the *Neuroptera*.

neū·rō′săl, *a.* [*neurosis* and *-al*.] of or like a neurosis.

neū·rōse′, *a.* [Gr. *neuron*, a nerve, and *-ose*.] possessing many nervures.

neū″rō·sen·sif′ĕr·ous, *a.* [*neuro-*, and L. *sensus*, sense, and *ferre*, to bear.] of or giving origin to both nerves and sense organs.

neū·rō′sis, *n.*; *pl.* **neū·rō′sēṣ** [Gr. *neuron*, a nerve, and *-osis*.]

1. formerly, a functional disorder of the nervous system.

2. any of various psychic, or mental, disorders characterized by special combinations of anxieties, compulsions, obsessions, phobias,

and motor or sensory manifestations, such as tics, without apparent organic or structural injury or change: it results only in partial disorganization of the personality and is less serious both in form and prognosis than a psychosis: also *psychoneurosis.*

neū′rō·sōme, *n.* [Gr. *neuron,* nerve, and *soma,* body.] any one of a group of minute particles in the ground substance of neural protoplasm.

neū·rō·sûr′ġẽr·y, *n.* the branch of surgery involving some part of the nervous system, including the brain and the spinal cord.

neū·rō·syph′i·lis, *n.* syphilis affecting the central nervous system.

neū·rō·ther·ȧ·peū′tiçs, *n.* the therapeutics of diseases of the nerves.

neū·rō·ther′ȧ·py, *n.* same as *neurotherapeutics.*

neū·rot′iç, *a.* 1. in neurology, of or pertaining to nerves; neural.

2. of, characteristic of, or having a neurosis.

neū·rot′iç, *n.* a neurotic person.

neū′rō·tōme, *n.* [*neuro-,* and Gr. *tomē,* a cutting.] a long and very narrow two-edged scalpel used in dissection of the nerves.

neū·rot′ō·mist, *n.* a specialist in neurotomy; one who dissects the nerves.

neū·rot′ō·my, *n.*; *pl.* **neū·rot′ō·mieṣ,** [*neuro-,* and Gr. *-tomia,* from *temnein,* to cut.]

1. the act or practice of dissecting nerves.

2. in medicine, the surgical severing, or cutting, of a nerve to obtain relief from pain, as in cases of neuralgia.

neū′rō·trans·mit′tẽr, *n.* a biochemical substance, as acetylcholine, that transmits nerve impulses from one nerve cell to another at a synapse.

neū′rụ·lȧ, *n.*; *pl.* **neū′rụ·lae,** [dim. from Gr. *neuron,* a nerve.] in some invertebrates, a form of embryo at the specific stage when the first band is developed.

Neūs′tri·ăn, *a.* designating or pertaining to Neustria, the western part of the kingdom of the Franks from the sixth to the eighth century, comprising Flanders and that part of France north of the Loire.

neū′tẽr, *a.* [L. *neuter,* neither; *ne,* not, and *uter,* either, one of two.]

1. neither the one thing nor the other: not adhering to either party; taking no part with either side, either when persons are contending or when questions are discussed; neutral. [Archaic.]

2. in biology, (a) having no sexual organs; asexual; (b) having undeveloped or imperfect sexual organs in the adult, as the worker bee.

3. in grammar, (a) designating or of one of the three genders of many highly inflected languages: most words of this gender designate or refer to things that are neither male nor female; (b) neither active nor passive; intransitive: said of verbs.

neū′tẽr, *n.* 1. a person or group who takes no part in a contest between individuals or nations; a neutral. [Archaic.]

> Damn'd *neuters,* in their middle way of steering,
> Are neither fish, nor flesh, nor good red herring. —Dryden.

2. a castrated animal.

3. in biology, a plant or animal lacking, or having undeveloped, sexual organs.

4. in grammar, (a) the neuter gender; (b) a neuter word.

neū′tẽr, *v.t.* to castrate or spay (an animal).

neū′trăl, *a.* [from *neuter,* neither one nor the other.]

1. (a) not taking part in either side of a quarrel; (b) not taking part in a war; giving no active aid to any belligerent.

2. of, belonging to, or characteristic of a nation not taking part in a war.

3. belonging to neither of two classes; in a middle position between extremes; not one thing or the other; indifferent.

4. (a) having little or no decided color; not vivid; (b) free from mixture of other colors.

5. in botany, without stamens or pistils.

6. in chemistry, giving neither acid nor alkaline reaction.

7. in electricity, neither negative nor positive; uncharged.

8. in phonetics, reduced in quality, especially through lack of stress: said of vowels, as *a* in *about.*

9. in zoology, neuter.

neutral axis; see under *axis.*

neutral equilibrium; in mechanics, that species of equilibrium in which a body, when moved slightly from a state of rest, has no tendency to continue in the direction moved nor to return to its original position; also, that condition of rest in which a slight disturbance will neither elevate nor depress the center of gravity; as, a smooth homogeneous sphere at rest on a smooth horizontal table is in *neutral equilibrium:* distinguished from *stable equilibrium* and *unstable equilibrium.*

neutral line; in physics, a line along which there is molecular equilibrium, as in a bar under flexion or in a symmetrical bar magnet transverse to its axis midway between its poles.

neutral spirits; ethyl alcohol of 190 proof or over, especially as used for blending with aged whiskeys, or with flavorings to make liqueurs, cordials, etc.

neū′trăl, *n.* 1. a nation not taking part in a war; neutral power.

2. a neutral person or a citizen of a neutral country.

3. a neutral color.

4. in mechanics, a disengaged position of gears; the position of gears when they do not transmit power from the engine to the operating parts.

neū′trăl·iṣm, *n.* a policy, or the advocacy of a policy, of remaining neutral, especially in international power conflicts.

neū′trăl·ist, *n.* 1. one who professes neutrality; a neutral.

2. an advocate of neutralism.

neū·tral′i·ty, *n.* 1. the quality, state, or character of being neutral.

2. the status, policy, or attitude of a nation not participating directly or indirectly in a war between other nations.

3. neutral status, as of a seaport in wartime.

armed neutrality; in time of war, the condition of a neutral state or nation which holds itself under arms prepared to resist by force any aggression of a belligerent power.

neū″trăl·i·zā′tion, *n.* the act of neutralizing or the condition of being neutralized.

neū′trăl·īze, *v.t.*; neutralized, *pt., pp.*; neutralizing, *ppr.* [Fr. *neutraliser.*]

1. to declare (a territory, nation, etc.) neutral; to declare open to all nations and inviolable from attack; to exempt from war or military operations.

2. to make ineffective; to paralyze, destroy, or counteract the effectiveness, force, disposition, etc. of.

3. in chemistry, to destroy the distinctive or active properties of; as, an alkali *neutralizes* an acid.

4. in electricity, to make electrically neutral.

neū′trăl·ī·zẽr, *n.* any neutralizing agent or agency.

neū′trăl·ly, *adv.* in a neutral manner.

neū·tret′tō, *n.*; *pl.* **neū·tret′tōṣ,** [from *neutron,* and It. dim. suffix *-etto.*] a neutral meson transformed from a positive meson that has collided with a neutron, or from a negative meson that has collided with a proton.

neū·trī′nō, *n.* in physics, a neutral particle, difficult to detect, having a mass approaching zero and no charge: it has almost no interaction with matter.

neū′trō·dȳne, *a.* [*neutro-* (from *neutral*), and *dyne.*] in radio, designating or of a high-frequency amplifying circuit that has a small condenser to neutralize the instability between the input and output circuits.

neū′trō·dȳne, *n.* such a circuit.

neū′tron, *n.* [from *neutral* and *-on* as in *electron.*] one of the fundamental particles of an atom: neutrons are uncharged and have approximately the same mass as protons: symbol, n.

neū′tron bomb, a small thermonuclear warhead for battlefield use, that would release large numbers of radioactive neutrons intended to disable or kill enemy soldiers without destroying buildings, vehicles, etc.

neū′tron stär, a heavenly object hypothesized to be a collapsed star consisting of immense numbers of densely packed neutrons: often equated with *pulsar.*

neū′trō·phīle, neū′trō·phil, *n.* [L. *neuter,* neither, and Gr. *philos,* loving.] in histology, a cell or structural element stainable by a neutral dye.

neū′trō·phīle, neū·trō·phil′iç, *a.* stainable by neutral dyes.

Ne·vȧd′ăn, *a.* of Nevada.

Ne·vȧd′ăn, *n.* a native or inhabitant of Nevada.

né·vé′ (nā-vā′), *n.* [Fr.] the granular, crystallized snow that accumulates in snowfields of glaciers and is later solidified into ice.

nev′en, *v.t.* to mention; to refer to; to name. [Obs.]

nev′ẽr, *adv.* [AS. *næfre; ne,* not, and *æfre,* ever.]

1. not ever; not at any time; at no time, past, present, or future.

2. in no degree; not at all; by no chance; in no case; under no conditions; as, to answer *never* a word.

Never is often used in the compounding of adjectives from present participles, as in *never*-ending, *never*-failing, *never*-dying, *never*-ceasing, *never*-fading, and in all such compounds it retains its usual meaning.

never so; to any or whatever degree; especially.

nev·ẽr·mōre′, *adv.* at no time to come; never again.

nev″ẽr-nev′ẽr, *n.* the installment plan. [Brit. Slang.]

nev″ẽr-nev′ẽr, *a.* imaginary, fantasized, unrealistic, etc.

never-never land; [after the fairyland in J. M. Barrie's *Peter Pan.*] an unreal, unrealistic, or fantasized place, state, or situation.

nev″ẽr·the·less′, *adv.* [compound of *never, the,* and *less.*] not the less; none the less; notwithstanding; still; yet; that is, in opposition to anything said or done; as, he declared that he would not yield; *nevertheless,* he yielded.

nē′void, nae′void, *a.* of or like a nevus or nevi.

nē′vus, nae′vus, *n.*; *pl.* **nē′vī, nae′vī,** [L.] in medicine, a pigmented patch on the skin, usually congenital; a birthmark.

new, *a.*; *comp.* newer; *superl.* newest, [AS. *niwe, neowe,* new; compare D. *nieuw,* Dan. and Sw. *ny,* Ice. *nyr,* Goth. *niujis,* O.H.G. *niwi, niuwi,* Lith. *naujas,* L. *novus,* Gr. *neos,* Sans. *navas,* new.]

1. never existing before; appearing, thought of, developed, made, produced, etc. for the first time.

2. (a) existing before, but known or discovered for the first time; as, a *new* planet; (b) recently observed, experienced, manifested, etc.; different; as, this is a *new* aspect of your personality; (c) strange; unfamiliar; foreign.

3. not yet familiar or accustomed; inexperienced; as, he is *new* to the work.

4. (a) designating the more or most recent of two or more things of the same class, though both may be old; as, *New* York; (b) taking the place of what has existed; recently appointed, acquired, etc.; as, a *new* teacher.

5. recently grown; fresh; as, *new* potatoes.

6. not previously used or worn.

7. modern; recent; fashionable; recently current.

8. more; additional.

9. beginning again; starting as a repetition of a cycle, series, etc.; making another start; as, the *new* moon.

10. having just come; having just reached a position, rank, place, etc.; as, a *new* arrival.

11. refreshed in spirits, health, etc.; as, a *new* man.

12. [N-] modern; in use since the Middle Ages: said of languages.

new birth; regeneration; spiritual rebirth; the beginning of a religious life.

new chum; in Australia, one recently arrived from another country.

New Church; same as *New Jerusalem Church.*

New Connexion; (a) formerly, a group of Methodists in England, who in 1797 separated themselves from the main body of the church and followed Alexander Kilham in certain matters of church government; (b) formerly, a branch of General Baptists in England.

New Deal; (a) the economic and political principles and policies adopted by President Franklin D. Roosevelt and his associates to advance the economic and social welfare of the American people; (b) the Roosevelt administration.

New Dealer; a supporter or advocate of the New Deal.

New Jerusalem; in the Bible, (a) the Holy City of Heaven: Rev. xxii. 2; (b) heaven.

New Jerusalem Church; the church that holds to the doctrines taught by Emanuel Swedenborg: the members are usually called *Swedenborgians.*

New Light; a member of any one of various denominations holding new, or liberal, views, as the Campbellites, the Reformed Presbyterian Church, etc.

new moon; (a) that phase of the moon when

it is between the earth and the sun, with the dark side of its disk toward the earth: it appears as a thin crescent curving toward the right; (b) the time of the new moon.

New Order; the fascist political and economic system that the Nazis set up in Germany and tried to establish throughout Europe.

New Style; the method of reckoning time in accordance with the Gregorian calendar.

New Testament; (a) in Christian theology, the promises of God to man that are embodied in the life and teachings of Jesus; (b) the part of the Bible that contains the life and teachings of Jesus and his followers, including the four Gospels, the Acts of the Apostles, the Epistles, and the Revelation of Saint John.

New Thought; a modern religious philosophy emphasizing the power of the mind over the body and its ills: also called *Higher Thought, Practical Christianity.*

new year; (a) the year just about to begin or just begun (usually with *the*); (b) the first day or days of the new year (with *the* or *a*); as, a fine *new year*: also *New Year's*; (c) something given or offered on New Year's Day.

New Year's Day; January 1, the first day of a calendar year, usually celebrated as a legal holiday: also *New Year's.*

New Year's Eve; the evening before New Year's Day.

Syn.—novel, fresh, modern, recent, young.

new, *adv.* 1. lately; newly; recently: often used in hyphenated compounds, as in *new*-made, *new*-grown, *new*-formed, *new*-found.

2. again.

new, *n.* something new.

new'bọrn, *a.* 1. just born, or of quite recent birth; as, a *newborn* babe.

2. reborn.

New'bŭrg, *a.* served in a specially prepared sauce.

new'çōme, *a.* just come; recently arrived.

new'çŏm″ẽr, *n.* one who has lately come; recent arrival.

New E·ġyp'tiăn (-shăn), the Hamitic language of the Copts; Coptic.

new'el, *n.* [OFr. *nuel, nouel,* from LL. *nucalis,* like a nut, from L. *nux, nucis,* a nut.]

1. in architecture, the central upright pillar around which the steps of a circular staircase wind. Winding stairs around a central well are said to have an open newel or hollow newel. The newel is sometimes carried through to the roof, to serve as a vaulting shaft, from which the ribs branch off in all directions.

2. in carpentry, the post at the head or foot of a flight of stairs, supporting a handrail: also *newel post.*

3. in civil engineering, a cylindrical pillar terminating the wing wall of a bridge.

4. in shipbuilding, an upright piece of timber to receive the tenons of the rails that lead from the breastwork of the gangway.

New Ĕng'lănd, [the name occurs on Italian maps antedating Captain John Smith, its reputed originator.] the six northeastern States of the United States: Maine, New Hampshire, Vermont, Massachusetts, Rhode Island, and Connecticut.

New Ĕng'lănd as'tẽr, a variety of aster that grows in the eastern part of North America, having a purplish flower.

New Ĕng'lănd boiled din'nẽr, a dish consisting of meat, usually beef, and whole potatoes, onions, carrots, etc., cooked together.

New Ĕng'lănd·ẽr, a native or inhabitant of New England.

New Ĕng'lish, [term popularized by Henry Sweet after G. *neuhochdeutsch,* New High German, etc.] Modern English, as distinguished from Early Modern English, Middle English, and Old English (Anglo-Saxon).

new'făn″gle, *a.* newfangled. [Dial.]

new'făn″gle, *v.t.* to change by introducing novelties. [Dial.]

new'făn″gled (-gld), *a.* 1. new; novel; newly done, made, etc.; formed with the affectation of novelty; as, *newfangled* devices.

2. inclined to affect things that are new or strange; tending toward the recent, different, or novel.

A contemptuous term.

new'făn″gled·ness, *n.* the quality of being newfangled; affectation of novelty.

new'făn″glist, *n.* one who affects novelty. [Obs.]

new'făn″gly, *adv.* in a newfangled manner. [Obs.]

new'-fash″iŏned (-und), *a.* 1. made in a new and different form or style.

2. recently or lately come into fashion.

New·found'lănd, *n.* a Newfoundland dog.

New·found'lănd dog, any of a North American breed of large, usually black, shaggy-haired dogs of above average intelligence.

New·found'lănd·ẽr, *n.* a native or inhabitant of Newfoundland.

New'gāte, *n.* a former prison in London, England: it was destroyed in 1902.

New Hīgh Ġẽr'măn (-hī), see *German.*

new'ing, *n.* yeast or barm. [Brit. Dial.]

new'ish, *a.* somewhat new; nearly new.

New Jẽr'ṣey·ite, a native or inhabitant of New Jersey.

New Lat'in, Modern Latin.

new'ly, *adv.* 1. lately; recently.

2. anew; afresh.

3. with a new form; differently.

new'ly·wed, *n.* a recently married person.

new'mär″ket, *n.* 1. a game of cards played with a full pack by any number of persons, in which the winner receives a chip for each card any player has left when a hand has been played.

2. a kind of close-fitting cloak with a long skirt formerly worn by a man while riding; also, a woman's close-fitting coat for outdoor wear, reaching to the floor: also *Newmarket coat.*

new math, an ordered system for teaching fundamental concepts of mathematics that emphasizes unifying themes, the development of the ability to solve problems, and preciseness in vocabulary and definition.

New Mex'i·căn, 1. of New Mexico.

2. a native or inhabitant of New Mexico.

new'-mod″el, *v.t.*; new-modeled, *pt., pp.*; new-modeling, *ppr.* to give a new form to; to remodel; to make over.

new·mōwn', *a.* freshly mown; just cut: said of hay or grass.

new'ness, *n.* the quality or the condition of being new.

newṣ, *n.pl.* [*construed as sing.*] [ME. *newes,* novelties (pl. of *newe,* adj.); after OFr. *noveles* (Fr. *nouvelles*) or ML. *nova,* pl. of *novum,* what is new; see *new.*]

1. new information about anything; information previously unknown; as, that's *news* to me.

2. recent happenings, especially those broadcast over the radio or television, printed in a newspaper, etc.

3. reports of such events, collectively.

4. a newspaper.

newṣ'boy, *n.* a boy who sells or delivers newspapers.

newṣ'çȧst, *n.* [*news* and broad*cast.*] a radio or television broadcast of news reports.

newṣ'çȧst, *v.t.* and *v.i.* to broadcast (news).

newṣ'çȧst″ẽr, *n.* a person who broadcasts news reports on radio or television.

newṣ'dēal″ẽr, *n.* a person who sells newspapers, magazines, etc.

newṣ'let″tẽr, *n.* 1. a bulletin issued at regular intervals to subscribers, containing recent news, particularly political and economic, and often including interpretations and predictions.

2. any similar report issued by a firm, governmental agency, etc. to keep employees or the public informed of pertinent matters.

newṣ'măn, *n.*; *pl.* **newṣ'men,** 1. a man who sells or delivers newspapers or periodicals.

2. a newspaper reporter.

newṣ'mŏn″gẽr, *n.* one who spends much time in hearing and telling news; a person who spreads news; especially, a gossip.

newṣ'pā″pẽr, *n.* 1. a publication regularly printed and distributed, usually daily or weekly, containing news, opinions, advertisements, and other items of general interest.

2. newsprint.

newṣ'pā″pẽr·dŏm, *n.* newspapers collectively; the interests or realm of newspapers.

newṣ'pā″pẽr·man, *n.*; *pl.* **newṣ'pā″pẽr·men,** one who owns, or is employed upon the staff of, a newspaper; especially, a writer for a daily newspaper, as an editor or reporter.

newṣ'pā″pẽr·wom″ăn (-woom″), *n*; *pl.* **newṣ-pā″pẽr·wom″en** (-wim″), a woman engaged in newspaper work; particularly, one who writes for publication in newspapers.

new'spēak, *n.* [coined (from *new,* and *speak*) by George Orwell in his novel *1984.*] [*sometimes* N-] the deliberate use of ambiguous and deceptive talk, as by government officials, in seeking to mold public opinion.

newṣ'print, *n.* a cheap, thin paper made mainly from machine-finished wood pulp and used for newspapers, etc.: sometimes called *print.*

newṣ'reel, *n.* a motion picture portraying current events.

newṣ'rọọm, *n.* 1. a reading room having newspapers, etc.

2. a room in a newspaper office containing the desks of reporters, copy editors, etc., where the news is written and edited: sometimes called *city room.*

3. a similar room for preparing news in a radio or television station.

newṣ'stand, *n.* a place for the sale of newspapers and periodicals.

newṣ stąll, a newsstand. [Brit.]

news vend'ŏr, a seller of newspapers.

newṣ'wŏr″thy, *a.* having the qualities of news; timely, important, and interesting.

news wrīt'ẽr, originally, a contributor to, or writer of, newsletters; in the modern use, a newspaper reporter.

newṣ'y, *a.*; *comp.* newsier; *superl.* newsiest, containing much news. [Colloq.]

newṣ'y, *n.*; *pl.* **newṣ'ieṣ,** a newsboy. [Colloq.]

newt, *n.* [ME. *newte,* a corruption of *an ewte*; *an,* indef. art., and *ewte, euete,* AS. *efete,* a lizard.] any of various small salamanders that can live both on land and in water; especially, any tailed animal of the genus *Triton.*

WARTY NEWT
(*Triton cristatus*)

New·tō'ni·ăn, *a.* pertaining to or agreeing with Sir Isaac Newton or his discoveries and theories.

Newtonian system; the system which explains the movements of the planets in their orbits, mainly by the law of gravitation.

Newtonian telescope; a form of the reflecting telescope, in which the rays are reflected from the surface of the object mirror and intercepted by a small oval mirror placed in the axis of the tube at an angle of 45°. The image which would have been formed in the axis is thereby deflected and is viewed by an eyepiece attached at a right angle to the side of the tube.

New·tō'ni·ăn, *n.* 1. an advocate of Newton's theories.

2. a Newtonian telescope.

New'tŏn'ṣ disk, a cardboard disk having radiating strips of paper of such dimensions and tints as to constitute five spectra. When the disk is rapidly rotated, the prismatic colors all blend together, the resultant being white or grayish-white.

New'tŏn'ṣ ringṣ, rings of color concentrically arranged, when a very thin lamina of anything transparent is subjected to light. The iridescence of a soap bubble is an instance.

new'-wŏrld, *a.* of or from the New World.

New Wŏrld, the Western Hemisphere.

New'-Wŏrld', *a.* of or from the New World.

New Yọrk'ẽr, a native or inhabitant of New York (State or, especially, City).

New Zēa'lănd·ẽr, a native or inhabitant of New Zealand.

New Zēa'lănd flax, a plant of the lily family, *Phormium tenax*; also, its fiber.

New Zēa'lănd tēa, the leaves of *Leptospermum scoparium,* a plant belonging to the order *Myrtaceæ,* sometimes used as a substitute for tea, and by some as a remedy for scurvy; also, the plant itself.

nex'ăl, *a.* in Roman law, of, subject to, or denoting nexum.

next, *a.* [AS. *nexta, nehsta,* from *nehst,* adv., superl. of *neăh,* nigh.] nearest; just before or after in place, time, rank, or degree; immediately preceding or following.

Let us go into the *next* towns, that I may preach there also. —Mark i. 38.

next door (*to*); in or at the next house, building, etc. (adjacent to).

next friend; in law, a person who, though not legally a guardian, acts for another unable to act for himself.

next, *adv.* 1. in the time, place, degree, or

rank nearest, or immediately preceding or following.
2. on the first subsequent occasion; as, when *next* we meet.
next, *prep.* beside; nearest or nighest to; in immediate proximity to.
next'-dōor, *a.* in or at the next house, building, etc.
next of kin, 1. a person's nearest relative or relatives.
2. in law, (a) the blood relatives who may be entitled to share in the estate of a person who dies without a will; (b) sometimes, the nearest relative by blood as defined in the law of the various States.
nex'um, *n.* in Roman law, the contract or obligation by which a debtor became subject to the will of the creditor in case of nonpayment of a debt.
nex'us, *n.*; *pl.* **nex'us·eṣ, nex'us,** [L., from pp. of *nectere*, to bind.]
1. a connection, tie, or link between individuals of a group, members of a series, etc.
2. the group or series connected.
Nez Per·cé' (nā pär-sā' *or Eng.* nez' pũrs'), *n.*; *pl.* **Nez Per·cés'** (pär-sā' *or Eng.* pũr'siz), [Fr., lit., pierced nose: from the practice of several western tribes (but not of this tribe,) of piercing the nose for insertion of a shell ornament.] a member of a tribe of North American Indians who lived in Idaho, Washington, and Oregon.
Ni, in chemistry, nickel.
nī'ȧ·cin, *n.* nicotinic acid.
Nī·ag'ȧ·rȧ pē'ri·ŏd, [so called from *Niagara* Falls where the rocks of this period are found.] in geology, a period embracing the Medina, Clinton, and Niagara epochs, the principal constituent of rocks belonging to the last-mentioned epoch being limestone.
ni·äre', *n.* the buffalo. [S. Afr.]
nī'ăs, *n.* an eyas; a fledgling hawk. [Obs.]
ni·ä'tȧ, *n.* a breed of small South American oxen.
nī'ȧ·tiṣm, *n.* the arrest of development in cattle, resulting in a variation of form and size resembling that of the niata.
nib, *v.i.* to nibble. [Dial.]
nib, *n.* [a variant of *neb*.]
1. the bill or beak of a bird.
2. (a) originally, the split and sharpened end of a quill pen; (b) the point of a pen, or the entire pen, meant to be inserted in a holder.
3. the projecting end of anything; a point; a sharp prong.
4. the short grip handles on the shaft of a scythe.
5. [*pl.*] crushed coffee or cocoa beans.
nib, *v.t.*; nibbed, *pt., pp.*; nibbing, *ppr.* 1. originally, to sharpen and split the end of (a quill) to make a pen.
2. to mend (a pen point).
3. to put a point on (a pen).
nibbed, *a.* having a nib or point.
nib'ble, *v.t.*; nibbled, *pt., pp.*; nibbling, *ppr.* [prob. from Late M.D. or M.L.G. *nibbelen* or base of *nip*, v., and freq. suffix *-le*.]
1. to eat (food) with quick bites, taking only a small amount at a time, as a mouse does.
2. to continue to bite (food) with small bites, gently and intermittently; as, a fish *nibbles* the bait.
nib'ble, *v.i.* 1. to take only small bites; to bite cautiously or gently (usually with *at*).
2. to show little interest in food by taking only small bites intermittently (usually with *at*).
nib'ble, *n.* 1. a small bite, morsel, or quantity.
2. act or instance of nibbling.
nib'blẽr, *n.* one who bites a little at a time.
nib'bling·ly, *adv.* in a nibbling manner.
Nī'be·lụng, *n.* [G.] in Norse mythology, (a) any of a race of dwarfs, the children of the mist, who owned a magic ring and a hoard of gold, taken from them by Siegfried; (b) any of Siegfried's followers; (c) any of the Burgundian kings in the Nibelungenlied.
Nī'be·lụng·en·liēd (-lēt), *n.* [G., song of the Nibelungs.] a Middle High German epic poem by an unknown author, written in the first decade of the thirteenth century and based on two main legends of the Burgundian kings, which were in turn ultimately based on various compilations of legends: Wagner's cycle of operas, *The Ring of the Nibelung*, is based chiefly on Norse variants of these legends.
nib'lick, *n.* a heavy, iron-headed golf club with much loft, used in sand and for short shots in which the ball must be stopped quickly: now usually called *number 8 iron*.
nibṣ, *n.* [earlier also *his nabs*; prob. var. of Brit. slang *nob* (wealthy, highly placed person).] a person of importance or authority (with *his*): said especially of self-important persons. [Colloq.]
nib'ung, *n.* [Malay.] a palm, *Oncosperma filamentosa*, native to the Malay Archipelago, having a tough wood useful in building.
Nī·cae'ăn, *n.* an adherent of the Nicene Council and Creed.
Nī·cae'ăn, *a.* same as *Nicene*.
Niç·ȧ·rä'guăn (-gwăn), *a.* of Nicaragua, its people, or their culture.
Niç·ȧ·rä'guăn, *n.* a native or inhabitant of Nicaragua.
niç·çol'iç, *a.* pertaining to nickel; containing or made of nickel.
niç·çō·lif'ẽr·ous, *a.* same as *nickeliferous*.
niç'çō·līte, *n.* [from *nickel* and *-ite*.] an arsenide of nickel (NiAs), copper-red and of metallic luster: also called *copper* nickel.
nīce, *a.*; *comp.* nicer; *superl.* nicest, [OFr. *nice, niche, nisce*, simple, foolish, impudent, ignorant, from L. *nescius*, ignorant, not knowing; *ne*, not, and *scire*, to know.]
1. very particular; fastidious; difficult to please or satisfy; very careful; refined.

To taste
Think not I shall be *nice*. —Milton.

2. delicate; minute; subtle; discriminative; exact; precise; as, *nice* proportions; *nice* workmanship; *nice* calculations.

The difference is too *nice*
Where ends the virtue or begins the vice. —Pope.

3. calling for delicacy, accuracy, or precision in handling, discrimination, or adjustment; calling for great care, tact, etc.; as, a *nice* problem.
4. (a) able to make fine or delicate distinctions; delicately skillful; finely discriminating; (b) minutely accurate, as an instrument.
5. having high standards of conduct; scrupulous.
6. (a) agreeable; pleasant; delightful; (b) attractive; pretty; (c) kind; thoughtful; considerate; (d) modest; well-mannered; reserved; (e) in good taste; (f) good; excellent. A generalized term of approval, having very wide application.
7. (a) ignorant; foolish; (b) wanton; (c) coy; shy. [Obs.]
Syn.—dainty, delicate, exquisite, fine, accurate, exact, correct, precise, particular, scrupulous, punctilious, fastidious, squeamish.
nīce'ly, *adv.* 1. in an attractive or pleasing manner.
2. exactly; precisely.
3. satisfactorily.
Nī'cēne, *a.* pertaining to Nicaea, a town of Asia Minor, or to the council held there in A.D. 325.
Nicene Councils; in church history, two councils held at Nicaea; the first in A.D. 325 under Pope Silvester I. on account of the Arian heresy. It drew up the Nicene Creed, and settled the controversy as to the keeping of Easter. The second, in A.D. 787, under Pope Adrian I., was convened to restore images, pass disciplinary measures, etc.
Nicene Creed; a summary of Christian faith, composed by the Council of Nicaea against Arianism, A.D. 325, altered and confirmed by the Council of Constantinople, A.D. 381, and in this form accepted by the Orthodox Eastern Church. The Roman Catholic Church uses a form containing one extra clause, and various Protestant denominations have accepted modifications of this.
nīce'ness, *n.* the state or quality of being nice; delicacy.
Nī·cē·nō-Çon·stan"ti·nō·pol'i·tăn, *a.* pertaining to Nicaea and Constantinople: applied to the Nicene Creed after its modification and confirmation by the Council of Constantinople in A.D. 381.
nī'cẽr·y, *n.* nicety. [Obs.]
nī'ce·ty, *n.*; *pl.* **nī'ce·tieṣ,** [ME. *nycete*; OFr. *nicete*, folly.]
1. the quality or state of being nice; specifically, (a) [Obs.] foolishness; (b) coyness; modesty; (c) excessive elegance; (d) scrupulosity; (e) precision; accuracy; minuteness; exactness, as of discrimination or perception; (f) fastidiousness; refinement; delicacy of taste.
2. the quality of calling for delicacy, accuracy, or precision in handling, discrimination, or adjustment.
3. anything involving or calling for delicacy, accuracy, or precision; subtle or minute detail, distinction, etc.
4. something choice, dainty, or elegant.
to a nicety; to a precise degree; exactly.
niche (nich), *n.* [Fr. *niche*, from L. *nidus*, a nest.]
1. a recess or hollow in a wall, usually intended for a statue, bust, or vase.
2. a place or position particularly suitable for the person or thing in it.

NICHE

niche, *v.t.*; niched, *pt., pp.*; niching, *ppr.* to place in or as in a niche.
nī'çhrōme, *n.* [*ni*ckel and *-chrome*.] an alloy of nickel, iron, and chromium, having high electrical and heat resistance: a trade-mark (*Nichrome*).
nicht wahr? (nikht vär), [G., lit., not true?] isn't that so?
Nick, *n.* the Devil; Satan: usually *Old Nick*.
nick, *v.t.* [prob. from M. L.G. *knicken*.]
1. to make a nick or nicks in.
2. to score or tally by means of notches.
3. to cut through or into.
4. to strike or catch at the exact or proper time; to hit, guess, grasp, etc. exactly.
5. (a) to catch off guard; (b) to trick; cheat; defraud. [Slang.]
6. to arrest; to nab. [Brit. Slang.]
nick, *n.* [from the v.]
1. a small notch or slit; especially, a small cut, indention, or chip on the edge or surface of wood, metal, china, etc.
2. any of certain winning throws or casts in a game of dice.
3. a channel cut in the bottom of a printing type.
4. a tally or record kept by notching something.
in the nick of time; at the critical moment.
nick'ăr nut, same as *nicker nut*.
nick'ăr tree, same as *nicker tree*.
nick'el, *n.* [Sw. *nickel*, an abbrev. of *kopparnickel*, copper nickel; so called because it was thought to be a base ore of copper.]
1. a hard, silver-white, malleable metallic chemical element, used extensively in alloys and for plating because of its resistance to oxidation: symbol, Ni; atomic weight, 58.69; atomic number, 28.
2. a United States or Canadian coin made of an alloy of nickel and copper and equal to five cents.
nick'el, *v.t.* to plate with nickel.
nick·el'iç, *a.* pertaining to or containing nickel, especially trivalent nickel.
niçk·el·if'ẽr·ous, *a.* [*nickel*, and L. *ferre*, to bear.] containing nickel: said of ore, etc.
nick'el·ine, *n.* same as *niccolite*.
nick·el·ō'dē·ŏn, *n.* [*nickel* and *odeon*, odeum.]
1. formerly, a motion-picture theater, variety show, etc. where admission was five cents.
2. a player piano or phonograph which can be operated by the insertion of a nickel in a slot.
nick'el·ous, *a.* containing nickel, especially bivalent nickel.
niçk'el-plāte, *v.t.* to plate with nickel by electrolysis, etc.
niçk'el plāte, a thin layer of nickel placed by electrolysis on objects made of other metal, to improve the finish and prevent rust.
niçk'el sil'vẽr, a hard, tough, ductile, malleable, silver-white alloy composed essentially of nickel, copper, and zinc: used in the manufacture of table ware, electric-resistance wire, etc.: also called *German silver*.
niçk'el steel, a steel alloy made harder and tougher than ordinary steel by the addition of small amounts of nickel.
nick'ẽr, *n.* [from *nick*, v.t.] a person or thing that nicks (esp. in sense 4); specifically, any of a group of eighteenth-century rowdies who broke windows by throwing copper coins.

nick'ẽr, *n.* and *v.i.* [prob. var. of *nicher, neigher,* freq. of *neigh.*]
1. neigh. [Chiefly Brit. Dial.]
2. laugh, snicker. [Chiefly Brit. Dial.]

nick'ẽr nut, a seed of the nicker tree: also called *bonduc seed.*

nick'ẽr·peck''ẽr, *n.* a woodpecker; especially, [Brit. Dial] the green woodpecker: also called *nickle.*

nick'ẽr tree, either of two leguminous climbing shrubs, *Cæsalpinia bonducella* and *Cæsalpinia bonduc,* growing in the tropics.

niç'kle, *n.* the nickerpecker. [Brit. Dial.]

nick'nack, *n.* same as *knickknack.*

nick'nack·ẽr·y, *n.* same as *knickknackery.*

nick'nāme, *n.* [ME. *ekename,* surname.]
1. an additional or substitute name given to a person, place, or thing: usually descriptive and given in fun, affection, or derision, as "Doc," "Shorty," etc.
2. a familiar form of a proper name, as "Freddy" for "Frederick," "Davey" for "David," etc.

nick'nāme, *v.t.*; nicknamed, *pt., pp.*; nicknaming, *ppr.* 1. to give a nickname to.
2. to call by a wrong name.

niç'ŏl, *n.* see *nicol prism* under *prism.*

Niç·ō·lā'i·tăn, *n.* [from *Nicolas,* a proselyte mentioned in Acts vi. 5.] one of certain corrupt persons in the early church at Ephesus who are censured in Rev. ii. 6, 15.

niç'ō·lō, *n.* [It.] a variety of bombardon used in the seventeenth century.

ni·çō'tiăn, *n.* tobacco. [Obs.]

Ni·çō·ti·ā'nȧ (-shi-), *n.* [Fr. *nicotiane,* the earliest name given to the tobacco plant in France.] a genus of chiefly American plants of the nighshade family, of which several species produce tobacco.

ni·çō'ti·ȧ·nin (*or* -shi-) *n.* [*nicotian* and *-in.*] a volatizable and fragrant crystalline substance obtained from tobacco.

ni·çot'iç, *a.* nicotinic.

niç'ō·tin, *n.* nicotine

niç'ō·tīne, *n.* [Fr., from Jacques *Nicot,* Fr. ambassador at Lisbon, who first introduced tobacco into France (1560).] a poisonous alkaloid, $C_{10}H_{14}N_2$, found in tobacco leaves, from which it is extracted as a colorless, oily, acrid, transparent liquid and used, ordinarily in an aqueous solution of its sulfate, as an insecticide.

niç'ō·tīned (*or* -tind), *a.* impregnated with nicotine.

niç·ō·tin'iç, *a.* [*nicotine* and *-ic.*] pertaining to or obtained from nicotine; as, *nicotinic* acid.

niç·ō·tin'iç ac'id, a white, odorless, crystalline substance, $C_6H_5O_2N$, found in protein foods like lean meat, eggs, whole-grain cereals, etc. and prepared synthetically by the oxidation of nicotine: it is a member of the vitamin B complex and is used in the treatment of pellagra: also called *niacin.*

niç'ō·tin·iṣm (*or* -tin-), *n.* a diseased condition caused by the ingestion of nicotine, as from tobacco; nicotine poisoning.

niç'ō·tin·ize (*or* -tin-), *v.t.,* nicotinized, *pt., pp.*; nicotinizing, *ppr.* to saturate with nicotine.

niç'tāte, *v.i.*; nictated, *pt., pp.*; nictating, *ppr.* [L. *nictatus,* pp. of *nictare,* to wink.] to wink; to nictitate.

niç'tāt·ing mem'brāne, a nictitating membrane.

niç·tā'tion, *n.* nictitation.

niç'ti·tănt, *a.* [L. *nictitans* (*-antis*), *ppr.* of *nictitare,* to wink.] in entomology, having the central spot lunate, as an ocellated spot.

niç'ti·tāte, *v.i.*; nictitated, *pt., pp.*; nictitating, *ppr.* [L. *nictitatus,* pp. of *nictitare,* freq. of *nictare,* to wink.] to wink or blink rapidly, as birds and animals with a nictitating membrane: also *nictate.*
nictitating membrane; a transparent third eyelid hinged at the inner side or lower lid of the eye of various animals, serving to keep the eye clean and moist: also *nictating membrane.*

niç·ti·tā'tion, *n.* a nictitating: also *nictation.*

nī'dăl, *a.* pertaining to a nidus.

nid·ȧ·men'tăl, *a.* [L. *nidamentum,* materials for a nest, from *nidus,* a nest.] pertaining to the protection of the egg and young: applied especially to the organs which secrete the materials of which many animals construct nests.

nid·ȧ·men'tum, *n.*; *pl.* **nid·ȧ·men'tȧ,** [L., materials for a nest.] an egg case.

nī'dȧ·ry, *n.* [L. *nidus,* a nest.] a nesting place. [Obs.]

nī·dā'tion, *n.* the development of the epithelial lining of the uterus during the intercatamenial period.

nid'dẽr·ing, nid'ẽr·ing, *n.* [popularized by Scott (*Ivanhoe*), from printer's error for ME. nithing, coward.] coward, wretch. [Archaic.]

nid'dẽr·ing, nid'ẽr·ing, *a.* base; cowardly. [Archaic.]

nīde *n.* [L. *nidus,* nest.] a brood of pheasants.

nīde, *v.i.*; nided, *pt., pp.*; niding, *ppr.* to nest. [Rare.]

nidġe, *v.t.*; nidged, *pt., pp.*; nidging, *ppr.* in masonry, to dress the face of (a stone) with a sharp-pointed hammer, instead of hewing it with a chisel and mallet: also written *nig.*

nidġ'et, *n.* [from OFr. *niger,* to trifle.] an idiot; a fool; a coward. [Archaic.]

nī'dī, *n.* pl. of *nidus.*

nid'i·fi·çāte, *v.i.*; nidificated, *pt., pp.*; nidificating, *ppr.* [L. *nidificatus,* pp. of *nidificare,* to build a nest.] to make a nest.

nid·i·fi·çā'tion, *n.* the act or operation of building a nest.

nid'i·fȳ, *v.i.*; nidified, *pt., pp.*; nidifying, *ppr.* to construct a nest; to nidificate.

nid'-nod, *v.t.* and *v.i.* to nod repeatedly, as when sleepy.

nī'dŏr, *n.* [L.] scent; savor; smell of cooked food.

nī'dŏr·ōse, *a.* nidorous. [Obs.]

nī·dŏr·os'i·ty, *n.* eructation with the taste of undigested meat.

nī'dŏr·ous, *a.* [L. *nidorosus,* steaming, from *nidor,* scent, savor.] resembling the smell or taste of roast meat. [Rare.]

nid'ū·lănt, *a.* [L. *nidulans* (*-antis*), ppr. of *nidulari,* to build a nest.] in botany, nestling; lying loose in pulp or cotton, within a berry or pericarp.

Nid·ū·lā'ri·ȧ, *n.* a genus typical of the family *Nidulariaceæ.*

Nid·ū·lā·ri·ā'çē·ae, *n.pl.* [L. *nidulus,* a little nest, dim. of *nidus,* a nest.] a family of small fungi, the structure of which is that of the hypogeal fungi reduced to single isolated cells. The species are small, growing on the ground among decaying sticks, dung, etc.

nid·ū·lā·ri·ā'ceous, *a.* pertaining to the *Nidulariaceæ.*

nid'ū·lāte, *v.i.*; nidulated, *pt., pp.*; nidulating, *ppr.* to build a nest; to nidificate. [Rare.]

nid'ū·lāte, *a.* same as *nidulant.*

nid·ū·lā'tion, *n.* the time of remaining in the nest, as of a bird. [Rare.]

nī'dus, *n.*; *pl.* **nī'dī, nī'dus·eṣ,** [L.] 1. a nest, especially one in which insects or spiders deposit their eggs.
2. a breeding place; specifically, (a) a place where spores or seeds are developed; (b) a source of infection or disease.

nieçe (nēs), *n.* [OFr. *niece, niepce,* from L. *neptis,* a granddaughter, niece.]
1. the daughter of one's brother or sister.
2. the daughter of one's brother-in-law or sister-in-law.
3. an illegitimate daughter, as of a medieval prelate: a euphemism.

ni·el'list, *n.* one who works in niello.

ni·el'lō, *n.*; *pl.* **ni·el'li, ni·el'lōṣ,** [It., from LL. *nigellum,* a blackish enamel, from L. *nigellus,* dim. of *niger,* black.]
1. any of a number of alloys of sulfur with silver, lead, copper, etc., characterized by a deep-black color and used to decorate objects of other metals by means of inlay.
2. the process of decorating with niello.
3. something decorated in this way.

ni·el'lō, *v.t.* to ornament by the niello method.

niē'pȧ bärk, [E. Ind. *niepa.*] the bark of *Samadera indica,* a tree of the quassia family.

Niē·rem·bẽrg'i·ȧ, *n.* [named after J. E. *Nieremberg,* Spanish Jesuit.] a genus of tropical American plants of the order *Solanaceæ,* having white or purple flowers: it includes about twenty species.

niēs'hout, *n.* [D.] a South African tree, *Ptæroxylon utile,* of the soapberry family.

Niē'tzsche·ăn (-che-), *a.* of Nietzsche or his philosophy.

Niē'tzsche·ăn, *n.* a follower of Nietzsche.

Niē'tzsche·iṣm, *n.* the doctrine of Friedrich W. Nietzsche (1844–1900), German philosopher, based on the theory that man can perfect himself through forcible self-assertion.

niēve, *n.* [ME. *neve*; ON. *hnefi.*] a fist or hand. [Archaic or Scot and Brit. Dial.]

nif'fẽr, *v.* and *n.* [freq. formation from ME. *neve,* nieve.] exchange; barter; trade. [Scot.]

nif'le (-l), *n.* a trifle. [Dial.]

Nĭ'fl·hẹim, Nĭ'fel·hẹim (niv'l-hām), *n.* [ON. *Niflheimr.*] in Norse mythology, the regions of darkness and cold, or realm of the dead; hell.

Nĭ'fl·hẹimr (-hām-ẽr), *n.* same as *Niflheim.*

nif'ty, *a.*; *comp.* niftier; *superl.* niftiest, [orig. theatrical slang; prob. from *magnificent.*] attractive, smart, stylish, enjoyable, etc.: a generalized term of approval. [Slang.]

nif'ty, *n.*; *pl.* **nif'tieṣ,** a clever remark. [Slang.]

nig, *v.t.*; nigged, *pt., pp.*; nigging, *ppr.* [prob. from *nig,* a chip.]
1. to clip off the edges of, as a coin. [Obs.]
2. to nidge.

nig, *v.i.* to be niggardly. [Obs.]

Nī·gel'lȧ, *n.* [dim. from L. *niger,* black; so called from the black seed.] a genus of annual plants of the order *Ranunculaceæ*; the fennel flowers. The seeds of *Nigella sativa* and *Nigella arvensis* are used as pepper.

Nī·ġē'ri·ăn, *a.* of Nigeria, its people, or their culture.

Nī·ġē'ri·ăn, *n.* a native or inhabitant of Nigeria.

Nī'ġẽr oil, an oil obtained from Niger seeds.

Nī'ġẽr seedṣ, [L. *niger,* black.]the small black seeds of *Guizotia oleifera.*

nig'gărd, *n.* [prob. from Norm. Fr.; the base prob. from ON.; compare Sw. *njugga,* to hoard.] a miserly, stingy fellow; a miser; a covetous person; one who is sparing or grudging of anything.

> Serve him as a grudging master,
> As a penurious *niggard* of his wealth.
> —Milton.

nig'gărd, *a.* 1. miserly; covetous; parsimonious.
2. sparing; wary.

> Most free of question but to our demands
> *Niggard* in his reply. —Shak.

nig'gărd, *v.t.* and *v.i.* to stint; to supply sparingly. [Obs.]

nig'gărd·iṣe, *n.* niggardliness. [Obs.]

nig'gărd·ish, *a.* somewhat covetous or niggardly.

nig'gărd·li·ness, *n.* the quality or state of being niggardly; parsimony; extreme avarice manifested in sparing expense.

> *Niggardliness* is not good husbandry.
> —Addison.

nig'gărd·ly, *a.* 1. like or characteristic of a niggard; covetous or avaricious; parsimonious; stingy; miserly.

> Where the owner of the house will be bountiful, it is not for the steward to be *niggardly.* —Hall.

2. small, few, or scanty, as if given by a niggard; as, a *niggardly* sum.

Syn.—miserly, sparing, penurious, stingy.

nig'gărd·ly, *adv.* sparingly; in the manner of a niggard.

nig'gărd·ness, *n.* niggardliness. [Obs.]

nig'gărd·ous, *a.* niggardly. [Obs.]

nig'gărd·ship, *n.* niggardliness; stinginess. [Obs.]

nig'gărd·y, *n.* niggardliness. [Obs.]

nigged, *a.* chipped or dressed with a pointed hammer, as building stone.

nig'gẽr, *n.* [earlier *neger*; Fr. *nègre*; Sp. *negro,* black, black person.]
1. a Negro.
2. a member of any dark-skinned people.
A vulgar, offensive term of hostility and contempt, as used by Negrophobes.

nig'gẽr·fish, *n.* a West Indian fish: also called *butterfish.*

nig'gẽr·head (-hed), *n.* 1. a round, black rock or boulder.
2. a kind of black chewing tobacco.

nig'gẽr·tōe, *n.* same as *Brazil nut.*

nig'gish, *a.* niggardly; stingy; mean. [Obs.]

> A most *niggish* and miserable man.
> —Copley.

nig'gle, *v.i.*; niggled, *pt., pp.*; niggling, *ppr.* [North Brit. dial.] to work fussily; to pay too much attention to details; to putter.

nig'glẽr, *n.* one who niggles.

nig'gling, *n.* excessive attention to detail; fussy or finicking work.

nīgh (nī), *a.* [AS. *neah, neh,* nigh, near.]
1. near; close.
2. direct or short.
3. on the left: said of animals, vehicles, etc.
4. parsimonious.
[Chiefly Archaic or Dial. in all senses.]

nīgh, *adv.* 1. near in time, place, etc. [Chiefly Archaic or Dial.]
2. nearly; almost. [Chiefly Archaic or Dial.]

nīgh, *prep.* near; near to. [Chiefly Archaic or Dial.]

nīgh (nī), *v.t.* and *v.i.* to approach; to advance or draw near. [Archaic.]

nīgh'ly, *adv.* nearly; almost. [Archaic.]

A cube and a sphere *nighly* of the same bigness. —Molyneaux.

nīgh'ness, *n.* nearness; proximity in place, time, or degree. [Archaic.]

nīght (nīt), *n.* [AS. *niht, neaht,* night; compare Ice. *nott,* Sw. *natt,* Dan. *nat,* Goth. *nahts,* D. and G. *nacht,* Lith. *naktis,* L. *nox, noctis,* Gr. *nyx, nyktos,* Sans. *nakti, nakta,* night.]

1. (a) the period from sunset to sunrise; (b) the period of actual darkness after sunset and before sunrise.

2. the darkness of this period.

3. any period or condition of darkness or gloom; specifically, (a) a period of intellectual or moral degeneration; (b) a time of grief; (c) death.

night and day; continuously or continually.

to make a night of it; to celebrate all or most of the night.

nīght, *a.* of or for the night.

nīght bell, a bell to be used at night.

nīght bīrd, a bird that flies or sings chiefly at night; specifically, (a) the moor hen; (b) the Manx shearwater; (c) an owl.

nīght blīnd'ness, imperfect vision in the dark or in dim light; nyctalopia: a sign of vitamin A deficiency.

nīght'-bloom"ing cē'rē·us, any of various kinds of cactus, especially one with large, white flowers that open at night.

nīght'çap, *n.* 1. a cap worn in bed to protect the head from cold.

2. an alcoholic drink taken just before going to bed. [Colloq.]

nīght cärt, a cart to remove night soil.

nīght'chŭrr, *n.* same as *nightjar.*

nīght clōthes, clothes to be worn in bed, as pajamas.

nīght çlub, a place of entertainment open at night for eating, drinking, etc., often having a floor show.

nīght crawl'ẽr, a large earthworm that comes out of the earth at night; nightwalker.

nīght çrōw, 1. a bird that cries in the night.

2. the nightjar.

nīght'dress, *n.* 1. a nightgown.

2. night clothes.

nīght'-eyed (-īd), *a.* capable of seeing in the darkness or at night; hence, sharp-eyed.

nīght'fall, *n.* the close of the day; dusk; early evening.

nīght'-fär"ing, *a.* traveling in the night.

nīght fīre, 1. ignis fatuus; will-o'-the-wisp. [Obs.]

2. fire burning in the night.

nīght flī'ẽr, a bird that flies by night.

nīght flow'ẽr, the night jasmine.

nīght glȧss, a field glass or telescope designed for use at night.

nīght'gown, *n.* 1. a loose gown, usually long, worn in bed by women or children.

2. a nightshirt.

3. a dressing gown. [Obs.]

nīght hag, a witch supposed to wander in the night.

nīght'hawk, *n.* 1. any of a group of birds, *Chordeiles virginianus,* related to the whippoorwill, with brown, mottled feathers and a broad, deeply cleft bill; goatsucker.

2. the European nightjar.

3. a petrel of the genus *Œstrelata.*

4. one who is habitually up or abroad at night; a night owl. [Colloq.]

nīght her'ŏn, any of various herons of the genus *Nycticorax,* most active at night or twilight.

nīght'ïē, *n.* a nightgown. [Colloq.]

nīght'in·gāle, *n.* [AS. *nihtegale,* lit., the night singer; *niht,* night, and *galan,* to sing; compare D. *nachtegaal,* Dan. *nattergal,* nightingale.] any of various small European thrushes of the genus *Daulias,* especially *Daulias luscinia,* which has a russet back and buff to white underparts: it is characterized by the varied, melodious singing of the male, especially at night during the breeding season.

NIGHTINGALE
(*Daulias luscinia*)

nīght'in·gāle, *n.* [from Florence Nightingale (1820–1910), famous English army nurse.] a kind of flannel scarf with sleeves, for persons confined to bed.

nīght'ish, *a.* pertaining to night. [Obs.]

nīght'jär, *n.* the European goatsucker, *Caprimulgus europæus.*

nīght jas'mine, a shrub, *Nyctanthes arbortristis,* of the East Indies, bearing fragrant white blossoms that open at night.

nīght kä'kȧ, the kakapo.

nīght kēy, a key for opening a night latch.

nīght latch, a spring lock for a door opened on the outside by a key, and on the inside by a knob.

nīght'less, *a.* having no night.

nīght let'tẽr, a telegram with a minimum charge for fifty words or fewer, sent at night to be delivered the next morning, and cheaper than a regular telegram: distinguished from *day letter.*

nīght līght, a small, dim light kept burning all night, as in the halls of rooming houses, etc.

nīght lock, a night latch.

nīght'lọng, *a.* continuing all night.

nīght'lọng, *adv.* during the entire night.

nīght'ly, *a.* 1. of, like, or characteristic of the night.

2. done or occurring every night.

nīght'ly, *adv.* 1. at night.

2. every night.

nīght'man, *n.*; *pl.* **nīght'men,** one who works at night.

nīght'māre, *n.* [ME. *nihtmare; niht,* night, and *mare,* demon, from AS. *mara,* incubus.]

1. formerly, an evil spirit that was believed to haunt and suffocate sleeping people.

2. a frightening dream, often accompanied by a sensation of oppression and helplessness.

3. any experience like a nightmare in its frightening or oppressing aspects.

nīght'mär·ish, *a.* like a nightmare.

nīght mŏn'key, a small nocturnal monkey of South America, belonging to the genus *Nyctipithecus.*

nīght mọth, a noctuid.

nīght owl, 1. an owl that is active almost exclusively at night.

2. a person who works at night or does not retire until very late.

nīght par'rŏt, the kakapo.

nīght pīēce, 1. a painting of a scene at night.

2. a poem or other literary work about night.

nīght rā'ven, any of various birds, as the night heron, that are most active at night. [Poet.]

nīght'rīd"ẽr, *n.* in the southern United States, any of a band of masked mounted men who perform lawless acts of violence and terror at night, generally to intimidate, punish, etc.

nīght rōbe, a nightgown.

nīghts, *adv.* at or by night. [Colloq. or Dial.]

nīght sçhọọl, a school held in the evening for people, usually adults, unable to attend by day.

nīght'shāde, *n.* [AS. *nihtscada,* lit., the shade or shadow of night; with reference to narcotic qualities.] any of various flowering plants of the genus *Solanum,* related to the potato and tomato; especially, *Solanum nigrum,* the black nightshade.

deadly nightshade; belladonna, a poisonous variety of nightshade.

stinking nightshade; henbane, a poisonous variety of nightshade.

three-leaved nightshade; see *trillium.*

woody nightshade; bittersweet.

nīght'shīrt, *n.* a loose, shirtlike garment reaching to the knees, worn in bed by men or boys.

nīght sīght (sīt), nyctalopia.

nīght soil, [from being collected at night.] excrement removed from a cesspool or privy and used as fertilizer.

nīght spell, a charm against accidents at night.

nīght'spot, *n.* a night club. [Colloq.]

nīght stand, a small table at the bedside.

nīght stick, a long, heavy club carried by a policeman, especially at night.

nīght swäl'lōw, the nightjar.

nīght sweats (swets), copious sweating in bed at night, as in tuberculosis.

nīght'tīde, *n.* nighttime. [Poetic.]

nīght'tīme, *n.* the space of time between the sunset of one day and the sunrise of the next.

nīght'walk"ẽr (-wak"), *n.* 1. one who walks in his sleep; a somnambulist.

2. one who roves about in the night, as a thief, prostitute, etc. [Rare.]

3. a large earthworm that comes out of the earth at night; a night crawler.

nīght'walk"ing, *n.* somnambulism.

nīght wän'dẽr·ẽr, one who roves at night.

nīght'-wän'dẽr·ing, *a.* wandering at night.

nīght war'blẽr, the sedge warbler of Europe, *Acrocephalus phragmitis.*

nīght'wȧrd, *a.* approaching toward night.

nīght wätch, 1. a watching or guarding during the night.

2. the person or persons doing such guarding.

3. the time of their guarding.

4. [*usually in pl.*] any of the periods into which the night was formerly divided for such guarding.

nīght wätch'ẽr, one who watches in the night.

nīght wätch'mȧn, one who watches the property of another at night to guard against theft, fire, or other damage.

nīght'weär, *n.* night clothes.

nīght witch, a night hag.

nīght'y, *n.*; *pl.* **nīght'ies,** a nightgown or nightshirt: a diminutive.

nī·gres'cence, *n.* [from *nigrescent.*]

1. the process of becoming black.

2. blackness, especially of the skin.

nī·gres'cent, *a.* [L. *nigrescens* (*-entis*), ppr. of *nigrescere,* to grow black.] growing black; changing to a black color.

nig'ri·çȧnt, *a.* same as *nigrescent.*

nig"ri·fi·çā'tion, *n.* the act or process of making black. [Rare.]

nig'ri·fȳ, *v.t.*; nigrified, *pt., pp.*; nigrifying, *ppr.* [L. *nigrificare,* from *niger,* black, and *facere,* to make.] to make black.

nī'grin, nī'grine, *n.* [L. *niger, nigris,* black, and *-in, -ine.*] in mineralogy, a ferriferous form of rutile.

Nī·gri'tiȧn, *a.* of or pertaining to Nigritia (former name for the Sudan), a district of Middle Africa inhabited by Negroes.

Nī·gri'tiȧn, *n.* a native or inhabitant of Nigritia (Sudan).

Nī·grit'iç, *a.* pertaining to or characteristic of Negroes or Negritos; Negritic.

nig'ri·tūde, *n.* [L. *nigritudo,* blackness, from *niger,* black.] blackness; the condition of being black.

nig'rō·man·cien, *n.* a necromancer. [Obs.]

nig'rō·man·cy, *n.* necromancy. [Obs.]

nī'grō·sïne, *n.* [L. *niger, nigris,* black, and *-ose,* and *-ine.*] in chemistry, a blue-black dye belonging to the induline group.

nī'guȧ (-gwȧ), *n.* [Sp.] the chigoe.

nī'hil, *n.* [L.] 1. nothing.

2. a thing of slight value or importance; a mere nothing.

nihil album; white oxide of zinc, a light, white powder formed by burning zinc.

nihil debet; (a) literally, he owes nothing; (b) in law, a plea denying a debt.

nihil dicit; (a) literally, he says nothing; (b) in law, a case in which the defendant makes no answer.

nī'hil·ism, *n.* [from L. *nihil,* nothing; *ne,* not, and *hilum,* a little thing, a trifle.]

1. in philosophy, (a) the denial of the existence of any basis for knowledge or truth; (b) the general rejection of customary beliefs in morality, religion, etc.: also *ethical nihilism.*

2. the belief that there is no meaning or purpose in existence.

3. in politics, (a) the doctrine that all social, political, and economic institutions must be completely destroyed in order to make way for new institutions; specifically, (b) [N–] a movement in Russia (c. 1860–1917) which advocated such revolutionary reform and attempted to carry it out through the use of some terrorism and assassination.

4. loosely, any violent revolutionary movement involving some use of terrorism.

nī'hil·ist, *n.* an advocate of any form of philosophical or political nihilism.

nī·hil·is'tiç, *a.* of, relating to, or characteristic of nihilism or nihilists.

nī·hil'i·ty, *n.* nothingness.

-nik, [from Russ. (chiefly via Yid.) *-nik,* equivalent to *-er.*] a suffix used to form slang or colloquial words, meaning *one who is or has to do with.*

Nī'kē, *n.* [Gr. *Nikē,* from *nikē,* victory.]

1. in Greek mythology, the goddess of victory, generally described and represented as a winged maiden carrying a palm branch: identified by the Romans with Victoria.

2. the goddess Athena as giver of victory.

Nī'kē Ap'tē·ros, [Gr., *apteros*, wingless.] Athena: a name used when referring or praying to her as the giver of victories; also, the temple of Nike Apteros at Athens.

Nī'kē of Sam'ō·thrāce, a statue of the Hellenes now in the Louvre. It represents a winged Victory standing on the prow of a ship. It was erected in 306 B.C. by Demetrius Poliorcetes to commemorate a naval victory over the Egyptians.

Nĭk'kō, *n.* Chinese blue.

Nĭk'kō fïr, a Japanese evergreen tree, *Abies homolepsis*, cultivated for ornamental purposes.

nik'les·īte, *n.* [from *Nicklesdorf*, in the Moravian valley.] a pyroxenite consisting of diallage, diopside, and enstatite.

nil, *n.* [L., a contr. of *nihil*, nothing.] nothing.

Nīle bïrd, 1. the wryneck.
2. the crocodile bird.

Nīle blūe, greenish blue.

Nīle goose, the Egyptian goose.

Nīle'-green', *a.* of Nile green.

Nīle green, yellow green.

nil'gaī, nil'ghaī (-gī), *n.*; *pl.* **nil'gaīs, nil'ghaīs** or **nil'gaī, nil'ghaī,** [Hind. and Per. *nīlgāw*, lit., blue cow, from Per. *nīl*, blue, and *gāw*, cow.] any of a group of large, slate-blue antelopes of India: also *nylghai, nylghau.*

nil'gau, nil'ghau (-ga), *n.*; *pl.* **nil'gaus, nil'ghaus** or **nil'gau, nil'ghau,** a nilgai.

nill, *v.t.* and *v.i.* [AS. *nillan*; *ne*, not, and *willan*, to will.] not to will (something); to refuse; to reject. [Archaic.]
And will you, *nill* you, I will marry you.
—Shak.

nil nī'sī bō'num, [L.] nothing but good.

Nī·lom'e·tēr, *n.* [Gr. *Neilometrion*; *Neilos*, the Nile, and *metron*, a measure.] an instrument for measuring the rise of water in the Nile during flood time: it consists of a graduated pillar with a water chamber.

Nī'lō·scōpe, *n.* same as *nilometer.*

Nī·lot'iç, *a.* 1. of the Nile or the Nile Valley.
2. designating or of the Sudanese Negroes who live in the valley of the White Nile.

nil'pō·tent, *a.* [L. *nil*, nothing, and *potens* (*-entis*), powerful.] in mathematics, vanishing on being raised to a certain power.

nim, *v.t.*; nam *or* nimmed, *pt.*; nomen *or* nome, *pp.*; nimming, *ppr.* [AS. *niman.*]
1. to take. [Obs.]
2. to steal; to filch. [Obs.]

nïm, *n.* the margosa: also spelled *neem.*

nimbed (nimbd), *a.* having or bearing a nimbus, as a head.

nim·bif'ēr·ous, *a.* [L. *nimbifer*; *nimbus*, a rainstorm, rain cloud, and *ferre*, to bear.] bringing rain clouds or stormy weather. [Rare.]

nim'ble, *a.*; *comp.* nimbler; *superl.* nimblest, [ME. *nimmel*, *nymel*; AS. *numol*, capable, quick at taking, from *niman*, to take.]
1. mentally quick; quick-witted; alert; as, a *nimble* mind.
2. showing mental quickness; as, a *nimble* reply.
3. moving or acting quickly and lightly.
Through the mid seas the *nimble* pinnace sails. —Pope.

nim'ble·ness, *n.* the quality of being nimble; lightness and agility in motion; quickness; celerity; speed; swiftness.
Ovid ranged over Parnassus with great *nimbleness* and agility. —Addison.

nim'ble Will, an American grass, *Muehlenbergia diffusa.*

nim'bly, *adv.* in a nimble manner; with agility; with light, quick motion.

nim'bōse, *a.* [L. *nimbosus*, from *nimbus*, a rainstorm, a cloud.] cloudy; threatening; stormy.

nim″bō-strā'tus, *n.* [from L. *nimbus*, a black-rain cloud, and *stratus*.] a low, gray cloud layer that covers the sky and brings rain or snow.

nim'bus, *n.*; *pl.* **nim'bus·es, nim'bī,** [L., a rain cloud, a storm.]
1. a bright cloud supposedly surrounding gods or goddesses when they appeared on earth.
2. an aura of splendor about any person or thing.
3. a halo or bright disk surrounding the heads of divinities, saints, and sovereigns on pictures, medals, etc.
4. a nimbo-stratus.

ni·mī'e·ty, *n.* [LL. *nimietas*, from L. *nimis*, too much.] the state of being too much; excess; redundancy.

nim'i·ny-pim'i·ny, *a.* [in imitation of mincing speech.] affectedly fine or delicate; mincing.

nim'i·ous, *a.* extravagant; excessive: used chiefly in Scottish law.

n'im·porte' (naṅ-pọrt'), [Fr.] it doesn't matter.

Nim'rod, *n.* 1. in the Bible, the son of Cush, referred to as a mighty hunter: Gen. x. 8–9.
2. a hunter; a keen sportsman.

nin'çŏm·poop, *n.* [perh. from *Nick* and D. *poep*, a fool.] a stupid, silly person; a fool; simpleton.

nīne, *a.* [ME. *nine*, *neghen*, *nighen*; AS. *nigon*, nine.] totaling one more than eight.
nine days' wonder; anything that arouses great excitement and interest for a short time.

nīne, *n.* 1. the cardinal number between eight and ten; 9; IX.
2. any group of nine persons or things; especially, a team of nine baseball players.
3. a playing card marked with the number 9 and nine spots of its suit.
the Nine; the Muses, nine in number.

nīne'bärk, *n.* an American shrub of the rose family, *Neillia*, or *Spiræa*, *opulifolia*, bearing white flowers and having bark that is composed of many thin layers.

nīne'-eyes (-īz), *n.* the lamprey. [Brit. Dial.]

nīne'fōld, *a.* 1. having nine parts.
2. having nine times as much or as many.

nīne'fōld, *adv.* nine times as much or as many.

nīne'hōles, *n.pl.* a game in which nine holes are made in the ground, into which a ball is to be bowled.

nīne'-kill″ēr, *n.* a shrike, the northern butcherbird: so called because it is supposed to kill nine birds in a day.

nīne'pence, *n.* 1. the sum of nine British pennies, equal to approximately eighteen American cents.
2. a British coin of this value.

nīne'pin, *n.* any of the pins used in the game of ninepins.

nīne'pins, *n.pl.* [*construed as sing.*] a game like tenpins, in which only nine pins are set up at one end of an alley and bowled at.

nīne'-point çïr'çle, in geometry, a circle passing through the three points in the sides of a given triangle at which the perpendiculars from each vertex meet the subtending sides or the sides produced, also through the middle points of the sides of the triangle, and through the middle points of these parts of the perpendiculars between each vertex and the common point of meeting.

nīne'sçōre, *a.* nine times twenty; one hundred and eighty.

nīne'sçōre, *n.* the product of nine times twenty; 180 units or objects.

nīne'teen', *n.* [AS. *nigontyne*; *nigon*, nine, and *tyn*, ten.]
1. the cardinal number between eighteen and twenty.
2. a symbol for nineteen, as 19 or XIX.

nīne'teen', *a.* nine more than ten.

nīne'teenth', *n.* [AS. *nigonteōtha.*]
1. any of the nineteen equal parts of something; $^1/_{19}$.
2. the one following the eighteenth.
3. in music, an interval of two octaves and a fifth.

nīne'teenth', *a.* 1. being one of nineteen equal divisions of anything.
2. next in order after the eighteenth.

nīne'teenth' hōle', any place, such as the locker room or bar of a clubhouse, where golfers meet for drinks and conviviality after playing a round of golf. [Colloq.]

nīne'ti·eth, *a.* 1. next in order after the eighty-ninth; 90th.
2. designating any of the ninety equal parts into which something is divided.

nīne'ti·eth, *n.* 1. the one following the eighty-ninth.
2. any of the ninety equal parts of something; $^1/_{90}$.

nīne'ty, *n.*; *pl.* **nīne'ties,** [AS. (*hund-*) *nigontig*, ninety; *nigon*, nine, and *-tig*, ten.]
1. the cardinal number between eighty-nine and ninety-one.
2. a symbol for ninety, as 90 or XC (or LXXXX).
the nineties; the years from ninety through ninety-nine (of a century or a person's age).

nīne'ty, *a.* nine times ten.

nin'ny, *n.*; *pl.* **nin'nies,** [prob. by syllabic merging and contr. of *an innocent.*] a fool; a simpleton.

nin'ny·ham″mēr, *n.* a simpleton.

nīnth, *a.* [AS. *nigonthe*, ninth.]
1. preceded by eight others in a series; 9th.
2. designating any of the nine equal parts of something.

nīnth, *n.* 1. the one following the eighth.
2. any of the nine equal parts of something; $^1/_9$.
3. in music, (a) an interval in pitch of an octave and a second; (b) the tone at the upper limit of such an interval; (c) the combination of this tone and of the tone at the lower limit of such an interval, written or sounded together.
ninth chord; in music, a chord consisting of the third, fifth, seventh, and ninth above the root.

nīnth'ly, *adv.* in the ninth place.

nin'ut, *n.* the magpie. [Brit. Dial.]

nī'ō·bāte, *n.* [*niob*ium and *-ate.*] a salt of niobic acid.

Nī'ō·bē, *n.* in Greek mythology, the daughter of Tantalus and wife of Amphion, king of Thebes: her children were slain by Artemis and Apollo when she boastfully compared herself to their mother, Leto: the weeping Niobe was changed by Zeus into a stone from which tears continued to flow.

NIOBE—ANTIQUE, FLORENCE

Nī·ō·bē'ăn, *a.* of or like Niobe.

nī·ob'iç, *a.* [*niob*ium and *-ic.*] of or relating to niobium.

nī'ō·bīte, *n.* same as *columbite.*

ni·ō'bi·um, *n.* [from L. *Niobe*, daughter of Tantalus.] a rare metallic chemical element with properties like those of tantalum, discovered by Hatchett in 1801, but more fully investigated by Rose, who named it: symbol, Nb; atomic weight, 92.91; atomic number, 41: formerly also called *columbium.*

ni·ō'pō, *n.* [S. Am.] a kind of snuff made from the roasted seeds of a leguminous tree, *Piptadenia peregrina*, in Venezuela.

ni·ō'pō tree, the tree bearing the seeds from which niopo is produced.

Nip, *n.* and *a.* Nipponese; Japanese: usually contemptuous. [Slang.]

nip, *v.t.*; nipped (nipt), *pt.*, *pp.*; nipping, *ppr.* [compare D. *knippen*, to nip, to clip, to snap, *nijpen*, to pinch, to nip, Ice. *kneppa*, to cut short, G. *kneipen*, *kneifen*, to pinch, to nip.]
1. to catch or squeeze between two surfaces, edges, or points; to pinch.
May this hard earth cleave to the Nadir hell,
Down, down, and close again, and *nip* me flat,
If I be such a traitress. —Tennyson.
2. to cut, bite, or pinch off (shoots, etc.); to pinch off with the ends of the fingers or a tool; to sever.
3. to check the growth or vigor of.
4. to benumb; to chill; to have a painful or injurious effect on; as, the frost *nipped* his ears.
5. to bite; to vex.
And sharp remorse his heart did prick and *nip.* —Spenser.
6. to satirize keenly; to taunt sarcastically. [Obs.]
7. (a) to steal; (b) to snatch. [Slang.]
8. in nautical usage, to tie or secure (a cable, etc.) with seizing.
to nip in the bud; to kill or destroy in the first stage of growth; to cut off before development.

nip, *n.* 1. the act of nipping; a pinch; a bite.
2. a piece nipped off; a small bit.
3. a stinging quality, as in cold or frosty air.
4. stinging cold; frost.
5. a stinging remark.
6. a tang in cheese.
7. a thief. [Obs.]
8. in nautical usage, (a) a short turn in a rope; (b) the part of a rope at the place where it is bound or caught by something.
nip and tuck; so close, even, or critical as to leave the outcome in doubt; neck and neck.

nip, *n.* [D. and L.G. *nippen*; Dan. *nippe*; G. *nipfen*, to sip.] a sip or small draught of liquor; as, a *nip* of brandy.

nip, *v.i.* and *v.t.*; nipped (nipt), *pt.*, *pp.*; nipping, *ppr.* to drink (liquor) in nips.

Nī'pă, *n.* [from native name in the Molucca Islands.] a genus of *Palmaceæ* with only one species, *Nipa fruticans*, growing in southern Asia and the Philippine Islands, its fiber being used for matting, and its leaves for thatching; also, the liquor made from its sap.

nī′pȧ pälm (päm), the sole species of the genus *Nipa*, an Asiatic palm, *Nipa fruticans*.

nip′pẽr, *n.* 1. anything that nips, or pinches.
2. [*pl.*] any of various tools for grasping or severing wire, etc., as pliers, pincers, or forceps.
3. any of certain organs of animals, used in biting, grasping, holding, etc.; specifically, (a) an incisor tooth of a horse; (b) the pincerlike claw of a crab.
4. a small boy. [Brit. Colloq.]
5. [*pl.*] (a) handcuffs; (b) leg irons. [Slang.]
6. a thief; a pickpocket. [Obs.]
7. a crab, *Polybius henslowi*: also called *nipper crab*.
8. a blue perch or cunner, *Ctenolabrus adspersus*.

nip′pẽr·kin, *n.* a small cup or measure for liquor. [Obs.]

nip′ping, *a.* 1. that nips, or pinches.
2. sharp; biting; nippy.
3. sarcastic.

nip′ping·ly, *adv.* in a nipping manner; as, she spoke *nippingly*.

nip′pi·tāte, *a.* good and strong: said of alcoholic liquor. [Obs.]

nip·pi·tā′tum, nip·pi·tā′tō, *n.* good and strong alcoholic liquor. [Obs.]

nip′ple, *n.* [earlier *neble*; prob. dim. of *neb*.]
1. the small protuberance on a breast or udder, through which the milk passes in suckling the young; teat; pap: it is rudimentary in the male.
2. a rubber cap with a teatlike part, for a baby's feeding bottle.
3. any projection, part, or thing resembling a nipple in shape or function; specifically, (a) a threaded piece of pipe at the end of a water line, to which is fastened a nozzle, faucet, etc.; (b) a short piece of pipe with both ends threaded; (c) a small projection on glass or metal.
nipple cactus; any cactus of the genus *Mamillaria*, bearing nipple-shaped tubercles upon its joints.

nip′ple·wört, *n.* an herb, *Lapsana communis*, formerly used as an external application to the breasts of women.

Nip·pŏn·ēse′, *a.* and *n.*; *pl.* **Nip·pŏn·ēse′,** [from *Nippon*, Japanese name for Japan.] Japanese.

nip′py, *a.*; *comp.* nippier; *superl.* nippiest.
1. nipping or tending to nip, or pinch; sharp; biting.
2. quick; active; nimble. [Brit. Colloq.]

nip′tẽr, *n.* [Gr. *niptēr*, a basin, a washing vessel, from *niptein*, to wash.] in the Orthodox Eastern Church, the ceremony of washing the feet of the poor on the day before Good Friday.

nir·vä′nȧ, *n.* [Sans. *nirvāṇa*, from *nirwā*, to blow.]
1. in Hinduism, a blowing out, or extinction, of the flame of life; reunion with Brahma.
2. in Buddhism, the state of perfect blessedness achieved by the extinction of individual existence and by the absorption of the soul into the supreme spirit, or by the extinction of all desires and passions.

nis, [contr. of *ne is*.] is not. [Obs.]

Nī′san, *n.* [Heb. *nisān*.] the seventh month of the Jewish year: early Hebrew name, *Abib*.

nī′sei′ (-sā′), *n.*; *pl.* **nī′sei′, nī′seis′,** [Japan., lit., second generation.] [also N–] a native American citizen born of immigrant Japanese parents and educated in the United States: distinguished from *issei*, *kibei*.

nī′sī, *conj.* [L. *nisi*; *ni*, not, and *si*, if.] if not; unless: used in law after *decree*, *order*, etc. to indicate that it shall take permanent effect at a specified time unless cause is shown why it should not, or unless it is changed by further proceedings.
nisi prius; [a legal phrase used originally in a writ directing a sheriff to summon a jury to Westminster on a certain date "unless before" that date the trial had been held in his own county.] in law, a civil action tried in a court of record before a judge and jury.

Nis′sen hut, [after P. N. *Nissen* (1871–), engineer in the Canadian Army.] a prefabricated shelter of corrugated metal shaped like a cylinder cut vertically in two and resting on its flat surface: it was first used by the British Army in World War II.

nis′try, *n.* [E. Ind.] a silkworm, *Bombyx mori*, of Bengal.

nī′sus, *n.*; *pl.* **nī′sus,** [L. *nisus*, effort, a striving, from *niti*, to strive.] a striving; an effort; an impulse; endeavor.

nit, *n.* [AS. *hnitu*; compare Ice. *gnit*, *nitr*, Sw. *gnet*, a nit.]
1. the egg of a louse or other small insect.
2. the young insect.

nī′ten·cy, *n.* [L. *nitere*, to shine.] brightness; luster. [Rare.]

nī′ten·cy, *n.* [L. *niti*, to strive.] endeavor; effort. [Rare.]

nī′tẽr, nī′tre (-tẽr), *n.* [Fr. *nitre*; L. *nitrum*; Gr. *nitron*, native soda, natron; compare Ar. *nitrūn*, *natrūn*, natron.]
1. potassium nitrate, a crystalline salt found in nature and used as a preservative, in making gunpowder, etc.; saltpeter.
2. sodium nitrate, a crystalline salt, used as a fertilizer, etc.; Chile saltpeter: also called *cubic niter*.

nī′tẽr bush, a thorny shrub of the genus *Nitraria*, found in North Africa, western Asia, and Australia.

nit grȧss, an annual grass of the genus *Gastridium*, whose spikelets resemble nits.

nith′ing, *n.* [AS. *nithing*, a wicked man.] a coward, a dastard; a poltroon. [Archaic.]

nit′id, *a.* [L. *nitidus*, bright, shining.]
1. bright; lustrous; shining.
2. gay; spruce; fine: applied to persons. [Rare.]

nit′id·ous, *a.* [L. *nitidus*, bright, shining.] nitid; bright; shining; lustrous.

nī′ton, *n.* [Mod. L., from L. *nitere*, to shine; and *-on* as in *argon*.] radon, a radioactive chemical element: symbol, Nt: former name.

nitr-, see *nitro-*.

nī·trȧ·nil′iç, *a.* [*nitr-* and chlor*anil* and *-ic*.] of, pertaining to, or derived from an aniline compound acted upon by nitric acid.

nī·tran′i·line, *n.* [*nitr-* and *aniline*.] in chemistry, any of several substances formed by the action of nitric acid on aniline compounds.

nī′trāte, *n.* [*nitric* and *-ate*.]
1. a salt or ester of nitric acid.
2. potassium nitrate or sodium nitrate, used as a fertilizer.
nitrate of silver; silver nitrate; a colorless crystalline salt prepared by dissolving silver in dilute nitric acid, and largely used in surgery, photography, etc.

nī′trāte, *v.t.*; nitrated, *pt.*, *pp.*; nitrating, *ppr.* to treat or combine with nitric acid or a nitrate; to make into a nitrate.

nī′trā·ted, *a.* combined with nitric acid.

nī·trā′tion, *n.* the process of nitrating; especially, the introduction of the NO_2 group into an organic compound.

nī′tre (-tẽr), *n.* same as *niter*.

nī′tri·ăr·y, *n.* [from *niter*.] an artificial bed of animal matter for the formation of niter; a place where niter is refined.

nī′triç, *a.* [L. *nitrum*, native soda.]
1. of, containing, or related to nitrogen.
2. designating or of compounds in which nitrogen has a higher valence than in the corresponding nitrous compounds.
nitric acid; a colorless, fuming acid, HNO_3, that is highly corrosive: it is prepared by heating equal parts of nitrate of potash and sulfuric acid.
nitric anhydride; an oxide of nitrogen recognized as the anhydride of nitric acid.
nitric bacteria; see *nitrobacteria*.
nitric oxide; a colorless gas, NO: it is obtained from the action of nitric acid on copper, etc.

nī′trid, *n.* a nitride.

nī′trīde, *n.* [*nitrogen* and *-ide*.] in chemistry, a combination of nitrogen with phosphorus, boron, silicon, etc.

nī·trif′ẽr·ous, *a.* [*niter* and *-ferous*.] containing or producing niter.

nī″tri·fi·cā′tion, *n.* a nitrifying.

nī′tri·fī·ẽr, *n.* any nitrifying agent.

nī′tri·fȳ, *v.t.*; nitrified, *pt.*, *pp.*; nitrifying, *ppr.* [Fr. *nitrifier*.]
1. to combine with nitrogen or nitrogen compounds.
2. to impregnate (soil, etc.) with nitrates.
3. to cause the oxidation of (ammonium salts, etc.) to nitrites and nitrates, as by the action of soil bacteria, etc.

nī′tri·fȳ, *v.i.* to be changed into niter.

nī′tril, *n.* a nitrile.

nī′trile, *n.* [from *niter*.] an organic cyanide of an alkyl group, yielding the corresponding acid and ammonia on hydrolysis.

nī′trīte, *n.* [*nitr-* and *-ite*.] in chemistry, a salt or ester of nitrous acid: called also *azotite*.

nī′trō, *a.* 1. designating certain compounds containing nitrogen and produced by the action of nitric or nitrous acid.
2. designating the NO_2 radical or compounds in which one or more NO_2 radicals have replaced atoms of hydrogen.

nī′trō-, [from L. *nitrum*; Gr. *nitron*, native soda.] a combining form used to indicate: (a) *the presence of nitrogen compounds made by the action of nitric* or *nitrous acid and other substances*, as in *nitro*cellulose; (b) *the presence of the NO_2 radical*, as in *nitro*benzene; (c) *niter*, as in *nitro*bacteria. Also, before a vowel, *nitr-*.

nī″trō·baç·tē′ri·ȧ, *n.pl.* [Mod.L.; *nitro-* and *bacteria*.] soil bacteria or other microorganisms which oxidize ammonia compounds into nitrites (*nitrous bacteria*), or nitrites into nitrates (*nitric bacteria*).

nī·trō·ben′zēne, *n.* [*nitro-* and *benzene*.] in chemistry, a poisonous yellow liquid, C_6H_5-NO_2, prepared by treating benzene with nitric acid, used in making dyes, perfumes, etc.: also called *essence of mirbane*.

nī·trō·ben′zōl, nī·trō·ben′zōle, *n.* [*nitro-* and *benzol*.] same as *nitrobenzene*.

nī·trō·çal′cīte, *n.* [*nitro-* and *calcite*.] in chemistry, a grayish-white chalky deposit on walls and cavernous rocks, resulting from efflorescence.

nī·trō·çär′bōl, *n.* same as *nitromethane*.

nī·trō·cel′lū·lōse, nī·trō·cel′lū·lōse, *n.* [*nitro-* and *cellulose*.] in chemistry, an amorphous yellow substance obtained by nitrating cellulose materials such as wood pulp, cotton waste, cotton wool, lint, and tissue paper, used in making explosives, photographic films, lacquers, etc.; cellulose nitrate.

nī·trō·chlō′rō·form, *n.* same as *chloropicrin*.

nī′trō çom′pound, a compound in which one or more atoms of hydrogen are replaced by an equivalent quantity of nitryl.

nī″trō·çot′tŏn, *n.* [*nitro-* and *cotton*.] nitrocellulose or cellulose nitrate made from cotton fibers; guncotton.

nī′trō·form, *n.* [*nitro-* and *formyl*.] a colorless, explosive, crystalline or oleaginous acid compound, derived from methane and allied to chloroform.

nī·trō·ġel′ȧ·tin, *n.* [*nitro-* and *gelatin*.] an explosive solution of camphor and guncotton in nitroglycerin.

nī′trō·ġen, *n.* [*nitro-* and Gr. *-genēs*, producing.] an odorless, colorless, tasteless gaseous chemical element forming four fifths of the atmosphere. It combines with oxygen, though indirectly, forming well-known compounds: symbol, N; atomic weight, 14.008; atomic number, 7.
nitrogen cycle; the cycle of processes by which atmospheric nitrogen is converted by natural agencies into compounds used by plants and animals in the formation of proteins, and is eventually returned to its original state.
nitrogen dioxide; same as *nitrogen peroxide*.
nitrogen fixation; (a) the conversion of atmospheric nitrogen into nitrates by soil bacteria (nitrogen fixers) found in the nodules of certain legumes; (b) the conversion of free nitrogen into nitrogenous compounds of commercial value by any of various processes.
nitrogen fixers; in chemistry, soil organisms which have the ability to assimilate free nitrogen from the air.
nitrogen pentoxide; in chemistry, an oxide of nitrogen, N_2O_5, which exists as a white solid.
nitrogen peroxide; in chemistry, a poisonous reddish-brown gas with the formula NO_2; nitrogen dioxide: when cooled, the gas changes to a light yellow liquid, nitrogen tetroxide (N_2O_4), and becomes a crystalline solid without color at −15.3° F.
nitrogen tetroxide; same as *nitrogen peroxide*.
nitrogen trioxide; in chemistry, an oxide of nitrogen, N_2O_3, obtainable at low temperatures as an unstable liquid having a deep-blue color: it rapidly decomposes into nitrogen peroxide and nitric oxide.

nī′trō·ġen-fix′ing, *a.* capable of nitrogen fixation: said of nitrobacteria, etc.

nī·trō·ġen′iç, *a.* same as *nitrogenous*.

nī·troġ′e·nīze (*or* **nī′trō·jen·īz″**), *v.t.*; nitrogenized, *pt.*, *pp.*; nitrogenizing, *ppr.* to combine or impregnate with nitrogen or its compounds.

nī·troġ′e·nous, *a.* of or containing nitrogen or nitrogen compounds.

nī·trō·glyc′ẽr·in, nī·trō·glyc′ẽr·ine, *n.* a heavy, pale-yellow, explosive oil, $C_3H_5(NO_3)_3$, obtained by dissolving glycerin in a mixture of fuming nitric and sulfuric acids, and precipitating with a large volume of water: it is used in medicine and as an ingredient of dynamite.

nī·trō·glyc′ẽr·ōl, *n.* nitroglycerin.

nī·trō·hȳ·drō·chlō′riç, *a.* pertaining to or containing nitric acid and hydrochloric acid.

nitrohydrochloric acid; a mixture of one part of concentrated nitric acid with three parts of concentrated hydrochloric acid, used as a solvent for gold and platinum: also called *aqua regia.*

nī′trōl, *n.* in chemistry, one of numerous hydrocarbons, in the carbon atoms of which the nitro group and the nitroso or isonitroso group are united.

nī·trō′lē·um, *n.* nitroglycerin.

nī·trō·lev′ū·lōse, *n.* levulose nitrate: used like nitroglycerin.

nī·trol′iç, *a.* designating or of any of a series of acids formed by the action of nitrous acid on nitroparaffin and containing the CH_2NO_2 group.

nī·trō·mag′nē·sīte, *n.* [*nitro-* and *magnes*ium and *-ite.*] nitrate of magnesium, a saline efflorescence, in appearance suggesting nitrate of calcium.

nī′trō·māne, *n.* in chemistry, a ferment that produces nitrification.

nī·trō·man′nī·tol, *n.* mannitol nitrate: used like nitroglycerin.

nī·trom′e·tẽr, *n.* [*nitro-*, and Gr. *metron*, a measure.] an instrument for measuring the quantity of nitrogen, or certain of its compounds, in a substance: called also *azotometer.*

nī·trō·meth′āne, *n.* in chemistry, nitrocarbol, a heavy, oily liquid derived from methane.

nī·trō·mū·ri·at′iç, *a.* in chemistry, pertaining to or containing nitric and muriatic (or hydrochloric) acids.

nī·trō·par′af·fin, *n.* a nitrogen compound derived from any member of the methane, or paraffin, series of hydrocarbons and containing an NO_2 group in place of one of the hydrogen atoms normally present in the hydrocarbon.

nī·trō·phē′nōl, *n.* in chemistry, any nitro derivative of phenol.

nī·trō·prus′siç, *a.* in chemistry, of, pertaining to, or containing nitric and prussic acids.

nī·trō·prus′sīde, *n.* [*nitroprussi*c and *-ide.*] in chemistry, nitroferricyanide, a salt of nitroprussic acid.

nī·trō·quī′nōl, *n.* [*nitro-* and *quin*ine and *-ol.*] in chemistry, a compound obtained by treating methyl ether with nitric acid.

nī·trō·saç′chȧ·rōse, *n.* a resinous explosive used like nitroglycerin.

nī·trō·sal·i·cyl′iç, *a.* pertaining to or derived from salicylic acid and nitric acid.

nī·trōs·am′in, *n.* a nitrosamine.

nī″trōs·ȧ·mīne′, *n.* [from *nitroso-* and *amine.*] any of a series of organic compounds derived from amines and containing the divalent =N·NO radical.

nī′trōse, *a.* nitrous. [Obs.]

nī·trō′sō, *a.* designating or containing the NO radical, or group.

nī·trō′sō-, [from L. *nitrosus*, full of natron, from *nitrum*, native soda.] a combining form used to indicate the presence of *the NO radical.*

nī″trō·sul·fū′ric, *a.* pertaining to or consisting of sulfuric acid and an oxide of nitrogen.

nī′trō·syl, *n.* [*nitroso-* and *-yl.*] in chemistry, the radical NO, known also as the *nitroso group.*

nī·trō·syl′iç, *a.* in chemistry, of, pertaining to, or containing nitrosyl.

nī′trous, *a.* 1. pertaining to, resembling, or containing niter.

2. designating or of compounds in which nitrogen has a lower valence than in the corresponding nitric compounds.

nitrous acid; an acid, HNO_2, known only in solution.

nitrous bacteria; see *nitro bacteria.*

nitrous oxide; in chemistry, N_2O, a sweet-tasting, colorless gas, obtained by heating a combination of ammonium sulfate and sodium nitrate: the resulting gas is collected over hot water or mercury and is used as an anesthetic: also called *laughing gas.*

nī·trox′yl, *n.* [*nitro-* and *oxygen* and *-yl.*] in chemistry, nitric peroxide in combination; nitryl, NO_2.

nī′trum, *n.* [L., natron, native niter.] natron; niter.

nī′try, *a.* nitrous; pertaining to niter; producing niter. [Obs.]

nī′tryl, *n.* nitroxyl, NO_2.

nit′tȧ tree, [African *nitta*, and E. *tree.*] an old-world leguminous tree, *Parkia africana*, both the seeds and the pulp of its pods furnishing food for the natives in Africa.

nit′tẽr, *n.* an insect that deposits nits on horses; the botfly.

nit′ty, *a.* full of nits.

nit′ty-grit′ty, *n.* [rhyming extension of *gritty.*] the actual, basic facts, elements, issues, etc. [Slang.]

nit′wit, *n.* [*nit* (from G. Dial. for G. *nicht*, not) or *nit* (louse), and wit.] a stupid person.

nī′văl, *a.* of, or growing under, snow.

niv′ē·ous, *a.* [L. *niveus*, snowy, from *nix, nivis*, snow.] snowy; resembling snow; partaking of the qualities of snow.

Ni·vôse (nē-vōz′), *n.* [Fr., from L. *nivosus*, abounding in snow.] the fourth month in the French Revolutionary Calendar, beginning December 21 and ending January 19.

nix, *n.* [G., a water sprite.] in Teutonic mythology, a frolicsome water spirit: also written *nis.*

nix, *adv.* [G. *nichts.*] 1. nothing. [Slang.]

2. no. [Slang.]

3. not at all. [Slang.]

nix, *interj.* an exclamation meaning (a) stop! (b) I forbid, refuse, disagree, etc.

nix′ie, nix′y, *n.* a female nix.

Ni·zäm′, *n.* [Hind. and Ar., from Ar. *nazama*, to arrange, to govern.]

1. the title of the native ruler in Hyderabad, India.

2. [*n-*] *pl.* **ni·zäm,** a Turkish soldier.

Njǫrd (nyǫrd), *n.* Njorth.

Njǫrth (nyǫrth), *n.* [ON. *Njörthr.*] in Norse mythology, a Vanir, the father of Frey and Freya.

Njör′thr (nyǫr′thr), *n.* Njorth.

nō, *a.* [from ME. *non*, from AS. *nan*, no, none, by loss of *n*, as in *a* for *an.*] not any; not a; not one; as, let there be *no* strife; *no* man can number the leaves of the forest.

nō, *n.*; *pl.* **nōeṣ,** 1. an utterance of *no*; refusal or denial.

2. a negative vote or a person voting in the negative.

nō, *adv.* [AS. *na*; *ne*, not, and *a*, ever.]

1. not; as, whether or *no.* [Scot. or Rare.]

2. not in any degree; not at all; as, he is *no* worse.

3. nay; not so: the opposite of yes, used to deny, refuse, or disagree.

nō, *n.*; *pl.* **nō** [Japan. *nō.*] a type of Japanese play with a highly stylized plot, almost no stage accessories, elaborate costuming, and much singing and dancing: also *no-gaku, noh.*

Nō·ā′çhi·ăn, *a.* [Gr. *Nōe*, from Heb. *Nōach*, lit., rest.]

1. relating to Noah or to the time in which he lived; as, the *Noachian* flood.

2. ancient; antique.

Nō·ạch′iç, *a.* Noachian.

Nō′ȧh, *n.* [Gr. *Nōe.*] the tenth male in descent from Adam, in the line of Seth; he was the son of Lamech, and the grandson of Methuselah. He received the divine command to build an ark, in which he and his family escaped the Deluge.

Noah's ark; (a) a child's toy in shape like the conventional ark of Noah and containing wooden figures of animals and men; (b) in zoology, a marine bivalve, *Arca noæ*, somewhat resembling a boat; (c) in botany, the large yellow flower of *Cypripedium pubescens*; (d) in meteorology, converging cirrus or cirro-stratus clouds produced probably by magnetic disturbances in the upper atmosphere.

nob, *v.t.* in boxing, to beat or strike on the head. [Slang.]

nob, *n.* [later form of *knob.*]

1. a knob.

2. the head. [Slang.]

3. in cribbage, the jack of the same suit as the card turned over by the dealer: it counts one point for the player holding it in his hand or playing it from the crib.

nob, *n.* [perh. contr. from *nabob.*] a person of wealth and high social status. [Slang.]

nō′-ball, *n.* in cricket, a ball that has not been bowled in the manner specified by the rules.

nob′bi·ly, *adv.* after the manner of a nob; stylishly. [Slang.]

nob′ble, *v.t.*; nobbled, *pt., pp.*; nobbling, *ppr.* [freq. of *nab.*]

1. to disable or harm (a horse) to keep it from winning a race, as by drugging, etc. [Brit. Slang.]

2. (a) to win (a race or other contest) by bribery or other underhand methods; (b) to win over by bribery. [Brit. Slang.]

3. to cheat; steal; bribe. [Brit. Slang.]

nob′blẽr, *n.* 1. a blow on the head; a finishing stroke. [Slang.]

2. a dram of spirits. [Australian.]

nob′blẽr, *n.* a thimblerigger's confederate. [Slang.]

nob′by, *a.*; *comp.* nobbier; *superl.* nobbiest.

1. of or for nobs; stylish; fashionable. [Slang.]

2. excellent; first-rate. [Slang.]

Nō·bel′ist, Nō·bel′list, *n.* a person who has been awarded a Nobel prize.

nō·bel′i·um, *n.* [after *Nobel* Institute in Stockholm, where discovered.] a radioactive chemical element produced by the nuclear bombardment of curium: symbol, No; atomic weight, 255(?); atomic number, 102.

Nō·bel′ prī′zeṣ, annual international prizes given by the Nobel Foundation for distinction in physics, chemistry, economics, medicine or physiology, and literature, and for promoting peace.

nō·bil′iȧ·ry, *a.* of or pertaining to nobles or the nobility; as, a *nobiliary* roll.

Nō′bi·lī′ṣ rings, [named after Leopold *Nobili*, an Italian physicist.] in electrolysis, a series of copper rings alternately dark and light, which may be produced by placing a drop of acetate of copper in solution on a silver plate and touching the middle of the drop with a piece of zinc.

nō·bil′i·tāte, *v.t.* to make noble; to ennoble; to dignify; to exalt. [Obs.]

nō·bil·i·tā′tion, *n.* the act of nobilitating or of making noble. [Obs.]

nō·bil′i·ty, *n.*; *pl.* **nō·bil′i·tieṣ,** [L. *nobilitas*, from *nobilis*, noble.]

1. the quality or state of being noble.

Sweet mercy is *nobility*'s true badge. —Shak.

2. high station or rank; especially, that distinction of rank in civil society which one derives from noble ancestors or from a title conferred.

3. those persons collectively who are of noble rank; the collective body of noble or titled persons in a state; in Great Britain, the peerage (usually with *the*).

Syn.—distinction, dignity, rank, peerage, lordship, loftiness, generosity, aristocracy.

nō′ble, *a.*; *comp.* nobler; *superl.* noblest. [ME.; OFr.; L. *nobilis*, well-known, famous, high-born, noble, from *noscere, gnoscere*, to know.]

1. famous, illustrious, or renowned; having eminence, dignity, fame, etc.

2. having or showing high moral qualities or ideals; lofty.

3. having excellent qualities.

4. grand; stately; splendid; magnificent; as, a *noble* view.

5. of high rank, title, or birth; of ancient lineage; aristocratic.

6. not corroding or deteriorating rapidly; precious; pure: said of metals, expecially gold, silver, etc.: distinguished from *base.*

Syn.—exalted, stately, majestic, grand, high, illustrious, imperial, august, generous, magnanimous.

nō′ble, *n.* 1. a person having hereditary rank or title; a nobleman; in England, a peer; a duke, marquis, earl, viscount, or baron.

2. formerly, an English gold coin equal (until 1461) to 6s. 8d. sterling.

NOBLE OF EDWARD III
A. actual diameter of the coin

3. a European fish, the lyrie or pogge, *Agonus cataphractus.*

4. a leader of men hired to break a strike. [Slang.]

nō′ble fīr, a variety of very large fir that grows in the western United States.

nō′ble·măn, *n.*; *pl.* **nō′ble·men,** a noble; a peer; a titled person; one of the nobility.

nō′ble-mīnd″ed, *a.* possessing a noble mind; honorable; magnanimous.

nō′ble·ness, *n.* 1. the state of being noble; excellence; grandeur; dignity; magnanimity; elevation of mind or of condition.

His purposes are full of honesty, *nobleness*, and integrity. —Taylor.

2. distinction by birth; honor derived from a noble ancestry; nobility. [Obs.]

nō·blesse′, *n.* [Fr. *noblesse*, from LL. *nobilitia*, from L. *nobilis*, noble.]

1. the nobility; persons of noble rank collectively.

2. noble birth or condition.

noblesse oblige; literally, nobility obliges; people of high rank or birth should behave nobly toward others: said sometimes of the rich in regard to charity.

nō′ble·wom″ăn (-woom″), *n.*; *pl.* **nō′ble·wom″en** (-wim″), a woman of noble rank; a peeress.

nō·bley′, *n.* [ME. *nobley*, *nobleie*; OFr. *noblee*, nobleness.]

1. the entire number of people composing the nobility. [Obs.]

2. superior birth, mind, or character. [Obs.]

nō′bly, *adv.* 1. with noble courage or spirit; gallantly.

2. (a) idealistically; loftily; (b) excellently; splendidly.

3. of titled birth; of the peerage.

nō′bod·y, *pron.* no person; no one.

nō′bod·y, *n.*; *pl.* **nō′bod·ieṣ**, a person of no consequence, influence, authority, or importance; as, a mere *nobody*.

nŏ′çāke, *n.* [Am. Ind. *nookik*, meal.] a food formerly used by the North American Indians made of parched maize pounded into meal.

nō′cent, *a.* 1. hurtful; mischievous; injurious; causing harm or injury; as, *nocent* qualities. [Obs. or Rare.]

2. criminal; guilty. [Obs. or Rare.]

nō′cent, *n.* one guilty of crime. [Obs.]

nō′cent·ly, *adv.* hurtfully; injuriously. [Obs.]

nō″ci·as·sō″ci·ā′tion, *n.* in medicine and surgery, unconscious discharge of nervous energy, as in surgical shock or under the influence of receiving wounds or other injuries.

nō′cive, *a.* hurtful; injurious. [Obs.]

nock, *n.* [ME. *nocke*; prob. from ON.]

1. a notch for holding the string at either end of a bow.

2. a similar notch in the end of an arrow, for the insertion of the bowstring.

3. in sailmaking, the foremost upper corner of boom sails, and of staysails cut with a square tack.

nock, *v.t.*; nocked (nokt), *pt.*, *pp.*; nocking, *ppr.*

1. to set (an arrow) into the bowstring.

2. to notch; to make a notch in (a bow or arrow).

noç·tam·bū·lā′tion, *n.* [L. *nox*, *noctis*, night, and *ambulare*, to walk.] same as *noctambulism*.

noç·tam′bū·liṣm, *n.* walking in one's sleep; somnambulism.

noç·tam′bū·list, *n.* one who walks in his sleep; a somnambulist; a sleepwalker.

noç·tam′bū·lō, *n.* a noctambulist. [Obs.]

noç′ti-, [from L. *nox*, *noctis*, night.] a combining form meaning *night*: also, before a vowel, *noct-*.

noç·tid′i·ăl, *a.* [L. *nox*, *noctis*, night, and *dies*, day.] comprising a night and a day. [Rare.]

noç·tif′ẽr·ous, *a.* [L. *nox*, *noctis*, night, and *ferre*, to bring.] bringing night. [Obs.]

noç·ti·flō′rous, *a.* [L. *nox*, *noctis*, night, and *flos*, *floris*, a flower.] blooming at night.

noç·til′i·ō·nid, *n.* an insectivorous bat, of the genus *Noctilio*.

noç·ti·lū′çȧ, *n.* [L. *nox*, *noctis*, night, and *lucere*, to shine.]

1. anything which shines in the darkness; phosphorus.

2. [N—] a genus of very small phosphorescent marine organisms that occur in vast numbers in the sea, causing parts of it to appear luminous at night.

3. any of these marine organisms.

noç·ti·lū′cent, *a.* shining by night.

noç·ti·lū′cid, *n.* any member of the genus *Noctiluca* or family *Noctilucidæ*.

noç·ti·lū′cin, *n.* the semifluid substance in noctiluca which causes light.

noç·ti·lū′cine, *a.* pertaining to the *Noctiluca*; shining by night.

noç·ti·lū′çous, *a.* [L. *nox*, *noctis*, night, and *lucere*, to shine.] shining in the night.

noç·tiv′ȧ·gănt, *a.* [L. *nox*, *noctis*, night, and *vagari*, to wander.] wandering in the night, as animals for prey.

noç·tiv·ȧ·gā′tion, *n.* a roving in the night.

noç·tiv′ȧ·gous, *a.* same as *noctivagant*.

noç′tō·grȧph, *n.* [L. *nox*, *noctis*, night, and Gr. *graphein*, to write.]

1. a writing frame for the blind.

2. an instrument or register which records the presence of watchmen on their beats.

noç′tū·ăr·y, *n.* [from L. *nox*, *noctis*, night.] an account of what passes in the night: the converse of *diary*. [Rare.]

noc′tū·id, *n.* [L. *noctua*, a night owl, from *nox*, *noctis*, night.] a moth of the family *Noctuidæ*.

noç′tū·id, *a.* pertaining to the noctuids.

Noç·tū′i·dae, *n.pl.* a large family of moths, comprising over 1,500 American species, including most of those flying into lighted houses, as the cutworm moth, dagger moth, etc.: their larvae are very destructive.

noç′tūle, *n.* [Fr. *noctule*, from L. *nox*, *noctis*, night.] a variety of large brown bat of Europe and the British Isles.

noç′tūrn, *n.* [ME. and OFr. *nocturne*; ML. *nocturna*, from L. *nocturnus*, by night, from *nox*, *noctis*, night.]

1. in the Orthodox Eastern and Roman Catholic churches, any of three divisions of the office of Matins; early morning service between midnight and daybreak.

2. in music, a nocturne.

noç·tūr′năl, *a.* [L. *nocturnus*, from *nox*, *noctis*, night.]

1. pertaining to night; as, *nocturnal* darkness.

2. done or happening at night; as, a *nocturnal* expedition or assault; a *nocturnal* visit.

3. nightly; functioning at night; active during the night.

From gilded roofs depending lamps display
Nocturnal beams, that emulate the day. —Dryden.

4. having blossoms that open at night, as the moonflower.

noç·tūr′năl, *n.* an instrument for taking the altitude of the stars at sea.

noç·tūr′năl·ly, *adv.* by night; nightly.

noç′tūrne, *n.* [Fr., from L. *nocturnus*, of the night.]

1. in art, a painting of a night scene.

2. in music, a composition of a romantic or dreamy character thought appropriate to night.

noç′ū·ment, *n.* [L. *nocumentum*, from *nocere*, to hurt.] harm; injury. [Obs.]

noç′ū·ous, *a.* [L. *nocuus*, injurious.] hurtful; harmful; poisonous; noxious.

noç′ū·ous·ly, *adv.* hurtfully; injuriously.

nod, *v.i.*; nodded, *pt.*, *pp.*; nodding, *ppr.* [ME. *nodden*; compare O.H.G. *hnoton*, *nuoton*, to shake.]

1. to bend the head forward slightly and raise it again quickly, as a sign of agreement, greeting, command, acknowledgment, or invitation.

2. to say "yes" by doing this.

3. to allow the head to fall forward involuntarily because of drowsiness; to be very sleepy.

4. to be guilty of oversights through carelessness; to be inattentive.

Nor is it Homer *nods*, but we that dream. —Pope.

5. to sway back and forth or up and down; as, *nodding* plumes.

nod, *v.t.* 1. to incline or bend (the head) forward slightly and raise it again quickly.

2. to signify by a nod; as, to *nod* approbation.

3. to convey a meaning to by a nod or nods.

nod, *n.* 1. a nodding, as of the head, treetops, etc.

Like a drunken sailor on a mast,
Ready with every *nod* to tumble down. —Shak.

2. a sign of affirmation, assent, agreement, etc.; as, he gave my plans the *nod*.

3. [N—] the imaginary realm of sleep and dreams: usually *land of Nod*.

nōd′ăl, *a.* pertaining to, or having the nature of, a node or nodes.

nodal line, nodal point; the line or point in a vibrating cord or plate that remains at comparative rest.

nō′dā·ted, *a.* [L. *nodatus*, from *nodus*, a knot.] knotted.

nodated hyperbola; in geometry, a certain curve having two branches intersecting each other.

nō·dā′tion, *n.* the act of making a knot, or state of being knotted. [Rare.]

nod′den, *a.* bent; inclined. [Obs.]

nod′dẽr, *n.* one who or that which nods.

nod′ding, *a.* in botany, having the top bent downward.

nod′ding aç·quāint′ănce, 1. a slight, not intimate, acquaintance with a person or thing.

2. a person whom one knows slightly.

nod′dle, *v.t.* and *v.i.* [freq. of *nod*.] to nod often; to nod slightly.

nod′dle, *n.* [ME. *nodle*.]

1. the head; the pate: a humorous term. [Colloq.]

Come, master, I have a project in my *noddle*. —L'Estrange.

2. the back part of the head or neck. [Obs.]

nod′dy, *n.*; *pl.* **nod′dieṣ**, [prob. from *nod*, and equivalent to one that nods; a sleepyhead; compare *noodle*.]

1. a simpleton; a fool.

2. any of several varieties of tame tropical sea birds, as *Anoüs stolida*: so called from being easily taken and hence considered stupid.

3. a game of cards resembling cribbage. [Obs.]

4. a sort of two-wheeled cab.

5. a form of inverted pendulum, the bob of which is supported by a vertical spring.

nōde, *n.* [L. *nodus*, a knot.]

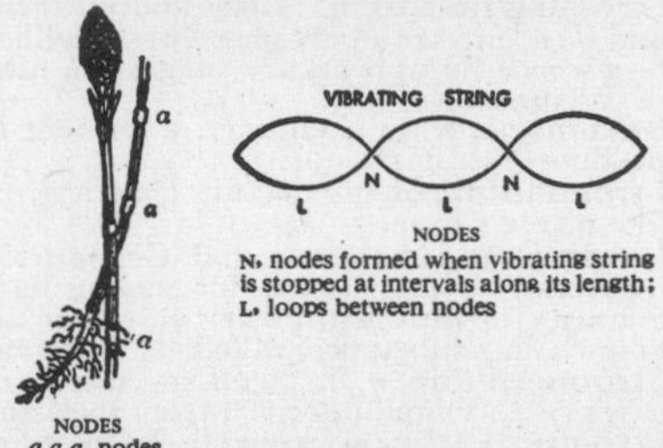

NODES
a a a, nodes

NODES
N, nodes formed when vibrating string is stopped at intervals along its length; L, loops between nodes

1. a knot, or what resembles one; a knob; a protuberance.

2. a dilemma or complication, as of a story or play.

3. a point of concentration; a central point.

4. in anatomy, a protuberance; a knotty, localized swelling.

5. in astronomy, (a) either point at which the orbit of a planet intersects the apparent path of the sun; (b) either point at which the orbit of a satellite intersects the plane of the orbit of its planet. The node at which a heavenly body passes to the north of the plane of the orbit with which its own orbit is compared is called the *ascending node*, or dragon's head; that where it passes to the south is called the *descending node*, or dragon's tail.

6. in dialing, a point or hole in the gnomon of a dial whose light shows the hour of the day, the parallels of the sun's declination and its place in the ecliptic, etc.

7. in botany, that part of a stem from which a leaf starts to grow; joint of a stem.

8. in geometry, the point where a continuous curve crosses or meets itself.

9. in physics, the point, line, or surface of a vibrating object, as a string, where there is comparatively no vibration.

line of nodes; a straight line that connects the two nodes of an orbit.

nodes of Ranvier; in anatomy, certain breaks or nodes at intervals along the course of peripheral medullated nerve fibers.

nod′iç·ăl, *a.* in astronomy, relating to the nodes: applied to a revolution from a node back to the same node again; as, the *nodical* revolutions of the moon.

nō′di·çorn, *a.* [L. *nodus*, a knot, and *cornu*, horn.] in zoology, having nodes or prominences at the joints of the antennae.

nō·dif′ẽr·ous, *a.* [L. *nodus*, a knot, and *ferre*, to bear.] in botany, having or causing nodes.

Nō·dō·sā′ri·ȧ, *n.* [L. *nodosus*, knotty, and *-aria*.] a genus of foraminifers, in which the buds or cells are thrown out from the primitive spherule in linear series so as to form a shell composed of numerous chambers arranged in a straight line. They occur as fossils in Chalk, Tertiary, and recent formations.

nō·dō·sär′i·ăn, *a.* and *n.* same as *nodosarine*.

nō·dō·sär′īne, *a.* of, relating to, or similar in form or structure to a foraminiferous shell of the genus *Nodosaria*.

nō·dō·sär′īne, *n.* one of the genus *Nodosaria*.

nō′dōse, *a.* [L. *nodosus*, from *nodus*, a knot.] knotted; knotty or knobby; having nodes: used specifically in botany and zoology.

nō·dos′i·ty, *n.* 1. the state or quality of being nodose or knotty; knottiness.

2. *pl.* **nō·dos′i·tieṣ**, a knotty swelling or protuberance; a knot.

 fāte, fär, fȧst, fąll, finăl, cãre, at; mēte, prẹy, hẽr, met; pīne, marïne, bïrd, pin; nōte, mōve, fọr, atŏm, not; mọọn, book;

It has all the *nodosities* of the oak without its strength; it has all the contortions of the sibyl without the inspiration.
—Burke.

nō'dous, *a.* nodose.
nod'ū·lăr, *a.* pertaining to, having, or in the form of a nodule or nodules.
nod'ū·lā·ted, *a.* same as *nodulose.*
nod·ū·lā'tion, *n.* the act or process of becoming nodular.
nod'ūle, *n.* [L. *nodulus*, dim. of *nodus*, a knot.]
1. a small knot or irregular, rounded lump.
2. in anatomy, a small node.
3. in botany, a small knot or joint on a stem or root.
4. in geology, a rounded, irregularly shaped mineral mass, as of ironstone.
nod'ūled, *a.* having little knots or lumps.
nod·ū·lif'ēr·ous, *a.* [L. *nodulus*, a little knot, and *ferre*, to bear.] bearing nodules.
nod'ū·lōse, nod'ū·lous, *a.* [L. *nodulus*, a little knot.] having nodules.
nō'dus, *n.* [ME.; L., a knot.] complication; difficulty; knotty situation, as in a play or story.
no·ël', no·ël' (nō-el' *or* nō'el), *n.* [from Fr. *noël*, replacing ME. *nowel*; OFr. *nowel, nouel*, from L. *natalis*, pertaining to birth, a birthday, from *natus*, born.]
1. an expression of joy used in Christmas carols.
2. a Christmas carol.
3. [N-] Christmas.
nō·ē·mȧ·tach'ō·gràph, *n.* [Gr. *noēma*, thought, *tachos*, swiftness, and *graphein*, to write.] an instrument for finding and registering the duration of certain mental operations of varying complexity.
nō·ē·mat'iç, nō·ē·mat'iç·ăl, *a.* [Gr. *noēma* (-*atos*), thought, understanding, from *noein*, to see, perceive.] of or pertaining to the understanding; mental.
nō·ē'sis, *n.* [Gr. *noēsis*, from *noein*, to perceive, from *nous*, the mind.]
1. comprehension by operation of the intellect alone.
2. cognition.
nō·et'iç, nō·et'iç·ăl, *a.* [Gr. *noētikos*, from *nous*, the mind.]
1. of, or existing or originating in, the intellect.
2. interested in intellectual activity.
nō·et'iç, *n.* an intellectual person.
nō'fault', *a.* 1. designating or of a form of insurance in which the victim as of an automobile accident or medical mishap collects damages without blame being established as to the cause of the accident.
2. designating a form of divorce granted without blame being sought or established.
nog, nogg, *n.* [from East Anglian dial.]
1. a kind of strong ale. [Brit.]
2. eggnog.
nog, *n.* [compare Dan. *knag, knage*, a wooden peg, the cog of a wheel; D. *knog*, a yardarm.]
1. a wooden pin; in ship carpentry, especially, a treenail driven through the heel of each shore that supports the ship on the slip.
2. a wooden pin or block set in a wall for nails, etc.
3. a brick-shaped piece of wood inserted in an internal wall; a timber brick.
4. a square piece of wood used to prop up the roof of a mine.
nog, *v.t.*; nogged, *pt., pp.*; nogging, *ppr.* 1. to fill in (a frame of wood) with brickwork.
2. in ship carpentry, to fasten or hold with wooden pegs or nogs.
nō'gä"ku (nōn'), *n.* no (Japanese drama).
nog'gin, *n.* [Ir. *noigin*; Gael. *noigean*, a noggin.]
1. a small mug or cup.
2. the contents of such a vessel.
3. a measure for ale or liquor equivalent to a gill.
4. the head. [Colloq.]
nog'ging, *n.* 1. in architecture, brickwork used to fill up the spaces of a wooden frame.
2. in ship carpentry, the act of securing the heels of the shores with treenails.
nogging pieces; horizontal pieces of timber fitting in between the quarters in brick nogging and nailed to them for strengthening the brickwork.
nō'-gō', *a.* [originally astronauts' jargon.] not functioning properly or not ready to go. [Slang.]
nōh, *n.* no (Japanese drama).
nō'how, *adv.* not at all; in no manner: generally regarded as substandard.
noil, *n.* [from SW. Yorkshire dial.; perh. from Walloon Fr.]
1. a short piece or knot of wool combed from the long staple.
2. shreds of wool, hair, or silk.
noint, *v.t.* to anoint. [Obs.]
noise, *n.* [Fr. *noise*, strife, quarrel, noise, perhaps from L. *noxia*, injury, hurt.]
1. (a) loud shouting; clamor; din; (b) any loud, discordant, or disagreeable sound or sounds.
2. (a) sound; as, the *noise* of the rain; (b) an unexpected or unusual sound; as, do you hear that *noise?*
3. frequent talk; much public conversation or discussion; stir. [Obs.]
Socrates lived in Athens during the great plague which has made so much *noise* in all ages, and never caught the least infection.
—Spectator.
4. bad report; rumor; scandal. [Obs.]
5. in radio, acoustics, etc., any sound that interferes with the sound impulse being communicated.
6. a set or company of musicians; a band. [Obs.]
Syn.—cry, outcry, clamor, din, clatter, tumult, uproar.
noise, *v.t.*; noised, *pt., pp.*; noising, *ppr.* 1. to spread about (a rumor or report).
It is *noised* he hath a mass of treasure.
—Shak.
2. to disturb with noise. [Obs.]
noise, *v.i.* 1. to talk much or loudly.
2. to make noise or a noise.
noise'fụl, *a.* loud; clamorous; making much noise or talk.
noise'less, *a.* 1. making or characterized by no noise; silent; as, the *noiseless* foot of time.
2. with much less noise than is expected; as, a *noiseless* streetcar, typewriter, etc.
noise'less·ly, *adv.* without noise; silently.
noise'less·ness, *n.* a state of silence.
noise'māk"ēr, *n.* a person or thing that makes noise; specifically, a horn, cowbell, etc. used for making noise in celebration, as on New Year's Eve.
noi·sette' (nwo-zet'), *n.* a variety of rose.
nois'i·ly, *adv.* in a noisy manner; with noise.
nois'i·ness, *n.* the quality or state of being noisy; loudness of sound; clamorousness.
noi'sŏme, *a.* [*noy* and *-some.*]
1. noxious to health; hurtful; harmful; as, *noisome* winds; *noisome* effluvia.
2. offensive to the smell or other senses; disgusting; fetid.
Foul breath is *noisome.* —Shak.
Syn.—noxious.
noi'sŏme·ly, *adv.* in a noisome manner.
noi'sŏme·ness, *n.* the state or quality of being noisome.
nois'y, *a.*; *comp.* noisier; *superl.* noisiest. 1. making a loud sound; accompanied by noise; as, the *noisy* crowd.
2. making more sound than is expected or customary.
3. full of noise; clamorous; turbulent.
O leave the *noisy* town. —Dryden.
Syn.—boisterous, clamorous, turbulent, uproarious, loud, blatant.
nō'-knock', *a.* designating or based on laws or provisions which permit police with search warrants to enter a private dwelling by force without announcing or identifying themselves.
Nō·lā'nȧ, *n.* [from LL. *nola*, a little bell.] a small genus of herbs, mostly aquatic, of the family *Nolanaceæ*, found in Chile and Peru.
Nol·ȧ·nā'cē·ae, *n.pl.* a group of South American perigynous exogens, allied to the *Solanaceæ*, with which they are now usually combined, consisting of herbaceous or shrubby plants, with alternate exstipulate leaves.
nō'lens vō'lens, [L.] unwilling (or) willing; whether or not one wishes to; willy-nilly.
nō'lī mē tan'ġe·rē, [L., touch me not.]
1. in botany, any of several plants whose ripe seed cases burst when touched; as, (a) any plant of the genus *Impatiens*, as the touch-me-not; (b) the squirting cucumber.
2. a warning against meddling.
3. a painting showing Jesus appearing to Mary Magdalene after his resurrection: from the Latin form of his caution to her: John xx. 17.
4. any of several skin diseases characterized by ulcers.
nō·li'tion (-lish'un), *n.* [L. *nolle*, be unwilling.] unwillingness: opposed to *volition.*
noll, *n.* the head. [Obs.]
nol·lē'i·ty, *n.* unwillingness. [Rare.]
nol'lē pros'e·quī, [L., to be unwilling to prosecute.] in law, (a) formal notice by the prosecutor that prosecution in a criminal case will be partly or entirely ended; (b) similar formal notice by the plaintiff in a civil suit
nō'lō çon·ten'de·rē, [L., to be unwilling to prosecute.] in law, a plea by the defendant in a criminal case declaring that he will not make a defense, but not admitting guilt: also *nolo.*
nol-pros', *v.t.*; nol-prossed, *pt., pp.*; nol-prossing, *ppr.* [from abbreviation of *nolle prosequi.*] to abandon (all or part of a suit) by entering a *nolle prosequi* on the court records.
nōlt, *n.* cattle. [Brit. Dial.]
nom (*or Fr.* nōn), *n.* [Fr., from L. *nomen*, name.] name.
nom de guerre; literally, war name; a fictitious name, or one assumed for a time; a pseudonym.
nom de plume; literally, pen name; a name assumed by an author or writer.
nō'mȧ, *n.*; *pl.* **nō'mae,** [Gr. *nomē*, a feeding, a corroding sore.] in medicine, a severe ulcerous condition of the mouth, occurring especially in young children, as after debilitating disease, and usually resulting in gangrene.
nō'mad, *n.* [Gr. *nomas* (-*ados*), living on pasturage, from *nemein*, to distribute, to divide, to feed, to pasture.]
1. a member of a tribe, nation, or race having no permanent home, but moving about constantly in search of food, pasture, etc.
2. any person who changes his residence frequently; wanderer.
nō'mad, *a.* nomadic; wandering.
nō'māde, *n.* same as *nomad.*
nō·mā'di·ăn, *n.* a nomad. [Rare.]
nō·mad'iç, *a.* [Gr. *nomadikos*, nomadic.] pertaining to, like, or characteristic of nomads or their way of life; as, the *nomadic* tribes of Asia.
nō·mad'iç·ăl·ly, *adv.* in a nomadic manner.
nō'mad·ism, *n.* the state of being a nomad.
nō'mad·ize, *v.i.*; nomadized, *pt., pp.*; nomadizing, *ppr.* to lead the life of a nomad.
nō'man·cy, *n.* [Fr. *nomancie*, abbrev. from *onomancie*; Gr. *onoma*, name, and *manteia*, divination.] the practice of allegedly divining the destiny of persons by the letters which form their names.
nō man's land, 1. a tract or district to which no one can lay a recognized or established claim; a region which is the subject of dispute between two parties; debatable land.
2. in nautical usage, a part of a ship of which no one has the specified care.
3. the area on a battlefield separating the combatants.
nom'ärch, *n.* [Gr. *nomarchēs*; *nomos*, a province, and *archein*, to rule.] the governor or ruler of a nome or nomarchy.
nom'ärch·y, *n.*; *pl.* **nom'ärch·ies,** a province governed by a nomarch, as in modern Greece; the jurisdiction of a nomarch.
nŏm'bles (-blz), *n.pl.* numbles. [Archaic.]
nom'bril, *n.* [Fr., the navel, for *l'ombril, ombril*, from L. *umbilicus*, the navel.] in heraldry, the point halfway between the fesse point, or center, of an escutcheon and the middle base point.
nōme, *n.* [Gr. *nomos*, a district, province, from *nemein*, to distribute, to graze.]
1. a province of ancient Egypt.
2. a province of modern Greece; a nomarchy.
nōme, *n.* [Gr. *nomos*, a usage, custom, musical strain, ode.] in ancient Greek music, a form of musical composition.
nō'men, *n.*; *pl.* **nom'i·nȧ,** [L.] a name; especially, the middle name of an ancient Roman, indicating his gens, as Caius *Julius* Caesar, of the Julian gens, or clan.
nō'men·clā·tŏr, *n.* [L., from *nomen*, name, and *calare*, to call.]
1. a person who calls things or persons by their names; as, in ancient Rome, (a) a person who informed candidates for office of the name of the persons they met whose votes it would be desirable to solicit; (b) a person who announced the names of guests or assigned them places at dinner.
2. an announcer of names, as at a reception.
3. a person who invents names for, or gives names to things, as in scientific classification.
4. a list, arranged alphabetically or otherwise, of the terms and technical words employed in any art or science. [Obs.]
nō·men·clā'tūr·ăl, *a.* pertaining or according to nomenclature.
nō'men·clā·tūre, *n.* [L. *nomen*, name, and *calare*, to call.]
1. a glossary or dictionary. [Obs.]
2. the system of names used in a branch of

learning or activity, for the parts of a mechanism or device, or by some person or group.

3. a name. [Obs.]

Nō′mex, *n.* a lightweight, fire-resistant nylon fiber made into garments, as for firemen and astronauts, aircraft upholstery, etc.: a trademark.

nō′mi·ăl, *n.* [from L. *nomen*, a name.] in algebra, a single term.

nom′iç, *a.* [Gr. *nomikos*, pertaining to custom or law, from *nomos*, usage, custom, law.] relating to the customary or conventional English spelling: opposed to *phonetic*.

nom′i·năl, *a.* [L. *nominalis*, pertaining to a name, from *nomen* (-*inis*), name.]

1. of, consisting of, having the nature of, or giving a name or names.

2. of or having to do with a noun or nouns.

3. in name only, not in fact; as, the *nominal* leader.

4. very small compared to expectations; slight; hardly worth mention; as, a *nominal* fee.

nom′i·năl, *n.* in linguistics, a nounlike word: nouns, adjectives, and pronouns are called *nominals*: distinguished from *verbal*.

nom′i·năl·iṣm, *n.* a doctrine of the late Middle Ages that all universal or abstract terms are mere necessities of thought or conveniences of language and therefore exist as names only and have no realities corresponding to them: opposed to (medieval) *realism*.

nom′i·năl·ist, *n.* a person who believes in nominalism.

nom′i·năl·ist, *a.* nominalistic.

nom″i·năl·is′tiç, *a.* of or relating to nominalism or the nominalists.

nom′i·năl·īze, *v.t.* to convert into a noun. [Obs.]

nom′i·năl·ly, *adv.* by name, or in name only.

nom′i·năl val′ūe, stated or par value, as for a stock certificate: distinguished from *actual* or *market value*.

nom′i·năl wāġ′eṣ, wages stated in terms of money paid, not in terms of purchasing power: distinguished from *real wages*.

nom′i·nāte, *v.t.*; nominated, *pt., pp.*; nominating, *ppr.* [L. *nominatus*, pp. of *nominare*, to name.]

1. originally, to name, call, or designate.

2. to name or appoint (a person) to an office or position.

3. to name (a person) as a candidate for election or appointment; to propose for office.

nom′i·nāte·ly, *adv.* by name; particularly. [Rare.]

nom·i·nā′tion, *n.* 1. the naming or appointing of a person to an office.

2. the naming of a person as a candidate for election or appointment to an office.

3. the state of being chosen or named for office, or of being named as a candidate.

nom″i·nā·tī′văl, *a.* in grammar, pertaining to or derived from the nominative case.

nom′i·nā·tive, *a.* [L. *nominativus*, belonging to a name, from *nomen*, a name.]

1. named or appointed to a position or office: distinguished from *elected*.

2. having the name of a person on it; as, a *nominative* will.

3. in grammar, designating or of the case of the subject of a finite verb and the words (appositives, predicate nouns or adjectives, and nouns of direct address) that agree with it; active or actor case.

nom′i·nā·tive, *n.* [L. *casus nominativus*, or *nominativus*, nominative case, from *nominare*, to name.] in grammar, (a) the nominative case; (b) a word in this case.

nominative absolute; a construction consisting of a noun or pronoun and a participle, expressed or understood, which together form a clause, independent of the remainder of the sentence, expressing time, cause, etc.

nom′i·nā·tive·ly, *adv.* in the manner of the nominative.

nom′i·nā·tŏr, *n.* one who nominates.

nom·i·nee′, *n.* 1. in English law, the person who is named to receive a copyhold estate on surrender of it to the lord: sometimes called the *surrenderee*.

2. a person named or designated by another to hold an office; also, one who has been nominated as a candidate for election.

3. the person named as recipient of an annuity.

nō′miṣm, *n.* [from Gr. *nomos*, law.] legalism in religion; the basing of conduct upon adherence to a law or holy scripture.

nō·mis′tiç, *a.* [Gr. *nomos*, law.] of, pertaining to, or derived from nomism.

nō·moç′ȧ·non, *n.* [Gr. *nomos*, a law, and *kanōn*, a rule, canon.] in the Eastern church, a collection of ecclesiastical canons, together with the civil enactments controlling matters in relation to the church.

nō·moç′rȧ·cy, *n.* [Gr. *nomos*, law, and *kratein*, to rule.] a state governed by a codified system of laws.

nō·mog′rȧ·phy, *n.* [Gr. *nomographia*; *nomos*, law, and *graphein*, to write.] the art of drafting or codifying laws, or a treatise upon laws or the art of drafting laws.

nō·mol′ō·ġy, *n.* [Gr. *nomos*, law, and *-logy*.]

1. the science of law and lawmaking.

2. the branch of a science, as of psychology, that investigates and formulates the principles governing its phenomena.

nom·ō·pel′mous, *a.* [Gr. *nomos*, law, and *pelma*, sole.] having a separate tendon, the flexor longus hallucis, by which the first toe is flexed, while the flexor perforans supplies the other three toes, as in most birds.

nom′ō·thēte, *n.* [Gr. *nomothetēs*, a legislator; *nomos*, law, and *tithenai*, to establish.] a lawgiver; especially, an Athenian juror chosen from the ecclesia.

nom·ō·thet′iç, nom·ō·thet′iç·ăl, *a.* 1. giving or enacting laws.

2. based on law.

3. of a science of general or universal laws.

-nō′my, [Gr. *-nomia*, from *nomos*, law.] a combining form meaning *the systematized knowledge of*, as in astro*nomy*, eco*nomy*.

non-, [from L. *non*, not.] a prefix meaning *not*, used to give a negative force, especially to nouns, adjectives, and adverbs, as in *non*resident: *non-* is less emphatic than *in-* and *un-*, which often give a word an opposite meaning (e.g., *non-American*, *un-American*); a hyphen may be used after *non-* and is generally used when the base word begins with a capital letter. The list below includes some of the more common compounds formed with *non-* that do not have special meanings; they will be understood if *not* is used before the meaning of the base word.

nonabsorbent
non-African
nonaggression
nonagreement
nonalcoholic
nonalgebraic
nonalphabetic
nonamendable
non-American
nonantagonistic
nonapologetic
nonapprehension
nonaquatic
non-Arab
nonarithmetical
non-Asiatic
nonassertive
nonassessable
nonassignable
nonassimilation
nonathletic
nonatmospheric
nonauthoritative
nonautomatic
nonbeliever
nonbelieving
nonbelligerent
nonbenevolent
non-Biblical
nonblooming
nonbreakable
nonbudding
nonburnable
nonbusiness
noncapitalistic
noncapsizable
noncategorical
noncelestial
noncellular
noncensored
noncentral
nonchemical
non-Christian
noncivilized
nonclassifiable
nonclerical
noncoercive
noncognitive
noncoherent
noncohesive
noncollaborative
noncollectable
noncombining
noncombustible
noncommercial
noncommunicant
noncompensating
noncompeting
noncompetitive
noncompressible
noncompulsion
nonconcentration
noncondensing
nonconducting
nonconfidential
nonconflicting
noncongealing
noncongenital
noncongestion
nonconnective
nonconnivance
nonconsecutive
nonconsent
nonconservative
nonconspiring
nonconstitutional
nonconstructive
noncontagious
noncontemplative
noncontiguous
noncontinental
noncontinuance
noncontinuous
noncontradiction
noncontradictory
noncontrolled
noncontroversial
nonconventional
nonconvertible
nonconviction
non-co-operative
non-co-ordinating
noncorrective
noncorroding
noncorrosive
noncreative
noncritical
noncultivation
noncumulative
nondamageable
nondecaying
nondeceptive
nondefamatory
nondefensive
nondeferential
nondefining
nondegeneration
nondemocratic
nondepartmental
nondeparture
nondependence
nondepositor
nonderivative
nonderogatory
nondestructive
nondetachable
nondetonating
nondevotional
nondialectal
nondifferentiation
nondiffractive
nondiffusing
nondiplomatic
nondirectional
nondischarging
nondisciplinary
nondiscrimination
nondispersion
nondistinctive
nondistributive
nondivergent
nondivisible
nondoctrinal
nondocumentary
nondogmatic
nondramatic
nondrying
nonearning
noneducational
nonefficacious
nonelective
nonelectric
nonelementary
nonemotional
non-English
nonentailed
nonephemeral
nonequal
nonequivalent
nonequivocating
nonerotic
noneternal
nonethical
non-Euclidean
noneugenic
non-European
nonevangelical
nonevasion
nonevolutionary
nonexchangeable
nonexclusive
nonexcusable
nonexecutive
nonexempt
nonexisting
nonexotic
nonexpansive
nonexperienced
nonexperimental
nonexploitation
nonexplosive
nonexportable
nonextended
nonextension
nonfactual
nonfading
nonfanatical
nonfanciful
nonfatal
nonfederal
nonfederated
nonfermentable
nonfertile
nonfiction
nonfictional
nonfiduciary
nonfigurative
nonfinancial
nonfireproof
nonfiscal
nonflowering
nonflowing
nonflying
nonforfeiture
nonformal
nonfraudulent
nonfreezing
nonfricative
nonfunctional
nonfundamental
nongaseous
nongelatinous
nongenerative
nongenetic
nongovernmental
nongranular
nongregarious
nonhabitable
nonhabitual
nonharmonious
nonhazardous
nonhereditary
nonheritable
nonhistoric
nonhostile
nonhuman
nonhumorous
nonidentical
nonidentity
nonimaginary
nonimitative
nonimmunized
nonimperial
nonimpregnated
nonincandescent
noninclusive
nonindependent
nonindustrial
noninfallible
noninfected
noninfectious
noninfinite
noninflammable
noninflammatory
noninflectional
noninformative
noninheritable
noninstructional
noninstrumental
nonintellectual
nonintelligent
noninterchangeable
noninterference
nonintermittent
noninternational
noninterrupted
nonintoxicating
noninverted
noniodized
nonionized
nonirradiated
nonirrigated
nonirritant
nonirritating
non-Islamic
non-Jewish
nonlegal
nonlicensed
nonlimiting
nonliquefying
nonliquidating
nonliterary
nonlocal
nonluminous
nonlustrous
nonmagnetic
nonmaintenance
nonmarital
nonmarriageable
nonmartial
nonmaterial
nonmaterialistic
nonmaternal
nonmathematical
nonmatrimonial
nonmechanical
nonmedicinal
nonmelodious
nonmetaphysical
nonmetropolitan
nonmigratory
nonmilitary
nonmineral
nonmobile
nonmortal
nonmunicipal
nonmystical
nonnautical
nonnavigable
non-Negro
nonneutral
nonnucleated
nonnutritious
nonobligatory
nonobservant
nonoccupational
nonoccurrence
nonodorous
nonofficial
nonoperative
nonoptional
nonoriental
non-Oriental
nonorthodox
nonoxidizing
nonpacific
nonpalatalization
nonpapal
nonpapist
nonparasitic
nonparental
nonparliamentary
nonparticipation
nonpartisanship
nonpaying
nonpensionable

nonperforated
nonperforming
nonperiodical
nonperishing
nonpermanent
nonpermissible
nonperpendicular
nonphilosophical
nonphysical
nonplausible
nonpoisonous
nonpolarizable
nonpolitical
nonporous
nonpredictable
nonpreferential
nonprejudicial
nonpriestly
nonproducer
nonprofessorial
nonprofiteering
nonprogressive
nonprophetic
nonproportional
nonprotective
nonpunishable
nonracial
nonradiating
nonradical
nonrational
nonreality
nonreciprocal
nonrecognition
nonrecoverable
nonrefillable
nonrefueling
nonregimented
nonregistered
nonregistrable
nonrelative
nonreligious
nonremission
nonrenewable
nonrepayable
nonrepentance
nonrepresentative
nonreproductive
nonresidential
nonresonant
nonrestricted
nonretentive
nonreturnable
nonrevealing
nonreversible
nonrevertible
nonrevolting
nonrevolving
nonrhyming
nonrhythmic
nonritualistic
nonrival
nonromantic
nonrotating
nonroyal
nonrural
nonrustable
nonsacred
nonsacrificial
nonsalable
nonsalaried
nonsalutary
nonscholastic
nonscientific
nonsecret
nonsecretory
nonsedentary
nonseditious
nonselective
nonservile
nonshattering
nonshrinkable
nonsmoker
nonsocial
nonsolid
nonsovereign
nonsparing
nonspecializing
nonspeculative
nonspherical
nonspiritual
nonstaining
nonstandardized
nonstarting
nonstationary
nonstrategic
nonstretchable
nonstriking
nonsubscriber
nonsuccessive
nonsupporting
nonsymbolic
nonsymmetrical
nonsympathizer
nonsymphonic
nonsystematic
nontarnishable
nontaxable
nonteachable
nontechnical
nonterritorial
nontheatrical
nonthinking
nontransferable
nontransitional
nontreasonable
nontributary
nontropical
nontuberculous
nontypical
nontyrannical
nonulcerous
nonunderstandable
nonuniversal
nonutilitarian
nonutilized
nonvegetative
nonvenomous
nonvernacular
nonvertical
nonviolation
nonvirulent
nonvisiting
nonvisual
nonvocational
nonvoting
nonvulcanizable
nonworker
nonyielding

non·ȧ·bil′i·ty, *n.* 1. a lack of ability.
 2. in law, any legal incapacity; as, the *nonability* of a lunatic or minor to make a contract.

non·aç·cept′ănce, *n.* failure to accept.

non·aç′cess, *n.* in law, lack of opportunity for sexual intercourse, especially between husband and wife; as, *nonaccess* may be shown as proof of bastardy of a child born in wedlock.

non·ac′id, *a.* not having acid qualities.

non·aç·quāint′ănce, *n.* lack of acquaintance.

non·ad·mis′sion (-mish′un), *n.* lack of admission.

non·ȧ·dult′, *a.* not adult; not mature; minor.

non·ā″ẽr·ō·bī·ot′iç, *a.* same as *anaerobiotic.*

non′āġe, *n.* [ME. *nounage;* OFr. *nonage.*]
 1. in law, the state of being under the lawful age for doing certain things, as making contracts, marrying, etc.; usually, the state of being under twenty-one.
 2. the period of immaturity; early stage.

nō′nāġe, *n.* [LL. *nonagium,* from L. *nonus,* ninth.] one-ninth of a deceased parishioner's movable property, formerly claimed by English clergy.

non·ȧ·ġē·nār′i·ăn, *n.* [from L. *nonaginta,* ninety.] a person between ninety and a hundred years old.

non·ȧ·ġē·nār′i·ăn, *a.* ninety years old, or between the ages of ninety and one hundred.

non·ȧ·ġes′i·măl, *a.* [L. *nonagesimus,* ninetieth.] pertaining to a nonagesimal or to the number ninety.

non·ȧ·ġes′i·măl, *n.* in astronomy, a point of the ecliptic ninety degrees from the horizon; usually the upper of two such points.

non·ag·gres′sion paçt, an agreement between two nations in which each guarantees not to aggress against the other, usually for a specified period of years.

non′ȧ·gon, *n.* [*nonus,* nine, and Gr. *gōnia,* an angle.] a plane figure having nine sides and nine angles.

non·ā′gri·ăn, *n.* a moth of the genus *Nonagria* or of an allied genus.

non·āl·ien·ā′tion (-yen-), *n.* lack of alienation.

nō′năn, *a.* [L. *nonus,* ninth, and *-an.*] recurring each ninth day or after eight-day intervals; as, a *nonan* fever. [Obs.]

non′āne, *n.* [L. *nonus,* nine.] one of various liquid hydrocarbons of the paraffin series, having the formula C_9H_{20}.

non·ap·pēar′ănce, *n.* default of appearance, as in court, to prosecute or defend.

non·ap·point′ment, *n.* neglect of appointment; failure to secure appointment.

non·ärç′ing, *a.* not allowing an alternating current arc to be maintained: said of metallic terminals.

non as·sump′sit, [L., he did not undertake.] in law, the general denial in an action of assumpsit.

non·at·tend′ănce, *n.* a failure to attend.

non·at·ten′tion, *n.* inattention.

non·bi·tū′mi·nous, *a.* containing no bitumen.

nonce, *n.* [same word as *once,* with an initial *n* derived by misdivision in such phrases as *for then anes, for then ones,* for the once; *then* is here the dat. sing. of the def. art.] the present occasion; the time being.
 for the nonce; for the present occasion; for the time.

nonce wŏrd, a word coined and use for one occasion.

non·çhȧ·länce′, *n.* [Fr.] indifference; coolness; unconcern.

non·çhȧ·länt′, *a.* [Fr., from *non,* not, and *chaloir,* to care for, to concern oneself with, from L. *calere,* to be warm or ardent.]
 1. lacking warmth or enthusiasm; not showing interest.
 2. casually indifferent; cool; unconcerned.

non·çhȧ·länt′ly, *adv.* in a nonchalant manner.

non′çlāim, *n.* a failure to make claim within the time limited by law; omission of claim.

non·çō·hē′sion, *n.* lack of cohesion.

non·çō·in′ci·dence, *n.* lack of coincidence.

non·çō·in′ci·dent, *a.* not coincident.

non′çom″, *n.* a noncommissioned officer. [Colloq.]

non·çom′bat·ănt, *n.* 1. a member of the armed forces whose duties do not include fighting, as a surgeon or a chaplain.
 2. a civilian in wartime.

non·çom′bat·ănt, *a.* 1. not involving combat.
 2. of noncombatants.

non·çŏm·mis′sioned, *a.* not having a commission.
 noncommissioned officer; see under *officer.*

non·çŏm·mit′tăl, *a.* not committing one to any point of view or course of action; not revealing one's position or purpose.

non·çŏm·mit′tăl, *n.* a state of not being committed or pledged; forbearance from committing oneself.

non·çŏm·mit′tăl·ly, *adv.* in a noncommittal manner.

non·çŏm·mūn′iŏn (-yun), *n.* neglect or failure of communion.

non·çŏm·plē′tion, *n.* lack of completion.

non·çŏm·plī′ănce, *n.* failure of compliance; refusal to agree, yield, etc.; obstinance.

non çom′pos men′tis, [L.] in law, not of sound mind; mentally incapable of handling one's own affairs: sometimes written *non compos.*

non·çŏn·clūd′ing, *a.* not ending or closing.

non·çŏn·çŭr′, *v.i.* to dissent or refuse to concur.

non·çŏn·çŭr′rence, *n.* a refusal to concur.

non·çŏn·duç′tion, *n.* failure or incapacity to conduct.

non·çŏn·duçt′ŏr, *n.* a material of low conductivity or of high resistance to the transmission of energy, especially electricity and heat.

non·çŏn·fọrm′ing, *a.* not conforming; specifically, dissenting from the established church.

non·çŏn·fọrm′ist, *n.* a person who does not act in harmony with the practices and doctrines of an established church; especially, [N–], a Protestant in England who is not a member of the Anglican Church; a Dissenter.

non·çŏn·fọrm′i·ty, *n.* 1. failure or refusal to act in conformity with generally accepted beliefs and practices; especially, [N–], refusal to accept the doctrines or follow the practices of the Anglican Church.
 2. the doctrines and rites of Nonconformists.

non çon′stat, [L.] it does not appear; it does not follow: used in law.

non·çŏn·tent′, *n.* in the British House of Lords, one who gives a negative vote, as not being satisfied with the measure: sometimes written *noncon.*

non·çŏn·trib′ū·tō·ry, *a.* not contributing.

non-çō-op·ẽr·ā′tion, *n.* 1. failure to work together or act jointly: refusal to work in unison with a person, group, or organization.
 2. refusal to perform civic duties, pay taxes, etc.: often used as a means of protest against a government, as by Gandhi formerly against the British government in India.

non′dȧ, *n.* [Australian.] an Australian tree, *Parinarium nonda,* or its fruit, resembling a plum.

non·deç′āne, *n.* [L. *nonus,* ninth, and *decem,* ten, so called from the number of carbon atoms it contains.] a paraffin hydrocarbon, $C_{19}H_{40}$, a white, waxy solid.

non·dē·cid′ū·āte, *a.* indeciduate.

non·dē·liv′ẽr·y, *n.* a failure to deliver.

non·dep·ō·si′tion, *n.* a failure to deposit.

non′dē·sçript, *a.* [L. *non,* not, and *descriptus,* described.] so lacking in recognizable character or qualities as to belong to no definite class or type; hard to classify or describe.

non′dē·sçript, *n.* a nondescript person or thing.

non·dē·vel′ŏp·ment, *n.* a failure to develop.

non·dis·çŏv′ẽr·y, *n.* lack of discovery.

non·dis·junç′tion, *n.* in biology, the failure of paired chromosomes to pass to separate cells in mitosis.

nŏne, *a.* [ME. *none, non;* AS. *nān; ne,* not, and *an,* one.] not any: used before a vowel; as, of *none* effect. [Obs.]

nŏne, *pron.* 1. no one; not anyone; as, *none* but Jack can do it.
 2. no persons or things; not any: usually used with a plural verb; as, there are *none* on the table.

nŏne, *n.* not any (of); no part; nothing; as, I want *none* of it.

nŏne, *adv.* in no way; not at all; as, he is *none* the stronger for it.
 none the less; nevertheless; notwithstanding.

non·ef·feçt′ive, *a.* not effective; also, unavailable for duty, as a soldier.

non·ē′gō, *n.* in metaphysics, whatever and all that is not the ego, or self; the objective as contrasted with the subjective; hence, the external world.

non·ē·las′tiç, *a.* without springiness or elasticity.

non·ē·leçt′, *n.* one who is not elected, or chosen, to salvation.

non·ē·leç′tion, *n.* failure of election.

non·em·phat′iç, *a.* having no emphasis; unemphatic.

non·em·phat′iç·ăl, *a.* nonemphatic.

non·en′ti·ty, *n.; pl.* **non·en′ti·tieṣ,** 1. the state of not existing.
 2. something without existence.
 3. a person considered of little importance; person having little influence or individuality.

non·ē·pis′çō·păl, *a.* not belonging to or vested in bishops or prelates: said of church polity.

nōneṣ, *n.pl.* [L. *nonæ,* from *nonus,* ninth, from *novem,* nine.]
 1. in the ancient Roman calendar, the ninth day before the ides of a month; the seventh of March, May, July, and October, and the fifth of the other months.
 2. in the early Christian Church, the fifth of the seven canonical hours, coming at the ninth hour of the day, or about 3:00 P.M.
 3. the service of this hour, now usually recited somewhat earlier than 3:00 P.M.

non·es·sen′tiăl, *a.* not essential; of relatively no importance; unnecessary.

non·es·sen′tiăl, *n.* a thing or person not essential; as, *nonessentials* may be omitted.

non est faç′tum, [L., it has not been done.] in law, the general issue in an action of debt on a bond or other deed, in which the defendant denies the deed to be his.

non est in·ven′tus, [L., he has not been found.] in law, the return of the sheriff on a writ, when the defendant is not to be found.

nŏne′such, *n.* 1. a person or thing that has no

equal; an extraordinary person or thing; a paragon.

2. any of certain plants, as *Medicago lupulina* and *Lychnis chalcedonica*; also, a variety of apple.

nō·net′, *n.* [L. *nonus*, ninth.] in music, a nine-part composition.

nō·nęt′tō, *n.* same as *nonet.*

non·ex·ē·çū′tion, *n.* neglect of execution; nonperformance.

non·ex·ist′ence (-egz-), *n.* 1. absence of existence; the negation of being.

2. a thing that has no existence or being.

non·ex·ist′ent, *a.* not having existence.

non·ex·pōr·tā′tion, *n.* a failure of exportation; the fact of not exporting goods or commodities.

non·ex·ten′sile, *a.* that cannot be stretched.

non·fēa′ṣănce, *n.* in law, a failure to perform a duty: distinguished from *malfeasance.*

non·fil′tēr·ă·ble (-bl), *a.* incapable of being filtered or obtained by filtration; as, a *nonfilterable* colloid, which is carried through filter paper together with its vehicle.

non·fọr′feit·ing (-fit), *a.* not liable to forfeiture: said of insurance policies and the like which do not lapse on failure to pay installments.

non·fụl·fill′ment, *n.* neglect or failure to fulfill.

nō·nil′liŏn, *n.* [L. *nonus*, ninth, and E. *million.*]

1. in the United States and France, the number represented by 1 followed by 30 zeros.

2. in Great Britain and Germany, the number represented by 1 followed by 54 zeros.

nō·nil′liŏn, *a.* amounting to one nonillion in number.

non·im·pōr·tā′tion, *n.* lack or failure of importation; the fact of not importing goods.

non·im·pōrt′ing, *a.* not importing; as, a *nonimporting* country.

non·in·duç′tive, *a.* in electricity, not inductive; as, a *noninductive* resistance.

non·in·hab′it·ănt, *n.* one not an inhabitant.

non·in′tēr·çōurse, *n.* lack of intercourse; in international affairs, suspension of commercial intercourse between parties of hostile countries.

non·in·tēr·ven′tion, *n.* a refraining from interference, as by one nation in the affairs of another.

non·in·trụ′ṣion·ist, *n.* in the Church of Scotland, one who was opposed to the forcible intrusion of unacceptable clergymen upon objecting congregations.

nō′ni·us, *n.* same as *vernier.*

non·join′dẽr, *n.* in law, a plea in abatement for the nonjoining of a person as codefendant.

non·jụ′rănt, *a.* nonjuring.

non·jụ′ring, *a.* 1. not swearing allegiance.

2. specifically, an epithet applied to the party in Great Britain that would not swear allegiance to William and Mary after the revolution of 1688.

non·jụ′rŏr, *n.* [*non-*, and L. *jurare*, to swear.] a person who refuses to take an oath of allegiance to his ruler or government; specifically, [N-] any of the clergymen of the Church of England who refused to take such an oath at the accession of William and Mary in 1689.

non·jụ′rŏr·iṣm, *n.* in English history, the principles or practices of nonjurors; Jacobitism.

non·lim·i·tā′tion, *n.* the condition of not being limited.

non lī′quet, [L.] in law, a verdict of indecision.

non·mă·lig′nănt, *a.* not malignant; benign; as, a *nonmalignant* tumor.

non·man·ū·faç′tūr·ing, *a.* not carrying on manufactures.

non·mem′bẽr, *n.* one not a member.

non·mem′bẽr·ship, *n.* state of not being a member.

non·met′ăl, *n.* any of those elements lacking the characteristics of a metal; specifically, any of the electronegative elements (e.g., oxygen, carbon, nitrogen, fluorine) whose oxides are not basic.

non·mē·tal′liç, *a.* not metallic; metalloid; belonging to a nonmetal.

non·mor′ăl, *a.* not connected in any way with morality and ethical precepts; not moral and not immoral; amoral.

non·nat′, *n.* a small food fish of the Mediterranean.

non·nat′ū·răl, *a.* not natural; outside of nature.

non·nat′ū·răl, *n.* a thing not natural; specifically, in old medicine, anything not immediately a part of the body, yet essential to the support of life, as air, water, sleep, etc.

non·nē·ces′si·ty, *n.* the quality of being not necessary.

non·nī·troġ′ē·nous, *a.* without nitrogen: said of foods.

non′ny, *n.*; *pl.* **non′nieṣ**, a ninny; a simpleton. [Dial.]

nō′-nō, *n.*; *pl.* **no′-nōeṣ**, [from *No! No!*, as said in admonishing a young child.] something that is forbidden or considered unwise to do, say, use, etc. [Slang.]

non·ō·bē′di·ence, *n.* neglect of obedience; disobedience.

non·ob·jeç′tive, *a.* nonrepresentational.

non·ob·ṣẽrv′ănce, *n.* neglect or failure to observe or fulfill.

non ob·stan′tē, [L.] 1. notwithstanding; in opposition to what has been stated or is to be stated or admitted.

2. formerly, a clause in statutes and letters patent importing a license from the king to do a thing which could not otherwise be legally done: abolished by the Bill of Rights, 1688.

non obstante veredicto; in law, a judgment given in opposition to the verdict of a jury.

non·pă·reil′ (-rel′), *n.* [Fr. *non*, not or no, and *pareil*, equal.]

1. a person or thing of unequaled excellence.

2. in printing, a size of type between minion and agate; 6 point.

3. a small bird of the United States, *Passerina ciris*: also called *painted bunting.*

non·pă·reil′, *a.* having no equal; peerless.

non·par′ous, *a.* [*non-* and *-parous.*] having borne no children.

non·pär·tic′i·pāt·ing, *a.* not participating; especially, in insurance, not giving the right to participate in the dividends from the profits or surplus of the company.

non·pär′ti·ṣăn, non·pär′ti·zăn, *a.* 1. not partisan; especially, not controlled or influenced by, or supporting, any single political party; as, a *nonpartisan* newspaper, *nonpartisan* league.

2. designating or having to do with an election in which candidates are not officially identified by party.

non·pāy′ment, *n.* neglect of payment.

non·pẽr·fọrm′ănce, *n.* a failure to perform.

non′pẽr·sŏn, *n.* a person completely ignored, as if he did not exist; specifically, one who is officially ignored by the government.

non′plus, *n.* [L. *non*, not, and *plus*, more, further.] a state in which one is unable to proceed or decide; inability to say or do more; puzzle: usually in the phrase, at a *nonplus.*

> They are at a loss, and their understanding
> is perfectly at a *nonplus*. —Locke.

non′plus, *v.t.*; nonplused *or* nonplussed, *pt.*, *pp.*; nonplusing *or* nonplussing, *ppr.* to bring to an embarrassing deadlock; to puzzle; to leave no opening for.

> That sin which is a pitch beyond all those
> must needs be such an one as must *non-*
> *plus* the devil himself to proceed farther.
> —South.

non pos′sū·mus, [L.] we cannot: used to signify the impossibility of doing something specified.

non·prep·ă·rā′tion, *n.* lack of preparation; state of being unprepared.

non·preṣ·en·tā′tion, *n.* neglect of presentation; the condition of not having been presented.

non·prō·duç′tion, *n.* a failure to produce or exhibit.

non·prō·duç′tive, *a.* not productive; specifically, (a) not resulting in the production of the goods sought or the realization of the effects expected; as, a *nonproductive* plan; (b) not directly related to the production of goods; as, clerks, salesmen, etc. are *nonproductive* personnel.

non·prō·fes′sion·ăl, *a.* not belonging to a profession; not done in a professional way.

non·prō·fi′cien·cy (-shen-), *n.* lack of proficiency.

non·prō·fi′cient, *a.* not proficient; not competent.

non·prof′it, *a.* not intending or intended to earn a profit; as, a *nonprofit* organization.

non″-pros′, *v.t.*; non-prossed (-prost′), *pt.*, *pp.*; non-prossing, *ppr.* to enter a judgment of *non prosequitur* against (a plaintiff or his suit).

non prō·seq′ui·tūr (-sek′wi-), [L., he does not prosecute.] in law, a judgment entered against a plaintiff who fails to prosecute: usually abbreviated to *non-pros.*

non·prō′tē·in, *n.* in biochemistry, a substance not protein; anything structurally less complex than protein, as the total nitrogenous composition of plant and animal tissues or fluids.

non·quō′tȧ, *a.* pertaining to anything or anyone that is not included in a certain quota; as, a *nonquota* immigrant.

non·rē·açt′ive, *a.* pertaining to or characterizing an electric circuit which offers only ohmic resistance to a current; having no inductance or capacity.

non·rē·çūr′rent, *a.* not occurring again.

non·rē·çūr′ring, *a.* nonrecurrent.

non·rē·dūç′ing, *a.* in chemistry, pertaining to or characterizing sugars which do not easily reduce Fehling solution.

non·rē′ġent, *n.* in the English universities, a master of arts whose regency has ceased.

non·reg·ū·lā′tion, *a.* not subject to certain rules as, formerly, in India, those provinces for which special regulations were made; not in keeping with existing rules or regulations, as *nonregulation* ordnance.

non″rep·rē·ṣen·tā′tion·ăl, *a.* not representational; specifically, designating or of art that does not attempt to represent in recognizable form any object in nature; abstract; nonobjective.

non·reṣ′i·dence, *n.* failure or neglect to reside at the place where one is stationed, or where official duties require one to reside, or on one's own lands.

non·reṣ′i·dent, *a.* not residing in a specified place; especially, having one's home in some locality other than where one works, attends school, etc.

non·reṣ′i·dent, *n.* one who does not reside on the lands owned by him, or in the place where official duties require; also, one who has his place of business or school, etc. in one place, as a county or state, and resides in another.

non·reṣ′i·dent·ẽr, *n.* one who is habitually absent from or does not live on an estate or benefice, as a clergyman.

non·reṣ·i·den′tiă·ry (-shă-), *n.* any nonresident dignitary of a church, benefice, or estate.

non·rē·ṣist′ănce, *n.* the fact or policy of not resisting; passive obedience; submission to authority, power, or usurpation without opposition.

non·rē·ṣist′ănt, *a.* making no resistance to power or oppression.

non·rē·ṣist′ănt, *n.* 1. a person who believes that force and violence should not be used to oppose arbitrary authority, however unjust.

2. a person who refuses to use force even to defend himself.

non·rē·ṣist′ing, *a.* making no resistance.

non·rē·strāint′, *n.* the absence of restraint; especially, in psychiatry, the management of psychotic persons without the use of a strait jacket or other physical restraint.

non·rē·striç′tive, *a.* in grammar, designating a clause, phrase, or word felt as not essential to the sense, or purely descriptive, and hence usually set off by commas (e.g., John, *who is six feet tall*, is younger than Bill): opposed to *restrictive.*

non·rē·vẽrs′ing, *a.* not making a change in direction or sign, as an electric current.

non·riġ′id, *a.* flexible; pliant; not rigid.

nonrigid airship; an airship whose form is maintained by the pressure of the gas contained within the envelope.

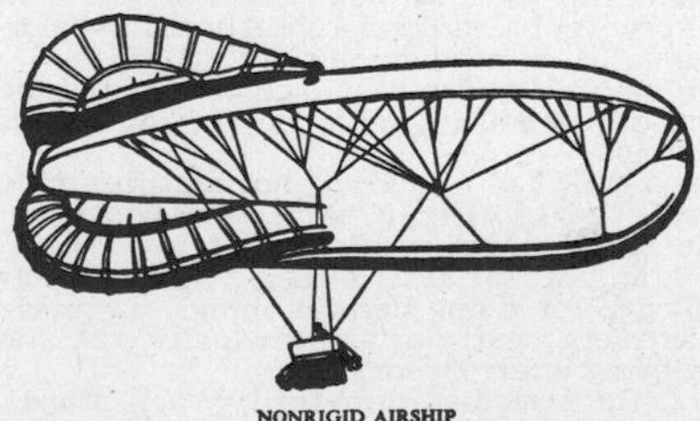

NONRIGID AIRSHIP

non·rụ′mi·nănt, *a.* not ruminating, as animals.

non·saç′çhȧ·rine, *a.* not sweet; not sugarlike; not containing saccharine.

non·sāne′, *a.* in law, unsound; not perfect; as, a person of *nonsane* memory.

non·sē·çrē′tion, *n.* lack of secretion.

non·seç·tār′i·ăn, *a.* not sectarian; not confined to or affiliated with any specific religion.

non'sense, *n.* [*non-* and *sense.*]
1. words or actions that convey an absurd meaning or no meaning at all.
2. things of relatively no importance or value; trivialities.
3. impudent, foolish, or evasive behavior; as, let's stop that *nonsense* right now.

non·sen'si·çăl, *a.* devoid of sense; unintelligible, absurd, foolish, silly, etc.

non·sen·si·çal'i·ty, *n.* nonsensicalness.

non·sen'si·çăl·ly, *adv.* in a nonsensical manner.

non·sen'si·çăl·ness, *n.* the quality of being nonsensical; also, that which is nonsensical.

non·sen'si·tive, *a.* not sensitive; wanting sense or perception.

non seq'ui·tūr (-wi-), [L., it does not follow.] in logic, a conclusion or inference which does not follow from the premises.

non·sex'ū·ăl, *a.* without sex; asexual; neuter.

non'skid', *a.* having the tread so constructed as to reduce skidding: said of a tire, etc.

non·sō·lū'tion, *n.* failure of solution or explanation.

non·sol'ven·cy, *n.* inability to pay debts.

non·sol'vent, *a.* not able to pay debts; insolvent.

non·sol'vent, *n.* an insolvent.

non'stop, *a.* and *adv.* without a stop.

non·strī'ā·ted, *a.* not striated; without striations, as muscle fiber.

non·sub·mis'sion, *n.* want of submission.

non·sub·mis'sive, *a.* not submissive.

non·sub·stan'tiăl·işm, *n.* nihilism; phenomenalism.

non·sub·stan'tiăl·ist, *n.* one who believes in nonsubstantialism.

nŏn'such, *n.* same as *nonesuch.*

Non·suç·tō'ri·ȧ, *n.pl.* an order of infusorians provided with tentacles which are not suctorial.

non'sūit, *n.* [ME. *noun suyt*; Anglo-Fr. *nonsute.*]
1. originally, the ending of a lawsuit by the voluntary withdrawal of the plaintiff.
2. a judgment against a plaintiff because of his failure to establish that he has a valid case or to produce adequate evidence.

non'sūit, *v.t.*; nonsuited, *pt., pp.*; nonsuiting, *ppr.* to bring a nonsuit against (a plaintiff or his case).

non'sūit, *a.* nonsuited. [Rare.]

non·sup·pōrt', *n.* failure to provide for a legal dependent.

non·ten'ūre, *n.* in law, a plea of a defendant, that he did not hold the land, as affirmed by the plaintiff.

non'tērm, *n.* a vacation between two terms of a court. [Brit.]

non'trō·nīte, *n.* [from *Nontron,* France, where it is found.] a hydrated silicate of iron.

nōn trōp'pō, [It.] in music, not too much; moderately: a direction to the performer, as in *allegro non troppo,* fast, but not too fast.

non·ū'ni·fọrm·ist, *n.* one who believes that past changes in the structure of the earth have proceeded from causes more violent than are now operating.

non·ūn'iŏn (-yun), *a.* 1. not belonging to a labor union.
2. not made or serviced by union workers or under conditions required by a labor union.
3. refusing to recognize, or sign a contract with, a labor union.

non·ūn'iŏn, *n.* failure to mend or unite: said of a broken bone.

non·ūn'iŏn·işm, *n.* theories and practices of those who oppose or refuse to accept labor unions.

non·ūn'iŏn·ist, *n.* 1. one who advocates nonunionism.
2. a person who is not a member of a labor union.

non'ū·plet, *n.* [Fr. *nonuple,* from L. *nonus,* ninth, and *-uple,* as in *quadruple,* and *-et.*] in music, nine notes played in the time of six or eight of the same kind.

non·ūş'ēr, *n.* 1. a person who is not a user.
2. in law, (a) neglect of official duty; default of performing the duties and services required of an officer; (b) neglect or omission to use an easement or other right.

non'vā·lent, *a.* [*non-,* and L. *valere,* to be able.] having no chemical valency; not capable of entering into chemical composition: said of the inert gases.

non·vī'ȧ·ble, *n.* not capable of living; said of the fetus after delivery.

non·vō'çăl, *a.* not vocal.

non·vōt'ēr, *n.* a person who does not vote or is not permitted to vote.

non'yl, *n.* [*non*ane and *-yl.*] the radical C_9H_{19}, derived from nonane: commonly used adjectively; as, *nonyl* alcohol.

non'y·lēne, *n.* [*non*ane and eth*ylene.*] a hydrocarbon, C_9H_{18}, of the ethylene series.

non·y·len'iç, *a.* relating to or containing nonylene; as, *nonylenic* acid.

nō·nyl'iç, *a.* relating to or containing nonyl; as, *nonylic* acid.

noo'dle, *n.* 1. a simpleton; fool.
2. the head. [Slang.]

noo'dle, *n.* [G. *nudel,* macaroni.] a flat, narrow strip of dry, rolled dough, usually containing egg and used in soup, etc.

nook, *n.* [ME. *nok.*] 1. a corner, especially of a room.
2. a secluded spot; a recess.

nook'-shot"ten, *a.* full of nooks and corners. [Archaic.]
That *nook-shotten* isle of Albion.—Shak.

nook'y, *a.* like a nook; full of nooks.

nō·ō·loġ'iç·ăl, *a.* pertaining to noology.

nō·ol'ō·ġist, *n.* one who is versed in noology.

nō·ol'ō·ġy, *n.* [Gr. *noos,* mind, and *-logy.*] the science of intellectual facts or phenomena.

noon, *n.* [AS. *non,* from L. *nona* (supply *hora,* hour), the ninth hour; originally applied to the service (nones) performed at that time and later it came to mean midday.]
1. twelve o'clock in the daytime; midday.
2. the highest point or culmination; time of greatest power, brilliance, etc.; as, in the *noon* of his life.
3. (a) twelve o'clock at night; midnight: now only in *noon of night*; (b) the position of the moon at this time. [Rare or Poet.]
apparent or *real noon*; the actual moment when the center of the sun is on the meridian.
high noon; see under *high.*
mean noon; see under *mean.*

noon, *a.* of or occurring at noon (midday).

noon'dāy, *n.* midday; twelve o'clock in the day.

noon'dāy, *a.* pertaining to midday; meridional; as, the *noonday* heat.

nō'-one (-wun), *pron.* no one.

no one, no person; not anybody; nobody.

noon'flow"ēr, *n.* in botany, the goat's-beard, *Tragopogon pratensis.*

noon'ing, *n.* 1. noon. [Archaic or Dial.]
2. a stop at midday for rest or food. [Archaic or Dial.]
3. a meal or refreshment at noon. [Archaic or Dial.]

noon'stead (-sted), *n.* the station of the sun at noon. [Obs.]

noon'tīde, *n.* [AS. *nontid*; *non,* noon, and *tid,* tide.] the time of noon; midday.

noon'tīde, *a.* pertaining to noon; meridional.
Summer's *noontide* air. —Milton.

noon'tīme, *n.* and *a.* the time of noon; midday.

noops, *n.* the cloudberry. [Brit. Dial.]

noose, *n.* [Languedoc *nous,* a knot, from L. *nodus,* a knot.]
1. a loop formed in a rope, cord, etc. by means of a slip knot so that the loop tightens as the rope is pulled: often used figuratively with reference to death by hanging.
2. anything that restricts one's freedom; tie, bond, snare, trap, etc.

noose, *v.t.*; noosed, *pt., pp.*; noosing, *ppr.* 1. to catch or hold in or as in a noose; to trap, ensnare, etc.
2. to form a noose in or of (a rope, cord, etc.).
3. to execute by hanging. [Rare.]

nō'păl, *n.* [Mex. *nopalli.*]
1. any one of several cactaceous plants from which the cochineal insect is collected.
2. the prickly pear.

nō'păl·ry, nō'păl·ēr·y, *n.*; *pl.* **nō'păl·ries, nō'păl·ēr·ies,** a plantation or nursery of nopals for rearing cochineal insects.

nō'-pär', *a.* having no stated par value; as, a *no-par* certificate of stock.

nōpe, *n.* the bullfinch. [Brit. Dial.]

nōpe, *adv.* no: a negative reply. [Slang.]

nor, *conj.* [ME. *nor,* contr. of *nother.*] and not; and not either: usually as the second of the correlatives *neither . . . nor,* implying negation of both parts of the statement, as, I can *neither* go *nor* stay; occasionally used in poetry or rhetoric: (a) without the preceding neither; as, he doesn't smoke, *nor* does he drink; (b) substituting for *neither* as the first in a pair of negative correlatives; as, *nor* flood *nor* fire.

nor, *conj.* [Northern ME.] than. [Dial.]

nor', nor, north: used especially in compounds, as in *nor'*western.

nō·rä'ghe (-gā), *n.* same as *nurhag.*

Nor'bērt·ine, *n.* same as *Premonstrant.*

nord'çä"pēr, *n.* the Atlantic right whale.

nor'den·skiol·dine (-shēl-), *n.* [from Baron *Nordenskiöld,* a Swedish geologist.] a crystalline borate of tin and calcium found in Norway.

Nor'diç, *a.* [ML. *Nordicus,* from G. or Fr. *nord,* north.] in ethnology, designating or of one of the three main divisions of the Caucasian, or white, race: term used to denote typically longheaded, tall, blond peoples of northern Europe, as the Scandinavians.

Nor'diç, *n.* a member of the Nordic division of the Caucasian race.

Nor'fōlk jack'et (-fōk), a singlebreasted, loose-fitting, belted jacket, with a boxpleat on both front and back.

nō'ri·ȧ, *n.* [Sp., from Ar. *nā'ōra,* a noria.] a water wheel with buckets at its circumference, used in Spain and the Orient to raise and discharge water.

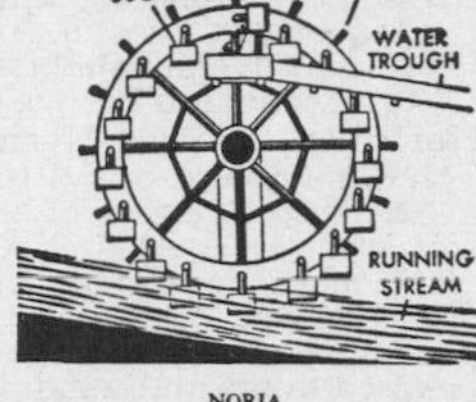

NORIA

nor'ice, *n.* a nurse. [Obs.]

nō'rie, *n.* the cormorant. [Brit.]

nor'i·mō"nō, nor'i·mon, *n.* [Japan.] a Japanese covered litter having the entrance at the side.

nō'rīte, *n.* [*Nor*way and *-ite.*] a rock consisting of plagioclase and hypersthene, with some orthoclase and diallage.

nor'lănd, *a.* and *n.* the land in the north.

nor'lănd·ēr, *n.* an inhabitant of the northland; a northerner.

norm, *n.* [L. *norma,* a carpenter's square, a rule.] a standard, model, or pattern for a group; especially, such a standard of achievement as represented by the median or average achievement of a large group.

nor'mȧ, *n.* [L., a carpenter's square, rule.]
1. a rule; a principle; a norm.
There is no uniformity, no *norma,* principle, or rule, perceivable in the distribution of the primeval natural agents through the universe. —J. S. Mill.
2. a square for measuring right angles, used by carpenters, masons, etc. to make their work rectangular.
3. a pattern; a gauge; a templet; a model.
4. [N—] the Square, a southern constellation, situated between Scorpio and Lupus. It contains twelve stars, all below the fourth magnitude.

nor'măl, *a.* [L. *normalis,* from *norma,* a carpenter's square, a rule.]
1. conforming with or constituting an accepted standard, model, or pattern; especially, corresponding to the median or average of a large group in type, appearance, achievement, function, development, etc.; natural; standard; regular.
2. in biology, (a) not immunized or otherwise exposed to an infectious agent; as, a *normal* animal; (b) happening naturally.
3. in chemistry, (a) designating or of a salt formed by replacing all the replaceable hydrogen of an acid with a metal or metals; (b) designating or of a solution which contains an amount of the dissolved substance chemically equivalent to one gram-atomic weight of hydrogen per liter of solution; (c) designating or of a fatty hydrocarbon, the chain of which is continuous rather than branched, in which no carbon atom is united directly to more than two others.
4. in economics, designating a price for a commodity approximately equal to the highest cost of production.
5. in mathematics, perpendicular; at right angles.
6. in psychology, average in intelligence or emotional stability.

nor'măl, *n.* 1. anything normal.
2. the usual state, amount, degree, etc.; especially, the median or average.
3. a normal school.
4. in mathematics, a perpendicular; especially, a perpendicular to a line tangent to a curve, at its point of tangency.

nor'măl·cy, *n.* normality; the state or fact of being normal.

nor·mal′i·ty, *n.* the state or fact of being normal.

nor″măl·i·zā′tion, *n.* reduction to a normal or standard state.

nor′măl·īze, *v.t.*; normalized, *pt., pp.*; normalizing, *ppr.* to make normal; to bring into conformity with a standard, pattern, model, etc.

nor′măl·ly, *adv.* 1. in a normal manner.
2. under normal circumstances; ordinarily.

nor′măl school, a school for training high-school graduates to become teachers.

nor′măl val′ūe, the average price of a commodity in a given market over a long period of time: distinguished from *market value.*

nor′măn, *n.* in nautical usage, a short wooden bar to be thrust into a hole of the windlass, on which to fasten the cable; also, a bar put through the head of the rudder, and a pin fixed to prevent the cable from falling off.

Nor′măn, *n.* [AS. *Northman,* lit., a Northman.]
1. any of the Northmen who occupied Normandy in the tenth century A.D.
2. a descendant of the Normans and French who conquered England in 1066.
3. Norman French.
4. a native or inhabitant of Normandy.
5. the modern French dialect of Normandy.

Nor′măn, *a.* 1. of Normandy, the Normans, their language, or culture.
2. designating or of the Romanesque style of architecture as it flourished in Normandy and, after the Norman Conquest, as developed in England: the style is characterized by massive construction, round arches over recessed doors and windows, and carving.

Nor′măn Con′quest (-kwest), the conquest of England by the Normans under William the Conqueror in 1066.

Nor·măn·esque′ (-esk′), *a.* in the style of the Normans.

Nor′măn-French′, *n.* Norman French.

Nor′măn-French′, *a.* 1. of or using Norman French.
2. of the Norman-French people.

Nor′măn French, 1. the French of the Normans or Normandy, as spoken in England by the Norman conquerors; Anglo-French: it was not imposed on the English as an official language at the Conquest, but gained legal and administrative currency after the accession of Eleanor of Aquitaine as queen (1152).
2. the later form of this language used as the legal jargon of England until the late seventeenth century; Law French.

Nor′măn·ism, *n.* an idiom of the Norman language; a habit or form of speech peculiar to the Normans.

Nor′măn·īze, *v.t.* and *v.i.*; Normanized, *pt., pp.*; Normanizing, *ppr.* to make or become Norman in style, character, language, customs, law, etc.

nor′mȧ·tive, *a.* 1. of or establishing a norm, or standard.
2. having to do with usage norms; as, *normative* grammar.

Norn, *n.* [ON. *norn.*] in Norse mythology, any of the three goddesses, Urth (the Past), Verthandi (the Present), and Skuld (the Future), who determined the destiny of gods and men.

nor·ō·pi·an′iç, *a.* obtained from opium.

Nor′roy, *n.* [*nord,* north, and *roy,* king.] the title of the third of the three English Kings of Arms, whose jurisdiction lies to the north of the Trent.

Norse, *a.* [prob. from D. *Noorsch,* a Norwegian, var. of *Noordsch*; *noord,* north, and *-sch,* -ish.]
1. Scandinavian.
2. West Scandinavian (Norwegian, Icelandic, and Faroese).

Norse, *n.* 1. the Scandinavian group of languages.
2. the West Scandinavian group of languages.
the Norse; (a) the Scandinavians; (b) the West Scandinavians.

Norse′măn, *n.*; *pl.* **Norse′men,** a member of the ancient Scandinavian people; a Northman.

Norsk, *a.* and *n.* Norse.

nor′te, *n.* [Sp. *norte,* the north, the north wind.] a norther.

nor′tel·ry, *n.* nurture; education; breeding. [Obs.]

north (*in nautical usage,* nor), *n.* [AS. *north*; cf. Ice. *northr,* G., Sw., and Dan. *nord,* north.]
1. the direction to the right of a person facing the sunset; the direction of the North Pole from any other point on the earth's surface: the needle of a compass points to the *magnetic north pole* rather than to the geographic pole.
2. the point on a compass at 0° or 360°, directly opposite south.
3. a region or district in or toward this direction.
4. [*often* N–] the northern part of the earth, especially the arctic regions.
5. the north wind. [Poet.]
the North; that part of the United States which is bounded on the South by Maryland, the Ohio River, and Missouri; the States opposed to the Confederacy in the Civil War.

north, *a.* 1. in, of, to, toward, or facing the north.
2. from the north; as, a *north* wind.
3. [N–] designating the northern part of a continent, country, etc.; as, *North* America, *North* India.

north, *adv.* in or toward the north; in a northerly direction.

north, *v.i.* in nautical usage, to move or veer toward the north.

North A·mer′i·cȧn, 1. of North America or its people.
2. a native or inhabitant of North America.

north′bound′, *a.* bound north; going northward.

north by̆ ēast, the direction, or the point on a mariner's compass, halfway between due north and north-northeast; 11°15′ east of due north.

north by̆ west, the direction, or the point on a mariner's compass, halfway between due north and north-northwest; 11°15′ west of due north.

North Car·ō·lin′i·ăn, 1. of North Carolina.
2. a native or inhabitant of North Carolina.

North Dȧ·kō′tăn, 1. of North Dakota.
2. a native or inhabitant of North Dakota.

north·ēast′, *n.* 1. the direction, or the point on a mariner's compass, halfway between north and east; 45° east of due north.
2. a region or district in or toward this direction.
the Northeast; the northeastern part of the United States, especially New England, but sometimes including New York City and its environs.

north·ēast′, *a.* 1. in, of, to, toward, or facing the northeast.
2. from the northeast, as a wind.
Northeast Passage; a passage for ships along the northern coasts of Europe and Asia to the Pacific Ocean. The first to make the complete voyage by this passage was the Swedish explorer Nordenskjöld, after it had been from time to time attempted in vain for upward of three centuries.

north·ēast′, *adv.* in, toward, or from the northeast.

north·ēast by̆ ēast, the direction, or the point on a mariner's compass, halfway between northeast and east-northeast; 11°15′ east of northeast.

north·ēast′ by̆ north, the direction, or the point on a mariner's compass, halfway between northeast and north-northeast; 11°15′ north of northeast.

north·ēast′ẽr, *n.* a storm or strong wind coming from the northeast.

north·ēast′ẽr·ly, *adv.* and *a.* 1. in or toward the northeast.
2. from the northeast.

north·ēast′ẽrn, *a.* 1. in, of, or toward the northeast.
2. from the northeast; as, a *northeastern* wind.
3. [N–] of or characteristic of the Northeast or New England.

north·ēast′wărd, *a.* and *adv.* toward the northeast.

north·ēast′wărd, *n.* a northeastward direction, point, or region.

north·ēast′wărd·ly, *a.* and *adv.* 1. toward the northeast.
2. from the northeast, as a wind.

north·ēast′wărds, *adv.* northeastward.

north′ẽr, *n.* a storm or strong wind from the north; especially, such a wind in the area about the Gulf of Mexico.

north′ẽr·li·ness, *n.* the state of being northerly.

north′ẽr·ly, *a.* 1. in, of, or toward the north.
2. from the north.

north′ẽr·ly, *adv.* 1. toward the north; as, to sail *northerly.*
2. from the north.

north′ẽrn, *a.* 1. pertaining to or being in the north; toward or facing the north.

Like a streamer of the *northern* morn,
Seen where the moving isles of winter shock
By night with noises of the *northern* sea.
—Tennyson.

2. from the north.
3. [N–] of or characteristic of the North.
Northern Cross; the northern constellation Cygnus, the brighter stars of which form a cross.
Northern Crown; the Corona Borealis, a small and bright constellation near Hercules.
Northern Hemisphere; that half of the earth north of the equator.
northern lights; the aurora borealis.
northern signs; those signs of the zodiac that are on the north side of the equator, viz., Aries, Taurus, Gemini, Cancer, Leo, and Virgo.
Northern Spy; a yellowish-red winter apple.

north′ẽrn, *n.* a northerner.

north′ẽrn·ẽr, *n.* 1. a native or resident of the north or northern part of a country, land, or province.
2. [N–] a native or inhabitant of the northern part of the United States.

north′ẽrn·ly, *adv.* toward the north. [Obs.]

north′ẽrn·mōst, *a.* situated at the point farthest north.

north′ing, *n.* 1. in astronomy, the distance in degrees that a heavenly body is north of the celestial equator; northern declination.
2. in navigation, the variation in latitude toward the north from the last reckoning of position.

north′land, *n.* 1. the northern region of a country; land in the north.
2. [N–] (a) the northern part of the earth; (b) the Scandinavian Peninsula. [Poetic.]

north′land·ẽr, *n.* a native or inhabitant of the northland.

North′măn, *n.*; *pl.* **North′men,** 1. a Norseman.
2. a native or inhabitant of the north of Europe.

north′mōst, *a.* situated farthest to the north; northernmost.

north′ness, *n.* the tendency of the end of a magnetic needle to point to the north. [Rare.]

north′-north·ēast′, *n.* the direction, or the point on a mariner's compass, halfway between due north and northeast; 22°30′ east of due north.

north′-north·ēast′, *a.* and *adv.* 1. in or toward north-northeast.
2. from north-northeast, as a wind.

north′-north·west′, *n.* the direction, or the point on a mariner's compass, halfway between due north and northwest; 22°30′ west of due north.

north′-north·west′, *a.* and *adv.* 1. in or toward north-northwest.
2. from north-northwest, as a wind.

North Pōle, the northern end of the earth's axis: its zenith (called the *north pole of the heavens*) is slightly more than 1° from Polaris, the North Star.

North Stär, Polaris, the bright star almost directly above the northern end of the earth's axis; the polestar.

North·um′bri·ăn, *a.* 1. of Northumbria, its people, or their dialect.
2. of Northumberland, its people, or their dialect.

North·um′bri·ăn, *n.* 1. a native or inhabitant of Northumbria.
2. the Anglo-Saxon dialect of Northumbria.
3. a native or inhabitant of Northumberland.
4. the dialect of Northumberland.

north′wărd, *n.* a northward direction, point, or region.

north′wărd, *a.* toward the north.

north′wărd, north′wărds, *adv.* toward the north.

north′wărd·ly, *a.* and *adv.* 1. toward the north.
2. from the north.

north′west, *n.* 1. the direction or the point on a mariner's compass, halfway between north and west; 45° west of due north.
2. a district or region in or toward this direction.
the Northwest; (a) the northwestern part of the United States when its western boundary was the Mississippi; (b) the northwestern

part of the United States, especially Washington, Oregon, and Idaho; (c) the northwestern part of Canada.

north·west′, *a.* 1. in, of, toward, or facing the northwest; as, the *northwest* coast.

2. from the northwest; as, a *northwest* wind.

Northwest Passage; a passage for ships from the Atlantic Ocean into the Pacific by the northern coastal waters of the American continent, long sought for, and at last discovered in 1850–1 by Sir R. McClure.

Northwest Territory; a region north of the Ohio, between Pennsylvania and the Mississippi, ceded (1783) by England to the United States: it now forms Ohio, Indiana, Illinois, Michigan, Wisconsin, and part of Minnesota.

north·west′, *adv.* in, from, or toward the northwest.

north·west′ bȳ north, the direction, or the point on a mariner's compass, halfway between northwest and north-northwest; 11°15′ north of northwest.

north·west′ bȳ west, the direction, or the point on a mariner's compass, halfway between northwest and west-northwest; 11°15′ west of northwest.

north·west′ẽr, *n.* a strong wind or storm from the northwest.

north·west′ẽr·ly, *a.* and *adv.* 1. in or toward the northwest.

2. from the northwest, as a wind.

north·west′ẽrn, *a.* 1. pertaining to or being in the northwest, or in a direction to the northwest; as, a *northwestern* course.

2. from the northwest; as, a *northwestern* wind.

3. [N–] of or characteristic of the Northwest.

north·west′wȧrd, *a.* and *adv.* toward the northwest.

north·west′wȧrd, *n.* a northwestward direction, point, or region.

north·west′wȧrd·ly, *a.* and *adv.* 1. toward the northwest.

2. from the northwest, as a wind.

north·west′wȧrds, *adv.* northwestward.

Nor′wāy rat, the common brown rat, which is larger than the black English rat.

Nor·wē′ġiăn (-jăn), *a.* of Norway, its people, their language, or culture.

Nor·wē′ġiăn, *n.* 1. a native or inhabitant of Norway.

2. either of two official forms of the North Germanic language of the Norwegians, one ("Book Language") derived from Danish, or the other ("New Norwegian") created c. 1850 from Norwegian dialects.

nōse, *n.* [AS. *nasu, nosu, næse*; compare Ice. *nōs*, Dan. *næse*, Sw. *näsa*, L. *nasus*, Sans. *nāsā, nasā*, nose.]

1. the part of the face between the mouth and the eyes, having two openings for breathing and smelling.

2. the part that corresponds to this in animals; snout; muzzle.

3. the sense of smell.

4. (a) scent; (b) power of tracking or perceiving by or as if by scent.

5. anything resembling a nose in shape or position; projecting or foremost part, as a nozzle, spout, prow of a ship, etc.

6. a spy; informer. [Brit. Slang.]

7. the arched portion of the frame of eyeglasses or spectacles, above the bridge of the nose.

by a nose; (a) in horse racing, etc., by the length of the animal's nose; hence, (b) by a very small margin.

nose of wax; one who is very easily controlled or influenced.

on the nose; (a) in racing, that (a specified horse, etc.) will finish first; (b) precisely; exactly. [Slang.]

to count noses; to count heads; to ascertain the number of people present, voting, etc.

to cut off one's nose to spite one's face; to injure one's own interests in a fit of anger, resentment, etc.

to follow one's nose; to move straight forward.

to lead by the nose; to dominate completely; to lead at will.

to look down one's nose at; to be disdainful of. [Colloq.]

to pay through the nose; to pay an unreasonable price.

to poke, stick, or *thrust one's nose into*; to interfere with; to pry into.

to put one's nose out of joint; (a) to secure the place of another in some person's favor; (b) to ruin one's plans, hopes, etc.

to turn up one's nose at; to show contempt for.

under one's (*very*) *nose*; in plain view.

nōse, *v.t.*; nosed, *pt., pp.*; nosing, *ppr.* 1. to discover or perceive by or as if by the sense of smell; to scent.

2. to touch or press against with the nose; as, the colt *nosed* its mother.

3. to oppose to the face; to face insolently

4. to utter in a nasal manner; to twang through the nose.

5. to make or push (a way, etc.) with the front forward; as, the ship *nosed* its way into the harbor.

6. to defeat by a very small margin (with *out*).

nōse, *v.i.* 1. to smell; to sniff.

2. to pry into what does not concern one.

3. to advance; to move forward.

to nose around; to sniff or smell over a surface, as a dog seeking a scent; also to pry secretly; to investigate in a stealthy manner, as one seeking information.

to nose over; in aviation, to turn over while taxiing by striking the front or nose of the ship against the ground.

nō·sē′ăn, *n.* [named after Karl W. *Nose*, a German geologist.] a silicate of aluminum of a brownish or bluish-gray color crystallizing in dodecahedrons.

nōse bag, same as *feed bag*.

nōse′band, *n.* that part of a bridle which comes over a horse's nose, and is attached to the cheek straps.

nōse bit, a bit similar to a gouge bit, having a cutting edge on one side of its end.

nōse′bleed, *n.* 1. a hemorrhage or bleeding from the nose.

2. any of several plants, as *Achillea millefolium*, birthroot, or wake robin.

nōse′bûrn, *n.* a tree, *Daphnopsis tenuifolia*, of the spurge laurels, indigenous to the West Indies.

nōse çōne, the cone-shaped foremost part of a rocket or missile, made to withstand intense heat.

nōsed, *a.* having a nose; especially, having a nose of a certain kind: mostly used in compounds, as in long-*nosed*.

nōse′-dīve, *v.t.*; nose-dived, *pt., pp.*; nose-diving, *ppr.* to make a nose dive.

nōse dive, 1. a swift, steep downward plunge of an airplane, with the nose toward the earth.

2. any sudden, sharp drop.

nōse drops, medication administered through the nose with a dropper.

nōse′fish, *n.* the batfish, *Malthe vespertilio*.

nōse′gāy, *n.* a bunch of flowers chosen for their fragrance; a small bouquet; a posy.

nōse′gāy tree, a tree of the dogbane family, as *Plumeria rubra*.

nōse guärd (gärd), in football, the defensive lineman whose position in a three-man or five-man line is directly opposite the offensive center.

nōse′hōle, *n.* a hole in the side of a glass furnace at which a globe of crown glass may be heated until soft enough to work.

nōse lēaf, a broad, thin, vertical expansion of the skin of the nose of certain bats, used as an organ of touch.

nōse′less, *a.* not having a nose.

nō′se·līte, *n.* same as *nosean*.

nōse′pieçe, *n.* 1. anything like a nose in form or position, as the nozzle of a hose or pipe.

2. in optics, that part which holds the object glass of a microscope.

3. a noseband.

4. a piece attached to a helmet and intended to protect the nose.

5. loosely, the bridge of a pair of glasses.

nōse pīpe, the inner nozzle of the blast pipe of a tuyère.

nōse ring, 1. a ring of bone or metal worn in the nose as an ornament.

2. a metal ring passed through the nose of an animal, as a bull, a pig, etc., for leading it about.

nōse taç′kle, same as *nose guard*; often, specifically, such a player in a three-man line.

nōse′thīrl, nōse′thrill, *n.* nostril. [Obs.]

nōs′ēy, *a.*; *comp.* nosier; *superl.* nosiest; nosy.

nosh, *v.t.* and *v.i.* [from Yid., from G. *naschen*, to nibble, taste.] to eat (a snack). [Slang.]

nosh, *n.* a snack. [Slang.]

nō′-shōw′, *n.* a person who makes a reservation, as for an airline flight, but fails to claim or cancel it. [Colloq.]

nōs′ing, *n.* [from *nose*, n. and *-ing*.]

1. the projecting edge of a step; that part of the tread which extends beyond the riser.

2. a strip, as of metal, for protecting this edge from wear.

3. any projection like a stair nosing.

nō′sīte, *n.* nosean. [Rare.]

no′sle, *n.* a nozzle. [Obs.]

nōs′ō-, [from Gr. *nosos*, disease.] a combining form meaning *disease*, as in *noso*logy: also, before a vowel, *nos-*.

nos·ō·çō′mi·ăl, *a.* [*noso-*, and Gr. *komein*, to care for.] relating to a hospital.

nō·sog′ē·ny, *n.* same as *pathogeny*.

nō·sog′rȧ·phy, *n.* [*noso-* and *-graphy*.] the science of the description of diseases.

nos·ō·log′iç·ăl, *a.* of or in nosology.

nō·sol′ō·ġist, *n.* one who classifies diseases.

nō·sol′ō·ġy, *n.* [*noso-* and *-logy*.]

1. a systematic arrangement or classification of diseases.

2. that branch of medical science which treats of the classification of diseases.

nos″ō·pō·et′iç, *a.* producing diseases. [Obs.]

nōst, a contraction of *ne wost*, knowest not. [Obs.]

nos·tal′ġi·ȧ, *n.* [Gr. *nostos*, a return, and *algos*, pain, grief.]

1. homesickness; a longing to go back to one's home, home town, or homeland.

2. a longing for something far away or long ago.

nos·tal′ġiç, *a.* of, having, or causing nostalgia.

nos·tal′ġy, *n.* nostalgia. [Rare.]

Nos′toç, *n.* [G. *nostok, nostoch*.] a genus of the lowest group of algae, abundant in fresh water and sometimes on other plants: known as *witches'-butter, fallen star, star spittle*, etc., because of suddenly swelling into a gelatinous mass after summer showers, and hence being thought to have fallen from the skies.

nos·tō·log′iç, *a.* of nostology.

nos·tol′ō·ġy, *n.* [Gr. *nostos*, a return, and *-logy*.] the scientific study of old age in man and animals; geriatrics.

nos·tō·mā′ni·ȧ, *n.* in psychiatry, excessive or abnormal nostalgia.

nos′tri·fi·çāte, *v.t.* [L. *noster*, our, and *facere*, to make.] to receive as, or to place on equal terms with, one's own: said of the degrees granted or diplomas given by another college, university, or the like.

nos′tril, *n.* [ME. *nosethril, nosethirl, nosethurle*; AS. *næsthyrl, nasthyrl*, lit., nosehole; *nosu, nasu*, nose, and *thyrl, thyrel*, hole.]

1. either of the external openings of the nose, through which air is inhaled and exhaled; a naris.

2. acuteness; perception. [Obs.]

nos′trum, *n.*; *pl.* **nos′trums,** [L., neut. of *noster*, ours.]

1. (a) a medicine the ingredients of which are kept secret for the purpose of restricting the profits of sale to the inventor or proprietor; (b) a quack medicine; (c) a patent medicine.

2. any quack device, scheme, or plan; a panacea.

nō′sy, *a.*; *comp.* nosier; *superl.* nosiest, provided with a large or conspicuous nose; also, prying; inquisitive. [Colloq.]

not, know not: a contraction of *ne wot*. [Obs.]

not, *a.* shaven; shorn. [Obs.]

not, *adv.* [ME. *not, noht, nought, naught*; AS. *naht, noht, nawiht*, lit., not a whit; *ne*, not, *a*, ever, and *wiht*, a thing.] a word that expresses negation, denial, refusal, or prohibition, or the reverse, opposite, or lack of the state, action, or condition of the word or phrase it modifies. It is sometimes used elliptically (e.g., whether you like it or *not*). In the Bible it is often used in the sense of *not living*; as, Rachel would not be comforted, for they (her children) were *not*.

nōt-, noto-.

nō′tȧ bē′nē, [L.] observe well; take particular notice: usually written *N. B.*

nō·tȧ·bil′i·ȧ, *n.pl.* [L.] notable things; things worthy of notice.

nō·tȧ·bil′i·ty, *n.*; *pl.* **nō·tȧ·bil′i·ties,** 1. notableness.

2. a remarkable or notable person or thing.

3. a noteworthy remark. [Obs.]

nō′tȧ·ble, *a.* [OFr. *notable*; L. *notabilis*, from *notare*, to mark, note, from *nota*, a mark.]

1. worthy of notice; remarkable; memorable; noted or distinguished.

2. conspicuous; easily seen or observed; manifest; observable. [Obs.]

3. notorious; well or publicly known.
A most *notable* coward, and infinite and endless liar. —Shak.
4. (*also* not'ȧ-ble), industrious, capable, or efficient in housekeeping: said of women. [Dial.]

nŏt'ȧ·ble, *n.* 1. a person, or rarely thing, of note or distinction.
2. [N–] in French history, one of the nobles or notable men selected by the king to form a parliament or representative body (Assembly of the Notables) in emergencies.

nŏt'ȧ·ble·ness, *n.* the state or quality of being notable.

nŏt'ȧ·bly, *adv.* 1. in a notable manner.
2. to a notable degree.

nō·tȧ·çan'thous, *a.* [Gr. *nōtos*, the back, and *akantha*, a spine.] having notal spines.

nō·tae'um, *n.* [Gr. *nōtaios*, of the back, from *nōtos*, the back.]
1. the back, as of a fowl.
2. a protective dorsal plate of certain tectibranchiates.

nō'tăl, *a.* [Gr. *nōtos*, the back.] belonging to the back; dorsal.

nō·tal'ġi·ȧ, *n.* [Gr. *nōtos*, the back, and *algos*, pain.] in pathology, pain in the back; irritation of the spine.

nō·tan'dum, *n.*; *pl.* **nō·tan'dȧ,** [L., from *notare*, to note, observe.] a thing to be observed or noted.

nō·tăr'i·ăl, *a.* 1. pertaining to a notary.
2. drawn up or executed by a notary.

nō·tăr'i·ăl·ly, *adv.* in a notarial manner.

nō'tȧ·rīze, *v.t.*; notarized, *pt., pp.*; notarizing, *ppr.* to certify or attest (a document) as a notary.

nō'tȧ·ry, *n.*; *pl.* **nō'tȧ·rieṣ,** [L. *notarius*, a clerk, secretary, writer, from *nota*, a mark.]
1. historically, a person employed to take notes of contracts, trials, and proceedings in courts among the Romans.
2. in modern usage, an official authorized to certify or attest documents, take depositions and affidavits, etc.

nō'tȧ·ry pub'liç, *pl.* **nō'tȧ·rieṣ pub'liç,** a notary.

nō'tāte, *a.* [L. *notatus*, pp. of *notare*, to mark.] in botany, marked with variously colored spots or lines.

nō·tā'tion, *n.* [L. *notatio* (-*onis*), from *notare*, to mark.]
1. the use of a system of signs or symbols to represent words, phrases, numbers, quantities, etc.
2. any such system of signs or symbols, as in arithmetic, algebra, music, etc.
3. a noting.
4. a note; an annotation.
5. etymological signification. [Obs.]

nō·tā'tion·ăl, *a.* of notation.

nō'tȧ·tive, *a.* self-explanatory, as distinguished from symbolical: used in referring to words, etc., that suggest their own characteristics.

notch, *n.* [a softened form of ME. *nock*, a notch.]
1. a V-shaped cut in an edge or across a surface; a nick; an indentation.
2. an opening or narrow passage, as through a mountain or hill; a defile.
3. a step; grade; degree; peg; as, his average dropped a *notch*. [Colloq.]
4. a depressed or indented portion of a bone; as, the ethmoidal *notch*.
the top notch; the highest point of attainment or effort; as, *the top notch* of prosperity.

notch, *v.t.*; notched (nocht), *pt., pp.*; notching, *ppr.* 1. to cut a notch or notches in; to nick; to indent; as, to *notch* a stick.
2. to place in a notch; to fit to a string by the notch, as an arrow.
3. to mark or score by notches.

notch'bōard, *n.* a board notched or grooved to receive the ends of the steps of a wooden stair.

notch'ing, *n.* 1. the act of cutting notches.
2. a notch or series of notches.
3. a system of excavating by a series of steps.
4. a mode of fastening timbers together in carpentry.

notch'weed, *n.* a plant, *Chenopodium vulvaria*: also called *stinking goosefoot*.

notch'wing, *n.* a kind of moth, *Rhacodia caudana*. [Brit.]

nōte, know not; a contraction of *ne wot*. [Obs.]

nōte, *n.* need. [Obs.]

nōte, *n.* nut. [Obs.]

nōte, *n.* [Fr. *note*, from L. *nota*, a mark, a sign, a shorthand character, a letter, from *notus*, pp. of *noscere*, to know.]
1. a mark or token by which a thing may be known; a visible sign; a symbol; a distinguishing characteristic; as, a *note* of power and grandeur.
2. importance, distinction, or eminence; as, a person of *note*.
3. any sign or character, other than a letter, used in writing or printing; as, a *note* of interrogation (?); a *note* of reference (*).
4. (a) a brief statement of a fact, experience, etc. written down for review, as an aid to memory, or to inform someone else; a memorandum; (b) [*pl.*] a record of experiences, etc.; as, the *notes* of a journey.
5. a comment, explanation, or elucidation, as at the foot of a page; an annotation.
6. notice; heed; observation; as, please take *note* of this.
7. any of certain types of correspondence, as a short informal letter or a formal diplomatic or other official communication.
8. any of certain commercial papers, some of which are negotiable, relating to the owing of debts or payment of money; as, a promissory *note*, a bank *note*.
9. a cry; call; sound.
10. the cry or call of a bird.
11. a signal or intimation; as, a *note* of admonition.
12. a melody, tune, or song. [Archaic or Poet.]
13. in music, (a) a tone of definite pitch, as made by a voice or musical instrument; (b) a symbol for a tone, indicating the duration by its form and the pitch by its position on the staff; (c) a key of a piano or similar musical instrument.
14. [*pl.*] the verbatim or condensed report of a discourse, an interview, court proceedings, etc., taken by a reporter or shorthand writer.
15. a small size of paper used for writing letters or notes.
16. reproach; shame; stigma. [Obs.]
17. account; intelligence; information. [Obs.]
to compare notes; to exchange views; to discuss.
to strike the right note; to say, write, or do what is specially suitable.
to take notes; to put facts, events, conversations, etc. in writing for later reference.

A B C D E F G H

MUSICAL NOTES
A, whole note; B, half notes; C, quarter notes; D, eighth notes; E, sixteenth notes; F, thirty-second notes; G, sixty-fourth notes; H, double notes

nōte, *v.t.*; noted, *pt., pp.*; noting, *ppr.* [L. *notare*, to mark, write in cipher, note, from *nota*, a mark, note.]
1. to observe; to notice with particular care; to heed; to attend to.
2. to set down in writing; to record; as, he *noted* down every word they said.
3. to mention particularly.
4. to indicate; to signify; to denote.
5. to furnish with notes; to anotate.
6. to write out in musical notes.
7. to charge, as with a crime: with *of* or *for*. [Obs.]
to note an exception; in law, to include in the minutes of proceedings any exception taken by counsel to a ruling of the court during a trial.
to note a protest; in maritime law, to serve notice before a consul or other official of the intention of the master of a vessel to enter a protest for damage to his vessel or loss of cargo as soon as the amount can be ascertained.

nōte'book, *n.* 1. a book in which notes, or memorandums, are written.
2. a record book for registering promissory notes.

nōt'ed, *a.* 1. observed; noticed.
2. remarkable; well-known by reputation or report; eminent; celebrated; as, a *noted* author.
Syn.—distinguished, illustrious, renowned, famous.

nōt'ed·ly, *adv.* conspicuously.

nōt'ed·ness, *n.* the quality of being noted.

nōte'fụl, *a.* serviceable. [Obs.]

nōte'less, *a.* 1. not attracting notice; not conspicuous.
2. unmusical; voiceless.

nōte'less·ness, *n.* the state of being noteless.

nōte'let, *n.* a short note.

note of hand, a promissory note.

nōte pā'pĕr, paper for writing notes (letters).

nōt'ĕr, *n.* 1. one who takes notice.
2. an annotator. [Rare.]

nōte'wŏr·thi·ly, *adv.* in a noteworthy manner; so as to be noteworthy.

nōte'wŏr·thi·ness, *n.* the quality or condition of being noteworthy.

nōte'wŏr·thy, *a.* worthy of observation or notice; outstanding; remarkable; notable.

not'-head"ed (-hed"), *a.* having the hair clipped close; shaven. [Obs.]

nŏth'ĕr, *a.* and *conj.* neither. [Obs.]

nŏth'ing, *n.* [AS. *nān thing*; *nān*, none, no, and *thing*, thing.]
1. not anything; no thing; not any being or existence: the opposite of *anything, something*; as, I opened the chest, but there was *nothing* in it.
2. (a) lack of existence; nonexistence; nothingness; (b) insignificance; unimportance.
3. a thing that does not exist.
4. (a) something of little or no value, seriousness, importance, etc.; triviality; (b) a person considered of no value or importance.
5. in mathematics, lack of any quantity either plus or minus; zero.
6. no part, quantity, or degree; as, the troops showed *nothing* of their fatigue.
for nothing; (a) free; at no cost; (b) in vain; uselessly; (c) without reason.
next to nothing; very little; nearly nothing.
nothing but; except; only; no other; as, he will buy *nothing but* the best of everything; a man who possesses *nothing but* worldly wealth is poor indeed.
nothing doing; (a) no: used as a refusal of a request to do something; (b) no result, accomplishment, etc.: an exclamation of disappointment. [Colloq.]
nothing less than; no less than; just the same as: also *nothing short of*.
nothing off; in nautical terms, a direction to the steersman to keep the ship close to the wind.
to make nothing of; (a) to treat lightly or as of little consequence; as, we *make nothing of* hardships endured to accomplish our selfish purposes; (b) to fail in understanding; as, I can *make nothing of* this puzzle; (c) to fail to use or do.
to think nothing of; to regard as unimportant, easy, etc.

nŏth'ing, *adv.* in no degree; not at all.
Adam, with such counsel *nothing* swayed. —Milton

nŏth·ing·ăr'i·ăn, *n.* a person who has no particular religious belief, or who belongs to no special sect; an unbeliever.

nŏth·ing·iṣm, *n.* nothingness; a theory or doctrine without a foundation of principles.

nŏth'ing·ness, *n.* 1. the quality or condition of being nothing; lack of existence; extinction.
2. lack of value or worth; uselessness; insignificance.
3. unconsciousness.
4. anything that is nonexistent, worthless, insignificant, etc.

nō'tice (-tis), *n.* [OFr. *notice*, from L. *notitia*, a being known, knowledge, from *notus*, pp. of *noscere*, to know.]
1. information, announcement, or warning; especially, formal announcement or warning, as in a newspaper; as, a legal *notice*.
2. a short article about a work of art, book, play, etc.
3. a written or printed sign giving some public information, warning, or rule.
4. (a) the act of observing; attention; regard; heed; cognizance; (b) courteous attention; civility.
5. a formal announcement or warning of intention to end an agreement, relation, or contract at a certain time; as, the tenant gave *notice*.
to serve notice; to give formal warning or information, as of intentions; to announce.
to take notice; to take cognizance; to become aware; to pay attention; to observe.

nō'tice, *v.t.*; noticed (-tist), *pt., pp.*; noticing, *ppr.* 1. (a) to mention; to refer to; to comment on; (b) to review briefly.
2. (a) to regard; to observe; to pay atten-

 fāte, fär, fȧst, fạll, finăl, cãre, at; mēte, prẹy, hēr, met; pīne, marïne, bïrd, pin; nōte, möve, fọr, atŏm, not; mọọn, book;

tion to; (b) to be courteous, civil, or responsive to.

3. to serve with a notice; to give formal warning to. [Rare.]

nō′tice·ȧ·ble, *a.* 1. capable of being observed; worthy of observation; significant.

2. easily seen; conspicuous.

nō′tice·ȧ·bly, *adv.* 1. in a noticeable manner;

2. to a noticeable degree.

nō′ti·cẽr, *n.* one who notices.

nō·ti·dā′ni·ăn, *n.* [Gr. *nōtidanos*, with pointed dorsal fin; *nōtos*, back, and *idanos*, fair, comely.] any shark of the *Hexanchidæ*, a family of sharks having six or seven gill openings.

nō·tid′ȧ·nid, nō·ti·dan′i·dăn, *n.* same as *notidanian.*

nō·tid′ȧ·nid, nō·ti·dan′i·dăn, *a.* same as *notidanoid.*

nō·tid′ȧ·noid, *a.* resembling a notidanian.

nō·tid′ȧ·noid, *n.* a notidanoid shark.

nō′ti·fī·ȧ·ble, *a.* of such a nature that notice must be given; as, scarlet fever is *notifiable* to the health board.

nō″ti·fi·cā′tion, *n.* 1. a notifying or being notified.

2. the notice given or received.

3. the writing used to convey such a notice; an advertisement, citation, etc.

nō′ti·fī·ẽr, *n.* a person or thing that notifies.

nō′ti·fȳ, *v.t.*; notified, *pt.*, *pp.*; notifying, *ppr.* [OFr. *notifier*, from L. *notificare*; *notus*, known, and *facere*, to make.]

1. to make known; to declare; to publish. [Chiefly Brit.]

2. to give notice to; to inform; to announce to.

3. to note; to observe. [Obs.]

nō′tion, *n.* [OFr. *notion*, from L. *notio* (*-onis*), an examination, conception, idea, from *notus*, pp. of *noscere*, to know.]

1. (a) conception; mental image; (b) a vague thought.

2. sentiment; opinion; view.

3. a desire; an inclination; a whim.

4. an intention; as, I have no *notion* of going yet.

5. [*pl.*] small, useful articles, as needles, thread, etc., sold in a store.

6. sense; understanding; intellectual power. [Obs.]

nō′tion·ăl, *a.* 1. of, expressing, or consisting of notions, or concepts.

2. imaginary; not actual; as, a *notional* value of one's own skills.

3. having visionary ideas; given to whims; fanciful.

4. in grammar, (a) having full lexical, as distinguished from relational, meaning; (b) of the meaning expressed by a linguistic form.

5. in semantics, presentive.

nō·tion·al′i·ty, *n.* the state or condition of being notional.

nō′tion·ăl·ly, *adv.* in a notional manner.

nō′tion·āte, *a.* notional. [Rare.]

nō′tion·ist, *n.* one who has whimsical notions.

nō′tist, *n.* a commentator. [Obs.]

nō′tō-, [from Gr. *nōton*, the back.] a combining form meaning *the back, dorsum*, as in *notochord*: also, before a vowel, *not-*.

Nō″tō·brañ·chi·ā′tȧ, *n.pl.* [*noto-*, and Gr. *branchia*, gills.]

1. same as *Dorsibranchiata.*

2. same as *Prosobranchiata.*

nō·tō·brañ′chi·āte, *a.* belonging or pertaining to the *Notobranchiata.*

nō′tō·chord, *n.* [*noto-*, and Gr. *chordē*, a string.]

1. a rod-shaped, elastic structure of cells forming the primitive supporting axis of the body in the lowest vertebrates.

2. a similar structure in the embryonic stages of higher vertebrates, which later develops into the backbone.

nō·tō·chor′dăl, *a.* 1. pertaining to the notochord.

2. having a notochord.

nō·tō·don′tiăn, *n.* [*not-*, and Gr. *odous*, *odontos*, a tooth.] any of various moths of which the larvae have a dorsal spine or hump.

nō·tō·don′tid, *a.* pertaining to the notodontians.

nō·tō·don′tid, *n.* same as *notodontian.*

nō·tō·don′toid, *a.* pertaining to or resembling notodontians.

nō·tō·don′toid, *n.* same as *notodontian.*

Nō·tō·gae′ȧ, *n.* [Mod. L., from Gr. *notos*, the south, and *gaia*, earth, land.] a primary zoological region of the earth's land area, including Australia, New Zealand, and the Neotropical regions.

Nō·tō·gae′ăn, Nō·tō·gē′ăn, *a.* of or from Notogaea.

nō·tō·neç′tăl, *a.* having the back below in swimming, as certain insects.

nō·tō·neç′tid, *n.* [*noto-*, and Gr. *nēktēs*, a swimmer.] a boat fly.

nō·tō·neç′tid, *a.* of or pertaining to a boat fly.

nō·tō·pō′di·um, *n.*; *pl.* **nō·tō·pō′di·ȧ,** [*noto-*, and Gr. *pous*, *podos*, foot.] the dorsal or upper lobe of a parapodium.

nō·tō·rhī′zăl (-rī′), *a.* [*noto-*, and Gr. *rhiza*, a root.] in botany, having the back of a cotyledon resting against the radicle.

nō·tō·rī′e·ty, *n.*; *pl.* **nō·tō·rī′e·tieṣ,** [Fr. *notoriété*, from LL. *notorius*, well known.]

1. the state or quality of being notorious; the state of being publicly or generally known.

2. a prominent or well-known person.

nō·tō′ri·ous, *a.* [L. *notorius*, pointing out, making known (LL., well-known), from *notus*, pp. of *noscere*, to know.]

1. well-known; publicly discussed. [Rare.]

2. widely but unfavorably known or talked about.

nō·tō′ri·ous·ly, *adv.* in a notorious manner.

nō·tō′ri·ous·ness, *n.* the state of being notorious.

Nō·tor′nis, *n.* [Gr. *notos*, the south or southwest, and *ornis*, a bird.] a genus of rare or extinct nonflying birds, formerly found in New Zealand and adjacent islands. The species resemble gallinules, but the wings are quite rudimentary.

Nō·tō·thē′ri·um, *n.* [Gr. *notos*, the south, and *thērion*, a wild beast.] an extinct genus of gigantic Australian marsupials.

Nō·tō·trē′mȧ, *n.* [*noto-*, and Gr. *trēma*, a perforation, hole.] a genus of South American marsupial frogs.

nō·tō·trem′ȧ·tous, *a.* having an aperture in the back for young, as a frog of the genus *Nototrema.*

nō′tō·trībe, *a.* [*noto-*, and Gr. *tribein*, to rub.] rubbing the back: applied to certain flowers having the styles and stamens so placed that they rub the backs of insects and assure cross-fertilization.

nō·tōur′, *a.* notorious; well-known: also written *nottour.* [Scot.]

Nō′tre Dāme′ (nō′tr dām′), [Fr.] 1. Our Lady (Mary, mother of Jesus).

2. a famous early Gothic cathedral in Paris: in full, *Notre Dame de Paris.*

nō′-trump, *a.* 1. without trumps.

2. in bridge, designating or of a bid to play with no suit being trumps.

nō′-trump, *n.* 1. a bid in bridge to play with no suit being trumps.

2. the hand so played.

not′self, *n.* the nonego.

nott, *a.* not. [Obs.]

not·tur′nō, *n.* [It.] in music, a nocturne.

nō′tum, *n.*; *pl.* **nō′tȧ,** [Gr. *nōton*, *nōtos*, the back.] in entomology, the back.

nō·tuñ′gū·lāte, *a.* [from Mod. L. *Notungulata*, name of the order.] of an extinct order of plant-eating mammals.

Nō′tus, *n.* [L.] the south or southwest wind.

not·with·stand′ing (*or* -with-), *prep.* in spite of; without hindrance or obstruction from; despite; as, they traveled on, *notwithstanding* the storm.

not·with·stand′ing, *adv.* nevertheless; however; as, they will do it, notwithstanding.

not·with·stand′ing, *conj.* although; in spite of the fact that.

nöu′găt (*or* -gä), *n.* [Fr., from L. *nux*, nut.] a confection of sugar and almonds or other nuts, stirred into a paste.

nought (nạt), *n.* [AS. *nowiht*, *nowhut*, from *ne*, not, and *owiht*, *awiht*, aught.]

1. nothing.

2. a person or thing considered of no value.

3. in arithmetic, the figure zero (0).

nought, *a.* worthless; useless.

nought, *adv.* in no way; not at all. [Archaic.]

nöuld, a contraction of *ne would*, would not. [Obs.]

nöu′mē·īte, nụ′mē·īte, *n.* [*Nouméa*, capital of New Caledonia, where it is found, and *-ite.*] same as *garnierite.*

nöu′mē·năl, *a.* in philosophy, of or pertaining to noumena or the noumenon: opposed to *phenomenal.*

nöu′mē·năl·iṣm, *n.* the doctrine maintaining the existence of noumena.

nöu′mē·năl·ly, *adv.* with respect to noumena.

nöu′mē·non, *n.*; *pl.* **nöu′mē·nȧ,** [Gr. *nooumenon*, anything perceived, neut. of *nooumenos*, ppr. pass. of *noein*, to perceive, from *noos*, the mind.] in Kantian philosophy, an object understood by intellectual intuition, without the aid of the senses: opposed to *phenomenon.*

noun, *n.* [OFr. *noun*, *nun*, *non*, *nom*, from L. *nomen*, name.]

1. in grammar, a name; a word used to denote a person, thing, action, quality, etc.

2. any word, phrase, or clause similarly used; a substantive.

noun′ăl, *a.* pertaining to a noun; having the character or qualities of a noun.

noun′ăl, *n.* a nominal.

noun′īze, *v.t.*; nounized, *pt.*, *pp.*; nounizing, *ppr.* to make a noun of, as an adjective, verb, etc.

noŭr′ice (nŭr′), *n.* a nurse. [Obs.]

noŭr′ish (nŭr′), *v.t.*; nourished, (-isht), *pt.*, *pp.*; nourishing, *ppr.* [ME. *norischen*, *norisen*, from OFr. *nurir*, *nurrir*, *norrir*, from L. *nutrire*, to nourish.]

1. to feed and cause to grow; to supply (any plant or animal) with matter necessary to life and growth.

2. to support; to maintain.

3. to supply the means of support and increase to; to encourage; as, to *nourish* rebellion.

4. to cherish; to comfort. [Obs.]

5. to educate; to instruct; to promote the growth of in attainments. [Obs.]

Nourished up in the words of faith.

—1 Tim. iv. 6.

nour′ish, *v.i.* 1. to promote growth; as, milk *nourishes.*

2. to gain nourishment. [Obs.]

nour′ish·ȧ·ble, *a.* 1. capable of being nourished; as, the *nourishable* parts of the body.

2. nutritious; capable of affording nourishment. [Obs.]

nour′ish·ẽr, *n.* one who or that which nourishes.

nour′ish·ing, *a.* promoting growth; nutritious; as, a *nourishing* diet.

nour′ish·ing·ly, *adv.* nutritively; in a nourishing manner.

nour′ish·ment, *n.* 1. a nourishing or being nourished; nutrition.

2. sustenance; nutriment; food; that which nourishes.

nöus, *n.* [Gr. *nous*, *noos*, mind, intelligence, perception.]

1. sharpness; wits; sense; understanding: often used humorously.

2. in philosophy, mind; understanding; intellect; reason.

nöu·veau′ riche (-vō′); *pl.* **nöu·veaux′ riches** (-vō′ rēsh), [Fr.] one who has recently become wealthy: often implying tasteless ostentation, lack of culture, etc.

nou·veau·té′ (nö-vō-tā′), *n.* [Fr.] a novelty.

nöu·velles′ (-vel′), *n.pl.* [Fr.] news.

nō′vȧ, *n.*; *pl.* **nō′vȧṣ, nō′vae,** [L., *nova* (*stella*), new (star), from *novus*, new.] in astronomy, a star that suddenly increases greatly in brilliance and then gradually grows fainter.

nō·vaç′ū·līte, *n.* [L. *novacula*, a razor, and *-ite.*] a hard, extremely fine-grained siliceous rock, supposedly sedimentary in origin: it is used for whetstones.

Nō′vȧ Sçō′tiăn, 1. of Nova Scotia, its people, or their culture.

2. a native or inhabitant of Nova Scotia.

Nō·vā′tiăn, *n.* a member of the religious sect founded by Novatianus, of Rome, in the third century.

Nō·vā′tiăn·iṣm, *n.* the beliefs or doctrines of the Novatians.

nō·vā′tion, *n.* [L. *novatio*, from *novare*, to make new, from *novus*, new.] in law, the substitution of a new obligation for an old one: any obligation may be legally terminated by novation.

nō·vā′tŏr, *n.* an innovator. [Rare.]

nov′el, *a.* [OFr. *novel*, *nouvel*, from L. *novellus*, dim. of *novus*, new.] new; of recent origin or introduction; not ancient; unusual; strange.

Syn.—new, rare, strange, uncommon, modern, unusual.

nov′el, *n.* [Fr. *nouvelle*, short story, or It. *novella*; both from L. *novella*, neut. pl. of *novellus*, dim. of *novus*, new; hence, orig., new things, news.]

1. [*usually in pl.*] a novella.

2. a relatively long fictional prose narrative with a more or less complex plot or pattern of events, about human beings, their feelings, thoughts, actions, etc.

3. the type or form of literature represented by such narratives (with *the*).

4. [*usually in pl.*] in Roman law, a new law or decree, specifically one made by Justinian supplementary to the Justinian Code.

nov·el·ette′, *n.* a short novel (usually about 30,000 to 50,000 words).

nov′el·iṣm, *n.* innovation. [Obs.]

nov'el·ist, *n.* 1. an innovator. [Obs.]
2. a writer of novels.
3. a writer of news. [Obs.]

nov·el·is'tiç, *a.* of, characteristic of, or like novels.

nov''el·i·zā'tion, *n.* a novelizing or being novelized.

nov'el·īze, *v.t.*; novelized, *pt., pp.*; novelizing, *ppr.* to give the form or characteristics of a novel to; to make into or like a novel.

nov'el·īze, *v.i.* to innovate. [Obs.]

nō·vel'lä, *n.*; *pl.* **nō·vel'le,** [It.] a short prose narrative, usually with a moral and often satiric, as any of the tales in Boccaccio's *Decameron*.

nov'el·ty, *n.*; *pl.* **nov'el·ties,** [L. *novellitas.*]
1. the quality of being new; newness; freshness.
Novelty is the great parent of pleasure. —South.
2. a new, fresh, or unusual thing; a change; innovation.
3. [*usually in pl.*] a small, often cheap, cleverly made article, usually for play or adornment.

nō'vem, *n.* [L., nine.] an old game of dice in which the two principal throws were nine and five.

Nō·vem'bēr, *n.* [L. *November,* or *Novembris* (supply *mensis,* month), the ninth month, according to the ancient Roman year, beginning in March, from *novem,* nine.] the eleventh month of the year, containing thirty days.

nō·vē'nȧ, *n.*; *pl.* **nō·vē'nȧs, nō·vē'nae,** [LL., neut. pl. of L. *novenus,* nine each.] in the Roman Catholic Church, the practicing of devotions during nine consecutive days, usually for some special religious purpose.

nov'ē·nār·y, *n.* [L. *novenarius,* from *novem,* nine.] nine units collectively.

nov'ē·nār·y, *a.* pertaining to the number nine.

nō'vēne, *a.* relating to or depending upon the number nine; proceeding by nines.

nō·ven'ni·ăl, *a.* [LL. *novennis,* of nine years, from *novem,* nine, and *annus,* a year.] occurring or done every ninth year.

nō·vēr'căl, *a.* [L. *noverca,* a stepmother.] pertaining to, like, or suitable to a stepmother.

nov'ice, *n.* [Fr., from L. *novicius,* new, fresh, from *novus,* new.]
1. one who has entered a religious group or order, but has not taken the final vows; a probationer.
2. one newly received into the church; specifically, one newly converted to the Christian faith.
3. one who is new in any business; one unacquainted or unskilled; a beginner; an inexperienced or untrained person.
I am young, a *novice* in the trade. —Dryden.
Syn.—beginner, learner, neophyte, tyro.

nō·vil·le'rō (-vil-lye'-), *n.*; *pl.* **nō·vil·le'rōs,** [Sp., from *novillo,* young bull, from L. *novus,* new.] a novice bullfighter.

nō·vi'ti·āte, nō·vi'ci·āte (-vish'i-), *n.* [L. *novitiatus,* novitiate, from L. *novicius,* new, fresh, from *novus,* new.]
1. the period of probation of a novice in a religious order.
2. the state or period of being a novice.
3. a novice.
4. the housing and training quarters of religious novices.

nov'i·ty, *n.* newness; novelty. [Obs.]

nō'vō·çain, nō'vō·çāine, *n.* [*novo-,* from L. *novus,* new, and *cocaine.*] an alkaloid compound resembling cocaine but less toxic and irritant, used as a local anesthetic; procaine: a trade-mark (*Novocain*).

nō'vum, *n.* same as *novem.*

nō'vus hō'mō, [L., a new man.] in ancient Rome, a man who had raised himself from obscurity to distinction without the aid of family connections; hence, a newly created noble; a parvenu; an upstart.

now, *adv.* [AS. *nu,* now.]
1. (a) at the present time; at this moment; (b) at once.
2. at the time referred to; then; next: usually in narrative, as, *now* a series of catastrophes occurred.
3. at a time very close to the present; specifically, (a) very recently; not long ago (with *just*); as, he left *just now*; (b) very soon (often with *just*); as, they are leaving *just now.*
4. given the situation; with things as they are; as, *now* we'll never know what happened.
Now is often used without any definite meaning, especially to introduce or emphasize; as, come *now,* don't be absurd.
now and again, now and then; at one time and another; occasionally; not often; at intervals.
now . . . now . . .; alternately; at this time . . . at another time . . . ; as, *now* up, *now* down.

now, *conj.* since; seeing that; as, *now* (that) the rain has come, we won't starve.

now, *a.* existing at the present; as, the *now* regime. [Obs.]

now, *n.* the present time or moment.
Nothing is there to come, and nothing past,
But an eternal *now* does ever last.
—Cowley.

now, *interj.* an exclamation expressing warning, reproach, etc.

now'ȧ·dāys, *adv.* in these days; at the present time; now.
What men of spirit *nowadays*
Come to give sober judgment of new plays?
—Garrick.

now'ȧ·dāys, *n.* the present time.

nō'wāy, *adv.* in no manner; by no means; not at all; nowise: now often written as two words (*no way*), pronounced with a rising stress, and used with the force of an interjection.

nō'wāys, *adv.* same as *noway.*

nōw'ed, *a.* [OFr. *nou,* a knot, from L. *nodus,* a knot.] in heraldry, knotted; tied in a knot, as a serpent or a lion's tail.

nōw·el, *n.* noel. [Archaic.]

now'el, *n.* [OFr. *noeil, nual,* the stone of a fruit, a newel, from L. *nucalis,* pertaining to a nut.]
1. a newel. [Obs.]
2. in iron founding, the inner portion, or core, of the mold for casting large hollow articles, as tanks, cisterns, etc.
3. the bottom, or drag, of a molding flask.

nō'whēre (-hwār), *adv.* not in any place or state.
nowhere near; not nearly; not by a wide margin.
to be (or *get*) *nowhere*; to have no success; to fail.

no'wheres (-hwārz), *adv.* nowhere. [Dial.]

nō'whith·ēr, *adv.* in no direction; toward no definite place.
Thy servant went *nowhither.*
—2 Kings v. 25.

nō'wīse, *adv.* [from *no* and *wise.*] not in any manner or degree; noway.

nowt, *n.pl.*; *sing.* **nowt,** [ON. *naut,* cattle.] cattle; oxen. [Scot. and Brit. Dial.]

now'y, *a.* [OFr. *noué,* knotted.] in heraldry, having a convex, thimble-shaped projection or curvature in or near the middle: said of a line, cross, or other bearing on a shield.

Nox, *n.* [L.] in Roman mythology, the goddess of night: identified with the Greek Nyx.

nox'ious (nok'shus), *a.* [L. *noxius,* from *noxa,* hurt, injury, from *nocere,* to hurt, injure.]
1. hurtful; harmful to health or morals; baneful; pernicious; injurious; unfavorable; destructive; unwholesome; insalubrious.
2. guilty; criminal. [Rare.]
Syn.—harmful, injurious, pernicious, baneful, pestilential, pestiferous, noisesome, insalubrious, unwholesome.

nox'ious·ly, *adv.* hurtfully; perniciously.

nox'ious·ness, *n.* hurtfulness; the quality that injures, impairs, or destroys; insalubrity.

no·yäde' (nwä-), *n.* [Fr., from *noyer,* to drown.] the act of drowning; specifically, the method of drowning political prisoners practiced at Nantes, France during the Reign of Terror. The prisoners were bound and dropped into the water from a boat with a movable bottom.

noy'ănce, *n.* annoyance. [Obs.]

noy·au' (nwä-yō'), *n.* [Fr. *noyau,* a stone of a fruit, from L. *nucalis,* like a nut, from *nux, nucis,* a nut.] a cordial made of brandy sweetened and variously flavored, as with orange peel, kernels of peach stones, bitter almonds, etc.

noz'zle, noz'le (-l), *n.* [dim. of *nose.*]
1. the small mouthpiece or spout of a hose, pipe, teakettle, pair of bellows, etc.
2. the nose; snout. [Slang.]

Np, in chemistry, neptunium.

-n't, a contracted and enclitic form of *not,* as in *aren't.*

nth (enth), *a.* 1. expressing the ordinal equivalent to *n.*
2. of the indefinitely large or small quantity represented by *n.*
to the nth degree (or *power*); (a) to an indefinite degree or power; (b) to an extreme.

nụ, *n.* [Gr. *ny.*] the thirteenth letter of the Greek alphabet, corresponding to English *N, n.*

nụ·änce', *n.* [Fr., a shading, from *nuer,* to shade, from *nue,* L. *nubes,* a cloud.]
1. each of the different gradations by which a color passes from its lightest to its darkest shade; shade.
2. a delicate degree of difference perceived by any of the senses, or by the mind; as, *nuances* of sound.

nub, *n.* [var. of *knob.*]
1. a knob; a lump.
2. the point of a story, etc.; gist. [Colloq.]

Nụ'bä, *n.*; *pl.* **Nụ'bä,** 1. a Nubian.
2. a member of a Negro tribe in the Sudan, related to the Nubians.
3. the language of the Nuba.

nub'bin, *n.* [dim. of *nub.*]
1. a small lump.
2. a small or imperfect ear of Indian corn.
3. an undeveloped fruit.

nub'ble, *n.* [dim. of *nub.*] a small knob or lump.

nub'bly, *a.*; *comp.* nubblier; *superl.* nubbliest; full of, or in the form of, nubbles.

nub'by, *a.*; *comp.* nubbier; *superl.* nubbiest; covered with small nubs, or lumps, as fabric with a rough, knotted weave.

nū·beç'ū·lȧ, *n.*; *pl.* **nū·beç'ū·lae,** [L. *nubecula,* a little cloud, dim. of *nubes,* a cloud.]
1. in astronomy, either of two clusters of nebulae in the southern hemisphere.
2. in medicine, (a) a speck or cloud in the cornea; (b) a cloudy appearance in the urine.

nū'bi·ȧ, *n.* [from L. *nubes,* a cloud.] a woman's light, fleecy, woolen wrap worn over the head and shoulders.

Nū'bi·ăn, *n.* 1. a member of a Negroid people of Nubia, in eastern Africa.
2. the language of Nubia.

Nū'bi·ăn, *a.* relating to Nubia, its people, or their language.

nū·big'e·nous, *a.* [L. *nubigena,* cloud-born; *nubes,* a cloud, and *-genus,* born.] produced by clouds.

nū'bi·lāte, *v.t.* [L. *nubilare,* to make cloudy, from *nubes,* a cloud.] to cloud; to obscure.

nū'bile, *a.* [L. *nubilis,* from *nubere*; to veil oneself, to marry.] marriageable: said of women, with reference to their age or physical development.

nū·bil'i·ty, *n.* the state of being nubile.

nū'bi·lous, *a.* [L. *nubilus,* from *nubes,* a cloud.]
1. cloudy; misty; foggy.
2. obscure; indefinite.

nū·cel'lăr, *a.* of a nucellus or nucelli.

nū·cel'lus, *n.*; *pl.* **nū·cel'lī,** [L. *nucella,* dim. of *nux, nucis,* a nut.] the central part of an ovule, in which the embryo is developed.

nū'çhȧ, *n.*; *pl.* **nū'çhae,** [LL. *nucha,* the nape of the neck.] the nape of the neck.

nū'çhăl, *a.* pertaining to or connected with the nucha; as, the *nuchal* region.

nū'ci-, [from L. *nux, nucis,* nut.] a combining form meaning *nut,* as in *nuciferous.*

nū·cif'ēr·ous, *a.* [*nuci-* and *-ferous.*] bearing or producing nuts.

nū'ci·form, *a.* [*nuci-* and *-form.*] formed like a nut; resembling a nut.

nū'çlē·ăl, *a.* same as *nuclear.*

nū'çlē·ăr, *a.* [L. *nucleatus,* having a kernel.] pertaining or relating to a nucleus; having the character of a nucleus; constituted by a nucleus; as *nuclear* fibers.

nū'çlē·ăr bomb, an explosive device that generates its energy by nuclear fission or fusion: see *atomic bomb* and *hydrogen bomb* under *hydrogen.*

nū'çlē·ăr fam'i·ly, a basic social unit consisting of parents and their children living in one household: cf. *extended family.*

nū'çlē·ăr fis'sion (fish'un), the splitting of the nuclei of atoms, accompanied by conversion of part of the mass into energy.

nū'çlē·ăr phys'içs, the branch of physics dealing with the structure of atomic nuclei and the energies involved in nuclear changes.

nū'çlē·ăr rē·aç'tŏr, a device for initiating and maintaining a controlled nuclear chain reaction in fissionable fuel for the production of energy or additional fissionable material.

nū'çlē·āte, nū'çlē·ā·ted, *a.* having a nucleus.

nū'çlē·āte, *v.t.*; nucleated, *pt., pp.*; nucleating, *ppr.* [L. *nucleatus,* pp. of *nucleare,* to become like a kernel, from *nucleus,* a little nut.] to form into or around a nucleus.

nū'çlē·āte, *v.i.* to form a nucleus.

nū·çlē·ā'tion, *n.* a nucleating or being nucleated.

nū'çlē·ī, *n.* plural of *nucleus.*

nū·çlē'iç ac'id, any of a group of acids occurring in organic nuclear material and consisting of a combination of phosphoric acid with a carbohydrate and a base.

nū·çlē'i·form, *a.* [L. *nucleus*, a kernel, and *forma*, form.] having the form of a nucleus.

nū'çlē·in, *n.* [*nucle*us and *-in*.] any of a group of colorless, amorphous protein substances found in all cell nuclei and consisting of nucleic acids combined with a base.

nū'çlē·ō-, [from L. *nucleus*, a kernel.] a combining form used in biology, physiology, etc. to denote *relation to* or *connection with a nucleus*; as, *nucleo*plasm.

nū″çlē·ō·al·bū'min, *n.* any one of a class of nucleins obtainable from the protoplasm of cells.

nū″çlē·ō·al·bū·min·ū'ri·à, *n.* the presence of nucleoalbumin in the urine.

nū'çlē·ō·brañçh, *n.* a mollusk of the order *Nucleobranchiata*, or *Heteropoda*.

nū'çlē·ō·brañçh, *a.* of or relating to the *Nucleobranchiata*, or *Heteropoda*.

nū″çlē·ō·his'ton, *n.* a phosphorized nucleoprotein obtained from the nuclei of lymphocytes.

nū·çlē'ō·lăr, *a.* of, or having the nature of, a nucleolus.

nū·çlē'ō·lāte, *a.* nucleolated.

nū·çlē'ō·lā·ted, *a.* having a nucleolus or nucleoli.

nū'çlē·ōle, *n.* same as *nucleolus*.

nū″çlē·ō·lī'nus, *n.* the nucleus of a nucleolus.

nū·çlē'ō·loid, *a.* resembling a nucleolus.

nū·çlē'ō·lus, *n.*; *pl.* **nū·çlē'ō·lī,** [L. *nucleolus*, dim. of *nucleus*, a little nut, kernel.] a conspicuous body, usually spherical, found in the nucleus of most cells.

nū'çlē·on, *n.* a proton or neutron in the nucleus of an atom.

nū·çlē·on'içs, *n. pl.* [*construed as sing.*], [*nucle*ar and electr*onics*.] the branch of physics dealing with nucleons or with nuclear action.

nū·çlē·op'ē·tăl, *a.* [*nucleo-*, and L. *petere*, to seek.] directed toward a nucleus.

nū'çlē·ō·plaşm, *n.* [from *nucleus* and *-plasm*.] the protoplasm that composes the nucleus of a cell.

nū″çlē·ō·plaş'miç, *a.* of, constituting, or like nucleoplasm.

nū″çlē·ō·prō'tē·in, nū″çlē·ō·prō'tē·id, *n.* from *nucleus* and *protein*.] any of a class of compound proteins found in the nuclei of plant and animal cells, consisting of a simple protein combined with a nuclein and either a pentose or a hexose.

nū'çlē·us, *n.*; *pl.* **nū'çlē·ī, nū'çlē·us·eş,** [L. *nucleus*, a little nut, kernel, dim. of *nux, nucis*, a nut.]

1. a thing or part forming the center, around which other parts or things are grouped or collected.

2. anything serving as a center of growth or development; as, the *nucleus* of an art collection.

3. in anatomy, a group of nerve cells in the brain or spinal column.

4. in astronomy, the bright central part of the head of a comet.

5. in biology, the central, spherical or egg-shaped mass of protoplasm present in most plant and animal cells and necessary to such functions as growth, reproduction, etc.

6. in botany, (a) a nucellus; (b) the kernel of a nut or seed; (c) the central point in a starch grain.

7. in chemistry and physics, the central part of an atom, the fundamental particles of which are the proton and neutron: it carries a positive charge and constitutes almost all of the mass of the atom.

8. in organic chemistry, a fundamental, stable arrangement of atoms (e.g., the benzene ring) that may occur in many compounds by atomic substitution without structural change.

Nū'çū·lȧ, *n.* [L., dim. of *nux, nucis*, a nut.] a genus of conchiferous mollusks of the family *Arcidæ*.

nū'çūle, *n.* [L. *nucula*, a little nut, dim. of *nux, nucis*, a nut.] in botany, a hard, small, one-seeded fruit; a small stone or seed.

nū'çū·lid, *n.* [L. *nucula*, a little nut.] a mollusk of the genus *Nucula*.

nū'çū·loid, *a.* relating to or having the appearance of a nuculid.

nū·dā'tion, *n.* [L. *nudatio (-onis)*, from *nudare*, to make bare or naked.] the act of stripping, or making bare or naked. [Rare.]

nūde, *a.* [L. *nudus*, naked.]

1. bare; naked; unclothed; specifically, in art, not covered with drapery.

2. in law, void; without consideration: said of contracts, etc.

3. in botany and zoology, bare; without leaves, hairs, feathers, or the external covering.

Syn.—naked, bare, unclothed, undraped.

nūde, *n.* [obs. Fr. *nud*, from L. *nudus*, naked.] a nude figure, especially as represented in painting, sculpture, etc.

the nude; (a) the nude human figure; (b) the representation of this in art; (c) the condition of being nude.

nudġe, *v.t.*; nudged, *pt., pp.*; nudging, *ppr.* to touch gently, as with the elbow, in order to call attention, hint slyly, etc.

nudġe, *n.* a slight push or touch with the elbow, etc.; jog.

nū'di-, [from L. *nudus*, naked, bare.] a combining form meaning *nude, bare*; as, *nudi*branchiate, *nudi*caul.

nū·di·braçh'i·āte, *a.* [*nudi-*, and L. *brachium*, the forearm.] with naked arms; in zoology, having tentacles but no vibratory swimming organs.

nū'di·brañçh, *n.* a nudibranchiate.

Nū·di·brañçh·i·ā'tȧ, *n.pl.* a suborder of mollusks lacking both a shell and true gills.

nū·di·brañ'çhi·āte, *a.* pertaining to the *Nudibranchiata*.

nū·di·brañ'çhi·āte, *n.* one of the *Nudribranchiata*.

nū·di·çau'dāte, *a.* [*nudi-*, and L. *cauda*, a tail.] having a naked tail.

nū'di·çaul, *a.* [*nudi-*, and L. *caulis*, a stem.] in botany, having leafless stems.

nū·di·çau'lous, *a.* same as *nudicaul*.

nū'dişm, *n.* the practice or cult of going nude for hygienic reasons.

nū'dist, *n.* a person who believes in nudism, or one who practices nudism.

nū'dist, *a.* of nudism or nudists.

nū·di·tăr'i·ăn, *n.* one who advocates the study of the nude.

nū'di·ty, *n.* [L. *nuditas*, from *nudus*, naked.]

1. the state, quality, or fact of being nude; nakedness.

2. *pl.* **nū'di·tieş,** anything nude.

nū'dum paç'tum, [L., nude contract.] in law, a contract made without any consideration and therefore void, or not valid according to the laws of the land; a nude pact.

nū·gac'i·ty, *n.* [L. *nugax*, from *nugæ*, trifles.] futility; trifling talk or behavior.

nū'gae, *n.pl.* [L.] trifles; trifling verses; light sayings.

nū·gā'tion, *n.* [L. *nugatus*, pp. of *nugari*, to jest, trifle.] the act or practice of trifling. [Obs.]

nū'gȧ·tō·ry, *a.* [L. *nugatorius*, trifling.]

1. trifling; vain; futile; insignificant; worthless.

2. of no force; inoperative; ineffectual; as, the laws are sometimes rendered *nugatory* by inexecution; any agreement may be rendered *nugatory* by something which contravenes its execution.

nug'găr, *n.* [Egypt.] a large Nile boat used for the transportation of freight and passengers.

nug'get, *n.* [prob. dim. of Brit. dial. *nug*, a lump.] a lump, block, or mass; especially, a lump of native gold.

nug'get·y, *a.* 1. having the shape of a nugget.

2. found in nuggets; containing many nuggets.

nū'gi·fȳ, *v.t.*; nugified, *pt., pp.*; nugifying, *ppr.* [L. *nugæ*, trifles, and *facere*, to make.] to make ridiculous; to make trifling. [Rare.]

nūi'sănce, *n.* [ME. *nusance*; OFr., from *nuisir, noisir*, from L. *nocere*, to annoy.] an act, condition, thing, or person causing trouble, annoyance, or inconvenience.

Syn.—offense, annoyance, plague, trouble, pest, dirtiness.

nūi'săn·cẽr, *n.* in law, one responsible for a nuisance.

nūi'sănce tax, a tax considered a nuisance because it is paid in very small amounts by the consumer.

nul, *a.* [Fr.] in law, no; not any; as, *nul* tort.

null, *v.t.* to annul.

null, *a.* [L. *nullus*, not any, none.]

1. without legal force; not binding; void; invalid.

2. amounting to nought; nit.

3. of no value, effect, or consequence; insignificant.

null and void; without legal force; invalid.

null method; a method of comparing or measuring physical quantities, in which the indicator of the testing device remains at zero when the quantities balance.

null, *n.* something that has no force or meaning; a cipher; a dummy. [Obs.]

nul'lȧh, *n.* [Hind. *nālā*, brook, ravine.] in India, etc., (a) a ravine; (b) a watercourse.

nul'lȧ-nul'lȧ, *n.* a wooden club used by the Australian natives: also written *nullah-nullah*.

nul″li·fi·çā'tion, *n.* [LL. *nullificatio*.]

1. a nullifying or being nullified.

2. in United States history, the refusal of a State to recognize or enforce within its territory any act of Congress held to be an infringement on its sovereignty.

nul·li·fid'i·ăn, *a.* [L. *nullus*, none, and *fides*, faith.] of no faith; of no religion.

nul·li·fid'i·ăn, *n.* a person having no religious faith.

nul'li·fī·ẽr, *n.* one who or that which nullifies.

nul'li·fȳ, *v.t.*; nullified, *pt., pp.*; nullifying, *ppr.* [L. *nullus*, none, and *facere*, to make.]

1. to annul; to make void; to render invalid; to deprive of legal force or efficacy; to invalidate.

2. to make valueless or useless; to bring to nothing.

nul·lip'ȧ·rȧ, *n.*; *pl.* **nul·lip'ȧ·rae,** [L. *nullus*, none, and *parere*, to bring forth.] in obstetrics, a woman who has not borne a child: said especially of a married woman.

nul·lip'ȧ·rous, *a.* of, or having the nature of, a nullipara; barren.

nul'li·pōre, *n.* [L. *nullus*, none, and *porus*, pore.] a red-spored, lime-secreting, seaweed.

nul'li·ty, *n.* [Fr. *nullité*, from L. *nullus*, none.]

1. the state, quality, or fact of being null.

2. *pl.* **nul'li·tieş,** anything that is null.

numb (num), *a.* [ME. *nomen, numen*, from AS. *numen*, pp. of *niman*, to take, seize.]

1. weakened in or deprived of the power of feeling or moving; benumbed; deadened; insensible; as, *numb* with cold, *numb* with grief.

2. having the nature of numbness, as a feeling.

numb, *v.t.*; numbed (numd), *pt., pp.*; numbing, *ppr.* to make numb.

numbed'ness (numd'), *n.* numbness. [Obs.]

num'bẽr, *n.* [ME. and OFr. *nombre*, from L. *numerus*, number.]

1. a symbol or word, or a group of either of these, showing how many or what place in a sequence: 1, 2, 3, 13, 23, 123 (one, two, three, thirteen, twenty-three, one hundred and twenty-three) are called *cardinal numbers*; 1st, 2d, 3d, 4th, 24th, 100th, 124th (first, second, third, fourth, twenty-fourth, one hundredth, one hundred and twenty-fourth) are called *ordinal numbers*. The symbol (#) is often used with a definite numeral, as in designating grade, size, rank, position, etc.

2. [*pl.*] arithmetic.

3. the sum of any collection of persons or things; amount of units; total; aggregate.

4. a collection of persons or things; company; assemblage.

5. (a) [*also pl.*] a certain, usually a considerable, company or collection; many; (b) [*pl.*] numerical superiority.

6. quantity, as consisting of units.

7. one of a series or group that is numbered or thought of as numbered; specifically, (a) a single issue of a periodical; as, the June *number* of a magazine; (b) a single or distinct part of a program of entertainment; any of a sequence of songs, skits, etc.

8. a person or thing singled out; as, this hat is a smart *number*. [Colloq.]

9. in grammar, (a) a difference of word form to show whether one or more than one person or thing is meant; (b) the form itself.

10. in music, (a) [*pl.*] measures; (b) rhythm.

11. in poetry, (a) [*pl.*] metrical feet, verses, or verse; (b) metrical rhythm.

a number of; an unspecified number of; several or many.

back number; an issue of a periodical other than the last one published; hence, any person or thing considered as old-fashioned or not up with the times.

beyond number; too numerous to be counted.

one's number is up; one's time to die, suffer, etc. has arrived. [Slang.]

the numbers; numbers pool.

to get one's number; to discover one's true character or motives. [Slang.]

to have one's number on it; to be assumed to have been marked by fate for the person whom it kills: said of a bullet, etc. [Slang.]

without number; too numerous to be counted.

num'bẽr, *v.t.*; numbered, *pt., pp.*; numbering, *ppr.* [OFr. *nombrer, numbrer*, from L. *num-*

erare, to number, count, from *numerus,* a number.]
1. to total the number of persons or things in; to count; to enumerate.
2. to give a number to; to designate by number.
3. to include as one of a group, class, collection, etc.
4. to fix or limit the number or the duration of; as, his days are *numbered.*
5. to have or comprise in number.
6. to add up to; to total; to equal.
7. to allot or appoint. [Obs.]

num'bẽr, *v.i.* 1. to total; to count; to enumerate.
2. to be numbered; to be included.

num'bẽr·ẽr, *n.* one who numbers.

num'bẽr·less, *a.* 1. that cannot be counted; innumerable.
2. without a number or numbers.

num'bẽr one (wun), 1. oneself. [Colloq.]
2. the first, usually the very best, quality or grade. [Colloq.]

Num'bẽrs, *n.pl.* [*construed as sing.*] [transl. of Gr. *Arithmoi*: so named from containing the census of the Hebrews after the Exodus.] the fourth book of the Old Testament.

num'bẽrs pool (or **game, rack'et**), an illegal lottery in which people place small bets on the order of certain numbers, usually the last three in some tabulation of game scores, financial reports, etc. published in the daily newspapers: also called *policy game.*

numb'fish (num'), *n.*; *pl.* **numb'fish** or **numb'fish·es,** *a.* fish that can give numbing shocks by means of its electric organs; an electric ray.

num'bles, *n.pl.* [Fr. *nombles,* numbles, from L. *lumbulus,* a dim. of *lumbus,* a loin.] the entrails of a deer, etc., used for food: also written *nombles.* [Archaic.]

numb'ness (num'), *n.* the state of being numb; that state of a living body in which it has not the power of feeling or motion.

nū'men, *n.*; *pl.* **nū'min·ȧ,** [L.] in Roman mythology, a presiding spirit; a divinity.

nū'mẽr·ȧ·ble, *a.* [L. *numerabilis,* from *numerare,* to number.] that can be numbered or counted.

nū'mẽr·ȧ·cy, *n.* the state of being numerate.

nū'mẽr·ăl, *a.* [L. *numeralis,* from *numerus,* a number.] of, expressing, or denoting number or numbers.

nū'mẽr·ăl, *n.* 1. a figure, letter, or word, or a group of any of these, expressing a number.
2. [*pl.*] the numerals of the year of graduation of one's class in college, etc., awarded and worn for participation in sports, etc.

nū'mẽr·ăl·ly, *adv.* numerically. [Obs.]

nū'mẽr·ăr·y, *a.* of a number or numbers.

nū'mẽr·āte, *v.t.*; numerated, *pt., pp.*; numerating, *ppr.* [L. *numeratus,* pp. of *numerare,* to count, number.]
1. to count; to enumerate.
2. to read (a number or numbers expressed in figures).

nū'mẽr·āte, *a.* [from L. *numerus,* number, and liter*ate.*] able to deal with scientific concepts, especially in a mathematical way; as, an increasingly *numerate* society. [Chiefly Brit.]

nū·mẽr·ā'tion, *n.* 1. a numbering or counting; calculation.
2. a system of numbering or of reading numbers expressed in figures.

nū'mẽr·ā·tive, *a.* of or pertaining to numbering; relating to numeration.

nū'mẽr·ā·tŏr, *n.* 1. that term of a fraction which shows how many of the specified parts of a unit are taken: in decimal fractions, it is written to the right of the decimal point; in common fractions, it is written above the line.
2. a person or thing that numbers.

nū·mer'iç, *a.* numerical.

nū·mer'iç·ăl, *a.* [Fr. *numérique,* from L. *numerus,* number.]
1. of, or having the nature of, number.
2. in or by numbers.
3. denoting (a) number.
4. expressed by a number or numbers, not by a letter or letters
5. in mathematics, designating or of value or magnitude regardless of sign; as, the *numerical* value of −3 is smaller than that of −7.
numerical aperture; in optics, the formula by which the illuminating and resolving power of high-power microscopic objectives is now calculated. It is expressed by the formula, *n* sin *u,* where *n* is the refractive index of the medium—air or fluid—and *u* the semiangle of aperture.

nū·mer'iç·ăl·ly, *adv.* in a numerical manner; in numbers; with respect to numerical quantity; as, parts of a thing *numerically* expressed; an algebraic expression *numerically* greater than another.

nū'mẽr·ō, *n.* number; the figure or mark by which any number of things is distinguished: usually abbreviated to *No.*; as, he rooms in *No.* 11.

nū·mẽr·ol'ō·ġy, *n.* [from L. *numerus,* a number; and *-logy.*] a system of occultism built around numbers, especially those giving birth dates, those which are the sum of the letters in one's name, etc.; divination by numbers.

nū·mẽr·os'i·ty, *n.* 1. numerousness.
2. harmony.

nú·me·ro ú'nō (nu'me rō), [Sp. and It.] the very best or the most important one. [Colloq.]

nū'mẽr·ous, *a.* [L. *numerosus,* from *numerus,* a number.]
1. being many, or consisting of a great number of persons or things; not few; as, a *numerous* army; a *numerous* people; *numerous* objects; attacked by *numerous* enemies.
My *numerous* footsteps nimbly to retrace.
—Robert Louis Stevenson.
2. very many.

nū'mẽr·ous·ly, *adv.* in or with great numbers.

nū'mẽr·ous·ness, *n.* the quality of being numerous or many; the state of consisting of a great number of persons or things; as, the *numerousness* of an army or of an assembly.

Nū·mid'i·ăn, *a.* of or pertaining to Numidia, an ancient kingdom on the northern coast of Africa, which forms the largest part of the territory now called Algeria; also, of or pertaining to its people and their language.
Numidian crane; a grallatorial bird, *Anthropoides virgo*: also called *demoiselle.*

Nū·mid'i·ăn, *n.* 1. a native or inhabitant of Numidia.
2. the Hamitic language of the Numidians.

nū·miṣ·mat'iç, nū·miṣ·mat'iç·ăl, *a.* [L. *numisma* (*-atis*), from Gr. *nomisma,* coin, money; lit., what is sanctioned by law, from *nomizein,* to sanction, to establish by law, from *nomos,* law or custom.]
1. pertaining to coins and medals.
2. pertaining to numismatics or numismatists.

nū·miṣ·mat'içs, *n.pl.* [*construed as sing.*] the study or collection of coins and medals.

nū·miṣ'mȧ·tist, *n.* a specialist in or collector of coins and medals.

nū·miṣ·mȧ·tog'rȧ·phy, *n.* same as *numismatics.*

nū·miṣ·mȧ·tol'ō·ġist, *n.* same as *numismatist.*

nū·miṣ·mȧ·tol'ō·ġy, *n.* same as *numismatics.*

num'mȧ·ry, *a.* [L. *nummus,* a coin.] of or pertaining to coins or money.

num'mū·lăr, *a.* [L. *nummularius,* from *nummulus,* dim. of *nummus,* a coin.] in medicine, (a) coin-shaped; (b) piled up like a roll of coins: said of agglutinating red blood cells.

num'mū·lăr·y, *a.* [L. *nummularius,* from *nummus,* a coin.]
1. pertaining to coin or money.
2. nummular.

num·mū·lā'tion, *n.* [L. *nummulus,* dim. of *nummus,* a coin.] in physiology, exhibition of nummular form.

num'mū·līte, *n.* [L. *nummulus,* a little coin, and *-ite.*] one of a class of nearly extinct one-celled animals, of the genus *Nummulites* or the family *Nummulinidæ,* having externally the appearance of a coin without any apparent opening, and internally a spiral cavity, divided by partitions into numerous chambers, communicating with each other by means of small openings.

Num·mū·lī'tēṣ, *n.* the genus of one-celled animals of which the nummulites are members.

num·mū·lit'iç, *a.* composed of or containing nummulites.

num'skull, *n.* [from *numb* and *skull.*] a dunce; a dolt; a stupid fellow.

num'skulled, *a.* dull in intellect; stupid; doltish.

num'ud, *n.* a thick Persian carpeting of felt with inlaid designs.

nun, *n.* [AS. *nunne,* a nun, from LL. *nonna,* a nun, *nonnus,* a monk; L.Gr. *nonna, nonnos*; compare Sans. *nana,* mother.]
1. a woman devoted to a religious life; especially, a member of a convent under vows, as of chastity, obedience, and poverty.
2. any of various birds, as the pigeon.

nūn, *n.* [Heb. *nūn,* lit., fish.] the fourteenth letter of the Hebrew alphabet, corresponding to English *N, n.*

Nunç Di·mit'tis, [L., now thou lettest depart: first words of the L. version.]
1. the song of Simeon, sung as a hymn or canticle in various liturgies: Luke ii. 29–32.
2. [n– d–] (a) departure or farewell, especially from life; (b) permission to depart; dismissal.

nun'cheŏn (-chun), *n.* [ME. *nonechenche.*] a portion of food taken between meals; a meal eaten about noon; a luncheon. [Obs.]

nun'ci·āte (-shi-), *n.* a messenger or nuncio.

nun'ci·ȧ·tūre, *n.* the office or term of office of a nuncio.

nun'ci·ō, *n.*; *pl.* **nun'ci·ōṣ,** [It. *nuncio, nunzio,* from L. *nuncius, nuntius,* a messenger.] the permanent official representative of the Pope to a foreign government; a papal ambassador.

nuñ'cle, *n.* [by syllabic merging of *mine uncle.*] uncle. [Dial.]

nun'çū·pāte, *v.t.* [L. *nuncupatus,* pp. of *nuncupare,* to call by name, to nominate, to vow in public; *nomen,* name, and *capere,* to take.]
1. to vow publicly and solemnly.
2. to dedicate; to inscribe.
3. to declare orally (a will or testament).

nun·çū·pā'tion, *n.* a naming.

nuñ'çū·pā·tive, *a.* 1. nominal; existing only in name. [Obs.]
2. oral; not written: said especially of wills.

nuñ'çū·pȧ·tō·ry, *a.* nuncupative. [Obs.]

nun'di·năl, *a.* [L. *nundinalis,* from *nundinæ,* a fair or market; originally, one held every ninth day from *novem,* nine, and *dies,* a day.] pertaining to a fair or to a market day.
nundinal letter; among the Romans, one of the first eight letters of the alphabet, which were repeated successively from the first to the last day of the year. One of these always expressed the market days, which returned every nine days.

nun'di·năl, *n.* a nundinal letter.

nun·di·nā'tion, *n.* buying and selling.

nun·nā'tion, *n.* [Mod. L. *nunnatio,* from Ar. *nun,* the letter *n.*] the addition of final *n* to words in which it does not historically occur, as in the declension of certain Arabic nouns.

nun'nẽr·y, *n.*; *pl.* **nun'nẽr·ieṣ,** [ME. and OFr. *nounerie.*] a community of nuns and the building or buildings in which they live; a convent.

nun'nish, *a.* relating to or characteristic of a nun or nuns. [Rare.]

nun'nish·ness, *n.* the habits or manners of nuns. [Rare.]

nun's veil'ing, a soft, loosely woven, untwilled woolen material, used for veils, light dresses, etc.

Nū'phär, *n.* [Gr. *nouphar,* a water lily.] a genus of plants of the water lily family growing on the margins of lakes and streams and bearing bright yellow flowers: also called *spatterdock* and *yellow water lily.*

nū'plex, *n.* [coined (1968) by the Atomic Energy Commission from *nu*clear com*plex.*] any of a number of proposed concentrations of industrial facilities clustered around a large nuclear reactor as their source of power.

nup'tiăl (-shăl), *a.* [L. *nuptialis,* from *nuptiæ,* marriage, from *nuptus,* pp. of *nubere,* to marry.] pertaining to marriage or a wedding; suggestive of or connected with a marriage or matrimony.

nup'tiălṣ, *n.pl.* a wedding; a marriage ceremony: this word now always has the plural ending, but earlier writers generally used *nuptial.*
This looks not like a *nuptial.* —Shak.

nù'rägh, nù'rhäg (-räg), *n.* [It.] one of numerous ancient stone towers found in Sardinia, used for tombs, temples, or forts of refuge.

nûrse, *n.* [ME. *nourse, norse, nourrice*; OFr. *norice, nourice,* a nurse, from L. *nutrix, nutricis,* a nurse, from *nutrire,* to nourish, to suckle.]
1. a woman who suckles a child not her own: now usually *wet nurse.*
2. a woman hired to take full care of another's young child or children.
3. a person trained to take care of the sick, injured, or aged, assist surgeons, etc.
4. a person or thing that nourishes, fosters, protects, or develops someone or something.
O Caledonia! stern and wild,
Meet *nurse* for a poetic child. —Scott.
5. the state of being nursed; as, to put a child to *nurse.*
Can wedlock know so great a curse
As putting husbands out to *nurse.*
—Cleaveland.

6. in horticulture, a shrub or tree which protects a young plant.

7. in zoology, (a) a shark, *Ginglymostoma cirrata*, common in the Gulf of Mexico; also, an arctic shark, *Læmargus microcephalus*; (b) a nurse frog; (c) a sexually incomplete worker bee or ant that cares for the young.

monthly nurse; a midwife.

nŭrse, *v.t.*; nursed (nŭrst), *pt., pp.*; nursing, *ppr.* 1. to suckle (an infant); to be wet nurse for.

2. to suck milk from the breast of.

3. to take care of (a child or children).

4. to bring up; rear.

5. to tend (the sick, injured, or aged).

6. to take special care of; to nourish, foster, develop, or cherish; as, she's *nursing* her anger.

7. to treat; to try to cure; as, he is *nursing* a cold.

8. (a) to use, operate, or handle cautiously or carefully, so as to avoid injury, pain, exhaustion, etc.; as, he's *nursing* his injured leg; (b) to drink slowly, so as to conserve; as, she *nursed* her highball.

9. to clasp; to hold carefully; to fondle.

10. in billiards, to keep (the balls) close together for a series of caroms.

nŭrse, *v.i.* 1. to be suckled; to feed at the breast.

2. to suckle a child.

3. to serve as a nurse.

nŭrse çrop, a crop planted with another to shelter it or promote its growth.

nŭrse frog, a male frog, *Alytes obstetricans*, which carries the eggs laid by the female, until they are hatched.

nŭrse'hound, *n.* a small shark, *Scylliorhinus catulus*.

nŭrse'ling, *n.* same as *nursling*.

nŭrse'māid, *n.* a girl or woman employed to tend a child or children.

nŭrse'pond, *n.* a pond for young fish.

nŭrs'ẽr, *n.* one who nurses, cherishes, encourages, or promotes; a nurse.

nŭrs'ẽr·y, *n.*; *pl.* **nŭrs'ẽr·ieṣ,** [ME. *norcery*; see *nurse*.]

1. (a) an infant's bedroom; (b) a room or apartment in a home, set aside for the children as a playroom, study, dining room, etc.; (c) specially equipped quarters, as in a theater or store, where parents may temporarily leave children with trained attendants while they shop, etc.; (d) a nursery school.

2. a place where young trees or other plants are propagated for experimental purposes, for transplanting, or for sale.

3. anything that nourishes, protects, develops, or fosters.

To see fair Padua, *nursery* of arts.—Shak.

4. the act of nursing. [Obs.]

nŭrs'ẽr·y·māid, *n.* same as *nursemaid*.

nŭrs'ẽr·y·man, *n.*; *pl.* **nŭrs'ẽr·y·men,** a man who owns, manages, or works in a nursery or place for young trees, shrubs, plants, etc.

nŭrs'ẽr·y rhȳme (rīm), a short, rhymed poem for children.

nŭrs'ẽr·y sçhool (sköl), a school for children of prekindergarten age (from three to approximately five years).

nŭrs'ing bot'tle, a bottle with a detachable rubber nipple, for feeding liquids to babies.

nŭrs'ing hōme, 1. a residence equipped and staffed to provide care for the infirm, chronically ill, disabled, etc.

2. a small private hospital. [Chiefly Brit.]

nŭrs'ling, *n.* 1. an infant still being nursed.

2. anything that is being carefully tended or cared for.

Also spelled *nurseling*.

nŭr'tūre, *n.* [ME. *nuriture*; OFr. *norreture*; LL. *nutritura*, from L. *nutrire*, to nourish.]

1. that which nourishes; food; nutriment.

2. the act or process of raising or promoting the development of; training; rearing; upbringing.

3. in sociology, all the environmental factors, collectively, to which the individual is subjected from conception onward, as distinguished from his nature, or heredity.

nŭr'tūre, *v.t.*; nurtured, *pt., pp.*; nurturing, *ppr.* 1. to feed; to nourish.

2. to raise or promote the development of; to educate; to bring or train up.

He was *nurtured* where he was born. —Wotton.

Syn.—nourish, cherish.—*Nourish* denotes to supply with food or cause to grow. To *nurture* is to train up with a fostering care; to *cherish* is to hold and treat as dear.

nut, *n.* [ME. *nutte, note*; AS. *hnutu, hnyt*; compare Ice. *hnot*, O.H.G. *nuz*, Dan. *nod*, G. *nuss*, nut.]

1. the dry, one-seeded fruit of any of various trees or bushes, consisting of a kernel, often edible, in a hard and woody or tough and leathery shell, more or less separable from the seed itself: walnuts, pecans, chestnuts, acorns, etc. are all *nuts*.

2. the kernel, or meat, of such a fruit.

3. loosely, any hard-shelled fruit that will keep more or less indefinitely; peanuts, almonds, and cashews are often called *nuts*.

4. a person, problem, or thing difficult to understand or handle.

5. a small block, usually of metal, with a threaded hole through the center, for screwing onto a bolt, etc.

6. (a) the head; (b) [*usually in pl.*] a testicle. [Slang.]

7. a queer, foolish, or demented person; an eccentric. [Slang.]

8. (a) a ridge of wood, ebony, etc. at the top of the fingerboard of a stringed instrument, over which the strings pass; (b) the small knob at the end of a violin bow, for tightening or loosening the hairs.

9. the projection near the eye of an anchor.

10. in firearms, the tumbler of a gunlock.

hard (or *tough*) *nut to crack*; (a) any problem, task, etc. that is difficult to solve or do; (b) a person who cannot be persuaded or convinced easily.

nuts and bolts; the basic elements or practical aspects of something. [Colloq.]

off one's nut; insane; crazy. [Slang.]

nut, *v.i.*; nutted, *pt., pp.*; nutting, *ppr.* to gather or hunt for nuts.

nū'tănt, *a.* [L. *nutans (-antis)*, ppr. of *nutare*, to nod.] nodding; having the top bent downward: said of plants.

nū·tā'tion, *n.* [L. *nutatio (-onis)*, a nodding, from *nutare*, to nod.]

1. in astronomy, a small vibratory movement of the earth's axis.

2. the act or an instance of nodding the head.

3. in botany, a slight rotatory movement in the stem of a growing plant, due to the varying rates of growth in the parts of the stem.

nut'breāk″ẽr, *n.* same as *nutcracker*, sense 2.

nut'-brown, *a.* dark brown, like some ripe nuts.

The spicy, *nut brown* ale. —Milton.

nut'çrack″ẽr, *n.* 1. [*sometimes pl.*] an instrument for cracking the shells of nuts, usually consisting of two hinged metal levers, between which the nut is squeezed.

2. (a) a white-spotted, dark-brown European bird of the crow family, that feeds on nuts; (b) a similar bird of western North America, with grayish plumage.

nut'gall, *n.* a small, nut-shaped gall on the oak and other trees.

nut'hatch, *n.* [ME. *notehach, nutlehache.*] any of various small, nut-eating birds of the genus *Sitta*, related to the creepers and titmice, having a sharp beak and a short

NUTHATCH
(*Sitta europæa*)

tail. The common European nuthatch, *Sitta europæa*, is a scansorial bird of shy and solitary habits, frequenting woods and feeding on insects chiefly. It also eats the kernel of the hazelnut, breaking the shell with great dexterity. The female lays her eggs in holes of trees, and hisses like a snake when disturbed. Also called *nutbreaker, nutjobber*, and *nutpecker*.

nut'hook, *n.* 1. a pole with a hook at the end, to pull down boughs for gathering the nuts.

2. formerly, a constable.

nut'job″bẽr, *n.* nuthatch. [Scot. and Brit. Dial.]

nut'let, *n.* 1. a small nut or nutlike fruit.

2. the pit, or stone, of a cherry, peach, plum, etc.

nut'mēat, *n.* the kernel of a nut, especially when edible.

nut'meg, *n.* [ME. *notemuge, nutmuge*; *nut*, nut, and OFr. *muge*, musk, from L. *muscus*, musk.]

NUTMEG
(*Myristica moschata*)

1. the hard, aromatic kernel of the seed of an East Indian tree, *Myristica moschata* or *fragrans*. This fruit is a nearly spherical drupe of the size and somewhat of the shape of a small pear. The fleshy part is of a yellowish color and opens into two nearly equal longitudinal valves, revealing the nut surrounded by its aril. The nut drops out and the aril withers. The nut is oval, the shell very hard and dark brown. The tree producing this fruit grows principally in the East Indies, and has been introduced into Sumatra, India, Brazil, and the West Indies. The nutmeg is grated and used as a spice.

2. the tree itself.

American nutmeg; a shrub of the custard apple family which bears a large pulpy fruit that contains aromatic seeds: also called *Jamaica nutmeg*.

Brazilian nutmeg; a tree, *Cryptocarya moschata*, producing an aromatic fruit.

California nutmeg; a tree, *Torreya californica*, which yields a fruit resembling the nutmeg.

nutmeg oil; a transparent oil, having a specific gravity of .948, an odor of nutmeg, and a burning, aromatic taste, obtained from the seeds of *Myristica fragrans* by distillation with water.

Peruvian nutmeg; a tree, *Laurelia sempervirens*, of South America, which yields an aromatic fruit.

nut'meg bīrd, an Indian finch or weaver bird, *Munia punctularia*.

nut'meg but'tẽr, a solid oil extracted from the nutmeg.

nut'meg flow'ẽr, an Egyptian plant, *Nigella sativa*, which yields small aromatic seeds.

nut'megged (-megd), *a.* prepared or seasoned with nutmeg.

nut'meg grāt'ẽr, a device used for grating nutmegs.

Be rough as *nutmeg graters*, and the rogues
obey you well. —Aaron Hill.

nut'meg·gy, *a.* smelling or tasting like nutmeg; having the appearance of nutmeg.

nut'meg liv'ẽr, in surgery, an abnormal condition of the liver, causing it to present a mottled appearance when cut.

nut'meg mel'ŏn, a small muskmelon having a green thickly-netted rind and a sweet, rich flavor.

nut'meg piġ'eŏn, an East Indian nutmeg-eating pigeon of the genus *Myristicivora*.

nut'peck″ẽr, *n.* same as *nuthatch*.

nut'pick, *n.* a small, sharp-pointed device for picking the kernels of nuts from the shells.

nut pīne, a pine tree yielding nutlike edible seeds, as *Pinus edulis* of New Mexico, and *Pinus pinea* of Europe.

nū'tri·ȧ, *n.* [Sp. *nutria, lutria, lutra*, from L. *lutra*, an otter.]

1. a beaverlike South American water-dwelling rodent; a coypu.

2. its short-haired, soft, brown fur, often dyed to look like beaver.

nū·tri·çā'tion, *n.* the manner of feeding or being fed. [Obs.]

nū'tri·ent, *a.* [L. *nutriens (-entis)*, ppr. of *nutrire*, to nourish.] nutritive; nourishing; promoting growth; nutritious.

nū'tri·ent, *n.* any substance which nourishes; anything nutritious.

nū'tri·fȳ, *v.i.* and *v.t.*; nutrified, *pt., pp.*; nutrifying, *ppr.* to nourish.

nū'tri·ment, *n.* [L. *nutrimentum*, from *nutrire*, to nourish.]
1. that which nourishes; that which promotes the growth or repairs the natural waste of animal bodies, or which promotes the growth of vegetables; food; aliment.
2. that which promotes growth or improvement; as, the *nutriment* of the mind.
Syn.—food, aliment, nourishment, sustenance, nutrition.

nū·tri·men'tăl, *a.* nutritious.

nū·tri'tiăl (-shăl), *a.* nutritious. [Obs.]

nū·tri'tion (-trish'un), *n.* [L. *nutrire*, to nourish.]
1. a nourishing or being nourished; especially, the series of processes by which an organism takes in and assimilates food for promoting growth and replacing worn or injured tissues.
2. that which nourishes; nourishment; food.
3. the science or study of proper, balanced diet to promote health, especially in human beings.

nū·tri'tiŏn·ăl, *a.* pertaining to nutrition.

nū·tri'tiŏn·ăl·ly, *adv.* with reference to nutrition.

nū·tri'tion·ist, *n.* an expert in nutrition.

nū·tri'tious, *a.* nourishing; promoting the growth or repairing the waste of organic bodies; containing or serving as nutriment.

nū·tri'tious·ly, *adv.* nourishingly.

nū·tri'tious·ness, *n.* the quality of being nutritious.

nū'tri·tive, *a.* 1. having to do with nutrition.
2. promoting nutrition; nutritious.

nū'tri·tive·ly, *adv.* nourishingly.

nū'tri·tive·ness, *n.* the quality of being nutritive.

nū'tri·tō·ry, *a.* pertaining to nutrition.

nū'tri·tūre, *n.* the act of nourishing; nourishment. [Obs.]

nut rush, a plant of the genus *Scleria*, belonging to the sedge family: it bears a fruit resembling a nut.

nuts, *a.* crazy; foolish. [Slang.]
to be nuts about; (a) to be greatly in love with; (b) to like very much; to be very enthusiastic about. [Slang.]

nuts, *interj.* an exclamation of disgust, scorn, disappointment, disapproval, refusal, etc. [Slang.]

nut sedge, a nut rush.

nut'shell, *n.* 1. the hard shell of a nut; the covering of the kernel; the pericarp.
2. figuratively, a thing of little size or of little value.
3. a bivalve of the family *Nuculidæ*.
in a nutshell; in brief form; in a few words; concisely.

nut'tĕr, *n.* one who gathers nuts.

nut'ti·ness, *n.* 1. the quality or state of being nutty.
2. a nutty flavor or consistency.

nut'ting, *n.* the act or process of gathering or hunting for nuts.

nut'ty, *a.*; *comp.* nuttier; *superl.* nuttiest, 1. containing or producing many nuts.
2. having a nutlike flavor.
3. (a) enthusiastic, often to excess; (b) queer, foolish, demented, etc. [Slang.]

nut wee'vil, a weevil, as *Balaninus nucum*, that infests nuts.

nux vom'i·cȧ, [L. *nux*, a nut, and *vomere*, to vomit.]
1. the poisonous, disklike seed of *Strychnos nux-vomica*, a loganiaceous tree of the East Indies. It contains strychnine and brucine, two poisonous alkaloids.
2. the tree which yields this fruit.
3. a medicine made from the seed, used as a heart stimulant.

NUX VOMICA

nuz'zĕr, *n.* [E. Ind.] in India, an offering or present to a superior.

nuz'zle, *v.t.*; nuzzled, *pt.*, *pp.*; nuzzling, *ppr.* [ME. *noselen*, *nuslen*, to thrust the nose in, to fondle, from *nose*, nose. The word has been confused with *noursle* and *nestle*.]
1. to push against or rub with the nose, snout, muzzle, etc.
2. to root up with the nose or snout: said of a pig, etc.
3. to foster; to rear; to nurse. [Obs.]
4. to nestle; to house, as in a nest. [Rare.]

nuz'zle, *v.i.* 1. to work with the nose, like swine in the mud; to push or rub closely against or into anything with the nose.
2. to go with the nose thrust out and down, like swine.
3. to lie close; to nestle; to snuggle.

nȳ, nor I; not I: contraction of *ne I*. [Obs.]

nȳ, *a.* and *adv.* nigh. [Obs.]

nyä'lȧ, *n.*; *pl.* **nyä'lȧ, nyä'lȧs,** [African.] any of several antelopes, genus *Strepsiceros*, of eastern Africa, with large, spiral horns.

nyän'zȧ, *n.* [African.] an expanse of water, as a lake or wide river.

nȳ'ăs, *n.* nias. [Obs.]

nyçh·thē'me·ron, *n.* [Gr. *nychthēmeros*, of a day and night; *nyx* (*nykt-*), night, and *hēmera*, day.] the whole day consisting of twenty-four hours.

nyct-, see *nycti-*.

Nyç″tȧ·ġi·nā'cē·ae, *n.pl.* same as *Nyctagineæ*.

nyç″tȧ·ġi·nā'ceous, *a.* pertaining to the *Nyctaginaceæ*.

Nyç·tȧ·ġin'ē·ae, *n.pl.* [Gr. *nyx*, *nyktos*, night, and L. *-ago*, a suffix used in some plant names.] a group of hypogenous exogens, consisting of herbs, shrubs, or trees, generally articulated with tumid nodes. They are native to the tropical parts of America and include the four-o'clock.

nyç·tȧ·lō'pi·ȧ, *n.* [Gr. *nyx*, *nyktos*, night, *alaos*, blind, and *ōps*, an eye.] night blindness.

nyç·tȧ·lop'iç, *a.* relating to or affected with nyctalopia.

nyç'tȧ·lops, *n.* [Gr. *nyktalōps*, able to see by night only; *nyx*, *nyktos*, night, and *ōps*, the eye.] one afflicted with *nyctalopia*.

nyç'tȧ·lō·py, *n.* same as *nyctalopia*.

Nyç·tan'thēs, *n.* [*nycti-*, and Gr. *anthos*, a flower.] a genus of plants of the family *Oleaceæ*, native to eastern India, with the single species, *Nyctanthes arbortristis*, a shrub bearing gamopetalous fragrant flowers which bloom and fall in the night: also called *night jasmine*.

nyç·thē'me·ron, *n.* same as *nychthemeron*.

nyç'ti-, [from Gr. *nyx*, *nyktos*, night.] a combining form meaning *of* or *at night*, as in *nyctitropic*: also *nycto-* and, before a vowel, *nyct-*.

nyç·ti·trop'iç, *a.* [*nycti-*, and Gr. *tropos*, a turning.] turning or bending into special positions at night: said of the movements of certain leaves, due to variations in the intensity of light.

nyç·tit'rō·pism, *n.* the tendency of the leaves of certain plants to be nyctitropic.

nyç'tō-, see *nycti-*.

nyç'tō·phīle, *n.* [*nycto-*, and Gr. *philos*, loving.] any Australian bat of the genus *Nyctophilus*, distinctive because of a rudimentary nasal appendage.

nyç·tō·phō'bi·ȧ, [*nycto-* and *-phobia*.] an unnatural or excessive fear of darkness or night.

nȳe, *n.* [contr. from *nide*.] a brood or flock of pheasants. [Dial.]

ny·en'tek, *n.* a small weasellike carnivorous mammal found in eastern Asia, the East Indies, and the adjacent islands. It has a strong musky odor and is marked with a white stripe along its back and across its shoulders.

nyl'ghai (-gī), *n.*; *pl.* **nyl'ghais** or **nyl'ghai,** a nilgai.

nyl'ghau, nyl'gau (-gạ), *n.*; *pl.* **nyl'ghaus** or **nyl'ghau, nyl'gaus** or **nyl'gau,** a nilgai.

nȳ'lon, *n.* [arbitrary formation.]
1. a highly elastic, very strong, synthetic material derived from coal, water, and air, and made into thread, bristles, sheets, etc.: a trade-mark (*Nylon*).
2. [*pl.*] stockings made of this.

nymph, *n.* [L. *nympha*; Gr. *nymphē*, a nymph.]
1. in Greek and Roman mythology, any of a group of minor nature goddesses, represented as beautiful maidens living in rivers, mountains, trees, etc.
2. (a) a lovely young woman; (b) a young woman; a maiden: literary or playful usage.
3. in entomology, (a) the young of an insect without complete metamorphosis; (b) a pupa.
4. any of the various nymphalid butterflies, including the purple, the fritillary, and the peacock butterflies.

nym'phȧ, *n.*; *pl.* **nym'phae,** 1. same as *nymph*, 3 (a).
2. [*pl.*] in anatomy, the labia minora.
3. in zoology, an impressed area behind the beak of a bivalve shell, strengthening the margin where the ligament is attached.

Nym·phae'ȧ, *n.* [L. *nymphæa*, a water lily.] a genus of aquatic plants belonging to the water lily family, having showy fragrant flowers of various colors, and including the white water lily and the Egyptian lotus: also called *Castalia*.

Nym·phae·ā'cē·ae, *n.pl.* a family of perennial polypetalous fresh-water lilies, the water-lily family, including the genera *Brasenia*, *Nelumbium*, *Nymphæa* (*Castalia*), and *Nuphar*.

nym·phae·ā'ceous, *a.* of or pertaining to the family *Nymphæaceæ*.

nymph'ăl, *a.* 1. of, like, or pertaining to a nymph or to nymphs.
2. in zoology, relating to a chrysalis or pupa.

nym'phȧ·lid, *a.* of or relating to the *Nymphalidæ*.

nym'phȧ·lid, *n.* one of the *Nymphalidæ*.

Nym·phal'i·dae, *n.pl.* a family of butterflies including several subfamilies and numerous genera, characterized by very short forelegs and, generally, brightly-colored wings.

nym·phē'ăn, *a.* pertaining to or like nymphs; inhabited by nymphs; as, a *nymphean* cave.

nymph'et, *n.* 1. a small or young nymph. [Obs.]
2. a pubescent girl, especially one who is sexually precocious.

nymph'iç, nymph'iç·ăl, *a.* nymphal.

nym·phip'ȧ·rous, *a.* [L. *nympha*, a nymph, and *parere*, to bring forth.] producing nymphs or pupas.

nymph'ish, *a.* somewhat like a nymph; pertaining to nymphs.

nym·phī'tis, *n.* in pathology, inflammation of the nymphae.

nymph'līke, *a.* resembling nymphs.

nymph'ly, *a.* nymphlike.

nym·phō·lep'si·ȧ, *n.* nympholepsy.

nym'phō·lep·sy, *n.* [Gr. *nymphē*, a nymph, and *lēpsis*, a taking, from *lambanein*, to take.]
1. in ancient times, a state of frenzy that was believed to seize any man who looked at a nymph.
2. a violent emotional state, especially that believed to result from desire for some unattainable ideal.

nym'phō·lept, *n.* a person who has nympholepsy.

nym·phō·lep'tiç, *a.* of, having, or pertaining to nympholepsy.

nym·phō·mā'ni·ȧ, *n.* [Gr. *nymphē*, a bride, and *mania*, madness.] excessive and uncontrollable sexual desire in the female.

nym·phō·mā'ni·aç, *a.* of, characteristic of, or having nymphomania.

nym·phō·mā'ni·aç, *n.* a woman having nymphomania.

nym'phō·mā·ny, *n.* same as *nymphomania*.

nym·phot'ō·my, *n.* [Gr. *nymphē*, a nymph, and *temnein*, to cut.] in surgery, the operation of removing the nymphae by cutting.

nys, is not. [Obs.]

Nys'sȧ, *n.* [L. *Nysa*; Gr. *Nysa*, the nurse or foster mother of Bacchus.] a widely scattered genus of trees or shrubs of the family *Cornaceæ*, including the tupelo, sour gum, and pepperidge.

nys·tag'miç, *a.* of, like, or characterized by nystagmus.

nys·tag'mus, *n.* [Gr. *nystagmos*, from *nystazein*, to nod, especially in sleep.] in pathology, an involuntary, rapid, movement of the eyeball; specifically, (a) a peculiar rhythmic eye movement, Cheyne's nystagmus; (b) a rolling of the eyes horizontally, or from right to left, lateral nystagmus; (c) the rotation of the eyes about the visual axis, rotatory nystagmus; (d) an up-and-down movement of the eyes, vertical nystagmus.
miners' nystagmus; an occupational nystagmus peculiar to miners, induced by continuous work in a dim light.

ny·ū'lȧ, *n.* in zoology, a species of ichneumon, *Herpestes nyula*, having handsome fur with zigzag markings.

Nyx, *n.* [Gr.] in Greek mythology, the goddess of night.

O

O, o (ō), *n.*; *pl.* **O's, o's, Os, os, oes** (ōz), 1. the fifteenth letter of the English alphabet: from the Greek *omega* (long *o*) and *omicron* (short *o*), both borrowed from the Phoenician.

2. a sound of O or o.
3. a type or impression for O or o.
4. the numeral zero; a cipher.
5. an object shaped like O or o.
6. *a symbol for* the fifteenth (or the fourteenth if J is omitted) in a sequence or group.
7. in physics, *the symbol for* ohm.

O, o (ō), *a.* 1. of O or o.
2. circular or oval in shape.
3. fifteenth (or fourteenth if J is omitted) in a sequence or group.

O (ō), *interj.* an exclamation variously used: (a) in direct address as, *O* God, save us!; (b) to express surprise, fear, wonder, pain, etc.: now usually *oh*; (c) at the end of a line in some ballads and songs.

O (ō), *n.*; *pl.* **O's** (ōz), any instance of the exclamation *O*. *O* and *oh* are now sometimes used interchangeably.

o' (ō), *prep.* an abbreviated form of: (a) of, as in o'clock, jack-o'-lantern; (b) [Archaic or Dial.] on.

O' (ō), [Ir. *ō*, descendant.] a prefix of some Irish surnames, meaning *a descendant of*, as in *O'*Reilly.

o-, in chemistry, ortho-.

o-, ob-: used before *m*, as in *o*mit.

O, 1. in chemistry, oxygen.
2. in mathematics, a medieval Roman numeral for 11: with a superior bar ($\bar{O}$), 11,000.

o, *a.* one. [Obs.]

ōad, *n.* woad. [Obs.]

ōaf (ōf), *n.*; *pl.* **ōafs** (ōfs), **ōaves** (ōvz), [earlier *auf, ouphe*, an elf, *aulf*, a changeling, an oaf, from Ice. *ālfr*, an elf.]

1. originally, a changeling; a child supposedly left by fairies in the place of another who is carried off by them.

The fairy left this *oaf*,
And took away the other. —Drayton.

2. a misshapen or idiotic child.
3. a stupid, clumsy fellow; a lout.

ōaf'ish, *a.* like or characteristic of an oaf; stupid; dull; doltish.

ōaf'ish·ness, *n.* the state or quality of being oafish; stupidity; dullness; folly.

ōak (ōk), *n.* [AS. *ac*, oak; compare Ice. *eik*, D. *eik*, L.G. *eeke*, Dan. *eeg*, Sw. *ek*, G. *eiche*, oak.]

1. in botany, any tree or shrub of the genus *Quercus*, bearing nuts called *acorns*. The species are very numerous, generally native to the more temperate parts of the Northern Hemisphere. They have alternate simple leaves, which are entire in some, but in the greater number variously lobed and sinuated or cut; evergreen in some, but more generally deciduous. The common oak attains a height of from 50 to 100 or even 150 feet, with a diameter of trunk of from four to eight feet. The wood is hard, tough, tolerably flexible, strong without being too heavy, not readily penetrated by water, and bears alternations of wetness and dryness better than other woods. The American white oak, *Quercus alba*, and the British oak, *Quercus robur*, have long been exceedingly valuable in shipbuilding. The bark of the oak tree is very useful, and is preferred to all other substances for the purpose of tanning. Gallic acid exists abundantly in the oak, and its leaves, etc. are useful in medicine. Cork is the bark of *Quercus suber*, or cork-oak. Galls are the produce of *Quercus infectoria*.

BRITISH OAK
(*Quercus robur*)

2. the wood of any of the oaks.
3. any of various plants resembling these trees; as, poison *oak*: in Australia the term *oak* is applied to some species of *Casuarina*.
4. a wreath of oak leaves.
5. woodwork, furniture, etc. made of oak.
6. a door, usually of oak. [Brit. University Slang.]

green oak; a condition of oak wood caused by its being impregnated with the spawn of *Peziza æruginosa*, a species of fungus which communicates a green tint, in which state it is much used for ornamentation.

the Oaks; a race for three-year-old fillies, run at Epsom, England, during the Derby week. The race was originated by the twelfth Earl of Derby in 1779, and received its name from Lambert's Oaks, formerly an estate adjacent to Epsom.

to sport one's oak; to shut one's door as a sign that one does not want visitors. [Brit. University Slang.]

ōak, *a.* of oak; oaken.

ōak ap'ple (or **gall**), an applelike gall on oak trees.

ōak bärk, the bark of the oak tree, used in tanning, dyeing, and in medicine.

ōak beau'ty (bū'), an English moth, *Biston prodromaria*, of the family *Geometridæ*, whose caterpillar feeds on the oak.

ōak'en (-n), *a.* 1. made of the wood of the oak or consisting of oak; as, an *oaken* plank or bench.
2. composed of oak trees, or leaves or branches of oak; as, an *oaken* bower; an *oaken* garland.

ōak fẽrn, in botany, a graceful and slender polypody, *Polypodium vulgare*.

ōak gall, see *oak apple*.

Ōak Lēaf Clus'tẽr, a bronze decoration consisting of a small cluster of oak leaves and acorns, awarded to the holder of a United States military decoration for any further award of the same medal.

ōak leath'ẽr (leth'), 1. oak-tanned leather.
2. a fungus growth, somewhat resembling white kid leather, found in the fissures of old oaks.

ōak'ling, *n.* a young oak.

ōak lungs, the lungwort, *Sticta pulmonacea*.

ōak pest, an insect injurious to the leaves of the oak, especially *Phylloxera rileyi*.

ōak prun'ẽr, a beetle, *Asemum mæstum*, the larvae of which infest oak trees.

ōak spañ'gle, a gall resembling a fungus growth, occurring on oak leaves.

ōak tree, the oak.

ōak'um, *n.* [AS. *acumba, æcemba, æcumba*, tow, oakum, from prefix *a-*, away, out, and *camb*, a comb, from *cemban*, to comb; lit., that which is combed out.]

1. the substance of old ropes untwisted and pulled into loose hemp, used for calking the seams of ships, stopping leaks, etc. That formed from untarred ropes is called white oakum.
2. the coarse part of hemp or flax, separated by hackling. [Obs.]

ōak wart, same as *oak gall*.

ōak'web, *n.* the cockchafer. [Brit. Dial.]

ōak'y, *a.* resembling oak; hence, hard; solid.

ōar, *n.* [AS. *ar*; compare Ice. *ar*, Dan. *aare*, Sw. *ara*, oar.]

1. a long piece of wood, flat at one end and round at the other, used in rowing or, sometimes, in steering a boat. The flat part, which is dipped into the water, is called the blade; the other end is the handle; and the part between the two is called the loom. The oar rests in a hole in the gunwhale, called the rowlock, or between two pins called thole pins. The action of an oar in moving a boat is that of a lever.
2. in brewing, a blade or paddle with which the mash is stirred.
3. an oarlike appendage or swimming organ of an animal, as the neuropodium of an annelid.
4. an oarsman; a rower; as, he is an excellent *oar*.

to boat oars; to cease rowing and lay the oars in the boat.

to lie on the oars; to suspend rowing, but without boating the oars; hence, figuratively, to cease from work; to rest.

to put one's oar in; to be meddlesome; to interfere.

to ship the oars; to place them in the rowlocks.

ōar, *v.t.* and *v.i.*; oared, *pt.*, *pp.*; oaring, *ppr.* to row.

ōared, *a.* equipped with oars: often used in hyphenated compounds, meaning *equipped with* (a specified number of) *oars*; as, a four-*oared* boat.

ōar'fish, *n.*; *pl.* **ōar fish** or **ōar fish'es,** any of a group of large, long deep-sea fishes, having long fins with flattened ends.

ōar-foot'ed, *a.* having feet capable of being used for swimming.

ōar'lap, ōar'lop, *n.* a rabbit having the ears at right angles to the head.

ōar'less, *a.* 1. having no oars: said of a boat.
2. not stirred or rippled by oars.

ōar'lock, *n.* a device, often U-shaped, for holding the oar in place in rowing or steering; a rowlock.

ōarṣ'măn, *n.*; *pl.* **ōarṣ'men,** one who rows; especially, an expert at rowing.

ōarṣ'măn·ship, *n.* [*oars-* and *man* and *-ship*.] the art of, or skill at, rowing.

ōar'y, *a.* like an oar in shape or function.

ō·ā'sis, *n.*; *pl.* **ō·ā'sēṣ,** [L., from Gr. *oasis*, a fertile spot; orig. Coptic.] a fertile place in a desert, due to the presence of water: often used figuratively.

My one *oasis* in the dust and drouth of city life. —Tennyson.

ōast, *n.* [AS. *ast*, a kiln.] a kiln to dry hops, tobacco, or malt.

ōat, *n.* [ME. *ote*; AS. *ate*.]

1. [*usually in pl.*] a common cereal plant, *Avena sativa*, or its edible seed, grown throughout the temperate zone.
2. any plant of the genus *Avena*, as (a) *Avena fatua*, the wild oat, having a small grain and held by some to be the original of the oats now in cultivation; (b) a grass, *Avena sterilis*, the animal or animated oat, the long irregularly coiled awns of which change in form with a change of moisture.
3. a simple musical pipe made of an oat stalk. [Obs. or Poet.]

to feel one's oats; (a) to be in high spirits; to be frisky; (b) to feel and act important. [Slang.]

to sow one's wild oats; to be promiscuous or dissolute in youth before settling down: usually said of a man.

ōat'çāke, *n.* a thin, flat, hard cake made of oatmeal.

ōat'en, *a.* of or made of oats, oatmeal, or oat straw.

ōat'fowl, *n.* a bird, the snow bunting. [Brit. Dial.]

ōat grȧss, any species of the genus *Avena* growing wild; by extension, any similar grass, as *Arrhenatherum avenaceum*, used to a limited extent for hay and pasture.

ōath, *n.*; *pl.* **ōathṣ** (*or* ōths), [ME. *oth*, AS. *ath*.]

1. (a) a solemn affirmation or declaration, made with an appeal to God or some revered person or object for the truth of what is affirmed; (b) the pattern of words used in such a declaration; (c) the thing declared or promised in this way.

2. in law, that kind of solemn declaration which is necessary as a condition to the filling of some office more or less public, or of giving evidence in a court of justice, being divided into two classes: (a) assertory oaths, or those by which something is asserted as true; (b) promissory oaths, or those by which something is promised; as, the *oath* of office; the *oath* of witnesses, etc.

3. the irreverent or profane use of the name of God or of a sacred thing to express anger or emphasize a statement.

4. a swearword; a curse.

to take oath; to promise or declare by making an oath; to swear solemnly.

ōath′à·ble, *a.* capable of having an oath administered. [Obs.]

ōat′mēal, *n.* 1. oats crushed into meal or flakes; rolled or ground oats.

2. a porridge made from such oats.

ob-, [from L. *ob*, prep.] a prefix meaning: (a) *to, toward, before*, as in *ob*ject; (b) *opposed to, against*, as in *ob*noxious; (c) *upon, over*, as in *ob*fuscate; (d) *completely, totally*, as in *ob*jurgate. In words of Latin origin, *ob-* assimilates to *oc-* before *c*, as in *oc*cur; *of-* before *f*, as in *of*fer; and *op-* before *p*, as in *op*press; it becomes *o-* before *m*, as in *o*mit.

Ō·bà·dī′ȧh, *n.* in the Bible, (a) one of the minor Hebrew prophets; (b) a book of the Old Testament containing his prophecies.

ob·am′bū·lāte, *v.i.* [L. *obambulare*; *ob*, about, and *ambulare*, to walk.] to walk about. [Rare.]

ob·am·bū·lā′tion, *n.* a walking about. [Rare.]

ob·bli·gä′tō, *a.* [It., lit., obliged; L. *obligatus*, pp. of *obligare*, to oblige; *ob-*, prep., and *ligare*, to bind.] in music, not to be left out; indispensable: said of an accompaniment that has its own character and importance and is necessary to the proper performance of a piece: also spelled *obligato*.

ob·bli·gä′tō, *n.*; *pl.* **ob·bli·gä′tōs, ob·bli·gä′ti,** an obbligato accompaniment: also spelled *obligato*.

ob·clā′vāte, *a.* [*ob-* and *clavate*.] inversely clavate.

ob·cŏm·pressed′, *a.* [*ob-* and *compressed*.] in botany, compressed so that the two sutures of a fruit are brought into contact; flattened, back and front.

ob·con′iç, *a.* in botany, conical, but having the apex downward.

ob·con′iç·ăl, *a.* obconic.

ob·çor′dāte, *a.* in botany, inversely cordate; shaped like a heart with the broad end opposite the attachment: said of leaves.

OBCORDATE LEAF

ob·del′toid, *a.* in botany, inversely deltoid.

ob·dip·lō·stem′ō·nous, *a.* displaying obdiplostemony.

ob·dip·lō·stem′ō·ny, *n.* a condition in which the stamens of a flower are arranged in two whorls, those of the inner whorl being opposite and equal in number to the sepals, and those of the outer whorl being opposite and equal in number to the petals.

ob·dor·mi′tion (-mish′un), *n.* 1. sleep; sound sleep. [Obs.]

2. numbness caused by pressure on a nerve.

ob·dūce′, *v.t.* to draw over, as a covering. [Obs.]

ob·duçt′, *v.t.* to draw over; to cover. [Obs.]

ob·duç′tion, *n.* the act of drawing over, as a covering. [Obs.]

ob′dū·rà·cy, *n.* the quality or state of being obdurate.

Syn.—stubbornness, doggedness, contumacy.

ob′dū·rāte, *a.* [L. *obduratus*, pp. of *obdurare*, to harden; *ob-*, intens., and *durare*, to harden, from *durus*, hard.]

1. not easily moved to pity or sympathy; hardhearted.

2. hardened and unrepenting; impenitent.

3. not giving in readily; stubborn; obstinate; inflexible.

Syn.—callous, hardened.—*Callous* denotes a deadening of the sensibilities; *hardened* implies a general and settled disregard for the claims of interest, duty, and sympathy; *obdurate* rises still higher and implies an active resistance against the pleadings of compassion and humanity.

ob′dū·rāte, *v.t.* and *v.i.* to make or become obdurate.

ob′dū·rāte·ly, *adv.* in an obdurate manner.

ob′dū·rāte·ness, *n.* obduracy.

ob·dū·rā′tion, *n.* obduracy.

ob·dūre′, *v.t.* to harden. [Obs.]

ob·dūre′, *a.* hardened; inflexible. [Obs.]

ōbe, *n.* in Greek history, a clan or a political subdivision among the ancient Athenians.

ō′bē·ȧh, *n.* [of W. Afr. origin.]

1. [*often* O-] a form of witchcraft or magic practiced by some Negroes in Africa, and formerly also in the West Indies.

2. a talisman or fetish used in such witchcraft.

Also *obi*.

ō′bē·ȧh, *v.i.* to practice obeah.

ō′bē·ȧh, *v.t.* to influence by the practice of obeah; to bewitch.

ō·bē′di·ence, *n.* [Fr. *obédience*, from L. *obedientia*, obedience.]

1. the act or habit of obeying; compliance with a command, prohibition, or known law and rule prescribed; submission to authority; as, *obedience* to a person or to a law.

2. in the Roman Catholic Church, (a) the Church's jurisdiction; (b) all those who submit to this jurisdiction.

3. a subordinate monastery or part of a monastery under the care of a prior; also, a written instrument by which a superior in a religious order communicates any special admonition.

canonical obedience; see under *canonical*.
passive obedience; see under *passive*.

ō·bē′di·ent, *a.* [L. *obediens* (*-entis*), ppr. of *obedire*, to obey.] submissive to authority; yielding willingly to commands, orders, or injunctions; performing what is required, or abstaining from that which is forbidden.

Syn.—compliant, dutiful, submissive; docile; tractable.

ō·bē·di·en′tiăl, *a.* in compliance with commands; as, *obediential* submission. [Rare.]

ō·bē′di·ent·ly, *adv.* with obedience.

ō·bei′sănce (*or* -bē′), *n.* [ME. *obeisaunce*; OFr. *obeissance*, from *obeissant*, ppr. of *obeir*, to obey.]

1. a gesture of respect or reverence, such as a bow or curtsy made by an inclination of the body or by bending the knee; also, homage; deference.

2. obedience. [Obs.]

ō·bei′sănt, *a.* showing or doing obeisance; respectful.

ō·bē′li·aç, *a.* pertaining to the obelion.

ō·bē′li·on, *n.* [from Gr. *obelos*, a spit.] the point at which the sagittal suture of the skull is crossed by the line connecting the parietal foramina.

ob·ē·lis′căl, *a.* in the form of an obelisk.

ob′e·lisk, *n.* [L. *obeliscus*; Gr. *obeliskos*, dim. of *obelos*, a spit.]

1. a tall, slender, four-sided pillar, gradually tapering as it rises, having the top in the form of a pyramid. The shaft in the Egyptian obelisks is a single stone often having on it inscriptions or hieroglyphics and erected in honor of distinguished persons or their achievements. Two of the Egyptian obelisks in existence, one now in New York and the other in London, are called *Cleopatra's needles*.

2. an obelus.

OBELISK

ob′e·lisk, *v.t.*; obelisked (-liskt), *pt.*, *pp.*; obelisking, *ppr.* to obelize.

ob′e·lize, *v.t.*; obelized, *pt.*, *pp.*; obelizing, *ppr.* [Gr. *obelizein*.] to mark with an obelus.

ob′e·lus, *n.*; *pl.* **ob′e·lī,** [ME.; LL.; Gr. *obelos*, a needle, a spit.]

1. a mark (— or ÷) so called from its resemblance to a needle: used in ancient manuscripts or old editions of the classics to indicate a suspected passage or reading.

2. in typography, a reference mark (†), used to indicate footnotes, etc.; a dagger.

ob·eq′ui·tāte (-ek′wi-), *v.i.* to ride about. [Obs.]

ob·eq·ui·tā′tion, *n.* the act of riding about. [Obs.]

Ō′bẽr·on, *n.* in early folklore, the king of the fairies.

ob·er·rā′tion, *n.* the act of wandering about. [Obs.]

ō·bēse′, *a.* [L. *obesus*.] stout; corpulent; very fat.

ō·bēse′ness, *n.* same as *obesity*.

ō·bēs′i·ty (or -bes′), *n.* [L. *obesitas*.] the quality or condition of being obese.

Syn.—fatness, fleshiness, corpulence, plumpness.

ō′bex, *n.* [L., from *objicere*, to throw before.]

1. an obstacle; a preventive. [Rare.]

2. in anatomy, a thickening of the ependyma at the point of the calamus scriptorius, the space at the lower part or floor of the fourth ventricle.

ō·bey′, *v.t.*; obeyed, *pt.*, *pp.*; obeying, *ppr.* [ME. *obeien*; OFr. *obeir*; L. *obedire*, to obey; Old L. *obœdire*; *ob*, before, and *audire*, to hear.]

1. to be obedient or submissive to; to comply with the commands, directions, or injunctions of; as, to *obey* one's parents.

2. to carry out (an instruction, order, etc.)

3. to follow the impulse, movement, power, or influence of; to be moved by; to submit to the direction or control of; as, a ship *obeys* her helm.

ō·bey′, *v.i.* to be obedient or submissive to authority; to do as directed: formerly followed by *to*, in accordance with the French idiom.

ō·bey′ẽr, *n.* one who yields obedience.

ō·bey′ing·ly, *adv.* in an obedient manner; complyingly; submissively.

ob·firm′āte, *v.t.* to make firm; to harden in resolution. [Obs.]

ob·fir·mā′tion, *n.* hardened resolution; obstinacy. [Obs.]

ob·fus′çāte, *a.* darkened; obscured; clouded. [Obs.]

ob·fus′çāte, *v.t.*; obfuscated, *pt.*, *pp.*; obfuscating, *ppr.* [L. *obfuscatus*, pp. of *obfuscare*, *offuscare*, to darken; *ob-*, intens., and *fuscare*, to obscure, from *fuscus*, dark.]

1. to darken; to obscure.

2. to stupefy; to confuse; to muddle.

ob·fus·çā′tion, *n.* 1. an obfuscating or being obfuscated.

2. something that obfuscates.

ō′bi, *n.* same as *obeah*.

ō′bi, *n.* [Japan.] a broad silk sash with a bow in the back, worn by Japanese women and children.

ob′i·it (*or* ō′bi-), [L.] he (or she) died.

ō·bis′pō, *n.* [Sp., a bishop.] the West Indian bishop ray.

ō′bit (*or* ob′it), *n.* [L. *obitus*, death, from *obire*, to go down, to fall, to die; *ob*, against, and *ire*, to go.]

1. death; decease; also, the time of a person's death. [Obs.]

2. a funeral ceremony; obsequies. [Obs.]

3. a service for the soul of a deceased person, celebrated on the anniversary of his death; especially, such a service by an institution memorializing its founder.

4. a notice of someone's death; an obituary.

ob′i·tẽr, *adv.* [L., from *ob*, along, and *iter*, a way.] in passing; incidentally; by the way.

ob′i·tẽr diç′tum, *pl.* **ob′i·tẽr diç′tȧ,** [L.]

1. an incidental opinion expressed by a judge, having no bearing upon the case in question, hence not binding.

2. any incidental remark.

ō·bit′ū·ăl, *a.* obituary. [Rare.]

ō·bit′ū·ăr·i·ly, *adv.* in the manner of an obituary.

ō·bit′ū·ăr·ist, *n.* one who writes an obituary.

ō·bit′ū·ăr·y, *a.* relating to or recording the death of a person or persons; as, an *obituary* notice.

ō·bit′ū·ăr·y, *n.*; *pl.* **ō·bit′ū·ăr·ieș,** [ML. *obituarius*, from L. *obitus*, death.]

1. an account or notice of someone's death, as in a newspaper, frequently accompanied with a brief biographical sketch.

2. in the Roman Catholic Church, a list of the dead, or a register of anniversary days when service is performed for the dead.

ob′jeçt, *n.* [ME.; ML. *objectum*, something thrown in the way; L. *objectus*, a casting before, orig. pp. of *objicere*, from *ob-*, ob-, and *jacere*, to throw.]

1. what is aimed at; that toward which the mind is directed in any of its states or activities; goal; aim; ultimate purpose; end.

The great *object* I desire to accomplish is to

open the avenues of scientific knowledge to youth. —Peter Cooper.

2. a person or thing to which action, thought, or feeling is directed.

Titus had, like every other human being, a right to justice, but he was not a proper *object* of mercy. —Macaulay.

3. anything visible or tangible; a material product or substance; as, he saw an *object* in the dark and felt it.

4. sight; appearance; representation. [Obs.]

5. a person or thing that excites pity or ridicule; a sight; as, she has made quite an *object* of herself. [Colloq.]

6. in grammar, a noun or substantive that directly or indirectly receives the action of a verb, or one that is governed by a preposition. In "Give me the book," *book* is the *direct object* and *me* is the *indirect object*.

7. in philosophy, anything that can be known or perceived by the mind.

Syn.—aim, end, design, purpose.

ob·jeçt′, *v.t.* 1. formerly, (a) to oppose; (b) to thrust in; to interpose; (c) to expose; (d) to bring forward as a reason, instance, etc.; to adduce.

2. to put forward in opposition; to state by way of objection; as, it was *objected* that the new tax law was unfair to property owners.

ob·jeçt′, *v.i.* 1. to put forward an objection or objections; to enter a protest; to be opposed.

2. to feel or express disapproval or dislike.

ob·jeçt′, *a.* opposed; presented in opposition. [Obs.]

ob·jeçt′a·ble, *a.* capable of being made or put forward as an objection. [Rare.]

ob·jeçt·ā′tion, *n.* reproach; caviling objection. [Rare.]

ob′jeçt ball, in billiards and pool, the ball that the player aims to hit with the cue ball, or any ball that may be hit by the cue ball.

ob′jeçt find′ẽr, a device in microscopes for registering the position of an object on a slide, so that it may be readily found again.

ob′jeçt glȧss, an objective (sense 4).

ob·jeç″ti·fi·çā′tion, *n.* the act of objectifying.

ob·jeç′ti·fȳ, *v.t.*; objectified, *pt., pp.*; objectifying, *ppr.* to give objective form to; to materialize; to make objective.

ob·jeç′tion, *n.* [ME. *objeccioun*; LL. *objectio* (*-onis*), from *objicere*, to throw before, to object.]

1. the act of objecting, urging, or bringing forward anything in opposition.

2. an adverse argument, reason, or charge; a ground or reason for objecting or opposing; a fault found or capable of being urged against anything; as, he raised many *objections* to the bill.

3. a feeling or expression of opposition, disapproval, or dislike.

Syn.—exception, cavil, scruple, difficulty, demurrer.

ob·jeç′tion·a·ble, *a.* justly liable to objection; hence, disagreeable; offensive; as, *objectionable* features.

ob·jeç′tion·a·bly, *adv.* in an objectionable manner; so as to be objectionable.

ob·jeç′ti·vāte, *v.t.* to objectify.

ob·jeç·ti·vā′tion, *n.* objectification.

ob·jeç′tive, *a.* [ML. *objectivus.*]

1. of or having to do with a known or perceived object as distinguished from something existing only in the mind of the subject, or person thinking.

2. being, or regarded as being, independent of the mind; real; actual.

3. determined by and emphasizing the features and characteristics of the object, or thing dealt with, rather than the thoughts, feelings, etc. of the artist, writer, or speaker; as, an *objective* description, painting, etc.

4. without bias or prejudice; detached; impersonal.

5. being the aim or goal; as, an *objective* point.

6. in grammar, designating or of the case of an object of a preposition or transitive verb.

7. in medicine, designating or of a symptom or condition perceptible to others besides the patient.

objective line; in perspective, a line drawn on the geometrical plane, the representation of which is sought in the draft or picture.

objective plane; any plane situated in the horizontal plane, whose perspective representation is required.

ob·jeç′tive, *n.* 1. anything external to or independent of the mind; something objective; reality.

2. something aimed at or striven for.

3. in grammar, (a) the objective case; (b) a word in this case.

4. in optics, the lens or lenses nearest to the object observed, in a microscope, telescope, etc.

endomersion objective; a kind of objective (sense 4) in which the chromatic aberration is removed by liquid placed between the lenses.

ob·jeç′tive·ly, *adv.* in an objective manner.

ob·jeç′tive·ness, *n.* the state of being objective; objectivity.

Is there such a motion or *objectiveness* of external bodies, which produceth light? —Hale.

ob·jeç′tiv·ism, *n.* 1. any of various philosophical doctrines that stress the objective reality of all that is known or perceived.

2. the use of objective methods in art or literature.

ob·jeç·tiv′i·ty, *n.* 1. the state or quality of being objective.

2. objective reality.

ob·jeç′tiv·īze, *v.t.*; objectivized, *pt., pp.*; objectivizing, *ppr.* to make objective; to objectify.

ob′jeçt·īze, *v.t.* to objectify.

ob′jeçt·less, *a.* 1. having no object; without purpose.

2. having no visible or concrete object; as, an *objectless* stretch of land.

ob′jeçt les′sŏn, an actual or practical demonstration or exemplification of some principle.

ob·jeçt′ŏr, *n.* one who objects.

ob′jeçt stȧff, same as *leveling rod.*

ob′jeçt tēach′ing, teaching by means of object lessons.

ọb·jet d'ȧrt′ (ọb-zhe-dȧr′), *pl.* **ọb·jets d'ȧrt′** (ọb-zhe-dȧr′), [Fr., lit., object of art.] a relatively small object of artistic value, as a figurine, vase, etc.

ob·jic′i·ent, *n.* an objector. [Rare.]

ob·jū·rā′tion, *n.* the act of binding by oath. [Rare.]

ob′jũr·gāte, *v.t.*; objurgated, *pt., pp.*; objurgating, *ppr.* [L. *objurgare*; *ob*, against, and *jurgare*, to chide.] to chide vehemently; to upbraid; to rebuke; to reprove.

ob·jũr·gā′tion, *n.* the act of objurgating; reproof; reprehension.

ob·jũr′gȧ·tō·ry, *a.* objurgating or tending to oburgate.

ob·lan′ce·ō·lāte, *a.* [*ob-* and *lanceolate.*] in botany, shaped like a lance point reversed, that is, having the tapering point next the leafstalk: said of certain leaves.

ob′läst, *n.* [Russ.] in the U.S.S.R., a regional congress of soviets.

ob′lāte (or ob-lāt′), *a.* [ML. *oblatus*, offered, thrust forward (in L., pp. of *offerre*, to offer.]

1. dedicated to a religious or monastic life.

2. [Mod. L. *oblatus*; *ob-*, and *-latus*, as in *prolatus*; see *prolate.*] in geometry, flattened at the poles; as, an *oblate* spheroid.

oblate ellipsoid or *spheroid*; see *ellipsoid of revolution* under *ellipsoid.*

ob′lāte, *n.* [L. *oblatus*, offered, devoted.] one dedicated to a religious or monastic life; specifically, in the Roman Catholic Church, (a) a secular person who, in the Middle Ages, devoted himself, his dependents, and estates, to some monastery, into which he was admitted as a kind of lay brother; (b) a member of a congregation of secular priests who live in community under a bishop; (c) a child dedicated by his parents to a religious life.

ob·lāte′ness, *n.* the quality or state of being oblate.

ob·lā′tion, *n.* [ME. *oblacioun*; OFr.; L. *oblatio* (*-onis*), an offering, from *offerre*, to bring forward, to offer.]

1. the act of offering. [Obs.]

2. an offering of a sacrifice, thanksgiving, etc. to God or a god.

3. the thing or things offered; especially, the bread and wine of the Eucharist.

4. in church history, a gift or contribution for the expenses of the Eucharist, or for the support of the clergy and the poor.

ob·lā′tion·ẽr, *n.* one who makes an oblation. [Obs.]

ob′lȧ·tō·ry, *a.* of an oblation.

ob·lā·trā′tion, *n.* a barking; a snarling; quarrelsome or snappish objection; caviling. [Obs.]

ob·leç′tāte, *v.t.* to delight; to please highly. [Rare.]

ob·leç·tā′tion, *n.* the act of pleasing highly; delight. [Rare.]

ob′li·gȧ·ble, *a.* capable of carrying out an obligation; worthy of confidence; reliable; trustworthy. [Rare.]

ob′li·gănt, *n.* in Scots law, a person who binds himself by a legal tie to pay or perform something.

ob′li·gāte, *v.t.*; obligated, *pt., pp.*; obligating, *ppr.* [L. *obligatus*, pp. of *obligare*, to bind, to bring under an obligation; *ob*, before, and *ligare*, to bind.] to bind by a contract, promise, sense of duty, etc.; to bring under obligation, legal or moral; to pledge.

ob′li·gāte, *a.* [ME., from L. *obligatus.*]

1. bound; obliged.

2. in biology, limited to a certain condition of life, as a parasite.

ob·li·gā′tion, *n.* [ME. *obligacioun*; OFr.; L. *obligatio.*]

1. an obligating or being obligated.

2. the contract, promise, moral responsibility, etc. binding one.

3. a duty imposed legally or socially; thing that one is bound to do as a result of a contract, promise, moral responsibility, etc.

4. the binding power of a contract, promise, moral responsibility, etc.

5. (a) the condition or fact of being indebted to another for a favor or service received; (b) a favor or service.

6. in law, (a) an agreement by which the *obligor* is bound under penalty of law to make payment or perform services for the benefit of the *obligee*; (b) the bond, contract, or other written document setting forth the terms of this agreement.

ob·li·gä′tō, *a.* same as *obbligato.*

ob·li·gä′tō, *n.*; *pl.* **ob·li·gä′tōs, ob·li·gä′ti,** same as *obbligato.*

ob·lig′a·tō·ri·ly (*or* ob′lig-), *adv.* because of obligation; in an obligatory manner.

ob·lig′a·tō·ri·ness, *n.* the quality or condition of being under obligation.

ob·lig′a·tō·ry, (*or* ob′lig-), *a.* [Late ME.; LL. *obligatorius.*]

1. legally or morally binding; constituting, or having the nature of, an obligation required.

2. in biology, obligate.

ō·blīge′, *v.t.*; obliged, *pt., pp.*; obliging, *ppr.* [ME. *obligen*; OFr. *obligier*; L. *obligare*, to bind, to oblige; *ob*, before, against, and *ligare*, to bind.]

1. to compel; to constrain by physical, legal, or moral force.

2. to do a favor for; to make indebted for a favor or kindness done; as, *oblige* us by attending to this matter promptly.

3. to bring under obligation.

To those hills we are *obliged* for all our metals. —Bentley.

Syn.—accommodate, compel, constrain.

ob·li·ġee′, *n.* [from *oblige* and *-ee.*]

1. a person obliged to do something for another: opposed to *obliger.*

2. in law, a person to whom another is bound by contract: opposed to *obligor.*

ō·blīge′ment, *n.* obligation. [Rare.]

ō·blī′ġẽr, *n.* a person who obliges.

ō·blī′ġing, *a.* 1. obligatory. [Rare.]

2. helpful; ready to be of service; civil; complaisant; accommodating; kind.

Syn.—kind, complaisant, amiable, pleasing. —One is *kind* who desires to see others happy; one is *complaisant* who endeavors to please; one who is *obliging* performs some actual service, or has the disposition to do so.

ō·blī′ġing·ly, *adv.* in an obliging manner.

ō·blī′ġing·ness, *n.* the state, quality, or condition of being obliging.

ob·li·gor′, *n.* [from *oblige* and *-or.*] in law, the person who binds himself to another by contract: opposed to *obligee.*

ob·li·quā′tion, *n.* [L. *obliquatio* (*-onis*), from *obliquus*, oblique.] declination from a straight line or course; a turning to one side; as, the *obliquation* of the eyes. [Rare.]

ob·lïque′ (-lēk′; *esp. in military use*, ō-blīk′), *a.* [L. *obliquus*; *ob*, before, against, and *liquis*, awry.]

1. having a slanting position or direction; neither perpendicular nor horizontal; not level or upright; inclined.

2. not straight to the point; not straightforward; indirect.

3. evasive, disingenuous, underhand, etc.

4. indirectly aimed at or attained, as results, etc.

5. in anatomy, designating or of any of certain muscles obliquely placed and attached.

6. in botany, having the sides unequal, as some leaves.

7. in grammar, designating or of any case except the nominative and the vocative (and sometimes the accusative).

8. in rhetoric, indirect: said of discourse.
oblique angle; any angle other than a right angle; an acute or obtuse angle.
oblique ascension; see under *ascension*.
oblique bridge; see *skew bridge* under *bridge*.
oblique circle; in projections, a circle whose plane forms an oblique angle with the primitive plane.
oblique motion; in music, a succession of chords in which one part sustains or repeats one tone while the other part ascends or descends.
oblique narration; indirect quotation.
oblique plane; in dialing, a plane which declines from the zenith, or inclines toward the horizon.
oblique sailing; a ship's movement in sailing on a course that forms an oblique angle with the meridian.
oblique sphere; in astronomy and geography, the celestial sphere seen by an observer when the apparent paths of the stars make oblique angles with the horizon; the celestial sphere as observed from any point on the earth other than at the equator or at one of its poles.

ob·lïque′, *v.i.*; obliqued (-lēkt′ *or* -līkt′), *pt., pp.*; obliquing, *ppr.* 1. to deviate from a direct line, or from the perpendicular; to slant; to slope.
Projecting his person toward it in a line which *obliqued* from the botton of his spine. —Scott.
2. in military usage, to change the original direction of march by approximately 45 degrees.

ob·lïque′-an″gled, (-gld), *a.* having oblique angles; as, an *oblique-angled* triangle.

ob·lïque′ly, *adv.* in a line deviating from a right line; not perpendicularly; indirectly; inferentially; deviously.

ob·lïque′ness, *n.* the condition of being oblique; obliquity.

ob·liq′ui·tous (-lik′wi-), *a.* characterized by or having obliquity.

ob·liq′ui·ty, *n.*; *pl.* **ob·liq′ui·tieș**, [L. *obliquitas*, from *obliquus*, oblique.]
1. the state or quality of being oblique.
2. a turning aside from moral conduct or sound thinking.
3. in astronomy, the angle between the planes of the earth's equator and orbit.
4. in mathematics, (a) deviation of a line or plane from the perpendicular or parallel; (b) the degree of this.

ob·lit′ẽr·āte, *v.t.*; obliterated, *pt., pp.*; obliterating, *ppr.* [L. *obliteratus*, pp. of *obliterare*, to blot out, to cause to be forgotten; *ob*, over, and *litera*, a letter.]
1. to efface; to erase or blot out, leaving no traces; to expunge.
2. to demolish; to wear out; to destroy all trace of.

ob·lit′ẽr·āte, *a.* in zoology, indistinct; scarcely discernible, as the markings of insects.

ob·lit·ẽr·ā′tion, *n.* the act of obliterating or effacing; also, the state of being obliterated; extinction.

ob·lit′ẽr·ā·tive, *a.* tending to obliterate; capable of obliterating.

ob·lit′ẽr·ā·tŏr, *n.* [LL.] one who or that which obliterates.

ob·liv′i·ŏn, *n.* [ME.; OFr.; L. *oblivio* (*-onis*), from *oblivisci*, to forget; *ob*, over, and prob. *livere*, to become black.]
1. a forgetting or having forgotten; forgetfulness.
Among our crimes *oblivion* may be set. —Dryden.
2. the condition or fact of being forgotten.
3. pardon of offenses or remission of punishment; amnesty or general pardon of crimes and offenses granted by a sovereign, by which punishment is remitted.

ob·liv′i·ous, *a.* [ME. *obliuyous*; L. *obliviosus*.]
1. causing forgetfulness; inducing oblivion.
The *oblivious* calm of indifference. —J. M. Mason.
2. forgetful; abstracted; inclined to forget; unmindful (with *of* or *to*).

ob·liv′i·ous·ly, *adv.* in an oblivious manner.

ob·liv′i·ous·ness, *n.* the quality of being oblivious.

ob′lŏng, *a.* [L. *oblongus*, rather long.]
1. longer than broad; specifically, retangular and longer in one direction than in the other.
2. in botany, elliptical and from two to four times as long as broad.

ob′lŏng, *n.* an oblong figure; anything oblong in form.

ob·lŏn·gā′tăl, *a.* pertaining to the medulla oblongata; myelencephalic; medullary.

ob′lŏng·ish, *a.* somewhat oblong.

ob′lŏng·ly, *adv.* in an oblong form. [Rare.]

ob′lŏng·ness, *n.* the state or quality of being oblong.

ob″lŏng-ō′vāte, *a.* both oblong and ovate.

ob·lō′qui·ous, *a.* containing obloquy. [Rare.]

ob′lō·quy, *n.*; *pl.* **ob′lō·quieș**, [L. *obloquium*, from *obloqui*, to speak against; *ob*, against, and *loqui*, to speak.]
1. verbal abuse of a person or thing; censure or vituperation, especially when widespread or general.
2. cause of reproach; disgrace. [Obs.]
3. the condition of being in disgrace; infamy; shame.
Syn.—contumely, odium, reproach, defamation.

ob·luç·tā′tion, *n.* a striving against; resistance. [Obs.]

ob·mū·tes′cence, *n.* loss of speech; a keeping silence. [Obs.]

ob·nox′ious (-nok′shus), *a.* [L. *obnoxius*, subject or liable, exposed to danger; *ob*, against, and *noxa*, harm, hurt, from root of *nocere*, to hurt.]
1. very unpleasant; objectionable; offensive.
2. (a) exposed or liable to injury, evil, or harm; (b) liable to punishment; censurable. [Archaic.]
3. in law, answerable; responsible.
Syn.—blameworthy, reprehensible, detestable.

ob·nox′ious·ly, *adv.* in an obnoxious manner.

ob·nox′ious·ness, *n.* the state or quality of being obnoxious.

ob·nū′bi·lāte, *v.t.* to cloud; to obscure. [Now Rare.]

ob·nū·bi·lā′tion, *n.* obscuration. [Now Rare.]

ō′bōe (*or* -boi), *n.* [It.; Fr. *hautbois*, hautboy; see *hautboy*.]
1. a double-reed wood-wind instrument having a range of nearly three octaves, and a high, penetrating, melancholy tone.
2. an organ stop producing an oboelike sound.
oboe da cacia; a tenor oboe or bassoon, now obsolete.
oboe d'amore; an alto oboe, now obsolete.

OBOE

ō′bō·ist, *n.* one who plays upon the oboe.

ob′ol, *n.* same as *obolus*.

ob′ō·lā·ry, *a.* having small coins only; poor.

ob′ōle, *n.* a small medieval French coin equal to half a denier.

ob′ō·līze, *v.t.* to obelize.

ob′ō·lus, *n.*; *pl.* **ob′ō·lī**, [L.; Gr. *obolos*.]
1. in ancient Greece, (a) a coin valued at 1/6 drachma; (b) a weight equal to 11 1/4 grains.
2. any of several small coins formerly current in Europe.

ob·ō·mē′goid, *a.* [*ob-* and *omegoid*.] obversely omegoid.

ob·ō′văl, *a.* obovate. [Rare.]

ob·ō′vāte, *a.* [*ob-* and *ovate*.] inversely ovate; having the shape of the longitudinal section of an egg, with the broad end at the top, as some leaves.

ob·ō′void, *a.* [*ob-* and *ovoid*.] egg-shaped, with the broad end at the top: said of some fruits, etc.

OBOVATE LEAF

ob·rep′tion, *n.* [L. *obreptio* (*-onis*), a creeping on, from *obrepere*; *ob*, on, and *repere*, to creep.]
1. the act of creeping upon by surprise. [Obs.]
2. in Scots law, the getting of gifts of escheat by falsehood.

ob·rep·ti′tious, *a.* done or obtained by surprise or by falsehood.

ob′rō·gāte, *v.t.* to repeal indirectly, as a law, by proclaiming another contrary to it.

ob·rok′, *n.* formerly, in Czarist Russia, the tax paid by a peasant when absent from his lord's property.

ob·scēne′ (-sēn′), *a.* [Fr. *obscène*; L. *obscenus*, *obscænus*, filthy, repulsive, ill-omened, obscene.]
1. offensive to modesty or decency; lewd; impure; as, *obscene* language or pictures.
2. foul; filthy; repulsive; disgusting.
3. inauspicious; ill-omened. [Obs.]
Syn.—impure, indecent, lewd, indelicate.

ob·scēne′ly, *adv.* in an obscene manner.

ob·scēne′ness, *n.* obscenity.

ob·scen′i·ty (*or* -sēn′), *n.* [Fr. *obscénité*; L. *obscenitas*.]
1. the state or quality of being obscene.
2. *pl.* **ob·scen′i·tieș**, something obscene, as language, conduct, a remark, an expression, an act, etc.

ob·sçūr′ănt, *n.* one who or that which obscures, especially one that tends to prevent human progress and enlightenment.

ob·sçūr′ănt, *a.* of or constituting an obscurant.

ob·sçūr′ănt·ișm, *n.* the principles or practice of an obscurant; opposition to human progress and enlightenment.

ob·sçūr′ănt·ist, *n.* a person who advocates obscurantism.

ob·sçūr′ănt·ist, *a.* of or like obscurantism or an obscurantist.

ob·sçū·rā′tion, *n.* [L. *obscuratio* (*-onis*), from *obscurare*, to darken, obscure.] the act of darkening; the state of being darkened or obscured; as, the *obscuration* of the moon in an eclipse.

ob·sçūre′, *n.* obscurity. [Rare.]

ob·sçūre′, *a.* [ME.; OFr. *obscur*; L. *obscurus*, dark, dusky, indistinct.]
1. dark; destitute of light; dim; gloomy.
2. living in darkness; as, the *obscure* bird.
3. not easily understood; not obviously intelligible; vague; ambiguous; as, an *obscure* passage in a writing.
4. in an inconspicuous position; hidden; retired; remote from observation; as, an *obscure* retreat.
5. not famous; unknown; humble; as, an *obscure* person.
6. not clear or distinct; as, an *obscure* idea.
7. not easily perceived or felt.
obscure rays; the nonluminous heat rays of the solar spectrum.
Syn.—dark, indistinct, abstruse, intricate, unknown, humble.

ob·sçūre′, *v.t.*; obscured, *pt., pp.*; obscuring, *ppr.* [L. *obscurare*, to darken, conceal, from *obscurus*, dark, shady.]
1. to make obscure; specifically, (a) to darken; to make dim; (b) to conceal from view; to hide; (c) to make less conspicuous; to overshadow; as, his success *obscured* his failures; (d) to make less intelligible; to confuse; as, his testimony *obscured* the issue.
2. in phonetics, to decrease the quality of (a vowel) to a more or less neutral sound, as that of (ə) or (i).

ob·sçūre′, *v.i.* to become obscure; also, to hide.

ob·sçūre′ly, *adv.* in an obscure manner.

ob·sçūre′ment, *n.* obscuration.

ob·sçūre′ness, *n.* obscurity.

ob·sçūr′ẽr, *n.* one who or that which obscures.

ob·sçū′ri·ty, *n.* [L. *obscuritas*, from *obscurus*, dark.]
1. the state or quality of being obscure.
2. *pl.* **ob·sçū′ri·tieș**, an obscure person or thing.

ob′sē·çrāte, *v.t.*; obsecrated, *pt., pp.*; obsecrating, *ppr.* [from L. *obsecratus*, pp. of *obsecrare*, to beseech.] to beseech; to entreat; to beg for (something). [Rare.]

ob·sē·çrā′tion, *n.* 1. entreaty; supplication.
2. any prayer or petition in the Litany beginning with *per* or *by*, and assigning a basis for the appeal.

ob′sē·quent, *a.* obedient; obsequious. [Obs.]

ob·sē′qui·ence, *n.* obsequiousness. [Obs.]

ob′sē·quieș, *n.* pl. of *obsequy*.

ob·sē′qui·ous, *a.* [Fr. *obséquieux*; L. *obsequiosus*, from *obsequium*, complaisance, from *obsequi*, to comply with.]
1. excessively willing to serve or obey; overly submissive; servile; toadyish; fawning.
2. compliant; devoted; dutiful. [Now Rare.]
3. of obsequies; funereal. [Obs.]
Syn.—attentive, yielding, cringing, deferential, slavish.

ob·sē′qui·ous·ly, *adv.* in an obsequious manner.

ob·sē′qui·ous·ness, *n.* 1. ready obedience.
2. servile submission; excessive and slavish complaisance.

ob′sē·quy, *n.*; *pl.* **ob′sē·quieș**, [ME.; OFr. *obseques*; ML. *obsequiæ*, by confusion with *exsequiæ*, funeral, from L. *obsequium*, complaisance.]
1. [*usually in pl.*] a funeral rite or ceremony.
2. obsequiousness. [Obs.]

ob·sėrv'à·ble, *a.* 1. that can be observed; specifically, (a) visible; discernible; noticeable; (b) that can be kept or celebrated; as, Lincoln's birthday is an *observable* holiday.
2. that should or must be observed; specifically, (a) deserving of attention; noteworthy; (b) that must be kept or celebrated.

ob·sėrv'à·ble·ness, *n.* the state of being observable.

ob·sėrv'à·bly, *adv.* so as to be observable.

ob·sėrv'ănce, *n.* 1. the act or practice of observing, or keeping a law, duty, custom, rule, etc.
2. a customary act, rite, ceremony, etc.
3. observation.
4. respectful attention; deference. [Archaic.]
5. in the Roman Catholic Church, (a) the rule or constitution to be observed by a religious order; (b) an order observing such a rule.
Syn.—form, ceremony, rite, custom.

ob·sėrv'ăn·cy, *n.* observance. [Rare.]

ob·sẽr·van'dum, *n.*; *pl.* **ob·sẽr·van'dȧ,** [L.] a thing to be observed.

ob·sėrv'ănt, *a.* [Fr., *ppr.* of *observer*, to observe.]
1. strict in observing, or keeping, a law, custom, duty, rule, etc. (often with *of*); as, *observant of* the rules of etiquette.
2. paying careful attention; keenly watchful.
3. perceptive or alert.

Ob·sėrv'ănt, *n.* 1. in the Roman Catholic Church, any member of a Franciscan order strictly observing the original rules, especially that of poverty.
2. [o–] one who observes a law, custom, etc. [Obs.]
3. [o–] a slavish attendant. [Obs.]
Syn.—heedful, listening, mindful, watchful, attentive.

Ob·sẽr·van'tine, *n.* an Observant.

ob·sėrv'ănt·ly, *adv.* in an observant manner.

ob·sẽr·vā'tion, *n.* [ME. *observacioun*; L. *observatio (-onis)*, a watching, noting.]
1. originally, observance, as of laws, customs, etc.
2. (a) the act, practice, or power of noticing; (b) something noticed.
3. the fact of being seen or noticed; as, let's try to avoid *observation*.
4. (a) the act or practice of noting and recording facts and events, as for some scientific study; (b) the data so noted and recorded.
5. a comment or remark based on something observed.
6. in navigation, (a) the act of determining the altitude of the sun, a star, etc., in order to find the ship's position at sea; (b) the result obtained.

ob·sẽr·vā'tion, *a.* for observing.

ob·sẽr·vā'tion·ăl, *a.* of or based on observation rather than experimentation.

ob·sẽr·vā'tion cär, a railway car at the end of a train with extra-large windows or, formerly, an open platform at the rear, for viewing the scenery along the route.

ob·sẽr·vā'tion pōst, an advanced military position from which movements of the enemy can be observed, artillery fire directed, etc.

ob·sėrv'à·tō·ry, *n.*; *pl.* **ob·sėrv'à·tō·rieș,** [Fr. *observatoire*.]
1. a building equipped for scientific observation, especially for astronomical or meteorological research.
2. any building or place providing an extensive view of the surrounding terrain.

ob·sėrve', *v.t.*; observed, *pt.*, *pp.*; observing, *ppr.* [ME. *observen*; OFr. *observer*; L. *observare*, to watch, note; *ob*, before, in front, and *servare*, to keep or hold.]
1. to adhere to, follow, keep, or abide by (a law, custom, duty, rule, etc.).
2. to celebrate or keep (a holiday, etc.) according to custom.
3. (a) to notice or perceive (something); (b) to pay special attention to; as, *observe* how I do this.
4. to say or mention casually; to remark.
5. to examine scientifically.

ob·sėrve', *v.i.* 1. to take notice.
2. to comment or remark (*on* or *upon*).
3. to act as an observer.

ob·sėrv'ẽr, *n.* a person who observes something; specifically, (a) a member of an aircraft crew whose job is to keep a lookout for the enemy and, often, to operate a machine gun; (b) a soldier manning an observation post.

ob·sėrv'ẽr·ship, *n.* the office of an observer.

ob·sėrv'ing, *a.* quick to perceive; attentive; as, *observing* eyes.

ob·sėrv'ing·ly, *adv.* attentively; carefully; with close observation.

ob·sess', *v.t.*; obsessed (-sest'), *pt.*, *pp.*; obsessing, *ppr.*[from L. *obsessus*, pp. of *obsidere*, to besiege.]
1. to haunt or trouble in mind; to beset; to harass; to preoccupy: usually in the passive voice, followed by *with* or *by*.
2. to besiege. [Obs.]

ob·ses'sion, *n.* [L. *obsessio*.]
1. originally, the act of an evil spirit in possessing or ruling a person.
2. (a) the fact or state of being obsessed with an idea, desire, emotion, etc.; (b) such an idea, desire, emotion, etc.
3. a siege. [Obs.]

ob·ses'sive, *a.* of, having the nature of, or causing an obsession or obsessions.

ob·sid'i·ăn, *n.* [L. *obsidianus*, from faulty reading of *obsianus* in early editions of Pliny: so called after a person named *Obsius*, who, according to Pliny, discovered it in Ethiopia.] a dark, hard, glassy volcanic rock, usually having the same composition as volcanic granite.

ob·sid'i·ō·năl, *a.* [L. *obsidionalis*, from *obsidio*, a siege.] pertaining to a siege.
obsidional coins; token metallic currency used within a beleaguered city.
obsidional crown; a crown or wreath of grass bestowed upon a Roman general who withstood or relieved a siege.

ob·sid'i·ō·nãr·y, *a.* obsidional.

ob·sig'nāte, *v.t.* [L. *obsignatus*, pp. of *obsignare*, to seal up.] to confirm; to seal. [Rare.]

ob·sig'nà·tō·ry, *a.* ratifying; confirming by sealing. [Rare.]

ob·sō·lesce', *v.i.*; obsolesced (-lest), *pt.*, *pp.*; obsolescing, *ppr.* to become obsolescent. [Rare.]

ob·sō·les'cence, *n.* the process or state of becoming obsolete.

ob·sō·les'cent, *a.* [L. *obsolescens (-entis)*, ppr. of *obsolescere*, to go out of use; *ob*, before, and *solere*, to use, be wont.] going out of use; becoming obsolete.

ob'sō·lēte, *a.* [L. *obsoletus*, pp. of *obsolescere*, to go out of use.]
1. no longer in use or practice; discarded: distinguished from *archaic*.
2. no longer in fashion; out of date; passé; as, *obsolete* equipment.
3. in biology, rudimentary or poorly developed as compared with its counterpart in other individuals of a related species, the opposite sex, etc.: said of an organ or the like.
Syn.—ancient, antique, antiquated, disused, obsolescent, old-fashioned, archaic.

ob'sō·lēte, *v.t.* to make obsolete. [Now Rare.]

ob'sō·lēte·ly, *adv.* in an obsolete manner.

ob'sō·lēte·ness, *n.* the state or condition of being obsolete.

ob'sō·lēt·ișm, *n.* an archaic word or phrase; a thing that is obsolete.

ob'stà·çle, *n.* [ME.; OFr.; L. *obstaculum*, an obstacle, from *obstare*, to withstand; *ob*, against, and *stare*, to stand.] anything that gets in the way or hinders; impediment; obstruction; hindrance.

ob'stà·çle rāce, a race in which the runners must surmount obstacles, such as fences, ditches, etc.

ob'stăn·cy, *n.* opposition; impediment; obstruction. [Obs.]

ob·stet'riç, ob·stet'riç·ăl, *a.* [L. *obstetrix*, a midwife; lit., she who stands before; *ob*, before, and *stare*, to stand.] of childbirth or obstetrics.
obstetrical toad; *Alytes obstetricans* and *Alytes cisternasi*, small toads of southwestern and central Europe, the males of which carry the strings of eggs laid by the female on their hind legs until they hatch.
obstetrical forceps; an instrument, resembling a forceps, used to facilitate childbirth.

ob·ste·tri'ciăn (-trish'ăn), *n.* a doctor who specializes in obstetrics.

ob·ste·tri'cious, *a.* obstetric. [Obs.]

ob·stet'riçs, *n.pl.* [*construed as sing.*], [from *obstetric*.] the branch of medicine concerned with the care and treatment of women during pregnancy, childbirth, and the period immediately following.

ob·stet'ri·cy, *n.* same as *obstetrics*.

ob'sti·nà·cy, *n.* [ME. *obstinacie*; LL. *obstinatio*, obstinateness.]
1. the state or quality of being obstinate; specifically, (a) stubbornness; (b) resistance to treatment; persistence, as of a disease.
2. *pl.* **ob'sti·nà·cieș,** an obstinate act, attitude, etc.
Syn.—firmness, resoluteness, inflexibility, persistency, pertinacity, stubbornness, perverseness, contumacy.

ob'sti·nāte, *a.* [ME.; L. *obstinatus*, pp. of *obstinare*, to set one's mind firmly on, to resolve on, from *obstare*, to stand against, to oppose; *ob*, against, and *stare*, to stand.]
1. unreasonably determined to have one's own way; not yielding to reason or plea; stubborn; dogged; mulish.
2. resisting remedy or treatment; as, an *obstinate* fever.
3. not easily subdued, ended, etc.
Syn.—contumacious, stubborn, headstrong, inflexible, opinionated, pertinacious, resolute.

ob'sti·nāte·ly, *adv.* in an obstinate manner.

ob'sti·nāte·ness, *n.* the quality or state of being obstinate; stubbornness; obstinacy.

ob·sti·nā'tion, *n.* obstinacy. [Rare.]

ob'sti·pănt, *n.* in medicine, any substance that causes obstipation.

ob·sti·pā'tion, *n.* [LL. *obstipare*, to stop up; *ob*, against, and *stipare*, to crowd.]
1. the act of stopping up, as a passage. [Rare.]
2. in medicine, extreme constipation.

ob·strep'ẽr·ous, *a.* [L. *obstreperus*, from *obstrepere*, to roar at; *ob-*, intens., and *strepere*, to make a noise, roar.] noisy; clamorous; vociferous; boisterous or unruly, especially in resisting or opposing.
Many a dull joke honored with much *obstreperous*, fat-sided laughter. —Irving.

ob·strep'ẽr·ous·ly, *adv.* in an obstreperous manner.

ob·strep'ẽr·ous·ness, *n.* the quality or state of being obstreperous.

ob·striç'tion, *n.* [from L. *obstrictus*, pp. of *obstringere*, to bind close.] obligation; bond; the state of being obligated.

ob·stringe', *v.t.* to place under obligation; to constrain; to oblige; to bind. [Rare.]

ob·struçt', *v.t.*; obstructed, *pt.*, *pp.*; obstructing, *ppr.* [L. *obstructus*, pp. of *obstruere*, to build before or against; *ob*, against, and *struere*, to pile up.]
1. to block or stop up (a passage) with obstacles or impediments; to dam; to bar.
2. to hinder (progress, an activity, etc.); to impede; to hamper; to check.
3. (a) to get in the way of; to cut off (an object) from view; (b) to block (the view).
Syn.—check, impede, retard, oppose, clog, arrest, stop.

ob·struçt'ẽr, *n.* one who obstructs.

ob·struç'tion, *n.* [L. *obstructio (-onis)*, a blocking up.]
1. the act of obstructing or the condition of being obstructed.
2. an obstacle; an impediment; anything that obstructs.
3. the checking of the vital functions; death. [Obs.]
Syn.—obstacle, impediment, hindrance, check, barrier.

ob·struç'tion·ișm, *n.* the action or policy of an obstructionist.

ob·struç'tion·ist, *n.* anyone who obstructs progress; especially, a member of a legislative group who hinders the passage of legislation by various technical maneuvers.

ob·struç'tion·ist, *a.* of obstructionists or obstructionism.

ob·struçt'ive, *a.* obstructing or intending to obstruct.

ob·struçt'ive, *n.* one who or that which obstructs.

ob·struçt'ive·ly, *adv.* in an obstructive manner.

ob·struçt'ive·ness, *n.* the quality or state of being obstructive.

ob·struçt'ŏr, *n.* an obstructer.

ob'strụ·ent, *a.* [L. *obstruens (-entis)*, ppr. of *obstruere*, to block up.] obstructing; especially, blocking up a natural passage of the body.

ob'strụ·ent, *n.* that which obstructs; an obstruction; specifically, an obstruction, as a kidney stone, in the natural passages of the body.

ob·stū·pē·faç'tion, *n.* stupefaction. [Obs.]

ob·stū·pē·faç'tive, *a.* stupefactive. [Obs.]

ob·stū'pē·fȳ, *v.t.* to stupefy. [Obs.]

ob·tāin', *v.t.*; obtained, *pt.*, *pp.*; obtaining, *ppr.* [ME. *obtenen*, *obteinen*; OFr. *obtenir*, from L. *obtinere*, to obtain, acquire, prevail, maintain; *ob*, upon, and *tenere*, to hold.]

1. to get possession of, especially by trying; to procure.
2. to arrive at; to reach; to achieve. [Archaic.]
Syn.—acquire, win, gain, attain, procure, get.

ob·tāin′, *v.i.* 1. to be in force or in general usage; to be established; to prevail; as, peace will *obtain*.
2. to succeed. [Archaic.]

ob·tāin′ȧ·ble, *a.* that can be obtained.

ob·tāin′ẽr, *n.* one who obtains.

ob·tāin′ment, *n.* an obtaining. [Rare.]

ob·tec̣t′ed, *a.* [L. *obtectus*, pp. of *obtegere*, to cover over; *ob*, over, and *tegere*, to cover.] enclosed in or covered with a hard outer shell: said of the pupae of certain insects.

ob·tem′pẽr, *v.t.* and *v.i.* [L. *obtemperare*, to comply with, obey.] to obey; specifically, in Scots law, to comply with (judgment of court). [Archaic.]

ob·tem′pẽr·āte, *v.t.* to obey. [Obs.]

ob·tend′, *v.t.* 1. to oppose; to hold out in opposition. [Obs.]
2. to pretend; to offer as the reason of anything. [Obs.]

ob·ten·ē·brā′tion, *n.* a darkening; the act of darkening; darkness. [Rare.]

ob·ten′sion, *n.* the act of obtending. [Obs.]

ob·test′, *v.t.* [L. *obtestari*, from *ob-*, ob-, and *testari*, to witness.]
1. to beg for; to beseech.
2. to call to witness.

ob·test′, *v.i.* to protest. [Rare.]

ob·tes·tā′tion, *n.* the act of obtesting. [Rare.]

ob·treç·tā′tion, *n.* slander; detraction; calumny. [Obs.]

ob·trụde′, *v.t.*; obtruded, *pt.*, *pp.*; obtruding, *ppr.* [L. *obtrudere*, to thrust or press upon; *ob*, upon, and *trudere*, to thrust.]
1. to thrust forward; to push out; to eject.
2. to offer or force (oneself, one's opinions, etc.) upon others without being asked or wanted.
Syn.—intrude.

ob·trụde′, *v.i.* to obtrude oneself (*on* or *upon*).

ob·trụd′ẽr, *n.* one who obtrudes.

ob·truñ′çāte, *v.t.*; obtruncated, *pt.*, *pp.*; obtruncating, *ppr.* [L. *obtruncatus*, pp. of *obtruncare*, to cut off.] to deprive of a limb; to lop.

ob·truñ·çā′tion, *n.* the act of lopping or cutting off.

ob·trụ′ṣion (-zhun), *n.* [L. *obtrusio* (*-onis*), a thrusting in.]
1. the act of obtruding; a thrusting upon others by force, or unsolicited; as, the *obtrusion* of crude opinions on the world.
2. that which is obtruded; violence offered.
He never reckons those violent and merciless *obtrusions*. —Milton.

ob·trụ′ṣion·ist, *n.* one who obtrudes; one who is of an obtrusive disposition.

ob·trụ′sive, *a.* 1. inclined to obtrude.
2. obtruding itself.
Not obvious, not *obtrusive*, but retired,
The more desirable. —Milton.

ob·trụ′sive·ly, *adv.* by way of obtrusion; in an obtrusive manner.

ob·trụ′sive·ness, *n.* the state of being obtrusive; forwardness.

ob·tund′, *v.t.*; obtunded, *pt.*, *pp.*; obtunding, *ppr.* [ME. obtunden; L. *obtundere*, to strike at or upon, to blunt; *ob*, upon, and *tundere*, to strike.] to dull; to blunt; to quell; to deaden; to reduce the edge, pungency, or violent action of.
Flattery is always at hand, to quiet conviction and *obtund* remorse. —Rambler.

ob·tund′ent, *n.* in medicine, a substance which sheathes or blunts irritation; usually, some bland, oily, or mucilaginous matter.

ob·tund′ẽr, *n.* that which obtunds.

ob′tū·rāte, *v.t.*; obturated, *pt.*, *pp.*; obturating, *ppr.* [L. *obturatus*, pp. of *obturare*, to stop up.]
1. to close (an opening); to stop up; to obstruct.
2. to close (a gun breech) so as to keep gas from escaping when the gun is fired.

ob·tū·rā′tion, *n.* an obturating or being obturated.

ob′tū·rā·tŏr, *n.* [Mod. L., from L., *obturare*, to stop up.] a thing that stops or closes an opening or passage; specifically, (a) a device on a gun breech to prevent the escape of gas on firing; (b) in surgery, a plate for closing a cleft palate or other abnormal opening.
obturator foramen; a large, oval interval between the pubes and the ischium; also called *thyroid foramen*.
obturator muscles; in anatomy, two muscles of the gluteal region.

ob·tūs″añ′gū·lȧr, *a.* same as *obtuse-angular*.

ob·tūse′, *a.* [L. *obtusus*, blunted, dull, ppr. of *obtundere*, to strike, to beat, to blunt.]
1. not sharp or pointed; blunt.
2. greater than 90 degrees: said of an angle.
3. slow to understand or perceive; insensitive.
4. not producing a sharp impression; not acute; dull, as pain, etc.

C 90° D A B E
OBTUSE ANGLES (ABE, DBE, CBE)

ob·tūse′-añ′gled (-gld), *a.* having one or more obtuse angles; as, an *obtuse-angled* triangle.

ob·tūse′-añ′gū·lȧr, *a.* having angles that are obtuse or larger than right angles.

ob·tūse′ly, *adv.* in an obtuse manner.

ob·tūse′ness, *n.* the state of being obtuse.

ob·tū′si-, a combining form meaning *obtuse*, as in *obtusi*pennate.

ob·tū′ṣion (-zhun), *n.* 1. the act of making obtuse. [Obs.]
2. the state of being dulled or blunted. [Obs.]
Obtusion of the senses, internal and external. —Harvey.

ob·tū·si·pen′nāte, *a.* [*obtusi-* and *pennate*.] having obtuse wings.

ob·tū′si·ty, *n.* obtuseness. [Rare.]

ob·um′brȧnt, *a.* [L. *obumbrans* (*-antis*), ppr. of *obumbrare*, to shade.] overhanging.

ob·um′brāte, *v.t.* [L. *obumbratus*, pp. of *obumbrare*, to overshadow, shade; *ob*, over, and *umbrare*, to shade, from *umbra*, a cloud.] to shade; to darken; to cloud. [Rare.]

ob·um′brāte, *a.* overhung; concealed by some overhanging or projecting part.

ob·um·brā′tion, *n.* the act of darkening or obscuring. [Rare.]

ob·ven′tion, *n.* [L. *obventio* (*-onis*), that which comes to a person's lot.] anything occasional; that which happens not regularly, but incidentally.

ob·vẽrs′ȧnt, *a.* familiar. [Obs.]

ob·vẽrse′, *a.* [L. *obversus*, pp. of *obvertere*, to turn toward.]
1. turned toward the observer: opposed to *reverse*.
2. narrower at the base than at the top; as, an *obverse* leaf.
3. forming a counterpart.

ob′vẽrse, *n.* 1. the side, as of a coin or medal, bearing the main design: opposed to *reverse*.
2. the front or main surface of anything.
3. a counterpart.
4. in logic, the negative counterpart of an affirmative proposition, or the affirmative counterpart of a negative; as, "no one is infallible" is the *obverse* of "everyone is fallible."

ob·vẽrse′ly, *adv.* in an obverse manner.

ob·vẽr′sion, *n.* 1. an obverting.
2. in logic, inference of the obverse.

ob·vẽrt′, *v.t.*; obverted, *pt.*, *pp.*; obverting, *ppr.* [L. *obvertere*, to turn toward; *ob*, toward, and *vertere*, to turn.]
1. to turn the main surface or a different surface of (a thing) toward.
2. in logic, to state the obverse of (a proposition).

ob′vi·āte, *v.t.*; obviated, *pt.*, *pp.*; obviating, *ppr.* [L. *obviatus*, pp. of *obviare*, to meet, withstand, prevent, from *obvius*, in the way so as to meet; *ob*, against, and *via*, a way.] to do away with or prevent by effective measures; to make unnecessary; to clear out of the way, as obstacles in reasoning, deliberating, or planning.
To lay down everything in its full light, so as to *obviate* all exceptions. —Woodward.

ob·vi·ā′tion, *n.* the act of obviating, or the state of being obviated.

ob′vi·ous, *a.* [L. *obvius*, in the way so as to meet.]
1. easy to see or understand; plain; evident.
2. standing or lying in the way. [Obs.]
3. meeting in opposition; fronting. [Archaic.]
I to the evil turn
My *obvious* breast. —Milton.
Syn.—clear, plain, manifest, apparent, evident.

ob′vi·ous·ly, *adv.* in an obvious manner; evidently; plainly; apparently; manifestly; naturally.

ob′vi·ous·ness, *n.* the state of being obvious, plain, or evident.

ob′vō·lūte, ob′vō·lū·ted, *a.* [L. *obvolutus*, pp. of *obvolvere*, to wrap round; *ob*, before, and *volvere*, to roll.]
1. overlapping; rolled or turned in or into; convolute.
2. in botany, having overlapping margins: said of leaves or petals.

ob·vō·lū′tion, *n.* the condition of being obvolute.

ob·vō·lū′tive, *a.* obvolute.

ob·vol′vent, *a.* [L. *obvolvens* (*-entis*), ppr. of *obvolvere*, to wrap round.] curved downward or inward, as the elytra of some beetles.

oç-, ob-: used before *c*, as in *occur*.

ō′çȧ, *n.* [Sp.; Peruv.] either of two wood sorrels, *Oxalis crenata* and *Oxalis tuberosa*, cultivated for its edible tubers.

oç·ȧ·rī′nȧ, *n.* [It., dim. of *oca*, a goose; L. *auca*, a goose: so called from its shape.] a small, simple wind instrument shaped like a sweet potato and usually made of terra cotta, with finger holes and a mouthpiece: it produces soft, hollow tones.

OCARINA

Oç′cȧm·iṣm, *n.* same as *Ockhamism*.

oç′çȧ·my, *n.* [a corruption of *alchemy*.] a kind of alloy.

oç·çā′ṣion (-zhun), *n.* [ME. *occasioun*; OFr.; [L. *occasio* (*-onis*), accidental opportunity, fit time, from *occasus*, pp. of *occidere*, to fall; *ob*, upon, and *cadere*, to fall.]
1. a favorable time or juncture; opportunity.
2. a fact, event, or state of affairs that is the immediate cause of something; as, a mere chance meeting was the *occasion* of the renewal of their friendship.
3. (a) a happening; occurrence; (b) the time at which something happens; particular time; as, on the *occasion* of our last meeting.
4. a special time or event.
5. need arising from circumstances.
6. [*pl.*] (a) [Obs.] needs; requirements; (b) [Archaic.] affairs; business.
on occasion; on suitable opportunity; once in a while; occasionally.
to rise to the occasion; to do whatever suddenly becomes necessary; to meet an emergency.
to take occasion; to take advantage of a situation or avail oneself of an opportunity.
Syn.—cause, reason, need, ground, exigency, necessity, opening, conjuncture, opportunity, time.

oç·çā′ṣion, *v.t.*; occasioned, *pt.*, *pp.*; occasioning, *ppr.* to be the occasion of; to give occasion to; to cause.

oç·çā′ṣion·ȧ·ble, *a.* that can be caused or occasioned.

oç·çā′ṣion·ăl, *a.* [Fr. *occasionnel.*]
1. occurring on a particular occasion.
2. of or for a special occasion.
3. acting only on special occasions.
4. of irregular occurrence; happening now and then; infrequent.
5. designating chairs, tables, etc. intended for occasional or auxiliary use.
occasional cause; in metaphysics, some circumstance preceding an effect, which, without being the real cause, becomes the occasion of the effect being produced by a truly efficient cause. Thus, the act of touching gunpowder with fire is the *occasional*, but not the efficient, *cause* of the explosion.
Syn.—casual, incidental, irregular.

oç·çā′ṣion·ăl·iṣm, *n.* in Cartesian philosophy, the doctrine that the interaction of mind and body is occasioned by God through His producing activities in one corresponding to those in the other.

oç·çā′ṣion·ăl·ist, *n.* one who adopts or defends the doctrine of occasionalism.

oç·çā·ṣion·al′i·ty, *n.* the state or quality of being occasional.

oç·çā′ṣion·ăl·ly, *adv.* in an occasional manner; now and then; sometimes; on occasion; as convenience requires or opportunity offers; not regularly; as, he was *occasionally* present at our meetings; we have *occasionally* lent our aid.

oç·çā′ṣion·āte, *v.t.* to occasion. [Obs.]

oç·çā′ṣion·ẽr, *n.* one who or that which occasions; a cause.

oç·cā'sive, *a.* [from L. *occasus*, sunset.] western; pertaining to the setting sun.

oç'ci·dent, *n.* [ME.; from L. *occidens* (*-entis*), ppr. of *occidere*, to fall; *ob*, before, and *cadere*, to fall.]
 1. the west. [Poetic.]
 2. [O-] the countries west of Asia; specifically, (a) formerly, Europe; (b) now, also, the Western Hemisphere.
 Opposed to *orient, Orient*.

oç·ci·den'tăl, *a.* 1. western.
 2. [O-] of the Occident, its people, or their culture; Western.
 Opposed to *oriental, Oriental*.

oç·ci·den'tăl, *n.* [*usually* O-] a native of the Occident, or a member of a people native to that region: opposed to *oriental, Oriental*.

Oç·ci·den'tăl·iṣm, *n.* the spirit, character, culture, customs, etc. of the Occident.

Oç·ci·den'tăl·ist, *n.* 1. one versed in or a student of Occidentalism.
 2. a native advocate of Occidentalism: opposed to *Orientalist*.

Oç·ci·den'tăl·īze, *v.t.*; occidentalized, *pt., pp.*; occidentalizing, *ppr.* to make Occidental in customs, spirit, etc.

oç·ci·den'tăl·ly, *adv.* in the occident or west; in the direction of the sun.

oç·cid'ū·ous, *a.* [L. *occiduus*.] western.

oç·cip'i·tăl, *a.* [from L. *occiput*, the back part of the head.] of the occiput or the occipital bone.
 occipital bone; the large, strong bone forming the base of the skull, enclosing and protecting the medulla oblongata and the cerebellum, and resting upon the atlas of the spinal column, with which it articulates in such a way as to allow the utmost freedom of motion of the head. Through an ample opening (*foramen magnum*) in the occipital bone near its lower margin the spinal column enters the cavity of the skull.
 occipital point; a point in the mesial plane on the outer surface of the occipital bone farthest from the ophryon.

oç·cip'i·tăl, *n.* the occipital bone.

oç·cip'i·tō-, a combining form meaning *occipital and*.

oç·cip"i·tō-ax'i·ăl, *a.* pertaining to the occipital bone and the spinal column; especially, pertaining to the occipital and the second vertebra; as. the *occipito-axial* ligaments.

oç'ci·put, *n.*; *pl.* **oç·ci'put·ȧ,** [L. *occiput*; *ob*, over, against, and *caput*, head.] the back part of the head or skull.

oç·ci'ṣion (-sizh'un), *n.* [L. *occisio* (*-onis*), from *occidere*, to kill.] a killing; the act of killing. [Obs.]

oç·çlūde', *v.t.*; occluded, *pt., pp.*; occluding, *ppr.* [L. *occludere*; *ob*, before, and *claudere*, to shut.] 1. to close, shut, or block (a passage).
 2. to prevent the passage of (something) by closing; to shut in or out.
 3. in chemistry, to absorb (a gas or liquid); as, palladium *occludes* hydrogen.

oç·çlūde', *v.i.* in dentistry, to meet with the cusps fitting close together: said of the upper and lower teeth.

oç·çlūd'ent, *a.* serving to occlude.

oç·çlūd'ent, *n.* anything which occludes.

oç·çlū'ṣion (-zhun), *n.* 1. an occluding or being occluded.
 2. in dentistry, the fitting together of the upper and lower teeth, or the way in which these fit together when the jaws are closed.
 occlusion of gases; the absorption of gases by metals, charcoal, etc.

oç·çlū'sive, *a.* occluding or tending to occlude.

oç·çlū'sŏr, *n.* anything that occludes; especially, in anatomy, an organ that closes any opening or passage.

oç·çult', *a.* [L. *occultus*, concealed, pp. of *occulere*, to cover over; *ob*, over, and root seen in *celare*, to conceal.]
 1. hidden; concealed.
 2. secret; esoteric.
 3. beyond human understanding; mysterious.
 4. designating or of certain mystic arts or studies, such as magic, alchemy, astrology, etc.
 occult crime; in Scots law, a crime committed in secret or privacy.
 occult line; in geometry, a line drawn to aid in construction, to be erased when the drawing is completed; a construction line; also, a dotted line.
 the occult; the occult arts, sciences, or studies.
 Syn.—latent, hidden, unrevealed, mysterious, secret, dark, unknown.

oç·çult', *v.t.* and *v.i.*; occulted, *pt., pp.*; occulting, *ppr.* to hide or become hidden from view; specifically, in astronomy, to hide by occultation.

oç·çul·tā'tion, *n.* [ME. *occultacioun*; L. *occultatio* (*-onis*), a hiding.]
 1. a hiding; the state of being hidden; disappearance.
 2. in astronomy, the disappearance of one heavenly body behind another.
 circle of perpetual occultation; see under *circle*.

oç·çult'ed, *a.* 1. hidden; concealed.
 2. in astronomy, hidden or concealed by the intervention of some other heavenly body; as, a star *occulted* by the moon.

oç·çult'iṣm, *n.* 1. belief in occult forces and powers.
 2. the study or practice of occult arts.

oç·çult'ist, *n.* one who practices occultism.

oç·çult'ly, *adv.* in an occult manner.

oç·çult'ness, *n.* the state of being occult, secret, or concealed from view; secretness.

oç'çū·păn·cy, *n.*; *pl.* **oç'çū·păn·cieṣ,** [from *occupant*.]
 1. (a) an occupying; a taking or keeping in possession; (b) the period during which a house, etc. is occupied.
 2. in law, the taking possession of a previously unowned object, thus establishing ownership.

oç'çu·pănt, *n.* [from Fr. or L.; Fr. occupant; L. *occupans* (*-antis*), ppr. of *occupare*, to occupy.]
 1. a person who occupies.
 2. a person who acquires a title to anything by occupancy.
 3. a prostitute. [Obs.]

oç'çū·pāte, *v.t.* [L. *occupare*.] to hold; to possess; to take up. [Obs.]

oç·çū·pā'tion, *n.* [ME. *occupacion*; OFr.; L. *occupatio* (*-onis*).]
 1. an occupying or being occupied.
 2. possession; a holding or keeping; tenure; use; as, lands in the *occupation* of a tenant.
 3. that which engages one's time and attention; employment; business; as, he devotes to study all the time that his other *occupations* will permit.

 No *occupation*, all men idle, all;
 And women, too, but innocent and pure.
 —Shak.

 4. the principal business of one's life; vocation; calling; trade; the business which one follows to procure a living or obtain wealth; as, he is a merchant by *occupation*.
 army of occupation; see under *army*.
 occupation bridge; a bridge connecting two parts of an estate separated from each other by some obstruction, such as a river, a railroad, or a canal.
 occupation road; a road made for the use of an occupier of premises; a private road.
 Syn.—calling, vocation, trade, profession, employment, pursuit, business, craft, office.

oç·çū·pā'tion·ăl, *a.* of occupation or an occupation.

oç·çū·pā'tion·ăl diṣ·ēaṣe', a disease commonly acquired by people in a particular occupation; as, silicosis is an *occupational disease* of miners.

oç·çū·pā'tion·ăl ther'ȧ·py, the treatment of mental and physical ailments by work designed to divert the mind or to correct a particular physical defect.

oç'çū·pā·tive, *a.* relating to occupation, especially to the right of occupation; as, an *occupative* right to hold.

oç'çū·pī·ẽr, *n.* one who occupies.

oç'çū·pȳ, *v.t.*; occupied, *pt., pp.*; occupying, *ppr.* [ME. *occupien*; OFr. *occuper*; L. *occupare*, to take possession of, to possess, to employ; *ob*, before, on, and *capere*, to seize or take.]
 1. to take possession of by settlement or seizure.
 2. to hold possession of by tenure; specifically, (a) to dwell in; (b) to hold (a position or office).
 3. to take up or fill up (space, time, etc.).
 4. to employ, busy, or engage (oneself, one's attention, mind, etc.).
 5. to take and use; to use; to lay out in traffic. [Obs.]
 6. to follow, as business or employment; to attend to. [Obs.]

 All the ships of the sea with their mariners were in thee to *occupy* thy merchandise.
 —Ezek. xxvii. 9.

 7. to have sexual intercourse with. [Obs.]

oç'çū·pȳ, *v.i.* 1. to be an occupant. [Obs.]
 2. to carry on business; to trade; to negotiate. [Obs.]

 Occupy till I come. —Luke xix. 13.

oç·çũr', *v.i.*; occurred, *pt., pp.*; occurring, *ppr.* [L. *occurrere*, to run, come up to, to meet; *ob*, before, and *currere*, to run.]
 1. to meet; to strike against; to clash. [Obs.]
 2. to come to mind; to be presented to the mind, imagination, or memory; to present itself; as, such a reflection has often *occurred* to me.

 There doth not *occur* to me any use of this experiment for profit. —Bacon.

 3. to befall; to happen, to take place.

 I shall travail for the new signature of your warrant for the same as soon as any opportunity shall *occur*. —Wyatt.

 4. to exist so as to be capable of being found or seen; to be found; to be or be met with; as, silver often *occurs* native.

 In Scripture, though the word heir *occur*, yet there is no such thing as heir in our author's sense. —Locke.

 5. to reply: with *to*. [Obs.]

 Before I begin that, I must *occur to* one specious objection against this proposition.
 —Bentley.

 6. to coincide in time; to conflict with one another: used of movable and immovable feasts; as, two holy days *occur*.

oç·çũr'rence, *n.* 1. the act or fact of occurring.
 2. something that occurs; an event; an incident.

 The ordinary course and *occurrences* of that life the young man is designed for.—Locke.

 3. the coincidence of two holy days or feasts falling on the same day.
 Syn.—happening, incident, event, circumstance, occasion, emergency.

oç·çũr'rent, *n.* 1. one who meets; an adversary. [Obs.]

 The weak part of their *occurrents*, by which they may assail and conquer the sooner.
 —Holland.

 2. an incident; anything that occurs. [Obs.]

 He did himself certify all the news and *occurrents* in every particular. —Bacon.

oç·çũr'rent, *a.* incidental; occurring. [Rare.]

ō'ceăn (ō'shăn), *n.* [ME. *occean*; L. *oceanus*, from Gr. *ōkeanos*, the ocean.]
 1. the great body of salt water that covers more than two thirds of the surface of the earth.
 2. any of its five principal geographical divisions; the Atlantic, Pacific, Indian, Arctic, and Antarctic Oceans.
 3. any great expanse or quantity.

ō'ceăn·ąut" (ō'shăn aut"), *n.* [from *ocean*, and Gr. *nautēs*, sailor.] same as *aquanaut*.

ō'ceăn·gō"ing (ō'shăn-), *a.* of, having to do with, or made for travel on, the ocean.

Ō·cē·an'i·ăn, Ō·cē·an'i·căn (-shē-), *a.* pertaining to Oceania, or Oceanica, or to its peoples.

Ō·cē·an'i·ăn, *n.* a native of Oceania.

ō·cē·an'iç (-shē-), *a.* 1. of, living in, or produced by the ocean.
 2. like the ocean; great in extent; vast.
 3. [O-] same as *Oceanian*.

Ō·cē'ăn·id (-sē'), *n.* [Gr. *Ōkeanis, Ōkeanidos*.] in Greek mythology, one of the three thousand ocean nymphs, daughters of Oceanus and Tethys.

ō"cē·ăn·og'rȧ·phẽr (-shē- *or* -shăn-), *n.* a student of or specialist in oceanography.

ō"cē·ăn·ō·graph'iç, *a.* of or connected with oceanography.

ō"cē·ăn·og'rȧ·phy, *n.* [from *ocean* and *-graphy*.] the branch of geography dealing with the ocean.

ō"cē·ăn·ol'ō·gy, *n.* [from *ocean* and *-logy*.] same as *oceanography*.

Ō·cē'ȧ·nus (-sē'), *n.* [L.; Gr. *Ōkeanos*.]
 1. a Titan who was god of the sea before Poseidon and father of the Oceanids.
 2. the great outer stream supposedly encircling the earth.

ō·cel'lăr, *a.* of an ocellus or ocelli.

oc'el·lāt·ed, oc'el·lāte (*or* ō-sel'), *a.* [L. *ocellatus*, from *ocellus*, a little eye.]
 1. like an ocellus.
 2. having an ocellus or ocelli.
 3. spotted.

oc·el·lā'tion, *n.* 1. the condition of being ocellated.
 2. an eyelike spot.

ō·cel'lī, *n.* pl. of *ocellus*.

ō·cel'li·cyst, *n.* [L. *ocellus*, a little eye, and Gr. *kystis*, bladder.] the eye of a hydrozoan.

oc·el·lif′ẽr·ous, *a.* [L. *ocellus*, a little eye, and *ferre*, to bear.] having a little eye; marked with eyelike spots of color; ocellate.

oc·el·lig′ẽr·ous, *a.* same as *ocelliferous*.

ō·cel′lus, *n.*; *pl.* **ō·cel′lī,** [L. *ocellus*, a little eye, dim. of *oculus*, eye.]

1. a small eye; especially, the simple, or rudimentary, eye of certain invertebrates, as distinguished from the compound eye of an insect.

2. an eyelike spot, as on a peacock's feathers.

ō′cē·loid, *a.* [*ocelot* and *-oid*.] like an ocelot.

ō′cē·lot, *n.*; *pl.* **ō′cē·lots** or **ō′cē·lot,** [Fr., from Mex. *ocelotl*, jaguar.] a large cat, *Felis pardalis*, of North and South America, with a yellow or gray hide marked with black spots.

OCELOT

ō′chẽr, ō′chre (-kẽr), *n.* [L. *ochra*; Gr. *ōchra*, from *ōchros*, pale, pale-yellow.]

1. an earthy clay containing iron ore, usually yellow or reddish brown in color: used as a pigment in paints.

2. the color of ocher; especially, dark yellow.

black ocher; a variety of mineral black.

ō′chẽr, ō′chre, *v.t.* to color or mark with ocher.

ō′chẽr·ous, ō′chrē·ous, *a.* 1. consisting of ocher; containing ocher; as, *ocherous* matter.

2. resembling ocher; as, an *ocherous* color.

ō′chẽr·y, ō′chry, *a.* pertaining to ocher; containing or resembling ocher.

och′i·dōre, *n.* a shore crab. [Brit.]

och′i·my, *n.* occamy. [Obs.]

och·lē′sis, *n.* [Gr., disturbance, from *ochlein*, to disturb as by a mob, from *ochlos*, a crowd, a mob.] any unhealthy condition caused by the crowding together of many persons.

och·let′iç, *a.* pertaining to or caused by ochlesis.

och·loç′rȧ·cy, *n.* [Fr. *ochlocratie*; Gr. *ochlokratia*; *ochlos*, the people or a multitude, and *kratein*, to govern.] a form of government in which the multitude or common people rule; mob rule.

och′lō·crat, *n.* a member of or believer in an ochlocracy.

och·lō·crat′iç, och·lō·crat′iç·ăl, *a.* of, like, or advocating ochlocracy.

och·lō·crat′iç·ăl·ly, *adv.* in the manner of an ochlocracy.

Och·nā′cē·ae, *n.pl.* [Gr. *ochnē*, a wild pear tree, and *-aceæ*: so called from the resemblance of the foliage to that of the pear tree.] a family of tropical trees or shrubs having a watery juice, alternate simple leaves, and panicles of large, showy flowers with elongated anthers.

och·nā′ceous, *a.* of or pertaining to the *Ochnaceæ*.

och·ōne′ (ukh-), *interj.* alas. [Scot. and Irish.]

ō′chrȧ, *n.* same as *okra*.

ō·chrā′ceous, *a.* same as *ocherous*.

ō′chre (-kẽr), *n.* and *v.t.*; ochred, *pt.*, *pp.*; ochring, *ppr.* ocher.

ō′chrē·ȧ, *n.* ocrea: erroneous spelling.

ō′chrē·āte, ō′chrē·ā·ted, *a.* see *ocreate*.

ō′chrē·ous, *a.* see *ocherous*.

ō′chrey, *a.* same as *ochery*.

och·rō·cär′pous, *a.* [Gr. *ōchros*, pale-yellow, and *karpos*, fruit.] having yellow fruit.

ō′chroid, *a.* [Gr. *ōchroeidēs*, pale, like ocher; *ōchros*, pale, pale-yellow, and *eidos*, form.] of an ocher color; resembling ocher.

och·rō·leū′çous, *a.* [Gr. *ōchros*, pale, pale-yellow, and *leukos*, white.] yellowish-white.

ō′chry, *a.* same as *ochery*.

-ock, [from AS. *-uc*.] a suffix originally used to form diminutives; as, bull*ock*, hill*ock*, butt*ock*.

Ock′ham·iṣm, *n.* the philosophical principles of William of Ockham, an English scholastic philosopher of the fourteenth century.

o′clock′, of, or according to, the clock.

Ō·çō′tē·ȧ, *n.* [native name.] a genus of trees of the order *Laurineæ*, including about 150 species, mostly found in the American tropics.

ō·çō·til′lō (-yō), *n.*; *pl.* **ō·çō·til′lōṣ,** [Sp., dim. of *ocote*.] (a) a candlewood, *Fouquieria splendens*, native to the southwestern United States and Mexico: it is a desert shrub with naked thorny branches and scarlet flowers; (b) also, a Mexican shrub of the thistle family, used in making charcoal.

ō′çrȧ, *n.* same as *okra*.

oç′rē·ȧ (*or* ō′krē-ȧ), *n.*; *pl.* **oç′rē·ae,** [L. *ocrea*, a greave, or legging.]

1. in botany, a tubelike covering around some stems.

2. in zoology, a sheath.

o, OCREA

ō′çrē·āte, ō′çrē·ā·ted, *a.* having an ocrea or ocreae; sheathed.

oct-, octa-.

oç′tȧ-, [Gr. *okta-*.] a combining form meaning *eight*, as in *octagon*: also *octo-*, *oct-*.

oç′tȧ·chord, *n.* [Gr. *oktachordos*, eight-stringed; *oktō*, eight, and *chordē*, string.]

1. a musical instrument having eight strings.

2. a system of eight sounds; especially, an octave of the diatonic scale.

oç·taç′ti·năl, *a.* [*oct-*, and Gr. *aktis* (*-inos*), a ray.]

1. in zoology, eight-rayed.

2. of or pertaining to the *Octactiniæ*.

Oç·taç·tin′ī·ae, *n.pl.* [*oct-*, and Gr. *aktis* (*-inos*), a ray.] a division of cœlenterates, the *Alcyonaria*.

oç′tad, *n.* [Gr. *oktas* (*-ados*), the number eight, from *oktō*, eight.]

1. a series or group of eight.

2. in chemistry, an element, atom, or radical with a valence of eight.

oç·tȧ·em′ẽr·on, *n.* [Gr. *oktaēmeron*, neut. of *oktaēmeros*, of the eighth day.] in the Greek church, a fast of eight days preceding a great festival.

oç′tȧ·gon, *n.* [Gr. *oktō*, eight, and *gōnia*, an angle.]

1. in geometry, a plane figure of eight sides and eight angles. When the sides and angles are equal, it is a regular octagon.

2. in fortification, a place with eight sides or bastions.

oç·tag′ō·năl, *a.* of, or having the form of, an octagon.

oç·tag′ō·năl·ly, *adv.* in the form of an octagon.

oç·tȧ·hē′drăl, *a.* of, or having the form of, an octahedron.

octahedral borax; borax crystallized in octahedrons, as distinguished from *prismatic borax*.

oç·tȧ·hē′drīte, *n.* [from LL. *oktaedros*, and *-ite*.] titanium dioxide, TiO_2, occurring in octahedral crystals.

oç·tȧ·hē′drŏn, *n.*; *pl.* **oç·tȧ·hē′drŏnṣ, oç·tȧ·hē′drȧ,** [Gr. *oktō*, eight, and *hedra*, a base.] a solid figure with eight plane surfaces.

OCTAHEDRON

oç·tam′ẽr·iṣm, *n.* the state of being octamerous.

oç·tam′ẽr·ous, *a.* [*octa-* and *-merous*.] having eight parts in each whorl: said of flowers: also written 8-*merous*.

oç·tam′ē·tẽr, *n.* [Gr. *oktametron*; *oktō*, eight, and *metron*, a measure.] a line of verse having eight metrical feet.

oç·tam′ē·tẽr, *a.* containing eight metrical feet.

oç′tan, *a.* [L. *octo*, eight, and *-an*.] recurring or happening every eighth day (counting both days of occurrence).

oç′tan, *n.* an octan fever, etc.

Oç·tan′dri·ȧ, *n.pl.* [*oct-*, and Gr. *anēr*, *andros*, man, male.] formerly, a Linnaean class of monoclinous or hermaphrodite plants, having eight stamens, which are distinct from each other, and distinct from the pistil.

oç·tan′dri·ăn, oç·tan′drous, *a.* pertaining to the class *Octandria*; having eight distinct stamens.

oç′tāne, *n.* [*oct-* and *-ane*.] an oily hydrocarbon, C_8H_{18}, occurring in petroleum, or any of a group of isomers of this substance.

oç′tāne num′bẽr (or **rāt′ing**), a number representing the antiknock properties of a gasoline, etc., determined by the percentage of 2·2·4-trimethylpentane that must be mixed with *n*-heptane to produce the knocking quality of the fuel being tested: the higher the number, the greater the antiknock properties.

oç′tañ·gle, *n.* [*oct-* and *angle*.] an octagon.

oç·tañ′gū·lăr, *a.* [*oct-* and *angular*.] having eight angles.

oç·tañ′gū·lăr·ness, *n.* the quality of having eight angles.

Oç′tanṣ, *n.* [Mod. L.] a southern constellation.

oç′tănt, *n.* [L. *octans* (*-antis*), an eighth part, from *octo*, eight.]

1. an eighth of a circle; 45° angle or arc.

2. an instrument like the sextant, for measuring angles.

3. in astronomy, the position of one heavenly body when it is 45° distant from another.

4. in mathematics, any of the eight parts into which a space is divided by three planes intersecting at a single point and at right angles to one another.

oç′tȧ·plȧ, *n.* [Gr. *oktaploos*, eightfold, from *oktō*, eight.]

1. a polyglot Bible printed in eight languages, usually in parallel columns, so as to present the different texts at one view.

2. any book published in eight different languages, printed in parallel columns.

oç·tap′ō·dy, *n.* [Gr. *oktapous* (*-podos*), eight feet long; *oktō*, eight, and *pous*, *podos*, foot.] same as *octameter*.

oç′tärch·y, *n.*; *pl.* **oç′tärch·ieṣ,** [*oct-* and *-archy*.]

1. government by eight rulers.

2. a group of eight governments or kingdoms: sometimes applied to the Heptarchy of Anglo-Saxon England.

oç·tȧ·roon′, *n.* same as *octoroon*.

oç·tȧ·sē′miç, *a.* [Gr. *oktasēmos*, of eight times; *oktō*, eight, and *sēmeion*, mark, sign.] in prosody, containing eight morae; marked by eight beats.

oç′tȧ·stich, oç·tas′ti·chon, *n.* [Gr. *oktastichon*; *oktō*, eight, and *stichos*, line, verse.] a poem containing eight verses or lines.

oç·tȧ·stroph′iç, *a.* [*octa-*, and Gr. *strophē*, strophe.] in prosody, containing or made up of eight stanzas or strophes.

oç′tȧ·style, *n.* [Gr. *oktastylos*; *oktō*, eight, and *stylos*, a pillar.] a building, as a temple, having eight columns in front: also spelled *octostyle*.

oç′tȧ·teūch (-tūk), *n.* [L.Gr. *oktateuchos*; *oktō*, eight, and *teuchos*, book.]

1. a collection or set of eight books.

2. [O-] the first eight books of the Old Testament.

oç·tā′văl, *a.* of or in an octave or octaves.

oç·tav′ȧ·lent, *a.* [*octa-* and *valent*.] in chemistry, having a valence of eight.

oç·tȧ·vār′i·um, *n.*; *pl.* **oç·tȧ·vār′i·ȧ,** [LL., from L. *octava*, an octave.] in the Roman Catholic Church, an office book of the collects, lections, etc., used during the octave of a festival.

oç′tāve, *a.* 1. consisting of eight, or an octave.

2. in music, producing tones an octave higher; as, an *octave* key.

oç′tāve (*or* -tiv), *n.* [Fr., from L. *octavus*, eighth, from *octo*, eight.]

1. (a) the eighth day following a church festival, counting the festival day as the first; (b) the entire period between the festival and this day.

2. a group of eight lines of verse; especially, the first eight lines of the Italian sonnet: also called *octet*.

3. any group of eight.

4. in fencing, a position of thrust or parry in which the hand is rotated with the palm up.

5. in music, (a) the eighth full tone above a given tone, having twice as many vibrations per second, or below a given tone, having half as many vibrations per second; (b) the interval of eight diatonic degrees between a tone and either of its octaves; (c) the series of tones contained within this interval, or the keys of an instrument producing such a series; (d) a tone and either of its octaves sounded together; (e) an organ stop producing tones an octave above those ordinarily produced by the keys struck.

6. a small cask of wine, the eighth part of a pipe.

octave coupler; an apparatus for coupling two octave notes, capable of being attached to the organ, piano, and other keyboard instruments.

octave flute; the piccolo.

oç·tā′vō (*or* -tä′), *n.*; *pl.* **oç·tā′vōṣ,** [L. *octavus*, eighth.]

1. the page size of a book made up of printer's sheets folded into eight leaves, each leaf being from 5 by 8 inches to 6 by 9 ½ inches.

2. a book consisting of pages of this size: also written 8vo or 8°.

oç·tā′vō, *a.* having eight leaves to the sheet;

 fāte, fär, fȧst, fạll, finăl, cāre, at; mēte, prey, hẽr, met; pīne, marīne, bīrd, pin; nōte, mōve, fọr, atŏm, not; mọọn, book;

of or equal to one leaf of printer's paper folded so as to make eight leaves.

oc'tēne, *n.* same as *octylene.*

oc·ten'ni·ăl, *a.* [L. *octo*, eight, and *annus*, year.]
 1. happening every eighth year.
 2. lasting for eight years.

oc·ten'ni·ăl·ly, *adv.* once in eight years.

oc·tet', oc·tette', *n.* [L. *octo*, eight.]
 1. any group of eight; especially, an octave (sense 2).
 2. in music, (a) a composition for eight voices or eight instruments; (b) the eight performers of this.

oc'tic, *a.* in mathematics, of the eighth order or degree.

oc'tic, *n.* in algebra, a quantic of the eighth degree.

oc'tile, *n.* same as *octant.*

oc·til'liŏn (-yun), *n.* [L. *octo*, eight, and Fr. *million.*]
 1. in the United States and France, the number represented by 1 followed by 27 zeros.
 2. in Great Britain and Germany, the number represented by 1 followed by 48 zeros.

oc·til'liŏn, *a.* amounting to one octillion in number.

oc'tō-, oc'tȧ-, oct-, [from L. *octo*, Gr. *oktō*, eight.] a combining form meaning *eight*, as in *octo*brachiate.

oc'tō·āte, *n.* [*octo*ic and *-ate.*] in chemistry, a salt of an octoic acid: also called *caprylate.*

Oc·tō'bēr, *n.* [L., from *octo*, eight; the eighth month of the primitive Roman year, which began in March.]
 1. the tenth month of the year, containing thirty-one days.
 2. ale made in October. [Brit.]

Oc·tō'bēr Rev·ō·lū'tion, the Russian revolution of November, 1917 (October, Old Style), in which the Kerensky government was overthrown by workers, peasants, soldiers, and sailors led by the Bolsheviks, or Communists, under Lenin, and the Soviet government was set up.

oc·tō·brach'i·āte, *a.* [*octo-*, and L. *brachium*, arm.] in zoology, having eight arms or rays; octocerous; octopod.

Oc·tō'brist, *n.* a Moderate Constitutionalist or Moderate Liberal in the Russian Duma; a member of a political group that supported the Czar's reform measures as proposed by him in October of 1905.

Oc·toc'ē·rȧ, Oc·tō·cer'ȧ·tȧ, *n.pl.* [*octo-*, and Gr. *keras*, horn.] a suborder of cephalopods, having eight sucker-bearing arms around the head; the *Octopoda.*

oc·toc'ēr·ous, *a.* of or pertaining to the *Octocera.*

Oc″tō·cō·ral'lȧ, *n.pl.* [*octo-*, and LL. *corallum*, coral.] the *Alcyonaria.*

oc·tō·cō·ral'līne, *a.* of or pertaining to the *Octocoralla.*

oc·tō·cō·ral'līne, *n.* one of the *octocoralla.*

oc·tō·dec'i·mō, *a.* [L. *octodecim*, eighteen.] having or consisting of eighteen leaves to a printer's sheet.

oc·tō·dec'i·mō, *n.*; *pl.* **oc·tō·dec'i·mōs,** 1. the page size of a book made up of printer's sheets folded into eighteen leaves, each leaf being approximately 4 by 6 1/4 inches.
 2. a book consisting of pages of this size: also called *eighteenmo*, and written 18*mo* or 18°.

oc·tō·den'tāte, *a.* [*octo-*, and L. *dentatus*, toothed.] having eight teeth.

oc'tō·dont, *a.* of or pertaining to the *Octodontidæ.*

Oc·tō·don'ti·dae, *n.pl.* [*octo-*, and Gr. *odous*, *odontos*, tooth.] a family of small rodents, including many South American species.

oc·tō·ē'chos, *n.* [Gr. *oktō*, eight, and *ēchos*, echo, tone.] in the Orthodox Eastern Church, a liturgical book attributed to St. John Damascene: it contains all troparia and canons for the Sunday service from the first vespers through the Liturgy in the order of their tones.

oc·tō·ed'ric·ăl, *a.* octahedral. [Obs.]

oc'tō·fid, *a.* [L. *octo*, eight, and *findere*, to cleave.] in botany, cleft or separated into eight segments, as a calyx.

oc'tō·foil, *n.* [*octo-* and *foil.*] in heraldry, a figure exhibiting eight leaves or lobes.

oc″tō·ġē·nâr'i·ăn, *a.* eighty years old; between eighty and ninety years of age.

oc″tō·ġē·nâr'i·ăn, *n.* a person eighty years of age; one between eighty and ninety years of age.

oc·toġ'e·nâr·y, *a.* [L. *octogenarius*, eighty years old, from *octoginta*, eighty.] octogenarian. [Rare.]

oc'tō·gild, *n.* [*octo-*, and AS. *gild*, payment.] in Anglo-Saxon law, a payment for an injury, reckoned at eight times its value.

Oc·tō·ġyn'i·ȧ, *n.pl.* [*octo-*, and Gr. *gynē*, female.] in botany, a former Linnaean order which has eight styles or pistils in a hermaphrodite flower.

oc·tō·ġyn'i·ăn, *a.* octogynous.

oc·toġ'y·nous, *a.* having eight pistils or styles.

oc·tō'ic, *a.* same as *caprylic.*

oc·tō·lat'ēr·ăl, *a.* [*octo-*, and L. *latus* (*-eris*), side.] having eight sides.

oc·tō·loc'ū·lăr, *a.* [*octo-*, and L. *loculus*, dim. of *locus*, a place.] in botany, having eight cells for seeds.

oc·tom'ēr·ăl, *a.* of or pertaining to the *Octomeralia*; having eight parts.

Oc″tō·mē·rā'li·ȧ, *n.pl.* [*octo-*, and Gr. *meros*, part.] in zoophytology, a subclass of *Scyphomedusæ.*

oc·tom'ēr·ous, *a.* same as *octamerous.*

oc'tō·năl, *a.* [L. *octoni*, eight each.] calculating by eights; pertaining to a system of eights.

oc·tō·naph'thēne, *n.* in chemistry, a hydrocarbon of the octylene series, found in Caucasian petroleum.

oc·tō·nâr'i·an, *a.* [L. *octonarius*, adj.] in prosody, consisting of eight feet.

oc·tō·nâr'i·an, *n.* in prosody, a verse of eight feet.

oc'tō·nâr·y, *a.* [L. *octonarius*, from *octoni*, eight each, from *octo*, eight.] of or consisting of eight or groups of eight.

oc'tō·nâr·y, *n.*; *pl.* **oc'tō·nâr·ies,** 1. a group of eight; an ogdoad.
 2. in prosody, a stanza of eight lines; octave.

oc·tō·nem'ȧ·tous, *a.* [*octo-*, and Gr. *nema* (*-atos*), thread.] having eight slender organs or parts.

oc·tō·noc'ū·lăr, *a.* [L. *octoni*, eight each, and *oculus*, eye.] having eight eyes.

oc·toon', *n.* a person having but one white grandparent. [Rare.]

oc'tō·ped, oc'tō·pēde, *n.* [*octo-*, and L. *pes*, *pedis*, foot.] an eight-footed animal.

oc·tō·pet'ăl·ous, *a.* [*octo-*, and Gr. *petalon*, a leaf.] having eight petals or flower leaves.

oc'tō·pine (*or* -pīn), *a.* pertaining to an octopus. [Rare.]

oc'tō·pod, *n.* [*octo-*, and Gr. *pous*, *podos*, foot.] any animal with eight limbs; specifically, the octopus; a member of the *Octopoda.*

oc'tō·pod, *a.* pertaining to the *Octopoda.*

Oc·top'ō·dȧ, *n.pl.* a section of the dibranchiate *Cephalopoda*, or cuttlefishes, including the families *Argonautidæ* and *Octopodidæ*, having eight arms.

oc·top'ō·dăn, *a.* same as *octopod.*

Oc·tō·pod'i·dae, *n.pl.* a family of octopods, including most of the cuttlefishes.

Oc'tō·pus, *n.* [Gr. *oktōpous*, eight-footed; *oktō*, eight, and *pous*, *podos*, foot.]

OCTOPUS (4-8 ft. across)

 1. a genus of dibranchiate *Cephalopoda*, the type of *Octopoda*, familiarly known as cuttlefishes, devilfishes, and poulps. They have eight arms covered with suckers, a soft, saclike body, and a large head with a mouth on the undersurface. *Octopus punctatus*, of the Pacific coast of North America, attains a length of sixteen feet. *Octopus vulgaris*, a Mediterranean species, is valued as food.
 2. [o–] *pl.* **oc'tō·pus·es, oc·top'ō·dēs, oc'tō·pī,** a member of this genus.
 3. [o–] anything supposedly like an octopus; especially, an organization with branches that reach out in a powerful and influential manner.

oc·tō·rā'di·ā·ted, *a.* [*octo-*, and L. *radius*, a ray.] having eight rays.

oc·tō·roon', *n.* the offspring of a quadroon and a white.

oc·tō·sep'ȧ·lous, *a.* [*octo-* and *sepal* and *-ous.*] in botany, having eight sepals.

oc·tō·spēr'mous, *a.* [*octo-*, and Gr. *sperma*, a seed.] containing eight seeds.

oc'tō·spō·rous, *a.* in botany, having eight spores.

oc·tos'ti·chous, *a.* [*octo-*, and Gr. *stichos*, a line, row.] in botany, having leaves arranged in eight vertical rows.

oc'tō·stȳle, *n.* see *octastyle.*

oc″tō·syl·lab'ic, *a.* [Gr. *oktōsyllabos*; *oktō*, eight, and *syllabē*, syllable.]
 1. containing eight syllables, as a line of verse.
 2. containing lines of eight syllables.

oc″tō·syl·lab'ic, *n.* an octosyllabic line or verse.

oc'tō·syl·lȧ·ble, *a.* octosyllabic.

oc'tō·syl·lȧ·ble, *n.* a word or line of eight syllables.

oc'tō·teūch, *n.* same as *octateuch.*

oc'tō·yl, *n.* in chemistry, a hypothetical radical, $C_8H_{15}O$, contained in octoic acid.

oc·troi' (-trwä'), *n.* [Fr., from *octroyer*, to grant.]
 1. a tax on certain goods entering a town.
 2. the place where this tax is collected.
 3. the official or officials collecting this tax.
 4. a grant or privilege, particularly a commercial privilege, as an exclusive right of trade, conceded by a government to a particular person or company; a concession.

oc'tū·or, *n.* same as *octet.*

oc'tū·ple, *a.* [L. *octuplus*; *octo*, eight, and *plicare*, to fold.]
 1. eightfold.
 2. consisting of eight parts.

oc'tū·ple, *n.* something eight times as great as something else.

oc'tū·ple, *v.t.*; octupled, *pt.*, *pp.*; octupling, *ppr.* to mutiply by eight.

oc'tū·ple, *v.i.* to become octuple.

oc'tū·plet, *n.* in music, a group of eight notes to be played in the time of six.

oc'tyl, *n.* [*oct-* and *-yl.*] in chemistry, a hypothetical hydrocarbon radical, C_8H_{17}, known only in combination.

oc·tyl·am'ine, *n.* [*octyl* and *amine.*] in chemistry, a colorless liquid compound obtained by heating alcoholic ammonia with iodide of octyl, and having the odor of fish.

oc'tyl·ēne, *n.* [*octyl* and *-ene.*] a hydrocarbon, C_8H_{16}: also called *octene.*

oc·tyl'ic, *a.* in chemistry, relating to, containing, or derived from octyl; as, *octylic* acid.

oc'ūl-, same as *oculo-.*

oc'ū·lăr, *a.* [L. *ocularis*, from *oculus*, the eye.]
 1. depending on the eye; by eyesight; as, *ocular* proof; *ocular* demonstration or evidence.
 2. in anatomy, of, for, or like the eye; optic.

oc'ū·lăr, *n.* the eyepiece of a microscope, telescope, or other optical instrument.

oc'ū·lăr·ly, *adv.* by the eye, sight, or actual view.

oc'ū·lā·ry, *a.* pertaining to the eye.

Oc·ū·lā'tȧ, *n.pl.* in arachnology, a division of spiders having eyes differing in size.

oc'ū·lāte, oc'ū·lā·ted, *a.* [L. *oculatus*, from *oculus*, the eye.]
 1. furnished with eyes.
 2. having spots resembling eyes; ocellated.

oc·ū·lau'di·tō·ry, *a.* [L. *oculus*, eye, and *auditorius*, pertaining to hearing.] combining sight and hearing, as the marginal organs of sense in some jellyfishes.

oc'ū·lī, *n.* plural of *oculus.*

oc·ū·lif'ēr·ous, *a.* [L. *oculus*, eye, and *ferre*, to bear.] eye-bearing.

oc'ū·li·form, *a.* [L. *oculus*, eye, and *forma*, form.] in the form of an eye; resembling the eye in shape; as, an *oculiform* pebble.

oc″ū·li·mō'tŏr, *a.* and *n.* same as *oculomotor.*

Oc·ū·lī'nȧ, *n.* [from L. *oculus*, eye.]
 1. in zoology, a type genus of *Oculinidæ.*
 2. [o–] a coral of this genus.

Oc·ū·lin'i·dae, *n.pl.* [*Oculina* and *-idæ.*] a family of *Zoantharia*, with several extinct and some surviving genera.

oc'ū·list, *n.* [from L. *oculus*, the eye.] a physician specializing in the treatment of abnormalities and diseases of the eye; an ophthalmologist.

oc'ū·lō-, [from L. *oculus*, the eye.] a combining form used to denote relation to the eye; as, *oculo*nasal: also *ocul-.*

oc″ū·lō·fron'tăl, *a.* [*oculo-* and *frontal.*] of or pertaining to the forehead and region of the eyes; as, an *oculofrontal* wrinkle.

oc″ū·lō·mō'tŏr, *a.* [*oculo-* and *motor.*] moving the eyeball; specifically, designating the third pair of cranial nerves, arising in the midbrain and supplying four of the six muscles that move each eyeball.

oc″ū·lō·mō′tŏr, *n.* the oculomotor nerve.

oc′ū·lus, *n.*; *pl.* **oc′ū·lī,** [L. *oculus*, the eye.]
1. the eye, or a spot shaped like an eye.
2. in botany, a leaf bud.
3. in architecture, a round window.

ō′cy·drōme, *n.* a bird of the genus *Ocydromus*.

Ō″cy·drō·mī′nae, *n.pl.* in ornithology, a subfamily of *Rallidæ*, represented by the ocydromes.

Ō·cyd′rō·mus, *n.* [Gr. *ōkydromos*, swift-running; *ōkys*, swift, and *dramein*, to run.] the typical genus of *Ocydrominæ*, swift-footed birds of Australia and New Zealand.

Ō·cyp′ō·dȧ, *n.* [Gr. *ōkys*, swift, and *pous*, *podos*, a foot.] a genus of swift-footed sand crabs, including the racer or horseman, a Brazilian crab.

ō′cy·pōde, *n.* a sand crab of the genus *Ocypoda*.

ō·cy·pō′di·ăn, *n.* same as *ocypode*.

O″cy·pō·doi′dē·ȧ, *n.pl.* a superfamily of crabs: also called *Grapsoidea*.

OD (ō-dē′), *n.*; *pl.* **ODs, OD's,** an overdose, especially of a narcotic. [Slang.]

OD (ō-dē′), *v.i.*; OD'd, ODed, *pt.*, *pp.*; OD'ing, ODing, *ppr.* to take an overdose, especially a fatal overdose of a narcotic. [Slang.]

Od, 'Od, *interj.* [*often* o-] a euphemism for God, used in oaths, etc: also spelled *Odd*. [Archaic.]

od (*or* ŏd), *n.*; *pl.* **od,** [G.; arbitrary formation.] a theoretical force formerly supposed by some to exist in nature and manifest itself in such phenomena as hypnotism, magnetism, light, etc.: also *odyl*, *odyle*.

Ō·dac′i·dae, *n.pl.* [from *Odax*.] a family of labroid fishes, typified by the genus *Odax*.

ō′dăl, ō′dăl·lēr, *n.* same as *udal*, *udaller*.

ō′dȧ·lisque (-lisk), **ō′dȧ·lisk,** *n.* [Fr. *odalisque*, from Turk. *ōdaliq*, a chamber companion, from *ōdah*, a chamber.] a female slave or concubine in an Oriental harem.

Ō′dax, *n.* a genus of small labroid fishes, found on the coasts of Australia and New Zealand.

Odd, *interj.* [*often* o-] Od.

odd, *a.*; *comp.* odder; *superl.* oddest, [Ice. *oddi*, a triangle, a point of land, an odd number, from *oddr*, the point of a weapon.]
1. being one of a pair of which the other is missing; as, an *odd* glove.
2. having a remainder of one when divided by two; not even: said of numbers.
3. characterized by an odd number; as, an *odd* month.
4. additional to a whole mentioned in round numbers; left over after taking a round number; as, a library of 5,000 and *odd* books; *odd* change.
5. with a relatively small amount or number over that specified; as, thirty *odd* years ago.
6. additional to what is usual, regular, habitual, accounted for, etc.; extra; occasional; incidental; as, *odd* jobs.
7. being one or more of a set, series, or group separated from the others; as, a few *odd* volumes of Dickens.
8. (a) not usual or ordinary; singular; peculiar; (b) queer; eccentric.
9. out of the way; retired; secluded; as, an *odd* corner.
10. at odds; on terms of enmity; as, to be *odd* with another. [Rare.]

Odd Fel′lōw, a member of the Independent Order of Odd Fellows, a fraternal and benevolent secret society, originated in England in the eighteenth century, and introduced in the United States in 1819.

odd′ish, *a.* somewhat odd; rather queer.

odd′i·ty, *n.* 1. the state or quality of being odd; strangeness; queerness; peculiarity; as, *oddity* of dress, manners, or appearance.
2. *pl.* **odd′i·ties,** an odd person or thing.

odd′ly, *adv.* 1. not evenly.
2. in an odd manner; strangely; unusually; as, *oddly* dressed.
oddly odd number; a number which contains an odd number an odd number of times.

odd′ment, *n.* 1. a fragment; an odd piece; a remnant; a scrap.
2. [*pl.*] in printing, parts of a book, as the title page, etc., not included in the text.

odd′ness, *n.* the state of being odd; the state of being not even; singularity; strangeness; peculiarity; irregularity; as the *oddness* of dress or shape; the *oddness* of an event or accident.

odd′-pin″nāte, *a.* in botany, pinnate with an odd, or single, terminal leaflet.

odds, *n.pl.* [*sometimes construed as sing.*], [from *odd*.]
1. unequal things; inequalities.
2. difference or amount of difference. [Rare.]
3. difference in favor of one side and against the other; advantage.
4. advantage given to a bettor or competitor in proportion to the assumed chances in his favor.
5. quarrel; dispute; disagreement: chiefly in *at odds*.
at odds; in disagreement; quarreling; antagonistic.
by (all) odds; by far.
odds and ends; small miscellaneous articles; remnants; scraps.
the odds are; the likelihood is; the chances are.

odds′māk″ēr, *n.* a person, usually an expert, who estimates the odds, or advantage, in betting or competing.

odds′-on′, *a.* having better than an even chance of winning; as, an *odds-on* bet, favorite, etc.

ōde, *n.* [LL. *ōde*; Gr. *ōdē*, an ode, song, or poem, from *aeidein*, to sing.]
1. originally, a poem written to be sung.
2. in modern use, a lyric poem, rhymed or unrhymed, usually addressed to some person or thing and characterized by lofty feeling, elaborate form, and dignified style, but sometimes simple in form and style.

-ōde, [from Gr. *hodos*, path, way.] a suffix meaning *way*, *path*, as in an*ode*, cath*ode*.

-ōde, [Gr. *-ōdēs*, *-odes*, from *-ō-*, ending of base or thematic vowel, and *-eidēs*, like, having the same form.] a suffix meaning *like* or *something like*, as in phyll*ode*.

ō·dē′on, *n.* same as *odeum*.

ō·dē′um, *n.* [L., from Gr. *ōdeion*, from *ōdē*, a song.] in ancient Greece and Rome, a roofed theater in which poets and musicians submitted their works to the approval of the public, and contended for prizes. The name is now sometimes applied to a hall or chamber for musical or dramatic performances. Called also *odeon*.

ōd′ic, *a.* of or forming an ode.

od′ic, *a.* of or relating to od.

od′ic·ăl·ly, *adv.* in an odic manner.

Ō′din, *n.* [Dan.; ON. *Odinn*.] in Norse mythology, the supreme deity, god of art, culture, war, and the dead: identified with the Teutonic Woden: also *Othin*.

Ō·din′ic, *a.* of or belonging to Odin.

ō′di·ous, *a.* [L. *odiosus*, from *odium*, hatred.] hateful; disgusting; offensive.

ō′di·ous·ly, *adv.* in an odious manner; hatefully; in a manner to deserve or excite hatred.

ō′di·ous·ness, *n.* the state of being odious.

ōd′ist, *n.* an ode writer.

ō′di·um, *n.* [L. *odium*, hatred, ill will, from *odi*, I hate.]
1. (a) hatred; (b) the state, quality, or fact of being hated.
2. the disgrace or infamy brought on by hateful action; opprobrium.
odium theologicum; the proverbial hatred of contending theologians.

ō′dō·grȧph, *n.* [Gr. *hodos*, way, road, and *-graph*.]
1. a device which measures the distance traveled by a person on foot or by a vehicle.
2. a device that records the number, length, and rapidity of steps taken by a pedestrian.

ō·dom′e·tēr, *n.* [Gr. *hodos*, a way, and *metron*, a measure.]
1. an instrument attached to the wheel of a vehicle to measure distance in traveling.
2. a surveyor's wheel for measuring distances.

ō·dō·met′ric·ăl, *a.* pertaining to an odometer or measurement by it.

ō·dom′e·try, *n.* the measurement of distances traveled by a vehicle.

Ō·don′ȧ·tȧ, *n.pl.* [Gr. *odōn*, *odontos*, tooth.] a division of insects of which the dragonflies are typical.

o·dont′-, see *odonto-*.

-ō·dont′, [from Gr. *odōn*, *odontos*, a tooth.] a combining form meaning *tooth*, as in macro*dont*.

ō·don·tal′gi·ȧ, *n.* [*odont-*, and Gr. *algos*, pain.] toothache.

ō·don·tal′gic, *a.* pertaining to toothache.

ō·don·tal′gic, *n.* a remedy for toothache.

ō·don·tal′gy, *n.* same as *odontalgia*.

ō·don·tī′ȧ·sis, *n.* [from Gr. *odontiăn*, to put forth the teeth.] the cutting of the teeth; dentition; also, any disorder caused by dentition.

ō·don′tic, *a.* pertaining to the teeth; dental.

ō·don·tī′tis, *n.* [*odont-* and *-itis*.] in pathology, inflammation of the teeth.

ō·don′tō-, [from Gr. *odōn*, *odontos*, a tooth.] a combining form meaning *tooth* or *teeth*, as in *odonto*blast, *odonto*stomatous: also, before a vowel, *odont-*.

ō·don′tō·blast, *n.* [*odonto-*, and Gr. *blastos*, germ.] one of the layers of connective tissue cells forming the outer surface of the pulp of a tooth: these cells secrete a substance which develops into dentine.

ō·don″tō·blas′tic, *a.* of an odontoblast.

Ō·don·tō·cē′tī, *n.pl.* [*odonto-*, and Gr. *kētos*, a whale.] the toothed whales; one of the divisions of the *Cetacea*.

ō·don′tō·clast, *n.* a cell which helps to absorb the roots of a milk tooth.

ō·don·tog′e·ny, *n.* [*odonto-*, and Gr. *-genēs*, producing.] generation, or mode of development, of the teeth.

ō·don·tō·glos′sum, *n.* [*odonto-*, and Gr. *glōssa*, tongue.] an extensive genus of orchids, natives to Central and South America, much prized by cultivators. There are more than eighty species.

ō·don′tō·grȧph, *n.* [*odonto-* and *-graph*.]
1. an instrument for laying out or marking gear teeth.
2. an instrument for recording irregularities of surface of tooth enamel.

ō·don·tō·graph′ic, *a.* pertaining to odontography.

ō·don·tog′rȧ·phy, *n.* [*odonto-* and *-graphy*.] the descriptive anatomy of the teeth.

ō·don′toid, *a.* [Gr. *odontoeidēs*; *odōn*, *odontos*, tooth, and *eidos*, form.]
1. toothlike.
2. designating or of a toothlike process, called the *odontoid peg* or *process*, projecting from the second vertebra of the neck, on which the top vertebra moves and rotates.
odontoid bone; same as the odontoid process when that exists as a separate bone, as in reptiles.

Ō·don·tol′cae, *n.pl.* [*odont-*, and Gr. *holkos*, a furrow.] an order of aquatic birds, now extinct, which resembled ostriches and had teeth set in grooves: spelled also *Odontholcæ* and *Odontoholcеæ*.

ō·don·tol′cāte, ō·don·tol′cous, *a.* pertaining to the *Odontolcæ*.

ō·don′tō·līte, *n.* [*odonto-*, and Gr. *lithos*, stone.] a fossil tooth; specifically, a fossil tooth or bone impregnated with oxide of copper, occurring in the Tertiary: used in making jewelry: also called *bone turquoise*.

ō·don·tō·log′i·căl, *a.* of or connected with odontology.

ō·don·tol′ō·gy, *n.* [*odonto-* and *-logy*.] the science dealing with the structure, growth, and diseases of the teeth; dentistry.

ō·don·tō′mȧ, *n.*; *pl.* **ō·don·tō′mȧ·tȧ,** [*odont-* and *-oma*.] a tooth tumor.

Ō·don·toph′ō·rȧ, *n.pl.* the division of mollusks, otherwise called *Encephala* or *Cephalophora*, comprising the classes *Gasteropoda*, *Pteropoda*, and *Cephalopoda*.

ō·don·toph′ō·răl, *a.* of an odontophore.

ō·don′tō·phōre, *n.* [*odonto-* and *-phore*.]
1. the ribbonlike tongue of certain mollusks having minute teeth; the radula.
2. a structure, usually protrusible, supporting the radula.

ō·don·toph′ō·rīne, *a.* of or like an odontophore.

ō·don·toph′ō·rous, *a.* having an odontophore.

ō·don′tō·plast, *n.* [*odonto-*, and Gr. *plassein*, to form, mold.] same as *odontoblast*.

Ō·don·top′te·ryx, *n.* [*odonto-*, and Gr. *pteryx*, a wing.] in paleontology, a genus of birds, probably belonging to the *Natatores*, and allied to the *Anatidæ*, from the Eocene. The jaws are furnished with denticulations of a compressed conical form and of two sizes, the larger resembling canine teeth.

Ō·don·tor′ni·thēs, *n.pl.* [*odont-*, and Gr. *ornis*, *ornithos*, a bird.] a subclass of extinct birds having the jaws furnished with true teeth sunk in distinct sockets or in a continuous groove.

ō·don·tor·rhā′gi·ȧ, *n.* hemorrhage following extraction of a tooth.

ō·don·tō·stom′ȧ·tous, *a.* [*odonto-*, and Gr. *stoma* (*-atos*), mouth.] having biting jaws: specifically applied to insects furnished with mandibles.

ō·don·tō·ther·ȧ·pī′ȧ, ō·don·tō·ther′ȧ·py, *n.* [*odonto-*, and Gr. *therapeia*, medical treatment.] the treatment of diseased teeth. [Obs.]

Ō·don·tō·tor′mae, *n.pl.* [*odonto-*, and Gr.

tormos, a socket.] a group of birds, now extinct, which had their teeth in sockets, like the *Ichthyornithes*.

ō′dŏr, ō′dŏur, *n.* [ME. via OFr., from L.]
1. that characteristic of a substance which makes it perceptible to the sense of smell; any smell, pleasant or unpleasant; fragrance; aroma.
2. a perfume.
to be in bad (or *ill*) *odor*; to have a poor reputation; be in ill repute.
Syn.—fragrance, perfume, incense, scent, smell.

ō′dŏr·ȧ·ment, *n.* a perfume; a strong scent. [Obs.]

ō′dŏr·ănt, *a.* fragrant. [Obs.]

ō′dŏr·āte, *a.* scented; having a strong scent, fetid or fragrant. [Obs.]

ō·dŏr·if′ẽr·ous, *a.* [L. *odorifer*; *odor*, odor, and *ferre*, to bear.]
1. giving off a scent; diffusing fragrance; fragrant; perfumed; usually, sweet of scent; as, *odoriferous* spices, *odoriferous* flowers.
2. bearing scent; as, *odoriferous* gales.

ō·dŏr·if′ẽr·ous·ly, *adv.* in an odoriferous manner.

ō·dŏr·if′ẽr·ous·ness, *n.* the quality of diffusing scent; fragrance; sweetness of scent.

ō′dŏr·in, *n.* an odoriferous product of the redistillation of the volatile oil obtained by distilling bone. [Obs.]

ō′dŏr·less, *a.* free from odor.

ō′dŏr·ous, *a.* having an odor; especially, sweet of scent; fragrant.

ō′dŏr·ous·ly, *adv.* sweetly; fragrantly.

ō′dŏr·ous·ness, *n.* the state of being odorous; the quality of diffusing scent or of exciting the sensation of smell; fragrance.

ō′dŏur, *n.* odor: British spelling.

Ods, Od′ș, *interj.* [*often* o-] a euphemism for *God's*, used in oaths, etc. [Archaic.]

-ō·dus, [Mod. L.; Gr. *-odous*, from *odōn*, *odontos*, tooth.] a combining form meaning *having teeth, toothed*.

od′yl, od′yle (*or* ōd′), *n.* same as *od*.

ō·dyl′iç, *a.* of or pertaining to od.

od′yl·ișm (*or* ōd′), *n.* the theory of od or odylic force.

od″yl·i·zā′tion (*or* ōd″), *n.* the process of transmitting odylic force from one individual to another.

ō″dyn·ȧ·çū′sis, *n.* [Gr. *odynē*, pain, and *akusis*, hearing.] painful hearing.

-ō·dyn′i·ȧ, [Gr. *-odynia*, from *odynē*, a pain.] a combining form meaning *pain in* (a specified organ or part), as in osteodynia.

od·yn·ō·phā′ġi·ȧ, *n.* [Gr. *odynē*, pain, and *phagein*, to eat.] the painful swallowing of food.

ō″dyn·ō·phō′bi·ȧ, *n.* [Gr. *odynē*, pain, and *phobos*, fear.] an extreme or abnormal fear of pain.

ō″dyn·ō·poe′iȧ, *n.pl.* [Gr. *odynē*, pain, and *poiein*, to make.] in obstetrics, agents for the induction of labor pains.

Od·ys·sē′ăn, *a.* of or like the (or an) Odyssey.

Ō·dys′seūs, *n.* [Gr. *Odysseus*.] the hero of the Odyssey, a king of Ithaca and one of the Greek leaders in the Trojan War; Ulysses.

Od′ys·sey, *n.* [L. *Odyssea*; Gr. *Odysseia*.]
1. an ancient Greek epic poem describing the wanderings of Odysseus during the ten years after the fall of Troy: it is generally attributed to Homer.
2. *pl.* **Od′ys·seyș,** [*sometimes* o-] any extended wandering or journey.

œ (ē *or* e), a diphthong in some Greek words, usually written *oe* or replaced by *e* in modern spelling of derived English words, as in *edema* (*oedema*).

oe′cist, *n.* [Gr. *oikistēs*, colonizer; *oikos*, house.] in ancient Greek history, one who founded a colony: also written *oekist*.

oe′çoid, *n.* [Gr. *oikos*, house, and *-oid*.] in anatomy, the colorless framework of a red blood corpuscle; ecoid.

oe·çō·log′iç·ăl, *a.* same as *ecological*.

oe·çol′ō·ġy, *n.* [Gr. *oikos*, house, and *-logy*.] same as *ecology*.

oe·çō·nom′iç·ăl, oe·çon′ō·my, etc. economical, economy, etc. [Obs.]

oeç·ū·men′iç, oeç·ū·men′iç·ăl, *a.* same as *ecumenic, ecumenical*.

oe·dē′mȧ, *n.*; *pl.* **oe·dē′mȧ·tȧ,** same as *edema*.

oe·dem′ȧ·tous, oe·dem′ȧ·tōse, *a.* same as *edematous*.

Oed′i·pus, *n.* [L.; Gr. *Oidipous*.] in Greek legend, the son of Laius and Jocasta, king and queen of Thebes, who, abandoned by his parents at birth because of the prophecy of an oracle, was raised by the king of Corinth, eventually returned to Thebes, and unwittingly killed his father and married his mother: subject of a tragedy by Sophocles.

Oed′i·pus çom′plex, in psychoanalysis, the unconscious tendency of a child to be attached to the parent of the opposite sex and hostile toward the other parent: its persistence in adult life results in neurotic disorders: sometimes restricted to a son's attachment, the term *Electra complex* being used for a daughter's.

oēil-de-boēuf′ (ẽy-de-bẽf′), *n.*; *pl.* **oēils-de-boēuf′** (ẽy-de-bẽf′), [Fr., an ox eye.] in architecture, a round or oval window in the frieze or roof of a large building.

oēil-de-per·drix′ (ẽy-de-pär-drē′), *n.* [Fr., a partridge eye.] in decorative art, a small round spot in a pattern; a dot.

oēil·lȧde′ (ẽy-yȧd′), *n.* an amorous or flirting glance; an ogle.

oeil·lère′ (ẽy-yär′), *n.* [Fr.] an opening in a helmet for the sight.

oe′kist, *n.* see *oecist*.

oe′lē·ō·blast, *n.* an excrescence on the embryo of certain tunicates.

oe′let, *n.* [dim., from Fr. *œil*, an eye.] an eyelet. [Obs.]

oe·nan′thāte, *n.* in chemistry, a salt of oenanthic acid.

oe·nan′thiç, *a.* [Gr. *oinanthē*, vine blossom; *oinē*, vine, and *anthos*, flower.] of, relating to, or imparting the odor peculiar to wine.
oenanthic acid; an acid obtained from oenanthic ether.
oenanthic ether; an oily liquid which gives to wine its characteristic odor.

oe·nan′thin, *n.* a poisonous and emetic resin from *Œnanthe fistulosa*, an herb of the parsley family.

oe·nan′thōl, *n.* a transparent, colorless oil, $C_7H_{14}O$, isomeric with butyrone, produced by the distillation of castor oil.

oe·nan′thyl, *n.* same as *heptyl*.

oe·nan′thyl·āte, *n.* in chemistry, a salt derived from oenanthylic acid.

oe·nan·thyl′iç, *a.* heptoic.

oe·nan·thyl′i·dēne, *n.* in chemistry, same as *heptine*.

oe·nan′thyl·ous, *a.* oenanthic. [Obs.]

oe·noch′ō·ē, *n.* see *oinochoe*.

oe′nō·lin, *n.* the red coloring matter of wine.

oe·nō·log′iç·ăl, *a.* of, by, or pertaining to oenology.

oe·nol′ō·ġy, *n.* [Gr. *oinos*, wine, and *-logy*.] the knowledge or study of wines.

oe′nō·man·cy, *n.* [Gr. *oinos*, wine, and *-mancy*.] a form of divination among the Greeks from the color, sound, etc. of wine when poured out in libations.

oe·nō·mā′ni·ȧ, *n.* [Gr. *oinos*, wine, and *mania*, madness.]
1. an abnormal craving for intoxicating drinks.
2. delirium tremens.

oe′nō·mel, *n.* [Gr. *oinos*, wine, and *meli*, honey.]
1. a drink resembling mead, composed of wine and honey, drunk by the ancient Greeks.
2. strong, sweet speech, thought, etc. [Poet.]

oe·nom′e·tẽr, *n.* an alcoholometer used for wines.

Oe·nō′nē, *n.* [L.; Gr. *Oinōnē*.] in Greek mythology, a nymph who became the wife of Paris and was deserted by him for Helen of Troy.

oe·noph′i·list, *n.* [Gr. *oinos*, wine, and *philein*, to love.] one who loves wine.

Oe·nō·thē′rȧ, *n.* [Gr. *oinothēras*, a plant, the root of which smells like wine.] a genus of American plants of the family *Onagraceæ*, containing about 100 species. *Oenothera biennis*, the evening primrose, is a common flower border plant.

ō′ẽr, *prep.* and *adv.* a contraction of *over*: chiefly used in poetry.

oẽr′sted, *n.* [named after Hans C. *Oersted* (1777–1851), a Danish physicist.]
1. formerly, the C.G.S. unit of magnetic reluctance.
2. the C.G.S. unit of magnetic intensity.

oe·soph′ăg-, oe·soph′ȧ·gō-, [from *oesophagus*.] a combining form meaning *the esophagus* or *the esophagus and*, as in *eosophagocele*: the forms *esophag-*, *esophago-* are also commonly used for the words listed below.

oe·soph·ăg·al′ġi·ȧ, *n.* [Gr. *oisophagos*, the gullet, and *algos*, pain.] pain in the esophagus: also spelled *esophagalgia*.

oe·sō·phaġ′ē·ăl, oe·sō·phaġ′ē·ăn, *a.* see *esophageal*.

oe·soph·ȧ·ġeç′tō·my, *n.* [Gr. *oisophagos*, and *ektomē*, excision.] excision of a portion of the esophagus: also spelled *esophagectomy*.

oe·soph·ȧ·ġiș′mus, *n.* [Gr. *oisophagos*, and *-ismos*.] spasm of the esophagus: also spelled *esophagismus*.

oe·soph·ȧ·ġī′tis, *n.* inflammation of the esophagus: also spelled *esophagitis*.

oe·soph′ȧ·gō-, see *oesophag-*.

oe·sō·phag′ō·cēle, *n.* [Gr. *oisophagos*, and *kēlē*, hernia.] abnormal distention or hernia of the esophagus: also spelled *esophagocele*.

oe·soph″ȧ·gō·mal·ā′ci·ȧ (-shi-), *n.* softening of the walls of the esophagus: also spelled *esophagomalacia*.

oe·soph·ȧ·gom′e·tẽr, *n.* [Gr. *oisophagos*, and *metron*, measure.] an instrument for measuring the length of the esophagus: also spelled *esophagometer*.

oe·soph″ȧ·gō·mȳ·cō′sis, *n.* [Gr. *oisophagos*, and *mykēs*, fungus.] any disease of the esophagus caused by fungi: also spelled *esophagomycosis*.

oe·soph′ȧ·gō·sçōpe″, *n.* [Gr. *oisophagos*, and *skopein*, to view.] an instrument for examining the interior of the esophagus by artificial light: also spelled *esophagoscope*.

oe·soph′ȧ·gō·spașm, *n.* [Gr. *oisophagos*, and *spasmos*.] spasm of the esophagus: also spelled *esophagospasm*.

oe·soph″ȧ·gō·stē·nō′sis, *n.* [Gr. *oisophagos*, and *stenōsis*, constriction.] stricture or constriction of the esophagus: also spelled *esophagostenosis*.

oe·soph·ȧ·gos′tō·mȧ, *n.* [Gr. *oisophagos*, and *stoma*, mouth.] an abnormal opening or passage leading into the esophagus: also spelled *esophagostoma*.

oe·soph·ȧ·got′ō·my, *n.* same as *esophagotomy*.

oe·soph′ȧ·gus, *n.* same as *esophagus*.

oes′tri·ăn, *a.* [Gr. *oistros*, the gadfly.] in zoology, relating to the botflies.

oes′tri·ăn, *n.* a botfly.

oes′trin, *n.* see *estrin*.

oes′troid, *a.* [Gr. *oistros*, gadfly, and *-oid*.] in zoology, of or resembling botflies.

oes′trous, *a.* see *estrous*.

oes′trū·ăl, *a.* see *estrual*.

oes′trū·āte, *v.i.* see *estruate*.

oes·trū·ā′tion, *n.* see *estruation*.

oes′trum, *n.* see *estrum*.

oes′trus, *n.* [L., from Gr. *oistros*, gadfly, hence a vehement impulse.]
1. see *estrus*.
2. [O–] a genus of dipterous insects, the type of the family *Œstridæ*. *Œstrus ovis* is the species whose larvae infest the nasal passages of sheep.
3. a gadfly.

oeu′vres (ũ′vr), *n.pl.* [Fr.] works, as of literature.

of (ov *or* uv), *prep.* [AS. *of* (also *af*), of, away from, out of, concerning; Ice., Sw., Dan., and D. *af*; Goth. *af*; O.H.G. *aba*, *apa*; G. *ab*; L. *ab*; Gr. *apo*; Sans. *apa*, from, away from.]
1. from; specifically, (a) derived or coming from; as, *of* good family, men *of* Ohio; (b) resulting from; caused by; through; as, he died *of* starvation; (c) at a distance from; apart from; as, a mile east *of* the river; (d) proceeding as a product from; by; as, the stories *of* Poe; (e) deprived, relieved, or separated from; as, cured *of* his disease, robbed *of* his money; (f) from the whole, or total number, constituting; as, he gave *of* his time; one *of* his brothers; (g) made from; using (a specified substance) as the material; as, a house *of* wood, made *of* plastic.
2. belonging to; as, the leaves *of* the book, the square root *of* a number.
3. (a) having; possessing; as, a man *of* property; (b) containing; as, a bag *of* peanuts.
4. that is; having the designation; specified as; as, the State *of* Utah, a height *of* six feet.
5. with (something specified) as object, goal, etc.; as, a reader *of* books.
6. having as a distinguishing quality or attribute; characterized by; as, a man *of* honor, a period *of* plenty.
7. having to do with; relating to; pertaining to; with reference to; concerning; about; as, don't think harshly *of* me.
8. set aside for; dedicated to; as, a week *of* festivities.
9. (a) during; as, *of* recent years; (b) on (a specified time); as, he came *of* a Saturday.
10. before: used in telling time; as, twenty *of* twelve.
11. by. [Archaic.]

When thou art bidden *of* any man to a wedding, sit not down in the highest room.
—Luke xiv. 8.

12. upon; on. [Obs.]
God's blessing *of* your good heart.—Shak.
13. with. [Obs.]
14. to; among; as, he was admitted *of* the council. [Obs.]
Of is also used in various idiomatic expressions (e.g., *of* course), many of which are entered in this dictionary under the key words.

of-, ob-: used before *f*, as in *offer*.

off, *adv.* [a Late ME. variant spelling of *of*, later generalized for all occurrences of *of* in stressed positions; *off* is thus merely *of* stressed.]
1. so as to be away, at a distance, to a side, etc.; as, he moved *off* toward the door.
2. so as to be no longer on, attached, united, in contact, etc.; as, he took *off* his coat, he tore a sheet *off*.
3. (a specified distance) away: (a) in space; as, the road is 200 yards *off*; (b) in time; as, my vacation is only two weeks *off*.
4. (a) so as to be no longer in operation, function, continuance, etc.; as, he turned the motor *off*; (b) to the point of completion or exhaustion; as, drink it *off*.
5. so as to be less, smaller, fewer, etc.; as, the number of customers dropped *off*.
6. away from one's work or usual activity; as, let's take the week *off*.
7. in nautical usage, away, as from the wind, etc.; as, to let a ship fall *off* a point or two.
Off is also used in various idiomatic expressions, many of which are entered in this dictionary under the key words.
from off; off from; as, a live coal taken *from off* the altar.
off and on; (a) not regularly; occasionally; now and then; (b) in nautical usage, on different tacks, now toward and now away from the shore.
to be off; to depart; to go away.
to get off; (a) to alight; to come down; (b) to escape; as, *to get off* easily from a trial; (c) to utter; as, *to get off* a joke.
to go off; (a) to depart; to desert; (b) to be discharged, as a gun.
to take off; (a) to take away; (b) to mimic or personate; (c) to go away.
to tell off; (a) in military tactics, to assign for a certain duty; as, ten men were *told off* for picket duty; (b) to count or reckon.

off, *interj.* go away! stay away!
off with! put off! take off! remove!
off with you! go away! depart!

off, *prep.* 1. (so as to be) no longer (or not) on, attached, united, etc.; as, it rolled *off* the table, the car is *off* the road.
2. from the substance of; on; as, he lived *off* the fat of the land.
3. coming or branching out from; as, an alley *off* Main Street.
4. free or relieved from; as, *off* duty.
5. not up to the usual level, standard, etc. of; as, badly *off* one's game.
6. no longer using, engaging in, supporting, etc.; abstaining from; as, he's *off* liquor for life. [Colloq.]
7. in nautical usage, away from (shore); as, a mile *off* shore.
8. from, as an indication of source; as, the thieves took $7 *off* him. [Colloq.]

off, *a.* 1. not on, attached, united, etc.; as, his hat is *off*.
2. not in operation, function, continuance, etc.; as, the motor is *off*.
3. gone away; on the way; as, the children are *off* to school.
4. less, smaller, fewer, etc.; as, profits are *off* this year.
5. away from work, etc.; absent; as, the office force is *off* today.
6. not up to the usual level, standard, etc.; as, an *off* season.
7. more remote; further; as, on the *off* chance, *off* side.
8. on the right: said of a horse in double harness, etc.
9. in (specified) circumstances; as, they are well *off*.
10. wrong; in error; as, you are *off* in your calculations.
11. in cricket, designating the side of the field facing the batsman.
12. in nautical usage, toward the sea; seaward.

off, *n.* 1. the fact or condition of being off; as, I've had my *offs* and ons.
2. in cricket, the off side.
Johnson, the young bowler, is getting wild, and bowls a ball almost wide to the *off*.
—T. Hughes.

off, *v.t.* to kill; murder. [Slang.]

off'făl, *n.* [lit., *off-fall*; so D. *afval*, Ice. *affall*, G. *abfall* are similarly formed, and with similar meanings.]
1. [*construed as sing. or pl.*] waste products; useless leftovers; especially, the entrails, etc. of a butchered animal.
2. rubbish; refuse; garbage.

off'bēat, *n.* in music, any of the beats of a measure that have weak, or secondary, accents.

off'bēat, *a.* in jazz, having the strong, or primary, accent on the second and fourth beats in 4/4 time; as, *offbeat* rhythm.

off'cȧst, off'-cȧst, *n.* and *a.* castoff.

off'chȧnce, *n.* a very slight chance; remote possibility.

off'-çŏl'ŏr, *a.* 1. varying from the usual, standard, or required color.
2. indelicate, indecent, or in bad taste; not quite proper; as, an *off-color* joke.

off'çut, *n.* 1. in bookbinding, a portion of printed sheets cut off for separate folding; as, the *offcut* of a 16-page form.
2. that which is cut off, as a surplus margin cut from paper.

of·fence', of·fence'fụl, etc. see *offense*, etc.

of·fend', *v.t.*; offended, *pt., pp.*; offending, *ppr.* [L. *offendere*, to strike against; *of* for *ob*, against, and Old L. *fendere*, to hit, thrust.]
1. to attack; to assail. [Obs.]
2. to hurt the feelings of; to insult; to displease; to make angry; to affront; to mortify.
For, indeed, the watch ought to *offend* no man. —Shak.
3. to be displeasing to (the taste, sense etc.).
A random string
Your finer, female sense *offends*.
—Tennyson.
4. to injure; to harm; to hurt. [Obs.]
5. to sin against; to transgress. [Obs.]
6. to draw to evil or hinder in obedience; to cause to sin or neglect duty. [Obs.]
If thy right eye *offend* thee, pluck it out.
—Matt. v. 29.
Syn.—anger, displease, wound, shock, annoy, affront.

of·fend', *v.i.* 1. to transgress the moral or divine law; to sin; to commit a crime or fault: sometimes used with *against*.
We have *offended against* the Lord already.
—2 Chron. xxviii. 13.
2. to cause dislike, resentment, or anger; to give offense.
3. to take offense; to be scandalized. [Obs.]
If meat make my brother to *offend*, I will eat no flesh. —1 Cor. viii. 13.

of·fend'ănt, *n.* an offender. [Rare.]

of·fend'ẽr, *n.* one who offends; one who violates any law, divine or human; a criminal; a trespasser; a transgressor; one who does an injury.
Syn.—delinquent, transgressor, culprit, evildoer.

of·fend'ress, *n.* a girl or woman who offends. [Rare.]

of·fense', *n.* [Fr. *offense*, from L. *offensa*.]
1. an offending; specifically, (a) the act of breaking the law; sin; crime; transgression; (b) the act of creating resentment, hurt feelings, displeasure, etc.
2. the condition of being offended, especially of feeling hurt, resentful, or angry; umbrage.
3. something that causes sinning or wrongdoing.
4. something that causes resentment, anger, etc.
5. the act of attacking or assaulting; aggression.
6. the person, team, army, etc. that is attacking.
7. harm; hurt; injury. [Obs.]
So shall he waste his means, weary his soldiers,
Doing himself *offense*. —Shak.
Also spelled *offence*.
to give offense; to offend; to anger, insult, displease, etc.
to take offense; to become offended; to feel hurt, resentful, angry, etc.
Syn.—crime, misdeed, misdemeanor, transgression, trespass, sin, scandal, resentment, fault, affront.

of·fense'fụl, *a.* giving displeasure; injurious: also spelled *offenceful*. [Rare.]

of·fense'less, *a.* 1. unoffending; innocent; inoffensive.
2. lacking or incapable of offense.
Also spelled *offenceless*.

of·fen'si·ble, *a.* liable to give offense. [Obs.]

of·fen'sive, *a.* 1. causing offense; specifically, (a) causing some degree of anger; giving provocation; irritating; as, you are *offensive* in your remarks; (b) disgusting; giving pain or unpleasant sensations; disagreeable; as, something *offensive* to taste or smell.
2. pertaining to offense; specifically, (a) of, for, or used in attack: opposed to *defensive*; as, an *offensive* weapon; (b) consisting in attack; proceeding by attack; assailant; invading: opposed to *defensive*; as, an *offensive* war.
We are not all arrayed in two opposite ranks: the *offensive* and the defensive.
—Dickens.
Syn.—displeasing, disagreeable, distasteful, obnoxious, abhorrent, disgusting, impertinent, rude, saucy, opprobrious, insulting, insolent, abusive, scurrilous.

of·fen'sive, *n.* the act of attacking; attitude, position, or operation of attack; aggressive attitude (often with *the*); as, to act on *the offensive*.

of·fen'sive·ly, *adv.* in an offensive manner.

of·fen'sive·ness, *n.* the quality or condition of being offensive; injuriousness; unpleasantness.

of'fẽr, *v.t.*; offered, *pt., pp.*; offering, *ppr.* [Fr. *offrir*, from L. *offerre*; *of* for *ob*, toward, and *ferre*, to bring.]
1. to present for acceptance or rejection; to tender; to proffer.
Servants placing happiness in strong drink, make court to my young master by *offering* him that which they love. —Locke.
2. to present to notice; to put forward for consideration; to suggest; to propose; as, several things *offer* themselves for our consideration.
3. to present to God or a god as an act of worship; to present devotionally: often with *up*; as, to *offer up* a prayer.
Thou shalt *offer* every day a bullock as a sin offering for atonement. —Ex. xxix. 36.
4. to attempt or threaten; to indicate intention of; to put in action; to set about; as, to *offer* violence; to *offer* an insult; to *offer* resistance.
You *offer* him, if this be so, a wrong
Something unfilial. —Shak.
5. to bid, as a price, reward, or wages.
Nor, shouldst thou *offer* all thy little store,
Will rich Iolas yield, but *offer* more.
—Dryden.
Syn.—propose, propound, move, proffer, tender, sacrifice, immolate.

of'fẽr, *v.i.* 1. to make a presentation or sacrifice in worship.
2. to present itself; to be at hand.
Th' occasion *offers*, and the youth complies.
—Dryden.
3. to make an attempt (*at*). [Archaic.]

of'fẽr, *n.* 1. the act of offering or presenting a proposal to be accepted or refused; a proffer; a tender.
A fire that will be sure to destroy the offering though mercy should spare the *offer*.
—South.
2. that which is offered; a proffer, presentation, suggestion, bid, proposal, etc.: sometimes used in the sense of a proposal of marriage.
I assure you, she has refused several *offers* to my own knowledge. —Goldsmith.
3. an attempt; an endeavor. [Archaic.]
One sees in it a kind of *offer* at modern architecture. —Addison.
4. in law, a proposal, the acceptance of which constitutes a contract.

of'fẽr·ȧ·ble, *a.* that can be offered.

of'fẽr·ẽr, *n.* one who offers.

of'fẽr·ing, *n.* 1. the act of making an offer.
2. something offered; specifically, (a) a gift or contribution; (b) presentation in worship; oblation; (c) something offered for sale; (d) a theatrical presentation.
The silly people take me for a saint,
And bring me *offerings* of fruit and flowers.
—Tennyson.

of'fẽr·tō·ry, *n.*; *pl.* **of'fẽr·tō·ries**, [Fr. *offertoire*, from LL. *offertorium*, place for offerings.]
1. that part of the Mass or Holy Communion during which the unconsecrated bread and wine of the Eucharist are offered to God: in the Anglican Church, alms are collected at this time.

2. the prayers recited or hymn sung at this time.
3. the alms collected at this time.
4. any money collected at a church service.

of′fẽr·tūre, *n.* offering. [Obs.]

off′hand′, *a.* 1. said or done offhand; extemporaneous; without previous preparation.
2. casual, curt, informal, brusque, etc.

off′hand′, *adv.* in an offhand manner; extemporaneously; informally.

off′hand′ed, *a.* same as *offhand.*

of′fice (-fis), *n.* [Fr., from L. *officium*, from *of* for prefix *ob-*, and *facere*, to make or do, or from *opus*, work, and *facere.*]
1. something performed or intended to be performed for another; (specified kind of) service; as, this was done through his good (or ill) *offices.*
2. a function or duty assigned to someone, especially as an essential part of his work or position.
3. a position of authority or trust, especially in a government, corporation, etc.; as, the *office* of president.
4. any of the branches of the United States Government ranking next below the departments; as, the Printing *Office.*
5. (a) the building, room, or series of rooms in which the affairs of a business, professional person, branch of government, etc. are carried on; (b) all the people working in such a place; staff; (c) all the administrative officers or executives of a business, etc.
6. [*pl.*] the rooms or buildings of a house or estate in which the servants carry out their duties.
7. a religious or social ceremony or rite; specifically, (a) the daily service of the Roman Catholic breviary: also called *Divine Office*; (b) the Morning and Evening Prayer of the Anglican Church; (c) the service of Holy Communion; (d) prayers or rites for any special purpose; as, the *Office* of the Dead.
houses of office; houses where official business is transacted.
little office; an office of lessons and hymns recited in the Roman Catholic Church in honor of the Virgin Mary.
office boy; a boy hired to do the small tasks in an office.
office copy; see *certified copy* under *copy.*
office found; in law, the finding of a jury in an inquest of office by which the crown becomes entitled to take possession of real or personal property. [Brit.]
office hours; the time of day during which an office is normally open for business.
office seeker; a person who tries to get himself oppointed to public office.
Syn.—service, duty, appointment, function, employment, station, business, post.

of′fice, *v.t.* to perform; to do; to discharge. [Obs.]

of′fice·hōld″ẽr, *n.* one who holds an office; especially, a government official holding office through political patronage.

of′fi·cẽr, *n.* [Fr. *officier*, from LL. *officiarius*, from L. *officium*, office.]
1. anyone elected or appointed to an office or position of authority in a government, business, institution, social club, etc.
2. a policeman or constable.
3. a person appointed to a position of authority in the armed forces of a country, especially one holding a commission or rank; a commissioned officer.
4. the captain or any of the mates of a ship.
5. in certain honorary societies, a member holding one of the higher grades.
noncommissioned officer; an enlisted person in the armed forces appointed by a proper authority to any of the ranks above private first class and below warrant officer: distinguished from *commissioned officer.*
officer of the day; in military usage, the officer having over-all charge of the interior guard and security of his garrison for any given day.
officer of the deck; the officer in temporary charge of the management of a ship.
officer of the guard; in military usage, an officer designated under the officer of the day to be in immediate command of the interior guard of a garrison.

of′fi·cẽr, *v.t.*; officered, *pt.*, *pp.*; officering, *ppr.*
1. to furnish with officers; to appoint officers over.

> Count Pulaski raised a legionary corps, which he *officered* principally with foreigners. —Marshall.

2. to act as an officer of; to command; to direct; to manage.

ŏf·fi′ciăl (-fish′ăl), *a.* [L. *officialis*; Fr. *officiel.*]
1. of or holding an office, or position of authority.
2. coming from the proper authority; authorized; as, an *official* reprimand.
3. befitting a person of authority in his capacity as an officer; formal; ceremonious.
4. in pharmacy, contained in the current pharmacopoeia; authorized for use in medicine.
Syn.—authentic, genuine, true, authoritative.

ŏf·fi′ciăl, *n.* 1. one who holds office, especially public office.
2. in English law, an ecclesiastical judge appointed by a bishop, chapter, archdeacon, etc., with charge of the spiritual jurisdiction.

ŏf·fi′ciăl·dŏm, *n.* 1. officials collectively.
2. excessive adherence to official routine; officialism.
3. the domain or position of officials.

ŏf·fi′ciăl·işm, *n.* 1. the characteristic practices and behavior of officials; especially, excessive adherence to official routine and regulations; red tape.
2. officials collectively; officialdom.

ŏf·fi·ci·al′i·ty (-fish-i-), *n.* same as *officialty.*

ŏf·fi′ciăl·ly, *adv.* in an official manner or capacity; by the proper officer; by virtue of the proper authority; in pursuance of the special powers vested; as, accounts or reports *officially* verified or rendered; letters *officially* communicated; persons *officially* notified.

ŏf·fi′ciăl·ty, *n.* the charge or office of an official.

ŏf·fi′ci·ănt (-fish-i-), *n.* an officiating priest, minister, etc.

ŏf·fi′ci·ā·ry, *n.*; *pl.* **ŏf·fi′ci·ā·rieş**, [ML. *officiarius.*] a group of officials.

ŏf·fi′ci·ā·ry, *a.* connected with or resulting from the holding of an office.

ŏf·fi′ci·āte, *v.i.*; officiated, *pt.*, *pp.*; officiating, *ppr.* [LL. *officiare.*]
1. to perform the duties of an office; to act as an officer.
2. to perform the functions of a priest, minister, etc.; to conduct a religious service.

ŏf·fi′ci·āte, *v.t.* to give, provide, or supply in discharge of an office or duty. [Obs.]

ŏf·fi·ci·ā′tion, *n.* the act of officiating.

ŏf·fi′ci·ā·tŏr, *n.* one who officiates.

ŏf·fic′i·năl, *a.* [ML. *officinalis*, from L. *officina*, workshop.] authorized and kept in stock in a pharmacy: said of drugs, etc.

ŏf·fic′i·năl, *n.* an officinal drug or preparation.

ŏf·fi′cious (-fish′us), *a.* [from Fr. or L.; Fr. *officieux*; L. *officiosus*, from *officium*, office.]
1. ready to serve; obliging. [Obs.]
2. offering unnecessary and unwanted advice or services; meddlesome.
3. in diplomacy, unofficial; informal.

ŏf·fi′cious·ly, *adv.* in an officious manner.

ŏf·fi′cious·ness, *n.* the state or quality of being officious.

ọff′ing, *n.* [from *off.*]
1. the distant part of the sea visible from the shore.
2. distance, or position at a distance, from the shore.
in the offing; (a) barely visible from shore; (b) far but in sight; (c) at some vague future time.

ọff′ish, *a.* shy; reserved; distant; inclined to remain aloof. [Colloq.]

ọff′let, *n.* a pipe by which water is discharged.

ọff′print, *n.* a separate reprint of an article, etc. that first appeared in a magazine or other larger publication.

ọff·print′, *v.t.*; offprinted, *pt.*, *pp.*; offprinting, *ppr.* to reprint (an excerpt, etc.) separately.

ọff′-pụt·ting, *a.* tending to put one off; distracting, annoying, etc. [Chiefly Brit.]

ọff·sad′dle, *v.t.*; offsaddled, *pt.*, *pp.*; offsaddling, *ppr.* to unsaddle. [S. African.]

ọff′scour·ing, *n.* [*usually pl.*] that which is scoured off; refuse; filth; garbage; rubbish.

ọff′-sēa·ṣŏn, *n.* a time of the year when the usual activity or business is reduced or not carried on.

ọff′set, *n.* 1. something that is set off, or has sprung or developed, from something else; offshoot; extension; branch; spur.
2. anything that balances, counteracts, or compensates for something else; compensation.
3. in architecture, a ledge or recess formed in a wall by a reduction in its thickness above.
4. in botany, a side shoot that takes root and starts a new plant.
5. in electricity, a branch off a main power line.
6. in mechanics, a curve or bend in a metal bar, pipe, etc. to permit it to pass an obstruction.
7. in printing, (a) offset printing; (b) an impression made by this process; (c) an ink smudge transferred from a freshly printed sheet to the one next to it.
8. in surveying, a short distance measured at right angles from the main line to help in computing the area of an irregular plot of ground.

ọff·set′, *v.t.*; offset, *pt.*, *pp.*; offsetting, *ppr.*
1. to balance, complement, counteract, compensate for, etc.
2. to make an offset in.
3. in printing, (a) to make (an impression) by offset printing; (b) to smudge with an offset.

ọff·set′, *v.i.* 1. to come out or develop as an offset.
2. in printing, to make an offset.

ọff′set print′ing, a printing process in which the matter to be reproduced is copied photographically upon a metal plate which, when placed upon the appropriate cylinder of an offset press, is inked, and makes an imprint of the text or illustration on a rubber-covered cylinder; this rubber-covered cylinder, in turn, prints upon sheets of paper which are automatically fed into the machine. Offset printing is especially useful in the preparation of large runs of profusely illustrated material, as advertising leaflets.

ọff′set sheet, in printing, an oiled sheet of paper used on the tympan of a press; also, a blank sheet, as of tissue paper, used between freshly printed sheets, as with engravings, to prevent offsets, or smudges.

ọff′shoot, *n.* anything that branches off, or derives from, a main source; specifically, a shoot or stem growing laterally from the main stem of a plant.

ọff′shōre, *adv.* 1. in or on the sea at a distance from the land; as, the boats anchored *offshore.*
2. from the land; away from the shore; as, the wind blows *offshore.*
3. outside the U.S.; as, to borrow money *offshore.*

ọff′shōre, *a.* 1. moving off or away from the shore; as, an *offshore* current.
2. of or situated at a part of the ocean away from the shore; especially, beyond the three-mile limit; as, the *offshore* fishing boats.
3. engaged in outside the U.S., as by U.S. banks or manufacturers; as, *offshore* investments; *offshore* assembly plants.

ọff′sīde, *a.* in certain sports, not in the proper position for play; specifically, in football, over the line of scrimmage or otherwise ahead of the ball before the play has properly begun, and hence subject to penalty: said of a player, team, or play.

ọff′sīde′, *adv.* into an offside position; as, to jump *offside.*

ọff′sīde, *n.* an offside play.

ọff′spring (*or* of′), *n.* [*sometimes construed as pl.*], [ME. and AS. *ofspring.*]
1. a child or children; descendant or descendants; progeny; issue; as, John is my only *offspring*, she has six *offspring.*
2. a product, outcome, or result.
Syn.—progeny, issue.

ọff′-stāġe′, *n.* that part of a stage not visible to the audience.

ọff′-stāġe′, *a.* in or from the off-stage; as, an *off-stage* whisper.

ọff′-stāġe′, *adv.* to the off-stage; as, he went *off-stage.*

ọff′tāke, *n.* a drainage channel; especially, a level for drainage in a mine; also, the point where such a channel leaves the place it is used to drain.

ọff′-track′, *a.* designating or of legalized betting on horseraces, carried on at places away from the racetrack.

ọff′wărd, *adv.* away from the shore; seaward.

ọff′-whīte′ (-hwīt), *a.* of an off shade of white; especially, grayish-white

ọft, *adv.* [ME.; AS.; akin to G. *oft.*] often. [Rare or Poet.]

ọf′ten (ọf′n), *adv.*; *comp.* oftener; *superl.* oftenest, many times; not seldom; frequently; on many occasions; repeatedly.

ọf′ten, *a.* frequent. [Archaic.]

> Use a little wine for thy stomach's sake and thine *often* infirmities. —1 Tim. v. 23.

ọf′ten·ness, *n.* frequency.

ọf′ten·tīmeş, *adv.* frequently; often.

ọft′tīmeş, *adv.* frequently; often. [Archaic or Poetic.]

ō′gak, ō′gaç, *n.* [Eskimo.] a codfish, the *Gadus ogac.*
og′dō·ad, *n.* [Gr. *ogdoas, ogdoados,* the number eight.]
1. the number eight.
2. any group or series of eight; especially, in Gnosticism, a group of eight eons or of eight divine persons.
og·dō·as′tich, *n.* [Gr. *ogdoas,* eight, and *stichos,* a verse.] a poem of eight lines. [Obs.]
ō·gee′, *n.* [ME. (pl.) *oggez;* OFr. *ogive, augive.*]
1. a molding having an S-shaped curve in profile.
2. any S-shaped curve or line.
3. an ogee arch.
ō·gee′ ärch, a pointed arch formed with the curve of an ogee on each side.
Ō·gee′chee līme, a sour red plumlike drupe of the *Nyssa capitata,* of the southern part of the United States; also, the tree on which it grows.
og·gȧ·ni′tion (-nish′un), *n.* a growling or snarling. [Obs.]
og′hăm, og′ăm, *n.* [Ir., Gael. *oidheam,* a line or character.]
1. a kind of writing used by the ancient Irish and some other Celtic races.

OGEE ARCH

OGHAM INSCRIPTION

2. one of the twenty characters used in this kind of writing. They consisted principally of straight lines, the significance of which depended on their position relative to a chief line, through, over, or under which they were drawn, singly or in groups, either perpendicularly or obliquely. The place of this chief line was sometimes filled by the edge of the substance, usually stone, on which the oghams were incised.
3. an inscription in such characters.
4. [O–] a dialect used by the ancient Irish.
ō·gī′văl, *a.* 1. of, or having the form of, an ogive; as, the *ogival* point of a projectile.
2. in architecture, having the distinctive features of a pointed arch or of a building with pointed arches; characterized by ogives.
ō′gīve, *n.* [Fr.] 1. in architecture, the diagonal rib or groin of a Gothic vault.
2. a pointed, or Gothic, arch.
ō′gle (ō′gl), *v.i.* and *v.t.;* ogled, *pt., pp.;* ogling, *ppr.* [prob. from L.G. *oegeln,* from *oog,* the eye.] to keep looking (at) with fondness or desire; to make eyes (at).
ō′gle, *n.* an ogling look.
ō′glẽr, *n.* one who ogles.
ō′gli·ō (-lē-), *n.* olio. [Rare.]
Og′pū, *n.* [Russ.] formerly, the state security police, or secret service, of the Soviet Union, succeeding the Cheka in 1922, and abolished in 1934: its functions were supplanted by those of the N.K.V.D. (1934–1946), which in turn was succeeded by the M.V.D.
ō′gre (ō′gũr), *n.* [Fr.; first used in Perrault's fairy tales and prob. coined by him.]
1. in fairy tales and folklore, a man-eating monster or giant.
2. a hideous, coarse, or cruel man.
ō′gre·ish, *a.* like or characteristic of an ogre.
ō′gre·iṣm, *n.* the character or habits of an ogre.
ō′gress, *n.* a female ogre.
ō′gress, *n.* in heraldry, a black roundel.
ō′grish, *a.* same as *ogreish.*
Ō·gyġ′i·ȧ, *n.* [L.; Gr. *Ōgygia.*] in Homer's Odyssey, the island of the sea nymph Calypso.
Ō·gyġ′i·ăn, *a.* 1. pertaining to Ogyges, an ancient mythical monarch in Greece, and to a great deluge in Attica in his reign.
2. of great and remote antiquity.
ōh, *interj.* an exclamation expressing surprise, fear, wonder, pain, etc.
ōh, *n.; pl.* **ōh′ṣ, ōhṣ** (ōz), any instance of this exclamation.
Ō·hī′ō·ăn, *a.* of Ohio.
Ō·hī′ō·ăn, *n.* a native or inhabitant of Ohio.
ōhm, *n.* [after George S. *Ohm* (1787–1854), German physicist.] the unit of electrical resistance, equal to the resistance of a circuit in which an electromotive force of one volt maintains a current of one ampere: symbol, Ω (no period).
ōhm′āġe, *n.* the electrical resistance of a conductor expressed in ohms.
ōhm′iç, *a.* 1. of or pertaining to an ohm.
2. measured in ohms.
ohmic resistance; actual resistance, as of a wire, as distinguished from spurious resistance produced by counter-electromotive force.
ōhm′mē″tẽr, *n.* an instrument for measuring electrical resistance in ohms; a resistance box.
Ōhm′ṣ lạw, see under *law.*
ō·hō′, *interj.* an exclamation expressing surprise, taunting, etc.
-oid, [Fr. *-oide;* L. *-oides;* Gr. *-o-eidēs,* from *eidos,* form, shape.] a suffix meaning *like, resembling,* as in typh*oid,* cellul*oid.*
-oi′de·ȧ, [Mod. L.; see *-oid.*] a combining form used in zoology to form the names of classes or superfamilies.
Ō·id′i·um, *n.* [dim. form of Gr. *ōon,* an egg.] in botany, a genus of exceedingly small fungi, as the vine mildew, which form a superficial growth on spoiled fruit, vegetables, etc.
oi·kol′ō·ġy, *n.* same as *ecology.*
oil, *n.* [ME. *oile;* OFr. *oile, oille;* L. *oleum,* oil.]
1. any of various kinds of greasy, combustible substances obtained from animal, vegetable, and mineral matter: oils are liquid at ordinary temperatures and soluble in certain organic solvents, as ether, but not in water.
2. petroleum.
3. any of various substances having the consistency of oil.
4. an oil color.
5. an oil painting.
6. flattery. [Colloq.]
animal oil, bone oil, or *Dippel's oil;* in old chemistry, an oil derived from the dry distillation of bones and other animal substances.
drying oil; see under *drying.*
essential oil; see under *essential.*
ethereal oil; see under *ethereal.*
ethereal oil of wine; see under *ethereal.*
fixed oil; see under *fixed.*
oil engine; an engine run by kerosene or one of the heavier oils.
oil of turpentine; a colorless, volatile oil distilled from the oleoresin of any of several trees, as the terebinth, pine, fir, etc., used in paints, varnishes, and disinfectants, in pharmacy, etc.: also *turpentine, spirits of turpentine.*
oil of vitriol; sulfuric acid.
oil of wine; see *oenanthic ether* under *oenanthic.*
to burn the midnight oil; see under *midnight.*
to pour oil on the fire; to intensify the conflagration; to add fuel to the flame; to aggravate differences, disagreements, etc.
to pour oil on troubled waters; to settle quarrels, differences, etc. by calm, soothing methods.
to strike oil; (a) to discover oil under the ground by drilling a shaft for it; (b) to become suddenly wealthy.
oil, *v.t.;* oiled, *pt., pp.;* oiling, *ppr.* 1. to smear, anoint, or rub over with oil; to lubricate with oil; to supply with oil.
2. to bribe.
oil, *v.i.* to turn into oil by melting.
oil, *a.* of, from, like, or yielding oil, or having to do with the production or use of oil.
oil bag, 1. a bag, cyst, or gland in animals, containing oil.
2. a bag containing oil.
3. a bag used in an oil press.
oil bee′tle, a species of coleopterous insects of the genus *Meloë* and the family *Cantharidæ,* named from the oillike matter which they exude from the joints of their legs.
oil′bīrd, *n.* 1. same as *guacharo.*
2. the frogmouth, an East Indian bird with a broad bill.
oil box, in machinery, a box containing a supply of oil for a journal and feeding it by means of a wick or other device.
oil bũrn′ẽr, anything which burns oil for fuel, as a heating device, engine, or locomotive; particularly, an apparatus in which oil is vaporized, mixed with air, and ignited.
oil çāke, a cake or mass of the compressed refuse seed of cotton, flax, mustard, etc. from which oil has been extracted: it is used as feed for cattle and as fertilizer.
oil′çan, *n.* a can for holding oil, usually with a spout for pouring it out, used for lubricating machinery, etc.
oil′çloth, *n.* cloth made waterproof by being coated with paint or treated with oil, used for covering tables, shelves, etc.
oil çol′ŏr, a color or paint made by grinding a pigment in oil, often linseed oil.
oil′çup, *n.* 1. in machinery, a cup-formed termination of the stuffing box, through which any rod, as a piston rod, works: it contains lubricating oil.
2. a cylindrical container (in a machine) for holding oil and releasing it gradually as lubrication for the moving parts.
oil der′rick, an apparatus used in boring oil wells, consisting of a strong wooden tower with machinery by means of which the various boring tools are operated.
oiled, *a.* smeared or anointed with oil; treated with oil; as, *oiled* silk; *oiled* paper.
oil′ẽr, *n.* 1. a person or thing that oils machinery, engines, etc.
2. an oilcan.
3. a ship for transporting oil; a tanker.
4. an oilskin coat. [Colloq.]
oil′ẽr·y, *n.* collectively, the things pertaining to the production of and trade in oil.
oil fiēld, a place where oil deposits of value are found.
oil gas, inflammable gas procured from fixed oils by intense heat and used for illuminating purposes.
oil gland, 1. a gland that secretes oil, especially the one at the rump of a bird from which it takes oil for preening its feathers.
2. a gland in certain plants secreting oil.
oil green, a yellowish green; malachite green.
oil′i·ly, *adv.* in an oily manner.
oil′i·ness, *n.* the quality or condition of being oily; unctuousness; greasiness.
oil′let, *n.* [Fr. *oeillet,* from *oeil,* eye.]
1. an eyelet.
2. an opening in a fortification for discharging missiles. [Obs.]
3. the eye or growing point of a plant. [Obs.]
oil′man, *n.; pl.* **oil′men,** 1. one who deals in oils.
2. one engaged in the business of producing oil.
3. a worker in the oil industries.
oil nut, 1. the butternut of North America; the white walnut.
2. the buffalo nut of the sandalwood family.
3. the castor-oil plant or its bean.
oil pāint′ing, 1. a picture painted in oil colors.
2. the art of painting in oil colors.
oil päłm (päm), any palm tree whose fruit yields oil, especially *Elæis guineensis.*
oil′pā″pẽr, *n.* paper made transparent and waterproof by treatment with oil.
oil′seed, *n.* any seed that yields oil, as cottonseed, flaxseed, the castor bean, etc.
oil shärk, any species of shark that yields a valuable oil.
oil′skin, *n.* 1. cloth made waterproof by treatment with oil.
2. [*often in pl.*] a garment made of this.
oil′stōne, *n.* a whetstone treated with oil.
oil stōve, a stove which burns oil as fuel, used chiefly in cooking.

OIL TANKER

oil tank′ẽr, a tank boat carrying oil.
oil test′ẽr, an apparatus designed, (a) to test the lubricating quality of oil; (b) to determine the temperature at which an oil will give off inflammable vapor.
oil tree, any one of several trees from which oil is obtained, as the oil palm, the illupi, the castor-oil plant, etc.
oil well, a well bored through layers of rock, etc. to a supply of petroleum.
oil′y, *a.; comp.* oilier; *superl.* oiliest, 1. of, like, consisting of, or containing oil.
2. covered with oil; fat; greasy.
3. too smooth; slippery; unctuous.
oil′y grāin, same as *benne.*
oi·noch′ō·ē, *n.* [Gr. *oinos,* wine, and *chein,* to pour.] in ancient Greece, a small pitcher or vase with a handle, of graceful shape and elaborate decoration, used for transferring wine by hand from the crater to the drinking cups: also written *oenochoe.*
oint, *v.t.* to anoint. [Archaic.]
oint′ment, *n.* [ME. *oinement;* OFr. *oignement;* Fr. *oindre,* from L. *unguere,* to anoint.] a fatty substance applied to the skin for healing or cosmetic purposes; salve; unguent.

Oir'each·tas (er'ekh-tȧs), *n.* [Ir.] the legislature of Ireland, consisting of the Dail Eireann (lower house) and the Seanad Eireann (upper house).

Ō·jib'wā, *a.* and *n.*; *pl.* **Ō·jib'wā, Ō·jib'wāş,** same as *Ojibway.*

Ō·jib'wāy, *a.* and *n.*; *pl.* **Ō·jib'wāy, Ō·jib'wāyş,** [Am. Ind. dial. *ojibway,* to roast till puckered: from the puckered seam on their moccasins.] same as *Chippewa.*

O.K., OK (ō'kā'), *a., adv., interj.* [orig. U.S. colloq.; first used in name of Democratic *O.K.* Club (earliest recorded meeting March 24, 1840), in which *O.K.* is abbrev. of *Old Kinderhook,* name of the native village of Martin Van Buren, whom the Club supported for a 2d term.] all right; correct: also spelled *okay.*

O.K., OK (ō'kā'), *n.* approval; endorsement: also spelled *okay.*

O.K., OK (ō-kā'), *v.t.*; O.K.'d, OK'd (-kād'), *pt., pp.*; O.K.'ing, OK'ing, *ppr.* to put an O.K. on; to approve; to endorse: also spelled *okay.*

ō'kȧ, *n.* [It. *oc(c)a*; Turk. *ōqah*; Ar. *ūqīyah*; Gr. *oungia,* an ounce.] in Turkey, Egypt, Bulgaria, etc., a unit of weight, equal to 2 ¾ pounds, or of liquid measure, equal to 1 ⅓ quarts: also *oke.*

ō·kä'pi, *n.*; *pl.* **ō·kä'piş** or **ō·kä'pi,** [native Afr. name.] an African animal related to the giraffe, but having a short neck.

ō'kāy', *a., adv., interj., n.* O.K. [Colloq.]

ō·kāy', *v.t.* O.K. [Colloq.]

ōke, *n.* same as *oka.*

ō'ken·īte, *n.* [named after Lorenz *Oken,* German naturalist.] a massive or fibrous mineral of a whitish color, consisting chiefly of hydrous silicate of lime.

ō'kẽr, *n.* ocher. [Obs.]

Ō'kie, *n.* [from *Oklahoma.*] a migratory agricultural worker, especially one forced to migrate from Oklahoma or other parts of the dust bowl through drought, farm foreclosure, etc., in the late 1930's.

Ō·klȧ·hō'măn, *a.* of Oklahoma.

Ō·klȧ·hō'măn, *n.* a native or inhabitant of Oklahoma.

ō'krȧ, *n.* [from W. Afr. (Tshi) name, *nkruman.*]
1. a tall plant, *Hibiscus esculentus,* with sticky green pods, used in soups, stews, etc.
2. the pod or pods of this plant.
3. a soup, stew, etc. made from these pods.
Also called *gumbo.*

OKRA (with pods)

-ōl, a suffix used in chemistry to mean: (a) [from *alcohol.*] *an alcohol* or *phenol,* as in menth*ol,* thym*ol*; (b) [from L. *oleum,* oil.] same as *-ole.*

Ol·ȧ·çā'cē·ae, *n.pl.* [LL. *olax, olacis,* smelling, from L. *olere,* to smell.] a family of tropical evergreen shrubs and trees, often climbing and thorny. They have a one-seeded fruit and the bad-smelling wood of some of the species is used as a remedy in fevers.

ol·ȧ·çā'ceous, *a.* of or relating to the family *Olacaceæ.*

ō'lāy, *n.* [Tamil *ōlai.*] the leaf of various species of palms, prepared so that it can be written upon with a steel-pointed stylus: also written *ola.*

ōld, *a.*; *comp.* older *or* elder; *superl.* oldest *or* eldest, [ME.; AS. *ald, eald.*]
1. advanced far in years or life; having lived beyond the middle period, or toward the end of the ordinary term of living; aged; as, an *old* man.
2. having been in use for a long time; shabby; trite; worn out; decayed by time; as, an *old* house, an *old* joke.
3. being of long standing; begun long ago; as, an *old* acquaintance.
4. made or produced some time ago; not new or fresh; as, *old* wine.
5. being of a former year's growth; not of the last crop; as, *old* hay.
6. ancient or medieval; belonging to the remote past; that existed in former ages; antiquated; as, *old* customs, an *old* civilization.
7. of a certain age or duration; as, the baby is six weeks *old,* I am *older* than you.
8. former; passed out of use; existing before something else; as, he built a new house on the site of the *old* one.
9. long practiced; experienced; hence, crafty; cunning; as, an *old* hand.
10. more than enough; great. [Obs.]
If a man were porter of hellgate, he should have *old* turning of the key. —Shak.
11. of or characteristic of aged people; having the feelings and thoughts of an older person; wise; as, she is *old* for her years.
12. known or enjoyed for a long time or a long time ago; customary; familiar; as, the good *old* days.
13. dear: a familiar term of affection or cordiality; as, cheer up, *old* man. [Colloq.]
14. designating the earlier or earliest of two or more; as, the *Old* Testament.
15. good; fine; excellent; as, a gay *old* time. [Colloq.]
16. designating a language in its early or earliest period or stage of development.
old age; the advanced years of human life, when strength and vigor decline.
Old Dominion; the State of Virginia.
Old Glory; the flag of the United States.
old gold; see under *gold.*
Old Harry; Satan; the devil.
old lady; (a) one's mother; (b) one's wife. [Slang.]
Old Lady of Threadneedle Street; a nickname for the Bank of England. [Brit.]
old man; (a) one's father; (b) one's husband; (c) any man in a position of authority, as the head of a business concern, captain of a vessel, military commander, etc.; (d) old Mr.—: used with reference to an elderly man, or to distinguish the father from the son. Also used as a term of address, as to a friend. [Slang.]
Old Man of the Mountain; the supreme spirit of a Moslem sect called Ishmaelites, or Assassins.
Old Man of the Sea; a bore; a tedious person; a burdensome attachment: in allusion to the old man in the *Arabian Nights* who jumped on the back of Sinbad the Sailor and clung to him.
old master; (a) any of the great European painters before the eighteenth century; (b) a painting by any of these.
Old Nick; same as *Old Harry.*
Old Probabilities; an epithet of the chief officer of the weather bureau: given at first somewhat in derision of the weather forecasts published. [Colloq.]
Old Red Sandstone; see under *sandstone.*
Old Scratch; same as *Old Harry.*
Old South; the South before the Civil War.
Old Testament; the first of the two general divisions of the Bible, containing the history of the Hebrews, the Mosaic law, the writings of the prophets, the Psalms, etc.
Syn.—ancient, antique, antiquated, old-fashioned, obsolete.—*Old* denotes what has long existed and still exists; *ancient* what existed at a distant period, but does not necessarily exist at present; *antique,* that which is ancient, either in fact or in style; *antiquated, old-fashioned,* and *obsolete,* that which has ceased to be used or esteemed. *Old* is opposed to *new*; *ancient, antiquated,* and *antique* are opposed to *modern*; *old-fashioned* is opposed to *fashionable*; *obsolete* is opposed to *current.*

Ōld Ar'ȧ·biç, Arabic in its oldest stage, chiefly as recorded in Northern Arabian inscriptions from the first century A.D. to the sixth, and in inscriptions of Mecca from 328 A.D. on.

Ōld Bāi'ley, formerly, the criminal court of London.

Ōld Çath'ō·liç, a member of a religious sect organized by Roman Catholics who, in 1870, refused to accept the doctrine of papal infallibility.

Ōld Cel'tiç, all the branches of the Celtic language as supposedly spoken at the close of the fourth century A.D.

Ōld Chũrch Slav'iç, see *Old Slavic.*

ōld cŏun'try, the country from which an immigrant came: said especially of a country in Europe.

Ōld Çym'riç, Cymric in its oldest stage.

Ōld Dăn'ish, the Danish language in its oldest recorded stage, as found in literary remains from the thirteenth century A.D., as conjectured from loan words in Middle English, and as preserved in certain Norman place names.

Ōld Dutch, the Dutch language in its oldest stage: it is actually recorded only on fragmentary relics, but may be reconstructed from Middle Dutch and from loan words in neighboring languages.

ōld'en, *a.* old; ancient; of old, or of former times. [Poet.]

ōld'en, *v.i.* to become old. [Rare.]

Ōld Eng'lish, 1. the West Germanic, Low German language of the Anglo-Saxons; the language spoken in England from the fifth century A.D. until shortly after the Norman Conquest (1066); Anglo-Saxon.
2. a style of black letter.

ōld'-fash'iŏned, *a.* formed or styled according to fashions, ideas, or customs of past times; out-of-date; antiquated; outmoded; as, an *old-fashioned* dress.
old-fashioned men of wit. —Addison.

Ōld Fash'iŏned, an iced cocktail containing whisky, a dash of soda, bitters, sweetening, and fruit.

Ōld·fiēl'di·ȧ, *n.* [named after R. A. *Oldfield,* an English official at Sierra Leone.] a genus of trees in West Africa with a single species, *Oldfieldia africana*: its wood is used in shipbuilding: also called *African teak.*

ōld'-fō'gy, ōld'-fō'gey, *a.* same as *old-fogyish.*

ōld fō'gy, ōld fō'gey, a person who is old-fashioned or overly conservative in ideas and actions.

ōld'-fō'gy·ish, ōld'-fō'gey·ish, *a.* of, like, characteristic of, or suitable for an old fogy.

Old French, the French language as spoken from the ninth century A.D. until modern French developed in the sixteenth century.

Ōld Fri'şiăn, a West Germanic language spoken from the eleventh century A.D. to the sixteenth, closely related to Anglo-Saxon and Old Saxon: the oldest documents date from the thirteenth century.

ōld"-gen'tle·măn·ly, *a.* pertaining to or like an old gentleman.

Ōld Guärd, 1. the imperial guard organized by Napoleon I in 1804.
2. any old group of defenders of a cause.
3. the conservative element of a group, party, etc.; specifically, the conservative or "stand-pat" element in the Republican Party.

ōld'hăm·īte (-ăm-), *n.* [named for Dr. Thomas *Oldham* (1816–1878), director of the Indian Geological Survey.] in mineralogy, a transparent calcium sulfide, occasionally found in meteorites.

ōld hat, old-fashioned: used predicatively. [Slang.]

Ōld Hīgh Gẽr'măn, the German language as spoken in southern Germany from the eighth century A.D. to the twelfth: it is the basis of literary Middle High German.

Ōld Ice·lan'diç, 1. Old Norse as spoken and written in Iceland.
2. loosely, Old Norse.

Ōld I·on'iç, a type of Greek spoken from the seventh to the fourth century B.C.

Ōld I'rish, the Gaelic Celtic of Ireland as spoken from the eighth century A.D. to the twelfth: it is recorded in many inscriptions and glosses, and in a long homily.

ōld'ish, *a.* somewhat old.

Ōld I·tal'iăn, the Italian language in its oldest stage, as recorded from 964 A.D. onward.

Ōld Lat'in, the Latin language from about the sixth to the first century B.C.: a late form appears in the comedies of Plautus.

Ōld Līght (līt), in Scottish church history, a member of a conservative party which favored the connection of church with state: opposed to *New Light,* or a seceder from this party; Auld Licht.

ōld'-līne, *a.* 1. with an old, well-established history.
2. following tradition in action, thought, etc.; conservative.

Ōld Lōw Frank'ish, the language of the Franks of the lower Rhine, the ancestor of Dutch, Flemish, etc.

Ōld Lōw Gẽr'măn, the language of northern Germany and the Netherlands from the eighth century A.D. to the twelfth, the ancestor of Modern Low German.

ōld māid, 1. a woman who is unmarried and seems likely to remain so.
2. a prim, prudish, fussy person.
3. a simple card game in which the players draw cards from one another's hands to match pairs.

ōld"-māid'ish, *a.* having the characteristics of an old maid; precise, orderly, prim, prudish, fussy, etc.

ōld"-māid'işm, *n.* the state of being an old maid.

ōld mōōn, the phase of the moon in which it

appears as a crescent curving toward the left; last quarter.

ōld′ness, *n.* old age; the state of being old; antiquity.

Old Nor′măn French, Norman French; Anglo-French.

Old Nọrse, the language spoken in Norway, Denmark, and Iceland from the eighth century A.D. to the fourteenth, recorded in the sagas, in the *Elder Edda*, and in the skaldic poetry: also called *Old Icelandic*.

Old Prus′siăn, a Baltic language spoken from the fifteenth century A.D. to the early eighteenth.

ōld′-rōṣe′, *a.* of old rose.

ōld rōṣe, a grayish or purplish red.

Old Sax′ŏn, a Low Germanic dialect once common in part of northern Germany, known chiefly from manuscripts of the ninth and tenth centuries A.D.: its chief literary monument is the *Heliand* ("savior"), a poem composed about 830 A.D.

ōld′-sçhọọl, *a.* designating a school or party belonging to a former time, or having the character, manner, or opinions of a bygone age, or having been succeeded by something different in teaching and doctrine.

ōld sçhọọl, a group of people who cling to traditional or conservative ideas, methods, etc.

Old Sẽr′bi·ăn, an old Bulgarian dialect that developed about the tenth century A.D., the ancestor of modern Serbian.

Old Slȧv′iç, Slavic in its oldest stage, as represented by Bible translations and other church documents recorded in the Bulgarian dialect of Salonika in the second half of the ninth century A.D.: as *Old Church Slavic*, it is still used in the liturgies of the Orthodox churches in Slavic-speaking countries.

ōld sledġe, the card game seven-up.

Old Span′ish, the Spanish language as spoken from the twelfth century A.D. to the sixteenth, first recorded in a document dated 1145.

ōld squạw, a sea duck common to northern regions.

ōld′stẽr, *n.* [formed to contrast with *youngster*.] an elderly person; one who is no longer a youngster. [Colloq.]

ōld′-stȳle, *a.* in or according to old style.

ōld stȳle, 1. in typography, an old style of type, modern varieties of which are in popular use.

2. [O– S–] the old method of reckoning time according to the Julian calendar, which was off one day every 128 years.

Old Teū·ton′iç, Germanic: the former name.

ōld′-tīme′, *a.* of, like, or characteristic of past times.

ōld′-tīm′ẽr, *n.* 1. a person who has been a resident, employee, member, etc. for a long time. [Colloq.]

2. a person who is old-fashioned. [Colloq.]

ōld′wīfe, *n.*; *pl.* **ōld′wīveṣ,** 1. an old woman.

2. an old squaw.

3. (a) any of several related fishes of the herring family, including the alewife and menhaden; (b) any of several species of triggerfishes found near the West Indies.

ōld wīveṣ′ tāle, a silly story or superstitious belief such as might be passed around by gossipy old women.

ōld′-wom′ăn·ish (-woom′), *a.* like, characteristic of, or suitable for an old woman; fussy.

ōld′-wom′ăn·ish·ness, *n.* the quality or state of being old-womanish.

ōld′-wŏrld′, *a.* 1. of or belonging to the ancient world.

2. characteristic of or belonging to former times.

3. of the Old World.

Old Wŏrld, the Eastern Hemisphere; the world of Europe, Asia, and Africa: opposed to *New World*.

Old′-Wŏrld′, *a.* of or from the Old World.

o·lé (ō-lā′), *interj.* and *n.* [Sp., probably from *hola*, hollo, echoic of shout.] a shout of approval, triumph, joy, etc., as at bullfights or flamenco dances.

-ōle, [from L. *oleum*, oil.] a suffix used in chemistry: (a) to indicate a closed-chain compound with five members, as in pyrr*ole*; (b) to form the names of certain aldehydes and ethers, as in anethole: also *-ol*.

O′lē·ȧ, [L., the olive tree.] a genus of trees of the olive family, native to the Old World.

O·lē·ā′cē·ae, *n.pl.* [from *Olea*, one of the genera.] a family of exogenous plants including about 300 species, native to the warm and temperate parts of the earth; the olive family. They are shrubs or trees and include the ash, lilac, forsythia, etc.

ō·lē·ā′ceous, *a.* pertaining to the *Oleaceæ*, or olive family.

ō·lē·aġ′i·nous, *a.* [Fr. *oléagineux*; L. *oleaginus*, from *oleum*, oil.]

1. having the qualities of oil; oily; unctuous.

2. figuratively, smoothly and hypocritically sanctimonious; affectedly fawning; oily.

The lank party who snuffles the responses with such *oleaginous* sanctimony.
—Farrar.

ō·lē·aġ′i·nous·ness, *n.* the condition of being oleaginous; oiliness.

ō·lē·an′dẽr, *n.* [Fr. *oléandre*; LL. *arodandrum*, in Isidore *lorandrum*, by corruption for *rhododendron*.] a plant of the genus *Nerium*; especially, *Nerium oleander*, the rose bay, an evergreen shrub, with fragrant flowers of white, pink, or red. Every part of the plant is poisonous.

ō·lē·an′dẽr fẽrn, a South American fern, *Oleandra neriiformis*.

ō·lē·an′drin, *n.* a glucoside from the oleander; also, an alkaloid from the same tree.

O·lē·ā′ri·ȧ, *n.* [said to be named after *Olearius*, a German botanist, but possibly from L. *olea*, olive tree.] a genus of composite plants containing between eighty and ninety species, native to Australia, New Zealand, and adjacent islands. *Olearia ilicifolia* is known as the New Zealand holly.

ō·lē·as′tẽr, *n.* [ME. *oliaster*; L. from *olea*, olive tree.] a southern European shrub resembling the wild olive, having fragrant, yellow flowers and olivelike fruit.

ō′lē·āte, *n.* 1. any salt or ester of oleic acid.

2. a solution of an alkaloid or a metallic oxide or salt dissolved in this.

ō·leç′rȧ·năl, *a.* pertaining to the olecranon.

ō·leç′rȧ·non, *n.* [Mod. L.; Gr. *ōlekranon*, from *ōlenē*, the ulna, and *kranion*, the head.] the part of the ulna projecting beyond the elbow joint.

ō·lē′fi·ănt, *a.* [Fr. *oléfiant*, from L. *oleum*, oil, and *facere*, to make.] producing or forming oil.

olefiant gas; ethylene: the former name.

ō′lē·fin, *n.* [from Fr. *oléfiant*, from L. *oleum*, an oil, and *-ficare* (from *facere*), to make.] any of a series of unsaturated open-chain hydrocarbons containing one double bond and corresponding in composition to the general formula C_nH_{2n}: similar compounds containing more than one double bond are called *diolefins*, *triolefins*, etc.

ō′lē·fine (*or* -fēn), *n.* same as *olefin*.

ō·lē′iç (*or* ō′lē-ik), *n.* [L. *oleum*, oil.] pertaining to or derived from oil.

oleic acid; an oily acid, $C_{17}H_{33}COOH$, present in the form of the glyceryl ester in most animal and vegetable fats and oils, used in making soap, ointments, etc.

ō·lē·if′ẽr·ous, *a.* [L. *oleum*, oil, and *ferre*, to bear.] producing oil; as, *oleiferous* seeds.

ō′lē·in, *n.* [Fr. *oléine*, from L. *oleum*, an oil.]

1. a liquid glyceride of oleic acid, present in olive oil and certain other oils and fats.

2. the liquid part of any fat, as distinguished from the solid part.

ō′lē·ō, *n.* same as *oleomargarine*.

ō′lē·ō-, [L., from *oleum*, an oil.] a combining form meaning *oil*, *olein*, or *oleic*, as in *oleo*margarine.

ō′lē·ō·ġrȧph, *n.* [L. *oleum*, oil, and *-graph*.]

1. a chromolithograph made in imitation of an oil painting.

2. the shape taken by a drop of oil when placed on the surface of water.

ō″lē·ō·graph′iç, *a.* of or like an oleograph or oleography.

ō·lē·og′rȧ·phy, *n.* 1. the act or art of making oleographs.

2. identification of oils by their oleographs.

ō″lē·ō·mär′ġȧ·rin (*occas.* -gȧ-), *n.* same as *oleomargarine*.

ō″lē·ō·mär′ġȧ·rine (*or* -rēn; *occas.* -gȧ-), *n.* [*oleo-* and *margarine*.] same as *margarine*.

ō·lē·om′e·tẽr, *n.* [L. *oleum*, oil, and Gr. *metron*, a measure.] an instrument for determining the weight and purity of oil; an elaeometer.

ō′lē·ō oil, a butterlike oil obtained from animal fat.

ō·lē·op′tēne, *n.* elaeoptene. [Rare.]

ō″lē·ō·reṣ′in, *n.* 1. a solution of a resin in an essential oil, as turpentine, occurring naturally in various plants.

2. a prepared mixture of an essential oil containing resin in solution.

ō″lē·ō·reṣ′in·ous, *a.* pertaining to or containing oleoresin.

ō″lē·ō·saç·çhȧ·rum, *n.* [L. *oleum*, oil, and LL. *saccharum*, sugar.] a mixture of oil and sugar.

ō′lē·ōse, *a.* oleous. [Rare.]

ō·lē·os′i·ty, *n.* the state of being fat or oily; oiliness. [Rare.]

ō′lē·ō strut, a shock-absorbing strut on airplanes, consisting of a telescopic cylinder containing oil.

ō′lē·ous, *a.* [L. *oleosus*, oily.] oily. [Rare.]

ol·ẽr·ā′ceous, *a.* [L. *oleraceus*, from *olus* (*-eris*), potherbs.] pertaining to potherbs; of the nature or qualities of herbs for cookery.

ol″ẽr·i·çul′tūr·ăl·ly, *adv.* with reference to olericulture.

ol′ẽr·i·çul″tūre, *n.* [L. *olus* (*-eris*), potherbs, and *cultura*, culture.] in horticulture, the cultivation of edible plants, as potherbs.

olf, *n.* [said to be a variant of *alp*.] the bullfinch.

ol·façt′, *v.t.* [L. *olfactare*, *olfacere*; *olere*, to smell, and *facere*, to make.] to smell. [Rare.]

ol·faç′tion, *n.* 1. the act of smelling.

2. the sense of smell.

ol·faç′tive, *a.* same as *olfactory*.

ol·faç·tom′e·tẽr, *n.* [L. *olfacere*, to smell, and Gr. *metron*, measure.] an apparatus for testing the sensitiveness of the sense of smell and the relative strengths of various odors.

ol·faç′tŏr, *n.* the nose. [Rare.]

ol·faç′tō·ry, *a.* [L. *olfactus*, pp. of *olfacere*, to smell; *olere*, to have a smell, and *facere*, to make.] pertaining to smelling; having the sense of smell; as, *olfactory* nerves.

ol·faç′tō·ry, *n.*; *pl.* **ol·faç′tō·rieṣ,** the sense of smell; also, the organ of smell: chiefly used in the plural.

ol′i·ban, *n.* olibanum. [Rare.]

ō·lib′ȧ·num, *n.* [ME.; ML., from L. *libanum*, from Gr. *libanos*.] true frankincense, a gum resin from various species of the genus *Boswellia*. It is used as an incense and medicine.

ol′i·bēne, *n.* in chemistry, a terpene of olibanum, obtained as an aromatic, colorless liquid.

ol′id, *a.* [L. *olidus*, from *olere*, to smell.] fetid; having a strong, disagreeable smell.

ol·i·gan′drous, *a.* [Gr. *oligos*, few, and *anēr*, *andros*, a male.] in botany, having fewer than twenty stamens.

ol·i·gan′thous, *a.* [Gr. *oligos*, few, and *anthos*, flower.] having few flowers.

ol′i·gärçh, *n.* [Gr. *oligarchēs*; *oligos*, few, and *archein*, to rule.] any of the rulers of an oligarchy.

ol·i·gär′çhăl, *a.* same as *oligarchic*.

ol·i·gär′çhiç, *a.* [Gr. *oligarchikos*.] of, constituting, or advocating an oligarchy.

ol·i·gär′çhiç·ăl, *a.* oligarchic.

ol′i·gär·çhist, *n.* one who advocates or supports oligarchical government.

ol′i·gär·çhy, *n.*; *pl.* **ol′i·gär·çhieṣ,** [Gr. *oligarchia*; *oligos*, few, and *archē*, rule.]

1. a form of government in which the supreme power is placed in the hands of a small exclusive class.

2. a state governed in this way.

3. the persons ruling such a state.

ol·i·ġid′ri·ȧ, *n.* [Gr. *oligos*, few, little, and *hidrōs*, sweat.] a deficiency in the secretion of the sweat.

ol′i·ġist, *n.* [Fr. *oligiste*, from Gr. *oligistos*, superl. of *oligos*, few, little.] a crystallized oxide of iron comprising the common specular iron ore and the micaceous specular iron ore; hematite having a crystalline structure.

ol·i·ġis′tiç, *a.* pertaining to oligist.

ol·i·ġis′tiç·ăl, *a.* oligistic.

ol′i·gō-, [Gr. *oligo-*, from *oligos*, small.] a combining form meaning *few*, *scant*, *small*, *a deficiency of*, as in *oligo*cythemia: also, before a vowel, *olig-*.

ol″i·gō·cär′pous, *a.* [*oligo-*, and Gr. *karpos*, fruit.] in botany, bearing few fruits.

Ol′i·gō·cēne″, *a.* [*oligo-*, and Gr. *kainos*, new, recent.] designating or of the second epoch of the Tertiary Period in the Cenozoic Era, characterized by the development of the higher mammals.

the Oligocene, the Oligocene Epoch or its rocks.

Ol″i·gō·çhae′tȧ, *n.pl.* [*oligo-*, and Gr. *chaitē*, hair.] a class of hermaphroditic worms, as the earthworm, having a segmented body and no distinct head.

ol″i·gō·çhae′tous, *a.* designating or of the Oligochaeta.

ol″i·gō·çhō′li·ȧ, *n.* [*oligo-*, and Gr. *cholē*, bile.] a lack or deficiency of the bile.

ol′i·gō·çhrōme″, *a.* [*oligo-*, and Gr. *chrōma*,

color.] *a.* painted or decorated in few colors, as a house.

ol′i·gō·chrōme″, *n.* a design showing but little variety of color.

ol″i·gō·chrō·mē′mi·ȧ, ol″i·gō·chrō·mae′mi·ȧ, *n.* [*oligo-*, and Gr. *chrōma*, color, and *haima*, blood.] insufficiency of hemoglobin in the blood.

ol′i·gō·clāse, *n.* [*oligo-*, and Gr. *klasis*, fracture.] a crystalline variety of feldspar, containing both sodium and calcium.

ol″i·gō·cys′tiç, *a.* [*oligo-*, and Gr. *kystis*, bladder, pouch.] containing only a few cysts.

ol″i·gō·cy̆·thē′mi·ȧ, ol″i·gō·cy̆·thae′mi·ȧ, *n.* [*oligo-*, and Gr. *kytos*, cell, and *haima*, blood.] a form of anemia characterized by a deficiency of red corpuscles in the blood.

ol″i·gō·gȧ·laç′ti·ȧ (-shi-ȧ), *n.* [*oligo-*, and Gr. *gala, galaktos*, milk.] in pathology, deficient secretion of milk.

ol·i·gom′ẽr·ous, *a.* [*oligo-*, and Gr. *meros*, a part.] in botany, consisting of fewer members than those of the other whorls.

ol·i·gō′my·oid, *a.* [*oligo-*, and Gr. *mys*, muscle, and *ōdē*, song.] possessing few or imperfectly differentiated syringeal muscles, as the *Oligomyodi*, a group of passerine birds.

ol″i·gō·pet′ăl·ous, *a.* [*oligo-*, and Gr. *petalon*, leaf.] in botany, having few petals.

ol·i·goph′yl·lous (*or* -gō-fil′), *a.* [*oligo-*, and Gr. *phyllon*, leaf.] in botany, having few leaves.

ol″i·gop′ō·ly, *n.*; *pl.* **ol″i·gop′ō·lieṣ,** [from *olig(o)-* and mono*poly*.] control of a commodity or service in a given market by a small number of companies or suppliers.

ol″i·gō·sep′ăl·ous, *a.* [*oligo-* and *sepal*.] having few sepals.

ol″i·gō·sid′ẽr·īte, *n.* [*oligo-* and *siderite*.] in mineralogy, a meteorite containing but little iron.

ol″i·gō·spẽr′mi·ȧ, *n.* [*oligo-*, and Gr. *sperma*, seed.] scantiness of the seminal secretion.

ol″i·gō·spẽr′mous, *a.* in botany, having few seeds.

ol″i·gō·stem′ō·nous, *a.* [*oligo-*, and Gr. *stēmon*, in the derived sense of stamen.] same as *oligandrous*.

ol·i·got′ō·kous, *a.* [*oligo-*, and Gr. *tokos*, issue.] in ornithology, not laying as many as five eggs.

ol·i·got′rō·phy, *n.* [*oligo-*, and Gr. *trophē*, nourishment.] insufficient nutrition.

ol″i·gū·rē′sis, *n.* same as *oliguria*.

ol·i·gū′ri·ȧ, *n.* [Mod. L.; see *oligo-*, and *-uria*.] a condition characterized by an abnormally small amount of urine secretion and a greatly decreased frequency of urination.

ō′li·ō, *n.*; *pl.* **ō′li·ōṣ,** [from Sp. *olla*, Port. *olha* (both pron. *olya*), a dish of meat boiled or stewed; L. *olla*, a pot.]

1. a highly spiced stew of meat and vegetables.

2. a mixture; a medley; a miscellany; especially, a collection of various musical pieces.

ol′i·phănt, *n.* 1. an elephant. [Obs.]

2. an ornamental ivory hunting horn. [Obs.]

ol′i·tō·ry, *a.* [L. *olitorius*; *olitor*, a gardener, from *olus*, potherbs.] belonging to a kitchen garden; as, *olitory* seeds.

ol′i·tō·ry, *n.*; *pl.* **ol′i·tō·rieṣ,** 1. a kitchen garden. [Obs.]

2. a potherb; any vegetable grown in a kitchen garden. [Obs.]

ō·lī′vȧ, *n.* [L., an olive.]

1. an olive shell; a gastropod having an olive-shaped, highly polished shell.

2. [O—] a genus of marine gastropods, the olive shells.

3. *pl.* **ō·lī′vae,** an olivary body.

ol·i·vā′ceous, *a.* like an olive; olive-green.

ol′i·văr·y, *a.* [Fr. *olivaire*; L. *olivarius*, from *oliva*, olive.] in anatomy, (a) shaped like an olive; (b) designating or of either of two oval bodies protruding from the sides of the medulla oblongata.

ol·i·vas′tẽr, *a.* [Fr. *olivâtre*, from L. *oliva*, olive.] of the color of the olive. [Obs.]

ol′ive, *n.* [L. *oliva*, olive.]

1. a low-branching evergreen tree, *Olea europæa*, reaching a height of from thirty to forty feet, with stiff, narrow, dark-green leaves and yellow flowers in small axillary bunches. It is native to Asia Minor and is cultivated along the Mediterranean, in California, in Australia, and in other warm, dry localities. Its chief value is in its edible fruit, but the wood is also extensively used in cabinetwork. Olive wreaths were used by the Greeks and Romans to crown the brows of victors.

2. the small, oval fruit of the olive, from which olive oil is obtained, and which is also much used as food, eaten green or ripe. Pickled olives are the unripe fruit deprived of part of their bitterness by being soaked in water containing potash and lime, and then preserved in an aromatized brine.

3. the wood of the olive tree.

4. an olive branch or wreath.

5. any of various trees allied to or resembling the olive.

6. a kind of yellowish green, as seen in the unripe fruit of the olive.

7. in anatomy, the olivary body.

8. in conchology, an oliva.

9. in ornithology, the oyster catcher. [Brit. Dial.]

10. an oval knob or button used with a loop of cord as a fastening for a coat or cloak.

American olive; the devilwood.

Bohemian olive; the oleaster.

mock olive; an ironwood, the *Notelæa longifolia* or the *Notelæa ligustrina*.

wild olive; the oleaster; also, any tree regarded as resembling the true olive.

ol′ive, *a.* 1. of the olive.

2. (a) olive-colored; (b) having a dark complexion tinged with this color.

ol′ive·back, *n.* a thrush, *Turdus swainsoni*.

ol′ive brȧnch, 1. a branch of an olive tree, traditionally a symbol of peace.

2. any peace offering.

3. [*pl.*] children: alluding to Ps. cxxviii. 3, in the Book of Common Prayer. [Humorous.]

ol′ived, *a.* decorated with olive trees or with their branches.

ol′ive-drab′, *a.* of olive drab.

ol′ive drab, 1. any of various shades of greenish brown, much used as a camouflage color in the armed forces.

2. woolen cloth dyed this color and used for uniforms by the United States Army: distinguished from *khaki*.

3. [*pl.*] a uniform of this cloth.

ol′ive green, the dull, yellowish-green color of the unripe olive.

ō·liv′en·īte, *n.* [G. *olivenerz*, olive ore; and *-ite*.] a native copper arsenate, CuO·As₂O₅·H₂O, usually of olive green.

ol′ive oil, a light-yellow oil pressed from the ripe fruit or pericarp of the olive. It is used in cooking, in salad dressings, in medicine, and in the manufacture of soaps and lubricants.

ol′ive ōre, same as *olivenite*.

ol′i·vẽr, *n.* a form of triphammer operated by the foot.

Ol′i·vẽr, *n.* [Fr. *Olivier*.] one of Charlemagne's twelve peers, a friend of Roland.

Ol·i·vē′ri·ăn, *n.* a follower of Oliver Cromwell.

ol′ive shell, any gastropod of the *Olividæ*.

ol′i·vet, *n.* an imitation or false pearl, used for barter with savages.

Ol′i·vet·ăn, *n.* one of an order of monks of the Roman Catholic Church, an offshoot of the great Benedictine order, founded in 1313 by Tolomei of Siena: also called *Monks of the Order of Mount Olivet*.

ol′ive wood, 1. the wood of the olive tree.

2. any of various trees of the genus *Elæodendron* or its wood.

ol′i·vil, ol′i·vile (*or* -vēl), *n.* an amylaceous crystalline substance obtained from the gum of the olive tree.

ol′i·vine (*or* -vēn′, -vin), *n.* [fr om*olive*, and *-ine*.] a silicate of magnesium and iron, $(MgFe)_2SiO_4$, existing usually as green crystals in many rocks and used as a semiprecious stone; green garnet; chrysolite.

ol′lȧ, *n.* [Sp., from L. *olla*, pot.]

1. a large-mouthed jar or pot of earthenware used in Spain and Latin America.

2. a porous jar of earthenware for holding water and cooling it by the evaporation of the moisture on the outer surface.

3. a highly spiced stew of meat and vegetables.

ol″lȧ-pō·drī′dȧ, *n.* [Sp., lit., rotten pot; *olla* (L. *olla*), pot, and *podrida* (L. *putridus*), rotten.]

1. an olla (stew).

2. any assortment, medley, or miscellany.

ol′lămh (-lăv), **ol′lăv,** *n.* [Ir. *ollamh*.] in ancient Ireland, a learned man; a teacher; a sage.

Ol′ney·ȧ, *n.* [after Stephen Olney, American botanist.] a genus of small, flowering trees of the bean family having but one species, *Olneya tesota*, ironwood, common to southern California and Arizona.

ol′ō·ġy, *n.*; *pl.* **ol′ō·ġieṣ,** [properly a suffix, from Gr. *logos*, description.] a branch of learning; a science: a humorous usage.

ō·lō′nȧ, *n.* a bush or shrub, *Touchardia latifolia*, the bark of which yields a fiber stronger than linen and very durable: much used by the natives of Hawaii for fish nets.

ol′pē, *n.* [Gr. *olpē*, a leathern oil flask.]

1. an ancient flask of leather.

2. a jug having no spout, but an even lip.

Ō·lym′pi·ad, *n.* [Gr. *Olympias, Olympiados*, from *Olympia*, a district in ancient Elis, where the Olympic games were held.]

1. in ancient Greece, a period of four years reckoned from one celebration of the Olympic games to another, by which the Greeks computed time from 776 B. C., taken as the first year of the first Olympiad.

2. a celebration of the modern Olympic games.

Ō·lym′pi·ăn, *n.* 1. in Greek mythology, one who dwelt on Mount Olympus; one of twelve major deities of the Greek religion, Zeus, Hera, Apollo, Artemis, Aphrodite, Athena, Ares, Hephaestus, Hermes, Hestia, Demeter, and Poseidon.

2. a native of Olympia.

3. any participant in the ancient or modern Olympic games.

Ō·lym′pi·ăn, *a.* 1. pertaining to Olympia (a district in ancient Elis) or to Mount Olympus.

2. like an Olympian god; exalted; celestial; majestic.

3. designating or of the Olympic games of ancient Greece.

Ō·lym′piç, *a.* same as *Olympian*.

Ō·lym′piç, *n.* 1. an Olympic game.

2. [*pl.*] the Olympic games (preceded by *the*).

Ō·lym′piç gāmeṣ, 1. in ancient Greece, a festival consisting of various contests in athletics, poetry, and music, held every four years at Olympia in honor of Zeus: also called *Olympian games*.

2. an international athletic competition of modern times, patterned after this festival and generally held every four years at some city chosen for this event: the competition, first held at Athens in 1896, includes track and field events, swimming, fencing, team games, etc.

Ō·lym′pus, *n.* 1. a mountain in northern Greece: in Greek mythology, the home of the gods.

2. heaven; the sky.

ōm, *n.* [Sans.] in Hinduism, a mantra characterizing the Supreme Power and used in formal worship to invoke Brahma.

-ō′mȧ, [Gr. *-ōma*.] a suffix meaning *morbid growth, tumor*, as in lymph*oma*, sarc*oma*.

om′ȧ·dhaun (-dạn), *n.* [Ir. and Gael. *amadan*, fool.] a fool or imbecile: an abusive term.

Ō′mȧ·hạ, *n.* a member of a tribe of Siouan Indians who migrated from the Ohio River Valley to northeastern Nebraska.

ō·man′dẽr wood, a variety of ebony produced from a tree, *Diospyros ebenum*, common to Ceylon.

ō·mā′sum, *n.*; *pl.* **ō·mā′sȧ,** [L., paunch.] the third division in the stomach of a cud-chewing animal, as the cow: also called *psalterium, manyplies*.

om′bẽr, om′bre (-bẽr), *n.* [Fr., from Sp. *hombre*; L. *homo*, man.]

1. a card game of Spanish origin, played with forty cards by three players: popular in England in the seventeenth and eighteenth centuries.

2. the player attempting to win the pool in this game.

om′brō·grȧph, *n.* [Gr. *ombros*, rainstorm, and *-graph*.] a rain gauge having an automatic recorder.

om·brom′e·tẽr, *n.* [Gr. *ombros*, rain, and *metron*, measure.] an instrument to measure the quantity of rain that falls; a rain gauge.

om′budṣ·măn, *n.*; *pl.* **om′budṣ·men,** [Swed.] an appointed public official who investigates activities of government agencies that may infringe on the rights of individuals.

ō·mē′gȧ (*or* -meg′), *n.* [Gr. *o*, and *mega*, great lit., the great or long *o*.]

1. the twenty-fourth and final letter of the Greek alphabet, corresponding to the English long *O, o*.

2. the last (of any series); the end.

ō·mē′goid, *a.* [Gr. *ōmega*, and *-oid*.] shaped like the Greek capital letter omega (Ω).

om′e·let, om′e·lette (*or* om′lit), *n.* [Fr. *omelette*, earlier *amelette*; by metathesis from *alemette*, from *alemelle*, from L. *lamella*, small plate.] a dish consisting of eggs beaten up, often with milk or water, and cooked in a frying pan.

ō'men, *n.* [L. *omen*, older *osmen*, from *os, oris*, the mouth, or else from *aus-* in *auscultare*, to hear.] a thing or occurrence thought to portend good or evil; a sign or indication of some future event; a prognostic; an augury; a presage.

Without a sign, his sword the brave man draws,
And asks no *omen* but his country's cause.
—Pope.

ō'men, *v.t.*; omened, *pt.*, *pp.*; omening, *ppr.* to be an omen of; to presage; as, to *omen* a successful end.

ō'mened, *a.* containing or accompanied by an omen or prognostic; as, ill-*omened* clouds.

ō·men'tăl, *a.* relating to or connected with the omentum.

ō·men·tī'tis, *n.* [L. *omentum*, and *-itis.*] an inflammatory condition of the omentum.

ō·men'tō·cēle, *n.* [L. *omentum*, and Gr. *kēlē*, tumor.] epiplocele.

ō·men'tum, *n.*; *pl.* **ō·men'tȧ,** [L.] a free fold of peritoneum connecting the stomach to the other visceral organs and supporting blood vessels, nerves, and lymphatics.

ō'mĕr, *n.* [Heb. *'ōmer.*] an ancient Hebrew dry measure equal to about 3.7 quarts; one tenth of an ephah.

om'i·çron, om'i·kron (*or* ō'mi-), *n.* [Gr. *o mikron*, lit., small o.] the fifteenth letter of the Greek alphabet, corresponding to English short *O, o.*

om'i·nāte, *v.t.* and *v.i.* [L. *ominari*, from *omen.*] to presage; to foreshow; to foretoken. [Obs.]

om·i·nā'tion, *n.* a foreboding; a presaging; prognostic. [Obs.]

om'i·nous, *a.* [L. *ominosus.*] of or serving as an omen; especially, having the character of an evil omen; threatening; sinister; menacing.

In the heathen worship of God, a sacrifice without a heart was accounted *ominous.*
—South.

Syn.—portentous, foreboding, premonitory, unpropitious.

om'i·nous·ly, *adv.* in an ominous manner.

om'i·nous·ness, *n.* the quality of being ominous.

ō·mis'si·ble, *a.* [L. *omissus*, pp. of *omittere*, to omit.] capable of omission; liable to be omitted.

ō·mis'sion (-mish'un), *n.* [Fr., from L. *omissio*, from *omittere*, to omit.]

1. an omitting or being omitted.

The most natural division of all offenses is into those of *omission* and those of commission.
—Addison.

2. that which is omitted.

ō·mis'sive, *a.* failing to do or include; omitting.

ō·mis'sive·ly, *adv.* in an omissive manner.

ō·mit', *v.t.*; omitted, *pt.*, *pp.*; omitting, *ppr.* [L. *omittere*; *ob*, by, and *mittere*, to send.]

1. to leave, pass by, or neglect; to fail or forbear to do or to use; as, he *omitted* to stop at the store.

2. to leave out; not to insert or mention; to fail to include; as, to *omit* an important word in a deed; to *omit* invidious comparisons; to *omit* a passage in reading or transcribing.

ō·mit'tănce, *n.* omission. [Obs.]

ō·mit'tĕr, *n.* one who omits.

om·mȧ·tē'ăl, *a.* in zoology, of or relating to an ommateum.

om·mȧ·tē'um, *n.*; *pl.* **om·mȧ·tē'ȧ,** [Gr. *omma* (*-atos*), eye.] in zoology, a compound eye, as of certain species of *Arthropoda.*

om·mȧ·tid'i·ăl, *a.* of an ommatidium.

om·mȧ·tid'i·um, *n.*; *pl.* **om·mȧ·tid'i·ȧ,** [Gr. *ommatidion*, dim. of *omma*, eye.] one of the elements forming the compound eye of an insect, etc., each element corresponding to a simple eye, or ocellus.

om·mat'ō·phōre, *n.* [Gr. *omma* (*-atos*), eye, and *pherein*, to bear.] a movable stalk to which the eye is attached, as in the mud puppy, snail, lobster, etc.

om·mȧ·toph'ō·rous, *a.* having an ommatophore.

Ōm·mī'ad, *n.*; *pl.* **Ōm·mī'adṣ, Ōm·mī'ȧ·dēṣ,** any of a dynasty of Moslem caliphs who ruled in Damascus from 661 to 750 A.D., or of a closely related branch ruling in Spain from 756 to 1031 A.D.

om·nē'i·ty, *n.* that which is essentially all; that which comprehends all.

om'ni-, [L., from *omnis*, all.] a combining form meaning *all, everywhere*, as in *omni*scient.

om'ni·ȧ vin'cit ā'mọr, [L.] love overcomes all (things): a quotation from Virgil.

om'ni·bus, *n.* [L., for all, dat. pl. of *omnis*, all.]

1. a large motor coach designed to carry a number of people as passengers, generally over a fixed route; a bus.

2. in glassmaking, a cover of sheet iron to protect the glass articles in a leer from drafts.

3. a book containing a collection of stories, essays, poems, etc., all written by the same author or bearing on the same subject; as, an *omnibus* of detective stories.

omnibus bill; a legislative bill containing many miscellaneous provisions, appropriations, etc.

omnibus box; a large box near and on a level with the stage of a theater.

om″ni·çọr·pō'rē·ăl, *a.* embracing or comprehending all matter; embracing the substance of all bodies. [Rare.]

om·ni·fâr'i·ous, *a.* [LL. *omnifarius*, of all sorts, from *omnis*, all, and *-farius.*] of all varieties, forms, or kinds.

om·nif'ĕr·ous, *a.* [L. *omnifer*; *omnis*, all, and *ferre*, to bear.] all-bearing; producing all kinds or varieties.

om·nif'iç, *a.* [*omni-*, and L. *facere*, to make.] all-creating.

om'ni·fọrm, *a.* [L. *omnis*, all, and *forma*, form.] having every form or shape.

om·ni·fọr'mi·ty, *n.* the quality of having every form.

om'ni·fȳ, *v.t.* to cause to become universal. [Rare.]

om·niġ'e·nous, *a.* [L. *omnigenus*; *omnis*, all, every, and *genus*, kind.] consisting of all kinds.

om·nil'e·ġent, *a.* [*omni-*, and L. *legens* (*-entis*), ppr. of *legere*, to read.] reading everything; given to much reading.

om·ni·pā'ri·ent, *a.* [L. *omniparens*; *omnis*, all, and *parens* (*-entis*), ppr. of *parere*, to bring forth.] bringing forth all things; producing all things. [Rare.]

om·ni·par'i·ty, *n.* [*omni-*, and L. *par*, equal.] equality of everything; general equality.

om·nip'ȧ·rous, *a.* [*omni-*, and L. *parere*, to produce.] producing or bringing forth all things; omniparient.

om·ni·pā'tient (-shent), *a.* [*omni-*, and L. *patiens* (*-entis*), ppr. of *pati*, to suffer.] patient in all things; possessed of unbounded endurance. [Rare.]

om″ni·pĕr·cip'i·ence, om″ni·pĕr·cip'i·en·cy, *n.* perception of everything.

om″ni·pĕr·cip'i·ent, *a.* [*omni-*, and L. *percipiens* (*-entis*), ppr. of *percipere*, to perceive.] perceiving everything.

om·nip'ō·tence, om·nip'ō·ten·cy, *n.* [L. *omnipotens*; *omnis*, all, and *potens*, powerful.]

1. the state or quality of being omnipotent; almighty power; unlimited or infinite power.

Will *Omnipotence* neglect to save
The suffering virtue of the wise and brave?
—Pope.

2. [O–] God.

om·nip'ō·tent, *a.* almighty; possessing unlimited power; all-powerful.

the Omnipotent; God.

om·nip'ō·tent·ly, *adv.* in an omnipotent manner.

om·ni·pres'ence, *n.* [*omni-*, and L. *præsens*, present.] the state or quality of being omnipresent; universal presence; ubiquity; as, *omnipresence* is an attribute of God.

om·ni·preṣ'en·cy, *n.* omnipresence. [Obs.]

om·ni·preṣ'ent, *a.* present in all places at the same time; ubiquitous; as, the *omnipresent* Jehovah.

om·ni·prev'ȧ·lent, *a.* prevalent everywhere; prevailing over all.

om·nis'cience (-nish'ens), *n.* [*omni-*, and L. *scientia*, knowledge.]

1. the quality or state of being omniscient; universal knowledge; knowledge unbounded or infinite; as, *omniscience* is an attribute of God.

2. [O–] God.

om·nis'cien·cy, *n.* omniscience. [Obs.]

om·nis'cient, *a.* having universal knowledge or knowledge of all things; infinitely knowing.

the Omniscient; God.

om·nis'cient·ly, *adv.* with omniscience; in an omniscient manner.

om'ni·sçōpe, *n.* a periscope (optical instrument).

om·ni·speç'tive, *a.* [*omni-*, and L. *spectare*, to see.] seeing, beholding, or capable of beholding everything; all-seeing. [Rare.]

om'ni·um, *n.* [L. *omnis*, all.] the aggregate value of different stocks in the public funds; the particulars included in the contract between government and the public for a loan. [Brit.]

om'ni·um-gath'ĕr·um, *n.* a miscellaneous collection of things or persons; a medley.

om·niv'ȧ·ġȧnt, *a.* [*omni-*, and L. *vagari*, to wander.] wandering anywhere and everywhere. [Rare.]

Om·niv'ō·rȧ, *n.pl.* a division of ungulate mammals, subsisting or capable of subsisting on both animal and vegetable food: it includes the hog and the hippopotamus.

om·niv'ō·rous, *a.* [*omni-*, and L. *vorare*, to devour.]

1. eating any sort of food, especially both animal and vegetable food.

2. taking in everything indiscriminately, as with the intellect; as, an *omnivorous* reader.

om·niv'ō·rous·ness, *n.* the quality of being omnivorous.

ō'mō-, [Gr. *ōmos*, shoulder.] a combining form meaning *shoulder.*

ō·mō·dyn'i·ȧ, *n.* [*omo-*, and Gr. *odynē*, pain.] in medicine, pain in the shoulder or shoulder joint.

ō·mō·hȳ'oid, *a.* [*omo-* and *hyoid.*] in anatomy, relating to the shoulder and the hyoid bone.

ō·mō·phā'ġi·ȧ, *n.* [Gr. *ōmophagia*, from *ōmos*, raw, and *phagein*, to eat.] the eating of raw flesh.

ō·mō·phaġ'iç, *a.* same as *omophagous.*

ō·moph'ȧ·ġist, *n.* an eater of raw flesh.

ō·moph'ȧ·gous, *a.* [Gr. *ōmophagos*, from *ōmos*, raw, and *phagein*, to eat.] eating raw flesh.

ō·mō·phō'ri·on, *n.*; *pl.* **ō·mō·phō'ri·ȧ,** [Gr. *ōmos*, shoulder, and *pherein*, to bear.] a vestment worn by bishops in the Orthodox Eastern Church, similar to the pallium of the Roman Catholic Church.

om'ō·plāte, *n.* [Gr. *ōmoplatē*; *ōmos*, shoulder, and *platē*, the flat surface of a body.] in anatomy, the shoulder blade, or scapula. [Rare.]

ō·mos'tē·ġīte, *n.* [Gr. *ōmos*, shoulder, and *stegos*, roof.] in zoology, the part of the carapace of a crustacean covering the thorax.

ō·mō·stĕr'năl, *a.* in anatomy, relating to the omosternum.

ō·mō·stĕr'num, *n.* [Gr. *ōmos*, shoulder, and *sternon*, the chest.] in anatomy, (a) in certain species of *Batrachia*, that part of the sternum projecting anteriorly between the clavicles; (b) a cartilage or bone situated between the clavicle and sternum in certain mammals.

om'phȧ·cine, *a.* [Gr. *omphakinos*, from **omphax**, unripe fruit.] pertaining to or expressed from unripe fruit; as, *omphacine* oil.

om'phȧ·cīte, *n.* [Gr. *omphakitēs*, of unripe fruit.] a variety of augite of a pale leek-green color.

Om'phȧ·lē, *n.* in Greek mythology, a queen of Lydia in whose service Hercules, dressed as a woman, spun wool and performed other womanly tasks for three years to appease the gods.

om·phȧ·leç'tō·my, *n.* [Gr. *omphalos*, the navel, and *ektomē*, a cutting out.] in medicine, the removal of the umbilicus by excision.

om·phal'iç, *a.* [Gr. *omphalos*, the navel.] pertaining to the navel.

om·phȧ·lī'tis, *n.* [*omphalo-* and *-itis.*] in medicine, inflammation of the umbilicus, or navel.

om'phȧ·lō-, [Gr. *omphalos*, the navel.] a combining form meaning *the navel, umbilicus*: also, before a vowel, *omphal-.*

om'phȧ·lō·cēle, *n.* [*omphalo-*, and Gr. *kēlē*, tumor.] a rupture at the navel; umbilical hernia.

om'phȧ·lōde, *n.* [Gr. *omphaloeidēs*, like the navel; *omphalos*, navel, and *eidos*, form.] same as *omphalodium.*

om·phȧ·lō'di·um, *n.* in botany, the central part of the hilum, through which the nutrient vessels pass into the endosperm.

om'phȧ·loid, *a.* resembling a navel.

om'phȧ·lō·man·cy, *n.* [*omphalo-*, and Gr. *manteia*, divination.] divination by means of the number of knots in the umbilical cord of a newborn child, to show how many more children its mother will supposedly bear.

om″phȧ·lō·mes·ȧ·rā'iç, *a.* [*omphalo-*, and Gr. *mesaraion*, the mesentery.] omphalomesenteric.

om″phȧ·lō·mes·en·ter'iç, *a.* [*omphalo-*, and Gr. *mesenterion*, the mesentery.] in anatomy, of or pertaining to the navel and the mesentery.

Om·phȧ·lop'sy·çhīte, *n.* [*omphalo-*, and Gr. *psychē*, spirit.] in Church history, one of a sect of mystics who practiced sitting with their eyes fixed on the navel; a Hesychast or Quietist.

om″phȧ·lor·rhā'ġi·ȧ, *n.* [*omphalo-*, and Gr. *rhegnynai*, to burst.] a bleeding or hemorrhage from the navel.

om′phȧ·los, *n.* [Gr., from L. *umbilus*, a form surviving only in *umbilicus*, the navel.] the navel.

om·phȧ·lot′ō·my, *n.* [*omphalo-*, and Gr. *temnein, tamein*, to cut.] the operation of dividing the umbilical cord.

-on, [Gr. *-on*, neuter suffix.] in chemistry, physics, etc., a suffix used to indicate an elementary particle or an inert gas as deut*on*, ne*on*.

on, *prep.* [ME.; AS. *on, an*; akin to G. *an.*]

1. upon; in a position above, but in contact with, as the surface or upper part of a thing, and supported by; placed or lying in contact with; as, my book is *on* the table; the table stands *on* the floor; the house rests *on* its foundation.

2. toward and to; in the direction of; as, rain falls *on* the earth.

Whosoever shall fall *on* this stone, shall be broken. —Matt. xxi. 44.

3. in contact with, as by touching or striking; as, to play *on* a harp, a violin, or a drum.

4. in addition to; besides; as, heaps *on* heaps; loss *on* loss.

5. at or near; by; indicating situation, place, or position; as, a ship is *on* the coast; *on* each side stands an armed man.

6. with the relation of reliance or dependence; as, to depend *on* a person for help; to rely *on*; hence, indicating the ground or basis of anything; as, *on* authority, *on* purpose.

7. at or in the time of; as, *on* the Sabbath we abstain from labor; *on* public occasions.

8. toward; for: indicating the object of some feeling; as, have pity, compassion, or mercy *on* him.

9. at the peril of, or for the safety of; as, *on* my life, I cannot tell.

10. noting the relation of a pledge or an engagement; as, he affirmed or promised *on* his word, or *on* his honor.

11. noting the relation of an imprecation or an invocation; to the account of.

His blood be *on* us, and *on* our children. —Matt. xxvii. 25.

12. after and in consequence of; immediately after and as a result; as, *on* the ratification of the treaty the armies were disbanded; he made a profit *on* the sale.

13. in reference or in relation to; as, *on* one side and *on* the other; *on* our part.

14. in betting, in support of the chances of; on the side of; as, I bet *on* the red against the black.

15. connected with; engaged in; as, *on* a trip; he is now *on* the staff of a magazine.

16. noting the relation of one to a state, condition, engagement, or occupation; as, *on* duty; *on* watch; *on* the outlook.

17. through the use of; as, to live *on* bread and water.

18. concerning or about; as, an essay *on* war.

19. chargeable to; at the expense of; as, a drink *on* the house. [Colloq.]

20. using; addicted to; as, to be *on* drugs. [Slang.]

21. carried by; as, to have no money *on* one. [Slang.]

on, *adv.* 1. forward; in advance; ahead; onward; as, move *on*; go *on*.

2. forward, in succession; as, from father to son, from the son to the grandson, and so *on*.

3. in continuance; without interruption or ceasing; as, sleep *on*; say *on*; write *on*.

4. in or into a situation or position of contacting, being supported by, or covering; as, put your shirt *on*.

5. in a direction to or toward; as, he looked *on*.

6. into operation, performance, or action; as, switch *on* the light.

off and on; once in a while; every now and then; intermittently.

on and on; continuously; without stopping or ceasing; as, he sailed *on and on*.

on, *a.* 1. in action, operation, or occurrence; as, the play is *on*, the light is *on*.

2. near or nearer.

3. in cricket, designating that side of the field, or of the wicket, where the batsman stands.

on to; aware of; cognizant of. [Slang.]

on, *n.* 1. the fact or state of being on.

2. in cricket, the on side.

on, *interj.* go on; advance; forward.

Charge, Chester, charge! *On*, Stanley, *on*!
Were the last words of Marmion.
—Sir W. Scott.

on′ȧ·gẽr, *n.*; *pl.* **on′ȧ·grī, on′ȧ·gẽrṣ,** [ME.; L., from Gr. *onagros*, a wild ass; *onos*, ass, and *agrios*, wild.]

1. a wild ass found in the deserts of Central Asia.

2. a catapult, used in ancient and medieval warfare, for throwing stones in the manner of a sling.

Ō·nā′grȧ, *n.* [Gr., also *oinagrc*; *oinos*, wine, and *agra*, hunting.] a former genus of plants which gave name to the family *Onagraceæ*, but now identical with *Œnothera*, the evening primrose.

On·ȧ·grā′cē·ae, *n.pl.* a family of annual or perennial dicotyledonous plants, comprising many genera and several hundred species: found principally in temperate zones. *Fuchsia* and *Œnothera* are well-known genera.

on·ȧ·grā′ceous, *a.* of or belonging to the evening primrose family of plants, *Onagraceæ*.

ō′năn·iṣm, *n.* [from *Onan* (Gen. xxxviii. 9).]

1. withdrawal in coition before ejaculation.

2. masturbation.

once (wuns), *adv.* [AS. *anes*, genit. of *an*, as G. *einst*, from *ein.*]

1. one time; as, opportunity calls but *once*.

2. one time, though no more; as, the mind *once* tainted with vice is prone to grow worse and worse.

3. at any time; at all; ever.

4. at some time in the past; formerly; as, *once* there was a man.

at once; at the same time; as, they all moved *at once*; also, immediately; without delay.

for once; at least one time, after many attempts and failures; as, he has succeeded *for once*.

once and again; repeatedly.

once (and) for all; for the last time; never to be repeated; decisively; conclusively.

once in a while; now and then; occasionally.

once or twice; not often; a few times.

once upon a time; a long time ago.

once, *conj.* as soon as; if ever; whenever; as, *once* he is tired he will quit.

once, *a.* former; quondam.

once, *n.* one time; as, let him go this *once*.

once′-ō′vẽr, *n.* a quick, comprehensive look or examination; a swiftly appraising glance; as, he gave her the *once-over*. [Slang.]

On·cid′i·um, *n.* [dim. of Gr. *onkos*, hook.] a large genus of tropical and subtropical plants belonging to the family *Orchidaceæ*. The species are common in tropical America. They have usually yellow flowers, spotted with a rich reddish-brown. One of the species is the butterfly plant, *Oncidium papilio*, so called because of its resemblance to a butterfly.

oñ′cō·grȧph, *n.* [Gr. *onkos*, bulk, and *-graph.*] a recording device attached to an oncometer.

oñ·çol′ō·ġy, *n.* [Gr. *onkos*, bulk, and *-logy.*] the study of tumors; also, a treatise on tumors.

oñ·çom′e·tẽr, *n.* [Gr. *onkos*, bulk, and *metron*, measure.] in anatomy and medicine, an instrument for measuring variations in the size of viscera.

oñ·cō·met′riç, *a.* pertaining to the oncometer or to measurements made with it.

on′çom·ing, *a.* coming nearer in position or time; approaching.

on′çŏm·ing, *n.* an approach.

oñ·çō·sim′e·tẽr, *n.* [Gr. *onkōsis*, swelling, and *metron*, measure.] an instrument for determining the specific gravity of a molten metal by means of an immersed metal ball of a known weight.

on′çost, *n.* overhead or overhead expenses. [Brit.]

oñ·çot′ō·my, *n.* [Gr. *onkos*, a tumor, and *tomē*, a cutting, from *temnein*, to cut.] in anatomy, the opening of an abscess with a cutting instrument; the excision of a tumor.

onde, *n.* [AS. *anda.*] zeal; malice; envy. [Obs.]

on′dine, *n.* [Fr.] an undine.

on′ding, *n.* [*on, adv.*, and dial. *ding*, to drive.] a heavy fall of snow or rain. [Scot.]

oṅ-dit (dē), [Fr., lit., one says.] they say; it is said; hence, a flying rumor; a piece of gossip.

on′dō·gram, *n.* the record made on an ondograph.

on′dō·grȧph, *n.* [from Fr. *onde* (from L. *unda*), a wave; and *-graph.*] in electricity, an instrument that records wave forms, as in alternating currents.

on·dom′e·tẽr, *n.* an instrument for measuring the frequency of an alternating current or radio carrier wave.

-ōne, [Gr. *-ōnē*, used to signify a female descendant of.] a suffix used in chemistry, meaning *a ketone*, as in acet*one*, butan*one*.

one (wun), *a.* [ME. *one, on*; AS. *an*; akin to G. *ein.*]

1. being a single thing or unit; not two or more; as, *one* man; *one* book; there is only *one* sun in our system of planets.

2. some or any; a certain; designating a single person or thing that is not clearly defined; as, *one* day you will repent your hasty speech.

3. denoting contrast: opposed to *another*; as, it is *one* thing to promise and *another* to fulfill.

4. single; unmarried. [Obs.]

5. noting one of two: opposed to *other*; as, stand on *one* side of me.

6. undivided; forming a whole; united.

The church is therefore *one*, though the members may be many. —Pearson.

7. single in kind; the same; as, all of *one* mind.

all one; (a) just the same; of no importance; as, it is *all one* what course you take; (b) united or agreed.

one with; of the same kind; identical with.

one with another; on an average; taken in the general run; as, *one with another*, the cattle are of good stock.

one, *n.* 1. the number expressing unity or designating a single unit: it is the lowest cardinal number and the first used in counting a series, etc.; 1; I.

2. a single thing or person.

at one; in unison; in agreement or concord.

in one; in union; in one united body.

one another; each person or thing the other: said of an action, relation, etc. reciprocally involving more than two individuals.

one by one; individually in succession.

one, *pron.* 1. a certain person or thing; some person or thing.

2. any person or thing; anybody or anything.

3. the same person or thing.

one, *v.t.* to combine into a whole; to unite; to make one of. [Rare.]

one′-bag′gẽr, *n.* a one-base hit. [Slang.]

one′-bāse hit, in baseball, a hit by which the batter can reach first base without benefit of an error: also called *single*.

one′ber″ry, *n.* an herb of the genus *Paris*.

one′-eȳed (-īd), *a.* having one eye only.

one′-horse, *a.* 1. drawn by one horse, as a vehicle; using only one horse.

2. small; petty; on a small scale; inferior; of little or no importance; as, a *one-horse* town; a *one-horse* business. [Colloq.]

Ō·neī′dȧ, *n.*; *pl.* **Ō·neī′dȧ, Ō·neī′dȧṣ,** one of a tribe of Iroquoian Indians formerly dwelling in the region about Oneida Lake, New York, the remnants of which are now scattered over New York, Wisconsin, and Canada.

ō·neī′rō-, [from Gr. *oneiros*, a dream.] a combining form meaning *dream*.

ō·neī·rō·çrit′iç, *n.* [*oneiro-*, and Gr. *kritikos*, discerning.] an interpreter of dreams.

ō·neī·rō·çrit′iç·ȧl, ō·neī·rō·çrit′iç, *a.* of, or having the power of, an oneirocritic.

ō·neī·rō·çrit′içs, ō·neī·rō·çrit′i·ciṣm, *n.* the art of interpreting dreams.

ō·neī·rō·dyn′i·ȧ, *n.* [*oneiro-*, and Gr. *odynē*, pain.] nightmare; disturbed dreams.

ō·neī·rol′ō·ġy, *n.* [*oneiro-* and *-logy.*] the interpretation or study of dreams; also, a treatise on dreams.

ō·neī′rō·man·cy, *n.* [*oneiro-*, and Gr. *manteia*, divination.] the art claiming to foretell the future by the interpretation of dreams.

ō·neī·ros′çō·pist, *n.* an interpreter of dreams; an oneirocritic.

ō·neī·ros′çō·py, *n.* [*oneiro-*, and Gr. *skopein*, to view.] the interpretation of dreams: also called *oneirocritics*.

one′-līn′ẽr, *n.* a short, witty remark.

ōne′ly, *a.* only. [Now Rare.]

one′-man′ (wun′), *a.* 1. pertaining to one man.

2. done by one man, or prepared by one man; as, a *one-man* crime; a *one-man* show.

3. devoted to one man; as, a *one-man* dog.

one′ment (wun′), *n.* the state of being one. [Obs.]

one′ness, *n.* 1. singleness in number; individuality; unity; the quality or state of being one.

Our God is one, or rather very *Oneness*. —Hooker.

2. unity of mind, feeling, or purpose.

3. sameness; identity.

one′-night′ stand, a single night performance of a show, lecture, etc. at a given town.

one′-on-one′, *a.* and *adv.* 1. in basketball, football, etc., contending individually against a single opposing player.

2. in direct, personal confrontation.

one′-pïece′, *a.* made in one piece; as, a *one-piece* undergarment.

on′ẽr (wun′), *n.* one who is distinct or distinguished; a good hand; an expert; as, he is a *oner* at billiards. [Slang.]

on′ẽr·ous, *a.* [L. *onerosus,* from *onus,* a load.]

1. burdensome; oppressive; laborious.

2. in law, involving a legal obligation; as, an *onerous* contract: opposed to *gratuitous.*

on′ẽr·ous·ly, *adv.* in an onerous manner.

one·self′ (wun-), *pron.* a person's own self; himself or herself: also *one's self.*

by oneself; alone; unaccompanied; withdrawn.

to be oneself; (a) to function physically and mentally as one normally does; (b) to be natural or sincere.

one′-sīd′ed, *a.* 1. on, having, or involving only one side.

2. larger or more developed on one side; leaning to one side.

3. favoring one side; uneven or unfair; partial; prejudiced.

one′-sīd′ed·ness (wun-), *n.* the state of being one-sided.

one′-step″, *n.* 1. a ballroom dance characterized by quick walking steps in two-four time.

2. music for this dance.

one′-step″, *v.i.* to dance the one-step.

one′-tīme″, *a.* at some past time; former.

one-tö-one′, *a.* 1. permitting the pairing of an element of one group uniquely with a corresponding element of another group.

2. in mathematics, designating a correspondence such that each member of one set has a partner in another set, and no element in either set is without a partner.

one′-track′, *a.* 1. having a single track.

2. able to deal with only one thing at a time; limited in scope; as, a *one-track* mind.

one′-wāy′, *a.* passing or moving in one direction only; also, permitting movement in one direction only; as, *one-way* traffic; a *one-way* street.

on′fall, *n.* an onset; a falling on.

on′gō″ing, *n.* 1. progression; the act of going on.

2. [*pl.*] current events; proceedings; affairs; goings on.

on′gō″ing, *a.* going on; advancing; progressing.

on′hang″ẽr, *n.* a hanger-on.

ŏn′iŏn (-yun), *n.* [ME.; OFr. *oignon;* L. *unio* (*-onis*), lit., oneness, then a kind of single onion, also a pearl; *unus,* one.]

1. a plant, *Allium cepa,* of the lily family, having an edible bulb with a strong, sharp smell and taste. It is a biennial herbaceous plant, with long tubulated leaves and a swelling, pithy stalk. The bulbous root is composed of a series of concentric coats, and varies in size according to the soil and climate, and in color, from a wine-red to white.

2. the bulb of this plant.

ŏn′iŏn-eyed (-īd), *a.* having the eyes filled with tears, as if from the effect of a peeled onion.

And I, an ass, am *onion-eyed.* —Shak.

ŏn′iŏn fly, either of two dipterous flies producing the onion maggot.

ŏn′iŏn mag′gŏt, the larva of the onion fly, feeding upon the interior of the root or bulb of the onion.

ŏn′iŏn shell, a species of oyster of roundish form.

ŏn′iŏn·skin, *n.* 1. the thin, translucent outer coating of an onion.

2. a tough, thin, translucent paper with a glossy surface.

ŏn′iŏn·y, *a.* having the characteristic smell or taste of the onion.

ō·nī·rō·crit′iç, *a.* same as *oneirocritic.*

ōn′li·ness, *n.* 1. uniqueness. [Rare.]

2. the state of being alone. [Rare.]

on′look″ẽr, *n.* one who looks on; a spectator.

on′look″ing, *a.* watching but not taking part; looking on.

on′look″ing, *n.* the act of looking on.

ōn′ly, *a.* [ME. *onli, onlich;* AS. *anlic.*]

1. single; by itself or by themselves; as, John was the *only* man present.

2. alone in its class; solitary; without a mate or peer; as, an *only* child.

3. pre-eminent; distinguished above all others.

He is the *only* man for music.—Johnson.

4. alone; without help, cooperation, or companionship. [Obs.]

With the *only* twinkle of her eye
She could or save or spill. —Spenser.

ōn′ly, *adv.* 1. in one manner or for one purpose alone; simply; merely; barely.

All who deserve his love he makes his own,
And to be loved himself, needs *only* to be known. —Dryden.

2. solely; no other than.

Every imagination of the thoughts of his heart was *only* evil continually. —Gen. vi. 5.

3. singly; without more; as, *only* begotten. *only too;* very; exceedingly.

ōn′ly, *conj.* but; were it not that; except that; as, he is remarkably like his brother in form and feature, *only* he is a little taller.

on·ō·cen′taur, *n.* [Gr. *onokentauros; onos,* ass, and *kentauros,* centaur.] a fabulous being like a centaur, but with the body of an ass.

On·ō·clē′ȧ, *n.* [Gr. *onos,* vessel, and *kleiein,* to close.] a genus of ferns found in the colder parts of the temperate zone.

on′ō·man·cy, *n.* [Gr. *onoma,* name, and *manteia,* divination.] divination by the letters of a name.

Destinies were superstitiously, by *onomancy,* deciphered out of names. —Camden.

on·ō·man′tiç, on·ō·man′tiç·ăl, *a.* relating to onomancy; predicting by names or the letters composing names.

on·ō·mas′tiç, *a.* of, pertaining to, or consisting of a name; specifically, in law, applied to the signature of an instrument where the body of it is in the handwriting of another person.

on·ō·mas′ti·çon, *n.* [Gr. *onomastikon,* from *onoma,* name.] a work containing nouns or names with their explanation, arranged in alphabetical or other order; a vocabulary, glossary, etc.

on″ō·mȧ·tol′ō·ġist, *n.* one versed in the history of names.

on″ō·mȧ·tol′ō·ġy, *n.* [Gr. *onoma* (*-atos*), and *-logy.*] a discourse or treatise on names, or the history of the names of persons.

ō·nom′ȧ·tōpe, *n.* [short form of *onomatopoeia.*] a word formed to resemble the sound made by the thing signified.

on″ō·mat·ō·poe′iȧ (*or* ō-nom″ȧ-tō-pē′ȧ), *n.* [LL.; Gr. *onomatopoiia; onoma, onomatos,* a name, and *poiein,* to make.]

1. the formation of a word by imitating the natural sound associated with the object or action involved (e.g., *tinkle, buzz, chickadee,* etc.).

2. a word formed in this way.

3. the use of such words, as in poetry or rhetoric.

on″ō·mat·ō·poe′iç, on″ō·mat″ō·pō·et′iç, *a.* of, having the nature of, or like onomatopoeia.

on″ō·mat″ō·poi·et′iç, *a.* same as *onomatopoeic.*

ō·nom′ȧ·tō·py, *n.* onomatopoeia. [Rare.]

ō·nom′ō·man·cy, *n.* onomancy.

On·on·dȧ′gȧ (*or* -dä′), *n.*; *pl.* **On·on·dȧ′gȧ, On·on·dȧ′gȧs,** [from Am. Ind.] a member of a tribe of Iroquoian Indians who lived near Onondaga Lake.

Ō·nō′nis, *n.* [Gr. *onōnis,* a plant, the rest harrow.] an extensive genus of annual and perennial trailing herbs and undershrubs, with trifoliate leaves and yellow or pink flowers, native to Europe, western Asia, and northern Africa.

On·ō·pọr′don, *n.* [Gr. *onos,* an ass, and *pordē,* flatulence, referring to the supposed effect when eaten by asses.] a genus of thistlelike herbs, chiefly biennial, containing about twelve species, native to Europe, northern Africa, and western Asia. They are tall plants with woolly-looking leaves, and large heads of purple or white flowers.

on′rush, *n.* a headlong dash forward; a strong onward flow.

on′set, *n.* 1. the act of setting or rushing on; an attack; an assault; an onslaught; especially, the attack of troops upon an enemy, fort, town, etc.

Barbaric armies suddenly retire
After some furious *onset.* —Grainger.

2. an attack of any kind.

The first impetuous *onsets* of his grief. —Philips.

3. a beginning; a setting out; a start.

on′set, *v.t.* to assault; to begin. [Obs.]

on′shōre′, *a.* 1. moving onto or toward the shore.

2. situated or operating on land; as, an *onshore* patrol.

on′shōre′, *adv.* toward the shore; landward.

on′sīde′, *a.* and *adv.* in football, hockey, etc., in the proper position for play, according to the rules.

on′slaught (-slạt), *n.* [prob. from D. *aanslag,* from *slagen,* to strike.] attack; onset; a furious assault.

on′stead (-sted), *n.* [equivalent to AS. *wunstede,* a dwelling place, from *wunian,* to dwell, and *stede,* a place.] a single farmhouse. [Scot. and Brit. Dial.]

On·tăr′i·ăn, *a.* of Ontario.

On·tăr′i·ăn, *n.* a native or inhabitant of Ontario.

on′tö, *prep.* 1. to and upon; to a position on; as, the passage opened *onto* a pleasant area.

2. aware of; cognizant of; as, father is *onto* you and your excuses. [Slang.]

Also *on to.*

on′tō-, [Gr. *ōn, ontos,* ppr. of *einai,* to be.] a combining form meaning *being, existence,* as in *onto*logy.

on·tō·ġen′e·sis, *n.* [*onto-,* and Gr. *genesis,* generation.] same as *ontogeny.*

on″tō·ġe·net′iç, *a.* of ontogeny.

on″tō·ġe·net′iç·ăl·ly, *adv.* with reference to ontogeny.

on·tō·ġen′iç, *a.* same as *ontogenetic.*

on·toġ′e·ny, *n.* [*onto-* and *-geny.*] the life cycle of a single organism; biological development of the individual: distinguished from *phylogeny.*

on·tō·loġ′iç·ăl, on·tō·loġ′iç, *a.* of ontology.

on·tō·loġ′iç·ăl ăr′gū·ment, in metaphysics, an a priori argument for the existence of God, based upon the widespread existence of the idea of God.

on·tō·loġ′iç·ăl·ly, *adv.* in the manner of ontology.

on·tol′ō·ġism, *n.* the philosophical doctrine that the knowledge of God is immediate and intuitive, and that all other knowledge springs from it.

on·tol′ō·ġist, *n.* one versed in ontology or who treats of or considers the nature and qualities of being in general.

on·tol′ō·ġy, *n.* [Mod. L. *ontologia;* see *onto-* and *-logy.*] the branch of metaphysics dealing with the nature of being or reality.

The science of *ontology* comprehends investigations of every real existence, either beyond the sphere of the present world or in any other way incapable of being the direct object of consciousness, which can be deduced immediately from the possession of certain feelings or principles and faculties of the human soul. —Archer Butler.

ō′nus, *n.* [L.] anything burdensome; a task; a responsibility.

ō′nus prō ban′dī, literally, the burden of proving; the burden of proof; the burden of proving what has been alleged.

on′wărd, on′wărds, *adv.* toward or at a position or point ahead in space or time; forward; progressively; in advance; as, to move *onward.*

Not one looks backward; *onward* still he goes. —Pope.

on′wărd, *a.* 1. advancing; moving forward or toward some desired end; as, an *onward* course.

2. advanced in progress; increased; improved. [Now Rare.]

on′wărd·ness, *n.* forward movement; advance; progress.

on′y, *a.* any. [Dial.]

on′yçh-, same as *onycho-.*

on′y·çhȧ, *n.* [LL., mussel; Gr. *onyx, onychos.*] the shell or cover of a species of mussel found in the lakes of India, which, when burned, emits a musky odor.

ō·nyçh′i·ȧ, *n.* [Gr. *onyx, onychos,* nail.] inflammation of the last phalanx of a finger or toe, generally near the base of the nail, accompanied with ulceration; a felon.

on′y·çhīte, *n.* [Gr. *onichitēs,* from *onyx,* onyx.] alabaster. [Obs.]

on·y·çhī′tis, *n.* same as *onychia.*

on′y·çhō-, on′yçh-, [from Gr. *onyx, onychos,* claw, nail.] combining forms meaning *claw* or *nail.*

on′y·çhō·man″cy, *n.* [*onycho-,* and Gr. *manteia,* divination.] divination by the fingernails.

on″y·çhō·path′iç, *a.* [*onycho-,* and Gr. *pathos,* suffering.] of, pertaining to, or producing onychosis.

on·y·chọph'ȧ·ġy, *n.* [*onycho-*, and Gr. *phagein*, to eat.] the habit of biting the fingernails.

On·y·chọph'ō·rȧ, *n.pl.* [*onycho-*, and Gr. *pherein*, to carry.] in zoology, a class of arthropods better known as *Malacopoda.*

on″y·chop·tō'sis, *n.* [*onycho-*, and Gr. *ptōsis*, a falling.] the loosening and falling away of the fingernails.

on·y·chō'sis, *n.* [*onycho-* and *-osis.*] disease of a fingernail or toenail.

on'ym, *n.* [Gr. *onyma*, name.] in biology, a technical name, as of a species or other group, according to some system of nomenclature.

on'y·my, *n.* the application of onyms; systematic nomenclature.

on'yx (*or* ō'niks), *n.* [Gr. *onyx*, the nail, from the color of the gem resembling that of the nail.]

1. a variety of agate with alternate layers of color used as a semiprecious stone. Onyx was valued highly by the ancients, and is much used for cameos, the figure being cut in one layer and the background consisting of the next layer.

2. an accumulation of pus, shaped like the fingernail, in the anterior chamber of the eye.

onyx marble; alabaster (sense 2).

ō·nyx'is, *n.* [Gr. *onyx*, a nail.] ingrowing of a fingernail.

ō'ō, *n.* [Haw.] a bird found in the Hawaiian Islands. Its bright yellow plumage is valued for dress ornamentation.

o'ö- (ō'ō), [from Gr. *ōion*, an egg.] a combining form meaning *egg* or *ovum*, as in *oö*gamous, *oö*logy.

o'ö·cyst (ō'ō-), *n.* 1. in biology, an encysted oöspore.

2. in zoology, an egg capsule.

o'ö·cyte (ō'ō-sīt), *n.* [*oö-* and *-cyte.*] in embryology, (a) an egg that has not yet undergone maturation; (b) in certain protozoans, an immature female gamete.

ọọ'dleṣ (-dlz), *n.pl.* [said to be dial. form of *huddle.*] a great amount; very many. [Slang.]

ō·oe'ci·um, *n.*; *pl.* **ō·oe'ci·ȧ,** [*oö-*, and Gr. *oikos*, a house.] the cells or saclike receptacles for the ova of many of the *Bryozoa.*

o·ög'ȧ·mous (ō-og'ȧ-), *a.* [*oö-* and *-gamous.*] in biology, having reproductive cells that are sexually differentiated; heterogamous.

o·ög'ȧ·my, *n.* [*oö-*, and Gr. *gamos*, marriage.] in biology, the union of reproductive cells that are sexually differentiated.

o·ö·gen'e·sis (ō-ō-jen') *n.* [*oö-* and *-genesis.*] in biology, the process by which the ovum is formed in preparation for its fertilization and development.

o″ö·ge·net'ic (ō″ō-jē-net'ik), *a.* of oögenesis.

o·ö·gle'a, o·ö·gloe'a (ō-ō-glē'ȧ), *n.* [*oö-*, and Gr. *gloia*, glue.] in zoology, egg glue.

o·ö·go'ni·um (ō-ō-gō'), *n.*; *pl.* **o·ö·go'ni·a** (-ȧ), **o·ö·go'ni·ums** (-umz), [Mod.L., dim., from *oö-*, and Gr. *gonos*, offspring.]

1. the female reproductive organ in thallophytic plants, consisting of a large cell in which the eggs (*oöspheres*) are developed.

2. in embryology, any of the cells from which the oöcytes derive.

o'ö·graph (ō'ō-gráf), *n.* [*oö-* and *-graph.*] an apparatus for reproducing the outline of a bird's egg.

ọọh, *interj.* an exclamation of surprise, delight, etc.

ō'oid, ō·oi'dăl, *a.* [Gr. *ōioeidēs*, from *ōion*, an egg, and *eidos*, form.] having the shape of an egg.

ọọ'lȧ·chan, *n.* the candlefish (sense 2): also written *eulachon.*

o'ö·lite (ō'ō-līt), *n.* [Fr. *oölithe*; see *oö-* and *-lite.*] a limestone composed of many small grains of carbonate of lime cemented together like fish eggs in a layer of sedimentary rock. They vary in size from that of small pinheads to that of peas. When the grains are very distinct and well-rounded, the rock is called *roestone*; when they are large and pealike, it is known as *pisolite*, *peagrit*, or *peastone.*

o·ö·lit'ic (ō-ō-lit'ik), *a.* of oölite.

ọọl'ly, *n.*; *pl.* **ọọl'lieṣ,** a small mass of steel just taken from the crucible: applied especially to wootz steel. [Ind.]

o·ö·log'ic·al (ō-ō-loj'ik-al), *a.* pertaining to oölogy: also *oölogic.*

o·öl'o·gist (ō-ol'ō-jist), *n.* 1. one who is versed in oölogy.

2. one who collects birds' eggs.

o·öl'o·gy (ō-ol'ō-ji), *n.* [*oö-* and *-logy.*] that branch of ornithology which deals with the study of birds' eggs, including size, shape, color, and other characteristics.

ọọ'lọng, *n.* [Chinese *oo*, black, and *lung*, dragon.] a Chinese variety of black tea that is partly fermented before being dried.

o·öm'e·ter (ō-om'e-tẽr), *n.* [*oö-* and *-meter.*] an apparatus for taking the measurements of eggs.

ọọ'mi·aç, ọọ'mi·ak, *n.* same as *umiak.*

oomph, *n.* [echoic of involuntary expression of approval.]

1. sex appeal. [Slang.]

2. vigor; energy. [Slang.]

O″ö·my·ce'tes (ō″ō-mī-sē'tēz), *n.pl.* [*oö-*, and Gr. *mykēs*, pl. *mykētes*, mushroom.] one of the main subgroups of the fungi *Phycomycetes.* They are parasitic or saprophytic, and reproduce sexually by oögonia and antheridia. The spores are either motile or nonmotile, and sexual or asexual.

o″ö·my·ce'tous (ō″ō-mī-sē'), *a.* of or pertaining to the *Oömycetes.*

ọọn, *a.* one; single. [Dial.]

ọọp, *v.t.* [form of *whip.*] to bind with thread; to join. [Scot.]

ọọ'pak, ọọ'paçk, *n.* a variety of black tea.

o″ö·pho·ral'gi·a (ō″ō-fō-ral'ji-ȧ), *n.* in medicine, neuralgia of the ovary.

o'ö·phore (ō'ō-fōr), *n.* [*oö-* and *-phore.*] same as *oöphyte.*

o″ö·pho·rec'to·my (ō″ō-fō-rek'tō-), *n.* [*oöphoro-* and *-ectomy.*] the surgical removal of one or both ovaries.

o·ö·phor'ic (ō-ō-for'ik), *n.* same as *oöphytic.*

o″ö·pho·rid'i·um (ō″ō-fō-), *n.*; *pl.* **o″ö·pho·rid'i·a** (-ȧ), in botany, same as *macrosporangium.*

o″ö·pho·ri'tis (ō″ō-fō-rī'), *n.* [Mod.L., from *oöphoro-* and *-itis.*] inflammation of an ovary or the ovaries.

o·öph'o·ro- (ō-oph'ō-rō) [from Mod.L. *oöphoron*, ovary, from Gr. *ōion*, an egg, and *phoros*, bearing.] a combining form meaning *ovary* or *ovaries*: also, before a vowel, *oöphor-.*

o'ö·phyte (ō'ō-fīt), *n.* [*oö-* and *-phyte.*] in plants undergoing alternation of generations, as ferns, mosses, etc., that generation in which the reproductive organs are developed.

o·ö·phyt'ic (ō-ō-fit'ik), *a.* pertaining to or having the nature of an oöphyte.

o'ö·pod (ō'ō-), *n.* [*oö-*, and Gr. *pous*, *podos*, a foot.] in zoology, one of the elements or parts of an ovipositor.

o·öp'o·dal (ō-op'ō-dăl), *a.* pertaining to an oöpod.

ọọ'ri·ăl, *n.* a wild sheep of northern India.

ọọ'rie, *a.* cold; dreary. [Obs.]

o'ö·scope (ō'ō-skōp), *n.* [*oö-*, and Gr. *skopos*, watcher, from *skopein*, to view.] a device for observing the development of the embryo in an egg.

o·ös'co·py (ō-os'kō-), *n.* observation with an oöscope.

o'ö·sperm (ō'ō-spẽrm), *n.* [*oö-*, and Gr. *sperma*, seed.]

1. in zoology, a zygote.

2. in botany, an oöspore.

o'ö·sphere (ō'ō-sfẽr), *n.* [*oö-* and *sphere.*] any of the unfertilized eggs that develop in the female reproductive organ of a thallophytic plant.

o″ö·spo·ran'gi·um (ō″ō-spō-ran'ji-), *n.*; *pl.* **o″ö·spo·ran'gi·a** (-ȧ), in botany, the single-chambered sac in certain algae in which motile spores are produced.

o'ö·spore (ō'ō-spōr), *n.* [*oö-* and *spore.*] an oösphere after it has been fertilized.

o·ö·spor'ic (ō-ō-spor'ik), *a.* same as *oösporous.*

o″ö·spo·rif'er·ous (ō″ō-spō-rif'ẽr-), *a.* [*oö-*, and Gr. *sporos*, seed, and *-iferous.*] bearing oöspores.

o·ös'po·rous (ō-os'pō-), *a.* pertaining to or bearing oöspores.

o·ös'tē·gite (ō-os'tē-jīt), *n.* [*oö-*, and Gr. *stegein*, to cover.] in some crustaceans, one of the platelike processes forming the wall of the case in which the ova are hatched.

o·ö·the'ca (ō-ō-thē'kȧ), *n.*; *pl.* **o·ö·the'cae,** [*oö-*, and Gr. *thēkē*, a case.]

1. in zoology, the case in which eggs are held.

2. in botany, the sporangium of ferns. [Obs.]

o·öt'o·coid (ō-ot'ō-koid), *n.* [*oö-*, and Gr. *tekein*, *tiktein*, to bear, and *-oid.*] a mammal of the *Implacentalia*, comprising the marsupials and monotremes.

o·öt'o·coid, *a.* implacental.

o·öt·o·coid'e·an (ō-ot-ō-koid'ē-ăn), *a.* and *n.* same as *oötocoid.*

o·öt'o·cous (ō-ot'ō-kus), *n.* oviparous.

o'ö·type (ō'ō-tīp), *n.* in worms of the division *Trematoda*, the section of the egg passage where the eggs are fertilized and the shells formed.

ọọze, *n.* [ME. *wose*, *wos*; AS. *wos*, sap, juice; akin to M.L.G. *wose*, scum.]

1. an infusion of oak bark, sumac, etc., used in tanning leather.

2. [from the *v.*] (a) an oozing; gentle flow; (b) something that oozes.

ọọze, *v.i.*; oozed, *pt.*, *pp.*; oozing, *ppr.* 1. to flow or leak out slowly, as a liquid through the pores of a substance, or through small openings.

The latent rill, scarce *oozing* through the grass. —Thomson.

2. to escape by degrees; to disappear gradually; as, his strength *oozed* away.

3. to give forth moisture, as through pores.

ọọze, *v.t.* to give forth, or exude (a fluid).

ọọze, *n.* [ME. *wose*, *wase*; AS. *wase.*]

1. soft mud or slime.

2. an area of muddy ground; a bog.

3. the deposit at the bottom of the ocean, consisting mostly of the calcareous shells of foraminifers.

ọọ'zi·ly, *adv.* in any oozy manner.

ọọ'zi·ness, *n.* an oozy quality or state.

ọọ'zy, *a.*; *comp.* oozier; *superl.* ooziest, oozing; giving forth moisture.

ọọ'zy, *a.*; *comp.* oozier; *superl.* ooziest, full of or like ooze; slimy.

op-, ob-: used before *p*, as in *op*pose.

ō·pā'çate, *v.t.* to make opaque. [Rare.]

ō·pac'i·ty, *n.* [Fr. *opacité*; L. *opacitas*, from *opacus*, shady.]

1. the state or quality of being opaque.

2. *pl.* **ō·pac'i·tieṣ,** something opaque.

ō·pā'çous, *a.* obscure; opaque. [Now Rare.]

ō'pȧh, *n.* a large sea fish, *Lampris guttatus*, of the Atlantic and Pacific oceans: it is brightly spotted with silvery dots.

ō'păl, *n.* [L. *opalus*; Gr. *opallios*, an opal; Sans. *upala*, a precious stone.] any of a large group of glassy, translucent silicas of various colors, capable of refracting light and then reflecting it in a play of colors: some varieties, used as semiprecious stones, include the *common opal*, with a generally milky appearance, the *black opal*, with a very dark-green background, and the *fire opal*, with flamelike colors.

ō·păl·esce' (-es'), *v.i.*; opalesced (-est'), *pt.*, *pp.*; opalescing, *ppr.* [*opal* and *-esce.*] to give forth a play of colors like the opal.

ō·păl·es'cence, *n.* the quality of being opalescent.

ō·păl·es'cent, *a.* resembling an opal in play of colors; iridescent.

ō'păl·ine, *a.* pertaining to or like opal.

ō'păl·ine, *n.* a translucent, milky variety of glass.

ō'păl·ize, *v.t.*; opalized, *pt.*, *pp.*; opalizing, *ppr.* to give the appearance of opal to.

ō'păl·oid, *a.* opaline; semitranslucent, as certain kinds of glass.

ō·pāque' (-pāk'), *a.* [ME. *opake*; L. *opacus*, shady.]

1. not letting light pass through; not transparent; as, chalk is an *opaque* substance.

2. not reflecting light; not shining or lustrous; dull or dark.

3. not allowing heat, electricity, etc. to pass through.

4. hard to understand; obscure.

5. slow in understanding; obtuse.

ō·pāque', *n.* 1. anything opaque.

2. a substance used to render anything opaque, as in preparing photographic negatives for printing.

ō·pāque'ness, *n.* opacity.

op (ärt), a style of abstract painting utilizing geometrical patterns or figures to create various optical effects, such as the illusion of movement.

ope, *a.* open. [Poet.]

ōpe, *v.t.* and *v.i.*; oped (ōpt), *pt.*, *pp.*; oping, *ppr.* to open: now used only in poetry.

Ope the sacred source of sympathetic tears. —Gray.

Op'-Ed', *a.* [*O*pposite *Ed*itorial page.] [*sometimes* op-ed] designating or appearing on a page in a newspaper, usually the one opposite the editorial page, that features columns, free-lance articles, letters, etc.

ō·peī'dō·sçope, *n.* [Gr. *ops*, *opos*, voice, *eidos*, form, and *skopein*, to view.] a device by which the vibrations due to various sounds are illustrated visually by the reflection of a beam of light from a sensitive diaphragm upon a screen.

ō'pen, *a.* [AS. *open*, open; D. *open*, open; Ice. *opinn*, lying on the back, open; Dan. *aaben*;

G. *offen*, open. It would seem to be a past participle of a verb formed from *up*, or at least to be based on *up*.]

1. in a state which permits entrance or exit; not closed, covered, clogged or shut; as, an *open* door; an *open* harbor; an *open* letter.

2. in a state which permits freedom of view or passage; not enclosed, fenced in, sheltered, screened, etc.; unobstructed; clear; as, an *open* field.

3. unsealed; unwrapped.

4. (a) not covered over; without covering, top, etc.; as, an *open* boat; (b) liable to attack, etc.; unprotected.

5. spread out; unfolded; unclosed; expanded; as, an *open* book.

6. having spaces between; having gaps, holes, interstices, etc.; as, *open* ranks.

7. free from ice; as, the lake is *open* in May.

8. free from frost; as, an *open* winter.

9. free to be entered, used, competed in, shared, visited, etc. by all; as, an *open* meeting or tournament.

10. free to be argued or contested; not settled or decided; as, an *open* question.

11. (a) free from prejudice or bigotry; not closed to new ideas, etc.; as, an *open* mind; (b) liberal; generous.

12. (a) free from restrictions; as, an *open* season; (b) free from effective regulation with respect to drinking, gambling, etc.; as, the city is wide *open;* (c) free from discriminatory restrictions based on race, religion, etc.; as, *open* housing; (d) not regulated, organized, or conducted along traditional or conventional lines; as, *open* marriage; *open* education.

13. characterized by social mobility, political freedom, diversity of opinion, etc.; as, an *open* society.

14. in force or operation; as, an *open* account.

15. (a) not already taken, occupied, or engaged; not filled; as, the job is still *open;* (b) free to be accepted or rejected.

16. not closed against access; accessible; available.

17. not hidden or secret; generally known; public; as, an *open* quarrel.

18. frank; candid; direct; honest; as, an *open* manner.

19. in music, (a) not stopped by the finger: said of a string; (b) not closed at the top: said of an organ pipe; (c) produced by an open string or pipe, or, in wind instruments, brasses, etc., without a slide or key: said of a tone.

20. in nautical usage, not hazy or foggy; clear.

21. in phonetics, (a) pronounced with the tongue as low as possible; low: said of a vowel; (b) pronounced with the organs of speech not in close contact; fricative: said of a consonant; (c) ending in a vowel or diphthong: said of a syllable.

22. in printing, designating or of a style of type the letters of which are cast in outline so that the inside of letters shows white.

23. ready to do, hear, see, or receive anything; fully prepared; attentive; as, *open* to advances; keep your ears *open*.

open chain; a molecular formation in which the chain of elements does not form a ring.

open circuit; in electricity, an interrupted circuit.

open communion; Holy Communion without restriction to those of a particular sect.

open diapason; an organ stop in which the metal pipes are shaped like the mouthpiece of a flageolet where the wind enters, and open at the other end.

open harmony; harmony of tones widely separated.

open hawse; a hawse in which the cables are not crossed.

open sea; (a) a sea not closed to any nation; (b) a part of the sea entirely outside the mainland, and away from bays, straits, breakers, and the like.

open to; (a) glad or willing to receive, discuss, etc.; (b) liable to; subject to; (c) available to or for.

open verdict; a verdict upon an inquest which finds that a crime has been committed, but does not specify the criminal; or which finds that a sudden or violent death has occurred, but does not find the cause proven.

ō'pen, *n.* an opening. [Now Rare.]

the open; (a) any open, unobstructed space on land or water; (b) an unenclosed area; the outdoors; (c) public knowledge; (d) in golf, any tournament open to both professionals and amateurs; (e) [O-] in golf, an open tournament played annually in the United States to decide the national championship: properly called the *National Open*.

ō'pen, *v.t.*; opened, *pt., pp.*; opening, *ppr.* [AS. *openian*; D. *openen*; G. *öffnen*.]

1. to make or cause to be open (senses 1, 2, 3); to unclose; to unfasten; as, *open* the door.

2. to make an opening or openings in; as, the doctor *opened* the abscess.

3. to make spaces between; to make less compact; to spread out; to expand; as, the soldiers *opened* their ranks.

4. to unclose; to unfold; to unroll; as, he *opened* the book.

5. to make available for use, competition, or participation, without restriction, taxation, fee, etc.

6. to free from prejudice and bigotry; to make liberal and generous.

7. to make known, public, etc.; to reveal; to disclose.

8. to begin; to enter upon; to start; to commence; as, he *opened* the session with a greeting.

9. to cause to start operating, going, etc.; as, he *opened* a new night club.

10. to undo, recall, set aside (a judgment, settlement, etc.), so as to leave the matter open to further action.

to open one's mouth; to speak.

to open out; (a) to make extended or larger; (b) to develop; (c) to disclose to view; to reveal.

to open up; (a) to make open; (b) to spread out; to unfold; (c) to start; to begin.

ō'pen, *v.i.* 1. to become open.

2. to spread out; to expand; to unroll; to unfold.

3. to become free from prejudice, etc.; to become liberal and generous.

4. to become revealed, disclosed, etc.; to come into view.

5. to be or act as an opening; to give access.

6. to begin; to start.

7. to start operating, going, etc.

8. to bark on scent or view of the game: a term used in hunting.

to open out; (a) to become extended or larger; (b) to develop.

to open up; (a) to become open; (b) to spread out; to unfold; (c) to start; to begin; (d) [Colloq.] to speak freely or with great feeling.

ō'pen-āir, *a.* outdoor.

ō'pen āir, out of doors.

ō'pen-and-shut', *a.* that can be clearly and easily determined or decided; simple; obvious; as, an *open-and-shut* case.

ō'pen·bill, *n.* an African or Asiatic bird of the genus *Anastomus*, related to the stork: also called *clapperbill, openbeak*, and *shell eater*.

ō'pen cit'y, a city which is a military objective but is completely demilitarized and left open to enemy occupation in order to gain immunity, under international law, from bombardment and attack.

ō'pen·dōor', *a.* designating or of the policy or principle of the open door.

ō'pen dōor, 1. unrestricted admission.

2. free and equal opportunity for all nations to trade with a given nation, without any restrictive terms.

ō'pen·ẽr, *n.* 1. one who or that which opens.

2. any of several devices for opening bottles, cans, etc.

3. the first game in a series.

4. that which separates; that which rends; specifically, a machine for opening cotton taken from the bales in which it has been closely compacted.

ō'pen-ēyed (-īd), *a.* 1. having the eyes open or wide-open; watchful; vigilant; wary; amazed.

2. done with the eyes widely open.

ō'pen-fāced, *a.* 1. with the face uncovered.

2. having a frank, honest face.

ō'pen·hand″ed, *a.* generous; liberal; munificent.

ō'pen·hand'ed·ness, *n.* the state or quality of being generous.

ō'pen·head″ed (-hed″), *a.* bareheaded. [Obs.]

ō'pen·heärt'ed, *a.* 1. candid; frank.

2. kindly; generous.

ō'pen·heärt'ed·ly, *adv.* in an openhearted manner.

ō'pen·heärt'ed·ness, *n.* the quality or condition of being openhearted.

ō'pen-heärth, *a.* 1. designating a furnace with a wide, saucer-shaped hearth and a low roof, used in making steel.

2. using a furnace of this kind; as, the *open-hearth* process.

open-hearth furnace; a reverberatory furnace using gas as fuel in the manufacture of steel.

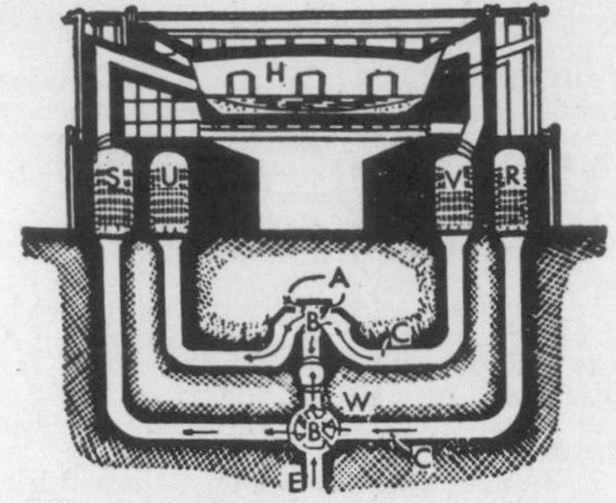

OPEN-HEARTH FURNACE
A, air valve; B, B, reversing valves; W, chimney; C, C, ports to chimney; E, gas main valve; H, hearth; R, S, U, V, regenerators

open-hearth process; a process in the manufacture of steel, melted cast iron being converted into steel by the addition of iron ore or wrought iron and manganese, and by exposure to heat in an open-hearth furnace.

ō'pen house, 1. a house that extends hospitality to all who wish to come.

2. an occasion when a school, institution, etc. is open to visitors for inspection and observation of activities.

ō'pen·ing, *n.* 1. the act of opening; the state of becoming opened.

2. an open place or part; a gap; an aperture; a hole or perforation.

3. a clearing in the midst of a wooded area.

4. (a) a beginning; first part; commencement; (b) start of operations; formal beginning.

5. a favorable chance or occasion; an opportunity.

6. an unfilled position, or office for which a person is wanted.

7. in chess, checkers, etc., the series of moves at the beginning of a game.

ō'pen let'tẽr, a letter written as to a specific person, usually in attack, criticism, etc., but published for everyone to read.

ō'pen·ly, *adv.* 1. in an open manner; publicly; not in private; without secrecy.

That justice that sees in secret and rewards
openly. —South.

2. plainly; evidently; without reserve or disguise.

ō'pen-mīnd'ed, *a.* having a mind open to new ideas; free from prejudice or bigotry.

ō'pen-mouthed' (*or* -moutht'), *a.* 1. having the mouth open.

2. gaping, as in astonishment.

3. greedy; ravenous.

4. clamorous; vociferous.

ō'pen·ness, *n.* 1. the quality or state of being open; freedom from obstruction; as, *openness* to the weather.

2. plainness; clearness; freedom from obscurity or ambiguity; as, deliver your answers with more *openness*.

3. freedom from prejudice or bigotry.

4. forthrightness; frankness; candor; as, *openness* of countenance.

5. unusual mildness; freedom from snow and frost; as, the *openness* of a winter.

ō'pen sēa'ṣŏn, any of various annual periods during which it is legal to kill or capture certain specified game, wild fowl, or fish.

ō'pen sē'çret, something supposed to be secret but known to almost everyone.

ō'pen ses'ȧ·mē, 1. magic words spoken to open the door of the robbers' den in the story of Ali Baba in the *Arabian Nights*.

2. any unfailing means of gaining admission, etc., as a password.

ō'pen shop, 1. a factory, business, etc. operating under the system of employing workers without regard to whether or not they are members of a union, or, especially, not knowingly employing any union members, and following an antiunion policy.

2. this system.

Distinguished from *closed shop, union shop*, etc.

ō'pen stock, merchandise sold in sets, the individual pieces of which are kept in stock in quantity so that replacements or additions are always available.

ō'pen·tīde, *n.* a period directly following the grain harvest, when the fields are open for the grazing of livestock. [Brit. Dial. or Obs.]

ō'pen-tim'bẽr, *a.* designating a roof, as of a church or public hall, in which the underside is ornamentally treated so as to form the ceiling of the apartment below.

ō'pen·wŏrk, *n.* ornamental work, as in cloth, metal, etc., which shows numerous openings through the material.

op'ẽr·ȧ, *n.* [It., Sp., and Fr., from L. *opera*, work, labor.]
1. a play having all or most of its text set to music with arias, recitatives, choruses, duets, trios, etc. sung to orchestral accompaniment, usually characterized by elaborate costuming, scenery, and choreography.
2. the branch of art represented by such plays.
3. the score, libretto, or performance of a musical drama.
4. a theater where operas are performed.
grand opera; an opera of high musical pretensions, serious or tragic in character, and accompanied by a full orchestra.
opéra bouffe; comic opera, especially if farcical.
opera buffa; an Italian comic opera.
opéra comique; French opera in which the dialogue is spoken: it may or may not be comic.

op'ẽr·ȧ·ble, *a.* 1. practicable.
2. that can be treated by a surgical operation.

op'ẽr·ȧ çlōak, a long, loose cloak, usually of rich material, worn by women over evening dress, as at the opera.

op'ẽr·ȧ dan'cẽr, one who dances in an opera; a ballet dancer.

op'ẽr·ȧ ġirls, a plant, *Mantisia saltatoria.*

op'ẽr·ȧ glass'eṣ, a small, binocular telescope used at the opera, in theaters, etc.

op'ẽr·ȧ hat, a tall, collapsible silk hat for men.

op'ẽr·ȧ house, a theater built especially for the performance of operas.

op·ẽr·am'ē·tẽr, *n.* [L. *opera*, work, and Gr. *metron*, measure.] an attachment to a machine to indicate the number of rotations of a shaft.

op'ẽr·ănce, *n.* the act of operating; operation.

op'ẽr·ăn·cy, *n.* same as *operance.*

op'ẽr·ănd, *n.* in mathematics, any symbol or quantity upon which an operation is performed.

op'ẽr·ănt, *a.* operating, or producing an effect or effects.

op'ẽr·ănt, *n.* one who or that which operates.

op'ẽr·ȧ sing'ẽr, a professional singer who performs in operas.

op'ẽr·āte, *v.i.*; operated, *pt., pp.*; operating, *ppr.* [L. *operatus*, pp. of *operari*, to work, from *opus, operis*, work.]
1. to act; to perform work; to be in action so as to produce an effect.
2. to have or produce a desired result or effect; to act effectively.
3. to carry on strategic military movements (usually with *against*).
4. in surgery, to perform an operation.
5. to buy and sell stocks on speculation: followed by *in*; as, to *operate in* corn. [Colloq.]
6. to act or produce effect on the mind; to exert moral power or influence.

op'ẽr·āte, *v.t.* 1. to effect; to produce or accomplish, as an agent; to cause.
2. to work; to set or keep in operation or activity; as, to *operate* a machine.
3. to superintend; to manage; to direct the affairs of; as, to *operate* a mine.

op·ẽr·at'iç, *a.* of or like opera.

op·ẽr·at'iç·ăl, *a.* operatic.

op·ẽr·at'iç·ăl·ly, *adv.* in an operatic manner.

op'ẽr·ā·ting tā'ble, a table on which a person who is to undergo a surgical operation is placed.

op·ẽr·ā'tion, *n.* [ME. *operacion*; OFr.; L. *operatio.*]
1. the act, method, or process of operating.
2. the condition of being in action or at work.
3. the power to act; force; influence.
4. a process or action that is part of a series in some work.
5. (a) any movement or series of movements made in carrying out strategic military plans; (b) any specific plan or project; as, *Operation* Cleanup.
6. any surgical procedure performed with or without the aid of instruments, usually to remedy a physical ailment or defect.
7. in mathematics, any process involving a change or transformation in a quantity; as, the *operations* of addition, subtraction, etc.
in operation; (a) in the act or process of making, working, etc.; (b) having an influence or effect; in force.

op·ẽr·ā'tion·ăl, *a.* 1. of, having to do with, or derived from the operation of a device, system, process, etc.
2. (a) that can be used or operated; (b) in use; operating.
3. of or ready for use in a military operation.

op·ẽr·ā'tionṣ rē·sẽarch', the systematic and scientific analysis and evaluation of problems, as in government, military, or business operations: also *operations analysis.*

op'ẽr·ā·tive, *a.* [Fr. *opératif*; LL. *operativus.*]
1. capable of, characterized by, or in operation.
2. accomplishing what is desired; effective.
3. connected with physical work or mechanical action.
4. in surgery, of or resulting from a surgical operation.

op'ẽr·ā·tive, *n.* 1. a skilled workman; an artisan; a mechanic.
2. a detective.

op'ẽr·ā·tive·ly, *adv.* in an operative manner.

op'ẽr·ā·tŏr, *n.* 1. one who or that which operates or produces an effect.
2. in surgery, the person who performs some act upon the human body by means of the hand, or with instruments.
3. in mathematics, a character that signifies an operation to be performed.
4. a person who works some machine; as, a telephone *operator.*
5. a person engaged in financial, commercial, or industrial operations; owner or manager of a mine, railroad, factory, etc.

ō'pẽr·cle, *n.* an operculum.

ō·pẽr'cū·lăr, *a.* of, or having the nature of, an operculum.

ō·pẽr'cū·lăr, *n.* in anatomy, the opercular bone of fishes.

Ō·pẽr·çū·lā'tȧ, *n.pl.* in conchology, a group of operculate gastropods.

ō·pẽr'cū·lāte, *a.* [L. *operculatus*, from *operire*, to cover.] having an operculum.

ō·pẽr'cū·lā·ted, *a.* operculate.

ō·pẽr·çū·lif'ẽr·ous, *a.* [*operculum* and *-iferous.*] in zoology, carrying an operculum.

ō·pẽr'cū·li·fŏrm, *a.* [from *operculum* and *-form.*] formed like an operculum.

ō·pẽr·çū·liġ'e·nous, *a.* [from *operculum* and *-genous.*] developing an operculum.

ō·pẽr·çū·liġ'ẽr·ous, *a.* [from *operculum* and *-gerous.*] having an operculum.

ō·pẽr'cū·lum, *n.*; *pl.* **ō·pẽr'cū·lȧ, ō·pẽr'cū·lumṣ,** [L., from *operire*, to close or shut.]
1. a lid or cover of various kinds.
2. the bony covering protecting the gills of fishes.
3. in many gastropods, the horny plate serving to close the shell when the animal is retracted.
4. the lid of the spore cases in mosses.
5. the lid of a pitcher-shaped leaf.

o'pe·rē ci·tā'tō, [L.] in the work cited, or quoted.

op·ẽr·et'tȧ, *n.* [It.] a short, light musical drama.

op'ẽr·ōse, *a.* [L. *operosus*, from *opera*, work.]
1. done with or requiring much toil.
2. very busy; industrious.

op'ẽr·ōse·ly, *adv.* laboriously.

op'ẽr·ōse·ness, *n.* the state of being operose.

op·ẽr·os'i·ty, *n.* operoseness.

op'ẽr·ous, *a.* operose. [Obs.]

Ō·phē'liȧ (-lyȧ), *n.* [prob. from Gr. *ōphelia*, a help, succor.] in Shakespeare's *Hamlet*, Polonius's daughter, in love with Hamlet.

oph'i·clēide (-klīd), *n.* [Gr. *ophis*, serpent, and *kleis*, key.] an early brass-wind instrument consisting of a long tube doubled back on itself. It usually has eleven keys and a range of about three octaves.

OPHICLEIDE

Ō·phid'i·ȧ, *n.pl.* [Gr. *ophidion*, dim. of *ophis*, a serpent.] an order of reptiles, comprising the snakes and serpents, characterized by an elongated and cylindrical body covered with horny scales, without breastbone, pectoral arch, and fore limbs, and rarely with rudimentary hind limbs.

ō·phid'i·ăn, *n.* [Gr. *ophidion*, a serpent.] a snake or serpent.

ō·phid'i·ăn, *a.* [Gr. *ophidion*, a serpent.] pertaining to the *Ophidia*; pertaining to or like a snake, or serpent.

ō·phid'i·oid, *a.* [Gr. *ophidion*, and *-oid.*] relating to or having the characteristics of the *Ophidiidæ*, a family of fishes having slender bodies and the ventral fin located on the lower jaw.

ō·phid'i·oid, *n.* an individual of the *Ophidiidæ.*

ō·phid'i·on, *n.*; *pl.* **ō·phid'i·ȧ,** same as *ophidium.*

ō·phid'i·ous, *a.* ophidian. [Rare.]

Ō·phid'i·um, *n.* 1. a genus of ophidioid fishes.
2. [o–] a fish of this genus.

Ō''phi·ō·glos·sā'cē·ae, *n.pl.* [Gr. *ophis*, serpent, and *glōssa*, tongue.] a family of ferns of which the genus *Ophioglossum* is the type; the adder's-tongue family.

ō''phi·ō·glos·sā'ceous, *a.* [Gr. *ophis*, serpent, and *glōssa*, tongue, and *-aceous.*] belonging to the *Ophioglossaceæ.*

Ō''phi·ō·glos'sum, *n.* [Gr. *ophis*, a serpent, and *glōssa*, the tongue.] a genus of cryptogamic plants belonging to the family *Ophioglossaceæ*, of which it is the type.

ō·phi·og'rȧ·phy, *n.* [Gr. *ophis*, serpent, and *-graphy.*] the exact and detailed description of serpents.

ō'phi·oid, *a.* [Gr. *ophis*, serpent, and *-oid.*] like or relating to serpents.

ō·phi·ol'ȧ·try, *n.* [Gr. *ophis*, serpent, and *latreia*, worship.] the worship of serpents.

ō'phi·ō·līte, *n.* [Gr. *ophis*, serpent, and *lithos*, stone.] rock composed of serpentine mixed with dolomite, magnesite, or calcite, of a clouded-green color, veined with white or pale green: also called *verd antique.*

ō''phi·ō·lit'iç, *a.* like or containing ophiolite.

ō''phi·ō·loġ'iç, ō''phi·ō·loġ'iç·ăl, *a.* pertaining to ophiology.

ō·phi·ol'ō·ġist, *n.* a student of or specialist in ophiology.

ō·phi·ol'ō·ġy, *n.* [Gr. *ophis*, serpent, and *logos*, discourse.] the branch of zoology dealing with snakes.

ō'phi·ō·man·cy, *n.* [Gr. *ophis*, a serpent, and *manteia*, divination.] the art of divining or predicting events by serpents, as by their manner of eating or by their coils. [Rare.]

Ō''phi·ō·mor'phȧ, *n.pl.* [Gr. *ophis*, a serpent, and *morphē*, shape.] a small order of amphibians, including only certain snakelike animals which are found in various tropical countries burrowing in marshy ground, something like gigantic earthworms.

ō''phi·ō·mor'phīte, *n.* [Gr. *ophis*, serpent, *morphē*, shape, and *-ite.*] a fossil shell having some resemblance to a snake; an ammonite.

ō''phi·ō·mor'phous, *a.* [Gr. *ophis*, serpent, and *morphē*, form.] having the form of a serpent.

ō·phi·oph'ȧ·gous, *a.* [Gr. *ophis*, serpent, and *phagein*, to eat.] eating or feeding on serpents, as certain birds and large serpents.

Ō·phi·oph'ȧ·gus, *n.* a genus of very venomous serpents, found throughout southern Asia, which devour smaller serpents. The *Ophiophagus elaps* is the largest cobra, sometimes growing to a length of twelve feet and easily killing men and even the large quadrupeds.

ō'phi·ō·sąur, *n.* [Gr. *ophis*, a serpent, and *sauros*, a lizard.] a lizard of the genus *Ophiosaurus*, or family *Ophiosauridæ.*

Ō'phir (-fẽr), *n.* [Heb. *ōphīr.*] in the Bible, a land rich in gold: 1 Kings ix. 28, x. 11, xxii. 48.

ō'phīte, *a.* [Gr. *ophis*, serpent.] pertaining to a serpent. [Rare.]

Ō'phīte, *n.* one of a Gnostic sect of the second century, who worshiped the serpent.

ō'phīte, *n.* [Gr. *ophis*, a serpent, whence *ophitēs*, a stone spotted like a serpent.] green porphyry or serpentine; a metamorphic rock of a dusky-green color.

ō·phit'iç, *a.* pertaining to ophite; consisting of feldspar crystals in a matrix of augite.

Ō·phi·ū'çhus, *n.* [Gr. *ophiouchos*; *ophis*, a serpent, and *echein*, to hold.] a southern constellation, one of the ancient asterisms, having Hercules on the north, Scorpio on the south, and Serpens on the west. It has about eighty stars visible to the naked eye.

Ō·phi·ū'rȧ, *n.* [Gr. *ophis*, serpent, and *oura*, tail.] a genus of sand stars with arms very long and adapted for creeping.

ō·phi·ū'răn, *a.* pertaining to the genus *Ophiura* or order *Ophiuroidea.*

ō·phi·ū'răn, *n.* one of the *Ophiuroidea.*

ō·phi·ū'rē·ae, *n.pl.* a division of the *Ophiuroidea*, including those species which have unbranched arms, as contrasted with the *Euryaleæ*, which have branching arms.

ō·phi·ū'rid, *n.* an ophiuran.

Ō·phi·ū'ri·dae, *n.pl.* a division of the *Ophiuroidea.*

ō·phi·ū'roid, *a.* of or relating to the *Ophiuroidea.*

ō·phi·ū'roid, *n.* one of the *Ophiuroidea*; an ophiuran.

Ō″phi·ū·roi'dē·ȧ, *n.pl.* [Gr. *ophis*, a serpent, *oura*, a tail, and *eidos*, form.] a class of echinoderms.

oph'ry·on, *n.* [LL., from Gr. *ophrys*, eyebrow.] in anatomy, the middle point of the transverse supraorbital line.

oph·ry·ō'sis, *n.* spasm of the eyebrow.

oph·thal·mal'ġi·ȧ, *n.* [Gr. *ophthalmos*, the eye, and *algos*, pain.] in pathology, pain in the eye.

oph·thal'mi·ȧ, *n.* [Gr., from *ophthalmos*, the eye, from a root *op*, signifying to see, akin to L. *oc* in *oculus*.] severe inflammation of the eyeball or of the conjunctiva.

varicose ophthalmia; a variety of ophthalmia with varicosity of the veins of the conjunctiva.

oph″thal·mi·at'riçs, *n.* [Gr. *ophthalmos*, the eye, and *iatreia*, treatment.] the treatment of eye diseases.

oph·thal'miç, *a.* 1. of or relating to the eyes.

2. pertaining to or suffering from ophthalmia.

oph·thal'mīte, *n.* in the *Crustacea*, the jointed segment which supports the compound eye, projecting from the surface of the head; an eyestalk.

oph·thal·mit'iç, *a.* pertaining to an ophthalmite.

oph·thal·mī'tis, *n.* [Gr. *ophthalmos*, the eye, and *-itis*.] inflammation of the eye; ophthalmia.

oph·thal'mō-, [from Gr. *ophthalmos*, the eye.] a combining form meaning the *eye* or *eyes*, as in *ophthalmo*scope: also, before a vowel, *ophthalm-*.

oph·thal·mō·blen·nor·rhē'ȧ, oph·thal·mō·blen·nor·rhoe'ȧ, *n.* [*ophthalmo-*, and Gr. *blenna*, mucus, and *rhoia*, flow.] gonorrheal or purulent ophthalmia.

oph·thal'mō·cēle, *n.* [*ophthalmo-*, and Gr. *kēlē*, tumor.] exophthalmia.

oph·thal·mō·çō'pi·ȧ, *n.* [*ophthalmo-*, and Gr. *kopos*, weariness.] asthenopia, or eyestrain; fatigue of the eyes.

oph·thal″mō·deṣ·mī'tis, *n.* [*ophthalmo-*, and Gr. *desmos*, ligament, and *-itis*.] inflammation of the ocular tendons.

oph·thal·mō·dī·ȧ·stim'ē·tēr, *n.* [*ophthalmo-*, and Gr. *diastēma*, interval, and *metron*, measure.] an instrument for determining the proper distance at which to place lenses for the eyes.

oph·thal·mō·dȳ·nȧ·mom'ē·tēr, *n.* an instrument for determining the near point of convergence.

oph·thal·mō·dyn'i·ȧ, *n.* [*ophthalmo-*, and Gr. *odynē*, pain.] pain in the eye.

oph·thal·mog'rȧ·phy, *n.* a description of the eyes.

oph·thal·mō·loġ'iç, *a.* ophthalmological.

oph·thal·mō·loġ'iç·ăl, *a.* pertaining to ophthalmology.

oph·thal·mol'ō·ġist, *n.* a specialist in ophthalmology.

oph·thal·mol'ō·ġy, *n.* [*ophthalmo-* and *-logy*.] the branch of medicine dealing with the structure, functions, and diseases of the eye.

oph·thal·mom'ē·tēr, *n.* [*ophthalmo-*, and Gr. *metron*, measure.] an instrument for measuring the eye; especially, one for determining its refractive powers and defects by measuring the size of the images reflected from the cornea and lens.

oph·thal·mom'ē·try, *n.* determination of the refractive powers and defects of the eye.

oph·thal'mō·phōre, *n.* [*ophthalmo-*, and Gr. *-phoros*, from *pherein*, to bear.] that section of the head of a gastropod in which the eye is located.

oph·thal·mō·phō'ri·um, *n.* same as *ophthalmophore.*

oph·thal·moph'ō·rous, *a.* pertaining to an ophthalmophore.

oph·thal·moph·thī'sis, *n.* [*ophthalmo-*, and Gr. *phthisis*, a wasting away.] shriveling of the eyeball.

oph·thal·mō·plē'ġi·ȧ, *n.* [*ophthalmo-*, and Gr. *plēgē*, a stroke.] paralysis of the eye muscles.

oph·thal'mō·sçōpe, *n.* [*ophthalmo-*, and Gr. *skopein*, to view.] an instrument used to examine the interior of the eye: it consists of a perforated mirror arranged to reflect light from a small bulb into the eye.

OPHTHALMOSCOPE

oph·thal·mō·sçop'iç, *a.* relating to the ophthalmoscope or to the use of it.

oph·thal·mos'çō·py, *n.* [*ophthalmo-*, and Gr. *skopein*, to view.]

1. a branch of physiognomy which deduces the knowledge of a person's temper and manner from the appearance of the eyes. [Rare.]

2. the examination of the interior of the eye with the ophthalmoscope.

oph·thal'mō·stat, *n.* [*ophthalmo-*, and Gr. *statos*, from *histanai*, to make to stand.] an instrument for holding the eye steady during operation.

oph·thal'my, *n.* same as *ophthalmia.*

-ō'pi·ȧ, [Gr. *-opia*, from *ops*, *opos*, an eye.] a combining form meaning *a* (specified kind of) *eye defect*, as in diplo*pia*: also *-opy*.

ō·pi·an'iç, *a.* pertaining to or obtained from opium; as, *opianic* acid.

ō'pi·ȧ·nīne, ō'pi·ȧ·nin, *n.* an alkaloid found in opium.

ō'pi·ȧ·nyl, *n.* same as *meconin.*

ō'pi·āte, *n.* [from *opium*.]

1. any medicine that contains opium or any of its derivatives, and acting as a sedative and narcotic.

2. that which induces rest or inaction; that which quiets uneasiness.

They chose atheism as an *opiate*.—Bentley.

ō'pi·āte, *a.* 1. containing opium.

2. inducing sleep; soporiferous; somniferous; narcotic; causing rest or inaction.

ō'pi·āte, *v.t.*; opiated, *pt.*, *pp.*; opiating, *ppr.* 1. to treat with an opiate. [Rare.]

2. to dull; to deaden. [Rare.]

ō'pi·ā·ted, *a.* mixed with opiates; under the influence of opiates.

ō'piē, *n.* opium or a drug which contains opium. [Obs.]

op'i·fice, *n.* workmanship. [Obs.]

ō·pif'i·cēr, *n.* one who performs any work. [Obs.]

ō·pīn'ȧ·ble, *a.* capable of being opined.

op·i·nā'tion, *n.* the act of thinking; opinion. [Obs.]

ō·pin'ȧ·tive, *a.* stubborn in opinion; opinionated. [Obs.]

ō·pin'ȧ·tive·ly, *adv.* in an opinative manner. [Obs.]

op'i·nā·tŏr, *n.* one who holds an opinion. [Obs.]

ō·pīne', *v.i.* and *v.t.*; opined, *pt.*, *pp.*; opining, *ppr.* [Fr. *opiner*; L. *opinari*, to think.] to think; to suppose; to hold or express (an opinion): now usually humorous.

ō·pīn'ēr, *n.* one who thinks or holds an opinion.

ō·pin·i·as'tēr, *a.* [Fr. *opiniâtre*.] unduly attached to one's own opinion, or stubborn in adhering to it. [Obs.]

ō·pin·i·as'trous, *a.* same as *opiniaster.* [Obs.]

ō·pin'i·āte, *v.t.* to express one's opinion. [Obs.]

ō·pin'i·ā·ted, *a.* unduly attached to one's own opinions. [Obs.]

ō·pin'i·ā·tive, *a.* opinionative. [Now Rare.]

ō·pin'i·ā·tive·ly, *adv.* in an opiniative manner. [Now Rare.]

ō·pin'i·ā·tive·ness, *n.* undue stubborness in opinion. [Now Rare.]

ō·pin'i·ā·tŏr, ō·pin'i·ā·tre (-tēr), *n.* one unduly attached to his own opinion. [Obs.]

ō·pin·i·ā'tre, *a.* opiniaster; obstinate. [Obs.]

ō·pin·i·āt'rē·ty, *n.* opiniativeness. [Obs.]

ō·pin'i·çus, *n.* [probably from L. *opinari*, to think; hence, imaginative.] a fictitious beast of heraldic creation, represented as having the body of a lion, the head and wings of an eagle, and a short tail resembling that of the camel.

OPINICUS

ō·pīn'ing, *n.* opinion; notion.

ō·pin'iŏn (-yun), *n.* [ME. *opinioun*; OFr.; L. *opinio*, from *opinari*, to think.]

1. a belief not based on absolute certainty or positive knowledge but on what seems true, valid, or probable to one's own mind; what one thinks; judgment.

2. an evaluation, impression, or estimation of the quality or worth of a person or thing.

3. the formal judgment of an expert on a matter in which his advice is sought.

4. in law, the formal statement by a judge, etc. of the law bearing on a case.

5. opinionativeness; conceitedness; obstinacy in a belief. [Obs.]

Syn.—notion, sentiment, conception, idea, estimation, belief.

ō·pin'iŏn, *v.t.* to think. [Obs.]

ō·pin'iŏn·ȧ·ble, *a.* admitting of opinion; capable of different views and beliefs; open to discussion: opposed to *dogmatic.*

ō·pin'iŏn·āte, *a.* same as *opinionated.*

ō·pin'iŏn·ā·ted, *a.* holding unreasonably or obstinately to one's own opinions.

Syn.—stubborn, dogmatic.

ō·pin'iŏn·āte·ly, *adv.* obstinately.

ō·pin'iŏn·ȧ·tist, *n.* an opinionated person. [Obs.]

ō·pin'iŏn·ȧ·tive, *a.* 1. opinionated.

2. of the nature of an opinion; consisting in opinion.

ō·pin'iŏn·ȧ·tive·ly, *adv.* with undue fondness for one's own opinions; stubbornly.

ō·pin'iŏn·ȧ·tive·ness, *n.* excessive attachment to one's own opinions; obstinacy in opinion.

ō·pin'iŏn·ā·tŏr, *n.* one who is opinionated. [Obs.]

ō·pin'iŏned, *a.* attached to particular opinions; opinionated. [Rare.]

ō·pin'iŏn·ist, *n.* one fond of his own notions; one unduly attached to his own opinions.

ō·pi·oph'ȧ·ġiṣm, *n.* [*opium*, and Gr. *phagein*, to eat.] the habitual use or eating of opium.

ō·pi·oph'ȧ·ġy, *n.* opiophagism.

ō·pip'ȧ·rous, *a.* sumptuous. [Obs.]

ō·pip'ȧ·rous·ly, *adv.* sumptuously; abundantly. [Obs.]

op·i·som'ē·tēr, *n.* [Gr. *opisō*, backward, and *metron*, measure.] a device for measuring the length of a line that is curved or irregular, as the lines upon a map, by means of a thin wheel mounted upon a threaded axle and rolled along the line to be measured, and afterward rolled backwards along a straight, scaled line until it has returned to its original position.

ō·pis'thi·on, *n.* [Gr., hinder part.] the midpoint of the lower border of the foramen magnum.

ō·pis'thō-, ō·pis'th-, [Gr. *opisthen*, behind.] combining forms meaning *behind.*

ō·pis'thō·branch, *n.* [*opistho-*, and Gr. *branchia*, gills.] a mollusk belonging to the *Opisthobranchiata.*

Ō·pis·thō·bran·chi·ā'tȧ, Ō·pis·thō·bran'chi·ȧ, *n.pl.* a large order of gastropods usually having the gills located behind the region of the heart.

ō·pis·thō·bran'chi·āte, *a.* pertaining to the *Opisthobranchiata.*

ō·pis·thō·bran'chi·āte, *n.* one of the *Opisthobranchiata.*

ō·pis·thō·coe'li·ăn, ō·pis·thō·coe'lous, *a.* [*opistho-*, and Gr. *koilos*, hollow.] in anatomy, concave behind; specifically, designating vertebrae that are hollow on the posterior side, or animals having such vertebrae, as in the saurians of the suborder *Opisthocœlia.*

ō·pis'thō·dōme, *n.* same as *opisthodomos.*

ō·pis·thod'ō·mos, *n.* [*opistho-*, and Gr. *domos*, house.] in architecture, the same as the Roman posticum, being the enclosed space in the rear of a Greek temple.

ō·pis'thō·dont, *a.* [*opistho-*, and Gr. *odous*, *odontos*, tooth.] having back teeth only.

Ō·pis·thō·glyph'i·ȧ, *n.pl.* [*opistho-*, and Gr. *gluphein*, to carve.] a division of snakes that have grooves in some of the posterior maxillary teeth.

ō·pis·thō·glyph'iç, *a.* 1. pertaining or belonging to the *Opisthoglyphia.*

2. having grooves in the back teeth.

op·is·thog'nȧ·thous, *a.* [*opistho-*, and Gr. *gnathos*, jaw.] having receding jaws: opposed to *prognathous.*

ō·pis'thō·grȧph, *n.* [*opistho-*, and Gr. *graphein*, to write.] something that has had writing inscribed upon both sides, as a monument, manuscript, slab, etc.

op·is·thog'rȧ·phy, *n.* [*opistho-*, and Gr. *graphein*, to write.] a writing on the opposite side of what has already been written on, as a leaf or sheet.

Op·is·thō′mī, *n.pl.* [*opisth-*, and Gr. *ōmos*, shoulder.] an order of fishes resembling eels, in which the scapular arch is free from the skull.

ō·pis·thō·pul′mō·nāte, *a.* [*opistho-*, and L. *pulmo* (*-onis*), lung.] having the pulmonary sac in a posterior position, as in certain gastropods.

op·is·thot′iç, *a.* [*opisth-*, and Gr. *ōtikos*, of the ear.] situated behind the ear.

op·is·thot′iç, *n.* the opisthotic bone.

op·is·thot′ō·nos, *n.* [*opistho-*, and Gr. *teinein*, to stretch.] a muscular spasm in which the body bends backward and becomes rigid.

ō·pit·ū·lā′tion, *n.* [L. *opitulatio*, from *opitulari*, to help.] help; aid. [Obs.]

ō′pi·um, *n.* [L. *opium*; Gr. *opion*, from *opos*, vegetable juice.] a narcotic drug prepared from the juice of the unripe seed capsules of the opium poppy: it contains such alkaloids as morphine, codeine, and papaverine, and is used as an intoxicant and medicinally to relieve pain and produce sleep. A full dose is intoxicating and exhilarating, but its effects are dangerous and fatal if taken in large quantities. It is heavy, of a dense texture, of a brownish-yellow color, has a faint smell, and its taste is bitter and acrid.

OPIUM POPPY (*Papaver somniferum*)

ō′pi·um·işm, *n.* 1. opium addiction.
2. the condition resulting from this.

ō′pi·um pop′py, a plant, *Papaver somniferum*, with grayish-green leaves and large white or purple flowers, the source of opium.

op·ō·bal′săm, op·ō·bal′sȧ·mum, *n.* [Gr. *opos*, juice, and *balsamon*, the balsam tree.] balm of Gilead.

op·ō·del′doç, *n.* [probably an arbitrary name coined by Paracelsus; the first part of the word is perhaps the Gr. *opos*, vegetable juice.]
1. a kind of plaster. [Obs.]
2. a saponaceous camphorated liniment; a solution of soap in ardent spirits, with the addition of camphor and essential oils.

ō·pop′ȧ·nax, *n.* [Gr., from *opos*, juice, and *panax*, a plant.]
1. a gum resin formerly of importance in medicine and still used to some extent in perfumery. It has a strong smell and an acrid taste and is obtained from the root of an umbelliferous plant, *Opopanax chironium*, being formerly imported from Turkey and the East Indies.
2. [O–] a genus of tropical and subtropical plants of the parsley family.

ō·por′i·cē, *n.* [from Gr. *opōra*, autumnal fruits.] a medicine composed of several autumnal fruits, particularly of quinces, pomegranates, etc., and wine, formerly administered in dysentery, diseases of the stomach, etc.

ō·pos′sum, *n.*; *pl.* **ō·pos′sumş** or **ō·pos′sum,** [N. Am. Ind., lit., white beast.] a small, tree-dwelling member of *Didelphys*, a genus of marsupial omnivorous mammals, characterized by three kinds of teeth, viz., incisors, canines, and molars, by posterior hands, and a long prehensile tail. They are fetid and nocturnal animals and pretend to be dead when trapped. The females have an abdominal pouch in which are the mammae, and in which they enclose their young. Also called *possum*.

OPOSSUM (15 in. long)

ō·pos′sum mouse, the pygmy petaurist, *Acrobates pygmæus*, a small Australian mammal.

ō·pos′sum shrimp, a shrimplike crustacean of the genus *Mysis*, the female of which carries her eggs in a pouch between the legs.

op·ō·ther′ȧ·py, *n.* in medicine, treatment of disease with animal extracts, chiefly of the glands of internal secretion, as the thyroid, adrenals, and pituitary body; organotherapy.

op′pi·dăn, *n.* [L. *oppidanus*, from *oppidum*, a city or town.]
1. an inhabitant of a town.
2. at Eton College in England, a student who boards in town.

op′pi·dăn, *a.* pertaining to a town; urban.

op·pig′nĕr·āte, *v.t.* to pledge; to pawn. [Obs.]

op′pi·lāte, *v.t.*; oppilated, *pt.*, *pp.*; oppilating, *ppr.* [L. *oppilare*; *ob*, before, and *pilare*, drive.] to fill with obstructions; to block, as the pores, bowels, etc.

op·pi·lā′tion, *n.* an oppilating or being oppilated.

op′pi·lā·tive, *a.* obstructive.

op·plēte′, op·plēt′ed, *a.* filled; crowded. [Obs.]

op·plē′tion, *n.* the act of filling up; the state of being full. [Obs.]

op·pōne′, *v.t.* to oppose. [Obs.]

op·pō′nen·cy, *n.* 1. opposition; resistance.
2. the opening of an academical disputation; the proposition of objections to a tenet, as an exercise for a degree. [Obs.]

op·pō′nenş, *n.*; *pl.* **op·pō·nen′tēş,** in anatomy, a muscle by the action of which a lateral digit of the hand or foot is placed in opposition to other digits; as, the *opponens pollicis*, which flexes and adducts the thumb.

op·pō′nent, *a.* [L. *opponens*, ppr. of *opponere*; *ob*, before or against, and *ponere*, to set, put, or lay; that is, to thrust against.]
1. opposite; standing in the front or way.
2. opposing; antagonistic; adverse; as, *opponent* lawyers.
3. in anatomy, bringing parts into opposition, as an opponens.

op·pō′nent, *n.* 1. one who opposes; one who supports the opposite side in a fight, game, cause, controversy, or argument; an adversary; an antagonist.

For, while his *opponents* were united, his adherents were divided. —Macaulay.

2. one who attacks some thesis or proposition; one who opens a dispute or argument by raising objections to a tenet or doctrine; correlative to *defendant* or *respondent*. [Obs.]

How becomingly does Philopolis exercise his office, and seasonably commit the *opponent* with the respondent, like a long practised moderator. —More.

op·pŏr·tūne′, *a.* [ME.; L. *opportunus*; literally, at or before the port; prefix *op* for *ob*, and *portus*, a port, harbor, haven.]
1. right for the purpose; fitting in regard to circumstances: said of time.
2. happening or done at the right time; seasonable; convenient; timely; well-timed.

The most *opportune* place, the strongest suggestion. —Shak.

op·pŏr·tūne′, *v.t.* to suit. [Obs.]

op·pŏr·tūne′ly, *adv.* in an opportune manner; seasonably; conveniently.

op·pŏr·tūne′ness, *n.* the state or quality of being opportune.

op·pŏr·tūn′işm, *n.* the policy or habit of adapting one's actions, thought, and utterances to circumstances, as in politics, in order to further one's immediate interests, without regard for basic principles or eventual consequences.

op·pŏr·tūn′ist, *n.* 1. one who endeavors to turn circumstances to his advantage; one who adopts the principles of opportunism.
2. [O–] a member of a section of the French Republican party led by Gambetta, advocating a policy in conformity to circumstances.

op·pŏr·tūn′ist, *a.* same as *opportunistic*.

op·pŏr·tūn·ist′iç, *a.* of an opportunist or opportunism.

op·pŏr·tū′ni·ty, *n.*; *pl.* **op·pŏr·tū′ni·tieş,** 1. fit or convenient time or occasion; a combination of circumstances favorable for the purpose; suitable time, combined with other favorable circumstances.

A wise man will make more *opportunities* than he finds. —Bacon.

2. convenience; fitness. [Obs.]
3. importunity; earnestness. [Obs.]

Syn.—occasion.—An *occasion* is that which falls in the way, or presents itself in the course of events; an *opportunity* is a convenience or fitness of time, place, etc., for the doing of a thing.

op·pōş·ȧ·bil′i·ty, *n.* the quality or condition of being opposable.

op·pōş′ȧ·ble, *a.* 1. capable of being opposed or resisted.
2. capable of being placed opposite something else.

op·pōş′ăl, *n.* opposition. [Obs.]

op·pōşe′, *v.t.*; opposed, *pt.*, *pp.*; opposing, *ppr.* [ME. *opposen*; OFr. *opposer*, from *poser*, to put in position; L. *pausare*, to pause, confused in meaning by association in LL. with *positus*, pp. of *ponere*, to place, put.]
1. to place in front; to offer to full view.

Her grace sat down
In a rich chair of state; *opposing* freely
The beauty of her person to the people. —Shak.

2. to set against; to place as an obstacle; to put in opposition, with a view to counterbalance or countervail.

I may without presumption *oppose* my single opinion to his. —Locke.

3. to act against; to resist, by physical force, by arguments, or other means; to withstand; to act as an opponent to; to object to.

It seems very senseless for a union to *oppose* piecework. —John Graham Brooks.

Syn.—combat, withstand, resist, contradict, deny, oppugn, contravene, check, obstruct.

op·pōşe′, *v.i.* to act adversely; to bring opposition: often with *to* or *against*.

A servant, thrill'd with remorse,
Opposed against the act. —Shak.

op·pōşe′less, *a.* irresistible. [Rare.]

op·pōş′ĕr, *n.* one who opposes; an opponent.

op·pos′it, *v.t.* and *v.i.* to deny; to assume the truth of the contrary. [Rare.]

op′pō·şite, *a.* [ME.; OFr.; L. *oppositus*, pp. of *opponere*; see *opponent*.]
1. opposed to.
2. set against; in a contrary position or direction (often with *to*).
3. characterized by hostility or resistance.
4. extremely different; exactly contrary; antithetical.
5. in botany, (a) growing in pairs, but separated by a stem; (b) having one part before another, as a stamen in front of a petal.
6. in logic, differing in quantity or quality, or in both, as propositions.

OPPOSITE LEAVES (*Veronica chamædrys*)

Syn.—opposed, hostile, antagonistic, facing, contradictory, contrary.

op′pō·şite, *n.* anything opposed.

op′pō·şite, *adv.* on opposing sides; in opposite positions; specifically, in the theater, in a complementary role (of the opposite sex) to; as, he played *opposite* her.

op′pō·şite, *prep.* fronting; across from.

op′pō·şite·ly, *adv.* in an opposite or adverse manner; in a situation to face each other; adversely; against each other.

op′pō·şite·ness, *n.* the state of being opposite.

op′pō·şite num′bĕr, a person having a position, rank, etc. comparable with that of another in a different place, organization, or situation.

op·pos″i·ti·fō′li·ous, *a.* opposite a leaf.

op·pō·şi′tion (-zish′un), *n.* [ME. *opposicioun*; OFr.; L. *oppositio*, from *oppositus*, pp. of *opponere*; see *opposite*.]
1. an opposing or being opposed.
2. resistance; contradiction; contrast; hostility.
3. anything that opposes.
4. [*sometimes* O–] a minority political party serving as a check on the party in power.
5. in astrology and astronomy, the position of two heavenly bodies when their longitudes differ by 180°; especially, such position of a planet with respect to the sun.
6. in law, the refusal of a creditor to assent to a debtor's release under the bankruptcy law.
7. in logic, the relation of exclusion or inclusion which exists between propositions having the same subject and predicate but differing in quality, quantity, or both.
8. in rhetoric, a counter proposition. [Obs.]
9. in chess, the position in which one king prevents the advance of the other king.
10. a position of guard in fencing.

Syn.—resistance, hostility, obstacle, obstruction, antipathy.

op·pō·şi′tion·ist, *n.* a member of the party opposing the administration.

op·pos″i·ti·pet′ăl·ous, *a.* opposite a petal: said of a stamen.

op·pos″i·ti·sep′ăl·ous, *a.* opposite a sepal: said of a stamen.

op·poş′i·tive, *a.* capable of being put in opposition.

op·press′, *v.t.*; oppressed (-prest), *pt.*, *pp.*; oppressing, *ppr.* [ME. *oppressen*; OFr. *oppresser*; ML. *oppressare*, from L. *oppressus*, pp. of *opprimere*, to press against.]
1. to weigh heavily on the mind, spirits, or senses of; to lie heavily on; to burden.

2. to keep down by the cruel or unjust use of power or authority; to burden with harsh, rigorous impositions; to tyrannize over.

3. (a) to crush; to trample down; (b) to overpower; to subdue. [Obs.]

4. to ravish. [Obs.]

op·pres′sion (-presh′un), *n.* 1. the act of oppressing; the imposition of unreasonable burdens, either in taxes or services; excessively rigorous government; severity.

2. the state of being oppressed or overburdened; misery.

3. that which oppresses; hardship; calamity.

4. depression; a feeling of being weighed down; physical or mental distress.

op·press′ive, *a.* 1. hard to put up with; burdensome.

2. cruelly overbearing; tyrannical.

3. weighing heavily on the mind, spirits, or senses; causing physical or mental distress.

Syn.—heavy, overpowering, unjust, galling, extortionate, grinding.

op·press′ive·ly, *adv.* in an oppressive manner.

op·press′ive·ness, *n.* the quality of being oppressive.

op·press′ŏr, *n.* one who oppresses; a tyrant.

op·pres′sūre (-presh′ẽr), *n.* oppression. [Obs.]

op·prō′bri·ous, *a.* 1. containing or expressive of opprobrium; reproachful and contemptuous; scurrilous; abusive.

2. deserving opprobrium; disgraceful; infamous.

Syn.—hateful, infamous, disgraceful, offensive, abusive, scurrilous.

op·prō′bri·ous·ly, *adv.* in an opprobrious manner.

op·prō′bri·ous·ness, *n.* opprobrium.

op·prō′bri·um, *n.* [L. *ob*, upon, and *probrum*, disgrace.]

1. the disgrace attached to shameful conduct or status; reproach mingled with contempt or disdain.

2. a source of disgrace; anything bringing shame.

Syn.—disgrace, ignominy, reproach.

op·prō′bry, *n.* opprobrium. [Obs.]

op·pūgn′ (-pūn′), *v.t.*; oppugned, *pt.*, *pp.*; oppugning, *ppr.* [L. *oppugnare*; *ob*, against, and *pugnare*, from *pugna*, a fight.] to oppose with argument; to reason against; to criticize adversely; to call in question; to controvert; to conflict with.

Syn.—oppose.

op·pug′năn·cy, *n.* the quality or state of being oppugnant; opposition; resistance.

op·pug′nănt, *a.* hostile; antagonistic; opposing; resisting.

op·pug′nănt, *n.* one who oppugns. [Rare.]

op·pug·nā′tion, *n.* opposition; resistance. [Rare.]

op·pūgn′ẽr (-pūn′), *n.* one who opposes or oppugns; that which opposes.

Ops, *n.* [L., lit., strength, riches.] in Roman mythology, the wife of Saturn and goddess of the harvest: identified with the Greek Rhea.

op·sim′ȧ·thy, *n.*; *pl.* **op·sim′ȧ·thieṣ**, [Gr. *opse*, late, and *mathein*, to learn.] late education; education late in life. [Rare.]

op·si·om′e·tẽr, *n.* [Gr. *opsis*, sight, and *metron*, measure.] an optometer.

-op′sis, [Gr. *-opsis*, from *opsis*, a sight, appearance.] a combining form meaning *sight* or *view*, as in syn*opsis*.

op·sō·mā′ni·ȧ, *n.* [Gr. *opson*, a dainty, and *mania*, madness.] the excessive love of some particular article of food.

op·sō·mā′ni·aç, *n.* one afflicted with opsomania.

op·son′iç, *a.* of, or having the effect of, opsonin.

op·son′iç in′dex, the ratio of the number of bacteria destroyed by phagocytes in an individual's blood serum to the number destroyed in a normal blood serum.

op·son″i·fi·çā′tion, *n.* the act, process, or result of opsonifying.

op·son′i·fȳ, *v.t.*; opsonified, *pt.*, *pp.*; opsonifying, *ppr.* to make bacteria more liable to destruction by phagocytes: said of opsonins.

op′sō·nin, *n.* in biology, a substance in the blood that renders pathogenic bacteria more liable to destruction by phagocytes.

op′sō·nīze, *v.t.*; opsonized, *pt.*, *pp.*; opsonizing, *ppr.* to form opsonins in.

opt, *v.i.*; opted, *pt.*, *pp.*; opting, *ppr.* [Fr. *opter*, from L. *optare*.]

1. to decide upon, or to choose.

2. to decide upon or choose one's citizenship: used in this sense in the case of an inhabitant of a territory which has been ceded to another country or government. The inhabitant then chooses either to remain a citizen of the first country holding this territory, or to change his citizenship.

op′tȧ·ble, *a.* desirable. [Obs.]

opt′ănt, *n.* 1. one who makes a choice; a chooser.

2. in central Europe, a citizen by choice.

op′tāte, *v.t.* to choose; to wish for; to desire. [Obs.]

op·tā′tion, *n.* a desiring; the expression of a wish. [Rare.]

op′tȧ·tive, *a.* [L. *optativus*, from *optare*, to desire.]

1. expressing wish or desire.

2. designating or of the grammatical mood in Greek, etc. which expresses wish or desire.

op′tȧ·tive, *n.* 1. something to be desired. [Obs.]

2. the optative mood of a verb.

3. a verb in this mood.

op′tȧ·tive·ly, *adv.* 1. in an optative manner; by desire.

2. by means of the optative mood; in the optative mood.

op′tiç, *a.* [Fr. *optique*, from Gr. *optikos*, from root *op*, seen in *opsomai*, I shall see.]

1. relating or pertaining to vision or sight; pertaining to the eye; ocular; as, an *optic* ganglion.

2. relating to the science of optics; optical. [Archaic.]

optic angle; (a) the angle included between the two lines drawn from the two extremities of an object to the optic center of the crystalline lens of the eye; the visual angle; (b) the angle which the optic axes of the eyes make with one another as they tend to meet at some distance before the eyes.

optic axis; in a crystal not having the same properties in all directions with regard to light, the direction or directions along which there is no double refraction.

optic foramen; the foramen of the sphenoid bone through which the optic nerves and vessels pass.

optic lobes; the corpora bigemina or quadrigemina, one or two pairs of lobes or tubercles in the brain of a mammal.

optic nerves; the second pair of nerves of the brain, springing from the crura of the medulla oblongata and passing thence to the retina of the eye; the nerves of sight.

optic thalamus; a mass of gray matter located at the base of the brain on either side, functioning as a visual center.

op′tiç, *n.* 1. an organ of sight; an eye. [Colloq.]

2. an eyeglass; a magnifying glass. [Obs.]

op′tiç·ăl, *a.* 1. of or connected with the sense of sight; visual; ocular.

2. of the relation between light and vision.

3. having to do with optics.

4. made to give help in seeing; as, *optical* instruments.

optical activity; the ability of certain substances to rotate the plane of polarization when transmitting polarized light.

optical circle; a circle graduated for use in optical investigations, as for determining the angle of refraction.

optical square; an instrument used in surveying, for laying out lines at right angles to each other. It consists of a circular brass box containing index and horizon glasses, fixed at an angle of 45°.

op′tiç·ăl·ly, *adv.* by optics or sight.

op·ti′ciăn (-tish′ăn), *n.* 1. one skilled in the science of optics. [Obs.]

2. one who makes or sells eyeglasses and other optical instruments.

op′tiçs, *n.pl.* [*construed as sing.*] that branch of physics which treats of the nature and properties of light and vision.

op′ti·grȧph, *n.* [Gr. *optikos*, of seeing, and *graphein*, to write.] a telescope made for the purpose of copying landscapes.

op′ti·mȧ·cy, *n.* [L. *optimates*, the nobility, from *optimus*, best.]

1. the body of nobles; the nobility. [Rare.]

2. government by the aristocracy. [Rare.]

op′ti·māte, *a.* [L. *optimates*, the nobility.] pertaining to the optimacy.

op′ti·māte, *n.* an aristocrat.

op·ti·mā′tēṣ, *n.pl.* [L.]

1. the Roman nobility.

2. an aristocracy.

op′ti·mē, *n.* [L., very well.] one who stands in the second or third rank of honors in the mathematical tripos, immediately after the wranglers, at Cambridge University, England.

op′ti·miṣm, *n.* [Fr. *optimisme*; L. *optimus*, best.]

1. in philosophy, (a) the doctrine of Leibnitz that the existing world is the best possible; (b) the doctrine or belief that good ultimately prevails over evil.

2. the tendency to take the most hopeful view of matters or to expect the best outcome in any circumstances; practice of looking on the bright side of things: opposed to *pessimism*.

op′ti·mist, *n.* 1. one who believes in optimism.

2. one who has a sanguine temperament; one who is hopeful.

op·ti·mis′tiç, *a.* 1. pertaining to optimism.

2. hopeful; cheerful; sanguine.

op·ti·mis′tiç·ăl·ly, *adv.* with optimism; in an optimistic manner.

op·tim′i·ty, *n.* the state of being best. [Rare.]

op′ti·mīze, *v.t.*; optimized, *pt.*, *pp.*; optimizing, *ppr.* to regard with optimism.

op′ti·mīze, *v.i.* 1. to hold or express the belief or doctrines of an optimist.

2. to make a practice of being optimistic; to be hopeful.

op′ti·mum, *n.*; *pl.* **op′ti·mumṣ, op′ti·mȧ**, [L., neut. of *optimus*, best.]

1. the best or most favorable degree, condition, amount, etc.

2. in biology, the amount of heat, light, moisture, food, etc. most favorable for growth and reproduction.

op′ti·mum, *a.* best; most favorable.

op′tion, *n.* [L. *optio*, option, from *optare*, to wish or desire.]

1. a choosing; choice.

2. the power, right, or liberty of choosing.

3. something that is or can be chosen.

4. the right, acquired for a consideration, to buy or sell something at a fixed price within a specified time.

5. in the Church of England, a choice which an archbishop had of any one ecclesiastical preferment in the gift of any of his suffragan bishops after they had been consecrated by him. The custom is now abolished.

6. a wishing; a wish. [Obs.]

op′tion·ăl, *a.* left to one's wish or choice; depending on choice or preference; not compulsory; elective.

op′tion·ăl, *n.* an elective course, study, or exercise.

op′tion·ăl·ly, *adv.* by or with the privilege of choice.

op′tō·coele, op·tō·coe′li·ȧ, *n.* a cavity in the optic lobe of the brain of certain animals.

op′tō·gram, *n.* an image on the retina due to bleaching of the visual purple.

op·tog′rȧ·phy, *n.* the act or process of producing an optogram.

op·tom′ē·tẽr, *n.* [Gr. *optikos*, of seeing, and *metron*, measure.] an instrument for measuring the range and power of distinct vision, and consequently for determining the focal lengths of lenses necessary to correct nearsightedness or farsightedness.

op·tom′ē·trist, *n.* one skilled in the science of optometry.

op·tom′ē·try, *n.* 1. the measurement of the range and power of vision.

2. examination of the eyes (without the use of drugs or medicine) for nearsightedness, farsightedness, etc., and the fitting of glasses to correct these defects; work of an optometrist.

op′tō·phōne, *n.* an instrument which, by combining a selenium cell and telephone apparatus, converts light energy into sound energy, enabling a blind person to locate and estimate varying degrees of light through the ear, and thus to read ordinary printed matter.

op·tō·tech′niçs, *n.* the technology of lenses, optometers, and other optical instruments and apparatus.

op′tō·tȳpe, *n.* [Gr. *optikos*, of seeing, and *typos*, type.] type by which to test the eyesight.

op′ū·lence, *n.* [L. *opulentia*, from *opes*, wealth.]

1. wealth; riches.

2. abundance.

op′ū·len·cy, *n.* opulence.

op′ū·lent, *a.* [L. *opulentus*.]

1. wealthy; rich; affluent; having a large estate or property.

2. profuse; copious; abundant; unstinted.

op′ū·lent·ly, *adv.* in an opulent manner.

Ō·pun′ti·ȧ (-shi-), *n.* [from *Opus*, a city of Locris, where some of the species are plentiful.]

1. a large genus of cacti with red, purple,

or yellow flowers and fleshy or dry berries, including the prickly pears, or Indian figs.

2. [o–] any plant of this genus.

ō·pun·ti·ā′cē·ae, *n.pl.* [*opuntia* and *-aceæ.*] same as *Cactaceæ.*

ō′pus, *n.*; *pl.* **op′e·rȧ,** now also **ō′pus·eṣ,** [L., a work.] a work; composition: the term when applied to a musical composition is followed by a number showing its place in order of composition or publication among the works of the composer.

ō·pus′çle, *n.* same as *opuscule.*

ō·pus′çūle, *n.* [L. *opusculum.*] a small or trivial work or composition.

ō·pus′çū·lum, *n.*; *pl.* **ō·pus′çū·lȧ,** same as *opuscule.*

-ō′py, -opia.

ō·quas′sȧ, *n.* [Am. Ind.] the blueback trout, *Salvelinus* or *Salmo oquassa,* a small trout with a red-spotted, dark-blue body, found in the lakes of Maine.

-ŏr, [ME. *-our*; OFr. *-our, -or, -eur*; L. *-or, -ator.*] a noun-forming suffix meaning *a person* or *thing that,* as in invent*or,* jur*or,* tract*or.*

-ŏr, [ME. and OFr. *-our*; L. *-or.*] a noun-forming suffix meaning *quality* or *condition,* as in horr*or,* err*or,* fav*or*: in British usage, often *-our.*

ọr, *conj.* [ME., in form a contr. of *other, auther,* either, but actually, from AS. *oththe* (in *āther... oththe,* either... or).] a co-ordinating conjunction introducing an alternative; specifically, (a) introducing the second of two choices; as, I'll offer him beer *or* wine; (b) introducing any of the choices in a series, but usually used only before the last; as, apples, (*or*) pears, (*or*) peaches, *or* plums; (c) introducing a synonymous word or phrase; as, botany, *or* the science of plants; (d) introducing the second of two choices when the first is introduced by *either* or *whether*; as, *either* go *or* stay, *whether* to go *or* stay; (e) in poetry, sometimes substituted for *either* as the first correlative; as, "*or* in the heart *or* in the head."

ọr, *conj.* and *prep.* [ME.; AS. *ar,* var. of *ær,* ere.] before; ere. [Archaic or Dial.]

or ever; before ever. [Archaic.]

ọr, *n.* [Fr. *or,* L. *aurum,* gold.] in heraldry, gold or yellow, represented in engraving by dots powdered over a plain field.

OR

ō′rȧ, *n.* plural of *os* (a mouth).

ō′rȧ, *n.* a money of account among the Anglo-Saxons, valued in the Domesday Book at twenty pence sterling.

ō·rȧ·bäs′sū, *n.* a small monkey of South America of the genus *Callithrix.*

or′ăch, or′ăche, *n.* [Fr. *arroche,* corrupted from L. *atriplex,* the orach.] a garden plant of the genus *Atriplex,* with red or green leaves, sometimes used as a vegetable.

or′ȧ·çle, *n.* [ME.; OFr.; L. *oraculum,* a divine announcement, an oracle, a prophecy, from *orare,* to speak, also to pray, beseech, entreat, from *os, oris,* the mouth.]

1. among the ancient Greeks and Romans, the place where or medium by which deities were consulted.

2. the revelation or response of a medium or priest.

3. (a) any person or agency believed to be in communication with a deity; (b) any person of great knowledge; (c) opinion or statements of such a person.

4. the holy of holies of the ancient Jewish Temple: 1 Kings. vi. 16, 19–23.

5. [*pl.*] the Scriptures.

or′ȧ·çle, *v.i.*; oracled, *pt., pp.*; oracling, *ppr.* to utter oracles. [Rare.]

ō·raç′ū·lăr, *a.* 1. uttering oracles; as, an *oracular* tongue.

2. of, or having the nature of, an oracle; grave; venerable; like an oracle; as, an *oracular* shade.

> They have something venerable and *oracular* in that unadorned gravity and shortness in the expression. —Pope.

3. very wise; prophetic; mysterious; obscure; ambiguous; like the oracles of classical deities.

ō·raç′ū·lăr·ly, *adv.* in the manner of an oracle; authoritatively; positively.

ō·raç′ū·lous, *a.* oracular. [Now Rare.]

ō′rad, *adv.* [L. *os, oris,* mouth, and *ad,* to.] toward the mouth.

ō′răl, *a.* [Fr., from L. *os, oris,* the mouth.]

1. uttered by the mouth, or in words; spoken, not written; as, *oral* traditions; *oral* testimony; *oral* law.

2. of speech; using speech.

3. of, at, or near the mouth.

4. in phonetics, having mouth resonance only: distinguished from *nasal.*

5. in zoology, on or of the same side as the mouth.

ō′răl, *n.* an oral examination, as in a university.

ō·rā′lē, *n.* [LL., from L. *os, oris,* mouth.] a striped veil worn by the Pope at some ceremonies: it is a form of the fanon.

ō′răl his′tō·ry, 1. historical data consisting of personal recollections, usually in the form of an interview recorded on magnetic tape.

2. the gathering and preservation of such data.

ō′răl·iṣm, *n.* the oral method of instruction of the deaf, etc.

ō′răl·ly, *adv.* 1. by word of mouth; in spoken words, without writing; as, traditions derived *orally* from ancestors.

2. by the mouth.

ō·ral′ō·ġy, *n.* the science that treats of the mouth, especially in regard to the teeth, their preservation, and prevention of decay.

ō·rang′, *n.* an orangutan.

or′ănġe (*or* -inj), *n.* [ME. and OFr. *orenge*; Pr. *auranja,* from Sp. *naranja,* from Ar. *nāranj,* an orange. The initial *n* was no doubt lost through a sort of confusion between it and the *n* of the article *une.*]

1. a tree of the genus *Citrus,* the *Citrus aurantium.* The orange is supposed to be native to India and China, but is now cultivated abundantly in the United States, Italy, Spain, Portugal, and other parts of the south of Europe, as also in the Azores. It is a middle-sized evergreen tree, with a greenish-brown bark and white, fragrant blossoms. The leaves are ovate, acute, pointed, and at the base of the petiole are winged. The fruit is globose and reddish-yellow and contains a pulp which consists of a collection of oblong vesicles filled with a sugary and refreshing juice; it is divided into eight or ten compartments, each containing several seeds. The principal varieties are the common sweet or China, the bitter or Seville, the Maltese or red-pulped, the Tangerine, the Mandarin or clove, and the St. Michael's. The leaves, flowers, and rind yield fragrant oils much used in perfumery. The wood is fine-grained, compact, susceptible of a high polish, and is employed in the arts. Several varieties of the orange are extensively grown in the United States, especially in the states of California and Florida.

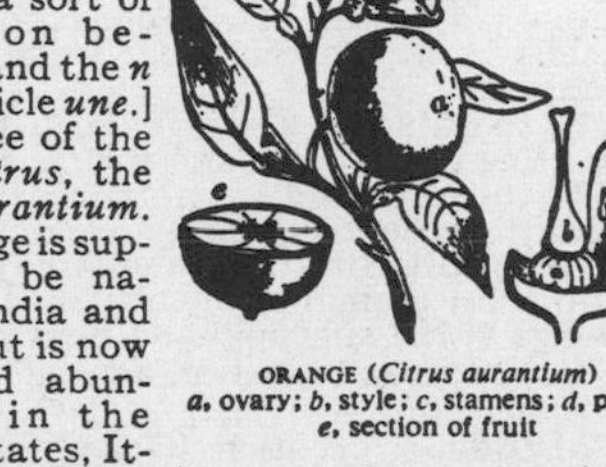

ORANGE (*Citrus aurantium*)
a, ovary; *b,* style; *c,* stamens; *d,* petal; *e,* section of fruit

2. the fruit of this tree.

3. any of several shrubs resembling this tree.

4. a reddish-yellow color, like that of an orange.

native orange; see *orange thorn.*

or′ănġe, *a.* 1. of or pertaining to an orange or oranges.

2. of the color of an orange; reddish-yellow.

or′ănġe·āde′, *n.* a drink made of orange juice mixed with water and sugar, usually iced.

or·ăn·geat′ (-zhat′), *n.* [Fr.] 1. orange peel covered with candy.

2. orangeade.

or′ănġe blos′sŏm, the pure white blossom of the orange tree, often worn by brides as typical of purity.

Or′ănġe·iṣm, *n.* the tenets or principles and practices of the Orangemen.

Or′ănġe·măn, *n.*; *pl.* **Or′ănġe·men,** [named after William III of England, Prince of *Orange.*] a member of a secret society instituted in northern Ireland in 1795, to uphold the Protestant religion and ascendancy.

or′ănġe oil, an oil obtained from the rind of the orange, used in perfumery.

or′ănġe peel, the rind or peel of an orange separated from the fruit. It is dried and candied, and used as a stomachic, and in flavoring puddings, cakes, etc.

or′ănġe pē′kōe, a black tea grown in Ceylon and India.

or′ăn·ġẽr, *n.* a ship engaged in carrying oranges. [Rare.]

or′ănġe·root, *n.* an American herb, *Hydrastis canadensis*: also called *goldenseal.*

or′ăn·ġẽr·y, *n.*; *pl.* **or′ăn·ġẽr·ieṣ,** [Fr. *orangerie.*] a place for raising oranges; a plantation of orange trees: usually with reference to a hothouse or other sheltered place used to grow orange trees in cooler climates.

or′ănġe sçāle, any scale insect, as *Mytilaspis citricola,* which infests the orange.

or′ănġe stick, a pointed stick of orangewood, used in manicuring.

or′ănġe-tąw″ny, *a.* of a color between yellow and brown.

or′ănġe-tąw″ny, *n.* a color between yellow and brown.

or′ănġe thorn, an Australian plant of the genus *Citriobatus.* Its fruit, which is about one and a half inches in diameter, is eaten by the natives: also called *native orange.*

or′ănġe tip, a butterfly having its wings tipped with orange.

or′ănġe wīfe, a woman who sells oranges.

or′ănġe·wood, *n.* the wood of the orange tree, used in woodwork, etc.

or′ănġe·wood, *a.* of orangewood.

or′ăn·ġīte, *n.* an orange-yellow variety of thorite found in Norway.

ORANGUTAN (4–5 ft. high)

ō·rang′ū·tan′, ō·rang′oū·tang′, *n.* [Malay *orangūtan*; *orang,* man, and *ūtan,* a forest, lit., man of the woods.] a large and powerful anthropoid ape, *Simia satyrus,* of Borneo and Sumatra. It is covered with reddish-brown hair, and, in structure, bears a close resemblance to man. It has very long arms, so that when the animal stands erect they reach nearly to the ground.

ō′rȧ prō nō′bis, [L.] pray for us: in the Roman Catholic liturgy, a plea to the Virgin Mary.

ō·rā′ri·ăn, *a.* [L. *orarius,* from *ora,* a shore.] pertaining to a coast.

ō·rā′ri·on, *n.*; *pl.* **ō·rā′ri·ȧ,** [from L. *orarium,* a napkin.] in the Orthodox Eastern Church, a deacon's stole.

ō·rāte′, *v.i.* and *v.t.*; orated, *pt., pp.*; orating, *ppr.* [L. *oratus,* pp. of *orare,* to speak.] to make (an oration); to indulge in high-sounding oratory; to say (something) in a pompous or bombastic manner: a humorously derogatory term.

ō·rā′tē frā′trēṣ, [L., pray, brethren.] in the celebration of Mass in the Roman Catholic Church, an exhortation to the people to pray to God for his acceptance of the Eucharistic oblation.

ō·rā′tion, *v.i.* to deliver an oration. [Colloq.]

ō·rā′tion, *n.* [ME. (Scot.) *oracione*; L. *oratio* (*-onis*), from *orare,* to speak.] an elaborate speech or discourse, composed according to the rules of oratory and delivered in public, and treating of some important subject in elevated and dignified language; an eloquent speech prepared beforehand and spoken in public: especially applied to a speech or discourse delivered on some important or special occasion.

> The great Athenian *orations.*—Macaulay.

Syn.—address, harangue, speech, discourse.

or′ȧ·tŏr, *n.* [ME. *oratour*; OFr. *orateur*; L. *orator.*]

1. a person who delivers an oration.

2. a public speaker, especially one who is eloquent and who has gained some distinction in the field of oratory.

3. in law, a petitioner; plaintiff.

4. in English universities, a public officer who acts as the spokesman of the university. He reads, writes, and records all letters of a public character, introduces distinguished personages on whom honorary degrees are about to be conferred, etc.

or·ȧ·tō′ri·ăl, *a.* oratorical. [Rare.]

or·ȧ·tō′ri·ăl·ly, *adv.* oratorically. [Rare.]

or·ȧ·tō′ri·ăn, *n.* a Father of the Oratory in the Roman Catholic Çhurch.

or·ȧ·tō′ri·ăn, *a.* oratorical. [Obs.]
or·ȧ·tor′iç, *a.* oratorical.
or·ȧ·tor′iç·ăl, *a.* 1. of or characteristic of orators or oratory; in the manner of an orator or oratory.
2. given to oratory.
or·ȧ·tor′iç·ăl·ly, *adv.* in an oratorical manner.
or·ȧ·tō′ri·ō, *n.*; *pl.* **or·ȧ·tō′ri·ōş,** [It., a small chapel, the place in which these musical compositions are said to have been first performed.]
1. a long, dramatic musical composition, usually on a religious theme, consisting of arias, recitatives, duets, trios, choruses, etc. sung to orchestral accompaniment: it is presented without stage action, scenery, or costumes.
2. the rendering of such a composition.
3. a chapel; an oratory.
or·ȧ·tō′ri·ous, *a.* oratorical. [Obs.]
or·ȧ·tō′ri·ous·ly, *adv.* oratorically. [Obs.]
or′ȧ·tŏr·īze, *v.i.*; oratorized, *pt.*, *pp.*; oratorizing, *ppr.* to act the orator; to give an oration. [Colloq.]
or′ȧ·tō·ry, *n.*; *pl.* **or′ȧ·tō·rieş,** [ME. *oratorie*; L. *oratoria.*]
1. the art of an orator; skill or eloquence in public speaking.
2. [ME. *oratorie*; LL. *oratorium*, from L. *oratorius*, of praying, from *orator.*] a small chapel, especially one for private prayer.
3. [O–] in the Roman Catholic Church, a religious society of secular priests, founded by Saint Philip Neri in 1564: also called *Fathers of the Oratory, Oratorians.*
or′ȧ·tress, *n.* an oratrix.
or′ȧ·trix, *n.* [L., f. of *orator*, speaker.] a woman orator.
ọrb, *n.* [OFr. *orbe*, blind, from L. *orbus*, bereft.] in architecture, a blind or blank window or panel. [Obs.]
ọrb, *n.* [from Fr. or L.; Fr. *orbe*; L. *orbis*, a circle.]
1. a sphere; globe.
2. (a) any of the heavenly spheres, as the sun, moon, etc.; (b) [Obs.] the earth; (c) [Obs.] the orbit of a planet, etc.
3. the eye or eyeball. [Poetic.]
4. a sphere surmounted by a cross, as a symbol of royal power.
5. (a) a sphere of activity; province; (b) rank; status. [Archaic.]
6. a collective body; organized whole.
7. anything circular in form; circle. [Rare.]
8. in astrology, the sphere of influence of a planet, star, or house.
9. one of the hollow and transparent globes or spheres, enclosed one within another and concentric, which were conceived by ancient astronomers to carry with them the planets in their revolutions. [Obs.]
10. a period or revolution of time. [Rare.]
ọrb, *v.t.*; orbed, *pt.*, *pp.*; orbing, *ppr.* 1. to form into a circle or sphere.
2. to enclose; to encircle; to surround. [Poet.]
ọrb, *v.i.* 1. to move in an orbit.
2. to be formed into an orb; to assume the appearance of an orb. [Poet.]
ọr′bāte, *a.* [L. *orbatus*, pp. of *orbare*, to bereave.] bereaved; fatherless; childless. [Obs.]
ọr·bā′tion, *n.* [L. *orbatio*, from *orbare*, to bereave.] privation of parents or children, or privation in general. [Obs.]
ọrbed, *a.* 1. round; circular; orbicular.
2. formed into the shape of an orb.
3. encircled or covered.
The wheels were *orbed* with gold.—Addison.
4. having orbs, or eyes; as, a bright-*orbed* maiden. [Poet.]
ọrb fish, a fish, *Chætodon orbis*, of a circular form, found in East Indian waters.
ọr′biç, *a.* spherical. [Rare.]
Ọr′biç·ū·lȧ, *n.* a genus of brachiopod shells, found in large masses on the coasts of Peru, Chile, and also in the northern seas. The shell consists of two unequal valves, one of which is round and conical, the other flat, and fixed on a rock. The animal has two short ciliated arms.
ọr·biç′ū·lăr, *a.* [Fr. *orbiculaire*, from L. *orbiculus*, a disk; *orbis*, circle.]
1. spherical; circular; in the form of an orb.
2. in botany, round and flat, as a leaf.
ọr·biç′ū·lăr·ly, *adv.* spherically.
ọr·biç′ū·lăr·ness, *n.* the state of being orbicular.
ọr·biç′ū·lāte, ọr·biç′ū·lā·ted, *a.* [L. *orbiculatus*, from *orbis*, circle.] orbicular.
ọr·biç′ū·lāte, *n.* anything in the form of an orb; specifically, in entomology, a round spot on the anterior wings of the noctuid moths.
ọr·biç·ū·lā′tion, *n.* the state of being made in the form of an orb.
Ọr·bil′i·us, *n.* a schoolmaster who is fond of whipping his pupils: so called after Orbilius, the tutor to Horace, the Roman poet.
ọr′bit, *n.* [Fr. *orbite*; L. *orbita*, a trace or track, from *orbis*, a wheel.]
1. in anatomy, the bony cavity in which the eye is situated.
2. in astronomy, the path described by a heavenly body in its periodical revolution; as, the *orbit* of Jupiter or Mercury; the *orbits* of the planets are elliptical.
3. the range of one's experience or activity; ordinary course of life.
4. in zoology, the skin which surrounds a bird's eye; the border around the compound eye of an insect.
ọr′bit·ăl, *a.* of or in an orbit.
orbital index; the ratio between the length and the greatest height of the orbit of the eye.
ọr′bit·ăr, *a.* orbital. [Rare.]
ọr′bit·ăr·y, *a.* orbital.
Ọr·bi·tē′lae, *n.pl.* [L. *orbis*, circle, and *tela*, web.] a division of spiders that spin round webs.
ọr′bi·tō-, [L. *orbis*, circle.] a combining form used to indicate *relation to* or *connection with an orbit*, particularly in medicine and anatomy.
Ọr″bi·tō·lī′tēş, *n.* [*orbito-*, and Gr. *lithos*, stone.] a genus of rhizopods having their shells in circular chamber form spirally arranged.
ọr″bi·tō·nā′şăl, *a.* [*orbito-*, and L. *nasus*, nose.] relating to the orbit and the nasal tract.
ọr″bi·tō·sphē′noid, *a.* relating to the orbit and the sphenoid bone.
ọr″bi·tō·sphē′noid, *n.* in anatomy, a bone of the third cranial segment, being one of the wings of the sphenoid and next to the orbit.
ọr″bi·tō·sphē·noid′ăl, *a.* relating to the orbitosphenoid.
ọr′bi·tūde, *n.* orbation. [Obs.]
ọrb′less, *a.* without an orb or orbs.
ọrb′līke, *a.* resembling an orb.
Ọr·bū·lī′nȧ, *n.* [L. *orbis*, circle.] a genus of very small rhizopods having round shells.
ọrb′y, *a.* 1. of, or having the form of, an orb.
2. revolving as an orb.
ọrç, ork, *n.* [L. *orca.*]
1. the grampus, or killer whale.
2. any dolphin whale resembling the grampus.
Ọr·çā′di·ăn, *a.* relating to or belonging to the Orkney Islands.
ọr′çȧ·net, *n.* same as *alkanet.*
ọr′cē·in, ọr′cē·ine, *n.* a red-brown dye, $C_{28}H_{24}O_7N_2$, obtained by treating orcinol with ammonia and oxygen.
ọr′chăl, ọr′chel, *n.* same as *orchil.*
ọr′chȧ·net, *n.* same as *alkanet.*
ọr′chărd, *n.* [ME.; AS. *orceard*, *ortgeard*; *ort* for *wyrt*, herb, and *geard*, garden.]
1. an area of land, generally enclosed, devoted to the cultivation of fruit trees, nut trees, etc.
2. such trees, collectively.
ọr′chărd grȧss, a heavy and high grass, *Dactylis glomerata*, growing most plentifully under shade and valuable as an early food for cattle.
ọr′chărd house, a hothouse in which fruit trees are grown: it is heated artificially when necessary, and is often placed with a southern exposure along a high wall.
ọr′chărd·ing, *n.* the cultivation of orchards.
ọr′chărd·ist, *n.* one who is skilled in or engaged in the cultivation of orchards.
ọr′chărd ō′ri·ōle, the common oriole of North America, *Icterus spurius*: also called *bastard Baltimore.*
ọr·chä′tȧ, *n.* a Spanish-American drink; milk of almonds.
ọr·chē·sog′rȧ·phy, *n.* [Gr. *orchēsis*, dance, and *-graphy.*] the theory of dancing; a treatise on dancing. [Rare.]
ọr′çhes·tĕr, *n.* same as *orchestra.*
ọr·çhes′ti·ăn, *n.* [Gr. *orchēstēs*, dancer.] a beach flea, or any of the crustacean amphipods of the genus *Orchestia.*
ọr′çhes·trȧ, *n.* [L.; Gr. *orchēstra*, from *orcheisthai*, to dance.]
1. in ancient Greek theaters, the semicircular space in front of the stage, used by the chorus.
2. in modern theaters, the narrow space in front of and below the stage, where the musicians sit: also called *orchestra pit.*
3. (a) the section of seats near the pit on the main floor of a theater; (b) the main floor of a theater.
4. (a) a group of musicians playing together; especially, a symphony orchestra; (b) the instruments of such a group.
ọr·çhes′trăl, *a.* pertaining to an orchestra; suitable for or performed by an orchestra; as, *orchestral* arrangement of music.
ọr′çhes·trāte, *v.t.* and *v.i.*; orchestrated, *pt.*, *pp.*; orchestrating, *ppr.* to compose or arrange (music) for an orchestra.
ọr·çhes·trā′tion, *n.* arrangement of music for an orchestra; instrumentation.
ọr′çhes·tre (-tĕr), *n.* same as *orchestra.*
ọr·çhes′triç, *a.* orchestral.
ọr·çhes·trī′nȧ, *n.* an orchestrion.
ọr·çhes′tri·ŏn, *n.* a large, mechanical musical instrument, somewhat like a barrel organ, intended to imitate the various instruments of an orchestra.
ọr′çhi-, orchido-.
ọr·çhi·al′ġi·ȧ, *n.* [Gr. *orchis*, testicle, and *algos*, pain.] pain in a testicle.
ọr′çhid, *n.* [Gr. *orchis* (assumed stem *orchid-*).]
1. any plant of the family *Orchidaceae*; an orchidaceous plant.
2. the flower of such a plant; especially, any of the brightly colored tropical varieties cultivated for wear by women and regarded as a symbol of luxury.
3. a light bluish red.

ORCHID
(*Orchis mascula*)

ọr′çhid, *a.* light bluish-red.
Ọr·çhi·dā′cē·ae, *n.pl.* [Mod. L.] one of the most highly developed and well-defined families of plants in the vegetable kingdom, found in almost all parts of the world, chiefly perennial, herbaceous, and epiphytic. The flowers are very irregular, the perianth being formed of three sepals and three petals, the lowest of the latter being often very different in shape and markings from the rest, and called the labellum, or lip: both sepals and petals are often richly and similarly colored.
ọr·çhi·dā′ceous, *a.* 1. pertaining to the orchids; belonging to the family *Orchidaceæ.*
2. like an orchid in showiness, beauty, etc.
ọr·çhid′ē·ăl, ọr·çhid′ē·ăn, ọr·çhid′ē·ous, *a.* same as *orchidaceous.*
ọr′çhi·dō- [from hyp. word *orchidos*, falsely assumed genit. of Gr. *orchis*, testicle.] a combining form meaning: (a) *testicle*, as in *orchidotomy*; (b) *orchid*, as in *orchidology*. Also *orchi-* and, before a vowel, *orchid-.*
ọr·çhid·ol′ō·ġist, *n.* one versed in the knowledge of orchids.
ọr·çhid·ol′ō·ġy, *n.* [*orchido-* and *-logy*] the special branch of botany or of horticulture dealing with the cultivation of orchids.
ọr·çhi·dot′ō·my, *n.* [*orchido-* and *-tomy.*] surgery on the testicles.
ọr′çhil, *n.* archil, a purple dye or the lichen from which it is obtained: also *orchal, orchel.*
ọr·çhil′lȧ weed, same as *orchil.*
ọr′çhi·ō·cēle, *n.* [Gr. *orchis*, *orchios*, a testicle, and *kēlē*, a rupture.] in pathology, one of various diseases of the testicle and its envelopes, as scrotal hernia, tumor of the testicle, and hernia humoralis.
Ọr′çhis, *n.* [Gr. *orchis*, a testicle, from the shape of the roots.]
1. a genus of hardy perennials, with tuberous fleshy roots, type of the *Orchidaceæ.*
2. [o–] an orchid; specifically, a variety with small purplish or white flowers growing in loose spikes.
ọr·çhī′tis, *n.* [Gr. *orchis*, testicle, and *-itis.*] inflammation of a testis.
ọr·çhot′ō·my, *n.* [Gr. *orchis*, testicle, and *temnein*, *tamein*, to cut.] the operation of extracting a testicle; castration or semicastration.
ọr′cin, ọr′cine, *n.* same as *orcinol.*
ọr′cin·ōl, *n.* [from It. *orcello*, archil; and *-in* and *-ol.*] a colorless, crystalline compound, $C_6H_3 \cdot CH_3(OH)_2$, obtained from aloes, some lichens, etc., used as a medicine or in making dyes.

Ọr′çus, *n.* [L.] in Roman mythology, (a) the lower world; Hades; (b) Pluto; Dis.

ọr·dāin′, *v.t.*; ordained, *pt., pp.*; ordaining, *ppr.* [ME. *ordeinen*; OFr. *ordener*; Fr. *ordonner*, from L. *ordinare*, to order, from *ordo, ordinis*, order.]

1. to set in order; to arrange; to prepare. [Obs.]

All things that we *ordained* festival
Turn from their office to black funeral.
—Shak.

2. to decree; to order; to establish; to enact; to appoint.

And doth the power that man adores
Ordain their doom? —Byron.

3. to appoint or admit to the Christian ministry.

Syn.—install, institute, appoint, enact, decree.

ọr·dāin′á·ble, *a.* capable or worthy of ordination.

ọr·dāin′ẽr, *n.* one who ordains.

ọr·dāin′ment, *n.* appointment; ordination.

ọr·dā′li·ăn, *a.* characteristic of an ordeal. [Obs.]

ọr·dēal′ (*or* -dē′ăl), *n.* [ME. *ordal*; AS. *ordal, ordel*, judgment, decision, ordeal; like D. *oordeel*, G. *urtheil*, a judgment, decision, formed from a prepositional prefix meaning out (AS. *or*, Ice. *or*, Goth. *us*), and a verb meaning to deal, divide, distribute.]

1. an ancient form of trial in which the accused was exposed to physical dangers, which were supposed to be harmless to him if he was innocent.

2. any painful or distressing trial or test, as that endured under severe affliction, calamity, or bereavement; a severe trial.

ọr·dēal′, *a.* relating to trial by ordeal.

ọr·dēal′ bēan, the seed of the Calabar bean tree, *Physostigma venenosum*, of the family *Leguminosæ*.

ọr·dēal′ rọot, the poisonous root of a species of *Strychnos*, used as an ordeal by the natives of western Africa.

ọr·dēal′ tree, any one of several trees of South Africa, the poisonous properties of which are used by the natives in applying ordeals, as by poisoning arrows, waters, etc.

ọr′dẽr, *n.* [ME. and OFr. *ordre*, from L. *ordo, ordinis*, a straight row, a regular series; from root *or*, seen in *oriri*, to rise.]

1. social position; rank in the community.

2. a state of peace and serenity; observance of the law; orderly conduct.

3. the sequence or arrangement of things or events; series; succession.

4. a fixed or definite plan; system; law of arrangement.

5. a group or class set off from others by some trait or quality.

6. (a) a group of men constituting a military or monastic brotherhood; as, the *Order* of Knights Templars, the Franciscan *Order*; (b) an organized group of persons united by common interests or for social purposes, often in the form of a secret organization or lodge; as, the *Order* of the Eastern Star.

7. (a) a group of persons distinguished by having received a certain award or citation, as for outstanding service to a state; as, the *Order* of the Purple Heart; (b) the insignia or badge of such a group.

8. a state or condition in which everything is in its right place and functioning properly.

9. condition or state in general; as, the motor was in very poor *order*.

10. a command, direction, or instruction, usually backed by authority.

11. a class; a kind; a sort; a group determined by distinction or uniqueness; as, sentiments of a high *order*.

12. an established method or system, as of conduct or action in meetings, worship, court, etc.

13. (a) a request or commission to make or supply something; as, have you received my *order* for books?; (b) the goods so made or supplied; as, I delivered her grocery *order*.

14. in architecture, (a) any of several classical styles of structure, determined chiefly by the type of column; (b) a style of building.

15. in finance, written instructions to pay money or surrender property.

16. in law, a decision of a court or judge, usually not a final judgment.

17. in mathematics, the degree or stage of complexity of a sum or figure.

18. in military science, (a) [*pl.*] commands or announcements issued by the War Department or by military commanders; (b) the position of a rifle following the command *order arms*.

19. in scientific classification, a group in botany or zoology next larger than the family and smaller than the class.

20. in theology, (a) one of the nine classifications or grades of angels; (b) any rank or grade in the Christian clergy; (c) [*pl.*] the position of ordained minister; as, he took holy *orders*; (d) the ceremony of ordaining a minister.

21. in rhetoric, the placing of words and members in a sentence in such a manner as to contribute to force and beauty of expression, or to the clear illustration of the subject.

22. in ecclesiastical affairs, a book containing a collection of forms or a service to be followed on certain occasions.

INSIGNIA OF THE ORDER OF ST. MICHAEL AND ST. GEORGE

Benevolent and Protective Order of Elks; a benevolent and social order founded in the year 1868.

by order; in observance of an order given by someone.

close order; a troop formation in which individuals or units are separated by normal intervals and distances: opposed to *extended order*.

in order; (a) in proper sequence or position; (b) in good condition; (c) in accordance with the rules, as of a meeting; (d) appropriate to the occasion; suitable.

in order that; so that; to the end that.

in order to; for the purpose of; as a means to; to.

in short order; in a short time; without delay; quickly.

military order; (a) an association of officers or soldiers who formerly served together; (b) an order issued by a military officer.

on order; ordered, or requested, but not yet supplied.

on the order of; somewhat resembling; similar to.

order in council; in England, an order issued by the sovereign, by and with the advice of the privy council.

order of battle; the arrangement and disposition of the different parts of an army for battle.

Order of the Bath; an order of British knighthood, instituted in 1725 by George I.

order of the day; (a) the business regularly set down for consideration at any particular session of a legislative body, etc.; (b) in military usage, a general order, usually one of an exceptional nature, issued by a commander to his troops.

Order of the Garter; the highest order of British knighthood, instituted about 1344 by Edward III.

Order of the Purple Heart; a United States military order of soldiers wounded in action: instituted by George Washington as a medal of merit and revived in its present form in 1932.

out of order; (a) out of proper sequence or position; (b) not in operation; in poor condition; (c) not in accordance with the rules, as of a meeting; (d) not appropriate to the occasion; not suitable.

religious orders; religious societies or communities bound by solemn vows.

standing orders; certain general rules and instructions laid down by a legislature, a court, etc., for its own guidance, and which are to be invariably followed unless formally suspended to meet some urgent case.

to call to order; (a) to request to be quiet and busy at work; (b) to start (a meeting).

to order; in accordance with the specifications made by the purchaser.

ọr′dẽr, *v.t.*; ordered, *pt., pp.*; ordering, *ppr.* [ME. *ordren*, D. *ordenen*, G. *ordnen*, L. *ordinare*, to arrange.]

1. to arrange; to organize; to put or keep in order.

2. to regulate; to manage; to subject to rules or laws.

3. to instruct (another) to do something; to direct; to command; as, the general *ordered* his troops to advance.

4. to deal with; to treat. [Obs.]

5. to ordain; to admit to holy orders.

6. to request (something) to be supplied; as, to *order* a carload of goods.

order arms; a military command to bring the rifle to an upright position with its butt on the ground beside the right foot, and remain at attention; also, the position of the soldier when the act is performed.

ọr′dẽr, *v.i.* 1. to give a command; to issue orders.

2. to request that something be supplied.

ọr′dẽr·ẽr, *n.* a person or thing that orders.

ọr′dẽr·ing, *n.* disposition; distribution; management.

ọr′dẽr·less, *a.* without order.

ọr′dẽr·li·ness, *n.* the quality or state of being orderly.

ọr′dẽr·ly, *a.* 1. methodical; regular; in order; neat; tidy; well-arranged.

2. not unruly; well-behaved; law-abiding; peaceable; observant of order.

3. having to do with the transmission of military orders.

orderly book; in military usage, a book for each company, in which general and regimental orders are kept. [Brit.]

orderly officer; the officer of the day.

orderly room; the office room of a company, where the company records are kept and company business is conducted.

orderly sergeant; the first sergeant in a company.

ọr′dẽr·ly, *adv.* methodically; according to due order; regularly; according to rule. [Rare.]

ọr′dẽr·ly, *n.*; *pl.* **ọr′dẽr·lieṣ,** 1. a soldier assigned to a superior officer to carry orders and messages, and perform personal services.

2. a male hospital attendant.

3. one who sweeps the public streets in England.

ọr·di·ná·bil′i·ty, *n.* capability of being appointed. [Obs.]

ọr′di·ná·ble, *a.* such as may be appointed; ordainable. [Obs.]

ọr′di·năl, *a.* [Fr. *ordinal*; L. *ordinalis*.]

1. denoting order; as, the *ordinal* numbers, first, second, third, etc.: distinguished from *cardinal*.

2. relating to an order of plants and animals.

ọr′di·năl, *n.* 1. an ordinal number.

2. [*often* O–] a book of prescribed forms used in church services or certain church ceremonies.

ọr′di·năl·iṣm, *n.* the quality of being ordinal.

ọr′di·nănce, *n.* [It. *ordinanza*; Fr. *ordonnance*.]

1. a direction or command of an authoritative nature.

2. a custom or practice established by usage or authority.

3. an established religious rite; specifically, the Communion.

4. in law, a statute enacted by the legislative department of a city government.

5. preparation. [Obs.]

6. rank. [Obs.]

ọr′di·nănd, *n.* one about to be ordained.

ọr′di·nănt, *n.* one who ordains.

ọr′di·nănt, *a.* [L. *ordinans*, ppr. of *ordinare*, to ordain.] ordaining; decreeing. [Rare.]

ọr′di·nãr·i·ly, *adv.* usually; as a rule; in most cases; as, a winter more than *ordinarily* severe.

ọr·di·nãr′i·ness, *n.* the quality or condition of being ordinary.

ọr′di·nãr·y, *a.* [L. *ordinarius*, from *ordo* (*-inis*), order.]

1. regular; customary; usual; normal.

2. common; familiar; unexceptional.

ordinary seaman; (a) a sailor not expert or fully skilled, and hence ranking below an able-bodied seaman; (b) formerly, in the United States Navy, a seaman second class.

ọr′di·nãr·y, *n.*; *pl.* **ọr′di·nãr·ieṣ,** [ME. *ordinarie*; L. *ordinarius*, from *ordo*, an order.]

1. an official of church or court whose power or jurisdiction is original and not that of a deputy.

2. a book containing the form or order for divine service.

3. a set meal served from day to day at the same price.

4. a tavern.

5. a prison chaplain.

6. an early type of bicycle having wheels of different size.

7. in heraldry, any one of the major devices used as heraldic distinctions.
8. the common Mass. [Obs.]
9. whatever is ordinary or generally used.
in ordinary; (a) in actual service or attendance; as, a physician or minister *in ordinary* to some personage; (b) out of commission: applied to ships of war.
ordinary of arms; a dictionary of heraldry.
Ordinary of the Mass; in the Roman Catholic Church, those portions of the Mass which are not changed from day to day.
ordinary of the season; a church service appointed for an ordinary Sunday or weekday between certain dates.
out of the ordinary; unusual; extraordinary.

or'di·nār·y·ship, *n.* the state of being an ordinary; the office of an ordinary.

or'di·nāte, *a.* [L. *ordinatus*, well-ordered, ordained, from *ordinare*, to order or arrange, from *ordo, ordinis*, order.]
1. regular. [Rare.]
2. orderly; temperate. [Rare.]
3. in entomology, arranged in rows; as, *ordinate* spots on the wing of an insect.

or'di·nāte, *n.* in mathematics, one of two lines used in fixing a point on a geometric graph.

ORDINATE

ME or YO, ordinate of point M; OE or YM, abscissa of M; NN, axis of ordinates; DD, axis of abscissas

or'di·nāte, *v.t.* to ordain; to direct. [Obs.]

or'di·nāte·ly, *adv.* in a regular, methodical manner. [Rare.]

or·di·nā'tion, *n.* 1. the act of disposing or arranging in regular order; order; arrangement.
2. an ordaining or being ordained.
3. admission to the Christian ministry.
angle of ordination; in analytical geometry, the angle between the axes of co-ordinates.

or'di·nā·tive, *a.* directing; giving order. [Rare.]

or'di·nā·tŏr, *n.* one who ordains.

ord'nănce, *n.* [contraction from *ordinance*, in restricted meaning.]
1. artillery.
2. (a) all weapons and ammunition used in warfare; (b) any equipment or supplies used in servicing weapons.
Ordnance Department; in the United States Army, the department which furnishes and distributes ordnance and ordnance supplies.
Ordnance Survey; the official survey of Great Britain, carried out at the expense of the country by the Royal Engineers.

or'dō, *n.*; *pl.* **or·di·nēs'**, [L., order.]
1. order; arrangement.
2. [O-] in the Roman Catholic Church, an annual calendar that gives directions for each day's Mass and Office.

or'dŏn·nănce, *n.* [Fr.] 1. in the fine arts, the arrangement of the parts either in regard to the whole composition or to the several parts.
2. in France and other European countries, an ordinance, law, or decree.

or'dŏn·nănt, *a.* [Fr.] relating to ordonnance.

Or·dō'vi·ăn, *a.* same as *Ordovician.*

Or·dō·vi'ciăn (-vish'ăn), *a.* [from *Ordovices*, the Roman name of an ancient Celtic tribe in Wales.] designating or of the fourth period of the Paleozoic Era, immediately following the Cambrian and preceding the Silurian, characterized by an abundance of invertebrate life and, in rock strata, by deposits of limestone, lead, and zinc.
the Ordovician; the Ordovician Period or its rocks.

or'dūre, *n.* [Fr. *ordure*; It. *ordura*, filth, from OFr. *ord*; It. *ordo*, filthy, from L. *horridus*, horrid.] dung; excrement; feces; filth.

As gardeners do with *ordure* hide those roots
That shall first spring and be most delicate.
—Shak.

or'dūr·ous, *a.* of or consisting of ordure.

ōre, *n.* [AS. *ār.*] grace; favor; glory. [Obs.]

ōre, *n.* [ME. *or*; AS. *ar*, brass, copper, identified with *ora*, unwrought metal; hence, the form is from the former, the meaning from the latter.]
1. any natural combination of minerals, especially one from which a metal or metals can be profitably extracted.
2. a natural substance from which a nonmetallic material, such as sulfur, can be extracted.

ōre, *n.* a seaweed. [Brit. Dial.]

ōre, *n.* a variety of fine English wool. [Obs.]

ö're (ō'rȧ), *n.*; *pl.* **ö're** [Sw., from ON. *aurar*, a unit of weight, coin, from L. *aureus*, a gold coin, from *aurum*, gold.]
1. the 100th part of a Swedish krona.
2. a coin of this value.

ø're (ō'rȧ), *n.*; *pl.* **ø're** [Dan. and Norw., from ON. *aurar*; see preceding entry.]
1. the 100th part of a Danish krone or a Norwegian krone.
2. a coin of either of these values.

ō'rē·ad, *n.* [Gr. *oreias, oreiados*, from *oros*, mountain.] in Greek mythology, a mountain nymph.

ō·reç'tiç, *a.* [from Gr. *oregein*, to stretch out for, desire.] in philosophy, of or characterized by desire or appetite.

ō·re'gȧ·nō, *n.* [Sp. *orégano*.] any of a number of plants of the mint family, especially *Origanum vulgare*, the fragrant leaves of which are used in seasoning.

Or'ē·gon grāpe, a small evergreen shrub, *Mahonia aquifolia*; also, its fruit. It grows wild in woods of the Pacific coast and is sometimes cultivated for its ornamental appearance.

Or·ē·gō'ni·ăn, *n.* 1. a native or inhabitant of Oregon.
2. a member of a linguistic family of American Indians who lived in the northwestern United States.

Or·ē·gō'ni·ăn, *a.* of Oregon.

Or'ē·gon pīne, the Douglas fir, *Pseudotsuga douglasii*, remarkable for its great height, often reaching 300 feet: also called *Oregon fir.*

Or'ē·gon Trāil, a former route extending northwest about 2,000 miles, from the Mississippi to the Columbia River in Oregon: it was used by pioneers (c. 1804–1850).

ō'rē·īde, *n.* see *oroide.*

o·reil·lère' (ō-rā-lyâr'), *n.* the earpiece of a helmet.

ō·reil·lette' (-rā-lyet'), *n.* [from Fr. *oreille*, the ear.] an earpiece; one of two pieces fixed on the side of a helmet or head covering and fastened upon it with a hinge. [Archaic.]

Ō'rē·ō·don, *n.* [Gr. *oros, oreos*, a mountain, and *odous, odontos*, a tooth.] a genus of fossil mammals found in the Miocene Tertiary of North America, having some of the characteristics of camels and swine.

Ō'rē·ō·dont, *a.* of or relating to the genus *Oreodon.*

Ō"rē·ō·dox'ȧ, *n.* [Gr. *oros*, mountain, and *doxa*, glory.] a small genus of tropical American palms: *Oreodoxa regia* is found in Florida.

ō"rē·ō·graph'iç, *a.* same as *orographic.*

ō·rē·og'rȧ·phy, *n.* same as *orography.*

Ō"rē·ō·sō'mȧ, *n.pl.* [Gr. *oros, oreos*, mountain, and *sōma*, body.] a genus of small oceanic fishes with tuberculated undersurface.

Ō·res'tēs, *n.* [Gr., from *oros*, mountain.] in Greek mythology, son of Agamemnon and Clytemnestra, who, with the aid of his sister Electra, avenged the murder of his father by killing his mother and her lover Aegisthus.

ōre'weed, ōre'wood, *n.* same as *oarweed.*

ō·rex'is, *n.* [Gr.] in medicine, a desire or appetite.

or'fe, *n.* [Fr.; Gr. *orphos*, perch.] a domesticated variety of the ide (fish), colored like a goldfish.

orf'gild, *n.* [AS. *orfgild*; *orf*, cattle, property, and *gild*, payment.] in Anglo-Saxon law, the restitution of or payment for stolen property, particularly cattle.

or'frāis, or'frāys, *n.* 1. embroidery. [Obs.]
2. same as *orphrey*. [Obs.]

or'frāy, *n.* the osprey. [Obs.]

or'găn, *n.* [L. *organum*, from Gr. *organon*, an instrument, implement, engine.]
1. a large wind instrument consisting of various sets of pipes which, as they are opened by their corresponding keys on the keyboard, allow passage to a column of compressed air that causes sound by vibration.

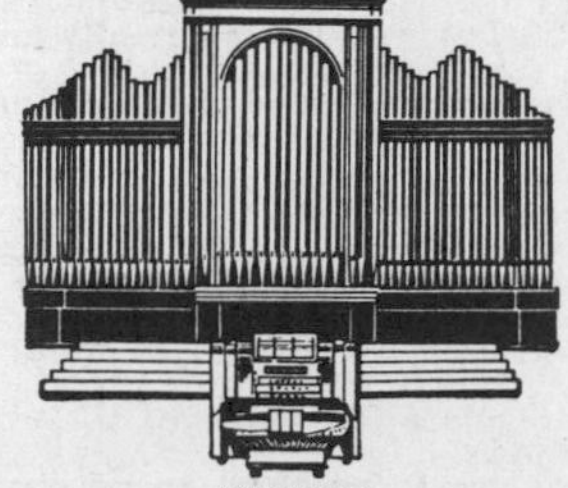

PIPE ORGAN

2. any of several other musical instruments resembling this instrument.
3. in animals and plants, a part composed of several tissues and adapted to the performance of a specific function or functions.
4. a means or instrument for the performance of some action.
5. a means of communicating ideas or opinions, as a periodical.
6. in phrenology, a portion of the brain considered as the seat of a particular function or faculty.
7. the voice or vocal organs as a whole regarded as an instrument of speech or music. [Rare.]
barrel organ; see under *barrel.*
organ gun; same as *orgue*, sense 2.
organ of Corti; a complex structure in the cochlea of the ear constituting the terminal acoustic apparatus, and including the rods of Corti and the auditory cells.

or'găn, *v.t.* to furnish with organs; to organize. [Obs.]

or'găn·bīrd, *n.* a Tasmanian bird having discordant organlike notes.

or'găn·dy, or'găn·die, *n.* [Fr. *organdi.*] a very sheer, stiff, lightweight cotton material, used for blouses, etc.

or'găn·dy, or'găn·die, *a.* made of organdy.

or'găn grīnd'ẽr, a person who makes a living by playing a barrel organ in the street.

or'găn hār·mō'ni·um, a harmonium or reed organ of great compass and power.

or·gan'iç, *a.* [L. *organicus*, from *organum*, implement.]
1. of or having to do with an organ.
2. inherent; inborn; constitutional.
3. organized; systematically arranged.
4. (a) designating or of any chemical compound containing carbon: some of the simple compounds of carbon, as carbon dioxide, are frequently classified as inorganic compounds; (b) designating or of the branch of chemistry dealing with carbon compounds.
5. of, having the characteristics of, or derived from living organisms.
6. in law, fundamental; as, the *organic* law of the United States is the Constitution.
7. in medicine, producing or involving alteration in the structure of an organ: opposed to *functional.*
8. in philosophy, having a complex but necessary interrelationship of parts, similar to that in living things.
organic analysis; in chemistry, the analysis of organic compounds.
organic disease; a disease caused or accompanied by an alteration in the structure of the tissues or organs.
organic electricity; see under *electricity.*

or·gan'iç·ăl, *a.* organic. [Obs.]

or·gan'iç·ăl·ly, *adv.* in an organic manner; so as to be organic.

or·gan'iç·ăl·ness, *n.* the state of being organical.

or·gan'i·cism, *n.* [Gr. *organon*, an organ.]
1. in medicine, (a) the theory that each bodily organ has its own constitution; (b) the theory that all disease is caused by organic lesions; (c) the theory that the bodily organs determine all symptoms.
2. in philosophy, the theory of biology that an organism's own dynamic system constitutes life: opposed to *mechanism, vitalism.*

or·găn·if'iç, *a.* [*organ* and *-ific.*] forming organs or an organized structure; forming an organism; acting through or resulting from organs.

or'găn·ism, *n.* 1. any living thing.
2. anything resembling a living thing in its complexity of structure or functions.

or'găn·ist, *n.* one who plays, or is skilled at playing, the organ.

or·găn·is'tiç, *a.* pertaining to an organ or organist.

or·gan'i·ty, *n.* organism. [Rare.]

or"găn·ī·zȧ·bil'i·ty, *n.* the quality or property of being organizable; capability for organization.

or'găn·ī·zȧ·ble, *a.* that can be organized.

or"găn·i·zā'tion, *n.* 1. an organizing or being organized.
2. organic structure; manner of being organized.
3. an organism.
4. any unified, consolidated group of elements; systematized whole; especially, a body of persons organized for some specific purpose, as a club, union, or society.
5. the administrative personnel or executive structure of a business.

6. all the functionaries, committees, etc. of a political party.

ọr'găn·īze, *v.t.*; organized, *pt.*, *pp.*; organizing, *ppr.* [ML. *organizare*, from L. *organum*; Gr. *organon*, organ.]
1. to provide with an organic structure; to systematize.
2. to arrange; establish; institute; bring into being.
3. (a) to enlist in, or cause to form, a labor union; (b) to enlist the employees of (an industry, store, etc.) in a labor union.

ọr'găn·īze, *v.i.* 1. to become organic or organized.
2. to form or join a labor union.

ọr'găn·ī·zẽr, *n.* a person who organizes; specifically, a labor-union official whose work is enlisting and orienting members.

ọr'găn loft, the loft where an organ stands, especially in a church.

ọr'gȧ·nō-, [Gr. *organon*, organ.] a combining form meaning *organ* or *organic*, as in *organography*.

ọr·gan'ō·ġen, *n.* [*organo-*, and Gr. *gennaein*, to beget.] in chemistry, any one of the elements carbon, hydrogen, oxygen, and nitrogen, regarded as the characteristic ingredients of an organic compound.

ọr"gȧ·nō·ġen'ē·sis, *n.* in biology, the origin and development of organs.

ọr"gȧ·nō·ġē·net'iç, *a.* organogenic.

ọr"gȧ·nō·ġen'iç, *a.* of or pertaining to organogeny.

ọr·gȧ·noġ'e·ny, *n.* [*organo-*, and Gr. *-geneia*, from *gignesthai*, to become.] organogenesis.

ọr"gȧ·nō·graph'iç, *a.* pertaining to organography.

ọr"gȧ·nō·graph'iç·ăl, *a.* organographic.

ọr·gȧ·nog'rȧ·phist, *n.* one who describes the organs of animal or vegetable bodies.

ọr·gȧ·nog'rȧ·phy, *n.* [*organo-*, and Gr. *graphein*, to describe, to write.] a scientific description of plant or animal organs.

ọr"gȧ·nō·lep'tiç, *a.* [*organo-*, and Gr. *lēpticos*, disposed to take, from *lambanein*, to take.]
1. making an impression on an organ of special sense.
2. capable of receiving a sense impression.

ọr"gȧ·nō·loġ'iç, *a.* pertaining to organology.

ọr"gȧ·nō·loġ'iç·ăl, *a.* organologic.

ọr·gȧ·nol'ō·ġist, *n.* one versed in organology.

ọr·gȧ·nol'ō·ġy, *n.* [*organo-* and *-logy*.]
1. the study of plant or animal organs, with reference to their form, structure, development, and functions.
2. phrenology.

ọr"gȧ·nō·mē·tal'liç, *a.* in chemistry, consisting of a metal in combination with an organic radical.

ọr'gȧ·non, *n.* [Gr.]
1. a method, means, or agency for communicating knowledge.
2. in philosophy, a system used in investigation.

ọr"gȧ·nō·nom'iç, *a.* pertaining to organonomy.

ọr·gȧ·non'ō·my, *n.* [*organo-*, and Gr. *nomos*, law.] the doctrine of the laws of organic life; also, the laws themselves.

ọr·gȧ·non'y·măl, *a.* pertaining to organonymy.

ọr"gȧ·nō·nym'iç, *a.* organonymal.

ọr·gȧ·non'y·my, *n.* [*organo-*, and Gr. *onyma*, name.] the nomenclature of organs.

ọr"gȧ·nō·plas'tiç, *a.* [*organo-* and *plastic*.] having the property of producing or evolving the tissues of the organs of animal or vegetable beings; as, *organoplastic* cells.

ọr·gȧ·nos'çō·py, *n.* [*organo-*, and Gr. *skopein*, to view.] phrenology.

ọr"gȧ·nō·ther"ȧ·peū'tiçs, *n.pl.* [*construed as sing.*] organotherapy.

ọr"gȧ·nō·ther'ȧ·py, *n.* [*organo-* and *therapy*.] the treatment of disease with extracts of animal organs, as of the glands of internal secretion.

ọr"gȧ·nō·troph'iç, *a.* [*organo-*, and Gr. *trephein*, to nourish.] pertaining to the nutrition of organs.

ọr'găn pīpe, any pipe of a pipe organ, or something resembling this.
organ-pipe coral; a coral of the genus *Tubipora*, consisting of cylindrical tubes united by horizontal plates.

ọr'găn point, in music, a passage in which the tonic or dominant is sustained continuously by one part, while the other parts move: also called *pedal point*.

ọr'găn stop, the stop of an organ: see *stop*, *n.*

ọr'găn·ūle, *n.* [dim. of *organ*.] a cell or element of an organ.

ọr'gȧ·num, *n.*; *pl.* **ọr'gȧ·nums, ọr'gȧ·nȧ,** [L.; Gr. *organon*, a tool.]
1. an organon.
2. in music, an early type of two-part harmony in which the voices are separated by an interval of a fourth or fifth.

ọr·gan'zȧ, *n.* a thin cotton material similar to organdy.

ọr'găn·zīne, *n.* [It. *organzino*; Fr. *organsin*.] silk twisted like a rope with different strands, so as to increase its strength.

ọr'gaṣm, *n.* [Gr. *orgasmos*, from *orgān*, to swell.] a frenzy; great excitement; especially, the climax or culmination of a sexual act.

ọr·gas'tiç, *a.* pertaining to or exhibiting orgasm.

ọr'ġeat (-zhat), *n.* [Fr., from *orge*, barley.] a liquor or sirup extracted from barley and sweet almonds, and used as a flavor for beverages and edibles, or medicinally as a mild demulcent.

ọr·ġi·as'tiç, *a.* of, resembling, or relating to an orgy or orgies.

ọrgue, *n.* [Fr.]
1. a long, thick piece of timber pointed and shod with iron, and hung over a gateway, to be let down in case of attack: used in medieval warfare.
2. a piece of ordnance composed of several musket barrels united, by means of which several explosions are made at once.

ọr'gū·lous, *a.* proud; haughty. [Archaic.]

ọr'ġy, *n.*; *pl.* **ọr'ġieṣ,** [Gr. *orgia*, secret rites, secret worship, from *orgē*, any violent passion, anger, wrath.]
1. [*usually in pl.*] in ancient Greece and Rome, feasting and wild celebration in worship of certain gods.
2. any wild, riotous merrymaking.
3. an overindulgence in any activity; as, an *orgy* of work.

Ọr·ġȳ'i·ȧ, *n.* [Gr. *orgyia*, length of outstretched arms, from *oregein*, to stretch.] a genus of lepidopterous insects: also called *vaporer moths*.

ō'ri·bi, *n.* [S. Afr. D., from Nama *arab*.] any of several species of African pygmy antelopes distinguished by a long tuft of hair growing from each knee.

or'i·chalç, *n.* same as *orichalch*.

or·i·chal'cē·ous, *a.* pertaining to or resembling orichalch.

or'i·chalch, *n.* [L. *orichalcum*, mountain brass; Gr. *oros*, a mountain, and *chalkos*, copper.] among the ancient Greeks and Romans, a metallic substance resembling gold in color, but inferior in value; a mixed metal resembling brass: also called *orichalcum* and *aurichalcum*.

ō'ri·el, *n.* [OFr. *oriol*; LL. *oriolum*, porch or gallery.] a large window built out from a wall and resting on a bracket or a corbel; a large bay window.

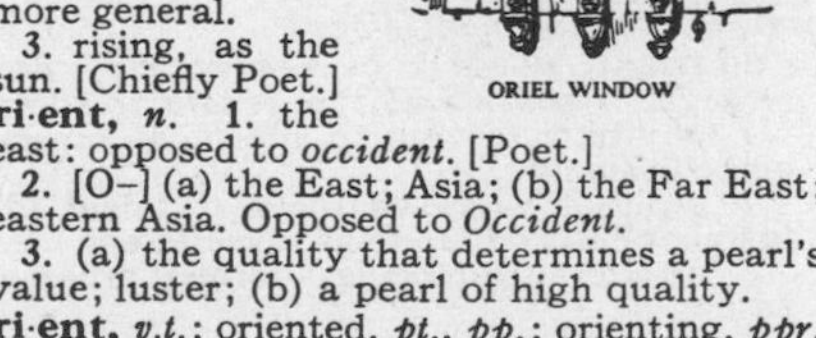
ORIEL WINDOW

ō'ri·en·cy, *n.* [*orient* and *-cy*.] brightness or strength of color.

ō'ri·ent, *a.* [L. *oriens*, from *oriri*, to arise.]
1. oriental; belonging to the east. [Poet.]
2. brilliant; shining; precious: originally of pearls, now more general.
3. rising, as the sun. [Chiefly Poet.]

ō'ri·ent, *n.* 1. the east: opposed to *occident*. [Poet.]
2. [O-] (a) the East; Asia; (b) the Far East; eastern Asia. Opposed to *Occident*.
3. (a) the quality that determines a pearl's value; luster; (b) a pearl of high quality.

ō'ri·ent, *v.t.*; oriented, *pt.*, *pp.*; orienting, *ppr.* [Fr. *orienter*.]
1. to cause to turn to or face the east.
2. (a) to set, as a map, in agreement with the points of the compass; (b) figuratively, to adjust or adapt to a particular situation (often used reflexively).
3. to show or establish relationship with others by placing or arranging in a certain manner.

ō'ri·ent, *v.i.* 1. to turn to or face the east.
2. to become adjusted to a situation.

ō·ri·en'tăl, *a.* 1. eastern: opposed to *occidental*.
2. [O-] of the Orient, its people, or their culture; Eastern: opposed to *Occidental*.

Ō·ri·en'tăl, *n.* [*sometimes* o-] a native of the Orient or a member of a people native to that region: opposed to *Occidental*.

Ō·ri·en'tăl·iṣm, *n.* 1. [*sometimes* o-] any trait, quality, mannerism, etc. usually associated with the people of the East.
2. study of Eastern culture.

Ō·ri·en'tăl·ist, *n.* [*sometimes* o-] a student of Eastern culture.

Ō"ri·en·tal'i·ty, *n.* the state or quality of being Oriental or Eastern.

Ō·ri·en'tăl·īze, *v.t.* and *v.i.*; Orientalized, *pt.*, *pp.*; Orientalizing, *ppr.* [*sometimes* o-] to make or become Oriental in character.

Ō·ri·en'tăl rug, any of various kinds of handmade rugs made in the Orient: also *Oriental carpet*.

ō·ri·en'tāte, *v.t.*; orientated, *pt.*, *pp.*; orientating, *ppr.* to orient.

ō·ri·en'tāte, *v.i.* 1. to turn or be directed toward the east, as a church.
2. to adjust to a situation.

ō"ri·en·tā'tion, *n.* 1. an orienting or being oriented.
2. (a) position with relation to the points of the compass; (b) the planning of church architecture so that the altar is in the east end.
3. familiarization with and adaptation to a situation or environment; specifically, in psychology, interpretation of the environment as to time, space, objects, and persons.
4. in zoology, the homing faculty or instinct of certain animals.

ō·ri·en·tā'tŏr, *n.* a person or thing that orientates; specifically, a contrivance consisting of a section of the fuselage of an airplane mounted on steel tubing so as to give student flyers in a safe way all the motions to which they will be subject in actual flight.

ō'ri·ent·ness, *n.* same as *oriency*.

or'i·fice, *n.* [Fr., from LL. *orificium*; L. *os*, *oris*, mouth, and *facere*, to make.] the mouth or aperture of a tube, pipe, etc.; an opening.

or'i·flamme, or'i·flamb, *n.* [Fr., from L. *auriflamma*, from *aurum*, gold, and *flamma*, a flame.]
1. the ancient royal standard of France, a red silk banner split at one end to form flame-shaped streamers, used as the early French kings' military ensign.
2. any battle standard.

ọ·ri·gä'mi, *n.* [Japan.]
1. a traditional Japanese art of folding paper to form flowers, animal figures, etc.
2. an object so made.

or'i·găn, *n.* a plant of the genus *Origanum*, especially wild marjoram.

Ō·rig'ȧ·num, *n.* [Gr. *oros*, a mountain, and *ganos*, splendor, joy, in allusion to the habitation of the plants.] a genus of labiate plants belonging to the mint family.

Or'i·ġen·iṣm, *n.* the doctrines of Origen of Alexandria (185–253 A.D.), an early Greek church father, who united the philosophy of the eclectic school of Neoplatonists with the doctrines of Christianity, holding that human souls existed before their union with bodies and that they were originally holy, but became sinful in the pre-existent state.

Or'i·ġen·ist, *n.* a follower of Origen.

or'i·gin, *n.* [Fr. *origine*; L. *origo*, *originis*, from *oriri*, to rise.]
1. a coming into existence or use; beginning.
2. parentage; birth; lineage.
3. that in which something has its beginning; source; root; cause.
4. in anatomy, the less movable of the two points of attachment of a muscle, usually the end attached to the more rigid part of the skeleton: opposed to *insertion*.
Syn.—source, beginning, cause, rise.

ō·rig'i·nȧ·ble, *a.* capable of being originated.

ō·rig'i·năl, *a.* [Fr. *originel*; L. *originalis*, from *origo*, origin or beginning.]
1. having to do with an origin; initial; first; earliest.
2. never having occurred or existed before; not copied; fresh; new; novel.
3. capable of or given to inventing or creating something new, or thinking or acting in an independent, individual, fresh way.
4. coming from someone as the originator, maker, author, etc.
5. being that or those from which reproductions, copies, etc. have been made.

ō·rig'i·năl, *n.* 1. a pristine form or primary type that has given rise to varieties.
2. an original work, as of art or literature,

in contradistinction to any reproduction, copy, etc.

3. the person or thing represented in a painting or the like.

4. a person of original mind, character, or behavior.

5. an eccentric person.

6. an originator. [Archaic.]

ō·rig′i·năl·ist, *n.* one who shows originality. [Rare.]

ō·rig·i·nal′i·ty, *n.* 1. the quality or state of being original.

2. *pl.* **ō·rig·i·nal′i·ties,** anything original.

ō·rig′i·năl·ly, *adv.* 1. with reference to origin, or beginning.

2. at or from the beginning; initially.

3. in the first place; chiefly.

4. in an original, independent, or novel manner.

ō·rig′i·năl·ness, *n.* the quality or state of being original; originality. [Rare.]

ō·rig′i·năl sin, a tendency to sin and depravity which, in Christian theology, is held to be inherent in mankind as a direct result of Adam's sin of rebellion and which, in Roman Catholicism, is held to have resulted in the loss of sanctifying grace.

ō·rig′i·nănt, *a.* originating.

ō·rig′i·nā·ry, *a.* [Fr. *originaire*; L. *originarius*, *from origo*, the beginning.] productive; causing existence. [Rare.]

ō·rig′i·nāte, *v.t.*; originated, *pt.*, *pp.*; originating, *ppr.* to cause to be; to bring into existence; to produce as new.

> The change is to be effected without a decomposition of the whole civil and political mass, for the purpose of *originating* a new civil order out of the elements of society. —Burke.

ō·rig′i·nāte, *v.i.* to come into being; to begin; to start.

ō·rig·i·nā′tion, *n.* 1. an originating or being originated.

2. origin.

ō·rig′i·nā·tive, *a.* having power or ability to originate; inventive; creative.

ō·rig′i·nā·tive·ly, *adv.* in an originative manner.

ō·rig′i·nā·tŏr, *n.* one who or that which originates.

ō·ril′liŏn, ō·ril′lŏn (-yun), *n.* [Fr. *orillon*, *oreillon*, from *oreille*, an ear, from L. *auricula*, dim. of *auris*, the ear.] in fortification, a curved projection formed by the face of a bastion overlapping the end of the flank, intended to protect the latter from oblique fire. [Obs.]

ō·ri·nā′ṣăl, *a.* [from L. *os*, *oris*, a mouth; and *nasal*.] in phonetics, pronounced with the nasal passage open to the breath.

ō·ri·nā′ṣăl, *n.* an orinasal sound, as a French nasalized vowel.

ō′ri·ōle, *n.* [OFr. *oriol*, from L. *aureolus*, dim. of *aureus*, golden.]

1. any bird of the family *Oriolidæ*, including the golden oriole, *Oriolus galbula*, with conspicuous plumage, bright yellow contrasted with black: it is found from Europe to Australia.

GOLDEN ORIOLE

2. one of various American birds of the family *Icteridæ*, as the Baltimore oriole, *Icterus galbula*, related to the starlings and characterized by bright-orange (or yellow) and black plumage and hanging nests.

Ō·rī′ŏn, *n.* [ME.; L.; Gr. *Ōriōn*, a mythological hunter, the handsomest of his race.]

1. in Greek and Roman mythology, a hunter whom Diana loved but accidentally killed: he was placed in the heavens by her as a constellation.

2. in astronomy, an equatorial constellation near Taurus, containing the first-magnitude stars Rigel and Betelgeuse.

Ō·ris′kȧ·ny, *a.* [from *Oriskany* in New York.] in geology, pertaining to or designating a formation well developed in Pennsylvania and Virginia and to some extent in New York, considered by some geologists to be Devonian.

ō·ris·mō·log′iç, ō·ris·mō·log′iç·ăl, *a.* pertaining to orismology.

ō·ris·mol′ō·gy, *n.* [Fr. *orismologie*, *horismologie*, from Gr. *horismos*, a bounding or defining, from *horizein*, to bound, *horos*, a boundary.] terminology.

or′i·ṣŏn, *n.* [ME. *oreisun*; OFr. *oreison*; L. *oratio*, from *orare*, to pray.] [*usually in pl.*] a prayer or supplication.

> Lowly they bowed adoring, and began
> Their *orisons*, each morning duly paid.
> —Milton.

or′i·ṣont, *n.* horizon. [Obs.]

ork, *n.* same as *orc*.

Ǫrk′ney·ăn, *a.* of or pertaining to the Orkney Islands.

ǫrle, *n.* [Fr., from LL. *orla*, from L. *ora*, border.]

1. in heraldry, (a) the inner border on an escutcheon, following the outline of the edge of the shield; (b) a wreath; a roll of cloth, silk or velvet, of two colors, sometimes jeweled, encircling a helmet, and supporting a heraldic crest.

ORLE

2. in architecture, same as *orlet*.

in orle; in heraldry, placed around the escutcheon, leaving the middle of the field vacant or occupied by something else: said of the charges.

Ǫr′lē·ăn·iṣm, *n.* the principles and policy of the Orleans family, descendants of a brother of Louis XIV of France, or of its adherents.

Ǫr′lē·ăn·iṣt, *n.* a supporter of the house of Orleans' claim to the French throne through the Duke of Orleans, a younger brother of Louis XIV.

Ǫr′lē·ăn·ist, *a.* pertaining to or characteristic of Orleanism.

ǫr′lē·ănṣ, *n.* [from *Orléans*, France.]

1. a dress goods made of cotton and worsted.

2. a variety of plum.

ǫr′let, *n.* in architecture, a fillet under the ovolo of a capital: called a cincture when it is at the top or bottom of a shaft.

ǫr′lon, *n.* a fabric of synthetic acrylic fiber somewhat similar to nylon: a trade-mark (*Orlon*).

ǫr′lop, *n.* [D. *overloop*; *over*, over, and *loopen*, to run.] the lowest deck of a ship, especially of a warship.

ǫr′lop deck, an orlop.

Ǫr′mazd, *n.* [Per. *Ormazd*; O.Per. *Auramazda*; Zend *Ahuro-Mazdao*, wise lord.] the supreme deity and creator of the world, in the Zoroastrian, or ancient Persian, religion: also spelled *Ormuzd*.

ǫr′mẽr, *n.* [Fr. *ormier*, shortened from *oreille de mer*; *oreille*, an ear, *de*, of, and *mer*, the sea.] an abalone shell; an ear shell.

ǫr′mō·lu̇, *n.* [Fr. *or moulu*; *or*, gold, and *moulu*, pp. of *moudre*, L. *molere*, to grind.]

1. an imitation gold consisting of an alloy of copper and tin, used in making ornaments, moldings, inexpensive jewelry, etc.

2. imitation gold leaf.

ǫr′mō·lu̇ vär′nish, a varnish used to imitate gold.

Ǫr′muzd, *n.* see *Ormazd*.

ǫrn, *v.t.* to ornament. [Obs.]

ǫr′nȧ·ment, *n.* [ME. *ournement*; OFr. *ornement*; L. *ornamentum*, from *ornare*, to adorn.]

1. anything serving to adorn; decoration; embellishment.

2. a person whose character or talent adds luster to his surroundings, society, etc.

3. an adorning or being adorned; ornamentation.

4. mere external display.

5. in ecclesiastical usage, an adjunct, accessory, or article of equipment.

6. in music, a tone or tones used to embellish a principal melodic tone.

ǫr′nȧ·ment, *v.t.*; ornamented, *pt.*, *pp.*; ornamenting, *ppr.* to adorn; to decorate; to beautify; to embellish.

ǫr·nȧ·men′tăl, *a.* serving to decorate; embellishing; of the nature of ornament.

ǫr·nȧ·men′tăl, *n.* something ornamental; specifically, a plant or shrub grown for its beauty or decorative effect.

ǫr·nȧ·men′tăl·ly, *adv.* in an ornamental manner.

ǫr·nȧ·men·tā′tion, *n.* 1. an ornamented condition or appearance.

2. an ornamenting or being ornamented.

3. ornaments collectively; decoration.

ǫr′nȧ·ment·ẽr, *n.* one who ornaments.

ǫr·nāte′, *a.* [ME.; L. *ornatus*, pp. of *ornare*, to adorn.]

1. heavily ornamented; overadorned.

2. flowery; showy; unnatural: said of literary style.

Syn.—embellished, garnished, florid.

ǫr·nāte′, *v.t.* to adorn; to ornament. [Obs.]

ǫr·nāte′ly, *adv.* in an ornate manner.

ǫr·nāte′ness, *n.* the quality of being ornate.

ǫr′nȧ·tūre, *n.* decoration.

ǫr′nẽr·y, *a.* [altered from *ordinary*.]

1. having an ugly or mean disposition. [Chiefly Dial.]

2. obstinate. [Chiefly Dial.]

3. base; low. [Chiefly Dial.]

4. ordinary. [Chiefly Dial.]

ǫr′nis, *n.* [Gr. *ornis*.] all the birds of a certain region; avifauna.

ǫr·nith′iç, *a.* [Gr. *ornithikos*, from *ornis*, *ornithos*, bird.] pertaining to birds; like birds.

ǫr·nith·iċh′nīte, *n.* [Gr. *ornis*, bird, and *ichnos*, track.] a fossil footmark, originally thought to be that of a bird, but now considered reptilian. [Obs.]

ǫr″nith·iċh·nol′ō·gy, *n.* [Gr. *ornis*, bird, *ichnos*, track, and *-logy*.] the scientific study of ornithichnites.

ǫr′ni·thin, *n.* same as *ornithine*.

ǫr′ni·thīne (*or* -thin), *n.* [from Gr. *ornis*, *ornithos*, bird; and *-ine*.] an amino acid, $C_5H_{12}O_2N_2$, found in the urine and excrement of birds.

ǫr′ni·thō-, [from Gr. *ornis*, *ornithos*, bird.] a combining form meaning *bird* or *birds*, as in *ornitho*logy: also, before a vowel, *ornith-*.

ǫr″ni·thō·ceph′ȧ·lous, *a.* [*ornitho-*, and Gr. *kephalē*, head.] shaped like the head of a bird, as some shells.

ǫr″ni·thō·cop′ros, *n.* [*ornitho-*, and Gr. *kopros*, dung.] guano; bird dung.

ǫr′ni·thō·delph, *n.* [*ornitho-*, and Gr. *delphys*, womb.] a member of the *Ornithodelphia*.

Ǫr″ni·thō·del′phi·ȧ, *n.pl.* the *Monotremata*.

ǫr″ni·thō·del′phid, *a.* of or pertaining to the *Ornithodelphia*.

Ǫr″ni·thō·gae′ȧ, *n.* [*ornitho-*, and Gr. *gaia*, land.] New Zealand considered as a zoogeographical region: so named because birds form a large part of its fauna.

Ǫr·ni·thog′ȧ·lum, *n.* [Gr. *ornithogalon*; *ornitho-*, and *gala*, milk.] a genus of bulbous herbs of the *Liliaceæ* with naked scapes crowned by white, blue, yellow, or purplish flowers.

ǫr′ni·thoid, *a.* [*ornith-* and *-oid*.] birdlike; resembling birds in appearance or structure.

ǫr·nith′ō·līte, *n.* [*ornitho-*, and Gr. *lithos*, stone.] a fossil bird or a fragment of one.

ǫr″ni·thō·lit′iç, *a.* pertaining to ornitholites.

ǫr″ni·thō·log′iç, *a.* same as *ornithological*.

ǫr″ni·thō·log′iç·ăl, *a.* pertaining to ornithology.

ǫr·ni·thol′ō·ġist, *n.* an expert in ornithology.

ǫr·ni·thol′ō·gy, *n.* [Mod.L. *ornithologia*, from Gr. *ornithologos*, bird study.] the branch of zoology dealing with birds; also, a treatise on birds.

ǫr′ni·thō·man″cy, *n.* [*ornitho-*, and Gr. *manteia*, divination.] divination by means of birds, their flight, etc.

ǫr′ni·thon, *n.* [Gr. *ornithōn*, an aviary.] an aviary.

Ǫr″ni·thō·pap′pī, *n.pl.* [*ornitho-*, and Gr. *pappos*, an ancestor.] an order of fossil birds represented by the archaeopteryx.

ǫr·ni·thop′i·lous, *a.* [*ornitho-*, and Gr. *philos*, loving.] bird-loving; bird-fertilized, as certain flowers.

ǫr′ni·thō·pod, *n.* [*ornitho-* and *-pod*.] one of the *Ornithopoda*.

ǫr′ni·thō·pod, *a.* 1. having birdlike feet.

2. pertaining to the *Ornithopoda*.

Ǫr·ni·thop′ō·dȧ, *n.pl.* a group of dinosaurs that walked upright on digitigrade hind feet.

ǫr·ni·thop′tẽr, *n.* an orthopter.

Ǫr·nith′ō·pus, *n.* [*ornitho-*, and Gr. *pous*, foot.]

1. a genus of the *Leguminosæ*, including the bird's-foot.

2. a genus of dinosaurs of the Triassic formation.

ǫr″ni·thō·rhyn′ċhous, *a.* beaked like a bird.

Ǫr″ni·thō·rhyn′ċhus, *n.* [*ornitho-*, and Gr. *rhynchos*, beak.]

1. a genus of monotrematous mammals of

which *Ornithorhynchus paradoxus* is the only known species. It lays an egg about one-half an inch broad by three-quarters of an inch in length, with a white, flexible shell.

2. [o–] a member of this genus; a duckbill; a platypus: also called *duck mole*, and *water mole*.

ọr′nith·ō·sa̤ur, *n.* a reptile of the *Ornithosauria*.

Ọr″ni·thō·sa̤u′ri·ȧ, *n.pl.* [*ornitho-*, and Gr. *sauros*, lizard.] same as the *Pterosauria*.

Ọr″ni·thō·scel′i·dȧ, *n.pl.* [*ornitho-*, and Gr. *skelos*, leg.] an order of reptiles including the *Compsognatha* and *Dinosauria*.

ọr·ni·thos′cō·py, *n.* [*ornitho-*, and Gr. *skopein*, to view.] the observation of birds, especially in order to foretell events; ornithomancy.

ọr″ni·thō·tom′iç·ăl, *a.* pertaining to ornithotomy.

ọr·ni·thot′ō·mist, *n.* one versed in ornithotomy.

ọr·ni·thot′ō·my, *n.* [*ornitho-*, and Gr. *tamein*, *temnein*, to cut.] ornithological anatomy.

ō′rō-, [from Gr. *oros*, mountain.] a combining form meaning *mountain*, as in *oro*graphy.

Ọr″ō·bañ·chā′cē·ae, *n.pl.* [Gr. *orobanchē*, parasitic plant, and *-aceæ*.] an order of monopetalous, exogenous, leafless plants, growing parasitically upon the roots of other species. Some species are pests of agriculture, destroying the useful plants. *Orobanche* is the type genus, including herbbane and broomrape.

ọr″ō·bañ·chā′ceous (-shus), *a.* of the broomrape family of leafless parasitic plants.

ọr·ō·ġen′e·sis, *n.* same as *orogeny*.

ọr·ō·ġen′iç, *a.* pertaining to orogeny.

ō·roġ′e·ny, *n.* [*oro-* and *-geny*.] the formation of mountains, especially through a disturbance in the earth's crust.

or·ō·graph′iç, *a.* relating to orography.

or·ō·graph′iç·ăl, *a.* orographic.

ō·rog′rȧ·phy, *n.* [*oro-* and *-graphy*.] the branch of physical geography which pertains to mountains and to features directly connected with mountains.

Or·ō·hip′pus, *n.* [Gr. *oros*, mountain, and *hippos*, horse.] a fossil genus of horses from the Eocene strata of North America, which had on each forefoot four toes and on each hindfoot three toes.

ō′rō·ide, ō′rē·ide, *n.* [Fr. *or*, from L. *aurum*, gold, and Gr. *eidos*, form.] an alloy, mainly of copper, tin, and zinc, which resembles gold in color and luster, used in inexpensive jewelry.

ō′rō·idc, *a.* made of the alloy called oroide.

ọr·ō·loġ′iç·ăl, *a.* pertaining to orology.

ō·rol′ō·ġist, *n.* a describer of mountains.

ō·rol′ō·ġy, *n.* [*oro-* and *-logy*.] the study of mountains.

ō·rom′ē·tēr, *n.* [*oro-* and *-meter*.] an aneroid barometer for measuring the altitudes of mountains, having an attachment with a scale for reading the elevation above sea level.

ọr·ō·met′riç, *a.* 1. of or for the measurement of the altitudes of mountains.

2. of an orometer.

ō·rō·nā′ṣăl, *a.* [from L. *os*, *oris*, the mouth, and *nasal*.] of or pertaining to the mouth and nose.

Ō·ron′ti·um (-shi-), *n.* [perhaps derived from Gr. *Orontes*, a river in Syria.] a genus of plants of the family *Arum*, with a single species, *Orontium aquaticum*, growing in the margins of rivers and ponds in the eastern part of the United States, closely related to skunk cabbage: also called *goldenclub*.

ō′rō·tund, *a.* [L. *os*, *oris*, the mouth, and *rotundus*, round, smooth.]

1. full; mellow; resonant; clear; strong: said of the voice.

2. showy; bombastic; pompous: said of a style of speaking or writing.

ō·rō·tun′di·ty, *n.* the quality of being orotund.

ọr′phȧ·line, *n.* and *a.* orphelin. [Obs.]

ọr′phăn, *n.* [Gr. *orphanos*, later *orphos*; L. *orbus*, bereaved.] a child whose father and mother are dead: sometimes applied to a child who has lost only one parent by death.

ọr′phăn, *a.* 1. being an orphan; bereaved of parents; as, an *orphan* child.

2. pertaining or belonging to an orphan; for orphans; as, an *orphan* home.

ọr′phăn, *v.t.*; orphaned, *pt.*, *pp.*; orphaning, *ppr.* to reduce to orphanhood; to cause to become an orphan; to bereave of parents or a parent.

ọr′phăn·āġe, *n.* 1. the condition of being an orphan.

2. an institution for orphans.

3. orphans collectively.

ọr′phăned, *a.* bereaved of parents; reduced to orphanhood.

ọr′phăn·et, *n.* a little orphan; a young orphan. [Obs.]

ọr′phăn·hood, *n.* the state of being an orphan.

ọr·phăn·ot′rō·phy, *n.* [Gr. *orphanos*, orphan, and *trephein*, to nourish.]

1. a hospital for orphans. [Rare.]

2. the support of orphans. [Rare.]

ọr·phā′ri·on, *n.* [Gr. *Orpheus*.] a musical instrument of the sixteenth and seventeenth centuries; a kind of large lute with metal strings in pairs and played with a plectrum.

Ọr·phē′ăn, *a.* of, like, or pertaining to Orpheus, the poet and musician; musical; melodious; charming; bewitching; as, *Orphean* hymns.

ọr′phe·lin, *n.* an orphan. [Obs.]

ọr′phe·lin, *a.* orphaned; bereaved of a parent or parents. [Obs.]

Ọr′phē·us, *n.* [L.; Gr. *Orpheus*.] in Greek mythology, a musician whose magic ability on the lyre affected beasts and even rocks and trees: when his wife Eurydice died, he obtained her release from the underworld on the condition that he would not look at her until they had reached the upper world, but he failed of his purpose at the last moment: the subject of operas by Monteverde, Gluck, etc.

Ọr′phiç, *a.* [L. *Orphicus*; Gr. *Orphikos*.]

1. of or characteristic of Orpheus or the mystic doctrines and rites in worship of Dionysus ascribed to him.

2. like the music attributed to Orpheus; entrancing.

3. [*also* o–] mystic; occult; oracular.

Ọr′phiṣm, *n.* the rites and religion ascribed to Orpheus as founder.

ọr′phrēy, *n.* [Fr. *orfroi*, from *or*, L. *aurum*, gold, and word equivalent to E. *frieze*.]

1. elaborate gold embroidery. [Obs.]

2. a broad band, usually of orphrey work, used in embroidering the front of certain ecclesiastical vestments.

ọr′phrēy wŏrk, gold embroidery; rich and costly embroidery of any kind.

ROCHET EMBROIDERED WITH ORPHREYS

ọr′pi·ment, *n.* [OFr., from L. *auripigmentum*; *aurum*, gold, and *pigmentum*.] trisulfide of arsenic, As_2S_3, found native and also manufactured artificially. The native orpiment appears in yellow, brilliant masses of various sizes, and forms the basis of a yellow paint called *king's yellow*.

ọr′pine, ọr′pin, *n.* [Fr. *orpin*, stonecrop, the French name being given to this species from the yellow flowers.] a succulent herbaceous plant, *Sedum telephium*, with fleshy leaves and stems, and white or purple flowers, found native in the northern parts of Europe, and also cultivated in country gardens in the United States. It has some reputation for its astringency, and the root and stem boiled in milk are a popular remedy for diarrhea. Also called *garden orpine* and *live-forever*.

Ọr′ping·tŏn, *n.* one of a valuable breed of heavy, full-bodied chickens having black, white, buff, or blue plumage, single combs, and unfeathered legs: originally bred at Orpington, Kent, England.

ọr′rȧ, *a.* [Scot. dial.; prob. from Gael.] odd (occasional, extra). [Scot.]

or′răch, *n.* orach. [Obs.]

or′rē·ry, *n.*; *pl.* **or′rē·rieṣ,** [so called after Charles Boyle, Earl of *Orrery*, for whom one was made.] a mechanical apparatus for illustrating, with balls of various sizes, the movements and the phases of the planets in the solar system; a planetarium.

or·rhor·rhē′ȧ, *n.* [Gr. *horros*, serum, and *rhein*, to flow.] in pathology, a watery or serous discharge.

or″rhō·ther·ȧ·peū′tiç, *a.* pertaining to or of the nature of orrhotherapy.

or·rhō·ther′ȧ·py, *n.* the therapeutic use of serums.

or′ris, or′rice, *n.* [corruption of *Iris*.] any plant of the iris family, having fragrant roots used in perfumes and medicine.

or′ris, *n.* [contr. from *orfrays*.] a sort of gold or silver lace.

or′ris oil, a volatile oil obtained from orrisroot, much used in the manufacture of perfumes and cosmetics.

or′ris·rōot, *n.* the rootstock of the orris, especially *Iris florentina*, which has a fragrance like that of violets: used, when pulverized, in perfumery or as a powder to whiten the hair in stage make-up.

ọr′se·dūe, ọrse′dew, *n.* [Fr. *or*, gold, and *séduire*, to mislead, to beguile.] Dutch metal. [Obs.]

ọr·sēille′ (-sāl′), *n.* [Fr.] same as *archil*.

ọr·sēil′lin (-sāl′in), *n.* [Fr.] a dyestuff giving a brownish-red color.

ọr·sel′liç, *a.* of or pertaining to orseille.

orsellic acid; a crystalline compound extracted from certain lichens: also called *lecanoric acid*.

ọr·sel·lin′iç, *a.* of, pertaining to, or containing orsellic acid.

orsellinic acid; a colorless crystalline substance derived from orsellic acid.

ọrt, *n.* [prob. from Early Mod. D. *oor-aete*, remains of food.] [*usually in pl.*] a fragment or scrap of food left from a meal; a piece or scrap of refuse. [Dial. or Obs.]

Ọr·tal′i·dae, *n.pl.* [LL., from Gr. *ortalis*, a young bird.] a family of flies having short antennae and the front bristly only above.

ọr·tȧ·lid′i·ăn, *n.* a fly of the family *Ortalidæ*.

Ọr′thi·çon, *n.* [*orth*(*o*)- and *Icono*scope.] an improved television pickup tube, developed from the Iconoscope: a trade-mark.

ọr′thid, *n.* in zoology, a shell of the *Orthis* and allied genera.

Ọr′this, *n.* [Gr. *orthos*, straight.] an extinct genus of molluscoid animals having a shell with a dorsal and a ventral valve, and a pair of armlike appendages rising from the sides of the mouth.

ọr′thīte, *n.* [Gr. *orthos*, straight.] a variety of allanite.

ọr′thō-, [from Gr. *orthos*, straight.]

1. a combining form meaning *straight*, *regular*, *upright*, as in *ortho*dontia, *ortho*gnathous.

2. a combining form meaning *right angle*, as in *ortho*rhombic.

3. a combining form meaning *proper*, *correct*, *standard*, as in *ortho*graphy.

4. in chemistry, a combining form meaning (a) *that acid* (*of a group containing the same nonmetallic element*) *which has the largest number of OH groups per atom of the nonmetal*, as in *ortho*phosphoric; (b) *characterized by substitutions in the* 1, 2 *position in the benzene ring*.

5. in medicine, a combining form meaning *correction of deformities*, as in *ortho*pedics.

Also, before a vowel, *orth-*.

ọr′thō·ax·is, *n.* [*ortho-* and *axis*.] same as *orthodiagonal*.

ọr″thō·çär·bon′iç, *a.* [*ortho-* and *carbonic*.] pertaining to, resembling, or containing a species of carbonic acid.

orthocarbonic ether; a liquid, $C(OC_2H_5)_4$, formed by the action of sodium ethylate on chloropicrin.

ọr·thō·cen′tēr, *n.* [*ortho-* and *center*.] the point of intersection of the three perpendiculars let fall from the angles of a triangle upon the subtending sides or the sides produced.

ọr″thō·cē·phal′iç (*or* -sef′ă-), *a.* [*ortho-* and *-cephalic*.]

1. having a skull whose height is 70 to 75 per cent of its length.

2. having a skull midway between brachycephalic and dolichocephalic; mesocephalic.

ọr·thō·ceph′ȧ·lous, *a.* orthocephalic.

ọr·thō·ceph′ȧ·ly, *n.* the condition of being orthocephalic.

Ọr·thoc′ē·ras, *n.* [*ortho-*, and Gr. *keras*, horn.] a genus of extinct tetrabranchiate cephalopods, typical of the family *Orthoceratidæ*. They have a straight shell, central siphuncle, and an aperture sometimes contracted.

ọr·thō·cer′ȧ·tid, *n.* an orthoceratite.

ọr·thō·cer′ȧ·tīte, *n.* a fossil cephalopod of the family *Orthoceratidæ*.

ọr·thō·cer·ȧ·tit′iç, *a.* pertaining to an orthoceratite; resembling an orthoceratite.

ọr·thō·cer′ȧ·toid, *a.* orthoceratitic.

ọr·thō·cer′ȧ·toid, *n.* an orthoceratite.

ọr″thō·çhrō·mat′iç, *a.* [*ortho-* and *chromatic*.] of, producing, or having tone values corresponding to natural colors, as a photographic film.

ọr·thō·çhrō′mȧ·tīze, *v.t.*; orthochromatized, *pt.*, *pp.*; orthochromatizing, *ppr.* in photography, to render orthochromatic.

ọr′thō·çlāṣe, *n.* [*ortho-*, and Gr. *klasis*, fracture.] a mineral of the feldspar family, having a vitreous luster and perfect cleavage: it occurs in igneous rocks.

or·thō·clas'tiç, *a.* having cleavage at right angles, as orthoclase.

orthoclastic feldspar; one of two divisions of feldspar, containing that which has rectangular cleavage.

or·thō·coe'liç, *a.* [*ortho-*, and Gr. *koilos*, hollow.] having the intestines arranged in parallel folds, as certain birds.

or·thō·cȳ'mēne, *n.* one of the three isomeric forms of cymene.

or"thō·dī·ag'ō·năl, *n.* [*ortho-* and *diagonal.*] in crystallography, the inclined lateral axis in a monoclinic crystal, at right angles to the vertical axis.

or"thō·dī·ag'ō·năl, *a.* pertaining to the orthodiagonal.

or·thō·dī'ȧ·gràph, *n.* [*ortho-*, Gr. *dia*, through, and *graphein*, to write.] an apparatus by means of which the true image of any object may be obtained in any desired position of the drawing plane. It is especially used for determining the exact shape and size of internal organs.

or"thō·dī"chlō·rō·ben'zēne, *n.* in chemistry, an organic compound, $C_6H_4Cl_2$, in which the two chlorine atoms are on adjacent carbon atoms in the benzene ring.

or'thō·dōme, *n.* [*ortho-*, and Gr. *domos*, house.] in crystallography, a dome parallel to the orthodiagonal axis.

or·thō·don'ti·ȧ (-shi-a), *n.* [Mod.L.] the branch of dentistry concerned with correcting and preventing irregularities of the teeth so as to bring about proper occlusion.

or·thō·don'tiç, *a.* of or for orthodontia.

or·thō·don'tist, *n.* a dentist specializing in orthodontia.

or'thō·dox, *a.* [from Fr. or LL.; Fr. *orthodoxe*; LL. *orthodoxus*; Gr. *orthodoxos*, from *orthos*, correct, and *doxa*, opinion, from *dokein*, to think.]

1. conforming to the usual beliefs or established doctrines, especially in religion; proper, correct, or conventional; as, *orthodox* ideas: opposed to *heterodox*.

2. conforming to the Christian faith as formulated in the early ecumenical creeds and confessions.

3. [O–] designating or of any of the churches comprised in the Orthodox Eastern Church.

or'thō·dox·ăl, *a.* orthodox. [Rare.]

or"thō·dox·al'i·ty, *n.* orthodoxy. [Rare.]

or'thō·dox·ăl·ly, *adv.* orthodoxly. [Rare.]

Or'thō·dox East'ērn Chūrch, the dominant Christian church in eastern Europe, western Asia, and northern Africa: originally it consisted of the four patriarchates of the Eastern Roman Empire that broke with the Roman See in 1054; now it includes the churches that recognize the primacy of the patriarchs of Constantinople, Alexandria, Antioch, and Jerusalem, as well as the autonomous churches of the Soviet Union, Greece, Romania, Bulgaria, Yugoslavia, etc., all of which agree in matters of dogma, ritual, and liturgy, and deny the supreme authority of the Pope: also called *Eastern Church*, *Orthodox Church*, and, less properly, *Greek* (*Orthodox*) *Church*.

or·thō·dox'iç·ăl, *a.* orthodox.

or'thō·dox·ly, *adv.* in an orthodox manner.

or'thō·dox·ness, *n.* the state or quality of being orthodox; orthodoxy.

or'thō·dox·y, *n.*; *pl.* **or'thō·dox·ieș,** [Gr. *orthodoxia*; *orthos*, right, true, and *doxa*, opinion, from *dokein*, to think.] quality, practice, or instance of being orthodox; orthodox belief, character, etc.

or·thō·drom'iç, *a.* pertaining to orthodromy.

or·thō·drom'içs, *n.* the art of sailing in a direct course, or on the arc of a great circle, which is the shortest distance between any two points on the surface of the globe.

or'thō·drom·y, *n.* [*ortho-*, and Gr. *dromos*, course.] the art or act of sailing on a great circle.]

or·tho·ĕp'ic (or-thō-ep'ik), *a.* of orthoëpy.

or·tho·ĕp'ic·al (-i-kăl), *a.* orthoëpic.

or·tho·ĕp'ic·al·ly (-i-kăl-y), *adv.* in an orthoëpic manner.

or·tho'ë·pist (or-thō'e-pist), *n.* a student of or expert in orthoëpy.

or·tho'ë·py (-py), *n.* [Gr. *orthoepeia*, from *orthos*, right, and *epos*, a word.]

1. the branch of grammar dealing with pronunciation; phonology.

2. the customary pronunciation of educated people; standard pronunciation.

or·thog'ȧ·mous, *a.* of or reproducing by orthogamy.

or·thog'ȧ·my, *n.* [*ortho-* and *-gamy.*] in biology, self-fertilization, as in some plants or animals.

or·thō·gen'e·sis, *n.* [Mod.L.]

1. in biology, progressive evolution in a certain direction, seen in successive generations and leading toward a definitely new form; determinate evolution.

2. in sociology, the theory that every culture or society follows the same fixed course of evolution, uninfluenced by environment.

or·thō·ġē·net'iç, *a.* of or by orthogenesis.

or·thog·nath'iç, *a.* same as *orthognathous*.

or·thog'nȧ·thism, *n.* the condition of being orthognathous.

or·thog'nȧ·thous, *a.* [*ortho-* and *-gnathous.*]

1. having the jaws straight or in line, with the lower jaw neither projecting nor receding.

2. designating a skull with the forehead and lower jaw in line.

or·thog'nȧ·thy, *n.* same as *orthognathism*.

or'thō·gon, *n.* [Gr. *orthos*, right, and *gōnia*, angle.] a rectangular figure, or one which has all its angles right angles.

or·thog'ō·năl, *a.* having to do with right angles; right-angled; rectangular.

orthogonal projection; same as *orthographic projection*.

or·thog'ō·năl·ly, *adv.* at right angles; perpendicularly.

or·thog'rȧ·phēr, or·thog'rȧ·phist, *n.* one who spells words correctly; one versed in correct spelling.

or·thō·graph'iç, or·thō·graph'iç·ăl, *a.* 1. of orthography.

2. characterized by correct spelling.

3. in geometry, of right angles and perpendicular lines.

or·thō·graph'iç prō·jeç'tion, in geometry and architecture, a projection in which the projecting lines are perpendicular to the plane of projection.

or·thō·graph'iç·ăl·ly, *adv.* 1. according to the rules of proper spelling.

2. in the manner of an orthographic projection.

or·thog'rȧ·phist, *n.* see *orthographer*.

or·thog'rȧ·phīze, *v.t.*; orthographized, *pt.*, *pp.*; orthographizing, *ppr.* 1. to spell correctly.

2. to correct the spelling of.

or·thog'rȧ·phy, *n.*; *pl.* **or·thog'rȧ·phieș,** [Gr. *orthographia*; *orthos*, right, and *graphē*, writing.]

1. correct spelling.
2. any style or way of spelling.
3. spelling as a subject or science.
4. orthographic projection.

or"thō·ker"ȧ·tol'ō·ġy, *n.* [*ortho-* and *kerato-* and *-logy.*] a branch of optometry that seeks to reduce certain refractive errors in the eye by altering the curvature of the cornea through the application of a series of graduated contact lenses over a period of time.

or·thol'ō·ġy, *n.* [*ortho-* and *-logy.*] the study of the correct use of words.

or·thō·met'riç, *a.* same as *orthorhombic*.

or·thom'ē·try, *n.* [*ortho-*, and Gr. *metron*, measure.] the art or practice of constructing verse correctly; the laws of correct versification.

or·thō·mor'phiç, *a.* [*ortho-*, and Gr. *morphē*, shape.] in descriptive geometry, having or preserving the right or original forms of the small parts of a figure, however the forms of the large parts may change.

or·thop'ȧ·thy, *n.* [*ortho-*, and Gr. *pathos*, from *paschein*, to suffer.] the treatment of disease without the use of drugs.

or·thō·pē'diç, or·thō·pae'diç, *a.* [from *ortho-*, and Gr. *paideia*, training of children, from *pais*, *paidos*, child; and *-ic.*] of or pertaining to orthopedics; used in orthopedics, as an *orthopedic* brace.

or·thō·pē'diçs, or·thō·pae'diçs, *n.pl.* [*construed as sing.*] [from *orthopedic.*] the branch of surgery dealing with the treatment of deformities, diseases, and injuries of the bones and joints.

or·thō·pē'dist, or·thō·pae'dist, *n.* an expert or specialist in orthopedics.

or"thō·phon'iç, *a.* [*ortho-*, and Gr. *phōnē*, sound, voice.] of or pertaining to correct speaking; characterized by the use of a cultured voice.

or·thō·phō'ri·ȧ, *n.* [*ortho-*, and Gr. *pherein*, to carry.] regular or correct sending of the optic axes or lines of sight.

or"thō·phos·phor'iç ac'id, [*ortho-* and *phosphoric.*] a clear, colorless, sirupy liquid or a colorless crystalline acid, H_3PO_4, produced from phosphorus or phosphate rock and used in the manufacture of fertilizers, textiles, etc.

or'thō·phȳre, *n.* [*ortho-* and *phyre*, contr. from *porphyry*, *porphyre*, Gr. *porphyra*, purple.] syenitic porphyry.

or·thō·pin'ȧ·çoid, *n.* [*ortho-* and *pinacoid.*] in crystallography, a plane of the monoclinic system parallel to the vertical and orthodiagonal axes.

or·thop'nē·iç, *a.* pertaining to or marked by orthopnea.

or·thop·nē'ȧ, or·thop'ny, *n.* [Gr. *orthopnoia*; *orthos*, right, erect, and *pnos*, breath; *pnein*, to breathe.] a disease in which respiration can be performed only when in an erect posture.

Or·thop'ō·dȧ, *n.pl.* [*ortho-*, and Gr. *pous*, *podos*, foot.] an extinct order of dinosaurians, with the feet, pelvis, and other parts resembling those of a bird, and having herbivorous habits.

or'thō·prax·y, or·thō·prax'is, *n.* [*ortho-*, and Gr. *praxis*, from *prassein*, to do.] the correction of bodily deformities by means of mechanical devices.

or'thō·prism, *n.* in crystallography, a prism in the monoclinic system, lying between the orthopinacoid and the unit prism.

or"thō·psȳ·chī'ȧ·try (-sī-kī'), *n.* [*ortho-* and *psychiatry.*] the study and treatment of disorders of behavior and personality, with emphasis on prevention.

or·thop'tēr, *n.* [Fr. *orthoptère*, from Gr. *orthos*, straight, and *pteron*, a wing.] a type of aircraft designed to be propelled by wing flapping, never proved practical: also *ornithopter*.

Or·thop'te·rȧ, *n.pl.* [Mod.L., from *ortho-*, and Gr. *pteron*, wing.] an order of insects having biting mouth parts and narrow, hard forewings that cover longitudinally folded, membranous hind wings: so named from the straight folding of their wings. The grasshoppers, cockroaches, and crickets are examples.

or·thop'tēr·ăn, *a.* same as *orthopterous*.

or·thop'tēr·ăn, *n.* a member of the insect order *Orthoptera*.

or·thop'tēr·on, *n.*; *pl.* **or·thop'tēr·ȧ,** one of the order *Orthoptera*.

or·thop'tēr·ous, *a.* pertaining to the order *Orthoptera*.

or·thop'tiç, *a.* [*orth-* and *optic.*]

1. correcting any deviations of the visual axis of the eye.

2. in mathematics, pertaining to tangents to a given curve which are perpendicular to each other.

or·thop'tiç ex'ēr·çīs·eș, the exercising of weakened eye muscles by the use of prisms to strengthen them and overcome any deviation.

or·thō·pyr'ȧ·mid, *n.* in crystallography, a monoclinic pyramid the intercept of which on the orthodiagonal is greater than that of the unit pyramid.

or·thō·rhom'biç, *a.* [*ortho-* and *rhombic.*] in crystallography, indicating crystallization distinguished by three unequal right-angled axes.

or'thō·sçōpe, *n.* [*ortho-* and *-scope.*] an instrument containing a layer of water which is held in contact with the eye, allowing an examination of the interior of the eye without the distortion due to corneal refraction.

or·thō·sçop'iç, *a.* [from *ortho-*, and Gr. *skopein*, to view; and *-ic.*] giving a true flat image without distortion.

or·thō·sil'i·çāte, *n.* [*ortho-* and *silicate.*] in mineralogy, a salt of orthosilicic acid: also known as *unisilicate*.

or"thō·si·lic'iç, *a.* [*ortho-* and *silicic.*] in chemistry, pertaining to or designating an acid of the highest hydroxyl value.

or·thō'sis, *n.* [Gr. *orthōsis.*] the correction of physical or mental distortion.

or·thō·spēr'mous, *a.* [*ortho-*, and Gr. *sperma*, seed.] in botany, having straight seeds.

or·thō·stat'iç, *a.* [*ortho-* and *static.*] caused by or pertaining to erect posture; standing upright.

or·thos'ti·chous, *a.* in botany, characterized by or arranged in orthostichies.

or·thos'ti·chy, *n.*; *pl.* **or·thos'ti·chieș,** [*ortho-*, and Gr. *stichos*, row.] in botany, a vertical arrangement of leaves or flowers on a stem.

or'thō·stȳle, *n.* [*ortho-*, and Gr. *stylos*, column.] in architecture, the arrangement of columns in a straight row.

or'thō·stȳle, *a.* in architecture, of or pertaining to the arrangement of columns in a straight row.

or·thō·tom'iç, *a.* in geometry, intersecting at right angles.

ọr·thot′ō·mous, *a.* [Gr. *orthos*, straight, and *temnein*, to cut.] same as *orthoclastic*.

ọr′thō·tōne, *a.* [*ortho-*, and Gr. *tonos*, tone.] retaining or acquiring an independent accent: said of certain particles, etc., as when used interrogatively.

ọr′thō·tōne, *n.* an orthotone word.

ọr·thot′ō·nus, *n.* [*ortho-*, and Gr. *tonos*, tension.] in pathology, the rigid straightening of the body, as in lockjaw.

ọr·thot′rō·pȧl, *a.* same as *orthotropous*.

ọr·thō·trop′iç, *a.* in botany, designating, of, or showing vertical growth.

ọr·thot′rō·piṣm, *n.* [*ortho-* and *-tropism*.] in botany, growth, or a tendency to grow, in a vertical direction or position.

ọr·thot′rō·pous, *a.* [*ortho-* and *-tropous*.] in botany, growing straight: said of a nucellus.

ọr·thot′y·pous, *a.* [*ortho-*, and Gr. *typos*, form.] in mineralogy, having a perpendicular cleavage.

ọr·thō·xy̆′lēne (-zī′), *n.* [*ortho-* and *xylene*.] in chemistry, xylene showing double substitution in contiguous carbon atoms.

ORTHOTROPOUS OVULE

ọr′thros, *n.* in the Orthodox Eastern Church, a canonical hour, similar to the Roman Catholic *lauds*, but having a more elaborate service.

ọr′tive, *a.* [L. *ortivus*, from *ortus*, pp. of *oriri*, to rise.] rising; eastern; orient; as, the *ortive* amplitude of a planet. [Rare.]

ọr′tō·lăn, *n.* [Fr.; Pr.; It. *ortolano*, a gardener, an ortolan; L. *hortulanus*, from *hortus*, a garden.]

1. an Old World bunting, prized as a table delicacy.
2. the bobolink.
3. the sora.

ọrts, *n.* plural of *ort*.

ọr′ty·găn, *n.* [Gr. *ortyx*, *ortygos*, quail.] any one of several East Indian birds of the genus *Turnix*, *Ortygis*, or *Hemipodius*.

ọr·vi·ē′tăn, *n.* [It. *orvietano*, from the town of *Orvieto*, where the inventor was born.] an antidote or counterpoison. [Obs.]

Ọr·vi·ẹ′tō, *n.* a white wine made near Orvieto, Italy.

-ō′ry, 1. [ME. *-orie*; OFr. *-oire*; L. *-orius*, *-oria*, *-orium*.] an adjective-forming suffix meaning *of, having the nature of*, as in hortat*ory*, commendat*ory*.

2. [ME. *-orie*; OFr. *-oire*, *-orie*; L. *-orium*.] a noun-forming suffix meaning *a place* or *thing for*, as in refect*ory*, direct*ory*.

or′yç·tēre, *n.* [Fr., from Gr. *oryktēr*, digger.] the aardvark.

ō·ryç′tēr·ōpe, *n.* an animal of the genus *Orycteropus*.

Or·yç·ter′ō·pus, *n.* [Gr. *oryktēr*, digger, and *pous*, a foot.] a genus of edentate insectivorous animals, resembling the anteater and the armadillo. The *Orycteropus capensis* has received the name of the aardvark, or earth hog, from the Dutch colonists at the Cape of Good Hope, from its habit of burrowing, and from its fancied resemblance to a small, short-legged hog. When full-grown it measures about five feet from the tip of the snout to the end of the tail.

or″yç·tog·nos′tiç, *a.* pertaining to oryctognosy. [Obs.]

or·yç·tog′nō·sy, *n.* [Gr. *oryktos*, fossil, and *gnōsis*, knowledge.] mineralogy. [Obs.]

or·yç·tog′rȧ·phy, *n.* oryctognosy. [Obs.]

or·yç·tō·loġ′iç·ȧl, *a.* pertaining to oryctology. [Obs.]

or·yç·tol′ō·ġist, *n.* one learned in oryctology. [Obs.]

or·yç·tol′ō·ġy, *n.* [Gr. *oryktos*, fossil, and *-logy*.] the science that deals with things dug up. [Obs.]

Ō′ryx, *n.* [ME. *orix*; ML.; L., gazelle; Gr. *oryx*, from *oryssein*, to dig: so called from its pointed horns.]

1. a genus of large antelopes having long, straight horns projecting backward and including *Oryx capensis*, the South African gemsbok, and *Oryx leucoryx*, the algazel.
2. [o–] *pl.* **ō′ryx·eṣ** or **ō′ryx,** any antelope of this genus.

Ō·ry̆′zȧ, *n.* [Gr. *oryza*, rice.] a genus of true grasses, mostly native to the tropics, and including the cultivated rice, *Oriza sativa*.

os, *n.*; *pl.* **os′sȧ,** [L.] in anatomy, a bone.

os, *n.*; *pl.* **ō′rȧ,** [L.] in anatomy, an opening, as a mouth; an entrance, as the orifice of the vagina.

os, *n.*; *pl.* **ō′sär,** [Sw. *as*.] in geology, a glacially deposited winding ridge of sand or gravel; an esker.

Ō′sȧġe, *n.* [Am. Ind. (Osage) *Wazhazhe*, war people.]

1. a member of a tribe of Siouan Indians who migrated from the Ohio River Valley to the Osage River in Missouri.
2. their Siouan language, closely allied to Omaha.

Ō′sȧġe or′anġe (-enj), 1. a small ornamental tree, *Maclura aurantiaca*, native to the Osage Mountains in Arkansas, and cultivated for hedges. It bears an inedible fruit somewhat resembling an orange. Its wood is hard and elastic and was formerly much used by the Indians in making bows, hence its popular name, *bowwood*.

2. its fruit.

ō·ṣan′nȧ, *n.* and *interj.* hosanna.

ōs′ȧ·zōne, *n.* in physiological chemistry, any one of a series of compounds obtained by heating sugar with phenyl hydrazine and acetic acid.

Os′căn, *a.* [L. *Oscus*.]

1. a member of an ancient people who lived in Campania, Italy.
2. the Italic language of the Oscans.

Os′căn, *a.* of the Oscans or their language.

Os′căr, *n.* any of the statuettes awarded annually in the United States for outstanding contributions to the motion-picture industry. [Slang.]

os′çhē·ō·cēle, *n.* [Gr. *oschē*, the scrotum, and *kēlē*, a tumor.] any tumor or swelling of the scrotum; also, scrotal hernia.

os′cil·lăn·cy, *n.* oscillation. [Rare.]

Os·cil·lȧ′ri·ȧ, *n.* a genus of algae typical of the family *Oscillariaceæ*.

Os·cil·lā·ri·ā′cē·ae, *n.pl.* a family of algae having blue-green filaments which, singly or massed, exhibit oscillating movements.

os·cil·lā·ri·ā′ceous, *a.* of or pertaining to the *Oscillariaceæ*.

os′cil·lāte, *v.i.*; oscillated, *pt.*, *pp.*; oscillating, *ppr.* [L. *oscillare*, to swing, from *oscillum*, a swing, lit., a little face or mask hung to a tree and swaying with the wind, dim. of *os*, the mouth, the face.]

1. to swing to and fro.
2. to be indecisive in purpose or opinion; to fluctuate; to vacillate.
3. in physics, to vary between maximum and minimum values, as an electric current.

os′cil·lāte, *v.t.* to cause to oscillate.

oscillating steam engine; an engine with a vibratory cylinder.

oscillating valve; a valve having axial vibration on a shaft.

os·cil·lā′tion, *n.* [L. *oscillatio*.]

1. an oscillating.
2. fluctuation; instability; variation.
3. in electricity, variation between maximum and minimum values, as of current or voltage.
4. in physics, a single swing of an oscillating object between the two extremes of its arc.

os′cil·lā·tive, *a.* having a tendency to oscillate.

os′cil·lā·tŏr, *n.* 1. one who or that which oscillates.

2. in electricity, an apparatus producing oscillations, as a radio-frequency generator.

Os″cil·lȧ·tō′ri·ȧ, *n.* same as *Oscillaria*.

os′cil·lȧ·tō·ry, *a.* moving backward and forward like a pendulum; oscillating.

os′cil·lō·grȧph, *n.* [L. *oscillare*, to swing, and Gr. *graphein*, to describe.] an instrument consisting usually of a galvanometer of strong field and high frequency of vibration, which registers oscillations of an electric current and photographically records the variation.

os·cil·lom′ē·tẽr, *n.* [L. *oscillare*, to swing, and Gr. *metron*, a measure.] an apparatus consisting of a telescope mounted to maintain a horizontal position, used to measure the degree of inclination of a rolling ship at sea.

os·cil′lō·sçōpe, *n.* [L. *oscillare*, to swing, and *-scope*.] a type of oscillograph that visually records an electrical wave on a fluorescent screen, as of a cathode-ray tube.

os′cine, *a.* of or pertaining to the *Oscines*.

os′cine, *n.* any of the *Oscines*.

Os′ci·nēṣ, *n.pl.* [L. *oscen*, singing bird; *obs*, old form of *ob*, before, and *canere*, to sing.] a special group of perching birds, as the finches, larks, shrikes, buntings, etc., with highly developed vocal organs and certain other structures in common: some do not sing.

os·cin′i·ăn, *a.* and *n.* same as *oscine*.

os·cin′i·ăn, *n.* any dipterous fly of the family *Oscinidæ*, including species destructive to grain.

os′ci·nine, *a.* pertaining to the *Oscines*.

os′ci·tăn·cy, *n.* [L. *oscitare*, to yawn, from *os*, the mouth, and *citare*, to move quickly, from *ciere*, to put in motion.]

1. the act of gaping or yawning.
2. apathy; stupor; drowsiness; dullness.

os′ci·tănt, *a.* 1. yawning; gaping.

2. sleepy; drowsy; dull; sluggish.

os′ci·tănt·ly, *adv.* in a sleepy, dull manner.

os′ci·tāte, *v.i.* [L. *oscitare*.] to yawn; to gape with sleepiness.

os·ci·tā′tion, *n.* the act of yawning or gaping from sleepiness.

Os′cō-Um′bri·ăn, *a.* designating or of the group of Italic languages comprising Oscan and Umbrian.

os′çū·lănt, *a.* [L. *osculans*, ppr. of *osculari*, to kiss.]

1. kissing.
2. touching; connecting.
3. in biology, intermediate; linking; shared: said of a characteristic common to two or more groups.

os′çū·lăr, *a.* 1. of the mouth or kissing.

2. in biology, of an osculum.

os′çū·lāte, *v.t.* and *v.i.*; osculated, *pt.*, *pp.*; osculating, *ppr.* [L. *osculari*, to kiss, from *osculum*, a little mouth, a kiss, dim. of *os*, the mouth.]

1. to kiss.
2. to touch closely.
3. in biology, to have (characteristics) in common.
4. in mathematics, to touch, as two curves, at three or more points.

os·çū·lā′tion, *n.* [L. *osculatio*, a kissing.]

1. a kissing or being kissed.
2. a kiss.
3. a close contact.
4. in mathematics, a contact between osculating curves, etc.

os′çū·lȧ·tō·ry, *a.* osculating.

os′çū·lȧ·tō·ry, *n.* in medieval church history, a tablet or board with a picture of Jesus, the Virgin Mary, or a saint, which was kissed by the priest, and then delivered to the congregation for the same purpose.

os·çū·lā′trix, *n.*; *pl.* **os·çū·lā′trix·eṣ,** in geometry, the invariable tangent of the osculating planes of a winding curve.

os′çūle, *n.* [L. *osculum*, a small mouth.] an osculum.

os′çū·lum, *n.*; *pl.* **os′çū·lȧ,** 1. any of the apertures by which water is expelled in sponges; a mouth.

2. a sucker on the head of a tapeworm.

-ōse, [Fr. *-ose*, from *glucose*.] a suffix meaning: (a) *a carbohydrate*, as in cellul*ose*, sucr*ose*; (b) *the product of a protein hydrolysis*, as in prote*ose*.

-ōse, [Fr. *-ose*, L. *-osus*.] a suffix meaning *full of, containing, like*, as in verb*ose*, glob*ose*.

ō′ṣel, *n.* same as *ouzel*.

ō·sel′lȧ, *n.* [It.] a silver medal instituted in 1521 and used by the doges of Venice for presentation to honored persons in the republic.

os′gas, *n.* same as *gecko*.

Ō·si·an′dri·ăn, *a.* pertaining to the teaching of Osiander, a Lutheran theologian (1498–1552).

Ō·si·an′dri·ăn, *n.* a follower of Osiander.

ō′ṣiẽr (-zhẽr), *n.* [Fr. *osier*; ML. *ausaria*, bed of willows.]

1. any of various related species of willow (*Salix*) whose twigs are used in making baskets. *Salix viminalis*, the European velvet osier, is the species most used.
2. a similar plant of some other genus.
3. one of the pliant twigs of the osier.

ō′ṣiẽr, *a.* consisting of or made of osiers.

ō′ṣiẽr āit, a small island for growing osiers.

ō′ṣiẽr bed, an osiery; a piece of ground planted with osiers.

ō′ṣiẽred (-zhẽrd), *a.* covered or decorated with osiers.

ō′ṣiẽr hōlt, [AS. *holt*, a wood.] in England, a place where willows for basketwork are cultivated.

ō′ṣiẽr·y, *n.*; *pl.* **ō′ṣiẽr·ieṣ,** a bed of osiers.

Ō·sī′ri·ăn, Ō·sī′ride, *a.* relating or belonging to Osiris.

Osirian column; an ancient Egyptian pillar upon which was placed a standing figure of Osiris.

Ō·sī′ri·fȳ, *v.t.*; Osirified, *pt.*, *pp.*; Osirifying, *ppr.* to deify or identify with Osiris.

Ō·sī′ris, *n.* [Gr. and L., from Egypt. *Ás-ár*.] the ancient Egyptian god of the lower world and judge of the dead, husband and brother of Isis.

-ō′sis, [Gr. *-osis*, condition.] a suffix meaning: (a) *state, condition, action*, as in osmosis; (b) *an abnormal* or *diseased condition*, as in neurosis.

-os′i·ty, [Fr. *-osité*; L. *-ositas*.] a suffix used to form nouns corresponding to adjectives ending in *-ose* or *-ous*.

Os·man′li, *a.* [from *Osman* or *Othman*, who founded the Ottoman Empire.] Turkish; Ottoman.

Os·man′li, *n.*; *pl.* **Os·man′lis,** 1. an Ottoman Turk.
2. the language of the Ottoman Turks.

os′mȧ·zōme, *n.* [Gr. *osmē*, odor, and *zōmos*, juice.] in old chemistry, a substance of an aromatic flavor, obtained from muscular fiber, and formed in the roasting of meat.

os·mē·tē′ri·um, *n.*; *pl.* **os·mē·tē′ri·ȧ,** in entomology, an organ for the production of a scent or odor.

os·mi·am′āte, *n.* a salt of osmiamic acid.

os·mi·am′iç, *a.* [*osmium* and *amide*.] containing nitrogen and osmium; as, *osmiamic* acid.
osmiamic acid; an acid obtained by decomposing barium salt with a solution of sulfuric acid.

os′miç, *a.* designating or of chemical compounds in which osmium has a higher valence than in the corresponding osmious compounds.

os·mi·drō′sis, *n.* [Gr. *osmē*, smell, and *hidrōsis*, perspiration.] in medicine, a condition in which the perspiration has an abnormally strong odor.

os′mi·ous, *a.* designating or of chemical compounds in which osmium has a lower valence than in the corresponding osmic compounds.

os·mi·rid′i·um, *n.* [*osmium* and *iridium*.] a very hard native alloy of iridium and osmium with a small amount of various other metals of the platinum group, used especially in pen points: also called *iridosmine, iridosmium*.

os′mi·um, *n.* [Gr. *osmē*, odor.] a bluish-white, amorphous, metallic chemical element of the platinum group: it occurs in the form of an alloy with platinum and iridium: symbol, Os; atomic weight, 190.2; atomic number, 76.

os′mō-, [from Gr. *osmē*, odor.] a combining form meaning *odor*.

os″mō·dys·phō′ri·ȧ, *n.* [*osmo-*, and Gr. *dys*, badly, and *pherein*, to bear.] an intense dislike for certain odors.

os·mom′ē·tēr, *n.* [Gr. *ōsmos*, impulsion, and *metron*, measure.]
1. in physics, a device for measuring the molecular pressure in different liquids.
2. [Gr. *osmē*, odor.] an instrument for measuring the acuteness of the sense of smell.

os·mom′e·try, *n.* 1. in physics, the measurement of osmotic force.
2. the measurement of the acuteness of smell.

os″mō·nos·ol′ō·ġy, *n.* [*osmo-*, and Gr. *nosos*, disease, and *logos*, description.] the branch of pathology that deals with diseases of the nose.

os′mōse, *v.i.*; osmosed (-mōst), *pt., pp.*; osmosing, *ppr.* to undergo osmosis.

os·mō′sis, *n.* [Gr. *ōsmos*, an impulse, a pushing, from *ōthein*, to push.]
1. the tendency of a fluid to pass through a semipermeable membrane, as the wall of a living cell, into a solution of lower concentration, so as to equalize concentrations on both sides of the membrane.
2. the diffusion of fluids through a membrane or porous partition.
electric osmose or *osmosis*; see under *electric*.

os·mot′iç, *a.* pertaining to or of the nature of osmosis.
osmotic pressure; the pressure produced by osmosis; the pressure in a solution due to the pressure of a dissolved substance.

os·mot′iç·ăl·ly, *adv.* by or according to osmosis.

os′mund, *n.* [Fr. *osmonde*; LL. *osmunda*.] a fern of the genus *Osmunda*.

Os·mun′dȧ, *n.* a genus of flowering ferns found throughout the northern temperate zone. It includes *Osmunda regalis*, the royal fern, or osmund royal, of North America.

Os·mun·dā′cē·ae, *n.pl.* an order of flowering ferns typified by *Osmunda*.

os·mun·dā′ceous, *a.* pertaining to or resembling the genus *Osmunda*.

os′nȧ·bŭrg, *n.* a kind of coarse, heavy cloth, originally of linen and now of cotton, used in making sacks, work clothes, etc.: it was made originally at Osnaburg, in Germany.

ō′sō·ber″ry, *n.* a small tree, *Nuttallia cerasiformis*, growing in California and Oregon.

os·phrā′di·um, *n.*; *pl.* **os·phrā′di·ȧ,** [Gr. *osphradion*, of the same root as *osmē*, smell.] the olfactory organ of certain mollusks.

os·phrē·si·ol′ō·ġy, *n.* [Gr. *osphrēsis*, smelling, and *-logy*.] the study of or a treatise on the sense of smell.

Os·phrō·men′i·dae, *n.pl.* a family of acanthopterygious fishes.

Os·phrom′e·nus, *n.* [Gr. *osphromenos*, ppr. of *osphrainesthai*, to smell.] a genus of fishes typical of *Osphromenidæ*.

os″phy·ō·mȳ″el·ī′tis, *n.* [Gr. *osphys*, loin, and *myelitis*.] inflammation of the spinal cord in the lumbar region.

os′prey (-pri), *n.*; *pl.* **os′preys,** [from L. *ossifraga*, the osprey; lit., the bone-breaker; *os*, a bone, and *frangere*, to break.] the fish-hawk, bald buzzard, or fishing eagle, *Pandion haliaëtus*, a bird of prey, of almost world-wide distribution, subsisting on fish. It is about two feet long, with a wing spread nearly three times as great. The plumage is glossy-brown on top, and the underparts are white with a brown band across the breast. Also called *fish hawk, ossifrage*.

OSPREY (*Pandion haliaetus*)

oss, *v.t.* and *v.i.* to presage; to predict. [Obs.]

oss, *n.* a prophecy. [Obs.]

os′sȧ, *n.* plural of *os* (bone).

os·sār′i·um, *n.*; *pl.* **os·sār′i·ȧ,** [LL., from L. *os*, bone.] an ossuary; a receptacle for the bones or ashes of the dead.

os′sȧ·tūre, *n.* [Fr., a skeleton, from L. *os*, bone.] in architecture, the frame or skeleton of a building or of some part of a building.

Os′sē·ī, *n.pl.* in zoology, same as *Teleostei*.

os′sē·in, *n.* [L. *os*, bone.] the organic basis of bone: also called *ostein*.

os′sē·let, *n.* [Fr., from L. *os, ossis*, a bone.]
1. an ossicle; a little bone.
2. in zoology, the bone or pen of a cuttlefish.

os′sē·ous, *a.* [L. *osseus*, from *os*, a bone.] bony; composed of or resembling bone; of the nature or quality of bone.
osseous labyrinth; the capsule of bone that encloses the passages to the inner ear.

os′sē·ous·ly, *adv.* as regards bones; in the way of bones.

Os′set, *n.* one of a people who live in the Caucasus, U.S.S.R.

os′sē·tēr, *n.* [Russ. *osetr′*.] a large sturgeon of Europe, *Acipenser guldenstadti*.

Os·sē′tiăn, *a.* 1. of the Ossets.
2. of Ossetia, a region in the Caucasus, U.S.S.R.

Os·sē′tiăn, *n.* an Osset.

Os·set′iç, *a.* same as *Ossetian*.

Os·set′iç, *n.* the Iranian language of the Ossets.

Os′siăn, *n.* in Gaelic folklore, a bard and hero of the third century A.D.: James MacPherson published pieces of rhythmic prose (1761–1765) which he claimed were his translations of Ossian's poetry from old Gaelic manuscripts.

Os·si·an′iç, *a.* 1. pertaining to or characteristic of Ossian, a Gaelic or Celtic poet, or the writings attributed to him.
2. of or like the supposed translations of Ossian by James MacPherson; pompous; flowery; bombastic.

os′si·çle, *n.* [L. *ossiculum*.] a small bone or bonelike structure; especially, any of the three small bones in the tympanic cavity of the ear.

os·siç′ū·lăr, *a.* pertaining to or like ossicles.

os·siç′ū·lāte, os·siç′ū·lā·ted, *a.* having ossicles, or small bones.

os·siç′ū·lum, *n.*; *pl.* **os·siç′ū·lȧ,** in zoology, same as *ossicle*.

os·sif′ẽr·ous, *a.* [L. *os*, a bone, and *ferre*, to produce.] containing bones, as a geologic deposit.

os·sif′iç, *a.* [L. *os*, a bone, and *facere*, to make.] having the power to ossify, or change tissue into bony substance.

os″si·fi·çā′tion, *n.* 1. an ossifying or being ossified.
2. any bone structure.
3. the pathological or abnormal conversion of soft tissue into bone.

os′si·fied, *a.* converted into bone, or a hard substance like bone.

os′si·frāġe, *n.* [L. *ossifraga*; *os*, bone, and *frangere*, to break.] a bird, the osprey; also, the European lammergeier.

os′si·fȳ, *v.t.* and *v.i.*; ossified, *pt., pp.*; ossifying, *ppr.* [L. *os*, bone, and *facere*, to form.]
1. in physiology, to change or develop into bone.
2. to settle or fix rigidly in a practice, custom, etc.

os′si·fȳ·ing, *a.* changing into bone; becoming bone.

os·siv′ō·rous, *a.* [L. *os*, bone, and *vorare*, to eat.] feeding on bones; eating bones.

os·sū·ār′i·um (*or* -shū-), *n.*; *pl.* **os·sū·ār′i·ȧ,** [L.] a receptacle for the bones of the dead.

os′sū·ăr·y, *n.*; *pl.* **os′sū·ăr·ies,** 1. a charnel house; a place where the bones of the dead are deposited.
2. a receptacle for the ashes or bones of the dead; an ossuarium.

ost, *n.* a kiln for drying hops or malt; an oast.

os′tē·ăl, *a.* [Gr. *osteon*, bone.] pertaining to or like bone; bony.

os′tē·in, *n.* same as *ossein*.

os·tē·it′iç, *a.* pertaining to or affected by osteitis.

os·tē·ī′tis, *n.* [Gr. *osteon*, bone.] inflammation of the bones or bony tissue: also *ostitis*.

os·tend′, *v.t.* and *v.i.* [L. *ostendere*, to show; *obs*, for *ob*, before, and *tendere*, to stretch.] to exhibit. [Obs.]

os·ten·si·bil′i·ty, *n.* the quality or state of being ostensible.

os·ten′si·ble, *a.* [It. *ostensibile*, from L. *ostendere*, to show.]
1. that may be shown; proper or intended to be shown. [Rare.]
2. apparent; seeming; shown; declared; avowed; evident.

> One of the *ostensible* grounds on which the proprietors had obtained their charter.
> —Ramsay.

Syn.—professed, apparent, avowed, specious.

os·ten′si·bly, *adv.* in an ostensible manner; in a declared or pretended manner; apparently; avowedly.

os·ten′sion, *n.* [L. *ostendere*, to show.] in the Roman Catholic Church, the placing of the Sacrament or Host on the altar for the purpose of adoration.

os·ten′sive, *a.* [Fr., from L. *ostendere*.]
1. ostensible; exhibiting; revealing.
2. in logic, characterized by proof through broad principle.

os·ten′sive·ly, *adv.* in an ostensive manner.

os·ten·sō′ri·um, os·ten′sō·ry, *n.* same as *monstrance*.

os·tent′, *n.* [L. *ostentum*, from *ostendere*, to show.]
1. appearance; air; manner; mien. [Obs.]
2. show; manifestation; token; portent. [Rare.]

> Goodly the *ostents* are to thee
> And pomps of time. —William Watson.

os′ten·tāte, *v.t.* [L. *ostentare*.] to make an ambitious display of; to show or exhibit boastfully. [Archaic.]

os·ten·tā′tion, *n.* [L. *ostentatio*.]
1. the act of making an ambitious display; pretentious or vain show; display of anything dictated by vanity or intended to invite praise or flattery.

> He knew that good and bountiful minds are sometimes inclined to *ostentation*.
> —Atterbury.

2. a show or spectacle. [Obs.]

Syn.—show, display, flourish, parade, pageantry, pomp, pomposity.

os·ten·tā′tious (-shus), *a.* characterized by or given to ostentation; boastful; showy; pretentious.

> Your modesty is so far from being *ostentatious* of the good you do. —Dryden.

os·ten·tā′tious·ly, *adv.* in an ostentatious manner.

os·ten·tā′tious·ness, *n.* the state or quality of being ostentatious.

os·ten·tā′tŏr, *n.* [L.] one who makes a vain show; a boaster. [Obs.]

os·ten′tive, os·ten′tous, *a.* ostentatious. [Obs.]

os′tē·ō-, [from Gr. *osteon*, a bone.] a combining form meaning *a bone* or *bones*, as in *osteo*path: also, before a vowel, *oste-*.

os′tē·ō·blast, *n.* [*osteo-*, and Gr. *blastos*, germ.] any cell which develops into bone or secretes substances producing bony tissue: also called *osteoplast*.

os″tē·ō·blas′tiç, *a.* of or relating to osteoblasts; characteristic of an osteoblast.

os′tē·ō·cēle, *n.* [*osteo-*, and Gr. *kēlē*, a rupture.]

a hernia in which the sac is cartilaginous and bony.

os·tē·oç′lȧ·sis, *n.* [*osteo-*, and Gr. *klasis*, fracture.]

1. the breaking of a bone to correct a deformity; especially, such breaking of a bone badly healed after a previous fracture.

2. the breaking down and absorption of bony tissue.

os′tē·ō·çlast, *n.* 1. any of the large multinuclear cells in developing bone which absorb bony tissue, thus forming certain hollow parts in the bone, as canals and marrow cavities.

2. an instrument used to perform osteoclasis.

os″tē·ō·çlas′tiç, *a.* relating to or characteristic of an osteoclast.

os″tē·ō·çol′lȧ, *n.* [*osteo-*, and Gr. *kolla*, glue: from its supposed quality of uniting fractured bones.] a carbonate of lime incrusting the stem of a plant.

os″tē·ō·çom′mȧ, *n.* [*osteo-* and *comma.*] one of the serial segments of bones of the vertebrate skeleton; a metamere of a skeleton; an osteomere.

os′tē·ō·çōpe, *n.* [*osteo-*, and Gr. *kopos*, labor, uneasiness.] pain in the bones; a sharp, prolonged pain in any part of a bone.

os″tē·ō·çop′iç, *a.* pertaining to osteocope.

os″tē·ō·crā′ni·um, *n.* [*osteo-* and *cranium.*] the osseous part of the cranium, as distinguished from the cartilaginous part.

os″tē·ō·den′tine, *n.* [*osteo-*, and L. *dens, dentis*, a tooth.] that modification of dentine found in the teeth of the cachalot and many fishes.

os″tē·ō·dēr′mȧ·tous, *a.* [*osteo-*, and Gr. *derma* (*-atos*), skin.] having an ossified skin, as certain animals.

os′tē·ō·ġen, *n.* the soft, transparent tissue that appears in developing bone.

os″tē·ō·ġen′e·sis, os·tē·oġ′e·ny, *n.* [*osteo-*, and Gr. *genesis*, generation.] the formation or growth of bone.

os″tē·ō·ġē·net′iç, *a.* relating to or characteristic of osteogenesis.

os·tē·ō·ġen′iç, *a.* same as *osteogenetic.*

os·tē·og′rȧ·phēr, *n.* an anatomist who describes the skeleton of the body; an osteologist.

os·tē·og′rȧ·phy, *n.* [*osteo-*, and Gr. *graphein*, to describe.] a description of the bones; osteology.

os′tē·oid, *a.* resembling bone; osseous.

Os·tē·ol′e·pis, *n.* [*osteo-*, and Gr. *lepis*, a scale.] a genus of ganoid fishes with a dermoskeleton of enameled bone, and an endoskeleton of cartilage.

os′tē·ō·līte, *n.* [*osteo-*, and Gr. *lithos*, stone.] a massive, impure variety of apatite.

os·tē·ol′ō·ġēr, *n.* an osteologist.

os″tē·ō·loġ′iç·ăl, os″tē·ō·loġ′iç, *a.* relating to osteology.

os″tē·ō·loġ′iç·ăl·ly, *adv.* according to osteology.

os·tē·ol′ō·ġist, *n.* one skilled in osteology.

os·tē·ol′ō·ġy, *n.* [*osteo-*, and Gr. *logos*, discourse.] that branch of anatomy which deals with the physical and chemical properties of osseous tissue, and with the form, development, articulations, etc. of the bones composing the skeletons of vertebrates.

os·tē·ol′y·sis, *n.* [*osteo-*, and Gr. *lysis*, from *lyein*, to loose.] in medicine, softening of bone; absorption of bone.

os″tē·ō·lyt′iç, *a.* pertaining to or characterized by osteolysis.

os·tē·ō′mȧ, *n.*; *pl.* **os·tē·ō′mȧṣ, os·tē·ō′mȧ·tȧ,** [Gr. *osteon*, a bone.] a bony tumor; an outgrowth from bone or cartilage.

os″tē·ō·mȧ·lā′ci·ȧ, *n.* [*osteo-*, and Gr. *malakia*, softness.] a softening of the bones in adults, the result of poor or faulty nutrition, in which the essential salts disappear from the bones.

os′tē·ō·man·ty, *n.* [*osteo-*, and Gr. *manteia*, prophecy.] divination by means of bones.

os′tē·ō·mēre, *n.* same as *osteocomma.*

os·tē·om′e·try, *n.* [*osteo-*, and Gr. *-metria*, from *metron*, measure.] the measurement of bones.

os″tē·ō·mȳ″e·lī′tis, *n.* [*osteo-* and *myelitis.*] inflammation of the bone marrow.

os′tē·ō·path, *n.* one who practices osteopathy.

os″tē·ō·path′iç, *a.* of or based on osteopathy.

os·tē·op′ȧ·thist, *n.* one believing in or practicing osteopathy; an osteopath.

os·tē·op′ȧ·thy, *n.* [*osteo-*, and Gr. *patheia*, from *pathos*, suffering.]

1. any form of bone disease.

2. a theory and system of treating ailments based on the belief that they generally result from the pressure of displaced bones on nerves, etc. and are curable by manipulation.

os′tē·ō·phōne, *n.* [*osteo-*, and Gr. *phōnē*, voice.] a hearing instrument for deaf persons: it is placed in contact with the upper teeth, the vibrations thus being transmitted to the auditory nerve through the medium of the bones of the skull.

os′tē·ō·phȳte, *n.* [*osteo-*, and Gr. *phyton*, tumor, growth.] in medicine, a small bony outgrowth.

os′tē·ō·plast, *n.* see *osteoblast.*

os″tē·ō·plas′tiç, *a.* 1. causing the formation and development of bone; as, *osteoplastic* cells.

2. in surgery, relating to the operation of replacing bone.

os′tē·ō·plas·ty, *n.* [*osteo-*, and Gr. *plassein*, to form.] in surgery, bone grafting.

os″tē·ō·pō·rō′sis, *n.* [*osteo-*, and Gr. *poros*, passage.] an absorption of bone, resulting in abnormally porous tissue.

os·tē·op·tēr·yġ′i·ous, *a.* [*osteo-*, and Gr. *pteryx, pterygos*, wing.] in zoology, designating certain fishes that have bones in the fins.

os″tē·ō·sär·çō′mȧ, *n.*; *pl.* **os″tē·ō·sär·çō′mȧ·tȧ,** [*osteo-* and *sarcoma.*] a disease of the bony tissue characterized by a fleshy or cartilaginous growth; a sarcoma of bone or one containing bony tissue.

os′tē·ō·tōme, *n.* [*osteo-*, and Gr. *tomē*, a cutting.] in surgery, a sawlike instrument for cutting bones.

os·tē·ot′ō·mist, *n.* one skilled in the science and practice of osteotomy.

os·tē·ot′ō·my, *n.* [*osteo-*, and Gr. *tomē*, a cutting.]

1. the dissection of bones; the anatomy of bones.

2. in surgery, the operation of cutting or dividing a bone in order to correct or remedy deformity, etc.

Os″tē·ō·zō′ȧ, *n.pl.* [*osteo-*, and Gr. *zōon*, animal.] same as *Vertebrata.*

os·tẹ·rï′ȧ, *n.* [It.] an inn; a hostelry.

Os′ti·ak, *n.* Ostyak.

os′ti·ăr·y, *n.*; *pl.* **os′ti·ăr·ieṣ,** [L. *ostium*, mouth.]

1. the mouth or opening by which a river discharges its waters into a sea or lake; an estuary. [Rare.]

2. a doorkeeper, particularly one who guards the door of a church.

3. in the Roman Catholic Church, (a) the lowest of the minor orders; (b) a member of this order.

Os′tiç, *a.* same as *Iroquoian.*

ọs·ti·nä′tō, *n.*; *pl.* **ọs·ti·nä′tōṣ,** [It., lit., obstinate.] in music, a short melodic phrase constantly repeated by the same voice or instrument and in the same pitch.

os′ti·ō·lăr, *a.* of an ostiole.

os′ti·ō·lāte, *a.* having ostioles; producing ostioles.

os′ti·ōle, *n.* [L., dim. of *ostium*, a door.] a small opening or orifice, as a pore.

os·tī′tis, *n.* same as *osteitis.*

os′ti·um, *n.*; *pl.* **os′ti·ȧ,** [L.] in anatomy, a mouth or orifice; a passage.

os′tlēr (-lēr), *n.* [ME. *osterlere*, var. of *hostelere*, with phonetic omission of mute *h.*] a hostler; stableman.

os′tlēr·ess, *n.* a woman hostler.

os′tlēr·y, *n.* a hostelry. [Obs.]

Ōst′märk, *n.*; *pl.* **Ōst′märk;** Eng. **Ōst′märks,** the monetary unit of the Soviet zone of occupation in Germany.

Ōst′men, *n.pl.* east men: the name formerly given to Danish and Norse settlers in Ireland.

os·tō′sis, *n.* [Gr. *osteon*, bone.] bone formation or development; ossification.

Os·trā′cē·ȧ (-shē-), *n.pl.* [LL., from Gr. *ostrakon*, shell.] in zoology, a family of bivalve mollusks in which are included the oysters and other related shells.

os·trā′ceăn (-shăn), *n.* a bivalve mollusk of the family *Ostracea.*

os·trā′ci·oid, *a.* [Gr. *ostrakon*, shell, and *-oid.*] relating to or resembling the *Ostracodermi.*

Os·trā′ci·on, *n.* [Gr. *ostrakon*, a shell.] a genus of fishes, in which the body is entirely enclosed, with the exception of the tail, in an immovable case composed of large ganoid plates firmly united to one another at their edges; trunkfishes.

os·trā′ci·ont, *n.* a fish belonging to the genus *Ostracion*, or some related genus.

os′trȧ·çiṣm, *n.* [Gr. *ostrakismos*, from *ostrakon*, a shell.]

1. in ancient Greece, the temporary banishment of a citizen by popular vote: ballots were cast on shells or potsherds.

2. a rejection or exclusion by general consent, as from society.

os′trȧ·çīte, *n.* [Gr. *ostrakitēs*, from *ostrakon*, a shell.] an oyster in its fossil state.

os′trȧ·çīze, *v.t.*; ostracized, *pt., pp.*; ostracizing, *ppr.* 1. in ancient Greece, to banish by popular vote.

2. to cast out or banish; to exclude; to subject to ostracism in social, political, or public life.

Os·traç′ō·dȧ, *n.pl.* [Gr. *ostrakōdēs*; *ostrakon*, shell, and *eidos*, form.] an order of entomostracous crustaceans, in which the body is entirely enclosed under a large shield having the form of a bivalve shell.

os″trȧ·çō·dēr′măl, os″trȧ·çō·dēr′mous, *a.*

1. of or pertaining to the *Ostracodermi.*

2. having the body covered with bony scales.

Os″trȧ·çō·dēr′mī, *n.pl.* [Gr. *ostrakon*, shell, and *derma*, skin.] a division of fishes which have the body encased in hard, rigid plates or scales. The typical genus is *Ostracion.*

os′trȧ·çoid, *a.* belonging or relating to the *Ostracoidea.*

os′trȧ·çoid, *n.* one of the *Ostracoidea.*

Os·trȧ·çoi′dē·ȧ, *n.pl.* [Gr. *ostrakon*, shell, and *-oid.*] an order of entomostracans which have a hard bivalve shell encasing most of the body.

Os′trē·ȧ, *n.* [L.] the genus of mollusks that includes the edible oysters.

os·trē·ā′ceous, *a.* pertaining to or characteristic of an oyster; shelly.

os″trē·i·çul′tūre, *n.* [L. *ostrea*, oyster, and *cultura*, culture.] the artificial cultivation of oysters.

os′trē·i·form, *a.* [L. *ostrea*, oyster, and *forma*, form.] shaped like an oyster.

os′trē·oid, *a.* [Gr. *ostreon*, oyster, and *-oid.*] relating to or characteristic of an oyster; ostreaceous.

os·trē·oph′ȧ·ġist, *n.* [Gr. *ostreon*, oyster, and *phagein*, to eat.] one who or that which eats or feeds on oysters.

os′trich, *n.* [OFr. *ostruche, ostruce*; Fr. *autruche*; Sp. *avestruz*, from L. *avis*, a bird, and *struthio*, Gr. *strouthiōn*, an ostrich.] a large bird of the genus *Struthio*, family *Struthionidæ.* The true, or African, ostrich, *Struthio camelus*, inhabits the sandy plains of Africa and Arabia, and is the largest of all existing birds, attaining a height of from 6 to 8 feet. It has a long neck, very long legs with two toes on each foot, and small, useless wings; the white tail and wing feathers of the male are used in millinery and as trimming. Its food consists of grass, grain, etc., and to pulverize this food the ostrich swallows large stones or other hard materials. Three South American birds of the same family, *Struthionidæ*, but of the genus *Rhea*, are very closely allied to the true ostrich, differing chiefly in having three-toed feet, each toe armed with a claw. The best known of the three is *Rhea americana*, the nandu of Brazil, which inhabits the pampas south of the equator and is considerably smaller than the true ostrich. *Rhea darwini*, a native of Patagonia, is still smaller. The third species is the ***Rhea macrorhyncha***, so called from its long bill.

AFRICAN OSTRICH (*Struthio camelus*)

os′trich färm, a farm or ranch where ostriches are raised.

os′trich fērn, a tall fern which grows in circular clumps in swamps and moist places in the United States and Canada.

os·trif′ēr·ous, *a.* [L. *ostrea*, oyster, and *ferre*, to bear.] containing or producing oysters.

Os′trō·goth, *n.* one of the eastern Goths, as

distinguished from the Visigoths, or western Goths.

Os·trō·goth′iç, *a.* [O.H.G. *ōstar*, east, and *Goth.*] relating or belonging to the Ostrogoths.

Os′ty·ak, *n.* 1. a member of a Finno-Ugric people living in western Siberia.
2. the Ugric language of the Ostyaks.
Also spelled *Ostiak*.

Os·wē′gō tēa, 1. a plant of the mint family, with red flowers and lance-shaped, saw-edge leaves.
2. the tea brewed from its leaves.

ot-, oto-.

ot·ȧ·çöus′tiç, *a.* [Gr. *ōta*, ears, and *akouein*, to hear.] assisting the sense of hearing; as, an *otacoustic* instrument.

ot·ȧ·çöus′tiç, *n.* an instrument to facilitate hearing, as an ear trumpet.

ot·ȧ·çöus′ti·çŏn, *n.* an otacoustic.

Ō·tȧ·hei′tē ap′ple, the fruit of a Polynesian tree, *Spondias dulcis*, about the size of a large apple, with the flavor of pineapple.

ō·tal′ġi·ȧ, *n.* [Gr. *ōtalgia*; *ous*, *ōtos*, ear, and *algos*, pain.] a pain in the ear; an earache.

ō·tal′ġiç, *n.* a remedy for earache.

ō·tal′ġiç, *a.* pertaining to otalgia.

ō·tal′ġy, *n.* otalgia.

Ō·tā′ri·ȧ, *n.* the typical genus of *Otariidæ*.

Ō·tȧ·rī′i·dae, *n.pl.* the family of seals with external ears; the otaries.

ō′tȧ·rīne, ō·tār′i·ine, *a.* pertaining to otaries.

ō·tā′ri·oid, *n.* one of the otaries.

ō·tȧ·ry, *n.*; *pl.* **ō′tȧ·rieṣ,** [Gr. *ōtaros*, large-eared, from *ous*, *ōtos*, an ear.] an eared seal; an animal of the family *Otariidæ*.

Ō tem′pō·rȧ! Ō mō′rēṣ!, [L.] O the times! O the customs!: a quotation from Cicero.

Ō·thel′lō, *n.* [It.] a tragedy (1604?) by Shakespeare in which the title character, a noble Moor, made madly jealous by the villainous Iago, kills his faithful and loving wife, Desdemona: subject of operas by Rossini (1816) and Verdi (1887).

ō·thē·mȧ·tō′mȧ, *n.* [Gr. *ous*, *ōtos*, ear, and *haima*, blood.] hematoma of the ear.

ō′thē·ō·sçōpe, *n.* [Gr. *ōthein*, to push, and *skopein*, to see.] an instrument akin to the radiometer, for showing the repulsion of radial energy in an exhausted space.

ŏth′ẽr, *conj.* either. [Obs.]

ŏth′ẽr, *a.* [AS. *other*; D. and G. *ander*; Goth. *anthar*; L. *alter*; Sans. *anyatara*, comp. of *anya*, other.]
1. (a) being the remaining one of two or more; as, the *other* foot; (b) being the remaining ones of several: used before a plural noun; as, his *other* books are better than this.
2. different or distinct from that or those referred to or implied; as, any *other* girl.
3. different in nature or kind; as, I wouldn't want it *other* than it is.
4. further or additional; as, he has no *other* coat.
5. former; as, *other* times had their own customs.
every other; every second; every alternate; as, *every other* day; *every other* week.
the other day (or *night*, etc.); not long ago; recently.

ŏth′ẽr, *pron.* 1. noting a mate or counterpart; as, I have one of my gloves; where is the *other?*
2. another or some other person or thing; as, how many *others* are there?: also used reciprocally with *each*, and applicable to any number of individuals.
They asked *each other* of their welfare.
—Ex. xviii. 7.
of all others; above all others.

ŏth′ẽr, *adv.* otherwise; differently; as, he can't do *other* than go.

ŏth′ẽr·gātes, *a.* different; other. [Obs.]

ŏth′ẽr·gātes, *adv.* in another manner. [Obs.]

ŏth′ẽr·guess (-ges), *a.* [var. of *othergates*.] of another kind; different. [Obs.]

ŏth′ẽr·guess, *adv.* in another way; differently; otherwise. [Obs.]

ŏth′ẽr·guīṣe (-gīz), *a.* of another kind.[Obs.]

ŏth′ẽr·ness, *n.* the quality of being not the same.

ŏth′ẽr·wāyṣ, *adv.* otherwise. [Obs.]

ŏth′ẽr·where (-hwâr), *adv.* in some other place; in other places. [Archaic or Dial.]

ŏth′ẽr·whīle (-hwīl), *adv.* at another time or at other times. [Archaic or Dial.]

ŏth′ẽr·whīleṣ, *adv.* otherwhile. [Archaic or Dial.]

ŏth′ẽr·wīṣe, *adv.* [*other* and *wise*, manner.]
1. in a different manner; in another way; as, he thought it right, but they held *otherwise*.
2. in other circumstances.
3. in all other respects; as, a good man *otherwise* may not be a good leader.

ŏth′ẽr·wīṣe, *a.* not like; different in any respect; as, he was regarded as honest, but proved to be *otherwise*.

ŏth′ẽr·wīṣe, *conj.* else; or; if not; as, keep to the right, *otherwise* you will be arrested.

ŏth′ẽr wŏrld, the world of the dead, or the supposed world after death.

ŏth′ẽr·wŏrld′li·ness, *n.* the condition or quality of being otherworldly.

ŏth′ẽr·wŏrld′ly, *a.* being apart from material or earthly interests; spiritual or concerned with life in a future world.

Ō′thin, *n.* same as *Odin*.

Oth′măn, *n.*; *pl.* **Oth′mănṣ,** same as *Ottoman*.

Oth′măn·ee, *a.* Turkish; Ottoman.

ō″ti·ȧ·trī′ȧ, *n.* same as *otiatrics*.

ō·ti·at′riçs, *n.* [Gr. *ous*, *ōtos*, ear, and *iatrikos*, medical.] the therapeutics of ear diseases. [Rare.]

ō·ti·at′rus, *n.* an aurist. [Rare.]

ō′tiç, *a.* [Fr. *otique*, from Gr. *ous*, *ōtos*, ear.] pertaining to the ear; aural.

-ot′iç, [Gr. *ōtikos*.] a suffix used to form adjectives corresponding to nouns ending in *-osis*, meaning: (a) *of* or *affected with*, as in sclerotic; (b) *producing*, as in narcotic.

Ō·tid′i·dae, *n.pl.* [from Gr. *ōtis*, *otidos*, the great bustard, and *-idæ*.] a family of grallatorial birds of the eastern hemisphere; the bustards.

ō·tid′i·um, *n.*; *pl.* **ō·tid′i·ȧ,** [LL., dim. from Gr. *ous*, *ōtos*, ear.] in conchology, the form of ear occurring in mollusks.

ō′ti·ōse (-shi-), *a.* [L. *otiosus*, from *otium*, leisure.]
1. unemployed; at one's ease; idle; indolent.
2. ineffective; futile; sterile.
3. useless; superfluous.

ō·ti·os′i·ty, *n.* the state or condition of being otiose.

Ō′tis, *n.* the typical genus of the *Otididæ*.

ō·tī′tis, *n.* [Gr. *ous*, *ōtos*, ear, and *-itis*.] inflammation of the ear.

ō·tī′tis mē′di·ȧ, inflammation of the middle ear.

ō′tō-, [from Gr. *ous*, *ōtos*, ear.] a combining form meaning *of* or *pertaining to the ear*, as in *oto*scope: also, before a vowel, *ot-*.

ō·tō′bȧ but′tẽr, ō·tō′bȧ fat, a substance obtained from the fruit of *Myristica otoba*, a species of nutmeg tree. It is nearly colorless, of the consistency of butter, and when fresh resembles nutmegs in odor.

ō·toç′ō·nīte, *n.* [LL. *otoconium*, and *-ite*.] a calcareous deposit found in the sacs of the vestibule of the ear.

ō·tō·çō′ni·um, *n.*; *pl.* **ō·tō·çō′ni·ȧ,** [LL., from Gr. *ous*, *ōtos*, ear, and *konis*, dust.] a small otolith: usually in the plural.

ō′tō·çrāne, *n.* [*oto-*, and Gr. *kranion*, the skull.] the bony structure containing the aural apparatus.

ō·tō·çrā′ni·ăl, ō·tō·çrā′niç, *a.* of or belonging to the otocrane.

ō′tō·cyst, *n.* [*oto-*, and Gr. *kystis*, bladder.] in zoology, any structure containing the necessary parts which go to make up a complete auditory apparatus; specifically, in invertebrates, a capsule of this description, having a secondary use in hearing.

ō·tō·cyst′iç, *a.* of or pertaining to the otocyst.

ō·tō·dyn′i·ȧ, *n.* same as *otalgia*.

ō·tog′rȧ·phy, *n.* [*oto-*, and Gr. *graphein*, to describe.] the science of the ear; a description of the ear.

ō″tō·lar″yn·gol′ō·ġy, *n.* [*oto-* and *laryngology*.] the study or treatment of ear, nose, and throat diseases; otology and laryngology combined for study or practice.

ō′tō·lith, ō′tō·līte, *n.* [*oto-*, and Gr. *lithos*, stone.] a small vibrating calcareous particle in the membranous cavity or labyrinth of the ear of some animals, especially of fishes and fishlike amphibia.

ō·tō·lith′iç, ō·tō·lit′iç, *a.* of or belonging to an otolith.

ō·tō·log′iç·ăl, *a.* of or belonging to otology.

ō·tol′ō·ġist, *n.* a specialist in otology.

ō·tol′ō·ġy, *n.* [*oto-*, and Gr. *logos*, discourse.] the branch of medicine dealing with the ear, its structure, disorders, and treatment.

ō″tō·mȳ·çō′sis, *n.* [*oto-*, and Gr. *mykēs*, mushroom.] in pathology, fungous growth in the auditory canal.

ō·top′ȧ·thy, *n.* [*oto-*, and Gr. *pathos*, disease.] in pathology, an abnormal condition of the ear; disease of the ear.

ō′tō·phōne, *n.* [*oto-*, and Gr. *phōnē*, sound.] a kind of ear trumpet.

ō′tō·plas·ty, *n.* [*oto-*, and Gr. *plastos*, from *plassein*, to form.] plastic surgery of the ear.

ō·tō·pȳ·or·rhē′ȧ, *n.* [*oto-*, and Gr. *pyon*, pus, and *rhein*, to flow.] a flowing of pus from the ear.

ō·tor·rhē′ȧ, *n.* a flowing from the ear.

ō′tō·sçōpe, *n.* [*oto-*, and Gr. *skopein*, to view.]
1. an instrument for examining the tympanic membrane and external canal of the ear.
2. a type of stethoscope for auscultating the middle ear.

ō·tō·sçop′iç, *a.* of or belonging to otoscopy.

ō·tos′çō·py, *n.* the scientific examination of the ear.

ō·tō′sis, *n.* [Gr. *ous*, *ōtos*, ear.] faulty hearing; also, a word mispronounced because of a mishearing.

ō·tos′tē·ăl, *a.* of or belonging to an otosteon.

ō·tos′tē·ăl, *n.* an otosteon.

ō·tos′tē·on, *n.* [*oto-*, and Gr. *osteon*, bone.] an ear stone; an auditory otolith; also, one of the bones of the ear.

Ō·tō·zō′um, *n.* [*Otos*, a giant in Gr. fable, and Gr. *zōon*, animal.] a genus of prehistoric dinosaurs: known only by fossil footprints in the sandstone of the Connecticut valley.

ot·tä′vä rï′mä, [It.] a stanza of eight lines with the rhyme scheme *abababcc*: the Italian form has eleven syllables in a line, the English, ten or eleven.

Ot′tȧ·wȧ, *n.* one of a tribe of Algonquian Indians that lived along the Ottawa River: formerly called *Algonquin*.

ot′tẽr, *n.* [AS. *ottor*, *otor*, *oter*; D. and G. *otter*; Ice. *otr*; Lith. *ûdra*; Russ. and Pol. *wydra*; Gr. *hydra*, water snake.]
1. an aquatic carnivorous mammal of the genus *Lutra* of which there are several species. They all have a large, flattish head, short ears, webbed toes, crooked nails, and a tail slightly flattened horizontally. The common river otter, the *Lutra vulgaris* of Europe, has short, strong, flexible, palmated feet, which serve as oars to propel it through the water, and a long and strong tail, which acts as a rudder. It inhabits the banks of rivers, and feeds principally on fish. The American otter is *Lutra canadensis*, furnishing a fur of great value.
2. the short, thick, lustrous fur of the otter.
3. same as *sea otter*.
4. the caterpillar of the ghost moth, frequently found upon hop vines.
5. a fishing tackle having a number of lines grouped about a float.

ot′tẽr çȧ·nöe′, a sharp-prowed kayak used by the Alaskan Indians in hunting otters.

ot′tẽr dog, a hound bred especially for the capture of otters.

ot′tẽr sheep, see under *ancon*.

ot′tẽr shell, a bivalve mollusk of the genus *Lutraria*, several species of which are eaten by the Indians.

Ot′tō·măn, *a.* of or belonging to the Sultan Othman, or Osman (1288–1326 A.D.); connected with the Othman dynasty or Ottoman empire; hence, Turkish.

Ot′tō·măn, *n.* a Turk.

ot′tō·măn, *n.* 1. a low, cushioned seat without a back or arms.
2. a kind of couch or divan, with or without a back.
3. a low, cushioned footstool.
4. a corded fabric of silk, rayon, etc., used for trimming.

ot′trel·īte, *n.* [*Ottrez*, and Gr. *lithos*, stone.] in mineralogy, a micaceous silicate, of uncertain crystallization, found at Ottrez, Luxemburg.

ouä·bä′in (wä-), *n.* a poison extracted from the ouabaio, used in medicine and as an arrow poison.

ouä·bä′iō, *n.* *Acocanthera ouabaia*, a plant of the nightshade family which yields ouabain.

ouä′bē oil, an oil extracted from *Omphalea triandra*, a West Indian plant of the spurge family.

ouä·kä′rï, *n.* a South American monkey of the genus *Uacaria*. *Uacaria calva* is the bald ouakari.

ouȧ·nȧ·nïçhe′, *n.* [Canadian Fr.] a fresh-water salmon related to the Atlantic salmon, found from New York to Labrador.

ou′bit, *n.* a hairy caterpillar, especially that of the tiger moth. [Brit. Dial.]

ou·bli·ette′, *n.* [Fr., from *oublier*, L. *oblivisci*, to forget.] a concealed dungeon with a trap door at the top as its only opening, formerly used for persons condemned to perpetual imprisonment or to perish secretly.

ouch, *n.* [ME. *anouche, a nouche*; OFr. *nousche,* collar, necklace, from Gmc.] a clasp or buckle; specifically, an ornamental brooch, especially when set with precious stones. [Archaic.]

ouch, *v.t.* to ornament with or as with ouches. [Archaic.]

ouch, *interj.* an exclamation of sudden pain.

ought (ạt), *n.* anything; whatever; aught.

ought (ạt), *adv.* to any degree; in any way; at all.

ought (ạt), *v. auxiliary* [originally the past tense of the verb *to owe*; AS. *agan,* to have or possess.] an auxiliary used with the infinitives of various verbs to express: (a) *obligation* or *duty*; as, he *ought* to pay his debts; (b) *desirability*; as, you *ought* to eat more slowly; (c) *expectancy* or *probability*; as, I *ought* to be through by Monday. Past time is expressed by combining *ought* with the perfect infinitive of the verb being used; as, I *ought* to have told you.

ought, *n.* a nought; cipher; zero.

ought'ness, *n.* the quality or state of being as a thing ought to be. [Rare.]

ouï (wē), *adv.* [Fr.] yes.

ouï'jà (wē'jà), *n.* [Fr. *oui,* yes, and G. *ja,* yes.] a device consisting of a planchette and a board bearing the alphabet and various other symbols, used in spiritualistic séances, etc., supposedly to convey and record messages from the spirits: a trade-mark (*Ouija*).

oul, *n.* an owl. [Obs.]

ö̆u'lŏng, *n.* same as *oolong.*

ö̆u·lor'rhà·gy (-rà-), *n.* [Gr. *oulon,* a gum, and *rhagē,* a fracture, from *rhēgnynai,* to break.] a sudden discharge of blood from the gums: also written *ulorrhagia.*

ounce, *n.* [L. *uncia,* the twelfth part of anything.]

1. a unit of weight equal to the twelfth part of a pound troy, and the sixteenth of a pound avoirdupois.

2. a very small quantity.

3. a fluid ounce.

fluid ounce; see under *fluid.*

ounce, *n.* [ME. *once, unce*; OFr. *l'once, lonce*; from L. *lynx.*] the rarely seen snow leopard, *Uncia uncia,* of the mountains of Central Asia and Siberia: it has wooly, gray-white fur marked with black.

ound'ed, *a.* oundy. [Obs.]

ound'ing, *n.* a waving; a curling. [Obs.]

oun'dy, *a.* waving; curly. [Obs.]

ouph, ouphe, *n.* [var. of *oaf.*] an elf; a goblin.

our, *pron.* [AS. *ūre,* of us, our, contr. from *ūser,* our, from *ūs,* us; G. *unser*; Goth. *unsar,* our.] possessive form of *we.*

our, *poss. pronominal a.* of, belonging to, or done by us.

ou·rà·nog'rà·phist, *n.* same as *uranographist.*

ou·rà·nog'rà·phy, *n.* same as *uranography.*

ö̆u·rä'rï, *n.* [Braz. native name.] curare.

Ö̆u·rà'tē·à, *n.* [LL., from native Guianian *oura-ara.*] a genus of trees, found in the tropical parts of South America and less abundantly in Asia and Africa, remarkable for bearing flowers with ten stamens.

ö̆u'rē·bï, *n.* a small African antelope, *Nanotragus scoparius,* which frequents open plains.

ou·ret'iç, *a.* same as *uretic.*

Our Lā'dy, the Virgin Mary.

Our Lā'dy's Wänd, in astronomy, Orion's Belt.

ourș, *pron.* [ME. *ures*; *ure,* and genit. *-s*; hence, in form, a double possessive.] that or those belonging to us: the absolute form of *our,* used without a following noun, often after *of*; as, a friend *of ours*; that book is *ours*; *ours* are better.

our·self', *pron.* myself: used, as in royal proclamations, of one person.

our·selveș', *pron.pl.* a form of the first person plural pronoun, used: (a) as an intensive; as, we went *ourselves*; (b) as a reflexive; as, we hurt *ourselves*; (c) as a quasi-noun meaning "our real, true, or actual selves" (e.g., we are not *ourselves* when we rage like that): in this construction *our* may be considered a possessive pronominal adjective and *selves* a noun, and they may be separated; as, *our* own sweet *selves.*

-ous, [ME. *-ouse*; It. *-oso*; L. *-osus.*]

1. a suffix meaning *having, full of, characterized by,* as in generous, gracious, religious, vicious.

2. in chemistry, a suffix meaning *having a valence lower than in a compound whose name ends in -ic,* as in sulfurous.

ö̆uṣe, *n.* and *v.* ooze. [Obs.]

ö̆u'ṣel, *n.* same as *ouzel.*

oust, *n.* same as *oast.*

oust, *v.t.*; ousted, *pt., pp.*; ousting, *ppr.* [OFr. *ouster*; Fr. *ôter,* supposed to be from LL. *haustare,* to remove, to draw out, a freq. from *haurire,* to draw out.] to force out; to expel; to drive out; dispossess; eject.

Multiplications of actions upon the case were rare, formerly, and thereby wager of law *ousted.* —Hale.

Syn.—eject, dispossess, evict, dislodge, remove.

oust'ẽr, *n.* [Anglo-Fr., inf. used as n.]

1. a person or thing that ousts.

2. in law, an ousting or being ousted, especially from real property, usually by illegal means.

ouster le main; a delivery of lands out of the hands of a guardian, or out of the king's hands, or a judgment given for that purpose.

out, *adv.* [AS. *ūt*; D. *uit*; G. *aus*; Sw. *ute*; Sans. *ud.*]

1. (a) away from, forth from, or removed from a place, position, or situation; as, *out* of the house; (b) away from home; (c) on strike.

2. into or in the open air; as, come *out* and play.

3. into or in existence or activity; as, disease broke *out.*

4. (a) to a conclusion or result; as, argue it *out*; (b) completely, fully, or to the point of exhaustion; as, tired *out,* dry *out.*

5. into sight or notice; as, the moon came *out.*

6. (a) into or in circulation; as, the firm put *out* a new line of shoes; (b) into or in society; as, this girl has just come *out.*

7. from existence, operation, or activity; as, fade *out,* burn *out,* die *out.*

8. forcefully; aloud; as, sing *out,* speak *out.*

9. beyond a regular or normal surface, condition, or position; as, stand *out,* eke *out,* lengthen *out.*

10. away from the interior, center, or midst; as, spread *out,* reach *out,* branch *out*: sometimes implying sharing or dividing; as, deal *out,* sort *out.*

11. from one state, as of composure, harmony, or agreement, into another, as of annoyance, discord, or disagreement; as, I felt put *out* about it; friends may fall *out.*

12. into or in disuse, retirement, or discard; as, new cars went *out* for the duration.

13. from a number, group, or stock; as, pick *out.*

14. out on or along; as, *out* our way. [Colloq.]

15. into or in unconsciousness; as, he passed *out.* [Slang.]

16. in baseball, etc., in a manner producing an out; as, he struck *out.*

all out; completely; wholeheartedly. [Colloq.]

day in, day out; day by day; from morning to night; every day.

out and away; by far; without comparison.

out and out; openly; completely; thoroughly.

out for; making a determined effort to get or do.

out from under; away from difficulty or danger. [Colloq.]

out of; (a) from inside of; (b) from the number of; (c) past the boundaries or scope of; beyond; (d) from (material, etc.); as, buildings made *out of* stone; (e) because of; as, *out of* spite; (f) given birth by: said of animals; (g) not in possession of; as, *out of* money; (h) so as to deprive or be deprived of; as, cheat *out of* money.

out of conceit with; displeased with.

out of frame; out of proper order; irregular.

out of mind; forgotten; beyond the reach of memory; as, time *out of mind.*

out of one's head; in an unsound mental state; delirious. [Colloq.]

out of one's time; having finished one's apprenticeship.

out of temper; in bad temper; irritated.

out of twist, wind, or *winding*; not warped: said of a surface which has been brought to a plane.

out to; making a determined effort to.

out, *a.* 1. external: usually in combination, as in *out*post, *out*field, *out*lying.

2. irregular: said of sizes of clothes, etc.

3. beyond regular limits.

4. outlying.

5. away from work, class, etc.; as, *out* because of sickness.

6. bared because of torn clothing, etc.; as, *out* at the elbow.

7. deviating from what is accurate or right; as, *out* in my estimates.

8. having suffered a financial loss; as, *out* five dollars.

9. not in effective use, operation, etc.

10. lacking enough practice; as, his hand is *out.*

11. in disagreement; at variance.

12. deliberating in order to reach a verdict; as, the jury is still *out.*

13. in baseball, (a) not at bat; fielding; (b) failing to get on a base.

out, *prep.* 1. forth from: usually after *from.*

2. on the outside of; as, *out* this window.

out, *n.* 1. something that is out.

2. a way out; a means of avoiding; excuse. [Slang.]

3. in baseball, (a) a failure to get on a base; retirement of a batter or of a player who has reached base; (b) [*pl.*] the players on the team not batting.

4. [*pl.*] in politics, the party not in office.

5. in printing, (a) the omission of a word or words; (b) the word or words omitted.

6. in tennis, a return that lands outside the court.

7. a nook or corner; a projecting angle; an open space; as, the ins and *outs* of a garden walk; hence, figuratively, the ins and *outs* of a question, that is, all its details.

8. an outing. [Brit. Dial.]

at (or *on*) *the outs*; on unfriendly terms. [Colloq.]

out, *v.t.* 1. to eject; to expel; to deprive by expulsion; to oust.

The French have been *outed* of their holds. —Heylin.

2. to make known. [Obs.]

3. to give out; to sell. [Obs.]

out, *v.i.* to go out; to come out; to become public; as, truth will *out*; murder will *out.*

out, *interj.* get out! away! begone!

out upon or *on!* shame upon; as, *out upon* the fellow! [Archaic or Dial.]

out-, [from *out.*] a combining form meaning: (a) *situated at* or *coming from a point away, outside, external,* as in *out*building, *out*patient; (b) *going away* or *forth, outward,* as in *out*bound, *out*cast; (c) *better, greater,* or *more than,* as in *out*run, *out*do, *out*sell: in this last sense *out-* is prefixed to many verbs, a few of which are listed below: some others may be found in their regular place in the dictionary.

outargue
outbabble
outbargain
outbeg
outbleat
outblow
outblush
outbluster
outbow
outbrazen
outbribe
outcant
outcheat
outclimb
outdare
outdazzle
outdrink
outequivocate
outfawn
outfeast
outfeat
outflatter
outfly
outfool
outjest
outjuggle
outknave
outlabor
outleap
outlearn
outluster
outmarch
outmeasure
outmove
outnoise
outparagon
outpray
outpreach
outrace
outreason
outreckon
outredden
outreign
outring
outrival
outromance
outsail
outscent
outscold
outscorn
outsee
outsin
outsing
outsleep
outsound
outsparkle
outspeed
outspend
outsport
outspring
outstep
outstorm
outstride
outsuffer
outswear
outswell
outswift
outtoil
outtravel
outvoice
outwait
outweave
outweep
outwrite

out·açt', *v.t.* to exceed in acting; to outdo.

Ö̆u·tà·gam'i, *n.*; *pl.* **Ö̆u·tà·gam'ieș,** a Fox (Indian).

out'ăge, *n.* [*out-* and *-age.*] an interruption; accidental suspension of operation; as, the power company reported an *outage* lasting two hours.

out'-and-out', *a.* complete; thorough.

out'-and-out'ẽr, *n.* one who or that which is out-and-out; one thorough or complete in his or its class; one pre-eminent in any respect. [Colloq.]

ö̆ut'ăs, *n.* [ME. *outhees*; AS. *ut,* out, and LL.

huesium, hue and cry.] an outcry; hue and cry. [Obs.]

out′back, *n.* [*also* O-] 1. the sparsely settled, flat, arid inland region of Australia.

2. any remote, sparsely settled region thought of as uncivilized.

out·bal′ănce, *v.t.* to be greater than in weight, value, etc.

out·bid′, *v.t.*; outbid, *pt.*, *pp.*; outbidding, *ppr.* to exceed in bidding; to bid more than (another).

For Indian spices, for Peruvian gold,
Prevent the greedy and *outbid* the bold.
—Pope.

out-bid′dẽr, *n.* one who outbids.

out′bōard, *a.* situated near or located on the outer surface of a water craft; being toward the outside of a vessel; outward; as, the *outboard* end of a boom.

outboard motor; a portable gasoline engine fastened to the stern of a small boat for the purpose of propelling it.

outboard motorboat; a small boat having an outboard motor.

out′bōard, *adv.* in a direction away from the center of a vessel.

out′bond, *a.* see *inbond*.

out′bound, *a.* outward bound; destined or proceeding from a country or harbor to another country or port; as, an *outbound* ship.

out′bounds, *n.pl.* the farthest boundaries or limits.

out′bōwed, *a.* having a convex surface.

out·brag′, *v.t.* to exceed in bragging.

out·brāve′, *v.t.*; outbraved, *pt.*, *pp.*; outbraving, *ppr.* 1. to overcome through bravery.

2. to defy.

I would outstare the sternest eyes that look,
Outbrave the heart most daring on the earth,
To win thee, lady. —Shak.

3. to exceed in splendid appearance.

The towers as well as men *outbrave* the sky.
—Cowley.

out·brāy′, *v.t.* 1. to surpass in braying.

2. to utter with great noise. [Obs.]

out′brēak, *n.* a bursting forth; eruption; breaking out; sudden occurrence, as of disease, looting, anger, etc.

The flash and *outbreak* of a fiery mind.
—Shak.

out′brēak·ing, *n.* 1. that which bursts forth.

2. the act of bursting forth.

out·breast′ (-brest′), *v.t.* to surpass in power of voice. [Obs.]

out·brēathe′, *v.t.* and *v.i.* to breathe out; to exhale.

out·breed′, *v.t.* and *v.i.*; outbred, *pt.*, *pp.*; outbreeding, *ppr.* to practice, or subject to, outbreeding.

out′breed·ing, *n.* 1. the breeding of unrelated stocks or individuals.

2. in sociology, a marrying out of the family or tribe because of a taboo against marriage of persons related by blood.

out·bring′, *v.t.* to bring or carry forth.

out·build′ (-bild′), *v.t.*; outbuilt, *pt.*, *pp.*; outbuilding, *ppr.* to surpass in building, or in durability of building.

out′build·ing, *n.* a subordinate building near a main building; an outhouse.

out·bŭrn′, *v.t.* to exceed in burning.

out·bŭrn′, *v.i.* to burn to ashes; to be consumed.

out′bŭrst, *n.* a breaking or bursting out; an outbreak; a violent issuing forth; as, an *outburst* of passion.

out′bȳ, out′bȳe, *adv.* 1. abroad; without; out from; at some distance. [Scot. and Brit. Dial.]

2. in mining, in the direction of the shaft or passage: opposed to *inby*.

out′ċast, *a.* driven or cast out; thrown away; rejected. [Rare.]

out′ċast, *n.* 1. one who or that which is cast out or expelled; an exile; one driven from home or country.

2. a worthless or degraded person.

3. an altercation; a disagreement. [Scot.]

Syn.—castaway, reprobate, vagrant, vagabond, exile.

out′ċaste, *n.* in India, a person expelled from his caste.

out·clȧss′, *v.t.* to surpass by a wide margin.

out′cōme, *n.* that which comes out of or results from something else; the issue; the result; the consequence.

The skepticism which forms the logical *outcome* common to them all.
—Herbert Spencer.

out·cŏm′pȧss, *v.t.* to exceed the bounds of.

out′çōurt, *n.* the exterior or outer court of a church; the precinct.

Such persons, who, like Agrippa, were almost Christians, and have been (as it were) in the skirts and *outcourts* of Heaven.
—South.

out′crī″ẽr, out′crȳ″ẽr, *n.* one who cries or proclaims; specifically, one who proclaims a sale; a public crier; an auctioneer.

To be sold by the common *outcryer* appointed for that purpose. —Baker.

out′crop, *n.* in geology, (a) the exposure of an inclined stratum at the surface of the ground; basseting; (b) the part so exposed.

out·crop′, *v.i.*; outcropped, *pt.*, *pp.*; outcropping, *ppr.* in geology, to come out to the surface of the ground: said of strata.

out′crȳ, *n.*; *pl.* **out′crīeṣ**, 1. a vehement or loud cry; cry of distress.

2. strong or noisy opposition or protest.

3. a sale at public auction.

out′çūrve, *n.* in baseball, a pitch curving away or out from the batter.

out·dāt′ed, *a.* 1. old-fashioned.

2. no longer popular.

out·dis′tănce, *v.t.*; outdistanced, *pt.*, *pp.*; outdistancing, *ppr.* 1. to leave behind in a race.

2. to get ahead of in any competition; to outstrip.

out·dö′, *v.t.*; outdid, *pt.*; outdone, *pp.*; outdoing, *ppr.* to excel; to surpass; to perform beyond another.

An imposture *outdoes* the original.
—L'Estrange.

to outdo oneself; (a) to do something better than one ever did before, or believed himself capable of doing; (b) to make a supreme effort.

out′dōor, *a.* 1. being outside of a building or shelter; open-air.

2. having to do with those activities of an institution, as a hospital, which are carried on outside its premises.

out′dōorṣ, *adv.* in or into the open; outside a building or shelter.

out′dōorṣ′, *n.* 1. any area or place outside a building or shelter.

2. the outdoor world.

out′dōorṣ′man, *n.*; *pl.* **out′dōorṣ′men**, a man who spends much time in the outdoors, as in camping, hunting, or fishing.

out·dōorṣ′wom″ăn, *n.*; *pl.* **out·dōorṣ′wom″en**, a woman who spends much time in the outdoors, as in camping, hunting, or fishing.

out′dōor′sy, *a.* of, characteristic of, or fond of the outdoors. [Colloq.]

out·drąw′, *v.t.* to draw out; to extract. [Rare.]

out·drēam′, *v.t.* to dream during the continuance of; to dream till a thing is past, as danger.

out′dwell″ẽr, *n.* a person owning land in a parish, but dwelling outside. [Brit.]

out′en, *prep.* out of. [Brit. Dial.]

out′ẽr, *a.* [ME. *outter*; new form, from *out* and *-er*, replacing *uttere*, from AS. *uterra*.]

1. located farther from a certain point or place than something else; external.

2. relatively far out or far removed; as, the *outer* regions: opposed to *inner*.

outer bar; in English courts, the junior barristers who plead outside the bar.

outer space; (a) space beyond the atmosphere of the earth; (b) space outside the solar system.

out′ẽr, *n.* 1. one who expels. [Rare.]

2. in law, dispossession; an ouster. [Rare.]

3. (a) that part of a target beyond the circles around the bull's-eye, and so nearer the outside; (b) a shot which strikes that part.

out′ẽr·ly, *adv.* 1. toward the outside. [Rare.]

2. absolutely; totally. [Obs.]

out′ẽr·mōst, *a.* and *adv.* in a position farthest from the inside or center.

out·fāce′, *v.t.*; outfaced (-fāst′), *pt.*, *pp.*; outfacing, *ppr.* 1. to stare down; to overcome or subdue with a look or stare.

2. to defy or resist.

out′fąll, *n.* 1. the mouth of a river; the lower end of a watercourse.

2. the point of discharge for a river, drain, culvert, or sewer.

out·fang′thef, *n.* [AS. *ūtfangen theóf*; *ūt*, out, *fangen*, pp. of *fōn*, take, *theóf*, thief.] in old law, a liberty or privilege, whereby a lord was enabled to call any man dwelling in his manor, and taken for felony in another place out of his fee, to judgment in his own court; also, the felon so taken. [Obs.]

out′fiēld, *n.* 1. distant or outlying farmland.

2. in baseball, (a) the playing area beyond the four lines connecting the bases; (b) the outfielders collectively.

3. in cricket, the part of the field farthest from the batsman.

4. any undefined or indefinite outlying region.

Distinguished from *infield*.

out′fiēld″ẽr, *n.* in baseball and cricket, any player who occupies a position in the outfield: distinguished from *infielder*.

out′fit, *n.* 1. (a) a set of articles for fitting out, or equipping; (b) the equipment used in any craft or activity; paraphernalia; as, a carpenter's *outfit*, camping *outfit*.

2. articles of clothing worn together; ensemble; as, a fall *outfit*.

3. a group of people associated in some undertaking or activity; especially, a military unit.

4. a fitting out; an equipping.

5. formerly, an allowance made by the United States government to a diplomatic representative when going to a foreign country.

out′fit, *v.t.*; outfitted, *pt.*, *pp.*; outfitting, *ppr.* to fit out; to equip.

out′fit·tẽr, *n.* one who supplies, sells, or makes outfits.

out·flaṅk′, *v.t.*; outflanked (-flaṅkt), *pt.*, *pp.*; outflanking, *ppr.* 1. to maneuver into a position on the flank, or side, of (a body of enemy troops); to go beyond or turn the flank of.

2. to thwart; outwit.

out′fling, *n.* a taunt; a gibe; a sarcasm.

out′flōw, *n.* 1. the act of flowing out.

2. (a) that which flows out; (b) the amount flowing out.

out·flōw′, *v.i.*; outflowed, *pt.*, *pp.*; outflowing, *ppr.* to flow forth.

out·foot′, *v.t.*; outfooted, *pt.*, *pp.*; outfooting, *ppr.* 1. to walk, run, etc. faster or farther than.

2. to sail faster than (another): said of a ship.

out·fox′, *v.t.*; outfoxed (-fokst), *pt.*, *pp.*; outfoxing, *ppr.* to outwit; outsmart.

out′gāte, *n.* an outlet; a passage outward. [Scot. and Brit. Dial.]

out·ġen′ẽr·ăl, *v.t.*; outgeneraled *or* outgeneralled, *pt.*, *pp.*; outgeneraling *or* outgeneralling, *ppr.* to exceed in generalship; to gain advantage over by superior military skill; to surpass in leadership or management.

out·gō′, *v.t.*; outwent, *pt.*; outgone, *pp.*; outgoing, *ppr.* 1. to go beyond; to go faster or farther than; to surpass; to excel.

2. to circumvent; to overreach. [Obs.]

out′gō, *n.*; *pl.* **out′gōeṣ**, 1. a going out.

2. whatever goes or is paid out; outflow or expenses: opposed to *income*.

out′gō″ẽr, *n.* one who goes out.

out′gō″ing, *a.* going out; as, an *outgoing* message, current, or tenant.

out′gō″ing, *n.* 1. the act of going out; departure.

2. utmost border; extreme limit. [Obs.]

3. whatever goes out; the outgo.

4. [*usually in pl.*] an outlay.

out′-group, *n.* all the people not belonging to a specific in-group.

out·grōw′, *v.t.*; outgrew, *pt.*; outgrown, *pp.*; outgrowing, *ppr.* 1. to surpass in growth; to grow faster or greater than.

2. to lose or get rid of by becoming mature; as, he *outgrew* his credulity.

3. to grow too large for; as, children *outgrow* their garments.

out′grōwth, *n.* 1. a growing out.

2. something that has its origin in something else; result; consequence; development.

3. an offshoot.

out′guärd (-gärd), *n.* a guard at a distance from the main body of an army; an outpost.

out·guess′ (-ges′), *v.t.* to outwit.

out′gush, *n.* a gushing out; an outburst.

out·gush′, *v.i.*; outgushed (-gusht), *pt.*, *pp.*; outgushing, *ppr.* to gush out.

out′haul, *n.* a rope by which a sail is hauled out, as upon a spar.

out·hees′, *n.* outas (hue and cry). [Obs.]

outh′ẽr, *conj.*, *a.*, and *pron.* other; either. [Obs.]

out-Her′ŏd, *v.t.*; out-Heroded, *pt.*, *pp.*; out-Heroding, *ppr.* 1. to be more violent or cruel than (Herod): Hamlet's reference to the usual characterization of Herod in the old mystery plays.

2. to surpass, as in excess.

out′house, *n.* a small building separate from but located near the main house; specifically, an outdoor latrine.

out'ing, *n.* [*out* and *-ing.*]
1. a pleasure trip or holiday spent outdoors or away from home.
2. an airing; a walk in the open air.
3. a sortie; a foray. [Obs.]
4. an overthrow; an expulsion; an ejection. [Obs.]

out'ing flan'nel, a warm cotton fabric in a plain or twill weave with a nap on both sides.

out'keep"ẽr, *n.* a device used to keep tally in surveying with a chain.

out'land, *n.* [ME.; AS. *utlond.*]
1. the outlying part of an estate.
2. a foreign land. [Archaic or Poet.]

out'land, *a.* 1. outlying.
2. foreign. [Archaic or Poet.]

out'land·ẽr, *n.* a foreigner; alien; stranger.

out·land'ish, *a.* 1. foreign; not native; alien. [Archaic.]
2. unfamiliar; strange; odd; barbarous; bizarre; grotesque; fantastic.
3. secluded; remote; out-of-the-way.

out·land'ish·ly, *adv.* in an outlandish fashion.

out·lȧst', *v.t.* 1. to endure longer than.
2. to outlive.

out·läugh' (-läf'), *v.t.*; outlaughed (-läft'), *pt. pp.*; outlaughing, *ppr.* 1. to laugh more or to greater effect than.
2. to laugh down; to overcome or embarrass by laughing. [Rare.]

out'law, *n.* [ME. *ullage*; AS. *utlaga*; ON. *ut-lagi*, lit., outlawed.]
1. originally, a person declared by a court of law to be deprived of legal rights and protection, generally for the commission of some crime: the killing of such a person was not a legal offense.
2. a habitual or notorious criminal; a fugitive from the law.
3. a fierce or uncontrollable animal.

out'law, *v.t.* 1. originally, to declare to be an outlaw.
2. in the United States, to remove the legal force of (contracts, etc.).
3. to declare unlawful or illegal.

out'law·ry, *n.*; *pl.* **out'law·rieṣ,** 1. an outlawing or being outlawed.
2. the state or condition of being an outlaw.
3. disregard or defiance of the law.

out'lāy, *n.* 1. a spending (of money).
2. money, or amount of money, spent.

out·lāy', *v.t.*; outlaid, *pt., pp.*; outlaying, *ppr.* to spend (money).

out'let, *n.* 1. a passage or vent for letting something out.
2. a means of expression; as, an *outlet* for the emotions.
3. in commerce, (a) a market for goods; (b) a store, agency, etc. that sells the goods of a specific manufacturer or wholesaler.
4. in electricity, any point in a wiring system at which current may be taken for consumption.

out'lick·ẽr, *n.* [D. *uitlegger*, outrigger.] in nautical usage, an outrigger. [Obs.]

out·līe', *v.i.* to lie in the open air; to camp out.

out'lī"ẽr, *n.* any person or thing that lies, dwells, exists, etc. away from the main body or expected place; specifically, (a) a person who resides away from his place of work or business; (b) a person who is excluded, or excludes himself, from some group; an outsider; (c) in geology, a mass of rock at some distance from the main formation as the result of the wearing away of the intermediate rock.

out'limb (-lim), *n.* an extremity of a body; a limb. [Obs.]

out'līne, *n.* 1. a profile line; line bounding the limits of an object.
2. a sketch showing only the contours of an object, without use of shading.
3. an undetailed general plan.
4. a summary of a subject, consisting of a systematic listing of its most important points.
Syn.—delineation, sketch, contour, draft, skeleton.

out'līne, *v.t.*; outlined, *pt., pp.*; outlining, *ppr.* 1. to draw a profile of; to draw in outline.
2. to give or write an outline of; to list or present the main points of; to sketch, as by an outline; as, to *outline* a story.

out·lin'ē·ăr, *a.* pertaining to or being in the form of an outline.

out·live', *v.t.*; outlived, *pt., pp.*; outliving, *ppr.* to live beyond; to survive; to live or endure longer than; to outlast; as, a man may *outlive* his children; a person may *outlive* his usefulness.

out·live', *v.i.* to live on; to continue to live. [Obs.]

out·liv'ẽr, *n.* a survivor. [Rare.]

out·look', *v.t.* 1. to face down; to browbeat; to stare out of countenance.
2. to select. [Obs.]

out'look, *n.* 1. a place for watching or looking out.
2. the view from such a place.
3. the act of looking out.
4. viewpoint; mental view.
5. expectation; prospect; probable result.
6. one who looks out.

out'lȳ"ing, *a.* relatively far out from a certain point or center; lying or being at a distance from the main body or design; remote.

out·man', *v.t.*; outmanned, *pt., pp.*; outmanning, *ppr.* 1. to surpass in number of men; to outnumber.
2. to outdo in manliness.

out·mȧ·neu'vẽr, out·mȧ·noeu'vre (-vẽr), *v.t.* to maneuver with better effect than; to outwit.

out·match', *v.t.* to be superior to; to outdo.

out·mōd'ed, *a.* no longer in fashion or accepted; obsolete.

out'mōst, *a.* farthest outward; most remote from the middle.

out·nāme', *v.t.* 1. to exceed in naming or describing. [Rare.]
2. to surpass in name, reputation, or degree.

out'ness, *n.* 1. the state of being outside.
2. in metaphysics, the quality or condition of being outside and distinguishable from the perceiving mind, by being possessed of material quality; objectivity; externality.

out·num'bẽr, *v.t.* to exceed in number; as, the troops *outnumbered* those of the enemy.

out'-ŏf-dāte', *a.* not current; obsolete; old-fashioned.

out'-ŏf-dōor', *a.* of or pertaining to the open air; outdoor.

out'-ŏf-dōorṣ', *a.* out-of-door.

out'-ŏf-dōorṣ', *n.* and *adv.* outdoors.

out'-ŏf-pock'et, *a.* designating unbudgeted expenses, or ready cash paid out, as for miscellaneous items.

out'-ŏf-the-wāy', *a.* 1. not near a frequented road or populous place; remotely situated; difficult of access; secluded.
2. unusual.
3. not conventional or proper.

out·pāce', *v.t.*; outpaced (-pāst), *pt., pp.*; outpacing, *ppr.* to outgo; to leave behind.

out'par"ish, *n.* a country or outlying parish as distinguished from a town parish.

out'pärt, *n.* a part remote from the center or main part.

out·pȧss', *v.t.* to pass beyond; to exceed in progress.

out'pā"tient (-shent), *n.* a nonresident patient; one who is not an inmate of a hospital but receives medical attention from it.

out·peer', *v.t.* to surpass or excel.

out·plāy', *v.t.* to play better than.

out'pock"et·ing, *n.* evagination.

out·point', *v.t.* 1. to score more points than.
2. in nautical usage, to get into a position closer to the wind than (another vessel).

out·poiṣe', *v.t.*; outpoised, *pt., pp.*; outpoising, *ppr.* to outweigh.

out'pọrch, *n.* an entrance.

out'pọrt, *n.* in Great Britain, a port at some distance from the seat of trade; specifically, any port but London.

out'pōst, *n.* 1. a post or station outside the limits of a camp, or at a distance from the main body of an army.
2. the troops placed at such a station.
3. a settlement on the border of a country or frontier.

out·pōur', *v.t.* and *v.i.* to pour out; to effuse.

out'pōur, *n.* a pouring out; effusion.

out'pụt, *n.* 1. the quantity of material put out, manufactured, or produced in a certain time; the amount or rate of production.
2. in mechanics, the amount of power or energy produced by a machine, etc.
3. in physiology, that which is thrown off from the body by the lungs, skin, or kidneys; the egesta other than the feces.

out'rāge, *v.t.* to rage in excess of; to excel in raging. [Rare.]

out'rāge, *v.t.*; outraged, *pt., pp.*; outraging, *ppr.* [Fr. *outrager.*]
1. to commit an outrage upon; to treat with violence and wrong; to do violence to; to abuse; to act with violence and roughness towards.

For in peace he continued to plunder and to *outrage* them. —Macaulay.

2. to commit a rape or indecent assault upon (a female).

out'rāge, *v.i.* to act outrageously; to be guilty of violence and rudeness; to go to excess. [Obs.]

out'rāge, *n.* [Fr. *outrage*; OFr. *oultrage*, from LL. *ultragium*; L. *ultra*, beyond.]
1. an extremely vicious or violent act.
2. a deep insult or offense.
3. any serious breach of legal or moral codes.
4. extravagance; excess; luxury. [Obs.]
Syn.—insult, abuse, affront, offense, indignity, injury.

out·rā'ġeous (-jus), *a.* [ME.; OFr. *outrageus*, from *outrage, oultrage*, outrage.]
1. having the nature of, involving, or doing great injury or wrong.
2. exceeding all bounds of decency or reasonableness; very offensive or shocking.
3. violent in action or disposition.
Syn.—excessive, wanton, flagrant, nefarious, heinous, atrocious, violent, infamous.

out·rā'ġeous·ly, *adv.* in an outrageous manner or degree.

out·rā'ġeous·ness, *n.* the quality or state of being outrageous.

out'rā·ġẽr, *n.* one who outrages.

ou·trănce', *n.* [Fr., from L. *ultra*, beyond.] the extreme limit; the utmost extremity.
combat à outrance; a desperate fight, often a duel, in which it is understood that one of the combatants must be killed before the combat ceases; a fight to the death.

out·rānġe', *v.t.* to have a greater range than, or to range beyond.

out·rank', *v.t.* to exceed in rank.

out·rāy', *v.i.* to spread out, as in rays. [Obs.]

out·rāy', *v.t.* to surpass. [Obs.]

ou·tré' (ö-trā'), *a.* [Fr.] 1. exaggerated.
2. eccentric; bizarre.

out·rēach', *v.t.* and *v.i.* 1. to reach farther (than); exceed; surpass.
2. to reach out; extend.

out·rēach', *a.* designating or of a branch office of a social agency, governmental department, etc. set up to accommodate those who cannot or will not utilize the services of the main offices.

ou·tre·cui·dănce' (-kwē-), *n.* [Fr. *outrecuidance*; *outre*, beyond, and *cuider*, to think, from L. *cogitare*, to think.] overweening presumption; arrogant or insulting conduct. [Archaic.]

out·rēde', *v.t.* to atrede. [Obs.]

out·rīde', *v.t.*; outrode, *pt.*; outridden, *pp.*; outriding, *ppr.* to ride faster than; to surpass in riding.

out'rīd"ẽr, *n.* 1. a summoner whose office was to cite men before the sheriff. [Obs.]
2. an attendant on horseback who rides out ahead of or beside a carriage on the highway.
3. a person who rides out or forth.

out'rig"gẽr, *n.* 1. any temporary support extending out from the main structure; as, a beam projecting outwardly from a wall to support a hoisting tackle.

OUTRIGGER

2. in gearing, a wheel or pulley outside the frame to receive a belt or other driving connection.
3. in machinery, the jib of a crane.
4. in nautical usage, any of a variety of frameworks extended beyond the rail of a ship for various purposes; as, (a) a spar for extending a sail or rope beyond the points of attachment furnished by the hull; (b) a boom rigged out from a vessel to which boats are secured when the vessel is at anchor; (c) a floating timber rigged out from the side of native canoes to prevent tipping; (d) a spar projecting over the stern of a boat for assistance in hauling out the clue; (e) an iron bracket fitted to the outside of a boat, and having an oarlock at the extremity, so as to increase the leverage of the rower.
5. a canoe or boat having an outrigger

(floating timber) or outriggers (projecting oarlocks).
6. a projection for supporting the lesser airfoils of an airplane.

out′right (rīt), *a.* 1. without reservation; downright.
2. straightforward.
3. complete; total; whole.

out′rīght′, *adv.* 1. entirely; wholly.
2. without reservation; openly.
3. at once.
4. straight ahead. [Obs.]

out·rīve′, *v.t.* to tear apart with force and violence. [Obs.]

out·rōar′, *v.t.* to exceed in roaring.

out′rọom, *n.* an outlying room. [Rare.]

out·rọot′, *v.t.* 1. to uproot.
2. to wipe out; to destroy; to eradicate; to extirpate.

out·run′, *v.t.*; outran, *pt.*; outrun, *pp.*; outrunning, *ppr.* 1. to leave behind in running; to run faster, longer, or better than.
2. to exceed; to go beyond; as, to *outrun* one's income.
3. to escape (a pursuer) by or as by running.

out′run″nēr, *n.* 1. a person or thing that runs out.
2. an attendant running alongside or in front of a carriage.
3. the leader of a team of dogs.
4. an offshoot. [Obs.]

out·rush′, *v.i.* to rush out quickly.

out·sçout′, *v.t.* to drive out; to outface. [Obs.]

out·sell′, *v.t.*; outsold, *pt.*, *pp.*; outselling, *ppr.* 1. to sell more easily or readily than.
2. to exceed in the number of sales; to sell more than.
3. to exceed or surpass in the selling price; to have a higher price than.

out′sen″try, *n.*; *pl.* **out′sen″trieṣ**, a sentry placed considerably in advance; a sentry who guards the approach to a place at a distance in advance of it.

out′set, *n.* 1. a setting out.
2. a beginning; a starting.
The *outset* of a political journey. —Burke.
Syn.—opening, start, commencement, exordium, beginning.

out′set″tlēr, *n.* one who settles at a distance from the main body.

out·shīne′, *v.t.*; outshone, *pt.*, *pp.*; outshining, *ppr.* 1. to shine more brightly or longer than (another).
2. to surpass.

out·shīne′, *v.i.* to shine out or forth.

out·shọot′, *v.t.*; outshot, *pt.*, *pp.*; outshooting, *ppr.* 1. to shoot more effectively than.
2. to shoot beyond.
3. to shoot out.

out·shọot′, *v.i.* to shoot out; to protrude.

out′shọot, *n.* 1. a shooting or being shot out.
2. that which shoots out, or protrudes.
3. in baseball, a pitch curving away or out from the batter.

out·shut′, *v.t.* to shut out or exclude.

out′sīde, *n.* 1. the external part of anything; the outer side or surface; the exterior; the superficies.

Thousands, careless of the damning sin,
Kiss the book's *outside*, who ne'er look within. —Cowper.

2. the unenclosed portion of anything partly enclosed.
3. (a) that part of an object which can be seen; (b) that which is obvious or superficial.
4. the extreme; the utmost; the farthest limit or estimate (with *the*); as, there are fifty at *the outside*.
5. one who or that which is without; a passenger traveling on the outside of a coach, or the like. [Brit. Colloq.]
at the outside; at the most; at the absolute limit.

out′sīde, *a.* 1. outer; having to do with, or located on, the outside.
2. originating, coming from, or situated beyond the limits of a given boundary or classification; as, the club would accept no *outside* help.
3. extreme; as, an *outside* estimate.
4. mere; slight; as, an *outside* chance.
5. in baseball, passing home plate beyond the side away from the batter.

out′sīde, *adv.* 1. externally; on the exterior.
2. to or toward the exterior.
3. beyond certain limits.
4. in or into the open air.
outside of; (a) outside; (b) [Colloq.] other than; with the exception of.

out·sīde′, *prep.* 1. on or to the outer side of.
2. outside the limits of.
3. except. [Colloq.]

out·sīd′ēr, *n.* 1. one who is outside, or not included; one who is unconnected or unacquainted with a matter in question; one who does not belong to or is not in sympathy with a given group, profession, or set.
2. [*pl.*] a pair of nippers with semitubular jaws, adapted to enter a keyhole and grasp the pin of a key, so as to unlock the door from the outside.
3. in horse racing, a horse which is not a favorite in the betting, or which has little chance of winning a given race.

out sis′tēr, a nun who manages the affairs of her order outside the convent.

out·sit′, *v.t.*; outsat, *pt.*, *pp.*; outsitting, *ppr.* 1. to sit longer than (another).
2. to sit beyond the time of.

out′sīze, *n.* 1. a size varying from the usual standard; an odd size; especially, an unusually large size.
2. a garment of such a size.

out′skirt, *n.* [*usually in pl.*] a part or district remote from the center or midst, as of a city.

out·smärt′, *v.t.* to overcome by cunning or cleverness; to outwit. [Colloq.]
to outsmart oneself; to have one's efforts at cunning or cleverness result in one's own disadvantage.

out·sōar′, *v.t.* to soar beyond or higher than.

out′sōle, *n.* the outer sole of a shoe or boot.

out·span′, *v.t.* and *v.i.*; outspanned, *pt.*, *pp.*; outspanning, *ppr.* [*out*, and D. *spannen*, to put horses to, from *span*, a team.] to unyoke (a team of oxen from a wagon); to unharness. [S. Afr.]

out′span, *n.* a place for or the act of unharnessing. [S. Afr.]

out·spēak′, *v.t.*; outspoke, *pt.*; outspoken, *pp.*; outspeaking, *ppr.* 1. to speak better, more loudly, or more forcibly than.
2. to say boldly or candidly.
3. to speak more than. [Obs.]

out·spēak′, *v.i.* to speak out; to speak up boldly or candidly.

Outspoke the hardy Highland wight,
I'll go, my chief, I'm ready. —Campbell.

out·spin′, *v.t.* to spin out; to exhaust.

out′spō″ken, *a.* 1. bold of speech; frank; candid.
2. spoken boldly or candidly.

out·spō′ken·ness, *n.* the quality of being outspoken.

out·spread′ (-spred′), *v.t.* and *v.i.*; outspread, *pt.*, *pp.*; outspreading, *ppr.* to extend; to spread out; to diffuse; to expand.

out′spread, *n.* a spreading out; extension; expansion.

out′spread, *a.* 1. extended; expanded.
2. diffused.

out·stand′, *v.t.*; outstood, *pt.*, *pp.*; outstanding, *ppr.* 1. to resist effectually; to withstand; to sustain without yielding.
2. to stand or stay beyond; to endure.

out·stand′, *v.i.* 1. to project outward from the main body; to stand out plainly.
2. to stand unpaid or not collected, as debts.
3. to leave port; to sail off from the coast, as a ship.

out·stand′ing, *a.* 1. projecting.
2. prominent; distinguished; conspicuous.
3. unfulfilled; unpaid; unsettled.
4. resisting.

out·stāre′, *v.t.* 1. to outdo in staring; to stare down.
2. to gaze at steadily without blinking.

out·stärt′, *v.i.* to start out.

out·stāy′, *v.t.* to stay longer than or beyond.

out·stretch′, *v.t.* 1. to extend; to stretch or spread out.
2. to extend beyond.

out·strīke′, *v.t.*; outstruck, *pt.*; outstruck *or* outstricken, *pp.*; outstriking, *ppr.* to surpass in striking.

out·strip′, *v.t.*; outstripped *or rare* outstript, *pt.*, *pp.*; outstripping, *ppr.* 1. to go at a faster pace than; to get ahead of.
2. to excel; surpass.

out′strōke, *n.* a stroke outward, as when an engine's piston goes out toward the crankshaft.

out·sweet′en (-n) *v.t.* to exceed in sweetness.

out′tāke, *n.* a scene, or take, photographed for a motion picture or television show, but not included in the shown version.

out·tāk′en, *prep.* except. [Obs.]

out·tạlk′ (-tạk′), *v.t.* to talk more skillfully, loudly, or forcibly than; to surpass in talking.

out·tell′, *v.t.*; outtold, *pt.*, *pp.*; outtelling, *ppr.* to tell or count in excess.

out′tērm, *n.* an outward or superficial manner, phrase, etc. [Obs.]

out·thrōw′, *v.t.*; outthrew, *pt.*; outthrown, *pp.*; outthrowing, *ppr.* to throw out or beyond; to exceed in throwing.

out·tŏngue′ (-tung′), *v.t.* to bear down by talk, clamor, or noise. [Rare.]

out·top′, *v.t.*; outtopped (-topt′), *pt.*, *pp.*; outtopping, *ppr.* to overtop.

out′tŭrn, *n.* output; quantity produced.

out·twīne′, *v.t.* to disentangle; to extricate; to disengage. [Obs.]

out·val′ūe, *v.t.*; outvalued, *pt.*, *pp.*; outvaluing, *ppr.* to exceed in price or value.

out·vīe′, *v.t.*; outvied, *pt.*, *pp.*; outvying, *ppr.* exceed; to surpass.

out·vil′lāin, *v.t.* to exceed in villainy.

out·vōte′, *v.t.*; outvoted, *pt.*, *pp.*; outvoting, *ppr.* to exceed in the number of votes given; to defeat or surpass in voting.

out·walk′ (-wạk′), *v.t.* to walk faster than; to leave behind in walking.

out′wall, *n.* an exterior wall.

out′wărd, *a.* [AS. *uteweard*; *ut*, out, and *weard*, -ward.]
1. having to do with the outside or exterior; outer.
2. obvious; observable; visible.
3. away from the interior; to or toward the outside.
4. having to do with the physical or the body as opposed to the mind or spirit.
5. concerning the surface only; superficial.
6. foreign. [Obs.]
Syn.—exterior, external, outer, outside, superficial.

out′wărd, *n.* 1. the outward part; the exterior.
2. the material or external world.
3. outward form or appearance.

out′wărd, out′wărdṣ, *adv.* 1. externally; on the outside.
2. away from the interior or from port; toward the outside.
3. visibly; openly; publicly.

out′ward, *n.* a detached ward in a hospital.

out′wărd·ly, *adv.* 1. toward or on the outside; externally.
2. in regard to external appearance or action.

out′wărd·ness, *n.* outward aspect.

out·wătch′ (-woch′), *v.t.* to surpass in watching.

out·weār′, *v.t.*; outwore, *pt.*; outworn, *pp.*; outwearing, *ppr.* 1. to last longer than (something else); to outlast.
2. to wear out; to use up.
3. to outgrow or outlive.
4. to exhaust, as in strength.

out·wēa′ry, *v.t.* to tire out; to exhaust. [Poet.]

out·weigh′ (-wā′), *v.t.* 1. to exceed in weight.
2. to exceed in value, influence, or importance.

out·well′, *v.t.* and *v.i.* to pour out.

out·went′, *v.* past tense of *outgo*.

out·whōre′ (-hōr′), *v.t.* to exceed in lewdness.

out·win′, *v.t.* to get out of. [Obs.]

out·wīnd′, *v.t.* to extricate by winding; to unwind. [Rare.]

out·wing′, *v.t.* to move faster on the wing; to outstrip; to outfly.

out·wit′, *v.t.*; outwitted, *pt.*, *pp.*; outwitting, *ppr.* 1. to overcome, or get the better of, by cunning or cleverness.
2. to be more intelligent than. [Archaic.]

out′wit, *n.* perceptive ability; experience. [Obs.]

out·wōe′, *v.t.* to surpass in woe. [Obs.]

out·wōre′, *v.* past tense of *outwear*.

out·wŏrk′, *v.t.* 1. to surpass in work, labor, workmanship, or skill; to outdo.
2. to work out to completion.

out′wŏrk, *n.* 1. in fortification, any work situated out beyond the principal defenses.
2. a shell, rind, carapace, or any outer protection. [Rare.]
3. outside work; outdoor work.

out·wọrn′, *v.* past participle of *outwear*.

ōu·vä′rō·vīte, *n.* same as *uvarovite*.

ōuze, *n.* and *v.* ooze. [Obs.]

ōu′zel, *n.* any of several blackbirds, thrushes, or related birds; especially, (a) the European blackbird; (b) *Turdus torquatus*, the ring ouzel; (c) *Cinclus aquaticus*, the water ouzel: also spelled *ousel*.

ō′vȧ, *n.* plural of *ovum*.

ō'văl, *a.* [Fr. *ovale*, from L. *ovum*, an egg.]
1. of the shape or figure of an egg; oblong and curvilinear.
2. resembling an egg in shape; ellipsoidal.
3. in botany and zoology, broadly elliptical.
4. pertaining to eggs; done in the egg. [Obs.]

ō'văl, *n.* 1. anything in the shape of an egg, or of an ellipse.
2. a race track or an enclosure of an oval form.
cassinian oval; see under *cassinian*.

ōv·al·bū'min, ōv·al·bū'men, *n.* the albumin or white of an egg, as distinguished from serum albumin.

ō·val'i·fọrm, *a.* ovoid.

ō'văl·ly, *adv.* so as to be oval.

ō'vănt, *a.* [L. *ovans* (*-antis*), ppr. of *ovare*, to celebrate a triumph.] triumphant; exulting. [Obs.]

ō·văr'i·ăl, *a.* same as *ovarian*.

ō·văr'i·ăn, *a.* of, in, or relating to an ovary; belonging to the female ovary.

ō·văr'i·ōle, *n.* a small ovary; a cylindrical ovarian gland in a composite ovary.

ō·văr·i·ot'ō·mist, *n.* one expert in ovariotomy.

ō·văr·i·ot'ō·my, *n.*; *pl.* **ō·văr·i·ot'ō·mieṣ**, [LL. *ovarium*, and Gr. *-tomia*, from *temnein*, to cut.]
1. a surgical operation on an ovary.
2. the surgical removal of an ovary.

ō·văr'i·ous, *a.* consisting of eggs. [Rare.]

ō·va·rī'tis, *n.* [LL. *ovarium* and *-itis*.] inflammation of an ovary.

ō·văr'i·um, *n.*; *pl.* **ō·văr'i·ȧ**, [L.] an ovary.

ō'vȧ·ry, *n.*; *pl.* **ō'vȧ·rieṣ**, [Fr. *ovaire*; LL. *ovarium*, from L. *ovum*, an egg.]
1. in anatomy and zoology, the female reproductive gland, in which the ova are formed.
2. in botany, the enlarged hollow part of a pistil in angiosperms, in which ovules are formed.

ō'vāte, *a.* [L. *ovatus*, from *ovum*, an egg.]
1. egg-shaped.
2. in botany, (a) having the shape of a longitudinal section of an egg; (b) having such a shape with the broader end at the base; as, an *ovate* leaf.

OVATE LEAF

ō'vāte-ȧ·çū'mi·nāte, *a.* ovate and tapering to a point.

ō'vāte-cyl·in·drā'ceous, *a.* between ovate and cylindraceous in form.

ō'vā·ted, *a.* ovate. [Rare.]

ō'vāte-lan'cē·ō·lāte, *a.* between ovate and lanceolate.

ō'vāte-ob'lọng, *a.* between ovate and oblong.

ō'vāte-rō·tund'āte, *a.* between round and ovate.

ō'vāte-sū'bū·lāte, *a.* between ovate and subulate.

ō·vā'tion, *n.* [L. *ovatio*, from *ovare*, to celebrate a triumph.]
1. in ancient Rome, a lesser ceremonial tribute allowed to a commander for a victory not deserving a full triumph.
2. an enthusiastic outburst of applause or an enthusiastic public welcome.

ō·vā'tō·ȧ·çū'mi·nāte, *a.* same as *ovate-acuminate*.

ō·vā'tō·cyl·in·drā'ceous, *a.* same as *ovate-cylindraceous*.

ō·vā'tō·ob'lọng, *a.* same as *ovate-oblong*.

ō·vā'tō·rō·tund'āte, *a.* same as *ovate-rotundate*.

ŏv'en, *n.* [AS. *ofen*; D. *oven*; Dan. *ovn*; Ice. *ofn*; G. *ofen*; Sw. *ugn*; Goth. *auhns*.]
1. a compartment or receptacle in which substances are baked, heated, or dried; a chamber in a stove or range in which food is baked. Ovens are used for various purposes, as the cooking of food, the baking of clay and ceramic ware, the annealing of glass, the roasting of ores, etc.
2. a furnace. [Obs.]

ŏv'en·bīrd, *n.* 1. any of various birds building a domelike nest resembling an oven, as (a) the golden-crowned thrush, *Siurus auricapillus*; (b) any one of a group of small South American passerine birds that build a two-chambered nest from clay.
2. in England, (a) the long-tailed titmouse; (b) the willow warbler.

ō'vẽr, *prep.* [AS. *ofer*, over, above, upon, beside, beyond; D. and Dan. *over*; Ice. *ofr*, *yfir*; G. *über*; L. *super*; Gr. *hyper*; Sans. *upari*, above, over.]
1. in, at, or to a position up from; higher than; above; as, the branch hung *over* the house.
2. so as to cover or close; as, they boarded *over* the window.
3. while occupied or engaged in; as, we'll discuss it *over* our dinner.
4. upon; upon the surface of; as, she spread the frosting *over* the cake.
5. upon, as an effect or influence; as, he cast a spell *over* the group.
6. above in authority, position, power, etc.; as, he will preside *over* the meeting.
7. in a course leading along or across, or above and to the other side of; as, *fly* over the lake.
8. on the other side of; as, a city *over* the border.
9. here and there in, or through all parts of; as, *over* the whole state.
10. during; through; as, the dictionary was in production *over* a period of several years.
11. more than, or above in degree, amount, number, etc.; as, it cost *over* five dollars.
12. up to and including; until after; as, stay *over* Easter.
13. in preference to.
14. concerning; about; regarding.
all over; (a) on or in every part of; (b) throughout.
over all; over the whole extent; from end to end; everywhere.
over and above; in addition to; more than; besides.
over there; in Europe: World War I expression. [Colloq.]

ō'vẽr, *adv.* 1. (a) above, across, or to the other side; (b) across the brim or edge.
2. more; in excess; beyond; as, they were gone three hours or *over*.
3. completely; covering the entire area; as, the wound healed *over*.
4. through; from start to finish; as, he took out his money and counted it *over*.
5. (a) from an upright position; as, the tree fell *over*; (b) upside down; into an inverted position; as, they turned the plank *over*.
6. again; another time; as, go back and do it *over*.
7. at or on the other side, as of an intervening space, or at an unspecified distance but in a specified direction or place; as, *over* in England, *over* by the park.
8. from one side, belief, viewpoint, etc. to another; as, the party's new policy won him *over*.
9. from one person, etc. to another; as, make your property *over* to her.
10. excessively; very; too; in a great degree.

The word symbol should not seem to be *over* difficult. —Baker.

all over; (a) so as to affect the whole of a surface; on or in every part; completely; as, splashed with mud *all over*; (b) throughout.
over again; once more; with repetition; anew.
over against; opposite to or in contrast with.
over and above; in addition to; besides; beyond what is supposed or limited.
over and over (*again*); time after time; repeatedly; once and again.
to give over; see under *give*.
to run over; see under *run*.
to throw over; see under *throw*.

ō'vẽr, *a.* 1. upper, outer, superior, excessive, or extra: often in combination, as in *over*coat, *over*seer, *over*supply.
2. finished; done with; past; as, the game is *over*.
3. having reached the other side; having got across.
4. having a surplus; as, he is three hours *over* for the week. [Colloq.]
all over (*with*); finished; ended.

ō'vẽr, *n.* 1. something in addition; an excess; a surplus.
2. in cricket, (a) the set number of balls bowled during a single turn at one end of the wicket; (b) the period of time during which this takes place.
3. in military usage, a shot that hits or explodes beyond the target.

ō'vẽr, *v.t.* and *v.i.* to pass above and across. [Poet.]

ō'vẽr-, a combining form meaning (a) *above in position*, *upper*, *superior*, *eminent*, as in *over*head, *over*bearing, *over*lord; (b) *excessive*, *too much*, *beyond the normal*, as in overrate, *over*sell, *over*sleep; (c) *passing across* or *beyond*, as in *over*shoot, *over*pass, *over*run; (d) *causing a change from the original position to one lower*, as in *over*set, *over*weigh, *over*whelm. The list below includes the more common compounds formed with *over-* that do not have special meanings; they will be understood if *too much* or *excessively* is used with the meaning of the base word.

overabound
overactive
overagitate
overambitious
overanxiety
overanxious
overanxiously
overattentive
overawful
overbarren
overbend
overbookish
overbounteous
overbreed
overbright
overburdensome
overburn
overbusy
overcareful
overcareless
overcaution
overcautious
overcautiously
overcautiousness
overcloy
overcolor
overconscientious
overconservative
overconsiderate
overcook
overcostly
overcredulous
overcritical
overcunning
overcurious
overdaring
overdeal
overdelicate
overdelighted
overdiligent
overdrink
overdry
overeager
overeagerly
overeagerness
overearnest
overearnestly
overearnestness
overelegant
overemotional
overemphasize
overempty
overenthusiastic
overexcite
overexercise
overexertion
overexpansion
overexposure
overexquisite
overfar
overfatigue
overfeed
overfierce
overfill
overfine
overfineness
overfish
overfond
overfondly
overfondness
overforward
overforwardness
overfree
overfreely
overfreight
overfrequent
overfruitful
overfull
overfullness
overgarrison
overgenerous
overgird
overgive
overglad
overgorge
overgreat
overgreatness
overgreedy
overgross
overhappy
overharden
overhardy
overhaste
overhastily
overhastiness
overhasty
overheavy
overhigh
overhighly
overindulge
overinfluence
overjealous
overkind
overknowing
overlabor
overlactation
overlade
overlarge
overlargeness
overlate
overlavish
overlearned
overlearnedly
overlearnedness
overliberal
overliberally
overlight
overlogical
overloud
overlove
overluscious
overlusty
overmagnify
overmeddle
overmellow
overmodest
overmodestly
overmoist
overmoisture
overneat
overnegligent
overnicely
overniceness
overnumerous
overobedient
overofficious
overpamper
overpassionate
overpassionately
overpassionateness
overpatient
overpeople
overperemptory
overplease
overply
overpolish
overponderous
overpopulate
overpopulation
overpotent
overpraise
overpraising
overprecise
overpressure
overprize
overprompt
overpromptly
overpromptness
overproud
overprovident
overprovoke
overquiet
overquietly
overquietness
overrack
overrank
overread
overreadily
overreadiness
overready
overrefine
overrefinement
overreligious
overrich
overrigged
overrighteous
overrigid
overrigorous
overripen
overroast
oversaturate
overscented
overscrupulous
overscrupulousness
overseason
oversensitive
oversentimental
overslight
overslow
oversorrow
overspecialize
overstimulate
overstore
overstrict
overstrong
overstudious
oversubtle
oversufficient
oversup
oversure
oversuspicious
overtalk
overtedious
overtempt

overtire overwary
overtoil overweak
overtroubled overwet
overvaluation overworry
overvehement overzealous

ō″vẽr·ȧ·bun′dȧnce, *n.* more than an abundance; superfluous plenty.

ō·vẽr·act′, *v.t.* and *v.i.* to act with exaggeration; to act or perform to excess.

ō·vẽr·āge′, *a.* 1. above a certain age set as a limit or standard.
2. so old as to be of no use.

ō′vẽr·āge, *n.* [*over-*, and *-age.*] a surplus or excess, as of goods.

ō′vẽr·all, *a.* 1. from end to end.
2. total; including everything.

ō′vẽr·all, *adv.* 1. from end to end.
2. in general.

ō′vẽr·all, *n.* an outer garment worn as a protection against dirt, wet, etc.; a coverall, smock, etc. [Brit.]

ō′vẽr·alls, *n.pl.* loose-fitting trousers, often with the front extending up over the breast, and usually of some strong cotton cloth, worn over other clothing as a protection against dirt and wear.

OVERALLS

ō·vẽr·ärch′, *v.t.* and *v.i.* to form an arch over (something).

ō′vẽr·ärm, *a.* overhand.

ō·vẽr·awe′ (-a̤′), *v.t.*; overawed, *pt.*, *pp.*; overawing, *ppr.* to restrain or subjugate by inspiring awe or fear.

ō·vẽr·bal′ance, *v.t.*; overbalanced, *pt.*, *pp.*; overbalancing, *ppr.* 1. to exceed in weight, value, or importance.
2. to cause to lose balance.

ō·vẽr·bal′ance, *n.* 1. excess of weight or value; something more than an equivalent; as, an *overbalance* of exports; an *overbalance* of probabilities.
2. something that outweighs or overbalances.

ō·vẽr·bat′tle (-tl), *a.* [*over-* and obs. *battel*, fertile.] too fruitful; exuberant. [Obs.]

ō·vẽr·beār′, *v.t.*; overbore, *pt.*; overborne, *pp.*; overbearing, *ppr.* 1. to press or bear down by weight or physical power.
2. to dominate, domineer over, overrule, or subdue.

ō·vẽr·beār′, *v.i.*, to be too fruitful; to bear to excess.

ō·vẽr·beār′ing, *a.* 1. inclined to disregard the wishes of others; domineering; arrogant.
2. of transcending importance; overriding.

ō·vẽr·beār′ing·ly, *adv.* in an overbearing manner.

ō·vẽr·bid′, *v.t.* and *v.i.*; overbade *or* overbid, *pt.*; overbidden *or* overbid, *pp.*; overbidding, *ppr.* 1. to outbid (another person).
2. to bid more than the worth of (a thing).

ō′vẽr·bid, *n.* a higher or excessive bid.

ō·vẽr·bīde′, *v.t.* to outlive. [Obs.]

ō′vẽr·bīte, *n.* faulty occlusion of the teeth in which the upper incisors and canines project over the lower to an abnormal extent.

ō·vẽr·blōw′, *v.i.* to blow with too much violence, as the wind. [Obs.]

ō·vẽr·blōw′, *v.t.*; overblew, *pt.*; overblown, *pp.*; overblowing, *ppr.* 1. to blow away, across, or down.
2. to cover with something blown, as sand.
3. in music, to force an overtone in (a wind instrument).

ō′vẽr·blōwn′, *a.* 1. blown away, across, or down.
2. in steelmaking, burnt by excessive blast.
3. past the stage of full bloom.

ō′vẽr·blōwn′, *a.* 1. stout; obese.
2. (a) overdone; excessive; (b) pompous or bombastic.

ō′vẽr·bōard, *adv.* 1. over the side of a ship.
2. from on board a ship into the water; as, to fall *overboard.*
to go overboard; to go to extremes; especially, to be wildly enthusiastic.
to throw overboard; to discard.

ō·vẽr·bōld′, *a.* impudent; unduly or excessively bold.

ō·vẽr·brim′, *v.i.*; overbrimmed, *pt.*, *pp.*; overbrimming, *ppr.* to overflow the brim.

ō·vẽr·brow′, *v.t.* to hang over.

ō·vẽr·build′ (-bild′), *v.t.*; overbuilt, *pt.*, *pp.*; overbuilding, *ppr.* 1. to build too many buildings in or on (a space or lot).
2. to build over or on top of.
3. to build too elaborately.

ō′vẽr·built′, *a.* having an excess of buildings.

ō·vẽr·bulk′, *v.t.* to oppress by bulk. [Obs.]

ō·vẽr·bũr′den, *v.t.* to load with too great weight; to burden oppressively.

ō′vẽr·bũr″den, *n.* something that overburdens.

ō′vẽr·bu̇y′, *v.t.* and *v.i.*; overbought, *pt.*, *pp.*; overbuying, *ppr.* 1. to buy at too dear a rate. [Obs.]
2. to buy more than is needed or justified by ability to pay.

ō·vẽr·çan′ō·py, *v.t.* overcanopied, *pt.*, *pp.*; overcanopying, *ppr.* to cover as with a canopy.

ō·vẽr·çap″i·tal·i·zā′tion, *n.* the act of overcapitalizing or state of being over capitalized.

ō′vẽr·çap′i·tal·īze, *v.t.* 1. to capitalize beyond what is warranted by the state of the business, etc.; to furnish too much capital for or overestimate the capital value of.
2. to set the nominal value of the capital of (a corporation) higher than is lawful or justifiable.

ō′vẽr·çāre, *n.* excessive care or anxiety.

ō·vẽr·çar′ry, *v.t.*; overcarried, *pt.*, *pp.*; overcarrying, *ppr.* to carry too far; to carry or urge beyond the proper point.

ō·vẽr·çȧst′, *v.t.*; overcast, *pt.*, *pp.*; overcasting, *ppr.* 1. (a) to overspread; (b) to cloud; to darken; to cover with gloom.
The clouds that *overcast* our morn shall fly.
—Dryden.
2. to cast or compute at too high a rate; to rate too high. [Rare.]
The king, in his account of peace and calms, did much *overcast* his fortunes—Bacon.
3. (ō′vẽr-cȧst) in sewing, to sew over; to take long, loose stitches over the raw edges of, to prevent raveling.
4. in fishing, to cast beyond the point intended.

ō′vẽr·çȧst, *n.* 1. a covering, especially of clouds.
2. an arch in a mine, supporting an overhead passage.
3. in fishing, a cast made to a point beyond the one intended.

ō′vẽr·çȧst, *a.* 1. covered over; coated.
2. cloudy; dark: said of the sky or weather.
3. in sewing, made with overcasting.

ō·vẽr·chärġe′, *v.t.*; overcharged, *pt.*, *pp.*; overcharging, *ppr.* 1. to charge too high a price for; to charge too much for.
2. to overload; to fill to excess.
Our language is *overcharged* with consonants.
—Addison.
3. to load with too great a charge, as a gun.
4. to exaggerate; as, to *overcharge* a statement.

ō′vẽr·chärġe, *n.* 1. an excessive charge.
2. a load or burden that is too full or heavy.

ō′vẽr·check, *n.* a checkrein that is passed over the head and between the ears of a horse.

ō′vẽr·clōthes (*or* -klōz), *n.pl.* outer garments worn over the usual clothing.

ō·vẽr·çloud′, *v.t.* 1. to darken or cover over with clouds; to obscure; to dim.
2. to make gloomy, angry, etc. in appearance; as, despair *overclouded* his face.

ō·vẽr·çloud′, *v.i.* to become cloudy, gloomy, etc.

ō′vẽr·çōat, *n.* a topcoat; a coat for outdoor use, worn over all other clothing for warmth.

ō′vẽr·çōld, *a.* cold to excess.

ō·vẽr·çōme′, *v.t.*; overcame, *pt.* overcome, *pp.*; overcoming, *ppr.* [ME. *overcomen*; AS. *ofercuman.*]
1. to get the better of in competition, struggle, etc.; to conquer.
2. to master, suppress, prevail over, surmount, or overwhelm; as, to *overcome* obstacles or temptations; to be *overcome* by grief.
3. to spread over or overrun. [Archaic.]
4. to come upon. [Obs.]
Syn.—subdue, vanquish, crush, defeat, surmount, conquer.

ō·vẽr·çōme′, *v.i.* to gain superiority; to be victorious.

ō·vẽr·çōm′ẽr, *n.* one who vanquishes or surmounts.

ō·vẽr·çōm′ing, *a.* vanquishing; subduing.

ō·vẽr·çōm′ing·ly, *adv.* with superiority.

ō·vẽr·çom′pen·sāte, *v.t.*; overcompensated, *pt.*, *pp.*; overcompensating, *ppr.* to give an excessive compensation to.

ō·vẽr·çom′pen·sāte, *v.i.* in psychology, to react to a real or imagined physical or psychological defect by a conscious or unconscious exaggerated drive to compensate for it.

ō·vẽr·çon′fi·dence, *n.* excessive confidence.

ō·vẽr·çon′fi·dent, *a.* confident without good reason; having too much confidence or trust.

ō·vẽr·çon′fi·dent·ly, *adv.* with overconfidence.

ō·vẽr·çount′, *v.t.* to rate above the true value; also, to outnumber.

ō·vẽr·çov′ẽr, *v.t.* to cover completely.

ō·vẽr·çrop′, *v.t.*; overcropped *or occas.* overcropt, *pt.*, *pp.*; overcropping, *ppr.* to deplete the fertility of (land) by overproduction of crops.

ō·vẽr·çrōw′, *v.t.* to crow over, as in triumph.

ō·vẽr·çrowd′, *v.t.* to crowd too many people in or on.

ō·vẽr·dāre′, *v.t.* and *v.i.* to exceed in daring; to dare too much or rashly; to be too daring.

ō·vẽr·dāte′, *v.t.* to date beyond the proper period. [Archaic.]

ō″vẽr·dē·vel′ŏp, *v.t.* 1. to develop too much.
2. in photography, to continue the process of developing for too long a time or to use too powerful an agent in developing.

ō·vẽr·dīght′ (-dīt′), *a.* decked over; overspread; covered over. [Obs.]

ō′vẽr·dö′, *v.t.*; overdid, *pt.*; overdone, *pp.*; overdoing, *ppr.*; 1. to do or perform too much, or to excess.
2. to overwork; to exhaust; to tire.
3. to spoil the effect of by exaggeration; to exaggerate; as, he *overdid* his part, and so made the pathetic scene ridiculous.
4. to excel; to exceed. [Archaic.]
5. to cook beyond the necessary time; as, the roast was *overdone.*

ō′vẽr·dö′, *v.i.* to do too much; to work too hard; to do more than necessary.

ō·vẽr·dö′ẽr, *n.* one who does too much.

ō′vẽr·dōse, *n.* too large a dose.

ō·vẽr·dōse′, *v.t.* to dose to excess.

ō′vẽr·drȧft, ō′vẽr·drȧught (-drȧft), *n.* 1. in banking, the act of drawing out by check or draft a sum of money exceeding the amount to one's credit; also, the amount of such excess.
2. a current of air passing over instead of through or under a fire, as in a furnace, or passing down through a kiln.

ō·vẽr·dra̤w′, *v.t.*; overdrew, *pt.*; overdrawn, *pp.*; overdrawing, *ppr.* 1. to draw upon for a larger sum than is due, or for a sum beyond one's credit in the books of a company; as, to *overdraw* one's account with a bank.
2. to exaggerate in representation, in writing, speech, or picture; as, to *overdraw* a tale of distress.
3. to draw (a bow, etc.) too far or too much.

ō·vẽr·dress′, *v.t.* and *v.i.* to dress extravagantly or beyond the call of good taste or the occasion.

ō′vẽr·drīve, *n.* a gear that at a certain speed automatically reduces an engine's power output without reducing its driving speed: used to lessen fuel consumption and engine wear.

ō·vẽr·drīve′, *v.t.*; overdrove, *pt.*; overdriven, *pp.*; overdriving, *ppr.* to drive too hard, or beyond strength.

ō′vẽr·dūe′, *a.* 1. past the time for payment; as, an *overdue* note.
2. delayed beyond the time set for arrival or for taking place; as, an *overdue* vessel; an *overdue* performance.
3. that should have come about sooner; as, *overdue* reforms.

ō·vẽr·dȳe′, *v.t.* 1. to subject too long to the dyeing process; to make too dark a color.
2. to dye over (a color previously dyed).

ō·vẽr·ēat′, *v.t.* and *v.i.*; overate, *pt.*; overeaten, *pp.*; overeating, *ppr.* 1. to eat too much or to excess; to surfeit: sometimes used reflexively.
2. to eat again. [Obs.]

ō′vẽr·est, *a.* uppermost. [Obs.]

ō·vẽr·es′ti·māte, *v.t.* to estimate too highly.

ō′vẽr·es′ti·māte, *n.* an estimate that is too high.

ō″vẽr·ex·cīte′ment, *n.* excess of excitement.

ō″vẽr·ex·ẽrt′, *v.t.* and *v.i.* to exert too much or too long (often used reflexively).

ō″vẽr·ex·pōse′, *v.t.* to expose too much or too long.

ō′vẽr·fa̤ll, *n.* 1. a cataract; a waterfall. [Obs.]
2. in nautical usage, a dangerous ridge or shoal hidden under the water; also, a turbulent sea current flowing over such ridges.

ō′vẽr·flīght, *n.* the flight of an aircraft over a specified area or beyond a specified place; especially, a flight over foreign territory for reconnaissance.

ō·vẽr·flōat′, *v.t.* to overflow; to inundate. [Obs.]

ō·vẽr·flour′ish, *v.t.* to make excessive display or flourish of. [Rare.]

ō·vẽr·flōw′, *v.t.*; overflowed, *pt.*, *pp.*; overflowing, *ppr.* 1. to flow or spread over or across; to inundate; to flood.

2. to cause to overflow; to pour in or upon beyond the capacity of.
3. to flow over the brim or edge of.
ō·vĕr·flōw′, *v.i.* 1. to flow or spread beyond the limits; to run over the surface; to swell and run over the brim.
2. to be more than full or complete; to be superabundant; to abound; to exuberate; as, *overflowing* plenty.
Syn.—abound, fill, overspread.
ō′vĕr·flōw, *n.* 1. an overflowing or being overflowed.
2. the amount that overflows; quantity in excess; superabundance.
3. an outlet; a vent for overflowing liquids.
Syn.—redundancy, exuberance, superabundance, deluge, inundation.
ō′vĕr·flōw bā′sin, a basin with an outlet which prevents its contents from rising above a fixed level.
ō·vĕr·flōw′ing, *a.* abundant; copious; exuberant.
ō·vĕr·flōw′ing, *n.* exuberance; copiousness.
ō·vĕr·flōw′ing·ly, *adv.* exuberantly; in great abundance.
ō′vĕr·flōw pīpe, a waste pipe, as in a cistern or basin, for carrying away all surplus water.
ō·vĕr·flush′, *v.t.* to flush to excess.
ō·vĕr·flut′tĕr, *v.t.* to flutter over.
ō′vĕr·flux, *n.* exuberance; excess. [Rare.]
ō·vĕr·flȳ′, *v.t.*; overflew, *pt.*; overflown, *pp.*; overflying, *ppr.* to pass over or cross by flight.
ō′vĕr·fōld, *n.* in geology, an anticlinal flexure, or inverted fold, so inclined from the vertical that one limb of the fold lies upon the other.
ō′vĕr·fōrce, *n.* violence; excess of force. [Rare.]
ō·vĕr·frïēze′, *v.t.* to cover with a frieze, or as with a frieze. [Rare.]
ō·vĕr·frŏnt′, *v.t.* to confront. [Obs.]
ō′vĕr·gär″ment, *n.* a garment worn over the rest of the clothes, as an overcoat or a cloak.
ō·vĕr·gāze′, *v.i.*; overgazed, *pt., pp.*; overgazing, *ppr.* to look over.
ō·vĕr·get′, *v.t.* to reach; to overtake. [Obs.]
ō·vĕr·glänce′, *v.t.*; overglanced, *pt., pp.*; overglancing, *ppr.* to glance over; to run over with the eye.
ō′vĕr·glāze, *n.* in ceramics, (a) a second glaze applied over the first; (b) a decoration applied over a glaze.
ō·vĕr·glāze′, *v.t.* to cover with a glaze or overglaze; to glaze over.
ō·vĕr·glo͝om′, *v.t.* to make gloomy; to cast a shadow over. [Rare.]
ō·vĕr·grāce′, *v.t.* to honor beyond what is deserved. [Rare.]
ō′vĕr·ground, *a.* above the ground: opposed to *underground*.
ō·vĕr·grōw′, *v.t.*; overgrew, *pt.*; overgrown, *pp.*; overgrowing, *ppr.* 1. to overspread or cover with growth or herbage.
2. to grow beyond; to rise above; to outgrow.
ō·vĕr·grōw′, *v.i.* 1. to grow too large or too fast.
2. to grow beyond the fit or natural size.
ō′vĕr·grōwn′, *a.* 1. overspread with foliage.
2. grown excessively or beyond normal size.
ō′vĕr·grōwth, *n.* exuberant or excessive growth.
ō·vĕr·hāil′, *v.t.* to overhaul. [Obs.]
ō′vĕr·hâir, *n.* the straight, smooth, comparatively rigid hair covering the fur of many mammals.
ō·vĕr·hāle′, *v.t.* to overhaul. [Obs.]
ō′vĕr·hand, *n.* 1. the upper hand; superiority; dominance. [Scot. and Brit. Dial.]
2. in sports, skill or style in performing or delivering overhand strokes.
ō′vĕr·hand, *a.* 1. descending; down from above; as, an *overhand* gesture.
2. performed with the hand raised above the elbow or the arm above the shoulder; as, an *overhand* pitch.
3. designating or of a style of sewing, or a seam, in which the stitches are passed over two edges to sew them together.
overhand knot; a kind of knot: see *knot*, illus.
ō′vĕr·hand, *v.t.* to sew overhand.
ō′vĕr·hand′, *adv.* in an overhand manner.
ō·vĕr·han′dle, *v.t.*; overhandled, *pt., pp.*; overhandling, *ppr.* to handle too much.
ō·vĕr·hang′, *v.t.*; overhung, *pt., pp.*; overhanging, *ppr.* 1. to hang over or above; to project beyond.
2. to impend; to threaten.
3. to decorate with hangings.
ō·vĕr·hang′, *v.i.* to hang over; to project or jut over something.
ō′vĕr·hang, *n.* 1. the projection of one thing over or beyond another.
2. the amount of such projection.
3. in architecture, a projection of one part of a structure over another.
4. the part of a ship which projects beyond the water line, as the bow or stern.
5. in machinery, that part which projects beyond another part beneath it.
6. in aeronautics, (a) the distance from the tip of the wings to the outer wing strut attachment; (b) one half the difference in length between two main airfoils: an overhang is said to be positive when the upper airfoil is longer than the lower.
ō′vĕr·haul, ō·vĕr·haul′ing, *n.* a thorough examination with a view to needed repairs; as, the vessel has received a thorough *overhaul*.
ō·vĕr·haul′, *v.t.* 1. to haul over, as for examination; hence, to examine thoroughly with a view to repairs.
2. to make all the repairs, adjustments, etc. needed to bring (a machine, etc.) into good working order.
3. to gain upon; to catch up with; to overtake.
to overhaul a ship; (a) to come up with or to gain upon a ship; (b) to search a ship for contraband goods.
ō′vĕr·head″ (-hed″), *n.* the general, continuing costs involved in running a business enterprise, as of breakage, rent, furnishings, lighting, heating, taxes, insurance, office expenses, etc.
ō·vĕr·head′, *adv.* aloft; above the level of the head; in the ceiling or story above.
ō′vĕr·head, *a.* 1. located or operating above the level of the head.
2. in the sky.
3. on a higher level, with reference to related objects; as, the machine had an *overhead* drive.
4. having to do with the overhead of a business.
overhead engine; an engine in which the cylinder is above the crank, the thrust motion being downward.
overhead work; shafting and gearing, collectively, when overhead.
ō·vĕr·hēar′, *v.t.*; overheard, *pt., pp.*; overhearing, *ppr.* 1. to hear (something spoken or a speaker) without the speaker's knowledge or intention; to hear by accident or stratagem.

I am invisible,
And I will *overhear* their conference.
—Shak.

2. to hear told over. [Obs.]

I stole into a neighbor thicket by,
And overheard what you shall *overhear*.
—Shak.

ō·vĕr·hēat′, *v.t.* to heat excessively; to make too hot.
ō·vĕr·hēle′, *v.t.* to cover over. [Obs.]
ō·vĕr·hend′, *v.t.* to overtake. [Obs.]
ō·vĕr·hip′, *v.t.*; overhipped (-hipt), *pt., pp.*; overhipping, *ppr.* to jump or leap over; to overpass. [Obs.]
ō·vĕr·hōld′, *v.t.* to overvalue; to estimate at too dear a rate. [Obs.]
ō·vĕr·hung′, *a.* 1. hung or covered over; adorned with hangings.

To him the upholsterer is no pontiff, neither is any drawing room a temple, were it never so begilt and *overhung*.—Carlyle.

2. hung from above; suspended from the top.
ō′vĕr·in·dul′ġence, *n.* excessive indulgence.
ō″vĕr·in·fọrm′, *v.t.* to inform or animate to excess.
ō′vĕr·is′sūe (-ish′ū), *n.* an excessive issue; an issue, as of bonds or stocks, that exceeds authorization, credit limits, etc.
ō·vĕr·is′sūe, *v.t.* to issue in too great a degree or quantity.
ō·vĕr·joy′, *v.t.* to give great or excessive joy to; to transport with gladness.
ō′vĕr·joy, *n.* joy to excess; transport.
ō·vĕr·jump′, *v.t.* to jump over; to overleap; to pass over; to pass without notice.
ō′vĕr·kill, *n.* the capacity of a nation's nuclear weapon stockpile to kill many times the total population of any given nation.
ō′vĕr·king, *n.* a king holding sway over several petty kings or princes.
ō·vĕr·lād′en, *a.* having too heavy a load; overloaded; overburdened.
ō′vĕr·land, *adv.* by way of, upon, or across land; as, the route lies *overland*.
ō′vĕr·land, *a.* lying over, on, or across the land; made by way of land; making a journey by way of land; as, an *overland* route.
ō′vĕr·land·ĕr, *n.* in Australia, one who makes an overland journey; specifically, one who drives cattle, etc. over a long distance.
ō·vĕr·lañ′guȧġed (-gwăjd), *a.* lacking conciseness; wordy.
ō·vĕr·lap′, *v.t.* and *v.i.*; overlapped, *pt., pp.*; overlapping, *ppr.* 1. to lap over; to lie upon and extend beyond (something or each other).
2. to extend over part of (a period of time, sphere of activity, etc.); to coincide in part (with).
ō′vĕr·lap, *n.* 1. an overlapping.
2. a part that overlaps.
3. the amount or extent of overlapping.
4. the place of overlapping.
5. in geology, the extension or spread of a superior stratum over an inferior so as to cover and conceal its edges.
ō·vĕr·lash′, *v.i.* to exaggerate; to proceed to excess. [Obs.]
ō·vĕr·lash′ing, *n.* extravagance; lavishness; excess. [Obs.]
ō·vĕr·lāve′, *v.t.*; overlaved, *pt., pp.*; overlaving, *ppr.* to bathe again or over.
ō·vĕr·lāy′, *v.t.*; overlaid, *pt., pp.*; overlaying, *ppr.* 1. to lay too much upon; to oppress; to burden; to weigh down.
2. to cover or overspread, as with a decorative layer of something.

See them *overlaid*
With narrow moon-lit slips of silver cloud.
—Tennyson.

3. to lay or spread over.
4. to smother with close covering or by lying upon; to overlie.

And this woman's child died in the night; because she *overlaid* it.—1 Kings iii. 19.

5. to obscure by covering; to cloud; to overcast

Physical astronomy eclipsed and *overlaid* theoretical mechanics. —Whewell.

6. to span; to join the opposite sides of. [Rare.]

And *overlay*
With this portentous bridge the dark abyss.
—Milton.

7. in printing, to place an overlay on.
ō′vĕr·lāy, *n.* 1. anything laid over another thing; a covering.
2. a decorative layer or the like, applied in overlaying.
3. in printing, a sheet of paper fastened on the printing surface of a press to make a heavier impression.
4. a cravat. [Scot.]
ō·vĕr·lāy′ing, *n.* a surface covering.
ō·vĕr·lēad′, *v.t.* to treat in a domineering manner. [Obs.]
ō′vĕr·lēaf, *adv.* on the other side of the leaf (of a book).
ō·vĕr·lēap′, *v.t.* 1. to leap over or across; to pass or move from one side to the other by leaping.

Overleaped all bound
Of hill or highest wall. —Milton.

2. figuratively, to omit or pass over; to ignore.
3. to leap farther than.
4. to overreach (oneself) by leaping too far.
ō′vĕr·leath″ĕr (-leth″), *n.* the upper leather of a shoe.
ō·vĕr·lïe′, *v.t.*; overlay, *pt.*; overlain; *pp.*; overlying, *ppr.* 1. to lie over or upon.
2. to stifle or smother by lying on.
ō′vĕr·light, (-līt), *n.* too strong a light.
ō′vĕr·li·ness, *n.* carelessness; superficiality. [Obs.]
ō·vĕr·liñ′gĕr, *v.t.* to cause to remain too long. [Obs.]
ō·vĕr·live′, *v.t.* to live longer than; to outlive; to survive.
ō·vĕr·live′, *v.i.* 1. to continue living or existing; to endure.
2. to live too long, too actively, or too luxuriously.
ō·vĕr·liv′ĕr, *n.* one who outlives.
ō·vĕr·lōad′, *v.t.* to load with too heavy a burden, charge, or cargo; to fill to excess; to overcharge; as, to *overload* the stomach or a vehicle.
ō′vĕr·lōad, *n.* too great a load.
ō′vĕr·lọng′, *a.* and *adv.* too long.
ō·vĕr·look′, *v.t.* 1. to look at from above.
2. to give a view of from above.
3. to rise above; to overtop.
4. (a) to look over or beyond and not see; (b) to ignore; neglect.
5. to pass over indulgently; to excuse.
6. to inspect; look over.
7. to oversee; supervise; manage.
8. to bewitch by looking at.
Syn.—condone, disregard, supervise, inspect, survey, review, pardon, forgive.

ō′vẽr·look, *n.* 1. a height from which to survey surroundings.
2. the view from such a height.
3. a viewing or surveying.
4. a leguminous climber, *Canavalia ensiformis*, of the tropics, planted as a watchman on plantation boundaries by the Negroes of the West Indies.

ō·vẽr·look′ẽr, *n.* one who overlooks.

ō′vẽr·lord, *n.* a lord ranking over other lords, especially in the feudal system.

ō′vẽr·lord·ship, *n.* the office or power of an overlord.

ō′vẽr·ly, *a.* 1. careless; negligent; superficial. [Obs.]
2. excessive; overmuch. [Obs.]

ō′vẽr·ly, *adv.* 1. superficially; carelessly. [Obs.]
2. excessively; too or too much; as, *overly* nice.

ō′vẽr·măn, *n.*; *pl.* **ō′vẽr·men,** 1. a man above others in power or authority; leader; foreman.
2. an arbitrator; referee.
3. (ō′vẽr-man), [transl. of G. *übermensch.*] a superman.

ō·vẽr·man′, *v.t.*; overmanned, *pt., pp.*; overmanning, *ppr.* to supply with more men than necessary.

ō′vẽr·man″tel, *n.* the ornamental work above a mantelpiece.

ō″vẽr·märch′, *v.t.* to pass over in marching; also, to go too far or fatigue by marching.

ō″vẽr·märk′, *v.t.* 1. to mark over, as by another mark.
2. to cause overmarking in (a horse).

ō′vẽr·märk′ing, *n.* the effect on a horse of overfeeding or overwork, marked by symptomatic constitutional changes and affection of the legs.

ō″vẽr·mȧsk′, *v.t.* to mask or to cover over as with a mask.

ō·vẽr·mȧst′, *v.t.* to furnish with a mast or with masts that are too long or too heavy. [Rare.]

ō·vẽr·mȧs′tẽr, *v.t.* to overpower; to subdue.

ō′vẽr·match, *n.* one superior in power.

ō·vẽr·match′, *v.t.* 1. to more than match; to exceed; to be too powerful for; to conquer; to subdue.
2. to give in marriage to a social superior. [Obs.]

ō″vẽr·mȧ·tūre′, *a.* past maturity.

ō′vẽr·meas′ūre (-mezh′), *n.* excess of measure; the amount that exceeds the measure proposed.

ō·vẽr·meas′ūre, *v.t.* to measure or estimate in excess of the proper measure.

ō′vẽr·mer″it, *n.* excessive merit.

ō·vẽr·mic′kle (-kl), *a.* and *adv.* overmuch. [Scot.]

ō·vẽr·mix′, *v.t.* to mix with too much.

ō′vẽr·mount, *n.* a mat used in picture framing.

ō·vẽr·mount′, *v.t.* to mount above; to surmount.

ō′vẽr·much′, *a.* and *adv.* too much.

ō′vẽr·much′, *n.* too great a quantity; an excessive amount.

ō·vẽr·mul′ti·plȳ, *v.t.* to repeat too often.

ō·vẽr·mul′ti·plȳ, *v.i.* to increase overmuch.

ō·vẽr·mul′ti·tūde, *v.t.* to outnumber. [Obs.]

ō′vẽr·nīce′, *a.* too nice; too fastidious, precise, etc.

ō′vẽr·nīght′ (-nīt′), *adv.* 1. during or through the night.
2. on or during the previous evening.

ō′vẽr·nīght′, *a.* 1. done, happening, or lasting during the night.
2. of the previous evening.
3. of or for only one night; as, an *overnight* guest.
4. of or for a short journey or visit; as, an *overnight* bag.

ō′vẽr·nīght, *n.* the previous evening.

ō·vẽr·pāint′, *v.t.* 1. to paint over.
2. to color or describe too strongly.

ō′vẽr·pȧss, *n.* a bridge or other passageway over or across a road, culvert, railroad track, or the like.

ō·vẽr·pȧss′, *v.i.* to pass over.

ō·vẽr·pȧss′, *v.t.*; overpassed, *pt., pp.*; overpassing, *ppr.* 1. to pass over, across, or through.
2. to overlook; to pass without regard; to ignore.
3. to transgress.
4. to surpass; to exceed; to outdo.

ō·vẽr·pāy′, *v.t.* and *v.i.* 1. to pay too much, or more than (the due or proper amount).
2. to pay too much to (someone).

ō·vẽr·peer′, *v.t.* to overlook; to hover over.

ō′vẽr·pēo′pled (-pē′pld), *a.* filled with too many people.

ō″vẽr·pẽr·suāde′ (-swād′), *v.t.* to persuade or influence against one's natural inclination or opinion; to win over by argument.

ō·vẽr·plāy′, *v.t.* 1. to overact or overdo.
2. in card games, to overestimate the strength of (one's hand) and be defeated as a result.
3. in golf, to hit (the ball) beyond the flag or green.

ō′vẽr·plus, *n.* [ME. *ouer*, over, and *pluse* (from L. *plus*), more; prob. after Late OFr. *surplus.*]
1. an amount left over; surplus.
2. too great an amount; excess.

ō·vẽr·poiṣe′, *v.t.* to outweigh.

ō′vẽr·poiṣe, *n.* preponderant weight.

ō·vẽr·pōst′, *v.t.* to hasten over quickly. [Obs.]

ō·vẽr·pow′ẽr, *v.t.*; overpowered, *pt., pp.*; overpowering, *ppr.* 1. to furnish with too much power, as the motorboat was *overpowered.*
2. to make helpless; to overwhelm; to vanquish by force; to subdue; to defeat.

ō′vẽr·pow·ẽr, *n.* too much power. [Rare.]

ō·vẽr·pow′ẽr·ing, *a.* that overpowers; overwhelming.

ō·vẽr·pow′ẽr·ing·ly, *adv.* with superior force.

ō·vẽr·press′, *v.t.* to bear upon with irresistible force; to crush; to overwhelm.

ō·vẽr·print′, *v.t.* to print over or on top of (a previously printed surface).

ō′vẽr·print, *n.* 1. anything overprinted.
2. (a) anything officially printed over the original design on a stamp; (b) a stamp so overprinted.

ō′vẽr·prō·dūce′, *v.t.* and *v.i.* to produce in a quantity that is too great or that exceeds demand.

ō′vẽr·prō·duc′tion, *n.* 1. the production of more than is necessary.
2. production that exceeds the demand.

ō′vẽr·proof′, *a.* having more alcohol than the standard proof spirit.

ō″vẽr·prō·pōr′tion, *v.t.* to make of too great proportion.

ō·vẽr·quell′, *v.t.* to subdue; to quell. [Rare.]

ō·vẽr·rāke′, *v.t.*; overraked (-rākt), *pt., pp.*; overraking, *ppr.* to sweep entirely from fore to aft; as, waves *overrake* a vessel when its head is to the wind.

ō·vẽr·rāte′, *v.t.*; overrated, *pt., pp.*; overrating, *ppr.* to rate, assess, or estimate too highly.

ō′vẽr·rāte, *n.* an excessive valuation. [Rare.]

ō·vẽr·rēach′, *v.t.*; overreached, *pt., pp.*; overreaching, *ppr.* 1. to reach or stretch beyond or above; to extend beyond.
2. figuratively, to extend beyond in time.
3. to spread over and cover.
4. to reach too far for and miss.
5. to cheat; to outdo by cunning.
to overreach oneself; (a) to fail because of trying to do more than one can; (b) to fail because of being too crafty or eager.

ō·vẽr·rēach′, *v.i.* 1. to reach too far.
2. to cheat.
3. to reach or stretch beyond or above something.
4. to strike the forefoot with the hind foot: said of hoofed animals.
5. in nautical usage, to sail too far on one tack.

ō′vẽr·rēach, *n.* the act of overreaching.

ō·vẽr·rēach′ẽr, *n.* one who overreaches.

ō·vẽr·reck′ŏn, *v.t.* to estimate too highly.

ō′vẽr·rē·fīned′ (-fīnd′), *a.* too refined.

ō·vẽr·rent′, *v.t.* to rent at too high a rate.

ō·vẽr·rīde′, *v.t.*; overrode, *pt.*; overridden, *pp.*; overriding, *ppr.* 1. to ride over.
2. to trample down.
3. to suppress, oppress, or domineer over.
4. to disregard; nullify; as, he *overrode* their objections.
5. to fatigue (a horse, etc.) by riding too long.
6. to pass or extend over.
7. in surgery, to overlap.

ō′vẽr·rīpe′, *a.* too ripe.

ō·vẽr·rụle′, *v.t.*; overruled, *pt., pp.*; overruling, *ppr.* 1. to set aside or decide against by virtue of higher authority; to rule out; annul; as, the major *overruled* the captain's order.
2. to have influence over or prevail over.

ō·vẽr·rụle′, *v.i.* to hold sway; to prevail.

ō·vẽr·rụl′ẽr, *n.* one who overrules.

ō·vẽr·rụl′ing·ly, *adv.* so as to overrule; in an overruling manner.

ō·vẽr·run′, *v.t.*; overran, *pt.*; overrun, *pp.*; overrunning, *ppr.* 1. to run or spread over; to grow over; to cover all over; as, thistles *overran* the field.
2. to spread over with a harmful result; to infest or swarm over, as vermin; also, to rove over; to harass by hostile incursions; to ravage; as, *overrun* by the Goths and Vandals.
3. to spread swiftly throughout, as ideas, a fad, etc.
4. to outrun; to run faster than (another) and leave (him) behind. [Rare.]
5. to run or extend beyond (certain limits); to run past; to exceed.
6. to tread down; to oppress. [Obs.]
7. in printing, to rearrange (lines of type, columns, or pages) by shifting words or letters from one line to another.

ō·vẽr·run′, *v.i.* 1. to overflow; to run over.
2. to run over or beyond certain limits.

ō′vẽr·run, *n.* 1. an overrunning.
2. the amount that overruns, or by which something overruns.

ō·vẽr·run′nẽr, *n.* one who overruns.

ō·vẽr·sāy′, *v.t.* to speak again; to repeat. [Obs.]

ō·vẽr·sçōre′, *v.t.*; overscored, *pt., pp.*; overscoring, *ppr.* 1. to put a line above (a word, sentence, etc.).
2. to mark lines through.

ō′vẽr·sçōre, *n.* a line over or through a word, sentence, etc.

ō′vẽr·sēa′, *a.* and *adv.* overseas.

ō·vẽr·sēarch′, *v.t.* to search over or through; to examine.

ō′vẽr·sēaṣ′, *adv.* abroad; over or beyond the sea.

ō′vẽr·sēaṣ′, *a.* 1. foreign; having to do with foreign countries.
2. from beyond the sea.
3. over or across the sea.

ō′vẽr·sēaṣ′ çap, a small, soft cap without a visor or brim, worn by U. S. forces since World War I.

ō·vẽr·see′, *v.t.*; oversaw, *pt.*; overseen, *pp.*; overseeing, *ppr.* [ME. *oversene*; AS. *oferseon.*]
1. to superintend; to supervise; to look or see after; to take care of.
2. to survey; to watch.
3. to examine; to inspect. [Obs.]
4. to overlook; to pass over or by; to neglect; to pass unheeded. [Obs.]

ō·vẽr·see′, *v.i.* to make an oversight; to overlook; to neglect to see or notice.

ō′vẽr·sē·ẽr, *n.* 1. one who watches over and directs the work of others; a supervisor.
2. in England, a parish official: in full, *overseer of the poor.*

ō·vẽr·sē′ẽr·ship, *n.* the office, position, or station of an overseer.

ō·vẽr·sell′, *v.t.*; oversold, *pt., pp.*; overselling, *ppr.* 1. to sell at too great a price.
2. to sell more of than is accessible or deliverable.
3. to sell to an excessive degree.

ō·vẽr·set′, *v.t.*; overset, *pt., pp.*; oversetting, *ppr.* 1. to overcome or upset.
2. to overturn or overthrow.
3. to set too great an amount of (type or copy), or too much type for (a given space).

ō·vẽr·set′, *v.i.* to turn or be turned over; to be overturned.

ō′vẽr·set, *n.* the act of oversetting or overthrowing; the state of being overset or overturned; overthrow; an upsetting.

ō′vẽr·sew (-sō *or* -sō′), *v.t.*; oversewed, *pt.*; oversewed *or* oversewn, *pp.*; oversewing, *ppr.* to sew together (two pieces of material) by passing small, close stitches over their coinciding edges; to overhand.

ō·vẽr·shāde′, *v.t.*; overshaded, *pt., pp.*; overshading, *ppr.* to overshadow.

ō·vẽr·shad′ōw, *v.t.*; overshadowed, *pt., pp.*; overshadowing, *ppr.* 1. to throw a shadow over.
2. to darken; obscure; dim.
3. to loom over, dominate, or be more significant or important than by comparison.
4. to shelter; to protect; to cover with protecting influence.

ō·vẽr·shad′ōw·ẽr, *n.* one who or that which overshadows.

ō·vẽr·shāke′, *v.t.* to shake excessively.

ō·vẽr·shīne′, *v.t.*; overshone, *pt., pp.*; overshining, *ppr.* 1. to shine over or upon; to illumine.
2. to outshine; to excel in luster.

ō′vẽr·shōe, *n.* a kind of shoe or boot of rubber or fabric, worn over the regular shoe as a protection from the wet or cold; a galosh; rubber.

ō·vẽr·shoot′, *v.t.*; overshot, *pt., pp.*; overshooting, *ppr.* 1. to shoot or pass beyond or over.
2. to go farther than (an intended or normal limit); to exceed.
3. to cause (a thing) to go beyond a proper limit.
to overshoot oneself; to venture too far; to assert oneself too much.

ō·vẽr·shoot′, *v.i.* to shoot or go too far; to fly beyond the mark.

ō′vẽr·shot, *a.* 1. with the upper part or half extending past the lower; as, an *overshot* jaw.

OVERSHOT WATER WHEEL

2. driven by water flowing onto the upper part; as, an *overshot* water wheel.

ō·vẽr·sīde′, *adv.* over the side, as of a ship.

ō′vẽr·sīde, *a.* discharging or working over the side, as a dredge.

ō′vẽr·sight (-sīt), *n.* 1. superintendence; watchful care; supervision.
2. an overlooking; failure to see or notice.
3. an unintentional, careless mistake or omission.
Syn.—supervision, management, inspection, superintendence, omission, mistake, error, inadvertence.

ō′vẽr·sīze′, *a.* 1. too large.
2. outsize; larger than the normal or usual.

ō′vẽr·sīze, *n.* an outsize; a size larger than regular sizes.

ō·vẽr·sīze′, *v.t.* to surpass in bulk. [Rare.]

ō·vẽr·sīze′, *v.t.* to cover with size. [Rare.]

ō′vẽr·skīrt, *n.* an outer skirt or the drapery for the skirt of a dress.

ō′vẽr·slaugh (-slạ), *n.* a bar in a river.

ō′vẽr·slaugh, *v.t.* [D. *overslaan*; *over*, over, and *slaan*, to strike, to slay.]
1. to pass over in favor of someone else.
2. to obstruct; to hinder; as, to *overslaugh* a bill in the legislature.

ō·vẽr·sleep′, *v.t.*; overslept, *pt.*, *pp.*; oversleeping, *ppr.* to sleep beyond; as, to *oversleep* the usual hour of rising.

ō·vẽr·sleep′, *v.i.* to sleep too long.

ō·vẽr·slīde′, *v.t.*; overslid, *pt.*; overslid *or* overslidden, *pp*; oversliding, *ppr.* to slip, slide, or pass by.

ō·vẽr·slip′, *v.t.* overslipped, *pt.*, *pp.*; overslipping, *ppr.* to slip or pass without notice; to pass undone, unnoticed, or unused; as, to *overslip* time or opportunity.

ō′vẽr·slop, *n.* an outer garment. [Obs.]

ō·vẽr·slōw′, *v.t.* to render slow. [Obs.]

ō′vẽrṣ·măn, *n.*; *pl.* **ō′vẽrṣ·men,** 1. an overseer.
2. in Scots law, an umpire appointed by a submission to decide where two arbiters have differed in opinion, or named by the arbiters themselves under powers given to them by the submission.

ō·vẽr·snōw′, *v.t.* to cover with or as with snow. [Rare.]

ō·vẽr·soon′, *adv.* too soon.

ō′vẽr·sōul, *n.* the spiritual element of the universe which is infinite and from which finite souls draw their being and support: a concept in the transcendentalist philosophy of Emerson and others.

ō′vẽr·sōw′, *v.t.*; oversowed, *pt.*; oversown *or* oversowed, *pp.*; oversowing, *ppr.* to sow over something already sown.

ō·vẽr·span′, *v.t.*; overspanned, *pt.*, *pp.*; overspanning, *ppr.* to reach or extend over.

ō′vẽr·spärred′, *a.* in nautical usage, having too large or too many spars: said of a ship.

ō·vẽr·spēak′, *v.t.* and *v.i.*; overspoke, *pt.*; overspoken, *pp.*; overspeaking, *ppr.* to speak too much; to describe verbosely.

ō·vẽr·spend′, *v.t.*; overspent, *pt.*, *pp.*; overspending, *ppr.* 1. to use till worn out; exhaust. [Rare.]
2. to spend more than.

ō·vẽr·spend′, *v.i.* to spend more than one can afford.

ō·vẽr·spent′, *a.* harassed or fatigued to an extreme degree. [Rare.]

ō·vẽr·spread′ (-spred′), *v.t.* and *v.i.*; overspread, *pt.*, *pp.*; overspreading, *ppr.* to spread over; to cover over; as, the deluge *overspread* the earth.

ō·vẽr·stand′, *v.t.* to outstay; to overstay. [Obs.]

ō·vẽr·stāre′, *v.t.* to stare wildly. [Obs.]

ō·vẽr·stāte′, *v.t.*; overstated, *pt.*, *pp.*; overstating, *ppr.* to give an extravagant or magnified account of (facts, truth, etc.); to exaggerate; to state in too strong terms.

ō·vẽr·stāte′ment, *n.* an exaggerated or extravagant statement.

ō·vẽr·stāy′, *v.t.* to stay beyond the time, limits, or duration of; as, to *overstay* one's time.

ō·vẽr·step′, *v.t.*; overstepped, *pt.*, *pp.*; overstepping, *ppr.* to step over or beyond: usually in a figurative application.

ō′vẽr·stock, *n.* too large a stock; superabundance; more than is sufficient.

ō·vẽr·stock′, *v.t.* to fill too full; to supply with more of than is wanted or can be readily used; as, the market is often *overstocked* with goods.

ō′vẽr·stō″ry, *n.* a clerestory. [Rare.]

ō·vẽr·strāin′, *v.i.* to strain to excess; to exert great effort; as, in his zeal he *overstrained*.

ō·vẽr·strāin′, *v.t.* to strain too much; to overwork; as, to *overstrain* one's eyes.

ō′vẽr·strāin, *n.* excessive strain.

ō·vẽr·stretch′, *v.t.* to stretch too far.

ō·vẽr·strew′, *v.t.*; overstrewed, *pt.*; overstrewed *or* overstrewn, *pp.*; overstrewing, *ppr.* to spread or scatter over.

ō·vẽr·strīde′, *v.t.*; overstrode, *pt.*; overstridden, *pp.*; overstriding, *ppr.* 1. to stride across or over; to go beyond.
2. to outdo; surpass.
3. to bestride.

ō′vẽr·strung′, *a.* too highly strung; tense; jittery.

ō·vẽr·stud′y, *v.t.* and *v.i.*; overstudied, *pt.*, *pp.*; overstudying, *ppr.* to study too hard or too much.

ō′vẽr·stud′y, *n.* too much study.

ō·vẽr·stuff′, *v.t.*; overstuffed, *pt.*, *pp.*; overstuffing, *ppr.* 1. to stuff to an excessive degree; to overfill or overburden.
2. to cover (furniture) completely with upholstery and to stuff it deeply or fully.

ō′vẽr·stuffed′ fũr′ni·tūre, furniture that is completely covered with upholstery which is deeply stuffed.

ō″vẽr·sub·scrībe′, *v.t.* and *v.i.*; oversubscribed, *pt.*, *pp.*; oversubscribing, *ppr.* to subscribe for more (of) than is available or asked.

ō″vẽr·sup·plȳ′, *v.t.*; oversupplied, *pt.*, *pp.*; oversupplying, *ppr.* to supply in excess.

ō′vẽr·sup·plȳ″, *n.*; *pl.* **ō′vẽr·sup·plīeṣ″,** too great a supply.

ō·vẽr·swāy′, *v.t.* to overrule; to bear down; to control. [Obs.]

ō·vẽr·swell′, *v.t.* to swell or rise above; to overflow. [Rare.]

ō′vẽrt (*or* ō-vẽrt′), *a.* [OFr. *overt*; Fr. *ouvert*, from *ouvrir*, to open; OFr. *ovrir*; Pr. *obrir*, *ubrir*; It. *obrire*, from L. *aperire*, to open.]
1. open to view; public; apparent; observable.
2. in law, done outwardly, without attempt at concealment and with evident intent.
3. in heraldry, spread out or open: applied to the wings of birds, etc.

ō·vẽr·tāke′, *v.t.*; overtook, *pt.*; overtaken, *pp.*; overtaking, *ppr.* 1. to come up with in a course, pursuit, progress, or motion; to catch up with; as, to *overtake* a fleeing enemy.
2. to come upon unexpectedly or suddenly.
Brethren, if a man be *overtaken* in a fault, ye which are spiritual, restore such an one in the spirit of meekness. —Gal. vi. 1.
3. to overcome the senses of; hence, figuratively, to intoxicate. [Dial.]
It mortified me to see a man in my coat so *overtaken*. —Swift.

ō·vẽr·task′, *v.t.* to impose too great or heavy a task or tasks upon.

ō·vẽr·tax′, *v.t.* 1. to tax too heavily.
2. to make excessive demands on.

ō′vẽr-thē-count′ẽr, *a.* 1. sold directly to buyers rather than through an exchange, as stocks and bonds.
2. sold or carried on in retail stores rather than by mail; as, *over-the-counter* sales.

ō·vẽr·thrōw′, *v.t.*; overthrew, *pt.*; overthrown, *pp.*; overthrowing, *ppr.* 1. to turn upside down; to throw down; to overturn.
His wife *overthrew* the table. —Taylor.
2. to defeat; to conquer; to ruin; to demolish; as, to *overthrow* an army or an enemy.
When the walls of Thebes he *overthrew*. —Dryden.
3. to subvert; to destroy (an established order); as, to *overthrow* a government.
4. to throw an object, as a ball, over or past (the intended receiver) so that it cannot be caught.
Syn.—destroy, subvert, upset, overturn, ruin, demolish, defeat, rout, overcome, discomfit, invert, overset, reverse.

ō′vẽr·thrōw, *n.* 1. the act of overthrowing or the state of being overthrown.
2. ruin; destruction; defeat; discomfiture.
Poor reason's *overthrow*. —Sir P. Sidney.

ō′vẽr·thrust, *n.* 1. a thrusting above.
2. in geology, a faulted structure in which there is a separation or thrusting apart of the rock masses on both sides of the overfolding fault.

ō′vẽr·thwart, *a.* 1. opposite; being over the way or street; crossing at right angles.
2. cross; perverse; adverse; opposing.

ō·vẽr·thwart′, *prep.* across; from side to side of.
Great trees felled *overthwart* each other. —Milton.

ō·vẽr·thwart′, *adv.* athwart; obliquely; from side to side.

ō′vẽr·thwart, *n.* that which is adverse; contradiction. [Obs.]

ō·vẽr·thwart′, *v.t.* to contend against; to run counter to. [Obs.]

ō·vẽr·thwart′ly, *adv.* across; transversely; perversely. [Obs.]

ō·vẽr·thwart′ness, *n.* the state of being athwart or lying across; perverseness. [Obs.]

ō·vẽr·tilt′, *v.t.* to tilt over; to overturn or overset. [Obs.]

ō′vẽr·tīme, *n.* 1. time beyond the established limit, especially beyond the regular number of working hours.
2. pay for such time.
3. in sports, an extra time period added to the game to decide a tie.

ō′vẽr·tīme, *a.* and *adv.* of, for, or during a period of overtime.

ō·vẽr·tīme′, *v.t.*; overtimed, *pt.*, *pp.*; overtiming, *ppr.* to exceed the proper limit in timing (a photographic exposure, etc.).

ō·vẽr·tī′tle, *v.t.* to give too high a title to. [Rare.]

ō′vẽrt·ly, *adv.* openly; in open view; publicly.

ō′vẽr·tōne, *n.* [transl. of G. *oberton*, contr., from *oberpartialton*, upper partial tone.]
1. any of the higher tones which faintly accompany the fundamental tone produced by a musical instrument, created by the vibration of small sections of the string or air column; upper partial; harmonic.
2. [*pl.*] implications; associations; suggestions; as, a reply full of *overtones*.
psychic overtone; the consciousness of a fringe or halo of associated relations which surrounds every image presented to the mind.

ō·vẽr·top′, *v.t.*; overtopped, *pt.*, *pp.*; overtopping, *ppr.* 1. to rise beyond or above.
2. to exceed in height; to tower over.
3. to excel; to surpass.
4. to obscure; to make of less importance by superior excellence.

ō·vẽr·tow′ẽr (-tou′) *v.t.* to tower over or above.

ō·vẽr·trāde′, *v.i.* to trade beyond one's capital; to purchase goods beyond the means of paying for or selling what is bought.

ō·vẽr·trād′ing, *n.* the act or practice of buying goods beyond the means of payment, or beyond the ability of the community to buy.

ō·vẽr·trāin′, *v.t.* and *v.i.* to train too long or too hard.

ō′vẽr·trick, *n.* in card games, a trick taken in excess of the number bid or needed to win the game.

ō·vẽr·trōw′, *v.i.* to trust excessively. [Obs.]

ō·vẽr·trump′, *v.t.* and *v.i.* in card games, to trump with a higher card than has been played.

ō·vẽr·trust′, *v.t.* to trust with too much confidence.

ō′vẽr·trust, *n.* excessive trustfulness.

ō′vẽr·tūre, *n.* [ME., an opening; OFr., from *ovrir*, to open.]
1. an aperture; an open place; a hole. [Obs.]
2. disclosure; discovery. [Obs.]
3. an introductory proposal or offer; an indication of willingness to negotiate.
4. (a) a musical introduction to an opera or other large musical work; (b) an independent orchestral composition of varying form.
5. in Presbyterian churches, (a) the submitting of a proposal or a question, as of doctrine, by the highest church court to the presbyteries for consideration preceding formal decision; (b) the proposal or question submitted.
6. an introductory section, as of a poem.

ō′vẽr·tūre, *v.t.* in Presbyterian churches, to lay before (an ecclesiastical body) an overture, or subject for consideration.

ō·vẽr·tũrn′, *v.t.*; overturned, *pt.*, *pp.*; overturning, *ppr.* 1. to overset; to turn or throw from a basis or foundation; as, to *overturn* a carriage or a building.
2. to subvert; to conquer; to defeat; to ruin; to destroy; as, to *overturn* plans.

ō·vẽr·tũrn′, *v.i.* to turn or tip over; to capsize.

ō′vẽr·tũrn, *n.* the act of overturning or the state of being overturned; overthrow.

ō·vẽr·tũrn′ȧ·ble, *a.* that can be overturned.

ō·vẽr·tũrn′ẽr, *n.* one who or that which overturns.

ō′vẽr·tȳpe, *a.* designating a dynamo having the armature bore above the field magnets to minimize leakage.

ō·vẽr·ūṣe′, *v.t.* to use too much, too long, or too often.

ō′vẽr·ūse′, *n.* too much use.

ō·vẽr·vāil′, *v.t.* to overveil. [Obs.]

ō·vẽr·val′ūe, *v.t.* to value too highly.

ō·vẽr·veil′, *v.t.* to cover or conceal as with a veil; to obscure; to veil.

The day begins to break, and night is fled;
Whose pitchy mantle *overveil'd* the earth.
—Shak.

ō′vẽr·view, *n.* a general review or survey.

ō·vẽr·vōte′, *v.t.* to outvote. [Rare.]

ō·vẽr·wạlk′ (-wạk′), *v.t.* to walk over or upon.

ō′vẽr·wăsh, *n.* in geology, the drift carried by a glacial stream and deposited on or beyond a frontal moraine.

ō·vẽr·wătch′, *v.t.* 1. to watch over.

2. to watch to the point of weariness or exhaustion.

ō′vẽr·weăr′, *v.t.*; overwore, *pt.*; overworn, *pp.*; overwearing, *ppr.* 1. to wear until no longer fit for use.

2. to outgrow.

ō·vẽr·wēa′ry, *a.* too weary; exhausted.

ō·vẽr·wēa′ry, *v.t.*; overwearied, *pt., pp.*; overwearying, *ppr.* to make overweary; to tire out.

ō·vẽr·weath′ẽr (-weth′), *v.t.* to cause to become bruised or battered by violence of weather.

ō·vẽr·ween′, *v.i.* to think too highly or too favorably; to think arrogantly or conceitedly.

My eye's too quick, my heart *o'erweens* too much,
Unless my hand and strength could equal them.
—Shak.

ō·vẽr·ween′ẽr, *n.* one who overweens; a conceited person.

ō′vẽr·ween′ing, *n.* self-assumption; arrogance.

ō′vẽr·ween′ing, *a.* [ME. *oferweninge*, ppr. of *oferwenen*; AS. *oferwenan*; *ofer*, over, and *wenan*, to hope.] esteeming oneself too highly; excessively proud; conceited; vain; as, *overweening* pride.

ō·vẽr·ween′ing·ly, *adv.* with too much vanity or conceit; in an overweening manner.

ō·vẽr·ween′ing·ness, *n.* the state or quality of being overweening; undue pride; arrogance; self-conceit.

ō′vẽr·weigh′ (-wā′), *v.t.*; overweighed, *pt., pp.*; overweighing, *ppr.* 1. to exceed in weight; to outweigh; to overbalance.

2. to burden; to oppress; to weigh down.

ō′vẽr·weight (-wāt), *n.* 1. more weight than is needed or allowed; extra or surplus weight.

2. a greater amount of importance or weight; preponderance.

ō′vẽr·weight′, *a.* above normal or legal weight: opposed to *underweight*.

ō′vẽr·weight′, *v.t.* to overweigh.

ō·vẽr·well′, *v.t.* to well over; to overflow; to inundate.

The water *overwelled* the edge.
—Blackmore.

ō·vẽr·whelm′ (-hwelm′), *v.t.*; overwhelmed, *pt., pp.*; overwhelming, *ppr.* [ME. *oferwhelmen*; *ofer*, over and *whelmen*, to turn.]

1. to pour down upon and cover over or bury beneath.

The sea *overwhelmed* their enemies.
—Ps. lxxviii. 53.

2. to make helpless; to overcome; to crush; to overpower.

His sorrows have so *overwhelmed* his wits.
—Shak.

3. to overthrow. [Obs.]

4. to overhang menacingly; to overlook gloomily. [Rare.]

Let the brow *o'erwhelm* it
As fearfully as doth a galled rock
O'erhang and jutty his confounded base.
—Shak.

5. to put over; to place over or around. [Obs.]

Then I *overwhelm* a broader pipe about the first.
—Papin.

Syn.—crush, overcome, overflow, drown, submerge.

ō·vẽr·whelm′, *n.* the act of overwhelming or state of being overwhelmed.

ō·vẽr·whelm′ing, *a.* that overwhelms; overpowering; resistless; crushing.

ō·vẽr·whelm′ing·ly, *adv.* in an overwhelming manner.

ō′vẽr·wind′, *v.t.* to wind too far or too tightly, as a winch.

ō·vẽr·wing′, *v.t.* to outflank; to extend beyond the wing of an army. [Obs.]

ō′vẽr·wīṣe′, *a.* too wise.

ō·vẽr·wīṣe′ly, *adv.* in an overwise manner.

ō·vẽr·wīṣe′ness, *n.* pretended or affected wisdom.

ō·vẽr·wit′, *v.t.* to defeat by superior wisdom or artifice; to outwit. [Obs.]

ō′vẽr·wŏrd′, *v.t.* to use too many words in describing.

ō·vẽr·wŏrd, *n.* the word or phrase which bears a meaning repeated and dwelt upon, as in songs; the refrain.

ō′vẽr·wŏrk′, *v.t.*; overworked *or* overwrought (-rạt), *pt., pp.*; overworking, *ppr.* 1. to work or use to excess; to work beyond the strength; to cause to labor too much; as, he *overworked* the horse; she *overworks* that excuse.

2. to cover the entire surface of, as with a design or embroidery: used only in past participle.

ō·vẽr·wŏrk′, *v.i.* to work more than the allotted time; to work beyond one's strength; to work too hard or too long.

ō′vẽr·wŏrk, *n.* 1. work that is severe or burdensome.

2. extra work; work done beyond the amount agreed upon; more work than one is able to do in the allotted time.

ō·vẽr·wọrn′, *a.* 1. worn out; subdued by toil.

2. used up by time.

ō·vẽr·wrest′ (-rest′), *v.t.* to wrench out of natural position.

ō·vẽr·wres′tle (-res′l), *v.t.* to subdue by superiority in wrestling.

ō·vẽr·wrīte′ (-rīt′), *v.t.*; overwrote, *pt.*; overwritten, *pp.*; overwriting, *ppr.* 1. to write over or again; to rewrite.

2. to write over, above, or on top of; to write over the surface of.

3. to write (something) over other writing.

4. to write in a forced or labored style; to use a literary style that is too pompous, too flowery, or too academic in writing about (some subject).

5. to write an excessive amount; to write too much; as, he *overwrote* himself.

6. to agree to pay a commission to (a general agent or a jobber) on the sales of subagents, brokers, local salesmen, etc.

ō·vẽr·wrīte′, *v.i.* to write too much for the good of one's style, reputation, position, etc.

ō′vẽr·wrīte, *n.* the commission granted to a general agent on the sales of his subagents, etc.

ō′vẽr·wrought′ (-rạt′), *a.* 1. overworked; fatigued.

2. nervous; strained; excited.

3. with the surface adorned.

4. too elaborate; ornate.

ō′vẽr·zēal, *n.* abundant ardor; unnecessary fervor.

ō′vi-, [from L. *ovum*, an egg.] a combining form meaning *egg* or *ovum*, as in *ovi*duct, *ovi*form.

ō·vi·çap′sūle, *n.* [*ovi-* and *capsule*.]

1. in anatomy, the external coat of a Graafian follicle.

2. in zoology, an egg sac; the oötheca.

ō′vi·cell, *n.* same as *ooecium*.

ō·vi·cel′lū·lăr, *a.* pertaining to an ovicell.

ō·viç′ū·lăr, *a.* [L. *ovum*, egg.] pertaining to an egg.

ō′vi·cyst, *n.* [*ovi-*, and Gr. *kystis*, pouch.] in some *Tunicata*, a pouch projecting into the atrial cavity, in which eggs incubate.

Ō·vid′i·ăn, *a.* belonging to or resembling the Latin poet Ovid or the style of his writings.

ō·vi·dū′çăl, *a.* [*ovi-*, and L. *ducere*, to lead.] of, relating to, or of the nature of an oviduct.

ō′vi·duçt, *n.* [*ovi-*, and L. *ductus*, a duct.] a duct or tube through which the ova pass from the ovary to the uterus or to the outside. Birds and all egg-bearing animals have but one developed oviduct, but in the higher mammals there are two, which are also called *Fallopian tubes*.

ō·vif′ẽr·ous, *a.* [*ovi-*, and L. *ferre*, to bear.] in anatomy and zoology, bearing, carrying, or producing ova.

ō′vi·fọrm, *a.* [*ovi-*, and L. *forma*, form.] having the form or figure of an egg; ovoid; egg-shaped.

ō·vig′ẽr·ous, *a.* [*ovi-*, and L. *gerere*, to carry.] same as *oviferous*.

ō′vile, *a.* same as *ovine*.

ō·vi·nā′tion, *n.* vaccination with ovine virus against sheep pox.

ō′vīne, *a.* [L. *ovinus*, from *ovis*, sheep.] pertaining to or having the characteristics of sheep; consisting of sheep.

ō·vin′i·ȧ, *n.* [L. *ovis*, sheep.] a disease of sheep resembling smallpox; sheep pox.

ō·vip′ȧ·rȧ, *n.pl.* that division of animals which lay eggs, as birds, fishes, etc.

ō·vi·par′i·ty, *n.* the quality or state of being oviparous.

ō·vip′ȧ·rous, *a.* [*ovi-*, and L. *parere*, to produce.]

1. producing eggs which hatch after leaving the body of the female.

2. designating or of this type of reproduction.

Opposed to *viviparous*.

ō·vi·poṣ′it, *v.i.*; oviposited, *pt., pp.*; ovipositing, *ppr.* to deposit or lay eggs: usually said of insects having an ovipositor.

ō·vi·poṣ′it·ing, *n.* same as *oviposition*.

ō″vi·pō·ṣi′tion, *n.* [*ovi-*, and L. *positio*, a depositing.] the laying or depositing of eggs, as with an ovipositor.

ō·vi·poṣ′i·tŏr, *n.* [*ovi-*, and L. *positor*, one who places, from *ponere*, to place.]

OVIPOSITOR
o, ovipositor of field cricket

1. a special organ of insects for depositing eggs in a suitable place, usually situated at the end of the abdomen.

2. an extension of the genital orifice of a fish.

ō′vi·saç, *n.* [*ovi-*, and L. *saccus*, sack.]

1. an egg capsule or case; oötheca.

2. an egg receptacle.

3. a Graafian follicle.

ō′vi·sçapt, *n.* [*ovi-*, and Gr. *skaptein*, to dig.] an ovipositor.

ō′viṣm, *n.* in biology, the former theory that the germs of all subsequent species were present in the primordial cell of each species.

ō·vi·spẽr′mȧ·ry, *n.* [*ovi-*, and LL. *spermarium*, from Gr. *sperma*, seed.] same as *ovotestis*.

ō′vist, *n.* same as *ovulist*.

ō′vō-, [from L. *ovum*, an egg.] a combining form meaning *ovum* or *ovally*.

ō·vō·gen′e·sis, *n.* [*ovo-*, and Gr. *genesis*, generation.] the production of an ovum or ova: also called *oögenesis*.

ō′void, ō·void′ăl, *a.* [*ovo-* and *-oid*.] egg-shaped.

ō′void, *n.* 1. anything of ovoid form.

2. a nonflagellated, or female, malarial microparasite.

ō·vō·lec′i·thin, *n.* a lecithin obtained from egg yolk.

ō′vō·lō, *n.*; *pl.* **ō′vō·lī,** [It., from LL. *ovulum*, dim. of L. *ovum*, egg.] in architecture, a convex molding, usually the quarter of a circle.

OVOLO

ō·vol′ō·ġy, *n.* [*ovo-*, and Gr. *logos*, description.] the branch of biology dealing with ova.

ō·von′iç, *a.* [after S. R. *Ov*shinsky, 1922– , American inventor, and electro*nic*.] designating, of, or utilizing various glassy, amorphous materials that undergo electronic or structural changes and act as semiconductors when subjected to voltage, light, etc.: used in computer memory elements, electronic switches, etc.

ō′vō·plaṣm, *n.* [*ovo-*, and Gr. *plasma*, something formed, from *plassein*, to form.] the protoplasmic substance of an ovum.

ō·vō·plaṣ′miç, *a.* protoplasmic.

ō·vō·tes′tis, *n.* [*ovo-*, and L. *testis*, testicle.] a structure which generates within itself both spermatozoa and ova; a hermaphrodite organ.

ō″vō·vi·vip′ȧ·rous, *a.* [*ovo-*, L. *vivus*, alive, and *parere*, to produce.] designating various animals which produce hard-shelled eggs that are hatched within the female's body, as some reptiles and fishes.

ō′vū·lăr, *a.* of, relating to, or springing from an ovule or ovum.

ō·vū·lăr′i·ăn, *a.* resembling an ovum.

ō′vū·lăr·y, *a.* same as *ovular*.

ō′vū·lāte, *a.* containing one or more ovules; ovuliferous.

ō′vū·lāte, *v.i.*; ovulated, *pt., pp.*; ovulating, *ppr.* to produce ovules or ova and expel them from the ovary.

ō·vū·lā′tion, *n.* the physiological act or process by which a mature ovum escapes from a ruptured Graafian follicle and leaves the ovary; the formation and discharge of ova from the ovary, which in the human female take place monthly.

ō′vūle, *n.* [LL. *ovulum,* dim. from L. *ovum.*]

1. in botany, a body borne by the placenta of a plant which develops into a seed.

2. in zoology, the immature ovum while still within the Graafian follicle.

3. any small egglike structure.

ō·vū·lif′ẽr·ous, *a.* [*ovule,* and L. *ferre,* to bear.] in biology, producing ovules.

ō·vū·liġ′ẽr·ous, *a.* [*ovule,* and L. *gerere,* to carry.] same as *ovuliferous.*

ō′vū·list, *n.* an adherent of the theory of ovism: also called *ovist.*

ō′vū·līte, *n.* a fossil egg. [Obs.]

ō′vū·lum, *n.*; *pl.* **ō′vū·lȧ,** an ovule.

ō′vum, *n.*; *pl.* **ō′vȧ,** [L., an egg.]

1. in biology, an egg; a female germ cell which, generally only after fertilization, develops into a new member of the same species.

2. in architecture, an ornament in the shape of an egg.

ōwe (ō), *v.t.*; owed, *pt., pp.*; owing, *ppr.* [ME. *owen, aghen*; AS. *agan,* to own, to possess, to have.]

1. to own; to possess; to have a right to. [Obs.]

Thou dost here usurp
The name thou *ow′st* not. —Shak.

2. to have an obligation to pay; to be indebted to the amount of.

There was a certain creditor who had two debtors; the one *owed* five hundred pence and the other fifty. —Luke vii. 41.

3. to be morally obligated to; as, I *owe* him my thanks.

4. to have or cherish (a certain feeling) toward another; bear; as, he *owed* ill will.

5. to be indebted to for the existence of.

Montague *owed* everything to his own merit and to the public opinion of his merit. —Macaulay.

ōwe, *v.i.* 1. to be obliged or bound; to be under an obligation or duty. [Obs.]

2. to be in debt.

ōw′el·ty, *n.* in law, the difference which is paid by one coparcener to another, for the purpose of equalizing a partition.

Ōw′en·īte, *n.* a follower of Robert Owen (1771–1858), an English industrialist, who attempted to reorgnize society by introducing a system of socialistic co-operation.

ōw′ing, *a.* 1. that owes.

2. due; unpaid; as, there are three dollars *owing.*

owing to; resulting from; caused by; on account of.

owl, *n.* [ME. and AS. *ule*; akin to G. *eule*: from echoic base seen also in L. *ulula,* owl, *ululare,* to howl.]

1. any of a group of night birds of prey found throughout the world, distinguished by a large head, eyes surrounded by stiff-feathered disks, a short hooked beak, feathered legs with sharp talons, and soft plumage which permits noiseless flight: applied figuratively to a person of nocturnal habits, solemn appearance, etc.

BARN OWL

2. a variety of the domestic pigeon, having a head resembling that of a true owl. There are African, English, and Chinese species.

burrowing owl; an owl found in the western United States and in Florida which inhabits holes in the ground, often those made by prairie dogs.

owl but′tẽr·flȳ, a large South American butterfly having two conspicuous spots resembling owl's eyes on the wings.

owl çär, a streetcar run late at night after regular service has stopped.

EUROPEAN HORNED OWL

owl′ẽr·y, *n.* the haunt or habitation of owls; a place where owls are kept.

owl′et, *n.* 1. a young or small owl.

2. a certain small European owl.

owl′-eȳed (-īd), *a.* having eyes like an owl's.

owl flȳ, an English stone fly.

owl′ish, *a.* resembling or having the characteristics of an owl.

owl light (līt), glimmering or imperfect light.

owl′like, *a.* like an owl in look or habits.

owl mon̄′key, a South American monkey; a night monkey.

owl moth, a very large Brazilian moth, *Thysania agrippina.*

owl par′rŏt, the kakapo, *Strigops habroptilus.*

owl′s-çlō′vẽr, *n.* a plant of the figwort family, with spikes of red or purple tubelike flowers.

owl trāin, a railway train that runs late at night after regular service has been discontinued.

ōwn, *a.* [ME. *owen, agen*; AS. *agen,* pp. of *agan,* to possess.] belonging, relating, or peculiar to oneself or itself: used to strengthen a preceding possessive, as, he wants his *own* book, he prefers his *own* doctor.

ōwn, *n.* that which belongs to oneself; as, that is his *own,* I'm on my *own.*

of one's own; belonging strictly to oneself.

on one's own; (a) by one's own efforts or on one's own initiative; (b) independent of help from others. [Colloq.]

to come into one's own; to receive what properly belongs to one, especially acclaim or recognition.

to hold one's own; to maintain one's place or condition in spite of criticism, illness, etc.

ōwn, *v.t.*; owned, *pt., pp.*; owning, *ppr.* [ME. *ohnen*; AS. *agnian,* from *agen,* one's own.]

1. to possess; to hold as personal property; to have.

2. to admit; recognize; acknowledge.

ōwn, *v.i.* to confess (with *to*).

to own up (*to*); to confess (to).

ōwn′ẽr, *n.* one who owns; the rightful proprietor; one who has the legal or rightful title, whether he is the possessor or not.

The ox knoweth his *owner.* —Isa. i. 3.

ōwn′ẽr·less, *a.* having no owner.

ōwn′ẽr·ship, *n.* 1. the state or fact of being an owner.

2. proprietorship; legal right of possession; legal or just claim or title (to something).

beneficial ownership; in law, the right to use property for one's own advantage, the legal title to which may be held by another.

owṣe, *n.* same as *ooze, n.* 1.

ox, *n.*; *pl.* **ox′en** (-n), [AS. *oxa,* pl. *oxan*; G. *ochs, ochse.*]

1. loosely, any animal of the bovine family (genus *Bos*).

2. a castrated bull.

grunting ox; the yak, *Bos grunniens,* of central Asia, of which there are several domesticated varieties.

Indian ox; the zebu, *Bos indicus.*

ox-, oxy-.

ox′ȧ-, in chemistry, a prefix indicating *the presence of oxygen, especially as replacing carbon in a ring.*

ox′ȧ·lan, *n.* a stable crystalline compound, $C_3N_3H_5O_3$, derived from alloxan.

ox·ȧ·lan′tin, *n.* a crystalline nitrogenous substance, reduced from alloxanic acid.

ox′ȧ·lāte, *n.* in chemistry, any salt or ester of oxalic acid.

ox·al′dē·hȳde, *n.* same as *glyoxal.*

ox·al·eth′yl·in, *n.* a poisonous aromatic liquid, $C_6H_{10}N_2$, used in medicine as a heart stimulant.

ox·al′iç, *a.* [Fr. *oxalique*; L. *oxalis*; Gr. *oxalis,* sorrel, from *oxys,* acid.]

1. having to do with or derived from the oxalis.

2. designating or of a colorless, poisonous, crystalline acid, $(COOH)_2$, found in oxalis and other plants or prepared synthetically: used in dyeing, bleaching, etc.

Ox·al·i·dā′cē·ae, *n.pl.* a family of plants including *Oxalis*; the sorrel family.

ox·al·i·dā′ceous, *a.* pertaining or belonging to the *Oxalidaceæ.*

ox′ȧ·lin, *n.* same as *glyoxalin.*

Ox′ȧ·lis, *n.* [Gr.] 1. a genus of plants typical of the *Oxalidaceæ,* with cloverlike leaves and flowers of white, red, etc. The wood sorrel, *Oxalis acetosella,* is also called *shamrock.*

2. [o—] a plant belonging to this genus; wood sorrel.

OXALIS (*Oxalis acetosella*)

ox′ȧ·līte, *a.* Humboldtine. [Obs.]

ox″ȧ·lūr·am′ide, *n.* same as *oxalan.*

ox·ȧ·lūr′āte, *n.* a salt or ester of oxaluric acid.

Ox·ȧ·lūr′i·ȧ, *n.* [*oxalic,* and Gr. *ouron,* urine.] the presence of an excessive amount of oxalic acid or of oxalates in the urine.

ox·ȧ·lūr′iç, *a.* pertaining to or designating an acid derivable from uric acid.

ox′ȧ·lyl, *n.* the bivalent radical of oxalic acid.

ox·am′āte, *n.* a salt or ester of oxamic acid.

ox·ȧ·meth′āne, *n.* ethylic oxamate, $C_4H_7NO_3$.

ox·ȧ·meth′yl·āne, *n.* methylic oxamate, a crystalline compound obtained by saturating methylic oxalate with dry ammonia.

ox·am′iç, *a.* pertaining to or designating a crystalline acid obtained from oxalic acid and ammonia.

ox·am′ide, *n.* a white compound obtained by the dry distillation of neutral ammonic oxalate.

ox·am′i·din, *n.* a crystalline compound known chiefly by its salts.

ox′an, *n.* a colorless gas of which there are two kinds: it is formed by the contact of nitrogen oxides and hot charcoal.

ox″ȧ·nil·am′īde, *n.* a white, flaky substance found among the products of the decomposition of a cyanogen by hydrochloric acid.

ox·an′i·lāte, *n.* a salt or ester of oxanilic acid.

ox·an·il′iç, *a.* contained in or derived from oxalic acid and aniline; as, *oxanilic* acid.

ox·an′i·lide, ox·an′i·lid, *n.* a crystalline substance, $(CONHC_6H_5)_2$, obtained by heating analine oxalate; diphenyl-oxamide.

ox an′tē·lōpe, a bubaline antelope, as the oryx.

ox′ȧ·zin, *n.* same as *oxazine.*

ox′ȧ·zīne, *n.* [*oxygen,* and *azine.*] any of thirteen compounds having a composition corresponding to the formula C_4H_5NO and composed of molecules which contain four atoms of carbon and one atom each of oxygen and nitrogen united in a ring structure.

ox bälm (-bäm), same as *horse balm.*

ox′bāne, *n.* a poisonous South African bulb of the genus *Buphane.*

ox′bird, *n.* 1. a cowbird: also called *oxbiter.*

2. an African weaver bird, *Textor alector.*

3. the sanderling, *Calidris arenaria.* [Brit. Dial.]

4. the dunlin, or red-backed sandpiper.

ox′bīt″ẽr, *n.* see *oxbird,* sense 1.

ox′blood (-blud), *n.* a deep red color.

ox bot, a botfly that infests cattle, boring under the skin; also, its larva.

ox′bōw, *n.* 1. the U-shaped part of an ox yoke which passes under and around the neck of the animal.

OXBOWS

YOKE WITH OXBOWS

2. a crescent-shaped bend in a river.

3. the land within such a bend.

Ox′bridġe, *n.* [from *Ox*ford, and Cam*bridge.*] Oxford and Cambridge universities thought of as forming a single entity in terms of their similar organization, traditions, and prestige.

Ox′bridġe, *a.* of or relating to Oxbridge.

ox′en, *n.* plural of *ox.*

ox′eȳe (-ī), *n.* 1. the oxeye daisy, *Chrysanthemum leucanthemum.*

2. any species of *Buphthalmum,* a plant cultivated in England.

3. one of the *Compositæ, Anthemis arvensis.*

4. in zoology, a titmouse, especially *Parus major,* the great titmouse, and *Parus cæruleus,* the blue titmouse.

5. a cloudy speck presaging a storm, often seen on the African coast.

creeping oxeye; a West Indian plant, *Wedelia carnosa.*

oxeye daisy; (a) a daisylike plant, *Chrysanthemum leucanthemum,* with flowers of white rays around a yellow disk: also called *whiteweed*; (b) the black-eyed Susan.

ox′-eȳed (-īd), *a.* having large full eyes, like those of an ox.

ox′flȳ, *n.* a fly hatched under the skin of cattle; an ox bot.

ox′fŏrd, sometimes **Ox′fŏrd,** *n.* 1. a type of low shoe laced over the instep: also *oxford shoe.*

2. a type of cotton cloth with a basketlike weave, used for men's shirts, etc.: also *oxford cloth.*

Ox'fŏrd çhrōme, oxide of iron used in painting.

Ox'fŏrd çlāy, in geology, a bed of clay underlying the coral and the accompanying sandy beds of the Middle Oölite.

Ox'fŏrd grāy, a very dark gray, approaching black.

Ox'fŏrd group mōve'ment, a religious movement started about 1921 by the Reverend Frank Buchman and based on early, or primitive, Christianity, emphasizing the fellowship of man and God, and the importance of confession: also called *Buchmanism.*

Ox'fŏrd mix'tūre, a woolen cloth of a very dark gray color: called also *Oxford gray.*

Ox'fŏrd mōve'ment, a movement begun at Oxford University in 1833 by certain Anglican clergymen to bring Catholic doctrine and ritual into the Anglican Church in opposition to the liberal movement in religion; Tracterianism.

Ox'fŏrd sçhool, the group of Anglican clergymen who supported the Oxford movement; also, their theories.

ox'gang, *n.* [*ox,* and AS. *gang,* a going.] bovate. [Obs.]

ox'head (-hed), *n.* 1. the head of an ox.
2. a stupid fellow; a blockhead; a dolt.

ox'hēal, ox'heel, *n.* a species of hellebore, *Helleborus fœtidus.*

ox'heärt, *n.* 1. a large cherry, shaped like a heart.
2. a kind of cabbage.

ox'hīde, *n.* 1. literally, the hide of an ox; also, the leather made from it.
2. in old English law, a hide of land.

ox'id, *n.* oxide.

ox″i·dȧ·bil'i·ty, *n.* ability to be changed into an oxide.

ox'i·dȧ·ble, *a.* same as *oxidizable.*

ox'i·dāṣe, *n.* [*oxidize* and *-ase.*] any of a group of enzymes which act as oxidizing agents.

ox'i·dāte, *v.t.* and *v.i.*; oxidated, *pt., pp.*; oxidating, *ppr.* to oxidize.

ox·i·dā'tion, *n.* 1. the union of a substance with oxygen.
2. the process of increasing the positive valence or of decreasing the negative valence of an element ion.
3. the process by which electrons are removed from atoms or ions.

ox'i·dā·tive, *a.* of or characterized by oxidation; able to oxidize.

ox'i·dā·tŏr, *n.* 1. an oxidizer. [Rare.]
2. a device for causing a current of air to impinge on the flame of an Argand lamp.

ox'īde, ox'id, *n.* [Fr., from Gr. *oxys,* sour, and Fr. *acide,* acid.] a binary compound of oxygen with some other element or with a radical.

ox'i·dī·zȧ·ble, *a.* that can be oxidized.

ox'i·dīze, *v.t.*; oxidized, *pt., pp.*; oxidizing, *ppr.*
1. to unite with oxygen.
2. to increase the positive valence or decrease the negative valence of (an element or ion).
3. to remove electrons from (an atom or ion).

ox'i·dīze, *v.i.* to become oxidized.
oxidized silver; silver on the surface of which a thin film of the silver sulfide has been formed.

ox'i·dīze·ment, *n.* oxidation.

ox'i·dī·zẽr, *n.* any substance that oxidizes or causes another to oxidize; oxidizing agent.

ox·id'ū·lā·ted, *a.* containing oxygen. [Obs.]

ox'īme, ox'im, *n.* [from *oxygen* and *imide.*] any of a series of compounds formed by the action of hydroxylamine on an aldehyde or ketone, in which the oxygen atom of the CHO group of the aldehyde, or of the CO group of the ketone, is replaced by the :NOH group.

ox·in'dōle, ox·in'dōl, *n.* a crystalline compound, C_8H_7NO, formed with sodium amalgam in acid solution. It forms crystallizable salts with acids and bases.

ox·i·od'iç, *a.* pertaining to or consisting of a compound of oxygen and iodine.

ox'līke, *a.* resembling an ox.

ox'lip, *n.* a plant of the primrose family, *Primula elatior,* resembling the common primrose or the cowslip: it has yellow flowers.

ox'ō·nāte, *n.* a salt of oxonic acid.

Ox·ō'ni·ăn, *a.* of or pertaining to the city or the University of Oxford, England.

Ox·ō'ni·ăn, *n.* 1. a native or inhabitant of Oxford, England.
2. a student or alumnus of Oxford University.

ox·on'iç, *a.* [from glyo*x*alic and carb*onic.*] pertaining to or designating an acid obtained as a potassium salt when a stream of air is passed through a solution of uric acid in potash.

ox'ō·zōne, *n.* an allotropic variety of oxygen believed to exist in ozone in solution.

ox·ō·zōn'īde, *n.* an organic oxidation product, obtained from unsaturated hydrocarbons.

ox'peck″ẽr, *n.* an African bird of the genus *Buphaga:* it destroys the parsites which infest the skin of cattle, antelopes, etc.

ŏx'rēim, *n.* [*ox,* and D. *riem,* thong or strap.] a strip of oxhide, flat or twisted, used in South Africa for halters, straps, etc.

ox'shōe, *n.* a shoe for oxen made of a flat piece of iron and nailed on the hoof.

ox'tāil, *n.* the tail of an ox, especially when skinned and used to make a soup.

ox'tẽr, [AS. *oxta.*] the armpit. [Scot. and Brit. Dial.]

ox'tŏngue (-tung), *n.* any of a number of related plants, as *Picris echioides,* having tongue-shaped leaves.

ox'y, *a.* like an ox; bovine.

ox'y-, [from Gr. *oxys,* sharp, acid.] a combining form meaning *sharp, pointed, acute,* or *acid,* as in *oxycephalic, oxymoron, oxygen.*

ox'y-, [from oxygen.] a combining form meaning *containing oxygen*: also, before a vowel, *ox-.*

ox″y·ȧ·çan'thous, *a.* [*oxy-,* and Gr. *akantha,* a spine.] having thorns or sharp spines.

ox″y·ȧ·cē'tiç, *a.* same as *glycolic.*

ox″y·ȧ·cet'y·lēne, *a.* [*oxy-* and *acetylene.*] of or using a mixture of oxygen and acetylene.

ox″y·ȧ·cet'y·lēne blōw'pīpe (or **tọrch**), a blowpipe in which the oxyacetylene flame produced is much hotter than an oxyhydrogen flame, used for cutting and welding steel.

ox·y·ac'id, *n.* [*oxy-* and *acid.*] an acid containing oxygen.

ox″y·aes·thē'si·ȧ, *n.* [*oxy-* and *æsthesia.*] same as *oxyesthesia.*

ox″y·am·mō'ni·ȧ, *n.* same as *hydroxylamine.*

ox·y·as'tẽr, *n.* [*oxy-* (pointed), and Gr. *astēr,* star.] a sponge spicule resembling a star in form, the rays of which have a point in common as an origin.

ox·y·ben'zēne, *n.* same as *phenol.*

ox·y·brō'miç, *a.* [*oxy-* and *bromic.*] of or containing oxygen and bromine.

ox″y·bū·tyr'iç, *a.* [*oxy-* and *butyric.*] of, pertaining to, or formed from hydroxyl and butyric acid.

ox·y·çal'ci·um, *a.* [*oxy-* and *calcium.*] of or pertaining to the combined action of oxygen and calcium.
oxycalcium light; a light produced by white-hot lime.

ox″y·ce·phal'iç, *a.* [*oxy-* and *cephalic.*] designating or having a skull coming to a more or less cone-shaped point on top.

ox·y·çhlō'riç, *a.* [*oxy-* and *chloric.*] of or derived from oxygen and chlorine.

ox·y·çhlō'rīde, *n.* [*oxy-* and *chloride.*] a basic chloride or compound of metallic chloride with the basic oxides of the same metals, produced by the action of water on certain metallic chlorides.

ox'y·çrāte, *n.* [Gr. *oxykraton,* sour wine mixed with water; *oxys,* sharp, and *kerannynai,* to mix.] a mixture of water and vinegar. [Rare.]

ox·y·cȳ'mēne, *n.* same as *carvacrol.*

ox'yd, *n.* same as *oxide.*

ox·y·daç'tyl, *a.* having slender toes or fingers.

Ox·y·daç'tyl, *n.* one of the *Oxydactyla.*

Ox·y·daç'tyl·ȧ, *n.pl.* [Gr. *oxys,* sharp, and *daktylos,* finger.] a group of batrachians, characterized by slender, tapering toes.

ox·y·dī'açt, *n.* [*oxy-,* and Gr. *di-,* two, and *aktis,* a ray.] a sponge spicule with only two of its axes developed.

ox″y·es·thē'si·ȧ, *n.* abnormal acuteness of sensation.

ox'y·ġen, *n.* [Gr. *oxys,* acid, and *gennān,* to generate.] a colorless, odorless, tasteless, gaseous chemical element, the most abundant of all elements: it occurs free in the atmosphere, forming one fifth of its volume, and in combination in water, sandstone, limestone, etc.; it is very active, being able to combine with nearly all other elements, and is essential to life processes and to combustion: symbol, O; atomic weight, 16.000; atomic number, 8.

ox'y·ġen ac'id, an acid that contains oxygen; oxyacid.

ox'y·ġen·āte, *v.t.*; oxygenated, *pt., pp.*; oxygenating, *ppr.* to unite or cause to combine with oxygen; to treat or impregnate with oxygen; to oxidize.

ox″y·ġen·ā'tion, *n.* the act, operation, or process of oxygenating; oxidation.

ox'y·ġen·ā·tŏr, *n.* an oxidizer.

ox·y·ġen'iç, *a.* pertaining to, containing, producing, or having some of the properties of oxygen.

ox·y·ġē'ni·um, *n.* oxygen. [Rare.]

ox'y·ġen·ī·zȧ·ble, *a.* that can be oxygenized.

ox'y·ġen·īze, *v.t.*; oxygenized, *pt., pp.*; oxygenizing, *ppr.* to oxygenate; oxidize.

ox'y·ġen·īze·ment, *n.* oxygenation. [Rare.]

ox·yġ'e·nous, *a.* oxygenic.

ox'y·ġen tent, a boxlike enclosure supplied with oxygen, in which a patient is kept to facilitate his breathing: used chiefly in cases of pneumonia and cardiac disease.

OXYGEN TENT

ox·y·ġeū'si·ȧ, *n.* [*oxy-,* and Gr. *geusis,* sense of taste.] excessive acuteness of the sense of taste.

ox·yg'nȧ·thous, *a.* [*oxy-,* and Gr. *gnathos,* jaw.] with jaws smooth or nearly so: said of certain mollusks, as land snails.

ox'y·gon, *n.* [*oxy-,* and Gr. *gōnia,* an angle.] a triangle having three acute angles. [Obs.]

ox·yg'ō·năl, *a.* oxygonial. [Obs.]

ox·y·gō'ni·ăl, *a.* having acute angles. [Obs.]

ox·y·haem·ȧ·cȳ'ȧ·nin, ox·y·haem·ō·cȳ'ȧ·nin, *n.* a substance in the blood of some invertebrates which becomes blue when oxygenated, because of the copper in it.

ox·y·hem'ȧ·tin, *n.* hematin when combined with oxygen.

ox·y·hēm·ō·glō'bin, ox·y·haem·ō·glō'bin, *n.* [*oxy-* and *hemoglobin.*] a substance found in the arterial blood, formed in the lungs by the loose union of hemoglobin with oxygen, which is thus carried to the body tissues.

ox·y·hȳ'drō·ġen, *a.* of or using a mixture or combination of oxygen and hydrogen; as, *oxyhydrogen* gas.
oxyhydrogen lamp; a lamp in which streams of oxygen and hydrogen in regulated quantities are commingled, the resulting flame being directed on a ball of quicklime and forming an extremely bright light.
oxyhydrogen light; light produced by burning some substance, as lime, in an oxyhydrogen flame.
oxyhydrogen microscope; a microscope in which the object is illuminated by oxyhydrogen light.

ox·y·hȳ'drō·ġen, *n.* oxyhydrogen gas.
oxyhydrogen torch (or *blowpipe*); a blowpipe which burns a mixture of oxygen and hydrogen at a very high temperature, used for cutting and welding steel.

ox'y·mel, *n.* [Gr. *oxys,* acid, and *meli,* honey.] a mixture of vinegar and honey.

ox·y·mō'ron, *n.* [Gr. *oxymōron,* a smart saying which at first view appears foolish, from *oxys,* sharp, and *mōros,* dull, foolish.] a figure of speech in which opposite or contradictory ideas or terms are combined (e.g., thunderous silence, sweet sorrow).

ox·y·mū'ri·āte, *n.* in old chemistry, a name for chloride: so called from the erroneous assumption that chlorine was a mixture of oxygen and muriatic acid.

ox·y·mū·ri·at'iç, *a.* [*oxy-* and *muriatic.*] in old chemistry, pertaining to or made of oxygen and muriatic acid.

ox·y·neū'rine, *n.* see *betaine.*

ox·yn'tiç, *a.* [Gr. *oxyntos,* verbal adj. of *oxynein,* to make sharp.] acid; secreting acid: said of certain glands.

ox·y·ō'pi·ȧ, ox'y·ō·py, *n.* [*oxy-,* and Gr. *ōps,* eye.] unusual acuteness of sight, arising from increased sensibility of the retina.

ox″y·os·phrē'si·ȧ, *n.* [*oxy-,* and Gr. *osphrēsis,* smell.] unusual acuteness of the sense of smell.

ox·y·phē'niç, *a.* [*oxy-* and *phenol* and *-ic.*] pertaining to or specifying oxyphenol or oxyphenic acid.

ox·y·phē'nōl, *n.* pyrocatechol, $C_6H_4(OH)_2$, obtained in the distillation of catechu.

ox'y·phile, ox'y·phil, *a.* same as *eosinophil.*

ox·y·phō′ni·ȧ, ox·yph′ō·ny, *n.* [*oxy-*, and Gr. *phōne*, sound.] an abnormally sharp quality of sound or pitch of voice.

ox·yph′yl·lous, *a.* [*oxy-*, and Gr. *phyllon*, leaf.] having leaves that end in a sharp point. [Rare.]

ox·y·quin′ō·line, ox·y·quin′ō·lin, *n.* [*oxy-* and *quinoline*.] a substance, C_9H_7NO, derived from quinoline.

ox′y·rhīne (-rīn), *a.* [*oxy-*, and Gr. *rhis, rhinos*, nose.] having a sharp-pointed snout; as, the *oxyrhine* frog.

ox′y·rhyn̄ch (-rin̄k), *n.* [*oxy-*, and Gr. *rynchos*, beak.] any of the *Oxyrhyncha* or *Maiidæ*, crabs with projecting or pointed beaks.

Ox·y·rhyn̄′chȧ, *n.pl.* the maioid crabs.

ox·y·rhyn̄′chous, *a.* same as *oxyrhine.*

ox′y·sa̤lt, *n.* a salt of an oxyacid.

ox″y·sul′fīde, ox″y·sul′fid, *n.* a compound formed of an element or positive radical with oxygen and sulfur, in which oxygen may be thought of as replacing a part of the sulfur.

ox·y·tō′ci·ȧ (-shi-), *n.* quickness of childbirth.

ox·y·toc′iç, *a.* [*oxy-*, and Gr. *tokos*, birth.] in medicine, promoting or hastening the process of childbirth by stimulating the contractions of the involuntary muscles of the uterus.

ox·y·toc′iç, *n.* an oxytocic medicine.

ox·y·tō′cin, *n.* [from Gr. *oxys*, quick, sharp, and *tokos*, birth, and *-in*.] one of the hormones of the posterior pituitary gland, serving to increase the contractions of the uterus during childbirth and to prevent or stop bleeding afterward.

ox·y·tol′ū·ēne, *n.* one of the cresols.

ox″y·tō·lū′iç, *a.* contained in or derived from oxygen and toluic acid; as, *oxytoluic* acid.

ox′y·tōne, *a.* [*oxy-*, and Gr. *tonos*, tone.] in Greek grammar, having an acute accent on the last syllable.

ox′y·tōne, *n.* an oxytone word.

ox·y·ton′iç·ăl, *a.* oxytone.

Ox·y·ū′ris, *n.* [Gr. *oxys*, sharp, and *oura*, tail.] a genus of internal parasitic worms (*pinworms*) related to the common *Ascaris*. They multiply with rapidity and pass from the intestine to other organs. *Oxyuris vermicularis* is often found in the human rectum and is usually about a quarter of an inch long.

ox·y·ū′rous, *a.* having a sharp-pointed tail, as certain birds. [Rare.]

ō′yẽr, *n.* [O. Norm. Fr. *oyer*, hearing; Fr. *ouïr*, L. *audire*, to hear.] a copy of a bond or other instrument that is the subject of a suit, given to the opposite party instead of being read aloud, as formerly.

oyer and terminer; a hearing and determining: used in the United States to designate the higher criminal courts. [Archaic.]

ō′yez, ō′yes, *interj.* [Fr. *oyez*, hear ye.] hear ye! attention!: usually cried out three times by officials to command silence before a proclamation is made.

ō′yez, ō′yes, *n.* a cry of *oyez.*

oys′tẽr, *n.* [OFr. *oistre, huistre*; Fr. *huitre*, from L. *ostrea, ostreum*, Gr. *ostreon*, an oyster, akin to *osteon*, a bone, and *ostrakon*, the hard shell of a shellfish.]

1. an edible mollusk belonging to the lamellibranchiate genus *Ostrea*, family *Ostreidæ*, characterized by an inequivalve shell composed of two irregular lamellated valves, of which the convex, or under one, adheres to rocks, to the shell of another mollusk, etc. The species are numerous and are found especially on the bottom of the sea. The common American oyster is *Ostrea virginica*, and the common European oyster is *Ostrea edulis.*

2. any of numerous similar bivalve mollusks, as the scallop, pearl oyster, etc.

3. the oyster-shaped bit of meat contained in a depression on each side of the pelvic bone of a fowl.

Applied figuratively to a taciturn person or to a thing from which profit or advantage can be extracted.

fresh-water oyster; a bivalve of the genus *Etheria*, or of some related genus, found in rivers of the Southern Hemisphere and somewhat resembling an oyster in form.

thorny oyster; any spiny bivalve of the genus *Spondylus.*

oys′tẽr bāy (or **bär**), an oyster shop; an eating place where oysters are served.

oys′tẽr bed, a place on the ocean floor naturally suited to, or artificially prepared for, the breeding and cultivation of oysters.

oys′tẽr catch′ẽr, any of several species of wading birds of the genus *Hæmatopus*, having a strong, wedge-shaped beak and stout legs, which feeds on marine animals. *Hæmatopus ostralegus*, the sea pie, is the European species, and *Hæmatopus palliatus*, the common American species.

OYSTER CATCHER (*Hæmatopus ostralegus*)

oys′tẽr ça̤b, a small crustacean often found living as commensals in the gill cavities of oysters; a pea crab, as the *Pinnotheres ostreum.*

oys′tẽr çrack′ẽr, a small, round cracker eaten with oyster stews, etc.

oys′tẽr dredġe (-drej), a dredge consisting of a heavy iron frame with a net of iron mesh, used to lift oysters from an oyster bed.

oys′tẽr färm, a place where oyster beds are maintained.

oys′tẽr·fish, *n.* 1. the tautog.

2. the toadfish.

oys′tẽr fish′ẽr·y, the business of fishing for oysters; also, the place from which oysters are dredged.

oys′tẽr·green, *n.* a seaweed; kelp.

oys′tẽr·ing, *n.* the act of taking oysters from an oyster bed.

oys′tẽr·ling, *n.* a small or young oyster.

oys′tẽr·măn, *n.*; *pl.* **oys′tẽr·men,** 1. a man whose business is fishing for, breeding, or selling oysters.

2. a vessel used in gathering oysters.

oys′tẽr plant, 1. salsify, a plant of the genus *Tragopogon*: so called from its taste when cooked: also called *vegetable oyster.*

2. the sea lungwort.

Spanish oyster plant; the *Scolymus hispanicus*, a prickly leaved plant of the *Compositæ*, having edible roots used like salsify.

oys′tẽr plŏv′ẽr, an oyster catcher.

oys′tẽr rāke, a rake with a long handle and curved teeth for gathering in oysters from shallow waters.

oys′tẽr ro̤ot, salsify.

oys′tẽr·shell, *n.* the shell of the oyster; especially, crushed shells of oysters for feeding to poultry.

oys′tẽr-shell sçāle (or **bärk louse**), a scale, *Mytilaspis pomorum*, injurious to the apple and to other fruits.

oys′tẽr stew, a dish consisting of whole oysters in a soup of heated milk or cream, butter, and seasoning.

oys′tẽr tongṣ, a kind of tongs used in oyster fishing.

oys′tẽr wench, an oysterwoman. [Archaic.]

oys′tẽr whīte (hwīt), a very light gray, with a creamy or yellowish cast.

oys′tẽr·wīfe, *n.* an oysterwoman. [Archaic.]

oys′tẽr·wom″ăn (-woom″), *n.*; *pl.* **oys′tẽr·wom″en** (-wim″), a woman whose business is selling oysters.

ō·zē′nȧ, ō·zae′nȧ, *n.* [Gr. *ozaina*, from *ozein*, to smell.] a fetid ulcer in the nostril.

ō·zō·çē′rīte, ō·zō·kē′rīte, *n.* [Gr. *ozein*, to smell, and *kēros*, wax.] a mineral wax consisting of natural paraffins, used in making candles, electrical insulation, etc.

ō′zō·nāte, *n.* [*ozone* and *-ate.*] in chemistry, any of a series of yellow or orange compounds formed by the action of oxygen containing ozone on alkalies: they slowly change to tetroxides on standing.

ō·zō·nā′tion, *n.* treatment with ozone; also, the act of forming ozone.

ō′zōne, *n.* [Gr. *ozein*, to smell.]

1. a blue gas, O_3, with a penetrating odor: it is an allotropic form of oxygen, formed usually by a silent electrical discharge in air, and is used as an oxidizing, deodorizing, and bleaching agent and in the purification of water.

2. pure air. [Slang.]

ō′zōne pā′pẽr, paper covered with moist starch and potassium iodide, becoming blue in the presence of ozone.

ō·zon′iç, *a.* pertaining to, like, or containing ozone.

ō·zon′iç ē′thẽr, a solution of ethylic ether, hydrogen peroxide, and alcohol, used as an antiseptic.

ō′zō·nid, *n.* an ozonide.

ō′zō·nīde, *n.* any of a series of compounds of ozone.

ō·zō·nif′ẽr·ous, *a.* [from *ozone* and *-ferous.*] having or containing ether.

ō·zō″ni·fi·çā′tion, *n.* [*ozone*, and L. *facere*, to make.] the act of producing ozone; treatment with ozone.

ō·zō·ni·zā′tion, *n.* ozonation.

ō′zō·nīze, *v.t.*; ozonized, *pt., pp.*; ozonizing, *ppr.* 1. to change (oxygen) into ozone.

2. to treat or impregnate with ozone.

ō′zō·nī·zẽr, *n.* a device for generating ozone.

ō·zō′nō·gra̤ph, *n.* [*ozone*, and Gr. *graphein*, to describe.] same as *ozonoscope.*

ō·zō·nom′ē·tẽr, *n.* [*ozone*, and Gr. *metron*, measure.] a device used to determine the relative amount of ozone in the air.

ō·zō·nō·met′riç, *a.* pertaining to ozonometry.

ō·zō·nom′e·try, *n.* the measurement of ozone.

ō·zō′nō·sçōpe, *n.* [*ozone*, and Gr. *skopein*, to view.] a device to determine the presence or amount of ozone in the air.

ō·zō·nō·sçop′iç, *a.* pertaining to the ozonoscope; revealing the presence of ozone in the air.

ō′zō·nous, *a.* ozonic.

ō·zos·tō′mi·ȧ, *n.* [Gr. *ozein*, to smell, and *stoma*, mouth.] bad-smelling breath.

P

P, p (pē), *n.*; *pl.* **P's, p's, Ps, ps** (pēz), 1. the sixteenth letter of the English alphabet: from the Greek *pi*, a borrowing from the Phoenician.

2. the sound of P or p: *p* is silent before *n* in words of Greek origin.

3. a type or impression for P or p.

4. *a symbol for* the sixteenth in a sequence or group (or the fifteenth if J is omitted).

P, p (pē), *a.* 1. of P or p.

2. sixteenth (or fifteenth if J is omitted) in a sequence or group.

P (pē), *n.* 1. an object shaped like P.

2. a Roman numeral for 400: with a superior bar (P̄), 400,000.

3. in genetics, *the symbol for* parental generation.

4. in chemistry, *the symbol for* phosphorus.

5. in mechanics, *the symbol for*: (a) power; (b) pressure.

P (pē), *a.* shaped like P.

p-, in chemistry, *para-*.

Pa, in chemistry, protactinium.

pä (*dial., often* pạ), *n.* father; **papa.** [Colloq.]

pä'ăġe, *n.* pedage. [Obs.]

paal'stab, *n.* same as *palstaff*.

Paas (pạs), *n.* the Passover; Pasch. [Obs.]

paas, *n.* pace. [Obs.]

pab'ū·lăr, *a.* pertaining to pabulum. [Rare.]

pab·ū·lā'tion, *n.* [L. *pabulatio*, from *pabulari*, to feed.]

1. the act of feeding or procuring food. [Rare.]

2. food; pabulum. [Rare.]

pab'ū·lous, *a.* affording food. [Rare.]

pab'ū·lum, *n.* 1. that which feeds or nourishes; food: often used figuratively of intellectual nourishment; food for the mind.

2. that which feeds a fire; fuel.

paç, *n.* [Am. Indian.] a shoe resembling a moccasin, made with the edges of the sole turned up and stitched to the upper.

pä'çȧ, *n.* [Port. and Sp., from Tupi *páca*.] any of a number of related short-tailed or tailless rodents of South and Central America, with spotted brown fur and hooflike toes.

pā'çȧ·ble, *a.* [L. *pacabilis*, from *pacare*, to pacify.] placable.

pā'çāte, *a.* [L. *pacatus*, pp. of *pacare*, to pacify.] peaceful; tranquil. [Obs.]

pā·çā'tion, *n.* the act of appeasing. [Rare.]

pāce, *n.* [OFr. *pas*, from L. *passus*, a step, lit., a stretching out of the feet in walking, from *pandere*, to stretch out. *Pass* has the same origin.]

1. a step in walking, running, etc.; a stride.

2. a conventional measure of length, approximately the distance covered in a step or stride: it is generally estimated at 2½ feet, or sometimes in measuring, 3 feet or 3.3 feet (⅕ of a rod). The regulation pace of the United States Army is 30 inches, or 36 inches for double time. The *Roman pace*, measured from the heel of one foot to the heel of the same foot in the next stride, was 5 Roman feet, or 58.1 inches: it is now known as a *geometric pace*, about 5 feet.

3. the rate of speed in walking, running, etc.

4. (a) rate of movement, progress, development, etc.; (b) an equal rate or speed; as, try to keep *pace* with me.

5. a particular way of walking, running, etc. (of a person or animal); walk; gait; as, a heavy *pace*.

> But on rode these strange horsemen,
> With slow and lordly *pace*.
> —Macaulay.

6. one of the gaits of a horse in which both legs on the same side are raised at the same time.

7. a step or measure. [Rare.]

> The first *pace* necessary for his majesty is to fall into confidence with Spain.
> —Temple.

8. in architecture, a deep step or platform; a part of the floor raised above the common level; a dais.

to keep (or *hold*) *pace with*; to keep up with; to go or move as fast as.

to put one through his paces; to test one's abilities, accomplishments, capabilities, etc.

to set the pace; (a) to go at a speed that others try to equal, as in a race; (b) to do or be something for others to emulate.

pāce, *v.t.*; paced, *pt., pp.*; pacing, *ppr.* 1. to measure by paces; as, to *pace* a piece of ground.

2. to regulate in motion; to guide; to train, as a horse.

> If you can, *pace* your wisdom
> In that good path that I would wish to go.
> —Shak.

3. to set the pace for (a runner, horse, etc.)

4. to walk or stride back and forth across; as, he *paced* the floor in silence.

to pace the web; in weaving with a hand-loom, to wind upon the beam a part of the cloth as it is woven.

pāce, *v.i.* 1. to walk or step slowly or with measured tread; to stride.

> *Pacing* through the forest,
> Chewing the food of sweet and bitter fancy.
> —Shak.

2. to move by lifting the legs on the same side together: said of a horse.

3. to make progress; to move on. [Obs.]

Syn.—amble, step, tread, walk.

pāce'bōard, *n.* a broad step or board at the foot of an altar; an altar footpace.

pāced (pāst), *a.* 1. having a specified pace: used in hyphenated compounds; as, slow-*paced* horses.

> But even-*paced* come round the years.
> —Whittier.

2. measured by paces or pacing.

3. in horse racing, having its pace set by a pacemaker.

pāce'māk″ẽr, *n.* 1. (a) a runner, horse, automobile, etc. that sets the pace for others, as in a race; (b) a person, group, or thing that leads the way or serves as a model. Also *pacesetter*.

2. in anatomy, (a) a dense network of interwoven fibers in the right atrium of the heart where the stimulus that initiates the heartbeat begins; (b) any of several similar sources of stimulus.

3. in medicine, an electronic device implanted into the body and connected to the wall of the heart, designed to provide regular, mild, electric shock that stimulates contraction of the heart muscles and restores normalcy to the heartbeat.

pāce'māk″ing, *n.* a setting of a pace, as by a runner, horse, etc.

pā'cẽr, *n.* 1. a horse whose normal gait is a pace.

2. a pacemaker (sense 1).

pȧ·chä', *n.* same as *pasha*.

Pä″chä·çȧ·mäç', *n.* [Peruv.] in Peruvian mythology, the creator of the universe.

pȧ·chäk', *n.* [E. Ind.] the fragrant roots of a plant, *Saussurea costus*, used by the Chinese as incense: the plant belongs to the composite family and grows in Kashmir, India.

pȧ·chä'liç, *n.* same as *pashalik*.

pȧ·chī'si, *n.* [Hind. *pacīsī*, from *pacīs*, twenty-five: so named from the highest throw.]

1. in India, a game for four players in which the moves of the pieces around a board are determined by the throwing of cowrie shells.

2. in England and the United States, a similar game in which dice replace the shells: also *parcheesi*, *parchesi*, *parchisi*.

paçh'nō·līte, *n.* [Gr. *pachnē*, hoarfrost, and *lithos*, stone.] a white, transparent compound, $H_2NaCaAlF_6O$.

pȧ·çhom'ē·tẽr, *n.* same as *pachymeter*.

pach'öu·li, *n.* same as *patchouli*.

paçh'y-, [Gr. *pachys*, thick.] a combining form meaning *thick*, as in *pachy*derm.

paçh·y·çär'pous, *a.* [*pachy-*, and Gr. *karpos*, fruit.] in botany, having a thick pericarp.

paçh″y·cē·phal'iç, paçh·y·ceph'ȧ·lous, *a.* [*pachy-*, and Gr. *kephalē*, head.] having an unusually thick skull.

paçh·y·daç'tyl, *n.* [*pachy-*, and Gr. *daktylos*, toe.] a bird or other animal having thick toes.

paçh·y·daç'tyl·ous, *a.* thick-toed or thick-fingered.

paçh'y·dẽrm, *n.* [Fr. *pachyderme*; Gr. *pachydermos*, thick-skinned, from *pachys*, thick, and *derma*, a skin.]

1. any of certain large, thick-skinned, hoofed animals, as the elephant, rhinoceros, and hippopotamus, formerly classified together.

2. a thick-skinned, insensitive, stolid person.

paçh·y·dẽr'măl, *a.* of or pertaining to the *Pachydermata*.

Paçh·y·dẽr'mȧ·tȧ, *n.pl.* in zoology, a former group of nonruminant, thick-skinned, hoofed animals, including the elephant, mastodon, hippopotamus, rhinoceros, tapir, horse, hog, etc.

paçh·y·dẽr'mȧ·tous, *a.* 1. pertaining to a pachyderm, or to the *Pachydermata*.

2. thick-skinned; insensitive to abuse or ridicule; dull; obtuse.

paçh·y·dẽr'mi·ȧ, *n.* [*pachy-*, and Gr. *derma*, skin.] hypertrophy or thickening of the skin.

pachydermia laryngis; a condition in which the laryngeal epithelium becomes thickened due to chronic catarrhal laryngitis.

paçh·y·dẽr'miç, *a.* characterized by abnormal thickness of the skin.

paçh·y·dẽr'moid, *a.* [*pachyderm* and *-oid*.] resembling a pachyderm; pachydermatous.

paçh·y·dẽr'mous, *a.* same as *pachydermatous*.

paçh·y·ē'mi·ȧ, paçh·y·ae'mi·ȧ, *n.* [*pachy-*, and Gr. *haima*, blood.] a thickening of the blood.

paçh·y·glos'săl, *a.* pachyglossate.

paçh·y·glos'sāte, *a.* [*pachy-*, and Gr. *glōssa*, tongue.] having a thick tongue, as lizards of the group *Pachyglossæ*.

paçh·y·glos'si·ȧ, *n.* abnormal thickness of the tongue.

paçh·yg'nȧ·thous, *a* [*pachy-*, and Gr. *gnathos*, jaw.] having thick jaws.

paçh·y·lō'sis, *n.* a chronic disease in which the skin becomes dry, thick, and harsh, especially on the legs.

paçh·y·mē'ni·ȧ, *n.* [*pachy-*, and Gr. *hymēn*, a membrane.] a thickening of the skin or a membrane.

paçh·y·mē'niç, *a.* having a thick skin.

paçh·y·men·in·ġit'iç, *a.* pertaining to or having pachymeningitis.

paçh·y·men·in·ġī'tis, *n.* [*pachy-* and *meningitis*.] inflammation of the dura mater, the outermost, toughest, and most fibrous of the membranes of the brain.

paçh·y·mē'ninx, *n.* [*pachy-*, and Gr. *mēninx*, membrane.] the tough membrane lining the cavity of the skull; the dura mater.

pȧ·çhym'ē·tẽr, *n.* [*pachy-*, and Gr. *metron*, measure.] an instrument for measuring the thickness of objects.

paçh'y·ō·dont, *a.* [*pachy-*, and Gr. *odous*, *odontos*, a tooth.] having thick teeth.

paçh'y·ōte, *n.* [*pachy-*, and Gr. *ous*, *ōtos*, ear.] a bat, as of the genus *Pachyotus*: so called because of its thick ears.

paçh'y·ōte, *a.* having thick ears.

paçh·y·ō′ti·à (-shi-à), *n.* marked thickness of the ears.

paçh″y·per·i·tō·nī′tis, *n.* [*pachy-* and *peritonitis.*] peritonitis with thickening of the affected membrane.

paçh′y·pod, *a.* [*pachy-*, and Gr. *pous, podos*, a foot.] having thick feet.

paçh·yp′tēr·ous, *a.* [*pachy-*, and Gr. *pteron*, a wing.] thick-winged or thick-finned: said of bats, insects, and fishes.

Paçh·y·san′drà, *n.* [*pachy-* and *-androus.*]
1. a genus of plants of the spurge family, having thick stamens. There are two species, one American and the other Japanese
2. [p–] a plant of this genus.

pac′i·fī·à·ble, *a.* capable of being pacified.

Pà·cif′iç, *a.* 1. designating, of, in, on, or near the Pacific Ocean.
2. on, along, or near the Pacific Coast of the United States.

pà·cif′iç, *a.* [Fr. *pacifique*; L. *pacificus*, from *pacificare*, to make peace.]
1. peacemaking; conciliatory; serving to make or restore peace; adapted to reconcile differences; mild; appeasing; as, to offer *pacific* proposals to a belligerent power.
2. calm; tranquil; not warlike; of a peaceful nature; as, a *pacific* temperament.
Syn.—peaceful, tranquil, calm, placid, smooth, still, conciliating, appeasing, gentle, reconciling.

pà·cif′iç·ăl, *a.* same as *pacific.*

pà·cif′iç·ăl·ly, *adv.* in a pacific manner.

pà·cif′i·çāte, *v.t.*; pacificated, *pt., pp.*; pacificating, *ppr.* to pacify.

pà·cif·i·çā′tion (*or* pas′i-fi-), *n.* [L. *pacificatio.*] a pacifying or being pacified.

pà·cif′i·çā·tŏr, *n.* [L.] a peacemaker; one who pacifies.

pà·cif′i·çà·tō·ry, *a.* tending to pacify, or make peace; conciliatory.

pà·cif′i·çişm, *n.* same as *pacifism.*

pä·cï′fï·çō, *n.*; *pl.* **pä·cï′fï·çōş,** [Sp.] a peaceful person; a nonresister; specifically, a native of Cuba or the Philippines who submitted to Spanish occupation.

Pà·cif′iç Stand′ărd Tīme, one of the four standard times in the United States, corresponding to the mean local time of the 120th meridian west of Greenwich, England: it is eight hours behind Greenwich time and three hours behind Eastern Standard Time.

pac′i·fī·ēr, *n.* 1. a person or thing that pacifies.
2. a nipple or teething ring for babies.

pac′i·fişm, *n.* opposition to all war and armed hostility; belief that national or international disputes should be settled by peaceful means rather than by force or war.

pac′i·fist, *n.* a person who advocates pacifism; one opposed to war or the use of force.

pac·i·fis′tiç, *a.* of pacifism or pacifists.

pac′i·fȳ, *v.t.*; pacified, *pt., pp.*; pacifying, *ppr.* [Fr. *pacifier*; L. *pacificare*; *pax, pacis*, peace, and *facere*, to make.]
1. to appease; to calm; to still; to quiet; to make peaceful or calm; as, to *pacify* an angry man.
2. to establish or secure peace in (a nation, etc.)
Syn.—appease, reconcile, conciliate, compose, assuage, mollify, still.

Pà·cin′i·ăn, *a.* relating to Pacini, an Italian anatomist (1812–1883), or to his discoveries.
Pacinian corpuscles; a set of small corpuscles in the subcutaneous cellular tissue of the fingers and toes, surrounding the terminations of the sensory nerves.

pack, *n.* [ME. *pakke*, from a L.G. form; cf. M.D., M.L.G. *pak*, M.Fl. *pac*: the word was carried throughout Europe via the Low Countries' wool trade.]
1. a large bundle of things wrapped or tied up for carrying, as on the back of an animal; a load; a burden; a bale.
2. a number of similar or related persons or things; specifically, (a) a number; group; collection; as, a *pack* of lies; (b) a package of a standard number; as, a *pack* of cigarettes; (c) a set of playing cards, usually 52; a deck; (d) a set of hunting hounds; (e) a number of wild animals living together; as, a *pack* of wolves; (f) a united group; a gang.
3. a mass of floating pieces of ice driven together.
4. (a) treatment by wrapping a patient in blankets or sheets that are wet or dry and hot or cold; (b) the blankets or sheets used; (c) a folded towel or cloth filled with crushed ice: also *ice pack.*
5. any of various cosmetic pastes applied to the skin and left to dry.
6. the amount of fish, meat, etc. put in cans, etc. in a season or year.
Syn.—bundle, group, package, lot, parcel, load.

pack, *v.t.*; packed, *pt., pp.*; packing, *ppr.* 1. to make a pack, or bundle, of.
2. (a) to put together compactly in a box, trunk, etc. for carrying or storing; (b) to fill (a box, trunk, etc.) for carrying or storing; as, he *packed* his bags.
3. (a) to put (food) in cans, boxes, etc. for preservation or sale; (b) to put food in (cans, boxes, etc.) for preservation or sale.
4. (a) to crowd; to fill closely; to cram; as, the audience *packed* the hall; (b) to crowd (people) together; to press together.
5. to fill in or surround tightly for protection, prevention of leaks, etc.; as, *pack* a joint.
6. to press together firmly; as, *packed* earth.
7. to load (an animal) with a pack.
8. to carry (goods, equipment, etc.) in or as in a pack: said of an animal.
9. to carry or wear as part of one's regular clothing, equipment, etc.; as, he *packs* a gun.
10. to wrap in a pack (sense 4b).
11. to send (*off*); as, they *packed* him *off* to school.
12. to deliver or be able to deliver (a blow, punch, etc.) with force. [Slang.]

pack, *v.i.* 1. to make up packs.
2. to put one's clothes, belongings, etc. into luggage for a trip; as, are you going to *pack* tonight?
3. to press, crowd, or throng together in a small space.
4. to admit of being folded compactly, put in a container, etc.; as, this suit *packs* well.
5. to depart in haste; to go off in a hurry: sometimes with *off* or *away.*
6. to gather or collect into a compact mass; as, wet snow *packs.*
7. to gather into packs, flocks, or bodies.
The frosty nights will cause the perch to *pack.* —Field.
to send packing; to send away in disgrace; to dismiss (a person) without delay.

pack, *v.t.* [from prec. *pack, v.t.*]
1. to put together, sort, or arrange (cards) so as to secure an unfair advantage in a game. [Archaic.]
There be that can *pack* cards and yet cannot play well. —Bacon.
2. to choose or arrange (a jury, committee, etc.) in such a way as to secure some advantage, or to favor some particular side or interest.
This *packed* and overawed Parliament. —Prynne.

pack, *a.* 1. (a) used in packing; (b) suitable for packing.
2. formed in a pack or packs.
3. used for carrying packs, loads, etc.

pack, *n.* [from *pack*, to choose a jury.] an agreement or plot. [Obs.]

pack′ăge, *n.* 1. the act or process of packing.
2. a wrapped or boxed thing or group of things; a parcel; a bundle.
3. a box, case, etc. in which things are packed.

pack′ăge stōre, a retail store where alcoholic beverages are sold by the bottle to be drunk off the premises.

pack an′i·măl, a pack-carrying animal.

pack′çlŏth, *n.* cloth, usually burlap, for packing goods.

pack′ēr, *n.* one who or that which packs; specifically, (a) a person who packs goods for preservation, transportation, or sale; (b) a person who owns or manages a packing house.

pack′et, *n.* [Anglo-Fr. *pacquet*, dim. of ME. *pakke*, pack.]
1. a small package or parcel.
2. a packet boat.

pack′et, *v.t.*; packeted, *pt., pp.*; packeting, *ppr.* 1. to make up into or wrap in a packet.
2. to transmit by packet boat. [Obs.]

pack′et, *v.i.* to ply with a packet or dispatch vessel. [Obs.]

pack′et bōat, pack′et ship, [so called from orig. carrying mail; cf. Fr. *paquebot.*] a boat that travels a regular route between ports, as along a coast or on a river, carrying passengers, freight, and mail.

pack′et dāy, the day for the sailing of a packet boat, or for delivering packages to be sent.

pack′et nōte, a kind of writing paper, $5^3/_4$ x 9 inches.

pack hŏrse, 1. a horse employed in carrying packs, luggage, etc.
2. a drudge.

pack′house, *n.* a house used for packing merchandise; a warehouse.

pack′ing, *n.* 1. the act or process of a person or thing that packs; specifically, (a) the canning of meats, fruits, or vegetables; (b) in medicine, the filling of a wound or cavity with gauze, etc. to permit drainage and prevent closure.
2. any material used in packing, as a fibrous substance placed around valves to make them watertight, etc.

pack′ing box, 1. a large wooden box for storing or shipping goods; a crate: also *packing case.*
2. a stuffing box.

pack′ing ef·feçt′, in physics, the loss of mass in the nucleus of an atom attributed to the loss of energy resulting in the building up of the nucleus from its component parts.

pack′ing house, a place where meats, and sometimes fruits, vegetables, etc., are prepared for future sale, by processing, canning, packaging, etc.

pack′ing press, any machine used for compressing solids; specifically, a press, usually hydraulic, for baling hay, cotton, etc.

pack′ing ring, an automatically expanding ring used in the packing of a piston.

pack′ing sheet, 1. a sheet of cloth, used for packing goods.
2. a sheet in which a patient is wrapped or packed, in hydropathic treatment.

pack′măn, *n.*; *pl.* **pack′men,** a man who carries a pack of goods for sale; a peddler.

pack mọth, a moth, *Anacampsis sarcitella*, having larvae that destroy woolen cloth.

pack nee′dle, a heavy needle used in sewing packcloth.

pack rat, a rat, *Neotoma cinerea*, with a bushy tail, living in the woods of North America, named from its habit of carrying and hiding small articles that it finds.

pack′sack, *n.* a traveling sack of canvas or leather, usually carried strapped on the shoulders.

pack sad′dle, a saddle designed to support the load carried by a pack animal.

pack′stȧff, *n.*; *pl.* **pack′stāveş,** a staff on which a traveler or a peddler supports his pack.

pack′thread (-thred), *n.* strong, thick thread or twine used for tying up parcels and for similar purposes.

pack trāin, a train, or procession, of pack animals.

pack wąll, in mining, a natural wall left standing for the support of the roof.

pack′wax, *n.* same as *paxwax.*

pack′wāy, *n.* a narrow path for pack animals.

pä′çō, pä′çōş, *n.* [Peruv.] a South American animal; the alpaca.

pä′çō, *n.* an earthy-looking ore, consisting of brown oxide of iron with small particles of native silver.

paçt, *n.* [ME.; OFr. *pacte*; L. *pactum*, from *pacisci*, to fix, settle, to make a bargain, to covenant.] a compact; an agreement or covenant.

paç′tion, *n.* [L. *pactio.*] an agreement or bargain. [Chiefly Scot.]

paç′tion·ăl, *a.* pertaining to an agreement; in accordance with a pact. [Chiefly Scot.]

Paç·tō′li·ăn, *a.* pertaining to Pactolus, a river in the ancient country of Lydia, famous for its golden sands.

pä′çū, *n.* a South American fish.

pad, *n.* [chiefly echoic, but influenced by *pad* (to travel).] the dull sound made by a footstep or staff on the ground.

pad, *n.* [D. *pad*, path.]
1. a footpath; a road; a way. [Brit. Slang or Dial.]
2. an easy-paced horse.
3. a footpad; a highwayman. [Rare.]

pad, *v.i.*; padded, *pt., pp.*; padding, *ppr.* [from *pad* (path).]
1. to travel on foot; to walk; tramp.
2. to walk or run with a soft, almost soundless, step: said especially of animals.
3. to rob on foot. [Obs.]

pad, *v.t.* to tread on; to travel over.

pad, *n.* [a variant of *pod.*]
1. anything resembling a cushion or used like a cushion; any mass of soft or elastic material used for support or for protection against impact, friction, etc., or for filling or stuffing.

2. a flat cushion used instead of a saddle; a treeless saddle.

3. a wadded shield or guard worn for protection, especially by players of football, cricket, and other athletic games; also, a guard for the leg of a horse.

4. the foot or footprint of certain animals, as the wolf, fox, etc.

5. a number of sheets of paper for writing or drawing, fastened together along one edge; a tablet.

6. a piece of timber used in shipbuilding just above the deck beams to give an arch to the deck.

7. an absorbent cushion soaked with ink for inking a rubber stamp.

8. the leather cushion that lines the valves of certain wind instruments.

9. the floating leaf of any water plant, as a lily *pad*.

10. in zoology, the thickening of the skin in a cushionlike form on the underside of the toes of some animals, birds, and insects.

11. a pallet or bed. [Slang.]

12. the room, apartment, etc. where one sleeps. [Slang.]

pad, *v.t.*; padded, *pt.*, *pp.*; padding, *ppr.* 1. to stuff, cover, or line with soft material.

2. to lengthen or expand with unnecessary material or words; as, to *pad* a book or a speech.

3. to fill (an expense account, etc.) with fraudulent or invented entries.

4. in dyeing, to imbue with a mordant.

pad çloth, a housing; a cloth or small blanket placed under a saddle.

pad′ded cell, a cell, or room, lined with heavy, soft material for the confinement of violently deranged patients or prisoners.

pad′dẽr, *n.* 1. a robber on foot; a highwayman. [Obs.]

2. a person who pads; also, anything used to pad out.

pad′ding, *n.* 1. the action of a person who pads; the operation or process of filling with a pad or with pads.

2. the material of which a pad is made, as cotton, felt, etc.

3. in dyeing, the impregnation of cloth with a mordant.

4. material, often unnecessary or irrelevant, inserted in a speech, writing, etc. in order to extend its length.

pad′dle (-l), *n.* [ME. *padell*, small spade; prob. var. of *patel*, shallow pan (from L. *patella*).]

1. a relatively short oar with a wide blade at one end or both ends, used, without an oarlock, to propel a canoe.

2. any of various implements shaped like this; specifically, (a) a metal tool for stirring iron in a furnace; (b) a small, flat, wooden instrument for working butter, stirring clay, etc.; (c) a wooden device used in washing clothes by hand; (d) a flat, wooden stick for administering punishment by beating; (e) a flat, rounded piece of wood with a short handle, used to hit a ball, as in table tennis or paddle ball.

3. any of the propelling boards in a water wheel or paddle wheel.

4. a small board for closing a lock gate or a sluice.

5. a tool used to clean plowshares.

6. in zoology, any flipper, as the paddle-shaped foot of a tortoise, a crocodile, or a seal.

pad′dle, *v.i.*; paddled, *pt.*, *pp.*; paddling, *ppr.* 1. to row slowly and gently.

2. to propel a canoe, etc. by means of a paddle or paddles.

pad′dle, *v.t.* 1. to propel (a canoe, etc.) by means of a paddle.

2. to punish by beating with or as with a paddle.

3. to stir, work, etc. with a paddle.

to paddle one's own canoe; to depend on one's own efforts; to be self-reliant.

pad′dle, *v.i.*; paddled, *pt.*, *pp.*; paddling, *ppr.* [prob. freq., from *pad*, v.i.]

1. to walk or move the feet in shallow water; to wade; to dabble.

2. to toy or play idly, as with the fingers (with *in*, *on*, or *about*).

3. to walk like a small child; to toddle.

pad′dle ball, a game similar to handball, but played with a short-handled, perforated paddle.

pad′dle bēam, in shipbuilding, one of the large beams in paddle-wheel vessels, extending beyond the side and forming part of the paddle box.

pad′dle bōard, same as *paddle*, n. 3.

pad′dle box, the semicircular structure often enclosing the upper portion of the paddle wheel of a steamboat.

pad′dle·fish, *n.*; *pl.* **pad′dle·fish** or **pad′dle·fish·eș**, a fish of the subclass *Ganoidei*, common to the Mississippi River, characterized by a large, spatulate snout: also called *spoon-billed cat* and *duck-billed cat*.

pad′dlẽr, *n.* a person or thing that paddles.

pad′dle shȧft, the driving shaft of a paddle wheel.

pad′dle stēam′ẽr, a steamboat having paddle wheels instead of a screw propeller.

pad′dle ten′nis, an outdoor game played with paddles and a rubber ball on a raised platform surrounded by a screen, combining elements of tennis, handball, and squash.

pad′dle wheel (hwēl), a water wheel used in propelling steamboats. It consists usually of a wheel with boards, or paddles, attached radially at its circumference, the wheel revolving on a horizontal rotating shaft. It is parallel to the length of the ship and is about half submerged. When single, it is placed at the stern; when there are two wheels, they are placed one on each side of the vessel toward the stern.

pad′dle·wood, *n.* the wood of a tree, *Aspidosperma excelsa*, native to tropical South America. The trunk is grooved and splits easily into planks, and the wood is light and elastic: also called *wheel tree*.

pad′dŏck, *n.* [phonetic alteration of AS. *pearruc*, enclosure.]

1. a small field or enclosure near a stable, in which horses are exercised.

2. an enclosure near a race track, where horses are assembled before a race.

3. in Australia, an enclosed piece of land.

pad′dŏck, *v.t.*; paddocked (-dŏkt) *pt.*, *pp.*; paddocking, *ppr.* to partition into paddocks or to enclose in a paddock.

pad′dŏck, *n.* [ME. *paddoke*, from *padde* (AS. *pad*, frog, toad), and *-ock*.]

1. a frog. [Obs. or Scot.]

2. a toad. [Obs.]

pad′dŏck stool, a toadstool. [Chiefly Scot.]

Pad′dy, *n.*; *pl.* **Pad′dieș**, [from *Pādraig*, Ir. form of *Patrick*, a frequent Christian name in Ireland, after St. *Patrick*.] an Irishman: a nickname. [Slang.]

pad′dy, *n.* [Malay *padi*.]

1. rice in the husk, growing or gathered.

2. rice in general.

3. *pl.* **pad′dieș**, loosely, a rice field.

pad′dy bird, same as *Java sparrow*.

pad′dy·mel·ŏn, *n.* same as *pademelon*.

pad′dy wag′ŏn, [prob. from *Paddy* (an Irishman).] a police wagon in which arrested persons are taken into custody. [Slang.]

pad′dy·whack (-hwak), *n.* [from *Paddy*, and *whack*; orig. Irishman.]

1. a rage; temper. [Brit. Dial.]

2. a beating. [Colloq.]

pad·ē·lī′ŏn, *n.* [Fr. *pas de lion*, lion's foot.] the plant *Alchemilla vulgaris*: also called *lion's-foot* or *lady's-mantle*. [Obs.]

pȧ·del′lȧ, *n.* [It., from L. *patella*, dim. of *patera*, cup.] a large bowl or saucer in which fat is burned by means of a wick: a kind of lamp used particularly in Italy.

pad′ē·mel·ŏn, *n.* the wallaby, a kangaroo native to Australia and Tasmania.

padġe, *n.* a barn owl. [Brit. Dial.]

pä′di·shäh, *n.* [Per. *pādshāh*, from *pati*, master, and *shāh*, shah.]

1. a great king; emperor.

2. [*often* P-] (a) the shah of Iran; (b) formerly, the sultan of Turkey; (c) formerly, the British sovereign as emperor of India.

pad′lock, *n.* [ME. *padlocke*; perhaps from *padde*, toad, frog, because of the shape.] a removable lock with a hinged or pivoted link to be passed through a staple, chain, or eye.

pad′lock, *v.t.*; padlocked (-lokt), *pt.*, *pp.*; padlocking, *ppr.* 1. to fasten with or as with a padlock; to furnish with a padlock or padlocks.

2. to close (a building) against entrance.

pad′nag, *n.* [from *pad*, to pace, and *nag*.] an easygoing, ambling nag.

pad′ōw, *n.* same as *paddock*.

pä′dre, *n.*; *pl.* **pä′dreș**, It. **pä′drī**, [Sp.; It.; Port., from L. *pater*, a father.]

1. father: the title of a priest in Italy, Spain, Portugal, and Latin America.

2. a chaplain. [Military Slang.]

3. in India, any clergyman or priest.

pȧ·drō′ne, *n.*; *pl.* **pȧ·drō′nī**, [It.; L. *patronus*, patron.]

1. patron; master; boss.

2. in Italy, (a) a master of a Mediterranean trading ship; (b) a person who employs street musicians, child beggars, etc.; (c) an innkeeper.

3. a contractor for Italian laborers in America.

pad′ū·ȧ·soy, *n.* [altered (after *Padua*, Italy) from Fr. *pou-de-soie*, earlier *poudesoy*.]

1. a corded silk cloth used extensively in the 18th century.

2. a garment made of this.

pad′ū·ȧ·soy, *a.* made of paduasoy.

Pȧ·dū′çȧh, *n.* Comanche (sense 1).

pae′ăn, *n.* [Gr. *Paian*, Apollo.]

1. in ancient Greece, a song of rejoicing in honor of Apollo, as the healer of evil; also, in later times, a song of praise to other gods.

2. a loud and joyous song; a song of triumph, joy, etc.

Also spelled *pean*.

pae′ăn·ișm, *n.* songs or shouts of triumph.

pae·deū′tiçs, *n.* [Gr. *paideutikos*; *paideuein*, to teach, from *pais*, *paidos*, child.] the science or art of education.

pae′dō- (*or* ped′ō), same as *pedo-*.

pae·dō·bap′tișm, *n.* same as *pedobaptism*.

pae·dō·ġen′e·sis, *n.* see *pedogenesis*.

pae″dō·ġē·net′iç, *a.* see *pedogenetic*.

pae′ŏn, *n.* [Gr. *paiōn*, song in honor of Apollo.] in Greek and Latin prosody, a foot consisting of one long syllable and three short syllables. The position of the long syllable can be varied in four ways, hence the paeon is said to be first, second, third, or fourth.

Pae·ō′ni·ȧ, *n.* a genus of plants of the crowfoot family, *Ranunculaceæ*, native to north temperate regions; the peonies.

pae·on′iç, *a.* pertaining to or equivalent to a paeon; consisting of paeons.

pae·on′iç, *n.* a paeonic verse; a paeon.

pae′ō·nin, *n.* a red resinous coloring matter, obtained by heating phenol with sulfuric and oxalic acids.

pae′ō·ny, *n.* same as *peony*.

pae·sän′ (pī-), *n.* same as *paesano*.

pae·sä′nō (pī-), *n.*; *pl.* **pae·sä′nī** or **pae·sä′nōș**, [It., from LL. *pagensis*, of the district, from *pagus*, district, country.]

1. a fellow countryman.

2. a fellow Italian.

pā′găn, *n.* [L. *paganus*, a peasant or countryman, from *pagus*, country.]

1. (a) formerly, a person who was not a Christian; (b) now, a person who is not a Christian, Moslem, or Jew; heathen.

2. a person who has no religion.

Syn.—gentile, heathen.—*Gentile* is applied to one who is not a Jew, or among Mormons, to one who is not a Mormon. *Pagan* is now applied to one of the ancient polytheistic peoples, as the Greek and Romans, and *heathen* is applied to any of the peoples regarded as uncivilized idolaters.

pā′găn, *a.* 1. of pagans or paganism; not Christian, Moslem, or Jewish.

2. not religious; heathen.

Pā·gȧ·nā′li·ȧ, *n.pl.* [L., from *paganus*, of a village.] in ancient Rome, an annual festival held in a rural community.

pā′găn·dŏm, *n.* 1. all pagans.

2. a place or all the places inhabited by pagans.

pā·gan′iç, *a.* paganish.

pā·gan′iç·ăl, *a.* paganic.

pā·gan′iç·ăl·ly, *adv.* in a paganic manner.

pā′găn·ish, *a.* of or like a pagan.

pā′găn·ișm, *n.* [Fr. *paganisme*.] 1. the state of being pagan.

2. pagan beliefs, customs, and attitudes.

pā·gan′i·ty, *n.* paganism. [Now Rare.]

pā′găn·īze, *v.t.* and *v.i.*; paganized, *pt.*, *pp.*; paganizing, *ppr.* to make or become pagan.

pā′găn·ly, *adv.* in a pagan manner.

pāġe, *n.* [ME.; OFr.; It. *paggio*; LL. *pagius*; perhaps from Gr. *paidion*, dim. of *pais*, *paidos*, child.]

1. formerly, a boy training for knighthood, who acted as an attendant on a knight.

2. (a) a boy attendant or servant, especially one serving a person of high rank, as in court; (b) a title of various officers of a royal household.

3. a boy, often in uniform, who runs errands, carries messages, etc., as in a hotel or office building.

4. an attendant in Congress or a legislature.

5. a contrivance for holding up the skirts of a lady's dress, to prevent their dragging on the ground.

6. in brickmaking, the track carrying the pallets that support the newly-molded bricks.

7. a lad; a boy; a child. [Obs.]

8. South American moth of the family *Uraniidæ*.

pāġe, *v.t.*; paged; *pt., pp.*; paging, *ppr.* 1. to attend as a page.

2. (a) to try to find, summon, or notify (a person) by calling his name, as in a hotel; (b) to have a page call the name of (a person).

pāġe, *v.i.* to serve as a page.

pāġe, *n.* [Fr., from L. *pagina*, a page, from *pangere*, to fasten.]

1. (a) one side of a leaf of a book, newspaper, etc.; also, in loose usage, a leaf; as, he accidentally tore three *pages* from the book; (b) the printing or writing on such a leaf.

2. [*often pl.*] a record; writing; as, the *pages* of history.

3. an episode; event or series of events that might fill a page; as, a colorful *page* in his life.

4. in printing, the type set up for one side of a leaf.

pāġe, *v.t.*; paged, *pt., pp.*; paging, *ppr.* to mark or number the pages of (a book or manuscript).

paġ′eant (-ent), *n.* [ME. *pagine, pagend, pagent*, scaffold for scenic exhibitions, also the exhibitions themselves; Anglo-L. *pagina*; prob. from base of L. *pangere*, to fix.]

1. (a) originally, an individual scene in a medieval mystery play; (b) [Anglo-L. *paganus*.] any of a series of movable outdoor platforms on which a mystery play was performed.

2. an elaborate display or exhibition devised for the entertainment of some important person or of the public; a spectacle; a showy display.

The Caesar's *pageant*, shorn of Brutus' bust. —Byron.

3. an outdoor drama celebrating a historical event or presenting, with local actors, the history of a community.

4. empty pomp or display; mere show.

paġ′eant, *a.* showy; spectacular; ostentatious.

paġ′eant, *v.t.* to exhibit in show; to represent. [Obs.]

paġ′eant·ry, *n.*; *pl.* **paġ′eant·rieṣ,** 1. pageants collectively.

What *pageantry*, what *feats*, what shows. —Shak.

2. grand spectacle; gorgeous display.

3. empty show or display.

Syn.—spectacle, parade, show, display, pomp, ostentation.

pāġe′hood, *n.* the state of being a page.

paġ′i·nȧ, *n.* in botany, a surface, as of a leaf, the thallus of a lichen, etc.

paġ′i·năl, *a.* [LL. *paginalis*.]

1. of a page or pages; consisting of pages.

2. page for page.

paġ·i·nā′tion, *n.* 1. the act of numbering the pages of a book, etc.

2. the figures and marks used in numbering the pages of a book.

3. the arrangement and number of pages, as noted in a catalogue.

pāġ′ing, *n.* the marking of the pages of a book.

pā′gle, pāi′gle, *n.* a plant, the primrose or the cowslip. [Brit. Dial.]

pag′ŏd, *n.* a pagoda. [Archaic.]

pȧ·gō′dȧ, *n.* [Port. *pagode*; prob. from Pers. *bulkadah*; *but*, idol, and *kadah*, temple.]

1. in India, China, Japan, and the Far East, a temple in the form of a pyramidal tower of several stories, commonly built over a sacred relic or as a work of devotion.

PAGODA

2. an idol worshiped in the Orient. [Obs.]

3. formerly, a gold coin of India.

pȧ·gō′dȧ sleeve, a broad, flaring cuff or oversleeve, turned back so as to expose a fine undersleeve, worn by women and afterward by men in the early part of the eighteenth century.

pȧ·gō′dȧ stōne, same as *pagodite*.

pȧ·gō′dȧ tree, any one of several tall trees of a form resembling a pagoda, as the *Sophora japonica* of China and Japan, and the *Ficus indica*, or banyan tree, of India.

pȧ·gō′dīte, *n.* a mineral out of which the Chinese carve figures of pagodas, images, and ornaments; a species of agalmatolite or pinite.

pȧ·gū′mȧ, *n.* a viverroid carnivore of the East Indies, resembling a weasel.

pȧ·gū′ri·ăn, *a.* of the family of crustaceans, *Paguridae*.

pȧ·gū′ri·ăn, pȧ·gū′rid, *n.* any crustacean of the family *Paguridæ*.

Pȧ·gū′ri·dae, *n.pl.* [L. *pagurus*; Gr. *pagouros*, a kind of crab, from *pag*, root of *pēgnynai*, to fix, *oura*, a tail, and *eidos*, resemblance.] a family of anomurous decapod crustaceans, of which the genus *Pagurus*, or hermit crabs, is the type. Most of the species of this family inhabit the deserted shells of mollusks, such as the whelk, which they change for a larger one as they increase in size.

pȧ·gū′roid, *a.* and *n.* same as *pagurian*.

Pȧ·gū′rus, *n.* the type genus of the *Paguridæ*.

päh, *interj.* bah; fie: an exclamation of disgust, contempt, or disbelief.

päh, *n.* 1. a New Zealand stockade.

2. a Maori camp or village.

pä′hĭ, *n.* a large canoe used in war by the natives of the Society Islands.

Päh′lȧ·vĭ, Päh′lẹ·vĭ, *n.* [Per., from O. Pers. *Parthava*, Parthia.] an Iranian language spoken and written in Persia from about the third to the tenth century A.D.; Middle Persian: the name is often restricted to the literary language of the Zoroastrian books, written c. 224–651 A.D., one form of which (Huzvarišn) writes Semitic words with Iranian inflections.

päh′lȧ·vĭ, *n.*; *pl.* **päh′lȧ·vĭ,** [Per., belonging to Riza Khan *Pahlavi*, Shah of Persia.] a gold coin of Iran, equivalent to 20 rials.

pä·hō′e·hō′e, *n.* [Hawaiian.] compact lava with a smooth surface.

Päh′-Ūte, *n.* same as *Paiute*.

pāid, *v.* past tense and past participle of *pay*.

pāid, *a.* 1. receiving pay; hired; as, a *paid* advisor.

2. (a) given in payment, as money (also with *out*); (b) discharged; settled, as a debt (also with *up*).

pī·jä′mȧṣ, *n.pl.* same as *pajamas*.

pāil, *n.* [OFr. *paile, paele, payelle*; Fr. *poele*, from L. *patella*, a pan, from root of *patere*, to lie open.]

1. a container made of wood, tin, etc., cylindrical and having a handle and sometimes a cover, used for carrying liquids, as water and milk.

2. a pailful.

pāil′fụl, *n.*; *pl.* **pāil′fụlṣ,** the quantity that a pail will hold.

pail·lasse′, pal·liasse′ (pal-yas′), *n.* [Fr., from *paille*, straw.] a mattress of straw, excelsior, or moss.

pail·lette′ (pal-yet′), *n.* [Fr. *paille*, straw.]

1. a piece of metal or foil used in enamel painting.

2. a small disk of shiny metal used in decorating women's dresses, etc.; a spangle.

pail·lon′ (pa-yọṅ′), *n.* [Fr. *paille*, straw.] a bright, glittering metal foil, used in enamelwork, showing through a thickness of enamel; also, the gilding beneath the enamel.

pāil-māil′ (*or* pel-mel′), *n.* pall-mall. [Obs.]

pāin *n.* [Fr., from L. *panis*.] bread. [Obs.]

pāin, *n.* [ME. *payne, peyne*, pain, trouble, from OFr. *peine, paine, poine, pœne*; Fr. *peine*, from L. *pœna*, expiation, penalty, punishment, and latterly, pain, torment.]

1. originally, penalty.

2. the sensations one feels when hurt, mentally, or physically, especially distress, suffering, great anxiety, anguish, grief, etc.: opposed to *pleasure*.

3. a sensation of hurting, or strong discomfort, in some part of the body, caused by an injury, disease, or functional disorder, and transmitted through the nervous system.

4. [*pl.*] the labor of childbirth.

She bowed herself and travailed; for her *pains* came upon her. —1 Sam. iv. 19.

5. [*pl.*] great care or effort in working; trouble which a person takes about something; as, to take *pains* to accomplish a work.

on (or *upon, under*) *pain of*; with the probability of suffering (death, punishment, etc.) unless a specified requirement, order, etc. is fulfilled.

to die in the pain; to die under torture. [Obs.]

Syn.—pang, agony, anguish, discomfort, misery.

pāin, *v.t.*; pained, *pt., pp.*; paining, *ppr.* 1. to cause uneasy sensations in; to torment: often used with an impersonal subject; as, it *pains* me to run.

2. to make uneasy; to distress; to make unhappy; as, his sins *pain* his mother; we are *pained* at the death of a friend.

I am *pained* at my very heart. —Jer. iv. 19.

3. to punish. [Obs.]

to pain oneself; to labor; to make toilsome efforts. [Obs.]

Syn.—hurt, grieve, afflict, torment, distress.

pāined (pānd), *a.* [pp. of *pain*.]

1. hurt or distressed; having the feelings hurt; offended.

2. showing hurt feelings or resentment; as, a *pained* expression.

pāin′fụl, *a.* 1. giving pain, uneasiness, or distress; as, a *painful* operation in surgery.

2. full of or suffering with pain; aching; as, a *painful* finger.

3. requiring labor or toil; difficult; irksome; as, a *painful* service; a *painful* march.

4. laborious; painstaking. [Archaic.]

pāin′fụl·ly, *adv.* in a painful manner.

pāin′fụl·ness, *n.* the state of being painful.

pāin′kill·ẽr, *n.* a medicine that relieves pain; especially, any patented tonic medicine. [Colloq.]

pāin′less, *a.* 1. free from pain.

2. not causing or involving pain; as, *painless* childbirth.

pāin′less·ly, *adv.* in a painless manner; without pain; as, the tooth was extracted *painlessly*.

pāin′less·ness, *n.* the state of being painless.

pāinṣ′tāk·ẽr, *n.* one who takes pains.

pāinṣ′tāk·ing, *a.* 1. taking pains; very careful; diligent.

2. characterized by great care.

pāinṣ′tāk·ing, *n.* the act of taking pains; great care or diligence.

pāint, *v.t.*; painted, *pt., pp.*; painting, *ppr.* [OFr. *paindre*, pp. *paint*; Fr. *peindre*, from L. *pingere*, to paint.]

1. (a) to make (a picture, design, etc.) in colors by means of pigments, brushes, etc.; (b) to depict or portray with paints; to represent in colors; as, he *painted* a landscape.

2. to describe colorfully or vividly; to picture in words for the mind.

3. to cover or decorate with paint; to color; as, he *painted* the walls.

4. to decorate with or as with colors, cosmetics, etc.; to adorn; to beautify.

5. (a) to apply (a medicine, etc.) like paint; (b) to treat in this way, as a wound.

to paint out; to cover up with or as with a coat of paint.

Syn.—delineate, color, picture, depict, portray, describe, adorn.

pāint, *v.i.* 1. to use cosmetics.

2. to practice the art of painting pictures.

pāint, *n.* 1. (a) a mixture of colored pigment with oil, water, etc., in liquid or paste form, applied as with a brush, roller, or spray gun, and used for protective covering or coloring of a surface or for making pictures on canvas, paper, etc.; (b) dry or solid pigment.

2. a dried coat of paint; as, this *paint* chips off.

3. coloring matter, such as lipstick, rouge, etc., used to ornament or beautify the face or body.

4. in the theater, grease paint.

pāint′box, *n.* a box with compartments for holding an artist's paints, brushes, etc.

pāint′brush, *n.* 1. a brush used for applying paint.

2. the painted cup, a plant.

pāint′ed, *a.* 1. represented in colors as a picture, likeness, etc.

2. coated with paint.

3. pretended; feigned.

4. highly colored.

painted beauty; an American butterfly, *Vanessa huntera*, having a variety of bright colors.

painted bunting; a bright colored variety of finch found in the southern United States.

painted clam; an edible clam, *Callista gigantea*, with a colored shell, found in the southern United States.

painted finch; same as *painted bunting*.

painted turtle; the American fresh-water tortoise, *Chrysemys picta*, common along streams and around ponds and small lakes: named from the brilliant markings of black and red on its carapace and about its head and neck.

pāint'ed çup, 1. a plant, *Castilleia coccinea*, of the figwort family, characterized by its brilliant scarlet stem leaves or bracts.

2. any one of several other figworts found in the valley of the Mississippi and westward.

pāint'ed gràss, ribbon grass, *Phalaris arundinacea*, sometimes cultivated for its leaves, which are striped longitudinally with white and green: also called *reed canary grass*.

pāint'ed lā'dy, a handsome butterfly, *Pyrameis cardui*, whose larvae feed on the thistle: also called *thistle butterfly*.

pāint'ẽr, *n.* one whose occupation is to paint; specifically, (a) one who artistically represents persons, scenes, or objects in colors on a suitable surface or material, as canvas, walls, ceilings, etc.; an artist; (b) one who covers surfaces with paint for their preservation; (c) one who draws ornamental designs, letters, etc., in colors; as, a sign *painter*.

pāint'ẽr, *n.* [OFr. *pentour*; ult. from L. *pendere*, to hang.] a rope at the bow of a boat, used to fasten it to a ship or other object.

to cut one's painter; to set one adrift; to leave one to his own resources.

pāint'ẽr, *n.* a cougar. [Dial.]

pāint'ẽr·ly, *a.* 1. originally, of or characteristic of a painter.

2. characterized by those qualities related to a painter's techniques in applying colors in masses, especially with a thick, rough surface texture, as distinguished from linear qualities that emphasize outline and contour.

pāint'ẽr·ly, *adv.* in the manner of a painter. [Rare.]

pāint'ẽr's çol'iç, a form of lead poisoning characterized by intense abdominal pains: also called *lead colic*.

pāint'ẽr·ship, *n.* the state of being a painter. [Rare.]

pāint'ẽr stāin'ẽr, a painter of coats of arms. [Brit.]

pāint'ing, *n.* 1. the act or occupation of covering surfaces with paint.

2. the act, art, or occupation of picturing scenes, objects, persons, etc. in paint.

3. a picture in paint, as an oil, water color, etc.

4. delineation that raises a vivid image in the mind; as, word-*painting*. [Obs.]

pāint'less, *a.* lacking paint.

pāint'root, *n.* the Carolina redroot, found in the southern United States, the root of which yields a red pigment.

pāin'tūre, *n.* [Fr. *peinture*.] painting. [Obs.]

pāint'y, *a.*; *comp.* paintier; *superl.* paintiest, 1. of, smeared, or covered with paint.

2. having more paint than necessary: said of a picture.

pāir, *n.*; *pl.* **pāirs,** sometimes, after a number, **pāir,** [OFr. *paire*, from L. *par*, equal.]

1. two things of a kind, similar in form, joined, associated, or used together; as, a *pair* of gloves or stockings; a *pair* of shoes.

2. a single thing composed essentially of two similar parts that must be used together; as, a *pair* or scissors; a *pair* of trousers.

3. two persons or animals; specifically, (a) a married or engaged couple; (b) two mated animals; (c) any two people considered as having something in common; as, a *pair* of rascals; (d) a brace; a span; as, a *pair* of horses; (e) two members of opposing parties in a legislative body who agree to withhold their vote on a given question; also, this agreement.

4. two playing cards of the same denomination.

5. a set or flight: used only in *a pair of stairs, a pair of steps*. [Rare or Dial.]

6. in mining, a gang of men.

7. in mechanics, two parts or elements, each acting upon the other to determine their relative motion, as a nut and screw, a cylinder and piston.

double pair royal; four of a kind, as playing cards.

pair royal; three of a kind, as three queens in some varieties of cribbage.

pāir, *v.i.*; paired, *pt.*, *pp.*; pairing, *ppr.* 1. to form a pair or couple; to match.

2. to join in marriage; to mate.

My heart was made to fit and *pair* with thine. —Rowe.

to pair off; (a) to depart from a company in pairs, or couples; (b) to abstain from voting on arrangement with a member of the opposite party to do the same: said of members of a deliberative body.

pāir, *v.t.*; paired, *pt.*, *pp.*; pairing, *ppr.* 1. to make a pair of (two persons or things) by matching, joining, grouping, mating, etc.

2. to arrange in pairs.

3. to provide with a partner (followed by *with*).

to pair off; to join or arrange (two people or things) in a pair.

pāir, *v.t.* and *v.i.* to impair. [Obs.]

pāired (pârd), *a.* 1. arranged in pairs on opposite sides, as the wings of an insect.

2. mated.

pāir'ẽr, *n.* one who impairs. [Obs.]

pāir'ing, *n.* impairment. [Obs.]

pāir'ing, *n.* the act of making a pair.

pāir'ing tīme, the time when animals pair to breed.

pāir'ment, *n.* impairment. [Obs.]

pāir'-ōar, *n.* a boat to be rowed by two persons who sit one behind the other, each using one oar.

pāir'-ōar, *a.* of a pair-oar.

pāis (pā), *n.* [Fr. *pays*, country.] in law, the people from among whom a jury is taken.

pāi·sän'ō, *n.*; *pl.* **pāi·sän'ōs,** [Sp., from Fr. *paysan*, from OFr. *païsent*, peasant.]

1. a fellow countryman.

2. a comrade; pal. [Slang.]

Also **pāi·sän'.**

pāiṣ'ley, *a.* [after *Paisley*, Scotland.]

1. [*also* P—] designating a shawl of soft wool, having an elaborate, colorful pattern, originally made in Paisley, Scotland.

2. designating cloth having the characteristic pattern of such a shawl.

3. made of such cloth or having the characteristic pattern of such cloth.

pāiṣ'ley, *n.* 1. paisley cloth.

2. a paisley shawl.

Pāi·ūte' (pī-ūt'), *n.* [orig. used of Corn Creek tribe in Utah.] a member of a tribe of Uto-Aztecan Indians that lived in Nevada, Utah, Arizona, and California.

pȧ·jä'mȧṣ, *n.pl.* [Hind. *pājāmā, paijāmā*, from Per. *pāi*, a leg, and *jāmah*, garment.]

1. [*sing.*] in the Orient, a pair of loose silk or cotton trousers.

2. a loose sleeping or lounging suit consisting of a jacket (or blouse) and trousers of silk, cotton, etc.

Also spelled *pyjamas*.

pā'jock, *n.* a word found in Shakespeare's *Hamlet*, act iii. scene 2, and usually explained as meaning *peacock*.

Pä·ki·stän'ī, *a.* of Pakistan or its people.

Pä·ki·stän'ī, *n.* a native or inhabitant of Pakistan.

pal, *n.* [Eng. Gypsy, brother, mate (for *prāl*, in dial. on European continent), from Sans. *bhrātr*, brother.] an intimate friend; comrade; chum. [Colloq.]

pal, *v.i.*; palled, *pt.*, *pp.*; palling, *ppr.* 1. to associate as pals. [Colloq.]

2. to be or become a pal with another. [Colloq.]

pal'ăce, *n.* [Fr. *palais*, from L. *Palatium*, one of the seven hills on which Rome was built, and that on which Augustus lived.]

1. the house in which an emperor, a king, or other distinguished person resides; as, a royal *palace*; a pontifical *palace*.

2. a splendid place of residence; a stately or magnificent mansion.

3. a large, ornate place of entertainment.

pal'ăce çăr, a passenger coach of especial elegance, as a sleeping car or parlor car.

Pal'ăce Çōurt, a domestic court of the kings of Great Britain, abolished in 1849, which administered justice between the king's domestic servants. It was held once a week before the steward of the household and knight marshal: its jurisdiction extended twelve miles in circuit from the palace at Whitehall.

pal'ȧ·din, *n.* [Fr.] 1. any of the twelve peers, or douzepers, of Charlemagne's court.

2. a knight; a heroic champion.

pā'lae-, same as *pale-*.

Pā·lae·ärç'tiç, *a.* pertaining to a large area including Europe, northern Asia, Arabia, and Africa.

pā'lae·ō-, same as *paleo-*.

pā''lae·ō·bot'ȧ·ny, *n.* same as *paleobotany*.

Pā''lae·ō·çar'i·dȧ, *n.pl.* [*paleo-*, and Gr. *karis*, a small lobster.] the *Merostomata*, in a wide sense.

Pā''lae·ō·çri·noi'dē·ȧ, Pā''lē·ō·çri·noi'dē·ȧ, *n.pl.* a suborder of crinoids. [Obs.]

pā''lae·ō·gae'ăn, pā''lē·ō·gae'ăn, *a.* [*paleo-*, and Gr. *gaia*, earth.] pertaining to the Old World or the Eastern Hemisphere.

pā·lae·og'rȧ·phẽr, *n.* same as *paleographer*.

Pā''lae·ō·sau'rus, *n.* [*paleo-*, and Gr. *sauros*, lizard.] a genus of fossil saurians found in magnesian limestone.

pā'lae·ō·thēre, *n.* an animal belonging to the genus *Palæotherium*.

pā''lae·ō·thē'ri·ăn, *a.* pertaining to the palaeotheres.

Pā''lae·ō·thē'ri·um, *n.* 1. a genus of extinct mammals of the Upper Eocene age.

2. [p—] an animal of this genus.

pā'lae·ō·tȳpe, pā'lē·ō·tȳpe, *n.* a universal phonetic system proposed in 1856 by Alexander John Ellis, an English philologist, to represent all spoken sounds by means of printing types.

pā''lae·ō·typ'iç·ăl, *a.* pertaining to the phonetic system called palaeotype.

pā''lae·ō·typ'iç·ăl·ly, *adv.* in a palaeotypical manner; by the system called palaeotype.

pȧ·laes'trȧ, *n.*; *pl.* **pȧ·laes'trae, pȧ·laes'trȧṣ,** [Gr. *palaistra*; *pale*, wrestling, from *pallein*, to throw.]

1. in ancient Greece, a public place for wrestling and athletics.

2. (a) a wrestling school; (b) a gymnasium. Also spelled *palestra*.

pȧ·laes'triç, pȧ·les'triç, *a.* pertaining to wrestling or to the palestra.

pȧ·lae''ti·ō·log'iç·ăl, pȧ·lē''ti·ō·log'iç·ăl, *a.* pertaining to paletiology.

pȧ·lae·ti·ol'ō·gist, pȧ·lē·ti·ol'ō·gist, *n.* a person versed in paletiology.

pȧ·lae·ti·ol'ō·gy, pȧ·lē·ti·ol'ō·gy, *n.* [*paleo-*, and *ætiology*.] the science which explains past events by the laws of causation.

pal'ȧ·fitte, *n.* [Fr.] in archaeology, a house built on piles over water, as those of the Switzerland lakes.

pȧ·lag'ō·nīte, *n.* [from *Palagonia* in Sicily, where it is found.] a basaltic rock forming a large part of many volcanic tuffs: it has a vitreous structure, a yellow or brown color, and a resinous luster.

pȧ·lag·ō·nit'iç, *a.* like or pertaining to palagonite.

pal'ȧ·mȧ, *n.* [Gr. *palamē*, the palm.] the membrane between the toes of birds.

pal'ȧ·māte, *a.* web-footed; having a palama.

Pal·ȧ·mē'dē·ae, *n.pl.* a family of South American birds, including the screamers.

pal·ăm·pōre', *n.* a kind of dimity or flowered cotton cloth made in India and used for bedspreads: also spelled *palempore*.

pȧ·lañ'kȧ, *n.* in Turkey, a permanent intrenched camp to protect a frontier fort.

pal·ăn·quin' (-kēn'), **pal·ăn·keen',** *n.* [Fr. *palanquin*; Javanese *palangki, palanghan*.] a

PALANQUIN

covered carriage used in the Orient, usually for one person, carried by poles on the shoulders of two or more men.

Pȧ·lap'te·ryx, *n.* [*palæo-*, Gr. *a*, priv., and *pteryx*, wing.]

1. in paleontology, a genus of birds of New Zealand, which resembled the ostrich.

2. [p—] one of the extinct birds of this genus.

pȧ·läs' (-läsh'), *n.* [Sans. *palāsa*.] a gum tree, *Butea frondosa*, of the East Indies: also, a tree of the same genus, *Butea superba*.

pal''ȧ·tȧ·bil'i·ty, *n.* the quality of being palatable.

pal'ȧ·tȧ·ble, *a.* 1. agreeable to the taste; savory.

2. pleasing to the mind; agreeable.
Syn.—tasteful, appetizing, delicious.

pal′á·tá·ble·ness, *n.* the quality of being agreeable to the taste; palatability.

pal′á·tá·bly, *adv.* in a palatable manner; agreeably.

pal′á·tăl, *a.* 1. pertaining to the palate.
2. in phonetics, pronounced with the front of the tongue raised against or near the hard palate: said of consonants, as *ch* in German *ich* or *y* in English *young*: the term is now often extended to include consonants produced by raising the main body of the tongue toward the palate (e.g., *ch* in *chill*) and also front vowels.

pal′á·tăl, *n.* a palatal sound.

pal″á·tăl·i·zā′tion, *n.* a palatalizing or being palatalized.

pal′á·tăl·īze, *v.t.*; palatalized, *pt., pp.*; palatalizing, *ppr.* in phonetics, to pronounce as a palatal sound; specifically, to change (a nonpalatal sound) into a palatal sound; as. the *t* in *nature* is now invariably *palatalized* to *ch.*

pal′āte, *n.* [L. *palatum.*]
1. the roof or upper part of the mouth, composed of a hard bony forward part (the *hard palate*) and a soft fleshy back part (the *soft palate*, or *velum*).
2. taste or sense of taste: the palate was incorrectly thought to be the organ of taste.
Hard task to hit the *palates* of such guests. —Pope.
3. liking; intellectual taste.
4. in botany, the convex base of the lower lip of a personate corolla.

pal′āte, *v.t.*; palated, *pt., pp.*; palating, *ppr.* to perceive by the taste. [Rare.]

pá·lā′tiăl (-shăl), *a.* [L. *palatium*, palace.] of, like, or suitable for a palace; hence, large and ornate; stately; magnificent; as, the *palatial* residences of New York and Chicago.

pá·lat′iç, *a.* palatal. [Rare.]

pá·lat′iç, *n.* palatal. [Rare.]

pá·lat′i·nāte, *n.* [Fr. *palatinat.*]
1. the territory ruled by a **palatine.**
2. the office of a palatine.
3. [P–] a native or inhabitant of the Palatinate, a district west of the Rhine.

pal′á·tīne, *a.* [Fr. *palatin*; L. *palatinus*, from *palatium*, palace.]
1. pertaining to a palace.
2. possessing royal privileges; as, a count *palatine.*
3. of or belonging to a count, earl, or county palatine.
4. [P–] of the Palatinate, a district west of the Rhine.

pal′á·tīne, *n.* 1. an officer of an imperial palace.
2. a medieval vassal lord having the rights of royalty in his own territory, or palatinate.
3. a fur piece covering the shoulders.
4. [P–] one of the seven hills on which Rome was built.
5. [P–] a native or inhabitant of the Palatinate, a district west of the Rhine.

pal′á·tīne, *a.* in anatomy, pertaining to the palate; as, the *palatine* bones.

pal′á·tīne, *n.* a bone of the hard palate.

pal·á·tī′tis, *n.* [L. *palatum*, palate, and *-itis.*] inflammation of the palate.

pal′á·tive, *a.* pleasing to the taste. [Rare.]

pal·á·ti·zā′tion, *n.* same as *palatalization.*

pal′á·tīze, *v.t.* same as *palatalize.*

pal″á·tō·glos′săl, *a.* [L. *palatum*, palate, and Gr. *glōssa*, tongue.] pertaining to the palate and the tongue.

pal·á·tog′ná·thous, *a.* [L. *palatum*, palate, and Gr. *gnathos*, jaw.] having a congenitally cleft palate.

pal′á·tō·gráph, *n.* [L. *palatum*, palate, and Gr. *graphein*, to write.] an instrument to record the movements of the palate in speech.

pal″á·tō·max′il·lăr·y, *a.* pertaining to the palate and the jaw or jawbone.

pal″á·tō·nā′rēs, *n.pl.* [L. *palatum*, palate, and *nares*, nostrils.] the posterior nares, or openings of the nasal fossae.

pal″á·tō·nā′săl, *a.* [L. *palatum*, palate, and *nasus*, nose.] pertaining to the palate and nose.

pal″á·tō·plē′gi·á, *n.* [L. *palatum*, palate, and Gr. *plēgē*, stroke.] paralysis of the palate.

pal″á·top·ter′y·goid, *a.* [L. *palatum*, palate, and *pterygoid.*] pertaining to the palate and the pterygoid bone.

pal·á·tor′rhá·phy (-rá-), *n.* [L. *palatum*, palate, and Gr. *rhaphō*, suture.] the joining together of a cleft palate.

pá·lā′tum, *n.* [L.] in anatomy, the palate.

pá·la′vẽr, *n.* [Port. *palavra*, a word, from L. *parabola*, parable.]
1. a discussion; a conference, especially among or with African tribes.
2. talk; chatter; superfluous or idle talk.
3. flattery; cajolery.

pá·la′vẽr, *v.t.*; palavered, *pt., pp.*; palavering, *ppr.* to flatter; to cajole.

pá·la′vẽr, *v.i.* to talk idly; to talk glibly or flatteringly.

pá·la′vẽr·ẽr, *n.* one who palavers.

pä·lay′ (-lī′), *n.* [E. Ind.] 1. a tree, *Wrightia tinctoria*, from the leaves of which an inferior kind of indigo is obtained.
2. a climbing plant, *Cryptostegia grandiflora*, of the milkweed family, the juice of which yields an inferior kind of rubber.

pä·läz′zō (-lät′sō), *n.*; *pl.* **pä·läz′zï** (-lät′sē), [It.] a palace or palatial building.

pá·läz′zō (-lät′sō), *a.* designating women's pajamas or pants with wide, billowy legs that flare broadly at the ankle.

pá·läz′zōş (-lät′sōz), *n.pl.* women's pants with wide, billowy legs that flare broadly at the ankle.

pāle, *a.*; *comp.* paler; *superl.* palest, [OFr. *pale, palle, pasle*; Fr. *pâle*, from L. *pallidus*, pale, from *pallere*, to be pale.]
1. white; pallid; wan; not ruddy; as, a *pale* face; *pale* cheeks; a *pale* blue.
Hands as *pale* as milk. —Shak.
2. not bright; lacking intensity or brilliance; dim; as, the *pale* light of the moon.
3. feeble; weak; faint; as, a *pale* imitation.

pāle, *v.i.*; paled, *pt., pp.*; paling, *ppr.* 1. to turn pale; to lose color; as, his cheeks *paled* suddenly.
2. to dim; to lessen in importance, significance, etc.; as, my work *paled* beside his.

pāle, *v.t.* to make pale; as, his face was *paled* by the shock.

pāle, *n.* [L. *palus*, originally *paglus*, a stake, from the root *pag*, seen in *pangere*, to fix.]
1. a pointed stake; a narrow, upright, pointed piece of wood, used in fencing by being fixed in the ground or joined above and below to a rail; a picket.
2. a fence; a boundary; a limit; a restriction: now chiefly used figuratively; as, outside the *pale* of the law.
Oft breaking down the *pales* and forts of reason. —Shak.
3. a space enclosed; limits; an enclosure: frequently in a figurative sense.
4. a stripe on cloth. [Obs.]
5. in heraldry, one third of the escutcheon bounded by two straight lines running vertically at equal distances from the sides of the escutcheon.

A PALE AZURE

the (*English*) *pale*; a district in eastern Ireland, around Dublin, included in the Angevin Empire of Henry II, and later regarded as English.

pāle, *v.t.* to enclose with pales; to enclose; to encompass.

pā′lē-, paleo-: words beginning with *pale-* are also spelled *palae-.*

pā′lē·á, *n.*; *pl.* **pā′lē·ae,** [L. *palea*, chaff.]
1. in botany, one of the bracts at the base of a floret of a composite flower; also, one of the inner bracts of the flowers of grasses.
2. in ornithology, a wattle; a dewlap.

pā·lē·ā′ceous, *a.* [L. *palea*, chaff.] having, consisting of, or resembling paleae.

Pā·lē·ärç′tiç, same as *Palaearctic.*

pāled, *a.* striped. [Obs.]

pā·lē·eth·nō·loġ′iç·ăl, *a.* of paleethnology.

pā″lē·eth·nol′ō·ġist, *n.* one versed in paleethnology.

pā″lē·eth·nol′ō·ġy, *n.* [*pale-* and *ethnology.*] the study of prehistoric races of man.

pāle′fāce, *n.* a white person: a term said to have been first used by American Indians.

pā·lē·iċh·thy·ol′ō·ġy, pā·lae·iċh·thy·ol′ō·ġy, *n.* [Gr. *palaios*, ancient, and *ichthyology.*] the study of extinct or fossil fishes: also written *paleoichthyology.*

pā′lē·i·form, *a.* [L. *palea*, chaff, and *-form.*] resembling chaff.

pāle′ly, *adv.* in a pale manner; with paleness.

pal·em·pōre′, pal·em·pōur′, *n.* same as *palampore.*

pāle′ness, *n.* the state or quality of being pale.

pā′lē·ō-, [from Gr. *palaios*, ancient.] a combining form meaning: (a) *ancient, historically early*, or *prehistoric*, as in *Paleo*zoic; (*b*) *primitive*, as in *paleo*lithic; (*c*) *paleontological*, as in *paleo*zoology. Also, before vowels, *pale-*. Words beginning with *paleo-* are also spelled *palaeo-.*

pā″lē·ō·an·throp′iç, pā″lae·ō·an·throp′iç, *a.* pertaining to the earliest races of men.

pā″lē·ō·bō·tan′iç, *a.* paleobotanical.

pā″lē·ō·bō·tan′iç·ăl, pā″lae·ō·bō·tan′iç·ăl, *a.* pertaining to paleobotany.

pā″lē·ō·bot′á·nist, pā″lae·ō·bot′á·nist, *n.* one versed in or a student of paleobotany.

pā″lē·ō·bot′á·ny, pā″lae·ō·bot′á·ny, *n.* the study of fossil plants.

Pā′lē·ō·cēne, *a.* [from *paleo-* and Gr. *kainos*, recent.] in some geological classifications, designating or of an epoch preceding the Eocene in the Tertiary Period.
the Paleocene; the Paleocene Epoch or its rocks.

pā″lē·ō·çlī·mat′iç, pā″lae·ō·çlī·mat′iç, *a.* pertaining to the earth's climate in early geological time.

pā″lē·ō·çoş′miç, pā″lae·ō·çoş′miç, *a.* pertaining to the ancient world, or to the earth during former geological periods.

pā″lē·ō·çrys′tiç, pā″lae·ō·çrys′tiç, *a.* [*paleo-*, and Gr. *kryos*, frost.] remaining frozen from antiquity: applied to the polar seas as perpetually covered with ice of unknown ages, or to such ice.

pā″lē·ō·eth·nō·loġ′iç·ăl, pā″lae·ō·eth·nō·loġ′iç·ăl, *a.* same as *paleethnological.*

pā″lē·ō·eth·nol′ō·ġist, pā″lae·ō·eth·nol′ō·ġist, *n.* same as *paleethnologist.*

pā″lē·ō·eth·nol′ō·ġy, pā″lae·ō·eth·nol′ō·ġy, *n.* same as *paleethnology.*

pā′lē·ō·gráph, pā′lae·ō·gráph, *n.* [*paleo-*, and Gr. *graphein*, to write.] an ancient manuscript.

pā·lē·og′rá·phẽr, pā·lae·og′rá·phẽr, *n.* one skilled in paleography.

pā″lē·ō·graph′iç, pā″lae·ō·graph′iç, *a.* pertaining to paleography.

pā″lē·ō·graph′iç·ăl, pā″lae·ō·graph′iç·ăl, *a.* same as *paleographic.*

pā·lē·og′rá·phy, pā·lae·og′rá·phy, *n.* 1. an ancient manner of writing; also, ancient writings collectively.
2. the art or science of decipering ancient inscriptions, writings, manuscripts, documents, etc.; the study of ancient writings.

pā″lē·ō·iċh″thy·ō·loġ′iç·ăl, pā″lae·ō·iċh″thy·ō·loġ′iç·ăl, *a.* paleichthyological.

pā″lē·ō·iċh·thy·ol′ō·ġist, pā″lae·ō·iċh·thy·ol′ō·ġist, *n.* a paleichthyologist.

pā″lē·ō·iċh·thy·ol′ō·ġy, pā″lae·ō·iċh·thy·ol′ō·ġy, *n.* paleichthyology.

pá·lē′ō·lá, *n.*; *pl.* **pá·lē′ō·lae,** [LL., dim. of L. *palea*, chaff.] in botany, a scale in the inflorescence of grasses; a small palea.

pā′lē·ō·lāte (*or* pá·lē′), *a.* supplied with paleolae.

pā′lē·ō·lith, pā′lae·ō·lith, *n.* [*paleo-*, and Gr. *lithos*, stone.] any unpolished stone implement of the paleolithic period.

pā″lē·ō·lith′iç, pā″lae·ō·lith′iç, *a.* designating or of the period of the Stone Age between the eolithic and the neolithic, or to its culture, characterized by the use of stone tools.

pā″lē·ō·lith′iç·ăl, pā″lae·ō·lith′iç·ăl, *a.* paleolithic.

pā″lē·ō·lith′iç man, in anthropology, any one of several kinds of man of the paleolithic period, including Cro-Magnon, Heidelberg, and Neanderthal man.

pā·lē·ol′ō·ġist, pā·lae·ol′ō·ġist, *n.* one versed in paleology.

pā·lē·ol′ō·ġy, pā·lae·ol′ō·ġy, *n.* the study or knowledge of antiquities; archaeology.

pā·lē·on·tō·graph′iç, *a.* paleontographical.

pā·lē·on·tō·graph′iç·ăl, pā·lae·on·tō·graph′iç·ăl, *a.* of or pertaining to paleontography.

pā″lē·on·tog′rá·phy, pā″lae·on·tog′rá·phy, *n.* [*paleo-*, Gr. *ōn, ontos*, being, and *-graphy.*] the description of fossils.

pā·lē·on·tō·loġ′iç, pā·lae·on·tō·loġ′iç, *a.* paleontological.

pā·lē·on·tō·loġ′iç·ăl, pā·lae·on·tō·loġ′iç·ăl, *a.* pertaining to paleontology.

pā·lē·on·tō·loġ′iç·ăl·ly, pā·lae·on·tō·loġ′iç·ăl·ly, *adv.* according to paleontology.

pā″lē·on·tol′ō·ġist, pā″lae·on·tol′ō·ġist, *n.* one versed in paleontology.

pā″lē·on·tol′ō·ġy, pā″lae·on·tol′ō·ġy, *n.* 1. the branch of geology that deals with prehistoric forms of life through the study of plant and animal fossils.
2. a treatise on this subject.

pā″lē·ō·phyt′iç, pā″lae·ō·phyt′iç, *a.* [*paleo-*, and Gr. *phyton*, plant.] relating to fossil plants; paleobotanical.

pā″lē·ō·phy̆·tō·loġ′iç·ăl, pā″lae·ō·phy̆·tō·loġ′iç·ăl, *a.* pertaining to paleophytology.

pā″lē·ō·phy̆·tol′ō·ġist, pā″lae·ō·phy̆·tol′ō·ġist, *n.* one versed in paleophytology.

pā″lē·ō·phy̆·tol′ō·ġy, pā″lae·ō·phy̆·tol′ō·ġy, *n.* paleobotany.

pā·lē·or″ni·thō·log′iç·ăl, pā·lae·or″ni·thō·log′iç·ăl, *a.* pertaining to paleornithology.

pā·lē·or·ni·thol′ō·ġy, pā·lae·or·ni·thol′ō·ġy, *n.* the science of fossil birds; that branch of paleontology which deals with fossil birds.

pā″lē·ō·teçh′niç, pā″lae·ō·teçh′niç, *a.* of or belonging to ancient art.

pā′lē·ō·thēre, pā″lē·ō·thē′ri·ăn, etc. same as *palaeothere*, etc.

pā″lē·ō·trop′iç·ăl, pā″lae·ō·trop′iç·ăl, *a.* of or relating to the tropical and subtropical regions of the eastern hemisphere, of which there are three arbitrary divisions, the Ethiopian or western, the Indian or middle, and the Australian or eastern.

pā′lē·ō·ty̆pe, *n.* same as *palaeotype*.

pā′lē·ous, *a.* [L. *palea*, chaff.] chaffy; like chaff; paleiform. [Rare.]

pā″lē·ō·vol·çan′iç, pā″lae·ō·vol·çan′iç, *a.* relating to or designating those eruptive rocks which are ascribed to a period preceding the Tertiary.

Pā″lē·ō·zō′iç, Pā″lae·ō·zō′iç, *a.* [*paleo-*, and Gr. *zōē*, life.]

1. designating or of the era between the Proterozoic and the Mesozoic, characterized by the development of fish and sea plants, the first amphibians, land plants, and reptiles, and later by temperature extremes which destroyed many of these: coal, oil, and many fossils were produced at this time.

2. of the rocks of this era.

the Paleozoic; the Paleozoic Era or its rocks.

pā″lē·ō·zō·ō·log′iç·ăl, pā″lae·ō·zō·ō·log′iç·ăl, *a.* pertaining to paleozoology.

pā″lē·ō·zō·ol′ō·ġy, pā″lae·ō·zō·ol′ō·ġy, *n.* that branch of paleontology which deals with fossil animals.

pale′ṣie, pale′ṣy, *n.* palsy. [Obs.]

Pal·es·tin′i·ăn, *a.* of or relating to Palestine or its people.

Pal·es·tin′i·ăn, *n.* a native or inhabitant of Palestine.

pȧ·les′trȧ, *n.*; *pl.* **pȧ·les′trae,** same as *palaestra*.

pȧ·les′trăl, *a.* palaestric.

pȧ·les′tri·ăn, *a.* palaestric.

pȧ·les′triç, *a.* same as *palaestric*.

pȧ·les′triç·ăl, *a.* palestric.

pal′et, *n.* same as *palea*.

pā·lē″ti·ō·log′iç·ăl, *a.* same as *palaetiological*.

pā·lē·ti·ol′ō·ġist, *n.* same as *palaetiologist*.

pā·lē·ti·ol′ō·ġy, *n.* same as *palaetiology*.

pal′ē·tōt (-tō), *n.* [Fr.] 1. an overcoat; greatcoat.

2. a loose jacket worn by women and children.

pal′ette, *n.* [Fr. *palette*, from LL. *paleta*, dim. from L. *pala*, a spade or shovel.]

1. a thin oval or oblong tablet or board, having a hole near one edge through which the thumb is inserted, used by artists for mixing or holding pigments.

PAINTER'S PALETTE

2. the set of colors used by a particular artist or for a particular painting.

3. in metalworking, the breastplate against which a person leans to furnish pressure for the hand drill.

4. in old armor, one of the protective plates for covering the junction of the armor at the armpits, the bend of the shoulder, and elbows. They were sometimes circular, and sometimes in the form of shields.

5. an adhesive disk-shaped organ on the tarsi of certain water beetles.

to set the palette; to lay pigments on the palette in certain order, selecting them according to the key in which the picture is to be painted.

ARMOR PALETTES

pal′ette knīfe (nīf), a knife with a thin, flexible, blunt-edged, steel blade, used by painters for mixing colors and for cleaning the palette.

pāle′wīṣe, *adv.* in heraldry, by vertical bands of alternating tinctures; as, divided *palewise*.

pa̤l′frey, *n.*; *pl.* **pa̤l′freyṣ,** [Fr. *palefroi*, older *palefrei*; LL. *parafredus*, from L. *paraveredus*, an extra post horse; Gr. *para*, beside, and L. *veredus*, a post horse, from *vehere*, to carry, and *reda*, a carriage.]

1. an ordinary riding horse as distinguished from a war horse. [Archaic.]

2. a small saddle horse for a woman. [Archaic.]

pa̤l′freyed (-frid), *a.* riding on or provided with a palfrey. [Archaic.]

pa̤l′grāve, *n.* same as *palsgrave*.

pā′lī, *n.* plural of *palus*.

Pä′lï, *n.* [Hind. *Pālī*.] the sacred language of the Buddhists, not now spoken, but used only in religious works. It was one of the Prakrit dialects of India.

Pal″i·çou′rē·ȧ, *n.* [etym. unknown.] in botany, a large genus of shrubs, family *Rubiaceæ*, native to tropical America and characterized by yellow or white flowers: some species are poisonous.

pal″i·fi·çā′tion, *n.* [L. *palus*, a stake or post, and *facere*, to make.] the act or practice of driving piles or posts into the ground to make a firm foundation. [Obs.]

pā′li·form, *a.* [L. *palus*, stake, and *-form*.] shaped like or resembling a palus; as, a *paliform* lobe.

pal′i·kär, *n.* [Gr. *palikari*, young man, from *pallēx*, a youth.]

1. a member of the Greek militia in the war against Turkey, waged from 1821 to 1828.

2. any soldier in the Greek or Albanian militia.

Pal·i·li′ci·um (-lish′), *n.* in astronomy, formerly, the entire cluster of the Hyades.

pȧ·lil′lō·ġy, *n.* [Gr. *palillogia*; *palin*, again, and *legein*, to speak.] in rhetoric, the repetition of a word or part of a sentence for greater emphasis; as,

Alone, alone, all, all alone,
Alone on a *wide, wide* sea. —Coleridge.

pal′imp·sest, *n.* [Gr. *palimpsēstos*, rubbed again; *palin*, again, and *psēn*, to rub.] a parchment, tablet, etc. that has been written upon or inscribed two or three times, the previous text or texts having been imperfectly erased and remaining, therefore, still visible.

pal′imp·sest, *a.* of or in the form of a palimpsest; written upon or engraved more than once.

pal′i·năl, *a.* [Gr. *palin*, backward.] relating to or characterized by backward motion of the lower jaw, as in the mastication of food: opposed to *proal*.

pal′in·drōme, *n.* [Gr. *palindromos*, running back; *palin*, again and *dromos*, a running.] a word, verse, or sentence that is the same when read backward or forward; as, *madam*, or *Roma tibi subito motibus ibit amor*.

pal·in·drom′iç, *a.* of or pertaining to a palindrome; of the nature of a palindrome; reading the same backward or forward.

pal·in·drom′iç·ăl, *a.* palindromic.

pȧ·lin′drō·mist, *n.* one who writes palindromes.

pā̤l′ing, *n.* 1. the action of making a fence of pales; fencing.

2. a fence made of pales.

3. pales collectively; material for fencing.

4. a strip of wood used in making a fence; a pale.

pāl′ing bōard, the outside part of a tree, taken from the sides to square the tree and fit it to be sawed up into boards. [Brit.]

pal″in·ġē·nē′si·ȧ, *n.* palingenesis.

pal·in·ġen′ē·sis, *n.* [Gr. *palin*, again, and *genesis*, generation.]

1. birth over again; regeneration.

2. the doctrine of successive rebirths; metempsychosis.

3. that phase in the development of an individual plant or animal which repeats the evolutional history of the group to which it belongs: opposed to *cenogenesis*.

4. the change in form and structure of an insect during its development; metamorphosis.

5. spontaneous generation. [Obs.]

pal·in·ġen′e·sy, *n.* palingenesis.

pal″in·ġē·net′iç, *a.* of or relating to palingenesis.

pal″in·ġē·net′iç·ăl·ly, *adv.* in a palingenetic manner; according to palingenesis.

pal′i·nōde, *n.* [Gr. *palinōdia*; *palin*, again, and *ōdē*, a song.] a song or poem in which the writer contradicts or retracts something said in a former one; hence, a recantation; a retraction.

pal·i·nō′di·ăl, *a.* relating to a palinode, recantation, or retraction.

pal′i·nō·dy, *n.* a palinode. [Archaic.]

Pal·i·nū′rus, *n.* [from *Palinurus*, a steersman in the Aeneid.] the single genus of the *Palinuridæ*, a marine family of decapods. The rock lobster, *Palinurus vulgaris*, is found along the western coasts of England.

pal·i·sāde′, *n.* [Fr. *palissade*; L. *palus*, stake.]

1. a fence or fortification consisting of a row of stakes or posts set firmly in the ground and sharpened on top, as a further defense against invasion.

2. the pales or timbers of which such a fence is constructed.

3. [*pl.*] a line of high cliffs, especially when they show basaltic columnar structure; specifically, [P–] a series of such cliffs on the western bank of the Hudson River.

pal·i·sāde′, *v.t.*; palisaded, *pt.*, *pp.*; palisading, *ppr.* to surround, enclose, or fortify with a palisade.

pal·i·sāde′ cell, one of the cells which compose the tissue of leaves. They are long and lie close to one another at right angles to the surface of the leaf.

pal·i·sāde′ wŏrm, a roundworm, *Strongylus armatus*, which is parasitic in the intestines and blood vessels of the horse, causing serious tumors.

pal·i·sād′ing, *n.* a row of stakes or palisades forming a defense; a palisade.

pal·i·sā′dō, *n.* [Sp.] a palisade. [Rare.]

pāl′ish, *a.* somewhat pale or wan; as, a *palish* face.

pal·is·san′dẽr, *n.* [Fr. *palissandre*.] Brazilian rosewood.

Pȧ·lis·sy′ (-sē′) **wāre,** the ware made by Bernard Palissy, a French potter of the sixteenth century. It is an enameled ware having figures of fish, reptiles, shells, etc., modeled in high relief.

päl′kee, *n.* same as *palanquin*

pa̤ll, *n.* same as *pawl*.

pa̤ll, *n.* [L. *pallium*, a cover (akin to *palla*, a robe, mantle).]

1. a black, purple, or white piece of velvet, etc. used to cover a coffin, hearse, or tomb.

2. a dark or gloomy covering; as, a *pall* of smoke.

3. a rich cloth or coverlet. [Obs.]

PALL

4. a cloak or mantle. [Obs.]

5. in Christian churches, (a) a piece of cloth, or cardboard covered with cloth, used to cover the chalice; (b) an altar cloth.

6. in heraldry, a figure suggestive of the Roman Catholic pallium.

pa̤ll, *v.t.* to cloak; to cover with or as with a pall.

pa̤ll, *v.i.*; palled (pa̤ld), *pt.*, *pp.*; palling, *ppr.* [ME: *pallen*, for *appallen*, appal.] to become vapid; to lose strength, life, spirit, or taste; to become insipid or cloying.

Beauty soon grows familiar to the lover,
Fades in the eye, and *palls* upon the sense.
—Addison.

pa̤ll, *v.t.* 1. to make vapid or insipid; to render spiritless; to weaken; to impair. [Obs.]

The more we raise our love,
The more we *pall*, and cool, and kill his ardor. —Dryden.

2. to cloy; to surfeit; as, to *pall* the appetite.

pa̤ll, *n.* nausea. [Rare.]

pal′lȧ, *n.* in ancient Rome, a large mantle or wrap worn by women.

Pal·lā′di·ăn, *a.* [L. *Palladius*, and *-an*.]

1. of Pallas Athena, Greek goddess of wisdom.

2. of wisdom or learning.

Pal·lā′di·ăn, *a.* relating to or designating a classical Roman style of architecture and decoration introduced by Andrea Palladio, a celebrated Italian architect (1518–80).

pal·lā′diç, *a.* designating or of chemical compounds containing palladium with a valence of four.

Pal·lā′di·um, *n.*; *pl.* **Pal·lā′di·ȧ,** [Gr. *palladion*, a sacred statue or image, from *Pallas*, the goddess.]

1. in ancient Greece and Rome, any statue of the Greek goddess Pallas Athena; specifically, the statue in Troy on the preservation of which the safety of the city was supposed to depend.

2. [p–] any safeguard, as of a city or institution.

3. [p–] an object or principle upon which the safety or security of something is dependent.

pal·lā′di·um, *n.* [Mod. L., from *Pallas*, the asteroid, from Gr. *Pallas*, the goddess.] a rare, silvery-white, ductile, malleable, metallic chemical element of the platinum group, which in powdered or spongy form is capable of absorbing large quantities of hydrogen and other gases: it is used as a catalyst, in alloys with gold, silver, and other metals, in jewelry, etc.: symbol Pd; atomic weight, 106.7; atomic number 46.

pal·lā′di·um·īze, *v.t.*; palladiumized, *pt., pp.*; palladiumizing, *ppr.* to coat with palladium; to treat with palladium.

pal·lā′dous, pal′ȧ·dous, *a.* designating or of chemical compounds containing palladium with a valence of two.

pal′lȧh, *n.* in zoology, a large bay-colored species of antelope, *Æpyceros melampus*, found in South Africa.

Pal′lȧs, *n.* [Gr.]

1. in Greek mythology, a name for Athena, the goddess of wisdom: also *Pallas Athena.*

PALLAS

2. one of the small planets, or asteroids, revolving between the orbits of Mars and Jupiter.

pal′lȧs·īte, *n.* an iron meteorite found by P. S. Pallas, Prussian naturalist, in Siberia in 1772, and carried to St. Petersburg.

pall′beâr″ẽr, *n.* [*pall* (cloth) and *bearer*: formerly, one who held the edges of the pall.] one of the persons who attend the coffin at a funeral.

päl′lẹ, *n.pl.* [It.] the six balls, five of which were red and the other white, used as a cognizance or distinguishing mark, and subsequently as heraldic bearings, by the Medici family. They frequently occur in Italian works of art.

pal·les′cence, *n.* [L. *pallescens* (*-entis*), ppr. of *pallescere*, to grow pale.] paleness; a turning pale. [Rare.]

pal′let, *n.* [Fr. *palette*, from LL. *paleta*, dim. from L. *pala*, a spade or shovel.] in heraldry, a diminutive of the pale, containing only one-half of it in breadth.

pal′let, *n.* [OFr. *pailet*, from *paille*, straw; L. *palea*, chaff.] a straw bed or mattress: often connoting a poor or inferior bed.

pal′let, *n.* [from Fr. *palette.*]

1. a wooden tool consisting of a flat blade with a handle; especially, such a tool used by potters for smoothing and rounding.

2. a painter's palette.

3. in bookbinding, a tool for printing letters on the binding of a book.

4. in mechanics, a part of a machine that changes back-and-forth motion to circular motion, or vice versa, by engaging the teeth of a ratchet wheel; a pawl; a click; especially, any of the clicks or pawls in the escapement of a clock or watch, which regulate the speed by releasing one tooth of a ratchet wheel at each swing of the pendulum or turn of the balance wheel.

5. a low, portable platform, usually double-faced, on which materials are stacked for storage or transportation, as in a warehouse.

pal′let·ed, *a.* in heraldry, conjoined by a pallet; as, a chevron *palleted.*

pal′lette, *n.* [Fr. *palette.*] a plate in the armpit of a suit of armor.

pal′li·ăl, *a.* pertaining to or produced by a mantle, especially the mantle of shellfishes.

pallial chamber; in zoology, the cavity enclosed by the mantle.

pallial impression or *line*; the mark formed in a bivalve shell by the pallium, or mantle.

pallial sinus; in zoology, a sinus or cavity in the pallial line of certain bivalve shells, showing where the siphons are withdrawn.

pal′li·ȧ·ment, *n.* [L. *pallium*, a cloak.] a dress; a robe. [Obs.]

pal′liȧrd (-yȧrd), *n.* [Fr.] 1. a lecher; a lewd person. [Obs.]

2. a vagabond. [Obs.]

pal·liasse′ (-lyas′), *n.* see *paillasse.*

pal′li·āte, *v.t.*; palliated, *pt., pp.*; palliating, *ppr.* [Fr. *pallier*, to cloak, palliate, from L. *pallium*, a cloak.]

1. to lessen the pain or severity of without curing; to alleviate; ease.

2. to make (a crime, offense, etc.) appear less serious than it is; to excuse; extenuate.

Syn.—cover, extenuate, gloss, soften.

pal′li·āte, *a.* 1. eased; mitigated. [Obs.]

2. cloaked as with a mantle; hidden; covered. [Obs.]

pal·li·ā′tion, *n.* 1. the act of palliating; extenuation, as of an offense, or alleviation, as of pain.

2. a thing that palliates.

pal′li·ā·tive, *a.* 1. extenuating; serving to extenuate by excuses or favorable representation.

2. mitigating; alleviating.

pal′li·ā·tive, *n.* 1. that which extenuates.

2. that which mitigates, alleviates, or abates the violence of pain, disease, or other evil.

pal′li·ā·tŏr, *n.* a person or thing that palliates.

pal′li·ȧ·tō·ry, *a.* palliative.

pal′lid, *a.* [L. *pallidus*, from *pallere*, to become pale.] pale; wan; faint in color; as, a *pallid* countenance; *pallid* blue.

pal·lid′i·ty, *n.* paleness.

pal′lid·ly, *adv.* in a pallid manner.

pal′lid·ness, *n.* paleness; wanness; pallidity.

pal′li·ō-, [from Latin *pallium*, mantle.] a combining form meaning *pallium.*

Pal″li·ō·brañ·ċhi·ā′tȧ, *n.pl.* [*pallio-* and *branchia*, gills.] in zoology, formerly, the *Brachiopoda.*

pal″li·ō·brañ′ċhi·āte, *a.* of or pertaining to the *Palliobranchiata.*

pal′liŏn (-yun), *n.* [It. *pallone*, ball.] a little pellet.

pal′liŏn, *n.* a pavilion. [Obs.]

pal″li·ō·ped′ăl, *a.* [*pallio-*, and L. *pes*, foot.] of or pertaining to the foot and the pallium.

pal′li·um, *n.*; *pl.* **pal′li·ȧ,** [L., cloak, mantle.]

1. in ancient Greece, a large, oblong mantle worn by men: also called *himation.*

2. in ecclesiastical usage, (a) an early form of mantle worn by various Christian devotees, as by a monk; (b) a form of vestment formerly worn by patriarchs and metropolitans of the Eastern Church; (c) in the Roman Catholic Church, a vestment consisting of a narrow band encircling the shoulders, and having two short vertical pieces, one of which rests upon the breast, the other on the back: it is given by the Pope to archbishops, to be worn only on certain high feasts; (d) an altar cloth.

3. in zoology, the mantle of a bivalve mollusk.

4. in anatomy, the entire cerebral cortex.

5. in meteorology, the sky when entirely and uniformly covered by cirro-stratus clouds.

pall′-mall′ (pel′mel′), *n.* [OFr. *palemail*; It. *pallamaglio*, from *palla*, a ball, and *maglio*, L. *malleus*, a mallet, a hammer.]

1. an old game in which a boxwood ball was struck by a mallet through an iron ring hung at the end of an alley.

2. the alley in which it was played.

pal·lō·met′riç, *a.* [Gr. *pallein*, to shake, and *metron*, measure.] of or relating to a means of measuring artificial vibrations of the earth's surface.

päl·lō′nẹ, *n.* [It.] a game in which a large leather ball is struck by the player's arm, which is encased in leather as a protection.

pal′lŏr, *n.* [L.] lack of color; unnatural paleness, as of the face.

pälm (päm), *n.* [L. *palma*, the palm of the hand; Gr. *palamē*, the palm of the hand.

1. the inner part or surface of the hand between the fingers and wrist.

2. the part of a glove, etc. that covers the palm.

3. the broad, flat part of an antler, as of a moose, deer, etc.

4. a unit of measure equal to either the width of the hand (3 to 4 inches) or its length (7 to 9 inches).

5. any broad, flat part at the end of an arm, handle, etc., as the blade of an oar.

6. a metal disk used by sailmakers over the palm of the hand to push a needle through canvas.

to grease the palm of; to bribe.

to have an itching palm; to desire money greedily. [Colloq.]

pälm, *v.t.*; palmed, *pt., pp.*; palming, *ppr.* 1. to conceal (something) in the palm of the hand, as in a sleight-of-hand trick.

2. to touch with the palm.

to palm off; to pass off by fraud or deceit.

pälm, *n.* [ME. *palme*; AS. *palm*; L. *palma*: so named because the fronded leaf somewhat resembles the palm of the hand.]

1. any of several kinds of tropical or subtropical trees having a tall, branchless trunk with a bunch of huge leaves at the top.

2. a leaf of this tree carried or worn as a symbol of victory, triumph, joy, etc.

3. victory; triumph.

4. a representation of a palm leaf or frond given in lieu of a second award of the same military decoration, as of the croix de guerre.

COCOANUT PALM (*Cocos nucifera*)

to bear (or *carry off*) *the palm*; to be the winner; to take the prize; to be supreme.

to yield the palm to; to acknowledge the superiority of; to admit to defeat by.

Pal·mā′cē·ae, *n.pl.* same as *Palmæ.*

pal·mā′ceous, *a.* pertaining to or resembling a palm tree.

pal′mȧ Ċhris′ti, [L., hand of Christ.] the castor-oil plant.

pal′mȧ·cīte, *n.* any fossil regarded as of the palms. [Obs.]

Päl′mae, *n.pl.* a family of monocotyledons, the palms, endogens chiefly inhabiting the tropics, having fleshy, colorless, six-parted flowers enclosed within spathes and a trunk that is usually unbranched, bearing a tuft of large leaves at the top: also called *Palmaceæ, Arecaceæ.*

pal′mãr, *a.* [L. *palmaris.*] of, in, or corresponding to the palm of the hand.

pal′mãr, *n.* 1. a palmar nerve or muscle.

2. in zoology, a joint or ossicle in the brachial skeleton of a crinoid.

pal′mȧ·ry, *a.* [L. *palmarius.*] bearing or worthy to bear the palm; pre-eminent; victorious.

pal′mȧ·ry, *a.* pertaining to the palm; palmar. [Rare.]

pal′māte, *a.* [L. *palmatus*, from *palma*, palm.] shaped like a hand with the fingers spread; specifically, (a) in botany, having veins or lobes radiating from a common center: said of some leaves; (b) in zoology, web-footed, as many water birds.

pal′mā·ted, *a.* same as *palmate.*

pal′māte·ly, *adv.* in a palmate manner.

PALMATE TUBERS

pal·mat′i·fid, *a.* [L. *palmatus*, palmate, and *fid*, root of *findere*, to split.] cleft palmately.

pal·mat′i·fọrm, *a.* [L. *palmatus* and *forma.*] palmate.

pal·mat·i·lō′bāte, *a.* [L. *palmatus*, and E. *lobate.*] lobed palmately.

pal·mat′i·lōbed, *a.* same as *palmatilobate.*

pal·mā′tion, *n.* 1. the state or quality of being palmate; palmate formation or structure.

2. a part or division of a palmate formation.

pal·mat·i·pär′tīte, *a.* [L. *palmatus*, and *partite.*] palmate with divisions more than halfway to the base.

pal·mat′i·seçt, *a.* [L. *palmatus* and *sectus*, pp. of *secare*, to cut.] palmate with divisions nearly to the base.

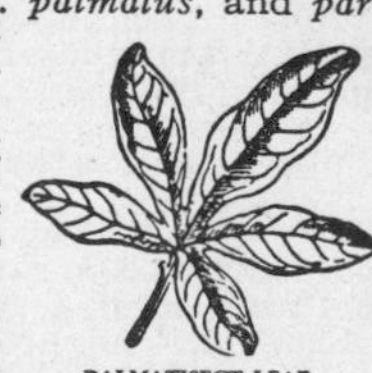

PALMATISECT LEAF

pälm′bärk tree (päm′), an Australian conservatory plant, *Melaleuca wilsoni*, of the myrtle family.

Pälm Bēach çloth, a lightweight cotton and mohair fabric used for men's summer suits: a trade-mark.

pälm bird, any bird nesting in palms, as a weaverbird.

pälm but'tēr, palm oil.

pälm çab'băge, the edible terminal bud of a cabbage palm.

pälm çat, a paradoxure.

pälm çrab, a tree crab, or purse crab of the genus *Birgus*.

pälmed, *a.* having the antlers palmate: said of a full-grown stag.

Pal·mel'là, *n.* [LL., dim. from Gr. *palmos*, vibration, from *pallein*, to shake.] a genus of green-spored algae in which the chlorophyll sometimes becomes red, as in gory dew, *Palmella cruenta*. They grow on damp surfaces, and propagate with great rapidity.

palmella stage or *condition*; a stage or phase in the development of certain algae in which colonies are formed surrounded by a gelatinous mass resembling species of *Palmella*.

pal'mel·lin, *n.* the substance giving the red color to gory dew (*Palmella cruenta*).

pälm'ēr, (päm'), *n.* [Anglo-Fr. *palmer*; ML. *palmarius*, from L. *palma*, the palm.]

1. a pilgrim who carried a palm leaf as a sign that he had been to the Holy Land; hence, any pilgrim.

2. a palmer worm; hence, in angling, a bait made in imitation of a hairy caterpillar: also called *palmer fly*.

3. a wood louse. [Rare.]

pälm'ēr, *n.* one who palms; a cheater.

pälm'ēr flȳ, a palmer (a bait).

pälm'ēr wọrm, 1. any of various hairy caterpillars, particularly that of the tiger moth, *Arctia caja*: so called because it wanders like a palmer, and devours leaves and herbage.

2. the larva of a small North American moth, *Ypsolophus pometellus*, which is very destructive to the leaves of the apple and other fruit trees.

pälm'ēr·y, *n.* a place where palms are grown.

pal·mette' (-met'), *n.* [Fr.] an architectural ornament somewhat resembling the leaf of a palm.

pal·met'tō, *n.* [Sp. *palmito*, dim. from L. *palma*, palm.]

1. any of several species of palm tree growing in the West Indies and in the southern part of the United States. The cabbage palmetto, *Sabal palmetto*, of the southern Atlantic coast of the United States is characterized by the hardness and durability of its wood, which is used for piles and for building wharves, and by the adaptability of the fiber in its leaves for making hats, fans, mats, etc.

2. the dwarf fan palm, *Chamærops humilis*, of southern Europe and northern Africa, the fiber of which is known as vegetable horsehair.

3. a hat made from the leaves of the palmetto.

palmetto flag; a flag bearing a palmetto tree on its canton; the flag of the state of South Carolina.

palmetto state; the state of South Carolina: so named from the species of the palmetto found within its borders.

royal palmetto; (a) the *Sabal umbraculifera* of the West Indies, the leaves of which are used for thatching and the trunk for making water pipes: it grows to a height of eighty feet or more: also called *big thatch* and *bull thatch*; (b) the silk-top palmetto.

pälm hŏn'ey, a syrup made from the sap of the coquito in Chile and used by the natives as a substitute for sugar.

pal'miç, *a.* same as *palmitic*.

pal·miç'ō·lous, *a.* [L. *palma*, palm, and *colere*, to inhabit.] attached to or living on palm trees; as, *palmicolous* insects or fungi.

Pal·mi·daç'ty·lēş, *n.pl.* [L. *palma*, palm, and Gr. *daktylos*, finger.] a group of web-footed birds distinct from *Natatores*.

pal·mif'ēr·ous, *a.* [L. *palma*, palm, and *ferre*, to bear.] bearing palms.

pal'mi·fọrm, *a.* same as *palmatiform*.

pal'mi·grāde, *a.* [L. *palma*, palm, and *gradi*, to walk.] walking on the whole sole of the foot; plantigrade, as the bear and some other mammals.

pal'mine, *n.* same as *palmitin*.

pal'mi·nērve, *a.* same as *palminerved*.

pal'mi·nērved, *a.* [L. *palma*, palm, and *nervus*, nerve.] having the nerves arranged palmately.

pal'mi·ped, pal'mi·pēde, *a.* [L. *palma*, palm, and *pes*, *pedis*, foot.] web-footed; having the toes connected by a membrane, as a water-fowl.

pal'mi·ped, pal'mi·pēde, *n.* a web-footed bird; one of the *Palmipedes*.

Pal·mip'e·dēş, *n.pl.* same as *Natatores*.

pälm'ist, *n.* [back-formation from *palmistry*.] a person who practices palmistry.

pal'mis·tēr, *n.* a palmist [Archaic.]

pälm'is·try (*formerly also* pal'), *n.* [ME. *paumestrie*.]

1. the pretended art of telling a person's fortune by the lines and marks of the palm of his hand.

2. a dexterous use of the hand; sleight of hand.

pal'mi·tāte, *n.* a salt or ester of palmitic acid.

pal'mīte, *n.* an aquatic plant of South Africa, *Prionium palmita*, belonging to the rush family, having long, notched leaves and stems which are used in making brushes.

pal·mit'iç, *a.* [from L. *palma*, the palm.] designating or of a colorless, crystalline fatty acid, $CH_3(CH_2)_{14}CO_2H$, found uncombined in palm oil and as the glyceryl ester in other vegetable and animal fats and oils.

pal'mi·tin, *n.* a colorless crystalline compound, $C_3H_5(C_{15}H_{31}COO)_3$, found in palm oil and many other fats: it is the glyceryl ester of palmitic acid.

pal'mi·tōne, *n.* the ketone of palmitic acid, $(C_{15}H_{31})_2CO$, formed by the distillation of calcium or barium palmitate with lime.

pal'mi·vẹined (-vānd), *a.* having the veins radiating from the apex of the petiole, as in the leaf of the linden.

pälm lēaf, the leaf of a palm tree, especially of one of the palmettos, used to make fans, hats, etc.

pal·mod'iç, *a.* [Gr. *palmōdēs*, pulselike; *palmos*, vibration, and *eidos*, form.] pertaining to or affected by palmus.

pälm oil, a yellow or reddish fat obtained from the fruit of several kinds of palms, especially the West African oil palm, used in making soap, candles, etc.

pälm sụg'ăr (shụg'ăr), sugar from the sap of certain palm trees.

Pälm Sun'dāy, the Sunday next preceding Easter, commemorating in Christian churches Jesus' entry into Jerusalem, when the people strewed palm branches before him.

pälm tree, any tree of the order *Palmæ*.

pal'mus, *n.* [LL., from Gr. *palmos*, palpitation, from *pallein*, to shake.] in medicine, a throb or twitch; specifically, a saltatory spasm.

pälm'y, *a.*; *comp.* palmier; *superl.* palmiest, 1. abounding in or shaded by palm trees.

2. of or like a palm or palms.

3. bearing or worthy to bear the palm; triumphant.

4. flourishing; prosperous; successful; as, *palmy* days.

Syn.—prosperous, glorious, distinguished, victorious, flourishing.

pal·mȳ'rà, *n.* [Port. *palmeira*, from L. *palma*, the palm: sp. affected by false association with *Palmyra*, a city in Syria.] the most common palm of India, *Borassus flabelliformis*, the wood of which is very hard, black, heavy, durable, and takes a high polish. It grows to a height of 40 to 60 feet. The large rounded leaves are shaped like a fan and are used to make thatching, matting, hats, etc. Also *palmyra palm*, *palmyra tree*.

pä'lō, *n.* same as *gulancha*.

pä'lō blañ'çō, a small tree, a variety of *Celtis occidentalis*, the American hackberry, found in the western part of the United States from Texas to Oregon.

pà·lō'lō, pà·lō'là, *n.* [native name.]

1. a dorsibranchiate marine annelid, *Palolo viridis*, found in great abundance in the sea near the coral reefs of the Samoan Islands.

2. [P–] the generic name of the palolo.

pä·lō·mẹ'tà, *n.* a fish, the pompano.

pal·ō·mī'nō, *n.* [Am. Sp., dim. of *paloma*, pigeon, dove: orig. applied to horses of a dovelike color.] a brownish-gray or golden horse that has a silvery-white or ivory mane and tail.

pà·loo'kà, *n.* [coined by Jack Conway (died 1928), one-time baseball player, and later writer for *Variety*.] in sports, an incompetent or easily defeated player. [Slang.]

palp, *n.* a feeler; a palpus.

palp, *v.t.* to feel; to have a feeling of.

pal·pà·bil'i·ty, *n.* the quality of being perceptible by the touch.

pal'pà·ble, *a.* [Fr., from L. *palpabilis*; *palpare*, to touch.]

1. that can be touched, felt, or handled; tangible.

2. easily perceived by the senses; audible, recognizable, perceptible, noticeable, etc.

3. clear to the mind; obvious; evident; plain.

Syn.—discernible, manifest, unmistakable, gross, plain.

pal'pà·ble·ness, *n.* the quality of being palpable; plainness; obviousness; grossness.

pal'pà·bly, *adv.* 1. in such a manner as to be perceived by the touch.

2. grossly; plainly; obviously.

pal'pāte, *v.t.*; palpated, *pt.*, *pp.*; palpating, *ppr.* to examine by touch, or palpation, as for medical diagnosis.

pal'pāte, *a.* provided with a palpus or palpi; having feelers.

pal·pā'tion, *n.* [L. *palpatio*, from *palpare*, to feel, to stroke.]

1. the act of feeling.

2. in medicine, the process of examining by means of touch.

pal·pā'tŏr, *n.* [L., from *palpare*, to stroke.]

1. in zoology, one of a suborder of clavicorn beetles with ovate glistening bodies and prominent hind coxae.

2. one of a suborder of arachnids characterized by slender, filiform palpi, a short sternum, free maxillary lobe of the first pair of legs, and genital opening near the mouth, as the daddy-longlegs.

pal'pē·brà, *n.*; *pl.* **pal'pē·brae,** [L.] the eyelid.

pal'pē·brăl, *a.* pertaining to the eyelids.

pal'pē·brāte, *a.* having eyelids.

pal·pē·brī'tis, *n.* blepharitis.

palped (palpt), *a.* provided with a palpus or palpi.

pal'pī, *n.* plural of *palpus*.

pal'pi·cil, *n.* [LL. *palpus*, feeler, and *cilium*.] any of the hairlike processes of the ectoderm carrying a tactile nerve filament.

pal'pi·çorn, *n.* [LL. *palpus*, feeler, and L. *cornu*, horn.] one of the *Palpicornia*, a group of beetles with short, club-shaped antennae and long, maxillary palpi.

pal'pi·çorn, *a.* having short, club-shaped antennae; belonging to the *Palpicornia*.

pal'pi·fēr, *n.* the part of an insect that carries a maxillary palpus.

pal·pif'ēr·ous, *a.* [LL. *palpus*, feeler, and *ferre*, to bear.] bearing palpi, especially maxillary palpi: said of insects and crustaceans.

pal'pi·fọrm, *a.* [LL. *palpus*, feeler, and L. *forma*, form.] having the form of palpi, or feelers.

pal'pi·ġēr, *n.* [LL. *palpus*, feeler, and *gerere*, to carry.] that part of an insect to which the labial palpus is attached.

pal·pig'ēr·ous, *a.* bearing palpi, or feelers.

pal'pi·tănt, *a.* palpitating; throbbing; trembling; showing palpitation.

pal'pi·tāte, *v.i.*; palpitated, *pt.*, *pp.*; palpitating, *ppr.* [L. *palpitare*, freq. of *palpare*, to feel.]

1. to beat rapidly; to pulsate violently; to flutter or move with slight throbs, as the heart.

2. to throb; to tremble; to quiver.

Syn.—pant, vibrate, throb, beat, flutter, tremble.

pal·pi·tā'tion, *n.* [L. *palpitatio*.]

1. a rapid, often irregular, beating of the heart from functional disorder, emotion, etc.

2. a trembling; palpitating; quivering; throbbing.

palp'less, *a.* without a palpus or palpi; having no feelers: said of insects and crustaceans.

pal'pō·cil, *n.* same as *palpicil*.

pal'pus, *n.*; *pl.* **pal'pī,** [from L. *palpus*, the soft palm of the hand.] in zoology, a jointed organ or feeler for touching or tasting, attached to the mouth of insects, lobsters, some worms, etc.

palş'grāve, *n.* [D. *paltsgrave*, from *palts*, from L. *palatium*, palace, and *graaf*, a count.] formerly, in Germany, a count or earl who had the superintendence of the king's palace; a count palatine.

palş'grà·vine, *n.* the wife or widow of a palsgrave.

pạl'şied, *a.* 1. having palsy; paralyzed.

2. shaking; tottering; trembling.

pal'stăff, *n.*; *pl.* **pal'stāveş,** in archaeology, an ax-shaped implement having a groove on each side terminating in a stop ridge and with lateral flanges designed to secure a hold on the handle.

pal'stēr, *n.* [D., from *pael*, stake.] a pilgrim's staff. [Obs.]

pạl'şy, *n.* [a contr. of *paralysis*.] paralysis in

any part of the body, sometimes accompanied with involuntary tremors.

Bell's palsy; paralysis of one side of the face, produced by a lesion of the facial nerve: named after Bell, the English surgeon who first described it.

scrivener's palsy; see *writer's cramp* under *writer*.

shaking palsy; a chronic degenerative disease of the central nervous system, characterized by tremors, muscular rigidity, weakness, and a masklike expression.

pal'sy, *v.t.*; palsied, *pt.*, *pp.*; palsying, *ppr.* 1. to paralyze; to affect with palsy.

2. to make powerless or helpless, as with fear.

pal'sy·wŏrt, *n.* the cowslip, *Primula veris*, which was once thought to be a remedy for palsy.

pal'tĕr, *v.i.*; paltered, *pt.*, *pp.*; paltering, *ppr.* [from dial. *palt*, a rag: the word prob. arose with reference to haggling over cloth prices.]

1. to talk or act insincerely; to deal crookedly; to prevaricate.

2. to trifle; to treat facts, decisions, etc. lightly or carelessly.

3. to quibble, as in bargaining.

pal'tĕr, *v.t.* to squander. [Obs.]

pal'tĕr·ĕr, *n.* one who palters.

pal'tĕr·ly, *a.* paltry. [Obs.]

pal'tock, *n.* [OFr. *paletoque*; Fr. *paletot*.] a man's doublet or jacket with sleeves. [Obs.]

pal'tri·ly, *adv.* in a paltry manner; despicably; meanly.

pal'tri·ness, *n.* the state or quality of being paltry.

pal'try, *a.*; *comp.* paltrier; *superl.* paltriest, [L.G. *paltrig*, *palterig*, *pultrig*, *pulterig*, ragged, from *palte*, *pulte*, a rag, a tatter.] mean; vile; worthless; despicable; trifling; of small value; as, a *paltry* trick, a *paltry* sum.

Syn.—petty, trivial, trifling, little, slight, mean, pitiful.

pȧ·lū'dăl, *a.* [L. *palus*, *paludis*, marsh.]

1. pertaining to marshes; marshy; swampy.

2. in medicine, caused by a marsh; malarial, as fever.

paludal fever; marsh fever; malarial fever.

pȧ·lū'dȧ·ment, *n.* same as *paludamentum*.

pȧ·lū·dȧ·men'tum, *n.* [L.] a military cloak worn by an ancient Roman general commanding an army, his principal officers, and his personal attendants, in contradistinction to the sagum of the common soldier, and the toga, or garb of peace. It hung loosely from the shoulders, reaching to the knees, and was fastened across the chest with a clasp.

Pal·ū·diç'ō·lae, *n.pl.* an order of marsh birds, including rails, cranes, etc.

pȧ·lū'di·çōle, *a.* [LL. *paludicola*; L. *palus*, *paludis*, marsh, and *colere*, to inhabit.] relating to the order *Paludicolæ*.

Pal·ū·dī'nȧ, *n.* a genus of fresh-water snails.

pal·ū·dī'năl, *a.* paludinous; paludine; inhabiting marshes, swamps, or ponds.

pal'ū·dine, *a.* [L. *palus*, *paludis*, marsh.] relating to a swamp or pond.

pȧ·lū'din·ous, *a.* pertaining to the *Paludina*; paludine.

pal'ū·diṣm, *n.* [L. *palus*, *paludis*, marsh.] in medicine, malaria.

pal'ū·dōse, *a.* [L. *paludosus*, from *palus*, *paludis*, marsh.] growing in swamps; marshy.

pal'ū·dous, *a.* malarial; marshy.

pal'ūle, *n.* [LL. *palulus*, dim. of L. *palus*, stake.] a palus.

pal'ū·lus, *n.* a palus.

pā'lus, *n.*; *pl.* **pā'lī,** [L., stake.] a thin vertical septum or lamina in the interior of certain polyp cells, as in some corals.

pȧ·lus'trăl, *a.* [L. *paluster* (*-ustris*).] paludal; marshy. [Rare.]

pȧ·lus'trine, *a.* paludinal; swampy. [Rare.]

pāl'y, *a.* pale; lacking color. [Poet.]

A dim gleam the *paly* lanthorn throws. —Gay.

pāl'y, *a.* [*pale*, a stake.] in heraldry, divided into four or more vertical stripes, or pales, of equal width, in alternating colors: said of the field of an escutcheon.

PALY

pāl'y-bend'y, *a.* having paly divisions cut by diagonal partition lines, either dexter or sinister.

pam, *n.* [from Fr. *pamphile*, from Gr. *pan*, all, and *philos*, beloved.]

1. in card playing, the jack of clubs, as in the game of loo.

2. a card game like napoleon in which the jack of clubs is the highest trump.

pam'ban·man'che, *n.* [Tamil.] a very long canoe, hollowed out of a single tree, used on the Malabar coast: also called *serpent boat*, *snake boat*.

PALY-BENDY

Pä'mir, *n.* Galcha, the Iranian language of the Pamiri.

Pä·mir'i, *n.*; *pl.* **Pä·mir'i,** a Galcha, one of the people living in the Pamirs.

pam'pȧṣ, *n.pl.* [Sp. Am.] extensive South American treeless plains; especially, those in Argentina and the southern regions.

pam'pȧṣ çat, a wildcat, *Felis pajeros*, having yellowish fur striped obliquely with a darker hue; the straw cat of the South American pampas.

pam'pȧṣ deer, a small deer inhabiting the pampas, *Cariacus campestris*, red-brown in color and bearing small antlers.

pam'pȧṣ grȧss, a variety of ornamental, bluish-green grass, *Gynerium argenteum*, common in the pampas of South America. The leaves grow to a length of six to eight feet, with flower stems ten to twelve feet high, bearing silky, silvery-white panicles, or plumes.

PAMPAS GRASS (*Gynerium argenteum*)

pam'pē·ăn, *a.* pertaining to the pampas or their Indian natives.

pam'pē·ăn, *n.* an Indian who lives in the pampas.

pam'pel·moose, *n.* see *pompelmous*.

pam'pĕr, *v.t.*; pampered, *pt.*, *pp.*; pampering, *ppr.* [ME. *pampren*; G. *pampen*, to stuff.]

1. originally, to indulge with rich food; to feed too much; to glut; to gratify to excess.

2. to give too many privileges to; to indulge to excess; as, to *pamper* a child.

Syn.—coddle, pet, indulge, spoil.

pam'pĕred·ness, *n.* the state of being pampered.

pam'pĕr·ĕr, *n.* one who pampers.

pam'pĕr·ize, *v.t.* to pamper. [Rare.]

pam·pe'rō, *n.*; *pl.* **pam·pe'rōs,** [Sp.] a violent west or southwest wind, usually dry and cold, that blows from the Andes across the South American pampas.

pam'phlet, *n.* [OFr. *Pamphilet*, familiar name of a popular ML. poem *Pamphilus, seu de Amore*.]

1. a small, thin, unbound book made up of sheets of paper stapled or stitched together and usually having a paper cover.

2. a treatise published in this form, usually as an argument on some topic of current interest.

pam'phlet, *v.i.* to write and publish a pamphlet or pamphlets.

pam'phlet, *v.t.* to report in a pamphlet or pamphlets.

pam'phlet·ȧge, *n.* pamphlets collectively.

pam'phlet·ăr·y, *a.* of, pertaining to, or like a pamphlet or pamphlets.

pam·phlet·eer', *n.* a writer or publisher of pamphlets.

pam·phlet·eer', *v.i.* to be a writer or publisher of pamphlets.

pam'phlet·ĕr, *n.* a pamphleteer.

pam·phlet'iç, *a.* of or like a pamphlet.

pam·phlet'i·căl, *a.* pamphletic.

pam'phlet·ize, *v.t.* and *v.i.*; pamphletized, *pt.*, *pp.*; pamphletizing, *ppr.* to pamphlet.

pam·pil'iŏn, *n.* 1. a kind of fur used in the fifteenth and sixteenth centuries.

2. a kind of coarse woolen cloth.

pam·pin'i·fōrm, *a.* [L. *pampinus*, tendril, and *forma*, form.] resembling a tendril: applied to a network of ovarian or spermatic veins.

pam·plē'ġi·ȧ, *n.* [Gr. *pan*, all, and *plēgē*, blow.] paralysis of the entire body.

pam'pre (-pĕr), *n.* [Fr.] an ornament composed of vine leaves and bunches of grapes: used for decorating the grooves of spiral columns.

pam·prō·daç'tyl·ous, *a.* [Gr. *pan*, all, *pro*, forward, and *daktylos*, finger.] with all four toes directed toward the front, as in the mousebird.

pan-, [from Gr. *pan*, *pantos*, all.] a combining form meaning: (a) *all*, as in *pan*chromatic, *pan*theism; (b) [P-] *of*, *comprising*, *embracing*, or *common to all* or *every*, as in *Pan*-American; (c) [P-] (*belief in*) *the cooperation, unity, or union of all members of* (a specified nationality, race, church, etc.), as in *Pan*-Americanism. In senses b and c, usually followed by a hyphen, as in *Pan*-Asiatic, *Pan*-European, *Pan*-Germanic, *Pan*-Islam, *Pan*-Slavic, *Pan*-Slavism.

Pan, *n.* [L.; Gr. *Pan*.] in Greek mythology, a god of fields, forests, wild animals, flocks, and shepherds, represented with the legs (and sometimes horns and ears) of a goat: identified by the Romans with Faunas.

PAN

pän, *n.* [Hind. *pān*; Sans. *parṇa*, a leaf, feather.]

1. a leaf of the betel palm.

2. a substance made of this leaf, chewed to increase the flow of saliva.

pan, *n.* [AS. *panne*; D. *pan*; G. *pfanne*, all; said to be early loan word from LL. *panna*, for *patna*, L. *patina*, a broad dish, a pan, from *patere*, to be wide.]

1. any of many kinds of dishes, usually broad, shallow, without a cover, and made of metal, and used for domestic purposes: often in combination; as, a frying *pan*, sauce*pan*, dish*pan*, etc.

2. any object or part of an apparatus shaped like a pan; specifically, (a) an open container for washing out gold, tin, etc. from gravel or the like, in mining; (b) either receptacle in a pair of scales; (c) a container for heating, evaporating, etc.

3. the amount a pan will hold; a panful.

4. a hollow, natural depression in the ground.

5. a layer of hard soil, impervious to water; hardpan.

6. a small ice floe.

7. the part of the flintlock that held the firing powder in old guns and pistols.

8. a face. [Slang.]

9. in carpentry, the socket for a hinge.

10. the rear part of the lower jaw of a whale.

pan, *v.t.*; panned, *pt.*, *pp.*; panning, *ppr.* 1. to cook in a pan.

2. to give an unfavorable criticism of; as, the critic *panned* the play. [Colloq.]

3. in mining, (a) to wash (gravel, etc.) in a pan, as for separating gold; (b) to separate (gold, etc.) from gravel by washing in a pan.

pan, *v.i.* 1. to search for gold by panning.

2. to yield gold as the result of panning.

to pan out; (a) in mining, to yield gold, as gravel, a mine, etc.; (b) [Colloq.] to turn out (in some way); to transpire; (c) [Colloq.] to turn out well; to succeed.

pan, *v.t.* and *v.i.*; panned, *pt.*, *pp.*; panning, *ppr.* [abbrev. from *panorama*.] to move (a motion-picture or television camera) in order to get a panoramic effect or to follow a moving object.

pan, *v.t.* and *v.i.*; panned, *pt.*, *pp.*; panning, *ppr.* [L. *pannus*, piece of cloth.] to join; to fit together. [Scot. or Brit. Dial.]

pan'ȧ·bāse, *n.* [Gr. *pan*, all, and *base*.] a gray copper ore; tetrahedrite. [Obs.]

pan·ȧ·cē'ȧ, *n.* [L., from Gr. *panakeia*; *pan*, all, and *akeisthai*, to cure.]

1. a supposed remedy, cure, or medicine for all diseases or ills; a cure-all.

2. an herb, allheal. [Obs.]

pan·ȧ·cē'ăn, *a.* curing all ills.

pȧ·nache', *n.* [Fr., from OFr. *pennache*; L. *penna*, feather.]

1. a bunch of feathers on a helmet; a plume.

2. dashing elegance of manner; carefree, spirited self-confidence; flamboyance.

3. in heraldry, an upright group of feathers.

4. in zoology, a bunch or tuft, as of hairs; a scopula.

5. in architecture, the triangular surface of a pendentive.

6. in astronomy, a plumelike projection above the solar chromosphere.

pȧ·nä'dȧ, *n.* [Sp. *panada*, from L. *panis*, bread.] a dish, generally for invalids, made of bread or crackers boiled to a pulp and flavored.

pȧ·nāde′, *n.* [ME.] a two-edged knife. [Obs.]

pan·aes·thē′si·ȧ, *n.* same as *panesthesia.*

pan·aes·thet′iç, *a.* same as *panesthetic.*

Pȧ·nā′gi·ȧ, *n.* [Gr. *panagios*; *pan*, all, and *hagios*, holy.]
1. in the Orthodox Eastern Church, a name for the Virgin Mary, signifying all-holy.
2. [p–] a medallion of the Virgin Mary worn as a breast ornament by bishops of the Orthodox Eastern Church.

Pan′ȧ·mä dis·ēase′, a destructive fungus disease affecting bananas, caused by *Fusarium cubense*, which stops up the water-conducting vessels.

Pan′ȧ·mä hat, 1. a fine, hand-plaited hat made from select leaves of a Central and South American palm tree.
2. any similar straw hat.

Pan·ȧ·mā′ni·ăn, *a.* of Panama.

Pan·ȧ·mā′ni·ăn, *n.* a native or inhabitant of Panama.

Pan″-Ȧ·mer′i·căn, *a.* [*pan-* and *American.*] relating to or including North, South, and Central America, or their peoples.

Pan″-Ȧ·mer′i·căn·işm, *n.* belief in, or any theory or policy of, political and economic co-operation, mutual social and cultural understanding, international alliance, etc. among the nations of North, Central, and South America.

Pan″-Ȧ·mer′i·căn Ūn′iŏn, the official international organization of the twenty-one American republics, established to develop closer co-operation among them.

Pan″-Añ′gli·căn, *a.* [*pan-* and *Anglican.*] relating to or including all Anglican and allied churches; as, a *Pan-Anglican* conference.

pȧ·nā′ris, *n.* [altered from *paronychium*, paronychia.] a felon; whitlow; paronychia.

pan′ȧ·ry, *a.* [L. *panis*, bread.] pertaining to bread.

pan·ȧ·tel′ȧ, pan·ȧ·tel′lȧ, *n.* [Am.Sp. *panatela*, originally, a long, narrow biscuit, from It. dim. of *pane*, bread.] a cigar of a long, slender shape.

Pan″ath·ē·nae′ȧ, *n.pl.* [Gr.] the most celebrated festival of ancient Athens, held in honor of Athena, the patroness of the city, and designed to remind the people of Attica of their union into one people by Theseus. Gynmastic games and musical competitions took place. There were two celebrations, the *Lesser Panathenaea*, held annually, and the *Greater Panathenaea*, held every fourth year.

Pan·ath·ē·nae′ăn, *a.* same as *Panathenaic.*

Pan·ath·ē·nā′iç, *a.* relating to or like the Panathenaea.

pan′broil, *v.t.* to fry in a pan with little or no fat.

pan′çāke, *n.* 1. a thin, flat cake of batter fried on a griddle or in a pan; a griddlecake.
2. anything thin and flat that has the appearance of a pancake.
3. a landing in which the airplane in a horizontal position drops almost vertically to the ground, after leveling off higher than for a normal landing.
pancake makeup; [from *Pan-Cake Make-Up*, a trade-mark.] a cosmetic or theatrical makeup made of a soluble, matte powder compressed into a thin cake and typically applied with a damp sponge.
Pancake Tuesday; Shrove Tuesday.

pan′çāke, *v.i.*; pancaked, *pt.*, *pp.*; pancaking, *ppr.* to land (an airplane) by keeping it level and descending in an almost vertical direction.

pan′çärte, *n.* a panchart. [Obs.]

pan′çhärt, *n.* [Fr., from LL. *pancharta*; Gr. *pan*, all, and L. *charta*, chart.] a royal charter confirming to a subject all his possessions. [Obs.]

pan′cheŏn, pan′chin, *n.* an earthenware pan; a panshon.

pan·çhrō·mat′iç, *a.* [*pan-* and *chromatic.*] sensitive to light of all colors; as, *panchromatic* film.

pan·çhrō′mȧ·tişm, *n.* the condition of being panchromatic.

panch′wāy, *n.* a Bengalese four-oared boat for passengers: also *pansway*, *paunchway.*

pan·çoş′mişm, *n.* [*pan-*, and Gr. *cosmos*, world.] the theory that the material universe constitutes all that exists.

pan·çrā′tiăn, *a.* pertaining to the pancratium; pancratic.

pan·çrā′ti·ast (-shi-), *n.* a combatant or competitor in the pancratium.

pan·çrā·ti·as′tiç (-shi-), *a.* pancratic.

pan·çrat′iç, *a.* [*pan-*, and Gr. *kratos*, strength.]
1. of the pancratium or pancratia; excelling in gymnastic exercises; very strong or robust.
2. having great range of power: applied to combinations of optical lenses.
pancratic eyepiece; a compound eyepiece in a microscope or a telescope that may be adjusted so as to give varying degrees of magnifying power.

pan·çrat′iç·ăl, *a.* pancratic.

pan′çrȧ·tist, *n.* same as *pancratiast.*

pan·çrā′ti·um (-shi-), *n.*; *pl.* **pan·çrā′ti·ȧ**, [Gr. *pankration*; *pan*, all, and *kratos*, strength.]
1. in ancient Greece and Rome, an athletic contest which combined boxing and wrestling.
2. [P–] in botany, a genus of plants of the amaryllis family having a funnel-shaped perianth with six long, narrow divisions.

pan′çrē·ȧs, *n.* [Gr. *pankreas*; *pan*, all, and *kreas*, flesh.] a large, elongated gland situated behind the stomach and secreting a digestive juice (*pancreatic juice*) into the small intestine: groups of differentiated cells (*islands of Langerhans*) in the gland produce the hormone insulin: the pancreas of animals, used as food, is also called *sweetbread.*

pan·çrē·at′iç, *a.* pertaining to or secreted from the pancreas; as, *pancreatic* juice.
pancreatic juice; the clear, alkaline juice secreted by the pancreas into the small intestine, where its constituent enzymes act on food passed down from the stomach.

pan′çrē·ȧ·tin, *n.* 1. any of the pancreatic enzymes or a mixture of these.
2. a commercial preparation of pancreas extract from cattle or hogs, used as an aid to digestion.

pan′çrē·ȧ·tīze, *v.t.*; pancreatized *pt.*, *pp.*; pancreatizing, *ppr.* in medicine, to mix or treat with pancreatin.

pan′çrē·ȧ·tō-, a combining form meaning *of the pancreas*, as in *pancreato*tomy: also, before a vowel, *pancreat-.*

pan″çrē·ȧ·tot′ō·my, *n.*; *pl.* **pan″çrē·ȧ·tot′ō·mieş**, surgical incision of the pancreas.

pan′dȧ, *n.* [from the native (Nepal) name.]
1. a small, reddish-brown animal, *Ælurus fulgens*, resembling a raccoon, native to the woody parts of the Himalaya Mountains of northern India: also called *wah.*
2. a white-and-black bearlike animal of Asia: also called *giant panda.*

GIANT PANDA (6 ft. long)

Pan·dā·nā′cē·ae, Pan·dā′nē·ae, *n.pl.* the screw pine family of which *Pandanus* is the type genus.

pan·dȧ·nā′ceous, *a.* of or pertaining to the *Pandanaceæ.*

Pan·dā′nus, *n.* [Malay *pandang*, conspicuous.]
1. a genus of Asiatic shrublike trees of the screw pine family.
2. [p–] any tree of this genus.

pan′dăr, *n.* same as *pander.*

pan·dä′ram, *n.* a low-caste Hindu priest of southern India; also, a mendicant of the Sudra, practicing severe asceticism.

pan′dăr·işm, *n.* same as *panderism.*

Pan′dȧ·rus, *n.* [L.; Gr. *Pandaros.*] one of the leaders of the Lycians in the Trojan War; in medieval romances and in Boccaccio, Chaucer, and Shakespeare, he acts as the go-between who arranges the meeting of Troilus and Cressida.

Pan·dē′ăn, *a.* of or pertaining to the god Pan.
Pandean pipes; same as *Panpipe.*

pan′deçt, *n.* [Fr. *pandecte*; L. *pandectæ*, from Gr. *pandektēs*; *pan*, all, and *dechesthai*, to contain, to receive.]
1. [P–] [*pl.*] a digest of Roman civil law in fifty books, compiled for the emperor Justinian in the 6th century A.D.: also called *the Digest.*
2. [*often pl.*] any complete body of laws; legal code.
3. any complete or comprehensive digest.

pan·dē′mi·ȧ, pan′dē·my, *n.* an epidemic that affects vast numbers or a majority of the inhabitants of a place at the same time.

pan·dem′iç, *a.* [*pan*,- and Gr. *dēmos*, people.] of all the people; prevalent over a whole area, country, etc.; universal; general; specifically, epidemic over a large region: said of a disease.

pan·dem′iç, *n.* a pandemic disease.

Pan·dē·mō′ni·aç, *a.* 1. of or relating to Pandemonium.
2. [p–] resembling pandemonium.

Pan·dē·mō′ni·um, *n.* [*pan-*, and Gr. *daimōn*, a demon.]
1. the abode of all demons: in *Paradise Lost* it is the palace built under Satan's orders as the capital of Hell.
2. hell.
3. [p–] any place or scene of wild disorder noise, or confusion.
4. [p–] wild disorder, noise, or confusion.

pan′dẽr, *n.* [from *Pandarus*, who performs the part of a pimp in the story of Troilus and Cressida.]
1. a go-between in a sexual intrigue; procurer; pimp.
2. a person who provides the means of helping to satisfy the ambitions, vices, etc. of another.

pan′dẽr, *v.t.*; pandered, *pt.*, *pp.*; pandering, *ppr.* to pimp for; to procure for. [Archaic.]

pan′dẽr, *v.i.* to act as a pander (with *to*).

pan′dẽr·āġe, *n.* the act of or the means employed in pandering.

pan′dẽr·işm, *n.* the employment, character, or vices of a pander.

pan′dẽr·ly, *a.* pimplike.

pan·dẽr′mīte, *n.* [from *Panderma*, a port on the Black Sea.] a calcium borate, closely resembling priceite.

pan′dẽr·ous, *a.* pertaining to or characteristic of a pander. [Rare.]

pan·diç·ū·lā′tion, *n.* [L. *pandiculari*, to yawn, to stretch.] the act of stretching and yawning.

pan′dit (pun′ *or* pan′), *n.* [var. of *pundit.*] in India, a learned man; scholar: used [P–] as a title of respect.

pan′dōor, *n.* same as *pandour.*

Pan·dō′rȧ, *n.* [Gr. *pan*, all, and *dōron*, a gift.]
1. in Greek mythology, the first mortal woman, sent by Zeus as a punishment to mankind for the theft of fire by Prometheus: Zeus gave her a box which she opened, letting out all human ills into the world (or, in a later version, letting all human blessings escape and be lost, leaving only hope).
2. in zoology, a genus of marine bivalves, with a thin inequivalve shell, pearly within, the valves close and attenuated behind the animal, with the mantle closed, except a small opening for the foot.
3. [p–] any member of this genus.

pan·dō′rȧ, pan′dōre, *n.* [Fr.] same as *bandore.*

pan′dour, *n.* [Croation *pandur*, constable; ML. *banderius*, one who follows a banner.]
1. a member of a force of Croatian soldiers organized in 1741 to quell frontier brigands and used in the Austrian army to fight the Turks: noted for their brutality.
2. any brutal soldier.

pan·dow′dy, *n.*; *pl.* **pan·dow′dieş**, deep-dish apple pie or pudding, having a top crust only.

pan′dū·rāte, *a.* [L. *pandura*, a bandore.] same as *panduriform.*

pan·dū′ri·form, *a.* in botany, shaped somewhat like a violin, as some leaves.

PANDURIFORM LEAF

pan′dy, *n.*; *pl.* **pan′dieş**, [L. *pande*, open (your hand), imperative of *pandere*, to extend, open.] a stroke or blow on the hand, as with a cane, for punishment. [Scot.]

pan′dy, *v.t.*; pandied, *pt.*, *pp.*; pandying, *ppr.* to punish by striking the hand, as with a cane. [Scot.]

pan·dy̆·nȧ·mom′ē·tẽr, *n.* [*pan-* and *dynamometer.*] a device for ascertaining the torsion of shafting, as a basis from which to compute the amount of power conveyed.

pāne, *n.* [ME.; OFr. *pane*, *panne*; L. *pannus*, piece of cloth.]
1. a piece or division, especially if flat and rectangular.
2. a flat side, or face, of something that has several sides, as of a nut, bolthead, cut diamond, etc.
3. (a) a single division of a window, etc., consisting of a sheet of glass in a frame; (b) the sheet of glass or a substitute.
4. a panel, as of a door, wall, etc.

pāne, *v.t.*; paned, *pt., pp.*; paning, *ppr.* to provide with panes or a pane; to set panes in.

pāned, *a.* provided with panes; composed of panes or squares.

pan·ē·ġyr′iç, *n.* [Fr. *panégyrique*; L. *panegyricus*, from Gr. *panēgyris*, a public meeting; *pan*, all, and *ageirein*, to bring together.]
1. a formal speech or writing in praise of some distinguished person or achievement; a formal or elaborate encomium.
2. encomium; eulogy; laudation; superlative praise bestowed on some person, action, or virtue; as, epitaphs replete with *panegyric*.

pan·ē·ġyr′iç, *a.* same as *panegyrical*.

pan·ē·ġyr′iç·ăl, *a.* of, or having the nature of, panegyric or a panegyric; eulogistic; praising.

pan·ē·ġyr′iç·ăl·ly, *adv.* in a panegyric manner.

pan·ē·ġyr′i·çon, pan·ē·ġyr′i·çum, *n.*; *pl.* **pan·e·ġyr′i·çȧ,** in the Orthodox Eastern Church, a collection of passages suitable for different festivals.

pȧ·neġ′y·ris, *n.* [Gr. *panēgyris.*] a festival; a public meeting. [Obs.]

pan′ē·ġyr·ist, *n.* one who writes or speaks panegyrics; a eulogist; an encomiast in writing or speaking.

pan′ē·ġy·rīze, *v.t.*; panegyrized, *pt., pp.*; panegyrizing, *ppr.* to write or speak a panegyric on; eulogize.

pan′ē·ġy·rīze, *v.i.* to write or speak panegyrics.

pan′ē·ġyr·y, *n.* a panegyris. [Obs.]

pan′el, *n.* [L. *pannus*, a piece of cloth.]
1. (a) a piece of cloth placed under a saddle; saddle lining; (b) a soft saddle.
2. a section or division of a wall, ceiling, or other surface; specifically, (a) a section of a fence or railing between two posts; (b) a flat piece of material, as wood or metal, usually rectangular, forming a part of the surface of a wall, door, cabinet, etc., and usually set off from the surrounding surface by being raised, recessed, framed, etc.; (c) a compartment or pane of a window; (d) an insulated board, or flat surface, for instruments or controls, as of an electric circuit, airplane, etc.
3. (a) a thin board used for oil painting; (b) a painting on such a board; (c) any picture very much longer than it is wide.
4. a list or group of persons selected for a specific purpose, as judging, discussing, etc.
5. in aeronautics, (a) one complete section of a wing; (b) in dirigibles, the quadrilateral area bounded by two adjacent longerons and transverses.
6. in dressmaking, a lengthwise strip, as of contrasting material, in a skirt or dress.
7. in law, (a) originally, a piece of parchment on which were recorded the list of persons summoned for jury duty; (b) later, the list itself; (c) the jurors as a whole.
8. in mining, a compartment of a mine.

pan′el, *v.t.*; paneled *or* panelled, *pt., pp.*; paneling *or* panelling, *ppr.* 1. to cover, provide, fit, or decorate with panels.
2. in law, to impanel (a jury).
3. in Scottish law, to indict.

pan·el·ā′tion, *n.* a paneling or being paneled.

pan′el dis·cus′sion, a discussion carried on by a selected group of speakers before an audience.

pāne′less, *a.* without panes.

pan′el gāme, theft or swindling by the use of secret panels, as in a panel house.

pan′el house, a house of prostitution having secret panels by entrance through which theft or swindling may be accomplished.

pan′el·ing, pan′el·ling, *n.* 1. the action of a person who panels.
2. panels collectively; series of panels in a wall, etc.

pan·el·lā′tion, *n.* same as *panelation*.

pan′el sa̤w, a saw used for cutting very thin wood.

pan′el thiēf, a thief who uses the panel game.

pan′el·wŏrk, *n.* panels collectively; paneling.

pan·es·thē′si·ȧ (-zhi-ȧ *or* -zhȧ *or* -zi-ȧ), *n.* the sum of all sensations experienced.

pan·es·thet′iç, *a.* pertaining to panesthesia.

pan·e·tel′ȧ, pan·e·tel′lȧ, [Sp.] a long, slender cigar.

pan fish, any small fish that can be fried whole in a pan.

pan′fish, *n.* a horseshoe crab.

pan′-frȳ, *v.t.*; pan-fried, *pt., pp.*; pan-frying, *ppr.* to fry in a shallow skillet or frying pan, with fat.

pan′ful, *n.*; *pl.* **pan′fuls̤,** the amount a pan can hold.

pang, *n.* [from ME. *prong.*] a sudden, sharp, and brief pain, physical or emotional; a spasm of agony or distress; as, the *pangs* of love.

Syn.—paroxysm, throe, agony, convulsion smart; anguish, pain, twinge.

pang, *v.t.* to torture; to give extreme pain to. [Now Rare.]

pan′ġēne, *n.* [*pan-* and *-gene.*] a protoplasmic unit supposedly constituting the physical basis of heredity.

pan·ġen′e·sis, *n.* [*pan-*, and Gr. *genesis*, generation.] an abandoned theory advanced by Darwin that each unit or cell of the body throws off very minute particles (*gemmules*) into the blood which circulate freely and undergo division and are collected in the reproductive cells; thus each part of the body is represented in the germ cell through these gemmules, which are regarded as the units of hereditary transmission.

pan·ġē·net′iç, *a.* pertaining to pangenesis.

Pan-Gẽr′măn, *a.* of or having to do with all Germans as a group or Pan-Germanism.

Pan-Gẽr′măn, *n.* an advocate of Pan-Germanism.

Pan-Gẽr′măn·işm, *n.* the theory of, or a movement toward, the political unification of all German peoples, especially by annexing to the German state all near-by territories inhabited by German-speaking peoples.

pang′ful, *a.* full of pangs; suffering. [Rare.]

pang′less, *a.* free from pangs; painless.

pan̄·gō′lin, *n.* [Malay.] any one of several species of edentate quadrupeds of the genus *Manis*, found in Asia and Africa; a scaly anteater, able to roll into a ball when attacked.

pan′han″dle, *n.* 1. the handle of a pan.
2. [*often* P–] a strip of land resembling the handle of a pan, as, in the United States, a narrow portion of a state lying between two other states; as, the *Panhandle* of Texas.

pan′han″dle, *v.t.* and *v.i.*; panhandled; *pt., pp.*; panhandling, *ppr.* to beg, especially on the streets. [Slang.]

pan′han″dlẽr, *n.* a beggar. [Slang.]

Pan·hel·len′iç, *a.* 1. of all the Greek peoples.
2. of Panhellenism.
3. of all Greek-letter fraternities and sororities.

Pan·hel′len·işm, *n.* formerly, the theory of, or a movement toward, the political union of all the Greek peoples.

Pan·hel′len·ist, *n.* a supporter or advocate of Panhellenism.

Pan·hel·lē′ni·um, *n.* the national assembly or council of Greece, organized by Hadrian.

pan′iç, *a.* [Fr. *panique*; Gr. *panikos*, of Pan, from *Pan*, Pan.]
1. literally, of Pan.
2. of sudden fear, as supposedly inspired by him.
3. having the nature of, or showing or resulting from, panic.

pan′iç, *n.* 1. a sudden, unreasoning, hysterical fear, often spreading quickly.
2. a widespread fear of the collapse of the financial system, resulting in unreasoned attempts to turn property into cash, withdraw money, etc.
3. a person or thing considered extremely humorous or entertaining. [Slang.]

pan′iç, *v.t.*; panicked (-ikt), *pt., pp.*; panicking, *ppr.* 1. to affect with panic.
2. to delight; to win laughter and applause from; as, the clown *panicked* the audience. [Slang.]

pan′iç, *n.* [L. *panicum.*] a grass, as millet, of the genus *Panicum*, used as fodder: also called *panic grass*.

pan′iç·ăl, *a.* panic. [Rare.]

pan′ick·y, *a.* 1. having the nature of, or showing or resulting from, panic.
2. liable or susceptible to panic; liable to be in a panic.

pan′i·çle, *n.* [L. *panicula*, a tuft on plants, a panicle, dim. of *panus*, Gr. *pēnos*, the thread wound on the bobbin in a shuttle.] a loose, irregularly branched flower cluster; a compound raceme.

PANICLE

pan′i·çled (-kld), *a.* furnished with panicles; arranged in panicles.

pan·ī′çō·grȧph, *n.* a paniconograph.

pan·i·çog′rȧ·phy, *n.* paniconography.

pan·i·çon′ō·grȧph, *n.* a printing plate made by a paniconographic process.

pan·i·çon·ō·graph′iç, *a.* pertaining to or made by paniconography.

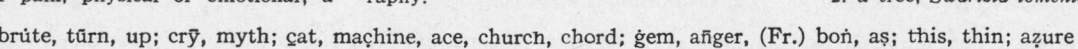

pan·ī·çō·nog′rȧ·phy, *n.* [*pan-*, and Gr. *eikōn*, image, and *-graphy.*] same as *photozincography*.

pan′iç-strick″en, pan′iç-struck, *a.* stricken with panic; badly frightened; hysterical and out of control from fear.

pȧ·niç′ū·lāte, *a.* in botany, panicled; arranged or growing in panicles.

pȧ·niç′ū·lā·ted, *a.* paniculate.

pȧ·niç′ū·lāte·ly, *adv.* in or with panicles.

Pan′i·çum, *n.* [L. *panicum*, panic grass.] a large genus of grasses; the panic grasses.

pan·id″i·ō·mor′phiç, *a.* having a structure characterized by idiomorphic development, as certain rocks.

pan′iẽr (-yẽr), *n.* same as *pannier*.

pan″i·fi·çā′tion, *n.* [L. *panis*, bread, and *facere*, to make.] breadmaking.

Pan·i·on′iç, *a.* in ancient Greece, pertaining to an assembly of all the Ionians.

Pan·is·lam′iç, *a.* pertaining to Panislamism, or to all Islam.

Pan·is′lăm·işm, *n.* a theory of, or movement toward, the political unification of all Islamic peoples.

pȧ·niv′ō·rous, *a.* [L. *panis*, bread, and *vorare*, to devour.] eating bread; subsisting on bread.

Pan·jä′bi (pun-), *n.* [Hind. *panjābī.*]
1. the Indic language spoken in the Punjab, India: also spelled *Punjabi*.
2. a native of the Punjab: usually *Punjabi*.

pan′jăm, *n.* [E. Ind.] a kind of cotton cloth manufactured in the south of India.

pan·jan′drum, *n.* [arbitrary formation from a nonsense story by Samuel Foote (1755).] a self-important, pompous official: a satirical title.

pan̄k, *v.i.* to pant. [Dial.]

pan′lō·ġişm, *n.* [*pan-*, and Gr. *logos*, a word, from *legein*, to speak.] in philosophy, the doctrine embodying the theory that the universe is the manifestation of the Logos.

pan·mix′i·ȧ, *n.* [*pan-*, and Gr. *mixis*, mixing.] in biology, the cessation of natural selection in generation.

pan·nāde′, *n.* the curvet of a horse. [Rare.]

pan′nāġe, *n.* in old English law, (a) the food of swine in the woods, as beechnuts, acorns, etc.: also called *pawnage*; (b) the money taken by agistors for the mast of the king's forests.

pan′nȧ·ry, *a.* same as *panary*.

pȧnne (pȧn), *n.* [Fr.] a fabric resembling velvet; a kind of plush, with a loose, flat nap.

pan′nel, *n.* and *v.* panel. [Obs.]

pan′ni·çle, *n.* the brainpan or skull. [Obs.]

pan·niç′ū·lus, *n.*; *pl.* **pan·niç′ū·lī,** [L., dim. of *pannus*, a cloth.] in anatomy, a layer of membrane.

panniculus adiposus; the subcutaneous layer of fat.

pan′niẽr (-yẽr *or* -ni-ẽr), *n.* [L. *panarium*, a bread basket, from *panis*, bread.]
1. a large basket; specifically, (a) a wicker basket for carrying loads on the back; (b) either one of a pair of baskets hung across the back of a mule, horse, etc. for carrying market produce.

PANNIERS

2. (a) a framework, as of whalebone, wire, etc., used to puff out a skirt at the hips; (b) a skirt extended or puffed at the hips to give the effect of a pannier.
3. in architecture, a corbeil.
4. a shield or cover of basketwork placed in front of medieval archers. [Obs.]

pan′niẽred (-yẽrd), *a.* loaded with panniers.

pan′ni·kin, *n.* 1. a small pan.
2. a metal cup.

pan′nōse, *a.* [from L. *pannus*, a cloth.] in botany, having a texture like coarse cloth.

pan′nōse·ly, *adv.* in a pannose manner.

pan′nus, *n.* [L. *pannus*, a cloth.] an abnormal membranelike vascularization of the cornea, due to granulation of the eyelids.

pan·nus·çō′ri·um, *n.* [L. *pannus*, a cloth, and *corium*, leather.] a soft, waterproof cloth used for the uppers of boots and shoes.

pȧ·nō′chȧ, pȧ·nō′che, *n.* [Mex.] a coarse sugar made in Mexico; also, a kind of candy made from this, resembling fudge: also *penuche*, *penuchi*.

pan·ō·çō′çō, *n.* [S. Am.] 1. a necklace tree, *Ormosia coccinea*.
2. a tree, *Swartzia tomentosa*, of the bean

family, growing in Guiana. Its wood is hard and durable.

pan·ō·is'tiç, *a.* [*pan-*, and Gr. *ōon*, egg, and *-istic.*] producing ova only, as the ovaries of certain insects.

pan·om·phē'ăn, *a.* [*pan-*, and Gr. *omphaios*, prophetic]. in Greek religion, uttering divinations: applied to Zeus as sender of all ominous and prophetic voices.

pan'ō·plied (-plid), *a.* having a panoply, or complete suit of armor; elaborately arrayed.

pan'ō·ply, *n.* [Gr. *panoplia*; *pan*, all, and *hopla*, arms.]

1. the entire equipment, complete armor, or full defense, as of a Greek foot soldier, medieval knight, etc.

2. any complete or magnificent covering or array.

We had need to take the Christian *panoply*,
to put on the whole armor of God.—Ray.

pan·op'tiç, *a.* including in one view everything in sight.

pan·op'ti·çon, *n.* [*pan-*, and Gr. *optikos*, of seeing.]

1. a prison so constructed that the inspector can see each of the prisoners at all times.

2. a room used as a museum, or for other exhibition purposes.

pan·ō·rä'mȧ (*or* -ra'mȧ), *n.* [*pan-*, and Gr. *horama*, view, from *horān*, to see.]

1. (a) a picture or series of pictures of a landscape, historical event, etc. presented on a continuous surface encircling the spectator; a cyclorama; (b) a picture unrolled before the spectator in such a way as to give the impression of a continuous view.

2. an unlimited view in all directions.

3. a comprehensive survey of a subject.

4. a continuous series of scenes or events; constantly changing scene.

pan·ō·ram'iç, pan·ō·ram'iç·ăl, *a.* of, or having the nature of, a panorama; specifically, (a) presenting an unlimited view in all directions; (b) passing before the eyes in a continuous picture or series of pictures.

panoramic camera; a camera having a wide-angle lens for taking a landscape picture in the form of a panorama.

panoramic sight; a kind of periscopic gun sight that provides a greatly enlarged field of view.

pan·ō·ram'iç·ăl·ly, *adv.* in a panoramic manner; as a panorama.

Pȧ·nor'pȧ, *n.* a genus of neuropterous insects, the type of the family *Panorpidæ*.

pȧ·nor'pi·ăn, *a.* of, pertaining to, or resembling the *Panorpa* or *Panorpidæ*.

pȧ·nor'pi·ăn, *n.* one of the *Panorpa* or *Panorpidæ*.

pȧ·nor'pid, *a.* and *n.* same as *panorpian*.

Pȧ·nor'pi·dae, *n.pl.* [from the genus *Panorpa*; Gr. *pan*, all, and *horpō* or *harpē*, a sickle.] a family of neuropterous insects, the type of which is the *Panorpa communis*, or scorpion fly. It has a long, curiously articulated anal appendage, somewhat resembling the tail of a scorpion, which gives it its common name.

pȧ·nöu'chi, *n.* same as *panocha*.

pan·phär'mȧ·çon, *n.* [*pan-*, and Gr. *pharmakon*, a medicine.] a universal medicine.

Pan'pīpe, *n.* a primitive musical instrument made of a row of reeds, or tubes of graduated lengths bound together lengthwise and played by blowing across the top, open ends: also called *Pandean pipes, Panpipes, Pan's pipes, syrinx*.

Pan″-Pres·by·tē'ri·ăn, *a.* relating to an assembly from all parts of the world of representatives of those who hold Presbyterian views.

pan'sied, *a.* having a covering of or abounding in pansies.

Pan-Släv'iç, *a.* of or pertaining to all the Slavic peoples or Pan-Slavism.

Pan-Släv'ism, *n.* a theory of, or movement toward, the political unification of all Slavic peoples.

Pan-Släv'ist, *n.* one who advocates or believes in Pan-Slavism.

pan·soph'iç, pan·soph'iç·ăl, *a.* of pansophy.

pan'sō·phism, *n.* [from Gr. *pansophos*, all-wise (from *pan*, all, and *sophia*, wisdom); and *-ism.*] pretension to universal wisdom or knowledge.

pan'sō·phy, *n.* [*pan-*, and Gr. *sophia*, wisdom.]

1. universal wisdom or knowledge.

2. a system or work embracing all knowledge.

pan·spẽr'mȧ·tism, *n.* [*pan-*, and Gr. *sperma*, seed, germ, and *-ism.*]

1. the germ theory; the assumption that germs have practically universal diffusion.

2. the doctrine that parent germs produce all microscopic organisms, such as bacteria.

pan·spẽr'mȧ·tist, pan'spẽr·mist, *n.* an advocate of the panspermic theory.

pan·spẽr'miç, *a.* relating to panspermy

pan'spẽr·my, *n.* same as *panspermatism*.

Pan's pīpes, same as *Panpipe*.

pan″stēr·ē·ō·rä'mȧ, *n.* [*pan-*, and Gr. *stereos*, solid, and *horān*, to see.] a model of a town or country in wood, cork, pasteboard, or other substance, showing every part in relief.

pan'sy, *n.*; *pl.* **pan'sies,** [Fr. *pensée*, fancy or thought, from *penser*, to think.]

1. a small plant of the violet family, with flat, broad, velvety petals in many colors: also called *heartsease*.

2. an effeminate man or male homosexual: contemptuous term. [Slang.]

pant-, same as *panto-*.

pant, *v.i.*; panted, *pt.*, *pp.*; panting, *ppr.* [from OFr. *pantaisier*, ult. from L. *phantasia*, nightmare, fantasy.]

1. to breathe rapidly and heavily; to gasp for breath, as from running fast.

2. to throb; pulsate; beat rapidly, as the heart.

3. to gasp with desire; to yearn eagerly (with *for* or *after*).

4. to give off steam, smoke, etc. in loud puffs, as an engine.

pant, *v.t.* 1. to utter hurriedly and breathlessly; to gasp out (often with *out* or *forth*); as, she *panted* a word in his ear.

2. to desire greatly. [Rare.]

pant, *n.* 1. any of a series of rapid, heavy breaths, as from exertion; a gasp.

2. a throb or pulsation, as of the heart.

3. a puff of an engine.

pan'tȧ-, same as *panto-*.

pan'tȧ·çosm, *n.* same as *cosmolabe*.

pan·tag'ȧ·my, *n.* [*panta-*, and Gr. *gamos*, marriage.] the relation between the sexes in a community in which every woman is the wife of every man and every man the husband of every woman.

pan'tȧ·grȧph, *n.* same as *pantograph*.

Pan·tag'rü·el, *n.* [Fr., coined by Rabelais, from Gr. *panta*, all, and *gruel*, athirst, hence, lit., all-thirsty.] the boisterous, young giant son of Gargantua in Rabelais' *Gargantua and Pantagruel*: he is a jovial drunkard characterized by rough, extravagant humor.

Pan″tȧ·grü·el'i·ăn, *a.* of, characteristic of, or having the nature of Pantagruel or Pantagruelism.

Pan·tȧ·grü'el·ism, *n.* rough, extravagant humor with a satirical intent, like that of Pantagruel.

pan·tȧ·lets', pan·tȧ·lettes', *n.pl.* [dim. of *pantaloon*.]

1. long, loose drawers frilled at the ankle and showing beneath the skirt, worn by women during the middle of the 19th century.

2. detachable ruffles for the legs of drawers.

pan·tȧ·lo͝on', *n.* [Fr. *pantalon*; It. *pantalone*, name of a character in an Italian comedy.]

1. [P–] (a) a stock character in an old Italian comedy, usually a slender, foolish old man, wearing tight trousers which extended to the feet; (b) a similar figure in modern pantomime, the butt of the clown's jokes.

2. [*pl.*] (a) formerly, tight trousers fastened below the calf or strapped under the boots; trousers and hose in one garment; (b) later, any trousers.

pan·tȧ·lo͝on'ẽr·y, *n.* buffoonery.

pan'tȧ·sçōpe, *n.* same as *pantoscope*.

pan·tȧ·sçop'iç, *a.* same as *pantoscopic*.

pan·tech'ni·çon, *n.* [*pan-*, and Gr. *technē*, art.]

1. originally, a bazaar where all kinds of things were sold.

2. a storage warehouse.

3. a furniture van: also *pantechnicon van*.

pan·tel'ē·grȧph, *n.* an apparatus by which a facsimile or copy of a chart, diagram, message, etc. is transmitted by telegraphy from one station to another.

pant'ẽr, *n.* one who or that which pants.

pant'ẽr, *n.* a keeper of the pantry. [Obs.]

pant'ẽr, *n.* [Fr. *pantière*, from L. *panther*, Gr. *panthēra*, a kind of net, from *pan*, all, and *thēr*, a wild beast.] a fowler's net. [Obs.]

Pan-Teū·ton'iç, *a.* same as *Pan-Germanic*.

Pan-Teū'tŏn·ism, *n.* same as *Pan-Germanism*.

pan'thē·ism, *n.* [*pan-* and *theism*.]

1. the doctrine or belief that God is not a personality, but that all laws, forces, manifestations, etc. of the self-existing universe are God; the belief that God is everything and everything is God.

2. the worship of all gods.

pan'thē·ist, *n.* a believer in pantheism.

pan·thē·is'tiç, pan·thē·is'tiç·ăl, *a.* of, or having the nature of, pantheism or pantheists.

pan·thē·is'tiç·ăl·ly, *adv.* in a pantheistic manner.

pan·thē·ol'ō·gist, *n.* a student of pantheology.

pan·thē·ol'ō·gy, *n.* [*pan-* and *theology*.] a universal system of theology.

Pan'thē·on, *n.* [L., from Gr. *pantheion*; *pan*, all, and *theos*, a god.]

1. a temple at Rome, dedicated to all the gods: used since 609 A.D. as a Christian church (*Santa Maria Rotunda*). It was built by Agrippa in 27 B.C., and rebuilt by Hadrian in the second century A.D.

2. [p–] the gods of a people taken collectively, or a treatise on them.

3. [*sometimes* p–] a temple or structure in which the great men of a nation are entombed or commemorated; as, Westminster Abbey is the *Pantheon* of the British.

pan'thẽr, *n.*; *pl.* **pan'thẽrs** or **pan'thẽr,** [L. *panthera*; Gr. *panthēr*.]

1. a puma; cougar; mountain lion.

2. a leopard, especially one of dark color.

3. a jaguar.

pan'thẽr çat, the ocelot.

pan'thẽr çow'rie, an East Indian cowry, *Cypræa pantherina*, spotted like a panther.

pan'thẽr·ess, *n.* a female panther.

pan'thẽr·ine, *a.* belonging to the panther, or resembling it in marking.

pan'thẽr·wood, *n.* same as *citronwood*.

pan'ties, *n.pl.* women's or children's short underpants.

pan'tīle, *n.* [*pan* (dish), and *tile*.] a roofing tile having an S curve, laid with the large curve of one tile overlapping the small curve of the next.

PANTILE

pan'tīle, *a.* of or designating Dissenters' chapels or congregations: so called because the chapels were often roofed with pantiles. [Obs.]

pant'ing·ly, *adv.* with palpitation or rapid breathing.

pan·ti·soç'rȧ·cy, *n.* [*panto-*, and Gr. *isos*, equal, and *kratein*, to rule.] a utopian community founded on the principle of equal rank and authority for all; the government of all by all.

pan·tis'ō·çrat, *n.* a pantisocratist.

pan″ti·sō·çrat'iç, *a.* of or pertaining to a pantisocracy.

pan·ti·soç'rȧ·tist, *n.* one who advocates pantisocracy or supports that theory of government.

pan'tlẽr, *n.* [Fr. *panetier*, from *pain*, L. *panis*, bread.] the employee in a great household who has charge of the bread and pantry. [Archaic.]

pan'tō-, [from Gr. *pantos*, genit. of *pan*, all.] a combining form meaning *all* or *every*, as in *panto*graph: also, before a vowel, *pant-*.

pan″tō·çhrō·nom'ē·tẽr, *n.* [*panto-* and *chronometer*.] an instrument which combines the properties of the compass, sundial, and the universal time dial.

pan'tō·fle, pan'tŏf·fle (-fl *or* -tof'l), *n.* [Fr. *pantoufle*; It. *pantofola*; MGr. *pontophellos*, whole cork, from Gr. *pantos*, whole, and *phellos*, a cork.] a slipper.

pan'tō·grȧph, *n.* [*panto-*, and *graph*.]

1. a mechanical device for reproducing a map, drawing, etc. on the same or a different scale, consisting of a framework of jointed rods in a roughly parallelogram form.

2. any similar framework, as an extendible arm for a telephone, a trolley on an electric locomotive, etc.

pan·tō·graph'iç, pan·tō·graph'iç·ăl, *a.* per-

taining to a pantograph; performed by a pantograph.
pan·tog′rȧ·phy, *n.* general description. [Rare.]
pan·tō·log′iç·ăl, *a.* pertaining to pantology.
pan·tol′ō·gist, *n.* one writing on or conversant with pantology.
pan·tol′ō·gy, *n.* [*panto-*, and Gr. *logos*, discourse.] a work of universal information; a systematic view of all branches of human knowledge.
pan·tom′ē·tēr, *n.* [*panto-*, and Gr. *metron*, a measure.] an instrument for measuring angles, elevations, and distances.
pan·tō·met′riç, *a.* pertaining to pantometry or the use of the pantometer.
pan·tom′ē·try, *n.* universal measurement. [Rare.]
pan′tō·mīme, *n.* [Fr.; L. *pantomimus*; Gr. *pantomimos*; *pan*, all, and *mimos*, a mimic.]
1. in ancient Rome, (a) an actor who played his part by gestures and action without words; (b) a drama played in action and gestures to the accompaniment of words sung by the chorus or music.
2. a dramatic representation in which the actors express their meaning without words, using action and gestures only.
3. action or gestures without words as a means of expression.
4. in England, a dramatic entertainment, usually performed at Christmas, relating to some popular story and containing dumb acting, burlesque dialogue, music, dancing, etc. It generally concludes with diverting farcical tricks performed by traditional characters called clown, pantaloon, harlequin, and columbine.
pan′tō·mīme, *a.* same as *pantomimic*.
pan′to·mīme, *v.t.* and *v.i.*; pantomimed, *pt.*, *pp.*; pantomiming, *ppr.* to express or act in pantomime.
pan·tō·mim′iç, pan·tō·mim′iç·ăl, *a.* of, or having the nature of, pantomime.
pan·tō·mim′iç·ăl·ly, *adv.* in the manner of pantomime.
pan′tō·mīm·ist, *n.* one who acts in pantomime; also, a writer or composer of pantomimes.
pan·tō·mor′phiç, *a.* [*panto-*, and Gr. *morphē*, form.] assuming all forms; of all shapes.
pan′tŏn, *n.* pantofle. [Now Dial.]
pan·toph′ȧ·ġist, *n.* an animal or person that eats everything.
pan·toph′ȧ·gous, *a.* [*panto-*, and Gr. *phagein*, to eat.] omnivorous; eating all kinds of food.
pan·toph′ȧ·ġy, *n.* omnivorousness; the habit or power of eating all kinds of food indiscriminately.
pan·tō·phō′bi·ȧ, *n.* [*panto-*, and Gr. *phobos*, fear.] a morbid fear of everything; a form of melancholia in which there is a generalized fear or terror.
Pan·top′ō·dȧ, *n.pl.* same as *Pycnogonida*.
pan′tō·sçōpe, *n.* [*panto-* and *scope*.]
1. a wideangle photographic lens.
2. a panoramic camera.
pan·tō·sçop′iç, *a.* [*panto-* and *-scope* and *-ic*.] having a wide range of view.
pantoscopic spectacles; same as *bifocals*.
Pan·tō·stō′mȧ·tȧ, *n.pl.* [*panto-*, and Gr. *stomata*, nom. pl. of *stoma*, mouth.] a division of infusorial protozoans, of the order *Flagellata*. It consists of those which have no special place for the ingestion of food.
pan″tō·then′iç ac′id, a B-complex vitamin, $C_9H_{17}O_5N$, widely distributed in animal and plant tissues and prepared synthetically: thought to be essential for cell growth and helpful in preventing gray hair.
pan·töum′, *n.* [Fr.; Malay *pantun*.] a verse form made up of quatrains rhyming *abab*, *bcbc*, *cdcd*, etc.: a European imitation of the Malayan pantun.
pan′try, *n.*; *pl.* **pan′trieṣ,** [ME. and OFr. *paneterie*; ML. *panetaria*, from L. *panis*, bread.]
1. a small room or closet off the kitchen, where cooking ingredients and utensils, china, etc. are kept.
2. a small room between the kitchen and dining room for serving meals and storing tableware: also called *butler's pantry*.
pants, *n.pl.* [abbrev. of *pantaloons*.]
1. an outer garment, extending from the waist to the knees or ankles and divided into separate coverings for the legs: more formally called *trousers*.
2. drawers or panties.
pan·tŭn′, *n.* [Malay.] a Malayan verse form, consisting of rhymed quatrains: see *pantoum*.
pan′ty·wāist, *n.* 1. originally, a child's two-piece undergarment that buttoned together at the waist.
2. a person considered as like a child in strength, courage, etc.; a weakling; sissy. [Slang.]
Pan·ŭrġe′, *n.* [Fr., from Gr. *panourgos*, ready to do anything; *pan*, all, and *-ourgos*, worker.] the gay, cowardly companion of Pantagruel in Rabelais' *Gargantua and Pantagruel*.
pan·ŭr′ġiç, *a.* capable of doing any kind of work; universally skilled.
pan′zēr (*G.* pän′tsēr), *a.* [G., armor; M.H.G. *panzier*; OFr. *pancier*, from It. *pancia*, belly; L. *pantex*, belly.] armored; as, a *panzer* division.
pan·zō′iṣm, *n.* [*pan-*, and Gr. *zōē*, life.] all the elements or factors which constitute vital energy or life.
pä′ō·lō, *n.* [L. *Paulus*, Paul.] an obsolete Italian coin: so called from Pope Paul V.
pap, *n.* [L. *papilla*.]
1. a nipple of the breast; a teat. [Archaic.]
2. something shaped like a nipple.
pap, *n.* [It. *pappa*; D. *pap*; L. *papa*.]
1. any soft or semiliquid food for babies or invalids.
2. the pulp of fruit. [Obs.]
3. any mash, paste, or pulp.
4. money or favors from public office; political patronage.
pap, *v.t.*; papped, (papt) *pt.*, *pp.*; papping, *ppr.* to feed with pap.
pä′pȧ (*or* pȧ·pä′), *n.* [like Fr. and L. *papa*, Gr. *pappas*, from baby talk.] father: a child's word, corresponding to *mamma* for *mother*: also *pa*, *paw*, *pop*, etc.
pä′pä, *n.* a parish priest of the Greek Church.
pā′pȧ·cy, *n.*; *pl.* **pā′pȧ·cieṣ,** [ME. *papacie*; ML. *papatia*, the papacy, from *papa*, the pope.]
1. the position, authority, or rank of the Pope.
2. the period of time during which a pope rules.
3. the succession of popes; popes collectively.
4. [*also* P–] the government of the Roman Catholic Church, headed by the Pope.
pȧ·pā′in, *n.* [*papaya*, and *-in*.] a protein-splitting enzyme obtained from the juice of unripe papaya and used as an aid to digestion.
pā′păl, *a.* 1. of or pertaining to the Pope; as, the *papal* chair, the *papal* crown.

> The progress of the *papal* policy took deeper root. —Blackstone.

2. of the papacy.
3. of or relating to the Roman Catholic Church.
pā′păl·in, *n.* a papist. [Obs.]
pā′păl·ist, *n.* one who favors papal power or doctrines.
pā·pal′i·ty, *n.* the papacy. [Obs.]
pā′păl·īze, *v.t.* and *v.i.*; papalized, *pt.*, *pp.*; papalizing, *ppr.* to make or become papal.
pā′păl·ly, *adv.* in a papal manner; popishly.
Pā′păl States, the lands in central and north central Italy that belonged to the Roman Catholic Church and were ruled by the Pope until 1870: also called *States of the Church*.
pā′păl·ty, *n.* the papacy. [Obs.]
pā·pȧ·phō′bi·ȧ, *n.* excessive or unreasonable fear, dread, or hatred of the Pope or of Roman Catholicism. [Rare.]
pā′pär·çhy, *n.* [LL. *papa*, pope, and Gr. *archein*, to rule.] government under a pope; papal rule.
pä′päs, pap′pȧs, *n.* [Gr.] in the Greek Church, a priest having charge of a parish; a papa.
Pȧ·pā′vēr, *n.* [L., poppy.] a genus of plants, the type of the poppy family, *Papaveraceæ*, having twelve known species, *Papaver rhœas* being the common red poppy of England.
Pȧ·pav·ēr·ā′cē·ae, *n.pl.* the poppy family, a family of hypogynous, exogenous herbs or shrubs, often with milky juice. They have alternate leaves, simple or divided, without stipules; peduncles long, one-flowered; sepals two or three, deciduous; petals four, or six, or multiples of four; stamens indefinite; ovary one-celled, with parietal placentae; fruit pod-shaped or capsular; seeds many.
pȧ·pav·ēr·ā′ceous, *a.* of or pertaining to the poppy family, *Papaveraceæ*.
pȧ·pav′ēr·in (*or* -pā′vēr-), *n.* same as *papaverine*.
pȧ·pav′ēr·ïne (*or* -pā′vēr-in), *n.* [L. *papaver*, poppy; and *-ine*.] a white, crystalline alkaloid, $C_{20}H_{21}NO_4$, derived from opium and used in medicine to relax muscles in spasms and as a local anesthetic.
pȧ·pav′ēr·ous, *a.* resembling the poppy; of the nature or qualities of poppies.
pa′pąw (*or* pȧ·pą′), *n.* [Sp. *papaya* (fruit), *papayo* (tree), from Carib. name.]
1. a papaya.
2. (a) a tree, *Asimina triloba*, of the custardapplefamily, growing in the central and southern United States and having an oblong, yellowish, edible fruit with many seeds; (b) its fruit.
Also *pawpaw*.

PAPAYA
(*Carica papaya*)

pȧ·pä′yȧ, *n.* [Sp., fruit of the pawpaw.]
1. a tropical tree, *Carica papaya*, of America, Hawaii, and the Philippines, resembling a palm, having a bunch of large leaves at the top, and bearing a large, oblong, yellowish-orange fruit like a melon.
2. its fruit, eaten raw or cooked, and also valued for its juice.
pȧ·pȳ′ō·tin, *n.* same as *papain*.
pap′bōat, *n.* 1. a dish shaped like a boat, used to hold children's pap.
2. a shell of *Turbinella rapha*, used on the Malabar coast, when scooped out internally and carved externally, to contain the sacred oil which is employed in anointing the priests.
pāpe, *n.* the Pope. [Scot.]
pä′pē·jāy, *n.* a popinjay. [Obs.]
pā′pēr, *n.* [ME. *papire*; OFr. *papier*; L. *papyrus*, Gr. *papyros*, an Egyptian reed, from the inner bark of which a kind of writing paper was made in ancient Egypt.]
1. a thin, flexible material made in leaves or sheets from a pulp of rags, straw, wood, or other fibrous material and used for writing or printing upon, for wrapping, and various other purposes.
2. a single piece, sheet, or leaf of such material.
3. a newspaper; a printed journal; a sheet appearing periodically; as, a daily *paper*, a Sunday *paper*.
4. a written or printed sheet of paper; a writing; specifically, an official document.
5. an essay or article on any subject; a dissertation, monograph, etc.
6. (a) negotiable papers, as promissory notes, bills of exchange, etc.: also *commercial paper*; (b) paper money.
7. wallpaper.
8. a free pass or free passes to any place of entertainment; also, the persons admitted by such passes; as, the house was filled with *paper*.
9. a written examination, report, theme, etc.
10. a small wrapper or card of paper, usually including its contents; as, a *paper* of pins.
11. any material like paper, as papyrus.
12. [*pl.*] (a) documents proving the identity of a person; credentials; (b) a collection of documents, letters, writings, etc., especially of one person; as, the Lincoln *papers*.
brown paper; see under *brown*.
business paper; same as *commercial paper*.
kraft paper; same as *kraft*.
on paper; (a) in written or printed form; (b) in theory.
pā′pēr, *a.* 1. of paper; made of or consisting of paper.
2. like paper; thin.
3. appearing or existing only in written or printed statements; theoretical; spurious; as, a *paper* army.
pā′pēr, *v.t.*; papered, *pt.*, *pp.*; papering, *ppr.*
1. to cover with paper, especially wallpaper.
2. to write down on paper; to describe in writing.
3. to wrap or enclose in paper.
4. to help to fill (a theater, etc.) by issuing free passes. [Slang.]
pā′pēr·back, *n.* a book bound in paper, instead of leather, cardboard, etc.
pā′pēr·bärk, *n.* an Australian tree, *Melaleuca leucadendron*.
pā′pēr birch, the North American birch, *Betula papyrifera*, with white or ash-colored, paperlike bark: also called *white birch*.
pā′pēr book, in English law, a copy of the

demurrer book which contains the pleadings on both sides in an action at law, when the issue is one not of fact but of law.

pā′pẽr·boy, *n.* a boy or man who sells or delivers newspapers.

pā′pẽr chāse, the game of hare and hounds, in which pieces of paper are scattered as "scent."

pā′pẽr çlamp, a contrivance for holding newspapers, sheet music, periodicals, etc. in convenient form for reference, and preserving them from injury by keeping them clean and flat.

pā′pẽr çlip, a flexible clasp, typically of metal wire, for holding loose sheets of paper together by pressure.

pā′pẽr çloth, same as *tapa*.

pā′pẽr çōal, a variety of Tertiary lignite: so named from its splitting into films or leaves not thicker than paper.

pā′pẽr çut′tẽr, 1. a machine for cutting and trimming paper to required dimensions.

2. a paper knife.

pā′pẽr·ẽr, *n.* one who papers.

pā′pẽr feed′ẽr, a device for delivering paper in single sheets, as to a printing press, ruling machine, etc.

pā′pẽr hang′ẽr, one whose occupation is to cover walls with wallpaper.

pā′pẽr hang′ings, same as *wallpaper*.

pā′pẽr hor′net, a hornet that makes its nest of a substance resembling paper, especially *Vespa crabro*: also called *paper wasp*.

pā′pẽr knīfe (nīf), a dull, narrow knife of metal, wood, ivory, etc., used to cut folded paper, as sealed envelopes or the uncut pages of books: also called *paper cutter*.

pā′pẽr ma̤·chīne′, a machine for manufacturing paper.

pā′pẽr mill, a mill in which paper is manufactured.

pā′pẽr mŏn′ey, noninterest-bearing notes issued by a government or its banks, circulating as a substitute for metallic money; as, a dollar bill is *paper money*.

pā′pẽr mul′ber·ry, a small tree, *Broussonetia papyrifera*: so named because the Japanese and the Chinese manufacture a kind of paper from its inner bark: also called *paper tree*.

pā′pẽr mus′lin, glazed muslin used for linings and the like.

pā′pẽr nau′ti·lus, an eight-armed mollusk related to the octopus: the female has a thin paperlike shell in which the young develop.

pā′pẽr reed, the papyrus.

pā′pẽr rūl′ẽr, one who or an instrument which traces straight lines on paper for various purposes.

pā′pẽr sāil′ŏr, the paper nautilus.

pā′pẽr shāle, a shale in which the lamination is so fine that laminae can be separated as thin as paper, from thirty to forty having been obtained in one inch.

pā′pẽr shell, anything having a thin shell resembling paper.

pā′pẽr spär, a kind of calcite formed in thin plates: also called *slate spar*.

pā′pẽr stock, material for manufacturing paper.

pā′pẽr tree, the paper mulberry.

pā′pẽr wäsh′ing, in photography, water in which silver photographic prints have been washed.

pā′pẽr wäsp, same as *paper hornet*.

pā′pẽr·weight (-wāt), *n.* any small, heavy object laid on loose papers to prevent them from being misplaced or blown away.

pā′pẽr wŏrk, the keeping of records, filing of reports, etc. that is incidental to some work or task; as, a teacher must spend several hours a day on *paper work*.

pā′pẽr·y, *a.* like paper; having the thinness and consistency of paper.

pap′e·terie (-tri *or Fr.* pȧp″trē′), *n.* [Fr., from *papetier*, paper-maker, from *papier*: see *paper*.] an ornamented case or box for holding paper and other materials for writing.

Pā′phi·ăn, *a.* 1. pertaining to Paphos, an ancient city of Cyprus, sacred to Venus and having one of her celebrated temples.

2. erotic.

Pā′phi·ăn, *n.* 1. one who was born or who lived in Paphos.

2. a prostitute.

pȧ·pier′ (-pyā′), *n.* [Fr.] paper.

pa·pier′ col·lé′ (pȧ-pyā′çol-lā′), *pl.* **pa·piers′ collés** (-pyā′ -lā′), [Fr., lit., pasted paper.] a kind of collage in which the pasted objects are grouped for pattern rather than for symbolism.

pa′pier-mȧ·ché′ (pā′pẽr-mȧ-shā′ *or Fr.* pȧ-pyā′mȧ-shā′), *n.* [Fr. *papier*, paper, and *mâché*, pp. of *mâcher*; L. *masticare*, to chew.] a material made of paper pulp mixed with rosin, oil, etc., that can be molded into various objects while moist.

Pȧ·pil′i·ō, *n.* [L.] a genus of butterflies, type of the *Papilionidæ*.

Pȧ·pil″i·ō·nā′cē·ae, *n.pl.* the legume family of plants: formerly so called from the fancied resemblance of the expanded superior petals to the wings of a butterfly.

pȧ·pil″i·ō·nā′ceous, *a.* 1. resembling the butterfly.

2. in botany, butterfly-shaped: used of a corolla, like that of the pea, in which there are five petals. The upper one, which is erect and more expanded than the rest, is the vexillum or standard; the two lateral ones are the alae or wings; and the two lower, which cohere by their inferior margin, the carina or keel.

Pȧ·pil·i·ō′nēṣ, *n.pl.* same as *Papilionidæ*.

Pȧ·pil·i·on′i·dae, *n.pl.* a family of butterflies, of which the genus *Papilio* is the type.

pȧ·pil′lȧ, *n.*; *pl.* **pa·pil′lae,** 1. (a) any small nipplelike projection or process of connective tissue, as the small elevations at the root of a developing tooth, hair, feather, etc. or the many and variously shaped elevations on the surface of the tongue; (b) the nipple.

2. in botany, a tiny, protruding cell.

pap′il·lăr, *a.* same as *papillary*.

pap′il·lăr·y, *a.* 1. pertaining to or resembling a papilla or papillae; covered with papillae.

2. having papillae; made up of papillae; as, the *papillary* surface of the tongue.

3. having the form of a papilla or of papillae; as, a *papillary* growth.

pap′il·lāte, *a.* same as *papillose*.

pap·il·lif′ẽr·ous, *a.* [L. *papilla*, and *ferre*, to bear.] bearing papillae.

pȧ·pil′li·fọrm, *a.* [L. *papilla*, and *forma*, form.] shaped like a nipple; having the form of a papilla.

pap·il·lī′tis, *n.* inflammation of the optic papilla.

pap·il·lō′mȧ, *n.*; *pl.* **pap·il·lō′mȧ·tȧ, pap·il·lō′mȧṣ,** [Mod. L., from *papilla*, and *-oma*.] a tumor of the skin or mucous membrane, consisting of a thickened and enlarged papilla or group of papillae, as a corn or wart.

pap·il·lom′ȧ·tous, *a.* of the nature of a papilloma.

pap′il·lon (*or Fr.* pȧ-pē-yọṅ′), *n.* [Fr., a butterfly: from the shape of the ears.] any of a breed of toy spaniel: one type has erect, fringed ears.

pap′il·lōse, *a.* covered with or having many papillae.

pap·il·los′i·ty, *n.* the quality of being papillose.

pap′il·lōte, *n.* [Fr.]

1. a small piece of paper for curling the hair; a curlpaper.

2. a paper frill placed on the end of the bone of a chop, cutlet, etc. before serving.

pap′il·lous, *a.* papillose. [Rare.]

pȧ·pil′lū·lāte, *a.* having papillules; especially, having papillules in the central parts of depressions or elevations, as on the surface of certain insects.

pȧ·pil′lūle, *n.* [Mod. L. *papillula*, dim.] a small papilla.

pā′pi·on, *n.* [Fr. *babouin*, a baboon.] any of various baboons.

pā′piṣm, *n.* Roman Catholicism: a hostile term.

pā′pist, *n.* a Roman Catholic; also, one who believes in papal supremacy: a hostile term.

pā′pist, *a.* Roman Catholic: a hostile term.

pȧ·pis′tiç, *a.* same as *papist*.

pȧ·pis′tiç·ăl, *a.* same as *papistic*.

pā′pist·ry, *n.* the beliefs and practices of the Roman Catholic Church: a hostile term.

pā′pīze, *v.t.* to make popish. [Obs.]

pap′mēat, *n.* infants' food. [Rare.]

Pamper him with *papmeat*, if ye will.
—Tennyson.

pa·pọọse′, *n.* [from Amer. Ind. (Algonquian) *papoos*.] a North American Indian baby.

pa·pọọse′rọọt, *n.* a plant, *Caulophyllum thalictroides*, of the barberry family, the root of which is used as an emmenagogue.

pap′păs, *n.* same as *papas*.

Pap′pē·ȧ, *n.* a genus of sapindaceous plants, the only species of which is *Pappea capensis*, a small tree about twenty feet high, native to the Cape of Good Hope.

pap·pif′ẽr·ous, *a.* [*pappus*, and L. *ferre*, to bear.] in botany, having a pappus, as in many composite flowers.

pap′pi·fọrm, *a.* [*pappus* and *form*.] having the form or appearance of a pappus.

pap·pọọse′, *n.* same as *papoose*.

pap·pōse′, *a.* in botany, provided or covered with pappus, or downy chaff, as the seeds of certain plants, as thistles, dandelions, etc.

pap′pous, *a.* same as *pappose*.

pap′pox, *n.* cowpox.

pap′pus, *n.*; *pl.* **pap′pī,** [Mod. L.; Gr. *pappos*, an old man or grandfather; hence, a substance resembling gray hairs.] in botany, a downy or feathery tuft of chaff or bristles on certain fruits, especially of the composite family, as on the seeds of the dandelion.

pap′py, *n.* papa; father. [Dial. or Colloq.]

pap′py, *a.* [from *pap* (soft food), and *-y*.] like pap; soft; succulent.

pap·rī′kȧ, pap·rī′çȧ (*or* pap′ri-), *n.* [G.; Hung.; Gr. *peperi*, a pepper.]

1. the fruit of the capsicum or various other pepper plants.

2. a mild, red condiment ground from it.

Pap test, [after George *Papanicolaou* (1883–1962), Am. anatomist who developed the test.] the microscopic examination of cells taken from the cervix of a woman, used as a test for uterine cancer in its early curable stage.

Pap′ū·ăn, *a.* [Malay, lit., frizzled, from the characteristic hair.] of Papua, its people, or their languages.

Pap′ū·ăn, *n.* 1. a member of the Negroid people living in New Guinea and near-by islands.

2. a member of any of the dark-skinned peoples of Oceania.

3. any of a number of languages spoken in New Guinea, New Caledonia, and elsewhere in the Southwest Pacific.

4. the Papuan family of languages.

pap′ū·lȧ, *n.*; *pl.* **pap′ū·lae,** [L.] 1. in medicine, a papule.

2. in zoology, a small papilla.

pap′ū·lăr, *a.* of or like a papule.

pap·ū·lā′tion, *n.* the production of papules.

pap′ūle, *n.* [L., akin to *papilla*, nipple.] a small, usually inflammatory, elevation of the skin; a pimple.

pap·ū·lif′ẽr·ous, *a.* [*papula*, and L. *ferre*, to bear.] having papules; covered with papules.

pap′ū·lōse, *a.* covered with papules; as, a *papulose* leaf or a *papulose* membrane.

pap′ū·lous, *a.* same as *papulose*.

pap·y·rā′ceous, *a.* made of or resembling papyrus or paper; papery.

pȧ·pyr′i·ăn, *a.* of, or made of, papyrus.

pȧ·pȳ′rī, *n.* plural of *papyrus*.

pap′y·rin, pap′y·rine, *n.* a tough, translucent imitation parchment made by treating paper with a sulfuric acid bath.

pȧ·pȳ′rō·grȧph, *n.* [*papyrus*, and Gr. *graphein*, to write.] any manifolding device, especially one in which a paper stencil is used.

pap·y·rog′rȧ·phy, *n.* manifolding by means of a papyrograph.

pap·y·rol′ō·gist, *n.* one versed in papyrology.

pap·y·rol′ō·gy, *n.* the study and translation of ancient manuscripts written on papyrus.

pȧ·pȳ′rō·type, *n.* a photolithographic process in which the picture to be reproduced is first printed upon specially prepared paper and then transferred to the stone or zinc.

pȧ·pȳ′rus, *n.*; *pl.* **pȧ·pȳ′rī, pȧ·pȳ′rus·eṣ,** [ME. *papirus*; L. *papyrus*; Gr. *papyros*, reed.]

1. a writing material made of strips of the pith of the papyrus plant laid evenly across similar strips in thin layers, the whole being soaked and then dried under pressure: used by the ancient Egyptians, Greeks, and Romans.

2. any ancient manuscript or document on papyrus.

3. a variety of tall water plant, the *Cyperus papyrus*, of the sedge family, formerly abundant in the valley of the Nile. Its soft pith was used for making the writing material.

PAPYRUS (3-12 ft. high)

Päque (päk), *n.* same as *Pasch*.

pär, *n.* same as *parr.*

pär, *n.* [L. *par*, an equal; whence *pair* and *peer.*]
1. the established or recognized value of the money of one country in terms of the money of another country, based on the same metal as standard of value.
2. an equal or common status, standing, footing, level, etc. (with *on* or *upon*); as, he is *on* a *par* with his associates in ability.
3. the average or normal state, condition, degree, etc.; as, his work is above *par.*
4. in commerce, the nominal, or face, value of stocks, bonds, etc.; as, the stock is at *par* when it can be sold for its face value.
5. in golf, the number of strokes established as an expert score for any given hole or for a whole course.

pär, *a.* 1. of or at par.
2. average; normal.

pär, *prep.* [Fr., from L. *per.*] by; by reason of: used in certain phrases taken from the French, as in *par exemple*, by (way of) example.

par-, same as *para-* (beside, etc.).

par'ȧ-, [Gr. *para-*, from *para*, at the side of, alongside, etc.] a prefix meaning: (a) *by the side of, beside, alongside of, by, past, beyond, to one side, aside from*, or *amiss*, as in *para*llel; (b) in chemistry, *an isomer, modification, polymer, derivative, etc. of* (a specified substance): used especially to designate a derivative of benzene in which two atoms or radicals are substituted in positions directly opposite each other in the ring, as in *para*dichlorobenzene; (c) in medicine, *in a secondary or accessory capacity*; (d) in medicine, *functionally disordered, abnormal*, as in *para*functional; (e) in medicine, *like* or *resembling*, as in *para*cholera. Also *par-.*

par'ȧ-, [Fr., from It. *para*, imperative of *parare*, to ward off; L. *parare*, to prepare.] a combining form meaning: (a) *a thing that protects from*, as in *para*chute, *para*pet; (b) *using a parachute*, as in *para*troop.

pä·rä', *n.* a small Turkish coin, the fortieth part of a piaster; also, a small Yugoslavian coin equal to $^1/_{100}$ dinar.

par″ȧ-ȧ·mi″nō·ben·zō'iç ac'id, [*para-* and *amino-* and *benzoic.*] a yellowish crystalline compound, $C_7H_7NO_2$, considered a member of the vitamin B complex, present in yeast and commercially prepared: a deficiency of this factor causes prematurely gray hair.

par'ȧ-an·al·gē'si·ȧ, *n.* analgesia of the lower part of the body.

par'ȧ-an·es·thē'si·ȧ (-zhi-ȧ *or* -zhȧ *or* -zi-ȧ), *n.* [*para-* and *anesthesia.*] anesthesia of both sides of the lower part of the body.

par'ȧ-ap·pend·i·çī'tis, *n.* appendicitis involving the nearby structures.

par·ȧ·ban'iç, *a.* [*para-*, carbamide, alox*an*, and *-ic.*] pertaining to or designating an acid derivable from uric acid by oxidation.

par·ȧ·bap'tism, *n.* baptism which has not been regularly or publicly performed; uncanonical baptism.

par·ab'ȧ·sis, *n.* in ancient Greece, the principal choral part in a comedy, being the poet's address to the audience delivered by the chorus.

par·ȧ·bē'mȧ, *n.*; *pl.* **par·ȧ·bē'mȧ·tȧ,** in Byzantine architecture, a chapel or sacristy separated from the bema or sanctuary by a wall.

par″ȧ·bē·mat'iç, *a.* relating to parabemata: applied, in Byzantine architecture, to a dome resting upon the walls of a parabema or of parabemata.

par'ȧ·blast, *n.* [*para-* (beside, etc.) and *-blast.*] in embryology, the nutritive yolk of a meroblastic ovum: distinguished from *archiblast.*

par·ȧ·blas'tiç, *a.* of or pertaining to the parablast.

par'ȧ·ble, *n.* [OFr. *parabole*, from L. *parabola*, from Gr. *parabolē*, from *paraballein*, to throw beside, to compare; *para*, beside, and *ballein*, to throw.]
1. a short, simple story from which a moral lesson may be drawn: it is usually an allegory.

And his disciples came unto him, saying,
Declare unto us the *parable* of the tares.
—Matt. xiii. 36.

2. an obscure or enigmatic saying. [Archaic.]

par'ȧ·ble, *v.t.*; parabled, *pt., pp.*; parabling, *ppr.* to represent by fiction or fable.

par·ȧ·blep'sis, *n.* in medicine, false or perverted vision.

pȧ·rab'ō·lȧ, *n.*; *pl.* **pȧ·rab'ō·lȧs,** [LL., from Gr. *parabolē*, so called from its axis being parallel to the side of the cone; *para*, beside, and *ballein*, to throw.] in geometry, a plane curve, the path, or locus, of a moving point that remains equally distant from a fixed point (*focus*) and from a fixed straight line (*directrix*); a curve formed by the intersection of a cone with a plane parallel to its side.

PARABOLA
A, focus; AX, axis; DR, directrix; P^1, P^2, P^3, points on the parabola; $P^3Y^3 = P^3A$, $P^2Y^2 = P^2A$, $P^1Y^1 = P^1A$

pȧ·rab'ō·lē, *n.* [Fr.] in rhetoric, similitude; comparison.

par·ȧ·bol'iç, *a.* of, in the form of, or expressed by a parable; allegorical.

par·ȧ·bol'iç, *a.* [LL. *parabolicus*, from *parabola*, a parabola.]
1. of, like, or having the form of a parabola; as, a *parabolic* curve.
2. generated by the revolution of a parabola; as, a *parabolic* conoid.
parabolic cylinder; a cylinder with a parabola for a directrix.
parabolic spindle; the solid generated by the revolution of a portion of a parabola cut off by a double ordinate, about such an ordinate.

par·ȧ·bol'iç·ăl, *a.* same as *parabolic* (allegorical).

par·ȧ·bol'iç·ăl·ly, *adv.* 1. in parables.
2. by means of parabolas.

par·ȧ·bol'i·form, *a.* [LL. *parabola*, a parabola, and L. *forma*, form.] resembling a parabola in form.

pȧ·rab'ō·list, *n.* one who narrates parables.

pȧ·rab'ō·līze, *v.t.*; parabolized, *pt., pp.*; parabolizing, *ppr.* 1. to tell in a parable or parables.
2. to make parabolic in shape.

pȧ·rab'ō·loid, *n.* [Gr. *parabolē*, a parabola, and *eidos*, form.] the surface or solid generated by the rotation of a parabola about its axis.

pȧ·rab·ō·loid'ăl, *a.* of, pertaining to, or in the form of, a paraboloid.

par·ȧ·bū'li·ȧ, *n.* [*para-*, and Gr. *boulesthai*, to will.] in medicine, abnormality of volitional action.

par·ȧ·bū'liç, *a.* pertaining to or affected with parabulia.

par·aç·an·thō'sis, *n.* [*para-*, and Gr. *acantha*, prickle.] an abnormal growth in the prickle layer of the skin.

par″ȧ·çȧ·thod'iç, *a.* [*para-* and *cathodic.*] of, relating to, or designating a cathode ray transformed by impingement upon the anticathode.

Par·ȧ·cel'si·ăn, *n.* a follower of Paracelsus, a Swiss physician of the sixteenth century who advocated observation and experiment.

Par·ȧ·cel'si·ăn, *a.* of or pertaining to the theories or practice of Paracelsus.

Par·ȧ·cel'sist, *n.* a Paracelsian.

par″ȧ·cen·tē'sis, *n.* [Gr. *parakentēsis*; *para*, through, and *kentein*, to pierce.] in surgery, the perforation of a cavity of the body to draw off any effused fluid; tapping.

par·ȧ·cen'triç, par·ȧ·cen'triç·ăl, *a.* [*para-*, and Gr. *kentron*, center.] deviating from circularity.
paracentric motion; the motion by which a revolving planet approaches nearer to, and recedes farther from, the sun, or center of attraction.

par·ȧ·ceph'ȧ·lus, *n.* [*para-*, and Gr. *kephalē*, head.] a fetus with a rudimentary or misshapen head, imperfect sense organs, and defective trunk or limbs.

par·ȧ·chol'li·ȧ, *n.* [*para-*, and Gr. *cholē*, bile.] in pathology, disordered bile secretion.

par·ȧ·chor'dăl, *a.* [*para-*, and Gr. *chordē*, chord.] situated close to the notochord.

par·ȧ·chor'dăl, *n.* the parachordal cartilage.

par·ȧ·chrō'mȧ·tin, *n.* linin, sense 1. [Obs.]

par·ȧ·chrō'mȧ·tism, *n.* [*para-*, and Gr. *chrōma* (*-atos*), color.] irregularity in color perception; color blindness.

pȧ·rach'rō·nism, *n.* [*para-*, and Gr. *chronos*, time.] an error in chronology; especially, the mistake of making the date of an event later than it was in reality.

par'ȧ·chrōse, *a.* [Gr. *parachrōsis*, false coloring.] in mineralogy, changing color by exposure to the weather.

par'ȧ·chute, *n.* [Fr.; *para-* (para-, protecting), and *chute*, a fall.]
1. a large cloth contrivance shaped like an umbrella when expanded, and used to retard the falling speed of a person or thing dropping from an airplane, etc.: it is generally carried folded in a pack, from which it is released by a rip cord or other device.
2. something shaped like or having the effect of a parachute.
3. in zoology, a fold of skin between the fore and hind limbs of flying squirrels, flying lizards, etc., enabling them to glide through the air; patagium.

PARACHUTE

par'ȧ·chute, *v.t.*; parachuted, *pt., pp.*; parachuting, *ppr.* to drop by means of a parachute.

par'ȧ·chute, *v.i.* to descend by means of a parachute.

par'ȧ·chut·ist, *n.* one who uses a parachute.

par'ȧ·clēte, *n.* [OFr. *paraclet*; LL. *paracletus*; Gr. *paraklētos*, from *parakalein*; *para*, to, and *kalein*, to call.] an advocate; one called to aid or support; a consoler, comforter, or intercessor; hence, [P–] in Christianity, the Holy Spirit, considered as comforter, intercessor, or advocate.

par'ȧ·clōse, *n.* same as *perclose.*

par·aç·mas'tiç, *a.* [*para-*, and Gr. *akmē*, point.] gradually declining.

par·aç'mē, *n.* [*para-*, and Gr. *akmē*, point.] the stage of decline or remission.

par·ȧ·con'scious (-shus), *a.* [Gr. *para-*, beside, and *conscious.*] independent of, but associated with, consciousness.

par″ȧ·çō·rol'lȧ, *n.* [*para-* and *corolla.*] in botany, an appendage of a corolla, often forming a nectary.

par·ȧ·çō'tō, *n.* the bark of a South American tree, used in medicine.

par·ȧ·çō'tō·in, *n.* a crystalline substance obtained from paracoto, used in the treatment of diarrhea.

par·ȧ·çou'si·ȧ, *n.* same as *paracusis.*

par·ȧ·çrē'sol, *n.* one of the three isomeric forms of cresol.

par·ȧ·çros'tiç, *n.* a poetical composition in which the first verse contains, in order, all the letters which commence the remaining verses of the poem.

par·ȧ·çū'sis, *n.* [*para-*, and Gr. *akousis*, hearing.] defective hearing.

par″ȧ·çȳ·an'ō·ġen, *n.* [*para-* and *cyanogen.*] a brownish-black insoluble substance, a polymer of cyanogen, which remains after the decomposition of cyanide of mercury by heat.

par·ȧ·çȳ'mēne, *n.* [*para-* (beside, etc.), and *cymene.*] a colorless liquid, $C_{10}H_{14}$, insoluble in water: made from oils of eucalyptus, cumin, thyme, etc., and used as a solvent.

par·ȧ·çys'tiç, *a.* [*para-*, and Gr. *kystis*, bladder.] situated near the bladder.

par″ȧ·çys·tī'tis, *n.* inflammation of the tissues around the bladder.

pȧ·rāde', *n.* [Fr. *parade*, show, display, a military parade, etc., from Sp. *parada*, a parade, a place for the exercise of troops, from L. *parare*, to set or place in order, to prepare.]
1. the ground or place where troops assemble for exercise or drilling, or where a review is held; parade ground.
2. military display; the assembly and orderly arrangement of troops for show, inspection, or the like.

The cherubim stood armed
To their night watches in warlike *parade.*
—Milton.

3. pompous exhibition; ostentatious display.

Be rich, but of your wealth make no *parade.*
—Swift.

4. any organized procession or march, as for display; a formal procession; as, a Labor Day *parade.*

The rites performed, the parson paid,
In state return'd the grand *parade.*—Swift.

5. (a) a public promenade or walk; (b) persons promenading; strollers.
on parade; on display.

pȧ·rāde', *v.t.*; paraded, *pt., pp.*; parading, *ppr.* 1. to bring together (troops, etc.) for inspection or display.

2. to march or walk through, as for display; as, the band *paraded* the streets.

3. to make a display of; to show off; as, he always *parades* his knowledge.

pȧ·rāde′, *v.i.* 1. to march in a parade or procession.

2. to walk about ostentatiously; to show off.

3. to assemble in military formation for review or display.

pȧ·rāde′ rest, in military usage, (a) a formal position of rest, distinguished by its prescribed stance from the informal position of *at ease*; (b) the command to assume this position.

par″ȧ·dī·chlō″rō·ben′zēne, *n.* [*para-* (beside, etc.), and *di-*, and *chloro-*, and *benzene.*] a white, crystalline compound, $C_6H_4Cl_2$, used as an insecticide, deodorant, etc.

par·ȧ·did′y·mis, *n.* in anatomy, a small group of convoluted tubes located above the epididymis, regarded as the remains of the posterior portion of the Wolffian body.

par′ȧ·digm (-dim *or* -dīm), *n.* [Fr. *paradigme*; LL. *paradigma*; Gr. *paradeigma*; *para*, and *deigma*, example, from *deiknynai*, to show.]

1. a pattern, example, or model.

2. in grammar, an example of a declension or conjugation, giving all the inflectional forms of a word.

par″ȧ·dig·mat′iç, par″ȧ·dig·mat′iç·ăl, *a.* of, or having the nature of, a paradigm; exemplary.

par″ȧ·dig·mat′iç, *n.* in church history, a writer of the memoirs of religious persons, as examples of Christian excellence. [Rare.]

par·ȧ·dig′mȧ·tīze, *v.t.* to set forth as a model or example. [Obs.]

par″ȧ·di·sā′iç, *a.* same as *paradisiac.*

par″ȧ·di·sā′iç·ăl, *a.* same as *paradisiacal.*

par·ȧ·dī′săl, *a.* same as *paradisiac.*

par′ȧ·dīse, *n.* [ME. and OFr. *paradis*; L. *paradisus*; Gr. *paradeisos*, a garden, from Old Per. *pairidaeza*, enclosure.]

1. [P–] the garden of Eden.

2. a place or state of bliss; a region or condition of supreme felicity or delight.

3. heaven.

4. a pleasure garden, with parks, animal sanctuaries, etc.

5. an enclosed court in front of medieval churches; also, a small room near an open space.

par′ȧ·dīse, *v.t.* to beatify; to enrapture. [Rare.]

par·ȧ·dis′ē·ăn, *a.* same as *paradisiac.*

par′ȧ·dīse ap′ple, a dwarf type of apple.

par′ȧ·dīse bird, a bird of paradise.

par′ȧ·dīse fish, a fish, *Macropus viridiauratus*, large-finned and brilliantly colored, native to the East Indies.

par′ȧ·dīse flȳ′çatch·ẽr, any passerine bird of the genus *Tersiphone*; especially, *Tersiphone paradisea*, of southern Asia.

par′ȧ·dīse graç′kle, any of various Asiatic grackles, usually of very dark plumage.

par′ȧ·dīse nut, the sapucaia nut.

par·ȧ·dis′i·aç, *a.* [L. *paradisiacus*; Gr. *paradeisiakos.*] pertaining to, like, or fit for paradise or a paradise.

par″ȧ·di·sī′aç·ăl, *a.* same as *paradisiac.*

par·ȧ·dis′i·ăl, *a.* same as *paradisiac.*

par·ȧ·dis′i·ăn, *a.* same as *paradisiac.*

par·ȧ·dis′iç, *a.* same as *paradisiac.*

par′ȧ·dos, *n.* [Fr., from *para-* (that protects) and *dos* (L. dorsum), the back.] in military usage, an embankment of earth at the back edge of a trench for protection against gunfire from the rear.

par′ȧ·dox, *n.* [Fr. *paradoxe*; Gr. *paradoxon*; *para*, beyond, and *doxon*, opinion; *dokein*, to think or suppose.]

1. a statement contrary to common belief. [Rare.]

2. a statement that seems contradictory, unbelievable, or absurd but that may actually be true in fact.

3. a statement that is self-contradictory in fact and, hence, false.

4. (a) something inconsistent with common experience or having contradictory qualities; (b) a person who is inconsistent or contradictory in character or behavior.

Syn.—contradiction, enigma, mystery, absurdity, ambiguity.

par′ȧ·dox·ẽr, *n.* one given to paradox.

par·ȧ·dox′iç·ăl, *a.* 1. of, having the nature of, or expressing a paradox or paradoxes.

2. fond of using paradoxes.

par·ȧ·dox′iç·ăl·ly, *adv.* in a paradoxical manner; in a manner seemingly absurd or impossible.

par·ȧ·dox′iç·ăl·ness, *n.* the state of being paradoxical.

Par·ȧ·dox′i·dēş, *n.* [Gr. *paradoxos*, incredible.] a genus of trilobites having a body two feet or more in length, a ringed thorax, and smooth reniform eyes. The genus is characteristic of the Middle Cambrian.

par·ȧ·dox′ist, *n.* same as *paradoxer.*

par·ȧ·dox′ūre, *n.* [Gr. *paradoxos*, incredible, and *oura*, tail.] any individual of the genus *Paradoxurus*, the palm cats. *Paradoxurus typus*, the common paradoxure, has a blackish body, with some obscure longitudinal bands on the flanks, a black tail, and a white spot below the eye. It is found in India.

par′ȧ·dox·y, *n.* the quality or state of being paradoxical.

par·aes·thē′si·ȧ, *n.* same as *paresthesia.*

par′ăf·fin, *n.* [G., from L. *parum*, little, and *affinis*, akin; from its resistance to chemical reagents.]

1. a white, waxy solid substance consisting of a mixture of hydrocarbons: it is obtained chiefly from the distillation of petroleum and is used for making candles, sealing preserving jars, waterproofing paper, etc.

2. in chemistry, any member of the methane series, the group of hydrocarbons having the general formula C_nH_{2n+2}.

par′ăf·fin, *v.t.* to coat or impregnate with paraffin.

par′ăf·fine (*or* -fēn), *n.* and *v.t.*; paraffined, *pt., pp.*; paraffining, *ppr.* paraffin.

par′ăf·fin oil, 1. any of the hydrocarbon oils formed with paraffin, used for fuel, lubrication, etc.

2. kerosene. [Brit.]

par′ăf·fin pā′pẽr, paper coated with paraffin and made waterproof.

par′ăf·fin sē′riēş, in chemistry, the methane series of hydrocarbons.

par′ăf·fin wax, solid paraffin.

par·ȧ·gas′tẽr, *n.* in zoology, one of two canals extending from the funnel of the *Ctenophora.* They run parallel to the digestive sac, one on each side, and terminate in the caecum before reaching the oral extremity.

par·ȧ·gas′triç, *a.* [*para-* and *gastric.*] of, relating to, or designating the paragaster.

par·ȧ·gas′trụ·lȧ, *n.* the sac resulting from the invagination of an amphiblastula, as in certain sponges.

par′āġe, *n.* [Fr., from LL. *paraticum*, from L. *par*, equal.]

1. in old English law, equality of birth and estate.

2. birth; parentage. [Obs.]

par″ȧ·ġe·nē′si·ȧ, *n.* same as *paragenesis.*

par·ȧ·ġen′e·sis, *n.* [Mod. L.; *para-* (beside, etc.), and *-genesis.*] the formation of minerals in close contact, with a resulting interlocking of their crystals, as in granite, marble, etc.

par″ȧ·ġē·net′iç, *a.* of or resulting from paragenesis.

par·ȧ·ġen′iç, *a.* same as *paragenetic.*

par·ȧ·ġeū′si·ȧ, par·ȧ·ġeū′sis (-gū′), *n.* [*para-*, and Gr. *geusis*, sense of taste.] in medicine, abnormality of the sense of taste.

par·ȧ·glob′ū·lin, *n.* [*para-* and *globulin.*] in physiological chemistry, same as *fibrinoplastin.*

par·ȧ·glos′sȧ, *n.*; *pl.* **par·ȧ·glos′sae,** [*para-*, and Gr. *glōssa*, tongue.] in zoology, a small appendage of the labium found in some insects.

par·ȧ·glos′sāte, *a.* of, pertaining to, or characterized by paraglossae.

par′ag·nath, *n.* in zoology, same as *paragnathus.*

pȧ·rag′nȧ·thous, *a.* in zoology, having equal mandibles, the points of which meet.

pȧ·rag′nȧ·thus, *n.*; *pl.* **pȧ·rag′nȧ·thī,** [*para-*, and Gr. *gnathos*, jaw.] in zoology, a toothlike jaw in certain of the *Annelida*; also, one of a pair of the lobes on the metastome of a crustacean.

par·ȧ·gō′ġe, *n.* [Gr. *paragōgē*, a drawing out; *para*, beyond, and *agein*, to lead.] in grammar, the addition of a letter or syllable at the end of a word, either functionally, as in drown*ed*, or unnecessarily, as in substandard drown*ded.*

par·ȧ·gog′iç, par·ȧ·gog′iç·ăl, *a.* of, having the nature of, or forming a paragoge.

par′ȧ·gon, *n.* [OFr. *paragon*; It. *paragone*, touchstone, from Gr. *parakonaein*, to test with a whetstone, from *para*, against, and *akonē*, whetstone.]

1. a model or pattern; a model of superior excellence or perfection; as, a *paragon* of beauty or eloquence.

2. a companion; a comrade; a mate. [Obs.]

3. emulation; rivalry. [Obs.]

4. a perfect diamond weighing a hundred carats or more.

5. in printing, a size of type, 20-point.

par′ȧ·gon, *v.t.* 1. to put side by side; to compare. [Poetic.]

2. to be equal to; to match. [Poetic.]

3. to surpass. [Obs.]

4. to set forth as a paragon. [Obs.]

par′ȧ·gon, *v.i.* to pretend to comparison or equality. [Rare.]

pȧ·rag′ō·nīte, *n.* [*paragon* and *-ite.*] a kind of mica, resembling muscovite but containing sodium instead of potassium.

pȧ·rag′ō·nīte sçhist, a mica schist found in the Alps, in which the mica is partly or wholly replaced by paragonite.

par′ȧ·gram, *n.* [Gr. *paragramma*, that which one writes beside; *para*, beside, and *gramma*, a writing.] a play upon words; a pun. [Rare.]

par·ȧ·gram′mȧ·tist, *n.* a punster. [Rare.]

par′ȧ·grȧph, *n.* [Fr. *paragraphe*; LL. *paragraphus*; Gr. *paragraphē*, a marginal note; *para*, beyond, and *graphein*, to write.]

1. a distinct section or subdivision of a chapter, letter, etc., usually dealing with a particular point: it is always begun on a new line and is often indented.

2. a mark (⁋ or ¶) used chiefly by proofreaders to indicate the beginning of a separate passage or paragraph, or a sign marking material referred to elsewhere.

3. a brief article, item, or note in a newspaper or magazine.

par′ȧ·grȧph, *v.t.*; paragraphed, *pt., pp.*; paragraphing, *ppr.* 1. to paragraph. [Obs.]

2. to separate or arrange in paragraphs.

3. to treat in a paragraph or paragraphs.

I am sneered at by my acquaintances and *paragraphed* by the newspapers.
—Sheridan.

par′ȧ·grȧph, *v.i.* to write paragraphs, especially for a newspaper.

par′ȧ·grȧph·ẽr, *n.* one who writes paragraphs; specifically, a writer of editorial paragraphs for a newspaper.

par·ȧ·graph′i·ȧ, *n.* [Mod. L., from *para-* (beside, etc.), and Gr. *graphein*, to write.] a mental disorder, generally due to cerebral injury, characterized by the unintentional omission, transposition, or insertion of letters or words in writing.

par·ȧ·graph′iç, *a.* pertaining to or forming a paragraph or paragraphs.

par·ȧ·graph′iç·ăl, *a.* paragraphic.

par·ȧ·graph′iç·ăl·ly, *adv.* by or in paragraphs.

par′ȧ·grȧph·ist, *n.* one who writes paragraphs.

par″ȧ·grȧ·phis′tiç·ăl, *a.* like or belonging to a paragraphist.

Pä·rä′ grȧss, in botany, a fine grass, *Panicum barbinode*, growing in tropical countries.

Par·ȧ·guāy′ăn (-gwā′), *a.* of or belonging to Paraguay, South America, its people, or culture; as, the *Paraguayan* language; a *Paraguayan* citizen.

Par·ȧ·guāy′ăn *n.* a native or inhabitant of Paraguay.

Par′ȧ·guāy tēa, 1. a beverage made from the leaves of a South American plant, *Ilex paraguayensis.*

2. this plant.

Also called *matē.*

PARAGUAY TEA (*Ilex paraguayensis*)

par·ȧ·hē·li·ot′rō·pişm, *n.* [*para-*, and Gr. *hēlios*, sun, and *trepein*, to turn.] in botany, the adjusting of the surface, as of a leaf, so as to be parallel with the rays of the sun; diurnal sleep of a leaf.

pȧ·raī′bȧ, *n.* [Braz.] a Brazilian plant of the genus *Simaruba.*

par′ȧ·keet, *n.* [OFr. *paroquet.*] any of certain small, slender parrots with long, tapering tails: also *parrakeet, parroket, paroquet, parroquet.*

par·ȧ·laç′tiç, *a.* [*para-* and *lactic.*] designating a modified form or condition of lactic acid, $C_3H_6O_3$.

paralactic acid; an acid isomeric with lactic acid, found in muscular tissue and in urine, bile, etc.

par·ȧ·lā′li·ȧ, *n.* [*para-*, and Gr. *lalia*, speech.] a speech disorder characterized by distortions of sound.

par·al′dē·hȳde, *n.* [*par-* and *aldehyde.*] a colorless liquid, $(CH_3CHO)_3$, produced by the polymerization of formaldehyde, having a strong, nauseating smell and used in medicine as a hypnotic and sedative.

par″ȧ·lē′găl, *a.* [*para-* and *legal.*] designating or of persons trained to aid lawyers but not licensed to practice law.

par″ȧ·lē′găl, *n.* a person doing paralegal work.

par·ȧ·leīp′sis, *n.* [Gr. *paraleipsis,* omission, from *para-,* beyond, and *leipein,* to leave.] in rhetoric, a device in which a point is stressed by suggesting that it is too obvious or well-known to mention, as in the phrase, "not to mention the expense involved."

par·ȧ·lep′sis, *n.* same as *paraleipsis.*

par·al·ġe′si·ȧ, *n.* [*par-,* and Gr. *algesis,* sense of pain, from *algos,* pain.] any condition marked by abnormal and painful sensations.

par″ȧ·li·pom′e·nȧ, *n.pl.* [Gr. *paraleipomena,* things omitted, from *paraleipein,* to omit; *para,* beyond, and *leipein,* to leave.]

1. things omitted; a supplement containing things omitted in the preceding work.

2. [P–] in the Douay version of the Bible, the Books of Chronicles, so called because they were regarded as supplemental to the Books of Kings.

Par″ȧ·li·pom′e·non, *n.pl.* same as *paralipomena,* sense 2.

par·ȧ·lip′sis, *n.* same as *paraleipsis.*

par·ăl·laç′tiç, par·ăl·laç′tiç·ăl, *a.* pertaining to a parallax.

par′ăl·lax, *n.* [Gr. *parallaxis,* from *parallassein,* to vary, to decline or wander; *para,* beyond, and *allassein,* to change.]

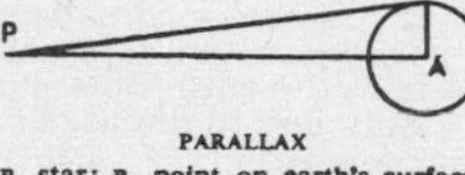

PARALLAX
P, star; R, point on earth's surface; A, center of the earth; angle RPA, parallax

1. the apparent change in the position of an object resulting from the change in the direction or position from which it is viewed.

2. the amount or angular degree of such change; specifically, in astronomy, the apparent difference in the position of a heavenly body with reference to some point on the surface of the earth and some other point, as the center of the earth (*diurnal,* or *geocentric, parallax*) or a point on the sun (*annual,* or *heliocentric, parallax*): the parallax of an object may be used in determining its distance from the observer.

binocular parallax; the difference between the position of an object as seen by one eye and that in which it is seen by the other, the head remaining unmoved.

horizontal parallax; the geocentric parallax of the sun, moon, or a planet when on the horizon.

optical parallax; same as *binocular parallax.*

stellar parallax; the annual parallax of a fixed star.

par′ăl·lel, *a.* [Fr. *parallèle;* L. *parallelus;* Gr. *parallēlos; para,* side by side, and *allēlōn,* of one another.]

1. extending in the same direction and at the same distance apart at every point, so as never to meet, as lines, planes, etc.: in modern non-Euclidian geometry, such lines and planes are considered to meet at infinity.

2. having parallel parts or movements, as some machines, tools, etc.

3. closely similar or corresponding, as in purpose, tendency, time, or essential parts.

4. in music, having consistently equal intervals in pitch, as two parts of harmony, a series of chords, etc.

parallel bar; (a) one of a pair of horizontal bars, parallel to each other, and supported by posts or a framework at a distance of from

PARALLEL BARS

four to six feet from the ground, used for gymnastic exercises; (b) in a steam engine, a rod parallel to the working beam, in the system of linkwork which converts reciprocating circular motion into rectilinear reciprocating motion.

parallel circles of a sphere; the circles of a sphere, having planes parallel to each other.

parallel columns; in printing, two or more passages of reading matter printed side by side in space the width of one ordinary column, for the purpose of illustrating their similarity or the difference between them.

parallel forces; mechanical forces which act in directions parallel to each other.

parallel motion; (a) a contrivance invented by Watt, for converting a reciprocating circular motion into an alternating rectilinear motion. The chief use to which the parallel motion is applied is to connect the pump rod and piston rod of a steam engine with the working beam in such a manner that while the points of the beam, to which these rods are attached, move in arcs of circles, the rods are made to move up and down in straight lines parallel to the sides of the cylinder; (b) in music, the movement of two or more parts at fixed intervals, as in a succession of thirds or sixths.

parallel rod; a coupling rod.

parallel ruler; a device for drawing lines parallel to each other, usually a pair of rulers so constructed and connected as to be parallel at all times at whatever distance apart they may be.

parallel sailing; the method of sailing when a ship's course lies along a degree or parallel of latitude.

parallel sphere; the position of the sphere in which, to an observer at either pole, the angle between the planes of the equator and the horizon vanishes.

parallel vise; a vise whose two jaws are always parallel.

Syn.—correspondent, congruous, correlative, analogous, concurrent, equidistant.

par′ăl·lel, *n.* 1. something parallel to something else, as a line or surface.

2. any person or thing essentially the same as, or closely similar or corresponding to, something else; counterpart.

3. the condition of being parallel; conformity in essential points.

4. any comparison showing the existence of similarity or likeness.

5. any of the imaginary lines parallel to the equator and representing degrees of latitude on the earth's surface.

6. such a line drawn on a map or globe.

7. in electricity, a hookup of lights, cells, etc. in which all positive poles or terminals are connected in one conductor and all negatives in another: also called *multiple circuit.*

8. in military science, a trench, usually one of a series, running parallel to and opposing a position.

9. [*pl.*] in printing, a sign (||) marking material referred to in a note.

parallel of altitude; in astronomy, one of the small circles of the sphere parallel to the horizon: also called *almucantars.*

parallel of declination; one of the small circles of the celestial sphere parallel to the equator.

parallel of latitude; a parallel (senses 5 and 6).

par′ăl·lel, *v.t.;* paralleled *or* parallelled, *pt., pp.;* paralleling *or* parallelling, *ppr.* 1. (a) to make (one thing) parallel to another; (b) to make parallel to each other.

2. to be parallel with; to extend parallel to; as, the highway *parallels* the river.

3. to compare (things, ideas, etc.) in order to show similarity or likeness.

4. to find a counterpart for; to match.

5. to be a counterpart for; to match; to equal.

par′ăl·lel, *v.i.* to be alike; to be parallel.

par′ăl·lel·ȧ·ble, *a.* capable of being made parallel or equal.

par·ăl·lel·ē·pī′ped, par·ăl·lel·ē·pip′e·don, *n.* [Gr. *parallēlos,* parallel, and *epipedos,* on the ground, on a level with it, plane, superficial; *epi,* upon, and *pedon,* the ground.] in geometry, a regular solid with six faces, each of which is a parallelogram.

PARALLELEPIPED

par′ăl·lel·iṣm, *n.* 1. the state of being parallel.

2. close resemblance; similarity.

3. in philosophy, the theory that mind and matter, though independent, function together in a parallel, but without an interactive causal relationship.

par·ăl·lel·is′tiç, *a.* having the nature of or illustrating parallelism.

par′ăl·lel·īze, *v.t.;* parallelized, *pt., pp.;* parallelizing, *ppr.* to make parallel.

par′ăl·lel·less, *a.* matchless; unrivaled; peerless. [Rare.]

par·ăl·lel′ō·drōme, *a.* [Gr. *parallēlos,* parallel, and *-dromos,* from *dramein,* to run.] in botany, having parallel veins, either longitudinally, as in grasses, or from the midrib to the margin, as in certain ferns.

par·ăl·lel′ō·gram, *n.* [Gr. *parallēlogrammon; parallēlos,* parallel, and *grammē,* a stroke in writing, from *graphein,* to write.] a plane figure with four sides, having the opposite sides parallel and equal.

PARALLELOGRAM

parallelogram of accelerations, forces, momenta, velocities, etc.; a diagrammatic representation of the resultant of two accelerations, forces, momenta, velocities, etc., by means of a parallelogram and its diagonal, the parallelogram representing, in terms of its sides, the respective accelerations, forces, momenta, velocities, etc., and the diagonal, their resultant.

par·ăl·lel″ō·gram·mat′iç, *a.* of or pertaining to a parallelogram.

par·ăl·lel·ō·gram′miç, par·ăl·lel·ō·gram′miç·ăl, *a.* parallelogrammatic.

par·ăl·lel·om′e·tēr, *n.* [Gr. *parallēlos,* parallel, and *metron,* measure.] an instrument for ascertaining the accuracy of parallel surfaces, especially of plate glass.

par·ăl·lel·ō·pī′ped, *n.* same as *parallelepiped.*

par·ăl·lel·ō·pip′ē·don, *n.* same as *parallelepipedon.*

par·ȧ·loġ′iç·ăl, *a.* [*para-* and *logical.*] illogical; dependent on paralogism.

pȧ·ral′ō·ġiṣm, *n.* [Gr. *paralogismos; para,* beyond, and *logismos,* reasoning; *logos,* discourse, reason.] in logic, a reasoning which is false in point of form; that is, in which a conclusion is drawn from premises which do not logically warrant it; faulty reasoning.

pȧ·ral·ō·ġis′tiç, *a.* of or by a paralogism; faulty in logic.

pȧ·ral′ō·ġīze, *v.i.;* paralogized, *pt., pp.;* paralogizing, *ppr.* to reason falsely or illogically.

pȧ·ral′ō·ġy, *n.* false reasoning; paralogism.

par′ȧ·lȳṣe, *v.t.* same as *paralyze.*

pȧ·ral′y·sis, *n.; pl.* **pȧ·ral′y·sēṣ,** [Gr. *paralysis,* from *paralyein,* to loosen, dissolve, or weaken at the side; *para,* beside, and *lyein,* to loose.] 1. (partial or complete) loss of the power of motion or sensation, especially voluntary motion, in some part or all of the body, as the result of injury to the nervous system or to some muscular mechanism.

2. a condition of helpless inactivity; a crippling of activities.

par·ȧ·lyt′iç, par·ȧ·lyt′iç·ăl, *a.* 1. of, or having the nature of, paralysis.

2. inclined or tending to paralysis.

3. having or subject to paralysis.

par·ȧ·lyt′iç, *n.* a person affected with paralysis.

par′ȧ·lȳ·zănt, *a.* causing paralysis.

par′ȧ·lȳ·zănt, *n.* anything that paralyzes.

par″ȧ·lȳ·zā′tion, *n.* the act of paralyzing; the state of being paralyzed.

par′ȧ·lȳze, *v.t.;* paralyzed, *pt., pp.;* paralyzing, *ppr.* 1. to cause paralysis in; to make paralytic.

2. to bring into a condition of helpless inactivity; to make ineffective or powerless.

Syn.—deaden, benumb, prostrate, enervate, debilitate, enfeeble.

par′ȧ·lȳzed, *a.* affected with paralysis.

par′ăm, *n.* a substance, CH_2N_2, produced by the action of carbonic anhydride on sodamide. It is isomeric with cyanamide, and crystallizes in groups of fine silky needles melting at 100°, and dissolving in water and alcohol.

par·ȧ·mag′net, *n.* any paramagnetic substance or thing.

par″ȧ·mag·net′iç, *a.* having a magnetic permeability greater than unity; having a capacity for magnetization greater than that of a vacuum.

par″ȧ·mag·net′iç·ăl·ly, *adv.* in a paramagnetic manner.

par·ȧ·mag′net·iṣm, *n.* the quality or condition of being paramagnetic.

par·ȧ·mas′toid, *a.* situated beside or near the mastoid process.

par·ȧ·mat′tȧ, *n.* [after *Paramatta,* Australia.] a light twilled dress goods of cotton and wool or, formerly, silk and wool: also spelled *parramatta.*

par·ȧ·mē′ci·um (-shi- *or* -si-) *n.; pl.* **par·ȧ·mē′ci·ȧ,** [Mod. L.; Gr. *paramēkēs,* oval.] any of a number of related one-celled, elongated animals, having a large mouth in a fold at the side and moving by means of cilia.

par'a·med·ic, *n.* a medic, especially a medical corpsman, who parachutes to combat or rescue areas.

par'a·med·ic, *n.* a person in paramedical work.

par·a·med'i·cal, *a.* designating or of auxiliary medical personnel, such as midwives, corpsmen, laboratory technicians, nurses' aides, etc.

par·a·mē'ni·a, *n.* [*para-*, and Gr. *mēnes*, menses.] disordered or difficult menstruation.

par'a·ment, *n.* [LL. *paramentum*, from L. *parare*, to prepare, adorn.] an ornamental drapery, piece of furniture, or other decorative article, especially in a state apartment; also, a rich and elegant robe of state. [Obs.]

par·a·men'tō, *n.* [Sp.] same as *parament.*

par'a·mēre, *n.* [*para-*, and Gr. *meros*, part.]
1. in biology, one of the symmetrical halves of a bilaterally symmetrical animal.
2. either one of the halves of a somite of a bilateral animal.
3. any radiated part or organ, as one of the rays of a starfish.

pa·ram'e·tēr, *n.* [LL. *parametrum*, from Gr. *para*, beside, and *metron*, measure.]
1. in mathematics, a quantity or constant whose value varies with the circumstances of its application, as the radius line of a group of concentric circles, which varies with the circle under consideration.
2. any constant, with variable values, used as a referent for determining other variables.

par·a·met'riç, *a.* [*para-*, and Gr. *mētra*, uterus.] near the uterus.

par"a·mē·trī'tis, *n.* [*para-*, Gr. *mētra*, uterus, and *-itis.*] inflammation of the parametrium.

par·a·mē'tri·um, *n.* the tissue that surrounds the uterus.

par'a·mide, *n.* in chemistry, a substance obtained by heating the ammonium salt of mellitic acid.

par·a·mil'i·tar·y, *a.* 1. designating, of, or having to do with forces working alongside of or in place of a regular military organization, usually as a semi-official, often secret, auxiliary.
2. designating or of a private, often secret, quasi-military organization.

par·a·mim'i·a, *n.* [LL., from Gr. *para*, beside, and *mimeisthai*, to imitate.] in pathology, loss of power to make natural or expressive gestures or movements.

par"a·mi·og'ra·phēr, *n.* [Gr. *paroimia*, proverb, and *graphein*, to write.] a writer of proverbs; one who collects proverbs. [Rare.]

par·a·mī'tōme, *n.* [*para-* and *mitome.*] the fluid portion of the cell substance contained within the meshes of the spongioplasm.

par·am·nē'si·a, *n.* [*para-*, and Gr. *mnēsi-*, remembering, from *mimnēskein*, to remind.] disorder or derangement of the memory; a state in which words are remembered but are used without due comprehension of their meaning.

pa'ra·mō, *n.*; *pl.* **pa'ra·mōs,** [Sp.] a high, treeless plain or plateau, as in the Andean range in South America, exposed to winds and generally enveloped in fog.

par·a·moe'ci·um (-shi-), *n.* same as *paramecium.*

par'a·morph, *n.* [*para-*, and Gr. *morphē*, shape.] a mineral that has undergone paramorphism.

par·a·mor'phi·a, par·a·mor'phine, *n.* same as *thebaine.*

par·a·mor'phiç, *a.* of, pertaining to, or characterized by paramorphism.

par·a·mor'phism, *n.* in mineralogy, the process by which some minerals undergo a change in physical character without change of their chemical composition.

par·a·mor'phous, *a.* same as *paramorphic.*

par'a·mount, *a.* [OFr. *paramont*; *par*, by, and *à mont*, uphill.] ranking higher than any other, as in power and importance; chief; supreme.

par'a·mount, *n.* a person having supreme power.

par'a·mount·cy, *n.* the quality or condition of being paramount.

par·a·mount'ly, *adv.* in a paramount manner.

par'a·mour, *n.* [Fr. *par amour*, with love; *par* (L. *per*), by, and *amour* (L. *amor*), love.]
1. a man's mistress or a woman's lover.
2. a sweetheart. [Archaic or Poetic.]

par"a·my·oç'lō·nus, *n.* [*para-*, and Gr. *mys, myos*, muscle, and *klonos*, confused motion.] a nervous disease in which the limbs are affected by sudden bilateral contractions of the muscles.

par·a·my·ō·sin'ō·gen, *n.* [*para-*, and *myosinogen.*] a protein found in muscle plasma.

par·a·naph'tha·lēne, *n.* anthracene. [Obs.]

par·a·neph'riç, *a.* 1. located near the kidney.
2. of a paranephros.

par"a·nē·phrī'tis, *n.* [*para-*, and *nephritis.*] inflammation of the paranephros.

par·a·neph'ros, *n.* [Gr. *para*, beside, and *nephros*, kidney.] an adrenal gland.

par·a·noi'a, *n.* [*para-*, and Gr. *nous*, mind.] in psychiatry, a mental disorder characterized by systematized delusions, as of grandeur or, especially, persecution.

par·a·noi'aç, *n.* one affected with paranoia.

par·a·noi'aç, *a.* of, like, or having paranoia.

par'a·noid, *a.* 1. of or like paranoia.
2. characterized by oversuspiciousness, grandiose delusions, or delusions of persecution.

par'a·noid, *n.* a person afflicted with paranoia.

par·ant·hē'li·on, *n.*; *pl.* **par·ant·hē'li·a,** [*par-*, Gr. *anti*, over, against, and *helios*, sun.] a diffuse image of the sun due to reflection from ice in the atmosphere; it has the same altitude as the sun and an angular distance from it varying from 90° to 140°.

par·an'thra·cēne, *n.* [*para-* and *anthracene.*] a crystalline isomer of anthracene.

par·a·nū'çlē·ar, *a.* of or pertaining to a paranucleus.

par·a·nū'çlē·in, *n.* [*para-* and *nuclein.*] a form of nuclein found in the nucleus of certain cells.

par·a·nū'çlē·us, *n.* [*para-* and *nucleus.*] an extranuclear body sometimes seen in cell protoplasm; an accessory nucleus.

Pä·rä' nut, same as *Brazil nut.*

par'a·nymph, *n.* [*para-*, and Gr. *nymphē*, bride.]
1. in ancient Greece, (a) a friend of the bridegroom who escorted him when he went to take his bride home; (b) a bridesmaid who escorted the bride to the bridegroom.
2. a best man or bridesmaid at a wedding.

par·a·nym'phal, *a.* of or pertaining to a paranymph. [Obs.]

par'a·pegm (-pem), *n.* [Gr. *parapegma*, tablet, from *para*, beside, and *pēgnynai*, to fix.] in ancient Greece, a table, usually of brass, fixed to a pillar, on which laws and proclamations were engraved; also, a table set in a public place, containing an account of the rising and setting of the stars, eclipses, seasons, etc.

par'a·pet, *n.* [Fr.; It. *parapetto*; *parare*, to guard, and *petto*, breast; L. *pectus.*]
1. a wall or bank used to screen troops from frontal enemy fire, sometimes placed along the top of a rampart.
2. a wall or railing to protect people from falling, as on a balcony or bridge.

par·a·pet'al·ous, *a.* [*para-*, and Gr. *petalon*, petal.] growing or standing by the side of a petal, as stamens in some plants.

par'a·pet·ed, *a.* having a parapet or parapets.

par'aph, *n.* [It. *paraffo*, paragraph.] a flourish made under one's signature, formerly used as a safeguard against forgery.

par'aph, *v.t.*; paraphed (-aft), *pt., pp.*; paraphing, *ppr.* to affix a paraph to; to sign, especially with the initials.

par·a·phā'si·a, *n.* [*par-* and *aphasia.*] a form of aphasia characterized by inability to express thoughts by the proper words.

par·a·phēr'na, *n.* [Gr. *parapherna*; *para*, beyond, and *phernē*, dower, from *pherein*, to bring.] in Roman law, the property which a wife brought with her at her marriage, or which she possessed beyond her dower or jointure, and which remained at her disposal after her husband's death.

par·a·phēr'nal, *a.* pertaining to or consisting in parapherna; as, *paraphernal* property.

par"a·phēr·nā'li·a, *n.pl.* [LL. *paraphernalia bona*, wife's own goods; Gr. *parapherna*; see *parapherna.*]
1. personal belongings.
2. any collection of articles, usually things used in some activity; equipment; apparatus; trappings; gear.
3. in law, formerly, property or possessions (other than dower) given over to the control, but not complete possession, of a wife.

par"a·phi·mō'sis, *n.* [Gr. *paraphimōsis.*] in pathology, a condition in which the opening of the prepuce is too small to allow it to be drawn back over the glans penis after it has been retracted.

par·a·phō'ni·a, *n.* [*para-*, and Gr. *phōnē*, voice.]
1. an abnormal alteration of voice.
2. in music, a melodic progression by the only consonances recognized in the Greek music, namely, fourths and fifths.

par·a·phos·phor'iç, *a.* pyrophosphoric. [Obs.]

par'a·phrase, *n.* [Gr. *paraphrasis*; *para*, beyond, and *phrasis*, phrase.]
1. a rewording of the thought or meaning expressed in something that has been said or written before.
2. the use or process of paraphrase as an educational or literary method.

par'a·phrase, *v.t.* and *v.i.*; paraphrased, *pt., pp.*; paraphrasing, *ppr.* to express in a paraphrase.

par·a·phrā'si·a (-zhi-), *n.* [*para-* and Gr. *phrasis*, utterance.] incoherent speech, an aphasic symptom or manifestation.

par'a·phrast, *n.* one who paraphrases.

par·a·phras'tiç, par·a·phras'tiç·al, *a.* [ML. *paraphrasticus*; Gr. *paraphrastikos.*]
1. of, having the nature of, or forming a paraphrase.
2. using paraphrase.

par·a·phras'tiç·al·ly, *adv.* in a paraphrastic manner; so as to paraphrase.

pa·raph'y·sāte, *a.* of, pertaining to, or designating paraphyses.

pa·raph'y·sis, *n.*; *pl.* **pa·raph'y·sēs,** [Gr., from *para*, beyond, and *phyein*, to produce.] a sterile filament found with the spore-bearing organs of some ferns and mosses.

par'a·plasm, *n.* [Gr. *paraplasma*, monster; *para*, beside, and *plasma*, anything formed.] a malformation of any kind.

par·a·plas'tiç, *a.* pertaining to or characterized by paraplasm.

par·a·plē'gi·a, par'a·plē·gy, *n.* [Gr. *paraplegia*, paralysis; *para*, beyond, and *plēgē*, stroke; *plēssein*, to smite.] motor and sensory paralysis of the entire lower part of the body, generally due to disease or lesion of the spine.

par·a·pleg'iç (*or* -plēg'), *a.* pertaining to or having paraplegia.

par·a·pleg'iç (*or* -plēg'), *n.* a person having paraplegia.

par·a·pleū'ra, *n.*; *pl.* **par·a·pleū'rae,** [*para-*, and Gr. *pleura*, rib.] a horny plate situated between the last part of the breastplate and the lateral plates in some insects.

par·a·pō'di·um, *n.*; *pl.* **par·a·pō'di·a,** [*para-*, and Gr. *pous, podos*, the foot.] one of the unarticulated lateral locomotive processes of many of the *Annelida.* It is sometimes called a *foot tubercle*, and may be used for either breathing, feeling, or moving about.

par·ap·ō·phys'i·al, *a.* pertaining to parapophysis.

par·a·poph'y·sis, *n.*; *pl.* **par·a·poph'y·sēs,** [Gr. *para*, beside, and *apophysis*, an outgrowth, an offshoot; *apo*, away, and *physis*, growth.] in comparative anatomy, the transverse process of a typical vertebra with which the end of the rib articulates.

par·a·prax'is, *n.*; *pl.* **par·a·prax'ēs,** [*para-*, and *praxis.*] an action in which one's conscious intention is not fully carried out, as in the mislaying of objects, slips of the tongue and pen, etc.: thought to be due to a conflicting unconscious intention.

par·a·prō·fes'sion·al, *n.* a worker trained to perform certain functions, as in medicine or teaching, but not licensed to practice as a professional.

pa·rap'si·dal, *a.* pertaining to a parapsis.

pa·rap'sis, *n.*; *pl.* **pa·rap'si·dēs,** [*para-*, and Gr. *hapsis*, loop.] one of the side plates of the back of the middle thoracic segment of an insect.

par"a·psy·chol'ō·gy (-sī-), *n.* the study that investigates the psychological aspect of apparently supernatural phenomena as telepathy, clairvoyance, extrasensory perception, etc.

pa·rap'tē·rum, *n.*; *pl.* **pa·rap'tē·ra,** [*para-*, and Gr. *pteron*, wing.] in entomology, one of the sclerites on each side of the thorax of an insect.

par'a·quet (-ket), *n.* a parakeet.

Par·arç·tā'li·a, *n.* in zoogeography, the temperate region of the northern ocean.

Pa·rá' rub'bēr (pä·rä'), crude rubber obtained from several South American trees.

par'a·sang, *n.* [Gr. *parasanges*; Per. *farsang.*] an ancient Persian measure of length, equal to thirty stadia, about 3½ miles.

par·a·scē'ni·um, *n.*; *pl.* **par·a·scē'ni·a,** [*para-*, and Gr. *skēnē*, stage.] in the Greek theater, a projecting wing on the side of the proscenium.

par'a·scēve, *n.* [Gr. *paraskeuē*, preparation.]

the day of preparation for, or the eve of, the Jewish Sabbath. [Rare.]

par″à·sçhē·mat′iç, *a.* [*para-*, and Gr. *schēma*, form.] of or designating words formed from others by means of inflections. [Rare.]

par″à·se·lē′ne, *n.*; *pl.* **par″à·se·lē′nae,** [*para-*, and Gr. *selēnē*, the moon.] a mock moon; a bright moonlike spot on a luminous ring or circle encompassing the moon.

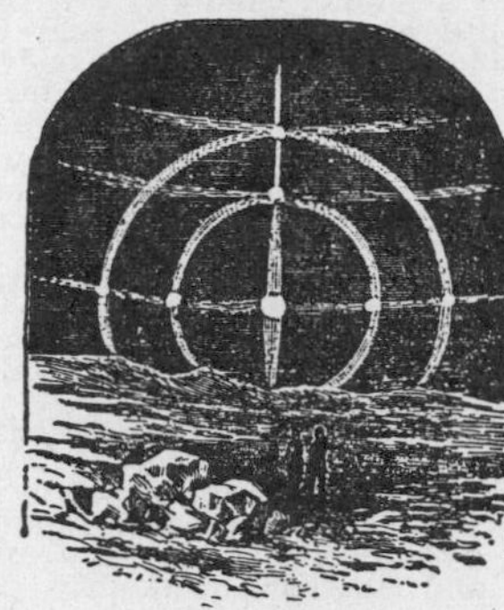

PARASELENAE

par′à·shäh, *n.*; *pl.* **par′à·shōth,** [Heb. *pārāshāh.*] a section of the Pentateuch read as part of the Jewish synagogue service on Sabbaths and holidays.

Par·à·sī′tà, *n.pl.* the parasitic animals. [Obs.]

par′à·sī·tăl, *a.* parasitic.

par′à·sīte, *n.* [Fr. *parasite*, from L. *parasitus*, from Gr. *parasitos*, one who eats beside or at the table of another, a parasite, a toady; *para*, beside, and *sitos*, food.]

1. in ancient Greece, (a) a person who flattered and amused his host in return for free meals; (b) a priest's helper who feasted with the priests after sacrificial rites.

2. a person who lives at the expense of another or others without making any useful contribution or return; a hanger-on.

3. in biology, a plant or animal that lives on or within another organism, from which it derives sustenance or protection without making compensation.

4. in mineralogy, a plumose variety of boracite, resulting from partial alteration.

Syn.—sycophant, fawner, flatterer, toady, wheedler.

par·à·sit′iç, par·à·sit′iç·ăl, *a.* 1. of or like a parasite; living at the expense of others.

2. caused by parasites, as a disease.

3. in phonetics, designating a sound which is attached to a word erroneously or by false analogy, as the *t* in tyran*t* and margen*t*.

par·à·sit′iç·ăl·ly, *adv.* in the manner of a parasite; by dependence on another.

par·à·sit′iç·ăl·ness, *n.* the quality of being parasitic.

par·à·sit′i·cīde, *a.* [from *parasite* and *-cide.*] that destroys parasites.

par·à·sit′i·cīde, *n.* anything used to destroy parasites.

par′à·sī·tism, *n.* 1. the state or condition of being a parasite.

2. the habits of a parasite.

3. in medicine, (a) the condition of being infested with parasites; (b) any of various diseases, as of the skin, caused by parasites.

par″à·sī·tol′ō·ġy, *n.* [*parasite*, and Gr. *logos*, discourse.] that branch of natural science which concerns itself with parasites.

par′à·sol, *n.* [Fr. *parasol*, from It. *parasole*; *parare*, Fr. *parer*, to ward off, and *sole*, L. *sol*, the sun.] a small umbrella used by women to protect themselves from the sun's rays.

par′à·sol, *v.t.* to screen with some covering like a parasol. [Rare.]

par′à·sol ȧnt, an ant that carries leaves; an umbrella ant.

par″à·sol·ette′, *n.* a small parasol or sunshade.

par′à·sol fīr, a Japanese tree, *Sciadopitys verticillata.*

par′à·sol mush′room, a large, edible mushroom, *Agaricus procerus.*

par·à·sphē′noid, *a.* pertaining to or situated near the sphenoid bone.

par·à·sphē′noid, *n.* a bone near the sphenoid.

pȧ·ras′tăs, *n.*; *pl.* **pȧ·ras′tȧ·dēṣ,** [Gr., from *para*, beside, and *histanai*, to stand.] in architecture, an anta; a column or pillar.

pȧ·ras′ti·chy, *n.*; *pl.* **pȧ·ras′ti·chieṣ,** [*para-*, and Gr. *stichos*, row.] in botany, a secondary spiral in a leaf or scale arrangement on an axis, stem, etc.

par·à·sym·pȧ·thet′iç, *a.* [*para-* (beside, etc.) and *sympathetic.*] in anatomy and physiology, designating or of that part of the autonomic nervous system whose nerves originate in the midbrain, the hindbrain, and the sacral region of the spinal cord and whose functions include the constriction of the pupils of the eyes, the slowing of the heartbeat, and the stimulation of certain digestive glands.

par″a·syn·ap′sis, *n.* [Mod. L.; *para* (beside, etc.) and *synapsis.*] the conjunction of chromosomes side by side.

par″à·syn·ax′is, *n.* [Gr.] unlawful meeting.

par·à·syn′the·sis, *n.* [Mod. L.; Gr. *parasynthesis*; *para-* (beside, etc.) and *synthesis.*] in linguistics, the process of forming words by both derivation and composition (e.g., *bighearted* from *big heart* and *-ed*, not from *big* and *hearted*).

par″à·syn·thet′iç, *a.* of or formed by parasynthesis.

par·à·taç′tiç, *a.* pertaining to or constituting parataxis; characterized by parataxis.

par·à·taç′tiç·ăl, *a.* same as *paratactic.*

par·à·tax′is, *n.* [Mod. L.; Gr. *parataxis*, a placing beside, from *para-*, beside, and *tassein*, to place.] the placing of related clauses, etc. in a series without the use of connecting words (e.g., "I came, I saw, I conquered."): opposed to *hypotaxis.*

pȧ·rath′ē·sis, *n.* [Gr., from *para*, beside, and *thesis*, placing, from *tithenai*, to place.]

1. in grammar, apposition.

2. in printing, parenthetical matter, printed within brackets.

3. in the Orthodox Eastern Church, a bishop's prayer for catechumens.

par·à·thet′iç, *a.* of or characterized by parathesis.

par·à·thȳ′roid, *a.* [*para-* (beside, etc.) and *thyroid.*]

1. situated alongside or near the thyroid gland.

2. designating or of any of four small, oval glands located on or embedded in the thyroid gland: they secrete a hormone that increases the calcium content of the blood.

par·à·thȳ′roid, *n.* a parathyroid gland.

pȧ·rat′ō·mous, *a.* [*para-*, and Gr. *temnein*, to cleave.] in mineralogy, having the faces of cleavage of an indeterminate number.

par·à·ton′iç, *a.* 1. caused by external stimuli, as certain plant movements.

2. checking, or retarding, growth, as light sometimes checks plant growth.

paratonic movements; movements in plants which result from such stimuli as heat, light, gravitation, etc.

pȧ·rȧ·ton·nerre′ (-nãr′), *n.* [Fr., from *parer*, to ward off, and *tonnerre*, thunder.] a pointed metallic rod used as a lightning conductor.

par′à·trọọp·ẽr, *n.* a soldier in the paratroops.

par′à·trọọps, *n.pl.* a unit of infantry soldiers trained and equipped to land behind enemy lines from airplanes by means of parachutes.

par·à·tȳ′phoid, *a.* [*para-* and *typhoid.*] designating, of, or causing an infectious disease closely resembling typhoid fever but usually milder and caused by a different bacillus.

par·à·tȳ′phoid, *n.* paratyphoid fever.

pȧ·rauque′ (-rōk′), *n.* a goatsucker found in tropical America.

par·à·vāil′, *a.* [OFr. *par*, by, and *aval*, below.] lowest; inferior: in feudal law the tenant *paravail* is the lowest tenant holding under a mean or mediate lord.

par′à·vāne, *n.* [*para-* (beside, etc.) and *vane.*]

1. one of a pair of large, torpedo-shaped devices towed under water on either side of a ship and equipped with sharp teeth for cutting the moorings of submerged mines, allowing them to float and be destroyed.

2. a similar device loaded with explosives for attacking submerged submarines.

par′à·vănt, par′à·väunt, *adv.* [Fr. *par*, and *avant*, before.] in front; first. [Obs.]

pȧr ȧ·vi·ōṅ′ (-vyōṅ′), [Fr., lit., by airplane.] by air mail.

par·à·xan′thin (-zan′), *n.* in chemistry, a crystalline substance found in urine.

par·ax′i·ăl, *a.* [*para-*, and L. *axis*, axis.] in anatomy, situated alongside an axis.

par·à·xȳ′lēne (-zī′), *n.* in chemistry, a colorless liquid compound of the aromatic series, a metamer of xylene.

pär′boil, *v.t.*; parboiled, *pt., pp.*; parboiling, *ppr.* [Fr. *parbouillir*; *par*, L. *per*, through, thoroughly, and *bouillir*, L. *bullire*, to boil.]

1. to boil until partly cooked: usually in preparation for roasting, etc.

2. to make uncomfortable by means of heat; to overheat.

3. to boil thoroughly. [Obs.]

pär·breăk′, *v.t.* and *v.i.* to vomit. [Obs.]

pär′buç·kle, *n.* [Early Mod. Eng. *parbunkel*, altered after *buckle.*]

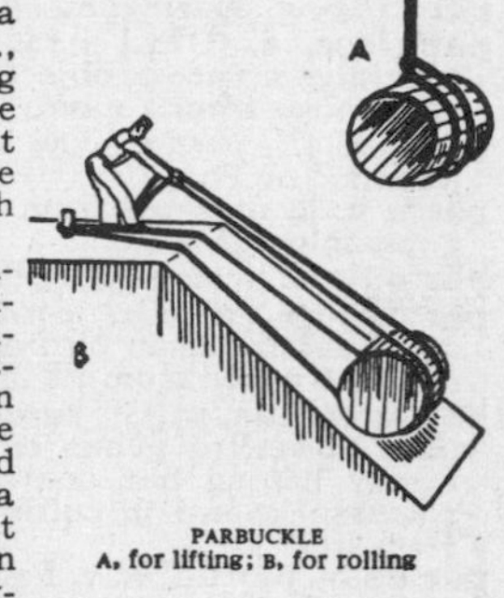

PARBUCKLE
A, for lifting; B, for rolling

1. a sling for a log, barrel, etc., made by passing a doubled rope around the object and pulling the rope ends through the loop.

2. a device consisting of a doubled rope, the middle of which is attached at a given height and the ends passed around either side of a cylindrical object which may then be raised or lowered by hauling in or paying out the rope ends.

pär′buç·kle, *v.t.*; parbuckled, *pt., pp.*; parbuckling, *ppr.* to hoist or lower by means of a parbuckle.

pärç, *n.* same as *park.*

Pär′cae, *n.pl.* in Roman mythology, the Fates.

pär·çase′, *adv.* percase. [Obs.]

pär′cel, *n.* [Fr. *parcelle*, from LL. *particella*, equivalent to L. *particula*, dim. of *pars*, *partis*, a part.]

1. a small, wrapped bundle; a package.

2. a quantity or a collection of items put up for sale; as, a *parcel* of books.

3. a group or collection; a pack; a bunch; as, a *parcel* of fools.

4. a piece, as of land, usually a specific part of a large acreage or estate.

5. a portion or part; especially, an inseparable or essential part: now only in *part and parcel.*

6. [*pl.*] in law, a description of property formally set forth in a conveyance, together with the boundaries thereof, so that it may be easily identified.

parcel post; that branch of the post office which carries and delivers parcels.

pär′cel, *v.t.*; parceled *or* parcelled, *pt., pp.*; parceling *or* parcelling, *ppr.* 1. to separate into parts and distribute; to apportion (with *out*).

2. to make up in or as a parcel.

3. in nautical usage, to wrap in canvas strips.

pär′cel, *a.* part or half; as, a *parcel* bawd.

pär′cel, *adv.* in part; partially.

pär′cel·ing, pär′cel·ling, *n.* 1. in nautical usage, long, narrow slips of canvas daubed with tar and bound about a rope to protect it.

2. a dividing into parcels, or a distributing in portions.

pär′cel·mēal, *adv.* in parcels; piecemeal. [Obs.]

pär′cē·nā·ry, *n.* [Anglo-Fr. *parcenier*, a parcener.] in law, coheirship; inheritance by two or more persons; partnership in inheritance.

pär′cē·nẽr, *n.* [Anglo-Fr. *parcenier*; ML. *partionarius*, from L. *partitio*, partition.] one of two or more persons sharing an inheritance; joint heir.

pärch, *v.t.*; parched (pärcht), *pt., pp.*; parching, *ppr.* [ME. *perchen*, *parchen*, contr. of *perischen*, to perish.]

1. to expose to great heat so as to dry or roast slightly, as corn, peas, etc.

2. to dry up with heat; to make hot and dry.

3. to make very thirsty.

4. to dry up and shrivel with cold.

pärch, *v.i.* 1. to be scorched or superficially burned; as, corn will dry and *parch* into barley.

2. to become very dry.

pär·chee′ṣi, *n.* same as *pachisi.*

pärch′ed·ness, *n.* the state of being scorched, or dried to extremity.

pär·chē′ṣi, *n.* same as *pachisi.*

pärch′ing·ly, *adv.* scorchingly.

pär·chī′ṣi, *n.* same as *pachisi.*

pärch′ment, *n.* [Fr. *parchemin*, from L. *pergamina* (*charta*, paper), parchment, lit., paper of Pergamus, from *Pergamos*, in Asia Minor.]

1. the skin of an animal, usually a sheep or

goat, prepared as a surface for writing or painting.
 2. a sheet of parchment used in this way; a document or manuscript on parchment.
 3. an imitation of this material used for lampshades, etc.
 4. a fine paper having a texture resembling parchment.

pärch′ment pā′pẽr, same as *papyrin.*

pär′ci·ty, *n.* sparingness. [Obs.]

pär′çlōșe, *n.* [OFr.] a railing or screen that separates a place or object from a larger body, as an altar from a nave. [Archaic.]

pärd, *n.* [L. *pardus.*] the leopard; a panther. [Archaic or Poet.]

pärd, *n.* [contracted from *partner.*] a partner; companion. [Slang.]

pär′dāle, *n.* a leopard. [Obs.]

pär′dȧ·lōte, *n.* [Gr. *pardalōtos*, spotted.] a small Australasian bird of the genus *Pardalotus*: so called from its distinct spots.

Pär·dan′thus, *n.* [Gr. *pardos*, leopard, and *anthos*, flower.] a genus of plants of the iris family having but one species, *Pardanthus sinensis*, known in cultivation as the *blackberry lily.*

pär′dȧ·ō, pär′dō, *n.* a Portuguese silver coin of Goa, India.

pär·dē′, pär·dī′, pär·dïe′, *adv.* and *interj.* same as *pardy.*

pär′dine, *a.* spotted like or resembling a pard.

pär′dō, *n.* see *pardao.*

pär′dŏn, *v.t.*; pardoned, *pt., pp.*; pardoning, *ppr.* [OFr. *perdoner, pardoner*; Fr. *pardonner*; It. *perdonare*, to pardon, from LL. *perdonare*, to pardon; L. *per*, through, quite, and *donare*, to give.]
 1. to release (a person) from punishment; not punish for crimes or offenses.
 2. to cancel or not exact penalty for (an offense); forgive.
 3. (a) to excuse or forgive (a person) for some minor fault, discourtesy, etc.; (b) to overlook (a discourtesy, etc.).

pär′dŏn, *v.i.* to grant pardon.
 Syn.—forgive, absolve, excuse, overlook, remit, acquit.

pär′dŏn, *n.* 1. a pardoning or being pardoned; forgiveness.
 2. an official document granting a legal or ecclesiastical pardon.
 3. in the Roman Catholic Church, a release from temporal purgatorial punishment; indulgence.

pär′dŏn·ȧ·ble, *a.* that can be pardoned, overlooked, or forgiven; as, the offender or the offense is *pardonable.*

pär′dŏn·ȧ·ble·ness, *n.* the quality of being pardonable; as, the *pardonableness* of sin.

pär′dŏn·ȧ·bly, *adv.* in a pardonable manner; so as to be pardonable.

pär′dŏn·ẽr, *n.* [ME. *pardonere*; OFr. *pardonaire.*]
 1. historically, a person authorized by the Roman Catholic Church to grant or sell ecclesiastical pardons, or indulgences.
 2. a person who pardons.

pär·dy′, pẽr·dy′, *adv.* and *interj.* [Fr. *par Dieu*, by God.] verily; indeed. [Archaic.]

pâre, *v.t.*; pared, *pt., pp.*; paring, *ppr.* [Fr. *parer*, to prepare, trim, pare, from L. *parare*, to prepare.]
 1. to cut or trim away the rind, skin, covering, rough surface, etc. of; to shave; peel.
 2. to cut or trim away (rind, skin, covering, rough surface, etc.) of anything.
 3. to reduce gradually; to make less, as savings.
 Syn.—peel, cut off, diminish.

pȧ·rē′cious (-shus), *a.* paroecious.

par·ē·gor′iç, *a.* [Gr. *parēgorikos*, from *para-*, beside, and *agora*, assembly.] mitigating; relieving pain; as, *paregoric* elixir.

par·ē·gor′iç, *n.* a medicine that soothes or lessens pain; specifically, a camphorated tincture of opium, used in cough mixtures and to relieve diarrhea.

pȧ·rei′rȧ brä′vȧ (-rā′), [Port. *parreira brava*, wild vine; *parreira*, vine, and *brava*, wild.] the root of a South American plant, used as a diuretic and tonic: also *pareira.*

par·ē·leç·trō·nom′iç, *a.* giving no response to electromotive stimuli.

par″ē·leç·tron′ō·my, *n.* [*par-*, *electro-*, and Gr. *nomos*, law.] in pathology, a muscular condition in which there is a reversal of electrical action while the structure of the tissue remains normal.

pȧ·rel′lȧ, *n.* one of several kinds of lichens yielding litmus, especially the crustaceous *Lecanora parella.*

pȧ·relle′, *n.* 1. same as *parella.*
 2. either of two species of dock, *Rumex patientia* or *Rumex hydrolapathum.*

pȧ·rem′bō·lē, *n.* [Gr. *paremballein*, to put in between.] in rhetoric, the parenthetic insertion of something in a period, but differing from parenthesis in being more closely connected with the context: also called *paremptosis.*

pâre′ment, *n.* same as *parament.*

par·emp·tō′sis, *n.* same as *parembole.*

pȧ·reñ′çhy·mȧ, *n.* [Gr. *parenchyma*, anything poured in beside; *para*, beside, and *enchyma*, an infusion, from *enchein*, to pour in; *en*, in, and *chein*, to pour.]
 1. in anatomy, the essential or functional tissue of an organ, as distinguished from its connective tissue, etc.
 2. in botany, a soft tissue of roundish, thin-walled cells in a plant stem or the pulp of fruits.
 3. in zoology, the endoplasm of a protozoan.

pȧ·reñ′çhy·măl, *a.* relating to or having the nature of parenchyma.

Par·eñ·çhym′ȧ·tȧ, *n.pl.* formerly, an order of *Entozoa*, including the tapeworms.

par·eñ·çhym′ȧ·tous, *a.* of, like, or containing parenchyma.

pȧ·reñ′çhy·mous, *a.* parenchymatous.

pȧ·ren′ē·sis, *n.* [Gr. *parainesis.*] exhortation; advice. [Rare.]

par·ē·net′iç, *a.* hortatory; admonitory. [Rare.]

par·ē·net′iç·ăl, *a.* parenetic.

pâr′ent, *n.* [L. *parens, parentis*, from *parere*, to bring forth, to bear, to beget.]
 1. a father or mother.
 2. any animal, organism, or plant in relation to another which it has produced.
 3. any cause or source.
 4. any relative. [Obs.]
 parent-teacher association; an organization in which the parents and the teachers of the children attending a certain school are joined because of their common interest in the education and progress of the pupils: commonly referred to as P.T.A.

pâr′ent, *a.* standing in the relation of a source, cause, or parent; resembling a parent; as, a *parent* speech; a *parent* nucleus.

pâr′ent·āġe, *n.* 1. origin; birth; extraction; derivation or descent from a parent or from any source considered as in the relation of a parent.
 2. parenthood.

pȧ·ren′tăl, *a.* 1. of or characteristic of a parent or parents.
 2. constituting the source or origin of something.
 3. in biology, of or designating the generation in which fertilization produces hybrids: symbol, P.

pȧ·ren′tăl·ly, *adv.* in a parental manner.

pâr·en·tā′tion, *n.* something done or said in honor of the dead. [Obs.]

pâr′ent cell, a cytula.

pâr′en·tēle, *n.* parentage; relationship. [Obs.]

pȧ·ren′tẽr·ăl, *a.* [*par-*, and Gr. *enteron*, intestine.] not intestinal; by some way other than through the digestive tract, as intravenous or intramuscular.

pȧ·ren′thē·sis, *n.*; *pl.* **pȧ·ren′thē·sēș**, [Gr. *parenthesis*; from *para*, beside, and *entithenai*, to insert.]
 1. an additional word, clause, etc. placed as an explanation or comment within an already complete sentence: in writing or printing it is usually marked off by curved lines, dashes, or commas.
 2. [*usually in pl.*] either or both of the curved lines () used to mark off parenthetic words, etc. or to enclose mathematical quantities that are to be treated as a single quantity.
 3. an episode or incident, often an irrelevant one; interlude.

pȧ·ren′thē·size, *v.t.*; parenthesized, *pt., pp.*; parenthesizing, *ppr.* 1. (a) to insert (a word, phrase, etc.) as a parenthesis; (b) to put into parentheses (sense 2).
 2. to place a parenthesis within; as, he *parenthesized* the rule with his own comment.

par·en·thet′iç, *a.* same as *parenthetical.*

par·en·thet′iç·ăl, *a.* 1. (a) of, or having the nature of, a parenthesis; (b) marked off or placed within parentheses.
 2. giving qualifying information or explanation.
 3. using or containing parenthesis.

par·en·thet′iç·ăl·ly, *adv.* in the manner or form of a parenthesis; by parenthesis.

pâr′ent·hood, *n.* the condition of being a parent; relation or authority of a parent.

pȧ·ren′ti·cīde, *n.* [L. *parens*, a parent, and *cædere*, to kill.]
 1. one who kills his own parent. [Rare.]
 2. the killing of one's own parent. [Rare.]

pâr′ent·ing, *n.* the work or skill of a parent in raising a child or children.

par·ep·i·did′y·mis, *n.* [*para-*, and Gr. *epi*, upon, and *didymos*, testicle.] a body on the spermatic cord above the epididymis, representing a vestige of part of the Wolffian body.

pâr′ẽr, *n.* one who or that which pares; specifically, (a) an instrument for paring, as vegetables or fruit; (b) a form of scraper or hoe.

par·ē·reth′e·sis, *n.* [*para-*, and Gr. *erethizein*, to excite.] extreme excitement.

pȧ·rẽr′gon, *n.*; *pl.* **pȧ·rẽr′gȧ**, [Gr. *para*, beyond, and *ergon*, work.] an incidental, subordinate, or subsidiary work.

pȧ·rē′sis, *n.* [Gr., from *parienai*, to relax.]
 1. partial paralysis.
 2. a disease of the brain caused by syphilis of the central nervous system and characterized by inflammation of the meninges, mental and emotional instability, paralytic attacks, etc.: usually *general paresis*: also called *general paralysis.*

par·es·thē′și·ȧ, par·aes·thē′și·ȧ (-zhi·ȧ *or* -zhȧ *or* -zi·ȧ), *n.* in medicine, abnormal sensation, as of pricking, tingling, and the like.

par·es·thet′iç, par·aes·thet′iç, *a.* of, like, or affected by paresthesia.

par·eth′moid, *a.* [*para-* and *ethmoid.*] located at the side of the ethmoid.

par·eth′moid, *n.* an ethmoturbinal bone; also, one of the nasal bones of some fishes.

pȧ·ret′iç, *a.* of, resulting from, or having paresis.

pȧ·ret′iç, *n.* a person having paresis.

pär ex·cel·lence′ (-loṅs′), [Fr., lit., by way of excellence.] in the greatest degree of excellence; beyond comparison; pre-eminently.

pär ex·em′ple (eg-zäṅ′pl), [Fr.]
 1. for example; for instance.
 2. really! well!: exclamation of surprise.

pär·fāit′ (-fā′), *n.* [Fr., perfect.]
 1. a dessert made of rich cream, eggs, sirup, etc. frozen together and served in a tall, narrow glass.
 2. a dessert of ice cream with crushed fruit or sirup, served in a similar glass.

pär′fleçhe, *n.* [Canadian Fr.] the prepared hide of an animal, as of a buffalo, dried on a frame after the hair has been removed; also, anything made of such hide.

pär·fō′çăl, *a.* [*par-* and *focal.*] arranged or mounted so that the eyepieces may be changed without disturbing the focus: applied to a microscope.

pär′gȧs·īte, *n.* [from *Pargas*, Finland.] a greenish variety of hornblende or amphibole.

pärġe′bōard, *n.* same as *bargeboard.*

pär′ġet, *v.t.*; pargeted *or* pargetted, *pt., pp.*; pargeting *or* pargetting, *ppr.* [OFr. *parjeter*; *par*, all over, and *jeter*, to throw.] to put plaster on, especially in a decorative way.

pär′ġet, *v.i.* to overlay walls, etc., with parget.

pär′ġet, *n.* 1. plaster or any similar wall coating.
 2. ornamental plasterwork on walls or ceilings.
 3. a kind of plaster used for lining chimneys.

pär′ġet·ẽr, *n.* a plasterer. [Obs.]

pär′ġet·ing, pär′ġet·ting, *n.* 1. ornamental plasterwork on walls or ceilings.
 2. plasterwork on the inside of chimneys.

pär·hē·lī′ȧ·căl, *a.* parhelic.

pär·hē′liç, *a.* relating to parhelia or a parhelion.

pär·hē′liç cīr′çle, a bright circular band or halo that appears to intersect the sun in a plane parallel to the horizon: also *parhelic ring.*

pär·hē′li·ŏn, *n.*; *pl.* **pär·hē′li·ȧ**, [*par-*, and Gr. *hēlios*, sun.] a mock sun, appearing in the form of a bright light near the sun, sometimes tinged with colors like the rainbow. Several parhelia sometimes appear simultaneously, connected with one another by a white arc or halo. They are the result of certain modifications which light undergoes when it falls on ice particles in the atmosphere.

pär·hē′li·um, *n.* same as *parhelion.*

pär·hi·drō′sis, *n.* excessive perspiration.

pär·hō·mol′ō·gous, *a.* [*par-* and *homologous.*]

seemingly homologous but not really so; relating to parhomology.

pär·hō·mol′ō·ġy, *n.* in biology, imitative homodynamy.

par·i-, [from L. *par, paris,* equal.] a combining form meaning *equal,* as in *pari*pinnate.

pȧ·rī′ȧh, *n.* [Tamil. *paraiyan,* drummer, from *parai,* drum: a pariah was a hereditary drumbeater.]

1. a member of one of the oppressed social castes in India.

2. any outcast; someone despised or rejected by others.

pariah dog; in India, a mongrel dog which has run wild.

pariah kite; a kite, *Milvulus govinda,* found in India.

pȧ·rī′ăl, *a.* of or arranged in pairs. [Rare.]

Pā′ri·ăn, *a.* 1. of Paros, a Greek island in the Aegean Sea.

2. (a) designating a fine, white marble found in Paros; (b) like this marble.

Pā′ri·ăn, *n.* 1. a native or inhabitant of Paros.

2. a fine, white porcelain that resembles Parian marble.

Par·i·dig·i·tā′tȧ, *n.pl.* the *Artiodactyla.*

par·i·dig′i·tāte, *a.* [L. *par,* equal, and E. *digitate.*] having an even number of fingers and toes.

par·i·drō′sis, *n.* same as *parhidrosis.*

pā′ri·ēṣ, *n.*; *pl.* **pȧ·ri′e·tēṣ,** [L. *paries,* a wall.]

1. in anatomy and botany, the inside walls of any cavity: usually in the plural; as, the *parietes* of the cranium; the *parietes* of a capsule.

2. in zoology, the middle part of each segment of the shell of a cirriped.

pȧ·rī′e·tăl, *a.* [L. *parietalis,* from *paries, parietis,* a wall.]

1. living within, or having to do with life within, a college. [Rare.]

2. in anatomy, of the parietes, or walls, of a hollow organ, cavity, cell, etc.; especially, designating either of the two bones between the frontal and occipital bones, forming part of the top and sides of the skull.

3. in botany, attached to the wall of the ovary, as the placenta in some plants.

pȧ·rī′e·tăl, *n.* 1. a parietal bone.

2. in zoology, a scale or plate that covers the back part of the head, as of a serpent.

Pȧ·rī·ē·tā′lēṣ, *n.pl.* a group of plants with parietal placentae. It includes several orders.

pȧ·rī′e·tăl lōbe, the part of each hemisphere of the brain between the frontal and the occipital lobes.

Pȧ·rī·ē·tā′ri·ȧ, *n.* [L. *parietaria,* the parietary.] a genus of plants of the nettle family, including seven or eight species widely distributed in temperate regions. *Parietaria officinalis,* the parietary, is the best-known species.

pȧ·rī′e·tā·ry, *n.* [Fr. *pariétaire,* from L. *paries, parietis,* a wall.] the wall pellitory, a plant of the genus *Parietaria.*

pȧ·rī′e·tēṣ, *n.* pl. of *paries.*

pā·ri·et′iç, *a.* pertaining to or obtained from the wall lichen, *Parmelia parietina.*

pȧ·rī′e·tō-, [from L. *paries (-etis),* a wall.] a combining form meaning *parietal and,* as in *parieto*mastoid.

pȧ·rī″e·tō·fron′tăl, *a.* pertaining to the parietal and frontal bones, gyri, or fissures: also written *frontoparietal.*

pȧ·rī″e·tō·mas′toid, *a.* of or belonging to the mastoid and to the parietal bones; as, the *parietomastoid* suture.

pȧ·rī″e·tō-oç·cip′i·tăl, *a.* pertaining to the parietal and occipital bones or lobes.

pȧ·rī″e·tō·quȧd′rāte, *a.* pertaining to the parietal and quadrate bones.

pȧ·rī″e·tō·sphē′noid, *a.* pertaining to the parietal and sphenoid bones.

pȧ·rī″e·tō·squȧ·mō′săl, *a.* pertaining to the parietal bone and the squamous portion of the temporal bone.

pȧ·rī″e·tō·tem′pō·răl, *a.* pertaining to the parietal and temporal bones or lobes.

par′i-mū′tū·el, *n.*; *pl.* **par′i-mū′tū·elṣ,** [Fr., lit., mutual stakes or bets.]

1. a system of betting on races in which those backing the winners divide, in proportion to their wagers, the total amount bet, after a percentage has been taken by the agency conducting the betting.

2. a machine used in registering such bets.

Par·i·nā′ri·um, *n.* [Braz.] a large genus of tropical trees of the rose family, comprising between thirty and forty species.

pãr′ing, *n.* 1. the act of cutting or trimming off a rind, skin, covering, etc.

2. that which is pared or shaved off; a clipping; rind.

pãr′ing chiṣ′el, a joiners' chisel having the bevel on one side, used in fitting and finishing.

pãr′ing ī′ron (-ũrn), a paring knife used by farriers.

pãr′ing plow, a plow for cutting sod or turf from the surface of the ground. [Brit. Dial.]

pā′rī pas′sū, [L.] 1. with equal pace; with equal speed.

2. in equal proportion.

3. at the same time.

par·i·pin′nāte, *a.* [L. *par,* equal, and *pinnatus,* winged.] in botany, equally pinnate; pinnate without a terminal leaflet or a tendril, as the leaf of the tuberous vetch.

Par′is, *n.* [from L. *par, paris,* equal, in allusion to the regularity of the parts.] a genus of plants of the lily family, native to the temperate regions of Europe and Asia. *Paris quadrifolia* was formerly used in medicine.

Par′is, *n.* [L.; Gr. *Paris.*] in Greek legend, a son of Priam, king of Troy: his kidnaping of Helen, wife of Menelaus, caused the Trojan War.

Par′is bā′sin, a series of Tertiary deposits lying in a cavity or depression in the Cretaceous rocks under and around Paris, France.

Par′is blūe, a bright blue coloring matter, obtained by heating aniline with stannic chloride.

Par′is dāi′ṣy, a species of chrysanthemum, *Chrysanthemum frutescens.*

Par′is green, see under *green.*

par′ish, *n.* [ME. *parissche, parisse*; OFr. *parosse, paroiche*; LL. *paræcia*; Gr. *paroikia*; *para,* beside, and *oikos,* dwelling.]

1. originally, a British church district with its own church and clergyman.

2. a district of British local civil government, often identical with the original church parish.

3. (a) an administrative district of various churches, especially a part of a diocese, under the charge of a priest or minister; (b) the members of the congregation of any church, without regard to the territory in which they live; congregation; (c) the territory in which the members of a congregation live.

4. a civil division in Louisiana, corresponding to a county.

5. the people of a parish (senses 1, 2, 3a, 4).

par′ish, *a.* 1. of or pertaining to a parish; connected with a parish; as, a *parish* church.

2. maintained by, or dependent on, a parish.

parish clerk; a person whose duty it is to lead the responses during the reading of the service in Anglican churches.

parish register; a book for recording every baptism, marriage, and death of the members of a parish.

par′ish·en, *n.* a parishioner. [Obs.]

pȧ·rish′iŏn·ăl, *a.* pertaining to a parish; parochial. [Rare.]

pȧ·rish′iŏn·ẽr, *n.* one who belongs to a parish.

Pȧ·ri′ṣiăn (-rizh′ăn), *n.* a native or resident of Paris, France.

Pȧ·ri′ṣiăn, *a.* relating to Paris, its people, or culture.

Pȧ·ri·ṣi·enne′ (-en′), *n.* [Fr.] a woman native or inhabitant of Paris.

par″i·syl·lab′iç, *a.* [L. *par,* equal, and *syllaba,* syllable.] having the same number of syllables in all inflections: said of Latin and Greek nouns.

par″i·syl·lab′iç·ăl, *a.* parasyllabic.

par′i·tŏr, *n.* an apparitor. [Archaic.]

par′i·ty, *n.* [Fr. *parité*; L. *paritas,* from *par,* equal.]

1. the state or condition of being the same in power, value, rank, etc.; equality.

2. resemblance; similarity.

3. the equivalent in value of a sum of money expressed in terms of another country's currency.

4. equality of value at a given ratio between different kinds of money, commodities, etc.

par′i·ty, *n.* [L. *parere,* to bear, and *-ity.*] in medicine, the state or fact of having borne offspring.

pärk, *n.* [OFr. *parc*; ML. *parricus,* from a Germanic equivalent of AS. *pearroc.*]

1. in English law, an enclosed area of land, held by authority of the king or by prescription, stocked and preserved for hunting.

2. an area of land containing pasture, woods, lakes, etc., surrounding a large country house or private estate.

3. an area of public land; specifically, (a) an area in or near a city, usually laid out with walks, drives, playgrounds, etc., for public recreation; (b) an open square in a city, with benches, trees, etc.; (c) a large area known for its natural scenery and preserved for public recreation by a state or national government.

4. a level, open area surrounded by mountains or forest.

5. a space set aside for leaving vehicles temporarily.

6. in military usage, (a) an area set aside for vehicles, supplies, and other equipment; (b) things kept in such an area; as, a *park* of tanks.

pärk, *v.t.* 1. to enclose in or as in a park.

2. to place or arrange (military equipment) in a park.

3. to leave (a vehicle) in a certain place temporarily.

4. to maneuver (a vehicle) into a space where it can be left temporarily.

5. to put or leave in a particular place; to deposit. [Slang.]

pärk, *v.i.* 1. to park a vehicle.

2. to drive in a park; to walk in a park.

3. to walk on a park drive and display fine style: said of horses.

pär′kȧ, pär′kee, *n.* [Aleutian.] a fur jacket or heavy, long, woolen shirt, often lined with pile or fleece, with an attached hood for protecting the head from the cold.

Pärk Av′e·nūe, a wealthy residential street in New York City, regarded as a symbol of high society, fashion, etc.

pärk′ẽr, *n.* the keeper of a park. [Obs.]

pärk′ing, *n.* the act or an instance of one who parks.

pärk′ing lot, an open space designed for the parking of a number of cars, usually for a fee.

pärk′ing mē′tẽr, a coin-operated timing device installed near a parking space for indicating the length of time that a parked vehicle has occupied the space.

pärk′ing ọr′bit, a temporary orbit of an artificial satellite or spacecraft around the earth or some other heavenly body, prior to carrying out a further maneuver.

pärk′ing tick′et, a police summons given for violating regulations concerning the parking of vehicles.

Pär·kin·sō′ni·ȧ, *n.* [after John *Parkinson* (1567–1650), a chemist in London, and author of some botanical works.] a widely scattered genus of spiny leguminous shrubs and trees, of which *Parkinsonia aculeata* is the type and chief representative.

pär′kin·sŏn·iṣm, *n.* 1. any of various brain disorders characterized by muscle rigidity as in Parkinson's disease, with or without tremor.

2. same as *Parkinson's disease.*

Pär′kin·sŏn's diṣ·ēaṣe′, [after James *Parkinson* (1755–1824), Eng. physician who first described it.] a degenerative disease of later life, characterized by a rhythmic tremor and muscular rigidity, caused by degeneration in the basal ganglia of the brain.

pärk′lēaveṣ, *n.* a plant, *Hypericum androsæmum*: also called *tutsan.*

pärk′wāy, *n.* 1. a broad roadway bordered or divided with plantings of trees, bushes, and grass.

2. the landscaped center strip or border.

pär′lănce, *n.* [OFr., from Fr. *parler,* to speak.]

1. conversation; speech; especially, parley or debate.

2. a style or manner of speaking or writing; language; idiom; as, military *parlance.*

pär·län′dō, pär·län′te, *a.* and *adv.* [It.] in music, to be sung in a style suggesting or approximating speech.

pär′lāy, *v.t.* and *v.i.*; parlayed, *pt., pp.*; parlaying, *ppr.* [Fr. and It. *paroli,* from *paro,* an equal.]

1. to bet (an original wager plus its winnings) on another race, contest, etc.

2. to exploit (an asset) successfully; as, he *parlayed* his voice into fame.

pär′lāy, *n.* a bet or series of bets made by parlaying.

pärle, *n.* conversation; talk. [Obs.]

pärle, *v.i.* [Fr. *parler.*] to converse. [Obs.]

pär′ley, *v.i.*; parleyed (-lid), *pt., pp.*; parleying, *ppr.* [Fr. *parler,* to speak; OFr. *paroler,* from LL. *parabolare,* to speak, from L. *parabola,* a comparison, later a word.] to speak with another; to discourse; to confer on some point of mutual concern; to discuss orally; hence, to confer with an enemy; to treat with by words, as on an exchange of prisoners or on the subject of peace.

pär′ley, *n.*; *pl.* **pär′leyṣ,** a talk or conference for the purpose of discussing a specific matter or of settling a dispute, as a military conference with an enemy, under a temporary truce, for discussing terms.

pär′lia̤·ment, *n.* [ME. and OFr. *parlement*, from *parler*, to speak.]

1. an official or formal conference or council, usually concerned with government or public affairs.

2. [P–] the national legislative body of Great Britain: it is composed of the House of Commons (elected) and the House of Lords (mostly hereditary).

3. [P–] any of several similar bodies in countries of the British Empire and in other countries.

4. any of several high courts of justice in France before 1789.

pär·lia̤·men′tăl, *a.* parliamentary. [Obs.]

pär″lia̤·men·tā′ri·ăn, *n.* 1. [P–] one of those who supported the Long Parliament in the time of Charles I; a Roundhead.

2. one versed in parliamentary rules, practice, or debate.

pär″lia̤·men·tā′ri·ăn, *a.* 1. [P–] serving the Parliament, in opposition to King Charles I.

2. pertaining to a parliament.

pär·lia̤·men′tā·ri·ly, *adv.* in a parliamentary manner.

pär·lia̤·men′tā·ry, *a.* 1. of or like a parliament.

2. decreed or established by a parliament.

3. conforming to the customs and rules of a parliament or other public assembly.

4. having or governed by a parliament.

parliamentary agent; a solicitor or lobbyist employed by interested private persons to explain and recommend claims, bills, etc. under consideration by Parliament.

parliamentary trains; in England, railway trains which, by act of Parliament, railway companies are required to run for the conveyance of third-class passengers at a cheap rate.

pär″lia̤·men·teer′, *n.* a parliamentarian. [Obs.]

pär′lŏr, *n.* [Fr. *parloir*, from *parler*, to speak.]

1. (a) originally, a room set aside for the entertainment of guests; formal sitting room; (b) now, any living room.

2. a small, semiprivate sitting room separate from the main lounges in a hotel, inn, etc.

3. (a) originally, a business establishment elegantly furnished to resemble a private sitting room; as, an ice-cream *parlor*; (b) now, a shop or business establishment, often with some special equipment or furnishings for personal services; as, a beauty *parlor*.

British spelling, *parlour*.

parlor pink; see under *pink*.

pär′lŏr bōard′ẽr, a privileged pupil who lives in the family of the principal of a boarding school.

pär′lŏr ça̤r, a railroad car for daytime travel, having comfortable individual chairs: it is more luxurious and expensive than a coach.

pär′lŏr·māid″, *n.* a maid who serves at table, answers the door, etc.

pär′lous, *a.* [old form of *perilous*.]

1. perilous; dangerous; risky. [Chiefly Archaic.]

2. dangerously clever; mischievous; shrewd. [Chiefly Archaic.]

pär′lous, *adv.* extremely; very. [Chiefly Archaic.]

pär·ma̤·cet′y, *n.* spermaceti. [Obs.]

Pär·mē′li·a̤, *n.* [L. *parma*; Gr. *parmē*, a small shield.] a large genus of lichens typical of the *Parmeliaceæ*.

Pär·mē·li·ā′cē·ae, *n.pl.* a family of gymnocarpous lichens bearing sessile shields and having their borders formed by the surface of the thallus.

pär·mē·li·ā′ceous, *a.* pertaining to or having a resemblance to the genus *Parmelia*, or to the *Parmeliaceæ*.

Pär·men·ti·ē′ra̤, *n.* [after Antoine A. *Parmentier* (1737–1813), an agriculturist of France.] a genus of Central American and Mexican trees.

Pär·mē·ṣan′, *a.* [Fr. *parmesan*; It. *parmigiano*, from *Parma*.] of or pertaining to Parma, in Italy.

Pär·mē·ṣan′, *n.* Parmesan cheese.

Pär·mē·ṣan′ cheeṣe, see under *cheese*.

pär·mi·gia̤′nä, *a.* [It. *Parmigiana*, Parmesan.] prepared with Parmesan cheese.

pär·mi·gia̤′nō, *a.* same as *parmigiana*.

Pär·nas′si·a̤, *n.* [Gr. *Parnassos*, Parnassus.] a genus of plants of the saxifrage family growing wild on wet banks and bearing large white flowers: also called *grass of Parnassus*.

Pär·nas′si·ăn, *a.* 1. of or pertaining to Mount Parnassus, in Greece, or the Parnassians.

2. of the art of poetry and the Muses.

3. [p–] any of the numerous species of butterflies belonging to the genus *Parnassius*.

Pär·nas′si·ăn, *n.* [Fr. *parnassien*.] a member of a school of late nineteenth century French poets: their first collection (1866) was titled *Le Parnasse contemporain*.

Pär·nas′sus, *n.* [Gr. *Parnasos*.]

1. a mountain in southern Greece: in ancient times it was sacred to Apollo and the Muses.

2. (a) poetry or poets collectively; (b) any center of poetic or artistic activity.

3. formerly, a common title for collections of poetry.

Pär′nell·īte, *n.* a follower of Charles Stewart Parnell (1846–1891), who led a movement in favor of home rule in Ireland.

par·oç·cip′i·tăl, *a.* [*par-* and *occipital*.] in anatomy, near the occipital bone.

pa̤·rō′çhi·ăl, *a.* [from LL. *parochia*, parish.]

1. of or in a parish or parishes.

2. restricted to a small area or scope; narrow; limited; provincial.

pa̤·rō′çhi·ăl·iṣm, *n.* 1. parochial government; management of a parish by a parochial board.

2. provincialism; narrowness of thought, interest, or activity.

pa̤·rō·çhi·al′i·ty, *n.* same as *parochialism*.

pa̤·rō′çhi·ăl·ly, *adv.* in a parish; by a parish.

pa̤·rō′çhi·ăl sçhool, a school supported and controlled by a church.

pa̤·rō′çhi·ăn, *a.* pertaining to a parish. [Obs.]

pa̤·rō′çhi·ăn, *n.* a parishioner. [Obs.]

pa̤·rod′iç, pa̤·rod′iç·ăl, *a.* having the nature of parody.

par′ō·dist, *n.* one who writes a parody.

par′ō·dy, *n.*; *pl.* **par′ō·dieṣ,** [Fr. *parodie*; Gr. *parōdia*; *para* and *ōdē*, ode.]

1. literary or musical composition imitating the characteristic style of some other work or of a writer or composer, but treating a serious subject in a nonsensical manner in an attempt at humor or ridicule.

2. a poor or weak imitation.

par′ō·dy, *v.t.*; parodied, *pt.*, *pp.*; parodying, *ppr.* to turn into a parody; to write a parody upon; to imitate, as a poem or song, in a ludicrous manner.

I have translated, or rather *parodied*, a poem of Horace. —Pope.

pa̤·roe′cious (-shus), *a.* [from *para-* (beside, etc.), and Gr. *oikia*, a house; and *-ous*.] in botany, having the male and female organs in the same flower cluster: also *parecious*, *paroicous*.

pa̤·roi′çous, *a.* same as *paroecious*.

par′ō·ket, *n.* same as *parakeet*.

pa̤·rōle′, pa̤·rōl′, *n.* [Fr. *parole*, a word; It. *parola*; LL. *parabola*, a parable, speech, word.]

1. word of honor; promise; especially, the promise of a military prisoner that, if released from captivity or given certain privileges, he will meet requirements made by his captors: usually a promise to take no further part in the fighting.

2. the condition of being on parole.

3. a release from prison, given to a prisoner before his sentence has expired, on condition of future good behavior: the sentence is not set aside and he remains under the supervision of a parole board.

4. the conditional freedom granted by such release, or the period of such freedom.

5. in military usage, a special password used as a check on the countersign for more complete identification.

on parole; at liberty under conditions of parole.

pa̤·rōle′, *v.t.*; paroled, *pt.*, *pp.*; paroling, *ppr.* to allow liberty to on parole; to release (a prisoner) on parole.

pa̤·rōle′, *a.* not committed to writing; oral; verbal; also, written but not sealed.

parole arrest; an arrest ordered of a person violating the law in the presence of a judge, magistrate, or other officer of the peace, as for an offense committed in open court.

pa̤·rōl″ee′, *n.* a person who has been released from prison on parole.

pär′ō·li, *n.* [Fr., a double stake.] in betting on horse races, a form of bet in which the possible winnings are wagered on subsequent races; in faro, a doubled bet. Also called *parlay*.

par·ō·mol′ō·ġy, *n.* [Gr. *paromologia*; *para*, beyond, and *homologein*, to admit.] in rhetoric, a figure by which an orator concedes something to an adversary in order to strengthen his own argument.

par″ō·nō·mā′si·a̤, *n.* [Gr., from *para*, beside, and *onomazein*, to name, from *onoma*, name.]

1. a pun.

2. the act or practice of punning.

par″ō·nō·mas′tiç, par″ō·nō·mas′tiç·ăl, *a.* of or by paronomasia; consisting in a play upon words.

par·ō·nom′a̤·sy, *n.* paronomasia. [Obs.]

par·ō·nyçh′i·a̤, *n.* [Gr. *parōnychia*; *para*, by, and *onyx*, the nail.]

1. a whitlow; a felon.

2. [P–] a genus of small plants having whorled leaves, scabrous stipules, and small flowers; the whitlowworts. *Paronychia argyrocoma*, the silver chickweed, is common in the eastern part of the United States.

par′ō·nym, *n.* a paronymous word.

par·ō·nym′iç, *a.* paronymous.

pa̤·ron′y·mous, *a.* [Gr. *parōnymos*; *para*, beside, and *onoma*, name.]

1. derived from the same root; cognate: said of words (e.g., *differ* and *defer*).

2. differing in spelling, origin, and meaning, but pronounced alike (e.g., *pair*, *pare*, and *pear*).

par·o·öph′o·ron (par-ō-of′ō-ron), *n.* [*para-*, and LL. *oöphoron*.] a vestigial structure in the broad ligament of the urinary portion of a Wolffian body. It is a tubular body corresponding to the paradidymis in the male.

par′ō·quet (-ket), *n.* same as *parakeet*.

pa̤·ror′çhis, *n.* [*para-*, and Gr. *orchis*, testicle.] in anatomy, the epididymis; a long canal or efferent duct constituting part of the excretory apparatus of the testicle: also written *parorchid*.

pa̤·ros′tē·ăl, *a.* of or relating to parostosis.

par·os·tō′sis, *n.* [*par-*, and Gr. *osteon*, bone.] tissue ossification outside of the periosteum.

par·os·tot′iç, *a.* parosteal.

pa̤·rot′iç, *a.* [*par-*, and Gr. *ous*, *ōtos*, ear.] situated or found near the ear.

pa̤·rot′id, *a.* [*par-*, and Gr. *ous*, *ōtos*, ear.] situated near or beside the ear; especially, designating or of either of the salivary glands situated below and in front of each ear.

pa̤·rot′id, *n.* a parotid gland.

par·ō·tit′iç, *a.* of or having parotitis, or the mumps.

par·ō·tī′tis, *n.* mumps; swelling or inflammation of the parotid.

pa̤·rō′toid, *a.* in zoology, designating or of skin glands forming warty growths near the ear in some frogs, toads, and related animals.

pa̤·rō′toid, *n.* a parotoid gland.

-păr′ous, [L. *-parus*, from *parere*, to bring forth, bear.] a combining form meaning *bringing forth*, *producing*, *bearing*, as in *viviparous*.

par·ō·văr′i·um, *n.* [*par-* and *ovarium*.] the remnant of the Wolffian body of the female.

par′ox·yṣm, *n.* [Gr. *paroxysmos*, from *paroxynein*, to excite or sharpen; *para*, beyond, in excess, and *oxynein*, to sharpen, from *oxys*, sharp.]

1. a sudden attack, or intensification of the symptoms, of a disease, usually recurring periodically.

2. any sudden convulsion, as of laughter, rage, sneezing, etc.; fit; spasm.

par·ox·yṣ′măl, *a.* 1. of, pertaining to, or characteristic of a paroxysm; as, *paroxysmal* pang; *paroxysmal* anger.

2. in geology, caused by any sudden or violent effect of natural agency, such as by the explosive eruption of a volcano, or the convulsive throes of an earthquake.

par·ox·yṣ′măl·ly, *adv.* in a paroxysmal manner.

par·ox′y·tōne, *n.* [*par-* and *oxytone*.] in Greek grammar, a word having an acute accent on the penult.

par·ox′y·tōne, *a.* having an acute accent on the penult.

pär·quet′ (-kā′ *or* -ket′), *n.* [Fr., dim. of *parc*, park.]

1. the main floor of a theater, especially that part from the orchestra to the parquet circle: usually called *orchestra*.

2. a flooring of parquetry.

3. in many European countries, the administrative branch of the law which deals with the prevention, investigation, and punishment of crime.

pär·quet′ (-kā′ *or* -ket′), *v.t.*; parqueted (-kād′ *or* -ket′id), *pt.*, *pp.*; parqueting, *ppr.* 1. to use parquetry to make (a floor, etc.).

2. to decorate the floor of (a room) with parquetry.

pär'quet·āġe, *n.* same as *parquetry.*

PARQUETRY

pär·quet' cĩr'çle, the part of a theater beneath the balcony and behind the parquet on the main floor: also called *orchestra circle.*

pär'quet·ry, *n.* [Fr. *parqueterie.*] inlaid woodwork in geometric or other patterns and generally of different colors: principally used for floors.

pär·quette' (-ket'), *n.* same as *parquet.*

pärr, *n.*; *pl.* **pärrṣ** or **pärr,** [perh. a Scot. dial. word.]

1. a young salmon before it enters salt water.

PARR

2. the young of certain other fish.

par'rȧ, *n.* [L. *parra*, barn owl.] same as *jacana.*

par'rȧ·keet, *n.* same as *parakeet.*

par'răl, *n.* same as *parrel.*

par·rä'quȧ (-kwȧ), *n.* [S. Am.] a gallinaceous bird, the guan, of the genus *Ortalida*; the chachalaca.

par·rȧ·mat'tȧ, *n.* paramatta.

par'rel, par'răl, *n.* [abbrev. of *apparel.*] in nautical usage, a band of rope, or now more generally an iron collar, by which the yards are fastened to the masts so as to slide up and down freely when required.

par'rel, par'ral, *v.t.* and *v.i.* to secure by using a parrel.

par'rel truck, a hard wooden ball, having a hole through its center through which the rope forming a parrel passes.

par·rhē'si·ȧ (par-rē'zhi-ȧ *or* -si-ȧ), *n.* [Gr. *parrēsia*; *para*, beside, and *rhēsis*, speech.] in rhetoric, boldness or freedom of speech.

par·ri·cīd'ăl, *a.* pertaining to or guilty of parricide.

par'ri·cīde, *n.* [Fr., from L. *parricida*, from *pater*, father, and *cædere*, to kill.]

1. a person who murders either or both of his parents or someone else who stands to him in a somewhat similar relationship.

2. the act of a parricide.

par'rŏck, *n.* [AS. *pearroc.*] a croft, or small field; a paddock. [Brit. Dial.]

par'rō·ket, par'rō·quet (-ket), *n.* same as *parakeet.*

par'rŏt, *n.* [Fr. *perrot*; prob. from *Perrot*, dim. of *Pierre*, Peter.]

1. a bird of the order *Psittaciformes*, or family *Psittacidæ*, with hooked bills, brightly colored feathers, and feet having two toes pointing forward and two backward. Several species can not only imitate the various tones of the human voice, but also repeat words and phrases. Parrots feed on fruits and seeds and are found in all warm countries.

ROSELLA PARROT (*Platycercus eximius*)

2. a person who mechanically repeats the words or acts of others without fully understanding what he does or says.

Carolina parrot; the parakeet of the Carolinas, *Conuropsis carolinensis*, now extinct.

par'rŏt, *v.t.* to repeat or imitate without understanding.

par'rŏt, *v.i.* to chatter like a parrot.

par'rŏt·bēak, *n.* same as *parrot's-bill.*

par'rŏt çōal, coal that burns with a crackling sound; cannel coal. [Brit. Dial.]

par'rŏt·ẽr, *n.* one who repeats or mimics what he hears.

par'rŏt fē'vẽr, psittacosis.

par'rŏt fish, a brightly colored, spoon-shaped fish of the genus *Scarus.* Most of the species are tropical, but one, *Scarus cretensis*, is found in the Mediterranean: all species have parrotlike jaws. Also called *parrot wrasse.*

par'rŏt green, a yellowish green.

par'rŏt·ry, *n.* acting the part of a parrot; servile imitation. [Rare.]

par'rŏt's-bill, *n.* see *Clianthus.*

par'rŏt weed, a shrubby plant, *Bocconia frutescens*, of tropical America, with very large leaves and small flowers.

par'rŏt wrasse (ras), see *parrot fish.*

par'ry, *v.t.*; parried, *pt.*, *pp.*; parrying, *ppr.* [Fr. *parer*; It. *parare*, to ward off, from L. *parare*, to prepare, keep off.]

1. to ward off; to deflect; as, to *parry* a thrust.

2. to avoid; to shift off; to elude; to evade. The French government has *parried* the payment of our claims. —E. Everett.

par'ry, *v.i.* to make a parry or evasion.

par'ry, *n.*; *pl.* **par'rieṣ,** 1. a warding off or a turning aside of an attack, blow, etc., as in fencing.

2. an evasion; evasive reply.

pärse, *v.t.*; parsed (pärst), *pt.*, *pp.*; parsing, *ppr.* [from L. *pars*, a part, in *Quæ pars orationis?* What part of speech?]

1. to break (a sentence) down into parts, explaining the grammatical form, function, and interrelation of each part.

2. to describe the form, part of speech, and function of (a word) in a sentence.

pärse, *v.i.* to be capable of being parsed.

pär'seç", *n.* [*par*allax and *sec*ond.] in astronomy, a unit used in measuring interstellar space; equivalent to the distance of a star having a heliocentric parallax of one second: it equals 3.26 light years, or 19,200,000,000,000 miles: also called *secpar.*

Pär'see, Pär'sï, *n.* [Per. and Hind. *pârsi*, a Persian, a fire worshiper.] a member of a Zoroastrian religious sect in India descended from a group of Persian refugees who fled from the Moslem persecutions of the seventh and eighth centuries.

Pär'see·iṣm, Pär'sï·iṣm, *n.* the Zoroastrian religion of the Parsees.

pärs'ẽr, *n.* one who parses.

Pär'sï, *n.* see *Parsee.*

Pär'si·fäl, *n.* [G.; M.H.G. *Parzival*; OFr. *Perceval.*] the title character in Wagner's music drama (1882) of the knights of the Holy Grail: he gets from Klingsor a magic spear with which he heals the wound of Amfortas.

pär·si·mō'ni·ous, *a.* characterized by parsimony; miserly; stingy; close.

Extraordinary funds for one campaign may spare us the expense of many years, whereas a long *parsimonious* war will drain us of more men and money. —Addison.

Syn.—saving, miserly, penurious, frugal, niggardly.

pär·si·mō'ni·ous·ly, *adv.* in a parsimonious manner.

pär·si·mō'ni·ous·ness, *n.* a very sparing use of money, or a disposition to save expense.

pär'si·mō·ny, *n.* [L. *parsimonia*, *parcimonia*, from *parcere*, to spare.] sparingness in expenditure; a disposition to avoid expense, unreasonable economy; extreme frugality; niggardliness; stinginess; miserliness; closeness in money matters.

Syn.—niggardliness, frugality, stinginess, closeness, penuriousness, economy, sparingness.

Pär'siṣm, *n.* same as *Parseeism.*

pärs'ley, *n.* [Fr. *persil*; L. *petroselinum*; Gr. *petroselinon*, rock parsley; *petros*, rock, and *selinon*, parsley.] a biennial herb, *Carum petroselinum* or *Petroselinum hortense*, used to flavor or garnish some foods. It has tripinnate, curled leaves and greenish-yellow flowers.

pärs'ley çam'phŏr, see *apiol.*

pärs'ley fẽrn, a fern, *Cryptogramma crispa* or *Allosorus crispus*, the leaves of which resemble parsley.

pärs'ley hạw, a tree, *Cratægus apiifolia*, of the southern part of the United States, having leaves resembling parsley leaves.

pärs'ley piẽrt, an herb, *Alchemilla arvensis*, of the rose family, formerly used in medicine.

pärs'nip, *n.* [OFr. *pastenaque*; L. *pastenaca*, parsnip, from *pastinum*, a two-forked dibble.]

1. a biennial herb of Europe, *Pastinaca sativa*, characterized by large, featherlike leaves, a long, thick, sweet, white root, and yellow flowers; it is poisonous in its wild state but cultivation has made it edible: varieties are the common, the Guernsey, the hollow-crowned, and the round or turnip-rooted parsnip.

2. the root, used as a vegetable.

pärs'nip chẽr'vil, a garden herb, *Chærophyllum bulbosum*, having an edible root.

pär'sŏn, *n.* [OFr. *persone*, from LL. *persona ecclesiæ*, the person of the church.]

1. a clergyman or minister in charge of a parish.

2. any clergyman or minister. [Colloq.]

pär'sŏn·āġe, *n.* 1. the dwelling provided by a church for the use of its parson, or minister.

2. in English ecclesiastical law, the land or income provided by a parish for its parson.

pär'sŏn bĩrd, same as *poebird.*

pär'sŏned, *a.* supplied with a parson or parsons.

pär·son'iç, *a.* of or relating to a parson; like a parson.

pär·son'iç·ăl, *a.* parsonic.

Pär'sŏnṣ tā'ble, [after *Parsons* School of Design, in New York.] [*also* p- t-] a lightweight, square-legged table of geometric design with no exposed joints, now often made of plastic.

pärt, *n.* [L. *pars*, *partis*, part.]

1. a portion or division of a whole; specifically, (a) any of several equal portions, quantities, numbers, pieces, etc. of which something is composed or into which it can be divided; as, an hour is the twenty-fourth *part* of a day; (b) an essential element or constituent; an integral portion which can be separated; as, an automobile *part*; (c) a portion detached or cut from a whole; a fragment; a piece; (d) a certain amount but not all; as, he lost *part* of his fortune; (e) a certain amount or section regarded as a separate division; as, which *part* of the book did you like best?; (f) a segment or organ of the body of men and animals; (g) a division of a literary work; (h) in mathematics, an aliquot part.

2. a portion assigned or given; a share; specifically, (a) something a person must do; business; duty; as, we do our *part*; (b) interest; concern; as, it was no *part* of his to interfere; (c) [*usually pl.*] talent; ability; as, a man of *parts*; (d) a character in a drama; a theatrical role; (e) the words, actions, etc. of a character in a play; (f) in music, the score for a particular voice or instrument in a concerted piece; also, any of the voices or instruments in a musical ensemble.

3. a region; area; especially, [*usually pl.*] a portion of a country; a district; a quarter; as, he left these *parts.*

4. one of the different sides or parties in a transaction, dispute, conflict, etc.

5. the dividing line formed by combing the hair in opposite directions.

aliquot part; see *aliquot.*

for one's part; so far as one is concerned.

for the most part; in the greatest part or to the greatest extent; mostly; generally.

in good part; good-naturedly; without offense.

in part; to a certain extent or degree; partly.

on the part of one; (a) as far as one is concerned; (b) by or coming from one.

part and parcel; an essential or necessary part: used emphatically.

to play a part; (a) to behave unnaturally in an attempt to deceive; (b) to participate or share: also *to take part.*

to take one's part; to support one in a struggle or disagreement; to side with one.

Syn.—portion, component, share, piece, constituent, fragment, section, member, division.

pärt, *v.t.*; parted, *pt.*, *pp.*; parting, *ppr.* [OFr. *partir*; L. *partire*, to divide, separate, from the noun.]

1. to break or divide into separate parts.

2. to comb (the hair) in opposite directions so as to leave a dividing line.

3. to break up (a connection or relationship) by separating the people or parties involved.

4. to separate (two or more persons or things); to break or hold apart; to put asunder.

5. to separate in the mind; to distinguish, as two theories.

6. to separate (substances) as by a chemical process.

7. to distribute; share; apportion. [Archaic.]

8. in nautical usage, to break or incur the breaking of (a hawser, chain, etc.).

pärt, *v.i.* 1. to break or divide into two or more pieces; to shift apart.

2. to separate and go different ways, as branches of a river.

3. to separate; to go away from each other; to cease associating.

4. to go away; to leave; to depart.

5. to die.

6. to have a share or part; to share. [Obs.]

to part from; to depart or separate from; to leave.

to part with; to give up; to let go; to relinquish.

pärt, *a.* less than a whole; as, *part* interest.

pärt, *adv.* partly; to some extent.

pärt'à·ble, *a.* partible. [Obs.]

pär·tage' (-tazh'), *n.* 1. division; severance.

2. part; share.

pär·tāke', *v.i.*; partook, *pt.*; partaken, *pp.*; partaking, *ppr.* [from *part taker*, translation of L. *particeps*, participant.]

1. to take part in an activity; to participate.

2. to take a portion; to eat or drink something, especially in company with others.

to partake of; (a) to take or have a share in, as a meal; to take; take of; take some of; (b) to have or show a trace or suggestion of; to have some of the qualities or nature of.

pär·tāke', *v.t.* 1. to take or have a part or share in, as a meal, responsibility, etc. [Rare.]

My royal father lives;
Let every one *partake* the general joy.
—Dryden.

2. to admit to a part; to share with. [Obs.]

3. to distribute; to impart; to communicate. [Obs.]

pär·tāk'ēr, *n.* 1. one who has or takes a part, share, or portion, in common with others; a sharer; a participator; usually followed by *of* or *in*.

If the Gentiles have been made *partakers of* their spiritual things. —Rom. xv. 27.

Wish me *partaker in* thy happiness.—Shak.

2. an accomplice; an associate. [Obs.]

When thou sawest a thief then thou consentedst with him, and hast been *partaker* with adulterers. —Ps. l. 18.

pär'tăn, *n.* a crab. [Scot. and Brit. Dial.]

pärt'ed, *a.* 1. divided; separated; split.

2. dead. [Archaic.]

3. in botany, divided almost to the base, as some leaves.

pärt'ēr, *n.* one who parts or separates.

pär·terre' (-târ'), *n.* [Fr., from *par*, by, and *terre*, L. *terra*, earth.]

1. an ornamental garden area in which the flower beds and paths form a pattern.

2. the part of a theater beneath the balcony and behind the parquet; parquet circle: also called *orchestra circle*.

pär·thē'ni·ad, *n.* a poem or song written in honor of a virgin. [Rare.]

pär·then'iç, *a.* [Gr. *parthenos*, virgin.] born of an unmarried woman: referring especially to the Spartan Partheniae, or sons of unmarried women.

Pär·thē'ni·um, *n.* [L., from Gr. *parthenios*, maidenly.] a genus of North American plants having small rays, a small, triangular, indehiscent pericarp containing one seed, and terminal panicles of white or yellow flowers

Pär"thē·nō·cis'sus, *n.* [Gr. *parthenos*, virgin, and *kissos*, ivy.] a genus of Asiatic and North American plants of the vine family, characterized by tiny flowers, perfectly formed and with distinct petals.

pär"thē·nō·ġen'e·sis, *n.* [Gr. *parthenos*, virgin, and *genesis*, origin.] reproduction by the development of an unfertilized ovum, seed, or spore, as in certain polyzoans, insects, algae, etc.: *artificial parthenogenesis* is the development of an ovum stimulated by chemical or mechanical means.

pär"thē·nō·ġē·net'iç, *a.* of, reproducing by, or reproduced by parthenogenesis.

pär"thē·nō·ġē·net'iç·ăl·ly, *adv.* in a parthenogenetic manner.

pär"thē·nō·ġen'i·tive, *a.* parthenogenetic.

pär·thē·nog'e·ny, *n.* parthenogenesis.

pär"thē·nō·gō·nid'i·um, *n.*; *pl.* **pär"thē·nō·gō·nid'i·ȧ,** [Gr. *parthenos*, virgin, and *gonidium*.] an individual produced by asexual generation and itself capable of reproduction by the same method.

pär·thē·nol'ō·ġy, *n.* [Gr. *parthenos*, virgin, and *logos*, discourse.] in medicine, the study of virginity, its health and disorders.

Pär'thē·non, *n.* [Gr. *parthenos*, a virgin (i.e., Athena).] the Doric temple of Athena built (5th century B.C.) on the Acropolis in Athens: sculpture is attributed to Phidias.

Pär·then'ō·pē, *n.* [Gr. *parthenos*, virgin, and *ōps*, *opos*, face.]

1. in Grecian mythology, one of the sirens who strove to beguile Ulysses with her songs and, failing, threw herself into the sea.

2. the city of Naples, Italy: so called from the legend that the body of Parthenope, the siren, was washed ashore there. [Obs. or Poetic.]

3. a minor planet between Jupiter and Mars, discovered in 1850 by M. de Gasparis of Naples.

Pär'thē·nos, *n.* [from Gr. *parthenos*, a virgin.] a virgin: an epithet of several Greek goddesses, especially of Athena.

pär'thē·nō·spērm, *n.* same as *parthenospore*.

pär'thē·nō·spōre, *n.* a reproductive body resembling the sexual spore of zygomycetous fungi: it is reproduced by parthenogenesis.

Pär'thi·ăn, *a.* of or pertaining to the ancient kingdom of Parthia, its people, or culture.

Parthian arrow or *shot*; an arrow shot at the enemy when retreating or fleeing, as the ancient Parthians did in their battles; hence, a parting shot or thrust.

Pär'thi·ăn, *n.* a native or inhabitant of Parthia, an ancient kingdom southeast of the Caspian Sea.

pär'tiăl (-shăl), *a.* [Fr., from L. *pars*, *partis*, part.]

1. favoring one person, faction, etc. more than another; biased; prejudiced.

2. of, being, or affecting only a part; not complete or total.

partial differential; see under *differential*.

partial fractions; the fractions into which a given fraction may be separated and whose sum equals the given fraction.

partial loss; a loss involving only a portion of the property or amount at risk.

partial to; fond of; having a liking for.

partial tone; in music and acoustics, any of the pure, or harmonic, tones forming a complex tone.

Syn.—favoring, inequitable, unfair, biased, prejudiced.

pär'tiăl, *n.* same as *partial tone* under *partial*, a.

pär'tiăl·işm, *n.* 1. partiality.

2. in theology, the doctrine that the atonement of Christ was made for only a part of mankind, that is, the elect; particularism.

pär'tiăl·ist, *n.* 1. one who is partial.

2. one who believes in partialism, or particularism.

pär·ti·al'i·ty (-shi-), *n.* 1. inclination to favor one party or one side of a question more than the other; an undue bias of mind toward one party or side, which is apt to warp the judgment.

2. a stronger inclination to one thing than to others; a particular fondness; a strong liking; as, a *partiality* for poetry or painting.

pär'tiăl·īze (-shăl-), *v.t.*; partialized, *pt.*, *pp.*; partializing, *ppr.* to render partial.

pär'tiăl·ly, *adv.* 1. with undue bias of mind to one party or side; with unjust favor or dislike; as, to judge *partially*.

2. in part; not totally; as, the story may be *partially* true; the sun and moon are often *partially* eclipsed.

pärt·i·bil'i·ty, *n.* susceptibility of division, partition, or severance; separability; as, the *partibility* of an inheritance.

pärt'i·ble, *a.* [LL. *partibilis*, from L. *partire*, to divide.] separable; that can be divided, separated, or parted; as, an estate of inheritance may be *partible*.

pär'ti·ceps çri'mi·nis, [L.] a partner in crime; an accomplice.

pär·tic'i·pȧ·ble, *a.* that can be divided, participated, or shared.

pär·tic'i·pănce, *n.* participation.

pär·tic'i·păn·cy, *n.* participance.

pär·tic'i·pănt, *a.* [L. *participans* (-*antis*), ppr. of *participare*.] participating.

pär·tic'i·pănt, *n.* a person who participates in something; one having a share or part.

pär·tic'i·pănt·ly, *adv.* in a participating manner.

pär·tic'i·pāte, *a.* acting together. [Rare.]

pär·tic'i·pāte, *v.i.*; participated, *pt.*, *pp.*; participating, *ppr.* [L. *participare*, *participatus*; *pars*, *partis*, a part, and *capere*, to take.] to have or take a part or share with others (*in* some activity, enterprise, etc.); to partake.

pär·tic'i·pāte, *v.t.* to have or take a part or share in. [Rare.]

Of fellowship I speak,
Such as I seek, fit to *participate*
All rational delight. —Milton.

2. to give a share of; to communicate [Obs.]

pär·tic·i·pā'tion, *n.* a participating; act or fact of sharing or partaking.

pär·tic'i·pā·tive, *a.* capable of participating.

pär·tic'i·pā·tŏr, *n.* one who participates.

pär·ti·cip'i·ăl (*or* -yăl), *a.* [L. *participialis*.]

1. having the nature and use of a participle.

2. formed from a participle; as, a *participial* noun.

pär·ti·cip'i·ăl, *n.* a verbal derivative (as a gerund or infinitive) used as a noun or adjective.

pär·ti·cip'i·ăl·īze, *v.t.* to form into a participle.

pär·ti·cip'i·ăl·ly, *adv.* as a participle; with participial function.

pär'ti·ci·ple, *n.* [ME.; OFr. *participe*, participle; L. *participium*, from *particeps*, participating, partaking; *pars*, *partis*, a part, and *capere*, to take: so named from participating in the nature of both verb and adjective.]

1. a word derived from a verb and having the qualities of both verb and adjective: a participle may be active (e.g., I am *asking*) or passive (e.g., I am *asked*) and is referred to as having tense (e.g., present, *asking*; past, *asked*; perfect, *having asked*) but does not indicate time except in relation to its context. Participles are used: (a) in various verb forms; (b) as adjectives (e.g., a club *used* in golf; a car *rushing* downhill); (c) in absolute constructions, modifying a whole sentence (e.g., generally *speaking*, these principles can be accepted). In any of these functions a participle may take an object or be modified by an adverb. The present participle is sometimes used with adverbial force (e.g., *raving* mad).

2. anything that partakes of the nature of different things. [Obs.]

pär'ti·çle, *n.* [ME. *partycle*; OFr. *particule*; L. *particula*, dim. of *pars*, *partis*, part.]

1. a minute part or portion of matter, the aggregation of which parts constitutes the whole mass.

There is not one grain in the universe, . . . nor so much as any one *particle* of it, that mankind may not be either the better or the worse for, according as it is applied. —L'Estrange.

2. any very small portion or part; a tiny fragment; the slightest trace; as, he has not a *particle* of patriotism or virtue.

From any of the other unreasonable demands, the houses had not given their commissioners authority in the least *particle* to recede. —Clarendon.

3. a small, individual section of written matter; a clause; an article in a document.

4. in grammar, (a) a short and indeclinable part of speech, as an article, preposition, conjunction, or interjection; (b) a prefix or suffix.

5. in physics, a piece of matter so small as to be considered without magnitude though having inertia and the force of attraction.

6. in the Roman Catholic Church, (a) a little piece of the consecrated Host; (b) any of the small Hosts given in the communion of the laity.

pär'ti-çol'ŏred, *a.* 1. having different colors in different parts.

2. showing variations or differences in form, quality, etc.; diversified; variegated.

Also spelled *party-colored*.

pär·tiç'ū·lăr, *a.* [ME. *particuler*; Fr. *particulier*; LL. *particularis*.]

1. pertaining to one and not to more; special; not general; as, this remark has a *particular* application.

One of the expedients of party to acquire influence, within *particular* districts, is to misrepresent the opinions and aims of other districts. —George Washington.

2. individual; single; specific; apart from others; considered separately; as, what *particular* fault do you refer to?

In what *particular* thought to work I know not. —Shak.

3. pertaining to a single person or thing; peculiar to one; distinct; characteristic; as, the *particular* properties of a plant.

4. personal; private; individual.

Thine own *particular* wrongs. —Shak.

5. unusual; special; worthy of attention and regard; not ordinary; notable; as, he brought no *particular* news.

6. dealing with particulars; itemized; detailed; as, a full and *particular* account of an accident.

I have been *particular* in examining the reason of children's inheriting the property of their fathers, because it will give us farther light in the inheritance of power. —Locke.

7. odd; singular; uncommon; marked; peculiar. [Obs.]

Lady Ruelle . . . had been something *particular*, as I fancied, in her behavior to me. —Graves.

8. singularly nice in taste; precise; fastidious; as, a man very *particular* in his diet or dress.

It was rather early in the day for a drinking bout. But the canting crew were not remarkably *particular*. —Ainsworth.

9. in law, separate or able to be separated; specific; special; definite.

10. in logic, designating a proposition which affirms or denies its predicate to a part of, but not to the whole of, a subject; limited in application to part of a class; as, "some people have red hair" is a *particular* proposition: opposed to *universal*.

Particular Baptists; a branch of the Baptist denomination accepting the doctrine of particularism.

particular lien; a right coming from a thing itself or connected with it by which a lien may be made upon that particular thing.

particular redemption; the theological doctrine of particularism.

Syn.—noteworthy, unusual, appropriate, circumstantial, distinct, exact, exclusive, nice, peculiar, specific.

pär·tiç′ū·lăr, *n.* 1. a separate and distinct individual, fact, item, or instance which may be classified or included under a generalization; single case.

2. a detail; item of information; point.

3. an individual; a private person. [Obs.]

4. private interest; personal relation. [Obs.]

5. private character; state of an individual; special peculiarity. [Obs.]

6. a minute and detailed account; as, a *particular* of premises, a *particular* of a plaintiff's demand, etc. [Now Chiefly Legal.]

The reader has a *particular* of the books wherein this law was written. —Ayliffe.

7. in logic, a particular proposition.

bill of particulars; see under *bill*.

in particular; especially; particularly.

pär·tiç′ū·lăr·işm, *n.* 1. the theological doctrine that redemption is possible only for certain individuals.

2. undivided adherence or devotion to one particular party, system, interest, etc.

3. the policy of allowing each member or state in a federation to function independently without regard for the whole.

pär·tiç′ū·lăr·ist, *n.* a believer in and advocate of particularism.

pär·tiç·ū·lăr·is′tiç, *a.* relating to the doctrine of particularism; having the character of particularism.

pär·tiç·ū·lar′i·ty, *n.*; *pl.* **pär·tiç·ū·lar′i·tieş,** [Fr. *particularité*; LL. *particularitas*.]

1. the state, quality, or fact of being particular; specifically, (a) individuality; characteristic quality: opposed to *generality, universality*; (b) the quality of being detailed or minute, as a description; (c) attention to detail; minute exactness; painstaking care; (d) the quality of being fastidious or hard to please.

2. something particular; specifically, (a) an individual trait or characteristic; a peculiarity, as of circumstance or detail; (b) a minute detail.

I saw an old heathen altar with this *particularity*, that it was hollowed like a dish at one end, but not the end on which the sacrifice was laid. —Addison.

pär·tiç·ū·lăr·i·zā′tion, *n.* a particularizing or being particularized.

pär·tiç′ū·lăr·īze, *v.t.*; particularized, *pt., pp.*; particularizing, *ppr.* to specify or mention distinctly; to give the particulars of; to enumerate or specify in detail; to itemize.

pär·tiç′ū·lăr·īze, *v.i.* to give particulars or details; as, it is needless, just now, to *particularize*.

pär·tiç′ū·lăr·ly, *adv.* 1. in a particular manner; distinctly; singly; so as to be particular; in detail.

Providence, that universally casts its eye over all the creation, is yet pleased more *particularly* to fasten it upon some. —South.

2. especially; unusually; extraordinarily; as, to be *particularly* pleased.

Syn.—especially, markedly, distinctly.

pär·tiç′ū·lāte, *v.t.* and *v.i.* to particularize. [Obs.]

pär·tiç′ū·lāte, *a.* 1. having the form of an atom or minute particle. [Rare.]

2. of or made up of particles. [Rare.]

pär′tim, *adv.* [L. *pars, partis*, a part.] in part; partially: used in noting names of species, genera, etc. which agree only in part.

pärt′ing, *a.* 1. serving to part; dividing; separating; breaking in pieces.

2. given, spoken, done, etc. at separation; as, a *parting* word.

3. departing; declining; hence, dying.

Parting day
Dies like the dolphin, whom each pang imbues
With a new color as it gasps away,
The last still loveliest. —Byron.

pärt′ing, *n.* 1. the act of dividing or separating; a division; a separation.

2. a place of division or separation; a dividing point or line.

3. something that separates or divides.

4. a separation of two or more persons; leavetaking.

5. a departure.

6. death.

7. in metallurgy, an operation by which gold and silver are separated from each other by different menstrua.

8. in geology, a fissure in strata; any thin subordinate layer occurring between two main beds.

pärt′ing bēad, a parting strip inserted into the center of the pulley style to keep apart the upper and lower sashes of a window.

pärt′ing çup, a drinking cup with two handles, used by two persons in drinking a toast at parting.

pärt′ing sand, in molding, dry sand placed between the two members of a mold to facilitate their separation.

pärt′ing strip, a thin strip of wood, metal, etc. for separating adjoining parts of a structure.

pȧr·tī′ pris′ (prē′), [Fr.] preconceived opinion.

pär′ti·ṣăn, *n.* [Fr.; It. *partigiano*, from *parte*, from L. *pars, partis*, a part.]

1. one who takes the side of or strongly supports a side, a party, or another person: often said of an unreasoning, emotional adherent.

John Locke hated tyranny and persecution as a philosopher; but his intellect preserved him from the violence of a *partisan*. —Macaulay.

2. in military affairs, (a) a member of a group of irregular troops engaged in guerrilla fighting, often behind enemy lines; (b) a person commanding such a party.

Also spelled *partizan*.

pär′ti·ṣăn, *a.* 1. of, like, or characteristic of a partisan, or adherent.

2. blindly or unreasonably devoted.

To those senators who were blinded by the promptings of supposed *partisan* advantage, we can in this hour afford to be charitable.

3. of or having to do with partisans or their type of fighting.

Also spelled *partizan*.

pär′ti·ṣăn, *n.* [OFr. *partizane, partisane*; It. *partesana, partigiana*; prob. from *pertugiare*, to pierce.] a variety of pike or halberd used by infantry in the sixteenth and seventeenth centuries.

pär′ti·ṣăn·ship, *n.* [*partisan* and *-ship*.]

1. the strong supporting or endorsement of a side, party, etc.

2. a strong, often unreasoning, attachment; blind loyalty.

pär′tīte, *a.* [L. *partitus*, pp. of *partire*, to part.] parted; having divisions; divided into parts: often in compounds, as tri*partite*.

pär·ti′tion (-tish′un), *n.* [ME. *particioune*; L. *partitio*, from *partire*, to divide, to part.]

1. the act of parting or dividing; the act of separating into portions and distributing; as, the *partition* of a kingdom among several other states.

2. the state of being divided; division; separation.

3. a part or section; a portion; a compartment.

4. that by which different parts are separated; as, (a) in architecture, a wall of stone, brick, timber, etc. which serves to divide one room from another; (b) in botany, the division of a partite leaf; also, the wall of a cell in an ovary or fruit; a dissepiment.

5. in law, the process of dividing property and giving separate title to those who previously had joint title.

6. in logic, the separation of a class into its elements or parts: a method of analysis.

7. in mathematics, division.

8. in music, the arrangement of the several parts of a composition on the same page or pages, above and under one another, so that they may be all under the eye of the conductor or performer: also called a *score*. [Now Rare.]

9. in heraldry, one of the several divisions made in a coat when the arms of several families are borne all together in one shield on account of intermarriages or otherwise.

partition lines; in heraldry, those lines by which the shield is cut or divided perpendicularly, diagonally, etc.; as, the party (*partition*) per pale, per bend, etc.

partition of numbers; in mathematics, the separation of numbers into parts satisfying some specified condition.

Syn.—barrier, division, enclosure, compartment, separation, distribution, apportionment.

pär·ti′tion, *v.t.*; partitioned, *pt., pp.*; partitioning, *ppr.* 1. to divide by walls or partitions.

2. to divide into shares or parts; to apportion; as, to *partition* an estate.

pär·ti′tion·ment, *n.* the act or the process of dividing; partition.

pär′ti·tive, *a.* [Fr. *partitif*; L. *partitus*, pp. of *partire*, to part.]

1. used in setting off or separating; making a division.

2. in grammar, restricting to or involving only a part of a whole.

pär′ti·tive, *n.* a partitive word or form (e.g., *few, some, any*).

pär′ti·tive·ly, *adv.* in a partitive manner.

pär·ti·vẽr′săl, *a.* in geology, denoting the condition of strata when the dip ranges through part of a circle: contrasted with *quaquaversal*.

pär′ti·zăn, *n.* and *a.* same as *partisan* (adherent).

pär′ti·zăn·ship, *n.* same as *partisanship*.

pärt′let, *n.* [earlier *pallet, palelet*; OFr. *patelette*, band of stuff, orig., dim. of *pate*, a paw.] a covering for the neck and upper chest, often ruffled or embroidered: popular in the sixteenth century.

pärt′ly, *adv.* in part; in some measure or degree; not wholly.

pärt mū′ṣiç, vocal music for two or more voices in independent parts, usually sung without the aid of instrumental accompaniment.

pärt′nẽr, *n.* [ME. *partener*; prob. from *parcener* (see *parcener*), influenced by *part*.]

1. one who has a share or part in anything with another or others; a sharer; a participator; a partaker; an associate.

Fair Fortune set me down
The *partner* of an emperor's crown. —Scott.

2. one who is associated with one or more persons in the same business and shares with them its profits and risks; a member of a partnership.

3. either of two persons dancing together.

Lead in your ladies every one; sweet *partner*,
I must not yet forsake you. —Shak.

4. either or any one of the players on the same side or team, especially one of two playing on the same side against two others, as in bridge.

5. a husband or wife.

The cottage where she dwelt;
And where yet dwells her faithful *partner*. —Wordsworth.

6. in nautical usage, one of the reinforcing timbers used to support a mast or other upright and to strengthen the deck at the point where the mast, etc. enters.

dormant partner; same as *silent partner*.

Syn.—associate, colleague, coadjutor, confederate, sharer, partaker, spouse, companion.

pärt′nẽr, *v.t.* 1. to join (others) together as partners.

2. to join with (another) as a partner; to be or provide a partner for.

pärt′nẽr·ship, *n.* 1. the state or condition of being a partner; participation.

He does possession keep,
And is too wise to hazard *partnership*. —Dryden.

2. the relationship of partners; joint interest; association.

3. (a) an association of two or more people who contribute money or property to carry on a joint business and who share profits or losses in certain proportion; (b) a contract by which such an association is created; (c) the people so associated.

general partnership; an association that functions for the joint profit and risk of all the partners regardless of the original contributions of each.

limited partnership; an association organized under a statute, with limited liability in some or all of the members.

mining partnership; a distinct association, with different rights and liabilities attaching to its members from an ordinary trading partnership. A member may convey his interest to another without dissolving the partnership, and the death or insolvency of a member will not result in a dissolution.

pärt of speech, in grammar, (a) any of the traditional form classes comprising the words of a language, to which a word is assigned according to its function (e.g., in Latin grammar, noun, verb, pronoun, adjective, adverb, preposition, conjunction, and interjection); (b) any word considered as belonging to one of these classes.

pär·took′, *v.* past tense of *partake*.

pär′tridġe (-trij), *n.*; *pl.* **pär′tridġ·eṣ** or **pär′tridġe,** [ME. *partryke, partriche, pertriche, partrys*; OFr. *pertrix, perdriz*; from L. and Gr. *perdix*, a partridge.]

RED-LEGGED PARTRIDGE (*Caccabis rufa*)

1. a rasorial bird of the genus *Perdix*. The common partridge, *Perdix cinerea*, is the most plentiful of all game birds in England and occurs in nearly all parts of Europe, in North Africa, and some parts of western Asia. It has a short strong bill, naked at the base, the upper mandible being convex and bent down at the tip. The wings and tail are short, the tarsi as well as the toes naked, and the tarsi not spurred. The upper parts of the plumage are ash-gray finely varied with brown and black. It feeds on grain and other seeds, and on insects and their larvae and pupae. Besides this species there are the red-legged, or Guernsey, partridge, *Caccabis rufa*, the Greek partridge, *Caccabis græca*, and various other species.

2. any of various American game birds resembling the true partridges, as the ruffed grouse, pheasant, quail, etc.

3. a tinamou.

4. in artillery, a large bombard formerly used in sieges and defensive works. [Obs.]

pär′tridġe·ber″ry, *n.*; *pl.* **pär′tridġe·ber″ries,** 1. a common plant, *Mitchella repens*, found in woods of eastern North America, having an edible, somewhat insipid berry of a scarlet color following fragrant, white paired flowers tinged with purple: also called *deerberry* and *hive vine*.

2. its berry.

3. the winter green.

pär′tridġe dŏve, a ground dove of Jamaica: also called *mountain witch*.

pär′tridġe pēa, an herb, *Cassia chamæcrista*, bearing a yellow flower, growing in sandy soils in the eastern United States.

pär′tridġe·wood, *n.* a tropical American wood, reddish in color and having dark-colored lines and streaks running longitudinally through it. It is used in the manufacture of canes and in cabinetwork.

pärt sing′ing, choral singing, as opposed to *solo singing*.

pärt sọng, a homophonic song for several voices, usually three or more, singing in harmony, generally without accompaniment.

pärt′-tīme, *a.* for, during, or by part time; as, he has a *part-time* job, working Tuesdays, Thursdays, and Fridays only.

pärt tīme, a part of the normal or customary time.

pär·tū′ri·āte, *v.i.* and *v.t.* [L. *parturire*, to desire to bring forth, to be in labor, from *partus*, birth, from *parere*, to bear.] to bring forth young. [Rare.]

pär·tū′ri·en·cy, *n.* the quality or condition of being parturient.

pär·tū′ri·ent, *a.* [L. *parturiens (-entis)*, ppr. of *parturire*, to be in labor.]

1. giving birth or about to give birth to young.

2. of childbirth, or parturition.

3. on the point of coming forth with a discovery, idea, etc.

pär·tū·ri·fā′cient (-shent), *a.* [from L. *parturire*, to be in labor; and *-facient*.] inducing or easing labor in childbirth.

pär·tū·ri·fā′cient, *n.* a parturifacient medicine.

pär·tū·ri′tion (-rish′un), *n.* [L. *parturitio, parturitionis*, from *parturire*, to be in labor.]

1. the act of bringing forth or being delivered of young; the act of giving birth; childbirth.

2. that which is born. [Obs.]

pär·tū′ri·tive, *a.* pertaining to parturition.

pär′ty, *n.*; *pl.* **pär′tieṣ,** [ME. and OFr. *parti, partie*, from *partir*, to divide; L. *partiri*, from *pars, partis*, a part.]

1. a part; a portion. [Obs.]

2. a group of people working together to establish, promote, or gain acceptance for, some kind of government, cause, opinion, etc. which they hold in common; especially, an organized political group which tries to elect its candidates to office.

Does the senator from Wisconsin object to my eulogizing members of his *party*?
—Senator Tilman.

3. the political practice of forming and supporting such groups.

4. a group of persons acting together; specifically, (a) a group sent out on a task or mission; as, a surveying *party*; (b) a group meeting together socially to accomplish a task; as, a quilting *party*; (c) a group assembled for amusement or recreation; as, the fishing *party* arrived early.

I saw our *party* to their trenches driven.
—Shak.

5. a gathering for social entertainment or the entertainment itself, often of a specific nature; as, a card *party*, cocktail *party*.

6. a cause; a side. [Now Rare.]

Three knights upon our *party* slain.—Shak.

7. an ally; a confederate. [Obs.]

His *parties*, his alliance. —Shak.

8. one of two litigants; the plaintiff or the defendant in a suit.

The cause of both *parties* shall come before the judges. —Ex. xxii. 9.

9. one who participates or is concerned in an action, proceeding, plan, etc. (often with *to*); as, I'll not be a *party* to the affair.

10. the certain individual or person referred to or under consideration; as, the old *party* spoke. [Now Slang.]

11. a person: often used facetiously. [Colloq.]

pär′ty, *a.* of, relating, or pertaining to a party, or faction; as, *party* policy.

pär′ty, *a.* in heraldry, parted or divided: in application to all divisions of the field or of charges; as, *party* per pale, when a field is divided by a perpendicular line; *party* per band, when a field is divided by a diagonal line from the dexter chief to the sinister base; *party* per fesse, when a field is divided by a horizontal line.

pär′ty-ċōat″ed, *a.* having a party-colored or motley coat.

pär′ty ċŏl′ŏr, variegated color.

pär′ty-ċŏl″ŏred, *a.* same as *parti-colored*.

pär′ty·iṣm, *n.* devotion to party.

pär′ty jụ′ry, a jury consisting half of aliens and half of citizens.

pär′ty līne, 1. a line marking the boundary between adjoining properties owned by two parties (sense 8).

2. a single circuit connecting two or more telephone users with the exchange.

3. [*usually in pl.*] a political tenet regarded as a line, or boundary, beyond which a political party or its members are not supposed to go; as, *party lines* are strictly drawn on this issue.

4. the line of policy followed by a political party, especially a Communist party.

pär′ty man, a faithful supporter of a political party.

pär′ty pol′i·tiċs, political acts and principles directed toward the interests of one political party or its members without reference to the common good.

pär′ty vẽr′diċt, a joint verdict. [Obs.]

Thy son is banish'd upon good advice,
Whereto thy tongue a *party verdict* gave.
—Shak.

pär′ty wạll, a wall separating and common to two buildings or properties: each owner has a partial right in its use.

pȧ·rụ′lis, *n.* [Gr. *paroulis*; *para*, beside, and *oulis, oulon*, gums.] a gumboil.

pär·um·bil′iç·ăl, *a.* [*par-* and *umbilical*.] in anatomy, situated near the umbilicus.

pȧ·rụre′, *n.* [ME. *parure, paroure*, from OFr., from L. *paratura*: the modern word is reborrowed from the Fr.] a number of pieces of jewelry, as earrings, bracelet, and necklace, intended to be worn as a set.

pär val′ūe, the value of a stock, bond, etc. fixed at the time of its issue; face value.

pär·vȧ·nim′i·ty, *n.* [L. *parvus*, small, and *animus*, mind.]

1. the state of having a little or ignoble mind; littleness of mind; meanness.

2. a person with a little or ignoble mind.

Pär′vȧ·tī, *n.* [Sans.] in Hindu mythology, a mountain goddess, the wife of Siva.

pär′vē·nū, *n.* [Fr.] a person who has suddenly acquired wealth or power, especially one who fails to conform to the established forms, customs, and habits of the class into which he has risen; a person considered an upstart.

pär′vē·nū, *a.* 1. being a parvenu.

2. like or characteristic of a parvenu.

pär′vis, *n.* [ME.; OFr. *parevis*; L. *paradisum*, lit., Paradise, name of the court before St. Peter's in Rome.]

1. an enclosed court or yard in front of a building, especially a church.

2. a portico or single line of columns in front of a church.

pär·vis′cient (-vish′ent), *a.* knowing little. [Rare.]

pär′vi·tūde, *n.* littleness. [Rare.]

pär′vō·lin, *n.* same as *parvoline*.

pär′vō·līne (*or* -lin), *n.* [from L. *parvus*, small, after Eng. *quinoline*: so named because of its low volatility.] any of the isomeric, liquid, basic compounds, $C_9H_{13}N$, derived from pyridine and found in decaying fish or meat.

pär′vūle, *n.* [L. *parvulus*, dim. of *parvus*, small.] a pellet; a small pill.

pȧ·ryph′ō·drōme, *a.* [*par-* and *hyphodrome*.] in botany, bordered by a strong vein: applied to leaves.

päs (pä), *v.t.* and *v.i.* to exceed; to surpass. [Obs.]

päs (pä), *n.* [Fr.] 1. a step or series of steps in dancing; also, a dance, as in *pas de deux*.

2. the right of going foremost; precedence; as, foreign ambassadors have the *pas*.

pas de deux; in ballet, a figure or dance for two persons.

pas seul; in ballet, a figure or dance by a single person.

to take the pas, to have the pas; to have precedence.

pā′ṣăn, *n.* the bezoar goat.

Pasḉh, Pas′ḉhȧ, *n.* [ME. *paske, pasche*; OFr. *pasque, pasche*; LL. and Gr. *pascha*, from Heb. *pesach*, passage, from *pasach*, to pass over.]

1. the Passover. [Chiefly Archaic.]

2. Easter. [Chiefly Archaic.]

pas′ḉhăl, *a.* 1. of or connected with the Passover.

2. of or connected with Easter.

paschal candle; in the Roman Catholic Church, a large wax candle blessed and placed on the altar on Holy Saturday, to remain lighted until Ascension Day.

paschal controversy; a controversy among early Christians as to the proper time to observe Easter.

paschal flower; same as *pasqueflower*.

paschal lamb; (a) in ancient times, the lamb slain and eaten at the Passover; (b) [P–L–], in the Christian Church, Jesus; hence, any of several symbolic representations of Jesus, as *Agnus Dei*.

paschal letters; letters written by the high dignitaries of the early church announcing the date of Easter.

pas′ḉhăl·ist, *n.* a controversialist of the early church who disputed as to the proper date of Easter.

pasḉh egg, Easter egg. [Scot. and Brit. Dial.]

pasḉh flow′ẽr, same as *pasqueflower*.

pas'ch̜īte, *n.* a Quartodeciman.

pas'cū·ȧge, *n.* [LL. *pascuagium*, from L. *pascuum*, pasture, from *pasci*, to feed.] in Old English law, the pasturing or grazing of cattle. [Rare.]

pas'cū·ous, *a.* [L. *pasci*, to feed.] found or growing in pastures.

pas'e·ăr, *n.* [Sp. Am.] an airing; a walk or promenade. [Colloq.]

pȧ·seng', *n.* same as *pasan*.

pash, *v.t.* and *v.i.* [ME. *passchen*, prob. echoic after *smash, dash, bash*, etc.] to hurl or be hurled violently so as to break or smash; to dash. [Obs. or Dial.]

pash, *n.* 1. a smashing blow. [Obs. or Dial.]
2. a heavy fall of snow or rain. [Brit. Dial.]

pash, *n.* [prob. from *pash*, v., with reference to blows on the head.] the head. [Obs. or Brit. Dial.]

pȧ·shä', *n.* (*or* pash'ȧ, päsh'ȧ), *n.* [Turk. *pāshā, bāshā*, prob. from *bāsh*, a head.] in Turkey, (a) a title of rank or honor placed after the name; (b) a high civil or military official. Also spelled *pacha, pashaw*.

pȧ·shä'lik, pȧ·shä'lic̜, *n.* [Turk. *pāshālik*; *pāshā*, and *-lik*, suffix of condition.] the jurisdiction of or area governed by a pasha: also spelled *pachalic*.

pashm, *n.* [Per.] a kind of fine wool for making shawls, obtained from Tibet.

pash·mi'nȧ, *a.* [Per.] made of pashm: also written *pushmina*.

Pasht, *n.* same as *Sekhet*.

Pash'tō (push'tō), *n.* Pushtu, language of Afghanistan.

pas·i·graph'ic̜, pas·i·graph'ic̜·ăl, *a.* of or pertaining to pasigraphy.

pȧ·sig'rȧ·phy, *n.* [Gr. *pas*, all, and *graphein*, to write.] a system of universal writing, especially one in which characters, e.g., mathematical symbols, represent ideas instead of words.

pas'i·lā·ly, *n.* [Gr. *pas*, all, and *lalein*, to talk.] a form of speech devised as a means of communication among all mankind; a universal language. [Rare.]

Pa·siph'a·ē (pȧ-sif'ȧ-ē), *n.* [L.; Gr. *Pasiphaē*.] in Greek mythology, the wife of Minos and mother of the Minotaur by a white bull belonging to Minos.

Pȧ·sit·e·lē'ăn, *a.* pertaining to or characteristic of a school of Greek sculpture founded by Pasiteles at Rome in the first century B.C.

Pask, *n.* same as *Pasch*.

Pas'pȧ·lum, *n.* [LL., from Gr. *paspalos*; *pas*, all, and *palē*, meal.] a large genus of swamp grasses, mostly tropical American.

Pasque (pask), *n.* [Fr.] same as *Pasch*.

pasque'flow''ẽr, *n.* [earlier *passeflower*; Fr. *passefleur*, from *passer*, to surpass, and *fleur*, a flower.] any of a number of related plants of the genus *Pulsatilla*, with hairy leaves and blue or purplish flowers shaped like cups: also *paschal flower*.

pas'quil (-kwil), *n.* same as *pasquinade*.

pas'quil, *v.i.* and *v.t.* to write pasquils. [Obs.]

pas'quil·ănt, *n.* a lampooner.

pas'quil·ẽr, *n.* same as *pasquilant*.

pas'quin, *n.* [It. *pasquino*.] a mutilated statue at Rome, in a corner of the palace of Ursini: said to be so called from a cobbler of that name who was remarkable for his sneers and gibes, and near whose shop the statue was dug up. On this statue it was once customary to paste satiric notices. Hence, a lampoon or a lampooner.

pas·quin·āde', *n.* [Fr.; It. *pasquinata*, from *Pasquino*.] a satire or sarcastic squib posted in a public place; lampoon.

pas·quin·āde', *v.t.*; pasquinaded, *pt., pp.*; pasquinading, *ppr.* to criticize or ridicule with such satire; a lampoon.

pȧss, *n.* [ME. *pas*: see *pace*.]
1. a narrow passage, opening, or way through, especially between mountains; a gap; a defile.
2. in a rolling mill, the opening which is formed by corresponding grooves in the rolls.

pȧss, *v.i.*; passed (past), *pt.*; passed *or*, *rare*, past, *pp.*; passing, *ppr.* [ME. *passen*; OFr. *passer*; LL. *passare*, from L. *passus*, step.]
1. to move forward; to go; to proceed from one place to another; as, a ship *passes* on or through the water; light *passes* from the sun to the planets.
2. to go from person to person; to circulate; to be handed on from one to another.
3. to go, shift, or be conveyed from one place, form, condition, circumstance, possession, etc. to another.
4. to be spoken or exchanged between persons, as greetings.
5. (a) to cease; to come to an end; as, the fever *passed*; (b) to go away; to depart.

Beauty is a charm, but soon the charm will *pass*. —Dryden.

6. to die.
7. to be spent; to go on or away progressively; to glide; to elapse.

The time when the thing existed is the idea of that space of duration which *passed* between some fixed period and the being of that thing. —Locke.

8. to be enacted; to receive the sanction of a legislative house or body by a majority of votes; as, the bill *passed* by a large majority.
9. to go or be accepted without dispute, question, or challenge; as, bank bills *pass* as a substitute for coin.

False eloquence *passeth* only where true is not understood. —Felton.

10. to be regarded; to be received in opinion or estimation.

This will not *pass* for a fault in him, till it is proved to be one in us. —Atterbury.

11. to get or make a way (with *through* or *by*).
12. to occur; to be present; to take place; as to notice what *passes* in the mind.
13. (a) to sit in inquest or judgment; (b) to determine; to give judgment or sentence.

Though well we may not *pass* upon his life. —Shak.

14. to be rendered or pronounced; as, the judgment *passed* against us.
15. to go through a trial, test, or examination successfully; to satisfy given requirements or standards.
16. to go unheeded or neglected; as, we saw the act, but let it *pass*.
17. in sports, to make a pass.
18. in card playing, to give the next player the option; to skip a bid or round of play.
19. to care or take heed. [Obs.]
20. to go beyond bounds; to surpass. [Obs.]
21. to run or extend, as a line or other thing; as, the north limit of Massachusetts *passes* north of the Merrimac.

to pass away; to move from sight; to vanish; hence, to come to an end; to cease; to die.
to pass for; to be accepted or looked upon as: said of an imitation or counterfeit.
to pass into; to unite and blend, as two substances or colors, in such a manner that it is impossible to tell where one ends and the other begins.
to pass off; (a) to come to an end; to cease; (b) to take place; to go through, as a transaction; (c) to be accepted or cause to be accepted as genuine, true, etc., especially by using deceit.
to pass on; (a) to proceed; (b) to give an opinion.
to pass over; to go or move from one side to the other; to cross; as, *to pass over* to the other side.

pȧss, *v.t.* 1. to go by, beyond, past, over, or through; specifically, (a) to leave behind; as, we have *passed* her house; (b) [Archaic.] to cross; traverse; (c) to omit the payment of (a regular dividend).
2. to experience; to undergo; to suffer.

She loved me for the dangers I had *passed*. —Shak.

3. to live through; to spend: used of time; as, she *passed* the winter in the South.

O, I have *pass'd* a miserable night.—Shak.

4. to let go by without care or notice; to take no notice of.

I *pass* their warlike pomp, their proud array. —Dryden.

5. to transcend; to exceed; to excel; to surpass.

Thy love to me was wonderful, *passing* the love of women. —2 Sam. i. 26.

6. to meet successfully the demands or requirements of; to undergo successfully, as an examination, ordeal, or the like; as, to *pass* an examination or a board of examiners; specifically, to obtain the legislative or official sanction of; to be enacted by.

Neither of these bills has yet *passed* the House of Commons. —Swift.

7. to cause to allow to go, move, or proceed; specifically, (a) to cause to move in a certain way; as, he *passed* his hand through his hair; (b) to guide into position; as, he *passed* the wire under the floor; (c) to cause to go through, or penetrate; (d) to cause to move past; (e) to cause or allow (a person or thing) to get by an obstacle, obstruction, etc.; (f) in baseball, to walk (a batter).
8. to transfer from one person, place, or condition to another; to cause to change hands; to hand over; to send; to circulate; to deliver; to make over; to communicate; as, to *pass* the news along; to *pass* title to property.

I had only time to *pass* my eye over the medals, which are in great number. —Addison.

9. to utter; to pronounce; as, to *pass* compliments; to *pass* sentence or judgment; to *pass* censure on another's works.
10. to put an end to; to cause to go by; to dispose of. [Obs.]

This night
We'll *pass* the business privately and well. —Shak.

11. to forward by degrees; to cause to advance by stages of progress; to carry on successfully through an examination, ordeal, or the like; specifically, to give legal or official sanction to; to enact; to ratify; to allow as valid or just.

My lord, and shall we *pass* the bill
I mentioned half an hour ago?—Tennyson.

12. to cause to obtain entrance or conveyance; as, to *pass* a friend into the theater; to *pass* one over a railroad.
13. to thrust; to make (a push) in fencing. [Obs.]

To see thee fight, to see thee *pass* thy puncto. —Shak.

14. to discharge from the intestinal canal or bladder; to void; to excrete.
15. to pledge. [Rare.]
16. to manipulate (cards, etc.) or trick (a person), as by sleight of hand.
17. to hit a tennis ball past (an opponent) so as to score a point.

to pass away; to spend; to waste; as, *to pass away* one's time.
to pass by; to pass near and beyond; to overlook; to excuse; to forgive; not to censure or punish; as, *to pass by* a crime or fault; also, to neglect; to disregard.
to pass in one's checks; to deliver checks for settlement at the close of a gambling game; hence, to go to a final reckoning; to die. [Slang.]
to pass off; to impose by fraud; to palm off.
to pass on or *upon*; to prartice artfully; to impose fraudulently; to put upon, as a trick; also, to give a decision upon; as, *to pass on* a case.
to pass over; to omit; to overlook or disregard.
to pass through; to experience or undergo, as the different phases of an illness.
to pass up; to reject, refuse, or let go, as an opportunity. [Slang.]

pȧss, *n.* [Fr. *passe*, from *passer*, to pass.]
1. an act of passing; passage.
2. (a) permission to pass, go, or come; (b) a license to pass; a passport; a ticket giving free admission or transit; (c) a written leave of absence for a brief period, given to a soldier.

A ship sailing under the flag and *pass* of an enemy. —Kent.

3. the successful completion of a scholastic course or examination, often without securing honors.
4. a mark, etc. indicating this.
5. a motion of the hands that is meant to deceive, as in card tricks or magic; sleight of hand.
6. a motion or stroke of the hand, as in mesmerism or hypnotism.
7. an attempt to embrace, caress, or kiss, often an improper or overfamiliar one. [Slang.]
8. in card games, a declining or refusal of a chance to bid or play a round, etc.
9. in sports, (a) an intentional transfer of the ball, puck, etc. to another player during play; (b) a lunge or thrust made in fencing; (c) a walk in baseball.
10. state; condition or extreme case; situation.

Matters have been brought to this *pass*. —South.

11. a sally of wit; a jest; a thrust. [Rare.]
12. character or estimation. [Obs.]
to bring to pass; to cause to happen.
to come to pass; to happen.

pȧss'ȧ·ble, *a.* 1. capable of being passed, traveled, or navigated; as, the roads are not *passable*; the stream is *passable* in boats.
2. that can be passed from person to person; current; receivable; that can be or is trans-

ferred from hand to hand; as, bills *passable* in lieu of coin.

3. such as can be allowed to pass without strong objection; tolerable; allowable; admissible; mediocre; adequate; moderate.

White and red well mingled on the face, make what was before but *passable* appear beautiful. —Dryden.

4. that can be enacted, as a proposed law.

Syn.—traversable, navigable, penetrable, admissible, tolerable, ordinary.

pȧss′ȧ·ble·ness, *n.* the state or quality of being passable.

pȧss′ȧ·bly, *adv.* tolerably; fairly; moderately.

päs·sȧ·çä′gliȧ (-lyȧ), *n.* [Sp. *pasacalle.*]

1. formerly, a slow, stately Italian dance, similar to the chaconne; also, the music for such a dance.

2. a musical form based on this dance, characterized by ³/₄ meter and a continuous ground bass.

päs·sȧ·çä′gliō (-lyō), same as *passacaglia.*

pas·sāde′, *n.* [Fr.; Pr. *passada* (It. *passata*): see *pass* and *-ade.*] in horsemanship, the movement of a horse backward and forward over the same course.

pas·sä′dō, *n.*; *pl.* **pas·sä′dōṣ, pas·sä′dōeṣ,** [altered from Fr. *passade*, from It. *passata* or Pr. *passada*, both from pp. of LL. *passare*, to pass.] in fencing, a thrust or lunge with one foot advanced.

pas′sȧġe, *n.* [ME.; OFr., from *passer*, to pass.]

1. the act of passing; specifically, (a) movement from one place to another; migration; as, birds of *passage*; (b) change or progress from one process or condition to another; transition; (c) the enactment of a law by a legislative body.

2. permission, right, or a chance to pass.

3. a journey by water; a voyage; a crossing.

4. (a) passenger accommodations on a ship; (b) the charge for this.

5. a way or means of passing; specifically, (a) a road; a path; an opening; (b) a hall or corridor that is an entrance or exit or onto which several rooms open; a passageway.

6. that which happens or takes place between persons; an interchange, as of blows or vows.

7. occurrence; event; incident; that which happens; as, a remarkable *passage* in the life of Newton. [Archaic.]

8. a passing away; decay; death. [Obs.]

Thy mortal *passage* when it comes. —Milton.

9. currency; reception; access. [Obs.]

Among whom I expect this treatise will have a fairer *passage* than among those deeply imbued with other principles. —Digby.

10. a portion of something spoken or written.

How commentators each dark *passage* shun. —Young.

11. in medicine, a bowel movement.

12. in music, (a) a run consisting of the tones of a scale or chord; (b) a short section of a composition.

13. an old game played by two persons throwing three dice.

in passage; in passing; in a hasty manner; cursorily.

Syn.—journey, thoroughfare, road, course, avenue, route.

pas′sȧġe, *v.i.*; passaged, *pt., pp.*; passaging, *ppr.* 1. to make a passage, or voyage; to journey.

2. to take part in a passage of arms.

pas′sȧġe, *v.t.* and *v.i.*; passaged, *pt., pp.*; passaging, *ppr.* in horsemanship, to sidle or cause to sidle.

pas′sȧġe grāve, in archaeology, a dolmen which is approached by a long passageway.

pas′sȧġe hawk, in falconry, a hawk which has been taken while migrating.

pas′sȧġe mon′ey, the charge for passenger accommodations on a ship.

pas′sȧġe of ärmṣ, 1. an exchange of blows; a fight.

2. an angry exchange of words; a quarrel.

pas′sȧ·ġēr, *n.* a passenger. [Archaic.]

pas′sȧġe·wāy, *n.* a narrow way for passage, as a hall, corridor, or alley; a passage.

pȧs·sȧ·mez′zō (-med′), *n.* an ancient Italian dance; also, the music for such dance.

pas′sȧnt, *a.* [ME. (only in sense "excelling, passing"), from OFr. *passant*, ppr. of *passer*, to go.]

1. in heraldry, represented as walking toward the (viewer's) left side of the shield with the right forepaw raised: said of an animal.

2. cursory; careless. [Obs.]

On a *passant* review of what I wrote to the bishop. —Sir Peter Pett.

3. rumored; current; generally received. [Obs.]

pȧss′book, *n.* 1. a customer's record in which a merchant or trader enters the articles sold on credit.

2. a bankbook.

pȧss box, in military usage, a wooden box used to carry cartridges from an ammunition chest to a gun.

pȧss check, a ticket of admission, as to an entertainment, or a ticket given to a person leaving before the end of an entertainment, entitling him to readmission.

pȧss dē·gree′, a scholastic degree indicating that the receiver has satisfied graduation requirements, but without any special distinction. [Chiefly Brit.]

pas·sé′, pas·sée′ (-sā′), *a.* [Fr., pp. of *passer*, to pass.] past the prime; out of date; old-fashioned.

pȧssed, *a.* 1. having satisfied some requirement, as for promotion; qualified.

2. left unpaid, as a dividend.

pȧssed ball, in baseball, a pitch that gets by the catcher when he could be expected to catch it, and allows a man on base to advance to another base.

passe′gärde (pas′gärd), *n.* [Fr.] in medieval armor, a ridge or projecting piece on the pauldron, or shoulder piece, to ward off the blow of a lance.

passe′ment, *n.* [Fr. *passement*, lace.] a piece of lace or silk sewed on clothes; hence, an external decoration. [Obs.]

passe·men′terie (-tri), *n.* [Fr., from *passement*, lace.] trimming made of gimp, cord, beads, braid, etc.

pas′sen·ġēr, *n.* [ME. and OFr. *passager*, one who makes a passage or journey. The *n* is an intrusive element, as in *messenger.*]

1. one who passes on his way, usually on foot; a traveler; a pilgrim; a wayfarer. [Rare.]

2. one who travels by some public conveyance, as an elevator, ship, railroad train, streetcar, coach, etc, especially one who has no part in the operation of the conveyance.

pas′sen·ġēr fal′çon, a kind of migratory hawk.

pas′sen·ġēr piġ′eon an extinct variety of North American pigeon, *Ectopistes migratorius*, which was distinguished from the common pigeon chiefly by its long, graduated tail.

PASSENGER PIGEON (*Ectopistes migratorius*)

passe pär·tōut′ (-tō′), [Fr., lit., pass everywhere.]

1. originally, that which passes or allows passage everywhere.

2. a key which will open various locks; a master key; a passkey.

3. a mat used in mounting pictures.

4. a frame for a picture, consisting of a light backboard, a sheet of glass, and sometimes a mat, bound together at the edges by narrow strips of gummed paper or cloth.

5. such gummed paper.

passe′pied (-pyā), *n.* [Fr., from *passer*, to pass, pace, and *pied*, a foot.]

1. a lively, seventeenth-century French dance, similar to the minuet but faster in tempo: now sometimes a movement in ballet.

2. the music for this.

pȧss′ēr, *n.* one who passes.

pȧss′ēr-bȳ′, *n.*; *pl.* **pȧss′ērṣ-bȳ′,** one who passes by without stopping; one who goes by or near.

As if he were afraid a *passer-by* might hear him. —Disraeli.

Pas′se·rēṣ, *n.pl.* [L., sparrows.] the largest order of birds, including more than half of all birds, chiefly perching songbirds.

Pas′sēr·ēṣ an·ī″sō·mȳ·ō′di, a suborder of *Passeres*, including the *Subclamatores* and *Clamatores.*

pas·sēr′i·form, *a.* [L. *passer*, sparrow, and *forma*, form.] relating to or having the form of passerine birds.

pas′sēr·ine (*or* -īn), *a.* [L. *passerinus*, from *passer*, a sparrow.] of a group of small or medium-sized, perching songbirds having grasping feet with the first toe directed backward: more than half of all birds belong to this group.

pas′sēr·ine, *n.* a passerine bird.

pas·si·bil′i·ty, *n.* a passible quality; aptness to feel or suffer.

pas′si·ble, *a.* [ME.] that can feel or suffer; sensible.

Apollinarius held even Deity to be *passible.* —Hooker.

pas′si·ble·ness, *n.* passibility. [Rare.]

Pas·si·flō′rȧ, *n.* [L. *passio*, passion, from *pati*, to suffer, and *flos, floris*, a flower.] a large genus of twining plants, belonging to the family *Passifloraceæ.* The genus includes a large number of species, chiefly found in tropical America. They have large, showy flowers and edible berries.

Pas″si·flō·rā′cē·ae, *n.pl.* the passionflower family, a family of chiefly climbing shrubs, with alternate simple or compound leaves, usually with tendrils and large flowers, of which the genus *Passiflora* is the type. It is very closely allied to *Cucurbitaceæ*, but is distinguishable by its peculiar filamentous crown and by its superior ovary.

pas″si·flō·rā′ceous, *a.* of the passionflower family, *Passifloraceæ.*

pas′sim, *adv.* [L.] throughout; in various parts (of a book, etc.).

pȧss′ing, *a.* 1. moving; proceeding; going by, beyond, past, over, or through.

2. lasting only a short time; fleeting; momentary.

One of those *passing* rainbow dreams. —Moore.

3. casual; cursory; incidental; as, a *passing* remark.

4. permitting one to go through a test, examination, course, etc. successfully; as, a *passing* grade.

5. that is happening; current.

6. surpassing; extreme; very. [Chiefly Archaic.]

pȧss′ing, *adv.* surpassingly; wonderfully; exceedingly; very. [Chiefly Archaic.]

Oberon is *passing* fell and wrath. —Shak.

pȧss′ing, *n.* 1. the act of a person or thing that passes.

2. a means or place of passing.

3. death. [Poetic.]

in passing; casually; incidentally.

pȧss′ing bell, a bell tolled to indicate death.

pȧss′ing·ly, *adv.* exceedingly. [Obs.]

pȧss′ing nōte, in music, a note that is not part of the harmonic scheme, but is introduced for ornamentation or to make the movement from one tone or chord to another smoother.

pȧss′ing tōne, same as *passing note.*

pas′sion, *n.* [ME.; OFr.; LL. *passio*, from L. *passus*, pp. of *pati*, to endure, suffer.]

1. originally, suffering or agony, as of a martyr.

2. [P–] (a) the agony and sufferings of Jesus during the Crucifixion or during the period following the Last Supper; (b) any of the gospel descriptions of this; (c) an artistic representation of this.

3. the state of being affected by an external agent or influence; the condition of being acted upon: opposed to *action.*

A body at rest affords us no idea of any active power to move, and when set in motion, it is rather a *passion* than an action in it. —Locke.

4. the power of receiving or being affected by outside influences.

The differences of moldable and not moldable, . . . and many other *passions* of matter, are plebeian notions. —Bacon.

5. (a) any one of the emotions, as hate, grief, love, fear, joy, etc.; (b) [*pl.*] all of these emotions.

6. extreme, compelling emotion; intense emotional drive or excitement; specifically, (a) great anger; rage; fury; (b) enthusiasm or fondness, as for music; (c) strong love or affection; (d) sexual drive or desire; lust.

7. the object of any strong desire or fondness.

Passion music; originally, music to which is chanted the gospel narrative of the Passion of Jesus; since the Reformation, an oratorio having the Passion for its theme.

Passion play; a medieval mystery play representing the Passion of Jesus; especially, the drama still presented every tenth year at Oberammergau, Bavaria. It was first given in

1634, in fullfillment of a vow made in thanksgiving for salvation from a plague.

Passion Sunday; the second Sunday before Easter, or the fifth Sunday in Lent; the first day of Passion Week.

Passion Week; (a) the week beginning on Passion Sunday; (b) formerly, the week before Easter; Holy Week.

Syn.—feeling, emotion, ardor, excitement, rapture, transport, vehemence, zeal, pathos, affection, love, devotion, tender emotion, attachment, anger, fury, indignation, wrath.

pas′sion, *v.i.* to show or be affected by passion.

pas′sion, *v.t.* to affect with passion.

pas′sion·ăl, *a.* of or pertaining to passion or the passions; exciting, catering to, or influenced by passion.

pas′sion·ăl, *n.* 1. a manuscript of the Gospels or first four books of the New Testament, used for administering the oath to English sovereigns at their coronation, from Henry I to Edward VI.

2. a book describing the sufferings of saints and martyrs: usually read during their festivals.

pas′sion·ăr·y, *n.* same as *passional*, sense 2.

pas′sion·āte, *a.* 1. easily aroused, excited, or agitated; capable of or susceptible to passion; especially, easily angered.

Homer's Achilles is haughty and *passionate*. —Prior.

2. expressing, resulting from, or tending to arouse strong emotion; ardent; intense; impassioned.

3. lustful; amorous.

4. strong; vehement: said of an emotion.

pas′sion·āte, *v.t.* to affect with passion; to express passionately. [Obs.]

pas′soin·āte·ly, *adv.* in a passionate manner.

pas′sion·āte·ness, *n.* the state of being passionate.

pas′sion·flow″er, *n.* any plant of the genus *Passiflora*, with white, red, purple, or orange flowers and yellow, egglike fruit: so named because parts of the flower are supposed to resemble Jesus' wounds, crown of thorns, etc.

pas′sion frụit, the pale-yellow, usually small, edible fruit of the passionflower.

Pas′sion·ist, *n.* a member of a religious order of the Roman Catholic Church, founded in Italy in the first half of the eighteenth century and introduced in the United States more than a hundred years later.

pas′sion·less, *a.* free from passion or emotion; impassive; calm.

Pas′sion·tīde, *n.* Passion Week and Holy Week; the last two weeks in Lent.

pas′sion vīne, the passionflower.

pas′sive, *a.* [L. *passivus*, from *passus*, pp. of *pati*, to suffer.]

1. receiving impressions from external agents; not acting; being the object of action rather than the subject.

The mind is wholly *passive* in the reception of all its simple ideas. —Locke.

2. unresisting; not opposing; receiving or suffering without resistance; as, *passive* submission to the laws.

3. mentally or physically inactive; lifeless; unenthusiastic; unresponsive.

4. in chemistry, inert.

5. in grammar, indicating that the subject is the receiver (object) of the action the verb denotes (e.g., in "the tree was struck by lightning," *was struck* is said to be in the passive voice).

6. in law and finance, noninterest-bearing, as certain bonds, shares, etc.

7. in medicine, designating certain abnormal conditions in which there is lowered activity and reaction.

passive congestion; in medicine, congestion caused by any difficulty met by the blood in returning to the affected part, either from some obstruction or from debility.

passive immunity; (a) immunity to a disease acquired by injecting into the blood stream serum from an individual who has acquired active immunity; (b) temporary immunity acquired by a child in the womb from antibodies transferred from the mother.

passive movement; in medicine, a movement of a part for exercise, effected by external force instead of by the usual voluntary muscular effort.

passive obedience; unqualified obedience or submission to the commands of another, whether such commands be lawful or unlawful, just or unjust. Passive obedience and nonresistance to authority have been at times taught as a political doctrine.

passive prayer; among mystics, a suspension of the activity of the soul or intellectual faculties, the soul remaining quiet and yielding only to the impulses of grace.

passive resistance; (a) in electricity, ohmic resistance; (b) opposition offered to a law, tax, or government by refusal to comply or obey or by such nonviolent acts as voluntary fasting.

Syn.—quiescent, resigned, submissive, unresisting, patient.

pas′sive·ly, *adv.* in a passive manner.

pas′sive·ness, *n.* the quality of being passive.

pas′siv·iṣm, *n.* 1. a passive quality or character.

2. the principle of or belief in being passive.

pas·siv′i·ty, *n.* the state or quality of being passive; inaction; submissiveness.

pȧss′kēy, *n.* 1. a key that will open every one of a group of locks, as those of a certain building; a master key.

2. any private key.

pȧss′less, *a.* having no pass; impassable.

pȧss′măn, *n.*; *pl.* **pȧss′men,** in British universities, a student who passes for his degree without honors.

Pȧss′ō·vẽr, *n.* [*pass* and *over*, used to transl. Heb. *pesaḥ*: see *Pasch.*]

1. a Jewish holiday (*Pesach*) commemorating the escape of the Hebrews in Egypt, when God, smiting the first-born of the Egyptians, *passed over* the houses of the Israelites, which were marked with the blood of the paschal lamb; also, the week following this holiday.

2. [p-] formerly, the paschal lamb.

pȧss′pōrt, *n.* [Fr. *passeport*, a safe-conduct, originally permission to leave or enter a port.]

1. a government document granting permission to a citizen to travel in certain specified foreign countries and certifying his identity and citizenship: it entitles the bearer to the protection of his own country and that of the countries visited.

2. a safe-conduct.

3. a government document permitting a vessel to leave or enter port.

4. that which enables one to be admitted, accepted, or successful.

His *passport* is his innocence and grace. —Dryden.

pas′sus, *n.*; *pl.* **pas′sus, pas′sus·eṣ,** [L., a step.] a part or section of a poem or story.

pȧss′wŏrd, *n.* a secret word or phrase used by the members of a certain group, as a military unit, to identify themselves, as in passing a guard.

pas′sy·meaṣ·ūre, *n.* passamezzo. [Obs.]

pȧst, *v.* alternative past participle of *pass*.

pȧst, *a.* 1. gone by or beyond; over; ended; accomplished.

2. having finished a term and retired; as, a *past* master of a lodge.

3. of a former time; bygone.

4. immediately preceding; just gone by; as, the *past* week.

5. in grammar, indicating a time or condition gone by or an action completed or in progress at a former time.

pȧst, *n.* 1. the history, former life, or experiences of a person, group, or institution: often used, with the indefinite article, to indicate a hidden or questionable past; as, the actress was found to have a *past*.

2. in grammar, (a) the past tense; (b) a verb form in this tense.

the past; something that has gone before; past time, state, or happenings.

pȧst, *prep.* 1. beyond in time; later than; as, *past* noon.

2. beyond; out of reach of; out of the scope or influence of; as, *past* belief.

3. beyond in space; farther on than; as, *past* the boundary.

4. beyond in amount or degree; above; more than; as, not *past* a mile to go.

to not put it past someone; to believe someone is likely (to do something specified).

pȧst, *adv.* to and beyond a point in time or space; so as to pass; by; as, ranks of infantry filed *past*.

päs′tȧ, *n.* [It., from LL., from Gr. *pastē*; see *paste*.]

1. the flour paste or dough used in making spaghetti, macaroni, ravioli, etc.

2. any food or foods made of this.

pāste, *n.* [OFr. *paste*; LL. *pasta*, paste, from Gr. *pastē*, a mess of barley porridge, from *passein*, to sprinkle.]

1. dough used in making rich pastry.

2. any of various soft, moist, smooth-textured substances; as, tooth *paste*, shoe *paste*.

3. a foodstuff, pounded or ground until fine and made creamy, soft, etc.; as, almond *paste*.

4. a jellylike candy.

5. a mixture of flour or starch, water, and occasionally alum, resin, etc., used as an adhesive for light materials, as paper.

6. the moistened clay used in manufacturing pottery and porcelain.

7. (a) a hard, brilliant glass containing oxide of lead: used in making artificial gems; (b) such a gem or gems.

8. a blow, or punch, as with the fist. [Slang.]

9. in mineralogy, the mineral substance in which other minerals are imbedded.

pāste, *v.t.*; pasted, *pt.*, *pp.*; pasting, *ppr.* 1. to fasten or make adhere, with or as with paste.

2. to cover with pasted material; as, he *pasted* the window with paper.

3. to hit; to beat; to punch. [Slang.]

pāste′bōard, *n.* 1. a stiff material formed of several single sheets of paper pasted one upon another, or by macerating paper and compressing it into sheets.

2. something made of pasteboard, as a playing card or visiting card. [Slang.]

pāste eel, a very small nematode worm.

pas′tel, *n.* [Fr.] 1. a plant whose leaves yield a blue dye.

2. this dye.

Also called *woad*.

pas·tel′, *n.* [LL. *pasta*, paste.]

1. (a) ground coloring matter mixed with gum and formed into a crayon; (b) a crayon so made.

2. a picture drawn with such crayons.

3. drawing with pastels as an art form or medium.

4. a light, brief prose work.

5. a soft, pale shade of some color.

pas·tel′, *a.* 1. soft and pale: said of colors.

2. of pastel.

pas·tel′, *v.t.* and *v.i.* to work with pastels.

pas′tel·ist, pas′tel·list, *n.* an artist who draws with pastels.

pāst′ẽr, *n.* 1. one who or that which pastes.

2. a printed slip of gummed paper prepared for pasting, as, to insert or alter a name on a ballot or to revise or add to a page in a reference work, as in annotated law reports.

pas′tẽrn, *n.* [OFr. *pasturon*, from *pasture*, a tether for cattle at pasture, from L. *pascere*, to feed.]

1. the part of a horse's foot between the fetlock and the hoof.

2. a hobble to prevent horses from straying from pasture. [Obs.]

pas′tẽrn joint, the joint between the fetlock and the hoof.

pas′tēur·iṣm, *n.* the theories or methods of Louis Pasteur; specifically, (a) pasteurization; (b) the Pasteur treatment for rabies.

pas″tēur·i·zā′tion (*or* pas″chẽr-ī-), *n.* [from *pasteurize* (*Pasteur*, and *-ize*), and *-ation*.] a method of destroying disease-producing bacteria, and checking the activity of fermentative bacteria, in milk, beer, etc. by exposing the liquid to a temperature of 142°–145° F. for thirty minutes.

pas′tēur·īze (*or* -chẽr-), *v.t.*; pasteurized, *pt.*, *pp.*; pasteurizing, *ppr.* 1. to subject (milk, beer, etc.) to pasteurization.

2. to give the Pasteur treatment to.

Pas·tēur′ trēat′ment, a method of preventing certain diseases, especially rabies, by successive inoculations with the specific virus in increasing strength: first used by Louis Pasteur.

päs·tic′ciō (-tēt′chō), *n.*; *pl.* **päs·tic′cī** (-chē), [It.; ML. *pasticius*; from LL. *pasta*, a paste.] same as *pastiche*.

pas·tiçhe′, *n.* [Fr.; It. *pasticcio*.]

1. (a) a literary, artistic, or musical composition made up of bits from various sources; potpourri; (b) such a composition.

2. a jumbled mixture; hodgepodge.

pas·tille′, pas′til, *n.* [Fr. *pastille*; L. *pastillus*, a little roll, a lozenge, from *pascere*, to feed.]

1. a pellet of aromatic paste for burning as a fumigator or deodorant.

2. a small tablet or lozenge containing medicine, flavoring, etc.

3. pastel for crayons.

4. a crayon of pastel.

pås′tīme, *n.* sport; amusement; diversion; that which serves to make time pass agreeably.

Syn.—recreation, entertainment, amusement, diversion, play, sport.

pås′tīme, *v.i.* to sport; to use diversion. [Obs.]

pāst′i·ness, *n.* a pasty state or quality.

påst mås′tẽr, 1. a person who formerly held the position of master, as in a lodge or club.

2. a person who has had long experience in some occupation, art, etc.; an expert.

pås′tŏr, *n.* [ME. *pastour*; OFr.; L. *pastor*, from *pascere*, to feed.]

1. a shepherd. [Obs.]

2. a clergyman or priest who has the charge of a church or congregation.

3. the locust bird.

pås′tŏr·ăl, *a.* [ME. *pastoralle*; L. *pastoralis*, from *pastor*, a shepherd.]

1. of shepherds or their work, way of life, etc.

2. of or portraying rural life, especially a conventionalized form of rustic life among shepherds, dairymaids, etc.

3. of pastoral literature or a pastoral.

4. characteristic of pleasant rural life; peaceful, simple, and natural.

5. of a pastor or his duties.

pastoral staff; a crosier.

pås′tŏr·ăl, *n.* 1. a piece of literature dealing with life in the country; especially, a poem, play, etc. treating the rustic lives and loves of shepherds in a conventionalized, artificial manner.

2. such writing as a literary form.

3. a pastoral picture or scene.

4. a book treating of the functions of a pastor.

5. a letter from a pastor to his congregation or from a bishop to his clergy.

6. a crosier.

7. in music, a pastorale.

pås·tō·rä′le, *n.*; *pl.* **pås·tō·rä′les, pås·tō·rä′lï,** [It.]

1. a musical composition in simple and idyllic style suggesting rural scenes.

2. a composition, as an opera or cantata, with a rural theme or subject.

pås′tŏr·ăl·iṣm, *n.* pastoral character or style.

pås′tŏr·ăl·ist, *n.* 1. a writer of pastorals.

2. one who makes a business of breeding and raising sheep. [Rare.]

pås′tŏr·ăl·ly, *adv.* in a pastoral manner.

pås′tŏr·āte, *n.* 1. the position, rank, or duties of a pastor.

2. (a) a group of pastors serving one locality; (b) pastors collectively.

3. a pastor's term of office with one church or parish.

pås·tō′ri·um, *n.* [Mod. L., from L. *pastorius*, of a shepherd, from *pastor*, a shepherd.] in the southern United States, a parsonage.

pås′tŏr·less, *a.* having no pastor.

pås′tŏr·ly, *a.* of or suiting a pastor.

pås′tŏr·ship, *n.* a pastorate.

pås·töu·relle′, *n.* the fourth figure in the quadrille.

påst pär′ti·ci·ple, a participle used usually with an auxiliary to indicate a time or state gone by or an action completed in the past (e.g., in "the garden has grown well because it has been properly tended," *grown* and *tended* are past participles).

påst pẽr′fect, 1. in grammar, expressing action completed before a given or implied time; pluperfect (e.g., in "he had locked the door before he left," *had locked* is past perfect).

2. a past perfect tense or form.

pås·trä′mi, *n.* [Yid.; Hung.] rolled beef, especially a shoulder cut, highly spiced and smoked.

pās′try, *n.*; *pl.* **pās′tries,** [from *paste.*]

1. flour dough or paste made with shortening and used for the crust of pies, tarts, etc.

2. articles of food made with this, as pies, tarts, etc.

3. in a broad sense, all fancy baked goods, including cakes, pies, tarts, etc.

pās′try çook, one whose occupation is to make pastry.

pås′tūr·à·ble, *a.* fit for pasture.

pås′tūr·āġe, *n.* [OFr. from *pasturer*, to pasture.]

1. pasture.

2. (a) the pasturing of cattle; (b) the right or business of pasturing cattle on certain ground.

pås′tūre, *n.* [ME.; OFr.; LL. *pastura*, from L. *pascere*, to feed.]

1. grass or other growing plants used as food by grazing animals.

2. ground suitable for grazing, or a field, plot, etc. set aside for this.

pås′tūre, *v.t.*; pastured, *pt.*, *pp.*; pasturing, *ppr.* 1. to put (cattle, etc.) out to graze in pasture.

2. to graze or feed on (grass, etc.).

3. to provide with pasture: said of land.

pås′tūre, *v.i.* to graze; to take food by eating growing grass or herbage.

pås′tūre·less, *a.* having no pasture.

pås′tūr·ẽr, *n.* one who pastures cattle, etc.

pås′tūre this′tle, a thistle common in the United States, growing in fields and along roadsides and bearing a sweet-scented purple or white flower.

pās′ty, *a.*; *comp.* pastier; *superl.* pastiest, of or like the color or consistency of paste; sticky.

pās′ty, *n.*; *pl.* **pās′ties,** [OFr. *paste*; Fr. *pâté.*] a pie, especially a meat pie covered with a paste, sometimes baked without a dish. [Chiefly Brit.]

pat, *a.* [prob. from *pat*, v.]

1. apt; timely; opportune; fit; convenient.

2. exactly suitable; as, a *pat* hand in poker.

pat, *adv.* aptly; perfectly; suitably; fitly; conveniently; timely.

to have (or *know*) *pat*; to know thoroughly. [Colloq.]

to stand pat; (a) to refuse to turn aside from an opinion, course of action, etc.; (b) in the game of poker, to take no card or cards in the draw; to play the hand held. [Colloq.]

pat, *n.* 1. a light, quick blow or stroke with the fingers or hand or with some flat implement.

2. a sound made by this.

3. a small mass or lump; as, a *pat* of butter.

pat, *v.t.*; patted, *pt.*, *pp.*; patting, *ppr.* [ME. *patte*; prob. echoic.]

1. (a) to tap, touch, or stroke quickly or gently, especially with the hand as in affection, sympathy, or encouragement; (b) to tap or stroke lightly with a flat surface.

2. to give a certain shape to, as mud, by patting.

to pat juba; to pat with the hands in a certain rhythmical way by striking them alternately against each other and against the thighs, thus furnishing the rhythm for a Southern Negro dance called juba.

pat, *v.i.* to make a patting sound, as in running.

på·tä′çà, *n.* [Port.] a coin of Portugal and Brazil.

pat′-à-çāke, *n.* 1. the opening words of a nursery rhyme.

2. a children's game played by clapping the hands in rhythm to this rhyme.

Also *patty-cake.*

på″täche′, *n.* a small boat formerly used to carry men or orders. [Obs.]

på·tā′ġi·um, *n.*; *pl.* **på·tā′ġi·à,** [L., the border of a dress.]

1. a fold of skin between the fore and hind limbs of flying squirrels, flying lizards, etc., enabling them to glide through the air.

2. a fold of skin between the shoulder and fore part of a bird's wing.

3. in entomology, a chitinous or scalelike appendage of the pronotum of lepidopterous insects.

Pat·à·gō′ni·ăn, *a.* of or pertaining to Patagonia, its people, or their culture.

Pat·à·gō′ni·ăn, *n.* a native of Patagonia; especially, a member of a tribe of very tall South American Indians living there.

pat′à·mär, *n.* a vessel employed in the coasting trade of Bombay and Ceylon: its stem and stern have great rake, and the draft of water is much greater at the head than at the stern: also spelled *pattemar.*

på·täs′ (-tä′), *n.* the West African red monkey, *Cercopithecus ruber.*

pat·à·vin′i·ty, *n.* the provincial style or diction of Livy, the Roman historian: so called from Patavium, modern Padua, the place of his nativity.

patch, *n.* a fool; a ninny: said of a peevish child or person. [Colloq. or Dial.]

patch, *n.* [ME. *pacche*, for *placce*, dial. G. *plakke*, patch.]

1. a piece of material applied to cover or mend a hole or tear or to strengthen a weak spot.

2. a dressing applied to a wound or sore.

3. a pad or shield worn over an injured eye.

4. a little piece of black paper, cloth, etc., put on a woman's face, back, etc. to emphasize the beauty or whiteness of her skin; a beauty spot.

5. a surface area differing from its surroundings in nature or appearance; as, *patches* of blue sky.

6. a small plot of ground; as, a potato *patch.*

7. a small piece of any material; a scrap; a bit; a remnant.

8. a small piece of greased leather or muslin used as packing in ramming home a rifle ball. [Obs.]

not a patch on; not to be compared with; not to be reckoned in the same class with; infinitely inferior to; as, Dick is *not a patch on* Tom for style. [Colloq.]

Peyer's patches; whitish patches of lymph follicles in the mucous and submucous layers of the small intestine.

patch, *v.t.*; patched (pacht), *pt.*, *pp.*; patching, *ppr.* 1. to put a patch or patches on.

2. to serve as a patch for.

3. to form or make by the use of patches, as a quilt.

4. to produce or bring together roughly, crudely, or hurriedly; to piece together (often with *up* or *together*).

He had thought it best to *patch up* a separate negotiation for himself.
—Sir W. Scott.

to patch up; to bring to an end; to make right; to settle, as differences or a quarrel.

patch′à·ble, *a.* in such a condition as to admit of patching.

patch′ẽr, *n.* one who patches.

patch′ẽr·y, *n.* bungling work; botchery.

patch′i·ly, *adv.* so as to be patchy; in patches.

patch′i·ness, *n.* the condition or quality of being patchy.

patch′ing *n.* 1. the act of repairing by means of patches.

2. the work accomplished by the act of repairing with patches.

3. material used in making patches for ramming home a rifle ball.

4. patchery. [Obs.]

patch′ing·ly, *adv.* in a bungling or imperfect manner.

patch′ou·li, patch′ou·ly (-oo- *or* pà-chö′), *n.* [Fr., from Tamil. *paccilai*, lit., green leaf.]

1. an East Indian labiate plant, *Pogostemon patchouli*, of the mint family.

2. the perfume extracted from its fragrant oil.

patch pock′et, a pocket made by sewing a patch of shaped material to the outside of a garment.

patch test, in medicine, a test for determining allergy to a specific substance, made by placing on the skin small pieces of cloth or blotting paper soaked in this substance and observing the reaction of the skin.

patch′wŏrk, *n.* 1. anything formed of irregular, incongruous, odd, or miscellaneous parts; a jumble.

2. needlework, as a quilt, made of odd patches of cloth, etc. sewn together at the edges.

3. any design or surface like this.

patch′y, *a.*; *comp.* patchier; *superl.* patchiest,

1. (a) made up of or characterized by patches; (b) forming or like patches.

2. giving the effect of patches; not consistent or uniform in quality; irregular.

pâ·té′ (pä-tā′), *n.* [Fr.] 1. a pie; a patty; a pasty.

2. a meat paste.

3. in fortification, a round or oval platform erected on marshy ground, for the defense of a gate.

pâté de foie gras; a paste made of the livers of fattened geese.

pâte (pät), *n.* [Fr.] paste; especially, the clay paste used in making porcelain or pottery.

pâte sur pâte; white paste applied over a dark or colored background, giving not only surface relief, but a contrast in coloring.

pâte tendre; a mild and easily fusible porcelain paste.

pāte, *n.* [ME.; prob. orig. euphemistic.]

1. the head.

2. the top of the head.

3. intelligence.

4. the skin of a calf's head.

A humorous or derogatory term.

-pāt′ed, a combining form meaning *having a* (specified kind of) *pate*, or *head*, as in bald-*pated.*

pa·tée′ (pä-tā′), *a.* in heraldry, same as *patté.*

pat·ē·fac′tion, *n.* [L. *patefactio* (-*onis*), from

patere, to be open, and *facere*, to make.] the act of opening or manifesting; open declaration. [Obs.]

pat′e·lȧ, *n.* [E. Ind.] a broad boat, with a flat bottom, used on the river Ganges: also written *puteli*.

PATELA

pȧ·tel′lȧ, *n.*; *pl.* **pȧ·tel′lȧs, pȧ·tel′lae,** [L., dim. of *patina*, a pan, from *patere*, to be open.]
1. the kneepan or kneecap.
2. [P–] a genus of gastropods including the limpets.
3. a small vase or dish; a small, shallow pan.
4. in botany, an orbicular apothecium in lichens, having a rim.
5. in botany and zoology, any panlike formation.

pȧ·tel′lȧr, *a.* in anatomy, of or belonging to the patella.

pȧ·tel′lȧr rē′flex, in medicine, a reflex kick with extension of the leg at the knee, produced by sharply tapping the tendon below the patella: it is a normal reaction in health: also called *knee jerk*.

pȧ·tel′lāte, *a.* having or like a patella.

pȧ·tel′li·fọrm, *a.* [from *patella* and *-form*.]
1. having the form of a flattened cone.
2. having the shape of a limpet shell.

pȧ·tel′loid, *a.* patelliform.

pȧ·tel′lū·lȧ, *n.*; *pl.* **pȧ·tel′lū·lae,** [LL., dim. of L. *patella*, dish.] a cuplike sucker on the tarsus of some insects, which enables them to adhere when climbing vertically.

pat′en, *n.* [L. *patina*, a broad dish, from *patere*, to be open.]
1. a metal plate or dish; especially, the plate holding the bread in the Eucharist.
2. a thin, flat piece of metal; a disk.
Also *patin, patina, patine*.

pȧ·tē′nȧ, *n.* a grassy area in the hilly parts of Ceylon.

pā′ten·cy (*or* pat′), *n.* 1. the condition or quality of being patent, or obvious.
2. in medicine, the condition of being open or unobstructed.

pat′ent (*or* pā′). *a.* [Fr., from L. *patens* (*-entis*), from *patere*, to be open.]
1. that can be examined by the public: said of a document granting some right, as, formerly, a commission to hold public office.
2. open to all; generally accessible or available.
3. obvious; plain; evident.
4. unobstructed.
5. (a) protected by a document (letters patent) granting exclusive right to the production, use, sale, and profit of an invention, process, etc.; (b) having received such a document, as an inventor.
6. new, unusual, practical, individual, etc.; as, a *patent* method of lighting a fire.
7. of high quality: said of flour.
8. in botany and zoology, spreading out or open; patulous.
patent ambiguity; see *latent ambiguity* under *latent*.
Syn.—obvious, evident, indisputable, plain, manifest.

pat′ent, *n.* 1. a document open to public examination and granting a certain right or privilege; letters patent; especially, a document granting the monopoly right to produce, use, sell, or get profit from an invention, process, etc. for a certain number of years.
2. (a) the right so granted; (b) the thing protected by such a right; patented article or process.
3. land or title to land granted by letters patent.
4. any exclusive right, title, or license; as, she had no *patent* on charm.

pat′ent, *v.t.*; patented, *pt., pp.*; patenting, *ppr.* 1. to secure exclusive right to produce, use, and sell (an invention or process) by a patent.
2. to grant a patent to or for. [Rare.]

pat′ent·ȧ·ble, *a.* that can be patented.

pat·ent·ee′, *n.* one to whom a grant is made or a privilege secured by patent.

pat′ent·ẽr, *n.* a patentee. [Obs.]

pat′ent leath′ẽr, leather having a hard, glossy, usually black finish: made by a process formerly patented.

pat′ent·ly, *adv.* clearly; obviously.

pat′ent med′i·cine, a trade-marked medical preparation usually containing secret ingredients or made by secret formula.

Pat′ent Of′fice, an office in the Department of Commerce which administers the patent and trade-mark laws.

pat′ent·ŏr, *n.* a person or agent who grants a patent.

pat′ent rīght (rīt), an exclusive privilege or right established by letters patent, especially the right to an invention.

pat′ent rōlls, the records or registers of patents, particularly the roll of letters patent issued by the crown in England. [Brit.]

pā′tẽr, *n.* [L.] father. [Chiefly Brit. Colloq.]

pat′e·rȧ, *n.*; *pl.* **pat′e·rae,** [L., from *patere*, to be open.]
1. a sacrificial plate, having as much depth as a shallow saucer, made of metal or pottery and used by the ancient Romans for liquid offerings.

GRECIAN PATERA

2. a bas-relief pattern in the form of an ornamented patera and common in ancient classical borders.

ARCHITECTURAL PATERAE

pā′tẽr·fȧ·mil′i·as, *n.*; *pl.* **pā′trēs·fȧ·mil′i·as,** [L., father of a family, *familias* being old genit. of *familia*, family.]
1. the father of a family; male head of a household: an expression used generally of a man when surrounded by his children or in his capacity of father.
2. in Roman law, the head of a patrician family; hence, the owner of the family estate and all belonging to it, its dependents, etc.

pȧ·tẽr′năl, *a.* [ML. *paternalis*; L. *paternus*, from *pater*, father.]
1. of, like, or characteristic of a father or fatherhood; fatherly.
2. derived, received, or inherited from a father.
3. on the father's side of the family; as, *paternal* grandparents.
paternal government; paternalism.

pȧ·tẽr′năl·ism, *n.* [*paternal* and *-ism*.] the principle or system of governing or controlling a country, group of employees, etc. in a manner suggesting a father's relationship with his children.

pȧ·tẽr·năl·is′tiç, *a.* of or characterized by paternalism.

pȧ·tẽr·năl·is′tiç·ăl·ly, *adv.* in a paternalistic manner; by paternalism.

pȧ·tẽr′năl·ly, *adv.* in a paternal manner.

pȧ·tẽr′ni·ty, *n.* [Fr. *paternité*; LL. *paternitas*.]
1. fatherhood; the state of being a father.
2. male parentage; the paternal origin of a child; the descent on the father's side.
3. authorship or origin in general.

pā′tẽr·nos′tẽr (*or* pat′), *n.* [L., our father.]
1. the Lord's Prayer, especially in Latin: often *Pater Noster*.
2. every eleventh bead of a rosary on which this prayer is said.
3. a rosary.
4. any muttered prayer or incantation.
5. a style of molding designed to resemble the large, or paternoster, beads of a rosary.
6. an angler's line having several small round sinkers and hooks baited with minnows placed at intervals.

pā′tẽr·nos′tẽr pump, a chain pump.

pā′tẽr·nos′tẽr wheel (hwēl), a paternoster pump.

pȧth, *n.*; *pl.* **pȧths,** [AS. *pæth*: akin to G. *pfad*.]
1. a track or way worn by footsteps; a trail.
2. a walk or way for the use of people on foot, as in a park or garden.
3. a line of movement; a course taken; as, the *path* of the meteor.
4. a course or manner of conduct or procedure.

pȧth, *v.t.*; pathed (patht), *pt., pp.*; pathing, *ppr.*
1. to make a path in or through, as by treading; to beat a path in, as in snow. [Obs.]
2. to push forward; to make or travel (a course, way, etc.). [Obs.]

pȧth, *v.i.* to walk abroad. [Rare.]

Pȧ·thän′ (-tän′), *n.* a member of a Moslem, Indo-Iranian people of Afghanistan.

path·ē·mat′iç, *a.* [Gr. *pathēma*, what is suffered.]
1. pertaining to or designating emotion. [Rare.]
2. relating to diseases and their characteristics.

pȧ·thet′iç, *a.* [Gr. *pathētikos*, from *pathos*, suffering.]
1. expressing, arousing, or intended to arouse pity, sorrow, sympathy, etc.; pitiful.
2. of the feelings or emotions.
pathetic fallacy; the literary device of portraying inanimate nature as having human feelings and character. Examples: "the angry sea," "a stubborn door."
pathetic muscle; the muscle used in moving up the eye; the upper oblique muscle of the eye.
pathetic nerve; the fourth cranial nerve, which directly supplies the pathetic muscle: sometimes called the *trochlear nerve*.
Syn.—affecting, touching, moving.

pȧ·thet′iç·ăl, *a.* pathetic. [Rare.]

pȧ·thet′iç·ăl·ly, *adv.* in a pathetic manner.

pȧ·thet′iç·ăl·ness, *n.* the quality of being pathetic.

path′e·tism, *n.* same as *hypnotism*.

path′e·tist, *n.* a hypnotist.

pȧth′fīnd″ẽr, *n.* a discoverer of new ways or routes where none had existed, as in an unknown region, wilderness, etc.; an explorer.

-path′i·ȧ, -pathy.

-path′iç, a combining form used to form adjectives corresponding to nouns ending in *-pathy*, as in osteo*pathic*, psycho*pathic*.

path′iç, *n.* [from Gr. *pathos*, suffering.] a male that commits pederasty. [Rare.]

path′iç, *a.* suffering.

pȧth′less, *a.* having no beaten way; without a path or track; untrodden; as, a *pathless* forest; a *pathless* coast.

path′ō-, [from Gr. *pathos*, from *pathein*, to suffer.] a combining form meaning *suffering, disease, feeling*, as in *path*ology: also, before a vowel, *path-*.

path′ō·gen, *n.* [*patho-* and *-gen*.] any microorganism or virus that can cause disease.

path′ō·ġēne, *n.* a pathogen.

path·ō·ġen′e·sis, *n.* the production or development of a disease.

path″ō·ġē·net′iç, path·ō·ġen′iç, *a.* of or causing pathogenesis.

pȧ·thoġ′e·ny, *n.* [*patho-*, and Gr. *-geneia*, from *-genēs*, producing.] pathogenesis.

pȧ·thog·nō·mon′iç, *a.* [*patho-*, and Gr. *gnōmōn*, one who knows, from *gignōskein*, to know.] indicating that which is inseparable from a disease, being found in that and no other; hence, indicating that by which a disease may be certainly known; characteristic; as, *pathognomonic* symptoms.

pȧ·thog′nō·my, *n.* [*patho-*, and Gr. *gnōmē*, means of knowing.] the study of the signs by which human passions are indicated.

path·ō·loġ′iç·ăl, path·ō·loġ′iç, *a.* 1. of pathology; of or concerned with diseases.
2. due to or involving disease.

path·ō·loġ′iç·ăl·ly, *adv.* of or with reference to pathology; in the manner of pathology.

pȧ·thol′ō·ġist, *n.* one who specializes in pathology; one versed in the nature of diseases.

pȧ·thol′ō·ġy, *n.* [*patho-*, and Gr. *logos*, discourse.]
1. that part of medicine that deals with the nature of diseases, their causes and symptoms,

and especially the structural and functional changes caused by disease.

2. *pl.* **pȧ·thol′ō·ġieṣ,** all the processes, results, or conditions produced by a particular disease.

path·ō·poe′iȧ (-pē′yȧ), *n.* [Gr. *pathopoiia.*] a speech, or figure of speech, contrived to move the passions.

pā′thos, *n.* [Gr. *pathos*, suffering, from root of *pathein*, *paschein*, to suffer.]

1. suffering. [Rare.]

2. the quality in something experienced or observed which arouses feelings of pity, sorrow, sympathy, or compassion.

3. the personal or emotional element in art: opposed to *ethos*.

pȧth′wāy, *n.* 1. a path; a way to be passed on foot.

2. a way; a course of life.

In the way of righteousness is life; and in the *pathway* thereof there is no death. —Prov. xii. 28.

-pȧ·thy, [from Gr. *pathos*, suffering.] a combining form meaning *feeling, suffering, disease, treatment of disease*, as in anti*pathy*, osteo*pathy*: also *-pathia*.

pat′i·ble, *a.* [L. *patibilis*, from *pati*, to suffer.] sufferable; tolerable; that can be endured. [Obs.]

pȧ·tib′ū·lăr·y, *a.* [Fr. *patibulaire*, from L. *patibulum*, gibbet.] of or relating to the gallows or to the death penalty. [Rare.]

pȧ·tib′ū·lā·ted, *a.* [L. *patibulum*, gibbet.] put to death on the gallows; subjected to the death penalty. [Rare.]

pā′tience (-shens), *n.* [Fr., from L. *patientia*, from *pati*, to suffer.]

1. the state, quality, ability, or fact of being patient; specifically, (a) the will or ability to wait or endure without complaint; (b) steadiness, endurance, or perseverance in performing a task.

2. any of a number of card games, usually for one player; solitaire. [Chiefly Brit.]

3. sufferance; permission. [Obs.]

4. a plant, a species of *Rumex* or dock.

Syn.—resignation, endurance, submission, perseverance.—*Patience* refers to the quietness or self-possession of one's own spirit; *resignation* to his submission to the will of another.

pā′tient (-shent), *a.* [Fr., from L. *patiens*, patient, ppr. of *pati*, to suffer.]

1. bearing or enduring pain, trouble, etc. without complaining, losing self-control, making a disturbance, etc.

2. refusing to be provoked or angered, as by an insult; forbearing; tolerant.

3. calmly tolerating delay, confusion, inefficiency, etc.; able to wait calmly.

4. showing or characterized by patience; as, a *patient* face.

5. steady; diligent; persevering, as a worker.

6. receiving action; passive. [Rare.]

patient of; (a) capable of bearing (fatigue, thirst, etc.); (b) admitting of or having (a particular meaning).

Syn.—calm, enduring, long-suffering.

pā′tient, *n.* 1. a person or thing that receives impressions from external agents; one who or that which is passively affected.

Malice is a passion so impetuous and precipitate, that it often involves the agent and the *patient*. —Henry More.

2. a person receiving care or treatment; especially, a person under the care of a doctor; as, the physician visits his *patient* morning and evening.

It is wonderful to observe how inapprehensive these *patients* are of their disease. —Blackmore.

pā′tient, *v.t.* to compose (oneself). [Obs.]

pā′tient·ly, *adv.* in a patient way.

pä′tï·ki, *n.* in zoology, a flounder found in New Zealand waters.

pat′in, *n.* a paten.

pat′i·nȧ, *n.*; *pl.* **pat′i·nae,** [L.] a paten.

pat′i·nȧ, *n.* [L. *patina*, a pan, a dish, also a kind of cake, from *patere*, to be open.]

1. a fine crust or film on bronze or copper: it is usually green or greenish-blue and is formed by natural oxidation: it is both preservative and ornamental. An artificial patina is produced by the forgers of antiquities by the use of acetic acid, but it is not durable.

2. any thin film, coloring, or mellowed appearance on the surface of an object as a result of age or use, as on the surface of old woodwork.

pat′i·nā·ted, *a.* in art, coated with patina.

pat′ine, *n.* a paten.

pä′tï·ō (*or Sp.* pä′tyō), *n.*; *pl.* **pä′tï·ōṣ** (*or Sp.* pä′tyōs), [Sp., probably from L. *patere*, to lie open.]

1. in metallurgy, a paved place where metals are separated from refuse, and assorted.

2. a courtyard or inner area open to the sky: common in Spanish and Spanish American architecture.

patio process; a process of amalgamation in which silver ore is mixed with salt, mercury, etc. and stirred up by mules driven through it on a patio.

pat′ly, *adv.* fitly; conveniently.

pat′ness, *n.* fitness; suitableness; convenience.

pat′ois (-wä *or Fr.* pȧ-twȧ′), *n.*; *pl.* **pat′oiṣ** (-wäz *or Fr.* pȧ-twȧ′), [Fr.]

1. a form of a language differing generally from the accepted standard, as a provincial or local dialect.

2. in linguistics, the blend of a provincial dialect with a standard form of a language.

pȧ·tonce′, *n.* in heraldry, a cross having the ends of the arms floreated.

pat′ri-, [L.; Gr. *patri-*, from *patēr*, father.] a combining form meaning *father*, as in *patri*mony.

pā′tri·ăl, *n.* [LL. *patrialis*; L. *patria*, native country.] in grammar, a noun derived from the name of a country, and denoting a native or inhabitant of that country, as *German*, a native or inhabitant of Germany.

pā′tri·ăl, *a.* in grammar, relating to a patrial.

pā′tri·ärch, *n.* [L. *patriarcha*, from Gr. *patriarchēs*; *patria*, a family, from *patēr*, father, and *archein*, to rule.]

1. the father and ruler of a family or tribe, as one of the founders of the ancient Hebrew families: in the Bible, Abraham, Isaac, Jacob, and Jacob's twelve sons were patriarchs.

2. a person regarded as the founder or father of a colony, religion, business, etc.

3. (a) a bishop in the early Christian Church, especially a bishop of Rome, Constantinople, Alexandria, Antioch, or Jerusalem; (b) in the Roman Catholic Church, a bishop who holds the highest rank, after the Pope, in the hierarchy of the jurisdiction: patriarchs with jurisdiction are the Pope as Patriarch of the West; those of Constantinople, Alexandria, Antioch, and Jerusalem; those of the Melkite, Syrian, Maronite, Armenian, Chaldean Churches, etc.; (c) in the Orthodox Eastern Church, the highest ranking bishop at Constantinople, Alexandria, Antioch, Jerusalem, Moscow, Bucharest, etc.; (d) the jurisdictional head of any of certain other churches, as the Coptic, Nestorian, Armenian, etc.

4. a man of great age and dignity.

5. the oldest individual of a class or group.

The monarch oak, the *patriarch* of trees. —Dryden.

pā·tri·är′chăl, pā·tri·är′chic, *a.* 1. of, ruled by, suitable to, or characteristic of a patriarch.

2. venerable.

3. having the position or jurisdiction of a patriarch.

patriarchal cross; in heraldry, a cross in which the shaft is twice crossed, the lower arms being longer than the upper ones.

pā′tri·är″chāte, *n.* 1. the office, dignity, position, rank, territory, or jurisdiction of a patriarch.

2. the residence of a patriarch.

3. a patriarchal government or system.

pā′tri·ärch″dŏm, *n.* the jurisdiction of a patriarch. [Rare.]

pā·tri·är′chiç, *a.* see *patriarchal*.

pā·tri·är′chiç·ăl, *a.* patriarchal.

pā′tri·ärch·iṣm, *n.* government by a patriarch or the head of a family.

pā′tri·ärch·ship, *n.* the office, dignity, or jurisdiction of a patriarch; a patriarchate.

pā′tri·ärch·y, *n.* 1. the jurisdiction of a patriarch.

2. a form of social organization in which the father or the eldest male is recognized as the head of the family or tribe, descent and kinship being traced through the male line: opposed to *matriarchy*.

3. government by men: opposed to *matriarchy*.

pȧ·tri′ciăn (-trish′ăn), *a.* [ME. *patricion*; OFr. *patricien*; L. *patricius*, pertaining to the patricians, from *pater*, father.]

1. of, pertaining to, or characteristic of patricians; as, *patrician* families.

2. noble; aristocratic.

pȧ·tri′ciăn, *n.* 1. in ancient Rome, (a) originally, a member of any of the ancient Roman citizen families; (b) later, a member of the nobility: opposed to *plebeian*; (c) a member of a class of honorary nobility of the later Empire; (d) a chief administrator in the Roman provinces in Africa and Italy.

2. a person of high rank in some medieval Italian republics and in certain Free Cities of the German Empire.

3. any person of high social rank; aristocrat.

pȧ·tri′ciăn·iṣm, *n.* the rank or character of patricians; also, the doctrine of privileged birth or unequal political conditions.

pȧ·tri′ci·āte (-trish′i-), *n.* 1. the aristocracy or nobility as a class; the patrician class.

2. the rank or position of a patrician.

pat′ri·cī·dăl, *a.* of or pertaining to patricide.

pat′ri·cīde, *n.* [L. *pater*, *patris*, father, and *caedere*, to kill.]

1. one who murders his father.

2. the act of killing one's own father; murder of a man by his child.

pat·ri·lin′ē·ăl, *a.* denoting or relating to descent through the male line or paternal ancestors: contrasted with *matrilineal*.

pat·ri·mō′ni·ăl, *a.* pertaining to a patrimony; inherited from ancestors; as, a *patrimonial* estate.

pat′ri·mō′ni·ăl·ly, *adv.* by inheritance.

pat·ri′mō·ny, *n.*; *pl.* **pat′ri·mō·nieṣ,** [L. *patrimonium*, from *pater*, *patris*, father.]

1. property inherited from one's father or ancestors.

2. property endowed to an institution, as a church.

3. anything inherited, as a trait or character.

pā′tri·ŏt (*or* pat′), *n.* [Fr. *patriote*; LL. *patriota*, fellow countryman; Gr. *patriōtēs*, from *patris*, fatherland.] a person who loves and loyally or zealously supports his own country.

pā′tri·ŏt, *a.* patriotic; devoted to the welfare of one's country; as, *patriot* zeal.

pā″tri·ŏt·eer′, *n.* an ostentatiously and volubly patriotic person, who makes a career of patriotism for his own benefit. [Colloq.]

pā·tri·ot′iç, pā·tri·ot′iç·ăl, *a.* 1. having or showing the qualities and feelings of a patriot.

2. characteristic of or suitable to a patriot; inspired by patriotism.

pā·tri·ot′iç·ăl·ly, *adv.* in a patriotic manner.

pā′tri·ŏt·iṣm, *n.* love and loyal or zealous support of one's own country, especially in all matters involving other countries; nationalism.

Pa′tri·ŏt's Day, April 19, a legal holiday in Maine and Massachusetts commemorating the battle of Lexington and Concord (1775).

Pā·tri·pas′siăn (-pash′ăn), *n.* [L. *pater*, father, and *passio*, suffering.] one of an ancient sect of religionists who taught that God the Father was born, suffered, and died with the Son.

Pā·tri·pas′siăn·iṣm, *n.* the doctrines or tenets of the Patripassians.

pā′trist, *n.* one versed in the lives or works of the fathers of the Christian Church.

pȧ·tris′tiç, pȧ·tris′tiç·ăl, *a.* [from L. *patres*, fathers.] of the early leaders, or fathers, of the Christian Church or the writings and doctrines attributed to them.

pȧ·tris′tiç·ăl·ly, *adv.* in a patristic manner.

pȧ·tris′tiçṣ, *n.* that branch of historical theology which is concerned with the doctrines, writings, and lives of the fathers of the Christian Church.

pā′tri·zāte, *v.i.* to imitate one's father. [Obs.]

pȧ·troc′i·nāte, *v.t.* to patronize; to favor; to support. [Obs.]

pȧ·troc·i·nā′tion, *n.* the act of countenancing, abetting, or patronizing. [Obs.]

pa·trō·clī′nous, *a.* designating or of characteristics inherited from the father.

Pȧ·trō′clus, *n.* [L.; Gr. *Patroklos.*] in Greek legend, a Greek warrior and friend of Achilles in the Trojan War: while wearing Achilles' armor he was mistaken for him and slain by Hector.

pa·trō·ġen′e·sis, *n.* reproduction in which the chromatin for the embryo is wholly supplied from the sperm or pollen cell.

pȧ·trōl′, *v.t.* and *v.i.*; patrolled, *pt.*, *pp.*; patrolling, *ppr.* [Fr. *patrouiller*, to paddle or puddle, to patrol, from *patte*, paw or foot.] to make a regular and repeated circuit of (an area, town, camp, etc.) in guarding or inspecting; as, an armed guard is *patrolling* the area.

pȧ·trōl′, *n.* [Fr. *patrouille.*]
1. a patrolling.
2. a person or persons patrolling.
3. a group of ships, airplanes, etc. used in guarding or gathering information about the enemy.
4. a group of eight boy scouts, constituting a subdivision of a troop.

pȧ·trōle′, *n.* and *v.* same as *patrol.*

pȧ·trōl′lẽr, *n.* a person who patrols.

pȧ·trōl′măn, *n.*; *pl.* **pȧ·trōl′men**, one who patrols; especially, a policeman assigned to make a circuit of a certain area.

pȧ·trol′ō·ġy, *n.* same as *patristics.*

pȧ·trōl′ wag′ŏn, a small enclosed truck used by the police in transporting prisoners.

pā′trŏn, *n.* [L. *patronus*, from *pater*, father.]
1. among the ancient Romans, a master who had freed his slave, and retained some rights over him after his emancipation; also, a man of distinction under whose protection another placed himself.
2. a person corresponding in some respects to a father; protector; benefactor.
3. a person empowered with the granting of an English church benefice.
4. a patron saint.
5. (a) a person, usually a wealthy and influential one, who sponsors and supports some person, activity, etc.; as, the book was dedicated to the author's *patron*; (b) a champion; advocate; supporter.
6. in nautical usage, the commander of a small vessel or passage boat; also, one who steers a ship's longboat.
Patrons of Husbandry; an order formed by farmers of the United States in 1867, having for its object the bringing together of producers and consumers of the products of the farm and of the factory in such a way as to do away with the services of middlemen and speculative traders: also called the *Grange.*
Syn.—benefactor, helper, protector, supporter, encourager, upholder.

pā′trŏn, *v.t.* to be a patron of. [Rare.]

pā′trŏn, *a.* acting the part of a patron; giving support and protection.
patron saint; a saint supposed to protect and promote the welfare of a particular person, community, state, or institution.

pā′trŏn·āġe (*or* pat′), *n.* 1. (a) the function or status of a patron; (b) support, favor, encouragement, sponsorship, etc. given by a patron.
2. the power to grant an English church benefice.
3. good will, favor, courtesy, etc. shown to people considered inferior; condescension.
4. (a) patrons collectively; clientele; (b) business; trade; custom.
5. the power to appoint to office or grant other favors, especially political ones.
6. offices or other favors distributed through this power.

pā′trŏn·āġe, *v.t.* to patronize or support. [Rare.]

pā′trŏn·ăl, *a.* [Fr.; LL. *patronalis.*] of or characteristic of a patron or patron saint; protective; guardian.

pā′trŏn·āte, *n.* the office, jurisdiction, or duty of a patron.

pā′trŏn·ess, *n.* a woman patron, especially one who sponsors or supports some activity, as the opera.

pā′trŏn·īze (*or* pat′), *v.t.*; patronized, *pt.*, *pp.*; patronizing, *ppr.* 1. to act as a patron toward; to sponsor; support; protect.
2. to show favor or kindness to in a condescending manner.
3. to be a regular customer of (a store, etc.); to give one's trade to.

pā′trŏn·ī·zẽr, *n.* one who patronizes.

pā′trŏn·ī·zing, *a.* defending; supporting; favoring; promoting; especially, showing condescension in favoring.

pā′trŏn·ī·zing·ly, *adv.* in a patronizing manner.

pā′trŏn·less, *a.* without a patron.

pat·rō·nom·ȧ·tol′ō·ġy, *n.* [Gr. *patēr*, father, *onoma*, name, and *logos*, discourse.] a systematic discussion of the origin, meaning, and modifications of family names. [Rare.]

pat·rō·nym′iç, *a.* [LL. *patronymicus*; Gr. *patēr*, father, and *onoma*, name.]
1. derived from the name of a father or ancestor.
2. showing such descent; as, a *patronymic* suffix.

pat·rō·nym′iç, *n.* 1. a name showing descent from a given person as by the addition of a prefix or suffix (e.g., *Stevenson*, son of Steven, *O'Brien*, descendant of Brien).
2. a family name; surname.

pȧ·troon′, *n.* [D. *patroon*, a protector; Fr. *patron.*]
1. a person who held a large estate with manorial rights in return for founding a colony under the old Dutch governments of New York and New Jersey.
2. a patron. [Obs.]

pȧ·troon′ship, *n.* the position of a patroon.

pat·té′, pat·tée′ (-tā′), *a.* [Fr. *patte*, paw.] in heraldry, designating a cross having the arms narrow at the center and expanding toward the ends.

pat′te·mär, *n.* see *patamar.*

pat′ten, *n.* [Fr. *patin*, a clog, patten, from *patte*, foot or paw.]
1. a thick wooden sandal mounted on an iron support, and worn in wet weather.
2. a wooden shoe or overshoe.

pat′tened, *a.* shod in pattens.

pat′tẽr, *v.t.* and *v.i.*; pattered, *pt.*, *pp.*; pattering, *ppr.* [ME. *patteren*, from *pater*, in *paternoster*, as pronounced in rapid and mechanical recitation.] to speak or mumble rapidly or glibly; recite mechanically or thoughtlessly, as prayers.

pat′tẽr, *n.* 1. language peculiar to a group, class, etc., and not generally understood by outsiders; cant; jargon.
2. the glib, rapid speech of salesmen, circus barkers, magicians, etc.
3. idle, meaningless chatter. [Colloq.]

pat′tẽr, *v.i.* [freq. of *pat*, to tap gently.]
1. to make a patter.
2. to move so as to make a patter.

pat′tẽr, *v.t.* to cause to patter.

pat′tẽr, *n.* a series of light, rapid taps; as, the *patter* of rain on dry leaves.

pat′tẽr, *n.* a person or thing that pats.

pat′tẽr·ẽr, *n.* one who patters.

pat′tẽrn, *n.* [OFr. *patron*, patron, hence something to be imitated.]
1. a person or thing so ideal as to be worthy of imitation or copying.
2. a model, guide, plan, etc. used in making things.
3. the full-scale model used in making a sand mold for casting metal.
4. something representing a class or type; example; sample.
5. an arrangement of form; disposition of parts or elements; design or decoration; as, wallpaper *patterns*, the *pattern* of a novel.
6. definite direction, tendency, or characteristics; as, behavior *patterns.*
7. (a) grouping or distribution, as of a number of bullets fired at a mark; (b) a diagram showing such distribution.
8. sufficient material for making a garment.
9. something made after a model; a copy. [Obs.]
10. in Ireland, a feast or merrymaking in honor of a patron saint.

pat′tẽrn, *v.t.*; patterned, *pt.*, *pp.*; patterning, *ppr.* 1. to make or do (something) in imitation of a model or pattern (with *on*, *upon*, or *after*).
2. to supply with a pattern or design; to put a pattern on.

pat′tẽrn bomb′ing (bom′), the simultaneous release of bombs from a formation of airplanes over an area containing individually assigned targets.

pat′tẽrn box, in weaving, (a) a box in a loom holding a number of shuttles, any of which may be projected along the shed. The shuttles are operated in due sequence by a pattern cylinder or pattern chain; (b) the box perforated for the cards in the Jacquard figure loom.

pat′tẽrn çärd, in weaving, one of the perforated cards in a Jacquard loom through which the needles pass. The pattern is determined by the perforations.

pat′tẽrn chāin, in weaving, a contrivance for automatically bringing the shuttles to the picker in proper order.

pat′tẽrn cyl′in·dẽr, in weaving, a method of operating the harness of a loom by means of a cylinder with projections, which come in contact in due order of time with the respective levers which work the shed.

pat′tẽrn·māk′ẽr, *n.* a person who makes patterns, especially patterns for molds: also *pattern maker.*

pat′tẽrn rēad′ẽr, one who arranges textile patterns.

pat′tẽrn wheel (hwēl), 1. in horology, a count wheel.
2. in weaving, a pattern cylinder.

pat′tẽr sǫng, in operettas, musical comedies, etc., a song with a simple tune and comic lyrics sung with great rapidity.

pat′tin·sŏn·īze, *v.t.*; pattinsonized, *pt.*, *pp.*; pattinsonizing, *ppr.* [from H.L. *Pattinson* of Newcastle on Tyne, who invented the process.] to separate silver from (argentiferous lead ore) by the fractional crystallization of the lead ore.

pat′ty, *n.*; *pl.* **pat′tieṣ**, [Fr. *pâté.*]
1. a small pie.
2. a small, flat cake of ground meat, fish, etc., usually fried.
3. any disk-shaped piece of food.

pat′ty-çāke, *n.* same as *pat-a-cake.*

pat′ty pan, a pan used for baking patties.

pat′ty shell, a puffy case or container made of pastry and used to hold light fillings of meat, vegetables, fruits, creams, etc.

pat′ū·lous, *a.* [L. *patulus*, from *patere*, to be open.] spreading somewhat widely apart; as, a *patulous* calyx.

pau·ci·den′tāte, *a.* [L. *paucus*, few, and *dentatus*, toothed, from *dens*, *dentis*, tooth.] having few teeth, as a leaf: also applied to animals.

pau·ci·flō′rous, *a.* [L. *paucus*, few, and *flos*, *floris*, flower.] in botany, having but few flowers.

pau·cil′ō·quent, *a.* [L. *paucus*, few, little, and *loquens* (*-entis*), ppr. of *loqui*, to speak.] uttering few words; saying but little. [Rare.]

pau·cil′ō·quy, *n.* [L. *paucus*, few, and *loqui*, to speak.] the utterance of few words. [Rare.]

pau·ci·rā′di·āte, *a.* [L. *paucus*, few, and *radius*, ray.] having few rays, as the fin of a fish.

pau·ci·spī′răl, *a.* [L. *paucus*, few, and *spira*, fold.] having few spirals or whorls; as, a *paucispiral* shell.

pau′ci·ty, *n.* [L. *paucitas*, from *paucus*, few.]
1. fewness; small number.
2. scarcity; dearth; insufficiency.

paul, *n.* an old silver coin of Italy: also called *paolo.*

paul, *n.* same as *pawl.*

Paul, *n.* in the Bible, a Jew of Tarsus, apostle of Christianity to the Gentiles; author of the Pauline Epistles: originally called *Saul*: also called *Saint Paul.*

Paul Bun′yăn, in American legend, a giant lumberjack who, with the help of his blue ox, Babe, performed various superhuman feats.

paul′drŏn, *n.* [Sp. *espaldaron*, from *espalda*; Fr. *épaule*, the shoulder; L. *spatula*, the shoulder blade.] in old armor, a shoulder plate of one piece.

a. PAULDRON

Pau′li·ăn, Pau′li·ăn·ist, *n.* a follower of Paul of Samosata, a heretic of the third century.

Pau·li′ciăn (-lish′un), *n.* one of a Christian sect of Asiatic origin, who appeared in Armenia in the seventh century. From the close of the seventh to the middle of the ninth century they suffered severe persecution.

pau′lin, *n.* same as *tarpaulin.*

Pau′line, *a.* pertaining to St. Paul or to his writings; written by St. Paul; as, the *Pauline* Epistles.

Pau′lin·iṣm, *n.* in church history, the teachings found in, or deducible from, the writings of St. Paul.

Paul′ist, *n.* 1. in India, a Jesuit.
2. a Roman Catholic priest belonging to the Missionary Society of St. Paul the Apostle, founded in New York in 1858.

Paul·lin′i·ȧ, *n.* [named by Linnaeus after Simon *Paulli*, professor of botany at Copenhagen, and author, in 1640 and 1648, of botanical works.] a genus of sapindaceous climbing shrubs, including about eighty species, chiefly native to the tropics of America.

pau·lō·çär′di·ȧ, *n.* [Gr. *paula*, pause, and *kardia*, heart.] the subjective sensation of intermission or momentary stoppage of the heartbeat.

Pau·lōw′ni·ȧ, *n.* [named after Anne *Paulowna*, a Russian princess.] a monotypic genus of trees of the order *Scrophulariaceæ*. It is native to Japan and has immense heart-shaped leaves and large purple flowers.

paum, *v.t.* to palm. [Obs.]

paunch (*or* ponch), *n.* [OFr. *panche*; Fr. *panse*, from L. *pantex*, *panticis*, the belly, the bowels.]

1. the abdomen or belly; especially, a large, protruding belly; a potbelly.
2. in cud-chewing animals, the first and largest stomach.
3. in nautical usage, a thickly thrummed mat of sennit wrapped around a spar or rope to keep it from chafing: also called *paunch mat.*

paunch (*or* **ponch**), *v.t.*; paunched, *pt., pp.*; paunching, *ppr.* 1. to pierce or rip the belly of; to eviscerate.
2. to overfeed. [Obs.]

paunch'y, *a.* having a large or fat paunch; big-bellied.

paune, *n.* pone. [Obs.]

pau'pẽr, *n.* [L., a poor person.]
1. a person who lives on charity, especially on tax-supported charity.
2. any person who is extremely poor.

pau'pẽr·ism, *n.* the state of being poor or destitute of the means of support; the state of indigent persons requiring support from the community; also, paupers collectively.
Syn.—poverty, indigence, penury, want, need, destitution, beggary.

pau·pẽr·i·zā'tion, *n.* a pauperizing or being pauperized.

pau'pẽr·ize, *v.t.*; pauperized, *pt., pp.*; pauperizing, *ppr.* to reduce to pauperism; to make a pauper of.

Pau·rop'ō·da, *n.pl.* [Gr. *pauros*, small, and *pous, podos*, foot.] an order of small myriapods with branched antennae.

paus'ăl, *a.* of or pertaining to a pause.

paus·ā'tion, *n.* [L. *pausatio.*] the act of pausing or stopping; a pause; a stop; a stay.

pause, *n.* [Fr., from L. *pausa*; Gr. *pausis*, a stopping, from *pauein*, to bring to an end, to stop.]
1. a short period of inaction; a temporary stop, break, or rest, as in speaking or reading.
2. hesitation; interruption; delay; as, pursuit without *pause.*
3. (a) a stop or break in speaking or reading to clarify meaning; (b) any mark of punctuation indicating this.
4. in music, a sign (◡ or ⌒) placed above or below a note or rest that is to be prolonged.
5. in prosody, a rhythm break or caesura.
to give one pause; to make one hesitant or uncertain.
Syn.—stop, cessation, suspension, halt, intermission, rest.

pause, *v.i.*; paused, *pt., pp.*; pausing, *ppr.* 1. to make a short stop; to cease speaking or action for a time; to stop temporarily.

Pausing a while, thus to herself she mused.
—Milton.

2. to dwell or linger (usually with *on* or *upon*); as, to *pause on* a point.

Tarry, *pause* a day or two,
Before you hazard. —Shak.

3. to hesitate; to hold back.
Syn.—cease, suspend, intermit, forbear, stay, wait, hesitate, demur, stop, desist.

paus'ẽr, *n.* one who pauses.

paus'ing·ly, *adv.* after a pause; by breaks; in an intermittent manner.

Paus'si·dae, *n.pl.* an anomalous family of beetles found in ants' nests and under stones and logs, chiefly in Asia, Africa, and Australia.

paut, *n.* [East Indian.] jute: also written *pat.*

paux'i, *n.* any of several South American birds, of the genus *Urax*, and family *Cracidæ*, the best-known species of which, *Urax galeata*, the galeated curassow, has a large, light blue tubercle at the base of the beak, nearly as large as the head.

pa·väde', *n.* same as *panade.*

pāv'ăge, *n.* a tax for the paving of streets or highways; a paving assessment.

pa·väis' (-vā'), *n.* same as *pavis.*

pav'ăn, *n.* [Fr. *pavane*; Sp. *pavana*, from *pavo*, peacock; L. *pavus.*]
1. a slow, stately court dance of Spanish or Italian origin, performed by couples.
2. the music for this.
Also *pavane, pavin, paven.*

pa·vé' (-vā'), *n.* [Fr.] 1. pavement.
2. a setting of jewelry in which the gems are placed close together so that no metal shows.

pāve, *v.t.*; paved, *pt., pp.*; paving, *ppr.* [Fr. *paver*; LL. *pavare, paviare*, from L. *pavire*, to ram, to beat, to pave.]
1. to cover over the surface of, as with concrete, asphalt, brick, etc.; as, a *paved* road makes travel easier.
2. to be the top surface or covering of.
3. to cover closely or thickly; to stud; to overlay.
to pave the way (*for*); to prepare the way (for); to facilitate the introduction (of).

pāve'ment, *n.* [L. *pavimentum*, from *pavire*, to beat down.]
1. a paved surface or covering, as of concrete, brick, etc.
2. a decorative and serviceable interior flooring of plain or variously shaped and colored tiles, stone, bricks, etc., often arranged in artistic or geometrical designs.
3. a paved street or road.
4. the material used in paving.

pāve'ment, *v.t.* to pave; to floor. [Rare.]

pav'en, *n.* same as *pavan.*

pāv'ẽr, *n.* 1. one who lays pavements, or whose occupation is to pave: also written *pavier, pavior*, and *paviour.*
2. a rammer used in laying pavements.
3. a paving stone, etc.

pav·e·säde', *n.* [Fr.] a canvas screen, designed to hide the operations on board a ship from the enemy during an engagement. [Obs.]

pav'id, *a.* [L. *pavidus.*] timid; afraid.

pa·vid'i·ty, *n.* fearfulness; timidity. [Rare.]

pāv'iẽr, *n.* same as *paver.*

pa'vi·in, *n.* same as *fraxin.*

pa·vil'iŏn (-yun), *n.* [Fr. *pavillon*; L. *papilio, papilionis*, a butterfly, also a tent, from the shape of the latter.]
1. a large tent, usually with a peaked top.
2. (a) a building or part of a building used for entertainment, exhibits, etc., as at a fair or park: often open-air and highly ornamented; (b) a decorative shelter or summerhouse.
3. part of a building jutting out from the main part and often ornamented.
4. any of the separate or connected parts of a group of related buildings, as of a hospital or sanitarium.
5. the auricle of the ear.
6. the part of a brilliant-cut gem between the girdle and the culet.
pavilion roof; a roof sloping or hipped equally on all sides.

pa·vil'iŏn, *v.t.*; pavilioned, *pt., pp.*; pavilioning, *ppr.* to furnish with or shelter in or as in a pavilion.

pa·vil·lon' (-vē-lyoṅ'), *n.* [Fr.] in music, the bell or mouth of a horn, trumpet, etc.
pavillon chinois; an instrument having a number of small bells in a frame attached to a staff: the bells are agitated by striking the staff on the ground.

pav'in, *n.* same as *pavan.*

pāv'ing, *n.* 1. the act of laying a pavement.
2. pavement or the material for a pavement.

pāv'iŏr, pāv'iŏur (-yẽr), *n.* same as *paver.*

pav'is, *n.* [OFr. *pavois*; It. *pavese*, from *Pavia*, Italy, where it was first made.] a large shield used in medieval warfare as a protection for the bearer and, sometimes, a companion archer: also written *pavais, pavise.*

PAVIS

pav'i·sẽr, *n.* a soldier who carried a pavis.

Pā'vō, *n.* [L., a peacock.]
1. a constellation near the southern pole, south of Sagittarius.
2. a genus of gallinaceous birds; the peacocks. The common peacock is *Pavo cristatus*, noted for the splendor of its tail.

pa·vōne', *n.* [L. *pavo, pavonis.*] a peacock. [Obs.]

pa·vō'ni·ăn, *a.* same as *pavonine.*

pav'ō·nīne, *a.* [L. *pavoninus*, from *pavo* (*-onis*), a peacock.]
1. resembling the tail of a peacock; iridescent.
2. of or resembling a peacock.

paw, *n.* [ME. *paue*; OFr. *poue.*]
1. the foot of a four-footed animal having claws.
2. a hand. [Colloq.]

paw, *v.t.* and *v.i.*; pawed, *pt., pp.*; pawing, *ppr.* 1. to touch, dig, strike, etc. with the paws or feet; as, the wild horse *pawed* the air.
2. to handle clumsily, roughly, or overintimately; to maul.

paw, *n.* pa; papa; father. [Dial.]

paw'ky, *a.*; *comp.* pawkier; *superl.* pawkiest, cunning; shrewd; crafty. [Scot. and Brit. Dial.]

pawl, *n.* a mechanical device allowing rotation in only one direction: one type consists of a hinged tongue, the tip of which engages the notches of a cogwheel, preventing backward motion.

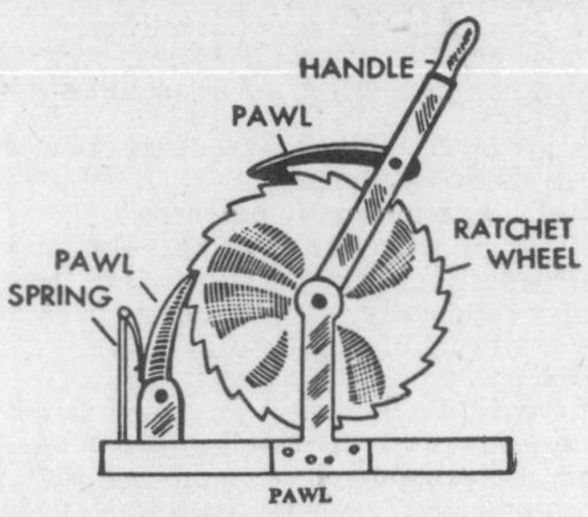

PAWL

pawl, *v.t.*; pawled, *pt., pp.*; pawling, *ppr.* to engage with or as with a pawl.

pawl bitt, a post to which the pawls of a ship's capstan are attached.

pawl rim, pawl ring, a ring at the base of a capstan furnished with ratchet teeth.

pawn, *n.* [ME. *poun*; OFr. *peon*; LL. *pedo*, foot soldier, from L. *pes, pedis*, a foot.]
1. a chessman of the lowest value: it can be moved only forward and but one square at a time (or two squares on the first move), but it captures with a diagonal move: symbol, P.
2. a person subject to the will of another; a tool.

pawn, *n.* [OFr. *pan, pant*; akin to G. *pfand.*]
1. anything given as security, as for a debt, performance of an action, etc.; a pledge; a guaranty.
2. a hostage.
3. the state of being pledged; as, his ring was in *pawn.*
4. the act of pawning.

pawn, *v.t.* 1. to give as security; to put in pawn.
2. to stake, wager, or risk; as, he *pawned* his honor.

pawn'a·ble, *a.* that can be pawned.

pawn'ăge, *n.* a pawning or being pawned.

pawn'brō·kẽr, *n.* a person licensed to loan money at a legally specified rate of interest on personal property left with him as security.

pawn'brō·king, *n.* the business of a pawnbroker.

pawn·ee', *n.* the person to whom a pawn is delivered as security; one who takes anything in pawn.

paw'nee, *n.* [Anglo-Ind., from Hind. *pānī.*] water.

Paw·nee', *n.* 1. *pl.* **Paw·nee', Paw·nees',** a member of a confederacy of North American Plains Indians of Caddoan linguistic stock, formerly living in the valley of the Platte River, Nebraska, and now in northern Oklahoma.
2. their language.

Paw·nee', *a.* of the Pawnee or their language.

pawn'ẽr, pawn'ŏr, *n.* one who pawns something.

pawn'shop, *n.* a pawnbroker's shop.

pawn tick'et, a receipt for goods in pawn.

paw'paw, *n.* same as *papaw.*

pax, *n.* [L. *pax*, peace.]
1. [P–] the Roman goddess of peace.
2. a small tablet representing the Crucifixion, the Virgin, a saint, etc.: formerly, during the Roman Catholic Eucharistic service, it was kissed by the celebrant and worshipers.

pax·il'la, *n.*; *pl.* **pax·il'lae,** [L. *paxillus*, a small stake.] a pillarlike process of certain echinoderms terminated by a cluster of spines.

pax'il·lāte, *a.* provided with paxillae.

Pax·il·lō'sae, *n.pl.* formerly, an order of starfishes, distinguished by the possession of paxillae.

PAX

pax'il·lōse, *a.* 1. relating to the *Paxillosæ.*
2. furnished with paxillae.
3. in geology, resembling a small stake.

pax·il'lus, *n.* a paxilla.

Pax Rō·mā'na, [L., Roman peace.]

1. the terms of peace imposed by Rome on any of its dominions.
2. a peace dictated to a subjugated people by a conquering nation.

pax vō·bis'çum, [L.] peace (be) with you.

pax'wax, *n.* [from AS. *feax*, hair, and *wax*, to grow.] a strong, elastic ligament running along the back of the neck, connecting the occiput with the prominences of the spine, as in an ox or horse. It supports the head in a horizontal position. Also called *faxwax*, *packwax*, *fixfax*, and *paxywaxy*.

pāy, *v.t.*; payed, *pt.*, *pp.*; paying, *ppr.* [OFr. *peier*, from L. *picare*, to cover with pitch, from *pix*, *picis*, pitch.] to daub, besmear, or cover with tar, pitch, tallow, resin, or other protective material; as, to *pay* a seam or spar.

pāy, *v.t.*; paid *or obs.* payed, *pt.*, *pp.*; paying, *ppr.* [ME. *paien*, *payen*, to pay, to please, to satisfy, from OFr. *paier*, *paer*; Fr. *payer*, to pay, originally, to please; It. *pagare*; from L. *pacare*, to pacify; *pax*, *pacis*, peace.]
1. to give to (a person) what is due, as for goods received, services rendered, etc.; to remunerate; to recompense.
2. to make return or recompense for; to repay; as, she *paid* kindness with evil.
3. to give (what is due or owed) in return, as for goods or services.
4. to discharge or settle (a debt, obligation, etc.) by giving something in return.
5. (a) to give or offer (a compliment, respects, attention, etc.); (b) to make (a visit, call, etc.).
6. to yield as a recompense or return; as, this job *pays* fifty dollars a week.
7. to give satisfaction or be profitable to; as, it will *pay* you to read the book.
to pay back; to repay.
to pay off; (a) to pay all that is owed on (a debt, etc.) or to (a person, as in discharging from employment); (b) to take revenge on (a wrongdoer) or for (a wrong done); (c) to turn (a ship's head) to leeward.
to pay one's way; to pay one's share of the expenses.
to pay out; (a) to give out (money, etc.); to expend; (b) to let out (a rope, cable, etc.).

pāy, *v.i.* 1. to give due or adequate compensation; to make payment.
2. to be profitable.
to pay as you go; to pay expenses as they arise.
to pay off; (a) to yield full recompense or return, for either good or evil; (b) in nautical usage, to veer to leeward: said of a vessel.
to pay up; to pay in full or on time.

pāy, *n.* [ME. *paye*; It. *paga*, from L. *pacare*, to pacify.]
1. a paying or being paid: said of wages, hire, etc.
2. compensation, especially money, for goods, services, etc.; wages or salary.
3. anything, good or evil, given or done in return.
4. a person regarded from the standpoint of his financial credit or willingness to pay.
full pay; the entire amount due; the maximum compensation for a certain office or rank.
in the pay of; employed and paid by.

pāy, *a.* 1. rich enough in minerals, etc. to make mining profitable; as, *pay* gravel.
2. having a mechanism that can be operated by depositing a specified coin or coins, as a telephone or public toilet.

pāy'à·ble, *a.* 1. that can be paid.
2. that is to be paid (on a specified date); due.
3. that is or can be profitable, as a mine or business venture.

pāy'dāy, *n.* the day when payment is to be made or debts discharged; especially, the day on which wages are paid.

pāy dīrt, soil, gravel, ore, etc. rich enough in minerals to make mining profitable.

pāy·ee', *n.* the person to whom money is to be paid or has been paid; the person named in a bill or note to whom the amount is promised or directed to be paid.

pāy'en, *a.* and *n.* pagan; heathen. [Obs.]

pāy'ẽr, *n.* a person who pays; particularly one who pays or should pay a bill, note, etc.

pāy lōad, a cargo, or the part of a cargo, producing income.

pāy'mȧs·tẽr, *n.* 1. a person who pays; one to whom is assigned the duty of paying employees.
2. formerly, an army officer whose duty is to pay the officers and soldiers their wages, and who is entrusted with money for this purpose.
3. formerly, a naval officer to whom the provisions, clothes, and money for his vessel are entrusted, and who has charge of their proper disbursement.

pāy'mȧs·tẽr ġen'ẽr·ăl, 1. formerly, an army officer having general supervision of the payment of officers and men.
2. formerly, the chief paying officer of the navy.

pāy'ment, *n.* [ME. and OFr. *paiement*.]
1. a paying or being paid.
2. something that is paid.
3. penalty or reward.

pāy'nim, *n.* [OFr. *paienisme*, *paianisme*, from LL. *paganismus*, pagnism.]
1. a pagan; a heathen. [Archaic.]
2. a non-Christian; especially, a Mohammedan. [Archaic.]
3. the pagan world. [Archaic.]

pāy'nim, *a.* 1. pagan; heathen. [Archaic.]
2. non-Christian. [Archaic.]

pāyn'īze, *v.t.*; paynized, *pt.*, *pp.*; paynizing, *ppr.* [after the inventor, *Payne*.] to treat (wood) with solutions of calcium sulfide and calcium sulfate, in order to harden and preserve.

pāy'-off'', *n.* 1. originally, the act or time of payment. [Colloq.]
2. settlement or reckoning. [Colloq.]
3. something that is unexpected or almost incredible, especially when coming as a climax or culmination. [Colloq.]

pāy'ŏr, *n.* payer. [Rare.]

pāy rōll, 1. a list of employees to be paid, with the amount due to each.
2. the total amount needed for this for a given period.

pāy'tine, *n.* a bitter crystallizable alkaloid, $C_{21}H_{24}N_2O$, obtained from the white bark of a Peruvian tree of the genus *Aspidosperma*.

Pb, *plumbum*, [L.] in chemistry, lead.

Pd, in chemistry, palladium.

pe̦, *n.* same as *peh*.

pēa, *n.*; *pl.* **pēaș** or Brit. dial. or archaic **pēașe,** [ME. *pese*, *pees*, a pea; AS. *pise*; L., *pisa*, pl. of *pisum*, a pea; Gr. *pison*, a pea.]
1. a plant of the genus *Pisum*, with white or pinkish flowers and green seed pods. The flower is papilionaceous, and the pericarp is a legume, called, popularly, a pod.
2. its small, round seed, used as a vegetable.
3. any of various leguminous plants of the same family as the pea; also, their seed.
as like as two peas; exactly alike.
hoary pea; any plant included in the genus *Tephrosia*: so named from the down growing on the leaves: also called *goat's rue*.
pea bean; a small variety of white bean, nearly round in shape.
pea coal; a size of coal smaller than nut, or chestnut: it is the smallest regular size in common use.

pēa'ber''ry, *n.*; *pl.* **pēa'ber''rieș,** a coffee bean, in size and shape resembling a pea, which grows singly.

pēa'bīrd, *n.* the wryneck, a bird of the genus *Iynx*. [Brit. Dial.]

pēa'bod·y bīrd, a white-throated sparrow, *Zonotrichia albicollis*, native to America.

pēace (pēs), *n.* [ME. *pees*, *pais*, from OFr. *pais*; Fr. *paix*, from L. *pax*, *pacis*, peace.]
1. freedom from war or civil strife.
2. a treaty or agreement to end war.
3. freedom from public disturbance or disorder; public security; law and order.
4. freedom from disagreement or quarrels; harmony; concord.
5. an undisturbed state of mind; absence of mental conflict; serenity.
6. calm; quiet; tranquillity.
at peace; (a) free from war; living in harmony; (b) in a state of quiet or repose.
to hold (or *keep*) *one's peace*; to be silent; to keep quiet.
to keep the peace; to avoid or prevent violation of law and good order.
to make one's peace with; to effect a reconciliation with.
to make peace; (a) to end hostilities; (b) to create harmony.
Syn.—quiet, tranquillity, calm, repose, pacification, order, calmness, reconciliation, harmony, concord.

pēace, *v.i.*; peaced (pēst), *pt.*, *pp.*; peacing, *ppr.* to be or become silent or quiet: now obsolete except in the imperative.

pēace, *v.t.* to make quiet. [Obs.]

pēace'à·ble, *a.* 1. in a state of peace; free from war or commotion; quiet; peaceful.
2. having a tendency or disposition toward peace; not quarrelsome.
Syn.—peaceful, calm, gentle, mild, pacific, quiet, serene, composed, undisturbed, amiable, friendly.

pēace'à·ble·ness, *n.* the state of being peaceable; quietness.

pēace'à·bly, *adv.* in a peaceable manner.

pēace'breāk''ẽr, *n.* one who violates or disturbs public peace.

pēace'breāk''ing, *n.* the act of disturbing public peace.

pēace çon'fẽr·ence, a conference for the purpose of ending a war or for seeking ways to establish lasting peace between or among nations.

pēace es·tab'lish·ment, in military science, that part of the military organization that a country maintains and supports during peacetime so that it may be available in time of war.

pēace'fụl, *a.* 1. quiet; undisturbed; not in a state of war or commotion; as, a *peaceful* time; a *peaceful* country.
2. pacific; inclined to peace; mild; calm; as, *peaceful* words; a *peaceful* temper.
3. pertaining to or associated with a state of peace; not used in war; as, a *peaceful* measure or proposition.

pēace'fụl·ly, *adv.* in a peaceful manner.

pēace'fụl·ness, *n.* the state of being peaceful.

pēace'less, *a.* without peace; disturbed.

pēace'māk''ẽr, *n.* one who makes peace by reconciling parties that are at variance.

pēace'māk''ing, *n.* the act of making peace.

pēace'māk''ing, *a.* that makes peace.

pēace'mŏn·gẽr, *n.* a peacemaker or an advocate of peace: used in a derogatory sense.

pēace of'fẽr·ing, 1. an offering or sacrifice in thanksgiving to God.
2. an offering made to maintain or bring about peace.

pēace of'fi·cẽr, any officer of the law charged with the preservation of the public peace, as a sheriff, constable, or policeman.

pēace pīpe, a ceremonial pipe smoked by American Indians as part of a peace conference; calumet.

pēace'tīme, *n.* a period or state of affairs when a country is not at war.

pēace'tīme, *a.* pertaining to a period or condition of peace.

pēach, *n.* chlorite and chloritic rocks, generally of a bluish-green color and rather soft. [Brit. Dial.]

pēach, *v.i.* [OFr. *empechier*.] to give evidence against another; to turn informer. [Slang.]

pēach, *v.t.* to impeach; to name in an indictment. [Obs.]

pēach, *n.* [Fr. *pêche*; It. *pesca*, *persica*, from L. *persica*, *Persicum* (*malum*), the Persian apple.]
1. a small tree (*Prunus persica*) with lance-shaped leaves, pink flowers, and round, juicy, orange-yellow fruit, with a fuzzy skin and a single, rough pit.
2. its fruit.
3. the orange-yellow color of this fruit.
4. any person or thing well-liked or admired. [Slang.]

PEACH (*Prunus persica*)

Guinea or *Sierra Leone peach*; a shrub or its fruit, *Sarcocephalus esculentus*, a tropical climber of western Africa.
native peach; the quandong.

pēach, *a.* 1. of the peach.
2. orange-yellow.

pēach'blōw, *n.* 1. a delicate, purplish-pink color.
2. a porcelain glaze of this color.

pēach bōr'ẽr, 1. a moth, *Ægeria exitiosa*, or

its larva, which bores the wood of peach trees and causes great destruction.
2. a beetle, *Dicerca divaricata*, or its larva, destructive to peach trees.
pēach bran'dy, brandy distilled from fermented peach juice.
pēach çŏl'ŏr, 1. the color of a ripe peach.
2. the color of a peach blossom.
pēach'-çŏl"ŏred, *a.* having the color of a peach or peach blossom.
pēach'ēr, *n.* one who peaches. [Rare.]
pēa'chick, *n.* the chick of the peafowl.
pēach'i·ness, *n.* the quality of being peachy.
pēach'wood, *n.* 1. a wood that dyes red and peach color.
2. the wood of the peach.
pēach'wŏrt, *n.* same as *lady's-thumb.*
pēach'y, *a.*; *comp.* peachier; *superl.* peachiest, 1. peachlike, as in color or texture.
2. fine, excellent, beautiful, etc. [Slang.]
pēa'çock, *n.*; *pl.* **pēa'çocks** or **pēa'çock,** [AS. *pawa*, and *cok*, a cock.]
1. any of a number of large, related birds, especially the male with a crest and a long

PEACOCK (body, 20 in. tall)

tail which has rainbow-colored, eyelike spots and can spread out like a fan: conventionally regarded as a symbol of vanity.
2. a vain person.
pēa'çock, *v.i.* to be vain; to strut.
pēa'çock-blūe', *a.* greenish-blue.
pēa'çock blūe, a greenish blue.
pēa'çock but'tēr·fly, a butterfly of the species *Vanessa io*: so called from the eyes on its wings resembling the eyes on peacocks' feathers.
pēa'çock çōal, a coal exhibiting iridescent colors. [Brit. Dial.]
pēa'çock fish, a fish, *Crenilabrus pavo*, characterized by the brilliancy of its hues, green, yellow, and red.
pēa'çock flow'ēr, a large tropical tree *Poinciana regia*, bearing bright yellow or orange blossoms.
pēa'çock·ish, *a.* like or characteristic of a peacock; vain; inclined to strut.
pēa'çock ōre, bornite, a copper ore.
pēa'çock pheaṣ'ănt (fez'), an Asiatic pheasant similar in color to the peacock.
pēa'çock·y, *a.* 1. colored like a peacock.
2. peacockish.
pēa çōmb (kōm), a form of the comb of a fowl, exhibited in the Brahma breeds. It consists of three parallel crests, closely notched.
pēa çrab, a small commensal crab that lives with a bivalve, especially a mussel.
pēa dŏve, the ground dove, common to the southern part of the United States.
pēa'fowl, *n.*; *pl.* **pēa'fowlṣ** or **pēa'fowl,** any fowl of the genus *Pavo*; a peacock or a peahen.
pēag, pēage (pēg), *n.* [Am. Ind.] wampum.
pēa'-green', *a.* light yellowish-green.
pēa green, a light yellowish green.
pēa'grit, *n.* a limestone whose structure is not unlike a mass of split peas concreted together.
pēa'hen, *n.* the female of the peafowl.
pēa jack'et, [from D. and *pije*, coarse, thick cloth.] a short coat of heavy woolen cloth, worn by sailors.
pēak, *n.* same as *peag.*
pēak, *n.* [var. of *pike* (peak, summit).]
1. a tapering part that projects; a pointed end or top, as of a cap, roof, etc.
2. part of the hairline coming to a point on a person's forehead; a widow's peak.
3. a promontory. [Rare.]
4. the crest or summit of a hill or mountain ending in a point.
5. a mountain with such a pointed summit.
6. the highest or utmost point of anything; height; maximum; as, the *peak* of production.
7. in electricity, the maximum value of a varying quantity during a specified period.
8. in nautical usage, (a) the top rear corner of a fore-and-aft (gaff) sail; (b) the narrowed part of the hull, front or rear.
pēak, *v.t.* and *v.i.*; peaked, *pt., pp.*; peaking, *ppr.* to bring or come to a vertical position; to tilt up, as a sail yard or spar.
pēak, *v.i.* to become sickly; to fade or waste away; to droop.
pēak ärch, a pointed arch.
pēaked (pēkt *or* pē'ked), *a.* pointed; ending in a point.
pēak'ed, *a.* having sharp features; thin and drawn, as from illness.
pēak'ish, *a.* 1. pertaining to peaks.
2. pointed.
pēak'ish, *a.* having pointed features, as from illness; sickly.
pēak'y, *a.* peaked from sickness. [Dial.]
pēal, *n.* a young salmon; a salmon peal. [Brit. Dial.]
pēal, *v.i.* to appeal. [Obs.]
pēal, *n.* [shortened from ME. *apel*, seen in *appeal.*]
1. the loud ringing of a bell or set of bells.
2. the ringing of changes on a set of bells.
3. a set of matched bells; a chime; a carillon.
4. any loud, prolonged sound, as of gunfire, thunder, laughter, etc.
pēal, *v.t.* and *v.i.* to sound in a peal; to resound; to ring.
pēa mọth, a European moth, *Semasia nebritana*, the larvae of which feed upon peas, being particularly active in wet seasons.
pēan, *n.* [OFr. *panne*, a skin, a fur.] in heraldry, one of the furs borne in coat armor, the ground of which is black, with ermine spots of gold.

PEAN

pē'ăn, *n.* same as *paean.*
pēa'nut, *n.* 1. an araceous trailing plant, *Arachis hypogæa*, of the pea family, with yellow flowers and brittle pods ripening underground and containing edible seeds.
2. the pod or its seed.

PEANUT (*Arachis hypogæa*)

pēa'nut but'tēr, a paste or spread made by grinding roasted peanuts.
pēa ōre, an argillaceous oxide of iron, occurring in round grains of the size of a pea.
pēar, *n.* [AS. *peru*; D. *peer*; Dan. *paere*; Fr. *poire*; It. and Sp. *pera*, from L. *pirum*, a pear.]
1. a tree of the genus *Pyrus*, the *Pyrus communis*, growing wild in many parts of Europe and Asia, and from which the numerous cultivated varieties have originated.
2. the fruit of *Pyrus communis*, soft and juicy, round at the base and narrowing toward the stem.
wooden pear; an Australian tree, *Xylomelum pyriforme*, having fibrous pear-shaped fruit.
pēar blīght (blīt), a highly destructive bacterial disease of the pear tree, caused by *Micrococcus amylovorus*.
pēar gāuġe, a gauge, consisting in part of a pear-shaped glass, which measures the exhaustion of an air-pump receiver.
pēar hạw, a species of haw, *Cratægus tomentosa*: so called because of its pear-shaped fruit.
pēa rī'fle, a rifle of small bore, using a small, round bullet about the size of a pea.
pēarl, *n.* [ME. *perle*; D. *paarl*; Fr. *perle*; LL. *perula*, from L. *perna*, kind of shellfish, lit., a ham: so called from the shape.]
1. a silvery or bluish-white, hard, smooth, lustrous substance, of a roundish, oval, or pear-shaped form, formed around a parasitic worm or other foreign body within the shell of certain mollusks. The presence of this body sets up an irritant action, resulting in the deposition of gradually increasing layers of nacreous material, the mother-of-pearl with which the inside of the shells is lined, over the particle. Chief among the pearl-producing mollusks are the pearl oyster, *Meleagrina margaritifera*, of the Indian seas, and the unios, or fresh-water mussels, of the rivers of the United States. The finest pearls are dived for and obtained in the Bay of Bengal, at Ceylon, in the Persian Gulf, etc. Pearls are used as precious gems.
2. anything pearllike in size, shape, color, beauty, value, etc.
3. the color of pearl, a bluish-gray.
4. in heraldry, white or silver color: also called *argent*.
5. a white speck or film growing on the eye; a cataract. [Obs.]
6. in printing, a size of type, 5 point, one of the smallest.
7. mother-of-pearl.
8. a tern of light color.
9. one of the bony tubercles forming the bur on a deer's antler.
10. a medicinal preparation consisting of a liquid enclosed in a capsule of gelatin, etc.
blown pearl; a hollow glass bead blown in imitation of a pearl.
Roman pearl; an imitation pearl produced by covering Oriental alabaster with white wax and varnishing.
to cast pearls before swine; to present something of great interest or value to someone incapable of appreciating it.
virgin pearl; a pearl of fine quality that has not been pierced.
pēarl, *a.* 1. relating to, made of, or containing a pearl or pearls; as, a *pearl* ring.
2. like a pearl in shape or color.
pēarl, *v.t.*; pearled, *pt., pp.*; pearling, *ppr.* 1. to set, cover, or adorn with pearls or pearllike drops; also, to ornament with mother-of-pearl.
2. to give the shape or color of pearls to.
pēarl, *v.i.* 1. to form pearls or pearllike drops.
2. to hunt for pearl-bearing mollusks, especially oysters.
pēarl, *n., v.t.* and *v.i.* purl.
pēarl·ā'ceous, *a.* resembling mother-of-pearl or pearl; having a pearllike appearance or quality.
pēarl'ash, *n.* potassium carbonate, obtained by calcining potashes upon a reverberatory hearth.
pēarl bär'ley, kernels of barley ground in the form of pearls, used in soups.
pēarl'ber"ry, *n.* a small South American shrub, *Margyricarpus setosus*, of the rose family, cultivated for its showy fruit, which is pearllike in color and shape.
pēarl'bụsh, *n.* an ornamental shrub of China, *Exochorda grandiflora*, belonging to the rose family and characterized by lance-shaped leaves and racemes of white flowers.
pēarl diṣ·ēaṣe', a form of tuberculosis occurring in cattle.
pēarl dīv'ēr (or **fish'ēr**), one who dives for pearl-bearing mollusks.
pēarl edġe, 1. thread edging, used as a border for lace.
2. an edge of small loops forming the border of certain kinds of ribbon.
pēarl eȳe, a cataract. [Obs.]
pēarl'-eȳed (-īd), *a.* afflicted with cataract. [Obs.]
pēarl'fish, *n.* any fish, as the bleak and whitebait, having scales which yield a certain pearllike pigment used in the manufacture of artificial pearls.
pēarl'fru̇it, *n.* same as *pearlberry*.
pēarl grāy, a pale blue-gray color.
pēarl'-grāy', *a.* pale bluish-gray.
pēarl'in, pēarl'ing, *n.* [Gael. *pearluinn.*] a lace of silk or thread. [Scot.]
pēarl'i·ness, *n.* a pearly quality or state.
pēarl'ing, *n.* the shaping of grain into the form of pearls, as in making pearl barley.
pēarl'īte, *n.* 1. same as *perlite*.
2. an alloy of carbon and iron used in making steel and cast iron.
pēarl mil'let, the Egyptian millet, *Pennicillaria spicata*, a tall cereal and forage grass having pearly white seeds.
pēarl mọss, same as *carrageen*.
pēarl mọth, a moth of the genus *Margaritia*.
pēarl oys'tēr, any of the oysters that yield pearls, as *Meleagrina margaritifera*.
pēarl pow'dēr, an oxychloride of bismuth, used as a cosmetic and also as a flux for certain enamels: also called *pearl white*.

pēarl sā′gō, sago reduced to small pearllike grains.
pēarl sin′tẽr, fiorite.
pēarl spär, brown spar, a variety of dolomite.
pēarl′stōne, *n.* same as *perlite.*
pēarl whīte (hwīt), 1. a cosmetic; subnitrate of bismuth, obtained by precipitation from nitrate of bismuth.
2. a silvery pigment from the scales of a fish, used in making artificial pearls.
pēarl′wŏrt, *n.* any species of plant of the genus *Sagina.*
pēarl′y, *a.*; *comp.* pearlier; *superl.* pearliest. 1. containing or yielding pearls; adorned or covered with pearls or mother-of-pearl; abounding with pearls; as, *pearly* shells; a *pearly* shore.
2. of or like a pearl; resembling pearls; clear; pure; transparent; as, the *pearly* flood; *pearly* dew; *pearly* teeth.
pēarl′y nau′ti·lus, a sea mollusk having a spiral chambered shell with a pearly lining.
peār′māin, *n.* [ME. *permayn*; OFr. *permain.*] a variety of apple embracing several subvarieties.
peār′-shāped (-shāpt), *a.* having the form of a pear.
peār shell, a pear-shaped tropical marine gastropod shell of the genus *Pyrula,* named from the shape of its shell.
peār slug, the larva of the sawfly: so called because it does great damage to the leaves of the pear tree.
pēart, *a.* [dial. form of *pert.*]
1. pert; lively; active; brisk; in good health and spirits. [Dial.]
2. clever. [Dial.]
peaṣ′ănt (pez′), *n.* [OFr. *païsant*; Fr. *paysan,* from *pays,* country; L. *pagus,* a district or country.]
1. in Europe, a worker who farms the land; agricultural worker; farmer; rustic.
2. a person considered inferior. [Obs.]
peaṣ′ănt, *a.* rustic; rural.
peaṣ′ănt·līke, *a.* resembling peasants.
peaṣ′ănt·ly, *a.* like a peasant. [Obs.]
peaṣ′ănt prō·prī′e·tŏr, a peasant who owns land.
peaṣ′ănt·ry, *n.* 1. peasants; rustics; country people collectively.
2. rusticity; a peasant's rank or condition.
pēaṣ′çod, *n.* same as *peasecod.*
pēaṣe, *n.* 1. *pl.* **pēaṣ′eṣ, pēaṣ′en,** a pea. [Obs.]
2. plural of *pea.* [Archaic or Brit. Dial.]
pēaṣe′çod, *n.* the legume or pod of the pea.
pēaṣe mēal, meal made of peas.
pēaṣe por′ridġe, porridge made of pease meal.
pēaṣe soup, pea soup.
pēa shell, same as *peasecod.*
pēa shell′ẽr, a mechanical device for shelling peas.
pēa′shoot″ẽr, *n.* a toy consisting of a tube through which dried peas, etc. are blown as a missile from a blowgun.
pēa sōup, 1. a heavy soup of which dried peas are the chief ingredient.
2. a dense, yellowish fog. [Slang.]
pēa′stōne, *n.* same as *pisolite.*
pēaṣ′weep, *n.* the pewit or lapwing; also, the greenfinch. [Scot.]
pēat, *n.* a small, delicate person; a pet. [Obs.]
pēat, *n.* [ME. *pete*; ML. *peta,* piece of turf; prob. specialized var. of *petia,* a piece, from Celt.]
1. partly decayed, moisture-absorbing plant matter found in ancient bogs and swamps, used as a plant covering or fuel.
2. a dried block of this used as fuel.
pēat bog, a bog or marshy place in which peat has been formed or is in process of formation.
pēat moss, 1. a kind of moss found abundantly among deposits of peat, especially of the genus *Sphagnum.*
2. any plant which becomes peat.
3. a peat bog.
pēa tree, any leguminous plant of the genus *Caragana.*
pēat reek, the smoke produced in the burning of peat.
peat reek flavor; the flavor imparted to whisky when peat is used as a fuel in distilling it. [Scot.]
pēat′y, *a.*; *comp.* peatier; *superl.* peatiest, composed of peat; resembling peat; having the odor of peat.
peau-d′ō-räṅge′ (pō-dō-räṅzh′), *a.* [Fr., orange skin.] having a surface similar in roughness to the skin of an orange: a term used in ceramics.
pēa′vey, *n.*; *pl.* **pēa′veyṣ,** [after its inventor, Joseph *Peavy.*] a lumberman's cant hook, having a spike fixed on the end of its lever.
pēa′vy, *n.*; *pl.* **pēa′vieṣ,** a peavey.
pēa vīne, 1. the common pea plant.
2. one of several leguminous plants, as the hog peanut, *Amphicarpæa monoica,* or any one of various species of vetch, as *Vicia americana.*
pēa wee′vil, an insect, *Bruchus pisi,* the larvae of which live in and feed on the growing pea.
pē′bȧ, *n.* [S. Am.] a small armadillo, *Dasypus peba,* found from Texas to South America.
peb′ble (-bl), *n.* [AS. *papol-stān,* pebblestone.]
1. a small stone rounded and made smooth, as by the action of water.

I bubble into eddying bays,
I babble on the *pebbles.*—Tennyson.

2. transparent and colorless rock crystal, as quartz, or a lens made from it.
3. a surface grain of pebbly appearance, artificially produced on leather, paper, etc.
Scotch pebble; one of a number of varieties of quartz, as agate, cairngorm, etc., regarded in Scotland as a stone of value.
peb′ble, *v.t.*; pebbled (-bld), *pt., pp.*; pebbling, *ppr.* to impart a grain to, as leather, so as to make its surface rough and pebbly.
peb′ble çrys′tăl, a crystal in the form of a pebble, found in a natural state.
peb′bled (-bld), *a.* 1. abounding with pebbles.
2. having a pebble surface or grain; as, *pebbled* leather.
peb′ble dash′ing, in plastering, mortar containing a mixture of pebbles.
peb′ble leath′ẽr (leth′), leather that has been pebbled.
peb′ble pāv′ing, paving laid with water-worn stones smaller than cobblestones.
peb′ble pow′dẽr, a slow-burning gunpowder pressed into pebble-sized grains.
peb′ble·stōne, *n.* a pebble; also, pebbles collectively.
peb′ble·wãre, *n.* in ceramics, a ware in which colored clays are mixed in the body of the paste; a kind of Wedgwood ware.
peb′bly, *a.*; *comp.* pebblier; *superl.* pebbliest. 1. full of pebbles; abounding with small, roundish stones.
2. having a pebble surface or grain.
pé·brinc′ (pā-brēn′), *n.* [Fr.] a bacterial disease of the silkworm.
pē·çan′ (*or* -kon′), *n.* [Sp. *pacana.*]
1. a species of hickory, *Carya olivæformis,* growing in parts of the United States and bearing the pecan nut of commerce.
2. the oval nut with a thin, smooth shell growing on this tree.

PECAN (*Carya olivæformis*)

peç′ȧ·ry, *n.* same as *peccary.*
peç·çȧ·bil′i·ty, *n.* the state of being peccable, or capable of sin.
peç′çȧ·ble, *a.* [L. *peccabilis*; *peccare,* to sin.] liable to or capable of sin.
peç·çȧ·dil′lō, *n.*; *pl.* **peç·çȧ·dil′lōeṣ, peç·çȧ·dil′lōṣ,** [Sp., dim. from *pecado*; L. *peccatum,* a sin; *peccare,* to sin.] a slight trespass or offense; a petty fault; a minor sin.
peç′căn·cy, *n.* 1. the state or quality of being peccant; sinfulness.
2. *pl.* **peç′căn·cieṣ,** offense; sin; trangression.
peç′cănt, *a.* [L. *peccans, peccantis,* ppr. of *peccare,* to sin.]
1. sinful; sinning; guilty of sin or transgression; criminal; as, *peccant* angels.
2. causing or signifying disease; morbid; not healthy; as, *peccant* humors.
3. breaking or disregarding a rule or practice; faulty; wrong; defective.
peç′cănt, *n.* an offender.
peç′cănt·ly, *adv.* in a peccant manner; sinfully.
peç′çȧ·ry, *n.*; *pl.* **peç′çȧ·rieṣ** or **peç′çȧ·ry,** [South Am.] a mammal belonging to the genus *Dicotyles* and related to the hog. There are two species, one, *Dicotyles torquatus,* inhabiting the eastern side of South America, and the other, *Dicotyles labiatus,* inhabiting Paraguay.

COLLARED PECCARY (*Dicotyles torquatus*)

peç·çā′vī, [L.] I have sinned.
peç·çā′vī, *n.*; *pl.* **peç·çā′vīṣ,** a confession of sin and guilt.
peç′çō, *n.* same as *pekoe.*
pē′cīte, *n.* a mixture of wax and plaster used as an insulating material in electrical work.
peck, *n.* [ME. *pekke*; Anglo-Fr. *pek,* chiefly of oats for horses.]
1. the fourth part of a bushel; a dry measure of eight quarts; as, a *peck* of wheat.
2. any container with a capacity of one peck.
3. a great deal; a large number or quantity, as, to be in a peck of trouble. [Colloq.]

A *peck* of uncertainties and doubts.
—Milton.

peck, *v.t.*; pecked (pekt), *pt., pp.*; pecking, *ppr.* [a form of *pick.*]
1. to strike with a pointed object, as with a beak.
2. to make by striking with the beak or a pointed instrument; as, to *peck* a hole.
3. to pick up with the beak; as, the chickens *pecked* the grains of corn.
peck, *v.i.* to use a beak or anything pointed in striking.
to peck at; (a) to make a pecking motion at; (b) [Colloq.] to eat very little of; to eat carefully or sparingly; (c) [Colloq.] to criticize or find fault with constantly.
peck, *n.* 1. a stroke made with a pointed object, as the beak.
2. a mark made by pecking.
3. a quick, casual kiss. [Colloq.]
peck′ẽr, *n.* 1. one who or that which pecks; specifically, a bird that pecks holes in trees; a woodpecker.
2. an instrument for pecking or making holes; a pick; a pickax.
3. courage; spirit. [Brit. Slang.]
peck′ish, *a.* inclined to eat; somewhat hungry. [Brit. Colloq.]
peç′kled (-kld), *a.* speckled. [Obs.]
Peck·sniff′i·ăn, *a.* [after *Pecksniff,* unctuous hypocrite in Dickens' *Martin Chuzzlewit.*] hypocritical; insincere; falsely moralistic.
Pē·çop′te·ris, *n.* [Gr. *pekein,* to comb, and *pteris,* a fern.] a genus of fossil ferns, named from the comblike arrangement of the leaflets.
pē·çop′tẽr·oid, *a.* of or resembling the *Pecopteris.*
Peç′ō·rȧ, *n.pl.* [L. *pecus,* a herd.] a large division of ruminating animals; the *Artiodactyla.*
Pe′çōs Bill, in American legend, the original cowboy, who performed such superhuman feats as digging the Rio Grande.
peç′tāse, *n.* [from *pectin* and *-ase.*] an enzyme found in fruits that is capable of converting pectin into pectic acid.
peç′tāte, *n.* in chemistry, a salt or ester of pectic acid.
pec′ten, *n.* [L. *pecten,* a comb, a kind of shellfish, from *pectere,* to comb; root *pek,* also in Gr. *pekein,* to comb.]
1. a comblike tissue on the eyes of birds, fishes, and reptiles, pleated with parallel folds resembling the teeth of a comb.
2. the pubic bone.
3. [P-] in zoology, a genus of marine bivalves belonging to the family *Pectinidæ,* or scallops.
4. any species of the genus *Pecten* or other related genera; a scallop.

PECTEN OR SCALLOP

pec′tic, *a.* [Gr. *pēktikos*, congealing, from *pēgnynai*, to fix.] pertaining to, characteristic of, or derived from pectin.
pectic acid; an acid, $C_{17}H_{24}O_{16}$, found in many vegetables: so called from its tendency to form a jelly when subjected to the action of a ferment.

pec′tin, *n.* a water soluble carbohydrate, a mixed polysaccharide obtained from certain ripe fruits, which yields a gel that is the basis of fruit jellies.

pec′tin·ăl, *a.* [from *pecten*.] pertaining to or resembling a comb.

pec′tin·ăl, *n.* a fish having bones resembling the teeth of a comb.

pec′tin·āte, pec′tin·ā·ted, *a.* [from *pecten*.] having toothlike projections like those on a comb.
pectinate claw; in zoology, a claw having a serrate edge, found in some birds, and supposed to be used in cleaning the feathers.
pectinate muscles; the muscular bands in the heart: so called from their resemblance to the teeth of a comb.

pec′tin·āte·ly, *adv.* in a pectinate manner.

pec·tin·ā′tion, *n.* 1. the state of being pectinated; anything pectinated.
2. the act of combing.
3. a structure resembling the toothing of a comb.

pec·tin′ē·ăl, *a.* 1. in anatomy, of or relating to the pecten.
2. of or pertaining to the pubic bone.

pec·tin′i·branch, *n.* [L. *pecten*, comb, and *branchiæ*, gills.] in zoology, any of the *Pectinibranchiata*.

pec·tin′i·branch, *a.* pertaining to or characteristic of a pectinibranch.

Pec″ti·ni·bran″chi·ā′tȧ, *n.pl.* in zoology, (a) the sixth of Cuvier's orders of *Gasteropoda* (b) an order including the *Ianthina*, the purple shells (*Murex*), the common shore shell (*Littorina*), whelk (*Buccinum*), cowries (*Cypræa*), etc.

pec″ti·ni·bran′chi·āte, *a.* having pectinate gills.

pec′tin·id, *n.* a pecten.

pec·tin′i·form, *a.* same as *pectinate*.

pic′tin·īte, *n.* a fossil pecten or scallop.

pec′tin·oid, *a.* of, pertaining to, or resembling the pectens.

pec′tīze, *v.i.* [Gr. *pēktos*, fixed.] to congeal; to thicken into a jelly or gelatinous mass.

pec′tō·līte, *n.* [L. *pecten*, a comb, and Gr. *lithos*, a stone.] a mineral consisting of a silicate of lime and soda. It is a tough, grayish or whitish mineral occurring in trap rocks and in aggregated crystals: also called *soda table spar*, *stellite*, and *Ratholite*.

pec′tō·rȧ, *n.* pl. of *pectus*.

pec′tō·răl, *a.* [L. *pectoralis*, from *pectus*, *pectoris*, breast.]
1. of or located in or on the breast or chest.
2. of or used in treating diseases of the chest or lungs.
3. worn on the chest or breast.
4. influenced by or resulting from personal feelings; subjective.
pectoral arch or *girdle*; in anatomy and zoology, the bony or cartilaginous structure to which the forelimbs (or arms) of a vertebrate are attached.
pectoral cross; a cross worn on the breast by bishops, abbots, and canons of the Roman Catholic and Greek churches.
pectoral fins or *pectorals*; the pair of fins just behind the head of a fish, corresponding to the forelimbs of a vertebrate.
pectoral rail; the land rail of Australia.
pectoral sandpiper; a variety of sandpiper with a heavily streaked breast, found in the Arctic.
pectoral theology; theology supposed to have its origin in the heart, and thus laying great stress on religious experiences and convictions as a foundation of spiritual truths.

pec′tō·răl, *n.* 1. a covering or armor for the breast.
2. a pectoral medicine.
3. a pectoral fin or muscle.
4. a sacerdotal habit or vestment worn in ancient times by the Jewish high priest; a breastplate.
5. a breastplate of gold, silver, or jeweled embroidery, or a pectoral cross, sometimes worn by dignitaries of the Greek and Roman Catholic churches, while celebrating Mass.

pec′tō·răl·ly, *adv.* in a manner regarding or pertaining to the breast.

pec″tō·ri·lō′qui·ăl, *a.* pertaining to or of the nature of pectoriloquy.

pec·tō·ril′ō·quism, *n.* pectoriloquy.

pec·tō·ril′ō·quous (-kwus), *a.* pectoriloquial.

pec·tō·ril′ō·quy, *n.* [L. *pectus*, *pectoris*, the breast, and *loqui*, to speak.] in medicine, a phase of disease in which the patient's voice, distinctly articulated, seems to proceed from the point of the chest on which the ear or a stethoscope is placed. It is caused by the resounding of the voice in cavities in the lungs.

pec′tōse, *n.* [from Gr. *pēktos*, congealed, from root of *pēgnynai*, to fix.] in chemistry, a substance contained in the pulp of fleshy, unripe fruit: the ripening process converts it into pectin.

pec·tō′sic, *a.* of or pertaining to pectose.
pectosic acid; an acid believed to be the chief constituent of pectin.

Pec·tos′trȧ·cȧ, *n.pl.* same as *Cirripedia*.

pec′tous, *a.* same as *pectosic*.

pec′tus, *n.*; *pl.* **pec′tō·rȧ**, [L.] the breast; especially, the breast of a bird.

pec′ul, *n.* same as *picul*.

pec′ū·lāte, *v.i.*; peculated, *pt.*, *pp.*; peculating, *ppr.* [L. *peculatus*, pp. of *peculari*, from *peculium*, private property, from *pecus*, cattle.] to steal or misuse (money or property entrusted to one's care, especially public funds); to embezzle.

pec·ū·lā′tion, *n.* the act of peculating; embezzlement.

pec′ū·lā·tŏr, *n.* [L.] one who peculates; an embezzler.

pē·cūl′iăr (-yẽr), *a.* [L. *peculiaris*, from *peculium*, one's own property, from *pecus*, cattle.]
1. distinctive; exclusive; characteristic; belonging to one person, nation, system, etc. and to no others.
2. particular; unique; special; as, a *peculiar* talent for distorting the truth.
3. out of the ordinary; queer; odd; strange.
peculiar people; (a) in the Bible, the Jews, considered as Jehovah's own and chosen people and so separated from other nations: Deut. xxvi. 18; (b) the followers of any of several Christian creeds, especially, a religious denomination founded during the first half of the nineteenth century at Plumstead, England: they believe in faith healing: also called *Plumstead Peculiars*.

pē·cūl′iăr, *n.* 1. that which belongs to a person in exclusion of others, as a privilege.
2. a particular parish or church under a jurisdiction other than that of the diocese in which it is located.
Court of Peculiars; in England, a branch of the Court of Arches. It has jurisdiction over all the parishes dispersed through the province of Canterbury, in the midst of other dioceses, which are exempt from the ordinary jurisdiction, and subject to the metropolitan only.

pē·cū·li·ar′i·ty, *n.* 1. the state or condition of being peculiar.
2. *pl.* **pē·cū·li·ar′i·ties**, something peculiar to a person or thing; that which belongs to or is found in one person or thing, and in no other; as, a *peculiarity* of style or manner of thinking; *peculiarity* in dress.
3. exclusive right. [Obs.]

pē·cūl′iăr·īze, *v.t.* to appropriate; to make peculiar. [Obs.]

pē·cūl′iăr·ly, *adv.* in a peculiar manner; strangely; particularly.

pē·cūl′iăr·ness, *n.* peculiarity.

pē·cū′li·um, *n.* [L.] 1. in Roman law, the property which a son, wife, or slave might hold as his own.
2. a private property or fund.

pē·cū′ni·ăl, *a.* pecuniary. [Obs.]

pē·cū′ni·ā·ri·ly, *adv.* in a pecuniary manner.

pē·cū′ni·ā·ry, *a.* [Fr. *pécuniaire*; It. *pecuniario*; L. *pecuniarius*, from *pecunia*, money, from *pecus*, cattle.]
1. relating to money; as, *pecuniary* affairs.
2. involving a money penalty, or fine; as, a *pecuniary* offense.

pē·cū′ni·ous, *a.* having money; rich.

ped, *n.* 1. a small packsaddle. [Brit. Dial.]
2. a basket; a hamper. [Brit. Dial.]

ped-, same as *pedo-* or *pedi-*.

-ped, same as *-pede*.

ped′āge, *n.* [OFr. *paage*; Fr. *péage*; It. *pedaggio*, from LL. *pedaticum*, from L. *pes*, *pedis*, a foot.] money given for passing through a country; a toll paid by travelers.

ped′ȧ·gog, *n.* a pedagogue.

ped·ȧ·gog′ic, *n.* same as *pedagogy*.

ped·ȧ·gog′ic, ped·ȧ·gog′ic·ăl, *a.* suiting, resembling, or pertaining to teachers or to education.

ped·ȧ·gog′ic·ăl·ly, *adv.* 1. in a pedagogic manner.
2. by means of or according to pedagogy.

ped·ȧ·gog′ics, *n.* pedagogy; the science and art of teaching.

ped′ȧ·gog·ism, *n.* 1. the characteristics, beliefs, or manners of a pedagogue, especially of a pedantic one; pedagogic quality.
2. the state of being a pedagogue.

ped′ȧ·gogue (-gog), *n.* [Gr. *paidagōgos*; *pais*, *paidos*, a child, and *agein*, to lead.]
1. a teacher; especially, a pedantic and dogmatic teacher.
2. among the ancient Greeks and Romans, a slave who attended the children of his master and conducted them to school, often acting also as a tutor.

ped′ȧ·gogue, *v.t.* to teach as a pedagogue.

ped′ȧ·gogu·ism (-gog-izm), *n.* pedagogism.

ped′ȧ·gō·gy, *n.* 1. the profession or function of a teacher; teaching.
2. the art or science of teaching; especially, instruction in teaching methods.

ped′ăl (*or for sense* 1, pē′dăl), *a.* [L. *pedalis*, from *pes*, *pedis*, a foot.]
1. pertaining to a foot or feet or to a footlike appendage, as of a gastropod.
2. pertaining to or operated by a pedal or pedals.
3. pertaining to or constituting a pedal curve or pedal surface; as, a *pedal* function.
pedal curve or *surface*; a curve or surface forming the locus of the feet of perpendicular lines drawn from a given point to the plane tangents of another curve or surface.
pedal note; (a) a holding note, generally the dominant, used to harmonize a passage in a fugue or other contrapuntal composition; (b) any note sounded by means of a pedal key.
pedal organ; that part of a large organ which is played by foot keys.
pedal pipe; a pipe in a pedal organ.

ped′ăl, *n.* 1. a lever operated by the foot, used in transmitting motion, as in a bicycle or sewing machine, or in changing the tone or volume of a musical instrument, as an organ or harp.
2. a fixed or stationary bass; a pedal bass or pedal point, over which various harmonies or contrapuntal devices are constructed, chiefly in fugues: also called *organ point*.
3. a curve or surface that is pedal or to which another is pedal.

ped′ăl, *v.t.* and *v.i.*; pedaled *or* pedalled, *pt.*, *pp.*; pedaling *or* pedalling, *ppr.* to move or operate by a pedal or pedals; to use the pedals (of).

ped′ăl bass, same as *pedal*, n. 2.

pē·dal′fẽr, *n.* [Gr. *ped*on, ground, and L. *al*umen, aluminum, and *fer*rum, iron.] soil containing alumina and iron oxide and lacking a layer of calcium and magnesium carbonates: usually found in areas having an annual rainfall of 25 inches or more.

Pē·dā·li·ā′cē·ae, *n.pl.* [Gr. *pēdalion*, rudder.] a family of soft herbs with a heavy smell, undivided lobed leaves, and large flowers, solitary or clustered. It is found in the tropics.

pē·dā·li·ā′ceous, *a.* pertaining to the *Pedaliaceæ*.

pē·dā′li·ăn, *a.* [L. *pedalis*, from *pes*, *pedis*, a foot.] pertaining to a foot or feet. [Rare.]

pē·dal′i·ty, *n.* [L. *pedalis*, from *pes*, *pedis*, foot.] measurement by paces. [Rare.]

Pē·dā′li·um, *n.* [Gr. *pēdalion*, rudder.] the typical genus of *Pedaliaceæ*, of which the only known species is *Pedalium murex*, found in India, especially near the sea.

ped′ăl·ō, *n.*; *pl.* **ped′ăl·ōs**, [arbitrary extension of *pedal*.] a small watercraft for one or two persons, on pontoons, with a paddle wheel propelled by foot pedals: also *pedallo*, *pedal boat*.

ped′ăl point, same as *pedal*, n. 2.

ped′ăl push′ẽrs, knee-length trousers for women or girls, used originally for bicycle riding.

ped′ănt, *n.* [Fr. *pédant*, a pedant, a schoolmaster; It. and Sp. *pedante*, contr. for *pedagogante*, from L. *pædagogans*, *pædagogantic*, ppr. of *pædagogare*, to educate.]
1. a schoolmaster; a pedagogue. [Obs.]
2. a person who overrates the importance of minor or trivial points of learning, displaying a scholarship lacking in judgment or sense of proportion.
3. a narrow-minded teacher who insists on exact adherence to a set of arbitrary rules.

pē·dan′tic, *a.* relating to pedants or pedantry;

making a display of learning; characterized by pedantry.
pē·dan′tiç·ăl, *a.* pedantic. [Rare.]
pē·dan′tiç·ăl·ly, *adv.* in a pedantic manner.
pē·dan′tiç·ly, *adv.* pedantically. [Rare.]
ped′ănt·ișm, *n.* pedantry.
ped′ănt·ize, *v.i.* to play the pedant.
ped·ăn·toç′rà·cy, *n.* [*pedant*, and Gr. *kratein*, to rule.] the rule or sway of a pedant or pedants; government by pedants.
ped′ănt·ry, *n.* [Fr. *pédanterie*.]
1. the qualities, characteristics, practices, beliefs, etc. of a pedant; display of narrow-minded and trivial scholarship or arbitrary adherence to rules and forms.
2. *pl.* **ped′ănt·rieș**, a pedantic act or expression.
ped′ănt·y, *n.* pedants collectively. [Obs.]
pē·dā′ri·ăn, *n.* [L. *pedarius*, from *pes*, *pedis*, foot.] in the Roman senate, one who was not a senator but was entitled to a seat by virtue of the office he held. He was not authorized to vote, but expressed his preference by walking over to the party with whose position he concurred.
Pē·dā′tȧ, *n.pl.* a family of holothurians characterized by having ambulacral feet.
ped′āte, *a.* [L. *pedatus*, from *pes*, *pedis*, the foot.]
1. in botany, in a fanlike arrangement with subdivided leaves, as the leaves of *Arum*, *Dracunculus*, and *Helleborus fœtidus*.
2. like or serving as a foot.
3. having feet.

PEDATE LEAF

ped′āte·ly, *adv.* in a pedate manner.
pē·da′ti- (*or* -dā′), a combining form meaning *pedately*, as in *pedatifid*.
pē·dat′i·fid, *a.* [L. *pes*, *pedis*, foot, and *findere*, to divide.] pedate, with the lobes divided at least halfway to the base.
pē·dat′i·nẽrved, *a.* having the ribs (of a leaf) pedate.
pē·dat″i·pär′tīte, *a.* pedate, with the lobes divided almost to the base.
pē·dat′i·seçt, *a.* same as *pedatipartite*.
ped′dẽr, ped′dăr, *n.* a peddler; a hawker. [Scot. and Brit. Dial.]
ped′dle, *v.i.*; peddled, *pt.*, *pp.*; peddling, *ppr.* [ME. *ped*, basket.]
1. to be busy about trifles; to piddle.
2. to travel from place to place selling small articles.
ped′dle, *v.t.* 1. to carry from place to place and offer for sale.
2. to deal in or dispense, especially in small amounts, as narcotics, gossip, etc.
ped′dlẽr, *n.* one who peddles: also spelled *pedlar*.
ped′dlẽr·ess, *n.* a woman peddler.
ped′dlẽr·y, *n.* 1. small wares sold by peddlers.
2. the business or occupation of a peddler.
3. trifling; trickery. [Obs.]
ped′dling, *a.* trifling; unimportant; petty.
-pēde, [from L. *pes*, *pedis*, a foot.] a combining form meaning *foot* or *feet*, as in centi*pede*: also *-ped*.
ped′ẽr·ast, *n.* [Gr. *paiderastēs*, from *pais*, *paidos*, a boy, and *erōs*, love.] a man who practices pederasty.
ped·ẽr·as′tiç, *a.* pertaining to pederasty.
ped′ẽr·as·ty, *n.* a form of sodomy between men, especially as practiced by a man with a boy: also spelled *paederasty*.
ped·ē·rē′rō, *n.* [Sp. *pedrero*, from *piedra*, a stone; L. *petra*; Gr. *petros*: so named from the use of stones in the charge, before the invention of iron balls.] a swivel gun: sometimes written *paterero*.
pē′dēș, *n.* pl. of *pes*.
pē·dē′sis, *n.* [Gr. *pēdēsis*, from *pēdān*, to leap.] the Brownian movement.
ped′es·tăl, *n.* [Sp. *pedestal*, from L. *pes*, *pedis*, the foot, and OSp. *estalo*, It. *stallo*, a place, from O.H.G. *stal* (AS. *stæl*), a place, a station.]
1. a base or bottom support, as for a lamp, column, statue, or vase.
2. any foundation, base, support, etc.
3. in mechanics, the standards of a pillow block, holding the brasses in which the shaft turns.
4. a casting fastened to the truck frame of a railway car, having vertical guides for the journal boxes of the axles, which rise and fall in the pedestals as the springs collapse and expand.
5. an iron socket on a bridge pier to resist the strain of the brace at the end of a truss.
to put (or *set*) *on a pedestal*; to regard with great or excessive admiration; to idolize.
ped′es·tăl, *v.t.*; pedestaled *or* pedestalled, *pt.*, *pp.*; pedestaling *or* pedestalling, *ppr.* to place on a pedestal; to support as a pedestal.
ped′es·tăl çoil, a coil or group of straight steam pipes, used as a radiator.
pē·des′tri·ăl, *a.* [L. *pedester*.] pertaining to the foot; serving as a foot; pedestrian. [Obs.]
pē·des′tri·ăl·ly, *adv.* in a pedestrial manner; on foot. [Obs.]
pē·des′tri·ăn, *a.* [L. *pedester*, from *pes*, *pedis*, the foot.]
1. going on foot; walking; also, performed on foot; as, a *pedestrian* journey.
2. lacking interest or imagination; prosaic; dull, as a literary style, etc.
pē·des′tri·ăn, *n.* one who journeys on foot.
pē·des′tri·ăn·ișm, *n.* 1. walking; the practice of walking, as for exercise.
2. a pedestrian quality, literary style, etc.
pē·des′tri·ăn·īze, *v.i.* to journey on foot.
pē·des′tri·ous, *a.* going on foot. [Obs.]
ped·ē·ten′tous, *a.* [L. *pes*, *pedis*, foot, and *tendere*, to stretch.] stepping cautiously; moving forward step by step; advancing tentatively. [Rare.]
pē·det′iç, *a.* relating to pedesis.
ped′i-, [from L. *pes*, *pedis*, a foot.] a combining form meaning *foot* or *feet*, as in *pedicure*: also, before a vowel, *ped-*.
pē′di·ăl, *a.* pertaining to a foot or to the feet.
pē·di·at′riç (*or* ped-i-), *a.* pertaining to pediatrics.
pē″di·ȧ·tri′ciăn, *n.* a specialist in pediatrics.
pē·di·at′riçs, *n.pl.* [*construed as sing.*] [Gr. *pais*, *paidos*, child, and *iatrikos*, relating to a physician.] the branch of medicine dealing with the care of children and the treatment of their diseases.
pē·di·at′rist, *n.* a pediatrician.
ped′i·at·ry, *n.* same as *pediatrics*.
ped′i·cab, *n.* [*pedi-*, and *cab*.] a three-wheeled passenger vehicle, especially in southeastern Asia, which the driver propels by pedaling like a bicycle.
ped′i·cel, *n.* [LL. *pedicellus*, dim. of L. *pediculus*, dim. of *pes*, *pedis*, foot.]
1. in botany, the stalk that supports one flower only, when there are several on a peduncle. Any short and small footstalk, although it does not stand upon another footstalk, is also called a pedicel.
2. in zoology, a footstalk or stem by which certain animals of the lower orders are attached, as zoophytes, etc.
3. in anatomy, a pedicle.

a, PEDUNCLE *bb*, PEDICELS

ped·i·cel′lăr, *a.* of or like a pedicel.
ped″i·cel·lā′ri·ȧ, *n.*; *pl.* **ped″i·cel·lā′ri·ae**, [LL. *pedicellus*, pedicel.] an external organ resembling a forceps, found in starfishes and sea urchins.
ped′i·cel·lāte, *a.* having a pedicel.
ped″i·cel·lī′nȧ, *n.* a minute marine mollusk, found attached by a pedicel to algae, zoophytes, and shells.
ped′i·cle, *n.* 1. in anatomy, the process which connects the lamina of a vertebra with the centrum.
2. a pedicel.
pē·diç′ū·lăr, *a.* 1. of lice.
2. infested with lice; lousy.
Pē·diç·ū·lā′ris, *n.* a genus of perennial herbs, commonly known as *lousewort*.
pē·diç′ū·lāte, *a.* [LL. *pediculatus*.]
1. supported by a pedicel, as a flower.
2. in zoology, relating to the *Pediculati*.
pē·diç′ū·lāte, *n.* a fish of the family *Pediculati*.
Pē·diç·ū·lā′tī, *n.pl.* a family of fishes having pectoral fins attached to an armlike base, including the angler, batfish, etc.
pē·diç·ū·lā′tion, *n.* same as *pediculosis*.
ped′i·çūle, *n.* a pedicel; a peduncle.
Pē·diç·ū·lī′nȧ, *n.pl.* [L. *pediculus*, louse.] a suborder of parasitic insects, including the lice proper.
pē·diç·ū·lō′sis, *n.* infestation with lice.
pē·diç′ū·lous, *a.* pertaining to or caused by lice; lousy.
pē·diç′ū·lus, *n.*; *pl.* **pē·diç′ū·lī**, [L.] 1. a louse.
2. [P–] a genus of true lice, including those that infest man.
ped′i·cūre, *n.* [L. *pes*, *pedis*, foot, and *cura*, care.]
1. a chiropodist.
2. chiropody.
3. [by analogy with *manicure*.] popularly, a cleaning, trimming, and polishing of the toenails.
ped′i·form, *a.* [L. *pes*, *pedis*, foot, and *forma*, form.] in the shape of a foot.
pē·diġ′ẽr·ous, *a.* [L. *pes*, *pedis*, foot, and *gerere*, to carry.] having feet.
ped′i·gree, *n.* [ME. *pedegru*, *pe de gre*, etc.; OFr. *pie de grue*, lit., crane's foot, from L. *pes*, foot and *grus*, a crane: so called from the lines in the genealogical tree.]
1. a list of ancestors; record of ancestry; family tree.
2. descent; lineage; ancestry.
3. a recorded or known line of descent, especially of a pure-bred animal.
ped′i·greed, *a.* having a known or recorded pedigree; as, a *pedigreed* dog.
ped·i·lā′vi·um, *n.* [L. *pes*, *pedis*, foot, and *lavare*, to wash.] the ceremony of washing the feet.
ped·i·lū′vi·um, *n.* [LL., from L. *pes*, *pedis*, foot, and *luere*, to wash.] a footbath; the bathing of the feet.
Pē·dim′ȧ·nȧ, *n.pl.* [L. *pes*, *pedis*, foot, and *manus*, hand.] a family of marsupials having hind feet shaped like hands, including the lemurs and opossums.
ped′i·māne, *n.* one of the *Pedimana*.
pē·dim′ȧ·nous, *a.* having feet shaped like hands, as monkeys.
ped′i·ment, *n.* [altered from earlier *periment* (alteration of *pyramid*) by association with L. *pes*, *pedis*, the foot.] in architecture, the low triangular mass resembling a gable, at the end of buildings in the Greek style, and especially over porticos surrounded with a cornice, and often ornamented with sculptures. The term is also applied to a similar triangular finishing over doors and windows. In the Roman style the same name is given to corresponding parts, though not triangular in their form, but circular, elliptical, or interrupted. In the architecture of the Middle Ages, small gables and triangular decorations over openings, niches, etc. are called pediments. These often have the angle at the apex more acute than the corresponding decoration of classic architecture.

PEDIMENT

ped·i·men′tăl, *a.* 1. of, or having the nature of, a pediment.
2. having the shape of a pediment.
ped′i·ment·ed, *a.* having a pediment.
ped′i·palp, *n.* [L. *pes*, *pedis*, a foot, and *palpare*, to feel.]
1. one of the *Pedipalpi*.
2. the pedipalpate feeler of an arachnid.
ped·i·pal′pāte, *a.* 1. pertaining to the *Pedipalpi*; having maxillary palpi.
2. having a pedipalp.
Ped·i·pal′pī, *n.pl.* [L. *pes*, *pedis*, foot, and *palpare*, to feel.] an order of pulmonate arachnids having the feelers in the form of pincers, including the whip scorpions and, in some classifications, the true scorpions. They have the abdomen distinctly segmented, but not separated from the cephalothorax by a well-marked constriction.
ped·i·pal′pous, *a.* same as *pedipalpate*.
ped·i·pal′pus, *n.*; *pl.* **ped·i·pal′pī**, one of a pair of palpi, or feelers, that are mouth appendages of arachnids: they are leglike in spiders and pincerlike in scorpions; a pedipalp.
ped′lăr, ped′lẽr, *n.* same as *peddler*.
pē′dō-, [from Gr. *pais*, *paidos*, a child.] a combining form meaning *child*, *children*, *offspring*, as in *pedo*baptism: also spelled *paedo-*: also, before a vowel, *ped-*.
pē·dō·bap′tișm, *n.* [*pedo-* and *baptism*.] the baptism of infants: also spelled *paedobaptism*.
pē·dō·bap′tist, *n.* one who believes in and practices infant baptism: written also *paedobaptist*.
pē·dō·don′ti·ȧ (-shi-ȧ), *n.* [*ped-*, and *-odont*, and *-ia*.] the branch of dentistry concerned with the care of children's teeth.
pē·dō·ġen′e·sis, *n.* reproduction by larvae, as of certain gallflies: also spelled *paedogenesis*.
pē″dō·ġē·net′iç, *a.* pertaining to or produced by pedogenesis: also spelled *paedogenetic*.

ped′ō·graph, *n.* [from Gr. *pedon*, the ground, and *-graph*.] an instrument which records the topography of the ground covered by a person carrying it while walking.

pē·dol′ō·gy, *n.* [Gr. *pedon*, ground, earth, and *logos*, a science.] the study of soils.

pē·dol′ō·gy, *n.* [*pedo-* and *-logy*.] the systematic study of the behavior and development of children.

ped′ō·man·cy, *n.* [L. *pes*, *pedis*, foot, and Gr. *manteia*, divination.] divination by the study of the lines on the soles of the feet.

pē·dom′ē·tēr, *n.* [Fr. *pédomètre*, from L. *pes*, *pedis*, the foot, and Gr. *metron*, measure.] an instrument which measures approximately distance covered in walking by recording the number of steps taken.

ped·ō·met′riç, ped·ō·met′riç·ăl, *a.* pertaining to or measured by a pedometer.

ped·ō·mō′tive, *a.* [L. *pes*, *pedis*, foot, and *motivus*, motive.] worked or driven by means of a treadle or pedal; moved by the foot.

pē·dot′rō·phy, *n.* [Gr. *pais*, *paidos*, child, and *trephein*, to nourish.] that branch of hygiene which treats of the nourishment and care of children.

ped′re·găl, *n.* [Sp., from *piedra*; L. *petrus*, stone.] in Mexico and the southwestern United States, a tract of land covered with stones or solidified lava.

pē′drō, *n.* [Sp., from L. *Petrus*, Peter.] in card games, a variety of seven-up in which the five of trumps counts five; also, the five of trumps in the game.

pē′dum, *n.*; *pl.* **pē′dȧ**, [L., a shepherd's crook, from *pes*, *pedis*, foot.] a pastoral staff; a crosier.

pē·duñ′çle, *n.* [Mod.L. *pedunculus*, dim. of L. *pes*, *pedis*, foot.]
1. a flower stalk.
2. in anatomy, a stalklike bundle of nerve fibers connecting various parts of the brain.
3. in zoology, a slender, stalklike part, as between the abdomen and middle section of an insect; pedicel.

pē·duñ′çled (-kld), *a.* having a peduncle or peduncles.

pē·duñ′çū·lăr, *a.* pertaining to or resembling a peduncle; as, a *peduncular* tendril.

Pē·duñ·çū·lā′tȧ, *n.pl.* in zoology, an order of cirripeds having peduncles.

pē·duñ′çū·lāte, pē·duñ′çū·lā·ted, *a.* having a peduncle; growing on a peduncle; as, a *pedunculate* flower.

pee, *v.i.* to look with one eye. [Obs.]

pee, *n.* the tip of the fluke of an anchor; the peak.

peek, *v.i.* [Early Mod. Eng. phonetic sp., from ME. *piken*, prob. var. of *kiken*, to peer, influenced by *peep*, etc.] to glance or peer quickly and furtively, especially through an opening or from behind something.

peek, *n.* a glance or look; a peep.

peek′ȧ·bo̤o̤, *n.* a child's game in which someone hides his face, as behind his hands, and then suddenly reveals it, calling "peekaboo!"

peel, *n.* [ME. and OFr. *pel*, a fort, stake; L. *palus*, a stake.] a fortified house or tower of a type built on the Scottish border during the sixteenth century. The lower part formed a lodging for the cattle, and was generally vaulted. The upper part served as a dwelling.

PEEL

peel, *v.t.*; peeled, *pt.*, *pp.*; peeling, *ppr.* [ME. *pelen*; OFr. *peler*, to strip, to pare; L. *pilare*, to make bald, from *pilus*, a hair.]
1. to strip of skin, bark, or rind; to strip by drawing or tearing off the skin; to bark; to flay; to decorticate; as, to *peel* a tree; to *peel* an orange.
2. to trim or cut away (rind, skin, covering, etc.) of anything.
3. to strip; to plunder; to pillage; as, to *peel* a province or conquered people. [Obs.]
to keep one's eyes peeled; to keep alert or on the watch. [Colloq.]

peel, *v.i.* 1. to shed skin or the outer surface; to become bare.
2. to come off; as, sunburned skin often *peels*.
3. to undress. [Slang.]
to peel off; in aviation, to veer away from a flight formation in order to make a dive at a target or to land.

peel, *n.* [from v. *peel*.] the skin or rind of fruit; as, the *peel* of an orange.

peel, *n.* [ME. and OFr. *pele*; L. *pala*, a spade.] a kind of long, wooden shovel used by bakers for moving bread into and out of the ovens.

pee′le, *n.* a South African antelope, with straight sharp horns.

peel′ēr, *n.* 1. one who peels, strips, or flays.
2. a plunderer; a pillager. [Obs.]

peel′ēr, *n.* [after Sir Robert *Peel*, who established a police force in Ireland and reorganized the London force.] a policeman. [Obs. Irish and Brit. Slang.]

peel′house, *n.* a peel, or fortified house.

peel′ing, *n.* anything peeled off, as an apple skin.

peen, *n.* [prob. var. dial. from ON.] the part of the head of a hammer opposite to the flat striking surface: it is often hemispherical or wedge-shaped.

peen, *v.t.*; peened, *pt.*, *pp.*; peening, *ppr.* to indent, bend, or alter in any way with a peen.

peenġe, *v.i.* to complain. [Scot. and Brit. Dial.]

peen ham′mēr, a hammer with a peen.

peep, *n.* [prob. suggested by rhyme with *jeep* and by dim. quality of sound made by small birds and chicks.] a jeep (sense 1): the more common name in some military units. [Military Slang.]

peep, *v.i.* [ME. *pepen*; prob. echoic formation.]
1. to make the short, high-pitched cry of a young bird or chick; to chirp; to cheep.
2. to speak in a small, weak voice, as from fear.

peep, *n.* a short, high-pitched sound like that made by a young bird; a chirp; a cheep.

peep, *v.i.* [ME. *pepen*; prob. symbolistic formation after earlier *keken* (*kiken*), to peep.]
1. to begin to appear; to make the first appearance; to issue or come forth gradually or partially, as though from hiding.
When flowers first *peeped*. —Dryden.
2. to look through a crevice; hence, to look narrowly, closely, or slyly; to take a hasty, furtive look.
Thou art a maid, and must not *peep*. —Prior.

peep, *v.t.* to cause to appear or protrude.

peep, *n.* 1. the first appearance; as, the *peep* of day.
2. a brief, hasty look or restricted view; a secret or furtive glimpse or glance.
3. an opening to peep through.
4. a peep sight.
Peep-o'-Day Boys; the Irish insurgents of 1784: so called from their early morning visits among the houses of their opponents in search of arms.

peep′ēr, *n.* 1. a person who peeps or pries.
2. an eye. [Slang.]

peep′ēr, *n.* 1. a person or thing that peeps, cheeps, chirps, etc.
2. any of several species of frogs.

peep′hōle, *n.* a hole or crevice through which one may peep or look without being discovered.

Peep′ing Tom, 1. in English legend, the Coventry tailor who was struck blind after peeping at Lady Godiva.
2. [p– T–] a person who gets pleasure, especially sexual pleasure, from watching others from a place of concealment.

peep show, a device containing a pictured scene or group of objects and a small opening, often with a magnifying lens, through which they may be viewed.

peep sīght, a rear sight for a firearm, usually consisting of an adjustable disk with a small opening in the center through which the front sight and target are lined up.

pee′pul tree, [Hind. *pīpal*.] the bo tree.

peer, *n.* [ME. *peir*, *peer*; OFr. *per*, *pair*; L. *par*, equal.]
1. an equal; one of the same rank, value, quality, ability, etc.; as, he was tried by a jury of his *peers*.
In song he never had his *peer*.—Dryden.
2. a companion; a fellow; an associate; a compeer. [Archaic.]
He all his *peers* in beauty did surpass. —Spenser.
3. a nobleman; especially, a British duke, marquis, earl, viscount, or baron.
peer of the realm; any of the class of British peers entitled to a seat in the House of Lords.

peer, *v.t.* 1. to match or equal.
2. to make a nobleman of.

peer, *v.i.* to assume equality. [Rare.]

peer, *v.i.*; peered, *pt.*, *pp.*; peering, *ppr.* [prob. contr. from *appear*.]
1. to appear. [Poet.]
2. to come out or show slightly; to come partly into sight.
See how his gorget *peers* above his gown. —Ben Jonson.
3. to look closely and searchingly, as in trying to see more clearly.
Peering in maps for ports, and piers, and roads. —Shak.

peer′ăge, *n.* 1. the rank or dignity of a peer, or nobleman.
2. the body of peers, collectively, of a particular country.
3. a book or list of peers with their lineage.

peer′dŏm, *n.* peerage (sense 1.)

peer′ess, *n.* 1. the wife of a peer.
2. a woman having the rank of peer in her own right.

peer′y, *a.* [from v. *peer*.] suspicious; prying; inquisitive; sharp; scrutinizing; as, two *peery* eyes.

peer′less, *a.* unequaled; having no peer or equal; as, *peerless* beauty or majesty.

peer′less·ly, *adv.* without an equal.

peer′less·ness, *n.* the state of having no equal.

peert, *a.* same as *peart*.

peet′weet, *n.* the spotted sandpiper, *Tringoides macularius*, common to North American shores.

peeve, *v.t.* and *v.i.*; peeved, *pt.*, *pp.*, peeving, *ppr.* to make or become peevish or bad-tempered. [Colloq.]

peeve, *n.* an object of dislike; annoyance. [Colloq.]

peeved, *a.* [pp. of *peeve*.] irritated; annoyed.

pee′vey, pee′vy, *n.* same as *peavey*.

pee′vish, *a.* [ME. *pevische*.]
1. fretful; petulant; apt to mutter and complain; easily vexed or fretted; querulous; hard to please.
She is *peevish*, sullen, froward. —Shak.
2. expressing discontent and fretfulness.
I will not presume
To send such *peevish* tokens to a king. —Shak.
3. silly; childish. [Obs.]
Syn.—captious, fretting, faultfinding, perverse, irritable.

pee′vish·ly, *adv.* fretfully; petulantly; with discontent and murmuring.

pee′vish·ness, *n.* fretfulness; petulance; irritability; sourness of temper; as, childish *peevishness*.
When *peevishness* and spleen succeed. —Swift.

pee′vit, pee′wit, *n.* same as *pewit*.

pee′wee, *n.* [said to be from Am. Ind. (Massachusett) *pewe*, little.] a person or thing that is unusually small. [Colloq.]

peg, *n.* [ME. *pegge*; prob. from L.G. source.]
1. a short, usually tapering or pointed piece used to hold parts together or to close an opening, as in a barrel.
2. a projecting pin or bolt used to hang things on, fasten ropes to, mark degrees of measurement or the score in a game, etc.
3. any of the pins which hold, and are used in regulating the tension of, the strings of a violin or other stringed instrument.
4. the distance between pegs.
5. a step or degree.
6. a point or prong for tearing, hooking, etc.
7. the foot or leg; as, he was knocked off his *pegs*. [Colloq.]
8. a tooth. [Colloq.]
9. an alcoholic drink, usually brandy and soda. [Brit.]
10. a shinny ball. [Scot.]
to take one down a peg; to lower one in estimation or in rank; to humiliate one.

peg, *v.t.*; pegged, *pt.*, *pp.*; pegging, *ppr.* 1. to put a peg or pegs into so as to fasten, secure, mark, etc.
2. to mark, as a score or distance, with pegs.
3. to strike with a peg so as to pierce or hook.
4. to maintain the price of, as a stock, by regulations or by buying and selling freely.
5. to throw; as, he *pegged* the ball to first base. [Colloq.]

peg, *v.i.* 1. to work, progress, etc. steadily and persistently; as, he's been *pegging* away at his studies.
2. to keep score with pegs, as in cribbage.
3. to hit a croquet peg, as in ending a game.
to peg out; (a) in cribbage, to win a game; (b) [Slang.] to die; to expire.

peg'ȧ·dọr, *n.* [Sp.] a fish, *Echeneis naucrates*; a remora that attaches itself to the shark; a sucking fish.

Pē·gā'sē·ăn, *a.* relating to Pegasus or to poetry. [Now Rare.]

peg'ȧ·soid, *a.* 1. resembling Pegasus.
2. of or pertaining to a family of fishes, the *Pegasidæ.*

Peg'ȧ·sus, *n.* [L., from Gr. *Pēgasos.*]
1. in Greek mythology, a winged horse, said to have sprung from Medusa when she was slain by Perseus and to have caused to spring from Mount Helicon the fountain of perpetual poetic inspiration called Hippocrene; hence, poetic inspiration.
2. a northern constellation near the vernal equinox.
3. a genus of fishes typical of the *Pegasidæ,* a family of marine fishes of the Indo-China seas; the flying sea horses.
4. [p-] any fish of this genus.

peg'gẽr, *n.* 1. one who pegs.
2. same as *pegging machine.*

peg'ging, *n.* 1. the act or the process of fastening with pegs.
2. pegs as a commodity, or the material for making pegs.

peg'ging mȧ·chïne', a machine for pegging shoes.

peg'gy, *n.* any of several small warblers. [Brit. Dial.]

peg lad'dẽr, a ladder made of a single pole, the rounds passing through and extending equally on both sides.

peg leg, a wooden leg; also, a person with a wooden leg. [Colloq.]

peg'mȧ·tīte, *n.* [Gr. *pēgma,* framework, and *-ite.*]
1. a very coarse igneous rock, usually granitic, containing large crystals of quartz, feldspar, and mica, usually found in fissures and cracks of other rocks.
2. graphic granite.

peg·mȧ·tit'iç, *a.* having the characteristics of pegmatite; made of pegmatite; resembling pegmatite.

peg'mȧ·toid, *a.* pegmatitic.

pegme (pem), *n.* a kind of moving machine or car in old pageants; also, a speech made from such a machine. [Obs.]

peg'ō·man·cy, *n.* [Gr. *pēgē,* fountain, and *manteia,* divination.] divination by means of a fountain or fountains.

peg'rọọts, *n.* same as *setterwort.*

peg tañk'ărd, a drinking vessel, formerly used, which was divided into parts of equal capacity by means of pegs as markers.

peg tọọth, a saw or gear tooth extending directly out of a gearwheel or saw blade: it is usually in the shape of a tapering peg and is not curved; a pivot tooth.

peg'-top, *a.* pear-shaped like a peg top; especially, designating trousers that are full at the hips and narrow at the cuffs.

peg top, 1. a child's spinning toy having a pear-shaped body with a metal tip; a top.
2. [*pl.*] peg-top trousers.

peh, *n.* the seventeenth letter of the Hebrew alphabet, corresponding to English *P, p*: also spelled *pe.*

peign·oir' (pān-wär'), *n.* [Fr., from *peigner,* to comb, from *peigne*; L. *pecten,* a comb.] a woman's dressing gown; a negligee.

pē·jō·rā'tion (*or* pej-ō-), *n.* 1. a worsening.
2. in linguistics, a change of meaning for the worse.
Opposed to *melioration.*

pē'jō·rā·tive (*or* pej'ō-), *a.* [from L. *pejoratus,* pp. of *pejorare,* to make worse, from *pejor,* worse.] making or becoming worse; disparaging or depreciative: applied in linguistics to words whose basic meaning has been changed for the worse (e.g., *silly, cretin*): opposed to *meliorative.*

pē'jō·rā·tive, *n.* a pejorative word or form: opposed to *meliorative.*

pek'ăn, *n.* [Canad. Fr., from Am. Ind. (Algonquian) name.]
1. a North American animal of the weasel family, with blackish fur above and brown or gray below.
2. its fur.

pē'kin', *n.* [Fr. *pékin,* from *Pékin,* Peking.] a patterned silk or satin material, originally from China.

Pē·kin·ēṣe', *a.* same as *Pekingese.*

Pē·kin·ēṣe', *n.*; *pl.* **Pē·kin·ēṣe',** same as *Pekingese.*

Pē'king' duck, a large, white, domesticated duck of a breed originating in China: also *Peking.*

Pē·king·ēṣe', *a.* of Peking, China, or its people.

Pē·king·ēṣe', *n.*; *pl.* **Pē·king·ēṣe',** 1. a native or inhabitant of Peking, China.
2. the Chinese dialect of Peking.
3. a small dog with long, silky hair, protruding eyes, short legs, and a pug nose: originally bred in China.

PEKINGESE (8 in. high at shoulder)

Pē'king' man, a type of primitive man of about 475,000 B.C. whose fossil remains were found near Peking, China, in 1929.

pē'kōe (*or Brit.* pek'ō), *n.* [from Chin. dial. *pek-ho,* lit., white down.] a black tea grown in Ceylon and India, made from the small leaves at the tips of the stem.

pe'lȧ, *n.* 1. a scale insect, *Ericerus pela,* of China, from the secretions of which is made Chinese wax.
2. Chinese wax.

pel'ȧġe, *n.* [Fr., from OFr. *pel,* hair; L. *pilus,* hair.] the hairy or furry covering of a mammal.

Pē·lā'ġi·ăn, *a.* relating to Pelagius, the founder of Pelagianism.

Pē·lā'ġi·ăn, *n.* a follower of Pelagius or a believer in Pelagianism.

Pē·lā'ġi·ăn·iṣm, *n.* the doctrines and teachings of Pelagius, a fourth-century British monk who denied the doctrine of original sin and maintained that man has freedom of will.

pē·laġ'iç, *a.* [L. *pelagicus*; Gr. *pelagikos,* from *pelagos,* the sea.] of the ocean surface or the open sea, especially as distinguished from coastal waters.

pel·ăr·gon'iç, *a.* 1. of or obtained from a pelargonium.
2. designating or of a monobasic organic acid, $CH_3(CH_2)_7CO_2H$, extracted from the leaves of a pelargonium.

Pel·ăr·gō'ni·um, *n.* [Mod. L., from Gr. *pelargos,* stork.]
1. a large genus of the order *Geraniaceæ,* divided into about fifteen subgenera. The flowers have a spurred calyx, a corolla generally with five, four, or two petals, and ten stamens, of which seven to ten are perfect. These plants are widely distributed, being commonly called *geraniums.*
2. [p-] a plant of this genus; a geranium.

Pē·laṣ'ġī, *n.pl.* [L., from Gr. *Pelasgoi,* from *Pelasgos,* the mythical founder of the race.] a prehistoric people believed to have lived in Greece, Asia Minor, and the Aegean Islands.

Pē·laṣ'ġi·ăn, *a.* of or pertaining to the Pelasgi.

Pē·laṣ'ġi·ăn, *n.* one of the Pelasgi.

Pē·laṣ'ġiç, *a.* 1. Pelasgian.
2. [p-] in zoology, wandering.

Pel·e·çan·i·fọr'mēṣ, *n.pl.* [LL. *pelecanus,* and L. *forma,* form.] an order of birds, also called *Totipalmatæ,* including the pelicans, the cormorants, the frigate birds, etc.

pel'e·çoid, *n.* [Gr. *pelekoeidēs*; *pelekys,* ax, and *eidos,* form.] a figure of a hatchet-shaped form, consisting of a semicircle and two inverted quadrantal arcs.

pel'ẽr·ine, *n.* [Fr. *pèlerine,* from *pèlerin,* pilgrim.] a woman's cape, usually of fur, tapering to long points in the front.

Pē'lē'ṣ hair, [Hawaiian.] fused lava drawn into long threads by the action of the wind: so called from the goddess of the volcano Kilauea.

Pē'leūs (*or* pē'li-us), *n.* in Greek legend, a king of the Myrmidons, father of Achilles.

pelf, *n.* [probably allied to *pilfer.*]
1. ill-gotten gains; booty. [Rare.]
2. mere money or wealth: a term of contempt.

Pē'li·ăs, *n.* in Greek mythology, a king of Thesalay: he was the uncle and guardian of Jason, whom he sent in search of the Golden Fleece.

pel'i·çăn, *n.* [ME. and AS. *pellicane*; LL. *pelicanus*; Gr. *pelekanos,* a pelican, from *pelekys,* a hatchet: so called from the shape of the bill.]
1. any of a number of large, related water birds of the genus *Pelecanus,* with completely webbed feet and a distensible pouch which hangs from the lower bill and serves to scoop up fish.

PELICAN (5 ft. long)

2. in old chemistry, a chemical glass vessel, or alembic, with a tubulated head, from which two opposite and curved beaks pass out and enter again at the belly of the cucurbit. It is designed for continued distillation and redistillation, the volatile parts of the substance distilling, rising into the head, and returning through the beaks into the cucurbit.
3. in dental surgery, an instrument formerly used for extracting teeth, curved at the end like the beak of a pelican.
pelican in her piety; in heraldry, the design of a pelican feeding her young with blood from her own breast.

pel'i·çăn fish, a deep-sea fish, *Eurypharynx pelecanoides,* with an extraordinarily large mouth and long head.

pel'i·çăn flow'ẽr, a West Indian creeper, *Aristolochia grandiflora,* or its blossom.

pel'i·çăn ī'bis, an Asiatic ibis of the genus Tantalus, having a white body with greenish-black wings and tail.

pel'i·çăn'ṣ-foot, *n.* same as *spoutshell.*

pel'ick, *n.* the common coot. [Dial.]

Pē·lī'dēṣ, *n.* 1. any male descendant of Peleus.
2. Achilles.

pel'i·kē, *n.* [Gr. *pelika.*] in archaeology, a Greek vase of the form of the hydria, the main points of difference being in the number of handles, the hydria having three and the pelike but two.

pē'li·om, *n.* same as *iolite.*

pē·li·ō'mȧ, *n.* [Gr., from *pelios,* livid.]
1. in mineralogy, peliom, or iolite.
2. same as *ecchymosis.*

pē·li·ō'sis, *n.* same as *purpura* (sense 1).

pe·lisse' (-lēs'), *n.* [Fr.; ML. *pellicia* (*vestis*), from L. *pellicius,* made of skins, from *pellis,* skin.] a long cloak or outer coat, especially one made or lined with fur.

pē'līte, *n.* [from Gr. *pelos,* earth, clay; and *-ite.*] any sedimentary rock, as shale, composed of minute particles of clay, mud, etc.

pē·lit'iç, *a.* [Gr. *pēlos,* clay.] of pelite; formed of or made up of mud.

pell, *n.* [L. *pellis*; It. *pelle*; G. *pelz,* a skin.]
1. a skin or hide. [Obs.]
2. a roll of parchment. [Obs.]
Clerk of the Pells; in England, a former officer of the exchequer, who entered every teller's bill on the parchment rolls, the roll of receipts, and the roll of disbursements. [Obs.]

Pel·lae'ȧ, *n.* [LL., from Gr. *pellos,* dark.] a widely distributed genus of ferns, the cliff brakes.

pell'ȧġe, *n.* [L. *pellis,* a skin.] custom or duty paid for skins of leather. [Obs.]

pel·lā'grȧ (*or* -lag'rȧ), *n.* [It., from *pelle* (L. *pellis*), the skin, and *agra,* hard, or *-agra,* from Gr. *agra,* seizure.] a chronic disease caused by a deficiency of nicotinic acid in the diet and characterized by gastrointestinal disturbances, skin eruptions, and nervous disorders: it is endemic in some parts of the world.

pel·lā'grin (*or* -lag'rin), *n.* one afflicted with pellagra.

pel·lā′grous (*or* -lag′rus), *a.* of or having pellagra.

pel′let, *n.* [ME. and OFr. *pelote*; ML. *pilota, pelota,* dim. of L. *pila,* a ball.]
1. a little ball or rounded mass, as of clay, paper, medicine, etc.
2. a crude projectile of stone, etc., as used in a catapult or early cannon.
3. a bullet.
4. a small lead shot.
5. in heraldry, a black roundel: also called *ogress* and *gunstone.*
6. in numismatics, a small circular boss.
pellet molding; in architecture, a flat band on which are circular flat disks, forming an ornament.

pel′let, *v.t.*; pelleted, *pt., pp.*; pelleting, *ppr.*
1. to make pellets of.
2. to shoot or hit with pellets.

pel′let·ed, *a.* consisting of pellets; furnished with pellets; made of or like pellets.
The discandying of this *pelleted* storm. —Shak.

pel′li·çle, *n.* [L. *pellicula,* dim. of *pellis,* skin.] a thin, skinlike substance, as a membrane, or the scum on a liquid.

pel·liç′ū·lăr, *a.* of, or in the form of, a pellicle.

pel·lī′lē, *n.* the redshank. [Brit. Dial.]

pel′li·tō·ry, *n.*; *pl.* **pel′li·tō·rieş,** [a corruption of L. *parietaria,* the wall plant, from *paries, parietis,* wall.]
1. any of a number of related climbing plants (genus *Parietaria*) of the nettle family.
2. a plant of the composite family whose root is used in medicine as a sedative, etc.; in full, *pellitory of Spain.*
3. the feverfew.
bastard pellitory; sneezewort.

pell′-mell′, pell′mell′, *adv.* [Fr. *pêle-mêle*; OFr. *pesle mesle,* redupl. from *mesler,* to mix.]
1. with confused violence; in a disorderly mass; in utter confusion.
The battle was a confused heap; the ground unequal; men, horses, chariots, crowded *pellmell.* —Milton.
2. in wild, disorderly haste; with reckless speed; headlong.

pell′-mell′, pell′mell′, *a.* 1. jumbled; confused; disorderly.
2. headlong.

pell′-mell′, pell′mell′, *n.* a jumble; confusion; disorder.

pel·lū′cid, *a.* [L. *pellucidus*; *pel,* for *per* intens., and *lucidus,* bright.]
1. transparent.
Such a diaphanous, *pellucid,* dainty body, as you see crystal glass is. —Howell.
2. admitting the passage of light; translucent; limpid; not opaque.
More *pellucid* streams; an ampler ether. —Wordsworth.
3. easy to understand; clear and simple in style; as, a *pellucid* explanation.

pel·lū·cid′i·ty, pel·lū′cid·ness, *n.* the quality or condition of being pellucid; as, the *pellucidity* of the air; the *pellucidness* of a gem.

pel·lū′cid·ly, *adv.* in a pellucid manner; transparently; clearly.

pel′mȧ, *n.*; *pl.* **pel′mȧ·tȧ,** the sole of the foot.

pel·mat′ō·gram, *n.* [Gr. *pelma* (-*atos*), sole of foot, and *-gram.*] an impression of the sole of the foot.

Pel″ō·pŏn·nē′siăn, *a.* pertaining to the Peloponnesus, the peninsula of southern Greece, or its people.

Pel″ō·pŏn·nē′siăn, *n.* a native or inhabitant of the Peloponnesus.

Pel″ō·pŏn·nē′siăn War, a war between Athens and Sparta (431–404 B.C.) ending with the victory of Sparta.

Pē′lops, *n.* [L.; Gr. *Pelops,* from *pelos,* dark, and *ops,* an eye.] in Greek mythology, the son of Tantalus: served up to the gods as food by his father and later restored to life by them.

pē·lō′ri·ȧ, *n.* [Gr. *pelōr,* a monster.] in botany, the appearance of regularity of structure in flowers of plants which normally bear irregular flowers, as the snapdragon and the toadflax, which, being normally irregular, assume a symmetrical form.

pē·lō′ri·āte, *a.* same as *peloric.*

pē·lō′riç, *a.* of or characterized by peloria.

pē·lō′rus, *n.* in nautical usage, an instrument for taking astronomical observations to correct errors in the compass: named after Pelorus, who is said to have guided Hannibal from Italy.

pe·lō′tȧ, *n.* [Sp., lit., a ball.] a Spanish game somewhat like handball, played in a walled court with a hard ball and a long, curved wicker basket strapped to the arm: in Spanish America, called *jai-alai.*

pelt, *n.* [ME.; prob. back-formation from OFr. *peleterie*: see *peltry.*]
1. the skin of a fur-bearing animal, especially when prepared for tanning.
2. an animal skin used as a garment.
3. the human skin: a humorous usage.
4. in falconry, the dead quarry of a hawk.

pelt, *v.t.*; pelted, *pt., pp.*; pelting, *ppr.* [ME. *pelten,* from L. *pultare,* form of *pulsare,* to strike.]
1. to strike with or as with missiles; to throw things at; as, to *pelt* with stones; *pelted* with hail.
2. to beat or pound heavily and repeatedly.
3. to throw or cast (missiles).

pelt, *v.i.* 1. to beat or strike heavily or steadily, as hard rain.
2. to rush or hurry.

pelt, *n.* 1. the act of pelting; a blow.
2. speed; tilt; as, running at full *pelt.*
3. rage; anger; passion. [Obs.]
Put her ladyship into a horrid *pelt,*
And made her rail at me. —E. Filmer.

pel′tȧ, *n.*; *pl.* **pel′tae,** [L.] 1. in ancient Greece, a small, light shield.
2. in lichens, a flat shield without any elevated rim, as in the genus *Peltigera*; also, a bract attached by its middle, as in peppers.

pel′tast, *n.* [Gr. *peltastēs.*] in ancient Greece, a soldier carrying a light shield.

pel′tāte, *a.* [L. *pelta,* a target.] shield-shaped, and fixed to the stalk by the center, or by some point distinctly within the margin; having the petiole inserted into the undersurface of the lamina, not far from the center: said of a leaf.

PELTATE LEAF

pel′tā·ted, *a.* peltate.

pel′tāte·ly, *adv.* in a peltate manner.

pel·tat′i·fid, *a.* cleft peltately.

pel·tā′tion, *n.* the quality or state of being peltate; also, a peltate form.

pelt′ẽr, *n.* one who pelts.

pel′tẽr, *n.* a mean, sordid, miserly person. [Obs.]

pelt′ẽr, *n.* one who deals in pelts.

pel′ti·fọrm, *a.* [L. *pelta,* a shield, and *forma,* form.] having simple veins arranged as in a peltate leaf; also, peltate.

Pel·tig′e·rȧ, *n.* [L. *pelta,* shield, and *gerere,* to carry.] a genus of lichens having shield-shaped apothecia.

pel·tig′e·rine, *a.* pertaining to or resembling the *Peltigera.*

pel′ti·nẽrved, *a.* [L. *pelta,* a target, and E. *nerve.*] in botany, having nerves radiating from a point at or near the center.

pelt′ing, *a.* mean; paltry. [Archaic.]

pelt rot, a disease in sheep in which the wool falls off.

pelt′ry, *n.*; *pl.* **pelt′rieş,** [Fr. *pelleterie,* from L. *pellis,* skin.]
1. pelts, or fur-bearing skins, collectively.
2. a pelt.

pelt′ry·wāre, *n.* peltry. [Obs.]

pelt wool, wool from the skins of dead sheep.

pē·lū′dō, *n.* [Sp., hairy, from L. *pilus,* hair.] the hairy armadillo, *Dasypus villosus,* from the pampas of South America. It is about fourteen inches long, with bands six or seven in number.

pel′vēş, *n.* plural of *pelvis.*

pel′vi-, [L., from *pelvis,* a basin.] a combining form meaning *pelvis, pelvic and,* as in *pelvimeter.*

pel′viç, *a.* of or situated near the pelvis.

pel′vi·fọrm, *a.* [*pelvi,* and L. *forma,* form.] basin-shaped; resembling a shallow cup.

pel·vim′ē·tẽr, *n.* [*pelvi-,* and Gr. *metron,* a measure.] an instrument to measure the dimensions of the pelvis.

pel·vim′ē·try, *n.* measurement of the pelvis.

pel′vis, *n.*; *pl.* **pel′vēş,** [L., a basin.]
1. in anatomy and zoology, any basinlike or funnel-shaped structure; specifically, (a) the basinlike cavity formed by the ring of bone in the posterior part of the trunk in many vertebrates: in man, it is formed by the ilium, ischium, pubis, and sacrum, supporting the spinal column and resting upon the legs; (b) these bones collectively: also *pelvic arch* (or *girdle*); (c) the funnel-shaped part of the kidney leading into the ureter.
2. the basal portion of the calyx of crinoids.

Pel″y·cō·saụ′ri·ȧ, *n.pl.* [Gr. *pelyx, pelykos,* a basin, and *sauros,* a lizard.] a division of extinct reptiles of the Carboniferous epoch.

pem′mi·căn, pem′i·căn, *n.* [from Am. Ind. (Cree) *pemikkân,* fat meat, from *pimiy,* fat.]
1. dried lean meat, pounded into a paste with fat and preserved in the form of pressed cakes.
2. dried beef, raisins, suet, and sugar prepared as a concentrated food, as for explorers.

pem′phi·goid, *a.* in medicine, having a likeness to pemphigus.

pem′phi·gus (*or* pem-fī′), *n.* [Mod. L., from Gr. *pemphix, pemphigos,* a bubble.] a disease of the skin characterized by the formation of watery blisters on the skin, which, after absorption, leave pigmented spots.

pen, *n.* [ME. *penne*; OFr. *penne, pene,* a pen, a feather, from L. *penna,* a feather. *Penna* is for *pesna,* which is from root *pet,* seen in Gr. *petomai*; Sans. *pet,* to fly, the root of E. *feather.*]
1. a feather; a quill; especially, a heavy wing feather. [Archaic.]
The proud peacock, overcharg'd with *pens.* —Ben Jonson.
2. (a) originally, a heavy quill or feather trimmed to a split point, used for writing with ink; (b) now, any of various devices used in writing or drawing with ink, usually with a half-tubular metal point split into two nibs: see also *ball point pen.*
3. the metal point for such a device.
4. (a) the pen regarded as an instrument of writing; hence, (b) literary style or expression; (c) writing as a profession; (d) a writer.
5. in zoology, the long, pen-shaped, internal shell of a squid.
6. a stylus; a graver. [Obs.]

pen, *v.t.*; penned, *pt., pp.*; penning, *ppr.* to write with or as with a pen; to compose.

pen, *n.* [ME.; AS. *penn.*]
1. a small yard or enclosure for domestic animals.
2. the animals so confined.
3. any small enclosure.

pen, *v.t.*; penned *or* pent, *pt., pp.*; penning, *ppr.* [AS. *pennan,* in *onpennan,* to unpin, to open.] to shut in or as in a pen; to confine in a small enclosure; to coop; to confine in a narrow place: usually followed by *up.*

pen, *n.* a female swan.

pen, *n.* a penitentiary. [Slang.]

Pē·nae′ȧ, *n.* [after the French botanist Pierre *Pena.*] the typical genus of the *Penæaceæ,* consisting of shrubs with small, flat, entire leaves and yellowish or reddish flowers.

Pen·ae·ā′cē·ae, *n.pl.* a family of evergreen shrubs having opposite leaves, and the flowers usually red and without corollas.

pen·ae·ā′ceous, *a.* pertaining to the *Penæaceæ.*

pē′năl, *a.* [ME.; L. *pœnalis,* relating to *pœna,* punishment.]
1. enacting punishment; specifying or prescribing the punishment of offenses.
The terror of any *penal* law. —South.
2. of, for, or constituting punishment, especially legal punishment.
Adamantine chains and *penal* fire. —Milton.
3. making a person liable to punishment; subject to a penalty; as, a *penal* offense.
4. used as a place of punishment; as, a *penal* settlement.
penal code; a code or body of law dealing with various crimes or offenses and their legal penalties.
penal laws; those laws which prohibit an act and impose a penalty for the commission of it.
penal servitude; imprisonment, usually at hard labor: the legal punishment for conviction of certain crimes.
penal statutes; those statutes which impose penalties or punishments for offenses committed.
penal sum; a sum declared by bond to be forfeited if the conditions of the bond be not fulfilled.

pē·nal′i·ty, *n.* penalty. [Obs.]

pē″năl·i·zā′tion (*or* pen″ăl-ī-), *n.* a penalizing or being penalized.

pē′năl·ize (*or* pen′ăl-), *v.t.*; penalized, *pt., pp.*; penalizing, *ppr.* 1. to make punishable; to set a penalty for, as an offense.
2. to impose a penalty on; specifically, to subject to a handicap, as in a contest, as penalty for the infraction of a rule.

pē′năl·ly, *adv.* in a penal manner.

pen′ăl·ty, *n.*; *pl.* **pen′ăl·tieş,** [ML. *pœnalitas,* from L. *pœna,* punishment.]
1. a punishment fixed by law, as for a crime or breach of contract.
2. the disadvantage, suffering, handicap, etc. imposed upon an offender, as a fine or forfeit.

3. any unfortunate consequence or result of an act or condition.

4. money recoverable by virtue of a penal statute.

Syn.—fine, forfeiture, mulct, punishment.

pen′ănce, *n.* [L. *pœnitentia*, penitence.]

1. a sacrament of the Roman Catholic Church involving the confession of sin, repentance, and submission to penalties imposed, followed by absolution by a priest.

2. any voluntary suffering or punishment to show repentance for a sin or wrongdoing.

3. repentance. [Obs.]

4. pain; sorrow. [Obs.]

pen′ănce, *v.t.*; penanced (-ănst), *pt., pp.*; penancing, *ppr.* to cause to undergo a penance.

pen′ănce·less, *a.* having no penance; free from penance.

pen′-ănd-ink′, *a.* 1. literary; in writing.

The last blow struck in the *pen-and-ink* war. —Craik.

2. made with a pen and ink: said of a drawing, sketch, etc.

pē·nang′-law″yẽr, *n.* a walking stick made from the stem of a palm, *Licuala acutifida*, imported from Penang.

pē·nang′ nut, the betel nut.

pen·an′nū·lăr, *a.* [L. *pene*, almost, and *annulus*, a ring.] nearly annular.

pē′nȧ·ry, *a.* penal. [Obs.]

pē·nā′tēs, *n.pl.* [L.] the household gods of the ancient Romans.

pence, *n.* [ME. *pens*, contr. of *penies*, pl. of *peny, pening.*] plural of *penny*: used also in compounds, as *twopence*. [Brit.]

pen′cel, *n.* [ME. *pencel, pensel*; OFr. *pennecel*, a pennon.] a small pennon, or narrow flag. [Archaic.]

pen′chănt (*or Fr.* päṅ-shäṅ′), *n.* [Fr., from *pencher*, to incline; from L. *pendere*, to hang.] a strong liking or fondness; inclination; taste.

pen′cil, *n.* [ME. *pencel*; OFr. *pincel*, from L. *penicellus*, a brush, dim. of *penis*, a tail; LL. *pinsellus*. The modern sense and form of *pencil* has been influenced by *pen* (writing instrument).]

1. originally, an artist's brush, especially a small, fine one.

2. the style or ability of a given artist.

3. a pointed, rod-shaped instrument of wood, metal, etc. with a center or core of graphite or crayon, used for marking, writing, and drawing.

4. something shaped or used like a pencil; specifically, (a) a small cosmetic stick for touching up the eyebrows; (b) a stick of some medicated substance; as, a styptic *pencil*.

5. in optics, an aggregate or set of rays of light diverging from or converging to a given point.

6. in geometry, a figure formed by lines converging to a point.

pen′cil, *v.t.*; penciled *or* pencilled, *pt., pp.*; penciling *or* pencilling, *ppr.* 1. to mark, write, or draw with or as with a pencil.

2. to use a pencil on.

pen′cil çāse, a holder for carrying pencils.

pen′cil çŏm′pȧss, a compass with a pencil on one branch, used in drawing.

pen′cil dī′ȧ·mŏnd, in glass cutting, a wooden handle set with a diamond chip at one end.

pen′ciled, pen′cilled, *a.* 1. written, drawn, or marked with a pencil.

2. radiated; having pencils of rays.

pen′cil·ẽr, pen′cil·lẽr, *n.* a person who pencils.

pen′cil flow′ẽr, an American herb of the genus *Stylosanthes*, characterized by a long style like a pencil.

pen′cil·i·form, *a.* [LL. *pencillus*, and L. *forma*, form.] resembling a pencil, as convergent rays of light, etc.

pen′cil·ing, pen′cil·ling, *n.* 1. the art of painting or sketching.

2. marks made with a pencil.

pen′cil lead (led), a small stick of graphite used in making pencils.

pen′cil tree, the groundsel tree.

pen′çrȧft, *n.* penmanship; chirography.

pend, *n.* a covered passageway into an interior court of a building. [Scot.]

pend, *v.i.* [L. *pendere*, to hang.]

1. to await judgment or decision.

2. to depend. [Dial.]

pend, *v.t.* to pen; to enclose. [Obs.]

pend′ănt, *n.* [ME.; OFr., ppr. of *pendre*, from L. *pendere*, to hang.]

1. a hanging object, as an earring, used as an ornament or decoration.

Some hang upon the *pendants* of her ear. —Pope.

2. the stem and ring of a pocket watch.

3. a suspended chandelier.

4. a pendulum. [Obs.]

5. anything hanging, as the pull chain on a lamp.

6. an appendix; an addition.

7. in architecture, a decorative piece suspended from a ceiling or roof: used especially in Gothic architecture.

8. match or parallel; one of a pair.

9. in nautical usage, a strap or short rope hanging from a masthead, and having thimbles for bearing the blocks, which transmit the effects of tackles to distant points, etc.: used especially in setting up masts and rigging.

Also spelled *pendent.*

PENDANT (sense 7)

pend′ănt, *a.* same as pendent.

pend′ănt bōw, the stem and ring by which a watch is suspended.

pend′ănt·ed, *a.* having a pendant or pendants.

pend′ănt·ing, *n.* in architecture, pendants arranged to form a design or group.

pend′ănt pōst, in architecture, a post resting on a corbel or other solid foundation, used to support any part of a roof.

pend′ănt switch, an electric switch hanging at the end of an electric cord.

pend′ănt tack′le, a form of tackle used on ships and attached to a short rope hanging from the masthead.

pend′en·cy, *n.* the state or condition of being pendent or pending.

pend′ent, *a.* [ME. *pendant, pendent*; L. *pendens*, ppr. of *pendere*, to hang.]

1. hanging; suspended from above; fastened at one end, the other being loose.

2. overhanging.

3. undecided; pending.

Also spelled *pendant.*

pendent post; in architecture, a short post placed against the wall, having its lower end supported on a corbel or capital, and its upper supporting the tie beam or hammer beam.

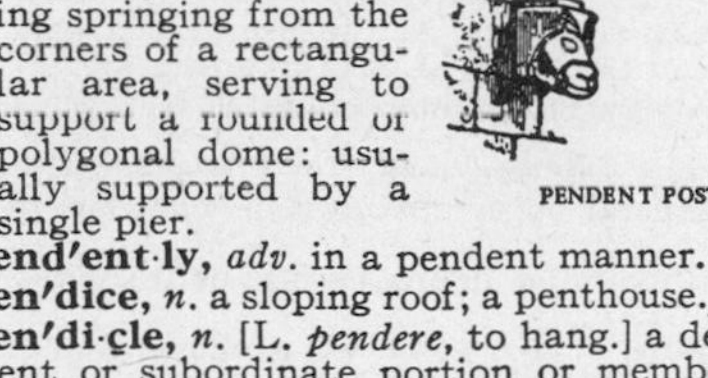

PENDENT POST

pend′ent, *n.* same as *pendant.*

pen·den′te lī′te, [L.] while a lawsuit or action is pending.

pen·den′tive, *n.* [Fr. *pendentif*, from L. *pendere*, to hang.] in architecture, one of the triangular pieces of vaulting springing from the corners of a rectangular area, serving to support a rounded or polygonal dome: usually supported by a single pier.

pend′ent·ly, *adv.* in a pendent manner.

pen′dice, *n.* a sloping roof; a penthouse. [Obs.]

pen′di·çle, *n.* [L. *pendere*, to hang.] a dependent or subordinate portion or member; an appendage; a pendant; specifically, a small farm that forms part of a large estate. [Scot.]

pen′di·clẽr, *n.* one who rents or farms a pendicle. [Scot.]

pend′ing, *a.* [L. *pendere*, to hang.]

1. remaining undecided; not determined; not established; as, a *pending* patent.

2. impending.

pend′ing, *prep.* 1. throughout the course or process of; during.

2. while awaiting; until; as, *pending* his arrival.

pen·drag′ŏn, *n.* [W. *pen*, head, and *dragon*, leader.] a supreme head or leader: a title used in ancient Britain.

pen′dū·lăr, *a.* same as *pendulous.*

pen′dū·lāte, *v.i.* to swing to and fro, as a pendulum.

pen′dūle, *n.* a pendulum.

pen′dū·line, *n.* [LL. *pendulinus.*] a European titmouse which builds a hanging nest.

pen·dū·los′i·ty, *n.* same as *pendulousness.*

pen′dū·lous, *a.* [L. *pendulus*, from *pendere*, to hang.]

1. hanging freely or loosely; fastened at one end, the other being free.

2. swinging.

pen′dū·lous·ly, *adv.* in a pendulous manner.

pen′dū·lous·ness, *n.* the quality or condition of being pendulous.

pen′dū·lum, *n.*; *pl.* **pen′dū·lumṣ,** [Mod. L., from L. *pendulus*, from *pendere*, to hang.] a body so suspended from or supported at a fixed point as to swing freely to and fro under the combined forces of gravity and momentum; especially, a body thus suspended in clocks and other machinery, to regulate the movement. The point A, about which the pendulum A B moves, is called the point of suspension or center of motion, the line C D, parallel to the horizon, is the axis of oscillation, and the arc B B B is called the arc of vibration.

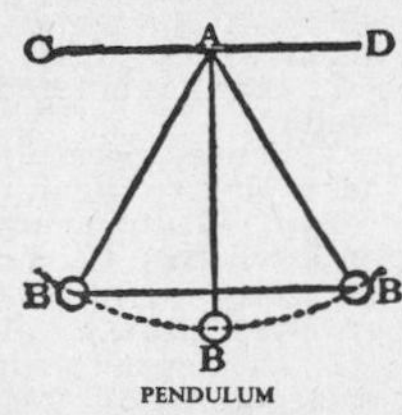

PENDULUM

compensation pendulum; a pendulum constructed so as to counteract the effect of heat and cold on metals, thus keeping the pendulum always of the same length.

compound pendulum; a body suspended by a string, rod, etc., free to move about a fixed horizontal axis, and acted upon by gravity only.

conical pendulum; a pendulum the movement of which is not limited to one plane, the center of gravity being limited only to the surface of a sphere.

gridiron pendulum; see under *gridiron.*

mercurial pendulum; a compensation pendulum having a quantity of mercury as a bob.

simple or *theoretical pendulum*; (a) an imaginary pendulum with the dimension of length only, and without weight except at the center of oscillation; (b) a pendulum consisting of a spherical body suspended at the end of a wire or cord.

pen′dū·lum bob, the weight attached to the lower end of a pendulum.

pen′dū·lum wheel (hwēl), the balance wheel of a watch.

pēne, *n.* and *v.t.* same as *peen.*

Pē·nel′ō·pē, *n.* 1. the faithful wife of Ulysses: during his absence she was courted by many suitors, who were asked to wait until she had woven a certain garment: it was never completed, since each night she secretly unraveled that day's work.

2. the type genus of the *Penelopinæ.*

Pē·nel·ō·pī′nae, *n.pl.* a subfamily of curassows; the guans.

pē′nē·plāin, pē′nē·plāne, *n.* [L. *pene, pæne*, almost; and *plain, n.*] land worn down by erosion almost to a level plain.

pen″ē·trȧ·bil′i·ty, *n.* the quality or condition of being penetrable.

pen′ē·trȧ·ble, *a.* [Fr., from L. *penetrabilis.*] that can be penetrated.

Let him try thy dart,
And pierce his only *penetrable* part. —Dryden.

I am not made of stone,
But *penetrable* to your kind entreaties. —Shak.

pen′ē·trȧ·ble·ness, *n.* same as *penetrability.*

pen′ē·trȧ·bly, *adv.* so as to be penetrable.

pen′ē·trăl, *n.* [L. *penetralia*, interior.] an interior part or place. [Now Rare.]

pen·ē·trā′li·ȧ, *n.pl.* [L.] 1. the recesses or innermost parts of any place, as of a temple or palace.

2. things concealed or secret; privacy.

pen′ē·trănce, pen′ē·trăn·cy, *n.* [L. *penetrans.*] the condition or quality of being penetrant; acuteness.

pen′ē·trănt, *a.* [Fr. *pénétrant*; L. *penetrans* (*-antis*), ppr. of *penetrare*, to penetrate.] sharp; acute; penetrating; as, *penetrant* oil, *penetrant* hatred.

pen′ē·trāte, *v.t.*; penetrated, *pt., pp.*; penetrating, *ppr.* [L. *penetratus*, pp. of *penetrare*; *penes*, within, and root *tra*, seen in *intrare*, to enter, *trans*, across.]

1. to enter by piercing; to find or force a way into or through; as, the dart *penetrated* his skin; oil *penetrates* wood.

2. to have an effect throughout; to spread through; to permeate.

3. to imbue; to cause to feel; to move deeply; as, to *penetrate* with grief.

4. to reach mentally; to understand; to

grasp the hidden meaning of; as, to *penetrate* his motives.

pen′ē·trāte, *v.i.* 1. to make a way into and through something; to pierce.

Born where heaven's influence scarce can *penetrate.* —Pope.

2. to have a marked effect on the mind.

pen′ē·trā·ting, *a.* 1. that can penetrate; sharp; piercing; as, a *penetrating* sound or smell.

2. that has entered deeply; as, a *penetrating* wound.

3. acute; discerning; quick to understand; as, a *penetrating* mind.

Syn.—acute, sharp, keen, astute, subtle.

pen′ē·trā·ting·ly, *adv.* in a penetrating manner; piercingly; discerningly.

pen·ē·trā′tion, *n.* 1. a penetrating.

2. the depth to which a projectile sinks into a target.

3. the extension of the influence of a country over a weaker one by means of commercial investments, loans, strong diplomatic posts, etc.

4. keenness of mind; discernment; insight.

Syn.—entrance, acuteness, discernment, comprehension.

pen′ē·trā·tive, *a.* penetrating.

pen′ē·trā·tive·ness, *n.* the quality of being penetrative.

pen′ē·tron, *n.* [Mod.L., from *penetrate,* and *electron.*] a meson.

pen feath′ẽr (feth′), a feather with a large quill that can be used as a pen.

pen′fish, *n.* 1. a squid.

2. a West Indian fish of the genus *Calamus.*

pen′fōld, *n.* same as *pinfold.*

pen′gö (pen′gē), *n.*; *pl.* **pen′gö, pen′gös** (-gēz), [Hung.] the former monetary unit of Hungary, replaced by the forint.

pen′gō·lin, *n.* same as *pangolin.*

pen′guin (-gwin), *n.* [perhaps from W. *pen,* head, and *gwyn,* white.]

1. a natatorial bird of the genus *Aptenodytes,* family *Aptenodytidæ,* or *Spheniscidæ,* related to the auks and guillemots. They are flightless birds found in the Southern Hemisphere, having webbed feet and paddlelike flippers for swimming and diving.

2. the great auk. [Obs.]

3. a training airplane having short wings and a small motor: it cannot be used for actual flight.

KING PENGUIN (*Aptenodytes patagonica*)

pen′guin, *n.* a species of West Indian *Bromelia,* the wild pineapple, the juice of which is used for making wine.

pen′guin·ẽr·y, *n.* a place where penguins congregate for breeding; a colony of penguins.

pen′hōld″ẽr, *n.* 1. the handle or holder into which a pen point fits.

2. a container or rack for a pen or pens.

pē′ni·ăl, *a.* pertaining to the penis.

pen′i·ble, *a.* 1. painful; laborious. [Obs.]

2. painstaking. [Obs.]

pen′i·cil, *n.* [L. *penicillus.*] in biology, a tuft of hairs resembling a painter's brush, as on a caterpillar.

pen·i·cil′lāte, *a.* [L. *penicillus,* a pencil or small brush.] having the form of a penicil; having a penicil or penicils.

pen·i·cil′li·fọrm, *a.* penicillate.

pen·i·cil′lin, *n.* a powerful antibiotic substance obtained from certain penicilliums and used in the treatment and prevention of some infections because of its ability to inhibit the growth of certain bacteria.

pen·i·cil′li·um, *n.*; *pl.* **pen·i·cil′li·ums, pen·i·cil′li·ȧ,** [Mod.L., from L. *penicillus*: so named because of the tuftlike ends of the conidiophores.]

1. any of a genus of fungi growing as green mold on stale bread, ripening cheese, decaying fruit, etc.: penicillin is derived from some species.

2. [P–] this genus of fungi.

pen·in′sū·lȧ, *n.* [L. *pene,* almost, and *insula,* an isle.]

1. a portion of land almost surrounded by water and connected with the mainland by an isthmus.

2. any land area projecting out into the water.

pen·in′sū·lăr, *a.* 1. of or forming a peninsula.

2. like a peninsula.

pen·in′sū·lāte, *v.t.*; peninsulated, *pt., pp.*; peninsulating, *ppr.* to almost isolate with water; to form into a peninsula.

pē′nis, *n.*; *pl.* **pē′nēș, pē′nis·eș,** [L., orig., a tail.] the male organ of sexual intercourse: in mammals it is also the organ through which urine is ejected.

pen′i·tence, pen′i·ten·cy, *n.* [Fr. *pénitence,* from L. *pœnitentia,* repentance.] the state of being penitent; regret for offense committed; sorrow, accompanied with the desire to atone.

Syn.—compunction, contrition, repentance.

pen′i·ten·cẽr, *n.* a priest specially appointed to hear confession; as, the king's *penitencer.* [Obs.]

pen′i·tent, *a.* [L. *pœnitens* (-*entis*) ppr. of *pœnitere,* to repent, from *pœna,* punishment.] regretting sin or offense and willing to atone; repentant; contrite; doing penance; as, *penitent* gifts.

pen′i·tent, *n.* 1. a penitent person; one who repents an offense or wrong committed.

2. in the Roman Catholic Church, a person undergoing the sacrament of penance.

pen·i·ten′tiăl (-shăl), *a.* of, expressing, or belonging to penitence; as, *penitential* tears.

pen·i·ten′tiăl, *n.* 1. a penitent.

2. a list or book of rules governing religious penitents and penance.

pen·i·ten′tiăl·ly, *adv.* in a penitential manner.

pen·i·ten′tiȧ·ry (-shȧ-), *a.* [ML. *penitentiarius,* from L. *pœnitentia,* repentance.]

1. of or for penance.

2. used in punishing, disciplining, and reforming; as, a *penitentiary* device.

3. that makes one liable to imprisonment in a penitentiary.

pen·i·ten′tiȧ·ry, *n.*; *pl.* **pen·i·ten′tiȧ·rieș,**

1. a prison; especially, a State or Federal prison for persons convicted of serious crimes.

2. a penitent. [Obs.]

3. a confession room in a monastery; also, the part of a church in which penitents were allowed during Mass or other worship. [Obs.]

4. in the Roman Catholic Church, (a) a papal court office or tribunal passing on certain cases, as of confession, penance, dispensation, absolution, etc., whose chief is the grand penitentiary, a cardinal appointed by the pope; (b) an officer vested with power from a bishop to give absolution in cases normally reserved to himself.

pen·i·ten′tiȧ·ry·ship, *n.* the office of one delegated as a penitentiary. [Rare.]

pen′i·tent·ly, *adv.* with penitence.

penk, *n.* same as *pink* (a fish).

pen′knīfe (-nīf), *n.*; *pl.* **pen′knīveș,** a small knife for the pocket: originally used to make quill pens.

pen′līght, pen′līte, *n.* a flashlight that is about as small and slender as a fountain pen.

pen′măn, *n.*; *pl.* **pen′men,** 1. a person employed to write or copy; a scribe.

2. one whose business is the use or teaching of penmanship, generally implying skill; a calligrapher.

3. an author; a writer.

pen′măn·ship, *n.* 1. the use of the pen in writing; the art or skill of handwriting.

2. a style or manner of handwriting; chirography.

pen′nȧ, *n.*; *pl.* **pen′nae,** [L.] a feather forming the general outer covering, or contour, of a bird.

pen·nā′ceous, *a.* characteristic of or similar to a penna.

pen′nach, *n.* [Fr. *panache.*] a plume or bunch of feathers. [Obs.]

pen nāme, a name used by an author in place of his true name; a nom de plume; a pseudonym.

pen′nănt, *n.* [from *pennon*; influenced by *pendant.*]

1. any long, narrow, usually triangular flag, as used for naval signaling, a school banner, etc.

2. any such flag symbolizing a championship, as in baseball.

3. a tackle for hoisting goods on board a ship; a pendant.

pen′nāte, pen′nā·ted, *a.* [L. *pennatus,* winged, from *penna,* a quill or wing.]

1. winged; plumed.

2. in botany, pinnate.

Pen·nat′ū·lȧ, *n.* [LL., provided with wings.]

1. a genus of polyps, family *Pennatulidæ,* having a calcareous midrib bladed like a feather; the sea pens.

2. [p–] any polyp of this genus.

Pen·nat·ū·lā′cē·ȧ, *n.pl.* a division of *Cœlenterata,* class *Actinozoa,* and order *Alcyonaria,* of which the sea pen (*Pennatula*) is the type.

pen·nat′ū·lid, *n.* any polyp of the family *Pennatulacea.*

pen·nat′ū·loid, *a.* characteristic of the *Pennatulacea.*

penned, *a.* 1. winged; having plumes. [Obs.]

2. written.

pen′nẽr, *n.* 1. a writer.

2. a pen case, carried at the girdle by medieval writers and illuminators. [Obs.]

pen′ni, *n.*; *pl.* **pen′ni·ȧ,** [Finn., from G. *pfennig*: see *penny.*] a Finnish coin equal to 1/100 markka.

pen′ni-, [from L. *penna,* a feather.] a combining form meaning *feather, featherlike,* as in *penni*form.

pen·nif′ẽr·ous, pen·nig′ẽr·ous, *a.* bearing feathers or quills.

pen′ni·fọrm, *a.* [L. *penna,* a feather or quill, and *forma,* form.] having the form or appearance of a quill or feather.

pen′ni·less, *a.* without even a penny; extremely poor.

pen′ni·less·ness, *n.* the state of being penniless.

pen′ni·nẽrved, *a.* nerved or veined pinnately, as some leaves.

pen′nŏn, *n.* [OFr. *penon*; L. *penna,* feather.]

1. a long, narrow, triangular or swallow-tailed flag used as an ensign by a knight or regiment of lancers.

2. any flag or pennant.

3. a pinion; a wing.

pen′nŏn·cel, pen′nŏn·celle, *n.* a pencel. [Obs.]

pen′nō·plūme, *n.* a feather plumule.

Penn·syl·vā′ni·ȧ-Dutch′, *a.* 1. of the Pennsylvania Dutch or their language.

2. designating or of a style of furniture, etc. characterized by carved or painted decorations of flowers, fruits, etc.

Penn·syl·vā′ni·ȧ Dutch, 1. the descendants of early German immigrants to Pennsylvania.

2. their German dialect.

Also called *Pennsylvania German.*

Penn·syl·vā′ni·ăn, *a.* 1. of Pennsylvania.

2. designating or of the second period of the Paleozoic Era in North America, characterized by the formation of coal deposits.

Penn·syl·vā′ni·ăn, *n.* a native or inhabitant of Pennsylvania.

the Pennsylvanian; the Pennsylvanian Period or its rocks.

pen′ny, *n.*; *pl.* **pen′nieș** or **pence,** [AS. *penig, pening,* a penny, a silver coin, probably of same origin as *pawn*; O.H.G. *pending*; G. *pfennig.*]

1. in the United Kingdom and certain Commonwealth countries, (a) a unit of currency equal to one twelfth of a shilling; (b) a unit in the new decimal monetary system (February, 1971), equal to one 100th part of a pound, or to 2.4 old penny: in full, *new penny.*

2. an insignificant coin or amount; a small sum.

I will not lend thee a *penny.* —Shak.

3. a sum of money; as, a pretty *penny.*

4. a cent (U. S. or Canadian); as, ten *pennies* make a dime.

a pretty penny; a large sum of money. [Colloq.]

to turn an honest penny; to make money fairly and honestly.

pen′ny, *a.* valued at a penny; as, a *penny* newspaper.

penny post; a post that conveys mail for a penny.]Brit.]

-pen′ny, a combining form meaning *costing* (a specified number of) *pennies,* as in six*penny*: formerly applied to nails to indicate the cost per hundred, but now simply a measure of their length.

pen′ny-ȧ-līne′, *a.* 1. receiving a penny per line of writing; i.e., having a low rate of pay.

2. of inferior quality; cheap: said of writing.

pen′ny-ȧ-līn′ẽr, *n.* a writer paid at a low rate, especially a hack writer.

pen′ny an′tē, a game of poker in which the ante is limited to one cent.

pen′ny är·çāde′, a public amusement hall with coin-operated game and vending machines.

pen′ny·çress, *n.* an herb of the mustard family, bearing round, flat pods resembling pennies.

pen′ny dog, a small shark or dogfish native to Europe.

pen′ny dread′fụl (dred′), a cheap book or magazine containing stories of crime, terror, the supernatural, etc.; a dime novel. [Brit. Colloq.]

pen′ny fā′thẽr, a miserly person. [Obs.]

pen'ny grȧss, any of several plants having round leaves or pods.

pen·ny·roy'ăl, *n.* 1. a hairy plant of the mint family.
 2. the oil it yields.
 bastard pennyroyal; see *blue curls.*
 false pennyroyal; a plant of the mint family.
 native pennyroyal; the mint plant of Australia.

pen'ny·wei̇ght (-wāt), *n.* a unit of weight, equal to 24 grains or $^1/_{20}$ ounce troy weight.

pen'ny-wīṣe', *a.* careful or thrifty in regard to small matters.
 penny-wise and pound-foolish; careful or thrifty in small matters but careless or wasteful in major ones.

pen'ny·wŏrt, *n.* any of various plants with small, round leaves, growing in crevices of rocks and walls or in marshy places.

pen'ny·wŏrth, *n.* 1. as much as is bought for a penny.
 2. the value of something bought, with regard to the price paid; as, a good *pennyworth.*
 3. a small quantity.

Pe·nob'sc̦ot, *n.* a member of a tribe of Algonquian Indians living around the Penobscot River and Penobscot Bay, Maine.

Pe·nob'sc̦ot, *a.* of the Penobscots.

pē·nō·lo̤g'iç·ăl, *a.* of penology.

pē·nol'ō·ġist, *n.* one who studies penology; a specialist in penology.

pē·nol'ō·ġy, *n.* [Gr. *poinē* (L. *pœna,* punishment), and *logos,* discourse.] the study of the reformation and rehabilitation of criminals and of the management of prisons: also spelled *poenology.*

pen pal, a person, especially a stranger in another country, with whom one arranges a regular exchange of letters.

pen'rack, *n.* a rack for penholders.

pen'sa·tive, *a.* pensive. [Obs.]

pen'sel, *n.* a pencil. [Obs.]

pen'sile, *a.* [L. *pensilis,* from *pendere,* to hang.]
 1. hanging; suspended; as, a *pensile* bell.
 2. having or building a hanging nest, as the Baltimore oriole.

pen'sion, *n.* [Fr., from L. *pensio* (*-onis*), a paying, from *pendere,* to weigh, to hang.]
 1. a payment, not wages, made regularly to a person (or to his family) who has fulfilled certain conditions of service, reached a certain age, etc.; as, a soldier's *pension,* old-age *pension.*
 2. a regular payment, not a fee, given to artists, etc. by patrons or benefactors; a subsidy.
 3. in England, a yearly payment in the Inns of Court.
 4. a payment of money; an allowance in the nature of tribute. [Obs.]
 5. in England, an assembly of the members of Gray's Inn.
 6. (pän-syōṅ'), in France and other Continental countries, a boarding school or boardinghouse.

pen'sion, *v.t.*; pensioned, *pt., pp.*; pensioning, *ppr.* to grant a pension to.
 to pension off; to dismiss from service with a pension.

pen'sion·ȧ·ble, *a.* having or giving a right to a pension; as, sixty-five is a *pensionable* age.

pen'sion·ãr·y, *a.* 1. maintained by a pension; receiving a pension; as, *pensionary* spies.
 2. dependent; hireling.
 3. of or constituting a pension; as, a *pensionary* provision for maintenance.

pen'sion·ãr·y, *n.*; *pl.* **pen'sion·ãr·ieṣ,** 1. a person who receives a pension.
 2. a hireling; a tool; a puppet.
 3. formerly, (a) the first magistrate of the republic of Holland, the presiding officer of the States General: commonly called the *Grand Pensionary*; (b) the chief municipal magistrate of a town in Holland.

pen'sion·ẽr, *n.* 1. one to whom a pension is granted; a dependent.
 2. in Cambridge University, England, an undergraduate who pays his own expenses.
 3. a gentleman-at-arms. [Obs.]

pen'sive, *a.* [ME. and OFr. *pensif,* from *penser,* to think or reflect; L. *pensare,* to weigh, to consider, freq. of *pendere,* to weigh.]
 1. thinking deeply or seriously, often of sad or melancholy things.

 Anxious cares the *pensive* nymph oppressed.
 —Pope.

 2. expressing or producing deep thoughtfulness, often with some sadness; as, *pensive* strains.

pen'sive·ly, *adv.* in a thoughtful or pensive manner; with seriousness or some degree of melancholy.

pen'sive·ness, *n.* the state or quality of being thoughtful or pensive; melancholy.

pen'stock, *n.* [*pen,* enclosure, and *stock.*]
 1. a gate or sluice used in controlling the flow of water.
 2. a tube or trough for carrying water to a water wheel.

pent, *v.* alternative past tense and past participle of *pen* (to shut in).

pent, *a.* [pp. of *pen.*] shut up; closely confined: often with *up.*

pen'tȧ-, [Gr. *penta-,* from *pente,* five.] a combining form meaning *five,* as in *penta*merous; also, before a vowel, *pent-.*

pen·tȧ·bā'siç, *a.* [*penta-* and *basic.*] in chemistry, having five atoms of hydrogen which may be displaced by a basic element or radical: applied to some acids.

pen·tȧ·çap'sū·lăr, *a.* [*penta-* and *capsular.*] in botany, bearing or made up of five capsules.

pen·tȧ·çhē'ni·um, *n.* [*pent-* and *achenium.*] in botany, a fruit having five cells or carpels, bound together by the calyx until maturity, when they separate.

pen·tȧ·çhlō'rīde, pen·tȧ·çhlō'rid, *n.* [*penta-* and *chloride.*] in chemistry, any chloride a molecule of which contains five atoms of chlorine.

pen'tȧ·çhord, *n.* [*penta-,* and Gr. *chordē,* a string.]
 1. an ancient musical instrument with five strings.
 2. a series or scale of five diatonic tones.

pen·tac'id, *a.* [*pent-* and *acid.*] in chemistry, containing five atoms of hydrogen which may be displaced by an acid; capable of neutralizing five molecules of a monobasic acid: applied to certain bases.

pen'tȧ·çle, *n.* [LL. *pentaculum,* from Gr. *pente,* five.] a five-pointed figure, composed of five straight lines interlacing to form a starlike shape. It was a popular design in medieval art, and was given a mystic significance by astrologers and magicians. The term has been enlarged to include figures of various forms, as the hexagram, triangle, etc.

pen·tȧ·çoç'çous, *a.* [*penta-,* and Gr. *kokkos,* a berry.] in botany, having or containing five grains or seeds, or having five united cells with one seed in each.

pen'tȧ·con·tẽr, *n.* same as *penteconter.*

pen·tā'çrȧ, *n.* pl. of *pentacron.*

pen·taç'ri·nīte, *n.* [*penta-,* and Gr. *krinon,* lily.] any crinoid or encrinite of the genus *Pentacrinus.*

pen·taç'ri·noid, *n.* [*penta-* and *crinoid.*] a crinoid of the genus *Antedon,* which when young is fixed by a stem, resembling an individual of the genus *Pentacrinus.*

Pen·taç'ri·nus, *n.* [*penta-,* and Gr. *krinon,* lily.] in zoology, a genus of crinoids, most of the species of which are fossil. The existing species are found in deep sea water; they are of large size and have pentagonal stalks.

pen·tā'çrŏn, *n.*; *pl.* **pen·tā'çrȧ, pen·tā'çrŏnṣ,** [*pent-,* and Gr. *akros,* topmost.] any solid figure having five points.

pen·tȧ·çros'tiç, *a.* [*pent-* and *acrostic.*] containing five acrostics of the same name.

pen·tȧ·cyç'liç (*or* -sȳ'klik), *a.* [*penta-,* and Gr. *kyklos,* circle.] in botany, having the members arranged in five cycles or whorls: said of certain flowers.

pen'tad, *n.* [Gr. *pentas* (*-ados*), the number five.]
 1. the number five.
 2. a series or group of five.
 3. a five-year period.
 4. in chemistry, an element or radical with a valence of five.

pen'tad, *a.* in chemistry, having the combining power of a pentad.

pen·tȧ·daç'tyl, pen·tȧ·daç'tyle, *a.* [*penta-,* and Gr. *daktylos,* finger.] in anatomy, having five fingers or toes on each hand or foot; having five parts or appendages resembling fingers or toes.

pen·tȧ·daç'tyl·iṣm, *n.* the state of having five fingers or toes.

pen·tȧ·daç'tyl·oid, *a.* [*pentadactyl* and *-oid.*] in anatomy, resembling or having the form of a pentadactyl limb.

pen·tȧ·deç'āne, *n.* [*penta-,* and Gr. *deka,* ten.] in chemistry, a liquid compound of the paraffin series, $C_{15}H_{32}$, contained in petroleum, tar, oil, etc. It takes its name from the fact that there are fifteen atoms of carbon in the molecule.

pen·tȧ·deç·ȧ·tō'iç, *a.* pertaining to, containing, or derived from pentadecane; as, *pentadecatoic* acid.

pen''tȧ·dē·cyl'iç, *a.* in chemistry, same as *quindecylic.*

pen·tȧ·del'phous, *a.* [*pent-,* and Gr. *adelphos,* brother.] in botany, having the stamens united in five clusters by their filaments, as the flowers of the linden.

pen'tȧ·fid, *a.* [*penta-,* and *fid,* root of L. *findere,* to split.] in botany, cleft or divided into five segments.

pen'tȧ·glot, *n.* [*penta-,* and Gr. *glōtta,* tongue.] a work written in five different languages.

pen'tȧ·glot, *a.* written in five languages.

pen'tȧ·gon, *n.* [*penta-,* and Gr. *gonia,* a corner.] in geometry, a plane figure having five angles and five sides.
 regular pentagon; a pentagon whose sides and angles are all equal.
 the Pentagon; the pentagonal building in Arlington, Virginia, in which the offices of the National Military Establishment are located.

PENTAGON

pen·tag'ō·năl, *a.* of, or having the form of, a pentagon.

pen·tag'ō·năl·ly, *adv.* with five angles; in pentagonal form.

pen·tag'ō·nous, *a.* pentagonal.

pen'tȧ·gram, *n.* [*penta-,* and Gr. *grammē,* a line, from *graphein,* to write.] a pentacle; also, any figure of five lines.

 Some figure like a wizard *pentagram.*
 —Tennyson.

pen'tȧ·grȧph, *n.* same as *pentograph.*

pen·tȧ·graph'iç, pen·tȧ·graph'iç·ăl, *a.* same as *pantographic,* etc.

Pen·tȧ·ġyn'i·ȧ, *n.pl.* [*penta-,* and Gr. *gynē,* a female.] in botany, a Linnaean order of plants having five styles.

pen·tȧ·ġyn'i·ăn, pen·taġ'y·nous, *a.* in botany, relating to the *Pentagynia*; having five styles.

pen·tȧ·hē'drăl, *a.* of, or having the form of, a pentahedron.

pen·tȧ·hed'riç·ăl, *a.* pentahedral.

pen·tȧ·hē'drŏn, *n.*; *pl.* **pen·tȧ·hē'drŏnṣ, pen·tȧ·hē'drȧ,** [*penta-,* and Gr. *hedra,* a side or base.] a solid figure having five plane surfaces.

pen·tȧ·hē'drous, *a.* pentahedral.

pen'tāil, *n.* a tree shrew, *Ptilocercus lowi,* inhabiting Borneo: so named from its long scaly tail, which has a feathery tip.

pen·tal'phȧ, *n.* [*pent-,* and Gr. *alpha,* the letter *A.*] a symbol in the form of a star with five points, suggesting five alphas united at the bases.

Pen·tam'e·rȧ, *n.pl.* in zoology, a large division of coleopterous insects, including those which have five joints on the tarsus of each leg. The division includes one half of the species of *Coleoptera.*

pen·tam'ẽr·ăn, *n.* in zoology, an individual of the division *Pentamera.*

pen·tam'ẽr·iṣm, *n.* the condition of being pentamerous.

PENTAMERAN

pen·tam'ẽr·ous, *a.* [*penta-* and *-merous.*] in botany and zoology, made up of five parts or divisions: also written *5-merous.*

Pen·tam'e·rus, *n.* a genus of brachiopods now extinct, formerly very plentiful in the Upper Silurian.

pen·tam'ē·tẽr, *n.* [Gr. *pentametros*; *pente,* five, and *metron,* measure.]
 1. a line of verse containing five metrical feet or measures; especially, English iambic pentameter. Example: "Yŏu blócks,| yŏu stónes, | yŏu wórse | thăn sénse | lĕss thíngs."
 2. verse consisting of pentameters; heroic verse.

pen·tam'ē·tẽr, *a.* having five metrical feet.

pen·tȧ·meth'yl·ēne, *n.* in chemistry, a hydrocarbon believed to consist of five methylene residues.

Pen·tan'dri·ȧ, *n.pl.* [*pent-,* and Gr. *anēr, andros,* a male.] in botany, a Linnaean class of hermaphrodite plants having five stamens with distinct filaments not connected with the pistil.

pen·tan'dri·ăn, *a.* in botany, pertaining to the *Pentandria*; having five stamens with distinct filaments not connected with the pistil.

pen·tan′drous, *a.* same as *pentandrian.*

pen′tāne, *n.* [Gr. *pente,* five.] any of three known isomeric, colorless hydrocarbons, C_5H_{12}, of the methane series, occurring in petroleum, etc.: two of these occur as liquids and the other as a gas, under ordinary conditions.

pen′tañ·gle, *n.* a pentagon.

pen·tañ′gū·lăr, *a.* [*pent-* and *angular.*] having five corners or angles.

pen·tȧ·pet′ăl·ous, *a.* [*penta-,* and Gr. *petalon,* a petal.] in botany, having five petals or flower leaves.

pen·taph′yl·lous, *a.* [*penta-,* and Gr. *phyllon,* a leaf.] in botany, having five leaves.

pen·tap′ō·dy, *n.* [*penta-,* and Gr. *pous, podos,* foot.] in prosody, a series composed of five metrical feet.

pen·tap′ō·lis, *n.* [*penta-,* and Gr. *polis,* city.] a confederacy of five cities.

pen′tap·tōte, *n.* [*penta-,* and Gr. *ptōtos,* fallen, declined, from *piptein,* to fall.] in grammar, a noun having five cases.

pen′tap·tyçh, *n.* [*penta-,* and Gr. *ptychē,* fold.] a picture or a set of pictures having a centerpiece and double-folding wings on each side.

pen′tärçh·y, *n.*; *pl.* **pen′tärçh·ieş,** [*pent-,* and Gr. *archē,* rule.]
1. a federation of five states, each under an individual leader or ruler.
2. government by five rulers.

pen·tȧ·sep′ăl·ous, *a.* [*penta-* and *sepal* and *-ous.*] in botany, having five sepals.

pen·tȧ·spẽr′mous, *a.* [*penta-,* and Gr. *sperma,* seed.] in botany, containing five seeds.

pen′tȧ·stiçh, *n.* [*penta-,* and Gr. *stichos,* verse.] a poem or stanza of five lines.

pen·tas′ti·çhous, *a.* in botany, arranged in five vertical rows: said of the leaves of such trees as the apple and cherry.

pen′tȧ·stōme, *n.* [Gr. *pentastomos; pente,* five, and *stoma,* mouth.] one of the *Pentastomida.*

Pen·tȧ·stom′i·dȧ, *n.pl.* in zoology, same as *Linguatulina.*

pen″tȧ·syl·lab′iç, *a.* [*penta-* and *syllabic.*] having or composed of five syllables.

Pen′tȧ·teūçh (-tūk), *n.* [*penta-,* and Gr. *teuchos,* an implement, a book.] the first five books of the Old Testament taken collectively: also called the *Books of Moses.*

Pen·tȧ·teū′çhăl, *a.* relating to the Pentateuch.

pen″tȧ·thī·on′iç, *a.* [*penta-* and *thionic.*] pertaining to or characteristic of a compound that contains five sulfur atoms.
pentathionic acid; acid derived from sulfurous acid by the action of hydrogen sulfide.

pen·tath′lon, *n.* [Gr., from *penta-,* five and *athlon,* a contest.] an athletic contest in which each contestant takes part in five events (broad jump, javelin throw, 200-meter dash, discus throw, and 1500-meter run): the winner is the contestant receiving the highest total of points.

pen·tȧ·tom′iç, *a.* [*pent-* and *atomic.*] in chemistry, (a) containing five atoms in the molecule; (b) containing five hydrogen atoms that can be replaced.

pen·tȧ·ton′iç, *a.* [*penta-* and *tonic.*] designating or of a musical scale having only five tones.

pen·tȧ·trē′mīte, *n.* any individual of the genus *Pentatremites.*

Pen″tȧ·trē·mī′tēş, *n.* [*penta-,* and Gr. *trēma,* a hole.] a genus of *Blastoidea.* The species were fixed to the sea bottom by a pedicel formed of solid polygonal plates, arranged in five ambulacral, and five interambulacral areas.

pen·tȧ·vā′lent (*or* -tav′ȧ-), *a.* 1. having a valence of five.
2. having five valences.
Also *quinquevalent.*

pen·tē·çon′tẽr, *n.* [Gr. *pentēkontoros* (*naus*), from *pentēkonta,* fifty.] an ancient Grecian vessel of fifty oars: also written *pentaconter.*

Pen′tē·çost, *n.* [Gr. *pentēkostē* (*hēmera*), the fiftieth (day), from *pentēkonta,* fifty, from *pente,* five.]
1. Shabuoth, the Jewish holiday.
2. a Christian festival on the seventh Sunday after Easter, celebrating the descent of the Holy Spirit upon the Apostles; Whitsunday.

Pen·tē·ços′tăl, *a.* pertaining to or taking place during Pentecost.

pen″tē·ços·tā′ri·ŏn, *n.* in the Orthodox Eastern Church, the book containing the offices used from Easter to the eighth day after Pentecost.

pen·tē·ços′tẽr, *n.* [Gr. *pentēkostēr,* from *pentēkonta,* fifty, from *pente,* five.] in ancient Greece, a military officer commanding fifty men.

pen·tē·ços′tys, pen·tē·ços′ty, *n.* [Gr. *pentēcostys.*] in ancient Greece, a body of fifty soldiers.

Pen·tel′iç, *a.* pertaining to or obtained from Mount Pentelicus, near Athens: applied to a variety of marble resembling Parian, but denser and finer grained. The Parthenon and other Athenian monuments were built of it.

Pen·tel′i·çăn, *a.* same as *Pentelic.*

pen′tēne, *n.* same as *amylene.*

pent′house, *n.* [altered from *pentice,* penthouse.]
1. a small structure, especially one with a sloping roof, attached to a larger building.
2. a sloping roof extending out from a wall or building.
3. a house or apartment built on the roof of a building.
4. anything like a penthouse, as a canopy or awning.

pent′house, *a.* overhanging. [Rare.]

pen′tice, *n.* [ME.; OFr. *apentis;* LL. *appendisium,* lit., an appendage.] penthouse. [Archaic.]

pen′tine, *n.* any of various isomeric hydrocarbons having the formula C_5H_8, and belonging to the acetylene series.

pent′land·īte, *n.* [after Joseph B. *Pentland.*] a bronze-yellow sulfide of nickel and iron, (FeNi)S, mined as an ore of nickel.

pen·tō·bar′bi·tal sō′di·um, *n.* [*pento-* for *penta-,* (because of methylbutyl five-carbon group) and *barbital.*] the soluble sodium salt of ethyl (1-methylbutyl) barbituric acid, used in medicine as a sedative, hypnotic, and analgesic.

pen′tōde, *n.* [*pento-* and electr*ode.*] in radio and communications, a five-electrode vacuum tube consisting of a cathode, an anode, and three other electrodes.

pen′tō·san, *n.* [from *pentose* and *-an.*] any of a group of plant carbohydrates which form pentoses upon undergoing hydrolysis.

pen′tō·sāne, *n.* pentosan.

pen′tōse, *n.* [*pent-* and *-ose.*] any of a group of monosaccharides having a composition corresponding to the formula $C_5H_{10}O_5$.

pen·tō·sū′ri·ȧ, *n.* [*pentose,* and Gr. *ouron,* urine.] the presence of pentose in the urine.

pen′tō·thal sō′di·um, [*pento-* for *penta-* (because of methylbutyl five-carbon group) and *thi*obarbiturate and *-al* (as in veron*al,* barbit*al*).] a drug, sodium ethyl-(1-methylbutyl)-thiobarbiturate, injected intravenously as an anesthetic and hypnotic: a trade-mark (*Pentothal Sodium*).

pen·tox′īde, *n.* [*pent-* and *oxide.*] an oxide, as of phosphorus or of antimony, in which there are five atoms of oxygen to the molecule.

pent rọọf, [Fr. *pente,* slope, and E. *roof.*] a roof formed like an inclined plane: the slope being all on one side: also called *shed roof.*

PENT ROOF

pen′trough (-trọf), *n.* a penstock.

Pent·stē′mŏn, *n.* [*pent-,* and Gr. *stēmōn,* warp, in modern botany, stamen.] a genus of herbs of the *Scrophulariaceæ,* in which the flower has five stamens, one of which is imperfect though conspicuous. Many species, with blue, purple, lilac, rose-colored, or yellow flowers, are cultivated.

pent·stē′mŏn, *n.* any plant of the genus *Pentstemon:* also called *beardtongue.*

pent′stock, *n.* a penstock.

pent′-up′, *a.* confined, suppressed, or penned up; held back; as, *pent-up* feelings.

pen′tyl, *n.* [*pent-* and *-yl.*] same as *amyl.*

pen′tyl·ēne, *n.* in chemistry, a local anesthetic obtained by the action of zinc chloride on amyl alcohol: it has a disagreeable odor.

pen·tyl′iç, *a.* pertaining to pentyl.

pen′tȳne, *n.* [*pent-* and *-yne.*] in chemistry, one of two normal hydrocarbons of the acetylene series having the formula C_5H_8.

pe·nụ′che, pe·nụ′chi, *n.* same as *panocha.*

pē′nuçh″le, pē′nuçk″le, *n.* same as *pinochle.*

pē′nult, *n.* [L. *penultima; pene,* almost, and *ultima,* last.] the next to the last; specifically, the second last syllable of a word.

pē·nul′ti·mȧ, *n.* same as *penult.*

pē·nul′ti·māte, *a.* 1. next to the last.
2. of the penult.

pē·nul′ti·māte, *n.* the penult.

pē·num′brȧ, *n.*; *pl.* **pē·num′brae, pē·num′brȧş,** [L. *pene,* almost, and *umbra,* shade.]
1. the partly lighted area surrounding the complete shadow of a body, as the moon, in full eclipse.
2. a partly lighted area around any area of full shadow, as of a sunspot.

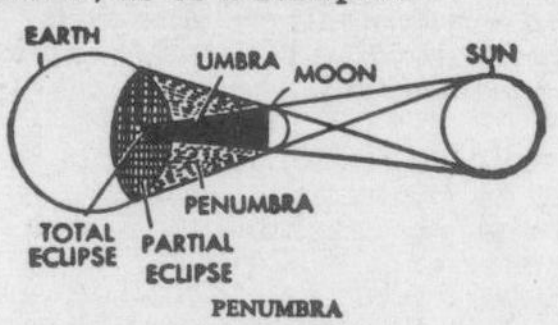

pē·num′brăl, *a.* pertaining to or resembling a penumbra; incompletely illuminated.

pē·num′brous, *a.* same as *penumbral.*

pē·nū′ri·ous, *a.* 1. excessively saving or sparing in the use of money; unwilling to part with money or possessions; mean; miserly; stingy; as, a *penurious* man.
2. scanty; barren; poorly supplied; as, a *penurious* spring.
3. without money; very poor. [Obs.]
Syn.—miserly, niggardly.

pē·nū′ri·ous·ly, *adv.* in a penurious manner.

pē·nū′ri·ous·ness, *n.* the state or quality of being penurious.

pen′ū·ry, *n.* [Fr. *pénurie;* L. *penuria,* want, scarcity.] lack of money or property; indigence; extreme poverty; privation; destitution.

Pe·nụ′ti·ăn, *n.* a conjectured family of western North American Indian languages.

pen′wīp″ẽr, *n.* a cloth or chamois used to wipe ink from a pen.

pen′wom″ăn (-woom″), *n.*; *pl.* **pen′wom″en** (-wim″), a literary woman; an authoress.

pē′ŏn, *n.* same as *poon.*

pē′ŏn, *n.* [from Sp. *peon,* a foot soldier, a day laborer, a pedestrian, from L. *pes, pedis,* the foot.]
1. in Latin America, (a) a member of the laboring class; (b) formerly, a person forced to work off a debt or to perform penal servitude.
2. in India, (a) a foot soldier; (b) a native policeman; (c) an attendant or footman.

pē′ŏn·ȧġe, *n.* 1. the condition of a peon.
2. the system by which debtors or legal prisoners are held in servitude to labor for their creditors or for persons who lease their services from the state.

pē′ō·ny, *n.*; *pl.* **pē′ō·nieş,** [L. *pæonia;* Gr. *paiōnia,* from *Paiōn,* an epithet of Apollo, who used this flower to cure the wounds of the gods.]
1. any plant and flower of the genus *Pæonia,* with large pink, white, red, or yellow, showy flowers.
2. the flower.

pēo′ple, *n.*; *pl.* **pēo′ple,** [ME. *peple, puple;* OFr. *pople, pueple;* Fr. *peuple,* from L. *populus,* people. The root is seen in L. *plebs,* the common people, and Gr. *polys,* many.]
1. *pl.* **pēo′pleş,** (a) all the persons of a racial, cultural, religious, or linguistic group; nation, race, etc.; (b) specifically, all the members of a group having in common traditional, historical, or cultural ties, as distinct from racial or political unity; as, the Jewish *people.*
2. the persons belonging to a certain place, community, or class; as, the *people* of Cleveland, *people* of wealth.
3. the members of a group under the leadership, influence, or control of a particular person or body, as a number of servants, royal subjects, etc.
4. the members of a person's class, set, race, tribe, etc.; as, the miner spoke for his *people.*
5. one's family; relatives; ancestry.
6. persons without wealth, influence, privilege, or distinction; populace.
7. the citizens or electorate of a state.
8. persons considered indefinitely; as, I don't care what *people* say.
9. *pl.* **pēo′pleş,** a tribe or kind, as of animals; a group of creatures; as, the ant *people,* fairies are the little *people.*
10. human beings, as distinct from other animals.
Syn.—nation, community, populace, mob, crowd, mass, persons, inhabitants, commonalty, tribe, race.

pēo′ple, *v.t.*; peopled, *pt., pp.*; peopling, *ppr.* to stock with inhabitants; to populate; to fill with or as with people.

pēo′ple·less, *a.* without people.

pēo'ple's frŏnt, popular front.

Pēo'ple's pär'ty, an American political party (1891–1904) advocating free coinage of gold and silver, public ownership of utilities, an income tax, and support of labor and agriculture: its members were called *Populists.*

Pē·ō'ri·à, *n.* one of a tribe of Indians native to what is now the state of Illinois.

pep, *n.* [abbrev. from *pepper.*] life; energy; spirited activity; verve; vigor; briskness. [Slang.]

pep, *v.t.*; pepped (pept), *pt., pp.*; pepping, *ppr.* to fill with pep; to invigorate; to animate: used with *up.* [Slang.]

pep'e·rine, *a.* of peperino.

pep·e·rī'nō, *n.* [It., from L. *piper,* pepper.] a volcanic rock, formed by the cementing together of sand, cinders, etc.

Pep·e·rō'mi·à, *n.* [Gr. *peperi,* pepper.] a large genus of tropical herbs of the pepper family, found chiefly in South America. Many are small creepers on the trunks of trees or wet rocks. *Peperomia pellucida* is used as a salad.

pe·pī'nō, *n.* [L. *pepo,* melon.] a cultivated shrub, *Philesia buxifolia,* of South Africa. It is of the lily family and has brilliant red flowers.

pep'lŏs, *n.* [Gr. *peplos.*] a large shawl or scarf worn draped about the body by women in ancient Greece: also spelled *peplus.*

pep'lum, *n.*; *pl.* **pep'lums, pep'là,** [L., from Gr. *peplos.*]
1. a peplos.
2. a flounce or short, flared skirt attached at the waist of a dress, blouse, coat, etc., and extending around the hips.

pē'pō, *n.* [L., large species of melon.] any fleshy gourd fruit with a hard rind and many seeds, as the melon, squash, etc.

pep'pẽr, *n.* [AS. *pipor, peppor,* from L. *piper*; Gr. *piperi*; Sans. *pippala.*]
1. (a) any of a number of related tropical shrubs of the capsicum family, especially a variety with a many-seeded, red or green, sweet or hot fruit; (b) the fruit.
2. (a) a pungent condiment prepared from any of a group of plants belonging to the genus *Piper*: *black pepper* is ground from the dried berries; *white pepper* consists of the dried seeds with the coatings removed; (b) any of these plants.

BLACK PEPPER (*Piper nigrum*)

3. cayenne; red pepper.
African pepper; (a) a tree of Western Africa; *Xylopia æthiopica,* or its pungent fruit, (b) cayenne pepper.
Chinese pepper; same as Japanese pepper.
Guinea pepper; same as *African pepper.*
Jamaica pepper; the allspice or pimento.
Japanese pepper; the aromatic fruit of a Japanese and Chinese shrub, *Xanthoxylum piperitum*; also, the shrub itself.
long pepper; (a) same as *kava*; (b) the spikes of *Piper longum* gathered before ripe to be used as the common black pepper of commerce.

LONG PEPPER (*Piper longum*)

Malaguetta or *Melegueta pepper*; same as *grains of paradise* under *grain.*
red pepper; see *capsicum.*

pep'pẽr, *v.t.* 1. to sprinkle or flavor with ground pepper.
2. to sprinkle freely or thickly.
3. to shower or pelt with many small objects; as, the lawn was *peppered* with hailstones.
4. to beat or thrash.

pep'pẽr, *v.i.* to fire shots at anything repeatedly.

pep'pẽr-ănd-sạlt', *a.* consisting of a fine weave or mixture of black with white, so as to appear grayish: said of cloth.

pep'pẽr·box, *n.* a small container with a perforated lid, used for sprinkling pulverized pepper on food.

pep'pẽr bush, a shrub of the heath family bearing fragrant flowers. It grows in the swamps of the Atlantic coast of the United States.

pep'pẽr cȧst'ẽr, a pepperbox; also, the bottle of a cruet stand designed to hold pepper.

pep'pẽr·çorn, *n.* 1. the dried berry of the black pepper: formerly used in a nominal payment of rent.
2. something insignificant or trifling.

pep'pẽr·çorn, *a.* of little value.

pep'pẽr dulse, *Laurencia pinnatifida,* an edible seaweed with a pungent taste. [Scot.]

pep'pẽr el'dẽr, one of various plants of the genus *Peperomia* or associated genera.

pep'pẽr·ẽr, *n.* 1. a grocer; one who sells pepper. [Obs.]
2. a person or thing that peppers.
3. a person who has a fiery temper. [Rare.]

pep'pẽr·gråss, *n.* 1. any plant of the genus *Lepidium,* as the garden cress, having white or greenish flowers formed like a cross, and leaves that are used in salads.
2. the European pillwort, *Pilularia globulifera.*

pep'pẽr·idġe, *n.* the tupelo or black gum, a tree with very tough wood, belonging to the genus *Nyssa.*
pepperidge bush; the barberry. [Brit. Dial.]

pep'pẽr·i·ness, *n.* a peppery quality.

pep'pẽr·mint, *n.* 1. a plant, *Mentha piperita,* of the mint family, with lance-shaped leaves and pink flowers.
2. an oil distilled from the peppermint herb, used for flavoring.
3. a confection, candy, or lozenge flavored with oil of peppermint.
peppermint camphor; same as *menthol.*

pep'pẽr·mint tree, any of a number of Australian eucalyptus trees yielding a peppermintlike oil, as *Eucalyptus piperita.*

pep'pẽr mọth, *Amphidasis betularia,* a white moth of Europe having black speckled wings.

pep'pẽr pot, 1. a pepperbox.
2. a West Indian stew of vegetables and meat or fish, flavored with cassava juice, red pepper, etc.
3. a thick, hotly seasoned stew of vegetables, dumplings, tripe, and other meat.
4. a soup of meat and vegetables flavored with hot spices.

pep'pẽr sạuce, small red peppers steeped in vinegar and used as a condiment.

pep'pẽr tree (or **shrub**), 1. a tropical or subtropical American tree, *Schinus molle,* having a pungent red drupe.
2. a Tasmanian tree, *Drimys aromatica,* the berries of which are used as pepper.

pep'pẽr·wŏrt, *n.* 1. peppergrass.
2. any plant of the *Marsileaceæ.*

pep'pẽr·y, *a.* 1. of, like, or highly seasoned with pepper.
2. sharp; fiery; hot, as speech or writing.
3. hot-tempered; easily angered; irritable.

pep'py, *a.*; *comp.* peppier; *superl.* peppiest; full of pep, or energy; brisk; vigorous; spirited. [Slang.]

pep'sin, *n.* [Gr. *pepsis,* digestion, from *peptein,* to digest.]
1. an enzyme secreted in the stomach, aiding in the digestion of proteins by splitting them into the less complex proteoses and peptones.
2. an extract of pepsin from the stomachs of calves, sheep, etc., used as a medicine in aiding digestion.

pep'sin·āte, *v.t.* pepsinated, *pt., pp.*; pepsinating, *ppr.* to treat, mix, or infuse with pepsin, as milk.

pep'sine, *n.* same as *pepsin.*

pep·sin·if'ẽr·ous, *a.* [*pepsin,* and L. *ferre,* to bear.] yielding pepsin.

pep·sin'ō·ġen, *n.* [from *pepsin* and *-gen.*] a pepsiniferous compound found in the gastric glands, which is changed to pepsin during digestion by the action of hydrochloric acid.

pep'tiç, *a.* [Gr. *peptikos,* from *peptein,* to digest.]
1. promoting digestion; relating to digestion.
2. having digestive powers.
3. of, pertaining to, or yielding pepsin.
4. caused by pepsin or other digestive secretions; as, a *peptic* ulcer.

pep'tiç, *n.* any substance which promotes digestion.

pep·tiç'i·ty, *n.* good peptic condition.

pep'tid, *n.* same as *peptide.*

pep'tīde, *n.* [*peptone* and *-ide.*] a combination of amino acids formed by the linkage of the amino groups of some of the acids with the carboxyl groups of others.

pep'tīze, *v.t.* and *v.i.*; peptized, *pt., pp.*; peptizing, *ppr.* [*pep*tone and *-ize.*] to change into a colloid, usually through the action of an added chemical; especially, to change (a sol) into a gel.

pep'tō·ġen, *n.* [*pep*tone and *-gen.*] any substance from which peptones can be derived.

pep·tō·ġen'iç, pep·toġ'e·nous, *a.* capable of producing or forming peptones.

pep"tō·hȳ"drō·çhlō'riç, *a.* of or pertaining to a compound of pepsin and hydrochloric acid.
peptohydrochloric acid; a hypothetical acid, formed when pepsin and dilute hydrochloric acid are mixed together, as in the process of digestion.

pep'tōne, *n.* [Gr. *peptos,* digested.] any of a group of soluble and diffusible simple proteins formed by the action of pepsin on albuminous substances, as in the process of digestion.

pep·tō·nē'mi·à, *n.* [*peptone,* and Gr. *haima,* blood.] a condition of the blood when peptones are present in it.

pep·ton'iç, *a.* of, like, or constituting a peptone.

pep"tō·ni·zā'tion, *n.* a peptonizing or being peptonized.

pep'tō·nīze, *v.t.*; peptonized, *pt., pp.*; peptonizing, *ppr.* to convert into peptones; to subject to the action of pepsin or other protein-converting agents.

pep'tō·noid, *n.* [*peptone* and *-oid.*] a substance resembling peptone or used instead of it.

pep·tō·nū'ri·à, *n.* [*peptone,* and Gr. *ouron,* urine.] the presence of peptones in the urine.

pep·tō·tox'in, *n.* [*pep*tone and *toxin.*] a poisonous alkaloid sometimes found in peptonized albumin, but disappearing as decomposition sets in.

Pē'quot, *n.* [from Am. Ind. (Algonquian) *Paquatauog,* destroyers.] a member of a tribe of Algonquian Indians that settled in Connecticut.

Pē'quot, *a.* of this tribe.

pẽr-, [from L. *per,* through.] a prefix meaning: (a) *through, throughout, away,* as in *per*ceive, *per*colate; (b) *thoroughly, completely, very,* as in *per*suade; (c) in chemistry, *containing* (a specified element or radical) *in its maximum, or a relatively high, valence,* as in *per*chlorate.

pẽr, *prep.* [L.] 1. through; by; by means of.
2. for each; for every; as, fifty cents *per* yard, the fare *per* mile.
per annum; by the year; annually.
per capita; for each person.
per diem; by the day; daily.
per se; by itself; considered in itself.

pẽr·ac'id, *n.* an acid containing a larger proportion of oxygen than other acids containing the same elements, as perboric acid, perchloric acid, etc.

pẽr·aċt', *v.t.* to perform; to accomplish. [Rare.]

pẽr·à·çūte', *a.* [L. *peracutus*; *per,* very, and *acutus,* sharp.] very sharp; very violent; as, a *peracute* fever. [Rare.]

pẽr·ad·ven'tūre, *adv.* [Fr. *par aventure*; *par,* L. *per,* by, and *aventure,* adventure.] by chance; also, perhaps; maybe. [Archaic.]

pẽr·ad·ven'tūre, *n.* chance; doubt; question; as, proved beyond *peradventure.* [Archaic.]

pe·rae'ō·pod, *n.* same as *pereiopod.*

per'à·grāte, *v.t.* [L. *peragrare*; *per,* through, over, and *ager,* a field.] to travel over or through. [Rare.]

per·à·grā'tion, *n.* the act of passing through any space; as, the *peragration* of the moon in her monthly revolution. [Rare.]

pẽr·am'bū·lāte, *v.t.*; perambulated, *pt., pp.*; perambulating, *ppr.* [L. *perambulare*; *per* and *ambulare,* to walk.]
1. to walk through, over, or around (a place).
2. to survey by passing over or around; to inspect.
3. to visit or traverse the boundaries of, as a parish or township.

pẽr·am'bū·lāte, *v.i.* to stroll.

pẽr·am·bū·lā'tion, *n.* a perambulating or that which is perambulated.

pẽr·am'bū·lā·tŏr, *n.* 1. a person who perambulates.
2. a wheeled instrument that measures the distance over which it is rolled: used by surveyors.
3. a baby carriage, or buggy. [Chiefly Brit.]

Per·à·mē'lēs, *n.* [Gr. *pēra,* bag, and L. *meles,* badger.] the typical genus of the family *Per-*

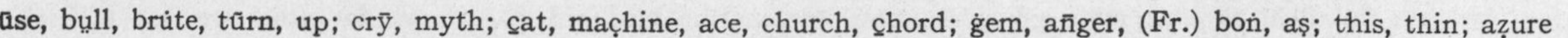

amelidæ, the bandicoots, small animals living on the ground in Australia and New Guinea.

pẽr′bend *n.* see *perpend.*

pẽr·bō′rāte, *n.* a salt of perboric acid.

pẽr·bō′riç ac′id, the hypothetical acid, HBO_3, whose salts, the perborates, are formed by the action of hydrogen peroxide on borates.

pẽr·brō′mīde, pẽr·brō′mid, *n.* a compound containing a high proportion of bromine.

Pẽr′çȧ, *n.* [L., a perch.] the perches, a Linnean genus of acanthopterygious fishes.

pẽr·çāle′, *n.* [Fr.] a closely woven cotton cloth, used for sheets, etc.

pẽr·çȧ·līne′, *n.* [Fr.] a fine cotton cloth, usually with a glazed finish and used for linings.

pẽr·çär′bīde, *n.* a compound of carbon in unusually large proportion. [Rare.]

pẽr·çär′bū·ret, *n.* a percarbide. [Obs.]

pẽr·çär′bū·ret·ed, *a.* combined with a maximum of carbon. [Obs.]

pẽr·çāse′, *adv.* [*per-* and L. *casus*, chance.] perhaps; perchance. [Obs.]

pẽrce, *v.t.* to pierce. [Obs.]

pẽr′ceȧnt (-sȧnt), *a.* piercing; penetrating. [Obs.]

pẽr·ceiv′ȧ·ble, *a.* that can be perceived.

pẽr·ceiv′ȧ·bly, *adv.* in a perceivable manner.

pẽr·ceiv′ănce, *n.* perception. [Obs.]

pẽr·ceive′, *v.t.* and *v.i.*; perceived, *pt., pp.*; perceiving, *ppr.* [Fr. *percevoir*; L. *percipere*, to take hold of, to feel, to perceive, to comprehend; *per*, through, and *capere*, to take.]

1. to grasp mentally; to take note (of); recognize; observe.

2. to become aware (of) through sight, hearing, touch, taste, or smell.

Syn.—discern, distinguish.

pẽr·ceiv′ẽr, *n.* one who perceives, feels, or observes.

pẽrce′ly, *n.* parsley. [Obs.]

pẽr·cent′, *n.* per cent.

pẽr cent, [L. *per centum.*] per hundred; by the hundred; in, to, or for every hundred; as, a 20 *per cent* casualty rate means that 20 in every 100 were casualties: symbol, %: also used as a noun meaning: (a) [Colloq.] percentage; (b) [*pl.*] bonds, government securities, etc. bearing regular interest of a (stated) per cent; as, three *per cents.*

pẽr·cent′ăge, *n.* [L. *per centum*, by the hundred.]

1. a given rate or proportion in every hundred.

2. any number or amount, as of interest, tax, etc., stated in per cent.

3. part; portion; share; as, only a small *percentage* of the people came.

4. use; advantage; profit; as, there's no *percentage* in worry. [Colloq.]

pẽr·cen′tile (*or* -tīle), *n.* in statistics, (a) any of the values in a series dividing the distribution of the individuals in the series into one hundred groups of equal frequency; (b) any of these groups.

pẽr·cen′tile, *a.* of a percentile or division into percentiles.

pẽr cen′tum, [L.] by the hundred: symbol, %.

pẽr′cept, *n.* [L. *perceptum*, from *percipere*, to perceive.] a recognizable sensation or impression received by the mind through the senses; something perceived.

pẽr·cep·ti·bil′i·ty, *n.* the state or quality of being perceptible; as, the *perceptibility* of light or color.

pẽr·cep′ti·ble, *a.* [Fr., from L. *percipere, perceptus*, to take up wholly.] that can be perceived.

pẽr·cep′ti·ble·ness, *n.* the state or quality of being perceptible.

pẽr·cep′ti·bly, *adv.* in a perceptible manner; so as to be perceptible.

pẽr·cep′tion, *n.* [L. *perceptio, perceptionis*, from *percipere*, to seize.]

1. consciousness; awareness.

2. the awareness of objects or other data through the medium of the senses.

3. the process or faculty of perceiving.

4. the result of this; knowledge, etc. gained by perceiving.

5. insight or intuition, as of an abstract quality.

pẽr·cep′tion·ăl, *a.* of or constituting perception.

pẽr·cep′tive, *a.* 1. of perception.

2. capable of perceiving; especially, perceiving readily.

pẽr·cep·tiv′i·ty, *n.* the state of being perceptive.

pẽr·cep′tū·ăl, *a.* of or involving perception.

Pẽr·ces′ō·çēs, *n.pl.* an order of fishes so named because of their similarity to perches and pikes: it includes mullets, sand smelts, silversides, etc.

pẽrch, *n.* [Fr. *perche*; L. *perca*; Gr. *perkē*, from *perknos*, dark-colored.]

1. any of several species of acanthopterygious fishes of the genus *Perca*, having powerful dorsal fins with strong and sharp spines. The common perch (*Perca fluviatilis*) is to be found in clear rivers and lakes throughout nearly the whole of the temperate parts of Europe; the common yellow perch of America is *Perca americana* or *flavescens.*

PERCH (*Perca fluviatilis*)

2. any of numerous fishes of related genera and families, as the surf fish of the *Embiotocidæ*, found on the Pacific coast.

black perch; any of several fishes, as the black bass.

blue perch; (a) the cunner; (b) the blue-banded perch of the Pacific coast.

gray perch; the fresh-water drum.

red-bellied perch; the long-eared sunfish, *Lepomis auritus.*

red perch; (a) the rosefish of the North Atlantic; (b) the garibaldi of California.

white perch; any of several species, especially *Morone americana*, common to the Atlantic coast of the United States and north to Nova Scotia.

pẽrch, *n.* [Fr. *perche*, from L. *pertica*, a pole, a staff.]

1. a horizontal pole provided as a roost for birds.

2. anything, as a branch or wire, upon which a bird rests.

3. any resting place or position, especially a high or insecure one.

4. a measure of length, equal to $5\frac{1}{2}$ yards; a rod.

5. a measure of area, equal to $30\frac{1}{4}$ square yards.

6. a cubic measure for stone, usually equal to $24\frac{3}{4}$ cubic feet.

7. a pole connecting the front and hind gear of a spring carriage.

pẽrch, *v.i.*; perched (pẽrcht), *pt., pp.*; perching, *ppr.* to sit or roost; to light or settle on or as on a perch; as, a bird *perches* on the limb of a tree.

Perched upon a bust of Pallas. —Poe.

pẽrch, *v.t.* 1. to place on or as on a fixed object or perch.

2. to inspect and remove imperfections from, as woolen cloth fresh from the loom. [Dial.]

pẽr·chȧnce′, *adv.* [L. *per*, by; and *chance.*] by chance; also, perhaps; possibly. [Archaic or Poet.]

pẽrch′ẽr, *n.* 1. one that perches; specifically, a bird of the order *Insessores.*

2. formerly, a wax candle placed on an altar. [Obs.]

3. one who perches rough cloth fresh from the loom.

Pẽr′çhe·ron, *n.* a large, fast-trotting draft horse of a breed from Perche, in France.

Pẽr′çhe·ron, *a.* relating to a kind of horse bred in Perche.

pẽrch′ing, *a.* designating a bird that perches; as, the robin is a *perching* bird.

pẽr·çhlō′rāte, *n.* a salt of perchloric acid.

pẽr·çhlō′riç, *a.* designating an acid, $HClO_4$, with a higher oxygen content for the same weight of chlorine than chloric acid.

pẽr·chlō′rīde, *n.* in a series, a chloride containing the highest percentage of chlorine.

pẽr·çhrō′miç, *a.* designating a compound containing chromium in its highest valence; as, *perchromic* acid.

pẽr′ci·fọrm, *a.* having the form of a perch; relating to the fishes classed as *Perciformes.*

pẽr′ci·fọrm, *n.* a perch; a percoid fish; one of the *Perciformes.*

Pẽr·ci·fọr′mēṣ, *n.pl.* a division of fishes characterized by compressed bodies and rather long dorsal fins, including the families *Percidæ, Sparidæ, Serranidæ*, and some others closely related.

pẽr·cip′i·ence, *n.* the act or power of perceiving; the state of being percipient; perception.

pẽr·cip′i·en·cy, *n.* percipience.

pẽr·cip′i·ent, *a.* perceiving; having the faculty of keen and ready perception.

pẽr·cip′i·ent, *n.* one who or that which perceives or has the faculty of perception.

Pẽr′ci·vāle, Pẽr′ci·văl, Pẽr′cē·văl, *n.* [OFr. *Perceval*; apparently coined by Chrétian de Troyes (12th century).] a knight of King Arthur's Round Table: he was one of the few to glimpse the Holy Grail.

pẽr·çlōṣe′, *n.* [OFr. *perclose*, from L. *per*, through, and *clausus*, pp. of *claudere*, to shut, end.]

1. conclusion. [Obs.]

2. a place closed, enclosed, or secluded. [Obs.]

3. in architecture, the raised back to a bench or seat of carved timber work; the parapet round a gallery; a screen or partition.

PERCLOSE

4. in heraldry, the lower part of the garter with the buckle, etc.: also called *demi-garter.* [Rare.]

Also *parclose.*

pẽr′çoid, *a.* [Gr. *perkē*, perch, and *-oid.*] resembling a fish of the perch family; belonging to the perch family.

pẽr′çoid, *n.* any fish of the perch family.

Pẽr·çoi′dē·ȧ, *n.pl.* same as *Perciformes.*

pẽr·çoi′dē·ăn, *a.* percoid.

pẽr′çō·lāte, *v.t.*; percolated, *pt., pp.*; percolating, *ppr.* [L. *percolare*, to strain.]

1. to pass (a liquid) gradually through small spaces or a porous substance; to filter.

2. to drain or ooze through (a porous substance); to permeate.

3. to brew (coffee) in a percolator.

pẽr′çō·lāte, *v.i.* to pass or ooze through small interstices; to filter; as, water *percolates* through a porous stone or a bed of sand.

pẽr′çō·lāte, *n.* a liquid product of percolation.

pẽr·çō·lā′tion, *n.* 1. the act of percolating.

2. in pharmacy, displacement.

pẽr′çō·lā·tŏr, *n.* 1. any device for percolating, as a porous vessel or a funnel lined with filter paper.

2. one who or that which filters.

3. a kind of coffeepot in which the boiling water repeatedly bubbles up through a tube and filters back to the bottom through the coffee grounds, which are held in a perforated container.

Pẽr·çō·mọr′phī, *n.pl.* [Gr. *perkē*, perch, and *morphē*, form.] an extensive class of spine-finned fishes including nearly all of the *Acanthopterygii.*

pẽr·çūr′rent, *a.* [L. *per*, through, and *currens* (*-entis*), *ppr.* of *currere*, to run.] in botany, running throughout the entire length: said of a midrib running from the stem to the apex of a leaf.

pẽr·çūr′sō·ry, *a.* [L. *percursus*, pp. of *percurrere*, to run through.] cursory; running over slightly or in haste. [Rare.]

pẽr·çuss′, *v.t.* [L. *percussus*, pp. of *percutere*, to strike.]

1. to strike forcibly. [Obs.]

2. in medicine, to subject to percussion.

pẽr·çus′sion (-kush′un), *n.* [L. *percussio* (*-onis*), a striking.]

1. the hitting or impact of one body against another, as the hammer of a firearm against a powder cap.

2. the shock, vibration, etc. resulting from this.

3. the impact of sound waves on the ear.

4. in medicine, the striking or tapping of the chest, back, etc. with the fingertips so as to determine from the sound produced the condition of any of the internal organs.

5. percussion instruments collectively.

center of percussion; see under *center.*

immediate percussion; in medicine, percussion of the body directly by the fingers.

mediate percussion; in medicine, percussion in which a pleximeter is employed, or a substance interposed between the fingers and the part struck.

pẽr·çus′sion bul′let, an explosive bullet, or one which bursts on impact.

pẽr·çus′sion çap, a small metal cap, containing fulminating powder, and used in a percussion lock to explode gunpowder.

pẽr·çus′sion çär′tridge (-trij), a cartridge exploding with slight impact.

pẽr·çus′sion fig′ūre, the figure formed by the cracks resulting when a hard, blunt object comes suddenly in contact with a flat crystal.

pẽr·çus′sion fūṣe, a fuse that explodes when struck or when striking an object.

pẽr·çus′sion in′strū·ment, a musical instrument in which the tone is produced when

some part is struck, as the drums, cymbals, tambourine, triangle, bells, xylophone, etc., and, broadly, the piano.

pẽr·çus'sion lock, a form of gunlock in which the cock or hammer strikes a fulminate to explode the charge.

pẽr·çus'sion match, a match which is ignited by percussion.

pẽr·çus'sion pow'dẽr, an explosive ignited by percussion.

pẽr·çus'sion sieve (siv), an apparatus for sorting ores, especially those of lead.

pẽr·çus'sion tā'ble, in metallurgy, a form of ore-separating apparatus consisting of a slightly sloping table on which stamped ore or metalliferous sand is placed to be sorted by gravity. A stream of water is directed over the ore, and the table is subjected to concussion at intervals.

pẽr·çus'sive, *a.* of or characterized by percussion.

pẽr·çū·tā'nē·ous, *a.* [L. *per*, through, and *cutis*, skin.]
1. going through the skin without breaking it.
2 acting through the skin.

pẽr·çū'tient (-shent), *a.* [L. *percutiens.*] striking or having the power to strike.

pẽr·çū'tient, *n.* one who or that which strikes or has power to strike.

Pēr·di·cī'nae, *n.pl.* [L. *perdix*, *perdicis*, and *-inæ.*] a subfamily of *Tetraonidæ*, including the partridges and quails. The legs are bare and the nostrils naked, with a small horny skin on the upper margin. The genera are numerous, and almost world-wide in distribution, being absent only from the Pacific islands.

pẽr·diē', *adv.* and *interj.* pardie. [Archaic.]

pẽr'di·foil, *n.* [L. *perdere*, to lose, and *folium*, leaf.] a plant that annually loses or drops its leaves: opposed to *evergreen.* [Rare.]

pẽr·di'tion (-dish'un), *n.* [L. *perditio* (*-onis*), from *perditus*, pp. of *perdere*, to lose, to ruin.]
1. complete and irreparable loss; ruin.
2. in theology, (a) the loss of the soul or of hope for salvation; damnation; (b) the place or condition of damnation; hell.

If we reject the truth, we seal our own *perdition.* —J. M. Mason.

3. loss. [Obs.]
4. the cause of ruin or destruction. [Obs.]

pẽr·di'tion·ȧ·ble, *a.* that can be ruined; fit for perdition. [Rare.]

Pẽr'dix, *n.* [Gr.] the typical genus of the *Perdicinæ*, including the partridges. The common European partridge is *Perdix perdix.*

pẽr·dū', pẽr·dūe', *n.* [Fr., pp. of *perdre*, to lose; L. *perdere.*] a soldier or group of soldiers sent on a forlorn hope, called in French *un enfant perdu* or *enfants perdus*; hence, one in a desperate situation. [Obs.]

To watch, poor *perdu*,
With this thin helm. —Shak.

pẽr·dū', pẽr·dūe', *a.* 1. out of sight; in hiding; concealed, as in military ambush.

The moderator, out of view,
Beneath the desk had lain *perdue.*
—Trumbull.

2. abandoned; employed on desperate purposes; accustomed to desperate purposes or enterprises. [Obs.]

pẽr·dū·el'liŏn (-yun), *n.* [L. *perduellio*; *per-* intens., and *duellum*, original form of *bellum*, war, from *duo*, two.] in law, treason. [Obs.]

pẽr·dūr·ȧ·bil'i·ty, *n.* durability.

pẽr·dūr'ȧ·ble, *a.* [Fr., from L. *perdurare*; *per*, through, and *durare*, to last.] very durable; lasting; continuing long.

pẽr·dūr'ȧ·bly, *adv.* in a perdurable manner.

pẽr·dūr'ănce, pẽr·dū·rā'tion, *n.* long continuance. [Rare.]

pẽr·dūre', *v.i.*; perdured, *pt.*, *pp.*; perduring, *ppr.* [L. *perdurare.*] to endure for a long time; to last indefinitely. [Rare.]

pẽr'dy, *adv.* [Fr. *par Dieu.*] certainly; verily; in truth. [Obs.]

pēre (pâr), *n.* [Fr., from L. *pater*, father.]
1. father: often used after the surname, like English *Senior*, as, Dumas *père.*
2. [P–] the title of certain priests.

pēre, *n.* a peer. [Obs.]

pẽr·ē'găl, *a.* [Fr. *per*, and *égal*, equal.] equal. [Obs.]

per'e·grin, *a.* peregrine.

per'ē·gri·nāte, *a.* traveled; foreign. [Rare.]

per'ē·gri·nāte, *v.i.*; peregrinated, *pt.*, *pp.*; peregrinating, *ppr.* [L. *peregrinatus*, pp. of *peregrinari*, from *peregrinus*, a traveler or stranger; *peragrare*, to wander; *per*, through, and *ager*, country.]
1. to travel from place to place, or from one country to another.
2. to live in foreign countries. [Obs.]

per'ē·gri·nāte, *v.t.* to follow (a route, etc.); to travel along.

per·ē·gri·nā'tion, *n.* 1. a traveling from one country to another; a wandering.
2. abode in foreign countries. [Obs.]

per'ē·gri·nā·tŏr, *n.* a traveler into foreign countries; one who wanders or travels about.

per'ē·grine, *n.* a species of large, swift falcon, *Falco peregrinus*, found in America, Europe, and Asia: also *peregrine falcon.*

per'ē·grine, *a.* [L. *peregrinus*; *per*, through and *ager*, field.] foreign; traveling or migratory.

per·ē·grin'i·ty, *n.* 1. the state of being peregrine.
2. travel; a wandering. [Rare.]

A new removal, what we may call his third *peregrinity*, had to be decided on.
—Carlyle.

pē·reī'on (-rī'), *n.* [LL., from Gr. *periiōn*, ppr. of *periienai*, to go about.] in crustaceology, the thorax.

pē·reī'ō·pod, *n.* [*pereion*, and Gr. *pous*, *podos*, foot.] a thoracic limb.

pe·rei'rȧ bärk, *n.* the medicinal bark of a tree, native to Brazil: used as a remedy for fevers and as a tonic: also *pereira.*

pe·rei'rine, pe·rei'rin (*or* -rin), *n.* an alkaloid powder, $C_{19}H_{24}N_2O$, obtained from pereira bark and used in medicine as a tonic and to reduce fevers.

pe·relle', *n.* [LL. *parella.*] a substance resembling litmus extracted from a lichen, *Lecanora parella*, and used in dyeing.

pẽr·empt', *v.t.* [L. *peremptus*, *perimere*, to kill.] in law, to defeat; to crush or destroy. [Obs.]

pẽr·emp'tion, *n.* [L. *peremptio.*] a defeat; a quashing; nonsuit. [Obs.]

pẽr·emp'tō·ri·ly, *adv.* in a peremptory manner; absolutely; positively; in a decisive manner.

pẽr·emp'tō·ri·ness, *n.* the state or quality of being peremptory; positiveness; absolute decision; dogmatism.

pẽr·emp'tō·ry, *a.* [Fr. *peremptoire*; L. *peremptorius*, from *peremptus*, pp. of *perimere*, to destroy.]
1. in law, barring further action, debate, question, etc.; final; absolute; decisive.
2. that cannot be denied, changed, delayed, opposed, etc., as a command.
3. intolerantly positive; dictatorial; dogmatic; imperious; as, a *peremptory* manner.

peremptory challenge; in law, an objection to seating a person as a juror that cannot be denied the party making it: in criminal cases, one or both parties may have a limited number of peremptory challenges, that is, they may disqualify a certain number of people from serving as jurors without giving reason or cause.

peremptory plea; in law, a plea in bar of the suit; a plea of defendant to the merits of action on the part of plaintiff.

peremptory writ; in law, a writ requiring the sheriff to cause the defendant to appear in court without any option, the plaintiff giving the sheriff security to effectually prosecute his claim.

Syn.—arbitrary, decisive, dictatorial, overbearing, absolute.

pẽr·en'nāte, *v.i.*; perennated, *pt.*, *pp.*; perennating, *ppr.* [L. *perennatus*, pp. of *perennare*; *perennis*, perennial.] to be perennial: said of plants.

pẽr·en'ni·ăl, *a.* [L. *perennis*; *per*, through, and *annus*, a year.]
1. lasting or continuing without cessation through the whole year.
2. lasting or continuing for a long time; as, a *perennial* youth.
3. returning or becoming active again and again; perpetual; unceasing; never failing.
4. in botany, having a life cycle of more than two years; as, a *perennial* root, a *perennial* plant.
5. in entomology, (a) living more than one year; (b) continuing existence from year to year by producing colonies, as the bee or the ant.

pẽr·en'ni·ăl, *n.* in botany, a plant that lives more than two years, whether it retains its leaves or not. One that retains its leaves during winter is called *evergreen*; one that casts its leaves *deciduous.*

pẽr·en'ni·ăl·ly, *adv.* in a perennial manner; every year; continually; without ceasing; from year to year.

pẽr·en'ni·brañch, *a.* [L. *perennis*, perennial, and *branchiæ*, gills.] pertaining to the *Perennibranchiata.*

pẽr·en'ni·brañch, *n.* an amphibian with gills that are retained throughout life; one of the *Perennibranchiata.*

Pẽr·en·ni·brañ·chi·ā'tȧ, *n.pl.* a division of urodelan amphibians which retain their gills through life.

pẽr·en·ni·brañ'chi·āte, *a.* same as *perennibranch.*

per·er·rā'tion, *n.* [L. *pererratus*, from *pererrare*, to wander.] a wandering or rambling through various places. [Obs.]

pẽr'feçt, *a.* [L. *perfectus*, pp. of *perficere*, to finish; *per*, through, and *facere*, to do.]
1. complete in all respects; without defect or omission; sound; flawless.
2. in a condition of complete excellence, as in skill or quality; faultless; most excellent: sometimes used comparatively; as, to create a more *perfect* union.
3. completely correct or accurate; exact; precise; as, a *perfect* copy.
4. without reserve or qualification; pure; utter; sheer; complete; as, a *perfect* fool, *perfect* stranger.
5. in botany, having stamens and pistils in the same flower; monoclinous.
6. in grammar, expressing or showing a state or action completed at the time of speaking or at the time indicated: verbs have three perfect tenses; simple (or present) perfect, past perfect (or pluperfect), and future perfect.
7. in music, (a) designating an interval (i.e., the fourth, fifth, or octave) whose character is not altered by inversion; (b) designating a cadence that satisfactorily ends a composition according to the standards of classical harmony.
8. quite certain; assured. [Obs.]

perfect cadence; in music, a cadence in which the dominant passes into the harmony of the tonic.

perfect chord; in music, a chord of the first, third, fifth, and octave.

perfect conductor; in electricity, any conductor which, when charged, has equal potential throughout the charge.

perfect game; (a) in baseball, a game in which no batter on the opposing team reaches base; (b) in bowling, a game in which a bowler scores twelve successive strikes.

perfect number; a number which is equal to the sum of all its different divisors; as, 28=1+2+4+7+14.

perfect participle; the past participle.

perfect rhyme; a rhyme of two words or syllables spelled or pronounced alike but differing in meaning, as *dear* and *deer*; rich rhyme.

pẽr·feçt' (*or* pẽr'fekt), *v.t.*; perfected, *pt.*, *pp.*; perfecting, *ppr.* 1. to finish or complete, so as to leave nothing wanting.
2. to make perfect or more nearly perfect according to a given standard, as by training or improvement.

If we love one another, God dwelleth in us, and his love is *perfected* in us.
—1 John iv. 12.

pẽr'feçt, *n.* 1. the perfect tense.
2. a verb form in this tense.

pẽr·feç'tȧ, *n.* [Sp., perfect.] a bet or betting procedure in which one wins if one correctly picks the first and second place finishers in a race.

pẽr·feçt'ẽr, *n.* one who perfects.

Pẽr·feç'tī, *n.pl.* [plural of L. *perfectus*, perfect.] a class of the Cathari, of the twelfth century, who practiced extreme asceticism, claiming to be the true church and therefore perfect.

pẽr·feç·ti·bil'i·ăn, *n.* an adherent to or believer in perfectibility.

pẽr·feç·tib'i·list, *n.* one who believes that perfectibility may be attained in this life.

pẽr·feçt·i·bil'i·ty, *n.* the capability of becoming or being made perfect.

pẽr·feçt'i·ble, *a.* capable of becoming or being made perfect.

pẽr·feçt'ing press, a printing press that receives and separates a sheet of paper from a roll, carries it along by means of rollers and guides, prints it on both sides, and delivers it folded and ready to be handled.

pẽr·feç'tion, *n.* [ME. *perfeccioun*; OFr.; L. *perfectio.*]
1. the act or process of perfecting; as, the *perfection* of the machine took many months.
2. the quality or condition of being perfect;

the extreme degree of excellence according to a given standard.

3. a person or thing that is the perfect embodiment of some quality.

4. a quality, endowment, or acquirement completely excellent, or of great worth.

to perfection; completely; perfectly; to the highest possible degree; in a manner not to be excelled; as, the machine does its work *to perfection*.

pẽr·fec̦′tion, *v.t.* to complete; to make perfect. [Rare.]

pẽr·fec̦′tion·ăl, *a.* of perfection. [Obs.]

pẽr·fec̦′tion·āte, *v.t.* to perfect. [Obs.]

pẽr·fec̦′tion·iṣm, *n.* any doctrine that holds that moral, religious, or social perfection can and should be attained in this life.

pẽr·fec̦′tion·ist, *n.* 1. a person who believes in a doctrine of perfectionism.

2. a person who strives for perfection.

3. [P–] one of a community founded by John H. Noyes (1811–1887) at Oneida, New York; a believer in the doctrine of Christian perfection as taught in the Oneida Community.

pẽr·fec̦′tion·ment, *n.* the state of being perfect; the act of perfecting. [Rare.]

pẽr·fec̦′tive, *a.* 1. conducing to make perfect; tending to bring to perfection: usually followed by *of*.

Praise and adoration are actions *perfective of* the soul. —More.

2. in grammar, designating an aspect of verbs, as in Russian, expressing completion of the action or state.

pẽr·fec̦′tive, *n.* 1. the perfective aspect.

2. a verb in this aspect.

pẽr·fec̦t′ive·ly, *adv.* in a manner that brings to perfection.

pẽr′fec̦t·ly, *adv.* 1. totally; completely; as, a thing *perfectly* new.

2. so as to be perfect; to a perfect degree; as, a proposition *perfectly* understood.

The apparatus was *perfectly* adjusted; the experiment began. —Von Blau.

Syn.—fully, wholly, entirely, completely, totally, exactly, accurately.

pẽr′fec̦t·ness, *n.* the state or quality of being perfect; perfection.

pẽr·fec̦′tō, *n.*; *pl.* **pẽr·fec̦′tōṣ,** [Sp., perfect.] a cigar of a standard shape, thick in the center and tapering to a point at either end.

pẽr·fẽr′vid, *a.* [L. *perfervidus*, for *præfervidus*, *præ*, very, and *fervidus*, ardent.] exceedingly fervid; ardent; too zealous.

pẽr·fi′cient (-fish′ent), *n.* [L. *perficiens*, ppr. of *perficere*, to do thoroughly.] one who perfects a lasting work; especially, one who endows a charity. [Obs.]

pẽr·fi′cient, *a.* making effective; actual. [Rare.]

pẽr·fid′i·ous, *a.* [L. *perfidiosus*, from *perfidia*, perfidy.]

1. violating good faith or vows; false to trust or confidence reposed; treacherous; as, a *perfidious* agent, a *perfidious* friend.

2. proceeding from treachery, or consisting in breach of faith; as, a *perfidious* act.

Syn.—unfaithful, traitorous, deceitful, untrustworthy.

pẽr·fid′i·ous·ly, *adv.* in a perfidious manner.

pẽr·fid′i·ous·ness, *n.* the quality of being perfidious; treachery; traitorousness.

pẽr′fi·dy, *n.*; *pl.* **pẽr′fi·dieṣ,** [L. *perfidia*; *per*, through, away from, and *fides*, faith.] the deliberate act of violating faith, a promise, a vow, or allegiance; treachery; the violation of a trust reposed.

pẽr′fit, *a.* perfect. [Obs.]

pẽr′fix, *v.t.* to fix. [Obs.]

pẽr′flȧ·ble, *a.* that may be blown through. [Obs.]

pẽr·flāte′, *v.t.* to blow through. [Obs.]

pẽr·flā′tion, *n.* the act of blowing through. [Obs.]

pẽr·fō′li·āte, *a.* [L. *per*, through, and *folium*, a leaf.]

1. in botany, having the base entirely surrounding the stem so that the stem appears to pass through it: said of a leaf.

2. in zoology, surrounded by flat expansions or discoid processes: said of certain forms of antennae.

PERFOLIATE LEAVES
A, perfoliate (of bellwort); B, connate perfoliate (of wild honeysuckle)

pẽr′fō·rȧ·ble, *a.* capable of being perforated.

Pẽr·fō·rā′tȧ, *n.pl.* 1. the perforate corals or *Porosa*, a group of the *Madreporaria*, characterized by porous reticulate walls.

2. a group of foraminifers having minute perforations in the shell through which the pseudopodia can protrude.

pẽr′fō·rāte, *v.t.*; perforated, *pt.*, *pp.*; perforating, *ppr.* [L. *perforatus*, pp. of *perforare*; *per*, through, and *forare*, to bore.]

1. to bore through; to pierce with a pointed instrument; to make a hole or holes through by boring or punching.

2. to pierce with holes in a row, as a pattern, sheet of stamps, etc.

pẽr′fō·rāte, *a.* 1. bored or pierced with holes, especially with a row of holes, as to facilitate tearing.

2. pertaining to the *Perforata*.

pẽr′fō·rā·ted, *a.* perforate.

pẽr′fō·rā·ting mȧ·chïne′, 1. a machine for making perforations in paper, to facilitate the separation of a portion, as between postage stamps.

2. a machine for making holes in paper for messages to be sent by the automatic method of telegraphy.

3. a machine for drilling rock.

pẽr·fō·rā′tion, *n.* 1. a perforating or being perforated.

2. a hole or any of a series of holes punched or drilled, as between postage stamps on a sheet.

pẽr′fō·rā·tive, *a.* that perforates readily.

pẽr′fō·rā·tŏr, *n.* one who or that which perforates.

pẽr·fōrce′, *adv.* [L. *per*, through, and *force*.] of or through necessity; necessarily.

pẽr·fōrce′, *v.t.* to compel; to coerce. [Obs.]

pẽr·fōrce′, *n.* necessity; compulsion. [Rare.]

pẽr·fo̤rm′, *v.t.*; performed, *pt.*, *pp.*; performing, *ppr.* [ME. *parfournen*, from OFr. *parfournir*, to perform, to consummate, from prefix *par*, *per*, and OFr. *fornir*, Fr. *fournir*, to accomplish, to furnish.]

1. to act on so as to accomplish or bring to completion; to execute; to do, as a task, process, etc.

2. to carry out; to meet the requirements of; to fulfill, as a promise or command.

3. to give a performance of; to render or enact, as a piece of music, dramatic role, etc.

pẽr·fo̤rm′, *v.i.* to carry out or execute an action or process; especially, to give a public exhibition of skill, as in music, drama, magic, etc.

pẽr·fo̤rm′ȧ·ble, *a.* that can be performed.

pẽr·fo̤rm′ănce, *n.* 1. the act of performing; execution; accomplishment.

2. operation or functioning, usually with regard to effectiveness, as of an airplane.

3. something done or performed; deed or feat.

4. a formal exhibition of skill or talent, as a play, musical program, etc.; a show.

pẽr·fo̤rm′ẽr, *n.* one who performs anything; particularly, one who takes part in a public entertainment or exhibition; as, a good *performer* on the violin; a celebrated *performer* in comedy or tragedy.

pẽr′fri·c̦āte, *v.t.* [L. *perfricare*.] to rub thoroughly. [Obs.]

pẽr·fri·c̦ā′tion, *n.* the act of rubbing vigorously; especially, of rubbing some substance, as ointment, into the skin. [Rare.]

pẽr·fū′mȧ·tō·ry, *a.* of or relating to perfumes. [Rare.]

pẽr·fūme′, *v.t.*; perfumed, *pt.*, *pp.*; perfuming, *ppr.* [Fr. *parfumer*; It. *perfumare*; L. *per-* intens., and *fumare* to smoke, from *fumus*, smoke.] to scent; to fill or impregnate with a fragrant or pleasing odor; as, to *perfume* an apartment; to *perfume* a garment.

pẽr′fūme, *n.* [Fr. *parfum*, from the v.]

1. a pleasing smell or odor; sweet scent, as of flowers; fragrance.

2. a substance producing a pleasing odor; especially, a liquid extract of the scent of flowers or a substance like this prepared synthetically.

Syn.—odor, scent, fragrance, smell, aroma, redolence, sweetness.

pẽr·fūm′ẽr, *n.* 1. one who or that which perfumes.

2. one who manufactures or sells perfumes.

pẽr·fūm′ẽr·y, *n.*; *pl.* **pẽr·fūm′ẽr·ieṣ,** 1. a perfume, or perfumes in general.

2. the trade of a perfumer.

3. a place where perfume is made or sold.

pẽr·func̦′tō·ri·ly, *adv.* in a perfunctory manner.

pẽr·func̦′tō·ri·ness, *n.* the quality or state of being perfunctory.

pẽr·func̦′tō·ry, *a.* [LL. *perfunctorius*; L. *per*, and *fungi*, *functus*, to get rid of, to perform; execute, do.]

1. done without care or interest or merely as a form or routine; superficial; as, a *perfunctory* examination.

2. without concern or solicitude; indifferent; as, a *perfunctory* lecturer.

pẽr·func̦′tū·rāte, *v.t.* to execute perfunctorily, or in an indifferent or mechanical manner. [Rare.]

pẽr·fūṣe′, *v.t.*; perfused, *pt.*, *pp.*; perfusing, *ppr.* [L. *perfusus*, pp. of *perfundere*; *per*, and *fundere*, to pour.]

1. to sprinkle, cover over, or permeate with or as with a liquid; to suffuse.

2. to pour or spread (a liquid, etc.) through or over something.

pẽr·fū′ṣion, *n.* a perfusing or being perfused.

pẽr·fū′sive, *a.* that perfuses readily.

pẽr·gȧ·mē′nē·ous, *a.* [L. *pergamena*, parchment.] in entomology, relating to any part consisting of a thin, tough, semitransparent substance somewhat resembling parchment; pergamentaceous.

pẽr·gȧ·men·tā′ceous, *a.* of the texture of parchment; pergameneous.

pẽr′gō·lȧ, *n.* [It. *pergola*, an arbor, from L. *pergula*, an arbor, a balcony, from *pergere*, to proceed, to continue.] a tunnel-shaped structure of latticework upon which climbing plants are grown.

pẽr·gun′nȧh, *n.* in Hindustan, a circle or territory comprising a limited number of villages.

pẽr·haps′, *adv.* [*per-* and *hap*, pl. *haps*.]

1. possibly; probably; maybe; as, *perhaps* we'd better go.

2. by chance; perchance; as, if, *perhaps*, he shouldn't come.

Syn.—possibly, peradventure, perchance.

per′i-, [Gr. *peri*, around.] a prefix meaning: (a) *around, about, encircling, surrounding*, as in *peri*scope; (b) *near*, as in *peri*gee.

pē′ri, *n.* [Per. *parī*.] in Persian mythology, an elf or fairy, represented as a descendant of fallen angels excluded from paradise till their penance is accomplished; hence, any fairylike or elfin being.

per·i·ad·ē·nī′tis, *n.* [*peri-*, Gr. *adēn*, gland, and *-itis*.] inflammation in the tissues contiguous to a gland.

per·i·ä′guȧ (-gwȧ), *n.* same as *piragua*.

per′i·anth, *n.* [*peri-*, and Gr. *anthos*, flower.] in botany, the envelope of a flower, especially one in which the calyx and corolla are combined so that they cannot be clearly distinguished from each other, as in many monocotyledonous plants, the tulip, orchid, etc. The perianth is called single when it consists of one verticil, and double when it consists of both calyx and corolla.

per·i·an′thi·um, *n.* same as *perianth*.

per′i·apt, *n.* [Gr. *periapton*, from *periaptein*, to fit or tie about.] an amulet; a charm worn to defend against disease or mischief.

per·i·är·tē·rī′tis, *n.* [*peri-* and *arteritis*.] inflammation in the sheathlike tissue about an artery.

per″i·är·thrī′tis, *n.* [*peri-* and *arthritis*.] an inflamed state of the tissues about a joint.

per″i·är·tic̦′ū·lăr, *a.* [*peri-* and *articular*.] relating to or surrounding a joint.

per·i·as′trăl, *a.* relating to the periastron.

per·i·as′tron, *n.* [*peri-*, and Gr. *astron*, star.] a point in the orbit of a star which revolves about another star where they are nearest to one another.

per·i·a̤u′gẽr, *n.* same as *piragua*.

per·i·ax′i·ăl, *a.* [*peri-*, and L. *axis*, axis.] in anatomy, surrounding an axis; used particularly in relation to the axis cylinder of a nerve.

per′i·blast, *n.* [*peri-*, and Gr. *blastos*, germ.] the cell substance surrounding the entoblast.

per·i·blas′tic̦, *a.* undergoing cell cleavage, as in the meroblastic egg.

per·i·blas′tū·lȧ, *n.* [*peri-* and *blastula*.] the blastula formed as the result of superficial cleavage in the periblastic ova.

per′i·blem, *n.* [Gr. *periblēma*, cloak; *periballein*, to throw round.] in botany, the undifferentiated embryonic tissue in the growing points of plant stems and roots which develops into the cortex.

pē·rib′ō·los, *n.* [Gr., from *peri*, around, and *ballein*, to throw.] a court entirely round a temple, surrounded by a wall.

per·i·brañ′chi·ăl, *a.* [*peri-* and *branchial*.] in

biology, relating to or surrounding the respiratory organs.

per·i·bron′chi·ăl, *a.* [*peri-* and *bronchial.*] located in the region of the bronchial tubes.

per·i·cae′căl, *a.* [*peri-*, and L. *cæcum*, the caecum.] related to or situated near the caecum, or vermiform appendix.

per·i·cam′bi·um, *n.* [*peri-* and *cambium.*] in botany, the layer of thin-walled cells lying next to the endodermis, and surrounding certain fibrovascular bundles.

per·i·căr′di·ăl, per·i·căr′di·aç, *a.* relating to the pericardium; surrounding the heart.
pericardial fluid; a serous fluid within the pericardium, by means of which the heart and pericardium glide upon one another without friction.

per·i·căr′di·ăn, *a.* relating to the pericardium; pericardial.

per·i·căr′diç, *a.* pericardial.

per″i·căr·dī′tis, *n.* [*pericardium* and *-itis.*] inflammation affecting the pericardium.

per·i·căr′di·um, *n.*; *pl.* **per·i·căr′di·ȧ,** [Gr. *perikardios*, from *peri*, around and *kardia*, heart.] the membranous sac that encloses the heart. It contains the pericardial fluid and consists of an outer layer of dense, fibrous tissue, derived from the sheet or band of tissue that invests the nerves, muscles, and blood vessels of the neck, and the epicardium, or inner serous layer which directly surrounds the heart. The epicardium folds back over the inside surface of the fibrous layer, forming the parietal pericardium which does not come into direct contact with the heart.

per′i·cărp, *n.* [*peri-*, and Gr. *karpos*, fruit.] in botany, the wall of a developed or ripened ovary, sometimes consisting of three distinct layers, the endocarp, mesocarp, and epicarp.

per·i·căr′pi·ăl, per·i·căr′piç, *a.* of or relating to a pericarp.

per·i·cel′lū·lăr, *a.* [*peri-* and *cellular.*] surrounding a cell or cellular tissue; as, *pericellular* lymph vessels.

per·i·cē·men·tī′tis, *n.* inflammation of the pericementum.

per″i·cē·men′tum, *n.* [*peri-*, and L. *cementum*, cement.] the layer of connective tissue surrounding the cement layer of a tooth.

per·i·cen′tẽr, *n.* [*peri-*, and Gr. *kentron*, center.] in astronomy, the point in its orbit where a satellite body most nearly approaches its center of attraction.

per′i·çhaete, *n.* same as *perichaetium*.

per·i·çhae′tiăl, *a.* pertaining to the perichaetium.

per·i·çhae′ti·um (-shi-), *n.* [*peri-*, and Gr. *chaite*, long hair.] in mosses, the cluster of leaves that surrounds the bulbous base of the stalk or seta of the seed vessel or sporangium.

per·i·çhae′tous, *a.* having the body encircled by hairlike processes or setae, as certain earthworms.

per′i·çhēte, *n.* same as *perichaetium*.

per·i·çhon′dri·ăl, *a.* of or characterized by perichondrium.

per″i·çhon·drī′tis, *n.* inflammation affecting the perichondrium.

per·i·çhon′dri·um, *n.*; *pl.* **per·i·çhon′dri·ȧ,** [*peri-*, and Gr. *chondros*, cartilage.] the membrane of white, fibrous connective tissue covering cartilage, except at the joints.

per·i·çhor′dăl, *a.* [*peri-*, and Gr. *chordē*, string.] surrounding or sheathing the notochord; as, *perichordal* tissue.

per′i·çlāse, *n.* [*peri-*, and Gr. *klasis*, fracture.] a mineral, MgO, occurring in greenish octahedrons, and composed principally of magnesia.

per·i·çlā′sīte, *n.* same as *periclase*.

Per·i·çlē′ăn, *a.* 1. of Pericles, an Athenian statesman of the fifth century B.C.
2. of the period of great intellectual achievement in Athens (c. 495–429 B.C.), in the lifetime of Pericles.

per′i·çlīne, *n.* [*peri-*, and Gr. *klinein*, to bend.] a variety of albite found in white, crystalline form.

per·i·çlin′i·um, *n.*; *pl.* **per·i·çlin′i·ȧ,** [Gr. *periklinon*, a couch all round a table.] in botany, the involucre of composite plants. [Rare.]

pē·riç′li·tāte, *v.t.* to endanger. [Obs.]

pē·riç·li·tā′tion, *n.* an exposing to peril; trial; the state of being endangered. [Rare.]

pē·riç′ō·pē, *n.* [Gr. *perikopē*; *peri*, about, and *koptein*, to cut.] a selected extract from a book or paper; especially, a passage from the Bible to be used in a formal service.

per·i·çrā′ni·ăl, *a.* pertaining to the pericranium.

per·i·çrā′ni·um, *n.*; *pl.* **per·i·çrā′ni·ȧ,** [*peri-*, and Gr. *kranion*, the skull.] the periosteum of the skull.

pē·riç′ū·lous, *a.* dangerous; hazardous. [Obs.]

pē·riç′ū·lum, *n.* [L., peril.] in law, a risk.

per′i·çȳ·çle, *n.* [*peri-* and Gr. *kyklos*, circle.] the outer layer of the stele in the root and stem of most plants.

per·i·çȳ′çlōne, *n.* [*peri-* and *cyclone.*] the ring around a cyclonic center, in which the atmospheric pressure is high.

per″i·çȳ·çlon′iç, *a.* pertaining to a pericyclone.

per′i·dẽrm, *n.* [*peri-* and *-derm.*] the outer bark and the layer of soft, growing tissue between the bark and the wood in plants.

per·i·des′mi·um, *n.* [*peri-*, and Gr. *desmos*, band.] the membranous sheath of a ligament.

pē·rid′i·ăl, *a.* of or constituting the peridium.

per″i·di·as′tō·lē, *n.* [*peri-* and *diastole.*] the slight period of time elapsing between the expansion and the contraction of the heart.

pē·rid′i·ōle, *n.* same as *peridiolum*.

per·i·dī′ō·lum, *n.*; *pl.* **per·i·dī′ō·lȧ,** [LL., dim. of *peridium.*] in botany, any of the spore cases within the peridium.

pē·rid′i·um, *n.*; *pl.* **pē·rid′i·ȧ,** [Mod. L., from Gr. *pēridion*, dim. of *pēra*, a leather pouch.] the outer coat of the spore-bearing organ in certain fungi.

per′i·dot, *n.* [Fr.] a kind of yellowish-green chrysolite, used as a gem: also called *olivine*.

per·i·dot′iç, *a.* of or like peridot.

per″i·dō′tīte, *n.* [Fr. *péridotite.*] a rare, dark, heavy rock of the igneous type, consisting of ferromagnesian minerals and olivine.

per′i·drōme, *n.* [Gr. *peridromos*; *peri*, around, and *dromos*, a course.] in Greek architecture, the open space between the columns and the wall of a temple, forming a promenade.

Per·i·ē′çiănṣ, *n.pl.* see *perioeci*.

per·i·en′te·ron, *n.* [*peri-*, and Gr. *enteron*, intestine.] the primitive cavity containing the viscera of an embryo.

per′i·ẽr·ġy, *n.* [Gr. *periergia*; *peri*, over, beyond, and *ergon*, work.] needless caution or diligence.

per·i·ē·sō·phaġ′ē·ăl, *a.* [*peri-* and *esophageal.*] around the esophagus; as, the *periesophageal* nerves.

per·i·gañ·gli·on′iç, *a.* [*peri-* and *ganglionic.*] around a ganglion.

per·i·gas′triç, *a.* [*peri-*, and Gr. *gastēr*, *gastros*, belly.] around the stomach.

per·i·gas′trū·lȧ, *n.* [*peri-* and *gastrula.*] a form of gastrula developed in superficial segmentation of the vitellus.

per·i·ġē′ăl, *a.* perigean.

per·i·ġē′ăn, *a.* of, or at the time of, the perigee.
perigean tides; the high tides which occur when the moon is in perigee.

per′i·ġee, *n.* [*peri-*, and Gr. *gē*, the earth.] that point in the orbit of a heavenly body, especially of the moon, in which it is at the least distance from the earth: opposed to *apogee*.

per·i·ġen′e·sis, *n.* [*peri-*, and *genesis.*] the dynamic theory of generation and reproduction advanced by Haeckel, which assumes that a form of growth force is transmitted from one generation to the next.

per·i·ġē·net′iç, *a.* pertaining to perigenesis.

per·i·ġē′um, *n.* perigee. [Rare.]

per·ig·nath′iç, *a.* [*peri-*, and Gr. *gnathos*, jaw.] around the jaw or jaws as in an echinoderm.

per′i·gōne, *n.* [*peri-*, and Gr. *gonē*, seed.]
1. the organ or organs enclosing the reproductive organs of plants, as the perianth in flowering plants, or the bracts in the mosses.
2. the walls of a spore cell in hydroids.

per·i·gō′ni·um, *n.* same as *perigone*.

per′i·grȧph, *n.* [*peri-*, and Gr. *graphē*, a writing.] a careless or inaccurate delineation of anything.

per·i·ġyn′i·um, *n.*; *pl.* **per·i·ġyn′i·ȧ,** [*peri-*, and Gr. *gynē*, a female.] the disk which is found in the flower of certain plants; also, the bristles or small scales that surround the pistil of some genera of *Cyperaceæ*, or sedges. These may be either distinct from each other, or more or less united by their margins.

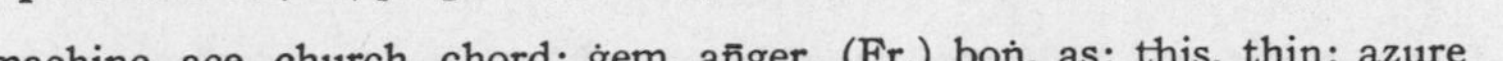

a

a, PERIGYNIUM OF A SEDGE

pē·riġ′y·nous, *a.* [*peri-*, and Gr. *gynē*, a female.]
1. growing in a ring around the pistil, as the stamens.
2. having stamens, etc. growing in this way: said of a flower.

pē·riġ′y·ny, *n.* the condition of being perigynous.

per·i·hē′li·ŏn, *n.*; *pl.* **per·i·hē′li·ȧ,** [Mod. L., from Gr. *peri-*, around, and *hēlios*, the sun.] that point in the orbit of a planet or comet, which is nearest the sun: opposed to *aphelion*.

per·i·hē′li·um, *n.* same as *perihelion*.

per′il, *n.* [Fr. *péril*, from L. *periculum*, *periclum*, danger, from root seen in *experiri*, to try, to attempt.]
1. danger; risk; jeopardy; exposure of person or property to injury, loss, or destruction.
2. in law, the risk, contingency, event, or cause of loss insured against, as in a policy of insurance.
at one's peril; at the risk of suffering harm of some kind.

per′il, *v.i.* to be in danger. [Obs.]

per′il, *v.t.*; periled *or* perilled, *pt.*, *pp.*; periling *or* perilling, *ppr.* to hazard; to risk; to expose to danger.

Pē·ril′lȧ, *n.* [E.Ind.] a genus of labiate plants cultivated for their purple foliage.

per′il·ous, *a.* involving danger; hazardous; full of risk; as, a *perilous* undertaking; a *perilous* situation.
Syn.—risky, precarious.

per′il·ous·ly, *adv.* in a perilous manner.

per′il·ous·ness, *n.* the state or quality of being perilous; hazardousness.

per′i·lymph, *n.* [*peri-* and *lymph.*] the liquid substance surrounding the most delicate parts of the inner ear.

per″i·lym·phan′ġi·ăl, *a.* [*peri-*, LL. *lympha*, lymph, and Gr. *angeion*, vessel.] surrounding a lymphatic.

per″i·lym·phat′iç, *a.* [*peri-* and *lymphatic.*] related to perilymph.

pē·rim′e·tẽr, *n.* [*peri-*, and Gr. *metron*, measure.]
1. the outer boundary of a figure or area; as, a fence marked the *perimeter* of the field.
2. the total length of this.
3. an optical instrument for testing the scope of vision and the visual powers of various parts of the retina.

per·i·met′riç, *a.* 1. relating to a perimeter, or boundary.
2. of or by a perimeter or perimetry.

per·i·met′riç, *a.* pertaining to the perimetrium.

per·i·met′riç·ăl, *a.* same as *perimetric*.

per″i·mē·trit′iç, *a.* of or related to perimetritis.

per″i·mē·trī′tis, *n.* [*peri-*, Gr. *mētra*, uterus, and *-itis.*] inflammation of the perimetrium.

per·i·mē′tri·um, *n.* the peritoneal covering of the uterus.

pe·rim′e·try, *n.* the practical use of the perimeter for testing the scope of vision.

per′i·mọrph, *n.* [*peri-* and *-morph.*] a mineral of one kind enclosing one of another kind.

per·i·mys′i·ăl, *a.* around a muscle; relating to the perimysium.

per·i·mys′i·um, *n.*; *pl.* **per·i·mys′i·ȧ,** [*peri-*, and Gr. *mys*, muscle.] the tissue which surrounds or encases a muscle or a muscular bundle.

per·i·nae′ăl, *a.* same as *perineal*.

per·i·nae′um, *n.* same as *perineum*.

per·i·nē′ăl, *a.* of or relating to the perineum.

per·i·nē′ō·plas″ty, *n.* [*perineum*, and Gr. *plastos*, verbal adj. of *plassein*, to mold.] plastic surgery of the perineum.

per″i·nē·or′rhȧ·phy (-rȧ-), *n.* [*perineum*, and Gr. *rhaphē*, suture, from *rhaptein*, to sew.] suturation of the perineum performed for the repair of a laceration.

per·i·neph′răl, *a.* pertaining to the immediate vicinity of the kidney.

per·i·neph′ri·ăl, *a.* situated or occurring around the kidney.

per·i·neph′riç, *a.* same as *perinephrial*.

per″i·nē·phrit′iç, *a.* relating to perinephritis.

per″i·nē·phrī′tis, *n.* [*perinephrium* and *-itis.*] inflammation of the perinephrium.

per·i·neph′ri·um, *n.* [*peri-*, and Gr. *nephros*, kidney.] the envelope of connective and fatty tissue surrounding the kidney.

per·i·nē′um, *n.*; *pl.* **per·i·nē′ȧ,** [LL., from Gr. *perineon.*] the region of the body between the thighs, at the outlet of the pelvis; specifically, the small triangular region including the anus and the vulva or the base of the penis.

per·i·neū′ri·ăl, *a.* pertaining to the perineurium.

per″i·neū·rī′tis, *n.* [*perineurium* and *-itis.*] inflammation of the perineurium.

per·i·neū′ri·um, *n.* [*peri-*, and Gr. *neuron*, nerve.] the sheath of dense connective tissue that envelops a bundle of nerve fibers composing a peripheral nerve.

pē·rin′i·um, *n.* [*peri-*, and Gr. *is*, *inos*, muscle.] the outer coat of the spore wall in certain

Hepaticæ, developed from the membrane of the special mother cells.

per·i·nū′clē·ăr, *a.* [*peri-* and *nucleus.*] around a nucleus; situated or occurring around a nucleus.

pē′ri·ŏd, *n.* [L. *periodus*, from Gr. *periodos*; *peri*, about, and *hodos*, way.]
 1. the interval between the successive occurrences of an astronomical event; as, the portion of time between two full moons is a *period*.
 2. the interval between certain happenings; as, a ten-year *period* of peace.
 3. a portion of time, often indefinite, distinguished by the existence of certain processes, characteristics, or conditions; a stage; as, a *period* of change, the present *period*.
 4. any of the portions of time into which an event of fixed duration, as a game or school day, is divided.
 5. the full course or one of the stages of a disease.
 6. the time of menstruation; menses.
 7. an end, completion, or conclusion or a point of time marking this; as, death put a *period* to his plans.
 8. in geology, a subdivision of a geological era, in which rock strata and fossils form a definite sequence.
 9. in grammar and rhetoric, (a) a complete sentence; (b) the natural pause, in speaking, or a mark of punctuation (.), in writing, used to indicate the end of a sentence; (c) the dot (.) following most abbreviations.
 10. in music, a group of measures, usually eight or sixteen, arranged in two phrases and forming a complete statement ending with a cadence.
 11. in physics, the interval of time necessary for a regularly recurring motion to make a complete cycle.
 12. in prosody, a rhythm group of two or more cola in the Greek system.
 Syn.—epoch, age, era, cycle, circuit, term, duration, end, limit, conclusion.

pē′ri·ŏd, *a.* of or like that of a certain period or age; as, *period* furniture or painting.

pē′ri·ŏd, *v.t.* and *v.i.* to put an end to; to come to an end; to cease. [Obs.]

pẽr·ī′ō·dāte, *n.* a salt of periodic acid.

pē·ri·od′iç, *a.* 1. occurring, appearing, or recurring at regular intervals; as, a *periodic* fever.
 2. occurring from time to time; intermittent.
 3. of or characterized by a period or periods; as, the *periodic* motion of a planet.
 4. of or characterized by periodic sentences.
 periodic comet; a comet known to have a period, in distinction from a comet which is not known to have revolved around the sun and which may or may not have a period; a comet which must have been observed at least twice in its passage around the sun.
 periodic curve; in physics, a curve made up of complex forms recurring at regular intervals.
 periodic function; in mathematics, a function in which equal values recur in the same order when the value of the variable is uniformly increased or diminished; any direct trigonometrical function; a function having a period.
 periodic law; the principle that the physical and chemical properties of the chemical elements recur periodically when the elements are arranged in increasing order of their atomic numbers.
 periodic sentence; a sentence in which the grammatical form and essential meaning are not completed until the end is reached: distinguished from *loose sentence*.
 periodic star; a variable star which shows periodic changes in brightness.
 periodic system; the system governing the classification of the elements: see *periodic law*.
 periodic table; an arrangement of the chemical elements according to their atomic numbers, to exhibit the periodic law: the vertical columns (*groups*) include elements having related properties; the aligned subgroups (*families*) in these columns include elements having more closely related properties; the horizontal columns (*periods*) show the periodic shift in the properties of the elements.
 periodic wind; a wind which has a period or periods of recurrence as to direction, as a monsoon.
 Syn.—stated, recurrent, regular, systematic.

pẽr·i·od′iç ac′id, [*per-* and *iodic.*] an oxygen acid, H_5IO_6, containing iodine in its highest valence.

pē·ri·od′iç·ăl, *a.* 1. periodic.
 2. published at regular intervals of more than one day.
 3. of a periodical.

pē·ri·od′iç·ăl, *n.* a publication appearing at regular intervals of more than one day, as a weekly magazine.

pē·ri·od′iç·ăl·ist, *n.* a publisher of or a writer for a periodical.

pē·ri·od′iç·ăl·ly, *adv.* 1. at regular intervals; at stated periods; as, a festival celebrated *periodically*.
 2. from time to time; recurrently.

pē·ri·od′iç·ăl·ness, *n.* the state of being periodical; periodicity. [Rare.]

pē″ri·ō·dic′i·ty, *n.*; *pl.* **pē″ri·ō·dic′i·ties**, 1. a tendency to recur at regular intervals, as of some fevers; periodic character or quality.
 2. in chemistry, the occurrence of similar properties in elements occupying similar positions in the periodic table.
 3. in electricity, frequency.

pẽr·ī′ō·dide, *n.* an iodide in which the proportion of iodine is relatively high as compared with other iodides of the same element.

per″i·ō·don′tăl, *a.* [*peri-*, and Gr. *odous*, *odontos*, tooth.] situated or occurring around a tooth.

pē·ri·od′ō·sçōpe, *n.* [*period*, and Gr. *skopein*, to view.] a calendar or dial indicating the probable date of childbirth.

Per·i·oe′cī, *n.pl.* [*peri-*, and Gr. *oikos*, a dwelling.]
 1. in ancient Greece, the original Achaean inhabitants of Laconia: so called by their Dorian conquerors.
 2. [p–] in geography, people who live in the same latitudes, but whose longitudes differ by 180°, so that when it is noon in one place it is midnight in the other.

per′i·ō·ple, *n.* [*peri-*, and Gr. *oplē*, hoof of a horse.] the outside, smooth, horny part of the hoof of a horse and of other hoofed mammals.

per·i·op′liç, *a.* of or related to the periople.

per·i·op′tiç, *a.* [*peri-* and *optic.*] in medicine, situated or occurring around the eye.

per·i·os′tē·ăl, *a.* of or belonging to the periosteum.

per·i·os·tē·ō′mȧ, **per″i·os·tō′mȧ**, *n.* a bony growth surrounding a bone.

per·i·os·tē·ot′ō·my, *n.* [*periosteum*, and Gr. *tomē*, a cutting.] surgical incision or slitting of the periosteum.

per·i·os′tē·um, *n.*; *pl.* **per·i·os′tē·ȧ**, [*peri-*, and Gr. *osteon*, bone.] the membrane of tough, fibrous connective tissue covering all bones except at the joints.

per″i·os·tī′tis, *n.* [*periosteum* and *-itis.*] inflammation of the periosteum.

per″i·os·tō′sis, *n.* [*periosteum* and *-osis.*] a tumor of the periosteum.

per·i·os·tos·teī′tis, *n.* [*periosteum*, Gr. *osteon*, a bone, and *-itis.*] simultaneous inflammation of the periosteum and bone.

per·i·os′trȧ·çum, *n.* [*peri-*, and Gr. *ostrakon*, shell.] the horny epidermis of shells.

per·i·ō′tiç, *a.* [*peri-* and *otic.*] in anatomy and zoology, surrounding the inner ear; specifically, of the bony structure (*periotic bone*) forming a capsule enclosing the labyrinth.

per·i·ō′tiç, *n.* a periotic bone or cartilage.

per″i·pȧ·tē′ciăn, *n.* a peripatetic. [Obs.]

per″i·pȧ·tet′iç, *a.* [Gr. *peripatētikos*, from *peripatein*, to walk about; *peri*, about, and *patein*, to walk.]
 1. walking about; itinerant.
 2. [P–] pertaining to Aristotle's philosophy, or to his followers; Aristotelian.

per″i·pȧ·tet′iç, *n.* 1. one who walks about, or moves from place to place; a pedestrian.
 2. [P–] a follower of Aristotle: so called because this philosopher and his followers disputed questions while walking in the Lyceum at Athens; an Aristotelian.

per″i·pȧ·tet′iç·ăl, *a.* peripatetic.

Per″i·pȧ·tet′i·çism, *n.* the philosophical system of Aristotle and his followers.

pē·rip′ȧ·toid, *a.* pertaining to or resembling a peripatus.

Pē·rip′ȧ·tus, *n.* 1. a genus of the *Malacopoda*. On each side of the body there are fourteen to thirty-three pairs of short legs which end in hooked claws. The head bears a pair of simple antennae and a pair of simple eyes. Several species are known, from the West Indies, the Cape of Good Hope, South America, and New Zealand.
 2. [p–] a myriapod of this genus.

per·i·pet′ăl·ous, *a.* [*peri-*, and Gr. *petalon*, leaf.] in botany and zoology, situated around the petals.

pe·riph′ẽr·ăl, *a.* 1. pertaining to, constituting, or of the nature of a periphery.
 2. in anatomy, outer; external; distal.

pe·riph′ẽr·ăl, *n.* a piece of equipment that can be used with a computer to increase its functional range or efficiency, as a printer, disc, etc.

pe·riph′ẽr·ăl·ly, *adv.* so as to be peripheral.

per·i·pher′iç, **per·i·pher′iç·ăl**, *a.* same as *peripheral*.

pe·riph′ẽr·y, *n.*; *pl.* **pe·riph′ẽr·ies**, [*peri-*, and Gr. *pherein*, to bear.]
 1. a boundary line, especially that of a rounded figure; a perimeter.
 2. an outside surface, especially that of a rounded object or body.
 3. surrounding space or area; environs.
 4. in anatomy, the area surrounding a nerve ending.

per′i·phrāșe, *n.* same as *periphrasis*.

per′i·phrāșe, *v.t.*; periphrased, *pt.*, *pp.*; periphrasing, *ppr.* to express by circumlocution.

per′i·phrāșe, *v.i.* to use circumlocution.

pē·riph′rȧ·sis, *n.*; *pl.* **pē·riph′rȧ·sēș** [Gr.]
 1. a method of speech lacking conciseness; roundabout or superlative language; circumlocution, as the use of the expression *the flaming orb of day* for *the sun*.
 2. a periphrastic expression.

per·i·phras′tiç, **per·i·phras′tiç·ăl**, *a.* 1. of, like, or expressed in periphrasis.
 2. in grammar, formed with a particle or auxiliary verb instead of by inflection (e.g., "she did sing" for "she sang" is a *periphrastic* construction).

per·i·phras′tiç·ăl·ly, *adv.* in a periphrastic manner.

pē·riph′y·sis, *n.*; *pl.* **pē·riph′y·sēș**, [Gr., a growing around; *peri*, around, and *phyesthai*, to grow.] a sterile filament arising from the hymenium of certain fungi.

per′i·plașm, *n.* [*peri-* and *plasm.*] a clear, protoplasmic layer surrounding another mass functionally different, as in some fungi.

per′i·plast, *n.* same as *periblast*.

per·i·plas′tiç, *a.* same as *periblastic*.

per·ip·neus′tiç, *a.* [*peri-*, and Gr. *pneustikos*, of breathing.] having certain thoracic stigmata functionally inactive, as various larvae.

per′i·proçt, *n.* [*peri-*, and Gr. *prōctos*, the anus.] the portion of the body wall surrounding the anus of an echinoderm.

per″i·proç·tī′tis, *n.* [*periproct* and *-itis.*] inflammation of the cellular connective tissues around the rectum and anus.

per·i·proç′tous, *a.* around the rectum; specifically, pertaining to the periproct.

per″i·prō·stat′iç, *a.* [*peri-* and *prostatic.*] about the prostate gland.

pe·rip′tẽr·ăl, *a.* [Gr. *peripteros*, from *peri*, around, and *pteron*, a wing, a row of columns.] in Greek architecture, surrounded by a row of columns: said of a building, especially of a temple in which the cella is surrounded by columns, those on the flank being distant one intercolumniation from the wall.

PLAN OF PERIPTERAL TEMPLE

pe·rip′tẽr·ous, *a.* [*peri-*, and Gr. *pteron*, a feather, a wing.]
 1. feathered on all sides.
 2. in architecture, peripteral.

per·ip′tẽr·y, *n.*; *pl.* **per·ip′tẽr·ies**, [Gr. *peripteros*, flying about.] that area around a moving body within which air currents are set up by the motion.

pe·rïque′ (-rēk′), *n.* a Louisiana tobacco, black when cured, and mostly used in mixtures to give a strong flavor.

per′i·särç, *n.* [*peri-*, and Gr. *sarx*, *sarkos*, flesh.] the chitinous protection of the soft parts of many of the *Hydrozoa*.

pē·ris′ciăn (-rish′ăn), *a.* relating to the periscii.

pē·ris′ciăn, *n.* one of the periscii.

pē·ris′ci ī, *n.pl.* [L. *periscii*; Gr. *periskioi*; *peri*, around, and *skia*, shadow.] the inhabitants of the polar circles, whose shadows move round, and at certain times of the year describe, in the course of the day, an entire circle.

per′i·sçōpe, *n.* [*peri-* and *-scope.*]
 1. a general view; a comprehensive summary. [Rare.]
 2. a periscopic lens.
 3. an optical instrument consisting of a

tube holding a system of lenses with a mirror at either end arranged so that a person looking through the eyepiece at one end can see objects reflected by the mirror at the other end: used on submerged submarines, etc.

per·i·sçop′iç, *a.* 1. viewing on all sides; specifically, providing clear lateral or oblique range of view, as certain lenses.
 2. of or by a periscope.

pē·ris′çō·pişm, *n.* the power or ability to see in all directions.

per′ish, *v.i.*; perished, *pt., pp.*; perishing, *ppr.* [Fr. *perir*, ppr. *périssant*, to perish, from L. *perire*, to go through, to perish or come to nothing; *per*, through, and *ire*, to go.]
 1. to die a violent or untimely death.
 2. to be destroyed; to be ruined.
 perish the thought! do not even consider such a possibility!

per″ish·ȧ·bil′i·ty, *n.* perishableness.

per′ish·ȧ·ble, *a.* that may perish; subject to decay and destruction; liable to spoil or deteriorate, as some foods.

per′ish·ȧ·ble, *n.* something liable to spoil or deteriorate, especially such a food.

per′ish·ȧ·ble·ness, *n.* the quality or state of being perishable.

per′ish·ȧ·bly, *adv.* in a perishable manner.

per·i·sō′mȧ, *n.*; *pl.* **per·i·sō′mȧ·tȧ,** [*peri-*, and Gr. *sōma*, body.] in zoology, the outer shell of the *Echinodermata*.

per″i·sō·mat′iç, *a.* relating to or characteristic of a perisoma.

per′i·spērm, *n.* [*peri-*, and Gr. *sperma*, seed.] in botany, the nutritive, fleshy part of the seed of plants, either entirely or partially surrounding the embryo.

per·i·spēr′miç, *a.* in botany, furnished with perisperm.

per·i·spher′iç, per·i·spher′iç·ăl, *a.* [*peri-*, and Gr. *sphaira*, sphere.] globular; having the form of a ball.

per″i·splē·nī′tis, *n.* [*peri-*, Gr. *splēn*, spleen, and *-itis*.] inflammation of the peritoneal membrane enveloping the spleen.

per′i·spōme, *a.* and *n.* same as *perispomenon*.

per·i·spom′e·non, *n.*; *pl.* **per·i·spom′e·nȧ,** [Gr. *perispōmenon*, drawn around; *peri*, around, and *spān*, to draw.] in Greek grammar, a word having the circumflex accent on the final syllable.

per·i·spom′e·non, *a.* in Greek grammar, having the circumflex accent on the final syllable.

per′i·spōre, *n.* [*peri-*, and Gr. *sporos*, seed.] in botany, the outer covering of a spore.

per′is·sad, *n.* [Gr. *perissos*, superfluous, odd; *peri*, beyond, and *-ad*.] in chemistry, an atom having an odd valence, as gold, which has a valence of one or three. [Obs.]

per′is·sad, *a.* not even; odd; having a valence represented by an odd number. [Obs.]

pe·ris·sō·daç′tyl, pe·ris·sō·daç′tyle, *a.* [Mod. L. *perissodactylus*, from Gr. *perissos*, uneven, and *daktylos*, finger.] having an uneven number of toes on each foot, as a horse, rhinoceros, etc.; of the *Perissodactyla*.

pe·ris·sō·daç′tyl, pe·ris·sō·daç′tyle, *n.* a hoofed animal with an uneven number of toes; one of the *Perissodactyla*.

Per·is·sō·daç′ty·lȧ, *n.pl.* an order of the *Ungulata*, or hoofed animals, including the rhinoceros, the tapir, the horse, etc. The hind feet are odd-toed in all, and the forefeet in all except the tapir. The horns, if present, are not paired. Usually there is only one horn, but if there are two these are placed in the middle line of the head, one behind the other. In neither case are the horns ever supported by bony horn cores. The stomach is simple, and is not divided into several compartments.

per·is″sō·daç·tyl′iç, *a.* same as *perissodactyl*.

per·is·sō·daç′tyl·ous, *a.* same as *perissodactyl*.

per·is·sō·log′iç·ăl, *a.* redundant in words.

per·is·sol′ō·ġy, *n.* [Gr. *perissologia*; *perissos*, redundant, and *logos*, discourse.] verbosity; much talk to little purpose.

per·is″sō·syl·lab′iç, *a.* [Gr. *perissos*, excessive, and E. *syllabic*.] having superfluous syllables.

per·is′tȧ·lith, *n.* [from Gr. *peri*, about, *histanai*, to stand, and *lithos*, a stone.] in archaeology, a series of standing stones surrounding an object, as a barrow or burial mound.

per·i·stal′sis, *n.*; *pl.* **per·i·stal′sēş,** [Gr., from *peri*, around, and *stellein*, to place.] the rhythmic, wavelike motion of the walls of the alimentary canal and certain other hollow organs, consisting of alternate muscular contractions and dilations that move the contents of the tube onward.

per·i·stal′tiç, *a.* [Gr. *peristaltikos*, from *peristellein*, to involve; *peri*, around, and *stellein*, to place.] of or characterized by peristalsis.

per·i·stal′tiç·ăl·ly, *adv.* in a peristaltic manner.

Per·is·tē′ri·ȧ, *n.* [Gr. *peristera*, dove.] a small genus of South American orchids: *Peristeria elata* is the dove plant, so called because the glumes of the orchidaceous flower are like a hovering dove.

pe·ris′tēr·īte, *n.* [Gr. *peristera*, dove, and *-ite*.] a variety of albite containing a small proportion of magnesia, and exhibiting when properly cut a bluish opalescence like the changing hues on a pigeon's neck.

per·is″tēr·ō·mor′phous, *a.* of, pertaining to, or like a pigeon or pigeons.

Per·is·tēr·op′ō·dēş, *n.pl.* [Gr. *peristera*, dove, and *pous*, *podos*, foot.] in old classifications, a group of birds having the hind toe low on the foot, as in pigeons.

per·is·tēr·op′ō·dous, *a.* having pigeonlike feet; of or pertaining to the *Peristeropodes*.

pē·ris′tō·lē, *n.* same as *peristalsis*.

pē·ris′tō·mȧ, *n.*; *pl.* **per·i·stom′ȧ·tȧ,** in zoology, a peristome.

per′i·stōme, *n.* [*peri-*, and Gr. *stoma*, mouth.]
 1. in botany, the fringe around the opening of the spore case in mosses.
 2. in zoology, the area or parts surrounding the mouth or a mouthlike part of an organism.

per·i·stō′mi·ăl, *a.* of or pertaining to a peristome.

per·i·stō′mi·um, *n.* same as *peristome*.

per·i·streph′iç, *a.* [*peri-*, and Gr. *strephein*, to turn.] turning round; rotary; revolving: applied to the paintings of a panorama.

per·i·stȳ′lăr, *a.* pertaining to a peristyle.

per′i·stȳle, *n.* [Gr. *peristylon*; *peri*, about, and *stylos*, a column.]
 1. a row of columns forming an enclosure or supporting a roof.
 2. any space or enclosure, as a court, so formed.

per″i·sy·nō′vi·ăl, *a.* enclosing the synovial membrane.

per·i·sys′tō·lē, *n.* [*peri-*, and Gr. *systolē*, contraction.] in physiology, the pause or interval between the systole, or contraction, and the diastole, or dilatation, of the heart.

pē·rīte′, *a.* [L. *peritus*.] skillful. [Obs.]

per·i·thē′ci·ăl, *a.* of or pertaining to the perithecium.

per·i·thē′ci·um (-shi- *or* -si-), *n.*; *pl.* **per·i·thē′ci·ȧ,** [*peri-*, and Gr. *thēkē*, a case.] in certain fungi, a flasklike case containing the spore sacs.

pē·rit′ō·mous, *a.* [*peri-*, and Gr. *temnein*, to cleave.] in mineralogy, cleaving in more directions than one parallel to the axis, the faces being all of one quality.

per″i·tō·nae′um, *n.* same as *peritoneum*.

per″i·tō·nae′ăl, *a.* same as *peritoneal*.

per″i·tō·nē′ăl, *a.* pertaining to the peritoneum.

per″i·tō·nē′um, *n.* [Gr. *peritonaion*; *peri*, about, and *teinein*, to stretch.] in anatomy, the transparent serous membrane lining the abdominal cavity and reflected inward at various places to cover the visceral organs.

per″i·tō·nī′tis, *n.* [*peritoneum* and *-itis*.] inflammation of the peritoneum. It may exist either as an acute or a chronic disease.

per·i·trā′chē·ăl, *a.* around the trachea.

per′i·trēme, *n.* [*peri-*, and Gr. *trēma*, a hole.]
 1. the raised margin which surrounds the breathing holes of insects.
 2. the peristome of a univalve shell.

Pē·rit′ri·chȧ, *n.pl.* [*peri-*, and Gr. *thrix*, *trichos*, hair.] a group of infusorians including those having cilia around the body in a circle.

per′i·troch, *n.* 1. a band of cilia.
 2. any organism having a band of cilia.

per·i·trō′chi·um, *n.* [*peri-*, and Gr. *trochos*, wheel.] a wheel or circle concentric with a cylinder, and movable together with it about an axis. [Obs.]

per·it′rō·păl, *a.* [*peri-*, and Gr. *trepein*, to turn.]
 1. rotary; circuitous; rotatory. [Rare.]
 2. peritropous. [Rare.]

per·it′rō·pous, *a.* directed from the axis to the horizon, as the embryo of a seed.

pe·rï′tus (*also Eng.* pȧ-rēt′ȧs), *n.*; *pl.* **pe·rï′tï,** [L.] an expert; specifically, a skilled theologian used as a consultant.

per″i·typh·lī′tis, *n.* [*peri-* and *typhlitis*.] the extension of typhlitis to adjacent parts: now generally diagnosed as appendicitis.

per·i·ū′tēr·ine, *a.* situated around the uterus.

per·i·vas′çū·lăr, *a.* surrounding a blood vessel.

per·i·vẽr′tē·brăl, *a.* situated around the vertebrae.

per·i·vis′cẽr·ăl, *a.* [*peri-*, and L. *viscera*, entrails.] surrounding the viscera.

per″i·vi·tel′line, *a.* [*peri-*, and L. *vitellus*, yolk.] surrounding the vitellus.

per′i·wig, *n.* [altered from Fr. *perruque*.] a wig; a peruke.

per′i·wig, *v.t.*; periwigged, *pt., pp.* periwigging, *ppr.* to dress with a periwig or with false hair.

per′i·wiñ·kle, *n.* [AS. *pinewincla*; L. *pinna*, a mussel, and AS. *wincle*, a winkle.]
 1. any of a number of small, related saltwater snails of the genus *Littorina* having a thick, brown or yellowish, cone-shaped shell with dark spiral bands.
 2. the shell of one of these snails.

per′i·wiñ·kle, *n.* [AS. *pervince*, from L. *pervinca*, the periwinkle.] a creeping plant of the genus *Vinca* with evergreen leaves and white or blue flowers; myrtle.

pẽr′jūre, *v.t.*; perjured, *pt., pp.*; perjuring, *ppr.* [ME. *parjuren*; OFr. *parjurer*; L. *perjurare*; *per*, through, and *jurare*, to swear.]
 1. to make (oneself) guilty of perjury.
 2. to prove guilty of perjury: in the passive.
 3. to make a false oath to; to deceive by false oaths or protestations. [Obs.]

pẽr′jūre, *n.* a perjured person. [Obs.]

pẽr′jūred, *a.* 1. having sworn falsely; guilty of perjury; as, a *perjured* villain.
 2. being sworn falsely. [Obs.]

pẽr′jūr·ẽr, *n.* one who commits perjury.

pẽr·jū′ri·ous, pẽr′jū rous, *a.* guilty of perjury. [Obs.]

pẽr′jū·ry, *n.*; *pl.* **pẽr′jū·rieş,** [ME. *perjurie*, *parjurie*; OFr. *parjurie*; L. *perjurium*, from *perjurus*, false, breaking oath, from *per*, through, and *jus*, *juris*, a right, justice.]
 1. in law, the willful telling of a lie while under oath to tell the truth in a matter material to the point of inquiry.
 2. the breaking of any oath or formal promise.

pẽrk, *v.i.*; perked (pẽrkt), *pt., pp.*; perking, *ppr.* [ME. *perken*; prob. from O.Norm.Fr. *perquer*, to perch.]
 1. to hold up one's head or straighten one's posture, as in acting jaunty.
 2. to become lively or animated; to recover one's spirits (with *up*).

pẽrk, *v.t.* 1. to raise, as the head, briskly or spiritedly (often with *up*).
 2. to make jaunty or smart in appearance (often with *up* or *out*).
 3. to give or restore freshness, vivacity, etc. to (usually with *up*).

pẽrk, *v.t.* and *v.i.* to percolate. [Colloq.]

pẽrk, *a.* perky.

pẽr′kin, *n.* [for *perrykin*, dim. of *perry*.] a kind of weak cider.

Pẽr′kin·işm, *n.* an obsolete treatment for rheumatism introduced by Dr. Elisha Perkins, of Connecticut, which consisted of applying to the diseased parts the ends of two rods made of different metals: also called *tractoration*.

pẽrk′y, *a.*; *comp.* perkier; *superl.* perkiest,
 1. spirited; aggressive.
 2. brisk; gay; saucy; jaunty.

Pẽr′lȧ, *n.* [LL.] the typical genus of *Perlidæ*.

pẽr·lā′ceous, *a.* like pearl; pearly.

pẽr′lid, *n.* any insect of the *Perlidæ*.

Pẽr′li·dae, *n.pl.* a family of insects having aquatic larvae; the stone flies.

pẽr′līte, *n.* [Fr., from *perle*, pearl.] a glassy volcanic rock with a pearly luster: it is a form of obsidian appearing as an aggregation of small, rounded masses.

pẽr·lit′iç, *a.* of, relating to, or resembling perlite.

pẽr·lus·trā′tion, *n.* [L. *perlustrare*; *per*, through, and *lustrare*, to survey.] the act of viewing all over.

pẽr′mȧ·frost, *n.* [*perma*nent, and *frost*.] permanently frozen subsoil.

pẽrm″al′loy, *n.* [*perm*eable and *alloy*.] any of various alloys of iron and nickel having a high magnetic permeability: a trade-mark (*Permalloy*).

pẽrm′al·loy, *a.* made of permalloy.

pẽr′mȧ·nȧ·ble, *a.* permanent; lasting; durable. [Obs.]

pẽr′mȧ·nence, *n.* the state or characteristic of being permanent; as, the *permanence* of a system of principles.

pẽr′mȧ·nen·cy, *n.* 1. permanance.
 2. *pl.* **pẽr′mȧ·nen·cieş,** something permanent.

pẽr′ma̤·nent, *a.* [L. *permanens*, pp. of *permanere*; *per-*, and *manere*, to remain.]

1. lasting or intended to last indefinitely without change; continuing in the same state or in the same place; stable; durable; abiding.

It is our true policy to steer clear of *permanent* alliances with any portion of the foreign world. —George Washington.

2. lasting a relatively long time; as, a *permanent* wave.

permanent blue; same as *ultramarine*.

permanent gases; formerly, gases such as oxygen, hydrogen, nitrogen, and others, once erroneously believed to be incapable of liquefaction.

permanent magnet; a magnet, usually of hard steel, which keeps most of its magnetism after it has once been magnetized.

permanent tooth; any of the 32 adult human teeth including those that replace the milk teeth: see *tooth*, illus.

permanent wave; a hair wave made to last for several months, produced by use of chemicals or heat.

permanent way; a finished railway, including a roadbed, switches, sidings, bridges, cattle guards, etc., in condition to carry on public traffic and transportation: opposed to *temporary way*.

permanent white; an artificially prepared barium sulfate used as a pigment: also called *constant white*.

Syn.—durable, abiding, lasting, unchangeable, irremovable, constant, changeless.

pẽr′ma̤·nent, *n.* a permanent wave. [Colloq.]

pẽr′ma̤·nent·ly, *adv.* in a permanent manner.

pẽr·man′ga̤·nāte, *n.* in chemistry, a salt of permanganic acid, generally dark purple.

pẽr·man·gan′iç ac′id, [*per-* and *manganic*.] an unstable acid, $HMnO_4$, that is a strong oxidizing agent in aqueous solutions.

pẽr·man′sion, *n.* [L. *permansio*.] continuance. [Obs.]

pẽr″mē·a̤·bil′i·ty, *n.* 1. the quality or state of being permeable.

2. in physics, (a) the measure of the ease with which magnetic lines of force are carried by a particular material; (b) the rate of diffusion of a fluid through a porous body under standard conditions of area, thickness, and pressure.

pẽr′mē·a̤·ble, *a.* [L. *permeabilis*.] that can be permeated; open to passage or penetration, especially by fluids.

pẽr′mē·a̤·bly, *adv.* in a permeable manner.

pẽr·mē·am′e·tẽr, *n.* [L. *permeare*, and Gr. *metron*, measure.] an instrument used for testing the magnetic permeability of substances.

pẽr′mē·ănce, *n.* 1. a permeating or being permeated.

2. the quality of being permeable.

pẽr′mē·ănt, *a.* permeating or tending to permeate.

pẽr′mē·āte, *v.t.*; permeated, *pt.*, *pp.*; permeating, *ppr.* [L. *permeare*, *permeatus*; *per*, through, and *meare*, to glide, flow, or pass.] to pass into and affect every part of; to penetrate and spread through; as, water will *permeate* blotting paper.

pẽr′mē·āte, *v.i.* to spread or diffuse; to penetrate (with *through* or *among*).

pẽr·mē·ā′tion, *n.* the act of permeating or being permeated.

pẽr′mē·ā·tive, *a.* permeating; diffusive.

pẽr men′sem, [L.] by the month.

Pẽr′mi·ak, *n.* one of a mixed Finnic people near Perm, Russia; also, their language.

Pẽr′mi·ăn, *a.* [after *Perm*, a province of Russia.] designating or of the geological period following the Pennsylvanian in the Paleozoic Era and preceding the Triassic in the Mesozoic: it was characterized by increased reptile life, major mountain building of the Appalachian ranges, and much glaciation, especially in the Southern Hemisphere.

the Permian; the Permian Period or its rocks.

Pẽr′mi·ăn, *a.* pertaining to Perm, Russia.

Pẽr′mi·ăn, *n.* a native of Perm; a Permiak; also, the language of the Permiaks.

pẽr·miss′, *n.* a permission of choice or selection. [Obs.]

pẽr·mis·si·bil′i·ty, *n.* the state or quality of being permissible.

pẽr·mis′si·ble, *a.* allowable; that can be permitted.

pẽr·mis′si·ble·ness, *n.* same as *permissibility*.

pẽr·mis′si·bly, *adv.* so as to be permissible.

pẽr·mis′sion, *n.* [L. *permissio*, from *permittere*, to permit.] the act of permitting or allowing; allowance; authority; formal consent; license or liberty granted.

pẽr·mis′sive, *a.* 1. giving permission; that permits.

2. allowing freedom; especially, tolerant of behavior or practices disapproved of by others; indulgent; lenient.

3. allowable and at one's option. [Archaic.]

pẽr·mis′sive·ly, *adv.* in a permissive manner; without prohibition or hindrance.

pẽr·mis′sō·ry, *a.* of, pertaining to, or done by permission: especially in law, said of acts or privileges accorded one by grant of some person or legislation in authority, as distinguished from an inherent right.

pẽr·mis′tion (-chun), *n.* permixtion. [Obs.]

pẽr·mit′, *v.t.*; permitted, *pt.*, *pp.*; permitting, *ppr.* [L. *permittere*; *per-*, and *mittere*, to send.]

1. to give permission to; to authorize; as, he is *permitted* to leave.

2. to allow by silent consent, or by not prohibiting; to suffer without giving express authority; to tolerate.

What God neither commands nor forbids, he *permits* with approbation to be done or left undone. —Hooker.

3. to give opportunity for; as, an intermission that *permits* conversation.

4. to leave; to give or resign. [Obs.]

Let us not aggravate our sorrows,
But to the gods *permit* the event of things.
—Addison.

Syn.—allow, let, suffer, tolerate.

pẽr·mit′, *v.i.* to give opportunity or possibility; as, if the weather *permits*, the journey will be made.

pẽr′mit (*or* pẽr-mit′), *n.* 1. permission.

2. a document granting permission to do something; a license; a warrant.

pẽr·mit′, *n.* [altered from Sp. *palometa*.] any of several fishes of the genus *Trachynotus*, found in the West Indies and Florida, and closely related to the pompano.

pẽr·mit′tănce, *n.* 1. the act of permitting; permission; allowance. [Obs.]

2. in electricity, electrostatic capacity, as of a condenser, residing in the dielectric, through whose power induction is assisted across it.

pẽr·mit·tee′, *n.* one to whom a permit is given or granted.

pẽr·mit′tẽr, *n.* one who permits.

pẽr·mit·tiv′i·ty, *n.* in electricity, specific capacity for induction.

pẽr·mix′, *v.t.* to mix together; to mingle. [Obs.]

pẽr·mix′tion (-chun), *n.* a mixing. [Obs.]

Pẽr·mō·cär·bŏn·if′ẽr·ous, *a.* in geology, pertaining to a transitional epoch between the Carboniferous and Permian periods; specifically, relating to a division of the Permian in the United States, making a transition to the Carboniferous.

pẽr·mū′ta̤·ble, *a.* capable of being changed or permuted.

pẽr·mū′ta̤·ble·ness, *n.* the state of being permutable.

pẽr·mū′ta̤·bly, *adv.* by interchange; in a permutable manner.

pẽr·mū·tā′tion, *n.* [L. *permutatio*.]

1. the act of permuting; the state of being permuted; intermutation; concurrent change; mutual change; interchange; rearrangement.

2. one of several possible arrangements of items in a group.

3. in mathematics, a change or a different combination of any number of quantities. Permutations differ from combinations in that the latter have no reference to the order in which the quantities are combined, whereas in the former this order is considered. Thus, the *permutations* of 1, 2, and 3, taken two at a time are 12, 21, 13, 31, 23, 32; the *combinations* are 12, 13, 23. If n represents the number of items within the group, the number of permutations that can be formed, taking two at a time, is $n(n-1)$, taking three at a time, is $n(n-1)(n-2)$, and so forth.

4. in civil law, barter; exchange. [Obs.]

5. in linguistics, formerly, the shifting of consonants according to Grimm's law: cf. *Grimm's law*.

pẽr·mū·tā′tion lock, a lock in which the moving parts are capable of transposition, so that being arranged in any certain order it becomes necessary before removing the bolt to arrange the tumblers.

pẽr·mūte′, *v.t.* [L. *permutare*; *per*, and *mutare*, to change.]

1. to make different; to alter.

2. to rearrange the order or sequence of.

3. to exchange; to barter. [Obs.]

pẽr·mūt′ẽr, *n.* one who permutes.

pẽrn, *n.* the honey buzzard, *Pernis apivorus*.

pẽr′năn·cy, *n.* a taking or reception, as the receiving of rents or tithes in kind.

pẽr·net′ti, *n.pl.* [It.] small supports placed under articles of pottery in firing; also, the indentations made by these supports.

pẽr·ni′ciŏn (-nish′ŏn), *n.* destruction. [Obs.]

pẽr·ni′cious, *a.* [L. *perniciosus*, from *pernicies*, destruction, from *pernecare*, to kill; *per*, thoroughly, and *necare*, to kill; *nex*, *necis*, death.]

1. destructive; having the power of killing, destroying, ruining, or injuring; fatal; deadly.

2. wicked; evil; as, intemperance is a *pernicious* vice. [Rare.]

Syn.—destructive, hurtful, mischievous, noisome, noxious, evil, deadly.

pẽr·ni′cious, *a.* [L. *pernix*, *pernicis*, swift, nimble.] quick. [Rare.]

pẽr·ni′cious a̤·nē′mi·a̤, a severe form of anemia characterized by a gradual reduction in the number of the red blood cells, general weakness, gastrointestinal and nervous disturbances, etc.: it can be successfully treated by the administration of liver or liver extracts.

pẽr·ni′cious·ly, *adv.* in a pernicious manner; with destructive effect.

pẽr·ni′cious·ness, *n.* the quality of being pernicious.

pẽr·nic′i·ty, *n.* [L. *pernicitas*, from *pernix*.] swiftness of motion; celerity. [Rare.]

pẽr·nick′et·y, pẽr·nick′et·ty, *a.* [from Scot. dial.; prob. echoic expansion of *pernicky* in same sense; perh. altered from *pertickie*, child's word for *particular*.]

1. too particular or precise; fastidious; fussy. [Colloq.]

2. showing or requiring extremely careful treatment. [Colloq.]

Also *persnickety*.

pẽr′ni·ō, *n.*; *pl.* **pẽr·ni·ō′nēṣ,** [L., from Gr. *perna*, the ham.] a chilblain.

pẽr·noç·tā′li·ăn, *n.* one who remains awake or watches all night. [Obs.]

pẽr·noç·tā′tion, *n.* [L. *pernoctare*, to pass the night; *per*, through, and *nox*, night.] the act of passing the whole night; a staying all night.

pẽr′nŏr, *n.* [OFr. *preneor*; L. *prendere*, to take.] in law, one who takes or receives anything, as rent or the profits of an estate.

Pẽr′not fũr′nāce, [after Charles *Pernot*, the inventor.] a reverberatory furnace having an inclined rotative bed, used in making steel.

pẽr′ny·ī mọth, [E. Ind.] the tusser moth of the East Indies and China, a silk-producing moth whose larva feeds on the oak: it has been introduced into Europe and the United States.

per·of′skīte, *n.* [after von *Perovski*, of Russia.] a hard, yellow, transparent titanate of lime, occurring in cubic crystals: written also *perovskite*.

pē·rōgue′ (-rōg′), *n.* same as *pirogue*.

Pē·rom′e·la̤, *n.pl.* same as *Ophiomorpha*.

pē·rom′e·lus, *n.* a malformation in which the extremities are incomplete.

per′ō·nāte, *a.* [L. *peronatus*, rough-booted, from *pero*, *peronis*, a kind of rough boot.] of the stipes of fungaceous plants which are thickly covered with a woolly or mealy substance.

per′ō·nē, *n.* [Gr. *peronē*, a brooch.] the fibula, a small bone of the leg: so called from its resemblance to the pin of a brooch.

per·ō·nē′ăl, *a.* of, pertaining to, or near the fibula; as, *peroneal* muscles.

Per·ō·nos′pō·ra̤, *n.* [Gr. *peronē*, brooch, and *sporos*, seed.] a large genus of parasitic fungi, typical of the order *Peronosporales*: many are injurious to cultivated plants.

per·ō·nos·pō·rā′ceous, *a.* of or pertaining to the *Peronospora*.

pē·rop′ō·dous, *a.* [Gr. *pēros*, maimed, and *pous*, *podos*, foot.] having rudimentary hind legs, as the pythons.

pē′rō·pod, *n.* a peropod snake.

per′ō·rāte, *v.i.*; perorated, *pt.*, *pp.*; perorating, *ppr.* [from L. *peroratus*.]

1. to make a speech; especially, to speak at some length; to harangue.

2. to sum up or conclude a speech.

per·ō·rā′tion, *n.* [L. *peroratio*, from *perorare*; *per*, through, and *orare*, to pray, to speak.]

1. the concluding part of a speech, in which there is a summing up and emphatic recapitulation.

2. a high-flown or bombastic speech.

pẽr·ox′id, *n.* peroxide.

pẽr·ox·i·dā′tion, *n.* the act or process of treating a compound with a peroxidizing agent, so that a peroxide will be formed.

pẽr·ox′īde, *n.* [*per-* and *oxide.*] any oxide containing the O_2 group in which the two atoms of oxygen are linked by a single bond; specifically, hydrogen peroxide.

pẽr·ox′īde, *v.t.*; peroxided, *pt., pp.*; peroxiding, *ppr.* to bleach with hydrogen peroxide.

pẽr·ox′īde, *a.* bleached with hydrogen peroxide; as, *peroxide* hair.

pẽr·ox′i·dīze, *v.t.*; peroxidized, *pt., pp.*; peroxidizing, *ppr.* to oxidize so as to form a peroxide.

pẽr·pend′, *v.t.* and *v.i.* [L. *perpendere*; *per,* and *pendere,* to weigh.] to weigh in the mind; to consider attentively; to ponder. [Archaic.]

pẽr′pend, *n.* [Fr. *parpaing, parpain,* from *par,* through, and *pan,* the side of a wall.] a large stone reaching through a wall from one side to the other, used as a binder: also called *perbend, perbend* (or *perpent*) *stone.*

pẽr·pend′ẽr, *n.* same as *perpend.*

pẽr·pen′di·çle, *n.* [Fr. *perpendicule,* from L. *perpendiculum.*] something hanging down in a direct line; a plumb line. [Obs.]

pẽr·pen·diç′ū·lăr, *a.* [L. *perpendicularis,* from *perpendiculum,* a plumb line; *per-* intens., and *pendere,* to hang.]

1. at right angles to a given plane or line.

2. exactly upright; vertical; straight up or down.

3. [P–] of or designating the third and latest style of English Gothic architecture of the fourteenth, fifteenth, and sixteenth centuries, characterized by vertical lines in its tracery.

P
H D R
PERPENDICULAR
P D perpendicular to HR

pẽr·pen·diç′ū·lăr, *n.* 1. a device used in finding or marking the vertical line from any point.

2. a line at right angles to the plane of the horizon.

3. a straight line at right angles to another line or plane.

4. a perpendicular or upright position.

pẽr·pen·diç·ū·lar′i·ty, *n.* the state or quality of being perpendicular.

pẽr·pen·diç′ū·lar·ly, *adv.* in a perpendicular manner; vertically; so as to fall on the plane of the horizon at right angles; in a direction toward the center of the earth or the center of gravity.

pẽr·pen′sion, *n.* [L. *perpendere,* to weigh carefully.] consideration. [Obs.]

per′pent, pẽr′pent stōne, same as *perpend.*

pẽr·pes′sion, *n.* [L. *perpessio,* from *perpeti,* to suffer; *per,* thoroughly, and *pati,* to endure.] suffering; endurance. [Obs.]

pẽr′pē·trā·ble, *a.* capable of perpetration.

pẽr′pē·trāte, *v.t.*; perpetrated, *pt., pp.*; perpetrating, *ppr.* [L. *perpetrare*; *per,* thoroughly, and *patrare,* to effect.] to do or perform (something evil, criminal, or offensive); to be guilty of; to commit (a blunder), impose (a hoax), etc.

pẽr·pē·trā′tion, *n.* 1. the act of perpetrating.

2. something perpetrated, as an offense.

pẽr′pē·trā·tŏr, *n.* one who perpetrates.

pẽr·pet′ū·a·ble, *a.* capable of being perpetuated.

pẽr·pet′ū·ăl, *a.* [Fr. *perpétuel*; L. *perpetuus*; *per,* through, and *petere,* to seek, to go on.]

1. lasting or enduring forever or for an indefinitely long time; eternal; permanent.

2. continuing indefinitely without interruption; unceasing; constant; as, a *perpetual* nuisance.

3. in gardening, blooming continuously throughout the growing season.

perpetual calendar; see under *calendar.*

perpetual canon; in music, a canon that will bear constant repetition without a break in time or rhythm.

perpetual motion; the motion of a hypothetical device which, once set in motion, would operate indefinitely by creating its own energy.

Syn.—continual, unceasing, endless, everlasting, incessant, constant, eternal, ceaseless, enduring, permanent, uninterrupted.

pẽr·pet′ū·ăl, *n.* a perpetual plant; especially, a variety of perpetual hybrid rose.

pẽr·pet′ū·ăl·ly, *adv.* 1. forever; eternally.

2. constantly; incessantly.

pẽr·pet′ū·ăl·ty, *n.* the state of being perpetual. [Obs.]

pẽr·pet′ū·āte, *v.t.*; perpetuated, *pt., pp.*; perpetuating, *ppr.* to make perpetual; to eternize; to cause to endure or to be continued indefinitely; to preserve from extinction or oblivion; as, to *perpetuate* the remembrance of a great event.

pẽr·pet′ū·āte, *a.* made enduring; perpetuated.

pẽr·pet·ū·ā′tion, *n.* the act of making perpetual or the state of being perpetuated.

pẽr·pet′ū·ā·tŏr, *n.* a person who perpetuates.

pẽr·pē·tū′i·ty, *n.*; *pl.* **pẽr·pē·tū′i·tieṣ,** [L. *perpetuitas*; from *perpetuus,* perpetual.]

1. the state or quality of being perpetual.

2. something perpetual, as an annuity or pension to be paid indefinitely.

3. unlimited time; eternity.

4. in law, (a) a limitation upon the transference of an estate: it is valid only for a legally specified period; (b) an estate so limited.

in perpetuity; forever.

pẽr·plex′, *v.t.*; perplexed (-plext′), *pt., pp.*; perplexing, *ppr.* [from L. *perplexus,* entangled, from *per-* intens., and *plexus,* pp. of *plectere,* to twist.]

1. to make intricate; to involve; to entangle; to make complicated and difficult to understand or unravel.

> What was thought obscure, *perplexed,* and too hard for our weak parts, will lie open to the understanding in a fair view. —Locke.

2. to make (a person) uncertain, doubtful, or hesitant; to confuse; to puzzle.

> We are *perplexed,* but not in despair. —2 Cor. iv. 8.

3. to plague; to vex. [Obs.]

Syn.—entangle, involve, complicate, embarrass, puzzle, bewilder, confuse, distract, harass, vex, plague, tease, molest, bother, confound, mystify.

pẽr·plex′, *a.* intricate; difficult. [Obs.]

pẽr·plexed′ (-plext′), *a.* 1. full of doubt or uncertainty; puzzled.

2. hard to understand; confusing.

pẽr·plex′ed·ly, *adv.* in a perplexed manner.

pẽr·plex′ed·ness, *n.* the quality or state of being perplexed.

pẽr·plex′ing, *a.* that perplexes.

pẽr·plex′ing·ly, *adv.* in a perplexing manner.

pẽr·plex′i·ty, *n.* [ME. *perplexite*; OFr. *perplexité*; LL. *perplexitas.*]

1. the condition of being perplexed; bewilderment; confusion.

2. *pl.* **pẽr·plex′i·tieṣ,** something that perplexes or is perplexed, as a complication or intricacy.

Syn.—bewilderment, doubt, embarrassment, intricacy, entanglement, confusion, anxiety.

pẽr·plex′ive·ness, *n.* the quality of being perplexing. [Obs.]

pẽr·plex′ly, *adv.* perplexedly. [Obs.]

pẽr′qui·ṣite, *n.* [from L. *perquisitus,* pp. of *perquirere,* to search diligently for.]

1. a fee, profit, compensation, or emolument in addition to the stated income, wages, or salary, resulting from one's employment or position, especially something customary or expected, as a tip or gratuity.

2. something to which a person, institution, etc. is entitled by virtue of status, position, or character; prerogative; right; as, the frank is a *perquisite* of congressmen.

3. in law, goods or property acquired by one's own exertions or bought with one's own money in distinction from inherited property.

pẽr·qui·ṣi′tion, *n.* [L. *perquirere,* to search carefully.] a thorough inquiry or search.

pẽr·rā′di·ăl, *a.* [*per-,* and L. *radius,* ray.] composing or relating to a primary ray, as the tentacles in certain hydrozoans.

per′rie, *n.* [Fr. *pierreries.*] jewelry; precious stones. [Obs.]

per′ri·ẽr, *n.* [OFr. *perriere*; LL. *petraria*; L. *petra,* stone.]

1. a medieval catapult for hurling stones. [Obs.]

2. a mortar to throw stone balls. [Obs.]

per′rŏn, *n.* [ME. *peroun*; OFr. *perron,* from *pierre*; L. *petra,* a stone.] an outside staircase, usually extending up the slope of a terrace, as to the front entrance of a building.

per·rō·quet′ (-ket′), *n.* [Fr.] same as *parakeet.*

pẽr·ruque′ (-rūk′), *n.* [Fr.] a peruke; a wig; a periwig.

pẽr·ru′qui·ẽr (-ki-), *n.* [Fr.] a wigmaker or hairdresser.

per′ry, *n.* [ME. *pereye*; OFr. *peré*; LL. *pera,* from L. *pirum,* pear.] the fermented juice of pears, prepared in the same way as cider.

pẽr′salt, *n.* a salt of a peracid.

pẽr·sçru·tā′tion, *n.* [L. *perscrutatio*; *perscrutari,* to search thoroughly.] a searching thoroughly; minute search or inquiry.

pẽrse, *a.* [ME.; OFr. *pers*; LL. *persus.*] grayish-blue.

pẽrse, *n.* grayish blue.

pẽr sē, [L.] by (or in) itself; inherently.

Pẽr·sē′ȧ, *n.* [Gr.] a genus of trees and shrubs of the laurel family. *Persea gratissima* is the true avocado; *Persea carolinensis* is the red bay of the southern part of the United States.

pẽr′sē·çūte, *v.t.*; persecuted, *pt., pp.*; persecuting, *ppr.* [Fr. *persécuter*; L. *persequi*; *per-,* through, and *sequi,* to follow.]

1. to afflict or harass constantly so as to injure or distress; to oppress cruelly, especially for reasons of religion, politics, or race.

2. to trouble or annoy constantly; as, *persecuted* by mosquitos.

Syn.—afflict, annoy, harass, oppress, torment, worry.

pẽr·sē·çū′tion, *n.* 1. the act or practice of persecuting; the infliction of pain, punishment, or death upon others, especially for reasons of religion, politics, or race.

2. the state of being persecuted.

3. annoyance by persistent unwelcome attentions or requests.

4. prosecution. [Obs.]

pẽr′sē·çū·tive, *a.* of, like, or constituting persecution.

pẽr′sē·çū·tŏr, *n.* one who persecutes.

pẽr′sē·çū·trix, *n.* a woman who persecutes.

Pẽr′sē·id, *n.* [from Mod.L. *Perseis,* daughter of Perseus.] any of a group of meteors seen annually about August 10 to 12, radiating from a point in the direction of the constellation Perseus.

pẽr′sē·ite, *n.* [*Persea* and *-ite.*] a substance found in the avocado, *Persea gratissima,* and also derived from mannose.

Pẽr·seph′ō·nē, *n.* in Greek mythology, the daughter of Zeus and Demeter, abducted by Hades (Pluto) and made his wife: identified by the Romans with Proserpina.

Pẽr′sē·us, *n.* [Gr.] 1. in Greek mythology, the son of Zeus and Danaë, who slew the Gorgon Medusa.

2. a northern constellation situated between Taurus and Cassiopeia.

pẽr·sev′ẽr, *v.i.* to persevere. [Obs.]

pẽr·sē·vẽr′ănce, *n.* [Fr., from L. *perseverantia.*]

1. the act of persevering.

2. the quality of one who perseveres; persistence.

> With steady *perseverance,* difficulties upon a mountain, as elsewhere, come to an end. —John Tyndall.

3. in Calvinistic theology, the doctrine that those who are elected to eternal life, justified, adopted, and sanctified, will never permanently lapse from grace or be finally lost: in full, *perseverance of the saints.*

Syn.—persistence, steadfastness, constancy, indefatigability, resolution, tenacity.

pẽr·sē·vẽr′ănt, *a.* persevering. [Rare.]

pẽr·sē·vēre′, *v.i.*; persevered, *pt., pp.*; persevering, *ppr.* [L. *perseverare,* from *perseverus,* very severe or strict; *per-* intens., and *severus,* severe, serious, grave, strict.] to persist in any business or enterprise undertaken; to pursue steadily any design or course once begun; to be steadfast in purpose.

> Thrice happy, if they know
> Their happiness, and *persevere* upright!
> —Milton.

> To *persevere* in any evil course makes you unhappy in this life. —Wake.

Syn.—continue, persist, insist, pursue.—*Continue* denotes to go on doing what one has done hitherto; to *persevere* is to continue in a given course in spite of difficulties, obstacles, etc.; to *persist* is to continue with a determination not to give up.

pẽr·sē·vẽr′ing, *a.* persistent; refusing to give up; showing perseverance; as, a *persevering* student.

pẽr·sē·vẽr′ing·ly, *adv.* in a persevering manner; with perseverance or continued pursuit of what is undertaken.

Pẽr′ṣiăn, *a.* of Persia, ancient or modern, its people, their language, or culture; Iranian.

Persian berry; the fruit of a species of buckthorn, used in making yellow dye.

Persian blinds; same as *persiennes.*

Persian cat; a variety of domestic cat with long, silky hair.

Persian drill; a drill operated by a drill holder which has a spiral groove, on which a grooved handle is pushed up and down.

Persian fire; same as *anthrax,* sense 1.

Persian insect powder; an insecticide made

from the flowers of *Pyrethrum corneum* or *roseum*, and reduced to a powder.

Persian lamb; (a) the lamb of certain Asiatic sheep; (b) its black, gray, or brown curly fleece, used for fur coats, etc.

Persian rug (or *carpet*); an Oriental rug made in Persia, having rich, soft colors in an intricate pattern.

Pēr'ṣiăn, *n.* 1. a native or inhabitant of Persia.

2. the Iranian language of the Persians: its historical forms are Old Persian, Avestan, and Pahlavi; the current form is known as Modern Persian.

3. a thin silk fabric, once used for linings.

4. in architecture, a male figure draped in the ancient Persian manner, and serving to support an entablature, in place of a column or pilaster.

Pēr'siç, *a.* characteristic of or relating to Persia or the Persian language. [Obs.]

pēr'si·çăr·y, *n.*; *pl.* **pēr'si·çăr·ieṣ,** [ML. *persicarius*, peach tree, from L. *persicum*, peach.] any of a group of plants of the knotweed family, characterized by jointed stems.

pēr'si·çot, *n.* [Fr., from L. *persica*, peach.] a cordial flavored with the kernels of apricots, nectarines, peaches, etc.

pēr·ṣi·enne' (-en'), *n.* [Fr., Persian.] cotton or silk painted or printed with designs.

pēr·ṣi·enneṣ' (*or Fr.* per-syen'), *n.pl.* [Fr., f. pl. of *persien*, Persian.] outside shutters for windows, having adjustable, horizontal slats like those on Venetian blinds: also *Persian blinds*.

pēr'si·flāge (-fläzh), *n.* [Fr., from *persifler*, to banter, from L. *per*, and Fr. *siffler*, to whistle, hiss; L. *sifilare*, *sibilare*, to hiss.]

1. a light, frivolous or flippant style of writing or speaking.

2. talk or writing of this kind; banter; raillery.

per·si·flēur' (-sē-flẽr'), *n.* [Fr.] one who indulges in banter.

pēr·sim'mŏn, *n.* [Am. Ind.]

1. any tree of the genus *Diospyros*, especially *Diospyros virginiana*, native to the United States, with white, cup-shaped flowers, hard wood, and yellow or orange-red, plumlike fruit.

2. the fruit, sour and astringent when green, but sweet and edible when thoroughly ripe.

3. any of various other species of *Diospyros*, as the black persimmon, *Diospyros texana*.

Japanese persimmon; (a) an Asiatic tree of the ebony family, bearing large, soft, edible, red or orange-colored fruit; (b) its fruit. Also called *kaki*, *date plum*.

pēr'sis, *n.* a kind of coloring matter prepared from lichens, drier than archil.

pēr·sist' (*or* -zist'), *v.i.*; persisted, *pt.*, *pp.*; persisting, *ppr.* [Fr. *persister*; L. *persistere*; *per*, through, and *sistere*, to cause to stand.]

1. to refuse to give up, especially when faced with opposition or difficulty; to continue firmly or steadily.

2. to continue insistently, as in repeating a remark or question.

3. to continue to exist or prevail; endure; remain; last.

Syn.—persevere, insist, endure, stay.

pēr·sist'ence, *n.* 1. the act of persisting; stubborn or enduring continuance, as in a chosen course or purpose.

2. a persistent or lasting quality; resoluteness; tenacity.

3. continuous existence; endurance, as of a headache.

4. the continuance of an effect after the cause which first gave rise to it is removed; as, *persistence* of vision causes visual impressions to continue upon the retina for some time.

pēr·sist'en·cy, *n.* same as *persistence*.

pēr·sist'ent, *a.* [L. *persistens*, ppr. of *persistere*, to persist.]

1. refusing to relent; continuing, especially in the face of opposition, etc.; stubborn; persevering.

2. continuing to exist or endure; lasting without change.

3. constantly repeated; continued.

4. in botany, remaining attached for a long time, as some withered leaves.

5. in zoology, remaining for life: said of such parts which in other animals disappear or wither at an early stage.

pēr·sist'ent·ly, *adv.* in a persistent manner.

pēr·sist'ing, *a.* continuing in the prosecution of an undertaking; persevering.

pēr·sist'ing·ly, *adv.* perseveringly; steadily.

pēr·sist'ive, *a.* inclined to persist; persistent.

pēr·snick'e·ty, *a.* pernickety. [Colloq.]

pēr'sŏn, *n.* [L. *persona*, lit., a face mask used by actors on the stage, hence, a character, a person, from *personare*, to sound through; *per*, through, and *sonare*, to sound.]

1. an individual human being, especially as distinguished from a thing or lower animal; an individual man, woman, or child.

> A zeal for *persons* is far more easy to be perverted than a zeal for things. —Sprat.

2. a common individual: used in slight or contempt.

3. (a) a living human body; (b) bodily form or appearance; as, she was neat and clean about her *person*.

> The rebels maintained the fight for a small time, and for their *persons* showed no want of courage. —Bacon.

4. personality; self; being; as, his very *person* is offensive.

5. in grammar, (a) division into three classes of pronouns and, in most languages, corresponding verb forms, the use of which indicates and is determined by the identity of the subject, thus: the *first person* (*I* or *we*) is used when the subject is the speaker; the *second person* (*you*) when the subject is spoken to; the *third person* (*he*, *she*, *it*, or *they*) when the subject is spoken of; (b) any of these three classes.

6. in law, any individual or incorporated group having certain legal rights and responsibilities.

7. in theology, one of the three modes of being (Father, Son, and Holy Ghost) in the Trinity.

8. a human being represented in dialogue, fiction, or on the stage; a character; as, a player appears in the *person* of King Lear. [Archaic.]

9. in biology, a bud or shoot of a plant; a polyp or zooid of any compound hydrozoan, anthozoan, etc.

in person; in the flesh; in bodily presence.

-pēr'sŏn, a combining form meaning *person* (of either sex) *in a specified activity*: used in coinages to avoid the masculine implication of "-man": as, chair*person*.

pēr·sō'nȧ, *n.*; *pl.* **pēr·sō'nae,** [L.] 1. person.

2. [*pl.*] the characters of a drama, novel, etc.

pēr'sŏn·ȧ·ble, *a.* 1. having a well-formed body or an attractive personal appearance; good-looking; handsome; comely.

2. in law, having the right to maintain pleas in court. [Obs.]

pēr'sŏn·āġe, *n.* [OFr.] 1. a person of importance or distinction

2. any person: often used ironically or contemptuously.

3. physical appearance; stature; air. [Archaic.]

4. a character assumed. [Obs.]

> The Venetians, naturally grave, love to give in to the follies of such seasons, when disguised in a false *personage*. —Addison.

5. a character in history, a play, novel, etc.

> Some persons must be found, already known in history, whom we may make the actors and *personages* of this fable. —Broome.

pēr·sō'nȧ grā'tȧ (*or* grä'), [L.] a person who is acceptable; one who is always welcome.

pēr'sŏn·ăl, *a.* [ME. *personele*; OFr. *personel*; L. *personalis*.]

1. belonging to human beings, not to things or abstractions.

> Every man so termed by way of *personal* difference only. —Hooker.

2. private; individual; affecting individuals; peculiar or proper to a certain person or to private actions or character; as, extreme *personal* annoyance.

> Character and success depend more on *personal* effort than on any external advantages. —J. Hawes.

3. pertaining to the person, body, or physical appearance; as, *personal* charms or accomplishments.

4. done in person or by oneself without the use of another person or outside agency; as, a *personal* interview.

> The immediate and *personal* speaking of God Almighty to Abraham, Job, and Moses. —White.

5. having to do with the character, personality, intimate affairs, conduct, etc. of a certain person; as, a *personal* remark.

6. tending to make remarks, or be inquisitive, about the private affairs of others.

7. of, like, or having the nature of a person, or rational, self-conscious being; as, a *personal* God.

8. in grammar, indicating grammatical person, as the inflectional endings of verbs in Latin and Greek: see also *personal pronoun*.

9. in law, of or constituting personal property.

personal action; in law, a suit or action in which a man claims a debt or personal duty, or damages in lieu of it, or in which he claims satisfaction in damages for an injury to his person or property; an action founded on contract or on tort, or wrong, as an action on a debt or promise, or an action for a trespass, assault, or defamatory words: opposed to *real actions*, one involving real property.

personal effects; same as *personal property*.

personal equation; same as *equation*, sense 2.

personal foul; in certain team games, a foul involving body contact with an opponent, as unwarranted roughness or hindering.

personal identity; in metaphysics, sameness of being, of which consciousness is the evidence.

personal pronoun; any of a group of pronouns referring to the speaker(s), the person(s) spoken to, or any other person(s) or thing(s). The English personal pronouns, nominative case form, are: I, we, you (*or archaic* thou, ye), he, she, it, and they.

personal property; in law, movables; chattels; any property that is movable or not attached to the land, as money, jewelry, furniture, etc.: opposed to *real property*.

pēr'sŏn·ăl, *n.* 1. a movable. [Obs.]

2. a local news item about a person or persons.

3. a brief newspaper advertisment concerning a personal matter.

pēr'sŏn·ăl·iṣm, *n.* the quality of being personal.

pēr·sŏn·al'i·ty, *n.*; *pl.* **pēr·sŏn·al'i·tieṣ,** [ME. *personalite*; OFr. *personalité*; ML. *personalitas*, from L. *personalis*, personal.]

1. the quality or fact of being a person.

2. the quality or fact of being a particular person; personal identity; individuality.

3. habitual patterns and qualities of behavior of any individual as expressed by physical and mental activities and attitudes; distinctive individual qualities of a person, considered collectively.

4. the sum of such qualities as impressing or likely to impress others; as, she has *personality*.

5. a person; especially, a notable person; personage.

6. [*usually pl.*] any remark, usually an offensive or disparaging one, aimed at or referring to a person.

7. in law, that which concerns the capacity, condition, and state of persons.

pēr'sŏn·ăl·ize, *v.t.*; personalized, *pt.*, *pp.*; personalizing, *ppr.* 1. to make personal; to apply to a specific person, especially to oneself; as, she *personalized* his general criticism of her group.

2. to personify; to endow with personality.

3. to have printed with one's name; as, *personalized* checks.

pēr'sŏn·ăl·ly, *adv.* 1. in person; by bodily presence; without the use of another person or an agent; as, to be *personally* present; to deliver a letter *personally*; the king opened Parliament *personally*.

2. as a person; particularly.

> She bore a mortal hatred to the house of Lancaster, and *personally* to the king. —Bacon.

3. with regard to personal existence or individuality.

> The converted man is *personally* the same he was before. —Rogers.

4. as though directed at one's person; as, she took his remarks *personally*.

5. in one's own opinion; as far as oneself is concerned; as, *personally* I have no feeling in the matter.

pēr'sŏn·ăl·ty, *n.*; *pl.* **pēr'sŏn·ăl·tieṣ,** [Anglo-Fr. *personaltie* for OFr. *personalité*: see *personality*.] personal property: opposed to *realty*.

pēr·sō'nȧ non grā'tȧ (*or* grä'), [L.] a person who is not acceptable; an unwelcome person.

pēr'sŏn·āte, *v.t.*; personated, *pt.*, *pp.*; personating, *ppr.* [from L. *personatus*, masked, from *persona*: see *person*.]

1. to act or play the part of, as in a drama or masquerade; to portray.

2. to personify, as in poetry.

3. in law, to assume the character or identity of with intent to defraud; to impersonate.
4. to counterfeit; to feign; as, a *personated* devotion. [Rare.]

pẽr′sŏn·āte, *v.i.* to play a part; to assume a character.

pẽr′sŏn·āte, *a.* having a single-petaled flower with two lips and a projection in its throat.

pẽr·sŏn·ā′tion, *n.* a personating or being personated; impersonation.
false personation; in law, the assumption of another's character or identity with intent to defraud, especially in the case of a detective or an officer making an arrest.

PERSONATE COROLLA

pẽr′sŏn·ā·tive, *a.* personating: especially, representing dramatically.

pẽr′sŏn·ā·tŏr, *n.* one who personates.

pẽr·sŏn·ē′i·ty, *n.* personality. [Rare.]

pẽr·son″i·fi·cā′tion, *n.* 1. a personifying or being personified.
2. a person or thing thought of as representing some quality, thing, or idea; embodiment; type; perfect example; as, the old man was the very *personification* of evil; Cupid is the *personification* of love.
3. a figure of speech in which a thing, quality, or idea is represented as a person.

pẽr·son′i·fī·ẽr, *n.* one who or that which personifies.

pẽr·son′i·fy, *v.t.*; personified, *pt., pp.*; personifying, *ppr.* [Fr. *personnifier*, from L. *persona*, a person, and *facere*, to make.]
1. to think or speak of (a thing) as having life or personality; to represent as a person; as, we *personify* a ship by referring to it as "she."
2. to symbolize (an abstract idea) by a human figure, as in art.
3. to be a perfect example of (some quality, thing, or idea); to typify; to embody.
4. to personate. [Rare.]

pẽr′sŏn·īze, *v.t.* to personify. [Rare.]

pẽr·sŏn·nel′, *n.* [Fr.] persons employed in any work, enterprise, service, establishment, etc.: distinguished in military usage from *matériel*.

pẽr·sŏn·nel′, *a.* of or in charge of personnel.
personnel director; (a) one who is in charge of the personnel of a business establishment: his duty is to supervise the selection, and sometimes training, of the personnel; (b) in a college, a vocational adviser.

pẽr·spec′tive, *a.* [ME. *perspectif*; LL. *perspectivus*, from L. *perspicere*, to look through, from *per*, through, and *spicere*, to look.]
1. pertaining to the science of optics; optical. [Obs.]
2. of perspective.
3. drawn in perspective.

pẽr·spec′tive, *n.* [ML. *perspectiva*, from LL. *perspectivus*, from L. *perspicere*, to look through.]
1. the art of picturing objects or a scene in such a way as to show them as they appear to the eye with reference to relative distance or depth.
2. (a) the appearance of objects or scenes as determined by their relative distance and positions; (b) the effect of relative distance and position.
3. the relationship or proportion of the parts of a whole, regarded from a particular standpoint or point in time.
4. a proper evaluation with proportional importance given to the component parts.
5. a picture in perspective.
6. a distant view; vista.
7. an optical instrument. [Obs.]

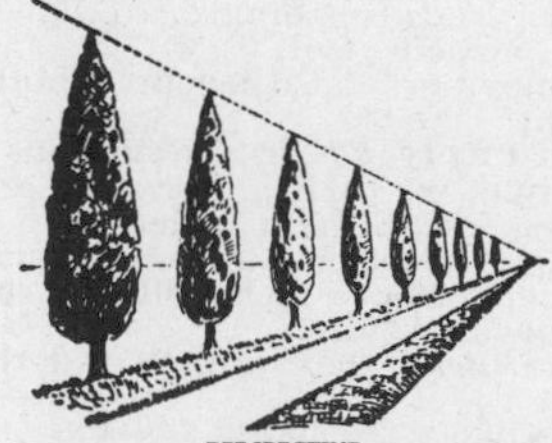
PERSPECTIVE

aerial perspective; the representation of space by gradations of the strength of light, shade, and colors of objects, according to their distances and the quantity of light falling on them, and to the medium through which they are seen.

pẽr·spec′tive·ly, *adv.* 1. optically. [Obs.]
2. according to the rules of perspective.

pẽr·spec′tō·graph, *n.* [L. *perspectus*, pp. of *perspicere*, to look through, and *-graph*.] an instrument for obtaining, or transferring to a picture, the points and outlines of original objects.

pẽr′spi·cā·ble, *a.* discernible. [Obs.]

pẽr·spi·cā′cious, *a.* [L. *perspicax*, *perspicacis*, from *perspicere*, to look through.]
1. having keen judgment or understanding.
2. having keen vision. [Archaic.]

pẽr·spi·cā′cious·ly, *adv.* in a perspicacious manner.

pẽr·spi·cā′cious·ness, *n.* the quality or state of being perspicacious.

pẽr·spi·cac′i·ty, *n.* [L. *perspicacitas*.]
1. acuteness of sight; keenness of sight. [Archaic.]
2. keenness of judgment or understanding.

pẽr′spi·cà·cy, *n.* perspicacity. [Obs.]

pẽr·spi′cience (-spish′ens), *n.* [L. *perspicientia*.] insight. [Obs.]

pẽr·spi·cū′i·ty, *n.* [Fr. *perspicuité*; L. *perspicuitas*, from *perspicere*, to look through.]
1. transparency. [Obs.]
2. the quality of being perspicuous; freedom from obscurity or ambiguity; lucidity; as, *perspicuity* is the first excellence of writing or speaking.
The *perspicuity* and liveliness of his style have been praised by Prior and Addison. —Macaulay.
Syn.—clearness, plainness, distinctness, explicitness.

pẽr·spic′ū·ous, *a.* [L. *perspicuus*.]
1. transparent; translucent. [Obs.]
2. clear in statement or expression; easily understood; lucid; not obscure or ambiguous; as, language is *perspicuous* when it readily presents to the reader or hearer the precise ideas which are intended to be expressed.

pẽr·spic′ū·ous·ly, *adv.* in a perspicuous manner; so as to be perspicuous.

pẽr·spic′ū·ous·ness, *n.* the quality or state of being perspicuous.

pẽr·spīr·à·bil′i·ty, *n.* the quality or state of being perspirable.

pẽr·spīr′à·ble, *a.* 1. capable of perspiring.
2. of or pertaining to perspiration.

pẽr·spi·rā′tion, *n.* 1. the act of perspiring; sweating.
2. moisture given off in perspiring; sweat.

pẽr·spīr′à·tive, *a.* perspiratory. [Rare.]

pẽr·spīr′à·tō·ry, *a.* of or causing perspiration.

pẽr·spīre′, *v.t.* and *v.i.*; perspired, *pt., pp.*; perspiring, *ppr.* [Fr. *perspirer*; L. *perspirare*; *per*, through, and *spirare*, to breathe.] to give forth (a characteristic salty moisture) through the pores of the skin; to sweat.

pẽr·stringe′, *v.t.* [L. *perstringere*.] to graze; to glance on. [Obs.]

pẽr·suād′à·ble, *a.* that can be persuaded.

pẽr·suād′à·bly, *adv.* so as to be persuaded.

pẽr·suāde′ (-swād′), *v.t.*; persuaded, *pt., pp.*; persuading, *ppr.* [Fr. *persuader*; L. *persuadere*; *per*, thoroughly, and *suadere*, to urge.]
1. to cause (someone) to do something, especially by reasoning, urging, or inducement; to prevail upon.
I should be glad if I could *persuade* him to write such another critic on anything of mine. —Dryden.
Almost thou *persuadest* me to be a Christian. —Acts xxvi. 28.
2. to induce (someone) to believe something; to convince.
Syn.—induce, win over, entice, prevail upon, exhort, influence, urge.

pẽr·suāde′, *v.i.* to use persuasion; to prevail by persuasion.

pẽr·suād′ẽr, *n.* 1. one who persuades or influences another.
2. that which incites or compels, as a weapon.
Hunger and thirst at once
Powerful *persuaders!* —Milton.

pẽr·suā·si·bil′i·ty, *n.* the state or quality of being persuasible.

pẽr·suā′si·ble, *a.* [ME.; L. *persuasibilis*.] that can be persuaded.

pẽr·suā′si·ble·ness, *n.* persuasibility.

pẽr·suā′ṣion (-swā′zhun), *n.* [L. *persuasio* (*-onis*), from *persuadere*, to persuade.]
1. a persuading or being persuaded.
2. the power of persuading.
For thou hast all the arts of fine *persuasion*. —Otway.
3. that of which one is persuaded or convinced; a settled or firm belief or conviction.
My firm *persuasion* is, at least sometimes,
That Heaven will weigh man's virtues and his crimes. —Cowper.
4. a particular religious belief or system or the persons adhering to this; religion.
He was of the Hebrew *persuasion*. —A. Trollope.
5. a particular party, sect, group, etc.
6. kind, sort, sex, etc.: used humorously. [Colloq.]
7. that which persuades or induces; a persuasive; a reason tending to persuade. [Obs.]
Syn.—conviction, inducement, opinion, creed, belief.

pẽr·suā′sive, *a.* [Fr. *persuasif*; ML. *persuasivus*, from L. *persuasus*, pp. of *persuadere*.] having the power of persuading; tending or intended to persuade; as, *persuasive* eloquence; *persuasive* evidence.

pẽr·suā′sive, *n.* that which persuades or tends to persuade; an inducement. [Rare.]

pẽr·suā′sive·ly, *adv.* in such a manner as to persuade or convince.

pẽr·suā′sive·ness, *n.* the quality of being persuasive.

pẽr·suā′sō·ry, *a.* persuasive. [Now Rare.]

pẽr·sul′fāte, *n.* [*per-* and *sulfate*.] a salt containing the S_2O_8 radical, produced by the electrolysis of a sulfate solution.

pẽr·sul′fīde, *n.* a sulfide in which there is a larger proportion of sulfur than is contained in any other sulfide of the same series.

pẽr·sul·fū′riç, *a.* designating an acid, $H_2S_2O_8$, obtained by electrolyzing sulfuric acid.

pẽr·sul·tā′tion, *n.* [L. *persultare*, to leap through.] an eruption of the blood from an artery. [Obs.]

pẽrt, *a.* [contr. from ME. and OFr. *apert*; L. *apertus*, open.]
1. forward; saucy; bold or impudent in speech or behavior.
A lady bids me in a very *pert* manner mind my own affairs. —Addison.
2. in good spirits; lively; brisk. [Dial.]
3. (a) expert; skilled; (b) clever. [Obs.]
4. comely; of fine appearance; neat. [Obs.]

pẽrt, *n.* one who is pert.

pẽrt, *v.i.* to behave with pertness; to be saucy. [Obs.]

pẽr·tāin′, *v.i.*; pertained, *pt., pp.*; pertaining, *ppr.* [ME. *partenen*; OFr. *partenir*; L. *pertinere*; *per-* intens., and *tenere*, to hold.]
1. to belong; to be connected or associated; to appertain; as, humidity *pertains* to the atmosphere.
2. to be appropriate or suitable; as, the grace that *pertains* to a lady.
3. to have reference or relevance; as, the statement *pertains* to an altogether different matter.
pertaining to; having to do with; belonging to; of.

pẽrth′īte, *n.* [from *Perth*, Ontario, and *-ite*.] a lamellar variety of feldspar.

pẽr·thit′iç, *a.* of or pertaining to perthite.

pẽr·ti·nā′cious, *a.* [L. *pertinax*, *pertinacis*; *per-* intens., and *tenere*, to hold.]
1. holding or adhering to some purpose, belief, or action; exhibiting unyielding purpose; obstinate; perversely resolute; as, *pertinacious* in opinion; a man of *pertinacious* confidence.
2. hard to get rid of; persistent, as an illness.
Syn.—unyielding, stubborn, determined, inflexible, obstinate, resolute.

pẽr·ti·nā′cious·ly, *adv.* obstinately; with firm or perverse adherence; as, he *pertinaciously* maintains his first opinion.

pẽr·ti·nā′cious·ness, *n.* same as *pertinacity*.

pẽr·ti·nac′i·ty, *n.* [Fr. *pertinacité*.] the state or quality of being pertinacious; firm or unyielding adherence to some purpose; obstinacy; as, he pursues his scheme with *pertinacity*.

pẽr′ti·nà·cy, *n.* pertinacity. [Obs.]

pẽr′ti·nāte, *a.* obstinate. [Obs.]

pẽr′ti·nāte·ly, *adv.* obstinately. [Obs.]

pẽr′ti·nence, *n.* the state or quality of being pertinent; justness of relation to the subject or matter in hand; fitness; relevance; appositeness; suitableness.

pẽr′ti·nen·cy, *n.* pertinence.

pẽr′ti·nent, *a.* [ME. *pertynent*; L. *pertinens*, ppr. of *pertinere*; *per-* intens., and *tenere*, to hold.] related to; just to the purpose; adapted to the end proposed; apposite; relevant; to the point; as, he used an argument not *perti-*

nent to his subject or design; he gave *pertinent* answers to the questions.

Syn.—apposite, appropriate, relevant, fitting, proper, suitable.

pẽr′ti·nent·ly, *adv.* in a pertinent manner.

pẽr′ti·nent·ness, *n.* the quality of being pertinent. [Rare.]

pẽr·tin′gent, *a.* [L. *pertingens*, ppr. of *pertingere*, to extend to; *per*, through, and *tangere*, to touch.] reaching to; touching. [Obs.]

pẽrt′ly, *adv.* in a pert manner.

pẽrt′ness, *n.* the quality of being pert.

Syn.—impertinence, flippancy.

pẽr·tụrb′, *v.t.*; perturbed, *pt., pp.*; perturbing, *ppr.* [ME. *perturben*; OFr. *perturber*; L. *perturbare*; *per*, through, and *turba*, turmoil.]

1. to cause to be alarmed, agitated, or upset; to disturb or trouble greatly.

2. to cause disorder or confusion in; to unsettle.

3. in astronomy, to cause perturbations in (a heavenly body).

pẽr·tụrb·ȧ·bil′i·ty, *n.* capability of being perturbed.

pẽr·tụrb′ȧ·ble, *a.* that can be perturbed.

pẽr·tụrb′ănce, *n.* agitation; disturbance; perturbation. [Rare.]

pẽr′tụr·bāte, *v.t.* to perturb. [Rare.]

pẽr′tụr·bāte, *a.* perturbed.

pẽr·tụr·bā′tion, *n.* [ME. *perturbacioun*; OFr. *perturbacion*; L. *perturbatio*.]

1. a perturbing or being perturbed.

2. something that perturbs; disturbance.

3. in astronomy, an irregularity in the motion or orbit of a heavenly body caused by some force other than that which determines its usual path.

Syn.—discomposure, trepidation, worry.

pẽr·tụr·bā′tion·ăl, *a.* relating to perturbation, especially to astronomical perturbation.

pẽr′tụr·bȧ·tive, *a.* producing or tending to produce perturbation.

pẽr′tụr·bȧ·tŏr, *n.* one who or that which disturbs or raises a commotion. [Rare.]

pẽr·tụrbed′, *a.* disturbed; agitated; disquieted.

pẽr·tụrb′ed·ly, *adv.* in the manner of one perturbed.

pẽr·tụrb′ẽr, *n.* one who perturbs or is the cause of perturbation.

pẽr·tūse′, *a.* [L. *pertusus*, pp. of *pertundere*; *per*, through, and *tundere*, to beat.]

1. punched; pierced with holes. [Rare.]

2. in botany, perforated or slitted, as a leaf. [Rare.]

pẽr·tū′ṣion, *n.* 1. the act of punching, piercing, or thrusting through with a pointed instrument. [Obs.]

2. a hole made by punching; a perforation. [Obs.]

pẽr·tus′săl, *a.* of or having pertussis.

pẽr·tus′sis, *n.* [Mod. L.; L. *per-* intens., and *tussis*, cough.] same as *whooping cough*.

pe·rụke′, *n.* [Fr. *perruque*.] a wig; a periwig.

pe·rụke′, *v.t.* to dress with a peruke. [Rare.]

per′ụ·lȧ, *n.*; *pl.* **per′ụ·lae,** same as *perule*.

per′ụ·lāte, *a.* pertaining to or having a perule or perules.

per′ụle, *n.* [L. *perula*, dim. of *pera*, a wallet.]

1. a scale of a leaf bud.

2. in certain orchids, a sac or pouch in the perianth.

pē·rụṣ′ȧ·ble, *a.* that can be perused.

pē·rụṣ′ăl, *n.* a perusing; a careful or thorough reading.

pē·rụṣe′, *v.t.*; perused, *pt., pp.*; perusing, *ppr.* [probably L. *per-* intens.; and *use*, v.]

1. to read with attention; to read carefully or thoroughly; to study.

2. to observe; to examine with careful survey; to inspect closely; to scrutinize. [Rare.]

3. to read.

pē·rụṣ′ẽr, *n.* one who peruses.

Pē·rụ′vi·ăn, *a.* of Peru, its people, or culture.

Pē·rụ′vi·ăn, *n.* a native or inhabitant of Peru, especially one of the aboriginal Indian stock.

Peruvian balsam; same as *balsam of Peru* under *balsam*.

Peruvian bark; cinchona.

Peruvian nutmeg; see under *nutmeg*.

pẽr·vāde′, *v.t.*; pervaded, *pt., pp.*; pervading, *ppr.* [L. *pervadere*; *per*, through, and *vadere*, to go.]

1. to pass through; to spread or be diffused throughout.

2. to be abundant or prevalent throughout.

pẽr·vā′ṣion, *n.* a pervading or being pervaded.

pẽr·vā′sive, *a.* tending or having power to pervade; permeating.

pẽr·vẽrse′, *a.* [ME. *peruers*; OFr. *pervers*; L. *perversus*, pp. of *pervertere*, to turn about.]

1. deviating from what is considered right or acceptable; wrong, improper, etc. or corrupt, wicked, etc.; perverted.

2. persisting in error or fault; stubbornly contrary.

3. obstinately disobedient or difficult; intractable.

4. characterized by or resulting from obstinacy or contrariness.

5. unlucky; unfortunate. [Obs.]

pẽr·vẽrsed′ (-vẽrst′), *a.* perverted. [Obs.]

pẽr·vẽrs′ed·ly, *adv.* perversely. [Obs.]

pẽr·vẽrse′ly, *adv.* in a perverse manner.

pẽr·vẽrse′ness, *n.* the state or quality of being perverse.

pẽr·vẽr′ṣion, *n.* [ME. *peruersion*; L. *perversio*, from pp. of *pervertere*.]

1. a perverting or being perverted.

2. something perverted; an abnormal form.

3. any of various sexual acts or practices deviating from what is considered normal.

pẽr·vẽr′si·ty, *n.* [Fr. *perversité*; L. *perversitas*, from *perversus*.]

1. the quality or condition of being perverse.

2. an instance of this.

pẽr·vẽr′sive, *a.* tending to pervert or corrupt.

pẽr·vẽrt′, *v.t.*; perverted, *pt., pp.*; perverting, *ppr.* [ME. *peruerten*; L. *pervertere*, *per-* intens., and *vertere*, to turn.]

1. to cause to turn from what is considered right, natural, or true; to misdirect; to lead astray; to corrupt.

He in the serpent had *perverted* Eve.
—Milton.

2. to turn to an improper use; to misuse.

3. to change or misapply the meaning of; to misinterpret; distort; twist.

4. to bring into a worse condition; to debase.

pẽr·vẽrt′, *v.i.* to become perverted. [Rare.]

pẽr′vẽrt, *n.* a perverted person; especially, a person who practices sexual perversions.

pẽr·vẽrt′ed, *a.* 1. deviating from what is considered right, natural, or true; characterized by perversion; misdirected.

2. of or practicing sexual perversions.

3. misinterpreted; distorted; twisted.

pẽr·vẽrt′ẽr, *n.* one who perverts.

pẽr·vẽrt′i·ble, *a.* capable of being perverted.

pẽr·ves′ti·gāte, *v.t.* to find out by research. [Obs.]

pẽr·ves·ti·gā′tion, *n.* thorough research. [Obs.]

pẽr′vi·ăl, *a.* pervious. [Obs.]

pẽr′vi·ăl·ly, *adv.* perviously. [Obs.]

pẽr·vi·cā′cious, *a.* [L. *pervicax*, headstrong; *per-* intens., and *vic*, root of *vincere*, to conquer.] obstinate; stubborn; willfully contrary or refractory. [Now Rare.]

pẽr·vi·cā′cious·ly, *adv.* in a pervicacious manner. [Now Rare.]

pẽr·vi·cā′cious·ness, *n.* the quality of being pervicacious. [Now Rare.]

pẽr·vi·caç′i·ty, *n.* willful obstinacy. [Obs.]

pẽr′vi·ȧç·cy, *n.* stubborness. [Obs.]

pẽr′vi·ous, *a.* [L. *pervius*; *per*, through, and *via*, way.]

1. allowing passage through; that can be penetrated by another body or substance; permeable; penetrable; as, glass is *pervious* to light.

2. having a mind open to influence, argument, or suggestion.

3. in zoology, perforate or open, as the nostrils of birds.

pẽr′vi·ous·ness, *n.* the quality of being pervious.

per′y, *n.* a pear tree. [Obs.]

pēṣ, *n.*; *pl.* **pē′dēṣ,** [L.] that part of the hind limb of a vertebrate which includes the ankle and the foot; also, any footlike organ.

Pe′sach (-säkh), *n.* [Heb. *pēsaḥ*, a passing over.] a Jewish holiday, the Passover.

pe·sāde′ (or -zäd′), *n.* [Fr., earlier *posade*; It. *posata*, a halt.] in horsemanship, the action of a horse in rearing, or bringing the forelegs up into the air without moving the hind legs.

pes′āġe, *n.* [Fr., from *peser*, L. *pensare*, to weigh.] a custom or rate paid for weighing merchandise. [Obs.]

pe·se′tȧ, *n.* [Sp., dim. of *pesa*, weight.] a monetary unit and silver coin of Spain, equal to 100 centimos.

Pe·shi′tō, Pe·shit′tä, *n.* [Syr. *peshîttâ*, simple.] the standard translation of the Old and New Testaments in ancient Syriac.

pes′ky, *a.*; *comp.* peskier; *superl.* peskiest, [prob. var. of *pesty*.] annoying; bothersome; vexatious; disagreeable. [Colloq.]

pe′sō, *n.*; *pl.* **pe′sōṣ,** [Sp., lit., weight, from L. *pensum*, something weighed.]

1. any of the monetary units and silver coins of certain Latin American countries, as of Mexico or Cuba.

2. a monetary unit and silver coin of the Philippines.

pes′sȧ·ry, *n.*; *pl.* **pes′sȧ·ries,** [LL. *pessarium*; Gr. *pessos*, an oval pebble.]

1. (a) an instrument placed in the vagina to support a displaced or weak uterus; (b) a somewhat similar contraceptive device.

2. a vaginal suppository.

pes′si·miṣm, *n.* [Fr. *pessimisme*; L. *pessimus*, worst.]

1. (a) the doctrine or belief that the existing world is the worst possible; (b) the doctrine or belief that the evil in life outweighs the good.

2. the tendency to expect misfortune or the worst outcome in any circumstances; the practice of looking on the dark side of things: opposed to *optimism*.

pes′si·mist, *n.* one who believes in or is given to pessimism.

pes′si·mist, *a.* pessimistic.

pes·si·mis′tiç, *a.* of or characterized by pessimism; expecting the worst.

pes·si·mis′tiç·ăl, *a.* pessimistic.

pes·si·mis′tiç·ăl·ly, *adv.* in a pessimistic manner.

pes′si·mīze, *v.i.*; pessimized, *pt., pp.*; pessimizing, *ppr.* to hold or advocate the opinion or doctrine of pessimism. [Rare.]

pes′sō·man·cy, *n.* [Gr. *pessos*, pebble, and *manteia*, divination.] divination by pebbles. [Rare.]

pes′sū·lus, *n.*; [L., the bolt of a door.] in ornithology, a thin membrane or cartilage in the lower larynx, at the bifurcation of the windpipe.

pest, *n.* [Fr. *peste*; L. *pestis*, plague.]

1. a plague; a pestilence; a fatal epidemic disease. [Now Rare.]

2. a person or thing that causes trouble, annoyance, discomfort, etc.; nuisance; specifically, any destructive insect or other small animal; vermin.

Of all virtues, justice is the best;
Valor without it is a common *pest*.
—Waller.

Pes·tȧ·loz′zi·ăn, *a.* of, relating to, or designating a system of elementary education instituted by Johann Heinrich Pestalozzi (1746–1827).

Pes·tȧ·loz′zi·ăn, *n.* one who follows the system of Pestalozzi.

Pes·tȧ·loz′zi·ăn·iṣm, *n.* the educational system of Pestalozzi.

pes′tẽr, *v.t.*; pestered, *pt., pp.*; pestering, *ppr.* [OFr. *empestrer*; Fr. *empêtrer*, originally to shackle the feet of a horse at pasture, to entangle, from LL. *pastorium*, footshackles, from L. *pascere*, *pastus*, to feed: meaning probably influenced by *pest*, a plague.]

1. to annoy constantly or repeatedly with petty irritations; to bother; vex.

2. to overcrowd. [Obs.]

pes′tẽr·ẽr, *n.* one who or that which pesters.

pes′tẽr·ment, *n.* the act of pestering; also, the condition of being pestered. [Obs.]

pes′tẽr·ous, *a.* encumbering; burdensome.

pest′fụl, *a.* pestiferous. [Rare.]

pest′hōle, *n.* [*pest* and *hole*.] a place infested or likely to be infested with an epidemic disease.

pest′house, *n.* [*pest*, and *house*.] a hospital for the isolation of people with contagious or epidemic diseases. [Archaic.]

pes′ti·cīde, *n.* [*pest*, and *-cide*.] any chemical used for killing insects, weeds, etc.

pes′ti·duçt, *n.* that which conveys contagion or infection. [Rare.]

pes·tif′ẽr·ous, *a.* [L. *pestiferus*, from *pestis*, plague, and *ferre*, to bear.]

1. (a) bringing or carrying disease; (b) infected with an epidemic disease.

2. dangerous to morals or to the welfare of society; noxious; evil.

3. annoying; mischievous; bothersome. [Colloq.]

pes·tif′ẽr·ous·ly, *adv.* in a pestiferous manner.

pes′ti·lence, *n.* [ME.; OFr.; L. *pestilentia*, from *pestilens*, *pestis*, plague.]

1. any virulent or fatal contagious disease.

2. an epidemic of such a disease; especially, the bubonic plague.

The *pestilence* that walketh in darkness.
—Ps. xci. 6.

Power like a desolating *pestilence*,
Pollutes whate'er it touches. —Shelley.

3. anything, as a doctrine, regarded as harmful or dangerous.

Profligate habits carry *pestilence* into the bosom of domestic society. —Mason.

pes′ti·lence·weed″, *n.* a plant, *Petasites officinalis*, the butterbur.

pes′ti·lent, *a.* [L. *pestilens*, from *pestis*, plague.]
1. likely to cause death; deadly.
2. (a) contagious; pestilential; (b) likely to produce a contagious disease. [Rare.]
A foul and *pestilent* congregation of vapors. —Shak.
3. pernicious; dangerous to morals or society; of evil effect or influence.
The world abounds with *pestilent* books, written against this doctrine. —Swift.
4. troublesome; mischievous; making disturbance; annoying; as, a *pestilent* fellow.

pes′ti·lent, *adv.* very: used as a mild expletive. [Obs.]
One *pestilent* fine. —Suckling.

pes·ti·len′tiăl (-shăl), *a.* [ME. *pestilencial*; ML. *pestilentialis*.]
1. of, causing, or likely to cause pestilence or infection.
2. like or constituting a pestilence; widespread and deadly.
3. pernicious; dangerous; harmful, as to morals.

pes·ti·len′tious (-shus), *a.* pestilential. [Obs.]

pes′ti·lent·ly, *adv.* in a pestilent manner.

pes′tle (-l), *n.* [ME. and OFr. *pestel*; L. *pistillum*, from *pinsere*, *pistus*, to pound or beat.]
1. an instrument for pounding and grinding substances in a mortar.
2. a short bludgeon, formerly carried by officers of the peace. [Obs.]
3. a leg of meat, especially of pork: so called from the shape. [Dial.]
4. in machinery, a vertically moving bar or hammer, usually designed for pounding.

pes′tle, *v.t.* and *v.i.*; pestled, *pt.*, *pp*; pestling, *ppr.* to pound, grind, crush, or mix with or as with a pestle.

pes′tō, *n.* [It. pp. of *pestare*, to pound, grind, from L. *pinsere*, to pound.] a sauce of ground fresh basil and garlic mixed with olive oil, used especially over pasta.

pet, *n.* [orig. Scot. dial.; perhaps connected with obs. Fr. *peton*, lit., little foot, or with Fr. *petit*, small.]
1. an animal that is tamed or domesticated and kept as a favorite or treated with affection.
2. a person who is treated with particular affection or indulgence; favorite; darling.
3. a cade lamb; a lamb brought up by hand. [Dial.]

pet, *a.* 1. kept or treated as a pet; as, a *pet* duck.
2. especially liked; favorite.
3. greatest; especial; particular: used humorously, as my *pet* peeve.

pet, *v.t.*; petted, *pt.*, *pp.*; petting, *ppr.* 1. to stroke or pat gently; to fondle; to caress.
2. to treat as a pet; to pamper. [Rare.]

pet, *v.i.* to make love; to kiss, embrace, fondle, etc. [Colloq.]

pet, *n.* [from obs. phr. *to take the pet*.] a state of sulky peevishness or ill-humor.

pet, *v.i.*; petted, *pt.*, *pp.*; petting, *ppr.* to be in a pet; to sulk.

pet′ăl, *n.* [Mod.L. *petalum*, from Gr. *petalon*, a leaf.]
1. any of the component parts, or leaves, of a corolla.
2. in zoology, an ambulacrum shaped like a petal.

a a a, PETALS

-pet′ăl, [from Mod. L. *-petus* (from L. *petere*, to seek), and *-al*.] a combining form meaning *moving toward*, *seeking*, as in centri*petal*.

pet′ăled, pet′ălled, *a.* having petals.

pet·ăl·if′ẽr·ous, *a.* [from *petal-* and *-ferous*.] having petals.

pet′ăl·ine (*or* -īne), *a.* pertaining to a petal; attached to a petal; as, a *petaline* nectary.

pet′ăl·işm, *n.* [Gr. *petalismos*.] a form of banishment among the ancient Syracusans, by which persons considered dangerous to the state were condemned to banishment for five years. Votes for such banishment were cast by writing the name of the suspected citizen on a leaf. Petalism in Syracuse was equivalent to ostracism in Athens.

pet′ăl·ite, *n.* [Gr. *petalon*, a leaf.] a rare mineral, a silicate of aluminum and lithium occurring in masses, having a foliated structure: its color is milk white or shaded with gray, red, or green.

pet·ă·lod′iç, *a.* of, like, or characterized by petalody.

pet′ăl·ō·dy, *n.* [Gr. *petalōdēs*, leaflike.] in botany, a transformation into petals of stamens or other parts of flowers, as in double flowers.

pet′ăl·oid, *a.* [Mod.L. *petaloideus*.] like a petal.

pet′ăl·ous, *a.* petaled; having petals.

pé·tãnque′ (pā-tänk′), *n.* [Fr. from Pr. *pès tanquès*, feet together (the required stance).] a French game similar to bowls.

pē·tär′, *n.* petard. [Obs.]

pē·tärd′, *n.* [Fr. *pétard*, from *péter*, to break wind behind, to bounce, from L. *pedere*, *peditus*, with same sense.]
1. a metal cone filled with explosives: in ancient warfare it was fastened to walls and gates and exploded to force an opening.
2. a kind of firecracker.
hoist with one's own petard; caught in one's own trap; involved in danger meant for others.

pet·är·deer′, pet·är·dīēr′, *n.* one who used a petard. [Obs.]

Pet·ȧ·sī′tēş, *n.* [Gr. *petasitēs*, from *petasos*, a broad-brimmed hat.] a genus of plants, of the family *Compositæ*. *Petasites vulgaris* is the butterbur.

pet′ȧ·sŏs, pet′ȧ·sus, *n.* [Gr. *petasos*, from *petannynai*, to spread out.]
1. a flat, broad-brimmed hat worn in ancient Greece.
2. the winged cap of Hermes.

pe·tä′te, *n.* dried palm leaves or grass used for plaiting into hats, mats, etc. in tropical America.

pē·tau′rist, *n.* [Gr. *petauristēs*, a vaulter, a rope dancer, from *petauron*, a roost for birds, a pole.] a member of any of several genera of flying marsupials, which take short flights in the air by extending the folds between the fore and hind extremities, as the flying phalanger and the flying mouse.

petch′ȧ·ry, *n.* one of the tyrant fly-catchers of the West Indies; the gray kingbird.

pet′çock, *n.* [perhaps from obs. *pett*, *pet*, breaking of wind, and *cock* (valve).] a small faucet or valve used in draining unwanted or excess water or air from pipes, radiators, steam boilers, etc.: also *pet cock*.

pē·teçh′i·ae, *n.pl.* [LL. *peteccia*, from L. *petigo* (*-inis*), scab, eruption.] purple spots which appear on the skin in malignant fevers, etc.

pē·teçh′i·ăl, *a.* spotted; like or characterized by petechiae.
petechial fever; a malignant fever accompanied with purple spots on the skin.

pē·teçh′i·āte, *a.* petechial; spotted.

Pē′tẽr, *n.* [L. *petrus*; Gr. *petros*, stone.]
1. in the Bible, one of the twelve Apostles, a fisherman on the Sea of Galilee; ?–67 A.D.; reputed author of two books of the New Testament that bear his name, considered first pope and founder of the Christian church: also called *Simon Peter*, *Saint Peter*.
2. either of the two Epistles of Peter in the New Testament.

pē′tẽr, *v.i.* [etym. uncertain.] to weaken; to lose power; to fail, to become exhausted; to vanish (with *out*); as, his strength *petered out*; the vein of gold *petered out*. [Colloq.]

pē′tẽr bōat, a fishing boat; a small boat shaped alike at stem and stern.

Pē′tẽr Funk, a by-bidder.

Pē′tẽr·măn, *n.*; *pl.* **Pē′tẽr·men,** a fisherman: from the occupation of St. Peter: an old name used on the Thames.

Pē′tẽr Pan, the title character of J. M. Barrie's play (1904), a little boy who ran away to "Never-Never Land" and never grew up.

Pē′tẽr Prin′ci·ple, [after *The Peter Principle* (1968) by L. J. Peter and R. Hull.] the facetious proposition that each employee in an organization tends to be promoted until he reaches his level of incompetence.

Pē′tẽr's fish, a name given to the haddock, from the spots on either side being supposed to be the marks of St. Peter's fingers, when he caught that fish for the tribute. It is also sometimes given to the sea bream and the John Dory, *Zeus faber*, both having similar marks.

pē′tẽr·shăm, *n.* [after Lord *Petersham*, who set the fashion of wearing it (c. 1812).]
1. a heavy, rough-napped woolen cloth.
2. formerly, an overcoat made of this.

Pē′ter's pence (or **pen′ny**), 1. an annual tax, originally of one penny, paid to the papal see by certain English property owners before the Reformation.
2. an annual voluntary donation made by Catholics to the papal treasury.
Also *Peter pence*, *Peter penny*.

peth, *n.* pith. [Now Dial.]

peth, *v.t.* to pith. [Now Dial.]

pet′i·ō·lăr, pet′i·ō·lăr·y, *a.* of or attached to the petiole; as, a *petiolar* tendril.

pet′i·ō·lāte, pet′i·ō·lā·ted, *a.* in botany and zoology, having a stalk or stalklike part.

pet′i·ōle, *n.* [Mod. L. *petiolus*, dim. from L. *pes*, *pedis*, foot.]
1. in botany, a leafstalk; the footstalk of a leaf, connecting the blade with the stem.
2. in zoology, a peduncle; a slender, stalklike part, as between the abdomen and middle section of an insect.

a, PETIOLE

pet′i·ōled, *a.* having a petiole; petiolate.

pet′i·ō·lū·lāte, *a.* provided with a petiolule.

pet′i·ō·lūle, *n.* a small petiole, such as belong to the leaflets of compound leaves.

pet′it (pet′i *or Fr.* pe-tē′), *a.* [ME.; OFr.; var. of *petty*.] of small importance; petty; minor: now used only in law.
petit constable; an inferior civil officer, subordinate to the high constable.
petit jury; see under *jury*.
petit larceny; same as *petty larceny* under *larceny*.
petit maître; [Fr., a little master.] a fop; a coxcomb.
petit mal; [Fr., little sickness.] a relatively mild form of epilepsy in which there are short attacks of unconsciousness without convulsions: distinguished from *grand mal*.
petit sergeanty; in English feudal law, the tenure of lands of the king, by the service of rendering to him annually some implement of war, as a bow, an arrow, a sword, lance, etc.
petit treason; in common law, formerly, the crime of killing a person to whom the offender owes duty or subjection, as for a wife to kill her husband, or a servant his lord or master: now treated as murder or manslaughter.

pe·tite′ (-tēt′), *a.* [Fr., f. of *petit*.] small and trim of figure: said of a woman.

pē·ti′tion, *n.* [L. *petitio*, *petitionis*, from *petere*, *petitus*, to seek, ask, make for, attack.]
1. an entreaty, supplication, or prayer; a solemn, earnest supplication or request, as one addressed to the Supreme Being, to a superior, or to a person or group in authority; also, a particular request or article among several in a prayer.
2. a formal writing or document embodying a request, addressed to a specific person or group and often signed by a number of petitioners.
3. something that is asked or entreated.
4. in law, a formal written request or plea in which specific court action is asked for; as, a *petition* in bankruptcy.
petition of right; (a) in English law, a petition to the crown seeking redress for injury, compensation for damages, or restoration of property from the crown, showing the petitioner's right or title by the facts stated in the document; (b) [P– R–] the statement by Parliament of the people's rights and liberties assented to in 1628, by Charles I.
Syn.—appeal, entreaty, prayer, request.

pē·ti′tion (-tish′un), *v.t.* to make a request to; to ask from; to solicit; particularly, to make supplication or application in writing in a formal manner, to a superior for some favor or right; as, to *petition* the legislature.

pē·ti′tion, *v.i.* to make a petition or entreaty.

pē·ti′tion·ăr·i·ly, *adv.* in a petitionary manner. [Rare.]

pē·ti′tion·ăr·y, *a.* 1. suppliant; begging. [Archaic.]
Pardon thy *petitionary* countrymen. —Shak.
2. of, like, or constituting a petition; as, a *petitionary* prayer; a *petitionary* epistle.

pē·ti·tion·ee′, *n.* a person cited to defend against a petition.

pē·ti′tion·ẽr, *n.* one who petitions.

pē·ti′tion·ing, *n.* the act of making a petition.

pe·ti′ti·ō prin·ci′pi·ī (-tish′i-ō), [L., lit., a begging of the question.] in logic, the fallacy of assuming in the premise of an argument the conclusion which is to be proved.

pet′i·tŏr, *n.* one who seeks or petitions. [Rare.]

pet′i·tō·ry, *a.* [L. *petitor*, plaintiff; *petere*, to seek.] petitioning; soliciting. [Now Rare.]
petitory suit or *action*; an action at law which seeks to gain a right to the title rather than to possession. In Scots law, an action by which the plaintiff seeks to enforce a contract made in his favor by the defendant.

pet′it point (pet′i), 1. any of various small stiches, as tent stitch, used in embroidering designs, pictures, etc. on canvas.
2. embroidery done in small stitches.

pe′tits fōurş (pet′i fōrz′ *or Fr.* pȧ-tē″ foor′), [Fr., small cakes, from *petits*, pl. of *petit*, small, and *fours*, pl. of *four*, lit., oven, from L.

furnus, oven.] cupcakes made of spongecake, etc., usually frosted.

pe·tïts″ pois′ (-tē″ pwȧ′), [Fr., little peas.] green peas, especially small ones.

pet nāme, a term of address used to express affection or love.

pet·ral′ō·ġy, *n.* same as *petrology.*

Pē·trär′ċhăn son′net, a sonnet composed of a group of eight lines (*octave*) with two rhymes *abba, abba,* and a group of six lines (*sestet*) with two or three rhymes variously arranged, typically *cdc dcd* or *cde cde*: the thought or theme is stated and developed in the octave, and expanded, contradicted, etc. in the sestet: also called *Italian sonnet.*

pet′rȧ·ry, *n.* [LL. *petraria;* L. *petra,* rock.] a machine used by the ancients in sieges for throwing stones.

pē′tre (-tẽr), *n.* same as *saltpeter.*

Pē′trē·ȧ, *n.* [after Lord *Petre,* English patron of botany.] a genus of climbing verbenaceous shrubs, native to tropical America, bearing opposite leaves and racemed flowers of various shades of blue and purple, the calyx enlarging when in fruit. Several species, especially the purple wreath, are cultivated in greenhouses.

pet′rel, *n.* [dim. of *Peter,* in allusion to St. Peter's walking on the sea.] any of various related small, dark, sea birds (family *Procellariidæ*) with long wings; especially, the stormy petrel.

diving petrel; a bird of the genus *Pelecanoides,* having short wings and nasal tubes opening upwards: it inhabits the oceans of the southern hemisphere.

pintado petrel; same as *Cape pigeon* under *cape* (promontory).

pē·tres′cent, *a.* [Gr. *petros,* a stone; L. *petra.*] converting into stone. [Now Rare.]

Pē·triç′ō·lȧ, *n.* [L. *petra,* rock, and *colere,* to inhabit.] a genus of bivalves of the family *Petricolidæ,* which bore their way into soft rock.

pē·triç′ō·lous, *a.* living in rocks, as some bivalves; of or relating to the *Petricola.*

pē′trï dish, [after Julius R. *Petri* (1852–1921), G. bacteriologist.] [*also* P- d-] a very shallow, cylindrical, transparent glass or plastic dish with an overlapping cover, used for the culture of microorganisms.

pet·ri·faç′tion, *n.* 1. a petrifying or being petrified.

2. something petrified.

pet·ri·faç′tive, *a.* tending to cause petrification.

pet′ri·fī·ȧ·ble, *a.* that can be petrified.

pē·trif′iç, *a.* petrifactive. [Archaic.]

pet′ri·fi·çāte, *v.t.* to petrify. [Obs.]

pet″ri·fi·çā′tion, *n.* same as *petrifaction.*

pet′ri·fȳ, *v.t.;* petrified, *pt., pp.;* petrifying, *ppr.* [Fr. *pétrifier,* from L. *petra,* a stone or rock, and *facere,* to make.]

1. to replace the normal cells of (organic matter) with silica or other mineral deposits; to change into a stony substance.

2. to make stiff or inflexible; to make callous or obdurate; to harden; to deaden; as, to *petrify* the heart

And *petrify* a genius to a dunce.—Pope.

3. to paralyze or stupefy, as with fear, astonishment, etc.

pet′ri·fȳ, *v.i.* 1. to change into stone or a stony substance.

2. to become hardened, lifeless, or callous.

Pē′trīne, *a.* of or characteristic of the Apostle Peter or his teachings; as, the *Petrine* liturgy.

Pē′trin·iṣm, *n.* the tenets believed by some scholars to have been insisted upon by St. Peter, that good works are powerful to save the soul.

pet′rō-, [from Gr. *petra,* a rock, or *petros,* a stone.] a combining form meaning *rock* or *stone,* as in *petrography.*

Pet·rō′bi·um, *n.* [Gr. *petros,* rock, and *bios,* life.] a monotypic genus of small trees of the aster family, consisting of a single species, native to the island of St. Helena. It is cultivated elsewhere as the rock plant of St. Helena.

Pet·rō·bru̇′si·ăn, *n.* [LL. *Petrobrusiani.*] a follower of Peter (Pierre) de Bruys, a Provençal, who in the beginning of the twelfth century preached against the doctrine of baptismal regeneration, the use of churches, altars, crucifixes, relics, etc., prayers for the dead, and the doctrine of the real presence.

pet″rō·ċhem′i·çăl, *n.* [from *petroleum,* and *chemical.*] a chemical derived ultimately from petroleum or natural gas, as ethylene glycol, the paraffin and aromatic hydrocarbons, etc.

pet′rō·dol″lărṣ, *n.pl.* [from *petroleum,* and *dollars.*] the revenue in terms of dollars, accumulated by oil-producing countries from the sale of petroleum and regarded as affecting the stability of the world financial system.

pē·trog′ȧ·lē, *n.* [Gr. *petros,* stone, and *galē,* weasel.] any kangaroo of the genus *Petrogale,* as the rock wallabee, *Petrogale penicillatus.*

pet′rō·glyph, *n.* [Gr. *petros,* stone, and *glyphē,* carving.] any inscription cut into the face of a cliff or rock; especially, a prehistoric carving of this kind.

pet·rō·glyph′iç, *a.* pertaining to petroglyphy.

pē·trog′ly·phy, *n.* [Gr. *petros,* stone, and *glyphein,* to carve.] the art or practice of carving petroglyphs.

pē·trog′rȧ·phẽr, *n.* one versed in petrography.

pet·rō·graph′iç, pet·rō·graph′iç·ăl, *a.* of or relating to petrography.

pet·rō·graph′iç·ăl·ly, *adv.* according to petrography.

pē·trog′rȧ·phy, *n.* [Gr. *petros,* stone, and *graphein,* to write.] the science dealing with the description or classification of rocks.

pet·rō·hȳ′oid, *a.* [Gr. *petros,* stone, and *hyoid.*] relating to the petrous region of the skull lying near the hyoid arch and the internal ear.

pet′rŏl, *n.* 1. petroleum. [Obs.]

2. gasoline. [Brit.]

pet·rō·lā′tum, *n.* [Mod.L., from *petroleum.*] a greasy, jellylike substance consisting of a mixture of semisolid hydrocarbons obtained from petroleum: it is used as a base for ointments, in leather-dressing, etc.

pē·trō′lē·um, *n.* [ML., from L. *petra,* rock, and *oleum,* oil.] an oily, liquid solution of hydrocarbons, yellowish-green to black in color, occurring naturally in the rock strata of certain geological formations: when fractionally distilled it yields paraffin, kerosene, benzene, naphtha, fuel oil, gasoline, etc.

pē·trō′lē·um ē′thẽr, an inflammable, volatile, liquid hydrocarbon produced by the fractional distillation of petroleum: it is the fraction that boils at 40°–60° C. and is used as a solvent.

pē·trō′lē·um jel′ly, petrolatum.

pē·trol′iç, *a.* pertaining to or produced from petroleum.

pet·rō·lif′ẽr·ous, *a.* [*petroleum,* and L. *ferre,* to bear.] containing or supplying petroleum.

pet′rō·lin, pet′rō·line, *n.* a variety of paraffin obtained from petroleum.

pet′rō·līze, *v.t.;* petrolized, *pt., pp.;* petrolizing, *ppr.* to treat with petroleum.

pet·rō·loġ′iç, pet·rō·loġ′iç·ăl, *a.* of or relating to petrology.

pet·rō·loġ′iç·ăl·ly, *adv.* in accordance with the science of petrology.

pē·trol′ō·ġist, *n.* one who has made petrology a special study.

pē·trol′ō·ġy, *n.* [Gr. *petros,* stone, and *-logy.*] the study of the composition, structure, and origin of rocks.

pet·rō·mas′toid, *a.* [Gr. *petros,* stone, and *mastoid.*] in anatomy, of or relating to the petrous and the mastoid bones.

pet·rō·mas′toid, *n.* the periotic bone.

pet·rō·mȳ′zont, *n.* [Gr. *petros,* stone, and *myzōn* (*-ontos*), ppr. of *myzein,* to suck.] a fish of the genus *Petromyzon;* a lamprey.

pet′rō·nel, *n.* [OFr. *petrinal,* from L. *pectus, pectoris,* the breast: so called from being discharged with the stock placed against the breast.] a carbinelike firearm of heavy caliber, used in the fifteenth to seventeenth centuries.

pet·rō′săl, *a.* [L. *petrosus,* rocky; *petra,* rock.]

1. pertaining to the petrous part of the temporal bone of the ear.

2. hard, like stone; flinty; stony.

petrosal bone; the petrous portion of the temporal bone; also, the hardest structure of the periotic capsule.

pet·rō′săl, pet·rō′sȧ, *n.* the hard, stony part of the temporal bone; especially, the vitreous bone surrounding the inner ear.

pet·rō·stē′ȧ·rin, *n.* [Gr. *petra,* rock, *stear,* tallow, and *-in.*] a mineral found in coal strata which consists of natural paraffins; mineral wax: it is used in the making of candles, and for other purposes: also spelled *petrostearine.*

pet′rous, *a.* [L. *petra,* a stone.]

1. of or like rock; hard; stony.

2. designating or of that part of the temporal bone which surrounds and protects the internal ear.

pet′ti·chaps, pet′ty·chaps, *n.* same as *beccafico.*

pet′ti·çōat, *n.* [*petty* and *coat.*]

1. a skirt, now especially an underskirt, worn by women and young children.

2. something suggestive of a petticoat, as any of the flanges of a petticoat insulator.

3. a woman or girl. [Colloq.]

pet′ti·çōat, *a.* 1. feminine; womanly.

2. of or by women; as, *petticoat* government.

pet′ti·çōat breech′eṣ (brich′), very loose breeches of a style fashionable in England and France about the middle of the seventeenth century.

pet′ti·çōat·ed, *a.* dressed in a petticoat or in petticoats.

pet′ti·çōat in′sū·lā·tŏr, a tumbler-shaped electric insulator with a flared base or ringed flanges around the center.

pet′ti·çōat pīpe, a bell-shaped piece placed over the nozzle of an exhaust pipe in the smoke box of a locomotive to equalize the draft.

pet′ti·çōat trouṣ′ẽrṣ, same as *petticoat breeches.*

pet′ti·fog, *v.i.;* pettifogged, *pt., pp.;* pettifogging, *ppr.* [*petty,* and Brit. dial. *fog,* to seek gain by mean practices.] to act as a pettifogger.

pet′ti·fog, *v.t.* to gain by pettifogging; as, to *pettifog* a case to a successful issue. [Colloq.]

pet′ti·fog·gẽr, *n.* a lawyer who handles petty cases, especially one who uses unethical methods in conducting trumped-up cases.

pet′ti·fog·gẽr·y, *n.* pettifogging.

pet′ti·fog·ging, *a.* tricky or dishonest, especially in petty matters.

pet′ti·fog·ging, *n.* petty dishonesty; trickery.

pet·ti·fog′ū·līze, *v.i.* to act the pettifog; to be tricky in the practice of law. [Rare.]

pet′ti·ly, *adv.* in a petty manner.

pet′ti·ness, *n.* the quality of being petty.

pet′tish, *a.* [from *pet.*] fretful; peevish; subject to ill temper.

pet′tish·ly, *adv.* in a pettish manner.

pet′tish·ness, *n.* fretfulness; petulance; peevishness.

pet′ti·tōeṣ, *n.pl.* [orig., giblets, and said to be from Fr. *petite oie,* little goose, goose giblets, understood as *petty toe.*]

1. pigs' feet as an article of food.

2. feet or toes, especially a child's.

pet′tō, *n.* [It., from L. *pectus,* the breast.] the breast; hence, *in petto,* in secrecy; not disclosed.

pet′ty, *a.; comp.* pettier; *superl.* pettiest. [Fr. *petit.*]

1. relatively worthless or unimportant; trivial; insignificant.

2. small-scale; minor.

3. tending to make much of small matters; narrow-minded; mean.

4. relatively low in rank; subordinate.

petty average; in a ship's voyage, the allowance for various items of expense, as pilotage, anchorage, and extra expenses of any kind.

petty cash; a cash fund from which small incidental expenses are paid.

petty jury; a petit jury: see under *jury.*

petty larceny; theft involving a sum smaller than that which constitutes grand larceny: see *larceny.*

petty officer; a naval enlisted man whose rank corresponds to that of a noncommissioned officer in the army.

Syn.—small, little, mean, paltry, ignoble, trifling, narrow, trivial, contemptible, insignificant, frivolous.

pet′ty·chaps, *n.* see *pettichaps.*

pet′ū·lănce, *n.* the quality or the condition of being petulant; peevishness; ill-humor.

pet′ū·lăn·cy, *n.* petulance.

pet′ū·lănt, *a.* [L. *petulans, petulantis,* forward, petulant, from root of *petere,* to make for, to aim at, to attack.]

1. (a) forward; immodest; (b) pert; insolent. [Obs.]

2. impatient or irritable, especially over a petty annoyance; peevish; bad-tempered.

Syn.—peevish, cross, irritable, fretful, querulous.

pet′ū·lănt·ly, *adv.* in a petulant manner.

Pē·tū′ni·ȧ, *n.* [Braz. *petun,* tobacco.]

1. a genus of plants of the nightshade family, having clammy pubescent herbage and large showy funnel-shaped flowers of various colors.

2. [p-] any flower of this genus, as the white petunia, *Petunia nyctaginiflora,* or the purple or red-rose petunia, *Petunia violacea.*

pe·tun′tse, pe·tun′tze, peh·tun′tse, *n.* [Chinese.] a powdered form of feldspar or partially decomposed granite, used by the Chinese in the manufacture of porcelain.

petz′īte, *n.* [named after the chemist *Petz,* who analyzed it.] a mineral telluride of gold and silver; a variety of hessite.

peu à peu (pē à pē′), [Fr.] little by little.

Peū·ced′ȧ·num, *n.* a genus of umbelliferous plants called hog's-fennel or sulfurwort, growing in salt marshes and characterized by large umbels and yellow flowers, long and extremely narrow leaves, and a sulfurous odor.

peu de chose (pēd″shōz′), [Fr.] a trifle; a thing of slight importance.

pew (pū), *n.* [OFr. *pui*; L. *podium*, balcony; Gr. *podion*, from *pous, podos*, foot.]
1. any of the rows of fixed benches with a back, in the auditorium of a church.
2. especially formerly, any of several box-like enclosures with seats, in a church, for the use of a particular family, etc.

pew, *n.* [Fr. *pieu*, stake.] a pole having at one end an iron spike, curved and pointed, used for pitching fish, as from a boat to a stage or wharf.

pew, *v.t.* to provide with pews. [Rare.]

pē′wee, *n.* [echoic of its call.]
1. the phoebe.
2. any of several other small flycatchers; especially, the wood pewee.

pew′fel″lōw (pū′), *n.* one occupying the same pew with another; hence, a companion; a chum. [Obs.]

pē′wit, pee′wit, *n.* 1. the lapwing.
2. the laughing gull, *Chroicocephalus ridibundus.*
3. a pewee.

pew′tēr, *n.* [OFr. *peutre, peautre, piautre.*]
1. an alloy of tin with lead, brass, or copper: it takes on a grayish, silvery luster when polished.
2. articles made of pewter collectively.

pew′tēr, *a.* made of pewter.

pew′tēr·ēr, *n.* one whose occupation is to make vessels and utensils of pewter.

pew′y, *a.* [from *pew.*] enclosed by fences; fenced in so as to form small fields: a British hunting term.

Peȳ′ēr·i·ăn, *a.* pertaining to, discovered by, or named after John Conrad Peyer (1653–1712), a Swiss anatomist.
Peyerian glands; lymphatic glands, chiefly of the ileum, in part solitary and partly in patches: also called *Peyer's patches.*

pe·yō′tē, *n.* [Sp., from Nahuatl *peyotl*, caterpillar, with reference to the down in the center.] any of various mescal cactuses of Mexico and the southwestern United States having buttonlike tops yielding an intoxicating drug.

Pē·zī′zȧ, *n.* [Gr. *pezis*, mushroom, without a stalk; perhaps from *peza*, foot.] in botany, a large genus of fungi characterized by their cuplike form and brilliant colors.

Pē·zī′zae, *n.pl.* an order of fungi of which the genus *Peziza* is the type.

pez′i·zoid, *a.* [*Peziza*, and Gr. *eidos*, form.] pertaining to or resembling the *Peziza* or *Pezizæ.*

pfen′nig (fen′), *n.* [G.] a small copper coin of Germany, equal to one-hundredth of a mark.

pH (pē′āch′), [from Fr. *p(ouvoir) h(ydrogène)*, lit., hydrogen power.] *a symbol for* the degree of acidity or alkalinity of a solution; originally, and still often, expressed as the logarithm of the reciprocal of the hydrogen ion concentration in gram equivalents per liter of solution, and now, in some cases, given other operational definitions: pH7 (.0000001 gram atom of hydrogen ion per liter), the value for pure distilled water, is regarded as neutral; pH values from 0 to 7 indicate acidity, and from 7 to 14 indicate alkalinity.

Phȧ·cē′li·ȧ, *n.* [Gr. *phakelos*, bundle.] in botany, a genus of American herbs of the waterleaf family, including about seventy or eighty species. Several species are cultivated for their flowers.

phȧ·cel′lȧ, *n.*; *pl.* **phȧ·cel′lae,** in zoology, a gastric filament of some hydrozoans.

phȧ·cel′lus, *n.*; *pl.* **phȧ·cel′lī,** same as *phacella.*

phaç′ō·çhoere, phaç′ō·çhēre, *n.* [Gr *phakos*, a lentil, a wart like a lentil, and *choiros*, hog.] the wart hog of Africa, marked by a large wart on each side of the face.

phaç′ō·līte, *n.* [Gr. *phakos*, lentil, and *lithos*, stone.] in mineralogy, a variety of chabazite occurring in lenticular forms arising from twinning: first found at Leipa, Bohemia.

phȧ·çom′e·tēr, *n.* an instrument for measuring the refractive power of lenses.

Phae·ā′ciăn (-shăn), *a.* pertaining to the Phaeacians, a mythical seafaring people described in Homer's Odyssey.

Phae′drȧ, *n.* [L.; Gr. *Phaidra.*] in Greek legend, the daughter of Minos and wife of Theseus: she killed herself and, through a suicide note, was responsible for the death of her stepson, Hippolytus, who had rejected her advances.

Phae·drȧ·nas′sȧ, *n.* [Gr. *Phaidranassa*, name of a nymph.] in botany, a genus of plants of the amaryllis family, comprising four species, native to mountainous parts of South America.

phae′nō·gam, phē′nō·gam, *n.* a plant of the class *Phænogamia.*

Phae·nō·gā′mi·ȧ, *n.pl.* same as *Phanerogamia.*

phae·nō·gam′iç, phē·nō·gam′iç, *a.* pertaining to phaenogams.

phae·nog′ȧ·mous, phē·nog′ȧ·mous, *a.* [Gr. *phainein*, to show, and *gamos*, marriage.] of or pertaining to the *Phænogamia*; having true flowers.

phae·nol′ō·ġy, *n.* same as *phenology.*

phae·nom′e·non, *n.* same as *phenomenon.*

phae·oçh′rous, *a.* [Gr. *phaios*, dusky, and *chrōs*, skin.] in zoology, dusky; dark.

phae′ō·spōre, *n.* [Gr. *phaios*, dusky, and E. *spore.*] a zoospore of the class *Phæosporeæ.*

Phae·ō·spō′rē·ae, *n.pl.* an extensive class of algae, including the olive and brown seaweeds.

phae·ō·spor′iç, *a.* pertaining to phaeospores.

Pha′ë·thon (fā′ȧ-thon), *n.* [Gr. *Phaethōn*, lit., shiner; *phaethein*, to shine, root as seen in *phōs*, light.]
1. in Greek and Roman mythology, the son of Helios, the sun god: he borrowed his father's sun chariot and, through careless driving, would have set the world on fire had not Zeus struck him down with a thunderbolt.
2. in ornithology, a genus of birds, the tropic birds.

phā′e·tŏn, pha′ë·ton (fā′e-tŏn), *n.* [Fr. *phaéton*, from L. *Phaethon.*]
1. a light, four-wheeled carriage, drawn by either one or two horses, with front and back seats and, usually, a folding top.
2. an open automobile with front and back seats and a folding top, usually furnished with side curtains; a touring car.

-phāġe, [from Gr. *phagein*, to eat.] a combining form meaning *eating* or *destroying*, as in xylo*phage.*

phaġ·ē·dē′nȧ, phaġ·ē·dae′nȧ, *n.* [Gr. *phagedaina*, from *phagein*, to eat.]
1. a rapidly spreading ulcer accompanied by sloughing, or the separation of dead tissue.
2. gangrene.

phaġ·ē·den′iç, *a.* characteristic of phagedena; of use in the treatment of phagedena.

phaġ·ē·den′iç, *n.* any medicine used to treat phagedena.

phaġ·ē·den′iç·ăl, *a.* phagedenic.

phaġ·ē·dē′nous, *a.* phagedenic.

-phā′ġi·ȧ, -phagy.

phag′ō- [from Gr. *phagein*, to eat.] a combining form meaning (a) *eating* or *destroying*, as in *phago*cyte; (b) *phagocyte.* Also, before a vowel, *phag-.*

phag′ō·çȳte, *n.* [Gr. *phagein*, to eat, and E. *cyte.*] any leucocyte that ingests and destroys other cells, microorganisms, or other foreign matter in the blood and tissues.

phag·ō·çyt′iç, *a.* of, relating to, or caused by phagocytes.

phag·ō·çyt′iç in′dex, the average number of bacteria ingested by a single leucocyte in an incubated mixture of normal or immune serum, bacteria, and normal leucocytes.

phag″ō·çȳ·tō′sis, *n.* the action or process of leucocytes attacking bacterial organisms.

-phȧ·gous, [from Gr. *phagein*, to eat.] a combining form used to form adjectives corresponding to nouns ending in *-phage*, as in xylo*phagous.*

-phȧ′ġy, [for G. *phagein*, to eat.] a combining form meaning *the practice of eating* (something specified), as in anthropo*phagy.*

phā″i·nō·pep′lȧ, *n.* [Gr. *phaeinos*, shining, and *peplos*, robe.] the black flycatcher or fly-snapper, *Phainopepla nitens.*

Phā′jus, *n.* [Gr. *phaios*, dusky.] a small genus of orchids, found in the tropics and characterized by fanlike leaves and variously colored flowers. The Chinese nunflower, *Phajus grandifolius*, is of this genus.

phak′ō·sçōpe, *n.* same as *phacoscope.*

Phȧ·lae′nȧ, *n.* [Gr. *phalaina*, moth.] the genus in which Linnaeus included the moths, now divided into several genera.

phȧ·lae′ni·ăn, phȧ·lae′nid, *n.* any moth of the family *Geometridæ.*

Phȧ·lae·nop′sis, *n.* [Gr. *phalaina*, moth, and *opsis*, appearance.] a genus of flowering orchids, native to East India, and common in cultivation in the United States and elsewhere. The moth orchid, *Phalænopsis amabilis*, is one of a number of similar plants bearing the same common name.

phȧ·laṅ′găl, *a.* phalangeal.

phal′ăṅġe (*or* fā-lanj′), *n.* [Gr. *phalangos.*]
1. in anatomy, a phalanx; any of the small bones of the fingers and toes.
2. in botany, a collection of several stamens joined by their filaments.
3. in zoology, a tarsal joint: applied especially to insects.

phȧ·lan′ġē·ăl, *a.* relating to the phalanges or a phalanx.

phȧ·lan′ġēr, *n.* [Mod. L.; from Gr. *phalanx*, bone between two joints (of the fingers or toes).] any animal of the genus *Phalangista*, a genus of marsupial quadrupeds inhabiting Australasia: also called *phalangists.* The hind feet have a large opposable thumb, which is nailless, with four toes armed with claws, and the second and third of the toes are joined together almost to the end. The phalangers are nocturnal in their habits, and live in trees, feeding on insects, leaves, fruits, etc.

phȧ·lan′ġēş, *n.* alternative plural of *phalanx.*

phȧ·lan′ġi·ăl, phȧ·lan′ġi·ăn, *a.* same as *phalangeal.*

phȧ·lan′ġi·ous, *a.* [Gr. *phalangion*, a spider.] pertaining to the *Phalangoidea.*

phȧ·lan′ġist, *n.* same as *phalanger.*

phal·an·ġis′tēr, phal·an·ġis′tine, *n.* a phalanger. [Obs.]

phal′an·ġīte, *n.* [Gr. *phalangitēs*, *phalanx*, *phalangos.*] a soldier belonging to a phalanx.

Phal·an·goi′dē·ȧ, *n.pl.* [from the LL. *Phalangium*, from Gr. *phalangion*, a venomous spider, from *phalanx*, a name given from the long joints of its legs.] a family of *Arachnida*, called *harvestmen* or *shepherd spiders.*

phal′ăn·stēre, *n.* same as *phalanstery.*

phal·ăn·stē′ri·ăn, *n.* a member of a phalanstery.

phal·ăn·stē′ri·ăn, *a.* of or relating to a phalanstery.

phal·ăn·stē′ri·ăn·işm, phȧ·lan′stēr·işm, *n.* same as *Fourierism.*

phal′ăn·ster·y, *n.*; *pl.* **phal′ăn·ster·ieş,** [Fr. *phalanstère*, formed from Gr. *phalanx*, a phalanx, on the analogy of *monastère*, monastery.]
1. a socialistic community of the type planned by F. M. C. Fourier.
2. any communal association.
3. the buildings housing one of these communities.

phā′lanx (-langks *or* fal′angks), *n.*; *pl.* **phā′lanx·eş** or **phȧ·lan′ġēş,** [Gr. *phalanx*, a line or order of battle, battle array.]
1. an ancient military formation of infantry in close and deep ranks with shields joined together and spears overlapping.
2. a massed group of individuals; a compact body.
3. a group of individuals united for a common purpose.
4. the people forming a phalanstery.
5. *pl.* **phȧ·lan′ġēş,** in anatomy, any of the bones forming the fingers or toes.

phal′ȧ·rōpe, *n.* [Gr. *phalaris*, coot, and *pous*, foot.] any of several species of small swimming and wading birds of the genus *Phalaropus.* They breed on the seashores, and resemble the sandpiper.

phal′liç, *a.* 1. relating to the phallus.
2. characteristic of phallicism.

phal′li·çişm, *n.* worship of the phallus as a symbol of the male generative power.

phal′li·cist, *n.* a person practicing phallicism.

phal′lişm, *n.* same as *phallicism.*

phal′list, *n.* a phallicist.

phal′loid, *a.* [Gr. *phallos*, penis, and *-oid.*] like a penis.

phal′lus, *n.*; *pl.* **phal′lī,** [Gr. *phallos.*]
1. a representation or image of the penis as the reproductive organ, worshiped as a symbol of generative power, as in the Dionysiac festivals of ancient Greece.
2. the penis or clitoris.
3. in psychoanalysis, the penis during the period of infantile sexuality.

-phāne, [from Gr. *phainein*, to appear.] a combining form meaning *resembling, appearing like*, as in allo*phane.*

phan″ēr·ō·çō·don′iç, *a.* [Gr. *phaneros*, visible, and *kōdōn*, bell.] having the body bell-shaped and the mouth open, as a gonophore.

phan″ēr·ō·çrys′tăl·line, *a.* [Gr. *phaneros*, visible, and E. *crystalline.*] plainly crystalline: the opposite of *cryptocrystalline.*

phan′ēr·ō·gam, *n.* [Gr. *phaneros*, visible, and *gamos*, marriage.] a flowering plant with distinctly developed pistils and stamens: opposed to *cryptogam.*

Phan″ẽr·ō·gā′mi·à, *n.pl.* a primary division of the vegetable kingdom comprising flowering plants.
phan″ẽr·ō·gā′mi·ăn, phan″ẽr·ō·gam′iç, *a.* phanerogamous.
phan·ẽr·og′à·mous, *a.* having visible flowers, containing stamens and pistils; flowering.
phan″ẽr·ō·glos′săl, *a.* [Gr *phaneros*, visible, and *glōssa*, tongue.] having a noticeable tongue, as certain frogs.
phan′tà·sçōpe, *n.* [Gr. *phantasma*, an image, and *skopein*, to view.] an apparatus for enabling persons to converge the optical axes of the eyes and thereby observe certain phenomena of binocular vision.
Phan·tā′ṣi·ast, *n.* [Gr. *phantasiastēs.*] one of an early Christian sect denying the reality of the body of Christ.
phan′taṣm, *n.* [Gr. *phantasma*, from *phantazein*, to show, from the stem of *phainein*, to show.]
1. a perception of something that has no physical reality; a figment of the mind; especially, a specter, or ghost.
2. a deceptive likeness (*of* something).
3. in philosophy, a mental image of a real person or thing.
Also spelled *fantasm*.
phan·taṣ′mà, *n.*; *pl.* **phan·taṣ′mà·tà,** [Gr.] a phantasm (sense 1).
phan·taṣ·mà·gō′ri·à, *n.* [Gr. *phantasma*, a phantasm, and *agora*, an assembly.]
1. a magic-lantern show consisting of various optical illusions in which objects rapidly change size, blend into one another, etc.
2. a rapidly changing series of things seen or imagined, as the figures or events of a dream.
phan·taṣ·mà·gō′ri·ăl, phan·taṣ·mà·gor′iç, *a.* relating to, characteristic of, or constituting a phantasmagoria.
phan·taṣ′mà·gō·ry, *n.*; *pl.* **phan·taṣ′mà·gō·rieṣ,** a phantasmagoria.
phan·taṣ′măl, *a.* of, constituting, or characteristic of a phantasm; unreal; shadowy.
phan·taṣ′mà·sçōpe, *n.* same as *phantascope*.
phan·taṣ·mà·tog′rà·phy, *n.* [Gr. *phantasma* (*-atos*), phantasm, and *-graphy*.] a treatise on celestial phenomena. [Rare.]
phan·taṣ′miç, *a.* phantasmal.
phan·tas′tiç, phan·tas′tiç·ăl, *a.* same as *fantastic*.
phan′tà·sy, *n.* same as *fantasy*.
phan′tŏm, *n.* [Fr. *fantôme*, from L. *phantasma*.]
1. something that seems to appear to the sight but has no physical existence; an apparition; vision; specter.
2. something that exists only in the mind; an illusion.
3. a person or thing that is something in appearance but not in fact; as, a *phantom* of a leader.
4. any mental image or representation; as, the *phantoms* of things past.
Also spelled *fantom*.
phantom circuit; in multiplex telegraphy, the circuit established, that in ordinary telegraphy calls for a one-wire conducting medium.
phantom tumor; a swelling, generally of the abdomen, a close counterfeit of an ordinary tumor, but unlike it in consisting of gaseous accumulations or the like, and quickly yielding to treatment.
-phăn·y, [from Gr. *phainein*, to appear.] a terminal combining form meaning *appearance* as in epi*phany*.
Phār′aōh (fâr′ō), *n.* [Egypt. *Pir-aa*, great house.] the title of the rulers of ancient Egypt: sometimes used as a proper name in the Bible.
Pharaoh's chicken; the Egyptian vulture.
Pharaoh's rat; the ichneumon.
Phăr·ā·on′iç, Phăr·ā·on′iç·ăl, *a.* pertaining to or resembling the Pharaohs, or kings of ancient Egypt.
phăre (făr), *n.* a lighthouse; also, formerly, a harbor lighted by a pharos.
Phar·i·sā′iç, Phar·i·sā′iç·ăl, *a.* 1. of the Pharisees.
2. [p–] emphasizing or observing the letter but not the spirit of religious law; self-righteous; sanctimonious.
3. [p–] pretending to be highly moral or virtuous without actually being so; hypocritical.
phar·i·sā′iç·ăl·ly, *adv.* in a pharisaic manner.
phar·i·sā′iç·ăl·ness, *n.* devotion to external rites and ceremonies; external show of religion without the spirit of it; hypocrisy.
phar′i·sā·iṣm, *n.* 1. [P–] the beliefs and practices of the Pharisees, as a sect.
2. rigid observance of external forms of religion without genuine piety; hypocrisy in religion; censoriousness or self-righteousness in matters pertaining to manners, morals, or religion.
Phar′i·see, *n.* [Gr. *pharisaios*, from Heb. *pārūsh*, separated, from *parash*, to cleave, divide, separate.]
1. a member of an ancient Jewish sect that rigidly observed the written law, but also insisted on the validity of the oral, or traditional, law, that had grown out of popular usage: opposed to *Sadducees*.
2. [p–] a pharisaic person.
phar′i·see·iṣm, *n.* same as *pharisaism*.
phär·mà·ceū′tiç·ăl, phär·mà·ceū′tiç, *a.* [Gr. *pharmakeutikos*, from *pharmakeuein*, to practice witchcraft, or use medicine; *pharmakon*, poison or medicine.]
1. of pharmacy or pharmacists.
2. of or by drugs; as, *pharmaceutical* cure.
phär·mà·ceū′tiç·ăl·ly, *adv.* in the manner of pharmacy.
phär·mà·ceū′tiçs, *n.pl.* [*construed as sing.*] pharmacy.
phär·mà·ceū′tist, *n.* a pharmacist.
phär′mà·cist, *n.* a person licensed to practice pharmacy; a druggist.
phär″mà·cō·dȳ·nam′içs, *n.* [Gr. *pharmakon*, medicine, and *dynamis*, power.] that branch of pharmacology which treats of or relates to the method of action and the effects of drugs or medicines.
phär″mà·çog·nos′tiçs, *n.* [Gr. *pharmakon*, drug, and *gnōsis*, knowledge.] that branch of pharmacology which treats of or considers the natural and chemical history of unprepared medicines or simples: also called *pharmacognosy*.
phär·mà·çog′rà·phy, *n.* a description of the characteristics and properties of drugs.
phär·maç′ō·līte, *n.* [Gr. *pharmakon*, drug, and *lithos*, stone.] a hydrous calcium arsenate, snow-white or milk-white, inclining to reddish or yellowish white. It occurs in small, reniform, botryoidal and globular masses, and has a silky luster.
phär″mà·cō·loġ′iç·ăl, *a.* of or by pharmacology.
phär·mà·çol′ō·ġist, *n.* one who is skilled in pharmacology.
phär·mà·çol′ō·ġy, *n.* [Gr. *pharmakon*, drug, and *legein*, to speak.]
1. the science or knowledge of drugs; the art of preparing medicines.
2. a treatise on the art of preparing medicines.
phär″mà·cō·mà·nī′aç·ăl, *a.* [Gr. *pharmakon*, drug, and *mania*, madness.] inordinately addicted to giving, trying, or using drugs.
phär′mà·çon, *n.* [Gr.] a drug; a poison.
phär″mà·cō·poe′ià, *n.* [Gr. *pharmakon*, drug, and *poiein*, to make.]
1. an official book issued by the proper authorities with a list of drugs and medicines and a description of their properties, preparation, and use.
2. a stock of drugs.
phär·mà·cō·poe′iăl, *a.* of a pharmacopoeia.
phär·mà·çop′ō·list, *n.* [Gr *pharmakon*, drug, and *pōlein*, to sell.] one who sells medicines; an apothecary
phär″mà·cō·sid′ẽr·īte, *n.* [Gr. *pharmakon*, drug, and *sidēros*, iron.] a hydrous ferric arsenate occurring principally in cubes associated with copper ores: also called *cube ore*.
phär′mà·cy, *n.* [Fr. *pharmacie*; Gr. *pharmakeia*, from *pharmakon*, drug.]
1. the art or profession of preparing, preserving, and compounding medicines and drugs and of dispensing them according to the prescriptions of physicians; the occupation of an apothecary or of a pharmaceutical chemist.
2. *pl.* **phär′mà·cieṣ,** a drug store; a place where pharmacy is practiced.
phà·rol′ō·ġy, *n.* [*pharos*, and Gr. *logos*, discourse.] the art or science of exhibiting light signals to ships for their guidance.
Phā′ros, *n.* [from Gr. *Pharos*, the name of a small island near Alexandria, in Egypt, on which Ptolemy Philadelphus built a famous lighthouse.]
1. the lighthouse on the island of Pharos, one of the Seven Wonders of the World.
2. [p–] any lighthouse or marine beacon.
phà·ryn̄′găl, *a.* pharyngeal.
phà·ryn′ġē·ăl (*or* far-in-jē′), *a.* of, or in the region of, the pharynx.
pharyngeal clefts or *slits*; the visceral clefts.
phar·yn·ġē′ăl, *n.* any part of or around the pharynx; specifically, one of various bones near the pharynx in some fishes.
phar·yn·ġeç′tō·my, *n.* [Gr. *pharynx*, *pharyngos*, pharynx, and *ektomē*, a cutting out.] removal of a portion of the pharynx by cutting.
phar·yn·ġiṣ′mus, *n.* spasmodic contraction of the pharyngeal muscles.
phar·yn·ġī′tis, *n.* [Gr. *pharynx*, *pharyngos*, pharynx, and *-itis*.] inflammation of the mucous membrane of the pharynx; sore throat.
phà·ryn̄′gō-, [from Gr. *pharynx*, *pharyngos*.] a combining form meaning *the pharynx* or *the pharynx and*, as in *pharyngo*logy: also, before a vowel, *pharyng-*.
phà·ryn̄·gō·bran̄′chi·ăl, *a.* [*pharyngo-* and *branchial*.] of or pertaining to both the pharynx and the gills, as in fishes.
Phà·ryn̄·gō·bran̄′chi·ī, *n.pl.* a family of fishes comprising only the lancelet: synonymous with *Leptocardii*.
phà·ryn̄′gō·cēle, *n.* [*pharyngo-* and *-cele*.] a hernia or pouchlike protrusion of the wall of the pharynx.
Phar·yn̄·gog′nà·thī, *n.pl.* [Gr. *pharynx*, *pharyngos*, the pharynx, and *gnathos*, the jaw.] an order of fishes, in which the inferior pharyngeal bones are ankylosed so as to form a single bone, which is usually armed with teeth. The order includes the wrasses, the parrot fishes, the garfish, saury pikes, and flying fish.
phà·ryn̄″gō·là·ryn′ġē·ăl, *a.* [*pharyngo-* and *laryngeal*.] pertaining to both pharynx and larynx.
phar·yn̄·gol′ō·ġy, *n.* [*pharyngo-* and *-logy*.] the branch of medicine dealing with the pharynx and its diseases.
Phà·ryn̄·gop·neū′tà, *n.pl.* [Gr. *pharynx*, *pharyngos*, pharynx, and *pneustos*, verbal adj. of *pnein*, to breathe.] a division of invertebrates formerly proposed to include the tunicates and *Balanoglossus*.
phà·ryn̄·gop·neū′tăl, *a.* of or pertaining to the *Pharyngopneusta*.
phà·ryn̄′gō·sçōpe, *n.* [*pharyngo-* and *-scope*.] a device used for examining the pharynx.
phar·yn̄·gos′çō·py, *n.* examination of the pharynx, especially with a pharyngoscope.
phà·ryn̄′gō·tōme, *n.* [Gr. *pharynx*, *pharyngos*, pharynx, and *temnein*, *tamein*, to cut.] a surgical instrument used to scarify inflamed tonsils, and to open abscesses which form in the pharynx.
phar·yn̄·got′ō·my, *n.* [*pharyngo-* and *-tomy*.] surgical incision of the pharynx.
phar′yn̄x (-ingks), *n.*; *pl.* **phar′yn̄x·eṣ, phà·ryn′ġēṣ,** [Mod. L.; Gr. *pharynx*, *pharyngos*, the throat.] the muscular and membranous cavity of the alimentary canal leading from the mouth and nasal passages to the larynx and esophagus.

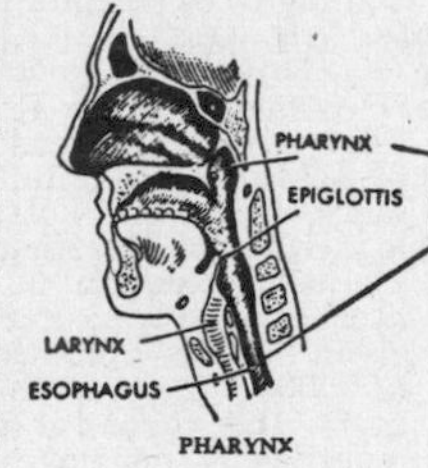

Phas·cō·lärç′tos, *n.* [Gr. *phaskōlos*, leathern bag, purse, and *arktos*, bear.] a genus consisting of the koala.
phas′cō·lōme, *n.* a wombat.
Phas·cō′lō·mys, *n.* [Gr. *phaskōlos*, leathern pouch, and *mys*, mouse.] a genus of marsupials including the wombat.
Phas′cum, *n.* [Gr. *phaskon*, tree moss.] a genus of minute mosses, some of them scarcely visible to the naked eye, growing on banks, clayfields, and the like. The leaves are costate and the flowers monoecious.
phāṣe, *n.* [Mod. L. *phasis*; Gr. *phasis*, from *phainesthai*, to appear.]
1. in astronomy, any of the stages of variation in the illumination or appearance of the moon or a planet.
2. any of the stages or forms in any series or cycle of changes, as in development.
3. any of the ways in which something may be observed, considered, or presented; aspect; side; part; as, this is but one *phase* of the subject.
4. in physical chemistry, a solid, liquid, or gaseous homogeneous form existing as a distinct part in a heterogeneous system; as, ice is a *phase* of H_2O.
5. the stage or progress of any cyclic movement, as of sound or light waves, alternating

electric current, etc., with reference to a standard position or assumed starting point.

6. in zoology, any of the characteristic variations in color of the fur or plumage of an animal, according to season, age, etc.

in (or *out of*) *phase*; in (or not in) a state of exactly parallel movements, oscillations, etc.; in (or not in) synchronization.

phase angle; in electricity, the angle which expresses phase relation.

phase splitter; an instrument for changing an incoming alternating current into currents of different phase.

phase transformation; in electricity, a change of phase effected by means of a transformer which transforms two-phase currents into three-phase currents, or the reverse.

phāșe, *v.t.*; phased, *pt., pp.*; phasing, *ppr.* 1. to plan, introduce, carry out, etc. in phases or stages (often with *in, into,* etc.)

2. to put in phase.

to phase out; to bring or come to an end, or withdraw from use, by stages.

phāșe, *v.i.* to move by phases.

phāșe'less, *a.* 1. without a visible form.

2. without variety; monotonous.

phȧ·sē'lin, *n.* a soluble albumin derived from two species of *Phaseolus.*

Phȧ·sē'ō·lus, *n.* [L. *phaseolus*; Gr. *phasēlos*, a kind of bean.] a genus of leguminous plants, including about sixty species, of which the kidney bean, the haricot, and the navy bean are the best known and most useful. *Phaseolus multiflorus* is the scarlet runner.

phā''sē·ō·man'nīte, *n.* see *inosite.*

phā'sēș, *n.* pl. of *phasis.*

-phā'și·ȧ (-zhȧ *or* -zhi-ȧ), [Mod. L., from Gr. *phanai*, to speak.] a combining form meaning *a* (specified) *speech disorder*, as in *aphasia.*

Phā''si·ȧ·nī'dae, *n.pl.* a family of gallinaceous birds including the pheasants.

phā'si·ȧ·nine, *a.* [Gr. *phasianos*, pheasant.] of or pertaining to the *Phasianidæ*; resembling a pheasant.

Phȧ·si·ā'nus, *n.* the typical genus of the *Phasianidæ.*

phā'sis, *n.*; *pl.* **phā'sēș,** [Mod.L.] a phase; aspect; way; stage.

phașm, phaș'mȧ, *n.* [Gr. *phasma*, from *phaein*, to shine.] a phantasm; fancied apparition; phantom. [Obs.]

Phaș'mȧ, *n.* a genus of insects typical of the *Phasmidæ.*

phaș'mid, *n.* one of the *Phasmidæ.*

phaș'mid, *a.* pertaining to the *Phasmidæ.*

Phaș'mi·dae, *n.pl.* [Gr. *phasma*, specter, and *eidos*, likeness.] a family of orthopterous insects allied to the *Mantidæ*, restricted to warm countries, and remarkable for their very close resemblance to the objects in the midst of which they live: also called *walking sticks, specter insects.*

phaș'moid, *a.* [*phasm*id and *-oid.*] relating to the *Phasmidæ.*

-phȧ'sy, -phasia.

pheaș'ănt (fez'), *n.*; *pl.* **pheaș'ănts** or **pheaș'ănt,** [L. *phasianus*; Gr. *phasianos*, from *Phasis*, a river of Asia, near the mouth of which these birds are said to have been numerous.]

GOLDEN PHEASANT (*Phasianus pictus*)

1. any of several birds of the genus *Phasianus*, family *Phasianidæ*, and order *Rasores* or *Gallinæ*, with a long, sweeping tail and brilliant feathers. The golden pheasant, *Phasianus pictus*, is native to China; the prevailing colors of its plumage are red, yellow, and blue, and it is distinguished by a crest upon the head. The silver pheasant, *Phasianus* or *Gallophasis nycthemerus*, is also native to China; its upper surface and tail are silver-white with black markings, hence its name.

SILVER PHEASANT (*Phasianus nycthemerus*)

2. one of various birds resembling the true pheasants, as the ruffed grouse.

pheaș'ănt çuck'oo, a large Australian bird, *Centropus phasianus.*

pheaș'ănt duck, the pintail; also, the merganser.

pheaș'ănt·ry, *n.*; *pl.* **pheaș'ănt·rieș,** a building or place for keeping and rearing pheasants.

pheaș'ănt's-eȳe (-ī), *n.* in botany, (a) an herb of the crowfoot family, *Adonis autumnalis*, with small, scarlet flowers and pale green leaves; (b) the common garden pink.

pheaș'ănt shell, a smooth, richly colored shell found in the tropics, having blotches of color resembling those of the pheasants.

phē'bē, *n.* the pewit: also written *phœbe.*

pheer, *n.* a companion. [Obs.]

pheeșe, *v.t.* and *v.i.* to feeze.

Phē·gop'te·ris, *n.* [Gr. *phēgos*, an oak (L. *fagus*, beech), and *pteris*, fern.] a genus of ferns, of which five species are found in America.

phel'lem, *n.* [from Gr. *phellos*, cork, and Eng. *-em*, as in *phloem.*] the layer of dead, corky cells produced externally by the cork cambium in the bark of woody plants.

phel'lō·dẽrm, *n.* [Gr. *phellos*, cork, and *-derm.*] in botany, a layer of soft, green tissue developed on the inner side by the phellogen.

phel·lō·dẽr'măl, *a.* of or like phelloderm.

phel'lō·ġen, *n.* [Gr. *phellos*, cork, and *-gen.*] in botany, the layer of embryonic tissue from which the cork and phelloderm are formed.

phel''lō·ġē·net'iç, *a.* phellogenic.

phel·lō·ġen'iç, *a.* of or like phellogen.

phel·lō·plas'tiçs, *n.* [Gr. *phellos*, cork, and *plassein*, to form, fashion, or make.] the art or process of modeling in cork.

phē·lō'ni·on, *n.* [Gr., for *phainolion*; L. *pænula*, a cloak.] a long, richly embroidered vestment, like a cope, worn by priests of the Orthodox Eastern Church.

phen-, [Fr. *phén-*, from Gr. *phainein*, to show, shine: term first used by Laurent, 19th-c. Fr. chemist, to indicate derivation from coal tar, a by-product in manufacturing illuminating gas.] a combining form meaning *of* or *derived from benzene*, as in *phen*azine.

phē'nȧ·çāine, *n.* [*phen*etidyl*a*cetphenetidine and co*caine.*] a colorless, odorless, crystalline compound, $C_{18}H_{22}N_2O_2 \cdot HCl$, used as a local anesthetic, especially for the eyes.

phē·nac'e·tin, phē·nac'e·tine, *n.* [*phen-* and *acetin.*] in chemistry, a compound derived from coal tar, $C_{10}H_{13}O_2N$, used in medicine as an antipyretic.

phē·nac·e·tū'riç, *a.* [*phen*yl and *acet*yl and hip*puric.*] designating an acid, $C_8H_7O \cdot NHCH_2CO_2H$, sometimes found in human urine.

phen'ȧ·cīte, *n.* [from Gr. *phenax, phenakos*, cheat; and *-ite*: so named because mistaken for quartz.] a silicate of glucinum: it is colorless or red, yellow, or brown with white streaks: used as a gem.

phen·ȧ·kis'tō·sçōpe, *n.* [Gr. *phenakistēs*, deceiver, and *-scope.*] an instrument which produces the representation of actual motion, as in walking, flying, etc., used for illustrating the persistence of impressions on the retina. The pictures may be reproduced on a screen.

phē·nan'thrēne, *n.* [*phen-* and *anthracene.*] a colorless, crystalline hydrocarbon, $C_{14}H_{10}$, an isomer of anthracene present in coal tar, used in making dyes and other products.

phē·nan'thri·dine, *n.* [*phenanth*rene and pyr*idine.*] a crystalline compound derived from benzoic aldehyde.

phē·nan'thrō-, phē·nan'thr-, phē·nan'thrȧ- (fē-), in chemistry, a combining form meaning *phenanthrene.*

phē·nan'thrōl, *n.* in chemistry, a derivative of phenathrene.

phē·nan'thrō·line, *n.* [*phenanthr*ene and quin*oline.*] one of several crystalline compounds, $C_{12}H_8N_2$, obtained from coal-tar derivatives.

phē'nāte, *n.* same as *phenolate.*

phen'ȧ·zin, *n.* phenazine.

phen'ȧ·zīne, *n.* a crystalline base, $C_6H_4N_2C_6H_4$, having a yellowish color: from it are obtained many important dyes.

phen'a·zōne, *n.* in chemistry, a crystalline base, yellowish in color and isomeric with phenazine, having the formula $C_6H_4N_2C_6H_4$.

phēne, *n.* same as *benzene.*

phē·net'i·din, *n.* same as *phenetidine.*

phē·net'i·dine, *n.* [*phen*ol and *-et-* and amido and *-ine.*] any of three isomeric compounds, $C_8H_{11}ON$, especially the para form, used in the manufacture of phenacetin.

phen'e·tōle, phen'e·tol, *n.* [*phen*ol and *-et-* and *-ole.*] a colorless liquid, $C_6H_5OC_2H_5$, the ethyl ether of phenol.

phen'ġīte, *n.* [Gr. *phengitēs*, from *phengein*, to shine.] a kind of alabaster.

phē'niç, *a.* [*phen*ol and *-ic.*] resembling or derived from phenol.

Phē·ni'ciăn (-nish'un), *a.* and *n.* same as *Phoenician.*

phen'i·cin, phen'i·cīne, *n.* [Gr. *phoinix*, purple.] a brown, amorphous powder produced by the action of nitrosulfuric acid on crystallized phenylic alcohol.

phē·ni'cious (-nish'us), *a.* pertaining to or having the color of phenicin.

phen·i·çop'tẽr, *n.* [Gr. *phoinix*, purple, and *pteron*, wing.] a flamingo: so named from its color, a bright red.

phē'nix, *n.* same as *phoenix.*

phē'nō-, phen-.

phē''nō·bär'bi·tal, *n.* [*pheno-* and *barbital.*] a white, colorless substance, $C_{12}O_3N_2H_{12}$, used as a sedative and soporific.

phē'nō·çop·y, *n.*; *pl.* **phē'nō·çop·ies,** [*pheno*type, and *copy.*] in genetics, an environmentally induced change in an organism that is similar to a mutation but is nonhereditary.

phē'nō·çryst, *n.* [Gr. *phainein*, to show, and *krystallos*, crystal.] in geology, an isolated or conspicuous crystal found imbedded in porphyritic rock.

phē'nō·gam, *n.* same as *phoenogam.*

Phē·nō·gā'mi·ȧ, *n.pl.* same as *Phanerogamia.*

phē·nō·gam'iç, phē·nog'ȧ·mous, *a.* same as *phoenogamic, phoenogamous.*

phē'nōl, *n.* 1. a white crystalline compound, C_6H_5OH, produced from coal tar, and used in making explosives, etc.: it is a strong, corrosive poison, and its dilute aqueous solution, commonly called carbolic acid, is used as an antiseptic.

2. any of a group of aromatic hydroxyl derivatives, similar in structure and composition to phenol.

phē'nō·lāte, *n.* a salt of carbolic acid (phenol in a dilute aqueous solution); carbolate.

phē·nol'iç, *a.* of, containing, or derived from phenol.

phenolic resin; any of a group of thermosetting resins formed by condensing phenol with various aldehydes, as formaldehyde: used to form molded and cast plastic items.

phē·nō·log'iç·ăl, phae·nō·log'iç·ăl, *a.* relating to phenology.

phē·nol'ō·gist, phae·nol'ō·gist, *n.* one skilled in the science of phenology.

phē·nol'ō·gy, phae·nol'ō·gy, *n.* [contr. of *phenomenology.*] the study of natural phenomena that recur periodically, as migration, blossoming, etc., and of their relation to climate and changes in season.

phē·nōl·phthal'ēin, phē·nōl-phthal'ēin (-thal'ēin *or* -fthal'i-in), *n.* [*phenol* and *phthalein.*] a white to pale-yellow, crystalline powder, $C_{20}H_{14}O_4$, used as a laxative, in making dyes, and as an acid-base indicator in chemical analysis: it is red in a solution containing a base and colorless in a solution containing an acid.

phē·nom'ē·nȧ, *n.* plural of *phenomenon.*

phē·nom'ē·năl, *a.* 1. of or constituting a phenomenon or phenomena.

2. extremely unusual; extraordinary; highly remarkable.

3. in philosophy, apparent to or perceptible by the senses.

phē·nom'ē·năl·ișm, *n.* the philosophic theory that knowledge is limited to phenomena, either because there is no reality beyond phenomena or because such reality is unknowable.

phē·nom'ē·năl·ist, *n.* a believer in and advocate of phenomenalism.

phē·nom''ē·năl·ist'iç, *a.* of or constituting phenomenalism.

phē·nom'ē·năl·ly, *adv.* in the manner of a phenomenon; wonderfully.

phē·nom'ē·nist, *n.* a phenomenalist.

phē·nom·ē·nol'ō·ġy, *n.* [*phenomenon* and *-logy.*]

1. the science dealing with phenomena as distinct from the science of being (*ontology*).

2. the branch of a science that classifies and describes its phenomena without any attempt at explanation.

phē·nom'ē·non, *n.*; *pl.* **phē·nom'ē·nȧ;** also, especially for 3 and 4, **phē·nom'ē·nonș,** [Gr. *phainomenon*, ppr. of *phainesthai*, to appear.]

1. any fact, circumstance, or experience that is apparent to the senses and that can be

scientifically described or appraised; as, an eclipse is a *phenomenon* of astronomy.
2. the appearance or observed features of something experienced as distinguished from reality or the thing in itself.
3. anything that is extremely unusual; extraordinary occurrence.
4. a person with some extraordinary quality, aptitude, etc.; a prodigy. [Colloq.]
phē'nōse, *n.* [*phen*yl and dextr*ose*.] benzene hexahydrate, $C_6H_{12}O_6$, an amorphous hygroscopic body.
phē'nō·type, *n.* [*pheno-* and *type.*]
1. in biology, a type distinguished by visible characters rather than by hereditary or genetic traits.
2. in biology, all the individuals belonging to such a type.
Opposed to *genotype.*
phē·nō·typ'iç, *a.* of or characteristic of a phenotype.
phē·nox'īde, *n.* phenolate.
phen'yl (*or* fē'nil), *n.* [*phen-* and *-yl.*] a monovalent radical, C_6H_5, forming the basis of phenol, benzene, aniline, and various other aromatic compounds.
phenyl hydrate; phenol [Obs.]
phenyl hydrazine; a colorless, oily nitrogenous base, $C_6H_5N_2H_3$, forming crystallized salts with acids, ketones, etc.
phen·yl·am'īde, *n.* same as *anilide.*
phen"yl·am·īne', *n.* same as *aniline.*
phen'yl·ēne, *n.* [*phenyl* and *-ene.*] a divalent radical, C_6H_4, derived from benzene by replacement of two hydrogen atoms.
phē·nyl'iç, *a.* relating to, containing, or derived from phenyl.
phē'on, *n.* in heraldry, the barbed iron head of a dart, arrow, or other weapon.
pheū (fū), *interj.* an exclamation expressing relief, disgust, surprise, etc.
phī, *n.* [Gr.] the twenty-first letter of the Greek alphabet, generally equivalent to English *ph* (*f*).

PHEON

phī'ăl, *n.* [ME. *fiole*; OFr. *fiole, phiole*; Pr. *fiola;* LL. *fiola*; L. *phiala*; Gr. *phialē*, broad, shallow drinking vessel.] a small glass bottle; a vial.
phī'ȧ·lē, *n.*; *pl.* **phī'ȧ·lae,** [Gr. *phialē*, a saucer.] in ancient Greece, a kind of shallow saucer-shaped vessel used in pouring libations; a patera.
phī'ăl·ine, *a.* having the shape of a saucer.
Phī Bę'ta Kap'pȧ, [from the initial letters of the Gr. words *philosophia biou kybernētēs*, philosophy the guide of life.] an honorary society composed of American college students of high scholastic rank: founded 1776.
Phid'i·ăn, *a.* of or characteristic of Phidias, a Greek sculptor of the fifth century B.C.
phil-, philo-.
-phil, -phile.
phil'ȧ·beg, *n.* same as *filibeg.*
Phil·ȧ·del'phi·ȧ law'yēr, a clever or shrewd lawyer, especially one skilled in the subtleties of legal technicalities: a somewhat opprobrious term connoting unscrupulous behavior. [Slang.]
Phil·ȧ·del'phi·ăn, *a.* [*philo-*, and Gr. *adelphos*, brother.] pertaining to one of the cities called Philadelphia or to Ptolemy Philadelphus.
Phil·ȧ·del'phi·ăn, *n.* 1. one of the Family of Love, a society of mystics which came into existence in the seventeenth century.
2. a native or resident of Philadelphia.
Phil·ȧ·del'phi·ȧ pep'pēr pot, same as *pepper pot.*
Phil·ȧ·del'phus, *n.* [Gr. *philadelphon*, a sweet-flowering shrub.] a genus of ornamental shrubs with sweet-scented flowers, many stamens, and an inferior ovary: also called *mock orange* and *syringa.*
phil·ȧ·lē'thist, *n.* [*philo-*, and Gr. *alētheia*, truth.] one who loves truth.
phi·lan'dēr, *n.* [from Gr. *philandros*, fond of men, from *philos*, loving, and *andros*, a man.]
1. a philanderer. [Rare.]
2. one of several marsupials, as (a) the Australian bandicoot, *Perameles lagotis*; (b) one of several species of South American opossums.
phi·lan'dēr, *v.i.* to engage lightly in passing love affairs; to make love insincerely: said of a man.
phi·lan'dēr·ēr, *n.* one who philanders.
phil'an·thrōpe, *n.* one who is philanthropic; a philanthropist.
phil·an·throp'iç, *a.* of, showing, or constituting philanthropy; charitable; benevolent; generous; humane.
phil·an·throp'iç·ăl, *a.* philanthropic.
phil·an·throp'iç·ăl·ly, *adv.* with philanthropy; benevolently; in a philanthropic manner.
phil·an·throp'i·niṣm, *n.* a system of education based on development of so-called natural principles, introduced in Dessau, Germany, by Basedow in 1774, but discontinued in 1793.
phil·an·throp'i·nist, *n.* a believer in or an advocate of the doctrine of philanthropinism introduced by Basedow, of Dessau.
phi·lan'thrō·pist, *n.* a person who practices philanthropy.
phi·lan·thrō·pis'tiç, *a.* having the characteristics of a philanthropist.
phi·lan'thrō·pīze, *v.t.*; philanthropized, *pt.*, *pp.*; philanthropizing, *ppr.* to deal with philanthropically.
phi·lan'thrō·pīze, *v.i.* to practice philanthropy.
phi·lan'thrō·py, *n.* [LL. *philanthropia*; Gr. *philanthrōpia*, from *philein*, to love, and *anthropos*, man.]
1. a desire to help mankind as indicated by acts of charity, etc.; love of mankind.
2. *pl.* **phi·lan'thrō·pieṣ,** something that helps mankind; philanthropic service, act, gift, institution, etc.
phil·ȧ·tel'iç, *a.* of or relating to philately.
phi·lat'e·list, *n.* a collector of postage stamps; one interested in philately.
phi·lat'e·ly, *n.* [Fr. *philatélie*, from Gr. *philos*, loving, and *ateleia*, exemption from tax; *a-* priv., and Gr. *telos*, tax.] the collection and study of postage stamps, postmarks, stamped envelopes, etc., usually as a hobby.
phil'au·ty, *n.* [Gr. *philautia*; *philein*, to love, and *autos*, self.] a selfish regard for oneself. [Obs.]
-phīle, [from Gr. *philos*, loving.] a combining form meaning *loving, liking, favorably disposed to*, as in Anglo*phile*: also *-phil.*
Phī·lē'mŏn, *n.* [L.; Gr. *Philemon*, lit., affectionate.]
1. the Epistle to Philemon, a book in the New Testament which was a message from the Apostle Paul to his convert Philemon.
2. in Greek mythology, an old man who, with his wife, Baucis, shared what little he had with the disguised Zeus and Hermes.
Phi·lē'si·ȧ, *n.* [Gr. *philēsis*, affection; *philein*, to love.] a genus of plants containing but one species, *Philesia buxifolia*, indigenous to Chile. It belongs to the lily family and bears showy red flowers. The common name is *pepino.*
phil·här·mon'iç, *a.* [Fr. *philharmonique*, after It. *filharmonico*, from Gr. *philos*, loving, and *harmonia*, harmony.]
1. loving or devoted to music.
2. of or by a philharmonic group or society.
Phil·här·mon'iç, *n.* 1. a society formed to sponsor a symphony orchestra.
2. an orchestra or concert sponsored by such a society. [Colloq.]
phil·här·mon'iç pitch, in music, the standard pitch, in which middle A has a frequency of 440 vibrations per second.
phil·hel'lēne, *n.* [*philo-*, and Gr. *Hellēn*, a Greek.] a friend of Greece or the Greeks; a supporter of the cause of Greece; especially, a supporter of the Greeks in their struggle for independence against the Turks.
phil·hel·len'iç, *a.* friendly toward or supporting the Greeks.
phil·hel'len·iṣm, *n.* the principles of the philhellenes; friendliness toward or support of Greece.
phil·hel'len·ist, *n.* a philhellene.
-phil'i·ȧ, [from Gr. *philos*, loving.]
1. a combining form meaning *tendency toward*, as in hemo*philia.*
2. a combining form meaning *abnormal attraction to*, as to copro*philia.*
phi·lī'ȧ·tēr, *n.* [Gr. *philiatros*, a friend of the science of medicine, from *philein*, to love, *iatros*, a physician, and *iasthai*, to heal.] an amateur medical student.
phil'i·beg, *n.* same as *filibeg.*
Phil'ip, *n.* one of the twelve Apostles.
phil'ip, *n.* a sparrow. [Brit. Dial.]
Phil·lip'pi·ăn, *a.* relating to the ancient town of Philippi in Macedonia, or to its inhabitants.
Phi·lip'pi·ăn, *n.* a native or inhabitant of Philippi.
Phi·lip'pi·ănṣ, *n.pl.* [*construed as sing.*] an Epistle to the Philippians, a book of the New Testament which was a message from the Apostle Paul to the Christians of Philippi.
Phi·lip'piç, *n.* 1. any of the orations of Demosthenes, the Grecian orator, against Philip, king of Macedon.
2. [p-] any discourse or declamation full of acrimonious invective.
Phil'ip·pīne, *a.* of the Philippine Islands or their people.
Phil'ip·piṣm, *n.* the teachings of Philip Melanchthon, German theologian of the sixteenth century.
phil'ip·pīze, *v.i.*; philippized, *pt.*, *pp.*; philippizing, *ppr.* 1. to write or deliver a philippic.
2. to side with or support the cause of Philip of Macedon.
Phi·lis'tēr, *n.* [G.] a person who has no university training; one not of the university set: name given by German university students to townspeople, etc.
Phi·lis'tine (*or* fil'is-tēn), *n.* [ME., also *Palestine*; LL. *Philistinus*, usually in pl. *Philistini*; Gr. *philistinoi*, *palaistinoi*; Heb. *p'lishtim*; akin to Eng. Palestine.]
1. a member of non-Semitic people who lived in southwestern Palestine from c. 1200 B.C. on: they repeatedly warred with the Israelites for control of the country.
2. [adapted by Matthew Arnold, from G. *Philister.*] a person regarded as smugly narrow and conventional in his views and tastes, lacking in and indifferent to cultural and aesthetic values, etc.
Phi·lis'tine, *a.* 1. of the ancient Philistines.
2. smugly conventional, lacking in culture, etc.
Phi·lis'tin·iṣm, *n.* the manners, habits, character, or mode of thinking of a Philistine (sense 2).
phil'lips·īte, *n.* [after the Eng. mineralogist, J. W. *Phillips.*] in mineralogy, a hydrous silicate of aluminum, potassium, and calcium, occurring in crystals.
phil·lyġ'e·nin, *n.* [*phyllyrin*, *-gen*, and *-in.*] a crystalline compound obtained from phillyrin.
Phil·lyr'ē·ȧ, *n.* [Gr.] in botany, a genus of evergreen shrubs of the olive family, found on the Mediterranean coast.
phil'ly·rin, *n.* a crystalline compound obtained from the bark of a species of *Phillyrea.*
phil'ō-, [from Gr. *philos*, loving.] a combining form meaning *loving, liking, having a predilection for*, as in *philology*: also *phil-.*
Phil·oç·tē'tēṣ, *n.* in Greek legend, the Greek warrior who killed Paris in the Trojan war with one of the poisoned arrows given into his custody by the dying Hercules.
Phil·ō·den'dron, *n.* [*philo-*, and Gr. *dendron*, tree.]
1. a genus of climbing plants of the family *Araceæ*, with coriaceous leaves and a dense spadix.
2. [p-] a plant of this genus.
phi·loġ'y·nist, *n.* [from *philogyny* and *-ist.*] a person who loves or is fond of women.
phi·loġ'y·nous, *a.* of or like a philogynist; fond of women.
phi·loġ'y·ny, *n.* [Gr. *philogynia*; *philein*, to love, *gynē*, woman.] love of or fondness for women: opposed to *misogyny.*
phil"ō·hel·lē'ni·ăn, *n.* same as *philhellene.*
phi·lol'ō·ġēr, *n.* same as *philologist.*
phil·ō·lō'ġi·ăn, *n.* a philologist.
phil·ō·loġ'iç, *a.* same as *philological.*
phil·ō·loġ'iç·ăl, *a.* of, or relating to philology.
phil·ō·loġ'iç·ăl·ly, *adv.* in a philological manner.
phi·lol'ō·ġist, *n.* one expert in philology: now generally replaced by *linguist.*
phi·lol'ō·ġīze, *v.i.*; philologized, *pt.*, *pp.*; philologizing, *ppr.* to study philology; to pursue the occupation of a philologist.
phil'ō·logue (-log), *n.* a philologist. [Rare.]
phi·lol'ō·ġy, *n.* [Gr. *philologia*, love of literature; afterward, study of words; *philein*, to love, and *logos*, word.]
1. originally, the love of learning and literature; study; scholarship.
2. the study of written records, especially literary texts, in order to determine their authenticity, meaning, etc.
3. linguistics: the current use.
phil'ō·math, *n.* [Gr. *philomathēs*; *philein*, to love, and *mathos*, *mathēsis*, learning; *manthanein*, *mathein*, to learn.] a lover of learning. [Rare.]
phil·ō·math·ē·mat'iç, *n.* a philomath. [Obs.]
phil·ō·math'iç, *a.* pertaining to the love of learning. [Rare.]
phi·lom'ȧ·thy, *n.* the love of learning. [Rare.]
phil'ō·mel, *n.* [ME. *Philomene*; OFr. *philomèle*; L. *Philomela.*] the nightingale. [Poet.]

Phil·ō·mē′lȧ, *n.* [L.; Gr. *Philomēla*, from *philein*, to love, and *melos*, song.]
1. in Greek mythology, the daughter of a king of Athens: her sister Procne's husband, Tereus, raped her and tore out her tongue; when, in revenge, the sisters killed his son and fled, the gods changed Philomela into a nightingale, Procne into a swallow, and Tereus into a hawk.
2. a nightingale; a philomel. [Poet.]

phil′ō·mēne, *n.* the nightingale. [Obs.]

phil′ō·mot, *n.* [corrupted from Fr. *feuille morte*, a dead leaf.] the color of a dead leaf. [Obs.]

phil·ō·mū′şiç·ăl, *a.* loving music.

phil·ō·pē′na, *n.* [altered from Fr. *philippine*, from G. *Philippchen*, little Philip, from *vielliebchen*, lit., sweetheart, pop. name for the joined kernels of nuts, hence the game played with such kernels; dim., from *viel*, much, and *lieb*, dear; influenced in Eng. by association with Gr. *philos*, loving and L. *poena*, a penalty, because of the forfeit paid to one of the "friends" playing the game.]
1. a nut with two kernels.
2. a game in which the two kernels of a nut are shared by two people, one of whom, if failing to fulfill a given condition, must pay a forfeit to the other.
3. the forfeit, usually a gift.

phil″ō·pō·lem′iç, *a.* [Gr. *philopolemos*, loving war; *philein*, to love, and *polemos*, war.] disputatious; liking controversy of strife. [Rare.]

phil″ō·pō·lem′iç·ăl, *a.* philopolemic. [Rare.]

phil″ō·prō·ġen′i·tive, *a.* [*philo-* and *progenitor* and *-ive*.]
1. productive of offspring; prolific.
2. loving offspring, especially one's own.
3. of such love.

phil″ō·prō·ġen′i·tive·ness, *n.* the quality or state of being philoprogenitive.

phil′ō·soph, *n.* a philosopher; also, a philosophaster.

phi·los′ō·phas·tẽr, *n.* a pretender to philosophy.

phi·los′ō·phāte, *v.i.*; philosophated, *pt., pp.*; philosophating, *ppr.* to play the philosopher; to philosophize. [Obs.]

phi·los·ō·phā′tion, *n.* philosophical discussion. [Obs.]

phi·los′ō·phēme, *n.* [Fr., from LL. *philosophema*.] a principle of reasoning; a theorem.

phi·los′ō·phẽr, *n.* [ME. *philosophre*, *filosofre*; OFr. *philosophe*; L. *philosophus*; Gr. *philosophos*, from *philos*, loving, and *sophos*, wise.]
1. a person who studies or is learned in philosophy.
2. a person who lives and thinks according to a system of philosophy.
3. a person who meets all events, whether favorable or unfavorable, with calmness and composure.
4. an alchemist, magician, etc. [Obs.]

phi·los′ō·phẽrş′ (or **phi·los′ō·phẽr′ş**) **stōne,** an imaginary substance sought for by alchemists in the belief that it would change base metals into gold or silver.

phil·ō·soph′iç, *a.* [L. *philosophicus*; Gr. *philosophikos*.]
1. of or according to a philosophy or a philosopher.
2. devoted to or learned in philosophy.
3. like or suited for a philosopher.
4. rational; sensibly composed; calm, as in a difficult situation.

phil·ō·soph′iç·ăl, *a.* same as *philosophic*.

phil·ō·soph′iç·ăl·ly, *adv.* in a philosophical manner; calmly; wisely; rationally.

phil·ō·soph′i·çō-, a combining form meaning *philosophical and*.

phil·ō·soph′i·çō·rē·li′ġious, (-jus), *a.* philosophical and religious.

phi·los′ō·phişm, *n.* [Fr. *philosophisme*, from *philosophe*.]
1. false or faulty philosophy; sophistry.
2. a philosophic proposition intended to deceive.

phi·los′ō·phist, *n.* a philosophaster; one who practices philosophism.

phi·los·ō·phis′tiç, phi·los·ō·phis′tiç·ăl, *a.* pertaining to philosophism; characteristic of a philosophist.

phi·los′ō·phīze, *v.i.*; philosophized, *pt., pp.*; philosophizing, *ppr.* to deal philosophically with abstract matter; to think or reason like a philosopher; to search into the reason and nature of; to investigate phenomena and assign rational causes for their existence.

phi·los′ō·phī·zẽr, *n.* one who philosophizes.

phi·los′ō·phy, *n.*; *pl.* **phi·los′ō·phieş,** [ME. and OFr. *philosophie*; L. *philosophia*; Gr. *philosophia*, from *philosophos*; see *philosopher*.]
1. originally, love of wisdom or knowledge.
2. a study of the processes governing thought and conduct; theory or investigation of the principles or laws that regulate the universe and underlie all knowledge and reality; included in the study are aesthetics, ethics, logic, metaphysics, etc.
3. the general principles or laws of a field of knowledge, activity, etc.; as, the *philosophy* of economics.
4. (a) a particular system of principles for the conduct of life; (b) a treatise covering such a system.
5. a study of human morals, character, and behavior.
6. the mental balance believed to result from this; calmness; composure.

phil·ō·stor′ġy, *n.* [*philo-*, and Gr. *storgē*, natural affection.] natural affection. [Obs.]

phil·ō·teçh′niç, phil·ō·teçh′niç·ăl, *a.* [*philo-*, and Gr. *technē*, art.] fond of the arts.

Phi·lō′tri·ȧ, *n.* in botany, a genus of submerged aquatic plants of North and South America.

-phi·lous, [from Gr. *philos*, loving; and *-ous*.] a combining form meaning *loving, having a liking for*, as in photo*philous*.

phil′tẽr, *n.* [Fr. *philtre*; Gr. *philtron*, from *philein*, to love.]
1. a potion or charm thought to cause a person to fall in love.
2. any magic potion.

phil′tẽr, *v.t.*; philtered, *pt., pp.*; philtering, *ppr.*
1. to impregnate with a love potion; as, to *philter* a draught.
2. to charm or bewitch with a philter.

phil′tre (-tẽr), *n.* a philter.

phil′tre, *v.t.*; philtred (-tẽrd), *pt., pp.*; philtring, *ppr.* to philter.

phil′trum, *n.*; *pl.* **phil′trȧ,** [LL., from Gr. *philtron*, a philter.]
1. in anatomy, the groove at the median line of the upper lip.
2. a philter.

phī·mō′sis, *n.* [Gr. *phimōsis*; *phimos*, a muzzle.]
1. an abnormal condition in which the foreskin of the penis is so tight as to prevent its being drawn back over the glans.
2. a similar condition of the clitoris.

phī′ton, *n.* a python. [Obs.]

phī′ton·ess, *n.* a pythoness. [Obs.]

phiz (fiz), *n.*; *pl.* **phiz′eş,** [contr. of *physiognomy*.] the face or facial expression. [Slang.]

phleb-, same as *phlebo-*.

phlē·beç·tā′si·ȧ, phlē·beç′tȧ·sis, *n.* [Gr. *phleps*, *phlebos*, vein, and *ectasis*, dilatation.] in medicine, dilatation of a vein or veins; a varicosity.

phlē·beç′tȧ·sy, *n.* phlebectasia.

phlē·ben·ter′iç, *a.* pertaining to phlebenterism.

phlē·ben′tẽr·işm, *n.* [Gr. *phleps*, *phlebos*, vein, and *enteron*, intestine.] in zoology, extension of the alimentary organs to the limbs.

phlē′bin, *n.* [Gr. *phleps*, *phlebos*, vein.] a pigment supposed to exist in venous blood.

phlē·bis′mus, *n.* [Gr. *phleps*, *phlebos*, vein.] in medicine, dilatation of veins, due to obstruction.

phlē·bit′iç, *a.* of or having phlebitis.

phlē·bī′tis, *n.* [Gr. *phleps*, *phlebos*, vein, and *-itis*.] in medicine, inflammation of a vein or veins.

phleb′ō-, [from Gr. *phleps*, *phlebos*, a vein.] a combining form meaning *vein*, as in *phlebotomy*: also, before a vowel, *phleb-*.

phleb′ō·gram, *n.* a tracing of the movements of a vein made by a phlebograph.

phleb′ō·grȧph, *n.* [*phlebo-*, and Gr. *graphein*, to write.] an instrument for recording the venous pulse.

phleb′ō·līte, phleb′ō·lith, *n.* [*phlebo-*, and Gr. *lithos*, stone.] a veinstone, a calculus or concretion in a vein.

phlē·bol′ō·ġy, *n.* [*phlebo-*, and Gr. *logos*, discourse.] the science of the veins. [Rare.]

phleb·ọr·rhā′ġi·ȧ, (-ra′), *n.* copious hemorrhage from a vein.

phleb″ō·sçle·rō′sis, *n.* [*phlebo-* and *sclerosis*.] hardening of the walls of a vein or veins.

phleb·ō·strep′sis, *n.* the surgical twisting of a vein.

phlē·bot′ō·mist, *n.* one who practices or believes in phlebotomy; a bleeder.

phlē·bot′ō·mīze, *v.t.* and *v.i.*; phlebotomized, *pt., pp.*; phlebotomizing, *ppr.* to let blood from a vein (of); to practice phlebotomy (on).

phlē·bot′ō·my, *n.* [Gr. *phlebotomia*; *phleps*, *phlebos*, a vein, and *temnein*, to cut.] the formerly common act or practice of opening a vein for letting blood as a therapeutic measure; venesection.

Phleg′ē·thon, *n.* [Gr. *phlegethōn*, ppr. of *phlegethein*, to burn.] in Greek mythology, a river of fire, one of the five rivers of Hades.

phlegm (flem), *n.* [Gr. *phlegma*, inflammation, hence, humors caused by inflammation, from *phlegein*, to burn.]
1. the thick, stringy mucus secreted by the mucous glands of the respiratory tract and discharged from the throat, as during a cold.
2. in early physiology, that one of the four humors of the body which was believed to cause sluggishness or dullness.
3. (a) sluggishness; apathy; (b) calmness; equanimity.
4. in old chemistry, the water of distillation. [Obs.]

phleg′mȧ·gogue (-gog), *n.* [Gr. *phlegma*, phlegm, and *agein*, to drive.] a medicine supposed to possess the property of expelling phlegm.

phleg·mā′si·ȧ, *n.* an inflammation or fever. *phlegmasia* (*alba*) *dolens*; milk leg.

phleg·mat′iç, *a.* 1. abounding in phlegm; as, a *phlegmatic* constitution.
2. hard to rouse to action; specifically, (a) sluggish; dull; apathetic; (b) calm; cool; imperturbable.
3. of, like, or producing the humor phlegm. [Obs.]
4. watery. [Obs.]

phleg·mat′iç·ăl, *a.* phlegmatic.

phleg·mat′iç·ăl·ly, *adv.* in a phlegmatic manner; coldly; heavily; apathetically.

phleg·mat′iç·ly, *adv.* phlegmatically.

phleg′mon, *n.* [Gr. *phlegmonē*, from *phlegein*, to burn.] inflammation, especially of the connective tissue, leading to ulceration or abscess.

phleg′mō·noid, *a.* characteristic of phlegmon.

phleg′mō·nous, *a.* having the nature or properties of phlegmon.

phlegm′y (flem′), *a.*; *comp.* phlegmier; *superl.* phlegmiest, 1. of, like, containing, or characterized by phlegm.
2. phlegmatic. [Rare.]

phlēme, *n.* a fleam. [Obs.]

Phlē′um, *n.* [Gr. *phleōs*, water plant.] a genus of grasses, chiefly native to Europe. Various species are known by the name of cat's-tail grass. Among these the *Phleum pratense*, meadow cat's-tail grass or timothy, is of considerable agricultural value as a fodder plant.

phlob′ȧ·phēne, *n.* [Gr. *phloios*, bark, and *baphē*, dyeing.] a reddish-brown coloring matter derivable from various barks.

phlō′em, [G., from Gr. *phloos*, the bark.] the cell tissue serving as a path for the distribution of food material in a plant; bast: also written *phloëm*.

phloe′um, *n.* [Gr. *phloios*, bark.] in botany, the cellular portion of bark lying immediately under the epidermis. [Obs.]

phlō·ġis′tiăn, *n.* a believer in the existence of phlogiston.

phlō·ġis′tiç, *a.* 1. of or pertaining to phlogiston.
2. fiery; flaming. [Obs.]
3. in medicine, inflammatory; of inflammation.

phlō·ġis′tiç·ăl, *a.* phlogistic.

phlō·ġis′ti·çāte, *v.t.*; phlogisticated, *pt., pp.*; phlogisticating, *ppr.* in old chemistry, to combine phlogiston with.

phlō·ġis·ti·çā′tion, *n.* the act or process of phlogisticating.

phlō·ġis′ton, *n.* [Gr. *phlogistos*, from *phlogizein*, to burn or inflame, *phlegein*, to burn.] in old chemistry, an imaginary element formerly believed to cause combustion and to be given off by anything burning; the principle or matter of fire in composition with other bodies. Stahl gave this name to a hypothetical element which he supposed to be pure fire fixed in combustible bodies, in order to distinguish it from fire in action or in a state of liberty.

phlō·gō·ġen′iç, *a.* phlogogenous.

phlō·goġ′e·nous, *a.* [Gr. *phlox*, *phlogos*, flame, and *-genēs*, producing.] in medicine, causing inflammation.

phlog′ō·pīte, *n.* [Gr. *phlox*, *phlogos*, flame, *ōps*, face, and *-ite*.] a magnesium mica having a pearly luster and various shades of copper and bronze color.

phlō·gō′sin, *n.* [Gr. *phlogōsis*, inflammation.] a crystallizable, nonnitrogenous substance obtained from cultures of the *Staphylococcus aureus*.

phlō·gō′sis, *n.* [Gr. *phlogōsis*, inflammation.]

inflammation, especially of the skin; erysipelas. [Now Rare.]

phlō·got′iç, *a.* of, having, pertaining to, or characteristic of phlogosis. [Now Rare.]

phlō·ram′ine, *n.* a compound obtained by the action of ammonia on phloroglucin.

phlō·ret′iç, *a.* of, relating to, or obtained from phloretin.

phlor′e·tin, *n.* [from *phlorizin.*] a bitter, white glucoside, $C_{15}H_{14}O_6$, derived from phlorizin, and used as a febrifuge.

phlō·rhi′zin (-ri′), *n.* phlorizin.

phlō·rid′zin, *n.* phlorizin.

phlor′i·zin, *n.* [Gr. *phloios*, bark, and *rhiza-*, root.] a bitter, white, crystalline glucoside, $C_{21}H_{24}O_{10}$, obtained from the root bark of the apple, pear, plum, and cherry trees, and used in medicine as a tonic and to combat periodic fevers, as in malaria.

phlor·ō·glū′cin, *n.* [*phlor*izin, and Gr. *glykys*, sweet.] a sweet crystalline phenol obtained from various barks, as that of the apple tree, and used as a test for woody fiber and for hydrochloric acid.

phlor·ō·glū′cin·ōl, *n.* same as *phloroglucin*.

phlō′rōl, *n.* an oily liquid derived from creosote.

phlō′rōne, *n.* [*phlor*ol and quin*one*.] a yellow crystalline compound obtained from beechwood and coal tar by distillation and from xylidine by oxidation.

Phlox, *n.* [Gr. *phlox*, a flame, from *phlegein*, to burn, from the appearance of the flowers.]

1. a North American genus of plants, family *Polemoniaceæ*, with small leaves and clusters of pink, blue, red, purple, or white flowers.

2. [p—] any plant of this genus.

phlox′in, *n.* [Gr. *phlox*, flame, and *-in*.] a coal-tar dyestuff, derivable from fluorescein.

phlox wŏrm, the larva of *Heliothis phlogophagus*, an American moth. It feeds on and is destructive to the phloxes.

phlyç·tae′nȧ, *n.*; *pl.* **phlyç·tae′nae,** a phlyctena.

phlyç·tē′nȧ, *n.*; *pl.* **phlyç·tē′nae,** [Mod.L.; Gr. *phlyktaina*, a blister, from *phlyein*, to swell.] a small blister or pustule.

phlyç·ten′ū·lăr, *a.* having or characterized by small vesicles, blisters, or pustules.

-phōbe, [Fr.; L. *-phobus*; Gr. *-phobos*, from *phobos*, a fear.] a combining form, used in forming adjectives and nouns, meaning *fearing* or *hating*, as in Franco*phobe*.

-phō′bi·ȧ, [Gr. *-phobia*, from *phobos*, a fear, flight.] a combining form meaning *fear*, *dread*, *hatred*, as in claustro*phobia*, Anglo*phobia*.

phō′bi·ȧ, *n.* [Gr. *phobos*, fear.] any persistent, irrational, and excessive fear of some particular thing or situation.

phō′biç, *a.* of, like, or constituting a phobia.

Phō′çȧ, *n.* [L.; Gr. *phōkē*, seal.] a genus of mammals typical of the *Phocidæ*, and including the harbor seals.

phō·çā′cē·ăn, *n.* a seal; any species of the genus *Phoca*.

phō·cā′çē·ăn, *a.* pertaining to the genus *Phoca*.

phō·cen′iç, *a.* [Gr. *phokaina*, a porpoise.] pertaining to or designating an oil obtained from porpoises or dolphins.

phocenic acid; valeric or valerianic acid.

Phō′ci·dae, *n.pl.* a family of aquatic mammals; the seals.

phō′cīne, *a.* [Gr. *phōkē*, seal.] of or relating to the seals; of or pertaining to the *Phocidæ*.

phō′çō·dont, *n.* [Gr. *phōkē*, seal, and *odous*, *odontos*, tooth.] one of the *Phocodontia*, a primary group of extinct whales.

Phoe′bē (fē′), *n.* [Gr. *Phoibē*.]

1. in Greek mythology, Artemis, goddess of the moon: identified by the Romans with Diana.

2. the moon. [Poetic.]

3. [p—] in zoology, a serranoid fish, *Haliperca phœbe*, of Cuban waters.

phoe′bē, *n.* [echoic; sp. influenced by *Phoebe*.] a small bird, one of the flycatchers, with a greenish-brown back, light-yellow breast, and a short crest: also called *pewit*, *pewee*.

Phoe·bē′ăn, *a.* characteristic of or relating to Phoebus Apollo.

Phoe′bus, *n.* [Gr. *Phoibos*, the bright one, from root of *phōs*, light.]

1. in Greek mythology, Apollo, the sun god.

2. the sun. [Poet.]

Phoe·ni′ciăn, Phē·ni′ciăn (-nish′un), *a.* of or pertaining to Phoenicia, its people, their language, or culture.

Phoe·ni′ciăn, *n.* 1. a native of Phoenicia, an ancient kingdom on the Mediterranean: the Phoenicians were famous as navigators and traders.

2. the extinct Northwest Semitic language of the Phoenicians, closely related to Moabite and Hebrew.

Phoe·ni·çop′tēr·us, *n.* [Gr. *phoinikopteros*, red-feathered; *phoinikos*, purple-red, and *pteron*, wing.] a genus of birds including the flamingos.

phoe′nix, phē′nix, *n.* [altered (after L.) from AS. and OFr. *fenix*; ML. *phenix*; L. *phoenix*; Gr. *phoinix*.]

1. in Egyptian mythology, a beautiful, lone bird which lived in the Arabian desert for 500 or 600 years and then consumed itself in fire, rising renewed from the ashes to start another long life: it is used as a symbol of immortality.

2. a person of singular distinction; a prodigy.

3. [P—] a southern constellation near the star Achernar.

4. in heraldry, a charge depicting a bird surrounded by flames.

5. a moth, *Cidaria ribesiaria*, the larvae of which feed on the gooseberry and the currant. [Brit.]

phō′lad, *n.* any member of the genus *Pholas*.

phō·lā′dē·ăn, phō·lā′di·ăn, *n.* same as *pholad*.

phō·lā′di·ăn, *a.* belonging or related to the genus *Pholas* or the family *Pholadidæ*.

Phō·lad′i·dae, *n.pl.* a family of lamellibranchiate, bivalve mollusks, comprising the genera *Pholas*, *Xylophaga*, and *Teredo*.

phō′lȧ·dīte, *n.* a petrified bivalve shell of the genus *Pholas*.

Phō′las, *n.* [Gr. *phōlas*, lurking in a hole, from *phōleos*, hole.]

1. a genus of marine lamellibranchiate bivalves of the family *Pholadidæ*, known as piddocks. They pierce wood, rocks, indurated clay, etc. by rasping with their shell, which is armed in front with file or rasplike imbrications; hence, also called *stoneborers*.

2. [p—] *pl.* **phō′lȧ·dēş,** a bivalve of this genus.

phol′i·dōte, *a.* [Gr. *pholidotos*, scaly, from *pholis*, *pholidos*, scale.] protected by a covering of scales. [Rare.]

phōn-, phono-.

phō′năl, *a.* [Gr. *phōnē*, voice.] of the voice.

phō·nas·cet′iċs, *n.* [Gr. *phōnaskein*, to practice the voice; *phōnē*, the voice, and *askein*, to practice.] systematic practice for strengthening the voice; treatment for improving or restoring the voice.

phō′nāte, *v.i.*; phonated, *pt.*, *pp.*; phonating, *ppr.* to utter a voiced sound; to vocalize.

phō·nā′tion, *n.* [Gr. *phōnē*, sound, the voice.] the act of phonating.

phō′nȧ·tō·ry, *a.* subserving or of phonation.

phō·nau′tō·gram, *n.* the tracing or diagram made by a phonautograph.

phō·nau′tō·grȧph, *n.* [*phon-* and *auto-* and *-graph*.]

1. an instrument which makes a graphic record of the vibrations set up by a sound.

2. a record or graph so made.

phō·nau·tō·graph′iç, *a.* like or pertaining to the phonautograph.

phōne, *n.*, *v.t.* and *v.i.*; phoned, *pt.*, *pp.*; phoning, *ppr.* [abbreviation of *telephone*.] telephone. [Colloq.]

phōne, *n.* [Gr. *phōnē*, sound, voice.] any single speech sound: a phoneme is composed of various *phones*.

-phōne, [from Gr. *phōnē*, a sound, voice.] a combining form meaning *producing*, or *connected with*, *sound*, as in saxo*phone*, mega*phone*.

phō·nei′dō·sçōpe, *n.* [Gr. *phōnē*, sound, *eidos*, form, and *skopein*, to view.] a device by which the vibrations of sound are made visible, to be studied by the eye.

phō′nēme, *n.* [Fr. *phonème*; Gr. *phōnēma*, a sound, from *phōnē*, a voice.] in linguistics, a class, or family, of closely related speech sounds (*phones*) regarded as a single sound and represented in phonetic transcription by the same symbol, as the sounds of *r* in *bring*, *red*, and *round*: the discernible phonetic differences between such sounds are due to the modifying influence of the adjacent sounds.

phō·nē′miç, *a.* 1. of or based on phonemes; as, a *phonemic* analysis of the sounds of a language.

2. of phonemics.

phō·nē′mi·cist, *n.* an expert in phonemics.

phō·nē′miçs, *n.pl.* [*construed as sing.*] the branch of language study dealing with the phonemic system of a particular language.

phō·nen′dō·sçōpe, *n.* [Gr. *phōnē*, voice, *endon*, within, and *skopein*, to see.] a stethoscope that intensifies auscultatory sounds.

phō·nē′sis, *n.* [Gr. *phōnēsis*, a sounding.] the making of voiced sounds; phonation.

phō·net′iç, *a.* [Gr. *phōnētikos*, from *phōnē*, sound.]

1. of speech sounds or the production or recording of these.

2. of phonetics.

3. conforming to pronunciation; as, *phonetic* spelling.

phonetic spelling; a system of orthography in which words are spelled according to their sound in pronunciation, and not according to tradition or conventionality.

phō·net′iç·ăl·ly, *adv.* in accordance with the principles of phonetics; so as to represent the sounds of speech.

phō·nē·ti′ciăn (-tish′un), *n.* an expert in phonetics.

phō·net′i·çişm, *n.* the quality of being phonetic; representation of spoken sounds by written signs.

phō·net′i·cist, *n.* a phonetist.

phō·net′içs, *n.pl.* [*construed as sing.*] 1. the branch of language study dealing with speech sounds, their production and combination, and their representation by written symbols.

2. the phonetic system of a particular language.

phō′nē·tişm, *n.* the science that symbolizes sounds by written characters.

phō′nē·tist, *n.* 1. an advocate or user of a system of phonetic spelling.

2. a phonetician.

phō·nē·ti·zā′tion, *n.* the art or practice of representing sounds phonetically. [Rare.]

phō′nē·tīze, *v.t.* to represent phonetically. [Rare.]

phō′ney, *a.* and *n.* phony. [Slang.]

-phō′ni·ȧ, -phony.

phon′iç (*or* fō′), *a.* [Fr. *phonique*; Gr. *phōnē*, sound.]

1. of, or having the nature of, sound; especially, of speech sounds.

2. voiced; sonant. [Rare.]

phon′içs (*or* fō′), *n.pl.* [*construed as sing.*] [from *phonic*.]

1. the science of sound; acoustics.

2. phonetics. [Rare.]

3. the use of elementary phonetics in teaching beginners to read or enunciate.

phō′ni·kon, *n.* a metal wind instrument.

phō′nişm, *n.* a sound or sensation of hearing produced by the effect of something seen, felt, tasted, smelt, or thought of.

phō′nō-, [from Gr. *phōnē*, a sound, voice.] a combining form meaning *sound*, *tone*, *speech*, as in *phono*logy: also, before a vowel, *phon-*.

phō·nō·çamp′tiç, *a.* [Gr. *phōnē*, sound, and *kamptein*, to inflect.] having the power to reflect sound, or turn it from its direction. [Rare.]

phō′nō·gram, *n.* [*phono-* and *-gram*.]

1. a sign or symbol representing a word, syllable, or sound, as in shorthand.

2. a phonograph record. [Now Rare.]

phō·nō·gram′iç, phō·nō·gram′miç, *a.* of or by a phonogram or phonograms.

phō′nō·grȧph, *n.* [*phono-* and *-graph*.]

1. a type or character for expressing a sound; a character used in phonography.

2. an instrument that records or, especially, reproduces sound from tracings made on a flat disk or, formerly, a cylinder.

phō·nog′rȧ·phēr, *n.* 1. one versed in phonography.

2. one who uses a phonograph. [Rare.]

phō·nō·graph′iç, phō·nō·graph′iç·ăl, *a.*

1. pertaining to or done by the phonograph.

2. of or pertaining to phonography.

phō·nō·graph′iç·ăl·ly, *adv.* 1. in a phonographic manner.

2. by means of a phonograph.

phō·nog′rȧ·phist, *n.* a phonographer.

phō·nog′rȧ·phy, *n.* [Gr. *phōnē*, sound, and *graphein*, to write.]

1. a written or printed representation of the sounds of speech; phonetic spelling or transcription.

2. any system of shorthand based on a phonetic transcription of speech; especially, the system invented by Isaac Pitman (1813–1897).

3. the use of a phonograph in recording or reproducing sound.

phō′nō·līte, *n.* [Gr. *phōnē*, sound, and *lithos*, stone.] a hard, compact, igneous rock consisting chiefly of alkali feldspar and nephelite and found in extensive masses among secondary rocks: also called *clinkstone* or *sounding stone*, on account of its ring when struck.

phō·nō·lit′iç, *a.* of or like phonolite.

phō·nol′ō·ġẽr, *n.* a phonologist. [Rare.]

phō·nō·loġ′iç, phō·nō·loġ′iç·ăl, *a.* pertaining to phonology.

phō·nol′ō·ġist, *n.* one versed in phonology; a phonemicist or phonetician.

phō·nol′ō·ġy, *n.* [Gr. *phōnē*, sound, voice, and *logos*, discourse.]
1. (a) phonetics; (b) phonemics; (c) phonetics and phonemics.
2. the study of the evolution of speech sounds, especially from one status to another within a particular language.

phō·nom′ē·tẽr, *n.* [Gr. *phōnē*, sound, voice, and *metron*, a measure.] an instrument for measuring the intensity and vibration frequency of sound.

phō·nō·mō′tŏr, *n.* an instrument in which the energy of sound waves produces motion by vibrating a membrane.

phō·nō·phō′bi·ȧ, *n.* morbid dread of speaking aloud.

phō′nō·phōre, *n.* 1. an ossicle of the ear.
2. a stethoscope that operates on the principle of an ear trumpet.
3. a device by means of which a telegraph wire may be used for telephoning without interfering with the transmission of telegrams.

phō·noph′ō·rous, *a.* conveying sound waves.

phō′nō·plex, *a.* [Gr. *phōnē*, voice, and *plex*, from L. *plectere, plexus*, to weave.] pertaining to or designating a telegraph system using phonophores.

phō′nō·pōre, *n.* same as *phonophore*.

phō·nop′si·ȧ, *n.* a subjective sensation as of seeing colors, caused by the hearing of sounds.

phō′nō·sçōpe, *n.* [Gr. *phōnē*, sound, and *-scope*.]
1. an instrument used to observe or exhibit the properties of a sounding body; especially, a device for testing the quality of strings for musical instruments.
2. an instrument that produces luminous figures corresponding to the vibrations of sounds or their differences in pitch.

phō·nō·te·lem′ē·tẽr, *n.* [Gr. *phōnē*, sound, and *tele*, far, and *metron*, measure.] an instrument for determining distance by recording the period of travel of a sound wave.

phō′nō·tȳpe, *n.* [Gr. *phōnē*, sound, and *typos*, mark, type.] a phonetic symbol or character, as used in printing.

phō·nō·typ′iç, phō·nō·typ′iç·ăl, *a.* of or pertaining to phonotypy or phonotypes; as, a *phonotypic* alphabet; *phonotypic* writing or printing.

phō·nō·typ′iç·ăl·ly, *adv.* in phonotypic characters.

phō′nō·tȳp·ist, *n.* one who is versed in or advocates phonotypy.

phō′nō·tȳp·y, *n.* a system of phonetic printing or writing, as some systems of shorthand.

phō′ny, *a.*; *comp.* phonier; *superl.* phoniest, [said to be altered from *Forney*, cheap jewelry, from *Forney rings*, brass rings made by a manufacturer named *Forney* for sale by street peddlers.] not genuine; false; counterfeit; spurious; fake; sham. [Slang.]

phō′ny, *n.*; *pl.* **phō′nieș,** 1. something not genuine; sham; fake. [Slang.]
2. a person who pretends to be what he is not; a charlatan; impostor. [Slang.]
Also spelled *phoney*.

-phō′ny, [from Gr. *phōnē*, a sound, voice.] a combining form meaning *a* (specified kind of) *sound*, as in caco*phony*: also *-phonia*.

Phō·rȧ·den′dron, *n.* [Gr. *phōr*, thief, and *dendron*, tree.] a large genus of American plants resembling the mistletoe, characterized by erect anthers and parasitic on trees. *Phoradendron flavescens*, the American mistletoe, is widely scattered through the warmer parts of North and South America.

-phōre, [Mod. L. *-phorus, -phorum*; Gr. *-phoros, -phoron*, from *pherein*, to bear.] a combining form meaning *bearer, producer*, as in carpo*phore*.

phor′minx, *n.* [Gr.] an ancient Grecian musical instrument, the cithara.

Phor′mi·um, *n.* [from Gr. *phormos*, a basket, from the purpose to which the plant is put in its native country.] the flax plant or flax lily, a genus of plants belonging to the family *Liliaceæ*. The principal species, *Phormium tenax*, is indigenous to New Zealand.

phō·rom′ē·tẽr, *n.* an instrument for measuring the relative strength of the muscles of the eyes.

phō′rōne, *n.* [cam*phor* and acet*one*.] a yellowish, oily substance derived from acetone, camphoric acid, etc.

Phō·rō′niș, *n.* [Gr.] a genus of marine worms with a dorsal circlet of tentacles.

phor·ō·nō′mi·ȧ, *n.* same as *phoronomics*.

phor·ō·nom′içs, *n.* [Gr. *phora*, a carrying, from *pherein*, to bear or carry, and *nomos*, a law.] that branch of mechanics which treats of motion in the abstract; kinematics. [Rare.]

phō·ron′ō·my, *n.* same as *phoronomics*.

phor′ō·sçōpe, *n.* [Gr. *phora*, a motion, and *-scope*.] an electrical device for transmitting a visual image to a distance.

phō′rō·tōne, *n.* [Gr. *phora*, motion, and *tonos*, tension.] an instrument for exercising the muscles of the eye.

-phōr′ous, [Mod. L. *-phorus*; Gr. *-phoros*, from *pherein*, to bear.] a combining form meaning *bearing, producing*.

phos′ġēne, *n.* [Gr. *phōs*, light, and *-gen*.] carbonyl chloride, $COCl_2$, a colorless gas formed by the reaction of carbon monoxide and chlorine in the sunlight: used in making dyes and other organic compounds, and as a lung irritant in warfare.

phos·ġen′iç, *a.* photogenic; light-producing.

phos′ġen·īte, *n.* a chlorocarbonate of lead, $Pb_2Cl_2CO_3$, occurring in white or yellowish crystals.

phosph-, phospho-.

phos′pham, *n.* [*phosph*orous and *am*monia.] a white compound derivable from phosphorus pentachloride by the action of ammonia gas.

phos′phȧ·tāse, *n.* [from *phosphate*, and *-ase*.] any of various enzymes found in body tissues and fluids that split the phosphate-carbohydrate compounds.

phos′phāte, *n.* 1. a salt or ester of phosphoric acid.
2. any substance containing phosphates, used as a fertilizer.
3. a soft drink made with soda water, sirup, and a few drops of phosphoric acid.

phos·phat′iç, *a.* relating to or containing phosphates.

phos′phȧ·tīze, *v.t.*; phosphatized, *pt., pp.*; phosphatizing, *ppr.* to change into, or treat with, a phosphate or phosphates.

phos″phat·op·tō′sis, *n.* [*phosphate*, and Gr. *ptōsis*, fall.] the spontaneous precipitation of phosphates from the urine.

phos·phȧ·tū′ri·ȧ, *n.* 1. an excess of phosphates in the urine.
2. phosphatoptosis.

phos·phȧ·tū′riç, *a.* of or characterized by phosphaturia.

phos′phēne, *n.* [Gr. *phōs*, light, and *phainein*, to show.] a bright visual image produced by mechanical stimulation of the retina, as by pressure on the eyeball through the closed eyelids.

phos′phid, *n.* a phosphide.

phos′phīde, *n.* the compound formed by trivalent phosphorus and a positive element or elements.

phos′phin, *n.* a phosphine.

phos′phīne, *n.* 1. hydrogen phosphide, PH_3, a colorless, poisonous gas with a garliclike odor.
2. a synthetic yellow dye.

phos′phīte, *n.* any salt or ester of phosphorous acid.

phos′phō-, [from *phosphorus*.] a combining form meaning *phosphorus*, as in *phospho*protein: also, before a vowel, *phosph-*.

phos′phō·līte, *n.* [*phosphor*, and Gr. *lithos*, a stone.] an earth united with phosphoric acid.

phos·phol′ō·ġy, *n.* the doctrine of the effect of excess or deficiency of oxidizable phosphorus compounds in the bioplasm.

phos·phon′iç, *a.* relating to or derived from phosphorous acid.
phosphonic acid; a compound of phosphorous acid in which a hydrocarbon replaces one of the hydrogen atoms.

phos·phō′ni·um, *n.* [*phosph*orus and ammo*nium*.] the monovalent radical PH_4, which is related to PH_3 as the ammonium radical NH_4 is related to NH_3.

phos·phō·prō′tē·in, *n.* any of a group of proteins in which the protein molecule is combined with some phosphorous compound other than lecithin or a nucleic acid, as casein of milk.

phos′phŏr, *n.* [Gr. *phōsphoros*; *phōs*, light, from *phaein*, to shine, and *pherein*, to bring.]
1. [P–] the morning star, or Lucifer; Venus, when it precedes the sun and shines in the morning. [Poetic.]
2. phosphorus or any other phosphorescent substance. [Archaic and Poet.]
3. in physics, any substance that gives off light when subjected to radiation.

phos′phŏr, *a.* phosphorescent. [Rare.]

phos′phō·rāte, *v.t.*; phosphorated, *pt., pp.*; phosphorating, *ppr.* to combine or impregnate with phosphorus.

phos′phōre, *n.* same as *phosphor*.

phos·phō·resce′ (-es′), *v.i.*; phosphoresced (-est), *pt., pp.*; phosphorescing, *ppr.* to shine, as phosphorus, by giving off light without noticeable heat or combustion.

phos·phō·res′cence, *n.* 1. the condition or property of giving off light without noticeable heat or combustion, as shown by phosphorus, decayed wood, etc.
2. such a light.

phos·phō·res′cent, *a.* showing phosphorescence.

phos·phō·res′cent, *n.* any substance having phosphorescence.

phos′phō·ret·ed, phos′phō·ret·ted, *a.* combined or impregnated with phosphorus: also *phosphureted, phosphuretted*.
phosphoreted hydrogen; a colorless gas, PH_3, smelling like decayed fish, prepared by boiling water-slaked lime and phosphorus.

phos·phor′iç, *a.* 1. of, like, or containing phsophorus, especially with a valence of five.
2. designating any of three oxygen acids of phosphorus, especially orthophosphoric acid, H_3PO_4, a colorless crystalline acid, soluble in water and used as a reagent.

phos·phor′iç·ăl, *a.* phosphoric. [Obs.]

phos′phō·rișm, *n.* chronic phosphorus poisoning.

phos′phō·rīte, *n.* 1. a fibrous variety of apatite.
2. any mineral phosphate used as fertilizer.

phos·phō·rit′iç, *a.* pertaining to phosphorite; of the nature of phosphorite.

phos′phō·rīze, *v.t.*; phosphorized, *pt., pp.*; phosphorizing, *ppr.* to phosphorate.

phos′phō·rō-, a combining form meaning *phosphorus* or *phosphorescence*, as in *phosphoro*scope: also, before a vowel, *phosphor-*.

phos·phor′ō·grȧph, *n.* [*phosphorus*, and Gr. *graphein*, to write.] a representation obtained by phosphorescence.

phos″phō·rō·graph′iç, *a.* of or relating to phosphorography.

phos·phō·rog′rȧ·phy, *n.* the act or art of taking phosphorographs.

phos·phor′ō·sçōpe, *n.* a device used in observing and measuring the persistence of phosphorescence after the source of light has been removed.

phos′phō·rous, *a.* 1. phosphorescent. [Rare.]
2. [Fr. *phosphoreux*.] of, like, or containing phosphorus, especially with a valence of three.
3. designating a white or yellowish, crystalline acid, H_3PO_3, that absorbs oxygen readily: used as a chemical reducing agent.
phosphorous anhydrid; a soft, white, readily volatile powder, P_2O_3, prepared by burning phosphorus in a limited supply of air.

phos′phō·rus, *n.*; *pl.* **phos′phō·rī,** [L., from Gr. *phōsphoros*; *phōs*, light, and *pherein*, to bear.]
1. [P–] the morning star, Phosphor.
2. any phosphorescent substance or object.
3. a nonmetallic chemical element, normally a white, phosphorescent, waxy solid, becoming yellow when exposed to light: it is poisonous and unites easily with oxygen so that it ignites spontaneously at room temperature: when heated in sealed tubes it is converted into a red form (*red*, or *amorphous, phosphorus*) which is nonpoisonous, and less inflammable than the white: when heated under a pressure of 15,000 atmospheres it is converted into a black powder: symbol, P.; atomic weight, 30.98; atomic number, 15.
phosphorus paste; a poisonous mixture containing phosphorus, used for vermin.

phos′phō·rus dis·ēașe′, a disease resulting from inhalation of the fumes of phosphorus, characterized especially by necrosis of the jaw.

phos′phō·ryl, *n.* in chemistry, the radical PO.

phos′phū·ret, *n.* phosphide. [Obs.]

phos′phū·ret·ed, phos′phū·ret·ted, *a.* phosphoreted.

phot (*or* fōt), *n.* [from Gr. *phōs, phōtos*, a light.] the C.G.S. unit of illumination, equal to one lumen per square centimeter, or the direct illumination produced by a uniform point source of one international foot-candle upon a surface one centimeter distant.

phō′tiç, *a.* [Gr. *phōs, phōtos*, light.]
1. of light.

2. in biology, having to do with the effect of light upon, or the production of light by, organisms.

phō′tiçs, *n.pl.* [*construed as sing.*] the science of light.

phō′tō, *n.*; *pl.* **phō′tōṣ,** [contr. of *photograph.*] a photograph. [Colloq.]

phō′tō-, [from Gr. *phōs, phōtos,* light.] a combining form meaning (a) *of or produced by light,* as in *photo*graphy, *photo*synthesis; (b) *of a photograph or photography,* as in *photo*play, *photo*montage.

phō″tō·aç·tin′iç, *a.* [*photo-* and *actinic.*] that can produce actinic effect, as ultraviolet rays.

phō″tō·bī·ot′iç, *a.* in biology, needing light for existence.

phō′tō·cell, *n.* a photoelectric cell.

phō·tō·çhem′iç·ăl, *a.* relating to or produced by the chemical action of light.

phō·tō·çhem′is·try, *n.* the branch of chemistry that relates to chemical changes produced by the action of light.

phō″tō·çhrō·mat′iç, *a.* relating to or derived from photochromy.

phō·tō·çhrō′miç, *a.* same as *photochromatic.*

phō″tō·çhrō·mog′rȧ·phy, *n.* [*photo-,* Gr. *chrōma,* color, and *graphein,* to write.] the printing of colored photolithographs.

phō·tō·çhrō′mō·sçōpe, *n.* [*photo-,* Gr. *chrōma,* color, and *-scope.*] an apparatus for reproducing color effects in photographs.

phō′tō·çhrō·my, *n.* [*photo-,* Gr. *chrōma,* color.] production of colored photographs; reproduction of natural colors in photographs; color photography.

phō·tō·çhron′ō·grȧph, *n.* [*photo-* and *chrono-* and *-graph.*]

1. an instrument that records motion, as of a bird, in a series of photographs taken at regular, extremely brief intervals.

2. a photograph so taken.

3. in physics, an instrument for recording the exact time of an event by exposing a moving photographic plate to the tracing of a thin beam of light synchronized with the event.

phō″tō·çŏn·duç′tive, *a.* designating or of a substance, as selenium, which exhibits changed electrical conductivity under varying amounts of radiation.

phō′tō·çop·y, *n.*; *pl.* **phō′tō·çop·ieṣ,** a copy of graphic material made by a device which photographically reproduces the original.

phō′tō·çop·y, *v.t.*; photocopied, *pt., pp.*; photocopying, *ppr.* to make a photocopy of.

phō″tō·dē·grȧd′ȧ·ble, *a.* [*photo-,* and *biodegradable.*] that will decompose under exposure to certain kinds of radiant energy, especially ultraviolet light, as certain plastics, insecticides, etc.

phō″tō·dis·in″tē·grā′tion, *n.* [*photo-* and *disintegration.*] in physics, the breaking down of the nucleus of an atom by the action of radiant energy.

phō′tō·drä·mȧ, *n.* a photoplay.

phō′tō·drōme, *n.* [*photo-,* and Gr. *dromos,* a running, from *dramein,* to run.]

1. a device for regulating light flashes so that a wheel or disk in rotation appears to be stationary or to have its motion reversed.

2. an instrument by which curious optical effects are produced, by throwing flashes of light upon revolving disks bearing various figures.

phō″tō·dȳ·nam′içs, *n.pl.* [*construed as sing.*]

1. the effect of light on living organisms, as in causing phototropism.

2. the science dealing with this.

phō″tō·ē·leç′triç, *a.* 1. of or having to do with the electric effects produced by light, especially as in the emission of electrons by certain substances when subjected to light or radiation of suitable wave length.

2. pertaining to the lowering of electrical resistance of some substances, as selenium, when exposed to certain wave lengths of light.

photoelectric cell; any device in which light controls the electron emission from a cathode, the electrical resistance of an element, or the electromotive force produced by a cell: it is usually incorporated in an electric circuit and used in controlling mechanical devices, as for opening doors: also called *electric eye.*

phō″tō·ē·leç·triç′i·ty, *n.* electricity as affected by light; difference of electric potential produced by the action of light.

phō″tō·ē·leç′tron, *n.* an electron ejected from a system by a photon striking it, or emitted as a result of radiation.

phō″tō·ē·leç′trō·tȳpe, *n.* an electrotype plate made by a photographic process.

phō″tō·ē·mis′sion (-mish′un), *n.* [*photo-,* and *emission.*] the ejection of one or more electrons from a substance, usually a metal, when subjected to light or other suitable radiation.

phō″tō·en·grāve′, *v.t.*; photoengraved, *pt., pp.*; photoengraving, *ppr.* to reproduce by the process of photoengraving.

phō″tō·en·grāv′ing, *n.* [*photo-* and *engraving.*]

1. a process by which photographs are reproduced on printing plates, especially one in which the reproduction is in relief.

2. a plate so made.

3. a print from such a plate.

phō·tō·etch′ (-ech′), *v.t.*; photoetched (-echt′), *pt., pp.*; photoetching, *ppr.* to produce by the process of photoetching.

phō·tō·etch′ing, *n.* the reproduction of a picture by any means in which an etching of the plate and photography are employed.

phō′tō fin′ish, a close finish of a game, competition, etc.: so called from horse racing, in which the finish of the race is photographed to determine the winner.

phō′tō·flash, *a.* in photography, designating, of, or using a lamp or light, especially a flashbulb, electrically synchronized with the shutter.

phō′tō·flash, *n.* a photoflash bulb, photograph, lamp, etc.

phō′tō·flood (-flud), *a.* 1. designating an electric bulb of low voltage which when connected to a circuit of standard voltage burns with a sustained intense light: used in photography.

2. (a) of or for such a bulb; (b) made with the aid of such a bulb.

phō′tō·flood, *n.* a photoflood bulb or photograph.

phō·tō·gas′trō·sçōpe, *n.* an instrument by means of which the interior of the stomach may be photographed.

phō·tō·ġel′ȧ·tin, *a.* of, designating, or produced by a photographic process in which prints are made from a film of hardened gelatin.

phō′tō·ġen, *n.* [*photo-* and *-gen.*] a light solvent or illuminating oil obtained from coal, shale, paraffin, etc. by distillation.

phō′tō·ġēne, *n.* photogen.

phō′tō·ġēne, *n.* an impression retained on the retina of the eye after the object itself has vanished; an afterimage.

phō·tō·ġen′iç, *a.* 1. due to or produced by light. [Rare.]

2. artistically suitable for being photographed; as, a *photogenic* face or figure.

3. in biology, producing or giving off light; phosphorescent.

phō·tō·ġen′iç·ăl·ly, *adv.* in a photogenic manner.

phō·tō·glyph′iç, *a.* [*photo-,* and Gr. *glyphein,* to engrave.] pertaining to photoglyphy.

phō·tog′ly·phy, *n.* 1. the art of engraving by means of photography.

2. photogravure.

phō·tō·gram′me·tẽr, *n.* a form of photographic camera employed in surveying.

phō·tō·gram′me·try, *n.* 1. the use of photography in surveying.

2. map-making from photographs.

phō′tō·grȧph, *n.* [*photo-* and *-graph.*] a picture or representation obtained by any process of photography.

phō′tō·grȧph, *v.t.*; photographed (-grȧft), *pt., pp.*; photographing, *ppr.* to take a picture of, by means of a camera; as, to *photograph* a scene or person.

phō′tō·grȧph, *v.i.* 1. to be a photographer; to practice photography.

2. to undergo being photographed, with reference to photogenic qualities; as, she *photographs* well.

phō·tog′rȧ·phẽr, *n.* one who photographs; especially, one whose business is taking photographs.

phō·tō·graph′iç, *a.* 1. of or like a photograph or photography; as, his *photographic* writing.

2. used in or made by photography, as equipment, records, etc.

3. retaining or recalling in precise detail; as, a *photographic* memory.

phō·tō·graph′iç·ăl, *a.* photographic.

phō·tō·graph′iç·ăl·ly, *adv.* 1. in a photographic manner.

2. by a photograph or photographs.

phō·tog′rȧ·phist, *n.* one who practises photography.

phō·tog′rȧ·phy, *n.* the art or practice of producing images of objects upon a photosensitive surface by the chemical action of light or other radiant energy.

phō″tō·grȧ·vūre′, *n.* [*photo-,* and Fr. *gravure,* engraving.]

1. a photoengraving process by which photographs are reproduced on intaglio printing plates or rolls from which they may be transferred to paper.

2. a print so made, usually with a velvety, satinlike finish.

phō″tō·grȧ·vūre′, *v.t.*; photogravured, *pt., pp.*; photogravuring, *ppr.* to reproduce by photogravure.

phō·tō·hē′li·ō·grȧph″, *n.* [*photo-* and *heliograph.*] a telescopic camera made especially for taking photographs of the sun.

phō·tō·jour′năl·iṣm, *n.* journalism in which news stories, etc. are presented mainly through photographs.

phō″tō·ki·nē′sis, *n.* [Mod. L.; *photo-,* and *kinesis,* motion, from Gr. *kinēsis,* from *kinein,* to move.] in physiology, movement in response to light.

phō″tō·ki·net′iç, *a.* of photokinesis.

phō·tō·lith′ō·grȧph, *n.* [*photo-* and *lithograph.*] a lithograph produced by photoengraving.

phō·tō·lith′ō·grȧph, *v.t.* to use photoengraving in the production or reproduction of.

phō″tō·li·thog′rȧ·phẽr, *n.* one who uses photolithography for producing pictures.

phō″tō·lith·ō·graph′iç, *a.* pertaining to, like, or obtained by photolithography.

phō″tō·li·thog′rȧ·phy, *n.* the art or process of making photolithographs.

phō·tol′ō·ġist, *n.* a person skilled in photology.

phō·tol′ō·ġy, *n.* the science of light; photics.

phō·tol′y·sis, *n.* 1. in chemistry, decomposition brought about by the action of radiant energy, particularly light.

2. in botany, the effect of light on the arrangement of chlorophyll.

phō·tō·lyt′iç, *a.* of photolysis.

phō″tō·mag·net′iç, *a.* pertaining to photomagnetism.

phō·tō·mag′net·iṣm, *n.* [*photo-* and *magnetism.*] the relation of magnetism to light.

phō′tō·map, *n.* a map made by piecing together aerial photographs.

phō″tō·mē·çhan′iç·ăl, *a.* [*photo-* and *mechanical.*] pertaining to any mechanical process of obtaining pictures by using photographic methods, as in photolithography or photogravure.

phō·tom′e·tẽr, *n.* [*photo-* and *-meter.*] an instrument for measuring the intensity of light, especially for determining the relative intensity of different lights; a light meter.

phō·tō·met′riç, *a.* of or by a photometer or photometry.

phō·tō·met′riç·ăl, *a.* same as *photometric.*

phō″to·mē·tri′ciăn (-trish′ăn), *n.* one skilled in photometry.

phō·tom′e·try, *n.* 1. the measurement of the intensity of light.

2. the branch of optics dealing with this.

phō·tō·mī′çrō·grȧph, *n.* [*photo-* and *micrograph.*]

1. a photograph taken through a microscope.

2. a very small photograph, usually requiring enlargement to bring out the details: usually *microphotograph.*

phō″tō·mī·çrog′rȧ·phy, *n.* the art or act of making photomicrographs.

phō·tō·mī′çrō·sçōpe, *n.* a microscope and camera used to make photomicrographs.

phō″tō·mī·çros′çō·py, *n.* photomicrography.

phō″tō·mon·täġe′ (-täzh′), *n.* montage done in photographs.

phō·tō·mū′răl, *n.* a large photograph used as a mural.

phō′ton, *n.* [*photo-,* and electr*on.*]

1. a quantum of electromagnetic energy having both particle and wave behavior: it has no charge or mass but possesses momentum: the energy of light, X rays, gamma rays, etc. is carried by photons.

2. a unit of retinal illumination equal to the illumination from a surface having a brightness of one candle per square meter seen through a pupil area of one square millimeter.

phō·tō·neū′tron, *n.* a neutron given off in the photodisintegration of an atomic nucleus.

phō′tō-off′set, *n.* a method of offset printing in which the pictures or text are photographically transferred to a metal plate from which inked impressions are made on the rubber roller.

phō″tō·ox·i·dā′tion, *n.* oxidation induced by light or some other form of radiant energy.

phō·toph′i·lous, *a.* [*photo-* and *-philous.*] in biology, thriving in light.

phō·tō·phō′bi·ȧ, *n.* [*photo-*, and Gr. *phobos*, fear.]
1. an abnormal fear of light.
2. in medicine, an abnormal sensitivity to light, especially of the eyes as in measles and certain eye conditions.

phō′tō·phōne, *n.* [*photo-*, and Gr. *phōnē*, sound.] an instrument for communicating sounds by the agency of a beam of light, usually employing a selenium cell.

phō·tō·phon′iç, *a.* pertaining to the photophone or to photophony.

phō·toph′ō·ny, *n.* the art, process, or operation of using the photophone, or of transmitting sound by light.

phō′tō·phōre, *n.* [*photo-*, and Gr. *pherein*, to bear.] in zoology, an organ that gives forth light.

phō″tō·phos″phō·res′cent, *a.* becoming phosphorescent upon exposure to light.

phō′tō·plāy, *n.* [*photo* and *play*.] a play presented in motion pictures; a screen play.

phō′tō·print, *n.* a picture printed by any photomechanical process.

phō′tō·proc·ess, *n.* a photomechanical process.

phō·top′si·ȧ, phō·top′sy, *n.* [*photo-*, and Gr. *opis*, sight.] a condition of the eye, in which the patient perceives luminous rays, lines, coruscations, etc.

phō·tō·rā′di·ō·gram″, *n.* a photograph reproduced at a distant receiving station by means of radio equipment.

phō″tō·rē·lief′, *n.* a picture or surface in relief, produced by a photomechanical process.

phō′tō·sçōpe, *n.* [*photo-* and *-scope*.]
1. any device for ascertaining the intensity of light.
2. any device for showing photographs.

phō·tō·sçop′iç, *a.* of or pertaining to a photoscope or its operation.

phō·tō·sçulp′tūre, *n.* [*photo-* and *sculpture*.] a rapid process of sculpturing statuettes, medallions, etc., by means of a pantograph which traces the outlines of a number of photographs taken simultaneously from different points of view.

phō·tō·sen′si·tive, *a.* reacting or sensitive to radiant energy, especially to light.

phō·tō·speç′trō·sçōpe, *n.* an instrument used in making a photographic record of spectra.

phō′tō·sphēre, *n.* the white-hot envelope of gas surrounding the sun.

phō·tō·spher′iç, *a.* of or pertaining to the photosphere.

phō′tō·stat, *n.* 1. a device used in making inexpensive photographic reproductions of printed matter, maps, drawings, etc.: the image is made directly as a positive upon special paper: a trade-mark (*Photostat*).
2. a reproduction or copy so made.

phō′tō·stat, *v.i.*; photostated *or* photostatted, *pt.*, *pp.*; photostating *or* photostatting, *ppr.* to produce or manufacture a photostat or photostats.

phō′tō·stat, *v.t.* to copy by means of a photostat.

phō·tō·stat′iç, *a.* of or by a phostat; having the appearance of a photostat.

phō·tō·syn′the·sis, *n.* 1. in chemistry and physiology, the synthesis of compounds by light.
2. in botany, the formation of carbohydrates in living plants from water and carbon dioxide, by the action of sunlight on the chlorophyll.

phō·tō·syn′the·sīze, *v.i.* and *v.t.* 1. in chemistry and physiology, to synthesize (compounds) by light.
2. in botany, to transform (carbon dioxide and water into carbohydrates) by means of photosynthesis.

phō″tō·syn·thet′iç, *a.* of or by photosynthesis.

phō·tō·taç′tiç, *a.* of or pertaining to phototaxis.

phō·tō·tax′is, *n.* [*photo-*, and Gr. *taxis*, arrangement.] the movement of an organism in response to stimulus from light.
negative phototaxis; a turning from the light.
positive phototaxis; a turning toward the light.

phō′tō·tax·y, *n.* phototaxis.

phō·tō·tel′ē·gràph, *v.t.* and *v.i.* to send by phototelegraphy.

phō·tō·tel′ē·gràph, *n.* something sent by phototelegraphy.

phō″tō·tē·leg′rȧ·phy, *n.* 1. communication by means of light, as by flashing reflections of the sun's rays.
2. the sending of photograph facsimiles by telegraphy.

phō·tō·tel′ē·sçōpe, *n.* a telescope equipped with a camera and used for photographing the heavenly bodies.

phō″tō·thē·od′ō·līte, *n.* same as *photogrammeter*.

phō·tō·ther·ȧ·peū′tiç, *a.* of or by phototherapy.

phō·tō·ther·ȧ·peū′tiçs, *n.pl.* [*construed as sing.*] phototherapy.

phō·tō·ther′ȧ·py, *n.* the treatment of disease, especially of certain skin diseases, by the use of light rays.

phō·tō·thẽr′miç, *a.* [*photo-* and *thermic*.] of both light and heat.

phō·tō·ton′iç, *a.* [*photo-*, and Gr. *tonos*, tension.] of or pertaining to phototonus.

phō·tot′ō·nus, *n.* in biology, the state of being responsive to or irritated by exposure to light.

phō·tō·trop′iç, *a.* of or by phototropism.

phō·tō·trop′iç·ăl·ly, *adv.* in a phototropic manner.

phō·tot′rō·piṣm, *n.* [*photo-* and *tropism*.] in biology, tropism toward or away from light.

phō′tō·tūbe, *n.* a photoelectric cell.

phō′tō·tȳpe, *n.* [*photo-*, and Gr. *typos*, a type.]
1. a type or plate upon which a photograph is reproduced.
2. the process by which such a plate is produced.
3. a print from such a block.

phō·tō·tȳp′iç, *a.* 1. of or like a phototype.
2. by phototype.

phō″tō·tȳ·pog′rȧ·phy, *n.* any mechanical printing process in which photographs are reproduced in relief for use with type.

phō′tō·tȳ·py, *n.* the art or act of producing or using phototypes.

phō″tō·vol·tā′iç, *a.* [*photo-* and *voltaic*.] photoelectric.

phō″tō·xȳ·log′rȧ·phy (-zī-), *n.* [*photo-*, Gr. *xylon*, wood, and *graphein*, to write.] the process of producing an impression on wood by photography and subsequent processes and then printing from the block.

phō·tō·ziñ′ço·gràph, *n.* [*photo-* and *zincograph*.] a plate or a print produced by photozincography.

phō″tō·ziñ·çō·graph′iç, *a.* of or pertaining to photozincography.

phō″tō·ziñ·çog′rȧ·phy, *n.* the use of a zinc plate in photoengraving.

phrag′mȧ, *n.*; *pl.* **phrag′mȧ·tȧ,** [Gr., a fence.] in botany and zoology, a false partition, or septum.

phrag′mō·çōne, *n.* [Gr. *phragma*, fence, and *konos*, cone.] the internal chambered cell of a fossil cephalopod.

phrag·mō·sī′phŏn, *n.* the siphon of a phragmocone.

phrāṣ′ăl, *a.* of or forming a phrase or phrases.

phrāṣe, *n.* [Gr. *phrasis*, from *phrazein*, to speak.]
1. a manner or style of speech, expression; phraseology.
2. a short, colorful, or forceful expression.
3. a connected series of movements in a formal dance.
4. in grammar, a sequence of a few words conveying a single thought or forming a separate part of a sentence but not containing a subject and predicate; specifically, in linguistics, a group of two or more words that can function as a grammatical structure (e.g., *of mine, giving parties, fresh milk.*)
5. in music, a short, distinct part or passage, usually of two, four, or eight measures.
6. in fencing, a short period in which there is a continual thrusting and parrying.
7. in shorthand, a group of characters joined in writing and indicating two or more words.

phrāṣe, *v.t.* and *v.i.*; phrased, *pt.*, *pp.*; phrasing, *ppr.* 1. to express in words or in a phrase.
2. in music, to mark off or divide (notes) into phrases.

phrāṣe′book, *n.* 1. a book explaining idiomatic phrases.
2. in shorthand, a book showing the outlines of various phrases.

phrāṣe′less, *a.* not to be expressed or described.

phrā′ṣē·ō·gram, *n.* [Gr. *phrasis*, *phraseōs*, a phrase, and *gramma*, a letter.] a mark or symbol representing a phrase, as in shorthand.

phrā′ṣē·ō·gràph, *n.* a phrase for which there is a phraseogram.

phrā″ṣē·ō·log′iç, *a.* same as *phraseological*.

phrā″ṣē·ō·log′iç·ăl, *a.* 1. expressing or expressed in phrases.
2. of phraseology.

phrā·ṣē·ol′ō·ġist, *n.* 1. a person who deals with, or pays much attention to, phraseology.
2. a person skilled at coining phrases, catchwords, etc.

phrā·ṣē·ol′ō·ġy, *n.*; *pl.* **phrā·ṣē·ol′ō·ġieṣ,** [Gr. *phrasis*, phrase, and *legein*, to speak.]
1. manner of expression; choice or pattern of words; diction.
2. a collection of phrases in a language; a phrasebook. [Obs.]

phrāṣ′ing, *n.* 1. the act or manner of making phrases; phraseology.
2. in music, the art or act of grouping notes into phrases.
3. in shorthand, the act or art of combining words so as to form a phrase or phrases.

phrā′try, *n.*; *pl.* **phrā′trieṣ,** [Gr. *phratria*, a tribe.]
1. a subdivision of an ancient Greek phyle, or tribe.
2. any of the similar units, as clans, of a primitive tribe.

phrē·at′iç, *a.* [Gr. *phrear* (*-atos*), a well.] in geology, underground; specifically, relating to the underground sources of water, as in a well.

phren-, phreno-.

phrē·net′iç, phrē·net′i·căl, *a.* 1. wild; delirious; insane; frenetic.
2. excessively excited; fanatic.

phrē·net′iç, *n.* a phrenetic person.

phrē·net′i·căl·ly, *adv.* in a phrenetic manner.

phren′iç, *a.* 1. belonging to the diaphragm.
2. pertaining to the mind.

phren·i·ceç′tō·my, *n.* surgical removal of the phrenic nerve.

phren·i·çot′ō·my, *n.* in surgery, the cutting of the phrenic nerve and its accessory to induce a paralysis of one side of the diaphragm: done to immobilize a diseased lung.

phren′içs, *n.* 1. mental philosophy.
2. mental diseases. [Obs.]

phrē′niṣm, *n.* mental activity; mind force; intellectual power.

phrē·nit′iç, *a.* of or having phrenitis.

phrē·nī′tis, *n.* [Gr., from *phrēn*, the mind.]
1. formerly, inflammation of the brain, with acute fever and delirium.
2. inflammation of the diaphragm.

phren′ō-, [from Gr. *phrēn*, *phrenos*, midriff, also mind, mental capacity (thought by the ancients to reside in the diaphragm).] a combining form meaning *the diaphragm* or *the diaphragm and*: also, before a vowel, *phren-*.

phrē·nō·gas′triç, *a.* pertaining to or connecting the stomach and diaphragm.

phrē′nō·gràph, *n.* [Gr. *phrēn*, *phrenos*, diaphragm, and *-graph*.] a device for determining the movement of the diaphragm in respiration.

phrē·nol′ō·gẽr, *n.* a phrenologist.

phren·ō·log′iç·ăl, phren·ō·log′iç, *a.* pertaining to phrenology.

phren·ō·log′iç·ăl·ly, *adv.* by the principles of phrenology.

phrē·nol′ō·ġist, *n.* one who practices phrenology.

phrē·nol′ō·ġy, *n.* [Gr. *phrēn*, the mind, and *logos*, discourse.] a system by which an analysis of character and of the development of faculties can allegedly be made by studying the shape and protuberances of the skull.

phren·ō·mag′net·iṣm, *n.* [Gr. *phrēn*, *phrenos*, the mind, and E. *magnetism*.] the power of exciting the organs of the brain through magnetic influence or through mesmerism.

phren·ō·path′i·ȧ, phrē·nop′ȧ·thy, *n.* [Gr. *phrēn*, *phrenos*, the mind, and *pathos*, suffering.] any mental disease or disorder.

phrē′nō·sin, *n.* [Gr. *phrēn*, *phrenos*, the mind.] a nitrogenous substance, $C_{34}H_{67}NO_8$, said to exist in the brain substance.

phren′ṣied, *a.* same as *frenzied*.

phren′ṣy, *n.*; *pl.* **phren′ṣieṣ,** same as *frenzy*.

phren′ṣy, *v.t.*; phrensied, *pt.*, *pp.*; phrensying, *ppr.* to frenzy.

phren′tiç, *a.* and *n.* phrenetic. [Obs.]

phron·tis·tē′ri·ŏn, phron′tis·tẽr·y, *n.* [Gr. *phrontistērion* from *phronein*, to think; *phrēn*, mind.] a school or seminary of learning. [Obs.]

phryg·ȧ·nē′id, *n.* an insect of the *Phryganeidæ*.

phryg·ȧ·nē′i·dae, *n.pl.* a family of insects including the caddis flies.

Phryġ′i·ăn, *a.* pertaining to Phrygia, an ancient country in central Asia Minor, or to its people, their language, etc.

Phryġ′i·ăn, *n.* **1.** a native or inhabitant of Phrygia.
2. the Indo-Hittite language of the ancient Phrygians, preserved only in fragmentary inscriptions: also *Thraco-Phrygian.*
3. in church history, a Montanist.

Phryġ′i·ăn cap, a close-fitting cap worn by the ancients and adopted as a symbol of liberty during the first French republic.

Phryġ′i·ăn mōde, a sprightly, bold kind of music among the ancient Greeks.

Phryġ′i·ăn stōne, a stone described by the ancients, used in dyeing; a light, spongy stone, resembling pumice, said to be drying and astringent.

Phrȳ′mȧ, *n.* [LL.] a genus of herbs of which the lopseed of eastern Asia and the eastern part of the United States is the only species.

phthal′āte (thal′ *or* fthal′), *n.* a salt derived from phthalic acid: also called *phthalamate.*

phthal′ēin (thal′ *or* fthal′ē-in), *n.* any one of a group of synthetic dyes manufactured from phenols and phthalic anhydride.

phthal′iç, (thal′ *or* fthal′), *a.* [*naphthal*ene and *-ic.*] derived from or contained in naphthalene.
phthalic acid; any of three isomeric acids, $C_6H_4(CO_2H)_2$; specifically, orthophthalic acid, which is produced by the oxidation of naphthalene and is used in the manufacture of dyes, medicines, phenolphthalein, synthetic perfumes, etc.
phthalic anhydride; a white, solid substance, $C_6H_4(CO)_2O$, produced by the oxidation of naphthalene and used to make the phthalein dyes, certain synthetic resins, and other products.

phthal′īde, phthal′id (thal′ *or* fthal′), *n.* [*phthal*yl and anhydr*ide.*] a white crystalline compound, $C_8H_6O_2$, obtained by distilling phthalic acid.

phthal′i·mīde, phthal′i·mid (thal′ *or* fthal′), *n.* [*phthal*ic and *imide.*] a colorless, crystalline compound, $C_8H_5O_2N$, obtained by treating phthalic anhydride with ammonia.

phthal′in (thal′ *or* fthal′), *n.* any of a series of compounds produced by the reduction of phthaleins.

phthal·ō·cȳ′ȧ·nīne, *n.* [from *phthalic* and *cyan-* and *-ine.*] any of a group of synthetic organic dyes of blue or green.

phthal′yl, (thal′ *or* fthal′), *n.* [*phthal*ic and *-yl.*] the bivalent radical of phthalic acid, $C_6H_4(CO)_2$.

phthan′īte (than′ *or* fthan′), *n.* [Gr. *phthanein,* to come first, and *-ite.*] a very compact micaceous or talcose quartz grit, occurring in numerous thin beds in the Cambrian and Silurian formations.

Phthär·tol′ȧ·trae (thär *or* fthär′), *n.pl.* [Gr. *phthartos,* corruptible, and *latreuein,* to worship.] a religious sect of the sixth century which believed that Christ's body, before the Resurrection, was corruptible; a Severian.

phthī′ō·cŏl (thī′), *n.* [from *phthisic* and *-ol,* with *-oc-* interpolated.] a yellow crystalline pigment, $C_{11}H_8O_3$, extracted from tubercle bacilli found in the body and used to prevent or stop hemorrhage.

phthi·rī′ȧ·sis (thi′ *or* thī′), *n.* [Gr. *phtheiriasis,* from *phtheir,* a louse.] infestation with lice; pediculation.

phthiṣ′iç, (tiz′), *n.* in pathology, phthisis.

phthiṣ′iç (tiz′), *a.* phthisical.

phthiṣ′iç·ăl (tiz′), *a.* pertaining to or suffering from phthisis.

phthiṣ′ick·y (tiz′), *a.* phthisical.

phthiṣ·i·ol′ō·ġy (thiz- *or* tiz-), *n.* [*phthisis,* and Gr. *logos,* discourse.] the study of phthisis.

phthiṣ″ip·neū·mō′ni·ȧ (thiz″), *n.* tuberculous pneumonia.

phthī′sis (thī′ *or* fthī′), *n.* [Gr. *phthisis,* decay, from *phthiein,* to waste away.] a wasting away of the body or any of its parts; especially, tuberculosis of the lungs; consumption: earlier usage.

phthoṅ′găl (thoṅg′ *or* fthoṅg′), *a.* [Gr. *phthongos,* voices.] using the voice; sonant. [Rare.]

phthoṅ·gom′ē·tẽr (thoṅg′ *or* fthoṅg′), *n.* [Gr. *phthongos,* sound, and *metron,* measure.] an instrument used for the measuring of vocal sounds.

phul·kä′ri, *n.* [Hind.]
1. embroidery done by natives of India, with a pattern of flowers.
2. the cloth so embroidered.

-phȳ′cē·ae, [Mod. L., from Gr. *phykos,* seaweed.] a combining form meaning *seaweed,* used in forming the botanical names of algae.

-phy′ceous (-shus), a combining form used to form adjectives derived from nouns ending in *-phyceae.*

phȳ′ċō·ċhrōme, *n.* [Gr. *phykos,* seaweed, and *chrōma,* color.] a bluish-green coloring matter found in certain algae.

phȳ·ċō·cȳ′ȧ·nin, phȳ·ċō·cȳ′ȧ·nīne, *n.* [Gr. *phykos,* seaweed, and *kyanos,* blue, and *-in.*] a blue pigment found in several red seaweeds.

phȳ″ċō·ē·ryth′rin, *n.* [Gr. *phykos,* seaweed, and *erthros,* red.] a red coloring matter found in several red seaweeds.

phȳ·cog′rȧ·phy, *n.* [Gr. *phykos,* seaweed, and *-graphy.*] a delineation or description of seaweeds.

phȳ·ċol′ō·ġist, *n.* one skilled in phycology.

phȳ·ċol′ō·ġy, *n.* [Gr. *phykos,* seaweed, and *logos,* discourse.] that branch of botany dealing with seaweeds or algae; algology.

Phȳ·ċō·mȳ′cēṣ, *n.* [Gr. *phykos,* seaweed, and *mykes,* fungus.] a genus of phycomycetous fungi, containing three species, of which the best known is *Phycomyces nitens.*

Phȳ″ċō·mȳ·cē′tē·ae, *n.pl.* a large division of fungi closely resembling the algae.

Phȳ″ċō·mȳ·cē′tēṣ, *n.pl.* the *Phycomyceteæ.*

phȳ″ċō·mȳ·cē′tous, *a.* belonging or pertaining to the *Phycomyceteæ.*

phȳ·ċō·phae′in, *n.* [Gr. *phykos,* seaweed, and *phaios,* dusky.] a reddish-brown pigment found in certain algae.

phȳ·ċō·xan′thin, phȳ·ċō·xan′thine (-zan′), *n.* [Gr. *phykos,* seaweed, and *xanthos,* yellow, and *-in.*] same as *diatomin.*

phyg·ō·gȧ·laç′tiç, *n.* [Gr. *phygein,* to avoid, and *galaktos,* milk.] anything which checks or arrests the secretion of milk.

phȳ′lȧ, *n.* plural of *phylon.*

phȳ′lȧ, *n.* plural of *phylum.*

phȳ·laç″ō·bī·ō·sis, *n.* [Gr. *phylaxis,* guardian, and *bios,* life.] in zoology, the living together, in close association, of a certain species of ant and a group of termites in the same nest: the ant is believed to protect its host.

phy·laç′tẽred, *a.* wearing a phylactery. [Obs.]

phyl·aç·ter′iç, phyl·aç·ter′iç·ăl, *a.* pertaining to phylacteries.

phy·laç′tẽr·y, *n.*; *pl.* **phy·laç′tẽr·ieṣ,** [Gr. *phylaktērion,* a fort, from *phylassein,* to defend or guard.]
1. a small, leather case holding slips inscribed with Scripture passages: one is fastened with leather thongs to the forehead and one to the left arm by men of orthodox Jewish faith during morning prayer: cf. Deut. xi. 18.
2. a reminder.
3. something worn as a charm or safeguard.

PHYLACTERIES

phy·laç′tō·cärp, *n.* [Gr. *phylaktos,* verbal adj. of *phylassein,* to guard, and *karpos,* fruit.] a branch-bearing gonangia, as in some hydroids.

Phy·laç·tō·lae′mȧ·tȧ, *n.pl.* [Gr. *phylaktos,* verbal adj. of *phylassein,* to guard, and *laimos,* throat.] an order of polyzoans, the *Lophopoda* or *Hippocrepia.*

phyl·aç·tō·lae′mȧ·tous, *a.* pertaining to the *Phylactolæmata.*

phȳ′lärċh, *n.* [Gr. *phylē,* tribe, and *archein,* to rule.] in Greek antiquity, the chief or governor of a tribe or clan.

phȳ′lärċh·y, *n.* in ancient Greece, government of a tribe or clan; the office of a phylarch.

phȳ·lax′is, *n.* [Gr. *phylaxis,* guarding.] in medicine, any of the body's natural defenses against infection, as immunity, phagocytosis, etc.

phȳ′lē, *n.*; *pl.* **phȳ′lae,** [Gr. *phylē,* a tribe.] a tribe, or clan; one of the divisions into which the ancient Athenians were divided. They were at first four in number, afterward ten.

phȳ·let′iç, *a.* in biology, of a phylum or subkingdom; racial.

phyll-, phyl′lō-, [from Gr. *phyllon,* a leaf.] a combining form meaning *leaf,* as in *phyllophagous.*

-phyll, [from Gr. *phyllon,* leaf.] a combining form meaning *leaf,* as in sporo*phyll.*

Phyl·lan′thus, *n.* [*phyll-,* and Gr. *anthos,* flower.] a large genus of plants of the spurge family, having alternate leaves and apetalous flowers. There are between four and five hundred species, widely dispersed throughout the tropics.

Phyl′lis, *n.* [L.; Gr. *Phyllis,* lit., green leaf, green bough.]
1. a country maiden in Virgil's *Eclogues.*
2. (a) any pretty country girl; (b) a sweetheart. [Poet.]
Also spelled *Phillis.*

phyl′līte, *n.* [Gr. *phyllon,* a leaf, and *-ite.*]
1. a greenish-gray to black mineral occurring in small shining scales or plates in a clay slate, the crystallization being probably monoclinic. It is essentially a hydrated silicate of aluminum, sesquioxide and protoxide of iron, protoxide of manganese, and potash.
2. a slaty rock intermediate between mica schist and ordinary clay slate.

phyl·lit′iç, *a.* pertaining to phyllite.

Phyl′li·um, *n.* [Gr. *phyllon,* a leaf.] a genus of orthopterous insects belonging to the family *Phasmidæ,* and popularly known as *leaf insects* or *walking leaves.* They are for the most part native to the East Indies, Australia, and South America. The males have long antennae and wings, and can fly; the females have short antennae and are incapable of flight.

phyl·lō·braṅ′ċhi·ȧ, *n.*; *pl.* **phyl·lō·braṅ′ċhi·ae,** a lamellar gill of a crustacean.

phyl·lō·braṅ′ċhi·ăl, *a.* pertaining to phyllobranchiae.

phyl·lō·braṅ′ċhi·āte, *a.* provided with phyllobranchiae, as a crustacean.

phyl′lō·ċlāde, phyl′lō·ċlad, *n.* [Gr. *phyllon,* a leaf, and *klados,* a branch.] a flattened branch or stem functioning as a leaf.

phyl·lō·ċlā′di·um, *n.*; *pl.* **phyl·lō·ċlā′di·ȧ,** a phylloclade.

phyl·lō·cȳ′ȧ·nin, *n.* [*phyllo-,* and Gr. *kyanos,* blue, and *-ine.*] a blue coloring matter existing in chlorophyll.

phyl′lō·cyst, *n.* [*phyllo-,* and Gr. *kystis,* bladder.] a cavity within the hydrophyllia of certain oceanic hydrozoans.

phyl·lō·cyst′iç, *a.* pertaining to a phyllocyst.

phyl′lōde, *n.* [Gr. *phyllōdēs,* leaflike, from *phyllon,* a leaf, and *eidos,* form.] a flat leaf stalk that functions as a leaf.

phyl·lō·din′ē·ous, *a.* pertaining to or like a phyllode.

phyl·lō·din·i·ā′tion, *n.* the condition of being phyllodineous.

phyl·lō′di·um, *n.*; *pl.* **phyl·lō′di·ȧ,** a phyllode.

phyl′lō·dy, *n.* [Gr. *phyllōdēs,* leaflike, from *phyllon* and *eidos,* form.] in botany, the transformation of floral organs into foliage leaves.

a, PHYLLODE (*Acacia heterophylla*)

phyl·loġ′e·nous, *a.* [*phyllo-* and *-genous.*] growing upon a leaf.

phyl′loid, *a.* [*phyll-* and *-oid.*] like a leaf.

phyl′lō·man·cy, *n.* [*phyllo-,* and Gr. *manteia,* divination.] divination by means of leaves.

phyl·lō·mā′ni·ȧ, *n.* [*phyllo-,* and Gr. *mania,* madness.] an abnormal development of leafy tissue; the production of leaves in unusual numbers or in unusual places.

phyl′lōme, *n.* [Gr. *phyllōma,* leafage.] in botany, a leaf or analogous member.

phyl·lom′iç, *a.* of a phyllome.

phyl″lō·mọr′phō·sis, *n.* [*phyllo-* and *morphosis.*] the study of the succession and variation of leaves during different seasons.

phyl′lō·mọr·phy, *n.* same as *phyllody.*

phyl·loph′ȧ·găn, *n.* [*phyllo-,* and Gr. *phagein,* to eat.] any individual of the *Phyllophaga,* a genus of hymenopterous insects containing the sawflies; any of the *Phyllophaga,* a division of lamellicorn beetles, feeding on leaves, etc., as, the chafers.

phyl·loph′ȧ·gous, *a.* [*phyllo-,* and Gr. *phagein,* to eat.] leaf-eating; feeding on leaves.

phyl·loph′ō·rous, *a.* [*phyllo-,* and Gr. *pherein,* to bear.] leaf-bearing; producing leaves.

phyl′lō·pod, *n.* a crustacean belonging to the order *Phyllopoda.*

phyl′lō·pod, *a.* pertaining to the *Phyllopoda.*

Phyl·lop′ō·dȧ, *n.pl.* [*phyllo-,* and Gr. *pous, podos,* foot.] an order of crustaceans of the division *Branchiopoda,* with leaflike, swimming feet.

phyl·lop′ŏ·dăn, *a.* and *n.* phyllopod.

phyl·lop′ō·dous, *a.* phyllopod.

phyl′lō·rhīne (-rīn), *a.* [*phyllo-,* and Gr. *rhis, rhinos,* nose.] of or pertaining to a subfamily of bats, *Phyllorhininæ,* having a leaflike membrane around the nostrils and but two phalanges to a toe.

phyl·lō·sō′mȧ, *n.* [*phyllo-*, and Gr. *sōma*, body.] the larval stage of certain crustaceans, as the spiny lobsters.

phyl·lō·stom′ȧ·tous, *a.* pertaining to the *Phyllostomatidæ*, a family of leaf-nosed bats of tropical America.

phyl′lō·stōme, *n.* [Gr. *phyllon*, a leaf, and *stoma*, a mouth.] a leaf-nosed bat, a member of the family *Phyllostomatidæ*.

phyl·los′tō·mīne (*or* -min), *a.* relating to the *Phyllostomatinæ*, a subfamily of leaf-nosed bats; phyllostomatous.

phyl·lō·taç′tiç, *a.* pertaining to phyllotaxis.

phyl′lō·tax·y, phyl·lō·tax′is, *n.* [*phyllo-*, and Gr. *taxis*, arrangement.]

1. the arrangement of the leaves on the stem of a plant. The three common positions are alternate, opposite, and verticillate.

2. the science of the distribution and arrangement of leaves.

phyl′lō·tax·y, *n.* phyllotaxis.

-phyl′lous, a combining form meaning *having* (a specified form or kind of) *leaves, leaflets*, etc., as in hetero*phyllous*.

phyl·lō·xan′thin (-zan′), *n.* [*phyllo-*, and Gr. *xanthos*, yellow, and *-in*.] same as *xanthophyll*.

Phyl·lox·ē′rȧ, *n.* [*phyllo-*, and Gr. *xēros*, dry.]

1. a genus of aphids, or plant lice. *Phylloxera vastatrix* is very destructive to grapevines.

2. [p–] a member of the genus *Phylloxera*.

phȳ·lō·ġen′e·sis, *n.* phylogeny.

phȳ″lō·ġē·net′iç, *a.* of or pertaining to phylogeny.

phȳ·lō·ġen′iç, *a.* of phylogeny.

phȳ·loġ′e·ny, *n.*; *pl.* **phȳ·loġ′e·niēs,** [Gr. *phylē*, tribe, and E. *genesis*.] the racial history or evolutionary development of any plant or animal species.

phȳ′lon, *n.*; *pl.* **phȳ′lȧ,** [Gr. *phylon*, race, tribe.] in biology, a phylum.

phȳ′lum, *n.*; *pl.* **phȳ′lȧ,** [Mod. L., from Gr. *phyllon*, tribe.]

1. any of the broad, basic divisions of the plant or animal kingdom.

2. any of the broad, basic divisions of the linguistic families.

phȳ′mȧ, *n.*; *pl.* **phȳ′mȧ·tȧ,** [Gr., from *phyein*, to produce.] a skin tumor or cutaneous nodule.

phȳ″mȧ·tō·rhȳ′sin (-rī), *n.* [Gr. *phyma* (*-atos*), tumor, and *rhousios*, reddish.] a dark pigment found in hair and melanotic tumors: a form of melanin.

-phȳre, [Fr., from *porphyre*.] a combining form meaning *a porphyritic rock*.

Phȳ′sȧ, *n.* [Gr. *physa*, a pair of bellows.] a genus of snails or gastropods with sinistral shells. There are about forty extinct and twenty living species, the latter found in North America, Europe, South Africa, India, and the Philippines.

Phȳ·sā′li·ȧ, *n.* [Gr. *physalis*, a bubble or bladder.] a genus of hydrozoa of the subclass *Siponophora* and family *Physaliidæ*, remarkable for size, brilliant color, and the severe burning pain produced by contact. The *Physalia atlantica* or *pelagica* is known as the Portuguese man-of-war. These hydrozoa are characterized by one or more large air sacs, by which they float on the surface of the tropical ocean.

phȳ·sā′li·ăn, *a.* of or pertaining to the *Physalia*.

phȳ·sā′li·ăn, *n.* any hydrozoan of the *Physaliidæ*.

Phys·ȧ·lī′i·dae, *n.pl.* a family of hydrozoans, being vesicular gelatinous bodies, having beneath them vermiform tentacles and suckers, intermingled with long filiform tentacles.

Phys′ȧ·lis, *n.* [Gr. *physalis*, bladder.] a genus of American herbs of the nightshade family, characterized by a bladdery calyx which encloses the globose edible fruit: also called *ground cherry*. The *Physalis alkekengi* is called *strawberry tomato*.

phys′ȧ·līte, *n.* [Gr. *physalis*, bladder.] a mineral of a greenish-white color, a variety of topaz: also called *pyrophysalite*.

phȳ·sē′tēr, *n.* [Gr. *physētēr*, blowpipe; *physān*, to puff out.]

1. a sperm whale; the cachalot.

2. a device for filtering worked by atmospheric pressure.

3. [P–] the typical genus of the subfamily *Physeterinæ* comprising the cachalots or sperm whales.

phyş·i·an′thrō·py, *n.* [Gr. *physis*, nature, and *anthrōpos*, man.] the study of the constitution of man, his diseases, and their remedies. [Rare.]

phyş·i·at′riçs, *n.* [Gr. *physis*, nature, and *iatreia*, healing.] the cure of disease by nature.

phyş′iç, *n.* [OFr. *phisique*, *phisike*; Fr. *physique*, from L. *physica*, natural science, from Gr. *physikē*, from *physis*, nature, from *phyein*, to produce.]

1. the art or science of healing diseases; the art of medicine and therapeutics. [Archaic.]

2. a medicine, especially a medicine that purges; a laxative or cathartic.

3. the science of physics. [Rare.]

phyş′iç, *v.t.*; physicked, *pt.*, *pp.*; physicking, *ppr.* 1. to dose with medicine, especially with a cathartic.

2. to cause to have a bowel movement.

3. to have a curative effect on; to heal; relieve.

phyş′iç·ăl, *a.* [Gr. *physikos*, pertaining to nature.]

1. of nature and all matter; natural; material: opposed to *spiritual, moral, mental*.

2. of natural science or natural philosophy.

3. of or according to the laws of nature; as, the force of gravity is a *physical* fact.

4. of, or produced by the forces of, physics.

5. of the body as opposed to the mind; as, *physical* exercise.

6. relating to the art of healing; as, a *physical* treatise. [Rare.]

7. medicinal; promoting the cure of diseases. [Obs.]

8. resembling medicine; as, a *physical* taste. [Obs.]

physical astronomy; the branch of astronomy which treats of the motions, masses, positions, etc. of celestial bodies.

physical chemistry; the branch of chemistry dealing with the physical properties of substances as they relate to the chemical properties and changes.

physical education; instruction in the exercise, care, and hygiene of the human body; especially, a course in gymnastics, athletics, etc., as in a school or college.

physical examination; an examination of the body to determine the health or condition of a person.

physical geography; the study of the features and nature of the earth's surface, atmosphere and climate, distribution of plant and animal life, etc.

physical science; any of the sciences that deal with inanimate matter or energy, as physics, chemistry, geology, etc.

physical signs; signs of the state of the body, as revealed by a medical examination, as eruptions, swellings, etc.

physical therapy, the treatment of disease, injury, etc. by physical means rather than with drugs, as by massage, infrared or ultraviolet light, electrotherapy, hydrotherapy, heat, or exercise: also called *physiotherapy*.

Syn.—natural, material, visible, tangible, substantial, corporeal, sensible.

phyş′iç·ăl·ly, *adv.* 1. with reference to the laws of nature; materially.

2. with regard to the body; corporeally.

phy·şi′ciăn (-zish′un), *n.* [ME. *phisicien*; OFr. *physicien*; It. *fisiciano*; L. *physicus*; Gr. *physikos*, a scientist, from *physis*, nature.]

1. a person licensed to practice medicine; a doctor of medicine.

2. a general medical practitioner, as distinguished from a surgeon.

3. any person or thing that heals, relieves, or comforts.

phy·şi′ciăned, *a.* licensed to practise medicine. [Obs.]

phyş′i·çişm, *n.* the practice of ascribing everything in the universe to physical or material causes; materialism.

phyş′i·cist, *n.* an expert in physics.

phyş′iç nut, the nut or seed of several species of *Jatropha*, a genus of the *Euphorbiaceæ*: also called *Barbados nut*.

phyş″i·çō·çhem′iç·ăl, *a.* caused by the action, or involving the principles, of both physics and chemistry.

phyş″i·çō·loġ′iç, *n.* logic illustrated by natural philosophy.

phyş″i·çō·loġ′iç·ăl, *a.* pertaining to physicologic.

phyş″i·çō·math·e·mat′içs, *n.* mathematics applied to the investigation and solution of physical conceptions and problems; mixed mathematics.

phyş″i·çō·phi·los′ō·phy, *n.* natural philosophy.

phyş″i·çō·thē·ol′ō·ġy, *n.* theology illustrated or enforced by physics or natural philosophy.

phyş″i·çō·ther″ȧ·peū′tiç, *a.* relating to physiotherapy, or physical therapy.

phyş″i·çō·ther″ȧ·peū′tiçs, *n.* physiotherapy, or physical therapy.

phyş″i·çō·ther′ȧ·py, *n.* physiotherapy, or physical therapy.

phyş′içs, *n.pl.* [*construed as sing. in senses* 1 *and* 2.] [Gr. *physika*, physical or natural things.]

1. originally, natural science or natural philosophy.

2. the science dealing with the properties, changes, interaction, etc. of matter and energy: physics is subdivided into mechanics, thermodynamics, optics, acoustics, etc.

3. a book or treatise on this.

4. physical properties or processes; as, the *physics* of flight.

phyş′i·ō-, [from Gr. *physis*, nature.] a combining form meaning *nature, natural*, as in *physio*graphy: also, before a vowel, *physi-*.

phyş·i·oç′rȧ·cy, *n.* the economic plan and doctrines of the physiocrats; physiocratism.

phyş′i·ō·çrat, *n.* [Gr. *physis*, nature, and *kratein*, to rule.] a believer in the economic theory that land and its products are the only true wealth and hence the only logical sources of revenue and that freedom of opportunity and trade and security of person and property are essential to prosperity.

phyş″i·ō·çrat′iç, *a.* of or pertaining to the theories of the physiocrats.

phyş·i·oç′rȧ·tişm, *n.* same as *physiocracy*.

phyş″i·ō·ġen′e·sis, *n.* same as *physiogeny*.

phyş″i·ō·ġē·net′iç, *a.* same as *physiogenic*.

phyş″i·ō·ġen′iç, *a.* pertaining to physiogeny; relating to physiological evolution and development.

phyş·i·oġ′e·ny, *n.* [Gr. *physis*, nature, and root of *gignesthai*, to come into being.] in biology, the science or history of the evolution of vital activities in the individual; the genesis of organic functions: a branch of ontogeny.

phyş·i·og′nō·mēr, *n.* see *physiognomist*.

phyş″i·og·nom′iç, *a.* pertaining to physiognomy.

phyş″i·og·nom′iç·ăl, *a.* same as *physiognomic*.

phyş″i·og·nom′iç·ăl·ly, *adv.* in accordance with the principles of physiognomy.

phyş″i·og·nom′içs, *n.* same as *physiognomy*.

phyş·i·og′nō·mist, *n.* a person who tries to judge character and mental qualities by observing the facial features.

phyş·i·og′nō·mīze, *v.t.*; physiognamized, *pt.*, *pp.*; physiognamizing, *ppr.* to study the physiognomy of. [Rare.]

phyş·i·og·nō·mon′iç, *a.* same as *physiognomic*.

phyş·i·og′nō·my, *n.* [from Gr. *physiognōmonia*; *physis*, nature, and *gnōmōn*, one who knows, from stem of *gignōskein*, to know.]

1. the practice of trying to judge character and mental qualities by observation of bodily, especially facial, features.

2. the face; facial features and expression, especially as supposedly indicative of character.

3. apparent characteristics; outward features or appearance.

phyş·i·oġ′ō·ny, *n.* [Gr. *physis*, nature, and *gonē*, generation.] the production or generation of nature.

phyş″i·og′rȧ·phēr, *n.* a specialist in physiography.

phyş″i·ō·graph′iç, *a.* pertaining to physiography.

phyş″i·ō·graph′iç·ăl, *a.* same as *physiographic*.

phyş·i·og′rȧ·phy, *n.* [Gr. *physis*, nature, and *graphein*, to describe.]

1. a description of the features and phenomena of nature.

2. physical geography.

phyş·i·ol′ȧ·try, *n.* [Gr. *physis*, nature, and *latreia*, worship.] the cult of the powers of nature; nature worship.

phyş·i·ol′ō·ġēr, *n.* a physiologist. [Rare.]

phyş″i·ō·loġ′iç, *a.* same as *physiological*.

phyş″i·ō·loġ′iç·ăl, *a.* 1. of physiology.

2. characteristic of or promoting normal, or healthy, functioning.

phyş″i·ō·loġ′iç·ăl·ly, *adv.* 1. according to the principles of physiology.

2. so as to be physiological.

phyş·i·ol′ō·ġist, *n.* a specialist in physiology.

phyş·i·ol′ō·ġīze, *v.i.*; physiologized, *pt.*, *pp.*; physiologizing, *ppr.* to engage in physiological speculation or investigation.

phys·i·ol′ō·gy, *n.* [Fr. *physiologie*; Gr. *physiologia*; *physis*, nature, and *logos*, discourse.]
 1. the branch of biology dealing with the functions and vital processes of living organisms or their parts and organs.
 2. a book or treatise on this subject.
 3. the functions and vital processes, collectively (*of* an organism).
 Distinguished from *anatomy, morphology.*

phys·i·os′ō·phy, *n.* a doctrine concerning the secrets of nature.

phys″i·ō·ther″ȧ·peū′tiç, *a.* relating to physiotherapy.

phys″i·ō·ther″ȧ·peū′tiçs, *n.* physiotherapy.

phys″i·ō·ther′ȧ·pist, *n.* one skilled in physiotherapy.

phys″i·ō·ther′ȧ·py, *n.* the treatment of disease, injury, etc. by mechanical and physical means, such as massage, electricity, exercise, heat, etc.; physical therapy.

phy·ṣique′ (-zēk′), *n.* [Fr.] the structure, form, constitution, strength, or appearance of the body.

phyṣ′nō·my, *n.* physiognomy. [Obs.]

phyṣ·ō·çlis′tiç, *a.* same as *physoclistous.*

phyṣ·ō·çlis′tous, *a.* [Gr. *physa*, bellows, and *kleistos*, that can be closed, from *kleiein*, to close.] pertaining to the *Physoclisti*, a group of fishes having the air bladder without a duct or closed.

phyṣ′ō·grāde, *n.* [Gr. *physa*, bellows, and L. *gradi*, to go.] one of a group of siphonophores which swim by means of air bladders; a jellyfish having a vesicular organ full of air, which buoys it up and enables it to float on the ocean.

Phȳ·sō·neç′tae, *n.pl.* [Gr. *physa*, bellows, and *nēktēs*, swimmer.] the *Physophoræ*.

Phȳ·soph′ō·rae, *n.pl.* [Gr. *physa*, bellows, and *pherein*, to bear.] an order of siphonophores having a pneumatophore.

phȳ·soph′ō·răn, *a.* same as *physophorous.*

phȳ·soph′ō·răn, *n.* a member of the *Physophoræ*.

phȳ·soph′ō·rous, *a.* pertaining to the *Physophoræ*.

phȳ′sō·pod, *n.* [Gr. *physa*, bellows, and *pous, podos*, foot.] in zoology, a member of the *Physopoda*.

Phȳ·sop′ō·dȧ, *n.pl.* the *Thysanoptera*. [Obs.]

phȳ·sō·stig′mīne, phȳ·sō·stig′min, *n.* [Gr. *physa*, bellows, and *stigma*, mark, and *-ine.*] a colorless or pinkish crystalline alkaloid, $C_{15}H_{21}O_2N_3$, extracted from the Calabar bean, used in medicine for stimulating intestinal muscles and for contracting the pupils of the eyes.

Phȳ·sos′tō·mī, *n.pl.* [Gr. *physa*, bellows, and *stoma*, a mouth.] an order of malacopterous fishes with the ventral fins abdominal or absent, and the air bladder when present provided with a duct.

phȳ·sos′tō·mous, *a.* in zoology, (a) of or pertaining to the *Physostomi*; (b) having an air bladder supplied with a duct.

phȳ·tal′bū·mōse, *n.* [Gr. *phyton*, plant; and *albumen*, and *-ose.*] an albumose of vegetable origin.

-phȳte, [from Gr. *phyton*, plant.] a combining form meaning *a plant growing in a* (specified) *way* or *place*, as in micro*phyte*.

Phȳ·tel′e·phas, *n.* [Gr. *phyton*, plant, and *elephas*, ivory.] a genus of plants inhabiting tropical America, the type of the family *Phytelephantinæ*. *Phytelephas macrocarpa*, the ivory plant of South America, resembles the palms in its fronds, which equal those of the cocoanut in dimensions, and also in the structure and weight of its fruit.

phȳ′ti·fọrm, *a.* [Gr. *phyton*, plant, and *-form.*] having the form of a plant.

phȳ′tin, *n.* [*phyt-* and *-in.*] a calcium-magnesium salt derived from the seeds of hemp, sunflowers, peas, beans, etc.

phȳ·tiv′ō·rous, *a.* [Gr. *phyton*, a plant, and L. *vorare*, to eat.] feeding on plants or herbage; herbivorous. [Rare.]

phȳ′tō-, phȳt-, [from Gr. *phyton*, a plant.] a combining form meaning *a plant, flora, vegetation*, as in *phyto*genesis, *phyto*geography, etc.

phȳ·tō·bī·ol′ō·gy, *n.* that branch of biology which treats of plants.

phȳ·tō·braṅ′chi·āte, *a.* provided with leaflike gills, as certain of the *Isopoda*.

phȳ·tō·chem′iç·ăl, *a.* pertaining to phytochemistry.

phȳ·tō·chem′is·try, *n.* [*phyto-* and *chemistry.*] the chemistry of plants.

phȳ′tō·chlōre, *n.* in botany, chlorophyll. [Obs.]

phȳ·tō·ġen′e·sis, *n.* the history of the development of plants.

phȳ″tō·ġē·net′iç, *a.* of or according to phytogenesis.

phȳ″tō·ġē·net′iç·ăl, *a.* phytogenetic.

phȳ·tō·ġen′iç, *a.* 1. of, or largely of, plant origin, as peat or coal.
 2. phytogenetic.

phȳ·toġ′e·nous, *a.* phytogenic.

phȳ·toġ′e·ny, *n.* phytogenesis.

phȳ″tō·ġē·og′rȧ·phẽr, *n.* an expert in phytogeography.

phȳ·tō·ġē·ō·graph′iç, *a.* pertaining to phytogeography.

phȳ·tō·ġē·ō·graph′iç·ăl, *a.* phytogeographic.

phȳ″tō·ġē·og′rȧ·phy, *n.* the geographical distribution of plants.

phȳ·tog′rȧ·phẽr, *n.* one skilled in phytography.

phȳ·tō·graph′iç, *a.* pertaining to phytography or the description of plants.

phȳ·tō·graph′iç·ăl, *a.* phytographic.

phȳ·tog′rȧ·phy, *n.* [*phyto-*, and Gr. *graphē*, description.] a description of plants, or that branch of botany which concerns itself with the rules to be observed in describing and naming plants.

phȳ′toid, *a.* [*phyt-*, and Gr. *eidos*, likeness.] plantlike; specifically, in zoology, applied to animals or organs having a plantlike appearance.

Phȳ·tō·laç′cȧ, *n.* [*phyto-*, and *lacca*, a Latinized form of *lac*, in allusion to the crimson color of the fruit.] a genus of tropical or subtropical herbaceous plants, with erect or occasionally twining stems, a thickish turnip-shaped root, alternate undivided broad leaves, and leafless erect racemes of flowers, succeeded by deep purple berries.

Phȳ″tō·laç·cā′cē·ae, *n.pl.* in botany, the pokeweed family, including 10 genera and some 60 species. The genus *Phytolacca* is the type of the order.

phȳ″tō·laç·cā′ceous, *a.* of or pertaining to the *Phytolaccaceæ*.

phȳ·tō·laç′cin, *n.* [from *Phytolacca.*] a concentration prepared from the root of *Phytolacca decandra*, and used in medicine.

phȳ′tō·līte, *n.* [*phyto-*, and Gr. *lithos*, a stone.] a fossil plant. [Obs.]

phȳ″tō·li·thol′ō·ġist, *n.* an expert in phytolithology.

phȳ″tō·li·thol′ō·gy, *n.* [*phyto-*, and Gr. *lithos*, stone, and *logos*, discourse.] the science dealing with fossil plants; paleobotany.

phȳ·tō·loġ′iç, *a.* of or according to phytology; botanical.

phȳ·tō·loġ′iç·ăl, *a.* phytologic.

phȳ·tol′ō·ġist, *n.* an expert in plants or in phytology; a botanist.

phȳ·tol′ō·gy, *n.* the scientific study of plants; botany. [Rare.]

phȳ′tō·mẽr, *n.* [*phyto-*, and Gr. *meros*, part.] in botany, a structural unit of a plant; a bud-bearing node.

phȳ·tom′e·ron, *n.*; *pl.* **phȳ·tom′e·rȧ,** a phytomer.

phȳ′ton, *n.* [Gr., plant.] a phytomer.

phȳ·ton′ō·my, *n.* [*phyto-*, and Gr. *nomos*, law.] the science of the origin and development of plants.

phȳ·tō·pā″lē·on·tol′ō·ġist, *n.* a paleobotanist.

phȳ·tō·pā″lē·on·tol′ō·gy, *n.* paleobotany.

phȳ·tō·path·ō·loġ′iç·ăl, *a.* pertaining to phytopathology.

phȳ″tō·pȧ·thol′ō·ġist, *n.* a student of or expert in phytopathology.

phȳ″tō·pȧ·thol′ō·gy, *n.* [*phyto-*, and Gr. *pathos*, suffering, and *logos*, discourse.] scientific knowledge relating to the diseases of plants.

Phȳ·toph′ȧ·gȧ, *n.pl.* [*phyto-*, and Gr. *phagein*, to eat.] in entomology, one of the divisions of hymenopterous insects, including the sawflies; also, a division of coleopterous beetles several species of which are very destructive.

phȳ·toph′ȧ·găn, *a.* phytophagous.

phȳ·toph′ȧ·găn, *n.* any individual of the *Phytophaga*: applied particularly to a beetle of that division.

phȳ·tō·phaġ′iç, *a.* phytophagous.

phȳ·toph′ȧ·gous, *a.* [*phyto-*, and Gr. *phagein*, to eat.]
 1. eating or subsisting on plants; herbivorous.
 2. pertaining to the *Phytophaga*.

phȳ·toph′ȧ·ġy, *n.* the eating of or subsisting on plants.

phȳ·toph′il·ous, *a.* [*phyto-*, and Gr. *philein*, to love.] attracted to plants, as some insects.

Phȳ·toph′thō·rȧ, *n.* [*phyto-*, and Gr. *phthora*, destruction.] a genus of parasitic fungi, the mycelium, which is uniseptate, ramifying deeply the tissues of higher plants. *Phytophthora infestans* is the potato blight, and *Phytophthora omnivora* destroys many kinds of garden and nursery plants.

phȳ·tō·phyṣ·i·ol′ō·gy, *n.* [*phyto-* and *physiology.*] the physiology of plants.

phȳ·tō′sis, *n.* [*phyt-* and *-osis.*] in medicine, any disease caused by vegetable parasites.

phȳ·tos′tẽr·in, *n.* [*phyto-* and *cholesterin.*] a fatty compound of the nature of cholesterin, occurring in the seeds and sprouts of plants.

phȳ·tot′ō·mist, *n.* one skilled in phytotomy.

phȳ·tot′ō·mous, *a.* cutting plants or their leaves: applied to some insects and birds.

phȳ·tot′ō·my, *n.* [*phyto-*, and Gr. *temnein*, to cut.] the anatomy or dissection of plants.

phȳ″tō·vi·tel′lin, *n.* [*phyto-* and *vitellin.*] a globulin; a vegetable proteid occurring in the kernels of oats, wheat, rye, etc.

phȳ·tō·zō′ȧ, *n.* plural of *phytozoon.*

Phȳ″tō·zō·ā′ri·ȧ, *n.pl.* [*phyto-*, and Gr. *zōon*, animal.] in zoology, one of the classes of protozoans usually called *Infusoria*.

phȳ·tō·zō′on, *n.*; *pl.* **phȳ·tō·zō′ȧ,** [*phyto-*, and Gr. *zōon*, animal.] a zoophyte.

phyz, *n.* same as *phiz.*

pī, pīe, *n.* 1. a mixed, disordered collection of printing type.
 2. any jumble or mixture.

pī, pīe, *v.t.*; pied, *pt.*, *pp.*; pieing, *ppr.* to mix or disarrange, as type; to make jumbled or disordered.

pī, *n.* [Gr.] the Greek letter (Π π) standing sixteenth in that alphabet, and corresponding to English *P, p*. It is used in mathematics to represent the ratio of the circumference of a circle to the diameter, the numerical value of which is 3.14159265+.

pī′ȧ, *n.* same as *pia mater.*

pī′ȧ, *n.* [Polynesian.] an Asiatic herb which is perennial, and has thick, tuberlike roots from which a kind of starch is obtained.

pi·ȧ·ça′ba (pē-ȧ-sä′vȧ), *n.* same as *piassava.*

pi·ȧ·çe′vō·le (-chā′), *adv.* [It.] in music, pleasingly; gaily; gracefully: a direction to the performer.

pī′ȧ·cle, *n.* [L. *piaculum.*] an enormous crime, or a sin; hence, that which requires expiation. [Obs.]

pī·aç′ū·lăr, *a.* [L. *piacularis*, from *piare*, to expiate.]
 1. expiatory; having power to atone.
 2. criminal; atrociously bad; requiring expiation.

pī·aç·ū·lar′i·ty, *n.* the condition of being piacular; the quality of wickedness; criminality.

pī·aç′ū·lous, *a.* same as *piacular.*

piaffe (pyaf), *v.i.*; piaffed, *pt.*, *pp.*; piaffing, *ppr.* to perform the piaffer.

piaf′fẽr (pyaf′), *n.* [substantive use of Fr. *piaffer*, to paw the ground, from Pr. *piafá*, to prance; of Gmc. origin.] a slow movement in horsemanship in which the animal simultaneously raises one forefoot and the opposite hind foot while standing in place.

pī′ăl, *a.* of or pertaining to the pia, or pia mater.

pī′ȧ·lyn, *n.* same as *steapsin.*

pī′ȧ mā′tẽr, [ML., from L., pious or gentle mother.] the vascular membrane immediately enveloping the brain and spinal chord and surrounded by the arachnoid and dura mater.

pī″ȧ-mā′trăl, *a.* of or pertaining to the pia mater.

pī·an′, *n.* same as frambesia.

pi·ȧ·nette′, *n.* a small upright piano.

pi·ȧ·nī′nō, *n.* [It., dim. of *piano.*] a pianette.

pi·ȧ·nis′si·mō, *a.* and *adv.* [It., superl. of *piano.*] in music, very soft: a direction to the performer.

pi·ȧ·nis′si·mō, *n.*; *pl.* **pi·ȧ·nis′si·mōṣ** or **pi·ȧ·nis′si·mī,** a passage to be performed pianissimo.

pi·an′ist (*or* pē′ȧ-), *n.* a person who plays the piano.

pi·ä′nō, *a.* and *adv.* [It., from L. *planus*, plain.] in music, soft: a direction to the performer.

pi·ä′nō, *n.*; *pl.* **pi·ä′nōṣ,** a passage to be performed piano.

pi·an′ō (*or* -än′), *n.*; *pl.* **pi·an′ōṣ,** [It., from *pianoforte.*] a large, stringed, percussion instrument played from a keyboard, each key of which operates a small, felt-covered hammer that strikes and vibrates a corresponding steel wire: the wires produce tones ranging over seven octaves and are mounted on a harp-shaped frame in a wooden case of various forms.

pi·an′ō·fōr·tē (*or* -fōrt), *n.* [It. *piano*, from L. *planus*, plain, smooth, and It. *forte*, L. *fortis*, strong.] a piano.

pi·an′ō·graph, *n.* [*piano*, and Gr. *graphein*, to write.] an electrically controlled apparatus used to record the notes played upon a piano.

Pi·ȧ·nō′lȧ, *n.* a device for playing a piano mechanically: a trade-mark.

pi·an′ō·logue (-lŏg), *n.* a comic performance on the piano, sometimes accompanied by humorous remarks by the player.

Pī′ȧ·rist, *n.* [LL., from *pius*, pious.] in the Roman Catholic Church, any member of a teaching order instituted at Rome at the beginning of the seventeenth century.

pï·ȧs·sä′bȧ, pï·ȧ·sä′bȧ, *n.* piassava.

pï·ȧs·sä′vȧ, pï·ȧ·sä′vȧ, *n.* [Port. *piaçaba.*]

1. the stiff, coarse fibers of the leafstalks of either of two palm trees, *Attalea funifera* or *Leopoldinia piassaba.*

2. either of the palms furnishing this fiber.

pi·as′tēr, pi·as′tre (-tēr), *n.* [Fr. *piastre*, It. and Sp. *piastra*, a thin plate of metal, a dollar, from LL. *plastra*, L. *emplastrum*, Gr. *emplastrum*, a plaster, from *emplassein*, to plaster up or over.]

1. the Spanish dollar. [Rare.]

2. a unit of currency equal to 1/100 of a pound in Egypt, Lebanon, Syria, and Sudan.

3. a monetary unit in South Vietnam.

4. a unit of money in Turkey, equal to 1/100 of a lira.

pi·ā′tion, *n.* [L. *piatio.*] the act of making atonement. [Rare.]

piät′tï (pyät′tē), *n.pl.* [It., plates.] cymbals.

pi·az′zȧ, *n.* [It.] 1. in Italy, an open, public square, especially one surrounded by buildings.

2. a covered gallery or arcade.

3. a large, covered porch; a veranda.

pib′çorn, *n.* [W.] a small reed instrument formerly used in Wales.

pi′broch, *n.* [Gael. *piobaireachd*, pipe music, from *piobair*, a piper, *piob*, a pipe, bagpipe.] a piece of music for the bagpipe, consisting of a theme with variations, usually martial in character but sometimes dirgelike.

piç, *n.* [Turk. *pik.*] a linear measure used in Turkey and other eastern countries: it is equal to from eighteen to twenty-eight inches.

piç, *n.* same as *pique.*

pī′çȧ, *n.* [L., a magpie.] an abnormal craving for certain unnatural foods, as clay or chalk, sometimes occurring in pregnancy, hysteria, and chlorosis.

pī′çȧ, *n.* [ML., directory, hence prob. applied to the type used in printing it.]

1. a size of type, 12 point.

This line is in pica.

2. the height of this type, about 1/6 inch: used as a measure.

piç′ȧ·dōr, *n.* [Sp., from *pica*, pike.] a horseman who participates in the early part of a bullfight, by irritating and enraging the bull with slight thrusts of a lance.

piç′ȧ·nin·ny, *n.* same as *pickaninny.*

Piç′ărd, *n.* one of a religious sect who in the fifteenth century attempted to renew the practices of the Adamites: so called from Picard, a native of Flanders.

piç·ȧ·resque′ (-resk′), *a.* [Sp. *picaresco*, from *picaro*, a rascal, orig., a Picard.]

1. of or dealing with sharpwitted vagabonds and their roguish adventures.

2. designating a style of fiction originating in Spain and having a roguish hero.

Pi·çā′ri·ae, *n.pl.* [LL., from *picus*, woodpecker.] a large order of birds, including almost all the nonpasserine carinate species, among them the kingfishers, rollers, trogons, and woodpeckers.

pi·çā′ri·ăn, *a.* belonging to or having the characteristics of the *Picariæ.*

pi·çā′ri·ăn, *n.* a bird of the order *Picariæ.*

piç·ȧ·roon′, *n.* [Sp. *picaron*, from *picaro*, a rogue.]

1. a rogue, adventurer, or thief.

2. a pirate.

3. a pirate ship.

piç·ȧ·roon′, *v.i.* to act as a pirate.

piç·ȧ·yūne′, *n.* [Fr. *picaillon*, a farthing.]

1. any coin of small value.

2. anything trivial or worthless.

piç·ȧ·yūne′, *a.* trivial; cheap; contemptible.

piç·ȧ·yūn′ish, *a.* picayune.

piç′çȧ·dil·ly, piç′çȧ·dill, *n.* [OFr. *picadille*, *piccadille*, from Sp. *picado*, pp. of *picar*, to pick.] a high collar or a kind of ruff worn in the seventeenth century.

PICCADILLY

piç′çāġe, *n.* [Norm. *pecker*, to break open; Fr. *piquer*, to pick.] formerly, in England, money paid at fairs as a tax for breaking ground for booths.

piç′çȧ·lil·li, *n.* [prob. from *pickle*; formerly also *piccalillo*, *pacolilla*, etc.] a relish, originally East Indian, of chopped vegetables, mustard, vinegar, and hot spices.

piç′çȧ·nin·ny, *n.*; *pl.* **piç′çȧ·nin·nieş**, same as *pickaninny.*

piç′çō·lō, *n.*; *pl.* **piç′çō·lōş**, [It. *piccolo*, small.]

1. a small instrument of the flute family pitched an octave above an ordinary flute.

2. an organ stop two feet long, having pipes of wood and a high piercing tone.

piç′çō·lō·ist, *n.* a player on the piccolo.

pīce, *n.* a small coin of India, equal to one fourth of an anna.

Pic′ē·ȧ, *n.* [L. *picea*, pine; Gr. *penkē.*] a genus of coniferous trees including the spruces.

pī′cēne, *n.* [L. *piceus*, from *pix*, *picis*, pitch.] a bluish fluorescent crystalline substance, $C_{22}H_{14}$, derived from coal tar and petroleum.

pic′ē·ous, *a.* [L. *piceus*, pitchy.] of the color of or like pitch; black; also, inflammable.

pi″chi·ci·ä′gō, *n.* [Sp.] a burrowing animal, *Chlamydophorus truncatus*, of South America, related to the armadillo but smaller.

pich′ū·rim, *n.* the seed or bean of a South American tree, *Nectandra puchurim*, used both medicinally and as a spice: also called *sassafras nut* and *pitchurim bean.*

Pī′cī, *n.pl.* [L.] a suborder of birds which includes the woodpeckers and the wrynecks.

pic′i·form, *a.* [L. *picus*, woodpecker, and *forma*, form.] of or pertaining to the *Piciformes.*

Pic·i·for′mēş, *n.pl.* [LL.] a division of picarian birds including the woodpeckers, toucans, kingfishers, hornbills, etc.

pī′cīne, *a.* [LL., from L. *picus*, woodpecker.] of or pertaining to the *Piciformes.*

pick, *v.t.* [var. of *pitch* (to throw).] in weaving, to throw (a shuttle); to cast.

pick, *n.* 1. one passage of, or the blow that drives, the shuttle of a loom.

2. one of the weft threads, or filling yarns.

pick, *v.t.* [from AS. *pycan*, to pick, to pull.]

1. to break up, pierce, or dig up (soil, rock, etc.) with something sharply pointed; to use a pick on.

2. to make or form, as a hole, with something pointed.

3. (a) to dig, probe, or scratch at with the fingers or with something pointed in an attempt to remove, as a scab; (b) to clear something from (the teeth, etc.) in this way.

4. to remove by pulling with or as with the fingers; specifically, to pluck or gather (flowers, berries, etc.)

5. to clear (something) in this way; specifically, (a) to prepare (a fowl) by removing the feathers; (b) to remove the fruit from (a tree).

6. to take up (food, etc.) in small pieces, as a bird with its bill; to peck.

7. to eat sparingly or daintily.

8. to pull apart, as fibers, rags, etc.

9. to choose; select; cull.

10. to look for and find excuse or occasion for (a quarrel or fight).

11. to look for purposefully and find; as, to *pick* flaws.

12. (a) to pluck (the strings on a guitar, etc.); (b) to play (a guitar, etc.) in this way.

13. to open (a lock) with a wire, etc. instead of a key, especially in a stealthy manner.

14. to steal from (one's pocket, purse, etc.).

to pick a bone with; see under *bone.*

to pick apart (or *to pieces*); (a) to separate or tear into many parts; (b) to find flaws in by examining critically.

to pick off; (a) to remove by picking or plucking; (b) to hit with a carefully aimed shot.

to pick one's way; to progress slowly, choosing each move with care, as in crossing muddy ground or in painstaking study.

to pick out; (a) to choose; to select; (b) to single out from or recognize among a group; to distinguish; (c) to make out (meaning or sense); (d) to play (a tune) note by note, as on a piano.

to pick over; to examine (a number of things) item by item; to sort out.

to pick up; (a) to break up (soil, etc.) with a pick; (b) to grasp and raise or lift; to take up; (c) to get; gain; find; to learn, especially by chance or in a casual manner; (d) to stop for and take or bring along; (e) to accelerate; to gain speed; (f) to bring into range of sight, hearing, radio reception, etc.; (g) to make a room, etc. tidy; (h) [Colloq.] to become acquainted with casually or informally; usually for purposes of love-making.

pick, *v.i.* 1. to eat sparingly or in a fussy manner.

2. to thieve or pilfer.

3. to use a pick.

4. to gather berries, flowers, etc. from the plants upon which they grow.

5. to be picked; as, grapes *pick* easily.

6. to select or choose, especially in a careful or fussy manner.

to pick and choose; to choose or select carefully.

to pick at; (a) to eat small portions of, especially in a dainty or fussy manner; (b) [Colloq.] to nag at; to find fault with; (c) to toy or meddle with; to finger.

to pick on; (a) to choose; to select; (b) [Colloq.] to single out for abuse, criticism, etc.; to annoy; to tease.

to pick up; to improve gradually; to gain strength.

pick, *n.* 1. the act of picking; a stroke or blow with something pointed.

2. the act of choosing or a thing chosen; choice.

3. the most desirable; the best; choicest.

4. the amount of a crop picked or gathered at one time.

pick, *n.* [var. of *pike* (weapon).]

1. a heavy, two-headed metal tool used in breaking up soil, rock, etc.: it is long, narrow, and slightly curved, and pointed at one or both ends, with a wooden handle fitted into its center.

2. any of several pointed tools or instruments for picking: usually in combination, as, ice*pick.*

3. a small, thin piece of metal, bone, etc., used in plucking the strings of a guitar, banjo, etc.; plectrum.

pick′ȧ·back, pick′back, *adv.* [form of *pickapack*, *pickpack*, a reduplication of *pack.*] on the back or shoulders; as, he carried the child *pickaback*: also *piggyback.*

pick′ȧ·back plāne, an airplane designed to be carried on the take-off by a larger plane and later released in mid-air.

pick′ȧ·ble, *a.* that may be picked.

pick′ȧ·nin·ny, *n.*; *pl.* **pick′ȧ·nin·nieş**, [dim., from Sp. *pequeño*, little.] a Negro baby or child: a patronizing or contemptuous term.

pick′ȧ·pack, pick′pack, *adv.* same as *pickaback.*

pick′ax, pick′axe, *n.* [corruption of OFr. *picquois*, pickax.] a pick with a point at one end of the head and a chisel-like edge at the other; a mattock.

pick′ax, pick′axe, *v.t.* and *v.i.*; pickaxed, *pt.*, *pp.*; pickaxing, *ppr.* to use a pickax (on).

pick′back, *adv.* see *pickaback.*

pick dress′ing, in stone cutting, a facing with small depressions made by a sharp tool.

PICKAX

picked (pikt), *a.* [from *pick*, to pierce.]

1. selected or chosen, especially with care; as, *picked* men.

2. gathered from plants rather than from the ground, as berries, apples, etc.

3. worked over with a pick or mattock.

pick′ed, *a.* 1. pointed; sharp. [Archaic.]

2. covered with spines; prickly; as, the *picked* dogfish. [Archaic.]

pick·eer′, *v.i.* [Fr. *picorer*, to maraud, originally to steal cattle, from L. *pecus*, *pecoris*, cattle.] to pillage; also, to skirmish, as soldiers. [Obs.]

pick′el·hau·be (-hou-bȧ), *n.*; *pl.* **pick′el·hau·ben**, [G.] a helmet formerly worn by the German army. It is crowned by a sharp metal point.

pick′ẽr, *n.* 1. one who or that which picks.
2. a machine for picking fibers.
3. in founding, a light steel rod, with a very sharp point, used for picking out small, light patterns from the sand.
4. in ordnance, a priming wire for clearing the vent.
5. in printing, a person who touches up defects in electroplates and stereotypes.

pick′ẽr, *n.* [from *pick*, to throw.] in weaving, the upper or striking portion of a picker staff which comes against the end of the shuttle and impels it through the shed of the warp.

pick′ẽr·el, *n.*; *pl.* **pick′ẽr·el** or **pick′ẽr·els,** any of a number of related, fierce fresh-water fishes of the pike family, especially a small variety with a narrow, pointed snout, projecting lower jaw, and sharp teeth. The common pickerel of the eastern part of the United States is *Esox reticulatus*. *Esox vermiculatus* is found chiefly in the Mississippi valley. The banded pickerel is *Esox americanus*.

pick′ẽr·el·weed″, *n.* any plant of the genus *Pontederia*, especially *Pontederia cordata*, having large, arrow-shaped leaves and spikes of blue-violet flowers.

pick′ẽr·ing, *n.* 1. a pickerel.
2. the sauger.

pick′ẽr·y, *n.* petty theft. [Scot.]

pick′et, *n.* [Fr. *piquet*, dim. of *pique*, a pike.]
1. a stake sharpened or pointed and used in fortification, encampments, etc.
2. a stalk or slat, usually pointed, used as an upright in a fence, a hitching post for animals, a marker, etc.
3. a group of soldiers or a single soldier used to guard a body of troops from surprise attack: a picket is usually stationed at an outpost.
4. a person, as a member of a labor union on strike, stationed outside a factory, store, public building, etc., often carrying a sign, to demonstrate protest, keep strikebreakers from entering, dissuade people from buying, etc.
5. a pointed stake or light metal rod used by surveyors to hold the end of a chain or to mark a station.
6. a guard sent out from a camp or barracks to arrest soldiers who have over-stayed their leave. [Rare.]
7. a game of cards; piquet.
8. an old military punishment in which the offender was made to stand with one foot on a pointed stake. [Obs.]
inlying picket; a detachment of troops held in camp or barracks, ready to move at once upon an alarm.
outlying picket; a picket stationed in the front of a body of troops.

pick′et, *v.t.*; picketed, *pt., pp.*; picketing, *ppr.*
1. to enclose, shut in, or protect with a picket fence or palisade.
2. to hitch (an animal) to a picket.
3. (a) to post as a military picket; (b) to guard (a body of troops) with a picket.
4. to place pickets, or serve as a picket, at (a factory, etc.)

pick′et, *v.i.* to serve as a picket (sense 3 or 4).

pick·e·tee′, *n.* same as *picotee*.

pick′et fence, a fence made of upright stakes or pales.

pick′et guärd (gärd), a guard stationed on the outskirts of a camp to give an alarm in case of the enemy's approach; also, one within a camp, fort, barracks, etc. prepared for instant service.

pick′et·ing, *n.* the act of guarding or watching with pickets; especially, the act of a labor organization in posting pickets during a strike.

pick′et līne, 1. the line outside a camp at which pickets are stationed.
2. in a military camp, the rope to which horses are tied while being groomed.
3. a line or cordon of people serving as pickets.

pick′et pin, 1. a short stake or pin driven into the ground and used as a post to which to tether horses.
2. any one of the many species of ground squirrels of the genus *Citellus* which, when sitting motionless in an upright position, resemble small stakes when at a distance. [Dial.]

pick′-fault, *n.* one who seeks out faults in others. [Obs.]

pick ham′mẽr, a pick with a point at one end of the head and a surface for hammering at the other.

pick′ing, *n.* 1. the act of a person who picks.
2. [*usually pl.*] something that is or may be picked, or the amount of this; specifically, (a) small scraps or refuse that may be gleaned; (b) something got by dishonest or unethical means; spoils; pilferings.
3. [*pl.*] finely broken shells of oysters used for footpaths. [Brit.]
4. in mining, rough sorting, as of ore.
5. a brick that is not burned correctly.
6. the finishing of an electrotype by removing defects.

pick′ing, *a.* 1. that picks.
2. discriminating; nice. [Obs.]

pick′ing peg, in weaving, the part of a handloom that operates the shuttle.

pick′le, piç′le (-l), *n.* a small piece of land surrounded by a hedge or wall; a close. [Obs.]

pick′le (-l), *n.* [D. and L.G. *pekel*; G. *pokel*, brine.]
1. any brine, vinegar, or spicy solution used to preserve or flavor food.
2. an article of food as a vegetable, specifically cucumber, preserved in such a solution.
3. a chemical bath used to clear metal of scale, to preserve wood, etc.
4. an awkward or difficult situation; plight. [Colloq.]
5. a troublesome or mischievous child. [Colloq.]
a rod in pickle; a punishment to be applied in the future should occasion offer.

pick′le, *v.t.*; pickled, *pt., pp.*; pickling, *ppr.*
1. to treat with or preserve in a pickle solution; as, to *pickle* herring.
2. to imbue highly with anything bad; as, a *pickled* rogue. [Obs.]
3. to subject to some treatment that gives an antique appearance: said of paintings in imitation of the old masters.

pick′led (-ld), *a.* 1. preserved in brine or pickle; as, *pickled* onions.
2. intoxicated; drunk. [Slang.]

pick′le-her″ring, *n.* 1. a merry-andrew; a zany; a buffoon. [Obs.]
2. a pickled herring. [Obs.]

pick′lẽr, *n.* one who pickles; specifically, one who pickles food.

pick′le·wŏrm, *n.* the larva of a moth, *Phacellura nitidalis*, which does great damage to green cucumbers and melons.

pick′lock, *n.* 1. an instrument for opening locks without a key.
2. on who picks locks; especially, one who enters houses to steal by picking the locks.

pick′maw, *n.* the black-headed gull of Europe. [Brit. Dial.]

pick′-mē-up, *n.* an alcoholic drink taken for quick stimulation. [Colloq.]

pick′nick, *n.* a picnic. [Obs.]

pick′pack, *adv.* pickaback.

pick′pen·ny, *n.*; *pl.* **pick′pen·nieṣ,** a miserly person. [Obs.]

pick′pock·et, *n.* one who steals from pockets; a picker of pockets.

pick′pũrse, *n.* one who steals the purse, or money from the purse, of another. [Obs.]

pick′thañk, *n.* a sycophant, flatterer, or informer. [Archaic or Dial.]

pick′up, *n.* 1. the act of picking up, as in fielding a rapidly rolling baseball.
2. the process or power of increasing in speed; acceleration.
3. a small, often open, truck used in collecting and delivering parcels, etc.
4. a casual or informal acquaintance, as one formed for purposes of love-making. [Colloq.]
5. improvement; recovery, as in trade. [Colloq.]
6. (a) a stimulant; bracer; (b) stimulation. [Colloq.]
7. (a) in an electric phonograph, a device that produces audio-frequency currents from the vibrations of the needle moving over the record; (b) the pivoted arm holding the needle and this device.
8. in radio and television, (a) the reception of sound or light for conversion into electrical energy in the transmitter; (b) the apparatus used for this; (c) any place outside a studio where a broadcast originates; (d) the electrical system connecting the program from this place to the broadcasting station.
9. in electricity, a device for picking up or gathering current from an electrically charged rail.
10. in printing, type matter kept ready for repeated or immediate use.
11. an attachment to an agricultural combine for picking up grain.

pick′up, *a.* used in picking up; also, picked up.

Pick′wick, Mr. (Sam′ū·el), the naive, benevolent president of the Pickwick Club in Dickens' *Pickwick Papers* (1836).

Pick·wick′i·ăn, *a.* 1. of or characteristic of Mr. Pickwick or the Pickwick Club.
2. used with a special or esoteric sense: said of a word or phrase.

piç′niç, *n.* [Fr. *piquenique*; prob. redupl., from *piquer*, to pick.]
1. a pleasure outing at which a meal is eaten outdoors.
2. any pleasant experience. [Slang.]

piç′niç, *a.* pertaining to or having the characteristics of a picnic; as, a *picnic* costume.

piç′niç, *v.i.*; picnicked (-nikt), *pt., pp.*; picnicking, *ppr.* to hold or attend a picnic.

piç′nick·ẽr, *n.* one who picnics; one of a picnic party.

pī′çoid, *a.* [L. *pica*, magpie, and *-oid*.] pertaining to or resembling the *Pici*, a suborder of birds.

piç′ō·lin, *n.* picoline.

piç′ō·līne, *n.* [L. *pix*, *picis*, pitch, *oleum*, oil, and *-ine*.] any of three isomeric, colorless, strong-smelling, liquid bases, C_6H_7N, found in the oil produced by the distillation of bones and coal, and used in medicine as a nerve sedative.

pī′çot (-kō), *n.*; *pl.* **pī′çots** (-kōz), [Fr., dim. of *pic*, a point, pike.] any of a number of small, threadlike loops forming an ornamental edging on lace, ribbon, etc.

pī′çot, *v.t* and *v.i.*; picoted (-kōd), *pt., pp.*; picoting, *ppr.* to trim or edge with picots.

piç·ō·tee′, *n.* [Fr. *picoté*, dotted, marked with dots.] a variety of carnation or clove pink, *Dianthus caryophyllus*, characterized by having the dark color only on the edge of the petals. The ground color is white or yellow, the color on the margin some shade of red or purple. The petals are slightly serrated or fringed at the edge.

PICOTEES

piç′ō·tīte, *n.* [after the French botanist, *Picot*.] a variety of spinel containing chromium.

piç′rȧ, *n.* [L. from Gr. *pikros*, sharp, bitter.] the powder of aloes with canella.

piç′rāte, *n.* a salt or ester of picric acid, usually highly explosive.

piç′riç aç′id, [from Gr. *pikros*, bitter; and *-ic*.] a yellow, crystalline, bitter acid, $C_6H_2(NO_2)_3OH$, obtained from the action of nitric acid on phenol, indigo, etc.: used in combination with butesin as an antiseptic, and in making dyes and explosives.

piç′rīte, *n.* [Gr. *pikros*, bitter, and *-ite*.] a dark, heavy, igneous rock which consists in large part of chrysolite, with hornblende, pyroxene, biotite, etc. and resembles peridotite.

piç′rō-, [from Gr. *pikros*, bitter.] a combining form meaning *bitter*: also, before a vowel, *picr-*.

piç·rō·çär′mine, *n.* [Gr. *pikros*, bitter; and *carmine*.] a coloring substance made of picric acid and carmine.

piç″rō·ē·ryth′rin, *n.* [Gr. *pikros*, bitter; and *erythrin*.] a substance, $C_{12}H_{16}O_7$, of crystalline form, obtained by boiling erythrin with water, alcohol, or alkali.

piç′rol, *n.* a colorless, bitter, crystalline compound, soluble in water, used in medicine as an antiseptic.

piç′rō·līte, *n.* [Gr. *pikros*, bitter, and *lithos*, stone.] a fibrous variety of serpentine.

piç·rō·tox′in, piç·rō·tox′ine, *n.* [Gr. *pikros*, bitter, and *toxikon*, poison.] a bitter, poisonous, crystalline compound, $C_{30}H_{34}O_{13}$, which exists in the seeds of *Cocculus indicus*, from which it is extracted by the action of water and alcohol. It resembles strychnine in properties and is used in medicine.

piç′ryl, *n.* [*picric* and *-yl*.] the hypothetic radical of picric acid, $C_6H_2(NO_2)_3$, analogous to phenyl.

Piçt, *n.* [Late ME.; LL. *Picti*, pl., said to be from L. *pictus*, pp. of *pingere*, to paint (hence, lit., painted people).] one of an ancient people of Great Britain, driven into Scotland by the Britons and Romans.

Piç′tish, *a.* pertaining to or resembling the Picts, their language, or their culture.

Piç′tish, *n.* the language of the Picts: its relationship is not established.

piç′tō·glyph, *n.* [L. *pictor*, painter, and Gr. *glyphein*, to engrave.] a colored glyph.

piç′tō-gràph, *n.* [L. *pictor,* painter, and Gr. *graphein,* to write.]
1. a picture representing an idea, as in primitive writing; hieroglyph.
2. writing of this kind.

piç-tō-graph′iç, *a.* pertaining to a pictograph.

piç-tog′rà-phy, *n.* writing by the use of pictographs.

Piç′tŏr, *n.* [L., painter.] a southern constellation.

piç-tō′ri-ăl, *a.* [L. *pictorius,* from *pictor,* a painter.]
1. of a painter or painting. [Rare.]
2. of, containing, or expressed in pictures.
3. invoking or suggesting a mental image or picture; vivid; graphic, as a description.

piç-tō′ri-ăl, *n.* a periodical featuring many pictures.

piç-tō′ri-ăl-ly, *adv.* with pictures; by means of pictures.

piç-tor′iç, piç-tor′iç-ăl, *a.* pictorial. [Rare.]

piç′tūr-à-ble, *a.* that can be pictured, or represented by a picture or painting; suitable for drawing or painting.

piç′tūr-ăl, *a.* pictorial.

piç′tūr-ăl, *n.* a picture. [Rare.]

piç′tūre, *n.* [L. *pictura,* from *pictus,* pp. of *pingere,* to paint.]
1. an image or likeness of an object, person, or scene produced on a flat surface, especially by painting, drawing, or photography.
2. a printed reproduction of any of these.
3. anything closely resembling or strikingly typifying something else; perfect likeness; image; as, she's the *picture* of her mother; that cat is the *picture* of laziness.
4. anything admired for beauty; as, the garden was a *picture.*
5. a mental image or impression; an idea.
6. a description; as, this is a poor *picture* of the times.
7. all the pertinent facts or conditions of an event.
8. a tableau.
9. a motion picture.
Syn.—effigy, image, likeness, portrait, representation.

piç′tūre, *v.t.*; pictured, *pt., pp.*; picturing, *ppr.*
1. to make a picture of by painting, drawing, photographing, etc.
2. to make visible; to show clearly; to reflect.
3. to describe or explain.
4. to form a mental picture or impression of; to imagine.

piç′tūred, *a.* furnished with or represented in pictures or a picture.

piç′tūre frāme, a frame, often ornamental, for forming a border around a picture.

piç′tūre gal′lēr-y, a place for exhibiting pictures.

piç′tūre hat, a woman's wide-brimmed hat with plumes, flowers, etc., like those seen in some famous paintings.

piç′tūr-ēr, *n.* a painter; one who makes pictures.

piç′tūre shōw, a motion picture or motion-picture theater.

piç-tūr-esque′ (-esk′), *a.* [Fr. *pittoresque;* It. *pittoresco,* from L. *pictura,* a picture.]
1. like or suggesting a picture; specifically, (a) having a wild or natural beauty, as mountain scenery; (b) pleasantly unfamiliar or strange; quaint; informal; as, a *picturesque* Indian village.
2. suggesting or calling up a mental picture; striking; vivid.
Syn.—comely, seemly, graceful, scenic, artistic, pictorial, graphic.

piç-tūr-esque′, *n.* that which is picturesque.
The lovers of the *picturesque* still regret the woods of oak and arbutus. —Macaulay.

piç-tūr-esque′ly (-esk′), *adv.* in a picturesque manner.

piç-tūr-esque′ness, *n.* the state or quality of being picturesque.

piç-tūr-esqu′ish (esk′), *a.* rather picturesque.

piç′tūre win′dōw, a large window, especially in a living room, that seems to frame the outside view.

piç′tūre wrīt′ing, 1. writing consisting of pictures or figures representing ideas.

EGYPTIAN PICTURE WRITING

2. the pictures or figures so used; pictographs; hieroglyphs.

piç″tūr-i-zā′tion, *n.* 1. a picturizing or being picturized.
2. something that is picturized.

piç′tūr-īze, *v.t.*; picturized, *pt., pp.*; picturizing, *ppr.* to make into a picture, especially a motion picture.

piç′ul, peç′ul, *n.* [Malay.] an Oriental weight varying from 130 to 140 pounds.

piç′ū-let, *n.* [L. *picus,* woodpecker.] any woodpecker of the *Picumninæ.*

Piç-um-nī′nae, *n.pl.* a group of small woodpeckers having short, straight bills, rounded wings, and short, soft, rounded tails.

Pī′çus, *n.* a genus of birds including the common woodpecker, the type genus of the *Picidæ.* There are numerous American species.

pid′dle (-dl), *v.t.* and *v.i.*: piddled, *pt., pp.*; piddling, *ppr.* [euphemistic dim., from base of *piss.*]
1. to dawdle or trifle (sometimes with *away*); as, he *piddles* the time *away.*
2. to urinate: child's term.

pid′dlēr, *n.* one who piddles.

pid′dling, *a.* frivolous; trifling; useless.

pid′dŏck, *n.* a boring mollusk of the genus *Pholas* or family *Pholadidæ.*

pidġ′eŏn, *n.* a pigeon. [Obs.]

pidġ′in, *n.* [Chin. pronoun. of *business.*] a mixed language or jargon, originally developed for purposes of trade, incorporating the vocabulary of one or more languages with a very simplified form of the grammatical system of one of these; pidgin English, Beach-la-Mar, or any similar jargon: also spelled *pigeon.*

pidġ′in Eñg′lish, a simplified form of English used by Orientals and South Pacific natives in dealing with foreigners: there are two forms, Chinese pidgin and Melanesian pidgin, the former based on the syntax of Chinese, the latter on the syntax of certain aboriginal languages of Melanesia and Northern Australia.

pīe, *n.* [ME.; prob. same word as *pie* (magpie), with reference to the magpie's habit of collecting oddments and to the miscellaneous character of the dish.]
1. a baked dish consisting of fruit, meat, etc., with either an under crust, an upper crust, or both.
2. a layer cake filled with custard, cream, jelly, etc.
3. (a) something extremely good or easy; (b) political graft. [Slang.]

pīe, *n.* [Fr., from L. *pica,* magpie.]
1. the magpie or a related bird.
2. a chatterer or gossip. [Obs.]

pīe, *n.* [from L. *pica.*] in England, a form or table of rules used before the Reformation in selecting the correct church service or office for the day: also spelled *pye.*

pīe, *n.* [Hind. *pa′i.*] a small bronze coin of India, equal to $^{1}/_{12}$ of an anna.

pīe, *n.* and *v.t.* same as *pi* (jumble).

pīe′bȧld, *a.* [from *pie,* a magpie, and *bald.*] covered with patches or spots of two colors, especially with white and black.

pīe′bȧld, *n.* a piebald horse or other animal.

pīēce (pēs), *n.* [Fr. *pièce;* OFr. *piece;* LL. *pecia.*]
1. a part or fragment broken or separated from the whole.
2. a section, division, or quantity regarded as complete in itself and distinct from the whole of which it is a part.
3. any single thing, amount, specimen, example, etc.; specifically, (a) an artistic work or composition, as of music, literature, painting, drama, etc.; (b) an action or its result; as, a *piece* of nonsense, business etc.; (c) a firearm; specifically, a rifle; (d) a coin; as, a fifty-cent *piece;* (e) one of a set, as of silver or china; (f) a counter or man, as used in various games; specifically, in chess, any man other than a pawn.
4. the quantity or size, as of cloth or wallpaper, that is manufactured as a unit.
5. an amount of work constituting a single job.
6. an amount of time or space, especially a small amount; bit. [Archaic or Dial.]
7. a person; individual. [Archaic or Dial.]
of a (or *one*) *piece;* like; consistent (*with*); as if taken from the same whole; as, they seemed all *of a piece.*
piece of eight; the obsolete Spanish or Spanish-American silver dollar, equal to eight reals.
to give a piece of one's mind; see under *mind.*
to go to pieces; (a) to break into pieces; to fall apart; (b) to lose all self-control, morally or emotionally.

pīēce, *v.t.*; pieced (pēst), *pt., pp.*; piecing, *ppr.*
1. to add a piece or pieces to, as in repairing or enlarging.
2. to join or put (*together*) the pieces of, as in mending.
3. to join or unite.
to piece out; to extend or enlarge by addition of a piece or pieces.

pīēce, *v.i.* 1. to unite by a coalescence of parts; to be compacted, as parts into a whole. [Obs.]
2. to eat between meals. [Colloq.]

pīēce brō′kēr, a dealer in shreds and remnants of cloth.

pīēced (pēst), *a.* mended or enlarged by a piece or pieces.

pièce de ré-sis-tance′ (pyes dẽ rā-zēs-täṅs′), [Fr., piece of resistance.]
1. the principal dish of a meal.
2. the main item or event in a series.

pīēce goodṣ, textiles made and sold in standard sizes.

pīēce′less, *a.* not made of pieces; consisting of an entire thing.

pīēce′ly, *adv.* piecemeal. [Obs.]

pīēce′mēal, *n.* [*piece,* and AS. *mæl,* part.] a small bit; a fragment. [Obs.]

pīēce′mēal, *a.* single; separate; made or done in parts or pieces.

pīēce′mēal, *adv.* 1. piece by piece; in small amounts or degrees.
2. into pieces or parts.

pīēce mōld, in sculpture, a mold used in bronze casting, composed of separate pieces which fit together but do not adhere.

pīē′cen, *v.t.* to add to or extend by parts. [Brit. Dial.]

pīēce′nēr, *n.* one who ties broken threads in a spinning mill. [Brit.]
The children whose duty it is to walk backward and forward before the reels on which the cotton, silk, or worsted is wound for the purpose of joining the threads when they break are called piecers or *pieceners.* —Mrs. Trollope.

pīēc′ēr, *n.* 1. one who pieces; a patcher.
2. same as *piecener.*

pīēce′wŏrk, *n.* work done and paid for by the piece or job.

pīed (pīd), *a.* [from *pie,* magpie.]
1. variegated with spots of different colors; spotted; piebald.
Meadows trim with daisies *pied.* —Milton.
2. wearing something of this description.
pied antelope; a piebald antelope, *Alcelaphus pygargus,* of South Africa.
pied blackbird; a thrush of the genus *Turdulus.*
pied finch; (a) the chaffinch; (b) the snow bunting. [Brit. Dial.]

pied-à-terre (pye-dȧ-tãr′), *n.* [Fr., lit., foot on the ground.] a place to live or rest, especially for a short time; lodging.

pīed′-billed, *a.* having a pied bill or beak.
pied-billed grebe; a small aquatic bird, the dabchick, *Podilymbus podiceps.*

pied-fort′ (pyā-fọr′), *n.* [Fr., lit., strong foot.] in numismatics, a coin pattern struck on a blank of unusual thickness.

pīed′mont, *a.* [from *Piedmont,* Italy; L. *Pedimontium,* from *pes, pedis,* a foot, and *mons, montis,* mountain.] at the base of a mountain or mountains; as, a *piedmont* stream.

pīed′mont, *n.* a piedmont area, plain, etc.

Pīēd-mont-ēṣe′, *a.* of Piedmont, Italy, its people, or culture.

Pīēd-mont-ēṣe′, *n.*; *pl.* **Pīēd-mont-ēṣe′,** a native or inhabitant of Piedmont, Italy.

pīēd′mont-īte, *n.* in mineralogy, a reddish-brown substance, containing manganese and allied to epidote, found in Piedmont, Italy.

pīed′ness, *n.* the quality of being pied.

pié-douche′ (pyā-dösh′), *n.* [Fr., from It. *peduccio,* a corbel; L. *pes, pedis,* foot.] a small pedestal for the support of busts, vases, etc.

Pīed Pīp′ēr (of Ham′el-in), in German legend, a musician who rid Hamelin of its rats by leading them with his piping to the river, where they drowned: in revenge for not receiving his reward, he later led the children of the village to a mountain where they disappeared: the subject of a poem by Robert Browning.

pie-droit′ (pyā-drwä′), *n.* [Fr. *pied-droit;* L. *pes directus,* lit., straight foot.] in architecture, a pier or square pillar, without base or capital, partly concealed within a wall. [Obs.]

pīe'-eȳed' (pī'-īd'), *a.* drunk; intoxicated. [Slang.]

pīe'măn, *n.*; *pl.* **pīe'men,** a baker or seller of pies.

piēnd, *n.* [Dan. *pind*, peg.] same as *Peen.*

pīe'plant, *n.* a species of garden rhubarb, the leafstalks of which are made into pies.

pīe'pow·dẽr, pīe'pöu·dre, *n.* [Fr. *pied*, foot, and *poudre*, dust.] an ancient court of record in England, having jurisdiction over all disputes arising in fairs or markets.

piēr, *n.* [OFr. *pere*; ML. *pera.*]
1. a heavy structure supporting the spans of a bridge, especially, as distinguished from an abutment, one supporting the adjacent ends of two center spans of a long bridge.
2. a structure built out over the water and supported by pillars or piles: used as a landing place, pleasure pavilion, etc.
3. in architecture, (a) a heavy column, usually square, used to support weight, as at the end of an arch; (b) the part of a wall between windows or other openings; (c) a reinforcing part built out from the surface of a wall; a buttress.

piēr'ăge, *n.* toll for using a marine pier.

piēr ärch, an arch supported by piers.

piērce (pērs), *v.t.*; pierced, *pt.*, *pp.*; piercing, *ppr.* [ME. *percen*; OFr. *percer.*]
1. to pass into or through as a pointed instrument does; to penetrate; to stab.
2. to affect sharply the senses or feelings of.
3. to make a hole in or through; to perforate; to bore.
4. to make (a hole), as by boring or stabbing.
5. to force a way into or through; to break through.
6. to sound sharply through; as, a shriek *pierced* the air.
7. to penetrate with the sight or mind.
Syn.—impale, penetrate, transfix.

piērce, *v.i.* to enter, as a pointed instrument; to penetrate; to force a way into or through anything: often used figuratively.

Her tears will *pierce* into a marble heart.
—Shak.

piērce'ȧ·ble, *a.* that can be pierced.

piērced (pērst), *a.* perforated; penetrated; entered by force; transfixed.

piēr'cel, *n.* an instrument like a gimlet for forming vents in casks; a piercer.

piēr'cẽr, *n.* 1. one who or that which pierces; specifically, (a) an instrument for making eyelets; a stiletto; (b) a piercel; (c) in founding, a wire used to vent a mold.
2. in zoology, (a) that organ of an insect with which it pierces bodies; the sting; the ovipositor; (b) an insect having an ovipositor.

piēr'cing, *a.* penetrating; perforating; entering, as a pointed instrument; making a way by force into another body; keen; cutting; poignant.
Syn.—acute, sharp, penetrating, discerning, keen.

piēr'cing, *n.* 1. the act of penetrating with force; penetration.
2. in metalworking, the process of sawing out a pattern, as distinguished from punching it out.

piēr'cing·ly, *adv.* in a piercing manner.

piēr'cing·ness, *n.* the quality of piercing or penetrating; sharpness; keenness.

piēr glȧss, a long mirror such as was formerly set in the pier, or wall section, between windows.

piēr'head (-hed), *n.* that part of a pier which forms a landing place; the outer end of a pier.

Pī·ē'ri·ăn, *a.* 1. of Pieria, a region of ancient Macedonia, where the Muses were worshiped.
2. of the Muses or the arts.

Drink deep, or taste not the *Pierian* spring.
—Pope.

pī'ẽr·id, *n.* [Gr. *Pieris* (*-idos*), sing. of *Pierides*, the Muses.] in zoology, any species of butterfly belonging to the genus *Pieris* and related genera.

Pī·ẽr'i·dēş, *n.pl.* [*Pieria*, the district, and *Pieros*, the mountain in Thessaly, sacred to the Muses.] in Greek mythology, the Muses.

pī·ẽr'i·dīne, *a.* of the genus *Pieris.*

Pī'ē·ris, *n.* a genus of small or medium-sized butterflies, usually white or yellow with dark markings, including the North American cabbage butterflies.

Pïer·rōt' (pye-rō'), *n.* [Fr., dim. of *Pierre* Peter.] a comedy character having a whitened face and wearing loose white pantaloons and a jacket with large buttons: originally a stock figure in French pantomime.

piēr tā'ble, a low table set in the pier, or wall section, between windows, often below a pier glass.

pī'et, *n.* [from *pie*, the bird.]
1. a magpie.
2. the dipper, or water ouzel.

Pie·tà' (pyā-tä'), *n.* [It.; L. *pietas*, piety.] a representation in painting, sculpture, etc. of Mary, the mother, grieving over the body of Jesus after the Crucifixion.

pī'e·tişm, *n.* 1. a system which stresses the devotional ideal in religion.
2. [P–] the principles and practices of the Pietists.
3. exaggerated pious feeling or attitude.

Pī'e·tist, *n.* [G., from L. *pietas*, piety; orig. used as a nickname for the followers of P. J. Spener (1635–1705), G. mystic.]
1. a member of a group of Germans who advocated a revival of the devotional ideal in the Lutheran Church.
2. [p–] a pious person.

pī·e·tis'tiç, pī·e·tis'tiç·ăl, *a.* of or characterized by pietism.

pi·e̦'trȧ dů'rȧ, [It., hard stone.] hard, fine stones, as jasper, carnelian, amethyst, etc., used in making mosaics, etc.

pī'e·ty, *n.*; *pl.* **pī'e·tieş,** [L. *pietas*, from *pius*, pious.]
1. devotion to religious duties and practices.
2. loyalty and devotion to parents, family, etc.
3. a pious act, statement, etc.
4. pity. [Obs.]

pīe'wīpe, *n.* the lapwing. [Brit. Dial.]

pī·ē″zō·ē·leç'triç, *a.* relating to or exhibiting piezoelectricity.

pī·ē″zō·ē·leç'tri·çăl·ly, *adv.* in a piezoelectric manner.

pī·ē″zō·ē·leç·tric'i·ty, *n.* [Gr. *piezein*, to press, and *electricity.*] charges of electricity induced in crystalline substance by the application of pressure.

pī·ē·zom'ē·tẽr, *n.* [Gr. *piezein*, to press, and *metron*, measure.]
1. any of various instruments for measuring the compressibility of liquids, pressure, sensitivity to pressure, etc.
2. a gauge connected to a water pipe to give the pressure at that point.

pī·ē″zō·met'riç, pī·ē″zō·met'ri·çal, *a.* 1. of piezometry.
2. determined by piezometry.

pī·ē·zom'e·try, *n.* the measurement of the compressibility of fluids.

pif'fe·rō, *n.* [It., a fife.] a musical instrument resembling a small oboe or flageolet; a fife: it is still used in some districts of Italy.

pif'fle, *v.i.*; piffled, *pt.*, *pp.*; piffling, *ppr.* 1. originally, to be squeamishly particular.
2. to talk nonsense. [Colloq.]

pif'fle, *n.* anything regarded as insignificant or nonsensical. [Colloq.]

pig, *n.* an earthenware crock: also written *pigg.* [Scot.]

pig, *n.*; *pl.* **pigş, pig,** [D. *big*; L.G. *bigge*, pig.]
1. a domesticated animal with a long, broad snout and a thick, fat body covered with coarse bristles; a swine; a hog.
2. a young hog.
3. meat from a pig; pork.
4. a person regarded as acting or looking like a pig; a greedy or filthy person. [Colloq.]
5. (a) an oblong casting of iron or other metal poured from the smelting furnace; (b) any of the molds in which these are cast; (c) pig iron collectively.
masked pig; see under *masked.*
pig iron; see under *iron.*
pig yoke; a quadrant or sextant. [Slang.]
to buy a pig in a poke; to buy, get, or agree to something without sight or knowledge of it in advance.

pig, *v.t.* and *v.i.*; pigged, *pt.*, *pp.*; pigging, *ppr.*
1. to bear pigs.
2. to live like pigs (usually with *it*).

pig bed, the bed of sand into which iron from a smelting furnace is run and cast into pigs.

pig'bōat, *n.* [so named from resembling suckling pigs when nosed against a tender.] a submarine. [Navy Slang.]

pig breāk'ẽr, one who breaks any of the crude metal castings, as pig iron, by hand or machine.

pig çärt, in Scotland, a cart on which crockery is transported from place to place and from which it is offered for sale.

pig deer, the *Babirussa babirussa* of the East Indies, a large animal resembling the pig and characterized by large, curved tusks.

pig'eŏn (pij'un), *n.*; *pl.* **pig'eŏnş, pig'eŏn,** [Fr. *pigeon*; It. *piccione*, from L. *pipio*, *pipionis*, a chirping bird, from *pipire*, to peep, to chirp, an imitative verb; compare Eng. *pipe*, *fife.*]

FANTAIL PIGEON

1. a bird with a small head, plump body, long, pointed wings, and short legs, of the order *Columbæ*, of which there are a great number of species widely distributed, as the stock dove, the ringdove, the turtledove, and the migatory or wild pigeon of America.
2. a simpleton; a person easily deceived. [Slang.]
blue pigeon; a sounding lead. [Slang.]
green pigeon; an old-world pigeon of the family *Treronidæ.*
imperial pigeon; a large fruit pigeon of Asia.

pig'eŏn, *v.t.* to swindle or cheat by tricks of gambling; to fleece; to pluck. [Slang.]

pig'eŏn, *n.* pidgin.

pig'eŏn·ber″ry, *n.* the fruit of the pokeweed; also, the pokeweed itself.

pig'eŏn breast (brest), a deformity of the human chest occurring in rickets, etc. and characterized by a sharply projecting sternum like that of a pigeon.

pig'eŏn-breast″ed, *a.* having a pigeon breast.

pig'eŏn·foot, *n.* a geranium, the dove's-foot.

pig'eŏn grȧss, a foxtail grass the seeds of which are eaten by pigeons and other birds.

pig'eŏn hawk, any of various small hawks; specifically, (a) the American falcon, *Falco columbarius*; (b) the sharp-shinned hawk.

pig'eŏn·heärt″ed, *a.* timid; easily frightened.

pig'eŏn·hōle, *n.* 1. a small recess or hole for pigeons to nest in, usually in a compartmented box, or dovecote.
2. a small open compartment or division, as in a desk, for papers, etc.: so named from their resemblance to the holes in a dovecote.

Abbe Sieyès has whole nests of *pigeonholes* full of constitutions already made, ticketed, sorted, and numbered. —Burke.

3. [*pl.*] an old English game in which balls were rolled through little cavities or arches. [Obs.]

pig'eŏn·hōle, *v.t.*; pigeonholed, *pt.*, *pp.*; pigeonholing, *ppr.* 1. to put in the pigeonhole of a desk, etc.
2. to put aside indefinitely, with the intention of ignoring; to shelve.
3. to arrange or classify systematically or logically.

pig'eŏn house, a house for pigeons; a dovecote.

pig'eŏn-liv″ẽred, *a.* mild in temper; soft; gentle.

pig'eŏn pēa, the seed of an East Indian shrub, a kind of edible pulse, often fed to pigeons.

pig'eŏn plum, a tree in Florida and the West Indies bearing racemes of edible berries; also the fruit itself.

pig'eŏn·ry, *n.* a place in which to keep pigeons; a dovecote.

pig'eŏn-tōed, *a.* having the toes or feet turning inward.

pig'eŏn trē'mex, see *tremex.*

pig'eŏn wing, *n.* 1. a fancy dance step performed by jumping and striking the feet together.
2. a figure in skating, outlining the spread wing of a pigeon.

pig'eŏn·wood, *n.* the wood of any of various West Indian trees.

pig'eŏn wood'peck·ẽr, the flicker.

pig'-eȳed (-īd), *a.* having small eyes set deep in the head.

pig'fish, *n.*; *pl.* **pig'fish, pig'fish·eş,** 1. a salt-water grunt that makes a grunting noise when taken out of water: also called *hogfish.*
2. a sculpin.

pig'foot, *n.* a salt-water fish of southern Europe, *Scorpæna porcus.*

pigg, *n.* a pig (vessel).

pig'gẽr·y, *n.*; *pl.* **pig'gẽr·ieş,** an enclosure in which pigs are kept and raised; a pigpen; a pigsty.

pig′gin, *n.* [Brit. dial.; dim. of *pig* in dial. and obs. sense "a pail."] a small wooden dipper; also, a small wooden pail with a long handle.
pig′gish, *a.* resembling a pig; greedy; filthy.
pig′gy, *n.*; *pl.* **pig′gies,** a little pig: also spelled *piggie.*
pig′gy, *a.* piggish.
pig′gy·back, *adv.* and *a.* same as *pickaback.*
pig′gy bank, 1. a small savings bank shaped like a pig with a slot in its back for receiving the coins.
2. any small savings bank.
pig′-head″ed (-hed″), *a.* obstinate; perverse.
pight (pīt), *a.* [from *pitch.*] pitched; fixed; determined. [Obs.]
pig′-jawed, *a.* in zoology, having the lower jaw receding, with the lower incisors behind those of the upper jaw.
pig′let, *n.* a little pig.
pig·mae′an, pig·mē′an, *a.* same as *pygmaean.*
pig′ment, *n.* [L. *pigmentum,* from the root of *pingere,* to paint.]
1. coloring matter, usually in the form of an insoluble powder, mixed with oil, water, etc. to make paints.
2. any coloring matter in the cells and tissues of plants or animals.
pig·men′tăl, *a.* pertaining to pigments or to pigmentation. [Rare.]
pig′men·tăr·y, *a.* of or containing pigment.
pigmentary degeneration; in medicine, the abnormal pigmentation of affected tissue.
pig·men·tā′tion, *n.* coloration in plants or animals due to the presence of pigment in the tissue.
pig′ment cell, a color-producing cell in a plant or animal; a chromatophore.
pig′ment·ed, *a.* having pigmentation; colored; filled with coloring matter; as, *pigmented* cells.
pig′men·tōse, *a.* filled with pigment. [Rare.]
pig′men·tous, *a.* pigmentose. [Rare.]
pig met′ăl, iron from the smelting furnace in the form of pigs.
Pig′my, *a.* and *n.*; *pl.* **Pig′mies,** pygmy.
pign′ŏn (pin′yun), *n.* [Fr. *pignon,* the kernel of a pine cone.] the edible seed of various pines, as *Pinus pinea,* native to southern Europe.
pig·nō·rā′tion, *n.* [L. *pignoratio, pigneratio,* a pledging, *pignerare,* to pledge, from *pignus, pignoris* or *pigneris,* a pledge.]
1. the act of pawning or the condition of being pawned.
2. in law, the impounding of cattle as security for damage done by them.
pig′nō·rā·tive, *a.* pledging; pawning. [Rare.]
pig′nus, *n.*; *pl.* **pig″nō·rȧ,** [L.] in law, the act of pawning personal property or the property so pledged.
pig′nut, *n.* 1. the thin-shelled nut of a kind of hickory, bitterish in taste, the fruit of *Carya porcina,* common in the United States.
2. the tree itself.
3. the tuber of *Bunium flexuosum,* a variety of European earthnut.
pig′pen, *n.* a pen or small enclosure for pigs; a sty; a pigsty.
pig′skin, *n.* 1. the skin of a pig.
2. leather made from this.
3. a football. [Colloq.]
4. a saddle. [Colloq.]
pigs′ney, pigs′ny, *n.* a darling: a word of endearment to a girl. [Archaic or Dial.]
pig′stick″ĕr, *n.* 1. one who slaughters pigs or hogs. [Slang.]
2. a pocketknife with a long pointed blade.
3. a hunter of wild boar; also, the spear used in hunting.
pig′stick″ing, *n.* 1. the slaughtering of pigs or hogs. [Slang.]
2. the hunting of wild boars with spears.
pig′stȳ, *n.*; *pl.* **pig′stīes,** a sty or pen for pigs.
pig′tāil, *n.* 1. a long braid of hair hanging at the back of the head.
2. a small roll of twisted tobacco.
pig′tāiled, *a.* having a tail like that of a pig; as, a *pigtailed* monkey.
pig′weed, *n.* any of a number of related coarse plants with tassellike heads of reddish flowers; any species of the genus *Chenopodium* of the goosefoot family, as lamb's-quarters or white goosefoot.
pig′widg·eŏn (-wij-un), *n.* anything or anyone unimportant or small: also spelled *pigwidgin.* [Obs.]
pī′kȧ, *n.* [from E. Siberian (Tungusic) name, *peeka.*] a small rodent of the genus *Lagomys* somewhat resembling a tailless rabbit and inhabiting mountainous regions in the northern part of Asia and North America: also called *rat hare, calling hare, cony, little chief hare.*
pīke, *n.* [short for *turnpike.*] 1. a gate or place on a road where a toll is paid.
2. the toll paid there.
3. a toll road.
pīke, *v.i.*; piked, *pt., pp.*; piking, *ppr.* to move quickly (usually with *along*). [Slang.]
pīke, *n.* [Fr. *pique,* from *piquer,* to pierce, prick, from *pic,* a pike, pickax.] a weapon, formerly used by foot soldiers, consisting of a metal spearhead on a long wooden shaft.
pīke, *v.t.*; piked, *pt., pp.*; piking, *ppr.* to pierce or kill with or as with a pike.
pīke, *n.* [ME. *pike*; AS. *piic,* a pickax; prob. from OFr. *pic,* a pick, pickax.] a spike; a point, as the pointed tip of a spear.
pīke, *n.* [ME.; prob. from ON. *pik.*]
1. a peaked summit. [Brit. Dial.]
2. a mountain or hill with a peaked summit. [Brit. Dial.]
pīke, *n.*; *pl.* **pīke, pīkes,** [ME. *pik* for *pikefish*: from the pointed head.]
1. any of various slender, fierce fresh-water fishes of the genus *Esox,* with a narrow, pointed snout, projecting lower jaw, and sharp teeth; specifically, *Esox lucius,* of North America, Europe, and northern Asia.

COMMON PIKE (*Esox lucius*)

2. any of several fishes with snouts resembling that of the pike, as the garfish, garpike, and others.
great pike; the muskellunge.
pīked (pīkt), *a.* ending in a point; acuminated; tipped with a sharp-pointed head.
pīke′let, *n.* a light cake or muffin. [Brit. Dial.]
pīke′măn, *n.*; *pl.* **pīke′men,** 1. a soldier armed with a pike.
2. a miner who handles a pike, or pick.
3. the keeper of a tollgate on a turnpike.
pīke pẽrch, a fresh-water fish resembling the pike, common to Europe and America, as the walleyed pike.
pīke pōle, a pole with a sharp iron attached to one end, for directing the course of floating logs.
pīk′ẽr, *n.* 1. one who tramps a turnpike; a tramp; a vagabond. [Old Slang.]
2. a person who does things in a petty or niggardly way; especially, one who gambles or speculates in an overly cautious way. [Slang.]
pīke′staff, *n.*; *pl.* **pīke′stāves,** 1. the staff or shaft of a pike.
2. a staff with a sharp iron or steel point, used by travelers and explorers; an alpenstock.
pīke′tāil, *n.* see *pintail.*
pīke whāle (hwāl), a rorqual whale, *Balænoptera rostrata.*
pik′rō·līte, *n.* same as *picrolite.*
pi·läf′, pi·läff′, *n.* pilau.
pī′lăr, *a.* [L. *pilus,* a hair.] pertaining to hair; hairy.
pi·las′tẽr, *n.* [Fr. *pilastre*; It. *pilastro*; from L. *pila,* a pile.] a rectangular support or pier treated architecturally as a column, with a base, shaft, and capital.

PILASTER

pi·las′tẽred, *a.* furnished with pilasters.
pi·lau′, pi·law′, *n.* [Turk.] a Turkish or Oriental dish consisting of boiled rice and mutton or fish with spices.
pilch, *n.* [AS. *pylce, pylece,* a furred garment, from LL. *pellicea,* from L. *pellis,* skin.] a furred gown or case; something lined with fur. [Obs.]
pil′chărd, *n.* [perh. from ME. *pilken, pilchen,* to pluck, pick.] a small fish of the herring family, *Clupea pilchardus,* that are caught on the southern coast of England in great numbers.

Fools are as like husbands as
pilchards are to herrings.
—Shak.

pilch′ẽr, pilch′ẽrd, *n.* same as *pilchard.*

PILCHARD (*Clupea pilchardus*)

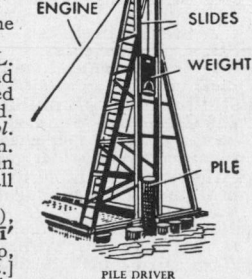

pil′çrōw, *n.* the paragraph symbol, ¶. [Obs.]
pīle, *n.* [ME.; OFr.; L. *pila,* a pillar.]
1. a mass of things heaped together; a heap.
2. a heap of wood or other combustible material on which a corpse or sacrifice is burned.
3. a large building or group of buildings.
4. a large amount or number. [Colloq.]
5. a lot of money; a fortune. [Slang.]
6. in electricity, (a) originally, a series of alternate plates of dissimilar metals with acid-saturated cloth or paper between them, for making an electric current; (b) any similar arrangement that produces an electric current; a battery.
7. in physics, a device for controlling the nuclear chain reaction in the production of atomic energy, consisting primarily of a latticework arrangement of uranium and some moderating material, as graphite.
pīle, *v.t.*; piled, *pt., pp.*; piling, *ppr.* 1. to put or set in a pile; to heap up.
2. to accumulate (with *up*).
3. to cover with a pile; to load.
pīle, *v.i.* 1. to form a pile or heap.
2. to move confusedly in a mass; to crowd (with *in, out, on, off,* etc.).
3. to accumulate (with *up*).
pīle, *n.* [AS. *pil,* a stake; L. *pilum,* a javelin.]
1. a long, heavy timber or beam driven into the ground, sometimes under water, to support a bridge, dock etc.
2. any similar supporting member, as of concrete.
3. in heraldry, a wedge-shaped charge with the point downward.
4. the head of an arrow; an arrow; a javelin. [Obs.]
cross and pile; see under *cross.*
pneumatic pile; see under *pneumatic.*
pīle, *v.t.*; piled, *pt., pp.*; piling, *ppr.* 1. to set or drive piles into.
2. to support, strengthen, or make a foundation for with piles.
pīle, *n.* [OFr. *peil*; Fr. *poil,* from L. *pilus,* a hair.]
1. a raised surface on material, produced by making yarn loops on the body of the cloth and, often, shearing them to produce a soft, velvety surface.
2. any of these loops.
3. soft, fine hair; down, wool, fur, etc.
Pī′lē·ȧ, *n.* same as *Adicea.*
pil′ē·āte, pil′ē·ā·ted, *a.* [L. *pileus,* a cap.]
1. having a pileus.
2. having a crest extending from the bill to the nape, as some birds.
pileated woodpecker; a North American woodpecker, *Ceophlœus pileatus,* with a red crest tapering to a point and a black and white body: also called *logcock.*
pīle bridge (brij), a bridge with a foundation of piles.
pīle çap, a beam that rests upon and forms a connection between the heads of piles.
pīled, *a.* having a pile, as certain textiles.
pīle drīv′ẽr, an engine with a drop hammer for driving piles: also *pile engine.*
pīle dwell′ing, same as *lake dwelling.*
pīle en′gine, same as *pile driver.*
pil′ē·i·fōrm, *a.* [L. *pileus,* cap, and *forma,* form.] shaped like a cap; pileated.
pi·lē′ō·lus, *n.*; *pl.* **pi·lē′ō·lī,** [L., dim. of *pileus,* cap.] in biology, a small cap, or crest.
pil″ē·ō·rhī′zȧ (-rī′), *n.*; *pl.* **pil″ē·ō·rhī′zae,** [L. *pileus,* cap, and Gr. *rhiza,* root.] the group of cells covering the growing end of a root; the rootcap.

CABLE TO ENGINE
PULLEY
SLIDES
WEIGHT
PILE
PILE DRIVER

pī′lē·ous, *a.* [L. *pilus,* hair.] hairy.

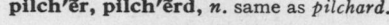

pīle′plank, *n.* a plank sharpened at the lower end used in making a cofferdam.

pīl′ẽr, *n.* [from *pile*, a heap.] one who piles or forms into a pile.

pīleṣ, *n.pl.* [LL. *pilæ*, pl. of L. *pila*, ball.] hemorrhoids; vascular tumors of the rectal mucous membrane; tumors formed by the dilatation of blood vessels in the region of the anus.

pī′lē-um, *n.*; *pl.* **pī′lē-ȧ,** [Mod. L.; from L. *pilleum*, felt cap.] the top of a bird's head from the bill to the nape.

pī′lē-us, *n.*; *pl.* **pī′lē-ī,** [L.] 1. in ancient Rome, a cap without a brim.
2. in botany, the cap of a mushroom.
3. in zoology, (a) the umbrella-shaped disk of a jellyfish; (b) the pileum.

pīle′wŏrm, *n.* a worm found in water-soaked timbers and piles; a shipworm; a teredo.

pīle′-wọrn, *a.* threadbare; having the pile worn off.

pīle′wŏrt, *n.* a plant of the crowfoot family, *Ranunculus ficaria*, whose tuberous roots have been used in poultices as a remedy for piles.

pil′fẽr, *v.i.*; pilfered, *pt.*, *pp.*; pilfering, *ppr.* [OFr. *pelfrer*, to plunder, from *pelfre*, goods, spoil, booty.] to steal in small quantities; to practice petty theft; as, he was caught *pilfering*.

pil′fẽr, *v.t.* to steal or gain by petty theft; to filch.
He would not *pilfer* the victory, and the defeat was easy. —Bacon.

pil′fẽr-ȧge, *n.* 1. a pilfering.
2. something pilfered.

pil′fẽr-ẽr, *n.* one who pilfers or practices petty theft.

pil′fẽr-ing-ly, *adv.* in a pilfering manner.

pil′fẽr-y, *n.* petty theft. [Obs.]

pil-gär′liç, *n.* [altered, from *pilled* (peeled) *garlic*.]
1. a bald-headed man.
2. a person regarded with contempt or pretended pity.

pil′grim, *n.* [Fr. *pelerin*; It. *pellegrino*, from L. *peregrinus*, a wanderer, a traveler in foreign parts, a foreigner; *per*, through, and *ager*, land.]
1. a wanderer; a sojourner.
2. a person who travels to a shrine or holy place.
3. [P–] a member of the band of English Puritans who founded Plymouth Colony in 1620.

pil′grim, *a.* of, like, or pertaining to a pilgrim; traveling; characteristic of pilgrims.
Pilgrim fathers; the Pilgrims.
pilgrim psalm; see *Song of Ascents* under *song*.

pil′grim, *v.i.* to behave as a pilgrim; to wander.

pil′grim-ȧge, *n.* 1. a journey undertaken by a pilgrim; specifically, a journey to some distant place, sacred and venerable for some reason, undertaken for devotional purposes.
Each did his patron witness make
That he such *pilgrimage* would take. —Scott.
2. figuratively, the journey of human life; the period between birth and death.
3. any long journey.
Syn.—journey, excursion, trip, expedition, tour.

pil′grim bot′tle, a flat bottle with a ring on each side to hold a cord: originally used by pilgrims.

pil′grim-īze, *v.i.* to wander about as a pilgrim. [Rare.]

pi-lī′, *n.* [Tag.] 1. the edible nut, somewhat like an almond, of a tropical tree of the Philippines.
2. the tree itself.

pī′lī, *n.* plural of *pilus*.

pil′i- [from L. *pilus*, a hair.] a combining form meaning *hair*, as in *piliform*.

pī-lid′i-um, *n.*; *pl.* **pī-lid′i-ȧ,** [L. *pileus*, cap, and Gr. *eidos*, appearance.] the helmet-shaped larvae of some nemertean worms, formerly regarded as a distinct genus.

pī-lif′ẽr-ous, *a.* [L. *pilus*, hair, and *ferre*, to bear.] bearing or producing hair or hairs, as a leaf.

pil′i-fọrm, *a.* [L. *pilus*, a hair, and *form*.] formed like a hair; hairlike.

pil′i-gȧ-nīne, pil′i-gȧ-nin, *n.* [Fr. *piligan*.] a yellowish, amorphous, poisonous alkaloid, $C_{15}H_{24}N_2O$, from *Lycopodium saussurus*, a South American plant.

pī-lig′ẽr-ous, *a.* [L. *pilus*, hair, and *gerere*, to bear.] bearing hair; covered with hair.

pīl′ing, *n.* 1. a supplying with piles.
2. piles collectively.
3. a structure of piles.

pill, *n.* the peel; the rind. [Obs.]

pill, *n.* [prob. M.D. *pille*, from L. *pilula*, dim. of *pila*, ball.]
1. a small ball or pellet of medicine to be swallowed whole.
2. anything unpleasant but unavoidable.
3. a baseball, golf ball, etc. [Slang.]
4. an unpleasant or boring person. [Slang.]
the pill or *the Pill*; any contraceptive drug for women. [Colloq.]

pill, *v.t.* 1. to dose with pills.
2. to form into pills.
3. to blackball. [Slang.]

pill, *v.t.* and *v.i.* [ME. *pilien*, *pillen*; Late AS. *pylian*; prob. from L. *pilare*, to make bare of hair, hence, fig., to peel, plunder, etc.]
1. to pillage; to plunder. [Archaic.]
2. to peel, skin, etc. [Archaic or Dial.]
3. to become or cause to become bald. [Obs.]

pil-laffe′, *n.* same as *pilau*.

pil′lȧġe, *n.* [Fr., from *piller*, to rob.]
1. a plundering.
2. that which is plundered; booty; loot.
Syn.—plunder, spoil, rapine.

pil′lȧġe, *v.t.*; pillaged, *pt.*, *pp.*; pillaging, *ppr.*
1. to deprive of money or property by violence; to loot.
2. to take as booty or loot.

pil′lȧġe, *v.i.* to take booty; to engage in plunder.

pil′laġ-ẽr, *n.* one who pillages; a plunderer.

pil′lăr, *n.* [ME. and OFr. *piler*; from L. *pila*, column.]
1. a column; a long, slender, vertical structure used to support a superstructure; also, such a column standing alone as a monument.
2. anything resembling a pillar or column in form or appearance; as, a *pillar* of fire.
3. figuratively, a supporter; one who sustains or supports; a mainstay.
4. in anatomy, a pillarlike fold, organ, part, etc.; as, the *pillars* of the abdominal ring; the *pillars* of the diaphragm.
5. in conchology, same as *columella*.
6. in ecclesiastical usage, a portable ornamental column carried before a cardinal as emblematic of his support to the church.
7. in firearms, a nipple.
8. in horsemanship, the center of the volt, ring, or manège ground, around which a horse turns. There are also pillars on the circumference or side, placed two and two at certain distances.
9. in horology, one of the posts in a watch or clock which separate and yet bind together the plates.
10. in mining, the mass of coal or ore left for the support of the ceiling of a mine.
11. in shipbuilding, a vertical post beneath a deck beam.
from pillar to post; from one predicament, place of appeal, etc. to another, usually under harassment.
Pillars of Hercules; the two points of land, Gibraltar and Jebel Musa, on either side of the Strait of Gibraltar.

pil′lăr block, same as *pillow block*.

pil′lăr box, a mail collection box. [Brit.]

pil′lăred (-lẽrd), *a.* 1. supported by pillars.
2. having the form of a pillar.

pil′lăr-et, *n.* a small pillar.

pil′lăr file, a narrow hand file with parallel sides and one safe edge.

pil′lăr-ist, *n.* same as *stylite*.

pil′lăr sāint, same as *stylite*.

pil-lau′, *n.* same as *pilau*.

pill bee′tle, a small round-bodied beetle of the genus *Byrrhus*.

pill′box″, *n.* 1. a small, shallow box, often cylindrical, for holding pills.
2. an enclosed gun emplacement of concrete and steel.

PILLBOX (fort)

3. a woman's short, cylindrical hat with a flat top.

pill bug, any of a number of related land crustaceans with a flat body, which has the ability to roll itself into a ball.

pilled (pild), *a.* 1. robbed. [Archaic.]
2. peeled. [Archaic or Dial.]
3. scant of hair; bald. [Obs.]

pil′lẽr-y, *n.*; *pl.* **pil′lẽr-ies,** pillage. [Obs.]

pil′liŏn (-yun), *n.* [from Gael. *peall*, a skin; L. *pellis*.]
1. a cushion attached behind a saddle for an extra rider, especially a woman.
2. an extra seat behind the driver's saddle on a motorcycle.

pill mil′lē-ped, in zoology, the pillworm.

pil′lō-rīze, *v.t.* to pillory.

pil′lō-ry, *n.*; *pl.* **pil′lō-rieṣ,** [Fr. *pilori*, from Pr. *espilori*.]
1. a device with holes for the head and hands, in which petty offenders were formerly locked and exposed to public scorn.
2. any exposure to public scorn, etc.

pil′lō-ry, *v.t.*; pilloried, *pt.*, *pp.*; pillorying, *ppr.*
1. to punish by placing in a pillory.
2. to hold up to public scorn, ridicule, or abuse.

pil′lōw, *n.* [ME. *pylwe*; AS. *pyle*; L. *pulvinus*, cushion.]
1. a cloth case filled with feathers, down, air, etc., used as a support for the head, as in sleeping.
2. any object used as a headrest.
3. anything like a pillow or cushion, as a pad on which certain laces are made.
4. anything that supports like a pillow, as the block supporting the inner end of a bowsprit.
5. a kind of coarse, twilled fustian.
pillow of a plow; a wooden crosspiece for raising or lowering the beam of a plow.

pil′lōw, *v.t.* 1. to rest on or as on a pillow.
2. to be a pillow for.

pil′lōw, *v.i.* to rest the head on or as on a pillow.

pil′lōw bär, the general background of pillow lace, consisting of threads which hold the pattern together.

pil′lōw biẽr, a pillowcase. [Obs.]

pil′lōw block, a block that supports the journal of a shaft, spindle, etc.

pil′lōw-çāse, *n.* a removable cotton or linen covering for a pillow.

pil′lōwed, *a.* supported by a pillow.

pil′lōw lāce, lace made by hand with bobbins over a pillow; bobbin lace.

pil′lōw sham, a decorative cover to be laid over a bed pillow.

pil′lōw-slip, *n.* a pillowcase.

pil′lōw-y, *a.* like a pillow; soft; yielding.

pill tīle, the plate on which a pharmacist rolls pills.

pill wil′let, [imitative.] in ornithology, the willet: also called *stone curlew*.

pill′wŏrm, *n.* in zoology, a myriapod of the genus *Iulus* or kindred genera, which rolls itself into the form of a pill; a gallyworm.

pī-lō-çär′pi-dīne, *n.* a siruplike alkaloid, $C_{10}H_{14}N_2O_2$, extracted from jaborandi.

pī-lō-çär′pīne, pī-lō-cär′pin, *n.* an alkaloid, $C_{11}H_{16}N_2O_2$, extracted from jaborandi, *Pilocarpus pinnatifolius*, and used in medicine to stimulate sweating.

Pī-lō-çär′pus, *n.* [Gr. *pilos*, cap, and *karpos*, fruit.] in botany, a genus of rutaceous shrubs of tropical America, bearing numerous small green or purple flowers.

pi-lō′ri rat, in zoology, the hutia of Cuba.

pī′lōse, *a.* [L. *pilosus*, from *pilus*, hair.] covered with or full of hair, especially fine, soft hair.

pī-los′i-ty, *n.* the condition of being pilose; hairiness.

pī′lŏt, *n.* [Fr. *pilote*; It. *pilota*, from Gr. *pedon*, an oar.]
1. a steersman; specifically, a person licensed to steer ships into or out of a harbor or through difficult waters.
Passengers in a ship always submit to their *pilot's* discretion. —South.
2. a guide; a director; one who directs the conduct of any person or undertaking; a spiritual guide.
3. a person who flies an airplane, airship, or balloon.
4. a device that guides the action of a machine or machine part.
5. the cowcatcher of a locomotive.
6. same as (a) *pilot cloth*; (b) *pilot light*.
7. a film (or videotape) of a single segment of a projected series of television shows, prepared for showing to prospective commercial sponsors: in full, *pilot film* (or *tape*).

8. an instrument for correcting compass error.

9. in railroading, one who directs the engineer of a locomotive through switching yards and other places where the system of tracks is complicated. [Brit.]

pī′lŏt, *v.t.*; piloted, *pt., pp.*; piloting, *ppr.* 1. to act as a pilot of, on, in, or over.

2. to guide; to conduct; to lead, as through dangers or difficulties.

pī′lŏt, *a.* 1. that serves as a guide or guiding device.

2. that serves as a device to start operation of a larger device; as, a *pilot* light.

3. that serves as a trial unit on a small scale for experimentation or testing.

pī′lŏt·āge, *n.* 1. a piloting.

2. the fee paid to a pilot.

3. the pilot's skill or knowledge of coasts, rocks, bars, and channels. [Rare.]

pī″lō·tax·it′iç, *a.* [Gr. *pilos*, felt, and *taxis*, an arranging, from *tassein*, to arrange.] consisting of slender microliths of feldspar, as certain volcanic rocks.

pī′lŏt bal·lo͝on′, a small balloon sent up to ascertain the velocity and direction of the wind.

pī′lŏt bīrd, a Caribbean bird whose presence indicates to sailors their approach to land.

pī′lŏt bis′cuit (-kit), hard biscuit used on ships; hardtack.

pī′lŏt bōat, a boat used by pilots for boarding ships near shore.

pī′lŏt bread (bred), pilot biscuit.

pī′lŏt bûrn′ẽr, pilot light.

pī′lŏt çloth, a heavy blue woolen cloth for overcoats and seamen's wear.

pī′lŏt en′ġine, a locomotive sent to clear the line in advance of a train, as a precaution.

pī′lŏt film, a film of a single segment of a projected series of television shows, prepared for showing to prospective commercial sponsors.

pī′lŏt fish, 1. a small pelagic fish, *Naucrates ductor*, about a foot long, of bluish color, marked with from five to seven broad dark vertical bars. It owes its name to its habit of accompanying large fish, generally sharks.

PILOT FISH (*Naucrates ductor*)

2. a fish, *Seriola zonata*.

3. a remora, or sucking fish.

4. a North American fresh-water fish, *Prosopium cylindraceum*.

pī′lŏt·house, *n.* an enclosed place on the upper deck of a ship, where the helmsman works the steering gear.

pī′lŏt·işm, *n.* pilotage; skill in piloting. [Rare.]

pī′lŏt jack, a flag or signal shown by a vessel when in need of a pilot.

pī′lŏt lamp, 1. an electric lamp which indicates the location of a switch or circuit breaker.

2. an electric lamp placed in an electric circuit to indicate when the current is on.

pī′lŏt līght, 1. a small gas burner which is kept lighted to rekindle the principal burner when needed: also *pilot burner*.

2. a pilot lamp.

pī′lŏt plant, a small factory or manufacturing unit for making experimental tests of new methods and techniques of production.

pī′lŏt·ry, *n.* same as pilotage.

pī′lŏt snāke, a large blacksnake, *Coluber obsoletus*, of North America.

pī′lŏt·weed, *n.* the compass plant.

pī′lŏt whāle (hwāl), the caaing whale.

pī′lous, *a.* same as *pilose*.

Pil′şẽner, Pil′şnẽr (pilz′nẽr, pils′-), *a.* [after *Pilsen*, city in Bohemia, where first made.] designating a light, Bohemian lager beer, traditionally served in a tall, conical, footed glass (*Pilsener glass*).

Pilt′down man, a supposed species of prehistoric man whose existence was presumed on the basis of bone fragments found in Piltdown (England) in 1911: exposed as a hoax in 1953.

pil′ū·lȧ, *n.*; *pl.* **pil′ū·lae,** [L., dim. of *pila*, ball.] in pharmacy, a pill.

pil′ū·lăr, *a.* pertaining to pills; like a pill; as, a *pilular* form.

pil′ūle, *n.* [Fr.; L. *pilula*.] a small pill.

pil′ū·lous, *a.* resembling a pill; small; of little importance. [Rare.]

pī′lum, *n.*; *pl.* **pī′lȧ,** [L.] 1. a heavy javelin used by the Roman infantry.

2. a pharmacists' pestle.

pī′lus, *n.*; *pl.* **pī′lī,** [L., hair.] a hairlike structure found on certain species of plants and animals.

pī′ly, *a.* [L. *pilus*, hair.] having the appearance or quality of pile, or fine, soft hair.

pī′ly, *a.* [L. *pila*, pillar.] in heraldry, divided into piles.

Pī′mȧ, *n.*; *pl.* **Pī′mȧ, Pī′mȧş,** a member of a tribe of Nahuatl Indians that live in the Gila and Salt River Valleys, Arizona.

Pī′mȧ, *a.* of the Pimas.

Pī′mȧ çot′tŏn, [after *Pima* County, Arizona.] a tough, strong, smooth, long-staple cotton grown in the southwestern United States.

Pī′măn, *n.* 1. one of the three branches of the Uto-Aztecan family of languages.

2. *pl.* **Pī′mănş, Pī′măn,** a Pima Indian.

Pī′măn, *a.* 1. of Piman.

2. of the Pimans.

pī·mar′iç, *a.* [L. *pinus*, pine, and *maritimus*, maritime, and *-ic*.] in chemistry, derived from the maritime pine or galipot; as, *pimaric* acid.

Pī·mē′lē·ȧ, *n.* [Gr. *pimelē*, fat.] a genus of Australian and New Zealand shrubs comprising about 80 species, several of which are cultivated in greenhouses under the name *rice flower*.

pī·mel′iç, *a.* [Gr. *pimelē*, fat.] in chemistry, derived from certain fatty bodies, as oleic acid.

pim·e·lī′tis, *n.* [Gr. *pimelē*, fat, and *-itis*.] inflammation of the adipose tissue.

Pim·e·lō′dus, *n.* [Gr. *pimelōdēs*, fatty.] the typical genus of the *Pimelodinæ*, a subfamily of Central and South American catfishes, having four mental and two maxillary barbels.

pī′ment, *n.* wine flavored with a mixture of spice or honey. [Obs.]

pi·men′tȧ, *n.* same as *pimento*.

pi·men′tō, *n.*; *pl.* **pi·men′tōş,** [Sp. *pimienta*.] 1. allspice; also, the tree producing it, which is cultivated in Jamaica.

2. the pimiento.

pi·men′tō cheeşe, a processed cheese to which pimentos have been added.

pi·mien′tō (-myen′), *n.*; *pl.* **pi·mien′tōş,** [Sp. *pimienta*.] a varity of garden pepper or its sweet red fruit, used as a relish, for stuffing olives, etc.; Spanish paprika.

pim′li·çō, *n.* [imitative.] the friarbird of Australia.

pimp, *n.* [prob. from or connected with OFr. *pimper*, to allure, entice (esp. by dressing smartly).] a go-between in illicit sexual affairs; especially, a prostitute's agent; a pander.

pimp, *v.i.* to act as a pimp.

pim′pẽr·nel, *n.* [ML. *pipinella*; L. *piperinus*, as if composed of peppercorns, from *piper*, pepper.] in botany, any plant of the genus *Anagallis*, of the primrose family. *Anagallis arvensis* bears small blue, purple, scarlet, or white flowers, which close at the approach of bad weather: also called *poor man's weatherglass*.

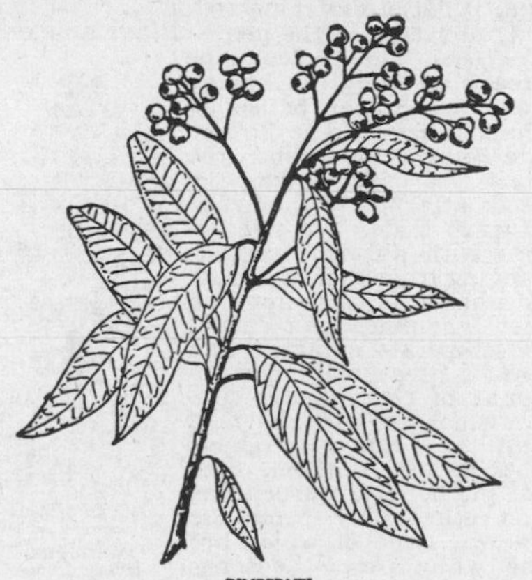

PIMPERNEL

bastard pimpernel; same as *chaffweed*.

false pimpernel; an American figwort, *Ilysanthes riparia*, which grows on damp ground.

pimp′pi·nel, *n.* in botany, the burnet saxifrage.

pimp′ing, *a.* 1. petty; mean. [Colloq.]

2. sickly; puny. [Colloq.]

pim′ple, *n.* [AS. *piplian*, to blister.]

1. any small, usually inflamed, swelling of the skin; papule or pustule.

2. any excrescence like a pimple.

pim′pled (-pld), *a.* having pimples.

pim′ple met′al, a by-product in the smelting of copper, containing about three-fourths copper.

pim′ply, *a.*; *comp.* pimplier; *superl.* pimpliest, pimpled; having pimples.

pin, *n.* [AS. pinn; akin to G. *pinne*.]

1. a peg of wood, metal, etc., used for fastening or holding things together, as a support for hanging things, etc.

2. a little piece of stiff wire with a pointed end and flattened or rounded head, for fastening things together.

3. something worthless or insignificant; trifle.

4. a pointed instrument for holding the hair, a hat, etc. in place.

5. a clothespin, hairpin, cotter's pin, rolling pin, etc.

6. anything like a pin in form, use, etc.

7. an ornament or badge having a pin or clasp with which it is fastened to the clothing.

8. [*usually pl.*] the leg. [Colloq.]

9. in bowling, one of the wooden clubs at which the ball is rolled.

10. in golf, the pole for the flag, at the hole of a green.

11. in music, a peg in a violin, cello, etc., for holding a string and regulating the tension.

12. in nautical usage, (a) a tholepin; (b) any of various pegs or bolts used in fastening the rigging.

on pins and needles; filled with anxiety; in a state of suspense or nervous anticipation.

pin, *v.t.*; pinned, *pt., pp.*; pinning, *ppr.* 1. to fasten with or as with a pin.

2. to pierce with a pin.

3. to hold firmly in one place or position.

4. to give one's fraternity pin to, as an informal token of betrothal. [College Slang.]

5. to pen; to enclose or keep in a pen. [Now Rare.]

to pin one down; to get a person to commit himself as to his opinion, a course of action, etc.

to pin (something) on one; to lay the blame of (something) on one. [Colloq.]

pī′nȧ, *n.* [from L. *pinea*, pine cone.] silver amalgam formed into a cone for use in a retort; also, such a cone after heating in a retort.

pī·nā′cē·ae, *n.pl.* the *Coniferæ*, the pine family of trees, including the pine, cedar, fir, etc.

pī·nā′ceous, *a.* of or like the *Pinaceæ*.

pi′ña çloth (pi′nyä), [Sp. *piña*, the pineapple.] a delicate, soft, transparent cloth with a yellowish tinge, made in the Philippine Islands from the fibers of the pineapple leaf.

pin′ȧ·çoid, *n.* [Gr. *pinax* (-*akos*), tablet, and *-oid*.] a plane to which two crystallographic axes are parallel.

pi·naç′ō·lin, *n.* [*pinacone*, and L. *oleum*, oil, and *-in*.] a derivative of pinacone, having the formula $C_6H_{12}O$. It is a colorless, oily liquid resembling peppermint in odor.

pin′ȧ·çōne, *n.* [Gr. *pinax* (-*akos*), tablet.] a derivative of acetone, having the formula $C_6H_{14}O_2$. It occurs in white crystals and also as a liquid.

pin″ȧ·çō·thē′çȧ, *n.* [Gr. *pinax* (-*akos*), a picture, and *thēkē*, a repository.] a picture gallery.

pin′ȧ·fōre, *n.* [*pin* and *afore*.] a sleeveless, apronlike garment worn especially by girls.

pi·nang′, *n.* [Malay.] the betel nut palm, *Areca cathecu*; also, its fruit.

pi·nas′tẽr, *n.* [L., from *pinus*, pine.] the cluster pine or seaside pine of the Mediterranean.

pi·ñā′tä (pi-nyä′tä), *n.* [Sp., orig., a pot, from It. *pignatta*, from L. *pinea*, a pine cone, from *pinus*, a pine tree.] in Mexico, a clay or papier-mâché container of various forms and shapes, hung from the ceiling on certain festivals and broken in a game by children with a stick so as to release its contents of toys and candy.

pin′ba̤ll mȧ·çhīne′, a game machine with an inclined board, typically containing a number of holes surrounded by numerous pins, springs, etc. and marked with scores credited to the player if he causes a number of spring-driven balls to strike the pins or roll into the holes.

pin bōr′ẽr, any of a number of small beetles which bore minute holes in trees, as bark beetles, etc.

pin boy, in bowling, a boy or man who sets up

the pins after each frame and returns the balls to the bowlers.

pin'çase, *n.* a case for holding pins.

pince'-nez (pans'nā), *n.*; *pl.* **pince'-nez,** [Fr., lit., nose-pincher.] eyeglasses kept in place on the nose by means of a spring.

pin'cērs, *n.pl.* [*occas. construed as sing.*] [OFr. *pincoir*, from *pincer*, to pinch.]

1. a tool having two jaws for gripping and two handles arranged as levers. Many forms are adapted for special work.

2. in zoology, the nippers of certain animals, as of insects and crustaceans; a chela. Also *pinchers.*

PINCERS

pin'cērs mōve'ment, a military movement in which simultaneous flank movements are used to converge upon an enemy force or stronghold and cut it off from support and supplies.

pinch, *v.t.*; pinched (pincht), *pt., pp.*; pinching, *ppr.* [Fr. *pincer.*]

1. to squeeze between a finger and the thumb or between two surfaces, edges, etc.

2. to press painfully upon (some part of the body).

3. to cause distress or discomfort to.

4. to cause to become thin, cramped, etc., as by hunger, pain, cold, etc.

5. to restrict closely; to straiten; to stint (often in the passive).

6. to steal. [Slang.]

7. to arrest or make a police raid on. [Slang.]

8. in nautical usage, to sail close-hauled.

pinch, *v.i.* 1. to squeeze painfully.

2. to be stingy or niggardly.

3. in mining, to become narrower; hence, to give (*out*): said of a vein of ore.

pinch, *n.* 1. a pinching; a squeeze or nip.

2. the quantity that may be grasped between the finger and thumb; a small amount.

3. distress; hardship; difficulty.

4. an emergency; an urgent situation or time.

5. a theft. [Slang.]

6. an arrest or raid. [Slang.]

7. a pinch bar.

pinch bär, a kind of crowbar having a pointed, projecting end, used in moving heavy weights, especially car wheels; a pinch.

pinch'beck, *n.* [after Christopher *Pinchbeck*, Eng. jeweler who invented it c. 1725.]

1. an alloy of copper and zinc used to imitate gold in cheap jewelry.

2. anything cheap or imitation.

pinch'beck, *a.* 1. made of pinchbeck.

2. cheap; imitation; spurious.

pinch'çock, *n.* any of various clamps for regulating the flow of a liquid through a compressible tube of rubber, etc.

pin'chem, *n.* [imitative.] the blue titmouse. [Brit. Dial.]

pinch'ẽr, *n.* one who or that which pinches.

pinch'ẽrs, *n.pl.* same as *pincers.*

pinch'fist, *n.* a miser; a niggard.

pinch'-hit, *v.i.*; pinch-hit, *pt., pp.*; pinch-hitting, *ppr.* 1. in baseball, to bat in place of the regular player when a hit is especially needed.

2. to act as a substitute in an emergency (*for*).

pinch hit'tẽr, one who pinch-hits.

pinch'ing bug, the hellgrammite. [Dial.]

pinch'ing·ly, *adv.* in a niggardly manner.

pinch'ing nut, a check nut, lock nut, or jam nut.

pinch'pen''ny, *n.*; *pl.* **pinch'pen''nies,** a miser; a grasping person. [Obs.]

Pin'ci·an (-shi-an), *a.* designating a small hill, formerly the Collis Hortorum, now known as Monte Pincio, just inside the walls of Rome, or a street and gate near by.

pin çlō'vẽr, a weed of the geranium family, *Erodium cicutarium*, common as a forage plant in California: also known as *pin grass, alfilerilla* or *alfilaria.*

pin'çoff''in, *n.* [after *Pincoff*, an English manufacturer.] a kind of garance prepared for commercial use: it produces deep violet shades.

piñç'piñç, *n.* [echoic of its note.] any of several African warblers of the genus *Drymæca.*

pin'çush''iŏn (-un), *n.* a small cushion in which pins and needles are stuck for convenience and safekeeping.

pin'dăl, pin'dăr, *n.* the groundnut, *Arachis hypogæa*; the peanut. [Dial.]

Pin·dar'iç, *a.* [L. *Pindaricus*; Gr. *Pindarikos.*]

1. of, characteristic of, or in the style of, Pindar.

2. elaborate or regular in metrical structure.

3. designating an ode in which the strophe and antistrophe have the same form, in contrast to the epode, which has a different form.

Pin·dar'iç, *n.* a Pindaric ode.

Pin·dar'iç·ăl, *a.* same as *Pindaric.*

Pin'dăr·işm, *n.* a style of writing imitating Pindar.

Pin'dăr·ist, *n.* one who adopts or attempts to adopt a Pindaric style of writing.

pin'dẽr, *n.* a poundkeeper. [Brit.]

pind'jä·jap (pin'), *n.* a boat of Sumatra and the Malay Archipelago, with one to three masts, generally two, carrying square sails, and having both the stem and stern much projected. Pindjajaps are used in carrying spices, cacao, and areca nuts to ports frequented by Europeans, and are also fitted out as pirate vessels.

PINDJAJAP

pin'dling, *a.* [euphemized var. of *piddling.*] puny; weak and undersized. [Dial.]

pin drill, a form of drill used as a counterbore. It has a pinlike end to center the drill in a hole previously bored.

pīne, *v.t.*; pined, *pt., pp.*; pining, *ppr.* [AS. *pīnian*, to torment, from *pīn*, L. *pœna*, pain.]

1. to wear out; to make to languish. [Dial.]

2. to afflict. [Obs.]

3. to grieve for; to bemoan; to mourn for. [Archaic.]

pīne, *v.i.* 1. to languish; to lose flesh or waste away through grief, pain, hunger, etc.; to grow thin or spiritless: followed sometimes by *away.*

> Ye shall not mourn nor weep; but ye shall *pine away* for your iniquities.
> —Ezek. xxiv. 23.

2. to languish with desire; to have an intense longing or desire; to yearn (with *for, after*, or an infinitive).

> Unknowing that she *pined for* your return.
> —Dryden.

Syn.—droop, fade, languish, waste.

pīne, *n.* woe; want; misery; wretchedness; torment. [Archaic.]

pīne, *n.* [L. *pinus*, pine tree.]

1. any tree of the genus *Pinus* and order *Coniferæ.* The typical pine tree is an evergreen having cones and clusters of needle-shaped leaves. The flowers are monoecious, and the fruit is a cone, having the seeds attached to the inside of each scale. The size varies with different species, ranging from that of a bush to a height of three hundred feet. The pines are plentiful in temperate climates, and are of great utility on account of the valuable timber which some species yield and the resinous products obtained from them, such as pitch, tar, turpentine, and resin. Many species are known, some of which are the white pine, the long-leafed pine, the yellow pine of the east (including the Georgia pine), and the nut pine, which has an edible fruit. The most important variety in Europe is the Scotch pine.

WHITE PINE (*Pinus strobus*)

2. any one of various trees of the order *Coniferæ*, but of a genus other than *Pinus*, as the black pine, *Callistris calcarata*, and the colonial pine, *Araucaria cunninghamii*; also, any plant or shrub resembling the pine.

STONE PINE (*Pinus pinea*)

3. the wood of a pine tree.

4. a pineapple. [Colloq.]

Aleppo or *Jerusalem pine*; *Pinus halepensis*, a low, spreading tree which ripens its cones in the autumn of the second year. It is found in the Apennines, in southern France, Dalmatia, Syria, Spain, and Asia Minor.

Amboina pine; *Dammara orientalis*, a huge tree with a smooth bark and straight trunk found in the mountains of Amboina and Ternate, and in the Molucca Islands, Java, and Borneo: also called *pitch tree.*

Austrian pine; *Pinus austriaca*, a large tree with spreading branches. Its timber is tough and resinous.

Balfour's pine; *Pinus balfouriana*, a straight tree of pyramidal shape, branching regularly from the ground and of thick foliage.

Bhutan pine; *Pinus excelsa*, a tree found principally in Nepal, also in Bhutan and thoughout the central zone bounded in part by the Himalayas. It is of immense height, with long horizontal branches, and has soft, white, compact timber, which furnishes a fragrant turpentine.

bishop's pine; *Pinus muricata*, a very distinct pine found in California. It is straight, short, and hardy.

black Austrian pine; same as *Austrian pine.*

black pine; a tree having a dark, fine-checked bark, leaves slightly colored by a whitish powder which, when broken, exhale an aromatic odor: also called *Sierra red-bark pine, Peninsula black pine*, and *Montana black pine.*

Brazil pine; *Araucaria brasiliensis*, a handsome pyramidal tree, covered with a smooth bark: it forms large forests in Brazil.

bull pine; same as *heavy-wooded pine.*

Calabrian cluster pine; *Pinus brutia*, a rare tree of medium height with thick, bright-green foliage.

Californian mountain pine; *Pinus monticola*, a tall tree with a dense head and short, glaucous leaves, abundant in northern California. It is also common throughout the Rocky Mountain regions.

Canary Island pine; *Pinus canariensis*, a large timber tree of the Canary Islands.

candlewood pine; *Pinus teocote*, a tall Mexican tree, with durable and resinous timber.

Chile pine; *Araucaria imbricata*, an immense tree growing on the western slopes of the Andes. Its nutritious seeds are eaten by the Indians.

Chinese pine; *Pinus sinensis*, a low, branching tree with a drooping appearance, found in China and Japan.

cluster pine; *Pinus pinaster*, a large tree which grows best when freely exposed to sea breezes. It is thickly set with foliage and is found in southern Europe and eastern Asia.

Corsican pine; *Pinus laricio*, an open pyramidal tree having a whitish wood, which becomes brown near the center. It is native to Corsica though found also in Greece, Crete, and Spain.

digger pine; *Pinus sabiniana*, a Californian tree with white, even-grained timber, not very durable.

dwarf Cembra pine; *Pinus cembra pygmæa*, a stunted pine of the Ural Mountains.

dwarf Corsican pine; a small variety of the Corsican pine.

dwarf Weymouth pine; a stunted Weymouth pine.

frankincense pine; same as *loblolly.*

Georgia pine; *Pinus palustris*, a large tree of the southern United States.

gigantic pine; same as *Lambert's pine.*

heavy-wooded pine; *Pinus ponderosa*, a tree of great size, found abundantly in the states of the Northwest: it furnishes a coarse-grained timber.

Highland pine; *Pinus sylvestris*, a tree of central Europe, Scotland, and North America, of a variety of types; the Scotch pine.

Hudson Bay pine; *Pinus banksiana*, a pine found near Hudson Bay: also called *Bank's pine* and *gray pine*.

Italian stone pine; *Pinus pinea*, the Tuscan tree which produces the Carpathian balsam.

Jersey or *New Jersey pine*; a low, spreading pine of North America, found principally in New Jersey.

knee pine; *Pinus mughus*, a pine of the Styrian Alps, which never grows more than three feet high.

Labrador pine; same as *Hudson Bay pine*.

Lambert's pine; *Pinus lambertiana*, a gigantic tree with an open, pyramidal head, found in the Northwest: also called *sugar pine*.

larch pine; same as *Corsican pine*.

maritime pine; same as *cluster pine*.

Moreton Bay pine; *Araucaria cunninghamii*, an Australian pine which yields a soft timber.

Mountain pine; same as *Californian mountain pine*.

Norfolk Island pine; *Araucaria excelsa*, a

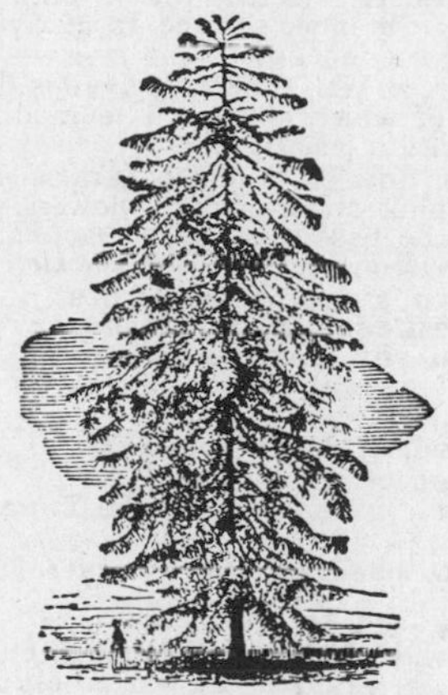

NORFOLK ISLAND PINE

majestic Australian pine with awl-shaped leaves.

Norway pine; *Pinus sylvestris*, a variety of the Scotch pine growing in Norway, Canada, etc.

old-field pine; same as *loblolly*.

Oyster Bay pine; an Australian pine of medium size.

parasol pine or *umbrella pine*; *Pinus sciadopitys*, a tree whose leaves are in whorls like an umbrella.

pond pine; *Pinus serotina*, a medium-sized tree which grows on the edges of swamps in Pennsylvania, the Carolinas, and New Jersey.

pumpkin pine; same as *Weymouth pine*.

red pine; a tree, *Pinus resinosa*, found at its

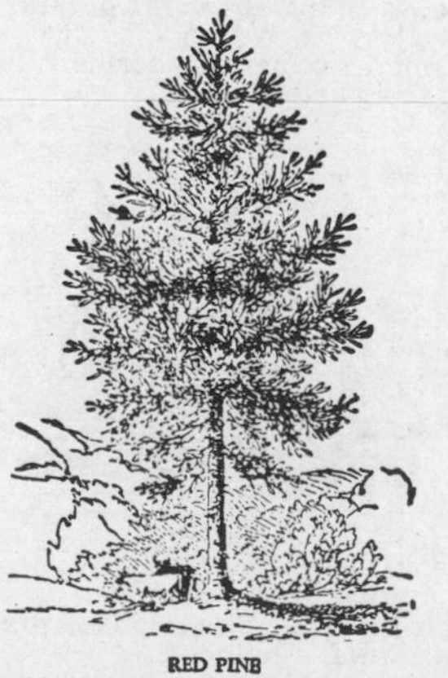

RED PINE

best in Minnesota and northern Wisconsin. It grows throughout Canada and in some parts of New England. It is valued for its wood, which is of a light reddish color, and combines qualities of hardness, toughness, and elasticity which make it highly suitable for general marine construction; also, the Norway pine, *Pinus rubra* or *sylvestris*, a variety of the Scotch pine.

Riga pine; same as *Highland pine*.

Scotch pine; *Pinus sylvestris*, of northern Europe and Asia, valuable for its timber: also called *Highland pine*.

Siberian pine; *Pinus cembra*, a lofty tree with leaves much shorter, more dense, and of a brighter green than those of the Swiss variety. Its seeds are large and edible.

star pine; same as *cluster pine*.

Swiss pine; *Pinus cembra*, a tree found in the highest regions of the Alps, of bluntish pyramidal shape, and thick foliage. Its timber is soft, fine in the grain, and resinous. Its seeds are large and edible.

thread-leaved pine; *Pinus filifolia*, a pine found in Guatemala, which is sixty feet high, with short, robust branches, and furnished with long, curved leaves. Its timber is light and of little value.

torch pine; same as *pitch pine*.

umbrella pine; see *parasol pine*.

Weymouth pine; a tall tree, *Pinus strobus*, with a smooth bark, found in Canada and New England: also called *Canadian white pine* and *pumpkin pine*. It derived its name from Lord Weymouth, who introduced the tree into England in 1705. Its timber is white, light, and easily worked.

yellow pine; any of several American pines having yellowish wood, which is close-grained, moderately resinous, durable, and widely used in manufacture.

pin′ē̤·ăl, *a.* [Fr. *pinéale*, from L. *pinea*, the cone of a pine, from *pinus*, a pine.]

1. pertaining to a pine cone; conical; shaped like a pine cone.

2. of or pertaining to the pineal gland.

pineal gland or *body*; a small, cone-shaped body or gland about the size of a pea, situated in the brain of all vertebrates having a cranium. It is supposed to be a vestigial sensory organ. Also called *epiphysis* and *conarium*.

pīne′ap″ple, *n.* [ME. *pinappel*, pine cone; mod. sense from shape of the fruit.]

1. a juicy, edible tropical fruit somewhat resembling a pine cone: it consists of the fleshy inflorescence of a collective fruit developed from a spike of flowers.

2. the plant, *Ananas sativus*, it grows on, having a short stem and spiny-edged recurved leaves from which a useful fiber is obtained.

3. a small dynamite bomb or hand grenade. [Slang.]

PINEAPPLE (*Ananas sativus*)

wild pineapple; the *Bromelia pinguin*, a tropical plant related to the pineapple, having violet flowers and yielding a valuable fiber.

pīne′ap″ple clo̤th, a delicate fabric made from the fiber of the pineapple leaf; piña cloth.

pīne′ap″ple flow′ẽr, any lilylike plant of the genus *Eucomis* and family *Liliaceæ*, resembling the pineapple in structure, and bearing ornamental fragrant flowers.

pīne′ap″ple mīte, a red mite, very destructive to the pineapple.

pīne bar′ren, a tract of poor land covered with pine trees.

pīne bōr′ẽr, any beetle whose larvae damage pines by boring under the bark or into the wood.

pīne′-clad, *a.* clad with pine trees.

pīne c̦one, the cone, or fruit, of the pine tree.

pīne′-c̦rowned, *a.* covered with pines, as hills.

pīne′drops, *n.*; *pl.* **pīne′drops,** a dark-red herb bearing white flowers but no leaves, parasitic on the roots of pine trees. It is native to the United States.

pīne finch, same as *pine siskin*.

pīne grōs′bēak, a beautiful finch of the Northern Hemisphere.

pīne gum, a resin obtained from trees of Australia of the genus *Callitris*.

pīne lin′net, same as *pine finch*.

pīne liz′ărd, a small lizard of North America; the fence lizard.

pīne mär′ten, 1. a beautifully colored marten of Europe.

2. the sable of America.

pīne mouse, an American field mouse.

pi·nen′c̦hy·mȧ, *n.* [LL., from Gr. *pinax*, tablet, and *enchyma*, infusion.] a tissue occurring in the epidermis of some plants, having cells which are broad and thin; tabular parenchyma.

pī′nēne, *n.* [*pine* (a tree) and *-ene*.] either of two isomeric terpenes, $C_{10}H_{16}$, occurring in oil of turpentine and other essential oils.

pīne nee′dle, one of the needlelike leaves of a pine tree.

pine-needle wo͝ol; a kind of fibrous material manufactured from pine needles: it is used for rough garments and as a filling for pillows.

pīne nut, 1. a pine cone.

2. the kernel of any of several species of pine.

pīne oil, an oil much like turpentine, a product of pine and fir trees, used in the manufacture of varnishes and colors.

pīne pest, a moth whose larvae are destructive to pines.

pīn′ẽr·y, *n.*; *pl.* **pīn′ẽr·ies̹,** 1. a plantation or hothouse in which tropical plants, as pineapples, are grown.

2. a locality in which pine trees grow; specifically, a pine forest yielding lumber, as in northern Minnesota, Wisconsin, and Michigan.

pīne′sap, *n.* a parasitic or saprophytic herb of the genus *Monotropsis* or *Schweinitzia*, found on the roots of pine trees. It grows from four to ten inches in height, is of a reddish or whitish color, and bears a cluster of flowers.

pīne sis′kin, a small, streaked, brown finch with yellow markings on the wings and tail: also *pine finch*.

pīne snāke, a harmless snake, native to North America.

pīne tär, a viscid, blackish-brown liquid prepared by the destructive distillation of pine wood and used in the preparation of expectorants, disinfectants, tar paints, roofing materials, etc.

pīne tree, a tree of the genus *Pinus*.

pine-tree money; silver coins stamped with the figure of a pine tree, coined in Massachusetts during the seventeenth century.

pī·nē′tum, *n.*; *pl.* **pī·nē′tȧ,** [L.] a grove or plantation of pine trees, particularly one intended for any special purpose.

pīne wa̤r′blẽr, a variety of small warbler living in the pine forests of the eastern United States.

pīne′weed, *n.* a small herb having little scale-like leaves and tiny flowers. It grows in sandy soils and is common in the eastern sections of the United States.

pīne wee′vil, a weevil whose larvae bore the wood of pine trees.

pīne wool, same as *pine-needle wool* under *pine needle*.

pīn′ey, *a.* piny.

pīn′ey, *n.* peony. [Dial.]

pin′-eyed″ (-īd), *a.* in botany, having the stigma visible at the throat of the corolla, and the stamens hidden from sight in the tube: opposed to *thrum-eyed*.

pin′feath″ẽr (-feth″), *n.* a small or undeveloped feather that is just emerging through the skin.

pin′feath″ẽred, *a.* having the feathers only beginning to emerge; not fully fledged.

pin′-fīre, *a.* designating a style of cartridge used in breech-loading guns, or a gun in which this form of cartridge is used.

pin′fish, *n.*; *pl.* **pin′fish** or **pin′fish·es̹,** any of various small fish of the porgy family, having a sharp dorsal spine and found in the South Atlantic along the southern coast of the United States, as the *Lagodon rhomboides*, *Diplodus holbrooki*, or *Lepomis pallidus*.

pin′fōld, *n.* [AS. *pyndan*, to pen, to pound, and *fold*.] a place in which stray animals are confined; an animal pound.

pin′fōld, *v.t.* to impound in a pinfold.

pin′-foot″ed, *a.* in ornithology, fin-footed; having the toes lobate.

ping, *n.* [imitative.]

1. the sound made by a bullet as it passes through the air.

2. the sound made by a bullet in striking something sharply.

ping, *v.i.* and *v.t.*; pinged, *pt.*, *pp.*; pinging, *ppr.* to travel or strike with a ping.

piñ′gle, *v.i.* 1. to eat with little appetite. [Scot. and Brit. Dial.]

2. to strive. [Scot. and Brit. Dial.]

piñ′gle, *n.* 1. a small enclosed place. [Obs.]

2. a difficulty. [Obs.]

ping′-pong″, *n.* [echoic.] a game somewhat like tennis in miniature, played on a large, rectangular table, usually indoors, with a small, hollow celluloid ball and small, racket-shaped paddles; table tennis: a trade-mark (*Ping-pong*).

pin grȧss, see *pin clover*.

pin′guē·fȳ, *v.t.*; pinguefied, *pt.*, *pp.*; pinguefying, *ppr.* to fatten. [Now Rare.]

pin·guiç′ū·lȧ (-gwik′), *n.* [L. *pinguiculus*, from *pinguis*, fat.]
1. in botany, same as *butterwort*.
2. a triangular yellowish patch on either side of the cornea in old age due to irritation from dust, etc.

piñ′guid (-gwid), *a.* [L. *pinguis*, fat.]
1. fat; unctuous.
2. rich; fertile: said of soil.

piñ·guid′i·nous, *a.* containing fat. [Obs.]

piñ·guid′i·ty, *n.* the quality or condition of being pinguid.

piñ′guin, *n.* same as *penguin*.

piñ′gui·tūde, *n.* [L. *pinguitudo*, from *pinguis*, fat.] fatness; a growing fat. [Rare.]

pin′head (-hed), *n.* 1. the head of a pin.
2. anything very small or trifling; a minute object.
3. a stupid or silly person.

pin′hōld, *n.* a place at which a pin holds or makes fast.

pin′hōle, *n.* 1. a small hole made by or as by the puncture or perforation of a pin; a very small aperture.
2. a hole into which a pin or peg goes.
3. in photography, a tiny transparent dot on the negative of a photograph from some fault or chemical defect.
false pinhole; in making lace, one of the inner pinholes in a rounded strip of lace, which is a guide to the outer curve: also called *false stitch*.
pinhole photography; photography in which, instead of a lens, the camera has a tiny aperture.

pī′niç, *a.* in chemistry, of, pertaining to, or derived from the pine.
pinic acid; abietic acid, obtained from the resin of the pine. [Obs.]

pī·niç′ō·line, *a.* [L. *pinus*, pine tree, and *colere*, to inhabit.] dwelling in or among conifers.

pī′ni·fôrm, *a.* [L. *pinus*, pine tree, and *forma*, form.] shaped like a pine cone.

pīn′ing·ly, *adv.* in a pining manner.

pīn′ings, *n.pl.* fallen or dry needles of the pine. [Poet.]

pin′iŏn (-yun), *n.* [Fr. *pignon* (in OFr., a battlement); ult., from L. *pinna*, a pinnacle.] a small cogwheel the teeth of which fit into those of a larger gear wheel or those of a rack.

PINION AND SPUR GEAR

pin′iŏn, *n.* [ME.; OFr. *pignon*; L. *pinna*, *penna*, a feather.]
1. the end joint of a bird's wing.
2. a wing.
3. any wing feather.
4. the anterior border of an insect's wing.
5. a fetter or band for the arm. [Obs.]
6. any of various moths.

pin′iŏn, *v.t.*; pinioned, *pt.*, *pp.*; pinioning, *ppr.*
1. to bind or confine the wings of; to confine by binding the wings or by cutting off the first joint of the wing.
2. to bind (the wings).
3. to disable or impede by binding the arms of.
4. to confine or shackle.

pin′iŏn bōne, the bones of a pinion collectively.

pin′iŏned, *a.* 1. furnished with wings.
2. having the wings or arms bound or confined.

pin′iŏn fīle, a thin file used by watchmakers.

pin′iŏn·ist, *n.* a winged animal; a bird. [Obs.]

pin′iŏn wīre, wire formed into the shape and size required for the pinions of clocks and watches.

pī·ni·pī′çrin, *n.* a bitter substance extracted from the needles and bark of the Scotch fir. It is a bright-yellow hygroscopic powder, soluble in water, alcohol, and ether alcohol.

pī·ni·tan′niç, *a.* designating a certain acid derived from the pine.

pīn′īte (*or* pin′), *n.* [from *Pini*, a mine in Saxony.] an amorphous mineral, found only in crystals as pseudomorphs and occurring in green, brownish, and reddish translucent to opaque masses. It is essentially a hydrous silicate of aluminum and potassium, the proportions being variable.

pīn′īte, *n.* same as *pinitol*.

Pī·nī′tēș, *n.pl.* [L. *pinus*, pine tree.] a group of fossil plants thought to be allied to the conifers, especially the genus *Pinus*, and occurring in the coal measures.

pī′ni·tōl, *n.* [Fr. *pinite*, *pinitol*, from L. *pinus*, pine (tree); and *-ol*.] a sweet crystalline compound, $C_6H_6(OH)_5OCH_3$, occurring in the resin of the sugar pine.

pink, *n.* [prob., from *pinkeye*, lit., little eye, a transl. of Fr. *oeillet*, the pink.]
1. any of a number of related plants of the genus *Dianthus* with five-petaled, pale-red flowers and sticky stems. *Dianthus plumarius* is the common garden pink and *Dianthus caryophyllus* is the clove pink, known in its cultivated form as the carnation.

PINK

2. any of various other plants superficially resembling these plants: the cushion pink is *Silene acaulis*; the moss pink, *Phlox subulata*; the sea pink, *Armeria vulgaris*.

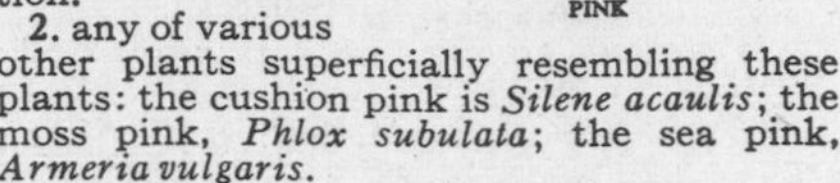

3. the flower of any of these plants.
4. the pale-red color of these flowers.
5. the highest or finest condition, example, degree, etc.
6. the scarlet worn by a fox hunter. [Brit.]
7. a fox hunter. [Brit.]
8. [*sometimes* P–] a person whose political views are somewhat radical: a derogatory term.
9. any one of several lakes of yellow or greenish color made by precipitating vegetable juices on a white earth, such as chalk or alumina; as, Italian *pink*, brown *pink*, rose *pink*, and Dutch *pink*. They are useful only in water colors.
Carolina pink; the pinkroot.
China pink; the *Dianthus chinensis*, a biennial flowering species having both single and double varieties.
fire pink; a scarlet-flowered annual plant, *Silene virginica*.
Indian pink; same as *China pink*.
parlor pink; a liberal or anyone advocating liberalism in theory; especially, one who has no intention of subsequently applying his views in action. [Slang.]

piñk, *v.t.* to dye or stain pink.

piñk, *a.* 1. pale-red.
2. mildly radical.

piñk, *n.* 1. a young salmon; a parr. [Brit.]
2. a minnow. [Brit. Dial.]
3. a young grayling. [Brit.]

piñk, *n.* [M.D. *pinke*.] a ship with a narrow stern: also *pinkie*, *pinky*.

piñk, *n.* the chaffinch. [Brit. Dial.]

piñk, *v.t.*; pinked (piñkt), *pt.*, *pp.*; pinking, *ppr.* [ME. *pinken*, from *picken*, pick.]
1. to ornament (cloth, leather, paper, etc.) by making perforations in a pattern.
2. to cut a saw-toothed edge on (cloth, etc.) so as to prevent unraveling or for decorative purposes.
3. to prick; stab.
4. to adorn; to embellish.

piñk, *n.* a stab. [Obs.]

piñk′ber″ry, *n.* *Cyathodes divarticata*, family *Epacridaceae*, a Tasmanian shrub characterized by very small flowers and leaves.

piñk bōll′wŏrm, the pink-colored larva of *Pectinophora*, a small, brown moth which is highly destructive to cotton crops wherever it is grown: it attacks the bolls and flowers, boring deeply into them.

piñk çock·a·tọọ′, the *Kakatoe leadbeateri*, a handsomely plumed and crested parrot of Australia.

piñk çūr′lew (-lọọ), the roseate spoonbill, *Ajaia ajaia*, characterized by pink plumage with the throat and head bare.

piñk diș·ēașe′, in plant pathology, a fungus disease affecting the bark of coffee, rubber, citrus, and other trees and caused by the fungus, *Corticium salmonicolor*.

piñked (piñkt), *a.* ornamented with holes or scallops; cut with pinking shears.

piñk′ēr, *n.* one who pinks.

Piñk′ēr·tŏn, *n.* a private detective; originally, an employee of a detective agency founded by Allan Pinkerton in 1850.

piñk′eȳe, *n.* an acute, contagious form of conjunctivitis in which the eyeball and the mucous membrane lining the eyelid become red and inflamed: also *pink eye*.

piñk′-eȳed (-īd), *a.* having small eyes.

piñk′-eȳed, *a.* having the eyes pink.

piñk′ie, *n.* the fifth, or smallest, finger: also spelled *pinky*.

piñk′ie, *n.* a pink (ship).

piñk′ing, *n.* the process of decorating the edges of a material with small holes and scallops by the use of pinking shears.

piñk′ing ī′ron (-ũrn), 1. an instrument with a curved zigzag edge, used for pinking edges, as of cloth or leather.
2. a sword. [Colloq.]

piñk′ing shēarș, shears with notched blades, used for pinking the edges of cloth, etc.

piñk′ish, *a.* somewhat pink.

piñk nee′dle, 1. a shepherd's bodkin.
2. a plant, the heron's-bill.

piñk′ness, *n.* the condition of being pink: also written *pinkiness*.

piñk′rọọt, *n.* 1. either of two related plants, *Spigelia marilandica* or *Spigelia anthelmia*, with tufted stems, stemless leaves, and red flowers with yellow throats.
2. the root of either of these plants, used as a vermifuge.

piñk sạlt, a mordant consisting of the double chloride of ammonium and tin.

piñk sạu′cēr, a saucer with a pink pigment covering the inner surface, formerly used for coloring the face, etc.

Piñk′stēr, *n.* [D., from G. *pfingsten*, lit., Pentecost, of which word it is a modification.] Whitsuntide. [Dial.]

piñk′stēr flow′ēr, a shrub, *Azalea nudiflora*, having pink, sweet-smelling flowers, purplish-red at the base: also called *mountain pink*, *purple azalea*, and *wild honeysuckle*.

piñk stērn, a narrow-sterned boat.

piñk′-stērned, *a.* having a very narrow stern.

piñk tēa, any frivolous social gathering, especially one attended largely by women. [Colloq.]

piñk′weed, *n.* the knotgrass.

piñk′wood, *n.* the tulipwood.

piñk′y, *a.* [from n. *pink*, the flower.] pink; pinkish.

piñk′y, *a.* small; blinking, as eyes. [Scot. and Brit. Dial.]

piñk′y, *n.*; *pl.* **piñk′ieș**, a pinkie.

piñk′y, *n.*; *pl.* **piñk′ieș**, a pink (ship).

pin′lock, *n.* a kind of lock whose bolt is a cylindrical pin.

pin mŏn′ey, 1. an allowance of money made by a husband to his wife for her own personal expenses, as clothing, etc.
2. any small sum of money, as for incidental small expenses.

pin′nȧ, *n.*; *pl.* **pin′nae**, **pin′nȧș**, [L., a feather, projection.]
1. in anatomy, the external ear; auricle.
2. in botany, one leaflet of a group arranged in feather fashion on a stem.
3. in zoology, a feather, wing, fin, or similar structure.

Pin′nȧ, *n.* [Gr., a kind of mussel.]
1. a genus of bivalve mollusks.
2. [p–] a large bivalve of this genus. The shell is attached by a strong byssus spun by the animal, which is sometimes mixed with silk and woven into cloth.

pin′năce, *n.* [Fr. *pinasse*; Sp. *pinaza*; L. *pinus*, pine tree.]
1. a small sailing ship formerly used as a tender, scout, etc.

PINNACE

2. a ship's boat.
3. a pimp; a procuress. [Obs.]

pin′nȧ·çle, *n.* [Fr. *pinacle*; LL. *pinnaculum*, from L. *pinna*, a pinnacle.]
1. in architecture, a small turret or spire that rises above the roof of a building, or that caps and terminates the higher parts of buildings or buttresses.

2. something resembling a pinnacle, as a slender, pointed formation at the top of some mountains; a peak; a sharp or pointed summit.

Three silent *pinnacles* of aged snow. —Tennyson.

3. the highest point; culmination; acme.

pin′nȧ·cle, *v.t.*; pinnacled, *pt.*, *pp.*; pinnacling, *ppr.* 1. to ornament or furnish with pinnacles.

2. to set on a pinnacle.

3. to form the pinnacle of.

pin·nad′i·form, *a.* [L. *pinna*, feather, and *forma*, form.] having the outline modified by the skin and scales lapping over the fins, as in the chaetodonts.

pin′nāge, *n.* poundage of cattle. [Obs.]

pin′năl, *a.* of or like a pinna.

pin′nāte, *a.* [L. *pinnatus*, from *pinna*, a feather or fin.]

1. in botany, having simple leaflets arranged on both sides of a common stem in a featherlike arrangement.

2. shaped like or resembling a feather.

abruptly pinnate; pinnate without a leaflet at the end. When a leaf has some of its pinnae much smaller than the others, it is said to be *interruptedly pinnate*.

PINNATE LEAF

pin′nā·ted′, *a.* pinnate.

pinnated grouse; the prairie chicken.

pin′nāte·ly, *adv.* in a pinnate manner.

pin·nat′i-, [from L. *pinnatus*, pinnate.] a combining form meaning *pinnately*, as in *pinnatifid*.

pin·nat′i·fid, *a.* [*pinnati-* and *-fid*.] in botany, having leaves in a featherlike arrangement, with narrow lobes whose clefts extend more than halfway to the stem.

pin·nat·i·lō′bāte, *a.* same as *pinnatilobed*.

pin·nat′i·lōbed, *a.* [*pinnati-* and *lobed*.] in botany, having the lobes arranged pinnately; specifically, pinnatifid, with the lobes divided to an uncertain depth.

PINNATIFID LEAF

pin·nā′tion, *n.* the condition or fact of being pinnate.

pin·nat·i·pär′tīte, *a.* [*pinnati-*, and L. *partitus*, divided.] in botany, pinnatifid, with the lobes separated almost to the stem.

pin·nat′i·ped, *a.* [*pinnati-*, and L. *pes* (*ped-*), foot.] having the toes bordered by lobed membranes, as some birds.

pin·nat′i·ped, *n.* any pinnatiped bird.

pin·nat′i·sect, *a.* [*pinnati-*, and L. *sectus*, pp. of *secare*, to cut.] in botany, pinnatifid with the lobes divided down to the midrib.

pin·nat′ū·lāte, *a.* [LL. *pinnatulatus*, dim. from L. *pinnatus*, pinnate.] again subdivided; having divided pinnules: said of a pinnate leaf. [Rare.]

pin′nȧ wool, cloth in which the byssus of the pinna is used.

pin′nẽr, *n.* 1. one who or that which pins or fastens.

2. a pin maker. [Obs.]

3. an apron with a bib pinned in front of the breast; a pinafore. [Dial.]

4. a woman's caplike headdress, having long flaps hanging down and pinned on either side, worn during the early part of the eighteenth century.

PINNER

pin′nẽr, *n.* an impounder. [Obs.]

pin′net, *n.* a pinnacle. [Obs.]

pin′ni·fọrm, *a.* [L. *pinna*, feather, and *forma*, form.] having the form of a fin or feather.

Pin·ni·grā′dȧ, *n.pl.* 1. same as *Pinnipedia*.

2. the *Crinoidea*. [Rare.]

pin′ni·grāde, *a.* moving by means of fins.

pin′ni·grāde, *n.* one of the *Pinnigrada*; a pinniped.

pin′ni·nẽrved, *a.* [L. *pinna*, feather, and E. *nerved*.] in botany, penninerved.

pin′ning, *n.* 1. the act of fastening with or as with a pin.

2. the low masonry that supports a frame of studwork.

pin′ni·ped, *a.* 1. having finlike feet or flippers.

2. of or relating to the *Pinnipedia*.

pin′ni·ped, *n.* [L. *pinna*, feather, and *pes* (*ped-*), foot.] a pinniped animal; specifically, one of the *Pinnipedia*.

Pin·nip′e·dēs, *n.pl.* 1. in ornithology, the *Steganopodes*.

2. in mammalogy, the *Pinnipedia*.

3. swimming crustaceans.

Pin·ni·pē′di·ȧ, *n.pl.* a suborder of aquatic carnivorous mammals, having flippers, including the seals and walruses.

pin·ni·pē′di·ăn, *a.* and *n.* pinniped.

pin·ni·tär′săl, *a.* having pinnate feet, as a swimming crustacean.

pin″ni·ten·taç′ū·lāte, *a.* provided with pinnate tentacles, as the *Alcyonaria*.

pin′nŏck, *n.* 1. a small bird, the tomtit. [Brit. Dial.]

2. the hedge sparrow. [Brit. Dial.]

pin′nō·īte, *n.* [named after *Pinno*, a German mineralogist.] a mineral found in nodules with boracite. It is a hydrous borate of magnesium and crystallizes in the tetragonal system.

pin′nō·thēre, *n.* a small crab of the genus *Pinnotheres*.

Pin·nō·thē′rēṣ, *n.* [L. *pinna*, a kind of shellfish, and Gr. *thērān*, to pursue.] a genus of small crabs, belonging to the brachyurous decapods: they are found during a portion of the year in different bivalve shells.

pin′nū·lȧ, *n.*; *pl.* **pin′nū·lae,** 1. in zoology, the barb of a feather.

2. a pinnule.

pin′nū·lăr, *a.* of or like a pinnule.

pin′nū·lāte, *a.* [LL. *pinnulatus*, from L. *pinnula*, dim. of *pinna*, feather.] having pinnules.

pin′nū·lā·ted, *a.* same as *pinnulate*.

pin′nūle, *n.* [L. *pinnula*, dim. of *pinna*, feather.]

1. in botany, any of the leaflets of a pinnate leaf.

2. in zoology, a small fin or finlike process; specifically, (a) any of the lateral branches of the arm of a crinoid; (b) in the mackerel, any of the short fin rays having no membranous connection with each other or with the fins.

pin′nū·lus, *n.*; *pl.* **pin′nū·lī,** [LL., from L. *pinnula*.] a sexradiate spicule of a sponge with a suppression of the proximal ray, and having the distal ray provided with spines which project forward.

pin′ny·wiñ·kle, pin′nie·wiñ·kle, *n.* a board with holes into which the fingers were thrust and pressed upon with pegs as a type of torture. [Scot.]

pin′ny·wiñks, *n.* same as *pinnywinkle*.

pin ōak, any of several oak trees found in the United States; especially, *Quercus palustris*, of the eastern part of the United States: also called *swamp Spanish oak* and *water oak*.

pï′noçh·le, pï′noç·le, *n.* [earlier also *penuchle*, *binochle*: the form of the word and the relation of the game to bezique suggest Fr. origin.]

1. a game of cards for two, three, or four persons, played with a special deck of 48 cards, consisting of a double deck of all cards above the eight (including the ace).

2. the combination of the queen of spades and the jack of diamonds in this game.

Also *penuchle*, *penuckle*.

double pinochle; a meld in pinochle consisting of both queens of spades and both jacks of diamonds, counting 300.

pi·nō′le, *n.* [Sp., from Nahuatl *pinolli*.]

1. flour made of ground corn, mesquite beans, etc. in the southwestern United States and Mexico.

2. an aromatic powder used in Italy for making chocolate.

piñ′on (pin′yŏn *or* pēn′yōn), *n.* [Sp.] any one of several species of pine trees of western North America, as *Pinus edulis*, *Pinus parryama*, and *Pinus monophylla*; also, the edible seeds of these trees.

pin′patch, *n.* the periwinkle, *Littorina littorea*. [Brit. Dial.]

pin′pil″lōw, *n.* the prickly-pear cactus of the West Indies, *Opuntia curassavica*.

pin′point, *v.t.* 1. to show the location of by sticking a pin into, as on a map.

2. to show the precise location of.

pin′point, *n.* 1. the point of a pin.

2. something trifling or insignificant.

pin′point bomb′ing (bom′), bombing directed precisely at a particular objective.

pin pọọl, a form of the game of pool played with two balls, with five small wooden pins placed in the form of a square in the center of the table.

pin′prick, *n.* 1. any tiny puncture made by or as by a pin.

2. a minor irritation or annoyance.

pin rāil, 1. a rack for belaying pins.

2. the ledge under an organ manual in which the key pins are held.

3. a rail with a row of pegs, hooks, etc., to be used as a rack for clothing, etc.

pinṣ and nee′dleṣ, paresthesia characterized by a tingling and prickling feeling in some parts of the body, as in the fingers and toes.

pin strīpe, a slender, light-colored stripe, about the width of a pin, as in the fabric of some suits.

pīnt, *n.* [ME. *pynte*; OFr. *pinte*, from M.D.] a measure of capacity (liquid or dry) equal to 1/2 quart.

pint, *n.* the laughing gull. [Brit. Dial.]

pin′tȧ, *n.* [Sp.] a contagious skin disease of tropical America, characterized by patches of various colors.

pin·tä′dō, *n.*; *pl.* **pin·tä′dōṣ** or **pin·tä′dōeṣ,** [Port., painted, pp. of *pintar*, to paint.]

1. a long, silvery food and game fish, *Scomberomorus regalis*, with brown spots and a widely forked tail: it is common in the waters surrounding Florida and Cuba.

2. the guinea fowl, *Numida meleagris*.

3. the pintado petrel, or Cape pigeon.

4. a kind of chintz. [Obs.]

pin·tä′dō, *a.* spotted, as if painted; pied.

pintado petrel; the Cape pigeon.

pin′tāil, *n.*; *pl.* **pin′tāilṣ** or **pin′tāil,** 1. a species of duck, *Dafila acuta*, the male having long, pointed, middle tail feathers. It is found in Europe, Asia, and North America. Also called *gray duck*, *piketail*, *pickettail*, *spiketail*, *sprigtail*, etc.

2. the sharp-tailed grouse, *Pediœcetes phasianellus*, of the Rocky Mountain region.

3. the ruddy duck, *Erismatura rubida*.

pin′tāiled, *a.* having the tail pointed, the central feathers being longest, as certain birds.

pin′tä′nō, *n.*; *pl.* **pin·tä′nōṣ,** a brightly colored fish found chiefly among coral reefs: also called *cow pilot*.

pin′tle, *n.* [ME. *pintil*, penis; AS. *pintel*.] a pin or bolt upon which some other part pivots or turns.

pin′tle hook, a hook attached to the rear of a limber to receive the lunette ring on the trail of the gun carriage when the gun is limbered up for transportation.

RUDDER
PINTLE
SOCKET
PINTLE

pin′tō, *a.* [Sp., from L. *pinctus*, painted.] marked with spots of two or more colors; mottled; piebald.

pin′tō, *n.*; *pl.* **pin′tōṣ,** 1. a pinto horse or pony.

2. the pinto bean.

3. [P—] an Indian of an extinct tribe formerly living in Texas and Mexico.

pin′tō bēan, a kind of mottled kidney bean that grows in the southwestern United States.

Pintsch gas (pinch), [after Richard *Pintsch* (1840–1919), G. inventor of the process.] a gas obtained by the destructive distillation of petroleum, used for lighting.

pin′-up, *a.* 1. that is or can be pinned up or otherwise fastened to a wall; as, a *pin-up* lamp.

2. designating a girl whose sexual attractiveness makes her a suitable subject for a picture to be displayed on a wall, as of a barracks. [Slang.]

pin′-up, *n.* a pin-up girl, picture, etc. [Slang.]

Pī′nus, *n.* [L., a pine tree.] a large and widely diffused genus of conifers, of the North Temperate Zone. Trees of the genus are characterized by having the primary leaves small and scalelike, and the secondary ones long, acicular, and in clusters of as many as seven, surrounded at the base by a sheath of scales.

pin′weed, *n.* a plant of the genus *Lechea*, with thin stems and leaves, and small, purplish or greenish flowers.

pin′wheel (-hwēl), *n.* 1. a crown wheel having pegs or pins in place of cogs.

2. a form of firework arranged on a wheel which rotates and throws off colored lights when set off.

3. a small wheel with variously colored vanes of paper, etc. pinned to a stick so as to revolve in the wind.

4. a cylindrical box having wooden pegs fixed in the inside, used for treating hides in tanning.

Also *pin wheel*.

pin'wŏrm, *n.* a small, threadlike worm with an unsegmented body, sometimes found as a parasite in the human rectum.

pin wrench (rench), a type of wrench with a projecting polygonal pin that fits into a corresponding hole in a nut, etc. so as to secure a firm hold.

pinx'it, *v.* [L., painted.] he (or she) painted (it): often placed after the artist's name on a painting.

pinx'tēr flow'ēr, same as *pinkster flower*.

pī'ny, *a.*; *comp.* pinier; superl. piniest, 1. abounding in pines.

2. of, relating to, or having some characteristic of the pine tree; as, a *piny* smell.

Also spelled *piney*.

piny resin; the resinous product of an East Indian tree of the genus *Dammarara*; dammar resin.

piny tallow; a fatty or oily substance obtained from the piny tree, and used in making candles.

piny tree; a tree, *Vateria indica*, of the East Indies, the seeds of which when roasted yield a fatty substance.

piny varnish; a resinous varnish made from the product of the piny tree.

pī'ny, *n.* peony. [Dial.]

pī·ō·neer', *n.* [Fr. *pionnier*; OFr. *peonier*, from *peon*, It. *pedone*, a foot soldier.]

1. a member of a military unit that precedes the main body and builds bridges, roads, trenches, etc.; a military engineer.

2. one who goes before into that which is unknown or untried, to prepare the way for others, as an early settler or a scientist doing original work.

3. a digger; a miner. [Obs.]

pī·ō·neer', *v.i.* to act as a pioneer.

pī·ō·neer', *v.t.*; pioneered, *pt.*, *pp.*; pioneering, *ppr.* 1. to go before and prepare (a way, etc.).

2. to be a pioneer in or of.

pī·ō·neer', *a.* being in advance of others.

pī'ō·ny, *n.* peony. [Obs.]

pī'ot, *n.* same as *piet*.

pī'ous, *a.* [L. *pius*, pious, devout, affectionate, good.]

1. having or showing religious devotion; zealous in the performance of religious obligations.

2. springing from actual or pretended religious devotion.

3. sacred, as distinguished from secular or profane.

4. having or showing a sense of duty and loyalty to parents, family, friends, etc. [Archaic.]

Syn.—devout, reverent, religious, godly, devotional, righteous.

pī'ous·ly, *adv.* in a pious manner.

pip, *n.* [abbrev. of *pippin*.]

1. a small seed, as of an apple, orange, or similar fruit.

2. a person or thing much admired. [Slang.]

pip, *n.* [earlier *peep*, of unknown origin.]

1. any of the figures or spots on playing cards, dominoes, dice, etc.

2. any of the diamond-shaped divisions of the skin of a pineapple.

3. a single rootstock or flower of the lily of the valley, peony, etc.

pip, *n.* [ME. and M.D. *pippe*; LL. *pipita*, for L. *pituita*, slime, phlegm, the pip in fowls.]

1. a contagious disease of fowls, in which there is a secretion of thick mucus in the mouth, which forms a horny scale on the tip of the tongue.

2. any minor human ailment: a humorous usage.

pip, *v.i.*; pipped (pipt), *pt.*, *pp.*; pipping, *ppr.* [prob. var. of *peep* (to cry).] to peep or chirp, as a young bird.

pip, *v.t.* to break through (the shell): said of a hatching bird.

Pī'pȧ, *n.* [LL.] 1. a genus of batrachians, the

PIPA

only known species of which is the Surinam toad, a native of Guiana and other warm parts of America. After the female has laid the eggs, the male places them upon her back, fecundates them, and then presses them into cellules, which at that period open for their reception and afterward close over them. In these cellules on the mother's back the eggs are hatched and the young pass their tadpole state.

2. [p—] the Surinam toad.

pīp'ăġe, *n.* 1. transportation, as of oil, water, gas, etc., through pipes.

2. the charge for such transportation.

3. a system of such pipes.

pī'păl, *n.* [Hind. *pīpal*; Sans. *pippala*.] a fig tree of India; bo tree: also *pipal tree*.

pīpe, *n.* [AS. and L.G. *pipe*, a pipe; G. *pfeife*; all of Romance or LL. origin; Fr. *pipe*; It., Port., and Sp. *pipa*, a pipe, from L. *pipare*, to cheep, chirp, or peep; an imitative word.]

1. a cylindrical tube, as of reed, straw, wood, or metal, for making musical sounds by the vibration of an air column; specifically, [*pl.*] (a) the Panpipe; (b) the bagpipe.

2. any of the wooden or metal tubes in an organ, that produce the tones.

3. (a) a boatswain's whistle; (b) the sounding of such a whistle to signal a ship's crew.

4. the voice in singing.

5. [*often pl.*] the singing voice.

6. the call, song, or note of a bird.

7. a long tube of clay, concrete, metal, wood, etc., for conveying water, gas, oil, or other fluids.

8. a tubular organ or canal of the body; especially, [*pl.*] the respiratory organs.

9. anything tubular in form.

10. (a) a tube with a small bowl at one end, in which tobacco, etc. is smoked; (b) enough tobacco to fill such a bowl.

11. something regarded as easy to accomplish. [Slang.]

12. in England, an enrolled account of a sheriff, etc. at the Exchequer, so called from resembling a pipe; also, the Exchequer itself. [Obs.]

13. a cask usually containing two hogsheads, or 126 gallons, used for wine, oil, etc.; also, this volume as a unit of measure.

14. in mining, a vein of ore that is cylindrical in form

Pan's pipes, *Pandean pipes*; same as *Panpipe*.

pīpe, *v.t.*; piped (pīpt), *pt.*, *pp.*; piping, *ppr.* 1. to play (a tune, etc.) on a wind instrument; as, to *pipe* a melody.

2. to utter in a shrill, reedy voice or tone; as, to *pipe* a song.

3. to affect or bring to some condition by or as by piping; as, he *piped* the children of Hamelin to their destruction.

4. to convey (water, gas, oil, etc.) by means of pipes.

5. to provide or equip with pipes; as, to *pipe* a building.

6. to trim with piping.

7. in nautical usage, to issue a call, as an order or a signal, to a crew by means of a boatswain's whistle.

pīpe, *v.i.* 1. to play on a pipe, fife, flute, or other tubular wind instrument of music.

We have *piped* to you, and ye have not danced. —Matt. xi. 17.

2. to utter shrill, reedy sounds or tones.

3. in metallurgy, to develop longitudinal cavities, as steel sometimes does in ingots and castings during solidification.

4. in nautical usage, to signal a ship's crew by sounding the boatswain's pipe.

to pipe down; to become quiet or quieter; to stop shouting, talking, etc. [Slang.]

to pipe up; to speak up or say in a piping voice.

pīpe çlāy, a white, plastic clay used for whitening and in making tobacco pipes and various kinds of earthenware.

pīpe'-çlāy, *v.t.* 1. to whiten with pipe clay; to clean and polish by the use of pipe clay; as, a soldier *pipe-clays* his gun or his sword.

2. to wipe out; to clear up; as, to *pipe-clay* one's debts.

pīped (pīpt), *a.* formed with a tube; tubular; as, a *piped* key.

pīpe drēam, a fantastic idea, vain hope, or impossible plan such as might be produced in the mind of an opium smoker. [Colloq.]

pīpe'fish, *n.*; *pl.* **pīpe'fish** or **pīpe'fish·eṣ,** any fish of the genus *Siphostoma* or *Syngnathus*, having a long and very slender, bony-scaled body with an elongated tubular snout.

PIPEFISH

pīpe fit'tēr, one who places pipes or fits them together.

pīpe fit'ting, a coupling, valve, or other contrivance used for joining pipes to each other or to the fixtures for which they are made.

pīpe'fụl, *n.*; *pl.* **pīpe'fụlṣ,** the amount (of tobacco, etc.) put in a pipe at one time.

pīpe'lāy″ēr, *n.* 1. one who lays pipes.

2. formerly, an intriguing politician. [Slang.]

pīpe'lāy″ing, *n.* the act or process of laying pipes.

pīpe līne, 1. a connected line of pipes equipped with machinery, for conveying oil, water, gas, etc. from one point to another, as from a refinery to a market.

2. any channel or means whereby something is conveyed; as, a *pipe line* of information.

pīpe'-līne, *v.t.* 1. to convey by a pipe line.

2. to supply with a pipe line.

pīpe'mouth, *n.* a fish of the genus *Fistularia*, characterized by a tubelike snout.

pīpe of'fice, formerly, an office in the English Court of Exchequer where grants of land from the crown, records of sheriffs, etc. were made out.

pīpe of pēace, a peace pipe; a calumet.

pīpe ọr'găn, a musical instrument with a keyboard that controls the flow of compressed air through one or more sets of pipes of varying length.

Pīp'ēr, *n.* the typical genus of the *Piperaceæ*.

pī'pēr, *n.* pepper. [Obs.]

pī'pēr, *n.* [ME. and AS. *pipere*.] 1. one who plays on a pipe, or wind instrument; especially, a bagpiper.

2. in zoology, (a) a bird, the sandpiper; (b) a fish, *Trigla lyra*, the lyre gurnard.

to pay the piper; to pay for one's pleasures or undertakings; to bear the consequences.

Pip·ēr·ā'cē·ae, *n.pl.* [L. *piper*, pepper.] a family of shrubby or herbaceous exogens, of which the genus *Piper* is the type. These plants are exclusively confined to the hottest parts of the world, and abound in tropical America and the Indian archipelago; they are generally aromatic, pungent, and stimulant.

pip·ēr·ā'ceous (-shus), *a.* [L. *piper*, pepper.] of or belonging to the *Piperaceæ*, or pepper family of plants.

Pip·ēr·ā'lēṣ, *n.pl.* an order of hypogynous exogens with naked flowers, minute embryos, and much outside mealy albumen: it includes the families *Piperaceæ*, *Chloranthaceæ*, and *Saururaceæ*.

pi·per'ȧ·zin, *n.* same as *piperazine*.

pi·per'ȧ·zīne, *n.* [*pipe*rine, and *az*ote, and *-ine*.] a crystalline compound $(C_2H_4NH)_2$, used in the treatment of gout.

pi·per'iç, *a.* produced from plants of the pepper family, or from piperine.

piperic acid; $C_{12}H_{10}O_4$, an acid produced by boiling piperine with potash.

pip'ēr·idġe, *n.* [perhaps a corruption of LL. *berberis*, barberry.]

1. the barberry. [Brit. Dial.]

2. same as *pepperidge*.

pi·per'i·dīne, *n.* [Fr., from *piperine*.] a colorless, liquid hydrocarbon, $C_5H_{11}N$, found in many alkaloids and obtained by treating piperine with alkalis.

pip'ēr·īne, pip'ēr·in, *n.* [L. *piper*, a pepper; and *-ine*.] a colorless, crystalline alkaloid, $C_{17}H_{19}O_3N$, found in black pepper and used in medicine to reduce fever.

pip'ēr·ō·năl, *n.* [G., from *piper*in, piperine, and *-on*, -one, and *al*dehyde.] an aldehyde, $C_8H_6O_3$, obtained from piperine and having a strong smell like that of heliotrope: used in making perfume.

pīpe'stem, *n.* 1. the long, slender stem of a tobacco pipe through which the smoke is drawn.

2. anything like this in form, as a very thin leg.

pīpe'stōne, *n.* a reddish, claylike stone used by the American Indians to make tobacco pipes.

pīpe tongṣ, a device for holding or turning a metal pipe, made of a pair of jaws and a pair of long handles for operating them.

pīpe tree, the lilac, *Syringa vulgaris.*

pi·pette′, pī·pet′ (*or* pi-), *n.* [Fr., dim. of *pipe.*] (a) a glass tube graduated and open at the top, the lower end having a small aperture and a stopcock, used for accurately measuring small quantities of a liquid; (b) a plain glass tube open at the top and with a small aperture at the lower end, used to transfer small quantities of a liquid by opening and closing the upper end with the finger.

pīpe′vīne, *n.* Dutchman's-pipe, a species of *Aristolochia.*

pīpe′wood, *n.* a shrub, *Leucothoe acuminata,* which grows in the swamps of the southern United States: so called from the straight hollow stems of which tobacco pipes are made.

pīpe′wŏrt, *n.* any plant of the family *Eriocauleæ,* very common in the marshes of Great Britain.

pīpe wrench (rench), a tool with a movable jaw which automatically clamps a pipe when the wrench is turned in the desired direction: used by gas fitters and plumbers.

pī′pī, *n.* [native name.] a plant of tropical America, *Cæsalpinia pipai,* the pods of which are used in tanning.

pīp′ing, *n.* 1. the act of a person who pipes.
2. the music made by pipes.
3. a shrill voice or sound.
4. a system of pipes.
5. material that resembles or can be used for pipes.
6. in cookery, ornamental pipelike lines of icing.
7. in dressmaking, etc., a pipelike fold of material with which edges or seams are trimmed.
8. a slip or cutting by which to propagate plants.

pīp′ing, *a.* 1. playing on a pipe; as, *piping* swains.
2. peaceful; quiet; characterized by pipe music rather than martial music; as, *piping* times of peace.
3. having a high, shrill sound; as, a child's *piping* voice.
piping crow or *piping crow shrike*; any Australian bird of the *Gymnorhina* or allied genera. They are often caged and taught to talk as well as sing.
piping frog; an American tree toad, *Hyla pickeringii.*
piping hare; the pika.

pīp′ing, *adv.* so as to hiss or sizzle; as, *piping* hot.

pip·is·trel′, pip·is·trelle′, *n.* [It. *pipistrello, vespistrello*; L. *vespertilio,* a bat.] a species of bat, *Vesperugo pipistrellus,* the smallest of its kind and common in Great Britain.

pip′it, *n.* [probably imitative of its cry.] any of a number of small related birds (genus *Anthus*) with a slender bill, streaked breast, and constantly wagging tail.

pip′kin, *n.* [dim. of *pipe.*]
1. a small earthenware pot.
2. a piggin.

pip′pin, *n.* [ME. *pipyn*; OFr. *pepin,* seed of fruit.]
1. any of a number of varieties of apple; as, Newtown *pippin,* fall *pippin,* golden *pippin.*
2. in botany, a seed.
3. a person or thing much admired. [Slang.]

pip′pi·ree, *n.* [Sp. *pipiri.*] a tyrant flycatcher of the West Indies.

pip′pul, pip′ul, same as *pipal.*

Pip′rȧ, *n.* [LL.] 1. a genus of small birds: also called *manakins*: they are common in Central and South America.
2. [p–] a manakin.

PIPRA (*Pipra aureola*)

pip′rine, *a.* of or pertaining to the genus *Pipra.*

pip·sis′se·wȧ, *n.* [Am. Ind. (Algonquian).] any of a number of related plants with pink or white flowers and jagged, leathery leaves, used in medicine as a diuretic and tonic.

pip′-squēak, *n.* [first applied to a small high-velocity shell used by the Germans in World War I: apparently echoic in origin.] anything or anyone regarded as small or insignificant.

pīp′y, *a.*; *comp.* pipier; *superl.* pipiest, 1. pipelike; tubular.
2. sounding like a pipe; shrill.

pī′quăn·cy (-kăn-), *n.* piquant quality, flavor, etc.

pī′quănt (-kănt), *a.* [Fr., from *piquer,* to prick or sting.]
1. agreeably pungent or stimulating to the taste; pleasantly sharp or biting.
2. exciting interest or curiosity; stimulating; provocative.
3. piercing or stinging; bitter. [Archaic.]
Syn.—spirited, lively, racy, smart, clever, charming.

pī′quănt·ly, *adv.* with sharpness or pungency; tartly; in a piquant manner.

pi·qué′ (pē-kā′), *n.* [Fr. *piqué,* pp. of *piquer,* to prick or pierce.] a firmly woven cotton fabric with vertical cords.

pïque (pēk), *n.* same as *chigoe.*

pïque (pēk), *n.* [Fr., grudge, from *piquer,* to sting.]
1. resentment at being slighted or disdained; ruffled pride.
Out of personal *pique* to those in service, he stands as a looker-on, when the government is attacked. —Addison.
2. a fit of displeasure.

pïque (pēk), *v.t.*; piqued (pēkt), *pt., pp.*; piquing, *ppr.* [Fr. *piquer.*]
1. to offend; to arouse resentment in, as by slighting; to ruffle the pride of.
I must first have a value for the thing I lose before it *piques* me. —Cibber.
2. to stimulate; to excite to action; to arouse; to provoke.
Piqued by Protogenes's fame,
From Cos to Rhodes Appelles came. —Prior.
3. to pride (oneself).
Men *pique* themselves on their skill in the learned languages. —Locke.
Syn.—offend, displease, irritate, fret, goad, stimulate.

pïque (pēk), *v.i.* to cause displeasure or offense.

pïque (pēk), *n.* [Fr. *pic.*] in the game of piquet, the scoring of thirty points by the elder hand, before the opponent scores at all.

pi·quet′ (-ket′), *n.* [Fr., a lance, a spade at cards.] a game of cards for two persons, played with thirty-two cards.

pī′rȧ·cy, *n.*; *pl.* **pī′rȧ·cieṣ,** [ML. *piratia*; Gr. *peiraleia,* from *peiratēs,* a pirate.]
1. the act, practice, or crime of robbing ships on the high seas; the taking of property from others by open violence and without authority on the sea.
2. the unauthorized publication or use of a copyrighted or patented work.

pi·rä′guȧ, *n.* [Sp.; see *pirogue.*]
1. a canoe made by hollowing out a large log: also *pirogue.*
2. a flat-bottomed, two-masted sailing boat.

pi·rä′nha (-rän′yȧ), *n.* [Braz. Port., from Tupi *piranha,* toothed fish, from *piro,* a fish, and *sainha,* a tooth.] any of a group of small, voracious South American fish that attack large mammals in the water, including man.

pi·raī′, *n.* same as *piranha.*

pī·ram′e·tẽr, *n.* [Gr. *peira,* trial, and *metron,* measure.] an instrument for measuring the amount of force expended in moving vehicles.

pī′răte, *n.* [ME.; L. *pirata*; Gr. *peiratēs,* from *peirān,* to attempt.]
1. a person who practices piracy; especially, a robber of ships on the high seas.
2. a ship used by pirates in attacking other vessels.

pī′răte, *v.i.* and *v.t.*; pirated, *pt., pp.*; pirating, *ppr.* 1. to practice piracy (upon).
2. to publish or use (a literary work, etc.) in violation of a copyright or patent.

pī′răte pẽrch, a spotted fish, *Aphredoderus sayanus,* common in still waters of some streams of the United States.

pī·rat′iç, *a.* same as *piratical.*

pī·rat′iç·ăl, *a.* [L. *piraticus*; Gr. *peiratikos,* pertaining to pirates, piratic, piratical.]
1. relating to a pirate; characteristic of a pirate or piracy; as, a *piratical* venture.
2. engaged in piracy.

pī·rat′iç·ăl·ly, *adv.* in a piratical manner.

pir′i·fọrm, *a.* [L. *pirum,* pear, and *forma,* form.] same as *pyriform.*

pi·ri·ri′guȧ, *n.* [native name.] a cuckoolike bird, *Guira guira,* found in South America.

Pi·rith′o·üs (pī-rith′ō-us), *n.* in Greek mythology, a king of the Lapithae who, with his friend Theseus, attempted to abduct Persephone from Hades: he was apprehended by Pluto and bound there to a rock.

pirl, *v.t.*; pirled, *pt., pp.*; pirling, *ppr.* [a form of *purl.*] to spin: to twist; to wind. [Scot. and Brit. Dial.]

pīrn, *n.* [ME. *pyrne.*] 1. the bobbin or spool of a weaver's shuttle.
2. a fishing reel. [Scot.]

pi·rōgue′ (-rōg′), *n.* [Fr. *pirogue*; Sp. *piragua*; originally a W. Ind. word.]
1. a canoe made by hollowing out a large log: also *piragua.*
2. any boat resembling a canoe in shape.

PIROGUE

pir·öu·ette′ (-et′), *n.* [Fr.] in dancing, a whirling on the toes.

pir·öu·ette′, *v.i.*; pirouetted, *pt., pp.*; pirouetting, *ppr.* to do a pirouette or pirouettes.

pir′ry, pir′rie, *n.* a rough gale of wind; a storm. [Obs.]

pī′ṣāy, *n.* same as *pisé.*

pis′çȧ·ry, *n.*; *pl.* **pis′çȧ·rieṣ,** [ML. *piscaria,* from L. *piscarius,* pertaining to fish or fishing, from *piscis,* a fish.]
1. in law, the right or privilege of fishing in another man's waters: now only in *common of piscary.*
2. a place for fishing.

pis·çā′tion, *n.* fishing. [Obs.]

pis·çȧ·tol′ō·ġy, *n.* [L. *piscatus,* pp. of *piscari,* to fish, and Gr. *logos,* discourse.] the art or science of fishing.

pis·çā′tŏr, *n.* [L.] one who fishes.

pis·çȧ·tō′ri·ăl, *a.* of fishes, fishermen, or fishing.

pis′çȧ·tō·ry, *a.* [L. *piscatorius,* from *piscator,* a fisherman.] same as *piscatorial.*

Pis′cēṣ, *n.* [ME.; L. *piscis,* a fish.]
1. a constellation south of Andromeda, supposedly resembling a fish in shape.
2. the twelfth sign of the zodiac, entered by the sun about February 21.
3. the class of vertebrates including the fishes.

pis′ci-, [from L. *piscis,* a fish.] a combining form meaning *fish,* as in *pisci*vorous.

pis′ci·çap·tūre, *n.* [L. *piscis,* fish, and *captura,* from *capere,* to take.] the taking or catching of fish by angling, netting, etc. [Rare.]

pis·ciç′ō·lous, *a.* [L. *piscis,* fish, and *colere,* to inhabit.] parasitic on fishes, as some crustaceans.

pis·ci·çul′tūr·ăl, *a.* relating to pisciculture.

pis′ci·çul·tūre, *n.* [*pisci-* and *culture.*] fish culture; the breeding and rearing of fish as an art or industry.

pis·ci·çul′tūr·ist, *n.* one who is skilled in or engaged in pisciculture; a breeder of fish.

Pis·cid′i·ȧ, *n.* [L. *piscis,* a fish, and *cædere,* to kill.] a genus of trees having but one species, *Piscidia erythrina,* of Jamaica.

pis·ci·fau′nȧ, *n.* [*pisci-* and *fauna.*] the fish of a given region.

pis′ci·fọrm, *a.* [*pisci-* and *-form.*] resembling a fish in form or structure; fishlike in characteristics.

pis·cī′nȧ (*or* -sē′), *n.* [L., fish pond, cistern, from *piscis,* a fish.] a basin with a drain, near the altar of a church, for the disposal of water used for sacred purposes.

PISCINA

pis′ci·năl, *a.* 1. belonging to a fish pond.
2. pertaining or belonging to a piscina.

pis′cīne (*or* -in), *a.* [L. *piscis,* a fish.] of or resembling fish.

Pis′cis Ạus·trī′nus (*or* **Ạus·trā′lis**), a southern constellation.

pis·civ'ō·rous, *a.* [*pisci-* and *-vorous.*] feeding or subsisting on fish; as, many species of aquatic birds are *piscivorous.*

pi·sé' (pē-zā'), *n.* [Fr., from L. *pisere,* to beat, to pound.] a method of forming walls of rammed clay. The conformation of the walls is given by means of boards on each side, and after one layer is formed and partially hardened, the boards are lifted to form bounds for another layer.

Pis'gȧh, Mount, [Heb. *pisgāh,* lit., prob., cleft.] the mountain ridge east of Jordan from which Moses saw the Promised Land.

pish, *interj.* and *n.* an exclamation of disgust or impatience.

A thing which causes many poohs and *pishes,*
And several oaths. —Byron.

pish, *v.i.* and *v.t.* to make an exclamation of disgust or impatience (at).

pi'shu, *n.* the Canada lynx.

pī'si·fọrm, *a.* [L. *pisum,* a pea, and *-form.*]

1. resembling a pea in shape and size.

2. designating a small round bone of the wrist.

pī'si·fọrm, *n.* the pisiform bone, a small bone of the carpus, connected with the tendon of the flexor on the ulnar side.

pisk, *n.* the common nighthawk of America.

pis'mīre, *n.* [ME. *pissemire; pisse,* urine, and *mire,* ant: so named because it discharges an irritant fluid popularly regarded as urine.] an ant.

pī'sō·līte, *n.* [Gr. *pison,* a pea, and *lithos,* a stone.] a limestone composed of pea-shaped pebbles.

pī·sō·lit'iç, *a.* composed of, containing, or having the appearance of pisolite.

Pī·sō'ni·ȧ, *n.* [after Dr. *Pison* (1611–1678), Dutch botanist.] a genus of trees and shrubs of the family *Nyctaginaceæ,* having flowers without petals, and stony fruits.

piss, *v.i.* [ME. *pissen;* OFr. *pissier;* prob. of echoic origin.] to urinate. [Now Vulgar.]

piss, *v.t.* to discharge as or with the urine. [Now Vulgar.]

piss, *n.* urine. [Now Vulgar.]

piss'ȧ·bed, *n.* the dandelion. [Dial.]

pis'sas·phạlt, *n.* [Gr. *pissasphalton; pissa,* turpentine, and *asphaltos,* asphalt; Sp. *pisasfalto.*] earth pitch; a soft bitumen of the consistency of tar, black, and of a strong smell.

pist, piste, *n.* [Fr. *piste,* from L. *pistus,* pp. of *pisere,* to beat, to pound.] a track or footprint; spoor.

pis·taçhe', *n.* same as *pistachio.*

pis·tä'çhi·ō (*or* -tash'), *n.; pl.* **pis·tä'çhi·ōṣ,** [It. *pistacchio;* L. *pistacium;* Gr. *pistakion,* from *pistakē,* pistachio tree.]

1. a small tree, *Pistacia vera,* of the cashew family.

2. its edible, greenish seed (*pistachio nut*).

3. the flavor of this nut.

4. a light yellow-green color.

Pis·tā'ci·ȧ (-shi-ȧ), *n.* [Gr. *pistakē,* pistachio.] a genus of small trees from fifteen to twenty feet high, with pinnate leaves and axillary panicles of small apetalous flowers. It includes the pistachio, the Mediterranean mastic tree, *Pistacia lentiscus,* and *Pistacia terebinthus,* which yield Cyprus turpentine.

PISTACHIO (branch bearing fruit)

pis'tȧ·cīte, *n.* in mineralogy, same as *epidote.*

pis·tȧ·reen', *n.* [dim. of *peseta,* dim. of *peso,* peso.] a former Spanish silver coin of the American colonies and the West Indies.

pis·tȧ·reen', *a.* concerned with petty affairs; trifling.

pis'tȧ·zīte, *n.* same as *pistacite.*

piste, *n.* see *pist.*

pis'tel, pis'til, *n.* an epistle. [Obs.]

Pis'ti·ȧ, *n.* [LL., from Gr. *pistos,* liquid; *pīnein,* to drink.] a genus of floating plants of the family *Araceæ.* The sole species, *Pistia stratiotes,* is widely distributed through the tropics.

pis'tiç, *a.* [Gr. *pistikos.*] pure: a word used in describing ointment. [Rare.]

pis'til, *n.* [LL. *pistillum,* a pistil.] the seed-bearing organ of a flower, consisting of the ovary, the stigma, and often also of a style. In the figure, *a* is the style, *b* the stigma; the ovary is concealed in the flower. Each modified leaf which forms the pistil is called a carpel, the two edges of which, coming into contact, cohere and form the placenta. The form of the pistil must depend on that of the carpels, on their number and on their arrangement. A simple pistil is formed of a single carpel, and a compound pistil of several carpels.

PISTIL

pis'til·lāte, *a.* in botany, having a pistil or pistils: said usually of a flower which has a pistil but is without a stamen.

pis'tōl, *n.* [Fr. and G. *pistole;* Czech *pist'al,* a pipe, pistol, from *pisk,* echoic word for a whistling sound.] a small firearm made to be held and fired with one hand: most pistols are now either revolvers or magazine-fed automatics.

pis'tōl, *v.t.;* pistoled *or* pistolled, *pt., pp.;* pistoling *or* pistolling, *ppr.* [Fr. *pistoler.*] to shoot with a pistol.

pis·tō·lāde', *n.* [Fr.] one or more pistol shots. [Obs.]

pis'tōl çär'bīne, a firearm with a detachable butt piece, which may be used either as a pistol or as a carbine.

pis·tōle', *n.* [Fr., lit., pistol (see *pistol*): so named in Fr., after a debasement of the coin, in punning allusion to a double use of the original name of the coin, *écu,* which also meant "shield."]

1. a former Spanish gold coin, valued at about $4.00.

2. any of various similar obsolete gold coins of Europe.

pis·tō·leer', pis·tō·liēr', *n.* formerly, a soldier armed with a pistol.

pis'tō·let, *n.* [Fr.] a pistol. [Obs.]

pis'tōl grip, the grip of the stock of a rifle, formed like the butt of a pistol and having corrugations to permit a firm grip of the hand.

pis'tōl pīpe, in a blast furnace, the blast pipe, conveying hot air.

pis'tōl shot, the firing of a pistol; also, the carrying distance of a shot fired from a pistol.

pis'tōn, *n.* [Fr. *piston;* It. *pistone,* piston, from *pestone,* a pestle, from *pistare, pestare,* to beat, pound; LL. *pistare,* from L. *pisere, pinsere,* to pound, beat.]

1. a disk or short cylinder closely fitted in a hollow cylinder and moved back and forth by the pressure of a fluid so as to transmit reciprocating motion to the piston rod attached to it, or moved by the rod so as to exert pressure on the fluid.

2. in music, a sliding valve moved in the cylinder of a brass-wind instrument to change the pitch.

PISTON
a, piston; *b b,* piston rod; *c c,* steam ports

pis'tōn·head (-hed), *n.* the part of a piston which is attached to the rod.

pis'tōn pack'ing, a material, such as hemp cord, or a device, such as metallic rings, springs, etc., placed around a piston to cause it to fit closely within its cylinder and at the same time allow its free backward and forward motion.

pis'tōn ring, a split metal ring placed around a piston to make it fit the cylinder closely.

pis'tōn rod, a rod which moves, or is moved by, the piston to which it is attached.

pis'tōn spring, a coil around or inside a piston, which, by expanding, acts as packing.

pis'tōn valve, a valve consisting of a circular disk reciprocating in a cylindrical chamber.

Pī'sum, *n.* [L.] a genus of plants of the bean family. *Pisum sativum* is the common garden pea.

pit, *n.* [D. *pit, pitte,* kernel, pith; akin to Eng. *pith.*] the hard stone, as of the plum, peach, cherry, etc., which contains the seed.

pit, *v.t.;* pitted, *pt., pp.;* pitting, *ppr.* to remove the pit from.

pit, *n.* [AS. *pitt, pytt,* a hole, a pit; D. *put;* Ice. *pittr,* a well, from L. *puteus,* a well.]

1. a hole or cavity in the ground, more or less deep, and either natural or made by digging, as (a) the shaft of a coal mine; also, the mine itself; (b) a vat for tanning; (c) a cavity in which charcoal is piled for burning; (d) an excavation in the soil for protecting plants, generally covered with a frame.

2. a deep or sunken place; an abyss; specifically, (a) [Obs. or Dial.] a grave; (b) the place of the dead or of evil spirits; hell.

3. a covered hole in the ground for catching wild animals; a pitfall.

4. any concealed danger; a trap; snare.

5. an indentation or depression on a part of the human body; as, an arm*pit.*

6. a small hollow in a surface; specifically, a depressed scar on the skin as that resulting from smallpox.

7. (a) the ground floor of a theater, especially the part at the rear; (b) the spectators in that section. [Brit.]

8. the small, often depressed, section in front of the stage where the orchestra sits.

9. an enclosed space or area in which cocks, dogs, etc. are set to fight.

What though her chamber be the very *pit*
Where fight the prime cocks of the game for wit. —B. Jonson.

10. the space on the floors of boards of trade and produce exchanges where a particular commodity is dealt in; as, the corn *pit.*

11. a pore in the cell walls of certain plants.

12. (a) an area in a garage, often below floor level, for repairing and servicing automobiles; (b) an area off the side of a speedway for servicing racing cars.

the pits; the worst possible thing, place, condition, etc. [Slang.]

pit, *v.t.;* pitted, *pt., pp.;* pitting, *ppr.* 1. to put, cast, or store in a pit.

2. to make pits in.

3. to mark with small scars; as, *pitted* by smallpox.

4. to set (cocks, etc.) in a pit to fight.

5. to set in competition (*against*).

pit, *v.i.* to become marked with pits.

pi'tȧ, *n.* [Sp., from Quechua *pita,* fine thread.]

1. any of a number of related agave plants, especially *Agave americana,* yielding a fiber used in paper and cord.

2. the fiber.

pi'tä, *n.* [Heb., from *pāt,* loaf, morsel.] a round, flat bread of the Middle East that can be split open to form a pocket for a filling: also called *pita bread*

pi·tȧ·hä'yȧ, *n.* [Sp.] a cactus, as *Cereus giganteus,* of tropical America, which yields an edible fruit.

pi·tȧ·hä'yȧ wood'peck·ẽr, the Gila woodpecker, *Melanerpes uropygialis,* of the southern part of Arizona.

pi·tañ'guȧ (-gwȧ), *n.* [Braz.] a tyrant flycatcher, *Megarhynchus pitangua,* of Brazil.

pit'ȧ·pat, *adv.* [redupl. of *pat.*] palpitatingly; with palpitation or quick succession of beats; as, his heart went *pitapat.*

pit'ȧ·pat, *n.* a rapid succession of beats or taps.

pit'ȧ·pat, *v.i.;* pitapatted, *pt., pp.;* pitapatting, *ppr.* to go pitapat; to palpitate.

Pit·çāir'ni·ȧ, *n.* [after Archibald *Pitcairne* (1652–1713), Scot. physician.] a genus of herbs of the pineapple family containing about seventy species indigenous to tropical America. Many of them are cultivated in greenhouses.

pitch, *n.* [ME. *pich;* AS. *pic;* L. *pix, picis,* pitch.]

1. a black, sticky substance formed in the distillation of coal tar, wood tar, petroleum, etc. and used for waterproofing, roofing, pavements, etc.

2. any of certain bitumens, as mineral pitch or asphaltum.

3. a resin found in certain evergreen trees.

Burgundy pitch; see under *Burgundy.*

Canada pitch; pitch obtained from the bark of the hemlock spruce in North America: also called *hemlock pitch.*

Jew's pitch; bitumen.

pitch, *v.t.;* pitched, *pt., pp.;* pitching, *ppr.* to smear, coat, or cover over with or as with pitch; as, to *pitch* the joints in a boat.

pitch, *v.t.* [ME. *picchen;* prob. form of *pick,* to strike.

1. to fix or plant in the ground, as a stake or pointed instrument; to fix firmly. [Now Rare.]

2. to set up; to erect; as, *pitch* a tent.

3. to set in orderly arrangement for battle: obsolete except in *pitched battle.*

4. to fix or set at a particular point, degree, level, etc.
5. to throw; to cast; to hurl; to toss; to fling; as, to *pitch* a quoit.
6. to pave or face with stones, as a road.
7. in baseball, to throw (the ball) to the batter.
8. in card games, (a) to lead (a card of a certain suit), thus establishing trump; (b) to establish (trump) thus.
9. in music, to determine or set the key of (a tune, an instrument, or the voice).
10. in brewing, to add yeast to (wort), in order to set up fermentation.

pitch, *v.i.* 1. to fix or pitch a tent or camp; to encamp.
Laban with his brethren *pitched* in the mount of Gilead. —Gen. xxxi. 25.
2. to light; to settle; to come to a state of rest.
3. to strike or come to the ground; as, the ball *pitched* halfway.
4. to pitch anything, as hay, a ball, etc.
5. to fall headlong.
Forward he flew, and *pitching* on his head,
He quiver'd. —Dryden.
6. to fix choice; to select; to decide on: followed by *on* or *upon.*
The words here *pitched upon* by me. —South.
7. to rear, as a horse. [Rare.]
8. to incline downward; to dip.
9. to plunge or toss with the bow and stern rising and falling: said of a ship.
10. to plunge forward; to lurch, as a person or animal does when off balance.
to pitch and pay; to pay ready money. [Obs.]
to pitch in; to begin; to set to work energetically. [Colloq.]
to pitch into; to attack; to assault. [Colloq.]

pitch, *n.* 1. the act or manner of throwing or pitching.
2. a toss; a throw; a cast; a jerk.
3. a plunging forward; especially, the rising and falling of the bow and stern of a ship in a rough sea.
4. anything pitched.
5. the amount pitched.
6. a place where a street hawker or carnival hawker sets up his stand.
7. a point or degree.
With what *pitch* of villainy it will be contented. —South.
8. the highest point or degree; height; loftiness. [Obs.]
The *pitch* and height of all his thoughts. —Shak.
9. size; stature; figure. [Obs.]
10. a slope, descent, or inclination, or the degree or rate of an inclination or slope.
11. a line of talk, such as a hawker uses. [Slang.]
12. in cricket, the ground between the wickets; also, the place on which the ball pitches when bowled.
13. in aeronautics, the distance advanced by a propeller in one revolution.
14. in architecture, the slope of the sides of a roof, expressed by the ratio of its height to its span.
15. in geology and mining, the dip of a stratum or vein.
16. in music, speech, etc., (a) that quality of a tone or sound determined by the frequency of vibration of the sound waves reaching the ear: the greater the frequency, the higher the pitch; (b) a standard of pitch for tuning instruments.
17. in machinery, (a) the distance between the threads of a screw measured on a line parallel to the axis; (b) the distance between the centers of two adjacent teeth in a cogwheel, measured on the pitch circle; (c) the distance apart from center to center of rivets; (d) the distance between the stays of marine and other steam boilers; in marine boilers, it is usually from twelve to eighteen inches.
18. a game of cards in which trump is determined by pitching, or leading, a card of a certain suit.
19. in electricity, the distance between successive corresponding conductors on a dynamo armature.
diametral pitch; a method of expressing the pitch of a toothed wheel in terms of its diameter. It is obtained by dividing the number of teeth by the pitch diameter; thus, the *diametral pitch* of a wheel 6 inches in diameter and containing 48 teeth would be 8.

pitch ănd toss, a game in which the players determine, by pitching coins at a mark, the order of tossing up the pennies of all the players and keeping those that fall heads up.

pitch'-black', *a.* black as pitch; very black.

pitch'blende, *n.* [G. *pechblende*; from *pech*, pitch, and *blenden*, to blind, dazzle.] a brown to black lustrous mineral containing uranium, radium, etc.

pitch chāin, a chain composed of metallic links riveted together to mesh with a toothed wheel.

pitch cĩr'çle, the circle formed by the pitch line of a circular gear.

pitch'-därk', *a.* extremely dark.

pitched bat'tle (picht), see under *battle.*

pitch'ẽr, *n.* [ME. *picher*; OFr. *pechier*; It. *bicchiere*; LL. *bicarium*; Gr. *bikos*, wine jar.]
1. a container, usually with a handle and lip, for holding and pouring liquids.
2. as much as a pitcher will hold.
3. in botany, a leaf, shaped somewhat like a pitcher, which attracts insects; ascidium.

pitch'ẽr, *n.* [*pitch*, v. and *-er.*]
1. one who pitches; especially, in baseball, the player who pitches the ball to the batter.
2. in golf, an iron club with the face slanted sharply backward.

pitch'ẽr·fụl, *n.* as much as a pitcher will contain.

pitch'ẽr mōld'ing, in ceramics, the art of molding earthenware articles in molds made of clay rather than plaster.

pitch'ẽr plant, any of a number of related plants with pitcherlike leaves which attract and trap insects, the best-known species being *Nepenthes distillatoria.*

PITCHER PLANT (*Nepenthes distillatoria*)

pitch'-fāced, *a.* in masonry, having the rock cut away or faced so as to show true edges along the arris line: said of a block of stone.

pitch fär'thing, same as *chuck farthing.*

pitch'fork, *n.* a large, long-handled fork used in throwing hay or sheaves of grain, as in loading or unloading carts and wagons.

pitch'fork, *v.t.* to lift and toss with or as with a pitchfork.

pitch'i·ness, *n.* the condition or quality of being pitchy; blackness; darkness.

pitch'ing, *a.* that pitches.

pitch'ing, *n.* 1. the act of throwing or tossing; as, good *pitching* in baseball.
2. the rough paving of a street with coarse blocks of stone.
3. a facing of dry stone laid upon a bank to prevent erosion by waves or currents.

pitch'ing piēce, a piece of timber supporting a staircase at the top.

pitch'ing tọọl, 1. in watchmaking, a tool used in placing wheels between the plates of a watch.
2. in mining, a kind of pick used in beginning a hole.

pitch līne, the hypothetical line in a toothed gear that has the same rolling velocity as the corresponding line in the gear with which it meshes.

pitch'măn, *n.*; *pl.* **pitch'men,** a person who makes his living by setting up small stands at carnivals or on city streets and hawking novelties, jewelry, etc.

pitch ōre, pitchblende.

pitch pīne, any of several resinous pines from which pitch or turpentine is obtained: one species, *Pinus rigida*, grows in the southeastern part of the United States.

PITCH PINE

pitch pīpe, a small metal pipe which produces a fixed tone used as a standard in tuning an instrument or establishing the pitch for a singer.

pitch'stōne, *n.* a glassy, lustrous volcanic rock with a pitchy appearance.

pitch tree, any of various resinous pines, as the kauri.

pitch wheel (hwēl), a gear wheel.

pitch'wŏrk, *n.* work done in mines by men who receive as their pay a certain proportion of the output. [Brit.]

pitch'y, *a.*; *comp.* pitchier; *superl.* pitchiest, 1. full of pitch; smeared with pitch.
2. resembling pitch in consistency or stickiness.
3. black; very dark.

pit çōal, mineral coal; coal dug from the earth.

pit'ē·ous, *a.* [ME. and OFr. *pitous*; L. *pietas*, piety, (later) pity.]
1. sorrowful; mournful; that may excite pity; as, a *piteous* look.
2. wretched; miserable; deserving compassion; as, a *piteous* condition.
3. compassionate; having or showing pity. [Archaic.]
4. pitiful; paltry. [Now Dial.]
Syn.—doleful, sad, wretched, sorrowful, miserable.

pit'ē·ous·ly, *adv.* in a piteous manner; with compassion; sorrowfully; mournfully.

pit'ē·ous·ness, *n.* the condition or quality of being piteous.

pit'fạll, *n.* 1. a pit slightly covered for concealment, intended as a trap for wild animals.
2. any hidden trap, danger, or temptation.

pith, *n.* [AS. *pitha*; D. *pit*, pith, kernel.]
1. the soft, spongy tissue, consisting of cellular tissue, in the center of certain plant stems.
2. the soft core of various other things, as of a bone, feather, etc.
3. the essential part; substance; gist.
4. strength; force; power; as, a leader of great *pith.*
5. energy; cogency; concentrated force; vigor; importance.
Enterprises of great *pith* and moment. —Shak.
6. in anatomy, the spinal cord. [Rare.]

pith, *v.t.*; pithed (pitht), *pt., pp.*; pithing, *ppr.*
1. to remove the pith from (a plant stem).
2. to pierce or sever the spinal cord of (an animal) in order to kill it or make it insensible for experimental purposes.

pith·ē·çan'thrōpe, *n.* a member of the genus *Pithecanthropus.*

pith·ē·çan'thrō·poid, *a.* [*Pithecanthropus* and *-oid.*] pertaining to the genus *Pithecanthropus.*

Pith″ē·çan·thrō'pus, *n.* [Gr. *pithēkos*, ape, and *anthrōpos*, man.] a hypothetical genus of primates, including *Pithecanthropus erectus*, an extinct early species of man, an apelike creature of the Pleistocene Epoch, some of whose remains have been found in Java: also called *Java man.*

Pi·thē'ci·ȧ, *n.pl.* [Gr. *pithēkos*, an ape.]
1. a division of mammals which comprises apes and monkeys.
2. the order *Primates.*

pith'ē·çoid, *a.* [Gr. *pithēkos*, ape, and *-oid.*]
1. of or pertaining to the *Pithecia.*
2. pertaining to anthropoid apes.

pith'fụl, *a.* pithy; full of or abounding in pith. [Rare.]

pith'i·ly, *adv.* in a pithy manner; with strength or force; cogently; with energy.

pith'i·ness, *n.* the condition or quality of being pithy; strength; concentrated force; as, the *pithiness* of a reply.

pith'less, *a.* having no pith; wanting strength or force.

pit'hōle, *n.* a pockmark.

pith pā'pẽr, rice paper.

pith'sŏme, *a.* pithy; vigorous; forcible. [Rare.]

pith'y, *a.*; *comp.* pithier; *superl.* pithiest, 1. of or like pith.
2. full of pith; as, a *pithy* nut.
3. full of substance, meaning, or force; as, a *pithy* style.
This *pithy* speech prevailed, and all agreed. —Dryden.
4. uttering energetic words or expressions.
In all these, Goodman Fact was very short, but *pithy.* —Addison.
Syn.—terse, laconic, pregnant, expressive.

pit'i·ȧ·ble, *a.* [Fr. *pitoyable.*]
1. deserving or arousing pity.
2. deserving contempt; despicable; mean.

pit'i·ȧ·ble·ness, *n.* the state of being pitiable.

pit'i·ȧ·bly, *adv.* in a pitiable manner.

pit'i·ẽr, *n.* a person who pities.

pit'i·fụl, *a.* 1. full of pity; tender; compassionate.
2. moving compassion; exciting pity; miserable; as, a sight most *pitiful*; a *pitiful* condition.

3. contemptible; despicable; mean.
That's villainous, and shows a most *pitiful* ambition in the fool that uses it.—Shak.

pit'i·ful·ly, *adv.* 1. with pity; compassionately.
Pitifully behold the sorrows of our hearts. —Common Prayer.
2. in a manner to excite pity.
They would sigh and groan as *pitifully* as other men. —Tillotson.
3. contemptibly; with meanness.

pit'i·ful·ness, *n.* 1. mercy; compassion.
2. contemptibleness.

pit'i·less, *a.* 1. without pity; hard-hearted; as, a *pitiless* master.
2. exciting no pity; as, a *pitiless* state.

pit'i·less·ly, *adv.* in a pitiless manner.

pit'i·less·ness, *n.* unmercifulness; insensibility to the distresses of others.

pit'măn, *n.* 1. *pl.* **pit'men,** a man who works underground or in a pit; especially, a coal miner.
2. *pl.* **pit'măns,** in machinery, a rod connecting a reciprocating part, as the cutting bar of a mower, with a rotary part.

pi'ton, *n*; *pl.* **pi'tons,** [Fr. from MFr., a spike, pointed object.] a metal spike with an eye to which a rope can be secured: it is driven into rock or ice for support in mountain climbing.

Pi·tōt' tūbe (-tō'), [after Henri *Pitot* (1695–1771), Fr. physicist, who invented the original instrument.] an instrument for measuring the velocity of flow of a fluid by differential pressure between openings at the tip and side: it is used on airplanes to measure air speed.

pit'pan, *n.* a long canoe with a flat bottom, used on the rivers of Central America.

pit'pat, *n.* and *adv.* same as *pitapat.*

pit'pit, *n.* [imitative.] an American tropical bird, commonly called *guitguit.*

pit'saw, *n.* a pit saw.

pit saw, a large saw worked by two men, one standing on the log, the other in a pit below it.

Pit'tà, *n.* [Telugu.]
1. a genus of brightly colored birds, common in the East Indies. They live chiefly on the ground and are often called ground thrushes, though they are not related to the true thrushes.
2. [p-] any bird of the genus *Pitta.*

pit'tănce, *n.* [Fr. *pitance,* a portion of food allowed a monk, from ML. *pietantia*; L. *pietas,* piety.]
1. a small or barely sufficient allowance of money.
2. a small amount or share, as of income.

pit'ted, *a.* 1. marked with little hollows or pits.
2. pock-marked.

pit'ted, *a.* having had the pits removed.

pit'tĕr, *n.* a device for removing the pits from fruit.

pit'tĕr, *v.i.* [echoic.] to murmur; to patter; as, *pittering* streams. [Obs.]

pit'tĕr-pat·tĕr, *n.* [ME. *pyter-pater*; echoic.] a rapid succession of light beating or tapping sounds.

pit'tĕr-pat·tĕr, *adv.* with a pitter-patter.

pit'ti·cite, *n.* [from Gr. *pittizein,* to be pitchy, from *pitta,* pitch.] pitchy iron ore; an arsenate and sulfate of iron occurring in reniform masses. It ranges from translucent to opaque and is brown and vitreous.

Pit"tō·spō·rā'cē·ae, *n.pl.* a family of trees and shrubs allied to *Polygalaceæ* and native to Australia. The family includes about a dozen genera, of which the best known are *Pittosporum, Billardiera,* and *Soltya.*

pit"tō·spō·rā'ceous, *a.* belonging to the order *Pittosporaceæ.*

Pit·tos'pō·rum, *n.* [Gr. *pitta,* pitch, and *sporos,* seed.] a large genus of evergreen trees and shrubs, type of the order *Pittosporaceæ,* of which several species are found in Australia and New Zealand.

pi·tū'i·tăr·y, *a.* [L. *pituita,* phlegm, rheum.]
1. of or secreting mucus.
2. of the pituitary gland.
3. designating a type of body structure characterized by large bones and abnormally long arms and legs, believed to be caused by excessive secretion by the pituitary gland.

pi·tū'i·tăr·y, *n.* 1. the pituitary gland.
2. any of various preparations made from extracts of either of the lobes of the pituitary gland.

pi·tū'i·tăr·y gland (or **bod'y**), a small, oval endocrine gland attached by a stalk to the base of the brain and consisting of an anterior and a posterior lobe: it secretes hormones influencing body growth, metabolism, etc.

pi·tū'i·tous, *a.* [L. *pituitosus.*] of, like, caused by, or discharging mucus.
pituitous fever; typhoid fever.

pit'ū·ri, *n.* an Australian plant, *Duboisia hopwoodii,* whose leaves and twigs are chewed by the natives as a stimulant.

pit vī'pĕr, any of a family *Crotalidae,* of poisonous snakes, as the rattlesnake, copperhead, etc., with a prominent, heat-sensitive pit on each side of the head.

pit'y, *n.*; *pl.* **pit'ies,** [Fr. *pitié,* from L. *pietas,* piety, from *pius,* pious.]
1. sympathy with the grief or misery of another; compassion or fellow suffering.
2. a cause for sorrow or regret.
3. piety. [Obs.]

pit'y, *v.t.*; pitied, *pt., pp.*; pitying, *ppr.* 1. to feel or express pity for; to have sympathy for; as, to *pity* a person or his misfortunes.
2. to excite pity in: used impersonally. [Obs.]
It would *pity* a man's heart to hear what I hear of the state of Cambridge. —Latimer.

pit'y, *v.i.* to be compassionate; to feel pity.

pit'y·ing·ly, *adv.* in a pitying manner.

pit·y·rī'ȧ·sis, *n.* [Gr. *pityron,* bran.]
1. any of various skin diseases characterized by the shedding of scaly flakes of epidermis.
2. a skin disease of domestic animals, characterized by the formation of dry scales.

più (pū), *adv.* [It., more; L. *plus.*] in music, more: a word prefixed to another in directions to the performer; as, *più allegro,* more quickly.

piv'ŏt, *n.* [Fr. *pivot,* a pivot; It. *piva,* a pipe.]
1. a pin, point, shaft, etc. on which anything turns.
2. a journal at the end of an arbor in a watch.
3. a person or thing on which any important matter turns or depends.
4. a pivoting movement.
5. the man on the flank of a line of soldiers on whom the rest of the line wheels; a pivot man.

piv'ŏt, *a.* pivotal.

piv'ŏt, *v.t.*; pivoted, *pt., pp.*; pivoting, *ppr.* to place on or as on a pivot; to provide a pivot for.

piv'ŏt, *v.i.* to turn on or as on a pivot.

piv'ŏt·ăl, *a.* of or belonging to a pivot; belonging to or constituting that on which anything turns; as, a *pivotal* question.

piv'ŏt bridge, a form of swing bridge moving on a vertical pivot underneath it.

pix, *n.* and *v.* same as *pyx.*

pix, *n.pl.* [from *pictures.*]
1. motion pictures. [Slang.]
2. photographs. [Slang.]

pix'i·lāt·ed, *a.* [from *pixy* and *titillated.*]
1. slightly unbalanced mentally.
2. drunk. [Slang.]

pix'y, pix'ie, *n.*; *pl.* **pix'ies** [from S.W. Brit. dial. *pixey, pisky.*] a fairy; an elf.

pix'y-led, *a.* led as by pixies; confused; bewildered.

pix'y stool, a toadstool; a mushroom.

pi·zazz', piz·zazz', *n.* [prob. echoic of exuberant cry.]
1. energy, vigor, vitality, spirit, etc. [Slang.]
2. smartness and dash; style, sparkle, flair, flash, etc. [Slang.]

piz'zä (pēt'sä), *n.* [It.] an Italian dish consisting of a breadlike crust covered with a spiced preparation of tomatoes and cheese and baked.

piz·ze·rì'ȧ (pēt-se-), *n.* [It.] a place where pizzas are prepared and sold.

piz·zi·çä'tō (pit-si-), *a.* [It., pp. of *pizzicare,* to pluck, pinch.] in music, plucked: a direction to performers on stringed instruments to pluck the strings with the fingers instead of running the bow across them.

piz·zi·çä'tō, *n.* 1. the act or art of plucking the strings on a violin, etc.
2. *pl.* **piz·zi·çä'tī,** a note or passage played in this way.

piz'zle, *n.* the penis of an animal, especially that of a bull, formerly used as a whip.

plā·çȧ·bil'i·ty (*or* plak-), *n.* the quality of being placable or appeasable.

plā'çȧ·ble (*or* plak'), *a.* [L. *placabilis,* from *placare,* to quiet, to soothe, to appease, to pacify; akin to *placere,* to please.] capable of being appeased or pacified; appeasable; willing to forgive.

plā'çȧ·ble·ness, *n.* same as *placability.*

plā'çȧ·bly, *adv.* in a placable manner.

plaç'ärd, *n.* [Fr., from *plaque,* plate; D. *plak,* a slice; L.G. *plakke,* a piece of turf.]
1. a notice posted in a public place; a bill posted up to draw public attention; a poster.
2. an edict, proclamation, or manifesto, issued by authority. [Obs.]
3. permission given by authority; a license. [Obs.]
4. a kind of jeweled stomacher worn in the fifteenth century and later.
5. in ancient armor, a placcate.

plȧ·çärd' (*or* plak'ärd), *v.t.*; placarded, *pt., pp.*; placarding, *ppr.* 1. to post placards on or in; to cover with placards.
2. to announce or give notice of by placards.
3. to display as a placard.

plā'çāte (*or* plak'), *v.t.*; placated, *pt., pp.*; placating, *ppr.* [L. *placare, placatus,* to appease] to appease or pacify; to quiet the anger of.

plā·çā'tion, *n.* the act of placating or the state of being placated.

plā'çȧ·tive, *a.* tending to placate.

plā'çȧ·tō·ry, *a.* [LL. *placatorius.*] serving or intended to placate.

plaç'çāte, *n.* 1. in armor, an extra plate upon the lower portion of the breastplate or backplate.
2. a doublet of leather having strips of steel as a lining.

plāce, *n.* [Fr., from L. *platea*; Gr. *plateia,* a street, from *platys,* broad.]
1. a square or court in a city.
2. a short, usually narrow street.
3. space; room.
4. a particular area or locality; region.
5. (a) the part of space occupied by a person or thing; (b) situation.
6. a city, town, or village.
7. a residence; dwelling; house and grounds.
8. a building or space devoted to a special purpose; as, a *place* of amusement.
9. a particular spot on or part of the body or a surface; as, a sore *place* in the back.
10. a particular passage or page in a book, magazine, etc.
11. position or standing as determined by others; as, his *place* in history is assured.
12. a step or point in a sequence; as, in the first *place.*
13. the customary, proper, or natural position, time, or character.
14. a space used, reserved, or customarily occupied by a person, as a seat in a theater, at a table, etc.
15. the space or position customarily or formerly occupied by another; as, a regent ruled in *place* of the boy king.
16. (another's) situation or state; as, you would have acted quite the same if you were in my *place.*
17. an office; employment; position.
18. official position.
19. the duties of any position.
20. the duty or business (of a person).
21. in arithmetic, the position of an integer, as in noting decimals; as, the third decimal *place.*
22. in racing, (a) a position among the leaders, usually first, second, or third, at the finish; (b) the second position at the finish.
23. in geometry, a locus. [Obs.]
24. in astronomy, the position of a heavenly body as defined by its location on the celestial sphere in terms of right ascension and declination.
25. in falconry, the greatest elevation which a bird of prey attains in flight. [Archaic.]
A falcon towering in her pride of *place.* —Shak.
in place; (a) in the customary, proper, or assigned place; (b) fitting; proper; timely.
in place of; instead of; as a substitute for.
out of place; (a) not in the customary, proper, or assigned place; (b) not fitting, proper, or timely.
to give place; to make room or way; also, to yield.
to go places; to achieve success. [Slang.]
to know one's place; to be conscious of one's (inferior) position or rank in life and act accordingly.
to put one in one's place; to humble a person who is overstepping bounds.
to take place; (a) to come to pass; to happen; to occur; (b) to take precedence or priority.
to take the place of; to be a substitute for.

plāce, *v.t.*; placed (plāst), *pt., pp.*; placing, *ppr.* [Fr. *placer.*]
1. to put in a particular place, condition, or relation.

2. to appoint, induct, or establish in an office or in any particular rank or station; as, to *place* a man in charge; to *place* an office seeker.

3. to arrange for a desired handling, treatment, or allocation of; as, he *placed* the whole shipment; the child was *placed* for adoption.

4. to repose (confidence, trust, hope, etc.) *in* a person or thing.

5. to identify by connecting with some place, time, circumstance, class, etc.

6. to pitch (the voice) in singing or speaking.

plāce, *v.i.* in sports, to finish among the first three in a contest; specifically, to finish second in a horse or dog race.

plȧ·cē'bō, *n.* [L., I will please.]

1. in the Roman Catholic Church, the vesper hymn for the dead, beginning *Placebo Domino.*

2. a medicine given merely to humor the patient; especially, a preparation containing no medicine but given for its psychological effect.

3. something said or done to win the favor of another.

to sing placebo; to agree; to humor someone by agreeing. [Archaic.]

plāce brick, a soft brick, imperfectly burned.

plāce ċärd, a small card bearing the name of a guest and placed at the seat that he is to occupy at table, as at a formal dinner.

plāce hōld'ēr, an officeholder.

plāce hunt'ēr, one who hunts after an office or post, especially a government office.

> The places in the gift of the crown were not enough to satisfy one twentieth part of the *place hunters.* —Macaulay.

plāce'-kick, *v.i.* to make a place kick.

plāce kick, in football, a kick performed while the ball is held in place on the ground, used in kicking off or, sometimes, in attempting to make a field goal or a point after a touchdown.

plāce'less, *a.* without place or office.

plāce'măn, *n.*; *pl.* **plāce'men,** one who has a government job: usually contemptuous. [Chiefly Brit.]

plāce'ment, *n.* 1. the act of placing; also, the condition of being placed.

2. the finding of employment for a person.

3. location or arrangement.

4. in football, (a) the setting of the ball on the ground in position for a place kick; (b) the position in which the ball is set.

plāce nāme, the name of a place, as of a city, province, etc.

plȧ·cen'tȧ, *n.* [L., lit., a cake.] 1. in anatomy and zoology, a vascular organ within the uterus, connected to the fetus by the umbilical cord: it serves as the structure through which the fetus receives nourishment from, and eliminates waste matter into, the circulatory system of the mother.

2. in botany, the part of the ovary from which the ovules arise. It generally occupies the whole or a portion of an angle of each cell.

plȧ·cen'tăl, *a.* 1. pertaining to the placenta.

2. of or pertaining to the *Placentalia.*

plȧ·cen'tăl, *n.* in zoology, one of the *Placentalia.*

Plac·en·tā'li·ȧ, *n.pl.* in zoology, a division of mammals identical with the *Monodelphia.*

plac'en·tăr·y, *a.* placental.

plȧ·cen'tāte, *a.* having a placenta.

plac·en·tā'tion, *n.* 1. in anatomy and zoology, the formation and mode of attachment of the placenta.

2. in botany, the manner in which the placenta is arranged in the ovary.

plac·en·tif'ēr·ous, *a.* [L. *placenta,* and *ferre,* to bear.] developing or possessing a placenta.

plȧ·cen'ti·form, *a.* [L. *placenta,* and *forma,* form.] in botany, formed like a placenta.

plac·en·tiġ'ēr·ous, *a.* same as *placentiferous.*

plȧ·cen'tious (-shus), *a.* gracious; amiable. [Obs.]

plȧ·cen'toid, *a.* placentiform.

plā'cēr, *n.* one who places, locates, or sets.

plac'ēr, *n.* [Sp., from *plaga,* a place.] a waterborne or glacial deposit of gravel or sand containing heavy ore minerals, as gold, platinum, etc., which have been eroded from their original bedrock and concentrated as small particles that can be washed out.

plac'ēr clāim, a mining claim covering a placer despoit.

plac'ēr mīn'ing, mining of placers (deposits) by washing, dredging, or other hydraulic methods.

plā'cet, *n.* [L., it pleases.]

1. the assent of the civil power to the publication and enforcement of an ecclesiastical order.

2. a vote of the governing body in a university, expressed by saying *placet.*

3. a vote of assent in an ecclesiastical council.

plac'id, *a.* [L. *placidus,* from *placere,* to please.] serene; mild; calm; quiet; tranquil; as, a *placid* sea, scenery, face, manner, etc.

plȧ·cid'i·ty, *n.* the state or quality of being placid.

plac'id·ly, *adv.* serenely; quietly; in a placid manner.

plac'id·ness, *n.* calmness; tranquillity; placidity.

plac'it, *n.* [L. *placitum,* that which pleases, a decree, from *placere,* to please.] a decree or decision. [Obs.]

plac'i·tō·ry, *a.* relating to pleas or pleading in courts of law. [Obs.]

plac'i·tum, *n.*; *pl.* **plac'i·tȧ,** [L.] 1. in the feudal ages, an assembly of all degrees of men, presided over by the sovereign, to consult upon important affairs of state.

2. [*pl.*] pleas, pleadings, or debate and trial at law.

plack, *n.* [Fr. *plaque,* a thin slice or sheet of metal.] a small copper coin, formerly current in Scotland, equal to one third of an English penny. [Scot.]

> While he has a *plack* in his purse, or a drap o' bluid in his body. —Scott.

plack'et, *n.* [var. of *placard,* in obs. sense "breastplate, top of skirt," etc.; the word *placard* is recorded in this sense.]

1. a slit at the top of a skirt to make it easy to put on and take off: also *placket hole.*

2. a pocket, especially in a woman's skirt.

3. a petticoat. [Archaic.]

plaç'ō·dērm, *a.* [Gr. *plax, plakos,* a plate, and *derma,* skin.] pertaining to the *Placodermi.*

plaç'ō·dērm, *n.* one of the *Placodermi,* a suborder of *Ganoidei.*

plaç·ō·dēr'măl, *a.* of or pertaining to the *Placodermi.*

Plaç·ō·dēr'mȧ·tȧ, *n.pl.* same as *placodermi.*

Plaç·ō·dēr'mī, *n.pl.* in paleontology, a group of fishes of the Paleozoic period; a suborder of *Ganoidei.*

plaç·ō·gan'oid, *a.* belonging to the *Placoganoidei.*

Plaç"ō·gȧ·noi'dē·ī, *n.pl.* same as *Placodermi.*

plaç'oid, *a.* [Gr. *plax, plakos,* plate, and *eidos,* appearance.] in zoology, (a) of or having bony, platelike scales; (b) belonging to the *Placoides.*

plaç'oid, *n.* any fish having placoid scales.

plȧ·çoid'ē·ăn, *a.* pertaining to the placoids; placoid.

Plȧ·çoi'dēs, *n.pl.* a former order of fishes having placoid scales, including the sharks: also called *Placoidei.*

Plȧ·çoph'ō·rȧ, *n.pl.* [Gr. *plax, plakos,* plate, and *pherein,* to bear.] a primary division of mollusks characterized by plated shells.

plȧ·çoph'ō·răn, *a.* of or relating to the *Placophora.*

plȧ·çoph'ō·răn, *n.* any mollusk belonging to the *Placophora.*

plȧ·çoph'ō·rous, *a.* placophoran.

plaç'ū·lȧ, *n.*; *pl.* **plaç'ū·lae,** [Gr. *plax, plakos,* plate.] a small plaque or plate; specifically, an embryo made up of several platelike cells arranged in the form of a disk.

plaç'ū·lăr, *a.* resembling a plate; of or relating to placulae; designating a discoid embryo made up of platelike cells.

plȧ·fond' (-fon'), *n.* [Fr.] 1. a decorated ceiling.

2. a painted or carved design on a ceiling.

3. same as *contract bridge.*

plā'gȧ, *n.*; *pl.* **plā'gae,** [L. *plaga,* blow or stripe.] in zoology, a colored band or stripe; a streak.

plā'găl, *a.* [Gr. *plagios,* oblique.]

1. in music, with its keynote in the middle of the compass, as a mode.

2. designating a cadence with the subdominant chord immediately preceding the tonic chord.

PLAGAL CADENCE

plagal melodies; certain melodies which have their principal notes lying between the fifth of the key and its octave.

plā'gāte, *a.* in zoology, of or relating to a plaga or to plagae; marked by plagae; as, transversely *plagate.*

plāġe, *n.* [L. *plaga.*] a region; a quarter of the globe. [Obs.]

plā'ġi·ȧ·riṣm, *n.* 1. the act of plagiarizing.

2. an idea, passage, plot, etc. that has been plagiarized.

plā'ġi·ȧ·rist, *n.* one who plagiarizes; a literary thief.

plā"ġi·ȧ·ris'tiç, *a.* of or characterized by plagiarism.

plā'ġi·ȧ·rīze, *v.t.*; plagiarized, *pt., pp.*; plagiarizing, *ppr.* 1. to take and pass off as one's own (the ideas, writings, etc. of another).

2. to take ideas, writings, etc. from and pass them off as one's own.

plā'ġi·ȧ·rīze, *v.i.* to be guilty of plagiarism.

plā'ġi·ȧ·ry, *n.*; *pl.* **plā'ġi·ȧ·rieṣ,** [L. *plagiarius,* a plagiary, from *plagium,* man-stealing, kidnaping, from *plaga,* a snare, trap, toil, from same root as Gr. *plekein,* to entwine.]

1. a plagiarist.

2. plagiarism.

3. a kidnaper. [Obs.]

plā'ġi·ȧ·ry, *a.* 1. stealing men; kidnaping. [Obs.]

2. practicing literary theft.

plā·ġi·hē'drăl, *a.* [Gr. *plagios,* oblique, and *hedra,* seat.] in crystallography, having an oblique arrangement of sides.

plā'ġi·ō-, [from Gr. *plagios,* oblique.] a combining form meaning *oblique, slanting,* as in *plagio*tropic: also *plagi-.*

plā·ġi·ō·cē·phal'iç, *a.* characterized by plagiocephaly.

plā·ġi·ō·ceph'ăl·iṣm, *n.* plagiocephaly.

plā·ġi·ō·ceph'ȧ·ly, *n.* [Gr. *plagios,* oblique, and *kephalē,* head.] an unsymmetrical, twisted condition of the head, usually produced by closure of half of the coronal suture.

plā'ġi·ō·çlāṣe, *n.* [Gr. *plagios,* oblique, transverse, and *klasis,* fracture.] any of a group of minerals of the feldspar family, containing varying proportions of calcium and sodium and having oblique cleavage.

plā·ġi·ō·çlas'tiç, *a.* 1. of the nature of, relating to, or containing plagioclase.

2. characterized by having oblique cleavage.

plā'ġi·ō·dont, *a.* [Gr. *plagios,* oblique, and *odous, odontos,* tooth.] having the teeth set obliquely toward each other; specifically, designating the arrangement of the teeth in certain snakes.

plā'ġi·ō·nīte, *n.* [Gr. *plagios,* oblique, and *-ite.*] a mineral of dark metallic luster; a sulfide of lead and antimony, $S_{17}Pb_6Sb_8$.

plā"ġi·ō·stom'ȧ·tous, *a.* same as *plagiostomous.*

plā'ġi·ō·stōme, *n.* a fish of the suborder *Plagiostomi.*

plā'ġi·ō·stōme, *a.* plagiostomous.

Plā·ġi·os'tō·mī, *n.pl.* [Gr. *plagios,* oblique, and *stoma,* mouth.] a suborder of cartilaginous fishes which have the mouth placed transversely beneath the snout. It includes the sharks and rays.

plā·ġi·os'tō·mous, *a.* relating to the *Plagiostomi.*

Plā"ġi·ō·trem'ȧ·tȧ, *n.pl.* same as *Lepidosauria.*

plā"ġi·ō·trop'iç, *a.* [Gr. *plagios,* oblique, and *tropos,* a turning, from *trepein,* to turn.] pertaining to or characterized by plagiotropism.

plā·ġi·ot'rō·piṣm, *n.* in botany, a modification of geotropism in which a plant or part of a plant, as a branch, root, or stem, grows or tends to grow away from a vertical line.

plāgue (plāg), *n.* [L. *plaga*; Gr. *plēgē,* a blow, misfortune.]

1. anything that afflicts or troubles; a calamity; a scourge.

2. divine punishment.

3. any contagious epidemic disease that is deadly; specifically, the bubonic plague.

4. a nuisance; an annoyance. [Colloq.]

a plague on or *upon*; a mild curse or denunciation expressive of weariness or petty annoyance.

black plague; see *black death* under *black.*

Siberian plague; anthrax, a destructive cattle disease.

plāgue, *v.t.*; plagued, *pt., pp.*; plaguing, *ppr.* 1. to vex; to tease; to harass; to trouble; to embarrass.

> We but teach
> Bloody instructions, which, being taught, return
> To *plague* the inventor. —Shak.

2. to bring disease upon; to afflict with a plague.

plāgue'ful, *a.* full of plagues; infected with plague; troublesome; vexatious. [Obs.]

plāgue'less, *a.* free from a plague or plagues.

plā′guẽr, *n.* one who plagues.

plā′gui·ly (-gi-), *adv.* with vexation; in a plaguy manner. [Colloq.]

plā′guy (-gi), *a.* troublesome; annoying; wearisome. [Colloq.]

plā′guy, *adv.* with vexation; plaguily. [Colloq.]

plāice, *n.*; *pl.* **plāice, plāic′es,** [LL. *platessa,* flatfish, from Gr. *platys,* broad.]

1. a food fish, *Pleuronectes platessa,* weighing eight or ten pounds or more.

2. any of various fishes having a flat, olive-brown body with white spots, especially the American flounder, *Paralichthys dentatus.*

Also spelled *plaise.*

plāice mouth, a small mouth drawn to one side like that of a plaice.

plaid (plad), *n.* [Gael. *plaide,* a blanket or plaid, said to be contr. from *peallaid,* a sheepskin, from *pealle,* a skin or hide.]

1. a long piece of twilled woolen cloth with a checkered or crossbarred pattern, worn over the shoulder by Scottish Highlanders.

2. cloth with a checkered or crossbarred pattern.

3. any pattern of this kind.

plaid, *a.* having the design of a plaid.

plaid′ed, *a.* 1. dressed in plaid; as, a *plaided* bagpiper.

2. with a plaid pattern; checkered; as, a *plaided* skirt.

3. made of plaid.

plaid′ing, *n.* plaid fabrics, collectively; material consisting of plaid; cloth with a plaid pattern.

plāin, *a.*; *comp.* plainer; *superl.* plainest, [Fr. *plain*; L. *planus,* plain.]

1. smooth; level; flat; free from depressions and elevations.

The crooked shall be made straight, and the rough places *plain.* —Isa. xl. 4.

2. open; clear; uninterrupted by anything; as, in *plain* view.

3. evident or clear to the understanding; manifest; obvious; not obscure; not liable to be mistaken or missed.

Lead me in a *plain* path. —Ps. xxvii. 11.

4. open; frank; plain-spoken; sincere; candid; blunt.

Give me leave to be *plain* with you. —Bacon.

5. free from difficulties or intricacies; as, it was all *plain* sailing.

6. free of ornament, show, or adornment; simple; unadorned.

Beneath
A *plain* blue stone, a gentle dalesman lies. —Wordsworth.

7. not dyed, colored, variegated, or ornamented with a pattern or figure; as, *plain* muslin.

8. not good-looking; homely; not handsome; as, a *plain* woman.

9. not rich; not luxurious; homely; simple; as, *plain* living, *plain* dress.

10. not of high rank or position; such as characterizes the common people; ordinary.

For us *plain* folks. —Cowper.

11. in card playing, not trumps.

plāin, *adv.* in a plain manner; clearly.

Sir, to tell you *plain,*
I'll find a fairer face not washed today. —Shak.

plāin, *n.* 1. level land; an extent of flat country.

2. a field of battle. [Obs.]

the Plain; the less radical party in the French legislature during the Revolution.

the Great Plains; the broad expanse of level land stretching westward from the Mississippi Valley.

plāin, *v.t.*; plained, *pt., pp.*; plaining, *ppr.* 1. to level; to make plain or even on the surface. [Obs.]

2. to make evident; to explain. [Obs.]

plāin, *v.i.* [OFr. *plaindre*; L. *plangere,* to beat the breast, lament.] to complain. [Archaic and Dial.]

plāin chȧnt, [Fr.] plain song.

plāin′clōthes man, a detective or policeman who wears civilian clothes on duty.

plāin′-dēal″ing, *a.* [*plain* and *deal.*] dealing with frankness and sincerity; honest; open.

plāin dēal′ing, straightforward dealing with others.

plāin′-heärt′ed, *a.* having a sincere heart; frank.

plāin′-heärt′ed·ness, *n.* the quality of being plain-hearted.

plāin′ing, *n.* complaint. [Obs.]

plāin′-lāid, *a.* made of three strands laid together with a right-handed twist: said of a rope.

plāin′ly, *adv.* in a plain or evident manner.

plāin′ness, *n.* the state of being plain.

plāin sāil′ing, 1. sailing on a smooth, clear course.

2. a smooth, clear course of action.

Plāins In′di·ăn, a member of any of the American Indian tribes formerly inhabiting the prairie region of the United States: they were of various linguistic stocks but shared certain culture traits in common, especially the nomadic following of bison herds.

plāins′măn, *n.*; *pl.* **plāins′men,** one living on the plains.

plāin sọng, [transl. of ML. *cantus planus.*]

1. early Christian church music, still used in Roman Catholic and Anglican services, in free rhythm and the limited Gregorian scale, sung in unison without accompaniment.

2. the simple notes of an air or melody without ornament or variation.

Also *plain chant.*

plāin spēak′ing, plainness, openness, or bluntness of speech; candor.

plāin′-spō″ken, *a.* speaking or spoken plainly or frankly.

plāint, *n.* [Fr. *plainte,* from *plaindre,* from L. *planctus,* lamentation, from *plangere,* to beat, to beat the breast in token of grief, to lament.]

1. lamentation; lament. [Poetic.]

His bursting passion into *plaints* thus poured. —Milton.

2. a complaint.

plāint′fụl, *a.* complaining. [Rare.]

plāin′tiff, *n.* [Fr. *plaintif,* mournful, making complaint.] a person who brings a suit before a court of law; a complainant: opposed to *defendant.*

plāin′tive, *a.* [Fr. *plaintif.*] lamenting; expressing sorrow or grief; mournful; sad.

plāin′tive·ly, *adv.* in a plaintive manner.

plāin′tive·ness, *n.* the quality or state of being plaintive.

plāint′less, *a.* without complaint; unrepining. [Rare.]

plāin wŏrk, plain needlework, as distinguished from embroidery.

plāise, *n.* same as *plaice.*

plāis′tẽr, *n.* a plaster. [Obs.]

plāit, *n.* [OFr. *ploit, pleit,* from L. *plicare,* to fold.]

1. a flattened fold, as of cloth doubled back on itself; a pleat.

2. a braid of hair, ribbon, etc.

plāit, *v.t.*; plaited, *pt., pp.*; plaiting, *ppr.* 1. to pleat.

2. to braid.

3. to make by braiding.

plāit′ed, *a.* folded; braided; interwoven.

plāit′ẽr, *n.* one who or that which plaits.

plan, *n.* [Fr., from L. *planus,* plane, level.]

1. an outline; a draft; a map.

2. a drawing or diagram showing the arrangement in horizontal section of a structure, piece of ground, etc.

3. a scheme for making, doing, or arranging something; a project; a program; a schedule.

4. in perspective, one of several planes thought of as perpendicular to the line of sight and between the eye and the object.

Syn.—draft, delineation, design, project, sketch, contrivance, method, scheme, device.

plan, *v.t.*; planned, *pt., pp.*; planning, *ppr.* 1. to make a plan of (a structure, piece of ground, etc.).

2. to devise a scheme for doing, making, or arranging.

3. to have in mind as a project or purpose.

Syn.—contrive, devise, design, draft.

plan, *v.i.* to make plans.

plan-, same as *plano-* (wandering).

plā′năr, *a.* of or pertaining to a plane; lying in a plane.

Plȧ·nā′ri·ȧ, *n.* a genus of turbellarian worms of oblong form, moving by means of cilia, typical of the family *Planariidæ.*

plȧ·nār′i·ăn, *n.* [L. *planus,* plane, flat.] an annelid of the suborder *Planarida.*

plȧ·nār′i·ăn, *a.* pertaining to the *Planarida.*

Plȧ·nar′i·dȧ, *n.pl.* a suborder of *Turbellaria*; the planarians.

plȧ·nar′i·dăn, *n.* a planarian.

plȧ·nar′i·dăn, *a.* planarian.

plȧ·nar′i·fọrm, *a.* [LL. *planarius,* flat, and L. *forma,* form.] having a form resembling a planarian.

plȧ·nār′i·oid, *a.* [LL. *planarius,* flat, and *-oid.*] planariform.

plā′nāte, *a.* [LL. *planatus*; L. *planus,* flat.] having a flat surface; flat or nearly flattened.

plȧ·nā′tion, *n.* the process by which a river erodes rocks to a level surface and covers them with an alluvial deposit.

planch′et, *n.* [Fr. *planchette.*] a flat piece of metal ready to be stamped as a coin.

plan·chette′, *n.* [Fr.] 1. a three-cornered board, often having as one of its supports a pencil, that is supposed to spell out a message as it moves with the fingers resting lightly on it.

2. a circumferentor.

planch′ing, *n.* the laying of floors in a building; also, a floor of boards or planks. [Dial.]

Plänck's çon′stănt, [named after Max *Planck,* Ger. physicist.] in physics, a universal constant (h) which gives the ratio of a quantum of radiant energy (E) to the frequency (ν) of its source: it is expressed by the equation $E = h\nu$ and its approximate numerical value is 6.625×10^{-27} erg second.

plāne, *n.* [ME. *playn*; OFr. *plasne*; L. *platanus*; Gr. *platanos,* from *platys,* broad: so called from its broad leaves.] any of a number of related trees with large leaves and streaky bark that sheds, as the sycamore.

plāne, *a.* [L. *planus.*] 1. without elevations or depressions; even; level; flat; as, a *plane* surface.

2. in mathematics, (a) lying on a surface that is a plane; (b) of such surfaces.

plane angle; an angle formed by two straight lines lying in the same plane.

plane chart; see under *chart.*

plane curve; a curve lying in a single plane.

plane figure; a portion of a plane limited by lines either straight or curved. When the bounding lines are straight the figure is rectilinear. When they are curved the figure is curvilinear.

plane geometry; that branch of geometry dealing with plane figures.

plane problem; a problem which can be solved by geometry.

plane scale; in surveying, a scale marked with graduated chords, sines, tangents, secants, geographical miles, etc.

plane surveying; ordinary field and topographical surveying, where only very limited portions of the earth's surface are considered, and its curvature is disregarded.

plane trigonometry; see *trigonometry.*

plāne, *n.* 1. a surface that wholly contains every straight line joining any two points lying in it.

2. a flat, level, or even surface.

3. a level of development, achievement, existence, etc.; as, a low *plane* of culture.

4. an airplane.

5. any airfoil; especially, a wing of an airplane.

Aeby's plane; a plane through the nasion and basion perpendicular to the median plane of the cranium.

Baer's plane; a plane through the upper border of the zygomatic arches.

Blumenbach's plane; a plane parallel with the base of a skull from which the lower jaw has been removed.

Morton's plane; a plane through the projecting points of the parietal and occipital protuberances.

objective plane; see under *objective.*

perspective plane; in perspective drawing, the theoretical surface upon which objects are

JACK PLANE

delineated, supposed to stand vertically between the eye of the spectator and the object.

plane of polarization; see under *polarization.*

SMOOTHING PLANE COMPASS PLANE

plane of projection; see *perspective plane.*

plane of refraction or *reflection*: in optics, the plane in which are contained the ray of refraction or reflection and the incident ray.

plāne, *n.* [Fr.; LL. *plana,* from *planare,* to plane, make level, from L. *planus,* level, flat.]

1. a kind of trowel used for smoothing the surface of sand, clay, etc.

RABBET PLANE

2. a carpenter's tool for leveling, smoothing, or removing wood, consisting of a smooth-soled stock with an aperture through which a piece of edged steel or a chisel passes obliquely. There are various kinds of planes:

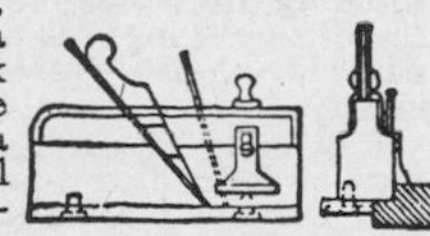
FILLISTER PLANE (side and end)

the *jack plane*, used for coarse work; the *jointer plane*, longer than the jack plane, used for obtaining very straight edges; the *smoothing plane* and *block plane*, chiefly used for final finished work; the *compass plane*, similar to the smoothing plane, has a convex undersurface, for forming a concave cylindrical surface; the *rabbet plane* and the *fillister plane*, chiefly used for making grooves and sharp corners; the *plow plane*, for sinking a channel or groove in a surface not close to the edge of it.

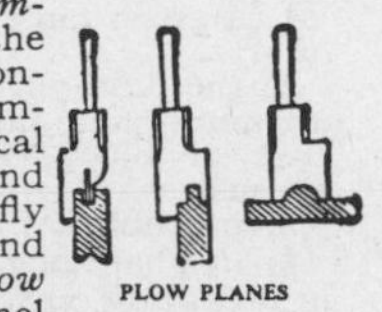
PLOW PLANES

plāne, *v.t.*; planed, *pt.*, *pp.*; planing, *ppr.* 1. to make smooth or level with or as with a plane.
2. to remove with or as with a plane (with *off* or *away*).

plāne, *v.i.* 1. to work with a plane.
2. to do the work of a plane.

plāne, *v.i.* [Fr. *planer*, from *plan*, a plane: from the position of a bird's wings while soaring.]
1. to soar or glide.
2. to rise partly out of the water while in motion at a high speed, as a hydroplane does.

plāne ī'ron (-ũrn), the iron blade of a carpenter's plane that cuts the wood.

plāne'-par″ăl·lel, *a.* in optics, having the opposite surface parallel, as a sheet of glass.

plān'ēr, *n.* 1. a person or thing that planes.
2. a machine that smooths or finishes the surface of wood or metal by planing.
3. in printing, a block of wood used to level type or in taking proofs.

plā'nēr tree, a tree, *Planera aquatica*, of the southern United States, having small, egg-shaped leaves and a nutlike fruit: it resembles the elm.

plāne sāil'ing, the act of determining a ship's position, on the supposition that it is moving on a plane instead of a spherical surface.

plan'et, *n.* [LL. *planeta*; Gr. *planētēs*, a wanderer, from *planan*, to wander.]
1. originally, any of the heavenly bodies with apparent motion (as distinguished from the fixed stars), including the sun, moon, Mercury, Venus, Mars, Jupiter, and Saturn.
2. now, any heavenly body that shines by reflected sunlight and revolves about the sun: the major planets, in their order from the sun, are Mercury, Venus, Earth, Mars, Jupiter, Saturn, Uranus, Neptune, and Pluto; the minor planets are the asteroids, or planetoids, which move in orbits between Mars and Jupiter.
3. in astrology, any heavenly body supposed to influence a person's life.

plȧ·nē'tȧ, *n.*; *pl.* **plȧ·nē'tae,** [LL.]
1. a garment worn by Roman officials and nobles in the fifth and sixth centuries.
2. in the Roman Catholic Church, a chasuble.

plāne tā'ble, an instrument used in land surveying, for plotting maps in the field: it consists of a drawing board mounted on a tripod with an alidade pivoted over its center.

plan·ē·tãr'i·um, *n.*; *pl.* **plan·ē·tãr'i·umṣ, plan·ē·tãr'i·ȧ,** [Mod.L., from LL. *planeta*, a planet.]
1. a model of the solar system in which, by means of clockwork, the relative motion of the planets around the sun can be demonstrated; an orrery.
2. an arrangement for projecting the images of the sun, moon, planets, and stars on the inside of a large hemispherical dome by means of a large, complex optical instrument which is revolved to show the principal celestial motions.
3. the room or building in which this is contained.

plan'et·ãr·y, *a.* [LL. *planetarius*.]
1. of a planet or the planets.
2. terrestrial; worldly.
3. wandering; erratic.
4. in astrology, under the influence of a planet.
5. in machinery, designating or of an epicyclic train of gears in an automobile transmission.
6. in physics, moving in an orbit, like a planet.
planetary days; the days of the week as allotted to the planets known to the ancient world.
planetary nebula; one of the six classes of nebulae, being circular or slightly oval in form and often colored.

plan·ē·tes'i·măl, *a.* [from *planet* and infinitesimal.] pertaining to minute spatial bodies that move in planetary orbits.

plan·ē·tes'i·măl, *n.* a planetesimal body.

plan·ē·tes'i·măl hȳ·poth'ē·sis, a hypothesis that the planets were formed by the uniting of planetesimals created by the tidal eruptions caused on the sun by the passage of a star close to it.

plan'et gēar'ing, gearing making use of planet wheels.

plȧ·net'iç, plȧ·net'iç·ăl, *a.* pertaining to planets. [Obs.]

plan'et·oid, *n.* [*planet* and *-oid*.] any of a group of minor planets the orbits of which lie between those of Mars and Jupiter; an asteroid.

plan·et·oid'ăl, *a.* pertaining to a planetoid.

plāne tree, same as *plane* (tree).

plan'et-strick'en, plan'et-struck, *a.* 1. stricken by the supposed influence of the planets; blasted.
2. panic-stricken.

plan'et·ūle, *n.* a little planet. [Rare.]

plan'et wheel (hwēl), a gear wheel that meshes with and revolves around another wheel in an epicyclic train.

plan'ġen·cy, *n.* the quality or state of being plangent.

plan'ġent, *a.* [L. *plangens* (-*entis*), ppr. of *plangere*, to beat.] beating with a loud or deep sound, as breaking waves, etc.

plan'i-, [from L. *planus*, flat, level.] a combining form meaning *level, plane, flat*, as in *planimeter*.

plan·i·fō'li·ous, *a.* [*plani-*, and L. *folium*, leaf.] flat-leaved.

plan'i·form, *a.* [*plani-*, and L. *forma*, form.] having the surfaces almost flat, as in a gliding joint.

plȧ·nim'e·tēr, *n.* [*plani-*, and Gr. *metron*, measure.] an instrument for measuring the area of a regular or irregular plane figure by tracing the perimeter of the figure.

plan·i·met'riç, plan·i·met'riç·ăl, *a.* of or by planimetry or a planimeter.

plȧ·nim'e·try, *n.* [L. *planus*, and Gr. *metrein*, to measure.] the measurement of plane surfaces; plane geometry.

plān'ing, *a.* leveling; smoothing.

plān'ing mȧ·chïne', 1. a machine for planing wood, acting by means of a rapidly revolving cutter which chips off the surface.
2. a planer for smoothing metals.

plā·ni·pen'nāte, *a.* of or pertaining to the *Planipennia*.

Plā·ni·pen'nēṣ, *n.pl.* [*plani-*, and L. *penna*, feather, wing.] a suborder of neuropterous insects, including those which have flat wings, of which the inferior pair almost equal the superior ones, and are simply folded underneath at their anterior margins. The ant lions and lacewings are examples of this group.

Plā·ni·pen'ni·ȧ, *n.pl.* same as *Planipennes*.

plan·i·pet'ăl·ous, *a.* [*plani-*, and Gr. *petalon*, petal.] flat-petaled.

plan·i·ros'trăl, *a.* [*plani-*, and L. *rostrum*, beak.] having a broad flat beak, as certain birds.

plan'ish, *v.t.*; planished, *pt.*, *pp.*; planishing, *ppr.* [OFr. *planir*, to flatten, from L. *planus*.] to render (a metallic surface) level and smooth, by pounding or rolling; as, to *planish* silver teaspoons or tin plate.

plan'ish·ēr, *n.* one who or that which planishes.

plan'ish·ing-rōll″ērṣ, *n.pl.* rollers used in planishing; in particular, those employed in the final rolling of sheets of metal to be used as coin blanks.

plan'i·sphēre, *n.* [*plani-* and *sphere*.]
1. a map or chart that is the projection of all or part of a sphere on a plane.
2. a projection of the celestial sphere on a plane with the zenith of the North Pole or of the South Pole as the center.

plan·i·spher'iç, *a.* pertaining to a planisphere.

plā·ni·spī'răl, *a.* [*plani-*, and L. *spira*, coil.] having the whorls coiled in one plane, as a flat spiral: also written *planospiral*.

plañk, *n.* [OFr. *planke*; Fr. *planche*; LL. *planca*, a board.]
1. a long, broad, thick board.
2. timber cut into planks; planking.
3. something that supports or forms a foundation.
4. any of the articles or principles in a platform, as of a political party.
to walk the plank; to walk blindfold off a plank projecting over the water from the side of a ship, as the victims of pirates were forced to do.

plañk, *v.t.*; planked, *pt.*, *pp.*; planking, *ppr.*
1. to cover, lay, or furnish with planks.
2. to broil and serve on a board, as fish or steak.
3. to lay or set down with force or emphasis. [Colloq.]
4. to pay (usually with *down* or *out*). [Colloq.]

plañk'ēr, *n.* in agriculture, a platform of heavy planks which is drawn over the soil in order to smooth and solidify it: also called a float.

plañk'ing, *n.* 1. the act of laying planks.
2. planks in quantity.
3. the planks of a structure.

plañk'-sheer, *n.* in shipbuilding, a timber extending around a vessel's hull at the line of junction with the deck.

plañk·tol'ō·ġy, *n.* [*plankton*, and Gr. *logos*, discourse.] that branch of biology which treats of plankton.

plañk'ton, *n.* [Gr. *planktos*, wandering, from *plazesthai*, to wander.] the microscopic animal and plant life found floating or drifting in the ocean or in bodies of fresh water, used as food by fish.

plañk·ton'iç, *a.* pertaining to the plankton.

plan'less, *a.* having no plan.

planned ē·çon'ō·my (pland), organization of the economy of a country by which all phases of production and distribution are planned as a whole by some central authority.

plan'nēr, *n.* one who plans or forms a plan.

plan'ō-, [from Gr. *planos*, *wandering*.] a combining form meaning wandering, as in *planoblast*: also, before a vowel, *plan-*.

plā'nō-, [from L. *planus*, level, flat.] a combining form meaning *plane, flat*, or *having one side plane and* (the other as specified), as in *plano*-concave.

plā'nō·blȧst, *n.* [*plano-*, and Gr. *blastos*, germ.] a tiny, free-swimming jellyfish; the medusa form of a hydroid.

plā·nō·blas'tiç, *a.* of or pertaining to planoblasts; medusoid.

plā″nō-çon'çāve, *a.* plane on one side and concave on the other.

plā″nō-çon'iç·ăl, *a.* plane on one side and conical on the other.

plā″nō-çon'vex, *a.* plane on one side and convex on the other; as, a *plano-convex* lens.

PLANO-CONCAVE LENS

plan'ō·gȧ·mēte″, *n.* in biology, same as *zoogamete*.

plā″nō·graph'iç, *a.* pertaining to planography.

plȧ·nog'rȧ·phy, *n.* [*plano-* and *-graphy*.] any method of printing from a flat surface, as lithography.

plȧ·nom'e·tēr, *n.* [*plano-*, and Gr. *metron*, a measure.] a plane hard surface used in machine making as a gauge for plane surfaces.

plȧ·nom'e·try, *n.* the act of measuring, making, or gauging plane surfaces; the act or art of using a planometer.

PLANO-CONVEX LENS

Plȧ·nọr'bis, *n.* [L. *planus*, flat, and *orbis*, a circle.] a genus of fresh-water shells of a discoidal form, resembling the ammonite, but not chambered.

plā·nō·spī'răl, *a.* planispiral.

plā″nō-sū'bū·lāte, *a.* smooth and shaped like an awl.

plant, *n.* [Fr. *plante*; L. *planta*, the sole.] the sole of the foot. [Obs.]

plant, *n.* [AS. *plante*; L. *planta*, a plant.]
1. a young tree, shrub, or herb, ready to put into other soil for growth to maturity; a slip, cutting, or set.
2. any living thing that cannot move voluntarily, has no sense organs, and generally makes its own food by photosynthesis; a vegetable organism, as distinguished from an animal organism; any tree, shrub, herb, etc.
3. a soft-stemmed organism of this kind, as distinguished from a tree or shrub.
4. the tools, machinery, fixtures, buildings, grounds, etc. of a factory or business.

5. the equipment, buildings, etc. used by any institution, as a hospital, school, etc.

6. the apparatus or equipment for a certain mechanical operation or process; as, the power *plant* of a ship.

7. a swindling scheme; a trick; trap. [Slang.]

8. a person placed or thing planned to trick, mislead, or trap. [Slang.]

plant, *v.t.*; planted, *pt., pp.*; planting, *ppr.* 1. to put into the ground to grow.

2. to set firmly; to fix in position.

3. to fix in the mind; to implant, as an idea.

4. to establish in a specified place, as a religion.

5. to settle; to found, as a colony.

6. to furnish; to stock, as a piece of land with plants or a body of water with fish.

7. to put a stock of (oysters, young fish, etc.) in a body of water.

8. to deliver (a punch, blow, etc.) on the spot aimed at. [Slang.]

9. to place (a person or thing) in such a way as to trick, mislead, or trap. [Slang.]

10. to hide (stolen articles, etc.). [Slang.]

plant, *v.i.* to set plants; to sow seed.

plan′tȧ, *n.*; *pl.* **plan′tae,** [L.]

1. the sole of the foot.

2. the back of the tarsus of a bird.

3. the first tarsal joint of some insects.

plant′ȧ·ble, *a.* that can be planted.

plant′ăġe, *n.* vegetation in general. [Obs.]

Plan·tag′ē·net, *n.* the ruling family of England (1154–1399) or any member of this family: also called *Anjou.*

Plan″tȧ·ġi·nā′cē·ae, *n.pl.* same as *Plantagineæ.*

plan″tȧ·ġi·nā′ceous, *a.* pertaining to the *Plantagineæ.*

Plan·tȧ·ġin′ē·ae, *n.pl.* a small order of plants belonging to the monopetalous exogenous series. It consists of herbaceous plants with alternate or radical, rarely opposite, leaves and inconspicuous flowers on scapes arising from the lower leaves. The common rib grass, *Plantago lanceolata,* is a type.

Plan·tā′gō, *n.* [L. *plantago* (*-inis*), plantain.] a genus of the *Plantagineæ,* including the plantain.

plan′tāin, *n.* [ME.; OFr.; L. *plantago,* from *planta,* sole of the foot: from the shape of the leaves.]

1. any of a number of plants of the genus *Plantago,* with leaves toward the bottom of the stem and spikes of tiny, greenish flowers.

2. a weed with broad, ribbed leaves.

English plantain; the common plantain, *Plantago lanceolata,* introduced into the United States from Europe.

Indian plantain; see under *Indian.*

ribwort plantain: same as *English plantain.*

plan′tāin, *n.* [OFr., plane tree.]

1. a plant, *Musa paradisiaca,* closely related to the banana, from which it differs in not having purple spots on its stem. The fruit also is larger and more angular. It is extensively cultivated throughout the tropics. The stem is herbaceous, reaching a height of fifteen feet, and is crowned by a cluster of broad leaves.

2. the fruit of the tree: it is usually eaten cooked before ripe, being similar to the potato.

PLANTAIN
(*Musa paradisiaca*)

plan′tāin ēat′ẽr, an African bird of the genus *Musophaga,* related to the cuckoo.

plan′tāin lil′y, the day lily, *Funkia.*

plan′tāin squīr′rel (skwīr′), a Javanese squirrel which feeds on plantains.

plant′ăl, *a.* belonging or relating to plants.

plan′tăr, *a.* [L. *plantaris.*] of or pertaining to the sole of the foot.

plan·tā′tion, *n.* [L. *plantatio,* from *plantare,* to plant.]

1. formerly, a colony or new settlement.

2. an area growing cultivated crops.

3. an estate, as in a tropical or semitropical region, cultivated by workers living on it; as, a sugar *plantation.*

4. a large, cultivated planting of trees; as, a rubber *plantation.*

plant bug, any bug injurious to the leaves of plants, as insects of the order *Capsidæ.*

plant çāne, the original plants of the sugar cane, or canes of the first growth, in distinction from the ratoons, or sprouts from the roots of canes which have been cut.

plant cell, any cell of a plant.

plant çut′tẽr, a South American bird which injures plants by cutting off buds and tender shoots with its serrated bill.

plant′-ēat″ing, *a.* eating or feeding on plants; phytophagous; as, a *plant-eating* bug.

plant′ẽr, *n.* 1. one who or that which plants, sets, or cultivates; as, a *planter* of corn.

2. one who settles in a new or uncultivated territory; a colonist; pioneer; as, the first *planters* in Virginia.

3. one who owns a plantation.

4. a person engaged in the fishing trade; specifically, in Newfoundland, one who operates a fishery plant.

plant′ẽr·ship, *n.* the business of a planter or the management of a plantation.

Plant′ẽr's Punch, [prob. so called because served by *planters* (plantation owners).] an alcoholic drink made by shaking Jamaica rum, lemon or lime juice, and sugar together with fine ice, served unstrained.

Plan·ti·grā′dȧ, *n.pl.* a subdivision of carnivorous animals, including those which walk on the whole sole of the foot, as the bears, badgers, etc.

plan′ti·grāde, *a.* 1. walking on the whole sole of the foot, as bears, man, etc.

2. of or pertaining to the *Plantigrada.*

plan′ti·grāde, *n.* [L. *planta,* the sole of the foot, and *gradi,* to walk.] a plantigrade animal.

plant′ing, *n.* 1. the act or operation of setting in the ground for propagation, as seeds, trees, shrubs, etc.

2. a plantation. [Brit. Dial.]

3. in architecture, the act of placing the first row of stone in a foundation. [Brit.]

plan·tiv′ō·rous, *a.* [L. *planta,* plant, and *vorare,* to eat.] feeding on plants, as certain caterpillars.

plant′let, *n.* a little plant.

plant louse, any of a number of related small, usually green, sucking insects harmful to plants; an aphid.

plan·toç′rȧ·cy, *n.* [L. *planta,* plant, and Gr. *-kratia,* from *kratein,* to rule.] government by planters; the body of planters collectively. [Rare.]

plan′tū·lȧ, *n.*; *pl.* **plan′tū·lae,** [LL., dim. of L. *planta,* sole of the foot.] a membranous lobe between the claws of many insects.

plan′tū·lăr, *a.* pertaining to a plantula.

plant′ūle, *n.* the embryo of a plant.

plan′ū·lȧ, *n.*; *pl.* **plan′ū·lae,** [LL., dim. of L. *planus,* flat.]

1. a stage in the development of the embryo, intermediate between the morula and gastrula.

2. the young, free-swimming larva of a coelenterate.

plan′ū·lăn, *n.* a planula.

plan′ū·lăr, *a.* pertaining to or resembling a planula.

plan′ū·lāte, *a.* planular.

plan′ū·li·fọrm″, *a.* [from *planula* and *-form.*] of the form of a planula.

plan′ū·loid, *a.* [from *planula* and *-oid.*] resembling a panula.

plȧ·nū′ri·ȧ, plan′ū·ry, *n.* [Gr. *planos,* straying, and *ouron,* urine.] the voiding of urine from an abnormal place.

plan̄x′ty, *n.* an Irish or Welsh melody, composed for the harp.

plap, *v.i.*; plapped (plapt), *pt., pp.*; plapping, *ppr.* to plop; to splash.

plȧque (plȧk), *n.* [Fr.] 1. any thin, flat piece of metal, wood, porcelain, terra-cotta, etc., used for ornamentation, as on a wall.

2. a platelike brooch or pin worn as a badge or ornament.

plȧ·quette′ (-ket′), *n.* [Fr.] a small plaque.

plash, *n.* [D. *plasch,* puddle.] a small body of standing water; a puddle.

plash, *v.t.*; plashed (plasht), *pt., pp.*; plashing, *ppr.* to splash or make a splashing sound in.

plash, *v.i.* to make a splashing noise.

plash, *n.* a splash.

plash, *v.t.* [OFr. *plassier*; L. *plectere,* to weave.] to cut partly, bend, and intertwine (branches, stems, etc.) so as to form a hedge; also, to strengthen (a hedge) by interweaving the boughs or twigs of.

plash, *n.* a plashed branch or hedge. [Obs. or Dial.]

plash′et, *n.* a puddle; a small pool. [Dial.]

plash′y, *a.*; *comp.* plashier; *superl.* plashiest; full of puddles; marshy; wet.

-plā′şi·ȧ (-zhi-ȧ), [Mod. L., from Gr. *plasis,* a molding, from *plassein,* to mold.] a combining form signifying *change, development,* as in cata*plasia*: also *-plasis, -plasy.*

plaşm, *n.* [Gr. *plasma,* from *plassein,* to form.]

1. a mold or matrix in which anything is cast or formed to a particular shape. [Obs.]

2. same as *plasma* (senses 1, 2, and 3).

-plaşm, [from Gr. *plasma.*] a terminal combining form meaning: (a) *the fluid substances of an animal* or *vegetable cell*; (b) *protoplasm,* as in ecto*plasm.*

plaş′mȧ, *n.* [LL., something shaped or molded; Gr. *plasma,* from *plassein,* to form, mold.]

1. a green somewhat translucent variety of quartz.

2. the fluid part of blood, lymph, milk, or intramuscular liquid; especially, the fluid part of blood, as distinguished from the corpuscles.

3. protoplasm.

4. in pharmacy, a glycerite of starch used in preparing ointments.

5. a high-temperature, ionized gas composed of electrons and positive ions in such relative numbers that the gaseous medium is essentially electrically neutral: confinement of plasma for thermonuclear reactions is achieved by magnetic fields.

muscle plasma; a liquid extracted from muscular tissue. It is sometimes injected subcutaneously as a restorative and stimulant.

plasma cells; cells derived from lymphocytes and found in connective tissue: they appear most often in disease, and stain deeply; their nuclei contain a great amount of chromatin arranged in a circular manner.

plaş″mȧ·pher′ē·sis, *n.* [*plasma,* and Gr. *aphairesis,* a removal.] in physiology and medicine, the removal of a considerable amount of blood from a living body, the corpuscles being reinjected after their separation from plasma by centrifuging.

plaş·mat′iç, plaş·mat′iç·ăl, *a.* 1. having the power of giving form. [Rare.]

2. in biology, of or relating to plasma.

plaş′miç, *a.* plasmatic.

-plaş′miç, a combining form used in forming adjectives derived from nouns ending in *-plasm,* as in proto*plasmic.*

plaş′mid, *n.* [*plasma* and *-id.*] a small, self-reproducing cytoplasmic element that exists outside the chromosome, as in some bacteria: it can alter a heredity characteristic when introduced into a foreign bacterium, as by changing its antibiotic resistance.

plaş′mō-, a combining form meaning *plasma,* as in *plasmo*lysis: also *plasm-.*

plaş′mō·çhin, *n.* [*plasmo-* and *china* bark.] an antimalarial drug, $C_{19}H_{29}N_3O$, prepared synthetically from quinoline: a trade-mark (*Plasmochin*): also *plasmoquine, plasmoquin.*

plaş′mō·cȳte, *n.* a white blood corpuscle.

plaş·mō′di·ăl, *a.* in biology, of, pertaining to, or resembling plasmodium.

plaş·mō′di·ō·cärp, *n.* [*plasmodium,* and Gr. *karpos,* fruit.] in botany, an irregular body which generates the spores of some slime fungi.

Plaş·mō·di·oph′ō·rȧ, *n.* [*plasmodium,* and Gr. *pherein,* to bear.] in botany, a genus of myxomycetous parasites, as *Plasmodiophora brassicæ,* which causes clubroot in turnips, cabbage, and other cruciferous plants.

plaş·mō′di·um, *n.*; *pl.* **plaş·mō′di·ȧ,** [Mod. L., from Gr. *plasma,* a molded figure, and *eidos,* appearance.]

1. a mass of protoplasm with many nuclei, formed by the fusion of a number of one-celled organisms.

2. any of various unicellular parasites found in red blood corpuscles: one variety causes malaria.

plasmodium malariæ; the hematozoon of malaria; a parasite existing in various forms in red blood corpuscles in malaria.

plaş·mol′ō·ġy, *n.* [Gr. *plasma,* a molded figure, and *-logy.*] the study of the most minute particles or ultimate corpuscles of living matter.

plaş·mol′y·sis, *n.* [Gr. *plasma,* molded form, and *lysis,* loosening.] a shrinking of the protoplasm of a cell due to loss of water by osmosis.

plaş·mō·lyt′iç, *a.* tending toward, pertaining to, or characterized by plasmolysis.

plaş′mō·lȳze, *v.t.* and *v.i.*; plasmolyzed, *pt., pp.*; plasmolyzing, *ppr.* to subject to or to undergo plasmolysis.

Plaş·mop′ȧ·rȧ, *n.* [Gr. *plasma,* a molded figure, and L. *parere,* to bring forth.] in botany, a genus of fungi which includes *Plasmopara viticola*, a mildew destructive to grapevines.

plaṣ′mō·quin, plaṣ′mō·quīne, *n.* plasmochin.

plaṣ′mō·sōme, *n.* [Gr. *plasma*, molded form, and *sōma*, body.] in biology, the true nucleolus of a cell.

plas′ōme, *n.* [Gr. *plassein*, to form.] in biology, a biophore.

-plast, [from Gr. *plastos*, formed, from *plassein*, to form.] a combining form meaning *a unit of protoplasm*, as in chromo*plast*.

plȧs′tẽr, *n.* [Fr. *plâtre*; OFr. *plastre*, from L. *emplastrum*; Gr. *emplastron*, plaster, from *emplassein*, to daub over; *en*, on, in, and *plassein*, to form, to mold, to shape.]

1. a pasty mixture of lime, sand, and water, hard when dry, for coating walls, ceilings, and partitions.

2. plaster of Paris.

3. a pasty preparation spread on cloth and applied to the body, used medicinally as a curative or irritant.

adhesive plaster; see under *adhesive*.

fibrous plaster; plaster of Paris containing some fiber, as hair, to prevent breaking.

plaster of Paris; a heavy white powder, a hemihydrate of calcium sulfate, made by calcining gypsum: when made into a thin paste by the addition of water, it soon hardens and slightly expands: used in making casts, in finishing plastered walls, in statuary, etc.

porous plaster; in medicine, a plaster perforated to render it pliable and to keep it from wrinkling.

plȧs′tẽr, *v.t.*; plastered, *pt., pp.*; plastering, *ppr.* 1. to cover, smear, overlay, etc. with or as with plaster.

2. to apply or affix like a plaster; as, we *plastered* posters on the walls.

plȧs′tẽr·bōard, *n.* a thin board formed of layers of plaster and paper, used in building walls, partitions, etc.

plȧs′tẽr çȧst, 1. a copy or mold of a statue or other object, cast in plaster of Paris.

2. in surgery, a rigid cast to hold a fractured bone in place and prevent movement, made by wrapping the limb or part with a bandage of gauze soaked in wet plaster of Paris.

plȧs′tẽred, *a.* intoxicated; drunk. [Slang.]

plȧs′tẽr·ẽr, *n.* 1. one who applies plaster or whose business is plastering.

2. one who makes plaster casts.

plȧs′tẽr·ing, *n.* 1. the act or process of applying plaster.

2. the plasterwork of a building; a covering of plaster.

plas′tẽr stōne, gypsum as found in its natural state.

plȧs′tẽr·wŏrk, *n.* any architectural work done in plaster.

plȧs′tẽr·y, *a.* of the nature of plaster; containing or resembling plaster.

plas′tiç, *a.* [Gr. *plastikos*, from *plassein*, to form.]

1. molding or shaping matter; formative.

2. that can be molded or shaped.

3. impressionable; easily influenced; flexible.

4. dealing with molding or modeling.

5. hypocritically false or synthetic; as, a *plastic* culture.

6. in biology, capable of undergoing metabolic changes.

7. in medicine, (a) of or helpful in the renewal of destroyed or injured tissue; (b) that can be so renewed.

8. in physics, capable of continuous and permanent change of shape in any direction without breaking apart.

plastic arts; any of the arts concerned with molding or modeling, as sculpture, ceramics, etc.

plastic bomb; a puttylike substance containing explosives, that will adhere to walls, etc. and is detonated by fuse or electricity, as in acts of terrorism.

plastic memory; the tendency of certain plastics to resume their original form when heated.

plastic operation; an operation in plastic surgery.

plastic surgery; surgery dealing with the repair or restoration of injured, deformed, or destroyed parts of the body, especially by transferring tissue, as skin or bone, from other parts or from another individual.

plastic wood; a synthetic product which dries and hardens to the consistency of wood when exposed to the air: used in repairing wooden articles or as a filler in cracks, etc.

plas′tiç, *n.* 1. any of various nonmetallic compounds, synthetically produced (usually from organic compounds by polymerization), which can be molded into various forms and hardened for commercial use.

2. any article made of plastic.

-plas′tiç, [from Gr. *plastikos*.] a combining form meaning: (a) *forming, developing*, as in cyto*plastic*; (b) *of* ——*plasty* or *a* ——*plast*, as in neuro*plastic*.

plas′tiç·ăl·ly, *adv.* in a plastic manner.

plas·tic′i·ty, *n.* the quality or state of being plastic.

plas′ti·cīze, *v.t.* and *v.i.*; plasticized, *pt., pp.*; plasticizing, *ppr.* to make or become plastic.

plas′ti·cīz″ẽr, *n.* any of various substances added to a plastic to keep it soft and viscous.

plas′tid, plas′tide, *n.* [LL. *plastidium*, from Gr. *plastos*, molded, from *plassein*, to form.]

1. a unit of protoplasm; a cell.

2. a granule of specialized protoplasm occurring in the cytoplasm of some cells.

plas′ti·dūle, *n.* [*plastid* and dim. -*ule*.] a hypothetical protoplasmic molecule.

plas′tin, *n.* [Gr. *plastos*, molded, from *plassein*, to form.] one of the proteides of the cell nucleus.

plas·tique′ (-tēk′), *n.* [Fr.]

1. same as *plastic bomb*.

2. the technique or action of making very slow movements in dancing or pantomime, like a statue in motion.

plas′trăl, *a.* of or relating to a plastron.

plas′trŏn, *n.* [Fr.; It. *piastrone*, from *piastra*, a piaster.]

1. a metal breastplate worn under a coat of mail.

2. a leather breastplate worn over the chest of fencers.

3. a trimming like a dickey, worn on the front of a woman's dress.

4. a starched shirt front.

5. the under shell of a turtle or tortoise.

-plasty, [from Gr. *plastos*, verbal adj. from *plassein*, to form.] a terminal combining form meaning: (a) *the act* or *means of forming, growth, development*, as in genio*plasty*, dermato*plasty*; (b) *plastic surgery in which a* (specified) *part of the body is involved*, as in thoraco*plasty*; (c) *plastic surgery in which tissue from a* (specified) *source is used*, as in auto*plasty*; (d) *plastic surgery for a* (specified) *purpose*, as in kine*plasty*.

plat, *v.t.*; platted, *pt., pp.*; platting, *ppr.* [a form of *plait*.] to weave; to form by weaving or interweaving; to braid; to plait; as, to *plat* a girdle, to *plat* the hair.

plat, *n.* a braid; a plait. [Dial.]

plat, *v.t.*; platted, *pt., pp.*; platting, *ppr.* to make a drawing or plan of; to plot; as, to *plat* a piece of land or a landscape.

plat, *n.* [var. of *plot*.] 1. a small piece of ground.

2. a map; a plan.

plat, *a.* flat; level. [Obs.]

plat-, platy-.

Plat·ȧ·nā′cē·ae, *n.pl.* [L. *platanus*, Gr. *platanos*, the plane tree, from *platys*, broad, in allusion to its broad, flat leaves.] an order of exogenous plants characterized by their round heads of monoecious flowers, their one-celled ovaries, containing one ovule, and the embryo lying in fleshy albumen. The leaves are alternate, with sheathing stipules opposite to the leaves. This order consists of the single genus *Platanus*, including the trees commonly called *buttonwood* and *sycamore*.

plat′ăn, plat′āne, *n.* the plane tree.

plat′ȧ·nist, *n.* [L. *platanista*, a fish of the Ganges.] the susu.

Plat′ȧ·nus, *n.* [L.] a genus of large trees of the plane tree family, containing six species.

plat′band, *n.* [Fr. *platebande*; *plat*, *plate*, flat, and *bande*, a band.]

1. a border of flowers in a garden, along a wall or the side of a parterre.

2. in architecture, (a) a plain flat ashlar or a molding on a capital from which an arch springs; an impost; (b) a flat fascia, band, or string having a projection less than its breadth; sometimes the lintel of a door or window; (c) the fillet between the flutes of the Ionic and Corinthian pillars.

plāte, *n.* [from OFr. *plate*, a metal plate; *plat*, flat, from Gr. *platys*, broad.]

1. a smooth, flat, relatively thin piece of any material, as metal.

2. sheet metal made by beating, rolling, or casting.

3. one of the thin pieces or sheets of metal used in armor.

4. armor made of these.

5. a thin flat piece of metal on which an engraving is, or is to be, cut.

6. an impression taken from the engraved metal.

7. loosely, a print of a woodcut, lithograph, etc., especially when used in a book.

8. a full-page book illustration of any kind, printed on paper of a stock different from that which carries the text.

9. dishes, utensils, and similar household articles of silver or gold.

10. metal dishes, utensils, etc. that are plated, or coated with gold or silver.

11. a shallow dish, usually circular, from which food is eaten.

12. a plateful.

13. the food in a dish; a course; as, a fruit *plate*.

14. food and service for an individual at a meal; as, dinner at three dollars a *plate*.

15. a dishlike object passed in churches, etc. for donations of money.

16. a thin cut of beef from the forequarter, just below the short ribs.

17. in anatomy and zoology, a thin layer, plate, or scale, as of bone, horny tissue, etc.; lamina; scute.

18. in architecture, a horizontal wooden girder that supports the trusses or rafters of a roof.

19. in baseball, the home base (usually a small five-sided piece of rubber, etc., set into the ground), beside which the batter stands and which a player must touch after a circuit of the bases in order to score a run.

20. in dentistry, (a) that part of a set of false teeth which fits to the mouth and holds the teeth; (b) loosely, a set of false teeth.

21. in electricity, the anode, or positive element, of an electron tube, a flat plate or cylinder toward which the stream of electrons flows.

22. in philately, the impression surface from which a sheet of postage stamps is printed.

23. in photography, a sheet of glass, metal, etc. coated with a film sensitive to light, upon which the image is formed.

24. in printing, a cast to be printed from, made from a mold of set type by the electrotype or stereotype process.

25. in sports, (a) a prize, originally a gold or silver cup, given to the winner of a race or contest; (b) loosely, a contest, especially a horse race, in which the prize is a plate: also called *plate race*.

plate armor; plates of iron or steel, generally having a case-hardened surface: used for defense, as of a battleship.

plate block; in philately, a block of postage stamps with a serial number in the margin.

plate girder; a girder formed of a single plate of metal or of a series of plates joined together.

plate glass; polished, clear glass in thick sheets, used for shop windows, mirrors, etc.

plāte, *v.t.*; plated, *pt., pp.*; plating, *ppr.* 1. to cover or overlay with any metal or metals in a thin layer by any of various processes, as by electrolysis, welding, or hammering.

2. to add metal plates, sheets, or strips to; to sheathe or dress with plates.

3. in printing, to make a stereotype or electrotype plate of.

4. to beat into thin, flat pieces or laminae.

5. in papermaking, (a) to finish with a high gloss; (b) to size heavily with a tint.

pla·teau′ (-tō′), *n.*; *pl.* **pla·teauṣ′** or **pla·teaux′** (-tōz′), [Fr.] an elevated tract of more or less level land; tableland: applied figuratively to a period in the evolution of something, as of an individual's learning, characterized by a relative absence of progress, as represented by a flat extent in a graph, etc.

plāte bōne, the shoulder blade; the scapula.

plāt′ed, *a.* 1. covered or protected with plates, as of armor.

2. knitted of two kinds of yarn, one forming the face and the other the back.

3. overlaid or coated with a metal, especially a precious one: sometimes used in hyphenated compounds, meaning *coated with* (a specified metal), as in silver-*plated*.

plāte′ful, *n.*; *pl.* **plāte′fulṣ,** as much as a plate will hold.

plāte′hōld·ẽr, *n.* in photography, the movable frame fitted with slides for containing a plate or plates for exposure in a camera.

plāte′lāy·ẽr, *n.* in railroad construction, one who lays down and secures rails.

plāte′let, *n.* any of certain round or oval disks, one-third to one-half the size of a red blood cell but containing no hemoglobin, found in the blood of mammals and associated with the process of blood clotting.

plāte märk, 1. a legal mark or symbol made on certain gold and silver articles for the purpose of indicating their degree of purity, place of manufacture, or the like; thus, the local mark for London is a leopard's head.
 2. the margin mark on an engraved plate.

plat′en, *n.* [Fr. *plat*, flat.]
 1. in a printing press, a flat metal plate or rotating cylinder that presses the paper against the inked type.
 2. in a typewriter, the roller against which the keys strike.
 3. in a machine tool, the table holding the work.

plāte pā′pẽr, a choice grade of paper having a treated surface specially adapted for engravings and fine plates.

plāte press, any press used in plate printing.

plāte print′ẽr, a printer using engraved plates.

plāte print′ing, printing from engraved plates instead of from type, stone, or otherwise.

plāt′ẽr, *n.* 1. one who or that which plates.
 2. the part of a papermaking machine calendering the paper.
 3. an inferior race horse: see *plate*, 24 b.

plat·ẽr·esque′ (-esk′), *a.* [Sp. *plateresco*, from *plata*, silver.] of, relating to, or designating architecture resembling silver tracing or work.

plāte tec·ton′ics, in geology, the theory that the earth's surface consists of plates, or large crustal slabs, whose constant motion accounts for continental drift, mountain building, etc.

plāte trā′cẽr·y, in architecture, a form of tracery, used at the beginning of early English architecture, in which the openings are formed or cut in the stonework, and have no projecting moldings.

PLATE TRACERY

plat′ē·trōpe, *n.* [Gr. *platys*, flat, and *trepein*, to turn.] in anatomy, one of two organs or parts bilaterally symmetrical.

plāte wheel (hwēl), a wheel having the rim and hub connected by a metal plate instead of by spokes.

plat′form, *n.* [Fr. *plateforme*, lit., flat form.]
 1. a raised horizontal surface of wood, stone, or metal; specifically, (a) a raised stage or flooring beside railroad tracks, streetcar tracks, etc.; (b) a vestibule at the end of a railway car, streetcar, etc.; (c) a raised flooring or stage for performers, speakers, etc.
 2. the statement of principles and policies of a political party or other organization.
 platform car; a railroad freight car without a roof or raised sides; a flatcar.
 platform scale; a large scale having a flat platform for the object to be weighed.

plat′form, *a.* 1. designating a shoe sole, from 1/2 to 3 inches thick, usually made of cork or wood.
 2. designating a shoe with such a sole.

plat′form, *v.t.* 1. to place on or as on a stage or platform.
 2. to make a plan of; to draw up; to outline. [Obs.]

plat′form ten′nis, same as *paddle tennis*.

Plat·hel·min′thēs, *n.pl.* same as *Platyhelminthes*.

plat′in-, see *platini-*.

plat′i·nȧ (*or* plȧ-tē′), *n.* [Mod. L.; Sp., dim. from *plata*, silver, orig. thin plate of metal.] platinum. [Obs. or Rare.]
 platina mohr; platinum black.

plāt′ing, *n.* 1. the art, act, or process of a person or thing that plates.
 2. an external layer of metal plates.
 3. a thin coating of gold, silver, tin, etc.

plat′i·ni-, plat′in-, plat′i·nō-, combining forms denoting *platinum*, as in *platini*ferous.

plȧ·tin′iç, *a.* of, like, or containing platinum, especially with a valence of four.

plat″i·ni·chlō′riç, *a.* characterizing the acid derived from a solution of platinum in aqua regia.

plat·i·nif′ẽr·ous, *a.* [*platini-* and *-ferous*.] having or yielding platinum.

plat″i·nī·rid′i·um, *n.* a native alloy of platinum and iridium, often containing other metals.

plat′i·nīze, *v.t.*; platinized, *pt.*, *pp.*; platinizing, *ppr.* to plate with platinum; to combine with platinum.

plat″i·nō·chlō′riç, *a.* characterizing the divalent compounds of platinum with chlorine, as platinum dichloride, $PtCl_2$.

plat′i·nō·chlō′ride, *n.* any chloride of platinum with another element or radical.

plat″i·nō·cy·an′iç, *a.* designating or of an acid containing platinum and the cyanogen radical.

plat″i·nō·cȳ′ȧ·nid, *n.* platinocyanide.

plat″i·nō·cȳ′ȧ·nīde, *n.* any cyanide of platinum with another element or radical: used in photography, etc.

plat′i·noid, *a.* resembling or characteristic of platinum.

plat′i·noid, *n.* 1. any of a group of metals with which platinum is invariably found associated. The platinoids include palladium, rhodium, iridium, osmium, and ruthenium.
 2. an alloy of copper, nickel, zinc, and wolfram (tungsten), used in electrical resistance coils, etc.

plat′i·nō·type, *n.* 1. a process of photography producing a picture in platinum black by using a platinum salt in the sensitizing solution or developer.
 2. the picture so obtained.

plat′i·nous, *a.* of, like, containing, or characteristic of platinum, especially with a valence of two; as, *platinous* oxide, PtO.

plat′i·num, *n.* [Sp. *platina*, from *plata*, silver.] a steel-gray, malleable, ductile metallic chemical element, highly resistant to corrosion and electricity: used as a chemical catalyst, for acid-proof containers, ignition fuses, jewelry, dental equipment, etc.: symbol, Pt; atomic weight, 195.23; atomic number, 78.
 platinum metal; one of a group of metals which resemble platinum in their physical and chemical properties: they include platinum, osmium, iridium, palladium, rhodium, and ruthenium, and, sometimes, rhenium and technetium.
 platinum sponge; metallic platinum in the form of a porous, dull-brown mass. It is used to occlude oxygen.

plat′i·num black, a black powder of finely divided metallic platinum, made by reduction of platinum salts and noted for its power to occlude gases, one volume absorbing 800 volumes of oxygen: it is used as a catalyst, as in organic synthesis.

plat′i·num blonde, a girl or woman who has very light pale-yellow hair.

plat′i·tūde, *n.* [Fr.] 1. commonplaceness; flatness; dullness; insipidity; as, there was much *platitude* in his remarks.
 2. a trite, dull, or commonplace remark, especially one uttered as if it were a novelty or matter of importance.

> An artless *platitude* is really more artificial than a clever paradox.
> —W. C. Brownell.

plat·i·tū·di·nãr′i·ăn, *n.* one who utters platitudes.

plat·i·tū′di·nīze, *v.i.*; platitudinized, *pt.*,*pp.*; platitudinizing, *ppr.* to write or speak platitudes.

plat·i·tū′di·nous, *a.* of or like a platitude; characterized by, full of, or using platitudes; trite; commonplace.

plat′ly, *a.* flatly; plainly. [Obs.]

plat′ness, *n.* flatness; plainness. [Obs.]

plat′oid, *a.* [Gr. *platys*, broad, and *-oid*.] flat.

plȧ·tom′ē·tẽr, *n.* same as *planimeter*.

Plȧ·ton′iç, *a.* [L. *Platonicus*; Gr. *Platōnikos*, from *Platōn*, Plato.]
 1. of, characteristic of, or pertaining to Plato, the philosopher (427–347 B. C.), or to his philosophy, his school, or his opinions.
 2. idealistic, visionary, or impractical.
 3. [*also* p–] not amorous or sensual but purely spiritual; as, *Platonic* love.
 Platonic bodies; the five regular geometrical solids, namely, the tetrahedron, hexahedron (or cube), octahedron, dodecahedron, and icosahedron.
 Platonic year; the great year; a period of time determined by the revolution of the equinoxes, or the space of time in which the stars and constellations return to their former places in respect to the equinoxes. This revolution, which is calculated by the precession of the equinoxes, is accomplished in about 26,000 of the earth's years.

Plȧ·ton′iç·ăl·ly, *adv.* after the manner of Platonists; in a Platonic manner.

Plā′tō·nism, *n.* [Mod. L. *platonismus*.]
 1. the philosophy of Plato and his followers: it is one kind of philosophical idealism.
 2. a doctrine or saying typical of Platonic philosophy.
 3. [*also* p–] the theory or practice of Platonic love.

Plā′tō·nist, *a.* of Plato, his ideas, or his school.

Plā′tō·nist, *n.* a follower of Plato, or a student of his philosophy.

Plā′tō·nīze, *v.t.*; Platonized, *pt.*, *pp.*; Platonizing, *ppr.* to explain on the principles of the Platonic philosophy; to make Platonic

Plā′tō·nīze, *v.i.* to follow the philosophy of Plato; to adopt Platonism; to philosophize in a Platonic manner.

Plā′tō·nīz·ẽr, *n.* one who Platonizes; a Platonist.

plȧ·toon′, *n.* [Fr. *peloton*, a ball, a group, a platoon, from *pelote*, a ball.]
 1. a military unit composed of two or more squads or sections, normally under the command of a lieutenant: it is a subdivision of a company, troop, etc.
 2. a group or unit like this; as, a *platoon* of police.
 3. in sports, any of the specialized squads (as the offensive and defensive squads in professional football) constituting a single team.
 4. formerly, a small body of soldiers or musketeers drawn out of a battalion of foot soldiers and formed into a hollow square to strengthen a formation, line, etc.

plȧ·toon′, *v.t.*; platooned, *pt.*, *pp.*; platooning, *ppr.* 1. to divide into platoons, or use as on a platoon.
 2. in sports, to alternate (players) at a position; as, to *platoon* two rookies in right field.

plȧ·toon′, *v.i.* in sports, (a) to be alternated with another player at a position; (b) to platoon players at a position.

Plätt′deutsch (-doich), *n.* the Low German vernacular language of northern Germany.

plat′ten, *v.t.* to form into plates, as glass.

plat′tẽr, *n.* one who plats or braids.

plat′tẽr, *n.* [ME. *plater*, from OFr. *plat*, flat.]
 1. a large, shallow dish, usually oval, for serving food.
 2. in baseball, the home base: also called *plate*. [Slang.]
 3. a phonograph record. [Slang.]

plat′tẽr-fāced (-fāst), *a.* having a broad face.

plat′ting, *n.* slips of bast, cane, straw, etc., woven or plaited, as for making into hats.

platt′nẽr·īte, *n.* [named after the German chemist, K. F. *Plattner*.] a mineral dioxide of lead found both massive and crystalline.

plȧ·tū′rous, *a.* [Gr. *platys*, broad, and *oura*, tail.] broad-tailed.

plāt′y, *a.* made of plates; like a plate. [Obs.]

plat′y-, [from Gr. *platys*, broad, flat.] a combining form meaning *broad* or *flat*, as in *platypus*; also *plat-*.

plat″y·cē·phal′iç, *a.* same as *platycephalous*.

plat·y·ceph′ȧ·lous, *a.* [*platy-*, and Gr. *kephalē*, head.] having a broad or flat head.

plat·y·ceph′ȧ·ly, *n.* the condition of being flat-headed.

plat·yç·nē′miç, *a.* [*platy-*, and Gr. *knēmē*, the lower leg.] of or displaying platycnemism.

plat·yç′nē·mism, *n.* the state or condition of having the tibiae abnormally compressed.

Plat·y·el′mi·ȧ, *n.pl.* same as *Platyhelminthes*.

Plat″y·el·min′thēs, *n.pl.* same as *Platyhelminthes*.

Plat·y·hel′mi·ȧ, *n.pl.* same as *Platyhelminthes*.

plat·y·hel′minth, *n.* a flatworm; any worm of the *Platyhelminthes*.

Plat″y·hel·min′thȧ, *n.pl.* same as *Platyhelminthes*.

Plat″y·hel·min′thēs, *n.pl.* [*platy-*, and Gr. *helmins*, *helminthos*, worm.] the flatworms; a phylum of worms including the *Trematoda*, the *Cestoidea*, and the *Turbellaria*, characterized by softness, and flatness of the body and indistinct segmentation: tapeworms, flukes, etc. are members.

plat·y·hī′er·iç, *a.* [*platy-*, and Gr. *hieron*, sacrum.] having the sacrum flat or broad.

plat·y·pel′liç, *a.* [*platy-*, and Gr. *pella*, a bowl.] having the pelvis flat or broad.

plat′y·pod, *n.* any animal having broad feet.

Plȧ·typ′ō·dȧ, *n.pl.* 1. a group of mammals having a bill like that of a duck; the duckbills.
 2. a group of rostriferous gastropods.

Plȧ·typ′tẽr·ȧ, *n.* [*platy-*, and Gr. *pteron*, wing.]

a genus of fishes of which the only species is *Platyptera aspro*, a fresh-water fish of the East Indies.

Plȧ·typ′tẽr·ȧ, *n.pl.* a division of pseudoneuropterous insects, including the stoneflies and termites.

plat′y·pus, *n.*; *pl.* **plat′y·pus·eṣ, plat′y·pī,** [*platy-*, and Gr. *pous*, foot.] a small Australian water mammal with brownish fur, a ducklike bill, and webbed feet: also called *duckbill, duckbilled platypus*.

plat′yr·rhīne, plat′y·rhīne, *a.* having a broad nose; pertaining to the *Platyrrhini*.

plat′yr·rhīne, plat′y·rhīne, *n.* a member of the *Platyrrhini*.

Plat·yr·rhī′nī, Plat·y·rhī′nī, *n.pl.* [*platy-*, and Gr. *rhis, rhinos*, nose.] a division of monkeys without a bony external auditory meatus. It includes all American monkeys.

plat·yr·rhin′i·ăn, *a.* [Mod. L. *platyrrhinus*, from *platy-* and Gr. *rhis*, rhinos, a nose.] having a broad, flat nose with the nostrils wide apart.

plat·yr·rhin′i·ăn, *n.* a platyrrhinian person, monkey, or skull.

Plat·y·stē′mon, *n.* [*platy-*, and Gr. *stemōn*, warp, stamen.] a genus of plants of the poppy family, consisting of a single species, *Platystemon californicus*, found in California and Arizona.

plat·y·stẽr′năl, *a.* [*platy-*, and Gr. *sternon*, breast.] having a broad, flat breastbone; ratite: said of a bird.

plȧ·tys′tō·mous, *a.* [*platy-*, and Gr. *stoma*, mouth.] having a broad mouth.

plaud, *v.t.* to applaud. [Obs.]

plau′dit, *n.* [L. *plaudite*, do you applaud, imper. of *plaudere*, to applaud, whence *applause*.] [*usually in pl.*] (a) an applauding or round of applause; (b) any expression of approval or praise.

Syn.—applause, approbation, encomium, acclamation.

plau′di·tō·ry, *a.* applauding; commending.

plau·ṣi·bil′i·ty, *n.*; *pl.* **plau·ṣi·bil′i·tieṣ,** 1. the quality of being plausible; plausibleness.

2. something deserving applause. [Obs.]

3. something plausible.

plau′ṣi·ble, *a.* [L. *plausibilis*, from *plaudere*, to clap hands in token of approbation.]

1. seemingly true, acceptable, etc.: often implying disbelief.

2. specious.

3. seemingly honest, trustworthy, etc.: often implying distrust; as, a *plausible* rogue.

4. deserving applause; praiseworthy. [Obs.]

Syn.—specious, colorable.

plau′ṣi·ble·īze, *v.t.* to make plausible. [Rare.]

plau′ṣi·ble·ness, *n.* plausibility.

plau′ṣi·bly, *adv.* in a plausible manner.

plau′sive, *a.* 1. applauding; showing praise.

2. plausible. [Obs.]

plāy, *v.i.*; played, *pt., pp.*; playing, *ppr.* [ME. *pleien*; AS. *plegan, plegian*.]

1. to move lightly, rapidly, or erratically; to frisk; to flutter; as, sunlight *plays* on the waves, a smile *played* on his lips.

2. to have fun; to amuse oneself; to take part in a game or sport; to engage in recreation.

3. to take part in a game for money; to gamble.

4. to make love playfully.

5. to handle anything carelessly or treat anyone lightly; to trifle (*with* a thing or person).

6. to perform on a musical instrument.

7. to give out musical sounds: said of an instrument.

8. to act in a specified way; as, *play* fast and loose.

9. to act in or as in a drama; to perform on the stage.

10. to lend itself to performance; as, the new piano *plays* well, that drama will *play*.

11. to be performed in a theater, on the radio, etc.; as, a new movie is *playing* tonight.

12. to move freely within limits, as parts of a machine.

13. to be ejected, discharged, or directed repeatedly or continuously, as a fountain, a gun, a spotlight, etc. (with *on, over*, or *along*).

to play at; (a) to participate in; (b) to pretend to be engaged in; (c) to perform or work at halfheartedly.

to play fair; (a) to play according to the rules; (b) to behave honorably.

to play for time; to maneuver so as to delay an outcome, gain a respite, etc.

to play into the hands of; to act or manage matters to the benefit or advantage of.

to play off; (a) to pretend; to simulate; (b) to show off; to display.

to play on or *upon*; to make adroit or unscrupulous use of (a person's feelings or susceptibilities) for one's own purposes.

to play on words; to pun.

to play up to; to try to please by flattery, etc. [Colloq.]

plāy, *v.t.* 1. to take part in (a game or sport).

2. to engage in a game or contest against.

3. to enter or use (a player, etc.) in a game or contest; as, the coach *played* Jones at center.

4. to do (something), often in fun or to deceive; as, *play* tricks.

5. (a) to bet; (b) to bet on; as, *play* the horses.

6. to cause to move, act, operate, etc.; to put into or keep in action; to wield; to ply.

7. to cause; effect; as, *play* hob, *play* havoc.

8. to perform (music).

9. to perform on (an instrument); cause to give out musical sounds.

10. to accompany or lead (a person or persons) with music (with *in, off, down*, etc.).

11. to perform (a drama or dramatic passage).

12. to act the part of; as, *play* Iago, *play* the fool.

13. to pretend or imitate for amusement; as, *play* soldier.

14. to give performances in; as, they *played* New York for a month.

15. to eject, discharge, or direct repeatedly or continuously, as a fountain, etc. (with *on, over*, or *along*).

16. to let (a fish) tire itself while hooked by tugging at the line.

played out; (a) finished; (b) worn out; exhausted; (c) out of date.

to play both ends against the middle; (a) to take chances on alternatives in order to win something no matter what the outcome; (b) to play off opposing factions, etc. against one another to one's own profit.

to play down; to attach little importance to; give little publicity to; minimize.

to play off; (a) to pit (a person or thing) against another; (b) to palm off; (c) in games, to break (a tie) by playing once more.

to play one's cards well; to manage one's business or resources in the most effective manner.

to play out; (a) to play to the finish; to end; (b) to play out (a rope, etc.).

to play second fiddle; to take a subordinate position.

to play up; (a) to begin playing; as, *to play up* a tune; (b) [Colloq.] to give prominence to; to advertise.

plāy, *n.* 1. action, motion, or activity, especially when free, rapid, or light; as, the *play* of muscles.

2. freedom or scope for motion or action.

3. action or exercise for amusement; recreation; sport.

4. fun; joking; as, do a thing in *play*: opposed to *earnest*.

5. the playing of a game.

6. the way of playing a game.

7. a maneuver, move, or act in a game.

8. gambling.

9. a dramatic composition or performance; a drama.

10. performance on an instrument of music. [Obs.]

11. the act or art of managing a fish with a line so as to tire it out and bring it to land.

a play on or *upon words*; the use of words or expressions the meaning of which may be construed in different ways; punning; a pun.

in or *out of play*; in sports, in (or not in) such a condition or position that play may legitimately be continued: said of a ball, etc.

play of colors; an appearance of several prismatic colors in rapid succession on turning an object, as a diamond.

to bring or *to come into play*; to bring or come into use or exercise.

to hold in play; to keep occupied or employed.

to make a play for; (a) to employ one's arts and wiles in order to fascinate; (b) to use all one's skill in order to obtain. [Colloq.]

plä′yȧ, *n.*; *pl.* **plä′yȧṣ,** [Sp.] a tract of hard clayey land which frequently becomes covered with water during heavy rains, and finally becomes dry again; a dried-up lake basin.

plāy′ȧ·ble, *a.* 1. capable of being played.

2. that can be played on; in suitable condition for playing.

plāy′-aćt″ing, *n.* the acting of plays or dramas.

plāy′-aç″tŏr, *n.* a stage player.

plāy′-aç″tŏr·iṣm, *n.* stage playing; histrionism.

plāy′back, *n.* 1. a playing back.

2. the part of an electric recorder that serves as a phonograph to play back transcriptions, etc.

plāy′bill, *n.* 1. a poster or circular advertising a play.

2. a printed program of a play, with the parts assigned to the actors.

plāy′book, *n.* a book of dramatic compositions.

plāy′boy, *n.* a man who is carefree, gay, and fond of playing; specifically, a well-to-do man who spends much time and energy in pleasure-seeking and dissipation. [Colloq.]

plāy′-bȳ-plāy′, *a.* of each play as it occurs; as, a *play-by-play* description of a game.

plāy′dāy, *n.* a day given to play or diversion; a day exempt from work; a holiday.

plāy′ẽr, *n.* 1. one who plays in any game or sport.

2. an idler; a trifler.

3. an actor in a drama.

4. one who performs on an instrument of music.

5. a gambler.

6. an apparatus for playing a musical instrument mechanically.

plāy′ẽr pi·an′ō, a piano that plays automatically.

plāy′fel″lōw, *n.* a playmate.

plāy′fụl, *a.* 1. fond of play or fun; frisky; sportive; indulging a sportive fancy; as, a *playful* child; a *playful* genius.

2. humorous; joking; merry.

Syn.—lively, sportive, jocund, frolicsome, gay, vivacious, sprightly.

plāy′fụl·ly, *adv.* in a playful manner.

plāy′fụl·ness, *n.* the state or quality of being playful.

plāy′gāme, *n.* a play or game of children.

plāy′gō″ẽr, *n.* one who goes to the theater frequently or regularly.

plāy′gō″ing, *a.* frequenting theaters.

plāy′gō″ing, *n.* the practice of going to theaters.

plāy′ground, *n.* a piece of ground set apart for outdoor games and recreation; especially, a piece of ground connected with a school, etc.

plāy′house, *n.* 1. a building used for dramatic performances; a theater.

2. a small house for children to play in.

3. a building used for recreation.

4. a child's toy house or doll house.

plāy′ing ćard, one of a pack of cards used for playing games: the cards are arranged in decks of four suits (hearts, diamonds, clubs, and spades).

plāy′let, *n.* a short drama.

plāy′māk″ẽr, *n.* a writer of plays; a playwright. [Rare.]

plāy′māte, *n.* a playfellow; a companion in games and recreations.

plāy′-off, *n.* in games, a match played to break a tie.

plāy′rọom, *n.* a room for playing or recreation.

plāy′sŏme, *a.* playful; wanton. [Rare.]

plāy′sŏme·ness, *n.* playfulness; wantonness. [Rare.]

plāyte, *n.* a plait. [Obs.]

plāy′thing, *n.* a toy; anything that serves to amuse.

> A child knows his nurse, and by degrees the *playthings* of a little more advanced age.
> —Locke.

plāy′tīme, *n.* time for amusement.

plāy′wrīght (-rīt), *n.* one who writes plays; a dramatist.

plä′zȧ, *n.* [Sp.] an open square or market place in a city or town for the use of the public.

plēa, *n.* [ME. *plee, plead, pleid*; OFr. *plai, plaid, plait*, a suit, a plea; Fr. *plaid*, the speech of a pleader; Norm. *plait, plaid*, plea, proceedings; from L. *placitum*, an opinion, a determination, from *placere*, to please.]

1. in law, (a) [Obs.] a suit or action; (b) a pleading or allegation; (c) a statement made by, or on behalf of, a defendant, either answering the charges or showing why he should not be required to answer.

2. that which is alleged in defense or justification; an excuse; an apology; as, the tyrant's *plea*.

When such occasions are,
No *plea* must serve; 'tis cruelty to spare.
—Denham.

3. an urgent prayer; an appeal; a request; an entreaty.

pleas of the crown; in English law, criminal actions.

Syn.—excuse, vindication, justification, defense, ground, apology, entreaty.

plēa bär′gain·ing, pretrial negotiations in which the defendant agrees to plead guilty to a lesser charge in exchange for having more serious charges dropped.

plēach, *v.t.* to bend; to interweave, as branches of trees; to plait.

plēad, *v.i.*; pleaded *or colloq. or dial.* plead, pled, *pt., pp.*; pleading, *ppr.* [ME. *plaiden*; OFr. *plaidier* from *plaid*; see *plea.*]

1. to present a plea in a law court; to argue the case of either party.

2. to make an earnest appeal; to supplicate; to beg; as, *plead* for mercy.

plēad, *v.t.* 1. to discuss or defend (a law case) by argument.

2. to declare oneself to be (guilty or not guilty) in answer to a charge.

3. to allege or adduce in proof, support, or vindication; as, the law of nations may be *pleaded* in favor of the rights of ambassadors.

4. to offer in excuse or defense; as, to *plead* ignorance.

I will neither *plead* my age nor sickness in excuse of faults. —Dryden.

Syn.—advocate, argue, ask, beg, beseech, entreat, implore, press, solicit, urge.

plēad′ȧ·ble, *a.* that can be pleaded; that can be alleged in proof, defense, or vindication; as, a right or privilege *pleadable* at law.

plēad′ẽr, *n.* 1. one who pleads in a law court; an advocate.

2. one who entreats or intercedes; one who offers reasons for or against; one who attempts to maintain by arguments.

So fair a *pleader* any cause may gain.
—Dryden.

plēad′ing, *n.* the act of supporting by arguments, or of reasoning to persuade.

plēad′ing·ly, *adv.* in a pleading manner; beseechingly.

plēad′ings, *n.pl.* in law, the statements setting forth to the court the claims or allegations of the plaintiff and the answer of the defendant.

pleaș′ănce (plez′), *n.* [ME. *plesaunce*; OFr. *plaisance*, from *plaisir*, to please.]

1. pleasure or pleasantry. [Archaic.]

2. a pleasure ground or garden, usually part of an estate.

pleaș′ănt, *a.* [Fr. *plaisant.*]

1. pleasing; agreeable to the mind or to the senses; as, a *pleasant* ride; a *pleasant* voyage; a *pleasant* view.

2. having an agreeable manner, appearance, etc.; amiable; cheerful; enlivening; as, *pleasant* society or company.

3. (a) gay; lively; merry; (b) jesting; jocular; playful.

Syn.—pleasing, gratifying, agreeable, cheerful, good-humored, enlivening, gay, lively, merry, sportive, humorous, jocose, amusing, witty, attractive.

pleaș′ănt, *n.* a wit. [Obs.]

pleaș′ănt·ly, *adv.* in such a manner as to please or gratify.

pleaș′ănt·ness, *n.* the state of being pleasant or agreeable; as, the *pleasantness* of a situation.

pleaș′ănt·ry, *n.*; *pl.* **pleaș′ănt·rieș,** [Fr. *plaisanterie.*]

1. the quality or state of being pleasant, or playful, in conversation; jocularity.

2. a humorous remark or action; a joke.

3. pleasure. [Archaic.]

plēaṣe, *v.t.*; pleased, *pt., pp.*; pleasing, *ppr.* [OFr. *plaisir*; Fr. *plaire*, from L. *placere*, to please.]

1. to excite agreeable sensations or emotions in; to gratify; to give pleasure to; to satisfy; as, to *please* the taste; to *please* the mind.

Leave such to trifle with more grace than ease,
Whom folly *pleases*, and whose follies *please*. —Pope.
What next I bring shall *please*
Thy wish exactly to thy heart's desire.
—Milton.

2. to be the will or wish of; as, it *pleased* him to remain.

please God; if it pleases God; if it is God's will.

to be pleased in or *with*; to approve; to have complacency in.

to please oneself; to do as one wishes.

Syn.—delight, gratify, humor, satisfy.

plēaṣe, *v.i.* 1. to be agreeable; to give pleasure; to satisfy; as, we aim to *please*.

2. to have the will or wish; to like; as, I'll do as I *please*: also used passively; as, you are *pleased* to scoff.

Spirits, freed from mortal laws, with ease
Assume what sexes and what shapes they *please*. —Pope.

Please is also used, followed by an infinitive, for politeness in requests or commands to mean "be obliging enough"; as, *please* (to) do this for me.

The first words that I learnt were to express my desire that he would *please* to give me my liberty. —Swift.

if you please; if you wish or like; if you permit: sometimes used in ironic exclamation.

plēaṣed, *a.* gratified; affected with agreeable sensations or emotions.

plēaṣ′ed·ness, *n.* the state of being pleased.

plēaṣe′măn, *n.* an officious person who courts favor servilely. [Obs.]

plēaṣ′ẽr, *n.* one who pleases or gratifies; one who courts favor by obeying, humoring, or flattering.

plēaṣ′ing, *a.* giving pleasure or satisfaction; agreeable; gratifying; as, a *pleasing* reflection.

Syn.—pleasant, agreeable.

plēaṣ′ing, *n.* the act of gratifying.

plēaṣ′ing·ly, *adv.* in such a mannner as to give pleasure.

plēaṣ′ing·ness, *n.* the quality of giving pleasure.

pleaș′ūr·ȧ·ble (plezh′), *a.* pleasing; giving pleasure; pleasant; enjoyable; agreeable.

pleaș′ūr·ȧ·ble·ness, *n.* the quality of giving pleasure.

pleaș′ūr·ȧ·bly, *adv.* in a pleasurable manner.

pleaș′ūre (plezh′), *n.* [Fr. *plaisir.*]

1. the gratification of the senses or of the mind; agreeable sensations or emotions: the excitement, relish, or happiness produced by enjoyment or the expectation of good; enjoyment; satisfaction: opposed to *pain*.

2. sensual or sexual gratification; diversion; sport; enjoyment.

3. what one's will dictates or prefers; will; choice; purpose; intention; command; as, use your *pleasure*.

4. a thing that gives delight and satisfaction; that which pleases.

Syn.—enjoyment, gratification, sensuality, self-indulgence, voluptuousness, choice, preference, will, inclination, purpose, determination, satisfaction, indulgence.

pleaș′ūre, *v.t.*; pleasured, *pt., pp.*; pleasuring, *ppr.* to give or afford pleasure to; to please; to gratify. [Archaic.]

pleaș′ūre, *v.i.* to seek pleasure; to devote one's time to pleasure; as, to go *pleasuring*. [Archaic.]

pleaș′ūre·fųl, *a.* full of pleasure; agreeable.

pleaș′ūre ground, any particular piece of land set aside for pleasure or amusement.

pleaș′ūre·less, *a.* without pleasure.

pleaș′ūre prin′ci·ple, in psychoanalysis, the automatic adjustment of the mental activity to secure pleasure, or gratification, and avoid pain, or unpleasantness.

pleaș′ūr·ẽr, *n.* a pleasure seeker.

pleaș′ūr·ing, *n.* the act of journeying for pleasure.

pleaș′ūr·ist, *n.* a person devoted to worldly pleasure. [Rare.]

plēat, *n.* [ME. *pleten*, var. of *playten*, a plait.] a flat double fold in cloth or other material, of uniform width and pressed or stitched in place.

plēat, *v.t.* to lay and press (cloth) in a pleat or series of pleats.

plēat′ẽr, *n.* a person or thing that pleats; specifically, an attachment on a sewing machine for making pleats.

pleb, *n.* 1. a plebian.

2. a plebe (sense 3).

plēbe, *n.* [Fr. *plèbe*; L. *plebs*, the common people.]

1. the Roman plebs. [Obs.]

2. the common people of a nation.

3. [short for *plebeian.*] a member of the lowest, or freshman, class at the United State Military Academy at West Point or the Naval Academy at Annapolis.

plē·bē′iăn (-yăn), *n.* [L. *plebeius*, of the common people.]

1. one of the common people, or a member of the lower class, in ancient Rome, as distinguished from a patrician.

2. one of the common people.

3. a vulgar, coarse person.

plē·bē′iăn, *a.* [Fr. *plébéien*; L. *plebeius*, from *plebs, plebis*, the common people.]

1. pertaining to or characteristic of the ancient Rome lower class or the common people; as, *plebeian* sports.

2. of low rank.

3. common; coarse; vulgar; as, a *plebeian* throng.

Syn.—low, vulgar, low-born, low-bred, coarse, ignoble.

plē·bē′iănce, *n.* plebeian quality. [Rare.]

plē·bē′iăn·ișm, *n.* 1. a plebeian characteristic, act, or remark.

2. plebeian quality or manners; vulgarity.

plē·bē′iăn·īze, *v.t.*; plebeianized, *pt., pp.*; plebeianizing, *ppr.* to cause to become plebeian; to vulgarize.

plē·biç′ō·list, *n.* [L. *plebicola*; *plebs*, the common people, and *colere*, to cultivate.] one who caters to vulgarity; one who seeks the favor of the common people; a demagogue. [Rare.]

pleb·i·fi·çā′tion, *n.* [L. *plebs*, the common people, and *facere*, to make.] the act of rendering plebeian. [Rare.]

pleb′i·fȳ, *v.t.*; plebified, *pt., pp.*; plebifying, *ppr.* [L. *plebs*, the common people, and *facere*, to make.] to cause to adopt the habits, tastes, and views of plebeians. [Rare.]

plē·bis·cī′tȧ, *n.* plural of *plebiscitum*.

plē·bis′ci·tăr·y, *a.* pertaining to a plebiscite.

pleb′i·scite, *n.* [Fr. *plébiscite*; L. *plebiscitum*, from *plebs, plebis*, the common people, and *scitum*, decree, neut. pp. of *scire*, to know.]

1. an expression of the people's will by direct ballot of all eligible voters on a political issue, as on choice of national sovereignty.

2. in Roman law, a plebiscitum.

plē·bis·cī′tum, *n.*; *pl.* **plē·bis·cī′tȧ,** [L.] in ancient Rome, a law enacted by an assembly of the plebs, presided over by a tribune or other plebeian magistrate independently of the senate.

plebș, *n.*; *pl.* **plē′bēș,** [L.] 1. in ancient Rome, the lower class in society: distinguished from *patricians*.

2. the common people; the masses.

pleç′tog·nath, *a.* pertaining to the *Plectognathi*.

pleç′tog·nath, *n.* one of the *Plectognathi*.

Pleç·tog′nȧ·thī, *n.pl.* [Gr. *plektos*, twisted, and *gnathos*, a jaw.] an order of fishes found in warm seas, having a small mouth with powerful jaws and bony or spiny scales.

pleç·tog·nath′iç, *a.* same as *plectognath*.

pleç·tog′nȧ·thous, *a.* same as *plectognath*.

pleç·tō·spon′dyl, *a.* pertaining to the *Plectospondyli*.

Pleç·tō·spon′dy·lī, *n.pl.* [Gr. *plektos*, twisted, and *spondylos*, backbone.] an order of fishes having the anterior vertebrae united, a complete gill cover, and an air bladder joined to the skull by ossicles.

pleç·tō·spon′dy·lous, *a.* same as *plectospondyl*.

pleç′tron, *n.* same as *plectrum*.

pleç′trum, *n.*; *pl.* **pleç′trumș, pleç′trȧ,** [L., from Gr. *plēktron*, from *plēssein*, to strike.]

1. a small, thin piece of metal, plastic, ivory, horn, etc., with which a player strikes or twangs the strings of a guitar, mandolin, etc.

2. in anatomy, (a) the styloid process of the temporal bone; (b) the uvula; (c) the tongue.

pled, *v.* colloquial or dialectal past tense and past participle of *plead*.

pledġe (plej), *n.* [OFr. *pleige*; LL. *plegium*, *plivium* (seen in *plevin*), possibly from L. *præbere*, to proffer.]

1. a promise or agreement; as, a candidate for election gives *pledges*, or promises, to support or oppose certain measures.

2. the condition of being given or held as security for a contract, payment, etc.; as, a thing held in *pledge*.

3. a person or thing given or held as security for the performance of a contract, as guarantee of faith, etc.; something pawned; a hostage.

4. a token or earnest.

5. a drinking of one's health to express good will or allegiance; a toast.

My heart is thirsty for that noble *pledge*.
—Shak.

6. in law, formerly, a surety whom a person was obliged to find in order to prosecute an action.

7. a person, usually a freshman in a college or university, who has promised to become a member of a fraternity, sorority, etc., and is in a trial period.

living pledge; in law, a conveyance, as of realty, in trust with power to collect.

to hold in pledge; to keep as security.

to put in pledge; to pawn.

to take the pledge; to commit oneself not to drink alcoholic liquor.

pledġe, *v.t.*; pledged, *pt.*, *pp.*; pledging, *ppr.* 1. to give as a pledge or pawn; to deposit in pawn; to hand over to another as a pledge or security for the repayment of money borrowed or for the performance of some obligation or engagement.

An honest factor stole a gem away;
He *pledg'd* it to the knight. —Pope.

2. to give or pass as a guarantee or security; to plight.

3. to bind to the performance of some engagement or obligation by giving a pledge or security; to engage solemnly.

4. to secure the performance of, by giving a pledge or security. [Obs.]

5. to drink a health to; to toast.

Pledge me, my friend, and drink till thou be'st wise. —Cowley.

6. to promise to join (a fraternity).

7. to accept (someone) as a candidate for membership in a fraternity.

pledġ·ee′, *n.* the person to whom anything is pledged.

pledġe′less, *a.* having no pledges.

pledġe′or, *n.* same as *pledgor*.

pledġ′ẽr, *n.* one who pledges.

pledġ′et, *n.* 1. a small wad of wool, cotton, or linen, used as a dressing for a wound or sore.

2. in nautical usage, a string of oakum used in calking.

pledġ′or, *n.* in law, a person who deposits something as security: distinguished from *pledgee*.

pleg·ȧ·phō′ni·ȧ, *n.* [Gr. *plēgē*, blow, and *phōnē*, sound.] auscultation of the chest during percussion of the larynx or trachea in cases in which the patient cannot or should not speak.

-plē′ġi·ȧ, [Gr. *-plēgia*, from *plēgē*, a stroke.] in medicine, a combining form meaning *paralysis*, as in para*plegia*.

-plē′ġy, same as *-plegia*.

Plē′iȧ·dēs (or plī′), *n.pl.*; *sing.* **Plē′iăd,** [L.] 1. in Greek mythology, the seven daughters of Atlas and Pleione, who were placed by Zeus among the stars.

2. in astronomy, a large group of stars in the constellation Taurus, six of which are visible and represent the daughters of Atlas, the seventh being "lost" (the *Lost Pleiad*).

plein-āir′, *a.* [Fr., lit., open air.] designating or of certain schools of French impressionist painting engaged mainly in representing effects of outdoor light and atmosphere.

Plei′ō·cēne, *a.* same as *Pliocene*.

pleī·ō·mor′phiç, *a.* having the property of or characterized by pleiomorphism.

pleī·ō·mor′phism, *n.* in biology, the occurrence at the same time and in the same place of independent forms or types of structure of the same organism: sometimes extended to the consideration of all the various genera of bacteria as polymorphous forms of certain species: also written *pleomorphism*.

pleī′ō·mor·phy, *n.* [Gr. *pleiōn*, more, and *morphē*, shape.]

1. pleiomorphism.

2. in botany, the change of a flower that is normally irregular to a form that is regular, by the growth of the members or parts previously defective: also written *pleomorphy*.

pleī·ō·phyl′lous, *a.* [Gr. *pleiōn*, more, and *phyllon*, leaf.] manifesting pleiophylly.

pleī′ō·phyl·ly, *n.* in botany, the state of having an increase in the number of leaves starting from one point, or an abnormally large number of leaflets in a compound leaf.

Pleī·ō·sau′rus, *n.* same as *Pliosaurus*.

Pleīs′tō·cēne, *n.* [Gr. *pleistos*, most, and *kainos*, recent.] designating or of the first epoch of the Quaternary Period in the Cenozoic Era, characterized by the rise and recession of continental ice sheets and by the appearance of man.

the Pleistocene; the Pleistocene Epoch or its rocks.

plem·y·ram′ē·tẽr, *n.* [from Gr. *plēmmyra*, flood tide.] an instrument by means of which the differences in level in a body of water can be measured.

plē′năl, *a.* plenary. [Obs.]

plē′nār·i·ly (*or* plen′ăr-), *adv.* in a plenary manner.

plē′nār·i·ness, *n.* fullness; completeness.

plen′ăr·ty, *n.* [OFr. *plenierte*.] the state of a benefice when occupied.

plē′nȧ·ry (*or* plen′ȧ-), *a.* [LL. *plenarius*; L. *plenus*, full.]

1. full; entire; complete; absolute.

2. attended by all members: said of an assembly.

plē′nȧ·ry in·dul′ġence, in the Roman Catholic Church, an indulgence remitting in full the temporal punishment incurred by a sinner.

plē′ni·çorn, *a.* [L. *plenus*, full, and *cornu*, horn.] having solid horns, as a deer.

plē′ni·çorn, *n.* a ruminant animal having solid horns.

plen·i·lū′năr, *a.* pertaining to the full moon.

plen·i·lū′nȧ·ry, *a.* plenilunar.

plen′i·lūne, *n.* [L. *plenilunium*; *plenus*, full, and *luna*, moon.] the full moon. [Chiefly Poet.]

plē·nip′ō·tence, *n.* [L. *plenus*, full, and *potentia*, power.] fullness or completeness of power. [Rare.]

plē·nip′ō·ten·cy, *n.* plenipotence. [Rare.]

plē·nip′ō·tent, *a.* [L. *plenipotens*.] possessing full power. [Rare.]

plen″i·pō·ten′ti·ăr·y (-shi- *or* -shi-ri), *a.* [ML. *plenipotentiarius*, from LL. *plenipotens*, from L. *plenus*, full, and *potus*, powerful.]

1. having or conferring full power or authority.

2. full; plenary: said of power, etc.

plen″i·pō·ten′ti·ăr·y, *n.*; *pl.* **plen″i·pō·ten′ti·ăr·ieṣ,** a person invested with full authority to act as representative of a government; an ambassador.

plen′ish, *v.t.* [from OFr. *pleniss-*, ppr. stem of *plenir*, to fill, from L. *plenus*, full.] to fill up; to furnish; to stock. [Scot. and Dial.]

plē′nist, *n.* [L. *plenus*, full.] one who maintains that all space is full of matter.

plen′i·tūde, *n.* [L. *plenitudo*, from *plenus*, full.]

1. repletion; animal fullness; plethora. [Obs.]

2. fullness; completeness; as, the *plentitude* of power.

3. abundance; plenty.

plen·i·tū·di·năr′i·ăn, *n.* a plenist. [Obs.]

plen·i·tū′di·năr·y, *a.* having fullness or completeness. [Obs.]

plen′tē·ous, *a.* [ME. *plenteus*, *plentevous*; OFr. *plentieus*, *plentevous*.]

1. abundant; copious; plentiful; sufficient for every purpose; as, a *plenteous* crop.

2. yielding abundance; fertile; productive; as, *plenteous* fields.

3. having an abundance; rich. [Archaic.]

plen′tē·ous·ly, *adv.* in abundance; copiously; plentifully.

plen′tē·ous·ness, *n.* the state of being plenteous; abundance; copious supply; plenty.

plen′ti·ful, *a.* 1. copious; abundant; adequate to every purpose; plenteous; as, a *plentiful* harvest.

2. having or yielding plenty; as, a *plentiful* year.

3. bestowing profusely; lavish. [Obs.]

Syn.—plenteous, abundant, copious, ample, full, bountiful.

plen′ti·ful·ly, *adv.* in a plentiful manner; abundantly; with ample supply.

plen′ti·ful·ness, *n.* the quality or state of being plentiful; abundance.

plen′ty, *n.*; *pl.* **plen′tieṣ,** [OFr. *plente*; L. *plenitas*, from *plenus*, full.]

1. the condition of being plentiful; the state of possessing an abundance.

2. abundance; copiousness; full or adequate supply; as, the garrison has *plenty* of provisions.

3. prosperity; opulence.

Syn.—abundance, exuberance, wealth, affluence.

plen′ty, *a.* plentiful; enough; ample: generally used in the predicate.

plen′ty, *adv.* fully; very; as, *plenty* good. [Colloq.]

plē′num, *n.*; *pl.* **plē′numṣ, plē′nȧ,** [L., neut. of *plenus*, full.]

1. space filled with matter: opposed to *vacuum*.

2. fullness.

3. a full assembly, as of all members of a legislative body.

4. an enclosed volume of gas under greater pressure than that surrounding the container.

plē′num, *a.* of any space in which there is a plenum.

plē·ō·çhrō′iç, *a.* possessing pleochroism; exhibiting different colors when seen from different directions.

plē·oçh′rō·iṣm, *n.* [Gr. *pleōn*, more, and *chroizein*, to color.] the property of certain crystals of exhibiting a variation of color when seen by transmitted light or in different directions.

plē″oçh·rō·mat′iç, *a.* same as *pleochroic*.

plē·ō·çhrō′mȧ·tiṣm, *n.* same as *pleochroism*.

plē·oçh′rō·ous, *a.* same as *pleochroic*.

plē′ō·dont, *a.* [Gr. *pleōs*, full, and *odous*, *odontos*, tooth.] in zoology, having teeth that are solid: opposed to *coelodont*.

plē·ō·mor′phiç, *a.* of or pertaining to pleomorphism.

plē·ō·mor′phiṣm, *n.* [Gr. *pleōn*, more, and *morphē*, form.]

1. polymorphism.

2. pleiomorphism.

plē·ō·mor′phous, *a.* exhibiting pleomorphism.

plē′ō·mor·phy, *n.* [Gr. *pleōn*, more, and *morphē*, form.]

1. polymorphism.

2. pleiomorphy.

plē′on, *n.* [Gr. *pleōn*, ppr. of *plein*, to sail, swim.]

1. the abdomen of any crustacean.

2. the telson of a king crab or other crab of the genus *Limulus*.

plē′ō·năl, *a.* of or pertaining to the pleon.

plē′ō·naṣm, *n.* [LL. *pleonasmus*; Gr. *pleonasmos*, from *pleōn*, *pleiōn*, more, comp. of *polys*, much.]

1. redundancy of words in speaking or writing; the use of more words than necessary in expressing ideas.

2. an instance of this.

3. the redundant word or expression.

plē′ō·nast, *n.* a person who uses pleonasm constantly in speech or writing. [Rare.]

plē′ō·naste, *n.* [L. Gr. *pleonastos*, abundant; from its four facets, sometimes found on each solid angle of the octahedron.] a dark-colored variety of spinel; ceylonite.

plē·ō·nas′tiç, *a.* of or pertaining to pleonasm; characterized by pleonasm; redundant.

plē·ō·nas′tiç·ăl, *a.* pleonastic. [Rare.]

plē·ō·nas′tiç·ăl·ly, *adv.* in a pleonastic manner.

plē′ō·pod, *n.* [Gr. *plein*, to swim, sail, and *pous*, *podos*, foot.] in zoology, an abdominal leg or appendage of a crustacean.

plē·op′ō·dīte, *n.* same as *pleopod*.

plē·rō′mȧ, *n.* [Gr. *plērōma*, a filling up; *plēroun*, to fill up, from *plērēs*, full.]

1. a state of abundance; fullness.

2. in Gnosticism, the spiritual world; the fullness of the Divine Being, and the eons which emanate from it.

3. in botany, plerome.

plē·rō·mat′iç, *a.* of or pertaining to the pleroma.

plē′rōme, *n.* [Gr. *plērōma*, a filling up.] the soft, cellular tissue forming the center of growing stems of dicotyledonous plants.

plē′rō·morph, *n.* [Gr. *plērēs*, full, and *morphē*, form.] in mineralogy, a pseudomorph produced by infiltration.

plē·roph′ō·ry, *n.* [Gr. *plērophoria*; *plērēs*, full, and *pherein*, to bear.] full certainty or confidence.

plē·rō′sis, *n.* [Gr. *plērōsis*, a filling up; *plēroun*, to fill up.] in medicine, the restoration of tissue, as in the regaining of flesh lost during sickness.

plē·rot′iç, *a.* [Gr. *plēroun*, to fill up.] restoring; filling up afresh.

plē·rot′iç, *n.* any medicine tending to restore tissue and produce fleshiness.

pleṣ′ănce, *n.* pleasance. [Obs.]

plē″si·ō·mor′phiṣm, *n.* [Gr. *plēsios*, near, and *morphē*, form.] the close resemblance in the form of crystallization of certain substances which are unlike in chemical composition.

plē″si·ō·mor′phous, *a.* nearly alike in form: said of crystals.

plē′si·ō·saur, *n.* an extinct animal belonging to the order *Plesiosauria*: also *plesiosaurus*.

Plē″si·ō·sau′ri·ȧ, *n.pl.* an order of fossil marine reptiles, occurring in the Mesozoic formations: it includes *Plesiosaurus*, *Pliosaurus*, and other genera.

plē″si·ō·sau′ri·ăn, *n.* a reptile of the extinct order *Plesiosauria*.

Plē″si·ō·sau′rus, *n.* [Gr. *plēsios*, near, and *sauros*, lizard.]

1. a genus of extinct marine animals of the order *Plesiosauria* of the Mesozoic Era, char-

acterized by a small head, long neck, short tail, and four paddlelike limbs. Specimens

PLESIOSAURUS (partially restored)

have been found from ten to twenty feet long.
  2. [p–] a member of this genus.

ples·sim′ē·tēr, *n.* same as *pleximeter.*

ples′sŏr, *n.* [from Gr. *plēssein,* to strike.] in medicine, a small hammer with a soft head, as of rubber, used in percussion: also *plexor.*

plēte, *v.t.* and *v.i.* to plead; to entreat. [Obs.]

pleth′ō·rȧ, *n.* [Gr. *plēthōrē,* from *plēthos,* fullness; same root as L. *plenus,* full.]
  1. the state of being too full; excess; overabundance; superfluity.
  2. an abnormal condition characterized by an excess of blood in the circulatory system or in some part of it.

pleth·ō·ret′iç, plē·thor′iç·ăl, *a.* plethoric. [Obs.]

plē·thor′iç (*or* pleth′ō-rik), *a.* [ML. *plethoricus;* Gr. *plēthōrikos.*]
  1. too full; swollen.
  2. bombastic.
  3. of or characterized by plethora; having an excess of blood.

plē·thor′iç·ăl·ly, *adv.* in a manner characterized by plethora.

pleth′ō·ry, *n.* plethora. [Now Rare.]

pleth′rŏn, pleth′rum, *n.;* *pl.* **pleth′rȧ,** [Gr. *plethron,* a measure.] in ancient Greece, a linear measure of 100 Greek feet (101 English feet); also, a square measure of 10,000 Greek square feet (10,201 English square feet).

plē·thyș′mō·grȧph, *n.* the instrument used in plethysmography to indicate and record by tracings the variations in size of an organ or part of the body.

plē·thyș·mō·grȧph′iç, *a.* pertaining to or obtained by means of the plethysmograph.

pleth·yș·mog′rȧ·phy, *n.* [Gr. *plēthysmos,* enlargement, from *plēthys,* full, and *graphein,* to describe.] in physiology, the study of the variations in size of an organ or part of the body, as produced by the quantity and circulation of blood in that part.

pleur-, see *pleuro-.*

pleū′rȧ, *n.;* *pl.* **pleū′rae,** [Gr. *pleura,* a rib, side.]
  1. in anatomy, a thin serous membrane, which covers the inside of the thorax and also envelops the lungs separately, forming two closed sacs.
  2. in zoology, a pleuron.

pleū′răl, *a.* 1. in anatomy, pertaining to the pleura or pleurae.
  2. in zoology, situated on the side; lateral; costal; thoracic.

pleū·ral′gi·ȧ, *n.* [Gr. *pleura,* the side, and *algos,* suffering.] pain in the sides or chest.

pleū·rap·ō·phyș′i·ăl, *a.* of or pertaining to a pleurapophysis.

pleū·rȧ·poph′y·sis, *n.;* *pl.* **pleū·rȧ·poph′y·sēș** [Gr. *pleuron,* rib, and *apophysis,* process.] one of the processes of a typical vertebra, projecting from the sides; the lateral part of the hemal arch, corresponding to a rib in the thoracic region.

pleū·reñ′çhy·mȧ, *n.* [Gr. *pleura,* the side, and *enchyma,* something poured in.] the cellular tissue which is the chief constituent of wood.

pleū′riç, *a.* pertaining to the pleura; pleural.

pleū′ri·sy, *n.* [Fr. *pleurésie;* LL. *pleurisis;* L. *pleuritis;* Gr. *pleuritis,* from *pleura,* the side.] inflammation of the pleura: it is accompanied by fever, pain, difficult respiration, a dry cough, and often by the exudation of liquid into the chest cavity.

pleū′ri·sy root, a plant of the milkweed family; butterfly weed.
  2. its root, formerly used as a cure for pleurisy.

pleū·rit′iç, pleū·rit′iç·ăl, *a.* of, indicating, or having pleurisy; as, *pleuritic* symptoms.

pleū·rī′tis, *n.* pleurisy.

pleū′rō-, [from Gr. *pleura,* a rib, side.] a combining form meaning: (a) *on* or *near the side,* as in *pleuro*dont; (b) *of* or *near the pleura,* as in *pleuro*tomy; (c) *pleural and,* as in *pleuro*pneumonia. Also, before a vowel, *pleur-.*

Pleū·rō·braçh′i·ȧ, *n.* [*pleuro-,* and Gr. *brachiōn,* arm.] a genus of *Cœlenterata,* family *Ctenophora,* possessing a transparent, colorless, gelatinous body that is melon-shaped. It has comblike groups of cilia, and long, flexible tentacles, which can be retracted.

pleū′rō·brañçh, *n.* a pleurobranchia.

pleū·rō·brañ′çhi·ȧ, *n.;* *pl.* **pleū·rō·brañ′çhi·ae,** [*pleuro-,* and Gr. *branchion,* a gill.] a gill attached to the body of a crustacean between the somites on the side of the thorax.

pleū·rō·brañ′çhi·āte, *a.* in zoology, having gills on the side; also, having pleurobranchiae.

pleū′rō·çärp, *n.* a pleurocarpous moss.

pleū·rō·çär′pous, pleū·rō·çär′piç, *a.* [*pleuro-,* and Gr. *karpos,* fruit.] in botany, having the fructification proceeding laterally from the axils of the leaves, as in some mosses.

pleū·rō·cen′trum, *n.;* *pl.* **pleū·rō·cen′trȧ,** [*pleuro-,* and Gr. *kentron,* center.] a lateral element in the centrum of a vertebra.

Pleū·rod′i·rȧ, *n.pl.* [*pleuro-,* and Gr. *dērē,* neck.] a group of fresh-water turtles found in regions south of the equator, characterized by having a neck that is nonretractile but folds laterally to come within the shell.

pleū′rō·dont, *a.* [*pleuro-* and *-dont.*] in zoology, having teeth growing from the side of the jawbone instead of from separate sockets, as some lizards.

pleū′rō·dont, *n.* a pleurodont lizard.

pleū·rō·dyn′i·ȧ, *n.* [*pleuro-,* and Gr. *odynē,* pain.] neuralgia in the side, resembling pleurisy, but caused by rheumatism in the intercostal muscles.

pleū′ron, *n.;* *pl.* **pleū′rȧ,** [Gr. *pleuron,* a rib.] either of the lateral plates on the thorax of an insect.

Pleū·rō·neç′ti·dae, *n.pl.* a family of flatfishes or flounders with both eyes on the upper side. They swim in a horizontal position.

pleū·rō·neç′toid, *a.* [*pleuro-,* Gr. *nēktēs,* a swimmer, and *-oid.*] of or pertaining to the *Pleuronectidæ.*

pleū·rō·ped′ăl, *a.* [*pleuro-,* and L. *pes, pedis,* foot.] uniting or relating to the side and the foot: applied especially to the nerve of a mollusk that connects the pleural and the pedal nerve ganglia.

pleū·rō·per·i·çär′di·ăl, *a.* [*pleuro-,* and LL. *pericardium.*] pertaining to or affecting the pleura and the pericardium.

pleū·rō·per″i·tō·nē′ăl, *a.* pertaining to the pleura and the peritoneum, or to the pleural and peritoneal cavities or membranes.

pleū·rō·per″i·tō·nē′um, *n.* [*pleuro-,* and Gr. *peritonaion.*] the serous membrane lining the pleural and peritoneal cavities; the membranous lining of the general visceral cavity when undivided, as in vertebrates having no diaphragm.

pleū″rō·pneū·mō′ni·ȧ (-nū-), *n.* [*pleuro-* and *pneumonia.*]
  1. pneumonia complicated by pleurisy.
  2. a contagious disease among cattle, in which there is inflammation of the pleura and the lungs.

Pleū·rō·sig′mȧ, *n.* [*pleuro-* and *sigma,* the Gr. letter.] a genus of *Diatomaceæ,* having elongated bodies doubly curved. Some forms are marked with lines so fine as to furnish a common test for the high powers of a microscope.

pleū·ros′tē·on, *n.;* *pl.* **pleū·ros′tē·ȧ,** [*pleur-,* and Gr. *osteon,* bone.] in the sternum of birds, a lateral element which joins on to the ribs.

pleū′rō·stiçt, *a.* [*pleuro-,* and Gr. *stiktos,* verbal adj. of *stizein,* to prick.] in zoology, having the spiracles of the abdominal segments situated pleurally, as in certain beetles.

pleū′rō·stiçt, *n.* any pleurostict beetle.

pleū·rō·thot′ō·nos, *n.* [Gr. *pleurothen,* from the side, and *tonos,* tension.] in medicine, tetanic contraction of the lateral muscles, causing the body to bend to one side.

Pleū·rot′ō·mȧ, *n.* [*pleuro-,* and Gr. *-tomos,* from *temnein,* to cut.] a genus of marine gastropods having the shell fusiform, with a long narrow slit in the outer lip and without an inner lip.

pleū·rot′ō·my, *n.;* *pl.* **pleū·rot′ō·mieș,** [*pleuro-* and *-tomy.*] in surgery, the making of an incision in the pleura to drain off exuded liquids.

pleū′rō·trībe, *a.* [*pleuro-,* and Gr. *tribein,* to rub.] in botany, rubbing or coming in contact with the side: applied to those irregular flowers that have the stamens and pistils so arranged as to touch the sides of any visiting insect, and thereby promote cross-pollination.

plev′in, *n.* in law, a warrant or assurance. [Obs.]

plex, *v.t.* and *v.i.;* plexed (plekst), *pt., pp.;* plexing, *ppr.* to form a plexus, or network.

plex′ăl, *a.* of or pertaining to a plexus.

plex′i·fọrm, *a.* [L. *plexus,* a fold, and *forma,* form.] in the form of network; complicated.

plex′i·glȧss, *n.* [from L. *plexus,* a twining, and *glass.*] a lightweight, transparent thermoplastic substance, used a a cockpit cover for aircraft, etc.: a trade-mark (*Plexiglas*).

plex·im′ē·tēr, plex·om′ē·tēr, *n.* [Gr. *plēxis,* percussion, and *metron,* a measure.] in medicine, a small, thin plate, as of ivory, placed against some part of the body and struck with a plessor in percussion.

plex′ŏr, *n.* same as *plessor.*

plex′ūre, *n.* [L. *plexus,* an interweaving, from *plexus,* pp. of *plectere,* to interweave.] an interweaving; a texture; also, that which is woven together.

plex′us, *n.;* *pl.* **plex′us·eș, plex′us,** [L., a twining, braid, from *plexus,* pp. of *plectere,* to twine, braid.] an interwoven arrangement of parts; a network; specifically, in anatomy, a network of blood vessels, lymphatic vessels, nerves, etc.; as, the solar *plexus* (of nerves) in the abdomen.

plī·ȧ·bil′i·ty, *n.* a pliable quality.

plī′ȧ·ble, *a.* [Fr. *pliable,* from *plier,* to bend, to fold, from L. *plicare,* to fold, to bend.]
  1. easily bent or molded; flexible; as, willow is a *pliable* plant.
  2. easily influenced or persuaded; readily yielding to influence, argument, persuasion, or discipline; adaptable; tractable.

> So is the heart of some men; when smitten
> by God it seems soft and *pliable.*
> —Taylor.

Syn.—pliant, flexible, supple, lithe, yielding, tractable, docile.

plī′ȧ·ble·ness, *n.* pliability.

plī′ȧ·bly, *adv.* in a pliable manner; yieldingly.

plī′ăn·cy, *n.* the state or quality of being pliant.

plī′ănt, *a.* [ME. *plyande;* OFr., ppr. of *plier,* to bend, fold, from L. *plicare,* to fold, bend.]
  1. capable of being easily bent; pliable; flexible; lithe; limber; as, a *pliant* twig.
  2. capable of being easily formed or molded to a different shape; plastic; as, *pliant* wax.

> Earth but new divided from the sky,
> And *pliant* still retain'd th' ethereal energy.
> —Dryden.

  3. readily influenced to good or evil; adaptable; compliant.

> The will was then more ductile and *pliant*
> to right reason. —South.

Syn.—flexible, limber, lithe, supple, bending, tractable, ductile, docile, obsequious.

plī′ănt·ly, *adv.* in a pliant manner; yieldingly; flexibly.

plī′ănt·ness, *n.* same as *pliancy.*

plī′çȧ, *n.;* *pl.* **plī′cae,** [LL. *plica,* from L. *plicare,* to fold.]
  1. in anatomy, a fold or folding, especially of the skin or mucous membrane.
  2. in medicine, a matted, diseased condition of the hair, in which it becomes covered with crusts and vermin.

plī′căl, *a.* of, pertaining to, or designating plica.

plī′çȧ pō·lon′i·çȧ, same as *plica,* sense 2.

plī·çā′tȧ, *n.;* *pl.* **plī·çā′tae,** [LL., f. of *plicatus,* pp. of *plicare,* to fold.] a folded chasuble used at certain penitential times by deacons in the Roman Catholic Church.

plī′çāte, plī′çā·ted, *a.* [L. *plicatus,* from *plicare,* to fold.] plaited; folded; arranged in pleats, as a fan.

plī′çāte·ly, *adv.* in a plicate, or folded, manner.

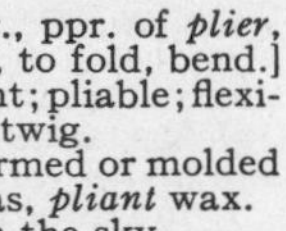

PLICATE LEAF

pliç′ȧ·tile, *a.* [L. *plicatilis,* from *plicare,* to fold.] capable of being folded; longitudinally folded when in repose: said of the wings of insects.

plī·çā′tion, *n.* [LL. *plicatio* (*-onis*); L. *plicare,* to fold.]
  1. a folding or being folded.
  2. a fold.
  3. in geology, a stratum fold.

pliç′ȧ·tive, *a.* [L. *plicatus,* pp. of *plicare,* to fold.] plaited; folded in plaits.

plī·çā′tŏr, *n.* [LL., from L. *plicare,* to fold.] a device for plaiting, attached to sewing machines; anything that makes folds.

pliç'ȧ·tūre, *n.* [L. *plicatura*, from *plicare*; to fold.] same as *plication.*

plic·i·den'tine, *n.* [LL. *plica*, fold, and L. *dens*, *dentis*, tooth.] a modified form of dentine folded so as to show fluted or sinuous lines on the surface of the tooth.

plī·cif'ẽr·ous, *a.* [LL. *plica*, fold, and L. *ferre*, to bear.] having plicae.

plic'i·form, *a.* [LL. *plica*, fold, and L. *forma*, form.] having a plaitlike or foldlike form.

plī'ẽr, *n.* one who or that which plies.

plī'ẽrṣ, *n.pl.* [from *ply* (to bend).] small pincers for handling small objects, cutting wire, etc.

plīght (plīt), *v.t.*; plighted, *pt.*, *pp.*; plighting, *ppr.* [ME. *plihten*; AS. *plihtan*, to pledge, to expose to danger, from *pliht*, a pledge, danger.]

1. to pledge or engage; as, to *plight* one's troth.

2. to bind (oneself) by a promise; to engage; betroth.

to plight one's troth; (a) to pledge one's truth; to give one's word; (b) to make a promise of marriage.

plīght, *n.* [AS. *pliht*, a pledge, obligation, danger.] that which is plighted or pledged; a security; a pledge; an assurance given. [Rare.]

That lord whose hand must take my *plight*. —Shak.

plīght, *n.* [ME. *plit*, a state, condition; Anglo-Fr. *plit*, for OFr. *ploit*, a fold, way of folding, condition.]

1. a condition, state of affairs, or situation; especially, now, a dangerous or awkward situation.

In this miserable loathsome *plight*. —Milton.

2. a fold; a plait. [Obs.]

Syn.—situation, condition, state, predicament, dilemma, difficulty.

plīght, *v.t.* to weave; to braid; to plait. [Obs.]

A *plighted* garment of divers colors. —Milton.

plīght'ẽr, *n.* one who or that which plights.

plim, *v.t.*; plimmed, *pt.*, *pp.*; plimming, *ppr.* to swell or expand; to fill out. [Brit. Dial.]

plim, *v.i.* to swell. [Brit. Dial.]

plim, *a.* [related to *plump*.] stout; swollen. [Brit. Dial.]

Plim'soll märk (or **līne**), [after Samuel *Plimsoll* (1824–1898), Brit. statesman who was instrumental in having legislation passed against overloading vessels.] a line on the outside of British merchant ships, showing the lawful submergence level: also *Plimsoll's mark* (or *line*).

plinth, *n.* [L. *plinthus*; Gr. *plinthos*, a brick, tile.]

1. the square block at the base of a column, pedestal, etc.

2. the rectangular or circular base on which a statue is placed.

a, PLINTH

plinth of a wall; two or three rows of bricks advanced from the wall, in the form of a platband; also, in general, any flat, high molding that serves in a front wall to mark the floors, to sustain the eaves of a wall, etc.

Plī'ō·cēne, *a.* [from Gr. *pleiōn*, *pleōn*, more, and *kainos*, recent, new.] designating or of the last epoch of the Tertiary Period in the Cenozoic Era, during which modern plants and animals developed: also spelled *Pleiocene.*

the Pliocene, the Pliocene Epoch or its rocks.

plī'ō·film, *n.* [from *pliable* and *film*.] a type of waterproof, transparent rubber sheeting used for raincoats, wrapping material, etc.: a trade-mark (*Pliofilm*).

Plī·ō·hip'pus, *n.* [*pliocene*, and Gr. *hippos*, horse.] an extinct genus of horses that existed in the Pliocene Period.

Plī·ō·saụ'rus, *n.* [*pliocene*, and Gr. *sauros*, lizard.] a genus of fossil marine reptiles now extinct, having a shortened neck.

plī'ō·tron, *n.* an electric detector and amplifier for fluctuating currents, consisting of a discharge tube in which is mounted a grid of wires between the incandescent cathode and the anode: a trade-mark (*Pliotron*).

plō'cē, *n.* [Gr. *plokē*, a plaiting, from *plekein*, to plait.] in rhetoric, a figure of speech which embodies the repetition of a word, generally with a modification of meaning: example, there are *medicines* and *medicines.*

plod, *v.i.*; plodded, *pt.*, *pp.*; plodding, *ppr.* [origin prob. echoic.]

1. to walk or move heavily and laboriously; to trudge.

A *plodding* diligence brings us sooner to our journey's end, than a fluttering way of advancing by starts. —L'Estrange.

2. to work steadily and monotonously; to toil; to drudge.

plod, *v.t.* to trudge over; to walk along in a heavy or laborious manner.

plod, *n.* 1. a plodding.

2. a heavy step.

3. the sound of this.

plod'dẽr, *n.* 1. one who plods.

2. a dull or stolid person.

plod'ding, *a.* that plods.

Syn.—painstaking, industrious, persevering, laborious, studious.

plod'ding·ly, *adv.* industriously; diligently.

-ploid, [from Gr. *-ploos*, -fold, and *-oid*.] a combining form meaning *of a* (specified) *multiple of chromosomes*, as in di*ploid.*

plop, *v.t.* and *v.i.*; plopped (plopt), *pt.*, *pp.*; plopping, *ppr.* [echoic.] to drop with a sound like that of something flat falling into water without splashing.

plop, *n.* 1. the sound made by something plopping.

2. a plopping.

plop, *adv.* with a plop.

plō'ṣion, *n.* [from *explosion*.]

1. the articulation of a plosive sound.

2. loosely, the final stage, or sudden release of breath, in the articulation of a plosive.

plō'sive, *a.* [from *explosive*.] designating or of a speech sound produced by the complete stoppage and sudden release of the breath, as the consonants *k*, *p*, and *t* when used initially.

plō'sive, *n.* a plosive sound.

plot, *n.* [a variant of *plat*.]

1. an area marked on a surface, usually of ground; a patch, a plot; as, a garden *plot.*

When we mean to build,
We first survey the *plot*. —Shak.

2. a chart, diagram, or map, as of a building, estate, etc.

3. a secret, usually evil, project or scheme; a conspiracy.

O, think what anxious moments pass between
The birth of *plots*, and their last fatal periods! —Addison.

4. the plan of action of a play, novel, poem, short story, etc.

If the *plot* or intrigue must be natural, and such as springs from the subject, the winding up of the *plot* must be a probable consequence of all that went before. —Le Bossu.

5. contrivance; deep reach of thought; ability to plot. [Obs.]

A man of much *plot*. —Denham.

6. a share in an intrigue or conspiracy. [Obs.]

7. a plan, purpose, or scheme. [Obs.]

Syn.—cabal, intrigue, combination, conspiracy.

plot, *v.t.*; plotted, *pt.*, *pp.*; plotting, *ppr.* 1. to draw a plan, chart, or map of (a building, ship's course, etc.).

2. to make secret plans for; as, to *plot* someone's destruction.

3. to plan the action of (a story, etc.).

4. in mathematics, (a) to represent (an equation) by locating points on a graph and joining them to form a curve; (b) to draw (the curve).

plot, *v.i.* 1. to form a scheme of mischief against another, or against a government or those who administer it; as, a traitor *plots* against his king.

2. to contrive a plan; to scheme.

The prince did *plot* to be secretly gone. —Wotton.

plot'fụl, *a.* abounding with plots.

Plō·tin'i·ăn, *a.* pertaining to the Plotinists, or the teachings of Plotinus.

Plō·tī'nist, *n.* one who believes in the teachings of Plotinus, a Neoplatonic philosopher of the third century A. D.

plot'proof', *a.* protected or secure from plots.

plot'tăge, *n.* the area of a plot of land.

plot'tẽr, *n.* one who plots or contrives; a contriver; a conspirator.

plot'tẽr, *v.i.* to plouter. [Scot. and Brit. Dial.]

plot'ting pā'pẽr, paper ruled into uniform small squares, for plotting graphs, etc.

plot'ting sçāle, a mathematical instrument used in plotting, or setting off the lengths of lines in surveying.

Plō'tus, *n.* a genus of birds consisting of the snakebirds.

plough (plow), *n.*, *v.t.* and *v.i.* same as *plow.*

plou'tẽr, *v.i.* [a form of *plod*.] to wade in water with a splashing noise; to dabble. [Chiefly Scot.]

plŏv'ẽr (*or* plō'), *n.*; *pl.* **plŏv'ẽrṣ** *or* **plŏv'ẽr,** [ME.; OFr. *plovier*, lit., the rain bird, from L. *pluvialis*, rainy; *pluere*, to rain.]

PLOVER

1. any of a number of related shore birds of North America, having a short tail, long, pointed wings, and, usually, brown or gray feathers mixed with white.

2. any shore bird similar to the true plovers, as the crab plover, the upland plover, and other sandpipers.

bastard plover; the lapwing.

stone plover; the black-bellied or black-breasted plover.

whistling plover; (a) the golden plover; (b) the black-bellied plover.

plow, plough (plow), *n.* [ME. *plowghe*; G. *pflug*.]

1. a farm implement for turning up, breaking, and preparing the ground for receiving the seed.

2. a device or implement resembling a plow in construction, used in a similar manner, or for like purposes, especially one used to remove snow.

3. a carpenter's instrument for grooving.

4. a plowland; as much land as one team can plow in a year. [Obs.]

5. [P-] in astronomy, a group of seven stars in the constellation Ursa Major; the Dipper; Charles's Wain.

6. in bookbinding, a tool used in preparing the edges of books.

7. in electricity, the rod of an underground trolley, moving in front of the car.

Plow Monday; the Monday after Twelfth Day, or the termination of the Christmas holidays, when, in ancient times, plowing began.

plow, *v.t.*; plowed, *pt.*, *pp.*; plowing, *ppr.* [ME. *ploghen*; G. *pflügen*.]

1. to cut and turn up (soil) with a plow.

2. to make furrows in (the earth, one's face, etc.).

3. to make by or as if by plowing; as, he *plowed* his way through the crowd.

4. to remove with a plow (with *up*).

5. to cut a way through (water); as, the ship *plows* the waves.

6. in carpentry, to groove; to cut a groove in, as for a shelf, an edge, or a tongue.

7. in bookbinding, to prepare the edges of a book with a bookbinders' plow.

Also spelled *plough.*

to plow in; to cover by plowing; as, *to plow in* wheat.

to plow up or *out*; to turn out of the ground by plowing.

plow, *v.i.* 1. to till the soil with a plow; to use a plow.

2. to take plowing; to be in a specified condition for plowing; as, the field *plows* well.

3. to cut a way (*through* water, snow, etc.), as a plow does.

4. to advance laboriously; to plod.

Also spelled *plough.*

to plow into; to begin work vigorously on (a job, etc.)

plow'ȧ·ble, *a.* capable of being plowed; arable.

plow älmṣ (ämz), in England, a penny formerly paid by every plowland to the church.

plow bēam, the horizontal part of the frame of a plow, to which the draft is attached.

plow'bōte, *n.* in English law, wood or timber allowed to a tenant for the repair of farming implements.

plow'boy, *n.* 1. a boy who drives or guides a team in plowing.

2. a country boy.

plow'ẽr, *n.* one who plows land; a cultivator.

plow'foot, *n.* 1. a handle of a plow. [Obs.]

2. an adjustable rod attached to a plow to regulate the depth to which it plowed. [Obs.]

plow'head (-hed), *n.* the draft iron at the end of a plow beam.

plow'land, *n.* 1. in medieval England, an assessment unit of land, approximately the area that could be plowed by a team of eight oxen in a year.

2. land being cultivated or suitable for cultivation.

plow'măn, *n.*; *pl.* **plow'men,** 1. one who plows or holds a plow; a cultivator of grain; a husbandman.

At last, the robber binds the *plowman*, and carries him off with the oxen. —Spelman.

2. a rustic; a farm worker.

plowman's spikenard; a British plant, the *Conyza squarrosa*. It is a soft and downy plant, with dull-yellow flowers, and grows in mountains, meadows, and pastures.

plow'point, *n.* a detachable piece of iron or steel at the extreme front end of a plow, the first part to enter the ground.

plow'shāre, *n.* [*plow* and *share*, shear.] the part of a plow that cuts the ground at the bottom of the furrow and raises the slice to the moldboard, which turns it over.

plow'staff, *n.* a kind of paddle used to clean a plowshare of weeds and earth.

plow'tāil, *n.* the hind part of a plow.

plow'tẽr, *v.i.* same as *plouter*.

plow'wright (-rīt), *n.* a maker or repairer of plows.

ploy, *n.* [prob. from *employ*.]

1. play; sport; frolic. [Scot.]

2. employment. [Scot.]

3. an action or maneuver intended to outwit or disconcert another person.

ploy, *v.i.* [abbrev. of *deploy*.] in military usage, to form from a line into a column.

ploy'ment, *n.* in military usage, the formation of a column from a line.

pluck, *v.t.*; plucked (plukt), *pt.*, *pp.*; plucking, *ppr.* [ME. *plukken*; AS. *pluccian*, perhaps from same source as It. *piluccare*, to pluck grapes.]

1. to gather; to pick; to pull off or out; as, to *pluck* flowers.

2. to strip of feathers; as, to *pluck* geese.

3. to pull with force; to tug; to twitch.

As they pass by, *pluck* Casca by the sleeve. —Shak.

4. to pull with force; to draw; to drag.

To *pluck* him headlong from the throne. —Shak.

5. to reject, as a candidate in an examination for degrees, etc., as not coming up to the required standard. [Brit.]

6. to pull at and release quickly with little jerking movements of the fingers, as the strings of a musical instrument.

7. to rob or swindle. [Slang.]

to pluck away; to pull away; to separate by pulling.

to pluck up; (a) to tear up by the roots; to eradicate; to exterminate; (b) to gain (courage): to take heart.

pluck, *v.i.* to pull; tug; snatch (with *at*).

pluck, *n.* 1. a pulling; tug.

2. an animal's heart, liver, and lungs, used for food.

3. courage; spirit; fortitude.

plucked (plukt), *a.* having pluck, courage, or endurance. [Brit. Colloq.]

You are a good-*plucked* fellow. —Thackeray.

pluck'ẽr, *n.* 1. one who or that which plucks.

2. a machine for straightening or cleaning long wool to make it fit for combing.

Plück'er (plük'ẽr) **tūbe,** a modification of a Geissler tube employed for studying the stratification of the light and the peculiarities of the space adjoining the negative electrode.

pluck'i·ly, *adv.* in a plucky or courageous manner; with pluck or spirit.

pluck'i·ness, *n.* the quality of being plucky.

pluck'less, *a.* without pluck; timid; fainthearted.

pluck'y, *a.*; *comp.* pluckier; *superl.* pluckiest, brave; spirited; resolute; courageous.

pluff, *v.t.* [imitative.] to throw or puff out (smoke) in quick whiffs; to throw out (hairpowder) in dressing the hair; to set fire to, as gunpowder. [Scot.]

pluff, *n.* 1. a puff, as of smoke; a small quantity of gunpowder set on fire. [Scot.]

2. a hairdressers' powder puff. [Scot.]

pluff'y, *a.* fluffy; flabby; puffy. [Scot. and Brit. Dial.]

plug, *n.* [M.D. *plugge*, a bung, plug, block.]

1. a piece of wood or other substance used to plug or stop a hole; a stopple.

2. a block of wood let into a wall of brick or other masonry, to afford a hold for nails in fixing the interior finishing.

3. a fireplug.

4. a cylindrical piece of soft steel whose end is turned to fit into a matrix: used in diesinking.

5. a filling for a carious tooth.

6. a spark plug.

7. (a) a flat, oblong cake of pressed tobacco; (b) a piece of chewing tobacco.

8. a plug hat. [Slang.]

9. an electrical device, as with projecting prongs, to be fitted into an outlet, etc., thus making contact or closing the circuit.

10. an inferior or worthless animal or thing; especially, an old, worn-out horse. [Slang.]

11. an advertisement, especially one interpolated in a radio or television program. [Slang.]

12. a recommendation, or boost, for someone or something. [Slang.]

13. in geology, an extrusive rock which has filled in the vent of a volcano and hardened: it is often exposed by erosion.

plug and feather; a device for splitting stones by means of a feather, or wedge.

plug center bit; a bit having a cylinder instead of a point, so as to fit within the hole around which a countersink or enlargement is to be made.

plug hat; a man's high silk hat. [Slang.]

plug, *v.t.*; plugged, *pt.*, *pp.*; plugging, *ppr.* 1. to stop up or fill (a hole, gap, etc.) by inserting a plug (usually with *up*).

2. to insert as a plug.

3. to shoot a bullet into. [Slang.]

4. to hit with the fist. [Slang.]

5. to advertise or recommend insistently. [Slang.]

6. to advertise or publicize (a song, etc.) by singing or playing frequently. [Slang.]

plug, *v.i.* 1. to work hard and steadily. [Colloq.]

2. to shoot or hit (at). [Slang.]

to plug in; to connect (an electrical device) with an outlet, etc. by inserting a plug into a socket.

plug çock, a cock having a perforated plug that will start or stop the flow according to how it is turned.

plug'gẽr, *n.* one who or that which plugs; specifically, (a) [Colloq.] one who keeps steadily and doggedly at work; (b) [Slang.] one who advertises or publicizes; as, a song *plugger*.

plug'ging, *n.* 1. the act of stopping with a plug.

2. the material of which plugs are made.

3. pins driven into the joints of brick or stone walls to receive the nails with which battens are fastened to the walls.

4. in electricity, the completion of a circuit by means of plugs.

5. in a telephone switchboard, the operation of making the connections by inserting plugs in the proper jack holes.

plug kēy, a key-shaped plug used for making electrical connections.

plug·ō'là, *n.* [*plug* (n. 11) and *-ola*, as in *Pianola*.] the paying of a bribe, or a bribe paid, for the underhanded promotion of something or someone on radio or television. [Slang.]

plug tree, a long rod suspended from the beams of single-acting pumping engines, provided with tappets for moving the handles of the equilibrium and steam-exhaust valves: also called *plug rod*.

plug'-ug''ly, *n.*; *pl.* **plug'-ug''lieș,** a city ruffian or gangster; a rowdy. [Slang.]

plug valve, a tapering valve opening and closing by means of a plug.

plum, *n.* [ME. and AS. *plume*; L. *prunum*; Gr. *prounon*, plum.]

1. any of a number of related trees of the genus *Prunus*, having smooth-skinned fruit with a smooth pit.

2. the fruit.

3. a raisin, when used in pudding or cake.

4. the dark bluish-red color of some plums.

5. a choice or desirable object.

6. the sum of £100,000 sterling; also, formerly, a person possessing this sum. [Brit. Slang.]

Chickasaw plum; an American tree, *Prunus angustifolia*, bearing a thin-skinned, red or yellow edible fruit.

plū'mȧ, *n.*; *pl.* **plū'mae,** [L.] a feather of pennaceous structure; a typical feather.

plū·mā'ceous, *a.* featherlike; pennaceous.

plū'măge, *n.* [ME.; OFr., from *plume*, a feather.] the feathers that cover a bird.

plū·mas·siẽr' (-syā'), *n.* [Fr.] one who prepares or deals in plumes or feathers for ornamental purposes.

plū'māte, *a.* [L. *pluma*, feather.] in zoology, resembling plumage or a feather.

Plū·mȧ·tel'lȧ, *n.* [LL., dim. from L. *pluma*, a feather.] in zoology, a typical genus of polyzoans. It has the coenoecium tubular, the tubes distinct, and the ectocyst pergamentaceous.

plumb (plum), *n.* [ME.; OFr. *plom*; L. *plumbum*, lead.]

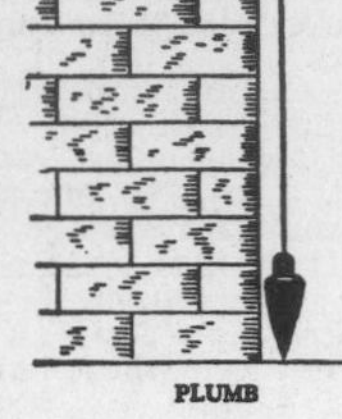
PLUMB

1. a lead weight hung at the end of a line, used to determine how deep water is or whether a wall, etc. is vertical: also called *plumb bob*.

2. a deep pool in a river or stream. [Scot.]

out of plumb; not vertical: also *off plumb*.

plumb, *a.* vertical; exactly perpendicular.

plumb, *adv.* 1. in a vertical direction.

2. exactly; directly; as, to hit a target *plumb*.

3. entirely; wholly; absolutely; as, he's *plumb* exhausted. [Colloq.]

plumb, *v.i.* [ME. *plumben*.]

1. to fall or sink straight down; to plump.

2. to hang vertically.

3. to work with lead, as a plumber.

plumb, *v.t.* 1. to test or sound with a plumb.

2. to discover the facts or contents of; to fathom; solve; understand.

3. to make vertical.

4. to weight or seal with lead.

5. to work on (pipes, etc.) as a plumber.

plum·bā'gin, *n.* [L. *plumbago* (*-inis*), from *plumbum*, lead.] the acrid principle of the root of *Plumbago europæa*.

plum·bag'i·nous, *a.* pertaining to or of the nature of plumbago; consisting of or containing plumbago.

plum·bā'gō, *n.*; *pl.* **plum·bā'gōș,** [L., from *plumbum*, lead (metal).] same as *graphite*.

plum'bāte, *n.* a salt of plumbic acid.

plumb bob, a pear-shaped or globular weight, ending in a point, suspended from the end of a plumb line.

plum'bē·ăn, *a.* like lead; leaden.

plum'bē·ous, *a.* [L. *plumbeus*, from *plumbum*, lead (metal).] of, like, or containing lead; leaden.

plumb'ẽr (plum'), *n.* [ME. *plomere, plummer*; OFr. *plommier*; L. *plumbarius*, lead-worker, from *plumbum*, lead (metal).]

1. one who works in lead. [Obs.]

2. a skilled worker who fits and repairs the pipes, fixtures, etc. of gas and water systems.

plumber's helper; a large, rubber suction cup with a long handle, used to free clogged drains. [Colloq.]

plumb'ẽr block, a metal box or case for supporting the end of a revolving shaft or journal: also called *pillow block*, *plummer block*, *plummer box*.

PLUMBER BLOCK

plumb'ẽr·y, *n.*; *pl.* **plumb'ẽr·ieș,** 1. a plumber's workshop.

2. a plumber's work.

plum'bic, *a.* pertaining to or containing lead, especially with a valence of four.

plum·bif'ẽr·ous, *a.* [from *plumbum* and *-ferous*.] producing or containing lead.

plumb'ing (plum'), *n.* [from *plumber*.]

1. the using of a plumb.

2. the work or trade of a plumber.

3. the pipes and fixtures with which a plumber works.

plum'bișm, *n.* lead poisoning.

plumb'less (plum'), *a.* unfathomable; not capable of being sounded with a plumb.

plumb līne, 1. a line directed to the earth's center of gravity.

2. a cord suspending a lead weight, or plumb, used in sounding and in determining vertical direction.

plum'bous, *a.* [L. *plumbum*, lead (metal).] of, containing, or pertaining to lead, especially with a valence of two.

plumb rūle, a narrow board having a plumb line suspended from its top and a mark through its middle parallel with its edges, and sometimes fitted with a cross level at its base: used by masons and carpenters in testing their work.

plum′bum, *n.* [L.] lead (the metal).

plum′çot, *n.* a fruit produced by cross-pollinating the plum and apricot.

plum duff, a flour pudding with raisins or currants in it, boiled in a cloth bag.

plụme, *n.* [ME.; OFr., from L. *pluma*, the downy part of a feather, a small soft feather.]
1. (a) a feather, especially a large and wavy one; (b) a group of such feathers.
2. an ornament made of a large feather or feathers, or of a feathery tuft of hair, especially when worn on a helmet, etc. as a mark of rank or distinction.
3. any token of worth or achievement; a prize.
4. plumage or down.
5. something like a plume in shape or lightness; as, a *plume* of smoke.
6. in botany, (a) a featherlike formation or part; (b) [Obs.] a plumule.
7. in zoology, (a) a plumate hair; (b) a plume moth; (c) a featherlike formation or part; as, the branchial *plume* of a crustacean.

plụme, *v.t.*; plumed, *pt., pp.*; pluming, *ppr.* 1. to pick and adjust the plumage of; to smooth its feathers: used reflexively, of a bird.
2. to strip of feathers. [Now Rare.]
3. to strip; to peel. [Now Rare.]
4. to provide, cover, or adorn with feathers or plumes.
5. to pride (oneself); as, he *plumes* himself on his skill.
6. to preen.

plụme bird, any of various birds whose feathers are used as ornaments; also, any bird having a conspicuous tuft of feathers, as the aigret or the bird of paradise.

plụme gràss, any species of grass with plumelike spikelets, as pampas grass.

plụme′less, *a.* without feathers, as a bird; having no plume or plumes.

plụme′let, *n.* 1. a small plume.
2. in botany, a plumule. [Obs.]

plụme′māk″ẽr, *n.* one who makes plumes; one who dresses and arranges feathers for ornament.

plụme moth, any moth of the family *Pterophoridæ*, characterized by having featherlike, divided wings.

plụme nut′meg, a large aromatic tree, *Atherosperma moschata*, of Australia and tropical America, bearing tufts of axillary flowers, each ovary having a persistent style with a terminal plume.

plụm′ẽr·y, *n.* plumes considered collectively; plumage; a mass of plumes. [Rare.]

plụ′mi·çorn, *n.* [L. *pluma*, feather, and *cornu*, horn.] in ornithology, either of a pair of earlike tufts of feathers, as on the head of an owl.

plụ′mi·form, *a.* [L. *pluma*, feather, and *-form*.] having the shape of a feather; resembling a feather or a plume.

plụ·miġ′ẽr·ous, *a.* [L. *pluma*, a feather, and *gerere*, to bear.] feathered; having feathers or a plume.

plụ′mi·ped, *a.* [L. *pluma*, feather, and *pes*, *pedis*, foot.] having feathered feet.

plụ′mi·ped, *n.* a bird that has feathered feet; a plumiped bird.

plụ′mist, *n.* one who deals in feathers or plumes; a plumemaker.

plum′met, *n.* [OFr. *plommet*, dim. of *plom*, *plum*; L. *plumbum*, lead.]
1. a weight attached to a plumb line; a plumb bob.
2. the line and bob together.
3. a thing that weighs heavily.
4. a piece of lead formerly used to rule paper for writing. [Obs.]
5. the hilt of a sword. [Obs.]

plum′met, *v.i.* to fall straight downward.

plum′my, *a.*; *comp.* plummier; *superl.* plummiest. 1. full of plums.
2. like a plum.
3. good; desirable. [Colloq.]

plụ′mōse, *a.* [L. *plumosus*, from *pluma*, feather.]
1. feathered.
2. like a feather; having hairs along the side like the barbs on a feather: said of bristles, pappus, etc.

plụ·mos′i·ty, *n.* the quality or state of being plumose.

plụ′mous, *a.* plumose. [Rare.]

plump, *a.* [Late ME.; M.D. *plomp*, unwieldy, balky, dull.]
1. full and rounded in form; chubby; fat; as, a *plump* boy; a *plump* habit of body.
2. blunt; dull. [Obs.]
Syn.—well-conditioned, well-rounded, chubby, strapping, bouncing, fleshy, round, full, fat, portly.

plump, *v.t.*; plumped, *pt., pp.*; plumping, *ppr.* to cause plumpness in; to make plump (sometimes with *up* or *out*).

plump, *v.i.* to become plump; to develop plumpness; to enlarge and become smooth and rounded or distended (sometimes with *up* or *out*).

plump, *n.* a cluster; a clump; a compact group; as, a *plump* of trees, a *plump* of fowls. [Archaic or Brit. Dial.]

plump, *v.i.* [ME. *plumpen*; M.D. *plompen*: origin echoic.]
1. to fall suddenly or with full impact.
2. to come in contact abruptly or heavily (*against* something).
3. to go or come in a rush (with *in* or *out*).
to plump for; (a) to vote for; (b) to support strongly.

plump, *v.t.* 1. to drop or throw; to put down heavily or all at once; as, to *plump* a ball against a floor or into water.
2. to utter or enunciate quickly and with emphasis: sometimes with *out*; as, to *plump* a question; to *plump out* a reply.

plump, *n.* 1. a falling, plunging, or colliding suddenly or heavily.
2. the sound of this.

plump, *adv.* 1. with a plump; suddenly; heavily.
2. straight down.
3. in plain words; bluntly.

plump, *a.* blunt; downright; straightforward.

plump′ẽr, *n.* one who or that which plumps; specifically, something carried in the mouth to plump out hollow cheeks.

plump′ẽr, *n.* 1. a plumping (dropping heavily).
2. a vote or votes for only one of several candidates running for the same office when two or more may be voted for.
3. a downright lie. [Slang.]

plump′ly, *adv.* in a plump manner.

plump′ness, *n.* the quality or state of being plump.

plum pud′ding, [orig. made with *plums*.]
1. a rich pudding made of suet, raisins, currants, etc., boiled or steamed, as in a linen bag.
2. a baked pudding containing similar ingredients in a crust. [Brit.]

plụ′mū·là, *n.*; *pl.* **plụ′mū·lae,** same as *plumule*.

plụ·mū·lā′ceous, *a.* of or like a plumule; downy.

plụ′mū·lăr, *a.* plumulaceous; downy.

plụ·mū·lā′ri·à, *n.* [L. *plumula*, a small feather.]
1. a polyp of the genus *Plumularia*.
2. [P–] a genus of hydroid polyps.

plụ·mū·lā′ri·ăn, *a.* of or like the genus *Plumularia*.

plụ·mū·lā′ri·ăn, *n.* a plumularia or a member of the family of which it is the type.

plụ′mū·lāte, *a.* having plumules.

plụ′mūle, *n.* [L. *plumula*.]
1. in botany, a little seed bud enclosed by the cotyledons of a dicotyledonous plant, or at one side of the cotyledon in a monocotyledonous one.
2. a small or downy feather.

P, PLUMULE

plụ′mū·lōse, *a.* like plumules; spreading laterally, as hairs on some insects.

plụm′y, *a.* 1. feathered; covered with feathers; also, feathery; downy.
2. adorned with plumes; as, a *plumy* crest.

plun′dẽr, *v.t.*; plundered, *pt., pp.*; plundering, *ppr.* [G. *plündern*, from *plunder*, trash, baggage.]
1. to rob or despoil (a person or place) by force, especially in warfare.
2. to take (property) by force or fraud.

plun′dẽr, *v.i.* to steal.

plun′dẽr, *n.* 1. the act of plundering; robbery; pillage.
2. that which is taken by force, theft, or fraud; loot; booty.
3. personal baggage, goods, or property. [Colloq.]

plun′dẽr·āġe, *n.* 1. robbery.
2. the embezzlement of property on board a ship.
3. the property embezzled.

plun′dẽr·ẽr, *n.* one who plunders.

plunġe, *v.t.*; plunged, *pt., pp.*; plunging, *ppr.* [ME. *plungen*; OFr. *plongier*, from a hypothetical Latin form *plumbicare*, from *plumbum*, lead; lit., to fall like lead or to fall plumb.]
1. to thrust into water or other fluid substance, or into any substance that is penetrable; to immerse in a fluid; to drive; to thrust.
2. to thrust or drive into any state in which the thing is considered as enveloped or surrounded; as, to *plunge* oneself into difficulties; to *plunge* a nation into war.
3. to baptize by immersion. [Obs.]

plunġe, *v.i.* 1. to pitch; to thrust or drive oneself into water or other fluid; to dive, or to rush in; as, to *plunge* into the river.
2. to fall or rush into any state or circumstances in which the person or thing is enveloped or overwhelmed; as, to *plunge* into debt or into war.
3. to throw the body forward and hind legs up, as an unruly horse.
4. to slope steeply; as, the cliff *plunged* down to the surf.
5. to move suddenly or with violence downward or forward; to leap, fall, or move, as with the entire weight; as, the automobile *plunged* forward.
6. to pitch, as a ship.
7. to hazard large sums on uncertain outcomes; to take undue risks; to be reckless in venturing or speculation. [Colloq.]

plunġe, *n.* 1. a place for plunging; a swimming pool.
2. (a) a dive or downward leap; (b) a swim.
3. any sudden, violent plunging motion.
4. a heavy, rash investment or speculation. [Colloq.]
to take the plunge; to start on some new and seemingly uncertain enterprise.

plunġe bȧth, a bath, as in a pool, in which a person can plunge wholly under water.

plunġe bat′tẽr·y, a voltaic cell or battery so arranged that the plates may be readily lowered into the liquid or raised from it when not required for use.

plun′ġẽr, *n.* 1. a person who plunges, or dives.
2. a person who acts hastily or recklessly; especially, a rash gambler or speculator. [Colloq.]
3. in mechanics, any cylindrical part that operates with a plunging motion, as a piston, dasher, firing pin, etc.
4. in pottery, a vessel in which clay is beaten by a wheel into the required consistency.

plun′ġẽr buck′et, a pump bucket having no valve.

plun′ġẽr pump, a pump with a solid cylindrical piston.

plun′ġing, *a.* that plunges; as, a *plunging* fire of missiles.

pluṅk, *v.t.* [echoic.] 1. to pluck or strum (a banjo, etc.).
2. to throw or put down heavily; to plump.

pluṅk, *v.i.* 1. to give out a twanging sound: said of a banjo, guitar, etc.
2. to fall or sink heavily.

pluṅk, *n.* 1. a plunking.
2. the sound made by plunking.
3. a hard blow. [Colloq.]
4. a dollar. [Slang.]

pluṅk, *adv.* 1. with a twang or thud.
2. exactly; as, *plunk* in the middle.

plụ·pẽr′feçt (*or* plụ′pẽr″), *a.* [abbrev. of L. *plus quam perfectum*, lit., more than perfect.] in grammar, denoting that an action or event was completed before a given or implied past time; past perfect.

plụ·pẽr′feçt, *n.* a pluperfect tense or form.

plụ′răl, *a.* [ME. and OFr. *plurel*; L. *pluralis*, from *plus*, *pluris*, more.]
1. of or including more than one.
2. of, involving, or being one of, a plurality of persons or things; as, *plural* marriage, a *plural* mate.
3. in grammar, (a) designating or of more than one (of what is referred to); (b) in languages having dual number, designating or of more than two (of what is referred to).

plụ′răl, *n.* in grammar, (a) the plural number; (b) a plural form of a word; (c) a word in plural form: distinguished from *singular*.

NOUN PLURALS IN ENGLISH.—The regular plural suffix is -(*e*)*s*. Even Latin, Greek, or other foreign words often have alternative plurals in this form, in addition to their original plurals. Words with alternative plurals in the regular -(*e*)*s* form are marked (*).

I. Regular English Plurals.
  A. Add -*s* in all cases except as noted below.
  B. Add -*es* after final -*ss*, -*sh*, and -*ch*: *glass-es, ash-es, witch-es.*
  C. Add -*es* after -*y* preceded by a consonant or by -*qu*-, and change the -*y* to -*i*: *fly, fli-es*; *army, armi-es*; *soliloquy, soliloqui-es*, etc. (Add -*s* after -*y* preceded by a vowel: *day, day-s*; *monkey, monkey-s*, etc.)
  D. Add -*es* to some words ending in -*o* preceded by a consonant: **buffalo-es*, **domino-es, echo-es, hero-es, potato-es*, etc. (Add -*s* to most words ending in -*o* preceded by a consonant, and to all words ending in -*o* preceded by a vowel: *piano-s, radio-s, studio-s*, etc.)

II. Minor English Plurals.
  A. Regular plural with change in preceding consonant: change *f* to *v* in many words, and add -(*e*)*s*: *half, self, life, leaf, *scarf, *wharf*, etc.
  B. Regular plural replaced:
    1. By -*en*: *ox-en.*
    2. By -*ren*: *child-ren.*
    3. By vowel change: *man, men*; *foot, feet*; *mouse, mice*, etc.
  C. Plural the same as the singular: *alms, barracks, Chinese, deer* (occas. *deers*), *forceps, gallows, gross, Iroquois, Japanese, means, moose, salmon, sheep, Swiss*, etc.
  D. Plural either different from or the same as the singular:
    1. Plural usually different, but sometimes the same, especially in the usage of hunters and fishermen:

albacore
albatross
anchovy
antelope
argali
badger
bear
beaver
bighorn
bittern
blackcock
blenny
boar
bobcat
bobwhite
bonito
brant
buck
buffalo
canvasback
carabao
caribou
cat
char
charr
chub
clam
cock
codling
coot
cougar
coyote
coypu
crake
crane
crappie
croppie
curlew
dhole
doe
dog
dotterel
dowitcher
duck
duiker
dunlin
eel
egret
elder
elephant
ermine
fisher
flounder
fowl
fox
gadwall
gannet
gazelle
giraffe
gnu
goat
goby
goldeneye
goose
goral
grebe
grouper
guanaco
gull
gurnard
gurnet
hare
hart
hartebeest
heron
herring
hind
hippopotamus
hog
horse
ibex
ibis
jack
jackal
jacksnipe
jaguar
kangaroo
killdee
killdeer
kittiwake
klipspringer
kudu
lemming
leopard
lion
llama
lobster
lynx
mallard
marten
meadow lark
merganser
mink
minnow
mouflon,
moufflon
mullet
murre
muskrat
musquash
nilgai, nilghai
nilgau, nilghau
nylghai, nylghau
ocelot
okapi
opossum
oryx
ostrich
otter
ox
panther
parr
partridge
peacock
peafowl
peccary
pheasant
pig
pigeon
pintail
plover
pochard
polecat
porcupine
porgy
porpoise
pronghorn
ptarmigan
puma
quail
rabbit
raccoon
rail
rhinoceros
robalo
roebuck
sable
sambar
sambur
sandpiper
sardine
scaup
scoter
seal
sheldrake
shiner
shrimp
skate
skipjack
skunk
smelt
snapper
snipe
squid
squirrel
stag
stilt
stint
stoat
stork
sturgeon
surmullet
swan
tapir
tarpon
teal
tench
tiger
tortoise
tunny
turkey
turtle
vicuña
wallaby
walrus
wapiti
waterfowl
weasel
whale
whippoorwill
whiting
widgeon
wigeon
wildcat
wildebeest
willet
wolverine
woodcock
yak
yellowtail
zebra
zebu

    2. Plural usually the same, but different if referring to different kinds, species, varieties, etc.: as, the *fishes* of the South Pacific:

barracuda
barramunda
barramundi
bass
beluga
blaubok
bleak
blesbok
blesbuck
bontebok
boschbok
boshbok
bream
brill
burbot
bushbuck
capelin
carp
cavalla
cavally
cero
cod
codling
cusk
dace
duikerbok
duikerbuck
eelpout
eland
elk
fish (and its compounds; as, *bluefish*)
gar
gemsbok
grayling
grilse
haddock
hake
halibut
holibut
ling
mackerel
perch
pickerel
pike
plaice
pollack
pollock
pout
quagga
reedbuck
roach
roe
salmon
scad
scup
shad
sheepshead
springbok
springbuck
steelhead
steenbok
steinbock
steinbok
torsk
trout
tuna
turbot
vendace
waterbuck

    3. Plural usually lacking, but given in -(*e*)*s* form when different kinds are referred to: as, the many *steels* produced.

barley
brass
coffee
copper
corn
fruit
iron
linen
millet
oak
pepper
pine
rye
silk
steel
tea
wheat
wool

    4. Plural and collective singular interchangeable: *cannons, cannon*, etc.

III. Forms Singular or Plural Only.
  A. Singular only (or when a generalized abstraction): *chess, clearness, fishing, information, knowledge, luck, music, nonsense, truth*, etc.
  B. Plural only (even when singular in meaning). This includes certain senses of nouns otherwise singular: *Balkans, blues* (depression), *bowels, glasses, lodgings, overalls, pliers, remains* (corpse), *scissors, tongs, trousers*, etc.
  C. Plural in form but construed as singular: *cards* (game), *checkers* (game), *measles, news*, etc.
  D. Nouns ending in -*ics* are singular when they denote scientific subjects, as *mathematics, physics*, etc., and plural when they denote activities or qualities as *acrobatics, acoustics*, etc.

IV. Latin and Greek Plurals.
  A. With suffix -*a* and loss of singular ending:
    1. Latin nouns in -*um*: *agendum, agend-a*; *datum, dat-a*; **medium, medi-a*, etc.
    2. Greek nouns in -*on*: *criterion, criteri-a*; *phenomenon, phenomen-a*, etc.
  B. With Latin suffix -*i* and loss of singular ending -*us*: *alumnus, alumn-i*; **focus, foc-i*; **radius, radi-i*, etc.
  C. With Latin suffix -*ae* and loss of singular ending -*a*; *alumna, alumn-ae*; **formula, formul-ae*, etc.
  D. With suffix -*es*:
    1. Latin nouns in -*ex* or -*ix* change the ending to -*ic* and add -*es*: **appendix, append-ices*; **index, ind-ices*, etc.
    2. Latin or Greek nouns in -*is* change -*is* to -*es*: *analysis, analys-es*; *axis, ax-es*, etc.
  E. Miscellaneous Latin plurals: **phalanx, phalang-es*; **stigma, stigma-ta*, etc.

V. Foreign Plurals.
  A. Hebrew: **cherub, cherub-im*; **seraph, seraph-im*, etc.
  B. Italian: **bandit, bandit-ti*; **prima donna, prim-e donn-e*; **dilettante, dilettant-i*; **virtuoso, virtuos-i*, etc.
  C. French: *bijou,bijou-x*; **château,château-x*;**portmanteau,portmanteau-x*,etc.

VI. Plurals of Numbers, Letters, Signs, Words (when thought of as things), etc. add -*'s*: *8's, B's, &'s, whereas's.*

plu̇'răl·iṣm, *n.* 1. the quality or condition of existing in more than one part or form.
  2. the holding by one person of more than one office or church benefice at the same time.
  3. in philosophy, the theory that reality is composed of a multiplicity of ultimate beings, principles, or substances: it opposes the position of monism that reality is ultimately one, but agrees in denying the dualism of mind and body.

plu̇'răl·ist, *n.* 1. one who holds two or more offices or church benefices at once.
  2. one who believes in pluralism.

plu̇·răl·is'tiç, *a.* of pluralists or pluralism.

plu̇·ral'i·ty, *n.*; *pl.* **plu̇·ral'i·tieṣ,** [ME. *pluralite*; OFr. *pluralité*, from L. *pluralis*, plural.]
  1. the condition of being plural or numerous.
  2. a great number; a multitude.
  3. the holding of two or more church benefices at the same time.
  4. any of the benefices so held.
  5. a majority.
  6. the number of votes in an election that the leading candidate obtains over his nearest rival.

plu̇"răl·i·zā'tion, *n.* the act of pluralizing; the attribution of plurality to a person or thing, as by the use of a plural pronoun.

plu̇'răl·īze, *v.t.*; pluralized, *pt.*, *pp.*; pluralizing, *ppr.* to make plural; to put into plural form.

plu̇'răl·īze, *v.i.* to hold two or more offices or church benefices at the same time.

plu̇'răl·ī·zẽr, *n.* a pluralist.

plu̇'răl·ly, *adv.* in a plural sense; so as to express a plural.

plu̇'ri-, [L., from *plus, pluris*, several.] a combining form meaning *several* or *many.*

plu̇·ri·çap'sū·lăr, *a.* [*pluri-*, and LL. *capsula*, capsule.] having more than one capsule.

plu̇'ri·ēṣ, *n.* in law, a writ issued in the third instance, after the first and the alias have been ineffectual: so called from the word *pluries*, often, which occurs in the first clause.

plu̇·ri·flō'rous, *a.* [*pluri-*, and L. *flos, floris*, flower.] in botany, having more than one flower.

plu̇·ri·fō'li·āte, *a.* [*pluri-*, and L. *folium*, leaf.] having many leaves.

plu̇·ri·lit'ẽr·ăl, *a.* [*pluri-*, and L. *litera*, letter.] in Hebrew grammar, containing more than three letters in the root.

plu̇·ri·lit'ẽr·ăl, *n.* in Hebrew grammar, a word containing more than three letters in the root.

plu·ri·loc'ū·lăr, *a.* [*pluri-*, and L. *loculus*, cell.] having many loculi; many-celled.

plu·ri·nom'i·năl, *a.* polynomial.

plu·rip'ȧ·rȧ, *n.* [*pluri-*, and L. *parere*, to bring forth.] a multipara.

plu·rip'ȧ·rous, *a.* multiparous.

plu·ri·pär'tīte, *a.* pluriseptate.

plu·ri·pres'ence, *n.* presence in several places. [Rare.]

plu·ri·sep'tāte, *a.* [*pluri-* and *septate.*] having many septa or divisions.

plu·ri·sē'ri·āte, *a.* in botany, arrayed in many series or rows.

plu·ri·spō'rous, *a.* [*pluri-*, and Gr. *sporos*, seed.] having several spores.

plus, *prep.* [L., more.]

1. added to; as, two *plus* two equals four (2 + 2 = 4): opposed to *minus*.

2. increased by; and in addition; as, the salary *plus* bonuses came to $3,000.

plus, *a.* 1. indicating or involving addition; as, a *plus* sign.

2. positive; as, a *plus* quantity.

3. somewhat higher than; as, a grade of B *plus*.

4. having something added, gained, etc.; as, I'm *plus* a dollar. [Colloq.]

5. and more; as, she has personality *plus*. [Colloq.]

6. in bookkeeping, credit; as, the *plus* column of an account.

7. in botany, designating or of a differentiation in physiology, found in fungi and some other plants, which is like maleness.

8. in electricity, positive: opposed to *negative*.

9. in golf, (a) already counted; as, a handicap of *plus* one; (b) having a handicap of (a specified number of strokes).

plus, *n.* 1. a plus sign.

2. an added or extra quantity or thing.

3. a plus quantity.

plus, *adv.* in electricity, positively.

plus fōurs, [orig. a tailoring term indicating added length of material for overlap below the knee.] loose knickerbockers worn for active sports.

plush, *n.* [Fr. *pluche*, *peluche*; It. *peluzzo*; L. *pilus*, hair.] a fabric having a soft pile over one-eighth of an inch long.

plush, *a.* 1. of or made of plush.

2. luxurious, as in furnishings. [Slang.]

plush'y, *a.*; *comp.* plushier; *superl.* plushiest; of or like plush.

plus sign (sīn), in mathematics, the sign (+), indicating addition or positive quantity: opposed to *minus sign* (−).

plu'tär·chy, *n.* [Gr. *ploutos*, wealth, and *archein*, to rule.] plutocracy.

plu'tē·ăl, *a.* of or belonging to a pluteus.

plu'tē·us, *n.*; *pl.* **plu'tē·ī,** [L., a breastwork to protect beseigers.]

1. in ancient Roman architecture, a low wall placed between columns.

2. in ancient Roman military usage, (a) boards or planks placed on the fortifications of a camp, on movable towers or other military engines, as a kind of roof for the protection of the soldiers; (b) a movable gallery on wheels, shaped like a sort of arched wagon, in which a besieging party made approaches.

3. in zoology, the name given to the larval form of the *Echinoidea*.

Plu'tō, *n.* [Gr. *Ploutōn.*] **1. in Greek and** Roman mythology, the god ruling over the lower world, son of Chronos and Rhea, and brother of Zeus (Jupiter) and Poseidon (Neptune). He is represented as an old man with a dignified but severe aspect, holding in his hand a two-pronged fork. He was generally called by the Greeks Hades, and by the Romans Orcus, Tartarus, and Dis. His wife was Persephone (Proserpine), daughter of Zeus (Jupiter) and Demeter (Ceres).

PLUTO AND PROSERPINE

2. the outermost planet of the solar system, discovered in 1930, ninth in distance from the sun: diameter, 7,600 mi.; period of revolution, 248.42 yrs.; symbol, ♇.

plu·toc'rȧ·cy, *n.*; *pl.* **plu·toc'rȧ·cies,** [Gr. *ploutos*, wealth, and *kratein*, to rule.]

1. government by the wealthy.

2. a government or state in which the wealthy rule.

3. a group of wealthy people who control or influence a government.

plu'tō·crat, *n.* [from Gr. *ploutos*, wealth; and *-crat.*]

1. a member of a wealthy ruling class.

2. a person whose wealth gives him control or great influence.

3. any wealthy person. [Colloq.]

plu·tō·crat'ic, *a.* pertaining to, like, or characteristic of a plutocracy or a plutocrat; as, *plutocratic* ideas; *plutocratic* government.

plu·tō·crat'i·căl, *a.* plutocratic.

plu·tol'ō·gist, *n.* a student of plutology.

plu·tol'ō·gy, *n.* [Gr. *ploutos*, wealth, and *logos*, discourse.] the science of wealth.

plu·tō·mā'ni·ȧ, *n.* [Gr. *ploutos*, wealth, and *mania*, madness.] in pathology, the insane belief of a patient that he is very rich.

Plu·tō'ni·ăn, *a.* of or like Pluto or the infernal regions.

plu·tō'ni·ăn, *n.* a plutonist.

Plu·ton'ic, *a.* [L. *Pluto* (*-onis*).]

1. Plutonian.

2. [*sometimes p-*] in geology, formed far below the earth's crust by the action of intense heat, and then crystallized; igneous; as, *Plutonic* rock.

Plutonic action; in geology, the influence of volcanic heat and other subterranean causes under pressure.

Plutonic rocks; in geology, granite, porphyry, and other igneous rocks, supposed to have consolidated from a melted state at a great depth from the surface.

Plutonic theory; the theory that the changes on the earth's surface are due to the action of intense heat far below the earth's crust.

plu'tō·nism, *n.* [L. *Pluto* (*-onis*).] the Plutonic theory.

plu'tō·nist, *n.* one who believes in the Plutonic theory.

plu·tō'ni·um, *n.* a radioactive chemical element obtained by bombarding uranium with neutrons. Symbol Pu, atomic weight 239, atomic number 94. It is a transformation product of neptunium.

Plu'tus, *n.* [Gr. *Ploutos*, from *ploutos*, wealth; root as seen in *pleōs*, more, L. *plus.*] in Greek mythology, the blind god of wealth, the son of Iasion and Demeter. Zeus is said to have blinded him, in order that he might not bestow his favors exclusively on good men, but that he might distribute his gifts without any regard to merit.

plu'vi·ăl, *a.* [L. *pluvialis*, from *pluvia*, rain.]

1. rainy; humid; of or having to do with rain; having much rain.

2. in geology, formed by rain.

plu'vi·ăl, *n.* [Fr. *pluvial.*] a priests' cope for protection against rain. [Obs.]

plu·vi·am'ē·tēr, *n.* [L. *pluvia*, rain, and Gr. *metron*, measure.] same as *pluviometer*.

plu″vi·ȧ·met'ric·ăl, *a.* same as *pluviometric*.

plu'vi·ăn, *n.* the crocodile bird.

plu'vi·ō·grȧph, *n.* [L. *pluvia*, rain, and Gr. *graphein*, to write.] a self-recording rain gauge.

plu·vi·og'rȧ·phy, *n.* 1. in meteorology, the art of obtaining the automatic registration of falls of rain, snow, etc.

2. the charting and graphic presentation of data pertaining to the precipitation of rain and snow.

plu·vi·om'ē·tēr, *n.* [L. *pluvia*, rain, and Gr. *metron*, measure.] a gauge for measuring the depth of a rainfall.

plu″vi·ō·met'ric, *a.* pertaining or relating to a pluviometer or pluviometry.

plu″vi·ō·met'ric·ăl, *a.* pluviometric.

plu″vi·ō·met'ric·ăl·ly, *adv.* in a pluviometric manner.

plu·vi·om'ē·try, *n.* the art of measuring rainfall.

plu'vi·ō·scōpe, *n.* [L. *pluvia*, rain, and Gr. *skopein*, to view.] a rain gauge.

Plu'vi·ōse, *n.* [Fr., lit., rainy month.] the fifth month (January 20—February 18) of the French Revolutionary Calendar, adopted in October, 1793, by the First Republic.

plu'vi·ous, *a.* [L. *pluvius.*] having abundance of rain; rainy; pluvial.

A moist and *pluvious* air.
—Sir T. Browne.

plȳ, *v.t.*; plied, *pt.*, *pp.*; plying, *ppr.* [ME. *plien*; OFr. *plier*, *ploier*; L. *plicare*, to fold.] to bend, twist, fold, or mold.

plȳ, *v.i.* 1. to bend or be bent. [Obs.]

2. to be pliable or adaptable; to yield or consent (*to* a person or thing). [Obs.]

plȳ, *n.*; *pl.* **plīes,** 1. a single thickness, fold, or layer, as of doubled cloth, plywood, etc.

2. one of the twisted strands in rope, yarn, etc.

3. the state of being bent or twisted.

4. bent, bias, or inclination.

plȳ, *a.* having (a specified number of) layers, thicknesses, or strands: usually in hyphenated compounds; as, *three-ply*.

plȳ, *v.t.*; plied, *pt.*, *pp.*; plying, *ppr.* [contr. from *apply.*]

1. to employ; to do work with; to use; as, to *ply* one's needle; to *ply* a hammer.

2. to practice or perform with diligence; to work at (a trade); to keep working on (*with* a tool, process, etc.).

Their bloody task, unwearied, still they *ply*.
—Waller.

3. to address (someone) urgently and constantly (*with* questions, etc.).

4. to keep supplying (*with* presents, food, etc.).

5. to sail back and forth across; as, boats *ply* the channel.

6. to press hard with blows or missiles; to assail briskly; to beset.

The hero stands above, and from afar
Plies him with darts and stones and distant war.
—Dryden.

plȳ, *v.i.* 1. to keep busy; to work (*at* something); to apply oneself (*to* something).

2. to sail or travel regularly back and forth (*between* places): said of ships, buses, etc.

3. to steer a course. [Poetic.]

4. in navigation, to sail in a zigzag course into the wind; to tack.

plȳ'ēr, *n.* 1. one who or that which plies.

2. [*pl.*] in old fortifications, a kind of balance used in raising and letting down a drawbridge, consisting of timbers joined in the form of a St. Andrew's cross.

3. [*pl.*] same as *pliers*.

Plym'ŏuth Breth'ren, Plym'ŏuth·ītes, *n.pl.* a sect of Christians, founded at Plymouth, England, in 1830. They have no formal creed or organization, and make the Bible their only guide. Also called *Brethren*, *Christian Brethren*, *Plymouthists*, and *Darbyites*.

Plym'ŏuth Col'ō·ny, the colony founded by the Pilgrims in 1620 on the shores of Massachusetts Bay.

Plym'ŏuth Rock, one of the breed of American chickens: the most common variety has gray and bluish-black striped feathers.

plȳ'wood, *n.* wood built up of two or more veneer sheets glued or cemented together under pressure, usually with their grains at right angles to one another.

Pm, in chemistry, promethium.

pnē″ō·dȳ·nam'ics (nē″), *n.* [Gr. *pnein*, to breathe, and *dynamis*, power.] that branch of physiology or animal mechanics which treats of respiration.

pnē·ō·gas'tēr, *n.* [Gr. *pnein*, to breathe, and *gastēr*, the stomach.] in anatomy, the respiratory tract.

pnē'ō·grȧph, *n.* [Gr. *pnein*, to breathe, and *graphein*, to write.] an instrument used for testing and tracing the character of lung expirations.

pnē″ō·mȧ·nom'ē·tēr, *n.* a pneumatometer.

pnē·om'ē·tēr, *n.* a spirometer.

pnē·om'ē·try, *n.* [Gr. *pnein*, to breathe, and *metron*, measure.] the measurement of air inhaled or exhaled by the lungs.

pnē'ō·scōpe, *n.* [Gr. *pnein*, to breathe, and *skopein*, to view.] an instrument for measuring and studying the movements of the thorax, as in breathing, etc.

pneū'mȧ (nū'), *n.* [Gr., from *pnein*, to breathe.]

1. soul; spirit; the breath of life.

2. in Christian theology, the Holy Spirit.

3. a breathing.

pneū·mat'ic, pneū·mat'ic·ăl, *a.* [Gr. *pneu-*

matikos, from *pneuma*, breath, *pnein*, to breathe.]

1. of or containing wind, air, or gases; gaseous; as, *pneumatic* pressure: opposed to *dense* or *solid*.

2. worked by or filled with compressed air.

3. equipped with pneumatic tires.

4. in theology, having to do with the spirit or soul; spiritual.

5. in zoology, having hollows filled with air, as the bones of certain birds.

6. pertaining to the science of pneumatics; as, a *pneumatic* experiment.

7. moved or played by means of air; as, a *pneumatic* instrument of music.

pneumatic pile; a pile that is driven into position by air pressure.

pneumatic pump; a forcing pump for exhausting air.

pneumatic syringe; in physics, a form of syringe used to prove the compressibility of gases.

pneumatic tire; a rubber tire inflated with compressed air.

pneū·mat′iç (nū-), *n.* 1. a pneumatic tire.

2. a vehicle with pneumatic tires.

pneū·mat′iç·ăl·ly, *adv.* in a pneumatic manner; especially, by air pressure.

pneū·mȧ·tic′i·ty, *n.* the state of being pneumatic; the character of being buoyant because of air cavities or air inflation; as, the *pneumaticity* of bones in birds.

pneū·mat′içs, *n.pl.* [*construed as sing.*], [from *pneumatic.*] 1. that branch of physics dealing with the properties, such as pressure, density, etc., of air and other gases.

2. in philosophy and theology, the doctrine of spiritual substances; pneumatology.

pneū′mȧ·tō- (nū′), [from Gr. *pneuma, pneumatos*, air, breath, spirit.] a combining form meaning: (a) *air, vapor*, as in *pneumato*lysis, *pneumato*phore; (b) *breathing*, as in *pneumato*meter; (c) *spirits*, as in *pneumato*logy.

pneū·mat′ō·cēle, *n.* [*pneumato-*, and Gr. *kēlē*, a tumor.]

1. in surgery, a distention of the scrotum by air.

2. hernia of the lungs.

pneū·mat′ō·cyst, *n.* [*pneumato-*, and Gr. *kystis*, a cyst.] in zoology, the air sac or float of certain of the oceanic *Hydrozoa* (*Physophoridæ*).

pneū·mat′ō·gram, *n.* [*pneumato-*, and Gr. *gramma*, a writing.] a tracing of the respiratory movements of the chest, obtained by a pneumatograph.

pneū·mat′ō·gráph, *n.* [*pneumato-*, and Gr. *graphein*, to write.] an instrument for recording movements of the chest during respiration.

pneū″mat·ō·lit′iç, *a.* same as *pneumatolytic.*

pneū″mȧ·tō·loġ′iç·ăl, *a.* pertaining to pneumatology.

pneū·mȧ·tol′ō·ġist, *n.* one versed in pneumatology.

pneū·mȧ·tol′ō·ġy, *n.* [*pneumato-* and *-logy.*]

1. in theology, the study or doctrine of spirits or spiritual phenomena.

2. in Christian theology, the doctrine of the Holy Ghost.

3. psychology. [Obs.]

4. pneumatics.

pneū·mȧ·tol′y·sis, *n.* the natural process that forms pneumatolytic ores and minerals.

pneū·mȧ·tō·lyt′iç, *a.* in geology, formed by steam pressure: said of ores and minerals found near igneous or volcanic formations: also spelled *pneumatolitic.*

pneū·mȧ·tom′ē·tẽr, *n.* [*pneumato-*, and Gr. *metron*, measure.] an instrument for determining the force of air from the lungs by measuring the amount of air breathed in or out at a single time.

pneū′mȧ·tō·phōre, *n.* [*pneumato-*, and Gr. *phoros*, from *pherein*, to bear.]

1. in botany, a porous structure, used as a breathing organ, on the roots of certain tropical plants.

2. in zoology, a cavity that contains air.

pneū″mȧ·tō·ther′ȧ·py, *n.* [*pneumato-* and *therapy.*] the treatment of disease by the use of rarefied or condensed air.

pneu″mȧ·tō·thō′rax, *n.* same as *pneumothorax.*

pneū·meç′tō·my, *n.* [from *pneumo-* and *-ectomy.*] the surgical removal of part of a lung.

pneū′mō- (nū′), pneumono-.

pneū″mō·bȧ·cil′lus, *n.*; *pl.* **pneū″mō·bȧ·cil′lī**, [Mod. L.; *pneumo-* and *bacillus.*] a bacillus found in some respiratory infections, but not regarded as the causative agent of pneumonia.

pneū′mō·cēle, *n.* same as *pneumonocele.*

pneū·mō·çoç′çăl, *a.* of or caused by pneumococci.

pneū·mō·çoç′ciç, *a.* pneumococcal.

pneū·mō·çoç′çus, *n.*; *pl.* **pneū·mō·çoç′cī**, [Gr. *pneumōn*, lung, and E. *coccus.*] a bacterium, occurring in a large number of strains, that is the causative agent of lobar pneumonia and certain other diseases.

pneū·mō·cō·ni·ō′sis, *n.* [from *pneumo-*, and Gr. *konia*, dust; and *-osis.*] any of various diseased conditions of the lungs characterized by fibrous hardening as a result of chronic inhalation of irritating dust particles, as by miners, etc.

pneū″mō·dȳ·nam′içs, *n.* [*pneumo-* and *dynamics.*] pneumatics.

pneū·mō·gas′triç, *a.* [Gr. *pneumōn*, lung, and *gastēr*, the stomach.] pertaining to the lungs and stomach; especially, designating or of the vagus nerve.

pneumogastric nerves; the vagus nerves.

pneū·mō·gas′triç, *n.* the vagus nerve.

pneū′mō·gram, *n.* same as *pneumatogram.*

pneū′mō·gráph, *n.* same as *pneumatograph.*

pneū·mog′rȧ·phy, *n.* [Gr. *pneumōn*, lung, and *graphein*, to write.] a scientific description of the lungs.

pneū·mol′ō·ġy, *n.* [Gr. *pneumōn*, lung, and *logos*, a discourse.] a treatise on the lungs; pneumography.

pneū·mom′ē·tẽr, *n.* [Gr. *pneumōn*, lung, and *metron*, measure.] same as *pneumatometer.*

pneū·mom′ē·try, *n.* same as *spirometry.*

pneū′mon- (nū′), pneumono-.

pneū·mō·neç′tō·my, *n.* the surgical removal of an entire lung.

pneū·mō′ni·ȧ, *n.* [Gr. *pneumōn*, lung, from *pnein*, to breathe.] a disease of the lungs in which the tissue becomes inflamed, hardened, and watery: there are several types of pneumonia, as lobar and bronchial.

catarrhal pneumonia; same as *bronchopneumonia.*

croupous pneumonia; the common pneumonia, an acute disease characterized by high fever and inflammation of the lungs: called also *lobar pneumonia.*

fibroid pneumonia; an inflammation of the connecting fibrous tissue of the lungs.

pneū·mon′iç, *a.* 1. pertaining to the lungs; pulmonary. [Rare.]

2. of, having, or relating to pneumonia.

pneū·mon′iç, *n.* a medicine for diseases of the lungs. [Rare.]

pneū·mō·nit′iç, *a.* pertaining to pneumonitis.

pneū·mō·nī′tis, *n.* [Gr. *pneumōn*, lung, and *-itis.*] inflammation of the lungs; pneumonia.

pneū′mō·nō- (nū′), [from Gr. *pneumōn, pneumonos*, lung.] a combining form meaning *lung* or *lungs*, as in *pneumono*phorous: also *pneumo-*, *pneumon-*.

pneū′mō·nō·cēle, *n.* [*pneumono-*, and Gr. *kēlē*, tumor.] hernial protrusion of lung tissue through the chest wall.

pneū″mō·nō·cir·rhō′sis, *n.* cirrhosis or hardening of a lung.

pneū″mō·nō·cō·ni·ō′sis, *n.* same as *pneumoconiosis.*

pneū″mō·nō·dyn′i·ȧ, *n.* [*pneumono-*, and Gr. *odynē*, pain.] pain in a lung.

pneū″mō·nō·mel·ȧ·nō′sis, *n.* melanosis of the lung tissue.

pneū·mō·nom′ē·tẽr, *n.* same as *pneumatometer.*

pneū·mō·nop′ȧ·thy, *n.* [*pneumono-*, and Gr. *pathos*, disease.] any lung disease.

pneū″mō·nō·phō′rous, *a.* [*pneumono-* and *-phorous.*] having lungs.

pneū′mō·ny, *n.* same as *pneumonia.*

pneū″mō·per·i·çär′di·um, *n.* the presence of air or gas in the pericardium.

pneū″mō·per·i·tō·nē′um, *n.* the presence of gas or air in the peritoneal cavity.

pneū″mō·per·i·tō·nī′tis, *n.* peritonitis with air or gas in the peritoneal cavity.

pneū′mō·pex·y, *n.* [*pneumo-*, and Gr. *pēxis*, fixation.] surgical fixation of the lung to the thoracic wall.

pneū″mō·pleu·rī′tis, *n.* inflammation of the lungs and pleura.

pneū·mor·rhā′ġi·ȧ (-rā′), *n.* [*pneumo-*, and Gr. *rhēgnynai*, to burst forth.]

1. hemorrhage from the lungs.

2. pulmonary apoplexy.

pneū·mō·skel′e·tŏn, *n.* the hard structure connected with the breathing organs of certain invertebrates. The shells of mollusks are pneumoskeletons.

pneū·mō·ther′ȧ·py, *n.* 1. the treatment of diseases of the lungs.

2. pneumatotherapy.

pneū·mō·thō′rax, *n.* [*pneumo-* and *thorax.*] an accumulation of air or gas in the pleural cavity: the air may enter as a result of a chest wound, a lung rupture, or diseased lung tissue or may be artificially induced for collapsing and immobilizing the lung in the treatment of tuberculosis.

Pneū·mot′ō·çȧ, *n.pl.* [Gr. *pneumōn*, lung, and *ōotokos*, egg-laying.] a division of oviparous air-breathing vertebrates, as birds and reptiles.

pneū·mō·tox′in, *n.* [*pneumo-* and *toxin.*] the toxin produced by the bacteria of pneumonia.

pnī·gā′li·on (nī-), *n.* [Gr. *pnigaliōn*, from *pnigein*, to choke.] a nightmare.

Pnyx (nix), *n.* in ancient Greece, a place near Athens, at which assemblies were held for oratory and for the discussion of political affairs of the state.

Po, in chemistry, polonium.

Pō′a, *n.* [Gr. *poa*, grass, or any plant that bears its leaves and seeds from the root.] a genus of grasses belonging to the family *Gramineæ*. The numerous species, as bluegrass, meadow grass, spear grass, wire grass, etc., chiefly native to the Northern Hemisphere, grow abundantly, and furnish valuable forage for cattle.

pō·ā′ceous, *a.* [from Gr. *poa*, grass; and *-aceous.*] in botany, of the grass family.

pōach, *v.t.*; poached, *pt.*, *pp.*; poaching, *ppr.* [OFr. *pochier*, to pocket, from *poche*, a pouch, a pocket.] to place the unbroken contents of (an egg) in boiling water, or in a small receptacle put over boiling water, and cook until the white of the egg coagulates.

pōach, *v.t.* [Fr. *pocher*; OFr. *pochier*, to tread upon, poach into, from M.H.G. *bochen, puchen*, to strike upon, to plunder.]

1. to soften, tear up, or make holes in (ground) by stamping; to trample.

2. to mix with water until smooth.

3. to trespass on (private property), especially for hunting or fishing.

4. to hunt or catch (game or fish) illegally.

5. to take (anything) by unfair or illegal methods; to steal.

6. to stab; to spear; to pierce. [Obs.]

7. to force or drive into; to plunge into. [Obs.]

pōach, *v.i.* 1. to sink into soft or wet earth when walking.

2. to become soggy or full of holes when trampled; to turn into mud.

3. to hunt or fish on another's property; to trespass.

4. to thrust; to stab; to poke.

pōach′ărd, *n.* a pochard. [Obs.]

pōach′ẽr, *n.* 1. one who poaches; one who steals game or kills game unlawfully.

2. the American widgeon.

3. a fish, the sea poacher.

pōach′i·ness, *n.* the state of being poachy.

pōach′y, *a.*; *comp.* poachier; *superl.* poachiest; wet and soft; swampy; easily trodden into holes by cattle: said of land.

pō′căn, *n.* the pokeweed, *Phytolacca decandra.*

pō·cā′sŏn, *n.* same as *pocosin.*

pō′chărd, *n.*; *pl.* **pō′chărds** or **pō′chărd**, [lit., the *poacher*, one that poaches or pokes.] a diving duck of the genus *Aythya*, native to the arctic seas, but found in winter on the coasts of America, Europe, and Asia. It has a brownish-red head and is related to the American widgeon and redhead. The common pochard, *Aythya ferina*, variously called *dunbird, red-headed poker*, and *red-eyed poker*, breeds in very northern regions, but visits the American coasts as far south as the Carolinas.

pock, *n.* [AS. *poc* or *pocc*; D. *pok*; G. *pocke*, a vesicle or pustule; pl. *pox*, for *pocks.*]

1. a pustule or pimple caused by smallpox and other eruptive diseases.

2. a scar or pit in the skin left by such a pustule.

pock′-ärred, *a.* pock-marked. [Brit. Dial.]

pock′-brō″ken, *a.* broken out with smallpox; pitted; pock-marked.

pock′et, *n.* [OFr. *poquette*, dim. of *poque*, pouch.]

1. a sack, especially when used to measure something. [Brit.]

2. a little bag or pouch, now usually when sewed into clothing, for carrying money and small articles.

3. any cavity or enclosure which holds or can hold something.

4. the condition of being surrounded and hemmed in, as in a race.
5. an atmospheric current or condition that causes an airplane to drop suddenly: also called *air pocket.*
6. an open pouch at the side or corner of a billiard or pool table.
7. in mining, (a) a cavity filled with ore; (b) a small deposit of ore.
8. in zoology, a sac or cavity in an animal's body.
9. figuratively, money; means; pecuniary resources.
10. in nautical usage, a piece of canvas sewed on a sail, designed to receive a light spar.
11. the trap of a weir in which fish are kept.
12. a hollow among mountains.
in one's pocket; completely under one's influence.
out of pocket; having lost money or spent it too freely.
pocket borough; see under *borough.*
to line one's pockets; to get or make much money.

pock'et, *a.* 1. that is or can be carried in a pocket.
2. small.

pock'et, *v.t.*; pocketed, *pt., pp.*; pocketing, *ppr.* 1. to put or conceal in the pocket; as, to *pocket* a penknife; to *pocket* a billiard ball.
2. to close in upon so that escape is difficult or impossible; to envelop or enclose; as, to *pocket* a horse in a race.
3. to take dishonestly or without right; to appropriate.
4. to submit to or put up with (an insult, gibe, etc.) without answering or showing anger.
5. to hide or suppress; as, *pocket* one's pride.
6. in politics, to prevent passage of (a bill) by the pocket veto.

pock'et bat'tle·ship, a small battleship: originally, one of the small battleships built by Germany after World War I, of 10,000 tons displacement and carrying heavier guns than a cruiser.

pock'et·book, *n.* 1. a case or folder, usually of leather, divided into compartments, and suitable for carrying money, papers, etc., in the pocket; a billfold.
2. a woman's purse or handbag.

pock'et book, a book small enough to be carried in one's pocket.

pock'et ē·di'tion (-dish'un), an edition, as of a periodical or book, suitable for carrying in the pocket.

pock'et flap, the piece of cloth which covers the pocket hole, as in a coat.

pock'et·fụl, *n.*; *pl.* **pock'et·fụls,** enough to fill a pocket; as much as a pocket will hold.

pock'et gō'phẽr, the *Geomys bursarius*, a gopher having large cheek pouches, not connected with the mouth; also, *Thomomys talpoides*, a gopher of the Pacific Coast.

pock'et ham'mẽr, a hammer adapted for carrying in the pocket; a geologist's hammer.

pock'et han'kẽr·chief (haṅ'), a handkerchief to be carried in the pocket.

pock'et hōle, the opening into a pocket.

pock'et·knīfe (-nīf) *n.*; *pl.* **pock'et·knīveṣ** (-nīvz), a knife suited for carrying in the pocket, with a blade or blades which fold into the handle.

pock'et lid, the flap over the pocket hole; a pocket flap.

pock'et mŏn'ey, money to be carried in the pocket; money for small expenses; small change.

pock'et mouse, any of several species of mice of the family *Saccomyidæ* having external cheek pouches.

pock'et piēce, a coin to be kept in the pocket and not spent: generally a coin not current.

pock'et pis'tŏl, 1. a pistol of a size convenient for carrying in the pocket.
2. a liquor flask for the pocket. [Humorous.]

pock'et rat, same as *pocket gopher.*

pock'et sher'iff, in England, a sheriff appointed by the sovereign, and not one nominated by the exchequer.

pock'et vē'tō, the method whereby the President of the United States can veto a bill passed by Congress and presented to him within ten days of its adjournment by failing to sign and return the bill by the time of adjournment.

pock'et·y, *a.* having the ore in pockets, as a lode.

pock'-fret"ten, *a.* pock-marked. [Obs.]

pock hōle, the pit or scar made by a pustule.

pock'i·ness, *n.* the state of being pocky.

pock'märk, *n.* a pit or scar in the skin left by a pustule, as in smallpox.

pock'-märked (-märkt), *a.* having, or marked with, pock-marks.

pock'-pit"ted, *a.* same as *pock-marked.*

pock pud'ding, a pudding cooked in a cloth bag. [Scot.]

pock'wood, *n.* a tree, *Guaiacum officinale*; lignum vitae: formerly used as a medicine in smallpox.

pock'y, *a.* 1. covered with pocks or pock-marks.
2. of or like a pock.
3. of or having the pox.
4. vile; low, contemptible. [Obs.]

pō'çō, *adv.* [It.] in music, a little; somewhat: a direction to the performer.

pō'çō, *n.* a little.

pō'çō ä pō'çō, [It.] in music, somewhat: a direction to the performer.

pō'çock, *n.* a peacock. [Obs.]

pō"çō·çū·ran'tē, *a.* [It., caring little.] caring little; indifferent; apathetic.

pō"çō·çū·ran'tē, *n.* a pococurante person; a trifler.

pō"çō·çū·ran'tē·iṣm, *n.* the attitude or behavior of a pococurante.

pō"çō·çū·ran'tiṣm, *n.* same as *pococuranteism.*

pō'çō·sin, pō·çō'sŏn, *n.* [Algonquian.] a marsh; a swamp: also written *poquoson* and *pocason.*

poç'ū·li·fọrm, *a.* [L. *poculum*, a cup, and *forma*, form.] cup-shaped.

-pod, [from Greek *pous, podos*, a foot.] a combining form used to form nouns and adjectives, meaning: (a) *foot*, as in pleo*pod*; (b) *(one) having* (a specified number or kind of) *feet*, as in tri*pod*: also *-pode.*

pod, *n.* [a form of *pad.*]
1. any of various different specific pericarps or dry seed vessels of plants, which split or burst open at maturity, such as the legume, the loment, the silique, the silicle, the follicle, the conceptacle, and the capsule; specifically, a legume.
2. a podlike container, as a cocoon, etc.
3. a pouch or bag.
4. the musk pouch of the musk deer as sold in the market.

pod, *v.i.*; podded, *pt., pp.*; podding, *ppr.* 1. to bear pods.
2. to swell out into a pod.

pod, *v.t.* to take (peas, etc.) out of pods; to shell.

pod, *n.* [prob. a special application of prec. *pod.*] a flock or school, as of birds, whales, etc.

pod, *v.t.* to herd (animals) together.

pod, *n.* [prob. var. of *pad*, in same sense.] in mechanics, (a) the sharp groove in certain boring tools, as the pod auger; (b) the socket for the bit in a brace.

-pod·a, in zoology, plural of *-pod.*

pō·dag'rȧ, *n.* [Gr., from *pous, podos*, foot, and *agra*, seizure.] gout, especially in a foot.

pō·dag'riç, *a.* [from *podagra.*]
1. gouty; partaking of the gout.
2. afflicted with gout.

pō·dag'riç·ăl, *a.* same as *podagric.*

pod'ȧ·grous, *a.* same as *podagric.*

pō·dal'ġi·ȧ, *n.* [Gr. *pous, podos*, foot, and *algos*, pain.] neuralgic pain or gout in the foot.

pō·dal'iç, *a.* [Gr. *pous, podos*, foot, and *-al* and *-ic.*] pertaining to the feet.
podalic version; changing the position of the fetus so that the feet shall be presented for delivery.

Pō·där'gus, *n.* [Gr. *pous, podos*, foot, and *argos*, swift.]
1. a genus of nocturnal birds native to Australia and some oriental countries. They are closely allied to the goatsuckers and are distinguished from them chiefly in having no connecting membrane at the base of the toes, and by the middle toe not being pectinated. They are known as *morepork, goatsucker, night hawk*, and *frogmouth.*
2. [p-] any bird of the genus *Podargus.*

pō·där'thrum, *n.* [Gr. *pous, podos*, foot, and *arthron*, joint.] a joint in a bird's foot.

pod ạu'gẽr, an auger formed with a pod.

pod bit, *n.* a semicylindrical bit having a hollow barrel, and a cutting lip which projects in front of the barrel.

pod'ded, *a.* having pods.

pod'der, *n.* [from *pod.*] a gatherer of pods. [Brit. Dial.]

-pōde, -pod.

pō·des'tȧ, *n.* [It. *podestà*; L. *potestas*, power, from *potis*, able.]
1. a governor or chief magistrate of a medieval Italian town.
2. a judge or minor official in an Italian town.
3. under Fascism, a chief executive, or mayor, of a commune.

pō·dē'ti·um (-shi-), *n.*; *pl.* **pō·dē'ti·ȧ,** [LL., from Gr. *pous, podos*, a foot.] the stalklike elongation of the thallus which supports the fructification of certain lichens.

pō'dex, *n.*; *pl.* **pod'i·cēṣ,** [L.] the anal region; the rump.
2. the pygidium of an insect.

podġe (poj), *n.* anything podgy. [Colloq.]

podġ'i·ness, *n.* the condition or quality of being podgy.

podġ'y, *a.*; *comp.* podgier; *superl.* podgiest, dumpy and fat; pudgy.

pō·dī'ȧ·trist, *n.* a specialist in podiatry.

pō·dī'ȧ·try, *n.* [from Gr. *pous, podos*, foot; and *-iatry.*] the branch of medicine having to do with the care of the feet and, especially, the treatment of foot disorders.

pod'i·çăl, *a.* [from *podex.*] pertaining to the podex, or rump; anal.

Pod'i·ceps, *n.* [from L. *podex*, rump, and *pes*, foot.] a genus of birds commonly called *grebes.*

pō·dit'ti, *n.* a kingfisher, *Syma flavirostris*, having a serrated yellow beak. [Australia.]

pō'di·um, *n.*; *pl.* **pō'di·ȧ,** [L., from Gr. *podion*, a little foot, dim. of *pous, podos*, foot.]
1. a low wall serving as a pedestal or foundation.
2. a wall separating the seats from the arena in an amphitheater.
3. a continuous bench projecting from the walls of a room.
4. a raised platform for the conductor of an orchestra; a dais.
5. in zoology, a structure or part serving as a foot.

-pō'di·um, [Mod. L., from Gr. *pous, podos*, a foot.] a combining form meaning *footstalk, supporting part*, as in mono*podium.*

pod'ō-, [from Gr. *pous, podos*, foot.] a combining form meaning *foot.*

pod'ō·branch, *n.* [*podo-*, and Gr. *branchia*, gills.] one of the gills attached to the legs of certain crustaceans; an epipodite.

pod'ō·çärp, *n.* [*podo-*, and Gr. *karpos*, fruit.] in botany, a stalk supporting the fruit.

Pod·ō·çär'pus, *n.* [*podo-*, and Gr. *karpos*, fruit.] a genus of coniferous trees of the yew family, chiefly of the Southern Hemisphere: so called because the fleshy seed is raised on a sort of stalk.

pod·ō·çeph'ȧ·lous, *a.* [*podo-*, and Gr. *kephalē*, head.] in botany, designating a plant having a head of flowers elevated on a long peduncle.

pod·ō·ġyn'i·um, *n.* [Gr. *pous, podos*, a foot, and *gynē*, a female.] same as *basigynium.*

Pod·oph·thal'mi·ȧ, *n.pl.* [*podo-*, and Gr. *ophthalmos*, eye.] the division of crustaceans in which the eyes are borne at the end of long movable footstalks, as lobsters, crabs, etc.

pod·oph·thal'miç, *a.* of or relating to the *Podophthalmia*; having the eye on a stalk.

pod·oph·thal'mīte, *n.* [*podo-* and *ophthalmite.*] the pedicel on which the eyes of a crustacean are borne.

pod·oph·thal'mous, *a.* podophthalmic.

pod·ō·phyl'lin, *n.* [*podo-*, *phyllum*, and *-in.*] a bitter, yellow, cathartic resin obtained from the rootstock of the mandrake.

pod·ō·phyl·lō·tox'in, *n.* [*podophyllum*, and Gr. *toxikon*, poison.] in medicine, an extract of the root of *Podophyllum*, used as a cholagogue.

pod·ō·phyl'lous, *a.* [*podo-*, and Gr. *phyllon*, leaf.] in entomology, having the feet or locomotive organs compressed into the form of leaves.

Pod·ō·phyl'lum, *n.* a genus of berberidaceous plants growing in the rich soil of open woods in the United States, represented by a single species, *Podophyllum peltatum*, which bears a single large white flower between its two broad shield-shaped leaves and produces a yellow pulpy plum-shaped edible fruit about one inch in diameter: also called *May apple* and *mandrake.*

pod'ō·sçaph, *n.* [*podo-*, and Gr. *scaphos*, something hollowed out, the hull of a ship, boat.] a kind of hollow apparatus like a small boat, attached one to each foot and used to support the body erect on the water.

pod'ō·spẽrm, *n.* [*podo-*, and Gr. *sperma*, seed.]

in botany, a threadlike stalk connecting an ovule with its placenta; a funicle. [Rare.]

Pod″ō·stē·mā′cē·ae, *n.pl.* [*podo-*, and Gr. *stēmōn*, warp, stamen, and *-aceæ*.] a family of small aquatic plants resembling moss or algae, growing in rivers and brooks, firmly attached to rocks under water: they are native to the tropical parts of America, Asia, and Africa.

pod″ō·stē·mā′ceous, *a.* belonging to or resembling the *Podostemaceæ*.

Pod·ō·stē′mon, *n.* [*podo-*, and Gr. *stēmōn*, warp, stamen.] a genus of aquatic plants, typical of the *Podostemaceæ*.

Pod·ō·stō′mȧ·tȧ, *n.pl.* [*podo-*, and Gr. *stoma*, *stomatos*, mouth.] a class of arthropods with footlike mouth parts.

pod·ō·thē′çȧ, *n.*; *pl.* **pod·ō·thē′cae,** [*podo-*, and Gr. *thēkē*, sheath.] the scalelike skin which covers the foot of a bird or reptile.

-pŏd′ous, [Gr. *-podos*, from *pous*, *podos*, a foot.] a combining form signifying *having* (a specified number or kind of) *feet*: used to form adjectives corresponding to nouns that end in *-pod* or *-poda*.

pod pep′pēr, one of the species of *Capsicum*.

Pō′duṅk″, *n.* [after *Podunk*, Massachusetts; of Am. Ind. origin.] an imaginary typical small town in the United States: humorous usage. [Colloq.]

Pō·dū′rȧ, *n.* the typical genus of the *Poduridæ*.

pō·dū′răn, *n.* any species of *Podura*.

pō·dū′răn, *a.* same as *podurous*.

pō·dū′rid, *n.* a species of *Podura* or some allied genus.

pō·dū′rid, *a.* same as *podurous*.

Pō·dū′ri·dae, *n.pl.* [*podo-*, and Gr. *oura*, tail, and *-idæ*.] a family of apterous insects belonging to the order *Thysanura*, distinguished from the *Lepismidæ*, the other family of the order, by an elastic forked caudal appendage which is folded under the body when at rest and by the sudden extension of which they are able to make long leaps. They are also called *springtails*.

pō·dū′roid, *a.* [*podura* and *-oid*.] resembling a podurid.

pō·dū′rous, *a.* of or relating to the genus *Podura*.

pod′zol, *n.* [Russ., lit., ashlike.] a type of relatively infertile soil found typically in forests and consisting of a thin, ash-colored layer overlaying a brown, acidic humus.

pō′ē, *n.* same as *poi*.

pō′ē·bīrd, a New Zealand bird, *Prosthemadera cincinnata*, belonging to the family of the honey eaters, about the size of a blackbird or small pigeon. Also called *tue* and *parson bird*.

Poe′ci·lē, *n.* [Gr.] the Porch in the agora of ancient Athens.

poe·ci·lit′iç, *a.* [Gr. *poikolos*, many-colored, and *-itic*.] spotted; dappled; variegated; in geology, designating rocks of the New Red Sandstone.

poe′ci·lō·cȳte, *n.* same as *poikilocyte*.

poe·cil′ō·pod, *n.* [Gr. *poikolos*, many-colored, and *pous*, *podos*, foot.] one of the *Pœcilopoda*.

poe·cil′ō·pod, *a.* of, relating to, or resembling the *Pœcilopoda*.

Poe·ci·lop′ō·dȧ, *n.pl.* [Gr. *poikolos*, many-colored, and *-poda*.] an order of entomostracan crustaceans.

pō′em, *n.* [Fr. *poeme*; L. *poema*; Gr. *poiēma*, anything made, a poem, from *poiein*, to make.]

1. an arrangement of words in verse; especially, a rhythmical composition, sometimes rhymed, expressing facts, ideas, or emotions in a style more concentrated, imaginative, and powerful than that of ordinary speech: some poems are in meter, some in free verse.

2. a composition, whether in verse or prose, having beauty of thought or language.

3. anything beautiful in a way suggesting a poem.

pō·em·at′iç, *a.* [Gr. *poiēma* (*-atos*), poem.] of the nature of a poem; poetical. [Rare.]

poe·nol′ō·ġy, *n.* see *penology*.

Pō·eph′ȧ·gȧ, *n.pl.* [Gr. *poē*, grass, and *phagein*, to eat.] a group of marsupials, so named from their herbivorous habits. The group includes the kangaroos and the kangaroo rats.

pō·eph′ȧ·gous, *a.* 1. grass-eating; herbivorous.

2. of or belonging to the *Poephaga*.

pō′e·sy, *n.*; *pl.* **pō′e·sieș,** [OFr. *poesie*; L. *poesis*; Gr. *poiēsis*, from *poiein*, to make.]

1. poetry; poems generally, or the art of writing poems. [Archaic.]

2. a poem. [Obs.]

3. a motto. [Obs.]

4. a nosegay. [Obs.]

pō′et, *n.* [Fr. *poète*; L., Sp., and It. *poeta*; Gr. *poiētēs*, one who makes, a poet, from *poiein*, to make.]

1. a person who writes poems or verses.

2. a person who writes or expresses himself with imaginative power and beauty of thought, language, etc.

pō′et·as·tēr, *n.* [*poet* and *-aster*.] a petty poet; a mediocre rhymer or writer of verses; one who merely dabbles in poetry.

pō′et·as·try, *n.* mediocre or poor poetry.

pō′et·ess, *n.* a woman poet.

pō·et′iç, *a.* [Gr. *poiētikos*; L. *poeticus*; Fr. *poetique*.]

1. of, characteristic of, like, or fit for a poet or poetry.

2. skilled in or fond of poetry.

3. written in verse.

4. having the beauty, imagination, etc. of good poetry.

5. imaginative.

pō·et′iç, *n.* poetics.

pō·et′iç·ăl, *a.* poetic: now used chiefly in reference to form, whereas *poetic* refers to the basic qualities of poetry.

pō·et′iç·ăl·ly, *adv.* in a poetic manner.

pō·et′iç jus′tice, justice, as in some plays, stories, etc., in which good is properly rewarded and evil punished; justice as one might wish it to be.

pō·et′iç lī′cense, a poet's or artist's right to deviate, for artistic effect, from literal fact and strict rules of form, grammar, etc.

pō·et′içs, *n.pl.* [*construed as sing.*] 1. the part of literary criticism that has to do with poetry; theory of poetry.

2. a treatise on poetry.

3. [P–] a famous treatise on poetic drama by Aristotle.

pō·et′i·cūle, *n.* a dabbler in poetry; a poetaster.

pō″et·i·zā′tion, *n.* the act of poetizing.

pō′et·īze, *v.i.*; poetized, *pt.*, *pp.*; poetizing, *ppr.* [Fr. *poétiser*.] to write poetry.

pō′et·īze, *v.t.* 1. to make poetic.

2. to express, or deal with, in poetry.

pō′et lau′rē·āte, *pl.* **pō′ets lau′rē·āte, pō′et lau′rē·ātes,** 1. the court poet of England, appointed by the monarch to write poems celebrating official occasions, national events, etc.

2. any official poet of a State, nation, etc.

pō′et·ress, *n.* a poetess. [Obs.]

pō′et·ry, *n.* [OFr. *poetrie*; LL. *poetria*, from L. *poeta*, poet.]

1. the writing of poems; the art of writing poems.

2. poems; poetical works.

3. something like poetry in quality or emotional effect; as, that acting is pure *poetry*.

4. poetic quality or spirit; as, the *poetry* of motion.

pog·ȧ·mog′găn, *n.* [Am. Ind.] a clublike weapon having a stone attached to one end of a flexible, wooden handle.

pogge, *n.* in zoology, *Agonus cataphractus*, a cottoid fish of the arctic seas.

pog′gy, *n.* same as *porgy*.

pō′gō, *n.* same as *pogo stick*.

pō·gō′ni·ȧ, *n.* [from Gr. *pōgōn*, a beard.]

1. a small orchid with a single white or pinkish flower having a lip tufted with yellow-brown hairs.

2. the flower.

pō·gō·nī′ȧ·sis, *n.* [Gr. *pōgōn*, beard, and *-iasis*.]

1. excessive growth of beard.

2. the growth of beard on a woman.

pō·gō′ni·āte, *a.* [Gr. *pōgōniatēs*, bearded, from *pōgōn*, beard.] bearded. [Rare.]

pog′o·nip, *n.* [from Shoshonean.] a heavy winter fog containing ice particles, occurring in the Sierra Nevada Mountains of the western United States.

pō′gō stick, [arbitrary coinage.] a stiltlike toy consisting of a strong stick with a metal spring at one end to which are fastened two pedals: by holding the stick in the hands and pushing down on the pedals with the feet, one can propel himself in a series of short jumps.

pō′grŏm (*or* pō-grom′), *n.* [Russ., devastation.]

1. an organized massacre of, or attack on, the Jews, as in Czarist Russia.

2. any similar persecution of a minority group.

pō·grom′, *v.t.* to slaughter or kill in a pogrom

pō·grom′ist, *n.* one who engages in pogroms.

pō′gy, *n.*; *pl.* **pō′gieș,** the menhaden, a kind of fish.

pōh, *interj.* same as *pooh*.

pō·hù·tù·kä′wȧ, *n.* [Maori.] in botany, a tree, *Metrosideros tomentosa*, of New Zealand, of the myrtle family. It has large spreading branches and its leaves are shining white below and green above.

po′i (poi *or* pō′i), *n.* a food of the Hawaiians made from the taro root by a process of baking and grinding. It is afterward mixed into a paste which is fermented.

pō′i, *adv.* [It.] in music, then; as, allegretto *poi* andantino: a direction to the performer.

Poi′ci·lē, *n.* same as *Poecile*.

-poi·et′iç, [from Gr. *poiēsis*, a making.] a combining form meaning *making, forming*, as in onomato*poietic*.

poign′ăn·cy (poin′), *n.* [from *poignant*.] the state or quality of being poignant.

poign′ănt, *a.* [Fr. *poignant*, from L. *pungens* (*-entis*), ppr. of *pungere*, to prick.]

1. sharp or biting to the smell or taste; tart; piquant.

2. sharply painful to the feelings; piercing.

3. keen; pointed; as, *poignant* wit.

poign′ănt·ly, *adv.* in a poignant manner.

poi′ki·lō·cȳte, *n.* [Gr. *poikilos*, many-colored, and *kytos*, cell.] a malformed and over-sized nonnucleated red blood corpuscle: also called *poecilocyte*.

poi″ki·lō·cȳ·tō′sis, *n.* [from *poikilocyte*.] a condition characterized by the presence of poikilocytes in the blood.

poi·kil·on′y·my, *n.* [Gr. *poikilos*, varied, and *onyma*, name.] the mingling of names or terms from different systems of nomenclature.

poi″ki·lō·thēr′măl, poi″ki·lō·thēr′miç, *a.* [Gr. *poikilos*, variegated, and *thermos*, warm.] having a body temperature that varies with the environmental temperature, as fish.

poi″ki·lō·thēr′mișm, *n.* the ability of bacteria, plants, and cold-blooded animals to adapt themselves to the temperature of their environment.

poi′lù (pwä′lü *or Fr.* pwȧ-lü′), *n.* [Fr., hairy, virile, bold, from *poil*, hair.] in World War I, a soldier in the French army. [Slang.]

poi·men′iç, *a.* [Gr. *poimēn*, shepherd.] pertaining to poimenics.

poi·men′içs, *n.* [Gr. *poimēn*, shepherd.] pastoral theology.

Poin·ci·ā′nȧ, *n.* [named after M. de *Poinci*, early governor of the Antilles.]

1. a genus of small tropical trees with showy red, orange, or yellow flowers. *Poinciana pulcherrima* is known as the flower fence.

2. [p–] a tree of this genus.

poind, *v.t.* [Middle Scot. *poynd*, var. of ME. *pinden*, from AS. *pyndan*, to enclose, impound.]

1. (a) to seize and sell (the property of a debtor) under a warrant; (b) to distrain the goods of (a debtor). [Scot.]

2. to impound. [Scot.]

poind, *n.* the act or an instance of poinding; distraint.

poind′ēr, *n.* one who poinds. [Scot.]

poin·set′ti·ȧ, *n.* [after Joel R. *Poinsett* (d. 1851), Am. ambassador to Mexico.]

1. a South American and Mexican shrub, Euphorbia or *Poinsettia pulcherrima*, of the spurge family, with yellow flowers surrounded by tapering red leaves resembling petals.

2. [P–] a genus including this shrub.

point, *v.t.* to appoint. [Obs.]

point, *n.* [ME.; OFr. *point*, a dot, prick, from L. *punctus*, pp. of *pungere*, to prick.]

1. a prick, speck, or dot.

2. a dot in print or writing, as a period, decimal point, vowel point, etc.

3. something thought of as having definite position in space, but no size or shape; location; as, a straight line is the shortest distance between two *points*.

4. the position of a certain player in cricket and other games.

5. the player.

6. a policeman's fixed station for duty, as distinguished from a beat. [Brit.]

7. a particular time; an exact moment; as, at this *point* she left the room, the *point* of death.

8. a stage or condition reached; as, boiling *point*.

9. a part of something; an item; a detail; as, he explained the problem *point* by *point*.

10. (a) a distinguishing feature; a characteristic; (b) a physical characteristic or quality of an animal, used as a standard in judging breeding.

11. a unit, as of measurement, value, game scores, etc.

12. a sharp or projecting end of something.

13. something with a sharp end.
14. needle-point lace.
15. a projecting or tapering piece of land; a promontory; a cape; a peak.
16. a small party before an advance guard or behind a rear guard in a military maneuver.
17. [*pl.*] a horse's extremities.
18. a branch of a deer's antler; as, a ten-*point* buck.
19. the exact or essential fact or idea under consideration (preceded by *the*).
20. a purpose; object; use; as, what's the *point* of acting like a child?
21. the important or main idea, as of a joke, speech, dispute, etc.
22. an impressive or telling argument, fact, or idea; as, you have a *point* there!
23. the posture of a hunting dog to show the presence and position of game.
24. a cord with metal tags, formerly used to lace up articles of clothing. [Archaic.]
25. in commerce, a standard unit of value, as $1 or 1¢, used in quoting current prices of stocks, commodities, etc.
26. in craps, the number that the thrower must make in order to win.
27. in education, a unit for grading school work; as, a grade of A is worth four *points*.
28. in electricity, (a) either of the two contacts, tipped with tungsten or platinum, that make or break the circuit in a distributor; (b) [Brit.] an outlet or socket.
29. in hunting, (a) a spot or landmark serving as the goal for a straight run; (b) a cross-country run.
30. in music, a short tune, sometimes sounded on an instrument as a military signal; as, *point* of war.
31. in navigation, (a) one of the thirty-two marks showing direction on the circumference of a compass card; (b) the corresponding position on the horizon; (c) the angle between two successive compass points.
32. in printing, a unit measure for type bodies, equal to about $^1/_{72}$ of an inch.
33. [*usually in pl.*] in railroading, a tapering rail in a switch. [Brit.]
34. in heraldry, one of the several different parts of the escutcheon, denoting the locations of figures.
35. in fencing, a stab with the tip of a sword.

at all points; in every detail; with completeness.

at the point of; very close to.

beside the point; not pertinent; irrelevant.

far point; the remotest point at which an object is clearly seen when the eye is at rest.

in point; appropriate; pertinent; apt.

in point of; in the matter of; as concerns.

multiple point; in geometry, a point in which two or more branches of a curve intersect each other. The analytical characteristic of a multiple point of a curve is that at it the first differential coefficient of the ordinate must have two or more values.

near point; the nearest point at which the eye can distinctly perceive an object; the nearest point of clear vision.

on the point of; almost in the act of; on the verge of.

point in perspective; one of the principal positions connected with the perspective of an object.

point lace; needle-point lace.

point of concurrence; a point common to two lines, but not a point of tangency or a point of intersection. Such, for instance, is the point in which a cycloid meets its base. In this case, the point of concurrence is also a cusp point.

point of contact; the point in a given line at which tangency takes place.

point of contrary flexure, or *point of inflexion*; a point at which a curve, from being convex toward a line not passing through it, becomes concave toward the same line, or the reverse.

point of curve; in a railroad curve, the beginning of the curve or that end first reached by the survey in its progress.

point of dispersion; in optics, that point at which the rays begin to diverge, commonly called the virtual focus.

point of honor; a matter affecting a person's honor.

point of incidence; in optics, that point upon the surface of a medium upon which a ray of light falls.

point of law; a question of law, as distinguished from a question of fact.

point of magnetic indifference; in physics, a point, as at the middle of a magnet, where no polarity exists.

point of order; in parliamentary practice, a question regarding the rules of debate.

point of sight; in perspective, the point at which, if the eye be placed, the picture will present the same dimensions as the object itself would: also called *point of view*.

point of tangent; in a railroad curve, the end of the curve opposite the point of curve.

point of view; (a) the place from which, or way in which, something is viewed or considered; (b) mental attitude or opinion.

point of vision; point of view.

point paper; paper with a pricked design for stenciling.

point rationing; a system of rationing food, clothing, etc., in which each item or a specified amount of a commodity is assigned a number of points, and each purchaser is permitted a fixed number of points for a given period of time.

points of the compass; (a) the thirty-two directional lines on the face of a compass; (b) the imagined points around the horizon corresponding to these.

point system; (a) in education, a system of averaging a student's grades by giving them equivalent numerical value in points: the average attained is called the *grade-point average*; (b) in typography, a system of graduating the sizes of type on a uniform scale of which the unit, called a *point*, is about $^1/_{72}$ inch: each type body is a multiple of the point unit and is designated by its number of points, as in *eight-point* type; (c) any system of writing or printing for the blind in which raised points or dots in certain combinations are used to represent the alphabet: Braille is a variety of this.

principal point; in perspective, the projection of the point of sight upon the perspective plane.

singular point; a point at which a curve possesses properties not possessed by other points of the curve.

to back a point; to point, as a dog does game, on seeing another dog do so.

to carry one's point; to succeed in a matter at issue; to convince by argument.

to come to points; to duel.

to make (or *gain*) *a point*; to accomplish an object; also, to advance a step in attaining an object.

to make a point of; to insist upon; to make (something) one's habit or purpose; as, *to make a point of* being punctual.

to score a point; to make a successful play in a game, and thus add a unit to a score.

to stand upon points; to stop for matters of but little importance.

to strain (or *stretch*) *a point*; to make an exception or concession.

to the point; pertinent; apt.

point, *v.t.*; pointed, *pt.*, *pp.*; pointing, *ppr.* [ME. *pointen*; OFr. *pointer*; LL. *punctare*, from L. *punctum*, point.]

1. to put punctuation marks or pauses in; as, *point* a sentence or a speech.
2. to mark off (parts of a sentence, sum, etc.) with points, as especially a decimal fraction from a whole number (with *off*).
3. to sharpen to a point, as a pencil.
4. to give (a story, remark, anecdote, action, etc.) force, purpose, or point (sometimes with *up*).
5. to show or call attention to (usually with *out*); as, *point* the way, he likes to *point out* the shortcomings of others.
6. to aim or direct (a gun, finger, etc.).
7. to show the presence and location of (game) by standing still and facing toward it: said of hunting dogs.
8. in linguistics, to put vowel points in (Hebrew writing).
9. in masonry, to fill the joints of (brickwork) with mortar.

to point a rope; in nautical usage, to prepare the end of a rope, so that it may reeve through a block, and not unlay. A few yarns are taken out of it, and a mat worked over it by its own yarn.

to point a sail; in nautical usage, to affix points through the eyelet holes of the reefs.

to point the yards (of a vessel); in nautical usage, to brace the yards so that the wind shall strike them obliquely.

to point up; to give more point to; to make more emphatic, as by a lengthier treatment, etc.

point, *v.i.* 1. to direct one's finger (*at* or *to* something).
2. to call attention (*to* something); to hint (*at* something).
3. to aim or be directed (*to* or *toward* something); to extend in a specified direction; to face.
4. to stand rigid and look in the direction of game: said of pointers and setters.
5. to come to a head, as an abscess. [Brit.]
6. in navigation, to sail close to the wind.

to point well; in nautical usage, to sail near to the wind, as a vessel.

point'ȧ·ble, *a.* 1. that can be pointed out.
2. that can be pointed.

point'ăl, *n.* same as *pointel*.

point'-blañk', *n.* the point at which the line of sight intersects the trajectory of a projectile.

point'-blañk', *a.* 1. in gunnery, (a) aimed horizontally, straight at a mark, without allowing for rise and fall in the projectile's flight; (b) of or suitable for this type of fire; as, *point-blank* range or distance.
2. straightforward; plain; blunt; as, a *point-blank* answer.

point'-blañk', *adv.* 1. straight; as, he fired the gun *point-blank* at the burglar.
2. without hesitation or quibbling; directly; bluntly; as, she refused *point-blank*.

point d'ap·pui' (pwañ då-pwē'), [Fr.] point of support, as for a battle line; basis; fulcrum.

point''-dē·vīce', point''-dē·vīse', *a.* [ME. *at point devis*; *at*, at, and *point*, a point, and *devis*, exact.] completely correct; precise. [Archaic.]

point''-dē·vīce', *adv.* to perfection; completely. [Archaic.]

point'ed, *a.* 1. having a sharp end; tapering.
2. sharp; incisive; to the point, as an epigram.
3. clearly aimed at, or referring to, someone, as a remark.
4. very evident; emphasized; conspicuous.

pointed arch; an arch having a pointed crown or apex.

pointed style; that style of architecture characterized by the pointed arch: generally called *Gothic*.

Syn.—acute, piquant, sharp, keen.

point'ed fox, red fox fur dyed black, with white hairs inserted, to simulate silver fox fur.

point'ed·ly, *adv.* in a pointed manner.

point'ed·ness, *n.* sharpness; also, epigrammatical keenness or smartness.

point'el, *n.* 1. in botany, the pistil of a plant. [Obs.]
2. a form of pencil or style used with the medieval tablets. [Obs.]

point'ẽr, *n.* 1. a person or thing that points.
2. a long, tapered rod used by teachers and lecturers for calling attention to things on a map, blackboard, etc.
3. an indicator on a clock, meter, scales, etc.
4. a large, lean hunting dog with a smooth coat, usually white with brown spots: it smells out game and then points until the hunter is ready to fire.

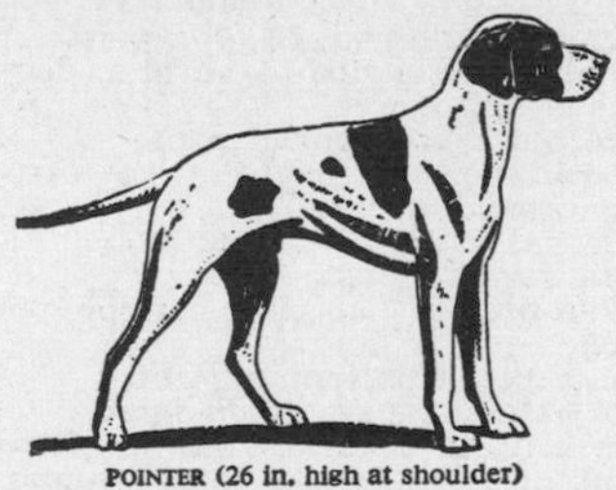

POINTER (26 in. high at shoulder)

5. a hint; clue; tip. [Colloq.]
6. [P–] [*pl.*] in astronomy, the two stars in the Big Dipper that are almost in a direct line with the North Star.
7. in shipbuilding, one of the pieces of timber fixed fore-and-aft and diagonally inside of a vessel's run or quarter, to connect the stern frame with the afterbody.
8. in bricklaying, a tool for clearing out to the required depth the old mortar between the courses of bricks in a wall, to be replaced by a fresh body of mortar.
9. a stone mason's chisel with a sharp point, used in spalling off the face of a stone in the rough.
10. the adjusting lever of a railway switch.

poin'til·lism (pwan'), *n.* [Fr. *pointillisme*, from *pointiller*, to mark with dots.] the method of painting of certain French impressionists, in which a white ground is systematically covered with tiny points of pure color that blend together when seen from a distance, producing a luminous effect.

point'ing, *n.* 1. the act of making sharp.
2. the act of calling attention to or designating, as by pointing the finger.
3. the act of filling the crevices of a wall with mortar, etc.; also, the material with which they are filled.
4. the act of rubbing off the points of wheat in the high-milling process.
5. the act or practice of punctuating; punctuation.
6. in sculpture, the art of measuring the surface of a piece of marble, at various intervals, for the purpose of forming a piece of statuary according to the measurements obtained.
7. in nautical usage, the process of pointing a rope and covering the pointed part with the yarns that have not been taken out.

point'ing·stock, *n.* an object of ridicule or scorn. [Obs.]

point'less, *a.* 1. without a point.
2. without meaning, relevance, or force; senseless; inane; dull.
Syn.—obtuse, blunt, stupid.

point'less·ly, *adv.* in a pointless manner.

point'let·ed, *a.* in botany, having a minute point; apiculate.

poin'trel, *n.* a tool used in engraving. [Obs.]

points'măn, *n.*; *pl.* **points'men,** in England, a man having charge of railroad switches; a switchman.

poise, *n.* [OFr. *pois*; Fr. *poids*; *peser*, to weigh.]
1. balance; stability.
2. ease and dignity of manner.
3. carriage; bearing, as of the body or head.
4. a suspension of activity in a condition of balance.
5. suspense; irresolution; indecision.

poise, *v.t.*; poised, *pt., pp.*; poising, *ppr.* [OFr. *poiser*; Fr. *peser*; L. *pensare*, to weigh out, from *pensus*, pp. of *pendere*, to weigh.]
1. to weigh mentally; to ponder. [Rare.]
2. to make (one thing) balance (*with* or *against* another); to equalize (two things). [Rare.]
3. to balance; to keep steady.
4. to suspend (usually passive or reflexive); as, the earth is *poised* in space.

poise, *v.i.* 1. to be suspended or balanced.
Breathless racers whose hopes *poise* upon the last few steps. —Keats.
2. to hover.

pois'ẽr, *n.* one who or that which balances; specifically, in zoology, the balancer of insects of the order *Diptera*.

poi'sŏn, *n.* [ME. *poisoun*, *puison*; OFr. *poison*; L. *potio (-onis)*, potion; *potare*, to drink.]
1. a substance, usually a drug, causing illness or death when eaten, drunk, or absorbed in relatively small quantities.
2. anything harmful or destructive to happiness or welfare, such as an idea, emotion, etc.; as, the *poison* of tyranny or jealousy.
Syn.—venom, virus, malignity.

poi'sŏn, *v.t.*; poisoned, *pt., pp.*; poisoning, *ppr.*
1. to give poison to; to harm or destroy by means of poison.
2. to put poison on or into.
3. to influence wrongfully; to corrupt; as, they *poisoned* his mind.

poi'sŏn, *v.i.* to act as poison.

poi'sŏn, *a.* poisonous.

poi'sŏn·ȧ·ble, *a.* 1. that can be poisoned. [Rare.]
2. capable of poisoning. [Obs.]

poi'sŏn ash, same as *poison sumac*.

poi'sŏn bāy, in botany, *Illicium floridanum*, a shrub of the magnolia family found in the southeastern part of the United States. Its leaves are supposed to be poisonous.

poi'sŏn bulb, either of two poisonous plants found in the tropics, *Crinum asiaticum* and *Buphane toxicaria*, belonging to the amaryllis family.

poi'sŏn çup, a cup formerly supposed to break when any poison was placed in it. [Archaic.]

poi'sŏn dog'wood, *n.* same as *poison sumac*.

poi'sŏn el'dẽr, same as *poison sumac*.

poi'sŏn·ẽr, *n.* one who or that which poisons.

poi'sŏn gas, any of several toxic chemical agents, in the form of gases, liquids, or solids, used in chemical warfare to kill or harass through inhalation or contact.

poi'sŏn hem'lock, in botany, *Conium maculatum*, a bad-smelling plant with finely cut leaves, small white flowers, and a very poisonous root.

poi'sŏn ī'vy, any of several American sumacs, as *Rhus toxicodendron*, having grayish berries and pointed leaves that grow in groups of three and can cause a skin rash if touched: also called *poison oak*.

POISON IVY

poi'sŏn nut, in botany, (a) the tree that yields nux vomica; (b) nux vomica.

poi'sŏn ōak, in botany, (a) the poison ivy; (b) *Rhus diversiloba*, a plant of western North America, resembling the poison ivy in its appearance and properties.

poi'sŏn·ous, *a.* that can injure or kill by or as by poison; containing, or having the effects of, a poison; venomous.
Syn.—venomous, corruptive, noxious, baneful.

poi'sŏn·ous·ly, *adv.* in a poisonous manner.

poi'sŏn·ous·ness, *n.* the quality of being poisonous.

poi'sŏn pēa, an Australian herb, *Swainsona greyana*, cultivated for its large pink flowers.

poi'sŏn plant, in botany, any one of several Australian plants of the bean family, particularly those of the genus *Gastrolobium*; also, *Swainsona greyana*, the poison pea, and *Lotus australis*.

poi'sŏn·sŏme, *a.* poisonous. [Obs.]

poi'sŏn sụ'maç (*or* shū'), in botany, *Rhus venenata*, a shrub growing in the swampy regions of North America, where it attains a height of from 6 to 18 feet. It bears berries of a greenish-white color and leaves made up of 7 to 13 gray leaflets. The shrub is poisonous to touch and can cause a severe rash. Also called *poison ash*, *poison dogwood*, and *poison elder*.

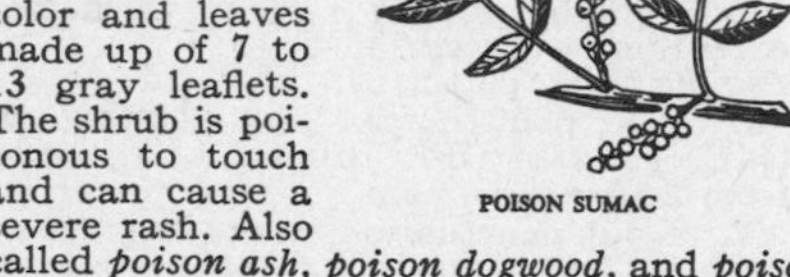
POISON SUMAC

poi'sŏn vīne, in botany, (a) the poison ivy; (b) same as *Virginia silk* under *silk*.

poi'sŏn·wood, *n.* in botany, (a) *Rhus metopium*, a tree of southern Florida and the West Indies having poisonous leaves: known also as *burnwood*, *coral sumac*, *mountain manchineel*, etc.; (b) *Sebastiania lucida*, a tree of the spurge family, found in Florida and the West Indies, having poisonous properties.

poi'sūre (-zhūr), *n.* weight. [Obs.]

poi'trel, *n.* [Fr. *poitrail*, from L. *pectorale*, from *pectus* (*pectoris*), the breast.] armor for the breast of a horse. [Obs.]

poize, *n.* poise. [Archaic.]

pōke, *n.* [ME.; OFr. *poke*.]
1. a sack; bag.
2. a pocket.
3. a baglike growth on the neck, especially of sheep.
[Archaic or Dial. in all senses.]

pōke, *n.* [Am. Ind.] same as *pokeweed*.

pōke, *v.t.*; poked (pōkt), *pt., pp.*; poking, *ppr.* [D. and L.G. *poken*, to poke.]
1. to push; to prod; to jab, as with a stick, an elbow, etc.; as, *poke* him in the ribs.
2. to hit with the fist. [Slang.]
3. to make by poking; as, she *poked* a hole in the wallpaper.
4. to stir up (a fire) by jabbing the coals with a poker (sometimes with *up*).
5. to thrust; to put forward; to intrude; as, *poke* the stake into the ground; don't *poke* your nose into my affairs.
to poke fun; to joke; to jest. [Colloq.]
to poke fun at; to make fun of; to ridicule. [Colloq.]

pōke, *v.i.* 1. to make jabs with a stick, poker, etc. (*at* something).
2. to intrude; to meddle.
3. to pry or search (sometimes with *about* or *around*).
4. to live or move slowly or lazily; to loiter; putter; dawdle (often with *along*).

pōke, *n.* 1. a poking; jab; thrust; nudge.
2. a blow with the fist. [Slang.]
3. a lazy or slow-moving person; dawdler; slowpoke.
4. a poke bonnet.
5. the projecting brim at the front of a poke bonnet.

pōke'ber"ry, *n.*; *pl.* **pōke'ber"rieş,** [*poke* (pokeweed) and *berry*.]
1. the reddish-purple berry of the pokeweed, containing poisonous seeds.
2. the pokeweed.

pōke bon'net, a large bonnet having a wide, projecting brim.

pōke'lō"ken, *n.* [Am. Ind.] a swamp that extends some distance from a river or lake.

pōk'ẽr, *n.* [from *poke*.] one who or that which pokes; specifically, a metal bar used in stirring a fire.

pōk'ẽr, *n.* [corresponds to G. *pochspiel*, from *pochen*, to brag; variety of older game *brag*.] a card game in which the players bet on the value of their hands, the bets forming a pool to be taken by the winner: there are several varieties (see *draw poker*, *stud poker*).

pōk'ẽr, *n.* [compare Dan. *pokker*, the devil, E. *puck*.] any frightful object, especially in the dark; a bugbear. [Rare.]

pōk'ẽr fāce, an expressionless face, as of a poker player trying to conceal the nature of his hand. [Colloq.]

pōk'ẽr·ish, *a.* 1. causing or exciting fear or alarm; as, a *pokerish* place. [Rare.]
2. stiff or rigid like a poker.

pōke'rọọt, *n.* same as *pokeweed*.

pōk'ẽr piç'tūre, a picture or drawing formed by applying a heated poker to the surface of wood.

pōke'weed, *n.* any of several North American weeds of the genus *Phytolacca*, with clusters of purplish-white flowers, reddish-purple berries, and smooth leaves and stems: the roots and berry seeds are poisonous.

pōk'ey, *a.* same as *poky*.

pōk'ing, *a.* drudging; servile. [Rare.]

pōk'ing stick, an instrument formerly used in stiffening the plaits of ruffs. [Obs.]

pōk'y, *a.*; *comp.* pokier; *superl.* pokiest, [from *poke*, to push.]
1. slow; dull; trifling.
2. small and uncomfortable; stuffy, as a place.
3. shabbily dressed; dowdy.

pō·laç'çȧ, *n.* [It. *polacca*; Fr. *polacre*, *polaque*.] a vessel with three masts, used in the Mediterranean. The masts are usually of one piece.

pō·laç'çȧ, see *polonaise*.

Pō'lack, *n.* [from Pol. *Polak*.]
1. a Pole. [Obs.]
2. a person of Polish descent: vulgar term of prejudice and contempt. [Slang.]

pō·lä'çre (-kẽr), *n.* same as first *polacca*.

Pō'lănd Chī'nȧ, an American breed of large hogs, usually black and white.

Pō'lănd·ẽr, *n.* a Pole; a native or inhabitant of Poland.

Pol·ȧ·nis'i·ȧ, *n.* [Gr. *polys*, many, and *anisos*, unequal; *an-* priv., and *isos*, equal.] a genus of plants of the order *Capparidaceæ*. The species are herbaceous plants, native to the warmer parts of Asia and America, with palmate leaves, and terminal clusters of showy flowers.

pō'lăr, *a.* [Fr. *polaire*; LL. *polaris*; L. *polus*, the pole.]
1. of, connected with, or near the North or South Pole.
2. of a pole or poles.
3. having polarity.
4. having two opposite natures, directions, etc.
5. central and guiding, like the earth's pole or the polestar.
polar angle; the angle at a pole formed by two meridians.
polar axis; that axis of an astronomical instrument, as an equatorial, set parallel to the axis of the earth.

polar bear; see *bear*, n.
polar body; a polar globule.
polar cell; a polar globule.
polar circles; the Arctic and Antarctic Circles.
polar co-ordinates; in mathematics, elements in a system of co-ordinates in which points are referred to a fixed point in a fixed straight line by means of a variable distance and a variable angle.
polar distance; the angular distance of any point on a sphere from one of its poles; specifically, the angular distance of a heavenly body from the elevated pole of the heavens.
polar equation; an equation that expresses the relation between the polar co-ordinates of every point of a line or surface.
polar front; in meteorology, the region, or belt, serving as the boundary or transition between the cold air of a polar region and the warmer air of the middle or tropical regions.
polar globule; in biology, one of the minute cells which separate from the ovum at maturation.
polar hare; a large arctic hare, *Lepus timidus*, the fur of which turns white on the approach of winter.
polar lights; (a) the aurora borealis: also called *northern lights*; (b) the aurora australis.
polar projection; the projection of part of the surface of a sphere on the plane of one of the polar circles, the point of projection being at the center of the sphere.
polar whale; the Greenland right whale.

pō′lăr, *n.* in analytical geometry, the reciprocal of a pole. The secant drawn through the points of contact of two intersecting tangents to a conic is called the *polar* of the point of intersection with respect to the conic, and the point is called the *pole* of the secant.

pō·lar′iç, *a.* polar.

pō′lăr·i·ly, *a.* with polarity; in a polary manner. [Obs.]

pō·lăr·im′e·tẽr, *n.* [*polar*, and Gr. *metron*, measure.] an instrument for measuring the degree of polarization in light, the amount of polarized light in a ray, or the amount of rotation of the plane of polarization.

pō·lăr·im′ē·try, *n.* the art or process of measuring or analyzing the polarization of light.

Pō·lā′ris, *n.* [LL.] the North Star; polestar; a star of the second magnitude, standing alone and forming the end of the tail of the constellation Ursa Minor: it marks very nearly the position of the north celestial pole.

pō·lar′i·sçōpe, *n.* [LL. *polaris*, and Gr. *skopein*, to view.] an optical instrument for exhibiting the polarization of light or for looking at things in polarized light.

pō·lar·i·sçop′iç, *a.* of, pertaining to, or obtained through the polariscope.

pō·lăr·is′çō·py, *n.* the art or process of using the polariscope.

pō·lăr·is′tiç, *a.* [*polar* and *-istic.*] pertaining to or exhibiting poles; arising from or dependent upon the possession of poles or polar characteristics; having a polar arrangement or disposition.

pō·lăr″i·strō·bom′ē·tẽr, *n.* [LL. *polaris*, polar, Gr. *strobos*, a whirling round, and *metron*, measure.] a form of polarimeter used in saccharimetry, the distinctive feature of which is the determination of certain parallel black lines appearing and disappearing according to the relative position of the polarizer and analyzer, used as a means of ascertaining the position of the rotated plane of polarization.

pō·lar′i·ty, *n.* 1. the property possessed by bodies having magnetic poles (one positive and attracting, one negative and repelling) of placing themselves so that their two extremities point to the two poles of the earth.
2. any tendency to turn, grow, think, feel, etc. in a certain way, as if because of magnetic attraction or repulsion.
3. the having or showing of two contrary qualities, powers, tendencies, etc.
4. in electricity, the condition of being positive or negative in relation to a magnetic pole.

pō′lăr·ī·zȧ·ble, *a.* that can be polarized.

pō″lăr·i·zā′tion, *n.* 1. the producing of polarity in something, or the acquiring of polarity.
2. in electricity, the production of a reverse electromotive force at the electrodes of a cell, by the depositing on them of gases produced during electrolysis.
3. in optics, (a) a condition of light or radiant heat, in which the transverse vibrations of the rays assume different forms in different planes; (b) the production of this condition.
elliptic polarization; polarization effected after a ray of light is reflected from a metal: also called *circular polarization*.
plane of polarization; that plane in which a ray of polarized light incident at the polarizing angle is reflected to the highest degree. When the polarization is produced by reflection, the plane of reflection is the plane of polarization.

pō′lăr·īze, *v.t.*; polarized, *pt.*, *pp.*; polarizing, *ppr.* to communicate polarity to; to produce polarization in.

pō′lăr·īze, *v.i.* to acquire polarity.

pō′lăr·ī·zẽr, *n.* that which polarizes; specifically, in optics, that part of a polariscope by which light is polarized: distinguished from *analyzer*.

pō′lăr·oid, *n.* a thin, transparent, filmlike material having marked properties of light polarization and a wide variety of uses in optics, scientific research, photography, etc.: a trade-mark (*Polaroid*).

pō·lȧ·tōuçhe′ (-tōsh′), *n.* [Fr., from Russ. *poletuchii*, flying.] a small flying squirrel, *Sciuropterus volans*, native to northern Europe and Asia.

pōl′dẽr, *n.* [D.] a tract of low land reclaimed from a lake, river, or sea by means of high embankments.

Pōle, *n.* a native or inhabitant of Poland.

pōle, *n.* [Fr. *pole*; L. *polus*, the pole of the heavens, the heavens, from Gr. *polos*, the axis of the sphere, the firmament, from *polein*, to be in motion.]
1. either end of any axis, as of the earth, of the celestial sphere, or of a cell nucleus.
2. a region contiguous to either end of the earth's axis, as the North and South Poles.
3. either of two opposed or differentiated forces, parts, or principles, such as the ends of a magnet, the terminals of a battery, cell, motor, or dynamo, or two extremes of opinion, etc.
4. a point of reference, as for a system of points or lines in mathematics, or for a series of arguments in logic.
5. the polestar. [Obs.]
6. the firmament; the sky. [Obs.]
poles apart; widely separated; having opposite natures, opinions, etc.; at opposite extremes.
poles of a circle of a sphere; the points in which the diameter of the sphere perpendicular to the plane of the circle pierces the surface of the sphere.

pōle, *n.* [ME.; AS. *pol*, *pal*; L. *palus*, a stake.]
1. a long, slender piece of wood, usually rounded; a long rod of any material; as, a tent *pole*, telephone *pole*.
2. a tapering wooden shaft attached to the front axle of a wagon or carriage and to the collars of the horses.
3. a unit of measure, equal to one rod in linear measure or one square rod in square measure.
under bare poles; (a) with all sails furled because of the force of a gale; (b) naked; stripped.

pōle, *v.t.*; poled, *pt.*, *pp.*; poling, *ppr.* 1. to furnish with poles for support; as, to *pole* beans.
2. to bear or convey on poles; as, to *pole* hay into a barn.
3. to impel by poles, as a boat; to push forward by the use of poles.
4. to stir with a pole.

pōle, *v.i.* to propel a boat or raft with a pole.

pōle′ax, pōle′axe, *n.* [from *pol* (poll), head, and *ax*.]
1. a long-handled battle-ax.
2. any ax with a spike, hook, or hammer opposite the blade.

POLEAXES

pōle′ax, pōle′axe, *v.t.* to attack or fell with or as with a poleax.

pōle bēan, any variety of bean trained upon poles, as the Lima bean or the scarlet runner.

pōle′bŭrn, *n.* a disease affecting tobacco while it is being cured.

pōle′çat, *n.* [prob. from Fr. *poule*, a hen, and *cat*.]
1. a small, bad-smelling European animal, *Putorius fœtidus*, akin to the marten, but with a broader head, a blunter snout, and a much shorter tail.
2. any of various small animals having a fetid odor, as a skunk.

pōle′çat weed, the skunk cabbage.

pōle çrab, a double loop on a carriage pole for receiving the breast straps or chains.

pōle·dā′vy, *n.* a sort of coarse canvas. [Obs.]

pōle floun′dẽr, a large flounder, *Glyptocephalus cynoglossus*, found in deep waters along the northern coasts of Europe and America, and greatly esteemed as food.

pōle hŏrse, a horse harnessed to the pole of a wagon, tandem, etc., and nearest the wheels.

pōle lāthe, a simple form of lathe in which the work is supported and turned by a strap that passes two or three times round it, the lower end of the strap being connected to the treadle, and the upper end to a spring pole above.

pōle′less, *a.* having no pole; as, a *poleless* chariot.

pol′e·märçh, *n.* [Gr. *polemarchos*; *polemos*, war, and *archē*, rule.] in ancient Greece, originally, the military commander in chief; later, a civil magistrate who had under his care all strangers and visitors in Athens.

pōle măst, a mast consisting of a single length.

pō·lem′iç, pō·lem′iç·ăl, *a.* [Gr. *polemikos*, from *polemos*, war.]
1. of or involving dispute; controversial; intended to maintain an opinion or system in opposition to others; as, a *polemic* treatise, discourse, or book; *polemic* divinity.
2. argumentative; engaged in supporting an opinion or system by contention; as, a *polemic* writer.

pō·lem′iç, *n.* 1. a person inclined to argument; a disputant; a controvertist; one who writes in support of an opinion or system in opposition to another.
2. an argument or controversial discussion.

pō·lem′iç·ăl·ly, *adv.* in a polemic manner; controversially.

pō·lem′i·cist, *n.* a skilled debater or writer of polemic discussions.

pō·lem′içs, *n. pl.* [*construed as sing.*] 1. the art or practice of disputation or controversy.
2. a dispute.
3. that branch of theological science dealing with the history of ecclesiastical controversy.

pol′e·mist, *n.* an argumentative person.

Pol·ē·mō·ni·ā′cē·ae, *n.pl.* a family of monopetalous exogens with a trifid stigma, three-celled fruit, and seeds attached to an axile placenta, the embryo lying in the midst of albumen. They consist for the most part of brightly-flowered herbaceous plants, native to temperate countries, and particularly abundant in the northwestern parts of America. The genera *Collomia*, *Phlox*, *Leptosiphon Gilia*, and *Polemonium* are cultivated for their showy blossoms.

pol·ē·mō·ni·ā′ceous, *a.* pertaining to the family *Polemoniaceæ*.

Pol·ē·mō′ni·um, *n.* [Gr. *polemōnion*, some kind of plant.] a genus of plants belonging to the family *Polemoniaceæ*. It includes the Greek valerian, or Jacob's-ladder, a blue-flowered British perennial, growing wild in some places in the north of England, and also cultivated in gardens.

pō·lem′ō·sçōpe, *n.* [Gr. *polemos*, war, and *skopein*, to view.] a perspective glass with an angled mirror, for seeing objects that do not lie directly before the eye.

pol′e·my, *n.* warfare; also, contention; opposition. [Obs.]

pō·len′tȧ, *n.* [It.] a porridge made of barley, chestnut meal, or corn meal, eaten especially in Italy.

pōle plāte, in carpentry, a timber laid on the ends of the tie beams of a roof to receive the rafters.

pōl′ẽr, *n.* 1. a pole horse.
2. one who poles a boat.

pōl′ẽr, *n.* an extortioner. [Obs.]

pōle′stär, *n.* 1. Polaris, a star that is vertical, or nearly so, to the pole of the earth: also called *North Star*.
2. that which serves as a guide or director.

pōle vąult, 1. an event in which the contestant leaps for height, vaulting over a bar with the aid of a long pole.
2. a leap so performed.

pōle′-vąult, *v.i.* to perform or compete in the pole vault.

pōle′wărd, *adv.* toward one of the poles of the earth.

pōle′wig, *n.* a fish, the European spotted goby. [Brit. Dial.]

pō′ley, *n.* same as *poly*.

pō′ley, *a.* having no horns; polled. [Brit. Dial.]

pō′ley·moun″tain (-tin), *n.* a plant of the genus *Teucrium.*

Pō′li·ăn, *a.* discovered by or named in honor of G. S. Poli, Italian naturalist.

Polian vesicles; caecal diverticula of the circular vessel of the ambulacral system of *Echinodermata.*

pō′li·ȧ·nīte, *n.* [Gr. *poliainesthai,* to grow white or gray.] a light steel-gray manganese dioxide occurring in tetragonal crystals of about the hardness of quartz.

Pol·i·an′thēṣ, *n.* [Gr. *polios,* gray, and *anthos,* a flower.] a genus of plants, one species of which, *Polianthes tuberosa,* is widely cultivated for its flowers.

pō·lïce′ (-lēs′), *n.* [Fr., from L. *politia,* Gr. *politeia,* government of a city (*polis*).]

1. the regulation of morals, safety, sanitation, etc.; public order; law enforcement.

2. the governmental department (of a city, state, etc.) organized for keeping order and for preventing, detecting, and punishing crimes.

3. an official body of persons, established and maintained for keeping order, etc.

4. [*construed as pl.*] the members of such a force or governmental department.

5. in the United States Army, (a) the act or duty of maintaining order or cleanliness in a camp, etc.; (b) the soldiers charged with maintaining order; (c) any nonmilitary duty or detail; as, kitchen *police.*

police commissioner; see under *commissioner.*

police constable or *police officer*; a policeman.

police court; an inferior court having jurisdiction over minor offenses and misdemeanors, and the power to hold for trial those charged with more serious crimes.

police dog; a dog specially trained to assist police, etc; especially, in popular use, a German shepherd (or German police).

POLICE DOG (German shepherd)

police inspector; an officer of the police having a rank just below that of superintendent.

police judge, justice, or *magistrate*; an officer presiding over a police court.

police jury; in the state of Louisiana, a body or board having charge of certain local police regulations and duties.

police offense; a minor offense against the order of the community, or one coming within the jurisdiction of a police judge.

police power; the power of the state, through all its agencies, to insure the lawful enjoyment of the rights of the citizen: it embraces the entire system of internal regulation.

police state, a government that seeks to intimidate and suppress political opposition by means of a secret police force.

police station; the headquarters of a local or district police force, where arrested persons are first charged.

pō·lïce′, *v.t.*; policed (-lēst′), *pt., pp.*; policing, *ppr.* 1. to place under the control of a police system; to keep in order with or as police or the like; as, *police* the street.

2. to make or keep (a military camp, etc.) clean or orderly (sometimes with *up*); as, to *police* a garrison.

pō·lïced′, *a.* regulated by laws; furnished with a regular system of laws and administration.

pō·lïce′măn, *n.*; *pl.* **pō·lïce′men,** a member of a police force; a peace officer; a constable.

pō·lïce′wom″ăn (-woom″), *n.*; *pl.* **pō·lïce′wom″en** (-wim″), a woman member of a police force.

pō·li′ciăl (-lish′al), *a.* pertaining to the police. [Rare.]

pol·i·clin′iç, *n.* [Gr. *polis,* city, and *klinē,* bed.] the department of a hospital where outpatients are treated: see also *polyclinic.*

pol′i·cy, *n.*; *pl.* **pol′i·cieṣ,** [OFr. *policie*; L. *politia*; Gr. *politeia,* polity, from *polis,* city.]

1. political wisdom or cunning; diplomacy; prudence; artfulness.

2. wise, expedient, or crafty conduct or management.

3. any governing principle, plan, or course of action.

4. in Scotland, the improved grounds about a country house. [Obs.]

5. polity. [Obs.]

pol′i·cy, *n.*; *pl.* **pol′i·cieṣ,** [Fr. *police*; It. *polizza*; ML. *apodixa*; Gr. *apodeixis,* proof, from *apodeiknynai,* to display, make known.]

1. a written contract in which one party guarantees to insure another against a specified loss or misfortune, in consideration of periodic payments called premiums: in full, *insurance policy.*

2. a gambling on lottery numbers: see *policy racket.*

3. a ticket or warrant for money in the public funds. [Obs.]

interest policy; a policy wherein the assured has a real interest in the thing insured.

open policy; a policy in which the value of the thing insured is left to be ascertained in case of loss.

valued policy; a policy in which a valuation is set in advance on the things insured.

wager or *wagering policy*; a policy or pretended insurance founded on risk wherein the assured, having no real interest in the thing insured, could sustain no loss by the happening of any of the contingencies against which the insurance was issued; a gambling policy.

pol′i·cy book, a record of policies, kept by insurance companies or their agents.

pol′i·cy·hōld″ẽr, *n.* one who holds an insurance policy or contract.

pol′i·cy rack′et, a lottery based on the appearance of a specific number in some daily statistical table: also *numbers pool.*

pol′i·cy shop, a place in which the gambling game of policy is played.

pol′i·cy slip, a ticket issued to the player in the game of policy as evidence of his bet.

pol″i·en·ceph·ȧ·lī′tis, *n.* [Gr. *polios,* gray, and E. *encephalitis.*] an inflammatory disease of the gray matter of the brain.

pol′i·gär, *n.* [E. Ind.] in Madras, a semi-independent feudal chieftain; also, the follower of such a chieftain.

pōl′ing, *n.* 1. support or propulsion by means of poles.

2. the planks, boards, or poles used to line a tunnel during its construction, to prevent the falling of earth or other loose material.

pō′li·ō (*or* pol′i-ō), *n.* poliomyelitis. [Colloq.]

pol″i·ō·mȳ″e·lī′tis, *n.* [Mod. L., from Gr. *polios,* gray, pale, and *myelos,* marrow.] inflammation of the gray matter of the spinal cord; especially, infantile paralysis.

Pōl′ish, *a.* of or pertaining to Poland, its people, their culture, or their language.

Pōl′ish, *n.* the West Slavic language of the Poles.

pol′ish, *v.t.*; polished (-isht), *pt., pp.*; polishing, *ppr.* [ME. *polischen*; Fr. *polissant,* ppr. of *polir*; L. *polire,* to polish.]

1. to make smooth and glossy, usually by friction; as, to *polish* glass, marble, metals, and the like.

2. to refine (manners, style, appearance, literary work, etc.); to remove crudity or vulgarity from; to make elegant and polite.

The Greeks were *polished* by the Asiatics and Egyptians. —S. S. Smith.

3. to complete or embellish; to finish; to perfect.

to polish off; (a) to finish (a meal, job, etc.) completely and quickly; (b) to overcome or get rid of (a competitor, enemy, etc.). [Colloq.]

to polish up; to improve. [Colloq.]

pol′ish, *v.i.* 1. to become smooth; to receive a gloss; to take a smooth and glossy surface.

Steel will *polish* almost as white and bright as silver. —Bacon.

2. to become polite and refined; to acquire elegance.

pol′ish, *n.* 1. a surface gloss, usually produced by friction.

Another prism of clearer glass and better *polish* seemed free from veins.—Newton.

2. anything used to produce a gloss or luster; a varnish; as, furniture *polish*; shoe *polish.*

3. refinement; elegance of manners.

What are these wondrous civilizing arts,
This Roman *polish?* —Addison.

4. a polishing or being polished.

pol′ish·ȧ·ble, *a.* capable of being polished.

pol′ished (-isht), *a.* 1. (a) made smooth and glossy, as by rubbing; (b) having a naturally smooth and shiny surface.

2. refined; elegant; polite.

3. without error or flaw; as, a *polished* performance.

pol′ished·ness, *n.* the state or characteristic of being polished or of being refined and elegant.

pol′ish·ẽr, *n.* one who or that which polishes.

pol′ish·ing, *n.* 1. the act of making or condition of being made smooth.

2. the act of refining or making elegant; refinement.

pol′ish·ing ī′ron (-ũrn), 1. an iron used to produce a gloss on shirt bosoms, collars, etc.

2. a tool used by bookbinders to finish the covers of books.

pol′ish·ing slāte, 1. a gray or yellow slate found in the coal regions of France and Bohemia, used for polishing glass, metal, etc.

2. a hone; an oilstone; a whetstone.

pol′ish·ing snāke, a variety of serpentine found in Scotland, formerly used for polishing lithographic stones.

pol′ish·ing wheel (hwēl), a wheel composed of or coated with material that polishes surfaces when it is rotated rapidly against them.

pol′ish·ment, *n.* refinement. [Rare.]

Po·lit′bū·rō, *n.* [from Russ. *Polit*cheskoe *Buro,* political bureau.] a leading committee of the Communist Party of the Soviet Union, having the responsibility of analyzing events, determining policy, etc. between sessions of the larger Central Committee: replaced by the Presidium in 1952.

pō·līte′, *a.*; *comp.* politer; *superl.* politest, [L. *politus,* pp. of *polire,* to polish.]

1. smooth; lustrous; glossy. [Obs.]

Rays of light falling on a *polite* surface. —Newton.

2. polished, cultured, elegant, correct, or refined in behavior; well-bred.

He marries, bows at court, and grows *polite.* —Pope.

3. courteous; having good manners.

Syn.—civil, courteous, genteel, polished, refined, well-bred, accomplished, finished.

pō·līte′, *v.t.* to make polite or polished; to refine. [Obs.]

pō·līte′ly, *adv.* 1. in a polite manner; with elegance of manners; genteelly; courteously.

2. with a polished or glossy surface; smoothly. [Obs.]

pō·līte′ness, *n.* 1. the quality of being polite; polish or elegance of manners; gentility; good breeding; ease and gracefulness of manners.

2. courteousness; complaisance.

3. smoothness; gloss. [Obs.]

Syn.—courtesy, affability, urbanity.

pol·i·tesse′, *n.* [Fr.] politeness.

pol′i·tiç, *a.* [L. *politicus*; Gr. *politikos,* relating to a citizen, *polites,* from *polis,* city.]

1. wise; prudent and sagacious in devising and pursuing measures; shrewd; diplomatic: applied to persons; as, a *politic* prince.

2. prudently or artfully contrived; well-devised; adapted to its end; expedient, as a plan, action, remark, etc.

This land was famously enriched
With *politic* grave counsel. —Shak.

3. crafty; unscrupulous; cunning; artful.

I have been *politic* with my friend, smooth with my enemy. —Shak.

4. political; consisting of citizens; constituting the state. [Rare.]

States or bodies *politic* are to be considered as moral persons having a public will, capable and free to do right and wrong. —Kent.

Syn.—prudent, wise, sagacious, provident, diplomatic, judicious, cunning, wary, well-devised, discreet.

pol′i·tiç, *n.* a politician. [Rare.]

pō·lit′i·çăl, *a.* [from L. *politicus.*]

1. of or concerned with government, the state, or politics.

2. having a definite governmental organization.

3. engaged in or taking sides in politics; as, *political* parties.

4. of or characteristic of political parties or politicians; as, *political* pressure.

5. artful; skillful; politic. [Obs.]

pō·lit'i·çăl, *n.* a political offender; a political prisoner.
pō·lit'i·çăl ē·çon'ō·my, economics.
pō·lit'i·çăl·iṣm, *n.* party spirit or zeal; political ardor.
pō·lit'i·çăl lib'ẽr·ty, the right to participate in determining the form, choosing the officials, making the laws, and carrying on the functions of one's government.
pō·lit'i·çăl·ly, *adv.* 1. with relation to the government of a nation or state.
2. with relation to politics.
3. in a political manner.
4. artfully. [Obs.]
pō·lit'i·çăl sci'ence (sī'), the science of political institutions, or of the principles, organization, and methods of government.
pō·lit'i·ças·tẽr, *n.* a petty politician.
pol·i·ti'ciăn, *a.* 1. cunning; using artifice. [Rare.]
2. pertaining to politicians or the methods of politics. [Rare.]
pol·i·ti'ciăn, *n.* [Fr. *politicien.*]
1. a person actively engaged in politics, especially party politics, professionally or otherwise; often, a person holding or seeking political office: frequently used in a derogatory sense, with implications of seeking personal or partisan gain, scheming, opportunism, etc., as distinguished from *statesman*, which suggests able, far-seeing, principled conduct of public affairs.
2. a person skilled or experienced in practical politics or political science. [Now Rare.]
pō·lit'i·cīze, *v.i.*; politicized, *pt., pp.*; politicizing, *ppr.* 1. to talk politics.
2. to take part in politics.
pō·lit'i·cīze, *v.t.* 1. to make political.
2. to discuss politically.
pō·lit'i·cist, *n.* one who writes on politics. [Rare.]
pol'i·tiç·ly, *adv.* in a politic manner.
pō·lit'i·çō, *n.* [Sp. *político* or It. *politico.*] a politician.
pō·lit'i·çō-, a combining form meaning *political and.*
pol'i·tiçs, *n.pl.* [*construed as sing. except in sense 6.*] [Fr. *politique*; Gr. *politikē*, from *polis*, city.]
1. the science and art of political government; political science.
2. [P–] a treatise on political science by Aristotle (384–322 B. C.).
3. political affairs.
4. the conducting of or participation in political affairs, often as a profession.
5. political methods, tactics, etc.
6. political opinions, principles, or party connections.
pol'i·ty, *n.*; *pl.* **pol'i·tieṣ**, [Gr. *politeia.*]
1. the form, constitution, system, or fundamental principles of government of any political body or other organization; the recognized principles on which any institution is based.

> He looked with indifference on rites, names, and forms of ecclesiastical *polity*. —Macaulay.

2. any body of persons having an organized system of government; a state or body politic.
3. policy; art; management; expediency. [Obs.]
Syn.—policy.—*polity* is confined to the structure of a government, as civil or ecclesiastical *polity*; while *policy* is applied to the management of both public and private affairs; as, foreign or domestic *policy*; business *policy*.
pō·litz"ẽr·i·zā'tion, *n.* [from Adam *Politzer*, an Austrian otologist.] the act of politzerizing.
pō·litz'ẽr·īze, *v.t.*; politzerized, *pt., pp.*; politzerizing, *ppr.* to force air into the nostrils of (a patient) to cause inflation of the tympanum and Eustachian tube, while the patient closes the pharynx by swallowing.
pōl'kȧ, *n.* [Fr. and G.; prob. from Czech *pulka*, half step.]
1. a fast dance for couples, developed in Bohemia in the early nineteenth century.
2. the basic step of this dance, a hop followed by three small steps.
3. music for this dance, in fast duple time.
pōl'kȧ, *v.i.* to dance the polka.
pōl'kȧ dot (pō'kȧ), 1. one of the small round dots regularly spaced to form a pattern on cloth.
2. a pattern or cloth with such dots.
pōl'kȧ jack'et, a knitted jacket for women.
Poll, poll, *n.* [*Polly*, for *Molly*, dim. of *Mary.*] a parrot: also called *Polly, poll parrot.* [Colloq.]
poll, *n.* [Gr. *pōlloi*, the many, the rabble.] at Cambridge University, one who receives no honors, but merely takes a degree. [Brit. Slang.]
pōll, *n.* [ME. *pol, polle*; M.D. *polle, pol*, top of the head, head.]
1. the head; especially, the crown, back, or hair of the head.
2. an individual person, especially one among several, as one of twelve jurors.
3. a counting, listing, or register of persons, especially of voters.
4. a voting or expression of opinion by individuals.
5. the amount of voting; the number of votes recorded.
6. [*usually in pl.*] a place where votes are cast and recorded.
7. a poll tax.
8. a canvassing of a selected sample group of people in an attempt to discover opinion on some question.
9. the blunt end of a hammer head.
pōll, *v.t.*; polled, *pt., pp.*; polling, *ppr.* [ME. *pollen.*]
1. to cut off or cut short.
2. to cut off or trim the wool, hair, horns, or branches of.
3. to take or register the votes of; as, to *poll* a county.
4. to receive (a certain number or proportion of votes); to receive the votes of (certain voters): said of a candidate.
5. to cast (a vote).
6. to canvass in a poll (sense 8).
to poll a jury; to ask each member of the jury individually for his verdict.
pōll, *v.i.* to vote at an election; to register a vote.
pol'lăck, *n.*; *pl.* **pol'lăck** or **pol'lăcks**, [Scotch *podlok.*] a salt-water food fish of the cod family closely allied to the whiting and coal fish, and belonging to the genus *Pollachius*: also spelled *pollock.* The common pollack of Europe, *Pollachius pollachius*, is also called *lob, leet, lythe, greenling, greenfish, green-cod, skeet*, and *whiting pollack. Pollachius virens* is the North Atlantic coalfish, or green pollack; *Pollachius chalcogrammus*, the Pacific pollack.

POLLACK (*Pollachius pollachius*)

pōl'ăġe, *n.* 1. a capitation or poll tax. [Rare.]
2. extortion; robbery. [Rare.]
pol'lăn, *n.* a whitefish, *Coregonus pollan*, found in some of the lakes of Ireland. It resembles the herring in appearance.
pol'lărd, *n.* [from *poll*, to cut off.]
1. a hornless animal, as a goat, deer, ox, etc.
2. a tree with its top branches cut back to the trunk, so as to cause a dense growth of new shoots.
3. a clipped coin; also, a spurious or counterfeit coin which was smuggled into England in the time of Edward I. [Obs.]
4. a coarse product of wheat, but finer than bran.
pol'lărd, *v.t.*; pollarded, *pt., pp.*; pollarding, *ppr.* to make a pollard of; to convert into a pollard by cutting off the top, as trees.
pōll'ax, pōll'axe, *n.* a poleax. [Obs.]
pōll' book, a book or list of registered voters in a precinct, county, etc.
pōlled, *a.* 1. with the branches cut off or trimmed; made into a pollard; lopped.
2. shorn of hair; cropped. [Archaic.]
3. having the antlers or horns removed, or being without antlers or horns; as, *polled* deer; *polled* cattle.
pōll·ee', *n.* a person questioned in a poll.
pol'len, *n.* [L. *pollen, pollis*, fine flour.] the yellow, powderlike male sex cells on the stamens of a flower.
pol'len bȧs'ket, a corbiculum; a concave basket-shaped area on the legs of a bee which serves to collect and carry pollen: also called *pollen plate.*
pol'len çȧ·tärrh' (-tär'), hay fever.
pol'len çount, the number of grains of a specified variety of pollen, usually ragweed, present in a given volume of air, usually a cubic yard, at a specified time and place.
pol'lened (-lend), *a.* covered with pollen.
pol'len fē'vẽr, hay fever: called also *pollen catarrh.*
pol·le·nif'ẽr·ous, *a.* same as *polliniferous.*
pol'len·īze, *v.t.*; pollenized, *pt., pp.*; pollenizing, *ppr.* same as *pollinize.*
pol'len mȧss, an agglutinated mass of pollen grains; a pollinium.
pol'len plāte, same as *pollen basket.*
pol'len saç, the cell or cavity of an anther in which pollen is developed.
pol'len tūbe, in botany, one of the tubular processes developed by the pollen when it comes in contact with the stigma.
pōll'ẽr, *n.* [from v. *poll.*]
1. one who polls; one who shaves or shears persons; a barber. [Obs.]
2. one who lops or polls trees.
3. a pillager; a plunderer; one who fleeces by extortion. [Obs.]
4. one who registers voters, or one who enters his name as a voter.
pōll ē'vil (-vl), a swelling or abscess on a horse's head, originating as an inflammation below the great ligament of the neck.
pol'lex, *n.*; *pl.* **pol'li·cēṣ**, [L.] in anatomy, the innermost of the five normal digits of the anterior limb of the higher vertebrates; the thumb in man.
pol'li·çăl, *a.* of or pertaining to the pollex.
pol·lic·i·tā'tion, *n.* [L. *pollicitatio*, from *pollicitari*, intens. of *polliceri*, to promise.]
1. a promise; a voluntary engagement or a paper containing it. [Rare.]
2. in Roman law, a promise without mutuality; a promise not yet accepted by the person to whom it is made.
pol'li·năr, *a.* [LL. *pollinaris.*] in botany, covered with a very fine dust resembling pollen.
pol·li·năr'i·um, *n.*; *pl.* **pol·li·năr'i·ȧ**, in phanerogams, same as *pollinium.*
pol'li·nāte, *v.t.*; pollinated, *pt., pp.*; pollinating, *ppr.* in botany, to convey pollen from the anther to the stigma of; as, some flowers are *pollinated* by the wind, others by the agency of insects.
pol·li·nā'tion, *n.* in botany, the conveyance of the pollen from the anther to the stigma.
pōll'ing, *n.* 1. the act of shearing, lopping, or clipping, as trees.
2. the act of plundering. [Obs.]
3. the act of voting or casting a ballot; also, the act of registering or placing one's name on the poll books.
pōll'ing bo͝oth, a polling place; also, a closet-like structure used at elections for the convenience and privacy of voters.
pol·li·nif'ẽr·ous, *a.* [L. *pollen*, and *ferre*, to produce.] bearing, yielding, or carrying pollen.
pol·lin'i·um, *n.*; *pl.* **pol·lin'i·ȧ**, [LL.] an agglutinated mass of pollen, as in the milkweed and some orchids; a pollen mass.
pol'li·nīze, *v.t.*; pollinized, *pt., pp.*; pollinizing, *ppr.* to pollinate.
pol'li·nōse, *a.* in entomology, covered with a substance resembling pollen, especially when yellow in color.
pol·li·nō'sis, *n.* [L. *pollen*, pollen, and *-osis.*] hay fever.
pol'li·wog, pol'li·wig, *n.* [ME. *polwygle*; from *poll* (the head) and *wiggle.*] a tadpole: also spelled *pollywog.*
pol'lŏck, *n.* see *pollack.*
poll par'rŏt, a parrot. [Colloq.]
pōll pick, a kind of pick used by miners: it has a stem or arm with a sledgelike head, or poll, which is used as a hammer for driving.
pōll'stẽr, *n.* a person who conducts polls (sense 8).
pōll tax, a tax per head: in some States payment of a poll tax is a prerequisite for voting.
poll'-tax, *a.* of, having, or advocating a poll tax, especially as a means of limiting the electorate.
pol'lụ·cīte, *n.* [L. *Pollux* (*-uctis*) and *-ite.*] an isometric mineral, hydrated cesium aluminum silicate, occurring in the granite of the island of Elba, having a vitreous luster on fractured surfaces but dull externally: it is colorless and transparent.
pŏl·lū'tănt, *n.* [*pollute* and *-ant.*] something that pollutes; especially, a harmful chemical or waste material discharged into the water or atmosphere.
pŏl·lūte', *v.t.*; polluted, *pt., pp.*; polluting, *ppr.* [L. *pollutus*, pp. of *polluere*, to pollute; *pol-*, for *por-* or *pro-*, forth, and *luere*, to wash.]
1. to make foul or unclean; to taint; to contaminate; to defile; to soil.
2. to corrupt or destroy the moral purity of.
Let not earth's kings *pollute* the work

That was done in their despite.—John Hay.
3. to render unclean or unfit for sacred services or uses; to desecrate.
Syn.—defile, soil, taint, debase, deprave, violate.

pŏl·lūte′, *a.* polluted. [Archaic.]

pŏl·lūt′ed·ly, *adv.* with pollution.

pŏl·lūt′ed·ness, *n.* the quality or state of being polluted; pollution; defilement.

pŏl·lūt′ẽr, *n.* one who pollutes, defiles, or profanes; a defiler.

pŏl·lūt′ing, *a.* adapted or tending to defile or infect; as, a *polluting* influence.

pŏl·lūt′ing·ly, *adv.* so as to pollute.

pŏl·lū′tion, *n.* [Fr., from L. *pollutio.*] a polluting or being polluted.

Pol′lux, *n.* [L.] 1. in Greek and Roman mythology, the son of Leda by Zeus, and twin brother of Castor.
2. one of the two bright stars in the constellation Gemini.
3. [p—] in mineralogy, same as *pollucite.*

Pol′ly, *n.* a parrot. [Colloq.]

Pol·ly·an′nȧ, *n.* [name of the young heroine of a novel by Eleanor H. Porter (1868–1920), Am. writer.] an excessively or persistently optimistic person.

pol′ly·wog, *n.* see *polliwog.*

pō′lō, *n.* [prob. from Tibet *pulu*, a ball.]
1. a game played on horseback by two teams of four players each, who attempt to drive a small wooden ball through the opponents' goal with long-handled mallets.
2. water polo.

pō′lō, *n.* [Sp.] a Spanish gypsy dance.

pō′lō çōat, a type of loose, tailored overcoat made of camel's hair or a similar fabric.

pō′lō·ist, *n.* a person who plays polo.

pō·lō·nāiṣe′, *n.* [Fr., fem. of *polonais*, Polish.]
1. a dress with the skirt divided in front and worn looped back over an elaborate underskirt: originally worn by Polish women.
2. a stately Polish dance in triple time, almost processional in character.
3. music for, or in the rhythm of, this dance.

POLONAISE

Pō·lō·nēṣe′, *n.* 1. the Polish language. [Obs.]
2. [p—] same as *polonaise*, 1.

pō·lō′ni·um, *n.* [Mod.L.: so named by its co-discoverer, Marie Curie, after her native land, Poland (ML. *Polonia*).] a radioactive chemical element formed by the disintegration of radium: symbol, Po; atomic weight, approximately 210; atomic number, 84: also called *radium F.*

Pō·lō′ni·us, *n.* in Shakespeare's Hamlet, a voluble, sententious old courtier, lord chamberlain to the king and father of Ophelia and Laertes.

pō·lō′ny, *n.* [probably a corruption of Bologna.] a kind of sausage.

pō′lō shirt, a short-sleeved, usually knitted, pull-over sport shirt for men and boys, somewhat like a T-shirt, but generally with a buttoned collar.

pōlt, *n.* [L. *pultare*, to strike.] a striking; a blow; a stroke. [Obs.]

pōl′tẽr·geist, *n.* [G.] literally, a noisy ghost; a ghost supposed to be responsible for table rappings and other mysterious noisy disturbances.

pōlt′foot, *n.* a clubfoot. [Archaic.]

pŏl·tin′nik, *n.*; *pl.* **pŏl·tin′ni·ky**, a Russian silver half ruble.

pol·troon′, *n.* [Fr. *poltron*; It. *poltrone*, an idle fellow, a coward, from O.H.G. *polstar, bolstar*, a pillow.] a thorough coward; a craven.

pol·troon′, *a.* cowardly; contemptible.

pol·troon′ẽr·y, *n.* cowardice.

pol·troon′ish, *a.* resembling a poltroon; cowardly; contemptible.

pol·troon′ish·ly, *adv.* in a poltroonish manner.

pol′vẽr·ine, *n.* [It. *polverino*, from L. *pulvis, pulveris*, dust.] the calcined ashes of a plant from the Levant, used in glassmaking.

pō′ly, *n.* [L. *polium*, from Gr. *polion*, from *polios*, white.] a labiate plant, *Teucrium polium*: it is an evergreen shrub, growing in southern Europe: also called *polymountain.* The name is sometimes applied to other plants of the same genus.

pol′y-, [from Gr. *polys*, much or many.] a combining form meaning: (a) *much, many, more than one*, as in *poly*chromatic, *poly*andry; (b) *more than usual, excessive*, as in *poly*phagia; (c) *in* or *of many kinds* or *parts*, as in *poly*morphous.

pol″y·ȧ·çan′thid, *a.* having many spines near the ambulacra, as certain starfishes.

pol″y·ȧ·çan′thous, *a.* [Gr. *polys*, many, and *akantha*, spine.] in botany, having many spines.

pol″y·ȧ·çöus′tiç, *a.* [*poly-* and *acoustic.*] capable of multiplying or increasing sound.

pol″y·ȧ·çöus′tiç, *n.* an instrument for multiplying or increasing sound.

pol″y·ȧ·çöus′tiçs, *n.* the art of multiplying or increasing sound.

pol′y·açt, pol·y·aç′ti·năl, *a.* [*poly-*, and Gr. *aktis*, ray.] having many rays, as a stellate sponge spicule.

Pol·y·aç′tis, *n.* in botany, a genus of hyphomycetous fungi, suborder *Mucedines. Polyactis vulgaris* is a common mold on decaying plants.

pol′y·ad, *n.* a multivalent element or radical.

pol′y·ȧ·delph, *n.* [*poly-*, and Gr. *adelphos*, brother.] a plant belonging to the class *Polyadelphia*, whose stamens are joined or bound in three or more bundles by the filaments.

POLYADELPH

Pol″y·ȧ·del′phi·ȧ, *n.pl.* [*poly-*, and Gr. *adelphos*, brother.] in the Linnean system, a class of plants having stamens united in three or more bodies or bundles by the filaments.

pol″y·ȧ·del′phous, pol″y·ȧ·del′phi·ăn, *a.* having stamens united in three or more bundles.

Pol·y·an′dri·ȧ, *n.* [*poly-*, and Gr. *anēr, andros*, a male.] in the Linnean system, a class of monoclinous or hermaphrodite plants having twenty or more stamens on the receptacle.

pol·y·an′dri·ăn, *a.* polyandrous.

pol·y·an′driç, *a.* relating to polyandry; having many husbands.

pol·y·an′drist, *n.* a person who practices polyandry.

pol·y·an′drous, *a.* 1. practicing polyandry.
2. of or characterized by polyandry.
3. in botany, having many stamens.

POLYANDRIA (*Anemone nemorosa*)
a, stamens and pistils

pol′y·an·dry, *n.* [Gr. *polyandria*, from *polys*, many, and *anēr, andros*, a man.]
1. the state or practice of having two or more husbands at the same time.
2. in botany, the presence of twenty or more stamens in one flower.
3. in zoology, the mating of one female animal with more than one male.

pol·y·an′thous, *a.* with many flowers; many-flowered.

pol·y·an′thus, pol·y·an′thos, *n.* [*poly-*, and Gr. *anthos*, flower.]
1. an ornamental plant of the genus *Primula* or primrose, having many flowers in an umbel: also called *cowslip* and *cowslip primrose.*
2. a kind of narcissus with many star-shaped flowers.

pol′y·är·çhist, *n.* one who believes in polyarchy.

pol′y·är·çhy, *n.*; *pl.* **pol′y·är·çhieṣ**, [*poly-*, and Gr. *archē*, government.] government by many persons, of whatever order or class: opposed to *monarchy.*

pol″y·ȧ·tom′iç, *a.* [*poly-* and *atomic.*]
1. having a valence of three or more.
2. having molecules consisting of three or more atoms.
3. designating or of an organic compound containing two or more hydroxyl groups.

pol″y·au·tog′rȧ·phy, *n.*; *pl.* **pol″y·au·tog′rȧ·phieṣ**, [*poly-*, and Gr. *autos*, self, and *graphein*, to write.] the act or practice of multiplying copies of manuscripts by engraving on stone, by mimeograph, or by other similar devices.

pol·y·bā′siç, *a.* 1. designating an acid having more than one hydrogen atom (per molecule) replaceable by basic atoms or radicals.
2. designating a salt having more than one atom (per molecule) of a monovalent metal.

pol·y·bā′sīte, *n.* [*poly-*, and *base*, and *-ite.*] an iron-black ore of silver, Ag_3SbS_3, a sulfide of silver and antimony.

Pol·y·brañ′çhi·ȧ, *n.pl.* [*poly-*, and Gr. *branchia*, gills.] a division of gastropods, particularly those having many branchial cerata on the back.

pol·y·brō′mīde, *n.* [*poly-* and *bromide.*] a bromide having two or more atoms of bromine in a molecule.

pol·y·cär′pel·lăr·y, *a.* [*poly-*, and LL. *carpellum*, carpel.] made up of many carpels, as the lemon.

pol·y·cär′piç, *a.* [*poly-*, and Gr. *karpos*, fruit.] bearing fruit many times, or year after year; fruiting again and again.

pol·y·cär′pous, *a.* with two or more carpels in the ovary or fruit.

pol·y·ceph′ȧ·lous, *a.* [*poly-*, and Gr. *kephalē*, head.] with many heads; bearing many heads, as a plant.

Pol·y·chae′tȧ, *n.pl.* [*poly-*, and Gr. *chaitē*, long hair.] a division of annelids, especially those with fascicles of setae.

pol·y·chae′tous, *a.* 1. having many setae.
2. of or resembling the *Polychæta.*

pol·y·çhā′si·um, *n.*; *pl.* **pol·y·çhā′si·ȧ**, [Mod. L., from *poly-* and Fr. *chasis*, division.] a broad cluster of flowers in which each main stem sends forth more than two branches.

pol·y·çhlō′rīde, *n.* a chloride having two or more atoms of chlorine in a molecule.

pol·y·çhoe′rȧ·ny (-kē′), *n.* [*poly-*, and Gr. *koiranos*, ruler.] a government having many chiefs. [Obs.]

pol′y·çhord, *a.* [*poly-*, and Gr. *chordē*, string.] having many chords or strings.

pol′y·çhord, *n.* a ten-stringed musical instrument resembling a bass viol, to be played with a bow or by the fingers.

pol′y·çhrest, *a.* [*poly-*, and Gr. *chrēstos*, useful; *chrēsthai*, to use.] useful in many conditions.

pol′y·çhrest, *n.* a medicine useful for many diseases.
polychrest salt; in medicine, potassium sulfate or tartrate of sodium and potassium. [Obs.]

pol·y·çhres′tiç, *a.* having many uses, as a drug, or as a word of many meanings.

pol′y·çhres·ty, *n.* [Gr. *polychrēstia.*]
1. the quality or character of being polychrestic.
2. the use of polychrestic expressions or of polychrestic drugs.

pol′y·çhrō·iṣm, *n.* same as *pleochroism.*

pol·y·çhrō′māte, *n.* the salt of any polychromic acid.

pol·y·çhrō′māte, *n.* any substance which is polychromatic.

pol″y·çhrō·mat′iç, *a.* changing in color; having many colors.
polychromatic acid; aloetic acid, derived from aloes by treatment with nitric acid.

pol′y·çhrōme, *n.* [*poly-*, and Gr. *chrōma*, color.]
1. a many-colored picture, bas-relief, etc.
2. esculin: so called because of its fluorescence in solution.

pol′y·çhrōme, *a.* 1. polychromatic.
2. done in several colors; as, *polychrome* painting.

pol·y·çhrō′miç, *a.* polychromatic.

pol·y·çhrō′mous, *a.* polychromatic; relating to polychromy.

pol′y·çhrō·my, *n.* [*poly-*, and Gr. *chrōma*, color.] the art of using many colors, especially when in harmonious combinations, as practiced by the Greeks in architecture and sculpture, and in modern color printing.

pol·y·çhrō′ni·ous, *a.* chronic. [Rare.]

pol·y·çlin′iç, *n.* 1. a medical institution in which instruction is given by clinics in various kinds of diseases.
2. a hospital for the treatment of various kinds of diseases.

pol·y·çon′iç, *a.* based upon or relating to many cones.
polyconic projection; a type of map projection in which the parallels are arcs of nonconcentric circles and the meridians are curves equally spaced from the central, straight meridian.

pol·y·çot·y·lē′dŏn, *n.* [*poly-* and *cotyledon.*] a plant having three or more cotyledons in the embryo.

pol·y·çot·y·led′ŏn·ăr·y, *a.* having the villi grouped into cotyledons or distinct masses, as the placenta in ruminants.

pol·y·çot·y·lē′dŏn·ous, *a.* having three or more cotyledons.

pō·lyç′rȧ·cy, *n.* [*poly-*, and Gr. *kratein*, rule.] polyarchy; power in many hands.

pol·y·çrot′iç, *a.* [*poly-*, and Gr. *krotos*, noise.] in physiology, having several beats; showing several secondary waves, as a pulse.

pol·yç′rō·tiṣm, *n.* in physiology, the condition of being polycrotic.

pol·y·çyç′liç, *a.* [*poly-*, and Gr. *kyklos*, circle.]
1. with many whorls, cycles, or volutions; as, a *polycyclic* shell.
2. in electricity, multiphase.

pol·y·cys′tiç, *a.* [*poly-*, and Gr. *kystis*, bag.] having many cysts.

pol·y·cys′tid, *n.* one of the *Polycystina* or *Polycystidea*.

pol·y·cys′tiç, *a.* of or relating to the *Polycystina* or *Polycystidea*.

Pol″y·cys·tid′ē·ȧ, *n.pl.* [*poly-*, and Gr. *kystis*, bag.] an order of sporozoans in which the endosarc has two or more chambers.

Pol″y·cys·tī′nȧ, *n.pl.* [*poly-*, and Gr. *kystis*, a bag.] a family of radiolarians having a siliceous instead of a calcareous shell. They are all minute, and are frequently found in great multitudes, forming a colored cloud on the surface of the sea.

pol·y·cys′tïne, *n.* an animal of the *Polycystina*.

pol·y·cys′tïne, *a.* relating to the *Polycystina*; designating a division of *Radiolaria*.

pol″y·cȳ·thē′mi·ȧ, *n.* [*poly-*, and Gr. *kytos*, cavity, and *haima*, blood.] superabundance of red blood corpuscles.

Pol″y·cyt·tā′ri·ȧ, *n.pl.* [*poly-*, and Gr. *kyttaros*, cell.] a group of radiolarians having numerous central capsules.

pol·y·daç′tyl, pol·y·daç′tyle, *a.* [*poly-*, and Gr. *daktylos*, finger, toe.] having more than the normal number of fingers or toes.

pol·y·daç′tyl, *n.* an animal or person exhibiting polydactylism.

pol·y·daç′tyl·iṣm, *n.* the condition of being polydactyl.

pol·y·dae′mŏn·iṣm, *n.* [*poly-*, and Gr. *daimōn*, demon.] a form of religion in which a multitude of demons or spirits are thought to govern natural phenomena.

pol·y·dip′si·ȧ, *n.* [*poly-*, and Gr. *dipsa*, thirst.] extreme thirst; continual craving for drink.

pol·y·ē′drous, *a.* same as *polyhedral*.

pol·y·eī′diç, *a.* [*poly-*, and Gr. *eidos*, form.] having several forms of larvae.

pol·y·eī′diṣm, *n.* the condition of being polyeidic.

pol·y·em′bry·ō·nāte, *a.* in botany, composed of or possessing several embryos; pertaining to polyembryony.

pol·y·em·bry·on′iç, *a.* same as *polyembryonate*.

pol·y·em′bry·ō·ny, *n.* [*poly-*, and Gr. *embryon*, an embryo.] the development of two or more embryos in a single ovule or ovum.

pol·y·ẽr′ġiç, *a.* [*poly-*, and Gr. *ergon*, work.] having the power of acting in many ways.

pol′y·es·tẽr, *n.* [*poly*mer, and *ester*.] any of several polymeric resins formed chiefly by condensing polyhydric alcohols with dibasic acids: used in making plastics, fibers, etc.

pol″y·eth′yl·ēne, *n.* [*poly*mer, and *ethylene*.] any of several thermoplastic resins $(C_2H_4)_n$, made by the polymerization of ethylene: used in making translucent, lightweight, and tough plastics, films, containers, insulation, etc.

pol′y·foil, *n.* [*poly-* and *foil*.] in architecture, a figure composed of more than five foils.

pol′y·foil, *a.* having more than five foils.

Pō·lyg′ȧ·lȧ, *n.* [*poly-*, and Gr. *gala*, milk.] **1.** a genus of plants of the family *Polygalaceæ*. The species abound in milky juice, and are found in most parts of the world. The root of *Polygala senega*, seneca root, or Virginian snakeroot, is used as a diuretic and expectorant. *Polygala vulgaris*, or milkwort, is a British plant, common in dry pastures.

POLYGALA
(*Polygala senega*)

2. [p—] a plant belonging to this genus.

Pol″y·gȧ·lā′cē·ae, *n.pl.* the milkwort family of polypetalous plants, characterized by the union of their stamens into a single body, by their one-celled anthers opening with a pore, and by their irregular petals, one of which is often bearded. The family consists of herbaceous plants or shrubs, the leaves of which are usually bitter and the root milky.

pol″y·gȧ·lā′ceous, *a.* pertaining to the *Polygalaceæ*.

pō·lyg′ȧ·liç, *a.* relating to or produced from *Polygala senega*.
polygalic acid; polygaline; saponin.

pō·lyg′ȧ·line, *n.* saponin.

Pol·y·gā′mi·ȧ, *n.pl.* [*poly-*, and Gr. *gamos*, marriage.] in the Linnean system, a class of plants bearing hermaphrodite and unisexual flowers on the same plant or on different plants.

pol·y·gā′mi·ăn, *a.* relating to the *Polygamia*.

pō·lyg′ȧ·mist, *n.* one who practices or upholds polygamy.

pō·lyg′ȧ·mīze, *v.i.*; polygamized, *pt., pp.*; polygamizing, *ppr.* to practice polygamy. [Rare.]

pō·lyg″ȧ·mō·dī·oe′cious, *a.* in botany, both polygamous and dioecious.

pō·lyg′ȧ·mous, *a.* 1. of, engaging in, or characterized by polygamy.
2. in botany, of or relating to *Polygamia*; having hermaphrodite and unisexual flowers on the same plant or on different plants.
3. in zoology, having more than one mate of the opposite sex.

pō·lyg′ȧ·my, *n.* [*poly-*, and Gr. *gamos*, marriage.] the state or practice of having two or more wives, husbands, or mates at the same time; plural marriage or mating.

pol′y·gär, *n.* same as *poligar*.

pol·y·ġen′e·sis, *n.* [*poly-* and *genesis*.] in biology, (a) derivation from more than one kind of germ cell; (b) the theory that different species are descended from different ultimate ancestors.

pol″y·ġē·net′iç, *a.* 1. having more than one source or origin.
2. in biology, of or characterized by polygenesis.

pol·y·ġen′iç, *a.* polygenetic.

pō·lyġ′e·niṣm, *n.* [*poly-*, and Gr. *genos*, kind.] the theory that the human species has been derived from more than one ancestral type.

pō·lyġ′e·nist, *n.* an advocate of polygenism.

pō·lyġ′e·nous, *a.* [*poly-*, and Gr. *genos*, kind.] consisting of many kinds of elements; as, a *polygenous* mountain is composed of strata of different kinds of rock.

pō·lyġ′e·ny, *n.* polygenism.

pol′y·glot, *a.* [*poly-*, and Gr. *glōtta*, tongue.]
1. having or containing many languages; as, a *polyglot* lexicon or Bible.
2. speaking or writing several languages; as, a *polyglot* people.

pol′y·glot, *n.* 1. a person who speaks or writes several languages.
2. a book written in several languages.
3. a mixture or confusion of languages.
Complutensian Polyglot; the first complete polyglot edition of the Bible: see *Complutensian*.

pol·y·glot′tiç, *a.* same as *polyglottous*.

pol·y·glot′tous, *a.* [Gr. *polyglōttos*; *polys*, many, and *glōtta*, tongue.] speaking or using many languages.

pol′y·gon, *n.* [*poly-*, and Gr. *gōnia*, an angle.] in geometry, a plane figure with several angles and sides, usually over four; as, an equilateral *polygon*; a regular *polygon*.
force polygon; in mechanics, a polygon formed by lines representing in order the direction and the magnitude respectively of a number of forces acting at a point in different directions, when these forces are in equilibrium.
funicular polygon; in mechanics, a polygon formed in a vertical plane by a series of weights suspended from a cord whose two ends are fixed.

Pol″y·gō·nā′cē·ae, *n.pl.* [*polygon*um and *-aceæ*.] a family of plants, the buckwheat family, characterized by alternate entire leaves, and stipules in the form of scarious or membranous sheaths at the strongly-marked, usually tumid, joints of the stem.

pol″y·gō·nā′ceous, *a.* of, pertaining to, or like the *Polygonaceæ*.

pō·lyg′ō·năl, *a.* of, or having the form of, a polygon.
polygonal numbers; in arithmetic, the successive sums of a series of numbers in arithmetical progression; figurate numbers.

Pol·y·gon′ȧ·tum, *n.* [*poly-*, and Gr. *gony*, *gonatos*, knee.] a genus of liliaceous plants with a recurved stem growing from a thick rootstock which is marked with a large round scar left by the previous stem: the typical species is called *Solomon's-seal*.

pol″y·gō·neū′tiç, *a.* [*poly-*, and Gr. *gonos*, offspring.] in zoology, producing several broods in a single year or season.

pol″y·gō·neū′tiṣm, *n.* the state of being polygoneutic.

pol″y·gō·nom′e·try, *n.* [*polygon*, and Gr. *metron*, measure.] the branch of mathematics dealing with polygons.

pō·lyg′ō·nous, *a.* same as *polygonal*.

Pō·lyg′ō·num, *n.* [*poly-*, and Gr. *gony*, *gonatos*, knee.] a genus of plants of the buckwheat family, of wide distribution in the temperate zones, represented by knotweed, prince's-feather, lady's-thumb, etc.

pō·lyg′ō·ny, *n.* any plant of the genus *Polygonum*, especially knotgrass, *Polygonum aviculare*.

Pol·y·gor′di·us, *n.* [*poly-*, and Gr. *Gordios*, king of Phrygia, with allusion to the Gordian knot.] a genus of marine worms typical of the family *Polygordiidæ*.

pol′y·gram, *n.* [*poly-*, and Gr. *gramma*, a writing.] a figure made by a polygraph.

pol′y·gràph, *n.* [*poly-*, and Gr. *graphein*, to write.]
1. a device for reproducing writings or drawings; especially, a gelatin copying pad.
2. a person who writes many works or many kinds of work.

pol·y·graph′iç, *a.* 1. pertaining to polygraphy; as, a *polygraphic* instrument.
2. done with a polygraph; as, a *polygraphic* copy or writing.

pol·y·graph′iç·ăl, *a.* same as *polygraphic*.

pō·lyg′rȧ·phy, *n.* the art of operating a polygraph.

pol′y·grōōve, *v.t.*; polygrooved, *pt., pp.*; polygrooving, *ppr.* to cut many grooves in, as in a column, a facing, or a piece of furniture.

pol′y·ġyn, *n.* a plant of the order *Polygynia*.

Pol·y·ġyn′i·ȧ, *n.pl.* [*poly-*, and Gr. *gynē*, a female.] in the Linnean system, an order of plants having many styles.

pol·y·ġyn′i·ăn, *a.* same as *polygynous*.

pō·lyġ′y·nist, *n.* one who believes in or practices polygyny.

pol″y·ġy·noe′ciăl (-shăl), *a.* [*poly-*, and LL. *gynoecium*, and *-al*.] in botany, produced by the massing of the gynoecia of many flowers, as in multiple fruits like the mulberry.

pō·lyġ′y·nous, *a.* 1. in botany, having many styles; pertaining to the order *Polygynia*.
2. characterized by or pertaining to polygyny.

pō·lyġ′y·ny, *n.* [*poly-*, and Gr. *gynē*, a female.]
1. the state or practice of having two or more wives or concubines at the same time.
2. the mating of a male animal with several females.

pol·y·ġy′răl, *a.* [*poly-*, and Gr. *gyros*, circle.] having many gyres or turns, as in the shell of a univalve mollusk.

pol·y·ġyr′i·ȧ, *n.* a condition in which there is an unusually large number of convolutions in the brain.

pol·y·hal′īte, *n.* [*poly-*, and Gr. *hals*, salt.] a mineral occurring in masses of a fibrous structure, of a brick-red color, being tinged with iron but essentially a hydrous sulfate of calcium, magnesium, and potassium.

pol·y·hē′drăl, *a.* [*polyhedr*an and *-al*.] of, or having the form of, a polyhedron.
polyhedral angle; an angle made by the passing of three or more planes through the same point.

pol·y·hē′driç, pol·y·hē′driç·ăl, *a.* same as *polyhedral*.

pol·y·hē′drŏn, *n.*; *pl.* **pol·y·hē′drŏnṣ, pol·y·hē′drȧ,** [*poly-*, and Gr. *hedra*, seat.]
1. in geometry, a solid figure with several plane surfaces, usually more than six.
2. in optics, a polyscope, or multiplying glass.
3. in botany, a cell of angular form in *Hydrodictyon utriculatum*, the water net.
conjugate polyhedra; two polyhedra of such form that each has a face for every vertex in the other, and vice versa.

pol·y·hē′drous, *a.* same as *polyhedral*.

pol·y·hē′mi·ȧ, pol·y·hae′mi·ȧ, *n.* [*poly-*, and Gr. *haima*, blood.] in medicine, excessive blood supply: also *polyemia*.

pol″y·hi·drō′sis, *n.* [*poly-*, and Gr. *hidrōs*, sweat.] excess in the secretion of sweat.

pol·y·his′tŏr, *n.* [*poly-*, and Gr. *histōr*, knowing.] one versed in varied learning; a universal scholar. [Rare.]

pol·y·hȳ′driç, *a.* [*poly-*, and *hydr*oxyl, and *-ic*.] in chemistry, a compound containing more than two hydroxyl groups.

Pol·y·hym′ni·ȧ, *n.* [L., from Gr. *Polymnia*; *polys*, many, and *hymnos*, hymn.] in Greek mythology, the Muse of sacred poetry: also *Polymnia*.

pol′y I:C (i′sē′), [*polyi*nosinic-polycytidylic acid.] a synthetic ribonucleic acid that promotes the production of a cellular protein that fights viruses.

pol·y·ī′ō·dīde, *n.* [*poly-* and *iodide.*] in chemistry, an iodide containing more than one atom of iodine to the molecule.

pol·y·lem′mȧ, *n.* [*poly-*, and Gr. *lēmma*, proposition.] a predicament; a dilemma with many equally objectionable alternatives.

pol·y·lep′i·dous, *a.* [*poly-*, and Gr. *lepis* (*-idos*), scale.] having many scales: said of a bud, an involucre, or a bulb.

pol′y·lith, *n.* [*poly-*, and Gr. *lithos*, stone.] a structure composed of many stones: the opposite of *monolith*.

pol·y·lith′iç, *a.* built of or containing many stones.

pō·lyl′ō·quent (-kwent), *a.* [*poly-*, and L. *loquens* (*-entis*), *ppr.* of *loqui*, to speak.] loquacious; talkative. [Rare.]

pol·y·mag′net, *n.* [*poly-* and *magnet.*] a combination of two or more electromagnets placed so that a variable magnetic field may be produced.

pol·y·mas′ti·ȧ, *n.* the presence of more than two mammae or breasts.

pol·y·mas′tiç, *a.* [*poly-*, and Gr. *mastos*, breast.] having an abnormal number of breasts or nipples.

pol′y·math, *n.* [Gr. *polymathēs*; *polys*, much, and *manthanein*, *mathein*, to learn.] a person having a wide range of knowledge; a polyhistor.

pol·y·math′iç, *a.* pertaining to polymathy; possessing varied learning.

pō·lym′ȧ·thy, *n.* the knowledge of many arts and sciences; acquaintance with many branches of learning or with various subjects.

pol·y·mē′li·ȧ, *n.* [*poly-*, and Gr. *melos*, limb.] the presence of supernumerary limbs.

pol·y·mē′li·ăn, *a.* pertaining to polymelia; having supernumerary limbs.

pol·y·mē′li·us, *n.* a fetus with more than the normal number of limbs.

pol′y·mē·ly, *n.* same as *polymelia*.

pol′y·mẽr, *n.* [from Gr. *poly*, many, and *meros*, a part.] any of two or more polymeric compounds, especially one with a higher molecular weight.

pol·y·mer′iç, *a.* composed of the same chemical elements in the same proportions by weight, but differing in molecular weight.

pō·lym′ẽr·īde (*or* -id), *n.* a polymer.

pō·lym′ẽr·işm, *n.* the condition of being polymeric or polymerous.

pol·y·mẽr·i·zā′tion, *n.* 1. the process of joining two or more like molecules to form a more complex molecule whose molecular weight is a multiple of the original and whose physical properties are different.

2. the changing of a compound into a polymeric form by this process.

pol′y·mẽr·īze, *v.t.* and *v.i.*; polymerized, *pt.*, *pp.*; polymerizing, *ppr.* [*polymer*ous and *-ize.*] to subject to or undergo polymerization.

pō·lym′ẽr·ous, *a.* [Gr. *polymerēs*; *polys*, many, and *meros*, part.]

1. in botany, consisting of many parts or having many members in each whorl.

2. in chemistry, polymeric. [Obs.]

pol·y·met·ȧ·mer′iç, *a.* [*poly-* and *metameric.*] in biology, pertaining to or connected with three or more metameres.

pō·lym′ē·tẽr, *n.* [*poly-*, and Gr. *metron*, measure.] an apparatus for measuring angles.

pol″y·me·tō′çhi·ȧ, *n.* [*poly-*, and Gr. *metochē*, a participle.] the frequent use of participles in speaking or writing.

pol·y·mī′çrō·sçōpe, *n.* a microscope in which a movable band is used as a support for the objects to be examined, so that shifts to various parts of the field can be made quickly.

pol·y·mig′nīte, *n.* [*poly-*, and Gr. *mignynai*, to mix, and *-ite.*] a shiny, black, crystalline mineral, containing titanium, zirconium, yttrium, cerium, calcium, iron, magnesium, manganese, potassium, and silica.

Pō·lym′ni·ȧ, *n.* 1. same as *Polyhymnia*.

2. a genus of the *Compositæ*, consisting of coarse shrubs or herbs having strong-scented, downy foliage and yellow flowers.

pol′ym·nīte, *n.* [*poly-*, and Gr. *mnion*, moss, and *-ite.*] a stone marked with dendrites and black lines which resemble rivers, marshes, and ponds.

pol′y·mọrph, *n.* [from Gr. *polymorphos*; from *poly-*, many, and *morphē*, shape.]

1. in biology, a polymorphous organism or one of its forms.

2. in chemistry and mineralogy, (a) a substance that can crystallize in two or more different forms; (b) one of these forms.

pol·y·mọr′phiç, *a.* same as *polymorphous*.

pol·y·mọr′phişm, *n.* the condition or quality of being polymorphous.

pol″y·mọr·phō′sis, *n.* [*poly-* and *morphosis.*] in zoology, the development of different structural forms having the same function, as in sponges.

pol·y·mọr′phous, *a.* [Gr. *polymorphos*; *polys*, many, and *morphē*, form.] having, occurring in, or passing through several or various forms.

pol′y·mọr·phy, *n.* same as *polymorphism*.

pō·ly·moun′tain (-tin), *n.* same as *poly*.

Pol″y·mȳ·ō′dī, *n.pl.* [*poly-*, and Gr. *mys*, muscle, and *ōdē*, song.] a group of singing birds having five pairs of vocal muscles in the syrinx: now classed as the *Oscines*.

pol″ȳ·my·ō′dous, *a.* pertaining to the *Polymyodi*; polymyoid.

pol·y·mȳ′oid, *a.* [*poly-*, and Gr. *mys*, muscle, and *-oid.*] having several pairs of vocal muscles, as the *Polymyodi*.

pol·y·mȳ·ō·sī′tis, *n.* [*poly-*, and Gr. *mys*, muscle, and *-itis.*] inflammation affecting several muscles.

pol′y·nēme, *n.* [*poly-*, and Gr. *nēma*, thread.] a sea fish of the genus *Polynemus*.

Pol·y·nem′i·dae, *n.pl.* a family of fishes represented by the genus *Polynemus*.

pol·y·nem′i·fọrm, *a.* shaped like a polyneme.

POLYNEME
(*Polynemus quadrifilis*)

pol·y·nē′moid, *a.* resembling or pertaining to the *Polynemidæ*.

Pol·y·nē′mus, *n.* [*poly*, many, and Gr. *nēma*, a thread.] a genus of fishes belonging to and typical of the family *Polynemidæ*, having the ventral fins abdominal instead of thoracic. The species have a compressed head entirely covered with deciduous scales, a blunt, prominent nose, and filiform appendages to the pectoral fins.

Pol·y·nē′şiăn, *a.* of Polynesia, its people, their language, or culture.

Pol·y·nē′şian, *n.* 1. a member of the brown people of Polynesia, including the Hawaiians, Tahitians, Samoans, and Maoris.

2. the group of Austronesian languages of Polynesia.

pol·y·neū′răl, *a.* [*poly-*, and Gr. *neuron*, nerve.] pertaining to or supplied by several nerves.

pol″y·neū·rī′tis, *n.* [*poly-* and *neuritis.*] neuritis affecting several nerves.

pō·lyn′i·ȧ, *n.* [Russ. *poluiniya*, an opening in an ice field.] an opening in a frozen sea.

Pol·y·nī′cēs, *n.* [L. *Polynices*; Gr. *Polyneikēs.*] in Greek legend, a son of Oedipus and the brother of Eteocles.

Pō·lyn′ō·ē, *n.* [*poly-*, and Gr. *nein*, to swim.] a genus of sea worms characterized by many segments covered with small paired scales.

pol′y·noid, *a.* [*polynoe* and *-oid.*] pertaining to the *Polynoe* and related genera.

pol′y·noid, *n.* a member of the genus *Polynoe*.

pol·y·nō′mi·ăl, *n.* [*poly-* and *binomial.*]

1. in algebra, an expression consisting of two or more terms; as, $x^2 - 2xy + y^2$ is a *polynomial*.

2. in biology, a species name consisting of more than two terms.

pol·y·nō′mi·ăl, *a.* of, belonging to, or constituting a polynomial.

pol·y·nō′mi·ăl·işm, *n.* nomenclature consisting of polynomials; a system using polynomials.

pol·y·nō′mi·ăl·ist, *n.* one who uses polynomials.

pol·y·nū′çlē·ăr, *a.* having many nuclei.

pol·y·ō′mȧ vī′rus, [*poly-*, and *-oma.*] a virus that causes various types of cancer in mice and other rodents.

pol·y·om′mȧ·tous, *a.* [*poly-*, and Gr. *omma* (*-atos*), eye.] having many eyes.

pol·y·on′ō·my, *n.* same as *polyonymy*.

pol′y·ō·nym, *n.* 1. a polynominal name.

2. a synonym. [Rare.]

pol″y·ō·nym′iç, *a.* polyonymous; polynomial.

pol·y·on′y·mous, *a.* many-titled; having many names.

pol·y·on′y·my, *n.* polynomialism; the giving of many names to the same thing.

pol·y·ō′pi·ȧ, *n.* [*poly-*, and Gr. *ōps*, *ōpos*, face.] double or multiple vision; the condition in which one object appears as two or more objects: also written *polyopsia*, *polyopsy*, *polyopy*.

pol″y·ō·rä′mȧ, *n.* [*poly-*, and Gr. *horama*, view, from *horān*, to see.] a view of many objects; also, an optical instrument presenting such views.

pol·y·ọr′çhis, *n.* [*poly-*, and Gr. *orchis*, testis.] a person with more than two testicles.

pol′yp, *n.* [L. *polypus*; Gr. *polypous*; *polys*, many, and *pous*, foot.]

1. any of a number of small, flowerlike water animals having a mouth fringed with many small, slender tentacles at the top of a tubelike body, as the sea anemone, hydra, etc.

2. a smooth projecting growth of hypertrophied mucous membrane in the nasal passages, bladder, rectum, etc.

3. an octopus. [Obs.]

pō·lyp′ȧ·rous, *a.* [*poly-*, and L. *parere*, to produce.] producing many seeds, eggs, or young at a time.

pol′y·pȧ·ry, *n.*; *pl.* **pol′y·pȧ·rieş,** [from *polyp.*] in zoology, the base or the connecting tissue to which each member of a colony of polyps is attached; a polypidom.

pol′ype, *n.* same as *polyp*.

pol·y·pē′ăn, *a.* pertaining to a polyp or polyps.

pol·y·pē′ăn, *n.* a polyp.

pol·y·pep′tīde, *n.* [*poly-*, and *peptide.*] a substance containing two or more amino acids in the molecule joined by peptide linkages.

Pol·y·pet′ȧ·lae, *n.pl.* a large group of plants characterized by having the corolla made up of many separate petals; a subdivision of dicotyledons.

pol·y·pet′ăl·ous, *a.* [*poly-*, and Gr. *petalon*, a petal.] in botany, having many separate petals; as, a *polypetalous* corolla.

pol·y·phā′ġi·ȧ, *n.* [Gr. *polyphagia*, from *poly*, many, and *phagein*, to eat.]

1. an abnormal or excessive desire for food.

2. the practice of subsisting on many kinds of food.

pol·y·phaġ′iç, *a.* [*poly-*, and Gr. *phagein*, to eat.] subsisting on many kinds of food.

pō·lyph′ȧ·gous, *a.* same as *polyphagic*.

pō·lyph′ȧ·ġy, *n.* polyphagia.

pol·y·phär′mȧ·cy, *n.* 1. a prescription made up of too many ingredients.

2. the practice of using an excessive number of ingredients in a prescription.

3. the use of many kinds of medicine at the same time.

pol′y·phāşe, *a.* in electricity, having or generating two or more phases.

polyphase armature; an armature so wound as either to produce polyphase currents or to be operated by such currents.

polyphase currents; currents differing in phase from one another by a definite amount, and suitable for the operation of polyphase motors or similar apparatus.

polyphase dynamo; a polyphase generator.

polyphase generator; an alternator which delivers two or more alternating currents definitely differing in phase.

polyphase motor; a motor operated by means of polyphase currents.

polyphase transmission; transmission of power by means of polyphase currents.

pol′y·phāş·ẽr, *n.* in electricity, a polyphase alternator or generator.

Pol·y·phē′mus, *n.* [L.; Gr. *Polyphēmos.*] in Greek legend, the Cyclops who confined Odysseus and his companions in a cave and ate two of them daily, until Odysseus blinded him with a stake as he slept and escaped along with those still alive.

Pol·y·phē′mus mọth, a large, yellowish-brown American bombycid moth, *Telea polyphemus*, with an eyelike spot on each hind wing.

pol′y·phōne, *n.* [*poly-*, and Gr. *phōnē*, voice, sound.] in phonetics, a polyphonic letter or other symbol.

pol·y·phon′iç, *a.* [Gr. *polyphōnos*, having many tones, from *poly*, many, and *phōnē*, a voice, sound.]

1. having or making many sounds.

2. in music, (a) of, having, or in polyphony; having two or more harmonized melodies; contrapuntal; (b) that can produce more than one tone at a time, as a piano.

3. in phonetics, representing more than one sound, as *c* in *cat* and *cereal*.

pō·lyph′ō·nism, *n.* same as *polyphony.*

pō·lyph′ō·nist, *n.* 1. one who is skilled in the art of the multiplication of sounds; an imitator of sounds; a ventriloquist.
2. in music, one skilled in polyphony.

pō·lyph′ō·nous, *a.* polyphonic.

pō·lyph′ō·ny, *n.* [*poly-*, and Gr. *phōnē*, voice.]
1. multiplicity of sounds, as in an echo.
2. in music, a combining of a number of individual but harmonizing melodies, as in a fugue, canon, etc.; counterpoint: opposed to *monody, homophony.*
3. in phonetics, the representation of two or more sounds by the same letter or symbol, as *c* in *ace* and *act.*

pol′y·phōre, *n.* [*poly-*, and Gr. *-phoros*, from *pherein*, to bear.] in botany, a receptacle bearing many ovaries. [Rare.]

pol′y·phōte, *a.* [*poly-*, and Gr. *phōs, phōtos*, light.] in electricity, of or designating arc lamps so constructed that more than one may be used on a single circuit.

pol″y·phy·let′iç, *a.* [*poly-* and *phyletic.*] in biology, derived from more than one ancestral type.

pol·y·phyl′lous, *a.* [*poly-*, and Gr. *phyllon*, leaf.] in botany, having many leaves; as, a *polyphyllous* calyx or perianth.

pol′y·phyl·ly, *n.* in botany, increase of the number of parts in a whorl.

pol·y·phy′ō·dont, *a.* [*poly-*, Gr. *phyein*, to produce, and *odous, odontos*, tooth.] having several sets of teeth.

pol·y·phy′ō·dont, *n.* an animal with several sets of teeth.

Pol′y·pī, *n.pl.* [from L. *polypus.*] the polyps as a group.

pol′y·pīde, *n.* [*polyp* and *-ide.*] any of the separate zooids of a polyzoarium.

pō·lyp′i·dŏm, *n.* [*polyp*, and Gr. *domos*, house.] a polypary.

pol′y·piēr, *n.* [Fr.] a polypary.

pol′y·pi·fēr, *n.* any of the *Polypifera*; a polyp.

Pol·y·pif′e·rȧ, *n.pl.* the *Polypi.*

pol·y·pif′ēr·ous, *a.* [*polyp*, and L. *ferre*, to bear.] producing polyps; bearing polypites.

pol′y·pi·form, *a.* of the form of a polyp.

pol·y·pig′ēr·ous, *a.* polypiferous.

pol·y·pip′ȧ·rous, *a.* [*polyp*, and L. *parere*, to bring forth.] polypiferous.

pol′y·pīte, *n.* [*polyp* and *-ite.*]
1. the fundamental element in the structure of a hydrozoan; a single zooid, consisting of a sac with an ingestive or oral opening at one end, leading into a digestive cavity; a hydranth.
2. a fossil polyp.
3. the manubrium of a medusa.

Pol″y·plȧ·çoph′ō·rȧ, *n.pl.* [*poly-*, and Gr. *plax, plakos*, tablet, and *pherein*, to bear.] an order of gastropods; the chitons.

pol′y·plāne, *n.* same as *multiplane.*

pol·y·plas′tiç, *a.* [*poly-* and *plastic.*] in biology, containing many structural or constituent elements; also, undergoing many changes of form.

pol·y·pleç′tron, pol·y·pleç′trum, *n.* [*poly-*, and Gr. *plēktron*, plectrum.] an old musical instrument in which the tones were produced by the friction of a number of slips of leather acting upon strings, and moved by pressing or striking keys, as in the piano; a kind of harpsicord.

pol′y·ploid, *a.* [*poly-* and *-ploid.*] having the number of chromosomes in the somatic cells more than twice the haploid number.

pol′y·ploid, *n.* a polyploid cell or organism.

pol·yp·noe′ȧ, *n.* [*poly-*, and Gr. *pnoia*, breathing, from *pnein*, to breathe.] a rapid or panting respiration.

pol′y·pod, *a.* [*poly-*, and Gr. *pous, podos*, foot.] having many feet, as a myriapod.

pol′y·pod, *n.* 1. a polypod animal; a myriapod.
2. in botany, a polypody.

Pol·y·pō·di·ā′cē·ae, *n.pl.* [*polypodium* and *-aceæ.*] a family of ferns, which can be taken as the type of the whole, having erect or creeping rootstocks and an elastic jointed ring nearly surrounding the spore cases.

pol·y·pō·di·ā′ceous, *a.* pertaining to the *Polypodiaceæ.*

Pol·y·pō′di·um, *n.* [L., *polypody.*] a genus typical of the *Polypodiaceæ.*

pol′y·pō·dy, *n.*; *pl.* **pol′y·pō·dieṣ,** [*poly-*, and Gr. *pous, podos*, foot.] a plant of the genus *Polypodium* or family *Polypodiaceæ*, having rather coarse and leathery leaves. *Polypodium vulgare* is the common polypody.

pol′y·poid, *a.* [*polyp* and *-oid.*] of the nature of or resembling a polyp or polypus.

Pol″y·pō·mē·dū′sae, *n.pl.* the hydrozoans.

Pol″y·pō·ri·ā′cē·ae, *n.pl.* [*polyporus* and *-aceæ.*] an order of fungi of which the genus *Polyporus* is the type.

pō·lyp′ō·roid, *a.* of or resembling the genus *Polyporus.*

pō·lyp′ō·rous, *a.* many-pored.

Pō·lyp′ō·rus, *n.* [*poly-*, and Gr. *poros*, pore, passage.] a genus of parasitical fungi.

pol′y·pō·stȳle, *n.* same as *dactylozooid.*

pol′y·pō·tōme, *n.* [*polypus*, and Gr. *-tomos*, from *temnein*, to cut.] a surgical instrument for removing a polypus.

pol′y·pous, *a.* of or like a polyp.

pol″y·prag·mat′iç, pol″y·prag·mat′iç·ăl, *a.* [*poly-* and *pragmatic.*] overbusy; overzealous; forward; officious. [Rare.]

pol″y·prag·mat′iç, *n.* a busybody; a meddler. [Rare.]

pol·y·prag′mȧ·ty, *n.* [*polypragmatic* and *-y.*] the state of being officious. [Rare.]

pol·y·prag′mŏn, pol·y·prag′mŏn·ist, *n.* a busybody. [Obs.]

pol′y·prism, *n.* a prism formed of several prisms of the same angle connected at their ends: a beam of light passing through the various component parts of such a prism is variously refracted and dispersed.

pol″y·priṣ·mat′iç, *a.* [*poly-* and *prismatic.*] in mineralogy, having crystals presenting many prisms in a single form.

pol·y·prō′tō·dont, *n.* one of the *Polyprotodontia.*

pol·y·prō′tō·dont, *a.* pertaining to the *Polyprotodontia.*

Pol·y·prō·tō·don′ti·ȧ (-shi-), *n.pl.* [*poly-*, and Gr. *prōtos*, first, and *odous, odontos*, tooth.] a division of marsupials having more than two lower incisors and well-developed canine teeth.

Pō·lyp·te·roi′dē·ī, *n.pl.* [*Polypterus*, and Gr. *eidos*, form.] a suborder of ganoid fishes with many dorsal fins: the genus *Polypterus* is the type.

Pō·lyp′te·rus, *n.* [*poly-*, and Gr. *pteron*, feather.] a genus typical of the *Polypteroidei*, including the bichir.

pol·yp·tō′ton, *n.* [*poly-*, and Gr. *ptōtos*, verbal adj. of *piptein*, to fall.] in rhetoric, a form of speech in which a word is repeated in different cases, numbers, genders, and the like. The following line is an example:

My own heart's heart, and ownest own, farewell. —Tennyson.

pol′yp·tyçh, *n.* [*poly-*, and Gr. *ptyx, ptychis*, fold.] any arrangement, as an altarpiece, having more than three leaves or panels hinged or folded together.

pol′y·pus, *n.*; *pl.* **pol′y·pī,** [*poly-*, and Gr. *pous, podos*, foot.] a polyp.

pol·y·rhī′zous (-rī′), *a.* [*poly-*, and Gr. *rhiza*, root.] having many rootlets.

pol·y·saç′çhȧ·rīde, *n.* [*poly-* and *saccharide.*] any of a group of carbohydrates that decompose by hydrolysis into more than three molecules of monosaccharides.

pol·y·sär′ci·ȧ, *n.* [*poly-*, and Gr. *sarx, sarkos*, flesh.] in medicine, corpulence or obesity.

pol·y·sär′çous, *a.* corpulent; obese.

pol·y·sçhe′ma·tist, *a.* [*poly-*, and Gr. *schēma* (*-atos*), form.] in ancient prosody, having many possible forms: said of meter.

pol′y·sçōpe, *n.* [*poly-*, and Gr. *skopein*, to view.]
1. a glass that makes a single object appear as many objects; a multiplying glass.
2. in surgery, an instrument for illuminating a body cavity and making it visible.

pol·y·sep′ăl·ous, *a.* [*poly-*, and LL. *sepalum*, sepal.] in botany, having the sepals separate from each other, as a calyx.

pol·y·sī′phŏn·ous, *a.* [*poly-*, and Gr. *siphōn*, tube.] having more than one siphon, as certain seaweeds.

pol″y·sō·mat′iç, *a.* [*poly-*, and Gr. *sōma* (*-atos*), body.] in mineralogy, having a grained structure.

pol″y·sō·mit′iç, *a.* [*poly-*, *somite*, and *-ic.*] made up of a collection of united somites, as the abdomen of an arthropod.

pol′y·spast, *n.* [Gr. *polyspastos*, drawn by many cords; *polys*, many, and *spān*, to draw.]
1. a machine consisting of many pulleys for raising heavy weights. [Obs.]
2. a similar apparatus formerly used in surgery to reduce dislocations. [Obs.]

pol′y·spērm, *n.* [*poly-*, and Gr. *sperma*, seed.] a tree whose fruit contains many seeds. [Obs.]

pol·y·spēr′mous, *a.* containing many seeds; as, a *polyspermous* capsule or berry.

pol′y·spēr·my, *n.* [*polysperm* and *-y.*] the entrance of more than one spermatozoon to one ovum.

pol″y·spō·ran′ġi·um, *n.* in botany, a sporangium with many spores. [Rare.]

pol′y·spōre, *n.* [*poly-*, and Gr. *sporos*, seed.] in botany, a spore with several cells. [Rare.]

pol·y·spōr′iç, *a.* polysporous.

pol·y·spōr′ous, *a.* having many spores.

pol·y·stau′ri·um, *n.* same as *stauracin.*

pol·y·stem′ō·nous, *a.* [*poly-*, and Gr. *stēmōn*, warp, stamen.] having many stamens; having stamens more than double the number of petals and sepals.

pō·lys′ti·çhous, *a.* [*poly-*, and Gr. *stichos*, row.] in biology, arranged in many rows or ranks: distinguished from *monostichous, distichous.*

pol′y·stigm (-stim), *n.* [*poly-*, and Gr. *stigma*, point.] a figure made up of several points.

Pol·y·stom′ȧ·tȧ, *n.pl.* [*poly-*, and Gr. *stoma* (*-atos*), mouth.] a section of the *Protozoa*, in which the inceptive apparatus consists of a considerable number of tentacular organs, each of which is used for grasping or as a tubular sucking mouth.

pol·y·stom′ȧ·tous, *a.* pertaining to the *Polystomata.*

pol′y·stōme, *a.* [*poly-*, and Gr. *stoma* (*-atos*), mouth.] polystomatous.

pol′y·stōme, *n.* any of the *Polystomata.*

pol′y·stȳle, *a.* [*poly-*, and Gr. *stylos*, column.] having a large number of columns; supported or surrounded by many columns.

pol·y·stȳ′lous, *a.* in botany, having many styles.

pol·y·stȳ′rēne, *n.* a clear, colorless plastic material, a polymer of styrene (C_8H_8).

pol·y·sul′fīde, *n.* [*poly-* and *sulfide.*] a binary compound of sulfur containing more atoms of sulfur than the valence of the combining element requires.

pol″y·syl·lab′iç, pol″y·syl·lab′iç·ăl, *a.* 1. having many, or more than three, syllables.
2. characterized by polysyllables.

pol·y·syl′lȧ·bism, pol″y·syl·lab′i·çism, *n.* the state or quality of being polysyllabic, or of having many syllables.

pol′y·syl·lȧ·ble, *n.* [*poly-* and *syllable.*] a word of more than three syllables.

pol·y·syl′lō·ġism, *n.* [*poly-* and *syllogism.*] in logic, a syllogism formed by a chain of connected syllogisms.

pol·y·syl·lō·ġis′tiç, *a.* having the character of a polysyllogism.

pol″y·sym·met′riç·ăl, *a.* [*poly-* and *symmetrical.*] capable of being divided into similar parts by more than one plane, as all regular flowers.

pol″y·sym·met′riç·ăl·ly, *adv.* in a polysymmetrical manner.

pol·y·sym′me·try, *n.* the state of being polysymmetrical.

pol″y·syn·det′iç, *a.* characterized by polysyndeton.

pol·y·syn′de·ton, *n.* [*poly-*, and Gr. *syndetos*, from *syndein*, to bind together.] in rhetoric, the use or repetition of conjunctions in close succession: opposed to *asyndeton.*

pol·y·syn′the·sis, *n.* polysynthetic character or structure; polysyntheticism.

pol″y·syn·thet′iç, *a.* in philology, compounded of several elements, each retaining a kind of independence; as, a *polysynthetic* word.

pol″y·syn·thet′iç·ăl, *a.* polysynthetic.

pol″y·syn·thet′i·çism, *n.* polysynthetic character or structure.

pol·y·teçh′niç, *a.* [*poly-*, and Gr. *technē*, art.] of or providing instruction in many scientific and technical subjects (and, formerly, arts).

pol·y·teçh′niç, *n.* a polytechnic institution, usually one offering instruction in engineering.

pol·y·teçh′niç·ăl, *a.* polytechnic.

pol·y·teçh′niçs, *n.* the science of the mechanical arts. [Rare.]

pol·y·tēr′pēne, *n.* any substance polymeric with a terpene, as gutta-percha.

Pol″y·thȧ·lā′mi·ȧ, *n.pl.* [*poly-*, and Gr. *thalamos*, a chamber.] an order of compound *Protozoa*, occupying compound chambered cells of microscopic size.

pol·y·thal′ȧ·miç, *a.* pertaining to the *Polythalamia.*

pol·y·thal′ȧ·mous, *a.* [*poly-*, and Gr. *thalamos*, chamber.] many-chambered, as the shells of cephalopods.

pol′y·thē·ism, *n.* [Fr. *polythéisme*; Gr. *polys*, many, and *theos*, god.] belief in or worship of many gods, or more than one god: opposed to *monotheism.*

pol′y·thē·ist, *n.* a person who believes in or practices polytheism.

pol″y·thē·is′tiç, pol″y·thē·is′tiç·ăl, *a.* 1. pertaining to or characterized by polytheism.
2. advocating or believing in polytheism.

pol″y·thē·is′tiç·ăl·ly, *adv.* in a polytheistic manner.

pol′y·thē·īze, *v.i.*; polytheized, *pt., pp.*; polytheizing, *ppr.* to believe in or teach the doctrine of polytheism.

pol·y·thē′liṣm, *n.* [*poly-*, and Gr. *thēlē*, nipple.] the occurrence of more than one nipple on a mammary gland.

pō·lyt′ō·çous, *a.* [*poly-*, and Gr. *-tokos*, from *tiktein*, to bring forth.] in zoology, multiparous; producing several eggs; bringing forth many at a birth.

pō·lyt′ō·mous, *a.* [*poly-*, and Gr. *tomē*, a cutting, from *temnein*, to cut.]
1. in botany, designating a leaf having narrow lobes not articulated with the midrib.
2. having more than two branches or parts.

pō·lyt′ō·my, *n.* [*poly-*, and Gr. *tomē*, a cutting.]
1. in logic, a division into several parts.
2. in biology, division into three or more branches at a place.

pol″y·tō·nal′i·ty, *n.* [*poly-* and *tonality*.] in music, the simultaneous use of several, or especially of two, keys in the various voices, or parts, of a composition.

pō·lyt′rō·chȧ, pol′y·troch, *n.* [*poly-*, and Gr. *trochos*, wheel.]
1. an embryo worm with several circles of cilia.
2. [P-] a division of *Rotifera* in which the cilia are arranged in several circles.

pol·y·trō′chăl, *a.* 1. pertaining to the *Polytrocha.*
2. characterized by several circles of cilia.

pol·y·troph′iç, *a.* [Gr. *polytrophos*, nutritious.] in bacteriology, obtaining nourishment from more than one kind of organic material, as many pathogenic bacteria.

pol·y·tung′stāte, *n.* a salt of any polytungstic acid.

pol·y·tung′stiç, *a.* [*poly-* and *tungstic*.] pertaining to or designating any one of several acids that contain more than one atom of tungsten in the molecule.

pol′y·tȳp·āġe, *n.* an old mode of stereotyping by which facsimiles of wood engravings, etc. are produced by pressing a woodcut into semi-fluid metal, thus producing an intaglio matrix. From this matrix, in a similar way, a polytype is obtained.

pol′y·tȳpe, *n.* [*poly-*, and Gr. *typos*, type.] a cast or facsimile of an engraving, matter in type, etc. produced by polytypage.

pol·y·typ′iç, *a.* having or involving several different types.

pol·y·typ′iç·ăl, *a.* same as *polytypic.*

pol″y·un·sat′ū·rā·ted, *a.* [*poly-*, and *unsaturated*.] containing more than one double or triple bond in the molecule, as certain vegetable and animal fats and oils.

pol″y·ū′rē·thāne, *n.* [*poly-*, and *urethane*.] any of several synthetic rubber polymers produced by the polymerization of a hydroxyl (OH) radical and an NCO group from two different compounds: used in cushions, insulation, molded products, etc.

pol·y·ū′ri·ȧ, *n.* [*poly-*, and Gr. *ouron*, urine.] excessive urination, as in certain diseases.

pol·y·ū′riç, *a.* of or characterized by polyuria.

pol·y·vā′lence, pol·y′vȧ·lence, *n.* the quality or state of being polyvalent.

pol·y·vā′lent, *a.* 1. in bacteriology, designating a vaccine containing two or more strains of the same species of bacteria.
2. in chemistry, having more than one valence.

pol·y·vī′nyl, *a.* designating or of any of a group of polymerized vinyl compounds.
polyvinyl resin; any of various plastics made from polymerized vinyl compounds or copolymers of vinyl and other resins, used in various molded or extruded products, coatings, adhesives, sizes, etc.

pol′y·vol′tine, *n.* [*poly-*, and It. *volta*, turn, time, and *-ine*.] a species of silkworm that produces cocoons several times in a season.

pol·y·wa̤′tẽr, *n.* [*poly*meric, and *water*.] a viscous laboratory substance, formed in minute quantities in capillary tubes, and variously identified as a hydrosol, a new form of water, contaminated water, etc.

Pō·lyx′ē·nȧ, *n.*; in Greek legend, a daughter of Priam and betrothed of Achilles.

Pol·y·zō′ȧ, *n.pl.* a class, mostly marine, of molluscoid invertebrates propagated by budding and living in colonies, or polyzoaria.

pol·y·zō′ăn, *n.* a member of the *Polyzoa.*

pol·y·zō′ăn, *a.* relating to or having the characteristics of *Polyzoa.*

pol″y·zō·ăr′i·um, *n.*; *pl.* **pol″y·zō·ăr′i·ȧ,** 1. an aggregation of individual polypides; a polyzoan colony.
2. its supporting skeleton.

pol·y·zō′ȧ·ry, *n.*; *pl.* **pol·y·zō′ȧ·rieṣ,** [*polyzoon* and *-ary*.] a polyzoarium.

pol·y·zō′iç, *a.* 1. of the polyzoans.
2. consisting of many zooids.
3. designating or of a spore that produces many sporozoites.

pol·y·zōn′ăl, *a.* [*poly-*, and Gr. *zōnē*, zone, belt.] consisting of many zones or rings; as, a *polyzonal* lens.

pol·y·zō′oid, *a.* [*poly-* and *zooid*.] resembling or pertaining to the *Polyzoa.*

pol·y·zō′on, *n.*; *pl.* **pol·y·zō′ȧ,** [*poly-*, and Gr. *zōon*, animal.] a polypide.

pŏm′āce, *n.* [LL. *pomacium*, cider; L. *pomum*, apple.]
1. the crushed pulp of apples or other fruit pressed for juice.
2. the crushed matter of anything pressed, as seeds for oil.

Pō·mā′cē·ae, *n.pl.* same as *Pomeæ.*

Pō·mȧ·cen′tri·dae, *n.pl.* [Gr. *pōma*, lid, and *kentron*, center.] a family of tropical pharyngognathous fishes of bright colors, found near coral formations: also called *coral fishes.*

pō·mȧ·cen′troid, *a.* belonging or pertaining to the *Pomacentridæ.*

pō·mā′ceous, *a.* [LL. *pomaceus*; L. *pomum*, apple.]
1. consisting of or pertaining to apples; as, *pomaceous* harvests. [Poetic.]
2. in botany, of or like the pomes.

pō·māde′, *n.* [It. *pomada*; LL. *pomatum*; L. *pomum*, apple.] a perfumed ointment, now usually one for the hair: said to have been made originally with apples.

pō·māde′, *v.t.*; pomaded, *pt., pp.*; pomading, *ppr.* to apply pomade to.

Pō·mȧ·der′ris, *n.* [Gr. *pōma*, cover, lid, and *derris*, skin.] a genus of hoary pubescent shrubs found in Australia and New Zealand, yielding a hard, close-grained wood.

pō·man′dẽr, *n.* [earlier *pomamber*; OFr. *pomme d'ambre*, apple or ball of amber.]
1. a ball made of a mixture of perfumes, formerly carried as a supposed safeguard against infection or bad luck.
2. a case for carrying this, as a perforated box, bag, or hollow ball.

pō′mȧ·rīne, *a.* [LL. *pomarinus*, from *pomatorhinus*; Gr. *pōma* (*-atos*), cover, and *rhis, rhinos*, nose.] having the nostrils covered or partly covered, as with scales: said of a bird.
pomarine jager; a gull-like bird, *Stercorarius pomarinus*, of the northern seas.

pō·mā′tum, *n.* [Mod. L.] pomade.

pō·mā′tum, *v.t.*; pomatumed, *pt., pp.*; pomatuming, *ppr.* to pomade.

pōme, *n.* [L. *pomum*, apple.]
1. in botany, any fleshy fruit containing a core and seeds, as the apple, pear, etc.
2. in medieval times, a small metal globe filled with hot water, used by a priest to keep his hands warm while handling the elements, so as to prevent accident on account of numbness.

pōme, *v.i.* [Fr. *pommer*, from *pomme*, apple.] to form a head in growing. [Obs.]

Pō′mē·ae, *n.pl.* a division of rosaceous plants in which the calyx tube becomes fleshy or pulpy and consolidated with from two to five ovaries to form a compound pistil and the kind of fruit called a pome; the apple family.

pōme′cit·rŏn, *n.* a citron apple; a citron. [Obs.]

pome′gran·āte, *n.* [L. *pomum*, an apple, and *granatum*, grained.]
1. a small tree, *Punica granatum*, of the family *Lythraceæ*, having oblong or lanceolate leaves, a leathery calyx shaped like a top, and many scarlet, white, or yellowish petals: it is native to western Asia or northern Africa.
2. the fruit of *Punica granatum*, about the size of an orange, covered with a hard rind, and containing many large seeds, each enclosed in juicy pulp of a reddish color and of an acid taste.
3. an ornament resembling a pomegranate.

A B

POMEGRANATE
A, leaves and fruit; B, cross section of fruit

pŏm′el, *n.* a pommel. [Obs.]

pom′e·lō, *n.*; *pl.* **pom′e·lōṣ,** 1. the shaddock.
2. the grapefruit.

pōme′ly, *a.* [Fr. *pommelé*, from *pomme*; L. *pomum*, an apple.] marked with round spots like apples; dappled. [Obs.]

Pom·e·rā′ni·ăn, *n.* 1. a native or inhabitant of Pomerania.
2. a dog of a small breed with long, silky hair, pointed ears and muzzle, and a bushy tail turned over the back.

Pom·e·rā′ni·ăn, *a.* of or pertaining to Pomerania, a former province of Prussia, or its people.

pome′roy, *n.* [Fr. *pomme*, apple, and *roi*, king.] a kind of apple. [Obs.]

pome·roy′ăl, *n.* pomeroy. [Obs.]

pōme′wa̤″tẽr, *n.* a sweet and juicy kind of apple. [Obs.]

pō′mey, *n.*; *pl.* **pō′meyṣ,** [Fr. *pommé*, grown round like an apple.] in heraldry, the figure of an apple or a roundel, always of a green color.

pom′fret, *n.* [Port. *pombo*.]
1. a fish of the genus *Stromateoides*, having the same compressed form as the dory, but the muzzle blunt and not retractile. The species are found in the Mediterranean and the Indian and Pacific Oceans.
2. the henfish, *Brama raji.*

pō′mi·çul·tūre, *n.* [L. *pomum*, apple, and E. *culture*.] cultivation of fruit.

pō·mif′ẽr·ous, *a.* [L. *pomum*, an apple, and *ferre*, to produce.] bearing fruit, especially pomes.

pō′mi·fo̤rm, *a.* [L. *pomum*, apple, and *forma*, form.] shaped like a pome or apple.

pom′māġe, *n.* same as *pomace.*

pŏmme blănçhe (blonsh), [Fr., white apple.] the prairie turnip.

pom·mée′ (-mā′), *a.* same as *pommetty.*

pŏm′mel (*or* pom′), *n.* [Fr. *pommeau*, dim. of *pomme*; L. *pomum*, an apple.]
1. a round knob on the end of the hilt of a sword, etc.
2. the rounded, upward-projecting front part of a saddle.
3. (a) a round knob on the frame of a chair; (b) a globular ornament, as at the top of a spire or turret; (c) the top (of the head). [Obs.]
4. a kind of club or bat. [Brit.]

pŏm′mel, *v.t.*; pommeled *or* pommelled, *pt., pp.*; pommeling *or* pommelling, *ppr.* to beat (formerly, with a sword pommel; now, usually, with the fists).

pŏm′meled, *a.* in heraldry, having pommels, as a sword or dagger.

pom·mĕl′iŏn (-yun), *n.* the cascabel or hindmost knob of a cannon. [Obs.]

pom′met·ty, *a.* [Fr. *pommetté*, from *pommette*, knob, dim. of *pomme*, apple.] in heraldry, having extremities terminated by a knob or by two knobs side by side, as a cross.

CROSS POMMETTY

pō·mō·log′iç·ăl, *a.* of pomology.

pō·mol′ō·gist, *n.* an expert in pomology.

pō·mol′ō·ġy, *n.* [L. *pommum*, apple, and *-ology*.] the art or science of raising fruit or fruit-bearing trees or shrubs.

Pō·mō′nȧ, *n.* [L. *pomum*, fruit.] in Roman mythology, the goddess of fruits and of fruit culture.

pomp, *n.* [Fr. *pompe*; L. *pompa*, from Gr. *pompē*, a solemn procession, from *pempein*, to send.]
1. stately or brilliant display; splendor; magnificence.
2. ostentatious or vain show.
3. a pageant. [Obs.]
Syn.—grandeur, splendor, magnificence, ostentation, display, pageantry.

pomp, *v.i.* to make ostentatious display. [Rare.]

pom′pȧ·dŏur, *n.* [after the Marquise de *Pompadour*, mistress of Louis XV.]
1. a woman's hairdo in which the hair is swept up high from the forehead, usually over a roll.

2. a man's hairdo in which the hair is brushed up straight from the forehead.
3. a style of dress with a square low-cut neck.

pom'pȧ·dŏur, *a.* of or pertaining to anything in the style of the Marquise de Pompadour.

pom'pȧ·nō, *n.*; *pl.* **pom'pȧ·nōs̨,** [Sp. *pampano.*]
1. one of several kinds of food fish belonging to the genus *Trachynotus,* having spiny fins and a widely forked tail.
2. a food fish of California, *Stromateus simillimus.*
3. *Gerres olisthostoma,* the Irish pompano found on the Florida coast.

pom'pȧ·nō shell, a small bivalve shell used as food by the pompano.

pom·pat'iç, *a.* pompous; ostentatious. [Obs.]

Pom·pē'iăn, *a.* pertaining to the ancient city or the people or culture of Pompeii in Italy, ruined and buried by an eruption of Vesuvius in A.D. 79, and excavated in recent times.
Pompeian red; a yellowish-red color found in wall decorations in Pompeii.

pom'pel·mous, *n.* [D.] the shaddock, especially some large form.

pom'pē·lō, *n.* same as *pompelmous.*

pom'pet, *n.* a printer's inking ball. [Obs.]

pom'phō·lyx, *n.* [Gr. *pompholyx,* a bubble, *pomphos,* a pustule.]
1. zinc oxide. [Obs.]
2. a variety of pemphigus.

pŏm'pi·ŏn, *n.* same as *pumpion.*

pom·pō'lē·ŏn, *n.* same as *pompelmous.*

pom'pom, *n.* [echoic.]
1. in World War I, a type of large machine gun firing one-pound shells.
2. in World War II, a rapid-firing, automatic antiaircraft gun firing explosive shells.

pom'pon, *n.* [Fr., from MFr. *pomper,* to exhibit pomp.]
1. an ornamental ball or tuft of silk, wool, feathers, etc., sometimes worn on women's or children's hats, or on the front of a soldier's shako.
2. (a) a kind of chrysanthemum with small, round flowers; (b) its flower.

pom·pos'i·ty, *n.*; *pl.* **pom·pos'i·ties̨,** [ML. *pompositas.*] quality or instance of being pompous; pompous behavior, speech, etc.; ostentation; self-importance.

pom·pō'sō, *a.* [It.] in music, grand and dignified: a direction to the performer.

pomp'ous, *a.* [Fr. *pompeux*; It. *pomposo,* from L. *pompa,* pomp.]
1. displaying pomp; showy with grandeur; splendid; magnificent; as, a *pompous* procession; a *pompous* triumph.
2. having or exhibiting marked self-importance; ostentatious; boastful; as, a *pompous* account of private adventures.
Syn.—vainglorious, arrogant, resplendent.

pomp'ous·ly, *adv.* in a pompous manner.

pomp'ous·ness, *n.* the state of being pompous; magnificence; splendor; great display; ostentatiousness.

Pomp'tine, *n.* same as *pontine.*

pom'wạ″tẽr, *n.* same as *pomewater.*

Poñ'çȧ, *n.*; *pl.* **Poñ'çȧ, Poñ'çȧs̨,** a member of a tribe of Siouan Indians of southwestern Minnesota.

Poñ'çȧ, *a.* of a tribe of Siouan Indians of southwestern Minnesota.

pon·ceau' (-sō'), *n.* [Fr.]
1. any aniline dye producing a red color.
2. a red poppy, *Papaver rhœas.*

ponce'let, *n.* [after the French engineer J. V. *Poncelet.*] a unit of activity equal to one hundred kilogrammeters per second, or approximately one kilowatt.

pon'chō, *n.*; *pl.* **pon'chōs̨,** [Sp., from Araucan *poncho.*]
1. a cloak like a blanket with a hole in the middle for the head, worn in Spanish America.
2. any similar garment, especially one of rubber, etc., worn as a raincoat.

pond, *n.* [form of *pound,* enclosure.] a body of standing water smaller than a lake, often artificially formed.

pond, *v.t.*; ponded, *pt. pp.*; ponding, *ppr.* to make into a pond; to collect in a pond by stopping the current of a river.

pond, *v.t.* to ponder. [Obs.]

pon'dẽr, *v.t.*; pondered, *pt.*, *pp.*; pondering, *ppr.* [L. *ponderare,* from *pondus, ponderis,* weight.]
1. to weigh in the mind; to consider carefully; to think deeply about.
Mary kept all these things, and *pondered* them in her heart. —Luke ii. 19.
2. to view with deliberation; to examine.
Ponder the path of thy feet. —Prov. iv. 26.
3. to weigh. [Obs.]

pon'dẽr, *v.i.* to think deeply; to deliberate; to meditate.

pon″dẽr·ȧ·bil'i·ty, *n.* the state or quality of being ponderable.

pon'dẽr·ȧ·ble, *a.* 1. that can be weighed.
2. that can be mentally weighed; appreciable.

pon'dẽr·ȧ·ble·ness, *n.* same as *ponderability.*

pon'dẽr·ăl, *a.* [from L. *pondus, ponderis,* weight.] estimated or ascertained by weight: distinguished from *numeral*; as, a *ponderal* drachma.

pon'dẽr·ănce, *n.* weight; gravity. [Rare.]

pon'dẽr·ȧ·ry, *a.* of or pertaining to weight. [Rare.]

pon'dẽr·āte, *v.i.*; ponderated, *pt.*, *pp.*; ponderating, *ppr.* to weigh; to have influence. [Rare.]

pon'dẽr·āte, *v.t.* to weigh in the mind; to consider. [Rare.]

pon·dẽr·ā'tion, *n.* the act of weighing. [Rare.]

pon'dẽr·ẽr, *n.* one who ponders, or weighs in his mind.

pon'dẽr·ing·ly, *adv.* with consideration or deliberation.

pon″dẽr·ō·mō'tive, *a.* [L. *pondus, ponderis,* weight, and *motive.*] pertaining to or having the power to move ponderable matter, as opposed to *electromotive.*

pon·dẽr·os'i·ty, *n.* the state or quality of being ponderous.

pon'dẽr·ous, *a.* [L. *ponderosus.*]
1. very heavy.
2. unwieldy because of weight.
3. that seems heavy; bulky; massive.
4. labored; dull; as, *ponderous* words.
ponderous spar; heavy spar, or barytes.
Syn.—heavy, lifeless, dull, inanimate.

pon'dẽr·ous·ly, *adv.* in a ponderous manner.

pon'dẽr·ous·ness, *n.* the state or condition of being ponderous; heaviness; gravity.

pond'fish, *n.* any fresh-water fish of the family *Centrarchidæ,* common in America and especially in New England: called also *pond perch, sunfish, bream,* and *sunny.*

pond lil'y, the water lily, an aquatic plant of the genus *Nymphæa,* growing in stagnant pools throughout Europe and the temperate zone. *Nymphæa advena* is the common yellow pond lily of middle and eastern North America.

pond pẽrch, see *pondfish.*

pond sçum, a mass of one-celled plants floating on the surface of ponds, etc., forming a green scum.

pond snāil, any snail of the genus *Limnæa,* or associated genera.

pond'weed, *n.* an aquatic herb of the genus *Potamogeton,* with straplike or long, grasslike leaves.
choke pondweed; an obstructive water weed of the genus *Anacharis.*
horned pondweed; a slender annual of the pondweed family, *Zannichellia palustris,* bearing small nuts.

pōne, *n.* [Am. Indian.] in the southern part of the United States, bread made of corn meal; also, a loaf or cake of this.

pō'nē, *n.* [L., imper. of *ponere,* to place.]
1. in old English law, (a) a writ whereby an action pending in an inferior court might be removed for trial to a superior one; (b) a writ whereby a sheriff was ordered to take security of a man for his appearance at a specified time.
2. (pōn), in certain card games, the player to the right of the dealer.

pō'nent, *a.* [It. *ponente,* the west.] western; as, the *ponent* winds. [Archaic.]

pon·ē·rol'ō·ġy, *n.* [Gr. *ponēros,* bad, and *-ology.*] the part of theology which deals with the doctrine of the origin and operation of evil or sin; diabolology.

pon·ġee', *n.* [from Chin. dial *pen-chi,* domestic loom.]
1. a soft, thin cloth of Chinese or Indian silk, usually left in its natural light-brown color.
2. a cloth, as of rayon, like this.

poñ'gō, *n.* [Borneo.] the orangutan.

pon'iărd (-yărd), *n.* [Fr. *poignard,* from *poing*; L. *pugnus,* fist.] a small dagger; a pointed instrument for stabbing, usually with a slender triangular or square blade.

pon'iărd, *v.t.*; poniarded, *pt.*, *pp.*; poniarding, *ppr.* to stab or pierce with or as with a poniard.

pons̨, *n.*; *pl.* **pon'tēs̨,** [L., a bridge.]
1. in anatomy and zoology, a narrow piece of tissue connecting two parts of an organ.
2. the pons Varolii.

pons̨ as·i·nō'rum, [L., bridge of asses.]
1. in geometry, the fifth proposition of the first book of Euclid (that the base angles of an isosceles triangle are equal).
2. any problem that is hard for beginners.

pons̨ Vȧ·rō'li·ī, [Mod. L., bridge of Varoli: after Costanzo *Varoli* (1542–1575), It. anatomist.] a broad band of nerve fibers that arch across the upper part of the medulla oblongata and connect the cerebrum, cerebellum, and medulla oblongata.

pon'taçq (-tak), *n.* [from *Pontacq,* in the Basses-Pyrénées, where it is made.] a kind of red wine.

pon'tăġe, *n.* [OFr., from LL. *pontaticum,* from L. *pons, pontis,* a bridge.] a duty paid for repairing bridges.

Pon·tē·dē'ri·ȧ, *n.* the type genus of the *Pontederiaceæ.*

Pon·tē·dē·ri·ā'cē·ae, *n.pl.* [after the Italian botanist, Giulio *Pontedera.*] a family of aquatic monocotyledons, native to the subtropical parts of America, Africa, and the East Indies. They are of the pickerel weed family, having leaves with parallel veins and flowers from a spathe.

pon·tē·dē·ri·ā'ceous, *a.* belonging or pertaining to the *Pontederiaceæ.*

Pon'tiç, *a.* [L. *Pontus*; Gr. *Pontos.*]
1. of Pontus, an ancient kingdom in Asia Minor on the Black Sea.
2. of the Black Sea.

pon'ti·fex, *n.*; *pl.* **pon·tif'i·cēs̨,** in ancient Rome, a member of the supreme college of priests, the Pontifical College.
Pontifex Maximus; the chief priest of the Pontifical College; also, the Pope.

pon'tiff, *n.* [L. *pontifex, pontificis,* a high priest.]
1. a pontifex.
2. a bishop.
3. the Pope.
4. a high priest.

pon·tif'iç, *a.* pontifical. [Rare.]

pon·tif'iç·ăl, *a.* [L. *pontificalis.*]
1. having to do with a pontifex, a high priest, or a bishop; episcopal.
2. having to do with the Pope; papal.
3. having the pomp, dignity, or dogmatism of a pontiff: often used to imply arrogance or haughtiness.
4. of or pertaining to bridge building. [Rare.]

pon·tif'iç·ăl, *n.* 1. a book directing ecclesiastical rites and ceremonies for a bishop.
2. [*pl.*] the insignia, garments, and ornaments of a pontiff or bishop.

pon·tif·iç·al'i·ty, *n.* the state and government of the pope; the papacy.

pon·tif'iç·ăl·ly, *adv.* in a pontifical manner.

pon·tif'i·çāte, *n.* [L. *pontificatus.*] the state, office, or term of office of a pontiff.
He turned hermit, in the view of being advanced to the *pontificate.* —Addison.

pon·tif'i·çāte, *v.i.*; pontificated, *pt.*, *pp.*; pontificating, *ppr.* 1. to officiate as a pontiff.
2. to behave in the manner of a pontiff; to be dogmatic.

pon'ti·fice (-fis), *n.* [L. *pons, pontis,* a bridge, and *facere,* to make.] bridgework; the erection or structure of a bridge. [Obs.]

pon·tif'i·cēs̨, *n.* plural of *pontifex.*

pon·ti·fi'ciăl (-fish'ăl), *a.* pontifical. [Obs.]

pon·ti·fi'ciăn (-fish'ăn), *n.* an adherent or supporter of the Pope or papacy; a papist. [Obs.]

pon'til, *n.* [Fr.; It. *pontello, puntello,* dim. of *punto,* a point.] a punty.

pon'tile, *a.* [LL. *pontilis,* of a bridge.] of or pertaining to a pons, particularly the pons Varolii.

Pon'tine, Pomp'tine, *a.* [L. *Pontinus, Pomptinus*; Fr. *Pontin*; It. *Pontino.*] pertaining or relating to a large marshy district, the Pontine Marshes, between Rome and Naples.

pont·lev'is, *n.* [Fr., a drawbridge.]
1. a drawbridge.
2. in horsemanship, a disorderly resisting action of a horse in disobedience to his rider, in which he rears up several times.

Pon·tō·ças'pi·ăn, *a.* [*Pontic* and *Caspian.*] relating to the region about the Black and Caspian Seas.

pon'tŏn, *n.* [Fr.] in the United States Army, a pontoon.

pon·tō·niēr' (-nēr'), *n.* [Fr. *pontonnier.*] a military engineer or other member of the armed forces who builds, or is in charge of building, a pontoon bridge.

pon·tọọn′, *n.* [Fr. *ponton*, from L. *pons, pontis*, a bridge.]

1. a flat-bottomed boat.
2. any of a number of these, or of some other floating objects, as hollow cylinders, used as supports for a temporary bridge.
3. either of two boatlike floats used on the landing gear of small airplanes to allow them to land on water.

pon·tọọn′ bridġe, a temporary bridge supported on pontoons: in military usage, usually *ponton bridge.*

PONTOON BRIDGE

pon·tọọn′ing, *n.* the art or operation of constructing pontoon bridges.

pon·tọọn′ trāin, the wagons, loaded with pontoon materials, which accompany an army when on the march.

pont″vō·lant′, *n.* [Fr., flying bridge.] a double-decked bridge, the upper portion of which may be projected first; a flying bridge: used in military operations to enable an attacking force to cross a moat. [Rare.]

pon′ty, *n.* same as *punty.*

pō′ny, *n.*; *pl.* **pō′nieṣ**, [Scot. *powny*; prob. from OFr. *poulenet*, dim. of *poulain*, a colt; LL. *pullanus*, from L. *pullus*, young animal.]

1. a horse of any of a number of small breeds, usually not over 14 hands high.
2. something small of its kind.
3. (a) a small liqueur glass; (b) the amount of liqueur, brandy, etc. this will hold. [Colloq.]
4. a literal translation of a literary work in a foreign language, used in doing schoolwork, often dishonestly; a crib. [Colloq.]
5. the sum of twenty-five pounds. [Brit. Racing Slang.]

pony cart; a low cart drawn by one or two ponies.

pony chaise; a pony cart.

pony engine; a small handy engine adapted to various uses.

pony express; a system of carrying and delivering mail by riders on swift ponies; specifically, such a system in operation from 1860 to 1861 between St. Joseph, Missouri, and Sacramento, California.

pony truck; a two-wheeled truck for a locomotive.

pō′ny, *v.t.* and *v.i.*; ponied, *pt., pp.*; ponying, *ppr.* to pay; to settle an account: followed by *up*; as, to *pony up.* [Slang.]

pọọ′à, *n.* [E. Ind.] an East Indian urticaceous plant, *Maoutia puya*, whose stem yields a valuable fiber: also spelled *pooah.*

pọọch, *n.* [coincides with dial. and obs. form of *pouch*; prob. with reference to appetite.] a dog, especially a mongrel. [Slang.]

pọọd, *n.* [Russ. *pud.*] a Russian weight, equivalent to approximately thirty-six pounds avoirdupois.

pọọ′dle, *n.* [G. *pudel*; L.G. *pudel, pudel-hund*, from *pudeln*, to splash.] any of a breed of medium-sized, white or black, curly-haired dogs.

POODLE
(15 in. high at shoulder)

pọọ′gyē, *n.* [Hind.] the nose flute of the Hindus.

pọọh, *interj.* [probably imitative.] an exclamation of contempt, disbelief, or impatience.

pọọh, *v.t.* to tire; to exhaust. [Slang.]

Pọọh′-bäh′, *n.* [from a character in W. S. Gilbert's comic opera, *The Mikado.*] one who fills several offices at one time; one who believes himself all-important.

pọọh″-pọọh′, *v.t.* and *v.i.* [reduplicative.] to express contempt (for); to make light (of); to disregard.

pọọh′-pọọh′, *interj.* an exclamation of contempt, disbelief, or impatience.

pọọh″-pọọh′, *n.* a pooh-poohing.

pọọ′jȧ, pụ′jȧ, *n.* [Sans. *pūjā*, honor.] a Hindu ceremony; any religious rite.

pọọ′kọọ, *n.* [African.] a large red African antelope, *Kobus vardoni.*

pọọl, *n.* [AS. *pol.*]

1. a small pond, as in a garden.
2. a puddle.
3. a swimming pool.
4. a deep, still spot in a river.

pọọl, *n.* [Fr. *poule*, pool, stakes, from LL. *pulla*, hen.]

1. the total amount of the players' stakes, played for in a card game, etc.
2. a container for this.
3. (a) any of several related games of billiards played with object balls numbered from 1 to 15 and a cue ball, on a table with six pockets; (b) [Brit.] a game of billiards for a pool (sense 1).
4. a combination of resources, funds, etc. for some common purpose or benefit; specifically, (a) the combined wagers of betters on a horse race, etc., the gains or losses from which are to be divided proportionately; (b) the combined investments of a group of persons or corporations undertaking, and sharing responsibility for, a joint enterprise; (c) a common fund of stockholders, for speculation, manipulation of prices, etc.
5. the persons or parties forming such a combination.
6. a combination of business firms for elimination of competition in, and for control of, a common market; a trust; a monopoly.
7. in fencing, a contest in which each member of a team successively competes with each member of the opposing team.

blind pool; a pool, or monopoly, the scope and purpose of which are known only to the originators, who retain entire control.

pọọl, *v.t.* and *v.i.*; pooled, *pt., pp.*; pooling, *ppr.* to contribute to a pool, or common fund; to make a common interest or form a pool (of).

pọọl′ẽr, *n.* a stick for stirring a tan vat.

pọọl′rọọm, *n.* 1. a room or establishment in which the game of pool is played.

2. a room or place where bets are made on sporting events.

pọọl sell′ẽr, one who sells pools on any event or contest.

pọọl tā′ble, a billiard table with a pocket at each corner and at the middle of both sides, for playing pool.

pọọn, *n.* [Singhalese.]

1. any of several East Indian trees, as the *Calaphyllum inophyllum*, whose seeds yield a bitter oil.
2. the wood of any of these trees.

Also *poon tree.*

pọọ′naç, *n.* [E. Ind.] the pulp cake remaining after the oil is pressed from the cocoanut.

pọọñ′gȧ oil, an oil obtained from the seeds of *Pongamia glabra*, in India, where it is used as a stimulant in medicine and as an illuminant.

pọọp, *n.* [L. *puppis*, the stern of a ship.]

1. originally, the stern section of a ship.
2. on sailing ships, a raised deck at the stern, sometimes forming the roof of a cabin: also *poop deck.*

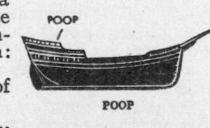

POOP

pọọp, *n.* the act of breaking wind.

pọọp, *v.t.*; pọọped, *pt., pp.*; pooping, *ppr.* 1. to break over the stern of, as a heavy sea: said of waves.

2. to receive (a wave) over the poop or stern.

pọọp, *v.i.* to break wind.

pọọp, *v.t.* [echoic.] to cause to become exhausted, out of breath, etc.: usually in the passive voice: also *pooh.* [Slang.]

pọọp ċab′in, the cabin under the poop deck.

pọọp deck, a deck built over the cabin of a ship, when the cabin is in the spar deck.

pọọped (pọọpt), *a.* having a poop.

pọọr, *a.*; *comp.* pọọrer; *superl.* poorest, [OFr. *poure, povre*; Fr. *pauvre*, from L. *pauper*, poor.]

1. lacking material possessions; having little or no means to support oneself; needy; impoverished.
2. indicating or characterized by poverty.
3. lacking in some quality.
4. lacking abundance; scanty; inadequate; as, *poor* crops.
5. lacking productivity; barren; sterile; as, *poor* soil.
6. lacking nourishment; feeble; emaciated; as, a *poor* body.
7. lacking excellence; paltry; mean; insignificant; inferior.
8. lacking good moral or mental qualities; mean-spirited; contemptible; as, he is a *poor* creature.
9. lacking pleasure, comfort, or satisfaction; as, we had a *poor* time.
10. worthy of pity; unfortunate.

Poor Clare; a Clarisse.

poor debtor; an insolvent debtor.

poor debtor's oath; an oath of poverty required of an imprisoned debtor before he may be released by taking insolvency proceedings under the law.

poor farm; a farm for paupers, supported by a county or other local government.

poor in spirit; humble; contrite; without pride.

poor john; a dried and salted hake. [Obs.]

poor laws; laws that provide for public relief and support of the poor.

poor man's weatherglass; the scarlet pimpernel, which opens its blossoms only in fair weather.

poor rate; in Great Britain, a tax levied in a parish to relieve the wants of the poor.

poor relief; material aid given to the needy, especially by local authority.

poor soldier; the Australian friarbird.

poor white; in the southern United States, a white person who lives in great poverty and ignorance, often as a tenant farmer: also, collectively, *poor white trash*: contemptuous term.

the poor; poor, or needy, people collectively.

Syn.—indigent, moneyless, impecunious, penniless, humble, meager, weak, insufficient, deficient, faulty, unsatisfactory, inconsiderable, thin, scanty.

pọọr, *n.* a small European fish, *Gadus minutus.*

pọọr′box, *n.* a box for receiving alms for the poor, especially one near the door of a church.

pọọr′house, *n.* a house or institution for paupers, supported from public funds; an almshouse.

pọọr′ish, *a.* somewhat poor; inferior.

pọọr′li·ness, *n.* the state of being poorly. [Rare.]

pọọr′ly, *adv.* 1. in a poor manner; scantily; badly; defectively.

2. with a low opinion; disparagingly; as, I think *poorly* of it.

poorly off; having little wealth.

pọọr′ly, *a.* somewhat ill; indisposed; in poor health. [Colloq.]

pọọr′màs″tẽr, *n.* a public officer who has charge of paupers. [Dial.]

pọọr′ness, *n.* the quality or state of being poor.

pọọr′-spir′it·ed, *a.* having or showing a poor spirit; cowardly; timorous; abject.

pọọr″-spir′it·ed·ness, *n.* the quality or state of being poor-spirited.

pọọrt, *n.* [D.] a mountain pass.

pọọr′will, *n.* an American bird, *Phalænoptilus nuttalli*, related to the whippoorwill.

pop, *n.* [imitative.]

1. a sudden, short, light, explosive sound.
2. a shot with a revolver, rifle, etc.
3. any carbonated, nonalcoholic beverage: so called from the sound produced when the cork, now generally replaced by a bottle cap, was removed from a bottle.

pop, *v.i.*; popped (popt), *pt., pp.*; popping, *ppr.* 1. to make a pop.

2. to burst with a pop.
3. to move, go, come, etc. suddenly and quickly, and usually unexpectedly; as, he *popped* into the room.
4. to open wide suddenly, or protrude, as with amazement: said of the eyes.
5. to shoot a pistol, etc.
6. in baseball, to be put out by hitting the ball high in the air so that it is easily caught: usually with *out* or *up.*

pop, *v.t.* 1. to cause to pop, as corn by roasting, etc.

2. to fire (a pistol, etc.).
3. to shoot.

4. to put suddenly, quickly, or unexpectedly; as, he *popped* his head in the door; they *popped* a question at him.
5. in baseball, to hit (the ball) high in the air, but in or near the infield, so that it is easily caught.
to pop the question; to make a proposal of marriage. [Colloq.]

pop, *adv.* with or like a pop.

pop, *n.* [from *papa.*] father: often a term of address to an elderly man. [Slang.]

pop (ärt), a realistic art style, especially in painting and sculpture, using techniques and popular subjects adapted from commercial art and the mass communications media, such as comic strips, posters, etc.

pop çon'cērt, a popular concert, chiefly of semiclassical and the light classical music.

pop'çorn", *n.* 1. a variety of Indian corn with small ears and hard grains which pop open into a white, puffy mass when heated.
2. the popped grains, eaten as a confection.

pop'dock, *n.* the foxglove.

pōpe, *n.* [AS. *papa,* from LL. *papa*; L.Gr. *papas,* father, bishop; Gr. *pappas,* father.]
1. [usually P-] the bishop of Rome; the head of the Roman Catholic Church.
2. a person who assumes, or is thought to have, popelike authority.
3. a parish priest of the Orthodox Eastern Church.
4. a small fish of the perch family, *Acerina cernua*: also called *ruff*.
5. the bullfinch. [Brit. Dial.]

pōpe'dŏm, *n.* the place, office, tenure, jurisdiction, or dignity of a pope.

pōpe'-hō"ly, *a.* hypocritical. [Obs.]

pōpe'hood, *n.* the office or function of a pope.

Pōpe Jōan, [from *Pope Joan,* the (fictitious) female pope of the ninth century.] an old game of cards played by any number of players with a deck from which the eight of diamonds has been removed.

pōpe'ling, *n.* an adherent of the Pope; a petty pope: used in contempt. [Obs.]

pope'lot, pop'let, *n.* [OFr. *poupette,* a puppet.] a darling. [Obs.]

pōp'ēr·y, *n.* the religion of the Roman Catholic Church, comprehending doctrines, beliefs, rituals, and practices: an opprobrious term.

pōpe's'-eȳe (-ī), *n.* the gland surrounded with fat in the middle of the thigh of an ox or sheep.

pōpe's head (hed), a large, round brush, with a long handle, for dusting ceilings.

pope's nōşe, the fleshy part of a bird's tail.

pop'et, *n.* a puppet. [Obs.]

pop'e·try, *n.* puppetry. [Obs.]

pop'eȳed (-īd), *a.* having popeyes.

pop'eȳeş, *n.pl.* wide, protuberant eyes.

pop'gun, *n.* a small toy gun that shoots harmless pellets or corks by air compression, with a pop.

pop'gun"nēr·y, *n.* the discharge of popguns; childish shooting.

pop'in·jāy, *n.* [OFr. *papegai*; LL. *papagallus,* a parrot.]
1. originally, a parrot.
2. the green woodpecker, a bird with a scarlet crown, native to Europe.
3. a gay, trifling young man; a talkative, vain person; a fop or coxcomb.

> But these gilt-edged purple *popinjays* do not speak for the Republic.
> —Edward Everett Hale.

4. formerly, a target in the shape of a parrot on a pole, for archery practice: also used for firearms at sixty to seventy paces.

pōp'ish, *a.* pertaining to the Pope, popery, or the Roman Catholic Church; as, *popish* tenets or ceremonies: a disparaging term.
Popish Plot; in English history, an alleged plot made known by Titus Oates in 1678. He asserted that two men had been told to assassinate Charles II, that certain Roman Catholics whom he named had been appointed to all the high offices of the state, and that the extirpation of Protestantism was intended. On the strength of his allegations, various persons, including Viscount Stafford, were executed.

pōp'ish·ly, *adv.* in a popish manner.

pōp'ish·ness, *n.* popery.

pop'joy·ing, *n.* pastime; sport. [Colloq.]

pop'lăr, *n.* [Fr. *peuplier*; L. *populus.*]
1. a tree of the genus *Populus,* of several species as the abele, the silver poplar, the white poplar, the black poplar, the aspen tree, etc. The species are all tall and fast-growing with small leaves and soft wood.
2. any one of several trees in some way resembling a poplar.
3. the wood of any of these trees.

POPLAR (*Populus alba*)

Carolina poplar; same as *cottonwood.*
downy poplar; the swamp cottonwood, *Populus heterophylla.*
gray poplar; a hybrid European white poplar which yields a superior timber.
Ontario poplar; same as *balsam poplar.*

pop'lăr birch, the American white birch, *Betula populifolia.*

pop'lăr bōr'ēr, a beetle, *Saperda calcarata,* whose larvae bore the trunks of poplars.

pop'lăred, *a.* covered or lined with poplars.

pop'lăr·wŏrm, *n.* any one of numerous larvae that feed on and destroy the poplar, willow, and cottonwood trees.

pop'lin, *n.* [Fr. *popeline.*] a silk, rayon, cotton, or woolen cloth with a ribbed surface, used for dresses, etc.
Irish poplin; a silk and worsted fabric made in Ireland.

pop·li·tē'ăl, pop·lit'iç, *a.* [L. *poples* (*-itis*), the ham.] pertaining to or near the ham, or that part of the leg behind the knee.

Pop'ō·crat, *n.* [*Pop*ulist and Demo*crat.*] a person who was considered to hold theories of both the Democratic and Populistic political parties.

pop'ō"vēr, *n.* a very light, puffy, hollow muffin made of a thin batter: so called because it rises over the baking tin.

pop'pēr, *n.* 1. a utensil for popping corn.
2. one who or that which pops.

pop'pet, *n.* [form of *puppet.*]
1. a poppethead.
2. a valve that moves up out of and down into its port, often used for regularly interrupted flow, as in a gasoline engine: also *poppet valve.*
3. a piece of wood on the gunwale of a boat, for supporting an oarlock.
4. one of several timbers used to shore up or support a vessel previous to launching.
5. (a) [Obs.] a doll; (b) [Brit. Dial.] a little person: term of endearment, as for a child.

pop'pet·head (-hed), *n.* the tailstock or headstock of a lathe.

pop'pied, *a.* 1. covered or mixed with poppies.
2. drugging or drugged, as with opium.

pop'ping crēase, in cricket, a line marking the batsman's position.

pop'ple, *v.i.*; poppled, *pt., pp.*; poppling, *ppr.* [ME. *poplen*; prob. of echoic origin.] to bob up and down, as a float on a fish line in rough water; to bubble; to ripple; to heave; to toss, as water in a choppy sea.

pop'ple, *n.* a poppling.

pop'ple, *n.* the poplar. [Dial.]

pop'py, *n.*; *pl.* **pop'pieş,** [AS. *popig*; It. *papavero*; L. *papaver.*]
1. any plant of the genus *Papaver,* having deeply cut leaves, a milky or colored juice, and pink, red, white, orange, or yellow flowers.
2. the flower of the poppy: in art, the symbol of sleep or death.
3. a pharmaceutical extract made from poppy juice.
4. opium.
5. poppy red.
California poppy; a plant, *Eschscholtzia californica,* bearing showy yellow flowers.
celandine poppy; a perennial herb, *Stylophorum diphyllum,* of the Mississippi valley, bearing yellow flowers.
giant poppy; same as *tree poppy.*
horned poppy; same as *horn poppy.*
prickly poppy; a prickly plant, *Argemone mexicana,* with yellow flowers.
water poppy; a tropical American aquatic plant, *Hydrocleys nymphoides,* having showy, yellow, poppylike flowers.
Welsh poppy; a European plant, *Meconopsis cambrica.*

pop'py bee, a bee that cuts the leaves of the poppy and uses the petals for lining its cells.

pop'py·çock, *n.* empty or foolish talk; bosh; buncombe; nonsense. [Colloq.]

pop'py·head (-hed), *n.* an ornament in the form of a small head, cluster of foliage, fleur-de-lis, finial, etc., carved at the top of pew ends or stall ends in Gothic churches.

POPPYHEADS

pop'py mal'lōw, any species of the genus *Callirrhoë,* with flowers resembling the poppy.

pop'py red, a yellowish red, the color of some poppies.

pop'py·seed, the small, dark seed of the poppy, used in cooking, especially as a flavoring or topping for bread, rolls, and the like.

pop'ū·lāce, *n.* [Fr., from It. *popolaccio,* from *popolo*; L. *populus,* people.] the common people; the masses.
Syn.—people, mob, commonalty, rabble.

pop'ū·lă·cy, *n.* the populace, or common people. [Obs.]

pop'ū·lăr, *a.* [Fr. *populaire*; L. *popularis.*]
1. of or carried on by the common people or all the people; as, *popular* opinion.
2. suitable or intended for the people at large; as, *popular* music.
3. within the means of the ordinary person; as, *popular* prices.
4. accepted among the people; common; prevalent; as, a *popular* misconception.
5. liked by the people or by most people; as, a *popular* magazine.
6. very well liked by one's friends and acquaintances.
7. courting popularity or the favor of the people. [Obs.]
8. plebeian; common; vulgar. [Obs.]
popular action; in law, an action to recover a penalty given by statute to a person suing for it.
popular etymology; folk etymology.
popular front; a coalition of leftist and centrist political parties and other groups, as in France (1936–1939), to combat fascism and promote social reforms: also *people's front.*
Syn.—common, current, vulgar, public, general, received, favorite, beloved, prevailing, approved, wide-spread, liked, fashionable.

pop·ū·lā'rēş, *n.pl.* [L.] in Roman history, the people's party, as distinguished from the senatorial party; also, the common people, as opposed to the *optimates.*

pop·ū·lar'i·ty, *n.* 1. the act of seeking the favor of the people. [Obs.]
2. the quality or state of being popular or pleasing to the people at large; the state of being in favor with or supported by the people.

> Without the help of Monmouth's immense *popularity,* it was impossible to effect anything. —Macaulay.

3. representation suited to vulgar or common conception; that which catches or is intended to catch the common people; claptrap. [Obs.]
4. vulgarity: commonness. [Obs.]

pop"ū·lăr·i·zā'tion, *n.* the act of popularizing or the state of being popularized.

pop'ū·lăr·īze, *v.t.*; popularized, *pt., pp.*; popularizing, *ppr.* to make popular; to render suitable or intelligible to the common people; to treat in a manner suited to the comprehension of the people at large.

pop'ū·lăr·ī·zēr, *n.* one who popularizes or renders anything intelligible to the populace.

pop'ū·lăr·ly, adv. 1. in a popular manner; in a manner to please or gain the favor of the people at large; so as to please the crowd.
2. commonly; generally; by the people.

pop'ū·lăr·ness, *n.* the quality or state of being popular; popularity.

pop′ū·lāte, *v.t.*; populated, *pt., pp.*; populating, *ppr.* [from ML. *populatus*, pp. of *populare*, to populate, from L. *populus*, the people.]
 1. to be or become the inhabitants of; to inhabit.
 2. to people; to furnish with people or inhabitants, either by natural increase or by immigration or colonization.

pop′ū·lāte, *v.i.* to propagate; to increase. [Obs.]

pop·ū·lā′tion, *n.* [LL. *populatio.*]
 1. all the people in a country, region, etc.
 2. the number of these.
 3. a (specified) part of the people in a given area; as, the Japanese *population* of Hawaii.
 4. a populating or being populated.
 5. in biology, all the organisms living in a given area.
 6. in statistics, a group of items or individuals.
 population explosion; the very great and continuing increase in human population in modern times.

pop′ū·lā·tŏr, *n.* one who populates or peoples.

pop′ū·lin, *n.* [L. *populus*, poplar, and *-in.*] a crystallizable substance found in the bark, root, and leaves of the *Populus tremula*, or aspen, along with salicin.

Pop′ū·lişm, *n.* [from L. *populus*, the people; and *-ism.*]
 1. the theory and policies of Populists.
 2. the Populistic movement.

Pop′ū·list, *n.* one belonging to the People's party.

Pop′ū·list, *a.* same as *Populistic.*

Pop·ū·list′iç, *a.* 1. of Populists or their views.
 2. having to do with the People's party.

pop′ū·lous, *a.* [L. *populosus.*] full of people; thickly populated.

pop′ū·lous·ly, *adv.* with many inhabitants in proportion to the extent of country.

pop′ū·lous·ness, *n.* the state of being populous.

Pop′ū·lus, *n.* [L., poplar.] a genus of trees which includes the common poplar. *Populus alba* is the European white poplar.

por′bēa″gle, *n.* [from Corn. dial.] any shark of the genus *Lamna*, especially *Lamna cornubica*, found in northern seas: it is large and fierce and brings forth living young rather than eggs.

por′çāte, por′çā·ted, *a.* [L. *porca*, a ridge.] ridged; formed in ridges.

pōr′ce·lain (-lin), *n.* [so called from its resemblance to the Venus shell, which is, in It., *porcellana*, from *porcella*, a little pig, the upper surface of the shell resembling the curve of a pig's back.]
 1. a fine, white, translucent, hard earthenware with a transparent glaze; china.
 2. porcelain dishes or ornaments, collectively.

pōr′ce·lain, *a.* made of porcelain.

pōr′ce·lain çrab, a crab having a very smooth, polished shell, as *Porcellana platycheles*, the broad-clawed species.

pōr′ce·lain·ized, *a.* altered by heating so as to resemble porcelain; in geology, metamorphosed so as to resemble white earthenware, as clays, shales, etc.

pōr′ce·lain jas′pēr, porcelanite.

pōr·ce·lā′nē·ous, pōr·cel·lā′nē·ous, *a.* of or resembling porcelain.

por′ce·lȧ·nīte, por′cel·lȧ·nīte, *n.* a semi-vitrified clay or shale, somewhat resembling jasper.

por′ce·lȧ·nous, por′cel·lȧ·nous, *a.* same as *porcelaneous.*

pōrch, *n.* [ME. and OFr. *porche*, from L. *porticus*, from *porta*, a gate, entrance, or passage.]
 1. a covered entrance to a building, usually projecting from the wall and having a separate roof.
 2. an open or enclosed gallery or room on the outside of a building; a veranda.
 3. a portico; a covered walk. [Obs.]
 the Porch; a portico in Athens where the Stoic philosopher Zeno taught his disciples.

pōrch çlīmb′ēr (klīm′), a burglar who gains entrance to a house by climbing the porch. [Slang.]

por′çīne, *a.* [L. *porcinus*, from *porcus*, hog.] of or like pigs or hogs.

por′çū·pīne, *n.*; *pl.* **por′çū·pīneş** or **por′çū·pīne,** [ME. *porkepyn, pork despyne*; OFr. *porc espin*, the spinous hog, or spine hog; L. *porcus*, and *spina*, a spine or thorn.] any of a number of related gnawing animals; specifically, (a) the old-world porcupine, *Hystrix cristata*, of the family *Hystricidæ*, bearing long, stiff, erectile spines sometimes a foot in length; (b) the North American porcupine, of the family *Erethizontidae*, which is armed with short, sharp quills or spines that may be easily detached from the body. The two species of this porcupine are *Erethizon dorsatus* of the eastern part of the United States and Canada, and *Erethizon epixanthus* of the West.

PORCUPINE

por′çū·pīne ant′ēat·ēr, an echidna, an ant-eating mammal resembling a porcupine.

por′çū·pīne çrab, a Japanese crab having long spines on its carapace and limbs; the *Lithodes hystrix.*

por′çū·pīne fish, a fish of the tropical seas, *Diodon hystrix*, which is covered with spines or prickles capable of being erected by its inflating the body; also, any fish with similarly erectile spines.

por′çū·pīne grȧss, the common prairie grass, *Stipa spartea*, of the United States.

por′çū·pīne wood, the outer wood of the cocoanut palm, which, when cut horizontally, presents markings resembling porcupine quills.

pōre, *n.* [ME. *pore, poor*; L. *porus*; Gr. *poros*, a passage, a pore, from *perān*, to pierce.]
 1. originally, a passage; a channel.
 2. a tiny opening, usually microscopic, as in plant leaves, skin, etc., through which fluids may be absorbed or discharged.
 3. a similar opening in rock or other substances.

pōre, *v.i.*; pored, *pt., pp.*; poring, *ppr.* [ME. *poren, pouren.*]
 1. to gaze intently or steadily.
 2. to look searchingly; to read carefully; to study minutely (with *over*); as, he *pored over* the book.
 3. to think deeply and thoroughly; to ponder; meditate (with *on, upon*, or *over*); as, he *pored on* the wonders of science.

pōr′ēr, *n.* one who pores.

por′gee, *n.* same as *porgy.*

por′gy (*or* -ji), *n.*; *pl.* **por′gieş** or **por′gy,** [prob. var. of *pogy.*] any of a large number of salt-water food fishes having spiny fins and a wide body covered with large scales.

Pō·rif′e·rȧ, *n.pl.* [*pore*, and L. *ferre*, to bear.] in zoology, a phylum of invertebrates which includes sponges.

pō·rif′ēr·ăn, *n.* any of the *Porifera.*

pō·rif′ēr·ous, *a.* 1. having pores.
 2. in zoology, of or related to the *Porifera.*

pō′ri·form, *a.* [L. *porus*, pore, and *form.*] resembling a pore.

pōr′i·ness, *n.* the state of being porous, or having numerous pores.

pō′rişm, *n.* [ME. *porysme*; ML. *porisma*; Gr. *porisma*, lit., a thing brought, from *porizein*, to bring.] in ancient mathematics, a geometrical proposition variously defined; specifically, (a) a proposition deduced from some other demonstrated proposition; a corollary; (b) a proposition that uncovers the possibility of finding such conditions as to make a specific problem capable of innumerable solutions.

pō·riş·mat′iç, *a.* pertaining to a porism; seeking to determine by what means and in how many ways a problem may be solved.

pō·riş·mat′iç·ăl, *a.* porismatic.

pō′rīte, *n.* a coral of the family *Poritidæ*, or of the genus *Porites.*

Pō·rī′tēş, *n.* [LL., from L. *porus*, pore.]
 1. in zoology, a genus of perforate madreporarian corals, having small twelve-rayed calicles and a very porous structure.
 2. a genus of millepores.

Pō·rit′i·dae, *n.pl.* a family of corals of which *Porites* is the type genus.

pōrk, *n.* [ME. and OFr. *porc*; L. *porcus*, a pig.]
 1. originally, a pig or hog.
 2. the flesh of a pig or hog, used, fresh or cured, as food.

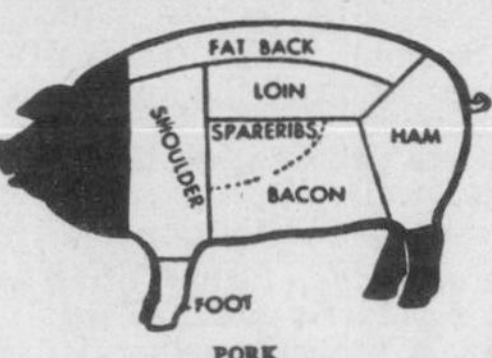

PORK

 3. money, position, etc. received from the government through political patronage. [Slang.]

pōrk bar′rel, government appropriations for political patronage, as for local improvements to please legislators' constituents. [Slang.]

pōrk′ēr, *n.* a hog, especially a young one, fattened for use as food.

pōrk′et, *n.* a young hog. [Rare.]

pōrk′fish, *n.*; *pl.* **pōrk′fish·eş** or **pōrk′fish,** a black grunt, *Anisotremus virginicus*, with yellow stripes, of the West Indies.

pōrk′i·ness, *n.* the state or quality of being porky.

pōrk′ling, *n.* a young pig.

pōrk pīe, 1. a meat pie made of chopped pork, usually eaten cold.
 2. a soft hat with a round, flat crown, worn by men: now often *porkpie.*

pōrk′pīe, *n.* same as *pork pie*, sense 2.

pōrk′y, *a.*; *comp.* porkier; *superl.* porkiest, 1. of or like pork.
 2. fat, as though overfed.
 3. saucy, cocky, presumptuous, impertinent, or the like. [Slang.]

por′nō, *n.* pornography. [Slang.]

por′nō, *a.* pornographic. [Slang.]

por·noç′rȧ·cy, *n.* [Gr. *pornē*, prostitute, and *kratein*, to rule.] government by prostitutes; domination, sway, or influence of profligate women; specifically, the government of Rome in the early part of the tenth century.

por·nō·graph′iç, *a.* of, or having the nature of, pornography; obscene.

por·nog′rȧ·phy, *n.* [Gr. *pornē*, prostitute, and *graphein*, to write.]
 1. originally, a description of prostitutes and their trade.
 2. writings, pictures, etc. intended to arouse sexual desire.
 3. the production of such writings, pictures, etc.

por·o·mēr′iç, *n.* [arbitrary coinage, prob. from *porous*, and poly*meric.*] a synthetic, leather-like, porous material, often coated or impregnated with a polymer.

pō·rō·phyl′lous, *a.* [Gr. *poros*, pore, and *phyllon*, leaf.] in botany, having leaves covered with transparent points or dots.

Pō·rō′sȧ, *n.pl.* same as *Perforata.*

pō·rōse′, *a.* [LL. *porosus*, full of pores.]
 1. porous.
 2. of or pertaining to the *Porosa.*

pō·ros′i·ty, *n.*; *pl.* **pō·ros′i·tieş,** [ME. *porositee*; ML. *porositas*, from *porosus*, from L. *porus*, a pore.]
 1. the quality or state of being porous.
 2. the ratio of the volume of a material's pores to that of its solid content.
 3. anything porous.
 4. a pore.

pō·rot′iç, *n.* [Gr. *pōros*, a callus.] any medicine which assists in the formation of callus.

pō′rous, *a.* [from *pore.*] full of pores, or tiny holes through which fluids, air, or light may pass; as, a *porous* skin; *porous* wood; *porous* earth.

pō′rous·ly, *adv.* in a porous manner.

pō′rous·ness, *n.* the quality or state of having pores; porosity; as, the *porousness* of the skin of an animal, or of wood.

por′pen·tīne, *n.* porcupine. [Obs.]

por·phy·rā′ceous, *a.* same as *porphyritic.*

por′phȳre, *n.* porphyry. [Obs.]

por′phy·rin, *n.* [from *hematoporphyrin*, from *hemato-*, and Gr. *porphyra*, purple, purple product of hemoglobin decomposition.] any of a group of pyrrole derivatives of hemoglobin and chlorophyll, containing no iron or magnesium.

por′phy·rīne (-rēn), *n.* a chemical substance, colorless and uncrystallized, obtained from the bark of an Australian tree, *Alstonia constricta.*

Por·phyr'i·ō, *n.* [Gr. *porphyriōn*, the purple gallinule, from *porphyra*, purple.]

1. a genus of birds of the rail family, including *Porphyrio hyacinthinus*, the purple or hyacinthine gallinule, a bird found in Europe, Asia, and Africa, having a strong beak and long legs.

2. [p-] a bird of this genus.

PORPHYRIO

por'phy·rīte, *n.* any rock of a porphyritic nature.

por·phy·rit'iç, *a.* [ME. *porphiritike*; ML. *porphyriticus*; L. *porphyrites*; Gr. *porphyritēs*, porphyry.]

1. composed of or pertaining to porphyry.

2. resembling porphyry; containing distinct crystals embedded in a fine-grained mass.

por"phy·ri·zā'tion, *n.* the act or process of porphyrizing, or the condition or quality of being porphyrized.

por'phy·rīze, *v.t.* to cause to resemble porphyry.

por'phy·rō·ġēne", *a.* [Gr. *porphyra*, purple, and *gennān*, to beget.] born to the purple or of royal descent.

por"phy·rō·ġē·net'iç, *a.* [Gr. *porphyritēs*, porphyry, and *gennān*, to beget.] of or relating to porphyrogenitism.

por"phy·rō·ġen'i·tişm, *n.* the mode of succession in some royal families, notably the Byzantine, whereby a younger son, if born in the purple, that is, after the accession of his parents to the throne, was preferred to an older son, who was born before the parents' accession.

por"phy·rō·ġen'i·tus, *n.* [Gr. *porphyra*, purple, and *gennētos*, from *gennān*, to beget.] a son born to a sovereign, especially in the Byzantine Empire.

por'phy·roid, *n.* a rock that resembles, or has the structure of, porphyry.

por'phy·ry, *n.*; *pl.* **por'phy·ries**, [ME. *purfire*, *porfirie*; OFr. *porfire*; ML. *porphyreus*, from Gr. *porphyros*, purple.]

1. originally, a hard Egyptian rock having red and white feldspar crystals embedded in a fine-grained, dark-red or purplish groundmass.

2. any igneous rock of similar texture.

por'phy·ry shell, a univalve shell of the genus *Murex*; also, a seashell, *Oliva porphyria*, that is spotted like porphyry.

Por'pi·tȧ, *n.* [Gr. *porpē*, brooch.] a genus of bright-colored, disk-shaped marine siphonophores.

por'poise (-pus), *n.*; *pl.* **por'pois·es** or **por'poise**, [ME. *porcpisce*, *porpesse*, *porpese*, *porpus*, lit., swine fish, from L. *porcus*, a pig or swine, and *piscis*, a fish.]

1. any of a number of small, related cetaceans of the genus *Phocæna*, dark above and white below, with a triangle-shaped fin on the back, a blunt snout, and many teeth.

PORPOISE

2. a dolphin or any of several other small cetaceans.

por'pō·rāte, *a.* arrayed in purple or royal raiment.

por'pus, *n.* a porpoise. [Dial.]

por·rā'ceous, *a.* [L. *porraceus*, from *porrum*, a leek or onion.] greenish; resembling the leek in color.

por·reçt', *a.* in zoology, denoting a part which extends forth horizontally.

por'reçt', *v.t.* [L. *porrectus*, pp. of *porrigere*, to extend.] to extend horizontally.

por·reç'tion, *n.* [L. *porrectio*, from *porrigere*; *por*, for *pro*, forward, and *regere*, to direct.] the act of stretching forth.

por'ret, *n.* [It. *porretta*; L. *porrum*, a leek.] a scallion; a leek or small onion. [Now Dial.]

por'ridġe, *n.* [altered from *pottage* by confusion with ME. *porrey*; OFr. *poree*; LL. *porrata*, leek broth, from L. *porrum*, leek.]

1. originally, pottage.

2. a soft food made of cereal or meal boiled in water or milk until thick. [Chiefly Brit.]

por'rin·ġēr, *n.* [earlier *pottanger*, *pottager*, from Fr. *potager*, soup dish: altered by association with *porridge*.]

1. a small metal vessel for porridge, etc., especially one from which children are fed.

2. a headdress in the shape of a porringer. [Rare.]

pōrt, *n.* [ME. *porte*, *port*; OFr. *porte*; L. *porta*, a door.]

1. a gateway; a portal. [Obs. except Scot.]

2. (a) a porthole; (b) the covering for this.

3. an opening, as in a cylinder face or valve face, for the passage of steam, gas, water, etc.

4. a mouthpiece of curved metal used in some bridle bits.

pōrt, *v.t.* [ME. *porten*; OFr. *porter*; L. *portare* to carry.]

1. originally, to carry.

2. to carry, hold, or place (a rifle or sword) diagonally in front of one, crossing the left shoulder, as for inspection.

pōrt, *n.* [ME. *porte*; OFr., from the v.]

1. the manner in which one carries oneself; carriage; deportment; demeanor.

2. the position of porting a weapon.

3. purport; meaning.

4. state; splendid or stately manner of living. [Obs.]

5. a piece of iron, somewhat in the shape of a horseshoe, fixed to the saddle or stirrup, and used to carry the lance when held upright. [Obs.]

pōrt, *n.* [ME., from OFr. and AS. *port*, port, haven, harbor, from L. *portus*, a haven; akin to L. *porta*, gate; Gr. *poros*, a passage.]

1. a harbor; a haven; any bay, cove, inlet, or recess of the sea or of a lake, or the mouth of a river, which ships or vessels can enter, and where they can lie safe from injury by storms.

2. a city or town with a harbor where ships arrive and depart, and load or unload cargoes.

3. a port of entry.

pōrt, *n.* [from *port* (harbor), with reference to the side opposite the steering oar.] the left-hand side of a ship or airplane as one faces forward, toward the bow; larboard: opposed to *starboard*.

pōrt, *a.* of or on the port, or left-hand side.

pōrt, *v.t.* and *v.i.* to move or turn (the helm) to the left.

pōrt, *n.* [from *Oporto*, Portugal.] a fortified sweet wine, usually dark-red, originally from Portugal.

pōr'tȧ, *n.*; *pl.* **pōr'tae**, [L.] the entrance for nerves and ducts into an organ.

pōrt·ȧ·bil'i·ty, *n.* the condition or quality of being portable.

pōrt'ȧ·ble, *a.* [L. *portabilis*.]

1. that can be carried.

2. easily carried.

3. bearable; endurable. [Obs.]

pōrt'ȧ·ble, *n.* anything portable.

pōrt'ȧ·ble·ness, *n.* the quality or state of being portable.

pōr'tăġe, *n.* [ME.; OFr.; ML. *portaticum*, from *portare*, to carry.]

1. the act of transporting or carrying.

2. the cost or price of transporting or carrying.

3. capacity for carriage; tonnage; burden. [Obs.]

4. a carrying or transporting of boats and supplies overland between navigable rivers, lakes, etc., as during a canoe trip.

5. any place or route over which this is done.

6. a sailor's wages.

pōr'tăġe, *v.t.* and *v.i.*; portaged, *pt.*, *pp.*; portaging, *ppr.* to carry or transport (boats, etc.) over a portage.

Pōr'tăġe fọr·mā'tion, a geological subdivision of the Upper Devonian of the United States. It is named after Portage township in New York State.

pōr'tȧ·gūe, *n.* an obsolete Portuguese coin.

pōr'tăl, *n.* [ME.; OFr.; ML. *portale*, orig. neut. of *portalis*, of a door, from L. *porta*, gate.]

1. a doorway or entrance, especially a large and imposing one.

2. in architecture, the lesser gate, where there are two gates of different dimensions.

3. formerly, a little square corner of a room, separated from the rest by a wainscot, and forming a short passage into a room.

4. any entrance: often figurative, as, the *portal* of wisdom. [Poetic.]

5. the portal vein.

pōr'tăl, *a.* [ML. *portalis*.] designating, of, or like the vein carrying blood from the intestines, stomach, etc. to the liver.

pōr'tăl-tō-pōr'tăl pāy, wages for workers based on the total time spent from the moment of entering the mine, factory, etc. until the moment of leaving it.

pōr·tȧ·men'tō, *n.*; *pl.* **pōr·tȧ·men'tï**, [It., from *portare*, to carry; L. *portare*.] in music, a continuous gliding from one note to another, sounding all intervening tones; a glide.

pōr'tănce, *n.* [Early Mod. Eng., from Fr. *portance*, from *porter*, to bear.] air; mein; carriage; port. [Archaic.]

pōr'tass, *n.* [OFr. *porte-hors*; *porter*, to carry, and *hors*, out of doors; so called from being easily portable.] a breviary; a prayer book. [Obs.]

pōr'tāte, *a.* [L. *portatus*, pp. of *portare*, to carry.] in heraldry, placed bendwise in an escutcheon; that is, lying as if carried on a person's shoulder, as a cross.

CROSS PORTATE

pōr'tȧ·tive, *a.* [ME. and OFr. *portatif*, lit., that is carried, from L. *portatus*, pp. of *portare*, to carry, and OFr. *-if*.]

1. of or having the power of carrying a load, charge, etc.

2. that can be carried; portable. [Obs.]

pōrt au·thor'i·ty, a governmental commission in charge of the traffic, regulations, etc. of a port.

port çap'tain (-tin), an official of a steamship company who assumes charge of vessels during their stay in port.

port chärġe, in commerce, a fee or duty charged for the privilege of keeping a ship or its cargo in a port.

pōrt'çlūse, *n.* a portcullis. [Obs.]

pōrt"çrāy'ŏn, *n.* [Fr. *porte-crayon*; *porter*, to carry, and *crayon*, pencil.] a small metallic handle with a clasp for holding a crayon, etc. when used in drawing.

pōrt·çul'lis, *n.* [ME. *portcoles*; OFr. *porte coleïce*; *porte*, a gate, and *coleïce*, f. of *coleïs*, sliding, from L. *colare*, to strain, filter.]

1. in fortification, a heavy grating or latticework of timber or iron with the lower ends pointed like the teeth of a harrow, suspended by chains over the gateway of a castle, fort, etc., to be let down to prevent the entrance of an enemy.

2. a coin used by the East India Company in the reign of Queen Elizabeth I: it had a design of a portcullis on one side. [Obs.]

PORTCULLIS

pōrt·çul'lis, *v.t.* to shut; to bar. [Rare.]

Pōrte, *n.* [the chief office of the Ottoman Empire was styled *Babi Ali*, lit., the High Gate, from the gate (*bāb*) of the palace at which justice was administered. The French translation of this term is *la Sublime Porte*: hence the use of this word.] the Ottoman Turkish government.

pōrte'-cō·chere' (-shār'), *n.* [Fr. *porte*, gate, and *cochère*, coach.]

1. a large porch outside the entrance of a building, under which vehicles may be driven.

2. a large entrance gateway through which vehicles are driven into a square or courtyard.

pōrt'ed, *a.* having gates. [Obs.]

pōrte'feuille' (-fē'ye), *n.* [Fr., from *porter*, to carry, and *feuille*, L. *folium*, leaf.] a portfolio.

pōr'tē·gūe, *n.* portague. [Obs.]

pōrte'-lù·miere" (-myār"), *n.* [Fr., from *porter*, to carry, and *lumière*, light.] a mirror that can be adjusted so as to cast rays of light in any required direction; a simple form of heliostat.

pōrte'mŏn·nāie" (-nā"), *n.* [Fr., from *porter* to carry, and *monnaie*, money.] a pocketbook for carrying money; a purse.

pōr·tend', *v.t.*; portended, *pt.*, *pp.*; portending, *ppr.* [L. *portendere*, *protendere*; *pro*, forth, and *tendere*, to stretch.]

1. to be an omen or warning of; to fore-

shadow; to presage; to indicate as about to happen: used especially of unpropitious or momentous events.

A moist and cool summer *portends* a hard winter. —Bacon.

2. to stretch forth. [Obs.]

pōr′tent, *n.* [L. *portentum.*]

1. something that portends an event about to occur, especially an unfortunate or evil event; an omen.

2. a portending; significance; as, a howl of dire *portent.*

3. something regarded as portentous; a marvel; prodigy.

pōr·ten′tion, *n.* the act of foreshowing; a portent.

pōr·tent′ive, *a.* foreshadowing; ominous; threatening. [Obs.]

pōr·tent′ous, *a.* [L. *portentosus.*]

1. ominous; portending evil.

2. marvelous; prodigious; wonderful.

No beast of more *portentous* size,
In the Hercynian forest lies.—Roscommon.

pōr·tent′ous·ly, *adv.* in a portentous manner; ominously.

pōr·tent′ous·ness, *n.* the state of being portentous.

pōr′tẽr, *n.* [ME.; OFr. *portier*; LL. *portarius,* from L. *porta,* a gate.] one who has the charge of a door or gate; a doorman; a gatekeeper.

pōr′tẽr, *n.* [ME. *portour, portere*; OFr. *porteour*; LL. *portator,* from L. *portare,* to carry.]

1. a carrier; a person who carries things; especially, a man who carries luggage, etc. for hire or as an attendant at a railroad station, hotel, etc.

2. a railroad employee who waits on passengers in a parlor car or sleeper.

3. in forging, a bar of iron attached to a heavy forging, whereby it is guided beneath the hammer or into the furnace, being suspended by chains from a crane above; also, a bar from whose end an article is forged.

4. a lever. [Obs.]

5. a supporting carriage for the sag of a wire rope running from a traction engine to a plow.

pōr′tẽr, *n.* [abbrev. of *porter's ale.*] a dark-brown beer resembling light stout, made from charred or browned malt.

pōr′tẽr·āġe, *n.* 1. a porter's work.

2. the charge for this.

pōr′tẽr·ess, *n.* same as *portress.*

pōr′tẽr·house, *n.* 1. formerly, a place where beer, porter, etc. (and sometimes steaks and chops) were served.

2. a porterhouse steak.

pōr′tẽr·house steāk, [said to be so named from having been a specialty at a former New York porterhouse.] a choice cut of beef from between the tenderloin and the sirloin.

pōr′tesse, *n.* a portass. [Obs.]

pōrt′fīre, *n.* [Fr. *porter,* to carry, and E. *fire.*] a composition formerly used for setting fire to powder, composed of saltpeter, sulfur, and mealed powder, mixed and sifted, well-rubbed, and stuffed into a case of strong paper.

pōrt·fō′li·ō (*or* -fōl′yō), *n.*; *pl.* **pōrt·fō′li·ōṣ,** [earlier *porto folio,* from It. *portafoglio,* from *portare* (L. *portare*), to carry, and *foglio* (L. *folium*), a leaf.]

1. a flat, portable case, usually of leather, for carrying loose sheets of paper, manuscripts, drawings, etc.; a brief case.

2. such a case for state documents.

3. the office of a minister of state; as, a minister without *portfolio.*

4. a list of the stocks, bonds, and commercial paper owned by a bank, an investor, etc.

pōrt′glāve, *n.* a sword bearer. [Obs.]

pōrt′grēve, pōrt′grāve, *n.* same as *portreeve.*

pōrt′hōle, *n.* 1. an opening in a ship's side to admit light and air, load cargo, or fire a gun through.

2. an opening to shoot through, in the wall of a fort, etc.; an embrasure.

3. an opening shaped somewhat like this, as in a furnace door.

PORTICO

pōrt′hook, *n.* one of the hooks in the side of a ship to which the hinges of a porthole cover are hooked.

Por′ti·ȧ (-shȧ *or* -shi-ȧ), *n.* the heroine of Shakespeare's *Merchant of Venice.*

pōr′ti·cō, *n.*; *pl.* **pōr′ti·cōes,** or **pōr′ti·cōṣ,** [It. *portico*; L. *porticus.*] in architecture, an open space covered by a roof supported on columns, sometimes detached, as a shady walk; in modern usage, a kind of porch before the entrance of a building fronted with columns. Porticos are called tetrastyle, hexastyle, octastyle, and decastyle, according as they have four, six, eight, or ten columns in front.

pōr′ti·cōed, *a.* having a portico.

pōr·tiere′, por·tière′ (pōr-tyâr′), *n.* [Fr., from *porte,* door.] a heavy curtain across an entrance or doorway.

pōr′tion, *n.* [ME. *porcioun*; OFr. *porcion*; L. *portio, portionis,* a portion; akin to *pars, partis,* a part, from *partiri,* to divide.]

1. a part of anything separated from it; that which is divided off, as a part from a whole.

We have come to dedicate a *portion* of that field, as a final resting place for those who here gave their lives that that nation might live. —Abraham Lincoln.

2. a part which, though not actually separated from the whole, is considered by itself.

Whatever facilitates intercourse between the different *portions* of the human family will promote the best interests of man. —Morse.

3. a part assigned; an allotment.

The priests had a *portion* assigned them by Pharaoh. —Gen. xlvii. 22.

4. the part of an estate given to a child or heir, or descending to him by law, and distributed to him in the settlement of the estate.

5. the part of a man's money or property contributed by his bride; a marriage portion; a dowry.

6. the part of experience supposedly allotted to a person by fate; one's lot; destiny.

7. the part of a meal or quantity of food served to a person; a serving; a helping.

Syn.—division, share, parcel, quantity, allotment, dividend.

pōr′tion, *v.t.*; portioned, *pt., pp.*; portioning, *ppr.* 1. to divide into portions.

2. to give as a portion to; to apportion.

And *portion* to his tribes the wide domain. —Pope.

3. to give a portion to; to endow with a portion; to dower.

pōr′tion·ẽr, *n.* one who gives or receives a portion. [Rare.]

pōr′tion·ist, *n.* 1. same as *postmaster,* sense 3.

2. the incumbent of a benefice which has more rectors or vicars than one.

pōr′tion·less, *a.* having no portion.

pōr′tise, *n.* a portass. [Obs.]

Pōrt′lănd cė·ment′, [so called from resemblance of the concrete made from it to stone quarried on the Isle of Portland, England.] a kind of cement that hardens under water, made by burning a mixture of limestone and clay or similar materials.

Pōrt′lănd stōne, brownstone; a compact sandstone from Portland, Connecticut, used extensively for building.

Pōrt′lănd väse, an ancient cinerary urn depicting in cameo the marriage of Peleus and Thetis. It was found in a tomb near Rome and is now in the British Museum.

pōrt′lȧst, *n.* the portoise. [Now Rare.]

pōrt′li·ness, *n.* the quality or state of being portly; corpulence.

pōrt′ly, *a.*; *comp.* portlier; *superl.* portliest, 1. originally, having a dignified and stately port or demeanor.

2. stout; obese.

pōrt′măn, *n.*; *pl.* **pōrt′men,** an inhabitant or burgess of a port town.

pōrt·man′teau (-tō), *n.*; *pl.* **pōrt·man′teauṣ, pōrt·man′teaux** (-tōz), [Fr. *portemanteau,* from *porter,* to carry, and *manteau,* a cloak.]

1. originally, a case or bag for carrying clothes on a trip.

2. a stiff leather suitcase that opens like a book into two compartments.

portmanteau word; a word that is a combination of two other words in form and meaning (e.g., *smog,* from *smoke* and *fog*).

pōrt·man′tle, *n.* a portmanteau. [Archaic and Dial.]

pōrt′mōte, *n.* [*port,* and AS. *gemot,* a meeting.] a court held in a port town. [Obs.]

pōrt of en′try, any place where customs officials are stationed to check the entry of foreign goods into a country.

pōr′toiṣe (-tiz), *n.* [OFr. *portoire,* from *porter,* to bear.] the gunwale of a ship: used only in the phrase *ȧ portoise.*

to ride ȧ portoise; to have the lower yards and topmasts struck or lowered down, when at anchor in a gale of wind.

Pōr′tō Ri′căn, *a.* and *n.* same as *Puerto Rican.*

pōr′tos, *n.* a portass. [Obs.]

pōrt′pāyne, *n.* [L. *portare,* to carry, and *panis,* bread.] a carrying cloth for bread, keeping it from the hands. [Obs.]

pōr′trāit, *n.* [Fr. *portrait,* pp. of *portraire,* to portray.]

1. originally, a drawn, painted, or carved picture of something.

2. a picture of a person, especially of his face, drawn, painted, photographed, etc. from life.

The *portrait* of George Washington had been the object of the most valuable years of my life. —G. C. Stuart.

3. a description, dramatic portrayal, etc. of a person.

pōr′trāit, *v.t.* to portray; to draw. [Obs.]

pōr′trāit bust, a bust representing the features of someone.

pōr′trāit·ist, *n.* one who makes portraits.

pōr′trāi·tūre, *n.* [ME. *purtreiture,* etc.; OFr.]

1. the process, practice, or art of portraying; hence, that which is portrayed; a portait.

2. portraits collectively.

pōr′trāi·tūre, *v.t.* to make a portrait of; to portray. [Obs.]

pōr·trāy′, *v.t.*; portrayed, *pt., pp.*; portraying, *ppr.* [ME. *purtreien*; OFr. *pourtraire, portraire*; L. *protrahere,* to draw forth.]

1. to make a picture or portrait of; to depict; delineate.

2. to make a word picture of; to describe graphically.

3. to picture on the stage.

4. to adorn with pictures; as, shields *portrayed.* [Obs.]

pōrtrāy′ăl, *n.* 1. the act of portraying.

2. a portrait; a description; a representation.

pōr·trāy′ẽr, *n.* one who or that which portrays.

pōrt′reeve, *n.* [*port* and *reeve.*] the chief magistrate of a town or borough.

pōr′tress, *n.* a women porter (doorkeeper).

Pōrt″-Roy′ăl·ist, *n.* one who was a scholar in the abbey at Port Royal, near Paris, which sheltered, in the seventeenth century, Arnauld, Pascal, and other celebrated scholars.

pōrt′sīde, *n.* 1. in nautical usage, the left side of a ship.

2. the left side of any person or thing. [Slang.]

Pōr′tū·guēṣe (-gēz), *a.* of or pertaining to Portugal, its people, their language, or culture.

Pōr′tū·guēṣe, *n.*; *pl.* **Pōr′tū·guēṣe,** 1. a native or inhabitant of Portugal.

2. the Romance language spoken in Portugal and Brazil.

Pōr′tū·guēṣe man-of-wạr′, any of several large, tubelike, warm-sea animals having a large, bladderlike sac, with a saillike structure on top, which enables them to float on the water.

Pōr·tū·laç′ȧ, *n.* [L., from *portare,* to carry, and *lac,* milk, from the juicy nature of the plants.]

1. a genus of fleshy plants with yellow, pink, or purple flowers.

2. [p-] any plant of this genus.

pōr″tū·lȧ·cā′ceous, *a.* of or relating to the purslane family of plants, *Portulaceæ,* or *Portulacaceæ.*

Pōr·tū·lā′cē·ae, *n.pl.* a small family of polypetalous exogens, consisting of annual, perennial, herbaceous, or shrubby plants, occurring in all the hotter or milder parts of the world: also written *Portulacaceæ.*

pōr′y, *a.* porous. [Now Rare.]

pō·sä′dȧ, *n.* [Sp.] a hotel.

Pō·ṣau′ne, *n.* [OFr. *buisine*; It. *buccina,* trumpet.] a kind of trombone.

po·sé′ (pō-zā′), *a.* [Fr., pp. of *poser,* to place.] in heraldry, standing, with none of the feet raised.

pōṣe, *n.* a cold in the head; catarrh. [Obs.]

pōṣe, *v.t.*; posed, *pt., pp.*; posing, *ppr.* [ME.; OFr. *poser,* to put in position; L. *pausare* (see *pause*), confused in meaning by association in LL. with *positus,* pp. of *ponere,* to place, put.]

1. to put forth; to lay down; to assert, as a claim, argument, etc.

2. to put forward or propose, as a question, problem, etc.
3. to put (an artist's model, etc.) in a certain attitude.

pōṣe, *v.i.* 1. to assume or hold a certain attitude, as in having one's portrait made.
2. to strike attitudes; to attitudinize; as, look at her *posing*.
3. to assume or maintain a mental attitude; to set oneself up; as, he *poses* as a scholar.

pōṣe, *n.* [OFr., from the v.]
1. a bodily attitude, especially one held for or pictured by an artist, photographer, etc.
2. a mental attitude assumed for effect; pretense.

pōṣe, *v.t.*; posed, *pt.*, *pp.*; posing, *ppr.* [abbrev. from *oppose* or *appose*.]
1. to embarrass by a difficult question; to baffle; to nonplus; to puzzle.
Learning was *posed*, philosophy was set,
Sophisters taken in a fisher's net.—Herbert.
2. to interrogate closely. [Obs.]

Pō·seī'dŏn, *n.* in Greek mythology, god of the sea and of horses: identified by the Romans with Neptune.

pōṣ'ẽr, *n.* a person who poses; an affected person.

pōṣ'ẽr, *n.* a baffling question or problem.

pō·ṣeūr', *n.* [Fr.] a poser (person who poses).

posh, *a.* [from obs. Brit. slang *posh*, a dandy, from ?] luxurious and fashionable; elegant. [Colloq.]

pō'ṣied, *a.* inscribed with a posy, or motto, as a ring.

pōṣ'ing·ly, *adv.* puzzlingly; in a manner to pose, or puzzle.

poṣ'it, *v.t.*; posited, *pt.*, *pp.*; positing, *ppr.* [L. *positus*, pp. of *ponere*, to place.]
1. to place in the proper relation to other objects; to dispose; to set; to put.
2. in logic, to state as a principle or fact; to assume; to postulate.

pō·ṣi'tion (-zish'un), *n.* [Fr.; L. *positio* (*-onis*), from *positus*, pp. of *ponere*, to place.]
1. a positing; a placing.
2. a person's mental attitude toward or opinion on a subject; stand; as, the senator's *position* on international affairs.
3. the place occupied by a person or thing; site; situation; location; as, the *position* of a building; the *position* of a figure in a picture.
4. the manner in which a person or thing is placed or arranged; posture; attitude; pose.
5. office; post; employment; situation; job; as, she has a fine *position*.
6. a positing of a proposition; an affirmation; a proposition advanced or affirmed as a fixed principle, or stated as the ground of reasoning, or to be proved; a stand taken in regard to some principle or dispute; as, to be in a false *position*; to define one's *position*.
Let not the proof of any *position* depend on the *positions* that follow, but always on those which precede. —Watts.
7. social status; relative rank or standing, especially high rank; as, he is a man of *position*.
8. a location or condition in which one has the advantage; as, to jockey for *position*; hence, a strategic military site.
9. in Greek and Latin prosody, the situation of a vowel before two consonants, or before a double consonant, causing a short vowel to become long.
10. the usual or proper place of a person or thing; station; as, the players were in *position*.
11. in arithmetic, a method of finding an unknown quantity by assuming various trial values for it until the true value is arrived at: also called *rule of trial and error*.
12. in music, (a) the arrangement of the notes of a chord with respect to their relative closeness or distance apart; as, open *position*; (b) the location of the left hand on the finger board of a violin; as, second *position*; (c) a corresponding location on a trombone slide.
angle of position; the angle which any line, such as that joining two stars, makes with a circle of declination or other fixed line.
Syn.—place, station, circumstance, posture, attitude, assertion, thesis, rank, office, employment, situation.

pō·ṣi'tion, *v.t.* 1. to put in a particular position; to place.
2. to locate. [Rare.]

pō·ṣi'tion·ăl, *a.* of or relating to position.

pō·ṣi'tion find'ẽr, a device by means of which a cannon may be aimed by a gunner who cannot see the object at which he is shooting.

poṣ'i·tive, *a.* [ME. and OFr. *positif*; L. *positivus*, from *positus*, pp. of *ponere*, to place.]
1. explicitly laid down; express; direct; explicit; precise; specific; as, he told us in *positive* words; we have his *positive* declaration to the fact.
2. independent of changes, circumstances, opinion, or taste; inherent; absolute; arbitrary; unqualified: distinguished from *comparative*, *relative*; as, beauty is not a *positive* thing, but depends on the different tastes of people.
3. absolute; real; existing in fact or by the presence of something and not by its absence: opposed to *negative*; as, *positive* good.
4. beyond all doubt, qualification, or denial; undeniable; sure; incontestable; express: opposed to *circumstantial*; as, *positive* proof.
5. confident; fully assured; firmly convinced; decided; as, the witness is very *positive* that he is correct.
6. dogmatic; overconfident in opinion or assertion.
Some *positive* persisting fops we know,
That, if once wrong, will needs be always so. —Pope.
7. settled by or dependent on arbitrary appointment; conventional; artificial: opposed to *natural*.
Although no laws but *positive* are mutable,
yet all are not mutable which are *positive*. —Hooker.
8. showing resolution or agreement; affirmative; certain; as, a *positive* answer.
9. tending in the direction regarded as that of increase, progress, etc.; as, clockwise motion is *positive*.
10. making a definite contribution; constructive; as, *positive* criticism.
11. concerned only with real things and experience; empirical; practical: distinguished from *speculative*, *theoretical*.
12. complete; downright; out-and-out; as, a *positive* devil. [Colloq.]
13. in bacteriology, showing the presence of a specific disease, condition, etc.
14. in biology, directed toward the source of a stimulus; as, *positive* tropism.
15. in electricity, (a) designating or of the kind of electricity generated on a glass rod when it is rubbed with a piece of silk; (b) of, generating, or charged with positive electricity. Opposed to *negative*.
16. in grammar, (a) of an adjective or adverb in its simple, uncompared form or degree; (b) of this degree. Distinguished from *comparative*, *superlative*.
17. in mathematics, greater than zero; plus.
18. in photography, with the lights and shades corresponding to those of the subject: opposed to *negative*.
positive crystal; in optics, a double-refracting crystal in which the index of refraction of the extraordinary ray is greater than that of the ordinary ray.
positive electricity; (a) electricity generated on a glass rod when it is rubbed with silk; (b) electricity appearing at the pole of the plate having the higher potential in a voltaic cell.
positive eyepiece; see under *eyepiece*.
positive law; same as *municipal law* under *law*.
positive philosophy; same as *positivism*, sense 3.

poṣ'i·tive, *n.* something positive, as a degree, quality, quantity, battery terminal, photographic print, etc.

poṣ'i·tive·ly, *adv.* 1. in a positive manner, as opposed to a negative manner.
2. certainly; assuredly; indubitably; explicitly; peremptorily.

poṣ'i·tive·ness, *n.* the quality or state of being positive.

poṣ'i·tiv·iṣm, *n.* [Fr. *positivisme*.]
1. the quality or state of being positive; certainty; assurance.
2. dogmatism.
3. a system of philosophy that is based solely on the positive data of sense experience; empiricism; especially, [also P–] a system of philosophy, originated by Auguste Comte, which is based solely on positive, observable, scientific facts and their relations to each other and to natural law: it rejects speculation on or search for ultimate origins.

poṣ'i·tiv·ist, *n.* a believer in or advocate of positivism.

poṣ'i·tiv·ist, *a.* same as *positivistic*.

poṣ''i·tiv·is'tiç, *a.* of or characteristic of positivism or positivists.

poṣ·i·tiv'i·ty, *n.* the quality of being positive.

poṣ'i·tron, *n.* [*positive* and *electron*.] the positive counterpart of an electron, having approximately the same mass and magnitude of charge.

poṣ'i·tūre, *n.* posture. [Obs.]

poṣ'net, *n.* [W. *posned*.] a little basin; a porringer, skillet, or saucepan. [Archaic or Dial.]

pos·ō·log'iç, pos·ō·log'iç·ăl, *a.* pertaining to posology.

pō·sol'ō·ġy, *n.* [Gr. *posos*, how much, and *-logy*.] in medicine, the science of doses; the art of making doses.

pos·pol'i·te, *n.* [Pol. *pospolite ruszenie*, a general call to arms against the enemy.] a kind of militia in Poland, which, in case of invasion, was summoned to arms for the defense of the country. [Obs.]

poss, *v.t.*; possed, *pt.*, *pp.*; possing, *ppr.* [form of *push*.] to dash; to push; to thrust. [Obs.]

pos'sē, *n.* [L., to be able.]
1. (a) the body of men liable to be summoned by a sheriff to assist him in keeping the peace, etc.; (b) a band of men, usually armed, so summoned: in full, *posse comitatus*.
2. any body of men armed with legal authority.
in posse; in the range of possibility, but not accomplished; potentially: opposed to *in esse*, in actual being.
posse comitatus; same as *posse*, sense 1.

poṣ·ṣess', *v.t.*; possessed, *pt.*, *pp.*; possessing, *ppr.* [OFr. *possessier*, from L. *possessus*, pp. of *possidere*, to possess; *port*, toward (conjectural), and *sedere*, to sit.]
1. to occupy in person; to have as occupant; to inhabit. [Obs.]
O, I have bought the mansion of a love,
But not *possess'd* it. —Shak.
2. to have as a piece of property or as a personal belonging; to be owner of; to own; as, to *possess* much money and property; also, to have as an attribute, quality, etc.; as, to *possess* many good qualities.
Share all that he doth *possess*. —Shak.
3. to become or make oneself master of; to seize; to gain; to win. [Archaic.]
The English marched toward the river Eske, intending to *possess* a hill called Under-Eske. —Hayward.
4. to gain strong influence or control over; to dominate.
Sin of self-love *possesseth* all mine eye—Shak.
5. to cause to be possessed, as by an evil influence, violent passion, etc. [Archaic.]
6. to put in possession of; to cause to have; to make master or owner: with *of* before the thing, and now generally used in the passive or with reflexive pronouns; as, to be *possessed of* a large fortune; to *possess* oneself *of* another's property.
Had *possessed* himself *of* the kingdom. —Shak.
7. to make acquainted with; to acquaint; to inform. [Archaic.]
Possess the people in Messina here how innocent she died. —Shak.
8. to keep control over; to maintain.
9. to furnish or fill; to imbue or instill into: with *with* before the thing [Archaic.]
It is of unspeakable advantage to *possess* our minds *with* an habitual good intention. —Addison.
10. to have knowledge or mastery of (a language, etc.).
11. to have sexual intercourse with.
Syn.—have, hold, occupy, own.

poṣ·ṣessed' (-zest'), *a.* 1. owned.
2. controlled by an evil spirit; crazed; mad.
possessed of; in possession of.

poṣ·ṣes'sion (-zesh'un), *n.* [ME.; OFr.; L. *possessio*.]
1. a possessing or being possessed; ownership, occupancy, hold, etc.
2. anything possessed.
3. [*pl.*] property; wealth.
4. any territory belonging to an outside country.
5. self-possession.
to put in possession; (a) to give possession to; (b) to place a person in charge of property recovered on ejectment or distraint.

poṣ·ṣes'sion, *v.t.* to provide with property. [Obs.]

poṣ·ṣes'sion·ăr·y, *a.* relating to or implying possession.

poṣ·ṣes'sion·ẽr, *n.* 1. one that has possession of a thing, or power over it. [Obs.]
2. a member of such religious communities as were endowed with lands, etc.: opprobrious term. The mendicant orders professed to live entirely upon alms. [Obs.]

poṣ·ṣes·sī'văl, *a.* in grammar, of or relating

to the possessive case; as, a *possessival* termination.

pos·ses′sive, *a.* [L. *possessivus.*]
1. of possession, or ownership.
2. showing, or characterized by a desire for, possession; as, a *possessive* person, *possessive* gestures.
3. in grammar, designating or of a case, form, or construction expressing possession or some like relationship: in English, this is expressed (a) by a final *s* (of nouns and some pronouns) preceded or followed by an apostrophe, or sometimes by an apostrophe only, following a final *s* sound (e.g., *John's* book, *men's* lives, *boys'* games, *conscience'* sake); (b) by change of form of pronouns (e.g., *my, mine, your, yours, his, her, hers, its, our, ours, their, theirs, whose*); (c) by *of* preceding a form in the objective case (e.g., the lives *of men*) or preceding a form in the possessive case (e.g., a play *of Shakespeare's*, a friend *of mine*—called a double possessive).

pos·ses′sive, *n.* in grammar, (a) the possessive case; (b) a possessive form or construction.

pos·ses′sive·ly, *adv.* in a manner denoting possession.

pos·ses′sŏr, *n.* [ME. and OFr. *possessour*; L.] one who possesses; an owner.
Syn.—proprietor, holder, master, owner.

pos·ses′sō·ry, *a.* 1. of, being, or characterizing a possessor.
2. of or based upon possession.
possessory action; in law, an action or suit in which the right of possession only, and not that of title, is contested.

pos′set, *n.* [ME. *poshote, poshoote, possot.*] a hot drink made of milk curdled with ale, wine, etc., usually spiced.

pos′set, *v.t.* 1. to curdle. [Rare.]
2. to pamper. [Rare.]

pos·si·bil′i·ty, *n.* 1. the quality or state of being possible.
2. *pl.* **pos·si·bil′i·ties,** that which is possible; a thing which may possibly happen, be, or exist.

pos′si·ble, *a.* [ME.; OFr.; L. *possibilis*, from *posse*, to be able.]
1. that can be; capable of existing.
2. that can be in the future; that may or may not happen: distinguished from *probable*.
3. that can be done, known, acquired, etc. by a person or thing expressed or implied.
4. that can be used, selected, done, etc., depending on circumstances; potential; as, a *possible* location.
5. that may be done, known, etc. if allowed; permissible.
6. that can be put up with; tolerable. [Colloq.]
Syn.—practicable, feasible, likely, potential.

pos′si·bly, *adv.* 1. in a possible manner; by any possible means: in any case; as, it can't *possibly* work.
2. perchance; perhaps; by some possibility; maybe; as, it may *possibly* be so.

pos′sum, *n.* an opossum. [Colloq.]
to play possum; to feign; to dissemble; in allusion to the opossum's habit of feigning death when attacked.
The Senate is *playing possum*—that is, it is playing politics. —Alfred Henry Lewis.

pōst, *n.* [ME.; AS.; L. *postis*, from *positus*, pp. of *ponere*, to place.]
1. a piece of wood, metal, etc., usually long and square or cylindrical, set upright and intended to support a building, sign, gate, etc.; a pillar; a pole; as, the *posts* of a house; the *posts* of a door.
2. the doorpost of a shop, on which the owner chalked up the debts of his customers; hence, a score; a debt. [Obs.]
3. anything resembling a post (sense 1) in shape or purpose.
4. any place originally marked by or associated with a post, as the starting point of a horse race.
from pillar to post; see under *pillar*.

pōst, *v.t.* 1. to put up (a poster, notice, etc.) on a wall, post, or other conspicuous place (also with *up*).
2. to announce, publicize, or advertise by posting notices, etc.; as, to *post* a reward.
3. to put posters, etc. on; to placard.
4. to warn persons against trespassing on (grounds, etc.) by posted notices.
5. to put (a person's name) on a posted or published list.
6. to denounce by a public notice.
7. to publish the name of (a ship) as lost or missing.

pōst, *n.* [Fr. *poste*; It. *posto*; LL. *postum*; contr. from L. *positum*, neut. pp. of *ponere*, to place.]
1. the place where a soldier is stationed.
2. a place where a body of troops is stationed or is in occupation.
3. the troops at such a place; garrison.
4. a local unit of a veterans' organization.
5. in the British Army, either of two bugle calls (*first post* and *last post*) sounded at tattoo.
6. a place where a person is stationed, as at a machine.
7. a position or job, especially one to which a person is appointed.
8. a trading post.

pōst, *v.t.* 1. to station at or assign to a post.
2. to appoint to a military post or command.

pōst, *n.* [Fr. *poste*; It. *posta*, orig., a station; LL. *posta*, for L. *posita*, f. pp. of *ponere*, to place.]
1. originally, one of a number of riders or runners posted at intervals to carry letters and packages in relays or stages along a route or, later, to provide fresh horses for a courier.
2. formerly, (a) a postrider or courier; (b) a stage of a post route; (c) a post horse or a station for one; (d) a packet (ship).
3. (a) (the) mail; (b) a post office; (c) a mail box. [Chiefly Brit.]
4. a postman. [Dial.]
5. a size of paper, approximately 16 by 20 inches: so called because the original watermark was a postman's horn.

pōst, *v.i.* 1. formerly, to travel in posts or stages.
2. to hasten; to travel with speed.
And *post* o'er land and ocean without rest. —Milton.
3. to rise and sink in the saddle in accordance with the motion of a horse, especially when trotting.

pōst, *v.t.* 1. originally, (a) to send by or as by post; (b) to hasten.
2. to mail; to put in a mailbox, etc. [Chiefly Brit.]
3. to inform, as of events (usually in the passive); as, he is kept well *posted*.
4. in bookkeeping, (a) to transfer (an item) from a daybook, etc. to the ledger; (b) to enter in the correct form and place; (c) to enter all necessary items in (a ledger, etc.).

pōst, *adv.* with post horses; hence, swiftly; expeditiously; expressly.
Sent from Media *post* to Egypt. —Milton.
to ride post; to be employed to carry dispatches and papers; hence, to hasten; to travel fast.

pōst, *prep.* and *adv.* [L.] after; behind; since: in English it occurs chiefly in phrases taken directly from Latin, as in *ex post facto*.

pōst-, [L., from *post*, behind, after.] a prefix meaning, (a) *after in time, later, following*, as in *post*graduate, *post*glacial; (b) *after in space, behind*, as in *post*axial.

pōst·ab·dō′men, *n.* a posterior part of, or part posterior to, the abdomen.

pōst′ȧ·ble, *a.* that can be posted. [Rare.]

pōst′ạge, *n.* [*post* (mail) and *-age.*] the amount charged for mailing a letter or package.

pōst′ạge stamp, a government stamp to be put on a letter or package as a sign that the postage has been prepaid: it is either a small printed gummed label or a design imprinted on an envelope, postal card, etc.

pōst′ăl, *a.* [Fr., from *poste.*] having to do with mail or post offices.
postal card; (a) a card with a printed postage stamp, issued by a government for sending messages at a rate lower than that for letters; (b) loosely, a post card.
postal money order; same as *money order*.
postal note; formerly, a postal money order.
Postal Union; a union entered into by different governments agreeing to stipulated postal rates in their several territories.

pōst·ā′năl, *a.* [*post-*, and L. *anus*, anus.] situated behind the anus.

pōst·ax′i·ăl, *a.* in anatomy and zoology, situated behind the axis of the body, as the posterior part of a limb.

pōst′bag, *n.* a mailbag.

pōst″-bel′lum, *a.* occurring after the war, specifically after the American Civil War.

pōst bel′lum, [L.] after the war.

pōst bill, a bill of letters mailed by a postmaster. [Obs.]

pōst′box, *n.* same as *mailbox*.

pōst′boy, *n.* 1. formerly, a man or boy who rode with the post.
2. a letter carrier.
3. a postilion.

pōst·cȧ·non′iç·ăl, *a.* written after the writings occurring in a canon.

pōst çap′tain (-tin), formerly, a naval officer commissioned as a captain.

pōst çärd, 1. a postal card.
2. an unofficial card, often a picture card, that can be sent through the mail when a postage stamp is affixed.

pōst·çā′vȧ, *n.*; *pl.* **pōst·çā′vae,** in anatomy, the ascending vena cava.

pōst·çā′văl, *a.* pertaining to the postcava.

pōst chāise, a closed, four-wheeled coach or carriage drawn by fast horses, which were changed at each post, formerly used to carry mail and passengers.

pōst·cī′băl, *a.* occurring after the taking of food.

pōst·clav′i·çle, *n.* a posterior bone in many fishes projecting backward from the clavicle.

pōst·clȧ·viç′ū·lăr, *a.* situated or occurring behind the clavicle.

pōst·com′mis·sūre, *n.* in anatomy, the posterior commissure of the brain.

Pōst·cŏm·mū′niŏn (-yun), *n.* 1. that part of the Communion service which follows after the people have taken Communion.
2. that part of the Mass which follows the Communion of the celebrant.

pōst·çor′nū, *n.* the posterior horn of the lateral ventricle.

pōst·dāte′, *v.t.*; postdated, *pt., pp.*; postdating, *ppr.* 1. to assign a later date to than the actual date.
2. to write such a date on; as, to *postdate* a contract, that is, to date it later than the true time of making the contract.
3. to be subsequent to.

pōst′dāte, *n.* a date attached to a writing or other document later than the real date.

pōst dāy, a day on which the mail arrives or departs. [Brit.]

pōst·dī·crot′iç, *a.* occurring after the dicrotic elevation of the sphygmogram.

pōst·di·lū′vi·ăl, *a.* same as *postdiluvian*.

pōst·di·lū′vi·ăn, *a.* [*post-*, and *diluvian.*] living or happening after the Flood.

pōst·di·lū′vi·ăn, *n.* a person who lived after the Flood.

pōst·dis·sēi′zin, *n.* in old law, a subsequent disseizin; also, a writ that lay for him who, having recovered lands or tenements by force of novel disseizin, was again disseized by the former disseizor. [Obs.]

pōst·dis·sēi′zŏr, *n.* a person who disseized another of lands which he had before recovered of the same person. [Obs.]

pōs′tē·ȧ, *n.* [L., afterward.] in common law, the entry made by the judge before whom a cause was tried, after the verdict, stating what was done in the cause.

pos′tel (pos′l), *n.* a doorpost or gatepost. [Obs.]

pōst″em·bry·on′iç, *a.* occurring after the embryonic stage.

pōst·en·ceph′ȧ·lon, *n.* in anatomy, the metencephalon, or afterbrain.

pōst′en·try, *n.* 1. a second or subsequent entry, at the customhouse, of goods which had been omitted by mistake.
2. in bookkeeping, an additional or subsequent entry.

pōst′ẽr, *n.* 1. originally, one who traveled by post, or rapidly.
2. a post horse.

pōst′ẽr, *n.* 1. a large printed bill or placard, often illustrated, to be posted in a public place as a notice or advertisement.
2. one who posts bills, notices, etc.

pōste res·tänte′, [Fr., remaining post.]
1. a notation on a letter asking that it be held at the post office until called for.
2. a department of the post office having charge of letters waiting to be called for. [Chiefly Brit.]

pos·tē′ri·ŏr, *a.* [L. *posterior*, comp. of *posterus*, from *post*, after.]
1. later or subsequent in time; following after: opposed to *prior*.
2. later in the order of proceeding or moving; coming after in order; succeeding.
3. situated behind, or toward the rear; hinder; rear: opposed to *anterior*.
4. in anatomy, at or toward the hind part of the body; dorsal.
5. in botany, on the side next to the main stem

pos·tē′ri·ŏr, *n.* [*sometimes pl.*] the buttocks.

pos·tēr·i·or'i·ty, *n.* [ME. *posteriorite*; ML. *posterioritas.*]
1. the condition or quality of being posterior.
2. posterior position in space or time.

pos·tēr'i·ŏr·ly, *adv.* in a posterior manner; so as to be posterior.

pos·ter'i·ty, *n.* [ME. *posterite*; MFr. *postérité*; L. *posteritas, posterus*, from *post*, after.]
1. all of a person's descendants: opposed to *ancestry*.
2. all succeeding generations; the future.

pōs'tērn (*or* pos'), *n.* [ME.; OFr. *posterne*, from LL. *posterna*, a secret gallery or means of exit, from L. *posterus*, behind, posterior, from *post*, behind.]
1. formerly, a back door or gate; a private entrance.
2. a hidden, often underground, entrance or exit to a castle.
3. a way of escape, refuge, dishonorable entrance, etc.

pōs'tērn, *a.* 1. of or resembling a postern.
2. rear; posterior.
3. lesser; inferior.
4. private; undercover.

pos'ter·ō-, [from L. *posterus*, following.] a combining form meaning *posterior and*.

Pōst Ex·chānge', a nonprofit general store at an army post or camp, for the sale of small articles for personal use, refreshments, etc.

pōst·ex·il'i·ăn (-egz-), *a.* [*post-*, and L. *exilium*, exile.] after the exile; specifically, of that period of Jewish history subsequent to the captivity of the Jews at Babylon (6th century, B.C.).

pōst·ex·il'iç, *a.* postexilian.

pōst·ex·ist' (-egz-), *v.i.* to live subsequently. [Rare.]

pōst·ex·ist'ence, *n.* subsequent or future existence.

pōst·ex·ist'ent, *a.* existing after. [Rare.]

pōst'façt, *n.* a fact that occurs after another. [Obs.]

pōst-faç'tum, *a.* ex post facto.

pōst·fē'bril, *a.* [*post-*, and L. *febris*, fever.] occurring after or resulting from a fever.

pōst'-fīne, *n.* in English law, a fine due to the king by prerogative: also called *king's fine*.

pōst'fix, *n.* [*post-* and af*fix*.] a letter, syllable, or word, added to the end of another word; a suffix.

pōst·fix', *v.t.*; postfixed (-fixt'), *pt., pp.*; postfixing, *ppr.* to suffix.

pōst'free', *a.* 1. that can be mailed free of charge.
2. postpaid. [Brit.]

pōst·frŏn'tăl, *n.* a bone behind the frontal region of the skull.

pōst·frŏn'tăl, *a.* situated behind the frontal region of the skull.

pōst·fūr'çȧ, *n.*; *pl.* **pōst·fūr'cae**, [*post-*, and L. *furca*, fork.] in zoology, an internal vertical process in the sternum of an insect to which some of the leg muscles are attached.

pōst·ġen'i·tūre, *n.* [*post-* and *geniture*.] the condition of being born after another of the same family, as the second-born of twins: opposed to *primogeniture*. [Rare.]

pōst·glā'ciăl (-shăl), *a.* existing or happening after the glacial, or Pleistocene, Epoch.

pōst·glē'noid, *a.* in anatomy, situated behind the glenoid fossa.

pōst·glē·noi'dăl, *a.* same as *postglenoid*.

pōst·grad'ū·āte, *a.* of or pertaining to studies pursued after being graduated or having received a degree.

pōst·grad'ū·āte, *n.* one who has pursued or is pursuing a postgraduate course.

pōst'hāste', *n.* great haste, as of a postrider. [Archaic.]

pōst'hāste', *adv.* with great haste; as, he traveled *posthaste*.

pos·thet'ō·my, *n.* [Gr. *posthē*, prepuce, and *-tomia*, from *temnein*, to cut.] circumcision.

pōst hoç, ẽr'gō prop'tẽr hoç, [L.] after this, therefore because of this: in logic, the fallacy of thinking that a happening which follows another must be its result.

pōst'hōle, *n.* a hole into which a post is sunk.

pōst hŏrn, formerly, a horn or trumpet carried and blown by a carrier of the public mail or by a coachman.

pōst hŏrse, formerly, one of a succession of horses stationed at post houses along a road for the rapid conveyance of couriers, passengers, etc.

pōst hour (our), the hour for posting letters.

pōst house, 1. a post office. [Now Dial.]
2. formerly, an inn or other place where post horses were kept.

post'hūme, *a.* posthumous. [Obs.]

post'hū·mous, *a.* [L. *postumus*, last, superl. of *posterus*, coming after, from *post*, behind.]
1. born after the death of the father; as, a *posthumous* son or daughter.
2. published after the death of the author; as, *posthumous* works.
3. arising or continuing after one's death.

post'hū·mous, *n.* a posthumous child. [Rare.]

post'hū·mous·ly, *adv.* after death.

pos'tiç, *a.* [L. *posticus*.] posterior. [Obs.]

pōs·tīçhe', *a.* [Fr.; It. *posticcio*; LL. *appositicius*, from L. *appositus*, pp. of *apponere*, to put near to, from *ad-*, to, and *ponere*, to put.]
1. counterfeit; artificial.
2. superfluously or inappropriately decorative.

pōs·tīçhe', *a.* 1. a substitute; counterfeit.
2. pretense.

pos·tī'çous, *a.* [L. *posticus*, hinder, back.] in botany, (a) situated on the posterior or outside; (b) extrorse; turned outward; opening on the outer side, as an anther.

pos·tī'çum, *n.* [L.] in ancient architecture, a portico or vestibule at the rear of a building; a postern; a reredos.

pos'til, *n.* [Fr. *postille*, from L. *post illa* (*verba*), after those (words).
1. a marginal note; a note in the margin of the Bible: so called because written after the text. [Obs.]
2. a homily or commentary to be read in a church service.

pos'til, *v.t.*; postiled, *pt., pp.*; postiling, *ppr.* to write marginal notes on; to gloss; to illustrate with marginal notes. [Obs.]

pos'til, *v.i.* to postillate; to comment. [Obs.]

pos'til·ẽr, *n.* one who writes marginal notes; one who illustrates the text of a book by notes in the margin. [Obs.]

pōs·til'iŏn (-yun), *n.* [Fr. *postillon*; *poste*, post.]
1. a person who rides the left-hand horse of the leaders of a four-horse carriage.
2. one who rides the left-hand horse of a two-horse carriage when there is no driver. Also spelled *postillion*.

pos'til·lāte, *v.i.*; postillated, *pt., pp.*; postillating, *ppr.* [from *postil*.]
1. formerly, to preach by expounding Scripture, verse by verse, in regular order. [Obs.]
2. to postil; to comment; to write a postil. [Rare.]

pos'til·lāte, *v.t.* to explain by postils. [Rare.]

pos·til·lā'tion, *n.* exposition of Scripture in preaching.

pos'til·lā·tŏr, *n.* one who expounds Scripture verse by verse. [Rare.]

pos'til·lẽr, *n.* same as *postiler*.

pōst·im·pres'sion·iṣm, *n.* the theory, practice, or methods of a group of late 19th-century painters who revolted against the objectivity and scientific naturalism of impressionism, and placed emphasis upon the subjective viewpoint of the artist rather than upon literal representation.

pōst·im·pres'sion·ist, *a.* of or characteristic of postimpressionism.

pōst·im·pres'sion·ist, *n.* an artist of the period or school of postimpressionism, as Cézanne, Van Gogh, or Gauguin.

pōst''im·pres·sion·is'tiç, *a.* postimpressionist.

pōst'ing, *n.* 1. the transferring of accounts to a ledger.
2. the act of traveling post or with post horses.

pos'tīque (-tēk), *a.* same as *postiche*.

pōst·lim'i·nȧ·ry, *a.* 1. same as *postliminiary*.
2. subsequent: opposed to *preliminary*.

pōst·li·min'i·ăr, *a.* same as *postliminiary*.

pōst·li·min'i·ăr·y, *a.* pertaining to *postliminium*.

pōst·li·min'i·ous, *a.* same as *postliminiary*.

pōst·li·min'i·um, pōst·lim'i·ny, *n.* [L. *post*, after, and *limen, liminis*, threshold.]
1. among the ancient Romans, the return to his own country of a person who had gone abroad or had been banished or taken by an enemy.
2. in international law, the rule by which persons and things taken by an enemy in war regain their former rights when coming again under the power of their own country.

pōst'lūde, *n.* [*post-*, and L. *ludus*, play.]
1. an organ voluntary played at the end of a church service.
2. a phrase or movement played at the end of a musical composition.

pōst'măn, *n.*; *pl.* **pōst'men**, a letter carrier.

pōst'măn, *n.* in England, formerly, an experienced and leading barrister in the Court of Exchequer: so called from the position of his seat in court. [Obs.]

pōst'märk, *n.* the mark or stamp of a post office put on mail canceling the postage stamp and recording the date, time, and place of sending or receving.

pōst'märk, *v.t.*; postmarked (-märkt), *pt., pp.*; postmarking, *ppr.* to stamp with a postmark.

pōst'mȧs''tẽr, *n.* 1. the official in charge of a post office.
2. originally, one who provided post horses.
3. in Merton College, Oxford, a scholar who is supported on the foundation.

pōst'mȧs''tẽr ġen'ẽr·ăl, *pl.* **pōst'mȧs''tẽrṣ ġen'ẽr·ăl, pōst'mȧs''tẽr ġen'ẽr·ălṣ**, the head of a government's postal system.

pōst'mȧs''tẽr·ship, *n.* the office or term of a postmaster.

pōst·me·rid'i·ăn, *a.* of or occurring in the afternoon, or after the sun has crossed the meridian; as, *postmeridian* sleep.

pōst mē·ri'di·em, [L.] after noon.

pōst mill, a windmill that rests on a vertical axis, and can be turned as the direction of the wind varies. In the figure, the post P has at its upper end a pivot working into a socket fixed in one of the strongest floor beams. The ladder L serves as a lever for turning the mill, and by dropping it on the ground and placing a weight on its lower end, it also serves to keep the mill steady when the right position is attained.

POST MILL

pōst''mil·lē·nār'i·ăn, *n.* one who adopts postmillennialism.

pōst''mil·lē·nār'i·ăn, *a.* pertaining to or denoting the doctrine of postmillennialism.

pōst''mil·lē·nār'i·ăn·iṣm, *n.* same as *postmillennialism*.

pōst·mil·len'ni·ăl, *a.* existing or happening after the millennium.

pōst·mil·len'ni·ăl·iṣm, *n.* the belief that the second coming of Christ will follow the millennium.

pōst·min'i·mus, *n.*; *pl.* **pōst·min'i·mī**, [*post-*, and L. *minimus* (*digitus*), the least (finger).] an extra or additional little toe or little finger, or a process resembling one.

pōst'mis''tress, *n.* a woman postmaster.

pōst''-mọr'tem, *a.* [L.] 1. happening, done, or made after death.
2. having to do with a post-mortem examination.

pōst''-mọr'tem, *n.* a post-mortem examination.

pōst''-mọr'tem ex·am·i·nā'tion, the examination of a human body after death; an autopsy.

pōst·nā'ris, *n.*; *pl.* **pōst·nā'rēṣ**, one of the posterior nares.

pōst·nā'tăl, *a.* after birth.

pōst'nāte, *a.* [L. *post*, after, and *natus*, born.] subsequent. [Obs.]

pōst·nā'tus, *n.*; *pl.* **pōst·nā'tī**, [L.] one born after a certain event; specifically, (a) a second son; (b) in the United States, one born after the American Revolution; (c) in Scotland, one born after the accession of James I to the English throne.

pōst''-Nī'cēne, *a.* subsequent to the general council at Nicaea, A. D. 325.

pōst nōte, [*post-* and *note*.] in commerce, a promissory note issued by a bank, and made payable to order at some future specified time.

pōst·nup'tiăl (-shăl), *a.* being or happening after marriage.

pōst″-ō′bit, *a.* being, or to be, in effect after a person's death.

pōst″-ō′bit, *n.* [L. *post*, after, and *obitus*, death.]
1. a bond given by a borrower pledging to pay his debt upon the death of a specified person from whom he expects to inherit money.
2. same as *post-mortem.*

pōst″ob·loṅ·gā′tȧ, *n.* the rear portion of the medulla.

pōst·oç′ū·lăr, *a.* and *n.* same as *postorbital.*

pōst′-of″fice, *a.* of a post office.

pōst of′fice, 1. a department of the government in charge of the mails.
2. an office or building where mail is sorted for distribution, postage stamps are sold, etc. *post-office order*; same as *money order.*

pōst·op′ẽr·ȧ·tive, *a.* existing or taking place after a surgical operation.

pōst·ō′răl, *a.* [*post-*, and L. *os*, *oris*, mouth.] situated behind the mouth.

pōst·or′bit·ăl, *n.* a bone or scale situated behind the orbit.

pōst·or′bit·ăl, *a.* situated behind the orbit.

pōst′pāid′, *a.* having the postage prepaid, as a letter.

pōst·pal′ȧ·tīne, *a.* located back of the palate or palatine bones.

pōst·pär′tum, *a.* [L.] subsequent to childbirth.

pōst″-Plī′ō·cēne, *n.* and *a.* same as *post-Tertiary.*

pōst·pōn′ȧ·ble, *a.* that can be postponed.

pōst·pōne′, *v.t.*; postponed, *pt.*, *pp.*; postponing, *ppr.* [L. *postponere*; *post*, after, and *ponere*, to put.]
1. to put off; to defer to a future or later time; to delay; as, to *postpone* the consideration.
2. to set below something else in value or importance. [Rare.]

pōst·pōne′, *v.i.* in medicine, to delay in coming on or recurring.

pōst·pōne′ment, *n.* a postponing or being postponed.

pōst·pōn′ẽr, *n.* one who postpones.

pōst·pōṣe′, *v.t.* to postpone. [Obs.]

pōst·poṣ′it, *v.t.* to postpone. [Obs.]

pōst·pō·ṣi′tion (-zish′un), *n.* 1. a placing after or being placed after.
2. a word placed after another word; especially, a word that has the function of a preposition but follows its object.

pōst·pō·ṣi′tion·ăl, *a.* pertaining to a postposition.

pōst·poṣ′i·tive, *a.* placed after or added to another word; enclitic; suffixed.

pōst·poṣ′i·tive, *n.* a postpositive word; a postposition.

pōst·poṣ′i·tive·ly, *adv.* in a postpositive manner.

pōst·pran′di·ăl, *a.* [*post-*, and L. *prandium*, dinner.] after-dinner; done or occurring after dining.

pōst·prē·diç′ȧ·ment, *n.* in logic, any one of the five categories dealing with forms of conceptions as treated by Aristotle after the discussion of his ten predicaments, comprising "movement," "possession," "before," "at once," and "the opposite."

pōst·prid′i·ē, *n.* [L. *post*, after, and *pridie*, day before.] in the Mozarabic liturgy, a prayer that follows the consecration of the Eucharistic elements.

pos·trē·mō·gen′i·tūre, *n.* [L. *postremus*, superl. of *posterus*, from *post*, after, and *geniture.*] in law, the rights of the last child born.

pōst·rē·mōte′, *a.* less remote in subsequent time or order.

pōst′rīd″ẽr, *n.* one who rides with the mails over a post road.

pōst rōad, 1. formerly, a road provided with post houses.
2. a road over which the post, or mail, is or formerly was carried.

pōs·trorse′, *a.* [L. *post*, back, and *versus*, turned: formed in imitation of *retrorse*, for *retroversus.*] directed or turned back: opposed to *antrorse.*

pōst rŏute, a road along which mail is carried.

pōst·sçap′ū·lȧ, *n.* the part of the scapula below or posterior to the spine.

pōst·sçap′ū·lăr, *a.* pertaining to or near the postscapula.

pōst·scē′ni·um (-sē′), *n.* [*post-*, and L. *scena*, a stage.] the part of a theater behind the scenes.

pōst·sçrībe′, *v.t.* to add a postscript to. [Rare.]

pōst′sçript, *n.* [L. *post*, after, and *scriptum*, written.] a paragraph or note added to a letter after it is concluded and signed; any addition made to a book or composition after it has been finished, containing something omitted, or something new occurring to the writer.

pōst·sçript′ăl, *a.* relating to or having the nature of a postscript.

pōst·sçū·tel′lum, *n.* [*post-* and *scutellum.*] the last of the four dorsal pieces into which the thoracic segment of an insect is divided.

pōst·sphē′noid, *a.* pertaining to or near the hinder part of the sphenoid bone.

pōst·sys·tol′iç, *a.* [*post-* and *systolic.*] in physiology, following the systole.

pōst·tem′pō·răl, *a.* situated back of the temporal bone.

pōst″tem′pō·răl, *n.* a bone that joins the supraclavicle to the skull in some fishes.

pōst″-Tẽr′ti·ăr·y (-shi-), *a.* following or later than the Tertiary.

pōst″-Tẽr′ti·ăr·y, *n.* in geology, a classification of phenomena sometimes called the Quaternary. It includes all deposits later than the Tertiary, particularly in glaciated regions.

pōst·ton′iç, *a.* [*post-*, and Gr. *tonos*, tone.] occurring after the accented syllable.

pōst town, 1. a town in which a post office is established by law.
2. a town in which post horses are kept. [Rare.]

pōst trād′ẽr, a trader formerly appointed by the Secretary of War for each military post.

pōst trā′gus, a growth behind the tragus, found in certain animals.

pōst·tym·pan′iç, *a.* situated behind the tympanum.

pos′tū·lănt, *n.* [L. *postulans* (*-antis*), ppr. of *postulare*, to demand.] a petitioner or candidate, especially one for admission into a religious order.

pos′tū·lāte, *n.* [L. *postulatum*, from *postulare*, to demand, from the root of *poscere*, to ask or demand.]
1. a position or supposition assumed without proof, or one that is considered as self-evident, or too plain to require illustration; a proposition of which the truth is demanded or assumed for the purpose of future reasoning; a necessary assumption.
2. in mathematics, a self-evident problem, answering to axiom, which is a self-evident theorem.
3. a prerequisite.
4. a basic principle.

pos′tū·lāte, *v.t.*; postulated, *pt.*, *pp.*; postulating, *ppr.* [L. *postulatus*, pp. of *postulare*, to demand.]
1. to claim; to demand; to require.
2. to assume without proof to be true, real, or necessary, especially as a basis for argument.
3. to assume; to take as self-evident or axiomatic.

The Byzantine emperors appear to have exercised, or at least to have *postulated*, a sort of paramount supremacy over this nation. —Tooke.

pos′tū·lāte, *a.* postulated. [Obs.]

pos·tū·lā′tion, *n.* [L. *postulatio.*]
1. the act of postulating or being postulated.
2. something postulated.

pos′tū·lā·tŏr, *n.* one who postulates.

pos′tū·lȧ·tō·ry, *a.* 1. assuming without proof.
2. assumed without proof. [Rare.]

pos·tū·lā′tum, *n.*; *pl.* **pos·tū·lā′tȧ,** [L.] a postulate.

pos′tūr·ăl, *a.* pertaining to posture; as, *postural* treatment.

pos′tūre, *n.* [Fr., from L. *positura*, a position, from *ponere*, to place.]
1. the position of the body or of parts of the body; carriage; bearing.
2. such a position assumed as in posing, etc.
3. the way things stand; condition with respect to circumstances; as, the delicate *posture* of foreign affairs.
4. an attitude of mind; frame of mind.

pos′tūre, *v.t.*; postured, *pt.*, *pp.*; posturing, *ppr.* to place in a particular manner; to pose.

pos′tūre, *v.i.* to assume a bodily or mental posture, as for effect; to pose; to attitudinize.

pos′tūre mȧs′tẽr, one who teaches or practices artificial postures of the body.

pos′tūr·ẽr, *n.* one who postures.

pos′tūr·īze, *v.t.*; posturized, *pt.*, *pp.*; posturizing, *ppr.* to posture.

pōst′wąr′, *a.* after the (or a) war.

pōst″zyg·ȧ·poph′y·sis, *n.*; *pl.* **pōst″zyg·ȧ·poph′y·sēs,** [*post-* and *zygapophysis.*] a posterior articular outgrowth of a vertebra.

pō′ṣy, *n.*; *pl.* **pō′ṣieṣ,** [contr. from *poesy.*]
1. originally, a sentiment in verse; especially, a motto inscribed in a ring, etc.
2. a flower or a bunch of flowers; a nosegay: so called probably from the use of flower imagery in posies (sense 1).

pō′ṣy ring, a ring having a posy inscribed in it.

pot, *n.* [AS. *pott*; akin to D. *pot*; prob. from *pod*; perh. named from the shape.]
1. a round vessel more deep than broad, made of earthenware, metal, or glass, used for holding liquids, cooking or preserving food, etc.
2. a pot with its contents.
3. a potful.
4. a pot of liquor; a drink; potation.
5. something resembling a pot in shape or use; as, a chimney *pot*, lobster *pot*.
6. (a) all the money bet at a single time pool; kitty; (b) a large amount of money. [Colloq.]
7. a pot shot. [Colloq.]
8. a size of writing paper.
9. a chamber pot.
10. marijuana. [Slang.]
to go to pot; to go to ruin; to become useless.

pot, *v.t.*; potted, *pt.*, *pp.*; potting, *ppr.* 1. to put into a pot.
2. to preserve in a pot or jar.
3. to cook in a pot.
4. to shoot (game) for food instead of for sport.
5. to hit or secure by or as by a pot shot.
6. to secure, win, or capture. [Colloq.]
7. to place or cover in pots of earth, as plants.
8. to put in casks for draining, as raw sugar.
9. in billiards, to pocket.

pot, *v.i.* 1. to tipple. [Obs.]
2. to take a pot shot; to shoot. [Colloq.]

pō′tȧ·ble, *a.* [Fr.; L. *potabilis*, from *potare*, to drink.] drinkable; suitable for drinking; as, water fresh and *potable.*

pō′tȧ·ble, *n.* [*usually in pl.*] something that may be drunk; a beverage.

pō′tȧ·ble·ness, *n.* the quality of being drinkable.

pot′ăġe, *n.* pottage. [Obs.]

pō·täġe′ (-täzh), *n.* [Fr.] soup; broth.

pot′ȧ·ġẽr, *n.* one who makes pottage. [Obs.]

pot āle, the refuse grain from a distillery, used to fatten swine. [Brit. Dial.]

pō·tā′mi·ăn, *n.* [Gr. *potamos*, river] a soft-shelled river tortoise.

Pot″ȧ·mō·ġē′ton, *n.* [Gr. *potamogeitōn*, pondweed; *potamos*, river, and *geitōn*, neighbor.] a genus of aquatic perennials of the *Naiadaceæ* or pondweed family, which grow in temperate regions and have long spikes of small flowers.

pot·ȧ·mog′rȧ·phy, *n.* [Gr. *potamos*, river, and *graphein*, to write.] a description of rivers; potamology.

pot·ȧ·mol′ō·ġy, *n.* [Gr. *potamos*, a river, and *-logy.*] a scientific treatise on rivers; the study of rivers; potamography.

pot·ȧ·mom′ē·tẽr, *n.* [Gr. *potamos*, river, and *metron*, measure.] a meter for measuring the speed of currents, as of a river or sea.

Pot″ȧ·mō·spon′ġi·ae, *n.pl.* [Gr. *potamos*, river, and *Spongiæ.*] the fresh-water sponges.

pō′tănce, *n.* same as *potence.*

pō·tär′gō, *n.* same as *botargo.* [Obs.]

pot′ash, *n.* [*pot* and *ash*; so called from being prepared for commercial purposes by evaporating the lixivium of wood ashes in iron pots.]
1. an oxide, K_2O, derived from natural brines, distillery waste from alcohol manufacture, flue dusts of blast furnaces, wood ashes, etc., used in fertilizer, soaps, etc.
2. a hard, white, brittle compound, strongly alkaline and caustic; caustic potash (potassium hydroxide).
3. potassium carbonate.

pō·tas′sȧ, *n.* potassium hydroxide.

pot·ass·am′ide, *n.* [*potass*ium and *amide.*] a yellowish-brown or white, crystalline compound, obtained by heating potassium in ammonia.

pō·tas′siç, *a.* [*potass*ium and *-ic.*] of or containing potassium.

pot·as·sif′ẽr·ous, *a.* [LL. *potassa*, potash, and L. *ferre*, to bear.] containing potash or potassium salts.

pō·tas′si·um, *n.* [Mod.L., from *potassa*; D. *potasch*, potash.] a soft, silver-white, waxlike metallic chemical element that oxidizes rapidly when exposed to air: it occurs abundantly in nature in the form of its salts, which are used in fertilizers, glass, etc.: symbol, K; atomic weight, 39.096; atomic number, 19.

potassium bitartrate; same as *cream of tartar.*
potassium bromide, a white, crystalline compound, KBr, used in photography, medicine, etc.
potassium carbonate; a strongly alkaline, white, crystalline compound, K_2CO_3, used in the manufacture of soap and glass, in medicine, etc.
potassium chlorate; a colorless, crystalline salt, $KClO_3$, a strong oxidizing agent used in the manufacture of explosives, matches, tooth pastes, etc.
potassium chloride; a colorless, crystalline salt, KCl, used in fertilizers, explosives, etc.; syenite.
potassium cyanide; an extremely poisonous, white, crystalline compound, KCN, used in metallurgy for extracting gold, in electroplating, as an insecticide, etc.
potassium dichromate; a yellowish-red, crystalline compound, $K_2Cr_2O_7$, used as an oxidizing agent and in photography, dyeing, etc.
potassium hydroxide; a white, crystalline salt or deliquescent solid, KOH, used in the manufacture of soap, glass, etc.: it is a very strong alkali and absorbs carbon dioxide from the air: also called *caustic potash.*
potassium myronate; a colorless, crystalline, glucoside salt, $KC_{10}H_{18}O_{10}NS_2$, extracted from the seeds of black mustard: it yields glucose by hydrolysis: also called *sinigrin.*
potassium nitrate; a colorless, crystalline compound, KNO_3, used in fertilizers, gunpowder, preservatives, etc., in medicine, and as a reagent and oxidizing agent in chemistry: also called *niter, saltpeter.*
potassium permanganate; a dark-purple, crystalline compound, $KMnO_4$, used as an oxidizer, disinfectant, etc.

pō'tāte, *a.* [L. *potatus*, pp. of *potare*, to drink.] potable; liquefied.

pō·tā'tion, *n.* [L. *potatio* (*-onis*), from *potare*, to drink.]
1. the act of drinking.
2. a draught or drink.
3. excessive drinking.
4. a liquor.

pō·tā'tō, *n.*; *pl.* **pō·tā'tōeṣ,** [Sp. *patata, batata*, the name originally applied to the sweet potato, from a Haitian word.]
1. originally, a sweet potato.
2. a common plant, *Solanum tuberosum*, or one of its starchy, brown-skinned or red-skinned tubers. It is native to the Andean region of South America, but it is now a staple food in most temperate countries. The tubers vary in form from roundish to an irregular oblong, have eyes more or less deeply set, and vary in weight up to a pound or more. The plants are raised from the eyes, which are planted in hills or rows. In addition to being used as food, potatoes are extensively used in the manufacture of spirits, starch, etc. Also called *white potato, Irish potato.*
indian potato; the ground nut.
native potato; an orchid of Tasmania and New South Wales, having a tuber somewhat resembling the potato.
potato whisky; an alcoholic liquor manufactured from potatoes.
wild potato; a Jamaican plant closely resembling the common sweet potato.

pō·tā'tō bēan, same as *yam bean.*

pō·tā'tō bee'tle (-tl), a black-striped, yellow beetle that eats the leaves of potatoes: also *potato bug.*

pō·tā'tō blīght (blīt), see *potato rot.*

pō·tā'tō bug, same as *potato beetle.*

pō·tā'tō chip, a very thin slice of potato fried crisp and then salted.

pō·tā'tō mil'dew, pō·tā'tō mōld, same as *potato rot.*

pō·tā'tŏr, *n.* [L.] a drinker. [Rare.]

pō·tā'tō rot, a disease attacking the potato, due to a fungus, *Phytophthora infestans*, causing the stem and leaves to turn black and the tubers to become affected and later decay: when confined to the stem and leaves it is also called *potato blight.*

pō'tȧ·tō·ry, *a.* [LL. *potatorius*; L. *potator*, drinker, from *potare*, to drink.] pertaining to drinking.

pō·tā'tō sçab, a diseased condition of potatoes caused by a fungus and characterized by rough, deep-seated scabs on the tubers.

pō·tā'tō vīne, 1. that part of the potato plant growing above ground.
2. the entire potato plant.

pot-au-feu' (pō-tō-fē'), *n.* [Fr., lit., pot on the fire.] beef stew with vegetables.

pot'bel''lied, *a.* having a protruding belly.

pot'bel''ly, *n.*; *pl.* **pot'bel''lieṣ,** a protruding belly; also, a person having such a belly.

pot'boil''ẽr, *n.* 1. a housekeeper. [Brit. Dial.]
2. any literary or artistic work done merely to make money rather than for artistic excellence or love of the work.

pot bot'tŏm, in mining, a concretion or large boulder in a roof slate, having an appearance similar to the rounded bottom of a pot.

pot'-bound'', *a.* having the roots so compact and matted as to allow no room for expansion: said of potted plants.

pot'boy, *n.* 1. a boy who carries pots of ale, etc. in a public house or inn. [Chiefly Brit.]
2. a person who serves customers, cleans up, etc. in a tavern. [Chiefly Brit.]

potch, *v.t.* in papermaking, to bleach (pulp).

potch, *v.t.* to poach; to boil. [Obs.]

pot cheeṣe, same as *cottage cheese* under *cheese.*

potch'ẽr, *n.* 1. one who potches. [Obs.]
2. same as *potcher engine.*

potch'ẽr en'ġine, in papermaking, a machine in which the pulp is bleached after being washed.

potch'ẽr·man, *n.* one who operates a potcher.

pot'-çlāy, *n.* a kind of fire clay from which melting pots used in glassmaking are made.

pot çŏm·pan'iŏn (-yun), an associate or companion in drinking.

pot'ē·çā·ry, *n.* an apothecary. [Obs.]

po·teen', *n.* [Ir. *poitin*, dim. of *poite*, a pot.] in Ireland, whisky that is illicitly distilled: also *potheen.*

pot'ē·line, *n.* a mixture of glycerin, gelatin, and tannin, used for sealing.

pō'tē·lot, *n.* in old chemistry and mineralogy, sulfuret of molybdenum.

pō'tence, *n.* [Fr.] 1. in heraldry, a cross whose ends resemble the head of a crutch. [Obs.]
2. same as *potency.*

pō'ten·cy, *n.*; *pl.* **pō'ten·cieṣ,** [L. *potentia*, from *potens*, powerful.]
1. the state or quality of being potent, or the degree of this; power; strength.
2. capacity for development; potentiality.
3. something or someone influential or powerful.
4. in heraldry, a potence, or cross.
5. in homeopathy, the power of a drug as induced by attenuation.

pō'tent, *a.* [L. *potens, potentis*, ppr. of *posse*, to be able; *potis*, able, and *esse*, to be.]
1. able to control or influence; having authority or power; mighty; as, a *potent* monarch.
2. convincing; cogent; influential; as, a *potent* argument.
3. effective or powerful in action, as a drug or drink.
4. able to perform sexual intercourse: said of a male.
5. in heraldry, resembling, composed of, or divided by a potent.
Syn.—forcible, powerful, strong, able, influential.

pō'tent, *n.* 1. a prince; a potentate. [Obs.]
2. a walking staff or crutch. [Obs.]
3. in heraldry, a T-shaped figure supposed to represent the head of a crutch; also, a fur composed of such figures arranged horizontally, and usually silver and blue in color.
potent counter-potent; a heraldic fur resembling the potent but having a different arrangement of the figures.

POTENT COUNTER-POTENT

pō'ten·tȧ·cy, *n.* sovereignty. [Obs.]

pō'ten·tāte, *n.* [Fr. *potentat*; LL. *potentatus*, from L. *potens*, powerful.] a person who possesses great power; a ruler; a monarch.

pō'tent·ed, *a.* in heraldry, with the outer edges formed into potents.

POTENTED

pō·ten'tiăl (-shăl), *a.* [LL. *potentialis*, from L. *potens* (*-entis*), powerful.]
1. originally, that has power; potent.
2. that can, but has not yet, come into being; possible; latent; unrealized; undeveloped: opposed to *actual.*
3. in grammar, expressing possibility, capability, or the like; as, the *potential* mood.
potential difference; the difference in potential between two points causing or tending to cause a current of electricity to pass between them.
potential energy; energy that is the result of relative position instead of motion, as in a coiled spring.
potential mood; same as *potential*, sense 3.

pō·ten'tiăl, *n.* 1. something potential; a potentiality.
2. in electricity, the relative voltage, amount of electric charge, or degree of electrification at a point in an electric circuit or field, as referred to some other point in the same circuit or field.
3. in grammar, (a) the potential mood or aspect; (b) a potential construction or form.
4. in physics, any scalar quantity in which energy is involved as a function of position or condition.
zero potential; the potential of a point at an infinite distance from all electrified bodies: in practice, the potential of the earth is used as a point of reference.

pō·ten·ti·al'i·ty (-shi-), *n.* 1. the state or quality of being potential; possibility or capability of becoming; latency.
2. *pl.* **pō·ten·ti·al'i·tieṣ,** something potential; a possibility of developing, coming to fruition, etc.

pō·ten'tiăl·ly (-shăl-), *adv.* 1. in a potential manner; possibly or hypothetically, but not yet actually.

This duration of human souls is only *potentially* infinite. —Bentley.

2. in a potent manner; powerfully. [Obs.]

pō·ten'ti·āte (-shi-), *v.t.*; potentiated, *pt., pp.*; potentiating, *ppr.* [L. *potentia*, power.] to endow with power; to make potent.

Pō·ten·til'lȧ, *n.* [L. *potens*, powerful, from the supposed medical qualities of some of the species.]
1. an extensive genus of herbaceous perennials of the family *Rosaceæ*, found chiefly in the temperate and cold regions of the northern hemisphere, containing about one hundred and twenty species. They are tall or procumbent herbs, rarely undershrubs, with saw-edged leaves, generally five, growing along the stem, and flowers of various colors.
2. [p–] any plant of this genus, as the cinquefoil or five-finger.

POTENTILLA
(*Potentilla anserina*)

pō·ten·ti·om'ē·tẽr (-shi-), *n.* [L. *potentia*, power, and Gr. *metron*, measure.] an instrument for measuring or controlling electromotive force or differences of electrical potentials.

pō'ten·tīze, *v.t.*; potentized, *pt., pp.*; potentizing, *ppr.* [*potent* and *-ize.*] to bring into active force and realize the latent power of.

pō'tent·ly, *adv.* 1. powerfully; with great force or energy.

You are *potently* opposed. —Shak.

2. with emphasis or assurance; very emphatically.

pō'tent·ness, *n.* the state or quality of being potent; powerfulness; strength; might; potency. [Obs.]

Pō·tē'ri·um, *n.* [Gr. *potērion*, a cup, *Poterium sanguisorba* being used in cooling drinks.] a genus of plants of the family *Rosaceæ*, having pinnate leaves and tall stems surmounted by dense heads of small, greenish flowers. The principal species is the *Poterium spinosum* of Italy, another being *Poterium canadense*, the wild burnet.

pō'tes·tāte, *n.* a potentate. [Obs.]

pō·tes'tȧ·tive, *a.* [from L. *potestas*, power.] authoritative. [Obs.]

pot'gun, *n.* 1. a cannon shaped like a pot; a mortar. [Obs.]
2. a popgun. [Obs.]

pot'hang''ẽr, *n.* a pothook.

poth'ē·çȧ·ry, *n.*; *pl.* **poth'ē·çā·rieṣ,** an apothecary. [Obs. or Dial.]

pō·theen', *n.* same as *poteen.*

poth'ẽr, *n.* [earlier *pudder*; vowel after *bother* or *potter.*]
1. bustle; confusion; tumult; fuss.
2. a suffocating cloud, as of dust or smoke.

poth'ẽr, *v.t.* and *v.i.*; pothered, *pt., pp.*; pothering, *ppr.* to bother; to worry.

pot'hẽrb (-ẽrb *or* -hẽrb), *n.* any plant whose leaves and stems are boiled and eaten, or used to flavor food.

pot'hōl''dẽr, *n.* a small pad, or piece of thick cloth, for holding and handling hot pots, etc.

pot'hōle, *n.* a deep hole or pit; especially, a deep, round basin worn in the rocks or rock bed of a stream by the grinding action of stones and gravel whirled around by the water.

pot′hook, *n.* 1. an S-shaped hook on which pots and kettles are hung over the fire.
 2. a hooked rod for lifting hot pots, etc.
 3. an S-shaped mark, as one made by children learning to write.

Pō′thos, *n.* [native name in Ceylon.] a genus of plants of the family *Araceæ*, which grow on trees like ivy. Some species are cultivated in hothouses.

pot′house, *n.* an alehouse or tavern, especially a disreputable one. [Brit.]

pot′hunt″ẽr, *n.* 1. a hunter who kills game indiscriminately, disregarding the rules of sport.
 2. a person who enters contests merely to win prizes.

pō·tiçhe′, *n.*; *pl.* **pō·tiçhes′** (-tēsh′), [Fr., from *pot*, a pot.] a vase or jar of porcelain, etc., with a rounded or polygonal body narrowing toward the top, and with a separate cover.

pot″i·çhō·mă′ni·ȧ, pot″i·çhō·mā′nie, *n.* [Fr. *potiche*, vase, and Gr. *mania*, madness.] the act or process of making glass vessels look like painted ware by coating the inner side with painted paper or linen.

pō′tion, *n.* [Fr., from L. *potio* (*-onis*), from *potare*, to drink.] a drink, especially of poison or medicine; a dose.

pot lāce, a lace having designs resembling baskets of flowers in the pattern.

pot′latch, *n.* [Am. Ind.]
 1. among some American Indians of the northern Pacific coast, (a) [*often* P-] a winter festival; (b) a distribution of gifts, as during such a festival.
 2. a ceremonial feast at which gifts are exchanged in a rivalry to display wealth.

pot lead (led), black lead, often used to reduce friction on the hulls of vessels.

pot′lid, *n.* the lid or cover of a pot.

pot′luck, *n.* whatever the family meal happens to be; as, will you take *potluck* with us?

pot′măn, *n.*; *pl.* **pot′men,** 1. a pot companion. [Obs.]
 2. a serving man, or waiter, as in a public house. [Brit.]

pot mar′i·gōld, any of a number of related plants of the daisy family, with showy yellow or orange flowers; calendula.

pot met′ăl, 1. originally, a mixture of copper and lead used in the manufacture of faucets and large pots.
 2. iron from which pots are manufactured.
 3. stained glass that is colored while molten.

pō·tō·mā′ni·ȧ, *n.* [L. *potus*, drinking, and E. *mania*.] same as *dipsomania*.

pō·tom′ē·tẽr, *n.* [Gr. *poton*, drink, and *metron*, measure.] an instrument by which the amount of moisture a paint absorbs is measured.

pō·tọọ′, *n.* [echoic.] a large, South American goatsucker, *Nyctibius grandis*.

pō·tō·rọọ′, *n.* the rat kangaroo of Australia and Tasmania.

pot′pīe, *n.* 1. a baked pie containing meat, made in a pot or deep dish.
 2. a similar dish that is stewed or boiled instead of baked; meat cooked with dumplings.

pot plant, 1. a plant growing in a pot.
 2. same as *pot tree*.

pōt·pöur·rī′ (pō-), *n.* [Fr.] 1. originally, a stew.
 2. a confused collection; a miscellaneous mixture; a medley; a hotchpotch.
 3. a mixture of dried flowers and spices for perfuming a room; also, the vase or jar holding the mixture.
 4. in music, a medley.
 5. in literature, an anthology.

pot rōast, meat, usually beef, cooked by braising.

pot′shärd, pot′shāre, *n.* a potsherd. [Obs.]

pot′shẽrd, *n.* [*pot* and *sherd* or *shard*; AS. *sceard*, a fragment, from *sceran*, to shear.] a piece or fragment of broken pottery.

pot shot, 1. originally, a pothunter's shot.
 2. an easy shot, as one at close range.
 3. a random shot.
 4. a haphazard try at something.

pot′stōne, *n.* a variety of steatite of which cooking vessels were made in prehistoric times.

pott, *n.* a pot (size of paper). [Obs.]

pot′tăģe, *n.* [Fr. *potage*; ME. *potage*, porridge, soup.] a kind of stew made of vegetables, or meat and vegetables; a thick soup.

pot′tāin, *n.* old pot metal. [Obs.]

Pot·tȧ·wät′ō·mie, *n.* a member of a tribe of North American Indians originally inhabiting Michigan and Wisconsin.

pot′ted, *a.* 1. put into a pot or pots.
 2. cooked or preserved in a pot or can.
 3. intoxicated; drunk. [Slang.]

pot·teen′, *n.* same as *poteen*.

pot′tẽr, *n.* [from *pot*.]
 1. one whose occupation is to make earthenware pots, dishes, and other vessels.
 2. a peddler of crockery. [Brit. Dial.]
 3. the red-bellied terrapin.
 4. one who pots meats, vegetables, or other food.
 potter's asthma; a disease of the lungs prevalent among persons who work in potteries.
 potter's clay; see under *clay*.
 potter's field; a piece of ground set aside as a burial place for criminals, paupers, and unknown or friendless persons: so named from a field near Jerusalem where strangers were buried, said to have been originally a potter's field.
 potter's ore; see *alquifou*.
 potter's wheel; a rotating horizontal disk, usually operated by a treadle or motor, upon which clay is molded into bowls, etc.

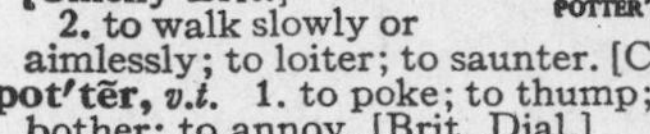

POTTER'S WHEEL

pot′tẽr, *v.i.*; pottered, *pt.*, *pp.*; pottering, *ppr.* [freq. of obs. *pote*, to push.]
 1. to employ oneself with trifles; to loiter about one's work; to trifle; to waste time in ineffectual efforts or work; to putter. [Chiefly Brit.]
 2. to walk slowly or aimlessly; to loiter; to saunter. [Chiefly Brit.]

pot′tẽr, *v.t.* 1. to poke; to thump; to push; to bother; to annoy. [Brit. Dial.]
 2. to dawdle or fritter (with *away*). [Chiefly Brit.]

pot′tẽr, *n.* a puttering. [Chiefly Brit.]

pot′tẽrn, *a.* of or pertaining to pottery or potters. [Obs.]
 pottern ore; a species of ore apt to vitrify like the glazing on pottery. [Obs.]

pot′tẽr wăsp, a small wasp, *Eumenes fraterna*, which builds globular cells or clay in which it stores insect larvae for its young.

pot′tẽr·y, *n.*; *pl.* **pot′tẽr·ieṣ,** [Fr. *poterie*, from *pot*, pot.]
 1. the vessels or ware made by potters of clay hardened by heat; earthenware.
 2. the place where earthen vessels are made; a potter's workshop or factory.
 3. the art or occupation of a potter; ceramics.

pot′tẽr·y tree, a South American tree of the family *Rosaceæ*, whose powdered bark is used in making pottery: also called *pottery-bark tree*.

pot′ting, *n.* 1. drinking; tippling. [Obs.]
 2. a placing or preserving in a pot.

pot′tle, *n.* [OFr. *potel*, dim. of *pot*, pot.]
 1. formerly, a liquid measure, equal to a half gallon.
 2. a pot or tankard having this capacity.
 3. the contents of such a pot.
 4. alcoholic liquor.
 5. a container or small basket for holding fruit.

pot′tō, *n.* a small, reddish-gray mammal, *Perodicticus potto*, of the lemur family: it is nocturnal in its habits, and native to the western part of Africa.

pot tree, any South American tree which bears monkeypots.

Pott's dis·ēaṣe′, [after Percival *Pott* (1714–1788), Eng. surgeon.] tuberculous caries of the vertebrae, resulting in curvature of the spine.

pot′ty, *a.*; *comp.* pottier; *superl.* pottiest, [from phr. *to go to pot*, or from notion of drunkenness.]
 1. trivial; petty. [Brit. Colloq.]
 2. slightly crazy. [Brit. Colloq.]

pot′ū·lent, *a.* fit to drink. [Obs.]

pot′-val′iănt (-yănt), *a.* [*pot* and *valiant*.] courageous and valiant from drunkenness; heated to valor by strong drink.

pot′-wäl′lŏp·ẽr, *n.* [*pot* and *wallop*, to boil.]
 1. in some English boroughs before the passing of the Reform Bill of 1832, a person considered a householder by virtue of owning a hearth, and therefore qualified to vote.
 2. a scullion. [Slang.]

pot wheel (-hwēl), a noria.

pouch, *n.* [ME. *pouche*; OFr. *pouche*, *poche*, forms of *poque*, to poke (sack).]
 1. a smallish bag or sack.
 2. a small bag for carrying ammunition.
 3. a small bag of leather, rubberized cloth, plastic, etc., for carrying pipe tobacco in one's pocket.
 4. a mailbag.
 5. anything shaped like a pouch.
 6. a pocket (in clothing). [Scot.]
 7. a purse. [Archaic.]
 8. in anatomy, any pouchlike cavity or part.
 9. in botany, a pod that looks almost square, with an upper and lower lid.
 10. in zoology, (a) a saclike structure on the abdomen of some animals, as the kangaroo and the opossum, used to carry young; (b) a baglike part, as of a pelican's bill or a gopher's cheeks, used to carry food.
 11. a partition in a ship's hold to prevent grain or other loose cargo from shifting.

pouch, *v.t.*; pouched (poucht), *pt.*, *pp.*; pouching, *ppr.* 1. to swallow.
 2. to pout.
 3. to put into a pouch.
 4. to make into a pouch; to make pouchy.
 5. to furnish with funds. [Brit. Slang.]
 6. to submit to; to put up with; to pocket, as a slight or affront.

pouch, *v.i.* to form a pouch or pouchlike cavity; to bag.

pouched (poucht), *a.* 1. having a pouch or pouches.
 2. pouchy.
 pouched dog; same as *thylacine*.
 pouched frog; a frog the female of which is furnished with a pouch in which the eggs are hatched and the tadpoles carried.
 pouched gopher; same as *pocket gopher*.
 pouched mouse; same as *pocket mouse*.
 pouched rat; same as *pocket gopher*.

pou′chet box, same as *pounce box*.

pouch mouth, a mouth with coarse protruding or swollen lips. [Obs.]

pouch′-mouthed, *a.* having a pouch mouth. [Obs.]

pouch shell, a small pond snail, *Bulinus hypnorum*, of Great Britain and America.

pouch′y, *a.*; *comp.* pouchier; *superl.* pouchiest, resembling a pouch; baggy.

pöu′dre (-dẽr), *n.* powder; very fine dust.

pöu′dre mär′chănt, [OFr.] a spice or flavoring powder. [Obs.]

pöu·drette′ (-dret′), *n.* [Fr., dim. of *poudre*, powder.] a very powerful manure made from night soil, dried and mixed with charcoal, gypsum, etc.

pöuf, pöuffe, *n.* [Fr.]
 1. an elaborate headdress worn by women, especially in the eighteenth century, and characterized by high rolls or puffs of hair.
 2. any part of a dress, etc. gathered into a puff, or projection.
 3. a kind of ottoman (sense 1).

pöu·lāine′, *n.* [OFr.] the long, pointed toe of a shoe worn in the Middle Ages.

pöu·lärd′, *n.* [Fr. *poularde*, from *poule*, hen.] a pullet which has had the ovaries removed to fatten it and prepare it for the table; hence, a fat pullet.

pōul′dā·vis, *n.* poledavy. [Obs.]

pōul′dẽr, *n.* and *v.* powder. [Obs.]

pōul′drŏn, *n.* pauldron. [Archaic.]

pöule, *n.* 1. pool (total amount of stakes).
 2. a position or figure in a square dance.

pöulp, pöulpe, *n.* [Fr. *poulpe*, from L. *polypus*.] same as *octopus*, the animal.

pōult, *n.* [Fr. *poulet*, dim. of *poule*, hen.] a young chicken, partridge, etc.

pöult″-de-soie′ (pö″de-swä′), *n.* [Fr.] a heavy silken material for dresses.

pōul′tẽr, *n.* a person who deals in poultry; a poulterer. [Archaic.]

pōul′tẽr·ẽr, *n.* [OFr. *pouletier*, from *poulet*, fowl.]
 1. one who makes a business of selling poultry, especially for the table. [Chiefly Brit.]
 2. formerly, in England, an officer of the king's household who had charge of the poultry.

pōult′foot, *a.* having distorted feet; clubfooted. [Obs.]

pōult′foot, *n.* a distorted foot; a clubfoot. [Obs.]

pōul′tice, *n.* [L. *puls, pultis,* thick pap.] a cataplasm; a soft, hot, moist mass, as of flour, mustard, meal, bran, flaxseed, or similar substances, applied to sores, inflamed parts of the body, etc.

pōul′tice, *v.t.*; poulticed (-tist), *pt., pp.*; poulticing, *ppr.* to cover with a poultice.

pōul′try, *n.* [OFr. *pouleterie,* from *poulet,* fowl; L. *pulla,* a hen.] domestic fowls which are propagated and fattened for the table, and for their eggs, feathers, etc., such as chickens, turkeys, ducks, guinea fowls, and geese.

pōul′try färm, a farm or piece of land devoted to the raising of poultry.

pōul′try feed′ẽr, an automatic machine which feeds grain to poultry in small quantities at a time.

pōul′try yärd, a yard or place where fowls are kept.

pounce, *n.* [Fr. *ponce*; L. *pumex (-icis),* pumice.]

1. a fine powder, as pulverized cuttlefish bone, formerly used to prevent ink from spreading on paper or to prepare the writing surface of parchment.

2. charcoal dust, etc. sprinkled over a stencil to make a design, as on cloth. This kind of pounce is used by embroiderers to transfer their patterns upon their stuffs, by lacemakers, and sometimes by engravers.

3. a perfumed toilet powder. [Obs.]

pounce, *v.t.*; pounced (pounst), *pt., pp.*; pouncing, *ppr.* 1. to sprinkle, finish, prepare, or rub with pounce.

2. to stencil with pounce.

pounce, *n.* [variant of *punch,* ultimately from L. *pungere,* to pierce.]

1. the claw or talon of a bird of prey.

2. a pouncing; a swoop, as by a bird of prey.

3. cloth worked in eyelet holes. [Obs.]

4. a punch or stamp. [Obs.]

pounce, *v.t.* 1. to strike or pierce with claws or talons. [Rare.]

2. to perforate; to punch holes in, as embroidery. [Obs.]

pounce, *v.i.*; pounced, *pt., pp.*; pouncing, *ppr.* to fall on suddenly; to fall on and seize with the claws; to spring or leap (*on, upon,* or *at* a person or thing) and, or as if to, attack or seize; as, a rapacious bird *pounces on* a chicken.

pounce box, a small box with a perforated lid, used for sprinkling pounce on paper or for holding perfume.

pounced (pounst), *a.* 1. furnished with claws or talons.

2. perforated. [Obs.]

poun′cẽr, *n.* 1. one who or that which pounces or perforates; specifically, an instrument for making eyelet holes in cloth; a bodkin.

2. in the medieval church in England, a bishop's thumbstall: also written *poncer, ponser, ponsir.* [Obs.]

poun′cet box, a small box with perforations on the top, to hold perfume for smelling. [Archaic.]

poun′cing, *n.* 1. the act of perforating or of punching holes.

2. falling suddenly on and seizing with the claws.

poun′cing, *n.* 1. sprinkling with pounce.

2. the transference of a pattern or design by means of pounce.

pound, *n.* [AS., Dan., Sw., Ice., and Goth. *pund*; G. *pfund*; L. *pondo,* a pound, akin to *pondus,* a weight used in a scale, from *pendere,* to cause to hang down.]

1. a unit of weight, equal to 16 ounces (7,000 grains) avoirdupois or 12 ounces (5,760 grains) troy.

2. the monetary unit of the United Kingdom, equal to 20 shillings or 100 (new) pennies: symbol, £.

3. the monetary unit of various other countries, including Cyprus, Egypt, Ireland, Lebanon, Malta, Israel, Syria, and Sudan.

4. in the New Testament, a mina.

5. a former Scottish monetary unit (*pound Scots*), originally equal to the British pound.

pound, *n.* [AS. *pund,* an enclosure.]

1. an enclosure, maintained by a town, etc., in which stray animals are confined when taken in trespassing or going at large in violation of law, and from which they may be redeemed by the payment of a fine; a pinfold.

2. an enclosure for keeping or sheltering animals.

3. an enclosure for trapping animals.

4. a place of confinement, as for arrested persons.

5. an enclosed area for catching or keeping fish.

6. a level stretch of water in a canal between the locks. [Dial.]

pound overt; an uncovered pound; a pound without a roof, in distinction from one which is covered.

pound, *v.t.* to confine in a pound; to impound.

pound, *v.t.*; pounded, *pt., pp.*; pounding, *ppr.* [AS. *punian,* to beat, bray: the *d* has become attached, as in *sound, compound.*]

1. to beat; to strike with some heavy instrument and with repeated, heavy blows, so as to make an impression; as, to *pound* meat to make it tender.

With cruel blows she *pounds* her blubbered cheeks. —Dryden.

2. to comminute and pulverize by beating; to bruise or break into fine parts by a heavy instrument; as, to *pound* spice or salt.

to pound out; (a) to flatten, smooth, etc. by pounding; (b) to play with a very heavy touch, as on a piano.

to pound the pavement; to walk the streets, as in looking for work. [Slang.]

pound, *v.i.* 1. to deliver repeated, heavy blows (*at* or *on* a door, etc.).

2. to move with heavy steps or come down heavily while moving; as, the horse *pounded* along the path.

3. to beat heavily; to throb.

pound, *n.* 1. a pounding.

2. a hard blow.

3. the sound of this; a thud; a thump.

pound′āġe, *n.* 1. a tax, rate, or commission, etc. per pound (sterling or weight).

2. in England, a subsidy of twelve pence in the pound, formerly granted to the crown on all goods exported or imported.

3. the commission paid to a sheriff or other officer upon the money realized by an execution.

pound′āġe, *v.t.* to assess and also to collect at a given rate per pound. [Rare.]

pound′āġe, *n.* 1. the condition of being impounded; confinement in or as in a pound, or enclosure.

2. the fee required for the release of animals in a pound.

pound′ăl, *n.* [from *pound,* weight.] a unit of force that, when applied for one second, will give to a weight of one pound a velocity of one foot per second, equal to 13,825 dynes.

pound breach, the breaking of a public pound for releasing beasts confined in it.

pound′cāke″, *n.* 1. a cake composed of a pound each, or equal quantities, of flour, butter, sugar, and eggs.

2. a cake resembling this.

pound′ẽr, *n.* a person or thing that pounds, or beats, as a pestle, a stamp in an ore mill, etc.

pound′ẽr, *n.* something weighing or worth a pound: often used in hyphenated compounds meaning *weighing, worth,* or *having to do with* (a specified number of) *pounds,* as *eight-pounder.*

pound′-fool′ish, *a.* foolish in the care of large sums of money: see phrase under *penny-wise.*

pound′ing, *n.* 1. the act of beating; a breaking into pieces; the act of raining blows (upon).

2. the sound which is produced by waves beating against rocks; as, the *pounding* of the surf against the headland.

3. [*pl.*] disintegrated or pulverized particles, as of rocks.

pound′keep″ẽr, pound′mȧs″tẽr, *n.* one who has the care of a pound, or enclosure.

pound′măn, *n.*; *pl.* **pound′men,** a fisherman who uses a pound in catching fish.

pound net, a fish trap consisting of nets arranged so as to form an enclosure with a narrow opening.

pound rāte, in England, a rate, assessment, or payment levied at a certain rate per pound.

pound scoop, a scoop net used to take fish out of a pound.

pound stẽr′ling, a pound (the British monetary unit).

pöu′pē-ton, *n.* an old dish made with layers of meat and fowl. [Obs.]

pöur, *a.* poor. [Obs.]

pōur, *v.i.* pore. [Obs.]

pōur, *v.t.*; poured, *pt., pp.*; pouring, *ppr.* [ME. *pouren*; prob. a dial word.]

1. to cause to flow in a continuous stream, either out of a vessel or into it; as, to *pour* water from a pail or into a pail; to *pour* wine into a decanter.

2. to emit; to send forth, as in a stream; to send out in profusion or great numbers.

London doth *pour* out her citizens. —Shak.

3. to utter, to give vent to, as under the influence of strong feeling; as, to *pour* out words, prayers, or sighs.

pōur, *v.i.* 1. to stream; to flow freely, continually, or copiously; to fall, or issue in a continuous stream or current; as, the torrent *pours* down from the mountain.

2. to rain heavily.

3. to rush in a crowd or in a constant stream; as, the people *poured* out of the church.

4. to assist in serving refreshments at a table; as, to *pour* at luncheon.

pōur, *n.* 1. a flow or pouring, as of a current of water.

2. a heavy fall of rain; a downpour.

pöur·boire′ (-bwär′), *n.* [Fr. *pour,* for, and *boire,* L. *bibere,* to drink.] a douceur; a gift; a tip or gratuity.

pōur′ẽr, *n.* one who or that which pours.

pöur′lieū, *n.* purlieu. [Obs.]

pöur·pär·ler′ (-lā′), *n.* [Fr. *pour,* for, and *parler,* to speak.] a preliminary, informal discussion, as a consultation held prior to a treaty for the purpose of discussing and framing it.

pöur·pär′ty, *n.* purparty. [Obs.]

pöur′point, *n.* [Fr., from *pour,* for, and *poindre*; L. *pungere,* to prick.] a stuffed and quilted close-fitting body garment, worn in the late Middle Ages: so named from the needlework upon it.

pöur·pres′tūre, *n.* purpresture. [Obs.]

pour·ri·dié′ (pö-rē-dyā′), *n.* [Fr., from *pourrir,* to rot.] any one of various fungous growths which decay the roots of vines.

pöur′sui·vănt (-swē-), *n.* same as *pursuivant.*

pöur·trāy′, *v.t.* to portray. [Obs.]

pöur·vey′ănce, *n.* purveyance. [Obs.]

pöus, *n.* pulse. [Obs.]

pous·sé′ (pö-sā′), *n.* [Fr. *poussée,* from *pousser,* to push.] in music, the upstroke of a bow on an instrument such as the violin.

pousse-ca·fé′ (pös-kȧ-fā′), *n.* [Fr., from *pousser,* to push, and *café,* coffee.]

1. a liqueur drunk with after-dinner coffee.

2. a drink made of several liqueurs, each forming its own layer in the glass.

pöus·sette′, *a.* [Fr., dim. of *pousse,* a push.] a dance figure in which a couple or several couples dance round and round with hands joined.

pöus·sette′, *v.i.*; poussetted, *pt., pp.*; poussetting, *ppr.* to perform a poussette.

pöu stō, [Gr. *pou sto,* where I may stand: from a saying of Archimedes, *dos moi pou sto, kai kino ten gen,* give me (a place) where I may stand, and I will move the earth.]

1. literally, a place to stand on.

2. a basis of operations.

pout, *n.*; *pl.* **pout** or **pouts,** [AS. *pute* (found only in compounds, as in *ælpute,* eelpout).] any of several fishes, as the horned pout, eelpout, or whiting pout.

pout, *n.* [a corruption of *poult.*] a young partridge or moorfowl; the young of any domesticated fowl; hence, a young child; a maiden. [Scot.]

pout, *v.i.* to shoot at young game birds, as grouse. [Scot.]

pout, *v.i.*; pouted, *pt., pp.*; pouting, *ppr.* [ME. *pouten.*]

1. to thrust out the lips, as in sullenness or displeasure.

2. to sulk.

3. to protrude, as the lips.

pout, *v.t.* 1. to thrust out (the lips or mouth).

2. to utter with a pout.

pout, *n.* 1. a pouting, or protrusion of the lips.

2. [*pl.*] a fit of sulking.

pout′ẽr, *n.* 1. one who or that which pouts.

2. a breed of long-legged pigeon that can distend its crop to produce a large, puffed-up breast.

pout′ing, *n.* childish sullenness.

pout′ing·ly, *adv.* in a pouting or sullen manner.

pov′ẽr·ty, *n.* [Fr. *pauvreté*; L. *paupertas.*]

1. the condition or quality of being poor; need; indigence; lack of means of subsistence.

2. deficiency in necessary properties or desirable qualities, or in a specific quality, etc.; inferiority; inadequacy.

3. unproductiveness, as of soil.
4. smallness in amount; scarcity; paucity; dearth; scantiness.

pov′ẽr·ty gràss, a name given to any of several slender, tufted grasses, especially *Danthonia spicata* and *Aristida dichotoma*, which grow in poor soils.

pov′ẽr·ty plant, a low-growing, heathlike shrub, *Hudsonia tomentosa*, which thrives on sandy shores.

pov′ẽr·ty-strick″en, *a.* 1. stricken with poverty; very poor.
2. characteristic of, or giving the appearance of, poverty.

pov′ẽr·ty-struck, *a.* poverty-stricken. [Now Rare or Obs.]

pōw, *n.* the poll (head). [Chiefly Scot.]

pow′ăn, pow′en, *n.* [a form of *pollan*.] a rare fresh-water fish peculiar to Loch Lomond, of the genus *Coregonus*, much resembling a herring, and often called the *fresh-water herring*.

pow′dẽr, *n.* [Fr. *poudre*; OFr. *pouldre*; It. *polvere*, from L. *pulvis, pulveris*, dust, powder.]
1. a dry substance composed of minute, dustlike particles, produced by crushing, grinding, etc.
2. a specific kind of powder; as, bath *powder*.
3. (a) a drug in the form of powder; (b) a packet or dose of this.
4. an explosive mixture of saltpeter, sulfur, and charcoal; gunpowder.
Brugère powder; a smokeless powder manufactured from picric acid and niter.
Dover's powder; a compound of ipecac, opium, and sulfate of potash, used as a sedative and sudorific: named from Dr. Dover, an English physician, who first compounded it.
progressive powder; a gunpowder that burns slowly until the projectile moves, after which it acts with full force.
talcum powder; see under *talcum*.
Vigo's powder; red oxide of mercury.

pow′dẽr, *v.t.*; powdered, *pt., pp.*; powdering, *ppr.* 1. to sprinkle, dust, or cover with or as with powder.
2. to ornament thus.
3. to make into powder; to pulverize.
4. to sprinkle with salt; to corn, as meat. [Chiefly Brit. Dial.]
5. to whiten with powder.

pow′dẽr, *v.i.* 1. to come violently. [Obs.]
2. to be made into powder, as by pulverization.
3. to use powder as a cosmetic.
4. to make a great commotion or stir; to hurry; to rush. [Now Chiefly Dial.]

pow′dẽr bar′rel, a barrel for storing or transporting powder, with a capacity of about 100 pounds.

pow′dẽr blōw′ẽr, same as *powder gun*.

pow′dẽr-blūe′, *a.* pale-blue.

pow′dẽr blūe, pale blue.

pow′dẽr box, a box in which face powder is kept.

pow′dẽr bũrn, a skin burn caused by exploding gunpowder.

pow′dẽr çärt, a cart that carries powder and shot for artillery.

pow′dẽr chām′bẽr, 1. that part of a gun in which the powder is exploded.
2. that portion of a military mine which contains the powder.

pow′dẽr chest, a small box or case charged with powder, old nails, etc., fastened to the side of a ship, to be discharged at an enemy attempting to board.

pow′dẽr di·vi′ṣion (-vizh′un), a part of the crew of a man-of-war detailed to supply ammunition during a sea fight.

pow′dẽr down, a powder or dust resulting from the falling off or removal of down feathers.

pow′dẽred, *a.* 1. reduced to powder; pulverized.
2. sprinkled with powder; corned; salted. [Brit. Dial.]
3. ornamented with a small pattern reduplicated.
4. in heraldry, same as *semé*.

pow′dẽred milk, milk which has been dried out by evaporation: also called *dried milk*.

pow′dẽred sṳ′gär (shṳ′), very fine sugar made by grinding granulated sugar: it includes *pulverized* sugar and *confectioner's* sugar.

pow′dẽr flag, a red flag hoisted at the masthead of a ship indicating that it is receiving or discharging explosives, etc.

pow′dẽr flȧsk, a small, flat, flask-shaped container in which gunpowder is carried.

pow′dẽr gun, 1. a gun that blows powder into crevices to get rid of insects.
2. an instrument for throwing medicinal powders upon an affected part.

pow′dẽr·hôrn, *n.* 1. a container for carrying gun powder, made of an animal's horn.
2. loosely, a powder flask.

pow′dẽr hōṣe, a flexible hose filled with powder, etc., and used by soldiers to fire a mine; a fuse.

pow′dẽr hoy, a vessel made for the purpose of conveying powder to a man-of-war or naval vessel.

pow′dẽr·ing tub, 1. a tub or vessel in which meat is corned or salted.
2. a tub in which a person with venereal disease was placed for treatment. [Obs.]

pow′dẽr mag·ȧ·zīne′, a fireproof vault or compartment for storing gunpowder and explosives.

pow′dẽr met′ăl·lũr·ġy, the science or process of working metals and alloys by reducing them to powder and shaping this into solids under great heat and pressure.

pow′dẽr·mill, *n.* a mill in which gunpowder is made.

pow′dẽr mīne, a cave or hollow in which powder is placed to be fired at a proper time.

pow′dẽr mŏn′key, formerly, a boy who carried powder from the magazine to the guns aboard a man-of-war.

pow′dẽr pā′pẽr, a paper pulp saturated with or made of an explosive substance; a substitute for powder.

pow′dẽr pōst, wood reduced to powder by insects or dry rot.

pow′dẽr-pōst′ed, *a.* affected with dry rot.

pow′dẽr prōv′ẽr, a machine for testing the explosive power of gun powder.

pow′dẽr puff, a soft pad for applying powder to the face or to the body, as after a bath.

pow′dẽr rọọm, 1. the apartment in a ship where gunpowder is kept.
2. a toilet or lavatory, especially one for women, as in a public building.

pow′dẽr sçut′tle, a hatchway or hole in the deck of a ship for conveying powder from the magazine to the guns.

pow′dẽr ves′sel, a vessel used for a magazine by a fleet.

pow′dẽr·y, *a.* 1. of, like, or in the form of, powder.
2. friable; easily crumbling to pieces.
3. dusty; sprinkled with powder.

pow′dīke, *n.* a marsh or fen dike. [Brit. Dial.]

pow′dry, *a.* same as *powdery*.

pow′ẽr, *n.* [OFr. *pooir*; Fr. *pouvoir*, from an old infinitive *podir*, from LL. *potere*, to be able, used for L. *posse*, to be able, from *potis*, able, and *esse*, to be.]
1. ability to do; capacity to act; capability of performing or producing.

> The brave men, living and dead, who struggled here, have consecrated it far above our poor *power* to add or detract.
> —Abraham Lincoln.

2. a specific ability or faculty; as, the *power* of hearing, beyond one's *powers*.
3. great ability to do, act, or affect strongly; vigor; force; strength.
4. (a) the ability to control others; authority; sway; influence; (b) legal ability or authority; (c) a document giving it.
5. physical force or energy; as, electric *power*.
6. the capacity to exert physical force or energy, usually in terms of the rate or results of its use; as, 60-watt *power*: symbol, P.
7. a person or thing having great influence, force, or authority.
8. a nation, especially one possessed of influence over other nations; as, the big *powers*.
9. national might or political strength.
10. a spirit or divinity.
11. an armed force; army; navy. [Archaic.]
12. a large number or quantity (of something specified). [Colloq.]
13. in mathematics, the product of the multiplication of a quantity by itself; as, 4 is the second *power* of 2 (2^2), 32 is the fifth power of 2 (2^5).
14. in optics, the degree of magnification of a lens, microscope, telescope, etc., expressed as a ratio of the diameters of image and object.
15. [*pl.*] in theology, one of the nine orders of angels.
16. in mechanics, that which produces or tends to produce motion: opposed to the weight, or that which is acted upon.
collateral power; in law, a power granted to a person in relation to land in which he has neither present nor future interest.
exchange of powers; the mutual submission by diplomats of the official documents authorizing them to act on the matters brought under their consideration.
in power; (a) in authority or control; (b) in office.
power of appointment; the authority granted by one person to another to dispose of his property.
power of attorney; a written statement legally authorizing a person to act for one.
power of sale; a clause in legal documents serving as securities for debt, giving the holder power to sell the subject so secured in default of payment.
stray power; in electricity, power lost by friction, eddy currents, etc. when running a dynamo.
the powers that be; the persons in control.

pow′ẽr·ȧ·ble, *a.* 1. possessing power; powerful. [Obs.]
2. possible; capable of being accomplished. [Rare.]

pow′ẽr·bōat, *n.* a motorboat, especially a fast one.

pow′ẽr çap′stăn, a capstan the power of which is increased by the use of gearing, at the same time the speed of its work is diminished.

pow′ẽr dīve, in aviation, a dive speeded by engine power.

pow′ẽr drill, 1. a portable drill operated by an electric motor.
2. a large drilling machine in which a vertical power-driven drill is lowered onto material by a lever.

pow′ẽr·fụl, *a.* 1. having great physical or mechanical power; strong; forcible; mighty; as, a *powerful* army or navy; a *powerful* engine.
2. having great moral power; able to persuade or convince the mind; as, a *powerful* reason or argument.
3. possessing great political and military power; strong in extent of dominion or national resources; potent; as, a *powerful* nation.
4. possessing or exerting great force or producing great effects; as, a *powerful* medicine.
5. in general, able to produce great effects; exerting great force or energy; as, *powerful* eloquence.
6. strong; intense; as, a *powerful* heat or light.

pow′ẽr·fụl, *adv.* very. [Dial.]

pow′ẽr·fụl·ly, *adv.* in a powerful manner; with great effect; forcibly: either in a physical or moral sense.

pow′ẽr·fụl·ness, *n.* the quality of having or exerting great power; force; power; might.

pow′ẽr·house, *n.* 1. a building where power, especially electric power, is generated.
2. a person with a great deal of energy, etc. [Slang.]

pow′ẽr·less, *a.* without power, force, or energy; weak; impotent; not able to produce any effect.

pow′ẽr·less·ness, *n.* the condition or quality of being without power.

pow′ẽr lọọm, a loom worked by water, steam, or some mechanical power.

pow′ẽr plant, 1. the entire apparatus serving as the source of power for some particular operation; as, the *power plant* of an automobile.
2. a factory, including all the buildings and equipment, for generating power, especially electric power.

pow′ẽr pol′i·tiçs, international political relations in which each nation attempts to increase its own power and interests by using military force or the threat of it.

pow′ẽr press, a printing press worked by electricity, steam, water, or other power.

pow′ẽr sçāle, a device for registering the amount of power transmitted.

pow′tẽr, *n.* a variety of the common domestic pigeon, with an inflated breast; the pouter.

pow′wow, *n.* 1. among the North American Indians, a priest or medicine man.
2. among North American Indians, a ceremony to conjure the cure of disease, success in war, etc., usually accompanied by magic, feasting, and noise.
3. a conference of or with North American Indians.

4. any conference. [Colloq.]
pow′wow, *v.i.* [Am. Ind.]
1. to hold a powwow.
2. to confer. [Colloq.]
pox, *n.* [form of pl. of *pock.*]
1. any of various diseases characterized by skin eruptions, as smallpox or chicken pox.
2. syphilis.
poy, *n.* [OFr. *apoi*; Fr. *appui*, support.]
1. a rope-dancers' pole. [Obs.]
2. a support or prop.
3. a pole used for steering or pushing boats against the stream. [Brit. Dial.]
poy′öu, *n.* [native name.] the South American six-banded armadillo, *Dasypus sexcinctus.*
poz·zō·lä′nä (pot-sō-), *n.* pozzuolana.
poz″zuō·lä′nä (pot″swō-), *n.* volcanic ashes, used in the manufacture of hydraulic cement.
Pr, in chemistry, praseodymium.
präam, *n.* 1. a flat-bottomed boat used in Holland and on the Baltic for conveying goods to or from a ship in loading or unloading.
2. in military affairs, a kind of floating battery.
prac′tic, *n.* practice. [Archaic.]
prac′tic, *a.* practical. [Obs.]
prac″ti·cȧ·bil′i·ty, *n.* the quality or state of being practicable; feasibility.
prac′ti·cȧ·ble, *a.* [LL. *practicus*, active, from *practicare*, to execute.]
1. capable of being done, effected, or performed; feasible; as, a *practicable* method.
2. capable of being practiced; as, a *practicable* virtue.
3. that can be used; usable; useful; as, a *practicable* road; a *practicable* weapon.
practicable breach; one that can be entered by troops.
Syn.—possible, practical.
prac′ti·cȧ·ble·ness, *n.* practicability.
prac′ti·cȧ·bly, *adv.* in a practicable manner.
prac′ti·căl, *a.* [L. *practicus*; Gr. *praktikos*, active, practical, from *prassein*, to do, to work.]
1. of, exhibited in, or obtained through practice or active use: opposed to *speculative*; as, a *practical* understanding; and in distinction from *ideal* and *theoretical*; as, *practical* chemistry.
2. that can be used in practice; that can be applied to use; as, *practical* knowledge.
3. designed for use; utilitarian; as, a *practical* dress.
4. concerned with the application of knowledge to useful ends, as distinguished from speculation, etc.; as, *practical* science, a *practical* mind.
5. given to or experienced from actual practice; as, a *practical* farmer.
6. of, concerned with, or dealing efficiently with everyday activities, work, etc.
7. that is so in practice whether or not in theory, intention, law, etc.; virtual.
8. matter-of-fact.
prac·ti·cal′i·ty, *n.* 1. the state or quality of being practical.
2. *pl.* **prac·ti·cal′i·ties,** something practical.
prac′ti·căl jōke, a trick played on someone, meant in fun.
prac′ti·căl·ly, *adv.* 1. in a practical way.
2. from a practical viewpoint.
3. for all practical purposes; in effect; virtually; as, he is *practically* the boss.
4. almost; nearly. [Colloq.]
prac′ti·căl·ness, *n.* the state or quality of being practical.
prac′ti·căl nũrse, an experienced nurse who is neither a graduate of a nursing school nor a registered nurse.
prac′tice, *v.t.*; practiced, *pt.*, *pp.*; practicing, *ppr.* [ME. *practisen*; OFr. *practiser*, from *practiquer*, *pratiquer*, from LL. *practicus*; Gr. *praktikos*, practical, from *prassein*, to do.]
1. to do or perform frequently, customarily, or habitually; to perform by a succession of acts; to make a habit or custom of; as, to *practice* gaming; to *practice* fraud or deception; to *practice* the virtues of charity and beneficence; to *practice* hypocrisy.
2. to use or exercise for instruction, discipline, or dexterity; to exercise oneself in; as, to *practice* music.
3. to put into practice; to use one's knowledge of; to work at, especially as a profession; as, she *practices* medicine.
4. to train; to teach by practice.
Also spelled *practise.*
prac′tice, *v.i.* 1. do something frequently or customarily, either for instruction, profit, or amusement; as, to *practice* with the broadsword; to *practice* with the rifle.
2. to form a habit of acting in any manner.
3. to put theoretical knowledge to practical use; to work at or follow a profession; as, a physician has *practiced* many years.
4. to scheme or intrigue. [Archaic or Rare.]
Also spelled *practise.*
prac′tice, *n.* 1. a practicing; specifically, (a) a frequent or usual action; habit; usage; as, he makes a *practice* of coming early; (b) a usual method; custom; convention; as, tipping is the *practice* in most restaurants: also used in the plural in a disapproving sense; as, the *practices* of a shyster.
2. repeated mental or physical action for the purpose of learning or acquiring proficiency; as, *practice* makes perfect.
3. proficiency or skill acquired through this; as, he's out of *practice.*
4. the doing of something, often as an application of knowledge; as, theory is useless without *practice.*
5. the exercise of a profession or occupation; as, the *practice* of law.
6. a business based on this, often regarded as a legal property; as, he bought their law *practice.*
7. a scheming, intriguing, or trickery.
8. (a) a scheme; an intrigue; (b) a stratagem; a maneuver.
9. in arithmetic, an abridged method of multiplying quantities of different denominations by the use of aliquot parts.
10. in law, an established method of court procedure.
prac′ticed (-tist), *a.* 1. expert by practice; skilled; experienced; as, a *practiced* eye.
2. learned or perfected by practice.
Also spelled *practised.*
prac′ti·cẽr, *n.* 1. one who practices; one who customarily performs certain acts.
2. one who exercises a profession; a practitioner.
Also spelled *practiser.*
prac·ti′ciăn (-tish′un), *n.* [*practic* and *-ian.*] a practitioner; one familiar with or skilled in anything by practice.
präc′ti·cō, *n.*; *pl.* **präc′ti·cōs,** [Sp., experienced.] a guide. [Sp. Am.]
prac′tise, *v.t.* and *v.i.*; practised, *pt.*, *pp.*; practising, *ppr.* to practice.
prac·ti′tiŏn·ẽr (-tish′un-), *n.* [formerly *practicioner*, from *practician* and *-er.*]
1. one who is engaged in the actual use or exercise of any art or profession, particularly in law or medicine.
2. one who does anything customarily or habitually.
3. one who practices sly or dangerous arts. [Obs.]
4. a Christian Science healer.
general practitioner; see under *general.*
prad, *n.* [D. *paard.*] a horse. [Brit. Slang.]
Prä′dō (*or Sp.* prä′thō), *n.* [Sp., meadow.] a fashionable boulevard in Madrid, Spain; hence, a boulevard like it elsewhere.
prae-, [L., from *prae*, before.] pre-: the preferred form in certain words, as *praenomen*, *praetor*, etc.
prae·cā′vȧ, *n.* same as *precava.*
prae·cā′văl, *a.* same as *precaval.*
praec′i·pē (pres′), *n.* [L., imper. of *præcipere*, to give rules.]
1. in law, a writ commanding a person to do a certain thing, or to show cause to the contrary.
2. the note of instructions delivered to the officer of the court who issues the writ.
prae·cō′ciăl, *a.* same as *precocial.*
prae·cog′ni·tum, *n.*; *pl.* **prae·cog′ni·tȧ,** [L., before known.] something previously known in order to understand something else.
prae·cor′ȧ·coid, *n.* same as *precoracoid.*
prae·cor′di·ȧ, *n.* [L. *præ*, before, and *cor*, *cordis*, the heart.] the precordial region.
prae·cor′di·ăl, *a.* same as *precordial.*
prae·cor′nū, *n.*; *pl.* **prae·cor′nū·ȧ,** [L. *præ*, before, and *cornu*, horn.] in anatomy, the anterior cornu of the lateral ventricle of the brain.
prae′di·ăl, *a.* [Fr. *prédial*, from L. *prædium*, a farm or estate.]
1. of land or stationary property; as, *praedial* estates.
2. attached to land or farms; as, *praedial* slaves.
3. growing or issuing from land; as, *praedial* tithes.
Also spelled *predial.*
prae′fect, *n.* a prefect.
prae·flō·rā′tion, *n.* in botany, the manner in which the floral envelopes are arranged in a flower before they expand; estivation.
prae·fō·li·ā′tion, *n.* [*pre-*, and L. *folium*, leaf.] in botany, vernation.
prae·lā′brum, *n.*; *pl.* **prae·lā′brȧ,** in entomology, the clypeus.
prae·max·il′lȧ, *n.* same as *premaxilla.*
prae·mō′lăr, *a.* and *n.* same as *premolar.*
prae·morse′, *a.* same as *premorse.*
prae·mū·nī′rē, *n.* [short for ML. *praemunire* (*facias*), (see to it) that you warn, used for L. *praemonere*, to forewarn.]
1. the offense of obeying other authority than that of the Crown.
2. a writ charging this offense.
3. the penalty for this offense, as imprisonment, forfeiture, etc.
prae·mū·nī′rē, *v.t.* to cause to incur the penalties of praemunire. [Obs.]
prae·mū′ni·tō·ry, *a.* same as *premunitory.*
prae·năr′is, *n.*; *pl.* **prae·năr′ēs,** same as *prenaris.*
prae·nā′săl, *a.* same as *prenasal.*
prae·nō′men, *n.*; *pl.* **prae·nom′i·nȧ,** [L.] among the Romans, a person's first, or personal, name, preceding the nomen and cognomen (e.g., *Marcus* Tullius Cicero).
prae·nom′i·năl, *a.* pertaining to a praenomen.
prae·ō·pẽr′cū·lăr, *a.* same as *preopercular.*
prae·ō·pẽr′cū·lum, *n.* same as *preoperculum.*
prae·ō′răl, *a.* same as *preoral.*
prae·pos′i·tŏr, *n.* 1. in Roman and civil law, a principal who puts a subordinate in charge.
2. same as *prepositor.*
prae·pos′tẽr, *n.* same as *prepositor.*
prae·pū′bis, *n.* same as *prepubis.*
prae·scap′ū·lȧ, *n.* same as *prescapula.*
prae·scū′tum, *n.* same as *prescutum.*
Prae·sē′pē, *n.* [L., from *præ*, and *sepire*, to fence.] a nebulous cluster of dim stars in the constellation Cancer.
prae·sẽr′tim, *n.* [L.] anything insisted upon, particularly with stress or emphasis.
prae′sēs, *n.* [L.] a college or university president.
prae·stō′mi·um, *n.*; *pl.* **prae·stō′mi·ȧ,** same as *prestomium.*
prae′tẽr-, same as *preter-.*
prae·tẽr·mit′, *v.t.* same as *pretermit.*
prae·tex′tȧ, *n.*; *pl.* **prae·tex′tae,** [L.] a white robe with a purple border, worn by a Roman boy before he was entitled to wear the toga virilis, or until about the completion of his fourteenth year, and worn by girls until their marriage; also, the white outer garment, bordered with purple, worn by higher magistrates.
prae′tŏr, prē′tŏr, *n.* [L. *prætor*; *præ*, before, and *ire*, to go.] a magistrate of ancient Rome, next below a consul in rank.
Prae·tō′rēs, *n.pl.* a group of butterflies which includes the satyrs.
prae·tō′ri·ăl, prē·tō′ri·ăl, *a.* of a praetor or the rank of a praetor.
prae·tō′ri·ăn, prē·tō′ri·ăn, *a.* 1. praetorial.
2. [*often* P-] designating or of the bodyguard (*Praetorian Guard*) of a Roman commander or emperor.
praetorian gate; in a Roman camp, that one of its four gates which lay next to the enemy, and in front of the praetor's tent.
prae·tō′ri·ăn, prē·tō′ri·ăn, *n.* 1. a man with the rank of a praetor or ex-praetor.
2. [*often* P-] a member of the Praetorian Guard.
prae·tō′ri·ăn·ism, prē·tō′ri·ăn·ism, *n.* the supremacy of the military; control of a government by soldiers.
prae·tō′ri·um, prē·tō′ri·um, *n.* [L. *prætorium*, from *prætor*, praetor, general.]
1. the tent of a Roman general; the headquarters of an encampment.
2. a building where causes were judged by a praetor.
3. the official residence of a Roman governor; hence, the country seat of a patrician.
prae′tŏr·ship, prē′tŏr·ship, *n.* the office or dignity of a praetor.
prae·zyg·ȧ·poph′y·sis, *n.* same as *prezygapophysis.*
prag·mat′ic, *a.* [L. *pragmaticus*; Gr. *pragmatikos*, from *pragma*, business; *prassein*, to do.]
1. (a) busy; active; (b) practical.
2. pragmatical; meddlesome, officious, conceited, etc.
3. having to do with the affairs of a state or community.
4. dealing with historical facts in their interrelations.

5. of or belonging to philosophical pragmatism.

pragmatic sanction; any of various royal decrees that had the force of fundamental law; specifically, (a) any of various decrees of the Roman emperors, regulating the interests of their subject provinces and towns; (b) a system of limitations set to the spiritual power of the Pope in Continental countries; as, the French *pragmatic sanction* of 1268, and that of 1438; (c) the instrument by which the German emperor Charles VI, being without male issue, endeavored to secure the succession to his female descendants, settling his dominions on his daughter Maria Theresa.

prag·mat′iç, *n.* 1. a pragmatic sanction.

2. a pragmatical person.

prag·mat′iç·ăl, *a.* 1. active; diligent; busy. [Obs.]

2. pertaining to business or to ordinary affairs; hence, material; commonplace; practical. [Obs.]

3. officious; meddlesome.

4. dogmatic; opinionated; conceited.

5. in philosophy, pragmatic.

prag·mat′iç·ăl·ly, *adv.* in a pragmatic manner.

prag·mat′iç·ăl·ness, *n.* the state or quality of being pragmatic.

prag′mȧ·tişm, *n.* 1. the quality or condition of being pragmatic.

2. an instance of this.

3. in philosophy, a system which tests the validity of all concepts by their practical results.

prag′mȧ·tist, *n.* 1. one who is pragmatic.

2. an adherent of pragmatism.

Prāi·rī·äl′, *n.* [Fr., from *prairie*.] the ninth month (May 20–June 18) of the French Revolutionary Calendar, adopted by the First Republic in 1793.

prāi′rie, *n.* [Fr. *prairie*, from LL. *prataria*, from L. *pratum*, meadow.] a large area of level or slightly rolling grassland, especially one in the Mississippi Valley.

prāi′rie an′tē·lōpe, the pronghorn.

prāi′rie breāk′ẽr, a heavy and strong plow used in breaking prairie land.

prāi′rie chick′en, 1. the pinnated grouse, *Tympanuchus americanus*, of the United States. The neck of the male has two posterior tufts, and two pendulous, wrinkled sacs capable of inflation: called also *prairie hen, prairie fowl, prairie grouse.*

2. the sharp-tailed grouse.

prāi′rie çlō′vẽr, any plant of the genus *Petalostemon*, of which several species grow on American prairies. They have small red or white flowers.

prāi′rie dock, a large, rough-leaved weed, *Silphium terebinthinaceum*, of the family *Compositæ*, which grows on American prairies.

prāi′rie dog, a small rodent, the *Cynomys ludovicianus*, related to the marmot and the squirrel, and found on the prairies west of the Mississippi. They live gregariously in burrows, and have a sharp bark, like that of a small dog. Also called *prairie marmot.*

PRAIRIE DOG (1 ft. long)

prāi′rie fowl, same as *prairie chicken.*

prāi′rie fox, a fox, *Vulpes velox.*

prāi′rie grouse, same as *prairie chicken.*

prāi′rie hāre, a jack rabbit, *Lepus campestris.*

prāi′rie hawk, the sparrow hawk.

prāi′rie hen, same as *prairie chicken.*

prāi′rie mär′mŏt, the prairie dog.

prāi′rie mōle, the *Scalops argentatus*, a large silvery mole of the prairies.

prāi′rie oys′tẽr, a raw egg seasoned with salt, pepper, and vinegar or spirits.

prāi′rie pig′eŏn, the golden plover or the upland plover.

prāi′rie plŏv′ẽr, the prairie pigeon.

prāi′rie rat′tle·snāke, the massasauga.

prāi′rie sçhoon′ẽr, a large covered wagon used by pioneers to cross the American prairies.

prāi′rie snāke, a snake, brown above, yellow below, large but harmless, the *Masticophis flavigularis.*

prāi′rie snīpe, same as *prairie pigeon.*

prāi′rie squir′rel (skwir′), any of various ground squirrels; as the common striped gopher; a rodent of the genus *Spermophilus*.

prāi′rie tũr′nip, the breadroot.

prāi′rie war′blẽr, a small American bird, *Dendrœca discolor*, olive-yellow on the back, spotted with red in the middle of the back, bright yellow underneath and round the eyes, black on the sides of the throat and in spots on the sides, and partly white on the tail.

prāi′rie wolf (-wulf), the coyote.

prāişe, *n.* [ME. *preis, preys.*]

1. a praising or being praised; commendation; approbation; glorification.

Pope was morbidly sensitive to slights, morbidly eager for *praise.*
—Hamilton Wright Mabie.

2. a reason or basis for praise. [Archaic.]

3. the object of praise. [Obs.]

to sing one's praise (or *praises*); to praise one highly.

Syn.—laudation, eulogy, applause, encomium, plaudit, panegyric, commendation.

prāişe, *v.t.*; praised, *pt., pp.*; praising, *ppr.* [ME. *preisen*; Fr. *priser*; It. *pregiare*; LL. *pretiare*, from L. *pretium*, price. *Price* and *prize* are variants of this word.]

1. originally, to set a price on; to appraise.

2. to commend; to applaud; to express approval or admiration of.

3. to extol in words or in song; to magnify; to glorify.

Praise him, all his angels; *praise* ye him, all his hosts.
—Ps. cxlviii. 2.

prāişe′less, *a.* without worth; without praise.

prāişe meet′ing, a devotional meeting consisting mainly in the singing of sacred songs. [Dial.]

prāiş′ẽr, *n.* one who praises.

prāişe′wŏr″thi·ly, *adv.* in a manner deserving praise.

prāişe′wŏr″thi·ness, *n.* the quality of deserving commendation.

prāişe′wŏr″thy, *a.* deserving praise; laudable; commendable; as, a *praiseworthy* action.

Prä′krit, *n.* [Sans. *prākrita*, vulgar, from *prakriti*, nature.] any of the several vernacular Indic languages used in India in the ancient and medieval period.

Prä·krit′iç, *a.* belonging or related to Prakrit; as, a *Prakritic* dialect.

prä′līne, *n.* [Fr.] a crisp candy, made from nut kernels boiled in sugar.

präll′tril·lẽr, *n.* [G.] in music, a figure in which a principal note is played, then the note above, and then the principal note again, all in very rapid succession: symbol, ∼, placed over the principal note: also called *inverted mordent.*

pram, *n.* 1. a perambulator. [Brit. Colloq.]

2. a hand cart used by milkmen. [Slang.]

prȧnce, *v.i.*; pranced (prȧnst), *pt., pp.*; prancing, *ppr.* [ME. *prauncen*; G. dial. *prangssen*, to assume airs.]

1. to rise up on the hind legs; especially, to move along in this way: said of a horse.

2. to ride on a prancing horse.

3. to move about in a way suggestive of a prancing horse; to caper.

4. to move or go gaily or arrogantly; to swagger; strut.

5. to ride gaily or arrogantly.

prȧnce, *v.t.* to cause (a horse) to prance.

prȧnce, *n.* a prancing or prancing movement.

prȧn′cẽr, *n.* a mettlesome, high-stepping horse.

pran′di·ăl, *a.* [L. *prandium*, early dinner.] of or belonging to a meal, especially dinner.

Pran̄′gos, *n.* in botany, a genus of umbelliferous plants of central Asia: one species, *Prangos pabularia*, yields a valuable kind of hay, its root and its seed being used as medicines.

pran̄k, *v.t.* pranked (pran̄kt), *pt., pp.*; pranking, *ppr.* [D. *pronken*; G. *prangen, prunken*, to make a show, from *pracht*, pomp.] to adorn in a showy manner; to dress up; to dress showily.

pran̄k, *v.i.* to present a showy appearance; to dress up.

pran̄k, *n.* 1. a mischievous trick; a practical joke.

2. a frolicsome movement of an animal.

pran̄k′ẽr, *n.* one who pranks.

pran̄k′ing·ly, *adv.* in a pranking manner.

pran̄k′ish, *a.* 1. full of pranks.

2. like a prank.

prāşe, *n.* [Gr. *prason*, leek.] a translucent quartz of a leek-green color.

prā″şē·ō·dym′i·um, *n.* [Mod.L., from Gr. *prasios*, green; and *didymium.*] a metallic chemical element of the rare-earth group, whose salts are generally green in color; symbol, Pr; atomic weight, 140.92; atomic number, 59.

prā′şē·ō·līte, *n.* [Gr. *prason*, leek, and *lithos*, stone.] a green mineral, chiefly silicate of aluminum, magnesium, iron, etc., closely related to iolite.

praş′i·nous, *a.* [L. *prasinus*, from Gr. *prason*, leek.] leek-green.

prā′şoid, *a.* [*prase* and *-oid.*] of the nature or appearance of prase.

prat, *n.* [*sometimes pl.*] the buttocks. [Slang.]

prā′tăl, *a.* [L. *pratum*, meadow.] of or relating to a meadow; growing in a meadow. [Rare.]

prāte, *v.i.*; prated, *pt., pp.*; prating, *ppr.* [D. *praten.*] to talk much and foolishly; to chatter; to babble.

To *prate* and talk for life and honor.
—Shak.

prāte, *v.t.* to utter foolishly; to tell or repeat idly; as, to *prate* a secret.

prāte, *n.* foolish or idle talk; chatter.

prāt′ẽr, *n.* one who prates.

prat′fall, *n.* a fall on the buttocks. [Slang.]

prat′in·çōle, *n.* [LL. *pratincola*; L. *pratum*, mea ow, and *incola*, inhabitant.] a ploverlike bird with a tail and wings like those of a swallow, as *Glareola pratincola*, or any bird of the same genus.

prāt′ing, *n.* foolish, idle talk.

prāt′ing·ly, *adv.* with much idle talk; with loquacity.

prat·ique′ (-ēk′), **prat′iç,** *n.* [Fr.] permission to carry on business with a port, granted to a ship that has complied with quarantine or health regulations.

prat′tle, *v.t.* and *v.i.*; prattled, *pt., pp.*; prattling, *ppr.* [dim. of *prate.*]

1. to prate.

2. to speak in a childish manner; to babble.

prat′tle, *n.* 1. prate.

2. babble.

prat′tlẽr, *n.* one who prattles.

prau, *n.* same as *proa.*

prav′i·ty, *n.* [L. *pravitas*, from *pravus*, crooked, evil.] moral perversion; corrupt state; depravity; as, the *pravity* of human nature; the *pravity* of the will. [Rare.]

prawn, *n.* [ME. *prayne, prane.*] a small, edible crustacean of the shrimp family, with a beak or snout bending upward and a thin, leathery shell with many reddish-brown dots. The common prawn is *Palæmon serratus*, and the term is extended to include any crustacean of the same or related genera.

prawn, *v.i.* to catch, or fish for, prawns.

prax·in′ō·sçōpe, *n.* [Gr. *praxis*, action, and *-scope.*] an optical instrument for representing moving images upon a screen.

prax′is, *n.* [Mod.L.; Gr. *praxis*, from *prassein*, to do.]

1. practice (sense 4): distinguished from *theory.*

2. established practice; custom.

3. a set of examples or exercises, as in grammar.

Prax·it·e·lē′ăn, *a.* relating to Praxiteles, the Greek sculptor, or to his works of art.

prāy, *v.t.*; prayed, *pt., pp.*; praying, *ppr.* [Fr. *prier*; It. *pregare*; L. *precari*, from *prex, precis*, prayer.]

1. originally, to beseech; to entreat; to implore: now seldom used except as the elliptical form of *I pray you*, as *pray* tell me.

2. to ask for by prayer or supplication; to beg for imploringly.

3. to bring about, get, etc. by praying.

Praying souls out of purgatory by masses said on their behalf became an ordinary office.
—Milman.

prāy, *v.i.* to ask very earnestly; to make supplication; to say prayers, as to God.

to pray in aid; in law, to call in aid one who has an interest in the cause.

prāy′ȧ, *n.* [Port. *praia*, beach, bank.] a road or driveway built upon an embankment along a shore or bank of a river, as in some cities of India.

prāy′ẽr, *n.* one who prays or supplicates.

prāyer (prâr), *n.* [OFr. *proiere*; Fr. *prière*, from LL. *precaria*, a prayer, from L. *precarius*, obtained by begging, from *precari*, to entreat.]

1. the act or practice of praying.

2. an earnest request; entreaty; supplication.

3. (a) humble entreaty addressed to God, to a god, etc.; (b) a request made to God, etc.; as, her *prayer* for his safe return; (c) any set formula for praying, as to God.

4. [*often pl.*] in some religions, a devotional service consisting chiefly of prayers.

5. any spiritual communion with God, etc.

6. something prayed for or requested, as in a petition.
7. that part of a petition or memorial to the sovereign or any authority, in which the request or thing desired to be done or granted is specified.
8. in a bill in equity, a request that the court will grant the relief desired; also, that part of the bill in which the request is made.
Syn.—request, petition, suit, entreaty, supplication.

prāyer bēad, a seed from the Indian licorice, *Abrus precatorius.*

prāyer book, 1. a book containing prayers or the forms of devotion, public or private.
2. [P–B–] the Book of Common Prayer.
3. in nautical usage, a small stone for scrubbing parts of a vessel.

prāyer′fụl, *a.* 1. devotional; given to frequent prayer.
2. like or expressive of prayer.

prāyer′fụl·ly, *adv.* in a prayerful manner.

prāyer′fụl·ness, *n.* the state of being prayerful.

prāyer′less, *a.* not using prayer; habitually neglecting the use of prayer.

prāyer′less·ly, *adv.* in a prayerless manner.

prāyer′less·ness, *n.* the state of being prayerless.

prāyer meet′ing, a meeting for prayer.

prāyer rug, the rug upon which a Moslem kneels at his devotions.

prāyer shawl, a tallith.

prāyer wheel, a revolving drum containing written prayers, used by Buddhists of Tibet.

prāy′ing, *n.* the act of offering prayer.

prāy′ing in′sect, a praying mantis, especially *Mantis religiosa.*

prāy′ing·ly, *adv.* supplicatingly.

prāy′ing mȧ·chïne′, a prayer wheel.

prāy′ing man′tis, any of a number of related long, slender, insects with grasping, spiny forelegs often held together as if in prayer.

prāy′ing wheel (hwēl), a prayer wheel.

prē-, [from Fr. or L.; Fr. *pré-*; L. *prae-*, from *prae*, before, in front of.] a prefix meaning (a) *before in time, earlier (than), prior (to),* as in *pre*suppose, *pre*war; (b) *before in place, in front (of), anterior (to),* as in *pre*axial; (c) *before in rank, superior, surpassing,* as in *pre*eminent; (d) *preliminary to, in preparation for,* as in *pre*school. See also *prae-*. Words formed with *pre-* are generally written without a hyphen unless the element following *pre-* begins with *e* or a capital letter.

prē″aç·cū·ṣā′tion, *n.* previous accusation.

prēace, *v.* and *n.* press. [Obs.]

prēach, *v.i.*; preached (prēcht), *pt., pp.*; preaching, *ppr.* [ME. *prechen*, from OFr. *precher, prechier*; Fr. *prêcher*, from L. *prædicare*, to declare in public; *præ*, before, and *dicare*, to proclaim; closely allied to *dicere*, to say.]
1. to deliver a public discourse on some religious subject; to deliver a sermon, as from the Gospel.
2. to discourse on moral or religious topics, especially in a tiresome manner; to advise or exhort like a preacher; as, you need not *preach* to me about it.

prēach, *v.t.* 1. to expound or proclaim by preaching.
2. to advocate by or as by preaching; to urge with earnestness upon a person or persons.

He oft to them *preached*
Conversion and repentance. —Milton.

3. to deliver (a sermon).
4. to advise or teach by preaching. [Obs.]
to preach down; to decry.
to preach up; to preach or discourse in favor of.

prēach, *n.* a religious discourse. [Colloq.]

prēach′ẽr, *n.* 1. one who discourses publicly on religious subjects; a clergyman.
2. one who inculcates anything with earnestness.

No *preacher* is listened to but time. —Swift.

prēach′ẽr bīrd, the toucan.

prēach′ẽr·ship, *n.* the office of a preacher.

prēach′i·fȳ, *v.i.*; preachified, *pt., pp.*; preachifying, *ppr.* to preach or moralize in a tiresome manner. [Colloq.]

prēach′ing, *n.* 1. the act or art of one who preaches.
2. an instance of this.
3. a sermon.

prēach′ing çross, a cross erected in some public or open place, where monks and others preached publicly.

PREACHING CROSS

prēach′măn, *n.* a preacher: used in contempt. [Obs.]

prēach′ment, *n.* a discourse or sermon, especially a long, tiresome one.

prēach′y, *a.*; *comp.* preachier; *superl.* preachiest; given to or resembling preaching. [Colloq.]

prē·aç·quāint′ (-kwānt′), *v.t.* to make acquainted with previously; to inform beforehand.

prē·aç·quāint′ănce, *n.* previous acquaintance or knowledge.

prē·açt′, *v.t.* to act beforehand.

prē·aç′tion, *n.* prior action.

prē·ȧ·dam′iç, *a.* prior to Adam.

prē·ad′ăm·ite, *n.* 1. an inhabitant of the earth who lived before Adam.
2. one who holds that there were persons inhabiting this world before Adam's time.

prē·ad′ăm·īte, *a.* 1. prior to Adam; that existed before Adam.
2. of or pertaining to the preadamites.

prē·ad·ăm·it′iç, *a.* same as *preadamite.*

prē·ad·just′ment, *n.* previous adjustment.

prē·ad·min·is·trā′tion, *n.* previous administration.

prē·ad·mon′ish, *v.t.* to admonish previously.

prē·ad·mō·ni′tion, *n.* previous admonition.

prē·ad′vẽr·tīṣe, *v.t.* to advertise previously; to preacquaint.

prē′am·ble, *n.* [Fr. *préambule*; L. *præ*, before, and *ambulare*, to go.]
1. an introduction, especially one to a constitution, statute, etc., stating its reason and purpose.
2. an introductory fact, event, etc.; a preliminary.

prē′am·ble, *v.t.* and *v.i.* to introduce with prefatory remarks; to serve as a preamble.

prē·am′bū·lăr·y, *a.* 1. having the character of a preamble; introductory. [Rare.]
2. pertaining to a preamble. [Rare.]

prē·am′bū·lāte, *v.i.* [L. *præ*, before, and *ambulare*, to walk.] to walk or go before. [Obs.]

prē·am·bū·lā′tion, *n.* 1. a preamble. [Obs.]
2. a walking or going before. [Obs.]

prē·am′bū·lȧ·tō·ry, *a.* going before; preceding. [Obs.]

prē·am′bū·lous, *a.* preambulary. [Obs.]

prē·am′pli·fī·ẽr, *n.* in a radio, phonograph, etc., an auxiliary amplifier for boosting the voltage of a weak signal before it reaches the first terminal of the main amplifier.

prē·ā′năl, prae·ā′năl, *a.* located in front of the anus.

prē·an″tē·pē·nul′ti·māte, *a.* indicating the fourth syllable from the end of a word; preceding the antepenultimate.

prē·ā·or′tiç, *a.* situated in front of the aorta.

prē·ap·point′, *v.t.* to appoint previously.

prē·ap·point′ment, *n.* previous appointment.

prē·ap·prē·hen′sion, *n.* an opinion formed before examination.

prē·ärm′, *v.t.* to forearm. [Obs.]

prē·ăr·rānge′, *v.t.* to arrange previously.

prē·ăr·rānge′ment, *n.* arrangement made beforehand.

prēase, *n.* a press; a crowd. [Obs.]

prē·ȧs·sụr′ănce (-shụr′), *n.* previous assurance.

prē·ȧ·tax′iç, *a.* [*pre-* and *ataxia* and *-ic.*] occurring before the advent of ataxia.

prē·ạu′di·ence, *n.* precedence or rank at the English bar among lawyers.

prē·ax′i·ăl, *a.* in anatomy, situated in front of the axis of the body; especially, of the radial side of the arm or the tibial side of the leg.

preb′end, *n.* [Fr. *prebende*, from LL. *præbenda*, things to be furnished or supplied, from L. *præbere*, to give, grant; *præ* before, and *habere*, to have.]
1. the part of the revenues of a cathedral or collegiate church paid as a clergyman's salary.
2. the property or tax yielding such revenue.
3. a prebendary or his benefice.

prē·ben′dăl, *a.* pertaining to a prebend or prebendary.

preb′en·dăr·y, *n.*; *pl.* **preb′en·dăr·ieṣ,** [ME. *prebendarie*; ML. *præbendarius.*]
1. a person receiving a prebend.
2. in the Church of England, an honorary canon with only the title of a prebend.
3. a prebend; a prebendaryship. [Obs.]

preb′en·dăr·y·ship, *n.* the office of a prebendary.

preb′en·dāte, *v.t.* to make a prebendary of.

preb′end·ship, *n.* a prebendaryship. [Obs.]

prē·bron′chi·ăl, *a.* in front of the bronchus: used especially in reference to two air sacs found in birds.

Prē″-Cam′bri·ăn, *a.* designating or of all the geologic time before the Cambrian Era: it is now divided into the Archeozoic and Proterozoic Eras.
the Pre-Cambrian; the Pre-Cambrian Era or its rocks.

prē·çan′cel, *v.t.*; precanceled *or* precancelled, *pt., pp.*; precanceling *or* precancelling, *ppr.* to cancel (a postage stamp) before use in mailing: chiefly in the past participle.

prē·çan′cel, *n.* a precanceled stamp.

prē′çănt, *n.* [L. *precans (-antis)*, ppr. of *precari*, to pray.] one who prays. [Rare.]

prē·çăr′i·ous, *a.* [L. *precarius*, depending on favor, from *precari*, to pray or entreat.]
1. depending on the will or pleasure of another; held by courtesy; liable to be changed or lost at the pleasure of another.
2. dependent upon circumstances; uncertain; insecure; as, a *precarious* living.
3. dependent upon chance; risky; dangerous; as, a *precarious* foothold.
4. dependent upon mere assumption; unwarranted; as, a *precarious* assertion.
Syn.—doubtful, uncertain, dubious, unsettled.

prē·çăr′i·ous·ly, *adv.* in a precarious manner.

prē·çăr′i·ous·ness, *n.* the quality or state of being precarious; as, the *precariousness* of life or health.

prē·çā′tion, *n.* [L. *precatio (-onis)*, from *precatus*, pp. of *precari*, to pray.] the offering of prayers; supplication; beseeching. [Obs.]

preç′ȧ·tive, *a.* [L. *precari*, to pray.] same as *precatory.*

preç′ȧ·tō·ry, *a.* of, having the nature of, or expressing entreaty.
precatory words; in law, expressions in a will praying or recommending that a thing be done; directions or commands that are not imperative.

prē·çau′dăl, *a.* situated in front of the coccygeal vertebrae.

prē·çau·ṣā′tion, *n.* same as *foreordination.*

prē·çau′tion, *n.* [L. *præcautio*, from *præcautus*, pp. of *præcavere*; *præ*, before, and *cavere*, to take care.]
1. caution or care taken beforehand; caution previously employed to prevent mischief or secure good in possession.

This *precaution* is intended to anticipate any conspiracy. —William E. Curtis.

2. a measure taken in advance to ward off possible danger, failure, etc., or to secure certain advantages; as, to take *precautions* against fire.
Syn.—forethought, provision, anticipation, prearrangement, care, providence.

prē·çau′tion, *v.t.* to warn or advise beforehand for preventing mischief or securing good.

prē·çau′tion·ăl, *a.* same as *precautionary.*

prē·çau′tion·ăr·y, *a.* of, advising, or using precaution; as, *precautionary* measures.

prē·çau′tious, *a.* taking preventive measures; using, or giving evidence of, precaution.

prē·çau′tious·ly, *adv.* with precaution.

prē·çau′tious·ness, *n.* the state of being precautious.

prē·çā′vȧ, *n.* [*pre*, before, and (*vena*) *cava.*] the superior vena cava of man and the corresponding vein of other animals.

prē·çā′văl, *a.* of or relating to the precava.

prē·çēde′, *v.t.*; preceded, *pt., pp.*; preceding, *ppr.* [L. *præcedere*; *præ*, before, and *cedere*, to move.]

1. to be, come, or go before in time, place, order, rank, or importance.

2. to introduce with prefatory remarks, etc.; to cause something to go before; to make to take place beforehand; to preface; used with *by* or *with*.

prē·cēde′, *v.i.* to be, come, or go before.

prē·cē′dence (*or* pres′e-), *n.* [from *precedent.*]

1. the act, right, privilege, or fact of preceding in time, place, order, or importance.

2. superiority in rank.

patent of precedence; in England, a crown grant to a barrister which entitles him to preaudience in the courts.

personal precedence; a precedence accorded to birth or family rank.

to take precedence of; to precede another by virtue of rank or importance.

Syn.—pre-eminence, preference, priority, antecedence, leadership.

prē·cēd′en·cy (*or* pres′e-den-), *n.*; *pl.* **prē·cēd′en·cieṣ**, precedence. [Rare.]

prē·cē′dent, *a.* [ME.; Early Fr. *précédent*, from L. *præcedens*, ppr. of *præcedere*; *præ-*, before, and *cedere*, to go.] going before in time; that precedes; antecedent; as, *precedent* services.

Our own *precedent* passions do instruct us. —Shak.

condition precedent; in law, a condition which must happen or be performed before an estate or some right can vest, and on failure of which the estate or right is defeated.

prec′e·dent, *n.* 1. something done or said that may serve or be adduced as an example, reason, or justification for a subsequent act of the like kind; a model instance.

Examples for cases can but direct as *precedents* only. —Hooker.

2. in law, a judicial decision, interlocutory or final, which serves as a rule for future determinations in similar or analogous cases; any proceeding, or course of proceedings, which may serve for a rule in subsequent cases of a like nature.

3. a prognostication; a presage; a sign. [Obs.]

4. the original draft of a writing. [Obs.]

Syn.—example, antecedent.—An *example* is a similar case which may serve as a guide, but has no authority within itself; a *precedent* is something which comes down to us from the past with the sanction of usage and of common consent.

prec′e·dent·ed, *a.* having a precedent; authorized by an example of a like kind.

prec·e·den′tiăl (-shăl), *a.* 1. suitable as an example for imitation; of, or having the nature of, a precedent.

2. having precedence; preliminary.

prē·cē′dent·ly, *adv.* beforehand; antecedently.

prē·cē′ding, *a.* 1. that precedes.

2. in astronomy, designating the direction toward which stars appear to move when viewed through a telescope.

Syn.—antecedent, anterior, foregoing, former, previous, prior.

prē·cel′, *v.t.* and *v.i.* to surpass in excellence; to excel. [Obs.]

prē·cel′lence, prē·cel′len·cy, *n.* excellence. [Obs.]

prē·cel′lent, *a.* surpassing; superior. [Obs.]

prē·cen′tŏr, *n.* [LL. *præcentor*; L. *præ*, before, and *canere*, to sing.]

1. the leader or director of the choir in a cathedral.

2. one who leads the congregational singing in any church.

prē·cen′tŏr·ship, *n.* the employment or office of a precentor.

prē′cept, *n.* [L. *præceptum*, from *præcipere*, to take beforehand, to admonish; *præ*, before, and *capere*, to take.]

1. a commandment or direction meant as a rule of action or conduct.

2. a rule of moral conduct; a maxim.

3. a rule or direction, as for doing something technical.

4. in law, a written order; a warrant; a writ.

Syn.—doctrine, law, principle, instruction, injunction, maxim, rule, warrant.

prē·cept′, *v.t.* to instruct by precept. [Obs.]

prē·cep′tiăl (-shăl), *a.* preceptive. [Obs.]

prē·cep′tion, *n.* a precept. [Rare.]

prē·cep′tive, *a.* [L. *præceptivus.*]

1. of, having the nature of, or expressing a precept.

2. giving precepts; instructive; didactic.

prē·cep′tŏr, *n.* [L. *præceptor.*]

1. a teacher; an instructor; the teacher of a school; sometimes the principal teacher of an academy or other seminary.

2. among the Knights Templars, the head of a preceptory.

prē·cep·tō′ri·ăl, *a.* 1. of or pertaining to a preceptor.

2. employing preceptors.

prē·cep′tō·ry, *a.* giving precepts; preceptive.

prē·cep′tō·ry, *n.*; *pl.* **prē·cep′tō·rieṣ**, [ML. *præceptoria*, estate of a preceptor, from L. *præceptor.*]

1. a provincial community or religious house of the medieval Knights Templars, subordinate to the London Temple.

2. its estates.

prē·çep′tress, *n.* 1. a woman preceptor.

2. a governess.

prē′cēṣ, *n.pl.* [L. *prex*, *precis*, prayer.] short responsive prayers in church worship.

prē·ces′sion (-sesh′un), *n.* [Fr. *précession*, from L. *præcedere*, pp. *præcessus*, to go before.]

1. a preceding; precedence.

2. the precession of the equinoxes.

3. in philology, a weakening of a vowel when unaccented: opposed to *progression*.

lunisolar precession; see under *lunisolar*.

planetary precession; the effect of the combined forces of the planets in producing precession of the equinoxes.

precession of the equinoxes; (a) the occurrence of the equinoxes earlier in each successive sidereal year, caused by the gradual westward movement of the equinoctial points along the ecliptic as the result of the change in direction of the earth's axis as it turns around the axis of the ecliptic so as to describe a complete cone approximately every 26,000 years; (b) the westward movement of the equinoctial points. Precession is the result of the action of the sun and the moon upon protuberances about the earth's equator.

prē·ces′sion·ăl, *a.* of or resulting from the precession of the equinoxes.

prē·ces′sŏr, *n.* a predecessor. [Obs.]

prē·çhor′dăl, *a.* [*pre-*, and L. *chorda*; Gr. *chordē*, chord.] (a) before the notochord in location; (b) prior to the development of the notochord.

pré·cieuse′ (prā-syēz′), *a.* [Fr.] fastidious; excessively precise.

pré·cieuse′, *n.*; *pl.* **pré·cieuses′** (-syēz′), a woman of polite society who puts on the air of a literary person; a pretentious woman of society.

prē′cinçt, *n.* [L. *præcinctus*, pp. of *præcingere*, to encompass; *præ*, and *cingere*, to surround or gird.]

1. an enclosure between buildings, walls, etc.; specifically, the grounds immediately surrounding a religious house or church.

2. [*usually pl.*] environs; a neighborhood.

3. a subdivision of a city, ward, etc.; as, police *precincts*.

4. any limited area, as of thought.

5. a boundary.

pre·ci·os′i·ty (presh-i-), *n.*; *pl.* **pre·ci·os′i·tieṣ**,

1. the quality of being precious. [Obs.]

2. great fastidiousness, overrefinement, or affectation, especially in language.

pre′cious (presh′us), *a.* [Fr. *précieux*; L. *pretiosus*, from *pretium*, price.]

1. of great price or value; costly.

2. of great desirability; held in high esteem; as, freedom is *precious*.

3. beloved; dear.

4. very fastidious, overrefined, or affected, as in behavior, language, etc.

5. egregious; arrant.

6. very great; as, a *precious* liar. [Colloq.]

7. worthless: used ironically. [Colloq.]

precious metals; the metals popularly regarded as rare and valuable, especially gold, silver, and platinum.

precious stone; any rare and valuable stone or gem.

Syn.—costly, valuable, beloved, dear.

pre′cious, *adv.* very. [Colloq.]

Pre′cious Blood (blud), 1. in the Roman Catholic Church, the blood shed by Christ for the redemption of mankind.

2. a devotion and feast celebrated on the first day of July.

pre′cious·ly, *adv.* in a precious manner.

pre′cious·ness, *n.* the state or quality of being precious.

prec′i·pice (-pis), *n.* [Fr. *précipice*; L. *præcipitium*, from *præceps*, headlong; *præ*, forward, and *ceps*, from *caput*, head.]

1. a sudden or headlong fall. [Obs.]

2. a vertical cliff; a very steep place; a bank or cliff extremely steep, or quite perpendicular or overhanging.

3. a hazardous situation.

prē·cip′i·ent, *a.* [L. *præcipiens.*] commanding; directing.

prē·cip″i·tȧ·bil′i·ty, *n.* the quality or state of being precipitable.

prē·cip′i·tȧ·ble, *a.* [L. *præcipitare*, from *præceps*, headlong.] capable of being precipitated or cast to the bottom, as a substance in solution.

prē·cip′i·tănce, *n.* quality, fact, or instance of being precipitant; headlong hurry; rash haste; haste in resolving, forming an opinion, or executing a purpose without due deliberation.

prē·cip′i·tăn·cy, *n.*; *pl.* **prē·cip′i·tăn·cieṣ**, same as *precipitance*.

prē·cip′i·tănt, *a.* [L. *præcipitans* (*-antis*), ppr. of *præcipitare*, from *præceps*, headlong.]

1. falling steeply or rushing headlong; rushing onward with velocity or recklessness.

They leave their little lives
Above the clouds, *precipitant* to earth.
—Philips.

2. acting very hastily or rashly; precipitate.

3. very abrupt, sudden, or unexpected.

prē·cip′i·tănt, *n.* in chemistry, a substance which, when added to a solution, causes the formation of a precipitate.

prē·cip′i·tănt·ly, *adv.* in a precipitant manner.

prē·cip′i·tănt·ness, *n.* the state or quality of being precipitant.

prē·cip′i·tāte, *v.t.*; precipitated, *pt.*, *pp.*; precipitating, *ppr.* [L. *præcipitare*, from *præceps*, headlong.]

1. to throw headlong; to hurl downward.

2. to cause to happen before expected, warranted, needed, or desired; to bring on; to hasten; as, he *precipitated* the crisis.

3. in chemistry, to cause (a slightly soluble substance) to become insoluble and separate out from a solution.

4. in meteorology, to condense (vapor, etc.) and cause to fall as rain, snow, sleet, etc.

prē·cip′i·tāte, *v.i.* 1. to fall headlong. [Rare.]

2. to hasten without preparation. [Rare.]

3. in chemistry, to be precipitated.

4. in meteorology, to condense and fall as rain, snow, sleet, etc.

prē·cip′i·tāte, *a.* 1. falling, flowing, or rushing, with steep and swift descent.

2. headstrong; acting, happening, or done very impetuously; overhasty; rashly hasty; as, the king was too *precipitate* in declaring war.

3. very sudden, unexpected, or abrupt; as, a *precipitate* case of disease.

prē·cip′i·tāte, *n.* in chemistry, a substance that is separated out from a solution as a solid by the action of chemical reagents, temperature, etc.

red precipitate; red oxide of mercury or mercuric oxide, HgO, a highly poisonous crystalline powder, soluble in acids and slightly soluble in water: commonly obtained by heating mercuric nitrate.

white precipitate; mercurammonium chloride, a colorless powdery substance, NH_2HgCl, obtained by the action of ammonia on mercuric chloride in solution.

prē·cip′i·tāte·ly, *adv.* in a precipitate manner.

prē·cip·i·tā′tion, *n.* [L. *præcipitatio* (*-onis*).]

1. the act of precipitating; the state of being precipitated.

2. a falling, flowing, or rushing down with violence and rapidity.

3. great hurry; rash, tumultuous haste; precipitance; impetuosity.

4. a bringing on suddenly; acceleration.

5. in chemistry, (a) a precipitating or being precipitated from a solution; (b) a precipitate.

6. in meteorology, (a) a depositing of rain, snow, sleet, etc.; (b) rain, snow, sleet, etc.; (c) the amount of this.

7. in spiritualism, materialization.

prē·cip′i·tā·tŏr, *n.* one who or that which precipitates.

prē·cip′i·tin, *n.* [*precipit*ate and *-in.*] an antibody produced in the blood of an animal injected with an antigen: when the antigen is added to the blood serum of such an animal, a precipitate is formed.

prec·i·pi′tious (-pish′us), *a.* precipitous. [Obs.]

prec·i·pi′tious·ly, *adv.* precipitously. [Obs.]

prē·cip′i·tous, *a.* [L. *præceps*, *præcipitis.*]

1. very steep; as, a *precipitous* cliff or mountain.

2. having precipices.
3. headlong; directly or rapidly descending; as, a *precipitous* fall. [Rare.]
4. hasty; rash; precipitate. [Rare.]

prē·cip′i·tous·ly, *adv.* in a precipitous manner; with violent haste.

prē·cip′i·tous·ness, *n.* the state or quality of being precipitous.

pré·cis′ (prā-sē′ *or* prā′sē), *n.*; *pl.* **pré·cis′** (-sēz′), [Fr.] a concise abridgement; a summary; an abstract.

pré·cis′, *v.t.* to make a precis of.

prē·cīse′, *a.* [L. *præcisus*, from *præcidere*, to cut off; *præ*, before, and *cædere*, to cut; lit., cut or pared away; that is, pared to smoothness or exactness.]
1. strictly defined; accurately stated; definite.
2. speaking definitely or distinctly.
3. with no variation; minutely exact; as, the *precise* amount.
4. (a) that strictly conforms to usage, etc.; scrupulous; fastidious; (b) overnice or finicky.
Syn.—accurate, definite, scrupulous, punctilious.

prē·cīse′ly, *adv.* in a precise manner; exactly: also used as an affirmative reply, equivalent to "I agree," "quite true."

prē·cīse′ness, *n.* the state or quality of being precise.

prē·ci′ṣiăn (-sizh′ăn), *n.* one who is punctilious and precise in observing customs, especially of religion; specifically, a sixteenth- or seventeenth-century English Puritan.

prē·ci′ṣiăn, *a.* exact; overprecise, or produced by the practice of formalism; as, *precisian* habits or expressions.

prē·ci′ṣiăn·iṣm, *n.* excessive exactness; formalism; specifically, Puritanism.

prē·ci′ṣiăn·ist, *n.* same as *precisian.*

prē·ci′ṣion (-sizh′un), *n.* [Fr., from L. *præcisio* (*-onis*).] the quality of being precise; exactness; accuracy of definition; definiteness; correctness of arrangement or adjustment; as, *precision* of thought, or in the use of an instrument.

prē·ci′ṣion bomb′ing, the dropping of bombs on narrowly defined targets with maximum accuracy obtained through the use of bombsights.

prē·ci′ṣion·ist, *n.* one who considers precision very important.

prē·cī′sive, *a.* 1. having or characterized by precision.
2. cutting off, separating, or defining (one thing or person) from another or other.

prē·ci′sō, *adv.* [It.] precisely; exactly.

prē·çlin′i·çăl, *a.* [*pre-* and *clinical.*] in medicine, of or in the period of a disease before any of the symptoms appear.

prē·çlūde′, *v.t.*; precluded, *pt.*, *pp.*; precluding, *ppr.* [L. *præcludere*, to shut off; *præ*, before, and *claudere*, to shut.]
1. to hinder, exclude, or prevent by logical necessity; to bar from access, possession, or enjoyment; to make impossible, especially in advance; as, these facts *precluded* his argument.
2. to hinder; to debar; to exclude; to keep out; as, to *preclude* ambassadors from a country.

prē·çlū′ṣion, *n.* the act of precluding or the condition of being precluded.

prē·çlū′sive, *a.* precluding or tending to preclude; preventive.

prē·çlū′sive·ly, *adv.* in a preclusive manner.

prē·çōce′, *a.* precocious. [Obs.]

prē·çō′ciăl (-shăl), *a.* designating or of birds whose newly hatched young are covered with down and are able to run about.

prē·çō′cious, *a.* [L. *præcox*, *præcocis*; *præ*, before, and *coquere*, to cook, mature.]
1. ripe before the proper or natural time; premature: said of plants, etc. [Rare.]
2. developed or matured earlier than usual, as a child or a child's mentality.
3. of or showing premature development.

prē·çō′cious·ly, *adv.* in a precocious manner.

prē·çō′cious·ness, *n.* precocity.

prē·çoc′i·ty, *n.*; *pl.* **prē·çoc′i·tieṣ,** the quality or condition of being precocious; premature development.

prē·çō·ē·tā′nē·ăn, *n.* a contemporary who is older than another. [Obs.]

prē·çog′i·tāte, *v.t.* to premeditate. [Obs.]

prē·çog·i·tā′tion, *n.* premeditation. [Rare.]

prē·çog·ni′tion, *n.* 1. previous knowledge; antecedent examination.
2. in Scottish law, an examination of witnesses to a criminal act, before a judge, justice of the peace, or sheriff, prior to prosecution of the offender, to decide whether there is ground for trial.

prē·çog′ni·zā·ble, *a.* capable of precognition.

prē·çog·nosce′ (-nos′), *v.t.* [L. *præcognoscere*; *præ*, beforehand, *cognoscere*, to know.] to hold a precognition on.

prē·çol·leç′tion, *n.* a collection previously made.

prē·çŏm·pōṣe′, *v.t.* to compose beforehand.

prē·çŏn·çēit′, *n.* an opinion or notion previously formed. [Obs.]

prē·çŏn·çēive′, *v.t.*; preconceived, *pt.*, *pp.*; preconceiving, *ppr.* to form a conception or opinion of beforehand.

prē·çŏn·çep′tion, *n.* 1. a preconceiving.
2. a preconceived idea or opinion.
3. prejudice.

prē·çŏn·çērt′, *v.t.*; preconcerted, *pt.*, *pp.*; preconcerting, *ppr.* to concert beforehand; to settle or arrange beforehand, as by agreement.

prē·çon′çērt, *n.* a previous agreement.

prē·çŏn·çērt′ed·ly, *adv.* by preconcert.

prē·çŏn·çērt′ed·ness, *n.* the state of being preconcerted.

prē·çŏn·çēr′tion, *n.* preconcert. [Rare.]

prē·çŏn·demn′ (-dem′), *v.t.* to condemn in advance. [Rare.]

prē·çon·dem·nā′tion, *n.* the act of condemning or the state of being condemned beforehand.

prē·çŏn·di′tion, *v.t.* to prepare (someone or something) to behave, react, etc. in a certain way under certain conditions.

prē·çŏn·di′tion, *n.* a previous or preliminary condition; a prerequisite.

prē·çŏn·fọrm′, *v.t.* and *v.i.* to conform in advance.

prē·çŏn·fọrm′i·ty, *n.* antecedent conformity.

prē·çon·i·zā′tion, *n.* 1. a proclamation.
2. in the Roman Catholic Church, the solemn public approbation by the Pope of the nomination by the College of Cardinals of any ecclesiastic to a church dignity.

prē′çŏn·īze *v.t.*; preconized, *pt.*, *pp.*; preconizing, *ppr.* [ME. *preconisen*; ML. *præconizare*, from L. *præco* (*-onis*), public crier.]
1. to proclaim or extol in public.
2. to approve and announce the name of (a new bishop) publicly: said of the Pope.

prē·çoñ′quēr (-kēr), *v.t.* to conquer beforehand. [Rare.]

prē·çon′scious, *a.* pertaining to the condition prior to consciousness.

prē·çŏn·sent′, *n.* consent given in advance.

prē·çŏn·sign′ (-sīn′), *v.t.*; preconsigned, *pt.*, *pp.*; preconsigning, *ppr.* to consign beforehand; to make a previous consignment of.

prē·çŏn·sol′i·dā·ted, *a.* consolidated beforehand.

prē·çon′sti·tūte, *v.t.*; preconstituted, *pt.*, *pp.*; preconstituting, *ppr.* to constitute or establish beforehand.

prē·çon′traçt, *n.* a previous contract, as, formerly, of marriage.

prē·çŏn·traçt′, *v.t.* 1. formerly, to betroth beforehand.
2. to agree to by advance contract.

prē·çŏn·traçt′, *v.i.* to contract or stipulate beforehand.

prē·çŏn·trīve′, *v.t.* and *v.i.* to contrive or plan in advance.

prē·çool′, *v.t.* to cool artificially before packing or shipment.

prē·çor′ȧ·çoid, *n.* a bone or cartilage situated in front of the coracoid bone or cartilage in some of the lower vertebrates.

prē·çor′di·ăl, *a.* pertaining to the praecordia, or parts in front of the heart.

prē·çrit′i·çăl, *a.* [*pre-* and *critical.*] in medicine, coming before the crisis (of a disease).

prē·çrū′răl, *a.* [*pre-*, and L. *crus*, *cruris*, leg.] situated in front of the leg or thigh.

prē·çŭr′rēr, *n.* a precursor. [Obs.]

prē·çŭrse′, *n.* [*pre-*, and L. *cursus*, a running.] a forerunning. [Obs.]

prē·çŭr′sive, *a.* same as *precursory.*

prē·çŭr′sŏr, *n.* [L. *præcursor*; *præ*, before, and *cursor*, a runner, from *cursus*, pp. of *currere*, to run.]
1. a forerunner; a harbinger; one who or that which goes before.
2. a predecessor, as in office.
Syn.—forerunner, harbinger, herald, messenger, predecessor, omen, sign.

prē·çŭr′sŏr·ship, *n.* the state, condition, or position of a precursor.

prē·çŭr′sō·ry, *a.* [L. *præcursorius.*]
1. serving as a precursor, or harbinger; indicating something to follow.
2. introductory; preliminary.

prē·çŭr′sō·ry, *n.* an introduction. [Obs.]

prē·dā′ceăn (-shăn), *n.* a carnivorous animal.

prē·dā′ceous, prē·dā′cious, *a.* [L. *præda*, prey.] preying on other animals; predatory.

prē·dac′i·ty, *n.* the condition or quality of being predaceous.

prē′dăl, *a.* [L. *præda*, prey.] plundering; predatory. [Rare.]

prē·dāte′, *v.t.* 1. to date before the actual date; as, to *predate* a letter.
2. to have an earlier date than; to antedate; as, one event *predates* another.

prē·dā′tion, *n.* [L. *prædatio*, a plundering.] the act of pillaging or plundering.

pred′ȧ·tŏr, *n.* a predatory person or animal.

pred′ȧ·tō·ri·ly, *adv.* in a predatory manner.

pred′ȧ·tō·ri·ness, *n.* the condition or quality of being predatory.

pred′ȧ·tō·ry, *a.* [L. *prædatorius*, from *præda*, prey.]
1. of, living by, or characterized by plundering or robbing; as, a *predatory* class of people.
2. predaceous.
3. destructive; wasteful. [Obs.]

prēde, *v.t.* to plunder; to loot. [Obs.]

prēde, *n.* plunder; loot; prey; booty. [Obs.]

prē·dē·çāy′, *n.* decay before the usual time; early decay.

prē·dē·çēase′, *v.t.* predeceased, *pt.*, *pp.*; predeceasing, *ppr.* [*pre-* and *decease.*] to die before (someone else or some event).

prē·dē·çēase′, *n.* decease before another.

pred·ē·ces′sive, *a.* being or going before; preceding. [Obs.]

pred′ē·ces·sŏr, *n.* [LL. *prædecessor*; L. *præ*, before, and *decessor*, a retiring officer; from *decessus*, pp. of *decedere*, to go away, to depart; *de*, from, and *cedere*, to go.]
1. one who precedes or preceded another, as in office.
2. a thing replaced by another thing, as in use.
3. a forefather; an ancestor.

prē·dē·çlāre′, *v.t.* to declare beforehand; to announce in advance.

prē·ded·i·çā′tion, *n.* a dedication previously made.

prē·dē·fīne′, *v.t.* to define or limit beforehand; to set a limit to previously.

prē·dē·lib·ēr·ā′tion, *n.* deliberation beforehand.

prē·dē·lin·ē·ā′tion, *n.* delineation beforehand; previous delineation.

prē·del′lȧ, *n.* [It.] 1. one of a series of steps rising one above another.
2. an altarpiece back of an altar, or a subdivision of such an altarpiece.

prē·dē·ṣign′ (-zīn′), *v.t.* to design beforehand; to predetermine.

prē·deṣ′ig·nāte, *a.* in logic, of propositions having their logical quantity expressed by one of the signs of quantity, *all*, *none*, etc.

prē·deṣ′ig·nāte, *v.t.* 1. to designate beforehand.
2, in logic, to prefix a sign of quantity, as *all*, *no*, *few*, etc., to.

prē·deṣ·ig·nā′tion, *n.* in logic, a sign, symbol, or word expressing logical quantity and prefixed to a proposition.

> He thinks that, in universal negation, the logicians employ the *predesignation* "all."
> —Sir W. Hamilton.

prē·deṣ′ig·nȧ·tō·ry, *a.* in logic, marking the logical quantity of a proposition.

prē·des·ti·nār′i·ăn, *a.* [*predestinate* and *-arian.*] of or believing in predestination.

prē·des·ti·nār′i·ăn, *n.* one who believes in the doctrine of predestination.

prē·des·ti·nār′i·ăn·iṣm, *n.* the doctrine of predestinarians; belief in predestination.

prē·des′ti·nāte, *a.* [L. *prædestinatus*, pp. of *prædestinare*, to predestine, foretell; *præ-*, before, and *destinare*, to determine.] predestinated; fated; foreordained.

prē·des′ti·nāte, *v.t.*; predestinated, *pt.*, *pp.*; predestinating, *ppr.* 1. in theology, to foreordain by divine decree or intent.
2. to predestine.
Syn.—foreordain, preordain, predestine, foredoom.

prē·des·ti·nā′tion, *n.* 1. in theology, (a) the act by which God supposedly foreordained everything that would happen; (b) God's predestinating of certain souls to damnation and others to salvation.
2. a predestinating or being predestinated; destiny; fate.

prē·des′ti·nā·tive, *a.* predestinating. [Rare.]

prē·des′ti·nā·tŏr, *n.* 1. one who predestinates.
2. a predestinarian. [Obs.]

prē·des′tine, *v.t.*; predestined, *pt., pp.*; predestining, *ppr.* [L. *prædestinare*; *præ*, before, and *destinare*, to appoint.] to destine or decree beforehand; to foreordain.

prē·dē·tẽr′mi·nȧ·ble, *a.* capable of being determined beforehand.

prē·dē·tẽr′mi·nāte, *a.* predetermined; as, the *predeterminate* counsel of God.

prē·dē·tẽr·mi·nā′tion, *n.* a predetermining or being predetermined.

prē·dē·tẽr′mine, *v.t.*; predetermined, *pt., pp.*; predetermining, *ppr.* [LL. *prædeterminare*; L. *præ*, before, and *determinare*, to bound, limit.]

1. to determine, decide, or decree beforehand.

2. to give a tendency to or impel beforehand; to prejudice.

prē·dē·tẽr′mine, *v.i.* to settle or determine beforehand.

prē″dē·tẽr′min·ẽr, *n.* one who predetermines.

prē″dē·tẽr′min·iṣm, *n.* the doctrine that individual development is predetermined by heredity.

prē·dē·vōte′, *a.* predevoted; of or pertaining to devotion assigned or given beforehand.

prē·dē·vōte′, *v.t.* 1. to foreordain.

2. to devote to beforehand.

prē′di·ăl, *a.* same as *praedial*.

prē·dī·as·tol′iç, *a.* in physiology, preceding the expansion of the heart.

pred″i·cȧ·bil′i·ty, *n.* the state or quality of being predicable, or capable of being affirmed.

pred′i·cȧ·ble, *a.* [Fr. *prédicable*; L. *prædicabilis*, from *prædicare*, to proclaim.] that can be predicated.

pred′i·cȧ·ble, *n.* 1. something predicable.

2. in logic, any of the several sorts of predicate that can be used of a subject: genus, species, difference, property, and accident are the five Aristotelian predicables.

pred′i·cȧ·bly, *adv.* in a predicable manner.

prē·diç′ȧ·ment, *n.* [LL. *prædicamentum*, from L. *prædicare*, to proclaim.]

1. in Aristotelian logic, same as *category*.

2. a condition or situation, especially one that is dangerous, unpleasant, embarrassing, or, sometimes, comical.

Syn.—category, contingency, condition, conjuncture, event, plight, situation.

prē·diç·ȧ·men′tăl, *a.* of, or having the nature of, a predicament.

pred′i·çănt, *a.* [L. *prædicans*, ppr. of *prædicare*, to proclaim.] predicating; proclaiming; preaching.

pred′i·çănt, *n.* one who predicates, affirms, or preaches; a preacher; a preaching friar.

pred′i·çāte, *v.t.*; predicated, *pt., pp.*; predicating, *ppr.* [L. *prædicatus*, pp. of *prædicare*, to proclaim; *præ*, before, and *dicere*, to say.]

1. to proclaim; preach; declare; affirm. [Rare.]

2. to affirm as a quality, attribute, or property of a person or thing; as, let us *predicate* greenness of grass.

3. to involve as a connotation; to imply; as, grass *predicates* greenness.

4. to affirm or base upon facts, arguments, conditions, etc.

pred′i·çāte, *v.i.* to make an affirmation or statement.

pred′i·çāte, *n.* 1. in logic, that which is affirmed or denied about the subject of a proposition. In these propositions, "paper is white," "ink is not white," whiteness is the *predicate* affirmed of paper and denied of ink.

2. in grammar, the word or words that make a statement about the subject of a clause or sentence: a predicate may be: (a) a verb of complete meaning; as, the wind *blows*; (b) a verb and its adverbial modifier; as, the wind *blows from the east*; (c) a transitive verb and its object; as, John *threw the ball*; (d) a linking verb and its complement; as, the grass *is green*, grass *is a plant*.

3. an appellation or title that asserts or affirms something.

pred′i·çāte, *a.* 1. predicated.

2. in grammar, of, having the nature of, or involved in a predicate; as, a *predicate* noun.

pred·i·çā′tion, *n.* [L. *prædicatio*.]

1. a predicating or being predicated.

2. a predicate.

pred′i·çā·tive, *a.* [L. *prædicativus*, from *prædicare*, to proclaim.]

1. predicating or expressing predication.

2. serving as or in a predicate.

pred′i·çā·tive·ly, *adv.* in a predicative manner.

pred′i·çȧ·tō·ry, *a.* [LL. *prædicatorius*, praising, from L. *prædicare*, to proclaim.]

1. preaching.

2. having to do with preaching.

3. preached.

prē·dī·çrot′iç, *a.* occurring before the dicrotic wave of the sphygmogram.

prē·diçt′, *v.t.*; predicted, *pt., pp.*; predicting, *ppr.* [L. *prædictus*, pp. of *prædicere*, to foretell; *præ*, before, and *dicere*, to tell.] to foretell; to prophesy; to prognosticate; to make known beforehand.

Syn.—foretell, prophesy, prognosticate, presage, forebode, foreshow.

prē·diçt′, *v.i.* to make a prediction or predictions.

prē·diçt′, *n.* a prophecy; a prediction. [Obs.]

prē·diçt′ȧ·ble, *a.* that can be predicted.

prē·diçt′ed, *a.* foretold; made known before the event.

prē·diç′tion, *n.* [L. *prædictio* (*-onis*).]

1. a predicting or being predicted.

2. a prophecy.

Syn.—prophecy, prognostication, foretelling, presage, augury.

prē·diç′tion·ăl, *a.* of the nature of a prediction.

prē·diçt′ive, *a.* foretelling; prophetic.

prē·diçt′ive·ly, *adv.* by way of prediction; prophetically.

prē·diçt′ŏr, *n.* 1. a person who predicts.

2. an antiaircraft aiming device that calculates flying speeds, courses, and altitudes of approaching planes.

prē·diçt′ō·ry, *a.* predictive; foretelling.

prē·di·ġest′, *v.t.*; predigested, *pt., pp.*; predigesting, *ppr.* to digest beforehand; specifically, to make (food) more digestible by an artificial process before it is eaten.

prē·di·ġes′tion (-jes′chun), *n.* 1. hasty digestion. [Obs.]

2. a predigesting or being predigested.

prē·di·leçt′, *a.* preferred; chosen. [Rare.]

prē·di·leç′tion, *n.* [Fr., *prédilection*, from ML. *prædiligere*, to prefer; L. *præ*, before, and *diligere*, to prefer.] a preconceived liking; partiality; preference.

prē·dis·çov′ẽr, *v.t.*; prediscovered, *pt., pp.*; prediscovering, *ppr.* to discover beforehand; to foresee.

prē·dis·çov′ẽr·y, *n.* prior discovery.

prē·dis·pō′nen·cy, *n.* a predisposition; the condition or state of being predisposed.

prē·dis·pō′nent, *a.* causing an inclination toward something; predisposing.

prē·dis·pō′nent, *n.* that which predisposes.

prē·dis·pōṣe′, *v.t.*; predisposed, *pt., pp.*; predisposing, *ppr.* 1. to dispose, or make receptive, beforehand; to make susceptible; as, fatigue *predisposes* one to colds.

2. to dispose of beforehand.

prē·dis·pō·ṣi′tion, *n.* 1. a predisposing.

2. the condition of being predisposed; previous inclination; tendency; predilection; susceptibility.

prē·dis·pō·ṣi′tion·ăl, *a.* of or relating to predisposition.

prē·dom′i·nănce, prē·dom′i·năn·cy, *n.* 1. the quality or condition of being predominant; prevalence over others; superiority in strength, power, influence, or authority; ascendancy.

2. in astrology, the superior influence of a planet.

prē·dom′i·nănt, *a.* [Fr. *prédominant*; L. *præ*, before, and *dominari*, to rule.]

1. having ascendancy, influence, or authority over others; superior; dominating; controlling; as, a *predominant* color.

2. most frequent, noticeable, etc.; prevailing; preponderant.

Syn.—prevalent, supreme, prevailing, overruling, ascendant, ruling, reigning, controlling.

prē·dom′i·nănt·ly, *adv.* in a predominant manner; so as to be predominant.

prē·dom′i·nāte, *v.i.*; predominated, *pt., pp.*; predominating, *ppr.* [from ML. *predominatus*, pp. of *predominari*, to rule.]

1. to have ascendancy, influence, or authority (*over* others); to be superior; to hold sway.

2. to be dominant over all others; to prevail; to preponderate.

So much did love to her executed lord
Predominate in this fair lady's heart.
—Daniel.

prē·dom′i·nāte, *v.t.* to rule over. [Rare.]

prē·dom′i·nā·ting, *a.* having superior strength or influence; ruling; controlling.

prē·dom′i·nā·ting·ly, *adv.* with predomination; predominantly.

prē·dom·i·nā′tion, *n.* a predominating.

prē·doom′, *v.t.* to doom beforehand.

prē·doomed′, *a.* doomed beforehand.

prē·dor′săl, *a.* situated immediately in front of the thoracic or dorsal region of the vertebral column.

prē·dread′naught (-dred′nạt), *n.* a battleship of extraordinary size that carries some large and some smaller guns, thus differing from the dreadnaught.

prē′dy, *a.* ready. [Obs.]

preef, *n.* proof. [Obs.]

prē-ē·leçt′, *v.t.* to choose or elect beforehand: also written *preëlect*.

prē-ē·leç′tion, *a.* occurring before an election: also written *preëlection*.

prē-ē·leç′tion, *n.* a previous choice: also written *preëlection*.

prē-em′i·nence, *n.* [LL. *præeminentia*.] the condition or quality of being pre-eminent: also written *preëminence*.

prē-em′i·nent, *a.* [L. *præeminens* (*-entis*), *ppr.* of *præeminere*, to project forward; *præ*, before, and *eminere*, to project.] eminent above others; excelling others, especially in a particular quality; prominent; surpassing: also written *preëminent*.

prē-em′i·nent·ly, *adv.* to a pre-eminent degree: also written *preëminently*.

prē-empt′, *v.t.*; pre-empted, *pt., pp.*; pre-empting, *ppr.* [back-formation from *preemption*.]

1. to acquire by pre-emption; to obtain the right of pre-emption, as by settlement upon (public land).

2. to seize before anyone else can, excluding others; to appropriate.

Also written *preëmpt*.

prē-emp′ti·ble, *a.* that can be pre-empted: also written *preëmptible*.

prē-emp′tion, *n.* [from ML. *preemptus*, pp. of *preemere*, to buy beforehand, from L. *præ*, before, and *emere*, to buy.]

1. the act or right of buying land, etc. before, or in preference to, others.

2. formerly, in England, the privilege or prerogative enjoyed by the king of buying provisions for his household in preference to others.

3. in international law, the right of seizing goods by a belligerent from a neutral upon compensation of the owner.

Also written *preëmption*.

prē-emp′tion·ẽr, *n.* a pre-emptor: also written *preëmptioner*.

prē-emp′tive, *a.* of, or having the nature of, pre-emption: also written *preëmptive*

prē-emp′tŏr, *n.* one who pre-empts: also written *preëmptor*.

prē-emp′tō·ry, *a.* pre-emptive: also written *preëmptory*.

preen, *n.* [AS. *preon*, a clasp.] a pin; a bodkin; a brooch. [Scot.]

preen, *v.t.*; preened, *pt., pp.*; preening, *ppr.* [var. of *prune* (to trim).]

1. to clean and trim (the feathers) with the beak: said of birds.

2. to make (oneself) trim; to dress up or adorn (oneself).

3. to show satisfaction with or vanity in (oneself).

preen, *v.i.* to prink; to primp.

prē-en·gāġe′, *v.t.*; pre-engaged, *pt., pp.*; pre-engaging, *ppr.* to engage by previous contract or influence; to preoccupy: also written *preëngage*.

prē-en·gāġe′ment, *n.* a prior engagement: also written *preëngagement*.

prē-Eṅg′lish, *n.* the Continental Low Germanic language from which Anglo-Saxon (Old English) developed; Anglo-Frisian.

prē-Eṅg′lish, *a.* 1. of pre-English.

2. of the peoples and languages of England before the Anglo-Saxon conquest.

prē-ē·reçt′, *v.t.* to erect previously: also written *preërect*.

prē-es·tab′lish, *v.t.* to establish beforehand: also written *preëstablish*.

prē-es·tab′lish·ment, *n.* settlement beforehand: also written *preëstablishment*.

prē-ex·am·in·ā′tion, *n.* previous examination: also written *preëxamination*.

prē-ex·am′ine, *v.t.* to examine beforehand: also written *preëxamine*.

prē-ex·il′i·ăn, *a.* [from *pre-*, *exile* (or L. *exilium*, exile), and *-an*.] of or in that period of Jewish history preceding the Babylonian exile (6th century B.C.): also written *preëxilian*.

prē-ex·il′iç, *a.* pre-exilian: also written *preëxilic*.

prē-ex·ist′, *v.i.* and *v.t.* to exist previously or before (another person or thing): also written *preëxist*.

prē-ex·ist′ence, *n.* 1. existence previous to something else.
2. the supposed existence of the soul before its union with the body, or before the body is formed.
Also written *preëxistence*.

pre-ex·ist′en·cy, *n.* pre-existence: also written *preëxistency*. [Obs.]

prē-ex·ist′ent, *a.* existing previously or before another person or thing: also written *preëxistent*.

prē-ex·ist′ent·iṣm, *n.* the philosophical doctrine that the soul has an existence prior to that in the human body: also written *preëxistentism*.

prē-ex·peç·tā′tion, *n.* previous expectation: also written *preëxpectation*.

prē·fab′ri·çāte, *v.t.*; prefabricated, *pt.*, *pp.*; prefabricating, *ppr.* 1. to fabricate beforehand.
2. to make or build in standardized sections for shipment and quick assembly, as a house.

pref′ăce, *n.* [OFr., from L. *præfatio*; *præ*, before, and *fari*, *fatus*, to speak.]
1. [*usually* P-] in Christian liturgy, the introduction to the Canon of the Mass.
2. a statement preliminary or introductory to an article, book, or speech, telling its subject, purpose, plan, etc.
3. something preliminary or introductory; a prelude.

pref′ăce, *v.t.*; prefaced (-ăst), *pt.*, *pp.*; prefacing, *ppr.* 1. to furnish or introduce with a preface; as, to *preface* a book or discourse.
2. to be or serve as a preface to; to begin.

pref′ăce, *v.i.* to say or write something introductory.

pref′ăc·ēr, *n.* the writer of a preface.

pref·ȧ·tō′ri·ăl, *a.* prefatory.

pref′ȧ·tō·ri·ly, *adv.* in a prefatory manner, as a preface.

pref′ȧ·tō·ry, *a.* of, like, serving as, or given as a preface; introductory.

prē′feçt, *n.* [L. *præfectus*, pp. of *præficere*, to set over; *præ*, before, and *facere*, to make.]
1. in ancient Rome, any of various high-ranking officials or chief magistrates. The prefect or warden of the city originally exercised the powers of the king or consuls during their absence; later, as a permanent magistrate, he was empowered to maintain peace and order in the city. The pretorian prefect was the commander of the pretorian guards. Under Constantine, the prefects became governors of provinces.
2. (a) the head of a department of France; (b) the chief of the Paris police.
3. in England, a monitor at certain public schools.
4. an ecclesiastical dean.
5. formerly, the person at the head of a department in China.
Also spelled *praefect*.

prē′feçt·ship, *n.* the position or office of a prefect.

prē·feç′tūr·ăl, *a.* of a prefecture.

prē′feç·tūre, *n.* [L. *præfectura*.] the office, authority, territory, or residence of a prefect.

prē·fēç·un·dā′tion, *n.* the conditions and changes prior to fecundation.

prē·fē·çun′dȧ·tō·ry, *a.* pertaining to prefecundation.

prē·fēr′, *v.t.*; preferred, *pt.*, *pp.*; preferring, *ppr.* [L. *præferre*, to place before; *præ*, before, and *ferre*, to bear or carry.]
1. to put before a magistrate, administrator, court, etc. for consideration, sanction, or redress; to set forth; to address; to present; as, he *preferred* charges against his assaulter.
2. to advance, as to an office or dignity; to raise; to promote; as, to *prefer* a person to a bishopric.
3. to set above something else in one's liking, opinion, etc.; to like better; to hold in greater esteem; to have a greater liking for; to incline more toward.
4. to offer or present; to proffer.
5. to recommend.
6. to surpass or outrank. [Obs.]

pref″ēr·ȧ·bil′i·ty, *n.* the quality or condition of being preferable.

pref′ēr·ȧ·ble, *a.* to be preferred; more eligible or more desirable (than something else).

pref′ēr·ȧ·ble·ness, *n.* preferability.

pref′ēr·ȧ·bly, *adv.* by preference; by choice.

pref′ēr·ence, *n.* [Fr. *préférence*; ML. *præferentia*, from L. *præferens*, ppr. of *præferre*, to place before.]
1. a preferring or being preferred; a greater liking.
2. the right, power, or opportunity of prior choice or claim; as, you have your *preference* of seats.
3. something preferred; one's first choice.
4. a giving of priority or advantage to one person, country, etc. over others, as in payment of debts or granting of credit.
Syn.—choice, selection, predilection, election.

pref·ēr·en′tiăl (-shăl), *a.* 1. of, giving, receiving, or having preference.
2. offering a preference; showing one's preference; as, a *preferential ballot*.

pref·ēr·en′tiăl·iṣm, *n.* the practice of giving preferences, as to certain countries in establishing tariffs.

pref·ēr·en′tiăl shop, a union shop in which the management by contract or agreement gives preference to union members, as in hiring, layoffs, promotion, etc.

pref·ēr·en′tiăl vōt′ing, a system of voting in which the voter indicates an order of preference for several candidates.

prē·fēr′ment, *n.* 1. the act of preferring, or of advancing to higher rank or dignity; advancement to a higher office, dignity, or station; promotion; preference.

> Neither royal blandishments nor promises of valuable *preferment* had been spared.
> —Macaulay.

2. an office, rank, or honor to which a person is advanced.

prē·fērred′ stock (-fērd′), stock on which dividends must be paid before those of common stock: it also has preference in the distribution of assets.

prē·fēr′rēr, *n.* one who prefers.

prē·fet′ (prā-fā′), *n.* [Fr.] in France, a prefect.

prē·fig′ū·rāte, *v.t.* to prefigure. [Rare.]

prē·fig·ū·rā′tion, *n.* 1. the act of prefiguring or the state of being prefigured.
2. something in which something else is prefigured; a prototype.

prē·fig′ūr·ȧ·tive, *a.* prefiguring.

prē·fig′ūre, *v.t.*; prefigured, *pt.*, *pp.*; prefiguring, *ppr.* [L. *præ*, before, and *figurare*, to fashion.]
1. to suggest or represent beforehand; to be an antecedent figure or type of; to foreshadow.
2. to figure to oneself, or imagine, beforehand.

prē·fig′ūre·ment, *n.* the act of prefiguring or that which is prefigured; a prefiguration.

prē·fīne′, *v.t.* [L. *præfinire*; *præ*, before, and *finire*, to limit; *finis*, limit.] to limit beforehand. [Obs.]

prē·fi′nīte, *a.* defined beforehand; prearranged. [Obs.]

pref·i·ni′tion (-nish′un), *n.* previous limitation. [Obs.]

prē·fix′, *v.t.*; prefixed (-fikst), *pt.*, *pp.*; prefixing, *ppr.* [ME. *prefyxen*; OFr. *prefixer*, from L. *præfixus*, pp. of *præfigere*; *præ*, before, and *figere*, to fix.]
1. to put or fix before, or at the beginning of another thing; as, to *prefix* a syllable to a word.
2. to set or appoint beforehand. [Rare.]
3. to settle; to establish beforehand. [Obs.]

prē′fix, *n.* [Mod. L., from L. *præfixus*; see the v.] a syllable, group of syllables, or word united with or joined to the beginning of another word to alter its meaning or create a new word; as, *pre-* is a *prefix* added to *cool* to form *precool*.

prē′fix·ăl (*or* prē-fik′săl), *a.* of or as a prefix.

prē·fix′iŏn (-fik′shun), *n.* a prefixing or being prefixed.

prē·fix′tūre, *n.* a prefix; also, a prefixing.

prē·fleç′tion, prē·flex′ion (-flek′shun), *n.* [L. *præ*, before, and *flection*, from *flexis*, to bend.] in philology, inflection based on prefixes.

prē·form′, *v.t.*; preformed, *pt.*, *pp.*; preforming, *ppr.* to form beforehand; also, to determine the shape of beforehand.

prē·fọr·mā′tion, *n.* 1. previous formation.
2. in biology, a former theory that every germ cell contains every part of the future organism in miniature, development being merely growth in size.

prē·fọrm′ȧ·tive, *n.* a formative letter at the beginning of a word.

prē·frŏn′tăl, *a.* situated in the anterior part of the frontal lobe or region.

prē·frŏn′tăl, *n.* the central part of the ethmoid bone.

prē·ful′ġen·cy, *n.* [L. *præfulgens*; *præ*, before, and *fulgere*, to shine.] superior brightness or effulgency. [Rare.]

prē·gāġe′, *v.t.* to pre-engage. [Obs.]

prē·glā′ciăl (-shăl), *a.* immediately preceding the glacial period.

preg·nȧ·bil′i·ty, *n.* the condition or quality of being pregnable.

preg′nȧ·ble, *a.* [ME. *prenable*, from Late OFr. *prenable*, from *prendre*; L. *prehendere*, to take.]
1. capable of being taken or won by force; liable to surrender when attacked.
2. that can be attacked or injured; assailable or vulnerable.

preg′nănce, *n.* pregnancy.

preg′năn·cy, *n.*; *pl.* **preg′năn·cieṣ**, 1. the condition, quality, or period of being pregnant.
2. a promising young person. [Obs.]
interstitial pregnancy; gestation in that part of the oviduct which is within the wall of the uterus.
mural pregnancy; interstitial pregnancy.

preg′nănt, *a.* [ME. *preignant*; L. *pregnans*, *pregnantis*, heavy with young; *præ*, before, and base of Old L. *gnasci*, to be born.]
1. having a fetus or fetuses growing in the uterus; that has conceived; with young or with child.
2. mentally fertile; prolific of ideas; inventive.
3. productive of results; fruitful; as, a *pregnant* cause.
4. full of or rich in meaning, significance, etc.
5. filled (*with*) or rich (*in*); abounding.
pregnant construction; in rhetoric, a construction in which more is implied than is said or seems.

preg′nănt·ly, *adv.* in a pregnant manner.

prē′grȧ·vāte, *v.t.* [L. *prægravare*, *prægravatus*, to press heavily; *præ-* intens., and *gravis*, heavy.] to bear down; to depress. [Obs.]

prē·gus′tănt, *a.* [L. *prægustans*.] tasting beforehand. [Rare.]

prē·gus·tā′tion, *n.* [L. *præ*, before, and *gustare*, to taste.] the act of tasting beforehand; anticipation. [Rare.]

prē·hal′lux, *n.* in zoology, an extra toe, wholly or partially developed, on the preaxial side of a hind limb.

prē·hēat′, *v.t.* to heat beforehand.

prē·hend′, *v.t.* [L. *prehendere*, to take or seize.] to lay hold of; to take; to seize. [Obs.]

prē·hen′si·ble, *a.* capable of being seized.

prē·hen′sile, *a.* [Fr. *préhensile*, from L. *prehensus*, pp. of *prehendere*, to take.] seizing; grasping; adapted to seize or grasp; as, the *prehensile* tails of some monkeys.

> His hands were small and *prehensile*, with fingers knotted like a cord.
> —Robert Louis Stevenson.

prē·hen·sil′i·ty, *n.* the state or quality of being prehensile.

prē·hen′sion, *n.* [L. *prehensio*.]
1. a taking hold; a seizing, as with the hand or other limb.
2. mental apprehension.

prē·hen′sŏr, *n.* one who or that which prehends, or seizes.

prē·hen′sō·ry, *a.* same as *prehensile*.

prē·his·tor′iç, *a.* relating to a period antecedent to the earliest period of recorded history.

> There are modern as well as ancient *prehistoric* races.
> —Wilson.

prē·his·tor′iç·ăl, *a.* same as *prehistoric*.

prē·his·tor′iç·ăl·ly, *adv.* before recorded history.

prē·his′tō·ry, *n.* history before recorded history, as learned from archaeology, etc.

prehn′īte (prен′), *n.* [named after Col. von *Prehn*, who discovered the stone at the Cape of Good Hope in 1774.] a pale-green mineral of a vitreous luster occurring in botryoidal or mammillary concretions and in small prismatic crystals, usually appearing as if made up of a series of small tables; a silicate of calcium and aluminum.

prehn·it′iç, *a.* of or resembling prehnite.

prē·ig·ni′tion, *n.* in an internal-combustion engine, ignition occurring before the intake valve is closed or before compression is at a maximum.

prē·in·çär′nāte, *a.* in theology, of or relating to existence previous to incarnation: applied especially to Jesus.

prē·in·deṣ′ig·nāte, *a.* [*pre-*, and *in-* priv., and *designate*.] in logic, having no sign to express the logical quantity; as, the *preindesignate* terms of a proposition.

prē″in·dis·pōṣe′, *v.t.* to make indisposed beforehand.

prē·in·struct′, *v.t.* to instruct previously.

prē·judge′, *v.t.* [Fr. *préjuger*; L. *præjudicare*; *præ*, before, and *judicare*, to judge.]

1. to judge in advance.

2. to judge and determine before a cause is heard; sometimes, to condemn beforehand.

prē·judg′ment, prē·judge′ment, *n.* [Fr. *préjugement.*] a prejudging or being prejudged.

prē·jū′di·ca·cy, *n.* prejudice; prepossession. [Obs.]

prē·jū′di·căl, *a.* prejudicial. [Obs.]

prē·jū′di·cănt, *a.* prejudging. [Obs.]

prē·jū′di·cāte, *a.* 1. decided in advance. [Obs.]

2. prejudiced; biased by opinions formed prematurely; as, a *prejudicate* reader. [Obs.]

prē·jū′di·cāte, *v.t.*; prejudicated, *pt., pp.*; prejudicating, *ppr.* [L. *præ*, before, and *judicare*, to judge.] to prejudge; to determine without fair hearing, especially adversely. [Obs.]

Our dearest friend
Prejudicates the business and would seem
To have us make denial. —Shak.

prē·jū′di·cāte, *v.i.* to form a judgment without due examination of the facts and arguments in the case. [Obs.]

prē·jū·di·cā′tion, *n.* 1. the act of judging without due examination of facts and evidence. [Rare.]

2. in Roman law, (a) judication from precedents involving the same points of law; (b) judication from precedents involving the same question between other parties; (c) judication from previous decisions of the same case between the same parties before inferior tribunals.

prē·jū′di·cā·tive, *a.* forming an opinion or judgment without examination. [Rare.]

prej′ū·dice, *n.* [ME.; OFr. *prejudice* [Fr. *préjudice*]; L. *præjudicium*, from *præ*, before, and *judicium*, a judgment, from *judex*, *judicis*, a judge.]

1. a judgment or opinion formed before the facts are known; preconceived idea, favorable or, more usually, unfavorable.

2. a judgment or opinion held in disregard of facts that contradict it; unreasonable bias; as, a *prejudice* against Northerners.

3. the holding of such judgments or opinions.

4. suspicion, intolerance, or hatred of other races, creeds, regions, occupations, etc.

5. injury or harm resulting as from some judgment or action of another or others.

6. foresight. [Obs.]

without prejudice to; in law, without dismissal of or detriment to a legal right, claim, or the like.

Syn.—bias, prepossession, detriment, unfairness, partiality.

prej′ū·dice, *v.t.*; prejudiced (-dist), *pt., pp.*; prejudicing, *ppr.* 1. to injure or harm, as by some judgment or action; as, his mistake *prejudiced* the outcome.

2. to cause to have prejudice; to cause to be prejudiced; to bias.

prej·ū·di′ciăl (-dish′ăl), *a.* [ME. *prejudiciall*; OFr. *prejudiciel*; Fr. *préjudiciel*, harmful, from L. *præjudicium*, a previous examination.]

1. biased or blinded by prejudices; as, a *prejudicial* eye. [Obs.]

2. causing prejudice, or harm; injurious; disadvantageous; detrimental; tending to obstruct or impair; as, a high rate of interest is *prejudicial* to trade; intemperance is *prejudicial* to health.

prej·ū·di′ciăl·ly, *adv.* in a prejudicial manner; injuriously, so as to warp the judgment.

prej·ū·di′ciăl·ness, *n.* the condition of being prejudicial.

prē·knowl′edge (-nol′ej), *n.* prior knowledge.

prē·lā′brum, *n.* same as *praelabrum.*

prel′ȧ·cy, *n.*; *pl.* **prel′ȧ·cies**, [ME. *prelacie*; ML. *prælatia.*]

1. the office or rank of a prelate.

2. the government of a church by prelates: often a hostile term.

3. prelates collectively.

prel′āte, *n.* [ME. and OFr. *prelat*; ML. *prælatus*, an ecclesiastical dignitary, from L. *prælatus*, pp. of *præferre*; *præ*, before, and *ferre*, to bear.] a high ranking ecclesiastic, having authority over the lower clergy, as an archbishop, bishop, etc.; a dignitary of the church.

prel′āte, *v.i.* to perform the duties of a prelate. [Obs.]

prel·ȧ·tē′i·ty, *n.* the prelacy; the theory of prelatic government. [Obs.]

prel′āte·ship, *n.* the office or tenure of a prelate.

prel′ȧ·tess, *n.* a woman prelate.

prē·lā′tiăl (-shăl), *a.* same as *prelatic.*

prē·lat′ic, *a.* pertaining to prelates or to prelacy; favoring prelacy; as, *prelatic* authority.

prē·lat′ic·ăl, *a.* same as *prelatic.*

prē·lat′ic·ăl·ly, *adv.* with reference to prelates.

prē·lā′tion, *n.* [L. *prælatio.*] preference; the setting of one above another. [Rare.]

prel′ȧ·tism, *n.* same as *prelacy*, sense 2.

prel′ȧ·tist, *n.* an advocate of prelacy or the government of the church by bishops.

I am an Episcopalian, but not a *prelatist.* —T. Scott.

prel′ȧ·tīze, *v.t.*; prelatized, *pt., pp.*; prelatizing, *ppr.* to bring under prelatic authority.

prel′ȧ·tīze, *v.i.* to come under prelatic authority. [Rare.]

prel′ȧ·tūre, *n.* [Fr. *prélature.*] same as *prelacy*, senses 1 and 3.

prel′ȧ·ty, *n.* episcopacy; prelacy. [Obs.]

prē·lect′, *v.i.* [L. *prælectus*, pp. of *prælegere*; *præ*, before, and *legere*, to read.] to lecture; to give lectures.

prē·lec′tion, *n.* [L. *prælectio.*] a lecture, especially at a university.

prē·lec′tŏr, *n.* a college or university lecturer. [Chiefly Brit.]

prē·lī·bā′tion, *n.* [L. *prælibare*; *præ*, before, and *libare*, to taste.]

1. foretaste; a tasting beforehand or by anticipation; as, the joy that proceeds from a belief of pardon is a *prelibation* of heavenly bliss.

2. a libation previous to tasting. [Rare.]

prē·lim′i·nȧr·i·ly, *adv.* in a preliminary manner; as a preliminary.

prē·lim′i·nār·y, *a.* [Fr. *préliminaire*; L. *præ*, before, and *limen*, threshold or limit.] serving as an introduction; going before the main business or major portion; prefatory; antecedent; as, the *preliminary* steps.

Syn.—introductory, preparatory, previous, prior, precedent.

prē·lim′i·nār·y, *n.*; *pl.* **prē·lim′i·nār·ies**, 1. a preliminary step, procedure, arrangement, etc.

2. a preliminary examination.

Syn.—introduction, preface, prelude, initiative.

prē·lim′it, *v.t.* to limit antecedently.

prē·lit′ēr·āte, *a.* [*pre-* and *literate.*] designating or of a culture developed before the invention of writing and, hence, leaving no written records.

pre′lūde (*or* prē′lūd), *n.* [Fr. *prélude*, from L. *præ*, before, and *ludus*, play.]

1. a thing serving as the introduction to a principal event, action, performance, etc.; preliminary part; preface; opening.

2. in music, (a) an introductory section or movement of a suite, fugue, etc.; (b) since the nineteenth century, any short romantic composition.

Syn.—preface, introduction, preliminary, forerunner, harbinger.

prel′ūde, *v.i.*; preluded, *pt., pp.*; preluding, *ppr.* 1. to serve as a prelude or introduction.

2. to play or provide a prelude.

prel′ūde, *v.t.* 1. to serve as or be a prelude to.

2. to introduce by or as by a prelude.

prē·lūd′ēr, *n.* one who or that which preludes.

prē·lūd′i·ăl, *a.* introductory; pertaining to a prelude.

prē·lūd′i·ous, *a.* preludial.

prē·lum′băr, *a.* in front of the lumbar vertebrae or loins.

prē·lū′sion (-zhun), *n.* [L. *prælusio.*] a prelude.

prē·lū′sive, *a.* introductory.

prē·lū′sive·ly, *adv.* in a prelusive manner.

prē·lū′sō·ry, *a.* prelusive.

prē·mȧ·tūre′, *a.* [L. *præmaturus*; *præ*, before, and *maturus*, ripe.]

1. ripe before the natural or proper time; as, the *premature* fruits of a hotbed. [Obs.]

2. happening, arriving, performed, or coming to pass before the proper or usual time; unexpectedly early; too early; as, a *premature* fall of snow in autumn; a *premature* birth.

Syn.—hasty, crude, too early, untimely, precocious, precipitate, rash, unseasonable.

prē·mȧ·tūre′ly, *adv.* in a premature manner; before the proper time; too soon.

prē·mȧ·tūre′ness, *n.* prematurity.

prē·mȧ·tū′ri·ty, *n.* the state of being premature.

prē·max·il′lȧ, *n.*; *pl.* **prē·max·il′lae**, [*pre-*, and L. *maxilla*, jawbone.] in anatomy and zoology, either of two bones in the upper jaw of vertebrates, situated between and in front of the maxillae, and fusing with them in the adult human being.

prē·max′il·lăr·y, *a.* relating to the premaxillae.

prē·max′il·lăr·y, *n.* the premaxilla.

prē·mē′di·āte, *v.t.* to plead; to advocate. [Obs.]

prē·med′i·căl, *a.* designating or of the studies preparatory to the study of medicine.

prē·med′i·tāte, *v.t.*; premeditated, *pt., pp.*; premeditating, *ppr.* [L. *præmeditari*, to think over.] to think out, plan, or scheme beforehand; as, to *premeditate* theft or robbery.

prē·med′i·tāte, *v.i.* to think, consider, or meditate beforehand; to deliberate.

prē·med′i·tāte, *a.* premiditated. [Obs.]

prē·med′i·tā·ted·ly, *adv.* in a premeditated manner.

prē·med′i·tāte·ly, *adv.* with premeditation. [Obs.]

prē·med·i·tā′tion, *n.* a premeditating; specifically, in law, a degree of planning and forethought sufficient to show intent to commit an act.

prē·med′i·tā·tive, *a.* that results from or shows premeditation.

prē·men′strū·ăl, *a.* occurring before menstruation.

prē·mer′it, *v.t.* to merit or deserve before hand.

prē′mi·ăl, *a.* premiant. [Rare.]

prē′mi·ănt, *a.* [L. *præmians*, *præmiantis*, ppr. of *præmiari*, to require a reward.] serving as a reward. [Rare.]

prē′mi·ēr (*or* prem′yēr), *a.* [Fr., from L. *primarius*, from *primus*, first.]

1. first in importance or rank; chief; foremost.

2. first in time; earliest.

prē·mier′ (*or* prē′mi-ēr), *n.* a chief official; specifically, a prime minister.

pre·mière′ (pri-mēr′; *or Fr.* prē-myär′), *a.* [Fr.] first; leading; as, a *première* danseuse.

pre·mière′ (pri-mēr′; *or Fr.* prē-myär′), *n.* 1. a first performance of a play, etc.

2. the leading lady (in the cast of a play, etc.).

prē·mier′ship (*or* prē′mi-ēr-), *n.* the office or term of a premier.

prē″mil·lē·nār′i·ăn, *a.* 1. occurring or living before the millennium.

2. designating or of the doctrine that the second coming of Christ will precede the millennium.

prē″mil·lē·nār′i·ăn, *n.* one who believes in premillennialism.

prē·mil·len′ni·ăl, *a.* of or happening in the period before the millennium.

prē·mil·len′ni·ăl·ism, *n.* the doctrine that the reappearance of Christ on earth will precede the millennium: opposed to *postmillennialism.*

prē·mil·len′ni·ăl·ist, *n.* same as *premillenarian.*

prē′mi·ous, *a.* [L. *præmium*, reward.] rich in gifts. [Rare.]

prem′ise, *n.* [ME. *premisse*; ML. *præmissa*, from L. *præmissus*, pp. of *præmittere*, to send before; *præ-*, before, and *mittere*, to send.]

1. a previous statement or assertion that serves as the basis for an argument.

2. [*pl.*] (a) the part of a deed or lease that states its reason, the parties involved, and the property in conveyance; (b) the property so mentioned.

3. [*pl.*] a piece of real estate; a house or building and its land; as, keep off the *premises.*

4. in logic, either of the two propositions of a syllogism from which the conclusion is drawn.

prē·mīse′, *v.t.*; premised, *pt.*; *pp.*; premising, *ppr.* 1. to state beforehand; to give as a premise.

2. to introduce or preface (a discourse, etc.), as with explanatory remarks.

prē·mīse′, *v.i.* to make a premise.

prem′iss, *n.* same as *premise.*

prē·mit′, *v.t.* to premise. [Obs.]

prē′mi·um, *n.*; *pl.* **prē′mi·ums**, [L. *præmium*, a reward, a recompense; *præ*, before, and *emere*, to take.]

1. a reward or prize, especially one offered as an added inducement to win, buy, etc.; a bonus.

2. an additional amount paid or charged; specifically, (a) an amount paid for a loan in addition to interest; (b) an amount paid, as for stock, above the nominal or par value.

3. a payment; specifically, (a) the amount payable or paid, in one sum or periodically, for an insurance policy; (b) a fee paid for in-

struction in a trade, etc.; (c) a fee paid by a borrower of stock to the lender.

4. very high value; as, he put a *premium* on punctuality.

5. in economics, the amount by which one form of money exceeds another (of the same nominal value) in exchange value, or buying power.

at a premium; (a) at a value or price higher than normal; (b) very valuable, usually because hard to get.

Syn.—reward, guerdon, encouragement, douceur, enhancement, bribe, recompense, bonus, prize, bounty.

prē·mō′lăr, *a.* designating or of any of the (bicuspid) teeth situated in front of the molars.

prē·mō′lăr, *n.* a premolar tooth.

prē·mon′ish, *v.t.* and *v.i.* to advise or caution beforehand. [Rare.]

prē·mon′ish·ment, *n.* previous warning or admonition; previous information. [Rare.]

prē·mō·ni′tion (-nish′un), *n.* [LL. *præmonitio*; L. *præ*, before, and *monere*, to warn.]

1. a forewarning.

We had been below but a short time when we had the usual *premonitions* of a coming gale. —Richard Henry Dana, Jr.

2. a foreboding; a presentiment.

prē·mon′i·tŏr, *n.* one who or that which gives forewarning or premonition.

prē·mon′i·tō·ri·ly, *adv.* in a premonitory manner.

prē·mon′i·tō·ry, *a.* giving previous warning or notice; serving as a premonition.

Prē·mon′strănt, *n.* [L. *præmonstrans*, ppr. of *præmonstrare*, to show beforehand.] in the Roman Catholic Church, one of a religious order of regular canons or monks of Prémontré, in France, instituted by St. Norbert in 1119: also called *White Canons.*

prē·mon′strāte, *v.t.* [L. *præmonstratus*, pp. of *præmonstrare*, to show beforehand.] to show beforehand. [Obs.]

Prē·mon·strā·ten′siăn, *n.* a Premonstrant.

prē·mon·strā′tion, *n.* a showing beforehand. [Obs.]

prē·mon′strā·tŏr, *n.* one who or that which premonstrates. [Obs.]

prē·morse′, *a.* [L. *præmorsus*, pp. of *præmordere*; *præ*, before, and *mordere*, to gnaw.] bitten off: applied in botany to a root or leaf terminating abruptly, as if bitten off.

prē·mō·sā′iç, *a.* pertaining to the time previous to Moses.

prē·mō′tion, *n.* previous motion or impulse to action.

prē·mun′dāne, *a.* antemundane.

prē·mū·nī′rē, *n.* same as *praemunire.*

prē·mū·nīte′, *v.t.* to guard against objection; to fortify or strengthen beforehand. [Obs.]

prē·mū·ni′tion, *n.* [L. *præmunitio*, from *præmunire*, to fortify beforehand.] the act of fortifying or strengthening beforehand against objections. [Obs.]

prē·năr′is, *n.*; *pl.* **prē·năr′ēş,** [*pre-*, before, and *naris*, nostril.] an anterior naris or nostril.

prē·nā′săl, *a.* in front of the nose.

prē·nā′tăl, *a.* existing or happening before birth.

prē·nā′tăl·ly, *adv.* before birth.

pren′dĕr, *n.* [Fr. *prendre*, to take, from L. *prehendere*, to seize.] in law, the right or power of taking a thing before it is offered.

prē·nō′men, *n.* same as *praenomen.*

prē·nom′i·năl, *a.* same as *praenominal.*

prē·nom′i·nāte, *a.* forenamed; named beforehand. [Obs.]

prē·nom′i·nāte, *v.t.*; prenominated, *pt.*, *pp.*; prenominating, *ppr.* to mention beforehand. [Obs.]

prē·nom·i·nā′tion, *n.* a naming or being named beforehand. [Obs.]

prē·nos′tiç, *n.* [irregularly formed from L. *præ*, before, and *noscere*, to know.] a prognostic; an omen. [Obs.]

prē·nōte′, *v.t.* to note or make out previously or beforehand. [Obs.]

prē·nō′tion, *n.* a preconception. [Rare.]

pren·sā′tion, *n.* [L. *prensatio*, from *prensare*, to seize.] the act of seizing with violence. [Obs.]

pren′tice, ′pren′tice, *n.* an apprentice. [Archaic or Dial.]

pren′tice, ′pren′tice, *a.* characteristic of an apprentice. [Archaic or Dial.]

pren′tice·hood, *n.* the state of an apprentice. [Obs.]

pren′tice·ship, *n.* apprenticeship. [Archaic or Dial.]

prē·nun·ci·ā′tion, *n.* [L. *prænunciatio.*] the act of telling before. [Obs.]

prē·ob·lon·gā′tȧ, *n.* the front portion of the medulla oblongata.

prē·ob·tāin′, *v.t.* to obtain beforehand.

prē·oç′çū·păn·cy, *n.*; *pl.* **prē·oç′çū·păn·cieş,** prior occupancy; preoccupation.

prē·oç′çū·pāte, *v.t.* 1. to anticipate; to take before. [Obs.]

2. to prepossess; to fill with prejudices. [Obs.]

prē·oç·çū·pā′tion, *n.* [L. *præoccupatio.*] a preoccupying or being preoccupied.

prē·oç′çū·pīed, *a.* 1. previously or already occupied.

2. occupied with or absorbed in one's thoughts; engrossed.

3. in biology, designating or of a name already used and hence no longer available.

prē·oç′çū·pȳ, *v.t.*; preoccupied, *pt.*, *pp.*; preoccupying, *ppr.* [L. *præoccupare*; *præ*, before, and *occupare*, to seize.]

1. to occupy the thoughts of; to engross; to absorb.

2. to occupy or take possession of before someone else or beforehand.

prē·oç′ū·lăr, *a.* in front of the eyes.

prē·oç′ū·lăr, *n.* a scale of a fish and of certain reptiles which is situated just in front of the eyes.

prē·om′i·nāte, *v.t.* [L. *præ*, before, and *ominari*, to prognosticate.] to prognosticate; to augur; to portend by omens. [Rare.]

prē·ō·pĕr′çū·lăr, *a.* pertaining to the preoperculum.

prē·ō·pĕr′çū·lum, *n.*; *pl.* **prē·ō·pĕr′çū·lȧ,** in fishes, the foremost opercular bone.

prē·ō·pin′iŏn (-yun), *n.* opinion previously formed; prejudice.

prē·op′tion, *n.* the right of first choice.

prē·ō′răl, *a.* in zoology, located in front of, or anterior to, the mouth.

prē·or′bit·ăl, *a.* in front of the orbit.

prē·or·dāin′, *v.t.*; preordained, *pt.*, *pp.*; preordaining, *ppr.* to ordain or decree beforehand; to predetermine.

prē·or′dĕr, *v.t.* to order or arrange beforehand; to prearrange; to foreordain.

prē·or′di·nănce, *n.* antecedent decree or determination. [Obs.]

prē·or′di·nāte, *a.* preordained. [Obs.]

prē·or·di·nā′tion, *n.* a preordaining or being preordained.

prep, *a.* preparatory; as, a *prep* school. [Colloq.]

prep, *n.* a preparatory school. [Colloq.]

prē·pāid′, *v.* past tense and past participle of *prepay.*

prē·pāid′, *a.* [pp. of *prepay.*] paid in advance, as postage of letters.

prē·pal′ȧ·tăl, *a.* in anatomy, in front of the palate; as, the *prepalatal* aperture.

prē·pal′ȧ·tine, *a.* same as *prepalatal.*

prep′ȧ·rȧ·ble, *a.* capable of being prepared.

prē·păr′ănce, *n.* preparation. [Obs.]

prep·ȧ·rā′tion, *n.* [L. *præparare*, to make ready.]

1. a preparing.

2. a being prepared; readiness.

3. something done to prepare; preparatory measure.

4. something prepared for a special purpose, as a medicine, cosmetic, condiment, etc.

5. in music, (a) the preparing for a dissonant chord by using the dissonant tone as a consonant tone in the immediately preceding chord; (b) a tone so used.

6. the day before a Jewish feast day, as the Sabbath; also, among Christians, the day preceding Holy Communion; the devotions of the celebrants, etc., on that day.

7. a force ready for combat, as an army or fleet. [Obs.]

8. accomplishment; qualification. [Obs.]

prē·par′ȧ·tive, *a.* [Fr. *preparatif.*] tending to prepare or make ready; having the power of qualifying or fitting; preparatory.

prē·par′ȧ·tive, *n.* 1. that which has the power of previously fitting for a purpose; that which prepares.

2. that which is done to prepare; preparation; as, *preparatives* for a voyage.

Their conversation is a kind of *preparative* for sleep. —Steele.

prē·par′ȧ·tive·ly, *adv.* by way of preparation.

prē·par′ȧ·tŏr, *n.* one who prepares subjects for scientific investigation, as bodies for dissection; a taxidermist.

prē·par′ȧ·tō·ri·ly, *adv.* in a preparatory manner.

prē·par′ȧ·tō·ry, *a.* 1. that prepares or serves to prepare; preliminary; introductory.

2. undergoing preparation, or preliminary instruction, especially for college entrance; as, a *preparatory* student.

Syn.—introductory, preparing, preparative, qualifying.

prē·pāre′, *v.t.*; prepared, *pt.*, *pp.*; preparing, *ppr.* [Fr. *préparer*; L. *præparare*, *præparatus*; *præ*, before, and *parare*, to set or place in order, to get ready.]

1. to make ready, usually for a specific purpose; to make suitable; to fit; to adapt; to train.

2. to make receptive; to dispose; to accustom; as, he *prepared* them for the bad news.

3. to equip or furnish with necessary provisions, accessories, etc.; to fit out; as, they *prepared* an expedition.

4. to put together or make out of materials, ingredients, parts, etc., or according to a plan or formula; to construct; to compound; as, they *prepared* dinner, he *prepared* the medicine.

5. in music, to use (a dissonant tone) in preparation (sense 5).

Syn.—fit, adjust, adapt, qualify, equip, provide, procure, form, make.

prē·pāre′, *v.i.* 1. to make all things ready; to put things in suitable order; as, *prepare* for dinner.

2. to make oneself ready; to hold oneself in readiness.

prē·pāre′, *n.* preparation. [Rare.]

prē·pāred′, *a.* fitted; made ready; provided; holding oneself in readiness.

As to being *prepared* for defeat, I certainly am not. —Farragut.

prē·pār′ed·ly, *adv.* 1. in a manner showing preparation.

2. in such a way as to be prepared.

prē·pār′ed·ness, *n.* the state of being prepared; specifically, possession of sufficient armed forces, matériel, etc. for waging war.

prē·pār′ĕr, *n.* one who or that which prepares, fits, or makes ready; as, a *preparer* of textbooks; a *preparer* of copy for the press.

prē·pāy′, *v.t.*; prepaid, *pt.*, *pp.*; prepaying, *ppr.* to pay or pay for in advance; as, to *prepay* the postage of a letter.

prē·pāy′ment, *n.* payment in advance, as of postage, rent, etc.

prē·pē′ni·ăl, *a.* situated in front of the penis.

prē·pense′, *a.* [L. *præ*, before, and *pensare*, to deliberate.] preconceived; premeditated; aforethought: usually placed after the word it qualifies, and now rarely used except in the phrase *malice prepense.*

Malice *prepense* is necessary to constitute murder. —Blackstone.

prē·pense′, *v.t.* and *v.i.*; prepensed, *pt.*, *pp.*; prepensing, *ppr.* to weigh or consider beforehand; to deliberate beforehand. [Obs.]

prē·pense′ly, *adv.* premeditatedly. [Rare.]

prē·plā·cen′tăl, *a.* preceding the placenta in origin and formation.

prē·pol′lence, prē·pol′len·cy, *n.* [L. *præpollens*, ppr. of *præpollere*, to be very powerful or strong; *præ*, before, and *pollere*, to be able.] prevalence; superiority of power. [Rare.]

prē·pol′lent, *a.* having superior gravity or power; prevailing.

prē·pol′lex, *n.*; *pl.* **prē·pol′li·cēş,** [*pre-*, and L. *pollex* (*-icis*), thumb.] an extra digit or rudiment of a digit on the preaxial side of the pollex in some animals.

prē·pon′dĕr, *v.t.* to outweigh. [Rare.]

prē·pon′dĕr·ănce, prē·pon′dĕr·ăn·cy, *n.* 1. the state or quality of preponderating or being preponderant; an outweighing; superiority in amount, weight, power, influence, importance, etc.

2. in gunnery, the excess of weight in the part of a gun behind the pivotal axis.

prē·pon′dĕr·ănt, *a.* that preponderates; greater in amount, weight, power, influence, importance, etc.; predominant.

prē·pon′dĕr·ănt·ly, *adv.* in a preponderant manner; so as to be preponderant.

prē·pon′dĕr·āte, *v.t.*; preponderated, *pt.*, *pp.*; preponderating, *ppr.* [L. *præponderare*, *præponderatus*; *præ*, before, and *ponderare*, to weigh, from *pondus*, *ponderis*, a weight.]

1. to outweigh; to overpower by weight. [Obs.]

An inconsiderable weight, by distance from the center of the balance, will *preponderate* greater magnitudes. —Glanvill.

2. to incline; to dispose; to decide. [Obs.]

prē·pon′dẽr·āte, *v.i.* 1. to weigh more than something else.
2. to sink or incline downward, as a scale of a balance.
3. to surpass in amount, number, power, influence, importance, etc.; to predominate.

prē·pon·dẽr·ā′ting·ly, *adv.* in a preponderating manner; preponderantly.

prē·pon·dẽr·ā′tion, *n.* the act or state of preponderating; preponderance.

prē·pōṣe′, *v.t.* to put before.

prep·ō·ṣi′tion (-zish′un), *n.* [ME. *preposicioun*; L. *præpositio*, from *præpositus*, pp. of *præponere*; *præ*, before, and *ponere*, to place.]
1. in some languages, a relation word, as English *in, by, for, with, to*, etc., that connects a noun, pronoun, or noun phrase to another element of the sentence, as to a verb (e.g., he went *to* the store), to a noun (e.g., the sound *of* tramping feet), or to an adjective (e.g., old *in* years).
2. any construction of similar function (e.g., *in back of*, equivalent to *behind*). The noun or pronoun usually following the preposition (as, *store, feet*, and *years*, in the preceding examples) is called its *object*.
3. a proposition; a discourse. [Obs.]

prep·ō·ṣi′tion·ăl (-zish′un-), *a.* of, functioning as, or formed with a preposition.

prep·ō·ṣi′tion·ăl·ly, *adv.* 1. as a preposition.
2. by means of a preposition.

prep·ō·ṣi′tion·ăl phrāṣe, a preposition and its object.

prē·poṣ′i·tive, *a.* in grammar, prefixed; put before; as, a *prepositive* letter or particle.

prē·poṣ′i·tive, *n.* a word put before another word; a prepositive word.

prē·poṣ′i·tŏr, *n.* [L. *præpositor.*] in some English public schools, a senior student with authority to discipline: also *praepositor, praepostor, prepostor.*

prē·poṣ′i·tūre, *n.* the office or function of a provost.

prē·pŏs·ṣess′, *v.t.*; prepossessed (-zest′), *pt., pp.*; prepossessing, *ppr.* 1. to take possession of or occupy beforehand or before another. [Rare.]
2. to possess or preoccupy beforehand to the exclusion of later thoughts, feelings, etc.
3. to prejudice; bias.
4. to impress favorably beforehand or at once.

prē·pos·ṣess′ing, *a.* that prepossesses, or impresses favorably; pleasing; attractive.
Syn.—attractive, alluring, charming, winning, taking, engaging.

prē·pos·ṣess′ing·ly, *adv.* in a prepossessing manner.

prē·pos·ṣes′sion (-zesh′un), *n.* a prepossessing or being prepossessed; predilection; bias.
Syn.—bent, bias.

prē·pos·ṣess′ŏr, *n.* one who prepossesses.

prē·pos′tẽr·ous, *a.* [L. *præposterus*; *præ*, before, and *posterus*, coming after.]
1. originally, with the first last and the last first; inverted.
2. contrary to nature, reason, or common sense; senseless; absurd; ridiculous.
Syn.—absurd, foolish, irrational.

prē·pos′tẽr·ous·ly, *adv.* in a preposterous manner.

prē·pos′tẽr·ous·ness, *n.* the quality of being preposterous; absurdity.

prē·pos′tŏr, *n.* same as *prepositor.*

prē·pō′ten·cy, *n.*; *pl.* **prē·pō′ten·cieṣ,** [L. *præpotentia*; *præ*, before, and *potentia*, power.]
1. the condition or quality of being prepotent.
2. in biology, the greater capacity of one parent to transmit certain characteristics to offspring.

prē·pō′tent, *a.* [L. *præpotens.*]
1. superior in power, force, or influence.
2. in biology, of or having prepotency.

prep′py, prep′pie, *n.*; *pl.* **prep′pies,** a student or former student at a private secondary school that prepares students to enter college.

prep′py, prep′pie, *a.*; *comp.* preppier; *superl.* preppiest; designating, of, or like the fashion in clothes associated with preppies.

prē·pū′biç, *a.* in front of the pubis; pertaining to the prepubis.

prē·pū′bis, *n.* a bone or cartilage in the median line and anterior to the pubic bones.

prē′pūce, *n.* [Fr., from L. *præputium.*] the foreskin; fold of skin covering the end (glans) of the penis or clitoris.

prē·pū′tiăl (-shăl), *a.* pertaining to the prepuce.

Prē-Raph′ȧ·el·iṣm, *n.* same as *Pre-Raphaelitism.*

Prē-Raph′ȧ·el·īte, *n.* 1. a member of the Pre-Raphaelite Brotherhood, a society of artists led by Dante Gabriel Rossetti, Holman-Hunt, and J. E. Millais, formed in England in 1848 to encourage painting with the fidelity to nature and delicacy of treatment characteristic of Italian art before the time of Raphael.
2. any modern artist with similar aims.
3. any Italian painter before Raphael.

Prē-Raph′ȧ·el·īte, *a.* 1. of or characteristic of the Pre-Raphaelites or their followers.
2. designating or of Italian painters or painting before Raphael.

Prē-Raph′ȧ·el·ī·tiṣm, *n.* the principles of the Pre-Raphaelites.

prē·reg′nănt, *n.* one who reigns before. [Rare.]

prē·rē·mōte′, *a.* more remote.

prē·rē·quīre′, *v.t.* to require previously. [Rare.]

prē·req′ui·ṣite (-rek′wi-), *a.* required beforehand, especially as a necessary condition for something following.

prē·req′ui·ṣite, *n.* something prerequisite.

prē·rē·ṣolve′, *v.t.* to resolve previously. [Rare.]

prē·rog′ȧ·tive, *n.* [L. *prærogativa*, called upon to vote first, from *prærogare*, to ask before; *præ*, before, and *rogare*, to ask.]
1. a prior or exclusive right or privilege, especially one peculiar to a rank, class, etc.
2. priority or precedence, as that derived from such a right or privilege.
3. a superior advantage.
prerogative court; (a) in Great Britain, formerly, a court for the trial of all testamentary causes, where the deceased had left effects of the value of five pounds, in two different dioceses; (b) in the state of New Jersey, the probate court.

prē·rog′ȧ·tive, *a.* of or having a prerogative.

prē·rog′ȧ·tived, *a.* having prerogative.

prē·rog′ȧ·tive·ly, *adv.* by exclusive privilege.

pre′sä, *n.*; *pl.* **pre′se,** [It., lit., a taking up, seizure, from pp. of *prendere* (L. *prehendere*), to take.] in music, a sign (:S:,+,※) showing where each successive voice enters in a canon.

pres′āge, *n.* [L. *præsagium*; *præ*, before, and *sagire*, to perceive.]
1. a sign or warning of a future event; an omen; portent; augury.
2. a foreboding; presentiment.
3. a prediction. [Rare.]
4. meaning; import; as, of ominous *presage.*

prē·sāġe′, *v.t.*; presaged, *pt., pp.*; presaging, *ppr.* 1. to give a presage, or warning, of; to portend.
2. to have a foreboding or presentiment of.
3. to predict.

prē·sāġe′, *v.i.* 1. to have a presentiment.
2. to make a prediction.

prē·sāġe′fụl, *a.* full of presages; containing presages.

prē·sāġe′ment, *n.* 1. a foreboding; foretoken. [Obs.]
2. a foretelling; prediction. [Obs.]

prē·sāġ′ẽr, *n.* a person or thing that presages.

prē·sā′ġious, *a.* full of presages; ominous. [Obs.]

preṣ′by·ōpe (*or* pres′), *n.* one affected with presbyopia; one who is farsighted; a presbyte.

preṣ·by·ō′pi·ȧ, *n.* [Gr. *presbys*, old, and *ōps*, eye.] a form of farsightedness occurring after middle age, caused by a diminished elasticity of the crystalline lens.

preṣ·by·op′iç, *a.* of or having presbyopia.

preṣ′by·ō·py, *n.* same as *presbyopia.*

preṣ′byte, *n.* same as *presbyope.*

preṣ′by·tẽr (*or* pres′), *n.* [LL., from Gr. *presbyteros*, comp. of *presbys*, old. *Priest* is the same word in a greatly altered form.]
1. in the early Christian church and in the Presbyterian Church, an elder.
2. in the Episcopal Church, a priest or minister.

preṣ·byt′ẽr·ăl, *a.* relating to a presbyter or presbytery; presbyterial.

preṣ·byt′ẽr·āte, *n.* 1. presbytery.
2. a presbytership.

preṣ′by·tẽr·ess, *n.* a woman presbyter.

preṣ·by·tē′ri·ăl, *a.* of or relating to a presbyter or to a presbytery; pertaining to government by presbyters.

preṣ·by·tē′ri·ăl·ly, *adv.* 1. in accordance with the rules of a presbytery.
2. [P–] in the manner of the Presbyterian Church or of Presbyterianism.

Preṣ·by·tē′ri·ăn, *a.* 1. [p–] having to do with church government by presbyters.
2. designating or of a church of a Calvinistic Protestant denomination governed by presbyters, or elders.

Preṣ·by·tē′ri·ăn, *n.* a believer in Presbyterianism or a member of a Presbyterian church.

Preṣ·by·tē′ri·ăn·iṣm, *n.* 1. church government by presbyters, or elders, of equal rank, over whom there is no higher authority.
2. the doctrines and beliefs of the Presbyterian churches.

preṣ·by·tē′ri·um, *n.* same as *presbytery*, sense 3.

preṣ′by·tẽr·ship, *n.* the office or position of a presbyter.

preṣ′by·tẽr·y, *n.*; *pl.* **preṣ′by·tẽr·ieṣ,** [LL. *presbyterium*, council of elders.]
1. a body of presbyters; specifically, in Presbyterian churches, an ecclesiastical court made up of all the ministers and one or two presbyters from each parish in a given district.
2. the district of such a court.
3. the part of a church reserved for the officiating clergy.
4. in the Roman Catholic Church, a priest's house.

preṣ·byt′i·ȧ, *n.* [Gr. *presbytēs*, an old person.] same as *presbyopia.*

preṣ·byt′iç, *a.* same as *presbyopic.*

preṣ′byt·iṣm, *n.* same as presbyopia.

prē·sçap′ū·lȧ, *n.*; *pl.* **prē·sçap′ū·lae,** in anatomy, that part of the scapula anterior to or above the spine: also written *praescapula.*

prē·sçap′ū·lăr, *a.* of or relating to the prescapula; situated in front of the long axis of the scapula.

prē·sçhool′ (-skọọl′), *a.* designating, of, or for a child between infancy and school age, or in the age group 2–4, 2–5, or 2–6.

prē′sçhool (-skọọl), *n.* a school for children of preschool age; a nursery school or kindergarten, or a school combining both.

prē′sci·ence (-shi-ens), *n.* foreknowledge; knowledge of events before they take place; as, absolute *prescience* belongs to God only.

prē′sci·ent (-shi-ent), *a.* [L. *præsciens, præscientis*, ppr. of *præscire*, to foreknow; *præ*, before, and *scire*, to know.] foreknowing; having prescience.

prē′sci·ent·ly, *adv.* in a prescient manner; with foresight; foreknowingly.

prē·scind′, *v.t.* prescinded, *pt., pp.*; prescinding, *ppr.* [L. *præscindere*; *præ*, before, and *scindere*, to cut.] to detach, abstract, or isolate (a meaning, one's mind, etc.).

prē·scind′, *v.i.* to withdraw one's own attention: usually with *from.*

prē·scind′ent, *a.* prescinding; abstracting. [Rare.]

prē′scious (-shus), *a.* prescient; having foreknowledge. [Obs.]

prē·sçrībe′, *v.t.*; prescribed, *pt., pp.*; prescribing, *ppr.* [L. *præscribere*; *præ*, before, and *scribere*, to write.]
1. originally, to write beforehand.
2. to set down as a rule or direction; to order; ordain; direct.
3. to order or advise as a medicine or treatment: said of physicians, etc.
4. in law, to invalidate or outlaw by negative prescription.

prē·sçrībe′, *v.i.* 1. to set down or give rules, directions, etc.
2. to give medical advice or prescriptions.
3. in law, (a) to claim a right or title through long use or possession (often with *to* or *for*); (b) to become invalidated or outlawed by negative prescription.
Syn.—direct, order, require, command, enjoin.

prē·sçrīb′ẽr, *n.* one who prescribes.

prē·sçript′, *a.* [L. *præscriptus*, pp. of *præscribere*, to write before.] directed; prescribed.

prē′sçript, *n.* [L. *præscriptum.*] something prescribed; an order; direction; rule.

prē·sçrip·ti·bil′i·ty, *n.* capability of being prescribed.

prē·sçrip′ti·ble, *a.* 1. that can be effectively prescribed for; as, a *prescriptible* illness.
2. acquired or acquirable by prescription (sense 5).

prē·sçrip′tion, *n.* [L. *præscriptio (-onis)*, from *præscriptus*, pp. of *præscribere*, to prescribe.]
1. a prescribing.
2. something prescribed; an order; direction; prescript.
3. a doctor's written direction for the preparation and use of a medicine.
4. a medicine so prescribed.
5. in law, (a) the acquirement of the title or right to something through its continued use or possession from time immemorial or over a long period; (b) a right or title so acquired.

prē·sçrip′tive, *a.* [LL. *præscriptivus*, pertaining to a prescript.]

1. that prescribes.
2. based on legal prescription.
3. prescribed by custom or long use.

prē·scrip′tive·ly, *adv.* by prescription.

prē·scū′tum, *n.* the anterior sclerite of the tergum of an insect.

prē′sē·ănce, *n.* priority of place. [Obs.]

prē·sē·leçt′, *v.t.* to select in advance.

prē·sem′i·năl, *a.* before fertilization or fecundation.

preș′ence, *n.* [L. *præsentia*, from *præesse*, to be present.]
1. the fact, condition, or quality of being present.
2. immediate surroundings; vicinity within close view; as, I was admitted to his *presence.*
3. attendance; company.
4. a person who is present, especially a royal person.
5. a person's bearing, personality, or appearance; as, he has a poor *presence.*
6. pleasing deportment; dignity; as, he has no *presence.*
7. an influence or supernatural spirit felt to be present; a ghost.
8. people present; an assemblage. [Archaic.]
9. a presence chamber. [Obs.]
saving your presence; though I apologize for saying or doing this in your presence.

preș′ence chām′bēr, the room in which a great personage receives company.

preș′ence of mind, ability to think clearly and act quickly and intelligently in an emergency.

preș′ence rọọm, same as *presence chamber.*

prē·sen·sā′tion, *n.* previous notion or idea; an anticipatory sensation. [Obs.]

prē·sen′sion, *n.* previous perception. [Rare.]

preș′ent, *a.* [L. *præsens (-entis)*, ppr. of *præesse*, to be present.]
1. being at the specified or understood place; at hand; in attendance: opposed to *absent.*
2. existing or happening now; in process: contrasted with *past, future.*
3. now being discussed, considered, written, read, etc.; as, the *present* writer.
4. self-possessed; collected; ready. [Archaic.]
5. prompt to act, understand, or assist; efficacious. [Obs.]
6. in grammar, designating or of a tense or verb form expressing action as now taking place or state as now existing (e.g., he *goes*), action that is habitual (e.g., he *speaks* with an accent), or action that is always true (e.g., two and two *is* four).

preș′ent, *n.* 1. the present time.
2. the present occasion.
3. in grammar, (a) the present tense; (b) a verb in it.
4. [OFr., in phr. *mettre en present à*, to put before (someone), present, offer, hence a gift.] something presented; a gift.
at present; now; at this time.
by these presents; in law, by this document.
for the present; for an indefinite time, beginning now; temporarily.

prē·șent′, *v.t.*; presented, *pt., pp.*; presenting, *ppr.* [Fr. *présenter*; L. *præsentare*, to place before, to present, to hold out, lit., to make present.]
1. to bring (a person) into the presence of another or others; to introduce, especially to a superior.
2. to offer to view or notice; to exhibit; display; show.
3. to offer for consideration.
4. to offer for acceptance; to make a gift of; bestow.
5. to make a gift or donation to; as, he *presented* the college with a library.
6. to represent (a character) on the stage; to act; perform.
7. to point, level, or aim, as a weapon.
8. to nominate to an ecclesiastical benefice.
9. in law, (a) to lay before a legislature, court, etc. for consideration; (b) to bring a charge or indictment against.
to present arms; in military usage, (a) to hold a rifle vertically in line with the middle of the body, with the muzzle up, at eye level, and the trigger away from the body: a position of salute; (b) this position or the command to assume it.

prē·șent′, *v.i.* in the church, to make a presentation (sense 4).

prē·șent′, *n.* in military usage, the attitude assumed by one in presenting arms; also, the position in which a rifle is held to be fired.

prē·șent·ȧ·bil′i·ty, *n.* the condition or quality of being presentable.

prē·șent′ȧ·ble, *a.* 1. capable of being presented; fit to be exhibited or offered; specifically, (a) fit to be introduced into society; fit to be shown or seen; (b) capable of being expressed, indicated, or revealed; as, *presentable* only in technical language.
2. in ecclesiastical usage, (a) capable of being presented to an ecclesiastical benefice; as, a *presentable* clergyman; (b) admitting of the presentation of a clergyman; as, a church *presentable.*

prē·șent′ȧ·bly, *adv.* in a presentable manner; so as to be presentable.

preș·en·tā′nē·ous, *a.* quick; rapid in effect; as, *presentaneous* poison. [Obs.]

preș·en·tā′tion, *n.* 1. a presenting or being presented.
2. something that is presented; specifically, (a) a performance, as of a play; (b) a gift.
3. in commerce, a presentment.
4. in ecclesiastical usage, (a) the naming of a clergyman to a benefice; (b) a request to the bishop to institute the clergyman named.
5. in obstetrics, the position of the fetus in the uterus at the time of delivery, with reference to the part presenting itself at the mouth of the uterus; as, an arm or breech *presentation.*
6. in philosophy and psychology, anything present in the consciousness at a single moment as an actual sensation or a mental image; perception.
Feast of the Presentation; in the Roman Catholic and Orthodox Eastern churches, a festival celebrated November 21 in honor of the presentation of the Virgin Mary in the Temple.

preș·en·tā′tion·ăl, *a.* 1. of (a) presentation.
2. presentive.

preș·en·tā′tion·ișm, *n.* in philosophy, the theory that in perception the mind is directly aware of an external object without any intervening medium: opposed to *representationism.*

prē·șent′ȧ·tive, *a.* 1. serving to present; presenting.
2. in ecclesiastical usage, designating a benefice to or for which a patron has the right of presentation.
3. in philosophy and psychology, capable of being known directly without the use of reason or reflective thought.

preș′ent-dāy′, *a.* of the present time.

preș·en·tee′, *n.* 1. a person presented, especially for institution to a benefice.
2. a person to whom something is presented.

prē·șent′ẽr, *n.* one who presents.

prē·șen′tiăl (-shăl), *a.* supposing actual presence; immediate; manifest. [Rare.]

prē·șen·ti·al′i·ty (-shi-), *n.* the state of being present. [Rare.]

prē·șen′tiăl·ly, *adv.* in a presential manner. [Rare.]

prē·șen′ti·āte (-shi-), *v.t.* to make present. [Obs.]

prē·sen′tient (-shent), *a.* perceiving beforehand.

prē·șent′i·ment, *n.* 1. previous conception, sentiment, or opinion; previous apprehension.
2. a belief, impression, or foreboding that something disastrous or distressing will soon happen; anticipation of imminent evil.

> A vague *presentiment* of impending doom
> Haunted him day and night.—Longfellow.

prē·șen·ti·men′tăl, *a.* relating to or having presentiment. [Rare.]

> A mysterious *presentimental* hell.
> —Thackeray.

prē·sen′tion, *n.* presension. [Obs.]

prē·șent′ive, *a.* presenting a conception of an object or idea directly to the mind; as, a *presentive* word: contrasted with *representative* or *symbolic.*

prē·șent′ive·ly, *adv.* in a presentive manner.

prē·șent′ive·ness, *n.* the state or quality of being presentive.

preș′ent·ly, *adv.* 1. at present; at this time; now.
2. in a little while; soon; shortly.
3. at once; instantly. [Archaic or Dial.]

prē·șent′ment, *n.* 1. presentation.
2. an exhibition; a thing presented to view.
3. in commerce, the producing of a note, bill of exchange, etc. for acceptance or payment at the proper time and place.
4. in law, the notice taken or report made by a grand jury of an offense on the basis of the jury's knowledge and without a bill of indictment.
5. in philosophy, a presentation.

preș′ent·ness, *n.* the state or quality of being present. [Rare.]

preș′ent par′ti·ci·ple, in grammar, a participle of present meaning (e.g., *running* in "running water").

preș′ent pẽr′feçt, in grammar, (a) expressing action or state as completed at the time of speaking but not at any definite time in the past; (b) the present perfect tense: it is formed in English by using the present tense of *have* with a past participle (e.g., he *has* gone); (c) a verb in this tense.

prē·șẽrv′ȧ·ble, *a.* that can be preserved.

preș·ẽr·vā′tion, *n.* the act of preserving, or keeping in safety or security from harm, injury, decay, or destruction; also, the state of being preserved; as, a picture in good *preservation.*

> Toward the *preservation* of your government it is requisite that you resist with care the spirit of innovation.
> —George Washington.

prē·șẽrv′ȧ·tive, *a.* having the power or quality of preserving.

prē·șẽrv′ȧ·tive, *n.* that which preserves or has the power of preserving; especially, a substance added to a food to keep it from spoiling or rotting.

prē·șẽrv′ȧ·tō·ry, *a.* preservative. [Rare.]

prē·șẽrv′ȧ·tō·ry, *n.*; *pl.* **prē·șẽrv′ȧ·tō·rieș,**
1. that which has the power of preserving; a preservative. [Obs.]
2. any place or apparatus for preserving food products.

prē·șẽrve′, *v.t.*; preserved, *pt., pp.*; preserving, *ppr.* [LL. *præservare*; L. *præ*, before, and *servare*, to keep.]
1. to keep from harm, damage, danger, evil, etc.; to protect; save.
2. to keep from spoiling or rotting.
3. to prepare (food), as by canning, pickling, salting, etc., for future use.
4. to keep up; to carry on; maintain.
5. to maintain and protect (game, fish, etc.) for private use in hunting or fishing.

Syn.—protect, guard, secure, defend, keep, save, maintain.

prē·șẽrve′, *v.i.* 1. to preserve fruit, etc.
2. to maintain a game preserve.

prē·șẽrve′, *n.* 1. [*usually pl.*] fruit preserved whole by cooking with sugar.
2. a place where game, fish, etc. are preserved.
3. something that preserves or is preserved.

prē·șẽrv′ẽr, *n.* 1. a person or thing that preserves; one who or that which saves or defends from destruction, evil, etc.
2. one who makes preserves of fruits.

prē·shōw′, *v.t.* to show beforehand; to foreshow. [Rare.]

prē′-shruñk′, *a.* shrunk by a special process in manufacture so that there is little or no shrinkage in laundering and dry cleaning.

prē·șīde′, *v.i.*; presided, *pt., pp.*; presiding, *ppr.* [L. *præsidere*; *præ*, before, and *sedere*, to sit.]
1. to be in the position of authority; to take charge of a meeting; to act as chairman.
2. to have control or authority.
3. to be in the leading place, as a featured instrumentalist, etc.

preș′i·dence, *n.* presidency. [Rare.]

preș′i·den·cy, *n.*; *pl.* **preș′i·den·cieș,** 1. the office or function of president.
2. the term during which a president is in office.
3. [*often* P–] the office of President of the United States.
4. [P–] formerly, any of the three original provinces of British India (Bengal, Bombay, and Madras), originally governed by presidents of the East India Company's holdings.
5. in the Mormon Church, (a) a council of three with local jurisdiction; (b) a council of three (*First Presidency*) that is the highest administrative body.

preș′i·dent, *n.* [Fr. *président*, from L. *præsidens (-entis)*, ppr. of *præsidere*, to preside.]
1. the highest officer of a company, society, university, club, etc.
2. [*often* P–] the chief executive of a republic.
3. the formal head of a republic, with little or no executive power, usually the presiding member of the legislative assembly or council.

preș′i·dent, *n.* a precedent. [Obs.]

preș′i·dent-ē·leçt′, *n.* an elected president who has not yet taken office.

preș·i·den′tiăl (-shăl), *a.* of or pertaining to a president or a presidency; as, the *presidential* chair, a *presidential* campaign.

pres'i·dent·ship, *n.* 1. the office, function, or dignity of a president; presidency.
2. the term for which a president holds his office.

prē·sīd'ēr, *n.* one who presides.

prē·sid'i·ăl, prē·sid'i·ā·ry, *a.* [L. *præsidium*, a garrison; *præ*, before, and *sedere*, to sit.] pertaining to a presidio, or garrison; having a garrison.

prē·sid'i·ō, *n.* [Sp., from L. *præsidium*, garrison.] a military post; a fortress or fortified place; a garrison.

prē·sid'i·um, *n.* [L. *præsidium*, a presiding over, protection.]
1. in the Soviet Union, (a) any of a number of permanent administrative committees meeting regularly and empowered to act for a larger body between its sessions; (b) [P–] the permanent administrative committee of the Supreme Soviet.
2. [P–] an administrative committee at the highest level of government in certain other countries, as Albania, Romania, etc.

prē·sig"ni·fi·cā'tion, *n.* the act of signifying or showing beforehand; also, that which presignifies.

prē·sig'ni·fȳ, *v.t.*; presignified (-fīd), *pt., pp.*; presignifying, *ppr.* to signify, or give an indication of, beforehand; to foreshadow.

prē·sphē'noid, *a.* designating or of the anterior portion of the body of the sphenoid bone.

prē·sphē'noid, *n.* the presphenoid bone.

prē·sphē·noid'ăl, *a.* presphenoid.

press, *n.* in zoology, an insectivore, *Tupaia ferruginea*, of the East Indies; a squirrel shrew.

press, *v.t.* [a confusion of obs. *prest*, to engage for military service by advance payment on wages, with *press*, to force.]
1. to force into military or naval service.
2. to force or urge into any kind of service.
3. to use in a way different from the ordinary.

press, *n.* 1. an impressment, or forcing into service, usually naval or military.
2. an order for impressing recruits.

press, *v.t.*; pressed (prest), *pt., pp.*; pressing, *ppr.* [OFr. *presser*, from L. *pressare*, a freq. of *premere*, to press.]
1. to act on with steady force or weight; to push steadily against; to squeeze.
2. (a) to extract juice, etc. from by squeezing; (b) to squeeze (juice, etc.) out; to express.
3. (a) to squeeze for the purpose of making smooth, compact, etc.; to compress; (b) to iron, as clothes.
4. to embrace closely.
5. to force; compel; constrain.
6. to urge or solicit earnestly or persistently; to entreat; importune.
7. to impose by persistent entreaty; to try to force; as, she *pressed* the gift on her friend.
8. to lay stress on; to be insistent about; to emphasize.
9. to distress; embarrass; straiten; as, they were *pressed* with want.
10. to urge on; to drive on.
11. to crowd; to throng. [Archaic.]
12. to oppress. [Obs.]
13. to print. [Archaic.]

press, *v.i.* to exert pressure; specifically, (a) to weigh down; to bear heavily; (b) to go forward with energetic or determined effort; (c) to force one's way; (d) to crowd; to throng; (e) to be urgent or insistent.

press, *n.* 1. a pressing or being pressed; pressure, urgency, crowding, etc.
2. a crowd; a throng.
3. an instrument or machine by which something is crushed, stamped, smoothed, etc. by pressure.
4. (a) any of various machines for printing; a printing press; (b) a printing establishment; (c) the art, business, or practice of printing; (d) newspapers, magazines, etc. in general, or the persons who write for them; journalism or journalists; (e) publicity, criticism, etc. in newspapers, magazines, etc.
5. an upright closet in which clothes or other articles are kept.
6. in photography, a printing frame.
7. in weight lifting, a lift in which the barbell is cleaned and then pushed steadily overhead until the arms are completely extended.
in press; in the printing process.
liberty of the press; same as *freedom of the press*.
press of sail or *canvas*; in nautical usage, as much sail as the ship can carry.
to go to press; to start to be printed.

press'ȧ·ble, *a.* that can be pressed.

press ā'gent, a person whose business is to advance the interests of a person, organization, etc., usually by getting publicity; publicity agent.

press bed, a folding bed; a bed built in solid woodwork, resembling a cupboard.

press'bōard, *n.* 1. a heavy glazed paper used to cover the cylinder or platen of printing presses.
2. a smooth board of stiff, heavy paper or wood, used in presses for finishing paper, books, etc.

press box, a box or group of seats at any public gathering, reserved for newspapermen.

press bū'reau (-rō), an establishment that acts as a press agent for theaters, lecturers, etc.

press çāke, in the manufacture of gunpowder, a mill cake; in sugar manufacturing, the residue from the filters; also, an oil cake.

press çon'fēr·ence, a collective interview granted to journalists, as by a celebrity or personage.

pressed duck, 1. the breast and legs of a roast duck served with a sauce prepared from juices obtained by squeezing the remainder of the carcass in a special press.
2. a Chinese dish of steamed duck, boned, pressed, deep-fried, and served with a sauce and toasted almonds.

press'ēr, *n.* 1. one who or that which presses.
2. a form of ironing machine.
3. one whose work is pressing newly made or freshly cleaned clothes.

press'ēr bär, the bar in a knitting machine which drives the barb of the needle into the groove of the shank in order to let off the loop.

press gal'lēr·y, a section set apart for journalists in a chamber where an official body meets.

press'gang, *n.* a press gang.

press gang, [for *prest gang*.] a group of men who round up other men and force them into naval or military service.

press'ing, *a.* [ppr. of *press* (to push against).]
1. calling for immediate attention; urgent.
2. persistent in request or demand; importunate.
Syn.—urgent, importunate.

press'ing bōard, in bookbinding, a board placed between layers of books when piled in the standing press.

press'ing·ly, *adv.* in a pressing manner; urgently.

press'ing·ness, *n.* the quality of being pressing.

pres'sion (presh'un), *n.* the act of pressing; pressure. [Rare.]

pres·si·ros'tēr, *n.* one of the *Pressirostres*.

pres·si·ros'trăl, *a.* having a compressed or flattened beak; pertaining to the *Pressirostres*.

Pres·si·ros'trēş, *n.pl.* [L. *pressus*, pressed, and *rostrum*, beak.] a group of wading birds characterized by the moderate length of the bill, which has a compressed tip. It includes the plovers and bustards. [Obs.]

pres'sive, *a.* 1. pressing; urgent; important. [Obs.]
2. oppressive. [Obs.]

press'ly, *adv.* with compression; closely; concisely. [Obs.]

press'măn, *n.*; *pl.* **press'men,** 1. one who operates a printing press.
2. a journalist; a reporter. [Brit.]

press'märk, *n.* a letter, number, etc. stamped on a book to show its place on a library shelf.

press mŏn'ey, same as *prest money*.

pres'sŏr (-ēr), *a.* [from *pressure*, after *motor*, a.]
1. increasing the pressure.
2. designating a nerve which, when stimulated, causes a rise in blood pressure and increased activity of some motor center.

press'pack, *v.t.* to compress or pack by means of a press.

press proof, the last proof examined before the matter is printed or the electrotype or stereotype is made.

press rē·lēase', in journalism, any material given or sent to a newspaper before a prearranged date of publication.

press'room, *n.* 1. any room in which presses for any purpose are kept.
2. the room in which printing presses are in use, as distinguished from the composing room.

pres'sūr·ăl, *a.* having the nature of pressure.

pres'sūre (presh'ēr), *n.* [L. *pressura*, from *pressus*, pp. of *premere*, to press.]
1. a pressing or being pressed; compression; squeezing.
2. a condition of distress; oppression; affliction.
3. a compelling influence; a constraining force; as, we all react to social *pressure*.
4. demands requiring immediate attention; urgency.
5. an impression; mark made by pressing. [Obs.]
6. in electricity, electromotive force.
7. in physics, force exerted against an opposing body; the thrust distributed over a surface: expressed in weight per unit of area: symbol P (no period).
atmospheric pressure; see under *atmospheric*.

pres'sūre, *v.t.*; pressured, *pt., pp.*; pressuring, *ppr.* to exert pressure, or compelling influence, on. [Colloq.]

pres'sūre blōw'ēr, a device which creates a blast by piston pressure, as distinguished from a *fan blower*.

pres'sūre çook'ēr, an airtight metal container for quick cooking by means of steam under pressure.

pres'sūre fil'tēr, a filter in which the liquid is forced by a pressure greater than that of its own weight.

pres'sūre gāuġe, 1. a manometer.
2. an instrument for determining the pressure of powder in a gun chamber.

pres'sūre grōup, any group that exerts pressure upon legislators and the public through lobbies, propaganda, etc. in order to affect legislation or policies.

pres'sūre point, any of a number of points on the body where an artery passes close to the surface and in front of a bony structure so that pressure applied there will check bleeding from a distal injured part.

pres'sūre spot, a point or spot on the surface of the body particularly sensitive to pressure.

pres'sūre sūit, a type of G-suit designed to maintain normal respiration and circulation, especially in space flights.

pres'sūr·īze, *v.t.*; pressurized, *pt., pp.*; pressurizing, *ppr.* to keep nearly normal atmospheric pressure inside of (an airplane, etc.), as at high altitudes, or in rising or descending.

press'wom"ăn (-woom"), *n.*; *pl.* **press'wom"en** (-wim-), a woman who is a member of the press; a newspaperwoman.

press'wŏrk, *n.* 1. the operation or management of a printing press.
2. work done by a printing press.
3. in cabinetmaking, the drying and pressing of superimposed veneers.

prest, *n.* [OFr. *prest*, from *prester*, to lend, afford, from L. *præstare*, to stand before.]
1. originally, a loan; an advance of money.
2. an advance of money to men enlisting in the British army or navy: also *prest money*.

prest, *a.* [from L. *præstare*.]
1. ready; prompt. [Obs.]
2. neat; proper. [Obs.]

prest'ȧ·ble, *a.* that can be paid. [Scot.]

pres'tănt, *n.* [L. *præstans* (-*antis*), ppr. of *præstare*, to stand before.] an organ stop; the open diapason.

pres·tā'tion, *n.* [L. *præstatio*.] in feudal law, a payment of money, as in toll; also, purveyance.

pres·tā'tion mŏn'ey, in feudal law, a sum of money paid yearly by archdeacons and other dignitaries to their bishop.

pres'tēr, *n.* [Gr. *prēstēr*, from *prēthein*, to kindle or inflame.]
1. a meteor or exhalation formerly supposed to be thrown from the clouds with such violence that by collision it was set on fire. [Obs.]
2. a swollen cervical vein, as in anger. [Obs.]

pres'tēr, *n.* [OFr. *prestre*, from L. *presbyter*, a priest.] a priest; a presbyter.
Prester John; a legendary medieval Christian king and priest thought to have ruled either in the Far East or in Ethiopia.

prē·stēr'năl, *a.* pertaining to the presternum.

prē·stēr'num, *n.* the anterior bone of the sternum.

pres·ti·dig'i·tăl, *a.* having light fingers.

pres·ti·dig·i·tā'tion, *n.* [L. *præsto*, at hand, prompt, and *digitus*, finger.] the performance of tricks by quick, skillful use of the hand; sleight of hand; legerdemain.

pres·ti·dig·i·tā'tŏr, *n.* an expert in prestidigitation.

pres·tiġe' (-tēzh' *or* pres'tij), *n.* [Fr., from L. *præstigium*, a delusion, an illusion, a juggler's trick, from *præstinguere*, to darken, to obscure.]

1. the power to command admiration or esteem.

2. reputation or distinction based on brilliance of achievement, character, etc.; renown.

pres·tiġ′i·āte, *v.t.*; prestigiated, *pt.*, *pp.*; prestigiating, *ppr.* to deceive, as by legerdemain. [Obs.]

pres·tiġ·i·ā′tion, *n.* the playing of legerdemain tricks; juggling. [Obs.]

pres·tiġ′i·ā·tŏr, *n.* a juggler; a cheat. [Obs.]

pres·tiġ′i·ā·tō·ry, *a.* juggling. [Obs.]

pres·tiġ′i·ous, *a.* [L. *præstigiosus*, full of deceitful tricks, from *præstigium*, delusion; see *prestige*.

1. having or imparting prestige or distinction.

2. practicing tricks. [Obs.]

pres′ti·mō·ny, *n.* [Fr. *prestimonie*, from LL. *præstimonium*, from L. *præstare*, to furnish; *præ*, before, and *stare*, to stand.] in canon law, a fund for the support of a priest, appropriated by the founder, but not erected into any title or benefice.

pres·tis′si·mō, *a.* and *adv.* [It.] in music, in very quick time; as fast as possible: a direction to the performer.

pres·tis′si·mō, *n.* a prestissimo musical passage or movement.

prest mŏn′ey, in the British army and navy, money loaned in advance to the men upon their enlistment.

pres′tō, *a.* and *adv.* [L. *præsto*, at hand, ready; *præ*, before, and *stare*, to stand.]

1. in music, in rapid tempo: a direction to the performer.

2. fast.

pres′tō, *n.* a musical passage or movement performed in fast tempo.

prē·stō′mi·um, *n.*; *pl.* **prē·stō′mi·ȧ**, the fore part of the head of an annelid.

prē′stressed′ çon′çrēte, concrete containing steel cables, wires, etc. under tension to produce compressive stress and lend greater strength.

prē·striç′tion, *n.* [L. *præstrictus*, pp. of *præstringere*, to bind fast, to obscure.] the condition of being dazzled or blinded. [Obs.]

prē·ṣūm′ȧ·ble, *a.* that may be presumed, or taken for granted; probable.

prē·ṣūm′ȧ·bly, *adv.* as may be presumed or taken for granted; probably.

prē·ṣūme′, *v.t.*; presumed, *pt.*, *pp.*; presuming, *ppr.* [ME. *presumen*; OFr. *presumer*; L. *præsumere*; *præ*, before, and *sumere*, to take.]

1. to take upon oneself without permission or authority; to dare (to say or do something); to venture.

2. to take for granted; to accept as true until proof to the contrary is furnished; to suppose; to presuppose.

3. to constitute reasonable evidence for supposing; as, a signed invoice *presumes* receipt of the shipment.

prē·ṣūme′, *v.i.* 1. to act presumptuously; to take liberties.

2. to rely too much (*on* or *upon*), as in taking liberties.

3. to take something for granted; to make suppositions.

prē·ṣūm′ed·ly, *adv.* as is or may be presumed; supposedly.

prē·ṣūm′ẽr, *n.* one who presumes.

prē·ṣūm′ing·ly, *adv.* confidently; arrogantly.

prē·ṣump′tion, *n.* [ME.; OFr. *presomption*; L. *præsumptio*, a taking beforehand.]

1. the act of presuming; specifically, (a) an overstepping of proper bounds; forwardness; effrontery; (b) the taking of something for granted.

2. the thing presumed; supposition.

3. a ground or reason for presuming; evidence that points to the probability of something.

4. in law, the inference that a fact exists, based on the proved existence of other facts.

presumption of fact; an argument which assumes certain propositions to be sufficiently proved when certain other propositions have been established.

presumption of law; a condition assumed to exist, which needs no proof or which may not be denied.

prē·ṣump′tive, *a.* 1. giving reasonable ground for belief; as, *presumptive* evidence.

2. based on probability; presumed; as, an heir *presumptive*.

presumptive evidence; same as *circumstantial evidence*.

presumptive heir; same as *heir presumptive*.

prē·ṣump′tive·ly, *adv.* by presumption or by supposition grounded on probability.

prē·ṣump′tū·ous, *a.* [LL. *præsumptiosus*, from L. *præsumere*, to take beforehand.]

1. bold and confident to excess; adventuring without reasonable ground of success; taking liberties; rash; insolent; audacious; as, a *presumptuous* commander; *presumptuous* behavior.

> There is a class of *presumptuous* men whom age has not made cautious, nor adversity wise. —Buckminster.

2. presumptive. [Obs.]

prē·ṣump′tū·ous·ly, *adv.* in a presumptuous manner; with presumption.

prē·ṣump′tū·ous·ness, *n.* the quality or state of being presumptuous.

prē·sup·pōṣ′ăl, *n.* a supposal previously formed; presupposition.

prē·sup·pōṣe′, *v.t.*; presupposed, *pt.*, *pp.*; presupposing, *ppr.* 1. to suppose or assume beforehand; to take for granted.

2. to require or imply as a preceding condition; as, a healthy body *presupposes* healthful living.

prē″sup·pō·ṣi′tion, *n.* [ML. *præsuppositio.*]

1. a presupposing.

2. the thing, fact, idea, etc. presupposed.

prē·sūr·mīṣe′, *v.t.*; presurmised, *pt.*, *pp.*; presurmising, *ppr.* to surmise beforehand.

prē·sūr·mīṣe′, *n.* a presentiment.

prē·sys′tō·lē, *n.* the time elapsing immediately before the systole.

prē·sys·tol′iç, *a.* before the systole of heart-contraction; pertaining to the beginning of the systole.

prē′tax′, *a.* before the payment of taxes.

prē′teen′, *n.* a child nearly a teen-ager.

prē·tem′pō·răl, *a.* situated in front of the temporal bone.

prē·tence′ (*or* prē′tens), *n.* pretense: British spelling.

prē·tend′, *v.t.*; pretended, *pt.*, *pp.*; pretending, *ppr.* [L. *prætendere*; *præ*, before, and *tendere*, to reach or stretch.]

1. to claim; profess; allege; as, he *pretended* ignorance of the law.

2. to claim or profess falsely; to feign; to simulate; as, he *pretended* that he was ill.

3. to suppose in play; to make believe; as, she *pretended* that she was a princess.

4. to reach or stretch forward. [Obs.]

5. to exhibit as a cloak or disguise for something. [Rare.]

6. to claim or put in a claim for; to allege a title to. [Now Rare.]

7. to design; to plan; to plot. [Obs.]

Syn.—feign, counterfeit, simulate, affect.

prē·tend′, *v.i.* 1. to put in a claim, truly or falsely: usually with *to*.

2. to make believe in play or in an attempt to deceive; to feign.

prē·tend′, *a.* make-believe; as, *pretend* jewelry. [Colloq.]

prē·tend′ănt, *n.* one who pretends.

prē·tend′ed, *a.* 1. not genuine; feigned.

2. reputed or alleged.

prē·tend′ed·ly, *adv.* with a mere pretense; in appearance only.

prē·tend′ence, *n.* pretense. [Obs.]

prē·tend′ẽr, *n.* 1. a person who pretends.

2. a claimant to a throne; specifically, [P–], in English history, the son (James Edward, called *Old Pretender*) or the grandson (Charles Edward, called *Young Pretender*) of James II.

3. an aspirant.

prē·tend′ẽr·ship, *n.* the right or claim of a pretender.

prē·tense′ (*or* prē′tens), *n.* [L. *prætentus*, later *prætensus*, pp. of *prætendere*, to pretend.]

1. a claim, as to some distinction or accomplishment; pretension; as, he made no *pretense* to being infallible.

2. a false claim or profession; as, under the *pretense* of friendship.

3. a false show of something.

4. something said or done for show.

5. a pretending, as at play; make-believe.

6. a false reason or plea; a pretext.

7. aim; intention. [Rare.]

8. pretentiousness.

9. a pretentious act or remark.

false pretenses; in law, deliberate misrepresentation of fact in speech or action in order to defraud someone of the title to a certain property or money.

Syn.—pretext, mask, appearance, color, show, excuse.

prē·tensed′ (-tenst′), *a.* pretended; feigned; as, a *pretensed* right to land. [Obs.]

prē·tens′ed·ly, *adv.* pretendedly. [Obs.]

prē·tense′less, *a.* without pretenses. [Rare.]

prē·ten′sion, *n.* [LL. *prætentio* (*-onis*), from L. *prætendere*, to pretend.]

1. a pretext or allegation.

2. a claim, as to a right, title, distinction, importance, dignity, etc.

3. assertion of a claim.

4. pretentiousness.

prē·ten′tȧ·tive, *a.* [*pre-*, and L. *tentare*, to try.] testing tentatively; experimental. [Archaic.]

prē·ten′tious (-shus), *a.* [Fr. *prétentieux.*]

1. making claims, explicit or implicit, to some distinction, importance, dignity, or excellence.

2. showy; ostentatious.

prē·ten′tious·ly, *adv.* in a pretentious manner.

prē·ten′tious·ness, *n.* the quality of being pretentious; false assumption of excellence.

prē′tẽr, *a.* past. [Obs.]

prē′tẽr, *n.* the past. [Obs.]

prē′tẽr-, prae′tẽr-, [L. *præter-*, from *præter*, beyond, past, compar. of *præ*, before, ahead.] a prefix meaning *past*, *beyond*, *outside the bounds of*, as in *preter*natural.

prē·tẽr·hū′măn, *a.* exceeding the human; especially, superhuman.

prē·tē′ri·ent, *a.* [L. *præteriens* (*-entis*), ppr. of *præterire*, to go by.] transient; passing by. [Rare.]

prē″tẽr·im·pẽr′fect, *a.* designating the imperfect tense. [Obs.]

pret′ẽr·ist, *n.* 1. one whose chief interest and pleasure is in the past.

2. in theology, one who believes that the prophecies of the Apocalypse have already been fulfilled.

pret′ẽr·ist, *a.* pertaining to preterists or their interpretation of the Scriptures.

pret′ẽr·it, pret′ẽr·ite, *a.* [L. *præteritus*, gone by, pp. of *præterire*; *præter*, beyond, and *ire*, to go.]

1. in grammar, expressing past action or state.

2. past; bygone; former. [Rare.]

pret′ẽr·it, pret′ẽr·ite, *n.* 1. in grammar, the past tense.

2. a verb in the past tense.

pret·ẽr·i′tion (-ish′un), *n.* [L. *præteritio*, from *præterire*, to pass by.]

1. a passing over; omission.

2. in law, an omitting of one or more legal heirs from a will.

3. in theology, the passing over by God of those not elect: a doctrine of Calvinism.

prē·tẽr′i·tive, *a.* in grammar, denoting past time; confined to past tenses, as certain verbs.

pret′ẽr·it·ness, pret′ẽr·ite·ness, *n.* the state of being past. [Rare.]

pret′ẽr·it-preṣ′ent, *a.* in grammar, having preterit form but present sense, as *ought*, *can*, etc.

prē·tẽr·lapsed′ (-lapst′), *a.* [L. *præterlapsus*, pp. of *præterlabi*; *præter*, beyond, and *labi*, to glide.] past; gone by; as, *preterlapsed* ages. [Obs.]

prē·tẽr·mis′sion (-mish′un), *n.* [L. *prætermissio*, from *prætermittere*, to let go by.] a pretermitting or being pretermitted.

prē·tẽr·mit′, *v.t.*; pretermitted, *pt.*, *pp.*; pretermitting, *ppr.* [L. *prætermittere*, to let go by; *præter*, beyond, and *mittere*, to send.]

1. to leave out or undone; to neglect or omit.

2. to let pass unnoticed; to overlook.

prē·tẽr·nat′ū·răl, *a.* 1. differing from or beyond what is natural; out of the ordinary.

2. supernatural.

prē·tẽr·nat′ū·răl·iṣm, *n.* 1. the quality or condition of being preternatural.

2. a preternatural occurrence.

3. a preternatural doctrine or system.

prē·tẽr·nat·ū·ral′i·ty, *n.* preternaturalness. [Rare.]

prē·tẽr·nat′ū·răl·ly, *adv.* in a preternatural manner.

prē·tẽr·nat′ū·răl·ness, *n.* the quality or condition of being preternatural.

prē·tẽr·pẽr′fect, *a.* [L. *præter*, beyond, and *perfectus*, perfect.] in grammar, preterit. [Rare.]

prē·tẽr·pẽr′fect, *n.* the preterit tense. [Rare.]

prē″tẽr·plū″pẽr′fect, *a.* [L. *præter*, beyond, *plus*, more, and *perfectus*, perfect.] in grammar, pluperfect. [Rare.]

prē″tẽr·plū″pẽr′fect, *n.* the pluperfect tense. [Rare.]

prē″tẽr·plū·ral′i·ty, *n.* numerousness; great number. [Rare.]

prē-Tẽr′ti·ăr·y (-shi-), *a.* in geology, before the Tertiary.

prē'test, *n.* 1. a test given a student before entering a course of instruction, to determine his fitness for the course.

2. a preliminary training test designed to acquaint a student with the methods of replying to test questions.

prē·test', *v.t.* and *v.i.* to test beforehand.

prē·tẽr·veç'tion, *n.* [L. *prætervectio* (*-onis*), from *prætervehere*, to carry beyond.] the act of carrying by or beyond. [Rare.]

prē·tex', *v.t.* to cloak; to conceal; to devise; to fabricate; to allege falsely. [Obs.]

prē·text', *v.t.* to employ as a cover or pretext.

prē'text, *n.* [L. *prætextum*, neut. of *prætextus*, pp. of *prætexere*, to weave before.] pretense; false appearance; ostensible reason or motive assigned or assumed as a color or cover for the real reason or motive.

We need not by silence give the least *pretext* for uncertainty. —Grover Cleveland.

Syn.—pretense, disguise, semblance, excuse.

prē·text'ed, *a.* applied or used as an excuse.

prē·tex'tūre, *n.* a pretext. [Obs.]

prē·thō·rac'iç, *a.* in anatomy, situated above or in front of the thorax: applied particularly to those vertebræ in front of or over those containing the thoracic ribs.

prē·tib'i·ăl, *a.* in anatomy, situated upon the front of the tibia; as, a *pretibial* muscle.

prē'ti·um (-shi-), *n.* [L.] the money or price paid for a thing.

pretium affectionis; in law, the price above its value set upon a thing by its owner because of his affection for it.

pretium laborum non vile; the value of the labor is not trifling: the motto of the Order of the Golden Fleece.

pretium periculi; a premium for insurance; the price given for a risk.

pretium puellae; in law, the price of a maiden: from a system formerly practiced by early Teutonic races, in which a woman could be given in marriage only after the payment of something of value to her guardian.

prē'tōne, *n.* the syllable or vowel which immediately precedes the accented syllable.

prē·ton'iç, *a.* 1. in music, preceding a tone; as, a *pretonic* note.

2. in philology, preceding the accent.

prē'tŏr, *n.* same as *praetor*.

prē·tō'ri·ăl, *a.* same as *praetorial*.

prē·tō'ri·ăn, *a.* and *n.* same as *praetorian*.

Prē·tō'ri·ȧ sē'ries, [named after *Pretoria* in South Africa.] in geology, the second uppermost subdivision of South African, pre-Devonian rocks of the Transvaal system: it is made up of beds of iron ore, lavas, shales, etc.

prē·tọr'tūre, *v.t.* to torture beforehand.

prē·trēat', *v.t.* to treat beforehand, as in some processes of manufacture in order to facilitate an operation or prevent damage or change.

prē·trēa'ty, *a.* before a treaty.

prē·trē·mat'iç, *a.* [L. *præ*, before, and Gr. *trēma*, *trēmatos*, a hole.] in zoology, situated in or pertaining to the front wall of the first gill cleft.

pret'ti·fȳ (prit'), *v.t.*; prettified, *pt.*, *pp.*; prettifying, *ppr.* to overembellish; to make pretty, especially in a finical way.

pret'ti·kin (prit'), *n.* [dim. from AS. *prætt*, a trick.] in the Orkney Islands, a feat or trick.

pret'ti·ly (prit'), *adv.* 1. in a pretty manner; with neatness and taste; pleasingly without magnificence or splendor; as, a woman *prettily* dressed.

2. with decency, good manners, and decorum.

Children kept out of ill company take a pride to behave themselves *prettily*. —Locke.

pret'ti·ness (prit'), *n.* the state or quality of being pretty; dainty beauty of feature; neatness and taste of finish; delicate harmony of sound.

pret'ty (prit'), *a.*; *comp.* prettier; *superl.* prettiest, [AS. *prættig*, crafty; possibly from LL. *practicus*, skilled.]

1. pleasing; attractive: implying daintiness, delicacy, or gracefulness rather than striking beauty, elegance, grandeur, or stateliness.

2. fine; good; nice: often used ironically.

3. foppish.

4. elegant. [Archaic.]

5. brave; bold; gallant. [Archaic or Scot.]

6. considerable; rather large in amount or extent. [Colloq.]

7. sly; crafty. [Obs.]

8. cunning; able. [Obs.]

Syn.—elegant, fine, dainty, handsome, agreeable.

pret'ty, *adv.* somewhat; to some extent or degree; tolerably; moderately; as, a farm *pretty* well stocked; a *pretty* wide river; a *pretty* good appetite.

pretty much; in a high degree; to a great extent; nearly all; as, a garment is *pretty much* worn out; the building is *pretty much* dilapidated; the cut of steak is *pretty much* bone. [Colloq.]

sitting pretty; in a favorable position. [Slang.]

Syn.—fairly.

pret'ty, *n.*; *pl.* **pret'tieṣ,** a pretty person or thing.

pret'ty-fāce, *n.* a small bulbous plant, *Calliprora lutea*, of the lily family, growing in California and characterized by its handsome umbellate yellow flowers shaped like stars.

pret'ty·ish, *a.* somewhat pretty.

pret'ty-spō''ken, *a.* spoken or speaking prettily; having an agreeable manner of speaking.

prē·typ'i·fȳ, *v.t.*; pretypified, *pt.*, *pp.*; pretypifying, *ppr.* to prefigure; to typify beforehand; to foreshadow.

pret'zel (-sel), *n.* [G.] a hard, brittle biscuit in the shape of a knotted ring made of slender rolls of dough, dipped in hot lye, and sprinkled with salt.

PRETZEL

prē·vāil', *v.i.*; prevailed, *pt.*, *pp.*; prevailing, *ppr.* [Fr. *prévaloir*; from L. *prævalere*; *præ*, before, and *valere*, to be strong or well.]

1. to overcome; to gain the victory or superiority; to gain the advantage: used often with *over* or *against*.

When Moses held up his hand, Israel *prevailed*. —Ex. xvii. 11.

This kingdom could never *prevail against* the united power of England. —Swift.

2. to be or become stronger or more widespread; to predominate.

3. to exist widely; to be in general use; to be prevalent.

4. to be effective; to produce or achieve the desired effect; to operate effectually; to succeed.

He had power over the angel, and *prevailed*. —Hos. xii. 4.

5. to persuade or induce: with *on*, *with*, or *upon*; as, they *prevailed on* the emperor to ratify the treaty; he *prevailed upon* his friend to accompany him.

prē·vāil'ing, *a.* [ppr. of *prevail*.]

1. being superior in strength or influence.

2. predominant.

3. widely existing; prevalent.

4. efficacious.

Syn.—predominant, dominant, ruling, efficacious, overcoming, prevalent, overruling, successful.

prē·vāil'ing·ly, *adv.* so as to prevail; with success.

prē·vāil'ment, *n.* prevalence. [Rare.]

prev'ȧ·lence, *n.* [Fr. *prévalence*; ML. *prævalentia*, from L. *prævalere*.]

1. predominance. [Rare.]

2. widespread existence; general practice, occurrence, or acceptance.

prev'ȧ·len·cy, *n.* prevalence.

prev'ȧ·lent, *a.* [L. *prævalens* (*-entis*), ppr. of *prævalere*, to prevail.]

1. prevailing; gaining or having the superiority; superior in force, influence, or efficacy; victorious; efficacious. [Rare.]

2. widely spread or current; generally received, adopted, or practiced; prevailing; as, a *prevalent* disease, opinion, rumor, belief, sentiment, etc.

prev'ȧ·lent·ly, *adv.* in a widespread manner.

prē·var'i·çāte, *v.i.*; prevaricated, *pt.*, *pp.*; prevaricating, *ppr.* [L. *prævaricari*, to prevaricate, to be guilty of collusion; *præ*, before, and *varicus*, straddling, from *varus*, bent.]

1. to quibble; to shift or turn aside from or evade the truth; to equivocate or speak evasively.

2. loosely, to lie.

3. in civil law, to collude, as where an informer colludes with the defendant and makes a sham prosecution. [Obs.]

4. in common law, to undertake a thing falsely and deceitfully with the purpose of defeating or destroying it. [Obs.]

Syn.—evade, equivocate.—One who *evades* a question ostensibly answers it, but really turns aside to some other point; he who *equivocates* uses words which have a double meaning, so that in one sense he can claim to have said the truth, though he does in fact deceive, and intends to do it; he who *prevaricates* talks all around the question, hoping to dodge it by confusing the issue and disclose nothing.

prē·var'i·çāte, *v.t.* to pervert; to corrupt; to evade by a quibble. [Obs.]

prē·var·i·çā'tion, *n.* 1. a prevaricating or quibbling to evade the truth or the disclosure of truth; the practice of some trick for evading what is just or honorable; a deviation from the plain path of truth and fair dealing.

2. in civil law, the collusion of an informer with the defendant for the purpose of making a sham prosecution. [Obs.]

3. in common law, a false or apparent undertaking of a thing for the purpose of defeating or destroying it. [Obs.]

4. a secret abuse in the exercise of a public office or commission. [Obs.]

prē·var'i·çā·tŏr, *n.* 1. one who prevaricates; a quibbler.

2. one who abuses a trust. [Obs.]

prēve, *v.t.* and *v.i.* to prove. [Obs.]

prēve, *n.* proof. [Obs.]

prev'ē·nănce, *n.* [Fr.] the act of going before.

prev'ē·năn·cy, *n.* [Fr. *prévenance*.] anticipatory courtesy or civility; readiness to oblige. [Rare.]

prē·vēne', *v.t.* [L. *prævenire*; *præ*, before, and *venire*, to come.] to come or go before; hence, to hinder. [Obs.]

prē·vēn'ience (-yens), *n.* the condition or fact of being prevenient.

prē·vēn'ient (-yent), *a.* [L. *præveniens* (*-entis*), ppr. of *prævenire*, to go before.]

1. going before; preceding.

2. anticipating; expectant.

3. antecedent to human action; as, *prevenient* grace.

prē·vent', *v.t.*; prevented, *pt.*, *pp.*; preventing, *ppr.* [L. *prævenire*, *præventus*, to anticipate; *præ*, before, and *venire*, to come.]

1. formerly, (a) to act in anticipation of (an event or a fixed time); (b) to anticipate (a desire, want, objection, etc.); (c) to anticipate in action; (d) to precede; (e) to forestall; balk; frustrate.

2. to stop or keep from doing something.

3. to keep from happening; to make impossible by prior action; to hinder.

4. to preoccupy (one's mind). [Obs.]

Syn.—block, stop, thwart, debar, repress, interrupt.

prē·vent', *v.i.* to come before the usual time. [Obs.]

prē·vent·ȧ·bil'i·ty, *n.* the quality or the condition of being preventable.

prē·vent'ȧ·ble, *a.* capable of being prevented or hindered: also spelled *preventible*.

prē·vent'ȧ·tive, *n.* and *a.* same as *preventive*.

prē·vent'ẽr, *n.* 1. one who goes before. [Obs.]

2. one who hinders; a hinderer; that which hinders; as, a *preventer* of evils or of disease.

3. in nautical language, any contrivance of rope, spar, cable, etc. to secure stays by bracing; as, a *preventer* stay to the mainmast.

preventer bolts or *preventer plates*; bolts or plates used for attaching stays or braces in the rigging of a ship.

preventer stay; an auxiliary stay used to strengthen a mast, etc.

prē·vent'ing·ly, *adv.* in such a manner or way as to hinder.

prē·ven'tion, *n.* [Fr. *prévention*; LL. *præventio*, from L. *præventus*, pp. of *prævenire*, to anticipate.]

1. the act of going before. [Obs.]

2. anticipation. [Obs.]

3. the act of hindering or preventing.

4. a means of preventing; hindrance; an obstacle.

5. prejudice; prepossession. [Obs.]

prē·ven'tion·ăl, *a.* tending to prevent. [Obs.]

prē·vent'ive, *a.* [Fr. *préventif*.] anticipating; preventing or serving to prevent; specifically, in medicine, preventing disease: also *preventative*.

preventive service; in England, a service rendered by armed men in preventing smuggling along the coast; the coast guard. [Obs.]

prē·vent'ive, *n.* that which prevents; specifically, in medicine, something administered to prevent disease; a prophylactic: also *preventative*.

prē·vent'ive·ly, *adv.* by way of prevention; in a manner that tends to hinder.

prē·vẽr'tē·brăl, *a.* situated in front of a vertebra.

prē'view (-vū), *n.* 1. a previous view or survey.

2. (a) a private showing of a motion picture, fashion show, etc. before exhibition to the public; (b) a showing of scenes from a motion picture in order to advertise its coming appearance: also spelled *prevue.*

prē·view′ (-vū′), *v.t.*; previewed, *pt., pp.*; previewing, *ppr.* 1. to show, as a performance or an exhibition, before exhibition to the public; as, they *previewed* the film and invited many actors to see it.

2. to view or see, as a performance or exhibition, before public showing; as, we were invited to *preview* the play.

prē′vi·ous, *a.* [L. *prævius*; *præ*, before, and *via*, way.]

1. going before in time or order; being or happening before something else; antecedent; prior; as, a *previous* intimation of a design; a *previous* notion; a *previous* event.

2. too early; premature. [Colloq.]

previous to; before.

Syn.—antecedent, preceding, anterior, prior, foregoing, former, preliminary, preparatory, introductory.

prē′vi·ous·ly, *adv.* at a previous time; beforehand; antecedently; as, a plan *previously* formed.

prē′vi·ous·ness, *n.* antecedence; priority in time.

prē′vi·ous ques′tion (-chun), the question whether a matter under consideration by a parliamentary body should be voted on immediately: in the United States, generally, a negative vote does not postpone further consideration of the matter as it does in England.

prē·vīşe′, *v.t.*; prevised, *pt., pp.*; prevising, *ppr.* [L. *prævisus*, pp. of *prævidere*, to foresee.]

1. to know or see beforehand. [Rare.]

2. to notify or warn beforehand. [Rare.]

prē·vi′şion (-vizh′un), *n.* [L. *prævisus*, pp. of *prævidere*, to foresee; *præ*, before, and *videre*, to see.]

1. foresight; foreknowledge; prescience.

2. a prophetic or anticipatory vision or prognostication.

prē·vi′şion·ăl, *a.* of prevision.

prē″vō·cā′tion·ăl, *a.* designating or pertaining to vocational training, instruction, or experience, as in the practical arts or in manual labor, required before admission to a vocational school, or sometimes given as an introductory course or courses.

prē·voy′ănt, *a.* [Fr. *prévoyant*, ppr. of *prévoir*, L. *prævidere*, to foresee.] having ability to foresee; prescient. [Rare.]

prē′vūe, *n.* same as *preview*, sense 2 b.

prē′wạr′, *a.* before the war.

prē·wạrn′, *v.t.*; prewarned, *pt., pp.*; prewarning, *ppr.* to warn beforehand. [Rare.]

prex′y, *n.*; *pl.* **prex′ies,** [contr. of *president.*] the president, especially of a college or university: also *prex.* [Slang.]

prēy, *n.* [L. *præda*, booty, from *prehendere*, to seize.]

1. originally, spoil; booty; plunder; goods taken by force from an enemy in war, sometimes including captives; as, Judah shall be a *prey.*

They brought the captives and the *prey.*
—Num. xxxi. 12.

2. an animal hunted or killed for food by another animal.

3. a person or thing that falls victim to someone or something.

4. the act or habit of seizing other animals for food; as, a bird of *prey.*

Hog in sloth, fox in stealth, lion in *prey.*
—Shak.

beast of prey; see under *beast.*

bird of prey; see under *bird.*

prēy, *v.i.*; preyed, *pt., pp.*; preying, *ppr.* 1. to plunder; pillage; rob.

2. to hunt or kill other animals for food.

3. to make profit from a victim by swindling, etc.

4. to have a wearing or destructive influence; to weigh heavily.

Generally used with *on* or *upon.*

prēy′ẽr, *n.* he who or that which preys; a plunderer; a waster; a devourer.

prēy′fụl, *a.* 1. full of prey; rich in game or booty. [Obs.]

2. of a preying disposition; given to prey; savage. [Obs.]

prī′ăl, *n.* pair royal. [Brit. Dial.]

Prī′ăm, *n.* [L. *Priamus*; Gr. *Priamos.*] in Greek legend, the last king of Troy, who reigned during the Trojan War, father of Hector and Paris.

Prī·ȧ·pē′ăn, *n.* [L. *Priapeia*, a collection of poems upon *Priapus* by various authors.] in ancient prosody, a species of hexameter divisible into two parts of three feet each, as follows:

—◡|—◡◡|—◡—||—◡|—◡◡|——|.

Prī·ȧ·pē′ăn, *a.* 1. of or relating to a Priapean.

2. relating to Priapus, the god of procreation.

Prī·ap′iç, *a.* same as *Priapean*, sense 2.

prī′ȧ·pişm, *n.* [from L. *Priapus.*] a pathological condition characterized by persistent and abnormal erection of the penis, usually without sexual desire.

Prī·ā′pus, *n.* [L.; Gr. *Priapos.*]

1. in Greek and Roman mythology, a god personifying the male function of generation, conceived as the son of Dionysus and Aphrodite; the god of procreation.

2. [p–] a representation or symbol of the male generative organ; a phallus.

3. [p–] the genitals of a male.

prīce, *n.* [OFr. *pris*; Fr. *prix*; L. *pretium*, price.]

1. the amount of money, etc. asked or given for something; cost; charge.

2. value; worth.

3. a reward for the capture or death of a person.

4. money or other consideration as a bribe; as, some people think that every man has his *price.*

5. the cost, as in life, labor, sacrifice, etc., of obtaining some benefit or advantage.

at any price; no matter what the cost.

beyond (or *without*) *price*; priceless; invaluable.

to make a price; to set a price for an object one has for sale.

to set a price on one's head; to offer a reward for the capture of a person, dead or alive.

Syn.—charge, cost, expense, expenditure, outlay, value, worth.

prīce, *v.t.*; priced (-prīst), *pt., pp.*; pricing, *ppr.* 1. to pay for. [Obs.]

2. to set a price on; to fix the price of; to appraise.

3. to ask for or find out the price of, as in shopping. [Colloq.]

prīce cŏn·trōl′, the establishment of ceiling prices on basic commodities by a government to prevent or combat inflation.

prīce çur′rent, a list or table containing the current prices of merchandise, stocks, specie, bills of exchange, rate of exchange, etc.

prīced (prīst), *a.* set at a value: used in hyphenated compounds: as, high-*priced*, low-*priced.*

prīce′-ēarn′ingş rā′tiō (-shō), the ratio of the current market price of a share of stock to the corporation's annual earnings per share.

prīce fix′ing, the setting or maintenance of prices at a certain level, especially by mutual agreement of competitors.

prīce′īte, *n.* [after Thomas *Price*, Am. metallurgist.] a chalky-white mineral, hydrous calcium borate, closely related to colemanite.

prīce′less, *a.* 1. invaluable; too valuable to admit of a price.

2. without value; worthless or unsalable. [Rare.]

3. very amusing or absurd. [Colloq.]

prīce list, 1. same as *price current.*

2. a list printed and used by a dealer in any special line of manufacture or merchandise; as, a *price list* of apparatus, fixtures, musical instruments, books, motors, etc.

prīce sup′pōrt, support of certain price levels at or above market values, especially by government action, as by buying up surpluses.

prīce wạr, a situation in which competitors, selling a certain commodity, successively lower prices, as to force one or more out of business.

prick, *n.* [AS. *prica*, point; Ir. *pricadh*, goad.]

1. a slender pointed instrument or substance, which is hard enough to pierce the skin; a thorn; a goad; a small sharp-pointed thing. [Archaic.]

Pins, wooden *pricks*, nails. —Shak.

2. a very small puncture or, formerly, dot, made by a sharp point.

No asps were discovered in the place of her death, only two small insensible *pricks* were found in her arm. —Browne.

3. a pricking.

4. a sharp pain caused by or as if by being pricked; figuratively, a stinging or tormenting thought; remorse.

5. a dot, point, or small mark; specifically, (a) the point on a target at which an archer shoots; (b) a mark on a dial noting the hour; (c) a mark denoting degree; pitch; (d) a mathematical point. [Obs.]

6. the print of the foot of a hare on the ground.

7. a small roll; as, a *prick* of spun yarn; a *prick* of tobacco.

prick, *v.t.*; pricked, *pt., pp.*; pricking, *ppr.* 1. to pierce with a sharp-pointed instrument or substance; to puncture; as, to *prick* one with a pin, a needle, a thorn, or the like.

2. to make (a hole) with a sharp point.

3. to fix by the point; as, to *prick* a knife into a board. [Obs.]

4. to hang on a point. [Obs.]

The cooks *prick* a slice on a prong of iron.
—Sandys.

5. to fasten by means of a pin or pointed instrument. [Obs.]

An old hat and the humor of forty fancies *pricked* in't for a feather. —Shak.

6. to designate or set apart by a puncture or mark: frequently with *off.*

Let the soldiers for duty be carefully *pricked off.* —Scott.

7. to spur; to goad; to incite: often with *on.* [Archaic.]

My duty *pricks* me *on* to utter that
Which else no worldly good should draw from me. —Shak.

8. to affect with sharp pain; to sting, as with remorse.

When they heard this they were *pricked* in their heart. —Acts ii. 37.

9. to mark or trace by dots or points; to trace by puncturing; as, to *prick* the notes of a piece of music; to *prick* a pattern for embroidery.

10. to render acid or pungent to the taste; as, the wine is *pricked.*

11. in nautical language, to run a middle seam through, as the cloth of a sail.

12. in horseshoeing, to pierce (a horse's foot) to the quick, causing lameness.

to prick the ship off; to mark or trace a ship's course or position on a chart.

to prick up; to rise erect; to point or stick up.

to prick up one's (or *its*) *ears*; (a) to raise the ears with the points upward; (b) to listen closely.

prick, *v.i.* 1. to give or feel a slight piercing or sharp pain.

2. to have a prickly or stinging sensation; to tingle.

3. in horticulture, to transfer seedlings from seed pans to shallow boxes (with *off* or *out*).

4. to become acid; as, cider *pricks* in the rays of the sun.

5. to dress oneself for show. [Dial.]

6. to spur on; to ride rapidly; to post. [Archaic.]

The fiery duke is *pricking* fast across St. André's plain. —Macaulay.

7. to aim at a point, mark, or place.

8. to stand erect.

prick, *a.* carried stiffly erect: said of a dog's ears.

prick′-ēared (-ērd), *a.* having the ears pointed or erect: an epithet commonly applied by the Cavaliers to the Puritans because, their hair being cut close all round, their ears stuck up prominently.

prick′ẽr, *n.* 1. that which pricks; a sharp-pointed instrument; a prickle; specifically, (a) in blasting and gunnery, a rod which makes an opening for the priming wire which makes a connection between the fuse or other igniting device and the charge; (b) in saddlery, a toothed instrument for marking or stabbing holes for sewing leather, etc.; (c) in nautical language, a small marlinespike for making and stretching the holes for points and rope bands in sails.

2. one who pricks; specifically, (a) a light-horseman; (b) one who tested whether women were witches by sticking pins into them; a witch-finder.

prick′et, *n.* 1. a wax candle or taper. [Obs.]

2. a spike on which to impale a candle for burning; also, a candlestick having such a spike.

3. a buck in his second year, with straight, unbranched antlers.

I said the deer was not a haud credo; 'twas a *pricket.* —Shak.

prick′ing, *n.* 1. the act or process of one that pricks.

2. a prickly feeling.

3. in farriery, the act of driving a nail into a horse's foot so as to cause lameness.

4. the making of an incision at the root of a horse's tail to make him carry it higher.

5. the prick or mark left by an animal's foot, as a hare; therefore, the act of tracing an animal by such a mark.

6. the condition of becoming acid, as wine.

pricking for sheriffs; the annual ceremony of making returns to the privy council by the judges of assize of three persons for each county in England and Wales from whom to select the sheriff for the ensuing year. The ceremony is so called from the appointment being made by marking a name with the prick of a pin.

pricking up; in building, the first coating of plaster upon lath; a scratch coat.

prick'ing nōte, a document delivered by a shipper of goods authorizing the receiving of them on board: so called from a practice of pricking holes in the paper corresponding to the number of packages counted into the ship. [Brit.]

prick'ing wheel (hwēl), a small-toothed wheel set in a handle, used by harness makers to mark the place for stitches, or by dressmakers in tracing patterns; a tracing wheel.

prick'le, *n.* [ME. *prykel*; AS. *pricel*, earlier *pricels*, from base of *prica*, a point, and *-els*, instrumental suffix.]

1. a small, sharply pointed growth; a spine; a thorn.

2. a prickly sensation; a stinging or tingling.

3. in botany, a small, sharply pointed process growing from the tissue under the outer layer of a plant.

prick'le, *v.t.*; prickled, *pt., pp.*; prickling, *ppr.*

1. to prick as with a spine or thorn.

2. to cause to feel a tingling sensation.

prick'le, *v.i.* to tingle.

prick'le, *n.* 1. a kind of basket. [Brit. Dial.]

The *prickle* is a brown willow basket, in which walnuts are imported into this country (England). —Mayhew.

2. a sieve of filberts, containing about a half hundredweight. [Brit. Dial.]

prick'le·back, *n.* a fish, the stickleback.

prick'le cell, a cell provided with delicate radiating processes which connect with similar cells; found chiefly in the deep layers of stratified pavement epithelium.

prick'le·fish, *n.* a fish, the stickleback.

prick'le lāy'ẽr, the lowest layer of the epidermis, being made up of prickle cells.

prick'li·ness, *n.* the state or quality of being prickly.

prick'ling, *a.* prickly.

prick'louse, *n.* a tailor: contemptuous term. [Obs.]

prick'ly, *a.*; *comp.* pricklier; *superl.* prickliest.

1. full of prickles, or sharp points.

2. stinging; smarting; tingling.

prick'ly ash, a shrub or small tree of the genus *Xanthoxylum*, the common prickly ash of the northern states being *Xanthoxylum americanum*, having prickles, yellowish flowers, downy leaves when young, and small pods resembling peppercorns. The southern prickly ash is *Xanthoxylum carolinianum*.

prick'ly·back, *n.* the prickleback.

prick'ly cē'dăr, a European juniper, *Juniperus oxycedrus*.

prick'ly hēat, a noncontagious, itching and prickling skin eruption caused by inflammation of the sweat glands, as in hot weather.

prick'ly peãr, 1. any cactus of the genus *Opuntia*, as *Opuntia vulgaris*, growing on barren ground in the eastern and southern parts of the United States, and having flat stems.

2. the pear-shaped fruit of these cactuses.

PRICKLY PEAR

prick'ly pōle, a slender palm of the West Indies, *Bactris plumeriana*, having long prickles on its trunk.

prick'ly pop'py, any of a number of related plants with prickles, yellow juice, and large flowers of various colors.

prick'ly withe, a climbing plant, *Cereus triangularis*, growing in Jamaica and Mexico.

prick'mad"ăm, *n.* any one of several varieties of stonecrop. [Obs.]

prick pōst, same as *queen post*.

prick punch, a pointed piece of tempered steel used to prick marks on cold iron or other metal.

prick shȧft, a shaft for hitting the prick, or mark, of a target; an arrow. [Obs.]

prick sọng, 1. music written down in pricks, or dots; written music. [Obs.]

2. counterpoint; descant.

prick'tim"bẽr, *n.* the spindle tree, *Euonymus europæus*, or the dogwood, *Cornus sanguinea*: so named from the use of the wood as skewers.

prick wheel (hwēl), same as *pricking wheel*.

prick'wood, *n.* same as *pricktimber*.

prick'y, *a.* prickly. [Dial.]

prīde, *n.* [AS. *pryte*, from *prȳt*, proud.]

1. an overhigh opinion of oneself; exaggerated self-esteem; conceit.

2. the showing of this in behavior; haughtiness; arrogance.

3. a sense of one's own dignity or worth; self-respect.

4. delight or satisfaction in one's achievements, possessions, children, etc.

5. a person or thing in which pride is taken; as, his daughters are his *pride*.

6. the best of a class, group, society, etc.; pick; flower; as, the *pride* of the Yankees.

7. the best part or time; prime; flowering; as, in the *pride* of manhood.

8. mettle (in a horse).

9. (a) magnificence; splendor; (b) ornament. [Archaic.]

10. sexual desire, or heat, especially in a female animal. [Obs.]

11. wantonness; extravagance; excess. [Obs.]

12. in heraldry, the state of having the tail expanded; as, a peacock in his *pride*.

13. a group, as of lions. [Archaic.]

14. lameness. [Brit. Dial.]

Syn.—vanity, conceit, self-esteem, self-satisfaction, self-respect, vainglory.

prīde, *v.t.*; prided, *pt., pp.*; priding, *ppr.* to make proud. [Rare.]

to pride oneself on; to be proud of.

prīde, *v.i.* to be proud. [Rare.]

prīde, *n.* the sand pride.

prīde'fụl, *a.* full of pride; insolent; proud; haughty.

prīde'fụl·ly, *adv.* in a prideful manner.

prīde'fụl·ness, *n.* the state or quality of being prideful.

prīde'less, *a.* lacking pride; without pride.

prīde ŏf In'di·ȧ, a tropical tree with purple or white flowers: also called *pride of China*.

Prīde's Pũrge, the expulsion in 1648 of over 100 Royalist and Presbyterian members from the English House of Commons: conducted by Thomas Pride.

prid'i·ăn, *a.* [L. *pridianus*; *prius*, before, and *dies*, day.] pertaining or belonging to the previous day. [Rare.]

prīd'ing·ly, *adv.* with pride; in pride of heart. [Rare.]

prīe, *v.i.* to pry. [Obs.]

priē-dieu' (-dyẽ'), *n.* [Fr. *prier*, to pray, and *dieu*, God.] a small, low reading desk with a ledge for kneeling at prayer.

priēf, *n.* proof. [Obs.]

prī'ẽr, *n.* one who pries: also spelled *pryer*.

priēst, *n.* [AS. *preōst*; Ice. *prestr*; Fr. *prêtre*; LL. *presbyter*, a presbyter, elder.]

1. originally, in the early Christian church, a presbyter, or elder.

2. in hierarchical Christian churches, a clergyman ranking next below a bishop and authorized to administer the sacraments and pronounce absolution.

3. any clergyman: distinguished from *layman*.

4. a minister of any religion.

5. a person whose function is to make sacrificial offerings and perform other religious rites.

6. a person whose duties, attitude, etc. are like a priest's.

priēst, *v.t.* to ordain as a priest.

priēst'çap, *n.* in fortification, an outwork with three salient and two entering angles.

priēst'crȧft, *n.* the craft, policies, methods, etc. of priests: often, in a derogatory sense, the scheming or intrigues of priests.

priēst'ẽr·y, *n.* the priesthood: used as a term of contempt. [Rare.]

priēst'ess, *n.* a girl or woman priest, as of a pagan religion.

priēst'fish, *n.* a fish of California, *Sebastichthys mystinus*; the black rockfish.

priēst'hood, *n.* 1. the office, rank, or characteristics of a priest.

2. the order composed of priests; priests collectively.

priēst'ing, *n.* the office of a priest. [Obs.]

priēst'işm, *n.* the tenets, policy, characteristics, or power of priests or of the priesthood: a term of contempt.

priēst'less, *a.* having no priest.

priēst'līke, *a.* resembling a priest; priestly.

priēst'li·ness, *n.* the quality or state of being priestly.

priēst'ly, *a.*; *comp.* priestlier; *superl.* priestliest; of, like, suitable for, or pertaining to a priest or to priests; sacerdotal; as, the *priestly* office.

priēst'-rid"den, *a.* managed, dominated, tyrannized, or governed by priests.

priēve, *v.t.* to prove. [Obs.]

prig, *n.* 1. originally, any person regarded with dislike.

2. a person who affects great preciseness or propriety in matters of learning or morals, to the annoyance of others; a smug, pedantic person.

prig, *n.* a thief or pickpocket. [Brit. Slang.]

prig, *v.t.*; prigged, *pt., pp.*; prigging, *ppr.* to steal. [Brit. Slang.]

prig, *v.i.* to haggle about the price of a commodity. [Scot. or Brit. Dial.]

prig'gẽr·y, *n.* the character or behavior of a prig; priggism.

prig'gish, *a.* like or characteristic of a prig; smug; overprecise.

Syn.—coxcombical, dandified, foppish, affected, prim, conceited.

prig'gish·ly, *adv.* in a priggish manner.

prig'gish·ness, *n.* the state or quality of being priggish.

prig'gişm, *n.* the manners of a prig; priggery; priggishness.

prill, *n.* a brill. [Obs.]

prill, *v.i.* to flow. [Obs.]

prill, *n.* a little stream. [Dial.]

prill, *n.* 1. the better portions of ore from which inferior pieces have been separated; also, a nugget of virgin metal.

2. a button of metal obtained from an assay of specimen ore. [Brit.]

pril'liŏn, *n.* tin extracted from slag.

prim, *n.* a plant, the privet.

prim, *a.*; *comp.* primmer; *superl.* primmest. [OFr. *prim*, prime, first; also, sharp, thin, slender, and hence neat; from L. *primus*, first; compare *prime*, to trim trees.] neat; stiffly formal, precise, or correct; proper; demure; affectedly nice.

The garden in its turn was to be set free from its *prim* regularity. —Walpole.

Syn.—formal, precise, demure, stiff, self-conscious, unbending.

prim, *v.t.*; primmed, *pt., pp.*; primming, *ppr.* to produce a prim expression on (one's face or mouth); to form with affected preciseness.

prim, *v.i.* to make oneself prim; to act in a prim or formal manner.

prī'mȧ, *a.* [It.] in music, first.

prī'mȧ·cy, *n.*; *pl.* **prī'mȧ·cieș,** [OFr. *primacie*, *primatie*; LL. *primatia*, primacy; L. *primus*, first.]

1. the state of being first in time, order, rank, importance, etc.; the fact of being primary; supremacy.

2. the rank, duties, or authority of a primate.

3. in the Roman Catholic Church, the supreme authority of the Pope.

prī'mȧ don'nȧ, *pl.* **prī'mȧ don'nȧș,** [It., lit., first lady.]

1. the principal woman singer in an opera or concert.

2. a temperamental, conceited, or vain person; especially, such a woman. [Colloq.]

prī'mȧ-fā'ci·ē (-shi-), *a.* in law, adequate to establish a fact or raise a presumption of fact unless refuted: said of evidence.

prī'mȧ fā'ci·ē (-shi-), [L.] at first sight; on first view; before further examination.

prī'măġe (-mij), *n.* [ML. *primagium*; perh. from It. *primo* (*legno*), keel.]

1. formerly, a small fee paid by a shipper to a ship's master and crew for loading and taking care of his freight.

2. now, a small percentage added to freight charge and paid to the ship's owner.

Also called *hat money*.

prī'măl, *a.* [LL. *primalis*, from L. *primus*, first.]

1. first in time; original; primitive; primeval.

The *primal* father of our line. —Blackie.

2. first in importance; chief; primary.

3. [P—] in geology, applied to the earliest Paleozoic series of the Appalachian basin.

prī·mal'i·ty, *n.* the state of being primal. [Rare.]

prī'mãr·i·ly (*or* prī-mãr'i-ly), *adv.* 1. at first; in the first instance; originally.

2. in the first place; principally.

prī'mãr·i·ness, *n.* the state of being first in time, act, or intention.

prī'mãr·y, *a.* [L. *primarius*, from *primus*, first.]

1. first in time or order of development; primitive; original; earliest; as, a *primary* instinct.

2. (a) from which others are derived; fundamental; elemental; (b) designating the colors regarded as basic, or as those from which

all others may be derived: the classification of colors as primary differs according to the point of view; thus, in color photography, red, green, and blue are considered primary, but in painting the term is applied to red, yellow, and blue.

3. of or in the first stage of a succession; elementary; preparatory; as, *primary* studies: distinguished from *secondary, tertiary*, etc.

4. first in importance; chief; principal; as, a *primary* policy.

5. in chemistry, (a) characterized by or resulting from the replacement of one atom or radical; (b) designating or characterized by one carbon atom united to not more than one other carbon atom in a molecule.

6. in electricity, designating or of an inducing current, circuit, or coil in an induction coil, etc.

7. in geology, designating or of the earliest periods, up through the Paleozoic Era.

8. in linguistics, (a) having as its fundamental form a base or other element that cannot be broken down: said of derivation; (b) referring to present or future time: said of Latin, Greek, and Sanskrit tenses.

9. in zoology, of the large, stiff feathers on the end joint of a bird's wing.

primary accent; (a) the heaviest accent, or stress, in pronouncing a word; (b) the mark for this, in this dictionary (ʹ), as in *plodʹding*.

primary amine; an amine in which one hydrogen atom is replaced by a univalent alkyl: distinguished from *secondary* and *tertiary amines*.

primary amputation; in surgery, an amputation performed just after the period of shock, just before the development of inflammation.

primary axis; in botany, the principal axis or stalk of any form of compound inflorescence.

primary battery; a single electric source comprising several separate primary cells.

primary cell; in electricity, a battery cell whose energy is derived from an irreversible electrochemical reaction and which is hence incapable of being recharged by an electric current.

primary coil; (a) that coil of an induction coil or transformer on which the primary electromotive force is impressed; (b) the driving coil of a transformer; (c) the coil that receives energy prior to transformation.

primary current; a current flowing in a primary circuit, as distinguished from a current flowing in a secondary circuit.

primary electromotive force; electromotive force applied to the primary coil of a transformer.

primary impedance; the impedance of the primary coil of a transformer or that of an induction machine.

primary meeting; a preliminary meeting of members of a political party to confer in regard to the nomination of candidates; a caucus.

primary nerves; in botany, the veins given off laterally from the midrib of a leaf.

primary pinna; in botany, a part of a compound leaf which branches from the main stem.

primary planets; see *primary* (n., 5).

primary qualities of bodies; qualities which are original and inseparable from bodies.

primary quills; in ornithology, the largest feathers of a bird's wings; the primaries.

primary rocks; in geology, the rocks of the Paleozoic Era and before.

primary salt; a salt in which the replacement of but one hydrogen atom by a basic radical has taken place in a polybasic acid.

primary school; a school providing elementary instruction; specifically, a school providing instruction for the first few years of the public-school course, as in the United States.

primary syphilis; syphilis in its first stage, characterized by a chancre and non-ulcerating buboes.

primary union; in surgery, healing by first intention; the union of two accurately apposed surfaces without any visible granulating process.

Syn.—first, primeval, primitive, chief, fundamental, original, radical.

prīʹmăr·y, *n.*; *pl.* **prīʹmăr·ieṣ,** 1. something first in order, quality, importance, etc.

2. in the United States, a local meeting of voters of a given political party to prepare for choosing candidates for public office, by selecting delegates to a nominating convention, etc.

3. [*often in pl.*] a direct primary election.

4. one of the primary colors.

5. in astronomy, a planet, etc. in relation to one or more smaller bodies (satellites) revolving around it.

6. in electricity, a primary coil.

7. in zoology, a primary feather.

8. in entomology, a fore wing of an insect.

prīʹmāte, *n.* [Fr. *primat*; LL. *primas*, of the first, from L. *primus*, first.]

1. a person with primacy. [Rare.]

2. an archbishop, or the highest-ranking bishop in a province, etc.

3. one of the *Primates*.

Primate of All England; the Archbishop of Canterbury.

Prī·māʹtēṣ, *n.pl.* [LL. *primas*, of the first; L. *primus*, first.] the most highly developed order of mammals, including man, the apes, lemurs, monkeys, etc.

prīʹmāte·ship, *n.* the rank or duties of an archbishop or primate.

prī·māʹtiăl (-shăl), *a.* [Fr., from ML. *primatia*, primacy.] pertaining to a primate.

prī·matʹiç·ăl, *a.* same as *primatial*.

prī·må·tolʹō·ġist, *n.* one versed in primatology.

prī·må·tolʹō·ġy, *n.* the branch of zoology dealing with primates, especially the apes, monkeys, and early hominids.

prīme, *a.* [L. *primus*, superl. of *prior*, former; same root as Gr. and L. *pro*, before.]

1. first in time; original; primeval; primitive.

2. first in rank, degree, influence, or dignity; as, *prime* minister.

3. first in importance or value; main; as, a *prime* advantage.

4. first in quality; of the highest excellence; as, a *prime* cut of beef.

5. early; blooming; being in the first stage. [Rare.]

His starry helm, unbuckled, showed him *prime*
In manhood, where youth ended.
—Milton.

6. from which others are derived; fundamental; elemental; as, the *prime* reason.

7. in mathematics, (a) that can be divided by no other whole number than itself or 1, as 3, 5, or 7; (b) that cannot be divided by the same whole number except 1; as, 9 and 16 are *prime* to one another.

8. marked by a sign (ʹ) called a prime mark.

prime conductor; see under *conductor*.

prime cost; the direct cost of labor and material in producing an article, exclusive of capital, overhead, etc.

prime factor; in arithmetic, a prime number which will exactly divide another number.

prime meridian; the meridian taken as a starting point from which to reckon longitude: it passes through Greenwich, England.

prime minister; in some countries, the chief executive of the government and, usually, head of the cabinet.

prime mover; (a) the original force in a series of transmissions of force; (b) any natural force applied by man to produce power, as muscular energy, flowing water, etc.; (c) a machine, as a turbine, that converts a natural force into productive power; (d) in Aristotelian philosophy, the first cause of all movement.

prime ribs; a choice cut of beef consisting of the seven ribs immediately before the loin.

prime time; in radio and television, the hours when the largest audience is regularly available; especially, the evening hours.

prime vertical; in astronomy, a great circle passing through the east and west points of the horizon and through the zenith.

prime vertical dial; a sundial projected on the plane of the prime vertical circle, or on one parallel to it.

prime vertical transit; a transit whose telescope revolves in the plane of the prime vertical.

prīme, *n.* 1. the earliest stage or beginning of anything; hence, the spring of the year.

2. the spring of life; youth; full health, strength, or beauty; hence, the highest or most perfect state or most flourishing condition of anything; as, the *prime* of life.

3. the best part; that which is best in quality.

4. in the Roman Catholic Church, the first daylight canonical hour, usually beginning at 6 A. M. or sunrise.

5. the first hour of the day, usually corresponding to this; dawn.

6. the best of several or many; pick; cream.

7. any of a number of equal parts, usually sixty, into which a unit of measure, as a degree, is divided, and which usually may in turn be subdivided in the same proportion.

8. in fencing, the first of the chief guards.

9. in chemistry, a number used in conformity with the theory of definite proportions, to express the ratios in which elements enter into combination.

10. same as *primero*.

11. in arithmetic, a prime number.

12. a mark or sign (ʹ) used with figures or letters to distinguish one from another of the same kind.

13. in music, (a) the tonic; (b) unison.

prīme, *v.t.*; primed, *pt., pp.*; priming, *ppr.* 1. to make ready; prepare.

2. to prepare (a gun) for firing by providing, formerly, with a charge of gunpowder, now, with a primer.

3. to get (a pump) into operation by pouring in water until the suction is established.

4. to undercoat, size, or otherwise prepare (a surface) for painting.

5. to provide (a person) beforehand with information, answers, etc.

6. to prune, as a tree. [Brit. Dial.]

7. in mathematics, to give a prime mark to.

prīme, *v.i.* 1. to prime a gun, pump, surface, person, etc.

2. in a steam engine, to let water in the form of spray mix with the steam forced from the boiler into the cylinder; as, the engine *primes*.

prīmeʹly, *adv.* 1. at first; originally; primarily. [Obs.]

2. excellently; in a prime manner or degree. [Colloq.]

prīmeʹness, *n.* the state or quality of being prime.

primʹẽr, *a.* first; original. [Obs.]

prīmʹẽr, *n.* 1. one who or that which primes.

2. a small tap, tube, etc. containing explosive, used to fire the main charge of a big gun.

primʹẽr, *n.* [Fr. *primaire*, elementary; L. *primarius*, from *primus*, first.]

1. originally, a small prayer book; also, a work of elementary religious instruction.

2. a small elementary book for teaching children to read or spell.

3. a textbook that gives the first principles of any subject.

4. in printing, one of two sizes of type, great primer (18 point) and long primer (10 point).

pri·me·rō (-mărʹō), *n.* [Sp., first.] an ancient game of cards.

primʹẽr·ōle, *n.* [OFr. *primerole, primverole*; LL. *primula veris*, primrose.] a primrose. [Obs.]

prīmʹẽr sēiʹzin, in feudal law, the right of the king, when a tenant in chief died seized of a knight's fee, to receive of the heir, if of full age, one year's profits of the land if in possession, and half a year's profits if the land was in reversion expectant on an estate for life.

prī·mēʹvăl, *a.* [L. *primævus*; *primus*, first, and *ævum*, age.] original; primitive; belonging to the first or earliest period; as, the *primeval* innocence of man.

Chaos and *primeval* darkness. —Keats.

prī·mēʹvăl·ly, *adv.* originally; in the earliest times or period.

prī·mēʹvous, *a.* primeval. [Rare.]

Primʹi·ăn·ist, *n.* one of the Donatists who followed Primianus, bishop of Carthage, in the fourth century.

prī·mi·ġēʹni·ăl, *a.* [L. *primigenius*; *primus*, first, and *gignere*, to beget.]

1. original; primary. [Obs.]

2. in zoology, designating or of a species of a primitive type.

prīʹmine, *n.* [L. *primus*, first.] in botany, the outer covering of an ovule.

prīmʹing, *n.* 1. the act of a person or thing that primes.

2. the gunpowder or other explosive used to fire a charge in a gun or in blasting.

3. an undercoat or first coat of paint, sizing, etc.

priming of the tide; the acceleration of the tide wave, or amount of shortening of the tide day in the second and fourth quarters of the moon.

prīmʹing horn, the powder horn of a miner or quarryman.

prīmʹing valve, a spring valve fitted to the end of a cylinder, to permit the escape of water without danger to the machinery from the shock of the piston against the incompressible fluid.

prīm'ing wire, a pointed wire used to penetrate the vent of a firearm for piercing the cartridge.

prī·mip'à·rȧ, *n.*; *pl.* **prī·mip'à·rae,** [L., from *primus*, first, and *parere*, to bear.] a woman who is pregnant for the first time or who has borne just one child.

prī·mi·par'i·ty, *n.* the fact or condition of being a primipara.

prī·mip'à·rous, *a.* [L. *primipara*; *primus*, first, and *parere*, to bring forth.] of or being a primipara or primiparae.

prī·mip'i·lăr, *a.* [L. *primipilaris*, from *primipilus*, the first centurion of a Roman legion.] pertaining to the first centurion or captain of the body of veterans that formed a regular portion of a Roman legion.

prī·mi'ti·ae (-mish'i-), *n.pl.* [L., from *primus*, first.] the first fruits of any production of the earth; specifically, the first year's profits of an ecclesiastical benefice.

prī·mi'tiăl (-mish'ăl), *a.* being of the first production.

prim'i·tive, *a.* [L. *primitivus*, from *primus*, first.]
1. pertaining to the beginning or the earliest times or ages; original; first; as, *primitive* civilizations.
2. characterized by or imitative of the earliest times; crude; simple; rough; as, *primitive* weapons.

This stern, never-to-be-changed, *primitive* idea. —Susan Keating Glaspell.

3. original; primary; underived; as, a *primitive* verb in grammar.
4. in biology, (a) primordial; (b) designating species, etc. very little evolved from early ancestral types.
5. in geology, of the earliest formation.

primitive chord; in music, a chord whose lowest note is of the same literal denomination as the fundamental bass of the harmony.

primitive circle; in the stereographic projection of the sphere, the circle on the plane of which the projection is made.

primitive colors; same as *primary colors*: see *primary* (a., 2).

primitive groove; a lengthwise furrow on the outer surface of the primitive streak.

primitive plane; in spherical projection, the plane upon which the projections are made, generally coinciding with some principal circle of the sphere.

primitive rocks; same as *primary rocks*.

primitive sheath; the neurilemma.

primitive streak or *trace*; a faint white trace at the uppermost end of the germinal area, formed by an aggregation of cells, and constituting the first indication of the development of the blastoderm.

Syn.—primeval, original, primordial, first, radical, pristine, simple, unsophisticated, archaic.

prim'i·tive, *n.* 1. a primitive person or thing.
2. an artist or a work of art that belongs to or is suggestive of an early period.
3. an original word; a form from which a word or other form is derived; root; base: distinguished from *derivative*.
4. in algebra and geometry, a form from which another is derived.

prim'i·tive·ly, *adv.* 1. originally; at first.
2. primarily; not derivatively.
3. according to the original rule or ancient practice.

prim'i·tive·ness, *n.* the state or quality of being primitive.

prim'i·tiv·işm, *n.* belief in or practice of primitive ways, living, etc.

prim'ly, *adv.* in a prim manner; precisely.

prim'ness, *n.* affected formality or niceness; stiffness; preciseness.

prī'mō, *a.* [It.] in music, first; leading; pertaining to the leading part.

prī'mō, *n.* in music, the leading or principal part.

prī·mō·ġē'ni·ăl, *a.* same as *primigenial*.

prī·mō·ġen'i·tive, *n.* primogeniture. [Obs.]

prī·mō·ġen'i·tive, *a.* of or pertaining to primogeniture.

prī·mō·ġen'i·tŏr, *n.* [L. *primus*, first, and *genitor*, father.]
1. an ancestor; a forefather.
2. the earliest ancestor of a family, race, etc.

prī·mō·ġen'i·tūre, *n.* [Fr. *primogéniture*, from L. *primus*, first, and *genitura*, a begetting, from *gignere*, to beget.]
1. the state of being born first of the same parents.
2. in law, the right of the eldest son to inherit the estate of his father.

prī·mō·ġen'i·tūre·ship, *n.* the state or privileges of one who is the firstborn. [Rare.]

prī·mọr'di·ăl, *a.* [L. *primordialis*; *primus*, first, and *ordiri*, to begin.]
1. first in time; existing from the beginning; primitive.
2. underived; fundamental; original.
3. in geology, of or pertaining to the Cambrian strata; showing the first traces of life.
4. in biology, first formed in the growth of an individual or organ; as, a *primordial* cell.

primordial cell; a cell having no cell wall.

primordial utricle; the layer of protoplasm which lines a vegetable cell.

prī·mọr'di·ăl, *n.* origin; first principle or element. [Rare.]

prī·mọr'di·ăl·işm, *n.* continuance of the primordial state.

prī·mọr·di·al'i·ty, *n.* the state or condition of being promordial.

prī·mọr'di·ăl·ly, *adv.* in a primordial manner.

prī·mọr'di·āte, *a.* original; existing from the first. [Rare.]

prī·mọr'di·um, *n.*; *pl.* **prī·mọr'di·ȧ,** [L., earliest beginning.] in embryology, the first recognizable aggregation of cells that will form a distinct organ or part of the embryo.

prim·os'i·ty, *n.* the state of being prim; prudery. [Rare.]

primp, *v.i.* and *v.t.*; primped (primpt), *pt.*, *pp.*; primping, *ppr.* [formed on *prink*, variant of prim.] to dress overcarefully or showily; to prink.

prim'rōşe, *n.* [OFr. *primerose*, altered (by association with *rose*) from *primerole*, dim. of *primule*, from LL. *primula*, from L. *primus*, first.]
1. an early flowering plant, *Primula veris*, of several varieties, as the white, the red, and the yellow, whose tubelike flowers have five lobes; also, any plant of the same genus, as the cowslip, polyanthus, oxlip, etc.
2. the flower of any of these plants.
3. a light yellow color.

Primrose League; an association of men and women formed in London in 1883, in the interest of the Conservative party, and named after the favorite flower of Benjamin Disraeli, Earl of Beaconsfield, the former leader of the party.

prim'rōşe, *a.* 1. of the color of the primrose; light-yellow.
2. abounding in or suggestive of primroses; flowery; gay.

prim'rōşed, *a.* bedecked with primroses.

prim'rōşe pȧth, [popularized after Shakespeare, *Hamlet*, I, iii.] the path of pleasure.

prim'sie, *a.* demure; prim. [Scot.]

Prim'ū·lȧ, *n.* [LL.] the genus of plants that includes the European primrose, *Primula veris*; also, [p—] a plant of this genus.

Prim·ū·lā'cē·ae, *n.pl.* [*Primula* and *-aceæ*.] a family of monopetalous exogenous herbs distinguished by having the stamens opposite to the lobes of the corolla, and by a superior capsule with a free central placenta.

prim·ū·lā'ceous, *a.* of or pertaining to the *Primulaceæ*.

Prim·ū·lā'lēş, *n.pl.* [LL., from *Primula*.] a series of gamopetalous plants comprising the families *Primulaceæ*, *Plumbaginaceæ*, and *Myrsineæ*.

prī'mum mo'bi·lē, [L.] in Ptolemaic astronomy, the tenth and outermost of the revolving spheres of the universe, which was supposed to give motion to all the others; hence, any great or original source of motion.

Prī'mus, *n.* [L., first.] in the Episcopal Church of Scotland, a bishop who presides at the meetings of the bishops and has certain privileges, but is without metropolitan authority.

prīm'y, *a.* being in its prime. [Rare.]

prince, *n.* [Fr., from L. *princeps*, *principis*, a prince, from *primus*, first, and *capere*, to take.]
1. one who holds the first or chief place or rank; a sovereign; the ruler of a country or state; especially, a king: originally applied to either sex.

The greatest *prince* that has ever ruled England. —Macaulay.

2. the ruler or sovereign of a principality, whose rank is below that of king.
3. the son of a sovereign, or the issue of a royal family; as, the *princes* of the blood. In English heraldic language, the courtesy title of prince belongs to dukes, marquises, and earls of Great Britain, but in ordinary use it is confined to members of the royal family.
4. the English equivalent of any of various titles of nobility in other languages.
5. the chief of any class or group; one who is pre-eminent in his class, profession, or vocation; as, a merchant *prince*; a *prince* of players.

Prince Albert; [after *Prince Albert*, consort of Victoria of England.] a long, double-breasted frock coat.

prince consort; the husband of a queen or empress who reigns in her own right.

Prince of Darkness; see under *darkness*.

Prince of Peace; Jesus Christ.

Prince of Wales; the oldest son of the reigning English sovereign.

prince royal; the oldest son of a king or queen.

prince, *v.i.* to play the prince. [Rare.]

prince'āġe, *n.* princes collectively. [Rare.]

prince'dŏm, *n.* 1. the rank or dignity of a prince.
2. the territory over which a prince rules; a principality.

prince'hood, *n.* the quality or rank of a prince.

Prince'īte, *n.* one of the Agapemone.

prince'kin, *n.* a princeling.

prince'less, *a.* having no prince.

prince'let, *n.* a princeling.

prince'līke, *a.* princely.

prince'li·ness, *n.* the state or quality of being a prince.

prince'ling, *n.* a young, small, or subordinate prince.

prince'ly, *a.*; *comp.* princelier; *superl.* princeliest, 1. that is a prince.
2. characteristic of a prince; liberal; generous.
3. of a prince; royal; grand; august; noble.
4. magnificent; rich; befitting a prince; lavish; as, a *princely* entertainment.

Syn.—imperial, munificent, magnificent, superb, august, regal, royal, supreme.

prince'ly, *adv.* in a princelike manner.

prin'ceps, *n.*; *pl.* **prin'ci·pēş,** [L., chief.]
1. one who or that which is first.
2. in ancient Teutonic history, a chieftain of a pagus.

prin'ceps, *a.* [L.] first; original; of the first edition.

prin'ce's·feath'ẽr (-feth'), *n.* in botany, either of two annual plants, *Polygonum orientale* or *Amarantus caudatus*, bearing apetalous flowers of a reddish color, arranged in long, paniculate, recurved spikes.

prin'ce's pīne, same as *pipsissewa*.

prin'cess, *n.* 1. originally, a woman sovereign.
2. a nonreigning female member of a royal family.
3. in Great Britain, a daughter of the sovereign or of a son of the sovereign.
4. the wife of a prince.
5. any woman regarded as having the characteristics, position, etc. of a princess.

princess royal; the oldest daughter of a sovereign.

prin·cesse' (*or* prin'ses), *a.* [Fr., princess.] in dressmaking, made long and close-fitting, with the skirt and waist in one, unbroken at the waistline; as, a *princesse* gown.

prin'cess·līke, *a.* having the characteristics or manner of a princess.

prin'cess·ly, *adv.* in the manner of a princess.

prince'wood, *n.* in botany, a brown, light-veined wood obtained from two small trees, *Cordia gerascanthoides* and *Hamelia ventricosa*, native to the West Indies.

princ'i·fīed, *a.* having the manner of a prince.

prin'ci·păl, *a.* [Fr., from L. *principalis*, from *princeps*, chief.]
1. chief; highest in rank, character, or respectability; as, the *principal* officers of a government.
2. chief; most important or considerable; as, the *principal* topics of debate; the *principal* points of law; the *principal* productions of a country.
3. pertaining to a prince; princely. [Obs.]

principal axis; same as *axis of a curve* under *axis*.

principal challenge; same as *challenge*, n. 7.

principal parts; the principal inflected forms of a verb, from which the other forms may be derived: in English, the principal parts are the present infinitive, the past tense, and the past participle (e.g., *drink, drank, drunk; go, went, gone; add, added, added*).

principal plane; same as *perspective plane* under *plane*.

principal ray; the line passing through the point of sight vertical to the perspective plane.

principal section; in crystallography, that section containing the optic axis.

Syn.—capital, important, cardinal, chief, main, essential, prime, first, leading, head, foremost.

prin'ci·păl, *n.* 1. a principal person or thing; specifically, (a) a chief; head; (b) a governing or presiding officer, as of a school; (c) a main actor or performer; (d) a combatant in a duel: distinguished from *second*.

2. one of the main end rafters of a roof, supporting the purlins, which in turn support the ordinary rafters.

3. in finance, (a) the amount of a debt, investment, etc. minus the interest, or on which interest is computed; (b) the face value of a stock or bond; (c) the main body of an estate, etc., as distinguished from income.

4. in law, (a) a person who employs another to act as his agent; (b) the person primarily responsible for an obligation: distinguished from *surety*; (c) a person who commits a crime or is present as an abettor to it: distinguished from *accessory*.

5. in music, (a) in German organs, the open diapason in 4-foot, 8-foot, 16-foot, and 32-foot stops; (b) in American and British organs, a 4-foot open diapason, or an 8-foot open diapason on the pedal; (c) the soloist in a concert; (d) the first player of any division of orchestral instruments except the first violins; (e) the subject of a fugue: opposed to *answer*.

6. the principal or main point. [Obs.]

7. the chief feature in a work of art, to which the rest are to be subordinate.

prin·ci·pal'i·ty, *n.*; *pl.* **prin·ci·pal'i·tieș,** [ME. and OFr. *principalite*.]

1. the state or quality of being principal or a principal. [Rare.]

2. the rank, dignity, or jurisdiction of a prince.

3. the territory ruled by a prince.

4. a country with which a prince's title is identified.

5. [*pl.*] in theology, one of the nine orders of angels.

prin'ci·păl·ly, *adv.* chiefly; mainly; above all.

prin'ci·păl·ness, *n.* the state of being principal or chief.

prin'ci·păl·ship, *n.* the position, duties, or term of a principal.

prin'ci·pāte, *n.* supreme rule; primacy. [Rare.]

prin'ci·pēș, *n.* pl. of *princeps*.

prin·cip'i·ȧ, *n.* pl. of *principium*.

prin·cip'i·ăl, *a.* elementary. [Obs.]

prin·cip'i·ănt, *a.* relating to principles or beginnings. [Obs.]

prin·cip'i·ănt, *n.* a beginner. [Obs.]

prin·cip·i·ā'tion, *n.* [from L. *principium*, beginning.] analysis into constituent or elemental parts. [Rare.]

prin·cip'i·um, *n.*; *pl.* **prin·cip'i·ȧ,** [L., from *princeps*, chief.]

1. a principle.

2. [*pl.*] first principles; fundamentals.

prin'ci·ple, *n.* [Fr. *principe*; L. *principium*, beginning.]

1. the ultimate source, origin, or cause of something.

2. a natural or original tendency, faculty, or endowment.

3. a fundamental truth, law, doctrine, or motivating force, upon which others are based.

4. a rule of conduct, especially of right conduct; as, the *principle* of racial equality.

5. (a) such rules collectively; (b) adherence to them; integrity; uprightness; as, a person of *principle*.

6. an essential element, constituent, or quality, especially one that produces a specific effect; as, the active *principle* of a medicine.

7. the law of nature by which a thing operates; as, capillary attraction is the *principle* of a blotter.

8. the method of a thing's operation; as, the *principle* of a gasoline engine is internal combustion.

9. a beginning. [Obs.]

10. in old chemistry, a component part; an element; as, the constituent *principle* of bodies. [Obs.]

prin'ci·ple, *v.t.*; principled, *pt.*, *pp.*; principling, *ppr.* to establish in a principle; to impress with any tenet. [Obs.]

prin'ci·pled (-pld), *a.* having principles, as of conduct: often in hyphenated compounds, as high-*principled*.

prin'çox, prin'cock, *n.* [earlier also *princocks*; the first element is prob. from *preen*, *v.*, the second, from *cox-*, *cocks-*, as in *coxcomb*.] a coxcomb; a fop. [Obs. or Dial.]

priñk, *v.i.*; prinked (prinkt), *pt.*, *pp.*; prinking, *ppr.* 1. to prank; to dress for show; to preen.

2. to fuss over one's appearance; to primp.

priñk, *v.t.* to dress oneself up.

print, *n.* [ME. *prente*, *preinte*; OFr. *priente*, *preinte*, from *prient*, pp. of *preindre*, from L. *premere*, to press.]

1. a mark made in or on a surface by pressing or hitting with an object; an impression; imprint; as, the *print* of a heel.

2. an object for making such a mark, as a stamp, die, seal, mold, etc.

3. an object or mass that has received such a mark; as, a *print* of butter.

4. a cloth printed with a design, or a dress made of this.

5. the condition of being printed.

6. printed letters, words, etc.; the impression made by inked type; typography; as, uneven *print*.

7. a picture or design printed from a plate, block, roll, etc., as an etching, woodcut, lithograph, etc.

8. printed material; as, news*print*.

9. a publication.

10. an edition or printing, as of a book.

11. a photograph, especially one made from a negative.

in print; (a) in printed form; published; (b) still for sale by the publisher.

out of print; no longer procurable for purchase from the publisher: said of books, etc.

print, *v.t.*; printed, *pt.*, *pp.*; printing, *ppr.* [ME. *prenten*, *printen*, from the *n.*]

1. to mark by pressing or stamping; to imprint; as, to *print* butter.

2. to press or stamp (a mark, letter, etc.) into or upon a surface; as, to *print* a kiss on one's cheek; *printing* their hoofs in the earth.

3. to draw, trace, carve, or otherwise make (a mark, letter, etc.) on a surface.

4. to produce on the surface of (paper, etc.) the impression of inked type, plates, etc. by means of a printing press.

5. to perform or cause to be performed all processes connected with the printing of (a book, etc.), as typesetting, presswork, binding, etc.

6. to publish (a manuscript, one's ideas, etc.) in print.

7. to write in letters resembling printed ones; as, *print* the name.

8. to produce (a photograph) by exposing sensitized paper to light passed through a negative.

9. in computers, to deliver (information) by means of a printer: often with *out*.

10. to impress upon the mind, memory, etc.

printed circuit; an electrical circuit formed by applying conductive material in fine lines or other shapes to an insulating sheet, as by printing with electrically conductive ink, by electroplating, etc.

printed goods; calicoes printed in designs.

print, *v.i.* 1. to practice the art or trade of printing.

2. to produce an impression, print, photograph, etc.; as, a negative *prints* well or badly.

3. to draw letters resembling printed ones.

4. to produce newspapers, books, etc. by means of a printing press.

print'ȧ·ble, *a.* 1. that can be printed or printed from.

2. fit to print.

print'ẽr, *n.* 1. a person whose work or business is printing.

2. a device that prints; especially, (a) one that makes copies by chemical or photographic means; (b) in computers, a device that produces information in printed or typewritten form.

printer's devil; see *devil*, n. 8.

print'ẽr·y, *n.*; *pl.* **print'ẽr·ieș,** 1. a printing shop.

2. a factory where cloth is printed.

print'ing, *n.* 1. the act of a person or thing that prints.

2. the production of printed matter.

3. the art of a printer; typography.

4. something printed; the printed part.

5. all the copies of a book, etc. printed at one time.

6. letters made like printed ones; lettering.

7. in photography, the act or art of obtaining a positive picture from a negative.

embossed printing; printing in relief, as in the stamp design of a stamped envelope.

printing in; the process of introducing into a photograph features from the negative of another photograph.

printing out; a method of photographic printing in which printing-out paper is used.

printing telegraph; a ticker; a telegraph that is self-recording.

print'ing frāme, a frame for holding the negative in contact with the sensitized paper during printing.

print'ing iñk, ink used in printing.

print'ing mȧ·çhïne', a power printing press. [Brit.]

print'ing of'fice, a place where the business of printing is carried on: also *printing house*.

print'ing-out, *a.* yielding a visible image by the direct action of actinic light: said of photographic papers.

print'ing pā'pẽr, paper to be used in printing.

print'ing press, a machine for printing from inked type, plates, or rolls.

print'less, *a.* having, making, or leaving no print or mark.

print'māk·ẽr, *n.* a person who makes prints, etchings, etc.

print'out, *n.* the output of a computer presented in printed or typewritten form.

print shop, 1. a shop where printing is done.

2. a shop where prints, etchings, etc. are sold.

print'wŏrks, *n.* a factory where calico is printed.

Prī·ō″nō·des·mā'cē·ȧ, *n.pl.* [Gr. *priōn*, saw, and *desmos*, band, and *-acea*.] a division of bivalves with serrated hinges.

prī·on'ō·dont, *a.* [Gr. *priōn*, saw, and *odous*, *odontos*, tooth.] having sawlike teeth.

prī'ŏr, *a.* [L., former, superior, comp. of Old Latin *pri*, before.] preceding in order, time, or importance; previous: earlier; former; antecedent; as a *prior* obligation: used with *to* in an adverbial sense; as, *prior* to her arrival.

prī'ŏr, *n.* [LL.; L. *prior*, former, superior.]

1. the head of a priory or other religious house.

2. in an abbey, the person in charge next below the abbot.

prī'ŏr·āte, *n.* 1. the rank, term, or office of a prior; a priorship.

2. a priory.

prī'ŏr·ess, *n.* 1. the woman head of a priory of nuns, etc.

2. in an abbey of nuns, the woman in charge next below the abbess.

prī·or'i·tīze″, *v.t.*; prioritized, *pt.*, *pp.*; prioritizing, *ppr.* 1. to arrange (items) in order of priority.

2. to assign (an item) to a particular level of priority.

prī·or'i·ty, *n.*; *pl.* **prī·or'i·tieș,** 1. the state of being prior, or of preceding something else; precedence in time, order, importance, etc.

2. (a) a right to precedence in obtaining travel reservations, purchasing certain commodities, etc.; (b) an order granting this.

3. in law, a precedence or preference in claims, etc.; as, certain debts are paid in *priority* to others.

4. something given prior attention.

prī'ŏr·ly, *adv.* antecedently.

prī'ŏr·ship, *n.* the rank, office, or term of a prior; priorate.

prī'ō·ry, *n.*; *pl.* **prī'ō·rieș,** a religious house of which a prior or prioress is the superior: sometimes a subordinate branch of an abbey.

priș'āge, *n.* [OFr., prizing, rating, valuing, from *priser*, to estimate, or meaning a share, rather from *prise*, a taking.]

1. a right of the English crown to take two tuns of wine from every ship importing twenty tuns or more: changed into a duty of two shillings for every tun imported by merchant strangers, and called *butlerage*.

2. the share which belongs to the Crown of merchandise taken as lawful prize at sea.

pris'çăn, *a.* pristine; primitive. [Rare.]

Pris·cil'liăn·ist, *n.* in church history, a follower of Priscillian, a Spaniard, bishop of Avila, who was put to death for heresy in 385. A.D. Priscillian's doctrine was substantially that of the Manicheans.

priṣe, *n.* and *v.t.*; prised, *pt.*, *pp.*; prising, *ppr.* prize (lever, etc.).

priṣm, *n.* [LL. *prisma*, from Gr. *prisma*, lit., something sawed, from *prizein*, to saw.]

1. in geometry, a solid figure whose ends are polygonal, equal in size and shape, and parallel, and whose sides are parallelograms.

2. a crystalline body having parallel faces.

3. anything that refracts light, as a drop of water.

TRIANGULAR PRISM

4. in optics, (a) a transparent body, as of glass, whose ends are equal and parallel triangles, and whose three sides are

parallelograms: used for refracting or dispersing light, as into the spectrum; (b) any similar body of three or more sides.

Nicol or *Nicol's prism*; a polarizer, invented by Prof. Nicol of Scotland, composed of two pieces of Iceland spar cemented together: it totally reflects the ordinary ray of light, allowing the extraordinary ray only to be transmitted.

priș·mat′iç, *a.* 1. of or resembling a prism.
2. that refracts light as a prism.
3. that forms or resembles prismatic colors.
4. many-colored; brilliant; dazzling.
5. orthorhombic.

prismatic colors; the seven primary colors of the spectrum, red, orange, yellow, green, blue, indigo, and violet, into which a ray of white light is separated in passing through a prism.

prismatic compass; a compass with a prism by the aid of which distant objects and the compass card can be seen at the same time.

prismatic spectrum; the spectrum given by light passed through a prism.

priș·mat′i·çăl, *a.* prismatic.

priș·mat′i·çăl·ly, *adv.* 1. through, or as if through, a prism.
2. with prismatic colors.

priș·mȧ·toid′ăl, *a.* [Gr. *prisma* (*-atos*), prism, and *-oid*, and *-al*.] having a prismlike form.

priș′moid, *n.* a prismlike solid whose ends are parallel but unequal polygons, and whose sides are consequently trapezoids instead of paralleograms.

priș·moid′ăl, *a.* of, or having the form of, a prismoid.

priș′my, *a.* pertaining to or like a prism.

priș′ŏn (priz′n), *n.* [Fr., from L. *prensio* (*-onis*), a taking, from *prendere*, short form of *prehendere*, to take.]
1. a place where persons are confined.
2. a building, usually with cells, where convicted criminals are confined or accused persons are held awaiting trial; a jail.
3. in the United States, a State prison: distinguished from *reformatory.*
4. imprisonment.

priș′ŏn, *v.t.*; prisoned, *pt.*, *pp.*; prisoning, *ppr.* to shut up in a prison; to confine. [Poet. and Dial.]

priș′ŏn brēach, the unlawful departure of a prisoner from custody.

priș′ŏn·ẽr (*or* priz′nẽr), *n.* 1. one who is confined in a prison.
2. a person under arrest or in custody, whether in prison or not; as, a *prisoner* at the bar of a court.
3. a captive; one taken by an enemy in war.
4. one whose liberty is restrained in any way; as, a *prisoner* of love.

prisoner's base; a children's game in which each side has a base to which captured opponents are brought: also called *prison bars, prison base,* and *prisoner's bars.*

priș′ŏn house, a house in which prisoners are confined; a jail: often used figuratively.

priș′ŏn·ment, *n.* imprisonment. [Rare.]

priș′ŏn ship, a ship for confining prisoners.

priș′ŏn van, a vehicle for the conveyance of prisoners.

pris′sy, *a.*; *comp.* prissier; *superl.* prissiest. [from *precise* or *prim*, and *sissy.*]
1. very prim or precise; fussy. [Colloq.]
2. overrefined; prudish. [Colloq.]

pris′täv (-täf), *n.* [Russ.] in Russia, an overseer, inspector, or commissioner of police.

pris′tin·āte, *a.* pristine; primitive; first. [Obs.]

pris′tīne, *a.* [L. *pristinus*; same root as *prior.*]
1. characteristic of the earliest, or an earlier, period or condition; original.
2. still pure or untouched; uncorrupted; unspoiled.

> Many noble monuments which have since been destroyed or defaced, still retained their *pristine* magnificence.—Macaulay.

pritch, *n.* [a softened form of *prick.*]
1. any sharp-pointed instrument; an instrument for making holes in the ground; also, an eelspear. [Brit. Dial.]
2. pique; offense taken. [Obs.]

pritch′el, *n.* [dim. of *pritch.*] a punch employed for making or enlarging the nail holes in a horseshoe, or for temporarily inserting into a nail hole to form a means of handling the shoe.

prith′ee, *interj.* [altered from *pray thee.*] I pray thee; please: also spelled *prythee.* [Archaic.]

prit′tle-prat″tle, *n.* empty talk; prattle: used in contempt or ridicule. [Now Rare.]

prī′vȧ·cy, *n.*; *pl.* **prī′vȧ·cieș,** 1. a state of being private; withdrawal from public view or company; seclusion.
2. a place of seclusion from company or observation; retreat; solitude; retirement.

> Her sacred *privacies* all open lie.—Rowe.

3. joint secret knowledge; privity. [Obs.]
4. a taciturnity. [Obs.]
5. secrecy; concealment of what is said or done.

pri·vä′dō, *n.* [Sp.] a secret or confidential friend. [Obs.]

Prī·vät′dō·cent′ (-tsent′), *n.*; *pl.* **Prī·vät′dō·cent′en,** [G., from L. *privatus*, private, and *docens* (*-entis*), ppr. of *docere*, to teach.] in European, especially German, universities, a lecturer paid only by his students' fees.

Prī·vät′dō·zent′ (-tsent′), *n.*; *pl.* **Prī·vät′dō·zent′en,** a Privatdocent.

prī′vāte, *a.* [L. *privatus*, belonging to oneself, not public or pertaining to the state, from *privare*, to separate, deprive, from *privus*, separate, peculiar.]
1. of, belonging to, or concerning a particular person or group of persons; not common or general; as, *private* property.
2. not open to, intended for, or controlled by the public; as, a *private* school.
3. not holding public office; as, a *private* citizen.
4. away from public view; secluded; as, a *private* dining room.
5. not known to the public; secret; confidential; as, one's *private* opinion.
6. unconnected with others; being by oneself; solitary. [Obs.]

> Away from light steals home my heavy son,
> And *private* in his chamber pens himself.
> —Shak.

7. participating in knowledge; privy. [Obs.]

> She knew them averse to her religion and *private* to her troubles and imprisonment.
> —Sir R. Naunton.

8. designating a common soldier or one not an officer or noncommissioned officer.

> I cannot put him to a *private* soldier that is the leader of so many thousands.
> —Shak.

private act or *statute*; a statute which operates on an individual or company only: opposed to a *general law*, which operates on the whole community.

private nuisance or *wrong*; a nuisance which affects an individual.

private way; (a) in law, a way or passage in which a man has an interest and right, though the ground may belong to another person; (b) a secret way, not known or public.

prī′vāte, *n.* 1. a secret message; private intimation. [Obs.]
2. personal interest. [Obs.]
3. privacy; retirement. [Obs.]
4. in the United States armed forces, the lowest rank of enlisted man: in the Army, there are two ranks of private, comprising the sixth and seventh grades of enlisted man (see *recruit*); in the Marine Corps and Air Force, it is the seventh, or lowest, grade.
5. an ordinary citizen; one not invested with a public office. [Obs.]
6. [*pl.*] the genitals.

in private; secretly; not openly or publicly.

prī·vȧ·teer′, *n.* 1. a ship or vessel of war owned and equipped by one or more private persons, and licensed by a government to seize or plunder the ships of an enemy in war; a ship carrying letters of marque and reprisal.
2. a commander or crew member of a privateer.

prī·vȧ·teer′, *v.i.*; privateered, *pt.*, *pp.*; privateering, *ppr.* to sail on or as a privateer.

prī·vȧ·teerș′măn, *n.*; *pl.* **prī·vȧ·teerș′men,** an officer or seaman of a privateer.

prī′vāte first çlȧss, in the United States armed forces, a rank of enlisted man, just below a corporal: in the Army, it is the fifth grade of enlisted man (formerly *corporal*); in the Marine Corps and Air Force, it is the sixth grade.

prī′vāte·ly, *adv.* 1. in a secret manner; not openly or publicly.
2. in a manner affecting an individual; in a personal or nonofficial manner.

prī′vāte·ness, *n.* the state or quality of being private; privacy. [Now Rare.]

prī·vā′tion, *n.* [L. *privatio* (*-onis*), from *privare*, to deprive.]
1. a depriving or being deprived; deprivation. [Rare.]
2. the absence of, or state of having lost, some quality or condition, or the quality or condition implicit in this; as, cold is the *privation* of heat.
3. the lack of usual necessities or comforts.

priv′ȧ·tive, *a.* 1. depriving or tending to deprive.
2. characterized by a taking away or loss of some quality.
3. in grammar, changing a positive term to give it a negative meaning.

priv′ȧ·tive, *n.* 1. that of which the essence is the absence of something; as, blackness and darkness are *privatives.*
2. in logic, a term denoting the absence of a quality usually possessed or that is in common or natural possession.
3. in grammar, (a) a prefix or suffix changing the sense of a word from positive to negative, as *un* in *un*well; (b) a nonpositive term which also involves the idea of the natural inherence of the lacking quality.

priv′ȧ·tive·ly, *adv.* in a privative manner.

priv′ȧ·tive·ness, *n.* the state of being privative.

priv′et, *n.* [earlier *primprint, primet*; form due to *private*, since the plant is chiefly used to screen.] an ornamental European shrub, *Ligustrum vulgare*, now naturalized in the United States, and much used in hedges.

barren privet; the semitropical European shrub *Rhamnus alaternus.*

Egyptian privet; a plant of the genus *Lawsonia.*

evergreen privet; the barren privet or alaternus.

Mock privet; a plant of the genus *Phillyrea.*

priv′i·leġe, *n.* [L. *privilegium*, an exceptional law made in favor of or against any individual, from *privus*, separate, peculiar, and *lex*, *legis*, a law.]
1. a right, immunity, benefit, or advantage granted to some person, group of persons, or class, not enjoyed by others and sometimes detrimental to them.
2. a basic civil right, guaranteed by a government; as, the *privilege* of equality for all.
3. in commerce, an option embracing puts and calls.

breach of privilege; see under *breach.*

question of privilege; a question affecting the privileges appertaining to the members of a legislative body.

writ of privilege; a writ to deliver a privileged person from custody when arrested in a civil suit.

priv′i·leġe, *v.t.*; privileged (-lejd), *pt.*, *pp.*; privileging, *ppr.* to grant a privilege or privileges to.

priv′i·leġed, *a.* enjoying a privilege or privileges; as, a *privileged* class.

privileged communication; in law, (a) a communication that one cannot legally be compelled to divulge, as that to a lawyer from his client; (b) a communication made under such circumstances, as in a legislative proceeding, that it is not actionable as slander or libel.

privileged debts; in law, debts payable before other debts, such as servants' wages, etc.

privileged witnesses; in law, those witnesses exempt from being required to testify in certain particulars, as a lawyer or doctor in regard to professional secrets.

priv′i·ly, *adv.* in a privy manner.

priv′i·ty, *n.*; *pl.* **priv′i·tieș,** [OFr. *priveté*; L. *privus*, private.]
1. (a) private or secret knowledge, as shared between persons; (b) participation in this.
2. in law, a successive relationship to or mutual interest in the same property, etc., established by law or legalized by contract, as between a testator and legatee, lessor and lessee, etc.
3. privacy. [Obs.]
4. [*pl.*] the genital organs. [Obs.]

priv′y, *a.* [Fr. *privé*; L. *privus*, private.]
1. originally, private; not public; confidential: now used only in such phrases as *privy* council.
2. hidden, secret, clandestine, surreptitious, or furtive. [Archaic.]
3. privately knowing; admitted to the participation of knowledge with another of a secret transaction (with *to*).

> Myself am one made *privy to* the plot.
> —Shak.

privy chamber; a private apartment; specifically, a secluded apartment in a royal or imperial residence. [Obs.]

privy council; a group of confidential counselors appointed by a ruler to advise him.

privy councilor; a member of a privy council.

privy purse; the money devoted exclusively to the personal use of a monarch; also, [P– P–] the title of the person who has the custody of such money: in full, *Keeper of the Privy Purse.*

privy seal or *signet*; the seal used by a king in granting privileges, sometimes along with the great seal and sometimes alone, as in matters of minor importance; also, [P– S–] an epithet of the person who has the custody of this seal: in full, *Lord Privy Seal.*

privy verdict; a verdict rendered to the judge out of court.

priv'y, *n.*; *pl.* **priv'ies,** 1. a toilet; especially, a small shelter outside of a house, etc., containing a toilet.

2. in law, one of the parties to a privity.

prix fixe (prē' fēks'), [Fr., fixed price.]

1. a meal for which a fixed price is charged; table d'hôte: distinguished from à la carte.

2. its price.

prīz'à·ble, *a.* having some value as a prize; desirable.

prīze, *v.t.*; prized (prīzd), *pt., pp.*; prizing, *ppr.* [ME. *pris*; var. of *price.*]

1. to set a value upon; to appraise; to price.

2. to value highly; to esteem.

prīze, *n.* 1. something offered or given to a person winning a contest.

2. something won in a game of chance, lottery, etc.

3. anything worth striving for; any enviable or highly valued possession.

prīze, *a.* 1. that has received a prize; as, a *prize* novel.

2. that could win a prize; first-rate; as, a *prize* answer: sometimes used ironically.

3. given as a prize.

prīze, *n.* [ME. *prise,* a taking hold, lever; OFr. *prise,* a taking, from *prise,* fem. pp. of *prendre,* to take; L. *prehendere.*]

1. originally, the act of capturing; seizure.

2. something taken by force, as in war; especially, a captured enemy warship or its cargo.

3. (a) an instrument for prying; a lever; (b) leverage. Also spelled *prise.* [Dial.]

prīze, *v.t.*; prized, *pt., pp.*; prizing, *ppr.* 1. to seize as a prize of war.

2. to pry, as with a lever: also spelled *prise.*

prīze, *n.* valuation. [Obs.]

prize çourt, a military court with jurisdiction to decide all questions arising from captures made at sea in wartime.

prīze fīght (fīt), a professional boxing match.

prīze fīght'ẽr, a professional boxer.

prīze fīght'ing, professional boxing.

prīze'măn, *n.*; *pl.* **prīze'men,** a winner of a prize.

prīze mȧs'tẽr, the officer in charge of a vessel captured from the enemy at sea, whose duty it is to bring it into port for judicial condemnation.

prīze mŏn'ey, part of the money from the sale of a ship and cargo captured in battle, usually divided proportionately according to rank among the officers and crew who made the capture.

prīz'ẽr, *n.* 1. one who estimates or sets the value of a thing. [Obs.]

2. a contestant for a prize. [Archaic.]

prīze ring, 1. a square platform or similar space, enclosed by ropes, where prize fights are held.

2. prize fighting.

prō-, [Gr. *pro-,* from *pro,* before; akin to Eng. *for.*] a prefix meaning, (a) *before in place* or *position,* as in *pro*strate; (b) *before in time,* as in *pro*phet.

prō-, [L., from *pro,* before, forward, for.] a prefix meaning, (a) *moving forward* or *ahead of,* as in *pro*gress; (b) *substituting for, acting for,* as in *pro*noun; (c) *defending, acting in behalf of,* as in *pro*locutor; (d) *favoring,* as in *pro*labor, *pro*-German.

prō, *prep.* [L.] on behalf of; in accordance with; for: used in some common Latin phrases.

pro bono publico; for the public good; for the commonweal.

pro confesso; literally, as confessed; the particular action in a court of equity on a part of the pleading where the pleading on the other side offers no denial.

pro rata; proportionately; in proportion.

pro re nata; as matters now stand; for the present.

prō, *adv.* [L. *pro,* for.] on the affirmative side; favorably: opposed to *con.*

pro and con; for and against; on this side and on that; as, I have examined it carefully, *pro and con.*

prō, *a.* favorable.

prō, *n.*; *pl.* **prōṣ,** 1. a person who favors the affirmative side of some debatable question.

2. an argument in favor of something; as, the *pros* and cons of the matter.

3. a vote for the affirmative.

prō, *a.* and *n.*; *pl.* **prōṣ,** [contr. from *professional.*] professional. [Colloq.]

prō'ȧ, *n.* [Malay *prāu.*] a long, narrow, swift Malayan canoe having a lateen sail and an outrigger.

PROA

prōach, *v.t.* to approach. [Obs.]

prō'ăl, *a.* [Gr. *pro,* before, and *-al.*] characterizing mastication which takes place by forward motion: opposed to *palinal.*

prō·am'ni·ŏn, *n.* the folded first form of the amnion around the head of the embryo.

prō·am·ni·ot'iç, *a.* of or pertaining to the proamnion.

prō·ȧ·naph'ō·rȧ, *n.* in the liturgy of the Orthodox Eastern and Coptic churches, that part of the ceremony immediately preceding the consecration of the elements.

prō·an'ġi·ō·spẽrm, *n.* an ancient fossil angiosperm supposed to be the ancestor of all modern angiosperms.

prō·at'lăs, *n.* a rudimentary bone in front of the atlas: found in some reptiles.

prō·ąu'li·on, *n.*; *pl.* **prō·ąu'li·ȧ,** [Gr., a court; *pro,* before, and *aulē,* a court, a hall.] an outer or supplementary porch of an Orthodox Eastern church or of a modern Greek church.

prob·ȧ·bil'i·ŏr·iṣm, *n.* [L. *probabilior,* more probable, and *-ism.*] in Roman Catholic theology, the doctrine that forbids action or interpretation of law in accordance with one's inclination unless there is a balance of probability in favor of such action or decision.

prob·ȧ·bil'i·ŏr·ist, *n.* a believer in and advocate of probabiliorism.

prob'ȧ·bi·liṣm, *n.* [L. *probabilis,* probable, and *-ism.*]

1. in the Roman Catholic Church, the doctrine that in matters concerning which there are two opinions, both probable but neither decisive, it is lawful to follow the one preferred: opposed to *rigorism.*

2. in philosophy, the doctrine that certainty in knowledge is impossible and that probability is a sufficient basis for action and belief.

prob'ȧ·bi·list, *n.* a believer in probabilism.

prob·ȧ·bil'i·ty, *n.*; *pl.* **prob·ȧ·bil'i·tieṣ,** [Fr. *probabilité*; L. *probabilitas.*]

1. likelihood; chance stronger than possibility but falling short of certainty; quality or state of being probable.

2. something probable.

3. in mathematics, the ratio of the chances favoring a certain happening to all the chances for and against it.

in all probability; very likely; quite probably.

Syn.—chance, likelihood, presumption.

prob'ȧ·ble, *a.* [Fr., from L. *probabilis,* from *probare,* to prove.]

1. likely; that can reasonably be expected or believed on the basis of the available evidence, though not proved or certain.

2. such as to establish a probability: said of evidence, etc.

3. that can be proved. [Rare.]

probable cause; in criminal law, reasonable grounds for presuming that a person on trial is guilty of the crime charged.

probable error; an error of such magnitude that is is reasonable to suppose that the real error is as likely to exceed as to fall short of it. Such error may be found by taking the average of a great number of different observations made by different means and by different observers under different environments and at different times.

Syn.—likely, presumable, credible, supposable.

prob'ȧ·ble, *n.* that which is likely to be so, or more likely to occur than not to occur.

prob'ȧ·bly, *adv.* most likely; with probability; as, the story is *probably* true; the account is *probably* correct.

prō·bal'i·ty, *n.* probability. [Obs.]

prō'bang, *n.* [earlier *provang,* from obs. *provet,* probe, and *fang.*] a flexible, slender rod with a ball, sponge, or tuft on the end, for removing obstructions from, or for treating diseases of, the esophagus or larynx.

prō'bāte, *n.* [L. *probatus,* pp. of *probare,* to prove.]

1. in law, (a) official proof, as of the genuineness or validity of a will or other document, ascertained by a judge or competent officer; (b) [Rare.] a copy of a proved will.

2. the right or jurisdiction of probating wills and administering estates. In the United States, the probate of wills belongs to a court of civil jurisdiction established by law, usually to a single judge, called a judge of probate or a surrogate: in some States, the right extends also to the appointing of guardians, the adoption of children, etc.

3. proof. [Obs.]

prō'bāte, *a.* of or relating to a probate, or probate court, or its jurisdiction.

probate court; in the United States, a court for probating wills and, when necessary, administering estates: in some States, its jurisdiction extends to the appointing of guardians, changing of names, etc.

probate duty; in English law, a tax imposed on property transferred by will.

prō'bāte, *v.t.*; probated, *pt., pp.*; probating, *ppr.* 1. to establish officially the genuineness or validity of (a will).

2. to put on probation; to suspend conditionally the sentence of.

prō·bā'tion, *n.* [L. *probatio* (*-onis*), a testing, from *probare,* to prove.]

1. a testing or trial, as of a person's character, his ability to meet certain requirements, or his fitness for a position.

2. the conditional suspension of sentence of a person convicted but not yet imprisoned: after promising good behavior he is placed under the supervision of a probation officer.

3. the status of a person being tested or on trial; as, several students are on *probation* because of low grades.

4. the period of testing or trial.

5. proof. [Rare.]

prō·bā'tion·ăl, *a.* probationary.

prō·bā'tion·ãr·y, *a.* of, serving for, or undergoing probation.

> All the *probationary* work of man is ended
> when death arrives. —Dwight.

prō·bā'tion·ẽr, *n.* 1. one who is on probation.

2. in Scotland, a student in divinity who is admitted to several trials and on acquitting himself well is licensed to preach.

prō·bā'tion·ẽr·ship, *n.* the state of being a probationer; novitiate. [Rare.]

prō·bā'tion·iṣm, *n.* the belief in a state of probation after death.

prō·bā'tion of'fi·cẽr, an officer appointed by a magistrate to watch and report on a person placed on probation.

prō·bā'tion·ship, *n.* a state of probation; novitiate; probation. [Rare.]

prō'bȧ·tive, *a.* 1. serving to test or try.

2. providing proof or evidence.

prō·bā'tŏr, *n.* [L.] 1. an examiner; an approver. [Obs.]

2. in old English law, an accuser; one who turns state's evidence in order to secure pardon for himself. [Obs.]

prō'bȧ·tō·ry, *a.* of or serving as proof; probative.

prō·bā'tum est, [L., it is proved.] it has been proved: an expression appended to a prescription or recipe, denoting that it had been tried or proved. [Obs.]

prōbe, *n.* [L. *probare,* to test, to prove.]

1. a slender, blunt surgical instrument for exploring a wound or the like.

2. the act of probing.

3. a searching investigation, as by a committee appointed for the purpose, of alleged corrupt practices, illegal transactions, and the like.

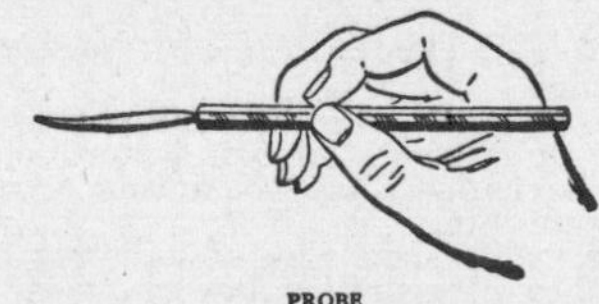

PROBE

prōbe, *v.t.*; probed, *pt., pp.*; probing, *ppr.* 1. to

examine, as a wound, ulcer, or some cavity of the body, with a probe.
 2. to search to the bottom; to investigate with great thoroughness.
prōbe, *v.i.* to search (with *into*).
prōb′i·ty, *n.* [L. *probitas*, from *probus*, honest, virtuous.] tried virtue or integrity; complete honesty; uprightness in one's dealings.
 Syn.—integrity, trustiness, uprightness, honesty.
prob′lem, *n.* [ME. *probleme*; L. *problema*, from Gr. *problēma* (*-atos*), from *proballein*, to throw forward; *pro*, forward, and *ballein*, to throw, to drive.]
 1. a question proposed for solution or consideration.
 2. a question, matter, situation, or person that is perplexing or difficult.
 3. in mathematics, anything required to be done, or requiring the doing of something.
prob·lem·at′i·căl, prob·lem·at′iç, *a.* 1. of the nature of a problem.
 2. uncertain.
prob·lem·at′i·căl·ly, *adv.* doubtfully; in a problematical manner.
prob′lem·ȧ·tist, *n.* one who is occupied with problems. [Rare.]
prō bō′nō pu′bli·cō, see under *pro*.
prō·bos′ci·dāte, *a.* having a proboscis.
Prō·bos·cid′ē·ȧ, *n.pl.* an order of mammals including the elephant and the extinct mastodon.
prō·bos·cid′ē·ăn, *a.* and *n.* same as *probiscidian*.
prō·bos·cid′i·ăl, *a.* same as *proboscidate*.
prō·bos·cid′i·ăn, *a.* in zoology, of a group of animals having tusks and a long, flexible, tubelike snout, as the elephant or the extinct mastodon.
prō·bos·cid′i·ăn, *n.* any member of the *Proboscidea*.
prō·bos·cid′i·fọrm, *a.* resembling a proboscis in shape or in use.
prō·bos′cis, *n.*; *pl.* **prō·bos′cis·eṣ, prō·bos′ci·dēṣ,** [L., from Gr. *proboskis* (*-idos*); *pro*, before, and *boskein*, to feed or graze.]
 1. an elephant's trunk, or a long, flexible snout, as of a tapir.
 2. a tubular sucking organ, as of some insects, worms, and mollusks.
 3. a person's nose: humorously so called.
prō·bos′cis mŏn′key, a large-sized monkey of Borneo having a long, thick, flexible nose; the kahau.
prō·çā′cious, *a.* [L. *procax* (*-acis*), from *procare*, to demand, akin to *precari*, to pray.] pert; petulant; saucy. [Rare.]
prō·çac′i·ty, *n.* [L. *procacitas*.] impudence; petulance. [Rare.]
prō·çāine′, *n.* [*pro-* and *cocaine*.] a synthetic crystalline compound, $C_{13}H_{20}O_2N_2{\cdot}HCl$, resembling, but less toxic than, cocaine, used as a local anesthetic in medicine and dentistry.
prō·çam′bi·ăl, *a.* of the procambium.
prō·çam′bi·um, *n.* the growing layer of plant tissue from which wood cells and cells conducting food and water are formed.
prō′çärp, *n.* [*pro-* and *-carp*.] in botany, a female reproductive organ in certain algae.
prō·çar′y·ōte, *n.* same as *prokaryote*.
prō·çat·ärç′tiç, *a.* [Gr. *prokatarktikos*, beginning beforehand, from *prokatarchein*, to begin first; *pro*, before, *kata*, used intensively, and *archein*, to begin.] of or pertaining to procatarxis. [Now Rare.]
prō·çat·ärx′is, *n.* formerly, in medicine, (a) a predisposing cause; (b) predisposition; also, the production of a disease partially as a result of predisposition.
prō·çȧ·thē′drăl, *n.* a church used as a temporary substitute for a cathedral.
prō·cē·den′dō, *n.* [L., abl. sing. gerundive of *procedere*, to proceed.] in law, a writ by which a cause that has been sent up from an inferior to a superior court is remanded to the lower court to be proceeded in there.
prō·cē′dūr·ăl, *a.* of or according to procedure.
prō·cē′dūr·ăl, *n.* a mystery novel in which much emphasis is placed on the procedures used, especially by police, in investigating a crime.
prō·cē′dūre, *n.* [Fr. *procédure*; L. *procedere*, to go forward.]
 1. the act, method, or manner of proceeding in some process or course of action.
 2. a particular course of action or way of doing something.
 3. the established way of carrying on the business of a legislature, law court, etc.
 4. that which proceeds from something; product. [Obs.]
prō·ceed′, *v.i.*; proceeded, *pt.*, *pp.*; proceeding, *ppr.* [ME. *proceden*; L. *procedere*; *prc*, forward, and *cedere*, to go.]
 1. to move, pass, advance, or go on, especially after stopping; as, a man *proceeds* on his journey; a ship *proceeds* on her voyage.
 2. to pass from one point, stage, or topic to another; as, the lawyer *proceeded* from one argument to another.
 3. to issue or come, as from a source or fountain; as, light *proceeds* from the sun; growth *proceeds* from cultivation.
 4. to be transacted or carried on. [Obs.]
 5. to make progress; to advance. [Obs.]
 6. to begin and carry on a series of actions or measures; as, he *proceeded* to eat his dinner.
 7. to take legal action (often with *against*.)
 8. to be the issue of; to be produced or propagated. [Obs.]
 From my loins thou shalt *proceed*.
 —Milton.
 9. to go on speaking, especially after an interruption.
prō·ceed′ẽr, *n.* one who proceeds.
prō·ceed′ing, *n.* 1. an advancing or going on with what one has been doing.
 2. action or course of action.
 3. a particular course of action.
 4. [*pl.*] transactions.
 5. [*pl.*] a record of the business transacted by a learned society or other organized group.
 6. (a) [*pl.*] legal action; (b) the taking of legal action.
 summary proceeding; the determination of a matter without a jury.
 Syn.—action, course, deed, measure, step, performance, process, transaction.
prō′ceedṣ, *n.pl.* that which proceeds or results, as from a transaction; especially, the sum derived from a sale, venture, etc.
proc″ē·leūs·mat′iç, *a.* [LL. *proceleusmaticus*; Gr. *prokeleusmatikos*; *pro*, before, and *keleusma*, mandate, incitement, from *keleuein*, to incite.]
 1. inciting; animating; encouraging; stirring: said of a song.
 2. in prosody, (a) consisting of four short syllables; (b) designating metrical feet of four short syllables each.
proc″ē·leūs·mat′iç, *n.* in prosody, a foot composed of four short syllables.
Proc·el·lā′ri·ȧ, *n.* [LL., from L. *procella*, a storm.] a genus typical of *Procellaridæ*.
proc·el·lār′i·ăn, *a.* belonging to the family *Procellaridæ*; resembling or related to a petrel.
proc·el·lār′i·ăn, *n.* a member of the genus *Procellaria*; a petrel of any kind.
Proc″el·lȧ·rī′dae, *n.pl.* a family of natatorial birds having tubular nostrils and webbed feet; the petrels.
prō·cel′lăs, *n.* [etym. unknown.] in glassmaking, a pair of tongs with flat jaws, used to reduce the outside diameter of a glass object or give it shape as it rotates on the pontil: also written *pucellas*.
prō·cel′lous, *a.* [L. *procellosus*.] stormy.
prō·cē·phal′iç, *a.* 1. of the forepart of the head; as, the *procephalic* lobe of an invertebrate animal.
 2. in ancient prosody, having an extra syllable in the first foot.
pro·cēre′ (-sẽr′), *a.* [L. *procerus*, tall.] lofty; tall. [Obs.]
prō·cer′ē·brăl, *a.* prosencephalic.
prō·cer′ē·brum, *n.* in anatomy, the forebrain; the prosencephalon.
proc′ẽr·ēṣ, *n.pl.* [L., chiefs, nobles.] the nobility.
proc′ẽr·īte, *n.* [Gr. *pro*, before, and *keras*, horn, and *-ite*.] the last segment of the antennae of some crustaceans, as lobsters.
prō·cer′i·ty, *n.* [L. *proceritas*; *procerus*, tall.] tallness; height; loftiness. [Rare.]
prō·cē′rous, *a.* [L. *procerus*, tall.] lofty; high. [Obs.]
prō·cē′rus, *n.* [Gr. *pro*, before, and *keras*, horn.] in anatomy, a muscle, the pyramidalis nasi.
proc′ess, *n.* [ME. and OFr. *proces*; L. *processus*, pp. of *procedere*, to proceed.]
 1. a proceeding or moving forward; progressive course; tendency; progress; procedure.
 2. the course of being done: chiefly in *in process*.
 3. course, as of time.
 4. a continuing development involving many changes; as, the *process* of digestion.
 5. a particular method of doing something, generally involving a number of steps or operations.
 6. in anatomy, a projection or outgrowth from a larger structure, usually a bone; as, the alveolar *process* of the jaw.
 7. in botany and zoology, an appendage or projecting part of an organism.
 8. in law, (a) an action or suit; (b) a writ or summons directing a defendant to appear in court; (c) the total of such writs in any action or proceeding.
 9. in printing, photomechanical or photoengraving methods collectively.
 10. a narrative; a story of events; also, a proclamation. [Obs.]
 basic process; the use of a Bessemer converter lined with basic material in making steel and certain kinds of iron.
 Deacon process; the process of making chlorine by passing hydrochloric acid gas over heated porous slag saturated with a solution of copper salt, usually copper chloride.
 final process; the writ of execution used to carry a judgment into effect.
 in (*the*) *process of*; in or during the course of.
 LeBlanc process; a process of manufacturing sodium carbonate by treating sodium sulfate with charcoal and lime.
 mesne process; in law, that which issues, pending the suit, upon some collateral or interlocutory matter.
 original process; in law, the means taken to compel the defendant to appear in court.
proc′ess, *v.t.*; processed (-sest), *pt.*, *pp.*; processing, *ppr.* 1. in law, (a) to prosecute; (b) to serve a process on.
 He was at the quarter sessions *processing* his brother.
 —Edgeworth.
 2. to prepare by or subject to a special treatment or process.
proc′ess, *a.* 1. prepared by a special treatment or process.
 2. of, made by, used in, or using photomechanical or photoengraving methods.
prō·ces′săl, *a.* of or relating to proceedings at law.
proc′ess·ẽr, *n.* same as *processor*.
proc′ess·ing tax, a tax levied on the processing of certain agricultural products.
prō·ces′sion (-sesh′un), *n.* [Fr., from L. *processio* (*-onis*), from *procedere*, to proceed.]
 1. the act of proceeding, especially in an orderly manner.
 2. a number of persons or things moving forward, ordinarily in a long line, in orderly fashion toward some set destination; as, a religious *procession*.
 3. a litany or hymn sung by persons moving in a religious procession.
 Syn.—train, march, caravan, file, cortége, cavalcade, retinue.
prō·ces′sion, *v.t.* and *v.i.* 1. to ascertain, mark, and establish the boundary lines of, as lands. [Dial.]
 2. to form or take part in a procession.
prō·ces′sion·ăl, *a.* [ME.; ML. *processionalis*.] of, or used in connection with, a procession or processions.
prō·ces′sion·ăl, *n.* 1. a book setting forth the ritual to be observed in processions of the church.
 2. a hymn sung at the beginning of a church service during the entrance of the clergy.
 3. any musical composition intended for performance in connection with a procession, as at a university convocation.
prō·ces′sion·ăl·ly, *adv.* in a processional manner; in solemn or formal march.
prō·ces′sion·ăr·y, *a.* processional.
 processionary moth; the *Cnethocampa processionea*, whose larvae feed gregariously on oaks, advancing in cuneate processionary order.
prō·ces′sion·ẽr, *n.* 1. a processionist.
 2. a processional; a handbook of processions. [Obs.]
 3. an officer appointed to procession lands. [Dial.]
prō·ces′sion flow′ẽr, same as *milkwort*.
prō·ces′sion·ist, *n.* one who takes part in a procession.
prō·ces′sive, *a.* [L. *processus*, pp. of *procedere*, to proceed.] proceeding; going forward; advancing.
proc′ess·ŏr, *n.* a person or thing that processes.
proc′ess print′ing, a method of printing colored reproductions of paintings, etc. by use of plates made from half tones.
proc′ess sẽrv′ẽr, in law, a policeman, sheriff, or deputy who delivers an official order, or process, to a person, commanding him to be in court at a time and place named in the order.

prō·ces′sū·ăl, *a.* in law, relating to some legal proceeding or judicial process.

prō·ces′sus, *n.*; *pl.* **prō·ces′sus,** [L.] in anatomy, a process.

pro·cès′-ver·bal′ (prō-se′-vär-bål′), *n.*; *pl.* **pro·cès′-ver·baux′** (-bō′), [Fr., a verbal process.] an authenticated official report of proceedings or facts; an authorized statement; minutes (of a meeting).

prō·chaiṅ′ (-shaṅ′), *a.* [Fr.] same as *prochein.*

prō′chein (-shen), *a.* [Fr. *prochain*; L. *proximus*, next.] in law, next; nearest.
prochein ami or *amy*; same as *next friend* under *next.*

prō·chlō′rīte, *n.* [*pro-* and *chlorite.*] a greenish chlorite containing silica and iron and occurring in laminated or granular masses.

prō·chon′drăl, *a.* [Gr. *pro*, before, and *chondros*, cartilage.] previous to the formation of cartilage.

prō′chō·os, *n.*; *pl.* **prō′chō·oi,** [Gr., from *prochein*, to pour forth.] an ancient Greek vase or pitcher like the oinochoē, but more slender, used for washing one's hands before meals.

prō·chor′dăl, *a.* in anatomy, anterior to the notochord.

prō·chō′ri·on, *n.* in biology, the primitive chorion; the zona pellucida.

prō·chō·ri·on′iç, *a.* of or pertaining to the prochorion.

prō′chrō·niṣm, *n.* [Gr. *pro*, before, and *chronos*, time.] an antedating; the dating of an event before the time it happened.

prō′chrō·nīze, *v.t.* to antedate. [Rare.]

proc′i·dence, proc·i·den′ti·ȧ (-shi-), *n.* [L. *procidentia*, from *procidere*, to fall down.] in pathology, a falling down; a prolapse.

proc′i·dent, *a.* affected by prolapse.

prō·cid′ū·ous, *a.* procident. [Obs.]

prō·ciṅct′, *n.* complete preparation for action. [Obs.]

prō·clāim′, *v.t.*; proclaimed, *pt.*, *pp.*; proclaiming, *ppr.* [ME. *proclame(n)*; OFr. *proclamer*; L. *proclamare*; *pro*, before, and *clamare*, to cry out.]
1. to announce officially; to announce to be; as, they *proclaimed* her queen.
2. to outlaw, ban, or otherwise restrict by a proclamation.
3. to show to be; as, her every act *proclaimed* her a snob.

prō·clāim′, *n.* a proclamation; a calling out. [Rare.]

prō·clāim′ẽr, *n.* one who proclaims.

proc·lȧ·mā′tion, *n.* [L. *proclamatio* (*-onis*), from *proclamare*, to proclaim.]
1. a proclaiming or being proclaimed.
2. that which is proclaimed, or announced officially.

prō·clit′iç, *a.* [Mod. L. *procliticus*, from Gr. *proklinein*, to lean forward; *pro*, forward, and *klinein*, to lean, incline.] pronounced, in ordinary speech, with the word that follows it, and so having no accent of its own: said of such words as *to* in a phrase like *to be or not to be*: distinguished from *enclitic.*

prō·clit′iç, *n.* a proclitic word.

prō·clīve′, *a.* inclined; proclivous. [Rare.]

prō·cliv′i·ty, *n.*; *pl.* **prō·cliv′i·tieṣ,** [Fr. *proclivité*; L. *proclivitas*; *pro*, before, and *clivus* slope.] a natural tendency in human nature; inclination, especially toward something discreditable; propensity; proneness; as, a *proclivity* to vice.

prō·clī′vous, *a.* [L. *proclivus*, sloping.] inclined: specifically applied to incisor teeth sloping forward.

Proç′nē, [L.; Gr. *Proknē.*] in Greek and Roman mythology, Pandion's daughter, transformed into a swallow by the gods.

prō·coe′li·ȧ, *n.* [Gr. *pro*, before, and *koilos*, hollow.] in anatomy, the lateral ventricle of the brain.

Prō·coe′li·ȧ, *n.pl.* [Gr. *pro*, before, and *koilos*, hollow.] in zoology, a suborder of *Crocodilia*, having procoelous vertebrae, and including all the existent crocodiles and alligators and many extinct ones.

prō·coe′li·ăn, *a.* having vertebrae hollowed in front; pertaining to or resembling the *Procœlia.*

prō·coe′li·ăn, *n.* a member of the *Procœlia.*

prō·coe′lous, *a.* concave on the anterior surface; procoelian.

prō·çon′sul, *n.* [L., from *pro*, for, and *consul.*]
1. a Roman official invested with consular authority who commanded an army in one or more of the provinces and often acted as a provincial governor.
2. a governing official in a modern British colony.

prō·çon′sū·lăr, *a.* [L. *proconsularis.*] 1. pertaining to a proconsul; as, *proconsular* powers.
2. under the government of a proconsul; as, a *proconsular* province.

prō·çon′sū·lăr·y, *a.* same as *proconsular.*

prō·çon′sū·lāte, *n.* the proconsular office, jurisdiction, or term of office.

prō·çon′sul·ship, *n.* same as *proconsulate.*

prō·cras′ti·nāte, *v.i.*; procrastinated, *pt.*, *pp.*; procrastinating, *ppr.* [from L. *procrastinatus*, pp. of *procrastinare*; *pro*, for, forward, and *crastinus*, belonging to the morrow, from *cras*, tomorrow.] to put off doing something until a future time; to postpone or defer taking action.
Syn.—postpone, defer, delay, put off.

prō·cras′ti·nāte, *v.t.* to defer; to postpone.

prō·cras·ti·nā′tion, *n.* [L. *procrastinatio* (*-onis*).] the act or habit of procrastinating.

prō·cras′ti·nā·tŏr, *n.* one who procrastinates, especially habitually.

prō·cras′ti·nȧ·tō·ry, *a.* tending to delay; dilatory.

prō′crē·ănt, *a.* [L. *procreans* (*-antis*), ppr. of *procreare*, to procreate.]
1. generating; producing young; productive; fruitful.
2. of procreation.

prō′crē·ănt, *n.* same as *procreator.*

prō′crē·āte, *v.t.* and *v.i.*; procreated, *pt.*, *pp.*; procreating, *ppr.* [L. *procreatus*, pp. of *procreare*, to procreate; *pro*, before, and *creare*, to create.]
1. to produce (young); to beget (offspring).
2. to produce or bring into existence.

prō·crē·ā′tion, *n.* [L. *procreatio* (*-onis*).] a procreating or being procreated.

prō′crē·ā·tive, *a.* 1. of procreation, or the producing of young.
2. productive.

prō′crē·ā·tive·ness, *n.* the power of generating.

prō′crē·ā·tŏr, *n.* one who procreates.

Prō·crus′tē·ăn, *a.* 1. of, pertaining to, or resembling Procrustes or his famous bedstead.
2. designed to secure strict conformity by violent measures; producing strict conformity by force or mutilation; drastic, as methods.

Prō·crus′tē·ăn·īze, *v.t.*; Procrusteanized, *pt.*, *pp.*; Procrusteanizing, *ppr.* to torture into conformity or uniformity.

Prō·crus′tēṣ, *n.* [L.; Gr. *Prokroustēs*, from *prokrouein*, to beat out.] in Greek mythology, a giant of Attica who seized travelers and tied them to an iron bedstead, after which he either cut off their legs or stretched his victims till they fitted it.

prō·cryp′tiç, *a.* [*pro-* and *cryptic.*] in zoology, serving to hide, conceal, or obscure in a protective way: said of animal coloration.

proct-, same as *procto-.*

proc·tal′ġi·ȧ, *n.* pain in the rectum.

proc·tī′tis, *n.* [Gr. *prōktos*, the anus, and *-itis.*] rectal inflammation.

proc′tō-, [from Gr. *prōktos*, anus.] a combining form meaning *rectum*, as in *proctology.*

proc′tō·cēle, *n.* [*procto-* and *-cele.*] hernia or prolapse of the rectum.

proc″tō·cys·tot′ō·my, *n.* cutting into the bladder by way of the rectum.

proc·tō·dae′um, *n.* [*procto-*, and Gr. *hodaios*, by the way; *hodos*, a way.] a portion of the posterior end of the alimentary canal, forming the anus and lower rectum, and produced by the invagination of the epiblast.

proc·tol′ō·gy, *n.* [*procto-* and *-logy.*] the branch of medicine dealing with the rectum and its diseases.

proc′tŏr, *n.* [ME. *proketour*; contr. from *procuratour*; L. *procurator*, a procurator.]
1. a person employed to manage the affairs of another; an agent.
2. a college or university official who maintains order, supervises examinations, etc.
3. in the Church of England, one of the clergymen elected to represent cathedral or other collegiate churches, and also the common clergy of every diocese in convocation.
4. a beggar. [Obs.]

proc′tŏr, *v.t.* 1. to manage as a proctor, or agent.
2. to supervise (an academic examination).

proc′tŏr·ăġe, *n.* management by or as by a proctor.

proc·tō′ri·ăl, *a.* of or employing a proctor or proctors.

proc·tor′i·căl, *a.* proctorial. [Rare.]

proc′tŏr·ship, *n.* the office or term of office of a proctor.

proc′tō·sçōpe, *n.* [*procto-* and *-scope.*] an instrument used for the direct examination of the interior of the rectum.

proc·tot′ō·my, *n.* [*procto-*, and Gr. *temnein*, to cut.] in surgery, a rectal incision.

pro·cum′bent, *a.* [L. *procumbens*, ppr. of *procumbere*, to lean forward; *pro*, forward, and *cubare*, to lie down.]
1. lying face down; prone.
2. in botany, trailing; prostrate; lying on the ground, but without putting forth roots; as, a *procumbent* stem.

prō·çūr′ȧ·ble, *a.* that can be procured, or obtained.

proç′ū·rȧ·cy, *n.*; *pl.* **proç′ū·rȧ·cieṣ,** 1. the office or act of a procurator.
2. a proxy or procuration. [Obs.]

prō·çūr′ănce, *n.* the act of procuring, obtaining, or bringing about; agency.

proç·ū·rā′tion, *n.* [L. *procuratio*, from *procurare*, to take care of.]
1. procurement; the act of procuring.
2. the management of another's affairs.
3. power of attorney.
4. a sum of money paid formerly to the bishop or archdeacon, now to ecclesiastical commissioners, by incumbents, on account of visitations: also called *proxy.* [Brit.]
procuration fee or *procuration money*; a fee for effecting loans of money.

proç′ū·rā·tŏr, *n.* 1. the manager of another's business or legal affairs.
2. in the Roman Empire, an official who managed the financial affairs of a province or acted as governor of a territory, as Judaea, without the status of a province.
procurator fiscal; in Scots law, a district attorney or public prosecutor.

proç″ū·rȧ·tō′ri·ăl, *a.* pertaining to a procurator or proctor; also, done by a proctor.

proç′ū·rā·tŏr·ship, *n.* the office of a procurator.

proç′ū·rȧ·tō″ry, *a.* [LL. *procuratorius*, belonging to a procurator.] of a procurator or procuration. [Rare.]

proç′ū·rȧ·tō″ry, *n.* [ML. *procuratorium.*] an authorization to act as a procurator.

prō·çūre′, *v.t.*; procured (-kūrd′), *pt.*, *pp.*; procuring, *ppr.* [ME. *procuren*; OFr. *procurer*, to procure, from L. *procurare*, to take care of, to attend to; *pro*, for, and *cura*, care.]
1. to obtain, as by effort, labor, or purchase; to get; to gain; to come into possession of; as, we *procure* favors by request; we *procure* money by borrowing; we *procure* titles to estates by purchase.
2. to cause to come on; to bring on; to attract; as, modesty *procures* love and respect. [Obs.]
3. to cause; to bring about; to effect; to contrive and effect. [Rare.]
Proceed, Solinus, to *procure* my fall.
—Shak.
4. to induce to do something. [Archaic.]
5. to obtain (girls) for the purpose of prostitution.
6. to solicit; to urge earnestly. [Obs.]

prō·çūre′, *v.i.* to obtain girls for the purpose of prostitution.

prō·çūre′ment, *n.* a procuring, or obtaining.

prō·çūr′ẽr, *n.* 1. one who procures, or obtains.
2. a man who obtains girls for the purpose of prostitution; a pimp; a pander.

prō·çūr′ess, *n.* a woman who obtains girls for the purpose of prostitution.

prō·çu·reūr′, *n.* [Fr., from L. *procurator.*] in French law, a procurator, or agent.

prō·çūr′sive, *a.* [L. *procursus*, pp. of *procurrere*, to run forward.] running forward.
procursive epilepsy; in medicine, a form of epilepsy in which the sufferer runs forward at the beginning of a seizure.

Prō′cy·on, *n.* [Gr., from *pro*, before, and *kyōn*, dog, i.e., rising before the dog star.]
1. in astronomy, a star of the first magnitude in the constellation Canis Minor, the Little Dog.
2. a genus of plantigrade carnivorous mammals consisting of the raccoons.

prod, *n.* [prob. merging of *prog* and *brod*, both of which mean "to stab."]
1. a thrust or dig with something pointed; a prodding.
2. something that serves to goad or urge on; as, many stockyards use an electric *prod* to keep the cattle moving.

prod, *v.t.*; prodded, *pt.*, *pp.*; prodding, *ppr.*
1. to prick or jab with something sharp and pointed; to poke; to goad.
2. to urge or rouse.

prō·dā′tȧ·ry, *n.*; *pl.* **prō·dā′tȧ·rieṣ,** [*pro-* and *datary.*] formerly, the presiding officer over the Roman datary when a cardinal in rank.

prod′dẽr, *n.* one who or that which prods.

prod′i·găl, *a.* [obs. Fr.; ML. *prodigalis*, from L. *prodigus*, prodigal, from *prodigere*, to drive forth or away, to get rid of; *pro*, forth, and *agere*, to drive.]

1. given to extravagant expenditures; expending money or other things without necessity; exceedingly or recklessly wasteful; not frugal or economical; as, a *prodigal* man, the *prodigal* son.

2. profuse; extremely abundant; as, the *prodigal* foliage of the jungle.

3. extremely generous; lavish (often with *of*); as, she was *prodigal of* praise.

prod′i·găl, *n.* one who expends money extravagantly or without necessity; one who wastes his means; a waster; a spendthrift.

prod·i·gal′i·ty, *n.*; *pl.* **prod·i·gal′i·ties,** [ME. *prodigalite*; OFr. *prodigalité*; LL. *prodigalitas.*]

1. reckless wastefulness.

2. abundant generosity or liberality; lavishness.

3. extreme abundance.

prod′i·găl·ize, *v.i.* and *v.t.*; prodigalized, *pt.*, *pp.*; prodigalizing, *ppr.* to be extravagant in expenditures (of); to spend lavishly.

prod′i·găl·ly, *adv.* in a prodigal manner.

prod′i·gence, *n.* waste; profusion; prodigality. [Obs.]

prō·di′gious (-dij′us), *a.* [L. *prodigiosus*, marvelous, from *prodigium*, portent.]

1. wonderful; amazing.

2. enormous; huge.

3. monstrous.

4. portentous. [Obs.]

Syn.—vast, immense, amazing, extraordinary, marvelous, miraculous, astonishing.

prō·di′gious·ly, *adv.* 1. in a prodigious manner; enormously; wonderfully; astonishingly; as, a number *prodigiously* great.

2. very much; extremely; as, he was *prodigiously* pleased. [Colloq.]

prō·di′gious·ness, *n.* the state or quality of being prodigious.

prod′i·gy, *n.*; *pl.* **prod′i·gies,** [L. *prodigium*; perhaps from *pro*, forth, and *dicere*, to tell.]

1. an extraordinary happening, thought to foretell good or evil fortune. [Rare.]

2. a marvel; a person, thing, or act so extraordinary as to inspire wonder; as, a child *prodigy.*

3. something monstrous.

Syn.—wonder, marvel, monster, enormity, miracle.

prō·di′tion (-dish′un), *n.* [L. *proditio*, from *prodere*, to betray.] treachery; treason; betrayal. [Now Rare.]

prod′i·tŏr, *n.* [L.] a traitor. [Obs.]

prod·i·tō′ri·ous, *a.* 1. treacherous; perfidious; traitorous. [Obs.]

2. apt to make disclosures. [Obs.]

prod′i·tō·ry, *a.* treacherous; perfidious. [Obs.]

prod′rō·măl, *a.* [*prodrome* and *-al.*] in medicine, of or being a prodrome; premonitory.

prō·drom′ȧ·tȧ, *n.pl.* [LL., from Gr. *prodromos*, a running before.] such symptoms as manifest themselves previous to the outbreak of a disease, and by their nature and severity give some clue as to the pathological condition.

prod·rō·mat′iç, *a.* of or relating to prodromata; prodromal.

prō′drōme, *n.* [Fr.; L. *prodromus*; Gr. *prodromos*, a forerunner; *pro*, before, and *dromos*, a running.] in medicine, an indication or symptom of the impending outbreak of some disease.

prō·drom′iç, *a.* same as *prodromal.*

prod′rō·mous, *a.* prodromal. [Rare.]

prod′rō·mus, *n.* [L., from Gr. *prodromos*, forerunner.]

1. same as *prodrome.*

2. a preparatory course or introductory treatise on any subject, to be followed by a larger work.

prō·dūce′, *v.t.*; produced (-dūst′), *pt.*, *pp.*; producing, *ppr.* [L. *producere*; *pro*, forward, and *ducere*, to lead or draw.]

1. to bring forward; to bring or offer to view or notice; to exhibit; as, to *produce* a witness or evidence in court.

Your parents did not *produce* you much into the world. —Swift.

2. to bring forth; to generate; to give birth to; to bear; to furnish; to yield; as, trees *produce* fruit; a well that *produces* oil.

3. to cause; to effect; to bring about; as, small causes sometimes *produce* great effects; vice *produces* misery.

4. to make; to manufacture; as, the manufacturer *produces* excellent wares.

5. to yield; to make accrue; as, money *produces* interest; capital *produces* profit.

6. to get ready and present (a play, motion picture, etc.) on the stage or screen.

7. in economics, to create (anything having exchange value).

8. in geometry, to extend (a line or plane).

prō·dūce′, *v.i.* to bring forth, manufacture, bear, or yield the customary product or products; as, the tree *produces* well.

prod′ūce, *n.* something that is produced; the outcome yielded by labor or natural growth; yield or production; especially, farm products collectively; as, the *produce* of a farm or of a country.

Syn.—product, yield, fruit, profit, effect, consequence, result, amount.

prō·dūced′ (-dūst′), *a.* extended; elongated.

prō·dūce′ment, *n.* production. [Obs.]

prō·dū′cent, *n.* one who brings forward, or offers to view or notice. [Obs.]

prō·dūc′ẽr, *n.* 1. a person who produces; specifically, in economics, one who produces goods and services: opposed to *consumer.*

2. a special type of furnace for making producer gas.

3. a person who is in charge of the production of a play, motion picture, etc.

prō·dūc′ẽr gas, a gas prepared by burning low-grade coal with a limited supply of air so that a combustible mixture of nitrogen and carbon monoxide is obtained.

prō·dūc′ẽrs′ goods, goods, such as raw materials and machines, that are used in producing consumers' goods.

prō·dūc·i·bil′i·ty, *n.* the condition, quality, or fact of being producible.

prō·dūc′i·ble, *a.* capable of being produced.

prō·dūc′i·ble·ness, *n.* the state or quality of being producible; as, the *producibleness* of salts.

prod′uçt, *n.* [L. *productus*, pp. of *producere*, to produce.]

1. that which is produced by nature or made by industry or art; as, the *products* of the season; the *products* of manufacture.

2. result; outgrowth; as, war is a *product* of greed.

3. in chemistry, any substance resulting from a chemical change.

4. in mathematics, the number obtained by multiplying two or more numbers together.

Syn.—fruit, result, issue, consequence, effect, emanation, work.

prō·duçt′, *v.t.* to produce. [Obs.]

prō·duçt·i·bil′i·ty, *n.* the state, quality, or fact of being productible.

prō·duçt′i·ble, *a.* producible; capable of being produced.

prō·duç′tile, *a.* capable of being drawn out or extended in length.

prō·duç′tion, *n.* [L. *productio* (*-onis*), from *producere*, to produce.]

1. the act or process of producing.

2. the rate of producing.

3. (a) something produced; product; (b) a work of art, literature, the theater, etc.

4. in economics, the creation of economic value; the producing of goods and services: opposed to *consumption.*

Syn.—evolution, formation, genesis, product, work.

prō·duç′tive, *a.* 1. having the quality or power of producing; bringing as a result; causing to exist (with *of*); as, *productive* genius; an age *productive of* great men.

2. fertile; producing abundantly; yielding large results; as, *productive* soil.

3. marked by abundant production; as, a *productive* time.

4. in economics, of or engaged in the creating of economic value, or the producing of goods and services.

prō·duç′tive·ly, *adv.* by production; in a productive manner.

prō·duç′tive·ness, *n.* the quality or state of being productive; as, the *productiveness* of land or labor.

prō·duç·tiv′i·ty, *n.* the quality or state of being productive; productiveness.

prō·duç′tress, *n.* a woman producer. [Rare.]

Prō·duç′tus, *n.* [L., pp. of *producere*, to produce.] a genus of fossil brachiopods, found in the Paleozoic rocks.

prō·ē·gū′me·năl, *a.* in old medicine, predisposing; rendering susceptible to. [Obs.]

prō′em, *n.* [ME. and OFr. *proeme*; L. *prœmium*; Gr. *prooimion*; *pro*, before, and *oimos*, way.] a brief preface or introduction; preliminary observations; preamble.

prō′em, *v.t.* to preface. [Obs.]

prō·em′bry·ō, *n.* [*pro-*, and Gr. *embryon*, embryo.] in botany, a cell series formed consequent upon fertilization but previous to the development of the embryo; also, in certain cryptogams, a growth from the spore upon which the young plant develops.

prō·ē′mi·ăl, *a.* of a proem; introductory; prefatory; preliminary.

prō·emp·tō′sis, *n.* [Gr., from *pro*, before, and *emptōsis*, the act of falling; *en*, in, and *ptōsis*, a fall, from *piptein*, to fall.] in chronology, the addition of a day every 300 years and another every 2400 years to the lunar calendar, to prevent the date of the new moon being set a day too soon.

prof, *n.* [contr. from *professor.*] a professor. [Colloq.]

prō·fāce′, *n.* [OFr. *prou face* or *prou fasse*, from *prou*, profit, and *faire*, to do.] may it do you good!: an exclamation of welcome or good wishes. [Obs.]

prof′ȧ·nāte, *v.t.* to violate, desecrate, or profane. [Obs.]

prof·ȧ·nā′tion, *n.* [L. *profanatio* (*-onis*), from *profanatus*, pp. of *profanare*, to profane.]

1. the act of violating sacred things or disrespectful or irreverent treatment of sacred or divine things; desecration.

2. the act of treating with abuse or disrespect; the rendering common of anything honorable; debasement.

prō·fan′ȧ·tō·ry, *a.* involving profanation; profaning.

prō·fāne′, *a.* [L. *profanus*; *pro*, before, and *fanum*, a temple; lit., forth from the temple, hence, not sacred, common, profane.]

1. not concerned with religion or religious matters; secular; as, *profane* art; *profane* history, that is, history other than biblical.

2. irreverent toward God or holy things; speaking, spoken, acting, or done in contempt of sacred things; blasphemous; as, *profane* words or language.

3. not hallowed or consecrated.

Nothing is *profane* that serveth to holy things. —Raleigh.

4. not initiated into certain mysterious rites.

Far hence be souls *profane*,
The sibyl cried, and from the grove abstain.
—Dryden.

Syn.—impious, godless, ungodly, irreverent, irreligious, unholy, unhallowed, unsanctified, secular, temporal, worldly.

prō′fāne, *n.* one who is profane.

prō·fāne′, *v.t.*; profaned, *pt.*, *pp.*; profaning, *ppr.* 1. to treat as if profane or not sacred; to violate; to treat with irreverence, impiety, or contempt; to pollute; to desecrate; as, to *profane* the name of God; to *profane* the Sabbath.

2. to put to a wrong use; to employ basely or unworthily; to debase.

I feel me much to blame,
So idly to *profane* the precious time.
—Shak.

prō·fāne′ly, *adv.* in a profane manner; specifically, (a) with irreverence to sacred things or names; impiously; as, to speak *profanely* of God or sacred things; (b) with abuse or contempt for anything venerable.

prō·fāne′ness, *n.* the state or quality of being profane; irreverence for sacred things.

prō·fān′ẽr, *n.* 1. one who profanes, or who by words or actions treats sacred things with irreverence; one who uses profane language.

There are a lighter ludicrous sort of *profaners*, who use Scripture to furnish out their jests. —More.

2. a polluter; a defiler.

Profaners of the temple. —Hooker.

prō·fan′i·ty, *n.* [LL. *profanitas.*]

1. the state or quality of being profane.

2. *pl.* **prō·fan′i·ties,** something that is profane, especially profane language.

prō·feç′tion, *n.* [L. *profectio.*] a going forward; advance; progression. [Obs.]

prō·feç·ti′tious, *a.* [LL., from *profectus*, pp. of *proficisci*, to proceed.] derived from an ancestor or ancestors. [Rare.]

prō′fẽrt, *n.* [L., he produces.] in law, a formal offer in a pleading to produce in court the documentary evidence on which the pleader's action is based.

prō·fess′, *v.t.*; professed (-fest′), *pt.*, *pp.*; professing, *ppr.* [L. *professus*, pp. of *profiteri*, to avow publicly; *pro*, before, and *fateri*, to avow.]

1. to make an open or public declaration of; to avow publicly; to acknowledge; to own freely; to affirm.

I *profess* in my career to have kept steadily in view the prosperity and honor of the whole country. —Daniel Webster.

2. to lay claim openly to the position or character of; to acknowledge oneself as being.

I *profess* myself an enemy. —Shak.

3. to practice as one's profession; to hold oneself out as proficient in; as, to *profess* medicine.

4. to affirm or avow faith in or allegiance to; to declare one's adherence to; as, to *profess* Christianity.

5. to make protestations or show of; to make a pretense of; to pretend.

6. to accept into a religious order.

Syn.—declare, affirm, proclaim, allege, avouch, avow, acknowledge, confess, pretend.

prō·fess′, *v.i.* 1. to make profession.

2. to make one's profession (sense 5).

prō·fessed′ (-fest′), *a.* 1. openly declared; avowed; acknowledged; as, a *professed* foe, a *professed* tyrant, a *professed* atheist.

2. insincerely avowed; pretended; as, their *professed* neutrality.

3. having made one's profession (sense 5).

prō·fess′ed·ly, *adv.* avowedly, allegedly, or ostensibly.

prō·fes′sion (-fesh′un), *n.* [Fr., from L. *professio* (*-onis*), a declaration.]

1. a professing, or declaring; avowal, whether true or pretended; as, a *profession* of faith.

2. (a) the avowal of belief in a religion; (b) a faith or religion professed.

3. a vocation or occupation requiring advanced training in some liberal art or science, and usually involving mental rather than manual work, as teaching, engineering, writing, etc.; especially, medicine, law, or theology (formerly called *the learned professions*).

The student who has read much in his *profession* is saved from innumerable blunders. —John Bach McMaster.

4. the collective body of persons engaged in or practicing a particular calling or vocation.

5. the act by which a novice becomes a member of a religious order or congregation.

prō·fes′sion·ăl, *a.* 1. of, engaged in, or worthy of the high standards of, a profession.

2. making some activity not usually followed for gain, such as a sport, the source of one's livelihood.

3. engaged in by professionals (sense 2); as, *professional* hockey.

4. engaged in a specified occupation for pay or as a means of livelihood; as, a *professional* writer.

5. having much experience and great skill in a specified role; as, a *professional* rabble-rouser.

prō·fes′sion·ăl, *n.* 1. a person belonging to one of the professions.

2. a person who makes some activity not usually followed for gain, such as a sport, the source of his livelihood.

prō·fes′sion·ăl·ism, *n.* 1. professional quality, status, etc.

2. the practice or fact of using professional players in organized sports.

prō·fes′sion·ăl·ist, *n.* a professional. [Rare.]

prō·fes′sion·ăl·ly, *adv.* in a professional manner.

prō·fes′sŏr, *n.* [ME. *professoure*; L., a teacher, from *professus*; see *profess*.]

1. a person who professes something; especially, one who openly declares his sentiments, religious beliefs, etc.

2. a teacher; specifically, a college teacher of the highest rank (*full professor*), usually in a specific field: see also *associate professor, assistant professor*.

3. any person claiming or assumed to be especially skilled or experienced in some art, sport, etc.: a popular or humorous usage.

prō·fes′sŏr·āte, *n.* 1. the position or office of a professor; professorship.

2. a body of professors; the professorial staff, as in a university.

3. the length of time during which a professor is in office.

prō·fes·sō′ri·ăl, *a.* [L. *professorius*.] of or characteristic of a professor; as, the *professorial* chair.

prō·fes·sō′ri·ăl·ism, *n.* the character, habits, or manner of thinking of a professor. [Rare.]

prō·fes·sō′ri·ăl·ly, *adv.* in a professorial manner; academically.

prō·fes·sō′ri·āte, *n.* 1. the professors of a school collectively.

2. a professorship.

prō·fes′sŏr·ship, *n.* the office or position of a professor.

prō·fes′sō·ry, *a.* professorial. [Rare.]

prof′fēr, *v.t.*; proffered, *pt.*, *pp.*; proffering, *ppr.* [ME. *profren*; Anglo-Fr. and OFr. *proffrir*, from *poroffrir*, *por-*, *pro-*, and *offrir*.]

1. to offer for acceptance; to make an offer of; as, to *proffer* a gift; to *proffer* services; to *proffer* friendship.

2. to essay or attempt of one's own accord. [Obs.]

prof′fēr, *n.* 1. an offer made; something proposed for acceptance by another; as, *proffers* of peace or friendship.

He made a *proffer* to lay down his commission of command in the army. —Clarendon.

2. essay; attempt. [Obs.]

prof′fēr·ēr, *n.* one who offers anything for acceptance.

prō·fi′cience (-fish′ens), *n.* proficiency. [Now Rare.]

prō·fi′cien·cy (-fish′en-), *n.*; *pl.* **prō·fi′cien·cies**, the state, quality, or fact of being proficient.

Syn.—expertness, adroitness, dexterity, skillfulness, advancement, improvement.

prō·fi′cient (-fish′ent), *a.* [L. *proficiens* (*-entis*), ppr. of *proficere*, to advance; *pro*, forward, and *facere*, to make.] highly competent; skilled.

prō·fi′cient, *n.* an expert.

prō·fi′cient·ly, *adv.* with proficiency.

prō·fiç′ū·ous, *a.* [LL. *proficuus*, from L. *proficere*, to advance.] profitable; advantageous; useful. [Obs.]

prō′file, *n.* [It. *profilo*, from L. *pro*, before, and *filum*, a thread, line, outline.]

1. a side view of the face.

2. a drawing of such a view.

3. outline; as, the *profile* of a distant hill.

4. a short, vivid biography, briefly outlining the most outstanding characteristics of the subject.

5. in architecture, a side or sectional elevation of a building or the like.

6. in engineering, a vertical section through a work or section of country to show the elevations and depressions.

7. in fortification, (a) a section perpendicular to the face of the work; (b) a light wooden frame set up to guide workmen in throwing up a parapet.

prō′file, *v.t.*; profiled, *pt.*, *pp.*; profiling, *ppr.* 1. to draw the outline of; to draw in profile or with a side view.

2. in mechanics, to work (an object) to an outline, as by chiseling, filing, etc.

3. to write a profile of.

prō′file çut′tēr, in woodworking, the cutting knife, usually made up of sections which correspond to parts of a given pattern of molding, and by which molding is cut in a machine.

prō′file pā′pēr, paper ruled into equal squares or rectangles and thus made suitable for laying out profiles in engineering.

prō′fil·ing mȧ·chine′, a machine having a rotory milling cutter which may be guided by a pattern or templet: used in making interchangeable parts.

prō′fil·ist, *n.* one who makes profiles.

prof′it, *n.* [ME.; OFr.; L. *profectus*, pp. of *proficere*, to profit, lit., to proceed forward, to advance; *pro*, forward, and *facere*, to make.]

1. proficiency; advancement; improvement. [Obs.]

My brother Jacques he keeps at school, and report speaks goldenly of his *profit*. —Shak.

2. advantage; gain; benefit.

3. [*often pl.*] (a) financial or monetary gain obtained from the use of capital in a transaction or series of transactions; (b) the ratio of this to the amount of capital invested; (c) proceeds from property or the like.

4. [*often pl.*] in economics, the net income, as of a business, or the difference between the income and the costs, direct and indirect.

5. a right to take a portion of the products of land: also called *profit à prendre*.

prof′it, *v.t.*; profited, *pt.*, *pp.*; profiting, *ppr.* to benefit; to advance the interest of; to be of advantage or service to.

'Tis a great means of *profiting* yourself, to copy diligently excellent pieces and beautiful designs. —Dryden.

prof′it, *v.i.* 1. to make progress; to improve, grow, prosper, advance, etc. [Obs.]

2. to benefit; to reap an advantage, financial or otherwise; as, to *profit* by trade or manufactures.

3. to be of advantage or benefit; to bring good.

prof′it·ȧ·ble, *a.* yielding or bringing profit or gain; gainful; lucrative; useful; advantageous; as, a *profitable* business, a *profitable* study.

Syn.—gainful, desirable, beneficial, productive, remunerative.

prof′it·ȧ·ble·ness, *n.* the state or quality of being profitable.

prof′it·ȧ·bly, *adv.* in a profitable manner; with profit, gain, or benefit.

prof′it-and-lọss′, *a.* of or showing profit and loss.

prof′it and lọss, the gain and loss from business transactions, etc.: applied especially to a bookkeeping account at the close of a fiscal period.

prof·it·eer′, *n.* one who takes unfair advantage of a shortage of supply, such as is produced by war, to make excessive profits by charging unreasonably high prices.

prof·it·eer′, *v.i.*; profiteered, *pt.*, *pp.* profiteering, *ppr.* to be a profiteer.

prof′it·ing, *n.* gain; advantage; improvement.

prof′it·less, *a.* without profit or gain.

prof′it-shār″ing, *a.* of profit sharing.

prof′it shār′ing, the practice of giving employees a share in the profits of a business, in addition to paying them stipulated wages.

prof′li·gȧ·cy, *n.* the quality or condition of being profligate.

prof′li·gāte, *a.* [L. *profligatus*, pp. of *profligare*, to rout, to ruin; *pro*, forward, and *fligere*, to drive or dash.]

1. abandoned to vice; lost to principle, virtue, or decency; vicious; shameless in wickedness.

2. extremely wasteful; recklessly extravagant.

3. beaten; overthrown; conquered. [Obs.]

Syn.—abandoned, dissolute, depraved, degenerate, corrupt, shameless.

prof′li·gāte, *n.* an abandoned or a depraved person; one who is profligate.

prof′li·gāte, *v.t.* to drive away; to disperse; to discomfit; to overcome. [Obs.]

prof′li·gāte·ly, *adv.* in a profligate manner.

prof′li·gāte·ness, *n.* the quality or state of being profligate; profligacy.

prof·li·gā′tion, *n.* defeat; rout. [Obs.]

prof′lu̇·ence, *n.* a progress or course. [Rare.]

prof′lu̇·ent, *a.* [ME.; L. *profluens*, ppr. of *profluere*; *pro-*, forth, and *fluere*, to flow.] flowing smoothly and copiously.

prō fọr′mȧ, [L.] for (the sake of) form; as a matter of form.

prō·found′, *a.* [ME.; OFr. *profund*, *profond*; It. *profondo*; L. *profundus*; *pro*, forward, and *fundus*, bottom.]

1. deep; descending or being far below the surface: mainly poetic when used of the physical features of the earth's surface; as, a gulf *profound*.

2. marked by intellectual depth; entering deeply into subjects; not superficial; as, *profound* reasoning.

3. deeply or intensely felt; as, a *profound* reverence for the Supreme Being.

4. thoroughgoing; as, *profound* changes in our mode of living.

5. unbroken; as, a *profound* silence.

Syn.—deep, penetrating, obscure, mysterious, humble.

prō·found′, *n.* 1. an abyss or deep, as of the ocean or of space. [Poet.]

2. that which is profound. [Poet.]

prō·found′, *v.i.* and *v.t.* to dive; to penetrate. [Obs.]

prō·found′ly, *adv.* in a profound manner.

prō·found′ness, *n.* the state or quality of being profound.

prō·ful′ġent, *a.* gleaming; brilliant; effulgent. [Poet.]

prō·fun′di·ty, *n.*; *pl.* **prō·fun′di·ties**, [ME. *profundite*; OFr. *profondite*; LL. *profunditas*, from L. *profundus*, deep.]

1. depth, especially great depth.

2. something profound, as a thought.

3. a very deep place; an abyss.

prō·fūse′, *a.* [ME.; L., *profusus*, pp. of *profundere*, to pour out; *pro*, forth, and *fundere*, to pour.]

1. poured forth, given, or produced freely and abundantly.

2. pouring forth or giving freely; generous, often to the point of excess (usually with *in*); as, she was *profuse in* her apologies.

Syn.—lavish, prodigal, extravagant, liberal. —*Profuse* denotes pouring out with great fullness or exuberance; *lavish* is stronger, implying unnecessary or wasteful excess; *prodigal* is stronger still, denoting unmeasured or reckless profusion.

prō·fūṣe′, *v.t.* to pour out. [Obs.]

prō·fūse′ly, *adv.* in a profuse manner.

prō·fūse′ness, *n.* the quality or state of being profuse.

prō·fū′ṣion, *n.* [Fr.; L. *profusio* (*-onis*), from *profusus*, lavish.]

1. a pouring forth or expending with great liberality or wastefulness.

2. great liberality or wastefulness.

3. abundant supply; abundance.

Syn.—copiousness, plenty, prodigality.

prō·fū′sive, *a.* lavish; profuse.

prog, *v.i.*; progged (progd), *pt.*, *pp.*; progging, *ppr.* [via dial., from ME. *prokken*, to beg (prob. from L.G.).] to prowl about, as in search of food or plunder; to forage. [Obs. or Brit. Dial.]

prog, *v.t.* to poke; to prod. [Scot. and Brit. Dial.]

prog, *n.* 1. food obtained as by progging. [Obs. or Brit. Dial.]

2. a goad; a prod. [Scot. and Brit. Dial.]

prō·gen′ẽr·āte, *v.t.* to beget. [Rare.]

prō·gen·ẽr·ā′tion, *n.* the act of begetting. [Rare.]

prō·gen′i·tive, *a.* [LL. *progenitivus.*] capable of begetting offspring; reproductive.

prō·gen′i·tŏr, *n.* [ME. *progenitour*; Fr. *progeniteur*; L., from *progignere*, to beget; *pro-*, forth, and *gignere*, to beget.] an ancestor in the direct line; a forefather.

prō·gen·i·tō′ri·ăl, *a.* pertaining to progenitors.

prō·gen′i·tŏr·ship, *n.* the state of being a progenitor.

prō·gen′i·tress, *n.* a woman progenitor.

prō·gen′i·trix, *n.* same as *progenitress.*

prō·gen′i·tūre, *n.* a begetting or birth. [Rare.]

prog′e·ny, *n.*; *pl.* **prog′e·nieṣ**, [ME. and OFr. *progenie*; L. *progenies*, descent, lineage, race, family, from *pro*, forth, and *gen*, root of *gignere*, to bring forth, to bear, seen also in *gender*, *generation*, *genus*, etc.] offspring, children, or descendants collectively; issue.

prō·gẽr·mi·nā′tion, *n.* [L. *progerminare*, to germinate.] birth; issue; origin. [Rare.]

prō·ges′tẽr·ōne, *n.* [*pro-*, and *ges*tation, and *ster*ol, and *-one.*] a crystalline hormone, $C_{21}H_{30}O_2$, secreted by the corpus luteum or prepared synthetically, serving to prepare the uterus for the reception and development of the fertilized ovum.

prō·ges′tin, *n.* [*pro-*, and *gest*ation, and *-in.*]

1. progesterone: the earlier name.

2. any substance whose action is like that of progesterone.

prog′gẽr, *n.* one who progs; a person who digs for clams. [Dial.]

prō·glos′sis, *n.* [Gr.] the tip of the tongue.

prō·glot′tiç, *a.* of, relating to, or forming a proglottid.

prō·glot′tid, *n.* any one of the joints of a tapeworm's body: each segment has both male and female reproductive organs and can become an independent organism.

prō·glot·tid′ē·ăn, *a.* same as *proglottic.*

prō·glot′tis, *n.*; *pl.* **prō·glot′ti·dēṣ**, [Gr. *proglōssis*, tip of the tongue; *pro*, before; and *glōssa*, tongue.] a proglottid; a single sexually mature segment of a tapeworm.

prog′nȧ·thī, *n.pl.* [Gr. *pro*, before, and *gnathos*, jaw.] prognathous people collectively.

prog·nath′iç, *a.* [Gr. *pro*, before, and *gnathos*, jaw.] prognathous.

prog′nȧ·thiṣm, *n.* in anatomy, the state of being prognathous, or a tendency toward this condition.

prog′nȧ·thous (*or* prog-nā′), *a.* [Gr. *pro*, before, and *gnathos*, jaw.]

1. having either or both jaws projecting abnormally.

2. projecting abnormally: said of a jaw.

prog′nȧ·thy, *n.* prognathism.

Prog′nē, *n.* [L., from Gr. *Proknē*, daughter of Pandion, changed into a swallow.]

1. a genus of swallows containing the purple martins, of which *Progne subis* is common in the United States.

2. [p–] an American butterfly whose hind wings show an L-shaped silver mark on the underside.

3. [p–] a swallow. [Poet.]

prog·nō′sis, *n.*; *pl.* **prog·nō′sēṣ**, [Gr. *prognōsis*; *pro*, before, and *gnōsis*, a knowing, from *gignōskein*, to know.] a forecast or forecasting; especially, in medicine, a judgment in advance concerning the probable course of a disease and the chances of recovery.

prog·nos′tiç, *n.* [Gr. *prognōstikos*; *pro*, before, and *gignōskein*, to know, to perceive.]

1. a sign or indication of things to come; an omen.

2. a foretelling; prediction.

Syn.—augury, forecast, foreshadowing.

prog·nos′tiç, *a.* 1. foretelling; predictive.

2. in medicine, of, or serving as a basis for, prognosis.

prog·nos′tiç, *v.t.* to prognosticate. [Obs.]

prog·nos′ti·çȧ·ble, *a.* of such a nature as to be prognosticated.

prog·nos′ti·çāte, *v.t.*; prognosticated, *pt.*, *pp.*; prognosticating, *ppr.* 1. to foretell; to predict.

2. to indicate beforehand.

Syn.—forebode, prophesy, forecast.

prog·nos′ti·çāte, *v.i.* to predict future events.

prog·nos·ti·çā′tion, *n.* 1. the act of foreshowing or foretelling a future course or event.

2. a prophecy or prediction.

prog·nos′ti·çā·tive, *a.* having the nature of or tending to prognostication.

prog·nos′ti·çā·tŏr, *n.* a foreteller of a future course or event; a predictor.

prō′gram, *n.* [Fr. *programme*, from Gr. *programma*, an edict; *pro*, before, and *graphein*, to write.]

1. originally, (a) a proclamation; (b) a prospectus or syllabus.

2. (a) a list of the events, pieces, performers, speakers, etc. of an entertainment, ceremony, or the like; (b) the events or pieces collectively.

3. an outline of work to be done; a prearranged plan of procedure; as, the *program* of the administration.

> He has the whole *program* of the war mapped out. —William McKinley.

4. a scheduled broadcast on radio or television.

5. all the activities that can be participated in at a community center, camp, etc.

6. (a) a logical sequence of operations to be performed by a digital computer in solving a problem or in processing data; (b) the coded instructions and data for such a sequence.

prō′gram, *v.t.*; programed *or* programmed, *pt.*, *pp.*; programing *or* programming, *ppr.* 1. to enter or schedule in a program.

2. (a) to plan a computer program for (a task, problem, etc.); (b) to furnish (a computer) with a program; (c) to incorporate in a computer program.

prō′gram, *v.i.* to plan or prepare a program or programs.

prō·gram′mȧ, *n.*; *pl.* **prō·gram′mȧ·tȧ**, 1. a proclamation or edict posted in a public place.

2. that which is written before something else; a prolegomenon.

prō·gram·mat′iç, *a.* of, or having the nature of, a program or program music.

prō′gramme, *n.*, *v.t.*, and *v.i.* Brit. spelling of *program.*

prō′gram·mẽr, *n.* one who prepares a program.

prō′gram mū′ṣiç, instrumental music that depicts or suggests a particular scene, story, etc.

prog′ress, *n.* [ME. *progresse*; OFr. *progres*; L. *progressus*, pp. of *progredi*, from *pro-*, before, and *gradi*, to step, go.]

1. an official journey, as of a sovereign. [Archaic.]

2. a moving forward or onward.

3. forward course; development.

4. improvement; advance toward perfection or to a higher state.

> In the modern world the intelligence of public opinion is the one indispensable condition of social *progress.* —President Eliot of Harvard.

Syn.—progression, advance, advancement.

prō·gress′, *v.i.*; progressed (-grest′), *pt.*, *pp.*; progressing, *ppr.* 1. to move forward or onward.

2. to continue toward completion; to come along.

3. to improve; to advance toward perfection or to a higher state.

prō·gress′, *v.t.* 1. to make progress in or pass through. [Obs.]

2. to push forward.

prō·gres′sion (-gresh′un), *n.* [L. *progressio*; see *progress.*]

1. a moving forward or onward; progress.

2. a sequence or succession, as of acts, happenings, etc.

3. in astronomy, direct planetary motion (as contrasted to retrograde).

4. in mathematics, a series of numbers increasing or decreasing by proportional differences.

5. in music, (a) the movement forward from one tone or chord to another; (b) a succession of tones or chords.

arithmetic progression; progression in a series of numbers having a common difference, as the increasing series, 1, 3, 5, 7, 9, etc., or the decreasing series, 9, 7, 5, 3, 1, etc., where the common differences are 2 and −2 respectively: generalized in the formula a, $a \pm d$, $a \pm 2d$, $a \pm 3d$, $a \pm 4d$, etc.

geometric progression; progression in a series of terms having a common ratio, as 2, 4, 8, 16, etc., or 16, 8, 4, 2, etc., where the ratios are 2 and $^1/_2$ respectively: generalized in the formula a, ar, ar^2, ar^3, or $a, \frac{a}{r}, \frac{a}{r^2}, \frac{a}{r^3}$, etc.

harmonic progression; progression in harmonic proportion, or such that of any three consecutive terms the first is to the third as the difference between the first and second is to the difference between the second and third; a progression in which the reciprocals of the terms taken in order form an arithmetic progression, as $^1/_1$, $^1/_4$, $^1/_7$, $^1/_{10}$, etc.

prō·gres′sion·ăl, *a.* of or involving progression.

prō·gres′sion·ist, *n.* 1. a person who believes in progress, particularly in the progress of human society toward desirable ends through natural processes or human effort.

2. one who holds that the existing species of animals and plants were not originally created but were gradually developed from simpler forms.

prog′ress·ist, *n.* a progressionist. [Now Rare.]

prō·gres′sive, *a.* [Fr. *progressif*, from *progres.*]

1. moving forward or onward.

2. continuing by successive steps; as, the *progressive* decline of Macbeth's fortunes.

3. marked by progress, reform, or a continuing improvement; as, a *progressive* people, *progressive* education.

4. favoring progress through political or other reform.

5. in bridge, involving certain regular changes of partners and tables after each game.

6. in grammar, indicating continuing action: said of certain verb forms, such as *am working* (as compared with the simple form *work*).

7. in medicine, becoming more severe or spreading to other parts: said of a disease.

8. [P–] in politics, of a Progressive Party.

prō·gres′sive, *n.* 1. a person who is a progressive, especially one who favors political progress or reform.

2. [P–] a member of a Progressive Party.

prō·gres′sive·ly, *adv.* in a progressive manner.

prō·gres′sive·ness, *n.* the state or quality of being progressive.

Prō·gres′sive Pär′ty, 1. an American political party organized in 1912 by followers of Theodore Roosevelt, with a program of direct primaries, extension of the franchise to women, the initiative, referendum, and recall, etc.: in full, *National Progressive Party.*

2. an American political party formed in 1924 under the leadership of Robert M. LaFollette.

3. an American political party formed in 1948, originally under the leadership of Henry A. Wallace.

prō·gres′siv·iṣm, *n.* the doctrines, principles, and practices of progressives.

prō·gres′sŏr, *n.* one who progresses.

prōgue, *v.i.* to prog. [Obs.]

prōgue, *n.* prog. [Obs.]

Prō·gym·nā′ṣi·um, *n.* in Germany, a preparatory school.

prō·gym′nō·spẽrm, *n.* [*pro-* and *gymnosperm.*] an archetypal gymnosperm.

prō′heme, *n.* a proem; a preface. [Obs.]

prō·hib′it, *v.t.* prohibited, *pt.*, *pp.*; prohibiting, *ppr.* [from L. *prohibitus*, pp. of *prohibere*, to prohibit; *pro*, before, and *habere*, to have.

1. to forbid, as by law; to refuse to permit; to interdict by authority; as, to *prohibit* a person from doing a thing; to *prohibit* a thing from being done.

2. to hinder; to debar; to prevent.

> Gates of burning adamant,
> Barred over us, *prohibit* all egress.
> —Milton.

prō·hib′it·ẽr, *n.* one who prohibits.

prō·hi·bi′tion (-bish′un), *n.* [ME. *prohibicion*; L. *prohibitio.*]

1. a prohibiting or being prohibited.

2. an order or law forbidding something to be done.

3. the forbidding by law of the manufacture, transportation, and sale of alcoholic liquors for beverage purposes.

writ of prohibition; a writ issuing from a superior tribunal, directed to the judges of an inferior court, commanding them to cease from the prosecution of a suit.

prō·hi·bi′tion·ist, *n.* 1. one who is in favor of prohibiting by law the manufacture and sale of alcoholic beverages.

2. [P–] a member of the Prohibition Party.

3. one who favors such heavy duties on certain goods as practically to prohibit their importation. [Rare.]

Prō·hi·bi′tion Pär′ty, an American political party, established in 1869, advocating the prohibition by law of the manufacture and sale of alcoholic drinks.

prō·hib′i·tive, *a.* 1. prohibiting or tending to prohibit something.

2. such as to prevent purchase, use, etc.; as, *prohibitive* prices.

prō·hib′i·tō·ry, *a.* [from L. *prohibitus*, pp. of *prohibere*, to prohibit.] prohibitive.

prohibitory index; same as *Index Librorum Prohibitorum* under *Index*.

proin, *v.t.* and *v.i.* to trim; to prune. [Obs.]

prō·jeçt′, *v.t.*; projected, *pt.*, *pp.*; projecting, *ppr.* [from L. *projectus*, pp. of *projicere*, to throw forth, to cast forward, to cause to jut out; *pro*, forward, and *jacere*, to throw.]

1. to propose (an act or plan of action).

2. to throw or hurl forward.

3. to send forth in one's thoughts or imagination; as, *project* yourselves into the world of tomorrow.

4. to cause to stick out.

5. to cause (a shadow, image, etc.) to fall or appear upon a surface.

6. in geometry, to represent (a solid, etc.) on a plane surface by means of lines of correspondence.

7. in psychology, to externalize (a thought or feeling) so that it appears to have objective reality.

prō·jeçt′, *v.i.* 1. to stick out; to protrude; to extend beyond something else; to jut; to be prominent; as, the cornice *projects*.

2. to make a plan; to scheme. [Rare.]

proj′eçt, *n.* 1. a scheme; a design; a proposal of something intended or devised.

2. in education, a unit of work involving constructive thought and action in connection with learning.

3. an undertaking, as a unit of work done by one of the various governmental agencies; as, a flood-control *project*.

4. in psychology, a sensory impression seen as existing away from and outside of the mind of an individual.

Syn.—device, scheme, plan, design.

prō·jeç′tile, [Fr., from L. *projectus*.]

1. an object, as a bullet, shell, rocket, etc., designed to be hurled or shot forward, as from a gun.

2. anything thrown or hurled forward.

prō·jeç′tile, *a.* 1. hurling or impelling forward; as, a *projectile* force.

2. given by impulse; impelled forward; as, *projectile* motion. [Rare.]

3. in zoology, that can be thrust out; protrusile; as, the *projectile* jaw of a fish.

4. intended to be used as a projectile; designed to be hurled forward.

prō·jeç′tion, *n.* [L. *projectio* (*-onis*), from *projectus*, pp. of *projicere*, to throw forward.]

1. a projecting or being projected.

2. something that projects, or sticks out.

3. something that is projected; specifically, in map making, the representation on a plane of the earth's surface (or the celestial sphere) or of a part thereof.

4. in psychiatry, the unconscious act or process of ascribing to others one's own ideas or impulses, especially when such ideas or impulses are considered undesirable.

5. in photography, (a) the process of causing an image to appear upon a screen, etc.; as, the *projection* of motion pictures; (b) the representation thus produced.

polar projection; a system of representation in which the plane of projection meets either the arctic or the antarctic circle.

powder of projection; the alchemic powder that supposedly transmuted prepared substances into gold.

projection of a point on a plane; the foot of a perpendicular let fall upon a plane from the given point.

projection of a straight line upon a plane; the line connecting the projections upon the plane of the extremities of the given line.

prō·jeç′tion bo͝oth, the small chamber at the rear of a motion-picture theater from which the pictures are projected onto a screen at the front.

prō·jeç′tion·ist, *n.* the operator of a motion-picture projector.

prō·jeç′tive, *a.* of, made by, or of the nature of projection.

prō·jeç′tive ġē·om′e·try, the branch of geometry dealing with those properties of a figure (projective properties) that do not vary when the figure is projected.

prō·jeçt′ment, *n.* design; contrivance. [Obs.]

prō·jeç′tŏr, *n.* 1. one who or that which projects; specifically, a machine for throwing an image on a screen; as, a motion-picture *projector*.

2. one who forms projects.

prō·jeç′tūre, *n.* a jutting out; a projection.

prō·jet′ (-zhe′), *n.* [Fr.] a plan proposed; the draft of a proposed measure.

prō·kar′y·ōte, *n.* [Gr. *pro*, before, and *karyōtis*, a date, from *karyon*, a nut.] an organism, as a bacterium, lacking a true nucleus in the cell and reproducing by fission.

prō·kar·y·ot′iç, *a.* of or having to do with prokaryotes.

prōke, *v.t.* and *v.i.* to urge; to prod; to poke. [Obs.]

prō·kei′mē·non, *n.* [Gr., neut. ppr. of *prokeisthai*, to lie or be placed before.] in the Orthodox Eastern Church, a short hymn or selection from the Psalms sung before the Epistle.

prō·laç′tin, *n.* in biochemistry, a pituitary hormone which influences milk secretion in mammals and gland secretions in birds.

prō′lan, *n.* [from L. *proles*, offspring, and *-an* as in pentos*an*.] a hormone found in the urine during pregnancy, hence serving to diagnose pregnancy in the early stages.

prō·lapse′, *n.* [L. *prolapsus*, pp. of *prolabi*, to fall forward.] in medicine, the slipping out of place or falling of some internal organ, as of the uterus or intestines.

prō·lapse′, *v.i.*; prolapsed, *pt.*, *pp.*; prolapsing, *ppr.* in medicine, to fall or slip out of place.

prō·lap′sus, *n.* prolapse.

prō′lāte, *a.* [L. *prolatus*, pp. of *proferre*, to bring forward.] extended at the poles; elongated: opposed to *oblate*; as, a *prolate* spheroid is produced by the revolution of an ellipse about its larger diameter.

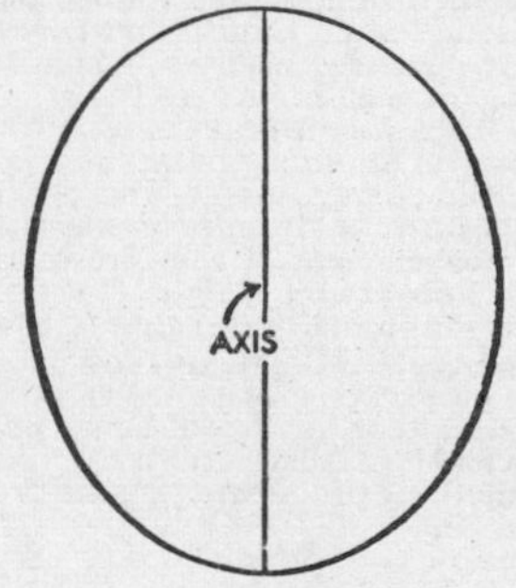

PROLATE SPHEROID

prō·lā′tion, *n.* [L. *prolatio* (*-onis*), a bringing forward, from *prolatus*, pp. of *proferre*, to bring forward.]

1. utterance; pronunciation. [Obs.]

2. delay; the act of deferring. [Obs.]

3. in music, the subdivision of a semibreve into minims.

prō′leg, *n.* [L. *pro*, for, and *leg*.] in zoology, any of the stubby, fleshy limbs attached to the abdomen of certain insect larvae.

prō·lē·gom′ē·non, *n.*; *pl.* **prō·lē·gom′ē·nȧ,** [Gr., from *pro*, before, and *legein*, to speak.] [*usually in pl.*] a preliminary observation or introductory remark; a foreword, as to a book or treatise.

prō·lē·gom′ē·nous, *a.* 1. preliminary; prefatory.

2. having or giving too lengthy prefatory matter.

prō·lep′sis, *n.*; *pl.* **prō·lep′sēs,** [L.; Gr. *prolēpsis*, an anticipating, from *prolambanein*, to take before; *pro-*, before, and *lambanein*, to take.] an anticipating; especially, the describing of an event as taking place before it could have done so, the treating of a future event as if it had already happened, or the anticipating and answering of an argument before one's opponent has a chance to advance it.

prō·lep′tiç, *a.* [Gr. *prolēptikos*, anticipating.]

1. pertaining to prolepsis; anticipatory.

2. in medicine, anticipating the usual time: applied to a periodical disease whose paroxysm returns at an earlier hour at every repetition.

prō·lep′ti·çăl, *a.* same as *proleptic*.

prō·lep′ti·çăl·ly, *adv.* by way of anticipation.

prō·lep′tiçs, *n.* the art and science of prognosis.

prō′lēs, *n.* [L.] 1. offspring.

2. in law, legal offspring.

prō·lē·tā′nē·ous, *a.* having numerous offspring. [Rare.]

prō·lē·tăr′i·ăn, *a.* of or characteristic of the proletariat.

prō·lē·tăr′i·ăn, *n.* a member of the proletariat; a worker; one of the masses; one whose only capital is his labor.

prō·lē·tăr·′i·ăn·iṣm, *n.* the political position of the proletarians.

prō·lē·tăr′i·ăn·īze, *v.t.* to bring to proletarianism.

prō·lē·tăr′i·ăt, *n.* [Fr. *prolétariat*.]

1. the class of lowest status in ancient Roman society.

2. the class of lowest status in any society or community. [Rare.]

3. the working class; especially, the industrial working class: the current sense, as in Marxism.

prō·lē·tăr′i·āte, *n.* same as *proletariat*.

prō′lē·tăr·y, *n.*; *pl.* **prō′lē·tăr·ies,** [L. *proletarius*, a citizen of the lowest class, who served the state only by having children, since he had no property, from *proles*, offspring.]

1. in ancient Rome, a member of the lowest class of citizens, who had no property.

2. a proletarian. [Obs.]

prō′lē·tăr·y, *a.* proletarian. [Obs.]

prō′li·cīde, *n.* [L. *proles*, offspring, and *cædere*, to slay.] the crime of destroying one's offspring either before or after birth.

prō·lif′ĕr·āte, *v.i.*; proliferated, *pt.*, *pp.*; proliferating, *ppr.* to reproduce or grow by multiplying new parts, as by budding, in quick succession.

prō·lif′ĕr·āte, *v.t.* to reproduce (new parts) in quick succession.

prō·lif·ĕr·ā′tion, *n.* a proliferating or being proliferated.

prō·lif′ĕr·ȧ·tive, *a.* characterized by proliferation.

prō·lif′ĕr·ous, *a.* [L. *proles*, *prolis*, offspring, and *ferre*, to bear.]

1. in botany, (a) multiplying freely by means of buds, side branches, etc.; (b) having leafy shoots growing from a flower or fruit.

2. in zoology, reproducing by budding, as coral.

proliferous cyst; in pathology, a cyst producing multiple daughter cysts, often malignant.

prō·lif′ĕr·ous·ly, *adv.* in a proliferous manner.

prō·lif′iç, *a.* [Fr. *prolifique*; L. *prolificus*, *proles*, *prolis*, offspring, and *facere*, to make.]

1. producing many young or much fruit: applied to animals and plants; as, a *prolific* female; a *prolific* tree.

2. fruitful; abounding (often with *in* or *of*); as, a controversy *prolific of* evil consequences.

3. turning out many products of the mind; as, a *prolific* scholar or poet.

> Jefferson was one of the most *prolific* of writers. —Paul Leicester Ford.

prō·lif′i·çȧ·cy, *n.* the quality or state of being prolific; fruitfulness; great productiveness.

prō·lif′i·çăl·ly, *adv.* in a prolific manner; fruitfully; with great increase.

prō·lif′i·çāte, *v.t.* to render prolific. [Obs.]

prō·lif·i·çā′tion, *n.* 1. the generation of young or of fruit.

2. in botany, the production of certain outgrowths, as of a second flower from the substance of the first. This is either from the center of a simple flower, or from the side of an aggregate flower.

prō·lif′iç·ness, *n.* the state or quality of being prolific.

prō·liġ′ĕr·ous, *a.* 1. producing offspring.

2. in botany, proliferous.

proligerous disk; the cellular layer embedding the germinal ovum of a nascent organism.

prō′lin, *n.* proline.

prō′līne, *n.* [from *pyrrole* and *-ine*.] an amino

acid, $C_6H_9O_3N$, formed by the decomposition of proteins.

prō·lix′ (*or* prō′liks), *a.* [L. *prolixus*, extended, prolix; *pro*, forth, and root of *liquere*, to flow.]
1. long; extended; of long duration. [Obs.]
2. long and wordy; extending or spread out to a great length; tedious; tiresome; diffuse; as, a *prolix* oration; a *prolix* poem.
3. given to or indulging in long and wordy discourses; tedious; prosy; discussing at great length; as, a *prolix* writer.
Syn.—diffuse, protracted, tedious, wordy, long, tiresome, wearisome, prolonged.

prō·lix′ious (-lik′shus), *a.* prolix. [Obs.]

prō·lix′i·ty, *n.*; *pl.* **prō·lix′i·ties** 1. length; extent. [Rare.]
2. the state or quality of being prolix; wordiness; great length; tediousness; tiresome length of speaking; as, *prolixity* in writings.

prō·lix′ly, *adv.* at great length.

prō·lix′ness, *n.* prolixity.

prōll, *v.t.* and *v.i.* to prowl. [Obs.]

prōll′ẽr, *n.* a prowler. [Obs.]

prō·loc′ū·tŏr, *n.* [L., from *proloqui*; *pro*, for, and *loqui*, *locutus*, to speak.]
1. the speaker or chairman of a convocation.
2. one who speaks for another person or for a group; a spokesman.

prō·loc′ū·tŏr·ship, *n.* the office or station of a prolocutor.

prō·loc′ū·trix, *n.* a female prolocutor; a spokeswoman.

prō′log, *n.* same as *prologue.*

prō′log·īze, *v.i.* see *prologuize.*

prō′logue, *n.* [Fr., from L. *prologus*, Gr. *prologos*; *pro*, before, and *logos*, discourse.]
1. an introduction to a poem, play, etc.; especially introductory lines or verses spoken, ordinarily by one of the principal members of the cast, before a dramatic performance.
2. the person who speaks such lines or verses.
3. a preliminary act or course of action foreshadowing greater events.
Also spelled *prolog.*

prō′logue, *v.t.*; prologued, *pt.*, *pp.*; prologuing, *ppr.* to introduce with a formal preface.

prō′logu·īze, prō′log·īze, *v.i.*; prologuized *or* prologized, *pt.*, *pp.*; prologuizing *or* prologizing, *ppr.* to compose or deliver a prologue.

prō·long′, *v.t.*; prolonged, *pt.*, *pp.*; prolonging, *ppr.* [Fr. *prolonger*, from L. *pro*, forth, and *longus*, long.]
1. to lengthen in time; to extend the duration of; to continue; as, to *prolong* life.
Generalities and abstractions do not demand our *prolonged* consideration.
—Rose Elizabeth Cleveland.
2. to put off to a distant time; to defer. [Obs.]
3. to extend in space or length; as, to *prolong* a straight line.
Syn.—extend, protract, continue, draw out.

prō·long′à·ble, *a.* capable of being prolonged.

prō·lon′gāte, *v.t.*; prolongated, *pt.*, *pp.*; prolongating, *ppr.* to prolong.

prō·lon·gā′tion, *n.* [Fr.] 1. the act of lengthening or state of being lengthened in time or space; as, the *prolongation* of life; the *prolongation* of a line.
2. extension of time by delay or postponement; as, the *prolongation* of a term of credit. [Obs.]
3. the part added in lengthening something; an extension.
Two remarkable processes or *prolongations* of the bones of the leg. —Paley.

prō·longe′, *n.* [Fr.] a strong rope having a hook and toggle, occasionally used in field artillery to drag a gun carriage without a limber, when it is necessary to retire firing through a street or narrow defile.

prō·longe knot, a kind of knot: see *knot* illus.

prō·long′ẽr, *n.* one who or that which lengthens in time or space.

prō·long′ment, *n.* the act of prolonging; the state of being prolonged; prolongation.

prō·lū′sion, *n.* [L. *prolusio* (-*onis*), a prelude, from *prolusus*, pp. of *proludere*, to play beforehand.]
1. a prelude to a game or entertainment.
2. a preliminary piece, essay, or exercise in which the writer treats briefly of a subject with which he intends to deal more fully at a future time; a literary composition of a preliminary or preparatory character.

prō·lū′sō·ry, *a.* [ML. *prolusorius.*] of, having the nature of, or serving as a prolusion; preliminary.

prom, *n.* [contr., from *promenade.*] a ball or dance, usually given by a particular group or class of students at a college, high school, etc. [Colloq.]

prom·à·nā′tion, *n.* [L. *pro*, forth, and *manatio* (-*onis*), a flowing, from *manare*, to flow.] the act of flowing forth; emanation. [Obs.]

prom·ē·nāde′ (*or* -näd′) *n.* [Fr., from *se promener*, to go for a walk, *promener*, to take for a walk, from LL. *prominare*, to drive (animals) onward; L. *pro-*, forth, and *minare*, to drive (animals), from *minari*, to threaten.]
1. a leisurely walk taken for pleasure, to display one's finery, etc.
2. a public place for walking, as an avenue, the deck of a ship, or the hall of a building.
3. in dancing, (a) a ball; (b) a march, ordinarily participated in by all the guests, beginning a formal ball; (c) a march introduced between the figures of a square dance.

prom·ē·nāde′, *v.i.*; promenaded, *pt.*, *pp.*; promenading, *ppr.* to take a promenade; to walk about for amusement, exercise, or show.

prom·ē·nāde′, *v.t.* 1. to take a promenade along or through.
2. to take or show on or as on a promenade; to parade.

prom·ē·nād′ẽr, *n.* one who promenades.

prō·mer′it, *v.t.* [L. *promeritus*, *promerere*, to be deserving of; *pro*, for, and *merere*, to merit.]
1. to oblige; to confer a favor on. [Obs.]
2. to deserve; to procure by merit. [Obs.]

prom′e·rops, *n.* [Gr. *pro*, before, and *merops*, a bird, the bee eater.] in zoology, any one of various species of birds of the genera *Promerops*, *Epimachus*, and other related genera, mostly native to Papua. They are closely allied to the birds of paradise. *Promerops cafer* is the Cape promerops.

Prō·mē′thē·ăn, *a.* 1. pertaining to, like, or suggestive of Prometheus.
2. having a life-giving, creative, or courageously original quality.

Prō·mē′thē·ăn, *n.* 1. a person who is Promethean in spirit or deeds.
2. [p-] an early kind of match, in use before the present-day friction match.

Prō·mē′theūs, *n.* [Gr. *Promētheus*, probably from *promēthēs*, forethinking; *pro*, before, and *mathein*, to learn.]
1. in Greek mythology, the son of the Titan Iapetus, who took pity on the misery of mankind and stole fire from heaven for their benefit. Zeus (Jupiter), enraged at the favor this gift procured him, caused him to be chained to a rock on Mount Caucasus, where a vulture each day devoured his liver, which was made whole again each night.
2. a large bombycid moth, *Callosamia promethea*, of America, the larvae of which feed on the wild cherry, maple, and other trees.

prō·mē′thi·um, *n.* [from *Prometheus.*] a metallic chemical element of the rare-earth group: symbol, Pm: atomic weight, 147(?); atomic number, 61: formerly designated as *illinium.*

prom′i·nence, *n.* [L. *prominentia*, from *prominere*, to project.]
1. the state or quality of being prominent; conspicuousness; distinction.
2. something prominent; as, the *prominence* of the nose.

prom′i·nen·cy, *n.* prominence.

prom′i·nent, *a.* [L. *prominens* (-*entis*), ppr. of *prominere*, to project.]
1. standing out beyond the line or surface of something; jutting; protuberant; projecting; as, a *prominent* figure on a vase.
2. conspicuous; noticeable at once; as, a *prominent* person.
3. eminent; widely and favorably known; as, a *prominent* character.
Syn.—jutting, protuberant, conspicuous, eminent, distinguished, main, important, leading.

prom′i·nent, *n.* in zoology, any bombycid moth of the family *Notodontidæ*, the larva of which has a projection on its back.

prom′i·nent·ly, *adv.* in a prominent manner.

prō·mis·cū′i·ty, *n.*; *pl.* **prō·mis·cū′i·ties,**
1. state, quality, or instance of being promiscuous, especially in sexual relations.
2. an indiscriminate mixture; a jumble.

prō·mis′cū·ous, *a.* [L. *promiscuus*; *pro*, forth, and *miscere*, to mix.]
1. mingled; consisting of elements united in a body or mass without order; confused; undistinguished; as, a *promiscuous* crowd or mass.
A wild, where weeds and flowers *promiscuous* shoot. —Pope.
2. characterized by a lack of discrimination; specifically, engaging in sexual intercourse indiscriminately or with many persons.
3. without plan or purpose; casual. [Colloq.]
Syn.—indiscriminate, confused, undistinguished.

prō·mis′cū·ous·ly, *adv.* in a promiscuous manner.
A few green islands, scattered about *promiscuously*, are occupied by barracks, villas, and plantations. —William E. Curtis.

prō·mis′cū·ous·ness, *n.* the state or quality of being promiscuous.

prom′ise, *n.* [L. *promissum*, from *promittere*, to send before or forward; *pro*, forth, and *mittere*, to send.]
1. an oral or written agreement to do or not to do something; a vow.
2. indication, as of a successful prospect or future; basis for expectation.
3. that which is promised; performance or grant of the thing promised.
Wait for the *promise* of the Father.
—Acts i. 4.
Syn.—assurance, engagement, word, contract, pledge, covenant, arrangement.

prom′ise, *v.t.*; promised (-ist), *pt.*, *pp.*; promising, *ppr.* 1. to make a promise of (something) to somebody.
2. to engage or pledge (followed by an infinitive or clause).
Temures *promised* the garrison of Sebastia that, if they would surrender, no blood should be shed. —Paley.
3. to give a basis for expecting; as, the year *promises* a good harvest.
4. to pledge to give in marriage.

prom′ise, *v.i.* 1. to make a promise.
2. to give a basis for hopes or expectations (often with *well* or *fair*).

Prom′ised Land; same as *Land of Promise.*

prom·is·ee′, *n.* a person to whom a promise is made.

prom′is·ẽr, *n.* one who promises.

prom′is·ing, *a.* giving promise or just grounds for expectation or hope of future distinction or excellence; likely to turn out well; as, a *promising* youth.
Syn.—auspicious, assuring, engaging.

prom′is·ing·ly, *adv.* in a promising manner.

prom′is·or, *n.* in law, a promiser.

prō·mis′sive, *a.* making a promise. [Rare.]

prom′is·sō·ri·ly, *adv.* by way of promise.

prom′is·sō·ry, *a.* 1. containing a promise.
2. having the nature of a promise.
promissory note; a written promise to pay a given sum of money to a certain person or bearer on demand or on a specified date.

prom′ont, *n.* a promontory. [Obs.]

prom′ŏn·tō·ry, *n.*; *pl.* **prom′ŏn·tō·ries,** [LL. *promontorium*; *pro*, forward, and *mons*, a mountain.]
1. a high point of land or rock projecting out over an expanse of water; a headland.
Like one that stands upon a *promontory.*
—Shak.
2. in anatomy, a prominent part; as, the *promontory* of the tympanum.

prō·mor·phō·log′i·căl, *a.* pertaining to promorphology.

prō·mor·phol′ō·gist, *n.* one who is versed in promorphology.

prō·mor·phol′ō·gy, *n.* [Gr. *pro*, before, and *morphē*, form, and *-logy.*] morphology in which the forms of organisms are considered geometrically.

prō·mōte′, *v.t.*; promoted, *pt.*, *pp.*; promoting, *ppr.* [L. *promotus*, pp. of *promovere*, to move forward; *pro*, forward, and *movere*, to move.]
1. to forward; to advance; to contribute to the growth, enlargement, or excellence of.
It is the duty of all ranks to *promote* the means of education. —John Adams.
2. to exalt; to elevate; to raise; to prefer in rank or honor; as, *promoted* to a foremanship.
3. to work actively and stir up interest for the accomplishment of (something); as, *promote* a new law.
4. in education, to move forward a grade in school.
5. to inform against. [Obs.]
Syn.—advance, encourage, forward, prefer, organize, equip.

prō·mōte′, *v.i.* to incite or urge on a person; also, to act as an informer. [Obs.]

prō·mōte′ment, *n.* promotion. [Rare.]

prō·mō′tẽr, *n.* 1. one who or that which promotes; as, a *promoter* of charity.

2. an informer. [Obs.]

3. a person who furthers a business enterprise; an organizer of capital; one who makes a business of organizing or financing any kind of financial, commercial, or manufacturing enterprise.

4. the plaintiff in a suit in an ecclesiastical court. [Brit.]

prō·mō′tion, *n.* [LL. *promotio* (*-onis*), from L. *promotus*, pp. of *promovere*, to advance.]

1. a promoting; furtherance.

2. the result of promoting; advancement.

3. the stirring up of interest in an enterprise.

prō·mō′tion·ăl, *a.* pertaining to promotion or advancement; preparatory to, or serving to bring about, promotion.

prō·mō′tive, *a.* tending to advance or promote.

prō·möve′, *v.t.* to advance; also, to incite. [Obs.]

prō·möv′ẽr, *n.* one who promotes. [Obs.]

prompt, *a.* [Fr. *prompt*, from L. *promptus*, brought out, hence at hand, ready, quick, from *promptus*, *promere*, to bring forth; *pro*, forth, and *emere*, to take.]

1. ready and quick to act as occasion demands; immediately or instantly at hand.

2. done at the appointed time; exact; as, *prompt* payment.

3. hasty; forward. [Obs.]

Syn.—active, alert, expeditious, apt, nimble, ready.

prompt, *v.t.*; prompted, *pt.*, *pp.*; prompting, *ppr.* 1. to incite; to move or excite to action or exertion; as, insults *prompt* anger or revenge.

2. to remind (a person) of something he has forgotten; to help with a cue.

3. to move or inspire by suggestion.

prompt, *n.* 1. the act of prompting.

2. in commerce, (a) the time limit specified for the payment of an account; (b) the contract in which the due date is specified.

3. any reminder or notice of payment due.

prompt′book, *n.* in the theater, a fully annotated copy of the script of a play, for the use of the director or prompter, containing full directions for action, settings, properties, etc.

prompt′ẽr, *n.* 1. one who prompts.

2. the person in an operatic or theatrical company whose task is to cue the actors or singers when they forget their words, entrances, etc.

promp′ti·tūde, *n.* [Fr., from L. *promptus*, ready.] the quality of being prompt.

prompt′ly, *adv.* readily; quickly; expeditiously.

prompt′ness, *n.* readiness; quickness.

prompt nōte, a note of reminder or statement sent to a purchaser, stating the amount due, the goods purchased, and the day on which payment becomes due.

prompt sīde, the side of the stage at which the prompter is stationed.

promp′tū·ăr·y, *n.* [Fr. *promptuaire*, from LL. *promptuarium*, a storehouse, from L. *promptus*, ready.] a place from which supplies are drawn; a storehouse; a magazine; a repository. [Obs.]

promp′tūre, *n.* suggestion; incitement; prompting. [Archaic.]

prō·mul′gāte, *v.t.*; promulgated, *pt.*, *pp.*; promulgating, *ppr.* [L. *promulgatus*, pp. of *promulgare*, to publish, the origin of which is uncertain.]

1. to publish or make known officially (a decree, church dogma, etc.); as, to *promulgate* a law.

2. (a) to make known the terms of (a new or proposed law or statute); (b) to put (a law) into effect by publishing its terms.

3. to make widespread; as, *promulgate* learning and culture.

Syn.—publish, declare, proclaim, announce, spread.

prō·mul·gā′tion, *n.* the act of promulgating; as, the *promulgation* of an edict or law.

prō′mul·gā·tŏr, *n.* one who promulgates.

prō·mulġe′, *v.t.*; promulged, *pt.*, *pp.*; promulging, *ppr.* to promulgate. [Archaic.]

prō·mul′ġẽr, *n.* same as *promulgator*.

prō·mus′cis, *n.* [altered from *proboscis*.] the proboscis of hemipterous insects.

prō·mȳ·cē′li·ăl, *a.* pertaining to the promycelium.

prō·mȳ·cē′li·um, *n.*; *pl.* **prō·mȳ·cē′li·ȧ,** [*pro*- and *mycelium*.] in botany, a short filament bearing sporidia, developed in spore germination.

prō·nā′os, *n.* [Gr. *pro*, before, and *naos*, temple.] the porch or vestibule of a temple; a portico.

prō′nāte, *a.* [LL. *pronatus*, pp. of *pronare*, to bend forward, from L. *pronus*, from *pro*, before.] more or less prone; leaning; inclined, as trees.

prō′nāte, *v.t.*; pronated, *pt.*, *pp.*; pronating, *ppr.* [from LL. *pronatus*, pp. of *pronare*, to bend forward, from L. *pronus*, from *pro*, before.]

1. to bend or turn face downward; to make prone.

2. to turn (the hand or forelimb) with the palm down or toward the body.

prō′nāte, *v.i.* to bow or bend forward; to assume a prone position.

prō·nā′tion, *n.* [from LL. *pronatus*: see *pronate*.]

1. a pronating; especially, in physiology, a turning of the hand so that the palm faces downward or a similar turning of the forelimb of an animal.

2. that position of the hand when the palm is turned downward.

Opposed to *supination*.

prō·nā′tŏr, *n.* a muscle of the forearm or forelimb by which pronation is effected: opposed to *supinator*.

prōne, *a.* [L. *pronus*, leaning forward, prone, from *pro*, before.]

1. lying or leaning face downward; pronated: opposed to *supine*.

2. lying flat or prostrate; in a horizontal position; as, he fell *prone* on the floor.

3. inclined; propense; disposed (with *to*); as, men *prone to* evil; *prone to* strife.

4. groveling; as, *prone* before tyranny.

5. leaning forward or sloping downward. [Poetic.]

prōne′ly, *adv.* in a prone manner or position.

prōne′ness, *n.* the state of being prone.

prō·neph′riç, *a.* of or pertaining to the pronephros.

prō·neph′ron, *n.* same as *pronephros*.

prō·neph′ros, *n.* [L. *pro*, before, and Gr. *nephros*, a kidney.] a primitive kidney, the most anterior of three pairs of renal organs in lower vertebrates, but appearing only transiently in the human embryo.

prọng, *n.* [nasalized form of *prog*, thrust.]

1. any pointed projecting part; as, the *prong* of an antler.

2. the tine of a fork or of a similar instrument.

3. a fork of a stream. [Dial.]

prọng, *v.t.* 1. to use a prong on; to pierce.

2. to break up (clods) with or as with a prong.

3. to furnish with prongs or tines.

prọng′buck, *n.* same as *pronghorn*.

prọnged, *a.* having prongs.

prọng hōe, a hoe with prongs to break the earth.

prọng′họrn, *n.*; *pl.* **prọng′họrnṣ** or **prọng′họrn,** a species of antelope, *Antilocapra americana*, which inhabits the western United States and Mexico. It frequents the plains in summer and the mountains in winter. It is one of the few hollow-horned ruminants and the only living one in which the horny branch is sheathed.

prō′ni·ty, *n.* same as *proneness*.

prō·nom′i·năl, *a.* [L. *pronomen*, a pronoun.] in grammar, belonging to or of the nature of a pronoun.

prō·nom′i·năl·īze, *v.t.*; pronominalized, *pt.*, *pp.*; pronominalizing, *ppr.* to use with the significance of a pronoun.

prō·nom′i·năl·ly, *adv.* as a pronoun.

prō·nō′tȧ·ry, *n.* prothonotary. [Obs.]

prō·nō′tum, *n.*; *pl.* **prō·nō′tȧ,** [LL., from Gr. *pro*, before, and *nōtos*, back.] the dorsal section of the prothorax of an insect.

prō′noun, *n.* [L. *pronomen*; *pro*, for, and *nomen*, noun.] in grammar, a word used in the place of or as a substitute for a noun: *I*, *you*, *he*, *she*, *it*, *we*, *they*, etc. are *pronouns*.

prō·nounce′, *v.t.*; pronounced (-nounst′), *pt.*, *pp.*; pronouncing, *ppr.* [Fr. *prononcer*; L. *pronuntiare*; *pro*, before, and *nuntiare*, to announce.]

1. (a) to utter or articulate (a sound or word); as, I *pronounce* it differently; (b) to utter or articulate (a word or sound) in the required or standard manner; as, he couldn't pronounce my name; (c) to indicate the pronunciation of (a word) with phonetic symbols.

2. to utter formally, officially, or solemnly; as, the court *pronounced* the sentence of death on the criminal.

3. to speak or utter rhetorically; to deliver; as, to *pronounce* an oration.

Speak the speech, I pray you, as I *pronounced* it to you. —Shak.

4. to declare or affirm; as, he *pronounced* the book to be a libel; he *pronounced* the signature to be a forgery.

prō·nounce′, *v.i.* 1. to speak with confidence or authority; to make a pronouncement (with *on*).

2. to articulate words; to give a pronunciation; as, to *pronounce* clearly.

Syn.—articulate, speak, utter.

prō·nounce′, *n.* declaration; pronouncement. [Obs.]

prō·nounce′ȧ·ble, *a.* capable of being pronounced or uttered.

prō·nounced′ (-nounst′), *a.* 1. of marked character; strongly marked or defined; as, a *pronounced* accent.

2. spoken or uttered.

3. decided; as, *pronounced* opinions.

prō·nounce′ment, *n.* 1. the act of pronouncing.

2. a formal announcement of fact, opinion, or judgment.

prō·noun′cẽr, *n.* one who pronounces.

prō·noun′cing, *a.* pertaining to, teaching, indicating, or serving as a guide in pronunciation; as, a *pronouncing* dictionary.

pron′tō, *adv.* [Sp., from L. *promptus*, brought out, hence at hand, ready, quick.] at once; quickly; immediately. [Slang.]

prō·nū′bi·ăl, *a.* [L. *pronubus*; *pro*, for, and *nubere*, to marry.] presiding over marriage. [Rare.]

prō·nū′çlē·us, *n.*; *pl.* **prō·nū′çlē·ī,** [*pro*- and *nucleus*.] in zoology, the nucleus of either the male or the female gamete, the former being called the spermatozoon and the latter the ovum: they unite in fertilization to form the double nucleus of the fertilized ovum.

prō·nun′ciăl (-shăl), *a.* pertaining to pronunciation.

prō·nun″ci·ȧ·men′tō (*or* -shi-), *n.*; *pl.* **prō·nun″ci·ȧ·men′tōṣ,** [Sp.] 1. a proclamation; a formal public announcement.

2. a manifesto.

prō·nùn″ciä·mien′tō (-thyä-myen′), *n.* same as *pronunciamento*.

prō·nun·ci·ā′tion, *n.* [L. *pronuntiatio* (*-onis*), from *pronuntiare*, to proclaim.]

1. the act or manner of pronouncing words with reference to the production of sounds, the placing of stress, intonation, etc.

2. the transcription in phonetic symbols of the accepted or standard pronunciation or pronunciations of a word; as, variant *pronunciations* are sometimes recorded here.

3. the manner of uttering a discourse or oration: generally called *delivery*. [Obs.]

prō·nun′ci·ȧ·tive (-shi- *or* -si-), *a.* 1. of or pertaining to pronunciation; pronunciatory.

2. uttering confidently; dogmatical. [Obs.]

The confident and *pronunciative* school of Aristotle. —Bacon.

prō·nun′ci·ā·tŏr, *n.* a pronouncer; one who pronounces.

prō·nun′ci·ȧ·tō·ry, *a.* relating to pronunciation.

prō·oe′mi·um, prō·oe′mi·on, *n.* [Gr. *prooimion*, proem.] an opening or introduction; the introduction to a poem or song; a preface; a proem.

prọọf, *n.*; *pl.* **prọọfs,** [OFr. *prueve*; LL. *proba*, proof; L. *probare*, to prove.]

1. any effort, process, or operation that attempts to establish truth or fact; a test; a trial; as, to make *proof* of the truth of a statement.

Only this *proof* I'll of thy valor make. —Shak.

2. something serving as evidence; that which proves or establishes; a convincing token or argument; a means of conviction.

Strong as *proofs* of holy writ. —Shak.

3. the thing proved or experienced; truth or knowledge gathered by experience. [Obs.]

'Tis a common *proof*,
That lowliness is young ambition's ladder. —Shak.

4. the state of having been tried and having stood the test; firmness or hardness that resists impression, or yields not to force.

5. the establishment of the truth of something; as, he is completing the *proof* of his theory.

6. a test or trial of the truth, worth, quality, etc. of something; as, the *proof* of the pudding is in the eating.

7. tested or proved strength, as of armor.

8. the relative strength of an alcoholic liquor with reference to the arbitrary standard for proof spirit, taken as 100 proof.

9. in engraving, a trial impression taken from a plate before its completion.

10. in law, all the facts, admissions, etc. which together operate to determine a verdict or judgment.

11. in mathematics, a process for testing the correctness or accuracy of a computation.

12. in printing, a printed trial sheet or impression, taken for comparison with the original manuscript to find and correct errors: called also *proof sheet.*

13. in photography, a trial print of a negative.

artist's proof; in engraving, one of the first proof impressions of an engraving or lithograph, taken before the plate is worn.

Syn.—demonstration, evidence, testimony, experience, trial, experiment, test, assay.

prọọf, *a.* 1. impenetrable; able to resist; of tested and proved strength: followed by *against.*

Proof against all temptation. —Milton.

2. pertaining to or used in proving, testing, or correcting; as, a *proof* sheet.

3. being of a standard alcoholic strength: said of liquors.

-prọọf, a suffix used in forming adjectives (and verbs) meaning: (a) *impervious to,* as in water*proof*; (b) *protected from* or *against,* as in fool*proof,* weather*proof*; (c) *as strong as,* as in armor*proof*; (d) *resistive to, unaffected by,* as in pity*proof,* woman*proof.*

prọọf′-ärm′, *v.t.* to arm as with proof; to arm so as to make secure. [Rare.]

A delicate, and knows it,
And out of that *proof-arms* herself.
—Beau. and Fl.

prọọf chärġe, a charge of powder, greater than the usual charge, fired in a gun or cannon to test the strength of the weapon.

prọọf′ing, *n.* 1. the act or process of making (something) proof, especially waterproof.

2. the chemical, etc. used in this process.

prọọf′less, *a.* lacking proof.

prọọf′less·ly, *adv.* without proof.

prọọf plāne, in electricity, a small, thin metallic disk, attached to an insulated handle, used in measuring the electrification of an object.

prọọf plān′ẽr, same as *planer,* sense 3.

prọọf press, a printing press used in taking proofs.

prọọf′-prọọf′, *a.* standing out against proof; unaffected by proof.

prọọf′rēad, *v.t.* and *v.i.* to read (printers' proofs, etc.) in order to make corrections.

prọọf′rēad·ẽr, *n.* one whose work is reading printers' proofs for the purpose of finding errors and correcting them.

prọọf′rēad·ing, *n.* the act or art of reading printers' proofs for the correction of errors.

prọọf sheet, a printer's proof.

prọọf spir′it, an alcoholic liquor, or a mixture of alcohol and water, containing 50 per cent of its volume of alcohol having a specific gravity of .7939 at 60° F.

prō·os′trȧ·çum, *n.*; *pl.* **prō·os′trȧ·çȧ,** [Gr. *pro,* before, and *ostrakon,* shell.] in zoology, the horny pen of the belemnite.

prō-ō′tiç, *a.* [Gr. *pro,* before, and *ous, ōtos,* the ear.] being in front of the ear or auditory capsule.

prō-ō′tiç, *n.* a pro-otic bone.

prop, *n.* a sea shell used in the game of props.

prop, *n.* [ME. *proppe*; M.D. *proppe,* a prop.]

1. a rigid support, as a beam, stake, or pole, placed under or against a structure or part.

2. a person who is one of the main supports of an enterprise, institution, etc.

prop, *v.t.*; propped (propt), *pt., pp.*; propping, *ppr.* 1. to support, hold in place, or prevent from falling by placing something under or against: often with *up*; as, to *prop* (*up*) a fence or an old building.

2. to lean (something) *against* a support.

3. to sustain; to bolster; as, to *prop* a declining state.

prop, *n.* a property (sense 7).

prō·pae·deū′tiç, prō·pae·deū′tiç·ăl, *a.* [Gr. *propaideuein,* to instruct beforehand, from *pro,* before, and *paideuein,* to instruct, to educate, from *pais, paidos,* a child.] pertaining to or having the nature of elementary or introductory instruction; instructing beforehand.

prō·pae·deū′tiç, *n.* an elementary or introductory subject or study.

prō·pae·deū′tiçs, *n.pl.* [*construed as sing.*] the preliminary learning connected with any art or science; the body of basic knowledge and of rules necessary for the study of some particular art, science, etc.

prop′ȧ·gȧ·ble, *a.* capable of being propagated.

Such creatures as are produced each by its peculiar seed constitute a distinct *propagable* sort of creatures. —Boyle.

prop·ȧ·gan′dȧ, *n.* [L., gerundive of *propagare,* to propagate.]

1. [P–] in the Roman Catholic Church, a committee of cardinals, the Congregation for the Propagation of the Faith, in charge of the foreign missions.

2. any organization or movement working for the propagation of particular ideas, doctrines, practices, etc.

3. the ideas, doctrines, practices, etc. spread in this way.

4. any systematic, widespread, deliberate indoctrination or plan for such indoctrination: now often used in a derogatory sense, connoting deception or distortion.

prop·ȧ·gan′diṣm, *n.* the art, system, or use of propaganda.

prop·ȧ·gan′dist, *n.* a person who propagandizes.

prop·ȧ·gan′dist, *a.* of, or having the nature of, propaganda.

prop·ȧ·gan′dīze, *v.t.*; propagandized, *pt., pp.*; propagandizing, *ppr.* 1. to spread (a doctrine or theory) by propaganda.

2. to subject (someone) to propaganda.

prop·ȧ·gan′dīze, *v.i.* to organize or conduct propaganda.

prop′ȧ·gāte, *v.t.*; propagated, *pt., pp.*; propagating, *ppr.* [L. *propagatus,* pp. of *propagare,* to peg down, to set, to propagate, to enlarge; *pro,* before, forward, and *pag,* root of *pangere,* to fasten.]

1. to cause (a plant or animal) to reproduce itself; to raise or breed.

2. to reproduce (itself); to multiply: said of a plant or animal.

3. to transmit (hereditary characteristics) by reproduction.

4. to spread (ideas, customs, etc.) from person to person or generation to generation.

5. to extend or transmit through space; as, to *propagate* light.

6. to cause to increase or multiply. [Obs. or Rare.]

Griefs of my own lie heavy in my breast,
Which thou wilt *propagate.* —Shak.

Syn.—multiply, continue, increase, spread, diffuse, disseminate, promote, circulate, beget, breed, engender, generate, originate, procreate.

prop′ȧ·gāte, *v.i.* to reproduce or multiply, as plants or animals.

prop′ȧ·gā·ting glȧss, a bell-shaped glass used by horticulturists to cover slips and seedlings in course of propagation.

prop·ȧ·gā′tion, *n.* [L. *propagatio* (*-onis*), a propagating.] a propagating or being propagated.

prop′ȧ·gā·tive, *a.* promoting or tending to promote propagation; of a propagating character.

prop′ȧ·gā·tŏr, *n.* [L.] one who propagates; any agent of propagation.

prop′ȧ·gā·tō·ry, *a.* propagative; serving for propagation.

prō·pā′gō, *n.* in horticulture, a branch laid down to take root; also, in botany, a bulblet.

prō·pag′ū·lum, *n.*; *pl.* **prō·pag′ū·lȧ,** [LL., dim. of L. *propago,* a shoot.]

1. a runner or sucker used in the asexual propagation of plants.

2. a gemma or bud in certain algae which serves as a means of asexual reproduction.

prō·pāle′, *v.t.* [LL. *propalare,* from L. *propalam,* openly.] to divulge publicly. [Archaic.]

prō·pal′i·năl, *a.* [Gr. *pro,* before, and *palin,* back, and *-al.*] moving forward and backward; relating to or characterized by a backward and forward movement, as the lower jaw in the process of mastication.

prō′pāne, *n.* [*prop*yl and meth*ane.*] a gaseous hydrocarbon of the methane series, $CH_3CH_2CH_3$, derived from crude petroleum.

prō·pär·ġyl′iç, *a.* same as *propiolic.*

prō·par·ox′y·tŏne, *a.* [*pro-* and *paroxytone.*] in Greek grammar, having an acute accent on the antepenult.

prō·par·ox′y·tōne, *n.* a proparoxytone word.

prō pā′tri·ȧ, [L.] for (one's) country.

prō·pel′, *v.t.*; propelled, *pt., pp.*; propelling, *ppr.* [L. *propellere*; *pro,* forward, and *pellere,* to drive.] to drive forward; to impel or press onward by force; as, wind or steam *propels* ships; the blood is *propelled* through the arteries and veins by the action of the heart.

Syn.—drive, push, urge, press, force.

prō·pel′lănt, *n.* a person or thing that propels; specifically, the explosive charge that propels a shell from a gun.

prō·pel′lent, *a.* propelling or tending to propel.

prō·pel′lent, *n.* a propellant.

prō·pel′lẽr, *n.* a person or thing that propels; specifically, any of various propellent devices on a ship or aircraft, consisting typically of a series of blades mounted at an angle in a revolving hub and serving to propel the craft forward by a driving action on the water or air.

prō·pel′lẽr well, a recess or chamber into which the propeller of a ship may be hoisted when not in use.

prō·pel′ment, *n.* 1. the act or process of propelling.

2. a mechanism for propelling the scape wheel of a clock.

prō·pend′, *v.i.* [L. *propendere*; *pro,* forward, and *pendere,* to hang.] to lean forward; to incline; to be disposed (*to* or *toward* something). [Obs.]

prō·pend′ent, *a.* inclining forward or toward; hanging down. [Rare.]

prō′pēne, *n.* same as *propylene.*

prō·pense′, *a.* [L. *propensus,* pp. of *propendere,* to incline.] leaning toward; inclined; prone; disposed; as, women *propense* to piety. [Archaic.]

prō·pense′ly, *adv.* with natural inclination; in a propense manner. [Archaic.]

prō·pense′ness, *n.* the state or condition of being propense; natural inclination. [Archaic.]

prō·pen′sion, *n.* [L. *propensio* (*-onis*).] the state of being propense; proclivity; propensity. [Rare.]

It requires critical nicety to find out the genius or *propensions* of a child.
—L'Estrange.

prō·pen′si·ty, *n.*; *pl.* **prō·pen′si·tieṣ,** [from L. *propensus,* pp. of *propendere,* to hang forward.]

1. a natural inclination or tendency; a bent.

2. favorable inclination; bias (with *for*). [Rare.]

Syn.—proclivity, aptitude, proneness, disposition, inclination, tendency, bent.

prop′ẽr, *a.* [Fr. *propre*; L. *proprius,* one's own.]

1. specially adapted or suitable to a specific purpose or specific conditions; appropriate; as, the *proper* tool for this job.

2. naturally belonging or peculiar (*to* a specified person or thing); as, this weather is *proper to* Florida.

3. conforming to an accepted standard or to good usage; correct.

4. fitting; seemly; right; as, it was *proper* for him to strike back.

5. decent; decorous; chaste; modest: often connoting exaggerated respectability.

6. understood in its most restricted sense; strictly so called: usually following the noun modified, as, the population of Cleveland *proper* (i.e., apart from its suburbs).

7. (a) fine; good; excellent; (b) becoming in appearance; handsome. [Archaic or Dial.]

8. complete; thorough; as, a *proper* scoundrel. [Brit. Colloq.]

9. one's own; belonging to oneself or itself. [Obs.]

10. in ecclesiastical usage, reserved for a particular day or festival: said of prayers, rites, etc.

11. in grammar, used to designate a specific individual, place, etc.: *Donald, Rover, Boston,* etc. are *proper* nouns, written with an initial capital letter.

12. in heraldry, represented in its natural colors.

in proper; in private; as one's own. [Obs.]

proper flower or *corolla*; a floret, as distinguished from the entire head of which it is a part.

proper fraction; in mathematics, a fraction in which the numerator is less, or of lower degree, than the denominator, as $^2/_5$ or x/x^2.

proper motion; in astronomy, that motion of a star by which it alters its place with reference to other stars near it; the actual change of place in a star, as determined by comparison with its former place.

proper nectary; a nectary not connected with the petals or other parts of the flower.

proper noun; a name designating a specific person, place, etc.

proper perianth or *involucre*; a perianth enclosing but a single flower.

proper receptacle; a receptacle supporting but a single fruit or flower.

Syn.—fit, just, right, suitable, fair, appropriate, adapted, meet, seasonable, correct, fitting.

prop'ẽr, *adv.* properly; very; exceedingly; as, *proper* angry; *proper* good. [Dial.]

prop'ẽr, *n.* 1. any part of a church service appointed for a certain day or season; as, the *proper* for Whitsunday.

2. in the Roman Catholic Church, the part of a breviary or missal which contains such propers.

prop'ẽr·āte, *v.t.* and *v.i.*; properated, *pt., pp.*; properating, *ppr.* [L. *properatus, properare,* to hasten.] to hasten; to come on amain. [Obs.]

Hurl them down on their pates,
Awhile to keep off death which *properates.*
—Vicars.

prop·ẽr·ā'tion, *n.* the act of properating or hastening; haste. [Obs.]

prō·per'i·spōme, *n.* [Gr. *properispōmenon,* from *properispān,* to circumflex the penult; *pro,* before, and *perispān,* to draw round, to mark a vowel or word with the circumflex; *peri,* around, and *spān,* to draw.] in Greek prosody, a word having the circumflex accent on the penult.

prō·per·i·spom'ē·non, *n.* same as *properispome.*

prop'ẽr·ly, *adv.* in a proper manner.

properly speaking; in a strict or literal sense; without qualifications.

prop'ẽr·ness, *n.* the quality or state of being proper.

prop'ẽr·tied, *a.* owning property.

prop'ẽr·ty, *n.*; *pl.* **prop'ẽr·tieṣ,** [OFr. *properte*; L. *proprietas,* from *proprius,* one's own.]

1. the right to possess, use, and dispose of something; ownership; as, *property* in land.

2. a thing or things owned; holdings or possessions collectively; especially, land or real estate owned.

3. a specific piece of land or real estate.

4. any trait or attribute proper to a thing or, formerly, to a person; characteristic quality; peculiarity; specifically, any of the principal characteristics of a substance, especially as determined by the senses; as, the *properties* of a chemical compound.

5. something regarded as being possessed by, or at the disposal of, a person or group of persons; as, that joke is common *property.*

6. in logic, an essential quality common to all members of a species or class.

7. in the theater and motion pictures, any of the movable articles used as part of the setting or in a piece of stage business, except the costumes, backdrops, etc.: also called *prop.*

private property; any property, real or personal, which the owner has the right to control, use, and dispose of as he wills.

property damage; in law, disturbance or injury to the intrinsic value of property.

Syn.—characteristic, attribute, essential, necessity, goods, ownership, possessions, right.

prop'ẽr·ty, *v.t.* 1. to endow with properties or qualities. [Obs.]

2. to appropriate; to seize and hold as one's own. [Obs.]

prop'ẽr·ty man, a man employed in a theater to take charge of the properties.

prop'ẽr·ty plot, a list for the property man of the properties required in a theatrical production.

prop'ẽr·ty rọọm, the room in a theater in which the properties are kept.

prō·phāne', *a.* and *v.* profane. [Archaic.]

prō'phāṣe, *n.* [*pro-* (before) and *phase.*] in biology, the first stage in mitosis, during which the chromatin is formed into chromosomes.

proph'ȧ·sis, *n.* [Gr. *prophasis,* from *prophainein,* to show beforehand; *pro,* before, and *phainein,* to show.] in medicine, prognosis; foreknowledge of a disease. [Rare.]

proph'e·cy, *n.*; *pl.* **proph'e·cieṣ,** [OFr. *prophecie, prophetie,* from LL. *prophetia*; Gr. *prophēteia,* from *prophētēs,* prophet.]

1. prediction of the future under the influence of divine guidance; act or practice of a prophet.

2. any prediction.

3. something prophesied or predicted; specifically, the utterance or utterances of a prophet.

4. a book of prophecies.

proph'e·sī·ẽr, *n.* one who prophesies.

proph'e·sȳ, *v.t.*; prophesied (-sīd), *pt., pp.*; prophesying, *ppr.* 1. to declare or predict (something) by or as by the influence of divine guidance.

2. to predict (a future event) in any way.

3. to foreshadow. [Rare.]

proph'e·sȳ, *v.i.* 1. to speak as a prophet; to utter or make prophecies.

2. to teach religious matters; to preach.

proph'et, *n.* [Fr. *prophète,* from LL. *propheta,* from Gr. *prophētēs*; *pro,* before, and *phanai,* to speak.]

1. a person who speaks for God or a god, or as though under divine guidance.

2. a religious teacher or leader regarded as, or claiming to be, divinely inspired.

3. a spokesman for some cause, group, movement, etc.

4. a person who predicts future events in any way.

school of the prophets; among the ancient Israelites, a school or college in which young men were educated to become teachers of religion among the people. These students were called *sons of the prophets.*

the Prophet; (a) in Moslemism, Mohammed; (b) in Mormonism, Joseph Smith.

the Prophets; (a) the writers of the prophetic books of the Old Testament; (b) these books, forming a division distinct from the Law and the Hagiographa.

proph'et·ess, *n.* a woman prophet.

proph'et flow'ẽr, a boraginaceous plant of the genus *Arnebia,* native to northern India.

proph'et·hood, *n.* the state, position, or powers of a prophet.

prō·phet'iç, prō·phet'i·çȧl, *a.* 1. of, or having the powers of, a prophet.

2. of, or having the nature of, prophecy or a prophecy.

3. containing a prophecy; as, a *prophetic* utterance.

4. that prophesies, predicts, or foreshadows.

And fears are oft *prophetic* of the event.
—Dryden.

prō·phet·i·çal·i·ty, *n.* propheticalness. [Rare.]

prō·phet'i·çȧl·ly, *adv.* by way of prediction; in the manner of prophecy.

prō·phet'i·çȧl·ness, *n.* the state of being prophetic. [Rare.]

proph'et·iṣm, *n.* the act or art of a prophet; the system or practice of prophecy.

proph'et·īze, *v.i.*; prophetized, *pt., pp.*; prophetizing, *ppr.* to give predictions; to prophesy.

proph'et·ship, *n.* prophethood.

prō·phor'iç, *a.* enunciative. [Rare.]

prō·phy·laç'tiç, *a.* [Gr. *prophylaktikos,* from *prophylassein,* to prevent, to guard against; *pro,* before, and *phylassein,* to preserve.] in medicine, preventive; protecting against disease.

prō·phy·laç'tiç, *n.* in medicine, a remedy, device, etc. that prevents disease.

prō·phy·laç'ti·çȧl, *a.* prophylactic.

prō·phy·lax'is, *n.* [LL., from Gr. *prophylassein,* to prevent.] in medicine, the prevention of disease; preventive treatment.

prō·pīce', prō·pīse', *a.* propitious; favorable. [Obs.]

prop·i·nā'tion, *n.* [L. *propinatio.*] the act of pledging, or drinking first, and then offering the cup to another. [Obs.]

prō·pīne', *v.t.* to drink, as a toast. [Obs.]

prō·pīne', *n.* 1. a present; a tip; drink money. [Scot.]

2. the power of giving. [Scot.]

prō·piṅ'qui·ty (-kwi-), *n.* [L. *propinquitas,* from *propinquus,* near.]

1. nearness in time or place.

2. nearness of relationship; kinship.

3. likeness or affinity of nature.

prō'pi·ō·nāte, *n.* a salt or ester of propionic acid.

prō'pi·ōne, *n.* in chemistry, the ketone of propionic acid, obtained in the distillation of some propionates.

prō·pi·on'iç, *a.* [Gr. *prōtos,* first, and *piōn,* fat, and *-ic.*] designating a colorless, sweet-smelling, liquid fatty acid, $C_2H_5CO_2H$, found in chyme and sweat, and produced in the distillation of wood.

Prō·pi·thē'çus, *n.* [LL., from Gr. *pro,* before, and *pithēkos,* ape.] a genus of animals of the lemur family, including the diadem lemur.

prō·pi'ti·ȧ·ble (-pish'i-), *a.* that can be propitiated.

prō·pi'ti·āte, *v.t.*; propitiated, *pt., pp.*; propitiating, *ppr.* [L. *propitiatus,* pp. of *propitiare,* to propitiate, from *propitius,* propitious.] to cause to become favorably inclined; to win or regain the good will of; to appease or conciliate.

prō·pi'ti·āte, *v.i.* to make atonement or propitiation. [Rare.]

prō·pi·ti·ā'tion, *n.* [Fr. *propitiation.*]

1. a propitiating or being propitiated.

2. something that propitiates.

prō·pi'ti·ā·tive, *a.* that propitiates or tends to propitiate.

prō·pi'ti·ā·tŏr, *n.* one who propitiates.

prō·pi'ti·ȧ·tō·ri·ly, *adv.* by way of propitiation.

prō·pi'ti·ȧ·tō·ry, *a.* having the power to propitiate or intended to propitiate; supplicatory; expiatory; as, a *propitiatory* rite or sacrifice.

prō·pi'ti·ȧ·tō·ry, *n.* 1. in ancient Jewish ritual, the mercy seat; the lid or cover of the ark of the covenant, lined within and without with plates of gold.

2. a propitiation; specifically, the propitiatory sacrifice of Jesus. [Obs.]

prō·pi'tious (-pish'us), *a.* [L. *propitius,* favorable, generally supposed to be formed from *pro,* before, forward, and *petere,* to seek, originally to fly, referring to a bird whose flight is of happy augury.]

1. favorably inclined or disposed; gracious; as, the gods were *propitious.*

2. favorable; boding well; auspicious; as, a *propitious* omen.

3. that favors or furthers; advantageous; as, *propitious* winds.

Syn.—auspicious, benign, helpful, gracious, favorable.

prō·pi'tious·ly, *adv.* in a propitious manner; favorably; kindly.

prō·pi'tious·ness, *n.* the quality of being propitious; favorableness; kindness.

prō'plaṣm, *n.* [Gr. *proplasma,* model.] a mold; a matrix, as that used by sculptors.

prō·plas'tiç, *a.* serving as a matrix or mold.

prō·pleū'rȧl, *a.* pertaining to the propleuron.

prō·pleū'ron, *n.*; *pl.* **prō·pleū'rȧ,** [Gr. *pro,* before, and *pleura,* side.] the lateral part of the prothorax of an insect.

prō·plex'us, *n.* the plexus of the procoelia, or lateral ventricle of the brain.

prō·pō'dē·um, *n.* [L. *podex,* fundament.] that part of the thorax of an insect above the insertion of the abdomen, as in hymenopters; originally, the basal segment of the abdomen.

prō·pō'di·ăl, *a.* 1. of or pertaining to the propodialia.

2. of or pertaining to the propodium.

prō·pō·di·ā'lē, *n.*; *pl.* **prō·pō·di·ā'li·ȧ,** [LL., from Gr. *propodios,* before the feet.] one of the proximal segment bones of the forearm or thigh; a femur or humerus.

prop'ō·dīte, *n.* [Gr. *pro,* before, and *pous, podos,* foot, and *-ite.*] in crustaceans, the penultimate joint of a maxilliped.

prop·ō·dit'iç, *a.* of or pertaining to a propodite.

prō·pō'di·um, *n.*; *pl.* **prō·pō'di·ȧ,** [Gr. *propodios,* before the feet.] the foremost division of the foot of a mollusk.

prop'ō·lis, *n.* [Gr. *pro,* before, and *polis,* city.] a brownish, waxy substance collected from the buds of certain trees by bees and used by them to cement or caulk their hives.

prop'ō·līze, *v.t.*; propolized, *pt., pp.*; propolizing, *ppr.* to secure or cover with propolis.

prō·pōne', *v.t.*; proponed, *pt., pp.*; proponing, *ppr.* [L. *pro,* forth, and *ponere,* to set.] to propound; to bring forward; to propose, as a plan or scheme. [Scot.]

prō·pō'nent, *n.* [L. *proponens (-entis),* ppr. of *proponere,* to set forth.]

1. a person who makes a proposal or proposition.

2. a person who supports a cause, etc.

3. in law, one who propounds something, especially a will for probate.

prō·pō'nent, *a.* proposing; offering proposals.

prō·pōr'tion, *n.* [L. *proportio*; *pro,* before, and *portio,* part or share.]

1. a part, share, or portion, especially in its relation to the whole; a quota.

2. the comparative relation between parts or things with respect to size, amount, quantity, etc.; ratio.

3. a harmonious relationship between parts or things; balance or symmetry.

4. size, degree, or extent relative to a standard.

5. [*pl.*] dimensions; as, a building of large *proportions.*

6. relation, other than of quantity, between things; comparison; analogy. [Rare.]

7. in mathematics, (a) an equality between ratios; a relationship between four quantities in which the quotient of the first divided by the second is equal to that of the third divided by the fourth (e.g., 2 is to 6 as 3 is to 9): also *geometrical proportion*; (b) a method for finding the fourth quantity in such a relation-

ship when three are given; rule of three.

compound proportion; the equality of the ratio of two quantities to another ratio, the antecedent and consequent of which are respectively the products of the antecedents and consequents of two or more ratios.

continued proportion; see *continued proportion* under *continued*.

geometrical proportion; same as *proportion* (sense 7a).

Syn.—symmetry, rate, relation, ratio, quota, size.

prō·pōr′tion, *v.t.*; proportioned, *pt.*, *pp.*; proportioning, *ppr.* 1. to adjust the comparative relation, harmony, or symmetry of (something) to another; as, *proportion* the penalty to the nature of the crime.

> In the loss of an object, we do not *proportion* our grief to its real value, but to the value our fancies set upon it.—Addison.

2. to arrange the parts of (a whole) so as to be harmonious or symmetrical.

prō·pōr′tion·ȧ·ble, *a.* in proper proportion; having due correspondence; proportional.

prō·pōr′tion·ȧ·ble·ness, *n.* the state of being proportionable. [Rare.]

prō·pōr′tion·ȧ·bly, *adv.* according to proportion or comparative relation. [Rare.]

prō·pōr′tion·ăl, *a.* [Fr. *proportionnel*, from L. *proportio* (*-onis*), proportion.]

1. having a due comparative relation; being in suitable proportion or degree; as, the parts of that building are *proportional*.

2. in mathematics, having the same or a constant ratio; as, the velocity of a moving body is *proportional* to the impelling force.

3. relating to or determined by proportion; relative; as, the *proportional* meanings of life and death.

proportional logarithms; same as *logistic logarithms* under *logarithm*.

proportional representation; a system of voting that gives minority parties representation in a legislature in proportion to their popular vote.

proportional scale; (a) a scale divided in proportion to the logarithms of the natural numbers; (b) a scale for changing the size of a drawing, etc., and at the same time preserving the proportion of the parts.

prō·pōr′tion·ăl, *n.* a quantity in a mathematical proportion.

prō·pōr·tion·al′i·ty, *n.* the quality of being proportional, or in proportion.

prō·pōr′tion·ăl·ly, *adv.* in proportion.

prō·pōr′tion·ate, *a.* [LL. *proportionatus*, from L. *proportio* (*-onis*).] in proper proportion; proportional.

prō·pōr′tion·āte, *v.t.*; proportionated, *pt.*, *pp.*; proportionating, *ppr.* to make proportionate; to adjust according to a settled rate or to due comparative relation; as, to *proportionate* punishments to crimes.

prō·pōr′tion·ate·ly, *adv.* in a proportionate manner.

prō·pōr′tion·ate·ness, *n.* the state or quality of being proportionate.

prō·pōr′tioned, *a.* 1. in proportion.

2. having specified proportions.

prō·pōr′tion·less, *a.* without proportion.

prō·pōr′tion·ment, *n.* the act of proportioning or the state of being proportioned.

prō·pōs′ăl, *n.* 1. a proposing.

2. a plan, scheme, etc. proposed.

3. an offer of marriage.

prō·pōse′, *v.t.*; proposed, *pt.*, *pp.*; proposing, *ppr.* [Fr. *proposer*; *pro-*, from L. *pro*, forth, and *poser*, from L. *positus*, pp. of *ponere*, to place.]

1. to put forth for consideration or acceptance.

2. to purpose; to plan; intend.

3. to present as a toast in drinking.

4. to nominate (someone) for membership, office, etc.

5. to set or place forth; to place out. [Obs.]

6. to place oneself before; to confront. [Obs.]

Syn.—design, project, plan, purpose.

prō·pōse′, *v.i.* 1. to form or announce an intention or design; to make a proposal; to purpose; to plan.

> Man *proposes*, but God disposes.
> —Thomas à Kempis.

2. to offer marriage.

3. to converse; to discourse; to speak. [Obs.]

prō·pōse′, *n.* a proposal. [Obs.]

prō·pōs′ẽr, *n.* one who proposes.

prop·ō·si′tion, *n.* [L. *propositio*, from *proponere*, to put forth publicly; *pro*, before, and *ponere*, to put.]

1. a proposing.

2. (a) something proposed; a proposal; a plan; (b) [Colloq.] an indecent or immoral proposal.

3. a setting forth; an offering. [Archaic.]

4. a project; a business undertaking. [Colloq.]

5. a person, problem, undertaking, etc. to be dealt with. [Colloq.]

6. in logic, an expression in which the predicate affirms or denies something about the subject.

7. in mathematics, a theorem to be demonstrated or a problem to be solved.

8. in rhetoric, a subject to be discussed or a statement to be upheld.

prop·ō·si′tion, *v.t.* to make an indecent or immoral proposal to. [Colloq.]

prop·ō·si′tion·ăl, *a.* 1. pertaining to a proposition.

2. having the character of a proposition.

prō·pos′i·tus, *n.* in law, the person from whom descent is reckoned.

prō·pound′, *v.t.*; propounded, *pt.*, *pp.*; propounding, *ppr.* [earlier *propone*; L. *proponere*, to put forth publicly.]

1. to propose; to offer for consideration; to put forward, as a question; as, to *propound* a rule of action.

2. to propose or name as a candidate for admission to communion with a church. [Rare.]

prō·pound′ẽr, *n.* one who propounds.

prō·prae′tŏr, prō·prē′tŏr, *n.* [L. *proprætor*.] in ancient Rome, a magistrate who was sent to govern a province after having served as praetor in Rome.

prō·prī′e·târ·y, *a.* [Fr. *propriétaire*, from LL. *proprietarius*; L. *proprietas*, property.]

1. belonging to a proprietor.

2. holding property.

3. of property or proprietorship.

4. held under patent, trade-mark, or copyright by a private person or company; as, a *proprietary* medicine.

prō·prī′e·târ·y, *n.*; *pl.* **prō·prī′e·târ·ies,** 1. a proprietor; an owner; one who has the exclusive legal right or title to anything.

2. a group of proprietors; as, the *proprietary* of a county.

3. in church history, a monk who had reserved goods and effects to himself, contrary to his vows.

4. proprietorship.

5. in American history, the owner of a proprietary colony.

6. a proprietary medicine.

prō·prī′e·târ·y col′ō·ny, in American history, any of certain North American colonies that were granted by the British Crown to an individual or group of individuals in whom all governing rights were vested.

prō·prī′e·tŏr, *n.* [Fr. *propriétaire*, from LL. *proprietarius*.]

1. a person who has a legal title or exclusive right to some property; an owner.

2. the owner of a proprietary colony.

prō·prī·e·tō′ri·ăl, *a.* of or pertaining to ownership; proprietary; as, a *proprietorial* right.

prō·prī′e·tŏr·ship, *n.* the state or condition of a proprietor; ownership.

prō·prī′e·tress, *n.* a woman proprietor or owner.

prō·prī′e·trix, *n.* same as *proprietress*.

prō·prī′e·ty, *n.*; *pl.* **prō·prī′e·ties,** [Fr. *propriété*; L. *proprietas*, from *proprius*, one's own.]

1. the quality of being proper, fitting, or suitable; fitness.

2. conformity with what is proper or fitting.

3. conformity with accepted standards of manners or behavior.

4. (a) peculiar or proper nature or state; (b) a peculiarity. [Obs.]

5. private property. [Obs.]

the proprieties; accepted standards of behavior in polite society.

Syn.—appropriateness, circumspection, decency, seemliness, correctness.

prō″pri·ō·cep′tive, *a.* [from L. *proprius*, one's own, and *-ceptive*, as in *inceptive*.] designating or of stimuli produced in body tissues, as the muscles or tendons, and received there by the proprioceptors.

prō″pri·ō·cep′tŏr, *n.* any of the sensory end organs in the muscles, tendons, etc. that are sensitive to the stimuli originating in these tissues by the movement of the body or its parts.

prō′pri·um, *n.* [L., neut. of *proprius*, one's own.]

1. in logic, same as *property*.

2. in Swedenborgianism, differentiation of personality; selfhood.

prō·proc′tŏr, *n.* an assistant or deputy proctor in an English university.

prop root, any root that helps support the plant stem, as on the mangrove or banyan tree.

props, *n.pl.* the property man in a theater. [Slang.]

props, *n.pl.* a gambling game played with four shells; also, the shells used in the game.

prop·tēr·yg′i·um, *n.*; *pl.* **prop·tēr·yg′i·ȧ,** the anterior of three basal cartilages in a pectoral fin of certain fishes.

prop·tō′sis, *n.* [Gr. *pro*, before, and *piptein*, to fall.] a forward displacement; protrusion, especially of the eyeball.

prō·pūgn′ (-pūn′), *v.t.* [L. *propugnare*; *pro*, for, and *pugnare*, to fight.] to defend; to vindicate; to contend for. [Obs.]

prō·pug′nȧ·cle, *n.* a fortress. [Obs.]

prō·pug·nac′ū·lum, *n.* a bulwark.

prō·pug·nā′tion, *n.* defense; vindication; means of combat. [Obs.]

prō·pūgn′ẽr (-pūn′), *n.* a defender; a vindicator. [Obs.]

prō·pulse′, *v.t.* to drive away or off; to repel; to keep at a distance. [Obs.]

prō·pul′sion, *n.* [L. *propulsus*, pp. of *propellere*, to propel.]

1. a propelling or being propelled.

2. something that propels; a propelling force.

prō·pul′si·ty, *n.* propulsion. [Rare.]

prō·pul′sive, *a.* having power to propel, tending to propel, or propelling.

prō·pul′sō·ry, *a.* same as *propulsive*.

prō·pū′pȧ, *n.* [L. *pro*, before, and LL. *pupa*.]

1. in entomology, a stage of development intermediate between larva and pupa; semipupa.

2. an insect in this stage of development.

prō′pyl, *n.* [*prop*ionic and *-yl*.] the monovalent radical C_3H_7, derived from propane.

prop·y·lae′um, *n.*; *pl.* **prop·y·lae′ȧ,** [Gr. *pro*, before, and *pylē*, a gate.] in Greek and Roman architecture, a portico, entrance, or vestibule before a building or group of buildings; especially [*pl.*], the architectural structure forming the entrance to the Acropolis of Athens.

prō·pyl·ȧ·mine′, *n.* a liquid amine or base, occurring in two forms, normal propylamine and isopropylamine.

prō′pyl·ēne, *n.* [*prop*ionic and *-yl* and *-ene*.] an unsaturated hydrocarbon, C_3H_6, a colorless gas obtained in the refining of petroleum: also called *propene*.

prō·pyl′ic, *a.* contained in or derived from propyl.

prō·pyl′i·dēne, *n.* an unsaturated hydrocarbon dyad radical, isomeric with propylene.

prop′y·līte, *n.* [Gr. *pro*, before, *pylē*, a gate, and *-ite*.] a type of volcanic rock found in silver-mining regions, a form of andesite.

prop′y·lon, *n.* [Gr. *propylon*, gateway; *pro*, before, and *pylē*, a gate.] a gateway standing before the entrance of an Egyptian temple or portico.

prō rā′tȧ, [L.] in proportion; proportionately.

prō·rāt′ȧ·ble, *a.* capable of being prorated.

prō·rāte′, *v.t.* and *v.i.*; prorated, *pt.*, *pp.*; prorating, *ppr.* to divide, assess, or distribute proportionally.

prōre, *n.* [L. *prora*.] the prow; the fore part of a ship. [Poetic.]

prō·rec′tŏr, *n.* [*pro-* and *rector*.] a presiding officer in a university.

prō·rec′tŏr·āte, *n.* the office of a prorector.

prō·rep′tion, *n.* [L. *pro-*, forward, and *repere*, *reptus*, to creep.] the act of creeping on or forward. [Rare.]

prō′rex, *n.* [L. *pro*, for, and *rex*, a king.] a viceroy. [Obs.]

prō·rhī′năl (-rī′), *a.* [*pro-* and *rhinal*.] in front of the nasal chambers.

prō′rō·gāte, *v.t.* and *v.i.*; prorogated, *pt.*, *pp.*; prorogating, *ppr.* same as *prorogue*.

prō·rō·gā′tion, *n.* [L. *prorogatio*.] a proroguing, as of a legislative assembly.

prō·rōgue′ (-rōg′), *v.t.*; prorogued, *pt.*, *pp.*; proroguing, *ppr.* [L. *prorogare*, to defer.]

1. to discontinue or end a session of (a legislative assembly, as the British Parliament).

2. to defer; to delay; to postpone. [Rare.]

3. to protract; to extend. [Obs.]

prō·rup′tion, *n.* the act of bursting forth; a bursting out. [Rare.]

prō·sā′ic, *a.* [L. *prosaicus*, from *prosa*, prose.]

1. pertaining to prose; resembling prose; unpoetic.

2. dull; uninteresting; ordinary; commonplace; as, a *prosaic* person.

Syn.—dull, tedious, commonplace, prolix, prosy, matter-of-fact.

prō·ṣā′i·çăl, *a.* prosaic.
prō·ṣā′i·çăl·ly, *adv.* in a prosaic manner.
prō·ṣā′i·çăl·ness, *n.* the quality or state of being prosaic.
prō·ṣā′i·cịṣm, *n.* a prosaic style or character; prosaicalness.
prō′ṣā·iṣm, *n.* 1. prosaic quality or style.
2. that which is in the form of prose writing; a prosaic expression.
prō′ṣā·ist, *n.* a writer of prose.
prōṣ′ăl, *a.* prosaic. [Obs.]
prō·scē′ni·um, *n.*; *pl.* **prō·scē′ni·ȧ,** [L., from Gr. *proskēnion*; *pro*, before, and *skēnē*, scene.]
1. the stage of the ancient Greek and Roman theater.
2. (a) the front area of the stage that is still visible to the audience when the curtain is lowered; (b) the curtain and the arch or framework that holds it.
prō·scē′ni·um box, a theater box on either side of and nearest to the proscenium.
prō·sciụt′tō (prō-shụ̈t′ō), *n.* [It., from *prosciugare*, to dry out, altered from LL. hyp. *perexsucare*, from *per-*, through, and *exsucare*, to extract juice from, from L. *exsuctus*, pp. of *exsugere*, to suck out.] a spicy Italian ham, cured by drying and served in very thin slices, often with melon.
prō·sçō′lex, *n.*; *pl.* **prō·sçō′li·cēṣ,** [Gr. *pro*, before, and *scōlex*, worm.] a redia or early form of larva found in some species of the *Trematodea*.
prō·scrībe′, *v.t.* proscribed, *pt.*, *pp.*; proscribing, *ppr.* [L. *proscribere*; *pro*, before, and *scribere*, to write.]
1. in ancient Rome, to publish the name of (a person) condemned to death, banishment, etc.
2. to deprive of the protection of the law; to outlaw.
3. to banish; to exile.
4. to denounce; to forbid; to interdict.
Syn.—banish, outlaw, prohibit, interdict, forbid, ostracize.
prō·scrib′ẽr, *n.* one who proscribes or prohibits.
prō′scrịpt, *n.* [L. *proscriptus*, pp. of *proscribere*, to proscribe.]
1. one who falls under a ban of proscription. [Rare.]
2. a proscription; a formal interdict. [Obs.]
prō·scrịp′tion, *n.* [L. *proscriptio*.]
1. a proscribing or being proscribed.
2. interdiction; prohibition.
prō·scrịp′tive, *a.* pertaining to or consisting in proscription; proscribing or tending to proscribe.
prō·scrịp′tive·ly, *adv.* in a proscriptive manner.
prō·sçū·tel′lum, *n.*; *pl.* **prō·sçū·tel′lȧ,** the scutellum of an insect's prothorax.
prōṣe, *n.* [Fr., from L. *prosa* for *prorsa* (*oratio*), direct (speech), from *prorsus*, forward, straight on; *pro*, forward, and *versus*, pp. of *vertere*, to turn.]
1. the ordinary form of written or spoken language, without rhyme or meter: opposed to *verse*, *poetry*.
2. dull, commonplace talk or expression.
3. in the Roman Catholic Church, a hymn sung after the gradual: also called *sequence*.
prōṣe, *a.* 1. of prose.
2. in prose.
3. dull; unimaginative; commonplace; prosaic.
prōṣe, *v.t.* and *v.i.*; prosed, *pt.*, *pp.*; prosing, *ppr.* 1. to speak, write, or express (one's thoughts, etc.) in prose.
2. to speak or write in a prosaic manner.
prō·sec′tŏr, *n.* [*pro-*, and L. *secare*, to cut.] one skilled in dissection who prepares subjects for anatomical demonstration.
pros′ē·çū·tȧ·ble, *a.* open to prosecution; that can be prosecuted.
pros′ē·çūte, *v.t.*; prosecuted, *pt.*, *pp.*; prosecuting, *ppr.* [L. *prosecutus*, pp. of *prosequi*; *pro*, before, and *sequi*, to follow.]
1. to follow or pursue with a view to reach, execute, or accomplish; to continue (something) so as to obtain or complete it; as, to *prosecute* a war with great vigor.
That which is morally good is to be desired and *prosecuted*. —Wilkins.
2. to carry on; to practice; to engage in; as, *prosecute* your studies.
3. to institute legal proceedings against, or conduct criminal proceedings in court against.
4. to seek to obtain, enforce, etc. by legal process; as, to *prosecute* a right in a court of law.
Syn.—pursue, follow, continue, carry on, arraign, sue.
pros′ē·çūte, *v.i.* 1. to institute and carry on a legal suit.
2. to act as prosecutor.
pros′ē·çūt·ing at·tŏr′ney, a public official who conducts criminal prosecutions on behalf of the State or people.
pros·ē·çū′tion, *n.* 1. a prosecuting, or following up.
2. the conducting of a lawsuit.
3. the party who institutes and carries on criminal proceedings in court.
pros′ē·çū·tŏr, *n.* 1. a person who prosecutes.
2. in law, (a) a person who institutes a prosecution in court; (b) a prosecuting attorney.
pros′ē·çū·trix, *n.* a woman prosecutor.
pros′e·lȳte, *n.* [Fr. *prosélyte*; Gr. *prosēlytos*, from *pros*, toward, and an aorist stem of *proserchesthai*, to come.] a person who has been converted from one religion, opinion, or party to another.
pros′e·lȳte, *v.t.* and *v.i.*; proselyted, *pt.*, *pp.*; proselyting, *ppr.* 1. to proselytize.
2. to persuade (an athlete), usually by an attractive offer, to attend and play for a certain school.
pros′e·lyt·iṣm, *n.* 1. the fact of becoming or being a proselyte.
2. the act or practice of proselytizing.
pros′e·lyt·īze, *v.t.*; proselytized, *pt.*, *pp.*; proselytizing, *ppr.* to make a convert of.
pros′e·lyt·īze, *v.i.* to make proselytes, or converts.
pros′e·lyt·īz·ẽr, *n.* one who makes proselytes.
prōṣe′măn, *n.* a man who writes prose. [Rare.]
prō·sem′i·nãr·y, *n.*; *pl.* **prō·sem′i·nãr·ieṣ,** a seminary in which pupils are prepared for a higher institution; a preparatory school.
prō·sem·i·nā′tion, *n.* propagation by seed. [Obs.]
pros″en·cē·phal′iç, *a.* pertaining to the prosencephalon.
pros·en·ceph′ȧ·lon, *n.* [Gr. *pros*, in front, and *en*, in, and *kephalē*, the head.] the forebrain in the embryo of man and other mammals.
pros·eñ′çhy·mȧ, *n.* [Gr. *pros*, toward, and *enchyma*, infusion, from *enchein*, to pour in.] in botany, a tissue made up of thick-walled elongated cells without much protoplasm, found in some plants; the woody tissue: distinguished from *parenchyma*.
pros·eñ·çhym′ȧ·tous, *a.* in botany, pertaining to, or having the nature of, prosenchyma.
prōṣ′ẽr, *n.* a person who writes proses; especially, one who talks or writes in a prosaic manner.
Prō·sẽr′pin·ȧ, *n.* [L.] in Roman mythology, the daughter of Ceres and wife of Pluto: identified with the Greek Persephone.
Prō·sẽr′pin·ē, *n.* Proserpina.
prō·sil′i·en·cy, *n.* [L. *prosiliens*, ppr. of *prosilire*, to leap forward.] a leaping forward. [Rare.]
prōṣ′i·ly, *adv.* in a prosy manner.
Prō·sim′i·ae, *n.pl.* a suborder of *Primates* including the lemurs.
prō·sim′i·ăn, *n.* any of the *Prosimiæ*; a lemur.
prō·sim′i·ăn, *a.* pertaining to the *Prosimiæ*.
prōṣ′i·ness, *n.* the quality of being prosy.
prōṣ′ing, *n.* dull and tedious minuteness in speech or writing.
prōṣ′ing·ly, *adv.* in a prosing manner.
prō·sī′phŏn, *n.* a tube found in the protoconch of an ammonite.
prō·sī′phŏn·ăl, *a.* pertaining to the prosiphon.
prō′sit, *interj.* [L.] to your health: a toast, especially among Germans.
prō·slāv′ẽr·y, *a.* in favor of slavery; especially, in United States history, in favor of preserving the institution of Negro slavery.
prō·slāv′ẽr·y, *n.* support or advocacy of slavery.
pros′ō·brañch, *n.* a prosobranchiate.
Pros·ō·brañ·chi·ā′tȧ, *n.pl.* [Gr. *prosō*, forward, and *branchia*, gills.] the most highly organized order of *Gastropoda*, including all those with gills anterior to the heart and with distinct sexes.
pros·ō·brañ′çhi·āte, *a.* pertaining to the *Prosobranchiata*.
pros·ō·brañ′çhi·āte, *n.* any of the *Prosobranchiata*.
pros′ō·cēle, pros′ō·coele, *n.* [Gr. *prosō*, forward, and *koilos*, hollow.] the ventricular cavity of the prosencephalon.
pros·ō·dī′ȧ·çăl, *a.* same as *prosodic*.
pros·ō·dī′ȧ·çăl·ly, *adv.* same as *prosodically*.
prō·sō′di·ăl, *a.* same as *prosodic*.
prō·sō′di·ăn, *n.* same as *prosodist*.
prō·sod′iç, *a.* pertaining to prosody or the rules of prosody.
prō·sod′i·çăl, *a.* prosodic.
prō·sod′i·çăl·ly, *adv.* 1. in a prosodic manner.
2. as regards prosody.
pros′ō·dist, *n.* one who is skilled in prosody.
pros′ō·dy, *n.*; *pl.* **pros′ō·dieṣ,** [L. *prosodia*, from Gr. *prosōdia*, a song sung to music; *pros*, to, and *ōdē*, a song.]
1. the science or art of versification, including the study of metrical structure, rhyme, stanza forms, etc.
2. a particular system of versification and metrical structure; as, Dryden's *prosody*.
prō·sō′mȧ, *n.*; *pl.* **prō·sō′mȧ·tȧ,** [Gr. *pro*, before, and *sōma*, body.] the forepart of the body of a cephalopod, etc.
pros·ō·pal′ġi·ȧ, *n.* [Gr. *prosōpon*, face, and *algos*, pain.] neuralgia of the face.
Prō·sō′pis, *n.* [Gr. *prosōpis*, a kind of plant, from *prosōpon*, face.] a genus of leguminous branching plants and shrubs, with bipinnate leaves, found in tropical regions. *Prosopis juliflora* is the mesquite.
prō·sō′pō·lep·sy, *n.* [Gr. *prosōpolēpsia*, respect of persons; *prosōpon*, a face, a person, and *lēpsis*, a taking, receiving, from *lambanein*, to take.] respect or acceptance of persons from external appearance. [Obs.]
prō·sō·pō·poe′iȧ (-yȧ), *n.* [Gr. *prosōpopoiia*, personification; *prosōpon*, person, and *poiein*, to make.]
1. a figure in rhetoric by which things are represented as persons, or by which things inanimate are spoken of as animated beings, or by which an absent person is introduced as speaking, or a deceased person is represented as alive and present.
2. personification.
pros′peçt, *n.* [ME. *prospecte*; L. *prospectus*, a lookout, from *prospicere*, to look forward.]
1. view of things within the reach of the eye; a scene.
Eden, and all the coast, in *prospect* lay. —Milton.
2. the view obtained from a particular point; outlook.
3. a place which affords an extended view. [Obs.]
4. a looking forward; anticipation; foresight.
Is he a prudent man as to his temporal estate, who lays designs only for a day, without any *prospect* to or provision for the remaining part of life?—Tillotson.
5. (a) something hoped for or expected; probable outcome; as, a *prospect* of a good harvest; *prospect* of preferment; (b) [*usually in pl.*] apparent chance for success, gain, etc.
6. a likely customer, candidate, etc.
7. in mining, (a) a place where a mineral deposit is sought or found; (b) a sample of gravel, earth, etc. tested for a particular mineral, or the resulting yield of mineral.
in prospect; expected.
pros′peçt, *v.t.* prospected, *pt.*, *pp.*; prospecting, *ppr.* to explore; to search or examine for minerals; as, to *prospect* a country.
pros′peçt, *v.i.* to search; to seek; to explore; as, to *prospect* for copper.
prō·speç′tion, *n.* the act of prospecting or looking forward.
prō·speç′tive, *a.* [LL. *prospectivus*, from L. *prospicere*, to look forward.]
1. looking forward in time; looking to the future.
2. pertaining to a prospect; perspective. [Obs.]
3. relating to the future; likely; anticipated; as, a *prospective* gift.
prō·speç′tive, *n.* 1. the scene before or around; prospect; outlook.
2. a glass for seeing places far away. [Obs.]
prō·speç′tive·ly, *adv.* in a prospective manner.
prō·speç′tive·ness, *n.* the state of being prospective.
pros′peç·tŏr, pros′peç·tẽr, *n.* one who prospects; specifically, one who searches and explores for minerals, oil, etc.
prō·speç′tus, *n.* a brief sketch or plan of some proposed commercial enterprise or undertaking, containing the details of the general plan or design; specifically, a document issued by the directors or promoters of a new company, association, or institution, containing the objects of the association, the amount of capital required, the security offered, the profits estimated, and such other details as may assist in judging the feasibility of the undertaking.
Syn.—program, plan, catalogue, announcement, scheme.
pros′pẽr, *v.t.*; prospered, *pt.*, *pp.*; prospering, *ppr.* [Fr. *prospérer*, to prosper, to thrive, from

L. *prosperare*, to make to prosper, from *prosperus*, favorable, fortunate; *pro*, before, and *spes*, hope.] to favor; to make prosperous, fortunate, or successful.

pros′pĕr, *v.i.* to be successful; to succeed; to be prosperous; to thrive; to flourish.

pros·per′i·ty, *n.*; *pl.* **pros·per′i·ties,** [L. *prosperitas.*] the state of being prosperous; advance or gain in anything good or desirable; successful progress in any business or enterprise; success; wealth; as, the *prosperity* of arts; national *prosperity*.

Syn.—success, weal, welfare, good fortune, well-being, good luck.

Pros′pĕr·ō, *n.* [It.] in Shakespeare's *The Tempest*, the deposed Duke of Milan, who by magic raises a tempest off the island which he inhabits with his daughter Miranda, and then acts as host to the shipwrecked malefactors.

pros′pĕr·ous, *a.* [L. *prosperus.*]

1. making gain or increase; thriving; successful; as, a *prosperous* trade; a *prosperous* voyage; a *prosperous* exhibition or undertaking.

2. favorable; helpful; propitious; as, a *prosperous* wind.

3. well-to-do; well-off.

Syn.—successful, fortunate, lucky, favorable, flourishing, propitious, well-off.

pros′pĕr·ous·ly, *adv.* in a prosperous manner.

pros′pĕr·ous·ness, *n.* the state of being prosperous; prosperity.

prō·spi′cience (-spish′ens), *n.* [L. *prospiciens*, ppr. of *prospicere*, to look forward.] the act of looking forward. [Rare.]

prō·spō·ran′ġi·um, *n.* [Gr. *pro-*, for, *spora*, a seed, and *aggeion*, a vessel.] in botany, a type of cell having protoplasm which develops into a vesicle in which the zoospores are formed.

pross, *n.* gossip; conversation. [Brit. Dial.]

pros′tăt-, same as *prostato-*.

pros′tāte, *a.* [Gr. *prostatēs*, standing before; *pro*, before, and stem, *sta*, to stand.] designating or of the prostate gland.

pros′tāte, *n.* a gland situated just before the neck of the bladder in males, and surrounding the first portion of the urethra: it secretes an alkaline fluid that is discharged with the sperm.

pros″tȧ·teç′tō·my, *n.* the surgical removal of all or part of the prostate gland.

prō·stat′iç, *a.* pertaining to the prostate gland.

pros·tȧ·tī′tis, *n.* inflammation of the prostate gland.

pros′tȧ·tō-, a combining form meaning *of the prostate*: also, before a vowel, *prostat-*.

pros·tẽr·nā′tion, *n.* dejection; depression. [Obs.]

prō·stẽr′num, *n.* the ventral sclerite of the prothorax of an insect.

prōs·then′iç, *a.* being proportionally stronger in the fore parts.

pros′thē·sis, *n.* [Gr., from *pros*, to, and *thesis*, the act of placing, from *tithenai*, to place.]

1. in medicine, (a) the replacement of a missing part of the body, as a limb, eye, or tooth, by an artificial substitute; (b) such a substitute.

2. in grammar, prothesis.

pros·thet′iç, *a.* pertaining to prosthesis.

pros·thet′iç den′tist·ry, prosthodontia.

pros·thet′içs, *n.pl.* [*construed as sing.*] the branch of surgery dealing with the replacement of missing parts, especially limbs, by artificial substitutes.

pros·thō·don′ti·ȧ (-shȧ), *n.* [Mod. L.] the branch of dentistry dealing with the replacement of missing teeth, as by bridges or artificial dentures.

pros·thō·don′tist, *n.* a specialist in prosthodontia.

pros′ti·tūte, *v.t.*; prostituted, *pt., pp.*; prostituting, *ppr.* [from L. *prostitutus*, pp. of *prostituere*; *pro*, before, and *statuere*, to cause to stand.]

1. to sell the services of (oneself or another) for purposes of sexual intercourse.

2. to sell (oneself, one's artistic or moral integrity, etc.) for low or unworthy purposes.

pros′ti·tūte, *a.* debased; corrupt; sold to wickedness or to base purposes.

Made bold by want and *prostitute* for bread.
—Prior.

pros′ti·tūte, *n.* 1. a woman who engages in promiscuous sexual intercourse for pay; whore; harlot.

2. a person, as a writer, artist, etc., who sells his services for low or unworthy purposes.

No hireling she, no *prostitute* to praise.
—Pope.

pros·ti·tū′tion, *n.* the act or practice of prostituting, or the fact of being prostituted; especially, the trade of a prostitute.

pros′ti·tū·tŏr, *n.* one who or that which prostitutes.

prō·stō′mi·ăl, *a.* pertaining to the prostomium; preoral.

prō·stō′mi·um, *n.*; *pl.* **prō·stō′mi·ȧ,** [Gr. *pro*, before, and *stoma*, mouth.] the preoral region of the head of certain invertebrates, as a mollusk or worm.

pros′trāte, *a.* [L. *prostratus*, pp. of *prosternere*, to lay flat.]

1. lying with the face downward in demonstration of great humility or abject submission.

2. lying flat, prone, or supine.

3. thrown or fallen to the ground.

4. laid low; completely subjugated; overcome; submissive.

5. in botany, growing on the ground; trailing.

6. in zoology, making a slight angle with the surface; not erect, as a hair.

pros′trāte, *v.t.*; prostrated, *pt., pp.*; prostrating, *ppr.* 1. to lay flat; to throw down; as, to *prostrate* the body; to *prostrate* trees or plants.

2. to throw down; to overthrow; to demolish; to ruin; as, to *prostrate* a village.

3. to throw (oneself) down; to cause (oneself) to fall or lie in humility or reverence: used reflexively.

4. in medicine, to reduce or cause to grow weak; as, a person *prostrated* by grief.

pros·trā′tion, *n.* 1. a prostrating or being prostrated.

2. great depression; dejection; as, a *prostration* of spirits.

prō′stȳle, *a.* [L. *prostylus*; Gr. *prostylos*; *pro-*, before, and *stylos*, pillar.] in architecture, having a portico whose columns, usually four in number, extend in a line across the front only, as in a Greek temple.

prō′stȳle, *n.* 1. a prostyle portico.

2. a prostyle building.

prōs′y, *a.*; *comp.* prosier; *superl.* prosiest, like prose; prosaic; hence, dull; tedious; boring.

prō·syl′lō·ġism, *n.* in logic, a syllogism so connected with another syllogism that the conclusion of the first becomes the premise of the second.

prō·taç′tiç, *a.* [Gr. *protaktikos*, placing or placed before; *pro*, before, and *tassein*, to arrange.] being placed at the beginning; introductory.

prō·taç·tin′i·um, *n.* [Mod. L., from *proto-* and *actinium.*] one of the four isotopes which together comprise the radioactive element number 91: it is the only one of the isotopes that can be isolated in significant amounts: symbol, Pa; atomic weight, 231; atomic number, 91: formerly called *protoactinium*.

prō′tȧ·gon, *n.* [Gr. *prōtos*, first, and *agōn*, ppr. of *agein*, to lead.] a phosphoreted fatty compound which forms a chief constituent of nervous tissue.

prō·tag′ō·nist, *n.* [Gr. *prōtagōnistēs*; *prōtos*, first, and *agōnistēs*, actor.] in the drama, the leading character or actor in a play, novel, or story, about whom the action centers; hence, a person who plays a leading or active part.

prō′tȧ·mīne, prō′tȧ·min, *n.* any of a class of simple proteins that are soluble in ammonia, do not coagulate by heat, and yield relatively few amino acids upon hydrolysis.

prō·tan′driç, *a.* [Gr. *prōtos*, first, and *anēr*, *andros*, male.] in zoology, having male sexual organs while young, but later developing female sexual organs.

prō·tan′driṣm, *n.* the state of being protandric.

prō·tan′drous, *a.* same as *proterandrous*.

prō·tär′sus, *n.*; *pl.* **prō·tär′sī,** in an insect, the tarsus of the first leg.

prot′ȧ·sis, *n.* [Gr. *protasis*, from *proteinein*, to stretch before, to present.]

1. a proposition; a maxim. [Rare.]

2. in grammar and rhetoric, the clause that expresses the condition in a conditional sentence, being the condition on which the main term (*apodosis*) depends, or notwithstanding which it takes place; as, if we run (*protasis*) we shall be in time (*apodosis*).

3. in classical drama, the first part of a play, in which the characters are introduced.

prō·tat′iç, *a.* pertaining to protasis; introductory.

Prō′tē·ȧ, *n.* [from *Proteus*, a self-transforming sea-god; in allusion to the diversity of appearance of the species.] a genus of plants belonging to the family *Proteaceæ*, of which it is the type. The species are chiefly native to South Africa and consist of a variety of shrubs, with very variable foliage and large heads of flowers, six or eight inches in diameter.

Prō·tē·ā′cē·ae, *n.pl.* a family of apetalous arborescent exogens, found chiefly in Australia and South Africa. They are shrubs or small trees, with hard, dry, opposite or alternate leaves, and often large heads of showy and richly colored flowers.

prō·tē·ā′ceous, *a.* pertaining to the *Proteaceæ*.

Prō′tē·ăn, *a.* 1. pertaining to Proteus, the god who could change his shape; hence, [p–] readily assuming different shapes; exceedingly variable.

She was sadly flustered by the *protean* act of the playwright.
—James O'Donnell Bennett.

2. [p–] an actor who has two or more parts in a play.

prō′tē·ăn·ly, *adv.* in a protean manner.

prō′tē·āse, *n.* in biochemistry, an enzyme active in the digestion of proteins.

prō·teçt′, *v.t.*; protected, *pt., pp.*; protecting, *ppr.* [L. *protectus*, pp. of *protegere*, to protect; *pro*, before, and *tegere*, to cover.]

1. to cover or shield from danger or injury; to defend; to guard; to preserve in safety.

2. in commerce, to set aside funds toward the payment of (a note, draft, etc.) at maturity.

3. in economics, to guard (domestic industry) by tariffs on imported products.

Syn.—defend, guard, shelter, shield.

prō·teçt·ee′, *n.* one who is protected. [Rare.]

prō·teçt′ing·ly, *adv.* in a protecting manner.

prō·teç′tion, *n.* 1. (a) the act of protecting; defense; shelter from evil; preservation from loss, injury, or annoyance; as, we find *protection* under good laws and an upright administration; (b) an instance of this.

2. one who or that which protects.

3. a writing that protects; a passport or other writing which secures from molestation.

4. (a) money extorted by racketeers as insurance against threatened violence; (b) extortion of this kind. [Colloq.]

5. in economics, a policy of stimulating industrial development by payment of bounty on domestic products or, usually, by protecting domestic producers from foreign competition in the home market by the laying of such discriminating import duties on foreign-made goods as will lessen their power to compete: opposed to *free trade*.

writ of protection; a writ by which the king of Great Britain exempted a person from arrest. [Obs.]

Syn.—defense, preservation, shelter.

prō·teç′tion·ăl, *a.* pertaining to protection.

prō·teç′tion·iṣm, *n.* in economics, the policy of aiding or protecting home industries by paying bounties on domestic products or, usually, by laying import tariffs on foreign products.

prō·teç′tion·ist, *n.* one who favors protectionism and is opposed to free trade.

prō·teç′tion·ist, *a.* of protectionists or protectionism.

prō·teç′tive, *n.* anything that protects.

prō·teç′tive, *a.* affording protection; sheltering; defensive; specifically, in political economy, serving or intended to protect domestic products, industries, etc. in competition with foreign products, industries, etc.; as, a *protective* tariff.

protective coloration (or *coloring*); the natural coloration of any of certain organisms by means of which it is blended in with its normal environment and is thus protected from detection by its enemies.

protective tariff; a tax or duty imposed on imported goods to protect domestic industry.

prō·teç′tive·ly, *adv.* after the manner of protection; in a protective manner.

prō·teç′tive·ness, *n.* the condition or quality of being protective.

Prō·teç′tō·grȧph, *n.* [L. *protectus*, protected, and Gr. *graphein*, to write.]

1. a trade-mark describing a machine which so perforates a portion of a check or draft while printing the amount thereon that alteration of or tampering with the check becomes impossible.

2. [p–] a machine for preventing alteration of checks.

prō·teç′tŏr, *n.* [LL., from L. *protectus*, pp. of *protegere*, to protect.]

1. one who or that which defends or shields

from injury, evil, or oppression; a defender; a guardian.

2. in English history, (a) one who formerly had the care of the kingdom during the minority, absence, or incapacity of the sovereign; a regent; (b) the title (in full, *Lord Protector*) held by Oliver Cromwell (1653–1658) and his son Richard (1658–1659), during the British Commonwealth.

prō·teç′tŏr·ăl, *a.* pertaining to a protector; as, *protectoral* power.

prō·teç′tŏr·āte, *n.* 1. government by a protector.

2. the office or term of office of a protector.

3. [P–] the government of England under Oliver Cromwell and his son Richard (1653–1659).

4. the relation of a strong state to a weaker state under its control and protection.

5. a state or territory so controlled and protected.

6. the authority exercised by the controlling state.

prō·teç·tō′ri·ăl, *a.* protectoral.

prō·teç′tŏr·less, *a.* having no protector.

prō·teç′tŏr·ship, *n.* the office or government of a protector or regent.

prō·teç′tō·ry, *n.*; *pl.* **prō·teç′tō·ries,** an institution for the protection of destitute or delinquent children.

prō·teç′tress, *n.* a woman who protects.

prō·teç′trix, *n.* a protectress.

pro′té·gé (prō′te-zhā *or Fr.* prō-tā-zhā′), *n.* [Fr., pp. of *protéger*, to protect.] one under the patronage, care, or protection of another.

pro′té·gée (-zhā *or Fr.* prō-tā-zhā′), *n.* a girl or woman under the patronage, care, or protection of another.

Prō·tē′i·dae, *n.pl.* a family of tailed amphibians typified by the genus *Proteus.*

prō′tē·ide, *n.* in zoology, one of the family *Proteidæ.*

prō′tē·īde, prō′tē·id, *n.* [*prote*in and *-ide.*] protein.

prō′tē·īde, prō′tē·id, *a.* containing proteins.

prō·tē′i·form, *a.* [from *proteus* and *form.*] of changeable form; protean.

prō′tē·in (*or* -tēn), *n.* [Gr. *prōtos*, first, and *in.*] any of a class of nitrogenous substances consisting of a complex union of amino acids and containing carbon, hydrogen, nitrogen, oxygen, and, frequently, sulfur: proteins occur in all animal and vegetable matter and are essential to the diet of animals.

prō″tē·i·nā′ceous, *a.* pertaining to or containing protein.

prō′tē·in·āse, *n.* any enzyme that promotes proteolysis.

prō′tē·in çrys′tăl, same as *crystalloid.*

prō·tē′i·nous, *a.* same as *proteinaceous.*

Prot′e·lēs, *n.* [LL., lit. complete in front, the forefeet being pentadactyl; Gr. *pro*, forward, and *teleios*, perfect.] a genus of South African animals consisting of a single species, the aardwolf, *Proteles lalandi.*

Prō·tel′i·dae, *n.pl.* [*Prote*les and *-idæ.*] a family of hyenalike carnivores, typified by the genus *Proteles.*

prō tem′pō·rē, [L.] for the time (being); temporary: shortened to *pro tem.*

prō·tend′, *v.t.* [L. *protendere*; *pro*, forth, and *tendere*, to stretch.] to hold out; to stretch forward; to reach ahead. [Obs.]

prō·tense′, *n.* extension. [Obs.]

prō·ten′sion, *n.* a reaching ahead; a stretching forward. [Obs.]

prō·ten′sive, *a.* extended; stretched out.

prō·tē·ol′y·sis, *n.* [*proteid*, and Gr. *lysis*, loosening.] in biochemistry, the chemical changes which take place in proteins during the processes of dissolving and digesting to form simple, soluble substances.

prō″tē·ō·lyt′iç, *a.* of or pertaining to the dissolving or digesting of proteins.

prō′tē·ōse, *n.* [*prote*id and *-ose.*] any of a class of water-soluble products formed in the hydrolysis of proteins, as albumose.

prō·tēr·an′drous, *a.* [Gr. *proteros*, fore, and *anēr, andros*, male.] characterized by proterandry.

prō′tēr·an·dry, *n.* in botany and zoology, the maturation of the male organs of reproduction in advance of those of the female.

prō·tēr·an′thous, *a.* [Gr. *proteros*, fore, and *anthos*, flower.] in botany, bearing flowers before leaves, as certain willows.

Prot·ēr·og′ly·phȧ, *n.pl.* [Gr. *proteros*, fore, and *glyphein*, to carve.] a group of poisonous snakes having erect poison fangs and grooved or perforated anterior maxillary teeth. The coral snakes, sea snakes, cobras, and asps are included in this group.

prot·ēr·og′y·nous, *a.* [Gr. *proteros*, fore, and *gynē*, female.] characterized by proterogyny.

prō·tēr·og′y·ny, *n.* in botany, the maturation of the stigmas in a hermaphrodite flower before the maturation of the pollen in the same flower: the opposite of *proterandry.*

Prot″ēr·ō·sau′rus, *n.* [Gr. *proteros*, fore, and *sauros*, lizard.] an extinct genus of lizardlike reptiles, found fossil in the Permian.

Prot″ēr·ō·zō′iç, *a.* [Gr. *proteros*, fore, and *zōē*, life.] designating or of the geological era following the Archeozoic and preceding the Paleozoic, characterized by the appearance of the simplest types of algae, widespread glaciation and mountain formation, and the laying down of iron and copper deposits: sometimes called *Cryptozoic.*

the Proterozoic; the Proterozoic Era or its rocks.

prō·tēr′vi·ty, *n.* [L.] peevishness; petulance.

prō·test′, *v.t.*; protested, *pt.*, *pp.*; protesting, *ppr.* [L. *protestari*; *pro*, forth, and *testari*, to affirm.]

1. to make a solemn declaration or affirmation of; to state positively; as, to *protest* one's innocence.

2. to call as a witness in affirming or denying, or to prove an affirmation. [Rare.]

3. to make objection to; to speak strongly against.

4. to make a written declaration of the nonpayment of (a bill of exchange or a promissory note).

prō·test′, *v.i.* 1. to affirm with solemnity; to make a solemn declaration of a fact or opinion; as, I *protest* to you I have no knowledge of the transaction.

2. to express opposition; to object; to dissent; as, he *protests* against your votes.

prō′test, *n.* 1. an objection; a remonstrance.

2. a document formally objecting to something; especially, a formal and solemn declaration of dissent from the proceedings of a legislative body; as, the *protest* of lords in Parliament.

3. in law, (a) a declaration made by a person of his belief in the illegality of some measure to which he is forced to submit, as the paying of a tax, etc., that he may go on record as having not complied with the measure voluntarily; (b) a formal declaration made by a notary public at the request of the payee or holder of a bill of exchange, for nonacceptance or nonpayment of the same, showing that it has not been honored by the drawer; (c) a writing, attested by a justice of the peace or consul, drawn by the master of a ship, stating the cause of damages or losses the ship has suffered, and showing that the damages were not due to the neglect or misconduct of the officers or crew.

Prot′es·tăn·cy, *n.* Protestantism. [Now Rare.]

prot′es·tănt, *n.* [Fr., from L. *protestans* (*-antis*), ppr. of *protestari*, to bear witness.]

1. [P–] originally, any of the German princes and free cities that formally protested to the Diet of Spires (1529), its decision to uphold the edict of the Diet of Worms against the Reformation.

2. [P–] any Christian not belonging to the Roman Catholic or Orthodox Eastern Church: in the seventeenth century the term was restricted to Lutherans and Anglicans.

3. (*or* prō-tes′), a person who protests.

prot′es·tănt, *a.* 1. [P–] of Protestants or Protestantism.

2. (*or* prō-tes′), protesting.

Prot′es·tănt Ē·pis′çō·păl Chŭrch, the Protestant church in the United States that conforms to the practices and principles of the Church of England.

prot·es·tant′i·çăl, *a.* Protestant. [Obs.]

Prot′es·tănt·işm, *n.* 1. the religion of Protestants.

2. Protestants or Protestant churches, collectively.

3. the state or condition of being a Protestant.

Prot′es·tănt·ly, *adv.* in conformity to Protestantism or the Protestants. [Obs.]

prot·es·tā′tion, *n.* [LL. *protestatio* (*-onis*), from L. *protestari*, to bear witness.]

1. a protesting; a strong declaration or affirmation.

2. a protest; an objection.

3. formerly, in law, a declaration in pleading, by which the party interposes an oblique allegation or denial of some fact, protesting that it does or does not exist.

prot′es·tā·tŏr, *n.* one who protests. [Obs.]

prō·test′ēr, *n.* 1. one who protests, or makes a solemn affirmation.

2. one who protests, or expresses objection.

3. one who protests a bill of exchange or promissory note.

prō·test′ing·ly, *adv.* by way of protesting.

prō·test′ŏr, *n.* same as *protester.*

Prō′teūs (-tūs *or* -tē-us), *n.* [Gr. *Prōteus.*]

1. in Greek mythology, a sea god, the son of Oceanus and Tethys, whose distinguishing characteristic was the power of assuming different shapes at will.

2. a changeable, shifty, or fickle person; one who readily changes his principles or appearance.

3. a genus of perennibranchiate amphibians. One species only has been discovered, the *Proteus anguinus*, found in subterranean lakes and caves in Illyria and Dalmatia. It attains a length of about one foot, and has four legs. The body is smooth, naked, and eellike, the legs are small and weak, the fore feet three-toed, the hind four-toed, and in addition to permanent external gills, it has lungs formed like slender tubes. Its eyes are rudimentary and covered by the skin.

4. a genus of bacteria that form amoeboid colonies and are pathogenic in the intestinal tracts of vertebrates.

prō″tē·van·ġel′i·um, prō″tē·van·ġel′i·on, *n.* [Gr. *prōtos*, first, and *euangelion*, gospel.] an Apocryphal gospel ascribed to St. James the Less.

prō·thȧ·lā′mi·on, prō·thȧ·lā′mi·um, *n.*; *pl.* **prō·thȧ·lā′mi·ȧ,** [Gr. *pro*, for, and *thalamos*, bridechamber.] a nuptial song.

prō·thal′lī, *n.* pl. of *prothallus.*

prō·thal′li·ăl, *a.* of a prothallium.

prō·thal′liç, *a.* pertaining to the prothallium; prothalline.

prō·thal′līne, *a.* having the nature of a prothallium.

prō·thal′li·um, *n.*; *pl.* **prō·thal′li·ȧ,** [L. *pro*, before, and *thallus.*] that part of a fern which bears the sex organs.

prō·thal′loid, *a.* resembling a prothallium.

prō·thal′lus, *n.*; *pl.* **prō·thal′lī,** same as *prothallium.*

proth′e·sis, *n.* [Gr. *prothesis*, from *protithenai*, to set before; *pro*, forth, forward, and *tithenai*, to place.]

1. in grammar, the addition of a letter, syllable, or phoneme to the beginning of a word, as of *be-* in *beloved*, *a-* in *ahead*: also *prosthesis.*

2. in the Orthodox Eastern Church, (a) the preparation and preliminary oblation of the elements of the Eucharist; (b) the table on which this is done; (c) the place where this table stands.

3. in surgery, same as *prosthesis.*

prō·thet′iç, *a.* pertaining to prothesis.

prō·thon·ō·tăr′i·ăl, *a.* of or belonging to a prothonotary.

prō·thon′ō·tăr·y, *n.*; *pl.* **prō·thon′ō·tăr·ieş,** [ML. *protonotarius*; Gr. *prōtos*, first, and L. *notarius*, a scribe.]

1. a chief notary or clerk.

2. the chief notary or clerk in the Byzantine Court.

3. in the Greek Church, the chief secretary of the patriarch of Constantinople.

4. in the Roman Catholic Church, one of the seven members of the College of Prothonotaries Apostolic, who are charged with registering the acts of the church, lives of the martyrs, etc.: sometimes held as an honorary title by other ecclesiastics.

5. formerly, in English law, a chief clerk in the Court of Common Pleas and in the King's Bench: there were formerly three such officers in the former court, and one in the latter. These offices are now abolished.

6. in the United States, a chief clerk of court in some of the States.

prothonotary warbler; a small warbling bird, *Protonotaria citrea*, yellow in general color, with olivaceous back and gray wings: found in the swamps of the southern United States.

prō·thon′ō·tăr·y·ship, *n.* the office of a prothonotary.

prō·thō·rac′iç, *a.* of or relating to the prothorax.

prō·thō′rax, *n.* [Mod. L.; *pro-*, before, in front, and *thorax.*] in zoology, that division of an insect's body nearest the head.

prō·throm′bin, *n.* [Mod. L., from Gr. *pro-*, before, and *thrombos*, a clod, curd.] a factor in the blood plasma that takes part in the blood-clotting process: believed to be a precursor of thrombin.

prō′tist, *n.* a member of the *Protista*; any one-celled plant or animal.

Prō·tis′tȧ, *n.pl.* [Gr. *prōtista*, neut. pl. of *prōtistos*, the very first, superl. of *prōtos*, first.] the one-celled organisms collectively.

prō·tis′tăn, *a.* of or belonging to the protists.

prō·tis′tăn, *n.* same as *protist*.

prō·tis′tiç, *a.* of the protists.

prō′ti·um (*or* -shi-), *n.* [Mod.L., from *proto-* and *-ium*, n. suffix.] the most common isotope of hydrogen, H^1, having a mass number of 1.

Prō′ti·um (-shi-), *n.* a genus of tropical drupaceous trees, some of them valuable for gum, others for timber, of which there are nearly fifty species, characterized by pinnate leaves and paniculate flowers.

prō′tō-, [Gr. *prōto-*, from *prōtos*, first.] a combining form meaning: (a) *first in time, original, primitive*, as in *proto*col, *proto*plast; (b) *first in importance, principal, chief*, as in *prot*agonist; (c) (of people, their language, etc.) *primitive, original*, as in *proto*-Arabic; (d) in chemistry, *being that member of a series of compounds having the lowest proportion of* (the specified element or radical); also, *being the parent form of* (a specified substance), as in *proto*actinium. Also *prot-*.

prō″tō·aç·tin′i·um, *n.* same as *protactinium*.

prō″tō·çȧ·non′i·çăl, *a.* [*proto-* and *canonical*.] relating to the first canon, containing the books of Scripture: distinguished from *deuterocanonical*.

prō·tō·çat·ē·chü′iç, *a.* [*proto-* and *catechuic*.] designating or of a colorless, crystalline acid, $C_7H_6O_4$, obtained from various resins.

prō·tō·cẽr′çăl, *a.* [*proto-*, and Gr. *kerkos*, tail.] having the tail fin consisting of a fold extending continuously around the end of the tail, as in the embryo of fishes.

prō·tō·chlō′rīde, *n.* the chloride having the smallest ratio of chlorine to the base, where a series of two or more chlorides exist.

Prō″tō·çoç·çā′cē·ae, *n.pl.* [*Protococcus* and *-aceæ*.] a group of algae of which *Protococcus* is the typical genus.

prō″tō·çoç·çā′ceous, *a.* pertaining to or resembling the *Protococcaceæ*.

prō·tō·çoç′çoid, *a.* resembling the algae of the genus *Protococcus*.

Prō·tō·çoç′çus, *n.* [*proto-*, and Gr. *kokkos*, berry.] the typical genus of the group *Protococcaceæ*. In one of the two conditions in which it occurs it is a spheroidal body consisting of a structureless, tough, transparent wall, enclosing viscid and granular protoplasm and chlorophyll which usually is green in color but frequently becomes red, as in *Protococcus nivalis*, the so-called "red snow."

prō′tō·çol, *n.* [Early Mod. Eng. *prothocoll*; OFr. *prothocole*; ML. *protocollum*, the first leaf glued to a manuscript, the first sheet of a legal instrument which was glued to the *scapus*, or cylinder, round which the document was rolled; Gr. *prōtos*, first, and *kolla*, glue.]

1. an original draft or record of a document, negotiation, etc.

2. [Fr. *protocole*.] in diplomacy, (a) a signed document containing a record of the points on which agreement has been reached by negotiating parties preliminary to a final treaty or compact; (b) the ceremonial forms and courtesies that are established as proper and correct in official intercourse between heads of states and their ministers.

prō′tō·çol, *v.t.* to put into the form of a protocol.

prō′tō·çol, *v.i.* to issue or write protocols.

prō′tō·çol·ist, *n.* one who draws up protocols.

Prō′tō·çolș of the El′dẽrș of Zī′ŏn, a set of forged writings created by Russian reactionaries in 1903 and circulated by anti-Semitic propagandists, purporting to be a record of a series of meetings in Basle in 1897 for plotting the overthrow of Christian civilization by Jews and Freemasons.

prō′tō·conçh, *n.* [*proto-*, and Gr. *konchē*, shell.] the embryonic shell of a cephalopod.

prō·tō-Dor′iç, *a.* in architecture, exhibiting primitive features of the Doric style.

prō·tō·gas′tẽr, *n.* [*proto-*, and Gr. *gastēr*, stomach.] in embryology, the archenteron, or primitive intestinal cavity.

prō·tō·ġ′e·năl, *a.* [*proto-*, and *-gen*, and *-al*.] primordial; primitive.

prō·tō·ġen′e·sis, *n.* abiogenesis. [Rare.]

prō″tō·ġē·net′iç, *a.* of protogenesis.

prō·tō·ġen′iç, *a.* pertaining to first origin: used in geology and botany.

prō′tō·ġine, *n.* [*proto-*, and Gr. *ginesthai*, *gignesthai*, to become.] a variety of granite with a foliated structure, found mainly in the Alps.

prō·tō·glob′ū·lōse, *n.* [*proto-* and *globulose*.] any albumose derived from globulin.

prō·tō·gos′pel, *n.* same as *protevangelium*.

prō·toġ′y·nous, *a.* same as *proterogynous*.

prō·toġ′y·ny, *n.* same as *proterogyny*.

Prō·tō·hip′pus, *n.* [*proto-*, and Gr. *hippos*, horse.] a genus of fossil *Equidæ* having three toes on each foot: found in the Lower Pliocene.

prō″tō·his·tor′iç, *a.* of or relating to primitive history and historical records.

prō·tō·lith′iç, *a.* [*proto-* and *-lithic*.] designating or of the earliest Stone Age; eolithic.

prō·tō·mär′tyr (-tūr), *n.* the first martyr (of some cause); especially, [P–] Saint Stephen, the first Christian martyr.

prō·tō·mer′is·tem, *n.* the primary meristem.

prō·tō·mẽr′īte, *n.* [*proto-*, and Gr. *meros*, part, and *-ite*.] the smaller anterior cell of a gregarine protozoan.

prō′tō·mọrph, *n.* [*proto-* and *-morph*.] in biology, a primitive form.

prō·tō·mọr′phiç, *a.* [*proto-* and *-morphic*.] in biology, primitive in form or character.

prō″tō·mȳ·os′i·nōse, *n.* [*proto-*, and *myosin*, and *-ose*.] an albumose derived from myosin.

prō′ton, *n.* [Mod. L., from Gr. *prōton*, neut. of *prōtos*, first.] the nucleus of an atom of the protium isotope of hydrogen, having a mass number of 1: it is considered to be one of the fundamental particles of the nuclei of all atoms and carries a unit positive charge of electricity.

prō·tō·nē′mȧ, *n.*; *pl.* **prō·tō·nē′mȧ·tȧ,** [Mod. L., from Gr. *prōto-*, first, and *nēma*, *nēmatos*, a thread.] a threadlike growth in mosses, developing small buds that grow into leafy moss plants.

prō·tō·nem′ȧ·toid, *a.* [from *protonema* and *-oid*.] resembling a protonema.

prō·tō·neph′ros, *n.* [LL., from Gr. *prōtos*, first, and *nephros*, kidney.] the primitive renal organ.

prō·ton′ō·tăr·y, *n.*; *pl.* **prō·ton′ō·tăr·ieș,** same as *prothonotary*.

prō·tō·ọr′găn·ișm, *n.* in biology, a protozoan or protophyte.

prō·tō·pap′ȧs, *n.* [*proto-*, and L.Gr. *papas*, a priest.] in the Greek Church, a chief priest; a priest of superior rank, corresponding to a dean or archdeacon.

prō·tō·path′iç, *a.* [*proto-* and *-pathic*.] in physiology, designating or of primary, or primitive, sensibility, which can perceive and localize only strong, gross stimuli, as pain.

prō·tō·pep′si·ȧ, *n.* [*proto-*, and Gr. *pepsis*, digestion.] primary digestion.

prō·tō·phlō′em, *n.* [*proto-* and *phloem*.] in botany, the primary phloem of a vascular bundle.

Prō·toph′y·tȧ, *n.pl.* in botany, a primary division of unicellular plants of the lowest and simplest organization.

prō′tō·phȳte, *n.* [*proto-* and *-phyte*.] a unicellular plant organism; one of the *Protophyta*.

prō·tō·phyt′iç, *a.* pertaining to the *Protophyta*.

prō·tō·phȳt′ŏn, *n.* same as *protophyte*.

prō′tō·pīne, *n.* [*proto-*, and *opium*, and *-ine*.] in chemistry, an alkaloid, $C_{20}H_{19}NO_5$, derived from opium. It possesses anodyne and hypnotic properties.

prō′tō·plașm, *n.* [G. *protoplasma*, from Gr. *prōtos*, first, and *plasma*, anything formed or molded, from *plassein*, to mold.]

1. a semifluid, viscous, translucent colloid, the essential matter of all animal and plant cells: it consists largely of water, proteins, lipoids, carbohydrates, and inorganic salts.

2. formerly, cytoplasm.

prō·tō·plaș′mȧ, *n.* protoplasm.

prō·tō·plaș′măl, *a.* protoplasmic.

prō″tō·plaș·mat′iç, *a.* protoplasmic.

prō·tō·plaș′miç, *a.* 1. in biology, pertaining to, resembling, or consisting of protoplasm.

2. pertaining to the primitive formation of organized beings.

prō′tō·plast, *n.* [Fr. *protoplaste*; LL. *protoplastus*; Gr. *protoplastos*, formed first, from *prōtos*, first, and *plastos*, formed, from *plassein*, to form].

1. a thing or being that is the first of its kind.

2. in biology, a unit of protoplasm, such as makes up a single cell; a plastid.

Prō·tō·plas′tȧ, *n.pl.* [LL.] a division of rhizopods found in fresh water.

prō·tō·plas′tiç, *a.* 1. first-formed.

2. protoplasmic; pertaining to a protoplast.

3. pertaining to the *Protoplasta*.

prō·top′ō·dīte, *n.* [*proto-*, and Gr. *pous*, *podos*, a foot, and *-ite*.] in zoology, the basal segment of the typical limb of a crustacean.

prō′tō·pōpe, *n.* [Russ. *protopop*′; L.Gr. *prōtopapas*, chief priest.] a protopapas.

prō·tō·preș′by·tẽr, *n.* a protopope. [Obs.]

prō′tō·prișm, *n.* in crystallography, a prism of the first order in the tetragonal system.

prō·tō·prō′tē·ōse, *n.* [*proto-* and *proteose*.] in biochemistry, one of the primary products of the gastric digestion of proteins.

prō·top′te·rus, *n.* [*proto-*, and Gr. *pteron*, wing.] an African food fish, the lepidosiren; a mudfish.

prō′tō·sạlt, *n.* in chemistry, that one of a series of salts of the same base which contains the smallest amount of the substance combining with the base.

prō·tō·sō′mīte, *n.* [*proto-* and *somite*.] a primitive segment of an animal's body.

prō′tō·spașm, *n.* in pathology, a spasm which begins in a limited area and extends to other parts.

prō′tō·stē·lē (*or* -stēl), *n.* [*proto-* and *stele*.] a simple central cylinder in the stems and roots of plants, through which food and liquids pass.

prō·tō·stē′liç, *a.* of or characterized by a protostele.

prō′tō·stōme, *n.* [*proto-*, and Gr. *stoma*, mouth.] in biology, the mouth opening into the invaginal cavity of a gastrula; the blastopore.

prō·tō·sul′fāte, *n.* in chemistry, that one of several sulfates of the same base which contains the least amount of sulfuric acid.

Prō·tō·thē′ri·ȧ, *n.pl.* in zoology, a group of mammals, the *Monotremata*.

Prō·tō·trā·çhē·ā′tȧ, *n.pl.* same as *Protracheata*.

prō·tō·troph′iç, *a.* [*proto-* and *trophic*.] nourished by uncombined elements, as the nitrogen-fixing bacteria.

prō′tō·tȳp·ăl, *a.* 1. having the nature of a prototype.

2. of a prototype.

prō′tō·tȳpe, *n.* [Fr., from Gr. *prōtotypos*; *prōtos*, first, and *typos*, type, form, model.] an original or model after which anything is formed; the first thing or being of its kind; a pattern; exemplar; archetype.

prō·tō·typ′iç, *a.* same as *prototypal*.

prō·tō·typ′i·çăl, *a.* prototypal.

prō·tō·vẽr′tē·brȧ, *n.* [*proto-*, and L. *vertebra*, vertebra.] in biology, a segment of the trunk of the embryo; an embryonic segment of the paraxial mesoblast; one of the segments composing the mesoblast.

prō·tō·vẽr′tē·brăl, *a.* of or belonging to the protovertebra.

prō·tō′vum, *n.*; *pl.* **prō·tō′vȧ,** [*proto-*, and L. *ovum*, egg.] in biology, the original undifferentiated ovum.

prō·tox′īde, prō·tox′id, *n.* that one of a series of oxides which contains the smallest proportion of oxygen.

prō·tox′i·dīze, *v.t.* to combine with oxygen, as any elementary substance, so as to form a protoxide. [Obs.]

prō·tō·xȳ′lem (-zī′), *n.* [*proto-* and *xylem*.] in botany, the primitive undifferentiated wood element in a fibrovascular bundle.

Prō·tō·zō′ȧ, *n.pl.* [Mod. L., pl. of *protozoon*, from Gr. *prōtos*, first, and *zōion*, an animal.] a phylum of one-celled, usually microscopic, animals, belonging to the lowest division of the animal kingdom. Protozoa reproduce by fission, and in some forms conjugation also takes place. The organs of locomotion are varied. In some of the higher forms, movements are effected by means of cilia, in others by long, whiplike bristles termed flagella; but the most characteristic organs of locomotion are processes named pseudopodia, consisting simply of prolongations of the protoplasmic substance of the body, which can be emitted and retracted. In a few, a thin marginal lamina propels the animal by its undulations. The Protozoa, with the exception of a few inhabiting the bodies of animals, are aquatic in their habits.

prō·tō·zō′ăn, *a.* of or belonging to the *Protozoa*.

prō·tō·zō′ăn, *n.* a member of the phylum *Protozoa*; any of a number of one-celled animals, usually microscopic, belonging to the lowest division of the animal kingdom.

prō·tō·zō′iç, *a.* 1. belonging to or containing the earliest forms of life; specifically, in zool-

ogy, of or pertaining to the *Protozoa*; protozoan.
2. in geology, designating the system of rocks in which the earliest traces of organic life have been found.

prō″tō·zō·ol′ō·ġy, *n.* that branch of zoology devoted to the study of the protozoans.

prō·tō·zō′on, *n.*; *pl.* **prō′tō·zō·ȧ,** in zoology, one of the *Protozoa*; a protozoan.

Prō·trā·chē·ā′tȧ, *n.pl.* one of the primary divisions of the *Arthropoda*: it includes the *Malacopoda*.

prō·tract′, *v.t.*, protracted, *pt.*, *pp.*; protracting, *ppr.* [L. *protractus*, pp. of *protrahere*; *pro*, forward, and *trahere*, to draw.]
1. to draw out or lengthen in time; to continue; to prolong; as, to *protract* an argument or a war.
2. to delay; to defer; to put off to a distant time; as, to *protract* the decision of a question. [Now Rare.]
3. to draw a plan or map of to scale, using a protractor and scale.
4. in zoology, to extend; to thrust out: opposed to *retract*.

prō·tract′, *n.* tedious continuance; delay. [Obs.]

prō·tract′ed, *a.* drawn out in time; prolonged.

prō·tract′ed·ly, *adv.* in a protracted manner.

prō·tract′ẽr, *n.* same as *protractor*.

prō·trac′tile, *a.* that can be protracted or thrust out; extensible.

prō·trac′tion, *n.* 1. a protracting; extension; as, the *protraction* of a debate.
2. a drawing to scale of any figure, plan, etc.
3. such a drawing.
4. extension by a protractor muscle.
5. the giving of a long quantity to a short syllable.

prō·trac′tive, *a.* protracting or tending to protract.

prō·trac′tŏr, *n.* 1. a mathematical instrument in the form of a graduated semicircle, for laying down and measuring angles.

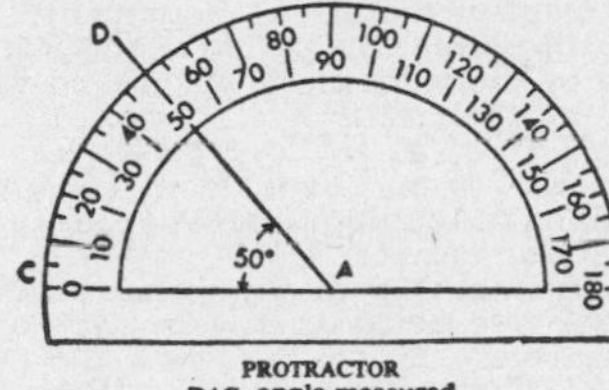

PROTRACTOR
DAC, angle measured

2. a form of tailors' pattern.
3. in anatomy, a muscle whose function is to extend a limb, organ, or other portion of a body.
4. in old surgery, an instrument for removing foreign substances from a wound.
5. one who protracts.

prō·trep′ti·căl, *a.* [Gr. *protreptikos*, fitted for urging on, hortatory, from *protrepein*, to urge on; *pro*, forward, and *trepein*, to turn.] hortatory; persuasive; intended to persuade.

prō·trūd′ȧ·ble, *a.* capable of protrusion.

prō·trūde′, *v.t.*; protruded, *pt.*, *pp.*; protruding, *ppr.* [L. *protrudere*; *pro*, forth, and *trudere*, to thrust.]
1. to thrust out or forth; to cause to move outward or to project, as from confinement or from a small opening; as, to *protrude* one's tongue.
2. to drive or force along; to thrust forward. [Rare.]

prō·trūde′, *v.i.* to jut out; to be thrust forward; to project.

prō·trūd′ent, *a.* protruding.

prō·trū′si·ble, *a.* [L. *protrusus*, pp. of *protrudere*, to thrust forth.] same as *protrusile*.

prō·trū′sile, *a.* capable of being protruded, or thrust out, as an elephant's trunk, a tentacle, etc.

prō·trū′sion, *n.* 1. a protruding or being protruded.
2. a protruding part or thing.

prō·trū′sive, *a.* 1. thrusting or impelling forward; as, *protrusive* motion. [Now Rare.]
2. jutting or bulging out; protruding.
3. obtrusive.

prō·trū′sive·ly, *adv.* in a protrusive manner.

prō·tū′bẽr·ănce, *n.* [LL. *protuberans*, ppr. of *protuberare*, to swell.]
1. the condition or fact of being protuberant.
2. a part or thing that protrudes; a projection; bulge; swelling.

prō·tū′bẽr·ăn·cy, *n.*; *pl.* **prō·tū′bẽr·ăn·cies,** same as *protuberance*.

prō·tū′bẽr·ănt, *a.* swelling or bulging out; protruding; prominent.

prō·tū′bẽr·āte, *v.i.*; protuberated, *pt.*, *pp.*; protuberating, *ppr.* [LL. *protuberare*, from L. *pro*, before, and *tuberare*, to swell, from *tuber*, a hump, a bump, a swelling, akin to *tumere*, to swell.] to bulge or swell out.

prō·tū·bẽr·ā′tion, *n.* a protuberating. [Obs.]

prō·tū′bẽr·ous, *a.* protuberant. [Rare.]

prō·tū′tŏr, *n.* in civil law, one who has acted as guardian or tutor without legal authority or without knowledge of his authority.

prō′tȳle (*or* -til), *n.* [from *prot-* and Gr. *hylē*, substance, stuff.] the hypothetical primordial substance from which all elements are supposed to be derived.

proud, *a.*; *comp.* prouder; *superl.* proudest, [AS. *prut*, proud, whence *pryte*, pride; Dan. *prud*, stately, magnificent.]
1. having or exhibiting pride; specifically, (a) having or showing inordinate self-esteem; possessing an unreasonably high conception of one's own excellence of body or mind, of one's achievements, position, or importance; hence, arrogant; haughty; supercilious; (b) having or showing an aversion to whatever is considered unworthy of one's reputation, character, or self-respect; (c) feeling or showing great pride or joy; elated; exultant; highly pleased; as, *proud* of one's country's greatness; *proud* to receive commendation.
2. that is an occasion or cause of pride; exciting pride; grand; magnificent; as, a *proud* day for Rome; *proud* temples; a *proud* array.
3. spirited; of high mettle; as, the *proud* Arabian steed.
4. arising from or caused by pride; presumptuous; as, a *proud* glance.
5. turgid or swollen, as a river in flood.
6. excited sexually: used of a female animal, as a cat. [Obs. or Dial.]
7. valiant. [Obs.]

proud flesh, [so called from the notion of swelling up.] an abnormal growth of flesh around a healing wound, caused by excessive granulation.

proud′ish, *a.* somewhat proud. [Rare.]

proud′ling, *n.* one who is proud, or haughty. [Obs.]

proud′ly, *adv.* in a proud manner; with pride.
Proudly he marches on and void of fear.
—Pope.

proud′ness, *n.* pride; the state or quality of being proud.

prōust′īte, *n.* [named after J. L. *Proust* (1754–1826), French chemist.] a ruby red sulfide of arsenic and silver, found in rhombohedral crystals: also called *ruby* or *red silver*.

prōv′ȧ·ble, *a.* capable of being proved; demonstrable.

prōv′ȧ·ble·ness, *n.* the quality of being provable.

prōv′ȧ·bly, *adv.* in a manner capable of proof.

prov′ănd, prov′ănt, *n.* provender or food. [Archaic.]

prō·vant′, *v.t.* to furnish with provisions. [Obs.]

prov′ănt, *a.* [OFr. *provende*; LL. *præbenda*, payment; L. *præbere*, to furnish.] furnished for general use, as in an army; hence, common in quality; of low grade. [Archaic.]

prōve, *v.t.*; proved, *pt.*; proved *or* proven, *pp.*; proving, *ppr.* [ME. *proven*; Late AS. *profian*; L. *probare*, to test, to show to be good; *probus*, good.]
1. to try; to ascertain, as some unknown quality or truth, by an experiment, or by a test or standard; to subject to a testing process; as, to *prove* the strength of a fabric by experiment; to *prove* cannon.
2. to evince, establish, or ascertain as truth, reality, or fact, by testimony or other evidence; as, the prosecutor must *prove* his charges against the accused.
3. to establish the genuineness or validity of; to verify; as, to *prove* a will.
4. to experience; to learn or know by suffering or encountering. [Archaic.]
Let him in arms the power of Turnus *prove*.
—Dryden.
5. in mathematics, to test or verify the correctness of (a calculation, etc.). Thus, in subtraction, if the difference between two numbers, added to the lesser number, makes a sum equal to the greater, the correctness of the subtraction is *proved*.
6. in printing, to take a trial impression or proof of (type, etc.).
the exception proves the rule; the exception puts the rule to the test.
Syn.—demonstrate, evince, manifest.—To *prove* is to give proof; to *demonstrate* is to give clear or visible proof; to *evince* is to show by convincing proof; to *manifest* is to make obvious to the understanding.

prōve, *v.i.* 1. to make trial; to essay. [Archaic.]
The sons prepare
To *prove* by arms whose fate it was to reign.
—Dryden.
2. to be found or ascertained to be by experience or trial; to turn out to be; as, a medicine *proves* beneficial; the operation *proved* fatal.
3. to succeed; to turn out as was anticipated.
to prove up; to furnish proof or fulfillment of the conditions of a grant, franchise, etc.; especially, in the western United States, to show compliance with the Homestead Act.

prō·vect′, *a.* advanced or carried forward. [Obs.]

prō·vec′tion, *n.* [LL. *provectio* (*-onis*), from L. *provectus*, pp. of *provehere*, to advance.] the act of carrying the terminal letter from a preceding word to the next succeeding one, when the latter begins with a vowel; as, *for the nonce* from *for then ones*.

prō·ved′i·tŏr, *n.* [It. *proveditore*, from *provedere*, to provide.]
1. a purveyor; one employed to procure supplies for an army, vessel, etc.; a provider.
2. in the Venetian republic, a governor.

prov′e·dōre, prov′e·dọr, *n.* [Port. *provedor*.] a purveyor; one who procures provisions for others.

prōv′en, *v.* alternative past participle of *prove*.

prov′e·nănce, *n.* [Fr.] derivation; origin.

Pro·ven·çal′ (prō-ven-säl′; *or Fr.* prō-vän-säl′), *a.* [Fr. *Provençal*, from L. *Provincialis*, from *provincia*, province.] of or pertaining to Provence, its people, their language, etc.

Pro·ven·çal′, *n.* 1. a native or inhabitant of Provence, in southern France.
2. the vernacular of southern France, a distinct Romance language comprising several dialects.
3. the medieval language of southern France: as cultivated by the troubadours, it was one of the great literary languages of Europe.

Prov′ence, (*or Fr.* prō-väns′), *a.* of or from Provence.
Provence or *Provins rose*; same as *cabbage rose*.

Prō·ven′ciăl (-shal), *a.* same as *Provençal*.

prov′end, *n.* provand. [Archaic.]

prov′en·dẽr, *n.* [ME. *provendre*; OFr. *provendre*, variant of *provende*; L. *præbenda*, payment.]
1. dry food for livestock; meal, or a mixture of meal and cut straw or hay; fodder.
2. food: used humorously. [Colloq.]

prov′en·dẽr, *v.t.* to provide with food; to feed; to fodder.

prō·vē′ni·ence (-ni-ens *or* -ni-yuns), *n.* [L. *provenire*, to come forth.] provenance; origin.

prov′ent, *n.* provand. [Obs.]

prō·ven·tric′ū·lăr, *a.* pertaining to the proventriculus.

prō·ven·tric′ū·lus, *n.* [*pro-*, and L. *ventriculus*, dim. of *venter*, stomach.]
1. the glandular stomach, situated between the crop and gizzard of a bird.
2. the ingluvies, or first stomach, of an insect.

prōv′ẽr, *n.* one who proves or tries; that which proves.

prov′ẽrb, *n.* [ME. and OFr. *proverbe*; L. *proverbium*; *pro*, before, and *verbum*, a word.]
1. a short saying in common use expressing a well-known truth or common fact ascertained by experience or observation; a maxim; an adage.
The *proverb* is true, that light gains make heavy purses; for light gains come often, great gains now and then. —Bacon.
2. a person or thing that has become commonly recognized as a type of specified characteristics; a byword.
3. in the Bible, an enigmatical saying in which a profound truth is cloaked; a parable; allegory: see also *Proverbs*.
4. [*pl.*] any of various games in which prov-

erbs are to be guessed by questioning, watching a dramatization, etc.

Syn.—aphorism, maxim, adage, byword, axiom, motto.

prov′ẽrb, *v.t.* 1. to describe in a proverb.

2. to make a byword of.

prov′ẽrb, *v.i.* to quote or utter proverbs. [Rare.]

prō·vẽr′bi·ăl, *a.* [ME.; LL. *proverbialis.*]

1. of, or having the nature of, a proverb.

2. expressed in a proverb.

3. that has become an object of common reference, as in a proverb.

prō·vẽr′bi·ăl·iṣm, *n.* a proverbial phrase. [Rare.]

prō·vẽr′bi·ăl·ist, *n.* one who composes or uses proverbs; one versed in proverbs.

prō·vẽr′bi·ăl·īze, *v.t.* and *v.i.* to proverb.

prō·vẽr′bi·ăl·ly, *adv.* 1. by means of, or as expressed in, a proverb.

2. to the point or degree of becoming a proverb; notoriously.

prov′ẽrb·īze, *v.t.* and *v.i.* to proverb. [Rare.]

Prov′ẽrbṣ, *n.pl.* [*construed as sing.*] a book of the Old Testament, containing various maxims ascribed to Solomon and others.

prō·vīd′à·ble, *a.* capable of being provided.

prō·vīde′, *v.t.*; provided, *pt., pp.*; providing, *ppr.* [ME. *providen*; L. *providere*; *pro*, before, and *videre*, to see.]

1. to procure beforehand; to get, collect, or make ready for future use; to prepare; as, to *provide* coal for winter.

2. to furnish: followed by *with*; as, to *provide* a person *with* money.

3. to make available; to supply; to afford.

4. to foresee. [Obs.]

5. to appoint to an ecclesiastical benefice before it is vacant. [Obs.]

Syn.—accouter, equip, prepare, supply, furnish.

prō·vīde′, *v.i.* 1. to furnish the means of support (usually with *for*).

2. to prepare (*for* or *against*) some probable or possible situation, occurrence, condition, etc.; as, to *provide against* the inclemencies of the weather.

> Government is a contrivance of human wisdom to *provide for* human wants. —Burke.

3. to stipulate; to make a condition.

prō·vīd′ed, *conj.* on condition; on these terms; this being understood, conceded, or established; if: frequently followed by *that*.

> *Provided that* you do no outrages.—Shak.

prov′i·dence, *n.* [ME.; L. *providentia*, foresight.]

1. the act of providing; provision; preparation. [Obs. or Dial.]

> *Providence* for war is the best prevention of it. —Bacon.

2. foresight; timely care; particularly, active foresight, or foresight accompanied with the procurement of what is necessary for future use, or with suitable preparation.

> A glance satisfied her that her Duc was where her benevolent *providence* had directed him to be. —Elizabeth Phipps Train.

3. skill or wisdom in management; prudence.

4. the care or benevolent guidance of God or nature.

5. an instance of this.

6. [P–] God.

prov′i·dent, *a.* [ME.; L. *providens* (*-entis*), ppr. of *providere*, to provide.]

1. providing for future needs or events; exercising or characterized by foresight.

2. prudent; economical.

Syn.—careful, frugal, foreseeing.

prov·i·den′tiăl (-shăl), *a.* 1. of providence.

2. decreed by Providence.

3. fortunate; lucky.

prov·i·den′tiăl·ly, *adv.* in a providential manner.

> Every animal is *providentially* directed to the use of its proper weapons. —Ray.

prov′i·dent·ly, *adv.* with prudent foresight; with wise precaution in preparing for the future.

prov′i·dent·ness, *n.* the state of being provident; providence; foresight; carefulness; prudence.

prō·vīd′ẽr, *n.* one who provides, furnishes, or supplies; one who procures what is wanted.

prō·vīd′ing, *conj.* [ppr. of *provide.*] on the condition or understanding (that); provided.

prov′i·dōre, *n.* same as *provedor*.

prov′ince, *n.* [ME.; OFr.; L. *provincia*, a province.]

1. a territory, outside Italy, governed by ancient Rome.

2. an administrative division of a country.

3. any of the British colonies in North America now administrative divisions of Canada.

4. any of certain British colonies now a part of the United States.

5. (a) a region; district; territory; (b) [*pl.*] the parts of a country removed from the capital and the populated, cultural centers.

6. in ecclesiastical usage, a division of a country under the jurisdiction of an archbishop or metropolitan.

7. a division of the world according to the plants or animals found there: it is smaller in size than a region.

8. proper duties or functions; sphere of action.

> It is the *province* of the court to judge of the law, that of the jury to decide on the facts. —Bouvier.

9. a division in any department of knowledge or speculation; a department; a branch of learning.

> Their understandings are cooped in narrow bounds, so that they never look abroad into other *provinces* of the intellectual world. —Watts.

Syn.—tract, region, department, section, sphere, domain, territory.

prō·vin′ciăl (-shăl), *a.* 1. of or belonging to the provinces or to a province; as, a *provincial* government; a *provincial* dialect.

2. having the ways, speech, attitudes, etc. of people in a province.

3. countrified; rustic; local.

4. narrow; limited; as, a *provincial* outlook.

prō·vin′ciăl, *n.* 1. a native of a province.

2. [*pl.*] troops raised in a province.

3. a provincial person.

4. a monastic superior who under the general of his order has the direction of all the religious houses of the same fraternity in a given district, called a *province* of the order.

prō·vin′ciăl·iṣm, *n.* 1. the condition or fact of being provincial.

2. narrowness of outlook.

3. a provincial custom, characteristic, etc.

4. a word, phrase, or pronunciation peculiar to a province.

prō·vin′ciăl·ist, *n.* one who lives in a province; also, one characterized by provincialism.

prō·vin·ci·al′i·ty (-shi-), *n.*; *pl.* **prō·vin·ci·al′i·tieṣ,** same as *provincialism*.

prō·vin′ciăl·īze (-shăl-), *v.t.*; provincialized, *pt., pp.*; provincializing, *ppr.* to cause to be or to become provincial.

prō·vin′ciăl·ly, *adv.* in a provincial manner; as in a province.

prō·vin′ci·āte (-shi-), *v.t.* to convert into a province.

prō·vin′çū·lum, *n.* [L. *pro-*, prefix denoting primitive, rudimentary, and *vinculum*, from *vincire, vincium*, to bend.] in zoology, a rudimentary hinge in certain mollusks, formed of very small teeth that are developed before the permanent teeth are formed.

prō·vīne′, *v.i.* [Fr. *provigner*, from *provin*, L. *propago, propaginis*, the layer of a vine; perh. influenced by Fr. *vigne*, a vine.] to lay a stock or branch of a vine in the ground for propagation.

pröv′ing, *n.* a testing; trying; establishing.

pröv′ing ground, a place used for the purpose of testing new equipment, theories, etc.

prō·vi′ṣion (-vizh′un), *n.* [ME. *provysion*; L. *provisio* (*-onis*), a foreseeing, from *providere, provisus*, to provide.]

1. a providing, preparing, or supplying of something.

2. something provided, prepared, or supplied for the future.

3. [*pl.*] a stock of food and other supplies assembled for future needs.

4. preparatory arrangements or measures taken in advance for meeting some future needs.

5. a clause, as in a legal document, agreement, etc., stipulating or requiring some specific thing; a condition.

6. in ecclesiastical usage, appointment to an office; especially, advance appointment by the Pope to a see or benefice that is not yet vacant.

Syn.—preparation, arrangement, produce, supply, anticipation, food, supplies, victuals, edibles, eatables.

prō·vi′ṣion (-vizh′un), *v.t.*; provisioned, *pt., pp.*; provisioning, *ppr.* to supply with provisions, especially with a stock of food; as, the ship was *provisioned* for a voyage of six months.

prō·vi′ṣion·ăl, *a.* provided for present need or for the occasion; temporarily established; having a conditional or temporary character; as, a *provisional* government or regulation; a *provisional* treaty.

prō·vi′ṣion·ăl·ly, *adv.* by way of provision; temporarily; for the present exigency.

prō·vi′ṣion·ăr·y, *a.* same as *provisional*.

prō·vi′ṣion·ẽr, *n.* one who supplies provisions.

prō·vī′ṣō, *n.*; *pl.* **prō·vī′ṣōṣ, prō·vī′ṣōeṣ,** [L. *provisus*, ablative *proviso*, it being provided.]

1. an article or clause in any statute, agreement, contract, grant, or other writing, making some stipulation or condition; a conditional stipulation that affects an agreement, contract, law, grant, etc.; as, the charter of the bank contains a *proviso* that the legislature may repeal it at pleasure.

2. any condition or stipulation.

Wilmot proviso; an amendment introduced in the U. S. House of Representatives in 1846 by David Wilmot of Pennsylvania to a bill under discussion for the purchase of certain territory from Mexico. The proviso was that slavery should forever be excluded from the territory in question.

prō·vī′ṣŏr, *n.* [L., a foreseer.]

1. a person appointed by the Pope to a benefice before the death of the incumbent.

2. the purveyor, steward, or treasurer of a religious house. [Obs.]

prō·vī′ṣō·ri·ly, *adv.* in a provisory or conditional manner; temporarily.

prō·vī′ṣŏr·ship, *n.* the office of a provisor.

prō·vī′ṣō·ry, *a.* 1. making temporary provision; provisional.

2. containing a proviso or condition; conditional.

prō·vī′tà·min, *n.* any substance in the body believed to be the precursor or source of a vitamin.

prov·ō·çā′tion, *n.* [ME. *provacacion*; L. *provocatio* (*-onis*), provocation.]

1. a provoking.

2. something that provokes; the cause of resentment or irritation; incitement.

the provocation; the period of the Jews' wandering in the wilderness, when God was provoked by their sins.

prō·voç′à·tive, *a.* [ME. *prouocatyue*, aphrodisiac; LL. *provocativus*, from L. *provocare.*] provoking or tending to provoke, as to action, thought, anger, etc.

prō·voç′à·tive, *n.* something that provokes.

prō·voç′à·tive·ness, *n.* the quality of being provocative.

prō·voç′à·tō·ry, *a.* provocative. [Rare.]

prō·vōk′à·ble, *a.* that can be provoked.

prō·vōke′, *v.t.*; provoked, *pt., pp.*; provoking, *ppr.* [ME. *provokin*; OFr. *provoquer*, to provoke, from L. *provocare*, to call forth; *pro*, forth, and *vocare*, to call.]

1. to challenge. [Obs.]

2. to stimulate to action; to move; to excite; to arouse.

> Beauty *provoketh* thieves sooner than gold. —Shak.

3. to call forth; to produce; to cause; to occasion; to instigate.

> Swelling passion doth *provoke* a pause. —Shak.

4. to excite to anger or passion; to exasperate; to irritate; to enrage.

> Nothing in the whole affair *provoked* him so much as the condolences of his friends. —Sterne.

5. to stir up (action or feeling).

Syn.—arouse, stir up, rouse, awake, cause, excite, move, induce, incite, stimulate, inflame, offend, irritate, anger, chafe, exasperate, incense, enrage.

prō·vōke′, *v.i.* 1. to appeal. [Obs.]

2. to produce anger.

prō·vōke′ment, *n.* provocation. [Obs.]

prō·vōk′ẽr, *n.* one who or that which provokes.

prō·vōk′ing, *a.* that provokes; especially, annoying; vexing; as, *provoking* words; *provoking* treatment.

prō·vōk′ing·ly, *adv.* in a provoking manner; so as to excite anger or annoyance.

prov′ŏst (*or* prō′vō), *n.* [AS. *profost, prafost*; OFr. *provost*; LL. *propositus*, for L. *præpositus*, chief, director, prefect, orig. pp. of *præponere*, to set before, place first; *præ-*, before, and *ponere*, to put, place.]

1. a superintendent; an official in charge.

2. the chief magistrate in a Scottish burgh.

3. a jailer. [Obs.]

4. in ecclesiastical usage, the head of a cathedral chapter or principal church.
5. in education, (a) the head of any of certain colleges in England and Ireland; (b) in certain American universities, an administrator concerned with educational matters.

prō′vōst çourt (prō′vō), a military court for trying soldiers or civilians charged with minor offenses in occupied territory.

prō′vōst guärd (prō′vō gärd), a detail of military police headed by a provost marshal.

prō′vōst mär′shăl (prō′vō), 1. in the army, an officer in charge of military police.
2. in the navy, an officer who has the custody of prisoners on trial by court-martial.

prō′vōst ser′ġeant (sär′jent), a sergeant who heads a detachment of military police.

prov′ŏst·ship, *n.* the office, rank, or authority of a provost.

prow, *a.*; *comp.* prower; *superl.* prowest, [OFr. *prou*; LL. *prode*, brave.] valiant; brave. [Archaic.]
As *prowest* knight and truest lover.
—Tennyson.

prow, *n.* [Fr. *proue*; Pr. *proa*; L. *prora*, from Gr. *prōira*, a prow.]
1. the forward part of a ship.
2. a part resembling this, as the front end of an airship.

prow, *n.* [OFr. *prou*; origin doubtful.] profit; advantage; benefit. [Obs.]

prow, *n.* same as *proa.*

prow′ess, *n.* [ME. *prowess*, from OFr. *prouesse*, prowess, from *prou*, brave; LL. *prode*, brave.]
1. bravery; valor; gallantry.
2. a valorous act.
3. superior ability, skill, ingenuity, or technique.

prowl, *v.t.*; prowled, *pt.*, *pp.*; prowling, *ppr.* [ME. *prollen, prolen*, to search about.]
1. to rove or wander over in a stealthy manner in search of prey; as, to *prowl* the woods or the streets.
2. to collect by plunder. [Obs.]

prowl, *v.i.* 1. to rove or wander stealthily, particularly for prey, as a wild beast; as, a *prowling* wolf.
2. to prey; to plunder. [Obs.]

prowl, *n.* a prowling.
on the prowl; prowling about.
prowl car; a squad car.

prowl′ẽr, *n.* one who or that which prowls.

prowl′ing, *a.* wandering about as if in search of prey or plunder.

prowl′ing·ly, *adv.* in a prowling manner.

prox′ē·nēte, *n.* a negotiator. [Rare.]

prox′ē·nus, *n.*; *pl.* **prox′ē·nī,** [Fr. *proxène*; Gr. *proxenos*, from *pro*, before, and *xenos*, a friend, a guest.] in ancient Greece, an official of one state who was appointed to represent the local interests of citizens of another state.

prox′i·mad, *adv.* toward the proximal part; proximally.

prox′i·măl, *a.* 1. proximate; next or nearest.
2. in anatomy, situated nearest the center of the body or the point of attachment of a limb, etc.

prox′i·măl·ly, *adv.* toward the proximal.

prox′i·măte, *a.* [L. *proximatus*, pp. of *proximare*, to come near, from *proximus*, nearest, superl. of *prope*, near.]
1. nearest or next in space, order, time, etc.
2. approximate.
proximate analysis; in chemistry, the separation of a complex substance into its constituent compounds.
proximate cause; a cause which immediately precedes and produces the effect, as distinguished from the *remote, mediate*, or *predisposing cause.*
proximate principles; organic compounds that are the constituents of more complex organizations and occur naturally in animal and vegetable tissues, such as proteins, fats, sugars, resins, etc.
Syn.—nearest, next, closest, immediate, direct.

prox′i·măte·ly, *adv.* immediately; by immediate relation or effect.

prox′ime, *a.* proximate. [Obs.]

prox·im′i·ty, *n.* [Fr. *proximité*; L. *proximitas*, nearness.] the state or quality of being next or near; nearness in place, time, or alliance.

prox′i·mō, *adv.* in or of the month following the present; as, the fair will be held on the 5th *proximo.*

prox′y, *n.*; *pl.* **prox′ieș,** [ME. *prokecye*, contr. form of *procuracy*; LL. *procuratia*, a caring for.]
1. the agency or function of a deputy.
2. the authority to act for another.
3. a document empowering a person to act for another, as in voting.
4. a person empowered to act for another.
5. an election; also, a ballot. [Dial.]
Syn.—agency, substitution, representation, agent, substitute, representative, deputy, commissioner, lieutenant, delegate.

prox′y·ship, *n.* the office or agency of a proxy.

prụde, *n.* [OFr. *prude, prode*, excellent; Fr. *prude*, prob. from L. *prudens*, prudent.] a person affecting a bearing and demeanor that is overly modest or proper.

prụ′dence, *n.* 1. the state or quality of being prudent; the habit of acting with deliberation and discretion; wisdom applied to practice.
It would be the point of *prudence* to defer forming one's ultimate irrevocable decision so long as new data might be offered.
—George Washington.
2. an instance of this.
3. careful management; economy.
Syn.—forecast, providence, considerateness, judiciousness, discretion, caution, circumspection, judgment.

prụ′den·cy, *n.* prudence. [Obs.]

prụ′dent, *a.* [Fr., from L. *prudens*, for *providens*, provident.]
1. capable of exercising sound judgment in practical matters.
2. cautious or discreet in conduct; circumspect; sensible; not rash.
3. characterized, dictated, or directed by prudence; as, *prudent* measures.
Syn.—circumspect, discreet, cautious, judicious, careful, considerate, sagacious, thoughtful, provident, frugal, economical.

prụ·den′tiăl (-shăl), *a.* 1. characterized by or proceeding from prudence; prudent; discreet; as, *prudential* motives.
2. exercising prudence, or sound judgment.
3. advisory; discretionary; superintending the discretionary concerns of a society; as, a *prudential* committee.

prụ·den′tiăl, *n.* a matter requiring prudence or discretion: chiefly used in the plural.

prụ·den′tiăl·ist, *n.* one who acts from or is governed by prudential motives. [Rare.]

prụ·den·ti·al′i·ty (-shi-), *n.* the quality or state of being prudential or being directed by prudential motives.

prụ·den′tiăl·ly, *adv.* in a prudential manner.

prụ′dent·ly, *adv.* in a prudent manner; judiciously; discreetly.

prụd′ẽr·y, *n.*; *pl.* **prụd′ẽr·ieș,** [Fr. *pruderie.*]
1. the quality or state of being prudish; the manners or characteristics of a prude; affected or excessive niceness or preciseness.
2. an instance of this.

prụ·d'homme′ (-dǫm′), *n.* [Fr., from OFr. *prud*, excellent, and *homme*, man.] a skillful or discreet man; specifically, in France, a member of a board composed of masters and workmen whose office is to arbitrate in trade disputes.

prụd′ish, *a.* like or characteristic of a prude; affectedly grave; overly modest or proper; as, a *prudish* woman; *prudish* manners.
Syn.—overmodest, overnice, squeamish, reserved, demure.

prụd′ish·ly, *adv.* in a prudish manner.

prụd′ish·ness, *n.* prudery.

prụ′i·nāte, *a.* same as *pruinose.*

prụ·i·nes′cence, *n.* the quality or state of being pruinose.

prụ′i·nōse, *a.* [L. *pruinosus*, from *pruina*, hoarfrost.] covered with a white, powdery substance or bloom.

prụ′i·nous, *a.* frosty.

prụne, *v.t.*; pruned, *pt.*, *pp.*; pruning, *ppr.* [ME. *proinen, prunen*, to trim, from OFr. *proignier, preugner*; contr. of *provigner*, to plant a slip or cutting of a vine, from L. *propago, propaginis*, a slip or sucker.]
1. to remove dead or living parts from (a plant) so as to increase fruit or flower production or improve the form.
2. to cut out or get rid of, as unnecessary parts.
3. to free from anything superfluous or overabundant.
One sees him clipping his apricots and *pruning* his essays. —Thackeray.

prụne, *v.i.* to cut away or remove unnecessary branches or parts.

prụne, *v.t.* and *v.i.*; pruned, *pt.*, *pp.*; pruning, *ppr.* [ME. *proinen*; OFr. *poroindre*; *por-* (for *pro-*) and *oindre* (from L. *ungere*), to anoint.] to preen or dress up. [Archaic.]
His royal bird
Prunes the immortal wing, and cloys his beak. —Shak.

prụne, *n.* [Fr., from L. *prunum*; Gr. *prounon*, a plum.]
1. a dried plum.
2. any kind of plum that can be easily dried without spoiling.
3. a person regarded as stupid, silly, or unpleasant. [Slang.]
South African prune; the fruit of *Pappea capensis*, a small tree of the soapberry family.

Prụ·nel′lȧ, *n.* [Fr. *prunelle, brunelle*, derived from G. *die bräune*, a disorder in the jaws and throat, which this plant was supposed to cure.] a genus of perennial herbs, native to the northern parts of America and of Europe, of the family *Labiatæ*. *Prunella vulgaris* was formerly valued for its vulnerary properties.

prụ·nel′lȧ, *n.* in medicine, (a) sore throat; (b) thrush; (c) angina pectoris. [Obs.]

prụ·nel′lȧ, *n.* [from Fr. *prunelle*, the ball of the eye.] a preparation of purified niter molded into cakes or balls: also called *prunella salt.*

prụ·nel′lȧ, *n.* [Fr. *prunelle, prunella*, prob. from its color resembling that of prunes.] a strong textile, usually a worsted twill, used for clerical, academic, and legal gowns, shoe uppers, etc.

prụ·nelle′, *n.* [Fr.] a small, yellow prune with the skin removed.

prụ·nel′lō, *n.* [Fr. *prunelle*, from *prune.*] a species of dried plum.

prụn′ẽr, *n.* 1. one who prunes or removes what is superfluous.
2. a beetle, the oak pruner.

prụne tree, 1. any tree bearing plums from which prunes are made.
2. a tree, *Prunus occidentalis*, of the West Indies.

prụ·nif′ẽr·ous, *a.* [L. *prunum*, a plum, and *ferre*, to bear.] bearing plums.

prụ′ni·fọrm, *a.* having the shape of a plum.

prụn′ing, *n.* 1. the act of lopping off superfluous branches; a trimming; a clearing of what is superfluous.
2. in falconry, that which is cast off by a bird when it preens its feathers; refuse; leavings.

prụn′ing chiș′el, a chisel for pruning trees.

prụn′ing hook, a pair of shears with one hooked blade, used in trimming trees, shrubs, and vines.

prụn′ing knīfe (nīf), a knife used for pruning trees and the like.

prụn′ing shearș, shears for pruning trees, etc.

Prụ′nus, *n.* [L., a plum tree.] a genus of arborescent plants, comprising several domestic fruits, as the cherry, peach, plum, damson, sloe, and apricot. There are about a hundred species, mostly native to the temperate regions of the northern hemisphere.

prụ′ri·ence, *n.* the condition or fact of being prurient.

prụ′ri·en·cy, *n.* prurience.

prụ′ri·ent, *a.* [L. *pruriens*, from *prurire*, to itch or long for a thing, to be lecherous.]
1. itching. [Rare.]
2. inclined or disposed to lewdness or lascivious thoughts; having lustful ideas or desires.
3. characterized by lewdness; lustful; lascivious; as, *prurient* longings.

prụ′ri·ent·ly, *adv.* in a prurient manner.

prụ·rig′i·nous, *a.* [L. *pruriginosis*, from *prurigo*, an itching, from *prurire*, to itch.] of, having the nature of, caused by, causing, or having prurigo.

prụ·rī′gō, *n.* a chronic, inflammatory skin disease, marked by the development of small pale-red papules and intense itching.

prụ·rit′iç, *a.* of, having, or pertaining to pruritus.

prụ·rī′tus, *n.* intense itching of the skin without eruption. It is a sympton of various skin diseases and may occur idiopathically as a neurosis.

Prus′siăn (prush′ăn), *a.* 1. of or pertaining to Prussia, its people, their language, etc.
2. like or characteristic of the Junkers and military caste of Prussia, regarded as harsh in discipline, militaristic, arrogant, etc.
Prussian blue; any of a group of dark-blue powders, ferrocyanides of iron, used as dyes or pigments; especially, ferric ferrocyanide, $Fe_4[Fe(CN)_6]_3$.
Prussian brown; an orange-brown color derived from Prussian blue.
Prussian carp; the gibel.
Prussian green; a blue-green color.

Prus′siăn, *n.* 1. originally, a member of a

Lettic people formerly living in the coastal regions of the southeastern Baltic.
2. a native or inhabitant of Prussia.
3. any of the German dialects of East or West Prussia.
4. Old Prussian.

Prus′siăn·iṣm, *n.* the principles, practices, and doctrines of the Prussians; specifically, the despotic militarism and harsh discipline of the Prussian ruling classes.

prus′si·āte (*or* prush′), *n.* [Fr.] 1. a salt of prussic acid; cyanide.
2. a ferrocyanide or ferricyanide.

prus′siç, *a.* related to or derived from Prussian blue.
prussic acid; hydrocyanic acid.

prus′sin, prus′sīne, *n.* cyanogen. [Obs.]

Prū·ten′iç, *a.* Prussian: used to denote certain astronomical tables of Erasmus Reinhold published in Prussia in the sixteenth century. [Obs.]

prȳ, *v.i.*; pried, *pt., pp.*; prying, *ppr.* [ME. *piren, prien*, to peer.] to inspect or look closely or inquisitively; to peer.

prȳ, *n.*; *pl.* **prīes,** 1. a prying; narrow inspection.
2. a person who is improperly curious or inquisitive.

prȳ, *n.*; *pl.* **prīeṣ,** [back-formation from *prize* (a lever).]
1. a lever, crowbar, etc.; a tool for raising or moving something by leverage.
2. leverage.

prȳ, *v.t.*; pried, *pt., pp.*; prying, *ppr.* 1. to raise, move, or force with a lever, crowbar, etc.
2. to draw forth with difficulty.

Pry·de′ri, *n.* in Brythonic mythology, a son of Pwyll and Rhiannon, and one of the gods of the Cymric otherworld. Witches kidnapped him as soon as he was born but later returned him to his parents.

prȳ′ēr, *n.* same as *prier.*

prȳ′ing, *a.* looking closely; peering; inquisitive; improperly curious.

prȳ′ing·ly, *adv.* in a prying or inquisitive manner.

prȳ′lēr, *n.* one who sweeps or removes scale from bars and sheets in a sheet steel rolling mill.

prȳ pōle, the pole forming the support of a hoisting gin.

pryt·ȧ·nē′um, *n.* [L., from Gr. *prytaneion.*] the public hall in ancient Greek states or cities; especially, the public hall at Athens, in which official hospitality was extended toward distinguished citizens, foreign ambassadors, envoys, etc. The prytanes, and others to whom the privilege was granted, also took their meals there at the public cost.

pryt′ȧ·nis, *n.*; *pl.* **pryt′ȧ·nēṣ,** 1. in ancient Greece, one of a governing committee of fifty, composed of five deputies chosen by lot from each of the ten phulai, or tribes, and so forming one tenth of the senate at Athens. Out of their number, one served as chief president for about one tenth of the year.
2. one of the chief magistrates in several of the Greek states, as at Corinth and Miletus.

pryt′ȧ·ny, *n.* in Athens, the period during which the presidency of the senate belonged to the prytanes of one section.

pryth′ee, *interj.* same as *prithee.*

psälm (säm), *n.* [ME. *psalme*; AS. *sealm*, from LL. *psalmus*; Gr. *psalmos*, a song sung to the harp, a pulling or twanging with the fingers.]
1. a sacred song or hymn.
2. any of the sacred songs or hymns constituting the Book of Psalms in the Old Testament.
Psalms of Zoroaster; same as *Gathas.*

psälm, *v.t.*; psalmed, *pt., pp.*; psalming, *ppr.* to sing, glorify, or praise in psalms.

psälm′book, *n.* a collection of psalms for use in religious worship.

psälm′ist (säm′ist), *n.* 1. a writer or composer of psalms.
2. formerly, a precentor, singer, or leader of music in the church.
the Psalmist; King David, to whom all or certain of the Psalms are variously attributed.

psälm′ist·ry, *n.* the singing of psalms; psalmody.

psal·mod′iç (sal-), *a.* of or relating to psalmody.

psal′mō·dist (*or* säm′), *n.* one who sings sacred songs; a person skilled in psalmody.

psal′mō·dīze, *v.i.* to sing psalms; to give praise.

psal′mō·dy, *n.* 1. the act, practice, or art of singing sacred songs.
2. psalms collectively.
3. the arrangement of psalms for singing.

psal·mog′rȧ·phēr (sal-), *n.* a writer of psalms.

psal·mog′rȧ·phist, *n.* same as *psalmographer.*

psal·mog′rȧ·phy, *n.* [Gr. *psalmos*, song, psalm, and *graphein*, to write.] the act or practice of writing psalms.

Psälmṣ (sämz), *n.pl.* [*construed as sing.*] a book of the Old Testament, consisting of 150 psalms; Book of Psalms.

Psąl′tēr (sąl′), *n.* [L. *psalterium*; Gr. *psalterion*, a stringed instrument.]
1. the Book of Psalms: often applied to a book containing the Psalms separately printed.
2. [also p-] a version of the Psalms for use in religious services, as in the Book of Common Prayer (in the Anglican Church) and the breviary (in the Roman Catholic Church).

psąl·tē′ri·ȧ (sąl-), *n.* pl. of *psalterium.*

psąl·tē′ri·ăl, *a.* pertaining to the psalterium.

psąl·tē′ri·um, *n.*; *pl.* **psąl·tē′ri·ȧ,** 1. the third stomach of ruminant animals; the omasum, or manyplies.
2. in anatomy, the lyra of the fornix.

psąl′tēr·y, *n.*; *pl.* **psąl′tēr·ieṣ,** 1. in the Middle Ages, a stringed instrument with a shallow sound box, plucked with the fingers or a plectrum.
2. a psalter.

PSALTERY

psam′mīte (sam′), *n.* [Gr. *psammos*, sand.] a kind of sandstone.

psam·mit′iç, *a.* pertaining to or like psammite.

psam·moph′i·lous, *a* growing or living in sandy areas or in sand.

psam·mō·ther′ȧ·py, *n.* a method of healing by means of sand baths.

psam′mous, *a.* sandy.

psar′ō·līte (sar′), *n.* [Gr. *psaros*, speckled, and *lithos*, a stone.] a tree fern found as a fossil in the Triassic sandstone.

psel′liṣm (sel′), *n.* [Gr. *psellieín*, to stammer.] any speech defect, as stammering or lisping.

psē·phiṣ′mȧ (sē-), *n.* [Gr. *psēphizein*, to reckon or count with pebbles.] in ancient Greece, a public vote of the people; also, a measure adopted by such a vote.

psē′phīte (sē′), *n.* [from Gr. *psēphos*, a pebble, and *-ite.*] conglomerate or fragmental rock.

pseū̄d- (sūd-), same as *pseudo-.*

pseū·dȧ·cū′sis (sū-), *n.* [LL., from Gr. *pseudēs*, false, and *akoustis*, a hearing.] in medicine, a subjective sensation of hearing, in which sounds are altered in pitch and quality.

pseū·daes·thē′ṣi·ȧ (-zhi-ȧ), *n.* same as *pseudesthesia.*

pseū·dap″ō·sē·mat′iç, *a.* [*pseudo-* and *aposematic.*] in biology, imitating in coloration or form an individual of another species having unpleasant or dangerous qualities.

pseū·dȧ·pos′tle (-pos′l), *n.* a pretended apostle.

pseū·dax′sis, *n.* [*pseud-* and *axis.*] in botany, a sympodium.

pseū·del′minth, *n.* [*pseud-*, and Gr. *helminthos*, a worm.] an organism erroneously supposed to be an endoparasitic worm of the group *Helminthes.*

pseū·dem′bry·ō, *n.* [*pseud-*, and Gr. *embryon*, an embryo.] an apparent embryo: said of certain larval forms, as the swarm gemmule of a sponge, and others.

pseū·dē·pig′rȧ·phȧ, *n.pl.* [*pseud-*, and *epi-*, and Gr. *graphein*, to write.] writings falsely attributed to Biblical characters, alleged to have been written in Biblical times, but never accepted as canonical.

pseū″dep·i·graph′iç, pseū″dep·i·graph′iç·ăl, *a.* pertaining to pseudepigraphy or pseudepigrapha.

pseū·dē·pig′rȧ·phous, *a.* of, or having the nature of, pseudepigrapha; spurious.

pseū·dē·pig′rȧ·phy, *n.* the false ascription of authorship to works.

pseū·dep″i·sē·mat′iç, *a.* [*pseud-*, and *epi-*, and Gr. *sematos*, sign.] in zoology, having a color or form that is deceptively similar to some object of prey.

pseū·des·thē′ṣi·ȧ (-zhi-ȧ), *n.* [*pseud-*, and Gr. *aisthēsis*, feeling.] in medicine, false sensory perception; imaginary feeling, as that of sensation in a region from which a part has been amputated.

pseū̄d·hē′măl (sūd-), *a.* [*pseud-*, and Gr. *haima*, blood.] pertaining or relating to the various simple vascular tracts and systems of the invertebrates.

pseū·di·mā′gō, *n.* same as *subimago.*

pseū·dī·sod′ō·mon, *n.* [*pseud-* and *isodomon.*] in ancient architecture, a form of masonry in which the height, length, and thickness of the courses, or layers, differ.

PSEUDISODOMON

pseū′dō-, [Gr. *pseudo-*, from *pseudēs*, false, from *pseudein*, to deceive.] a combining form meaning: (a) *fictitious, pretended, sham*, as in *pseudo*nym; (b) *counterfeit, spurious*, as in *pseud*epigrapha; (c) *closely* or *deceptively similar to* (a specified thing), as in *pseudo*morph; (d) *not corresponding to the reality, illusory*; (e) in chemistry, *an isomer* or *related form of* (the specified compound). Also, before a vowel, *pseud-.*

pseū′dō, *a.* sham; false; spurious; pretended; counterfeit.

The *pseudo* mole was put on to stay until time wore it off.—Elizabeth Robinson.

pseū′dō ȧ·pos′tle (-pos′l), same as *pseudapostle.*

pseū″dō·ȧ·quat′iç, *a.* having a moist or wet habitat, but not truly aquatic.

pseū″dō·bȧ·cil′lus, *n.* an exceedingly small rodlike poikilocyte resembling a microorganism.

pseū″dō·baç·tē′ri·um, *n.* any inorganic bacteroid particle of a nutrient or excretory nature simulating bacteria; a cell that resembles a bacterium; a pseudobacillus.

pseū·dō·blep′sis, *n.* [*pseudo-*, and Gr. *blepsis*, vision.] a condition of false or distorted vision.

pseū′dō·branch, *n.* an accessory gill.

pseū·dō·brañ′chi·ȧ, *n.*; *pl.* **pseū·dō·brañ′chi·ae,** an accessory or false gill; a formation which has the appearance of a gill.

pseū·dō·brañ′chi·ăl, *a.* of, relating to, or resembling a pseudobranch.

pseū′dō·bulb, *n.* a modified aerial internode in which food material is stored, as in many orchids.

pseū·dō·bulb′il, *n.* in ferns, a prothallus which sometimes replaces the sporangia.

pseū′dō·cärp, *n.* [*pseudo-*, and Gr. *karpos*, fruit.] in botany, a fruit which consists of more than the ripened ovary proper, as the apple, strawberry, pineapple, and many other fruits.

pseū·dō·cär′pous, *a.* of or like a pseudocarp.

pseū·dō·chī′nȧ, *n.* a plant of the smilax family, *Smilax pseudochina*, with a tuberous rootstock.

pseū·dō·chrys′ȧ·lis, *n.* a transitional form of certain insects assumed when passing from the larval to the pupal phase; a pseudopupa.

pseū·dō·clas′siç, *a.* pretending, or falsely seeming, to be classic.

pseū′dō·coele, pseū·dō·coe′li·ȧ, *n.* [*pseudo-*, and Gr. *koilos*, hollow.] the fifth ventricle in the brain of mammals.

pseū·dō·coe′liç, *a.* of or pertaining to the pseudocoele.

pseū·dō·çōne, *n.* a gelatinous refractory cone in the compound eyes of some insects, replacing the crystalline cones.

pseū·dō·çor′nē·ous, *a.* having antlers or horns composed of cornified hairs, as the rhinoceros.

pseū·dō·ços′tāte, *a.* [*pseudo-*, and L. *costa*, rib.] of or pertaining to a leaf with marginal venation.

pseū·dō·çū′mēne, *n.* an aromatic liquid hydrocarbon derived from coal tar and isomeric with cumene.

pseū″dō·cȳ·ē′sis, *n.* [*pseudo-*, and Gr. *kyesos*, pregnant.] a false pregnancy.

pseū″dō·diph·thē′ri·ȧ (-dif-), *n.* a sort of diphtheria in which a false membrane is developed, not due to the diphtheria bacillus.

pseū″dō·diph·thē·rit′iç, *a.* of or pertaining to pseudodiphtheria.

pseū·dō·dip′tēr·ăl, *a.* [*pseudo-*, and Gr. *dipteros*, two-winged.] of or relating to a temple with a peripheral row of columns only, those pertaining to the inner part being omitted.

pseū′dō·dont, *a.* having horny teeth derived from the buccal mucous membrane, as the monotremes.

pseū′dō·dox, *a.* [*pseudo-*, and Gr. *doxa*, opin-

ion]. designating or of a false or erroneous opinion.
pseū'dō·dox, *n.* a false opinion.
pseū"dō·fi·lā'ri·ȧ, *n.*; *pl.* **pseū"dō·fi·lā'ri·ae,** [*pseudo-*, and L. *filum*, thread.] the protoplasmic process formed from the cell substance of the spores of a gregarina, which becomes the embryo.
pseū"dō·fō·li·ā'ceous, *a.* of or relating to leaflike outgrowths in the lower plants.
pseū"dō·gȧ·lē'nȧ, *n.* false galena: also called *blende, blackjack,* and *sphalerite.*
pseū·dō·ġē'nus, *n.* [*pseudo-*, and L. *genus*, birth.] a spurious genus based on forms that are really stages in the development of some species.
pseū·dō·geū'si·ȧ, pseū·dō·geūs'ti·ȧ, *n.* [*pseudo-*, and Gr. *geusis*, sense of taste.] an abnormal state of the sense of taste; false taste.
pseū'dō·grȧph, *n.* a false writing; a forgery.
pseū·dog'rȧ·phy, *n.* wrong spelling; incorrect writing.
pseū'dō·ġȳne, *n.* [*pseudo-*, and Gr. *gynē*, female.] a parthenogenetic aphid or plant louse.
pseū'dō heärt, in brachiopods, an organ between the body cavity and the pallial chamber, formerly described as a heart.
pseū"dō·hex·ag'ō·năl, *a.* apparently hexagonal; simulating a hexagon, as certain twinned crystals.
pseū"dō·hȳ·pēr·troph'iç, *a.* [*pseudo-*, and *hyper-*, and Gr. *trophikos*, nursing.] of or pertaining to an increase in the size of any organ not produced by growth, but by the accumulation of fat.
pseū·dō·lā'bi·um, *n.* [*pseudo-*, and L. *labium*, lip.] a median plate behind the labium in the *Myriapoda*, which carries the poison claws.
pseū·dol'ō·ġist, *n.* one who speaks an untruth; a liar. [Rare.]
pseū·dol'ō·ġy, *n.* [*pseudo-*, and Gr. *logos*, word.] speech or statements simulating truth; lying.
pseū·dō·mal'ȧ·chīte, *n.* a hydrous phosphate of copper resembling malachite.
pseū·dō·mā'ni·ȧ, *n.* a kind of insanity in which the patient accuses himself of crimes which he has not committed.
pseū·dō·mem'brāne, *n.* a tissue resembling a membrane.
pseū"dō·mē·tal'liç, *a.* semimetallic, as the luster in certain minerals, such as quartz, calcite, etc.
pseū"dō·mon"ō·çot·y·lē'dŏn·ous, *a.* [*pseudo-*, *mono-*, and Gr. *kotylēdōn*, socket.] or or pertaining to dicotyledonous plants that have fused cotyledons, as the live oak.
pseū'dō·mọrph, *n.* [*pseudo-*, and Gr. *morphē*, form.]
1. any false, irregular, or deceptive form.
2. a mineral possessing the external form characteristic of another, as when quartz has the form of fluorite.
pseū·dō·mọr'phiç, *a.* same as *pseudomorphous.*
pseū·dō·mọr'phism, pseū"dō·mọr·phō'sis, *n.* 1. the state or quality of being pseudomorphous.
2. the formation or occurrence of pseudomorphs.
pseū·dō·mọr'phous, *a.* relating to or exhibiting the qualities of a pseudomorph.
pseū"dō·nav·i·cel'lȧ, *n.*; *pl.* **pseū"dō·nav·i·cel'lae,** [*pseudo-*, and L. *navicula*, a small boat.] an elliptical spore case of certain parasitic protozoans, which contains several spores, as in most *Sporozoa.*
Pseū"dō·neū·rop'te·rȧ, *n.pl.* [*pseudo-*, and Mod.L. *Neuroptera.*] a former group of insects with partial metamorphosis, many of the species having aquatic larvae, while the adult is winged and aerial. It embraced the white ants, May flies, dragonflies, etc.
pseū·dō·nyçh'i·um, *n.*; *pl.* **pseū·dō·nyçh'i·ȧ,** [*pseudo-*, and Gr. *onyx*, a claw.] an empodium.
pseū'dō·nym, *n.* [Fr. *pseudonyme*, from Gr. *pseudēs*, and *onyma*, name.] a borrowed or fictitious name, especially one adopted by an author; a pen name.
pseū·dō·nym'i·ty, *n.* 1. the condition of being pseudonymous.
2. the use of a pseudonym.
pseū·don'y·mous, *a.* 1. bearing a pseudonym, as an author.
2. written under a pseudonym.
pseū·don'y·mous·ly, *adv.* in a pseudonymous manner.
pseū·don'y·mous·ness, *n.* the state or quality of being pseudonymous.
pseū"dō·pȧ·ren'çhy·mȧ, *n.* [*pseudo-*, and Gr. *parenchein*, to pour into.] an aggregate of closely interwoven hyphae forming a definite body, as in the mushrooms.
pseū·dō·pēr'çū·lum, *n.* [*pseudo-*, and L. *operculum*, a lid.] an epiphragm.
pseū"dō·pē·rid'i·um, *n.* a cuplike false peridium.
pseū·dō·pē·ri·od'iç, *a.* quasi-periodic.
pseū"dō·pē·rip'tēr·ăl, *a.* falsely peripteral: applied to a temple having the columns on its sides attached to the walls, instead of being arranged as in a peripteral temple, and having a portico only at the front.
pseū'dō·pod, *n.* a pseudopodium.
pseū·dō·pō'di·ăl, *a.* pertaining to a pseudopodium.
pseū·dō·pō'di·um, *n.*; *pl.* **pseū·dō·pō'di·ȧ,**
1. in zoology, a temporary projection consisting of an irregular prolongation of the protoplasm of a unicellular organism, capable of being withdrawn again into the general mass of the body, and serving as a means of moving about or for taking in food.
2. the caudal end of a rotifer.
3. a stalklike pedicel supporting the sporangium of some mosses.
pseū·dop'si·ȧ, *n.* same as *pseudoblepsis.*
pseū·dō·pū'pȧ, *n.*; *pl.* **pseū·dō·pū'pae,** a stage in the development of some insects, preceding the pupa.
pseū·dō·rā'mōse, *a.* having or forming false branches.
pseū·dō·ram'ū·lus, *n.* a false branch or filament of some algae.
pseū'dō·sçōpe, *n.* [*pseudo-*, and Gr. *skopein*, to view.] an optical instrument somewhat on the principle of the stereoscope, but producing effects directly opposite, namely, reversing the reliefs so that what is nearest appears farthest, a globe appearing as a basin, a convex body concave, and a picture on a wall as if sunk into a deep recess.
pseū·dō·sçop'iç, *a.* pertaining to the pseudoscope.
Pseū·dō·sçọr·pi·ō'nēş, *n.pl.* a family of *Arachnida* the maxillary palpi of which are of large size, and are converted into nipping claws, thus giving the animal the appearance of a scorpion in miniature. The abdomen is segmented, but there is no post abdomen as in the true scorpions.
pseū"dō·sē·mat'iç, *a.* colored in such a manner as to attract prey or repel enemies.
pseū·dō·sep'tāte, *a.* having a false septum.
pseū·dō·sī'phŏn, *n.* a false siphon, as in many fossil cephalopods.
pseū·dō·sī'phun̄·çle, *n.* a pseudosiphon.
pseū·doş'mi·ȧ, *n.* [*pseudo-*, and Gr. *osmē*, odor.] an imaginary sensation of smell.
pseū'dō·sphēre, *n.* 1. a surface with a constant negative curvature.
2. the figure in non-Euclidean space which corresponds to the sphere in ordinary space.
pseū'dō·spōre, *n.* same as *teliospore.*
pseū·dos'tō·mȧ, *n.*; *pl.* **pseū·dō·stom'ȧ·tȧ,** [*pseudo-*, and Gr. *stoma*, mouth.]
1. a closed space between the cells of a serous membrane.
2. the mouth of the larva of an echinoderm.
pseū"dō·sym·met'riç, *a.* having pseudosymmetry.
pseū·dō·sym'me·try, *n.* the apparent symmetry of compound or twin crystals by which they resemble another crystalline type.
Pseū"dō·tē·tram'ēr·ȧ, *n.pl.* a division of beetles having five-jointed tarsi, though there appear to be but four joints.
pseū·dō·trā'çhē·ȧ, *n.* [*pseudo-*, and Gr. *tracheia*, windpipe.] a tracheal space in the oral parts of some insects.
Pseū·dō·tsū'gȧ, *n.* [*pseudo-*, and LL. *tsuga*, from Japan., larch.] a genus of trees of the pine family, having but one species, *Pseudotsuga douglasii*, growing widely as a forest tree of the United States: commonly known as the *Douglas fir.*
pseū·dō'vȧ·ry, *n.*; *pl.* **pseū·dō'vȧ·ries,** [*pseudo-* and *ovary.*] in certain insects, the ovary in which the pseudova are formed.
pseū·dō'vum, *n.*; *pl.* **pseū·dō'vȧ,** [*pseudo-*, and L. *ovum*, egg.] in zoology, one of the egglike bodies from which the young of the viviparous aphid are produced. They differ from true ova only in being produced in organs which lack certain important parts of the fully-formed female reproductive system, and in undergoing development without impregnation.
pshąw (shą), *interj.* and *n.* an expression of contempt, disdain, or impatience.
pshąw, *v.t.* and *v.i.*; pshawed, *pt.*, *pp.*; pshawing, *ppr.* to express impatience, contempt, etc. at, for, or to (someone or something) by saying "pshaw."

My father traveled homewards in none of the best of moods, *pshawing* and pishing all the way down. —Sterne.

psī (sī *or* Gr. psē), *n.* [Gr.] the twenty-third letter of the Greek alphabet, corresponding to English *ps*, as in li*ps* (usually pronounced in English derivatives simply as *s*, as in *psychology*).
Psid'i·um (sid'), *n.* [Gr. *sidion*, pomegranate peel.] a genus of tropical plants belonging to the family *Myrtaceæ*, and including the guava.
psī·lan·throp'iç (sī-), *a.* relating to or of the nature of psilanthropy.
psī·lan'thrō·pişm, *n.* psilanthropy.
psī·lan'thrō·pist, *n.* [Gr. *psilos*, bare, mere, and *anthrōpos*, man.] one who believes in psilanthropy.
psī·lan'thrō·py, *n.* the doctrine that Jesus was merely a human being.
psī'lō- (sī'), [from Gr. *psilos*, naked, bare.] a combining form meaning *mere, bare.*
psī·lol'ō·ġy, *n.* [*psilo-*, and Gr. *logos*, word.] love of chatter or idle talk.
psī·lom'e·lāne, *n.* [*psilo-*, and Gr. *melas*, black.] a mineral, essentially manganese oxide, occurring in smooth botryoid forms, and having a color nearly steel gray.
Psī·lō·pae'dēş, *n.pl.* [*psilo-*, and Gr. *paides*, children.] a group of birds the young of which upon leaving the egg are only covered with down.
psī·lō·paed'iç, *a.* of or pertaining to the *Psilopædes.*
psī·lō'sis, *n.* [Mod.L.; Gr. *psilōsis*, from *psiloun*, to strip bare, from *psilos*, bare, mere.]
1. a falling out of hair.
2. sprue.
psī·los'ō·phēr, *n.* [*psilo-*, and Gr. *sophos*, wise.] a sham philosopher. [Rare.]
psit·tā'ceous (sit-), *a.* [L. *psittacus*, from Gr. *psittakos*, a parrot.] belonging or relating to the parrot family of birds.
Psit'tȧ·cī, *n.pl.* a monotypic order of birds including the true parrots which are mostly inhabitants of tropical America and green in color. Many of the African species are gray. Other forms are the macaws, lories, cockatoos, and parakeets.
psit'tȧ·cid, *a.* same as *psittaceous.*
Psit·tac'i·dae, *n.pl.* the parrot family.
psit'tȧ·cīne, *a.* same as *psittaceous.*
psit·tȧ·çō'sis, *n.* [Mod.L. *psittacus*, from Gr. *psittakos*, parrot.] an acute infectious virus disease peculiar to parrots but transmissible to humans: it is characterized by pulmonary disorders and high fever: also called *parrot fever.*
psō'ȧs (sō'), *n.* [Mod.L.; acc. pl. of Gr. *psoa*, muscle of the loins.] either of two muscles of the loin that connect the spinal column and the thighbone.
psō'rȧ, *n.* [L.; Gr. *psōra*, an itch.] any itching disease of the skin, especially psoriasis or scabies.
Psō·rā'lē·ȧ, *n.* [LL., from Gr. *psoraleos*, scabby, mangy.]
1. a genus of leguminous plants containing over 100 widely distributed species and characterized by pink, purple, or white flower clusters and short pods with single seeds.
2. [p—] any plant of this genus.
psō·rī'ȧ·sis, *n.* [Mod.L.; Gr. *psōriasis*, from *psōra*, an itch.] a chronic skin disease characterized by scaly, reddish patches.
psō'riç, *a.* pertaining to, connected with, or suffering from psora.
psō'roid, *a.* resembling psora or scabies.
psō·roph·thal'mi·ȧ, *n.* [Gr. *psōra*, itch, and *ophthalmia.*] marginal blepharitis.
Psō·rop'tēş, *n.* [Gr. *psōra*, itch, mange, and *pteron*, a wing.] a genus of mites.
psō·rō'sis, *n.* [Mod.L., from Gr. *psōra*, an itch; and *-osis.*] a plant disease affecting citrus fruit trees: also called *scaly bark.*
psō'rō·spērm, *n.* a unicellular organism belonging to the *Protozoa.*
psō·rō·spēr'mi·ăl, *a.* psorospermic.
psō·rō·spēr'miç, *a.* of psorosperms.
psō'rous, *a.* pertaining to psora.
psȳ·chȧ·gog'iç (sȳ-), *a.* persuasive; winning.
psȳ'chȧ·gogue (-gog), *n.* [*psycho-*, and Gr. *agein*, to lead.] a conjurer; a necromancer. [Rare.]
psȳ'çhăl, *a.* [Gr. *psychē*, soul, and E. suffix *-al.*] psychic. [Rare.]

psy̆·çhal′ġi·ȧ, *n.* [Gr. *psychē*, soul, and *algos*, pain.] mental strain.

psy̆çh·as·thē′ni·ȧ (sīk-), *n.* a type of neurosis characterized by obsessions, morbid anxieties, etc.

Psy̆′çhē (sī′), *n.* [Gr. *psychē*, the soul.]
1. in Greek and Roman mythology, a nymph, the personification of the soul. Her great beauty excited the jealousy and hatred of Venus, who ordered Cupid to inspire her with love for some contemptible being. Cupid, however, fell in love with her himself, and after many persecutions by Venus, a reconciliation was effected, and Psyche was made immortal.
2. [p–] the human soul.
3. [p–] the mind; especially, in psychiatry, the mind considered as an organic system reaching all parts of the body and serving to adjust the total organism to the needs or demands of the environment.
4. a genus of moths, family *Psychidæ*.
5. [p–] a cheval glass. [Now Rare.]

psy̆″çhe·del′iç, *a.* [from *psyche* (mind) and Gr. *delein*, to make manifest.]
1. of or causing extreme changes in the conscious mind, as hallucinations, delusions, intensification of awareness and sensory perception, etc.
2. simulating the auditory or visual effects of the psychedelic state.

psy̆″çhe·del′iç, *n.* a psychedelic drug.

Psy̆′çhē knot (not), a woman's coiffure in which a knot or coil of hair projects from the back of the head.

psy̆·çhī′ȧ·tẽr, *n.* same as *psychiatrist*.

psy̆·çhi·at′riç, *a.* 1. pertaining to psychiatry; as, a *psychiatric* clinic.
2. employing psychiatry; as, *psychiatric* care.

psy̆·çhi·at′ri·çăl, *a.* psychiatric.

psy̆·çhī′ȧ·trist, *n.* an expert in psychiatry.

psy̆·çhī′ȧ·try, *n.* [from Gr. *psychē*, the soul, and *iatreia*, healing.] the branch of medicine concerned with the study and treatment of mental disorders, including psychoses and neuroses.

psy̆′çhiç, *a.* [from Gr. *psychikos*, of the soul, from *psychē*, the soul.]
1. of the psyche, or mind.
2. beyond natural or known physical processes.
3. apparently sensitive to forces beyond the physical world.

psy̆′çhiç, *n.* 1. a person who is supposedly sensitive to forces beyond the physical world.
2. a spiritualistic medium.

psy̆′çhi·çăl, *a.* psychic.

psy̆′çhi·çăl·ly, *adv.* in a psychical manner.

psy̆′çhişm, *n.* 1. the doctrine of Quesne, that a certain fluid everywhere diffused is the animating principle in all living things.
2. the condition of being psychic.

psy̆′çhō- (sī′), [from Gr. *psychē*, soul, mind.] a combining form meaning *the mind* or *mental processes*, as in *psycho*logy, *psycho*analysis: also *psych-*.

psy̆′çhō, *a.* and *n.* psychoneurotic. [Colloq.]

psy̆·çhō·ȧ·çöus′tiçs, *n.pl.* [*construed as sing.*] [*psycho-*, and *acoustics*.] the study of how sounds are heard subjectively and of the individual's response to sound stimuli.

psy̆·çhō·aç′tive, *a.* designating or of a drug, chemical, etc. that has a specific effect on the mind.

psy̆·çhō·ȧ·nal′y·sis, *n.* 1. a method, developed by Freud and others, of treating neuroses and some other disorders of the mind: it is based on the assumption that such disorders are the result of the rejection by the conscious mind of factors that then persist in the unconscious as dynamic repressions, causing conflicts which may be resolved by discovering and analyzing the repressions through the use of such techniques as free association, dream analysis, etc.
2. the theory or practice of this.
Often shortened to *analysis*.

psy̆·çhō·an′ȧ·lyst, *n.* one who specializes in psychoanalysis.

psy̆·çhō·an·ȧ·lyt′iç, *a.* of, pertaining to, or characterized by psychoanalysis.

psy̆″çhō·an·ȧ·lyt′i·çăl, *a.* psychoanalytic.

psy̆″çhō·an·ȧ·lyt′i·çăl·ly, *adv.* 1. in a psychoanalytic manner.
2. from a psychoanalytic standpoint.

psy̆·çhō·an′ȧ·lyze, *v.t.*; psychoanalyzed, *pt.*, *pp.*; psychoanalyzing, *ppr.* to treat or investigate by means of psychoanalysis.

psy̆″çhō·bī·og′rȧ·phy, *n.* a biography dealing with the psychodynamic processes that have affected the development of the subject.

psy̆″çhō·bī·ol′ō·ġy, *n.* 1. that branch of biology dealing with the interrelationship of the mental processes and the anatomy and physiology of the individual.
2. psychology as investigated by biological methods.

psy̆·çhō·çhem′i·çăl, *n.* any of various drugs or chemical compounds, as LSD, capable of affecting mental activity.

Psy̆·çhō′dȧ, *n.pl.* [Gr. *psychē*, a butterfly, and *eidos*, form.] the typical genus of the *Psychodidæ*, a family of nemocerous dipterous insects.

psy̆′çhō·drä·mȧ, *n.* in psychiatry, a form of cathartic therapy in which a patient acts out by spontaneous improvisation situations related to his problem, often with others who represent persons near his problem.

psy̆″çhō·dy̆·nam′iç, *a.* of or relating to psychodynamics.

psy̆″çhō·dy̆·nam′içs, *n.* the science dealing with the laws of mental action.

psy̆″çhō·ed·ū·çā′tion·ăl, *a.* designating or of psychological methods, as intelligence tests, used in evaluating learning ability.

psy̆·çhō·eth′i·çăl, *a.* relating to inherent moral ideas.

psy̆·çhō·ġen′e·sis, *n.* 1. origination and development within the psyche, or mind.
2. the origin and development of the psyche, or mind.

psy̆·çhō·ġē·net′iç, *a.* psychogenic.

psy̆″çhō·ġē·net′i·çăl, *a.* relating to psychogenesis.

psy̆″çhō·ġē·net′i·çăl·ly, *adv.* with respect to psychogenesis.

psy̆·çhō·ġen′iç, *a.* of psychic origin; caused by mental conflicts.

psy̆·çhoġ′e·ny, *n.* 1. psychogenesis.
2. the doctrine of the source of mind.

psy̆·çhog′nō·sis, *n.* any investigation or diagnosis of the psyche. [Rare.]

psy̆′çhō·gràph, *n.* 1. in psychology, a graphic chart outlining the relative strength of the fundamental personality traits in an individual.
2. a device for recording psychic processes.
3. a psychological analysis of a person.
4. an image supposedly made by a spirit on a photographic plate.

psy̆·çhog′rȧ·phy, *n.* 1. writing said by spiritualists to be done by spirits; spirit writing.
2. descriptive psychology. [Now Rare.]

psy̆·çhō·his′tō·ry, *n.* 1. the study of historical events by applying psychological theory and methods.
2. same as *psychobiography*.

psy̆″çhō·ki·nē′si·ȧ, *n.* [*psycho-*, and Gr. *kinēsis*, motion.] violent cerebral action due to defective inhibition.

psy̆·çhō·loġ′iç, *a.* psychological

psy̆·çhō·loġ′i·çăl, *a.* 1. of psychology.
2. of the mind; mental.
psychological moment; (a) the moment when the mind is most willing to accept a fact, suggestion, etc.; most propitious time to act; (b) the critical moment.
psychological warfare; the use of propaganda or other psychological means to influence or confuse the thinking, undermine the morale, etc. of an enemy or opponent.

psy̆·çhō·loġ′i·çăl·ly, *adv.* 1. in a psychological manner.
2. from a psychological standpoint.

psy̆·çhol′ō·ġist, *n.* one who studies or is versed in psychology.

psy̆·çhol′ō·ġīze, *v.t.* psychologized, *pt.*, *pp.*; psychologizing, *ppr.* to analyze psychologically.

psy̆·çhol′ō·ġīze, *v.i.* 1. to study psychology.
2. to reason psychologically.

psy̆·çhol′ō·ġy, *n.*; *pl.* **psy̆·çhol′ō·ġieş**, 1. (a) the science dealing with the mind and mental processes, feelings, desires, etc.; (b) the science of human and animal behavior.
2. the sum of a person's actions, traits, attitudes, thoughts, etc.; as, the *psychology* of the adolescent.
3. a treatise on psychology.
4. a system of psychology.
comparative psychology; the method of study which consists in comparing mental phenomena as found in the various classes of animal life, including man.
physiological psychology; psychology dealing with physiological phenomena.

psy̆·çhom′ȧ·çhy, *n.* [*psycho-*, and Gr. *machē*, a battle.] a conflict of the soul with the body. [Obs.]

psy̆·çhō·met′riç, *a.* of or pertaining to psychometry.

psy̆·çhom′ē·trīze, *v.t.* to practice psychometry on.

psy̆·çhom′e·try, *n.* 1. the supposed faculty of divining knowledge about an object, or about a person connected with it, through contact with the object.
2. the measurement of the duration, force, precision, etc. of mental processes.

psy̆·çhō·mō′tŏr, *a.* of the motor effects of mental processes.

psy̆″çhō·neū·rō′sis, *n.*; *pl.* **psy̆″çhō·neū·rō′sēş**, a neurosis.

psy̆″çhō·neū·rot′iç, *a.* and *n.* neurotic.

psy̆·çhon′ō·my, *n.* [*psycho-*, and Gr. *nomos*, law.] the science of the laws of mental activity.

psy̆·çhō·pan′ny·çhişm, *n.* [*psycho-*, and Gr. *pannychios*, all night long; *pan*, all, *nux*, night, and *-ism*.] the doctrine or belief that the soul falls asleep at death, and does not awake until the resurrection of the body.

psy̆·çhō·pan′ny·çhist, *n.* a believer in psychopannychism.

psy̆′çhō·path, *n.* a person affected with psycopathy; specifically, a psychopathic personality.

psy̆·çhō·path′iç, *a.* pertaining to psycopathy.

psy̆·çhō·path′iç pẽr·sŏn·al′i·ty, 1. a person characterized by emotional instability, lack of sound judgment, perverse and impulsive (often criminal) behavior, inability to learn from experience, amoral and asocial feelings, and other serious personality defects: he may or may not have psychotic attacks or symptoms.
2. the personality of such a person.

psy̆·çhop′ȧ·thist, *n.* a psychiatrist. [Obs.]

psy̆″çhō·pȧ·thol′ō·ġy, *n.* the science dealing with diseases and abnormalities of the mind.

psy̆·çhop′ȧ·thy, *n.* mental disorder.

psy̆·çhō·phyş′iç, *a.* psychophysical.

psy̆·çhō·phyş′i·çăl, *a.* pertaining to psychophysics.

psy̆·çhō·phyş′i·cist, *n.* one who studies or specializes in psychophysics.

psy̆·çhō·phyş′içş, *n. pl.* [*construed as sing.*] the branch of psychology dealing with the functional relations between the body and the mind.

psy̆·çhō·phyş″i·ō·loġ′i·çăl, *a.* pertaining to psychophysiology.

psy̆·çhō·phyş·i·ol′ō·ġy, *n.* the physiology of the mental organs; physiological psychology.

psy̆′çhō·plaşm, *n.* [*psycho-*, and Gr. *plasma*, anything formed.] the supposed physical basis of consciousness.

psy̆′çhō·pomp, *n.* [*psycho-*, and Gr. *pompos*, leader, conductor.] a guide or conductor of departed souls: a name given to Hermes.

psy̆·çhō·sex′ū·ăl, *a.* pertaining to the emotional constituents of the sexual instinct.

psy̆·çhō′sis, *n.*; *pl.* **psy̆·çhō′sēş**, [Gr., a giving of life or soul to.]
1. in psychiatry, any mental disorder in which the personality is very seriously disorganized: psychoses are of two sorts, (a) functional (characterized by lack of apparent organic cause, and principally of a schizophrenic or manic-depressive type), and (b) organic (characterized by a pathological organic condition, such as general paresis, brain tumor, alcoholism, etc.).
2. in psychology, any mental state or process.

psy̆·çhō·sō′ciăl (-shăl), *a.* pertaining to or concerning the mental factors or activities which determine the social relations of an individual.

psy̆·çhō·sō·mat′iç, *a.* 1. designating or of a physical disorder of the body originating in or aggravated by the psychic or emotional processes of the individual.
2. designating the branch of medicine using a psychological approach to the study of the causes and treatment of physical disorders.

psy̆′çhō·thē·işm, *n.* [Gr. *psychē*, spirit, and *theos*, God.] the doctrine that God is pure spirit.

psy̆·çhō·ther·ȧ·peū′tiçs, *n.pl.* [*construed as sing.*] the science of psychotherapy.

psy̆·çhō·ther′ȧ·py, *n.* the application of various forms of mental treatment, as hypnosis, suggestion, psychoanalysis, etc., to nervous and mental disorders.

psy·chot′ic, *a.* 1. of, or having the nature of, a psychosis.
2. having a psychosis.

psy·chot′ic, *n.* a person who has a psychosis.

Psy̆·chō′tri·ȧ, *n.* [Gr. *psychōtria*, vivifying.] a genus of tropical American shrubs, typical of the family *Psychotrieæ*: several of the species yield dyestuffs.

psy̆·chō·zō′ic, *a.* [*psycho-*, and Gr. *zōē*, life, and *-ic*.] pertaining to both mind and animal life.

psy̆′chrō- (sī′), [from Gr. *psychros*, cold.] a combining form meaning *cold*, as in *psychro*meter.

psy̆″chrō·es·thē′si·ȧ (-zhi-ȧ, -zhȧ, *or* -zi-ȧ), a state in which a part of the body, though warm, seems cold.

psy̆·chrom′e·tẽr, *n.* [*psychro-* and *-meter*.] an instrument with wet and dry bulb thermometers, for measuring the amount of moisture in the air.

psy̆·chrō·met′ric, *a.* pertaining to a psychrometer or to psychrometry.

psy̆·chrō·met′ri·căl, *a.* psychrometric.

psy̆·chrom′e·try, *n.* the art of determining the amount of moisture in the air by the use of the psychrometer; hygrometry.

psy̆·chrō·phō′bi·ȧ, *n.* [from *psychro-* and *-phobia*.] fear of cold, especially of cold water.

psy̆′chrō·phōre, *n.* [*psychro-* and *-phore*.] a double catheter for applying cold to the urethra.

psy̆·chrō·ther′ȧ·py, *n.* [*psychro-* and *therapy*.] treatment of disease by the application of cold.

psych′tic *a.* (sik′), having the power to reduce temperature; refrigerant.

psych′tic, *n.* a cooling medicine.

psy̆′chŭr·gy (sī′), *n.* [Gr. *psychē*, the soul or mind.] mental activity or mind-using.

Psyl′lȧ (sil′), *n.* [Gr. *psylla*, a flea.] a genus of plant lice typical of the family *Psyllidæ*, with twenty-seven species: the head is moderately notched in front, the antennae are slender, and the wing covers are membranous.

psyl′lid, *a.* pertaining to the *Psyllidæ*.

psyl′lid, *n.* one of the *Psyllidæ*.

Psyl′li·dae, *n.pl.* a family of insects comprising the genus *Psylla* and several others. They have antennae containing eight or ten joints, short legs, and leathery fore wings.

psyl′loid, *a.* resembling a psyllid.

Pt, in chemistry, platinum.

Ptae·rox′y·lon (tē-), *n.* [Gr. *ptairein*, to sneeze, and *xylon*, wood.] a genus of small polypetalous South African trees of the order *Sapindaceæ*, typified by the single species *Ptæroxylon utile*, a valuable timber tree: popularly called *sneezewood*.

Ptäh (p′tä *or* p′täkh), *n.* [Egypt. *Ptaḥ*.] the chief god of ancient Memphis, in Egypt, creator of gods and men.

ptär′mic (tär′), *a.* [Gr. *ptarmikos*, causing to sneeze, from *ptairein*, to sneeze.] causing to sneeze.

ptär′mic, *n.* a medicine which causes sneezing; snuff.

Ptär′mi·cȧ, *n.* in botany, a genus of *Anthemideæ*, sometimes placed under *Achillea*, including the sneezewort and some other species which are used in the Swiss Alps for tea and as the basis of an aromatic liquor.

ptär′mi·găn, *n.*; *pl.* **ptär′mi·găns** or **ptär′mi·găn,** [from Scot. *tarmachan*: wrongly spelled with a *p*, because of supposed Greek origin.] a bird of the genus *Lagopus*, and belonging to the grouse family, *Tetraonidæ*, that undergoes seasonal changes of color. It is distinguished from the true grouse, *Tetrao*, by having the toes as well as the tarsi feathered. The common European ptarmigan, or white grouse, is *Lagopus vulgaris* or *mutus*. It is a native of the north, or elevated and alpine regions, and is especially plentiful in Scandinavia. The willow ptarmigan or willow grouse, *Lagopus saliceti*, occurs in great abundance in the arctic regions of America and in Norway.

EUROPEAN PTARMIGAN

PT bōat, a patrol torpedo boat.

Ptē′lē·ȧ (tē′), *n.* [Gr., elm.] in botany, a genus of the rue family. *Ptelea trifoliata* is the shrubby trefoil of North America: its bitter and aromatic fruits have been used for hops.

ptē′lē·in, *n.* a stimulant and tonic extracted from the root bark of *Ptelea trifoliata*.

Ptē·nō·glos′sȧ, *n.pl.* [Gr. *ptēnos*, feathered, and *glōssa*, tongue.] a division of gastropod mollusks, comprising four families, with pointed teeth arranged in long transverse rows.

ptē·nō·glos′sāte, *a.* of or pertaining to the *Ptenoglossa*.

Ptē·ran′ō·don, *n.* [Gr. *pteron*, wing, and *anodontos*, toothless.]
1. a genus of American pterodactyls of *Pterosauria*, typical genus of *Pteranodontia*. The species are of gigantic size, toothless, and have a short, slender tail.
2. [p–] any pterodactyl of this genus.

Ptē·ran·ō·don′ti·ȧ (-shi-), *n.pl.* a distinct section of *Pterosauria*, with two genera, *Pteranodon* and *Nyctisaurus*, both from the Chalk of North America.

Ptē·ras′pis, *n.* [Gr. *pteron*, a wing, and *aspis*, a shield.] a genus of fossil fishes, the *Placodermi*, having a finely-grooved shield composed of seven pieces. It is thought to be the most ancient fish form and is characteristic of the Upper Silurian, and the Lower Devonian.

Ptē·rich′thys, *n.* [Gr. *pteron*, wing, and *ichthys*, fish.] a genus of fishes, typical of the family *Pterichthyidæ*, discovered by Hugh Miller in the Old Red Sandstone. The head and anterior part of the trunk were defended by a buckler of large ganoid scales united by sutures; the rest of the body was covered with small ganoid scales. The genus is characteristic of the Lower and Upper Devonian.

ptē·rid′i·um, *n.* same as *samara*.

pter·i·dog′rȧ·phy (ter-), *n.* [Gr. *pteris*, *pteridos*, a fern, and *graphein*, to write.] a description of or a treatise on ferns; the science of ferns.

pter·i·dol′ō·gist, *n.* one who studies, writes upon, or is versed in pteridology.

pter·i·dol′ō·gy, *n.* [Gr. *pteris*, *pteridos*, a fern, and *logos*, a description.] that branch of botany dealing with ferns.

Pter·i·doph′y·tȧ, *n.pl.* [Gr. *pteris*, *pteridos*, a fern, and *phylon*, plant.] in botany, the division of plants, the vascular cryptogams, which represents the highest type of flowerless plants.

pter′i·dō·phy̆te″, *n.* a fern or related plant having no seeds and included in the *Pteridophyta*.

pter″i·dō·phyt′ic, *a.* of or belonging to the pteridophytes.

pter·i·doph′y·tous, *a.* of or pertaining to the *Pteridophyta*.

ptē′ri·on (tē′), *n.* [LL., from Gr. *pteron*, wing or feather.] in anatomy, the junction of the frontal, the temporal, and the great wing of the sphenoid bones.

Ptē′ris, *n.* [Gr. *pteris*, a fern.] a genus of ferns including about eighty species, of world-wide distribution. *Pteris aquilina* is the common brake. *Pteris esculenta* is the Tasmanian fern root, eaten raw by animals, and, when roasted, by the natives.

ptẽr′nȧ (tẽr′), *n.*; *pl.* **ptẽr′nae,** [Gr., the heel.] the sole of a bird's foot at the parting of the toes; the heel pad.

pter′ō-, [from Gr. *pteron*, feather, wing.] a combining form meaning *feather, wing*, as in *ptero*dactyl.

Pter·ō·bran′chi·ȧ, *n.pl.* [*ptero-*, and Gr. *branchia*, gills.] a section of *Polyzoa*, with two genera, *Cephalodiscus* and *Rhabdopleura*.

pter·ō·bran′chi·āte, *a.* belonging to or connected with the *Pterobranchia*.

Pter·ō·cär′pus, *n.* [*ptero-*, and Gr. *karpos*, fruit.] a genus of large tropical trees, having a thin wing at the edge of the fruit. *Pterocarpus marsupium*, *Pterocarpus indicus*, and *Pterocarpus macrocarpus* furnish East Indian kino, and *Pterocarpus erinaceus*, African kino, *Pterocarpus draco* and *Pterocarpus santalinus*, red sandalwood, *Pterocarpus dalberggioides*, a good Indian wood, and *Pterocarpus indicus*, the excellent Andaman redwood. Cattle and goats feed on the leaves of *Pterocarpus marsupium*.

Pter·ō·cau′lŏn, *n.* [*ptero-*, and Gr. *kaulos*, stem.] a genus of herbaceous composite plants native to subtropical regions. *Pterocaulon undulatum*, the blackroot, is found in the southern states.

Ptē·roc′e·răs (tē-), *n.* [*ptero-*, and Gr. *keras*, a horn.] a scorpion-shelled genus of gastropods, having a shell, when young, like that of *Strombus*; afterward the outer lip becomes prolonged into several long claws, one of them forming a posterior canal: they are found in India or China: the paleontological species are numerous from the Lias to the Upper Chalk.

Pter′ō·clēs (ter′), *n.* [*ptero-*, and Gr. *kleis*, key, tongue of a buckle.] in ornithology, the typical genus of the *Pteroclidæ*, a family of birds found mostly in Africa and Asia. *Pterocles arenaria* is the common sand grouse.

pter·ō·dac′tyl, *n.* [*ptero-*, and Gr. *daktylos*, finger or toe.] any of a number of related flying reptiles of the genus *Pterodactylus*, extinct at the end of the Mesozoic Era, having wings of skin stretched along the body between the hind limb and a very long digit of the fore-limb.

PTERODACTYL

Pter·ō·dac′ty·lus, *n.* a genus of extinct reptiles; the flying dragons.

pter·ō·glos′săl, *a.* [*ptero-*, and Gr. *glōssa*, tongue.] in zoology, having a tongue finely notched along the margins, causing it to resemble a feather or a wing.

pter·ō·graph′ic, *a.* of or relating to pterography.

ptē·rog′rȧ·phy (tē-), *n.* [*ptero-*, and Gr. *graphein*, to write.] a description of or treatise on feathers.

ptē′roid, *a.* [Gr. *pteris*, a fern.] relating to or characteristic of a fern; fernlike.

ptē′roid, *n.* a bone in the anterior limb of a pterodactyl extending from the carpus toward the humerus.

pter·ō·log′i·căl (ter-), *a.* of or relating to the science of pterology.

ptē·rol′ō·gy (tē-), *n.* that branch of knowledge concerning the structure of the wings of insects.

ptē·rō′mȧ, *n.*; *pl.* **ptē·rō′mȧ·tȧ,** [Gr., wing of a temple, from *pteroūn*, to furnish with feathers.] in Grecian architecture, the part of a temple or other similar structure lying between the main wall and the columns of the peristyle.

Pter′ō·mys (ter′), *n.* [*ptero-*, and Gr. *mūs*, mouse.] a genus of rodent animals of the flying squirrel family, *Sciuridæ*, of Europe and Asia: their fore and hind legs are united by winglike folds of skin which enable them to make long, gliding leaps.

ptē′ron (tē′), *n.*; *pl.* **ptē′rȧ,** 1. in anatomy, same as *pterion*.
2. in Grecian architecture, a row of columns, as in a peristyle; a portico.

pter·ō·pae′dēs (ter-), *n.pl.* [*ptero-*, and Gr. *pais*, *paidos*, child.] birds that are able to fly shortly after they are hatched, as the mound bird of Australia.

pter·ō·pae′dic, *a.* having the characteristics of the *Pteropædes*.

pter′ōpe, *n.* an animal of the genus *Pteropus*; specifically, a fruit bat or flying fox.

pter·ō·pē′gum, *n.*; *pl.* **pter·ō·pē′gȧ,** [*ptero-*, and Gr. *pēgos*, fastened.] the socket in which the wing of an insect articulates.

Pter·oph′ō·rȧ, *n.pl.* an extensive division of insects including all hexapods with wings.

pter′ō·phōre, *n.* any insect of the genus *Pterophorus*, especially a moth.

Ptē·roph′ō·rus (tē-), *n.* a genus of *Lepidoptera*, common in North America.

pter′ō·pod (ter′), *n.* [*ptero-*, and Gr. *podos*, foot.] any mollusk belonging to the *Pteropoda*.

pter′ō·pod, *a.* having the characteristics of a pteropod.

Ptē·rop′ō·dȧ (tē-), *n.pl.* a group of gastropod mollusks, naked or bearing fragile shells, that swim about by means of winglike lobes on the foot.

ptē·rop′ō·dăn, *a.* and *n.* pteropod.

pter·ō·pō′di·ăl (ter-), *a.* of or relating to a pteropodium.

pter·ō·pō′di·um, *n.*; *pl.* **pter·ō·pō′di·ȧ,** the foot of a pteropod.

ptē·rop′ō·dous (tē-), *a.* of or relating to the *Pteropoda.*

Pter′ō·pus (ter′), *n.* [Gr. *pteropous,* wing-footed.] a genus typical of the *Pteropodidæ,* or flying fox family, and including the large fruit bats. *Pteropus eautis* of Java has wings measuring five feet from tip to tip.

pter′ō·rhine, (-rin), *a.* [*ptero-,* and Gr. *rhinos,* nose.] having feathered nostrils: said of birds, as the auk and others.

pter′ō·saur, *n.* a pterodactyl.

Pter·ō·sau′ri·ȧ, *n.pl.* [*ptero-,* and Gr. *sauros,* lizard.] an order of extinct flying Mesozoic reptiles with batlike wings, containing the pterodactyls; the *Ornithosauria.*

pter·ō·sau′ri·ăn, *a.* of or relating to the *Pterosauria*; like a pterosaur.

pter·ō·sau′ri·ăn, *n.* a flying reptile; a member of the *Pterosauria.*

pter·ō·sau′roid, *a.* like a pterosaur.

Pter·ō·spẽr′mum, *n.* [*ptero-,* and Gr. *sperma,* seed.] a genus of tropical trees and shrubs of the family *Sterculiaceæ,* having large single fragrant white flowers and winged seeds. Some species are called *wingseed.*

pter·ō·stig′mȧ, *n.*; *pl.* **pter·ō·stig′mȧ·tȧ,** [*ptero-,* and Gr. *stigma,* a spot.] a thickened colored or opaque space peculiar to the wings of certain insects; a wing mark.

pter·ō·thē′çȧ, *n.*; *pl.* **pter·ō·thē′cae,** [*ptero-,* and Gr. *theka,* case.] the part of a chrysalis which covers the future wings of an insect.

ptē·rō′tiç (tē-), *n.* [*ptero-,* and Gr. *ous, otos,* ear.] a bone in the skull of teleostean fishes; the ossified periotic capsule.

ptē·rō′tiç, *a.* pertaining to the pterotic.

-pter′ous (-ter′), [*ptero-* and *-ous.*] a combining form meaning *having* (a specified number or kind of) *wings,* as in homo*pterous.*

ptē·ryġ′i·um (tē-), *n.*; *pl.* **ptē·ryġ′i·ȧ** or **ptē·ryġ′i·umṣ,** [L., from Gr. *pterygion,* a little wing.]

1. a vascular growth spreading from the cornea over the surface of the eye.

2. the hypothetically perfect limb of a vertebrate.

3. one of the lateral lobes at the end of the snout in some beetles, as in weevils.

pter′y·gō- (ter′), [from Gr. *pterygion.*] a combining form meaning *wing, fin,* as in *pterygoblast.*

pter′y·gō·blȧst, *n.* [*pterygo-,* and Gr. *blastos,* shoot or sprout.] a fin ray of a fish before development; a germinal ray of a fin.

pter″y·gō·brañ′chi·āte, *a.* [*pterygo-,* and Gr. *branchia,* gills.] having featherlike gills: said of certain isopods.

pter·y·gō′dȧ, *n.pl.* [Gr. *pterygōdēs,* winglike.] the small appendages above the base of the wings of an insect; tegulae.

pter′y·gōde, *n.* one of the pterygoda; a pterygoid.

pter′y·goid, *a.* [*pterygo-,* and Gr. *eidos,* form.]

1. like a wing.

2. designating, of, or near either of two winglike processes in the skull that descend from the sphenoid bone.

pter′y·goid, *n.* any wing-shaped part, as a bone or a muscle; a pterygoid bone.

pterygoid bone; in all vertebrates except mammals, a bone which connects the palatine bones with the lower jaw. It corresponds to the inner plate of the pterogoid process of the human skull.

pterygoid plate; one of the two bone plates which unite at their distal end to form a pterygoid process.

pterygoid process; one of the winglike bony processes descending from either side of the sphenoid bone and enclosing the pterygoid fossa.

pter″y·gō·max′il·lȧ·ry, *a.* of or relating to a pterygoid bone and a maxillary bone.

pter″y·gō·pal′ȧ·tine, *a.* relating to or connected with the pterygoid processes and the palatine bones.

pter″y·gō·pō′di·um, *n.*; *pl.* **pter″y·gō·pō′di·ȧ,** [*pterygo-,* and Gr. *podion,* dim. of *podos,* foot.] a modification of the ventral fin in the males of elasmobranch fishes; a clasper.

pter″y·gō·quäd′rāte (-kwod′), *a.* of, pertaining to, or connected with the quadrate and the pterygoid bones.

pter·y·gos′ti·um, *n.*; *pl.* **pter·y·gos′ti·ȧ,** [*pterygo-,* and L. *ostium,* a mouth.] any vein or rib in an insect's wing.

Pter·y·gō′tȧ, *n.pl.* same as *Pterophora.*

pter′y·gōte, *a.* [Gr. *pterygōtos,* winged.] having wings or parts resembling wings; alate; belonging to the *Pterygota.*

pter′y·lȧ, *n.*; *pl.* **pter′y·lae,** [Gr. *pteron,* feather, and *hylē,* wood.] one of the definitely limited feather tracts of the skin of a bird: opposed to *apterium,* a naked area.

pter″y·lō·graph′iç, *a.* relating to pterylography or to pterylosis.

pter″y·lō·graph′i·çăl, *a.* pterylographic.

pter·y·log′rȧ·phy, *n.* [*pteryla,* and Gr. *graphein,* to write.] the description or the science of the arrangement of feathers on a bird.

pter·y·lō′sis, *n.* the grouping of pterylae; the distribution of feathered tracts.

Ptil·ō·cẽr′çus (til-), *n.* [Gr. *ptilon,* feather, and *kerkos,* tail.] a genus of shrews of a single species, *Ptilocercus lowi,* characterized by a long tail resembling a feather; the pentails.

ptil′ō·cẽrque (-sẽrk), *n.* a shrew of the genus *Ptilocercus*; a pentail.

ptil·ō·pae′dēṣ, *n.pl.* [Gr. *ptilon,* down, and *pais, paidos,* child.] a group of birds including such as are clothed with down when hatched, not only on the pterylae but on the apteria: a division virtually coextensive with *Præcoces.*

ptil·ō·pae′diç, *a.* of, like, or relating to the *Ptilopædes.*

pti·lō′sis (ti-), *n.* [Gr. *ptilon,* feather, wing.]

1. the plumage of birds.

2. in medicine, a falling out or loss of the eyelashes.

ptin′id (tin′), *n.* [Gr. *phthinein,* to decay, waste, destroy.] a beetle of the genus *Ptinus.*

ptī′noid (tī′), *a.* like a ptinid; of the genus *Ptinus.*

Ptī′nus, *n.* an extensive and widespread genus of beetles, including many species of which the larvae and the beetles themselves are destructive to furs, books, papers, and even such substances as tobacco, pepper, spices, etc.

ptis′ăn (tis′ *or* ti-zan′), *n.* [L. *ptisana*; Gr. *ptisanē,* peeled barley, also a drink made from it, barley water, from *ptissein,* to peel, to husk.]

1. a drink made by boiling down barley with water and other ingredients; barley water.

2. any similar decoction, as of herbs.

3. the unpressed juice of grapes, resulting from drainage.

ptō·çhoç′rȧ·cy (tō-), *n.* [Gr. *ptōchos,* a beggar, and *kratein,* to rule.] government by paupers: the converse of *plutocracy.* [Rare.]

Ptol·e·mā′iç (tol-), *a.* 1. of or pertaining to Ptolemy, the Alexandrian astronomer and geographer.

2. of the Ptolemies of the Greco-Egyptian dynasty (323–30 B.C.).

Ptolemaic system; in astronomy, the theory systematized by Ptolemy, who supposed the earth to be fixed in the center of the universe, and the sun and stars to revolve around it.

Ptol·e·mā′ist, *n.* a believer in the Ptolemaic system of astronomy.

ptō′māine, ptō′māin (tō′mān *or* tō-mān′), *n.* [Gr. *ptōma,* corpse.] any of a class of alkaloid substances, some of which are poisonous, found in decaying animal or vegetable matter.

ptō′māine poi′ṣŏn·ing, an acute digestive disorder caused by the eating of putrid or rancid food containing certain toxic bacilli (formerly believed to be ptomaines).

ptō·mat′rō·pīne, *n.* a poison whose effects resemble atropine.

ptō′sis, *n.* [Gr. *ptōsis,* a fall, a falling, from *piptein* (verb. adj. *ptōtos*), to fall.] in medicine, (a) a paralytic drooping of the upper eyelid; (b) the prolapse of an organ or part.

ptō′tiç, *a.* of, having, or relating to ptosis.

ptȳ′ȧ·lin, ptȳ′ȧ·line (tī′), *n.* [Gr. *ptyalon,* spittle, from *ptyein,* to spit.] an enzyme contained in the saliva of man (and some lower animals) that converts starch into dextrin and maltose.

ptȳ′ȧ·liṣm, *n.* [Gr. *ptyalismos,* a spitting, from *ptyalizein,* to spit often.] excessive secretion of saliva.

ptȳ′ȧ·līze, *v.t.*; ptyalized, *pt., pp.*; ptyalizing, *ppr.* to cause ptyalism in.

ptȳ·al′ō·gogue (-gog), *n.* [Gr. *ptyalon,* saliva, and *agōgos,* leading, from *agein,* to induce.] a medicine which causes salivation or a flow of saliva.

Ptȳ·çhō·spẽr′mȧ, *n.* [Gr. *ptychē,* a fold, and *sperma,* seed.] a genus of palms, native to the Malay Archipelago, Australia, and the Pacific islands. They are of decorative value only, the dwarf species, as *Ptychosperma seemani,* and others in greenhouse cultivation being known as feather palms. Many species reach a considerable height.

ptyx′is (tix′), *n.* [Gr. *ptyxis,* a folding, from *ptyssein,* to fold.] in botany, the manner of folding in the bud of a leaf or flower. [Rare.]

Pu, in chemistry, plutonium.

pub, *n.* [contr., from public (house).]

1. a bar; a tavern. [Brit. Slang.]

2. a hotel; an inn. [Brit. Slang.]

pub′ble, *a.* [comp. Gael. *plub,* an unwieldly lump or mass.] pudgy; fat. [Obs.]

pū′bẽr·ăl, *a.* [L. *pubes, puber,* adult.] pertaining or relating to puberty.

pū′bẽr·ty, *n.* [L. *pubertas,* from *pubes, puber,* of ripe age, adult.]

1. the state of physical development at which persons are first capable of begetting or bearing children. In law, the age of puberty is usually fixed at fourteen in the male, and twelve in the female.

2. in botany, the period when a plant first begins to bear flowers. [Obs.]

pū·ber′ū·lent, *a.* in botany, covered with fine, short, and nearly imperceptible down.

pū′bēṣ, *n.* [L., the hair which appears on the body at the age of puberty.]

1. the hair appearing on the body at puberty; especially, the hair at the lower part of the abdomen surrounding the external genitals.

2. the region of the abdomen covered by such hair.

3. in botany, the down of plants; a downy or villous substance which grows on plants; pubescence.

pū′bēṣ, *n.* plural of *pubis.*

pū·bes′cence, pū·bes′cen·cy, *n.* 1. the reaching of the state of being sexually mature.

2. a filmy covering of soft short hairs found upon many plants and some animals, such as insects, snails, etc.

pū·bes′cent, *a.* [L. *pubescentis,* reaching the age of puberty, becoming downy.]

1. arriving or having arrived at puberty.

2. in botany, covered with pubescence, as the leaves of plants.

3. in zoology, covered with very fine, recumbent, short hairs.

pū′biç, *a.* of or in the region of the pubis or the pubes; as, the *pubic* area.

pū·biġ′e·rous, *a.* same as *pubescent.*

pū·bi·ot′ō·my, *n.* [L. *pubis,* and Gr. *tomia,* from *temnein,* to cut.] in surgery, the operation of cutting through the pubic bone.

pū′bis, *n.*; *pl.* **pū′bēṣ,** in anatomy, either of two bones that, together with a third bone between them, make up the front arch of the pelvis.

pub′liç, *a.* [L. *publicus,* from *populus,* people.]

1. of, belonging to, concerning, or pertaining to the people of a nation, state, or community as a whole; as, the *public* welfare; *public* good; *public* property; the *public* service.

2. open to common use; for the use or benefit of all; as, a *public* road; *public* parks.

3. acting in an official capacity on behalf of the people as a whole; as, a *public* prosecutor.

4. known by, or open to the knowledge of, all or most people; as, he will make this information *public.*

> Joseph, her husband, being a just man, and
> not willing to make her a *public* example,
> was minded to put her away privily.
> —Matt. 1. 19.

public act or statute; in law, an act or statute which concerns the public and of which judicial notice is taken by the courts.

public credit; the confidence which men entertain in the ability and disposition of a nation to make good its engagements with its creditors; also, a similar confidence on the part of the public toward those in business.

public debt; the debt of a government or nation to individual creditors; national debt.

public enemy; (a) a government with which one's country is at war; (b) a hardened criminal or other person who is a menace to society.

public enemy number 1; a particularly notorious underworld character. [Colloq.]

public holiday; same as *legal holiday.*

public house; (a) a bar; a tavern; (b) an inn. [Brit.]

public lands; land which is the property of a government or people, especially that which is open to settlers.

public opinion; the opinion of the people generally, especially as a force in determining social conduct and political action.

public orator; same as *orator,* sense **4.**

public relations; relations with the general public through publicity; those functions of a corporation, organization, branch of military service, etc. concerned with informing the public of its activities, policies, etc. and attempting to create favorable public opinion.

public school; (a) in the United States, an elementary or secondary school that is part of a system of schools maintained by public taxes and supervised by municipal, county, or State authorities, offering education, usually free, to the children and youth of the district; (b) in England, originally, any nonprofit grammar school endowed for the general use of the public; (c) in England, now, any of several private, expensive, endowed boarding schools for boys, offering instruction preparatory to college or the public service, as Eton and Rugby.

public servant; a person who serves the people, as in civil service or elective office.

public spirit; interest in matters concerning the public.

public stores; naval and military supplies, or stores.

public utility; (a) an organization supplying water, electricity, transportation, etc. to the public, operated by a private corporation under a government franchise, or by the government directly; (b) [*usually pl.*] shares or stock issued by public utilities.

public works; works such as roads, railways, bridges, etc. constructed for public use or service at public cost.

to be in the public line; to be engaged in a public-house business. [Brit. Colloq.]

Syn.—open, notorious, common, social, national, exoteric, general.

pub′liç, *n.* 1. the general body of a nation, state, or community; the people as a whole; the community at large.

> The *public* is more disposed to censure than to praise. —Addison.

2. a specific part of the people; those people considered together because of some common interest or purpose; as, the sporting *public*, an author's *public*.

3. a public house. [Brit. Colloq.]

in public; in open view; before the people at large; not in private or secrecy.

pub′liç-ad·dress′ sys′tem, an electronic amplification system, used in auditoriums, theaters, or the like, so that announcements, music, etc. can be easily heard by a large audience.

pub′li·căn, *n.* [L. *publicanus*, from *publicus*.]

1. in ancient Rome, a collector of public revenues, tolls, etc.; a farmer of the taxes and public revenues: the inferior officers of this class were deemed oppressive.

> As Jesus sat at meat in the house, behold, many *publicans* and sinners came and sat down with him and his disciples. —Matt. ix. 10.

2. the keeper of an inn or public house; one licensed to retail beer, spirits, or wine. [Brit.]

pub·li·çā′tion, *n.* [L. *publicatio* (*-onis*), a making public.]

1. a publishing or being published; public notification.

2. the printing and distribution, usually for sale, of books, magazines, newspapers, etc.

3. something published, as a book, periodical, article, etc.

publication of a libel; in law, the exposing of a libel so that one person at least besides the person libeled may be aware of it.

publication of banns; in law, the announcing in a parish church of a forthcoming marriage.

pub′liç-heärt″ed, *a.* public-spirited. [Rare.]

pub′li·cist, *n.* 1. a student of or specialist in international law; one who treats of the rights of nations.

2. one who writes on current affairs; a writer for the public, especially on political topics.

3. a publicity agent.

pub·lic′i·ty, *n.* [Fr. *publicité*.]

1. the state of being public, commonly known, or open to the knowledge of a community.

2. any information, usually printed, which brings a person, place, thing, or cause to the notice or attention of the public.

3. notice by or attention of the public.

4. any procedure or act that seeks to gain this.

publicity bureau; an office or agency specializing in preparing publicity; as, the *publicity bureau* of a concert management.

publicity man; one who obtains or writes publicity; a press agent.

publicity manager; same as *publicity man*.

publicity stunt; any act performed for the purpose of gaining notoriety or attracting public attention.

to do publicity; to write publicity or to obtain material for it.

pub′li·cīze, *v.t.*; publicized, *pt.*, *pp.*; publicizing, *ppr.* to announce publicly, especially in the newspapers; to give publicity to.

pub′liç·ly, *adv.* 1. in a public manner; openly; with exposure to popular view or notice; without concealment; as, property *publicly* offered for sale; an opinion *publicly* avowed; a declaration *publicly* made.

2. by, or by consent or agency of, the public; in the name of the community.

pub′liç-mīnd″ed, *a.* disposed to promote the public interest; public-spirited.

pub′liç-mīnd″ed·ness, *n.* the quality of being public-minded.

pub′liç·ness, *n.* 1. the state of being public, or open to the view or notice of people at large; publicity; as, the *publicness* of a sale.

2. the state of belonging to the community; as, the *publicness* of property.

pub′liç-sçhool′, *a.* of or for public schools.

pub′liç-sẽrv′ice çor·pō·rā′tion, a privately owned corporation that supplies certain common needs of the public, as water, electricity, gas, or transportation.

pub″liç-spir′it·ed, *a.* 1. having or exercising a disposition to advance the interest of the community; disposed to make private sacrifices for the public good; as, *public-spirited* men.

2. dictated by a regard for the public good; as, a *public-spirited* project or measure.

pub″liç-spir′it·ed·ly, *adv.* in a public-spirited manner.

pub″liç-spir′it·ed·ness, *n.* a disposition to advance the public good; a willingness to make sacrifices of private interest to promote the common weal.

pub′lish, *v.t.*; published, *pt.*, *pp.*; publishing, *ppr.* [ME. *publischen*, from OFr. *publier*; L. *publicare*, to make public.]

1. to make public or known, either by words, writing, or printing, as what before was private or unknown; to notify publicly; to divulge, as a private transaction; to promulgate or proclaim, as a law.

2. to cause to be printed and offered for sale; to issue from the press to the public; to put into circulation.

3. to utter, pass, or put into circulation; as, to *publish* counterfeit paper.

4. to make known by posting, or by reading in a church; as, to *publish* banns of matrimony.

to publish a will; in law, to acknowledge, before witnesses, that it is the last will and testament of the testator.

Syn.—announce, advertise, declare, proclaim, divulge, disclose.

pub′lish·ȧ·ble, *a.* fit for publication.

pub′lish·ẽr, *n.* a person or firm that publishes; especially, one that prints and issues to the public newspapers, books, and other literary matter, maps, engravings, music, and the like, for sale.

pub′lish·ment, *n.* publication; the act of making known publicly; specifically, a notice of intended marriage.

pū′bō-, [from L. *pubes*.] a combining form meaning *pubic and*.

pū″bō·çoç·cyġ′ē·ăl, *a.* pertaining to or connected with the coccyx and the pubis.

pū·bō·fem′ō·răl, *a.* of or pertaining to the region of the pubis and the thigh.

pū·bō·il′ĭ·aç, *a.* of or pertaining to the ilium and the pubis.

pū·bō·is′çhi·aç, *a.* of or pertaining to the ischium and the pubis.

pū·bō·tib′ĭ·ăl, *a.* pertaining to or connected with the tibia and the pubis.

Puç·cin′ĭ·ȧ, *n.* [LL., from T. *Puccini*, an Italian anatomist.] in botany, a genus of fungi, the rusts: *Puccinia graminis* is the common rust of wheat that attacks the stems and leaves.

puç·çoon′, *n.* [Am. Ind.]

1. a red or yellow vegetable pigment used by the North American Indians.

2. any plant yielding this pigment, as (a) *Lithospermum canescens*, the hoary puccoon; (b) *Lithospermum hirtum*, the hairy puccoon; (c) *Sanguinaria canadensis*, the bloodroot or red puccoon.

pūce, *n.* [Fr. *puce*, a flea, from L. *pulex*.] brownish purple.

pūce, *a.* of a puce color.

pū′cel·ăġe, *n.* virginity. [Rare.]

pū·cel′lăs, *n.* same as *procellas*.

pū·celle′, *n.* [ME., from OFr. *pulcelle*, from L. *pullus*, a young animal, a chick.] a virgin; a maid; also, satirically, a wanton; a harlot. [Obs.]

La Pucelle; Joan of Arc, the Maid of Orleans.

pū·ce·ron′, *n.* [Fr., from *puce*, a flea.] the aphis, vine fretter, or plant louse.

pū′çhẽr·īte, *n.* [from *Pucher*, a mine in Saxony, and *-ite*.] a reddish-brown orthorhombic mineral occurring in small crystals with bismite and consisting of vanadate of bismuth.

pū·çhe′rō, *n.* [Sp., mess (of food).] a South American edible plant, *Talinum patens*, of the purslane family.

puck, *n.* [ME. *puke*; AS. *puca*; akin to ON. *puki*, a devil.]

1. a mischievous sprite; goblin; elf.

2. [P–] the mischievous sprite in Shakespeare's *Midsummer Night's Dream*; Robin Goodfellow.

puck, *n.* [from dial. *puck*, to strike.] in ice hockey, the hard rubber disk which the players strike with their sticks and try to drive into the opponents' goal.

puck′ȧ, *a.* [Hind. *pakkā*, ripe, of full weight.]

1. good or first rate of its kind.

2. genuine; firm; solid; permanent; real.

Also spelled *pukka*.

puck′bạll, *n.* [from *puck*.] a mushroom, the puffball.

puck′ẽr, *v.t.* and *v.i.*; puckered, *pt.*, *pp.*; puckering, *ppr.* [a freq. form of *poke*, a pocket.] to draw or gather into wrinkles or small folds.

puck′ẽr, *n.* 1. a fold or wrinkle, or a number of folds running together.

2. a state of anxiety; perplexity; agitation; bother. [Colloq.]

puck′ẽr·ẽr, *n.* one who or that which puckers.

puck′ẽr·y, *a.* 1. astringent; causing the mouth to wrinkle up.

2. full of puckers; tending to pucker.

puck′fist, *n.* 1. a puffball.

2. a mean wretch. [Archaic.]

puck′ish, *a.* resembling Puck; mischievous; elfish: also *Puckish*.

pū′çras, *n.* an Oriental pheasant of the genus *Pucrasia*, having the bill short, the nostrils nearly concealed by feathers, and the head covered with a long crest: also spelled *pukras*.

pụd, *n.* same as *pood*.

pud, *n.* [OFr. *pote*, paw.] the fist; the hand. [Colloq.]

pụd′den·ing, *n.* 1. a thick, spindle-shaped pad of rope used as a fender on shipboard.

2. a bunch of rope yarn or soft material to prevent chafing, as between spars.

pud′dẽr, *n.* a tumult; a confused noise; a bustle. [Obs.]

pud′dẽr, *v.i.* to make a tumult. [Obs.]

pụd′ding, *n.* [ME. *poding*.]

1. a sausage made of intestine stuffed with meat, suet, etc., and boiled. [Scot. and Dial.]

2. a soft, sweetened food, usually made with flour or some cereal as a base and variously containing eggs, milk, fruit, meat, etc.

3. anything like this in appearance or consistency.

pụd′ding çloth, any cloth in which a pudding is boiled.

pụd′ding-fāced (-fāst), *a.* having a large, fat face.

pụd′ding fish, the bluefish of Florida, *Platyglossus radiatus*, having the body deep steel-blue, with oblique blue streaks on the cheek, and blue spots on the ventrals.

pụd′ding grȧss, pennyroyal.

pụd′ding·head″ed (-hed″), *a.* stupid; fat-headed. [Colloq.]

pụd′ding pīe, 1. a pudding with meat baked in it.

2. a kind of open cheese cake with currants.

pụd′ding sleeve, a full sleeve drawn tight at the wrist.

pụd′ding stōne, conglomerate, a coarse sandstone in which pebbles are embedded like plums in a pudding.

pụd′ding tīme, 1. the time of dinner, pudding being formerly the first dish eaten. [Obs.]

2. the nick of time; a favorable time.

pụd′ding·wīfe, *n.* same as *pudding fish*.

pud′dle, *n.* [ME. *podel*, dim. of AS. *pudd*, a ditch.]

1. a small pool of water, especially stagnant or spilled water.

2. a thick mixture of clay, and sometimes sand, with water.

pud′dle, *v.t.*; puddled, *pt.*, *pp.*; puddling, *ppr.* 1. to make muddy.

2. to make a thick mixture of (wet clay and sand).
3. to keep water from penetrating by the use of such a mixture.
4. to treat (iron) by puddling.
5. in agriculture, to work (soil) while it is wet, as in rice cultivation.

pud'dle, *v.i.* to dabble or wallow in dirty or muddy water.

pud'dle ball, the ball or mass of iron which while in a pasty condition is taken from the puddling furnace to be worked.

pud'dle bär, the bar of malleable iron as it leaves the last of the grooves in the finishing series of puddle rolls.

pud'dle duck, the common domestic duck.

pud'dlẽr, *n.* one who or that which puddles; specifically, a person who puddles clay or iron.

pud'dle rōlls, a pair of heavy, grooved iron rollers used in making puddle bars.

pud'dle wall, a wall of well-rammed impervious soil, such as gravelly clay, reaching from the top to several feet below the base of an embankment, to prevent leaking either through or beneath it.

pud'dling, *n.* 1. the process of working clay or a similar substance with water so as to make a mixture which moisture cannot penetrate.
2. the process of making wrought iron from pig iron by heating and stirring it in the presence of oxidizing agents.

pud'dling fũr'nāce, a kind of reverberatory furnace for puddling iron, so constructed that it is only the heated gases that are allowed to play upon the surface of the metal.

pud'dly, *a.*; *comp.* puddlier; *superl.* puddliest, 1. like a puddle.
2. having puddles.

pud'dŏck, *n.* a paddock. [Dial.]

pū'den·cy, *n.* [L. *pudens*, bashful, modest.] modesty; embarrassment; bashfulness.

pū·den'dăl, *a.* relating to the pudenda.

pū·den'dum, *n.*; *pl.* **pū·den'dȧ,** [L.] 1. the external genitals of the female; the vulva.
2. [*pl.*] the external genitals of either sex.

pudġ'i·ness, *n.* a pudgy quality or condition.

pudġ'y, *a.*; *comp.* pudgier; *superl.* pudgiest, [Scot.] fat and short; thick; fleshy: also spelled *podgy, pudsy.*

A *pudgy* hand was laid on his shoulder.
—Thackeray.

pū'diç, pū'di·çăl, *a.* [L. *pudicus*, modest.] pudendal.

pū·dic'i·ty, *n.* [Fr. *pudicité*; L. *pudicitia.*] modesty; chastity.

pú'dú, *n.* [S. Am., native name.] a small red deer, *Pudua humilis*, which inhabits the mountains of Chile.

pueb'lō (pweb'), *n.*; *pl.* **pueb'lōs,** [Sp., a town or people.]
1. a type of communal village built by certain Indians of the southwestern United States and parts of Latin America, consisting of one or more flat-roofed structures of stone or adobe, arranged in terraces and housing a number of families.
2. [P–] any Indian of the tribes inhabiting such villages, as the Zuñi and the Hopi, characterized by a peaceful agricultural life and a culture related to that of the Aztec, Mayan, and Toltec Indians.
3. an Indian village.
4. in Spanish America, a village or town.
5. in the Philippines, a municipality; a town or township.

Pueb'lō, *a.* of the Pueblo Indians.

pū'ẽr·ile, *a.* [Fr. *puéril*, from L. *puerilis*, from *puer*, a boy.] childish; silly; immature; trivial; as, a *puerile* amusement.

Syn.—juvenile, boyish, childish, infantile.

pū'ẽr·ile·ly, *adv.* childishly; triflingly.

pū'ẽr·il·ism, *n.* childishness, especially, in psychiatry, as a symptom of psychoneurosis.

pū·ẽr·il'i·ty, *n.* [Fr. *puérilité*; L. *puerilitas*, from *puer*, a boy.]
1. the quality or condition of being puerile; childishness.
2. *pl.* **pū·ẽr·il'i·ties,** an instance of this.
3. in civil law, the period of life from the age of seven years to that of fourteen (for boys) and twelve (for girls).

pū·ẽr'pẽr·ăl, *a.* [L. *puerpera*, a woman in labor, from *puer*, a boy, and *parere*, to bear.] pertaining to childbirth; as, a *puerperal* fever.

pū·ẽr'pẽr·ăl fē'vẽr, septic poisoning sometimes occurring during childbirth.

pū·ẽr·pē'ri·um, *n.* [L., childbirth.] the period or state of confinement during and immediately after childbirth.

pū·ẽr'pẽr·ous, *a.* bearing children. [Rare.]

Puer'tō Ri'çăn (pwer'), 1. of Puerto Rico, its people, or culture.
2. a native or inhabitant of Puerto Rico. Formerly *Porto Rican.*

pū'et, *n.* same as *pewit.*

puff, *n.* [ME. *puf*, from the verb.]
1. (a) a short, sudden gust, as of wind, or expulsion, as of breath; (b) the sound of this; (c) a bit of vapor, smoke, etc. expelled at one time.
2. a draw at a cigarette, etc.
3. a swelling, or a protuberance caused by swelling.
4. a shell of soft, light pastry filled with whipped cream, etc.
5. a soft, bulging mass of material, full in the middle and gathered in at the edges.
6. a soft roll of hair on the head.
7. a soft pad for dabbing powder on the skin or hair.
8. a quilted bed covering with cotton, wool, or down filling.
9. undue or exaggerated praise, as in the advertisement of a book, etc.

puff, *v.i.*; puffed (puft), *pt., pp.*; puffing, *ppr.* [ME. *puffen*; AS. *pyffan.*]
1. to blow in puffs.
2. (a) to give forth puffs of smoke, steam, etc.; (b) to breathe rapidly and hard, as from strenuous exercise.
3. to move, giving forth puffs (with *away, out*, or *in*).
4. to come in puffs.
5. to inflate with air or pride; to swell (with *out* or *up*).
6. to take a puff or puffs at a cigarette, etc.

puff, *v.t.* 1. to blow, drive, give forth, etc. in or with a puff or puffs.
2. to swell; distend; inflate.
3. to praise unduly.
4. to write or print a puff or puffs of (a book, etc.).
5. to smoke (a cigarette, etc.).
6. to set in soft, round masses or rolls, as the hair.

puff, *a.* vain.

puff ad'dẽr, 1. an African snake, *Bitis arietans*, or any snake of the same genus, so named from its power of distending the body. It is very poisonous, but sluggish in its nature, and attains a length of four or five feet.
2. a harmless North American snake, *Heterodon platyrrhinos*, which has distensive powers: also called *flathead, spreading adder*, and *blowing adder.*

puff'ball, *n.* 1. any of a number of related round, white-fleshed, mushroomlike fungi of the genus *Lycoperdon*, that burst at the touch and discharge a brown powder.
2. the feathery tuft of the dandelion.

puff'bĩrd, *n.* a barbet: so called from its habit of puffing out the feathers.

puff'ẽr, *n.* 1. a person or thing that puffs.
2. any of various fishes capable of expanding by swallowing air, as the swellfish, globefish, etc.

puff'ẽr·y, *n.* extravagant praise.

puf'fin, *n.* [from *puff*, in allusion to its puffed-out beak.]

COMMON PUFFIN (*Fratercula arctica*)

1. any of the marine diving birds of the genus *Fratercula*, of the auk family, characterized by a brightly colored triangular beak. The common puffin is *Fratercula arctica*, the horned puffin, *Fratercula corniculata*, and the tufted puffin, *Lunda cirrhata.*
2. in botany, the puffball.

puff'i·ness, *n.* state or quality of being puffy.

puff'ing ad'dẽr, see *puff adder.*

puff'ing pig, the porpoise.

puff'-leg, *n.* any hummingbird of the genus *Eriocnemis*, characterized by tufts resembling powder puffs on its legs.

puff pāste, a rich dough for light, flaky pastries.

puff'y, *a.*; *comp.* puffier; *superl.* puffiest, 1. blowing or coming in puffs.
2. panting; shortwinded.
3. puffed up; swollen; inflated.
4. fat; obese.

pug, *v.t.*; pugged, *pt., pp.*; pugging, *ppr.* [echoic of pounding.]
1. to mix or fill in with wet, plastic clay.
2. to tamp; to fill, as a floor or wall with mortar, clay, sawdust, etc., in order to deaden sound.

pug, *n.* clay that has been prepared by mixing with water and grinding, as for molding into bricks, etc.

pug, *n.* [a form of *puck.*]
1. an elf; a goblin. [Obs.]
2. a small, short-haired dog with a wrinkled face, snub nose, and curled tail.
3. a pug nose.
4. any moth of the genus *Eupithecia*: also *pug moth.*

pug, *n.* [Hind. *pag*, foot.] a track or footprint. [Anglo-Ind.]

pug, *v.t.* and *v.i.* to track, as an animal, by footprints; to track animals. [Anglo-Ind.]

pug, *n.* [contr. of *pugilist.*] a pugilist. [Slang.]

pug'ȧ·ree, *n.* same as *puggree.*

pug'-fāced (-fāst), *a.* having a face like a pug dog.

pug'gȧ·ree, *n.* same as *puggree.*

pug'gẽr, *v.t.* to pucker. [Obs.]

pug'ging, *n.* 1. the preparation of clay for molding into bricks, etc.
2. in architecture, clay, mortar, sawdust, etc. used for soundproofing: also called *deafening.*

pug'ging, *a.* thieving. [Obs.]

pug'gree, pug'gry, *n.* [Hind. *pagrī*, a turban.] a light scarf wrapped around the crown of a sun helmet and hanging behind to protect the back of the neck.

pŭgh (pọọ), *interj.* an exclamation of disgust or contempt.

pū'ġil, *n.* [L. *pugillus*, a handful.] as much as is taken up between the thumb and first two fingers. [Archaic.]

pū'ġil·ism, *n.* [from L. *pugil*, a boxer, pugilist; same stem as *pugnus*, a fist.] the art or practice of fighting with the fists; prize fighting; boxing.

pū'ġil·ist, *n.* a boxer; one who fights with his fists, especially in matched contests; a prize fighter.

pū·ġil·is'tiç, *a.* pertaining to pugilists or to prize fighting.

pū·ġil·is'tiç·ăl·ly, *adv.* in a pugilistic manner.

pug'mill, *n.* a mill by which clay is worked, to blend its materials and render it plastic for bricks or pottery.

pug·nā'cious (-shus), *a.* disposed to fight; inclined to fighting; quarrelsome; combative.

pug·nā'cious·ly, *adv.* in a pugnacious manner.

pug·nā'cious·ness, *n.* the quality of being pugnacious; pugnacity.

pug·nac'i·ty, *n.* inclination to fight; quarrelsomeness.

pug nōse, a short, thick nose, slightly turned up at the end; a snub nose.

pug'-nōsed', *a.* having a pug nose.
Pug-nosed eel; a deep-sea eel, *Simenchelys parasiticus.*

pug'ree, *n.* a puggree.

pū̆is'ne (pū'ny), *a.* [OFr.; *puis*, since, afterward, and *ne*, born.]
1. in law, inferior in rank; junior; as, three *puisne* judges.
2. later in date. [Obs.]
3. puny. [Obs.]

pū̆is'ne, *n.* an inferior; a junior; specifically, in law, a judge of inferior rank.

pū̆is'ny, *a.* puisne. [Obs.]

pū'is·sȧnce, *n.* power; strength; might; force. [Archaic or Poetic.]

pū'is·sȧnt, *a.* [Fr. *puissant*, powerful; formed as if from a participle *possens*, from L. *posse*, to be able.] powerful; strong; mighty; forcible; as, a *puissant* empire. [Archaic or Poetic.]

pū'is·sȧnt·ly, *adv.* powerfully; with great strength. [Archaic or Poetic.]

pū'is·sȧnt·ness, *n.* the condition of being puissant; power. [Archaic or Poetic.]

pú'já, pú'jáh, *n.* [Sans. *pūjā*, worship.] a Hindu prayer ritual.

pūke, *v.i.* and *v.t.*; puked (pūkt,) *pt., pp.*; puking, *ppr.* [akin to G. *spuchen*, to spit.] to vomit.

pūke, *n.* 1. an emetic; a medicine that induces vomiting.
2. the act of vomiting; also, that which is vomited.

3. a disgusting person. [Slang.]

pūk′ẽr, *n.* 1. one who vomits.
2. a medicine causing vomiting.

puk′kȧ, *n.* same as *pucka.*

pu·läs′ (-läsh′), *n.* same as *palas.*

pul′chri·fȳ, *v.t.*; pulchrified, *pt., pp.*; pulchrifying, *ppr.* [L. *pulcher*, beautiful.] to make beautiful. [Rare.]

pul′chri·tūde, *n.* [L. *pulchritudo*, from *pulcher*, beautiful.] physical beauty.

pul·chri·tū′di·nous, *a.* possessing physical beauty.

pūle, *v.i.*; puled, *pt., pp.*; puling, *ppr.* [echoic.] to whine; to cry, as a complaining child; to whimper.

pū′lẽr, *n.* one who pules; a weakling.

Pū′lex, *n.* [L., a flea.] a genus of insects, including the fleas. *Pulex irritans* is the common flea.

pul′i·cat, *n.* [from *Pulicat*, India, where it is made.] a kind of handkerchief.

pū′li·cēne, *a.* of or having fleas.

Pū·lic′i·dae, *n.pl.* [L. *pulex, pulicis*, a flea, and Gr. *eidos*, likeness.] the fleas, a family of insects coextensive with the order *Aphaniptera*, parasitic upon different animals. The genus *Pulex* is the type, *Pulex irritans* being the common flea.

pū′li·cīne, *a.* pertaining to the *Pulicidæ*.

pū′li·coid, *a.* of or resembling fleas.

pū′li·cōse, *a.* [L. *pulicosus*, from *pulex*, a flea.] full of fleas.

pū′li·cous, *a.* same as *pulicose.*

pūl′ing, *a.* whimpering; whining; as, a *puling* babe.

pūl′ing·ly, *adv.* in a puling manner; with whining or complaint.

pū′li·ol, *n.* [L. *puleium*, fleabane.] a plant, pennyroyal. [Obs.]

pū′lish, *n.* the ant thrush of Africa, *Pitta angolensis.*

Pul′it·zẽr Prīze (*or, now often*, pūl′it-sẽr), any of a number of yearly prizes for outstanding work in journalism and literature, established by Joseph Pulitzer.

pul′kȧ, *n.* [Lappish *pulkke*.] a Laplander's traveling sled or sledge: it is shaped somewhat like a boat, made of light materials, covered with reindeer skin, and drawn by a single reindeer.

LAPLANDER IN THE PULKA

pull, *v.t.*; pulled, *pt., pp.*; pulling, *ppr.* [ME *pullen*; AS. *pullian*.]
1. to exert force on in such a way as to cause to move toward or after the source of the force; to drag, tug, draw, attract, etc.
2. (a) to draw, or pluck, out; as, he had two teeth *pulled*; (b) to pluck and gather; as, she *pulled* several roses.
3. to draw apart; rip; tear; as, the seam of her dress is *pulled*.
4. to stretch (taffy, etc.) back and forth repeatedly.
5. to stretch or strain to the point of injury; as, he *pulled* a muscle in the game.
6. to draw the entrails from (a fowl). [Dial. or Rare.]
7. to put into effect; perform; do; as, the police *pulled* a raid. [Colloq.]
8. to hold back the force of deliberately; to restrain; as, he's *pulling* his punches. [Colloq.]
9. (a) to arrest (someone); (b) to make a police raid on. [Slang.]
10. in baseball, golf, etc., to hit (the ball) so as to cause it to curve to the left or, if the player is left-handed, to the right.
11. in horse racing, to rein in, or restrain (a horse), to keep it from winning.
12. in printing, to take (a proof) on a hand press.
13. in rowing, (a) to work (an oar) by drawing it toward one; (b) to transport by rowing; (c) to be rowed normally by; as, this boat *pulls* four oars.
to pull a long face; to look dejected.
to pull apart; to find fault with; to criticize.
to pull down; (a) to tear down, demolish, or overthrow; (b) to degrade; to humble; (c) to reduce.
to pull off; to bring about or accomplish. [Colloq.]
to pull oneself together; to collect one's faculties; to regain one's poise, courage, etc.
to pull the wool over one's eyes; to deceive one by preventing the discovery of the truth. [Colloq.]
to pull through; to get through or over (an illness, difficulty, etc.).
to pull up; (a) to uproot; (b) to bring to a stop.

pull, *v.i.* 1. to exert force in or for dragging, tugging, or attracting something.
2. to take a deep draft of a drink or puff at a cigarette, etc.
3. to be capable of being pulled.
4. to move (*away, ahead*, etc.).
to pull apart; to separate by pulling; as, a rope will *pull apart.*
to pull for; to cheer on, or hope for the success of. [Colloq.]
to pull over; to move to or toward the curb, as a motor vehicle. [Colloq.]
to pull up; (a) to come to a stop; (b) to move ahead.

pull, *n.* 1. the act, force, or result of pulling (in various senses); specifically, (a) a dragging, tugging, attracting, etc.; (b) the act or an instance of rowing; (c) a drink; (d) a puff at a cigarette, etc.; (e) the effort used in climbing, etc.; (f) any difficult, continuous effort; (g) in sports, the act or an instance of pulling a ball.
2. something to be pulled, as the handle of a drawer, etc.
3. influence or special advantage. [Slang.]
4. a contest; a struggle. [Obs.]
5. in printing, a single impression taken by pulling the handle of a hand press.

pul′lāile, *n.* poultry. [Obs.]

Pul·las′trae, *n.pl.* [LL., dim. pl. form of *pullus*, young chicken.] a group of gallinaceous birds that includes the pigeons and other birds that have the toes all on the same level.

pul·las′tri·form, *a.* same as *pullastrine.*

pul·las′trine, *a.* relating or belonging to the *Pullastræ.*

pull′back, *n.* 1. a pulling back.
2. a retarding or hindering force, situation, etc.
3. a device for pulling something back.
4. in architecture, an iron hook used to hold a casement in any particular position.

pull′down, *n.* a wire attached to the under side of the pallet of an organ, by which the pallet is opened as the key of the manual is depressed.

pulled bread (bred), the crumb or inside of stale bread, broken up into small bits and lightly browned.

pul′len, *n.* [Fr. *poule*, L. *pullus*, a hen.] poultry. [Obs. or Dial.]

pull′ẽr, *n.* one who or that which pulls.

pul′let, *n.* [Fr. *poulette*, dim. from *poule*, L. *pullus*, a hen.] a young hen, usually not more than a year old.

pul′let spẽrm, the chalaza of an egg. [Obs.]

pul′ley, *n.*; *pl.* **pul′leys,** [ME. and OFr. *polie*; ML. *poleia*; prob. *poulie*, a pulley, from Gr. hyp. *polidion*, dim. of *polos*, pulley, hinge.]
1. a small wheel, sometimes turning in a block, with a grooved rim in which a rope runs, as to raise weights by being pulled down.
2. a combination of such wheels, used to increase the applied power.
3. a wheel that turns or is turned by a belt so as to transmit or apply power.

PULLEY

conical pulley; a cone pulley.
fast pulley; a pulley firmly attached to the shaft from which it receives or to which it communicates motion.
idle pulley; a pulley used to alter the direction in which a belt moves.
loose pulley; a pulley running free on the shaft to receive the belt and allow it to traverse without being affected by or affecting the motion of the shafting.
parting pulley; a pulley made in sections so that a shaft need not be dismounted in order to receive it.
split pulley; a parting pulley.

pul′ley, *v.t.* to raise or hoist by means of a pulley.

pul′ley block, a shell or block which contains a pulley or pulleys.

pul′ley stīle, that part of a window frame into which a pulley is fixed and along which a sash moves.

pul′li·cat, *n.* same as *pulicat.*

pull′ing bōat, a rowboat.

Pull′măn, *n.* a Pullman car.

Pull′măn cär, [after George M. *Pullman* (1831–1897), Am. inventor.] a railroad car with private compartments or chairs that can be made up into berths for sleeping.

pul′lock, *n.* a kind of porpoise.

pull′-off, *n.* the trigger pressure required to discharge a gun.

pul·lō′rum dis·ēase′, [L. *pullorum*, genit. pl. of *pullus*, chicken.] a highly destructive bacterial disease of poultry, often transmitted in the egg.

pull′-out, *n.* a maneuver in which an airplane levels out into horizontal flight after a dive.

pull′-ō·vẽr, *a.* that is put on by being pulled over the head.

pull′-ō·vẽr, *n.* a pull-over sweater, shirt, etc.

pul′lū·lāte, *v.i.*; pullulated, *pt., pp.*; pullulating, *ppr.* [L. *pullulatus*, from *pullulare*, to spread out, sprout.]
1. to sprout out; germinate; bud.
2. to breed quickly.
3. to spring up in abundance; to teem or swarm.

pul·lū·lā′tion, *n.* a pullulating.

pull-up, *n.* a maneuver in which an airplane goes into a short, sudden climb from level flight.

pul′lus, *n.*; *pl.* **pul′lī,** [L., a young animal.] a young bird covered with down; a nestling.

pul′mō-, [from L. *pulmo*, lung.] a combining form meaning (a) *lung*; (b) *pulmonary and.*

pul′mō·branch, *n.* one of the *Pulmobranchiata.*

Pul·mō·bran′chi·ȧ, *n.pl.* [*pulmo-*, and LL. *branchiæ*, gills.] same as *Pulmonifera.*

pul·mō·bran′chi·ȧ, *n.*; *pl.* **pul·mō·bran′chi·ae,** a lung sac or modified gill of mollusks, etc.

pul·mō·bran′chi·ăl, *a.* pulmobranchiate.

Pul·mō·bran·chi·ā′tȧ, *n.pl.* same as *Pulmonifera.*

pul·mō·bran′chi·āte, *a.* of or pertaining to the *Pulmobranchiata.*

pul·mō·bran′chi·ate, *n.* any member of the order *Pulmobranchiata.*

pul″mō·cū·tā′nē·ous, *a.* [*pulmo-*, and L. *cutis*, skin.] of or pertaining to the lungs and skin.

Pul·mō·gas·tẽr·op′ō·dȧ, *n.pl.* [*pulmo-*, and Gr. *gastēr*, stomach, and *pous, podos*, foot.] same as *Pulmonifera.*

Pul·mō·grā′dȧ, *n.pl.* [*pulmo-*, and L. *gradus*, a step.] in zoology, an order of the old subclass *Acalephæ*, including the *Discophora* and in part the *Lucernarida.*

pul′mō·grāde, *a.* of or relating to the *Pulmograda.*

pul′mō·grāde, *n.* a member of the *Pulmograda.*

pul·mom′e·tẽr, *n.* an instrument for measuring respiration; a spirometer.

pul·mom′e·try, *n.* [*pulmo-*, and Gr. *metron*, measure.] the determination of lung capacity.

pul′mō·năr, *a.* 1. of or pertaining to the *Pulmonariæ* or *Pulmonata.*
2. having lungs or air-breathing organs.

Pul·mō·nā′ri·ȧ, *n.* [from former medicinal use.] a genus of plants generally known as lungwort.

Pul·mō·nā′ri·ae, *n.pl.* same as *Pulmonata.*

pul·mō·năr′i·ăn, *a.* of or pertaining to the *Pulmonariæ* or *Pulmonata.*

pul·mō·năr′i·ăn, *n.* any arachnid with lunglike organs for respiration.

pul′mō·năr·y, *a.* [L. *pulmonarius*, from *pulmo, pulmonis*, a lung.]
1. of, like, or affecting the lungs.
2. having lungs or lunglike organs.
3. designating the artery conveying blood from the heart to the lungs, and the vein conveying blood from the lungs to the heart.
pulmonary cavity or *sac*; the cavity of a pulmonate mollusk or arachnid which serves for respiration.
pulmonary consumption; tuberculosis of the lungs.
pulmonary valves; the three valves of the right cardiac ventricle.

pul′mō·năr·y, *n.* a plant, lungwort.

Pul·mō·nā′tȧ, *n.pl.* [L. *pulmo, pulmonis,* a lung.]
 1. a division of pulmonary arachnidans, including scorpions and spiders.
 2. same as *Pulmonifera.*

pul′mō·nāte, *a.* having lungs, or organs that act as lungs.

pul′mō·nāte, *n.* one of the *Pulmonata.*

pul′mō·nāt·ed, *a.* pulmonate.

pul·mon′iç, *a.* [Fr. *pulmonique,* from L. *pulmo,* a lung.]
 1. pulmonary.
 2. of pneumonia; pneumonic.

pul·mon′iç, *n.* 1. a medicine for diseases of the lungs.
 2. one affected by a disease of the lungs.

pul·mon′i·fēr, *n.* an animal having lungs; specifically, a member of the *Pulmonifera.*

Pul·mō·nif′ēr·ȧ, *n.pl.* [L. *pulmo,* a lung, and *ferre,* to bear.] an order of *Gasteropoda* having the simplest form of lung, resembling the bronchial chamber of the stomach of the sea snail, but lined with a network of respiratory vessels; also having the foot broad, and, generally, a spiral shell. The order contains the land snails and slugs.

pul·mō·nif′ēr·ous, *a.* 1. having lungs, or organs which act as lungs; pulmonate.
 2. pertaining or belonging to the *Pulmonifera.*

pul′mō·tŏr, *n.* [from L. *pulmo,* a lung.; and *motor.*] an apparatus used in applying artificial respiration to persons who are in danger of death from drowning, suffocation, etc.: a trade-mark (*Pulmotor*).

pul·mō·trā′çhē·āte, pul·mō·trā′çhē·ăl, *a.* [*pulmo-,* and L. *trachea,* windpipe.] pulmonate; having lunglike organs, as the spiders.

pulp, *n.* [Fr. *pulpe;* L. *pulpa,* flesh, pulp of fruit.]
 1. a soft, moist, formless mass that sticks together.
 2. the soft, juicy part of a fruit.
 3. the soft, spongy pith inside the stem of a plant.
 4. the soft, sensitive substance underneath the enamel and dentine of a tooth.
 5. a mixture of ground-up, moistened cellulose material, as wood, linen, rags, etc., from which paper is made.
 6. ore ground to a powder and mixed with water.
 7. [*usually in pl.*] a magazine printed on rough, inferior paper stock made from wood pulp, usually containing sensational stories of love, crime, etc. [Slang.]

pulp, *v.t.*; pulped, (pulpt) *pt., pp.*; pulping, *ppr.*
 1. to remove the pulp from.
 2. to reduce to pulp.

pulp, *v.i.* to become pulp.

pul·pȧ·toon′, *n.* [Fr.] a French stew. [Obs.]

pulp di·gest′ēr, in papermaking, a machine for eliminating extraneous matter from fibrous material.

pul·pē·fac′tion, *n.* [L. *pulpa,* pulp, and *facere,* to make.] the act of converting into pulp.

pulp en′ġine, a machine for converting raw materials into paper pulp: also called *pulp machine.*

pulp′i·fȳ, *v.t.*; pulpified, *pt., pp.*; pulpifying, *ppr.* to make pulp of.

pulp′i·ness, *n.* the state or quality of being pulpy.

pụl′pit, *n.* [L. *pulpitum,* a stage, scaffold.]
 1. a raised platform from which a clergyman preaches in a church.
 2. preachers collectively; (*the*) ministry.
 3. preaching.
 4. an iron bow on the end of the bowsprit of a whaling vessel, used to support the harpooner.

pụl′pit, *a.* belonging, pertaining, or suited to the pulpit; as, *pulpit* eloquence.

pụl·pit·eer′, *n.* a preacher: a term of contempt.

pụl′pit·ēr, *n.* a preacher.

pụl·pit′i·căl, *a.* pertaining to the pulpit; associated with or suited to the pulpit. [Rare.]

pụl·pit′i·căl·ly, *adv.* in a manner suited to the pulpit. [Rare.]

pulp′ī·tis, *n.* an inflamed condition of the dental pulp.

pụl′pit·ish, *a.* pertaining to or like the pulpit, or a pulpit performance. [Rare.]

pụl′pit·ry, *n.* the teaching of the pulpit. [Obs.]

pulp′less, *a.* without pulp.

pulp′ous, *a.* consisting of pulp; pulpy.

pulp′ous·ness, *n.* the quality or state of being pulpous.

pulp′wood, *n.* 1. soft wood used in the manufacture of paper; especially, the wood of spruce and aspen trees.
 2. wood ground to pulp for papermaking.

pulp′y, *a.*; *comp.* pulpier; *superl.* pulpiest; of, having the nature of, or like pulp; as, the *pulpy* covering of a nut; the *pulpy* substance of a peach or cherry.

pul′que (-kā), *n.* [Sp.; prob. of Mex. Ind. origin.] a fermented drink, popular in Mexico, made from the juice of an agave.

pul′sär, *n.* [*pulse,* and *-ar.*] any of several small, heavenly objects in the Milky Way that emit radio pulses at regular intervals.

pul′sāte, *v.i.*; pulsated, *pt., pp.*; pulsating, *ppr.* [L. *pulsatus,* from *pulsare,* to beat.]
 1. to beat or throb, as the heart.
 The heart of a viper or frog will continue to *pulsate* long after it is taken from the body. —Darwin.
 2. to vibrate; to quiver; to thrill.

pul′sȧ·tile, *a.* [LL. *pulsatilis,* from *pulsare,* to beat.]
 1. played by beating, as a drum.
 2. in medicine, beating as a pulse; throbbing; pulsating: applied to tumors.

pul′sȧ·tile, *n.* an instrument of music which is played by beating.

pul·sȧ·til′lȧ, *n.* [LL., dim. from L. *pulsatus,* pp. of *pulsare,* to beat.] the pasque flower, *Anemone pulsatilla;* also, a preparation obtained from several species of the genus *Anemone,* used in medicine in cases of asthma, bronchitis, epididymitis, etc.

pul·sā′tion, *n.* [L. *pulsatio.*]
 1. a pulsating; rhythmical beating or throbbing.
 2. a beat; throb; vibration.

pul′sȧ·tive, *a.* pulsating.

pul·sā′tŏr, *n.* 1. a beater; a striker.
 2. any device or machine part that pulsates.

pul′sȧ·tō·ry, *a.* characterized by pulsation; throbbing.
 pulsatory current; in electricity, a current whose direction remains constant, but whose intensity is subject to sudden changes.

pulse, *n.* [ME. *pous;* OFr. *pols, pouls;* L. *puls,* a porridge of beans, peas, etc.]
 1. the edible seeds of peas, beans, lentils, and similar plants having pods.
 2. any plant producing pulse.

pulse, *n.* [ME. *pous;* OFr. *pouls;* L. *pulsus,* a beating, striking.]
 1. the regular beating in the arteries, caused by the contractions of the heart.
 2. any beat that is regular or rhythmical.
 3. the perceptible underlying feelings of the public, group of people, etc.
 4. a variation, characterized by a rise, limited duration, and decline, of a quantity whose value normally is constant; specifically, (a) in electricity, a brief surge of voltage or current; (b) in radio, a very short burst of electromagnetic waves.
 to feel (or *take*) *one's pulse;* (a) to ascertain the condition of the pulse by pressing the fingers on the radial artery at the wrist; (b) figuratively, to sound one out; to try to discover one's opinions, views, or feelings.

pulse, *v.i.*; pulsed (pulst), *pt., pp.*; pulsing, *ppr.* to beat, as the arteries; to throb; to pulsate.

pulse, *v.t.* to drive, as by a pulsation of the heart. [Obs.]

pulse glȧss, a device for indicating the boiling of certain liquids at low temperatures.

pulse′-jet″, *n.* an aeropulse, a type of jet engine.

pulse′less, *a.* having no pulsation.

pulse′less·ness, *n.* cessation of the pulse; the state of being pulseless.

pulse wāve, in physiology, an arterial movement produced by the successive contractions of the heart.

pul·sif′iç, *a.* exciting the pulse; causing pulsation. [Rare.]

pul·sim′e·tēr, *n.* [L. *pulsus,* pulse, and *-meter.*] an apparatus for measuring the force and rate of the pulse.

pul′sion, *n.* the act of driving forward: opposed to *suction* or *traction.* [Rare.]

pul′sive, *a.* impelling; propulsive.

pul·som′e·tēr, *n.* [L. *pulsus,* pulse, and *-meter.*]
 1. a type of pistonless pump for raising water by the condensation of steam, in a vessel situated at such elevation above the water supply that the atmospheric pressure will raise the water to the chamber and operate the valves: also called vacuum pump.
 2. a pulsimeter.

pul·tā′ceous, *a.* [L. *puls,* porridge, and *-aceous.*] macerated; softened; nearly fluid.

pụ′lụ, *n.* [Haw.] a fine, silky fiber of one or more species of tree fern. It is exported and used for the stuffing of mattresses, etc. It is also employed in surgery as a styptic, acting mechanically by its great absorbent powers. The tree ferns yielding the fiber are of the genus *Cibotium,* also found in tropical Asia.

pul′vēr·ȧ·ble, *a.* [from L. *pulverare,* to cover with dust, and *-able.*] pulverizable.

pul·vēr·ā′ceous, *a.* in botany, having a dusty or powdered surface; pulverulent.

pul′vēr·āte, *v.t.*; pulverated, *pt., pp.*; pulverating, *ppr.* to pulverize. [Obs.]

pul·vē′rē·ous, *a.* powdery; pulverulent.

pul′vēr·in, pul′vēr·ine, *n.* ashes of barilla.

pul′vēr·ī·zȧ·ble, *a.* capable of being pulverized.

pul″vēr·i·zā′tion, *n.* a pulverizing or being pulverized.

pul′vēr·īze, *v.t.*; pulverized, *pt., pp.*; pulverizing, *ppr.* [Fr. *pulvériser.*]
 1. to crush, grind, etc. into a powder or dust.
 2. to break down completely; to demolish.

pul′vēr·īze, *v.i.* to be crushed, ground, etc. into powder or dust.

pul′vēr·īz·ēr, *n.* one who or that which pulverizes.

pul′vēr·ous, *a.* consisting of dust or powder; like powder.

pul·vēr′ū·lence, *n.* the state or quality of being pulverulent; dustiness.

pul·vēr′ū·lent, *a.* [L. *pulverulentus,* from *pulvis, pulveris,* dust.]
 1. consisting of or covered with a powder; powdery.
 2. crumbling to powder or dust.

pul′vil, *n.* a sweet-scented powder; a sachet bag: written also *pulville.* [Obs.]

pul′vil, *v.t.* to sprinkle with a perfumed powder; to apply pulvil to. [Obs.]

pul′vil·lăr, *a.* 1. pulvinar.
 2. pertaining to the pulvillus of an insect.

pul·vil′li·fọrm, *a.* resembling a pulvillus.

pul·vil′li·ō, pul·vil′lō, *n.* pulvil. [Obs.]

pul·vil′lus, *n.*; *pl.* **pul·vil′lī,** [L. *pulvillus,* a little cushion.] a pad or cushionlike part on the foot of an insect.

pul·vī′năr, *n.* [L. *pulvinus,* a cushion.]
 1. a pillow or cushion. [Obs.]
 2. a prominence on the back part of the optic thalamus.

pul·vī′năr, *a.* of, relating to, or like a pillow or pad; resembling a cushion or pillow.

Pul·vi·nā′ri·ȧ, *n.* 1. a genus of scale insects or bark lice of the family *Coccidæ,* many species of which are injurious to trees and small plants, as the grapevine. The females are large, circular, and flat, with a cushion-shaped waxy egg mass.
 2. [p—] any insect of this genus.

pul′vi·nāte, *a.* 1. cushion-shaped.
 2. in botany, shaped like a cushion; having a leafstalk with a swollen base.

pul′vi·nāt·ed, *a.* pulvinate.

pul·vin′i·fọrm, *a.* in botany, pulvinar.

pul·vin′ū·lus, *n.*; *pl.* **pul·vin′ū·lī,** same as *pulvillus.*

pul·vī′nus, *n.*; *pl.* **pul·vī′nī,** in botany, a cushion or enlargement, as on the stem below the leaf; also, the enlargement of the base of a petiole.

pul′vi·plụme, *n.* [L. *pulvis,* dust, and *pluma,* feather.] a powder-down feather.

pū′mȧ, *n.*; *pl.* **pū′mȧṣ** or **pū′mȧ,** [Peruv. *puma.*]
 1. a long-tailed, slender, tawny-brown animal of the cat family, found in North and South America; cougar; mountain lion.
 2. its fur.

pum′e·lō, *n.* in botany, same as *pomelo.*

pū′mi·çāte, *v.t.*; pumicated, *pt., pp.*; pumicating, *ppr.* [L. *pumicatus,* from *pumex, pumicis,* pumice.] to make smooth with pumice. [Rare.]

pum′ice, *n.* [L. *pumex,* pumice.] a spongy, light, porous, volcanic rock, used in solid or powdered form for removing stains, smoothing, and polishing: also *pumice stone.*

pum′ice, *v.t.*; pumiced (-ist), *pt., pp.*; pumicing, *ppr.* to clean, polish, etc. with pumice.

pum′iced (-ist), *a.* in farriery, affected with an abnormal spongy growth between the coffin bone and the wall of the hoof, producing laminitis.

pū·mi′ceous (-mish′us), *a.* pertaining to or having the nature of pumice.

pū·mic′i·fọrm, *a.* resembling or having the form of pumice. [Rare.]

pum′i·çōse, *a.* pumiceous.

pum′māce, *n.* same as *pomace.*

pum′mel, *n.* and *v.t.*; pummeled *or* pummelled, *pt., pp.*; pummeling *or* pummelling, *ppr.* same as *pommel*.

pump, *n.* [prob. from Fr. *pompe*, ornament.] a low-cut shoe without straps or ties.

pump, *n.* [ME. *pumpe, pompe*; MD. *pompe*; Sp. *bomba*; prob. of echoic origin.] any of various machines that force a liquid or gas into, or draw it out of, something, as by suction or pressure.

circulating pump; a pump used for sending a current of cold water through a surface condenser.

PUMP

pump, *v.t.*; pumped (pumpt), *pt., pp.*; pumping, *ppr.* 1. to raise or move (fluids) with a pump.
2. to remove water, etc. from.
3. to inflate (a rubber tire) by pumping air into it.
4. to force or draw out, move up and down, pour forth, eject, etc. in the manner of a pump; as, her eyes were *pumped* dry of tears.
5. to question closely and persistently.
6. to get (information) out of a person in this way.
7. to work with the same action as a pump handle or piston does.

pump, *v.i.* 1. to work a pump.
2. to raise or move water, etc. with a pump.
3. to move up and down like a pump handle or piston.

pump′āge, *n.* the aggregate of what is pumped; as, the daily *pumpage* of an oil well.

pump box, 1. the chamber in which the piston of a pump works.
2. the piston of a pump.

pump brāke, the arm or lever of a pump; a pump handle.

pump dāle, a long hose or wooden trough to convey water from a chain pump across a ship and through the side; any similar contrivance for carrying water from a pump.

pump′ẽr, *n.* 1. one who or that which pumps.
2. an oil well in which a pump must be used to raise the oil, in distinction from a gusher.

pump′ẽr·nick·el, *n.* [G., from *pumpern*, to pass wind, and *Nickel*, a goblin.] a coarse, dark bread made of unsifted rye.

pum′pet ball, formerly, a padded ball of soft leather used by printers for inking the types. [Obs.]

pump han′dle, the lever for working the piston rod of a pump up and down.

pum′pi·ŏn, *n.* a pumpkin. [Obs.]

pump′kin (*also commonly* puñ′kin), *n.* [OFr. *pompon*, from L. *pepo*, Gr. *pepōn*, a kind of melon, lit., something ripened by the sun.]

PUMPKIN (*Cucurbita pepo*)

1. a plant, *Cucurbita pepo*, or its fruit; the leaves are large, rough, and heart-shaped, the flowers large, yellow, and solitary, while the fruit is gourdlike, dull orange-yellow, and melon-shaped with depressed ends, having an edible fleshy layer beneath the rind. It is widely cultivated in the tropics, and also in the United States. It is much used as food, prepared in a variety of ways, as in pumpkin pie, and also fed to stock.
2. the vine on which it grows.

pump′kin head (hed), a thick-headed lout; a blockhead.

pump′kin·seed, *n.* 1. the seed of the pumpkin.
2. any of a number of related small freshwater fishes of North America, greenish-olive above and orange-yellow below; the sunfish.
3. a boat with a flat bottom, for use in shallow water, and either rowed or sailed.

pump rod, the rod by which the engine is connected with the piston of a pump; any piston rod in a pump.

pump spēar, the rod suspended from the end of the pump handle and attached at its lower end to the bucket.

pump rōom, 1. a room in connection with a mineral spring, in which the waters are drunk.
2. the room or place, as in a waterworks pumping station, where the pumping apparatus is placed.

pump stock, the solid part or body of a pump.

pump well, a compartment extending from a ship's bottom to the lower or the upper deck, as the case may be, to contain the pump stocks.

pun, *n.* [17th-c. clipped form; perh. from It. *puntiglio*, fine point, hence, verbal quibble.] the humorous use of a word, or of words which are formed or sounded alike but have different meanings, in such a way as to play on two or more of the possible applications; a play on words.

pun, *v.i.*; punned, *pt., pp.*; punning, *ppr.* to make a pun or puns.

pun, *v.t.* to bring to a specified state by punning.

pū′nȧ, *n.* [Peruv.] a cold, dry, elevated tableland, as in the Peruvian Andes.

punch, *n.* [a shortened form of old *punchon*, a dagger, from OFr. *poinson*, a bodkin, from L. *punctio*, a puncturing, from *pungere*, to prick.]
1. a tool driven or pressed against a surface that is to be pierced, shaped, or stamped, or a nail, bolt, etc. that is to be worked in or out.
2. a tool for driving nailheads below the surface.
3. a hardened piece of steel, with the design projecting from its face, used to make impressions in the faces of dies, etc., as in type founding.
4. an extension piece on the end of a pile, when the latter is beyond the stroke of the monkey.
5. studding used to support a roof. [Brit.]

punch, *v.t.*; punched (puncht), *pt., pp.*; punching, *ppr.* to pierce, shape, stamp, etc. with a punch.

Syn.—perforate, pierce, puncture, bore.

punch, *n.* [Hind. *pāc*, five, from its consisting originally of five ingredients.] a sweetened drink flavored with fruit juices, spices, etc., often mixed with wine or liquor.

Punch, *n.* [from It. *pulcinello*, a clown.] the buffoon or harlequin of a puppet show "Punch and Judy," a hooknosed, humpbacked figure.

pleased as Punch; greatly pleased or gratified.

punch, *n.* 1. a well-set horse, with a short back, thin shoulders, broad neck, and well covered with flesh. [Brit. Dial.]
2. a short, fat fellow. [Brit. Dial.]

punch, *v.t.* [ME. *punchen*.]
1. to prod or poke with a stick.
2. to herd (cattle) by or as by prodding.
3. to strike with the fist.
4. to pierce or perforate with a punch.
5. to make (a hole) with a punch.
6. to cut out (a piece) by punching.

punch, *n.* 1. a blow or thrust with or as with the fist.
2. force, vigor; as, the scene opened with a *punch*. [Colloq.]

to pull one's punches; (a) in boxing, to deliver blows that are intentionally ineffective; (b) to attack, criticize, etc. in an intentionally ineffective manner. [Slang.]

Punch-and-Jū′dy shōw, a puppet show in which the quarrelsome Punch constantly fights with his wife, Judy.

pun·chay′et, *n.* [Hind.] in India, an elective village council.

punch′bōard, *n.* a board or card with holes containing concealed slips or disks to be punched out, used in games of chance, raffles, etc.: the slips bear numbers, names, prize designations, or the like.

punch bōwl, a bowl in which punch is made or served.

punch ċard, a card with holes or notches positioned in it for interpretation by an automatic data-processing machine or for quick mechanical selection.

punch′-drunk, *a.* 1. having or showing a condition resulting from numerous blows on the head and marked by an unsteady gait, slow muscular movements, hesitant speech, mental confusion, etc.
2. acting in a hazy, bewildered manner; thoroughly dazed. [Colloq.]

pun′cheŏn, *n.* [Fr. *poinçon*, a bodkin, a punch, from L. *punctio, punctionis*, from *punctus*, pp. of *pungere*, to prick, to puncture.]
1. a short, upright wooden post used in framework.
2. a heavy, broad piece of roughly dressed timber with one side hewed flat.
3. any of various devices for punching, perforating, or stamping; especially, a figured die used by goldsmiths, etc.

pun′cheŏn, *n.* [Late ME. *pwncion*; OFr. *ponçon, poinchon*; identical in form with *puncheon* (punch, die, etc.).]
1. a large cask of varying capacity (72–120 gallons), for beer, wine, etc.
2. as much as such a cask will hold.

punch′ẽr, *n.* one who or that which punches.

pun·chi·nel′lō, *n.*; *pl.* **pun·chi·nel′lōs, pun·chi·nel′lōeṣ,** 1. a prototype of Punch.
2. a buffoon; a clown.

punch′i·ness, *n.* the state or condition of being punchy.

punch′ing bag, a stuffed or inflated leather bag hung up so that it can be punched as an exercise in boxing.

punch′ing mȧ·chïne′, a punch press.

punch′ing press, a punch press.

punch lā′dle, a small ladle used for serving punch from a bowl into a glass.

punch plī′ẽrṣ, an instrument or tool used by shoemakers to perforate leather, by railroad conductors to mark tickets to prevent their being used a second time, and the like.

punch press, a machine for impressing or cutting a design on or of metal, for shaping metal or stamping a die; a press machine for working with metal.

punch′y, *a.* short and thick; fat; paunchy. [Colloq.]

punc′tāte, *a.* [L. *punctus*.]
1. pointed.
2. in botany and zoology, having dots scattered over the surface; dotted.

punc′tāt·ed, *a.* same as *punctate*.

punc·tā′tion, *n.* 1. the condition of being punctate.
2. a dot.
3. a marking with many dots.
4. a statement of points to be negotiated.

punc·tā′tŏr, *n.* one who marks with dots; specifically, applied to the Masorites, who invented the Hebrew vowel points.

punc·tic′ū·lāte, *a.* marked by dots. [Rare.]

punc′tid, *n.* one of the *Punctidæ*.

Punc′ti·dae, *n.pl.* [*punctum* and *-idæ*.] a family of pulmonate gastropods having a heliciform shell, laminate jaw, and narrow reflexed teeth: it is typified by the genus *Punctum*.

punc′ti·fọrm, *a.* [L. *punctum*, point, and *-form*.] having the form of a point.

punc·til′i·ō (*or* -yō), *n.*; *pl.* **punc·til′i·ōṣ,** [Sp. *puntillo*; It. *puntiglio*; from L. *punctum*, a point.]
1. a nice point of conduct, manners, ceremony, or honor.
2. observance of petty formalities.

punc·til′i·ous (*or* -yus), *a.* 1. careful in the observance of the nice points of behavior, ceremony, etc.
2. very exact; scrupulous.

punc·til′i·ous·ly, *adv.* in a punctilious manner.

punc·til′i·ous·ness, *n.* the quality or state of being punctilious; exactness in the observance of forms or rules.

punc′tion, *n.* [L. *punctio*.] a puncture; a pricking. [Obs.]

punc′tist, *n.* a punctator.

punc′tō, *n.* punto. [Obs.]

punc′tū·ȧl, *a.* [Fr. *ponctuel*; It. *puntuale*; Sp. *puntual*, from L. *punctum*, a point.]
1. of or like a point; minute.
2. punctilious.
3. carefully observant of an appointed time; on time; prompt.

Syn.—prompt, timely, precise, exact.

punc·tū·ȧl·ist, *n.* one who is very exact in observing forms and ceremonies. [Obs.]

punc·tū·al′i·ty, *n.* 1. the quality or condition of being punctual.
2. *pl.* **punc·tū·al′i·tieṣ,** an instance of this.

punc′tū·ȧl·ly, *adv.* nicely; exactly; with scrupulous regard to time, appointments, promises, or rules.

punc′tū·ȧl·ness, *n.* exactness; punctuality.

punc′tū·āte, *v.t.*; punctuated, *pt., pp.*; punctuating, *ppr.* [from L. *punctum*, a point.]
1. to insert punctuation marks in (written or printed matter) in order to clarify the meaning.
2. to interrupt from time to time.
3. to emphasize.

punc′tū·āte, *v.i.* to use punctuation marks.

punc·tū·ā′tion, *n.* 1. the act, practice, or system of using certain standardized marks

and signs in writing and printing, as to separate sentences, independent clauses, parenthetical phrases, etc., in order to make the meaning more easily understood: the marks of punctuation, originally conventionalized from normal speech patterns of pause, pitch, and stress, no longer correspond with these in detail.
2. punctuation marks.

punc·tū·ā'tion märk, any of the marks and signs used in punctuation, chief among which are the period (.), the comma (,), the colon (:), the semicolon (;), the interrogation mark (?), the exclamation mark (!), the apostrophe ('), quotation marks (" "), (' '), parentheses (( )), the dash (—), the hyphen (-), and brackets ([ ]).

punc'tū·ā·tive, *a.* 1. pertaining to punctuation.
2. serving to punctuate.

punc'tū·ā·tŏr, *n.* one who punctuates.

punc'tū·ist, *n.* a punctator.

punc'tū·lȧ, *n.* plural of *punctulum.*

punc'tū·lāte, *a.* marked with small spots; minutely punctate.

punc'tū·lāt·ed, *a.* same as *punctulate.*

punc·tū·lā'tion, *n.* the state of being punctulate; puncturation.

punc'tūle, *n.* [L. *punctum,* a point.] a minute puncture, dot, or pit.

punc'tū·lum, *n.;* *pl.* **punc'tū·lȧ,** same as *punctule.*

punc'tum, *n.;* *pl.* **punc'tȧ,** [L., a point.]
1. a point; in anatomy, a dot, spot, or pit.
2. [P-] a genus of minute gastropods, typical of the family *Punctidæ.*
punctum coecum; same as *blind spot.*
punctum saliens; a prominent point; in embryology, the first pulsating point or heart.
punctum vegetationis; the terminal cell of a leaf bud; the vegetating point.

punc'tūr·ȧ·ble, *a.* that can be punctured.

punc·tūr·ā'tion, *n.* 1. the state of being punctured; a collection or set of punctures.
2. in surgery, same as *acupuncture.*

punc'tūre, *n.* [LL. *punctura,* a pricking, from L. *pungere,* to pierce.].
1. the act of perforating or pricking with a pointed instrument.
2. a small wound, as by the insertion of a needle in the skin; a hole, as in an automobile tire.
3. in zoology, a pit or depression; a punctum.
exploratory puncture; the piercing of a cavity or tumor to secure contents for examination.
lumbar puncture; the tapping of the spinal membranes in the lumbar regions to secure cerebrospinal fluid for examination.

punc'tūre, *v.t.;* punctured, *pt., pp.;* puncturing, *ppr.* 1. to perforate or pierce with a sharp point.
2. to reduce or put an end to, as if by a puncture; as, his pride was *punctured.*

punc'tūre, *v.i.* to make punctures or to be punctured.

punc'tūred, *a.* pierced; incised; having the surface pitted or indented.

punc'tūre·less, *a.* having a smooth surface without punctures.

punc'tus, *n.* [L.] 1. in medieval music, a note.
2. a dot, pit, or point.

pund, *n.* a pound. [Scot.]

pun'dit, *n.* [Sans. *pandita,* a learned man, from *pand,* to heap up or collect.]
1. in India, a learned Brahman; one learned in the Sanskrit language, and in Hindu philosophy, law, and religion.
2. a person of great learning; an authority: often used humorously.

pun·dō·nor', *n.* [Sp., contraction of *punto de honor.*] a point of honor.

pū·nēse', *n.* same as *punice.*

pung, *n.* [from earlier *tom pung,* altered from *toboggan* or its Am. Ind. source.] a rude sort of sleigh or oblong box, made of boards and placed on runners. [Dial.]

puñ'gär, *n.* [Gr. *pagouros.*] a crab. [Brit. Dial.]

pun'gence, *n.* same as *pungency.*

pun'gen·cy, *n.* the quality or condition of being pungent; acridness; keenness; sharpness; causticity; raciness; acrimoniousness.

pun'gent, *a.* [L. *pungens,* ppr. of *pungere,* to prick, to puncture.]
1. producing a sharp sensation of taste and smell; acrid.
2. sharp and piercing; poignant; painful.
3. sharply penetrating; expressive; biting; as, *pungent* language.
4. keenly clever; stimulating.
5. in botany, ending in a hard, sharp point, as some leaves.
Syn.—biting, acute, penetrating, severe, stinging.

pun'gent·ly, *adv.* in a pungent, sharp, or biting manner; with pungency.

puñ'gi, *n.* [E. Ind.] a Hindu nose flute made of leather, gourd, etc., used by snake charmers and jugglers.

puñ'gled (-gld), *a.* shriveled; shrunk: applied specifically to grain whose juices have been extracted by the wheat midge, *Thrips cerealium.*

pung'y, *n.;* *pl.* **pung'ies,** a small sloop or shallop or a large boat with sails: mainly used in the Chesapeake Bay by oyster fishermen.

Pū'nic, *a.* [L. *Punicus,* from *Puni* or *Pæni,* the Carthaginians.]
1. of ancient Carthage or its people.
2. like or characteristic of the Carthaginians, regarded by the Romans as faithless and treacherous.
Punic Wars; the three wars between the Romans and the Carthaginians: the first (264–241 B. C.), for the possession of Sicily, ended by the Carthaginians having to withdraw from the island; the second (218–201 B. C.), in which Hannibal gained his great victories in Italy, was a death struggle between the two rival powers, which ended with a decisive victory to the Romans; the third (149–146 B. C.) resulted in the destruction of Carthage.

Pū'nic, *n.* the West Semitic language of ancient Carthage, closely related to Phoenician: it consists of Old Punic, spoken from about the fifth century B.C. to 146 B.C., and New Punic, spoken in parts of the Western Roman Empire from 146 B.C. until about 550 A.D.

Pū'ni·cȧ, *n.* [L. *Punica* (*arbor*), a pomegranate tree, so called because first found at Carthage.] a genus of polypetalous, showy, loosestrife plants, including *Punica granatum,* the pomegranate.

pū·nice', *n.* [Fr. *punaise.*] the bedbug.

pū'ni·cin, *n.* [L. *punica* and *-in.*] a red coloring matter obtained from the bark of the pomegranate, *Punica granatum.*

pū'ni·ness, *n.* [from *puny.*] a puny quality or condition.

pun'ish, *v.t.;* punished (-isht), *pt., pp.;* punishing, *ppr.* [Fr. *punir, punissant,* from L. *punire,* to punish, from *pœna,* punishment, penalty.
1. to cause (a person) to undergo pain, loss, or suffering for a crime or wrongdoing.
2. to impose a penalty on a criminal or wrongdoer for (an offense).
3. to treat in a harsh or greedy manner; to deplete in quantity, as food or drink. [Colloq.]

pun'ish, *v.i.* to deal out punishment.
Syn.—chastise, correct, discipline, whip.

pun''ish·ȧ·bil'i·ty, *n.* the quality or condition of being punishable.

pun'ish·ȧ·ble, *a.* 1. deserving of punishment.
2. liable to punishment; capable of being punished by law or right: applied to persons or offenses: as, a man is *punishable* for robbery or for trespass; a crime is *punishable* by law.

pun'ish·ȧ·ble·ness, *n.* the quality of deserving or being liable to punishment.

pun'ish·ēr, *n.* one who punishes.

pun'ish·ment, *n.* 1. a punishing or being punished.
2. a penalty imposed on an offender for a crime or wrongdoing.
3. rough handling. [Colloq.]

pū·ni'tion (-nish'un), *n.* [Fr., from L. *punitio,* from *punire.*] punishment. [Rare.]

pū'ni·tive, *a.* 1. inflicting punishment.
2. concerned with or directed toward punishment.

pū'ni·tō·ry, *a.* punitive.

Pun·jä'bi, *n.* [Per. *panj,* five, and *ab,* water.] a native or inhabitant of the Punjab, a region of northwestern India; also, the dialect of this district: also spelled *Panjabi.*

puñk, *n.* [Am. Ind.]
1. decayed wood or dried fungus used for tinder.
2. any substance that smolders when ignited, usually in the form of a stick used to light fireworks, etc.

puñk, *n.* [etym. uncertain.]
1. a prostitute. [Obs.]
2. (a) a catamite; (b) a male homosexual; (c) a young gangster or hoodlum; (d) any person, especially a youngster, regarded as inexperienced, insignificant, etc. [Slang].

puñk, *a.* poor or bad in quality. [Slang.]

puñ'kȧh, puñ'kȧ, *n.* [Hind. *pankha,* a fan.] in India, a large fan made from the palmyra leaf, or a large, swinging fan consisting of canvas stretched over a rectangular frame and hung from the ceiling.

puñk'ie, *n.* [D. *punki,* from Am. Ind.] a tiny fly with piercing and sucking mouth parts, found in some mountain regions of the United States.

puñ'kin, *n.* pumpkin. [Slang.]

puñk'ling, *n.* a young prostitute. [Obs.]

puñk rock, [from *punk, n.* 2 (c).] a form of simple rock music, often with coarse lyrics, typically performed in a hostile, deliberately offensive way.

puñ'ky, *n.;* *pl.* **puñ'kies,** a punkie.

pun'nēr, *n.* a punster.

pun'net, *n.* a small, shallow basket, for displaying fruit or flowers.

pun'stēr, *n.* one who puns habitually or continually.

punt, *v.i.;* punted, *pt., pp.;* punting, *ppr.* [Fr. *punter;* It. *puntare,* from L. *punctum,* a point.]
1. in certain card games, to bet against the dealer or banker.
2. to gamble.

punt, *n.* [AS. *punt,* from L. *ponto,* a punt, a pontoon, from *pons, pontis,* a bridge.] a square-built, flat-bottomed boat, without masts, usually propelled by a long pole.

punt, *v.t.;* punted, *pt., pp.;* punting, *ppr.* 1. to propel (a punt) by pushing with a pole against the bottom of a shallow lake or stream.
2. to convey in a punt.

punt, *v.i.,* to go in a punt.

punt, *n.* [prob. from dial. *bunt,* to strike, kick.] in football, a type of kick in which the ball is dropped from the hands and then kicked before it strikes the ground.

punt, *v.t.* and *v.i.* to kick (a football) in a punt.

punt'ēr, *n.* one who punts, or gambles.

pun'til, pun'tel, *n.* same as *pontil.*

pun'tō, *n.* [It., from L. *punctum,* a point.]
1. a pontil.
2. a thrust in fencing.

pun'ty, *n.;* *pl.* **pun'ties,** [Fr. *pontil;* It. *pontello,* dim. of *punto,* a point.] a metal rod on which the molten glass is handled in glassmaking; a pontil.

pū'ny, *a.;* *comp.* punier; *superl.* puniest, [from Fr. *puiné,* younger.]
1. of inferior size, strength, or importance; weak; slight.
2. puisne. [Obs.]

pū'ny, *n.;* *pl.* **pū'nies,** a young, inexperienced person; a novice. [Obs.]

pup, *n.* [contr. of *puppy.*] 1. a young dog.
2. a young seal.

pup, *v.i.;* pupped (pupt), *pt., pp.;* pupping, *ppr.* to give birth to pups.

pū'pȧ, *n.;* *pl.* **pū'pae, pū'pȧs,** [L. *pupa,* a girl, a doll, a puppet.]
1. an insect in the stage of development between the larval and adult forms.
2. [P-] a former genus of land snails, so called from the resemblance of the shell to the pupa or chrysalis of an insect.

pū'pȧl, *a.* of or relating to a pupa.

pū·pā'ri·um, *n.* the outer shell covering a coarctate pupa.

pū'pāte, *v.i.;* pupated, *pt., pp.;* pupating, *ppr.* to become a pupa.

pū·pā'tion, *n.* 1. the act or condition of becoming a pupa.
2. the stage in insects between the larval and adult forms.

pup'fish, *n.;* *pl.* **pup'fish, pup'fish·es,** any of several small, minnowlike, nearly extinct fishes of the genus *Cyprinodon,* found in desert springs and pools of western North America.

pū'pi·form, *a.* shaped like a pupa.

pū·pig'ēr·ous, *a.* forming a puparium; coarctate, as a pupa.

pū'pil, *n.* [L. *pupilla,* dim. of *pupa,* a girl.]
1. the contractile circular opening, apparently black, in the center of the iris of the eye.
2. in zoology, the dark central spot of an ocellus.

pū'pil, *n.* [Fr. *pupille;* L. *pupillus,* dim. of *pupus,* a boy.]
1. a person, especially a young person, who is being taught under the supervision of a teacher or tutor, as in school.
2. in civil law, a minor under the care of a guardian.
Syn.—scholar, learner, student, tyro, novice, ward.

pū′pil·ăġe, pū′pil·lăġe, *n.* the state or period of being a pupil.

pū′pil·āte, pū′pil·lāte, *a.* having a spot, resembling the pupil of the eye, within another spot, as the feathers of some birds.

pū′piled, pū′pilled, *a.* pupilate.

pū′pil·īze, pū′pil·līze, *v.i.*; pupilized, *pt., pp.*; pupilizing, *ppr.* to teach; to have the care of pupils.

pū·pil·lar′i·ty, pū·pil·ar′i·ty, *n.* [Fr. *pupillarité.*] in Scots law, the interval from birth to puberty.

pū′pil·lăr·ry, *a.* of the pupil of the eye.

pū′pil·lăr·y, *a.* [Fr. *pupillaire*; L. *pupillaris.*] of a person who is a pupil.

pū·pil·lom′e·tĕr, *n.* an instrument for measuring the pupil of the eye.

Pū·pip′ȧ·rȧ, *n.pl.* [LL. *pupa*, pupa, and L. *parere*, to bear.] a division of dipterous insects whose eggs are hatched in the matrix of the mother: the young are not born until they are ready to become pupae.

pū·pip′ȧ·rous, *a.* pertaining to the *Pupipara*; producing the young in the pupal state, as the horse tick.

Pū·piv′ō·rȧ, *n.pl.* [LL. *pupa*, pupa, and L. *vorare*, to devour.] a division of hymenopterous insects, comprising those of which the larvae live parasitically in the interior of the larvae and pupae of other insects, as the *Ichneumonidæ.*

pū·piv′ō·rous, *a.* feeding on the pupae of insects.

pū′poid, *a.* resembling a pupa; pupiform.

pup′pet, *n.* [Fr. *poupée*; L. *pupa*, a puppet.]

1. a small figure that is a likeness of the human form; a doll.
2. such a figure moved by attached strings or wires, or by the hands, in a puppet show.
3. a person whose actions, ideas, etc. are controlled by another.

pup·pet·eer′, *n.* a person who operates, designs, or costumes puppets, or produces puppet shows.

pup′pet·ish, *a.* like a puppet.

pup′pet·mȧs″tĕr, *n.* one who manages or performs in a puppet show.

pup·pet·o͞on, *n.* [*puppet* and *-oon* as in *cartoon.*] a motion picture made by arranging jointed puppets into the successive stages of some motion and photographing each stage separately.

pup′pet plāy, same as *puppet show.*

pup′pet plāy′ĕr, one who works puppets in a puppet show.

pup′pet·ry, *n.* 1. puppets or their actions; mummery.
2. the art of producing puppet shows.

pup′pet shōw, a play or performance with puppets.

pup′pet valve, same as *poppet*, sense 2.

Pup′pis, *n.* [L., stern of a ship.] in astronomy, a subdivision of the constellation Argo, near Canis Major.

pup′py, *n.*; *pl.* **pup′pieṣ,** [from Fr. *poupée*, a doll, a puppet; L. *pupa*, a puppet.]

1. a young dog.
2. the young of the shark and some other animals.
3. a conceited, affected, or impertinent young man.

pup′py, *v.i.*; puppied, *pt., pp.*; puppying, *ppr.* to bring forth puppies, or whelps; to pup.

pup′py·doġ, *n.* a puppy.

pup′py·fish, *n.* same as *angelfish.*

pup′py·hood, *n.* the period or condition of being a puppy.

pup′py·ish, *a.* of or like a puppy.

pup′py·iṣm, *n.* affectation, impertinence, or conceit.

pup′py lŏve, calf love.

pup tent, a shelter tent.

pũr, *n., v.i.* and *v.t.*; purred, *pt., pp.*; purring, *ppr.* purr.

pụ·rä′nȧ, *n.* [Sans. *purā*, past, former.] in Hinduism, one of a class of sacred poetical writings in the Sanskrit tongue, which treat chiefly of the creation, destruction, and renovation of worlds, the genealogy and deeds of gods, heroes, and princes, the reigns of the Manus, etc.

pụ·rän′iç, *a.* pertaining to the puranas.

Pũr′beck bedṣ, the uppermost members of the Oölite proper, or, according to some writers, the basis of the Wealden formation, deriving their name from the peninsula of Purbeck on the coast of Dorsetshire, England, where they are typically displayed. They consist of argillaceous and calcareous shales and fresh-water limestones and marbles. They are noted for their layers of fossil vegetable earth (dirt beds) enclosing roots, trunks, and branches of cycads and conifers.

Pũr′beck mär′ble, an impure, fresh-water, brown limestone obtained from the Purbeck beds. Also called *Purbeck stone.*

pũr′blīnd, *a.* [ME. *pur*, quite, and *blind*, blind.]

1. partly blind.
2. slow in perceiving or understanding.
3. totally blind. [Archaic.]

pũr′blīnd·ly, *adv.* in a purblind manner.

pũr′blīnd·ness, *n.* the state or quality of being purblind.

pũr′chăs·ȧ·ble, *a.* 1. that can be purchased.
2. open to bribery.

pũr′chăse, *v.t.*; purchased (-chăst), *pt., pp.*; purchasing, *ppr.* [Fr. *pourchasser*, to seek, to pursue; *pour*, for, and *chasser*, to chase.]

1. to obtain, acquire, or gain in any way or by any means. [Archaic.]
2. in law, to acquire (land, buildings, etc.) by means other than inheritance or descent.
3. to obtain or acquire by payment of money or its equivalent; to buy for a price; as, to *purchase* a hat.
4. to obtain or gain by an expenditure of labor, danger, or other sacrifice.

It was necessary to *purchase* concession by concession. —Macaulay.

5. to redeem; to expiate; to pay for. [Obs.]
6. to raise or move by applying mechanical power.

pũr′chăse, *v.i.* 1. to put forth efforts to obtain anything; to strive. [Obs.]
2. to buy.
3. to grow wealthy. [Obs.]

pũr′chăse, *n.* 1. the acquisition of anything by any means; possession; acquirement. [Obs.]

Prize and *purchase* of his lustful eye. —Shak.

2. anything obtained by buying.
3. the act of buying.
4. income; return; as, worth a decade's *purchase.*
5. a fast hold applied to move something mechanically or to keep from slipping.
6. any apparatus with which such a hold is applied.
7. in law, the acquisition of land, buildings, etc. by means other than inheritance or descent.
8. an attempt to acquire; an endeavor. [Obs.]
9. robbery or that which is gained by robbery; pillage; plunder. [Obs.]

worth or *at* (so many) *years' purchase*; worth or at a sum that a property would bring in, in the specified time. Thus, to buy an estate *at twenty years' purchase* is to buy it for a sum equivalent to the total return from it for twenty years.

pũr′chăse mŏn′ey, the money paid, or contracted to be paid, for anything bought.

pũr′chăs·ĕr, *n.* 1. one who obtains or acquires property by paying an equivalent in money or other exchange value.
2. in law, one who acquires or obtains by conquest, deed, or gift, or in any manner other than by descent or inheritance.

pũr′chăs·ing pow′ĕr, the value of a specified monetary unit in terms of the amount of commodities or services that can be bought with it.

pũr′dȧh, *n.* [Hind. and Per. *pardah*, a veil.]

1. in India, a curtain used to screen off the part of the house where women are secluded.
2. the Hindu system of secluding women.

pūre, *a.*; *comp.* purer; *superl.* purest, [Fr. *pur*, from L. *purus*, pure.]

1. free from anything that adulterates, taints, impairs, etc.; unmixed; clear; as, *pure* water; *pure* clay; *pure* air; *pure* gold.
2. simple; mere.
3. utter; absolute; sheer.
4. free from defects; perfect; faultless.
5. free from sin or guilt; blameless.
6. virgin or chaste.
7. of unmixed stock; pure-blooded.
8. restricted to the abstract or theoretical aspects; as, *pure* physics: contrasted with *applied.*
9. in the Bible, ceremonially undefiled.
10. in biology, conforming accurately to the parental type with respect to certain characters; homozygous.
11. in Kantian philosophy, free from empiricism.
12. in phonetics, having an unchanging sound made by keeping the oral speech organs in a fixed position for the duration of the sound.

Syn.—clear, unmixed, simple, genuine, sheer, mere, absolute, unadulterated, uncorrupted, unsullied, unblemished, chaste, real, clean, spotless, immaculate, undefiled, unspotted, guileless, innocent, guiltless.

pūre, *v.t.* to purify; to cleanse. [Obs.]

pūre, *n.* that which is pure (with *the*). [Poet.]

pūre′bred′, *a.* belonging to a breed with recognized characteristics maintained through generations of unmixed descent.

pūre′bred′, *n.* a purebred plant or animal.

pūre çul′tūre, see under *culture.*

pūred, *a.* purified. [Obs.]

pu·rée′ (pū-rā′ *or* pūr′ā), *n.* [Fr., from OFr. *purer*, to strain; L. *purare*, to purify, from *purus*, pure.]

1. food prepared by straining the boiled pulp through a sieve.
2. a thick soup.

pu·rée′, *v.t.* to prepare a purée from.

pūre līne, in genetics, a breed or strain of animals or plants that maintains a high degree of consistency in certain characteristics as a result of continued inbreeding for generations.

pūre′ly, *adv.* 1. in a pure manner; unmixed with anything else.
2. perfectly; thoroughly. [Obs.]
3. merely.
4. innocently.
5. completely; totally; as, the meeting was *purely* accidental.

pūre′ness, *n.* the condition or quality of being pure; purity.

pũr′file, *n.* purfle. [Obs.]

pũr′fle, *v.t.*; purfled (-fld), *pt., pp.*; purfling, *ppr.* [ME. *purfilen*; OFr. *pourfiler*; *pour*, L. *pro*, for, before, and *fil*, L. *filum*, a thread.]

1. to decorate the border of.
2. to border or ornament with metallic thread, beads, lace, etc.

purfled work; in Gothic architecture, ornamental work resembling purfle. [Archaic.]

pũr′fle, *n.* an ornamental border or trimming.

pũr′fling, *n.* fancy ornamentation of a border; specifically, inlaid bordering of a musical instrument, as a violin.

pũr′gȧ, *n.* a Siberian blizzard in the region of the lower Yenisei River.

pũr′gȧ·ment, *n.* [L. *purgamentum*, offscourings.] an excretion. [Obs.]

pũr·gā′tion, *n.* [ME. *purgacioun*; OFr. *purgacion*; L. *purgatio* (*-onis*), a purging.]

1. a purging.
2. in old law, the act of clearing oneself of an alleged crime or suspicion of guilt. Canonical purgation required the accused party to make oath to his own innocence, and then the twelve clerks or compurgators swore that they believed he spoke the truth, after which other witnesses were examined upon oath on behalf of the prisoner only. Vulgar purgation was performed by the ordeal of fire or water or by combat.

pũr′gȧ·tive, *a.* [ME. *purgatyf*; LL. *purgativus*, from L. *purgare*, to cleanse.]

1. purging.
2. causing bowel movement.

pũr′gȧ·tive, *n.* 1. a substance that purges.
2. a cathartic.

pũr′gȧ·tive·ly, *adv.* in a purgative manner.

pũr·gȧ·tō′ri·ăl, *a.* [from L. *purgatorius*, and *-al.*]

1. serving to atone for sins; expiatory.
2. of or like purgatory.

pũr·gȧ·tō′ri·ăn, *a.* same as *purgatorial.*

pũr·gȧ·tō′ri·ăn, *n.* a believer in the doctrine of purgatory.

pũr′gȧ·tō·ry, *n.*; *pl.* **pũr′gȧ·tō·ries,** [ME. *purgatorie*, from OFr. and ML.; OFr. *purgatoire*; ML. *purgatorium*, from LL. *purgatorius*, cleansing, from L. *purgare*, to cleanse.]

1. in Roman Catholic theology, a state or place in which those who have died in the grace of God expiate their sins by suffering.
2. any state or place of temporary punishment, expiation, or remorse.

pũr′gȧ·tō·ry, *a.* same as *purgative.*

pũrġe, *v.t.*; purged, *pt., pp.*; purging, *ppr.* [ME. *purgen*; OFr. *purgier*; L. *purgare*, to cleanse, from *purus*, clean, and *agere*, to do, to act.]

1. to cleanse or purify by separating and carrying off whatever is impure, foreign, or superfluous; as, to *purge* a city of accumulated filth.

2. to cleanse of guilt, sin, or ceremonial defilement.

3. to clear or rid (a nation, political party, etc.) of individuals held to be disloyal or undesirable.

4. in law, to free from a charge or imputation of guilt.

5. in medicine, (a) to empty (the bowels); (b) to cause (a person) to empty his bowels.

6. to clarify; to defecate, as liquors.

7. to remove by cleansing: followed by *out*, *away*, or *off*; as, *purge away* our sins.

pũrġe, *v.i.* 1. to become pure, clean, or clear.

2. to have or effect a thorough bowel movement.

pũrġe, *n.* 1. a purging.

2. that which purges; especially, a purgative, or cathartic.

3. the process of ridding a nation, political party, etc. of individuals held to be disloyal or undesirable.

pũrġ'ẽr, *n.* one who or that which purges.

pũr'ġẽr·y, *n.*; *pl.* **pũr'ġẽr·ieṣ,** the portion of a sugarhouse where the sugar from the coolers is placed in hogsheads or in cones, and allowed to drain off its molasses.

pũr'ġing, *n.* 1. the act of cleansing; purgation.

2. diarrhea or dysentery; looseness of the bowels.

3. that which is evacuated or excreted; a deposit.

pũr'ġing ag'ȧ·riç, a fungus, *Polyporus officinalis*, used as a cathartic.

pũr'ġing flax, in botany, the dwarf flax, *Linum catharticum*, growing wild in Europe, from which a purgative is made.

pũr'ġing nut, in botany, a small tree of the genus *Jatropha*, belonging to the spurge family.

pū″ri·fi·çā'tion, *n.* [Fr., from L. *purificatio* (*-onis*), a purifying.]

1. the act of purifying; the act or operation of separating and removing from anything that which is polluted or foreign to it; as, the *purification* of liquors or of metals.

2. the act or operation of cleansing ceremonially by removing any pollution or defilement.

3. a cleansing from guilt or the pollution of sin; the extinction of sinful desires, appetites, and inclinations.

Purification of St. Mary the Virgin; same as *Candlemas*.

pū″ri·fi·çā'tion flow'ẽr, the snowdrop, *Galanthus nivalis*.

pū'ri·fi·çā″tive, *a.* same as *purificatory*.

pū'ri·fi·çā·tŏr, *n.* 1. one who or that which purifies.

2. in the Roman Catholic and Anglican churches, a cloth for wiping the chalice and paten: also called *mundatory*.

pū·rif'i·çȧ·tō″ry, *a.* having a purifying effect.

pū·rif'i·çȧ·tō″ry, *n.* a purificator. [Rare.]

pū'ri·fī·ẽr, *n.* one who or that which purifies.

pū'ri·fọrm, *a.* [L. *pus*, *puris*, pus, and *form*.] like pus; in the form of pus.

pū'ri·fȳ, *v.t.*; purified, *pt.*, *pp.*; purifying, *ppr.* [ME. *purifien*; OFr. *purifier*; L. *purificare*; *purus*, pure, and *facere*, to make.]

1. to rid of impurities or polluting matter; as, to *purify* liquors or metals; to *purify* the air.

2. to free from guilt, sin, or ceremonial uncleanness.

3. to free from foreign or corrupting elements.

4. to purge (*of* or *from*).

Syn.—cleanse, refine, clarify, chasten, wash.

pū'ri·fȳ, *v.i.* to be purified.

Pū'rim, *n.pl.* [*construed as sing.*], [Heb. *pūrim*, lit., lots.] a Jewish holiday, the Feast of Lots, commemorating the deliverance of the Jews by Esther from a general massacre inspired by Haman: Est. ix. 21.

pū'rīne, pũr'in, *n.* [G. *purin*, from L. *purus*, pure, and Mod. L. *uricum*, uric acid.]

1. a colorless, crystalline compound, $C_5H_4N_4$, the parent substance of which many of the uric-acid group of compounds are derivatives.

2. any of several basic substances produced by the decomposition of nucleoproteins.

pū·rī'rī, *n.* [Maori.] in botany, *Vitex littoralis*, a tree of New Zealand, whose brown wood is very hard and durable.

pūr'iṣm, *n.* [Fr. *purisme*, from *pur*; L. *purus*, pure.]

1. strict observance of or insistence upon precise usage or purity in language, style, etc.

2. an instance of this.

pūr'ist, *n.* [Fr. *puriste*.]

1. one who practices or advocates purism.

2. one who maintained that the New Testament was written in pure Greek. [Rare.]

pū·ris'tiç, pū·ris'ti·çăl, *a.* relating to purism or to purists.

Pū'ri·tăn, *n.* [from L. *puritas*, purity.]

1. a member of a group in England and the American colonies who, in the 16th and 17th centuries, wanted a greater reformation of the Church of England than that established by Elizabeth, in order to purify it further from elaborate ceremonies and forms.

2. [p–] a person regarded as extremely or excessively strict in matters of morals and religion.

Pū'ri·tăn, *a.* 1. of the Puritans or Puritanism.

2. [p–] puritanical.

pū·ri·tan'iç, *a.* same as *puritanical*.

pū·ri·tan'i·çăl, *a.* 1. [P–] of the Puritans or Puritanism.

2. extremely or excessively strict in matters of morals and religion.

pū·ri·tan'i·çăl·ly, *adv.* in a puritanical manner.

Pū'ri·tăn·iṣm, *n.* 1. the doctrines or practices of the Puritans.

2. [p–] extreme or excessive strictness in matters of morals and religion.

Pū'ri·tăn·īze, *v.i.*; Puritanized, *pt.*, *pp.*; Puritanizing, *ppr.* to conform to the notions of Puritans; to affect or teach Puritanism.

pū'ri·ty, *n.* [ME. *purete*, *purte*; OFr. *purté*, *pureté*; L. *puritas*, from *purus*, pure.] the state or quality of being pure; specifically, (a) freedom from adulterating matter; as, the *purity* of water; the *purity* of drugs; the *purity* of metals; (b) cleanness; freedom from foulness or dirt; as, the *purity* of a garment; (c) freedom from evil or sin; innocence; as, *purity* of heart or life; (d) freedom from any sinister or improper views; as, the *purity* of motives or designs; (e) freedom from foreign elements: said of language, style, etc.; (f) freedom from mixture with white; color saturation.

Syn.—cleanness, chastity, innocence, sinlessness, uprightness, integrity, virtue.

Pũr·kin·jē'ăn, *a.* in physiology, relating to or named after J. E. Purkinje, a Bohemian physiologist (1787–1869).

Purkinjean cells; in anatomy, reticulated moniliform fibers in the cerebellar cortex.

Purkinjean figures; sets of dark lines on a yellowish background, seen by candlelight in the eye and produced by the retinal vessels.

Purkinjean vesicle; the germinal vesicle.

pũrl, *n.* [earlier *pyrle*, from a Romance source.]

1. an embroidered and puckered border; the plait or fold of a ruff or band.

2. an inversion of the stiches in knitting which gives a ribbed effect: also spelled *pearl*.

3. twisted metal thread, as of gold or silver, used in embroidery.

4. a small loop, or a chain of loops, made on the edge of lace: also spelled *pearl*.

pũrl, *v.t.* and *v.i.* 1. to purfle.

2. to edge (lace) with a chain of small loops: also spelled *pearl*.

3. to invert (stitches) in knitting: also spelled *pearl*.

pũrl, *n.* [from *pearl*, alluding to the beady surface of the drink.] originally, beer or ale with an infusion of wormwood: now applied to beer heated to the boiling point and flavored with gin, sugar, and ginger.

pũrl, *n.* the common tern. [Brit Dial.]

pũrl, *v.i.*; purled, *pt.*, *pp.*; purling, *ppr.* [echoic.]

1. to move in ripples or with a murmuring sound.

2. to run or rise in circles or eddies; to swirl.

Thin winding breath which *purled* up to the sky. —Shak.

pũrl, *n.* 1. a purling stream or rill.

2. the murmuring sound of purling water.

pũr'lieū, *n.* [altered (after Fr. *lieu*, a place) from Anglo-Fr. *puralee*, *poralee*, from *puraler*, to go through, from *pur-*, *por-* (from L. *pro-*, for), and *aler*, to go.]

1. an outlying part of a forest, exempted from forest laws and returned to private owners.

2. a place that one visits often or habitually; haunt.

3. [*pl.*] bounds; limits.

4. an outlying part, as of a city.

5. [*pl.*] environs.

pũr'lin, pũr'line, *n.* [ME. *purlyn*.] a piece of timber laid horizontally to support the common rafters of a roof.

pũr·loin', *v.t.* and *v.i.*; purloined, *pt.*, *pp.*; purloining, *ppr.* [ME. *purlognen*; OFr. *porloignier*, *purloignier*, from L. *prolongare*, to prolong.] to steal; to take by theft.

pũr·loin'ẽr, *n.* a thief; one who purloins.

pũr·loin'ing, *n.* theft; a pilfering.

pũr'pär·ty, *n.* [Fr. *pour*, for, and *partie*, part.] in law, a share, part, or portion of an estate, allotted to a coparcener by partition.

pũr'ple, *n.* [ME. *purpel*, *purpre*; AS. *purpl*(*e*).]

1. a dark color that is a blend of red and blue.

2. in ancient times, crimson cloth or clothing, especially as an emblem of royalty or high rank.

3. the rank or office of a cardinal.

4. [*pl.*] same as *purpura*.

5. [*pl.*] same as *earcockle*.

6. [*pl.*] a kind of orchid with purple flowers. [Brit. Dial.]

purple of Cassius; [after A. *Cassius*, 17th-c. German physician.] a purple pigment made up of colloidal gold and stannic oxide: used for coloring glass or enamel.

purple of mollusca; a viscid liquor, secreted by certain mollusks, as the *Purpura lapillus*, which dyes wool, etc. a purple color, and is supposed to be the substance of the famous Tyrian dye.

the purple; royal or high rank.

to be born in or *to the purple*; to be of royal or high birth.

pũr'ple, *a.* 1. of the color purple.

2. colored or stained as with blood. [Archaic.]

I view a field of blood,
And Tiber rolling with a *purple* flood.
—Dryden.

3. imperial; regal: so used because purple was the Roman imperial color.

4. ornate; elaborate; as, a *purple* passage in a book.

purple avens; a rosaceous plant, *Geum rivale*, having purple flowers, common in the United States: also called *water avens*.

purple azalea; an ericaceous plant, *Azalia nudiflora*, common to the eastern and southern parts of the United States, growing in swampy places: also called *pinkster flower*.

purple copper ore; same as *bornite*.

pũr'ple, *v.t.*; purpled (-pld), *pt.*, *pp.*; purpling, *ppr.* to dye a purple or deep red color; as, hands *purpled* with blood.

When morn
Purples the east. —Milton.

pũr'ple, *v.i.* to become purple; to assume a purple color; as, he fairly *purpled* with rage.

pũr'ple fish, a gastropod, *Murex purpurea*.

pũr'ple-fringed ọr'çhis, either of two North American orchids with purple-fringed flowers.

pũr'ple·heärt, *n.* a purplish, strong, elastic, durable wood taken from the heart of a leguminous tree, *Copaifera martii* or *Copaifera bracteata*, of South America, used for inlaid work, ramrods, etc.

Pũr'ple Heärt, a medal of the Order of the Purple Heart.

pũr'ple mär'tin, a large American swallow with bluish-black plumage.

pũr'ple med'iç, alfalfa, a plant with small, purple flowers.

pũr'ple sçāle, same as *orange scale*.

pũr'ple·wood, *n.* same as *purpleheart*.

pũr'plish, *a.* somewhat purple; having a purple tinge.

pũr'ply, *a.*; *comp.* purplier; *superl.* purpliest, somewhat purple; purplish.

pũr·pōrt', *v.t.* [Anglo-Fr. *purporter*; OFr. *pourporter*, *porporter*, from *pur-*, *por-* (L. *pro-*), forth, and *porter* (L. *portare*), to bear.]

1. to profess or claim as its meaning.

2. to give the appearance, often falsely, of being, intending, etc.

pũr'pōrt, *n.* 1. meaning; tenor; sense; as, the *purport* of a word or phrase.

2. intention; object; as, the *purport* of Plato's dialogue.

pũr'pōrt·less, *a.* having neither meaning nor purport.

pũr'pōse, *v.t.* and *v.i.*; purposed (-pust), *pt.*, *pp.*; purposing, *ppr.* [ME. *purposen*; OFr. *purposer*; L. *propositus*, from *proponere*; *pro*, before, and *ponere*, to place.] to intend; to design; to resolve; to determine on, as some end or object to be accomplished.

I have *purposed* it, I will also do it.
—Isa. xlvi. 11.

Syn.—intend, determine, design, propose, resolve, mean.

pŭr′pŏse, *n.* 1. that which a person sets before himself as an object to be reached or accomplished; aim; intention; design.

2. end in view; the object for which something exists or is done; as, what good *purpose* will this answer? men often employ their time, talents, and money for very evil *purposes.*

3. resolution; determination.

4. instance; example. [Obs.]

on purpose; with previous design; with the mind directed to that object.

to the purpose; relevant; pertinent.

Syn.—intention, design, mind, meaning, view, object, aim, end, scope, point, resolve.

pŭr′pŏsed·ly (-pust-), *adv.* purposely.

pŭr′pŏse·fu̇l, *a.* 1. characterized by a definite purpose; determined.

2. full of meaning.

pŭr′pŏse·fu̇l·ly, *adv.* in a purposeful manner; determinedly.

pŭr′pŏse·less, *a.* having no effect or purpose; aimless.

pŭr′pŏse·less·ness, *n.* the state of being purposeless.

pŭr′pŏse·ly, *adv.* by design; intentionally; with predetermination; with a definite purpose; deliberately.

pŭr′pŏs·ẽr, *n.* one who purposes.

pŭr′pŏs·ive, *a.* 1. serving some purpose.

2. having a purpose.

pŭr·pres′tūre, *n.* [Fr. *pour* and *pris*, pp. of *prendre*, to take.] in law, a nuisance, consisting in an enclosure of or encroachment on land that belongs to the public or has common rights.

pŭr′pū·rȧ, *n.* [L., purple.]

1. a disease characterized by purplish patches on the skin or mucous membranes, caused by the subcutaneous escape of blood from its vessels.

2. [P—] a genus of mollusks, some of which yield a purple dye.

pŭr·pū·rā′ceous, *a.* purple in color; purpurate. [Rare.]

pŭr′pū·rāte, *a.* pertaining to purpura.

pŭr′pū·rāte, *n.* a salt or ester of purpuric acid.

pŭr′pūre, *n.* in heraldry, purple, represented in engraving by diagonal lines downward from sinister to dexter.

pŭr·pū′rē·ăl, *a.* purple in color.

pŭr·pū′rē·ō-, [L. *pupureus*, purple.] a combining form used specifically in chemistry to designate certain *purple compounds.*

pŭr·pū·res′cent, *a.* tinged with purple.

pŭr·pū′riç, *a.* 1. of or having purpura.

2. in chemistry, of, relating to, or designating the hypothetical acid formed by the action of nitric acid upon uric acid.

pŭr·pū·rif′ẽr·ous, *a.* [L. *purpura*, purple, and *ferre*, to bear.] same as *purpuriparous.*

pŭr·pū′ri·fọrm, *a.* pertaining to the genus *Purpura.*

pŭr·pū·rig′e·nous, *a.* [L. *purpura*, purple, and *gignere*, to bear.] producing purple.

pŭr′pū·rin, pŭr′pū·rine, *n.* a red coloring matter obtained from madder in the same way as alizarin.

pŭr·pū·rip′ȧ·rous, *a.* [L. *purpura*, purple, and *parere*, to bring forth.] producing a purple secretion.

pŭr·pū·rog′e·nous, *a.* having the power to produce purple.

pŭr′pū·roid, *a.* same as *purpuriform.*

pŭrr, *n.* [echoic.] 1. a low, vibratory sound made by a cat when it seems to be pleased.

2. any sound resembling this.

Also spelled *pur.*

pŭrr, *v.i.*; purred, *pt., pp.*; purring, *ppr.* to make a soft murmuring sound, as a cat when pleased: also spelled *pur.*

pŭrr, *v.t.* to show or express by purring: also spelled *pur.*

The secretary *purred* delighted approval.
—Kingsley.

pŭrre, *n.* a bird, the dunlin. [Brit. Dial.]

pŭrre mąw, the roseate tern. [Brit. Dial.]

pŭrse, *n.* [ME.; AS. *purs*; LL. *bursa, byrsa*, a purse, from Gr. *byrsa*, a skin, a hide.]

1. a small bag, pouch, or case in which money is carried.

2. treasury; resources; finances; as, to exhaust the public *purse.*

3. a sum of money offered as a prize, or collected as a present; as, the *purse* in this race is $5000.

4. in the Orient, a specific sum of money; as, in Turkey, a *purse* of silver is equal to 500 piasters.

5. a women's handbag.

6. anything like a purse in shape, use, etc.

light purse or *empty purse*; poverty, or lack of resources.

long purse or *heavy purse*; wealth; riches.

pŭrse, *v.t.*; pursed (pŭrst), *pt., pp.*; pursing, *ppr.* 1. to put in a purse. [Archaic.]

2. to contract into folds or wrinkles; to pucker; knit: often with *up*; as, to *purse up* the mouth.

Thou didst contract and *purse* thy brow.
—Shak.

pŭrse, *v.i.* to steal. [Obs.]

pŭrse çrab, a crustacean, as *Birgus latro*, or other crabs of the same genus, found in the eastern islands of the Indian Ocean.

pŭrse′fu̇l, *n.* as much as a purse will hold.

pŭrse line, the line used to close a purse seine.

pŭrse net, a net whose mouth may be closed or drawn together like a purse.

pŭrse prīde, pride of money; insolence proceeding from the possession of wealth.

pŭrse′-proud, *a.* proud of wealth; overbearing because of the possession of money or riches.

pŭrs′ẽr, *n.* a ship's officer in charge of the accounts, freight, tickets, etc., especially on a passenger vessel.

pŭrse rat, same as *pocket gopher.*

pŭrs′er·ship, *n.* the position of a purser.

pŭrse sẹine, same as *purse net.*

pŭrse spī′dẽr, a spider that weaves a web like a purse. [Dial.]

pŭrse strings̹, strings drawn to close a purse.

to hold the purse strings; to be in control of the money.

pŭrs′et, *n.* a purse. [Obs.]

pŭr′si·ness, *n.* the quality or condition of being pursy.

pŭr′sive, *a.* pursy. [Obs.]

pŭr′sive·ness, *n.* pursiness. [Obs.]

pŭrs′lāin, *n.* same as *purslane.*

pŭrs′lāne, *n.* [ME. *purcelane*; OFr. *porcelaine*; It. *porcellana*, from L. *porcilaca*, purslane.] any of a number of related weeds, especially an annual plant, *Portulaca oleracea*, with fleshy, succulent leaves, formerly used as a pot herb and for salads, garnishing, and pickling. It is especially persistent, growing close to the ground and crowding out growing plants. Also called *pusley* or *pusley weed.*

black purslane; a kind of spurge somewhat resembling common purslane.

wild purslane; a trailing plant, *Euphorbia peplis*, growing on sandy shores of Europe.

pŭrs′lāne tree, a shrub of South Africa, *Portulacaria afra.*

pŭr·sū′ȧ·ble, *a.* capable of being pursued.

pŭr·sū′ăl, *n.* pursuit.

pŭr·sū′ănce, *n.* the act of pursuing; pursuit.

pŭr·sū′ănt, *a.* [ME. and OFr. *poursuiant*, ppr. of *poursuir*, to pursue.] carrying out; following.

pursuant to; (a) following upon; (b) in accordance or compliance with.

pŭr·sū′ănt·ly, *adv.* so as to carry out, conform, or accord (with *to*).

pŭr·sūe′, *v.t.*; pursued, *pt., pp.*; pursuing, *ppr.* [ME. *pursuen*; OFr. *poursuir*; L. *prosequi*; *pro*, forth, and *sequi*, to follow.]

1. to follow in order to kill, capture, or overtake; to follow after; to chase.

2. to attend; to accompany. [Rare.]

3. to proceed along or follow, as a specified course, action, plan, etc.

4. to try to find; to strive for; to seek.

5. to follow as an occupation, profession, or study.

6. to continue; to carry on.

7. to continue to annoy or distress.

pŭr·sūe′, *v.i.* 1. to follow after another; to go in pursuit.

2. to go on; to proceed; to continue.

3. to follow a matter in a legal manner; to be a prosecutor. [Obs.]

pŭr·sū′ẽr, *n.* 1. one who pursues.

2. in Scots law, a plaintiff; a prosecutor.

pŭr·sūit′, *n.* [ME. *purseute*; OFr. *poursuite.*]

1. the act of following with a view to overtaking; a following with haste, either for sport or in hostility; as, the *pursuit* of game; the *pursuit* of an enemy.

2. a following with a view to reaching, accomplishing, or obtaining; an endeavor to attain to or gain; as, the *pursuit* of knowledge; the *pursuit* of happiness.

3. the thing pursued; occupation or the like ordinarily followed; as, mercantile *pursuits*; literary *pursuits.*

4. in law, prosecution. [Obs.]

curve of pursuit; the path of a point moving with uniform velocity in the direction of another point which is also moving with uniform velocity in a given curve.

pŭr·sūit′ plāne, a fast, maneuverable military plane.

pŭr′sui·vănt (-swi-), *n.* [ME. *pursevante*; OFr. *poursuivant.*]

1. a follower; an attendant.

2. in the British College of Heralds, an officer ranking below a herald. There are four pursuivants attached to the British College of Arms: Rouge Croix, Blue Mantle, Rouge Dragon, and Portcullis.

pŭr′sui·vănt, *v.t.* to follow or overtake with a pursuivant. [Obs.]

pŭr′sy, *a.*; *comp.* pursier; *superl.* pursiest, [earlier *pursive;* ME. *purcyfe*; OFr. *polsif*, from *pourcer, poulser*, Fr. *pousser*, to push, also to breathe or pant, from L. *pulsare*, to beat.]

1. short-winded; fat and short-winded; asthmatic.

Grown fat and *pursy* by retail. —Butler.

2. puffed up or swollen with pampering.

pŭr′te·nănce, *n.* [ME.; OFr.] the viscera of an animal. [Archaic.]

pū′ru̇·lence, pū′ru̇·len·cy, *n.* [L. *purulentus*, from *pus, puris*, matter.] the quality or state of being purulent; generation of pus or matter; also, pus.

pū′ru̇·lent, *a.* of, like, containing, or discharging pus.

pū′ru̇·lent·ly, *adv.* in a purulent manner.

pū′ru̇·loid, *a.* resembling pus.

pŭr·vẹy′, *v.t.*; purveyed, *pt., pp.*; purveying, *ppr.* [ME. *pourveien*; OFr. *proveoir, porveoir*, from L. *providere*, to foresee.]

1. to provide or supply (a person) *with* something. [Archaic.]

2. to furnish or supply (food or provisions).

3. to foresee. [Obs.]

pŭr·vẹy′, *v.i.* 1. to purchase and supply provisions, especially for a number of people.

2. to pander. [Obs.]

pŭr·vẹy′ănce, *n.* 1. a purverying.

2. provisions; the things purveyed.

3. formerly, in England, the royal prerogative of buying up provisions and other necessaries, and of impressing carriages and horses for the conveyance of timber, baggage, etc., at a rate fixed by the King's agent: abolished in 1660.

pŭr·vẹy′ŏr, *n.* 1. one who purveys, or supplies provisions, etc.

2. in English history, an officer who formerly provided or exacted provisions for the king's household, under purveyance (sense 3).

3. a procurer; a pimp; a bawd.

pŭr′view (-vū), *n.* [Anglo-Fr., for OFr. *pourveü*, provided, pp. of *pourveir*, to purvey; n. use from occurring in legal phrases "*purveu est*," it is provided, "*purveu que*," provided that.]

1. the body and scope of an act or bill.

2. the extent or range of control, activity, or concern; province.

3. range of sight or understanding.

4. a condition or proviso. [Obs.]

pus, *n.* [L., from same root as in *putrid*, *putrefy.*] the yellowish-white matter produced by an infection, consisting of bacteria, white corpuscles, serum, etc.

Pū′s̹ey·is̹m, *n.* [from Rev. E. B. *Pusey*, 1800–1882, Brit. leader of the movement.] Tractarianism.

Pū·s̹ey·is′tiç, *a.* of or relating to Puseyism; Tractarian.

Pū′s̹ey·īte, *n.* an adherent of Puseyism.

Pū′s̹ey·īte, *a.* same as *Puseyistic.*

pu̧sh, *v.t.*; pushed (pu̧sht), *pt., pp.*; pushing, *ppr.* [ME. *posshen*; Early Fr. *pousser*; OFr. *poulser*, from L. *pulsare*, to beat; a freq. from *pellere, pulsum*, to beat, to drive.]

1. to thrust or press against (a thing) so so as to move it away.

2. to move by exerting force in this way.

3. to thrust, shove, or drive up, down, in, out, forward, etc.

4. to urge forward or on; to impel; to press.

5. to follow up vigorously, as a campaign, claim, etc.

6. to extend; to expand; as, the Genoese *pushed* their trade to the Far East.

7. to press hard upon; as, he was *pushed* for time.

8. to urge or promote the use, sale, success, etc. of.

9. to butt; to strike with the end of the

horns; to thrust the points of horns against. [Dial.]

10. in baseball and golf, to hit (the ball) so that it goes to the right or, if one is left-handed, to the left.

pụsh, *v.i.* 1. to press against a thing so as to move it.
2. to press or thrust forward vigorously.
3. to put forth great effort.
4. to advance against opposition.
5. to make an attack; to make a thrust; as, to *push* with a sword. [Obs.]
to push off; to set out; to depart.
to push on; to proceed.
Syn.—press, drive, impel, shove, press against, propel, butt, thrust, urge, expedite, accelerate.

pụsh, *n.* 1. a pushing; shove, thrust, etc.
2. a thing to be pushed in order to work a mechanism.
3. a vigorous effort.
4. an advance against opposition.
5. pressure of affairs or of circumstances.
6. an emergency.
7. aggressiveness; enterprise; drive; force. [Colloq.]
8. a crowd or clique. [Slang.]
9. a little swelling or pustule. [Brit. Dial.]

pụsh'bạll, *n.* 1. a game, played by two teams, in which a large ball about six feet in diameter is to be pushed across the opponent's goal.
2. the ball used in this game.

pụsh but'tŏn, a small knob or button which when pushed makes or breaks an electric circuit.

pụsh'çärt, *n.* a cart pushed by hand: used by street peddlers or venders.

pụsh'ẽr, *n.* 1. one who or that which pushes.
2. an airplane with the propeller mounted behind the engine, usually at the trailing edge of the wing: also *pusher airplane.*

pụsh'ing, *a.* 1. aggressive; enterprising; energetic.
2. forward; officious.

pụsh'ing·ly, *adv.* in a pushing manner.

pushm, *n.* [Per.] same as *pashm.*

push·mï'nȧ, *a.* same as *pashmina.*

pụsh'-ọff, *n.* 1. the act of pushing off.
2. in electricity, a structural compression member (rod, bar, etc.) used for holding a transmission wire in its proper position.

pụsh'ō·vẽr, *n.* 1. a person, group, etc. whose resistance can be overcome with little effort. [Slang.]
2. anything very easy to do. [Slang.]

pụsh'pin, *n.* 1. a child's game played with pins.
2. anything trivial.
3. a tacklike pin with a prominent head, used as a map marker, etc.

Push'tu̇, *n.* an Iranian language, the principal one spoken in Afghanistan: also *Pashto.*

pū″sil·lȧ·nim'i·ty, *n.* [LL. *pusillanimitas*, faintheartedness.] the quality or state of being pusillanimous.
Syn.—cowardliness, fear, timidity, pusillanimousness.

pū·sil·lan'i·mous, *a.* 1. irresolute; fainthearted; cowardly; as, a *pusillanimous* governor.
2. proceeding from or showing a lack of courage; as, *pusillanimous* counsels.

pū·sil·lan'i·mous·ly, *adv.* in a pusillanimous manner; with lack of courage.

pū·sil·lan'i·mous·ness, *n.* lack of courage or spirit; pusillanimity.

pus'ley, *n.* same as *purslane.*

pụss, *n.* [D. *poes*; L.G. *puus*; Gael. and Ir. *pus*: prob. imitative of the spitting of a cat.]
1. a cat: pet name or child's term
2. a hare. [Brit.]
3. a puss moth.
4. a girl or young woman: term of affection.
puss-in-the-corner; a game played chiefly by children, in which all the players except one have corners or stations which they must exchange constantly, the object of the cornerless player being to secure a corner or station during such exchange, leaving some other player without a corner.

pụss, *n.* 1. the face. [Slang.]
2. the mouth. [Slang.]

pụss çlō'vẽr, rabbit-foot clover, *Trifolium arvense.*

puss'ley, puss'ly, *n.* same as *purslane.*

pụss mọth, a European bombycid moth, *Cerura vinula*, having whitish fore wings with black spots and gray markings, and hind wings white in the male, clouded with gray in the female, both having a dark central lunule. The larva is dark green, with two projecting caudal appendages, and feeds on sallows, poplars, and willows.

pus'sy, *a.* containing or like pus.

pụss'y, *n.*; *pl.* **pụss'ies,** 1. a cat.
2. a catkin, as of the pussy willow. [Colloq.]

pụss'y·çat, *n.* [L.G. *pusekätte.*]
1. a cat; a puss.
2. the catkin of the pussy willow.

pụss'y·foot, *v.i.* 1. to move with stealth or caution, as a cat does. [Slang.]
2. to avoid committing oneself or making one's position clear. [Slang.]

pụss'y·foot, *n.* a person who pussyfoots. [Slang.]

pụss'y wil'lōw, any willow producing silky catkins in the early part of spring; specifically, a common small American willow, *Salix discolor.*

pus'tū·lȧnt, *a.* causing pustulation.

pus'tū·lănt, *n.* an agent that causes pustulation.

pus'tū·lăr, *a.* 1. of, or having the nature of, pustules.
2. covered with pustules.

pus'tū·lāte, *v.t.* and *v.i.*; pustulated, *pt., pp.*; pustulating, *ppr.* [L. *pustulare*, to blister.] to form into pustules.

pus'tū·lāte, *a.* covered with pustules.

pus'tū·lāt·ed, *a.* pustulate.

pus·tū·lā'tion, *n.* 1. the formation of pustules.
2. a pustule.

pus'tūle, *n.* [L. *pustula*, a blister or pimple.]
1. a small, inflamed elevation of the skin, containing pus.
2. any small elevation like a pimple or blister.
malignant pustule; anthrax.

pus'tū·li·fọrm, *a.* resembling a pustule in form.

pus'tū·lōse, *a.* in botany, having prominences resembling blisters; pustular.

pus'tū·lous, *a.* full of or covered with pustules; pustular.

put, *n.* [W. *pwt*, a short, thick person.] a rustic; a clown; a silly fellow. [Archaic.]

pụt, *v.t.*; put, *pt., pp.*; putting, *ppr.* [ME. *putten, puten*; AS. *putian*, to push, thrust.]
1. to place, set, lay, deposit, bring, or cause to be in any position, place, or situation; as, *put* the book on the table.
2. to bring to, or place in any state or condition; as, to *put* to shame; to *put* to silence; to *put* to death.

> This question asked
> *Puts* me in doubt. —Milton.

3. to apply, as in any effort, exercise, or use; to direct with steady attention.

> The great difference in the notions of mankind is from the different use they *put* their faculties to. —Locke.

4. to oblige; to force; to constrain; to push to action.

> We are *put* to prove things which can hardly be made plainer. —Tillotson.

5. to impose; as, to *put* a tax on luxuries.
6. to set before one for consideration, deliberation, judgment, acceptance, or rejection; to propose; to offer; as, to *put* the question.
7. to state; to express; as, *put* it in plain language.

> These verses, originally Greek, were *put* in Latin. —Milton.

8. to lay down; to give up; to surrender. [Obs.]
9. to cast or throw with an overhand thrust from the shoulder; as, to *put* the shot.
10. to push; to thrust; to drive; to impel.
11. to attribute; to ascribe; as, to *put* the proper interpretation on the clause of a contract.
12. to place in estimation; to appraise.
13. to adapt or fit, as words to music.
14. to wager; to bet.
to be put upon; to be imposed on; to be victimized.
to put about; (a) in nautical usage, to change the course of; (b) to put to inconvenience; as, he was much *put about* by that occurrence.
to put across; (a) to cause to be understood or accepted; (b) to carry out with success; (c) to perpetrate. [Slang.]
to put an end to; to stop; to bring to a conclusion.
to put away; (a) [Colloq.] to consume (food or drink); (b) [Slang.] to kill. (c) to renounce; to discard; to expel; (d) [Obs.] to divorce.
to put back; (a) to hinder; to delay; (b) to restore to the original place; (c) to refuse; to say no to.
to put by; (a) to turn away; to thrust aside; (b) to place in safekeeping; to save or store up; as, *to put by* something for a rainy day.
to put down; (a) to repress; to crush; as, to *put down* a rebellion; (b) to degrade; to deprive of authority, power, or place; (c) to attribute (to); (d) to write; to subscribe; as, *to put* one's name *down* for a sum.
to put forth; (a) to propose; to offer; (b) to stretch out; to reach; (c) to shoot out; to send out, as a sprout; (d) to exert; to bring into action; (e) to publish, as a book.
to put forward; to advance or present, as a claim.
to put in; (a) to introduce among others; to interpose; (b) to insert; as, *to put in* a passage or clause; *to put in* a scion; (c) to conduct (a ship) into a harbor; (d) [Colloq.] to spend (time) in a specified manner.
to put in mind; to remind.
to put in (or *into*) *practice*; to apply; to make use of; to exercise.
to put off; (a) to postpone; delay; (b) to discard; (c) to evade; divert.
to put on or *upon*; (a) to impute; to charge; as, *to put* one's own crime or blame *on* another; (b) to clothe, adorn, or cover oneself with; as, *to put on* a cloak; (c) to assume or pretend; as, *to put on* a grave countenance; (d) [Obs.] to forward; to promote; (e) to impose; to inflict; (f) to apply, as a brake; (g) to stage (a play).
to put out; (a) to place at interest; (b) to send; to emit; to shoot, as a bud or sprout; (c) to extend; to reach out; to protrude; (d) to drive out; to expel; to dismiss; (e) to publish; to make public; (f) to confuse; to disconcert; as, *to put* one *out* in reading or speaking; (g) to gouge out (an eye); (h) to extinguish (a fire or light); (i) to distress; to vex; (j) in baseball, to retire (a batter or runner).
to put over; (a) to refer; to send; (b) to defer; to postpone; as, the court *put over* the cause to the next term; (c) [Colloq.] to accomplish (something) against odds or by craft.
to put through; (a) to perform successfully; to carry out; (b) to cause to do or undergo.
to put to; (a) to add; to unite; as, *to put* one sum *to* another; (b) to refer to; to expose; as, *to put* the fate of the army or nation *to* a battle.
to put to it; to distress; to press hard; to perplex; to give difficulty to.
to put up; (a) to expose; to offer publicly; as, *to put up* goods for sale at auction; (b) to start from a cover; (c) to hoard; (d) to preserve or can; as, *to put up* apples for winter; (e) to pack in containers; as, *to put up* pork, beef, or fish; (f) to hide or lay aside; (g) to advance, provide, or stake (money); as, *to put up* money on a race; (h) [Colloq.] to incite (a person) to some action; (i) [Archaic.] to sheath (one's sword).

pụt, *v.i.* 1. to go or move; to take one's course (with *in, out, for, back, to*, etc.).
2. to shoot; to germinate. [Now Dial.]
to put forth; to set out from a port.
to put in; (a) to enter a harbor; to sail into port; (b) to offer a claim; as, A *puts in* for a share of profits.
to put in for; to offer oneself; to stand as a candidate for.
to put up; (a) to take lodgings; to lodge; (b) to offer oneself as a candidate.
to put up with; to overlook or suffer patiently; to tolerate.

pụt, *n.* 1. a thrust; a push; a cast; a throw.
2. the act of throwing a stone or weight overhand.
3. an old game of cards played by two, three, or four players, in which the whole pack is used, but only three cards are dealt at a time.
4. a forced action to avoid something; an action of distress. [Obs.]
5. in commerce, the right or option that one party buys of another to deliver to him a certain amount of a commodity or stock at or within a certain time at a stipulated price: opposed to *call.*

pụt, *a.* fixed; as, stay *put.* [Colloq.]

pū'tāge, *n.* prostitution. [Rare.]

pū·tā'men, *n.* [L.] the hard stone of certain fruits, as of the peach.

pū·tam'i·nous, *a.* relating to a putamen.

pū'tă·nişm, *n.* [Fr. *putanisme.*] lewdness or prostitution of a woman.

pū·tā'tion, *n.* 1. the act of considering; estimation.
2. a trimming; pruning. [Obs.]

pū′tȧ·tive, *a.* [Fr. *putatif;* It. *putativo,* from L. *putare,* to suppose.] supposed; reputed; commonly considered or deemed; as, the *putative* father of a child.

pụt·chuk′, pụt·chock′, *n.* [E. Ind.] the costus root of India, which is exported to China to be used as incense. It is used medicinally in India.

pū′tē·ăl, *n.* [L., from *puteus,* a well.] a well curb.

pụt′ē·li, *n.* a broad boat, with a flat bottom, used on the Ganges river.

pū′tēr·y, *n.* [Fr. *puterie.*] putage. [Obs.]

pū′tid, *a.* [L. *putidus,* from *putere,* to have an ill smell.] mean; worthless; rotten.

pū·tid′i·ty, *n.* same as *putidness.*

pū′tid·ness, *n.* the condition of being rotten, worthless, or low.

pụt′log, *n.* any of the short pieces of timber on which the planks forming the floor of a scaffold are laid.

pụt′-ọff, *n.* an excuse; a shift for evasion or delay.

pụt′-out, *n.* in baseball, a play in which the batter or runner is retired, or put out.

pū·tred′i·nous, *a.* [L. *putredo,* from *putris,* rotten.] proceeding from putrefaction, or partaking of the putrefactive process; having an offensive smell; rotten; putrid. [Rare.]

pū·trē·fac′tion, *n.* [Fr., from L. *putrefactio, putris,* putrid, and *facere,* to make.]
1. the decomposition of organic matter by bacteria, fungi, and oxidation, resulting in the formation of foul-smelling products; a rotting.
2. the state of decay; rottenness.
3. rotting or putrid matter.

pū·trē·fac′tive, *a.* 1. pertaining to or characterized by putrefaction; as, the *putrefactive* smell or process.
2. tending to promote putrefaction; causing putrefaction.

pū·trē·fac′tive·ness, *n.* the state or character of being putrefactive.

pū′trē·fī·ȧ·ble, *a.* liable to become putrid; subject to putrefaction.

pū′trē·fī·ẽr, *n.* any agent of putrefaction.

pū′trē·fȳ, *v.t.;* putrefied, *pt., pp.;* putrefying, *ppr.* 1. to cause to be decomposed; to cause to rot; as, heat and moisture soon *putrefy* dead flesh or vegetables.
2. to corrupt; to make foul; as, to *putrefy* the air. [Rare.]

pū′trē·fȳ, *v.i.* to rot; to become putrid.

pū·tres′cence, *n.* [from L. *putrescens,* a decaying.]
1. the condition of being putrescent.
2. putrescent matter.

pū·tres′cent, *a.* 1. becoming putrid; putrefying; rotting.
2. of or pertaining to putrefaction; as, a *putrescent* smell.

pū·tres′ci·ble, *a.* that may be putrefied; liable to become putrid; as, *putrescible* substances.

pū·tres′ci·ble, *n.* a substance liable to decay by putrefaction, as green vegetables or fresh meat.

pū·tres′cine, *n.* a liquid, poisonous, and ill-smelling ptomaine, $C_4H_{12}N_2$, from decaying animal tissues and from cultures of the comma bacillus and the bacteria of the feces.

pū′trid, *a.* [Fr. *putride;* L. *putridus,* from *putris,* rotten.]
1. decomposed; rotten and foul-smelling.
2. causing, showing, or proceeding from decay.
3. morally corrupt; depraved.
4. very disagreeable or unpleasant. [Colloq.]

pū·trid′i·ty, *n.* 1. the state of being putrid; decay; rottenness.
2. matter that is putrid.

pū′trid·ness, *n.* the state of being putrid.

pū′tri·fact·ed, *a.* putrefied.

pū″tri·fi·cā′tion, *n.* putrefaction. [Obs.]

pū′tri·fȳ, *v.t.* and *v.i.* to putrefy. [Obs.]

pū′tri·lāge, *n.* [Fr.; L. *putrilago,* putrefaction.] putrid matter from putrefying substances; matter undergoing putrefaction.

Pụtsch (pụch), *n.* an uprising; an unsuccessful rebellion; a riot.

pụtsch′ist, *n.* one who participates in a Putsch; a rioter.

putt, *n.* in golf, a light stroke made on the putting green in an attempt to get the ball into the hole.

putt, *v.t* and *v.i.;* putted, *pt., pp.;* putting, *ppr.* [from *put,* v.] in golf, to hit (the ball) with a light stroke on the putting green, so as to get the ball in a hole.

put·tee′, *n.* [Hind. *paṭṭī,* a bandage; Sans. *paṭṭa,* a strip of cloth.] a covering for the lower leg, in the form of a cloth or leather gaiter or a cloth strip wound spirally: also *puttie, putty.*

putt′ẽr, *n.* in golf, a club with a short shaft and a straight face, designed for strokes on the putting green; also, the player using the club.

pụt′tẽr, *n.* one who or that which puts or places, as (a) in athletics, one who puts or throws a heavy shot; (b) one who hauls coal from the place where it is mined to the hoisting shaft.

put′tẽr, *v.i.* [var. of *potter.*] to busy oneself or proceed in a trifling, ineffective, or aimless way; to dawdle (often with *over, along, around,* etc.): also *potter.*

put′tẽr, *v.t.* to dawdle or fritter (with *away*): also *potter.*

put′tẽr, *n.* a puttering: also *potter.*

pụt′tẽr-on, *n.* one who incites or instigates.

pụt′ti, *n.pl.; sing.* **pụt′tō,** [It., children, from L. *putus,* a child.] figures of Cupidlike children used in architectural adornment.

put′ti·ẽr, *n.* a person who works with putty, as a glazier.

pụt′ting, *n.* the action of one who puts (in various senses).

put′ting green, in golf, the area of smooth, closely mowed turf in which the hole is sunk.

pụt′ting stōne, a heavy globular stone used in the athletic exercise of putting.

put′tŏck, *n.* [according to Skeat from *pout, poult,* and *hawk,* the chicken hawk.] (a) the European kite; (b) the marsh harrier; (c) the buzzard.

put′tọọ, *n.* [E. Ind.] a species of fabric made in Kashmir and neighboring regions, of the long and coarse wool of the goat.

put′ty, *n.* [Fr. *potée,* calcined tin, brass, etc., putty powder, from *pot,* a pot, because putty powder was made of old pots.]
1. a soft plastic material compounded of finely powdered chalk and linseed oil and used in fastening glass in sashes, filling small cracks, etc.
2. any substance like this in consistency, use, etc.
3. putty powder.
4. a cement of quicklime and water, mixed with plaster of Paris or sand for use as a finishing coat in plastering.
jeweler's putty; same as *putty powder.*

put′ty, *v.t.;* puttied, *pt., pp.;* puttying, *ppr.* to cement, fix, cover, or fill with putty.

put′ty çōat, in plastering, a finishing coat of putty (sense 4).

put′ty eȳe (ī), the eye of a pigeon: so named on account of the puttylike appearance of its orbit.

put′ty knīfe (nīf), a knife for applying putty.

put′ty pow′dẽr, powdered oxide of tin, or of tin and lead, used for polishing glass or metals.

put′ty·rọọt, *n.* a North American orchid, *Aplectrum hiemale,* having yellowish-brown flowers, one leaf at the base of the stem, and a solid bulb filled with strong glutinous matter.

pụt′-up, *a.* arranged beforehand and in a clandestine way; as, a *put-up* job. [Colloq.]

puy (pwē), *n.* same as *poy.*

puy, *n.* any hill or cone of volcanic origin; specifically, one in Auvergne, France.

puz′zel, *n.* a pucelle. [Obs.]

puz′zle, *v.t.;* puzzled, (-zld) *pt., pp.;* puzzling, *ppr.* [freq. from ME. *posen,* to pose (a question, etc.).]
1. to perplex; to confuse; to nonplus.
2. to make intricate; to entangle.
3. to solve; to work out: followed by *out;* as, he finally *puzzled* it *out.*

puz′zle, *v.i.* 1. to be bewildered or perplexed; to be in doubt.
2. to work or try to work, as a puzzle: followed by *over;* as, to *puzzle over* his meaning.
Syn.—perplex, complicate, bewilder, confuse, involve, confound.

puz′zle, *n.* 1. the state of being puzzled; perplexity; bewilderment.
2. a toy or problem purposely arranged to test mental ingenuity.
3. a question, problem, etc. that puzzles.
Syn.—embarrassment, bewilderment, enigma, confusion, conundrum, intricacy, labyrinth.

puz′zle·dŏm, *n.* the state or condition of being puzzled; bewilderment.

puz′zle-head″ed (-hed″), *a.* having the head full of confused notions.

puz′zle·ment, *n.* the state of being puzzled or perplexed; also, a thing that puzzles; a puzzle.

puz′zle mŏn′key, the monkey puzzle.

puz′zlẽr, *n.* one who or that which puzzles.

puz′zling·ly, *adv.* in a puzzling manner.

puz·zō·lä′nȧ, puz·zō·lä′nō, *n.* same as *pozzuolana.*

pȳ-, same as *pyo-.*

pȳ·ae′mi·ȧ, *n.* same as *pyemia.*

pȳ·ae′miç, *a.* same as *pyemic.*

Pyç·nan′thē·mum, *n.* [Gr. *pyknos,* thick, and *anthemon,* blossom.] a genus of labiate plants containing about a dozen species including the mountain mint.

pyç′nid, *n.* same as *pycnidium.*

pyç·nid′i·um, *n.; pl.* **pyç·nid′i·ȧ,** in certain fungi, a sort of sac in which spores are produced.

pyç′nīte, *n.* [Gr. *pyknos,* compact, and *-ite.*] a variety of topaz occurring in aggregations of columnar crystals.

Pyç·noç′ō·mȧ, *n.* [Gr. *pyknos,* thick, and *komē,* hair.] a genus of tropical trees of the spurge family, found in Africa and the Mascarene Isles.

pyç″nō·çō·nid′i·um, *n.; pl.* **pyç″nō·çō·nid′i·ȧ,** a spore or conidium produced within a pycnidium.

pyç′nō·dont, *n.* [Gr. *pyknos,* thick, and *odous, odontos,* tooth.] any of the *Pycnodontidæ.*

pyç′nō·dont, *a.* pertaining to the *Pycnodontidæ.*

Pyç·nō·don′ti·dae, *n.pl.* the principal family of the *Pycnodonti.*

Pyç·nō·don′tī, *n.pl.* an extinct group of ganoid fishes having the body compressed, and covered with rhombic scales.

Pyç·nō·gon′i·dȧ, *n.pl.* a group of marine arthropods; the sea spiders.

pyç·nog′ō·noid, *n.* [Gr. *pyknos,* thick, and *gona,* knee.] any of the *Pycnogonida.*

pyç·nom′e·tẽr, *n.* [Gr. *pyknos,* thick, dense, and *-meter.*] a vessel for determining the densities of liquids or solids.

pyç′nō·spōre, *n.* [Gr. *pyknos,* thick, and *sporos,* seed.] a stylospore.

pyç′nō·stȳle, *n.* [Gr. *pyknos,* close, and *stȳlos,* column.] see *intercolumniation.*

pȳe, *n.* [Fr. *pie,* from L. *pica,* a woodpecker.] a magpie. [Brit. Dial.]

pȳe, *n.* a pie (table).

pȳe′bald, *a.* same as *piebald.*

pȳ·ē·lī′tis, *n.* [Gr. *pyelos,* a pan or trough, and *-itis.*] inflammation of the pelvis or the kidney.

pȳ′e·lō·gram″, *n.* an X-ray picture taken by pyelography.

pȳ′e·lō·grȧph″, *n.* same as *pyelogram.*

pȳ·e·log′rȧ·phy, *n.* [from Gr. *pyelos,* basin; and *-graphy.*] the art of taking X-ray pictures of the kidney and ureter after filling them with some radio-opaque solution.

pȳ·ē′mi·ȧ, *n.* [Mod. L.; *py-,* and *-emia,* from Gr. *-aimia,* from *haima,* blood.] a condition of infection caused by the presence in the blood of pus-producing micro-organisms that are carried to various parts of the body, producing abscesses, fever, chill, etc.: also spelled *pyaemia.*

pȳ·ē′miç, *a.* pertaining to or affected with pyemia.

pȳ·en′gȧ·dụ, *n.* same as *acle.*

pȳ′et, *n.* same as *piet.*

pȳ′găl, *a.* of, pertaining to, or situated near the region of the rump: applied especially to the carapace of tortoises.

pȳ′găl, *n.* [Gr. *pygē,* rump, and *-al.*] a pygal shield.

pȳ′gärg, pȳ·gär′gus, *n.* [L. *pygargus.*]
1. a quadruped, probably a species of antelope or gazelle.
2. the osprey or fishhawk. [Obs.]

pȳ·ġid′i·ăl, *a.* pertaining to the pygidium.

pȳ·ġid′i·um, *n.; pl.* **pȳ·ġid′i·ȧ,** [Gr. *pygē,* rump, and dim. *-idion.*] the caudal shield or tail of a trilobite; also, the posterior segment of an insect.

pyg·mae′ăn, pyg·mē′ăn, *a.* pertaining to or resembling a pygmy.

Pyg′my, *n.; pl.* **Pyg′mies,** [L. *Pygmæus;* Gr. *Pygmaios,* from *pygmē,* the distance from the elbow to the knuckles, about 13½ inches.]
1. any of several races of African and Asiatic dwarfs described in ancient history and legend.
2. a person belonging to any of several modern races of African (Negrillo) and Asiatic (Negrito) dwarfs.

3. [p–] any person, animal, or plant abnormally undersized; a dwarf.

4. [p–] an insignificant person or thing.

Also spelled *Pigmy*.

Pyg'my, *a.* 1. of the Pygmies.

2. [p–] very small.

3. [p–] insignificant.

Also spelled Pigmy.

pygmy antelope; the kleenebok.

pygmy goose; any of a group of very small geese.

pygmy owl; the gnome owl.

pygmy parrot; a very small green parrot, not larger than a sparrow, of the genus *Nasiterna* and native to New Guinea and the adjacent islands.

pyg'my·weed, *n.* a minute, annual plant, *Tillæa simplex*, having inconspicuous solitary white flowers, sessile in their axils.

Pȳ·gō·bran'chi·ȧ, *n.pl.* [Gr. *pygē*, rump, and *branchia*, gills.] a group of gastropods having a wreath of gills around the anus.

pȳ'gō·pod, *n.* [Gr. *pygē*, rump, and *podos*, foot.] any bird of the *Pygopodes*.

Pȳ·gop'ō·dēs, *n.pl.* an order of web-footed birds in which the legs are placed far back of the middle, causing the body to be nearly erect when standing. The grebes, loons, auks, and divers are included in this order.

Pȳ·gō·pod'i·dae, *n.pl.* a family of lizards having no forelegs and undeveloped hind legs. They are native to Australia.

pȳ·gop'ō·dous, *a.* pertaining to or resembling the *Pygopodes*.

pȳ'gō·stȳle, *n.* [Gr. *pygē*, rump, and *stylos*, column.] a plate of bone made up of caudal vertebrae joined together and forming the last bone of the spinal column in most birds; the vomer.

pȳ'iç, *a.* [Gr. *pyon*, pus, and *-ic*.] of pus; purulent.

pȳ'in, *n.* [Gr. *pyon*, pus.] a mixture of proteins found in pus.

py·jä'mȧs, *n.pl.* pajamas: British spelling.

pyk'ăr, *n.* a kind of fishing boat. [Obs.]

pyk'niç, *a.* [from Gr. *pyknos*, compact, solid; and *-ic*.] in psychology, designating or having a body type characterized by roundness of contour, squatness, fleshiness, etc.

pyk'niç, *n.* a person of the pyknic type.

pyk·nom'e·tēr, *n.* same as *pycnometer*.

pȳ'lȧ, *n.*; *pl.* **pȳ'lae** or **pȳ'lȧs,** [Gr. *pylē*, a gate.] the duct between the iter and the third ventricle of the brain.

pyl'ȧ·gōre, *n.* [Gr. *Pylagoras*, from *pylē*, a gate, and *ageirein*, to collect.] in ancient Greece, a delegate or representative of a city, sent to the Amphictyonic council.

pȳ·lan'gi·ăl, *a.* of or pertaining to the pylangium.

pȳ·lan'gi·um, *n.* [Gr. *pylē*, gate, and *angeion*, a vessel.] the first and unsegmented part of the arterial trunk in the lower vertebrates.

pȳ''leph·lē·bī'tis, *n.* [Gr. *pylē*, gate, and *phleps*, *phlebos*, vein, and *-itis*.] inflammation of the portal vein.

pȳ'lon, *n.* [Gr. *pylōn*, a gateway.]

1. a gateway.

2. a truncated pyramid, or two of these, serving as a gateway to an Egyptian temple.

3. any slender, towering structure flanking an entranceway, supporting telegraph wires, marking a course in an air race, etc.

pȳ·lō·reç'tō·my, *n.* [Gr. *pylōros*, gatekeeper, and *ektomē*, a cutting out.] the surgical removal of the pyloric end of the stomach.

pȳ·lor'iç, *a.* pertaining to or situated near the pylorus; as, the *pyloric* artery.

pȳ·lō'rus, *n.*; *pl.* **pȳ·lō'rī,** [Gr. *pylōros*, a gatekeeper.]

1. the opening from the stomach into the duodenum, the first part of the small intestine.

2. a structure separating the gastric and somatic cavities in siphonophores.

pȳ'ō-, [from Gr. *pyon*, pus.] a combining form meaning: (a) *pus*, as in *pyogenic*; (b) *suppurative*, as in *pyosis*. Also *py-*, as in *pyemia*.

pȳ'ō·cēle, *n.* [*pyo-*, and Gr. *kēlē*, hernia.] a hernia which contains pus.

pȳ·ō·cy'ȧ·nin, *n.* a blue or violet ptomaine found in pus and caused by the growth of *Bacillus pyocyaneus*.

pȳ'ō·cyst, *n.* a cyst containing pus.

pȳ'ō·cȳte, *n.* [*pyo-*, and Gr. *kytos*, a hollow, cell.] a pus corpuscle.

pȳ''ō·dĕr·mȧ·tī'tis, *n.* [*pyo-*, Gr. *derma*, skin, and *-itis*.] any purulent skin disease.

pȳ·ō·gen'e·sis, *n.* [*pyo-*, and Gr. *genesis*, origin, beginning.] in medicine, the formation of pus; pyosis.

pȳ''ō·gē·net'ic, *a.* pertaining to pyogenesis; producing or secreting pus.

pȳ·ō·gen'iç, *a.* same as *pyogenetic*.

pȳ'oid, *a.* [*pyo-*, and Gr. *eidos*, form.] of or resembling pus.

pȳ''ō·nē·phrī'tis, *n.* [*pyo-* and *nephritis*.] purulent nephritis.

pȳ''ō·pneū·mō·thō'rax (-nū-), *n.* [*pyo-*, and Gr. *pneumōn*, lung, and E. *thorax*.] a collection of pus and air or gas in the pleural cavity.

pȳ''ō·poi·ē'sis, *n.* [*pyo-*, and Gr. *poiein*, to make.] pyogenesis.

pȳ·ŏr·rhē'ȧ, pȳ·ŏr·rhoe'ȧ (-rē'), *n.* [*pyo-*, and Gr. *rhein*, to flow.] a discharge of pus; especially, pyorrhea alveolaris.

pȳ·ŏr·rhē'ȧ al·vē''ō·lā'ris, an infection of the gums and tooth sockets, characterized by the formation of pus and, usually, by loosening of the teeth.

pȳ·ŏr·rhē'ăl, pȳ·ŏr·rhoe'ăl, *a.* of, having the nature of, or characterized by pyorrhea.

pȳ''ō·sap·rē'mi·ȧ, *n.* [*pyo-*, Gr. *sapros*, rotten, and *haima*, blood.] purulent infection of the blood.

pȳ·ō'sis, *n.* [Gr.] the formation or discharge of pus; suppuration.

pȳ'ōt, *n.* same as *piet*.

pȳ·ō·thō'rax, *n.* an accumulation of pus in the pleural cavity; empyema.

pȳ·ō·xan'thōse (-zan'), *n.* [*pyo-*, and Gr. *xanthos*, yellow.] a brownish-red to yellow pigment found in pus.

pȳr-, pyro-.

pȳ'rȧ·çanth, *n.* [Gr. *pyr*, fire, and *akanthos*, thorn.] an evergreen species of thorn, *Cratægus pyracantha*, with flame-colored berries, found in the south of Europe.

pȳ'răl, *a.* pertaining to a pyre. [Rare.]

pyr'ȧ·lid, *n.* [LL. *pyralis*, from Gr. *pyr*, fire.] any moth of the family *Pyralidæ*.

Pȳ·ral'i·dae, *n.pl.* a family of moths of which there are many species, mostly small and injurious, as the bee moth, meal moth, etc.: they have narrow, triangular forewings, broader hind wings, and long legs.

pȳ·ral'i·dăn, *a.* and *n.* same as *pyralidid*.

pȳ·ral'i·did, *a.* of the *Pyralidae* family.

pȳ·ral'i·did, *n.* a moth of the family *Pyralidae*.

pyr'ȧ·loid, *a.* of or resembling the pyralids.

pyr'ȧ·mid, *n.* [Fr. *pyramide*; L. *pyramis*; Gr. *pyramis*, *pyramidos*, a pyramid; ME. had *piramis*, from L.]

1. a huge structure with a square base and four triangular sides meeting at a point, built by the ancient Egyptians as a royal tomb.

2. an object or formation shaped like a pyramid.

3. in crystallography, a form in which the faces intersect the vertical and lateral axes.

4. in geometry, a solid figure having a polygonal base, the sides of which form the bases of triangular surfaces meeting at a common vertex.

5. a tree grown or trained in pyramidal form.

6. in anatomy, a conical bony projection on the posterior wall of the tympanum, immediately behind the oval aperture (fenestra ovalis) of the ear.

7. [*pl.*] a game, pyramid pool.

pyramid pool; a form of pool in which the balls are racked in a triangular form instead of being spotted at the diamonds of the table.

the (Great) Pyramids; the three large pyramids at El Gîza, Egypt: the largest is the Pyramid of Cheops.

pyr'ȧ·mid, *v.t.* and *v.i.* 1. to build up in the form of a pyramid; to collect in a mass or heap.

2. to engage in (a series of buying or selling operations) during an upward or downward trend in the stock market, working on margin with the profits made in the transactions.

py·ram'i·dăl, *a.* [Fr. *pyramidal*; It. *piramidale*.]

1. of, pertaining to, or of the form of a pyramid.

2. in biology, conical; pointed, as the prickles of some roses.

3. in crystallography, same as *tetragonal*.

pyramidal numbers; the third order of figurate numbers.

py·ram'i·dāle, *n.* in anatomy, the cuneiform bone of the carpus.

py·ram'i·dăl·ly, *adv.* 1. in the form of a pyramid.

2. extremely; exceedingly; supremely. [Obs.]

py·ram'i·dāte, *a.* pyramidal. [Rare.]

pyr·ȧ·mid'iç, pyr·ȧ·mid'iç·ăl, *a.* pyramidal.

pyr·ȧ·mid'iç·ăl·ly, *adv.* in a pyramidal manner.

pyr·ȧ·mid'iç·ăl·ness, *n.* the state of being pyramidical.

pyr·ȧ·mid'i·on, *n.*; *pl.* **pyr·ȧ·mid'i·ȧ,** the apex of an obelisk, resembling a pyramid.

py·ram'i·doid, *n.* [Gr. *pyramis*, a pyramid, and *eidos*, form.] a solid resembling a pyramid.

pyr'ȧ·mis, *n.*; *pl.*, **py·ram'i·dēs,** a pyramid. [Obs.]

pyr'ȧ·moid, *n.* pyramidoid. [Rare.]

Pyr'ȧ·mus and This'bē, [L.; Gr. *Pyramos* and L.; Gr. *Thisbē*.] Babylonian lovers whose story is told in Ovid's *Metamorphoses*: Pyramus, believing Thisbe killed by a lion when he finds her blood-stained veil at their trysting place, kills himself; and Thisbe, when she finds him dying, kills herself.

pȳ'ran, *n.* [from *pyrone*.] any of a group of closed-chain compounds, C_5H_6O, the ring of which contains one oxygen atom and five carbon atoms.

pȳ·rär'gy·rīte, *n.* [Gr. *pyr*, fire, and *argyros*, silver.] a lustrous, dark-red or black sulfide of silver and antimony, $3Ag_2S{\cdot}Sb_2S_3$, with hexagonal crystallization.

pȳre, *n.* [Gr. *pyr*, fire.] a heap of combustible materials arranged for the burning of a corpse or corpses; a funeral pile.

pȳ·rē'nȧ, *n.*; *pl.* **pȳ·rē'nae,** same as *pyrene* (seed).

pȳ·rē·när'i·um, *n.*; *pl.* **pȳ·rē·när'i·ȧ,** in botany, a pome, particularly one having pyrenes. [Rare.]

pȳ'rēne, *n.* [Gr. *pyrēn*, stone of a fruit.] the stone or seed of apples, pears, etc.

pȳ'rēne, *n.* [Gr. *pyr*, fire, and *-ene*.] one of the hydrocarbons, $C_{16}H_{10}$, obtained in the dry distillation of fats, resins, and coal.

Pyr·ē·nē'ăn, *a.* [Fr. *Pyrénées*, the Pyrenees.] of or pertaining to the Pyrenees, a range of mountains separating France from Spain.

pyr·ē·nem'ȧ·tous, *a.* [Gr. *pyrēn*, stone of a fruit, and *haima*, blood.] having nucleated red blood corpuscles.

pȳ·rē'nin, *n.* a substance found in the nucleoli of cells.

pȳ·rē'noid, *n.* [Gr. *pyrēn*, stone of a fruit, and *eidos*, form.] a rounded granule found in the chromatophores of *Protozoa* and *Protophyta*, and specially active in the formation of starch.

pȳ·rē'noid, *a.* resembling a wart in form.

Pȳ·rē''nō·my·cē'tēs, *n.pl.* [Gr. *pyrēn*, stone of a fruit, and *mykētes*, mushrooms.] a group of ascomycetous fungi, chiefly parasitic and very injurious to plants, the ergot, *Claviceps purpurea*, being an example.

pȳ·reth'rin, *n.* [L., from Gr. *pyrethron*, feverfew.] a soft resin extracted from *Radix pyrethri* by alcohol and ether. Later researches have shown it to be a mixture of two oils and a resin.

pȳ·reth'rine, *n.* an alkaloid found in the root of *Anacyclus pyrethrum*, the pellitory of Spain.

Pȳ·reth'rum, *n.* [L., from Gr. *pyrethron*, feverfew.]

1. a section of the genus *Chrysanthemum*, including various garden plants.

2. [p–] any plant of this genus; also, insect powder made from certain of these flowers.

pȳ·ret'iç, *a.* [Gr., from *pyr*, fire.]

1. of or causing fever.

2. feverish.

pȳ·ret'ic, *n.* a medicine for fever; a febrifuge. [Rare.]

pyr'ē·tō-, [from Gr. *pyretos*, burning heat, fever.] a combining form meaning *fever*, as in *pyretology*: also, before a vowel, *pyret-*.

pyr''ē·tō·gen'e·sis, *n.* the origin of fever.

pyr''ē·tō·gen'iç, *a.* of or pertaining to the origin of fevers.

pyr·ē·tol'ō·gy, *n.* the branch of medicine which deals with fevers.

pȳ'rex, *n.* [from *pie*, and L. *rex*, king; spelled as if from Gr. *pyr*, a fire, *pyra*, hearth.] a heat-resistant glassware for cooking, etc.: a trademark (*Pyrex*).

pȳ·rex'i·ȧ, *n.* [Mod. L., from Gr. *pyrexis*, feverishness.] fever.

pȳ·rex'i·ăl, *a.* of or having a fever; feverish.

pȳ·rex'iç, pȳ·rex'iç·ăl, *a.* pyrexial.

pyr'gom (pĩr'), *n.* same as *fassaite*.

pyr·hē·li·om'ē·tēr (pĩr-), *n.* [Gr. *pyr*, fire, and *hēlios*, sun, and *metron*, measure.] an instrument to measure the amount of energy given off by the sun.

pȳ·rid′iç, *a.* derived from or related to pyridine.

pyr′i·dīne, pyr′i·din, *n.* a colorless or pale-yellow liquid, C_5H_5N, obtained from coal tar and bone oil by destructive distillation and having a sharp, pungent odor. It is used as a solvent, alcohol denaturant, antiseptic, etc.

pyr·i·dox′ine, *n.* a complex pyridine compound, one of the B complex vitamins, found in various foods and prepared synthetically, usually as the hydrochloride: known to prevent nutritional dermatitis in rats: also called *vitamin B_6*.

pyr′i·dyl, *n.* the monovalent radical, C_5H_4N.

pyr′i·form, *a.* [L. *pyrum* or *pirum*, a pear.] shaped like a pear.

py·rim′i·dīne, *n.* a colorless, crystalline organic compound, $C_4H_4N_2$, the fundamental form of a group of bases, some of which are constituents of nucleic acid.

pyr·i·tā′ceous (-shus), *a.* pertaining to pyrites. [Rare.]

pȳ′rīte, *n.*; *pl.* **pȳ·rī′tēṣ** (*or* pī′rīts), [L. *pyrites*, from Gr. *pyritēs*, flint or millstone.] iron sulfide, FeS_2, a lustrous, yellow mineral occurring abundantly as a native ore and serving principally as a source of sulfur in the manufacture of sulfuric acid: also called *iron pyrites, fool's gold.*

pȳ·rī′tēs (*or* pī′rīts), *n.* any native metallic sulfide. The name was originally given to iron pyrites, the mineral pyrite, alluding to its property of giving sparks when struck with steel.

arsenical pyrites; arsenopyrite.
copper pyrites; chalcopyrite.
hair pyrites; millerite.
magnetic pyrites; pyrrhotite.
tin pyrites; stannite.
white iron pyrites; marcasite.

pȳ·rit′iç, pȳ·rit′i·çăl, *a.* of, containing, or resembling pyrites.

pyr·i·tif′ėr·ous, *a.* bearing or producing pyrites.

pyr′i·tīze, *v.t.*; pyritized, *pt.*, *pp.*; pyritizing, *ppr.* to change or convert into pyrites.

pyr·i·tō·hē′drŏn, *n.* [Gr. *pyritēs*, and *hedra*, base.] the pentagonal dodecahedron, a crystalline form often assumed by pyrite.

pyr·i·tol′ō·ġy, *n.* [from Gr. *pyritēs*, of fire (from *pyr*, a fire); and *-logy*.] the science of analyzing compounds by means of the blowpipe.

pyr′i·tous, *a.* consisting of pyrites; pyritic.

pȳ′rō-, pȳr-, [from Gr. *pyr*, *pyros*, a fire.] a combining form meaning: (a) *fire, heat*, as in *pyro*mania, *pyro*meter; (b) in chemistry, *a substance derived* (from the specified substance) *by* or *as if by the action of heat*, as in *pyro*gallol; (c) in geology, *a formation due to the action of heat*, as in *pyro*xenite.

pȳ′rō, *n.* in photography, pyrogallic acid. [Colloq.]

pȳ·rō·ȧ·cē′tiç, *a.* of or relating to an acetone derived from acetates by distillation, or to pyroacetic ether.

pȳ·rō·ac′id, *n.* an acid derived from another acid by the action of heat.

pȳ·rō·an·ti·mō′nāte, *n.* a salt of pyroantimonic acid.

pȳ·rō·an·ti·mon′iç, *a.* designating or of an acid of antimony similar to pyrophosphoric acid.

pȳ·rō·är′sē·nāte, *n.* a salt of pyroarsenic acid.

pȳ·rō·är·sen′iç, *a.* designating or of an acid derived from arsenic acid by heat.

pȳ·rō·bō′rāte, *n.* any salt of pyroboric acid.

pȳ·rō·bō′riç, *a.* designating or of an acid obtained from boric acid by heat.

pȳ·rō·çat′ē·chin, *n.* pyrocatechol.

pȳ·rō·çat′ē·çhōl, *n.* [*pyro-*, and *catechu*, and *-ol*.] a white, crystalline substance, $C_6H_4(OH)_2$, occurring naturally in plants or produced by dry distillation of catechu, etc.

pȳ·rō·çhem′i·çăl, *a.* of chemistry at high temperatures.

pȳ′rō·çhlōre, *n.* [*pyro-*, and Gr. *chlōros*, green.] a brownish or yellowish mineral with resinous luster, usually occurring in octahedrons.

pȳ·rō·cit′riç, *a.* obtained from citric acid by distillation: said of citraconic acid.

pȳ·rō·çlas′tiç, *a.* [*pyr-*, and Gr. *klastos*, broken.] made up of rock material broken into fragments through volcanic or igneous action.

pȳ·rō·çon·duç·tiv′i·ty, *n.* conductivity effected in certain electric insulators when they are subjected to high temperatures.

pȳ·rō·çrys′tăl·line, *a.* crystallized from molten rock material.

pȳ′rō·din, pȳ′rō·dīne, *n.* $C_6H_5{\cdot}NH{\cdot}NH{\cdot}CO{\cdot}CH_3$, a crystalline compound: it is used like chrysarobin in skin diseases and also as an antipyretic.

pȳ″rō·ē·leç′triç, *a.* of, pertaining to, or exhibiting pyroelectricity.

pȳ·rō·ē·leç′triç, *n.* a pyroelectric substance.

pȳ·rō·ē·leç·tric′i·ty, *n.* the development of electric polarity in certain crystals by a change of temperature.

pȳ·rō·gal′lāte, *n.* a salt or ester of pyrogallol.

pȳ·rō·gal′liç ac′id, pyrogallol.

pȳ·rō·gal′lōl (*or* -lol), *n.* a white, crystalline phenol, $C_6H_3(OH)_3$, a product of the dry distillation of gallic acid, used in medicine, as a developer in photography, etc.

pȳ′rō·ġen, *n.* [*pyro-*, and Gr. *-genēs*, producing.]

1. a product of the action of heat on an organic substance; a pyroacid. [Obs.]
2. any cause of fever, as a ptomaine from decomposing meat. [Obs.]
3. electricity. [Obs.]

pȳ·rō·ġen′e·sis, *n.* the process of developing heat.

pȳ·rō·ġē·net′iç, *a.* evolving or developing heat; heat-producing.

pȳ·rō·ġen′iç, *a.* 1. producing, or produced by, heat or fever.
2. in geology, igneous.

pȳ·roġ′ē·nous, *a.* pyrogenic.

pȳ·rog·nos′tiç, *a.* [*pyro-*, and Gr. *gnōstikos*, knowing.] of or produced by the use of heat.

pȳ·rog·nos′tiçs, *n. pl.*; the properties of a mineral made known when heat is applied to it, such as flame coloration, fusibility, etc.

pȳ·rog′rȧ·phėr, *n.* one skilled in pyrography.

pȳ·rō·graph′iç, *a.* of or relating to pyrography.

pȳ·rog′rȧ·phy, *n.* [*pyro-* and *-graphy*.]

1. the art or process of burning designs on wood or leather by the use of heated tools.
2. a design so made.

pȳ″rō·grȧ·vūre′, *n.* the art of engraving or making a design, as on wood, by means of a hot point; also, the engraving or design thus made; pyrography.

Pyr·ō′lȧ, *n.* a genus of ericaceous plants of the subfamily *Pyroleæ*, including the wintergreen and shinleaf.

Pyr·ō·lā′cē·ae, *n.pl.* same as *Pyroleæ*.

pȳ·rol′ȧ·tėr, pȳ·rol′ȧ·tŏr, *n.* a fire worshiper.

pȳ·rol′ȧ·try, *n.* fire worship.

Pȳ·rō′lē·ae, *n.pl.* a subfamily of ericaceous plants including the genera *Pyrola*, or shinleaf, *Moneses*, or one-flowered wintergreen, and *Chimaphila*, or pipsissewa.

pȳ·rol′ē·tėr, *n.* [*pyro-*, and Gr. *oletēr*, destroyer.] an apparatus for extinguishing fire by the use of carbon dioxide generated by the union of sodium bicarbonate and hydrochloric acid.

pȳ·rō·lig′nē·ous, pyr·ō·lig′niç, *a.* [*pyro-*, and L. *lignum*, wood.]

1. produced by the destructive distillation of wood.
2. designating or of a reddish-brown liquid (*pyroligneous acid*), chiefly acetic acid and methyl alcohol, obtained by the destructive distillation of wood.
3. designating or of methyl alcohol, especially when obtained from wood.

pȳ·rō·lig′nīte, *n.* a salt of pyroligneous acid.

pȳ·rō·lig′nous, *a.* pyroligneous.

pȳ·rō·lith′iç, *a.* cyanuric. [Obs.]

pȳ·rol′ō·ġist, *n.* one versed in or a student of pyrology.

pȳ·rol′ō·ġy, *n.* pyritology.

pȳ·rō·lū′site, *n.* [*pyro-* and Gr. *louein*, to wash.] MnO_2, a native manganese dioxide having a metallic luster and a dark, steel-gray color: used in glassmaking and as an oxidizing agent in varnish.

pȳ·rol′y·sis, *n.* [Mod. L.; *pyro-* and *-lysis*.] chemical decomposition by heat.

pȳ·rō·lyt′iç, *a.* of pyrolysis.

pȳ″rō·mag·net′iç, *a.* of or produced by the combined action of heat and magnetism.

pyromagnetic generator; an induction machine in which the strength of current is made to vary by alternately heating and cooling its field magnets.

pȳ′rō·man·cy, *n.* [*pyro-*, and Gr. *manteia*, a divination.] divination by means of flame or fire.

pȳ·rō·mā′ni·ȧ, *n.* [*pyro-*, and Gr. *mania*, madness.] a persistent compulsion to start destructive fires.

pȳ·rō·mā′ni·aç, *n.* a person having pyromania.

pȳ·rō·mā′ni·aç, *a.* of or affected with pyromania.

pȳ″rō·mȧ·nī′ȧ·çăl, *a.* pyromaniac.

pȳ·rō·man′tiç, *a.* of or pertaining to pyromancy.

pȳ·rō·man′tiç, *n.* one who divines or pretends to divine by fire.

pȳ″rō·mel·lit′iç, *a.* derived from mellitic acid by heat.

pȳ·rō·met·ȧ·mor′phiṣm, *n.* metamorphism produced or chiefly produced by the action of heat.

pȳ·rom′ē·tėr, *n.* [*pyro-* and *-meter*.]

1. formerly, an instrument for measuring the expansion of bodies by heat. [Obs.]
2. an instrument for measuring degrees of heat above those indicated by ordinary thermometers, as by the change of electric current.

pȳ·rō·met′riç, pȳ·rō·met′riç·ăl, *a.* of or registered on a pyrometer.

pȳ·rom′ē·try, *n.* the act or the process of using a pyrometer; the branch of physics which treats of the measurement of temperatures over 1500°C.

pȳ·rō·mor′phīte, *n.* [*pyro-*, and Gr. *morphē*, form.] a lead salt occurring mostly in veins with other ores of lead; a chlorophosphate of lead, $3Pb_3(PO_4)_2{\cdot}PbCl_2$, occurring naturally in any of various colors.

pȳ·rō·mor′phous, *a.* capable of being made crystallizable by heat.

pȳ·rō·mū′çāte, *n.* a salt of pyromucic acid.

pȳ·rō·mū′ciç, *a.* designating an acid derived by distillation from mucic acid.

pȳ·rō·naph′thȧ, *n.* an illuminant distilled from petroleum in Russia.

pȳ′rōne, *n.* in chemistry, $CO(CH)_4O$, an unsaturated, closed-chain compound from which several yellow dyes are derived.

pȳ·rō·nom′içs, *n.* [*pyro-*, and Gr. *nomos*, law.] the science pertaining to heat and its laws. [Rare.]

pȳ′rōpe, *n.* [Gr. *pyr*, fire, and *ōps*, eye.] a variety of garnet, deep red to black in color, containing aluminum and used as a gem.

pyr′ō·phāne, *n.* an opaque opal which becomes temporarily transparent when immersed in a hot bath of wax, but loses its transparency as it cools. [Obs.]

pȳ·roph′ȧ·nous, *a.* [*pyro-*, and Gr. *phanein*, to show.] becoming transparent by heat.

pȳ·rō·phō′bi·ȧ, *n.* [*pyro-*, and Gr. *phobos*, to fear.] an irrational fear of fire.

pȳ′rō·phōne, *n.* [*pyro-*, and Gr. *phōnē*, sound.] a musical apparatus consisting of a series of glass tubes graduated in length, each containing a jet of burning hydrogen by which its tones are produced: also called *chemical harmonicon*.

pȳ·rō·phor′iç, *a.* capable of igniting spontaneously when exposed to air.

pȳ·roph′ō·rus, *n.* any compound which takes fire spontaneously.

Pȳ·roph′ō·rus, *n.* [Gr. *pyrophoros*, fire-bearing, from *pyr*, fire, and *pherein*, to bear.] a genus of beetles, the elaters, of the family *Elateridæ*, native to tropical America and including the *Pyrophorus noctilucus* of South America and the West Indies.

pȳ·rō·phos′phāte, *n.* a salt of pyrophosphoric acid.

pȳ″rō·phos·phor′iç, *a.* derived from phosphoric acid by heat.

pyrophosphoric acid; a viscous liquid acid, $H_4P_2O_7$, which crystallizes when left standing at ordinary temperatures and is easily converted to orthophosphoric acid upon dilution with water.

pȳ·rō·phō·tom′ē·tėr, *n.* [*pyro-* and *photometer*.] an optical instrument for the measurement of extremely high temperatures.

pȳ·rō·phyl′līte, *n.* [*pyro-* and *phyll-* and *-ite*.] a hydrous aluminum silicate, $Al_2O_3{\cdot}4SiO_2{\cdot}H_2O$, resembling talc in structure and color, used for polishing rice, as a filler for slate pencils, etc.

pȳ·rō·punç′tūre, *n.* puncture by the use of hot needles.

pȳ″rō·rȧ·cē′miç, *a.* derived from racemic acid by heat: applied to acetoformic acid, $C_3H_4O_3$.

pȳ′rō·sçōpe, *n.* [*pyro-* and *-scope*.] an instrument to measure the intensity of heat radiating from a body. It resembles a differential thermometer, having two bulbs, one covered with thick silver leaf.

pȳ·rō′sis, *n.* [Gr., a burning.] a condition characterized by a burning sensation in the stomach and esophagus and the belching of an acid fluid; heartburn.

pȳ·ros′mȧ·līte, *n.* [*pyro-*, and Gr. *osmē*, a smell.] a mineral found in some iron mines in Wermland, Sweden. It is of various shades from pale liver-brown to blackish-green, and consists of a hydrated silicate of iron and manganese with chloride of iron. When heated, it gives the odor of chlorine.

pȳ'rō-sōme, *n.* any sea animal of the *Pyrosomidæ.*

Pȳ-rō-sōm'i-dae, *n.pl.* [*pyro-,* and Gr. *sōma,* body.] a family of the compound ascidians having but one genus, *Pyrosoma,* with three species. They unite in great numbers, forming a large hollow cylinder, from two to fourteen inches in length, and from half an inch to three inches in circumference, open at one end and closed at the other, swimming in the ocean by the alternate contraction and dilatation of its component individual animals. They are brilliantly phosphorescent.

pȳ-rō-sō'moid, *a.* resembling a pyrosome.

pȳ'rō-stat, *n.* [*pyro-,* and Gr. *statos,* from *histanai,* to stand.]
1. a device that automatically puts into action a mechanism sounding an alarm when a fire breaks out near by.
2. a high-temperature thermostat.

pȳ-rō-sul'fāte, *n.* a salt of pyrosulfuric acid: also called *disulfate.*

pȳ''rō-sul-fūr'iç ac'id, a strong, crystalline acid, $H_2S_2O_7$, prepared commercially as a heavy, oily, fuming liquid: also called *disulfuric acid.*

pȳ''rō-tär-tar'iç, *a.* derived from tartaric acid by heat: applied to an acid, $C_5H_8O_4$.

pȳ-rō-tär'trāte, *n.* a salt of pyrotartaric acid.

pȳ-rō-tech'ni-ăn, *n.* a pyrotechnist. [Rare.]

pȳ-rō-tech'niç, *a.* [*pyro-,* and Gr. *technē,* art.]
1. of or pertaining to pyrotechnics.
2. brilliant; dazzling.

pȳ-rō-tech'niç-ăl, *a.* pyrotechnic.
pyrotechnical sponge; same as *amadou.*

pȳ''rō-tech-ni'cian (-nish'un), *n.* a pyrotechnist. [Rare.]

pȳ-rō-tech'niçs, *n.pl.* [*construed as sing.*]
1. the art of making and using fireworks.
2. a display of fireworks.
3. a dazzling display, as of eloquence, wit, etc.

pȳ-rō-tech'nist, *n.* one skilled in pyrotechnics.

pȳ-rō-tech'ny, *n.* [Fr. *pyrotechnie.*] pyrotechnics (senses 1 and 2).

pȳ''rō-tē-reb'iç, *a.* obtained from terebic acid by heat: applied to an acid, $C_6H_{10}O_3$, of the acrylic series.

pȳ-roth'ō-nide, *n.* [*pyro-,* and Gr. *othonē,* fine linen.] an oily liquid produced by the destructive distillation of cellulose, as linen, hemp, or cotton rags: also called *rag oil* and formerly used as a gargle.

pȳ-rot'iç, *a.* caustic.

pȳ-rot'iç, *n.* a caustic remedy.

pȳ-rō-tox'in, *n.* 1. a toxin developed during fevers.
2. a toxin that induces fever.

pȳ-rō-ū'riç, *a.* same as *cyanuric.*

pȳ-rō-xan'thine (-zan'), *n.* [*pyro-,* and Gr. *xanthos,* yellow.] a yellow crystalline substance produced by the action of alkalis on one of the substances contained in crude wood spirit.

pȳ'rox-ēne, *n.* [Fr. *pyroxène,* from *pyro-,* and Gr. *xenos,* a stranger: so named (by Haüy, Fr. mineralogist) as being foreign to igneous rocks.] a complex silicate mineral, containing iron, magnesium, and calcium, found in igneous rocks.

pȳ-rox-en'iç, *a.* pertaining to or consisting of pyroxene.

pȳ-rox'e-nīte, *n.* a dark-colored, granular, igneous rock composed chiefly of pyroxene.

pȳ-rox'yle, *n.* same as *pyroxylin.*

pȳ-rox-yl'iç, *a.* obtained from wood by heat: an old term used to designate methylic alcohol.

pȳ-rox'y-lin, pȳ-rox'y-line, *n.* [*pyro-,* and Gr. *xylon,* wood.] nitrocellulose, especially in less highly nitrated and explosive forms than guncotton, used in the manufacture of paints, lacquers, collodion, celluloid, etc.

Pyr'rhȧ (-rȧ), *n.* [L.; Gr. *Pyrrha.*] in Greek mythology, a survivor of a great deluge.

pyr'rhiç (-rik), *a.* [Gr. *pyrrhichē,* a war dance, from *Pyrrhichus,* the inventor of the dance.]
1. of or pertaining to a certain Greek martial dance.
2. consisting of two short syllables, or of pyrrhics; as, a *pyrrhic* verse.

pyr'rhiç, *n.* 1. a war dance of the ancient Greeks. It was danced by boys in armor, accompanied by the lute or lyre.
2. a metrical foot consisting of two short or unstressed syllables.

Pyr'rhiç, *a.* pertaining to Pyrrhus, king of Epirus.
Pyrrhic victory; a too costly victory: in reference to the victory of Pyrrhus over the Romans at Asculum in 279 B.C., in which the losses were extremely heavy.

pyr'rhi-cist, *n.* a dancer of the pyrrhic.

pyr'rhō-līte (-rō-), *n.* same as *pyrrhotine.*

Pyr-rhō'ni-ăn, *a.* same as *Pyrrhonic.*

Pyr-rhon'iç, *a.* pertaining to Pyrrhonism.

Pyr'rhō-nism, *n.* 1. the doctrine taught by Pyrrho (365–275 B.C.), the Greek Skeptic, that all knowledge, including the testimony of the senses, is uncertain.
2. extreme skepticism.

Pyr'rhō-nist, *n.* an advocate of Pyrrhonism.

pyr'rhō-tine, *n.* same as *pyrrhotite.*

pyr'rhō-tīte, *n.* [from Gr. *pyrrhotēs,* redness (from *pyrrhos,* flame-colored, from *pyr,* a fire); and *-ite.*] any of several bronze-colored, lustrous native sulfides of iron, often containing small amounts of copper, cobalt, and nickel.

pyr'rhous (-rus), *a.* reddish; flame-colored.

Pyr'rhus, *n.* in Greek legend, Achilles' son.

pyr-rōle', pyr-rōl', *n.* [*pyr-,* and L. *oleum,* oil.] a colorless, pungent, slightly basic liquid, C_4H_5N, derived from coal tar, bone oil, etc. by destructive distillation. It is soluble in alcohol and ether, and is found in bile pigments, chlorophyll, and hematin.

Pyr'ū-lȧ, *n.* [L. *pyrum,* a pear.] a genus of gastropods, so called from the pyriform shell; the fig shells; the pear shells.

pȳ-rū'riç, *a.* cyanuric.

Pȳ'rus, *n.* [L., a pear tree.] a genus of the *Rosaceæ,* consisting of ornamental and fruit trees. They have deciduous simple leaves and white or pink flowers. The pear, *Pyrus communis,* and the apple, *Pyrus malus,* are the most numerous species. The genus also includes the quince, the mountain ash, the beam tree, the chokeberry, and the service tree.

pȳ-rū'viç ac'id, a colorless, liquid organic acid, CH_3COCO_2H, obtained by the dry distillation of racemic acid or ether.

Py-thag-ō-rē'ăn, *n.* a disciple of Pythagoras.

Py-thag-ō-rē'ăn, *a.* pertaining to Pythagoras, his philosophy and teachings, or his followers.
Pythagorean letter; the letter Y, so called because Pythagoras employed it to signify the bifurcation of the good and evil ways of men; also taken as symbolic of the triad formed by the monad giving rise to the duad.
Pythagorean system; in astronomy, a primitive conception of the solar system, not unlike that of Copernicus, as formulated by Pythagoras.
Pythagorean theorem or *proposition;* the forty-seventh proposition of the first book of Euclid's Elements, that in a right-angled triangle the sum of the squares of the legs is equal to the square of the hypotenuse.

Py-thag-ō-rē'ăn-ism, *n.* the philosophy of Pythagoras, the main tenets of which were the transmigration of the soul and the belief in numbers as the ultimate elements of the universe.

Pyth-ȧ-gor'iç, Pyth-ȧ-gor'iç-ăl, *a.* Pythagorean. [Rare.]

Py-thag'ō-rism, *n.* same as *Pythagoreanism.*

Py-thag'ō-rīze, *v.i.;* Pythagorized, *pt., pp.;* Pythagorizing, *ppr.* to speculate after the manner of Pythagoras.

Pyth'i-ȧ, *n.* [Gr.] in ancient Greece, the high priestess of Apollo at Delphi, who was believed to hold communion with the god and to voice his oracles.

Pyth'i-ad, *n.* [Gr.] the interval of four years between one celebration of the Pythian games and another.

Pyth'i-ăn, *a.* [L. *Pythius;* Gr. *Pythios,* pertaining to Pytho, the older name of Delphi and its environs.]
1. of Apollo as patron of Delphi and the oracle located there.
2. designating or of the games held at Delphi every four years by the ancient Greeks in honor of Apollo.
Pythian verse; in Greek prosody, dactylic hexameter.

Pyth'i-ăs, see *Damon and Pythias.*

Pyth'i-ăn, *n.* one who is frenzied, like the Delphic priestess; also, a devotee of Apollo.

Pyth'iç, *a.* pertaining to Pythia or her prophecies.

pyth'id, *n.* one of the *Pythidæ.*

Pyth'i-dae, *n.pl.* [L.] a family of small heteromerous beetles of the subtribe *Trachelia,* found in the North Temperate Zone.

pȳ-thō-ġen'e-sis, *n.* [Gr. *pythein,* to rot, and *genesis,* origin.] generation or production by means of filth.

pȳ''thō-ġē-net'iç, *a.* pythogenic.

pȳ-thō-ġen'iç, *a.* produced by filth.
pythogenic fever; any fever produced by filth; specifically, typhoid fever.

Pȳ'thon, *n.* [Gr. *Pythō,* the older name for *Delphi.*]
1. a genus of very large, nonpoisonous snakes of Burma, Indo-China, etc. that crush their prey to death, the typical genus of the family *Pythonidæ.*
2. in classic mythology, a monster serpent inhabiting the caves of Parnassus and preying upon the people of Delphi and their flocks: it was slain by Apollo.
3. [p–] any large snake that crushes its prey, as the boa.
4. [p–] any snake of the genus *Python* or of the family *Pythonidæ.*

pȳ'thō-ness, *n.* [Fr. *pythonisse,* from LL. *pythonissa,* from *Pytho,* a familiar spirit.]
1. the priestess of Apollo at Delphi.
2. any woman soothsayer; a prophetess.
Like Saul, to run to a *pythoness.*
—Jeremy Taylor.

pȳ-thon'iç, *a.* [Gr. *Pythōnikos,* relating to Pytho.] pertaining to the prediction of future events; oracular; prophetic.

pȳ-thon'iç, *a.* of or like a python.

pȳ'thŏn-id, *n.* one of the *Pythonidæ.*

Pȳ-thon'i-dae, *n.pl.* [*Python* and *-idæ.*] a family of peropod snakes, having intermaxillary teeth and rudimentary hind limbs; the rock snakes.

pȳ-thon'i-form, *a.* having the form of a python; pythonoid.

pȳ'thŏn-ine, *a.* of or pertaining to the *Pythonidæ.*

pyth'ō-nism, *n.* the art of predicting events after the manner of Pythia.

pȳ'thŏn-oid, *a.* [L. *Python,* and Gr. *eidos,* form.] pertaining to or resembling a python; pythoniform.

pȳ'thŏn-oid, *n.* one of the *Pythonoidea.*

Pȳ-thō-noi'dē-ȧ, *n.pl.* a division of large nonvenomous peropod snakes, having rudimentary hind limbs but no pelvis, including the families *Boidæ, Charinidæ,* and *Pythonidæ.*

pȳ'thō-nō-morph, *n.* one of the *Pythonomorpha.*

Pȳ''thō-nō-mor'phȧ, *n.pl.* [*Python,* and Gr. *morphē,* form.] same as *Mosasauria.*

pȳ''thō-nō-mor'phiç, *a.* pythonomorphous.

pȳ''thō-nō-mor'phous, *a.* pertaining to the *Pythonomorpha;* mosasaurian.

pȳ-ū'ri-ȧ, *n.* [Gr. *pyon,* pus, and *ouron,* urine.] the presence of pus in the urine.

pyx, *n.* [L. *pyxis* or *puxis;* Gr. *pyxis,* a box.]
1. (a) the container in which the consecrated wafer of the Eucharist is kept; (b) a small container for carrying the Eucharist to the sick.
2. a box in the British mint that holds the sample coins until the annual test for purity and weight.
3. the box that holds a ship's compass; the binnacle. [Rare.]
4. in anatomy, the pyxis.
Also spelled *pix.*
trial of the pyx; in the English mint, the annual trial of the sample standard coins of gold and silver.

PYX (twelfth century)

pyx, *v.t.* to test coins as to fineness and weight. [Brit.]

pyx cloth, a veil of precious stuff covering the pyx.

pyx'i-dāte, *a.* [Gr. *pyxidion,* dim. of *pyx.*] furnished with a pyxidium.

pyx-id'i-um, *n.; pl.* **pyx-id'i-ȧ,** [Gr. *pyxidion,* a writing tablet.]
1. in botany, a seedcase with two parts, the upper acting as a lid.
2. the theca of mosses. [Rare.]

PYXIDIUM

pyx'ie, *n.* same as *pixy.*

pyx'ie, *n.* [prob. from the botanical name, *Pyxidanthera barbulata.*] a creeping evergreen plant with small, leathery leaves and white, starshaped flowers.

Pyx'is, *n.* [L., box (mariner's).] formerly, in astronomy, a subdivision of the constellation Argo.

pyx'is, *n.*; *pl.* **pyx'i·dēș,** [L.; Gr. pyxis, a box.]
1. a vase with a cover, used by the ancient Greeks and Romans.
2. a small box or case.
3. a pyxidium.
4. the acetabulum of the hip joint.

Q

Q, q (kū), *n.pl.* **Q's, q's, Qs, qs** (kūz), 1. the seventeenth letter of the English alphabet: from the Roman adoption of the early Greek *koppa*, a borrowing from the Phoenician.
2. the sound of Q or q: normally, in English, *q* is followed by *u*, and is pronounced (*kw*), as in *queen* (kwēn), or occasionally (*k*), as in *conquer* (koṅ'kẽr).
3. a type or impression for Q or q.
4. a symbol for the seventeenth in a sequence or group (or the sixteenth if J is omitted).

Q, q, *a.* 1. of Q or q.
2. seventeenth (or sixteenth if J is omitted) in a sequence or group.

Q, *n.* 1. an object shaped like Q.
2. a medieval Roman numeral for 500.

Q, *a.* shaped like Q.

qăt (kät), *n.* [Ar.] a plant, *Catha edulis*, of the staff-tree family, found in Africa and Arabia: the fresh leaf is chewed for its stimulating effects or used in tea.

Q'-bōat", *n.* same as *mystery ship.*

Q fē'vẽr, [from *q*uery: so named because of many unanswered questions about the disease when first identified.] a mild illness characterized by fever, headache, muscular pains, and pneumonia, transmitted by contact or ticks, and caused by a rickettsia, *Coxiella burnetii.*

qi'vi·ut (kē'vē-), *n.* [Esk.]
1. the fine, soft, light-brown under layer of hair on the musk ox.
2. yarn spun from this hair.

qoph (kọf), *n.* same as *koph.*

Q.T., quiet: usually in *on the Q.T.*, in secret. [Slang.]

quā (*or* kwä), *adv.* [L.] in the capacity, function, or character of; as being; as, he spoke not *qua* a public official, but *qua* a private person.

Quāā'lūde, *n.* methaqualone: a trade-mark.

quack, *v.i.*; quacked (kwakt), *pt., pp.*; quacking, *ppr.* [echoic, cf. D. *kwaaken, kwakken*, G. *quaken*, Dan. *qvākke*, to croak, to quack.] to utter the sound or cry made by a duck or goose, or a sound like it.

quack, *n.* the cry uttered by a duck, or any sound resembling it.

quack, *n.* [short for *quacksalver.*]
1. one who, with little or no foundation, pretends to have skill or knowledge in a particular field.
2. an untrained pretender to medical skill he does not possess; a fraudulent practitioner.
Syn.—charlatan, empiric, impostor, mountebank, pretender.

quack, *a.* 1. characterized by pretentious claims with little or no foundation.
2. dishonestly claiming to effect a cure.

quack, *v.i.* 1. to engage in quackery.
2. to talk with a pretension to knowledge one does not have.

quack'ẽr·y, *n.*; *pl.* **quack'ẽr·ieș,** the actions, claims, or methods of a quack, especially in medicine; empiricism; charlatanry; humbug; imposture.

quack grȧss, same as *couch grass.*

quack'ish, *a.* 1. like or characteristic of a quack.
2. boastfully pretentious; boasting of skill not possessed.

quack'ișm, *n.* the practice of quackery.

quaçk'le, *v.t.* and *v.i.* to strangle; to choke. [Dial.]

quack'sal"vẽr, *n.* [D. *kwaksalver*; L.G. *quaksalver*; G. *quacksalber*, lit., a quack that deals in salves.] a quack; a charlatan.

quăd, *n.* in printing, a quadrat.

quăd, *n.* a quadrangle or court, as of a college. [Colloq.]

quăd, *n.* a prison; a jail: usually written *quod.* [Chiefly Brit. Slang.]

quăd, *a.* quadraphonic. [Colloq.]

quădr-, quadri-.

quăd'rȧ, *n.*; *pl.* **quăd'rae,** [L., a square or plinth, a fillet.] in architecture, (a) a square frame or border enclosing a bas-relief; also, any frame or border; (b) the plinth of a podium; (c) one of the fillets above and below the scotia of the Ionic base.

quăd'rȧ·ble, *a.* [L. *quadrare*, to square; written as if *quadrabilis.*] in mathematics, capable of being squared, as a surface.

quăd"rȧ·ġē·nār'i·ăn, *a.* [L. *quadragenarius*, from *quadrageni*, forty each.] forty years old, or between the ages of forty and fifty.

quăd"rȧ·ġē·nār'i·ăn, *n.* a person of this age.

quăd"rȧ·ġē·nār'i·ous, *a.* same as *quadragenarian.*

Quăd·rȧ·ġes'i·mȧ, *n.* [L. *quadragesimus*, fortieth, from *quadraginta*, forty, from *quattuor*, four.]
1. the forty days of Lent. [Obs.]
2. Quadragesima Sunday.
Quadragesima Sunday; the first Sunday in Lent.

quăd·rȧ·ġes'i·măl, *a.* 1. lasting forty days: said of Lent.
2. [Q-] Lenten; of or suitable for Lent.

quăd·rȧ·ġes'i·mălș, *n.pl.* offerings formerly made by a church to the mother church on Mid-Lent Sunday.

quăd'rañ·gle, *n.* [L. *quadrus*, a square, from *quattuor*, four, and *angulus*, angle.]
1. in geometry, a plane figure having four angles, and consequently four sides.
2. an area surrounded on its four sides by buildings.
3. the buildings surrounding a quadrangle.
4. the area of land charted on each of the atlas sheets published by the United States Geological Survey.

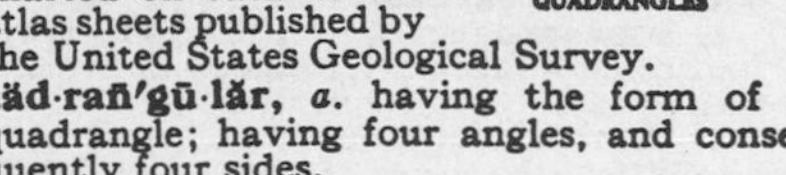
QUADRANGLES

quăd·rañ'gū·lăr, *a.* having the form of a quadrangle; having four angles, and consequently four sides.

quăd·rañ'gū·lăr·ly, *adv.* in the shape of a quadrangle.

quăd'ranș, *n.*; *pl.* **quăd·ran'tēș,** an ancient Roman copper coin, the fourth part of the as.

quăd'rănt, *n.* [L. *quadrans*, a fourth part.]
1. a fourth part; a quarter. [Obs.]
2. a fourth part of the circumference of a circle; an arc of 90°.
3. a quarter section of a circle.
4. any piece or part shaped like a quarter section of a circle.
5. an instrument for measuring angular elevations or altitudes, variously constructed and mounted for different specific uses in astronomy, navigation, surveying, etc., consisting originally of a graduated arc of 90°, with a movable index or vernier, and either plain or telescopic sights, along with a plumb line or spirit level for fixing the vertical or horizontal direction. Its principle and application are the same as that of the sextant, by which it is superseded.
6. in analytic geometry, any of the four parts formed by rectangular co-ordinate axes on a plane surface: the quadrants are designated as first, second, third, and fourth in counterclockwise order, starting with the upper right-hand section.

HADLEY'S QUADRANT

quăd·ran'tăl, *a.* 1. of or pertaining to a quadrant; included in a quadrant; as, *quadrantal* space.
2. shaped like a quadrant.
quadrantal triangle; a spherical triangle having one side equal to a quadrant.

quăd·ran'tăl, *n.* 1. a cube. [Rare.]
2. a cubical vessel used by the Romans, and containing a cubic foot.

quăd'rănt çŏm'pȧss, a carpenter's compass, with an arc and a binding screw.

quăd·rȧ·phon'iç, *a.* [from L. *quadra*, a square, and *phonic.*] designating or of sound reproduction, as on records or tapes or in broadcasting, using four channels to carry and reproduce through separate speakers a blend of sounds from separate sources.

quăd·rȧ·son'iç, *a.* same as *quadraphonic.*

quăd'răt, *n.* [Fr., from L. *quadratus*, squared.]
1. in printing, a block of type metal lower than the face of the type, and used for filling out lines, spacing between words, etc. There are four sizes: en (■), em (■), two-em (■■), and three-em (■■■) quadrats. Commonly shortened to *quad.*
2. a mathematical instrument, chiefly used in finding heights or depths: also called *geometrical square.* [Obs.]

quăd'rāte, *a.* [L. *quadratus*, squared, pp. of *quadrare*, to make square; *quadrus*, a square, from *quattuor*, four.]
1. square or nearly square; rectangular.
2. in zoology, designating a bone or cartilage of the skull in birds, fishes, and reptiles, to which the lower jaw is joined.
3. in astrology, designating an aspect of heavenly bodies in which they are 90° distant from each other.
4. square; equal; exact. [Obs.]
5. suited; fitted; applicable; correspondent. [Obs.]

quăd'rāte, *n.* [Late ME.; L. *quadratum*, from *quadratus.*]
1. a square or rectangle.
2. a square or rectangular space, thing, etc.
3. in zoology, the quadrate bone.
4. in astrology, an aspect of the heavenly bodies, in which they are 90° distant from each other.

quăd'rāte, *v.i.*; quadrated, *pt., pp.*; quadrating, *ppr.* to square; to suit; to correspond; to agree: followed by *with.*

quăd'rāte, *v.t.* 1. to trim, as a ship's gun on its carriage and its trucks; to adjust, as a gun for firing on a level range. [Obs.]
2. to make square; to make (something) conform (*to*).

quăd·rat'iç, *a.* [from *quadrate* and *-ic.*]
1. square.
2. in algebra, pertaining to or involving the square or second power of an unknown quantity, but no higher power.
3. in crystallography, dimetric: applied to the system that includes the square prism and related forms.

quäd·rat′iç, *n.* a quadratic term, expression, or equation.

quäd·rat′i·căl·ly, *adv.* by means of quadratics; to the second degree.

quäd·rat′iç ē·quā′tion, in algebra, an equation in which the second power, or square, is the highest to which the unknown quantity is raised.

quäd·rat′iç̧s, *n.pl.* [*construed as sing.*] that branch of algebra dealing with quadratic equations.

quäd·rā·tō·jụ′găl, *a.* of, connected with, or common to the quadrate and jugal bone.

quäd·rā·tō·jụ′găl, *n.* a bone, generally long and slender, lying between the quadrate bone and jugal bone of birds.

quäd·rā′trix, *n.*; *pl.* **quäd·rā′tri·cēṣ,** [LL. trans. from Gr. *tetragōnizousa*, a mechanical line.] in geometry, a mechanical line by means of which we can find right lines equal to the circumference of circles or other curves and their several parts.

quäd·rā′tum, *n.*; *pl.* **quäd·rā′tȧ,** 1. in zoology, the quadrate bone.
2. in old music, a breve.

quäd′rȧ·tūre, *n.* [LL. *quadratura.*]
1. the act of squaring.
2. the determining of the dimensions of a square equal in area to a given surface.
3. a quadrate; a square. [Obs.]
4. in astronomy, the position of one heavenly body in respect to another, when 90° distant from it, as the moon, when at an equal distance from the points of conjunction and opposition.
5. in physics, a phase difference of ninety degrees.
quadrature of the circle; the famous problem of the squaring of the circle; that is, finding a square equal in area to a given circle, now known to be insoluble.

quäd′rel, *n.* [LL. *quadrellus*, dim. of L. *quadrus*, a square.]
1. a square stone, brick, or tile. [Obs.]
2. a kind of artificial stone made of chalky earth dried in the sun: so called from the square shape. [Obs.]
3. a piece of turf or peat cut in a square form. [Brit. Dial.]

quäd·relle′ (-rel′), *n.* [Fr.] an iron mace with a head of four projections, carried at the saddle bow in the fifteenth century.

QUADRELLE

quäd·ren′ni·ăl, *a.* [L. *quadriennium*, from *quattuor*, four, and *annus*, year.].
1. lasting or comprising four years; as, a *quadrennial* period.
2. occurring once in four years; as, *quadrennial* games.

quäd·ren′ni·ăl, *n.* a quadrennial event.

quäd·ren′ni·ăl·ly, *adv.* once in four years.

quäd·ren′ni·um, *n.*; *pl.* **quäd·ren′ni·ȧ,** [L.] a space or period of four years.

quäd′ri-, [from L. *quadri-*, *quadru-*, and *quatri-*, from *quattuor*, four.] a combining form meaning *four times, fourfold*; also, before a vowel, *quadr-*.

quäd·ri·bā′siç, *a.* in chemistry, designating an acid having four hydrogen atoms which may be replaced by basic atoms or radicals.

quäd′ri·ble, *a.* quadrable. [Obs.]

quäd′riç, *a.* in mathematics, of the second degree: used of a function with more than two variables.

quäd′riç, *n.* [LL. *quadrus*, a square, from L. *quattuor*, four.] in mathematics, a quantic of the second degree.

quäd·ri·çap′sū·lăr, *a.* [*quadri-*, and L. *capsula*, a capsule.] in botany, having four capsules.

quäd″ri·cen·ten′ni·ăl, *n.* [*quadri-* and *centennial.*] a 400th anniversary or its celebration.

quäd″ri·cen·ten′ni·ăl, *a.* of a quadricentennial.

quäd′ri·ceps, *n.* [*quadri-*, and L. *-ceps*, from *caput*, head.] in anatomy, the great extensor muscle of the thigh, which functions to extend the leg when contracted.

quäd·ri·cip′i·tăl, *a.* of or pertaining to the quadriceps.

quäd′ri·çorn, *n.* [*quadri-*, and L. *cornu*, horn.] any animal having four horns or antennae.

quäd·ri·çor′nous, *a.* having four horns or antennae.

quäd·ri·ços′tāte, *a.* [*quadri-*, and L. *costa*, rib.] having four ribs.

quäd′ri·cȳ·çle, *n.* a four-wheeled cycle, or velocipede.

quäd·ri·den′tāte, *a.* [*quadri-*, and L. *dens*, *dentis*, a tooth.] having four teeth or parts resembling teeth.

quäd·ri·en′ni·ăl, *a.* same as *quadrennial.*

quäd·ri·fār′i·ous, *a.* [*quadri-*, and L. *-farius*, from *fari*, to speak.] arranged in four rows or ranks.

quäd′ri·fid, *a.* [L. *quadrifidus*; *quadri-*, four, and *findere*, to divide.] in botany, divided into four parts, as a leaf or petal.

quäd·ri·fō′li·āte, *a.* [*quadri-*, and L. *folium*, a leaf.] having four leaves attached laterally to a common stalk.

quäd·ri·fō′li·ō·lāte, *a.* [*quadri-*, and L. *foliolus*, a leaflet.] of or designating a compound leaf having four leaflets.

quäd·ri·fūr′çāte, quäd·ri·fūr′çā·ted, *a.* doubly dichotomous.

quäd·rī′gȧ, *n.*; *pl.* **quäd·rī′gae,** [*quadri-*, and L. *jugum*, a yoke of oxen, a team.] in ancient Rome, a two-wheeled car or chariot drawn by four horses, which were harnessed all abreast, and not in pairs.

quäd·ri·ġem′i·nȧ, *n.pl.* [L. *quadrigeminus*, fourfold.] in anatomy, two pairs of rounded eminences of the brain separated by a crucial depression, above the passage leading from the third to the fourth ventricle of the cerebrum: more fully called *corpora quadrigemina.*

quäd·ri·ġem′i·năl, *a.* fourfold; specifically, in anatomy, designating the quadrigemina.

quäd·ri·ġem′i·nous, *a.* [L. *quadri-*, *quattuor*, four, and *geminus*, born with another.] of, relating to, or designating the quadrigemina.

quäd″ri·ġē·nār′i·ous, *a.* [L. *quadrigeni*, contr. from *quadringeni*, four hundred each.] consisting of four hundred.

quäd·ri·jụ′gāte, *a.* in botany, bearing four pairs of leaflets, as the petiole of a pinnate leaf.

quäd·ri·jụ′gous, *a.* same as *quadrijugate.*

quäd·ri·lat′ẽr·ăl, *a.* having four sides, and consequently four angles.

quäd·ri·lat′ẽr·ăl, *n.* [*quadri-*, and L. *latus*, *lateris*, side.]
1. in geometry, a figure having four sides and four internal angles.
2. a four-sided area.
3. a space within and defended by four fortresses.

QUADRILATERALS

quäd·ri·lat′ẽr·ăl·ness, *n.* the condition of being quadrilateral.

quäd·ri·liñ′guăl (-gwăl), *a.* [from *quadri-*, and L. *lingua*, the tongue; and *-al.*]
1. written in, or involving, four languages.
2. using or speaking four languages.

quäd·ri·lit′ẽr·ăl, *a.* [*quadri-*, and L. *litera*, letter.] consisting of four letters.

quȧ·drille′ (*or* kȧ-dril′), *n.* [Fr. *quadrille*; Sp. *cuadrilla*, a group of four persons, *cuadrillo*, a small square, from L. *quadra*, *quadrum*, a square, from *quattuor*, four.]
1. a square dance of French origin, in which four couples take part, formerly of five movements, each complete in itself.
2. the music for a quadrille.

quȧ·drille′, *v.i.*; quadrilled, *pt.*, *pp.*; quadrilling *ppr.* to dance or play a quadrille.

quȧ·drille′, *n.* [Fr., altered (after *quadrille*, the dance, from Sp. *cuartillo*, dim., from *cuarto*, fourth, from L. *quartus*, from base of *quattuor*, four.] a game of cards, popular in the eighteenth century, played by four persons with the forty cards remaining after the tens, nines, and eights are discarded.

quȧ·drille′, *v.i.* to play quadrille. [Obs.]

qua·dril·lé′ (kȧ-drē-yā′), *a.* [Fr.] having a pattern of small squares; ruled or marked in small squares; as, *quadrillé* ruling of paper for engineers.

quäd·ril′liŏn (-yun), *n.* [*quadri-* and *million.*]
1. in France and the United States, the fifth power of a thousand; 1 followed by fifteen zeros.
2. in Great Britain and Germany, the fourth power of a million; 1 followed by twenty-four zeros.

quäd·ril′liŏn, *a.* amounting to one quadrillion in number.

quäd·ri·lō′bāte, quäd′ri·lōbed, *a.* [*quadri-*, and L. *lobus*, Gr. *lobos*, a lobe.] in biology, having four lobes; as, a *quadrilobed* leaf.

quäd·ri·loç′ū·lăr, *a.* [*quadri-*, and L. *loculus*, a cell.] in biology, having four cells or parts resembling cells; as, a *quadrilocular* pericarp.

quäd′rin, quäd′rine, *n.* [LL. *quadrinus.*] a small piece of money worth about a farthing. [Obs.]

quäd·ri·nōd′ăl, *a.* [*quadri-*, and L. *nodus*, a knot.] having four nodes.

quäd·ri·nō′mi·ăl, *a.* [*quadri-*, and L. *nomen*, name.] in algebra, consisting of four terms.

quäd·ri·nō′mi·ăl, *n.* in algebra, a quadrinomial expression.

quäd·ri·nom′i·năl, *a.* and *n.* same as *quadrinomial.*

quäd·ri·pär′tīte, *a.* [L. *quadripartitus*, pp. of *quadripartire*, to divide into four.]
1. made up of or divided into four parts.
2. shared in or formulated by four persons, nations, etc.; as, a *quadripartite* pact.

quäd·ri·pär′tīte·ly, *adv.* in four divisions.

quäd″ri·pär·ti′tion (-tish′un), *n.* a division by four or into four equal parts; also, the taking of the fourth part of any quantity or number.

quäd·ri·pen′nāte, *a.* [*quadri-*, and L. *penna*, a wing.] having four wings, as an insect.

quäd·riph′yl·lous, *a.* [*quadri-*, and Gr. *phyllon*, a leaf.] having four leaves, as a plant.

quäd·ri·plā′năr, *a.* [*quadri-*, and LL. *planum*, a plane.] in geometry, formed by or made up of four planes.

quäd·ri·pul′mō·năr·y, *a.* [*quadri-*, and L. *pulmo*, a lung.] having two pairs of pulmonary sacs, as certain spiders.

quäd·ri·quäd′riç, *a.* of a quartic curve, which is formed by the intersection of two quadric surfaces.

quäd′ri·rēme, *n.* [L. *quadriremis*, from *quattuor*, four, and *remus*, an oar.] in ancient Greece and Rome, a galley having four benches or ranks of oars or rowers.

quäd′ri·seçt, *v.t.* [from *quadri-*, and L. *sectus*, pp. of *secare*, to cut.] to divide into four equal parts.

quäd·ri·seç′tion, *n.* a section or division into four equal parts.

quäd·ri·sẽr′i·ăl, *a.* [*quadri-*, and L. *series*, a row, a succession.] having four series or rows.

quäd·ri·sul′çāte, *a.* having four grooves or furrows; specifically, of mammals, having four toes on each foot or a four-parted hoof.

quäd″ri·syl·lab′iç, *a.* pertaining to or having the nature of a quadrisyllable.

quäd″ri·syl·lab′i·căl, *a.* quadrisyllabic.

quäd·ri·syl′lȧ·ble, *n.* a word consisting of four syllables.

quäd·ri·ū′rāte, *n.* a mixture of urates and uric acid.

quäd·ri·vā′lence, *n.* [*quadri-*, and L. *valens*, ppr. of *valere*, to be strong.] the quality or state of being quadrivalent.

quäd·ri·vā′len·cy, *n.* same as *quadrivalence.*

quäd·ri·vā′lent, *a.* 1. having a valence of four.
2. having four valences.
Also, especially for 1, *tetravalent.*

quäd′ri·valve, *a.* [*quadri-*, and L. *valva*, a door.] having four valves.

quäd·ri·val′vū·lăr, *a.* in botany and zoology, having four valves or valvelike parts.

quäd·riv′i·ăl, *a.* [*quadri-*, and L. *via*, a road.]
1. having four roads meeting in a point.
2. leading in four directions: said of roads or ways.
3. of or pertaining to the quadrivium. [Obs.]

quäd·riv′i·ăl, *n.* one of the arts constituting the quadrivium.

quäd·riv′i·um, *n.* in the Middle Ages, four of the seven liberal arts; namely, arithmetic, music, geometry, and astronomy.

quäd·ri·vol′tine, *a.* [*quadri-*, and It. *volta*, turn, time.] producing four times annually: said of a silkworm.

quäd·ri·vol′tine, *n.* a silkworm that makes four cocoons a year.

quäd·rọọn′, *n.* [Sp. *cuarterón*, from L. *quartus*, fourth, *quattuor*, four.] the offspring of a mulatto and a white; a person who has one Negro grandparent.

quäd′rụ·māne, *n.* one of the *Quadrumana*; any of the primates except man.

Quäd·rụ′mȧ·nȧ, *n.pl.* [L. *quadru-*, four, in composition, and *manus*, the hand.] a group of mammals having four feet that function as hands, as monkeys.

quäd·rụ′mȧ·nous, *a.* 1. having all four feet adapted to function as hands.

2. relating to or resembling the *Quadrumana.*

quäd·rum′vi·rāte, *n.* [*quadr-*, and tri*umvirate.*]
1. government by four persons.
2. any group of four persons associated in office or authority.

quäd′rụ·ped, *a.* [L. *quadrupes; quadru-, quattuor,* four, and *pes,* foot.] having four legs and feet; walking on all fours.

quäd′rụ·ped, *n.* an animal, especially a mammal, having four legs and feet; an animal that walks on all fours, as a dog or a horse.

quäd·rụ′pē·dăl, *a.* 1. walking on all fours.
2. pertaining to a quadruped.

quäd′rụ·ple, *a.* [Fr. *quadruple;* L. *quadruplus.*]
1. consisting of or including four.
2. four times as much or as many; fourfold.
3. in music, having four beats to the measure, the first and third beats being accented.

quäd′rụ·ple, *adv.* four times as much or as many.

quäd′rụ·ple, *n.* an amount four times as much or as many.

quäd·rụ′ple, *v.t.*; quadrupled, *pt., pp.*; quadrupling, *ppr.* [Fr. *quadrupler;* LL. *quadruplare,* from L. *quadruplus,* fourfold.] to make four times as much or as many.

quäd·rụ′ple, *v.i.* to become four times as much or as many.

quäd′rụ·plet, *n.* 1. a combination or compound of four, usually of one kind.
2. a bicycle for carrying four riders.
3. one of four offspring born at one birth; also, [*pl.*] four offspring born at a single birth.

quäd′rụ·ple tīme (or **meaṣ′ūre**), in music, (a) a measure having four beats, of which the first and third are accented; (b) the rhythm resulting from this.

quäd′rụ·plex, *a.* [L.] fourfold; folded twice; specifically, designating or of a telegraph system which transmits four messages, two in each direction, over a wire at the same time.

quäd′rụ·plex, *n.* an instrument for quadruplex transmission.

quäd·rụ′pli·cāte, *v.t.*; quadruplicated, *pt., pp.*; quadruplicating, *ppr.* [L. *quadruplicare,* to quadruple.] to make fourfold; to make four identical copies of.

quäd·rụ′pli·cāte, *a.* 1. fourfold; four times repeated; as, a *quadruplicate* ratio or proportion.
2. in mathematics, raised to the fourth power.

quäd·rụ′pli·cāte, *n.* one of four copies all alike.

quäd″rụ·pli·cā′tion, *n.* the act of quadruplicating; also, the result of this.

quäd·rụ′pli·cȧ·tūre, *n.* same as *quadruplication.*

quäd·rụ·plic′i·ty, *n.* fourfoldness; the state of being quadruplex.

quäd′rụ·ply, *adv.* to a fourfold degree; as, to be *quadruply* recompensed.

quae′rē, *v. imperative* [L., imper. of *quærere,* to seek, seek to learn, question.] inquire; find out: used to express doubt or to suggest that certain information be sought.

quae′rē, *n.* a query; a question.

quae·sī′tum, *n.*; *pl.* **quae·sī′tȧ,** [L., neut. of *quæsitus,* pp. of *quærere,* to seek, to ask.] an object of search.

quaes′tŏr (kwes′ *or* kwēs′), *n.* [L., contr. from *quæsitor,* from *quæsitus,* pp. of *quærere,* to inquire.] in ancient Rome, (a) originally, an official who judged certain criminal cases; (b) later, any of certain state treasurers: also *questor.*

quaes·tō′ri·al, *a.* of a quaestor.

quaes′tŏr·ship, *n.* the position, rank, or duties of a quaestor.

quȧff (kwȧf), *v.t.* and *v.i.* [prob. from L.G. *quassen,* to overindulge.] to drink or swallow in large quantities and with pleasure.

quȧff, *n.* a drink; also, the act of quaffing.

quȧff′ẽr, *n.* one who quaffs.

quag, *n.* a quagmire.

quag′gȧ, *n.*; *pl.* **quag′gȧ** *or* **quag′gȧṣ,** [Hottentot *quagga,* a name derived from the cry.] a South African mammal, *Equus quagga,* resembling the donkey and the zebra, having a striped head, neck, and shoulders, a brown back, and a whitish-gray belly and legs: now extinct.

QUAGGA
(*Equus quagga*)

quag′gle, *n.* an unsteady motion. [Brit. Dial.]

quag′gy, *a.*; *comp.* quaggier; *superl.* quaggiest,
1. like a quagmire; boggy; soft and miry.
2. soft; flabby.

quag′mīre, *n.* [formerly *quakemire.*]
1. soft, wet, miry ground that shakes or yields under the feet.
2. a difficult position, as of one sinking or stuck in a quagmire.
Syn.—swamp, marsh, morass, bog, slough.

quạ′hog, quạ′hạug, *n.* [Am. Ind. (Narragansett) *poquauhock.*] a large species of clam or bivalvular mollusk, *Venus mercenaria,* having a very hard, solid shell.

quāiçh, quāigh (kwāk), *n.* [Ir. *cuach,* a cup or bowl; compare Eng. *quaff.*] a shallow cup or drinking vessel: also written *quegh.* [Scot.]

Quāi d'Or·sāy′ (kā; *Fr.* ke dọr-se′), [Fr., lit., quay of Orsay (former Fr. general).]
1. a quay on the Seine in Paris, toward which the building housing the French Foreign Office faces.
2. the French Foreign Office.

quāil, *v.i.*; quailed, *pt., pp.*; quailing, *ppr.* [ME. *quelen;* AS. *cwelan,* to die: *cwellan,* to kill, to quell.]
1. to draw back in fear; to lose heart, courage, or spirits.
2. to fade; to wither. [Obs.]
Syn.—shrink, cower, tremble, quake, yield, blench.

quāil, *v.t.* to crush; to depress; to sink; to subdue; to cause to shrink or lose heart. [Obs.]

quāil, *v.i.* [Fr. *cailler;* It. *quagliare,* to curdle; W. *caul,* a calf's maw, rennet, chyle, a curd; *ceulaw,* to curdle.] to curdle; to coagulate, as milk. [Obs.]

quāil, *n.*; *pl.* **quāilṣ** *or* **quāil,** [It. *quaglia;* Fr. *caille;* ML. *cuacula.*] any of various gallinaceous game birds, of America, Europe, Africa, and Asia of several genera and species; specifically, (a) *Coturnix coturnix,* and others of the same species in Europe; (b) *Lophortyx californica californica,* a bird of California; (c) *Colinus virginianus virginianus,* the bobwhite, valued as a game bird.

EUROPEAN QUAIL
(*Coturnix coturnix*)

quāil çall, a quail pipe.

quāil dŏve, a ground pigeon of the genus *Starnænas.*

quāil hạwk, the sparrow hawk of New Zealand.

quāil pīpe, a pipe or call formerly used for luring quails into a net.

quāil snīpe, 1. the dowitcher.
2. a small bird of the *Thinocoridæ* of South America, related to the plovers.

quāil′y, *n.*; *pl.* **quāil′ieṣ,** in Canada, the upland plover.

quāint, *v.t.* to acquaint. [Obs.]

quāint, *a.* [ME. *queint, cointe,* from OFr. *coynt, coint,* neat, fine, trim, dainty, from L. *cognitus,* known.]
1. pleasingly odd and antique.
2. singular; unusual; curious.
3. fanciful; whimsical.
4. artificially elegant; ingeniously contrived; trim; pretty; neat; finespun; pleasant. [Archaic.]
5. artful; subtle; wily. [Obs.]
6. prim; shy; squeamish. [Obs.]
7. noted; notable; remarkable. [Obs.]

quāin′tise, *n.* guile; cunning; craft. [Obs.]

quāint′ly, *adv.* in a quaint manner.

quāint′ness, *n.* the quality of being quaint.

quāir, *n.* a quire; a book. [Obs.]

quāke, *v.i.*; quaked (kwākt), *pt., pp.*; quaking, *ppr.* [AS. *cwacian;* G. *quackeln,* to shake, to agitate.]
1. to shake; to be agitated with quick, short motions continually repeated; to shudder; as, he *quaked* with fear.
2. to shake, tremble, move, or quiver, as land in an earthquake.

quāke, *v.t.* to frighten; to throw into agitation. [Obs.]

quāke, *n.* 1. a shaking or tremor.
2. an earthquake.

quāk′ẽr, *n.* 1. one who quakes.
2. [Q–] [orig. derisive: so called from Fox's admonition to "quake" at the word of the Lord.] a member of a religious sect, the Society of Friends, founded by George Fox, an Englishman, about 1650: Friends believe in plainness of dress, manners, and religious worship, and are opposed to military service and the taking of oaths; they do not use the term *Quaker* of themselves.
3. [Q–] a Quaker gun.
4. any grasshopper of the genus *Œdipoda*: so called from the quaking noise made in flying.
5. any of several dull-hued noctuid moths, as *Agrotis castanea.*
6. the sooty albatross.

quāk′ẽr but′tŏnṣ, nux vomica seeds.

Quāk′ẽr·ess, *n.* a Quaker woman or girl.

Quāk′ẽr gun, see *Quaker gun* under *gun.*

Quāk′ẽr·ish, *a.* like a Quaker in manner, dress, principles, etc.

Quāk′ẽr·iṣm, *n.* the principles and ways of the Quakers.

Quāk′ẽr-lā″dieṣ, *n.pl.* the pale-blue flowers of the bluet, *Houstonia cærulea.*

Quāk′ẽr·ly, *a.* resembling Quakers.

Quāk′ẽr·ly, *adv.* in the manner of Quakers.

Quāk′ẽr meet′ing, 1. a religious meeting of Quakers, characterized by long periods of silence.
2. any meeting or assembly in which there are many silent moments. [Colloq.]

Quāk′ẽr·y, *n.* Quakerism. [Obs.]

quāke′tāil, *n.* the wagtail. [Brit. Dial.]

quāk′i·ly, *adv.* in a quaky manner.

quāk′i·ness, *n.* the quality or condition of being quaky.

quāk′ing ȧsp′en, *Populus tremuloides,* an American poplar having its leaves attached by petioles so slender that any movement of air will make them quiver: also called *trembling aspen.*

quāk′ing grȧss, 1. any of various species of graminaceous plants belonging to the genus *Briza,* whose spikelets make a quaking or rattling sound in the wind.
2. rattlesnake grass, *Glyceria canadensis.*

quāk′ing·ly, *adv.* tremblingly.

quāk′y, *a.*; *comp.* quakier; *superl.* quakiest, quaking; shaky.

quäl′i·fī·ȧ·ble, *a.* capable of being qualified.

quäl″i·fi·çā′tion, *n.* [Fr., from L. *qualificare,* to qualify.]
1. the act of qualifying or the state of being qualified.
2. any quality, knowledge, ability, experience, or acquirement that fits a person for a position, office, profession, etc.; a requisite.
3. a condition that must be met in order to exercise certain rights.
4. modification; restriction; limitation; diminution; abatement; as, to use a word without *qualification.*
5. in logic, the addition of a negative or affirmative quality to the subject or predicate of a proposition.
property qualification; the ownership of a fixed amount of property as a prerequisite to exercising certain rights, as voting, jury duty, holding office, etc.

quäl′i·fi·çā″tive, *n.* a modifying clause, phrase, or word.

quäl′i·fi·çā″tive, *a.* having power to modify; qualifying.

quäl′i·fi·çā″tŏr, *n.* [LL. *qualificator,* from *qualificare,* to qualify.] in the Roman Catholic Church, an officer who examines and prepares cases for trial in an ecclesiastical court.

quäl′i·fīed, *a.* 1. having met conditions or requirements set.
2. having the necessary or desirable qualities; fit; competent.
3. limited; modified; as, he gave only *qualified* approval.
4. empowered to be invested with two benefices. [Obs.]
qualified fee; in law, a base fee, or an estate which has a qualification annexed to it, the fee ceasing with the qualification.
Syn.—capable, competent, fit.

quäl′i·fīed·ly, *adv.* with or by way of qualification.

quăl′i·fied·ness, *n.* the state of being qualified.

quăl′i·fi·ẽr, *n.* 1. one who or that which qualifies.
2. a word, as an adjective or adverb, that modifies or limits the meaning of another word.

quăl′i·fȳ, *v.t.*; qualified, *pt., pp.*; qualifying, *ppr.* [Fr. *qualifier*; ML. *qualificare*, from L. *qualis*, of what kind, and *facere*, to make.]
1. to describe by giving the qualities or characteristics of.
2. to render fit for an office, occupation, exercise of a right, etc.
3. to furnish with legal power or capacity.
4. to abate; to soften; to diminish; to moderate.
5. to ease; to assuage. [Obs.]
6. to modify; to restrain; to limit by exceptions; as, to *qualify* words or expressions, or to *qualify* the sense of words or phrases.
7. to modulate; to vary; as, to *qualify* sounds.
8. to change the strength of (a liquor, etc.).
9. in grammar, to limit or modify the meaning of (a word).

quăl′i·fȳ, *v.i.* to be or become qualified.

quăl′i·tā·tive, *a.* [LL. *qualitativus*, from L. *qualitas*, *qualitatis*, quality.] relating to quality or qualities: distinguished from *quantitative*.
qualitative analysis: the branch of chemistry dealing with the determination of the elements or ingredients of which a substance is composed: distinguished from *quantitative analysis*.

quăl′i·tā·tive·ly, *adv.* in a qualitative manner.

quăl′i·tied, *a.* having a quality or qualities.

quăl′i·ty, *n.*; *pl.* **quăl′i·tieṣ,** [L. *qualitas*, *qualitatis*, quality.]
1. that which belongs to something and makes or helps to make it what it is; characteristic element; attribute; as, purity of tone is an important *quality* of music.
2. any character or characteristic which may make an object good or bad, commendable or reprehensible; the degree of excellence which a thing possesses; as, a fabric of poor *quality*.
3. superiority; excellence; as, a person of *quality*.
4. basic nature; character; kind.
5. character; position; as, the attorney advised him in the *quality* of a friend, not professionally.
6. in phonetics, the character of a vowel sound as determined by the resonance of the vowel chords and the shape of the passage above the larynx when the sound is produced.
7. in logic, the nature of a proposition as affirmative or negative.
8. in acoustics, character of sounds, apart from pitch and intensity, depending upon the various combinations of overtones; timbre.
9. position in society. [Archaic.]
10. people of superior rank or station; as, he belongs to the *quality*. [Archaic or Dial.]

I shall appear at the masquerade dressed up in my feathers, that the *quality* may see how pretty they will look in their traveling habits. —Addison.

Syn.—attribute, character, nature, characteristic, peculiarity, property.

quăl′i·ty cŏn·trōl′, a system for maintaining desired standards in production or in a product, especially by inspecting samples of the product.

qualm (kwäm), *n.* [AS. *cwealm*, pestilence, destruction, death; Dan. *qvalm*, qualm, vapor, smoke.]
1. a fit of nausea; a sudden fit or seizure of sickness or faintness; as, *qualms* of heartsick agony.
2. a scruple; a twinge of conscience.
3. a sudden feeling of uneasiness or doubt; a misgiving.

quälm′ish, *a.* 1. having qualms.
2. having the nature of a qualm.
3. of such a nature as to produce qualms.

quälm′ish·ly, *adv.* in a qualmish manner.

quälm′ish·ness, *n.* the state or condition of being qualmish.

quäm′ash, *n.* same as *camass*.

Quȧ·mā′ṣi·ȧ (-zhi-ȧ *or* -si-ȧ), *n.* same as *Camassia*.

Quam′ō·clit, *n.* [Mex.] a genus of plants merged with the genus *Ipomæa*.

quan′dȧ·ry, *n.*; *pl.* **quan′dȧ·rieṣ,** [origin obscure; prob. from scholastic L., from L. *quando*, when (interrogative).] doubt; uncertainty; a state of difficulty or perplexity; a predicament; a dilemma.

quan′dong, quan′dang, *n.* [native name.]
1. an Australian tree, *Fusanus acuminatus*, of the family *Santalaceæ*.
2. the edible fruit of this tree, having a single stone, or seed: also called *native peach*.
3. the stone or seed of the quandong.
Also *quantong*.

quan′net, *n.* [etym. uncertain.] a kind of flat file with a handle usually placed along the side: it is used like a plane.

quant, *n.* [perh. from L. *contus*, from Gr. *kontos*, boat pole.] a pole with a disk near the end, for propelling a small boat: the disk prevents sinking in the mud. [Brit.]

quant, *v.t.* and *v.i.* to propel (a boat) with a quant. [Brit.]

quan′tȧ, *n.* plural of *quantum*.

quan′tiç, *n.* [L. *quantus*, how much.] in mathematics, a homogeneous integral function of two or more variables. They are classified according to their dimensions, as quadric, cubic, quartic, quintic, etc., denoting quantics of the second, third, fourth, fifth, etc. degrees. They are further distinguished as binary, ternary, quaternary, etc., according as they contain two, three, four, etc. variables.

quan″ti·fi·çā′tion, *n.* [LL. from *quantificare*, to quantify.] the act or process of quantifying.

quan′ti·fȳ, *v.t.*; quantified, *pt., pp.*; quantifying, *ppr.* [ML. *quantificare*, to quantify, from L. *quantus*, how much, and *facere*, to make.]
1. to determine or express the quantity of; to indicate the extent of.
2. to express in quantitative terms, or as a numerical equivalent.
3. in logic, to make the quantity of (a term) clear and explicit, as by using *all*, *none*, or *some*.

quan′ti·tā·tive, *a.* [ML. *quantitativus*, from L. *quantitas*, *quantitatis*, quantity.]
1. having to do with quantity: distinguished from *qualitative*.
2. capable of being measured.
3. having to do with the quantity of a speech sound.
quantitative analysis; the branch of chemistry dealing with the accurate measurement of the amounts or percentages of the various components of a substance or compound: distinguished from *qualitative analysis*.

quan′ti·tive, *a.* same as *quantitative*.

quan′ti·tive·ly, *adv.* so as to be measurable by quantity.

quan′ti·ty, *n.*; *pl.* **quan′ti·tieṣ,** [OFr. *quantite*; L. *quantitas*, quantity, extent, from *quantus*, how great, from *quam*, how.]
1. that property of anything which can be determined by measurement; that attribute of anything by which it is greater or less than some other thing; extent; measure; size; greatness; magnitude.
2. (a) an amount; a portion; (b) any indeterminate weight or measure.
3. an exact amount of a particular thing.
4. a large sum, number, mass, or portion.
5. a small portion; anything very little or diminutive. [Obs.]

If I were sawed into *quantities*, I should make four dozen of such. —Shak.

6. in mathematics, (a) a thing that has the property of being measurable in dimensions, amounts, etc., or in extensions of these which can be expressed in numbers or symbols; (b) a number or symbol used to express a mathematical quantity. Thus, number is a quantity; time, space, mass, force, weight, etc. are also quantities. A *simple quantity* is expressed by a single term, as *a* or *b*; a *compound quantity* by two or more terms connected by the signs + (plus) or — (minus). Quantities which have the sign + prefixed to them are called *positive* or *affirmative quantities*; those to which the sign — is prefixed are called *negative quantities*.
7. in logic, that character which is determined by the extension of the subject of a proposition as universal or particular.
8. in music, the relative length of a tone.
9. in philosophy, that aspect of things to which measure applies and according to which they can be compared with one another.
10. in phonetics and prosody, the relative length or brevity of a vowel, continuant consonant, or syllable, with reference to the time needed to utter it.
11. in electricity, strength of current, or the amount passing through a conductor in a given time, as distinguished from the potential.
quantity of estate; in law, the time during which the right of enjoyment of an estate continues.

quan·ti·vā′lence (*or* -tiv′ȧ-lens), *n.* in chemistry, valence. [Now Rare.]

quan′tong, *n.* same as *quandong*.

quan′tum, *n.*; *pl.* **quan′tȧ,** [L., neut. sing. of *quantus*, how much, how many.]
1. quantity, or amount.
2. a specified quantity; a portion.
3. in the quantum theory, a (or the) fixed, elemental unit, as of energy, angular momentum, etc.
quantum jump (or *leap*); (a) a sudden alteration in the energy level of an atom or molecule together with the emission or absorption of radiant energy; (b) any sudden and extensive change or advance, as in a program or policy.
quantum mechanics; a mathematical theory in physics which starts with the assumption that energy is not infinitely divisible and deals with atomic structure and phenomena by the methods of quantum theory.
quantum meruit; whatever he deserved; in law, an action grounded on a promise that the defendant would pay the plaintiff for his service as much as he would deserve.
quantum number; a number indicating a quantum condition and given to each energy level in an atom.
quantum sufficit; enough; sufficient.
quantum theory; the theory that energy is not absorbed nor radiated continuously but discontinuously, in definite units called *quanta*.
quantum valebat; whatever it was worth; in law, an action to recover of defendant, for goods sold, as much as they were worth.

Quạ′pạw, *n.* a member of the Sioux tribe of Indians formerly living in Arkansas.

quā·quȧ·vẽr′săl, *a.* [L. *quaqua*, in all directions, and *versus*, pp. of *vertere*, to turn.] in geology, directed from a common center toward all points of the compass; turning or dipping in all directions.

quar·ăn·tīn′ȧ·ble, *a.* subject to quarantine.

quar′ăn·tīne, *n.* [It. *quarantina*, a space of forty days, from *quaranta*, contr. from L. *quadraginta*, forty, from *quatuor*, four.]
1. a period of forty days; specifically, in English law, a period of forty days, during which the widow of a man dying seized of land had the privilege of remaining in her husband's mansion house, and during which time her dower was to be assigned.
2. a period, originally of forty days, during which a vessel arriving from an infected port, or being suspected of carrying a contagious disease on board, is detained in port in strict isolation.
3. the place where such a vessel is stationed.
4. any isolation or restriction on travel or passage imposed to keep contagious diseases, insect pests, etc. from spreading.
5. a place where persons, animals, or plants having contagious diseases, insect pests, etc. are kept in isolation, or beyond which they are prohibited from travel or passage.
quarantine flag; a yellow flag displayed to indicate the presence of infectious diseases: also called *yellow jack*.

quar′ăn·tīne, *v.t.*; quarantined, *pt., pp.*; quarantining, *ppr.* 1. to put under quarantine; to cause to undergo quarantine.
2. to isolate politically, commercially, etc., as an aggressor nation.

quark, *n.* [arbitrary use of a word coined by James Joyce in *Finnegans Wake*.] any of three hypothetical particles postulated as forming the building blocks of baryons and mesons and accounting in theory for their properties.

quar′rel, *n.* [ME. *quarel*, *quarell*, *querel*; OFr. *querele*; L. *querela*, *querelæ*, from *queri*, to complain, to lament.]
1. a cause for dispute.
2. a dispute or disagreement, especially one marked by anger and deep resentment.
3. a falling out; a breaking up of friendly relations.

Syn.—contention, fuss, altercation, wrangle, feud, strife, bickering.

quar′rel, *v.i.*; quarreled *or* quarrelled, *pt., pp.*; quarreling *or* quarrelling, *ppr.* 1. to dispute heatedly, or with loud and angry words; to wrangle; to contend; to squabble.
2. to find fault; to cavil.
3. to have a breach in friendship.

quar′rel, *v.t.* 1. to quarrel with. [Obs.]
2. to compel by a quarrel.

quär'rel, *n.* [LL. *quadrellus*, from L. *quadrus*, a square.]
1. a square-headed missile or arrow used in ancient crossbows.
2. any of the small diamond-shaped or square panes of glass in a latticed window.
3. anything with a square-headed part, as a stonemason's chisel.
4. a glaziers' diamond.
5. a square or diamond-shaped paving stone.

QUARREL

quär'rel·ẽr, quär'rel·lẽr, *n.* one who quarrels.

quär'rel·et, *n.* in architecture, a small quarrel, or lozenge. [Obs.]

quär'rel·ing, *a.* disposed to quarrel; scolding; wrangling.

quär'rel·ing·ly, *adv.* in a quarreling manner.

quär'rel·ous, *a.* quarrelsome. [Obs.]

quär'rel·sōme, *a.* inclined to quarrel.
Syn.—choleric, irascible, petulant, litigious, pugnacious, brawling, fiery, hot-tempered, contentious, irritable.

quär'rel·sōme·ly, *adv.* in a quarrelsome manner; with a quarrelsome temper; petulantly.

quär'rel·sōme·ness, *n.* the quality or condition of being quarrelsome.

quär'ri·ẽr, *n.* a worker at a quarry.

quär'ry, *n.*; *pl.* **quär'ries,** [ME. *quarry, quarrey, quarre*, square, thick, from L. *quadrus*, a square.]
1. an arrow with a square head; a quarrel. [Obs.]
2. a small pane of glass; a small square tile.

quär'ry, *a.* square; quadrate. [Obs.]

quär'ry, *n.*; *pl.* **quär'ries,** [ME. *querre*; OFr. *cuiree*; Fr. *curée*, quarry, from *cuir*, L. *corium*, hide.]
1. a part of the refuse of a slain animal placed on the hide and given to the hounds. [Obs.]
2. an animal that is being hunted down; especially, the game which a hawk is pursuing.
3. any object of pursuit.

quär'ry, *v.i.* to prey, as a vulture.

quär'ry, *n.*; *pl.* **quär'ries,** [OE. *quarrere, quarere*, from OFr. *quarriere*; Fr. *carrière*, a place where stones are hewn for building, lit., a place where they are squared, from LL. *quadraria*, from L. *quadrare*, to square.] a place where stone or slate is excavated, as by cutting or blasting, for building purposes, etc.: it is usually open to the light, and in this respect differs from a mine.

quär'ry, *v.t.*; quarried, *pt., pp.*; quarrying, *ppr.*
1. to excavate or take from a quarry; as, to *quarry* marble.
2. to make a quarry in (land).

quär'ry-fāced (-fāst), *a.* having a rough or unfinished face: said of a building stone which has its face rough, as when taken from the quarry, and not pointed.

quär'ry·măn, *n.*; *pl.* **quär'ry·men,** a man who works in a quarry; a quarrier.

quart, *n.* the fourth part; a quarter. [Obs.]

quart, *n.* [OFr. *quarte*, a fourth part, from L. *quartus*, fourth, from *quattuor*, four.]
1. a liquid measure, equal to $^1/_4$ gallon (57.75 cubic inches).
2. a dry measure, equal to $^1/_8$ peck.
3. any container with a capacity of one quart.
4. in music, the interval of a fourth.

quärt (kärt), *n.* 1. in card games, a sequence of four cards of the same suit.
2. carte, a position in fencing: also *quarte*.

quar'tăl, *a.* [*quarter* and *-al*.] in music, designating or of harmony based on intervals of fourths instead of the usual thirds.

quar'tăn, *a.* [L. *quartanus*, the fourth.] designating the fourth; occurring every fourth day, counting both days of occurrence: said of a fever.

quar'tăn, *n.* 1. a type of malaria in which the paroxysms occur every fourth day.
2. a measure containing the fourth part of some other measure.

quar'tāne, *n.* [L. *quartanus*, pertaining to a fourth, from *quartus*, fourth.] in chemistry, butane, an inflammable compound, having four carbon atoms to each molecule. [Rare.[

quar·tā'tion, *n.* [L. *quartus*, the fourth: so named from the fact that usually enough silver is alloyed with the gold to make the amount of the latter equivalent to a quarter of the alloy.] in chemistry and metallurgy, the alloying of one part of gold that is to be refined with three parts of silver, by which means the nitric or sulfuric acid separates the gold from the inferior metals originally associated with it: also called *inquartation*.

quärte (kärt), *n.* [Fr.] carte, a position in fencing: also *quart*.

quar'tẽr, *n.* [ME. *quartre*; OFr. *quarter, quartier*; L. *quartarius*, a fourth part, from *quartus*, fourth, from *quattuor*, four.]
1. one of four equal parts into which anything is capable of being divided; a fourth part or portion of anything; as, a *quarter* of an hour, a *quarter* of a dollar, three *quarters* of a yard.
2. a fourth part of a hundredweight: 25 pounds in the United States, 28 pounds in England.
3. a measure of grain, equal to eight bushels ($^1/_4$ ton); as, a *quarter* of wheat; also, the fourth part of a chaldron of coal.
4. one fourth of a yard, or 9 inches; a span.
5. one fourth of a mile.
6. one fourth of a year; three months.
7. a school or college term of instruction, usually one fourth of a school year.
8. (a) one fourth of an hour; 15 minutes; (b) the moment marking the end of each fourth of an hour.
9. (a) one fourth of a dollar; 25 cents; (b) a silver coin of the United States and Canada equal to 25 cents.
10. one leg of a four-legged animal, with the adjoining parts.
11. (a) any of the four main points of the compass; (b) any of the four divisions of the horizon as marked off by the four main compass points; (c) any of the regions thought of as under these divisions; any part or region of the earth.
12. a particular district or section in a city; as, the Chinese *quarter*.
13. [*pl.*] lodgings; place of abode.
14. a particular person or group of persons, or a previously identified place, direction, point, etc.; as, this information comes from the highest *quarters*.
15. the part forming the side of a shoe from the heel to the vamp.
16. in astronomy, (a) the period of time in which the moon makes one fourth of its revolution around the earth; (b) the phase of the moon when it is half lighted.
17. in football, etc., any of the four periods into which a game is divided.
18. in heraldry, (a) any of the four equal divisions into which a shield is divided; (b) the charge occupying such a division.
19. in military usage, etc., mercy granted to a surrendering foe.
20. in nautical usage, (a) the afterpart of a ship's side; (b) the post or station assigned to one on a ship; (c) one fourth of a fathom; (d) one fourth of the distance between any two of the 32 points on the compass: also *quarter point*.

QUARTER (sense 18)

21. in farriery, that part of a horse's foot between the toe and the heel, being the side of the coffin.
22. in architecture, a small upright post in partitions; a stud.
23. proper station; assigned or allotted position.

Swift to their several *quarters* hasten then. —Milton.

24. treatment shown to an enemy; indulgence; particularly, the remission or sparing of the life of a captive or an enemy when in one's power and when no longer able to defend himself.

He magnified his own clemency, now they were at his mercy, to offer them *quarter* for their lives, if they would give up the castle. —Clarendon.

Lambs at the mercy of wolves must expect no *quarter*. —L'Estrange.

25. friendship; amity; concord. [Obs.]
false quarter; a cleft in the quarter of a horse's hoof reaching from top to bottom.
grand quarter; in heraldry, any one of the four quarters of an escutcheon.
on the quarter; in nautical usage, in a direction considerably abaft the beam; as, the wind was *on the quarter*.
to come to close quarters; to engage in a direct struggle or a hand-to-hand fight, as with an enemy.
to cry quarter; to beg for mercy.
to keep quarter; to keep one's place and so maintain a friendly relationship with everybody. [Obs.]
to show or *give quarter*; to refrain from slaying, as a defeated enemy.
Syn.—region, district, locality, territory, mercy, forbearance, pity.

quar'tẽr, *v.t.*; quartered (-tẽrd), *pt., pp.*; quartering, *ppr.* 1. to divide into four equal parts.
2. loosely, to separate into any number of parts.

Then sailors *quartered* heaven. —Dryden.

3. to provide lodgings for; specifically, to assign (soldiers) to lodgings; as, to *quarter* troops in the city.

They mean this night in Sardis to be *quartered*. —Shak.

4. to defile (the body of a person put to death) by dismembering it into four parts.
5. to cover (an area) by passing back and forth over it in many directions: said of hounds searching for game.
6. in heraldry, (a) to place or bear, as different coats of arms, on the quarters of a shield; (b) to add (a coat of arms) to a shield in a quarterly arrangement.
7. in mechanics, to set (a crank, etc.) at right angles to the connecting part.

quar'tẽr, *v.i.* 1. to lodge; to have a temporary residence (with *at* or *with*); as, the general *quarters at* a hotel in Church Street.
2. to range over a field, etc. in search of game: said of hounds in hunting.
3. in nautical usage, to blow on the quarter of a ship: said of the wind.
4. to drive a vehicle along a thoroughfare so that the wheels shall not fall into ruts. [Brit.]

quar'tẽr·āge, *n.* [ME.; OFr., from *quartier*, a quarter.]
1. a payment made or received every quarter of the year.
2. the quarters provided for troops, etc.
3. (a) the provision of quarters; (b) the expense of this.

quar'tẽr as'pect, in astrology, same as *quadrate*, sense 4.

quar'tẽr·back, *n.* in football, (a) the player whose position is behind the line of scrimmage together with the fullback and halfbacks, and who generally calls the signals; (b) the position played by a quarterback.

quar'tẽr bend, a bend of 90° in a pipe or rod.

quar'tẽr bill, in the navy, a list of the officers and crew of a ship, showing the various posts allotted to each in time of action.

quar'tẽr block, in nautical usage, a block attached to the quarter of a yard, through which are reeved the sheets and clue lines.

quar'tẽr bōards, in nautical usage, the boards heightening the bulwarks of the quarter; a topgallant bulwark.

quar'tẽr boot, a leather boot to protect the forefoot of a horse which overreaches, and to prevent it from being injured by the hind foot.

quar'tẽr-bound', *a.* in bookbinding, a term applied to a book the back only of which is cloth or leather bound.

quar'tẽr crack, a fissure in the lateral part of the wall of a horse's hoof, usually causing lameness.

quar'tẽr dāy any of the four days regarded as beginning a quarter of the year; hence, the day on which a quarterly payment, as rent, is made. The quarter days in England are Lady Day (March 25), Midsummer Day (June 24), Michaelmas Day (September 29), and Christmas Day (December 25).

quar'tẽr-deck, quar'tẽr·deck, *n.* [so called because orig. half the length of the half deck.] the afterpart of the upper deck of a ship, usually reserved for officers: it was originally between the poop and the mainmast.

QUARTER-DECK

quar'tẽr-deck·ẽr, *n.* 1. a ship's officer who is believed to pay more attention to rules and etiquette than to efficiency. [Naval Slang.]
2. in zoology, any marine shell of the genus *Crepidula*.

quar'tẽred, *a.* 1. separated or divided into four equal parts; divided into fourths.
2. provided with quarters; having shelter; as, we were comfortably *quartered*.

3. sawed into quarters, as a log, and cut to show the grain; as, *quartered* oak.
4. in heraldry, divided into quarters; as, a cross *quartered*.

quar′tẽr ē′vil, a disease of cattle caused by a bacillus: also known as *symptomatic anthrax*.

quar′tẽr fāce, a face in a portrait, etc. so turned that one quarter only is visible.

quar·tẽr-fī′năl, *a.* in sports, designating or of the round of matches immediately preceding the semifinals in a tournament.

quar·tẽr-fī′năl, *n.* a quarter-final match.

quar·tẽr-fī′năl·ist, *n.* in sports, a person or team competing in a tournament and qualifying for the quarter-final round.

quar′tẽr·foil, *n.* same as *quatrefoil*.

quar′tẽr gal′lẽr·y, formerly, a balcony on a ship's quarter, sometimes extended over the stern.

quar′tẽr grāin, the grain of wood, particularly of oak, as it looks when quartersawed.

quar′tẽr guärd, in the British military service, a guard stationed in camp directly on the arrival of each division of a regiment or battalion.

quar′tẽr gun′nẽr, in ships of war, formerly, a petty officer, under the gunner, who had charge of a number of the guns, their ammunition, etc.

quar′tẽr-hour′ (-our′), *n.* 1. fifteen minutes.
2. the point on a clock marking the first quarter or third quarter of an hour.
Also *quarter hour*.

quar′tẽr ill, same as *quarter evil*.

quar′tẽr·ing, *a.* 1. blowing on the afterpart of a ship's side: said of the wind.
2. in machinery, set at right angles to each other, as the cranks of a locomotive.

quar′tẽr·ing, *n.* 1. a dividing into quarters.
2. the providing of quarters for soldiers, etc.
3. in heraldry, (a) the division of a shield into quarters; (b) any of these, or the coat of arms on it.
4. in architecture, a series of quarters, or small upright posts.

QUARTERINGS

quartering block; a block on which the body of one condemned to be quartered was cut in pieces.

quar′tẽr līne, a line fastened to the lower side of a seine by which it is dragged to the shore.

quar′tẽr·ly, *a.* 1. containing or consisting of a quarter; as, *quarterly* seasons.
2. occurring or appearing at regular intervals four times a year; as, *quarterly* payments of rent; the society requires *quarterly* reports from its officers.

quar′tẽr·ly, *adv.* 1. once every quarter of the year; as, the returns are made *quarterly*.
2. in heraldry, in or by quarters, as a shield.

quar′tẽr·ly, *n.*; *pl.* **quar′tẽr·lies,** a publication issued every three months.

quar′tẽr·măn, *n.*; *pl.* **quar′tẽr·men,** one who has charge of or superintends a number of workmen in a navy yard.

quar′tẽr·mȧs″tẽr, *n.* 1. in military usage, (a) an officer whose duty it is to assign quarters to troops and provide them with clothing, equipment, etc.; (b) any member of the Quartermaster Corps.
2. in nautical usage, a petty officer who attends to the steering, ship's compass, signals, etc.

Quar′tẽr·mȧs″ter Cōrps (kōr), that branch of the United States Army concerned with supplying food, clothing, etc. to soldiers.

quar′tẽr·mȧs″tẽr ġen′ẽr·ăl, *pl.* **quar′tẽr·mȧs″tẽrs ġen′ẽr·ăl, quar′tẽr·mȧs″tẽr ġen·ẽr·ăls,** 1. in the United States Army, the general heading the Quartermaster Corps.
2. in the British service, a staff officer of high rank, whose department is charged with all orders relating to the marching, embarking, disembarking, billeting, quartering, and cantoning of troops, and to encampments and camp equipage.

quar′tẽr·mȧs″tẽr sẽr′ġeănt (sär′jent), formerly, in the United States Army, a noncommissioned officer who acted as assistant to a quartermaster.

quar′tẽrn, *n.* [ME.; OFr. *quarteron*, from LL. *quartero, quarteronis*, from L. *quartus*, fourth.]
1. a fourth part; a quarter.
2. one fourth of a pint; a gill.
3. one fourth of a peck.
4. one fourth of a stone, or 3 ½ pounds.
5. a loaf of bread weighing about four pounds.

quar′tẽr net′ting, netting hung along the quarter rails of a vessel for the storage of hammocks.

quar′tẽrn lōaf, a loaf of bread weighing about four pounds; a loaf of bread made of a quarter of a stone of flour.

Who makes the *quartern loaf* and Luddites rise? —H. Smith.

quar′tẽr nōte, in music, a note having one fourth the duration of a whole note: also called *crotchet*.

quar′tẽr·on, *n.* [Fr.] a quarter; particularly, a quarter of a pound, or of a hundred.

quar′tẽr·on, quar′tẽr·ọọn, *n.* same as *quadroon*.

quar′tẽr·pāce, *n.* the platform of a staircase, when it occurs at a right-angle turn of the stairs.

quar′tẽr-phāse, *a.* in electricity, generating, carrying, or run by, two alternating currents whose phases differ by 90 degrees: also called *diphase*.

quar′tẽr piēce, in ships, one of several pieces of timber near the taffrail at the after part of the quarter gallery.

quar′tẽr plāte, in photography, (a) a plate 3¼ by 4¼ inches in size; (b) a picture made from such a plate.

quar′tẽr point, a fourth part of the distance between any two points of the mariner's compass; a quarter.

quar′tẽr rāil, in ships, that part of the rail from the stern to the gangway guarding the quarter deck: also called *quarter railing*.

quar′tẽr round, in architecture, an ovolo.

quar′tẽr·saw, *v.t.*; quartersawed, *pt.*; quartersawed *or* quartersawn, *pp.*; quartersawing, *ppr.* to saw (a log) lengthwise into quarters and then into boards, for the purpose of showing the grain and in order that the board or plank may not warp to any appreciable extent.

quar′tẽr sēal, in Scotland, a seal, now in the form of one half of the great seal, but formerly one fourth of it, held by the director of the Chancery and attached to certain writs, grants, etc.

quar′tẽr seç′tion, one fourth of a section of land, approximately ¼ sq. mi., or 160 acres.

quar′tẽr ses′sions (sesh′unz), 1. in England, a local court that sits quarterly and has limited criminal jurisdiction along with authority in ordinary civil proceedings.
2. in the United States, any of various courts that sit every three months.

quar′tẽr sling, in nautical usage, a sling on either side of the center of a yard to support it.

quar′tẽr·stȧff, *n.*; *pl.* **quar′tẽr·stāves,** 1. a stout, iron-tipped wooden staff, six to eight feet long, formerly used in England as a weapon: it was held by one hand at the middle and the other at a point about halfway between the middle and the end.
2. fighting or play with such a staff.

quar′tẽr step (or **tōne**), in music, an interval of one quarter of a whole tone.

quar′tẽr tim′bẽr, in shipbuilding, one of the timbers in the quarter.

quar′tẽr tũrn, in machinery, a turn or twist of 90°, as in a belt which transmits motion between pulleys on shafts which are at right angles to each other.

quar′tẽr wätch (woch), in nautical usage, one half of the watch on duty.

quar′tẽr wind, in nautical usage, a wind that blows upon the quarter of a vessel.

quar·tet′, quar·tette′, *n.* [Fr. *quartette*; It. *quartetto*, a quartet, from L. *quartus*, fourth.]
1. in music, (a) a composition in four parts, each performed by a single voice or instrument; (b) the set of four persons who perform a musical composition containing four parts.
2. any group of four persons or things.

quar′tiç, *a.* [L. *quartus*, fourth.] in mathematics, of the fourth degree.

quar′tiç, *n.* in mathematics, a quantic of the fourth degree.

quar′tīle, *a.* [ML. *quartilis*, from L. *quartus*, a fourth.]
1. in astrology, designating an aspect of heavenly bodies in which they are 90° distant from each other.
2. in statistics, (a) designating any of the values in a series dividing the distribution of the individuals in the series into four groups of equal frequency; (b) designating any of these groups.

quar′tīle, *n.* 1. in astrology, a quartile aspect.
2. in statistics, a quartile point or group.

quar′tō, *n.*; *pl.* **quar′tōs,** [L., short for *in quarto*; *in*, in, and *quarto*, abl. of *quartus*, fourth.]
1. the page size of a book made up of sheets each of which is folded into four leaves, or eight pages, about nine by twelve inches in size.
2. a book made of pages folded in this way.

quar′tō, *a.* having four (quarto) leaves to the sheet.

Quar·tō·dec′i·măn, *n.* [L. *quartus*, fourth, and *decimus*, tenth.] one of a group of Christians in the early church who, in accordance with the custom of the Jews, celebrated Easter on the fourteenth day of the paschal moon, whether that day fell on a Sabbath or not. This practice led to what was called the paschal controversy and was finally condemned by the Council of Nicaea, A.D. 325.

quartz, *n.* [G. *quarz*, quartz.] a brilliant, crystalline mineral, silicon dioxide, SiO_2, occurring in abundance, most often in a colorless, transparent form, but also as variously colored semiprecious stones. When crystallized it generally occurs in hexagonal prisms, terminated by hexagonal pyramids.

quartz·if′ẽr·ous, *a.* [*quartz* and *-(i)ferous*.] consisting of or yielding quartz.

quartz′īte, *n.* [*quartz* and *-ite*.] a massive, hard, light-colored rock with a flinty sheen: it is a metamorphosed sandstone: also called *quartz rock*.

quartz lamp, a mercury-vapor lamp having a tube made of quartz so that most of the ultraviolet rays are transmitted.

quartz′oid, *n.* [*quartz*, and Gr. *eidos*, likeness.] in crystallography, a crystal composed of two six-sided single pyramids base to base.

quartz′ōse, *a.* containing quartz; having the nature or qualities of quartz; resembling quartz.

quartz′ous, *a.* same as *quartzose*.

quartz plāte, in electricity, a piece of quartz crystal having electric polarity.

quartz′y, *a.* same as *quartzose*.

quā′sär, *n.* [*quasi*-stell*ar* radio source.] any of a number of starlike, celestial objects that emit immense quantities of light or of powerful radio waves, or both, and that appear to be extremely distant from the earth.

quäsh, *v.t.*; quashed, *pt.*, *pp.*; quashing, *ppr.* [ME. *quashen*; OFr. *quasser*, from L. *quassare*, to shake, shatter, shiver, intens. from *quassus*, pp. of *quatere*, to shake, to break.]
1. to beat down or beat in pieces; to crush.
2. to crush; to subdue; to suppress forcibly or summarily; as, to *quash* a rebellion.

quäsh, *v.i.* 1. to shake. [Rare.]
2. to make the noise of water when dashed about or shaken. [Obs.]

quäsh, *v.t.* [OFr. *quasser*, from LL. *cassare*, to annihilate, destroy, from L. *cassus*, empty.] in law, to abate, annul, overthrow, make void, or set aside; as, to *quash* an indictment.

quäsh, *n.* same as *squash* (the plant).

Quäsh′ee, *n.* a Negro; specifically, a Negro of the West Indies.

quā′sī (*or* kwā′zī), *adv.* [L.] as if; in a manner; in a certain sense or to a certain degree; seemingly: often hyphenated as a prefix to an adjective or adverb, as in *quasi*-judicial.

quā′sī, *a.* [L.] seeming; as, a *quasi* wisdom: often hyphenated as a prefix to a noun.

quā′sī çon′traçt, in law, an obligation to do something imposed upon someone by law but bearing the force of a contract and subject to legal action as a contract: now imposed chiefly to prevent unfair gain at the expense of another.

quā′sī çor·pō·rā′tion, a body that exercises some of the functions of a corporation, though not expressly incorporated under the law.

quā′sī dē·liçt′, in civil law, the action of one doing damage or evil voluntarily; an act that resembles an offense, and produces the same result to the extent of incurring a penalty.

quā″sī-jụ̈·di′ciăl (dish′ăl), *a.* having to do with powers that are to some extent judicial, as those of certain boards and commissions of the Federal government.

Quas·i·mō′dō, *n.* in the Roman Catholic Church, the first Sunday after Easter: so called because the introit for that day begins with the words *quasi modo geniti infantes*, as newborn babes: also called *Low Sunday*.

quā′sī-pēr·i·od′iç, *a.* in mathematics, noting a function which reproduces itself to within a factor or an additive quantity when its arguments are subjected to certain linear substitutions; designating a function in which the increase of the variable by a fixed amount is equivalent to the multiplication of the whole function by another function.

quā'sī rē'ăl·ty, in law, things which are fixed in contemplation of law to realty but movable in themselves, as heirlooms, title deeds, court rolls, etc.

quā'sī·ten'ănt, in law, an undertenant who is in possession at the determination of an original lease, and is permitted by the reversioner to hold over.

quā'sī trus·tee', in law, a person who reaps a benefit from a breach of trust and so becomes answerable as a trustee.

quȧss, *n.* same as *kvass.*

quas·sā'tion, *n.* [L. *quassatio, quassationis,* a shaking, a beating, from *quassare,* to shake.] the act of shaking; concussion; the state of being shaken. [Rare.]

Quäs'si·ȧ (kwosh'i-ȧ), *n.* [Mod. L., from Graman *Quassi,* Surinam Negro who prescribed it as a remedy for fever, c. 1730.]

1. a genus of South American tropical plants, consisting of trees of the family *Simarubaceæ. Quassia amara,* native to Panama, Venezuela, Guiana, and northern Brazil, is a small tree with crimson flowers; *Quassia excelsa* (*Picræna excelsa,* Lindley), a native of Jamaica, is a tree fifty feet high, something like an ash, having inconspicuous greenish flowers and black shining drupes the size of a pea.

2. [q–] any plant of this genus.

3. [q–] the wood of any of these plants.

4. [q–] a drug or medicinal preparation from these trees, the active principle of which has been termed quassin, or quassite, a neutral substance readily soluble in alcohol. Quassia is a pure and simple bitter, possessing marked tonic properties. It is generally given in the form of infusion and was formerly substituted by some brewers for hops.

quäs'sin, *n.* the bitter principle of quassia crystallizing from aqueous solutions in very small white prisms: also written *quassiin.*

quäs'sīte, *n.* same as *quassin.*

quȧt, *n.* 1. a pustule or pimple. [Obs. or Dial.]

2. figuratively, a shabby, diminutive, troublesome, or worthless person. [Obs. or Dial.]

quȧt, *v.t.* [a form of *quit, quite, quiet.*] to satiate. [Obs. or Dial.]

quä'tȧ, *n.* same as *coaita.*

quätch, *a.* [origin obscure.] squat; flat. [Obs.]

quā'tērn, *a.* [L. *quaterni,* four each, by fours, distributive from *quattuor,* four.]

1. fourfold; quadruple. [Obs.]

2. consisting of, having, or growing in fours. [Obs.]

quȧ·tēr'nȧ·ry, *a.* [L. *quaternarius,* from *quattuor,* four.]

1. consisting of four; in sets of four.

2. [Q–] designating or of the geological period following the Tertiary in the Cenozoic Era, comprising the Pleistocene and Recent Epochs.

quȧ·tēr'nȧ·ry, *n.*; *pl.* **quȧ·tēr'nȧ·rieṣ,** 1. the number four.

2. a set of four.

the Quaternary; the Quaternary Period or its rocks.

quȧ·tēr'nāte, *a.* [ME.; LL. *quaternio,* a body or group of four, from L. *quaterni,* four each, by fours.] consisting of four; arranged in sets of four; as, a *quaternate* leaf.

quȧ·tēr'ni·ŏn, *n.* [LL. *quaternio,* a body or group of four, the number four.]

1. the number four. [Rare.]

2. a set of four.

He put him in prison, and delivered him to four *quaternions* of soldiers.—Acts xii. 4.

3. a quadrisyllable, or word of four syllables.

4. in mathematics, (a) a factor which, by multiplication, changes one vector into another: it is expressible by a quadrinomial; (b) [*pl.*] the form of calculus using the quaternion.

quȧ·tēr'ni·ŏn, *v.t.* to divide into files, companies, or sets of four. [Rare.]

quȧ·tēr'ni·ty, *n.* [Fr. *quaternité,* from L. *quaternitas, quaternitatis,* from *quaterni,* four each.] the number four; the condition of making up the number four.

The *quaternity* of the elements.—Browne.

quȧ'tēr·on, *n.* a quadroon. [Obs.]

quat'ŏr·zāin (kat'ēr-zān *or* kȧ-tọr'zān), *n.* [OFr. *quatorzaine,* the number fourteen.]

1. a sonnet.

2. any poem of fourteen lines.

quȧ·torze' (kȧ-), *n.* [Fr. fourteen.] in the game of piquet, four aces, kings, queens, jacks, or tens held in one hand: so called because each quatorze counts fourteen points.

quät'rāin, *n.* [Fr., from *quatre*; L. *quattuor,* four.] a poem or stanza of four lines, usually rhyming *abab* or *abba.*

quä'tre (kä'tēr), *n.* [Fr., from L. *quattuor,* four.] a playing card, a die, or a domino having four spots, or pips.

quat're·foil (kat'ēr- *or* kat'rȧ-), *n.* [ME. *quaterfoyle*; OFr. *quatrefeuille*; *quatre* (L. *quattuor*), four, and *feuille* (L. *folium*), a leaf.]

1. a flower with four petals.

2. a leaf with four leaflets.

3. in architecture, a leaflike ornament having four lobes.

QUATREFOILS

4. in heraldry, a representation of a four-leaved flower, used as a bearing.

quät·trō·cen'tist (-chen'), *n.* a follower or advocate of the type of art developed in Italy in the fifteenth century; a Pre-Raphaelite.

quät·trō·cen'tō (-chen'), *n.* [It. *quatro,* four, and *cento,* a hundred; lit., four-hundredth, but used for fourteen-hundredth] the fifteenth century as a period in Italian art and literature.

quät·trō·cen'tō, *a.* pertaining to fifteenth-century art and literature in Italy.

quät'ū·ọr, *n.* [from L. *quattuor,* four.] in music, a quartet.

quāve, *n.* a quaver. [Dial.]

quāve, *v.i.* [a word allied to *quake*; L.G. *quabbeln,* to quiver, to tremble.] to quiver; to shake. [Dial.]

quāve'mīre, *n.* a quagmire. [Obs.]

quā'vēr, *v.i.*; quavered, *pt., pp.*; quavering, *ppr.* [ME. *quaveren,* freq. of Early ME. *cwafien,* to shake, tremble.]

1. to shake or tremble.

2. to be tremulous: said of the voice.

3. in music, to make a trill or trills in singing or playing.

quā'vēr, *v.t.* 1. to utter in a tremulous voice; as, to *quaver* a few words.

2. in music, to sing or play with a trill or trills.

quā'vēr, *n.* 1. a tremulous quality in a voice or tone.

2. in music, an eighth note; half of a crotchet.

quā'vēr·ēr, *n.* one who quavers.

quā'vēr·y, *a.* quavering; shaky; tremulous.

quay (kē), *n.* [ME. *kei*; OFr. *cai, caie.*] a wharf, usually of concrete or stone, with facilities for loading and unloading ships.

quay (kē), *v.t.* to furnish with quays.

quay'āge (kē'), *n.* [Fr.] 1. the charge made for using a quay.

2. space on a quay.

3. quays collectively.

quēach, *n.* a thicket. [Obs. or Dial.]

quēach'y, *a.* 1. shaking; moving, yielding, or trembling under the feet, as moist or boggy ground. [Obs. or Dial.]

2. thick; bushy. [Obs.]

quēan, *n.* [ME. *quene, queyne*; AS. *cwene.*]

1. a bold, brazen, or impudent girl or woman.

2. an immoral woman; a slut.

3. a girl or unmarried woman. [Scot.]

quēa'ṣi·ly, *adv.* in a queasy manner.

quēa'ṣi·ness, *n.* a queasy quality or state.

quēa'ṣy, *a.*; *comp.* queasier; *superl.* queasiest, [ME. *quesye*; akin to ON. *kveisa,* ulcer, boil, Ice. *kveisa,* pain in the stomach, Norw. *kveis,* sickness, nausea.]

1. causing nausea.

2. sick at the stomach; affected with nausea; inclined to vomit.

3. squeamish; qualmish; easily nauseated.

4. uncomfortable; embarrassed.

5. difficult to please; fastidious.

6. troublous; hazardous.

quẹ·brä'chō (kā-), *n.*[Sp., contr. from *quiebrahacha,* ax breaker, because of the hardness of the wood; *quebrar,* to break, and *hacha,* ax.]

1. any of a number of tropical American trees, especially *Aspidosperma quebracho* and *Quebrachia lorentzii,* whose bark and wood are variously used in medicine, tanning, and dyeing.

2. the bark or wood.

queb'rith (kweb'), *n.* sulfur. [Obs.]

qued, *a.* evil; bad. [Obs.]

queen (kwēn), *n.* [ME. *quen*; AS. *cwēn,* wife, woman.]

1. the wife of a king.

2. a woman who rules over a monarchy in her own right; female counterpart of a king.

3. a woman foremost among others in certain attributes or accomplishments, as beauty, etc.

4. a place or thing that is regarded as the best or most beautiful of its kind; as, Cuba is called the *Queen* of the Antilles.

5. the fully developed, reproductive female in a colony of bees, ants, or termites.

6. in cards, a playing card with a conventionalized picture of a queen on it.

7. in chess, the most powerful piece, permitted to move any number of unoccupied spaces in a straight or diagonal direction.

Queen Anne's Bounty; in English history, a trust fund founded by Queen Anne from the revenue obtained from the first year's income and used to increase the amounts given to underpaid clergy: now greatly augmented by private gifts and grants from Parliament, the fund is mainly used to keep benefices in repair and to provide mortgage loans.

Queen Anne's lace; a wild plant of the carrot family, with fine leaves and small, delicate, white flowers in flat-topped clusters.

Queen Anne style; (a) a style of architecture developed in England during the early 18th century, characterized by construction in red brick, the modification of classical architecture to meet domestic needs, and the use of simple, dignified ornamentation; (b) a style of furniture developed in the same period, characterized by simple lines and the use of upholstery.

queen bee; the fully developed, reproductive female bee in a hive or nest. It lays two or three thousand eggs daily during the height of summer, or more than a million during its lifetime, which is about five years.

QUEEN BEE

queen consort; the wife of a reigning king.

queen dowager; the widow of a king.

Queen Mab; in English folklore, a fairy queen who governs people's dreams.

Queen mother; a queen dowager who is also mother of the reigning sovereign.

Queen of May; same as *May queen.*

queen regent; (a) a queen reigning in behalf of another; (b) [Rare.] a queen regnant.

queen regnant; a queen reigning in her own right.

Queen's Counsel; see *King's Counsel.*

queen's English; see *king's English.*

queen's evidence; see *king's evidence.*

queen, *v.t.* 1. in chess, to make a queen of (a pawn that has been moved to the opponent's end of the board).

2. to supply a queen to, as a beehive.

3. to make (a girl or woman) a queen.

to queen it; to play the queen; to domineer.

queen, *v.i.* to reign as queen.

queen cell, a large cell, in which the larval queen bee is developed.

queen çonçh, a large conch, *Strombus gigas,* much used for making cameos.

queen'çrȧft, *n.* skill or craft in policy on the part of a queen.

Queen Dāy, same as *Lady Day.*

queen'dŏm, *n.* 1. the rule or realm of a queen.

2. queenhood.

queen'fish, *n.*; *pl.* **queen'fish** or **queen'fish·eṣ,** an edible fish, *Seriphus politus,* of the Pacific coast of North America.

queen gōld, a royal duty or revenue formerly belonging to every queen of England during her marriage to the king.

queen'hood, *n.* the state, rank, position, or dignity of a queen.

queen'ing, *n.* 1. a kind of apple; as, the scarlet *queening.*

2. the act of supplying a bee colony with a queen.

queen'let, *n.* a petty queen.

queen lil'y, any one of various plants of the genus *Phædranassa.*

queen'li·ness, *n.* the state or condition of being queenly; the characteristics of a queen; queenly nature or quality; dignity; stateliness.

queen'ly, *a.*; *comp.* queenlier; *superl.* queenliest, 1. of or like a queen.
2. suitable to a queen.

queen'ly, *adv.* in a queenly manner.

queen ŏf the mead'ōw (med'), the meadowsweet of Europe; any of several species of *Spiræa*.

queen ŏf the prāi'rie, a plant of the rose family, with clusters of small pink flowers and large leaves.

queen ol'ive, a large olive with a long, slender pit.

queen pōst, in carpentry, either of a pair of two vertical posts set between the rafters and the base, or tie beam, of a truss, at equal distances from the apex: distinguished from *king post*.

QUEEN POSTS

queen'ṣ'-dē-light' (-līt'), *n.* a euphorbiaceous plant, *Stillingia sylvatica*, found in the southern United States.

queen'ṣ'-flow"ẽr, *n.* the bloodwood, *Lagerstræmia speciosa*; also, its flower.

queen'ship, *n.* the state, position, or dignity of a queen.

Queenṣ'land nut, the nut of *Macadamia ternifolia*, a tree of Queensland, Australia.

queen'ṣ met'ăl, an alloy made by fusing under charcoal a mixture of nine parts of tin and one part each of antimony, lead, and bismuth.

queen'ṣ pig'eŏn (pij'un), a large ground pigeon of the genus *Goura*, especially *Goura victoriæ*.

queen'ṣ'-root, *n.* same as *queen's-delight*.

queen'ṣ wāre, glazed earthenware of a creamy color.

queen'ṣ yel'lōw, same as *turpeth*, sense 3.

queen truss, in carpentry, a truss framed with queen posts.

queer, *a.*; *comp.* queerer; *superl.* queerest, [L.G. *queer*, across; *quere*, obliquity; G. *quer*, transverse; *querkopf*, a queer fellow.]
1. strange; odd; behaving, acting, or appearing in a manner other than the ordinary, normal, or usual manner; singular; droll; peculiar; as, a *queer* manner.
2. not very well; qualmish; giddy; as, I feel very *queer*.
3. doubtful; suspicious; as, things look very *queer*. [Colloq.]
4. counterfeit; spurious. [Slang.]
5. having mental quirks; eccentric. [Colloq.]
6. homosexual. [Slang.]
Syn.—odd, whimsical, quaint, cross, strange, crotchety, singular, eccentric, droll, erratic, unique.

queer, *v.t.* 1. to banter; to ridicule. [Slang.]
2. to puzzle. [Brit. Dial.]
3. to spoil, as the smooth operation or success of; as, to *queer* one's business. [Slang.]
4. to put (oneself) into an unfavorable position. [Slang.]

queer, *n.* 1. counterfeit money. [Slang.]
2. a homosexual. [Slang.]

queer'ish, *a.* rather queer.

queer'ly, *adv.* in a queer manner.

queer'ness, *n.* 1. the state or quality of being queer.
2. something queer.

queest, *n.* the ringdove, *Columba palumbus*.

queġh (kwākh), *n.* same as *quaigh*.

queint, *a.* quaint. [Now Dial.]

queint, *v.* obsolete past participle of *quench*.

quein'tiṣe, *n.* quaintness. [Archaic.]

Quē'lē·ȧ, *n.* [native name.] a genus of birds found in Africa.

quell, *v.i.* to die; to be abated. [Obs.]

quell, *v.t.* [ME. *quellen*; AS. *cwellan*, to kill; Dan. *qvæler*, to stifle, suffocate, choke; G. *qualen*, kill.]
1. to crush; to subdue; to cause to cease; as, to *quell* an insurrection or riot.
2. to quiet; to allay; to reduce to peace; as, to *quell* the tumult of the soul.
3. to destroy; to kill. [Obs.]

quell, *n.* murder. [Obs.]

quell'ẽr, *n.* one who quells.

quelque-chōṣe' (kelk-shōz'), *n.* [Fr., something.] a trifle; a kickshaw.

quēme, *v.t.* and *v.i.* to please. [Obs.]

quēm'ful, *a.* pleasing; becoming. [Obs.]

quench, *v.t.*; quenched (kwencht), *pt., pp.*; quenching, *ppr.* [ME. *quenchen*; AS. *cwencan*, to quench.]
1. to extinguish; to put out; as, water *quenched* the fire.
2. to still; to quiet; to repress; as, to *quench* a passion or emotion.
3. to satisfy; to slake; as, to *quench* thirst.
4. to cool suddenly, as heated iron or steel, by plunging into water, oil, etc.

quench, *v.i.* to cool; to become cool; to lose zeal.

quench'ȧ·ble, *a.* capable of being quenched.

quench'ẽr, *n.* 1. one who or that which quenches.
2. a drink. [Slang.]

quench'less, *a.* that cannot be quenched or repressed; inextinguishable; as, *quenchless* fire or fury.

quench'less·ly, *adv.* in a quenchless manner.

quench'less·ness, *n.* the state of being quenchless.

quē·nelle' (kē-nel'), *n.* [Fr., from G. *knödel*, dumpling.] minced chicken or veal, mixed with eggs and bread crumbs in the shape of a ball, fried in fat, and served as an entree or a garnish.

quē·nöuille' trāin'ing (kē-nö'y'), [Fr. *quenouille*; LL. *conucula*, *colucula*, a distaff, dim. of L. *colus*, a distaff.] in horticulture, a method of training a tree or a shrub by clipping and bending its branches so as to make it conical or spindle-shaped in outline.

quẽr·cet'iç (*or* -sē'tik), *a.* of or derived from quercetin.

quẽr'cē·tin, *n.* [L. *quercetum*, an oakwood, from *quercus*, an oak.] the yellow, crystalline dyestuff, $C_{15}H_{10}O_7$, extracted from the inner bark of the black oak and also produced synthetically.

quẽr'cine, *n.* [LL. *quercinus*, from L. *quercus*, oak.] of the oak.

quẽr·ci·tan'iç, *a.* same as *tannic*.

quẽr'cite, *n.* [L. *quercetum*, an oakwood.] a saccharine substance of the starch group, $C_6H_{12}O_5$, derived from acorns.

quẽr'ci·tin, *n.* same as *quercetin*.

quẽr'cit·rin, *n.* [L. *quercus*, an oak, and *citrina*, lemon-colored.] the coloring matter, $C_{21}H_{22}O_{12}\cdot 2H_2O$, of quercitron bark.

quẽr'cit·rŏn, *n.* [L. *quercus*, an oak, and *citrus*, a tree of the lemon kind.]
1. the *Quercus tinctoria*, black oak, or dyer's oak, which grows from Canada to Georgia, and west to the Mississippi. It frequently attains the height of seventy or eighty feet, and is one of the largest trees of the forests in the Mississippi basin.
2. the bark of the quercitron.
3. the yellow dye derived from this bark.

quẽr'cit·rŏn bärk, same as *quercitron*.

quẽr·civ'ō·rous, *a.* [L. *quercus*, oak, and *vorare*, to devour.] in zoology, subsisting upon the oak: said of insects and their larvae.

Quẽr'çus, *n.* [L.] a genus of trees of which the oak is the type.

quē·rē'lȧ, *n.*; *pl.* **quē·rē'lae,** [L., a complaint.] a suit filed in a court of justice; also, the bill containing the complaint preferred.

quer'ēle, *n.* querela. [Obs.]

quē'rent, *n.* the complainant; the plaintiff. [Obs.]

quē'rent, *n.* an inquirer. [Obs.]

quer·i·mō'ni·ous, *a.* [L. *querimonia*, complaint, from *queri*, to complain.] complaining; querulous; apt to complain.

quer·i·mō'ni·ous·ly, *adv.* with complaint; querulously.

quer·i·mō'ni·ous·ness, *n.* a disposition to complain; a complaining temper.

quer'i·mō·ny, *n.*; *pl.* **quer'i·mō·nieṣ,** a complaint.

quē'rist, *n.* [from L. *quærere*, to inquire.] one who inquires, or asks questions.

quẽrk'en, *v.t.* to choke. [Brit. Dial.]

quẽrl, *v.t.* [G. *querlen*.] to twirl; to turn or wind round; to coil; as, to *querl* a cord, thread, or rope. [Dial.]

quẽrl, *n.* a coil. [Dial.]

quẽrn, *n.* [AS. *cwyrn*, *cweorn*; D. *kweern*; Dan. *kværn*; Sw. *qvarn*, a millstone, a quern.]
1. a primitive hand mill for grinding grain, consisting of two stone disks, one upon the other, the upper stone of which was turned by hand.
2. a small hand mill in which spices are ground.

quẽr'pō, *n.* cuerpo. [Obs.]

quẽr'quē·dūle, *n.* [L. *querquedula*, a kind of teal.] an aquatic fowl; a species of teal.

quer'ū·lent, *a.* given to unfounded suspicions.

quer'ū·lous, *a.* [L. *querulus*, from *queri*, to complain.]
1. inclined to find fault; fretful; peevish; habitually complaining; as, a *querulous* man or people.
2. expressing complaint; characterized by complaining; as, a *querulous* tone of voice.

quer'ū·lous·ly, *adv.* in a complaining manner.

quer'ū·lous·ness, *n.* disposition to complain; the habit or practice of finding fault.

quē'ry, *n.*; *pl.* **quē'rieṣ,** [a modified form of L. *quære*, 2d pers. sing. imper. of *quærere*, to ask, to inquire.]
1. a question; a point to be answered or solved; an inquiry.
2. a doubt.
3. the mark or sign of interrogation; a question mark (?), used to indicate that the sentence to which it is appended contains a question or used to express doubt as to the correctness, accuracy, etc. of written or printed matter.

quē'ry, *v.t.*; queried, *pt., pp.*; querying, *ppr.* 1. to call in question; to ask about; to seek by questioning; to endeavor to ascertain by inquiry; as, to *query* a motive.
2. to examine by questions; to question (a person).
3. to express doubt concerning the correctness, etc. of (written or printed matter) by marking with question marks; to express a desire to examine into the truth or correctness of; to mark with a query.

quē'ry, *v.i.* 1. to ask a question or questions.
Each prompt to *query*, answer, and debate.
—Pope.
2. to express doubt.

que·säl' (ke-), *n.* same as *quetzal*.

quest, *n.* [ME. *queste*; OFr. *queste*; L. *quæsita*, a thing sought for, f. or neut. pl. of *quæsitus*, pp. of *quærere*, also *quæsere*, to seek, ask, inquire.]
1. the act of seeking; search; hunt; pursuit, as, to rove in *quest* of game; to go in *quest* of a lost child; in *quest* of property.
2. a journey in search of adventures, as those undertaken by knights-errant in medieval times; heroic expedition in search of a particular object; as, the *quest* of the Golden Fleece.
3. a jury of inquest. [Rare.]
4. the group of persons participating in a quest; searchers, collectively.
5. inquest. [Obs.]
6. request; desire; solicitation. [Rare.]
Gad not abroad at every *quest* and call
Of an untrained hope or passion.—Herbert.

quest, *v.t.*; quested, *pt., pp.*; questing, *ppr.* to search or seek for. [Rare.]

quest, *v.i.* 1. to go in search; to search; to seek. [Rare.]
2. to go begging.
3. to follow the track of game, or to bay in pursuit of game, as a hound on the trail.
To bay or *quest* as a dog. —Florio.

quest'ănt, *n.* a candidate, competitor or aspirant. [Obs.]

quest'ẽr, *n.* a seeker.

ques'tion (-chun), *n.* [Fr.; L. *quæstio*, *quæstionis*, a seeking, inquiry, question.]
1. an asking; inquiry.
2. something that is asked; interrogative sentence; query.
3. doubt; uncertainty; as, there is no *question* of his veracity.
4. something in controversy before a court.
5. a problem; matter open to discussion or inquiry.
6. a matter or case of difficulty; as, it's not a *question* of money.
7. a point being debated or a resolution brought up for approval or rejection before an assembly.
8. the procedure of putting such a matter to a vote.
9. trial; examination; judicial trial or inquiry.
He that was in *question* for the robbery.
—Shak.
10. examination by torture, or the application of torture to prisoners under criminal accusation in order to extort confession.
11. conversation; speech; talk. [Obs.]
12. in logic, a proposition, or that which is to be established as a conclusion, stated by way of interrogation.
beside the question; not related to the subject under discussion.
beyond (*all*) *question*; beyond dispute.
in question; in debate; in the course of examination or discussion; being at present dealt with; as, the matter or point *in question*.
out of question; doubtless.
out of the question; not to be considered; impossible; not to be thought of.

to call in question; (a) to take exception to; to challenge; (b) to doubt; to cast doubt on.

ques′tion, *v.i.*; questioned, *pt., pp.*; questioning, *ppr.* 1. to ask a question or questions; to inquire by interrogatory or proposition to be answered.

2. to debate; to consider. [Obs.]

ques′tion, *v.t.* 1. to ask questions of; to interrogate; to put queries to; as, to *question* a witness.

2. to doubt; to be uncertain of; to have no confidence in; to treat as doubtful.

3. to challenge; to call in question.

Syn.—inquire, interrogate.—We *inquire* for the sake of information; as, to *inquire* one's way; we *question* with a series of questions in order to gain the whole truth; as, to *question* a witness; we *interrogate* with a systematic examination; as, to *interrogate* a prisoner of war.

ques″tion·ȧ·bil′i·ty, *n.* questionableness.

ques′tion·ȧ·ble, *a.* 1. that can be questioned; doubtful; uncertain; disputable.

It is *questionable* whether Galen ever saw the dissection of a human body.—Baker.

2. of dubious repute; suspected of being immoral, not respectable, etc.

Syn.—doubtful, dubious, equivocal, uncertain.

ques′tion·ȧ·ble·ness, *n.* the quality or state of being questionable.

ques′tion·ȧ·bly, *adv.* in a questionable manner; doubtfully.

ques′tion·ãr·y, *a.* inquiring; asking questions; as, *questionary* epistles.

ques′tion·ãr·y, *n.*; *pl.* **ques′tion·ãr·ieṣ,** a questionnaire.

ques′tion·ẽr, *n.* one who asks questions; an inquirer.

ques′tion·ist, *n.* 1. a questioner; an inquirer.

2. a candidate for honors or degrees at some universities.

ques′tion·less, *adv.* beyond a question or doubt; unquestionably; certainly.

ques′tion·less, *a.* 1. unquestionable; indubitable.

2. asking no questions; without a question; unquestioning.

ques′tion märk, the interrogation mark (?).

ques·tion·nâire′, *n.* [Fr.] a written or printed form used in gathering information on some subject or subjects, consisting of a list of questions to be submitted to one or more persons.

quest′măn, *n.*; *pl.* **quest′men,** one legally empowered to make quest of certain matters; specifically, (a) a person chosen to inquire into abuses and misdemeanors, especially with regard to weights and measures; (b) a collector of parish rates; (c) a person chosen annually to assist the churchwardens; (d) a juryman. [Obs.]

quest′mŏn″gẽr, *n.* a person who conducts inquests as a business. [Obs.]

ques′tŏr, *n.* [L. *quæstor*, the Roman financial magistrate.] a quaestor.

ques′tŏr·ship, *n.* quaestorship.

ques′trist, *n.* a seeker; a pursuer. [Obs.]

ques′tū·ãr·y, *a.* [L. *quæstuarius*, from *quæstus*, gain, profit.] studious of profit. [Obs.]

ques′tū·ãr·y, *n.* one employed to collect profits. [Obs.]

quet, *n.* a guillemot. [Brit. Dial.]

quet·zäl′ (ket-säl′), *n.* [Sp.; Nahuatl *quetzaltototl*, from *quetzalli*, tail feather.]

1. a crested bird of Central America, a member of the trogons, *Pharomacrus mocinno*, usually brilliant green above and red below, with long, streaming tail feathers (in the male).

2. *pl.* **quet·zäl′eṣ** (ket-sä′lās), the gold monetary unit of Guatemala. Also *quezal*.

queūe (kū), *n.* [Fr., from L. *cauda*, tail.]

1. a plait of hair worn hanging from the back of the head; a pigtail; the tie of a wig.

2. a line or file of people or things waiting to be served or brought into service.

3. in heraldry, the tail of a beast.

4. in music, the tail or stem of a note.

5. a tailpiece, as of a violin.

6. a support for a lance. [Obs.]

queūe, *v.i.*; queued, *pt., pp.*; queuing, *ppr.* to form in a line or file while waiting to be served, etc. (often with *up*). [Chiefly Brit.]

queūe (kū), *v.t.* to braid (hair) in a queue.

quey, *n.* [Ice. *kviga*; Sw. *qviga*, heifer.] a heifer. [Scot.]

que·zäl′ (ke-säl′), *n.* a quetzal.

quib, *n.* [W. *chwip*, a flirt, a quirk, or *qwib*, a quick course or turn.] a sarcasm; a bitter taunt; a quip; a gibe. [Obs.]

quib′ble, *n.* [dim., from *quib*, from L. *quibus*, abl. pl. of *qui*, who, which: *quibus* was common in legal documents and suggested sharp legal practice.]

1. a play on words. [Rare.]

2. a petty evasion or cavil.

quib′ble, *v.i.*; quibbled, *pt., pp.*; quibbling, *ppr.* 1. to evade the point in question, or plain truth, by artifice, play upon words, or any cavil; to trifle in argument or discourse.

2. to pun. [Obs.]

quib′blẽr, *n.* one who quibbles.

quib′bling, *n.* a cavil.

quib′bling·ly, *adv.* triflingly; evasively.

quī′cȧ (kē′), *n.* [native name.] an opossum of small size found in Brazil and Guiana.

quick, *a.* [AS. *cwic*, *cuc*, living, lively; D. *kwik*; Ice. *kvikr*, *kykr*; Dan. *qvik*; Sw. *qvick*; L.G. *queck*, *quik*, all with similar meanings.]

1. alive; living: opposed to *dead*; as, *quick* flesh. [Archaic.]

2. (a) swift; hasty; speedy; rapid; as, a *quick* walk; (b) done with promptness; prompt; as, a *quick* reply.

3. occurring in a brief space of time; as, a *quick* glance.

4. prompt to understand or learn; sharp in discernment; as, a *quick* mind.

5. sharply curved.

6. uncontrolled; hasty; easily stirred; fiery; passionate; sharp; as, a *quick* temper.

7. sensitive; discerning; acutely perceptive; alert; as, a *quick* ear or eye.

8. pregnant; with child: specifically said of a pregnant woman when the motion of the fetus is felt.

9. bracing; refreshing; keen; invigorating.

Syn.—active, swift, nimble, agile, alert, brisk, lively.

quick, *adv.* nimbly; with celerity; quickly; with haste; speedily; without delay; as, run *quick*.

quick, *n.* [Sw. *qviga*, a heifer; Dan. *qvæg*, cattle, from *quik*, living.]

1. the living, especially in *the quick and the dead*.

2. the sensitive flesh under a toenail or fingernail.

3. the center of the feelings; as, her sarcasm cut him to the *quick*.

4. a living plant; especially, (a) the hawthorn; (b) the couch grass; (c) quickset.

quick, *v.t.* 1. to revive; to animate; to invigorate. [Archaic.]

2. in electroplating, to prepare (a metallic surface) by treatment with a solution of a salt of mercury.

quick as′sets, in accounting, cash on hand and all readily marketable merchandise.

quick′bēam, *n.* a tree, the rowan, or mountain ash.

quick bread (bred), any bread, as muffins, cornbread, etc., leavened with baking powder, soda, etc., so that it may be baked as soon as the batter is mixed.

quick′en, *v.t.*; quickened, *pt., pp.*; quickening, *ppr.* [AS. *cwician*, from *cwicu*, alive.]

1. to animate; to enliven; to make alive; to vivify; to revive or resuscitate, as from death or an inanimate state.

2. to hasten; to accelerate; as, to *quicken* motion.

3. to sharpen; to give keener perception to; to arouse; to stir; to stimulate; to incite; as, to *quicken* the appetite.

4. in shipbuilding, to make more curved.

Syn.—accelerate expedite, refresh, stimulate, revive.

quick′en, *v.i.* 1. to become enlivened; to revive.

2. (a) to begin to show signs of life, as a fetus in the womb; (b) to enter the stage of pregnancy in which the movement of the fetus can be felt.

3. to move more rapidly; as, the pulse *quickens* with fear.

quick′en·ẽr, *n.* one who or that which quickens.

quick′en·ing, *n.* 1. the act of hastening or increasing activity.

2. in pregnancy, the time at which the fetus quickens, usually about the eighteenth week.

quick′enṣ, *n.* couch grass. [Scot. and Brit. Dial.]

quick′en tree, the quickbeam, or rowan.

quick′-fīre, *a.* firing, or designed for firing, in quick succession.

quick fīre, shots fired in quick succession.

quick′-fīr′ing, *a.* quick-fire.

quick′-freeze′, *v.t.*; quick-froze, *pt.*; quick-frozen, *pp.*; quick-freezing, *ppr.* to subject (raw or freshly cooked food) to such sudden freezing that the flavor and natural juices are retained and the food can be stored at low temperatures for a long time.

quick gräss, couch grass.

quick′hatch, *n.* [Am. Ind.] the wolverine.

quick′ie, *n.* anything done or made quickly and cheaply; especially, a motion picture made in this way. [Slang.]

quick′lime, *n.* calcium oxide; unslaked lime.

quick′ly, *adv.* 1. in a living or lively manner. [Obs.]

2. with haste or speed; rapidly.

quick märch, a march in the rhythm of quick time.

quick match, a combustible preparation formed of cotton strands dipped in a boiling composition of alcohol, saltpeter, and mealed gunpowder, used by artillerymen.

quick′ness, *n.* the state or quality of being quick.

quick′sand, *n.* [ME. *quyykkesand*; prob., from M.D. or M.L.G.] a loose, wet, deep sand deposit in which a person or heavy object may easily be engulfed.

quick′-scent″ed, *a.* having acute perception by the nose.

quick′set, *n.* 1. a live slip or cutting, especially of hawthorn, planted, as for a hedge.

2. any plant growing in a hedge.

3. a hedge, especially of hawthorn.

quick′set, *v.t.* to plant with living shrubs or trees for a hedge or fence; as, to *quickset* a ditch. [Obs.]

quick′set, *a.* made of growing shrubs, as a hedge; planted with hawthorn.

quick′-sīght′ed (-sīt′), *a.* having quick sight.

quick″-sīght′ed·ness, *n.* quickness of sight or discernment.

quick′sil″vẽr, *n.* [ME. *quyksilver*; AS. *cwicseolfor*; *cwicu*, living, and *seolfor*, silver.] mercury (the metal).

quicksilver water; same as *quick water*.

quick′sil″vẽr, *v.t.*; quicksilvered, *pt., pp.*; quicksilvering, *ppr.* to cover with mercury, as a mirror.

quick′sil″vẽr·ing, *n.* the amalgam of tinfoil and mercury on the back of a mirror.

quick′step, *n.* 1. the step used for marching in quick time.

2. in music, a march in the rhythm of quick time.

3. a spirited dance step.

quick′-tem′pẽred, *a.* easily angered.

quick tīme, the normal rate of marching (in the United States Army), 120 paces a minute, each pace being 30 inches.

quick vin′ē·gãr, vinegar produced by exposing the fermenting liquid in thin layers to the action of the ferment, as by trickling over shavings.

quick wą′tẽr, a dilute solution of mercury nitrate.

quick′-wit′ted, *a.* having ready wit; keen; nimble of mind.

quick″-wit′ted·ness, *n.* readiness of wit.

quick′wŏrk, *n.* in wooden ships, the short planking between portholes.

quid, *n.* 1. a cud.

2. a portion suitable to be chewed; specifically, a piece of tobacco chewed and rolled about in the mouth.

quid, *v.t.* and *v.i.* to drop food from the mouth when partly masticated: said of horses.

quid, *n.*; *pl.* **quid,** a sovereign, or one pound sterling. [Brit. Slang.]

quī′dam, *n.* [L.] somebody; one unknown.

quid′dȧ·ny, *n.* [L. *cydonium*, quince juice.] a confection of quinces prepared with sugar. [Obs.]

quid′dȧ·tive, *a.* same as *quidditative*.

quid′dit, *n.* a subtlety; an equivocation. [Archaic.]

quid′di·tā·tive, *a.* constituting the essence of a thing.

quid′di·ty, *n.*; *pl.* **quid′di·tieṣ,** [L. *quid*, what.]

1. the essence or essential quality of a thing, comprehending both the substance and the qualities; that which distinguishes a thing from others, and makes it what it is.

2. a trifling distinction; a cavil; a captious question.

quid′dle, *n.* one who spends time in trifling niceties; a dawdler.

quid′dle, *v.i.*; quiddled, *pt., pp.*; quiddling, *ppr.* [L. *quid*, what.] to spend or waste time in trifling employments, or to attend to useful subjects in a trifling, superficial manner.

quid'dlẽr, *n.* a quiddle.

quid'nunc, *n.* [L., what now?] one who is curious to know everything that happens; a busybody.

quid prō quō, [L., something for something.]
1. one thing in return for another.
2. something equivalent; a substitute.

¿quién sa'be? (kyen sä'be), [Sp.] who knows?

quī·esce', *v.i.*; quiesced (-est'), *pt., pp.*; quiescing, *ppr.* [L. *quiescere*, to rest, to keep quiet.]
1. to be silent, as a letter; to have no sound.
2. to become quiet; to become calm or hushed.

quī·es'cence, quī·es'cen·cy, *n.* [LL. *quiescentia*, rest, quiet; L. *quiescens* (*-entis*), ppr. of *quiescere*, to repose, to rest.] the quality or condition of being quiescent.

quī·es'cent, *n.* in philology, a silent letter.

quī·es'cent, *a.* 1. resting; being in a state of repose; still; not moving; as, a *quiescent* body or fluid.
2. silent; not sounded; having no sound; as, a *quiescent* letter.

quī·es'cent·ly, *adv.* in a quiescent manner.

quī'et, *a.*; *comp.* quieter; *superl.* quietest, [OFr. *quiet*; L. *quietus*, from *quiescere*, to keep quiet, from *quies* (*-etis*), rest.]
1. still; calm; motionless.
2. (a) not noisy; hushed; (b) not speaking; silent.
3. not agitated in motion; gentle; as, a quiet sea.
4. not easily excited or disturbed; as, a *quiet* disposition.
5. not ostentatious or pretentious; as, *quiet* furnishings.
6. not forward; unobtrusive; as, a *quiet* manner.
7. secluded; as, a *quiet* den.
8. serving to relax and soothe; as, a *quiet* evening at home.
9. in commerce, not busy; as, a *quiet* day on the stock exchange.
Syn.—pacific, peaceful, tranquil, still, calm, placid, smooth, unruffled, contented, satisfied, meek.

quī'et, *n.* 1. a quiet state or condition; calmness; inactivity; rest; repose; stillness; freedom from noise, etc.
2. a quiet or peaceful quality; tranquillity; peace; freedom from disturbance or agitation.
in quiet; quietly.
on the quiet; secretly. [Slang.]
Syn.—rest, silence, tranquillity, repose, calmness.

quī'et, *v.t.*; quieted, *pt., pp.*; quieting, *ppr.* to make quiet; to calm; to appease; to pacify; to stop motion in; to still; to reduce to a state of rest; to silence.
Syn.—allay, pacify, tranquilize, soothe, calm.

quī'et, *v.i.* to become quiet or calm: usually followed by *down*.

quī'et, *adv.* in a quiet manner.

quī'et·āġe (-ij), *n.* peace; quietness. [Obs.]

quī'et·en, *v.t.* and *v.i.* to make quiet; to become quiet. [Brit. or Dial.]

quī'et·ẽr, *n.* one who or that which quiets.

quī'et·ism, *n.* [It. *quietismo*, from L. *quietus*; see *quiet* and *-ism*.]
1. a form of religious mysticism that involves complete extinction of the human will, drawing away from worldly things, and passive contemplation of God and divine things: it was taught by the 17th-century Spanish priest Molinos.
2. any religious mysticism of this sort.
3. tranquillity of the spirit or quietness of life.

quī'et·ist, *n.* a person who believes in or practices quietism.

quī'et·ist, *a.* of quietism or quietists.

quī·et·is'tiç, *a.* pertaining to a quietist or to quietism.

quī'et·ive, *a.* tending to quiet.

quī'et·ive, *n.* in medicine, a sedative.

quī'et·īze, *v.t.* to render quiet. [Rare.]

quī'et·ly, *adv.* 1. in a quiet state; without motion, in a state of rest; as, to lie or sit *quietly*.
2. without tumult, alarm, dispute, or disturbance; peaceably; as, to live *quietly*.
3. calmly; without agitation or violent emotion; patiently; as, submit *quietly* to unavoidable evils.
4. without noise; in a silent manner; unobtrusively; as, she *quietly* slipped away.

quī'et·ness, *n.* the state, quality, or condition of being quiet; stillness; freedom from motion; noiselessness; calmness; repose.

quī'et·sōme, *a.* calm; still; undisturbed. [Obs.]

quī'e·tūde, *n.* [Fr.] a state of being quiet; calmness; rest; repose; quiet; tranquillity.

quī·ē'tus, *n.* [ML. quit (in the formula *quietus est*, he is quit; L., he is quiet).]
1. discharge or release from debt, obligation, or office.
2. discharge or release from life; death.
3. anything that kills.
4. anything that serves to quiet, curb, or end an activity.

quī'-hī', *n.* [Anglo-Ind., from Hind. *koī hai*, is anyone there?: the customary call for a servant.] an Anglo-Indian, especially one stationed or resident in Bengal.

Qui·ī'nȧ, *n.* [native name in Guiana.] a genus of plants of the gamboge family, native to tropical America. They are characterized by having two seed lobes, opposite or whorled stipulate leaves, small flowers occurring in clusters, and baccate fruit.

quill, *n.* [ME. *quil*, hollow stalk; prob. from M.L.G. or M.D.]
1. one of the large, stiff feathers of a bird; especially, a feather from the wing or the tail of a bird and having a stout horny shaft fit for use as a pen or as a toothpick: also called *quill feather*.
2. the stout, horny, cylindrical part of a large stiff feather; calamus.
3. a pen for writing made of a quill: also called *quill pen*.
4. the spine or prickle of a porcupine or hedgehog; also, the pen of a squid.
5. a plectrum with which musicians pluck the strings of certain instruments.
6. a musical pipe made of a hollow stem, reed, or cane.
7. a weaver's spindle.
8. in pharmacy, a small roll of dried bark, as of cinchona, cinnamon, etc.
9. that which has the form of a quill or some resemblance to a quill, as (a) a hollow shaft used in machinery; (b) the fold of a plaited ruff.

quill, *v.t.*; quilled, *pt., pp.*; quilling, *ppr.* 1. to plait or to form with small ridges like quills or reeds; as, a woolen stuff *quilled*.
2. to wind on a quill (sense 7).

quil·laī' (ki-lī'), *n.* [Chilean *quillai*, so called from its soaplike qualities, from *quillean*, to wash.]
1. a Chilean tree, *Quillaja saponaria*, whose inner bark is used instead of soap in washing silks, woolens, etc.
2. its inner bark: also called *quillai bark*, *soapbark*.

quil·laī'ȧ bärk (ki-lī'ȧ *or* kwi-lā'yȧ), same as *quillai* (*bark*).

Quil·lā'jȧ (-yȧ), *n.* a genus of trees found in South America: its bark has soaplike qualities.

quill'back, *n.* [so called because the anterior rays of its dorsal fin are elongated and curved like a quill.] a fresh-water fish belonging to the genus *Carpiodes*, found in American waters, especially in those of the Mississippi Valley: also called *carp sucker*, *sailfish*, and *spearfish*.

quill bit, a shell bit; a gouge bit.

quill çŏv'ẽrt, one of the feathers which cover the bases of the quills of the wings and tail of a bird.

quill drīv'ẽr, 1. a clerk; a writer.
2. an author: a term of contempt or ridicule.

quill drīv'ing, writing: a contemptuous term.

quilled, *a.* 1. furnished with or having the shape of quills.
2. in botany, having quill-like corollas or florets.
quilled suture; in surgery, a suture in which a double thread is employed and tied over quills or a soft catheter in order that the sutures may be relaxed when the tension becomes too great.

quil'let, *n.* [L. *quidlibet*, what you please.] a quibble; a subtlety; nicety; fraudulent distinction. [Archaic.]

quil'let, *n.* [origin obscure.] a small piece of land. [Brit. Dial.]

quill'ing, *n.* a narrow bordering of ribbon or lace plaited so as to resemble a row of quills; also, one of the plaits comprising such a band.

quill nib, a small pen made of quill to be placed in a holder.

quill pen, a pen for writing, made of a stout feather, the shaft of which serves as a holder: used generally before the invention of metal pens.

quill'wŏrt, *n.* any plant of the genus *Isoetes*, of the club-moss family, characterized by a tuft of quill-like leaves growing from a corm under water: one of the best-known species is *Isoetes lacustris*.

quill'y, *a.* having or resembling quills.

quilt, *n.* [OFr. *cuilte*, *coutre*, *coultre*, from L. *culcitra*, *culcita*, a bed, a mattress, a pillow.]
1. a bedcover made of two layers of cloth filled with down, cotton, wool, etc. and stitched together in lines or patterns.
2. anything used as a quilt.
3. any material made up like a quilt.

quilt, *v.t.*; quilted, *pt., pp.*; quilting, *ppr.* 1. to stitch together, as two pieces of cloth, with a soft material between.
2. to stitch in lines or patterns like those used in quilts.
3. to sew up or fasten between two pieces of material.
4. to line or pad like a quilt.

quilt, *v.i.* to make a quilt or quilts.

quilt'ed, *a.* stitched together, as two pieces of cloth, with a soft substance between them.

quilt'ẽr, *n.* one who quilts; also, an attachment to sewing machines used in quilting.

quilt'ing, *n.* 1. the act or process of making a quilt or of stitching in a similar manner to that employed in quilt making.
2. a quilting bee.
3. the material used in making quilts; quilted work.

quilt'ing bee, a social gathering of women at which they work together sewing quilts.

quin, *n.* a scallop. [Brit. Dial.]

quin'ȧ·crīne, *n.* [*quin*ine and *acr*id and *-ine*.] atabrine, a synthetic drug: in full, *quinacrine hydrochloride*.

quin·al'dīne, *n.* [*quin*oline and *ald*ehyde and anil*ine*.] in medicine, a liquid antiperiodic derivative, $C_{10}H_9N$, of aniline and paraldehyde.

quin·am'i·cīne, *n.* an amorphous artificial alkaloid, $C_{19}H_{24}N_2O_2$, obtained from quinamine.

quin·am'i·dīne, *n.* an artificial alkaloid, isomeric with quinamicine, prepared from quinamine.

quin'ȧ·mīne, *n.* a crystallizable alkaloid, $C_{19}H_{24}N_2O_2$, obtained from various cinchona barks.

qui·nār'i·ăn, *a.* [L. *quinarius*, from *quini*, five each, from *quinque*, five.] quinary; in parts or groups of five; specifically, designating an obsolete system of classification or division of the animal kingdom which regarded all groups as naturally consisting of five primary parts.

qui·nār'i·ăn, *n.* an advocate of the quinary system; one who applies the quinary system in classification.

quī'nȧ·ry, *a.* [L. *quinarius*, from *quinque*, five.] consisting of five; arranged by fives; as, a *quinary* number.
quinary system; in zoology, an obsolete system of grouping founded on the fancied natural division of every group into five primary types.

quī'nȧ·ry, *n.*; *pl.* **quī'nȧ·rieṣ,** a group, number, class, or any entirety made up of five similar parts.

quī'nāte, *a.* [L. *quini*, five each, and *-ate*.] in botany, arranged in or bearing a set of five similar parts: said of a petiole bearing five radiating similar leaflets, as in *Ampelopsis quinquefolia*.

quin'āte, *n.* any salt of quinic acid.

quin·ȧ·tox'īne, *n.* in chemistry, one of several toxic, ketonic bases obtained from cinchona bark or cinchona alkaloids: it is also prepared synthetically.

quin·az'ō·līne, *n.* in chemistry, $C_8H_6N_2$, a colorless, crystalline compound which is thought to be derived from quinoline by substituting an atom of nitrogen for a CH group occupying the 3 position.

quince (kwins), *n.* [OFr. *cooin*; L. *cotonium*, *cydonium*; Gr. *kydōnion mēlon*, a quince, from *Kydōnia*, Cydonia, a town on the north coast of Crete.] the golden, apple-shaped fruit of *Cydonia vulgaris*, of the rose family, with hard

QUINCE (*Cydonia vulgaris*)

flesh, cultivated widely for use in preserves, etc.

2. the tree on which the fruit grows.

Bengal quince; same as *bel*.

Japan quince; a shrub, *Pyrus japonica*, cultivated for its showy rose or scarlet flowers which appear before the leaves in early spring.

quince slug, same as *pear slug*.

quince tree, the tree, *Cydonia vulgaris*, which produces the quince.

quinch, *v.i.* [prob. from *wince* or *winch*.] to stir, wince, or flounce. [Obs.]

quin·çun′ciăl (-shăl), *a.* [from L. *quincunx*, five twelfths of anything; *quinque*, five, and *uncia*, a twelfth part.]

1. having the form of a quincunx.

2. in botany, having five parts, two outer, two inner, and one covering the latter by one of its sides: said of petals or of leaves in the bud.

quincuncial phyllotaxy; a spiral arrangement of leaves on a stem such that five leaves constitute one turn of the spiral and the angular distance between any two consecutive leaves is two fifths of the circumference.

quin·çun′ciăl·ly, *adv.* in a quincuncial manner or order.

quin′çuñx, *n.*; *pl.* **quin′çuñx·eş,** [L. *quinque*, *five*, and *uncia*, a twelfth.]

1. an arrangement of five objects in a square, one at each corner and one in the middle; especially, an arrangement, as of trees in such squares, thus ∴∵, continuously. A collection of trees in such squares forms a regular grove or wood, presenting parallel rows or alleys in different directions, according to the spectator's position.

2. in botany, a quincuncial arrangement of the petals of a flower.

3. in astrology, the condition of planets when the angular distance between them is five signs, 150°.

quin·deç′ȧ·gon, *n.* [L. *quinque*, five, Gr. *deka*, ten, and *gōnia*, angle.] in geometry, a plane figure with fifteen angles and fifteen sides.

quin·dē·cem′vir, *n.* [L. *quinque*, five, *decem*, ten, and *vir*, man.] in Roman history, one of an ecclesiastical college of fifteen men whose chief duty was to care for the Sibylline books.

quin·dē·cem′vi·rāte, *n.* the body or office of the quindecemvirs.

quin·dē·cen′ni·ăl, *a.* [from L. *quindecim*, fifteen, and *-ennial* as in *biennial*.]

1. happening once in a period of fifteen years.

2. lasting for fifteen years.

quin·dē·cen′ni·ăl, *n.* 1. a fifteenth year of existence or duration; fifteenth anniversary.

2. the celebration of this.

quin·dē·cyl′iç, *a.* [L. *quindec*im, fifteen, *-yl*, and *-ic*.] in chemistry, of, relating to, or designating a compound, as of the fatty acid series, having fifteen atoms of carbon. [Rare.]

quin′diṡm, *n.* a fifteenth. [Obs.]

quin·hȳ′drōne, *n.* [*quin*one and *hydro*quinone.] a compound produced by treating an aqueous solution of quinone with a limited quantity of sulfurous acid, and by mixing solutions of quinone and hydroquinone.

quin′i·ȧ, *n.* [ML., from Sp. *quina*.] quinine.

quin′i·ble, *n.* in music, an interval of a fifth; a part sung with such intervals; a descant in fifths. [Archaic.]

quin′iç, *a.* derived from or contained in quinine.

quin′iç ac′id, a colorless, crystalline acid, $C_6H_7(OH)_4·COOH$, prepared from cinchona bark, coffee beans, etc.

quin′i·cīne, *n.* an alkaloid isomeric with quinine and quinidine, and produced by the molecular transformation of either of these bases. It is very bitter, possesses febrifugal properties, and turns the plane of polarization to the right.

quin′i·dīne, quin′i·din, *n.* a colorless, crystalline alkaloid, $C_{20}H_{24}N_2O_2$, isomeric with quinine, and occurring associated with it in some cinchona barks.

quin′in, *n.* quinine.

qui·nī′nȧ (ki-), *n.* quinine.

quī′nīne (*or* kwi-nēn′ *or* kwin′ēn), *n.* [LL. *quinina*, from Sp. *quina*, Peruvian bark.]

1. a bitter, crystalline alkaloid, $C_{20}H_{24}N_2O_2$, extracted from cinchona bark.

2. any compound of this, as quinine sulfate, used in medicine for various purposes, especially in the treatment of malaria.

qui·nin′iç, *a.* of or derived from quinine.

quī′nin·iṡm, *n.* see *cinchonism*.

quī′niṡm, *n.* see *cinchonism*.

qui·niz′ȧ·rin, *n.* a red crystalline compound; an isomer of alizarin.

quin′nat salm′ŏn (sam′un), *n.* [Am. Indian.] a fish, *Oncorhynchus quinnat*, the king salmon, or chinook salmon.

qui·nō′ȧ (kē-), *n.* [native name.] a South American plant, *Chenopodium quinoa*, cultivated in Peru and Chile for its seeds, which are used in making broth and a kind of cake.

quin′ō·ġen, *n.* a ketonic compound formed from quinine.

qui·noi′dīne, qui·noi′din, *n.* [*quinoid* and *-ine*.] a brownish substance containing a mixture of alkaloids formed in the process of extracting quinine from cinchona, used as a substitute for quinine.

quin′ōl, *n.* a compound obtained by reduction of quinone.

quin′ō·līne, quin′ō·lin, *n.* [*quin*ine and *-ol* and *-ine*.] a colorless, liquid compound, C_9H_7N, obtained by the destructive distillation of bones, coal tar, and various alkaloids, or by synthesis: it is used in making antiseptics, dyes, etc.: also spelled *chinoline*.

qui·nol′ō·ġist, *n.* one who studies or is versed in quinology.

qui·nol′ō·ġy, *n.* the branch of science which deals with the cultivation and use of the cinchonas and quinine.

qui·nōne′ (*or* kwin′ōn), *n.* [*quin*ic acid and *-one*.]

1. either of two isomeric compounds, $C_6H_4O_2$, especially the yellow, crystalline isomer used in making dyes.

2. any of a series of compounds of this type.

qui·non′i·mīne, *n.* [from *quinone* and *imine*.] a crystalline compound, C_6H_5NO, derived from a quinone by the replacement of an oxygen atom by an imino group.

quin′ō·noid, *a.* [*quinone* and *-oid*.] like quinone in structure, properties, etc.

qui·nō′viç, *a.* derived from or containing quinovin.

qui·nō′vin, *n.* [LL. *quina nova*, a kind of tree.] a bitter substance obtained from cinchona.

quin′ō·yl, *n.* [*quin*one and *-yl*.] a bivalent radical, $C_6H_2O_2$, of which quinone is the hydride.

quin″quȧ·ġē·nār′i·ăn, *a.* [from L. *quinquaginta*, fifty.] fifty years old, or between the ages of fifty and sixty.

quin″quȧ·ġē·nār′i·ăn, *n.* a person fifty years old or between the ages of fifty and sixty.

Quin·quȧ·ġeṡ′i·mȧ, *n.* [L., f. of *quinquagesimus*, fiftieth.]

1. a period of about fifty days between the Sunday before Lent to Easter Sunday. [Obs.]

2. the Sunday before Lent: also *Quinquagesima Sunday*.

quin·quañ′gū·lăr, *a.* [L. *quinque*, five, and *angulus*, angle.] having five angles or corners. [Obs.]

quin′que-, [from L. *quinque*, five.] a combining form meaning *five* or *a multiple of five*, as in *quinque*valent: also, before a vowel, *quinqu-*.

quin·quē·añ′gled (-gld), *a.* having five angles.

quin·quē·çap′sū·lăr, *a.* [*quinque-* and *capsular*.] in biology, having five capsules.

quin·quē·den′tāte, quin·quē·den′tā·ted, *a.* [*quinque-* and *dentate*.] having five teeth.

quin·quē·făr′i·ous, *a.* [*quinque-* and *-farious* as in *multifarious*.] in biology, arranged in five rows, ranks, or columns.

quin′quē·fid, *a.* [*quinque-*, and L. *findere*, to split.] in botany, five-cleft; cut about halfway from the margin to the base into five segments, with linear sinuses and straight margins, as a leaf.

quin·quē·fō′li·āte, quin·quē·fō′li·ā·ted, *a.* [*quinque-*, and L. *folium*, leaf.] having five leaves or leaflets.

quin·quē·lit′ẽr·ăl, *a.* [*quinque-*, and L. *litera*, letter.] consisting of five letters.

quin·quē·lō′bāte, quin′quē·lōbed, *a.* [*quinque-*, and LL. *lobus*, lobe.] five-lobed; divided about to the middle into five distinct parts, with convex margins, as a leaf.

quin·quē·loç′ū·lăr, *a.* [*quinque-*, and L. *loculus*, a cell.] five-celled; having five cells, as a pericarp.

quin′quē·nẽrved, *a.* [*quinque-*, and L. *nervus*, a nerve.] having five nerves.

quin·quen·nā′li·ȧ, *n.pl.* [L., neut. pl. of *quinquennalis*, that takes place every five years; from *quinque*, five, and *annus*, year.] in Roman history, public games celebrated every five years.

quin·quen′ni·ad, *n.* a quinquennium.

quin·quen′ni·ăl, *a.* 1. occurring once in five years.

2. lasting five years.

quin·quen′ni·ăl, *n.* a quinquennial event.

quin·quen′ni·um, *n.*; *pl.* **quin·quen′ni·ȧ,** [L. *quinquennis*, of five years.] a period of five years.

quin·quē·păr′tīte, *a.* [L. *quinque*, five, and *partitus*, pp. of *partire*, to divide.]

1. in botany, divided into five parts almost to the base.

2. consisting of five parts.

quin′quē·rēme, *n.* [L. *quinque*, five, and *remus*, oar.] a galley having five banks or rows of oars.

quin·quē·syl′lȧ·ble, *n.* a word having five syllables.

quin·quē·vā′lence, *n.* [*quinque-* and *valence*.] the quality or state of being quinquevalent.

quin·quē·vā′len·cy, *n.* quinquevalence.

quin·quē·vā′lent, *a.* 1. having five valences.

2. having a valence of five.

Also, especially for 2, *pentavalent*.

quin′quē·valve, quin·quē·valv′ū·lăr, *a.* having five valves, as a pericarp.

quin′quē·vir, *n.*; *pl.* **quin·quev′i·rī,** in ancient Rome, one of five commissioners appointed for some special object.

quin·quī′nȧ (*or* kin-kē′), *n.* cinchona bark.

quin′qui·nō (kin′ki-), *n.* [S. Am.] a tall, flowering leguminous tree, *Myroxylon pereiræ*, yielding the balsam of Peru.

quin′şy, *n.* [from LL. *cynanche*; Gr. *kynanchē*, an inflammation of the throat.] an inflammation of the tonsils, accompanied by the formation of pus.

quin′şy·ber″ry, *n.* the black currant, whose berries yield a jelly used as a medication for quinsy.

quin′şy·wŏrt, *n.* a European herb, *Asperula cynanchica*, once used as a gargle.

quint, *n.* [L. *quintus*, fifth.]

1. in music, (a) an interval of a fifth; (b) an organ stop producing tones a fifth above those sounded by the keys that are pressed; (c) the E string of a violin.

2. in piquet, a sequence of five cards in the same suit.

quint, *n.* a quintuplet. [Colloq.]

quin′tȧ, *n.* [Sp. and Port.] a country house or suburban residence.

quin′tāin, *n.* [Fr. *quintaine*, LL. *quintana*, a quintain, prob. from L. *quintana* (*via*), street in the camp intersecting the legions so as to separate the fifth maniple from the sixth; later, market place, from *quintanus*, fifth, belonging to the fifth, from *quintus*, fifth.] in medieval sports, an object supported by a crosspiece on an upright post, used as a target in tilting.

quin′tăl, *n.* [Fr. *quintal*; It. *quintale*, from the root of L. *centum*, a hundred.]

1. a hundredweight (100 pounds in the United States, 112 pounds in Great Britain).

2. a metric unit of weight, equal to 100 kilograms (220.46 pounds).

quin′tăn, *a.* [L. *quintanus*, from *quintus*, fifth.] happening or recurring every fifth day (counting both days of occurrence); as, a *quintan* fever.

quin′tăn, *n.* a quintan fever, etc.

quint·es′sence, *n.* [L. *quinta essentia*, fifth essence.]

1. the fifth essence, or ultimate substance, of which the heavenly bodies were thought to be composed, in ancient and medieval philosophy: distinguished from the four elements, air, fire, water, and earth.

2. the pure, concentrated essence of anything.

3. the most perfect manifestation or embodiment of a quality or thing.

quint·es′sence, *v.t.* to extract as a quintessence; to distill. [Obs.]

quin·tes·sen′tiăl (-shăl), *a.* of the quintessence; purest; most perfect.

quin·tet′, quin·tette′, *n.* [L. *quintus*, fifth.]

1. any group or set of five persons or things.

2. in music, (a) a composition for five voices or five instruments, as for string quartet and piano; (b) the five performers of such a composition.

quin′tiç, *a.* [L. *quintus*, fifth.] relating to or of the fifth order.

quin′tiç, *n.* in algebra, a function or quantic of the fifth degree.

quin′tile, *a.* [L. *quintus*, fifth.] in astrology, designating an aspect of heavenly bodies in which they are 72 degrees, or one fifth of a circle, distant from each other.

quin′tile, *n.* a quintile aspect.

Quin·til′li·ăn (-yăn), *n.* [L. *Quintilla*, fem. name, f. of *Quintillus*, dim. of *quintus*, fifth.] a member of a division of the Montanists led by Quintilla, a prophetess.

quin·til′liŏn, *n.* [L. *quintus,* fifth, and Eng. *million.*]
1. in the United States and France, a number represented by 1 followed by 18 zeros.
2. in Great Britain and Germany, a number represented by 1 followed by 30 zeros.

quin·til′liŏn, *a.* amounting to one quintillion in number.

quin′tōle, *n.* [It. *quinto,* from L. *quintus,* fifth.] in music, five notes in a group to be played in the time of four.

quin·troon′, *n.* [Sp. *quinterón,* from L. *quintus,* fifth.] the offspring of a white and an octoroon.

quin′tū·ple, *a.* [L. *quintuplus,* fivefold; *quintus,* fifth, and *plicare,* to fold.]
1. fivefold; five times as much or as many.
2. consisting of or including five.

quin′tū·ple, *v.t.* and *v.i.*; quintupled, *pt., pp.*; quintupling, *ppr.* to make or become five times as much or as many; to multiply by five.

quin·tū′ple, *n.* a number, etc. five times as great as another.

quin′tū·ple-nẽrved, quin′tū·ple-ribbed, *a.* same as *quintuplinerved.*

quin′tū·plet, *n.* 1. (a) any of five offspring born at a single birth; (b) [*pl.*] five offspring born at a single birth.
2. a collection or group of five, usually of one kind.

quin·tū′pli·cāte, *v.t.*; quintuplicated, *pt. pp.*; quintuplicating, *ppr.* to make fivefold; to quintuple.

quin′tū·pli·nẽrved, *a.* in botany, having five nerves, all proceeding from above the base of the lamina: said of certain leaves.

quin·zaine′ (kan-zen′), *n.* [Fr., the number of fifteen, a fortnight, from *quinze,* fifteen.] the fourteenth day after a feast day, or the fifteenth if the day of the feast is included.

quinze, *n.* [Fr., fifteen, from L. *quindecim,* fifteen.] a card game in which the aim is to accumulate cards that total as near to fifteen as possible without exceeding it.

quip, *n.* [contr. from earlier *quippy,* from L. *quippe,* indeed, forsooth.]
1. a witty or sarcastic expression or allusion; a gibe; a jest.
2. a quibble.
3. something curious or odd.

quip, *v.t.*; quipped (kwipt), *pt., pp.*; quipping, *ppr.* to direct quips at.

quip, *v.i.* to utter quips.

quip′stẽr, *n.* a person who quips.

quī′pu (kē′), *n.* [Peruv. *quipu,* a knot.] a device consisting of knotted cords of various colors, used by the ancient Peruvians to record events, keep accounts, send messages, etc.

quīre, *n.* a choir. [Archaic.]

quīre, *v.t.* and *v.i.*; quired, *pt. pp.*; quiring, *ppr.* to choir. [Archaic.]

quīre, *n.* [ME. *quair;* OFr. *quaer,* book of loose pages, from LL. *quaternum,* from L. *quattuor,* four.] one twentieth of a ream of paper, consisting of 24 or 25 sheets of paper of the same size and stock.

Quir′i·năl, *n.* [L. *Quirinalis,* from *Quirinus.*] the Italian civil government, as distinguished from the Vatican, or papal government: from the palace on the Quirinal Hill, one of the seven hills of Rome.

Quir′i·năl, *a.* 1. of or situated on the Quirinal Hill in Rome.
2. of Quirinus.

Quir·i·nā′li·ȧ, *n.pl.* [L., neut. pl. of *quirinalis,* from *Quirinus.*] an ancient Roman festival observed on February 17, in honor of Romulus, who became identified with Quirinus.

qui·riñ′çȧ podș, [native name.] pods of a South American tree, *Acacia cavenia,* containing tannin.

Quir·ī′nus, *n.* [L.; akin to *Quirites*] in Roman mythology, an early god of war: identified by the Romans with Romulus.

quir′is·tẽr, *n.* a chorister. [Obs.]

quir·i·tãr′i·ăn, *a.* [L. *quiritare,* to raise a plaintive cry, from *queri,* to complain.] in Roman law, legal: distinguished from *bonitarian.*

Qui·rī′tēș, *n.pl.* [L., from *Cures,* the ancient Sabine capital.] in ancient Rome, the people as civilians: the name *Quirites* was used in addition to *Romani,* the latter designation applying to the people in their political and military capacity.

quirk, *n.* [perh. from ON. *kuerk,* a crop, bird's neck (via dial.).]
1. a sudden twist, turn, or stroke, as a flourish in writing.
2. an evasion, subterfuge, quibble, or equivocation.
3. a clever turn of speech; a sally; a quip.
4. a peculiarity, peculiar trait, or mannerism.
5. in architecture, a groove running lengthwise in a molding.
6. in building, a space taken out of any regular ground plot or floor to make a court, yard, etc.
7. a quirk bead or quirk molding.
8. a guide on a grooving plane.
9. a diamond-shaped pane of glass.

quirk, *v.t.* in architecture, to form with a quirk.

quirk′ish, *a.* 1. consisting of quirks.
2. resembling a quirk.

quirk mōld′ing, in architecture, a molding having a quirk on one or both sides of the bead, ovolo, ogee, etc.

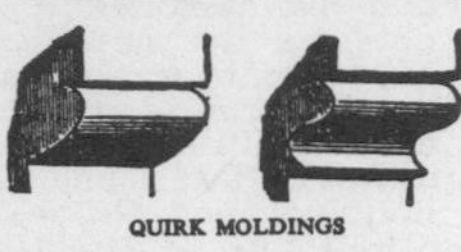
QUIRK MOLDINGS

quirk′y, *a.*; *comp.* quirkier; *superl.* quirkiest; having quirks.

quirl, *n.* a querl; a twirl; a twist; a coil.

quirt, *n.* [Mex. Sp. *cuarta,* a quirt, long whip, from *cuarta,* guide mule, lit., fourth (of a four-mule team), fem. of Sp. *cuarto* (L. *quartus*), fourth.] a riding whip with a braided leather lash and a short handle.

quirt, *v.t.* to strike with a quirt.

quish, *n.* a cuisse. [Obs.]

quiș′ling, *n.* [after Vidkun *Quisling* (1887–1945), Norw. politician who betrayed his country to the Nazis and became its puppet ruler.] a person who betrays his own country by helping an enemy to invade and occupy it; a traitor.

quit, *v.t.*; quit *or* quitted, *pt., pp.*; quitting, *ppr.* [OFr. *quiter;* ML. *quittare,* from LL. *quietare,* to set free, from L. *quietus,* quiet, at rest, satisfied.]
1. to free (oneself) *of.*
2. to discharge (a debt or obligation); to repay.
3. to stop having, using, or doing (something); to give up.
4. to let go (something held).
5. to leave; to depart from.
6. to stop or discontinue, as work.
7. to conduct (oneself). [Archaic.]
to quit cost; to pay; to reimburse.
to quit scores; to make even.
Syn.—abandon, leave, forsake, relinquish, cease.

quit, *v.i.* 1. to go away.
2. to stop or discontinue doing something; to give up an undertaking.
3. to give up one's position of employment; to resign. [Colloq.]

quit, *a.* free; clear; discharged; absolved.

quit, *n.* [echoic.] any of various birds of Jamaica, as the banana quit, *Certhia flaveola,* the blue quit, *Euphonia jamaica,* the grass-quit, *Spermophila olivacea,* and the orange quit, *Tanagrella ruficollis.*

quit, *n.* in astronomy, the point in the heavens from which the earth or any of the heavenly bodies is moving at a given time.

quī tam, [L. *qui,* who, and *tam,* as well.] in law, an action in which a man prosecutes an offender for the state, as well as for himself as informer.

quitch, *n.* [AS. *cwice,* from base of *cwicu,* alive: so named supposedly from the great vitality of the plant.] a long-rooted grass, growing in lawns, etc. as a weed: also *quitch grass.*

quit′çlāim, *v.t.*; quitclaimed (-klāmd), *pt., pp.*; quitclaiming, *ppr.* [OFr. *quiteclamer,* to release, to give up.] to give up a claim to (some property or right).

quit′çlāim, *n.* 1. the release or relinquishment of a claim.
2. a deed or other legal paper in which a person relinquishes to another a claim to some property or right.

quite, *v.t.* and *v.i.* to quit. [Obs.]

quīte, *adv.* [Fr. *quitte,* free, clear.]
1. completely; entirely.
2. really; truly; positively.
3. to a considerable degree or extent; very. [Colloq.]
quite a few; more than a few. [Colloq.]
quite so; certainly.

quīte′ly, *adv.* quite. [Obs.]

quit′rent, *n.* a rent paid in lieu of required feudal services: also *quit rent.*

quits, *a.* [from *quit, a.*] on even terms, as by discharge of a debt, retaliation in vengeance, etc.
to cry quits; to declare oneself even with another; to agree to stop competing.

quit′tȧ·ble, *a.* that can be quit. [Rare.]

quit′tăl, *n.* return; repayment. [Obs.]

quit′tănce, *n.* [Fr.] 1. discharge from a debt or obligation.
2. a document certifying this; a receipt.
3. recompense; repayment; reprisal.

quit′tănce, *v.t.* to repay. [Obs.]

quit′tẽr, *n.* one who quits or gives up easily, without trying hard. [Colloq.]

quit′tẽr, *n.* 1. same as *quittor.*
2. scoria of tin.
3. a purulent discharge. [Obs.]

quit′tŏr, *n.* [OFr. *cuiture,* cooking.] any of various foot diseases of horses, mules, etc., characterized by tissue degeneration and the formation of a slough.

qui va là? (kē vȧ lȧ), [Fr.] who goes there?: a sentry's challenge.

quiv′ẽr, *a.* [AS. *cwifer-.*] nimble; active. [Obs. or Dial.]

quiv′ẽr, *v.i.*; quivered, *pt., pp.*; quivering, *ppr.* [ME. *quivere(n),* prob. from base of *quaver.*] to shake or tremble; to quake; to shudder; as, to *quiver* with fear or anger, leaves *quiver* in the breeze.

quiv′ẽr, *n.* the act of quivering; a tremulous motion; a tremor; a shiver.

quiv′ẽr, *n.* [OFr. *quivre, cuivre;* AS. *cocer,* a case, a sheath.]
1. a case for holding arrows.
2. its contents.

quiv′ẽred, *a.* 1. furnished with a quiver.
2. sheathed, as in a quiver.

quiv′ẽr·ing·ly, *adv.* in a quivering manner.

quiv′ẽr tree, an aloe plant of South Africa, *Aloe dichotoma.*

quī vīve? (kē vēv), [Fr., lit., who lives?] who goes there?: a sentry's challenge.
to be on the qui vive; to be on the lookout; to be on the alert.

quix·ot′iç, quix·ot′i·çăl, *a.* [Sp., from Don *Quixote.*]
1. [*sometimes* Q–] like or befitting Don Quixote.
2. extravagantly chivalrous or romantically idealistic; visionary; impractical or impracticable.

quix·ot′i·çăl·ly, *adv.* in a quixotic manner.

quix′ŏt·ișm, *n.* 1. quixotic character or practice.
2. a quixotic act or idea.

quix′ŏt·ry, *n.* quixotism.

quiz, *n.* [prob. an arbitrary formation; perh. suggested by L. *quis,* who, which, what, *quid,* how, why, wherefore.]
1. a queer or eccentric person. [Rare.]
2. a practical joke; a hoax.
3. a questioning; especially, an informal oral or written examination to test one's knowledge.

quiz, *v.t.*; quizzed, *pt., pp.*; quizzing, *ppr.* 1. to make fun of (someone or something).
2. to ask questions of (a person) to test his knowledge.

quiz, *v.i.* to hold or conduct a quiz.

quiz prō′gram, a type of radio or television program in which a group of experts or members of the audience compete in answering questions.

quiz seç′tion, in some colleges and universities, a small group of students who meet with an instructor to discuss and be examined on the content of lectures.

quiz′zẽr, *n.* one who quizzes.

quiz′zẽr·y, *n.* the act or habit of quizzing. [Rare.]

quiz′zi·căl, *a.* 1. odd; comical.
2. given to making fun of others; bantering.
3. perplexed; questioning.

quiz·zi·çal′i·ty, *n.* the quality of being quizzical.

quiz′zi·çăl·ly, *adv.* in a quizzical manner.

quiz′zing glȧss, a monocle.

quiz′zișm, *n.* the act of quizzing; quizzery.

quō′ad hoc, [L.] 1. to this extent.
2. with respect to this.

quō an′i·mō? [L., lit., with what mind?] with what intent?

quod, *n.* [a form of *quad,* contr. of *quadrangle.*] prison; as, sent to *quod.* [Chiefly Brit. Slang.]

quod, *v.t.*; quodded, *pt., pp.*; quodding, *ppr.* to send to or confine in prison. [Chiefly Brit. Slang.]

quōd, *v.* obsolete form of *quoth.*

quod′dy, *n.*; *pl.* **quod′dieș,** [abbrev. of *Passa-*

maquoddy.] a variety of herring found in Passamaquoddy Bay, Maine.

quod er'at dem·ŏn·stran'dum, [L.] which was to be demonstrated or proved.

quod er'at fā·ci·en'dum (-shi-), [L.] which was to be done.

quod est, [L.] which is.

quod'li·bet, *n.* [L., also *quidlibet,* what you please, neut. of *quilibet,* any one you please, any one at all.]
1. a nice point; a subtlety.
2. in music, a fantasia.

quod'li·bet·ăl, *a.* composed of quodlibets. [Rare.]

quod"li·bē·tãr'i·ăn, *n.* one who talks and disputes about quodlibets. [Rare.]

quod·li·bet'iç, quod·li·bet'i·çăl, *a.* 1. not restrained to a particular subject; discussed at pleasure for curiosity or entertainment.
2. given to subtle or fine distinctions.

quod·li·bet'i·çăl·ly, *adv.* in an academic or subtle manner.

quod vī'dē, [L.] which see.

quoil, *n.* a coil. [Dial.]

quoin (koin *or* kwoin), *n.* [Fr. **coin,** a corner.]
1. the external corner of a building; especially, any of the large, squared stones by which the corner of a building is marked.
2. a wedgelike piece of stone, etc., such as the keystone or one of the pieces of an arch.
3. a wedge-shaped wooden or metal block used to lock up type in a galley or form, to keep casks from rolling, to fix the position of a gun breech, etc.

QUOINS

hollow quoin; a quoin of brick or masonry built hollow, to receive a quoin post.

quoin, *v.t.* 1. to secure with a quoin.
2. to furnish with quoins, or corners.

quoin pōst, the heelpost of a lockgate.

quoit, *n.* [ME. *coite, coyte;* OFr. *coite,* a cushion.]
1. a ring of rope or flattened metal, used in the game of quoits.
2. [*pl.*] a game in which players throw such rings at a peg in the ground, the object being to encircle it or come as close to it as possible.

quoit, *v.i.* to throw quoits; to play at quoits. [Rare.]

quoit, *v.t.* to throw like a quoit; to hurl.

quō jụ'rē? [L.] by what right?

quō mō'dō, [L.] 1. in what manner?
2. in the manner that.

quōk, quōke, *v.* obsolete past tense of *quake.*

quon'dam, *a.* [L.] having been formerly; former; as, a *quondam* friend.

quon'dam, *n.* one who formerly occupied an official or other position. [Obs.]

Quō'ni·am, *n.* [L.] that part of the Gloria in Excelsis which begins with *Quoniam tu solus sanctus* (For thou only art holy); also, a musical setting of these words.

Quon'set hut, [from *Quonset,* R. I., where they were first manufactured.] a prefabricated shelter of corrugated metal shaped like a cylinder cut vertically in two and resting on its flat surface: it is similar to the British Nissen hut and was first used by the U. S. Army in World War II.

quō'rum, *n.* [L., genit. pl. of *qui,* who.]
1. (a) originally, the number of justices of the peace required to be present at sessions of English courts; (b) later, English justices of the peace, collectively.
2. a select group or company.
3. the minimum number of members required to be present at an assembly before it can validly proceed to transact business.

quō'tȧ, *n.; pl.* **quō'tȧṣ,** [L., f. of *quotus,* of what number, how many.] a share or proportion which each of a number is called upon to contribute, or which is assigned to each; a proportional share.

quōt·ȧ·bil'i·ty, *n.* the quality or state of being quotable; fitness for quotation.

quōt'ȧ·ble, *a.* that can be quoted or cited; suitable for quotation.

quō·tā'tion, *n.* 1. the act or practice of quoting or citing.
2. the words or passage quoted or cited; the part of a book or writing named, repeated, or adduced as evidence or illustration.
3. in commerce, (a) a statement of the current price of a stock, bond, commodity, etc.; (b) the price itself.

quō·tā'tion·ist, *n.* one who makes or is given to making quotations.

quō·tā'tion märk, either of a pair of punctuation marks ("...") used to enclose a direct quotation: a quotation within a quotation is enclosed in single marks ('...'): in British usage, this procedure is usually reversed.

quote, *v.t.;* quoted, *pt., pp.;* quoting, *ppr.* [Late OFr. *coter,* to mark according to the order of the numbers or letters; LL. *quotare,* to give chapter and verse for, from L. *quotus,* of what number.]
1. to reproduce or repeat a passage from or statement of; as, the teaçher *quoted* Chaucer.
2. to reproduce or repeat (a passage from a book, a statement, etc.).
3. to cite; to refer to as authority or an example.
4. in commerce, to state (the price of something).
5. in printing, to enclose in quotation marks.
6. to mark; to observe; to note, as in writing. [Obs.]
Syn.—cite, repeat, adduce.

quōte, *v.i.* to repeat the words of another; to make a quotation.

quōte, *n.* 1. a quotation. [Colloq.]
2. a quotation mark. [Colloq.]

quōt'ẽr, *n.* one who quotes.

quōth, *v.t.* [AS. *quæth,* pret. of *cwethan,* to speak, to say.] said; spoke: used in the first and third persons in the past tense, followed instead of preceded by its subject, and taking as its object the words being repeated. [Archaic.]
How now, Sir John, *quoth* I. —Shak.

quōth'ȧ, *interj.* [from *quoth I* or *quoth he.*] forsooth! indeed!: used ironically. [Archaic.]

quō·tid'i·ăn, *a.* [L. *quotidianus,* daily, from *quotidie,* daily; *quot,* as many as, and *dies,* day.] occurring or returning every day; daily; as, a *quotidian* fever.

quō·tid'i·ăn, *n.* 1. a fever whose paroxysms recur every day.
2. anything that recurs daily.

quō'tient (-shent), *n.* [L. *quoties, quotiens,* how often, how many times, from *quot,* how many.] in arithmetic, the number resulting from the division of one quantity by another, and showing how often one number is contained in another; as, the *quotient* of ten divided by five is two.

quō·tī'e·ty, *n.* [L. *quoties,* how often.]
1. the relation of an object to number.
2. the proportionate frequency of an event.

quō'tŭm, *n.* a quota, portion, or share. [Rare.]

quō wär·ran'tō, *pl.* **quō wär·ran'tōṣ,** [L. *quo,* ablative of *qui,* who, which, and LL. *warrantus,* a guarantee, warrant.]
1. originally, a writ ordering a person to show by what right he exercises an office, franchise, or privilege.
2. (a) a legal proceeding undertaken to recover an office, franchise, or privilege from the person in possession, initiated upon an information; (b) the information.

Qụ·rän' (koo-), *n.* see *Koran.*

R

R, r (är), *n.; pl.* **R's, r's, Rs, rs** (ärz), 1. the eighteenth letter of the English alphabet: from the Greek *rho,* a borrowing from the Phoenician.
2. the sound of R or r.
3. a type or impression for R or r.
4. *a symbol for* the eighteenth in a sequence or group (or the seventeenth if J is omitted).

R, r, *a.* 1. of R or r.
2. eighteenth (or seventeenth if J is omitted) in a sequence or group.
the three R's; reading, writing, and arithmetic, regarded as the basic elementary studies and the fundamentals of an education: so called from the humorous spelling *reading, 'riting,* and *'rithmetic.*

R, *a.* shaped like R.

Rä, *n.* [Egypt. *Rā, Rē',* sun.] the sun god, principal god of the ancient Egyptians, usually depicted as having the head of a hawk and wearing the solar disk as a crown: also *Re.*

Ra, in chemistry, radium.

rȧ·äd', *n.* [Ar. *ra'ād,* thunder.] the electric catfish, *Malapterurus electricus.*

räad (rät), *n.* [D.] a former legislative body in the Boer states in South Africa.

rab, *n.* [Heb.] teacher; master: used [R–] as a Jewish title of respect for a teacher of the law.

rȧ·ban'nȧ, *n.* [Native.] in Madagascar, a cloth woven from raffia.

rȧ·bat', *n.* [Fr., ruff or band.]
1. a neckband worn by French priests.
2. a clerical collar having a piece of cloth in front which reaches to the chest.

rab'at, *n.* a polishing material made of potters' clay incompletely baked.

rȧ·bā'tō, *n.* [Fr. *rabat.*] formerly, a large collar of linen, lace, etc. worn turned down so as to fall over the shoulders.

rab'băn, *n.* [Heb.] lord; master: a Jewish title higher in dignity than *rabbi,* formerly applied to heads of the Sanhedrin.

rab'băn·ist, *n.* a rabbinist.

rab'băn·ite, *n.* a rabbinist.

rab'bet, *n.* [ME. *rabet, rabbot,* from Fr. *raboter,* to plane, from OFr. *rabouter,* to thrust back.]
1. a groove or cut made in the edge of a board, etc. in such a way that another piece may be fitted into it to form a joint.

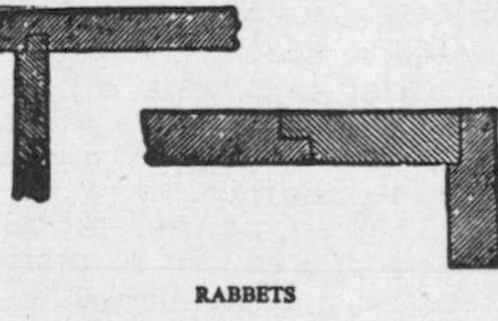

RABBETS

2. a rabbett plane.
3. a rabbett joint.

rab'bet, *v.t.* 1. to cut a rabbet in.
2. to join in a rabbet (joint).

rab'bet, *v.i.* to be joined by a rabbet.

rab'bet joint, the joint made by rabbeting.

rab'bet plāne, a plane used in making rabbets.

rab'bī, *n.; pl.* **rab'bīṣ, rab'bīeṣ,** [Heb., master, lord.] an ordained teacher of the Jewish law, authorized to decide questions of law and ritual and to perform marriages, etc., now usually the spiritual head of a congregation: the term is also used in respectful address.

rab′bin, *n.* [Fr.; ML. *rabbinus.*] a rabbi.

rab′bin·āte, *n.* 1. the position or office of rabbi.

2. rabbis collectively.

rab·bin′iç, *a.* same as *rabbinical.*

Rab·bin′iç, *n.* the Hebrew language or dialect of the rabbis, used in their writings in the Middle Ages.

rab·bin′iç·ăl, *a.* of the rabbis, their doctrines, learning, language, etc., especially in the early Middle Ages.

rab·bin′iç·ăl·ly, *adv.* in a rabbinical manner.

rab′bin·işm, *n.* a rabbinical expression or phraseology; a peculiarity of the language of the rabbis.

rab′bin·ist, *n.* one who adhered to the Talmud and the traditions of the rabbis, in opposition to the Karaites, who rejected the traditions.

rab·bin·is′tiç, *a.* of, or in the tradition of, the rabbis.

rab′bin·īte, *n.* same as *rabbinist.*

rab′bit, *n.* [OE. *rabet*; O.D. *robbe, robbeken,* a rabbit. Connections doubtful.]

1. a burrowing rodent, *Lepus cuniculus,* of the hare family, smaller than most hares and characterized by soft fur, long ears, and a bobbed tail; also, its fur.

2. loosely, any hare.

3. a dish of melted cheese and toast: see *Welsh rabbit,* below.

Angora rabbit; a variety of rabbit that has long, soft fur and is domestic.

Welsh rabbit; cheese toasted or melted, usually with ale, and served on toast.

rab′bit, *v.i.* to hunt rabbits.

rab′bit ban′di·cọọt, a marsupial of Australia, having highly developed hind legs and long ears.

rab′bit-ber″ry, *n.* same as *Buffalo berry.*

rab′bit brush, a shrub, *Bigelovia graveolens,* of the *Compositæ,* common in the plains of western North America: so named because its dense growths are frequented by jack rabbits.

rab′bit·ẽr, *n.* one who or that which hunts rabbits.

rab′bit fē′vẽr, same as *tularemia.*

rab′bit fish, any of various fishes, as (a) *Lagocephalus lævigatus,* having front teeth like those of a rabbit; (b) *Chimæra monstrosa*; (c) the streaked gurnard.

rab′bit mọth, a moth, *Lagoa opercularis,* covered with rabbit-colored furry down.

rab′bit·mouth, *n.* a fish, the cutlips or harelipped sucker.

rab′bit punch, in boxing, a short, sharp blow to the back of the neck.

rab′bit rat, a rodent of Australia, *Hapalotis albipes.*

rab′bit·rọọt, *n.* the wild sarsaparilla.

rab′bit·ry, *n.*; *pl.* **rab′bit·rieş,** a place where domesticated rabbits are kept; rabbit hutch.

rab′bit's (or **rab′bit) foot,** the hind foot of a rabbit, used superstitiously as a talisman, or good-luck charm.

rab′bit squir′rel (skwĩr′), a chincha

rab′bit wär′ren, a place in which rabbits are kept and bred.

rab′ble, *n.* [L. *rabula,* a brawler, from *rabere,* to rave.] a throng of noisy people; a mob; a disorderly crowd.

the rabble; the common people; the masses: a term of contempt.

rab′ble, *v.t.*; rabbled, *pt., pp.*; rabbling, *ppr.* to attack with a mob.

rab′ble, *a.* pertaining to or made up of a rabble; disorderly; vulgar; noisy.

rab′ble, *n.* [OFr. *roable*; Fr. *râble,* an implement for stirring or mixing, a poker, from L. *rutabulum,* LL. *rotabulum,* a poker or shovel.] a bent bar of iron used in stirring or skimming melted iron in puddling.

rab′ble, *v.t.*; rabbled, *pt., pp.*; rabbling, *ppr.* to stir or skim with a rabble, as molten iron.

rab′ble·ment, *n.* a noisy disturbance like that made by a rabble, or mob.

rab′blẽr, *n.* one who rabbles, as in puddling iron; also, the iron bar used in rabbling.

rab′ble rouş′ẽr, a demagogue; one who seeks to stir up people into violent action by appealing to their emotions, prejudices, etc.

rab·bō′nī, *n.* [Heb., my great master.] a title of very high honor among the Jews.

Rab·e·lāi′şi·ăn, *a.* of or like Francois Rabelais, French satirist and humorist (1494?–1553), or his works; broadly and coarsely humorous, satirical, etc.

Rab·e·lāi′şi·ăn, *n.* a person who imitates, admires, or studies Rabelais.

rab′ī, *n.* [Hind.] the crop in India that is sown in the fall and harvested in the spring.

rab′iç, *a.* pertaining to rabies.

rab′id, *a.* [L. *rabidus,* from *rabere,* to rage.]

1. furious; raging; mad.

2. affected with rabies, or hydrophobia.

3. excessively or extravagantly enthusiastic or zealous; fanatical.

Syn.—frantic, furious, mad, infuriated, raging, fanatical.

rȧ·bid′i·ty, *n.* rabid state or quality.

rab′id·ly, *adv.* in a rabid manner.

rab′id·ness, *n.* a rabid state or condition.

rā′bi·ēş, *n.* [L., madness.] an infectious virus disease of the central nervous system in dogs and other flesh-eating animals: it can be transmitted to man by the bite of an infected animal and is characterized by choking, convulsions, inability to swallow liquids, etc.; it is fatal if not treated immediately: also called *hydrophobia.*

rā·bi·et′iç, *a.* of or characterized by rabies.

rȧ·bif′iç, *a.* communicating or of a character such as to communicate rabies or hydrophobia; as, a *rabific* virus.

rab′i·net, *n.* [etym. obscure.] formerly, a small cannon.

rȧ·çä′, *a.* [Gr. *rhaka,* from Aram. *rēqā,* contemptible.] beggarly; foolish: a term of contempt.

raç′çȧ·hout, *n.* [Fr., from Ar. *rāqaut.*] a starch or meal prepared from the edible acorns of the Barbary oak, *Quercus ballota.*

raç·çọọn′, *n.*; *pl.* **raç·çọọnş′** or **raç·çọọn′,** [corruption of the Am. Ind. name, *arrathkune, arathcone,* formerly in use.] a small, tree-climbing, carnivorous mammal of North America, belonging to the genus *Procyon,* the common raccoon being *Procyon lotor.* It is active largely at night and is characterized by long, yellow-black fur, black masklike markings across the eyes, and a long, black-ringed tail; also, its fur. Also spelled *racoon.*

RACCOON
(*Procyon lotor*)

raç·çọọn′ dọg, a small wild dog of Asia, having long, loose fur, a thick tail, and raccoonlike rings about the eyes.

raç·çọọn′ fox, the cacomistle.

raç·çọọn′ oys′tẽr, a wild oyster of little or no commercial value: also called *coon oyster.* [Dial.]

rāce, *n.* [Fr. *race*; It. *razza,* race, family; perh. from L. *generatio,* a begetting.]

1. (a) any of the major biological divisions of mankind, distinguished by color and texture of hair, color of skin and eyes, stature, bodily proportions, etc.: many ethnologists now consider that there are only three primary divisions, the Caucasian (loosely, *white race*), Negroid (loosely, *black race*), and Mongoloid (loosely, *yellow race*), each with various subdivisions: the term has acquired so many unscientific connotations that in this sense it is often replaced in scientific usage by *ethnic stock* or *group*; (b) mankind.

2. a population that differs from others in the relative frequency of some gene or genes: a modern scientific use.

3. any geographical, national, or tribal ethnic grouping.

4. (a) the state of belonging to a certain ethnic stock, group, etc.; (b) the qualities, traits, etc. belonging, or supposedly belonging, to such a division.

5. any group of people having the same activities, habits, ideas, etc.; as, the *race* of dramatists.

6. a group of people having a common parentage; the descendants collectively of a common ancestry; family; clan.

7. (a) a breed; a stock; a large division or class, the species and genera of which are traceable to a common origin; (b) in zoology, a subspecies or variety.

8. characteristic strength or flavor indicating the origin of some natural product; as, the *race* of a wine. [Rare.]

Syn.—breed, family, nation, people, tribe.

rāce, *a.* 1. [of recent origin with euphemistic intent.] Negro.

2. racial.

rāce, *n.* [AS. *ræs,* a rush, a rapid course, a stream; Ice. *rás,* a race, a running.]

1. a competition of speed in running, skating, riding, etc.

2. [*pl.*] a series of such competitions for horses, on a regular course.

3. (a) any contest of speed in acting, thinking, etc.; as, a *race* for power; (b) any contest; as, the *race* for mayor.

4. a steady onward movement or course.

5. the span of life; as, the old man's *race* was run.

6. (a) a swift current of water; (b) the channel for a current of water, especially one built to use the water industrially; as, a mill*race.*

7. a channel or groove for the moving parts of a machine, as the groove for the balls in a ball bearing.

8. in aeronautics, the slip stream.

rāce, *v.i.*; raced (rāst), *pt., pp.*; racing, *ppr.* 1. to run swiftly; to contend in running; as, the animals *raced* over the ground.

2. to take part in a competition of speed.

3. in machinery, to move or revolve with too great speed because of diminished resistance, as the flywheel of a steam engine, or the driving wheel of a locomotive when it slips on the track in starting.

rāce, *v.t.* 1. to cause to engage in a race; as, to *race* a horse or a dog.

2. to compete with in a competition of speed.

3. (a) to cause to go swiftly; (b) to cause (an engine) to run too swiftly without engaging the gears.

rāce, *n.* a root or rhizome, especially of ginger; as, *race* ginger.

rāce çärd, a printed card containing the program of and information about a race or races.

rāce çlọth, a cloth with pockets for holding the prescribed weights, worn by a race horse.

rāce′çourse, *n.* 1. the track on which a race, especially a horse race, is run.

2. same as *millrace.*

rāce ġin′ġẽr, [OFr. *raïs,* from L. *radix,* a root.] gingerroot.

rāce glȧss, a field glass used for viewing races.

rāce họrse, 1. a horse bred and trained for racing.

2. a mantis.

3. the steamer duck.

rāce knīfe (nīf), a scribing tool having a U-shaped blade.

rac′ē·māte, *n.* in chemistry, a salt of racemic acid.

rac·ē·mā′tion, *n.* [L. *racemus,* a cluster.]

1. a cluster, as of grapes. [Obs.]

2. the cultivation or harvesting, as of clusters of grapes. [Obs.]

rȧ·cēme′, *n.* [L. *racemus,* a cluster of grapes.] a variety of flower cluster in which single flowers grow individually on small stems arranged at intervals along a single larger stem, as in the lily of the valley.

RACEMES
a, of red currant; *b,* of lily of the valley

compound raceme; a raceme with the lower pedicels developed into secondary racemes.

rȧ·cēmed′, *a.* having racemes; arranged in racemes.

rȧ·cē′miç, *a.* [*raceme* and *-ic.*]

1. designating or of an optically inactive form of tartaric acid.

2. (a) consisting of an optically inactive, equimolecular mixture of the dextrorotatory and levorotatory forms of certain substances; (b) designating or of a compound formed of such a mixture.

rac·ē·mif′ẽr·ous, *a.* [L. *racemus,* a cluster, and *ferre,* to bear.] bearing racemes, as the currant.

rȧ·cem′i·fọrm, *a.* formed or shaped like a raceme.

rac′ē·miṣm, *n.* same as *racemization.*

rac″ē·mi·zā′tion, *n.* the conversion of an optically active substance into a racemic form.

rac′ē·mōse, *a.* growing in the form of, or bearing, a raceme or racemes.

rac′ē·mōse·ly, *adv.* so as to appear like racemes.

rac′ē·mous, *a.* racemose.

rac′ē·mūle, *n.* [LL. *racemulus,* dim. of L. *racemus,* a cluster.] a small raceme.

rȧ·cem′ū·lōse, *a.* like a racemule.

rāce plāte, a circular platform of iron or steel on which a cannon is moved, and over which it moves backward in recoil.

rā′cẽr, *n.* 1. any person, animal, airplane, etc. that takes part in races.

2. any of several snakes; especially, the American blacksnake.

3. a revolving turntable on certain gun carriages, by which the gun can be aimed.

rāce rī′ŏt, fighting and violence in a community, characterized by racist hostility.

rāce sū′i·cīde, the gradual dying out of a people as a result of the deliberate failure of its members to maintain a birth rate equal to the death rate.

rāce track, a racecourse.

rāce′wāy, *n.* 1. a narrow channel for water.

2. a tube for carrying and protecting electric wires.

Rā′chel, *n.* [LL.; Gr. *Rhachēl*; Heb. *rāḥēl,* lit. ewe.] in the Bible, the younger of the two wives of Jacob, and mother of Joseph and Benjamin.

rā·ḉhi·al′ġi·ȧ, *n.* [Gr. *rhachis,* spine, and *algos,* pain.] pain in the spine.

rā·ḉhi·al′ġiç, *a.* suffering from rachialgia.

raḉh′i·dēṣ, *n.* pl. of *rachis.*

rȧ·ḉhid′i·ăl, *a.* pertaining to a rachis.

rȧ·ḉhid′i·ăn, *a.* rachidial.

Rā·ḉhi·glos′sȧ, *n.pl.* [*rachi-,* and Gr. *glossa,* tongue.] a division of the *Gasteropoda* with three longitudinal series of teeth on the radula. It includes the whelks, purpuras, etc.

rā·ḉhi·glos′sāte, *a.* pertaining to the *Rachiglossa.*

rȧ·ḉhil′lȧ, *n.* in botany, the zigzag center upon which the florets are arranged in the spikelets of grasses.

rā′ḉhi·ō-, rā′ḉhi-, [from Gr. *rhachis, rhachios,* spine.] a combining form meaning *of* or *relating to the spine.*

rā′ḉhi·ō·dont, *a.* having a series of vertebral processes that serve as teeth, as some snakes.

rā·ḉhi·om′e·tẽr, *n.* an instrument for measuring the spine.

rā′ḉhis, *n.*; *pl.* **rā′ḉhis·eṣ, raḉh′i·dēṣ,** [Gr. *rhachis,* spine.]

1. in anatomy, the spinal column.

2. in botany, a branch that proceeds nearly in a straight line from the base to the apex of a raceme.

3. in zoology, (a) the central portion of an odontophore; (b) the shaft of a feather, especially that part bearing the barbs.

RACHIS *Lolium perenne* (rye grass)

rȧ·ḉhit′iç, *a.* pertaining to or affected with rickets.

rȧ·ḉhī′tis, *n.* [Gr. *rhachis,* the spine, and *-itis.*]

1. rickets.

2. in botany, abortion of the fruit or seed.

rā′ḉhi·tiṣm, *n.* a tendency toward rickets.

rā′ḉhi·tōme, *n.* [*rachi-,* and Gr. *tomos,* a cutting, from *temnein,* to cut.] a surgical instrument for opening the spinal cord.

ra·ḉhit′ō·mous, *a.* in paleontology and zoology, pertaining to or characterized by vertebrae, whose central portions remain separate.

rȧ·ḉhit′ō·my, *n.* in surgery, the cutting or opening of the spinal column.

Raḉh·y·cen′tri·dae, *n.pl.* [Gr. *rhachis,* spine, *kentron,* a sharp point, and *-idae.*] a genus of fish of which the sergeant fishes are typical.

rā′ciăl (-shăl), *a.* of or pertaining to race, family, or descent; of or pertaining to the races of mankind; ethnological.

rā′ciăl·iṣm, *n.* a doctrine or feeling of racial differences or antagonisms, especially with reference to supposed racial superiority, inferiority, or purity; racial prejudice.

rā′ciăl·ly, *adv.* in a racial manner.

rā′ci·ly, *adv.* in a racy manner.

rā′ci·ness, *n.* the quality of being racy.

rā′cing çal′en·dăr, a list of races run or to be run.

rā′cing çrab, a crab of the family *Ocypodoidea.*

rāc′iṣm, *n.* 1. racialism.

2. program or practice of racial discrimination, segregation, persecution, and domination, based on racialism.

rāc′ist, *a.* of or characterized by racism.

rāc′ist, *n.* a person who believes in the doctrine of racialism or who advocates or practices racism.

rack, *n.* [ME. *racke*; prob. from M.D. *rek,* framework, from *recken,* to stretch.]

1. a framework, grating, case, stand, etc. for holding or displaying various articles; specifically, (a) a grating for holding hay, etc. to feed cattle; (b) a frame for holding hay, straw, etc. on a wagon; (c) a frame with hooks for hanging clothes; (d) a row of pigeonholes for holding sorted papers, etc.; (e) a framework for holding aerial bombs in an airplane; (f) a frame for arranging billiard balls in a triangle at the beginning of a game; (g) in printing, a frame for holding cases of type.

2. an instrument of torture which consists of a large, open wooden frame, within which the victim is laid on his back, with his wrists and ankles fastened by cords to two rollers at the ends of the frame. These rollers are then drawn or moved in opposite directions until the limbs of the victim are forced from their sockets.

3. any great mental or physical torment, or its cause.

4. a wrenching or upheaval, as by a storm.

5. a toothed bar whose pitch line is straight, adapted to mesh with the teeth of a gear wheel, worm gear, etc.

RACK AND PINION

6. a pair of antlers.

7. in mining, an inclined frame or table, open at the foot, upon which ores are placed and exposed to a stream of water, which washes off the lighter portions.

8. in nautical usage, a frame of wood with belaying pins or a row of sheaves for reeving the running rigging.

off the rack; ready-made: said of clothing.

to put on the rack; to torture; to torment; to put in a very difficult or painful situation.

rack, *v.t.* 1. to torture, as on the rack.

2. to torment; to torture physically or mentally.

3. to arrange in or on a rack.

4. (a) to oppress by unfair demands, especially by exacting exorbitant rents; (b) to raise (rents) to an exorbitant degree.

5. in mining, to wash (ores) on the rack.

6. in nautical usage, to bind together, with cross turns, as two ropes.

to rack a tackle; in nautical usage, to bind together two ropes of a tackle to retain it at a tension and prevent the ropes from reeving back through the blocks.

to rack one's brains (or *memory,* etc.); to try very hard to remember or think of something.

to rack up; (a) to be credited with; to gain, score, or achieve; as, to *rack up* a victory; (b) to be the victor over or beat decisively; (c) to knock down, as with a punch.

Syn.—torment, torture, harass, rend.

rack, *n.* [prob. var. of *track* with loss of *-t.*] a gait used by horses, the single-foot.

rack, *v.t.* to move with a rack: said of a horse.

rack, *n.* [var. of *wrack.*] destruction; wreckage: now only in the phrase *to go to rack and ruin,* to become ruined.

rack, *n.* [ME. *rac, rakke*; prob. from ON.] a broken mass of clouds blown by the wind: also spelled *wrack.*

rack, *v.i.* to be blown by the wind: said of clouds: also spelled *wrack.*

rack, *v.t.* [Late ME.; Pr. *arracar,* from *raca,* husks and stems of grapes, thick dregs.] to draw off (cider, wine, etc.) from the dregs.

rack, *n.* same as *arrack.*

rack, *n.* [AS. *hracca,* the back part of the head.] the neck and spine of a forequarter of veal, pork, or mutton. [Rare.]

rack′ȧ·bōneṣ, *n.* a very thin, bony person or animal. [Colloq.]

rack băr, in nautical usage, a billet of wood used to twist the bight of a rope in order to bind together the parts of a raft.

rack block, in nautical usage, a range of sheaves cut in one piece of wood for running ropes to lead through.

rack′ẽr, *n.* one who or that which racks, or tortures.

rack′et, *n.* [probably echoic.]

1. a noisy confusion; loud and confused talk or activity; uproar.

2. a period of gay, exciting merrymaking or revelry.

3. (a) an obtaining of money illegally, as by bootlegging, fraud, or, especially, threats of violence; (b) any dishonest scheme or practice; (c) any business, profession, or occupation; as, selling is a good *racket.* [Slang.]

rack′et, *v.i.* 1. to make a racket; to take part in a noisy activity.

2. to frolic noisily; to revel.

rack′et, *n.* [Fr. *raquette,* from Sp. *raqueta,* a racket, from Ar. *rāhat,* the palm of the hand.]

1. a light bat for tennis, badminton, etc., with a network of catgut, silk, nylon, etc. in an oval or round frame attached to a handle.

2. a snowshoe.

3. [*pl.*] same as *racquets.*

4. a broad wooden shoe for a horse, to enable him to step on marshy or wet ground.

rack′et, *v.t.*; racketed, *pt., pp.*; racketing, *ppr.* to strike with or as with a racket. [Obs.]

rack·et·eer′, *n.* [*racket* (uproar), sense 3, and *-eer.*] a person who obtains money illegally, as by bootlegging, fraud, or, especially, threats of violence.

rack·et·eer′ing, *n.* the practice or methods of a racketeer.

rack′et·ẽr, *n.* one who makes a racket, or noisy confusion.

rack′et·tāil, *n.* a species of hummingbird of the genus *Steganura,* with two tail feathers shaped like rackets.

rack′et·y, *a.*; *comp.* racketier; *superl.* racketiest, 1. making a racket.

2. fond of or engaging in frequent revelry, etc.

rack′ing, *n.* 1. the act of torturing by means of the rack.

2. in nautical usage, a piece of spun yarn used in racking a tackle.

rack rāil′wāy, a railway for climbing an inclined plane, as a mountain, having a toothed rail (*rack rail*) between the regular rails for engaging with cogwheels on the locomotive.

rack′-rent, *v.t.* to exact rack rent from.

rack rent, [*rack* (to stretch) and *rent.*] a rent whose annual amount is equal, or almost equal, to the value of the property.

rack′-rent″ẽr, *n.* 1. one who is subjected to the payment of rack rent.

2. a person who exacts rack rent.

rack saw, a saw with wide teeth.

rack′wŏrk, *n.* a mechanism having a rack (toothed bar).

raç·on·teur′ (*or Fr.* rȧ-kōṅ-tẽr′), *n.*; *pl.* **raç·on·teurṣ′** (-tẽrz′ *or Fr.* -tẽr′), [Fr.] one skilled in the narration of anecdotes or stories; one given to telling anecdotes.

ra·çoon′, *n.* a raccoon.

Rȧ·çō′vi·ăn, *n.* [from *Racow,* a town of Poland.] a native of Racow, Poland; also, one of the sect of Socinians having headquarters there in the seventeenth century.

raç′quet (-ket), *n.* a racket (bat).

raç′quet·ball, *n.* a game similar to handball, but played with a short-handled racket.

raç′quets (-kets), *n.pl.* [*construed as sing.*] a game like court tennis, played in an enclosure with four walls.

rā′cy, *a.*; *comp.* racier; *superl.* raciest, [from *race* (tribe) and *-y.*]

1. having the characteristic taste, flavor, or quality associated with the original or genuine type; as, a *racy* fruit.

2. lively; spirited; vigorous.

3. piquant; pungent.

4. somewhat indecent; suggestive; risqué; as, a *racy* novel.

rā′dăr, *n.* [*ra*dio *d*etecting *a*nd *r*anging.] any of several systems or devices using transmitted and reflected radio waves for detecting a reflecting object, as an aircraft, and determining its direction, distance, height, or speed, or in storm detection, navigation, etc.

radar beacon; a beacon with its transmitter and other components that emits radar waves for reception and display, indicating its range or bearing, or both, from a receiving set.

rā′dăr·sçōpe, *n.* an oscilloscope that visually records the reflected radio beams picked up by a radar receiver.

rad′dle (-dl), *n.* [Anglo-Fr. *reidele,* cart rail; M.H.G. *reidel, reitel,* a cudgel.]

1. a long stick used in making hedges; also,

a hedge formed by interweaving such sticks. [Obs. or Dial.]

2. a wooden bar, with a row of upright pegs set in it, used by weavers to keep the warp of a proper width and to prevent it from becoming entangled when it is wound upon the beam of the loom. [Obs.]

rad′dle, *v.t.*; raddled, *pt., pp.*; raddling, *ppr.* to interweave.

rad′dle, *n.* reddle; red ocher; hence, any red pigment.

rad′dle, *v.t.*; raddled, *pt., pp.*; raddling, *ppr.* to color as with raddle.

rad′dŏck, *n.* the ruddock. [Brit. Dial.]

rāde, *n.* a road; also, a raid. [Scot. or Obs.]

rāde, *v.* past tense of *ride.* [Scot.]

rȧ·deau′ (-dō′), *n.*; *pl.* **rȧ·deaux′** (-dōz′), [Fr., from L. *ratis*, raft.] a raft.

rā′di·ăl, *a.* [Fr., from L. *radius*, a ray, a rod, a spoke.]

1. (a) of or like a ray or rays; spreading or branching out in all directions from a common center; (b) having or characterized by parts that branch out in this way.

2. of or situated like a radius.

3. in anatomy, of or near the radius, or forearm.

radial artery; in anatomy, the lesser branch of the two parts into which the brachial artery divides after passing the elbow: it can be felt as the radial pulse at the wrist.

radial curves; in geometry, curves of the spiral kind, whose ordinates all terminate in the center of the including circle and appear like so many semidiameters.

radial engine; an internal-combustion engine with the cylinders arranged radially around the crankshaft instead of in tandem: used in some airplanes.

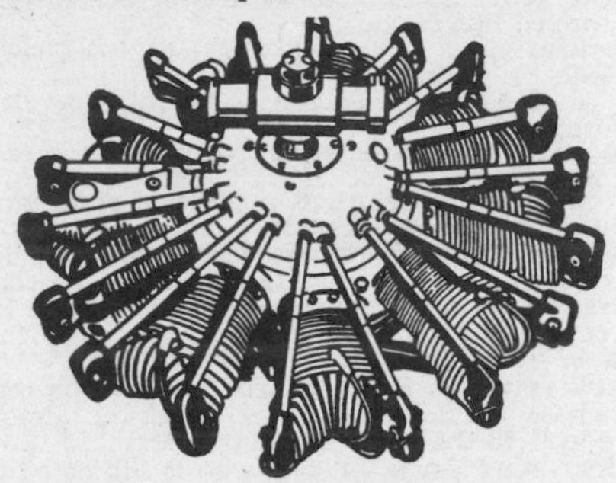

RADIAL ENGINE

radial motor; same as *radial engine.*

radial symmetry; see under *symmetry.*

rā′di·ăl, *n.* 1. in anatomy, same as *radiale.*

2. in zoology, (a) any one of a median circle of plates in the body of a crinoid; (b) a hypercoracoid.

3. a ray; a radiating part.

rā·di·ā′lē, *n.*; *pl.* **rā·di·ā′li·ȧ,** 1. in anatomy, an articulating element on the radial side of the carpus; the scaphoid bone in the human body.

2. a ray or radial of the cup of a crinoid.

3. a hypercoracoid.

rā′di·ăl·ly, *adv.* in a radial manner; so as to be radial.

rā′di·ăn, *n.* 1. an arc in any circle, equal in length to the radius of the same circle.

2. the angle at the center of a circle formed by two radii cutting off such an arc, equal to 57.295+ degrees.

rā′di·ănce, *n.* [L. *radians*, beaming.]

1. the quality or state of being radiant; brightness.

2. radiation. [Rare.]

Syn.—brilliance, luster, splendor, resplendence.

rā′di·ăn·cy, *n.* same as *radiance.*

rā′di·ănt, *a.* 1. sending out rays of light; shining brightly.

2. filled with light; bright; as, the *radiant* morning.

3. showing pleasure, joy, well-being, etc.; beaming; as, a *radiant* smile.

4. issuing (from a source) in or as in rays; radiated; as, *radiant* energy.

radiant energy; any form of energy radiating from a source, as electromagnetic waves, sound, heat, light, X rays, gamma rays, etc.

radiant heat; heat radiating from a heated body, as distinguished from that transmitted by intervening media.

radiant heating; a method of heating a building by means of electric coils, hot-water or steam pipes, etc. installed in the floors or walls.

radiant point; a point from which rays are emitted.

rā′di·ănt, *n.* 1. in optics, the point or object from which light proceeds.

2. in geometry, a straight line proceeding from a given point, or fixed pole, about which it is conceived to revolve.

3. in astronomy, the point in the heavens from which a shower of meteors seems to proceed.

rā′di·ănt·ly, *adv.* in a radiant manner.

Rā·di·ā′tȧ, *n.pl.* an obsolete division of the animal kingdom, including those animals having radial instead of bilateral symmetry, including the *Echinodermata, Acalephæ, Entozoa, Polypi,* and *Infusoria.*

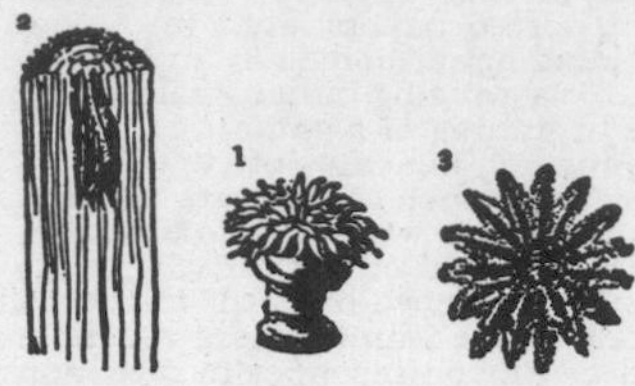

RADIATA
1. the sea anemone; 2. jellyfish; 3. starfish

rā′di·āte, *n.* an animal having radial symmetry.

rā′di·āte, *v.i.*; radiated, *pt., pp.*; radiating, *ppr.* [L. *radiare.*]

1. to send out rays of heat, light, etc.

2. to come forth or spread out in rays; as, heat *radiates* from the stove.

3. to branch out in lines from a center; as, highways *radiate* from the city.

rā′di·āte, *v.t.* 1. to send out (heat, light, etc.) in rays.

2. to give out or spread (happiness, love, etc.) as if from a center.

rā′di·āte, *a.* 1. having rays or lines proceeding from or as from a center; adorned with rays; radiated.

2. in botany, (a) diverging from a common center; (b) bearing ray flowers, as the sunflower.

3. in mineralogy, having crystals or fibers diverging as from a center.

4. in zoology, having the organs of circulation and sensation arranged in radial symmetry around a central axis.

rā′di·ā·ted, *a.* adorned with rays or radiations; rayed; radiate.

rā′di·āte·ly, *adv.* in a radiate manner.

rā′di·āte-vẹined (-vānd), *a.* in botany, having palmate nervation.

rā·di·at′i·fọrm, *a.* in botany, radiate in appearance, as the heads of *Centaurea cyanus.*

rā·di·ā′tion, *n.* [L. *radiatio.*]

1. the act or process of radiating; specifically, the process in which energy in the form of rays of light, heat, etc. is sent out from atoms and molecules as they undergo internal change.

2. the rays sent out; radiant energy.

3. the treatment of disease by radium or other radioactive material.

4. radial arrangement of parts.

direct radiation; the radiation of heat from a bank of pipes carrying steam or hot water.

obscure radiation; radiation of energy by means of waves not recognizable by the eye, as those below the red and above the violet of the spectrum.

solar radiation; the radiation of the sun as estimated by the amount of energy that reaches the earth.

terrestrial radiation; the radiation of heat from the earth into the space surrounding it.

rā·di·ā′tion fog, fog formed over damp places in the evening by the condensation of vapor in the warm humid atmosphere.

rā′di·ā·tive, *a.* of, capable of, or characterized by radiation.

rā′di·ā·tŏr, *n.* anything that radiates; specifically, (a) a series of pipes or coils through which hot water or steam circulates so as to radiate heat into a room, etc.; (b) loosely, a hot-air register; (c) a water-filled apparatus, as in an automobile, for radiating superfluous heat and thus cooling the engine.

rad′i·çăl, *a* [Fr., from LL. *radicalis*, having roots, from L. *radix*, root.]

1. of or from the root or roots; going to the center, foundation, or source of something; fundamental; basic; as, a *radical* principle.

2. (a) favoring fundamental or extreme change; specifically, favoring such change of the social structure; very leftist; (b) [R–] designating or of any of various modern political parties, especially in Europe, ranging from mildly leftist to conservative in program.

3. in botany, of or coming from the root.

4. in mathematics, having to do with the root or roots of a number or quantity.

radical quantity; in algebra, a quantity to which the radical sign is prefixed.

radical sign; the sign ($\surd \sqrt{\ }$) placed before any quantity, signifying that its root is to be extracted, thus $\surd a$ or $\sqrt{a+b}$.

Syn.—entire, complete, primitive, original, essential, extreme, positive, fundamental.

rad′i·çăl, *n.* 1. (a) a basic or root part of something; (b) a fundamental.

2. (a) a person having radical views; (b) [R–] a member or adherent of a Radical political party.

3. in chemistry, a group of two or more atoms that acts as a single atom and goes through a reaction unchanged, or is replaced by a single atom: symbol, R.

4. in linguistics, a word, or part of a word, serving as a base, or root, on which other words have been or can be formed.

5. in mathematics, (a) any quantity from which the root is to be extracted; (b) the radical sign.

compound radical; same as *radical*, n. 3.

rad′i·çăl·ịsm, *n.* 1. the quality or state of being radical, especially in politics.

2. radical principles, ideals, methods, or practices.

rad·i·cal′i·ty, *n.* the quality of being radical.

rad′i·çăl·ly, *adv.* 1. (a) as regards root or origin; as, English is *radically* a Germanic language; (b) from the very origin or foundation; fundamentally; basically; completely; as, *radically* mistaken.

2. in a manner characterized by radicalism.

rad′i·çăl·ness, *n.* the state of being radical.

rad·i·çand′, *n.* [L. *radicandus*, taking root.] the quantity under a radical sign.

rad′i·çănt, *a.* [Fr., from L. *radicare*, to take root.] in botany, rooting; as, a *radicant* stem.

rad′i·çāte, *v.t.*; radicated, *pt., pp.*; radicating, *ppr.* [L. *radicatus*, rooted.] to root; to plant deeply and firmly; as, *radicated* opinions. [Now Rare.]

rad′i·çāte, *v.i.* to take root; to become grounded permanently; to be established. [Now Rare.]

rad′i·çāte, *a.* 1. radicated.

2. in botany, rooted.

rad′i·çā·ted, *a.* rooted. [Now Rare.]

rad·i·çā′tion, *n.* the process of taking root deeply; as, the *radication* of habits. [Obs.]

rad′i·cel, *n.* [from L. *radex, radicis*, root.] in botany, a rootlet; a branchlike extension of a root.

rad′i·cēș, *n.* alternative plural of *radix.*

rad·i·çiç′ō·lous, *a.* in zoology, attacking or subsisting on roots.

rȧ·dic·i·flō′rous, *a* in botany, flowering from a rootstalk.

rȧ·dic′i·fọrm, *a.* in shape and appearance like a root.

rad′i·çle, *n.* [L. *radicula*, dim. of *radix*, a root.]

1. in anatomy, the rootlike beginning of a nerve, vein, etc.

2. in botany, (a) the lower part of the axis of an embryo seedling; strictly, the root part; often, the hypocotyl, sometimes together with the root; (b) a radicel or rudimentary root.

3. in chemistry, a radical.

rȧ·diç′ō·lous, *a.* same as *radicicolous.*

rȧ·diç′ū·lăr, *a.* of or relating to roots.

rad′i·çūle, *n.* radicle. [Rare.]

rȧ·diç′ū·lōse, *a.* having many rootlets.

rā′di·ī, *n.* alternative plural of *radius.*

rā′di·ō-, [from L. *radius*, a rod, hence radius.] a combining form meaning: (a) *ray, raylike*, as in *radio*larian; (b) *by radio*, as in *radio*telegraphy; (c) in anatomy, *the radius and*; (d) in medicine, *by means of radiant energy*, as in *radio*therapy; (e) in physics and chemistry, *radioactive*, as in *radio*thorium.

rā′di·ō, *n.*; *pl.* **rā′di·ōș,** [contr. of *radiotelegraphy, radiotelephony*, etc.]

1. the practice or science of communicating over a distance by converting sounds or signals into electromagnetic waves and transmitting these directly through space, without connecting wires, to a receiving set, which changes them into sounds; wireless telephony or telegraphy.

2. such a receiving set, especially one adapted for receiving the waves of the assigned fre-

quencies of certain transmitters or broadcasting stations.

3. (a) broadcasting by radio as a business, entertainment, art, etc.; (b) all the facilities and related activities of such broadcasting.

4. a message sent by radio; a radiogram.

rā'di·ō, *a.* 1. of, using, used in, sent by, or operated by radio.

2. having to do with electric frequencies of more than 15,000 cycles per second.

rā'di·ō, *v.t.* and *v.i.*; radioed, *pt., pp.*; radioing, *ppr.* to send (a message, etc.) or communicate with (a person, etc.) by radio.

rā″di·ō·aç'tive, rā″di·ō-aç'tive, *a.*[*radio-* and *active.*] giving off, or capable of giving off, radiant energy in the form of particles or rays, as alpha, beta, and gamma rays, by the disintegration of atomic nuclei: said of certain elements, as radium, thorium, and uranium, and their products.

radioactive dating; the determination of the age of an object or material based on the known rates of decay of radioactive isotopes of various elements.

radioactive series; the series of isotopes of various elements successively formed by a radioactive substance before it comes to a stable state.

rā″di·ō·aç·tiv'i·ty, *n.* the property or process of being radioactive.

rā'di·ō as·tron'ō·my, that branch of astronomy which deals with radio waves in space in order to obtain data and information about particular regions in the universe.

rā'di·ō·au'tō·gräph, *n.* [*radio-* and *autograph.*] a picture produced on photographic film, etc. by the rays from a radioactive substance in the thing being photographed.

rā'di·ō bēa'çŏn, a radio transmitter that gives off special signals to help ships or aircraft determine their positions or come in safely, as at night or in a fog.

rā'di·ō bēam, a constant stream of radio signals sent in a given direction from a radio beacon to serve as a course for incoming airplanes, etc.: also *beam.*

rā″di·ō·broad'çast, *v.t.* to broadcast by radio.

rā″di·ō·broad'çast, *n.* a broadcast by radio.

rā″di·ō·çhem'is·try, *n.* the branch of chemistry dealing with radioactive phenomena.

rā'di·ō çŏm'pȧss, a device for determining the direction of incoming radio waves: used in navigation, etc.

rā'di·ō çŏn·trōl', the directional control of pilotless aircraft, missiles, etc. by means of radio waves.

rā″di·ō·dẽr·mȧ·tī'tis, *n.* [*radio-* and *dermatitis.*] in pathology, inflammation of the skin due to prolonged exposure to X rays or other forms of radiation.

rā″di·ō·dē·teç'tŏr, *n.* an apparatus (usually a vacuum tube or a crystal) which rectifies high-frequency electric currents.

rā″di·ō·el'e·mĕnt, *n.* a radioactive element.

rā″di·ō-frē'quen·cy, *a.* of or using a radio frequency.

rā'di·ō frē'quen·cy, in electricity, a frequency of more than 15,000 vibrations per second.

rā″di·ō·ġen'iç, *a.* [*radio-* and *-genic.*] produced by radioactivity.

rā'di·ō·gram, *n.* 1. a message sent by radio: also *radiotelegram.*

2. a radiograph.

rā'di·ō·gräph, *n.* [*radio-* and *-graph.*] a picture produced on a sensitized film or plate by rays other than light rays, especially by X rays.

rā'di·ō·gräph, *v.t.* to make a radiograph of.

rā'di·ō·gräph, *v.i.* 1. to make a radiograph.

2. to send a radiogram.

rā·di·og'rȧ·phẽr, *n.* a person who makes, or is an expert in, radiographs.

rā″di·ō·graph'iç, *a.* of radiography.

rā″di·ō·graph'i·çăl·ly, *adv.* by means of radiographs or radiography.

rā·di·og'rȧ·phy, *n.* the art, process, or act of producing radiographs.

rā'di·ō·im″mū·nō·as'sāy, *n.* the technique of immunoassay in which radioactive tracers are introduced into the substance to be analyzed.

rā″di·ō·ī'sō·tōpe, *n.* an artificially created radioactive isotope of a chemical element that is normally nonradioactive, used in biological research, in the treatment of various diseases, etc.

Rā″di·ō·lā'ri·ȧ, *n.pl.* [Mod. L., from *radiolus,* dim. of L. *radius,* rod.] an order of one-celled sea animals with long, slender pseudopodia and a perforated outer skeleton of silica.

rā″di·ō·lãr'i·ăn, *n.* one of the *Radiolaria.*

rā'di·ō·līte, *n.* [L. *radius,* a ray, and *-lite.*] any of a genus of fossil lamellibranchiate mollusks, the Radiolites. They are striated externally. The inferior valve is in the form of a reversed cone, and the superior, is convex.

rā″di·ō·lō·çā'tion, *n.* the use of radar or radiolocators in finding the location and direction of enemy aircraft, etc.

rā″di·ō·lō'çā·tŏr, *n.* a British device similar to the American radar.

rā·di·ol'ō·ġist, *n.* a person skilled in the use of X rays; particularly, a physician so skilled

rā·di·ol'ō·ġy, *n.*[*radio-* and *-ology.*] the branch of science dealing with radiant energy and its uses, as in the treatment of disease by X rays.

rā″di·ō·met·ăl·log'rȧ·phy, *n.* the study of the structure of metals and alloys by X rays.

rā″di·ō·mē'tē·ŏr·ō·gräph, *n.* a radiosonde.

rā·di·om'ē·tẽr, *n.* [*radio-* and *-meter.*] an instrument for detecting, and measuring the intensity of, radiant energy, as by exposing to sunlight a set of vanes blackened on one side and suspended on an axis in a vacuum, and measuring their speed of rotation (i.e., the mechanical energy into which the radiant energy has been converted).

RADIOMETER

rā″di·ō·met'riç, *a.* of or pertaining to the radiometer; denoting experiments performed by the radiometer.

rā″di·om'e·try, *n.* the art or act of using a radiometer.

rā″di·ō·mī·çrom'ē·tẽr, *n.* a sensitive instrument, modified from the thermopile, for indicating minute fluctuations in radiant heat.

rā″di·ō·pāque', *a.* [*radio-,* and *opaque.*] not allowing the passage of X rays, gamma rays, or other forms of radiant energy.

rā'di·ō·phāre, *n.* a radio station formerly used for determining the location of ships.

rā'di·ō·phōne, *n.* 1. a wireless telephone; telephone operated by radio: also *radiotelephone.*

2. in physics, any instrument for transforming radiant energy into sound.

rā'di·ō·phōne, *v.t.* and *v.i.*; radiophoned, *pt., pp.*; radiophoning, *ppr.* to send (a message) by radiophone (sense 1): also *radiotelephone.*

rā″di·ō·phon'iç, *a.* pertaining to a radiophone.

rā·di·oph'ō·ny, *n.* 1. in physics, the transformation of radiant heat energy into sound.

2. in communications, the science or practice of radiotelephony.

rā″di·ō·phō'tō·gräph, *n.* a photograph transmitted by radio equipment; a photoradiogram.

rā″di·ō·phō'tō·gräph, *v.t.* to make a radiophotograph of (a person or thing).

rā″di·ō·phō'tō·gräph, *v.i.* to transmit photographs by radio equipment.

rā″di·ō·phō·tog'rȧ·phy, *n.* the art or science dealing with the transmission and reception of photographs by means of radio.

rā″di·os'çō·py, *n.* [*radio-* and *-scopy.*] the direct examination of the inside structure of opaque objects by means of X rays or rays from radioactive substances.

rā″di·ō·sen·si·bil'i·ty, *n.* in medicine, sensitivity to radioactive influence.

rā″di·ō·sen'si·tive, *a.* in medicine, sensitive to radiant energy; relating to that which may be destroyed by radioactive substances.

rā″di·ō·sen·si·tiv'i·ty, *n.* same as *radiosensibility.*

rā'di·ō set, the apparatus by means of which radio broadcasts are transmitted or received; usually, a receiving set.

rā'di·ō·sonde, *n.* [Fr., from *radio,* and *sonde,* a sounding lead, from *sonder,* to sound.] a compact package of meteorological instruments and a radio transmitter, carried aloft by a small balloon to measure and transmit to ground observers temperature, pressure, and humidity data from the upper atmosphere by means of special radio signals.

rā'di·ō speç'trum, the complete range of frequencies or wave lengths of electromagnetic waves, specifically those used in radio and television.

rā'di·ō stā'tion, a broadcasting station.

rā″di·ō·teçh·nol'ō·ġy, *n.* 1. the science or study of radio engineering.

2. the application of X rays and other forms of radiation to industrial purposes.

rā″di·ō·tel'ē·grăm *n.* same as *radiogram,* sense 1.

rā″di·ō·tel'ē·gräph, *n.* an apparatus by means of which radiotelegrams may be transmitted.

rā″di·ō·tel'ē·gräph, *v.t.* and *v.i.* to send (a message) by radiotelegraphy.

rā″di·ō·tel″ē·gräph'iç, *a.* of or by a radiotelegraph or radiotelegraphy.

rā″di·ō·tē·leg'rȧ·phy, *n.* the sending and receiving of messages by a radiotelegraph.

rā″di·ō·tel'ē·phōne, *n.* same as *radiophone,* n. 1.

rā″di·ō·tel'ē·phōne, *v.t.* and *v.i.* to radiophone.

rā″di·ō·tel″ē·phon'iç, *a.* of or by a radiotelephone or radiotelephony.

rā″di·ō·tē·leph'ō·ny, *n.* telephony by radio, without connecting wires.

rā″di·ō·tel·lū'ri·um, *n.* an isotope of tellurium which has radioactive properties.

rā″di·ō·thal'li·um, *n.* an isotope of thallium which has radioactive properties.

rā″di·ō·ther″ȧ·peū'tiç, *a.* of or pertaining to radiotherapeutics.

rā″di·ō·ther″ȧ·peū'tiçs, *n.* therapeutics as concerned with or making use of radium or radioactive energy in the treatment of disease.

rā″di·ō·ther'ȧ·py, *n.* the treatment of disease by the use of X rays or rays from a radioactive substance, as radium.

rā″di·ō·thẽr'miçs, *n.pl.* [*construed as sing.*] [from *radio-,* and Gr. *thermē,* heat; and *-ics.*] the science of heat generation by radio-frequency currents.

rā'di·ō·thẽr″my, *n.* the treatment of disease or alleviation of pain by using the heat given off by radioactive substances; short-wave diathermy.

rā″di·ō·thō'ri·um, *n.* [Mod. L.] a radioactive isotope of thorium, formed from mesothorium 2.

rā'di·ō tūbe, a type of vacuum tube used in radio, etc.

rā'di·ous, *a.* made up of rays; radiant. [Obs.]

rā'di·ō wāve, an electrical impulse sent through the atmosphere at radio frequency.

rad'ish, *n.* [Fr. *radis,* a radish, from L. *radix,* a root.]

1. a plant of the genus *Raphanus,* particularly *Raphanus sativus,* a common garden plant with an edible red or white root.

2. the pungent root, eaten raw as a relish or in a salad.

rā'di·um, *n.* [Mod. L., from L. *radius,* ray.] a radioactive metallic chemical element, found in very small amounts in pitchblende and certain other uranium minerals, which undergoes spontaneous atomic disintegration through several stages, finally forming an isotope of lead: it was discovered by Pierre and Marie Curie in 1898 and is used in the treatment of cancer and some skin diseases: symbol, Ra, formerly Rd; atomic weight, 226.05; atomic number, 88.

rā'di·um A, a substance formed from radon by atomic disintegration: by further disintegration it gives rise to *radium B* (an isotope of lead), which in turn gives rise to *radium C* (an isotope of bismuth), followed successively by the forms *C', D, E, F* (polonium), and *G* (an isotope of lead).

rā'di·um bäth, in medicine, water treated with some radioactive matter, to be used for therapeutic bathing.

rā'di·um em·ȧ·nā'tion, radon.

rā'di·um paint, a kind of paint that glows in the dark due to the addition of mesothorium to the paint mixture.

rā″di·um·ther'ȧ·py, *n.* in medicine, the care, management, and treatment of disease with radium and other radioactive substances: used chiefly in treating malignant cancer, etc.: also *radium therapy.*

rā'di·us, *n.*; *pl.* **rā'di·ī, rā'di·us·eṣ,** [L., a ray, a rod, a beam, a spoke.]

1. a ray or raylike part; specifically, (a) any of the rays of a composite flower; (b) the pivoted arm of a quadrant, sextant, etc.; (c) a spoke of a wheel.

2. any straight line extending from the center to the periphery of a circle or sphere: symbol, R.

CA. CD. CB. CE. RADII

3. the circular area or distance limited by the sweep of such a line; as, there was no house within a *radius* of five miles.

4. any limited extent, scope, range, etc.; as, within the *radius* of my experience.

5. (a) the shorter and thicker of the two bones of the forearm on the same side as the thumb; (b) a corresponding bone of the forelimb of a four-legged animal.

radius of curvature of a curve at any point; the radius of the circle which has the same curvature as the curve at that point.

radius of gyration; the distance from a fixed axis to the center of mass of a given body.

radius vector; pl. *radii vectores, radius vectors*, (a) the distance, or a straight line representing this distance, from a fixed point to a variable point on a curve or curved surface; (b) in astronomy, the line joining the center of an attracting body, as the sun, with the center of each of the bodies revolving around it.

rā′di·us bär, one of the guiding rods in a parallel motion, jointed to the connecting links, to counteract the vibratory motion communicated by the beam, by guiding the links so that the head of the piston rod may reciprocate in a line sensibly straight.

rā′dix, *n.*; *pl.* **rad′i·cēs, rā′dix·es,** [L., a root.]
1. in linguistics, a root, base, or etymon.
2. in mathematics, a number made the base of a system of numbering.
3. in algebra, a finite expression, from which a series is derived. [Rare.]
4. in anatomy, the root or portion of anything inserted into another, as the root of a tooth; the insertion of a nerve or its branches.
5. the root of any plant.

rā′don, *n.* [*rad*ium and *-on* as in *neon.*] a radioactive gaseous chemical element formed, together with alpha rays, as a first product in the atomic disintegration of radium, and used in the treatment of cancer: also called *radium emanation*: symbol, Rn; atomic weight, 222; atomic number, 86.

radon seed; in medicine, a sealed tube of glass or gold containing a small amount of radon: it is used for treatment of cancer and is inserted into the diseased tissue.

rad′ū·lȧ, *n.*; *pl.* **rad′ū·lae,** [L., a scraper, from *radere*, to scrape.] in zoology, the file or rasplike organ in the mouth of the gastropodous mollusks used to tear up food and take it into the mouth: sometimes applied to the odontophore itself, but properly confined to that portion which is armed with toothlike processes.

rad′ū·lăr, *a.* pertaining to a radula.

rad′ū·lāte, *a.* having a radula.

rad·ū·lif′ĕr·ous, *a.* radulate.

rȧ·dū′li·fọrm, *a.* [L. *radula*, a scraper.] shaped like a rasp; as, *raduliform* teeth in some fishes.

răff, *v.t.* to sweep. [Obs.]

răff, *n.* [ME. *raf*; OFr. *raffe.*]
1. a heap; a jumble; a large number, collection, or quantity.
2. the dregs of society; rabble; mob: contemptuous term.
3. rubbish; trash. [Scot. or Brit. Dial.]

Raf″fā·el·esque′, *a.* same as *Raphaelesque.*

raf′fi·ȧ, *n.* [from Malagasy native name.]
1. a Madagascar palm, *Raphia ruffia*, having large pinnate leaves, furnishing a fibrous material used for mats, hats, tie bands in agriculture, and for other purposes.
2. the fiber from its leaves, woven into hats, etc.
3. a related palm tree; also, its fiber.

raf′fi·nōse, *n.* [Fr. *raffiner*, to refine.] a sweetish, crystalline trisaccharide, $C_{18}H_{32}O_{16}\cdot5H_2O$, derived from sugar beets, cottonseed, etc.

raff′ish, *a.* 1. disreputable; disgraceful.
2. tawdry; flashy; cheap.

raf′fle, *n.* [Fr. *rafle*; OFr. *raffle*, a kind of game at dice; *rafler*, to snatch.]
1. a kind of lottery in which each participant buys a chance to win the prize.
2. an old game of dice in which three dice were thrown, the one who threw three alike winning, or in default of such a throw, the one who threw the highest pair winning. [Obs.]

raf′fle, *v.i.*; raffled; *pt., pp.*; raffling, *ppr.* to participate in or conduct a raffle.

raf′fle, *v.t.* to offer as a prize in a raffle (often with *off*).

raf′fle, *n.* rubbish; raff. [Archaic.]

raf′flĕr, *n.* one who raffles.

Raf·flē′ṣi·ȧ, *n.* [after Sir Stamford *Raffles* (1781–1826), the discoverer of the first known species.]
1. a genus of parasitic plants, the type of the family *Rafflesiaceæ*, native to Sumatra and Java, having scales in place of leaves, and exhibiting in some degree the structure both of flowering and flowerless plants.
2. [r–] any of a number of related species of this genus, having large stemless flowers and a bad smell.

Raf·flē·ṣi·ā′cē·ae, *n.pl.* a family of rhizogens, the species of which are found in the East Indies, Java, Sumatra, and South America.

raf·flē·ṣi·ā′ceous, *a.* of or pertaining to the *Rafflesiaceæ.*

rȧft, *n.* [ME. *rafte*, a beam; ON. *raptr*, a log.]
1. a number of logs, boards, barrels, etc. fastened together into a sort of platform and floated on water, used as a means of transportation or as a device for conveying the component logs, boards, etc.
2. an accumulation of logs, fallen trees, etc. in a stream, obstructing navigation. [Colloq.]
3. an aggregation of the eggs of certain insects, as the cockroach, which adhere to each other, forming a mass.

raft bridge; (a) a bridge supported by rafts; (b) a floating bridge of timbers fastened together.

rȧft, *v.t.*; rafted, *pt., pp.*; rafting, *ppr.* 1. to carry or transport on a raft.
2. to form or make into a raft.

raft, *v.i.* to control or to be employed on a raft; to travel on a raft.

rȧft, *n.* [from *raff.*] a large number, collection, or quantity; lot. [Colloq.]

rȧft, *v.* obsolete past tense and past participle of *reave.*

rȧft dog, an iron bar with ends bent over and pointed, for securing logs together in a raft.

rȧft duck, any of several ducks noted for their swimming in a compact group resembling a raft; as, (a) the big scaup duck, *Aythya marila*; (b) [Dial.] the American redhead, *Aythya americana.*

rȧft′ĕr, *n.* [AS. *ræfter*; ON. *raptr*, a beam, a log.] in building, a roof timber, a piece of timber that extends from the ridge of a roof to the eaves and serves to give slope to and to support the covering of the roof.

rȧft′ĕr, *v.t.* 1. to form into rafters, as lumber.
2. to provide with rafters, as a house.
3. to plow in ridges. [Brit. Dial.]

rȧft′ĕr bĭrd, the spotted flycatcher. [Brit. Dial.]

rȧft pōrt, a port in the side of a vessel for loading or unloading timber and other bulky articles.

rȧfts′măn, *n.*; *pl.* **rȧfts′men,** a man who manages or is employed on or operates a raft.

rȧf′ty, *a.* damp; musty. [Brit. Dial.]

rag, *n.* [ME. *ragge*; AS. *ragg-*, from ON. *rögg*, tuft of hair.]
1. a waste piece of cloth, especially one that is torn or uneven.
2. a small piece of cloth for dusting, cleaning, washing, etc.
3. anything more or less resembling a rag, considered of little value: used contemptuously or humorously.
4. [*pl.*] old, worn clothes.
5. [*pl.*] any clothes: used humorously.
6. the axis and white, tough membrane of citrus fruits.
7. in metalworking, a jagged or ragged edge.
8. one of several lichens, as *Parmelia saxatilis.*
9. a catkin.

to chew the rag; to chat or converse. [Slang.]

rag, *a.* made of rags; resembling rags; as, a *rag* carpet.

rag, *v.i.* 1. to become tattered or ragged. [Obs.]
2. to dress finely or conspicuously: followed by *out*; as, she *ragged out* in her best. [Slang.]

rag, *v.t.*; ragged, *pt., pp.*; ragging, *ppr.* 1. to separate or sort (ore).
2. to cut roughly, as in stone dressing.

rag, *n.* [prob. var. of *rag* (torn piece).] a kind of slate with one rough surface, used in roofing.

rag, *v.t.* [from 19th-c. Brit. university slang; prob. from phr. *like a red rag to a bull* and derivatives *bullyrag*, etc.]
1. to tease. [Slang.]
2. to scold. [Slang.]
3. to play a practical joke or jokes on. [Brit. Slang.]

rag, *n.* a ragging. [Brit. Slang.]

rag, *n.* ragtime. [Slang.]

rag, *v.t.* and *v.i.* to play in the style of ragtime. [Slang.]

rag′ȧ·bash, rag′ȧ·brash, *n.* an idle; ragged person. [Scot. and Brit. Dial.]

rag′ȧ·muf·fin, *n.* [ME. *Ragamofin*, a demon in mystery plays: demons were often described as *ragged*, i.e., shaggy.]
1. a dirty, ragged person; tatterdemalion; especially, a dirty, ragged child.
2. a titmouse. [Brit. Dial.]

rag bōlt, a bolt with barbs on its shank to retain it in place after it is driven in; a barb bolt.

RAG BOLTS

rāġe, *n.* OFr. *rage*, from L. *rabies*, rage, madness, from *rabere*, to rave, to be mad.]
1. insanity; amentia. [Obs.]
2. a furious uncontrolled anger; raving fury.
3. a great force, violence, or intensity, as of the wind.
4. strong emotion, enthusiasm, or desire.
5. anything arousing general enthusiasm or desire; a craze; fad.

Syn.—anger, choler, fury.

rāġe, *v.i.*; raged, *pt., pp.*; raging, *ppr.* 1. to show violent anger in action or speech.
2. to be forceful, violent, agitated, etc.; as, the sea *raged.*
3. to spread unchecked, as a disease.

Syn.—rave, storm, fume, be furious, be violent.

raġ′ee, *n.* same as *raggee.*

rāġe′fụl, *a.* filled with rage, apt to rage. [Obs.]

rā′ġĕr·y, *n.* rage; wantonness. [Obs.]

rag′ġed, *a.* [from *rag* (torn piece) and *-ed.*]
1. shabby or torn from wear; as, a *ragged* shirt.
2. dressed in shabby or torn clothes.
3. uneven; rough; jagged; as, a *ragged* edge.
4. shaggy; unkempt; as, *ragged* hair.
5. not finished; imperfect; as, a *ragged* style.
6. harsh; strident; as, a *ragged* voice.

rag′ġed edġe, the extreme edge, as of a precipice; verge; as, on the *ragged edge* of poverty.

on the ragged edge; precariously close to loss of self-control, mental stability, etc.

rag′ġed·ly, *adv.* in a ragged manner; roughly.

rag′ġed·ness, *n.* the state or quality of being ragged.

rag′ġed rob′in, a common English plant of the pink family, *Lychnis flos-cuculi*, introduced into parts of the United States.

rag′ġed sāil′ŏr, same as *Prince's-feather.*

rag′ġed sçhọọl, in England, a school providing instruction and religious training for the poor.

rag′ġee, *n.* [Hind. *rāgī*; Sans. *rāgin*, red.] a cereal grass of the East Indies (*Eleusine coracana*) whose grain is a staple food in parts of Asia: also spelled *raggi, raggy, ragi.*

rag′ġing, *n.* in metallurgy, a process of grading slimes: also called *framing.*

rā′ġing·ly, *adv.* with fury; with violent impetuosity.

rag′lăn, *n.* [after Lord *Raglan* (1788–1855), British commander in chief in the Crimean war.] a loose overcoat or topcoat with sleeves that continue in one piece to the collar, so that there are no shoulder seams.

rag′lăn, *a.* designating or of such a sleeve.

rag′man, *n.*; *pl.* **rag′men,** a man who collects or deals in rags, old paper, etc.

rag′man rōll, the record, contained on rolls of parchment, of those instruments by which the Scottish nobility and gentry subscribed allegiance to Edward I of England, in 1296; hence, any similar roll or catalogue, as an official list. [Obs.]

Răg′nȧ·rok′ (-rok′ *or* -rĕk′), *n.* [ON. *ragna rök*, judgment of the gods; *ragna*, genit. pl. of *regin*, god, and *rök*, judgment, reason; confused with *ragnarœker*, twilight of the gods (G. *götterdämmerung*).] in Norse mythology, the destruction of the world in the last great conflict between the gods and the forces of evil: also written *Ragnarök* (-rĕk′).

ra·gōut′ (-gō′), *n.* [Fr. *ragoût.*] a stew of highly seasoned meat and vegetables.

ra·gōut′, *v.t.*; ragouted (-gōd′), *pt., pp.*; ragouting (-gō′ing), *ppr.* to make into a ragout.

rag′pick″ĕr, *n.* 1. one who makes his living by collecting and selling rags and junk.
2. in papermaking, a machine for reducing rags to staple.

ragpickers' disease; see *malignant pustule* under *malignant.*

rag′shag, *n.* a ragamuffin. [Colloq.]

rag′stōne, *n.* a siliceous stone having a rough fracture, found in Kent, Northumberland, and other places in England.

rag′tag, *n.* [*rag* (torn piece) and *tag.*] the rabble; the lowest classes, as in *ragtag and bobtail*: contemptuous term.

rag′tīme, *n.* [from *ragged time*, term first applied (c. 1890) to New Orleans music as played by Negro orchestras on Mississippi River boats.]

1. a type of American dance music, popular from about 1890 to 1915, characterized by strong syncopation in fast, even time: it is regarded as an early form or predecessor of jazz.
2. its syncopated rhythm.

rag′tīme, *a.* played in or denoting ragtime; as, a *ragtime* melody.

rag′ū·ly, *a.* in heraldry, designating a charge or ordinary that is jagged or notched in an irregular manner: also written *raguled, ragulé.*

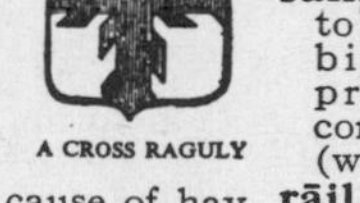

A CROSS RAGULY

rag′weed, *n.* [so called from the tattered appearance of the leaves.] a plant of the genus *Ambrosia;* specifically, *Ambrosia trifida,* the great ragweed, or *Ambrosia artemisiæfolia,* hogweed, the pollen of which is a cause of hay fever.

rag wheel (hwēl), 1. in machinery, a wheel having a notched or serrated margin.
2. a polishing wheel.

rag wool, shoddy, especially that made from woolen cloth.

rag′wŏrk, *n.* 1. masonry built with undressed flat stones of about the thickness of a brick, and leaving a rough exterior.
2. carpet, or material similar to carpet, made from strips of rag.

rag′wŏrm, *n.* any worm of the genus *Nephthys.*

rag′wŏrt, *n.* a tall plant of the genus *Senecio,* having irregularly toothed leaves and yellow flowers.

räh, *interj.* hurrah.

rä′iȧ (-yȧ), *n.* [Fr., from Turk. *ra'āya,* from Ar. *ra'īyah,* flock.] a non-Moslem inhabitant of a Moslem country, as formerly in Turkey: also spelled *rayah.*

Rā′iȧ, *n.* [L., a ray.] a genus of marine fishes including the skates or rays.

Rā′iae (-ē), *n.pl.* a family of fishes including and typified by the genus *Raia.*

rāid, *n.* [North Eng. form of *road,* preserving etym. sense, "a riding"; used orig. of an incursion along the Border; popularized by Scott.]
1. a sudden, hostile attack, especially by troops, military aircraft, etc., or by armed, usually mounted, bandits intent on looting.
2. any sudden invasion of some place by police, for discovering and dealing with violations of the law.
3. a deliberate attempt by one or more operators to cause a quick, unexpected fall in stock-market prices.

rāid, *v.t.;* raided, *pt., pp.;* raiding, *ppr.* to make a raid or raids on.

rāid, *v.i.* to take part in or conduct a raid or raids.

rāid′ẽr, *n.* a person or thing that makes a raid; specifically, (a) a ship or airplane making a quick, unexpected attack; (b) [*often* R-] a member of any of various battalions of the United States Marine Corps especially trained in close combat.

rāil, *n.* [ME.; OFr. *reille;* L. *regula,* a rule.]
1. a bar of wood, metal, etc. placed horizontally between upright posts to serve as a guard or support.
2. a fence or railing.
3. any of a series of parallel metal bars laid upon crossties or in the ground to make a track for railroad cars, streetcars, etc.
4. a railroad as a means of transportation; as, he went by *rail.*
5. a horizontal piece of wood separating the panels in doors or wainscoting.
6. in nautical usage, a narrow wooden piece at the top of a ship's bulwarks.
continuous or *combined rail;* a rail having a side mortise which permits its connection without forming a joint.
girder rail; a guard rail.
to ride on a rail; to place on a rail and carry out of the community: extralegal punishment in which the victim was usually tarred and feathered beforehand.
T rail; a rail the cross section of which approximates a **T** in form.

rāil, *v.t.;* railed, *pt., pp.;* railing, *ppr.* to supply with rails or a railing; to fence.

rāil, *v.i.* to fish over the rail of a ship or boat. [Colloq.]

rāil, *v.t.* [ME. *railen;* G. *regeln,* from L. *regula,* a rule.] to set in line or order. [Obs.]

rāil, *n.* [ME. *reil;* AS. *hrægel,* from *wrigan,* to put on.] a garment; a robe or dress. [Obs.]

rāil, *n.; pl.* **rāils** or **rāil,** [OFr. *rasle, raale,* a rail.] any of a number of small wading birds of the family *Rallidæ,* resembling the cranes and living in marshes: they are characterized by short wings and tail, long toes, and a harsh cry.

RAIL
(*Rallus aquaticus*)

rāil, *v.i.* [Fr. *railler,* to banter.] to speak bitterly or reproachfully; to complain violently (with *against* or *at*).

rāil, *v.t.* to have an effect on by railing; to force, remove, etc. by railing. [Rare.]

rāil′bīrd, *n.* 1. a bird, the Carolina rail, *Porzana carolina.*
2. a hanger-on at race tracks; also, one who secretly clocks race horses in their private trials.

rāil chāir, the iron or steel block used to secure the rails to the sleepers.

rāil çoup′ling, a bar connecting parallel rails to prevent spreading, as at a curve in a railroad.

rāil′ẽr, *n.* one who rails, or complains violently.

rāil guärd, 1. in England, a device for throwing aside obstructions from the rail of a railway consisting of a stout rod reaching within two inches of the rail, one being placed before each of the front wheels of the locomotive.
2. a guardrail.

rāil′head (-hed), *n.* 1. the farthest point to which rails have been laid in a railroad under construction.
2. in military usage, the point on a railroad in a theater of operations at which supplies are unloaded and sent to troops at the front by other means of transportation.

rāil′ing, *n.* 1. material for rails.
2. rails collectively.
3. a fence or balustrade made of rails and posts.

rāil′ing·ly, *adv.* in a railing, or reviling, manner.

rāil′lẽr·y, *n.; pl.* **rāil′lẽr·ieṣ,** [Fr. *raillerie.*]
1. light, good-natured ridicule or satire; banter.
2. a teasing act or remark.

rȧil·lëur′ (rȧ-yẽr′), *n.* [Fr.] a banterer; a jester; a mocker.

rāil′rōad, *n.* 1. a road laid with parallel steel rails along which cars carrying passengers or freight are drawn by locomotives.
2. a complete system of such roads, including land, rolling stock, stations, etc.
3. the persons or corporation owning and managing such a system.
inclined railroad; a railroad having a steep grade, requiring cogged rails or a chain or cable to haul the cars.
underground railroad; (a) in the United States before 1861, a system set up by certain opponents of slavery to help fugitive slaves from the South escape to free States and Canada; (b) a railroad in a subway or tunnel.

rāil′rōad, *v.t.* 1. to transport by railroad.
2. to furnish with railroads.
3. to rush through quickly, especially so quickly as to prevent careful consideration; as, he *railroaded* the motion through the committee. [Colloq.]
4. to cause to go to prison on a trumped-up charge or with too hasty a trial. [Slang.]

rāil′rōad, *v.i.* to work on a railroad.

rāil′rōad·ẽr, *n.* one engaged in railroading.

rāil′rōad eū′chre (-kẽr), a game of euchre in which four players may participate and which allows any provision for rapid scoring.

rāil′rōad·ing, *n.* 1. the building or operation of railroads.
2. the act or process of one that railroads (in various senses).

rāil′-split″tẽr, *n.* one who splits logs into rails, as for fences.
the Rail-Splitter; Abraham Lincoln.

rāil′wāy, *n.* 1. a railroad for light vehicles; as, a street *railway.*
2. any railroad. [Brit.]
3. any track with rails for guiding wheels.

rāi′ment, *n.* [contr. from OFr. *arrayment.*] that which serves as clothing; vesture; dress; attire. [Archaic or Poet.]

rāin, *n.* [ME. *rein, raine;* AS. *regn.*]
1. water falling to earth in drops that have been condensed from the moisture in the atmosphere.
2. the falling of such drops; a shower or rainstorm.
3. (a) rainy weather; (b) [*pl.*] seasonal rainfalls; the rainy season (preceded by *the*).
4. a rapid falling or propulsion of many small particles or objects; as, a *rain* of ashes.

rāin, *v.i.* 1. to fall: said of rain, and usually in an impersonal construction; as, it is *raining.*
2. to fall like rain; as, bullets *rained* about him.
3. to cause rain to fall: said of the heavens, God, etc.

rāin, *v.t.* 1. to pour down (rain or something likened to rain).
2. to give in large quantities; as, they *rained* praises on him.
to rain cats and dogs; to rain heavily. [Colloq.]

rāin′band, *n.* a dark band in the yellow part of the solar spectrum caused by water vapor in the atmosphere.

rāin′bīrd, *n.* any of various birds whose cries or actions are considered to presage rain, as the rain crow.

rāin′bōw, *n.* [AS. *regnboga.*] a bow, or an arc of a circle, consisting of the colors of the spectrum in consecutive bands, formed by the refraction and reflection of rays of light from drops of rain or vapor, appearing in the part of the sky opposite to the sun. A similar phenomenon is sometimes seen in the spray of waterfalls, etc. It often presents the appearance of two concentric circles, the inner of which is called the *primary rainbow* and the outer the *secondary rainbow.*
lunar rainbow; an arc resembling a rainbow formed by moonlight.
marine rainbow; an arc similar to a rainbow seen in the spray at sea.
supernumerary rainbow; a rainbow other than the primary or secondary bow, smaller and with fewer colors.

rāin′bōw därt′ẽr, any bright-hued darting fish, as the blue darter, *Pœcilichthys cæruleus,* of the Mississippi Valley.

rāin′bōw fish, any of several fishes of bright or variegated hues.

rāin′bōw-tint″ed, *a.* having tints like those of a rainbow.

rāin′bōw trout, a bright-hued trout, *Salmo irideus,* native to the mountain streams and coastal waters of the Pacific States: so called from its color.

rāin′bōw wrasse (ras), a European wrasse of brilliant coloring.

rāin çheck, a ticket stub which, in case of a postponement or halting of any outdoor performance or game on account of rain, entitles the holder to admission on a future occasion: also used figuratively.

rāin′çōat, *n.* a waterproof coat for giving protection from rain.

rāin çrōw, a species of cuckoo the cries of which are supposed to presage rain.

rāin′drop, *n.* a single drop of rain.

rāin′fąll, *n.* 1. a falling of rain; a shower.
2. the amount of water falling in the form of rain, snow, etc. over a given area in a given period of time, usually a year: it is stated in terms of the inches in depth of water that has fallen into a rain gauge.

rāin gāuġe, an instrument for measuring or gauging the quantity of rain which falls at a given place: also called *pluviometer, udometer.*

rāin′i·ness, *n.* the quality or state of being rainy.

rāin′less, *a.* having no rain; as, a *rainless* region.

rāin′prọọf, *a.* waterproof in case of rain; raintight; shedding rain.

rāin′prọọf, *v.t.* to make rainproof.

rāin quāil, a bird, *Coturnix coromandelicus,* of India and South Africa.

rāin′stŏrm, *n.* a storm with a heavy rain.

rāin′-tīght (-tīt), *a.* so tight as to exclude rain; as, a *rain-tight* roof.

rāin wą′tẽr, water that has fallen or is falling as rain, containing relatively little soluble mineral matter.

rāin′y, *a.; comp.* rainier; *superl.* rainiest, 1. characterized by rain, especially by much rain; as, the *rainy* season.
2. wet with rain.
3. bringing rain; as, *rainy* winds.

rāin′y dāy, a possible future time of difficulty or need.

rā′ioid (-yoid), *a.* [L. *raia,* a ray.] pertaining to or resembling the *Raiæ,* or rays.

rā′ioid, *n.* one of the *Raiæ*; a ray or skate.
rāip, *n.* a rope. [Scot.]
rāiṣ′ȧ·ble, *a.* capable of being raised.
rāiṣe, *v.t.*; raised, *pt., pp.*; raising, *ppr.* [ME. reisen; ON. *reisa*, exactly akin to AS. *ræran*, caus. of *risan*, to rise.]
1. to cause to rise; to take or bring from a lower place to a higher; to put, place, or remove higher; to lift or move upward; to elevate; to heave; as, to *raise* a weight; a foot-pound is the work done against gravity in *raising* a pound one foot.
2. to bring to a higher condition or situation; to elevate in social position, rank, dignity, and the like; to exalt; to enhance (fame, reputation, etc.); to promote; to advance.

Satan exalted sat, by merit *raised*
To that bad eminence. —Milton.

3. to increase in size, value, amount, etc.; as, he *raised* his prices.
4. to increase the intensity, strength, power, or vigor of; to intensify the vehemence or ardor of; to invigorate; to excite; to heighten; as, to *raise* the pulse by stimulants; to *raise* the courage or spirits; to *raise* one's voice.
5. to bring, call up, or summon from the lower regions; to cause to appear from the world of spirits; to recall from death; to restore to life; to give life to.

If the dead rise not, then is not Christ *raised*. —1 Cor. xv. 16.
These are the specters the understanding *raises* to itself, to flatter its own laziness. —Locke.

6. to cause to assume an upright position or stand erect; to set upright; to lift up from a horizontal to a vertical position; as, to *raise* a mast or a pole.
7. to cause to stand or spring up from a recumbent position, from a state of quiet, sleep, or the like; to awaken.

When Annie would have *raised* him Enoch said
Wake him not; let him sleep.—Tennyson.

8. to rouse to action; to incite, as to tumult, struggle, or war; to stir up; to excite; as, to *raise* the populace; to *raise* the country; to *raise* a mutiny.

He sowed a slander in the common ear, . . .
Raised my own town against me in the night. —Tennyson.

9. to set into commotion; to bring into an active state; as, to *raise* the sea.

He commandeth and *raiseth* the stormy wind. —Ps. cvii. 25.

10. to cause to arise into existence, grow up, or come into being; to give rise to; to originate; to produce.
11. to form by the accumulation or heaping up of materials or constituent parts; to build up; to erect or construct (a building, etc.).

Raise thereon a great heap of stones. —Josh. viii. 29.

12. to bring together; to get together or obtain for use or service; to gather; to collect; to levy; as, to *raise* money; to *raise* an army.
13. to cause to grow; to cause to be produced, bred, or propagated; to rear; to grow; as, to *raise* wheat, oats, turnips, etc.; to *raise* cattle, pigs, sheep, etc.
14. to give vent or utterance to; to utter; to strike up; as, to *raise* the song of victory.
15. to cause to appear; to call up; to provoke; to inspire; as, the remark *raised* a laugh.
16. to bring to attention; to bring forward for consideration; as, to *raise* an objection.
17. to heighten or elevate in pitch or degree; as, a sharp *raises* a note half a tone; to *raise* the temperature of a room.
18. in law, to create, originate, or constitute; as, to *raise* an action or a use.
19. to cause to swell and become light and spongy; as, to *raise* dough or paste by yeast or leaven.
20. to rear and bring up (children); as, I was *raised* in Kentucky.
21. to bring to an end; to remove; as, we have *raised* the siege.
22. to make angry or excited; to madden. [Scot.]
23. in commerce, to increase by fraud the face value of (a check, etc.).
24. in nautical usage, to cause (land, another ship, etc.) to appear to rise over the horizon by coming nearer; to come within sight of.
25. in poker, etc. (a) to bet more than (the highest preceding bet); (b) to bet more than (the preceding better).
to raise Cain (or *the devil, hell, a rumpus, the roof*, etc.); to create a disturbance; to cause trouble. [Slang.]
to raise steam; to produce steam, as in a boiler, of sufficient pressure to drive an engine.
to raise the market on one; to charge one a higher than the current or regular price.
to raise the wind; figuratively, to obtain ready money by some shift or other, as pawning property, by accommodation bills, and the like. [Old Slang.]
Syn.—lift, erect, hoist, elevate, exalt, arouse, call forth, produce, excite, cause, collect, levy, heighten, grow, aggravate, heave, increase, aggrandize, rear, set up, uplift.
rāiṣe, *v.i.* 1. to rise or arise. [Dial.]
2. to cough up phlegm. [Colloq.]
3. in poker, etc., to increase the bet.
rāiṣe, *n.* 1. the act of raising.
2. an increase in amount; specifically, an increase in salary or wages.
3. in mining, a rise or riser.
rāiṣed, *a.* [pp. of *raise*.]
1. made in low relief; embossed.
2. made light and fluffy with yeast or other leavening agent: said of bread, etc.
raised beach; in physical geography, a former beach, as of a sea or lake, now above high-water level.
rāiṣ′ẽr, *n.* 1. one who or that which raises; one who builds; one who levies or collects; one who begins, produces, or propagates; as, a *raiser* of cattle or of revenue.
2. in building, a riser.
rāi′ṣin (-zn), *n.* [OFr. *reisin*, from L. *racemus*, a cluster of grapes.]
1. any of various kinds of sweet, dried grapes, usually seedless.
2. a bunch of grapes. [Obs.]
rāiṣ′ing, *n.* 1. the act of elevating, raising, or lifting.
2. any substance used for rendering bread light, as yeast.
3. in printing, an overlay.
rāiṣ′ing bee, a gathering of neighbors for putting together the framework of a building, as a house or a barn. [Obs.]
rāiṣ′ing bōard, in leathermaking, a ribbed and grooved board on which to rub the surface of tanned leather in order to raise the grain.
rāiṣ′ing ham′mẽr, a hammer with a smooth convex face used for making sheet metal cup-shaped by hammering it on one side only.
rāiṣ′ing knīfe (nīf), a cooper's knife used in setting the staves of a barrel together.
rāiṣ′ing plāte, in building, the plate or longitudinal timber on which the roof stands or is raised or placed: also called *upper plate*.
rāi′ṣin grāpe, any variety of grape, as the Malaga, suitable for making raisins, as distinguished from *table grape* and *wine grape*.
rai·son′ d'être (rā-zoṅ′ de′tr′), [Fr.] reason for being; justification for existence.
rai·son·né′ (rā-zō-nā′), *a.* [Fr.] logically or systematically arranged.
rāi′vel *n.* ravel. [Scot.]
räj, *n.* in India, rule; dominion.
Rä′jȧ, *n.* same as *Raia*.
rä′jȧh, rä′jȧ, *n.* [Hind. *rāja*; Sans. *rāja*; L. *rex, regis*, ruler, king.] a prince or chief in India, the East Indies, etc.
rä′jȧh·ship, rä′jȧ·ship, *n.* the rank or principality of a rajah.
Raj′pụt, Raj′pọọt, *n.* [Hind., prince, from *Rājan*, king, and *putra*, son.] a member of a strong Hindu military and ruling caste of northern India.
rāke, *n.* [AS. *raca*, a rake.] any of various long-handled tools with teeth or prongs at one end, used for gathering loose grass, hay, leaves, etc., or for smoothing broken ground.
rāke, *v.t.*; raked, *pt., pp.*; raking, *ppr.* 1. to gather or scrape together with or as with a rake.
2. to gather with great care.
3. to scratch or smooth with a rake, as in leveling broken ground.
4. to search through minutely; to scour.
5. to direct gunfire along the length of (a line of troops, the deck of a ship, etc.): often used figuratively.
rāke, *v.i.* 1. to use a rake.
2. to search as if with a rake.
3. to scrape or sweep (with ***over, across***, etc.).
rāke, *n.* in mining, a rent or fissure in strata, vertical or highly inclined; a rake vein. [Scot. and Brit. Dial.]
rāke, *n.* [contr. from *rakehell*.] a dissolute, debauched man; a roué.
rāke, *v.i.*; raked, *pt., pp.*; raking, *ppr.* [akin to Sw. *raka*, to project, G. *ragen*, Eng. *rock*; prob. from a Scand. word used in the international language of the sea.] to be slightly inclined; to have a rake, or slant, as a ship's masts, etc.
rāke, *v.t.* to give a slant to.
rāke, *n.* 1. a slanting or inclination from the perpendicular.
2. the angle made by the edge of a cutting tool and a plane perpendicular to the surface that is being worked.
3. a cutting away of the outer tip of the trailing edge of an airplane wing so that it is shorter than the leading edge.
rāke, *v.i.*; raked, *pt., pp.*; raking, *ppr.* [AS. *racian*, to speed forward.]
1. to fly after game: said of a hawk.
2. to run after game with the nose to the track instead of in the wind: said of a hunting dog.
rāke′hell, *n.* [from *rake* (to gather) and *hell* (as if so evil as to be found only by raking hell).] a dissolute, debauched man; a rake.
rāke′hell, rāke′hell·y, *a.* immoral; dissolute; debauched.
rāke′ọff, *n.* [*rake* (to gather) and *off*.] a commission, rebate, or share, especially when received in an illegitimate transaction. [Slang.]
rā′kẽr, *n.* one who or that which rakes; specifically, (a) formerly, one who raked and removed filth from the streets; a scavenger; (b) a machine used to rake hay or the like; (c) a piece of iron having two points bent at right angles, used for picking out mortar from the joints of old walls preparatory to pointing or replacing by new mortar; (d) an instrument for raking out ashes; especially, an automatic contrivance for cleaning the grate of a locomotive; (e) a rakelike organ, as the pharyngeal bones of some fishes; (f) a gun so placed as to rake an enemy.
rā′kẽr·y, *n.* lewdness; debauchery. [Rare.]
rāke′shāme, *n.* a vile, dissolute wretch. [Obs.]
rāke′stāle, *n.* [E. *rake*, and AS. *stele*, stalk.] a rake handle.
rāke vein, an inclined mineral vein; a rake.
rak′ī, rak′ee, *n.* [Turk. *rāqi*; Ar. *'araq*.] an aromatic alcoholic liquor resembling brandy, made from grape juice, grain, etc. in southern Europe and the Near East.
rāk′ing, *n.* 1. the act of using a rake; the act of collecting, cleaning, or smoothing with a rake.
2. the space of ground raked at one time; also, the quantity of hay, etc., collected by raking.
3. a critical or censorious overhauling; a scoring.
rāk′ish, *a.* given to a dissolute life; debauched.
rāk′ish, *a.* [from *rake* (to slant), and *-ish*.]
1. having a trim, neat appearance, suggesting speed: said of a ship.
2. dashing; jaunty.
rāk′ish·ly, *adv.* in a rakish manner.
rāk′ish·ness, *n.* the quality or state of being rakish.
räk′shȧ·sȧ, *n.* [Hind.] in Hindu mythology, an evil spirit or goblin.
rä′kụ wãre, a variety of pottery formerly made in Japan, with a dark glaze.
râle (räl), *n.* [Fr., from *râler*, to rattle.] in medicine, an abnormal rattling or bubbling sound accompanying the normal sound of breathing, and usually indicating a diseased condition of the lungs or bronchi.
rȧl·len·tȧn′dō, *a.* and *adv.* [It.] in music, gradually slower: also written *rallentato*: a direction to the performer.
ral′li·ănce, *n.* the act of rallying. [Rare.]
ral′li·ẽr, *n.* one who rallies.
ral′li·fọrm, *a.* [from Mod. L. *rallus*, a rail (bird); and *-form*.] like the rails (birds) in appearance, structure, etc.
Ral·lī′nae, *n.pl.* a subfamily of birds including the rails and containing about sixty species.
ral′line, *a.* pertaining to the rails (*Rallinæ*).
Ral′lus, *n.* [LL., from Fr. *râle*, a rail.] a genus of the *Rallinæ*, including the rails or marsh hens. They inhabit sedgy places, the banks of streams, and moist cornfields and meadows.
ral′ly, *v.t.*; rallied, *pt., pp.*; rallying, *ppr.* [Fr. *rallier*.]
1. to bring back together and put in a state of order, as retreating troops.
2. to summon or bring together for a common purpose; as, the leader *rallied* the workers.
3. to bring back to action; to revive; as, he *rallied* his energy.
ral′ly, *v.i.* 1. to come back to a state of order; as, the soldiers *rallied*.
2. to come together for a common purpose.

3. to come in order to help; as, he *rallied* to his defeated friend.

4. to come back to action, normal strength, etc.; to revive; as, the patient *rallied* from the coma.

5. in badminton, tennis, etc., to take part in a rally.

6. in commerce, to rise in price after having fallen: said of stocks, etc.

7. in sports, to come from behind in scoring.

ral′ly, *n.*; *pl.* **ral′lieṣ**, 1. a rallying or being rallied; specifically, a gathering of people for a common purpose; a mass meeting.

2. an organized automobile run, especially of sports cars on public roads, designed to test driving skills: also spelled *rallye*.

3. in badminton, tennis, etc., an exchange of several strokes before the point is won.

ral′ly, *n.* raillery. [Rare.]

ral′ly, *v.t.* and *v.i.*; rallied, *pt.*, *pp.*; rallying, *ppr.* [Fr. *railler*, to banter.] to tease or mock in mild derision; to ridicule; to banter.

ral′ly·ing·ly, *adv.* in a rallying manner.

ral′stŏn·īte, *n.* [after J. G. *Ralston*, Norristown, Pa.] a pseudoisometric mineral, consisting of a hydrated fluoride of aluminum, sodium, calcium, and magnesium, and occurring in small octahedral crystals.

ram, *n.* [AS. *ramm*, *ram*, a ram.]

1. a male sheep.

2. a battering-ram.

3. (a) formerly, a sharp metal beak on the prow of a ship, used to batter against or pierce enemy vessels; (b) a ship with such a beak.

4. a pump that raises water by the force of the water itself falling through a pipe: also called *hydraulic ram*.

5. the weight, or striking part, of a pile driver.

6. the plunger of a force pump.

7. [R–] (a) the constellation Aries; (b) the zodiacal sign of this constellation.

ram's horn; a semicircular work in the ditch of a fortified place, and sweeping the ditch, being itself commanded by the main work. [Rare.]

ram, *v.t.*; rammed, *pt.*, *pp.*; ramming, *ppr.* [ME. *rammen*, D. *rammen*, to batter.]

1. to strike against with great force; to drive into.

2. to force into place; to press or drive down; as, *ram* the charge into the gun.

3. to stuff or cram (*with* something).

4. to force (an idea, legislative bill, etc.) to be accepted: often with *across* or *through*.

ram, *v.i.* to use a ram; to drive; to pound.

Rä′mȧ, *n.* [Sans. *Rāma*.] any of three of the incarnations of the Hindu god Vishnu, especially the seventh.

Rä″mȧ·chan′drȧ (-chun′), *n.* [Sans. *Rāmacandra*.] Rama, the seventh incarnation of the Hindu god Vishnu: he is the hero of the Ramayana.

Ram·ȧ·dän′, *n.* [Ar. *ramadān*, from *ramad*, to be hot, the hot month.] the great annual fast of the Mohammedans, kept through their ninth month, which is also called *Ramadan*.

ram′ăġe, *n.* 1. branches of trees, collectively.

2. the warbling of birds sitting on boughs. [Obs.]

ram′ăġe, *a.* [OFr., wild, belonging or pertaining to branches, from L. *ramus*, a branch.] wild; shy; untrained, as a hawk. [Obs.]

rā′măl, *a.* 1. pertaining to or situated on a branch; rameal.

2. pertaining to or like a ramus.

Rä·mä′yȧ·nȧ, *n.* [Sans. *Rāmāyaṇa*.] one of the two great epic poems of India, written in Sanskrit some time after the Mahabharata.

Ram·ȧ·zän′, *n.* [Turk.] same as *Ramadan*.

ram′bĕrge, *n.* [OFr., from *rame*, an oar, and *barge*.] formerly, a large war galley used in the Mediterranean.

ram′ble, *v.i.*; rambled, *pt.*, *pp.*; rambling, *ppr.* [ME. *romblen*.]

1. to move, especially to walk about idly, without any special goal; to stroll; roam.

2. to talk or write aimlessly, without connection of ideas.

3. to grow or spread in all directions; as, vines *rambled* over the fence.

Syn.—rove, roam, wander, range, stroll, stray.

ram′ble, *n.* a rambling; an aimless stroll.

ram′blĕr, *n.* a person or thing that rambles; especially, any of certain climbing roses.

ram′bling, *a.* that rambles; disconnected, straggling, wandering, etc.

ram′bling, *n.* a roving; an irregular excursion.

ram′bling·ly, *adv.* in a rambling manner.

ram′bo͝oze, *n.* same as *rumbooze*.

Ram′bouil·let (-boo-lā *or Fr.* rän″bo͞o-yā′), *n.* [after *Rambouillet*, France.] a variety of merino sheep originally bred in France, now raised in the western United States for both its wool and mutton.

ram bow, a ship's bow that projects and is used for ramming.

ram·buṅç′tious (-shus), *a.* [from *robustious*.] wild, disorderly, boisterous, unruly, etc. [Colloq.]

ram·bus′tious (-chus), *a.* same as *rumbustious*.

ram·bụ′tăn, ram·bo͞o′tăn, *n.* [Malay *rambut*, hair.]

1. the spiny fruit produced by an East Indian and Malayan tree, *Nephelium lappaceum*, of the soapberry family. It is oval in shape, of a bright red color, and has an edible acid pulp.

2 the tree on which this fruit grows.

rā′mē·ăl, *a.* pertaining to or growing upon a branch; rameous.

Rā′mē·ăn, *n.* and *a.* same as *Ramist*.

rāmed, *a.* [OFr. *raim*, a branch, stake, from L. *ramus*, a branch.] framed on the stocks, as a ship having the frame, stem, and sternpost adjusted.

ram′ee, *n.* same as *ramie*.

ram′e·kin, ram′e·quin (-kin), *n.* [Fr. *ramequin*, from G. *rahm*, cream.]

1. a kind of hash made chiefly of bread crumbs, cheese, and eggs, and baked in individual baking dishes.

2. such a baking dish.

3. any food mixture prepared or served in such a dish.

rā′ment, *n.* [L. *ramentum*, a chip, shaving, scale, from *radere*, to scrape.]

1. a chip, scale, or shaving. [Obs.]

2. [*pl.*] in botany, same as *ramenta*.

ram·en·tā′ceous, *a.* in botany, covered with weak, shriveled, brown, scalelike processes, as the leaves of many ferns.

rȧ·men′tum, *n.*; *pl.* **rȧ·men′tȧ**, [L.] a thin, brown scale appearing on young shoots and on the stems of many ferns.

rā′mē·ous, *a.* [L. *ramus*, a branch.] in botany, belonging to a branch; growing on or shooting from a branch.

ram·fee′zled (-zld), *a.* fatigued; exhausted. [Scot.]

ram′head (-hed), *n.* an iron lever for hoisting heavy stones. [Obs.]

rā′mī, *n.* plural of *ramus*.

ram′i·çorn, *n.* [LL. *ramicornis*, from L. *ramus*, branch, and *cornu*, horn] an insect having branched antennae.

ram′i·çorn, *a.* having branched antennae: said of some insects; pertaining to the *Ramicornes*.

Ram·i·çor′nēs, *n.pl.* a group of insects having ramicorn antennae.

ram′iē, ram′ee, *n.* [Malay *rami*.]

1. an Asiatic plant with many rodlike stems and heart-shaped flowers.

2. the fine fiber, somewhat resembling that of cotton, made from the young shoots of the plant and used for making fine cloth.

rȧ·mif′ĕr·ous, *a.* producing branches.

ram″i·fi·çā′tion, *n.* [Fr., from L. *ramus*, a branch.]

1. a ramifying or being ramified; specifically, the arrangement of branches or offshoots, as on a plant.

2. the result of ramifying; specifically, (a) a branch or offshoot; (b) a subdivision, consequence, or result; as, the *ramifications* of an act.

point of ramification; see *critical point*, sense (a), under *critical*.

ram′i·fīed, *a.* in anatomy and zoology, having branches; branched

ram′i·form, *a.* [from L. *ramus*, a branch; and *-form*.] branched or resembling a branch.

ram′i·fȳ, *v.t.*; ramified, *pt.*, *pp.*; ramifying, *ppr.* Fr. *ramifier*, from L. *ramus*, a branch, and *facere*, to make.] to divide into branches or branchlike parts; as, to *ramify* an art, a subject, or scheme.

ram′i·fȳ, *v.i.* 1. to be divided into branches, as the stem of a plant.

2. to be divided or subdivided; to have offshoots or branches.

Ram′i·liē, *n.* an article or mode of dress, especially a cocked hat, a peculiar wig, etc., named in honor of the victory of the British over the French at Ramillies in Belgium in 1706: also used attributively; as, a *Ramilie* hat.

Rā′miṣm, *n.* the philosophical and dialectical system of Pierre de la Ramée (better known by his Latinized name, Ramus), royal professor of rhetoric and philosophy at Paris. He was born in 1515, and was one of the victims of the massacre of St. Bartholomew (1572). He was a strong opponent of scholasticism, and of the dialectics of Aristotle.

Rā′mist, *a.* belonging to or connected with Ramism; Ramean.

Rā′mist, *n.* a follower of Ramus; a Ramean.

ram′jet, *n.* a jet engine in which the air is continuously compressed by being rammed into the open front end: also called *athodyd*.

ram′līne, *n.* a line or small rope, formerly used to secure a straight center line from stem to stern when building a boat.

ram′mel, *n.* [ME. *ramel*, rubbish, from OFr. *ramaille*, branches, twigs.] useless or refuse matter; rubbish. [Obs.]

ram′melṣ·bĕrg·īte, *n.* [after K. F. *Rammelsberg* (1813–1899), the German chemist and mineralogist.] an orthorhombic form of nickel arsenide, having the formula $NiAs_2$.

ram′mĕr, *n* 1. one who rams or drives.

2. an instrument for driving anything with force; as, a *rammer* for driving stones or piles.

3. a ramrod

ram′mish, *a.* characteristic of a ram; buckish; strong-scented; hence, lustful; lascivious.

ram′mish·ness, *n.* the state or quality of being rammish.

ram′my, *a.* like a ram; rammish.

rā′mōse, *a.* [L. *ramosus*, branched, from *ramus*, a branch.]

1. bearing many branches.

2. branching.

rā′mous, *a.* 1. ramose.

2. branchlike.

ramp, *v.i.*; ramped (rampt), *pt.*, *pp.*; ramping, *ppr.* [ME. *rampen*; OFr. *ramper*, to creep or climb.]

1. to stand upright on the hind legs, as a lion in heraldry.

2. to assume a threatening position or posture.

3. to move or rush threateningly, violently, or with fury; to rampage; to storm.

4. to climb, as a plant; to creep up. [Archaic and Dial.]

5. to prance; to gambol; as, children romp and *ramp* around. [Now Dial.]

ramp, *n.* a ramping.

ramp, *n.* [Fr. *rampe*, from *ramper*, to climb.]

1. a sloping passage, usually curved, joining different levels of a building, road, etc.

2. a concave bend or curve where a handrail or coping changes its direction, as at a staircase landing.

3. a means for boarding or leaving an airplane, as a staircase on wheels rolled up to the door.

4. a sloping runway for launching boats, as from trailers.

5. any sloping roadway or passage.

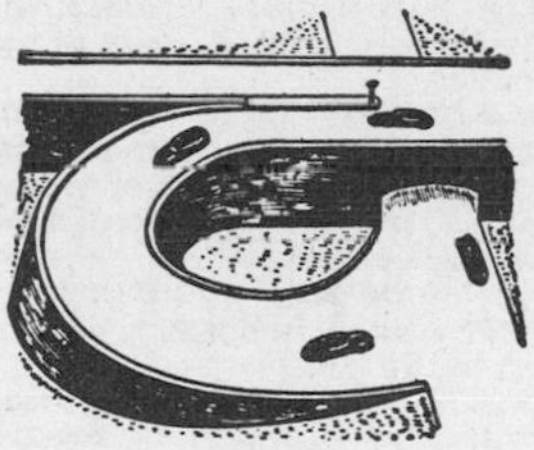

RAMP

ram′pāġe, *v.i.*; rampaged, *pt.*, *pp.*; rampaging, *ppr.* [from Scot. dial. *ramp*, v., and *rage*.] to rush violently about; to rage; to act violently.

ram′pāġe, *n.* an outbreak of violent, raging behavior: usually in *on the* (or *a*) *rampage*.

ram·pā′ġeous, *a.* rampaging; unruly or boisterous; not easily controlled.

ram·pā′ġeous·ness, *n.* the quality of being rampageous.

ram·pal′liăn, ram·pal′liŏn (-yun), *n.* a rapscallion; a mean wretch. [Obs.]

ram′păn·cy, *n.* the condition or quality of being rampant; exuberance.

ram′pănt, *a.* [OFr., from *ramper*, to climb.]

1. growing luxuriantly; flourishing; as, *rampant* plants.

2. spreading unchecked; widespread; rife.

3. violent and uncontrollable in action, manner, speech, etc.

4. in architecture, having one abutment higher than the other: said of an arch or vault.

5. in heraldry, rearing up on the hind legs,

usually in profile, with one forepaw raised above the other, as a lion, etc.

rampant gardant; in heraldry, same as *rampant*, but with the animal full-faced.

RAMPANT ARCH

rampant passant; in heraldry, of or designating an animal when walking with the dexter forepaw raised somewhat higher than the mere passant position.

rampantregardant; in heraldry, rampant, but with the animal's head turned round toward the tail.

rampant sejant; in heraldry, designating or of an animal when in a sitting posture with the forelegs raised.

ram′pănt·ly, *adv.* in a rampant manner.

ram′pärt (*or* pẽrt), *n.* [Fr. *rempart*, a rampart, from *remparer*, to fortify a place; *re*, again, *em* for L. *in*, in, and *parer*, to defend, from L. *parare*, to prepare.]

1. an embankment of earth surmounted by a parapet and encircling a castle, fort, etc., for defending it from attackers.

2. anything that defends or protects; as, courage forms a *rampart* against troubles.

rampart gun; a large piece of artillery fitted for use on a rampart and not for field purposes.

Syn.—bulwark, defense, guard, security, mound, embankment.

ram′pärt, *v.t.*; ramparted, *pt., pp.*; ramparting, *ppr.* to fortify or defend with or as with ramparts.

ram′pick, ram′pīke, *n.* a dead tree or stump. [Dial.]

ram′pi·ŏn, *n.* [from L. *rapum*, a turnip, rape, through some Romance form; compare Fr. *raiponce*; It. *ramponzolo*.] a plant, *Campanula rapunculus*, belonging to the bellwort family, indigenous to Europe. Its thick, fleshy, white root is eaten like a radish. The American evening primrose, *Œnothera biennis*, and certain other plants of the bellwort family, are sometimes called rampions.

ram′pīre, *n.* a rampart. [Obs.]

ram′plẽr, *n.* a rambler; a rover. [Scot.]

ram′plẽr, *a.* roving; traveling. [Scot.]

ram′rod, *n.* 1. a metal rod used for ramming down the charge in a gun that is loaded through the muzzle.

2. a rod for cleaning a rifle bore.

ram′shaç″kle, *a.* [back-formation from *ramshackled*, for earlier *ransackled*, pp. of *ransackle*, freq. of *ransack*.] loose and rickety; likely to fall to pieces; shaky; as, a *ramshackle* old building.

ram′s′-head (-hed), *n.* in botany, a North American orchid, *Cypripedium arietinum*.

ram′sŏn, *n.* [AS. *hramsa*, *hramse*, wild garlic.]

1. a species of garlic, *Allium ursinum*, with broad leaves.

2. [*usually in pl.*] its root, used in salads.

ram′stead, ram′sted, *n.* same as *ranstead*.

ram′til, *n.* [Hindu.] a plant of tropical India, *Guizotia oleifera*, from the seeds of which a valuable oil is extracted.

ram′ūle, *n.* in botany, a ramulus.

ram·ū·lif′ẽr·ous, *a.* in botany, bearing branchlets, or ramuli.

ram′ū·lōse, *a.* [L. *ramulosus*, from *ramulus*, dim. of *ramus*, a branch.] having many small branches, or ramuli.

ram′ū·lous, *a.* same as *ramulose*.

ram′ū·lus, *n.*; *pl.* **ram′ū·lī,** [L.] a branchlet or small ramus, as of coral or an artery.

rā′mus, *n.*; *pl.* **rā′mī,** [L.] in biology, a branch or branching part.

rȧ·mus′cūle, *n.* [Fr., from L. *ramusculus*, dim. of *ramus*, a branch.] a little ramus; a branchlet; a ramulus.

ran, *v.* past tense of *run*.

also ran; (a) competed without placing first, second, or third: said of a race horse, etc.; (b) competed without winning: said of a contestant, candidate, etc.

Rän, *n.* [ON. *Rān*.] in Norse mythology, the goddess of the sea and of drowning persons.

ran, *n.* a length of twine.

Rā′nȧ, *n.* [L., a frog.] a genus of amphibian vertebrates, including the various species of frogs.

rā′năl, *a.* in botany, relating to the *Ranunculaceæ*.

Rȧ·nā′lēş, *n.pl.* an order of hypogynous, polypetalous herbs having indefinite stamens and a minute embryo enclosed in a large quantity of albumen.

rȧ·nā′ri·um, *n.*; *pl.* **rȧ·nā′ri·ȧ,** [from L. *rana*, a frog.] a place where live frogs are kept.

rance, *n.* [OFr. *ranche*, a stick or wooden pin, from L. *ramex*, staff.] a strut, shore, or prop. [Scot.]

rance, *n.* [Fr.] a kind of dull-red marble with markings of pale blue and white, found in Belgium.

ran·ces′cent, *a.* [L. *rancescere*, to be rank.] becoming rancid or sour. [Rare.]

ranch, *n.* [Sp. *rancho*, a small farm.]

1. a large farm used for breeding and pasturing cattle, horses, or sheep; a stock farm.

2. any large farm devoted to the raising of a particular crop or livestock; as, a fruit *ranch*.

3. all the people living and working on a ranch.

ranch, *v.i.* to work on or manage a ranch.

ranch, *v.t.* to put (an animal) to graze on a ranch.

ranch′ẽr, *n.* one who owns or manages a ranch; also, a cowboy.

ràn·chẹ·rī′ȧ, *n.* [Sp.] 1. the dwelling place of a rancher.

2. an Indian hamlet. [Dial.]

ran·chẹ′rō (*or Sp.* rän-che′rọ), *n.*; *pl.* **ran·chẹ′rōş,** [Sp.] in the southwestern United States and Mexico, a rancher.

ranch′măn, *n.*; *pl.* **ranch′men,** a rancher.

ràn′chō, *n.*; *pl.* **ràn′chōş,** [Sp., a small farm, a mess, soldiers' quarters.] in Spanish America, a hut or huts used by ranch workers for shelter or lodging; also, a ranch.

ran′cid, *a.* [L. *rancidus*, from *rancere*, to be rank.] having the rank smell and sour taste of stale fats or oils; not fresh; spoiled; as, *rancid* butter.

ran·cid′i·fȳ, *v.t.* and *v.i.*; rancidified, *pt., pp.*; rancidifying, *ppr.* to cause to become rancid; to become rancid. [Rare.]

ran·cid′i·ty, *n.* the quality or condition of being rancid.

ran′cid·ly, *adv.* in a rancid manner.

ran′cid·ness, *n.* rancidity.

rañ′çŏr, *n.* [L., from *rancere*, to be rank.] a continuing and bitter hate or ill will; deep spite or malice.

> In the wildest exhibition of partizan *rancor* the party cannot be accused of reactionary opposition. —Grover Cleveland.

Syn.—enmity, ill will, harshness, spite, hatred, malevolence.

rañ′çŏr·ous, *a.* full of, or showing, rancor.

rañ′çŏr·ous·ly, *adv.* with deep spite or malice.

rañ′çŏur, *n.* rancor: British spelling.

rand, *n.* [ME. *rand*; AS. *rand*, *rond*, edge, border, shield; Ice. *rönd*, a stripe, a shield.]

1. in shoemaking, a leather strip used to level off the back part of a sole before the heel is put on.

2. a long fleshy piece of beef cut out between the flank and the buttock. [Dial.]

3. a border; edge; margin. [Rare or Dial.]

4. a strip, as of leather.

rand, *v.t.* in shoemaking, to fit with rands.

rand, *v.i.* to rant. [Archaic.]

ran′dăll gràss, a tall nutritive meadow grass, *Festuca elatior*.

Ran′dăll·īte, *n.* a member of the sect of New England Freewill Baptists, founded in 1780 by Benjamin Randall.

ran′dăn, *n.* 1. a boat propelled by three rowers using four oars, the midship rower having two sculls, the bowman and strokesman one oar each.

2. a drinking fit; a spree: used only in the phrase *on the randan*. [Brit. Dial.]

Ran′di·ȧ, *n.* [after Isaac *Rand*, an eighteenth century London botanist.] a large genus of erect or climbing, sometimes spiny trees and shrubs, of the family *Rubiaceæ*, with opposite entire leathery leaves, and white or yellow axillary flowers, native to the tropics.

rand′ing, *n.* 1. in military usage, a sort of basketwork for gabions.

2. the act of preparing and attaching rands to shoes.

ran′dŏm, *n.* [OFr. *à randon*, at random; *randon*, an impetuous course or efflux, vivacity, violence; *randoner*, *randir*, to run rapidly.]

1. a roving motion or course without direction; want of direction, rule, or method: used only in the phrase *at random*, without careful choice, aim, plan, etc.; haphazardly.

2. range of a gun, etc.; as, the farthest *random* of a missile. [Obs.]

3. in mining, the course of a vertical mineral vein.

4. violence; force. [Obs.]

ran′dŏm, *a.* without aim or purpose; haphazard; as, a *random* shot; a *random* guess.

ran′dŏm·ly, *adv.* at random; without aim or purpose.

ran′dŏn, *n.* random. [Obs.]

ran′dŏn, *v.i.* to move at random. [Obs.]

ran′dy, *a.* coarse; crude; vulgar. [Scot.]

ran′dy, *n.*; *pl.* **ran′dieş,** 1. an impudent, threatening beggar. [Scot.]

2. a coarse, vulgar, quarrelsome woman; a shrew. [Scot.]

rä′nee, *n.* same as *rani*.

Rȧ·nel′lȧ, *n.* [LL.] a genus of the order *Nuricidæ*, having ovate operculum, lateral nucleus, and two rows of continuous varices.

rang, *v.* past tense of *ring* (to sound, as a bell).

rānġe, *v.t.*; ranged, *pt., pp.*; ranging, *ppr.* [ME. *rengen*; OFr. *renger*; Fr. *ranger*, to array, range.]

1. to set in a row or in rows; to place in a regular line, lines, or ranks; as, to *range* troops in the order of battle.

2. to put in proper classes, orders, or divisions; to classify; as, to *range* plants and animals in genera and species.

3. to roam about; to pass over or through; as, to *range* the coast for the enemy.

4. to place (oneself or another) with others in a cause, party, etc.; as, he *ranged* himself with the rebels.

5. to put in a line with the target or object, at a proper angle of elevation; to train (a gun, telescope, etc.).

6. to put out (cattle, etc.) to graze on a range.

7. to uncoil (the cable of an anchor) and arrange on deck.

8. to sift. [Obs.]

rānġe, *v.i.* 1. to roam; to wander without restraint or direction.

2. to be placed in order; to be ranked or classified.

3. to extend, reach, or lie in a particular direction; to correspond in direction; to lie alongside; as, the front of the house *ranges* with the line of the street.

4. to pass from one point to another; to vary between stated limits; as, the price *ranges* between 10 and 15 cents.

5. to exist in a certain region, as a plant or animal.

6. to roam through an area for a special purpose; as, the dog *ranges* for game.

7. to have a specified range; to be able to project over a specified distance; as, the gun *ranged* five miles.

8. in gunnery, to determine the range of a target by firing alternate rounds beyond and before it.

Syn.—rove, roam, ramble, wander, stroll.

rānġe, *n.* [ME. *reng*; OFr. *rangie*, a range, row, or line.]

1. a rank; a row; a series of things in a line; as, a *range* of hills; a *range* of buildings.

2. a class, kind, or order.

> The next *range* of beings above him are the immaterial intelligences. —Hale.

3. a wandering, roving, or roaming.

4. space or extent taken or passed over; command; scope; as, the *range* of one's ability.

5. the step of a ladder; a rung. [Obs.]

6. in U. S. public surveying, a row of townships lying between two consecutive meridian lines, which are six miles apart, and numbered in order east and west from the principal meridian of each survey, the townships in the range being numbered north and south from the base line, which runs east and west; as, township No. 6 N., *range* 7 W., from the fifth principal meridian.

7. a kitchen grate. [Obs.]

8. a bolting sieve to sift meal. [Brit. Dial.]

9. a series of connected mountains considered as a single system.

10. a line of direction; as, the tree is in *range* with the house.

11. a large, open area of land over which livestock can wander and graze.

12. the limits of possible variations of amount, degree, etc.; as, the *range* of price was narrow.

13. in botany and zoology, the region in which a plant or animal is normally found.

14. in statistics, the difference between the greatest and smallest values in a series of variable quantities.

15. in gunnery, (a) the horizontal distance from a gun to its target; (b) the maximum effective horizontal distance that a gun can

fire its projectile; (c) a place where gun or rifle practice is carried on.

16. in music, the whole ascending or descending series of sounds capable of being produced by a voice or instrument; the compass or register of a voice or instrument.

17. in nautical usage, (a) a length of cable a little in excess of the depth of water, ranged on deck ready to run out when the anchor is let go; (b) a large cleat in the waist for belaying the sheets.

18. a cooking stove.

range of accommodation; in physiology and optics, the difference between the far point and the near point for which an eye may become accommodated.

rānġe, *a.* of a range or open grazing place; as, *range* livestock.

rānġe fīnd'ẽr, any of various instruments for determining the distance of a target or object from an observer, from a gun, etc.

rānġe'heads (-hedz), *n.pl.* in nautical usage, the bitts of a windlass.

rānġe līght (līt), either of two or more lights placed as at the entrance to a harbor, by means of which a ship, when keeping them in line, may be guided into port.

rān'ġẽr, *n.* 1. one who ranges; a rover; a wanderer.

2. one of a body of mounted troops for patrolling a region.

3. [R–] any of a group of American soldiers trained for raiding and close combat behind enemy lines.

4. in the United States, a warden who patrols government forests.

5. a dog that searches for game.

6. in England, formerly, a sworn officer of a forest, appointed by the king's letters patent, to walk through the forest, watch the deer, prevent trespasses, etc.; now, the chief official of a royal park or forest.

rān'ġẽr·ship, *n.* the position of a park or forest ranger.

rānġe'wŏrk, *n.* stonework in which the squared stones are placed in even rows.

rān'ġing, *n.* the act of one who ranges.

rañ'gle, *v.i.* to range about irregularly; to stray. [Obs.]

rān'ġy, *a.*; *comp.* rangier; *superl.* rangiest.

1. roving; capable of ranging about, as cattle.

2. commodious; roomy; as, a *rangy* stable. [Colloq.]

3. long-limbed and slender; as, *rangy* cattle.

rä'nī, rä'nee, *n.* [Hind.] in India, a reigning princess or queen; also, the wife of a rajah, king, or prince.

rā'nīne, *a.* [L. *rana*, a frog.]

1. pertaining or belonging to the frogs.

2. in anatomy, pertaining to the lower surface of the tongue.

rȧ·niv'ō·rous, *a.* living on frogs; frog-eating, as certain birds.

rañk, *a.* [ME. *ranke*; AS. *ranc*, strong, proud.]

1. overly luxuriant; being of vigorous growth; as, *rank* grass; *rank* weeds.

2. causing vigorous growth; producing luxuriantly; very rich and fertile; as, *rank* land.

3. strong and offensive in smell or taste; rancid; musty; as, oil of a *rank* smell.

4. in sexual heat. [Obs.]

5. in bad taste; coarse; indecent.

6. complete; extreme; utter; as, *rank* pride; *rank* enmity: used contemptuously.

7. in law, excessive; exceeding the actual value; as, a *rank* modus.

8. in mechanics, projecting so as to cut deeply; as, to set the iron of a plane *rank*, that is, to set it so as to take off a thick shaving.

rañk, *adv.* rankly; violently; strongly. [Obs.]

rañk, *n.* [ME. *renk, reng*, pl. *renges*, class, order, a row or line; OFr. *renc, reng*.]

1. a line; a row; a range; a series of things in a line.

2. an orderly arrangement.

3. a social division; a class; an order.

4. degree of dignity, eminence, or excellence; comparative station or position in civil, military, or social life; relative place; as, a lawyer of high *rank*; a writer of the first *rank*.

5. an official grade or position; as, the *rank* of captain; the *rank* of admiral.

6. high social position; eminence; excellence; distinction; high degree; as, a man of *rank*.

7. any of the horizontal rows of squares on a chessboard.

8. in miltary usage, (a) a row of soldiers, vehicles, etc. placed side by side, or abreast of one another: opposed to *file*; (b) [*pl.*] an army; (c) [*pl.*] the body of soldiers of an army, as distinguished from the officers; as, he rose from the *ranks*.

9. in organ building, a row of pipes belonging to one stop.

rank and file; (a) the body of soldiers of an army, as distinguished from the officers; (b) the ordinary people forming the large part of some group; common people, as distinguished from leaders, etc.

to pull one's rank on; to take advantage of one's rank in enforcing commands to (a subordinate). [Military Slang.]

rañk, *v.t.*; ranked (rañkt), *pt., pp.*; ranking, *ppr.* 1. to place abreast, or in a line.

2. to place in a rank or ranks.

Poets were *ranked* in the class of philosophers. —Broome.

3. to assign a certain rank, or position, to; to place in suitable order.

Ranking all things under general and special heads. —Watts.

4. to outrank; to take precedence over.

rañk, *v.i.* 1. to hold the highest rank, or grade; as, the *ranking* member of the embassy.

2. to hold a certain rank or position; to be held in a certain degree of esteem; as, he *ranks* with the best class of writers.

rañk'ẽr, *n.* 1. one who ranks.

2. (a) a commissioned officer in the British army who has served in the ranks; (b) a British soldier in the ranks.

rañ'kle, *v.i.*; rankled, *pt., pp.*; rankling, *ppr.* [ME. *ranclen*; OFr. *rancler*, from *raoncle, draoncle*; ML. *dracunculus*, a fester, ulcer; ult. from L. *draco*, dragon.]

1. to become inflamed or cause inflammation; to fester; as, a *rankling* wound.

A malady that burns and *rankles* inward. —Rowe.

2. to become bitter; to cause bitterness or self-torment; to cause continual mental pain, resentment, etc.; as, *rankling* malice.

Syn.—fester, smolder, burn, irritate, gall.

rañ'kle, *v.t.* to make sore; to inflame; to irritate. [Rare.]

rañk'ly, *adv.* in a rank manner.

rañk'ness, *n.* the quality or state of being rank.

ran'nel, *n.* a strumpet. [Obs.]

ran'ny, *n.* the shrewmouse. [Obs.]

ran'pīke, *n.* same as *rampick*.

ran'sack, *v.t.*; ransacked (-sakt), *pt., pp.*; ransacking, *ppr.* [ON. *rannsaka*, from *rann*, a house, and *-saka*, from *sækja*, to seek.]

1. to plunder; to pillage completely.

2. to search thoroughly; to enter and search every place or part of; as, to *ransack* a building.

ran'sack, *v.i.* to search thoroughly.

ran'sack, *n.* 1. the act of ransacking; the state of being searched. [Archaic.]

2. sack; pillage. [Obs.]

ran'sack·ẽr, *n.* one who ransacks; a pillager.

ran'sŏm, *n.* [ME. *ranson, ransom*, etc.; OFr. *raenson, raanson*; L. *redemptio* (*-onis*), redemption, from *redimere*; *re-*, back, and *emere*, to buy.]

1. release from captivity or bondage by payment of money or compliance with other demands.

2. the price paid or demanded which procures the release of a captive or of property seized and restores the former to liberty and the latter to the original owner.

3. in theology, a means of freeing from sin; redemption.

4. in old English law, a sum paid for the pardon of some great offense, and the discharge of the offender; a fine paid in lieu of corporal punishment.

ran'sŏm, *v.t.* 1. to obtain the release of (a captive, property, etc.) by paying the demanded price.

2. to release after such payment.

3. in theology, to free from sin; to redeem.

4. to hold at ransom; to demand or exact a ransom from; to exact a fine or payment from. [Rare.]

Syn.—free, release, rescue, deliver, redeem.

ran'sŏm·ȧ·ble, *a.* that can be ransomed.

ran'sŏm bill, a war contract by which it is agreed to pay money for the ransom of property captured at sea, and for its safe conduct into port.

ran'sŏm·ẽr, *n.* one who redeems.

ran'sŏm·less, *a.* free from ransom; without ransom; also, that cannot be ransomed.

ran'stead (-sted), *n.* [*ranstead's weed*, from a Mr. *Ranstead* of Philadelphia, who introduced it.] in botany, the toadflax, *Linaria vulgaris*.

rant, *v.i.*; ranted, *pt., pp.*; ranting, *ppr.* [O.D. *ranten*, to be enraged; Gael. and Ir. *ran*, to make a noise.]

1. to talk in a loud, wild, extravagant way; to declaim violently; to rave.

2. to be boisterously merry. [Brit. Dial.]

rant, *v.t.* to say or declaim in a ranting manner (often with *out*); as, he *ranted out* his denunciation.

rant, *n.* 1. loud, wild, extravagant speech.

2. a boisterous merrymaking. [Brit. Dial.]

rant'ẽr, *n.* 1. a noisy talker; a boisterous orator.

2. [R–] [*pl.*] a religious sect which sprang up in 1645. They called themselves *Seekers*, their members maintaining that they were seeking for the true church and its ordinances, and the Scriptures, which were lost; also, the Primitive Methodists, who seceded from the Wesleyan Methodists on the ground of their deficiency in fervor and zeal.

Rant'ẽr·iṣm, *n.* the practice or the tenets of the Ranters.

rant'ing·ly, *adv.* in a ranting manner.

rant'i·pōle, *a.* wild; roving.

rant'i·pōle, *n.* a rude, romping boy or girl.

rant'i·pōle, *v.i.* to run about wildly.

Rant'iṣm, *n.* the practice or tenets of Ranters.

rant'y, *a.* wild; noisy; boisterous. [Brit. Dial. and Scot.]

ran'ū·lȧ, *n.* [L., a little frog, dim. of *rana*, a frog.] a swelling of a salivary gland under the tongue.

Rȧ·nuñ·çū·lā'cē·ae, *n.pl.* [from *Ranunculus*, one of the genera.] a very large family of exogenous polypetalous plants, the crowfoot or buttercup family, including the larkspur, peony, anemone, etc., in almost all cases herbaceous. They have radical or alternate leaves, often regular or irregular flowers, and fruits consisting of one-seeded achenes or many-seeded follicles. *Ranunculus* is the chief genus.

rȧ·nuñ·çū·lā'ceous, *a.* resembling or belonging to the *Ranunculaceæ*.

Rȧ·nuñ'çū·lus, *n.* [LL., from L. *rana*, a frog.] a genus of herbaceous plants, the type of the *Ranunculaceæ*. They have entire, lobed, or compound leaves, and usually panicled, white or yellow flowers.

rȧ·nuñ'çū·lus, *n.*; *pl.* **rȧ·nuñ'çu·lus·eṣ, rȧ·nuñ'çu·lī,** any plant of the genus *Ranunculus*.

ränz dḙs vȧches (räṅz dā väsh), [Fr., lit., the ranks or rows of the cows.] any of various simple melodies of the Swiss mountaineers, commonly played on a long trumpet called the alpenhorn.

rap, *v.t.*; rapped (rapt), *pt., pp.*; rapping, *ppr.* [ME. *rappen*; prob. Gmc.]

1. to strike with a quick blow; to tap; as, to *rap* one's knuckles.

2. to utter with sudden violence; to say sharply (with *out*); as, to *rap out* an oath.

3. to give a rap with; as, to *rap* a stick against a door.

rap, *v.i.* 1. to give a quick sharp blow; to knock quickly and sharply.

2. to swear; to take a false oath. [Slang.]

rap, *n.* 1. a quick smart blow; a knock; as, a *rap* on the knuckles.

2. the sound made by or as by knocking.

3. blame or punishment; specifically, a judicial sentence, as to a prison term: usually in *beat* (escape) or *take* (receive) *the rap*. [Slang.]

rap, *v.t.*; rapt *or* rapped (rapt), *pt., pp.*; rapping, *ppr.* [prob. back-formation from *rapt*.]

1. to affect with ecstasy or rapture; to carry away with rapture: now only in the past participle. [Obs. or Rare.]

2. to snatch; to seize. [Obs. or Rare.]

to rap and rend; to seize and steal.

rap, *n.* [cf. G. *rappe*, small coin.]

1. originally, a counterfeit Irish halfpenny of the time of George I.

2. the least bit: now usually in *not care* (or *give*) *a rap*, not care (or give) anything at all. [Colloq.]

Rȧ·pā'cēṣ, *n.pl.* Raptores. [Obs.]

rȧ·pā'cious, *a.* [L. *rapax, rapacis*, from *rapere*, to seize.]

1. given to plunder; seizing by force.

2. subsisting on captured prey: said of animals or birds.

3. voracious; ravenous; excessively greedy.

That robbers' roost, hideous and of a dark, *rapacious* architecture, has cost $18,000,000 and the end is not yet. —Alfred Henry Lewis.

rȧ·pā'cious·ly, *adv.* in a rapacious manner.

rȧ·pā'cious·ness, *n.* the quality of being rapacious.

ra·pac′i·ty, *n.* the quality, act, or practice of being rapacious.

rāpe, *n.* [from *rap*, to seize, to snatch, the meaning being influenced by L. *rapere, raptum*, to seize.]
 1. the act of snatching or carrying off by force.
 2. something taken or seized and carried away by force.
 3. the crime of having sexual intercourse with a woman or girl forcibly and without her consent. If the act is committed when the woman is stupefied by drugs or liquors, deceived as to nature of the act, or overcome by duress or threats, or if she is below the age of consent, it is rape.
 4. the plundering or violent destruction (*of* a city, etc.), as in warfare.
 5. any outrageous assault or flagrant violation.

rāpe, *v.t.*; raped (rāpt), *pt., pp.*; raping, *ppr.*
 1. to seize and carry off by force.
 2. to affect with rapture; to transport. [Archaic.]
 3. to ravish; to commit rape on (a woman or girl); to violate.
 4. to plunder or destroy (a city, etc.), as in warfare.

rāpe, *n.* [Fr. *râpe*; ML. *raspa*; ult. from O.H.G. *raspon*, to scrape together.]
 1. the stalks and skins of grapes from which juice has been extracted.
 2. a filter used in vinegar manufacturing to separate the mucilaginous matter from the vinegar.

rāpe, *n.* [of uncertain origin.] one of the six divisions of the county of Sussex, England.

rāpe, *n.* [L. *rapa*, turnip.] either of two plants of the mustard family, *Brassica campestris*, the summer rape, or *Brassica napus*, the winter rape. The seeds are the source of rape oil and the leaves are used as fodder.

rāpe, *v.i.* and *v.t.* [ME. *rapen*; Ice. *hrapa*, to fall, to hasten.] to hasten; to hurry. [Obs.]

rāpe, *n.* haste; a precipitate course. [Obs.]

rāpe, *n.* rope. [Dial.]

rāpe but′tėr·fly̆, the cabbage butterfly. [Brit.]

rāpe çāke, the refuse remaining after the oil has been extracted from the rapeseed.

rāpe oil, the thick oil extracted from rapeseed, used for lubricating, etc.; colza oil: also *rapeseed oil.*

rāpe′seed, *n.* 1. the seed of the rape plant.
 2. the plant.

rāpe′seed oil, same as *rape oil.*

rāpe wīne, a thin wine from the last dregs of grapes which have been pressed.

rap′-fųll′, *a.* filled with wind: said of a sail.

rap′-fųll′, *n.* state of having the sails bellied by the wind.

Raph′ā·el (*or* rā′fi-), *n.* an archangel mentioned in the Apocrypha.

Raph″ā·el·esque′ (-esk′), *a.* [from *Raphael* (*Raffaello* Santi), the celebrated Italian painter, 1483–1520.] like the style of the painter Raphael; in the manner of Raphaelism.

Raph′ā·el·iṣm, *n.* the theory of art or manner of execution displayed in the paintings of Raphael.

Raph′ā·el·īte, *n.* an advocate of Raphaelism.

Raph′ȧ·nus, *n.* [Gr. *rhaphanos*, radish.] a genus of cruciferous plants including the common radish.

rā′phē, *n.* [Gr. *rhaphē*, a seam or suture.]
 1. in anatomy, a seamlike joining of the two lateral halves of an organ, as of the tongue, etc.
 2. in botany, (a) a cord of tissue forming a seam along the body of certain ovules; (b) a median line, rib, or slot on a diatom valve or cell wall.

Rā′phi·a, *n.* [LL., from Malagasy native name *raffia.*] in botany, a genus of African palms, having pinnate leaves and bearing large fruit.

raph′i·dēṣ, *n.pl.* [Mod. L., from Gr. *raphis, raphidos*, a needle.] the needle-shaped crystals developed in plant cells.

rā′phis, *n.* singular of *raphides.*

rap′id, *a.* [Fr. *rapide*, from L. *rapidus*, rapid, from *rapere*, to seize and carry, or hurry away.]
 1. swift; quick; moving, progressing, or done with speed.
 2. steep; abrupt; as, a *rapid* rise in the highway.

rap′id, *n.* 1. [*usually in pl.*] a part of a river where the water moves swiftly, as because of a sudden drop in the river bed.
 2. a rapid transit car, train, or system.

rap′id-fīre′, *a.* 1. firing or capable of firing shots in rapid succession: said of guns.
 2. done, delivered, proceeding, or carried on swiftly and sharply; as, a *rapid-fire* talk.

rap′id-fīr′ing, *a.* same as *rapid-fire.*

rȧ·pid′i·ty, *n.* [Fr. *rapidité*, from L. *rapiditas*, rapidity.] the quality or state of being rapid; swiftness in movement or progress; celerity; speed; as, the *rapidity* of a current, the *rapidity* of his speech.
 Syn.—rapidness, dispatch, fleetness.

rap′id·ly, *adv.* in a rapid manner; with great speed, celerity, or velocity; swiftly; with quick progression; as, to run *rapidly.*

rap′id·ness, *n.* swiftness; speed; rapidity.

rap′id trans′it, a system of rapid public transportation in an urban area, using electric trains running along an unimpeded right of way, as in a subway.

rā′pi·ėr, *n.* [Fr. *rapière*; prob. from *raspiere*, a name given in contempt, meaning a rasper or poker.]
 1. originally, a slender, two-edged sword with a large cup hilt, used chiefly for thrusting.
 2. later, a light, sharp-pointed sword used only for thrusting.

rā′pi·ėred, *a.* provided with or wearing a rapier.

rap′ine, *n.* [Fr., from L. *rapina*, plundering.] the act of plundering; the seizing and carrying away of things by force; pillage; plunder.

rāp′ist, *n.* one who has committed rape.

rap′pāge, *n.* in ironworking, the process of loosening a pattern in the foundry sand previous to its withdrawal, effected by inserting the pointed end of an iron bar in a hole bored in the pattern and striking it heavily sideways with a hammer.

rap·pȧ·ree′, *n.* [Ir. *rapaire*, robber, or noisy fellow.]
 1. formerly, an Irish freebooting soldier.
 2. a plunderer or robber.

rap·pee′, *n.* [Fr. *râpé*, from *râper*, to rasp or scrape.] a strong snuff made from the coarser, darker tobacco leaves.

rap·pel′, *n.* [Fr. *rappeler*, to repeal, revoke.]
 1. in military usage, the beat of a drum, summoning to arms.
 2. an ancient musical instrument, still used in Egypt. It is of the rattle variety.
 3. a descent by a mountain climber, as down a sheer face of a cliff, by means of double rope belayed above and arranged around the climber's body so that the slide downward can be controlled.

rap·pel′, *v.i.*; rappelled, *pt., pp.*; rappelling, *ppr.* to descend by a rappel.

rap′pėr, *n.* 1. one who or that which raps; specifically, a door knocker.
 2. an oath or a lie. [Now Dial.]

rap′ping, *n.* 1. the act of making a sound by a rap.
 2. the sound of raps supposed to be produced by spirits through mediums; spirit rapping.
 3. same as *rappage.*

Rapp′ist, *n.* same as *Harmonist.*

rap·pōrt′ (*or Fr.* rȧ-pōr′), *n.* [Fr., from *rapporter*, to refer, from *re-*, again, and *apporter*, from L. *apportare*, to bring, from *ad-*, to, and *portare*, to carry.] relationship; especially, a close or sympathetic relationship; agreement; harmony.

rap·proche·ment′ (rȧ-prōsh-mäṅ′), *n.* [Fr.] an establishing or, especially, a restoring of harmony and friendly relations.

rap·sçal′liŏn, *n.* [from earlier *rascallion*, extension of *rascal.*] a rascal; a scamp; a rogue.

rapt, *v.* past tense and past participle of *rap*, to seize. [Obs. or Rare.]

rapt, *a.* [L. *raptus*, pp. of *rapere*, to snatch, seize.]
 1. carried away in a body or spirit (*to* heaven, etc.).
 2. carried away with joy, love, etc.; enraptured.
 3. completely absorbed or engrossed (*in* meditation, study, etc.).
 4. resulting from or showing rapture; as, a *rapt* look.

rapt, *v.t.* 1. to transport or ravish. [Obs.]
 2. to seize and carry away by force. [Obs.]

rapt, *n.* 1. an ecstasy; a trance. [Obs.]
 2. rape or rapine. [Obs.]

rap·tȧ·tō′ri·ăl, *a.* preying on other animals; predatory.

rap′tėr, *n.* a ravisher. [Obs.]

rap′tŏr, *n.* [L. *raptor.*] 1. a plunderer; a ravisher. [Obs.]
 2. a raptorial bird.

Rap·tō′rēṣ, *n.pl.* [LL., pl. of L. *raptor*, plunderer.] in a former classification, an order of birds of prey which live on other birds and animals and are characterized by a strong curved sharp-edged and sharp-pointed beak, robust short legs, with three toes before and one behind, and armed with long, strong, and crooked talons. The eagles, vultures, and falcons are examples.

rap·tō′ri·ăl, *a.* [L. *raptor*, plunderer, from pp. of *rapere*, to snatch; and *-ial.*]
 1. of or pertaining to the *Raptores.*
 2. adapted for seizing and holding prey; as, *raptorial* claws.
 3. living on prey; predatory: applied especially to birds.

rap′tūre, *n.* [L. *raptus*, *rapere*, to carry away.]
 1. a seizing by violence. [Obs.]
 2. the state of being carried away with joy, love, etc.; ecstasy.
 3. an expression of great joy, pleasure, etc.
 4. a carrying away or being carried away in body or spirit. [Rare.]
 5. an attack of intense excitement; delirium; hysterics; paroxysm. [Obs.]
 Syn.—ecstasy, bliss, delight, transport, joy.

rap′tūre, *v.t.*; raptured, *pt., pp.*; rapturing, *ppr.* to enrapture; to fill with ecstasy; as, a *raptured* soul. [Poet.]

rap′tūre of the deep, reduction in the ability to think clearly and react quickly, caused by the inhalation of too much nitrogen, as by deep-sea divers: so called from its initial intoxicating effect.

rap′tūr·īze, *v.t.* to enrapture; to put into a state of ecstasy. [Rare.]

rap′tūr·īze, *v.i.* to be in a state of rapture.

rap′tūr·ous, *a.* ecstatic; feeling or showing rapture; as, *rapturous* joy, pleasure, or delight.

rap′tūr·ous·ly, *adv.* with rapture; ecstatically.

rā′rȧ ā′vis, *pl.* **rā′rae ā′vēṣ,** [L., lit., strange bird.] a rarity; an unusual person; a most remarkable thing of any kind.

rāre, *a.* early. [Obs.]

rāre, *a.* [earlier *rear*; ME. *rere*; AS. *hrere*, lightly boiled.] nearly raw; not completely cooked; underdone; as, *rare* beef or mutton.

rāre, *a.*; *comp.* rarer; *superl.* rarest, [Fr.; L. *rarus*, thin, few, rare.]
 1. uncommon; not frequently found; scarce; unusual; as, a *rare* event; a *rare* phenomenon.
 Some claim that all musical aptitude is *rare* and exceptional. —Waldo S. Pratt.
 2. unusually excellent; remarkably fine.
 3. not close together; scattered. [Obs.]
 4. thin; porous; not dense; rarefied: applied especially to the atmosphere; as, mountain air is *rare.*

rāre′bit, *n.* [altered from (*Welsh*) *rabbit.*] Welsh rabbit; a dish of melted cheese over toast.

rāre ēarth, any of certain basic oxides much alike in physical and chemical properties; specifically, any of the oxides of the rare-earth metals.

rāre′-ēarth′ met′ălṣ, a group of rare metallic chemical elements with consecutive atomic numbers of 57 to 71 inclusive: also *rare-earth elements.*

rār′ee shōw, [from pronun. (by Savoyard showmen) of *rare show.*]
 1. a portable peep show.
 2. any street show.

rār·ē·fac′tion, *n.* [Fr.] a rarefying or being rarefied.

rār·ē·fac′tive, *a.* characterized by or causing rarefaction.

rār′ē·fī·ȧ·ble, *a.* capable of being rarefied.

rār′ē·fy̆, *v.t.* and *v.i.*; rarefied, *pt., pp.*; rarefying, *ppr.* [Fr. *raréfier*; L. *rarefacere*; *rarus*, rare, and *facere*, to make.]
 1. to make or become thin, or less dense.
 2. to make or become purer, or more refined.

rāre gas, in chemistry, any one of the group of inert gases.

rāre′ly, *adv.* 1. seldom; not often; infrequently; as, things *rarely* seen.
 2. beautifully; excellently; with consummate skill.
 3. uncommonly; exceptionally; extremely.

rāre′ness, *n.* the state or quality of being rare, or scarce, excellent, etc.

rāre′ness, *n.* the state of being rare, or underdone.

rāre′rīpe, *a.* [prob. from ME. *rathripe*, early ripe.] early ripe; ripe before others, or before the usual season.

rāre′rīpe, *n.* a fruit or vegetable that ripens

early; particularly, a kind of peach which ripens early.

rãr″i·fi·çā′tion, *n.* same as *rarefaction.*

rãr′i·fȳ, *v.t.* and *v.i.* same as *rarefy.*

rãr′i·ty, *n.* [L. *raritas.*]

1. the quality or condition of being rare; specifically, (a) uncommonness; scarcity; (b) excellence; (c) lack of density; thinness.

2. *pl.* **rãr′i·tieṣ,** something remarkable or valuable because of its scarcity.

räs, *n.* [Ar.] 1. in Ethiopia, a prince.

2. a headland, cape, or promontory: a term prefixed to the names of headlands on the coasts of Arabia and Africa.

ras·à·mä′là, *n.* [Malay.] a large timber tree, *Altingia excelsa,* of the East Indies, belonging to the witch-hazel family and allied to the sweet gum of the United States, growing to the height of one hundred feet before branching. It yields a valuable balsam.

rā′ṣȧnt, *a.* [Fr., from *raser,* to shave.] sweeping; so low as to sweep or graze: applied to a style of fortification in which the command of the works over the country is kept very low, so that the shot may scour or sweep the ground with more effect. [Rare.]

ras′çȧl, *n.* [ME. *rascaile;* OFr. *rascaille,* scrapings, dregs, the rabble, also refuse beasts, especially a worthless lean deer; from LL. *rasicare,* from L. *radere,* to shave or scrape, whence also Sp. *rascar,* It. *rascare,* to scrape.]

1. a scoundrel; a rogue; a scamp: sometimes used jokingly or affectionately; as, stop laughing, you little *rascal.*

2. in hunting, a lean or a worthless animal, as a deer.

3. one of the rabble. [Obs.]

ras′çȧl, *a.* 1. pertaining to the rabble. [Obs.]

2. low; dishonest; base. [Rare.]

ras′çȧl·dŏm, *n.* the state of being a rascal; the dominion of rascals.

ras′căl·ess, *n.* a woman rascal. [Rare.]

ras·çal′i·ty, *n.* 1. the rabble; the lower classes.

2. mean trickishness or dishonesty; the character or quality of being rascally or a rascal.

3. *pl.* **ras·çal′i·tieṣ,** a low, mean, or dishonest act.

ras·çal′liŏn (-yun), *n.* same as *rapscallion.*

ras′çăl·ly, *a.* of or like a rascal; base; dishonest; mean.

ras′çăl·ly, *adv.* in a rascally manner.

rāṣe, *v.t.*; rased, *pt., pp.*; rasing, *ppr.* [Fr. *raser,* from LL. *rasare,* freq. of L. *radere,* to scrape.]

1. to pass along the surface of; to scratch; to graze; to raze. [Obs.]

2. to erase; to scratch or rub out; to blot out; to cancel. [Obs.]

3. to level to the ground: in this sense now always spelled *raze.*

rāṣe, *n.* 1. a cancel; an erasure. [Obs.]

2. a slight wound; a scratch. [Obs.]

rash, *v.t.* [OFr. *esrachier;* Fr. *arracher,* to tear up or away, from L. *exradicare; ex,* out, and *radix,* a root.] to tear or pull violently; to tear asunder. [Obs.]

rash, *n.* [OFr. *rasche,* rash, scurf, itch, from L. *radere,* to shave.] an eruption of red spots on the skin, usually of a temporary nature.

rash, *n.* [It. *rascia.*] formerly, a kind of inferior cloth of silk and worsted fabric.

rash, *a.*; *comp.* rasher; *superl.* rashest, [ME. *rasch.*]

1. too hasty in acting or speaking; reckless; as, a *rash* commander.

2. characterized by too great haste or recklessness; as, *rash* words, *rash* measures.

3. requiring haste; urgent. [Obs.]

4. acting quickly; speedy. [Obs.]

5. so dry in the straw as to fall out with handling, as grain. [Brit. Dial.]

Syn.—adventurous, foolhardy, hasty, precipitate, thoughtless, headlong, headstrong, indiscreet, careless, incautious, reckless.—A man is *adventurous* who incurs risk or hazard from a love of the arduous and the bold; a man is *rash* who does it from the mere impulse of his feelings without counting the cost; a man is *foolhardy* who throws himself into danger in disregard or defiance of the consequences. *Reckless* is close in meaning to *rash,* but more directly indicates absence of care for, or regard to, consequences.

rash′ẽr, *n.* [prob. from obs. *rash,* to cut.] a thin slice of bacon or, rarely, ham, to be fried or broiled.

rash′ẽr, *n.* a vermilion-colored rockfish, *Sebastichthys miniatus,* found in California.

rash′fụl, *a.* rash. [Rare.]

rash′ly, *adv.* in a rash manner; hastily.

rash′ness, *n.* the state or quality of being rash.

Syn.—temerity, hastiness, precipitancy.

rā′ṣing ī′ron (-ũrn), in nautical usage, a tool for removing oakum and pitch from the seams of a wooden vessel before recalking.

Ras·kol′nik, *n.* [Russ., from *raskolo,* a division.] in Russia, a dissenter from the Orthodox Church.

Rà·sō′rēṣ, *n.pl.* [from L. *rasus,* pp. of *radere,* to scrape.] in a former classification, an order of birds equivalent to the *Gallinæ.*

rà·sō′ri·ȧl, *a.* characteristically scratching the ground to find food, as a chicken; gallinaceous.

ràsp, *v.t.*; rasped (raspt), *pt., pp.*; rasping, *ppr.* [OFr. *rasper;* Fr. *râper,* to scrape or rasp, like Sp. *raspar;* It. *raspare,* to scrape, grate, rasp, from O.H.G. *raspon,* to scrape together.]

1. to rub or scrape with or as with a rasp or file; as, to *rasp* wood to make it smooth; to *rasp* bones to powder.

2. to utter in a rough, grating tone.

3. to grate harshly upon; to irritate; as, the baby's crying *rasped* her nerves.

ràsp, *v.i.* 1. to rub roughly against something; to annoy by or as by grating; as, the boat *rasped* along the wharf; her nature *rasped* against his.

2. to make a rough, grating sound.

ràsp, *n.* 1. a type of rough file with raised points instead of lines.

2. a machine used in a process of reducing material to a pulp or mass by action resembling that of a rasp.

3. the feel of a rough surface; also, the sound of grating or rubbing rough surfaces together.

4. the act of rasping.

5. the lingual ribbon of a mollusk.

ràsp, *n.* the raspberry. [Now Chiefly Dial.]

ràsp, *v.i.* to belch. [Obs. or Dial.]

ràsp′à·tō·ry, *n.*; *pl.* **ràsp′à·tō·rieṣ,** a surgeon's rasp.

raṣp′ber″ry (raz′), *n.*; *pl.* **raṣp′ber″rieṣ,** [earlier *raspis berry,* from *rasp, raspis,* raspberry; prob. same word as ME. *raspis,* kind of wine.]

1. any of a group of prickly shrubs of the genus *Rubus,* belonging to the rose family. The plant grows wild in wooded places, and the present cultivated varieties are improvements of the original wild shrubs. The fruit is red, purple, or black, differing from the blackberry in having the mass of drupes constituting the fruit separable from the receptacle.

2. the small, juicy, edible fruit of this plant, used for desserts, preserves, and jellies.

3. [from rhyming slang *raspberry tart.*] a sound of derision, contempt, etc. made by expelling air forcibly so as to vibrate the tongue between the lips. [Slang.]

dwarf raspberry; a kind of raspberry, *Rubus triflorus,* resembling a blackberry.

flowering raspberry; one of two American shrubs: (a) *Rubus nutkanus,* bearing white flowers; (b) *Rubus odoratus,* with purplish flowers which persist during the summer months.

ràsped (ràspt), *a.* 1. affected with hoarseness, as the voice; nervous or irritated, as if grated upon by a rasp.

2. in bookbinding, having the cover edges rubbed down but not beveled.

ràsp′ẽr, *n.* 1. one who or that which rasps; a scraper.

2. in hunting, a high or difficult fence.

ràsp′ing, *a.* 1. scraping or rubbing with a rasp.

2. having a grating or scraping sound.

A great *rasping* laugh. —O. W. Holmes.

3. in hunting, difficult to leap one's horse over: said of a fence.

ràsp′ing·ly, *adv.* in a rasping manner.

ras′pis, *n.* the raspberry. [Obs.]

ràsp′y, *a.*; *comp.* raspier; *superl.* raspiest, 1. rasping; grating; resembling a rasp; especially, having a sound like that of a rasp; grating.

2. easily irritated.

rasse, *n.* [Javanese *rasa,* a sensation of the palate or nostrils; Sans. *rasa,* taste.] a carnivorous quadruped of the genus *Viverricula,* closely allied to the civet, spread over a great extent in Asia, including Java and other localities: a civetlike perfume is obtained from a glandular secretion of the rasse: also called *lesser civet.*

ras′tẽr, *n.* [G., a screen.] in television, the group of closely spaced parallel lines appearing on the cathode-ray tube when there is no incoming signal: the image is formed by modulating the brightness of the different parts of these lines.

rā′ṣūre (-zhũr), *n.* [L. *rasura,* a scraping.]

1. the act of scraping; the act of erasing.

2. the mark by which a letter, word, or any part of a writing or print is erased, effaced, or obliterated; an erasure. [Obs.]

rat, *n.* [ME. *ratte;* AS. *ræt;* akin to G. *ratte, ratze.*]

1. any of several kinds of black, brown, or gray, long-tailed rodents, resembling, but larger than, the mouse. Most of them belong to the genus *Rattus* (formerly, *Mus*). The name is popularly applied to certain other rodents, as the muskrat.

2. a small pad used in certain styles of women's coiffures to make the hair look thicker. [Colloq.]

3. a sneaky, contemptible person; specifically, (a) an informer; stool pigeon; (b) a worker who betrays or scabs on his fellow workers. [Slang.]

pouched rat; same as *pocket gopher.*

to smell a rat; to suspect a trick, plot, etc.

rat, *v.i.*; ratted, *pt., pp.*; ratting, *ppr.* 1. to hunt for rats, especially with dogs.

2. (a) to desert one's companions, especially one's fellow workers, as rats are reputed to desert a sinking ship; (b) to act as a stool pigeon. [Slang.]

rat, *v.t.* to displace union workers in; as, to *rat* a factory. [Slang.]

rä′tȧ, *n.* [Maori.] a large New Zealand forest tree, *Metrosideros robusta;* also, the wood of the tree, which is used by the Maoris for war clubs, canoe paddles, etc.

rāt·à·bil′i·ty, *n.* the state or quality of being ratable; ratableness.

rāt′à·ble, *a.* 1. capable of being rated, or estimated, etc.

2. liable or subjected by law to taxation; as, *ratable* property. [Brit.]

3. estimated proportionally; figured at a certain rate; proportional; as, *ratable* payments.

Also spelled *rateable.*

rāt′à·ble·ness, *n.* the state of being ratable; ratability.

rāt′à·bly, *adv.* by rate or proportion; proportionally.

rat·à·fee′, *n.* same as *ratafia.*

rat·à·fi′à, *n.* [Fr.; perhaps of Creole origin.]

1. a liqueur or cordial flavored with the kernels of almonds or fruit, particularly of cherries, apricots, and peaches: also written *ratifia.*

2. a fancy cake or sweet biscuit served with the drink; a macaroon: in full, *ratafia biscuit.* [Brit.]

rà·tan′, *n.* and *v.t.* same as *rattan.*

rat′à·ny, *n.* same as *rhatany.*

rat·à·plan′, *n.* [Fr.; echoic of drumming.] the beating of a drum, or a sound like this.

rat·à·plan′, *v.i.*; rataplanned, *pt., pp.*; rataplanning, *ppr.* to make a sound as of the beating of a drum.

rat·à·plan′, *v.t.* to make a sound on as of the beating of a drum.

rä″tà·touille′ (rä″tä-twē′), *n.* [Fr., from *ra-,* intensive, and *ta-* reduplicated syllable, and *touiller,* to mix, from L. *tudiculare,* to stir about, from *tudicula,* device for crushing olives, dim. of *tudes,* a hammer, from root of *tundere,* to strike.] a vegetable stew of eggplant, zucchini, tomatoes, etc. flavored with garlic and served hot or cold.

rat′bīte fē′vẽr (or **diṣ·ēaṣe′**), an infectious disease caused by certain spirochetes and transmitted by the bite of a rat: it is characterized by a bluish-red rash, attacks of fever, and muscular pain.

rat′çatch″ẽr, *n.* one whose work is catching rats.

ratch, *v.t.* to stretch; to rend. [Obs.]

ratch, *n.* [var. of *ratchet.*] a ratchet.

ratch′et, *n.* [Fr. *rochet,* from It. *rochetto,* bobbin, spindle, dim. of *rocca,* distaff.]

1. a hinged catch, or pawl, arranged so as to engage with a toothed wheel or bar whose teeth slope in one direction, thus imparting forward movement and preventing backward movement.

2. such a wheel or bar.

3. such a catch and wheel (or bar) as a unit.

ratch′et brāce, a boring brace in which the spindle carrying the bit is rotated by means of a ratchet wheel and a spring pawl on a hand lever. It is used for drilling a hole in a narrow place where there is not sufficient room to use the common brace.

ratch′et drill, a drill whose rotatory movement is derived from a ratchet and pawl actuated by a lever.

ratch'et wheel (hwēl), a wheel having inclined teeth for receiving a ratchet or detent, by which motion is imparted or arrested. The teeth are of such shape as to revolve and pass the detent in one direction only. Also called *ratchet.*

ratch'et wrench (rench), a wrench operated by a ratchet and pawl, so that it may be turned continuously, without removal from the bolt or nut to which it is applied, by a backward and forward movement of the handle.

rāte, *n.* [ME.; OFr.; L. *rata* (supply *pars*, part), from *ratus*, reckoned.]
1. the amount, degree, etc. of anything in relation to units of something else; as, a *rate* of forty miles per hour.
2. price or amount stated or fixed on anything with relation to a standard; a fixed ratio; a settled proportion; as, the *rate* of interest is six per cent.
3. settled and regular allowance; as, a daily *rate* of provisions. [Obs.]
4. a price or value; specifically, the cost per unit of some commodity, service, etc.; as, an electricity *rate*, insurance *rate*.
5. speed of movement or action; as, he read at a moderate *rate*.
6. a class; rank; as, of the first *rate*.
7. amount; quantity. [Obs.]
8. standard of action, conduct, etc.; particular style in which anything is done; manner of doing anything. [Obs.]
9. a local property tax: often in the plural; as, parish *rates*, town *rates*. [Brit.]
10. in the navy, (a) the order or class of a ship, which is called first, second, third, etc. *rate*, according to its size, strength, etc.; (b) classification, as of men, according to rank and pay.
11. in horology, the gain or loss of a timepiece in a unit of time.
at any rate; (a) in any event; (b) at least; anyway.
Syn.—proportion, ratio, price, degree, valuation.

rāte, *v.t.*; rated, *pt., pp.*; rating, *ppr.* 1. to estimate the value of; to value; to appraise; to set a certain value on; to value at a certain price or degree of excellence.

Instead of *rating* the man by his performances, we too frequently *rate* the performance by the man. —Johnson.

2. to fix the relative scale, rank, or position of; as, to *rate* a ship, to *rate* a seaman.
3. to determine the rate of in respect to a variation from a standard: said of a timepiece; as, to *rate* a chronometer.
4. to consider; esteem; as, he is *rated* as an important national figure.
5. to determine the rates for shipping (goods), as by rail or air.
6. to deserve; as, he *rates* the best. [Colloq.]
Syn.—compute, calculate, estimate, value, appraise.

rāte, *v.i.* 1. to be classed or ranked; as, the ship *rates* as a ship of the line.
2. to have value, status, or rating.

rāte, *v.t.* and *v.i.*; rated, *pt., pp.*; rating, *ppr.* [ME. *raten*, *araten*; prob. from OFr. *rater*, *areter*, to scold, from L. *ad-*, to, and *reputare*, to count: but cf. Sw. *rata*, to find fault, to blame; Norw. *rata*, to reject.] to chide with vehemence; to reprove; to scold severely; to censure violently.

rāte, *v.t.* to ratify. [Obs.]

rāte'ȧ·ble, *a.* same as *ratable.*

rāte'ȧ·bly, *adv.* same as *ratably.*

rāte bāse, in economics, the value of public property, as appraised by an authorized body in order to fix upon reasonable rates.

rāte çap, an outlet cap affixed to a gas meter in order to regulate the flow of gas in units of time.

rä'tel, *n.* [S. Afr. D., short for *rateldas*, from D. *raat*, a honeycomb, and *das*, a badger.] a carnivorous quadruped of the genus *Mellivora*, native to India and Africa. It is somewhat like a badger.

rāte'pāy"ēr, *n.* one who pays rates, or local taxes. [Brit.]

-rāt'ēr, a combining form used in hyphenated compounds, meaning *one of a* (specified) *rate*, or *class*, as in second-*rater*.

rāt'ēr, *n.* one who scolds or chides.

rāt'ēr, *n.* one who sets a value or makes an estimate; an appraiser.

rat'fish, *n.* an American cartilaginous fish of the Pacific coast, the *Chimæra colliæi*.

rath, *n.* [Ir. *rath*, a hill, mount, or fortress.] in ancient Ireland, an earthwork or fortification.

rath, *a.* and *adv.* rathe. [Obs. or Poet.]

rāthe, *a.* [ME.; AS. *hræth*, var. of *hræd*, quick, speedy, after *hræthe*, *hrathe*, *adv.*, speedily.]
1. quick; prompt; eager. [Obs. or Poet.]
2. coming or happening early in the day, year, etc.; especially, blooming or ripening early in the season: said of flowers, plants, etc. [Obs. or Poet.]

rāthe, *adv.* 1. quickly; promptly. [Obs. or Poet.]
2. early, or too early, in the day, season, etc. [Obs. or Poet.]

rat hāre, a small rodent; a pika.

rath'ēr (*or* rä'thēr), *adv.* [ME., comp. of *rathe*, quickly; AS. *hrathe*, comp. *hrathor*.]
1. more readily or willingly; preferably; as, he would *rather* go than stay.
2. more quickly; sooner. [Obs. or Brit. Dial.]
3. with more justice, logic, reason, etc.; as, I, *rather* than you, should take the risk.
4. more accurately; more precisely; as, it was in the morning, or *rather*, the early afternoon.
5. on the contrary; quite conversely; as, we have not lost; *rather*, we have won.
6. somewhat; to some degree; as, I *rather* enjoy singing.
7. certainly; assuredly: used as an answer. [Chiefly Brit. Colloq.]
had rather; would choose to; would prefer that.
the rather; especially; for better reason; all the more.

räths'kel·lēr (räts' *or* rath'skel-), *n.* [G., from *rat*, council, town hall, and *keller*, cellar.] a restaurant of the German type that serves beer, whisky, wine, etc., usually below the street level.

rat"i·fi·cā'tion, *n.* [Fr.; ML. *ratificatio*, from pp. of *ratificare.*] a ratifying or being ratified; approval; sanction; confirmation.

rat'i·fī·ēr, *n.* a person or group that ratifies.

rat'i·fȳ, *v.t.*; ratified, *pt., pp.*; ratifying, *ppr.* [Fr. *ratifier*; ML. *ratificare*, from L. *ratus*, firm, and *facere*, to make.] to approve or confirm; especially, to give formal sanction to; as, to *ratify* an agreement or treaty.
Syn.—confirm, sanction, authorize.—To *ratify* is to make valid, usually by authoritative approval; to *sanction* implies countenance or support; to *confirm* is to validate by formal assent.

rat"i·hȧ·bi'tion (-bish'un), *n.* [L. *ratihabitio* (-*onis*).] ratification; approval.

ra·ti·né' (rat-ȧ-nā'), *n.* [Fr., frizzed, tufted: of the nap.] a coarse, loosely woven fabric of cotton, wool, rayon, etc., with a nubby or knotty surface.

rāt'ing, *n.* [see *rate* (to appraise).] 1. a rank, class, or grade, as of enlisted men in an army or navy.
2. a placement in a certain rank or class.
3. an expression in horsepower, etc. of the working power of an engine or other machine.
4. an evaluation of the credit or financial standing of a businessman, firm, etc.
6. an amount determined as a rate, or grade.

rāt'ing, *n.* [see *rate* (to scold).] a rebuke; a scolding; a tongue lashing.

rā'tiō (-shō *or* -shi-ō), *n.*; *pl.* **rā'tiōṣ,** [L., account, reckoning, reason.]
1. a fixed relation in degree, number, etc. between two similar things; proportion; as, in our class there is a *ratio* of three boys to two girls.
2. in finance, the relative value of gold and silver in a currency system based on both.
3. in mathematics, the quotient of one quantity divided by another of the same kind, and usually expressed as a fraction.
direct ratio; ratio considered directly; as, the lengths of two lines are in *direct ratio* to the numbers expressing those lengths.

ra·ti·oc'i·nāte (rash-i-os'), *v.i.*; ratiocinated, *pt., pp.*; ratiocinating, *ppr.* [L. *ratiocinari*, from *ratio*, reason.] to reason; especially, to reason using formal logic.

ra·ti·oc·i·nā'tion, *n.* [L. *ratiocinatio.*]
1. the act or process of reasoning, or of deducing consequences from premises.
2. an instance of reasoning.

ra·ti·oc'i·nā·tive, *a.* of or characterized by ratiocination.

ra·ti·oc'i·nȧ·tō·ry, *a.* ratiocinative. [Rare.]

ra'tion (rash'un *or* rā'shun), *n.* [Fr., from L. *ratio* (-*onis*), proportion.]
1. a fixed portion; share; allowance.
2. a fixed allowance or allotment of food or provisions.
3. a fixed daily allowance of food for one person (or one animal) in an army or navy.
4. [*pl.*] something to eat; food. [Military Slang.]

ra'tion, *v.t.* 1. to give a ration or rations to.
2. to distribute (food, clothing, etc.) in rations, as in times of scarcity.

ra'tion·ăl (rash'un-), *a.* [L. *rationalis.*]
1. of, based on, or derived from reasoning; as, *rational* powers.
2. able to reason; reasoning; as, an infant is not yet *rational.*
3. showing reason; not foolish or silly; sensible; as, a *rational* argument.
4. in mathematics, designating a number or quantity expressible without a radical sign as an integer or as a quotient of an integer.
Syn.—reasonable.

ra'tion·ăl, *n.* 1. a rational being. [Rare.]
2. the breastplate of a Jewish high priest.

ra·tion·ale' (rash-un-al' *or* -ā'lē), *n.* [L., neut. of *rationalis*, rational.]
1. the fundamental reasons, or rational basis, of something.
2. a statement, exposition, or explanation of reasons or principles.

ra'tion·ăl·iṣm, *n.* [*rational* and *-ism.*]
1. the principle or practice of accepting reason as the only authority in determining one's opinions or course of action.
2. in philosophy, the theory that the reason, or intellect, is the true source of knowledge, rather than the senses.
3. in theology, the doctrine that rejects revelation and the supernatural, and makes reason the sole source of knowledge.

ra'tion·ăl·ist, *n.* one who believes in or practices rationalism.

ra"tion·ăl·is'tiç, ra"tion·ăl·is'tiç·ăl, *a.* of rationalism or rationalists.

ra"tion·ăl·is'tiç·ăl·ly, *adv.* in a rationalistic manner.

ra·tion·al'i·ty, *n.* [LL. *rationalitas.*]
1. the quality or condition of being rational; the power or faculty of reasoning; possession of reason; reasonableness.
2. *pl.* **ra·tion·al'i·tieṣ,** a rational act, belief, etc.

ra"tion·ăl·i·zā'tion, *n.* a rationalizing or being rationalized.

ra'tion·ăl·īze, *v.t.*; rationalized, *pt., pp.*; rationalizing, *ppr.* 1. to make rational; to make conform to reason.
2. to explain or interpret on rational grounds.
3. to apply modern methods of efficiency to (an industry, agriculture, etc.).
4. in mathematics, to remove the radical signs from (an equation) without changing the value.
5. in psychology, to devise superficially rational, or plausible, explanations or excuses for (one's acts, beliefs, desires, etc.), usually without being aware that these are not the real motives.

ra'tion·ăl·īze, *v.i.* 1. to think in a rational or rationalistic manner.
2. to rationalize one's acts, beliefs, etc.

ra'tion·ăl·ī·zēr, *n.* one who rationalizes.

ra'tion·ăl·ly, *adv.* in a rational manner; reasonably.

ra'tion·ăl·ness, *n.* the state of being rational or consistent with reason.

Rȧ·tī'tae, *n.pl.* [L. *ratis*, a raft. a division of birds comprising all that cannot fly, such as the ostriches, emus, and cassowaries. It is characterized by the fact that the sternum, or breastbone, has no median ridge or keel for the attachment of the great pectoral or wing muscles. The breastbone is flat, or raftlike, hence the name of the order.

rat'īte, *a.* pertaining to the *Ratitæ.*

rat'īte, *n.* any bird belonging to the *Ratitæ.*

rat'line, rat'lin, *n.* [folk-etym. form; earlier also *ratling*; Late ME. *radeling*, from *raddle*, to interlace, with reference to the appearance of the shrouds.]
1. any of the small, relatively thin pieces of rope which join the shrouds of a ship and serve as a ladder for climbing the rigging.
2. the light, tarred rope used for this.

rȧ·tōōn', *n.* [Sp. *retoño*; Hind. *ratun.*] a shoot growing from the root of a plant (especially the sugar cane) that has been cut down: also spelled *ratoon.*

rȧ·tōōn′, *v.i.*; ratooned, *pt., pp.*; ratooning, *ppr.* to grow new shoots, or grow as a new shoot, from the root of a plant that has been cut down: also spelled *rattoon.*

rat rāce, a frantic scurry or mad scramble. [Slang.]

rats′bāne, *n.* rat poison; especially, trioxide of arsenic.

rat snāke, a large snake, especially *Ptyas mucosus* of India, which kills rats, fowls, etc., and often enters houses.

rat′s′-tāil, *n.* same as *rattail.*

rat′tāil, *n.* 1. a horse's tail when bare.
2. an excrescence growing from the pastern to the middle of the shank of a horse.
3. a fish, the grenadier fish.
4. in botany, any plant having flower spikes resembling the tail of a rat, as the common plantain, *Plantago major.*

rat′tāil, *a.* slender, round, and tapering.

rat′-tāiled, *a.* 1. having a tail resembling that of a rat.
2. having a slender, tapering form like that of a rat's tail.
rat-tailed larva; the grub of *Eristalis tenax*, the drone fly, which inhabits stagnant water, and breathes by means of a telescopic, tubular tail.
rat-tailed serpent; the fer-de-lance.
rat-tailed shrew; the Indian shrew: also called *musk shrew, muskrat.*

rat·tan′, rȧ·tan′, *n.* [Malay *rotan.*]
1. any of various species of *Calamus* and *Rhapis*, climbing palms having perennial, long, round, solid, jointed, unbranching stems, extremely tough and pliable.
2. a stem of any of these trees used in making wickerwork, chair seats, walking sticks, thongs, ropes, cables, etc.
3. a small cane or walking stick made of rattan.
ground rattan; a rattan palm having small and tough stems, as the *Rhapis flabelliformis.*

rat·tan′, rȧ·tan′, *v.t.* [Malay *rotan.*]
1. to cover with or construct of rattan, as a chair seat.
2. to punish with or as with a rattan cane.

rat-tat′, *n.* a sharp knocking or beating, as the rattle of a drum.

rat·teen′, *n.* [Fr. *ratine.*] a heavy, twilled woolen cloth like frieze. [Obs.]

rat′ten, *n.* a rat. [Brit. Dial.]

rat′ten, *v.t.* and *v.i.* [lit., to play a rat's trick upon, from prov. *ratten*, a rat.] to destroy or remove machinery, tools, etc. in order to compel (an employer) to agree to certain trade-union demands. [Brit. Slang.]

rat′tẽr, *n.* 1. (a) a person hired to catch or destroy rats; (b) a dog that is especially skilled at catching rats.
2. a betrayer or deserter. [Slang.]

rat·ti·net′, *n.* [dim. of *ratteen*; Fr. *ratine.*] a woolen cloth similar to, but thinner than, ratteen.

rat′ting, *n.* 1. the act of deserting one's party and going over to the opposite party. [Brit.]
2. the act of working for less than the established prices; also, the act of taking a striker's place. [Slang.]
3. the sport of setting a dog on rats in a rat pit.

rat′tish, *a.* 1. of or infested with rats.
2. like or characteristic of a rat.

rat′tle, *v.i.*; rattled, *pt., pp.*; rattling, *ppr.* [ME. *ratelen*; prob. of echoic origin.]
1. to make a series of sharp, short sounds in quick succession; as, the window *rattles* in the wind.
2. to go or move with such sounds; as, the wagon *rattled* over the stones.
3. to talk rapidly and incessantly; to chatter (often with *on*).

rat′tle, *v.t.* 1. to cause to make a rattling sound, or a rapid succession of sharp sounds; as, to *rattle* a chain.
2. to stun with noise; to affect with sharp sounds rapidly repeated. [Obs.]
3. to utter or perform rapidly; as, to *rattle* off a message.
4. to scold; to rail at clamorously. [Obs.]
5. to confuse; to cause to become irritated or agitated; to disconcert. [Colloq.]

rat′tle, *n.* 1. a rapid succession of sharp, short sounds; as, the *rattle* of a drum.
2. a rapid succession of words sharply uttered; loud, rapid talk; a noisy uproar.
3. a rattling noise made by air passing through the mucus of a partly closed throat, often heard in a dying person.
4. (a) a series of horny rings at the end of a rattlesnake's tail, used to produce a rattling sound; (b) any of these.
5. a device, especially a baby's toy, intended to rattle when shaken.
6. a person who talks rapidly, noisily, or foolishly.
7. any of various plants; specifically, (a) *Pedicularis palustris*, a lousewort; (b) *Rhinanthus crista-galli*, the yellow rattle.

rat′tle, *v.t.* to provide with ratlines, as the rigging of a vessel.

rat′tle·box, *n.* 1. a plant of the genus *Crotalaria.*
2. a plant, the yellow rattle.
3. a child's rattle.

rat′tle·brāin, *n.* a silly, talkative person.

rat′tle·brāined, *a.* of, or having the nature of, a rattlebrain; silly; frivolous; harebrained.

rat′tle·head (-hed), *n.* a silly chatterer.

rat′tle·head″ed, *a.* noisy; giddy; unsteady.

rat′tle·pāte, *n.* same as *rattlebrain.*

rat′tle·pāt″ed, *a.* same as *rattlebrained.*

rat′tlẽr, *n.* 1. one who or that which rattles.
2. a rattlesnake.

rat′tle·snāke, *n.* any of various poisonous American snakes of the family *Crotalidæ*, having a series of articulated horny rings at the end of the tail that make a rattling sound when shaken. There are several species, including *Crotalus horridus*, the best-known

RATTLESNAKE (2–8 ft. long)

species; *Crotalus durissus*, the striped rattlesnake; *Crotalus dryinus*, the wood rattlesnake; and *Crotalus miliarius*, the ground rattlesnake. All these species inhabit America. The *Crotalus horridus* sometimes attains a length of eight feet.

rat′tle·snāke fẽrn, an American fern, *Botrychium virginianum*, having a panicle of spore cases somewhat resembling the rattles of a rattlesnake.

rat′tle·snāke grȧss, a tall American marsh grass, *Glyceria canadensis*: called also *quaking grass.*

rat′tle·snāke mȧs′tẽr, any American plant the juice of which was once thought to cure the bite of the rattlesnake; specifically, *Agave virginica, Eryngium yuccæfolium*, or button snakeroot, and *Liatris squarrosa*, or blazing star.

rat′tle·snāke plan′tāin, a variety of orchid with spotted leaves and yellowish-white flower spikes.

rat′tle·snāke rōōt, any of a number of related plants with composite flowers of various colors and a thick, bitter root, formerly considered a cure for snake bite.

rat′tle·snāke weed, 1. any of a number of related plants, especially a variety of the hawk weed, *Hieracium venosum*, with one purple-veined leaf to a stem.
2. a rattlesnake plantain.

rat′tle·trap, *n.* [*rattle* and *trap* (carriage).]
1. anything worn out, rickety, or rattling, especially such a wagon, automobile, etc.
2. (a) a person who talks much; (b) the mouth: now usually *trap.* [Slang.]

rat′tle·weed, *n.* any plant of the genus *Astragalus.*

rat′tle·wŏrt, *n.* a leguminous plant, *Crotalaria sagittalis*, having a coriaceous inflated pod in which the seeds rattle when dry: also called *rattlebox.*

rat′tling, *a.* 1. that rattles.
2. very fast, good, lively, etc.; as, a *rattling* pace. [Colloq.]

rat′tling, *adv.* very; as, *rattling* good. [Colloq.]

rat′tly, *a.* that rattles or tends to rattle; noisy.

rat·tōōn′, *n.* and *v.i.* same as *ratoon.*

rat′trap, *n.* 1. a trap for catching rats.
2. a hopeless situation; a desperate predicament.

rat′ty, *a.*; *comp.* rattier; *superl.* rattiest, 1. of or like rats.
2. full of rats.
3. dilapidated. [Slang.]

rau′ci·ty, *n.* [L. *raucus*, hoarse, rough.] a raucous quality or condition.

rau′çous, *a.* harsh; hoarse; rough-sounding.

rau′çous·ly, *adv.* in a raucous manner; with a harsh sound.

raught (rąt), *v.* obsolete past tense and past participle of *reach.*

Rau·wol′fi·ȧ, *n.* [after Leonhard *Rauwolf* 17th-c. German botanist.] a genus of tropical shrubs of the dogbane family, with opposite or whorled leaves and corymbose flowers: some of its species yield valuable medicines.

rav′ăge, *n.* [Fr., from *ravir*, to rob or carry off.]
1. the act or practice of violently destroying.
2. desolation; destruction; devastation from any cause; ruin; havoc; as, the *ravages* of time.

rav′ăge, *v.t.*; ravaged, *pt., pp.*; ravaging, *ppr.* [Fr. *ravager.*] to spoil; to plunder; to pillage; to sack; to waste by violent force; to devastate by any means; as, fields *ravaged* by swarms of locusts.

rav′ăge, *v.i.* to commit ravages.

rav′ȧ·gẽr, *n.* one who or that which ravages; a plunderer; a spoiler.

rāve, *n.* [etym. unknown.] an upper side piece of timber of the body of a cart or other vehicle.

rāve, *v.t.* to rive; to tear. [Obs. or Dial.]

rāve, *v.i.*; raved, *pt., pp.*; raving, *ppr.* [OFr. *raver*, to be delirious, to revel.]
1. to talk incoherently or wildly, as a delirious or demented person.
2. to talk with excessive enthusiasm (*about* someone or something).
3. to rage or roar, as a storm.

rāve, *v.t.* to utter incoherently or with excessive enthusiasm; as, to *rave* heresy.

rāve, *n.* 1. the act or condition of raving.
2. a raving action or speech.
3. (a) an excessively enthusiastic commendation: often used attributively, as, *rave* reviews; (b) an infatuation. [Slang.]

rāve, *v.* obsolete past tense of *rive.*

rāve′hook, *n.* in nautical usage, an implement with a hooked end, used in ship carpentry for cleaning and dressing cracks and joints to be filled with oakum.

rav′el, *v.t.*; raveled *or* ravelled, *pt., pp.*; raveling *or* ravelling, *ppr.* [M.D. *ravelen* (D. *rafelen*, to snatch away).]
1. originally, to make complicated or tangled; to involve.
2. to separate the parts, especially threads, of; untwist; unweave; unravel.
3. to make clear; to disentangle.
Syn.—disentangle, separate, undo, untwist, unwind.

rav′el, *v.i.* 1. to become separated into its parts, especially threads; to fray (usually with *out*).
2. to become complicated or tangled. [Rare.]

rav′el, *n.* 1. a raveled part, especially a thread; a raveling.
2. a tangled mass or complication.

rav′el·ẽr, rav′el·lẽr, *n.* one who ravels.

rave′lin (rav′), *n.* [Fr. *ravelin*, from It. *ravellino, revellino*; prob. from L. *re*, back, and *vallum*, a rampart set with palisades.] a detached fortification with two embankments projecting outward and forming a salient angle.

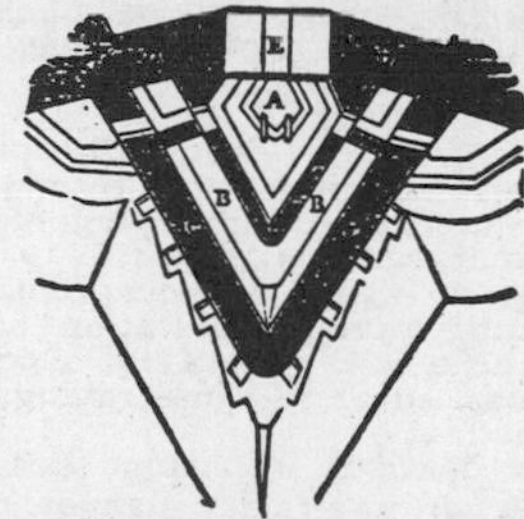

RAVELIN
A, redout; BB, ravelin; CC, ditch; DD, main ditch; E, passage of access from fortress to ravelin

rav′el·ing, rav′el·ling, *n.* 1. the act of something that ravels or is raveled.
2. anything raveled; especially, a thread raveled from a knitted or woven material.

rav′el·ly, *a.* raveled or inclined to ravel.

rā′ven (-vn), *n.* [AS. *hræfn, hrefn* or *ræfn*; Ice. *hrafn*; Dan. *ravn.* Prob. from its cry.] a large bird, *Corvus corax*, of the crow family, having lustrous black feathers and a straight, sharp beak, inhabiting the north temperate regions of the world, characterized by intelligence and the power of uttering articulate sounds in a hoarse ominous voice.

Quoth the *raven*, Nevermore!
—Edgar Allan Poe.

rā'ven (-vn), *a.* very black and lustrous; as, *raven* locks.

rav'en (-n), *v.t.*; ravened, *pt.*, *pp.*; ravening, *ppr.* [OFr. *ravine*; L. *rapina*, plunder, rapine.]
1. to devour with great eagerness; to eat with voracity.
Like rats that *raven* down their proper bane.
—Shak.
2. to obtain or capture by violence; to seize forcibly. [Obs.]
Also spelled *ravin*.

rav'en, *v.i.* 1. to prowl hungrily; to search for prey or plunder.
Benjamin shall *raven* as a wolf.
—Gen. xlix. 27.
2. to devour food or prey greedily.
3. to have a voracious appetite.
Also spelled *ravin*.

rav'en, *n.* ravin.

Rav·e·nā'lȧ, *n.* [native name.] a genus of trees containing only two species, the best-known being *Ravenala madagascariensis*, a fine large, palmlike, musaceous tree of Madagascar, with leaves six to eight feet long. It is called traveler's tree because of the refreshing water found in the cuplike sheaths of the leafstalks. Its leaves are used for thatch and the leafstalks for partitions. The seeds are edible and the blue pulpy fiber surrounding them yields an essential oil.

rav'en·ẽr, *n.* 1. one who ravens or plunders.
2. a bird of prey, as the owl, kite, hawk, or vulture. [Obs.]

rav'en·ing, *a.* 1. preying with rapacity; voraciously devouring; as, a *ravening* wolf.
2. demented; mad.

rav'en·ing, *n.* ravin.

rav'en·ing·ly, *adv.* in a ravening manner.

rav'en·ous, *a.* [OFr. *ravinos*, from *ravine*; see *raven*, v.]
1. greedily hungry; voracious.
2. very eager for gratification of some desire; as, *ravenous* for praise.
3. very rapacious.

rav'en·ous·ly, *adv.* in a ravenous manner.

rav'en·ous·ness, *n.* the state of being ravenous.

rā'ven·ry, *n.* 1. a place where ravens roost or breed.
2. a place where ravens are bred or kept.

Rav·en·sā'rȧ, *n.* [Malagasy *ravin-dzara*, a good leaf.] a genus of the laurel family, found chiefly in Madagascar: its bark, leaves, and fruit are aromatic and used for spice. The kernel of the fruit of *Ravensara aromatica* is called clove nutmeg.

rā'ven's-duck, *n.* [G. *ravenstuch*.] a species of hempen sailcoth: also called *ravens*.

rā'ven·stōne, *n.* a place of execution; a gallows. [Poet.]

rāv'ẽr, *n.* one who raves or is furious.

rav'in, rav'ine, *n.* [ME. and OFr. *ravine*; see *raven*, v.]
1. a violent preying or plundering; rapine.
2. anything captured; prey or plunder.
Also spelled *raven*.

rav'in, *a.* ravenous. [Obs.]

rav'in, rav'ine, *v.t.* and *v.i.* to raven.

rȧ·vīne', *n.* [Fr. *ravine*, a ravine, a hollow worn by floods, from L. *rapina*, rapine, violence, from *rapere*, to seize or carry away.]
1. a raging torrent. [Obs.]
2. a long, narrow, deep gully, or hollow, in the earth's surface, worn by a stream or flood of water; a large gully; a gorge.

rȧ·vīne' deer, same as *chikara*.

rāv'ing, *a.* 1. raging; delirious; frenzied.
2. exciting raving admiration or praise; notable; as, a *raving* beauty. [Colloq.]

rāv'ing, *adv.* so as to cause raving; as, he's *raving* mad.

rāv'ing, *n.* delirious, incoherent speech.

rāv'ing·ly, *adv.* in a raving manner.

rav·i·ō'li, *n.pl.* [*usually construed as sing.*] [It., pl. of *ravi(u)olo*, from dial. *rava*; ult., from L. *rapum*, turnip, beet.] small casings of dough, often square, containing highly seasoned chopped meat and, sometimes, spinach, cooked and served usually in a savory sauce.

rav'ish, *v.t.*; ravished (-isht), *pt.*, *pp.*; ravishing, *ppr.* [Fr. *ravissant*, ppr. of *ravir*, to carry away; L. *rapere*, to seize.]
1. to seize and carry away by violence and force.
2. to have sexual intercourse with (a woman) by force and against her consent; to rape; to deflower.
3. to carry away with emotion; to fill with great joy or delight; to transport; to enrapture.

Syn.—charm, entrance, enrapture, violate, force, deflower.

rav'ish, *n.* rapture; ravishment. [Obs.]

rav'ish·ẽr, *n.* one who ravishes; one who or that which takes by force.

rav'ish·ing, *a.* causing great joy; charming; enchanting; delighting; entrancing; captivating.

rav'ish·ing, *n.* ravishment.

rav'ish·ing·ly, *adv.* in a ravishing manner.

rav'ish·ment, *n.* 1. the act of forcing a woman to have sexual intercourse without her consent; rape.
2. a being carried away with delight or joy; rapture; transport of delight; ecstasy; pleasing effect on the mind or senses.
3. the act of seizing and carrying away forcibly; abduction; as, the *ravishment* of children from their parents, of a ward from his guardian, or of a wife from her husband.

rạw, *a.* [AS. *hreaw*, *hræw*; akin to G. *roh*, raw. Same root as L. *crudus*, raw, having originally had an initial guttural.]
1. not roasted, boiled, or cooked; not prepared by heat; as, *raw* meat.
2. with the skin rubbed or torn off; bare, sore, and inflamed; as, a *raw* cut.
3. unseasoned; inexperienced; not yet developed or trained; having no skill; as, *raw* recruits in the army or navy
4. bleak; chilly; uncomfortably cold and damp; as, a *raw* day; a *raw*, cold climate.
5. in its natural condition; not changed by art, dilution, manufacture, aging, etc.; as, *raw* silk, *raw* whisky.
6. indecent; bawdy; somewhat obscene. [Colloq.]
7. harsh or unfair; as, he received *raw* treatment. [Slang.]
8. in ceramics, unbaked.
raw edge; the unhemmed end or edge of cloth.
raw material; material of any kind in its original or natural state, not yet subjected to manufacturing processes; as, cotton in the bale is the *raw material* of cotton fabrics.
raw silk; silk reeled from the cocoon but not yet spun.
Syn.—uncooked, unprepared, unfinished, unripe, crude, unseasoned, inexperienced, fresh, green, unpracticed, untried, bare, exposed, galled, chill, bleak, piercing.

rạw, *n.* 1. in commerce, an unmanufactured or uncooked article, as oysters, sugar, etc.
2. a part of the body made raw by chafing; a fresh sore place; a raw or inflamed spot on the body.
in the raw; (a) in the natural or original state; without cultivation, refinement, etc.; (b) naked; nude.

rạw'bōne, *a.* rawboned. [Obs.]

rạw'bōned, *a.* having little flesh or fat covering the bones; gaunt; lean.

rạw'head (-hed), *n.* a specter mentioned to frighten children; as, *rawhead* and bloody bones.

rạw'hīde, *n.* 1. an untanned or only partially tanned cattle hide.
2. a whip made of this.

rạw'ish, *a.* somewhat raw.

rạw'ish·ness, *n.* the state of being rawish.

rạw'ly, *adv.* in a raw manner (in several senses).

rạw'ness, *n.* the state of being raw in any sense; as, the *rawness* of flesh.

rax, *v.t.* and *v.i.* to reach; to reach for something. [Scot. and Brit. Dial.]

rāy, *n.* [L. *raia*, a ray.] in zoology, any one of the many fishes of the class *Elasmobranchii*, order *Batoidei*, as the electric ray, skate, etc., with the body flattened dorsally and ventrally, excessively developed pectoral fins radiating from its sides and head, the eyes located on the upper surface of the body, and the clefts of the gills and mouth on the under side. The tail is very slender and whiplike in form and there is no anal fin. Some types are viviparous while others are oviparous.

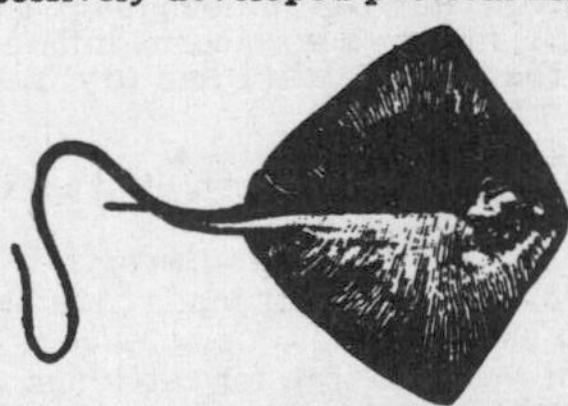

STING RAY (3 ft. wide)

rāy, *n.* [OFr. *ray*, from L. *radius*, a ray or beam.]
1. (a) any of the thin lines, or beams, of light that appear to come from a bright source; (b) a graphic representation of one of these, as in heraldry.
2. any of several lines radiating from a center; a radius.
3. a disclosure of mental or spiritual enlightenment; as, a *ray* of intelligence.
4. a tiny amount; a slight trace; as, a *ray* of hope.
5. in botany, (a) a ray flower; (b) any of the pedicels, or flower stalks, of an umbel; (c) a medullary ray.
6. in physics, (a) a stream of particles given off by a radioactive substance; (b) a straight line along which any part of a wave of radiant energy is regarded as traveling from its source to any given point.
7. in zoology, (a) any of the bony spines supporting the fin membrane of a fish; (b) a radiating limb, as the arm of a starfish; (c) one of the longitudinal veins in the wing of an insect.
8. a look; a glance; sight. [Archaic.]
9. in geometry, an unlimited straight line.
Becquerel rays; invisible rays emitted by radioactive substances, as uranium, radium, thorium, etc.: named after their discoverer, Henri Becquerel.

rāy, *v.i.*; rayed, *pt.*, *pp.*; raying, *ppr.* 1. to shine forth in rays.
2. to radiate.

rāy, *v.t.* 1. to send out in rays; to emit.
2. to subject to the action of X rays, radium rays, etc., as in the treatment of disease.
3. to irradiate.
4. to supply with radiating lines.

rāy, *v.t.* 1. to foul; to beray. [Obs.]
2. to array. [Obs.]

rä'yȧh, *n.* [Ar. *raiya*, a peasant.] a raia.

rāyed, *a.* 1. adorned or ornamented with rays; having rays; striped; radiated.
2. in botany, radiate.

rāy flow'ẽr, any of the flowers around the margin of the head of certain composite flowers, as the daisy: also *ray floret*.

rāy grȧss, *Lolium perenne*, rye grass; darnel.

Rāy'lēigh wave, [after J. W. Strutt (1842–1919), 3d Baron *Rayleigh*, Eng. physicist who first described them.] any of the undulating surface waves present in a solid having uniform properties; especially, any such wave on the earth's surface, caused by an earthquake.

rāy'less, *a.* 1. without rays of light; dark; gloomy; not illuminated.
2. without sight; blind. [Obs.]
3. in botany and zoology, having no rays.

Ray·naud's' dis·ēase' (re-nōz'), [named after A. G. M. *Raynaud* (1834–1881), French physician.] a disease of the nerves, parts of the body becoming cold, pale, and painful, sometimes gangrenous: it especially affects the fingers and toes.

rāy oil, oil made from the livers of rays.

rāy'on, *n.* [arbitrary coinage suggested by *ray* as descriptive of its sheen.]
1. any of various textile fibers synthetically produced by pressing cellulose acetate or some other cellulose solution through very small holes and solidifying it in the form of filaments.
2. any of various woven or knit fabrics made of such fibers.

rāy'on ac'ē·tāte, rayon which has been treated with acetate to give it weight and glossiness.

rāy'ŏn·nănt, *a.* [Fr. *rayon*, a ray.] in heraldry, emitting rays.

rāy point, the point where a pencil of rays converges, or the point from which radiant lines emanate.

rāze, *v.t.*; razed, *pt.*, *pp.*; razing, *ppr.* [Fr. *raser*; L. *rasus*, from *radere*, to raze, scrape.]
1. originally, to scrape or graze; to wound slightly.
2. to scrape or shave off; to erase.
3. to tear down completely; to level to the ground; to demolish: the current sense.
Also spelled *rase*.
Syn.—destroy, demolish, level, wreck, ruin.

rāze, *n.* a swinging fence or cattle guard in a stream. [Brit. Dial.]

rāzed, *a.* 1. striped in a pattern. [Archaic.]
2. in heraldry, raguly.

rā·zee', *n.* an armed ship having the upper deck cut down, and thus reduced to a lower rating. [Obs.]

rā·zee', *v.t.*; razeed, *pt.*, *pp.*; razeeing, *ppr.* 1. to remove the upper deck or decks of (a ship); to cut down to an inferior rate or class.
2. to abridge or reduce, as by cutting parts.

rā'zŏr, *n.* [Fr. *rasoir*, from *raser*; L. *radere*, to scrape.]

1. an exceedingly keen-edged instrument with a thin blade, used for shaving.
2. a tusk of a boar.

rā′zŏr·ȧ·ble, *a.* fit to be shaved. [Obs.]

rā′zŏr·back, *n.* 1. a wild or semiwild hog of the southern United States, with a slender body, a ridged back, and long legs.
2. same as *finback*.

rā′zŏr-backed (-bakt), *a.* having a sharp thin back, as a lean animal, or having dorsal fins, as some fishes.

rā′zŏr·bill, *n.* 1. an aquatic fowl, the common auk, *Alca torda*.
2. the cutwater, or skimmer.

rā′zŏr çlam, a bivalve of the family *Solenidæ*.

rā′zŏr fish, 1. a small fish of the Mediterranean, very thin and sharp; also, a labroid fish of Florida and the West Indies, with blue and red marks.
2. the razor clam.

rā′zŏr gràss, a West Indian plant, *Scleria scindens*, which derives its name from the sharp edges of its leaves and triangular stems.

rā′zŏr-grīnd″ēr, *n.* 1. the Australian flycatcher.
2. the European goatsucker. [Brit. Dial.]

rā′zŏr shell, a bivalve shellfish, of the genus *Solen*, having a shell long and narrow like the handle of a razor: also called *razor clam* and *razor fish*.

rā′zŏr strop, a strop, or strap, of leather, etc., used to sharpen razors.

rā′ẓūre, *n.* [Fr. *rasure*; L. *rasura*, from *radere* to scrape.] the act of erasing or effacing; obliteration. [Obs.]

razz, *v.t.* and *v.i.* [contr. from *raspberry*.] to tease, ridicule, deride, heckle, etc. [Slang.]

razz, *n.* a raspberry (derisive sound). [Slang.]

raz′zi·ȧ, *n.* [Fr.] a predatory incursion; a foray.

raz′zle-daz″zle, *v.t.* to make drunk or confused. [Slang.]

raz′zle-daz″zle, *n.* 1. a state or event of confusion, bewilderment, bustling, etc.
2. a game of cards.

Rb, in chemistry, rubidium.

r′-çŏl″ŏr (är′), *n.* in phonetics, the acoustic quality produced by retroflex articulation: also *r-quality*.

Rd, in chemistry, radium: now generally *Ra*.

Rę, *n.* Ra.

rę, *n.* [It., from L. *resonare*; see *gamut*.] in music, a syllable representing the second tone of the diatonic scale.

rē, *prep.* [L., abl. of *res*, thing.] in the case or matter of; as regards: used in law, etc., for *in re*.

Re, in chemistry, rhenium,

rē-, [from Fr. or L.; Fr. *re-*, *ré-*; L. *re-*; *red-*, back, backward.]
1. a prefix meaning *back*, as in *re*pay, *re*store.
2. a prefix meaning *again, anew, over again*, as in *re*appear, *re*tell.

When hyphenated, it is used (a) to distinguish between a word in which the prefix means simply *again* or *anew* and a word of similar form having a special meaning or meanings (e.g., *re-sound, resound*); (b) to avoid ambiguity in forming nonce words, as in *re-urge*; and (c) before elements beginning with *e*, as in *re-edit, re-elect* (such words are also written *reëdit, reëlect*, etc.). The following list contains some of the more common words in which *re-* means simply *again* or *anew*. Words with special meanings are entered in their proper alphabetical places in the vocabulary.

reaccommodate
reaccompany
reaccusation
reaccuse
reacquire
reacquisition
readjourn
readjournment
readmittance
readopt
readorn
readvance
reafforest
reafforestation
reagree
reallege
realliance
reamputation
reannex
reannexation
reanoint
reapparel
reapply
re-argue
re-argument
reassemblage
reassembly
reassess
reassimilate
reassimilation
reassociate
reassume
reassumption
reattach
reattachment
reattack
reattain
reattainment
reattempt
reavow
reawake
reawaken
rebanish
rebellow
rebeloved
rebending
rebind
rebless
rebloom
reblossom
reblue
reboil
rebrace
rebreathe
rebury
recalculate
recapacitate
recarriage
recarry
recelebrate
recelebration
rechange
recharter
rechase
rechasten
recheck
rechoose
rechristen
recircle
reclasp
reclassify
reclean
reclose
reclothe
recoagulation
recolonization
recolonize
recombination
recombine
recommission
recommunicate
recompact
recompile
recomplete
recompletion
recondensation
recondense
reconduct
reconfirm
reconjoin
reconsecrate
reconsecration
reconsign
reconsolidate
reconsolidation
reconstitute
recontinuance
recontinue
recopy
recoronation
recorporification
recouch
recross
recrown
recrucify
recrystallization
recrystallize
recultivate
recultivation
redamage
redare
redeceive
redecide
redecorate
redecoration
rededicate
rededication
redeliberate
redemonstrate
redeny
redescend
redescent
redescribe
redetermine
redigest
rediminish
rediscover
rediscoverer
rediscovery
redispose
redisposition
redissolution
redissolve
redistill
redistrainer
redivide
redivision
redo
redrive
redrop
redry
re-edify
re-edit
re-elaborate
re-elevate
re-embark
re-embarkation
re-embody
re-embrace
re-emerge
re-emergence
re-emigrate
re-emphasize
re-encourage
re-encouragement
re-endow
re-engage
re-engagement
re-engrave
re-enjoy
re-enjoyment
re-enkindle
re-enlist
re-enlistment
re-enslave
re-enslavement
re-enstamp
re-enthrone
re-enthronement
re-enthronize
re-erect
re-erection
re-exhibit
re-expel
re-experience
re-explain
re-expulsion
refertilize
refilm
refire
refold
refoment
reformulate
reformulation
refortification
refortify
refreeze
refurnish
refurnishment
regalvanize
regather
regear
regerminate
regermination
reget
regild
regird
regive
reglaze
reglorify
reglue
regraft
regrasp
rehandle
reharden
rehead
rehear
reheat
reheater
reheel
rehire
rehypothecate
rehypothecation
reidentify
reignite
reillume
reilluminate
reillumination
reillumine
reimbody
reimportune
reimpregnate
reimprint
reimprison
reimprisonment
reinaugurate
reincense
reincorporate
reincur
reinduce
reinfection
reinflame
reinform
reinfuse
reinfusion
reingratiate
reinhabit
reinoculate
reinoculation
reinquire
reinscribe
reinsist
reinspect
reinspection
reinspire
reinstruct
reinter
reinterment
reinterpret
reinthrone
reintrench
reintroduce
reintroduction
reinundate
reinvent
reinvestigate
reinvestigation
reinvite
reinvolve
relabel
relade
reland
relaunch
relaunder
relearn
relend
reline
reliquidate
reliquidation
relisten
reloan
relocate
relocation
relodge
remap
remast
remelt
remerge
remigrate
remigration
remix
remodification
remodify
remold
remolten
remultiply
rename
renationalize
renavigate
renerve
renominate
renumber
renumerate
reobtain
reobtainable
reoccupy
reoppose
repacify
repack
repacker
repaganize
repaper
repave
repenalize
reperception
repercolation
reperusal
reperuse
rephotograph
replait
replant
replantable
replantation
replaster
replay
replead
repledge
repledger
replunge
repolarization
repolish
reponder
repopularize
repopulate
repopulation
repot
repour
reprime
reproceed
reprocess
reproclaim
repromulgate
repromulgation
reprune
republish
repurge
repurify
repursue
requicken
reradiate
reread
re-refer
re-refine
re-reflect
rereign
re-reiterate
re-resolve
re-restitution
rerise
reroll
resaddle
resail
resalute
reseed
reseek
resegregate
reseizure
resell
reshake
reshape
resharpen
reshuffle
resift
resmooth
resolder
resolidify
resow
respace
respade
resplice
resplit
respot
respread
restart
restem
restipulate
restipulation
restrengthen
restrike
restring
restrive
restudy
restuff
resubject
resubjection
resummon
resummons
resupply
resurprise
retaker
retaunt
reteach
retear
retell
retemper
retest
rethink
retie
retoss
retrain
retraverse
retrial
retrim
retune
retwist
reunify
re-urge
re-use
reutilize
reutter
revaccinate
revaccination
revaluate
revaluation
revalue
revarnish
revegetate
revegetation
reverification
reverify
revote
rewarm
rewash
rewater
reweigh
rewin
rewind
rework

rē·ȧb·sọrb′, *v.t.*; reabsorbed, *pt., pp.*; reabsorbing, *ppr.* to draw in or suck up again what has been emitted or thrown off; as, to *reabsorb* chyle, lymph, blood, gas, etc.

rē·ȧb·sọrp′tion, *n.* the act or process of reabsorbing.

rē·aç′cess, *n.* a second access or approach; a visit renewed.

rēach, *v.t.*; reached (rēcht), *pt., pp.*; reaching, *ppr.* [ME. *rechen*; AS. *ræcan*.]
1. to extend; to stretch; to thrust out: sometimes followed by *out* or *forth*; as, to *reach out* the arm.

2. to extend to by thrusting out, throwing something, etc.; to touch by extending either the arm alone, or with an instrument in the hand; as, to *reach* a book on the shelf; the seaman *reaches* the bottom of the river with a pole or a line.
3. to carry as far as; to penetrate to; to extend to.
4. to obtain and deliver to someone else with the hand, by extending the arm; to hand; as, he *reached* me an orange.
5. to go as far as; to arrive at; to come to; as, to *reach* a destination.
6. to attain to or arrive at by effort, labor, or study; hence, to gain or obtain.

The heights by great men *reached* and kept
Were not attained by sudden flight.
—Longfellow.

7. to extend to so as to include or comprehend; to have influence on; to affect.

The law *reached* the intention of the promoters, and this act fixed the natural price of money. —Locke.

8. to establish contact with; to get in touch with, as by telephone.

rēach, *v.i.* 1. to thrust out the hand, foot, etc.
2. to stretch, or be extended, in amount, influence, space, time, etc.; as, his power *reaches* into other lands.
3. to carry; to penetrate, as sight, sound, etc.
4. to try to obtain something; to make an attempt.
5. in nautical usage, to sail on a reach.
Syn.—extend, thrust, stretch, obtain, attain, gain, grasp, penetrate, strain.

rēach, *n.* 1. the act of reaching.
2. the power of reaching, touching, or taking with the hand stretched out, or with an instrument managed by the hand.
3. the distance or extent to which one can reach, stretch, obtain, influence, etc.; as, the book is out of my *reach*.

Be sure yourself and your own *reach* to know. —Pope.

4. a contrivance; an artful scheme. [Obs.]
5. a continuous, uninterrupted extent, expanse, or stretch; as, a *reach* of desert land.
6. a stretch of water, as (a) the straight course of a river between two bendings or bights; (b) a channel; a strait; an arm of the sea; (c) that portion of a canal between two locks, having a uniform level.
7. a rod or bar that connects the rear axle of a vehicle with the bolster.
8. a narrow shoal extending out into the water; a promontory; a point. [Dial.]
9. in nautical usage, a tack sailed with the wind coming more or less from abeam: it may be a *close reach*, with the wind forward of the beam; a *beam reach*, with the wind abeam; or a *broad reach*, with the wind abaft the beam.

rēach′à·ble, *a.* within reach; capable of being reached.

rēach′ēr, *n.* 1. one who or that which reaches.
2. an exaggeration. [Obs.]

rēach′less, *a.* beyond reach; unattainable.

rēach′-mē-down″, *a.* ready-made; also, cast-off; secondhand. [Brit. Colloq.]

rēach′-mē-down″, *n.* a ready-made or secondhand garment. [Brit. Colloq.]

rē-aċt′, *v.t.*; re-acted, *pt., pp.*; re-acting, *ppr.* to act or perform again, or a second time; as, to *re-act* a play; the same scenes were *re-acted* at Rome.

rē·aċt′, *v.i.* [*re-* and *act.*]
1. to act in return or reciprocally.
2. to act in opposition.
3. to act in a reverse way; to go back to a former condition, stage, etc.
4. to respond to a stimulus; to be affected by some influence, event, etc.
5. in chemistry, to act with another substance in producing a chemical change.

rē·aċt′, *v.t.* to cause to react; specifically, to produce a chemical change in.

rē·aċt′ănce, *n.* [*react* and *-ance.*] in electricity, the opposition to the flow of alternating current made by an inductance coil or a condenser.

rē·aċt′ănt, *n.* any of the substances participating in a chemical reaction.

rē·aċ′tion, *n.* 1. a return or opposing action, influence, etc.
2. a response, as to a stimulus or influence.
3. a movement back to a former or less advanced condition, stage, etc.; countertendency; especially, such a movement or tendency in economics or politics; extreme conservatism.
4. a chemical change.
5. in medicine, (a) an action induced by resistance to another action; (b) a depression or exhaustion of energy following nervous tension, overstimulation, etc.; (c) an increased activity following depression.
6. in physiology and psychology, an organic response to a stimulus.
acid reaction; the turning of blue litmus paper red: an indication of the presence of an acid.
alkaline reaction; the turning of red litmus blue: an indication of the presence of an alkali.

rē·aċ′tion·ăr·y, *a.* of, characterized by, proceeding from, tending toward, or favoring reaction, especially in politics.

Should a *reactionary* temper assert itself in that variable quantity, French politics.
—Elizabeth Phipps Train.

rē·aċ′tion·ăr·y, *n.*; *pl.* **rē·aċ′tion·ăr·ies,** one who favors or promotes reaction; specifically, one who seeks to check, undo, or reverse political progress.

rē·aċ′tion·ist, *n.* and *a.* reactionary.

rē·aċ′tion pē′ri·ŏd, reaction time.

rē·aċ′tion tīme, in psychology, the time that elapses between the application of a stimulus and the beginning of the response.

rē·aċ′tion wheel (hwēl), a wheel to which a rotary motion is imparted by the action of streams of water escaping from its sides under the pressure of a head of water entering it from the center, as in a turbine.

rē·aċ′ti·vāte, *v.t.*; reactivated, *pt., pp.*; reactivating, *ppr.* to make active again; specifically, to place (an inactivated military unit, ship, etc.) back on an active status.

rē·aċ′ti·vāte, *v.i.* to be reactivated.

rē·aċt′ive, *a.* 1. tending to react.
2. of, caused by, or showing reaction.
reactive circuit; in electricity, a circuit containing either inductance or capacity alone, or both inductance and capacity.
reactive current; that portion of the current in an alternating circuit which is at right angles to the electromotive force.

rē·aċt′ive·ly, *adv.* by reaction.

rē·aċt′ive·ness, *n.* the quality of being reactive.

rē·aċ·tiv′i·ty, *n.* the state of being reactive.

rē·aċ′tŏr, *n.* 1. a person or thing that reacts or undergoes a reaction.
2. in electricity, a device inserted in a circuit to add reactance.
3. in medicine, a person or animal having a positive reaction to a particular foreign substance.
4. in nuclear physics, an atomic pile in which there is control of the atomic energy produced.

rēad, *n.* [AS. *ræd*, counsel.]
1. counsel. [Obs.]
2. a saying. [Obs.]

rēad, *n.* rennet. [Brit. Dial.]

read (red), *a.* instructed or knowing by reading; versed in books; learned: usually in hyphenated compounds; as, *well-read* in history.

rēad, *n.* a reading. [Archaic.]

rēad, *v.t.*; read (red), *pt., pp.*; reading, *ppr.* [AS. *rædan*, to discern, to advise, to read; Ice. *rátha*, to advise, to explain, to read.]
1. to get the meaning of (something written, printed, etc.) by interpreting its characters or signs.
2. to utter aloud (printed or written matter).
3. to learn the true meaning of; to understand the nature or significance of as if by reading; as, you *read* a person's character in his face.
4. to interpret, as dreams, signs, etc.
5. to foretell (the future).
6. to interpret or understand (a printed passage, etc.) as having a particular meaning.
7. to have or give as a reading in a certain passage; as, this edition *reads* "show," not "shew."
8. to get knowledge of; to learn from printed matter; as, he *read* the account yesterday.
9. to apply oneself to; to study; as, he *read* a subject for examination.
10. to record and show; to register; as, the speedometer *reads* fifty miles per hour.
11. to put into a (specified) state by reading.
12. to advise; to counsel. [Obs.]
13. to declare; to tell. [Obs.]
14. to suppose; to imagine. [Obs.]
to read into (or *in*); to attribute a particular meaning to; to interpret in a certain way.
to read oneself in; in the Church of England, to read the Thirty-nine Articles and repeat the declaration of assent prescribed by law, as required of every clergyman on the first Sunday on which he officiates in his benefice.
to read out of; to dismiss or expel from (a political party, society, etc.) by public reading of dismissal.

rēad, *v.i.* 1. to read something written, printed, etc., as words, music, books, etc.
2. to utter or repeat aloud the words of written or printed matter.
3. to learn by reading (with *about* or *of*).
4. to study.
5. to have or give a particular meaning when read; as, the paragraph *reads* to the effect that all men are equal.
6. to contain, or be drawn up in, certain words; as, the sentence *reads* as follows.
7. to admit of being read: followed by *well*, *poorly*, etc.
8. to advise; to counsel. [Obs.]
9. to tell; to declare. [Obs.]
to read between the lines; to discover or detect a hidden meaning in a phrase or statement; to perceive something not directly obvious, as a motive, intention, etc.

read (red), *v.* past tense and past participle of *read*.

rēad·à·bil′i·ty, *n.* readableness.

rēad′à·ble, *a.* 1. capable of being read; legible.
2. fit to be read; interesting, agreeable, and attractive in style; enjoyable.

rēad′à·ble·ness, *n.* the quality or state of being readable.

rēad′à·bly, *adv.* so as to be readable.

rē·ăd·dress′, *v.t.* 1. to address or occupy (oneself) anew.
2. to change the address on (a letter, etc.).
3. to address or speak to once more.

rē·à·dept′, *v.t.* to regain; to recover. [Obs.]

rē·à·dep′tion, *n.* a regaining; recovery, as of something lost. [Obs.]

rēad′ēr, *n.* 1. one who reads; especially, one who reads much; one studious in books.
2. a reciter of literary works in public; one who reads aloud and interprets.
3. a person who reads lessons, prayers, etc. aloud in church.
4. a person who reads manuscripts for a publisher and advises as to their merit.
5. a person who corrects proofs for a printer.
6. a person who records the readings of meters, etc., as for a public utilities company.
7. a book with selected passages for practice and instruction in reading.
8. a lecturer or instructor in a university. [Chiefly Brit.]
9. an assistant who corrects examinations, themes, etc. for a professor.

rēad′ēr·ship, *n.* 1. the people who read a particular publication, author, etc. or the estimated number of these.
2. the state or position of being a reader.

read′i·ly (red′), *adv.* [ME. *redili.*]
1. without hesitation; willingly.
2. without delay; quickly.
3. without difficulty.

read′i·ness, *n.* the state or quality of being ready.
Syn.—quickness, expedition, promptitude, aptness, knack, skill, expertness, promptness, facility, aptitude, dexterity, ease, willingness, alacrity, alertness.

rēad′ing, *a.* 1. inclined to read or study; addicted to reading; as, a *reading* community.
2. made or used for reading.
a reading man; in English universities, a student who is entirely devoted to his studies.

rēad′ing, *n.* 1. the act or practice of one who reads; perusal, as of books.
2. in legislation, the formal recital of a bill by the proper officer before the house which is to consider it; as, the bill passed the second *reading*.
3. the act of repeating aloud the words of printed or written matter, especially for public entertainment.
4. the study of books; academic learning.
5. any material printed or written to be read.
6. a recording of information on a barometer, thermometer, etc.
7. the form of a specified word, sentence, etc. in a particular edition of a literary work; as, there were several *readings* for the passage.
8. a particular interpretation, as of something written.

That word *reading*, in its critical use, always charms me. An actress's *reading* of a chambermaid, a dancer's *reading* of a hornpipe, a singer's *reading* of a song, a marine paint-

er's *reading* of the sea, the kettledrum's *reading* of an instrumental passage, are phrases ever youthful and delightful.
—Dickens.

rēad'ing book, a book containing exercises in reading; a reader.

rēad'ing desk, 1. a desk with a sloping top on which a book is supported while being read.
2. a lectern.

rēad'ing glȧss, a large magnifying lens, set in a frame furnished with a handle, used to assist in reading.

rēad'ing rọom, a room (in a club, library, etc.), furnished with newspapers, periodicals, etc., for writing and reading.

rē·ad·just', *v.t.* to settle again; to put in order again, as what was discomposed; to rearrange.

rē·ad·just'ẽr, *n.* 1. one who readjusts.
2. [R–] a member of a political faction in Virginia that wanted to readjust the state debt by legislative action in 1878.

rē·ad·just'ment, *n.* 1. a readjusting or being readjusted.
2. in finance, rearrangement of the structure of a corporation: often distinguished from *reorganization*.

rē·ad·mis'sion, *n.* a readmitting or being readmitted.

rē·ad·mit', *v.t.* to admit again.

rēad'out, *n.* 1. the act of retrieving information from storage in a digital computer.
2. information taken out of a computer and displayed visually or recorded, as by typewriter or on tape, for immediate use.
3. information immediately displayed or recorded from other sources, as from electrical instruments.

rēad'out, *a.* of or pertaining to any device that presents data output, as in numbers, letters, etc., for immediate use.

read'y (red'), *a.*; *comp.* readier; *superl.* readiest, [OE. *redi, rædi*; AS. *ræde*, ready; Dan. *rede*; Sw. *reda*; Ice. *reithi*; G. (*be*)*reit*.]
1. prepared or equipped to act immediately; waiting to be used; as, she is *ready* to sing, the house is *ready* for occupancy.
2. prepared in mind; unhesitant; willing.
3. (a) likely or liable immediately (usually with an infinitive); (b) apt; inclined (usually with an infinitive); as, he is always *ready* to blame us.
4. clever and skillful mentally or physically; dexterous.
5. done or made without delay; prompt; as, a *ready* reply.
6. convenient or handy to use; available immediately; as, *ready* cash.
7. at hand; present: used in response to a roll call. [Obs.]
all ready; ready in every sense of the word; wholly prepared.
to make ready; (a) to prepare; to put everything in readiness; (b) to dress.
Syn.—apt, dexterous, facile, prompt, expeditious, skillful, handy, expert, prepared.

read'y, *adv.* in a state of preparation so as to need no delay; readily. [Archaic.]
We ourselves will go *ready* armed before the house of Israel. —Num. xxxii. 17.

read'y, *n.* 1. ready money; cash at hand (usually with *the*). [Colloq.]
2. in military science, the position of a rifle just before aiming and firing.

read'y, *v.t.*; readied, *pt., pp.*; readying, *ppr.* to prepare; to get or make ready (often used reflexively).

read'y-māde', *a.* 1. made so as to be ready for immediate use or for sale to any buyer, rather than to individual order; as, *ready-made* suits: opposed to *custom-made*.
2. commonplace; stock; not original; as, *ready-made* opinions.

read'y-mix, *a.* ready to be used after the addition of liquid; as, *ready-mix* concrete.

read'y reck'ŏn·ẽr, a book having tables for computing interest, prices, etc. already figured out for convenience.

read'y-tö-weãr', *a.* ready-made: said of clothes.

read'y-wit'ted, *a.* having ready wit; mentally quick; quick in thought or understanding.

rē·ȧf·firm', *v.t.*; reaffirmed, *pt., pp.*; reaffirming, *ppr.* to affirm again or a second time.

rē·ȧf·firm'ȧnce, *n.* a second affirmation

rē″af·fir·mā'tion, *n.* a reaffirming or being reaffirmed.

rē·ā'ġent, *n.* in chemistry, any substance employed to detect or measure another substance or to convert one substance into another by means of the reaction that it causes.

rē″ag·grȧ·vā'tion, *n.* in Roman Catholic ecclesiastical law, the last monitory, published after three admonitions and before the last excommunication.

rēak, *n.* a seaweed or rush. [Obs.]

rēaks, *n.pl.* tricks; pranks. [Obs.]

rē'ăl, *a.* [OFr., from LL. *realis*, from L. *res*, a thing.]
1. existing or happening as or in fact; actual, true, objectively so, etc.; not merely seeming, pretended, imagined, fictitious, nominal, or ostensible.
2. authentic; genuine.
3. in law, of or relating to permanent, immovable things; as, *real* property: opposed to *personal*.
4. in mathematics, not imaginary: said of a number or quantity.
5. in optics, of or relating to an image made by the actual meeting of light rays at a point.
6. in philosophy, existing objectively; actual (not merely possible or ideal), or essential, absolute, ultimate (not relative, derivative, phenomenal, etc.).
7. relating to things, not persons. [Obs.]
Many are perfect in men's humors, that are not greatly capable of the *real* part of business. —Bacon.
chattels real; such chattels as concern real estate.
real action; in law, an action which concerns real property.
real assets; assets consisting in real estate; lands and tenements descending to an heir.
real presence; in Christian theology, the doctrine of the actual presence of the body and blood of Christ in the Eucharist.
real property; same as *real estate*.
real wages; wages measured by how much they can buy, rather than by monetary value.
Syn.—genuine, actual, authentic, true.

rē'ăl, *adv.* really; very. [Colloq. or Dial.]

rē'ăl, *n.* 1. a realist. [Obs.]
2. anything that actually exists, or reality in general (with *the*).

rē'ăl (*or Sp.* re-äl'), *n.*; *pl.* **rē'ălṣ** or Sp. **re·äl'es,** [Sp. and Port., lit., royal, from L. *regalis*.]
1. a former monetary unit and silver coin of Spain.
2. a former Spanish monetary unit, equal to about one quarter of a peseta.

re·äl', *n.* singular of *reis*.

rē'ăl, *n.* the saury.

rē'ăl, *a.* regal; royal. [Obs.]

rē'ăl-es·tāte″, *a.* having to do with real estate or dealing in real estate.

rē'ăl es·tāte', 1. land, including the buildings or improvements on it and its natural assets, as minerals, water, etc.
2. ownership of or property in land, etc.

rē·al'găr, *n.* [Fr. *réalgar*; Sp. *rejalgar*, from Ar. *rahj*, powder, *al*, the, and *ghār*, a mine.] an orange-red mineral, arsenic sulfide, with a resinous luster, used for making fireworks.

rē'ăl·işm, *n.* 1. a tendency to face facts and be practical rather than imaginary or visionary.
2. in art and literature, the attempted picturing of people and things as they really are; effort at faithful reproduction of nature.
3. in philosophy, (a) the doctrine that universals have objective reality: opposed to *nominalism*; (b) the doctrine that material objects exist in themselves, apart from the mind's consciousness of them: opposed to *idealism*.

rē'ăl·ist, *n.* 1. a person concerned with real things and practical matters rather than those that are imaginary or visionary.
2. a believer in or advocate of realism.
3. an artist or writer whose work is characterized by realism.

rē·ăl·is'tiç, *a.* 1. of, having to do with, or in the style of realism or realists.
2. tending to face facts; practical rather than visionary.

rē·ăl·is'tiç·ăl·ly, *adv.* in a realistic manner.

rē·al'i·ty, *n.*; *pl.* **rē·al'i·tieş,** [Fr. *réalité*.]
1. the quality or state of being real.
2. a person or thing that is real; a fact.
3. the quality of being true to life; fidelity to nature.
4. in philosophy, that which is real: see *real*, *a.*, sense 6.
5. realty (real estate or fidelity). [Obs.]
in reality; in fact; actually.

rē'ăl·ī·zȧ·ble, *a.* that may be realized.

rē″ăl·i·zā'tion, *n.* [Fr. *réalisation*.]
1. the act of realizing; also, the condition of being realized.
2. something realized.
Syn.—fruition, gratification, enjoyment.

rē'ăl·īze, *v.t.*; realized, *pt., pp.*; realizing, *ppr.* [Fr. *réaliser*.]
1. to make real; to bring into being; to achieve.
2. to make appear real.
3. to understand fully; to apprehend; as, I *realize* the difficulties.
4. to convert (assets, rights, etc.) into money.
5. to gain; to obtain; as, the company *realized* a profit.
6. to be sold for; to bring as profit: said of property.

rē'ăl·īze, *v.i.* to sell property, a right, etc. for ready money.

rē'ăl·ī·zẽr, *n.* one who realizes.

rē'ăl·ī·zing·ly, *adv.* in such a manner as to realize. [Rare.]

rē'ăl·ly, *adv.* 1. in a real manner; in reality; in fact and not in appearance only; actually; as, it *really* happened.
2. indeed; as, *really*, you mustn't say that.
Why, *really*, sixty-five is somewhat old. —Young.
3. truly or genuinely; in truth; as, a *really* hot day.
Syn.—veritably, truly, indeed, actually, unquestionably.

rē·ăl·lȳ', *v.t.* to reunite; to ally again.

realm (relm), *n.* [OFr. *realme*, from hypothetical LL. *regalimen*, from L. *regalis*, royal, from *rex, regis*, a king.]
1. a royal jurisdiction or extent of government; a kingdom; a king's dominions.
2. figuratively, a province; a department; a region; a sphere; a domain.
Truth and right are above utility in all *realms* of thought and action. —Charles W. Eliot.
3. in zoogeography, a division of the earth's surface; a faunal or floral area.

rē'ăl·ness, *n.* the state or quality of being real; reality.

rē'ăl num'bẽr, in mathematics, any rational or irrational number.

Rẹ·äl'pō·li·tik', *n.* [G.] practical politics: usually a euphemism for *power politics*.

rē'ăl·tŏr (*or* -tọr), *n.* a real-estate broker who is a member of a local board affiliated with the National Association of Real Estate Boards.

rē'ăl·ty, *n.* [OFr. *realte*, from L. *regalitas*, royalty.] royalty. [Obs.]

rē'ăl·ty, *n.* [*real*, *a.* and *-ty*.]
1. real estate.
2. fidelity; honesty. [Obs.]
3. reality. [Obs.]

rēam, *n.* [AS. *reám*, cream.] cream; also, the creamlike froth on ale. [Scot. and Brit. Dial.]

rēam, *v.i.* to cream; to foam. [Scot. and Brit. Dial.]

rēam, *n.* [OFr. *raime*; It. *risma*; Sp. *resma*, a ream of paper, from Ar. *rizmat*, a bale, a packet, especially a ream of paper, from *razama*, to pack together.]
1. a quantity of paper varying from 480 sheets (20 quires) to 516 sheets ($21^1/_2$ quires, called a *printer's ream*).
2. [*pl.*] a great amount. [Colloq.]

rēam, *v.t.*; reamed, *pt., pp.*; reaming, *ppr.* [ME. *remen*; AS. *ryman*, to widen; Ice. *ryma*, to make room.]
1. (a) to enlarge (a hole) in something; (b) to enlarge the bore of (a gun). Often with *out*.
2. to countersink or taper (a hole): with *out*.
3. to get rid of (a defect) by reaming (with *out*).
4. to remove the juice from (a lemon, orange, etc.).
5. in nautical usage, to open, as a seam, for calking.

rēam'ẽr, *n.* a person or thing that reams; specifically, (a) a sharp-edged tool for enlarging or tapering holes; (b) a device for squeezing the juice from lemons, oranges, etc.; (c) an implement for reaming pipe bowls.

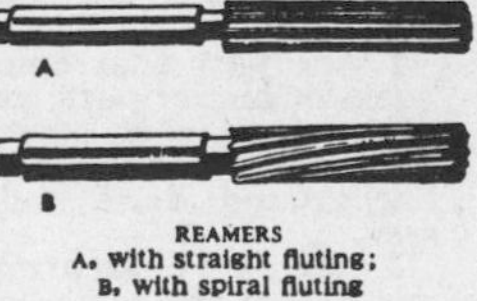

REAMERS
A, with straight fluting;
B, with spiral fluting

rēam'ing ī'ron (-ũrn), in nautical usage, a blunt chisel used for opening the seams between the planking of a ship, preparatory to calking them.

rē·an'i·māte, *v.t.* 1. to revive; to resuscitate; to restore to life, as a person apparently dead; as, to *reanimate* a drowned person.

2. to revive when dull or languid; to invigorate; to infuse new life, courage, strength, etc. into; as, to *reanimate* disheartened troops; to *reanimate* drowsy senses or languid spirits.

rē·an·i·mā'tion, *n.* the act or operation of reviving from apparent death; the act or operation of giving fresh spirits, courage, or vigor; also, the condition of being reanimated.

rē·an'swēr (-sēr), *v.t.* 1. to answer again.
2. to correspond to; to repay; to compensate. [Obs.]

rēap, *v.t.*; reaped, *pt., pp.*; reaping, *ppr.* [AS. *ripan*, to reap; closely allied to Goth. *raupjan*, to pluck, as also to D. *rapen*, to glean, to gather.]
1. to cut down, as grain, with a sickle, scythe, or reaping machine.
2. to cut down and gather (a crop, harvest, etc.) when ripe and ready.
3. to cut down and gather the crop of; to clear of a crop, especially of a grain crop; as, to *reap* a field.
4. to gain or obtain as the reward of action, conduct, work, etc.; as, to *reap* a benefit from exertions; to *reap* the whirlwind.

rēap, *v.i.* 1. to perform the act or operation of reaping grain, a harvest, etc.
2. to get a return or reward; to receive the fruit of labor or works.
They that sow in tears shall *reap* in joy.
—Ps. cxxvi. 5.

rēap, *n.* a small bundle of grain. [Brit. Dial.]

rēap'ēr, *n.* 1. one who reaps.
2. a machine used in reaping; a reaping machine.
the (Grim) Reaper; death.

rēap'ing hook, a curved blade of steel set in a short handle, used for reaping; a sickle.

rēap'ing mȧ·chïne', a machine for harvesting a crop of grain, the essentials of which are a means for cutting the standing grain and, often, a mechanism for disposing of it when cut, automatically placing the grain in unbound or bound bundles.

REAPING MACHINE

rē·ăp·pēar', *v.i.* to appear again.

rē·ăp·pēar'ănce, *n.* a second appearance.

rē"ap·pli·cā'tion, *n.* a second application; the act of applying again; also, the state of being applied again.

rē·ăp·point', *v.t.* to appoint again.

rē·ăp·point'ment, *n.* a second or new appointment.

rē·ăp·pōr'tion, *v.t.* to apportion again.

rē·ăp·pōr'tion·ment, *n.* a second or renewed apportionment.

rē·ăp·prōach', *v.t.* and *v.i.* to approach again.

rēar, *adv.* early. [Obs.]

rēar, *n.* [OFr. *riere*; Pr. *reire*, from L. *retro*, behind; *re-*, back, and suffix *-tro*, direction or motion.]
1. the part that comes last in order; the back, or hinder part; as, the *rear* of a car.
2. the place or position behind or at the back; the part lying back of and beyond; the background; as, a building standing in the *rear*.
3. the part of an army or of a fleet farthest away from the battle front: opposed to *van*.
to bring up the rear; to come at the end (of a procession); to be last in order.

rēar, *a.* being in or at the back part; of or occupying a place in the rear; as, a *rear* rank.

rēar, *a.* rare. [Obs.]

rēar, *v.t.*; reared, *pt., pp.*; rearing, *ppr.* [AS. *ræran*, to raise, caus. of *risan*, to rise.]
1. to cause to rise or become erect, etc.; to lift up; to elevate; to raise; as, a serpent *rears* its head.
2. to bring up or to raise to maturity; to foster; to cherish; to nurse; to educate; to instruct; as, to *rear* children.
Delightful task! to *rear* the tender thought,
To teach the young idea how to shoot.
—Thomson.
3. to exalt; to elevate. [Obs.]
4. to rouse; to stir up. [Obs.]
5. to raise; to breed; to grow, as animals or plants.
6. to build up; to construct; as, to *rear* a monument.

rēar, *v.i.* 1. to rise or stand on the hind legs, as a horse.
2. to rise up in anger, etc. (usually with *up*).
3. to rise high, as a mountain peak.

rēar ad'mi·răl, a naval officer next in rank above a captain and below a vice admiral.

rēar'ēr, *n.* 1. one who raises; a breeder.
2. a horse that rears.

rēar guărd, the detachment that marches in the rear of the main army to protect it.

rēar'hørse, *n.* the mantis.

rēar'ing bit, a bit that prevents a rearing horse from raising his head.

rēar līne, the line at the rear of an army.

rē·ärm', *v.t.* and *v.i.* 1. to arm again.
2. to arm with new or more effective weapons.

rē·är'mȧ·ment, *n.* the act of rearming or the state of being rearmed.

rēar'mōst, *a.* farthest from the front; last.

rēar'mouse, *n.* same as *reremouse.*

rē·ăr·rānġe', *v.t.* 1. to arrange again.
2. to arrange differently.

rē·ăr·rānġe'ment, *n.* 1. the act of rearranging; the condition of being rearranged.
2. a new arrangement.
3. in chemistry, a redistribution of atoms, or atomic groups within a molecule, forming the molecule of a different substance.

rēar sīght (sīt), the sight on a firearm nearest the breech, often with a movable part that can be adjusted to the desired range of fire.

rēar'wȧrd, *n.* [ME. *rerewarde*; Anglo-Fr. *rerewarde.*]
1. a position in the rear. [Rare.]
2. the rear (sense 3). [Archaic.]

rēar'wărd, rēar'wărdṣ, *adv.* toward the rear; backward.

rēar'wărd, *a.* at, in, or toward the rear; coming last.

rē·ȧs·cend', *v.t.* and *v.i.* to rise, mount, or climb again.

rē·ȧs·cen'sion, *n.* the act of reascending; a remounting.

rē·ȧs·cent', *n.* another ascent.

rēa'ṣŏn, *n.* [OFr. *reson, raisun*, from L. *ratio, rationis*, reason, plan.]
1. an explanation or justification of an act, idea, etc.
2. a cause; a motive.
3. the ability to think, form judgments, draw conclusions, etc.
4. sound thought or judgment; good sense.
5. normal mental powers; a sound mind; sanity.
6. in logic, one of the premises of an argument, especially the minor.
7. ratio; relation between quantities; proportion. [Obs.]
by reason of; because of.
in reason; (a) justifiably; (b) reasonable.
out of all reason; unreasonable.
to bring to reason; to make reasonable.
to stand to reason; to be logical or reasonable.
with reason; justifiably; rightly.
Syn.—ground, consideration, motive, principle, sake, account, object, purpose, design.

rēa'ṣŏn, *v.i.*; reasoned, *pt., pp.*; reasoning, *ppr.*
1. to think coherently and logically; to draw inferences or conclusions from facts known or assumed.
2. to argue or talk in a logical way.
And they *reasoned* among themselves.
—Matt. xvi. 7.
Syn.—deduce, establish, prove, infer.

rēa'ṣŏn, *v.t.* 1. to analyze; to think logically about; to think out systematically.
2. to argue; to discuss.
3. to support, justify, etc. with reasons.
4. to persuade or bring by reasoning (with *into* or *out of*).
to reason that; to conclude or infer that.

rēa"ṣŏn·ȧ·bil'i·ty, *n.* the quality or condition of being reasonable; reasonableness.

rēa'ṣŏn·ȧ·ble, *a.* 1. able to reason; having the faculty of reason; endowed with reason; as, a *reasonable* being.
2. amenable, conformable, or agreeable to reason; just; rational.
3. not immoderate; not excessive; not unjust; tolerable; moderate; sensible; sane.
4. not expensive.
reasonable doubt; in criminal law, that condition of mind in which there is a sincere doubt as to whether a person charged with a crime has been proved guilty.

rēa'ṣŏn·ȧ·ble·ness, *n.* the quality or state of being reasonable; conformity to the dictates of reason.

rēa'ṣŏn·ȧ·bly, *adv.* 1. in a reasonable manner; in conformity to the dictates of reason.
2. to a reasonable degree.

rēa'ṣŏn·ēr, *n.* one who reasons or argues; as, a fair *reasoner*; a close *reasoner*; a logical *reasoner.*

rēa'ṣŏn·ing, *n.* 1. the drawing of inferences or conclusions from known or assumed facts; the act or process of exercising the faculty of reason; as, the *reasoning* taxed his exhausted brain.
2. facts, reasons, and proofs produced in a course of reasoning or argumentation; as, the *reasoning* embraces a wide field of knowledge.

rēa'ṣŏn·ist, *n.* a rationalist. [Obs.]

rēa'ṣŏn·less, *a.* 1. not able to reason; as, a *reasonless* man or mind.
2. not warranted or supported by reason; illogical or senseless.

rē·ȧs·sem'ble, *v.t.* and *v.i.* to collect again.

rē·ȧs·sērt', *v.t.* to assert again; to maintain after suspension or cessation.

rē·ȧs·sēr'tion, *n.* a second assertion of the same thing.

rē·ȧs·sess'ment, *n.* an assessment made in addition to one already made.

rē·ȧs·sīgn' (-sīn'), *v.t.* to assign again; to transfer a person or thing that has been assigned.

rē·ȧs·sīgn'ment, *n.* the act of reassigning.

rē·ȧs·sūr'ănce (-shūr'), *n.* 1. assurance or confirmation repeated.
2. same as *reinsurrance.*
3. restoration of confidence; removal of doubt.

rē·ȧs·sūre', *v.t.*; reass ıred, *pt., pp.*; reassuring, *ppr.* 1. to restore confidence to; to remove doubt or hesitation from; to relieve from fear.
2. same as *reinsure.*
3. to assure again or anew.

rē·ȧs·sūr'ēr, *n.* one who reassures.

rē·ȧs·sūr'ing·ly, *adv.* in a reassuring manner.

rēast, *v.t.* to cure with smoke, as bacon. [Scot. Dial.]

rēast, *v.i.* 1. to become offended. [Brit. Dial.]
2. to become rancid. [Obs.]

rēast'ed, *a.* rancid. [Obs.]

rēas'ti·ness, *n.* rancidness. [Obs.]

rēas'ty, *a.* rancid. [Obs.]

rē·ä'tȧ, *n.* [Sp.] a lariat.

rēate, *n.* the floating water crowfoot, *Ranunculus fluitans*; also, any of various other water weeds. [Obs.]

rē'aume, *n.* realm. [Obs.]

Re'au·mur, Ré'au·mur (rā'ō-mūr), *a.* [after R. A. *Réaumur*, the inventor.] designating or of a thermometer which registers the boiling point of water at 80° and the freezing point at 0°.

Re'au·mur, Ré'au·mur, *n.* a Reaumur thermometer.

rēave, *v.t.*; reaved or reft, *pt., pp.*; reaving, *ppr.* [AS. *reafian*, to steal or rob.]
1. to take away by stealth or violence; to bereave; to seize. [Archaic.]
2. to tear up. [Obs.]

rēave, *v.i.* to act as a plunderer or robber; to carry off goods taken by robbery. [Archaic.]

rēav'ēr, *n.* a robber; one who plunders. [Archaic.]

rē·bap'tiṣm, *n.* a rebaptizing or being rebaptized.

rē·bap'tist, *n.* one who baptizes or is baptized again; specifically, an Anabaptist. [Obs.]

rē"bap·ti·zā'tion, *n.* rebaptism. [Obs.]

rē·bap·tīze', *v.t.* 1. to baptize a second time.
2. to give a new name to.

rē·bap·tīz'ēr, *n.* one who baptizes again.

rē·bär"bȧ·ri·zā'tion, *n.* the state of being rebarbarized.

rē·bär'bȧ·rīze, *v.t.* to cause to return to barbarism.

rē'bāte, *v.t.*; rebated, *pt., pp.*; rebating, *ppr.* [Fr. *rebattre*; *re* and *battre*, from LL. *batere*, to beat.]
1. (a) to give back (part of an amount paid); (b) to make a deduction from (a bill).
2. to reduce; to lessen. [Rare.]

3. to blunt; to beat to obtuseness; to deprive of keenness. [Archaic.]

rē'bāte, *v.i.* to abate. [Obs.]

rē'bāte, *n.* [Fr. *rabat,* from the *v.*] a deduction; return of part of an amount paid, as for goods.

rē'bāte (*or* rab'it), *n.* and *v.t.*; rebated, *pt., pp.*; rebating, *ppr.* rabbet.

rē'bāte, *n.* 1. a kind of hard freestone used in pavements. [Obs.]

2. a piece of wood fastened to a long stick for beating mortar. [Obs.]

rē'bā·ted, *a.* in heraldry, having the points broken off or cut short.

rē·bāte'ment, *n.* 1. a rebate. [Obs.]

2. in heraldry, a diminution or abatement of the bearings in a coat of arms. [Obs.]

3. a narrowing [Obs.]

rē·bä'tō, *n.* same as *rabato.*

rē'beç, *n.* [Fr., from OFr. *rebebe,* from Ar. *rabāb,* a kind of musical instrument.] an old form of stringed instrument somewhat similar to the violin, having three or four strings tuned in fifths, and played with a bow; also spelled *rebeck.*

REBEC

rē'beck, *n.* an old woman; a hag. [Obs.]

Rē·beç'çȧ, *n.* in the Bible, the wife of Isaac and mother of Jacob and Esau: also spelled *Rebekah.*

reb'el, *n.* [OFr. *rebelle;* L. *rebellis,* rebel, rebellious, from *rebellare;* see the *v.*] a person who openly resists authority or opposes any control.

reb'el, *a.* 1. rebellious.

2. of rebels.

rē·bel', *v.i.*; rebelled, *pt., pp.*; rebelling, *ppr.* [OFr. *rebeller;* L. *rebellare,* to make war again.]

1. to resist authority, government, etc. openly and by force.

2. to oppose any authority or control.

3. to feel or show strong aversion; as, his mind *rebels* at the prospect of such drudgery.

reb'el clō'vẽr, *Lespedeza striata,* an annual plant resembling clover, valued as a soil-improving and pasture crop: also called *Japan clover.*

reb'el·dŏm, *n.* 1. the actions and behavior of rebels; rebellious conduct.

2. rebels collectively.

3. any territory held by rebels.

rē·bel'lẽr, *n.* one who rebels. [Rare.]

rē·bel'liŏn (-yun), *n.* [Fr., from L. *rebellio* (*-onis*), a renewed war.]

1. an act or state of armed, open resistance to authority, government, etc.

2. a defiance of or opposition to any control.

3. a rebelling.

commission of rebellion; in English law, one of the abolished processes of contempt in the High Court of Chancery.

Syn.—insurrection, sedition, revolt, mutiny, resistance, contumacy, anarchy, revolution.

rē·bel'lious (-yus), *a.* 1. resisting authority; engaged in rebellion.

2. of or like rebels or rebellion.

3. opposing any control; defiant.

4. in medicine, difficult to treat; resisting cure; as, a *rebellious* growth.

rē·bel'lious·ly, *adv.* in a rebellious manner.

rē·bel'lious·ness, *n.* the quality or state of being rebellious.

rē·bĩrth', *n.* 1. a new or second birth.

2. a reawakening; renaissance; revival.

rē·bīte', *v.t.*; rebit, *pt.*; rebitten, rebit, *pp.*; rebiting, *ppr.* to bite again; specifically, to deepen the lines in (an etched plate) by subjecting again to the action of the corroding fluid.

reb'ō·ănt, *a.* [from L. *reboare,* from *re-,* and *baore,* to bellow.] resounding or reechoing loudly; bellowing back again. [Poet.]

reb·ō·ā'tion, *n.* a loud, re-echoing sound. [Poet.]

rē·boiṣe', *v.t.*; reboised, *pt., pp.*; reboising, *ppr.* to reconvert into a forest.

rē·boiṣe'ment, *n.* the re-establishment of a forest by planting trees on land from which trees have been removed.

rē·bọrn', *a.* born again; having new life, spirit, etc.

rẹ·bō'ṣō, *n.* same as *rebozo.*

rē·bound', *v.i.*; rebounded, *pt., pp.*; rebounding, *ppr.* 1. to bound, leap, or spring back upon impact with another body.

2. to re-echo; to reverberate; to resound.

3. to take bounds or leaps; to bound.

4. in basketball, to seize a rebound.

rē·bound', *v.t.* 1. to make bound or spring back. [Rare.]

2. to return (a sound). [Rare.]

rē'bound, *n.* 1. a rebounding; recoil: sometimes figurative; as, he married Jane on the *rebound* when Betty jilted him.

2. in sports, (a) a basketball that bounces off the backboard or the rim of the basket, or a hockey puck that bounds back after an attempted goal; (b) a play made by recovering such a rebound.

rẹ·bō'zō, *n.* [Sp.] a scarf or long shawl worn over the head and shoulders by women in Spain, Mexico, etc.

rē·broad'cȧst, *v.t.* and *v.i.* 1. to broadcast again.

2. to broadcast (a program, etc. received in a relay system from another station).

rē·broad'cȧst, *n.* 1. a rebroadcasting.

2. a program, etc. that is being or has been rebroadcast.

rē·buff', *n.* [Fr. *rebuffade;* It. *ribuffo,* a check, a chiding.]

1. an abrupt, blunt refusal of offered advice, help, etc.

2. any check or repulse.

The strong *rebuff* of some tumultuous cloud. —Milton.

Syn.—rebuke, discouragement, repulsion, check.

rē·buff', *v.t.*; rebuffed (-buft'), *pt., pp.*; rebuffing, *ppr.* 1. to refuse bluntly; to snub.

2. to check; to repulse.

3. to blow or drive back. [Rare.]

Syn.—rebuke, repel, oppose.

rē·build' (-bild'), *v.t.*; rebuilt, *pt., pp.*; rebuilding, *ppr.* to build again; to renew or remodel a structure; to build or construct what has been demolished; as, to *rebuild* a house, a wall, a wharf, or a city.

rē·built', *a.* reconstructed; built again.

rē·būk'ȧ·ble, *a.* worthy of rebuke.

rē·būke', *v.t.*; rebuked, *pt., pp.*; rebuking, *ppr.* [Anglo-Fr. *rebuker;* OFr. *rebuchier; re-,* back, and *buchier, buschier,* to beat, from *busche,* a log.]

1. to address in sharp and severe disapproval; to reprimand.

2. to force back; to check. [Obs.]

rē·būke', *n.* a sharp reprimand; a chiding; reproof for faults; reprehension.

Why bear you these *rebukes* and answer not? —Shak.

rē·būke'fụl, *a.* containing or full of rebukes.

rē·būke'fụl·ly, *adv.* with reproof or reprehension.

rē·būk'ẽr, *n.* one who rebukes; a chider; one who reprimands.

rē·būk'ing·ly, *adv.* by way of rebuke.

rē'bus, *n.*; *pl.* **rē'bus·eṣ,** [L., ablative plural of *res,* a thing; lit., by things: so named because the meaning is indicated by things.]

1. a kind of puzzle consisting of pictures of objects, signs, etc. which by the sound of their names suggest words or phrases; as, a picture of a bedspring followed by a picture of a meadow is a *rebus* for Springfield.

2. in heraldry, a device intended to represent a personal name; a bearing or bearings on a coat of arms conveying an allusion to the name of the person, as castles for Castleton, three cups for Butler.

rē'bus, *v.t.* to indicate in the form of a rebus.

rē·but', *v.t.*; rebutted, *pt., pp.*; rebutting, *ppr.* [OFr. *rebuter, rebouter,* to put or thrust back; *re,* back, and *bouter,* to put, to thrust.]

1. to contradict, refute, or oppose, especially in a formal manner by argument, proof, etc.

2. to force back; to repel. [Obs.]

rē·but', *v.i.* 1. to retire; to draw back; to recoil. [Obs.]

2. to make answer, as to a plaintiff's surrejoinder.

The plaintiff may answer the rejoinder by a surrejoinder; on which the defendant may *rebut.* —Blackstone.

rē·but'tȧ·ble, *a.* capable of being rebutted.

rē·but'tăl, *n.* 1. in general, the act of refuting.

2. in debate, refutation of an opponent's argument.

3. in law, the refuting of, or effort to refute, testimony previously introduced by the opposing side.

rē·but'tẽr, *n.* 1. in law pleadings, the answer of a defendant to a plaintiff's surrejoinder.

2. one who or that which rebuts.

rē·çal'ci·trănce, *n.* 1. the quality or state of being recalcitrant; refractoriness.

2. recalcitrant action or conduct.

rē·çal'ci·trăn·cy, *n.* recalcitrance.

rē·çal'ci·trănt, *a.* [L. *recalcitrare,* to kick back.] making obstinate opposition; refusing to obey authority, custom, regulation, etc.; stubbornly defiant; noncompliant; refractory.

rē·çal'ci·trănt, *n.* a recalcitrant person; one who refuses submission.

rē·çal'ci·trāte, *v.i.*; recalcitrated, *pt., pp.*; recalcitrating, *ppr.* [L. *recalcitrare,* to kick back; *re-,* back, and *calcitrare,* to kick, from *calx, calcis,* the heel.] to refuse to obey; to be stubborn in opposition; to show repugnance or resistance.

rē·çal'ci·trāte, *v.t.* to kick back. [Rare.]

rē·çal·ci·trā'tion, *n.* the act of recalcitrating or the state of being recalcitrant; opposition; repugnance.

rē·çȧ·lesce' (-les'), *v.i.*; recalesced, *pt., pp.*; recalescing, *ppr.* [*re-,* and L. *calescere,* to grow hot.] to become warm again; to exhibit recalescence.

rē·çȧ·les'cence, *n.* the act of growing warmer or glowing again; specifically, the phenomenon exhibited by hot steel or iron when there is a sudden and temporary increase in glow and temperature upon reaching a particular stage in the cooling process: opposed to *decalescence.*

rē·çȧ·les'cent, *a.* [L. *recalescens.*] having or showing recalescence.

rē·çall', *v.t.*; recalled, *pt., pp.*; recalling, *ppr.*

1. to call back; to bid return; specifically, to ask purchasers to return (an imperfect or dangerous product), often so that a manufacturing defect can be corrected.

2. to remember; to recollect.

3. to take back; to cancel; annul; revoke; withdraw.

4. to remove from office by the process of recall.

5. to bring back in awareness or attention, as to the immediate situation.

6 to revive. [Poet.]

rē·çall', *n.* 1. the act of calling back.

2. revocation; abrogation.

3. the power of recalling, revoking, or annulling; as, a deed past *recall.*

4. a calling back to mind; recollection.

5. nautically, a flag hoisted as a signal for a boat to rejoin a ship or for a ship to rejoin a squadron.

6. a drumbeat or trumpet call to order the return of soldiers to camp or ranks.

7. in political science, the process of removing, or right to remove, an official from office by popular vote.

rē·çall'ȧ·ble, *a.* capable of being recalled; subject to recall.

Delegates *recallable* at pleasure. —Madison.

rē·çall'ment, *n.* the act of recalling; recall. [Rare.]

rē·çant', *v.t.*; recanted, *pt., pp.*; recanting, *ppr.* [L. *recantare,* to sing back, from *re-,* back, and *cantare,* freq. of *canere,* to sing.]

1. to withdraw or renounce (beliefs, statements, etc. formerly held), especially in a formal or public manner; to abjure.

2. to repeat in songs. [Obs.]

rē·çant', *v.i.* to make a formal or public withdrawal or renunciation of beliefs, statements, etc. formerly held.

Syn.—repudiate, disavow, renounce.—To *renounce* is to abandon an opinion or doctrine; to *recant* is formally and distinctly to disavow it as a serious error. It of course implies the adoption of the opposing truth.

rē·çan·tā'tion, *n.* the act of recanting; formal disavowal; retraction.

rē·çant'ẽr, *n.* one who recants.

rē·çap', *v.t.*; recapped, *pt., pp.*; recapping, *ppr.* [*re-* and *cap.*] to cement, mold, and vulcanize a strip of rubber on the outer surface of (a worn pneumatic tire).

rē'çap, *n.* a recapped tire.

rē·çap'i·tăl·īze'', *v.t.* to capitalize again; specifically, in commerce, to change the capital or capitalization of.

rē·çȧ·pit'ū·lāte, *v.t.*; recapitulated, *pt., pp.*; recapitulating, *ppr.* [LL. *recapitulare,* to go over the main points again.] to repeat in outline, as a discourse, treatise, or essay; to restate briefly; to summarize.

It is not my purpose to *recapitulate* all the topics that should find a place in Democracy's message to the people. —Grover Cleveland.

rē·ca̤·pit′ū·lāte, *v.i.* to repeat in brief what has been said previously.

Syn.—repeat, reiterate, summarize.

rē·ca̤·pit·ū·lā′tion, *n.* 1. the act of recapitulating.

2. a summary or concise statement or enumeration of the principal points or facts in a preceding discourse, argument, essay, etc.

3. in biology, the repeating in an individual's development, especially in the embryo, of the evolutionary stages of the species.

4. in music, reprise.

rē·ca̤·pit′ū·lā·tive, *a.* 1. of or pertaining to recapitulation; consisting of a summary.

2. recapitulating.

rē·ca̤·pit′ū·lā·tŏr, *n.* one who recapitulates.

rē·ca̤·pit′ū·la·tō″ry, *a.* repeating again; containing or of the nature of recapitulation.

rē·ca̤p′pẽr, *n.* a device or tool for applying fresh percussion caps or primers to cartridge shells when reloading them.

rē·ca̤p′tion, *n.* the retaking of one's own goods, chattels, wife, or children, without force or violence, from one who has taken them and wrongfully detains them; reprisal.

writ of recaption; a writ to recover property taken by a second distraint, pending a replevin for a former distraint for the same rent or service.

rē·ca̤p′tŏr, *n.* one who retakes or recaptures; one who takes a prize which was previously taken.

rē·ca̤p′tūre, *v.t.*; recaptured, *pt., pp.*; recapturing, *ppr.* 1. to capture again; to retake, particularly a prize which had been previously taken.

2. to get by recapture (sense 2).

3. to remember.

rē·ca̤p′tūre, *n.* 1. a recapturing or being recaptured.

2. the taking by the government of a fixed portion of all earnings exceeding a certain percentage of property value.

3. that which is recaptured.

rē·cär″bū·ri·zā′tion, *n.* the act of restoring carbon after decarburization.

rē·cär′bū·rīze, *v.t.* to carbonize again; to restore carbon to, as to steel, after decarburization; as, to *recarburize* iron in converting it into steel: also *recarbonize.*

rē·ca̤st′, *v.t.*; recast, *pt., pp.*; recasting, *ppr.* 1. to cast, or mold, anew or again; as, to *recast* cannon.

2. to throw again or a second time.

3. to remodel and improve by changing form, style, or arrangement; to reconstruct; as, to *recast* an argument.

4. to compute a second time; to calculate or count again; as, to *recast* an account.

5. to provide a new cast for (a play).

rē·ca̤st′, *n.* 1. a recasting.

2. a new form produced by recasting; that which is remodeled or cast anew.

rec̜′che, *v.i.* and *v.t.* to reck. [Obs.]

rec̜′che·les, *a.* reckless. [Obs.]

rē·cēde′, *v.i.*; receded, *pt., pp.*; receding, *ppr.* 1. to move back; to retreat; to fall away; as, the high water *receded.*

2. to withdraw a claim or pretension; to desist; to relinquish what had been proposed or asserted: usually with *from*; as, to *recede from* a demand, to *recede from* terms or propositions.

3. to slope backward; as, a *receding* forehead.

4. to become more distant, and hence indistinct; as, memories of childhood *recede.*

Syn.—retire, withdraw, retrograde.

rē·cēde′, *v.t.* to cede back; to grant or yield to a former possessor; as, to *recede* conquered territory.

rē·cē′dence, *n.* the act of receding; recession.

rē·cēipt′ (-sēt′), *n.* [OFr. *recete, recepte*; Fr. *recette*, from L. *receptus*, pp. of *recipere*, to receive.]

1. a recipe.

2. a receiving or being received.

3. a written acknowledgment that something has been received, as goods, money, etc.

4. (a) that which is received; (b) [*pl.*] the amount received.

5. the place of receiving. [Obs.]

Matthew, sitting at the *receipt* of custom.
—Matt. ix. 9.

6. a reception; welcome; hospitality; as, the kind *receipt* of a friend. [Obs.]

7. power or capability of receiving; capacity. [Obs.]

A place of great *receipt.* —Evelyn.

8. admission; a taking in. [Obs.]

The most convenient place . . . for such *receipt* of learning. —Shak.

gross receipts; receipts from all sources; the entire receipts: opposed to *net receipts*, the sum remaining after deduction of all expenses.

return receipt; the receipt given a postmaster by the addressee of registered mail, which is returned by him to the sender.

Syn.—acknowledgment, voucher.

rē·cēipt′ (-sēt′), *v.t.*; receipted, *pt., pp.*; receipting, *ppr.* 1. to give a receipt for; as, to *receipt* goods delivered by a sheriff.

2. to write or stamp a receipt on; to mark (a bill) paid.

rē·cēipt′, *v.i.* to give a receipt, as for money paid.

rē·cēipt′a·ble, *a.* capable of being receipted.

rē·cēipt′ book, a book containing blank forms for making out receipts.

rē·cēipt′ment, *n.* in old English law, the act of willfully or knowingly harboring a felon.

rē·cēipt′ŏr, *n.* a person who receipts; specifically, in law, one who receipts as bailee for property which has been taken by the sheriff.

rē·cēiv·a·bil′i·ty, *n.* the quality or state of being receivable.

rē·cēiv′a·ble, *a.* [ME. *resceyuable*; Anglo-Fr.; OFr. *recevable*; also from *receive* and *able.*]

1. that can be received.

2. due; requiring payment.

3. suitable for acceptance.

rē·cēiv′a·ble·ness, *n.* same as *receivability.*

rē·cēiv′a·bles̜ (-blz), *n.pl.* accounts or bills receivable.

rē·cēive′, *v.t.*; received, *pt., pp.*; receiving, *ppr.* [OFr. *receiver*; Fr. *recevoir*, from L. *recipere*, to receive; *re-*, back, and *capere*, to take.]

1. to take into one's possession (something given, offered, sent, etc.); to get; accept; acquire.

2. to encounter; experience; as, she *received* much acclaim.

3. to undergo; submit to; suffer; have inflicted on one; as, he *received* punishment.

4. to bear; to take the effect or force of; as, all four wheels *receive* the weight equally.

5. to take from another by hearing or listening; as, his confession was *received* by the priest.

6. to apprehend mentally; to get knowledge of or information about; to learn; as, they *received* the news.

7. to accept mentally as authentic, valid, etc.

8. (a) to let enter; admit; (b) to have room for; hold; contain; as, a cistern receives rain water.

9. to give admittance to or greet (visitors, guests, etc.).

10. to take (goods) from a thief, knowing them to be stolen.

Syn.—accept, admit, obtain, secure, take, hold.—To *receive* describes simply the act of taking; to *accept*, the taking cordially or for the purpose for which a thing is offered.

rē·cēive′, *v.i.* 1. to get, accept, take, or acquire something; to be a recipient.

2. to receive guests or visitors; to be a host.

3. in radio and television, to convert incoming electromagnetic waves into sound or light, thus reproducing the sounds or images being transmitted.

4. in religious usage, to receive the Eucharist.

5. in tennis, etc., to return, or prepare to return, a served ball; to be the striker.

rē·cēiv′ed·ness, *n.* the quality or state of being generally received, allowed, or acknowledged; general allowance. [Rare.]

rē·cēiv′ẽr, *n.* 1. a person who receives; specifically, (a) a person who officially receives money, etc. for others; a collector; a treasurer; (b) a person who knowingly receives stolen goods for gain or concealment; a fence; (c) in baseball, a catcher; (d) in law, a person appointed by a court to administer or hold in trust property in bankruptcy or in a lawsuit.

2. a thing that receives; specifically, (a) a receptacle; especially, in chemistry, a receptacle connected with a retort, tube, etc., into which a distilled product passes; (b) an apparatus or device for receiving electrical waves, signals, etc. and converting them into sound or light, as a radio or television receiving set, or that part of a telephone which is held to the ear; (c) the glass receptacle on the table of an air pump; (d) a vessel which is adapted to collect or contain gas; (e) a sheet iron vessel lined with firebricks and clay from which the melted iron in a foundry is conducted into the mold: it also acts as a receptacle for large quantities of melted iron of fifteen or twenty tons weight which exceed the capacity of the foundry ladles.

exhausted receiver; the receiver, as of an air pump, from which the air has been pumped out.

intermediate receiver; a vessel or casing employed on some compound steam engines as a steam chamber or reservoir between the high- and low-pressure cylinders. It is rendered necessary when the cranks of the two cylinders are set at right angles to each other, so that when one piston is at full the other is at midstroke. Its effect is also to equalize the back pressure in the high-pressure cylinder and to diminish the variations in its temperature.

rē·cēiv′ẽr·ġen′ẽr·ăl, *n.*; *pl.* **rē·cēiv′ẽrs̜·ġen′ẽr·ăl,** in some states and countries, an official in charge of the public revenues.

rē·cēiv′ẽr·ship, *n.* in law, (a) the duties, office, or position of a receiver; (b) the state of being administered or held by a receiver.

rē·cēiv′ing set, in radio and television, an apparatus for converting incoming electromagnetic waves into sound or light, thus reproducing the sounds or images being transmitted; a receiver.

rē·cēiv′ing ship, a ship stationed in a harbor to receive recruits, who are ultimately to be transferred to the naval service.

rē′cen·cy, *n.* [L. *recens*, recent.] the quality or state of being recent.

rē·cense′, *v.t.* [*re-*, and L. *censere*, to count.] to review; to revise.

rē·cen′sion, *n.* 1. review; examination; enumeration. [Rare.]

2. a revision of a text, based on a critical examination of sources.

3. a text established by such a critical revision.

rē·cen′sion·ist, *n.* one who makes a recension.

rē′cent, *a.* [Fr. *récent*, from L. *recens* (*-entis*), recent.]

1. done, made, etc. just before the present time; modern; new.

2. of a time just before the present.

3. [R—] in geology, designating or of the present epoch, extending from the close of the Pleistocene.

the Recent; the Recent Epoch.

rē′cent·ly, *adv.* at a recent time; lately; not long since; as, *recently* received news, a town *recently* built.

rē′cent·ness, *n.* the state or quality of being recent.

rē′cept, *n.* [*re-*, again, and *-cept* as in *concept.*] in psychology, a mental image formed by successive sense impressions of the same or closely allied objects.

rē·cep′ta·c̜le, *n.* [Fr. *réceptacle*; L. *receptaculum*, from *recipere*, to receive.]

1. that which receives, admits, or contains things; a place or vessel in which anything is received and contained; a container; a repository.

2. in botany, the enlarged part of the stalk on which the flower grows; the torus. The term is used by botanists in different senses. Thus, it is used to signify the axis of the theca among ferns; that part of the ovarium from which the ovula arise, commonly called the placenta; also, that part of the axis of a plant which bears the flowers when it is depressed in its development, so that it forms a flattened area over which the flowers are arranged, as in *Compositæ*: this is called the *clinanthium.* A proper receptacle belongs only to one set of parts of fructification; a common receptacle bears several florets or distinct sets of parts of fructification. Among the coarser algae, the term is applied to those podlike bodies which contain spores.

RECEPTACLES
1a. hollow receptacle of *Matricaria*; 2a. dry receptacle of the raspberry, bearing fleshy ovaria; 3a. succulent receptacle of the strawberry, bearing dry ovaria

rē·cep·tac̜′ū·lăr, *a.* in botany, pertaining to or growing on a receptacle.

rē·cep·tac̜′ū·līte, *n.* a fossil organism belonging to the extinct family *Receptaculitidæ*, found in the seas of the Silurian and Devonian periods. By many they have been classified as sponges.

rē·cep·tac̜′ū·lum, *n.*; *pl.* **rē·cep·tac̜′ū·la̤,** in anatomy, a receptacle.

rec′ep·tȧ·ry, *a.* accepted generally but not proved. [Obs.]

rec′ep·tȧ·ry, *n.* a thing popularly accepted. [Obs.]

rē·cep·ti·bil′i·ty, *n.* the quality or state of being receptible; receivableness.

rē·cep′ti·ble, *a.* capable of or suited for receiving or being received; receivable.

rē·cep′tion, *n.* [Fr., from L. *receptio (-onis)*, a receiving.]

1. the act of receiving; the getting or receiving of a thing sent, offered, given, or communicated; as, the *reception* of news.

2. the state of being received or admitted; admission.

3. the manner of receiving on arrival; treatment at first coming; welcome; as, a hearty *reception*, a cold *reception*.

4. a social function, often formal, for the receiving of guests.

5. the act of mentally accepting or approving; admission, credence, or allowance, as of an opinion or doctrine; sanction.

As extravagant opinions as even common *reception* countenanced. —Locke.

6. in radio and television, the manner of receiving and reproducing, with reference to the relative quality of the reproduction; as, the storm caused poor *reception*.

Syn.—admission, admittance, acceptance, acceptation.

rē·cep′tion·ist, *n.* a person employed in an office to receive callers, make appointments, give information, etc.

rē·cep′tion rọọm, a room in a house, office, etc. for receiving visitors as they arrive.

rē·cep′tive, *a.* [ML. *receptivus*, from L. *receptus*.]

1. receiving or tending to receive, take in, admit, or contain.

2. inclined to the favorable reception of a request, suggestion, etc.

3. able or ready to receive new ideas, etc.

4. of reception or receptors.

rē·cep′tive·ness, *n.* the state or quality of being receptive; receptivity.

rē·cep·tiv′i·ty, *n.* 1. the state or quality of being receptive.

2. the ability or capacity of the mind for receiving impressions.

rē·cep′tŏr, *n.* [L.] 1. a receiver; anyone or anything that receives.

2. in physiology, a sense organ; the peripheral cells, nerve endings, etc. which receive and transmit external stimuli.

rē·cep′tō·ry, *n.* a receptacle. [Obs.]

rē·cess′ (*also, esp. in sense 5*, rē′ses), *n.* [L. *recessus*, from *recedere*, to withdraw.]

1. a withdrawing or retiring; departure. [Obs.]

2. a receding; recession; as, the *recess* of the tides.

3. a receding or hollow place, as in a surface, wall, etc.; a niche.

4. [*usually in pl.*] a secluded, withdrawn, or inner place; as, subterranean *recesses;* the *recesses* of the subconscious.

5. (a) a temporary withdrawal from or halting of work or business, as at school; (b) the state or time of this; as, the court was in *recess*.

6. in anatomy, a small cavity, hollow, indentation, etc. in an organ or part.

7. privacy; seclusion from the world or company; a state of retirement; as, lords in close *recess*. [Obs.]

8. secret or abstruse part; as, the difficulties and *recesses* of science.

9. a decree of the Imperial Diet of the old German Empire.

rē·cess′, *v.t.*; recessed (-cest′), *pt., pp.*; recessing, *ppr.* 1. to make into a recess; to make a recess in.

2. to place or set in a recess.

rē·cess′, *v.i.* to take a recess.

rē·ces′sion (-sesh′un), *n.* [L. *recessio (-onis)*, from *recedere*, to withdraw.]

1. the act of receding; a going back or backward; withdrawal.

2. the procession of the clergy and choir from the chancel to the vestry at the end of the service.

3. a receding part, as of a wall.

4. in economics, a temporary falling off of business activity during a period when such activity has been generally increasing, as during that after a depression.

rē·ces′sion, *n.* a cession or granting back; as, the *recession* of conquered territory to its former sovereign.

rē·ces′sion·ăl, *a.* 1. of or pertaining to a recession.

2. of a parliamentary recess. [Brit.]

rē·ces′sion·ăl, *n.* 1. a recessional hymn.

2. music for such a hymn.

rē·ces′sion·ăl hymn (him), a hymn sung at the end of a church service during the recession (sense 2).

rē·ces′sive, *a.* [from L. *recessus*, and *-ive*.]

1. receding or tending to recede.

2. tending to move from the last toward the first syllable of a word: said of stress, or accent.

3. in genetics, designating or relating to that one of any pair of opposite Mendelian characters which, when factors for both are present in the germ plasm, remains latent: opposed to *dominant*.

rē·ces′sive, *n.* 1. in genetics, a recessive character or factor.

2. an organism having such characters.

Reçh′ȧ·bīte, *n.* 1. one of a family descended from Jonadab, the son of Rechab, bound to the continuance of the nomadic life and adhering to several rules, the chief of which were: to abstain from wine, from building houses, from sowing seed, and from planting vineyards. These rules were observed by the Rechabites with great strictness.

2. a member of a secret benefit society composed of total abstainers from intoxicating drinks, called the Independent Order of Rechabites: it was founded in England in 1835.

rē·chärġe′, *v.t.* and *v.i.*; recharged, *pt., pp.*; recharging, *ppr.* to charge again (in various senses).

rē′chärġe, *n.* a recharging.

ré·chauf·fé′ (rā-shō-fā′), *n.*; *pl.* **ré·chauf·fés′** (-fā′), [Fr., pp. of *réchauffer*, to warm over, from *ré-*, again, and *échauffer*, to heat.]

1. a dish of leftover food reheated.

2. any used or old material, especially literary material, worked up in a new form; a rehash.

rē·chēat′, *n.* [Fr. *requête*, older *requeste*, a note on the horn to recall the dogs.] in hunting, a strain blown to call back the hounds. [Archaic.]

re·cher′ché (rē-shär′shā), *a.* [Fr., pp. of *rechercher*.]

1. sought out with care; rare; choice; uncommon.

2. having refinement or studied elegance.

3. too refined; too studied.

reçh′less, *a.* reckless. [Obs.]

rē·cid′i·vāte, *v.i.* to backslide. [Obs.]

rē·cid·i·vā′tion, *n.* [L. *recidivus*, a falling back.]

1. a backsliding. [Obs.]

2. habitual return to former criminal practices; recidivism.

rē·cid′i·viṣm, *n.* [from L. *recidivus*, from *recidere*, to fall back, from *re-*, back, and *cadere*, to fall; and *-ism*.] habitual or chronic relapse, or tendency to relapse, into crime or antisocial behavior patterns.

rē·cid′i·vist, *n.* a habitual criminal; a person characterized by recidivism; one who returns to criminal practices habitually.

rē·cid′i·vous, *a.* liable to backslide; especially, characterized by or tending to recidivism.

rec′i·pē, *n.* [L., imperative of *recipere*, to take.]

1. a formula for a medical prescription: symbol, ℞: now usually called *prescription*.

2. a medicine made up according to such a formula; a prescription.

3. a list of materials and directions for preparing a dish or drink; a receipt.

4. anything proposed as a remedy, for doing something, or for producing a desired result.

rē·cip′i·añ·gle, *n.* [L. *recipere*, to take, and *angulus*, an angle.] in engineering, an instrument formerly used for measuring angles, especially in fortification.

rē·cip′i·ence, *n.* 1. a receiving; reception.

2. the condition of being recipient; receptivity.

rē·cip′i·en·cy, *n.* same as *recipience*.

rē·cip′i·ent, *a.* receiving, or ready, willing, or able to receive.

rē·cip′i·ent, *n.* [L. *recipiens (-entis)*, ppr. of *recipere*, to receive.]

1. a receiver; one to whom or that to which anything is communicated or given.

2. a receiver (sense 2a). [Obs.]

rē·cip′i·ō·mō″tŏr, *a.* in physiology, receiving a motor stimulus.

rē·cip′rō·çăl, *a.* [L. *reciprocus*; Fr. *réciproque*, alternating, going backward and forward.]

1. done, felt, given, etc. in return; as, *reciprocal* tolerance.

2. on both sides; each to the other; mutual; as, they felt a *reciprocal* affection.

3. corresponding but reversed or inverted.

4. corresponding; equivalent or interchangeable; complementary.

5. in grammar, (a) expressing mutual action or relation; as, *each other* is a *reciprocal* pronoun; (b) formerly, reflexive.

6. in mathematics, of the reciprocals of quantities, or their relations.

7. reciprocating; alternate. [Obs.]

reciprocal equation; one which has the same form if the reciprocal of the unknown quantity is substituted for the quantity itself.

reciprocal figures; two figures of the same kind, as triangles, parallelograms, prisms, etc., so related that two sides of one form the extremes of a proportion of which the means are the two corresponding sides of the other.

reciprocal proportion; same as *inverse proportion* under *inverse*.

reciprocal quantities; those quantities which multiplied together produce unity.

reciprocal ratio; same as *inverse ratio* under *inverse*.

reciprocal terms; terms which have the same value and may be used for each other.

Syn.—interchangeable, mutual.—The distinctive idea of *mutual* is that the parties unite by interchange in the same act; as, a *mutual* covenant. The distinctive idea of *reciprocal* is that one party acts by way of return or response to something previously done by the other party; as, a *reciprocal* kindness.

rē·cip′rō·çăl, *n.* 1. anything that has a reciprocal action on or relation to another; a complement, counterpart, equivalent, etc.

2. in mathematics, the quantity (with reference to a given quantity) resulting from the division of 1 by the given quantity; as, the *reciprocal* of 7 is $^1/_7$.

rē·cip·rō·çal′i·ty, *n.* the state or quality of being reciprocal.

rē·cip′rō·çăl·ly, *adv.* in a reciprocal manner.

reciprocally proportional; designating two quantities when both being variable the ratio of the one to the reciprocal of the other is constant. This requires that their product should be constant.

rē·cip′rō·çăl·ness, *n.* same as *reciprocality*.

rē·cip′rō·çănt, *n.* in mathematics, a differential invariant. [Rare.]

rē·cip′rō·çāte, *v.i.*; reciprocated, *pt., pp.*; reciprocating, *ppr.* [from L. *reciprocatus*, pp. of *reciprocare*, from *reciprocus*.]

1. to move alternately back and forth; to interchange position.

2. to give and get reciprocally; to interchange.

3. to make some sort of return for something done, given etc.

4. to be correspondent or equivalent.

reciprocating engine; that form of engine in which the piston and piston rod move back and forth in a straight line, absolutely, or relatively to the cylinder: distinguished from *rotary engine*, (a).

reciprocating motion; in mechanics, motion alternately backward and forward, or up and down, as of a piston rod.

rē·cip′rō·çāte, *v.t.* 1. to cause to move alternately back and forth.

2. to give and get, do, feel, etc. reciprocally; to interchange; as, they *reciprocate* enmity.

3. to give, do, feel, etc. in return; to return in kind or degree; as, we *reciprocate* her affection.

4. to make correspondent or equivalent. [Rare.]

rē·cip·rō·çā′tion, *n.* [L. *reciprocatio*.] the act or fact of reciprocating (in various senses).

rē·cip′rō·çā·tive, *a.* 1. reciprocating or tending to reciprocate.

2. characterized by reciprocation.

rē·cip′rō·çā·tŏr, *n.* a person or thing that reciprocates.

rec·i·proc′i·ty, *n.* [Fr. *réciprocité*.]

1. reciprocal state or relationship; mutual action, dependence, etc.

2. a reciprocating; interchange; mutual exchange; especially, exchange of special privileges between two countries, to the advantage of both, as mutual reduction of tariffs.

reciprocity treaty; a treaty entered into for the purpose of securing commercial reciprocity between two nations.

rē·cip·rō·çor′nous, *a.* [L. *reciprocus*, backward and forward, and *cornus*, having horns.] having horns turned first backward and then forward, as those of a ram.

rē·cip′rō·cous, *a.* reciprocal. [Obs.]

rec′i·prōque (-prōk), *a.* [Fr. *réciproque.*] reciprocal. [Obs.]

rē·ci′ṣion (-sizh′un), *n.* [L. *recisio*, from *recidere*, to cut off.]
1. the act of cutting off. [Rare.]
2. a rescinding, or annulling.

rē·cīt′ăl, *n.* 1. the repetition of the words of another, or of a writing; as, he gave a *recital* of selections from Byron.
2. a reciting; a telling of facts, events, etc. in detail.
3. a detailed statement, as of facts or events.
4. that which is recited; a story, account, description, narration, etc.; as, a harrowing *recital.*
5. in law, that part of a deed which recites the facts, arguments, etc. which may be necessary to explain the reasons upon which it is founded.
6. a musical entertainment given by a soloist, soloists, or small ensemble; as, an organ *recital.*
Syn.—rehearsal, narration, account, recitation, description, explanation, narrative.

rẹ·cĭ·tăn′dō (rā-chē-), *a.* and *adv.* [It.] in music, in the style of recitative; in a declamatory way: a direction to the performer.

rec·i·tā′tion, *n.* [L. *recitatio* (*-onis*), a recital.]
1. a reciting, as of facts, events, etc.; a recital.
2. an account, story, etc.
3. (a) the speaking aloud in public of something memorized; (b) a piece of prose or verse so memorized and spoken.
4. (a) a reciting by pupils of answers to questions on a prepared lesson, etc.; (b) a class meeting or period in which this occurs.

rec′i·tā·tive, *a.* [from *recite* and *-ative.*] reciting; of, or having the nature of, recital, as of facts, events, etc.

rec″i·tȧ·tīve′, *n.* [It. *recitativo*, from L. *recitare.*]
1. in music, a type of declamatory singing, free in rhythm and tempo, used in the prose parts and dialogue of operas and oratorios.
2. a work or passage in this style.
3. music for such passages.

rec″i·tȧ·tīve′, *a.* having the nature, or in the style or manner, of recitative or declamation.

rec″i·tȧ·tīve′ly, *adv.* in the manner of recitative.

rẹ″cĭ·tȧ·tī′vō (rā″chē-), *n.*; *pl.* **rẹ″cĭ·tȧ·tī′vī,** [It.] in music, a recitative.

rē·cīte′, *v.t.*; recited, *pt.*, *pp.*; reciting, *ppr.* [L. *recitare*; *re-*, again, and *citare*, to call or name.]
1. to repeat or speak aloud from or as from memory, especially in a formal way, as lessons in class or a poem, speech, etc. before an audience.
2. to tell in detail; to give an account of; narrate; relate.
3. to enumerate.
4. in law, to cite; to set out in a written instrument.
Syn.—rehearse, repeat, relate, quote.

rē·cīte′, *v.i.* 1. to to repeat or speak aloud before an audience something memorized, as a literary composition.
2. to recite a lesson or part of a lesson before a teacher; to answer questions orally in class; as, the pupil *recites* well.

rē·cīte′, *n.* a recital. [Obs.]

rē·cīt′ẽr, *n.* one who recites or rehearses; a narrator; also, a book containing recitations.

rē·cīt′ing nōte, in a chant, a note representing the tone of several consecutive syllables.

reck, *v.i.* and *v.t.*; recked, *pt.*, *pp.*; recking, *ppr.* [ME. *reknen, rekenen*; AS. *gerecnian, recenian*; Dan. *regne*; Ice. *reikna*, to reckon, number, esteem.]
1. to have care or concern (for) or take heed (of); as, he *recks* not of the peril. [Archaic or Poet.]
2. to concern or be of concern; to matter (to); as, it *recks* him not. [Archaic or Poet.]

reck′less, *a.* 1. careless; heedless.
2. not regarding consequences; headlong and irresponsible.
Syn.—incautious, foolhardy, thoughtless, rash, overventuresome, inconsiderate, improvident.

reck′less·ly, *adv.* in a reckless manner.

reck′less·ness, *n.* the quality of being reckless.

reck′ling, *n.* the smallest and weakest in a brood of animals or of the children of a family. [Brit. Dial.]

reck′ŏn, *v.t.*; reckoned, *pt.*, *pp.*; reckoning, *ppr.* [ME. *rekenen, reknen*, from AS. *ge-recenian*, to explain. A derivative verb allied to AS. *gereccan*, to rule, direct, order, explain, tell; D. *rekenen*; Ice. *reikna*, to reckon.]
1. to count; to figure up; to compute; to calculate.
I *reckoned* above two hundred and fifty on the outside of the church. —Addison.
2. to consider as; to regard as being; to repute.
He was *reckoned* among the transgressors. —Luke xxii. 37.
3. to make account or reckoning of. [Obs.]
Faith was *reckoned* to Abraham for righteousness. —Rom. iv. 9.
4. to judge; to consider; to estimate.
5. to suppose, think, or believe; as, I *reckon* it will rain. [Colloq. or Dial.]

reck′ŏn, *v.i.* 1. to count up; to figure.
2. to depend; to rely (with *on*).
3. to settle an account.
4. to pay a penalty; to be answerable. [Obs.]
If they fail in their bounden duty, they shall *reckon* for it one day. —Sanderson.
to reckon for; to be answerable or responsible for.
to reckon with; (a) to balance accounts and make a settlement with; (b) to take into consideration.
to reckon without one's host; to ignore, in a transaction, one whose co-operation is essential; hence, to reckon without considering some important factor or factors.

reck′ŏn·ẽr, *n.* 1. one who or that which reckons or computes.
Reckoners without their host must reckon twice. —Camden.
2. something that assists a person to reckon, as a book containing a series of tables; a ready reckoner.

reck′ŏn·ing, *n.* 1. the act of computing, counting, or calculating; computation.
It were a pity you should get your living by *reckoning*, sir. —Shak.
2. a settlement of accounts with another; a comparison of accounts with a view to settlement.
3. an account of the time of pregnancy. [Now Rare.]
Canst thou their *reckonings* keep? —Sandys.
4. the charge, account, or bill; charge by the landlord of an inn, etc.
I never scorn to be treated by any that are kind enough to pay my *reckoning*. —Goldsmith.
5. a settlement of rewards or penalties for any action; a charge generally; cost incurred.
He deems a thousand, or ten thousand lives, An easy *reckoning*. —Cowper.
6. a measuring of possibilities for the future; calculated guess.
7. in nautical usage, (a) the determination of the position of a ship; (b) the position so determined.
8. esteem; estimation; account. [Obs.]
day of reckoning; (a) a time when accounts must be settled; (b) the Last Judgment.
Syn.—calculation, computation, estimate, charge, bill.

reck′ŏn·ing book, an account book. [Obs.]

rē·çlāim′, *v.t.*; reclaimed, *pt.*, *pp.*; reclaiming, *ppr.* to claim back; to attempt to recover possession of; to demand to have returned.
A tract of land (Holland) snatched from an element perpetually *reclaiming* its prior occupancy. —Coxe.

rē·çlāim′, *v.t.* [ME. *reclaimen*; OFr. *reclamer*; L. *reclamare.*]
1. to rescue or bring back (a person or people) from error, vice, savagery, etc. to ways of living or thinking regarded as right; to reform.
2. to make (wasteland, desert, etc.) capable of being cultivated or lived on, as by filling, ditching, or irrigating.
3. to obtain (useful materials, etc.) from waste products.
4. to call back; specifically, in falconry, to bring (a hawk) to the wrist by a certain call. [Obs.]
5. to call out repeatedly to; to call back; to call to a halt. [Obs.]
The headstrong horses hurried Octavius along, and were deaf to his *reclaiming* them. —Dryden.
6. to reduce from a wild to a tame or domestic state; to tame; to make gentle; as, to *reclaim* a hawk. [Obs.]
7. to bring under restraint or close limits; to check; to restrain; to hold back. [Obs.]
By this means also the wood is *reclaimed* and repressed. —Holland.
8. to gainsay or contradict. [Obs.]
Syn.—reform, restore, amend, correct.

rē·çlāim′, *v.i.* 1. to cry out; to exclaim against anything. [Obs.]
2. to effect reformation. [Obs.]
3. to draw back; to give way. [Obs.]
4. in Scots law, to appeal.

rē·çlāim′, *n.* the act of reclaiming; recovery; reclamation; as, he's past *reclaim.*

rē·çlāim′ȧ·ble, *a.* capable of being reclaimed, reformed, or tamed.

rē·çlāim′ănt, *n.* one who reclaims.

rē·çlāim′ẽr, *n.* one who reclaims.

rē·çlāim′less, *a.* not to be reclaimed. [Rare.]

reç·lȧ·mā′tion, *n.* [Fr. *réclamation*, a reclaiming or bringing back.]
1. a reclaiming or being reclaimed; recovery or restoration to a better or useful state, as of wasteland, desert, etc. by ditching, filling, or irrigating.
2. the process or industry of obtaining useful materials from waste products.
3. demand for or challenge of something to be restored; claim made in opposition or remonstrance.

ré·clame′ (rā-klȧm′), *n.* [Fr., from *réclamer.*]
1. publicity.
2. a seeking for publicity.

rē·çlī′nănt, *a.* leaning backward; bending backward.

reç′li·nāte, *a.* in botany, reclined, as a leaf bent downward, so that the point of the leaf is lower than the base.

reç·li·nā′tion, *n.* 1. the act of leaning or reclining.
2. in dialing, the angle which the plane of the dial makes with a vertical plane which it intersects in a horizontal line. [Obs.]
3. an old operation for cataract; couching.

rē·çlīne′, *v.t.*; reclined, *pt.*, *pp.*; reclining, *ppr.* [L. *reclinare*; *re-*, back, and *clinare*, to lean.] to lay back; to cause to lean or lie back or down; to cause to assume a recumbent position; as, to *recline* the head on a pillow.

rē·çlīne′, *v.i.* to lie back or down; to lean back; to rest or repose lying down (often with *on* or *upon*); as, to *recline on* a couch.

rē·çlīne′, *a.* leaning; being in a leaning posture. [Rare.]
They sat, *recline*,
On the soft, downy bank damasked with flowers. —Milton.

rē·çlīned′, *a.* in botany, same as *reclinate.*

rē·çlīn′ẽr, *n.* one who or that which reclines.

reç′li·vāte, *a.* in entomology, forming a double curve. [Rare.]

rē·çlūde′, *v.t.* to open. [Obs.]

rē·çlūse′, *a.* [Fr. *reclus*, from LL. *reclusus*, pp. of *recludere*, to shut up, but in L. with a signification directly opposite.] shut up; sequestered; retired from the world or from public notice; solitary; secluded; as, a *recluse* monk or hermit; a *recluse* life.

re′çlūse (*or* rē-klūs′), *n.* 1. a person who lives apart from the world for religious contemplation; an anchorite or anchoress.
2. a person who lives a secluded, solitary life.
3. a place of retirement or seclusion. [Obs.]

rē·çlūse′, *v.t.* to seclude; to retire. [Obs.]

rē·çlūse′ly, *adv.* in retirement or seclusion from society.

rē·çlūse′ness, *n.* retirement; seclusion from society.

rē·çlū′ṣion, *n.* 1. the condition or fact of becoming or being a recluse.
2. the condition or fact of being in solitary confinement.

rē·çlū′sive, *a.* 1. giving reclusion.
2. living in reclusion; recluse.

rē·çlū′sō·ry, *n.*; *pl.* **rē·çlū′sō·rieṣ,** a hermitage; the habitation of a recluse.

rē·çoçt′, *a.* revamped; made over; recooked.

rē·çoç′tion, *n.* a second coction or preparation.

reç·ŏg·ni′tion (-nish′un), *n.* [L. *recognitio* (*-onis*), a recognition.]
1. a recognizing or being recognized; acknowledgment; admission, as of a fact; acknowledgment and approval, gratitude, etc.; as, in *recognition* of your services.
2. formal acceptance by a government of the independence and sovereignty of a state newly created, as by secession, or of a government newly set up, as by revolution, in another state.
3. identification of something as having been known before or as being of a certain kind; identification of a person as being known to one.

4. notice, as in passing; greeting; salutation.
rē·çog′ni·tŏr, *n.* in early English law, one of a jury upon an assize.
rē·çog′ni·tō·ry, *a.* pertaining to or connected with recognition, or acknowledgment.
reç·ŏg·nī·zȧ·bil′i·ty, *n.* the state of being recognizable.
reç′ŏg·nī·zȧ·ble, *a.* capable of being recognized.
reç′ŏg·ni·zȧ·bly, *adv.* 1. in such a way as to be recognizable.
2. to a recognizable degree or extent.
rē·çog′ni·zănce (*or* -kon′), *n.* [OFr. *recognoissance*; LL. *recognoscentia*, an acknowledgment, obligation, from L. *recognoscere*, to recall to mind.]
1. in law, (a) a bond or obligation of record entered into before a court or magistrate, binding a person to do or not do something, be in court at a certain time, etc.; (b) a sum of money pledged and subject to forfeit if this obligation is not fulfilled.
2. the act of recognizing; acknowledgment of a person or thing; avowal; recognition.
Distance of *recognizance* bereaves. —Keats.
3. mark or badge of recognition; token; symbol. [Obs.]
That *recognizance* and pledge of love,
Which I first gave her, a handkerchief. —Shak.
rē·çog·ni·zā′tion, *n.* the act of recognizing or of being recognized. [Obs.]
reç′ŏg·nīze, *v.t.*; recognized, *pt., pp.*; recognizing, *ppr.* [back-formation from *recognizance.*]
1. to know again; to identify as known before, or as the same as that known.
2. to know by some detail, as of appearance; as, *recognize* dachshunds by their short legs.
3. to perceive; to identify; as, *recognize* the omens of defeat.
4. to acknowledge the existence, validity, or genuineness of; as, *recognize* a claim.
5. to accept as a fact; to admit; to accept; as, *recognize* defeat.
6. to acknowledge as worthy of appreciation or approval; as, *recognize* devotion.
7. to acknowledge the legal standing of, as a government or state, by some formal action or by entering into dealings with it.
8. to show acquaintance with (a person) by greeting.
9. to grant (a person) the right of speaking in a meeting, assembly, etc.
reç′ŏg·nīze, *v.i.* in law, to enter an obligation of record before a proper tribunal.
rē·çog′nīze, *v.t.* to review; to take cognizance of anew. [Rare.]
rē·çog·ni·zee′ (*or* -kon-), *n.* the person to whom a recognizance is made.
reç′ŏg·nī·zẽr, *n.* one who recognizes.
reç′ŏg·nī·zing·ly, *adv.* with recognition or appreciation.
rē·çog·ni·zọr′ (*or* -kon-), *n.* in law, one who enters into a recognizance.
reç′ŏg·nosce, *v.t.* to recognize. [Obs.]
rē·çoil′, *v.i.*; recoiled, *pt., pp.*; recoiling, *ppr.* [Fr. *reculer*, from L. *re-*, back, and *culus*, the buttocks.]
1. to retreat; to draw back, fall back, or stagger back.
2. to start or shrink back, as in fear, surprise, disgust, etc.
3. to fly back when released, as a spring, or kick back when fired, as a gun.
4. to return to or as to the starting point or source; to react (with *on* or *upon*); as, our acts *recoil upon* ourselves.
5. to degenerate. [Obs.]
rē·çoil′, *v.t.* to drive back. [Obs.]
rē·çoil′ (*of weapons, usually* rē′koil), *n.* 1. the state of having recoiled; reaction.
2. a recoiling, especially of firearms when discharged.
3. the distance through which a gun, spring, etc. recoils.
recoil atom; in physical chemistry, the rapidly moving, heavy remainder of a radioactive atom: the motion is due to the recoil action caused by the emission of an alpha or beta particle.
recoil dynamometer; an apparatus by means of which the force of recoil in a gun can be accurately measured.
recoil escapement; in horology, an escapement in which, after the pallets leave the teeth at each oscillation of the pendulum, the extremities of the teeth slide along the surfaces of the pallets, and thereby give an impulse to the pendulum or balance: the vertical escapement of a watch is a recoil escapement, and the word is used as distinguished from a *deadbeat escapement.*
rē·çoil′, *v.t.* and *v.i.* to coil anew or again.
rē·çoil′ẽr, *n.* one who recoils; one who falls or turns back from a promise or profession.
rē·çoil′ing, *n.* the act of starting or falling back; a shrinking; revolt.
rē·çoil′ing·ly, *adv.* in a recoiling manner; with starting back or retrocession.
rē·çoil′ment, *n.* the act of recoiling; a recoil. [Rare.]
rē·çoil′ pal′let, one of the parts of a recoil escapement.
rē·çoil′ spring, a spring for controlling recoil.
rē·çoin′, *v.t.*; recoined, *pt., pp.*; recoining, *ppr.* to coin anew or again; as, to *recoin* gold or silver.
rē·çoin′ăġe, *n.* 1. the act of coining anew.
2. that which is coined anew.
rē·çoin′ẽr, *n.* one who recoins.
Reç′ŏl·leçt, *n.* same as *Recollet.*
reç·ŏl·leçt′, *v.t.*; recollected, *pt., pp.*; recollecting, *ppr.* [*re-*, and L. *colligere*, to collect.]
1. to recall to memory; to recover or recall the memory or knowledge of, to bring back to mind or memory; to remember; as, to *recollect* an appointment.
2. to recall to (oneself) something temporarily forgotten; as, "Now I know!" he exclaimed, *recollecting* himself.
3. to recover or regain control of, as oneself after excitement: a reflexive use: usually written *re-collect.*
Syn.—recall, remember, bethink.
reç·ŏl·leçt′, *v.i.* to have a recollection; to remember.
rē-çŏl·leçt′, *v.t.* [orig. from L. *recollectus*, pp. of *recolligere*; later felt as, from *re-* and *collect.*]
1. to gather together again (what has been scattered).
2. (a) to collect or rally (one's thoughts, strength, courage, etc.); (b) to recover or compose (oneself): in this sense sometimes written *recollect.*
rē·çŏl·leçt′, *v.i.* to come together again; to reunite.
reç·ŏl·leçt′ed·ness, *n.* regained composure; self-possession.
reç·ŏl·leç′tion, *n.* [L. *recollectio* (*-onis*), from *recolligere*, to collect again.]
1. the act of recollecting, remembering, or recalling to the memory; the operation or process by which objects are recalled to the memory, or ideas revived to the mind; reminiscence; memory.
2. the power of recalling ideas to the mind; the period over which such power extends; remembrance; memory; as, within my *recollection.*
3. that which is recollected or recalled to mind; a reminiscence.
4. the act, process, or habit of collecting or concentrating the mind or thoughts; concentration of thought; collectiveness. [Rare.]
reç·ŏl·leç′tive, *a.* 1. of or characterized by recollection.
2. having the power of recollecting.
Reç′ŏl·let (*or Fr.* rā-kō-lā′), *n.* [Sp. and Port. *recoleto.*] in the Roman Catholic Church, a monk of a reformed order of Franciscans; a friar of the Observants.
Reç′ŏl·let, *a.* of or pertaining to the Recollets; as, a *Recollet* friar.
rē·çŏl′ŏr, *v.t.* and *v.i.* to color or dye anew; to color again; to blush again.
rē·çŏm′fŏr·tūre, *n.* renewed or restored comfort. [Obs.]
rē·çŏm·mence′, *v.t.* and *v.i.*; recommenced (-menst′), *pt., pp.*; recommencing, *ppr.* to commence, or begin, again or anew.
Recommencing our voyage about the 5th of June. —Cook.
rē·çŏm·mence′ment, *n.* the act or state of commencing anew or afresh; a fresh commencement.
reç·ŏm·mend′, *v.t.*; recommended, *pt., pp.*; recommending, *ppr.* [Fr. *recommander*, from L. *re-*, and *com-*, from *cum* intensive, and *mandare*, to order; lit., to order back or commend strongly.]
1. to give in charge or care; to commit; to entrust; as, I *recommend* him to your care.
2. to name or speak favorably as suited for some use, function, position, etc.; as, *recommend* a book.
3. to make acceptable or pleasing; as, his diligence *recommends* him.
4. to advise; to counsel; as, *recommend* that something be done.
Harmony and a liberal intercourse with all nations are *recommended* by policy, humanity and interest. —George Washington.
to recommend itself; to make itself approved; to present a favorable appearance; to be agreeable.
Syn.—commend, confide, praise, applaud, approve, advise.
reç·ŏm·mend′, *n.* a verbal or written recommendation. [Colloq.]
reç·ŏm·mend′ȧ·ble, *a.* fit or suitable to be recommended; worthy of recommendation; commendable.
reç·ŏm·mend′ȧ·ble·ness, *n.* the quality of being recommendable.
reç·ŏm·mend′ȧ·bly, *adv.* in a recommendable manner or degree; so as to deserve recommendation; commendably.
reç″ŏm·men·dā′tion, *n.* [LL. *recommendare*, to recommend.]
1. a recommending; a calling attention to a person or thing as suited for some purpose.
2. anything that recommends; specifically, a letter recommending a person or thing.
3. qualities, abilities, etc. that make a person or thing acceptable or pleasing.
4. advice; counsel.
5. a state of favor or high repute. [Obs.]
reç·ŏm·mend′ȧ·tive, *n.* that which recommends or serves to recommend; a recommendation. [Obs.]
reç·ŏm·mend′ȧ·tō·ry, *a.* 1. serving or tending to recommend; recommending.
2. having the nature of recommendation.
reç·ŏm·mend′ẽr, *n.* one who or that which recommends.
reç·ŏm·mend′um, *n.* commendation; praise; recommendation. [Obs.]
rē·çŏm·mit′, *v.t.*; recommitted, *pt., pp.*; recommitting, *ppr.* 1. to commit again or anew, as by placing in custody again; as, to *recommit* a person to jail.
2. to refer again or back; to refer again, as a question, bill, etc., to a committe; as, to *recommit* a bill in Congress.
rē·çŏm·mit′ment, *n.* the act of recommitting; the state of being recommitted.
rē·çŏm·mit′tăl, *n.* same as *recommitment.*
rē″çom·pen·sā′tion, *n.* 1. the act of recompensing; recompense. [Obs.]
2. in Scots law, the pursuer's plea in a case in which one pursues for a debt, and the defender pleads compensation, to which the pursuer replies by pleading compensation also.
reç′ŏm·pense, *v.t.* recompensed, *pt., pp.*; recompensing, *ppr.* [OFr. *recompenser*, from L. *re-*, and *compensare*, to reward.]
1. to repay (a person, etc.); to reward; to compensate.
2. to make repayment or requital for; to compensate, as a loss.
reç′ŏm·pense, *v.i.* to make recompense or compensation.
Syn.—requite, remunerate, reward, indemnify, satisfy, repay, reimburse, compensate.
reç′ŏm·pense, *n.* 1. something given or done in return for something else; repayment, remuneration, requital, or reward.
2. something given or done to make up for a loss, injury, etc.; compensation.
Syn.—compensation, satisfaction, remuneration, reward.
reç′ŏm·pense·ment, *n.* recompense. [Obs.]
reç′ŏm·pen·sẽr, *n.* one who or that which recompenses.
reç′ŏm·pen·sive, *a.* serving to recompense; compensatory.
rē″çom·pi·lā′tion, *n.* the act of recompiling; also, the result of being recompiled; a new digest.
rē·çŏm·pīle′ment, *n.* 1. the act of recompiling; the state of being recompiled.
2. a second compilation; a redigest.
rē·çŏm·pōṣe′, *v.t.*; recomposed, *pt., pp.*; recomposing, *ppr.* 1. to quiet anew; to restore to composure; to compose or tranquilize, as that which is ruffled or disturbed; as, to *recompose* the mind.
2. to compose anew or again; to rearrange, recombine, or reconstitute; to form or adjust again.
A lovely purple, which we can destroy or *recompose* at pleasure. —Boyle.
rē·çŏm·pōṣ′ẽr, *n.* one who or that which recomposes. [Rare.]
rē·çom·pō·ṣi′tion (-zish′un), *n.* the act of recomposing or the state of being recomposed.
rē·çon·cen·trä′dō, *n.* [Sp., lit., brought to a center.] a person who has been reconcentrated; specifically, during the Cuban revolution of 1895-1898, a dweller in the country

who was compelled by the Spaniards to remain within certain limits.

rē·con′cen·trāte, *v.t.*; reconcentrated, *pt., pp.*; reconcentrating, *ppr.* 1. to concentrate again or thoroughly.

2. to gather into fortified or guarded camps; as, Gen. Weyler *reconcentrated* the Cubans in camps.

rē·con·cen·trā′tion, *n.* the act of reconcentrating; specifically, the method employed by the Spanish governor of Cuba, prior to 1898, in order to prevent the native Cubans from joining the revolutionary forces in the field.

rec·ŏn·cīl·ȧ·bil′i·ty, *n.* the quality or condition of being reconcilable.

rec′ŏn·cī·lā·ble, *a.* capable of being reconciled; capable of renewed friendship; as, the parties are not *reconcilable.*

rec′ŏn·cī·lā·ble·ness, *n.* the quality of being reconcilable.

rec′ŏn·cī·lā·bly, *adv.* in a reconcilable manner; so as to be reconcilable.

rec′ŏn·cīle, *v.t.*; reconciled, *pt., pp.*; reconciling, *ppr.* [Fr. *reconcilier*; L. *reconciliare*; *re-*, and *conciliare*, to conciliate.]

1. to make friendly again or win over to a friendly attitude.

2. to settle (a quarrel, etc.) or compose (a difference, etc.).

3. to make (arguments, ideas, texts, etc.) consistent, compatible, etc.; to bring into harmony.

4. to make content, submissive, or acquiescent (*to*); as, we became *reconciled to* our lot.

5. in shipbuilding, to join (one piece of work) evenly with another: used especially in reference to the reversion of curves.

rec′ŏn·cīle, *v.i.* to become reconciled. [Rare.]

rec′ŏn·cīle·ment, *n.* reconciliation.

rec′ŏn·cī·lẽr, *n.* one who reconciles.

rec·ŏn·cil·i·ā′tion, *n.* [Fr., from L. *reconciliatio* (*-onis*), reconciliation.] a reconciling or being reconciled (in various senses).

Syn.—reconcilement, reunion, adjustment, appeasement, pacification, expiation, atonement.

rec·ŏn·cil′i·ȧ·tō·ry, *a.* reconciling or tending to reconcile.

rec′ŏn·dīte, *a.* [L. *reconditus*, hidden.]

1. beyond the grasp of the ordinary mind or understanding; profound; abstruse.

2. dealing with abstruse or difficult subjects.

3. obscure; concealed.

rē″cŏn·di′tion, *v.t.*; reconditioned, *pt., pp.*; reconditioning, *ppr.* 1. to bring back to working order; to put back in good condition; to repair, readjust, and renew parts of; as, this machine, when it is *reconditioned*, will be as good as new.

2. to cause to respond to a new or different stimulus or to a series of new and related stimuli; to re-educate (an individual) by reforming the emotional attitudes, habits, and responses (of the individual).

rē·con′di·tō·ry, *n.* a repository; a storehouse. [Obs.]

rē·cŏn·duc′tion, *n.* in law, a renewal of a lease.

rē·con′nāis·sănce, rē·con′nŏis·sănce, *n.* [Fr., earlier *reconnoissance.*]

1. in military science, the act or process of obtaining information about an enemy area, the troops in it, etc., by examination or survey.

2. a survey of a region for some other purpose, as, in engineering, to prepare for triangulation, or, in geology, to learn its features.

reconnaissance in force; a military demonstration or attack by a large body of men to ascertain the strength or position of the enemy.

rec·ŏn·noi′tẽr, rec·ŏn·noi′tre (*or* rē-kŏ-), *v.t.*; reconnoitered, reconnoitred, *pt., pp.*; reconnoitering, reconnoitring, *ppr.* [OFr. *reconnoitre*, from L. *recognoscere*; *re-*, again, and *cognoscere*, to know.]

1. in military science, to inspect or survey (an enemy position, etc.).

2. to make an examination or survey of (an area, region, etc.).

3. to survey; examine; explore.

rec·ŏn·noi′tẽr, rec·ŏn·noi′tre (*or* rē-kŏ-), *v.i.* to make a reconnaissance.

rec·ŏn·noi′tẽr·ẽr, rec·ŏn·noi′trẽr (*or* rē-kŏ-), *n.* a person who reconnoiters.

rē·con′quẽr (-kẽr), *v.t.*; reconquered, *pt., pp.*; reconquering, *ppr.* to conquer again; to recover by conquest.

rē·con′quest (-kwest), *n.* a second conquest.

rē·cŏn·sid′ẽr, *v.t.* 1. to consider again; to think over.

2. to think or argue over again with a view to changing a decision.

3. to take up again in a meeting (a matter discussed before and settled).

rē·cŏn·sid′ẽr, *v.i.* to reconsider a matter.

rē·cŏn·sid·ẽr·ā′tion, *n.* the act of reconsidering; the state of being reconsidered.

rē·cŏn·sīgn′ment (-sīn′), *n.* 1. a consigning again or anew.

2. in commerce, a change (made in transit) in the route, destination, or consignee as indicated in the original bill of lading.

rē·con·sti·tū′tion, *n.* the act of re-forming, or forming anew; a restoration.

rē·cŏn·struct′, *v.t.*; reconstructed, *pt., pp.*; reconstructing, *ppr.* 1. to construct again; to rebuild; to make over.

2. to build up, from remaining parts and other evidence, an image of what something was in its original and complete form.

rē·cŏn·struc′tion, *n.* 1. the act of constructing again.

2. [R–] (a) the process after the Civil War, of reorganizing the Southern States which had seceded and re-establishing them in the Union; (b) the period of this (1867–1877).

3. something reconstructed.

rē·cŏn·struc′tive, *a.* tending to reconstruct; reconstructing.

rē·cŏn·vēne′, *v.t.* to convene or call together again.

rē·cŏn·vēne′, *v.i.* to assemble or come together again.

rē·cŏn·vẽr′sion, *n.* 1. a reconverting or being reconverted; especially, the changing (of a nation, industry, etc.) back from a wartime to a peacetime basis.

2. the period during which this goes on.

rē·cŏn·vẽrt′, *v.t.* and *v.i.* [*re-* and *convert.*]

1. to change back, as to a former status, religion, opinion, etc.

2. to change, as a nation or industry, back from a wartime to a peacetime basis.

rē·con′vẽrt, *n.* one who has been reconverted.

rē·cŏn·vẽrt′i·ble, *a.* capable of being reconverted.

rē·cŏn·vey′, *v.t.* 1. to convey back or again, as to a former place; as, to *reconvey* goods.

2. to convey back or again, as to a former owner; as, to *reconvey* an estate.

rē·cŏn·vey′ănce, *n.* the act of reconveying or the state of being reconveyed.

rē·cord′, *v.t.*; recorded, *pt., pp.*; recording, *ppr.* [LL. *recordare*, to call to mind, to remember; *re-*, and *cor, cordis*, the heart or mind.]

1. to set down, as in writing; to preserve an account of; as, *record* the day's events.

2. to register in some permanent form, as on a graph or chart, an indication of (a motion or event) as it occurs; as, a seismograph *records* earthquakes.

3. to serve as evidence of; to tell of; as, the marks on the houses *record* the height of the flood waters.

4. (a) to transform (sound) by electrical or mechanical means and register it in some permanent form, as the grooved track of a phonograph record, the magnetization of fine wire, etc., so that it can be reproduced at will by a reverse process; (b) to register thus the performance of (a singer, orchestra, piece of music, etc.).

5. to show; indicate.

6. to set down or have set down in a register; as, *record* a vote.

7. to imprint deeply on the mind or memory; as, to *record* the sayings of another in the heart. [Obs.]

8. to recite; to repeat; also, to sing. [Obs.]

9. to call to mind; to remind; to remember. [Obs.]

rē·cord′, *v.i.* 1. to sing a tune; to carol; to warble. [Obs.]

2. to make a record; to record something.

3. to admit of being recorded.

rec′ŏrd, *n.* [ME.; OFr., from the verb.]

1. a recording or being recorded; preservation in or as in writing.

2. anything that is written down and preserved as evidence; account of events; anything that serves as evidence of an event, etc.

3. anything that the written evidence is put on or in, as a register, monument, etc.

4. an official written report of public proceedings, as in a legislature or court of law; documents preserved as evidence of proceedings, as of court.

5. the known or recorded facts about anything, as about conduct, performance, one's career, etc.

6. a flat disk, cylinder, paper roll, etc. on which sound has been recorded.

7. the best performance, as the highest speed, greatest amount, highest rate, etc., reached and publicly recorded.

8. witness; testimony; as, to bear *record.* [Obs.]

court of record; a court whose acts and judicial proceedings are written down for permanent keeping.

debt of record; a debt which appears to be due by the evidence of a court of record, as upon a judgment.

off the record; not for publication.

on record; recorded; publicly declared.

to break a record; to excel the best previous performance.

to go on record; to state one's opinions publicly.

trial by record; a trial in which a matter of record is pleaded, and the opposite party pleads that there is no such record. In this case, the trial is by inspection of the record itself, no other evidence being admissible.

Syn.—registry, entry, enrollment, list, index, catalogue, register, schedule, roll, scroll, enumeration, inventory, instrument, archive, memorandum, remembrance, tracing.

rec′ŏrd, *a.* making a record; being the largest, fastest, etc. of its kind; as, a *record* audience, *record* crop.

rē·cord′ănce, *n.* recollection; remembrance. [Obs.]

rec·ŏr·dā′tion, *n.* 1. remembrance. [Obs.]

2. record.

rē·cord′ẽr, *n.* 1. one who records.

2. an officer appointed or elected to keep records of deeds or other official papers.

3. in some cities, a judge who has the same criminal jurisdiction as a police judge.

4. (a) a machine that records; (b) the part of a machine that records what goes on in the rest of the machine.

5. an early form of flute, with eight finger holes and a fipple, held straight up and down when played.

RECORDER

rē·cord′ẽr·ship, *n.* the position or term of office of a recorder.

rē·cord′ing, *a.* that records; writing down or registering; keeping a record or an account of.

recording angel; the angel said to be keeping a record of the good and evil deeds of each individual.

recording secretary; a secretary who writes the minutes, recording the important facts of a meeting, as of a club or any organization.

rē·cord′ing, *n.* 1. the act of one that records.

2. what is recorded, as on a phonograph record.

3. the record itself.

4. the registering of sound, as on a phonograph record, with reference to the relative quality of reproduction afforded.

rē-count′ (*or* rē′kount), *n.* a repeated count; a second or additional count, as of votes: also written *recount.*

rē-count′, *v.t.* to count again as votes: also written *recount.*

rē·count′, *v.t.*; recounted, *pt., pp.*; recounting, *ppr.* [OFr. *reconter*; *re-*, and *conter*, to tell, *compter*, to count, to tell, from L. *computare*, to sum up, to compute.]

1. to relate; to rehearse; to recite; to tell or describe in detail; to give an account of; to narrate.

2. to tell in order or one by one; as, she *recounted* her sins.

rē·count′ăl, *n.* a recounting.

rē·count′ment, *n.* the act of recounting; recital. [Obs.]

rē·coup′, *v.t.*; recouped (-köpt′), *pt., pp.*; recouping, *ppr.* [Fr. *recouper*, to cut again; *re-*, and *couper*, to cut.]

1. to get back an equivalent for; to make up for; as, *recoup* a loss.

2. to pay back; to reimburse.

3. in law, to deduct or hold back (a part of what is due), having some reasonable claim to do so.

rē·coup′, *n.* the act of recouping.

rē·coupe′, *v.t.* to recoup. [Obs.]

rē·coup′ẽr, *n.* one who recoups.

rē·coup′ment, *n.* 1. the act of recouping or state of being recouped.

2. something recouped.

rē′course (*or* rē-kōrs′), *n.* [Fr. *recours*; L. *recursus*, a running back, a return; *re-*, back, and *currere*, to run.]

1. recurrence; return; fresh attack. [Obs.]
2. repeated course; frequent or repeated flowing or passage. [Obs.]
3. access; admission (to a person). [Obs.]
4. a going or applying to, as for help, protection, etc.; a turning to a person or line of action in time of difficulty, danger, need, or perplexity; as, he had *recourse* to a new source of information.
5. that to which one turns seeking aid, safety, etc.; as, his one *recourse* was the law.
6. in commerce and law, the right to demand payment from the maker or endorser of a commercial paper, as a bill of exchange: usually in *without recourse*, without obligation to pay (added by the endorser to a bill of exchange to protect himself from liability).

rē·çourse′, *v.i.* to recur; also, to resort. [Obs.]

rē·çŏv′ēr, *v.t.* to cover again or anew.

rē·çŏv′ēr, *n.* recovery. [Obs.]

rē·çŏv′ēr, *v.t.*; recovered, *pt., pp.*; recovering, *ppr.* [OFr. *recovrer*; Fr. *recouvrer*, from L. *recuperare*, to make good again; perhaps from same root as *cupere*, to desire.]
1. to get back (something lost, stolen, etc.); to regain (health, consciousness, etc.).
2. to compensate for; to make up for; as, *recover* losses.
3. to get back for (oneself) a state of control, balance, good physical or mental health, etc.; as, he *recovered* himself quickly in the hospital.
4. to catch or save (oneself) from a slip, stumble, betrayal of feeling, tactless remark, etc.
5. to reclaim, as land from the sea, useful substances from waste, or a person from a bad state.
6. in law, to get or get back by final judgment in a court; as, *recover* damages, *recover* judgment against someone.
7. in sports, to get back to (a position, as of guard, balance, or readiness).
8. to reach; to come to; to gain. [Obs.]
recover arms; in military usage, formerly, a command requiring a firearm to be brought back from the "aim" to the "ready" position.

rē·çŏv′ēr, *v.i.* 1. to regain health after sickness; to grow well again: often followed by *of* or *from.*

The man *recover'd of* the bite,
The dog it was that died.—Goldsmith.

2. to regain a former state or condition, as after misfortune or disturbance of mind; as, to *recover* from a state of poverty or depression.
3. to catch or save oneself from a slip, stumble, self-betrayal, etc.
4. in sports, to get back to a position of guard, readiness, etc., as after a lunge in fencing or a stroke in rowing.
5. to obtain a judgment in law; to succeed in a lawsuit; as, the plaintiff has *recovered* in his suit.
6. to return; to arrive. [Obs.]

rē·çŏv′ēr·ȧ·ble, *a.* 1. capable of being regained or recovered.
2. capable of being brought back to a former condition.
3. capable of being recovered or obtained back from a holder, possessor, or debtor; as, the debt is *recoverable.*
4. capable of being restored to health or revived, as from sickness, faintness, or danger.

rē·çŏv′ēr·ȧ·ble·ness, *n.* the condition of being recoverable.

rē·çŏv′ēr·ănce, *n.* recovery. [Archaic.]

rē·çŏv·ēr·ee′, *n.* in law, the tenant or person against whom a judgment is obtained in common recovery.

rē·çŏv′ēr·ēr, *n.* 1. one who recovers.
2. a recoveror. [Obs.]

rē·çŏv′ēr·ŏr, *n.* in law, the demandant or person who obtains a judgment in his favor in common recovery.

rē·çŏv′ēr·y, *n.*; *pl.* **rē·çŏv′ēr·ieș**, [Anglo-Fr. *recoverie.*]
1. the act or power of regaining, retaking, or conquering again; a recovering or reclaiming; as, to offer a reward for the *recovery* of stolen goods.
2. a getting well again, coming or bringing back to consciousness, revival of a person from weakness, etc.
3. a regaining of balance, of former position or condition, etc.; a return to soundness.
4. the time needed for recovering.
5. the thing or amount gained in recovering.
6. in sports, a return to a position of guard, readiness, etc., as after a lunge in fencing or a stroke in rowing.
7. in law, the obtaining of right to something by a verdict and judgment of court from an opposing party in a suit; as, the *recovery* of debt, damages, and costs by a plaintiff; the *recovery* of cost by a defendant; the *recovery* of land in ejectment.
common or *feigned recovery*; formerly, in law, a fictitious real action, carried on to judgment, and founded on the supposition of an adverse claim, a proceeding formerly resorted to by tenants in tail for the purpose of barring their entails, and all remainders and reversions consequent thereon, and making a conveyance in fee simple of the lands held in tail.
Syn.—restoration.

reç′rē·ănce, *n.* same as *recreancy.*

reç′rē·ăn·cy, *n.*; *pl.* **reç′rē·ăn·cieș**, [from *recreant.*]
1. a cowardly giving up; cowardice.
2. an abject failure to keep faith; treason or disloyalty.

reç′rē·ănt, *a.* [OFr. *recreant*, from LL. *recredere*, to give in, to give up, *recredere se*, to confess oneself vanquished in a fight or action at law; L. *re-*, back, again, and *credere*, to believe.]
1. (a) crying out for mercy; hence, (b) cowardly; craven.
2. unfaithful to duty; disloyal; traitorous; apostate; false; faithless.

reç′rē·ănt, *n.* 1. one who yields in combat and cries craven; one who begs for mercy; hence, a coward; a craven.
2. a disloyal person; a traitor.

reç′rē·ănt·ly, *adv.* in a recreant or cowardly manner; basely; falsely.

rē-crē·āte′, *v.t.* to create or form anew; to remake.

reç′rē·āte, *v.t.*; recreated, *pt., pp.*; recreating, *ppr.* [from L. *recreatus*, pp. of *recreare*, to create anew.] to revive or refresh, especially after toil or exertion, by some form of play, amusement, or relaxation; to reanimate, as languid spirits or exhausted strength; to amuse; to divert; to gratify.

reç′rē·āte, *v.i.* to take recreation.

reç·rē·ā′tion, *n.* [ME. *recreacioun*; OFr.; L. *recreatio.*]
1. refreshment in body or mind, as after work, by some form of play, amusement, or relaxation.
2. any form of play, amusement, or relaxation used for this purpose, as games, sports, hobbies, reading, walking, etc.
3. refreshment; food. [Obs.]
Syn.—amusement, diversion, entertainment, pastime, sport.

rē-crē·ā′tion, *n.* 1. a re-creating or being re-created.
2. something re-created.

reç·rē·ā′tion·ăl, *a.* of, having the nature of, or providing recreation.

reç·rē·ā′tion ground, any place set apart for recreation.

reç·rē·ā′tion rọọm, a room, as in the basement of a home, equipped for amusement and relaxation.

reç′rē·ā·tive, *a.* tending to recreate; refreshing; giving new vigor or animation; giving relief after labor or pain; amusing; diverting.

rē″-crē·ā′tive, *a.* having the power or tendency to create or form anew.

reç′rē·ā·tive·ly, *adv.* in a recreative manner; with recreation or diversion.

reç′rē·ā·tive·ness, *n.* the quality of being recreative, refreshing, or diverting.

reç′rē·ment, *n.* [L. *recrementum*; *re-*, back, and *cernere*, to separate.]
1. superfluous or useless matter separated from that which is useful; dross; scoria.
2. in physiology, any substance which, after having been secreted in the body by an organ of secretion, is reabsorbed into the blood, as saliva.

reç·rē·men′tăl, *a.* consisting of, having the nature of, or pertaining to recrement; recrementitious.

reç″rē·men·ti′tiăl (-tish′ăl), *a.* of or pertaining to recrement; recrementitious.

reç″rē·men·ti′tious, *a.* recrementitial.

rē·çres′cence, *n.* [*re-*, and L. *crescere*, to grow.] in zoology, regrowth; replacement of an excised or lost member, as in *Protozoa*, etc.

rē·çrew′, *v.t.* to recruit. [Obs.]

rē·çrim′i·nāte, *v.i.*; recriminated, *pt., pp.*; recriminating, *ppr.* to return one accusation with another; to charge an accuser with some fault, in return.

rē·çrim′i·nāte, *v.t.* to accuse (someone) in return. [Now Rare.]

rē·çrim′i·nā·ting, *a.* recriminatory.

rē·çrim·i·nā′tion, *n.* 1. the act of recriminating; the meeting of one accusation with another.
2. in law, an accusation brought by the accused against the accuser; a countercharge.

rē·çrim′i·nā·tive, *a.* of the nature of recrimination; recriminatory.

rē·çrim′i·nā·tŏr, *n.* one who recriminates.

rē·çrim′i·nȧ·tō·ry, *a.* 1. that recriminates.
2. of, having the nature of, or involving recrimination.

reç rọọm, a recreation room. [Colloq.]

rē·çrossed′ (-krọst′), *a.* in heraldry, (a) having the ends crossed; (b) indicating a cross crosslet.

rē·çrụ′den·cy, *n.* same as *recrudescence.*

rē·çrụ·desce′, *v.i.*; recrudesced, *pt., pp.*; recrudescing, *ppr.* [L. *recrudescere*; *re-*, again, and *crudescere*, to become harsh or raw, from *crudus*, raw, crude.] to break out afresh after a period of latency or relative inactivity; to become active again, as a disease.

rē·çrụ·des′cence, *n.* [from L. *recrudescens*; *re-*, again, and *crudescere*, to grow raw; *crudus*, raw.]
1. the state of being recrudescent.
2. a renewal; a fresh outbreak.
3. in medicine, an increase of a disease after a temporary remission; a relapse after a partial recovery.

rē·çrụ·des′cen·cy, *n.* recrudescence.

rē·çrụ·des′cent, *a.* recrudescing; breaking out anew; coming into fresh life or vigor.

rē·çrụit′, *v.t.*; recruited, *pt., pp.*; recruiting, *ppr.* [OFr. *recruter*, from L. *re-*, again, and *crescere*, to increase.]
1. to raise or strengthen (an army, navy, etc.) by enlisting personnel.
2. to enlist (personnel) into an army or navy.
3. to enlist (new members) for a party, organization, etc.
4. to increase, strengthen, or maintain by supplying anew. [Rare.]
5. to revive or restore, as health, strength, etc.
6. to supply with provisions, as a ship. [Obs.]

rē·çrụit′, *v.i.* 1. to enlist new personnel for a military force.
2. to get new supplies of something, as in replacement.
3. to regain health, strength, etc.
4. to put into port for supplies, as a vessel. [Obs.]

rē·çrụit′, *n.* 1. the supply of anything wasted; a reinforcement. [Now Rare.]
2. a recently enlisted soldier, sailor, etc.; specifically, in the United States Army, formerly, the seventh, or lowest, grade of enlisted man (now *private*).
3. a new member of any group, body, or organization.

rē·çrụit′ăl, *n.* the act of supplying anew; that which is supplied.

rē·çrụit′ēr, *n.* one who or that which recruits.

rē·çrụit′ing, *n.* the business of enlisting new men for an army or navy.

rē·çrụit′ment, *n.* the act or process of recruiting or state of being recruited; especially, the act of enlisting new men for an army or navy.

reç′tȧ, *n.* plural of *rectum.*

reç′tăl, *a.* of, for, pertaining to, or situated near the rectum.
rectal alimentation; liquid food injected into the large intestine through the rectum.
rectal chemise; a catheter used in surgery when tamponing the rectum.
rectal diaphragm; the sheet of muscles closing the lower and posterior part of the pelvis.

reç·tal′ġi·ȧ, *n.* same as *proctalgia.*

reç′tañ·gle, *n.* [Fr., from LL. *rectiangulum*; L. *rectus*, right, and *angulus*, angle.]
1. any four-sided plane figure with four right angles; a quadrilateral figure having all its angles right angles, and thus its opposite sides equal and parallel. When the adjacent sides are equal it becomes a square. Every rectangle is said to be contained by any two of the sides about one of its right angles; thus if A and B represent the sides about one of the right angles, the figure is said to be contained by A and B, and sometimes it is said to be the rectangle under A and B. The area of a rec-

RECTANGLES

tangle is numerically expressed by the product of the two numbers which express the lengths of its adjacent sides; thus, if the lengths of two adjacent sides be expressed by 6 feet and 4 feet respectively, the area is equal to 6×4=24 square feet.

2. a right angle. [Obs.]

reç′tañ·gle, *a.* right-angled. [Obs.]

reç′tañ·gled (-gld), *a.* 1. having one or more right angles; right-angled.

2. in heraldry, having the line of length interrupted by right angles.

reç·tañ′gū·lãr, *a.* 1. shaped like a rectangle; having four sides and four right angles.

2. having right-angled corners, or a base in the form of a rectangle, as a building.

3. right-angled.

rectangular co-ordinates; in analytical geometry, co-ordinates at right angles to each other.

rectangular solid; in geometry, a solid whose axis is perpendicular to its base.

reç·tañ·gū·la′ri·ty, *n.* the quality or condition of being rectangular.

reç·tañ′gū·lãr·ly, *adv.* in a rectangular manner; with or at right angles.

reç·tañ′gū·lãr·ness, *n.* rectangularity.

reç′ti-, [LL., from L. *rectus*, straight.] a combining form meaning *straight, right*, as in *recti*linear: also, before a vowel, *rect-*.

reç′ti·fī·ȧ·ble, *a.* 1. capable of being rectified, corrected, or set right; as, a *rectifiable* mistake.

2. in geometry, admitting the construction of a straight line of equal length: said of a curve.

reç″ti·fi·çā′tion, *n.* a rectifying or being rectified.

rectification of a globe; in astronomy, the adjustment of a globe preparatory to the solution of a proposed problem.

reç′ti·fi·çā·tŏr, *n.* same as *rectifier*.

reç′ti·fī·ẽr, *n.* 1. one who or that which rectifies.

2. an instrument formerly used for determining the variations of the compass in order to rectify the course of a ship.

3. any attachment or device for correcting, setting, or adjusting machinery, etc.

4. in electricity, any device, as a commutator or a vacuum tube, which converts alternating current to direct current.

reç′ti·fȳ, *v.t.*; rectified, *pt., pp.*; rectifying, *ppr.* [Fr. *rectifier*, from L. *rectus*, right, and *facere*, to make.]

1. to make right; to correct that which is wrong, erroneous, or false; to amend; as, to *rectify* errors, to *rectify* an opinion.

2. to adjust, as in movement or balance; to adjust by calculation.

3. in chemistry, to refine or purify by distillation, especially by distilling again and again.

4. in electricity, to change (alternating current) to direct current.

5. in mathematics, to find the length of (a curve).

to rectify a globe; to adjust a globe in order to prepare for the solution of a proposed problem.

Syn.—amend, correct, improve, refine, purify, adjust.

reç·ti·lin′ē·ăl, *a.*. rectilinear.

reç·ti·lin′ē·ăl·ly, *adv.* in a rectilineal manner.

reç·ti·lin′ē·ãr, *a.* [L. *rectus*, right, and *linea*, line.]

1. moving in a straight line.
2. forming a straight line.
3. bounded or formed by straight lines.
4. characterized by straight lines.
5. in optics, corrected so as not to distort straight lines: said of a type of lens.

reç·ti·lin·ē·ar′i·ty, *n.* the condition of being rectilinear.

reç·ti·lin′ē·ãr·ly, *adv.* in a rectilinear manner.

reç·ti·lin′ē·ous, *a.* rectilinear. [Obs.]

reç′ti·nẽrved, *a.* in botany, having straight nerves or veins, as a leaf.

reç′tion, *n.* in grammar, same as *government* (sense 5).

reç″ti·pet·al′i·ty, *n.* in botany, a natural tendency to grow in a straight line. [Rare.]

reç·ti·ros′trăl, *a.* in zoology, having a straight bill or beak.

reç·ti·sē′ri·ăl, *a.* 1. arranged in straight lines or rows.

2. in botany, designating phyllotaxy in which leaves stand in a vertical line or lines.

reç·tī′tis, *n.* [LL. *rectum*, and *-itis.*] inflammation of the rectum; proctitis.

reç′ti·tūde, *n.* [Fr., from L. *rectus*, right, straight.]

1. rightness of principle or practice; uprightness of character; conduct according to moral principles; strict honesty.

2. straightness. [Rare.]

3. correctness of method or judgment.

Syn.—honesty, justice, integrity, uprightness.

reç′tō-, [from LL. *rectum*.] a combining form used in medicine meaning *rectal, pertaining to the rectum*.

reç′tō, *n.* in law, a writ of right. [Obs.]

reç′tō, *n.*; *pl.* **reç′tōs̹,** [L., abl. of *rectus*, right.] in printing, a right-hand page of a book, usually an odd-numbered page; the front side of a leaf: opposed to *verso*.

reç′tō·cēle, *n.* [*recto-* and *-cele.*] a hernial protrusion of the rectum into the vagina.

reç′tŏr, *n.* [L. *rector*, a ruler, governor.]

1. a ruler or governor. [Obs.]

2. in the Protestant Episcopal Church, a minister in charge of a parish.

3. in the Church of England, a clergyman who holds the rights and tithes of his parish: distinguished from *vicar*.

4. in the Roman Catholic Church, (a) the head priest of a parish; (b) the head of a religious institution or school.

5. in certain schools, colleges, and universities, the head or headmaster.

reç′tŏr·ăl, *a.* same as *rectorial*.

reç′tŏr·āte, *n.* the position, office, or term of office of a rector.

reç′tŏr·ess, *n.* 1. the wife of a rector. [Rare.]

2. a woman ruler; a governess. [Obs.]

reç·tō′ri·ăl, *a.* pertaining to a rector or rectors.

reç′tŏr·ship, *n.* the office or rank of a rector.

reç′tō·ry, *n.*; *pl.* **reç′tō·ries̹,** [ML. *rectoria*.]

1. the house in which an Episcopal minister lives.

2. in the Church of England, (a) a benefice held by a rector; (b) the house in which a rector lives: distinguished from *vicarage*.

reç′tō·sçōpe, *n.* a speculum for inspecting the rectum.

reç·tō-ū′tẽr·ine, *a.* relating to the rectum and uterus.

reç·tō·vaġ′i·năl, *a.* relating to the rectum and vagina.

reç·tō·ves′i·căl, *a.* relating to the rectum and bladder.

reç′tress, *n.* a rectoress.

reç′trix, *n.*; *pl.* **reç·trī′cēs̹,** [L. *rectrix*, f. of *rector*, a ruler.]

1. a governess; a rectoress. [Rare.]

2. in zoology, any of the large tail feathers of a bird.

reç′tum, *n.*; *pl.* **reç′tȧ,** [L. *rectum* (*intestinum*), lit., straight (intestine).] the lowest segment of the large intestine, extending, in man, from the sigmoid flexure to the anus.

reç′tus, *n.*; *pl.* **reç′tī,** [L.] a straight muscle, as of the eye, neck, abdomen, thigh, etc.

reç′ū·bănt, *a.* recumbent; lying down. [Rare.]

reç·ū·bā′tion, *n.* [L. *recubare*; *re-*, back, and *cubare*, to lie.] the act of lying down. [Obs.]

rē·çuile′, *n.* recoil. [Obs.]

rē·çuile′ment, *n.* recoil. [Obs.]

rē·çūle′, *v.i.* to recoil. [Obs.]

rē·cumb′ (-kum′), *v.i.* [L. *recumbere*; *re-*, back, and *cumbere*, to lie.] to lean; to recline; to repose. [Obs.]

rē·cum′bence, *n.* [L. *recumbens*, lying down.] recumbency. [Rare.]

rē·cum′ben·cy, *n.* 1. the position of leaning, reclining, or lying.

2. rest; repose; a state of idleness.

rē·cum′bent, *a.* 1. leaning; reclining; lying down; specifically, in biology, designating a part that leans or lies.

2. reposing; inactive; idle.

rē·cum′bent·ly, *adv.* in a recumbent position.

rē·çū′pẽr·ȧ·ble, *a.* recoverable. [Obs.]

rē·çū′pẽr·āte, *v.t.*; recuperated, *pt., pp.*; recuperating, *ppr.* [L. *recuperare*, to obtain again.]

1. to restore to health, strength, etc.; to make well again.

2. to recover; to regain; as, to *recuperate* losses or strength.

3. to reimburse; to recoup. [Rare.]

rē·çū′pẽr·āte, *v.i.* 1. to convalesce; to regain health, strength, and vigor.

2. to recover losses, etc.

rē·çū·pẽr·ā′tion, *n.* [L. *recuperatio*, recovery.] a recuperating; recovery from disease, surgery, financial loss, etc.

rē·çū′pẽr·ȧ·tive, *a.* [L. *recuperativus*.] promoting recovery; pertaining to recovery.

He had shown surprising *recuperative* power.
—Morgan Robertson.

rē·çū′pẽr·ā·tŏr, *n.* 1. one who or that which recuperates or is recuperating.

2. a regenerator in a furnace or engine.

rē·çū′pẽr·ȧ·tō·ry, *a.* recuperative.

rē·çũr′, *v.i.*; recurred, *pt., pp.*; recurring, *ppr.* [L. *recurrere*; *re-*, back, and *currere*, to run.]

1. to return, as in thought, talk, or memory; as, *recurring* to an earlier question.

2. to occur again, as in talk or memory; to come up again for consideration.

3. to happen or occur again, especially after some lapse of time; to appear at intervals.

4. to resort; to have recourse; to return for help. [Rare.]

rē·çūre′, *v.i.* to recover, as from sickness. [Obs.]

rē·çūre′, *v.t.* to get back; to recover. [Obs.]

rē·çūre′, *n.* cure; recovery. [Obs.]

rē·çūre′less, *a.* incapable of cure or remedy. [Obs.]

rē·cur′rence, *n.* [from *recurrent*.]

1. a bringing up again, as in thought or discussion (with *to*).

2. a coming up or back; reappearance; return; repetition.

3. resort; recourse. [Rare.]

rē·cur′ren·cy, *n.* recurrence. [Rare.]

rē·cur′rent, *a.* 1. recurring; returning from time to time or periodically; as, *recurrent* pains of a disease.

2. in anatomy, turning back in the opposite direction; running back or toward the source, as a nerve or artery.

3. in entomology, deflected or turned toward the base; as, a *recurrent* nervure.

4. in geology, occurring in alternate series, as fossil fauna.

recurrent fever; same as *relapsing fever*.

recurrent pulse; a pulse reappearing in an artery beyond a point at which it is compressed.

recurrent sensibility; sensibility exhibited in the anterior root of a spinal nerve when the distal portion is stimulated after division.

recurrent stricture; a stricture which may be mechanically dilated, but which will soon return to its contracted condition: also called *contractile stricture*.

Syn.—returning, intermitting.

rē·çur′rent, *n.* in anatomy, a recurrent artery or nerve.

rē·çur′rent·ly, *adv.* in a recurrent manner.

rē·çur′ring dec′i·măl, a decimal in which two or more consecutive figures are repeated indefinitely, as .278278278 . . .; a circulating decimal.

rē·çũr′sănt, *a.* [L. *recursare*, freq. of *recurrere*, to run back.] in heraldry, displayed in a position contrary to the usual one, as an eagle with the back presented.

rē·çũr′sion, *n.* return. [Obs.]

rē·çũr′vănt, *a.* in heraldry, coiled with the head poised, as a snake.

rē·çũr′vāte, *v.t.* [L. *recurvare*; *re-*, back, and *curvare*, to bend.] to recurve. [Now Rare.]

rē·çũr′vāte, *a.* bent back; recurved.

rē·çũr·vā′tion, *n.* the act of recurving; the state of being recurved; recurvature. [Rare.]

rē·çũr′vȧ·tūre, *n.* recurvation. [Rare.]

rē·çũrve′, *v.t.* and *v.i.* [L. *recurvare*.] to curve or bend back or backward; to bend down; to render recurved.

rē·çũrved′, *a.* curved backward.

rē·çũr·vi·ros′tẽr, *n.* [L. *recurvus*, bent back, and *rostrum*, a beak.] a bird whose beak or bill bends upward, as the avocet.

rē·çũr·vi·ros′trăl, *a.* in ornithology, having the beak bent upward.

rē·çũr′vi·ty, *n.* recurvation. [Obs.]

rē·çũr″vō·pat′ent, *a.* in botany, bent backward and expanding.

rē·çũr′vous, *a.* [L. *recurvus*.] bent backward; recurved. [Rare.]

reç′ū·săn·cy, *n.* nonconformity; the condition of being recusant; refusal to obey or conform, especially in religious matters.

reç′ū·s̹ănt, *n.* [L. *recusans*, ppr. of *recusare*, to reject.]

1. a person who refuses to obey or conform to an established authority or its regulations.

2. in English history, a person, especially a Roman Catholic, who refused to attend the services of the Church of England or recognize its authority.

reç′ū·s̹ănt, *a.* 1. disobedient of authority, especially in religious matters; dissenting; nonconformist.

2. in English history, refusing to attend the services or recognize the authority of the Church of England.

reç·ū·s̹ā′tion, *n.* in law, formerly, the act of refusing a judge, or challenging that he shall not try the cause, on account of his supposed partiality. [Obs.]

rē-cū′ṡȧ-tive, *a.* denying; privative; refusing. [Rare.]

rē-çūṡe′, *v.t.*; recused, *pt.*, *pp.*; recusing, *ppr.* [ME. *recusen*; L. *recusare*.] in law, to challenge (a judge, juror, or court) as prejudiced or otherwise incompetent to act. [Rare.]

rē-çus′sion (-kush′un), *n.* the act of beating or striking back. [Rare.]

red-, a combining form meaning ***again*** or ***back***: variant of *re-*.

-red, [from AS. *rǣden*, condition, rule.] a combining form meaning ***condition*** or ***state***; as in kind*red*, hat*red*.

red, *n.* [ME. *red*, *redde*; AS. *read*; akin to G. *rot*, ON. *rauthr*: from same root come also L. *rutilus*, *rufus*, *ruber*, Gr. *erythros*, W. *rhwdd*, Ir. and Gael. *ruadh*, also Sans. *rudhira*, blood.]

1. a primary color, or any of a spread of colors at the lower end of the visible spectrum, varying in hue from that of blood to pale rose or pink.

2. a pigment producing this color.

3. [*often* R-] [senses *a* and *b* from the red flag symbolizing revolutionary socialism.] (a) a political radical or revolutionary; especially, a communist; (b) a citizen of the Soviet Union; (c) [*pl.*] North American Indians.

4. a red object, as a red space on the board or wheel used in various games of chance, a red chessman, or a red piece in checkers.

5. a red cent; as, I don't care a *red*. [Slang.]

6. [*pl.*] in medicine, the menses. [Obs.]

7. the nest or spawning trench of fishes. [Brit. Dial.]

Adrianople red; same as ***Turkey red***.

aniline red; same as ***fuchsin***.

hypericum red; extract of hypericum, a resinous red dyestuff.

Indian red; see under ***Indian***.

in the red; (a) losing money, as a business; (b) in debt.

Mars red; a pigment used by artists.

to see red; to be or become angry. [Colloq.]

red, *a.*; *comp.* redder; *superl.* reddest. 1. having or being of the color red or any of its hues.

2. having red hair.

3. having, or considered to have, a reddish or coppery skin, as the North American Indians.

4. [*often* R-] (a) politically radical or revolutionary; especially, communist; (b) of the Soviet Union.

red admiral; a purplish-black European and North American butterfly with white spots near the tips of the forewings and bright-orange bands across the forewings and bordering the hind wings.

red algae; a group of red, brownish-red, purple, or greenish seaweeds, ranging from delicately filamentous to coarse forms.

red ant; (a) the ordinary ant that infests houses; (b) a larger ant of the slave-making species.

red antimony; kermesite.

red ash; an American ash, ***Fraxinus pubescens***, valuable for its timber.

red bark; the bark or the preparation from the bark of the red cinchona, ***Cinchona succirubra***.

red bass; the red drum.

Red Book; in England, formerly, a book containing the names of all the persons in the service of the state.

Red Book of the Exchequer; an old English record book.

red brass; an alloy of eight parts of copper with three parts of zinc.

red cedar; (a) the common red cedar of the eastern part of the United States, ***Juniperus virginiana***, with red, fragrant heartwood; (b) the gigantic cedar, ***Thuya gigantea***, of the region of Puget Sound; (c) the toon tree, ***Cedrela toona***, of the East Indies; (d) the wood of any of these trees.

red clover; a kind of clover with flowers in reddish, ball-shaped heads, grown for fodder.

red coral; a coral, used in jewelry.

red deer; (a) a kind of stag of the European and Asian temperate zones; (b) the Virginia, or American, deer (in its reddish summer coloring).

red drum (or ***drumfish***); a large, edible drumfish of the Atlantic coast of the United States.

red duck; a reddish-brown duck of Europe.

red fir; (a) any of various evergreen trees with cones, needlelike leaves, and reddish wood, including the red silver fir and the California red fir; (b) the wood of any of these trees; (c) the Douglas fir.

red fire; any of various substances, especially, one containing strontium nitrate, which burn with a bright red light and are used in fireworks, flares, etc.

red flag; see under ***flag***.

red fox; (a) the common European fox, with reddish fur; (b) the similar related fox of North America; (c) the fur of either of these.

red grouse; the ptarmigan.

Red Hand; in heraldry, a left hand appaumée, fingers erect, borne on an escutcheon.

red hat; (a) the official hat, or biretta, of a cardinal, the symbol of his rank; (b) the rank or position of a cardinal; (c) a cardinal.

red heat; see under ***heat***.

red herring; (a) a smoked herring; (b) something used to confuse, or to divert attention from something else: from the practice of drawing a herring across the trace in hunting, to distract the hounds.

red hind; the cabrilla, a serranoid food fish.

red horse; a large red sucker found in the fresh waters of America.

red Indian; a North American Indian, having reddish or coppery skin.

red-ink plant; the pokeweed.

red lattice; an alehouse, or tavern: formerly marked by red lattices on the windows. [Archaic.]

red liquor; a solution of aluminum acetate, used to fix the colors in dyeing.

red louse; the harvest tick.

red maggot; the wheat midge's larva.

red man; a North American Indian.

red manganese; same as ***rhodochrosite***.

red meat; beef or mutton, as distinguished from pork, veal, etc.

red mite; same as ***red spider***.

red mullet; a mullet with reddish scales and two long chin barbels; surmullet.

red oak; (a) any of several oaks whose foliage is dark red in the autumn; (b) the hard wood of such a tree.

red ocher; an earthy hematite, red in color, used as a pigment: also called ***ruddle, reddle, raddle***.

red osier; a kind of dogwood with dark-red branches and white or bluish fruit.

red pepper; (a) a plant with a red, many-seeded fruit, as the sweet pepper or cayenne; (b) the fruit; (c) the ground fruit or seeds, used for seasoning.

red phosphorus; see under ***phosphorus***.

red pine; see under ***pine***.

red plague or ***red pestilence***; a form of the plague characterized by red spots or ulcerations.

Red Polled; any of a British breed of hornless, reddish dairy and beef cattle: also ***Red Poll***.

red precipitate; see under ***precipitate***.

red ribbon; the decoration of the English Order of the Bath.

red rockfish; a large fish of California.

red sandstone; see ***New*** and ***Old Red Sandstone*** under ***sandstone***.

red scale; a scale insect of a reddish color that injures oranges.

red silver; silver ore of a dark red color.

red snapper; a salt-water food fish with a reddish, blue-streaked, oblong body, found in the Gulf of Mexico and off the east coasts of Florida and Georgia.

red snow; patches of snow in cold regions colored by minute algae.

red spider; a red mite very destructive to plants.

red squirrel; a small squirrel of North America, of a rusty red color.

to paint the town red; to have a noisy good time, as by visiting bars, night clubs, etc. [Slang.]

red, *v.t.*; redded, *pt.*, *pp.*; redding, *ppr.* to make red; to redden. [Obs.]

red, *v.* obsolete past tense of ***read***.

red, *v.t.* to redd, or put in order. [Colloq. or Dial.]

rē-daçt′, *v.t.* [L. *redactus*, pp. of *redigere*, to bring into a certain condition, to reduce to order; *red-*, back, and *agere*, to drive, bring.]

1. to write out or draw up; to frame (a proclamation, government order, etc.).

2. to arrange in proper form for publication; to edit.

ré-dac-teur′ (rā-dȧk-tẽr′), *n.* same as ***redactor***.

rē-daç′tion, *n.* [from Fr. and LL.; Fr. *rédaction*; LL. *redactio*.]

1. the preparation of written work for publication; editing, re-editing, or revision.

2. an edited work; especially, a reissue; new edition.

rē-daç′tŏr, *n.* one who prepares or revises matter for publication; an editor.

rē-daç-tō′ri-ăl, *a.* pertaining to redaction; editorial.

rē-dan′, *n.* [Fr. *redan*; OFr. *redent*, from L. *re-*, back, and *dens*, *dentis*, a tooth; from its shape.] in fortification, a kind of rampart consisting of two walls or parapets in the form of a V having its angle toward the enemy and open at the back: two or more are often joined by walls or trenches.

REDANS

rē-dan′līne, in fortification, a line of redans joined by trenches.

red-ăr′gūe, *v.t.* [L. *redarguere*, to disprove, to refute; *red-*, *re-*, back, and *arguere*, to make clear, to prove, to argue.] to refute; to disprove; to convict. [Obs.]

rẹd-ăr-gū′tion, *n.* refutation; conviction; disproof. [Obs.]

red-ăr′gū-tō-ry, *a.* pertaining to or containing redargution; tending to refute. [Obs.]

Red Är′my, the army of the Soviet Union, commanded by the Communists who, since 1918, have controlled the government of the U. S. S. R.; any similar Communist armed forces in other countries.

red′back, *n.* a species of sandpiper; the dunlin.

red′bāit″, *v.t.* and *v.i.* [from *red*, *a.*, 4, and *bait*, *v.t.*, 4.] to make verbal attack on or utter denunciations of (a person or group) as being red, or communist.

red′bāit″ẽr, *n.* one who redbaits; one who ridicules, attacks, denounces, or discredits a person or group as being red, or communist.

red′bāit″ing, *n.* the ridiculing, attacking, denouncing, or discrediting of a person or group as being red, or communist.

red bāy, a tree of the laurel kind, *Persea caroliniensis*, growing in the United States from Delaware south.

red′bēard, *n.* a red sponge that grows on oyster shells and stones.

red′bel″ly, *n.* in zoology, (a) the red char; (b) the red terrapin; (c) the red-bellied sunfish; (d) the red grouper; (e) the red-bellied minnow.

red′ber″ry, *n.* in botany, any one of several species of Australian plants of the genus *Rhagodia*, bearing panicles of red berries: also called *seaberry*.

red′bīne, *n.* in botany, a species of hop of Flemish origin.

red′bĩrd, *n.* any one of several birds, as (a) the European bullfinch; (b) an East Indian bird, *Pericrocotus speciosus*; (c) the cardinal bird; (d) the summer tanager; (e) the scarlet tanager.

red blood cell, a red corpuscle; erythrocyte.

red′-blood′ed, *a.* 1. high-spirited and strong-willed; vigorous: said of persons.

2. full of action; exciting: said of novels, etc.

red′breast (-brest), *n.* 1. any of several birds with a reddish breast; especially, (a) the American robin; (b) the European robin; (c) the red-breasted snipe or knot: also called *robin snipe*.

2. a fish, the red-breasted bream.

red′-breast″ed brēam, a kind of sunfish with a red belly, found in the eastern United States.

red′buck, *n.* same as ***pallah***.

red′bud, *n.* any of a number of related trees with small, pink, budlike flowers and heart-shaped leaves; Judas tree.

red′bug, *n.* 1. a tick of the southern part of the United States which burrows in the human skin and causes inflamed red spots with intense burning and itching; the chigger.

2. a red insect living in clusters on tree trunks.

3. same as ***cotton stainer***.

red′çap″, *n.* 1. [R-] a specter with long teeth; a wraith that haunted old castles. [Scot.]

2. the European goldfinch.

3. a porter in a railway station, bus station, etc.

4. a military policeman. [Brit. Colloq.]

red cär′pet, a European carpet moth.

red cent, a cent; penny; especially in ***not worth a red cent, not give a red cent***, etc. [Colloq.]

red′çōat″, *n.* a British soldier (of the period

when a red coat was part of the British uniform, as during the American Revolution).

Red Çres′cent, in Turkey, an organization equivalent to the Red Cross, giving medical and other aid in time of war or disaster: its symbol is a red crescent.

red çross, 1. St. George's cross, red on a white ground, the national emblem of England.
2. [R– C–] a red Greek cross on a white ground (Geneva Cross), emblem of neutrality in war, adapted from the Swiss flag, with colors reversed, and used since 1864 to mark hospitals, ambulances, etc. in time of war.
3. [R– C–] (a) an international society for the relief of suffering in time of war or disaster; (b) any national branch of this.

redd, *v.t.*; redd *or* redded, *pt., pp.*; redding, *ppr.* [ME. (North and Scot.) *redden*; akin to and prob., from M.L.G. *redden* in the same sense.] to put in order; to make tidy (often with *up*). [Colloq. or Dial.]

red′de, *v.* obsolete past tense of *read* or *rede.*

red′den (red′n), *v.t.*; reddened, *pt., pp.*; reddening, *ppr.* to make red.

red′den, *v.i.* 1. to grow or become red.
2. to blush or flush.

red·den′dō, *n.* in Scots law, a clause in a charter specifying a vassal's obligations.

red·den′dum, *n.* [L., returned.] in law, the clause by which rent is reserved in a lease; a clause in a deed which specifies a reservation.

red′dēr, *a.* comparative of *red.*

red′dest, *a.* superlative of *red.*

red′ding, *n.* 1. material for reddening grate paints.
2. same as *reddle.* [Dial.]

red′ding çōmb, a coarse-toothed comb for combing the hair.

red′ding·īte, *n.* in mineralogy, a hydrous manganese phosphate.

red′dish, *a.* somewhat red; moderately red.

red′dish·ness, *n.* redness in a moderate degree.

red·di′tion (-dish′un), *n.* [Fr., from L. *reddere,* to give back.]
1. a returning of anything; restitution; surrender.
2. explanation; representation. [Obs.]

red′di·tive, *a.* [L. *redditivus,* from *reddere,* to return.] in grammar, making reply; answering to an interrogative. [Obs.]

red′dle, *n.* [var. of *ruddle.*] in mineralogy, red ocher: also called *red chalk, ruddle, raddle.*

red′dle, *v.t.*; reddled (-dld), *pt., pp.*; reddling, *ppr.* to color with red ocher: also *ruddle, raddle.*

red′dle·măn, *n.*; *pl.* **red′dle·men,** a person who sells reddle.

red′dŏck, *n.* same as *ruddock.*

red dog, the lowest grade of flour in the high milling process.

red′dŏur, *n.* redour. [Obs.]

rēde, *n.* [ME. *rede*; AS. *ræd,* from base of *rædan,* to interpret.]
1. counsel; advice.
2. plan; scheme.
3. a story; tale.
4. an interpretation.
[Archaic, Poet., or Dial. in all senses.]

rēde, *v.t.*; reded, *pt., pp.*; reding, *ppr.* [the same word as *read,* v., with retained ME. sp.]
1. to advise; counsel.
2. to explain; interpret, as dreams.
3. to narrate; tell.
[Archaic, Poet., or Dial. in all senses.]

red′edġe, *n.* a Florida bivalve, *Codakia tigerina.*

rē·deem′, *v.t.*; redeemed, *pt., pp.*; redeeming, *ppr.* [L. *redimere,* to buy back, to ransom; *red-, re-,* back, and *emere,* to obtain or purchase.]
1. to buy back; to repurchase.
2. to get back; to recover, as by paying a fee.
3. to pay off (a mortage or note).
4. to convert (paper money) into coin.
5. to rescue, ransom, or liberate from captivity or bondage, or from any liability or obligation to suffer or be forfeited, by the payment of an equivalent; to pay a ransom or equivalent for.
6. to deliver; to rescue; to save in any manner.

Sufficient to *redeem* the modern race. —Cowper.

7. to perform, as a promise; to make good by performance.
8. to make amends for; to atone for; to compensate.

They hope that you will now *redeem* what you must feel to be an error. —Macaulay.

9. in law, to recall, as an estate, or to regain, as mortgaged property, by payment of what may be due according to the terms of the mortgage.
10. in theology, to deliver from sin and its penalties, as by a sacrifice made for the sinner.
to redeem the time; to use time to the best advantage.

Redeeming the time because the days are evil. —Eph. v. 16.

Syn.—recover, rescue, deliver, ransom, reclaim.

rē·deem·ȧ·bil′i·ty, *n.* redeemableness.

rē·deem′ȧ·ble, *a.* 1. capable of being redeemed; admitting redemption.
2. that will be bought back, as bonds, stock, etc.

rē·deem′ȧ·ble·ness, *n.* the state of being redeemable.

rē·deem′ēr, *n.* 1. one who redeems.
2. [R–] Jesus Christ, regarded as the Saviour of the world.

rēde′less, *a.* lacking counsel. [Obs.]

rē·dē·liv′ēr, *v.t.* 1. to deliver back; to restore.
2. to deliver again; to liberate a second time.
3. to repeat, as a message; to report.

rē·dē·liv′ēr·ănce, *n.* a second deliverance.

rē·dē·liv′ēr·y, *n.* the act of delivering back; also, a second delivery or liberation.

rē·dē·mȧnd′, *v.t.* 1. to demand back; to demand the return of.
2. to demand again.

rē·dē·mȧnd′, *n.* a demanding back; a renewed demand; a redemanding. [Rare.]

rē·dē·mīșe′, *v.t.* to convey or transfer back, as an estate in fee simple, fee tail, for life, or a term of years.

rē·dē·mīșe′, *n.* reconveyance; the transfer of an estate back to the person who has demised it; as, the demise and *redemise* of an estate in fee simple, fee tail, or for life or years, by mutual leases.

rē·demp′ti·ble, *a.* redeemable.

rē·demp′tion, *n.* [OFr., from L. *redemptio (-onis),* a buying back.]
1. the act of redeeming; the state of being redeemed; ransom; release; deliverance; rescue; repurchase.
2. something that redeems.
3. in commerce, repurchase by the issuer of notes, bills, bonds, or other evidence of debt, by paying their value in money to the holders.
4. in law, the liberation or freeing of an estate from a mortgage; the repurchase of the right to re-enter upon an estate on performance of the terms or conditions on which it was conveyed; the right of redeeming and re-entering into possession.
5. in theology, the purchase of God's favor by the death and sufferings of Christ; the ransom or deliverance of sinners from the bondage of sin and the penalties of God's violated law.

In whom we have *redemption* through his blood. —Eph. i. 7.

rē·demp′tion·ēr *n.* 1. one who redeemed himself.
2. in Colonial days, one who, wishing to emigrate from Europe to America, paid for his passage by a stipulated period of service as a bond-servant in America.

rē·demp′tion·ist, *n.* a Trinitarian (sense 2).

rē·demp′tive, *a.* 1. serving to redeem.
2. of or relating to redemption.

Rē·demp′tŏr·ist, *n.* a member of the Congregation of the Most Holy Redeemer, a Roman Catholic order founded in Naples in 1732 by St. Alphonsus Liguori, devoted to the education of the ignorant, the poor, and the neglected.

rē·demp′tō·ry, *a.* redemptive.

rē·demp′tūre, *n.* a redeemer. [Obs.]

rē·dent′ed, *a.* formed like the teeth of a saw; indented. [Obs.]

rē·dē·ploy′, *v.t.* to move (troops) from one front to another, as from Europe to the Pacific.

rē·dē·poș′it, *v.t.* to deposit again.

rē·dē·poș′it, *n.* something deposited again.

rē·dē·vel′ŏp, *v.t.* and *v.i.*; redeveloped, *pt., pp.*; redeveloping, *ppr.* to develop again; specifically, in photography, to intensify or tone (a developed negative or image) by putting through a second process of development.

rē·dē·vel′ŏp·ment, *n.* a redeveloping or being redeveloped.

red′eȳe (-ī), *n.* 1. any of several fishes with red eyes, as the rudd.
2. the red-eyed vireo.
3. a species of sunfish, *Lepomis cyanellus.*
4. strong, inferior whisky. [Slang.]

This same moonshine is equally well known in the south as *redeye.* —Bryan.

Also *red eye.*

red′fin, *n.* any of a group of fresh-water food fishes of the carp family, with the lower fins red or orange, found in the east central States; especially, the dace, *Notropis megalops*: also called *shiner* and *red dace.*

red′finch, *n.* the European linnet.

red′fish, *n.* any one of certain fishes, as (a) the red drum, *Sciæna ocellata*; (b) a Californian food fish, *Trochocopus pulcher*; (c) the blueback salmon; (d) the rosefish.

red gum, 1. a disease of infants; an eruption of red pimples in early infancy.
2. a disease of grain, rust.

red gum, a tree of the genus *Eucalyptus,* found in Australia.

red′-hãired′, *a.* having hair of a reddish color.

red′-hand′ed, *a.* 1. having hands red with blood.
2. in the act, or fresh from the scene, of a crime.
3. bloody; violent: said of actions.

red′head″ (-hed″), *n.* 1. a person with red hair.
2. a North American diving duck the male of which has a red head: it resembles the related canvasback.
3. the redheaded woodpecker.

red′head″ed, *a.* having red hair, as a person, or a red head, as a bird.

red′head″ed wood′peck″ēr, a North American woodpecker with a bright-red head and neck, black back,and white underparts.

red·hi·bi′tion (-bish′un), *n.* in civil law, an action allowed to a purchaser by which to annul the sale of some movable, and oblige the seller to take it back again upon the purchaser's finding it damaged, or that there was some deceit, etc.

red·hib′i·tō·ry, *a.* of or pertaining to redhibition.

red′hoop, *n.* a male bullfinch. [Brit. Dial.]

red′horn, *n.* a butterfly of the family *Rhodoceridæ,* usually having the antennae red.

red′-hot, *n.* a hot dog. [Colloq.]

red′-hot′, *a.* 1. red with heat; hot enough to glow; very hot; as, *red-hot* iron.
2. very ardent; extreme; very excited, as with anger or enthusiasm; as, a *red-hot* argument.
3. very new; up-to-the-minute: said of news, etc.

rē′di·ȧ, *n.*; *pl.* **rē′di·ae,** [from *Redi,* an Italian naturalist.] an early larval stage in the development of some flukeworms, preceding the cercaria form.

rē′di·ent, *a.* [L. *rediens,* ppr. of *redire,* to return.] returning. [Rare.]

red′iñ·gōte, *n.* [Fr.; altered from Eng. *riding coat.*]
1. formerly, a man's full-skirted, double-breasted overcoat.
2. a long, unlined, lightweight coat, open down the front, worn by women.

TYPES OF REDINGOTE

red·in′tē·grāte, *v.t.*; redintegrated, *pt., pp.*; redintegrating, *ppr.* [L. *redintegrare*; *red-, re-,* back, again, and *integrare,* to renew, from *integer,* whole.] to make whole or perfect again; to reunite; to re-establish; to renew; to restore to a perfect state.

red·in′tē·grāte, *a.* renewed; restored to wholeness or a perfect state. [Obs.]

red·in·tē·grā′tion, *n.* 1. a redintegrating or being redintegrated; renovation; restoration to a whole or sound state.
2. in chemistry, the restoration of any mixed body or matter to its former nature and constitution. [Obs.]
3. in psychology, (a) that characteristic of the mind by which associated events are remembered as a group when one of the group is recalled; (b) the tendency to respond to a later stimulus in the same way as to an earlier complex stimulus of which the later one was a part.

rē·di·reçt′, *a.* in law, of or designating the examination of one's own witness again, following the cross-examination by the opposing lawyer.

rē·di·reçt′, *v.t.* to direct again; to give a new direction to; as, to *redirect* a letter.

rē·di·reç'tion, *n.* a redirecting.
rē·dis·bûrse', *v.t.* to repay or refund.
rē·dis'çount, *v.t.* in banking, to discount again; to subject to a second discount: said of commercial paper.
rē·dis'çount, *n.* 1. a rediscounting.
2. [*usually pl.*] rediscounted commercial paper.
rē·dis·sēize', *v.t.* to disseize again or anew.
rē·dis·sēi'zin, *n.* in law, a disseizing or being disseized a second time.
rē·dis·sēi'zŏr, *n.* a person who disseizes lands or tenements a second time, or after a recovery of the same from him in an action of novel disseizin.
rē·dis·trib'ūte, *v.t.* to distribute again; to deal back again.
rē·dis·tri·bū'tion, *n.* a dealing back, or a second distribution.
rē·dis'triçt, *v.t.* to divide into new districts, especially in order to reapportion electoral representatives; to make a new arrangement of the districts of.
red·i·vī'vus, *a.* [L.] brought to life again; restored.
red lead (led), red oxide of lead, Pb_3O_4, derived from massicot, used in making paint, in glassmaking, etc.; minium.
red lead ōre, a mineral, crocoite, a red chromate of lead: also called *red lead spar.*
red'legs, red'leg, *n.* 1. any of various birds; as, (a) the redshank; (b) the turnstone, *Strepsilas interpres*; (c) the red-legged partridge of Europe.
2. a plant, the bistort.
red'-let'tẽr, *a.* happy; memorable; as, a *red-letter* day.
red-letter day; a fortunate, happy, or auspicious day: so called because the holy days, or saints' days, were marked on the old calendars with red letters; a day of notable events or occurrences; a day to be remembered in a special manner.
red light (līt), 1. a danger signal.
2. a signal used to bring trains, automobiles, etc. to a stop; stop light.
red'-light' dis'triçt, a section of a town or city in which there are many houses of prostitution: so called because, formerly, it was customary to display a red light above the doors of such houses.
red'lin·ing, *n.* [from the practice of outlining such areas in red on a map.] the systematic refusal by some lending institutions or insurance companies to issue mortgage loans or insurance on property in certain neighborhoods regarded by them as deteriorating.
red'ly, *adv.* in a red manner; with a red color.
red mō·roç'çō, a plant, the pheasant's-eye.
red'mouth, *n.* a fish, the grunt.
red'ness, *n.* the quality of being red; red color.
red'ō·lence, red'ō·len·cy, *n.* the quality or state of being redolent; sweet scent; fragrance.
red'ō·lent, *a.* [L. *redolens, redolentis,* ppr. of *redolere,* to emit a scent; *red-, re-,* and *olere,* to smell.]
1. sweet-smelling; fragrant.
2. smelling (*of*); as, *redolent of* flowers.
3. suggestive (*of*).
rē·dŏu'ble, *v.t.*; redoubled (-bld), *pt., pp.*; redoubling, *ppr.* [Fr. *redoubler.*]
1. to make twice as much or twice as great; to increase two-fold.
2. to repeat; to do or say again.
3. to echo or re-echo.
4. to refold; to double back.
5. in bridge, to double the doubled bid of (one's opponent).
rē·dŏu'ble, *v.i.* 1. to become twice as great or twice as much.
2. to re-echo; resound.
3. in bridge, to double a bid that an opponent has already doubled.
rē·dŏu'ble, *n.* in bridge, a redoubling.
rē·doubt' (-dout'), *v.t.* to regard with fear; to dread. [Rare.]
rē·doubt', *n.* [Fr. *redoute*; It. *ridotto*; ML. *reductus,* a refuge, orig. pp. of L. *reducere.*]
1. in military science, (a) a temporary outlying fortification or breastwork, used to secure hilltops, passes, or the flanks of entrenchments; (b) in permanent fortifications, a breastwork surrounded by a parapet and dominated by guns from the heavier fortifications behind it.
2. a stronghold.
rē·doubt'ȧ·ble, *a.* [OFr. *redoubtable,* from *redoubter,* to fear or dread; L. *re-,* again, and *dubitare,* to doubt.]
1. formidable; that is to be dreaded; terrible; fearsome.
2. deserving of respect; as, a *redoubtable* opponent.
rē·doubt'ȧ·bly, *adv.* in a redoubtable manner; so as to be redoubtable.
rē·doubt'ed, *a.* formidable; redoubtable. [Archaic.]
rē·doubt'ing, *n.* honor; reverence. [Obs.]
rē·dound', *v.i.*; redounded; *pt., pp.*; redounding, *ppr.* [Fr. *redonder*; L. *redundare,* to overflow; *red-, re-,* and *undare,* to surge, swell, from *unda,* a wave.]
1. to have a result or effect (to the credit or discredit, etc. of someone or something); as, this work will *redound* to his credit.
2. to come back; to react; to recoil (*upon*): said of honor or disgrace.
3. to flow back, as waves. [Obs.]
4. to be redundant; to overflow. [Obs.]
rē·dound', *n.* 1. a coming back by way of consequence; return; result; requital.
2. reverberation; rebound. [Rare.]
red'ōw·ȧ, *n.* [Fr., from Bohem. *rejdowák,* a kind of dance, from *rejdowati,* to turn.]
1. either of two ballroom dances of the 19th century, one form of which resembles the polka, but is of a more lively nature, the other form resembling the waltz.
2. the music for either of these.
red'pōll, *n.* [*red* and *poll* (the head).]
1. any of a number of finches of the genus *Acanthis,* the males of which usually have a red patch on the head.
2. any of several other birds, as (a) the European linnet; (b) the redpoll warbler, *Dendrœca palmarum.*
rē'drȧft (*or* rē-drȧft'), *n.* 1. a second or later draft or framing, as of a legislative bill.
2. a draft on the drawer or endorser of a protested bill of exchange, for the amount of the bill plus charges and costs.
rē·drȧft', *v.t.* to draft anew or again.
rē·dra̤w', *v.t.*; redrew, *pt.*; redrawn, *pp.*; redrawing, *ppr.* to draw again; to make a second draft or copy of.
rē·dra̤w', *v.i.* to draw a new bill of exchange, as the holder of a protested bill, on the drawer or endorsers.
rē-dress', *v.t.* to dress again: variously applied; as, to *re-dress* a wound; to *re-dress* a doll.
rē·dress', *v.t.*; redressed (-drest), *pt., pp.*; redressing, *ppr.* [Fr. *redresser,* to straighten.]
1. to correct and compensate for, as evils, abuses, afflictions, etc.
2. to correct; to remedy, as a fault.
3. to compensate; to make amends to.
4. to adjust; as, *redress* the balances.
5. to place upright; to erect. [Obs.]
rē'dress (*or* rē-dres'), *n.* 1. compensation; satisfaction, as for a wrong done.
2. a redressing.
3. reformation; amendment. [Obs.]
4. one who or that which redresses. [Obs.]
Syn.—remedy, relief, amends, compensation, reparation.
rē·dress'ăl, *n.* redressment.
rē·dress'ẽr, rē·dres'sŏr, *n.* one who redresses.
rē·dress'i·ble, *a.* capable of being redressed, relieved, or indemnified.
rē·dress'ive, *a.* affording or giving relief; tending to redress. [Rare.]
rē·dress'less, *a.* without relief; incapable of being redressed; irremediable. [Rare.]
rē·dress'ment, *n.* the act of redressing; redress; redressal.
red rib'bŏn, same as *band fish.*
red'-rōan, *a.* red with a thick sprinkling of gray or white: said of horses.
red'rob'in, the wheat rust, *Puccinia graminis.*
red'ro̤ot, *n.* any of several plants, as (a) New Jersey tea, *Ceanothus americanus*; (b) stoneweed, *Lithospermum tinctorium*; (c) *Lachnanthes tinctoria,* a herbaceous plant of the bloodwort family having a red root, sword-shaped leaves, and orange-yellow flowers; (d) bloodroot.
red rust, a fungous disease appearing on the leaves and stem of growing grain.
red'sēar, *v.i.* to break or crack when too hot, as iron under the hammer; to be red-short. [Obs.]
red'seed, *n.* small crustaceans, as copepods, etc., which float near the sea surface and are eaten by various fishes.
red'shañk, *n.* 1. any bird of the snipe family belonging to the genus *Totanus*: so called from its red legs. *Totanus calidris* is about 11 inches long, lives in the British Isles all the year, but is known also as a summer bird of passage in the most northern parts of Europe and Asia, occurring in winter as far south as India. The spotted redshank, *Totanus fuscus,* visits Great Britain in spring and autumn on its migrations north and south.

SPOTTED REDSHANK (*Totanus fuscus*)

2. the fieldfare, *Turdus pilaris.*
3. a Highlander: so called in derision of his bare legs.
A generation of Highland thieves and *redshanks.* —Milton.
red·shâre', *a.* red-short. [Obs.]
red'-shŏrt', *a.* brittle when red-hot: said of iron or steel with too much sulfur in it.
red-shŏrt'ness, *n.* the quality of being brittle when red-hot: said of certain kinds of iron.
red'sīdes, *n.* a small cyprinoid American fish, *Notropis ardens*; the redfin.
red'skin, *n.* a North American Indian: so called from the reddish or coppery color of the skin.
Red Stär, an international organization having for its objective the humane treatment of animals: it had its inception in Switzerland.
red'stärt, *n.* [*red* and *start* (from AS. *steort*), tail.]
1. a small, handsome, singing bird, *Ruticilla phœnicura,* belonging to the warbler family, *Sylviadæ,* nearly allied to the nightingale, but having a more slender form and bill, a reddish tail, and a peculiar darting flight. It is widely diffused over Europe, Asia, and the north of Africa. It is found in almost all parts of Great Britain as a summer bird of passage. It has a soft and sweet song, which is continued during the breeding season far into the night. The black redstart, *Ruticilla tithys,* is distinguished from the common redstart by being sooty-black on the breast and belly where the other is reddish-brown.

REDSTART (*Ruticilla phœnicura*)

2. an American fly-catching warbler, red, black, and white, a small bird of the family *Muscicapidæ,* or flycatchers, common in most parts of North America.
Also called *redtail, firetail, fireflirt,* and *brantail.*
blue-throated redstart; same as bluethroat.
red'strēak, *n.* 1. a sort of apple so called from its red streaks.
2. cider pressed from redstreak apples.
red'tāil, *n.* 1. the red-tailed hawk or buzzard, *Buteo borealis,* of North America: also called *hen hawk,* and *red-tailed buzzard.*
2. same as *redstart.*
red'-tāiled', *a.* having a red tail, as various birds.
red-tailed hawk; same as *redtail,* sense 1.
red'-tāpe", *a.* of, pertaining to, or characterized by red tape, or official routine, formality, delay, etc.; as, *red-tape* statesmen.
red tāpe, [after the tape commonly used to tie official paper.]
1. official forms and routines.
2. rigid application of regulations and routines, resulting in delays and exasperations in getting business done.
red'-tāped' (-tāpt'), *a.* pertaining to or affected by red tape.
red"-tāp'ẽr·y, *n.* same as *red-tapism.*
red"-tāp'ism, *n.* the system of red tape or excessive official routine; strict or punctilious adherence to official formalities.
red"-tāp'ist, *n.* 1. one employed in a public office who ties his papers with red tape; hence, a mere government clerk.

2. one who adheres strictly to the forms and routine of office.

Pompous *red-tapists.* —Lord Lytton.

red'thrōat, *n.* 1. a small brown singing bird, *Pyrrholæmus brunneus*, of Australia, having a red spot at the center of the throat.

2. a fish of the West Indies, of the genus *Hæmalon*, belonging to the family *Sciænidæ*: so called from the portion of the under jaw which is covered by the upper when the mouth is closed being of a bright red color.

red'top, *n.* [from the reddish panicle of some forms.] a species of bent grass, *Agrostis vulgaris*, cultivated and highly valued in eastern North America for pasturage and hay: also called *English grass* and *herd's-grass.*

false redtop; the fowl meadow grass, *Poa serotina*, having narrow leaves and bearing some resemblance to true redtop.

tall redtop; a reddish grass, *Triodia cuprea*, common in the United States.

rē·dub', *v.t.* to repair or make reparation for; to repay; to requite. [Obs.]

rē·dub'bẽr, *n.* a person who bought stolen cloth and turned it into some other color or fashion, that it might not be known again. [Obs.]

rē·dūce', *v.t.*; reduced (-dūst), *pt., pp.*; reducing, *ppr.* [L. *reducere*, to lead back; *re-*, back, and *ducere*, to lead.]

1. to bring back; to lead back to a former place or condition; restore. [Obs.]

2. to atone for; to repair; to redress. [Obs.]

3. to lessen in any way, as in size, weight, amount, value, price, etc.; to diminish.

4. to bring into a certain order; to classify.

5. to break up into constituent elements by analysis.

6. (a) to change to a different form, as by putting something said into writing; (b) to change to a different physical form, as by melting, crushing, grinding, etc.

7. to lower, as in rank or position; to degrade.

8. to bring to order, attention, obedience, etc., as by persuasion or force.

9. to subdue or conquer, as a city or fort by siege or attack; to bring under control.

10. (a) to bring into difficult or wretched circumstances; as, *reduced* to poverty; (b) to compel by need to do something: used in the passive; as, he was *reduced* to stealing.

11. to weaken in bodily strength; to make thin; as, *reduced* to skin and bones.

12. to thin (paint), as with oil.

13. in arithmetic, to change in denomination or form without changing in value; as, *reduce* fractions to their lowest terms.

14. in biology, to cause (a cell) to undergo meiosis.

15. in chemistry, (a) to decrease the positive valence of (an element or radical); (b) to increase the negative valence of (an element or radical); (c) to remove the oxygen from; to deoxidize; (d) to combine with hydrogen; (e) to bring into the metallic state by removing nonmetallic elements.

16. in photography, to make less dense, as a negative.

17. in surgery, to restore (a broken bone, displaced organ, etc.) to its normal position or condition.

18. in military affairs, (a) to strike from the pay roll; (b) to assign or degrade to a lower rank.

to reduce a figure, design, or *draft*; to make a copy of it smaller than the original, preserving the form and proportion.

to reduce an equation; to subject an equation to the process of reduction.

to reduce an expression; in algebra, to secure an equivalent expression in simpler form.

to reduce a square; in military tactics, to alter the formation of troops from the hollow square to the line or column.

to reduce to the ranks; in military usage, to degrade a sergeant or corporal for misconduct to the rank of a private.

Syn.—lower, lessen, decrease, abate, diminish, degrade, subdue, conquer, impoverish, shorten, abridge, curtail, classify, modify, alter.

rē·dūce', *v.i.* 1. to become reduced.

2. to lose weight, as by dieting.

rē·dūce'ȧ·ble, *a.* same as *reducible.*

rē·dūced' (-dūst'), *a.* changed in form; brought to a former state; brought into any lesser state or condition; diminished; subdued; impoverished; classified; modified.

reduced iron; metallic iron in a fine state of division: it is obtained by deoxidation of an oxide of iron by exposing it to or heating it in hydrogen.

rē·dūce'ment, *n.* the act of reducing; reduction. [Obs.]

rē·dū'cent, *a.* tending to reduce.

rē·dū'cent, *n.* that which reduces.

rē·dū'cẽr, *n.* 1. one who or that which reduces.

2. in mechanics, a pipe fitting threaded to connect two different sizes of pipe.

3. in photography, (a) a developing agent; (b) an oxidizing solution for reducing negatives.

rē·dū·ci·bil'i·ty, *n.* the condition or quality of being reducible.

rē·dū'ci·ble, *a.* that can be reduced.

rē·dū'ci·ble·ness, *n.* the quality of being reducible.

rē·dū'ci·bly, *adv.* in a reducible manner; so as to be reducible.

rē·dū'cine, *n.* a basic substance or alkaloid found in urochrome.

rē·dū'cing ā'gent, in chemistry, any substance that reduces another substance, or brings about reduction, and is itself oxidized in the process.

rē·dū'cing fũr'nȧce, a furnace in which ores are deprived of their oxygen and reduced to the metallic state by the action of intensely heated vapors containing carbon, sometimes assisted by other reagents. It is used in the reduction of litharge, the treatment of copper ore in several stages, and for obtaining the precious metals.

rē·dū'cing glȧss, a double-concave lens used for reducing the visual size of something viewed through it.

rē·dū'cing pīpe, a pipe having different dimensions, or, sometimes, also different shapes at its opposite ends. It is used to connect pipes of unequal sizes or of different shapes.

rē·dū'cing sçāle, in geometry, a scale by means of which figures are copied on a scale smaller than the original, but preserving the form and proportion.

rē·dū'cing valve, a valve constructed for the regulation of steam pressure between a boiler and its connections. A weighted lever regulates the opening of the valve.

rē·duçt', *v.t.* [L. *re-* and *ductus*, from *ducere*, to lead.] to reduce, or bring back. [Obs.]

rē·duç'tāse (*or* -tāz), *n.* [*reduc*tion and *-ase.*] any enzyme that speeds up chemical reduction.

ré·duc·teur' (rā-duk-tẽr'), *n.* [Fr.] in electricity, a multiplying coil or multiplier of a voltmeter.

rē·duç·ti·bil'i·ty, *n.* the quality of being reducible. [Rare.]

rē·duç'ti·ō ad ab·sũr'dum (-shi-ō), [L., lit., reduction to absurdity.] in logic, the proof of a proposition by showing its opposite to be foolish or impossible, or the disproof of a proposition by showing its consequences to be impossible or absurd when it is carried to its logical conclusion.

rē·duç'tion, *n.* [Fr., from L. *reductio* (*-onis*), reduction.]

1. a reducing or being reduced.

2. the act of bringing back or restoring. [Obs.]

3. the act of bringing into subjection; conquest; subjugation; as, the *reduction* of a kingdom or fortress.

4. the act of diminishing in size, dimensions, value, quantity, force, etc.; diminution; abatement; as, the *reduction* of expenses; the *reduction* of forces.

5. anything made or brought about by reducing, as a smaller copy, lower price, etc.

6. the amount, value, quantity, etc. by which anything is reduced or lessened; as, he made a *reduction* of 5 per cent.

7. the act or process of making a copy of a figure, map, plan, design, etc. on a smaller scale than the original, but preserving the form and proportion.

8. in algebra, the act or process of clearing equations from all superfluous quantities, bringing them to their lowest terms, and separating the known from the unknown, till the unknown quantity alone is found on one side, and the known quantities on the other.

9. in arithmetic, (a) the operation or process of finding an equivalent expression in terms of a different unit; (b) the rule by which such operations are performed.

10. in astronomy, (a) the correction of observations for known errors of instruments, etc.; (b) the collection of observations to obtain a general result.

11. in biology, meiosis.

12. in geometry, the operation of constructing a figure similar to a given figure, either greater, less, or equivalent.

13. in logic, the process of bringing a syllogism in one of the imperfect modes to a mode in the first figure.

14. in Scots law, an action for setting aside a deed, writing, etc.

15. in surgery, the operation of restoring a fractured or dislocated bone to its proper place or state.

reduction ascending; in arithmetic, the changing of numbers of a lower denomination into a higher, as of cents into dimes.

reduction descending; in arithmetic, the changing of numbers of a higher denomination into a lower, as of dimes to cents.

Syn.—decrease, curtailment, diminution, contraction, abatement, abridgment.

rē·duç'tion·ȧl, *a.* of reduction.

rē·duç'tion wŏrks, a plant for rendering ore marketable by a process of reduction.

rē·duç'tive, *a.* [Fr. *réductif.*]

1. of reduction.

2. having the power of reducing; tending to reduce.

rē·duç'tive, *n.* that which has the power of reducing.

rē·duç'tive·ly, *adv.* by reduction; by consequence.

rē·duç'tŏr, *n.* in chemistry, any apparatus for carrying out the reduction of a metallic solution for purposes of analysis; specifically, a long tube filled with granular zinc for reducing a ferric solution to its ferrous salt.

ré·duit' (rā-dwē'), *n.* a central fortification within a larger fort.

rē·dun'dănce, *n.* redundancy.

rē·dun'dăn·cy, *n.* 1. the quality or state of being redundant; superfluity; excess; superabundance.

2. *pl.* **rē·dun'dăn·cieș,** that which is redundant or in excess, as, a part or quantity; anything superfluous or superabundant.

The *redundancy* and dreariness which have overwhelmed our declarations, have no redeeming quality. —Grover Cleveland.

3. in law, impertinent or foreign matter inserted in a pleading.

rē·dun'dănt, *a.* [L. *redundans* (*-antis*), *ppr.* of *redundare*, to flow back or overflow.]

1. more than enough; over-abundant; excessive.

2. excess; superfluous; as, a *redundant* foot in a line of verse.

3. wordy; as, a redundant literary style.

4. unnecessary to the meaning: said of words.

5. in grammar, designating or of a verb having alternative forms, as for the past tense or participle (e.g., *awake, dive*).

Syn.—excessive, superfluous, superabundant, copious, plentiful, exuberant.

rē·dun'dănt·ly, *adv.* with superfluity or excess; superfluously; superabundantly.

rē·dū'pli·çāte, *v.t.* [L. *reduplicatus*, pp. of *reduplicare*; *re-*, and *duplicare*, to duplicate.]

1. to double; to double again; to multiply; to repeat.

2. in linguistics, (a) to double (a root syllable or other element) so as to form an inflected or derived form of a word, sometimes with certain changes, as of the vowel (e.g., *chitchat, helter-skelter, tom-tom*); (b) to form (words) by such repetition.

rē·dū'pli·çāte, *v.i.* to be or become reduplicated.

rē·dū'pli·çāte, *a.* 1. redoubled; repeated; reduplicative.

2. in botany, having the edges of the sepals or petals folded back so that they project or are turned outward.

rē·dū'pli·çāte, *n.* something reduplicated.

rē·dū·pli·çā'tion, *n.* 1. the act of doubling; the state of being doubled.

2. something produced by reduplicating, as a word containing a reduplicated element.

3. the element added in a reduplicated word form.

4. in rhetoric, a figure in which a verse ends with the same word with which the following begins.

5. in anatomy and zoology, a folding of a part or organ; a fold, as in a membrane; reduplicature. [Rare.]

rē·dū'pli·cȧ·tive, *a.* 1. reduplicating or tending to reduplicate.

2. of or characterized by reduplication.

3. in botany, reduplicate.

rē·dū′pli·cȧ·tūre, *n.* in anatomy and zoology, reduplication.

rē·dū′vi·oid, *n.* [L. *reduvia*, a hangnail.] a predaceous bug of the family *Reduviidæ*. Some species suck the blood of certain animals.

red′wãre, *n.* [*red* and *ware* (ME. and AS. *war*), seaweed.] in botany, a large, brown, leathery seaweed, *Laminaria digitata*; the tangle.

red wa̤′tẽr, a disease in cattle: so called from a bloodlike appearance in the urine.

red′weed, *n.* the corn poppy [Brit. Dial.]

red′wing, *n.* 1. a north European songbird, *Turdus iliacus*, the smallest of the thrush family, named from the deep orange-red color of its underwing coverts.

2. the red-winged blackbird.

red′-wiñged″ black′bird, any of a species of North American blackbirds with a bright-red patch on each wing, near the shoulder, the *Agelæus phæniceus*: also known as the *marsh blackbird*.

red′withe, *n.* in botany, *Combretum jacquini*, a climbing vine of the West Indies.

red′wood, *n.* 1. any of a number of trees with wood of a red color, as (a) an Indian dyewood, the *Pterocarpus santalinus*; (b) the *Cornumascula*, the redwood of the Turks; (c) *Gordonia hæmatoxylon*, the redwood of Jamaica; (d) *Pterocarpus dalbergioides*, or Andaman wood; (e) *Ceanothus colubrinus*, the redwood of the Bahamas; (f) *Sequoia sempervirens*, a coniferous tree of California, the redwood of the timber trade. This last tree attains gigantic dimensions, being frequently more than 300 feet high.

2. the wood of any of these trees.

red′-yel′lōw, *n.* a color betewen red and yellow in the spectrum; orange.

red′-yel′lōw, *a.* of the color red-yellow; orange.

ree, *v.t.* [dial. spelling of *rid, riddle*.] to riddle; to sift; to separate or throw off. [Brit. Dial.]

ree′bok, *n.* [D., lit., roebuck.] a species of South African antelope, *Pelea capreola*.

rē-eçh′ō, *v.t.* and *v.i.*; re-echoed, *pt., pp.*; re-echoing, *ppr.* to echo back; to reverberate again; as, the hills *re-echo* the roar of cannon; the sound *re-echoes*: also *reëcho*.

rē-eçh′ō, *n.*; *pl.* **rē-eçh′ōeṣ,** the echo of an echo: also *reëcho*.

reech′y, *a.* reeky; grimy; smoky. [Obs.]

reed, *a.* red. [Obs.]

reed, *v.t.* to thatch.

reed, *n.* [ME. *rede, reed*; AS. *hreōd*; akin to G. *riet*.]

1. any of various tall, broad-leaved, related grasses with jointed, hollow stems which grow along the banks of streams, as the bamboo; specifically, any plant of the genera *Arundo, Ammophila*, and *Phragmites*, especially *Phragmites communis*, the common reed. This is the largest of all the grasses of northern climates, and one of the most universally diffused. It is used for thatching, for protecting embankments, for roofing, etc.

2. a mass of these, growing or dried.

3. a rustic musical instrument made from a hollow stem or stalk and played by blowing through it: used as the symbol of pastoral poetry.

4. an arrow. [Poetic.]

5. in architecture, a small, rounded molding.

6. in the Bible, a unit of length equal to 6 cubits: Ezek. xl. 3, 5.

7. in music, (a) in certain wind instruments, as the clarinet, a thin strip of some flexible substance, as cane, reed, wood, metal, etc., placed against the opening of the mouthpiece so as to leave a narrow opening: when vibrated by the breath, it produces a musical tone; (b) an instrument with a reed or reeds; (c) in an organ, a similar contrivance that vibrates in a current of air; (d) a reed, stop.

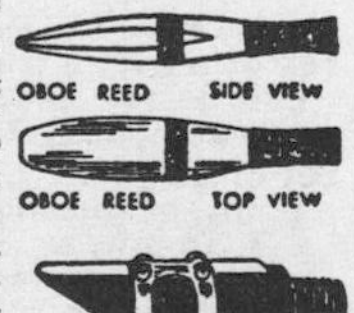

REEDS

8. straw prepared for thatching; thatch. [Brit. Dial.]

9. a weaver's instrument for separating the threads of the warp, and for beating the weft up to the web. It is made of parallel slips of metal or reeds, called dents, which resemble the teeth of a comb. The dents are fixed at their ends into two parallel pieces of wood set a few inches apart.

10. in mining, the tube conveying the train of gunpowder to the charge in the blasthole.

Egyptian reed; the papyrus.

free reed; a reed with edges that do not strike the wind aperture.

great reed or *Italian reed*; a large grass found in the southern part of North America and Europe; the *Arundo donax*.

reed bent grass; any species of the genus *Calamagrostis*.

reed canary grass; a wild grass, *Phalaris arundinacea*.

reed, *v.t* 1. to thatch with reeds.

2. to decorate with reeds.

reed, *n.* the abomasum. [Obs.]

reed bab′blẽr, an Asiatic bird of the genera *Eurycercus* and *Schænicola*.

reed′bird, *n.* a bird, (a) the bobolink; (b) the reed babbler; (c) the reed warbler.

reed′buck, *n.*; *pl.* **reed′buck** or **reed′bucks,** [transl. of D. *rietbok*.] any of several small, marsh-dwelling African antelopes with widely spread hooves and, in the males, backward-sloping, ringed horns turned inward and forward near the tips.

reed bun′ting, one of the British buntings, *Emberiza schœniclus*, a small insessorial bird that frequents reeds, fens, etc. It has a black head, brown back, and white underparts, and feeds on seeds and small mollusks. Also called *reed sparrow* or *black-headed bunting*.

reed′ed, *a.* 1. covered with reeds.

2. formed with channels and ridges like reeds.

reed′en, *a.* consisting of a reed or reeds, as pipes. [Rare.]

reed grȧss, any of various species of reedlike grasses.

reed′i·ly, *adv.* in a reedy manner.

reed′i·ness, *n.* the condition or quality of being reedy.

reed′ing, *n.* 1. the nurling on the edge of coins.

2. (a) a small, rounded molding resembling a reed; (b) a set of such moldings, as on a column.

3. ornamentation consisting of such moldings.

4. decoration by the use of woven reeds.

reed in′strụ·ment, any instrument whose sound is produced by the vibration of a reed, or thin strip of flexible substance: reed instruments include the oboe, clarinet, saxophone, English horn, and bassoon.

reed′less, *a.* without reeds; as, *reedless* banks.

reed′ling, *n.* [*reed* and *-ling*.] a small European bird with a long tail and orange-brown, black, and white plumage, found in reedy places, as marshes: the male has a black tuft on each side of the face.

reed mãce, the cattail.

reed o̤r′găn, an organ having free metal reeds instead of pipes to produce the tones.

reed pīpe, an organ pipe in which the tone is produced by a current of air striking a vibrating reed in an opening in the pipe: distinguished from *flue pipe*.

reed spar′rōw, the reed bunting.

reed stop, 1. a set of reed pipes (in an organ) controlled by one knob.

2. the knob.

rē-ed′ū·çāte, *v.t.*; re-educated, *pt., pp.*; re-educating, *ppr.* to educate again or anew; especially, to rehabilitate (a handicapped person, etc.) by special training or schooling: also *reëducate*.

reed wa̤r′blẽr, any of various small warblers of Europe and Asia living in marshes and swamps, as (a) the *Salicaria arundinacea* of the family *Sylviadæ*, frequenting marshy places and building its nest on reeds; (b) *Acrocephalus turdoides*, sometimes called the *reed wren*.

reed′wŏrk, *n.* the reed stops of an organ, collectively.

reed′y, *a.*; *comp.* reedier; *superl.* reediest, 1. full of reeds.

2. made of reed or reeds.

3. like a reed.

4. sounding like a reed instrument; thin; piping.

reef, *n.* [ME. *riff*; O.N. *rif*, lit., a rib.]

1. a line or ridge of sand or rock lying at or near the surface of the water; as, a coral *reef*.

2. in mining, a bed of ore; a lode; a vein.

3. a kind of sponge.

reef, *n.* [Early Mod. Eng. phonetic sp. of ME. *riff*.]

1. a part of a sail which can be folded together and tied down in order to reduce the area exposed to the wind.

2. the act of reefing.

close reef; the last reef in a sail; the last part to be fastened to the yard or boom.

French reef; the reefing of canvas in which the ordinary reef points are replaced by some other device, as jackstays.

to take a reef or *reefs in*; to reduce or contract the extent of, as of a sail, by folding a part of it and fastening it to the yard.

reef, *v.i.*; reefed (rēft), *pt., pp.*; reefing, *ppr.* to take in a reef or reefs; to contract or reduce the extent of a sail by rolling or folding a certain portion of it and making it fast to the yard.

reef, *v.t.* 1. to cut down the size of (a sail) by taking in and tying down part of it.

REEFING A SAIL

2. to lower (a spar); to shorten (a mast or bowsprit) by taking part of it in, lowering it, etc.

to reef paddles; to remove the floats of a paddle wheel nearer to the center of the wheel as to lessen the amount of dip.

reef band, a strong horizontal strip of canvas extending across a sail at right angles to the lengths of cloth and pierced with holes for the reef points, by which it is tied to the yard in shortening sail.

reef build′ẽr (bild′), one of the corals by which coral reefs are formed.

reef′ẽr, *n.* 1. a person who reefs: formerly a slang term for a midshipman.

2. a short, thick, double-breasted coat, worn especially by sailors.

3. a woman's form-fitting, double-breasted coat, similar to this.

4. [from the rolled appearance of a *reef* (of a sail).] a marijuana cigarette. [Slang.]

reef′ẽr, *n.* an oyster growing on reefs; a worthless oyster.

reef′ing, *n.* the process of taking in and reducing; in upholstery and decoration, the process of looping or festooning, as in curtains, lambrequins, wreaths, and the like.

reef′ing bow′sprit, a bowsprit fitted so as to allow reefing or sliding inboard.

reef jig, in nautical usage, a small tackle used to make the reef band taut before knotting the points in.

reef knot (not), a common square knot; in nautical usage, a knot in which the ends fall always in a line with the outer parts, formed by passing the ends of the two parts of one rope through the loop formed by another whose two ends are similarly passed through a loop on the first: used in fastening reef points: see *knot*, illus.

reef līne, a line formerly used in reefing. It passes spirally around the yard and through the eyelets in the reef band successively, so as to draw the latter up to the yard when the line is hauled upon.

reef point, in a sail, one of a series of cords fastened in the eyelets of the reef band and used in fastening the reefed sail to the yard.

reef taç′kle, a tackle by which the reef cringles, or rings, of a sail are hauled up to the yard for reefing.

reef tīe, same as *reef point*.

reef′y, *a.*; *comp.* reefier; *superl.* reefiest, full of reefs or rocks; having many reefs; as. a *reefy* bay.

reek, *n.* [ME. *reke*; AS. *rec*; akin to G. *rauch*; only Gmc.]

1. vapor; fume.

2. a strong, unpleasant smell.

3. smoke. [Dial.]

reek, *v.i.* [ME. reken, from the *n.*]

1. to give off steam or smoke.

2. to have a strong, offensive smell.

3. to be permeated with anything very unpleasant.

reek, *v.t.* 1. to expose to the action of smoke, etc.

2. to emit or exude (vapor, fumes, etc.).

reek, *n.* a rick of hay. [Obs.]

reek'le, *a.* same as *reeky.*

Auld Reekie; Edinburgh, Scotland.

reek'y, *a.*; *comp.* reekier; *superl.* reekiest, full of or giving off reek.

reel, *n.* [AS. *hreol, reol,* a reel; Ice. *hræll,* a weavers' rod or sley; also Gael. *ruidhil,* a reel for winding yarn on.]

1. any frame or spool on which thread, wire, film, nets, etc. may be wound: it usually turns on an axle, often by the power of a hand crank.

2. the quantity of wire, thread, etc. usually wound on one reel.

3. a machine on which yarn is wound and at the same time measured into skeins and hanks.

4. a frame attached to a harvesting machine which holds the stalks of grain so that they can be readily cut with the blades.

5. a moving-picture film, usually 1,000 feet long, wound on one reel.

6. a mechanically mounted spool fitted to the handle of a fishing rod for holding and controlling an angler's line; as, a rod and *reel.*

off the reel; fluently; easily; without hesitation.

reel-and-bead molding; in architecture, a kind of ornamental molding consisting of a series of reels or spindles separated from each other by a bead or beads and capable of being arranged in either straight or curved lines, much used in Greek and Roman architecture, and, in modified forms, in other styles.

reel oven; a bakers' oven in which bread is baked in pans suspended from arms attached to a rotating reel.

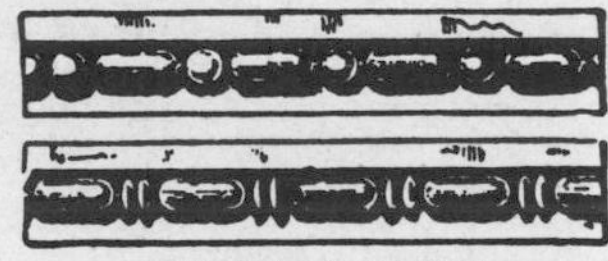

REEL-AND-BEAD MOLDINGS

reel, *v.t.*; reeled, *pt., pp.*; reeling, *ppr.* 1. to wind on or off a reel (with *in* or *out*).

2. to pull in (a fish) by winding a line on a reel (with *in*).

3. to tell, write, produce, etc. fluently and easily (with *off*).

4. to roll. [Obs.]

reel, *v.i.* [OE. *reile, rele,* to roll, to reel; perhaps from Ice. *rithlask,* to reel to and fro, to waver.]

1. to give way; to fall back; to sway, swing, or stagger from shock; as, the line of battle *reeled.*

2. to stagger; to lurch violently in moving; to swing; to sway, as from drunkenness.

3. to go around and around; to whirl.

4. to be dizzy; to have a sensation of spinning or whirling.

reel, *v.t.* to cause to reel (whirl).

reel, *n.* [ME. *rele*; AS. *hreol.*] a reeling; whirl; swaying motion; stagger.

reel, *n.* [from *reel* (a whirl): from the movement.]

1. a lively Scottish dance, forerunner of many others.

2. the Virginia reel.

3. music for any of these dances.

reel, *v.i.* to perform the dance called a reel.

reel çot'tŏn, sewing cotton wound on reels or spools, not made up into balls, skeins, or the like.

rē-ē-leçt', *v.t.* to elect again; as, to *re-elect* the former governor: also *reëlect.*

rē-ē-leç'tion, *n.* election a second time, or repeated election; as, the *re-election* of a former representative: also *reëlection.*

reel'ẽr, *n.* [imitative.]

1. the cricket bird or grasshopper warbler: so called from its peculiar, shrill note. [Brit. Dial.]

2. one who reels silk, linen, or other threads.

rē-el''i·ġi·bil'i·ty, *n.* the quality of being re-eligible: also *reëligibility.*

rē-el'i·ġi·ble, *a.* capable of being elected again to the same office: also *reëligible.*

reem, *n.* the wild ox: Hebrew name mentioned in Job xxxix. 9, and formerly translated as *unicorn.*

reem, *v.i.* to moan; to lament. [Obs.]

rē-em·bat'tle, *v.t.* to array again for battle; to arrange again in the order of battle: also *reëmbattle.*

reem'ing, *n.* [AS. *rȳmen,* to enlarge.] the opening of the seams between the planks of vessels with a calking iron, for the purpose of calking or recalking them with oakum.

rē-en·açt', *v.t.* to enact again: also *reënact.*

rē-en·aç'tion, *n.* re-enactment: also *reënaction*

rē-en·açt'ment, *n.* the enacting or passing of a law a second time; the renewal of a law: also *reënactment.*

rē-en·fōrce', *v.t.* and *n.* reinforce: also *reënforce.*

rē-en·fōrce'ment, *n.* reinforcement: also *reënforcement.*

rē-en'tẽr, *v.i.* 1. to enter again or anew (in various senses).

2. in law, to make a re-entry.

Also *reënter.*

rē-en'tẽr, *v.t.* to enter anew; as, to *re-enter* an item in legal paper; to *re-enter* a claim, etc.: also *reënter.*

rē-en'tẽr·ing, *a.* entering again: also *reëntering.*

re-entering angle; an angle in a geometric figure with its point turning back into the figure rather than out from it.

re-entering polygon; a polygon with a re-entering angle or with re-entering angles.

rē-en'tẽr·ing, *n.* in calico printing, the process of applying secondary colors to the cloth after the primary colors are printed: also *reëntering.*

rē-en'trănce, *n.* the act of entering again; a re-entering; re-entry: also *reëntrance.*

rē-en'trănt, *a.* re-entering; pointed inward: said of angles, etc.: also *reëntrant.*

rē-en'trănt, *n.* a re-entrant angle or part: also *reëntrant.*

rē-en'try, *n.*; **rē-en'trieṣ,** 1. a re-entering; specifically, a coming back, as of a space vehicle, into the earth's atmosphere.

2. a second or repeated entry.

3. in bridge and whist, a card that will win a trick and recover the lead.

4. in law, a coming into possession again under a right reserved in a prior transfer of property.

Also *reëntry.*

reer'mouse, *n.* same as *reremouse.*

rē-es·tab'lish, *v.t.* to establish anew; to fix or confirm again; as, to *re-establish* a covenant; to *re-establish* health: also *reëstablish.*

rē-es·tab'lish·ẽr, *n.* one who establishes again: also *reëstablisher.*

rē-es·tab'lish·ment, *n.* the act of establishing again; the state of being re-established; restoration: also *reëstablishment.*

rē-es·tāte', *v.t.* to re-establish. [Obs.]

reeve, *n.* a bird, the female of the ruff (sandpiper).

reeve, *v.t.*; reeved *or* rove, *pt.*; reeved, rove, *or* roven, *pp.*; reeving, *ppr.* [prob. from D. *reven,* to reef, in sense "use a rope in or as in reefing".]

1. in nautical usage, to slip (a rope end, etc.) through a block, ring, or cleat.

2. in nautical usage, (a) to pass in, through, or around something; (b) to fasten by so doing.

3. in nautical usage, to pass a rope through (a block or pulley).

reeve, *n.* [ME. *refe,* earlier *irefe*; AS. *gerefa*; prob. from base of *refan,* to call out.]

1. in English history, (a) the chief officer, under the king, of a town or district; (b) the overseer of a manor; steward; bailiff.

2. in Canada, the president of a village or town council.

rē-ex·am'i·nȧ·ble (-egz-), *a.* that may be re-examined or reconsidered: also *reëxaminable.*

rē-ex·am·i·nā'tion, *n.* 1. a renewed or repeated examination.

2. in law, the questioning of a witness by the side for which he has been testifying, after, and about what has been said in, the cross-examination.

Also *reëxamination.*

rē-ex·am'ine, *v.t.* 1. to examine anew.

2. in law, to subject to re-examination.

Also *reëxamine.*

rē-ex·chānġe', *v.t.* to exchange again or anew: also *reëxchange.*

rē-ex·chānġe', *n.* 1. a renewed exchange.

2. in commerce, the expense chargeable on a bill of exchange or draft which has been dishonored in a foreign country, and returned to that country in which it was made or endorsed, and then taken up.

Also *reëxchange.*

rē-ex·pōrt', *v.t.* to export again; to export after importation: also *reëxport.*

rē-ex'pōrt, *n.* 1. a re-exporting.

2. what is re-exported.

Also *reëxport.*

rē-ex·pōr·tā'tion, *n.* the act of exporting what has been imported: also *reëxportation.*

rē-ex·tent', *n.* in English law, a second extent made to correct imperfection in the first. [Obs.]

ref, *n.* and *v.t.* and *v.i.* referee. [Colloq.]

rē·fāce', *v.t.*; refaced, *pt., pp.*; refacing, *ppr.* to put a new face, facing, or surface on.

rē·faç'tion, *n.* satisfaction; retributive justice. [Obs.]

rē·fait' (-fe'), *n.* [*re-,* and Fr. *faire,* to do.] an indecisive or drawn game; specifically, in rouge et noir, the condition when the cards dealt to opposing players are equal in value.

rē·fash'iŏn, *v.t.* to fashion, form, or mold into shape a second time.

rē·fash'iŏn·ment, *n.* a refashioning; the act of repeating a fashioning.

rē·fȧs'ten (-n), *v.t.* to fasten again.

rē·feçt', *v.t.* [L. *refectus,* from *re-,* and *facere,* to make.] to refresh with food or drink; to restore after hunger or fatigue. [Obs.]

rē·feç'tion, *n.* [Fr., from L. *refectio* (*-onis*), a restoring.]

1. refreshment; food or drink taken after hunger or fatigue.

2. a light meal; lunch; repast.

3. in civil law, restoration of property to good condition. [Rare.]

rē·feç'tion·ẽr, *n.* in church usage, a keeper of a refectory.

rē·feç'tive, *a.* refreshing; restoring. [Obs.]

rē·feç'tive, *n.* that which refreshes. [Obs.]

rē·feç'tō·rẽr, *n.* a keeper of a refectory. [Rare.]

rē·feç'tō·ry, *n.*; *pl.* **rē·feç'tō·rieṣ,** [Fr. *réfectoire.*] a room of refreshment; especially, a hall or apartment in a convent, college, or monastery which serves as a dining hall.

rē·feç'tō·ry tā'ble, 1. a long, narrow, rectangular table used in a dining hall, especially of a monastery or convent.

2. a dinner table of similar shape, now usually with extensible leaves which may be concealed under the ends.

rē·fel', *v.t.* [L. *refellere,* to overthrow; *re-,* and *fallere,* to deceive.] to refute; to disprove. [Obs.]

rē·fẽr', *v.t.*; referred, *pt., pp.*; referring, *ppr.* [L. *referre,* to bring back; *re-,* and *ferre,* to bear.]

1. to carry back. [Obs.]

2. to assign (*to*); to regard as caused by or originated in; as, he *referred* his troubles *to* the war.

3. to assign, or regard or name as belonging (*to* a kind, class, date, etc.).

4. to submit (a quarrel, question, etc.) for determination or settlement.

5. to send or direct (a person) *to* someone or something for aid, information, etc.

6. to betake oneself; to appeal: used with the reflexive pronoun. [Obs.]

I do *refer me* to the oracle. —Shak.

7. to reduce or bring in relation, as to some standard. [Obs.]

8. to defer; to put off. [Obs.]

rē·fẽr', *v.i.* 1. to relate, or be concerned (with): used with *to*; as, the book *referred* only *to* fish.

2. to direct attention, or make reference or allusion (with *to*); as, he *referred* lightly *to* his wound.

3. to turn for information, aid, authority, etc. (with *to*); as, *refer to* a map.

ref'ẽr·ȧ·ble, *a.* capable of being referred; that can be referred, assigned, or attributed; assignable; attributable.

ref·ẽr·ee', *n.* 1. one to whom any matter, point, or question is referred for decision.

2. in law, a person appointed by a court to study, take testimony in, and report his judgment on, a matter.

3. in sports, an umpire; judge of a game, as of a boxing match.

ref·ẽr·ee', *v.t.*; refereed, *pt., pp.*; refereeing, *ppr.* to act as referee in.

ref·ẽr·ee', *v.i.* to act as referee.

ref'ẽr·ence, *n.* 1. a referring or being referred; submission of a problem, dispute, etc. to a person, committee, or authority for settlement.

2. relation; regard; as, with *reference* to his reply.

3. the directing of attention to a person or thing.

4. a mention or allusion.
5. an indication, as in a book or article, of some other work or passage to be consulted.
6. the work or passage so indicated.
7. the mark or sign, as a number or letter, directing the reader to a footnote, etc.
8. (a) the giving of the name of another person who can offer information or recommendation; (b) the person so indicated.
9. a written statement of character, qualification, or ability; testimonial.
10. use or consultation to get information, as an aid in research, etc.: often attributive; as, *reference* books.
11. in law, the act, order, or paper by which a matter is committed to one or more persons for investigation and report.
12. assignment; appointment; apportionment. [Obs.]
reference Bible; a Bible in which brief explanations of the text or references to parallel passages are arranged on the margins of the pages.
reference mark; any symbol used in printing and writing to mark a reference, as *, †, ‡, ¶, §.
to make reference to; to refer to; to mention.
work of reference; a work, such as a cyclopedia, dictionary, and the like, intended to be consulted when occasion requires.

ref·ĕr·en′dȧ·ry, *n.* 1. a referee. [Obs.]
2. formerly, an officer who delivered the royal answer to petitions.
3. in early history, an officer charged with the duty of procuring and dispatching diplomas and decrees.
4. in the Orthodox Eastern Church, an intermediary between the civil authorities and the patriarch at Constantinople.

ref·ĕr·en′dum, *n.*; *pl.* **ref·ĕr·en′dums, ref·ĕr·en′dȧ,** [L., a carrying back, from *referre*; *re-* and *ferre*, to bear.]
1. the submission of a law, proposed or already in effect, to a direct vote of the people.
2. the right of the people to vote directly on such laws, superseding or overruling the legislature.
3. the vote itself.
4. a note sent by a diplomatic agent to his own government, asking for instructions about a particular matter.

ref′ĕr·ent, *n.* [L. *referens*, ppr.] what is referred to; especially, in semantics, the object referred to by a term.

ref·ĕr·en′tiăl (-shăl), *a.* [from *reference* (as if from hyp. L. *referentia*) and *-al*.]
1. having reference (*to* something).
2. containing a reference or references.
3. used for reference.

ref·ĕr·en′tiăl·ly, *adv.* in a referential manner.

rē·fēr′ment, *n.* a referring or being referred. [Obs.]

rē·fēr·ment′, *v.t.* and *v.i.* to ferment again.

rē·fēr′rȧ·ble, *a.* referable.

rē·fēr′răl, *n.* a referring or being referred.

rē·fēr′rēr, *n.* one who refers.

rē·fēr′ri·ble, *a.* referable.

rē·fig′ūre, *v.t.* 1. to figure again.
2. to correct or restore the figure of, as a parabolic mirror in a telescope.

rē·fill′, *v.t.* to fill again.

rē′fill, *n.* a new filling or charge; especially, a unit made to replace the contents of a container that is not itself discarded after use; as, a *refill* for a ball-point pen.

rē·find′, *v.t.* to find again; to experience anew.

rē·fīne′, *v.t.*; refined, *pt., pp.*; refining, *ppr.* [Fr. *raffiner*; *re-* and *affiner*, to purify; *af*, L. *ad*, to, and *finer*, to fine.]
1. to bring or reduce to a pure state; to free from impurities, dross, alloy, sediment, etc.; to clarify; to purify; as, to *refine* liquor, sugar, or the like.
2. to remove in purifying; to take out (with *out* or *away*).
3. to free from what is imperfect, common, gross, coarse, debasing, low, vulgar, inelegant, rude, clownish, and the like; to make elegant; to raise or educate, as the taste; to give culture to; to polish; to improve, as, to *refine* the manners, taste, language, style, intellect, or moral feelings.

rē·fīne′, *v.i.* 1. to become fine or pure; to become free from impurities, etc.
2. to become more polished or elegant.
3. to use niceties and fine distinctions; to be subtle, as in language.
to refine on (or *upon*); to improve, as by adding refinements.

rē·fīned′, *a.* [pp. of *refine*.]
1. purified; separated from extraneous matter; freed from alloy, etc., as metals; clarified, as liquors.
2. characterized by cultivation or elegance; free from vulgarity or coarseness: said of manners, speech, character, etc.
3. characterized by more than ordinary subtlety, exactness, precision, etc.

rē·fīn′ed·ly, *adv.* with nicety or elegance, especially excessive nicety or elegance.

rē·fīn′ed·ness, *n.* the state of being refined; purity; refinement; also, affected purity.

rē·fīne′ment, *n.* 1. the act or process of refining or state of being refined; a purifying or clearing from extraneous matter; purification; clarification; specifically, the process of freeing metals, liquids, or other substances from impurities or crudities which impair their quality or unfit them for their appropriate uses.
2. the result of being refined or purified.
3. the state of being free from all that is gross, coarse, debasing, low, vulgar, rude, clownish, or the like; elegance or delicacy of taste, manners, language, etc.; high culture; polish.

That sensibility of pain, with which
Refinement is endued. —Cowper.

4. a development; improvement; elaboration; as, his solicitude was a *refinement* of cruelty.

rē·fīn′ēr, *n.* 1. one who refines metals, liquors, sugar, or other substances.
2. one who or that which refines, educates, or polishes the taste, manners, etc.; as, a *refiner* of language.
3. an inventor of superfluous subtleties; one who is overnice in discrimination, in argument, reasoning, philosophy, etc.

rē·fīn′ēr·y, *n.*; *pl.* **rē·fīn′ēr·ies,** 1. a place, establishment, or plant where oil, sugar, metals, liquors, etc., are refined.
2. an apparatus for removing impurities or crudities from metals, spirits, oil, sugar, etc.

rē·fit′, *n.* the repairing or renewing of what is damaged or worn out; specifically, the repair of a ship.

rē·fit′, *v.t.*; refitted, *pt., pp.*; refitting, *ppr.* 1. to make fit for use again; to repair, where damaged or worn out.
2. to fit out or provide anew.

rē·fit′, *v.i.* to repair damages, especially to a ship.

rē·fit′ment, *n.* the act of refitting; a second fitting out.

rē·fix′, *v.t.* to fix a second time; to fix or establish anew.

rē·flāme′, *v.i.* to burst again into flame.

rē·flāte′, *v.i.* and *v.t.*; reflated, *pt., pp.*; reflating, *ppr.* to reinflate.

rē·flect′, *v.t.*; reflected, *pt., pp.*; reflecting, *ppr.* [L. *reflectere*; *re-* and *flectere*, to bend.]
1. to bend or throw back, as light, heat, or sound.
2. to give back an image of; to mirror or reproduce.
3. to cast or bring back as a consequence (with *on*); as, his deeds *reflect* honor *on* the nation.
4. to fold or turn back. [Rare.]

rē·flect′, *v.i.* 1. to be bent or thrown back; as, the light *reflected* from the water into his eyes.
2. to bend or throw back light, heat, sound, etc.
3. (a) to give back an image or likeness; (b) to be mirrored.
4. to think seriously; contemplate; ponder (with *on* or *upon*).
5. to cast blame or discredit (with *on* or *upon*).

rē·flect′ed, *a.* 1. thrown back; returned, as by reflection.
2. in anatomy, bending or turning away from the general line of direction of a part; also, turned or folded back.

rē·flect′ent, *a.* reflecting. [Obs.]

rē·flect′i·ble, *a.* capable of being reflected or thrown back.

rē·flect′ing, *a.* 1. throwing back light, heat etc., as a mirror or similar surface.
2. given to reflection; meditative; reflective; as, a *reflecting* mind.
reflecting circle; an instrument for measuring altitudes and angular distances, constructed on the principle of the sextant, the graduations, however, being continued completely round the limb of the circle.

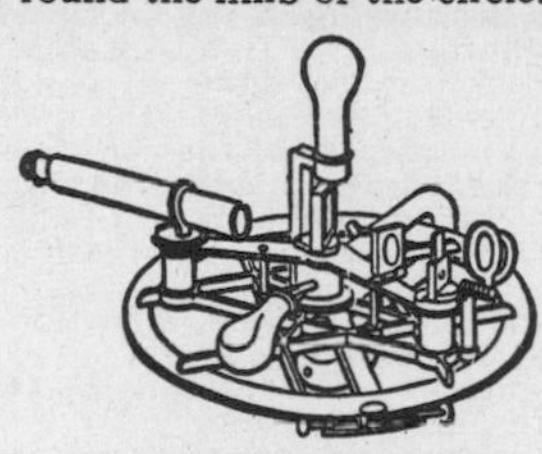

REFLECTING CIRCLE

reflecting galvanometer; a galvanometer invented by Sir W. Thomson, in which a delicately poised and adjusted magnet is attached to a mirror reflecting a ray of light upon a scale in such a manner as to indicate the strength of an electric current.
reflecting goniometer; see under *goniometer*.
reflecting telescope; see under *telescope*.

rē·flect′ing·ly, *adv.* with reflection.

rē·flec′tion, *n.* 1. the act of reflecting, or the state of being reflected.
2. in physics, the change of direction which a ray of light, radiant heat, sound, or other form of radiant energy, experiences when it strikes upon a surface and is thrown back into the same medium from which it approached. When a perfectly elastic body strikes a hard and fixed plane obliquely it rebounds from it, making the angle of reflection equal to the angle of incidence.
3. anything reflected.
4. an image; likeness.
5. the fixing of the mind on some subject; serious thought; contemplation.
6. the result of such thought; an idea or conclusion, especially if expressed in words.
7. blame; discredit.
8. a remark or statement imputing discredit or blame.
9. an action bringing discredit.
10. in anatomy and zoology, a turning or bending back on itself.
Also spelled *reflexion*.
Syn.—meditation, contemplation, rumination, cogitation, consideration, musing, thinking, censure, reproach.

rē·flec′tion·ăl, *a.* of reflection.

rē·flect′ive, *a.* 1. throwing back rays or images; reflecting; as, a *reflective* mirror.
2. of or produced by reflection.
3. (a) taking cognizance of the operations of the mind; capable of exercising thought or judgment; as, *reflective* reason; (b) exercising thought or reflection; meditative; thoughtful.
4. in grammar, (a) reflexive; (b) reciprocal.

rē·flect′ive·ly, *adv.* by reflection.

rē·flect′ive·ness, *n.* the state or quality of being reflective.

rē·flec·tiv′i·ty, *n.* the quality or condition of being reflective.

rē·flec′tŏr, *n.* 1. a person or thing that reflects; especially, a surface, object, etc. that reflects light, sound, heat, or the like, as a

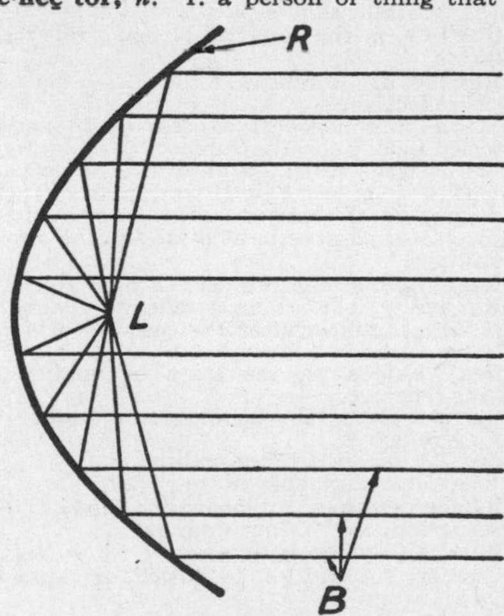

PARABOLIC REFLECTOR
R, parabolic reflecting surface; *L*, light source at focus; *B*, reflected parallel light rays

piece of glass or metal, highly polished and usually concave, which reflects and directs rays or a beam of light.

2. in photography, an adjustable, movable screen used to reflect and control light.

3. a reflecting telescope, the speculum of which is an example of the converse application of the parabolic reflector, the parallel rays proceeding from a distant body being in this case concentrated into the focus of the reflector.

rē·flet′ (-flē′), *n.* [Fr. *reflet*, reflection, from L. *reflectere*, to reflect.]

1. brightness or iridescence of surface, as a metallic glaze on pottery.

2. a tile or other piece of pottery having such a glaze.

rē′flex, *a.* [L. *reflexus*, reflected.]

1. turned, bent, or reflected back.

2. coming in reaction or reflection; as, a *reflex* effect; especially, in physiology, designating or of an involuntary action, as a sneeze, resulting when a stimulus is carried by an afferent nerve to a nerve center and the response is reflected along an efferent nerve to some muscle or gland.

REFLEX ANGLE

3. in geometry, designating an angle greater than a straight angle.

4. in radio, designating or of an apparatus in which some device functions in a double capacity, as a receiving set in which the same tube is both audio-frequency and radio-frequency amplifier.

5. in biology, bent back; reflexed.

reflex arc; in physiology, the entire nerve path involved in a reflex action.

rē′flex, *n.* 1. (a) reflection, as of light; (b) light or color resulting from reflection.

2. a reflected image, likeness, or reproduction.

3. in art, light reflected from a lighted to a shaded surface.

4. in physiology, a reflex action.

5. in radio, a reflex apparatus.

conditioned reflex; see under *conditioned*.

rē·flex′, *v.t.*; reflexed (-flekst), *pt., pp.*; reflexing, *ppr.* 1. to reflect. [Obs.]

2. to bend back; to turn back; to fold back.

3. to cause to undergo a reflex process.

rē′flex ça̤m′ẽr·ȧ, a camera in which the image formed by the lens is reflected by a mirror onto a ground-glass plate to help in focusing the lens.

rē·flexed′, *a.* bent backward; turned abruptly backward, as a petal; turned or bent up; curving back.

rē·flex·i·bil′i·ty, *n.* the quality of being reflexible.

rē·flex′i·ble, *a.* capable of being reflected or thrown back.

> The light of the sun consists of rays differently refrangible and *reflexible*. —Cheyne.

rē·flex′iŏn (-flek′shun), *n.* 1. reflection.

2. in anatomy, etc., a bending or folding back on itself, as of a part.

rē·flex′i·ty, *n.* the capacity of being reflected. [Rare.]

rē·flex′ive, *a.* 1. reflex.

2. reflective.

3. in grammar, (a) expressing an action turned back upon the subject; designating a verb whose subject and direct object are identical (e.g., *wash* in "I wash myself"); (b) designating a pronoun used as the direct object of such a verb, as *myself* in the above example.

rē·flex′ive, *n.* a reflexive verb or pronoun.

rē·flex′ive·ly, *adv.* 1. in a reflexive manner.

2. in grammar, after the manner of a reflexive verb.

rē·flex′ive·ness, *n.* the state or quality of being reflexive.

rē·flex·iv′i·ty, *n.* the condition or quality of being reflexive.

rē·flex′ly, *adv.* in a reflex manner.

rē′flōat, *n.* reflux; ebb. [Rare.]

rē·flō·res′cence, *n.* a blossoming anew.

rē·flŏur′ish, *v.i.* to flourish anew.

rē·flōw′, *v.i.* to flow back; to ebb.

rē·flow′ẽr, *v.t.* and *v.i.* to flower, or cause to flower, again.

rē·fluç·tū·ā′tion, *n.* a flowing back.

ref′lū·ence, ref′lū·en·cy, *n.* a flowing back.

ref′lū·ent, *a.* [L. *refluens*; *re-*, back, and *fluere*, to flow.] flowing back; ebbing; as, the *refluent* tide.

rē′flux, *a.* flowing back.

rē′flux, *n.* [Fr., the ebb of the sea, from L. *re-*, back, and *fluere*, to flow.] a flowing back; ebbing; as, the flux and *reflux* of the tides.

rē·foc′il·lāte, *v.t.* to refresh; to revive; to give new vigor to. [Obs.]

rē·foc·il·lā′tion, *n.* the act of refreshing or giving new vigor; restoration of strength by refreshment. [Obs.]

rē·for′est, *v.t.* and *v.i.* to plant new trees on (land once forested); to reafforest.

rē·for·es·tā′tion, *n.* the act of reforesting or the state of being reforested.

rē″for·es·ti·zā′tion, *n.* reforestation.

rē·for′est·īze, *v.t.* same as *reforest*.

rē·fōrġe′, *v.t.* to forge again or anew; to form anew; to make over by forging.

rē·fōr′ġẽr, *n.* one who reforges.

rē·fo̤rm′, *v.t.*; reformed, *pt., pp.*; reforming, *ppr.* [ME. *reformer*; OFr. *reformer*; L. *reformare*.]

1. to make better by removing faults and defects; to correct.

2. to make better by putting a stop to abuses or malpractices, or by introducing better procedures, etc.

3. to put a stop to (abuses, etc.).

4. to bring (a person) by force or persuasion to give up misconduct and behave better.

rē·fo̤rm′, *v.i.* to become or behave better; to abandon that which is evil or corrupt and return to a good state; to be amended or corrected; as, a man of settled habits of vice will seldom *reform*.

Syn.—amend, correct, better, mend, improve.

rē·fo̤rm′, *n.* 1. an improvement; correction of faults or evil, as in politics.

2. an improvement in character and conduct; reformation.

3. a movement aimed at removing corruption from politics.

4. in sociology, action by individuals or groups aimed at preventing crime or at eliminating or mitigating poverty by means of new laws.

Reform Act; any of various acts passed by the British Parliament largely increasing popular representation in the House of Commons: also called *Reform Bill*.

reform school; a reformatory for juveniles.

rē-fo̤rm′, *v.t.* and *v.i.* to form again or anew; as, to *re-form* a body of troops.

rē·fo̤rm′ȧ·ble, *a.* having capacity for reform; of a character such as to admit of reform.

ref·o̤r·mä′dō, ref·o̤r·mäde′, *n.* [Sp., from L. *re-*, again, and *formare*, to form.] an officer removed from command but still bearing his rank and, sometimes, drawing his pay. [Obs.]

ref·o̤r·mā′tion, *n.* 1. the act of reforming or the state of being reformed; correction or amendment of life, manners, or of anything vicious or corrupt; as, the *reformation* of manners, *reformation* of abuses.

2. [R—] in church history, the movement started by Martin Luther in the sixteenth century that aimed at reforming the Roman Catholic Church and resulted in the establishment of Protestantism.

Syn.—reform.—*Reformation* is a more thorough and comprehensive change than *reform*. It is applied to subjects that are more important, and results in changes which are more lasting. A *reformation* usually involves and is followed by many particular *reforms*.

rē-fo̤r·mā′tion, *n.* the act of forming anew; a second forming in order; as, the *re-formation* of a column of troops into a hollow square.

ref·ŏr·mā′tion·ăl, *a.* of reformation.

rē·fo̤rm′ȧ·tive, *a.* reforming or tending to reform.

rē-fo̤rm′ȧ·tive, *a.* forming again; having the quality of renewing form.

rē·fo̤rm′ȧ·tō·ry, *a.* reforming or tending to produce reformation.

rē·fo̤rm′ȧ·tō·ry, *n.*; *pl.* **rē·fo̤rm′ȧ·tō·rieṣ**, an institution where young offenders convicted of lesser crimes are confined for training and discipline intended to reform rather than punish them.

rē·fo̤rmed′, *a.* [pp. of *reform*.]

1. improved or corrected, as in behavior or morals, or made better by the removal of errors, abuses, etc.

2. [R—] designating or of a Protestant church or churches, especially Calvinist as distinguished from Lutheran.

3. [R—] designating a form of Judaism, introduced in the 19th century, which does not require strict observance of the traditional ritual of Orthodox Judaism.

4. in the English army, designating an officer who after his company has disbanded is retained on either half or full pay. [Obs.]

rē·fo̤rm′ẽr, *n.* 1. a person who reforms, or tries to reform, something, as morals, customs, institutions, etc.

2. any of the leaders of the Reformation, as Luther, Melanchthon, Zwingli, and Calvin.

rē·fo̤rm′ist, *n.* 1. [*often* R—] one who is of the Reformed religion. [Obs.]

2. a person who practices, believes in, or advocates reform, as of some doctrine, ideology, etc.

rē·fo̤rm′ist, *a.* of or characteristic of reformists.

rē·fos′sion (-fosh′un), *n.* the act of digging up anew. [Obs.]

rē·found′, *v.t.* to found or cast anew; to recast; as, to *refound* a bell.

rē·found′, *v.t.* to found again; to re-establish; to put on a new basis.

rē·found′, *v.* past tense and past participle of *refind*.

rē·found′ẽr, *n.* one who refounds.

rē·fraçt′, *v.t.*; refracted, *pt., pp.*; refracting, *ppr.* [L. *refractus*, pp. of *refringere*, to turn aside, to bend aside, from *re-* and *frangere*, to break.]

1. to bend (a ray or wave of light, heat, or sound) as it passes from one medium into another: said of the medium, as, glass *refracts* light.

2. in optics, to measure the degree of refraction of (an eye or lens).

rē·fraçt′ȧ·ble, *a.* capable of being refracted; refrangible.

rē·fraçt′ed, *a.* 1. turned from a direct course, as rays of light.

2. in botany and zoology, bent back at an acute angle; as, a *refracted* corolla.

rē·fraçt′ing, *a.* turning rays from a direct course; as, a *refracting* medium.

refracting telescope; see under *telescope*.

rē·fraç′tion, *n.* 1. a refracting or being refracted; the bending of a ray or wave of light, heat, or sound, as it passes obliquely from one medium to another of different density, in which its speed is different, or through layers of different density in the same medium.

2. in astronomy, the bending of the rays of light from a star or planet, greatest when the star or planet is lowest in the sky, so that it seems higher than it really is.

REFRACTION OF LIGHT RAY
RAY, light ray in straight line; RAP, refracted light ray

3. in optics, (a) the ability of the eye to refract light entering it, so as to form an image on the retina; (b) the measuring of the degree of refraction of the eye.

angle of refraction; the angle made by the refracted part of a light ray with a line perpendicular to the surface of the refracting medium through the point of incidence of the refracted ray.

axis of refraction; see under *axis*.

conical refraction; the refraction of a single ray of light, under certain conditions, into an infinite number of rays in the form of a hollow, luminous cone, and consisting of two kinds, *external conical refraction* and *internal conical refraction*: the ray in the first case issues from the refracting crystal as a cone with its vertex at the point of emergence; in the second case, the ray is converted into a cone on entering the crystal, and issues as a hollow cylinder.

differential refraction; the refraction that causes apparent change of place of an object relative to some other object.

double refraction; in optics, the refraction of light in two directions and the consequent production of two distinct images. The power of double refraction is possessed by all crystals except those of the isometric system.

index of refraction; see under *index*.

plane of refraction; the plane passing through the refracted ray and the perpendicular to the refracting surface at the point of incidence.

refraction of altitude and declination, of ascension and descension, of latitude and longitude; the change in the altitude, declination, etc. of a heavenly body due to the effect of atmospheric refraction.

terrestrial refraction; that refraction which makes terrestrial objects appear to be farther from the horizon than they are in reality. This arises from the air being denser near the surface of the earth than it is at higher elevations, its refractive power increasing as the density increases.

rē·fraç′tion·ăl, *a.* of refraction.

rē·fraç′tion cîr′çle, a device for measuring the various degrees of refraction by means of a graduated circle.

rē·fraç′tion·ist, *n.* one skilled in correcting errors in ocular refraction.

rē·fraçt′ive, *a.* 1. refracting or having power to refract.

2. of, caused by, or pertaining to refraction.

refractive index; same as *index of refraction* under *index*.

rē·fraçt′ive·ness, *n.* same as *refractivity*.

rē·fraç·tiv′i·ty, *n.* 1. the power of refraction; the measure of capacity for refraction.

2. the condition or quality of being refractive.

rē·fraç·tom′ē·tēr, *n.* [*refraction*, and Gr. *metron*, a measure.] an instrument for measuring refraction, as of the eye.

rē·fraçt′ŏr, *n.* anything that refracts; specifically, a refracting telescope.

rē·fraç′tō·ri·ly, *adv.* in a refractory manner; perversely; obstinately.

rē·fraç′tō·ri·ness, *n.* [L. *refractus*, broken.] the quality or state of being refractory.

rē·fraç′tō·ry, *a.* [Fr. *réfractaire*; L. *refractarius*, stubborn, obstinate.]

1. stubborn; obstinate; hard to manage: said of a person or animal.

2. resistant to heat; hard to melt or work: said of ores or metals.

3. not yielding to treatment, as a disease.

4. able to resist disease.

Syn.—contumacious, perverse, ungovernable, unruly, obstinate.

rē·fraç′tō·ry, *n.* 1. one who or that which is refractory.

2. in ceramics, a substance fusing at a very high temperature, used with a flux in glazing.

rē·fraç′tūre, *n.* in surgery, the act or process of rebreaking a bone which has been badly set.

ref′rȧ·gȧ·bil′i·ty, *n.* the quality that renders refragable. [Rare.]

ref′rȧ·gȧ·ble, *a.* [LL. *refragabilis*, from L. *refragari*, to oppose, to resist; *re-*, and *frangere*, to break.] that may be refuted; refutable. [Rare.]

ref′rȧ·gȧ·ble·ness, *n.* the quality of being refragable or refutable. [Rare.]

ref′rȧ·gāte, *v.i.* to oppose. [Obs.]

rē·frāin′, *v.t.*; refrained, *pt.*, *pp.*; refraining, *ppr.* [Fr. *refréner*, to bridle in, to curb; from *re-*, and LL. *frenare*, to curb; *frenum*, a rein.]

1. to hold back; to restrain; to keep from action. [Archaic.]

> Then Joseph could not *refrain* himself before all them that stood by.
> —Gen. xlv. 1.

2. to abstain from; to stop; to give up. [Obs.]

rē·frāin′, *v.i.* to hold back; to abstain; to keep oneself (*from*); to forbear (often with *from*).

> *Refrain from* these men, and let them alone.
> —Acts v. 38.

Syn.—withhold, cease.

rē·frāin′, *n.* [Fr. *refrain*, from OFr. *refraindre*; L. *refringere*; *re-*, and *frangere*, to break.]

1. a phrase or verse repeated at intervals in a song or poem.

2. music for this.

rē·frāin′ēr, *n.* one who refrains.

rē·frāin′ment, *n.* the act of refraining. [Rare.]

rē·frāme′, *v.t.* to frame again; to construct again; to remodel.

ref·rȧ·nā′tion, *n.* in astrology, the nonappearance of an expected planetary aspect. [Obs.]

rē·fran·gi·bil′i·ty, *n.* the state or quality of being refrangible.

rē·fran′gi·ble, *a.* [*re-*, and L. *frangere*, to break.] capable of being refracted or turned out of a direct course in passing from one medium to another, as rays of light.

rē·fran′gi·ble·ness, *n.* the state or quality of being refrangible.

ref·rē·nā′tion, *n.* refranation. [Obs.]

rę·fres′ço, *n.* [Sp.] in Spanish America, a sweet, cool, refreshing, fruit-flavored drink.

rē·fresh′, *v.t.*; refreshed (-fresht), *pt.*, *pp.*; refreshing, *ppr.* [Fr. *refraîchir*; *re-*, and *fraîcher*, from *fraîsche*, fresh.]

1. to make fresh by cooling, wetting, or airing, as a room, etc.

2. to make (a person) feel cooler, stronger, more energetic, etc. than before, as by food, drink, or sleep: also used reflexively.

3. to renew; to replenish, as by new supplies, etc.; to revive, as the memory.

4. to improve by new touches; to repair; to restore. [Obs.]

Syn.—cool, renew, revive, recruit, restore, invigorate, reinvigorate.

rē·fresh′, *v.i.* 1. to revive or become fresh again.

2. to take refreshment, as food or drink.

3. to put in a stock of fresh provisions; as, a ship *refreshes* for a voyage.

rē·fresh′ēr, *n.* 1. one who or that which refreshes, revives, or invigorates.

2. in law, an extra fee paid to a lawyer for services that have been unusually protracted, as during an adjournment from one term of court to the next.

rē·fresh′ēr çourse, a course of study reviewing material previously studied.

rē·fresh′fụl, *a.* refreshing; having qualities that refresh.

rē·fresh′fụl·ly, *adv.* in a refreshful manner.

rē·fresh′ing, *a.* 1. that refreshes; cooling; invigorating; reviving; reanimating.

2. pleasingly new or different.

rē·fresh′ing·ly, *adv.* so as to be refreshing.

rē·fresh′ing·ness, *n.* the quality of being refreshing.

rē·fresh′ment, *n.* 1. the act of refreshing or the state of being refreshed; new strength or vigor received after fatigue.

2. something that refreshes, as food, drink, rest, etc.

3. [*pl.*] food or drink or both, especially as a light meal.

Refreshment Sunday; the fourth Sunday in Lent. It is probably so called because the Gospel for that day relates the story of feeding the five thousand.

rē·frig′ēr·ănt, *a.* [L. *refrigerans*, *refrigerantis*, ppr. of *refrigerare*, to make cool or cold.]

1. refrigerating; cooling or freezing something.

2. reducing heat or fever.

rē·frig′ēr·ănt, *n.* 1. a medicine used to reduce fever.

2. a substance used in refrigeration, as ice or solid carbon dioxide.

3. any of various liquids that vaporize at a low temperature, used in mechanical refrigeration.

rē·frig′ēr·āte, *v.t.*; refrigerated, *pt.*, *pp.*; refrigerating, *ppr.* [L. *refrigerare*, to make cool or cold.]

1. to make or keep cool or cold; to chill.

2. to preserve (food, etc.) by keeping cold or freezing.

rē·frig′ēr·āt·ing mȧ·chïne′, an apparatus which utilizes the heat-absorbing properties of an expanding gas to lower the temperature of a substance to be cooled.

rē·frig·ēr·ā′tion, *n.* [L. *refrigeratio*.] a refrigerating or being refrigerated; a making or keeping cold or freezing for preservation, as food.

electric refrigeration; refrigeration by means of a cooling cycle driven by an electric motor.

gas refrigeration; refrigeration by means of a cooling cycle driven by a gas flame.

mechanical refrigeration; refrigeration by means of a refrigerating machine.

rē·frig′ēr·ā·tive, *a.* refrigerating or serving to refrigerate; cooling.

rē·frig′ēr·ā·tŏr, *n.* something that refrigerates or cools; specifically, (a) a box, room, etc. used to cool provisions and keep them from spoiling, as by ice or mechanical refrigeration; (b) a chamber in which ice creams are artificially made; (c) in brewing, a cooling apparatus of any description; (d) in marine engines, a casing with connecting tubes, through which feed water passes on its way to the boiler; (e) a form of condenser, in which the injection water is cooled by a surface application of cold sea water; (f) a refrigerant.

refrigerator car; a railway car built as a refrigerator for use in carrying perishable goods as fruits, fresh meats, and the like.

rē·frig′ēr·ȧ·tō·ry, *a.* cooling; refrigerating.

rē·frig′ēr·ȧ·tō·ry, *n.*; *pl.* **rē·frig′ēr·ȧ·tō·rieș,** a refrigerator; a refrigerant; anything cooling.

rē·frin′ġen·cy, *n.* [L. *refringere*, to break up; from *re-*, back, and *frangere*, to break.] the power of a substance to refract a ray; refringent or refractive power.

rē·frin′ġent, *a.* possessing the quality of refractiveness; refractive; refracting; as, a *refringent* prism.

reft, *v.* alternative past tense and past participle of *reave*.

reft, *a.* robbed or bereft (*of* something).

rē·fū′el, *v.t.* to supply again with fuel.

rē·fū′el, *v.i.* to take on a fresh supply of fuel.

ref′ūġe, *n.* [Fr., from L. *refugium*, a refuge, from *refugere*, to retreat; *re-*, back, and *fugere*, to flee.]

1. shelter or protection from danger or distress.

2. a person or thing that gives shelter, help, or comfort.

3. a place of safety; a shelter; a safe retreat; a stronghold which protects by its strength, or a sanctuary which secures safety by its sacredness; any place inaccessible to an enemy or evil; an asylum.

4. action taken to escape consequences; an expedient to secure protection or defense; a resort; a shift; a subterfuge.

cities of refuge; among the Israelites, certain cities appointed to secure the safety of such persons as might commit homicide without design. Of these there were three on each side of the Jordan.

harbors of refuge; harbors or ports which afford shelter to vessels in stormy weather; places of refuge for merchant vessels from the cruisers of an enemy in time of war.

house of refuge; an institution affording shelter to the destitute or homeless.

ref·ū·ġee′, *n.* [Fr. *réfugié*.]

1. one who flees to a shelter or place of safety.

2. one who in times of war, political or religious persecution, etc. flees to a foreign power or country for safety; as, the French *refugees* who left France after the revocation of the Edict of Nantes, and settled in Flanders and America.

ref·ū·ġee′, *v.i.* to seek refuge.

rē·fū′gi·um, *n.*; *pl.* **rē·fū′gi·ȧ,** [L., refuge.] a small, isolated area that has escaped the extreme changes undergone by the surrounding area, as during a period of glaciation, allowing the survival of plants and animals from an earlier period.

rē·ful′ġence, *n.* the state or quality of being refulgent; splendor; brilliance.

rē·ful′ġen·cy, *n.* refulgence.

rē·ful′ġent, *a.* [L. *refulgens*, *refulgentis*, ppr. of *refulgere*, to reflect a light; *re-*, back, and *fulgere*, to shine.] casting a bright light; shining brightly; glittering; brilliant; splendid; radiant; as, *refulgent* beams, *refulgent* arms.

rē·ful′ġent·ly, *adv.* in a refulgent manner.

rē·fund′, *v.t.*; refunded, *pt.*, *pp.*; refunding, *ppr.* [L. *refundere*, to pour back, to restore; *re-*, back, and *fundere*, to pour.]

1. to pour back. [Obs.]

2. to repay; to give back or pay back (money, etc.) in restitution, in compensation for overpayment, etc.; as, the store offers to *refund* the purchase price if the customer is not satisfied.

3. to make repayment to; reimburse (a person).

rē·fund′, *v.i.* to make repayment.

rē′fund, *n.* a refunding or the amount refunded; repayment.

rē·fund′, *v. t.* to fund again or anew; specifically, in finance, (a) to use borrowed money, especially the proceeds from the sale of a bond issue, to pay back (a loan); (b) to replace (an old bond issue) with a new bond issue, usually at a lower rate of interest.

rē·fund′ēr, *n.* one who refunds.

rē·fund′ment, *n.* the act of refunding; that which is refunded.

rē·fûr′bish, *v.t.* [*re-* and *furbish*.] to brighten, freshen, or polish up again; to renovate.

rē·fūș′ȧ·ble, *a.* that may be refused.

rē·fūș′ăl, *n.* 1. the act of refusing; denial of anything demanded, solicited, or offered for acceptance.

2. the right or chance to accept or refuse something before it is offered to another; option; preemption.

3. in engineering, the resistance to further driving offered by a pile.

rē·fūșe′, *v.t.*; refused, *pt.*, *pp.*; refusing, *ppr.* [OFr. *refuser*; LL. (hyp.) *refusare*, from L. *refusus*, pp. of *refundere*, to pour back.]

1. to decline to accept; to reject.

2. (a) to decline to do, give, or grant; (b) to decline (*to* do something); as, *refuse to* go.

3. to decline to accept or submit to (a command, etc.); to decline to undergo.

4. to stop short at (a fence, etc.) without jumping it: said of a horse.

5. to renounce; disavow; disown. [Obs.]

6. in military usage, to bring back out of line (the center or a flank) to protect against possible enemy attack from that sector.

7. to repel; to fail to take; as, a lithographic stone *refuses* the ink except where touched by the chalk.

rē-fūṣe′, *v.i.* to decline to accept, agree to, or do something.

ref′ūse, *a.* [OFr. *refus*, refusal, denial, that which is denied.] refused; rejected; worthless; of no value; left as useless or worthless; as, *refuse* stone or timber.

ref′ūse, *n.* that which is refused or thrown away as worthless or useless; rubbish; trash; waste matter; as, the *refuse* of a factory.

Syn.—offal, scum, dregs, sediment, recrement, sweepings, trash, offscourings, debris, remains, dross.

rē-fūṣe′, *n.* refusal. [Obs.]

rē-fūṣe′, *v.t.* and *v.i.* to remelt; to fuse again.

rē-fūṣ′ēr, *n.* one who refuses or rejects.

rē-fū′ṣion, *n.* [L. *refusio* (*-onis*), an overflowing, from *refusus*, pp. of *refundere*, to pour back, from *re-*, back, and *fundere*, to pour.] a pouring back; reinfusion. [Obs.]

rē-fū′ṣion, *n.* a repeated or second fusion.

rē-fūt-ȧ-bil′i-ty, *n.* the state of being refutable.

rē-fūt′ȧ-ble *a.* that may be refuted or disproved; that may be proved false or erroneous.

rē-fūt′ȧ-bly, *adv.* in a refutable manner; so as to be refutable.

rē-fūt′ăl, *n.* refutation; a refuting.

ref-ū-tā′tion, *n.* [L. *refutatio*, *refutationis*, a refutation.]

1. the act or process of refuting, or disproving; the act of proving to be false or erroneous; the overthrowing of an argument, opinion, testimony, doctrine, or theory, by argument or countervailing proof.

2. something that refutes, as an argument.

rē-fūt′ȧ-tō-ry, *a.* tending to refute.

rē-fūte′, *v.t.*; refuted, *pt.*, *pp.*; refuting, *ppr.* [L. *refutare*, to repel, repress, check.]

1. to prove (a person) to be wrong; to confute.

2. to prove (an argument or statement) to be false or wrong, by argument or evidence.

Syn.—confute, disprove, confound.

rē-fūt′ēr, *n.* one who or that which refutes.

rē-gāin′, *v.t.* [Fr. *regagner.*]

1. to gain anew; to get into one's possession again; to recover (what has been lost).

2. to come to again; to get back to; to succeed in reaching again.

Syn.—repossess, recover, retrieve, reobtain.

rē′găl, *a.* [L. *regalis*, kingly, from *rex*, *regis*, a king, from *regere*, to rule.]

1. of a king; royal.

2. characteristic of, like, or fit for a king; splendid, stately, magnificent, etc.

rē′găl, *n.* [OFr. *regale.*]

1. an old musical instrument, a sort of portable organ, played with the fingers of the right hand, the bellows being worked with the left. It had generally only one row of pipes, and was chiefly used to support the treble voices. It was much in use in the sixteenth and seventeenth centuries.

2. a set of reed stops in some organs.

rē-gā′lē, *n.* [L.] a prerogative of royalty: obsolete except in plural: see *regalia*.

rē-gāle′, *n.* [Fr. *régal*, earlier *régale*, from *ré-*, and OFr. *gale*, joy, pleasure.]

1. a feast. [Obs.]

2. a choice food; a delicacy. [Obs.]

3. refreshment. [Obs.]

rē-gāle′, *v.t.*; regaled, *pt.*, *pp.*; regaling, *ppr.* [Fr. *régaler*, from the n.]

1. to entertain; to provide a splendid feast for.

2. to delight with something pleasing.

rē-gāle′, *v.i.* to feast; to fare sumptuously.

rē-gāle′ment, *n.* a regaling or being regaled; refreshment; entertainment; gratification.

rē-gāl′ēr, *n.* one who entertains or regales.

rē-gā′li-ȧ, *n.pl.* [L. *regalia*, royal, regal things, nom. pl. neut. of *regalis*, regal, royal.]

1. the privileges, prerogatives, and rights belonging, in virtue of office, to a king.

2. ensigns of royalty; the emblems and insignia of kingship, as the crown, scepter, etc.

3. the insignia or decorations of any rank or position, or of an order or society, as of Freemasons, etc.

4. splendid clothes; finery.

rē-gā′li-ȧ, *n.* [Cuban Sp. *regalía*, a fine grade of cigar.] a cigar of good quality and large size.

rē-gā′li-ăn, *a.* [Fr. *régalien*, belonging to royalty.] pertaining to a sovereign; regal; pertaining to regalia.

rē′găl-iṣm, *n.* the doctrine or principle of royal supremacy, especially in ecclesiastical matters.

rē-gal′i-ty, *n.*; *pl.* **rē-gal′i-tieṣ**, [ME. *regalite*; OFr. *regalite*; LL. *regalitas*, *regalitatis*, royalty; L. *regalis*, kingly, regal.]

1. royalty; sovereignty; kingship.

2. a country or area subject to the authority of a king; a kingdom.

3. a right or privilege belonging to a king.

4. [*pl.*] regalia. [Obs.]

rē′găl-ly, *adv.* in a royal manner.

rē-gā′lō, *n.* [It., Sp., Port. *regalo.*] a dainty or delicacy given as a present; a feast. [Obs.]

Rē′găn, *n.* in Shakespeare's *King Lear*, the younger of Lear's two wicked daughters, married to the Duke of Cornwall: see *Goneril*, *Cordelia*.

rē-gärd′, *v.t.*; regarded, *pt.*, *pp.*; regarding, *ppr.* [Fr. *regarder*, to regard, observe, keep in view; *re*, back, and *garder*, to guard, keep.]

1. to observe or look at with a firm, steady gaze; to look at attentively.

2. to take into account; to consider.

3. to give attentive heed or respect to.

4. to hold in affection and respect; as, he *regards* his brothers highly.

5. to consider in a certain light or as being something; as, I *regard* this as a nuisance.

6. to have relation to; to concern; to have reference to; as, this proposal *regards* your welfare.

7. to care for. [Obs.]

8. to look toward; to have an aspect or prospect toward. [Obs.]

as regards; concerning.

Syn.—consider, respect, esteem, value, remark, observe, estimate, mind.

rē-gärd′, *v.i.* 1. to look; to gaze; to notice.

2. to pay heed or attention.

rē-gärd′, *n.* 1. a firm, fixed look; a gaze; aspect directed to another.

2. prospect; view. [Obs.]

3. attention, as to a matter of importance; consideration; thought; concern; as, with special *regard* for your safety.

4. that feeling or view of mind which springs from anything that excites admiration; respect; esteem; reverence; affection.

An object worthier of *regard* than he.
—Wordsworth.

5. repute, whether good or bad; account; note; reputation. [Obs.]

6. reference; relation; respect; as, in *regard* to your question.

7. matter demanding notice; consideration; point; particular; as, he will obey in this *regard*.

8. [*pl.*] respects; compliments; good wishes; affection: often used as a complimentary close to a letter; as, give my kind *regards* to your mother.

9. in old English forest law, a view or inspection of a forest.

10. aspect; appearance. [Obs.]

at regard of; with regard to; in respect to; in comparison of. [Obs.]

without regard to; not taking into account.

with regard of; with regard or respect to; as regards. [Obs.]

Syn.—consideration, notice, respect, observance, heed, care, concern, estimation, esteem, attachment, reverence.

rē-gärd′ȧ-ble, *a.* observable; worthy of notice. [Obs.]

rē-gärd′ănt, *a.* [OFr., ppr. of *regarder*, to look at, to regard.]

1. regarding; looking to; looking behind or backward; watching.

2. in heraldry, looking backward with the face in profile: applied to any animal whose face is turned toward the tail in an attitude of vigilance.

LION REGARDANT PASSANT

rē-gärd′ēr, *n.* 1. one who regards.

2. in old English law, an officer whose business was to inspect the forest.

rē-gärd′fụl, *a.* 1. taking notice; heedful; attentive; observant; mindful (often with *of*).

2. showing regard; respectful or considerate.

rē-gärd′fụl-ly, *adv.* in a regardful manner.

rē-gärd′ing, *prep.* in (or with) regard to; respecting; concerning; relating to.

rē-gärd′less, *a.* 1. not looking or attending to; heedless; careless; without regard; unmindful (often with *of*); as, *regardless of* life or *of* health; *regardless of* consequences.

2. not regarded; slighted. [Obs.]

Syn.—heedless, inconsiderate, careless, unmindful, inattentive, unobservant, disregarding, indifferent.

rē-gärd′less, *adv.* without regard for, or in spite of, objections, difficulties, etc.; anyway. [Colloq.]

rē-gärd′less-ly, *adv.* in a regardless manner; heedlessly; carelessly.

rē-gärd′less-ness, *n.* heedlessness; inattention.

rē-gat′tȧ, *n.* [It. *regatta.*] 1. originally, a gondola race in Venice.

2. (a) any sailing or rowing race in which a number of yachts or boats contend for prizes; (b) a series of such races.

rē′ge-lāte, *v.i.*; regelated, *pt.*, *pp.*; regelating, *ppr.* to unite by freezing together again.

rē-ge-lā′tion, *n.* [L. *re-*, again, and *gelatio* (*-onis*), a freezing, from *gelare*, to congeal, from *gelu*, frost.] in physics, the union, by freezing together, of two pieces of ice with moist surfaces when placed in contact under pressure at a temperature above the freezing point. A snowball is formed by the regelation of the particles composing it, as are the snow bridges spanning chasms on high mountains.

rē′ġence, *n.* regency. [Obs.]

rē′ġen-cy, *n.*; *pl.* **re′ġen-cieṣ**, [L. *regens*, *regentis*, ruling, from *regere*, to rule.]

1. rule; government; authority.

2. specifically, the office, function, authority, or jurisdiction of a regent or group of regents; regentship.

3. a group of men appointed to carry on the government while a king or other hereditary ruler is out of the country, too young, or mentally or physically unable to do so himself.

4. the district, country, or territory governed by a regency.

5. the time during which the government is carried on by a regent or regency.

6. [R–] (a) in England, the period between 1811 and 1820; (b) in France, the period between 1715 and 1723, characterized in art by scrollwork combined with natural forms, many curves, and strict balance and proportion.

Rē′ġen-cy, *a.* designating or of a style of furniture developed in France between 1715 and 1723, characterized by scrollwork combined with natural forms, many curves, and strict balance and proportion.

rē-ġen′ēr-ȧ-cy, *n.* the state or condition of being regenerate.

rē-ġen′ēr-āte, *v.t.*; regenerated, *pt.*, *pp.*; regenerating, *ppr.* [L. *regenerare*, to generate again; *re-*, again, and *generare*, to generate.]

1. to cause to be spiritually reborn, as by a religious conversion.

2. to cause to be completely reformed or improved.

3. to form or bring into existence again; to re-establish on a new basis.

4. in electricity and radio, to amplify by feeding energy back from the output into the input circuit.

5. in mechanics, to make use in any way of (heat, energy, pressure, etc. which would otherwise be wasted).

6. in botany and zoology, to grow (a part) anew, as a replacement for one hurt or lost.

rē-ġen′ēr-āte, *v.i.* 1. to form again; to be made anew.

2. to be regenerated; to be reborn spiritually; to be reformed or reconstituted.

3. to have a regenerative effect.

rē-ġen′ēr-āte, *a.* 1. spiritually reborn.

2. renewed; restored; made better, especially after a decline to a low or abject condition.

rē-ġen′ēr-āte-ness, *n.* the state of being regenerate.

rē-ġen-ēr-ā′tion, *n.* [ME. *regeneracioun*; OFr.; LL. *regeneratio.*]

1. a regenerating or being regenerated; a being renewed, reformed, or reconstituted.

2. a spiritual rebirth or conversion.

3. in botany and zoology, the renewal or replacement of any hurt or lost organ or part, as the arm of a starfish or claw of a lobster.

4. in radio, the amplification of a radio signal by feeding energy from the output back into the input circuit.

rē-ġen′ēr-ȧ-tive, *a.* [Fr. *régénératif*; ML. *regenerativus.*]

1. regenerating or tending to regenerate.

2. of regeneration.

3. having a regenerator, as a furnace, or utilizing the principle of a regenerator; as, a *regenerative* system of heating.

rē·gen′ẽr·ā·tive·ly, *adv.* in a regenerative manner.

rē·gen′ẽr·ā·tŏr, *n.* 1. one who or that which regenerates.

2. in a furnace, a chamber or chambers in which exhaust gases and products of combustion are utilized by being taken through layers of brickwork in order to heat the incoming current of air or gas; also, the metal gauze of a hot air engine through which the exhaust hot air passes and which then heats the incoming cold air.

rē·gen′ẽr·ā·tŏr fûr′năce, a furnace using a regenerator.

rē·gen′ẽr·ā·tō·ry, *a.* regenerative; having the power to renew; tending to reproduce or renovate.

rē·gen′e·sis, *n.* the state of being renewed or reproduced; renewal.

rē′gent, *a.* [L. *regens, regentis,* ppr. of *regere,* to rule.]

1. ruling; governing; acting as ruler. [Rare.]

2. exercising vicarious authority; acting in place of a king or ruler; as, prince *regent.*

rē′gent, *n.* 1. a governor; a ruler. [Obs.]

2. a person appointed to carry on a government while a king or other hereditary ruler is out of the country, too young, or mentally or physically unable to do so himself.

3. a member of a board appointed to govern a university or other institution, usually educational.

4. any of certain other university officers.

5. in English universities, a resident master of arts with certain duties of instruction or government.

rē′gent bĩrd, the *Sericulus chrysocephalus,* an

REGENT BIRD (*Sericulus chrysocephalus*)

Australian bird belonging to the family *Meliphagidæ* or honey eaters. The color of the plumage is golden-yellow and deep velvety black. It was discovered during the regency of George IV and was named in compliment to him.

rē′gent·ship, *n.* the power, position, or term of office of a regent; a regency.

reg′gae, *n.* [origin unknown.] a form of popular music of Jamaican origin, characterized by a strong, syncopated rhythm and influenced by rock-and-roll and calypso.

rē′gi·ăn, *n.* a royalist; one who upholds kingly authority. [Obs.]

reg·i·cī′dăl, *a.* pertaining to or having the nature of regicide or of a regicide; tending to regicide.

reg′i·cīde, *n.* [It. and Sp. *regicida*; Fr. *régicide*; L. *rex,* king, and *cædere,* to slay.]

1. the killing or murder of a king or sovereign.

2. one who kills, or is responsible for the killing of, a king or sovereign, especially of his own country; specifically, [R–] one of those who tried and executed Charles I of England.

re·gi·dōr′ (rā-hē-), *n.* [Sp., from *regir,* to rule; L. *regere.*] a magistrate or alderman of a Spanish municipality.

re·gime′ (rā-zhēm′), *n.* [Fr. *régime*; L. *regimen,* government.]

1. a political system.

2. a social system; a social order.

3. a course of treatment, as of diet and rest; regimen.

Also *régime.*

ancient regime; a former system of government or social system; especially, the political and social system which prevailed in France prior to the revolution of 1789.

reg′i·men, *n.* [L., rule, government, from *regere,* to rule.]

1. (a) government; administration; rule; (b) a particular system of government; a regime. [Archaic.]

2. a regulated system of diet, exercise, rest, and general hygiene, intended to maintain or improve the health or to have some specific result.

3. any regulation or procedure which is intended to produce beneficial effects by gradual operation.

4. in grammar, government; the influence of one word over the case or mood of another. [Rare.]

reg′i·ment, *n.* [ME. *regiment, regement*; OFr. *regiment, regement,* government, later a regiment of soldiers; LL. *regimentum,* rule, government; L. *regimen,* rule, from *regere,* to rule.]

1. a military unit, now usually consisting of three battalions and service and administrative units: it is normally commanded by a colonel and is the basic component of a division.

2. a large number (of persons, etc.).

3. rule; government. [Obs.]

4. a district or region ruled. [Obs.]

reg′i·ment, *v.t.*; regimented, *pt., pp.*; regimenting, *ppr.* 1. to form into a regiment or regiments.

2. to assign to a regiment or group.

3. to form into an organized or uniform group or groups; to organize systematically.

4. to organize and subject to strict discipline and control.

reg·i·men′tăl, *a.* of or belonging to a regiment.

reg·i·men′tăl·ly, *adv.* by regiments.

reg·i·men′tălș, *n.pl.* 1. the uniform and insignia worn by a particular regiment.

2. military uniform or clothing.

reg″i·men·tā′tion, *n.* a regimenting or being regimented; making people think and act alike.

rē·gim′i·năl, *a.* of or pertaining to regimen.

Rē·gī′nȧ, *n.* [*also r–*] queen: the official title of a reigning queen, as Victoria *Regina.*

rē·gī′năl, *a.* [ML. *reginalis,* from L. *regina,* a queen.] of, like, or characteristic of a queen; queenly: equivalent to *regal.*

rē′giŏn, *n.* [Fr. *région*; OFr. *regium*; L. *regio* (*-onis*), from *regere,* to rule.]

1. a large and indefinite part of the surface of the earth; a district.

2. an area; place; space.

3. a particular part of the world or universe.

4. a sphere; realm, as of art or science.

5. a division or part of an organism, often called after its main part or organ; as, the abdominal *region.*

6. any of the levels into which the atmosphere or ocean is thought of as being divided.

7. a division of the world according to the plants or animals found there.

8. an administration division of a district, as in the Roman Empire, or district under civil or ecclesiastical administration.

rē′giŏn·ăl, *a.* 1. of or pertaining to a whole region, not just a locality.

2. of some particular region, district, etc.; local; sectional.

rē′giŏn·ăl·ișm, *n.* 1. (a) the division of a country into small administrative regions; (b) the principle of this.

2. regional quality or character.

3. in literature, (a) the use of a particular region of a country as the setting of stories, plays, etc., representing it as affecting the lives of the characters; (b) the tendency to emphasize and value the qualities of life in a particular region, especially an agrarian region as opposed to an urban and industrial one.

rē′gi·ous, *a.* royal. [Obs.]

reg′is·tẽr, *n.* [ME. *regester*; OFr. *registre*; LL. *registrum,* a register, altered form of *regestum,* from L. *regesta,* records, neut. pl. of *regestus,* pp. of *regerere,* to record.]

1. (a) a record or list of events, items, etc., often kept by an official appointed to do so; (b) a book in which this is kept.

2. an entry in such a book or record.

3. a person who keeps such a record, especially one legally appointed to do so; a registrar.

4. registration; registry; enrollment.

5. a device for recording; specifically, (a) a meter or counter, as of fares paid, money deposited, etc.; as, a cash *register*; (b) the part of a meter that indicates the amount of gas, electricity, or water used; (c) that part of a telegraphic instrument which records the message received; (d) a device for automatically indicating the number of revolutions made or the amount of work done by machinery.

6. (a) a lid, stopper, or sliding plate in a furnace, stove, etc., for regulating the admission of air and the heat of the fire; (b) the damper plate of a locomotive; (c) a perforated plate governing the opening into a duct which admits warm air into a room for heat or fresh air for ventilation, or which allows foul air to escape.

7. in photography, exact matching in position of the focusing screen and the sensitive film or plate which replaces it.

8. in printing, (a) exact matching in position of pages, lines, etc. on opposite sides of a single sheet; (b) exact placing of successive colors as they are printed over each other; (c) the inner part of the mold in which types are cast.

9. in music, (a) a musical range or compass, or a particular portion of the compass of an instrument or voice, of which all the tones are produced in the same manner or are similar in quality; as, head *register*; (b) a stop or set of pipes in an organ; (c) [Rare.] the knob or handle by means of which the performer controls any given stop.

10. in commerce, a document issued by the customhouse, containing a description of a vessel, its name, tonnage, country, ownership, etc., always to be kept on board on a foreign voyage, as evidence of its nationality.

Army Register; an official list, issued periodically, containing the names of United States Army officers, their service records, etc.

hotel register; the book in which guests enter their names upon their arrival at a hotel.

Navy Register; an official list, issued periodically, of the ships of the United States Navy and their officers.

parish register; a book in which are recorded the births and baptisms of children and the marriages and burials of the parish.

social register; see under *social,* a.

Syn.—list, archives, chronicle, record.

reg′is·tẽr, *v.t.*; registered, *pt., pp.*; registering, *ppr.* [LL. *registrare,* to register.]

1. to enter in a record or list; to enroll; to record officially.

2. to indicate on or as on a scale; as, the thermometer *registers* 50 degrees.

3. to show, as by facial expression; as, to *register* surprise, anger, etc.

4. to safeguard (mail) by having its committal to the postal system recorded, on payment of a fee.

5. in printing, etc., to cause to be in register.

reg′is·tẽr, *v.i.* 1. to enter one's name in a register, as of a hotel.

2. to have one's name placed on the list of those eligible to vote in an election, by making application in the prescribed way.

3. to make an impression. [Colloq.]

4. in printing, etc., to be in register.

reg′is·tẽred, *a.* [pp. of *register.*] officially recorded or enrolled; specifically, (a) designating bonds, etc. having the owner's name listed in a register; (b) designating dogs, horses, etc. having pedigrees certified and listed by authorized breeders' associations; (c) legally certified or authenticated.

registered letter; a letter the address of which is registered at a post office, for which a special fee is paid in order to secure its safe transmission.

registered nurse; a nurse who has completed her training and has passed a State examination which qualifies her as a nurse in that State.

reg′is·tẽr·ing, *a.* recording; enrolling.

registering instruments; machines or instruments which register or record, such as gauges, indicators, and telltales.

reg′is·tẽr·ship, *n.* the office of register.

reg′is·trȧ·ble, *a.* that can be registered.

reg′is·trănt, *n.* one who registers; especially, one who makes official record of an invention or trade-mark and thereby secures a right to it.

reg′is·trär, *n.* [ME. *registrere*; ML. *registrarius,* one who keeps a register.]

1. a person charged with keeping a register; especially, a person responsible for the records in a college, court, etc.

2. a trust company charged with keeping the records of stock transfers, etc.

reg′is·trär·ship, *n.* the office of registrar.

reg′is·trā·ry, *n.* a registrar: now applied only to the registrar of Cambridge University.

reg′is·trāte, *v.t.* to register; to enroll. [Obs.]

reg·is·trā′tion, *n.* [LL. *registratio, registrationis,* a registering, from *registrare,* to register.]

1. a registering or being registered.
2. an entry in a register.
3. the number of persons registered.
4. the selection and combination of organ stops used in playing a specific composition.

reg′is·try, *n.*; *pl.* **reg′is·tries,** 1. registration; the act of recording or writing in a register; enrollment.
2. an office or place where a register or registers are kept.
3. a register; a series of facts recorded.

rē′gi·um dō′num, [L. *regium*, neut. of *regius*, royal, and *donum*, gift.] a royal gift; especially, a sum of money formerly granted yearly by the English crown in aid of the Presbyterian clergy of Ireland.

rē′gi·us, *a.* [L., from *rex, regis*, a king.]
1. royal: designating certain British and Scottish university professorships founded or appointed by royal command.
2. designating a professor holding such a professorship.

rē′gle (-gl), *v.t.* to rule. [Obs.]

reg′le·ment (reg′l-), *n.* regulation. [Obs.]

reg·lē·men′tȧ·ry, *a.* [OFr. *reglementaire.*] of, pertaining to, or embodying regulations; regulative; as, a *reglementary* charter. [Rare.]

reg′let, *n.* [Fr. *reglet*, from *regle*, rule; L. *regula*, from *regere*, to rule.]
1. a flat, narrow molding, used chiefly to separate the parts or members of compartments or panels from one another, or to form knots, frets, or other ornaments.
2. a flat strip of wood or metal, lower than the type face, used by printers to separate lines of type. It is made to correspond to the different sizes of type, and is known as pica *reglet*, nonpareil *reglet*, etc.
3. (a) reglets collectively; (b) material used in making these.

reg′mȧ, *n.*; *pl.* **reg′mȧ·tȧ,** [Gr. *rēgma*, fracture, from *rēgnynai*, to break.] in botany, a dry fruit consisting of three or more carpels, each of which bursts from the axis with elasticity into two valves when ripe, as in *Euphorbia*.

reg′mȧ·cärp, *n.* [Gr. *rēgma*, fracture, and *karpos*, a fruit.] any kind of dry, dehiscent fruit. [Rare.]

rē′năl, *a.* [LL. *regnalis*, from L. *regnum*, kingdom, rule.] of or relating to a sovereign, sovereignty, or reign.
regnal years; the years a sovereign has reigned.

reg′năn·cy, *n.* the act or state of being regnant; rule; predominance.

reg′nănt, *a.* [L. *regnans* (*-nantis*), ppr. of *regnare*, to be king, to rule.]
1. reigning; ruling; exercising regal authority; as, a queen *regnant*.
2. predominant; having the chief power.
3. prevalent; widespread.

regne (rān), *n.* and *v.* reign. [Obs.]

rē·gorge′, *v.t.*; regorged, *pt., pp.*; regorging, *ppr.* [Fr. *regorger*, to overflow.]
1. to vomit up; to eject from the stomach; to throw back or out.
2. to swallow again. [Rare.]

rē·gorge′, *v.i.* to flow back; to gush back, as water.

rē·grāde′, *v.t.* and *v.i.* to grade again or anew.

rē·grāde′, *v.i.* to retire; to go back. [Rare.]

rē·grȧnt′, *v.t.* to grant again; to renew the grant of.

rē·grȧnt′, *n.* 1. the act of granting back to a former proprietor.
2. a new, renewed, or fresh grant.

rē·grāte′, *v.t.* in masonry, to remove the outer surface of, as of an old hewn stone, so as to give it a fresh appearance.

rē·grāte′, *v.t.* to offend; to shock. [Obs.]

rē·grāte′, *v.t.*; regrated, *pt., pp.*; regrating, *ppr.* [Fr. *regratter*, to scratch or scrape again, to regrate, or drive a huckster's trade; *re-* and *grater*, to grate, to scratch.]
1. to buy up (commodities, especially marketable foods) for resale in or near the same market at a higher price: formerly a public offense.
2. to sell(commodities so bought) again.

rē·grāt′ẽr, rē·grāt′ŏr, *n.* [ME. *regratere*; OFr. *regratier*; Fr. *regrattier*, a huckster, a regrater.] one who buys provisions and sells them at a higher price in the same market.

rē·grāt′ẽr·y, *n.* the act of regrating. [Obs.]

rē·grā′ti·ȧ·tō·ry (-shi-), *n.* a giving of thanks. [Obs.]

rē·grāt′ing, *n.* in masonry, the process of removing the outer surface of an old hewn stone, so as to give it a fresh appearance.

rē·grēde′, *v.i.* to go back; to retrograde, as the apsis of a planet's orbit. [Rare.]

rē·grē′di·ence, *n.* a going back; a return; a retrogression. [Obs.]

rē·greet′, *v.t.* to greet again; to resalute.

rē·greet′, *n.* a return or exchange of salutation. [Obs.]

rē′gress, *n.* [L. *regressus*, pp. of *regredi*, to go back, to return.]
1. a going or coming back.
2. the right or privilege of this.
3. backward movement; retrogression.

rē·gress′, *v.i.* [L. *regressio* (*-onis*), a going back.] to go back; to return to a former place or state; to move backward.

rē·gres′sion (-gresh′un), *n.* [L. *regressio.*]
1. a regressing; a going back; return; movement backward.
2. retrogression.
3. in biology, reversion to an earlier or simpler form, or to a general or common type.
4. in psychoanalysis, reversion to earlier behavior patterns, as to escape from an unpleasant situation.

rē·gres′sive, *a.* 1. regressing or tending to regress.
2. of, like, or characteristic of regression.

rē·gres′sive·ly, *adv.* in a backward way or manner; by return.

rē·gres′sŏr, *n.* a person or thing that regresses.

rē·gret′, *n.* [Fr. *regret*, regret, *regretter*; OFr. *regreter*, to regret; prob. from a Teutonic verb base seen in Ice. *grâta*, Goth. *grêtan*, AS. *grœtan*, Sw. *grata*, to weep.]
1. sorrow or remorse over something that has happened, especially over something that one has done or left undone.
2. sorrow over a person or thing gone, lost, etc.
3. dislike; aversion. [Obs.]
regrets; (a) feelings of sorrow over what has happened, something gone or lost, etc.; (b) a polite expression of regret, as at declining an invitation.
Syn.—sorrow, grief, concern, remorse, lamentation, repentance.

rē·gret′, *v.t.*; regretted, *pt., pp.*; regretting, *ppr.*
1. to feel sorrow over; to mourn for (a person or thing gone, lost, etc.).
2. to feel sorrow or remorse over (something that has happened, one's own acts, etc.).

rē·gret′fu̇l, *a.* feeling or expressing regret; full of regret.

rē·gret′fu̇l·ly, *adv.* with regret.

rē·gret′tȧ·ble, *a.* admitting of regret; fit to produce regret; unfortunate.

rē·gret′tȧ·bly, *adv.* 1. in a regrettable manner.
2. to a regrettable extent.

re·gret′tẽr, *n.* a person who regrets.

rē·gröup′, *v.t.* and *v.i.* to group again; specifically, in military usage, to reassemble or reorganize (one's forces), as after a battle.

rē·grōw′, *v.t.* and *v.i.* to grow anew.

rē·grōwth′, *n.* the act of regrowing; a new growth.

rē·guärd′ănt, *a.* regardant. [Obs.]

rē·guẽr′dŏn, *n.* a reward; a recompense. [Obs.]

rē·guẽr′dŏn, *v.t.* to reward. [Obs.]

reg′ū·lȧ·ble, *a.* admitting of regulation; that can be regulated.

reg′ū·lăr, *a.* [OFr. *regulier*; L. *regularis*, from *regula*, a rule, from *regere*, to rule.]
1. conforming in form, build, or arrangement to a rule, principle, type, standard, etc.; orderly; symmetrical; as, *regular* ranks, *regular* features.
2. characterized by conformity to a fixed principle or procedure.
3. usual; customary; as, he sat in his *regular* place.
4. consistent or habitual in action; as, a *regular* customer; *regular* in one's coming and going.
5. not changing; uniform; as, *regular* speed, a *regular* pulse.
6. conforming to a standard or to a generally accepted rule or mode of conduct; proper.
7. properly qualified; as, a *regular* doctor.
8. thorough; complete; as, a *regular* nuisance. [Colloq.]
9. pleasant, amiable, dependable, etc. [Colloq.]
10. in botany, having all similar parts of the same shape and size; symmetrical: said of flowers.
11. in ecclesiastical usage, being of a religious order or monastic community and adhering to its rule: opposed to *secular*.
12. in grammar, conforming to the usual type in inflection, formation, etc.; having no forms peculiar to itself or to only a few similiar words: said mainly of verbs.
13. in international law, designating soldiers recognized as legitimate combatants in warfare.
14. in mathematics, (a) having all angles and sides equal, as a polygon; (b) having all faces exactly the same, as a polyhedron; (c) governed by one law throughout, as an equation.
15. in military usage, designating or of the permanently constituted, or standing, army of a country.
16. in politics, designating, of, or loyal to the recognized party leadership, candidates, etc.
Regular Army; the permanent, or standing, army of the United States; the United States Army: see also *Army of the United States*.
regular polygon; in geometry, a polygon with equal sides and angles.
regular polyhedron; a polyhedron whose faces are equal regular polygons, and whose polyhedral angles are all equal to one another.
Syn.—customary, normal, ordinary, orderly, recurrent, periodical, systematic, methodical, established, recognized, formal, symmetrical, certain.

reg′ū·lăr, *n.* 1. one of the regular clergy; a member of a religious order, as a monk, friar, etc.
2. a regular soldier.
3. one who is regular, as in habits. [Colloq.]
4. in politics, a person who is loyal to the recognized party leadership, candidates, etc.
5. in astrology, a fixed number attached to each month, which assists in ascertaining on what day of the week the first day of each month fell, and also the age of the moon on the first day of each month. [Obs.]

Reg·ū·lā′ri·ȧ, *n.pl.* [LL., neut. pl. of L. *regularis*, regular.] in zoology, a division of sea urchins having a centric mouth and opposite anus.

reg·ū·lar′i·ty, *n.*; *pl.* **reg·ū·lar′i·ties,** the state, instance, or quality of being regular; conformity to certain principles or to established order; method; steadiness or uniformity in a course; as, *regularity* of a plan or of a building; *regularity* of features; the watch goes with great *regularity*.

reg′ū·lăr·īze, *v.t.*; regularized, *pt., pp.*; regularizing, *ppr.* to make regular; to regulate.

reg′ū·lăr·ly, *adv.* 1. in a regular manner.
2. at regular times or intervals.

reg′ū·lăr·ness, *n.* regularity.

reg′ū·lā·tȧ·ble, *a.* capable of being regulated; admitting of regulation.

reg′ū·lāte, *v.t.*; regulated, *pt.,pp.*; regulating, *ppr.* [L. *regulatus*, pp. of *regulare*, to rule, to direct, to regulate.]
1. to control, direct, or govern according to a rule, principle, or system.
2. to adjust to a particular standard, rate, degree, amount, etc.; as, *regulate* the heat.
3. to adjust so as to make operate accurately, as a clock.
4. to make uniform, methodical, orderly, etc.

reg·ū·lā′tion, *n.* 1. the act of regulating; the act of reducing to order, or of disposing in accordance with rule or established custom.
2. the state of being regulated.
3. a rule, law, order, or direction from a superior or competent authority regulating action or conduct; a governing or prescribed course of action.

reg·ū·lā′tion, *a.* 1. ordered or required by regulation; in accordance with rules or regulations; prescribed; as *regulation* uniform.
2. usual; normal; ordinary; regular.

reg′ū·lā·tive, *a.* 1. regulating; tending to regulate.
2. assumed by the mind as the basis or condition of all other knowledge; furnishing fundamental or guiding principles.

reg′ū·lā·tŏr, *n.* 1. one who or that which regulates.
2. any mechanical contrivance for regulating or equalizing the movement of machinery, the flow of liquids, gases, electricity, steam, etc.; specifically, (a) a timepiece keeping accurate time, used for regulating other timepieces; (b) the device by which a pendulum bob is elevated or depressed; (c) the fly of the striking part of a clock or of a musical box, or the like; (d) the part of the works of a watch or clock by which its speed is adjusted, as an arm which determines the length of the

hairspring of a watch; (e) the governor of a steam engine; (f) a device for admitting steam in regulatable quantity to the valve chamber of a steam cylinder; (g) the brake band of a crab or crane; (h) a cataract; (i) a throttle valve; (j) a thermostat; (k) a damper; (l) a register; (m) a device for maintaining the proper distance between the carbons of an arc light; (n) a device for controlling the current in a circuit, as of a dynamo or in a series of lights.

3. a member of an unauthorized committee formed for the punishment or restraint of crime and disorder where regular law enforcement is not yet established.

reg′ū·line, *a.* pertaining to regulus.

reg′ū·līze, *v.t.* to reduce to regulus. [Rare.]

reg′ū·lus, *n.*; *pl.* **reg′ū·lus·eṣ, reg′ū·lī,** [L., a petty king.]

1. a kinglet; the golden-crested wren.

2. [R-] a genus of insessorial birds closely allied to the wren. They are the smallest birds of the family *Sylviadæ*, inhabiting the woods and thickets of the colder and temperate regions of both hemispheres.

3. in chemistry and metallurgy, (a) metallic antimony: formerly so called because of its ready combination with gold, the "king of metals"; (b) impure metal produced by the smelting or reduction of various ores; (c) partly purified metal that sinks by its weight to the bottom of a crucible when ore is smelted.

4. [R-] a fixed star of the first magnitude in the constellation Leo: sometimes called *Cor Leonis* or *lion's heart*.

rē′gŭr, rē′gär, *n.* [Hind.] the rich, loamy cotton soil of India, covering at least one third of southern India, chiefly the high plateaus of the Deccan. It is bluish-black, greenish, or dark-gray, and is extremely fertile.

rē·gũr′ġi·tănt, *a.* regurgitating; characterized by regurgitation.

rē·gũr′ġi·tāte, *v.i.*; regurgitated, *pt.*, *pp.*; regurgitating, *ppr.* [LL. *regurgitatus*, pp. of *regurgitare*, to regurgitate; *re-*, back, and *gurgitare*, to flood.] to rush, surge, or flow back.

rē·gũr′ġi·tāte, *v.t.* to cause to surge or flow back; specifically, to bring (partly digested food) from the stomach back to the mouth.

rē·gũr·ġi·tā′tion, *n.* [ML. *regurgitatio*.]

1. a regurgitating; specifically, (a) the return of partly digested food from the stomach to the mouth, as in a ruminant animal; (b) a backward flow of blood due to the imperfect closure of a heart valve.

2. the act of swallowing again. [Obs.]

rē·hȧ·bil′i·tāte, *v.t.*; rehabilitated, *pt.*, *pp.*; rehabilitating, *ppr.* [LL. *rehabilitatus*, pp. of *rehabilitare*, to restore; *re-*, again, and *habilitare*, to make suitable, from L. *habilis*, suitable.]

1. to restore to rank, privileges, or property which one has lost.

2. to restore the good name or reputation of; to reinstate in good repute.

3. to put back in good condition; to reestablish on a firm, sound basis.

4. in sociology, to restore (a dependent, defective, or criminal) to a state of physical, mental, and moral health through treatment and training.

rē·hȧ·bil·i·tā′tion, *n.* the act of rehabilitating or the state of being rehabilitated.

rē·hȧ·bil·i·tā′tion cen′tẽr, a place where injured, wounded, or shocked workers or soldiers receive treatment to help restore them to normal activity.

rē·hash′, *v.t.*; rehashed (-hasht), *pt.*, *pp.*; rehashing, *ppr.* [*re-* and *hash*.] to work up again, as old materials for publication, or go over again, as old, familiar arguments.

rē′hash, *n.* 1. a rehashing.

2. something rehashed.

rē·hēar′ing, *n.* in law, a second hearing or trial.

rē·hẽars′ăl, *n.* 1. a rehearsing, reciting, or recounting; a repeating in order; as, a *rehearsal* of her troubles.

2. a drilling or repeating for practice and future performance.

3. a practice performance of a play, concert, etc., or of part of it, in preparation for a public or formal performance.

in rehearsal; being rehearsed, as a play.

rē·hẽarse′, *v.t.*; rehearsed (-hẽrst), *pt.*, *pp.*; rehearsing, *ppr.* [OE. *reherce*, *reherse*, from OFr. *rehercer*, *reherser*, to repeat what one has already said; *re-*, again, and *hercer*, *herser*, to harrow; *herce*, *herse*, a harrow.]

1. to repeat aloud as heard or read, as the words or writings of another; to recite; to tell over again.

2. to relate in detail; to tell or describe in sequence and at length; to narrate; to recount.

3. to act or perform in private for practice, as a play, etc., before giving a public presentation; as, to *rehearse* a tragedy.

4. to drill or train (a person) by practice in what he is to do.

rē·hẽarse′, *v.i.* to repeat what has been already said, written, or gone over; to go through some performance in private, before giving a public presentation.

rē·hẽars′ẽr, *n.* one who rehearses.

rē·hi·bi′tion, *n.* same as *redhibition*.

rē·hib′i·tō·ry, *a.* redhibitory.

rẹi, *n.* occasional, but erroneous, singular form of *reis*, pl. of *real*, a former Portuguese and Brazilian money of account.

Reịch (*or G.* rīkh), *n.* [G.; akin to AS. *rice*, L. *rex*.]

1. the Holy Roman Empire, from its establishment in the 9th century to its dissolution in 1806 (*First Reich*).

2. Germany or the German government; specifically, (a) the German Empire, from 1871 to 1919 (*Second Reich*); (b) the German republic from 1919 to 1933 (*Weimar Republic*); (c) the German fascist state under the Nazis from 1933 to 1945 (*Third Reich*).

Reịchs′baṅk (*or G.* rīkhs′bäṅk), *n.* [G. *Reich*, empire, and *Bank*, a bank.] the national bank of Germany.

Reichs′füh″rer (rīks′fůr″ẽr *or G.* rīkhs′fůr″ẽr) *n.* [G. *Reich*, empire, and *Fuhrer*, leader.] leader of the empire: title assumed by Adolf Hitler during the Third Reich: also spelled *Reichsfuehrer*.

reịchs′märk (*or G.* rīkhs′), *n.*; *pl.* **reịchs′märks, reịchs′märk,** [G. *Reich*, empire, and *mark*.] the monetary unit of Germany, reconstituted and issued in November, 1924; mark: see *Deutschemark*, *Ostmark*.

reịchs′pfen″nig (-fen- *or G.* rīkhs′pfen″ikh) *n.*; *pl.* **reịchs′pfen″nigṣ** or G. **reịchs′pfen·ni·ge** (rīkhs′pfen″i-gȧ), [G. *Reich*, empire, and *pfennig*, penny.] a minor bronze coin of Germany, equal to 1/100 reichsmark; pfennig.

Reịchs′rät, Reịchs′räth (rīkhs′rät), *n.* [G., genit. of *Reich*, and *Rat*, *Rath*, council.]

1. the appointive upper house of the German legislature under the Weimar Republic.

2. formerly, the parliament of the Austrian Empire, excluding Hungary: it was composed of a house of nobles (upper house) and a house of elective deputies (lower house).

Reịchs′städt (*or G.* rīkhs′shtät), *n.* [G. *Reich*, empire, and *Stadt*, city.] a city of the empire: the designation given to the several free cities which, under the old German Empire, held their charters directly from the empire, and were represented in the diets.

Reịchs′täg (*or G.* rīkhs′täkh), *n.* [G. *Reich*, empire, and *Tag*, a day.]

1. the Imperial Diet of the First Reich, a formal assembly of councilors; also, sometimes, any similar informal assembly.

2. in the Weimar Republic, the lower house of Parliament: its members, 647 in number, were chosen every four years on a proportional basis and by universal election.

Reịchs′wehr (rīkhs′vār), *n.* [G. *Reich*, empire, and *Wehr*, defense, weapon.] the German army.

rēif, *n.* plunder. [Scot.]

rē′i·fȳ, *v.t.*; reified, *pt.*, *pp.*; reifying, *ppr.* [from L. *res*, thing; and *-fy*.] to treat (an abstraction) as substantially existing, or as a concrete material object.

rẹign (rān), *v.i.*; reigned, *pt.*, *pp.*; reigning, *ppr.* [OFr. *regner*; Fr. *régner*; from L. *regnare*, to rule, from *regnum*, a kingdom.]

1. to possess or exercise sovereign power or authority; to rule as a king or queen; to hold supreme power.

Behold, a king shall *reign* in righteousness.
—Isa. xxxii. 1.

2. to be predominant; to prevail; as, silence *reigned* for a while.

Syn.—govern, rule, control, prevail, dominate.

rẹign, *n.* [OFr. *reigne*; Fr. *règne*, from L. *regnum*, a kingdom, from *regere*, to rule; *rex*, *regis*, a king (whence *regal*, *regent*, etc.).]

1. royal authority; supreme power; sovereignty; rule; dominion.

2. dominance; prevalence; sway; as, the *reign* of fashion.

The blessed *reign* of bigotry
And rags might still be ours! —Moore.

3. the period or time during which a king, queen, or emperor possesses supreme authority; as, the *reign* of Queen Victoria.

4. kingdom; dominion. [Rare.]

rẹign′ẽr, *n.* one who reigns. [Obs.]

Rẹign ŏf Ter′rŏr, the period of the French Revolution from about March, 1793, to July, 1794, during which many persons, including Louis XVI, were beheaded.

rēim, *n.* same as *riem*.

rē·im·bũrs′ȧ·ble, *a.* that may be repaid; repayable.

rē·im·bũrse′, *v.t.*; reimbursed (-bũrst), *pt.*, *pp.*; reimbursing, *ppr.* [Fr. *rembourser*; *re-* and *embourser*; *en*, in, and *bourse*, a purse.]

1. to pay back (money spent).

2. to pay back to (a person) money spent; to compensate (a person) for damages, time lost, etc.

rē·im·bũrse′ment, *n.* a reimbursing or being reimbursed; repayment (of money spent) or compensation (for time lost, damage suffered, etc.).

rē·im·bũrs′ẽr, *n.* one who reimburses; one who repays or refunds what has been lost or expended.

Reī′mẽr-Tiē′männ rē·aç′tion, [after Carl L. *Reimer* and Ferdinand *Tiemann*.] in chemistry, a reaction in which aromatic hydroxy aldehydes are produced by the action of chloroform and caustic alkali on phenols.

rē·im·plant′, *v.t.* to implant again.

rē·im·plan·tā′tion, *n.* in surgery, replacement of a part that has been taken out, as of a tooth.

rē·im·pōrt′, *v.t.* to import again; to carry back to the country of exportation; especially, to import as finished products (goods previously exported as raw materials).

rē·im′pōrt, *n.* 1. a reimporting or being reimported.

2. something reimported.

rē″im·pōr·tā′tion, *n.* 1. the act of reimporting or the state of being reimported.

2. that which is reimported.

rē·im·pōṣe′, *v.t.* to impose anew; as, the court *reimposed* the sentence.

rē·im·press′, *v.t.* to impress anew.

rē·im·pres′sion (-presh′un), *n.* a second or repeated impression; specifically, a reprint, as of a book, from the original, unchanged plates.

rẹin, *n.* [OFr. *resne*; Fr. *rêne*; It. *redina*, from a hypothetical L. noun *retina*, from *retinere*, to retain; *re-* and *tenere*, to hold.]

1. [*usually in pl.*] a narrow strap of leather attached to each end of the bit in the mouth of a horse, and held by the rider or driver to control the animal.

2. [*pl.*] a means of guiding, controlling, checking, or restraining; as, the *reins* of government.

to draw rein; (a) to tighten the reigns; (b) to slacken speed; to stop. Also *to draw in the reins*.

to give (free) rein (or reins) to; to allow to act without restraint.

to keep a rein on; to keep a check or control on or over.

rẹin, *v.t.*; reined, *pt.*, *pp.*; reining, *ppr.* 1. to put a rein or reins on.

2. to guide, control, check, or restrain with or as with reins.

rẹin, *v.i.* 1. to cause to stop or slow down with or as with reins (with *in* or *up*).

2. to submit to or be controlled by reins: said of a horse. [Rare.]

rẹi′nȧ, *n.* see *rena*.

rē·in·cär′nāte, *v.t.* to incarnate again; to give another or different body to (a soul or spirit).

rē″in·cär·nā′tion, *n.* 1. rebirth (of the soul) in another body.

2. a new incarnation.

3. the doctrine that the soul reappears after death in another and different bodily form.

rē·in·cīte′, *v.t.* to incite again; to reanimate.

rē·in·çrēase′, *v.t.* to increase again; to augment.

rẹin′deer, *n.*; *pl.* **rẹin′deer,** occas. **rẹin′deerṣ,** [AS. *hran*, *hrandeor*, borrowed from the Scandinavian; Sw. *ren*, *rendjur*, Dan. *rensdyr*, a reindeer.] any of several species of large deer found in northern regions, as the *Rangifer tarandus*. It has large, recurved, round, branching antlers that are shed and renewed annually, the antlers of the male being much larger than those of the female. The reindeer is strong, keen of sight, and swift of foot, and is domesticated as a beast of burden and as a source of milk, meat, and hides. The North American species, *Rangifer caribou*, is called *caribou*.

REINDEER (*Rangifer tarandus*)

Reindeer period; in geology, that part of the paleolithic era during which the reindeer flourished in Europe.

rein'deer moss, a lichen, *Cladonia rangiferina*, which constitutes almost the sole winter food for reindeer in high northern latitudes. Its nutritive properties depend chiefly on the gelatinous or starchy matter of which it is largely composed. Its taste is slightly pungent and acrid, and when boiled it forms a jelly.

REINDEER MOSS (*Cladonia rangiferina*)

rei·nette' (re-), *n.* [Fr.] a kind of apple; a rennet.

rē·in·fect', *v.t.* to infect again.

rē·in·fec'tious (-shus), *a.* capable of infecting again.

rē·in·fōrce', *v.t.*; reinforced, *pt.*, *pp.*; reinforcing, *ppr.* [*re-* and *inforce*, var. of *enforce*.]
1. to strengthen (a military or naval force) by sending new troops or ships.
2. to increase the number or amount of.
3. to strengthen or make stronger, as by patching, propping, adding new material, etc.
4. to make stronger or more compelling; as, he *reinforced* his arguments.
Also spelled *re-enforce*, *reënforce*.

rē·in·fōrce', *n.* anything that strengthens, as the thicker part of a gun barrel, where the explosion occurs: also spelled *re-enforce*, *reënforce*.

rē·in·fōrced' (-fōrst'), *a.* made stronger; augmented; strengthened; as, the wall was *reinforced* by additional masonry.
reinforced concrete; concrete masonry in which steel bars or mesh are so embedded that the two materials act together in resisting forces.

rē·in·fōrce'ment, *n.* 1. the act of reinforcing or the state of being reinforced.
2. anything that reinforces; specifically, [*pl.*] additional troops, warships, etc. to reinforce those already sent.
Also spelled *re-enforcement*, *reënforcement*.

rē·in·fōr'cēr, *n.* one who reinforces: also spelled *re-enforcer*, *reënforcer*.

rē·in·fund', *v.i.* [*re-*, and L. *infundere*, to flow in.] to pour in again, as a stream. [Obs.]

rein'less, *a.* without rein; without restraint; unchecked.

reins, *n.pl.* [OFr. *reins*; L. *renes*, pl. of *ren*, kidney.]
1. the kidneys, region of the kidneys, or loins.
2. the seat of the affections and passions, formerly supposed to lie in the region of the kidneys, or loins.
3. the emotions and affections.
[Archaic in all senses.]
reins of a vault; in architecture, the sides or walls that sustain the arch.

rē·in·sērt', *v.t.* to insert a second time.

rē·in·sēr'tion, *n.* the act of inserting again.

reins'măn, *n.*; *pl.* **reins'men**, one skilled in driving horses.

rē·in·spir'it, *v.t.* to inspirit anew.

rē·in·stall', *v.t.* to install again; to seat anew.

rē·in·stall'ment, rē·in·stal'ment, *n.* a fresh installment.

rē·in·stāte', *v.t.* to place again in possession, or in a former state; to restore to a state, condition, position, etc. from which one had been removed; as, to *reinstate* a king.

rē·in·stāte'ment, *n.* a reinstating or being reinstated; the act of putting in a former state; re-establishment.

rē·in·stā'tion, *n.* a reinstating; the act of reinstating.

rē·in·sūr'ănce (-shūr'), *n.* 1. a renewed insurance of property already insured; a second insurance of the same property.
2. a contract in which the insurer becomes protected by effecting insurance upon a risk that he, as first insurer, has assumed.
3. the amount of this.

rē·in·sūre' (-shūr'), *v.t.* to insure a second time, especially under a contract by which the first insurer transfers all or part of the risk to another insurer; to grant reinsurance upon.

rē·in·sūr'ēr, *n.* one who grants a reinsurance.

rē·in'tē·grāte, *v.t.* [LL. *reintegratus*, pp. of *reintegrare*, from L. *redintegrare*, to restore, to renew.] to renew with regard to any state or quality; to restore; to make whole again.

rē·in·tē·grā'tion, *n.* a renewing or making whole again.

rē·in·ter'rō·gāte, *v.t.* to interrogate again; to question repeatedly.

rē·in·vēr'sion, *n.* in surgery, restoration of an inverted organ to its normal place; especially, restoration of an inverted uterus.

rē·in·vest', *v.t.* [LL. *reinvestire*, to invest again.] to invest anew.

rē·in·vest'ment, *n.* the act of investing anew; a second or repeated investment.

rē·in·vig'ŏr·āte, *v.t.* to revive vigor in; to reanimate.

reis, *n. pl.*; *sing.* **re·äl'**, [Port.] formerly, a Portuguese and Brazilian money of account, equal to $^1/_9$ and $^1/_{18}$ cent respectively.

reīs, *n.* [Ar.] a title of authority used in Moslem countries, especially of a ship's captain.
Reis Effendi; formerly, a Turkish minister, or secretary of state.

Reiss'nēr's mem'brāne, a thin membrane of the inner ear, between the cochlear canal and the scala vestibuli.

rē·is'sū·ȧ·ble (-ish'ū-) *a.* suitable to be issued again.

rē·is'sūe (-ish'ū), *v.t.* to issue again.

rē·is'sūe, *n.* a second or repeated issue.

reit, *n.* sedge; seaweed. [Obs.]

reit'bok, *n.* same as *reedbuck*.

rei'tēr, *n.* [G., a rider.] a German cavalryman of the fourteenth and fifteenth centuries.

rē·it'ēr·ănt, *a.* [OFr. *reiterant*; Fr. *réitérant*; L. *reiterans* (-*antis*), ppr. of *reiterare*, to repeat.] of a reiterating character.

rē·it'ēr·āte, *v.t.*; reiterated, *pt.*, *pp.*; reiterating, *ppr.* [L. *reiteratus*, pp. of *reiterare*; *re-*, again, and *iterare*, to say again, to repeat.] to repeat (something done or said); to repeat, say, or do again and again; as, to *reiterate* requests.
Syn.—repeat.—To *repeat* is to utter or express a second time; to *reiterate* is to repeat again and again.

rē·it'ēr·āte, *a.* reiterated.

rē·it'ēr·ā·ted·ly, *adv.* repeatedly.

rē·it·ēr·ā'tion, *n.* a reiterating or being reiterated; repetition.

rē·it'ēr·ā·tive, *n.* 1. a word in which there is reiteration, as of a letter or a syllable; a reduplication; as, fiddle-faddle is a *reiterative* of fiddle.
2. in grammar, a verb expressing reiterated action, as tittle-tattle.

rē·it'ēr·ā·tive, *a.* repetitious.

rēive, *v.i.* to reave (rob). [Scot. and Brit. Dial.]

rēiv'ēr, *n.* a reaver; a robber. [Scot. and Brit. Dial.]

rē·ject', *v.t.*; rejected, *pt.*, *pp.*; rejecting, *ppr.* [L. *rejectare*, to throw or cast back, a freq. of *reicere*, *rejicere*, to throw or fling back; *re-*, back, and *jacere*, to throw.]
1. to refuse to take, agree to, accede to, use, believe, etc.
2. to discard; to throw out or away as worthless, useless, or substandard; to cast off or out.
3. to throw up (food); to vomit.
4. to rebuff.
Syn.—decline, refuse, repudiate, repel, spurn, discharge.

rē'ject, *n.* something rejected or thrown away.

rē·ject'ȧ·ble, *a.* that can be rejected.

rē·jec·tȧ·men'tȧ, *n.pl.* [Mod. L., from L. *rejectare*, freq. of *rejicere*, to throw or fling back; *re-*, back, and *jacere*, to throw.]
1. things thrown out or away as worthless or useless.
2. excrement

rē·jec·tā'nē·ous, *a.* [L. *rejectaneus*, that is to be rejected, rejectable.] not chosen or received; rejected. [Obs.]

rē·ject'ed, *a.* thrown away; cast off; refused; slighted.

rē·ject'ēr, *n.* one who rejects or refuses.

rē·jec'tion, *n.* 1. a rejecting or being rejected; the act of throwing away; the act of casting off or forsaking; refusal to accept or grant.
2. something rejected.

rē·jec·ti'tious (-tish'us), *a.* that may be rejected; requiring rejection. [Obs.]

rē·ject'ive, *a.* that rejects or tends to cast off.

rē·ject'ment, *n.* matter thrown away. [Rare.]

rē·joice', *v.i.*; rejoiced, *pt.*, *pp.*; rejoicing, *ppr.* [OE. *rejoisse*, *rejoyse*, from OFr. *rejoïr*, *rejoïssant*; Fr. *réjouir*, *réjouissant*; *re-*, and *ējouir*, older, *esjoïr*; from L. *ex*, out of, from, and *gaudere*, to rejoice.] to experience joy and gladness in a high degree; to be exhilarated with lively and pleasurable sensations; to exult; to be full of joy (often with *at* or *in*).
I will *rejoice in* thy salvation. —Ps. ix. 14.

rē·joice', *v.t.* to make joyful; to gladden; to delight; to animate with lively, pleasurable sensations; to exhilarate.
Syn.—delight, glory, exult, joy, gladden, cheer, please, enliven, gratify.

rē·joice', *n.* the act of rejoicing. [Obs.]

rē·joice'ment, *n.* rejoicing.

rē·joic'ēr, *n.* one who rejoices.

rē·joic'ing, *n.* 1. the act of expressing joy and gladness.
2. the subject of joy. [Obs.]
Thy testimonies have I taken as a heritage forever, for they are the *rejoicing* of my heart. —Ps. cxix. 111.
3. the experiencing, feeling, or expressing of joy or gladness.
4. an occasion for joy.

rē·joic'ing·ly, *adv.* with joy or exultation.

rē·join', *v.t.*; rejoined, *pt.*, *pp.*; rejoining, *ppr.* [prob. *re-* and *join*.]
1. to join together again; to reunite after separation.
2. to meet again; to come into the company of again; as, I will *rejoin* you soon.

rē·join', *v.i.* to become joined together again; to be reunited.

rē·join', *v.t.* [Late ME. *rejoyne*; prob. from Anglo-Fr. *rejoyner* (Fr. *rejoindre*).] to say in answer.

rē·join', *v.i.* 1. to answer to a reply.
2. in law, to answer the plaintiff's replication.

rē·join'dēr, *n.* 1. (a) an answer to a reply; (b) a reply; an answer.
2. in law, the defendant's answer to the plaintiff's replication.
Syn.—reply, answer, replication.

rē·join'dēr, *v.i.* to make a rejoinder. [Obs.]

rē·join'dūre, *n.* the act of joining again. [Obs.]

rē·joint', *v.t.* to reunite the joints of.

rē·joint'ing, *n.* the filling up of the joints of stones in buildings when the mortar has been dislodged by age or weathering.

rē·jōlt', *n.* a reacting jolt or shock. [Obs.]

rē·jōlt', *v.t.* to jolt or shake the second time or again.

rē·jōurn', *v.t.* to adjourn to another hearing or inquiry. [Obs.]

rē·jōurn'ment, *n.* adjournment. [Obs.]

rē·judge', *v.t.* to judge again; to re-examine; to review; to call to a new trial and decision.

rē·jū'vē·nāte, *v.t.*; rejuvenated, *pt.*, *pp.*; rejuvenating, *ppr.* [from *re-*, and L. *juvenis*, young, and *-ate*.]
1. to make young or youthful again; to bring back to youthful strength, appearance, etc.
2. in geology, (a) to increase the grade and speed of flow of (a stream), usually by uplift of the surrounding land; (b) to give youthful land forms to (a region), as steep slopes.

rē·jū'vē·nā·ted, *a.* made young again.

rē·jū·vē·nā'tion, *n.* the act of rejuvenating or the state of being rejuvenated; a making young again; rejuvenescence.

rē·jū'vē·nā·tŏr, *n.* a person or thing that rejuvenates.

rē·jū·vē·nes'cence, *n.* [L. *re-*, again, and *juvenescens* (-*entis*), ppr. of *juvenescere*, to grow young, from *juvenis*, youth.] a renewing of youth; the state of being young again.

rē·jū·vē·nes'cen·cy, *n.* rejuvenescence. [Obs.]

rē·jū·vē·nes'cent, *a.* becoming or causing to become young again; rejuvenating.

rē·jū'vē·nīze, *v.t.*; rejuvenized, *pt.*, *pp.*; rejuvenizing, *ppr.* to make young again; to rejuvenate.

rē-kin'dle, *v.t.* 1. to kindle anew, as a fire that has gone out.
2. to arouse or inflame anew.

rek'ne, *v.t.* to reckon. [Obs.]

rē-lāid', *v.* past tense and past participle of *relay.*

re·lāis' (-lā'), *n.* [Fr.] in fortification, a narrow walk ouside of a rampart, to receive the earth that may be washed down, and prevent its falling into the ditch.

rē·lapse', *v.i.*; relapsed (-lapst), *pt., pp.*; relapsing, *ppr.* [L. *relapsus,* pp. of *relabi,* to fall, or slide back; *re-,* back, and *labi,* to slide.]
1. to slip or slide back; to return. [Obs.]
2. to slip or fall back into a former condition, especially after improvement or seeming improvement; specifically, (a) to fall back into illness after recovery or seeming recovery; (b) to fall back into bad habits, wrongdoing, error, etc.; to backslide.

rē·lapse', *n.* 1. the act or an instance of relapsing.
2. the recurrence of a disease after apparent recovery.

rē·laps'ēr, *n.* one who relapses.

rē·laps'ing fē'vēr, any of various acute infectious diseases caused by certain spirochetes transmitted by ticks or lice, and characterized by alternate attacks of fever and chills.

rē·lāte', *v.t.*; related, *pt., pp.*; relating, *ppr.* [Fr. *relater,* to state, to mention, from L. *relatum,* pp. of *referre,* to refer, to bring back; *re-,* back, and *ferre, latum,* to bring or bear.]
1. to tell the story of; to recite; to narrate the particulars of; as, to *relate* the story of Priam.
2. to ally by connection or kindred; to connect or associate, as in thought or meaning; to show as having to do with; to show a relation between; as, *relate* theory and practice.

rē·late', *v.i.* 1. to have some connection or relation (*to*).
2. to have reference (*to*).

rē·lāt'ed, *a.* [pp. of *relate.*]
1. narrated; recounted; told.
2. connected; associated.
3. connected by origin, kinship, marriage, etc.; of the same kind, family, etc.
4. in music, closely connected melodically or harmonically: said of tones, chords, etc.

rē·lāt'ed·ness, *n.* the state of being related.

rē·lāt'ēr, *n.* one who relates; a relator.

rē·lā'tion, *n.* [ME. *relacion,* from OFr. or L.; OFr. *relation*; L. *relatio.*]
1. a narrating, recounting, or telling.
2. what is narrated or told; a narrative; an account; a recital.
3. connection or mode of connection, as in thought, meaning, etc.; as, the *relation* of theory and practice, the *relation* of the individual to society.
4. connection of persons by blood or marriage; kinship.
5. a person connected with another or others by blood or marriage; a member of the same family; a relative; a kinsman or kinswoman.
6. [*pl.*] the connections between or among persons in business or private affairs; as, his *relations* with his friends are good.
7. [*pl.*] the connections between or among groups, peoples, nations, states, etc.; as, foreign and trade *relations.*
8. reference; regard; as, this work was outlined with *relation* to available funds.
9. in law, (a) the statement of a relator at whose complaint an action is begun; (b) the referring of an act or proceeding to a time before its completion or enactment, as the time of its taking effect.
10. in mathematics, ratio; proportion; something in common by means of which two quantities may be compared; any dependence of one quantity upon another.
11. in architecture, the direct conformity to each other, and to the whole, of the different parts of a building.
in (or *with*) *relation to*; concerning; regarding; about.
Syn.—reference, aspect, connection, recital, rehearsal, account, narrative, tale, detail, description, narration, proportion, bearing, affinity, homogeneity, association, relevancy, pertinency, fitness, harmony, ratio, relative.

rē·lā'tion·ăl, *a.* 1. of relation or relations.
2. showing or specifying relation.
3. in grammar, (a) showing relations of syntax: said of conjunctions, prepositions, relative pronouns, etc.; (b) having to do with grammatical relations that frequently recur; as, the dative, genitive, etc. are *relational* cases.

rē·lā'tion·ship, *n.* [*relation* and *-ship.*]
1. connection; a being related.
2. connection by blood or marriage; kinship.

rel'ȧ·tive, *a.* [Fr. *relatif*; LL. *relativus,* from L. *relatus,* pp. of *referre,* to refer.]
1. related each to the other; dependent upon or referring to each other; as, we ended in the same *relative* positions.
2. having to do with; pertinent; relevant; as, his letter was *relative* to this matter.
3. regarded in relation to something else; comparative; as, *relative* wages.
4. involving or expressing relations; meaningful only in relationship; as, cold is a *relative* term.
5. in grammar, (a) designating a word that introduces a subordinate clause and refers to an antecedent; as, *which* is a *relative* pronoun in "the hat which you bought"; (b) introduced by such a word; as, a *relative* clause.
6. in music, designating a key having the same signature.
relative major; in music, the major key whose tonic is the third degree of a specified minor key.
relative minor; in music, the minor key whose tonic is the sixth degree of a specified major key.
relative terms; in logic, terms which imply relation, as guardian and ward, master and servant, husband and wife.
relative to; (a) relevant to; concerning; about; (b) corresponding to; in proportion to.

rel'ȧ·tive, *n.* 1. something considered in its relation to something else; one of two things having a certain relation.
2. a person connected by blood or marriage; especially, one allied by blood; a relation; a kinsman or kinswoman.
3. in grammar, a word which relates to or represents another word called its antecedent, or refers back to a sentence or member of a sentence, or to a series of sentences, constituting its antecedent; a relative pronoun.
4. in logic, a relative term.

rel'ȧ·tive·ly, *adv.* 1. in a relative manner; in relation to or compared with something else; not absolutely; as, a *relatively* unimportant matter.
2. in relation or proportion (*to*).

rel'ȧ·tive·ness, *n.* the state of having relation, or of being relative.

rel'ȧ·tiv·ism, *n.* the theory of ethics or knowledge which maintains that the basis of judgment is relative, differing according to events, persons, etc.

rel'ȧ·tiv·ist, *n.* 1. a person who believes in relativism.
2. a person who believes in relativity.

rel·ȧ·tiv'i·ty, *n.* 1. the condition, fact, or quality of being relative.
2. the close dependence of one occurrence, value, quality, etc. on another.
3. in philosophy, existence only in relation to a thinking mind.
4. in physics, the fact, principle, or theory of the relative, rather than absolute, character of motion, velocity, mass, etc., and the interdependence of matter, time, and space; as developed and mathematically formulated by Albert Einstein and H. A. Lorentz in the *special* (or *restricted*) *theory of relativity* and by Einstein in the *general theory of relativity* (an extension covering the phenomena of gravitation), the theory of relativity includes the statements that: (a) there is no observable absolute motion, only relative motion; (b) the velocity of light is constant and not dependent on the motion of the source; (c) no energy can be transmitted at a velocity greater than that of light; (d) the mass of a body in motion is a function of the energy content and varies with the velocity; (e) time is relative; (f) space and time are interdependent and form a four-dimensional continuum; (g) the presence of matter results in a "warping" of the space-time continuum, so that a body in motion passing near by will describe a curve, this being the effect known as gravitation, as evidenced by the deflection of light rays passing through a gravitational field.
relativity of knowledge; in philosophy, the theory that all knowledge is relative to the mind, or that things can be known only through their effects on the mind, and that consequently there can be no knowledge of reality as it is in itself.

rē·lā'tŏr, *n.* [L.]
1. a person who relates, or tells; a narrator.
2. in law, a private person at whose prompting or complaint a public action is begun to bring in question the exercise of an office, franchise, etc.

rē·lā'trix, *n.* in law, a woman relator.

rē·lax', *v.t.*; relaxed (-lakst), *pt., pp.*; relaxing, *ppr.* [L. *relaxare,* to loosen, to slacken, to relax; *re-,* back, and *laxare,* to loosen, to widen, from *laxus,* wide, loose, open.]
1. to slacken; to make less tense or rigid; to loosen; to make less close or firm; as, to *relax* a rope or cord; to *relax* the muscles or sinews.
2. to make less severe or rigorous; to remit or abate in strictness; as, to *relax* a law or rule of justice.
3. to remit or abate in respect to attention, assiduity, effort, or labor; to reduce; as, to *relax* study; to *relax* exertions or efforts.
4. to reduce the concentration or application of; to relieve from attention or effort; to afford a relaxation to; as, conversation *relaxes* the mind of the student.
5. to relieve from constipation; to loosen; to open; as, fruits *relax* the bowels.
Syn.—slacken, loosen, remit, abate, mitigate.

rē·lax', *v.i.* 1. to become looser or less firm, as the muscles.
2. to become less tense or stern, as one's features.
3. to become less strict; to become milder, as discipline.
4. to become easier in manner; to become less stiff.
5. to rest from effort, application, or work.

rē·lax'ȧ·ble, *a.* that may be relaxed or remitted.

rē·lax'ănt, *n.* a medicine that relaxes or opens.

rē·lax·ā'tion, *n.* [L. *relaxatio* (*-onis*), a relaxing, from *relaxare,* to loosen, to relax, from *laxus,* loose, open.]
1. a relaxing or being relaxed; a loosening, lessening of severity, etc.
2. permission not to pay part of a penalty, duty, tax, etc.
3. a lessening of or rest from work or effort.
4. recreation; amusement.

rē·lax'ȧ·tive, *a.* and *n.* laxative.

rē·lax'ed·ly, *adv.* in a relaxed manner.

rē'lāy, *n.* [OFr. *relais,* pl., orig., hounds kept as reserves at points along the course of a hunt, from *relaier,* to leave behind; *re-,* again, and *laier,* to leave, let.]
1. a fresh supply of dogs, horses, etc. kept in readiness to relieve others in a hunt, on a journey, etc.
2. a crew of workers relieving others at work; a shift.
3. a device operated by a relatively weak force but capable of producing a stronger force, used to control a relatively powerful apparatus.
4. in electricity, a device by means of which a change of current or a variation in conditions of an electric circuit causes a change in conditions of another circuit or operates another or other devices in the same or another circuit; used in telegraphy, etc.
5. in sports, (a) a relay race; (b) any of the legs, or laps, of a relay race.

rē·lāy', *v.t.*; relayed, *pt., pp.*; relaying, *ppr.* 1. to convey by relays.
2. to convey as if by relays; to receive and pass on (a message, news, etc.).
3. to supply or replace with a relay or relays.
4. in electricity, to control, operate, or send on by a relay.

rē″-lāy', *v.t.*; re-laid, *pt., pp.*; re-laying, *ppr.* to lay again or anew: also written *relay.*

rē'lāy rāce, a race between two or more teams, each member of which goes a certain part of the distance.

rē·lēas'ȧ·ble, *a.* capable of being released.

rē·lēase', *v.t.*; released (-lēst), *pt., pp.*; releasing, *ppr.* [ME. *relessen*; OFr. *relesser, relaisser,* to release, to relinquish; *re-,* again, and *laisser,* to leave, from L. *laxare,* to loosen, from *laxus,* loose, lax.]
1. to set loose again; to set free from restraint, confinement, or servitude; to liberate; to free; to set at liberty.
2. to free from pain, care, trouble, grief, or other evil; to relieve.
3. to free from obligation, tax, or penalty; as, to *release* another from a debt.
4. to unfasten and let go, as something snagged, a bomb, arrow, etc.
5. to permit to be issued, shown, published, etc.

6. in law, to give up or surrender to someone else (a claim, right, etc.).

Syn.—free, loose, liberate, discharge, quit, acquit, exempt, extricate, disengage.

rē·lēase′, *n.* 1. the act of releasing, liberating, or freeing from restraint, confinement, or servitude; the state of being released; liberation.

2. liberation or freeing from pain, care, trouble, grief, or other evil.

3. liberation or discharge from obligation, penalty, responsibility, or claim of any kind; acquittance.

4. a written discharge, as from an obligation, from prison, etc.

5. a letting go of something caught, held in position, etc.

6. a device, as for starting or stopping a machine, used to release some other device.

7. (a) a releasing to the public, as of a book, film, news, etc.; (b) the book, film, etc. released.

8. in jazz music, the third group of four measures in a common form of sixteen-bar chorus, which supplies a bridge between repetitions of the melody.

9. in law, (a) a giving up or surrender to someone else, as of a claim or right; (b) the document by which this is done.

10. in a steam engine, the opening of the exhaust port before the stroke is finished to lessen the back pressure.

rē″-lēase′, *v.t.* to lease again.

rē·lēas″ee′, *n.* a person to whom a release is given.

rē·lēase′ment, *n.* the act of releasing from confinement or obligation.

rē·lēas′ẽr, *n.* one who or that which releases.

rē·leas′ŏr, *n.* in law, one who executes a release.

rel′ē·gāte, *v.t.*; relegated, *pt.*, *pp.*; relegating, *ppr.* [L. *relegatus*, pp. of *relegare*, to send away; *re-*, away, back, and *legare*, to send.]

1. to banish; to send into exile, usually to a specified place.

2. to consign or assign to an inferior position.

3. to assign to a class, sphere, realm, etc.; to classify (something) as belonging to a certain order of things.

4. to refer, commit, or hand over for decision, as to a person.

rel·ē·gā′tion, *n.* a relegating or being relegated; the act of banishment; exile.

rē·lent′, *v.i.*; relented, *pt.*, *pp.*; relenting, *ppr.* [from L. *relentescere*, to become soft, from *re-*, again, and *lentus*, pliant, flexible, slow; akin to *lenis*, soft, smooth, pliant.]

1. to soften in temper, resolution, etc.; to become less severe, stern, or stubborn; to become more mild and tender; to feel compassion.

2. to melt. [Obs.]

rē·lent′, *v.t.* to cause to relent. [Obs.]

rē·lent′less, *a.* 1. not relenting; harsh; unmoved by pity; unpitying; insensible to the distress of others; destitute of tenderness; as, a prey to *relentless* despotism.

2. persistent; unremitting.

rē·lent′less·ly, *adv.* in a relentless manner.

rē·lent′less·ness, *n.* the quality or state of being relentless.

rē·lent′ment, *n.* the act of relenting or the condition of having relented.

rē·les·sor′, *n.* the person who executes a release; a releasor. [Rare.]

rē·let′, *v.t.* to let anew, as a house.

rel′ē·vănce, *n.* the state or quality of being relevant; pertinence.

rel′ē·văn·cy, *n.* 1. relevance.

2. in Scots law, sufficiency to infer the conclusion.

rel′ē·vănt, *a.* [L. *relevans* (*-antis*), ppr. of *relevare*, to lift up again, to relieve.]

1. relieving. [Rare.]

2. bearing upon or relating to the matter in hand; to the point; pertinent; applicable; as, the testimony is *relevant* to the case; the argument is *relevant* to the question: opposed to *irrelevant*.

3. in Scots law, sufficient to support the cause.

Syn.—important, pertinent, applicable.

rel′ē·vănt·ly, *adv.* in a relevant manner.

rē·lī·ȧ·bil′i·ty, *n.* the state or quality of being reliable.

rē·lī′ȧ·ble, *a.* that can be relied on; dependable; to be trusted; worthy of confidence; trustworthy; as, a *reliable* servant.

rē·lī′ȧ·ble·ness, *n.* the quality that renders reliable.

rē·lī′ȧ·bly, *adv.* 1. in a reliable manner.

2. to a reliable degree.

rē·lī′ănce, *n.* 1. rest or repose of mind resulting from a full belief in the veracity or integrity of a person, or in the certainty of a fact; trust; confidence; dependence.

2. the act or the fact of relying.

3. what is relied on; anything upon which the mind rests in confidence.

rē·lī′ănt, *a.* 1. relying; having or showing trust, dependence, or confidence.

2. self-reliant.

rel′iç, *n.* [OFr. *relique*, L. *reliquiæ*, remains; *re-*, back, and *linquere*, to leave, from root *liq*, akin to *lip* in Gr. *leipein*, to leave.]

1. an object, custom, etc. that has survived, wholly or partially, from the past; often, something that has historic interest because of its age and associations with the past, or that serves as a keepsake, or souvenir.

2. [*pl.*] remaining fragments; surviving parts; ruins.

3. [*pl.*] the body, or parts of the body, of a dead person; remains. [Obs. or Poet.]

4. in ecclesiastical usage, the body or part of the body of, or an object kept and reverenced as a memorial of, a saint, martyr, etc., as in the Roman Catholic and Orthodox Eastern churches.

5. a memento; something left by a departed friend.

rel′iç·ly, *adv.* in the manner of relics. [Rare.]

rel′içt, *n.* [L. *relictus*, pp. of *relinquere*, to leave, to forsake.]

1. a widow or widower; particularly, a woman whose husband is dead. [Rare.]

2. a plant or animal living on in a particular area as a survival from an earlier period.

rē·liçt′, *a.* surviving the death of another; especially, widowed. [Archaic.]

rē·liçt′ed, *a.* in law, left uncovered, as land by the recession of the sea or other water. [Rare.]

rē·liç′tion, *n.* in law, land left uncovered by the recession of the sea or other water.

rē·liēf′, *n.* [ME. *relef*; OFr. *relief*, from *relever*; see *relieve*.]

1. an easing, as of pain, discomfort, or anxiety; setting free from some cause of distress in body or mind; lightening of a burden, as of taxation, oppression etc.

2. anything that lessens tension or strain, or offers a pleasing change, as to the mind or eye; as, the lakes were a *relief* after the dry countryside.

3. aid in the form of goods or money given by an agency, or by the state, city, county, etc., to persons out of work or in need.

4. any aid given in times of need or danger, as supplies sent into a beseiged area or troops sent to take the place of tired forces.

5. (a) release from work or duty; (b) the person or persons bringing such release by taking over a post.

6. [It. *rilievo*, from *rilevare*, [to raise.] in architecture and sculpture, (a) the projection of figures and forms from a flat surface, so that they stand wholly or partly free; (b) a work of art so made. Relief is of three kinds: high relief (*alto-relievo*), low relief (*basso-relievo*), and middle or half relief (*mezzo-relievo*). The difference is in the degree of projection. High relief is that in which the figures project at least one half of their apparent circumference from the background. Low relief is a representation of one or more figures, raised upon a flat surface or background, in such a manner, however, that no part of them shall be entirely detached from it, as in medals, festoons, foliages, and other ornaments. Middle or half relief is the third kind between the two described. Also *relievo*, *rilievo*.

HIGH RELIEF

7. in feudal law, a payment made by the heir of a vassal to the overlord on taking over an estate.

8. in physical geography, (a) the differences in height, collectively, of land forms in any particular area; (b) these differences as shown by lines or colors on a map.

9. in literature and drama, (a) sharp contrast, as of ideas, actions, or events; (b) comic scenes in a serious drama or motion picture: in full, *comic relief*.

LOW RELIEF

10. in painting, the apparent solidity or projection of objects, obtained by modeling and graduation in color, etc.

11. distinctness of outline; contrast.

12. in fortification, the height of a parapet from the bottom of the ditch.

in relief; carved or molded so as to project from a surface.

on relief; totally or partially supported by a temporary government allowance, as when unemployed.

Syn.—succor, support, release, extrication, alleviation, mitigation, aid, help, assistance, remedy, redress, exemption, deliverance, refreshment, comfort, consolation.

rē·liēf′fụl, *a.* giving relief; able to relieve. [Rare.]

rē·liēf′ glōbe, a globe representing in relief the surface of the earth.

rē·liēf′less, *a.* having no relief; also, without remedy.

rē·liēf′ map, 1. a map representing in relief a part of the surface of the earth, especially illustrating the systems of mountains, rivers, and lakes.

2. a map showing by lines, shading, or color the different heights of land forms, as hills and valleys.

rē·lī′ẽr, *n.* one who relies.

rē·liēv′ȧ·ble, *a.* capable of being relieved; worthy of being relieved.

rē·liēve′, *v.t.*; relieved, *pt.*, *pp.*; relieving, *ppr.* [OFr. *relever*, from L. *relevare*, to lift up again; *re-*, again, and *levare*, to raise, from *levis*, light.]

1. to ease; lighten; reduce, as pain, anxiety, etc.

2. (a) to free (a person) from pain, discomfort, anxiety, etc.; (b) to restore (a part of the body, the mind, etc.) to well-being.

3. to give aid or assistance to; as, *relieve* the poor; to bring or send help to; as, *relieve* a besieged city.

4. (a) to set free from a burden, obligation, grievance, etc.; (b) to remove (a burden, etc.).

5. to set free from duty, work, or responsibility, by sending someone, or coming oneself, to take it over; as, she *relieved* the nurse.

6. to make less tedious, monotonous, or unpleasant by being or providing a pleasing change.

7. to set off by contrast; to make sharply distinct or prominent.

8. to ease (oneself) by passing bodily waste matter.

9. to raise or lift again. [Obs.]

Syn.—alleviate, mitigate, succor, ease, relax, free.

rē·liēv′ẽr, *n.* one who relieves; any agent of relief.

rē·liēv′ing ärch, same as *discharging arch*.

rē·liēv′ing taç′kle, a tackle temporarily attached to the end of a ship's tiller to assist the helmsman in bad weather, and to act as a guard in case of accident to the tiller ropes or wheel; also, a tackle from a wharf passed beneath a vessel when careened, and secured to the opposite side, to act as a guard against upsetting and to assist in righting.

rē·liē′vō, *n.*; *pl.* **rē·liē′vōṣ**, [It.] a relief (sense 6).

rē·light′ (-līt′), *v.t.*; relighted, *pt.*, *pp.*; relighting, *ppr.* to light anew; to rekindle.

rē·lī″ġiēuṣe′ (rē-lē″zhyēz′), *n.*; *pl.* **rē·lī″ġiēuṣes′** (-zhyēz′), [Fr.] a woman member of a religious order; a nun.

rē·lī″ġiēux′ (-zhyē′), *a.* [Fr.] religious; pious.

rē·lī″ġiēux′ (-zhyē′) *n.*; *pl.* **rē·lī″ġiēux′** (-zhyē′), a man who has taken monastic vows; a member of a religious order; a monk.

rē·li′ġiŏn (-lij′un), *n.* [OFr. *religion*, from L. *religio* (*-onis*), religion, piety, conscientiousness, scrupulousness, from *religare*, to bind back; *re-*, and *ligare*, to bind, to bind together.]

1. belief in a divine or superhuman power or powers to be obeyed and worshipped as the creator(s) and ruler(s) of the universe.

2. expression of this belief in conduct and ritual.

3. (a) any specific system of belief, worship, conduct, etc., often involving a code of ethics and a philosophy; as, the Christian *religion*, the Buddhist *religion*, etc.; (b) loosely, any system of beliefs, practices, ethical values, etc. resembling, suggestive of, or likened to such a system; as, humanism is his *religion*.

4. a state of mind or way of life expressing love for and trust in God, and one's will and effort to act according to the will of God, especially within a monastic order or community; as, he achieved *religion*.

5. any object of conscientious regard and pursuit; as, cleanliness was a *religion* to him.

6. (a) the practice of religious observances or rites; (b) [*pl.*] religious rites. [Obs.]

7. a religious order or state; a monastery. [Obs.]

to experience religion; to have personal conscious evidence of the favor of God in the forgiveness of sin and a change of heart; to be converted.

to get religion; to become religious; to be converted. [Colloq.]

to profess religion; (a) to unite publicly with the church; (b) to take monastic vows.

Syn.—godliness, piety, devotion, holiness.

rē·li′ġiŏn·ăr·y, *a.* relating to religion; religious. [Rare.]

rē·li′ġiŏn·ăr·y, rē·li′ġiŏn·ẽr, *n.* a religionist. [Obs.]

rē·li′ġiŏn·işm, *n.* 1. excessive religious zeal.

2. pretended or affected religious zeal.

rē·li′ġiŏn·ist, *n.* one devoted to religion; a religious zealot or enthusiast; a fanatic.

rē·li′ġiŏn·īze, *v.t.*; religionized, *pt., pp.*; religionizing, *ppr.* to convert; to make religious.

rē·li′ġiŏn·less, *a.* without any religion.

rē·liġ·i·os′i·ty, *n.* [LL. *religiositas* (*-atis*), from L. *religiosus*, religious.]

1. the quality of being religious, especially of being extremely or excessively religious.

2. an affectation of this.

rẹ·lï·ġiō′sō (-jō′), *adv.* in music, with a religious expression; in a devout manner: a direction to the performer.

rē·li′ġiŏus (-lij′us), *a.* [L. *religiosus*, religious.]

1. of, concerned with, appropriate to, teaching, or relating to religion; as, a *religious* society; a *religious* sect; a *religious* place; *religious* subjects.

2. characterized by adherence to religion; pious; godly; devoted or conforming to religion; as, a *religious* man.

3. careful; scrupulous; conscientiously exact; strict; such as religion requires; as, a *religious* observance of vows or promises.

4. engaged by vows to a monastic life; belonging to a monastic order; as, a *religious* man.

Syn.—devout, pious, moral, godly, devotional.

rē·li′ġious, *n.*; *pl.* **rē·li′ġious,** a person bound by monastic vows or sequestered from secular concerns and devoted to a life of piety and devotion; a monk or friar; a nun.

the religious; religious people collectively.

rē·li′ġious·ly, *adv.* in a religious manner; exactly; strictly.

I *religiously* followed the doctor's mandate.
—Jerome K. Jerome.

rē·li′ġious·ness, *n.* the quality or state of being religious.

rel′ike, rel′ik, *n.* a relic. [Obs.]

rē·liñ′quent (-kwent), *a.* relinquishing. [Rare.]

rē·liñ′quent, *n.* one who relinquishes. [Rare.]

rē·liñ′quish, *v.t.*; relinquished (-kwisht), *pt., pp.*; relinquishing, *ppr.* [L. *relinquere*, to leave.]

1. to give up; to abandon, as a plan, policy, etc.

2. to renounce or surrender (something owned, a right, etc.).

3. to let go (a grasp, etc.).

Syn.—renounce, forego, leave, quit, abandon, resign.

rē·liñ′quish·ẽr, *n.* one who leaves or quits.

rē·liñ′quish·ment, *n.* a relinquishing or being relinquished; the act of leaving or quitting; a forsaking; the renouncing of a claim.

rel′i·quār·y, *n.*; *pl.* **rel′i·quār·ieş,** [Fr. *reliquaire*, from L. *reliquiæ*, relics.] a small chest, box, shrine, or casket, in which a relic or relics are kept and shown.

rel′ique (-ik *or* re-lēk′), *n.* a relic. [Archaic.]

re·liq′ui·ae (-wi-), *n.pl.* [L.] 1. remains, as of fossil organisms.

2. in botany, same as *induviæ*.

re·liq′ui·ăn, *a.* characteristic of or pertaining to relics. [Rare.]

rel′ish, *n.* [ME. *reles*; OFr. *reles*, *relais*, something remaining, from *relaisser*.]

1. (a) a flavor; taste; (b) distinctive or characteristic flavor; as, a *relish* of garlic in the stew.

2. a trace or touch (of some quality); hint or suggestion; as, there was a *relish* of malice in his action.

3. an appetizing flavor; a pleasing taste.

4. pleasure; enjoyment; zest; as, he eats with *relish*.

5. anything that gives pleasure, zest, or enjoyment; attractive quality.

6. pickles, chutney, or the like, served with meat, etc. to make it more appetizing.

7. inclination; taste; fondness; appetite; liking: usually followed by *for*; as, to have a *relish for* reading.

Syn.—appetite, taste, gusto, fondness, liking, appreciation, zest.

rel′ish, *v.t.*; relished (-isht), *pt., pp.*; relishing, *ppr.* 1. to give a relish, or agreeable flavor or taste to.

2. to like or enjoy the taste or flavor of; to partake of with pleasure or gratification.

3. to be pleased with; to enjoy.

rel′ish, *v.i.* 1. to have a pleasing taste.

2. to give pleasure.

3. to taste or have the relish or flavor (*of* something).

rel′ish, *n.* in carpentry, the projection at the base of a tenon.

rel′ish, *v.t.* in carpentry, to shape the shoulders of (a tenon).

rel′ish·a·ble, *a.* having an agreeable taste; capable of being relished.

rē·live′, *v.i.* to live again; to revive.

rē·live′, *v.t.* to recall to life. [Obs.]

rē·lōad′, *v.t.* to load again, as a wagon, gun, ship, etc.

rē·lū′cent, *a.* [L. *relucens* (*-entis*), ppr. of *relucere*, to shine back or out.] shining; bright; luminous; reflecting light.

rē·luçt′, *v.i.* [L. *reluctari*, to oppose, resist, from *re-*, back, and *luctari*, to struggle.]

1. to struggle or strive (*against*); to revolt (at). [Rare.]

2. to offer resistance or opposition; to show reluctance. [Rare.]

rē·luç′tănce, *n.* [L. *reluctans* (*-antis*), ppr. of *reluctari*, to oppose, resist.]

1. the state or quality of being reluctant; a feeling of not wanting to do or agree to something; unwillingness; repugnance: with *to* or sometimes *against*.

I wondered at my own *reluctance*.
—W. A. Fraser.

2. opposition; revolt. [Rare.]

3. in electricity, (a) resistance to the passage of magnetic lines of force; magnetic resistance; (b) in a magnetic circuit, the ratio of the magneto-motive force to the total magnetic flux.

rē·luç′tăn·cy, *n.* reluctance.

rē·luç′tănt, *a.* [L. *reluctans*, ppr. of *reluctari*, to resist: *re-*, against, and *luctari*, to struggle.]

1. unwilling; opposed in mind; disinclined.

2. marked by unwillingness; as, a *reluctant* answer.

3. struggling against; resisting; opposing. [Rare.]

Syn.—unwilling, disinclined, loath, averse.

rē·luç′tănt·ly, *adv.* in a reluctant manner.

rē·luç′tāte, *v.i.* to reluct. [Rare.]

rē·luç′tāte, *v.t.* to struggle against. [Rare.]

rel·uç·tā′tion, *n.* resistance. [Rare.]

rel·uç·tiv′i·ty, *n.* in electricity, the specific magnetic resistance of a medium; the reluctance of a one-centimeter cube of a given material.

rē·lūme′, *v.t.*; relumed, *pt., pp.*; reluming, *ppr.* [*re-* and il*lume*.]

1. to rekindle; to light again. [Archaic.]

2. to light up again; to illuminate or shine on again. [Archaic.]

rē·lū′mine, *v.t.*; relumined, *pt., pp.*; relumining, *ppr.* same as *relume*.

rē·lȳ′, *v.i.*; relied (-līd′), *pt., pp.*; relying, *ppr.* [OFr. *relier*, *ralier*; L. *religare*, to bind back; *re-*, again, and *ligare*, to bind.]

1. to rest or lean physically. [Obs.]

2. to rest or lean with confidence, as when satisfied of the truth or certainty of facts, evidence, or future events, or of the veracity and trustworthiness of a person or a statement, or of the ability and willingness of a person to do any act, fulfill a promise, etc.; to depend; to trust: followed by *on* or *upon*.

Syn.—trust, depend, repose, confide.

REM, *n.*; *pl.* **REMş,** [*r*apid *e*ye *m*ovement.] in psychology, the periodic, rapid, jerky movement of the eyeballs under closed lids during stages of sleep associated with dreaming.

rem, *n.*; *pl.* **rem,** [*r*oentgen *e*quivalent, *m*an.] a dosage of any ionizing radiation that will produce a biological effect approximately equal to that produced by one roentgen of X-ray or gamma-ray radiation.

rē·māde′, *v.* past tense and past participle of *remake*.

rē·māin′, *v.i.*; remained, *pt., pp.*; remaining, *ppr.* [OFr. *remaindre*, from L. *remanere*, to remain; *re-*, back, behind, and *manere*, to remain.]

1. to be left or left over when the rest has been taken away, destroyed, or disposed of in some way.

2. to stay while others go; to stay in the same place; as, he *remained* in the house.

3. to continue; to go on being; as, he *remained* a cynic.

4. to continue to exist; to endure; to persist; to last; as, the old house still *remains*.

5. to be left to be dealt with, done, said, etc.

Syn.—continue, wait, endure, last, stay.

rē·māin′, *n.* 1. the act or state of remaining; stay; abode. [Obs.]

2. something which remains to be done. [Obs.]

3. [*chiefly in pl.*] that which remains or is left; what is left after use, destruction, etc.; a remainder; a remnant.

4. [*pl.*] vestiges; traces.

5. [*pl.*] objects, buildings, monuments, etc. surviving from the past.

6. [*pl.*] that which remains of a human body after life has ceased; a corpse; a dead body.

7. [*pl.*] writings left unpublished at the death of an author.

8. [*pl.*] surviving works, as of an ancient writer.

rē·māin′dẽr, *n.* 1. those remaining.

2. the rest; what is left when a part is taken away; as, he ate the *remainder* of the candy.

3. a copy or copies of a book still held by a publisher when the sale has fallen off, usually disposed of very cheaply.

4. in law, an estate in expectancy but not in possession, as when land is conveyed by the same deed to one person during his lifetime, and at his death to another and his heirs: distinguished from *reversion*.

5. in mathematics, (a) what is left when a smaller number is subtracted from a larger; (b) what is left in addition to the quotient when a dividend is divided by a divisor that is not one of its factors.

Syn.—rest, residue, balance, remnant.

rē·māin′dẽr, *a.* remaining; left over.

rē·māin′dẽr, *v.t.* to sell (books, etc.) as remainders.

rē·māin′dẽr·man, *n.*; *pl.* **re·māin′dẽr·men,** in law, one who has a remainder.

rē·māin′ẽr, *n.* one who remains. [Obs.]

rē·māke′, *v.t.*; remade, *pt., pp.*; remaking, *ppr.* to make again or anew.

rē·māke, *n.* 1. a remaking.

2. something remade, as a motion picture.

rē·man′, *v.t.*; remanned, *pt., pp.*; remanning, *ppr.* 1. to man again, as a boat.

2. to give new manliness or courage to.

rē·mȧnd′, *v.t.*; remanded, *pt., pp.*; remanding, *ppr.* [Fr. *remander*; L. *re-*, and *mandare*, to order.]

1. to send back; to order to go back.

2. in law, (a) to send (a prisoner or accused person) back to jail, as to investigate the charges against him further; (b) to send (a case) back to a lower court, with directions concerning additional proceedings.

rē·mȧnd′, *n.* the state of being remanded; the act of remanding.

rē·mȧnd′ment, *n.* a remanding.

rem′ȧ·nence, rem′ȧ·nen·cy, *n.* a remaining; continuance. [Rare.]

rem′ȧ·nent, *n.* the part remaining. [Obs.]

rem′ȧ·nent, *a.* remaining; left over.

remanent magnetism; the magnestism in a core after the exciting current ceases to flow; residual magnetism.

rem′ȧ·net, *n.* [L., it remains.] in English law, a case postponed or held over.

rē·märk′, *v.t.*; remarked (-märkt), *pt., pp.*; remarking, *ppr.* [Fr. *remarquer*, to remark.]

1. to notice; observe; perceive.
2. to comment; to say or write as an observation or comment.
3. to mark; distinguish; indicate. [Obs.]

Syn.—observe, notice.—To *observe* is to keep or hold a thing distinctly before the mind; to *remark* is simply to mark or take note of whatever may come up; to *notice* implies still less continuity of attention.

rē·märk′, *v.i.* to make an observation or comment (with *on* or *upon*).

rē·märk′, *n.* [Fr. *remarque*.]

1. a noticing, perceiving, or observing; as, to elude conjecture and *remark*.
2. a brief statement taking notice of or referring to something; a casual observation; a comment; a note.
3. noticeable quality. [Obs.]
4. in engraving, remarque.

rē·märk′, *v.t.* to mark over; to mark a second time.

rē·märk′ȧ·ble, *a.* [Fr. *remarquable*.]

1. observable; worthy of notice or remark.
2. extraordinary; unusual; that deserves particular notice, or that may excite admiration or wonder; as, the *remarkable* properties of the element radium.

Syn.—observable, noticeable, extraordinary, unusual, rare, striking, noteworthy, notable.

rē·märk′ȧ·ble·ness, *n.* observableness; worthiness of remark; the quality of deserving particular notice.

rē·märk′ȧ·bly, *adv.* in a manner or degree worthy of notice; to a remarkable extent; notably.

rē·märk′ẽr, *n.* an observer; one who makes remarks.

rē·märque′ (-märk′), *n.* [Fr.] 1. in engraving, any mark made on the margin of a plate and appearing only on proofs, to identify a particular stage of the plate.

2. a small design or sketch etched on the margin of a plate, to be removed after a number of early proofs have been taken.
3. a plate, print, or proof bearing such a mark.

rē·mar′riaġe (-rij), *n.* a second marriage; the marriage ceremony repeated.

rē·mar′ry, *v.t.* and *v.i.* to marry again or a second time.

rē·mas′ti·ċāte, *v.t.* to chew or masticate again; to chew over and over, as in chewing the cud.

rē·mas·ti·ċā′tion, *n.* the act of masticating again or repeatedly.

rem′bẽrġe, *n.* a ramberge. [Obs.]

rem·blai′ (roṅ-ble′), *n.* [Fr., from *remblayer*, to fill up an excavation, to embank, from OFr. *emblaer*, to embarrass, to hinder; *em*, *en*, in, and *blaer*, to sow with wheat, from Fr. *blé*, wheat; LL. *bladum*, grain.]

1. in fortification, the earth or materials used in filling up a trench.
2. in engineering, the earth used for filling a depression, as for a railroad grade.

rē·meaṣ′ūre (-mezh′), *v.t.* to go over again; to measure over.

rē·mēde′, *n.* remedy. [Archaic.]

rē·mē′di·ȧ·ble, *a.* [OFr., from L. *remediabilis*, capable of being remedied, from *remediare*, to remedy.] that can be remedied or cured.

rē·mē′di·ȧ·bly, *adv.* in a remediable manner; so as to be susceptible of remedy or cure.

rē·mē′di·ăl, *a.* [L. *remedialis*.] providing or intended to provide a remedy.

> The *remedial* part of law is so necessary a consequence of the declaratory and directory, that laws without it must be very vague and imperfect. Statutes are declaratory or *remedial*. —Blackstone.

rē·mē′di·ăl·ly, *adv.* in a remedial manner; so as to remedy.

rē·mē′di·āte, *a.* remedial. [Obs.]

rē·mē·di·ā′tion, *n.* in education, the act or process of remedying or overcoming learning disabilities or problems.

rē·mē·di·ā′tion·ăl, *a.* of, or having the nature of, remediation.

rem′e·di·less, *a.* that cannot be remedied; incurable; irreparable; as, a *remediless* disease; a loss or damage is *remediless*.

rem′e·di·less·ly, *adv.* in a manner precluding a remedy.

rem′e·di·less·ness, *n.* the state or quality of being without a remedy.

rem′e·dy, *n.*; *pl.* **rem′e·dieṣ,** [L. *remedium*, that which heals again, from *re-*, again, and *mederi*, to heal.]

1. any medicine or treatment that cures, heals, or relieves a disease or bodily disorder, deadens pain, or tends to restore health.
2. something that corrects, counteracts, or removes an evil or wrong; relief; redress.
3. in coinage, variation allowed at the mint in weight and fineness of metal of a coin; tolerance.
4. in law, a means, as court action by which violation of a right is prevented or compensated for; legal redress.

civil remedy; redress afforded by a civil court for a private injury.

Syn.—cure, restorative, counteraction, reparation, redress, relief, help, specific, antidote.

rem′e·dy, *v.t.*; remedied, *pt., pp.*; remedying, *ppr.* [Fr. *remédier*, from L. *remedium*, that which heals again.]

1. to cure; to heal; as, to *remedy* a disease.
2. to put right; to put back in proper condition.
3. to correct or remove (an evil, etc.).
4. to redress (a person) in a legal matter. [Obs.]

rē·mem′bẽr, *v.t.*; remembered, *pt., pp.*; remembering, *ppr.* [OFr. *remembrer*, *se remembrer*, to call to mind, to remember, from LL. *rememorare*; L. *re-*, back or again, and *memorare*, to bring to remembrance, from *memor*, *memoris*, mindful.]

1. to have (an event, thing, person, etc.) come to mind again; to think of again; as, he suddenly *remembered* an appointment.
2. to bring back to mind by an effort; to recollect; to recall; as, he tried to *remember* the name.
3. to bear in mind; to keep in the memory; to be careful not to forget.
4. to keep (a person) in mind with some feeling, as of pleasure, gratitude, etc.
5. (a) to keep (a person) in mind for a present, legacy, etc.; (b) to give a present or tip to; as, *remember* the waiter.
6. to mention (a person) to another as sending regards or greetings; as, *remember* me to your mother.
7. to remind. [Obs.]

rē·mem′bẽr, *v.i.* 1. to bear in mind or call back to mind.

2. to have memory; to have the use of one's memory.

rē·mem′bẽr·ȧ·ble, *a.* capable of being remembered; memorable.

rē·mem′bẽr·ȧ·bly, *adv.* so as to be remembered.

rē·mem′bẽr·ẽr, *n.* one who remembers.

rē·mem′brănce, *n.* [ME. *remembrance*, *remembraunce*; OFr. *remembrance*, *remembraunce*; Fr. *remembrance*, from L. *rememorare*, to remember.]

1. the act of remembering or the state of being remembered; recognition; recollection; reminiscence.
2. power of remembering; retention.
3. the limit of time encompassed by one's memory; as, before one's *remembrance*.
4. a recollection; a memory.
5. an object that serves to bring to mind or keep in mind some person, event, etc.; a souvenir; a keepsake; a memento.
6. a reminder; a memorandum. [Obs.]
7. a memorial. [Now Rare.]
8. [*pl.*] greetings.
9. the state of being mindful; thought; regard; consideration. [Obs.]
10. a thing to be remembered; admonition. [Obs.]

Syn.—recollection, memory, reminiscence, token, memento, souvenir.

rē·mem′brăn·cẽr, *n.* [Anglo-Fr.] 1. a person who reminds another of something; especially, one who reminds or appointed to do so.

2. [*usually* R-] in England, (a) formerly, any of several officers of the Court of Exchequer; (b) an officer of the Supreme Court who is responsible for collecting debts due to the king or queen: also called the *King's* (or *Queen's*) *Remembrancer*; (c) an officer of the corporation of the City of London.
3. a reminder; a souvenir; a memento.

rē·mem′ō·rāte, *v.t.* to remember. [Obs.]

rē·mem·ō·rā′tion, *n.* remembrance. [Obs.]

rē·mem′ō·rȧ·tive, *a.* reminding. [Obs.]

rē′mex, *n.*; *pl.* **rem′i·ġēṣ,** [L., a rower, an oarsman, from *remus*, oar, and *agere*, to move.] a large quill feather of a bird's wing; a flight feather: chiefly used in plural.

rem′i·form, *a.* [L. *remus*, an oar, and *forma*, form.] oar-shaped.

rem′i·ġēṣ, *n.* plural of *remex*.

Rē·mig′i·ȧ, *n.* the typical genus of the family *Remigiidæ*, noctuid moths of tropical America.

rē·mig′i·ăl, *a.* relating to a remex or remiges.

Rē·mij′i·ȧ, *n.* [after *Remijo*, a Brazilian physician.] a genus of gamopetalous plants of the tribe *Cinchoneæ*, the bark of some species of which is used as a substitute for cinchona.

rē·mil′i·tȧ·rīze, *v.t.* to equip or supply again with arms, military and naval strength, etc.; to rearm.

rē·mīnd′, *v.t.*; reminded, *pt., pp.*; reminding, *ppr.* [*re-* and *mind*, v.] to put (a person) in mind (*of* something); to cause (a person) to remember; as, *remind* me of it.

rē·mīnd′ẽr, *n.* one who or that which reminds; a remembrancer; a thing to help one remember something else.

rē·mīnd′fụl, *a.* 1. reviving memory; reminding; reminiscent; tending or adapted to remind.

2. mindful; remembering.

rem′ing·tŏn·īte, *n.* [after Edward *Remington*, discoverer.] a rose-colored, hydrated carbonate of cobalt occurring as an incrustation on serpentine.

rem·i·nisce′, *v.i.*; reminisced (-ist), *pt., pp.*; reminiscing, *ppr.* [back-formation, from *reminiscence*.]

1. to call past events or experiences to mind.
2. to talk or write about remembered events or experiences.

rem·i·nis′cence, *n.* [L. *reminiscens* (*-entis*), ppr. of *reminisci*, to remember.]

1. a remembering; a recollecting; a recalling to mind.
2. memory; recollection.
3. [*pl.*] an account, written or spoken, of remembered events.
4. something that suggests or recalls something else; a reminder.
5. in psychology, the tendency of an experience to become more firmly fixed in the mind with the passage of time since its occurrence.

rem·i·nis′cen·cy, *n.* reminiscence. [Obs.]

rem·i·nis′cent, *a.* [L. *reminiscens*, ppr. of *reminisci*, from *re-*, again, and *memini*, to remember.]

1. having the nature of or characterized by reminiscence; remembering.
2. recalling the past and telling about it; given to dwelling on the past.
3. bringing to mind something else; suggestive (*of*).

rem·i·nis′cent, *n.* one who calls to mind and records past events.

rem″i·nis·cen′tiăl (-shăl), *a.* pertaining to reminiscence or recollection.

rem″i·nis·cen′tiăl·ly, *adv.* in a reminiscential manner.

Rem·i·nis′ce·rē Sun′dāy, [L. *reminiscere*, remember thou, imper. of *reminisci*, to remember.] the second Sunday of Lent: so called from the Latin word beginning the Psalm for the day.

rem·i·nis′ci·tō·ry, *a.* reminiscential.

rem′i·ped, *a.* [LL. *remipes*, oar-footed, from L. *remus*, an oar, and *pes*, *pedis*, a foot.] having oar-shaped feet or feet used like oars.

rem′i·ped, *n.* an animal whose feet serve as oars, as certain crustaceans and certain coleopterous insects.

rē·mīṣe′, *v.t.*; remised, *pt., pp.*; remising, *ppr.* [OFr. *remise*, delivery, from L. *remissa*, f. of *remissus*, pp. of *remittere*, to remit, release.]

1. in law, to give or grant back; to release a claim to; to resign or surrender by deed.
2. to send back; to remit. [Obs.]

rē·mīṣe′, *n.* 1. in law, a surrender or release, as of a claim.

2. in fencing, a second thrust, which touches the mark, given after one has missed, and before he returns to guard.
3. a livery carriage usually protected in a carriage house, or remise, in distinction from a fiacre, or ordinary hackney coach of the street stands. [Now Rare.]
4. a carriage house. [Now Rare.]

rē·miss′, *a.* [L. *remissus*, slack, remiss, pp. of *remittere*, to remit, slacken.]

1. careless or negligent at work; irresponsible; lax in the performance of duty.
2. characterized by carelessness or negligence; poorly or shoddily done.
3. not energetic; languid; sluggish.

rē·miss′, *n.* remissness; negligence; failure. [Obs.]

rē·miss′fụl, *a.* forgiving; pardoning; lenient. [Rare.]

rē·mis·si·bil′i·ty, *n.* the condition or quality of being remissible.

rē·mis′si·ble, *a.* capable of being remitted.

rē·mis′sion (-mish′un), *n.* [L. *remissio* (-*onis*), from *remittere*, pp. *remissus*, to send back, remit.]

1. the act of remitting (in various senses); a releasing, resigning, relinquishing, surrendering, etc.

2. forgiveness; pardon, as of sins or crimes.

3. cancellation of or release from a debt, tax, penalty, etc.

4. a lessening; abating; diminution, as of heat or cold.

5. a temporary lessening of a disease or pain.

6. a lessening of tension; relaxation. [Obs.]

7. the act of sending back. [Rare.]

8. the act of remitting or sending, as money, in payment; remittance.

remission of sins; forgiveness of or deliverance from the guilt and penalty of sin.

Remission Thursday; same as *Maundy Thursday*.

Syn.—relinquishment, release, forgiveness, pardon, remittance, abatement, cessation.

rē·mis′sive, *a.* 1. remitting; forgiving. [Rare.]

2. tending to abate; relaxing.

rē·miss′ly, *adv.* in a remiss manner; slackly; carelessly; negligently.

rē·miss′ness, *n.* the state or quality of being remiss.

rē·mis′sō·ry, *a.* tending to remission; pertaining to remission. [Rare.]

rē·mit′, *v.t.*; remitted, *pt.*, *pp.*; remitting, *ppr.* [L. *remittere*, to send back; *re-* and *mittere*, to send.]

1. to resign; to give up; to relinquish; to surrender. [Obs.]

2. to pardon or forgive (sins, etc.).

Whose soever sins ye *remit*, they are *remitted* unto them. —John xx. 23.

3. to restore; to replace; to put back, as into a state or position.

4. to relax or diminish in intensity; to make less violent; to abate; to decrease; to let slacken.

5. (a) to refrain from exacting (a payment, tax, etc.); (b) to refrain from inflicting (a punishment) or enforcing (a sentence); to cancel.

6. to submit or refer (a matter) for consideration, judgment, or action, especially to someone whose business it is to look after such things.

7. to refer (one) for guidance, assistance, etc.

8. to put off; to postpone.

9. to send or pay (money).

10. to send back to jail; to recommit. [Rare.]

11. in law, to send back (a case) to a lower court for further action.

Syn.—absolve, release, relax, pardon, acquit, relinquish, forward, forgive, exonerate.

rē·mit′, *v.i.* 1. to diminish; to become less intense or rigorous; to moderate in force or intensity; to abate by growing less earnest, eager, or active; specifically, in medicine, to abate in violence, as a fever.

2. to send or transmit money, as in payment; to pay.

rē·mit′ment, *n.* the act of remitting; the state of being remitted; pardon. [Obs.]

rē·mit′tȧ·ble, *a.* that can be remitted.

rē·mit′tăl, *n.* remission; a remitting.

rē·mit′tănce, *n.* 1. in commerce, the act of transmitting money, bills, or the like, as by mail, to a distant place, as in payment for goods.

2. the sum or thing remitted.

remittance man; a man who lives abroad supported principally by remittances received from home.

rē·mit·tee′, *n.* a person to whom a remittance is forwarded.

rē·mit′tent, *a.* [L. *remittens* (-*entis*), ppr. of *remittere*, to remit.] remitting; having periods of abatement and of exacerbation, but never entire cessation; as, a *remittent* fever.

rē·mit′tent, *n.* a remittent fever.

rē·mit′tẽr, *n.* 1. one who remits, or makes remittance; one who pardons or forgives.

2. restoration, as to a previous state or right.

3. in law, (a) the transfer of a case to another court, usually a lower one, for decision; (b) the principle or act of adjudging a person to hold property by an earlier and more valid title to it than the later but defective one by which he took it over.

rē·mit′ti·tŭr, *n.* [L.] in law, (a) a voluntary relinquishment of part of the damages found by a jury, done to avoid taking chances on a new trial; (b) the order of a court of review by which the record of a case is sent back to a lower court, with instructions as to subsequent procedure, as for execution or a new trial.

rē·mit′tŏr, *n.* in law, a person who makes a remittance.

rem′nănt, *n.* [contr. from ME. *remenant, remanent*; OFr. *remenant, remenaunt*, from L. *remanere*, to stay, to remain.]

1. what is left over; remainder; residue.

2. a small remaining part, quantity, or number; a fragment left over.

3. a trace; a last remaining indication of what has been; as, a *remnant* of his former pride.

4. a piece of cloth, ribbon, etc. left over or unsold, as at the end of a bolt.

Syn.—residue, remainder, balance, rest, leavings.

rem′nănt, *a.* remaining; yet left.

rē·mod′el, *v.t.*; remodeled *or* remodelled, *pt.*, *pp.*; remodeling *or* remodelling, *ppr.* 1. to model again.

2. to make over; to rebuild.

rę·mō·läde′, *n.* rémoulade, a French salad dressing somewhat resembling mayonnaise.

rē·mol′li·ent, *a.* [Fr.] emollient. [Obs.]

rē·mon′ē·ti·zā′tion, *n.* the act or process of remonetizing or the state of being remonetized.

rē·mon′ē·tīze, *v.t.*; remonetized, *pt.*, *pp.*; remonetizing, *ppr.* to restore to standing as legal tender, or lawful money; as, to *remonetize* silver.

rē·mon′strănce, *n.* [OFr. *remonstrance*; LL. *remonstrantia*; *remonstrans* (-*antis*), ppr. of *remonstrare*, to remonstrate.]

1. the act of demonstrating or manifesting demonstration; show; display. [Obs.]

2. declaration; statement. [Obs.]

3. act or instance of remonstrating or expostulating; a strong representation of reasons or facts against something complained of or opposed; expostulation; hence, a paper or document containing such representation or expostulation.

4. in the Roman Catholic Church, a monstrance.

rē·mon′strănt, *a.* [LL. *remonstrans* (-*antis*), ppr. of *remonstrare*, to remonstrate.]

1. remonstrating; expostulatory; urging strong reasons against an act.

2. [R—] of or pertaining to the Remonstrants.

rē·mon′strănt, *n.* 1. one who remonstrates.

2. [R—] one of the Dutch Protestants, who, after the death of Arminius (A. D. 1609), continued to maintain his views, and in 1610 presented to the States of Holland, at Friesland, a remonstrance in five articles formulating their points of departure from Calvinism. The Remonstrants still form a small sect in Holland.

rē·mon′strănt·ly, *adv.* in a remonstrant manner.

rē·mon′strāte, *v.i.*; remonstrated, *pt.*, *pp.*; remonstrating, *ppr.*. [LL. *remonstratus*, pp. of *remonstrare*, to demonstrate, from L. *re-*, again, and *monstrare*, to show.] to exhibit or present strong reasons against an act, measure, or any course of proceedings; to expostulate; to protest; to object.

Syn.—expostulate.—We *expostulate* when we unite argument and entreaty to dissuade some one from the course he has chosen; when we *remonstrate* we use argument and protest in demonstrating to another that he is wrong or blameworthy.

rē·mon′strāte, *v.t.* 1. to say or plead in protest, objection, complaint, etc.

2. to point out; to show. [Obs.]

rē·mon·strā′tion, *n.* the act of remonstrating.

rē·mon′strȧ·tive, *a.* remonstrating.

rē·mon′strā·tŏr, *n.* one who remonstrates.

rē·mon′tănt, *a.* [Fr., ppr. of *remonter*, to remount.] in horticulture, blooming again in the same season: said of roses.

rē·mon′tănt, *n.* any of the hybrid perpetual roses which bloom more than once in a season.

rem·ȯn·toir′ (-twor′), *n.* [Fr., from *remonter*, to wind up.] a mechanism, as in a clock, designed to render the force which sustains the movement of the escapement perfectly even.

remontoir escapement; an escapement in which the scape wheel is driven by a small weight raised by the clock, usually at intervals of thirty seconds, or by a spiral spring on the scape-wheel arbor, wound up a quarter or half turn at the said intervals.

rem′ō·rȧ, *n.* [L., a delay.]

1. a delay; a hindrance; an obstacle. [Obs.]

2. a sucking fish; any species of the genus *Echeneis*, especially *Echeneis remora*, about eight inches long, common in the Mediterranean. By means of the suctorial disk, a transformation of the spinous dorsal fin, the species can attach themselves to any flat surface. The adhesion is so strong that the fish

REMORA (*Echeneis remora*)

can only be dislodged with difficulty. They attach themselves to vessels, or to animals having greater power of locomotion than themselves, as sharks or turtles, but they cannot be regarded as parasites, as they do not obtain their food at the expense of their host: also called *shark sucker*.

3. in medicine, (a) a stoppage or stagnation, as of the blood; (b) an instrument to retain parts in place, as to maintain a fracture in place or a luxation reduced. [Rare.]

rem′ō·rāte, *v.t.* to hinder; to delay. [Obs.]

rē·mọrd′, *v.t.* to rebuke; to excite to remorse. [Obs.]

rē·mọrd′, *v.i.* to feel remorse. [Obs.]

rē·mọrd′en·cy, *n.* compunction; remorse. [Obs.]

rē·mọrse′, *n.* [LL. *remorsus*, a biting again; from L. *remorsus*, pp. of *remordere*; *re-*, again, and *mordere*, to bite, to gnaw.]

1. a deep, torturing sense of guilt felt for one's actions; the keen pain or anguish excited by a sense of guilt; compunction of conscience for an evil act committed; self-reproach.

Remorse bears the same relation to repentance, as rage does to anger, or agony to pain. —C. Darwin.

2. sympathetic sorrow; pity; compassion: now only in *without remorse*, pitilessly.

Syn.—compunction, regret, repentance, contrition.

rē·mọrsed′ (-mọrst′), *a.* feeling remorse or compunction. [Obs.]

rē·mọrse′fụl, *a.* 1. full of remorse; feeling, expressing, or caused by remorse.

2. compassionate; feeling tenderly. [Obs.]

3. pitiable. [Obs.]

rē·mọrse′fụl·ly, *adv.* with remorse of conscience.

rē·mọrse′fụl·ness, *n.* the state of being remorseful.

rē·mọrse′less, *a.* without remorse; unpitying; cruel; relentless; merciless; insensible to distress; implacable.

rē·mọrse′less·ly, *adv.* in a remorseless manner.

rē·mọrse′less·ness, *n.* the quality or state of being remorseless; insensibility to distress.

rē·mōte′, *a.*; *comp.* remoter; *superl.* remotest, [ME. *remote*; OFr. *remot*, masc., *remote*, f., from L. *remotus*, pp. of *removere*, to remove.]

1. distant in place; not near; far off; far away; as, a *remote* country; a *remote* people.

2. far off and hidden away; secluded.

3. distant in time, past or future; as, *remote* antiquity.

4. distant; primary; not proximate or immediate; far removed in influence; as, the *remote* causes of a disease.

5. distant in connection, relation, bearing, or the like (*from* some matter); alien; foreign; not agreeing; as, a proposition *remote from* reason.

6. abstracted; as, the mind placed by thought among or *remote* from all bodies.

7. distant in consanguinity or affinity; as, a *remote* kinsman.

8. distant in human relations; aloof; as, *remote* and cold in his manner.

9. slight; inconsiderable; faint; as, a *remote* analogy between cases; a *remote* resemblance in form or color.

10. in botany and zoology, separated by intervals or spaces greater than the ordinary.

Syn.—distant, indirect, unconnected, unrelated, foreign, alien, heterogeneous, separate.

rē·mōte′ çŏn·trōl′, control of aircraft, missiles, or other apparatus from a distance, as by radio waves.

rē·mōte′ly, *adv.* in a remote manner.

rē·mōte′ness, *n.* the state or quality of being remote.

rē·mō′tion, *n.* 1. the act of removing; removal.
2. the act of departing; departure. [Obs.]
3. remoteness. [Obs.]

ré·mou·lade′ (rā-mu̧-läd′), *n.* [Fr., from It. *remolata.*] a spicy sauce made with the yolks of hard-boiled eggs, vinegar, oil, etc., and served with cold dishes or as a salad dressing: also *remolade.*

rē′mount″, *n.* the opportunity or means of remounting; specifically, a fresh horse with its furnishings; a supply of fresh horses for cavalry.

rē·mount′, *v.t.*; remounted, *pt., pp.*; remounting, *ppr.* to mount again (in various senses).

rē·mount′, *v.i.* 1. to mount again (in various senses).
2. to go back, as in time or in researches.

rē·mŏv·ȧ·bil′i·ty, *n.* the quality or fact of being removable, as from an office or station; capacity of being displaced.

rē·mŏv′ȧ·ble, *a.* capable of being removed, as from an office or station, or from one place to another.

rē·mŏv′ȧ·bly, *adv.* so as to be removable.

rē·mŏv′ăl, *n.* a removing or being removed; especially, (a) a taking away or being taken away; (b) dismissal from an office or position; (c) a change of place, residence, etc.

rē·mŏve′, *v.t.*; removed, *pt., pp.*; removing, *ppr.* [L. *removere*, to remove; *re-* and *movere*, to move.]
1. to move (something) from where it is; to lift, push, or carry away, or from one place to another.
2. to take off; as, *remove* your coat.
3. to take (a person) away by death; to kill; to assassinate.
4. to dismiss, as from an office or position.
5. to wipe out; to get rid of; to eliminate; as, *remove* the causes of war.
6. to take, extract, separate, or withdraw (*from*).
7. in law, to transfer, as a cause, from one court to another by appeal or by change of venue. [Obs.]
Syn.—displace, separate, abstract, transport, carry, transfer, eject, oust, dislodge, suppress.

rē·mŏve′, *v.i.* 1. to move or move away; to change place in any manner; to go from one place to another; to change the place of residence; as to *remove* from New York to Philadelphia.
2. to go away. [Poet.]
Syn.—move, migrate, depart—We do not apply *remove* to a mere change of posture, without a change of place or the seat of a thing. A man *moves* his head when he turns it, or his finger when he bends it, but he does not *remove* it. *Remove* usually or always denotes a change of place in a body, but we never apply it to a regular continued course or motion. We never say, that the wind or water or a ship *removes* at a certain rate by the hour; but we say, that a ship was *removed* from one place in a harbor to another.

rē·mŏve′, *n.* 1. the translation of one to the place of another. [Obs.]
2. the state of being removed. [Obs.]
3. the act of moving a man in chess or other games. [Obs.]
4. a removing (in various senses).
5. the space or distance across which, or interval of time in which, a move is made.
6. a step; space; interval; as, we are but one short *remove* from war.
7. a change or transfer of one's furnishings to another residence or place of business; a move. [Brit.]
8. a dish or course following another at a meal. [Brit.]
9. the act of resetting a horse's shoes or putting on new ones. [Dial.]

rē·mŏved′, *a.* [pp. of *remove.*]
1. changed in place; carried to a distance; displaced from office; placed far off.
2. remote; separate from others; distant (with *from*).
3. distant by (a specified number of degrees of relationship); as, one's cousin once *removed* is the child of one's first cousin.

rē·mŏv′ed·ness, *n.* the state of being removed; remoteness.

rē·mŏv′ẽr, *n.* 1. one who or that which removes something; as, a *remover* of landmarks.
2. in law, the removal of a suit from one court to another by a writ of error.

Rem′phan, Rē′phan, *n.* [LL. *Rempham*; Gr. *Rhemphan.*] an idol worshiped by the Israelites while they were in the wilderness.

rem·pli′ (räṅ-plē′), *a.* [Fr., filled up, pp. of *remplir*, to fill up; L. *implere*, to fill up.] in heraldry, denoting a chief filled with any other metal or color, leaving only a border of the first tincture round the chief.

CHIEF REMPLI

rem·plis·sāġe′ (räṅ-plē-säzh′), *n.* [Fr.] something used to fill up with; padding: a term used in art, musical, or literary criticism.

rē·mū′ȧ·ble, *a.* changeable; inconstant; fickle; that may be removed; removable. [Obs.]

rē·mūe′, *v.t.* to remove. [Obs.]

rē·mū′ġi·ent, *a.* [L. *remugiens* (*-entis*), *ppr.* of *remugire*: *re-*, again, and *mugire*, to bellow.] bellowing again or a second time. [Rare.]

rē·mū″nẽr·ȧ·bil′i·ty, *n.* the capacity of being rewarded.

rē·mū′nẽr·ȧ·ble, *a.* capable of being rewarded; fit or proper to be recompensed.

rē·mū′nẽr·āte, *v.t.*; remunerated, *pt., pp.*; remunerating, *ppr.* [L. *remuneratus*, pp. of *remunerari, remunerare*, to reward, remunerate; *re-*, again, and *munus, muneris*, a service, an office, a present, a gift.]
1. to reward; to recompense; to requite; to pay an equivalent to for any service, loss, expense, or other sacrifice; as, to *remunerate* troops for services or sufferings; to *remunerate* men for labor.
2. to make up for; to compensate; as, his efforts were *remunerated.*
Syn.—reward, recompense, compensate, satisfy, requite, repay, pay, reimburse.

rē·mū·nẽr·ā′tion, *n.* 1. a remunerating; the act of paying an equivalent for services, loss, or sacrifices.
2. the equivalent given for services, loss, or sufferings; that which remunerates; reward; pay; recompense; compensation.
Syn.—reward, recompense, compensation, pay, payment, repayment, satisfaction, requital.

rē·mū′nẽr·ȧ·tive, *a.* 1. remunerating; tending to reward; as, *remunerative* justice.
2. yielding a sufficient return; affording ample remuneration; profitable; as, a *remunerative* position.

rē·mū′nẽr·ȧ·tive·ly, *adv.* in a remunerative manner; so as to remunerate.

rē·mū′nẽr·ȧ·tive·ness, *n.* the quality of being remunerative.

rē·mū′nẽr·ȧ·tō·ry, *a.* remunerative. [Rare.]

rē·mŭr′mŭr, *v.t.*; remurmured, *pt., pp.*; remurmuring, *ppr.* [L. *remurmurare*, to murmur back; *re-*, back, and *murmurare*, to murmur.] to utter back in murmurs; to return in murmurs; to repeat in low, hoarse sounds. [Poet.]

rē·mŭr′mŭr, *v.i.* to murmur back; to return or echo a low, rumbling sound. [Poet.]

Rē′mus, *n.* [L.] in Roman mythology, the twin brother of Romulus.

rē·mū·tā′tion, *n.* a returning to a previous form or quality; a changing back. [Rare.]

ren, ren′ne, *v.i.* to run. [Obs.]

rẹ′nȧ, rẹi′nȧ, *n.* [from Sp. *reina*, a queen.] a small, deep-water rockfish, *Sebastichthys elongatus*, of California.

ren′ȧ·ble, ren′ni·ble, *a.* [ME. *renable, resnable, resonable.*]
1. reasonable. [Obs.]
2. talkative; glib; loquacious. [Brit. Dial.]

ren′ȧ·bly, *adv.* 1. in a loquacious manner. [Brit. Dial.]
2. reasonably. [Obs.]

ren·ȧis·sänce′ (*or* -ȧ-zäns′ *or* rē-nā′sȧns), *n.* [Fr. *renaissance*; OFr. *renaissance, renaiscence*, from LL. *renascentia*, new birth.]
1. a new birth; rebirth; revival; renascence.
2. [R–] (a) the great revival of art, literature, and learning in Europe in the 14th, 15th, and 16th centuries, which began in Italy and spread gradually to other countries: it marked the transition from the medieval world to the modern; (b) the period during which this revival occurred; (c) the style and forms of art, literature, architecture, etc. of this period; (d) any similar revival or period of art, literature, or learning; as, the Provençal *Renaissance.*

Ren·ȧis·sänce′, *a.* 1. of, characteristic of, or in the style of, the Renaissance; as, *Renaissance* painting, the *Renaissance* mind.
2. designating or of a style of architecture developed in Italy and western Europe between 1400 and 1600, characterized by the revival and adaptation of classical orders and design, harmonious repetition of details, the use of horizontal lines, and delicate carving.

Ren·ȧis·sänt′, *a.* [Fr., ppr. of *renaître*, to be born again; L. *renasci.*] of or pertaining to the Renaissance.

rē′năl, *a.* [L. *renalis*, from *renes*, the kidneys.] of, near, or pertaining to the kidneys; as, the *renal* arteries.
renal calculus; a nodule of solid matter formed in the excretory passages of the kidneys.
renal glands or *capsules*; the adrenal glands: also called the *suprarenal glands* or *capsules.*

rē′năl-pōr″tăl, *a.* being both renal and portal.

Ren′ărd, *n.* Reynard (the fox).

Ren′ărd·ine, *a.* [*Renard* and *-ine.*] of or pertaining to Reynard, the fox, or the tales in which he is mentioned.

rē·nas′cence, *n.* [from *renascent.*]
1. a new birth; revival; renaissance.
2. [R–] the Renaissance.

rē·nas′cen·cy, *n.* renascence. [Obs.]

rē·nas′cent, *a.* [L. *renascense* (*-entis*), newborn; *re-*, again, and *nasci*, to be born.] being reborn; showing new life and strength; reviving; springing or rising into being again; reproduced.

rē·nas′ci·ble, *a.* capable of being reproduced; able to spring again into being. [Rare.]

rē·nāte′, *a.* revived; born again; renewed. [Obs.]

rē·nāy′, rē·nȳ′, *v.t.* to deny; to disown. [Obs.]

ren·çon′tre (-tẽr *or Fr.* räṅ-kōṅ′tr), *n.* [Fr.] same as *rencounter.*

ren·çoun′tẽr, *n.* [ME. *rencontre*; OFr. *rencontrer*, to encounter, meet, from *re-*, again, and *encontrer*, to meet.]
1. a hostile meeting; a meeting in opposition or contest, as a battle, duel, or debate.
2. a collision; an impact. [Obs.]
3. a casual meeting, as with a friend.

ren·çoun′tẽr, *v.t.*; rencountered, *pt., pp.*; rencountering, *ppr.* 1. to meet unexpectedly or casually, as a friend, without enmity or hostility. [Rare.]
2. to meet in or as in battle. [Rare.]

ren·çoun′tẽr, *v.i.* 1. to meet an enemy in or as in battle; to clash; to come in collision; to skirmish with another; to fight hand to hand. [Rare.]
2. to meet someone casually. [Rare.]

rend, *v.t.*; rent, *pt., pp.*; rending, *ppr.* [AS. *rendan, hrendan*, to tear, to rend.]
1. to tear, pull apart, rip up, or separate into parts with force or sudden violence; to tear asunder; to split; as, powder *rends* a rock in blasting; lighting *rends* an oak: often used figuratively; as, a roar *rends* the air.
2. to tear, pull, rip, separate, or part with violence (with *from, off, away*, etc.).

I will surely *rend* the kingdom *from* thee.
—1 Kings xi. 11.

Syn.—tear, split, break, rupture, lacerate, crack, burst.

rend, *v.i.* to tear; to burst; to split apart; to go to pieces.

rend′ẽr, *n.* one who tears by violence.

ren′dẽr, *v.t.*; rendered, *pt., pp.*; rendering, *ppr.* [Fr. *rendre*; It. *rendere*, from L. *reddere*, to restore, by the insertion of nasal *n* before *d*; *red-*, back, and *dare*, to give.]
1. to give, hand over, deliver, present, or submit, as for approval, consideration, payment, etc.; as, *render* an account of your actions; to *render* a bill.
2. to give up; to surrender (often with *up*); as, they *rendered up* the city to the enemy.
3. to give in return or requital; as, *render* good for evil.
4. to give back; to restore (often with *back*); as, I *render back* your gold.
5. to give or pay, as something due or owed; as, *render* thanks, *render* obedience.
6. to cause to be or become; to make; as, the heat *renders* me helpless.
7. (a) to give or provide (aid, etc.); (b) to do (a service, etc.).
8. to represent; to depict.
9. to perform or interpret by performance; to recite (a poem, etc.), play (music), treat (a subject, as in painting), act out (a role), etc.
10. to express in other words, as in another language; to translate.

11. to melt the fat from (bacon, etc.); to clarify, as lard.

12. in law, to make (a payment) in money, goods, or service.

13. in plastering, to cover (brickwork, etc.) with a first coat of plaster.

14. in architectural drawing, to apply a material to a drawing to bring out its form and accentuate its design: ink or crayons are the materials most commonly used.

Syn.—give, present, return, restore, apportion, assign, surrender, pay, requite, deliver.

ren′dẽr, *v.i.* 1. to furnish an account; to explain or confess. [Obs.]

2. in nautical language, to slip or run easily; as, the rope *renders* well.

ren′dẽr, *n.* 1. a surrender; a giving up. [Obs.]

2. a payment, sometimes in money but usually in goods or services, as for rent.

3. a first coat of plaster applied directly to a wall.

ren′dẽr·ȧ·ble, *a.* that may be rendered; ready for rendering.

ren′dẽr·ẽr, *n.* one who renders.

ren′dẽr·ing, *n.* 1. version; translation.

2. the act of laying the first coat of plaster on brick or stonework; also, the coat thus laid on.

3. the presentation of an idea in art.

4. the process of melting out animal fats.

ren′dez·vöus, (rän′de-vö *or Fr.* rän̄-dā-vö′), *n.*; *pl.* **ren′dez·vöus,** (-vöz *or Fr.* -vö′), 1. a place for a meeting or assembling, as of troops, ships, etc.

2. a place where people are in the habit of meeting or gathering.

3. (a) an agreement or appointment between two or more persons to meet at a certain time or place; (b) a meeting held by or as by appointment.

This generation of Americans has a rendezvous with destiny.
—Franklin D. Roosevelt.

4. a refuge. [Obs.]

5. a place for enlisting seamen into the naval service. [Obs.]

6. an assembly; a meeting. [Rare.]

ren′dez·vöus, *v.i.*; rendezvoused (-vöd), *pt., pp.*; rendezvousing (-vö-ing), *ppr.* to assemble or meet at a particular place or time, as troops, ships, etc.

ren′dez·vöus, *v.t.* to assemble or bring together (troops, ships, etc.) at a certain place or time.

rend′i·ble, *a.* 1. that may be rent or broken. [Obs.]

2. that may be translated. [Obs.]

ren·di′tion (-dish′un), *n.* [obs. Fr.; after L. *redditio* (from pp. of *reddere*) with *-n-*, from Fr. *rendre.*] a rendering or result of rendering; specifically, (a) a performance or interpretation (of a piece of music, a role, etc.); (b) a translation or version; (c) [Archaic.] a surrender; a giving up.

rend′rock, *n.* a kind of explosive used in blasting rock.

ren′ē·gāde, *n.* [Sp. *renegado*; Fr. *renégat*; LL. *renegatus*, one who denies his religion; L. *re-*, again, and *negatus*, pp. of *negare*, to deny.]

1. a person who abandons his religion for another; an apostate.

2. a person who abandons his party, principles, people, etc. for another or others; a traitor; turncoat; deserter.

ren·ē·gā′dō, *n.*; *pl.* **ren·ē·gā′dōes,** a renegade. [Archaic.]

ren′ē·gāte, *n.* a renegade. [Obs.]

ren′ē·gāte, *a.* apostate; traitorous. [Obs.]

ren·ē·gā′tion, *n.* [LL. *renegatus*, pp. of *renegare*, to deny, from L. *re-*, again, and *negare*, to deny.] denial; apostasy. [Rare.]

rē·nēge′ (*or* rē-nig′), *v.t.* to deny; to disown; to renounce. [Archaic.]

rē·nēge′, *v.i.*; reneged, *pt., pp.*; reneging, *ppr.* [ML. *renegare.*]

1. in card games, to play a card of another suit, against the rules of the game, when holding any of the suit called for.

2. to back out of an agreement; to go back on a promise. [Colloq.]

3. to deny. [Obs.]

rē·nēge′, *n.* in card games, a failure to follow suit; reneging.

rē·new′, *v.t.*; renewed, *pt., pp.*; renewing, *ppr.* [ME. *renewen*, from *re-* and *newe*, after L. *renovare*, to renew.]

1. to make new or as if new again; to make young, fresh, or strong again; to bring back into good condition.

2. to give new spiritual strength to; to make better in spirit.

3. to cause to exist again; to re-establish.

4. to begin again; to take up again; to resume.

5. to go over again; to say again; to repeat; as, to *renew* a promise.

6. to replace by something new of the same kind; to put in a fresh supply of; as, to *renew* provisions.

7. to refill with a fresh supply.

8. to give or get an extension of; as, to *renew* a lease.

Syn.—rejuvenate, recreate, rebuild, refresh, reclaim, revive, invigorate, renovate.

rē·new′, *v.i.* 1. to become restored or new again; to be renewed; to freshen.

2. to begin again; to start over.

rē·new·ȧ·bil′i·ty, *n.* capability of being renewed.

rē·new′ȧ·ble, *a.* capable of being renewed; as, a lease *renewable* at pleasure.

rē·new′ăl, *n.* the act of renewing or the state of being renewed; as, the *renewal* of a treaty.

rē·new′ed·ly, *adv.* again; once more.

rē·new′ed·ness, *n.* the state of being renewed.

rē·new′ẽr, *n.* one who or that which renews.

re·nęye′ (-nā′), *v.t.* to deny or renounce. [Obs.]

renge, *n.* a row or rank. [Obs.]

ren′i- (*or* rē′ni-), [from L. *ren, renis.*] a combining form meaning *kidney, kidneys*, as in *reni*form: also *reno-*.

ren·i·çär′di·aç, *a.* [*reni-*, and L. *cardiacus*, cardiac.] of or pertaining to the heart and kidneys.

rē·niç′ū·lus, *n.*; *pl.* **rē·niç′ū·lī,** [LL., dim. of L. *renes*, the kidneys.] a small reniform spot.

rē·nid″i·fi·çā′tion, *n.* [*re-*, and L. *nidus*, nest, and *facere*, to make.] the act of building another nest.

ren′i·fọrm, *a.* [*reni-*, and L. *forma*, form.] having the form or shape of a kidney.

rē·nig′, *v.i.* to renege. [Colloq.]

rē′nin, *n.* [from L. *ren*, kidney.] a protein formed in the kidneys and thought to be associated with some forms of hypertension in man.

ren·i·per·i·çär′di·ăl, *a.* [*reni-*, and LL. *pericardium.*] of, relating to, or designating the nephridium and the pericardium of a mollusk: also spelled *renopericardial.*

ren·i·pōr′tăl, *a.* of, relating to, or designating the portal system of the kidneys, by which the circulation of venous blood is effected in the kidneys before going to the heart.

rē·nī′ten·cy, rē·nī′tence, *n.* state, quality, or instance of being renitent; the resistance of a body to pressure; moral resistance; reluctance.

rē·nī′tent, *a.* [L. *renitens* (*-entis*), resistant, from *re-*, back, and *niti*, to struggle.]

1. resistant; resisting pressure or the effect of it; acting against impulse by elastic force.

2. opposing stubbornly; recalcitrant; obstinate.

ren′net, *n.* [ME. *rennen*, to run, because rennet causes the milk to run, that is, to coagulate or congeal; G. *rinnen*, to run, to curdle; O.D. *rinsel, runsel, renninge*, curds, rennet, from *rinnen*, to press, to curdle.]

1. the membrane that lines the fourth stomach of a calf or the stomach of some other young animals.

2. (a) a preparation or extract of this membrane, used to curdle milk, as in making cheese or junket; (b) anything used to curdle milk.

3. a substance containing rennin, found in the stomach of a calf.

4. rennin.

ren′net, *n.* [according to Diez, Fr. *reinette*, dim. of *reine*, L. *regina*, a queen, and so queen of apples; but Mahn gives it from *raine*, a green or tree frog, from L. *rana*, a frog, because the apple is spotted like this frog.] a variety or one of several subvarieties of apples having a more or less spotted fruit. [Brit.]

ren′net bag, the fourth stomach of a ruminant.

ren′net·ed, *a.* made by the use of rennet; containing or treated with rennet. [Obs.]

ren′net fẽr′ment, rennin.

ren′net·ing, *n.* rennet (apple). [Obs.]

ren′nin, *n.* [*renne*t and *-in.*] a coagulating enzyme that can curdle milk, found in the gastric juice of the calf, etc.

ren′ō- (*or* rē′nō-), reni-.

re·nō·mee′, *n.* renown. [Obs.]

rē·nounce′, *v.t.*, renounced (-nounst), *pt., pp.*, renouncing, *ppr.* [Fr. *renoncer*; L. *renuntiare*; *renunciare*, from *re-*, back, and *nuntiare, nunciare*, to tell, from *nuntius*, a messenger.]

1. to give up, usually by a formal public statement (a claim, right, opinion, etc.).

2. to give up, as a habit, practice, etc.; to cease to have or show (a feeling, etc.); as, he *renounced* all honor.

3. to cast off; to disown; to deny all responsibility for or allegiance to (a person); as, to *renounce* a son.

4. in card games, to indicate a lack of (a certain suit) by playing a card from another.

5. in law, to give up formally (a right, claim, or trust, especially one bestowed by a will).

Syn.—abandon, abjure, disown, disclaim, abdicate, forsake.

rē·nounce′, *v.i.* 1. in card games, to fail to follow suit, having no cards of the suit led.

2. in law, to give up a right, trust, etc.

rē·nounce′, *n.* in card playing, the failure to play the suit led.

rē·nounce′ment, *n.* a renouncing; the act of disclaiming or rejecting; renunciation.

rē·noun′cẽr, *n.* one who disowns or disclaims.

ren′ō·vāte, *v.t.*; renovated, *pt., pp.*; renovating, *ppr.* [L. *renovatus*, pp. of *renovare*, to renew; *re-*, again, and *novare*, to make new, from *novus*, new.]

1. to make new or like new; to clean up, replace worn and broken parts in, repair, etc.; to restore to good condition.

2. to refresh; to revive.

ren′ō·vāte, *a.* renovated. [Archaic.]

ren·ō·vā′tion, *n.* a renovating or being renovated.

ren′ō·vā·tŏr, *n.* one who or that which renovates.

rē·nov′el, *v.t.* to renew. [Obs.]

rē·nov′el·ănce, *n.* renovation. [Obs.]

ren′ō·vīze, *v.t.* and *v.i.*; renovized, *pt., pp.*; renovizing, *ppr.* to renovate; to restore to the first state or to a good condition.

rē·nown′, *n.* [OE. *renowme*, from Fr. *renom*, from L. *re-*, again, and *nomen*, a name.]

1. fame; celebrity; exalted reputation derived from the extensive praise of great achievements or accomplishments.

Well may the world cherish the author's *renown.* —Irving.

2. report or rumor. [Obs.]

rē·nown′, *v.t.*; renowned, *pt., pp.*; renowning, *ppr.* to make famous. [Obs.]

rē·nowned′, *a.* famous; celebrated for great achievements, for distinguished qualities, or for grandeur; eminent; as, a *renowned* author, a *renowned* city.

Syn.—famed, famous, distinguished, eminent, remarkable.

rē·nown′ed·ly, *adv.* with fame or celebrity.

rē·nown′ẽr, *n.* one who imparts or extends renown.

rē·nown′fụl, *a.* renowned; illustrious. [Rare.]

rē·nown′less, *a.* without renown; inglorious.

rens′se·laẽr·īte, *n.* [after Stephen Van *Rensselaer.*] a variety of talc found in New York state and Canada, of a fine compact texture: it can be worked on a lathe.

rent, *v.* past tense and past participle of *rend.*

rent, *a.* torn or split.

rent, *n.* 1. a fissure; a break or breach made by force; a hole or tear; as, a *rent* made in the earth, in a rock, or in a garment.

2. a breach of relations, as between persons or in an organized group; a schism; a separation; as, a *rent* in the church.

rent, *v.t.* to tear. [Obs. or Dial.]

rent, *v.t.*; rented, *pt., pp.*; renting, *ppr.* [ME. *renten*; OFr. *renter*; Sw. *ränta*, to give rent or revenue.]

1. to get temporary possession and use of (a house, land, etc.) in return for stated payments, usually at fixed intervals.

2. to give temporary possession and use of in return for such payments; to lease or let for rent (often with *out*).

rent, *v.i.* to be leased or let for rent; as, the room *rents* for $10 a week.

rent, *n.* [Fr. *rente*, rent, revenue, from It. *rendita*, a nasalized form of L. *reddita* (*pecunia*), money paid, f. sing. of *redditus*, pp. of *reddere*, to give back, to render.]

1. a stated return or payment for the temporary possession or use of a house, land, or other property, made, usually at fixed intervals, by the tenant or user to the owner.

2. in economics, (a) income from the ownership of real estate; the return yielded by land under cultivation minus the cost of production; (b) a return or profit realized from a differential advantage in production,

as the difference in yield between relatively good land and the poorest land under cultivation in similar conditions.
3. real estate or other property yielding an income. [Obs.]
4. revenue or income. [Obs.]
black rent; see under *black*, a.
for rent; available to be rented.
sleeping rent; a fixed sum as rent: distinguished from a rent contingent upon the amount of profits.
white rent; rent to be paid in a coin of silver or other white metal: opposed to *black rent*.

rent′á·ble, *a.* capable of being rented.
rent′ȧġe, *n.* rent. [Obs.]
rent′ăl, *n.* 1. an amount paid or received as rent.
2. an income from rents received.
3. a list, or schedule, of rents.
4. a house, apartment, etc. offered for rent.
rent′ăl, *a.* of, in, or for rent.
rent′ăl lī′brăr·y, a collection of popular books any of which can be borrowed for a small fee.
rent chärġe, a rent forming a charge upon land, reserved by deed (with a clause giving power to distrain for rent in arrears) in a conveyance of land.
rente (roṅt), *n.*; *pl.* **rentes** (roṅt), [Fr.]
1. annual income or revenue; annuity.
2. [*usually pl.*] (a) the bonds, stocks, etc. representing the consolidated governmental debt of France; (b) interest paid on this.
rent′ẽr, *n.* 1. a person who pays rent for the use of another's property.
2. a person who owns and rents out property.
ren′tẽr, *v.t.*; rentered, *pt.*, *pp.*; rentering, *ppr.* [Fr. *rentraire*; L. *retrahere*; *re-*, again, and *trahere*, to draw.]
1. to fine-draw; to sew together, as the edges of two pieces of cloth without doubling them, so that the seam is scarcely visible. [Obs.]
2. in tapestry, to work new warp into so as to restore the original pattern or design. [Obs.]
ren′tẽr·ẽr, *n.* one who renters. [Obs.]
rent′-free′, *a.* and *adv.* without payment of rent.
ren·tier′, (roṅ-tyā′), *n.* [Fr.] one who has a fixed income, as from lands, stocks, etc.
rent′-rōll, *n.* a rental; a list or account of rents or income.
rent seck, formerly, rent reserved by deed, but without any clause of distress.
rent sẽrv′ice, rent having some corporeal service incident to it, as fealty.
ren′ūle, *n.* [LL. *renulus*, dim. of *ren*, the kidney.] one of the small lobules of a kidney.
rē·nun·ci·ā′tion, *n.* [L. *renuntiatio* (*-onis*), a renouncing, from *renuntiatus*, pp. of *renuntiare*, to renounce.]
1. the act of disowning; rejection; repudiation.
2. a renouncing or giving up formally or voluntarily, often at a sacrifice, as of a right, claim, title, etc.
3. a written statement or declaration of this.
Syn.—abnegation, relinquishment, abandonment.
rē·nun′ci·ȧ·tō·ry, *a.* pertaining to, characterized by, or containing renunciation; declaring a renunciation.
ren·vẽrse′, *v.t.* to reverse. [Obs.]
ren·vẽrsé′, *a.* in heraldry, inverted; set with the head downward, or contrary to the natural posture.
ren·vẽrse′ment, *n.* the act of reversing. [Obs.]
ren·voy′, *v.t.* to send back. [Obs.]
ren·voy′, *n.* a sending back; a returning. [Obs.]
rē·om′e·tẽr, *n.* same as *rheometer*.
rē·ō′pen, *v.t.* and *v.i.* 1. to open again.
2. to begin again; to resume.
rē·ọr·dāin′, *v.t.* to ordain again, as when the first ordination is defective.
rē·ọr′dẽr, *v.t.* 1. to give a reorder for; to order again.
2. to put in order again.
rē·ọr′dẽr, *v.i.* to order goods again.
rē·ọr′dẽr, *n.* a second or repeated order for the same goods from the same dealer.
rē·ọr·di·nā′tion, *n.* a second ordination.
rē·ọr″găn·i·zā′tion, *n.* 1. the act of reorganizing or the state of being reorganized; as, repeated *reorganization* of the troops.
2. in finance, a thorough reconstruction of a business corporation, comprising a considerable change in capital structure, as effected after, or in anticipation of, a failure and receivership.

rē·ọr′găn·īze, *v.t.* and *v.i.*; reorganized, *pt.*, *pp.*; reorganizing, *ppr.* to organize again or anew; to effect a reorganization (of); as, to *reorganize* a society or an army.
rē·ō′ri·ent, *a.* rising anew. [Rare.]
rē·ō′ri·ent, *v.t.* and *v.i.* to orient again or anew.
rē·ō″ri·en·tā′tion, *n.* a reorienting or being reoriented; new orientation.
rē′ō·stat, *n.* same as *rheostat*.
rē′ō·trōpe, *n.* same as *rheotrope*.
rep, *n.* [prob. a corruption of *rib*.] a fabric formed with a finely ribbed surface, the ribs running transversely and not lengthwise: made of silk, wool, cotton, rayon, etc.: also written *repp*, *reps*.
rep, *a.* having a transversely ribbed surface: said of certain fabrics.
rē·pāce′, *v.t.* to pace again.
rē·pāid′, *v.* past tense and past participle of *repay*.
rē·pāint′, *v.t* and *v.i.* to paint again.
rē′pāint, *n.* 1. anything repainted, as a part of a picture, a car, etc.
2. a repainting.
rē·pāir′, *v.i.* [OFr. *repairer*, from LL. *repatriare*; whence also Sp. *repatriar*, It. *ripatriare*; L. *re-*, back, and *patria*, one's native country, because a haunt is as one's *patria* or country.]
1. to go (*to* a place); to betake oneself; to resort; as, to *repair to* a sanctuary for safety.
Go, mount the winds, and *to* the shades *repair*. —Pope.
2. to go often, customarily, or in numbers; as, they *repaired* daily to the park.
3. to return. [Obs.]
rē·pāir′, *n.* 1. the act of betaking oneself to a place. [Archaic.]
2. a place to which a person or persons go often or customarily; a resort; a haunt. [Archaic.]
rē·pāir′, *v.t.*; repaired, *pt.*, *pp.*; repairing, *ppr.* [Fr. *réparer*; L. *reparare*, from *re-*, again, and *parare*, to get, to make ready.]
1. to restore to a sound or good state after decay, injury, dilapidation, or partial destruction; to mend; as, to *repair* a house, a wall, or a ship; to *repair* roads and bridges.
2. to renew; restore; revive; as, to *repair* one's health.
3. to amend; set right; remedy; as, *repair* the mistake.
4. to make amends for; to make up for; to compensate for (a wrong, injury, etc.).
rē·pāir′, *n.* 1. the act, process, or work of repairing; restoration to a sound or good state after decay, waste, injury, or partial destruction.
2. [*usually in pl.*] an instance, piece, or result of repairing.
3. the state of being repaired, or fit for use; as, the car was kept in *repair*.
4. state with respect to repairing; as, the house is in bad *repair*.
rē·pāir′á·ble, *a.* that may be repaired; reparable.
rē·pāir′ẽr, *n.* one who or that which repairs, restores, or makes amends; as, the *repairer* of decay.
rē·pāir′man, *n.*; *pl.* **rē·pāir′men,** a man whose work is repairing things.
rē·pāir′ment, *n.* the act of repairing. [Obs.]
rē·pand′, *a.* [L. *repandus*, bent back, turned up; *re-*, back, and *pandis*, bent, crooked.] in botany, having an uneven, slightly wavy margin, as the leaf of *Solanum nigrum*, or common nightshade.

REPAND LEAF (*Solanum nigrum*)

rē·pand′ous, *a.* [L. *repandus*, bent back.] bent upward; convexedly crooked. [Obs.]
rep″ȧ·rȧ·bil′i·ty, *n.* [L. *reparabilis*, that may be repaired.] the state or quality of being reparable.
rep′ȧ·rȧ·ble, *a.* [Fr. *réparable*; L. *reparabilis*, that may be repaired.] that can be repaired, mended, remedied, etc.; that can be restored to a sound or good state; capable of reparation; as, a *reparable* injury.
rep′ȧ·rȧ·bly, *adv.* so as to be reparable.
rep·ȧ·rā′tion, *n.* [LL. *reparatio* (*-onis*), a restoration, from L. *reparare*, to restore.]
1. a repairing or being repaired; restoration to good condition.
2. repairs.
3. a making of amends; a making up for a wrong or injury.
4. anything paid or done to make up for something else; compensation; specifically, [*usually pl.*], compensation by a defeated nation for damage done to civilians and their property in a war, payable in money, labor, goods, etc.
Syn.—recompense, atonement, indemnity, satisfaction, remuneration, restitution, repair.
rē·par′ȧ·tive, *a.* 1. having the quality or power of repairing; tending to repair.
2. of or involving reparation.
rē·par′ȧ·tive, *n.* that which repairs. [Obs.]
rē·par′el, *n.* a change of apparel. [Obs.]
rep·ăr·tee′, *n.* [Fr. *repartie*, from *repartir*, to return quickly a thrust or a blow, to reply; *re-*, and *partir*, from L. *partire*, to share, part, from *pars*, *partis*, a part.]
1. a quick, witty reply.
2. quick, witty conversation.
3. skill in making such replies.
A majority is always better than the best *repartee*. —Disraeli.
Syn.—retort, reply, answer.
rep·ăr·tee′, *v.i.* to make smart and witty replies. [Rare.]
re·pär·ti·mi·en′tō, *n.* [Sp.] a partition or distribution; especially, a grant of land given as a fief to the conquerors of Spanish America; also, an assessment of taxes.
rē·pär·ti′tion, *n.* 1. a partitioning; distribution.
2. a partitioning again; redistribution.
rē·pär·ti′tion, *v.t.* to effect a repartition of.
rē·påss′, *v.t.* to pass again; to pass or travel back again over; as, to *repass* a bridge or a river.
rē·påss′, *v.t.* to pass or go back or again; to move back; as, troops passing and *repassing* before our eyes.
rē·pas′sȧġe, *n.* 1. the act of repassing.
2. the right or privilege of repassing.
3. in gilding, the applying of a second coat of flat size as a finish to a mat surface.
rē·pas′sănt, *a.* [Fr., *ppr.* of *repasser*, to repass.] in heraldry, counterpassant.
rē·påst′, *n.* [Fr. *repas*, from LL. *repastus*; L. *re-*, and *pascere*, to feed.]
1. (a) food and drink for a meal; (b) a meal.
2. (a) the eating of food, as at a meal; (b) mealtime. [Archaic.]
From dance to sweet *repast* they turn. —Milton.
3. food; victuals. [Obs.]
4. figuratively, any refreshment, as sleep, repose, etc. [Obs.]
rē·påst′, *v.t.* to supply with food. [Obs.]
rē·påst′, *v.i.* to partake of food. [Obs.]
rē·påst′ẽr, *n.* a person who takes a repast. [Obs.]
rē·pås′tūre, *n.* food; entertainment. [Obs.]
rē·pā′tri·āte, *v.t.* and *v.i.*; repatriated, *pt.*, *pp.*; repatriating, *ppr.* [LL. *repatriatus*, pp. of *repatriare*; L. *re-*, back, and *patria*, native land.] to send back or return to the country of birth, citizenship, or allegiance; as, prisoners of war were *repatriated*.
rē·pā·tri·ā′tion, *n.* [ML. *repatriatio*.] a repatriating or being repatriated; return or restoration to one's own country.
rē·pāy′, *v.t.*; repaid, *pt.*, *pp.*; repaying, *ppr.* [OFr. *repaier*.]
1. to pay back (money); to refund.
2. to pay back (a person).
3. to make some return for; to compensate; as, to *repay* a kindness.
4. to give or make some return or recompense to (a person), as for some service.
5. to do or give (the same as has been received); as, to *repay* a visit.
Syn.—remunerate, reimburse, recompense, reward, requite, refund, restore.
rē·pāy′, *v.i.* 1. to make a repayment or return.
2. to reward or punish.
Vengeance is mine; I will *repay*. —Rom. xii. 19.
rē·pāy′, *v.t.* and *v.i.* to pay again or a second time.
rē·pāy′á·ble, *a.* that can or must be repaid; as, money lent *repayable* at the end of sixty days.
rē·pāy′ment, *n.* 1. a repaying or being repaid; reimbursement.
2. the money, thing, or amount repaid.
rē·pēal′, *v.t.*; repealed, *pt.*, *pp.*; repealing, *ppr.* [Fr. *rappeler*, to recall; L. *re-*, and *appellare*, to call upon, to speak.]
1. to recall, as from banishment, exile, or disgrace. [Obs.]
2. to withdraw officially or formally; to recall, as a deed, law, or statute; to abrogate by authority; to revoke; to rescind; to annul.
Until that act of parliament be *repealed*. —Shak.

Syn.—abrogate, annul, cancel, nullify, recall, reverse.

rē·pēal, *n.* 1. recall, as from exile. [Obs.]
2. a repealing; revocation; abrogation; as, the *repeal* of a statute.

rē·pēal·ȧ·bil′i·ty, *n.* the quality or state of being repealable.

rē·peal′ȧ·ble, *a.* capable of being repealed.

rē·pēal′ȧ·ble·ness, *n.* repealability.

rē·pēal′ēr, *n.* one who or that which repeals; one who advocates repeal; specifically, one who agitated for a repeal of the union between Great Britain and Ireland.

rē·pēal′ment, *n.* recall, as from banishment. [Obs.]

rē·pēat′, *v.t.*; repeated, *pt., pp.*; repeating, *ppr.* [Fr. *répéter*, from L. *repetere*; *re-*, again, and *petere*, to seek.]
1. to say or utter again; to reiterate; as, to *repeat* a remark.
2. to say over or through; to recite, as a poem.
3. to say after someone else.
4. to tell to someone else; as, to *repeat* a secret.
5. (a) to do or make again; to do over again; as, to *repeat* an operation; (b) to make happen again or undergo again; as to *repeat* an adventure.
6. to say again what has been said before by (oneself); as, he *repeats* himself.
7. to present (itself or themselves) again; as, these things have a way of *repeating* themselves.
Syn.—reiterate, rehearse, recapitulate, relate, recite, quote.

rē·peat′, *v.i.* 1. to do or say something a second time or again.
2. to recur; as, experiences *repeat*.
3. to vote more than once in an election: an illegal and punishable act.
4. to strike again the hour last struck, when a spring is pressed, as some timepieces equipped with striking apparatus.
5. to return, as undigested food, from the stomach to the mouth soon after eating, without the ordinary efforts of vomiting; to regurgitate.

rē·pēat′, *n.* 1. the act of repeating; a doing or saying again; repetition.
2. that which is repeated; anything said, done, or occurring again.
3. in music, (a) a passage repeated in playing; (b) the symbol for this (:||), placed after, and often before, (||:), a passage to be repeated.

rē·pēat′ed, *a.* [pp. of *repeat.*] said, made, done, or happening again, or again and again.

rē·pēat′ed·ly, *adv.* more than once; again and again; frequently.
Syn.—frequently, often.

rē·pēat′ēr, *n.* 1. a person or thing that repeats.
2. a watch or clock, especially a watch, which can be made to strike whatever hour (or, sometimes, quarter-hour) it has struck last.
3. a person who has been in jail for the same crime, or in the same jail, more than once.
4. a person who fraudulently votes more than once in the same election.
5. in education, a student who takes again a course or courses in which he has previously failed.
6. in mathematics, a repeating decimal.
7. formerly, a vessel, usually a frigate, appointed to attend each admiral in a fleet, and to repeat every signal he made, with which it immediately sailed to the ship for which it was intended, or the whole length of the fleet when the signal was general: also called *repeating ship*.
8. a repeating rifle or pistol.
9. in calico printing, a figure appearing at equal intervals in a pattern.
10. a flag indicating that a certain flag in a display of signals is to be repeated.
11. in telegraphy, a device whereby the relay, sounder, or registering apparatus is caused to repeat the signals received, by opening and closing another circuit with which it is suitably connected.

rē·pēat′ing, *a.* performing the same functions over again.
repeating circle; an instrument constructed on the principle of the sextant, for measuring angular distances.
repeating decimal; (a) a decimal in which one digit is repeated infinitely (e.g., .23333 . . .); (b) a circulating decimal: see *circulate, v.i.* 4.
repeating firearm; a firearm which may be caused to fire a number of successive shots without reloading.
repeating instrument; in astronomy, surveying, etc. an instrument upon which several successive measurements of the angle may be taken, each beginning at the point where the last measurement ended. The object of the method is to eliminate as far as possible errors of graduation.
repeating relay; in telegraphy, a relay for repeating the signals through a second line.
repeating ship; see *repeater*, 7.
repeating sounder; in telegraphy, a sounder which repeats a message into another circuit.
repeating telegraphic station; a station on a long telegraphic line, at which the currents received from one section of the line are repeated into the other section by means of a repeater.
repeating telephone coil; an induction coil with two equal windings, each one being connected to a telephone circuit, thus obtaining close inductive association.

rep·ē·dā′tion, *n.* [LL. *repedatus*, pp. of *repedare*, to step back; L. *re-*, back, and *pes, pedis*, foot.] retrogression. [Obs.]

rē·pel′, *v.t.*; repelled, *pt., pp.*; repelling, *ppr.* [ME. *repellen*; It. *repellere*, from L. *repellere*, to drive back; *re-*, back, and *pellere*, to drive.]
1. to drive back; to force to return; to check the advance of; to ward off; as, to *repel* an enemy or an assailant.
2. to refuse; to reject; as, to *repel* advances.
3. to refuse to accept (a person); to spurn; as, to *repel* a suitor.
4. to cause distaste or dislike in; as, the odor *repels* me.
5. to be resistant to, or present an opposing force to; as, a plastic coating *repels* moisture.
6. to fail to mix with; as, water *repels* oil.
Opposed to *attract* (in senses 4, 5, 6).

rē·pel′, *v.i.* 1. to drive off, or offer an opposing force to, something.
2. to cause distaste, dislike, or aversion.
Syn.—repulse, reject, refuse, defeat, oppose, resist.

rē·pel′lence, *n.* 1. the quality or state of being repellent.
2. capacity of repelling.

rē·pel′len·cy, *n.* repellence.

rē·pel′lent, *a.* [L. *repellens (-entis)*, ppr. of *repellere*, to drive back.]
1. repelling; pushing away or driving back.
2. causing distaste, dislike, or aversion; repulsive.
3. able to repel water; waterproof; as, *repellent* cloth.

rē·pel′lent, *n.* something that repels; specifically, (a) a waterproof fabric; (b) any substance, as lime, oil, etc., used to drive away plant pests or other insects; (c) in medicine, anything used to reduce a tumor, swelling, etc.

rē·pel′lēr, *n.* one who or that which repels.

rē′pent, *a.* [L. *repens (-entis)*, ppr. of *repere*, to creep.]
1. in botany, creeping; lying flat on the ground and emitting roots.
2. in zoology, reptant; creeping or crawling.

rē·pent′, *v.i.*; repented, *pt., pp.*; repenting, *ppr.* [OFr. *repentir*, from L. *re-*, again, and *pœnitere*, to repent (used impersonally), from *pœna*, punishment.]
1. to feel pain, sorrow, or regret for something one has done or left undone; to be conscience-stricken or contrite (often with *of*).
2. to change one's mind about some past action, intention, etc. in consequence of regret or dissatisfaction; as, he *repented* of his generosity.
3. in theology, to feel such sorrow for sin as leads to amendment of one's ways; to be penitent.

rē·pent′, *v.t.* 1. to remember with sorrow; to feel contrition or remorse for (an error, sin, etc.); as, to *repent* rash words.
2. to feel such regret or dissatisfaction over as to change one's mind about; as, he *repented* his generosity.
3. to be sorry; to regret: used reflexively. [Archaic.]
4. to cause to have regret: used impersonally. [Archaic.]

rē·pent′ȧ·ble, *a.* capable of being repented of; admitting of repentance.

rē·pent′ănce, *n.* [OFr. *repentance, repentaunce*; LL. *repenitens (-entis)*, penitent.] the act of repenting or the state of being penitent; sorrow or regret for what has been done or left undone by oneself; especially, sorrow and contrition for sin; such sorrow for the past as leads to amendment of one's ways; penitence; contrition.
Syn.—compunction, regret; remorse, sorrow, self-reproach, self-condemnation.

rē·pent′ănt, *a.* 1. feeling or experiencing repentance or sorrow for past conduct or words; contrite; penitent.
2. expressive of or indicating repentance or sorrow for the past; springing from or caused by repentance.

rē·pent′ănt, *n.* one who repents; a penitent. [Obs.]

rē·pent′ănt·ly, *adv.* in a repentant manner.

rē·pent′ēr, *n.* one who repents.

rē·pent′ing·ly, *adv.* with repentance.

rē·pent′less, *a.* without repentance. [Rare.]

rē·pēo′ple, *v.t.* [Fr. *repeupler.*] 1. to people anew; to provide with new inhabitants.
2. to restock with animals.

rē·pēr·çuss′, *v.t.* to beat back. [Obs.]

rē·pēr·çus′sion (-kush′un), *n.* [L. *repercussio*, from pp. of *repercutere*, to rebound, strike back.]
1. a driving back or being driven back by something resistant; rebound; recoil.
2. reflection, as of light or sound; reverberation; echo.
3. a reaction; action set in motion by an event or action, often very remote; as, the explosion of the first atomic bomb had *repercussions* all over the world.
4. in medicine, (a) the action of a repellent in reducing a swelling, tumor, etc.; (b) ballottement.
5. in music, (a) reiteration of a tone or chord; (b) reappearance of the subject and answer after an episode in a fugue.

rē·pēr·çus′sive, *a.*]Fr. *répercussif.*] causing, caused by, or having the nature of, repercussion; reverberating or reverberated.

rē·pēr·çuss′ive, *n.* in medicine, a repellent. [Obs.]

rep′ēr·toire (-twär), *n.* [Fr.] a repertory; the stock of operas, dramas, etc. which can be readily performed by a company, from their familiarity with them; those parts, songs, etc. which are usually performed by an actor or vocalist; hence, generally, a number of things which can be readily and efficiently done by a person in consequence of his familiarity with them.

rep′ēr·tō·ry, *n.*; *pl.* **rep′ēr·tō·ries,** [LL. *repertorium*, an inventory, from *repertor*, a discoverer, from L. *repertus*, pp. of *reperire*, to find out, to discover.]
1. an index; a list; a catalogue. [Obs.]
2. that which contains a store or collection of things; a storehouse; a treasury; a magazine; a repository.
3. the things stored; stock; collection.
4. a repertoire.

rep′ēr·tō·ry thē′ȧ·tēr, a theater in which a permanent acting company presents a varied selection of plays.

rep′ē·tend, *n.* [L. *repetendus*, to be repeated, gerundive of *repetere*, to repeat.]
1. in mathematics, the digit or digits repeated indefinitely in a repeating or circulating decimal.
2. in music, a repeated sound or phrase, as a refrain.

rep·ē·ti′tion (-tish′un), *n.* [L. *repetitio (-onis)*, a demanding back, from *repetere*, to seek again, repeat.]
1. the act of repeating; the act of doing or saying the same thing a second time or again and again; iteration of the same act, word, or idea.
2. recitation, as of something memorized.
3. that which is repeated or made by repeating; specifically, a reproduction, copy, or replica.
4. in music, the frequent and rapid iteration of the same tone or chord in such a manner as to produce a continuous sound.
5. in rhetoric, the iteration or repeating of the same words, or of the meaning in different words, for the purpose of making a deeper impression on the audience.
6. in Scots law, the repayment of money paid in error.
7. in surveying and astronomy, the use of a series of successive observations in measuring an angle.
Syn.—iteration, reiteration.

rep·ē·ti′tion·ăl, *a.* containing repetition. [Rare.]

rep·ē·ti′tion·ăr·y, *a.* same as *repetitional.*

rep·ē·ti′tious (-tish′us), *a.* containing or characterized by repetition; marked by useless or tiresome repetition.

rē·pet′i·tive, *a.* of or containing repetition; repeating; repetitious.

rē·phrāṣe′, *v.t.* to phrase again, anew, or in a different way.

rē·pīne′, *n.* discontent; murmur. [Obs.]

rē·pīne′, *v.i.*; repined, *pt., pp.*; repining, *ppr.* [OE. *repoyne*; OFr. *repoindre*, to prick again, from L. *re-*, again, and *pungere*, to prick; influenced in its form by E. *pine*, to languish.]

1. to fret oneself; to be discontented; to complain discontentedly (often with *at*).

2. to fail; to grow less or weaker. [Obs.]

rē·pīn′ēr, *n.* one who repines.

rē·pïque′ (-pēk′), *v.t.*; repiqued, *pt., pp.*; repiquing, *ppr.* to score a repique against.

rē·pïque′, *v.i.* at piquet, to count thirty points in hand before the adversary counts one.

rē·pïque′, *n.* [Fr. *repic*, repique; *re-*, and *piquer*, to prick, thrust.] at piquet, a scoring of thirty points in hand before the adversary can count one, entitling the player to an initial score of ninety.

rē·plāce′, *v.t.*; replaced (-plāst), *pt., pp.*; replacing, *ppr.* 1. to put again in or restore to a former place, position, rank, office, etc.

2. to put back or pay back; to repay; to refund; to return; as, to *replace* a sum of money borrowed.

3. to fill the place of with a substitute or equivalent; to provide an equivalent for; as, to *replace* a worn tire.

4. to take the place of; to supplant; to be a substitute for; to succeed to; to supersede; to displace.

Syn.—restore, substitute, reinstate.

replaced crystal; a crystal with one or more planes in the place of its edges or angles.

rē·plāce′á·ble, *a.* capable of being replaced.

rē·plāce′ment, *n.* 1. the act of replacing or the state of being replaced.

2. a person or thing that takes the place of another, especially of one that has worn out, broken down, etc.

3. a member of the armed forces who is available for assignment to fill a vacancy or complete a quota; reinforcement.

4. in crystallography, the replacing of an angle or edge by one face or more.

rē·plāc′ēr, *n.* one who or that which replaces.

rē·plēad′ēr, *n.* [*re-* and obs. *pleader*; cf. Fr. *replaider*, OFr. *repledoier.*] in law, (a) a second pleading; (b) the right or privilege of pleading again; (c) a court order requiring the parties to plead again from that point in the pleading where an error first occurred.

rē·plen′ish, *v.t.*; replenished, *pt., pp.*; replenishing, *ppr.* [OFr. *replenissant*, ppr. of *replenir*, to fill again, from L. *re-*, again, and *plenus*, full.]

1. to make full or complete again, as by furnishing a new supply; as, *replenish* the stock of goods.

2. to supply again with fuel or the like.

3. to repeople.

Be fruitful, and multiply, and *replenish* the earth. —Gen. i. 28.

4. to finish; to complete; to consummate. [Obs.]

Syn.—fill, refill, restock, supply.

rē·plen′ish, *v.i.* to recover former fullness. [Obs.]

rē·plen′ish·ēr, *n.* 1. a person or thing that replenishes.

2. in electricity, an electrostatic influence machine for charging a quadrant electrometer or other electrostatic device.

rē·plen′ish·ment, *n.* 1. a replenishing or being replenished.

2. a fresh supply.

rē·plēte′, *a.* [L. *repletus*, pp. of *replere*, to fill again; *re-*, again, and *plere*, to fill.]

1. well filled; plentifully supplied; as, his words *replete* with guile.

2. stuffed, as with food; gorged.

rē·plēte′, *v.t.*; repleted, *pt., pp.*; repleting, *ppr.* to fill full; to surfeit. [Obs.]

rē·plēte′ness, *n.* the state of being replete.

rē·plē′tion, *n.* [Fr., from L. *repletio.*]

1. the state of being replete; a being completely filled or too full.

2. in medicine, fullness of blood; plethora.

rē·plē′tive, *a.* filling; replenishing.

rē·plē′tive·ly, *adv.* in a replete manner; fully.

rē·plē′tō·ry, *a.* repletive; relating to repletion; filling. [Rare.]

rē·plev′i·á·ble, *a.* in law, that can be replevied.

rē·plev′ied, *v.* past tense and past participle of *replevy.*

rē·plev′in, *n.* [OFr. *replevin*, from *replevir*, to warrant, to pledge.] in law, (a) the recovery by a person of goods claimed to be his, on his promise to test the matter in court and give the goods up again if defeated; (b) the writ by which he takes over the goods.

rē·plev′in, *v.t.*; replevined, *pt., pp.*; replevining, *ppr.* to replevy.

rē·plev′i·sá·ble, *a.* repleviable.

rē·plev′y, *v.t.*; replevied, *pt., pp.*; replevying, *ppr.* [OFr. *replevir*; LL. *replegiare*, to give bail, surety, from *plegium*, pledge, bail, security.]

1. to obtain or recover possession of by an action of replevin; to take back (goods) by a writ of replevin.

2. to release (a man) from prison when he has found bail to guarantee his return later. [Rare.]

rē·plev′y, *n.* replevin.

rep′li·çȧ, *n.* [It. *replica*, a reply, a repetition, from L. *replicare*, to repeat, to reply; *re-*, back, and *plica*, fold.]

1. a reproduction or copy of a work of art; especially, a copy made by the maker of the original.

2. any very close reproduction or copy; facsimile.

3. in music, a passage to be repeated; a repeat.

con replica; in music, with repetition.

rep′li·çănt, *n.* [L. *replicans* (*-antis*) ppr. of *replicare*, to fold back.] one who replies; a replier. [Obs.]

rep′li·çāte, *v.t.*; replicated, *pt., pp.*; replicating, *ppr.* [L. *replicatus*, pp. of *replicare*, to fold back; *re-*, back, and *plicare*, to fold.]

1. to fold or bend back, as a leaf.

2. to reply. [Rare.]

3. to repeat. [Rare.]

rep′li·çāte, *a.* in botany and entomology, folded back on itself, as a leaf in estivation or vernation, or a wing of an insect.

rep′li·çāte, *n.* in music, a tone repeated one or more octaves higher or lower than another.

rep′li·çāt·ed, *a.* replicate.

rē·pliç′á·tile, *a.* in entomology, of such a nature as to admit of folding back upon itself: said of the wing of an insect.

rep·li·çā′tion, *n.* [L. *replicatio* (*-onis*).]

1. an answer; a reply; especially, a reply to an answer.

2. in law pleadings, the reply of the plaintiff to the defendant's plea.

3. return or repercussion of sound; an echo.

4. a copying.

5. a copy; a repetition; a replica.

6. a doubling or folding over of a surface; a fold.

7. in music, the employment of a replicate or replicates. [Obs.]

8. in logic, the repetition of a term in the same proposition. [Obs.]

rep′li·çā·tive, *a.* accomplishing or containing replication.

rē·plī′ēr, *n.* one who answers; one who speaks or writes in reply to something spoken or written; a replicant.

rep′lum, *n.* in botany, the persistent frame of a pod after the valves fall away, as in certain cruciferous plants.

rē·plūme′, *v.t.* to preen; to rearrange and clean, as feathers.

rē·plȳ′, *v.i.*; replied, *pt., pp.*; replying, *ppr.* [Fr. *réplier*, to fold or double back, formerly to reply (though in French *répliquer* is to reply), from L. *replicare*, to fold back, to make a reply; *re-*, back, and *plicare*, to fold.]

1. to answer; to make a return in words or in writing to something said or written by another.

O man, who art thou that *repliest* against God? —Rom. ix. 20.

2. in law, to answer a defendant's plea.

3. to give answer by some action; as, to *reply* to an enemy's guns.

4. to echo.

Syn.—retort, answer, respond, rejoin, return.

rē·plȳ′, *v.t.* to return for an answer; to say in answer; as, he knows not what to *reply.*

rē·plȳ′, *n.*; *pl.* **rē·plīeṣ′,** 1. an answer; that which is said or written in answer to what is said or written by another; a response.

2. the making of an answer by means of some action.

3. in law, a response to a plea.

4. in music, the answer to the leading theme, subject, or principal in a fugue.

Syn.—rejoinder, answer.—A *reply* is a distinct response to a formal question or attack; a *rejoinder* is a second reply (a reply to a reply) in a protracted discussion or controversy.

ré·pon·dez′ s'il vous plaît (rā-pōṅ-dā′ sēl vo͞o ple′) [Fr.] please reply: placed on formal invitations: abbreviated *R.S.V.P.*, *r.s.v.p.*

rē·pōne′, *v.t.* [L. *reponere*, to place or put back.] in Scots law, to replace.

rē·pōrt′, *v.t.*; reported, *pt., pp.*; reporting, *ppr.* [Fr. *reporter*, to carry back; also *rapporter*, to carry back, to relate or report; the former from L. *reportare*; *re-*, again, and *portare*, to carry.]

1. to give an account of, often at regular intervals; to give information about, as something seen or investigated; to say.

2. to carry and repeat (a message, etc.).

3. to write an account of for presentation to others or for publication, as in a newspaper.

4. to give a formal statement or account of; to announce formally, as the results of an investigation.

5. to present or return (something referred for study, action, etc.) with the conclusions reached or recommendations made (often with *out*); as, the committee *reported* the bill *out.*

6. to complain about; to denounce to a person in authority; as, *report* a rudeness, *report* a salesgirl to the manager.

7. to tell or relate from one to another; to circulate publicly, as a story, as in the common phrase, it is *reported.*

8. to return, as sound; to give back. [Obs.]

9. to picture; to describe in a graphic manner. [Obs.]

10. to appeal to for information or credit. [Obs.]

Syn.—announce, relate, circulate, notify, recite, communicate, declare.

rē·pōrt′, *v.i.* 1. to make a report or a statement of facts; as, the committee will *report* at twelve o'clock.

2. to work as a reporter; to furnish for publication an account of a meeting, the words of a speech, etc.

3. to present oneself; to announce one's presence or whereabouts, etc.; to fulfill an engagement or appear for duty.

rē·pōrt′, *n.* 1. rumor; gossip; common talk; as, *report* has it that you are married.

2. reputation; as, a man of good *report.*

3. a statement or account brought in and presented, often for publication; as, a *report* of a battle.

4. a formal or official presentation of facts or of the record of something, as an investigation, law case, etc.

5. an account or statement of a judicial opinion or decision, or of a case argued and determined in a court of law or chancery.

6. [*pl.*] books containing a record of court cases, decisions, etc.

7. the noise made by an explosion; as, the *report* of a gun.

8. connection; rapport; reference; relation. [Obs.]

Syn.—tidings, announcement, narration, recital, communication, declaration, news, rumor, fame, repute, noise, reverberation.

rē·pōrt′á·ble, *a.* that can be reported; deserving to be reported.

rē·pōrt′ăġe, *n.* report. [Obs.]

rē·pōrt′ çärd, a written report of a pupil's grades, deportment, etc., sent to his parents or guardian at regular intervals.

rē·pōrt′ēr, *n.* [ME. *reportour*; OFr. *reporteur.*] a person who reports; especially, (a) a person authorized to report legal or legislative proceedings; as, a court *reporter*; (b) a person who gathers information and writes reports for publication in a newspaper, magazine, etc.

rē·pōrt′ing, *n.* the occupation or business of a reporter, especially of one who reports news for a newspaper or the official proceedings of a court; the business of securing reports.

rē·pōrt′ing·ly, *adv.* by report or common fame. [Obs.]

rep·ōr·tō′ri·ăl, *a.* of, characteristic of, like, or pertaining to a reporter or to reporting, especially to newspaper reporters and their work; as, a *reportorial* staff; *reportorial* ability.

rē·pōṣ′ăl, *n.* 1. the act of reposing or resting; as, the *reposal* of a trust.

2. that on which one reposes. [Obs.]

His pillow and chief *reposal.* —Burton.

rē·pōṣ′ănce, *n.* the act of reposing; repose. [Obs.]

rē-pōṣe′, *v.t.* and *v.i.* to pose again or anew.

rē·pōṣe′, *v.t.*; reposed, *pt., pp.*; reposing, *ppr.* [ME. *reposen*, from L. *repositus*, after verbs in *-pose*, as *dispose*.]
 1. to place; put. [Rare.]
 2. to place (trust, confidence, etc. *in* someone).

rē·pōṣe′, *v.t.*; reposed, *pt., pp.*; reposing, *ppr.* [Fr. *reposer*, to settle, to rest, from L. *re-*, again, and *pausare*, to pause, to rest.] to lay or put to rest: often reflexive; as, *repose* yourself on the bed.

rē·pōṣe′, *v.i.* 1. to lie at rest.
 2. to rest from work, travel, exercise, etc.
 3. to rest in a grave; as, he *reposes* at Arlington Cemetery.
 4. to rest in confidence; to depend; to rely; followed by *in, on,* or *upon*; as, to *repose on* the faith and honor of a friend. [Archaic.]
 5. to lie quiet and calm; as, the land *reposes* in the dusk.
 6. to lie, rest, or be supported; as, the shale *reposes on* a bed of limestone.
 Syn.—recline, lie, slumber, rest, settle.

rē·pōṣe′, *n.* [Fr. *repos*; It. *riposo*; Sp. *reposo*, repose.]
 1. the act or state of reposing; a lying at rest.
 2. (a) rest; (b) sleep.
 3. peace of mind; freedom from uneasiness, worry, or troubles.
 4. calm, ease, or composure of manner.
 5. calm; tranquillity; peace.
 6. harmony of form or color, giving an effect of tranquillity, as in a painting.
 angle of repose; that angle at which one body will just rest upon another without slipping, and which varies, of course, with the natures of the bodies in contact, but is constant for the same bodies.
 Syn.—quietness, peace, calmness, tranquillity, rest.

rē·pōṣed′, *a.* exhibiting repose; calm; settled.

rē·pōṣ′ed·ly, *adv.* in a reposed manner; composedly; quietly.

rē·pōṣ′ed·ness, *n.* the state of being reposed.

rē·pōṣe′fụl, *a.* full of repose; affording repose or rest.

rē·pōṣ′ẽr, *n.* one who reposes.

rē·poṣ′it, *v.t.*; reposited, *pt., pp.*; repositing, *ppr.* [L. *repositus*, pp. of *reponere*, to lay up, to put back; from *re-*, back, and *ponere*, to place.]
 1. to lay up; to store; to deposit (*in* some place), as for safety or preservation.
 2. to replace. [Rare.]

rē·pō·ṣi′tion (-zish′un), *n.* 1. the act of repositing or the state of being reposited.
 2. the act of replacing, as a part of the body in a surgical operation.
 3. in Scots law, retrocession, or the returning back of a right from the assignee to the person granting the right. [Archaic.]

rē·poṣ′i·tŏr, *n.* 1. one who or that which replaces.
 2. a surgical instrument used to replace some organ, as in prolapse.

rē·poṣ′i·tō·ry, *n.*; *pl.* **rē·poṣ′i·tō·rieṣ,** [L. *repositorium*, from *reponere*.]
 1. a box, chest, closet, or room in which things may be placed for safekeeping.
 2. a building for safekeeping; a museum. [Rare.]
 3. a warehouse or shop.
 4. a burial vault; a sepulcher.
 5. anything thought of as a place of accumulation or storage.
 6. a person to whom something is entrusted or confided; a confidant.

rē·poṣ′i·tō·ry, *a.* pertaining to or adapted to storage.

rē·poṣ·sess′, *v.t.*; repossessed (-zest), *pt., pp.*; repossessing, *ppr.* 1. to possess again; to regain ownership of.
 2. to put in possession again; as, they *repossessed* him of his house.

rē·poṣ·ṣes′sion (-zesh′un), *n.* a repossessing or being repossessed.

rē·pō′ṣūre, *n.* a state of repose; quietness. [Obs.]

re·pöus″sāġe′ (-pö″säzh′), *n.* [Fr. *repousser*, to beat back.] the art or process of making repoussé work.

re·pous″sé′ (re-pö″sā′), *a.* [Fr., pp. of *repousser*, to push back; *re-*, back, and *pousser*.]
 1. formed in relief, as a pattern on thin metal beaten up from the underside.
 2. shaped or decorated with patterns made in this way.

re·pous″sé′, *n.* 1. a repoussé pattern or surface.
 2. the art or process of hammering metal in this way.

repp, *n.* rep (fabric).

repped (rept), *a.* corded or ribbed transversely.

rē·preef′, rē·prēfe′, *n.* reproof; censure. [Obs.]

rep·rē·hend′, *v.t.*; reprehended, *pt., pp.*; reprehending, *ppr.* [L. *reprehendere*, to hold back, to check, to blame; *re-*, back, and *prehendere*, to hold, seize.]
 1. to reprimand; to rebuke; to reprove.
 2. to find fault with; to censure; to blame.
 3. to convict of fallacy. [Obs.]
 Syn.—chide, blame, reprimand, rebuke.

rep·rē·hend′ẽr, *n.* one who reprehends, blames, or censures.

rep·rē·hen·si·bil′i·ty, *n.* the state or quality of being reprehensible; reprehensibleness.

rep·rē·hen′si·ble, *a.* [L. *reprehensus*, pp. of *reprehendere*, to reprehend.] blamable; culpable; censurable; deserving reproof; as, a *reprehensible* person; *reprehensible* conduct.

rep·rē·hen′si·ble·ness, *n.* culpableness; blamableness.

rep·rē·hen′si·bly, *adv.* 1. in a reprehensible manner.
 2. to a reprehensible degree.

rep·rē·hen′sion, *n.* [L. *reprehensio* (*-onis*), from *reprehensus*, pp. of *reprehendere*, to reprehend.] the act of reprehending; reproof; censure; open blame.

rep·rē·hen′sive, *a.* containing reproof; having the nature of, or conveying, reprehension; censuring. [Now Rare.]

rep·rē·hen′sive·ly, *adv.* reprovingly. [Now Rare.]

rep·rē·hen′sō·ry, *a.* reprehensive. [Now Rare.]

rē·prē·mi·ā′tion, *n.* a rewarding. [Obs.]

rep·rē·ṣent′, *v.t.*; represented, *pt., pp.*; representing, *ppr.* [Fr. *représenter*; L. *repræsentare*, to place or bring before one, to show, to manifest, from *re-*, again, and *præsentare*, to hold out, to present, from *præsens*, present.]
 1. to present or picture to the mind; to put clearly before the mind.
 2. (a) to present a likeness or image of; to portray; to depict; (b) to be a likeness or image of, as a picture or statue is.
 3. to present in words; to describe, state, or set forth; often, to do so forcibly or earnestly, so as to influence action, persuade hearers, make effective protest, etc.; as, he *represented* the war as already lost.

 The managers of the bank at Genoa have been *represented* as a second kind of senate. —Addison.

 4. (a) to be a sign for; to stand for; to denote; to designate; to symbolize; as, x *represents* the unknown; (b) to denote or express by symbols, characters, etc.; as, *represent* mathematical quantities by letters.
 5. to be the equivalent of; to correspond to, as in a different place or time; as, a cave *represented* home to these people.
 6. (a) to present, produce, or perform (a play, etc.); (b) to play the part of; to impersonate (a character), as in a drama.
 7. to act or stand in place of; to be an agent, proxy, or substitute for.
 8. to speak and act for by duly conferred authority, as an ambassador for his country or a legislator for his constituents.
 9. to serve as a specimen, example, type, or instance of; to exemplify or typify.
 Syn.—portray, delineate, reproduce, exhibit, personate, state, describe, indicate, embody, enact, illustrate, denote, play, dramatize, resemble.

rē-prē·ṣent′, *v.t.* to present again; to present anew.

rep·rē·ṣent·ȧ·bil′i·ty, *n.* the quality of being representable.

rep·rē·ṣent′ȧ·ble, *a.* capable of being represented.

rep″rē·ṣen·tā′men, *n.* [L. *repræsentare*, to represent.] an object which is the consequence of representation.

rep·rē·ṣent′ănce, *n.* representation; likeness. [Obs.]

rep·rē·ṣent′ănt, *a.* [L. *repræsentans* (*-antis*), ppr. of *repræsentare*, to place or bring before one, to show, to manifest.] representing another; acting or appearing for another. [Rare.]

rep·rē·ṣent′ănt, *n.* a representative. [Rare.]

rep·rē·ṣen·tā′tion, *n.* [L. *repræsentatio* (*-onis*), a showing, exhibiting, manifesting, from *repræsentatus*, pp. of *repræsentare*, to represent.]
 1. act or instance of representing, or the state, fact, or mode of being represented (in various senses).
 2. a likeness, image, picture, etc.
 3. any exhibition of the form or operations of a thing by something resembling it.
 4. [*often in pl.*] a description, account, or statement of facts, allegations, or arguments, especially one intended to influence action, persuade hearers, make protest, etc.
 5. presentation, production, or performance of a play, etc.
 6. the part performed by a representative, delegate, agent, or deputy; especially, the functions of a representative in a legislative assembly; the system according to which communities, districts, counties, etc. are represented in such assemblies.
 7. a number of delegates or representatives collectively.
 8. the standing in the place of another, as an heir or in the right of taking by inheritance.
 9. in law, a statement or implication of fact, oral or written, as made by one party to induce another to enter into a contract.
 Syn.—description, show, delineation, portraiture, likeness, resemblance, exhibition.

rē-prē·ṣen·tā′tion, *n.* the act or process of re-presenting; presenting anew or again.

rep″rē·ṣen·tā′tion·ăl, *a.* of or characterized by representation.

rep″rē·ṣen·tā′tion·ăr·y, *a.* pertaining to or characterized by representation; representative. [Rare.]

rep·rē·ṣent′ȧ·tive, *a.* [Fr. *représentatif*; LL. *repræsentativus*, from L. *repræsentare*, to represent.]
 1. representing or serving to represent; specifically, (a) picturing; portraying; reproducing; (b) acting or speaking, especially by due authority, in the place, or on behalf, of another or others; serving as an agent, deputy, or delegate, especially in a legislative assembly.
 2. composed of persons duly authorized, as by election, to act and speak for others; as, a *representative* assembly.
 3. of, characterized by, or based on representation of the people by elected delegates; as, *representative* government.
 4. being an example or type of a certain class or kind of thing; typical; as, Detroit is a *representative* American city.
 5. in botany and zoology, corresponding to, or taking the place of, some other form of plant or animal, as in a different area.

rep·rē·ṣent′ȧ·tive, *n.* 1. a person or thing enough like the others in its class or kind to serve as an example or type of the class or kind.
 2. a person duly authorized to act or speak for another or others; agent, delegate, deputy, etc., as a member of an elected legislative body.
 3. [R–] a member of the lower house of Congress (*House of Representatives*) or of a State legislature.
 4. in law, one who stands in the place of another as heir or in the right of succeeding to an estate of inheritance.
 5. that by which anything is exhibited or shown. [Obs.]
 House of Representatives; the lower branch of the legislature of: (a) the United States; (b) most of the States of the United States; (c) Australia; (d) New Zealand; (e) Mexico.
 Syn.—agent, commissioner, proxy, deputy, substitute, embodiment, personation, delegate, vicar, vicegerent, principal.

rep·rē·ṣent′ȧ·tive·ly, *adv.* 1. in the character of another; by a representative.
 2. by substitution; by delegation of power.

rep·rē·ṣent′ȧ·tive·ness, *n.* the state or quality of being representative.

rep·rē·ṣent′ẽr, *n.* 1. one who shows, exhibits, or describes.
 2. a representative; one who acts by deputation. [Obs.]

rep·rē·ṣent′ment, *n.* representation; image; an idea proposed as exhibiting the likeness of something. [Rare.]

rē-press′, *v.t.* to press anew.

rē·press′, *v.t.*; repressed (-prest′), *pt., pp.*; repressing, *ppr.* [L. *repressus*, pp. of *reprimere*, to check, hold back; *re-*, back, and *premere*, to press.]
 1. to crush; to quell; to put down; to subdue; to suppress; as, to *repress* sedition or rebellion; to *repress* the first risings of discontent.

2. to check; to keep down; to hold back; to restrain.
3. to prevent the natural development or expression of; to control too strictly or severely; as, the parents *repressed* their child.
4. in psychiatry, (a) to force (ideas, impulses, etc. painful to the conscious mind) into the unconscious, where they still modify behavior or remain dynamic; (b) to prevent (unconscious ideas, impulses, etc.) from reaching the level of consciousness.

rē·press′, *n.* the act of repressing. [Obs.]

rē·pressed′ (-prest′), *a.* [pp. of *repress.*] affected by, showing, or resulting from repression.

rē·press′ēr, *n.* one who or that which represses.

rē·press′i·ble, *a.* capable of being repressed.

rē·pres′sion (-presh′un), *n.* 1. the act of repressing or the condition of being repressed; as, the *repression* of tumults.
2. in psychiatry, what is repressed.

rē·press′ive, *a.* having power to repress; tending or serving to repress.
The task of medieval municipality was no merely *repressive* one. —W. J. Ashley.

rē·press′ive·ly, *adv.* in a repressive manner.

rē·press′ŏr, *n.* one who represses.

rē·prēv′ȧ·ble, *a.* reprovable. [Obs.]

rē·prēve′, *v.t.* to reprove. [Obs.]

rē·prēve′, rē·priēfe′, *n.* reproof. [Obs.]

rē·priēv′ăl, *n.* respite; reprieve. [Obs.]

rē·priēve′, *v.t.*; reprieved (-prēvd′), *pt., pp.*; reprieving, *ppr.* [earlier *repry*, from Fr. *repris*, pp. of *reprendre*, to take back.]
1. to delay the punishment of (a person); especially, to postpone the execution of (a person condemned to death); as, to *reprieve* a criminal for thirty days.
2. to give temporary relief to, as from pain.
Company, though it may *reprieve* a man from his melancholy, yet cannot secure a man from his conscience. —South.
3. to postpone; to defer (something evil).
4. to acquit. [Obs.]

rē·priēve′, *n.* a reprieving or being reprieved; specifically, (a) postponement of a penalty, especially that of death, or a warrant ordering this; (b) a temporary relief or escape, as from pain or evil.

rep′ri·mȧnd, *n.* [OFr. *reprimande*, from L. *reprimenda*, a thing that ought to be repressed, f. gerundive of *reprimere*, to repress.] severe reproof for a fault; especially, a formal rebuke by a person in authority.

rep′ri·mȧnd, *v.t.*; reprimanded, *pt., pp.*; reprimanding, *ppr.* 1. to reprove severely; to reprehend; to chide for a fault.
2. to reprove publicly and officially in execution of a sentence; as, the court ordered the officer to be *reprimanded*.

rep′ri·mȧnd·ēr, *n.* one who reprimands.

rē·prīm′ēr, *n.* a machine for applying a fresh primer to a cartridge shell, enabling it to be used again.

rē·print′, *v.t.*; reprinted, *pt., pp.*; reprinting *ppr.* 1. to print again; to print a new or further edition or impression of, usually without change.
2. to renew the impression of. [Rare.]

rē′print, *n.* 1. something reprinted; specifically, (a) a new or further impression or edition, usually without change, of something previously printed, as a book, pamphlet, etc.; especially, such an impression or edition issued by another publisher and intended for sale at a lower price; (b) a separately printed excerpt, as of an article published in a magazine; an offprint; (c) in philately, a stamp, not to be used for postage, printed from the original plate, often with different paper and ink, after the issue of the stamps has ceased.
2. a reprinting.
3. copy in the form of printed matter, as distinguished from *manuscript*.

rē·print′ēr, *n.* one who reprints.

rē·prī′ṣăl, *n.* [Fr. *représaille*, from LL. *reprisaliæ*, from L. *reprehendere*, to take back.]
1. originally, the forcible seizure of property or subjects in retaliation for an injury inflicted by another country.
2. the act or practice of using force, short of war, against another nation to obtain redress of grievances.
3. injury done, or the doing of injury, in return for injury received, with intent to inflict at least as much harm as has been suffered; retaliation or an act of retaliation, especially in war, as the killing of prisoners.
4. whatever is taken from an enemy to indemnify an owner for something of his which the enemy has seized. [Obs.]
5. recaption; a retaking of a man's own goods wrongfully taken from him or detained by another. [Obs.]
letters of marque and reprisal; see under *letter*.

rē·prīṣe′, *n.* [ME.; OFr., from *repris*, pp. of *reprendre*, to take.]
1. a taking by way of retaliation. [Obs.]
2. a ship or other property recaptured from a pirate or a foe. [Obs.]
3. [*usually pl.*] in English law, annual deductions and duties paid from the income of a manor or land, as rents, annuities, pensions, etc.
4. (*or* rē-prēz′) in music, repetition: now usually restricted to the repetition of or return to the first subject, or theme, of a sonata movement, after the development; recapitulation.

rē·prīṣe′, *v.t.* 1. to take again. [Obs.]
2. to recompense; to pay. [Obs.]

rē·pris′ti·nāte, *v.t.* to restore to its original condition; to rejuvenate. [Rare.]

rē·pris·ti·nā′tion, *n.* the act of restoring to an original state or the condition of being so restored; rejuvenation. [Rare.]

rē·prīve′, *v.t.* 1. to reprove. [Obs.]
2. to reprieve. [Obs.]

rē·prīze′, *v.t.* to reprise. [Obs.]

rē-prīze′, *v.t.* to prize anew.

rē·prīz′eṣ, *n.pl.* reprises (deductions). [Obs.]

rē·prōach′, *v.t.*; reproached (-prōcht′), *pt., pp.*; reproaching, *ppr.* [Fr. *reprocher*; OFr. *reprochier*; Pr. *repropchar*, to reproach, referred to a LL. *repropiare*, from L. *re-*, back, and *prope*, near.]
1. to accuse of and blame for a fault; to rebuke; to reprove; to censure; to upbraid.
2. to bring shame and disgrace upon; to be a cause of discredit to; as, this crime will *reproach* him.
Syn.—reprove, rebuke, upbraid, revile, condemn, blame, accuse.

rē·prōach′, *n.* 1. a source or cause of shame, disgrace, discredit, or blame.
2. shame, infamy, disgrace, discredit, or blame incurred.
Give not thine heritage to *reproach*. —Joel ii. 17.
3. a blaming or reproving; censure; rebuke.
4. an expression of blame, reproof, or censure.
5. an object of blame, censure, scorn, etc.
Come, and let us build up the wall of Jerusalem, that we may be no more a *reproach*. —Neh. ii. 17.

rē·prōach′ȧ·ble, *a.* 1. deserving reproach.
2. expressing reproach. [Obs.]

rē·prōach′ȧ·ble·ness, *n.* the state of being reproachable.

rē·prōach′ȧ·bly, *adv.* in a reproachable manner.

rē·prōach′ēr, *n.* one who reproaches.

rē·prōach′fụl, *a.* 1. containing or expressing reproach, or blame, censure, etc.; upbraiding; as, *reproachful* words.
2. worthy or deserving of reproach; shameful; bringing or casting reproach; infamous; base; vile; as, *reproachful* conduct. [Obs.]
3. opprobrious; scurrilous. [Obs.]
Syn.—censorious, contemptuous, upbraiding.

rē·prōach′fụl·ly, *adv.* in a reproachful manner.

rē·prōach′fụl·ness, *n.* the quality of being reproachful.

rē·prōach′less, *a.* being without cause for reproach; irreproachable.

rep′rō·bȧ·cy, *n.* the state of being a reprobate.

rep′rō·bănce, *n.* reprobation. [Obs.]

rep′rō·bāte, *a.* [L. *reprobatus*, disapproved, pp. of *reprobare*, to disapprove, reject, condemn.]
1. depraved; vicious; unprincipled.
2. in theology, rejected by God; excluded from salvation and lost in sin.
3. disallowed; disapproved; rejected. [Obs.]
4. expressive of censure; condemnatory. [Obs.]
Syn.—depraved, corrupt, wicked, profligate, base, vile, castaway.

rep′rō·bāte, *n.* one who is very reprobate; a depraved, vicious person.

rep′rō·bāte, *v.t.*; reprobated, *pt., pp.*; reprobating, *ppr.* 1. to disapprove with detestation or marks of extreme dislike; to contemn strongly; to condemn.
2. to reject.
3. in theology, to reject and abandon as beyond saving; to foreordain (a person) to damnation: said of God.
Syn.—condemn, reprehend, censure, disown, abandon, reject.

rep′rō·bāte·ness, *n.* the state or quality of being reprobate.

rep′rō·bā·tēr, *n.* one who reprobates.

rep·rō·bā′tion, *n.* 1. the act of reprobating, or of disapproving with marks of extreme dislike.
2. the state of being reprobated; condemnation; censure.
3. rejection as worthless.
4. in theology, rejection by God, as beyond saving.
5. in ecclesiastical law, the propounding of exceptions either to facts, persons, or things.
6. in military tactics, disqualification for or ejection from office as a punishment.

rep·rō·bā′tion·ēr, *n.* one who believes in the doctrine of the reprobation of the nonelect. [Rare.]

rep′rō·bā·tive, *a.* of, relating to, or expressing reprobation, or disapproval; severely condemnatory.

rep′rō·bȧ·tō·ry, *a.* reprobative.

rē·proc′essed wool, wool cloth that has been respun and rewoven from the raveled fibers of cloth previously woven but never used, as the waste or clippings from a garment factory.

rē·prō·dūce′, *v.t.*; reproduced (-dūst′), *pt., pp.*; reproducing, *ppr.* to produce again; to make, form, or bring into existence again or anew in some way; specifically, (a) to produce by generation or propagation; to bring forth one or more other individuals of (the kind or species) by sexual or asexual processes; (b) to make grow again, as a lost part or organ; (c) to bring about or promote the reproduction of (plants or animals); (d) to make a copy, close imitation, duplication, etc. of (a picture, sound, or the like); (e) to bring before the mind again, as a past scene; to recreate mentally by imagination or memory; (f) to repeat; (g) to put (a play, etc.) on again; to repeat the performance or presentation of.

rē·prō·dūce′, *v.i.* 1. to produce offspring; to bring forth others of its kind.
2. to undergo reproduction, or copying, etc.

rē·prō·dūc′ēr, *n.* 1. one who or that which reproduces.
2. the part of any apparatus which reproduces; specifically, the reproducing diaphragm of a phonograph.

rē·prō·dūc′i·ble, *a.* capable of being reproduced.

rē·prō·duç′tion, *n.* 1. a reproducing or being reproduced.
2. something made by reproducing; a copy, close imitation, duplication, etc.
3. the process, sexual or asexual, by which animals and plants produce new individuals.

rē·prō·duç′tive, *a.* 1. reproducing or tending to reproduce.
2. of or for reproduction.

rē·prō·duç′tive·ness, *n.* the state or quality of being reproductive.

rē·prō·duç′tō·ry, *a.* reproductive. [Rare.]

rē·prọọf′, *n.* [ME. *reprove*; OFr. *reprouve.*]
1. a reproving; rebuking; censuring.
2. an expression of censure; a rebuke.
3. disproof or refutation. [Obs.]
Syn.—censure, chiding, rebuke, reprehension.

rē·pröv′ȧ·ble, *a.* worthy of reproof; deserving censure; blamable.

rē·pröv′ȧ·ble·ness, *n.* the state of being reprovable.

rē·pröv′ȧ·bly, *adv.* in a reprovable manner.

rē·pröv′ăl, *n.* reproof.

rē·pröve′, *v.t.*; reproved, *pt., pp.*; reproving, *ppr.* [Fr. *réprouver*; L. *reprobare*; *re-* and *probare*, to prove.]
1. to blame; to censure; to condemn; to disapprove of; to find fault with.
2. to speak to in disapproval; to rebuke; to charge with a fault; to chide; to reprehend.
3. to refute; to disprove. [Obs.]
4. to convict or convince. [Obs.]
Syn.—rebuke, reprimand, reprehend.—To *reprove* implies calmness and self-possession; to *rebuke* implies a more excited and personal feeling. A *reprimand* proceeds from a person invested with authority, and is a formal act.

rē-pröve′, *v.t.* to prove again or anew.

rē·pröv′ēr, *n.* one who or that which reproves.

rē·pröv′ing·ly, *adv.* in a reproving manner.

rep sil′vēr, formerly, in England, money paid by a tenant, who thus canceled his obligation to pay his rent by reaping the landlord's crops: also written *reap silver.*

rep'tănt, *a.* [L. *reptans* (*-antis*), ppr. of *reptare,* to crawl, creep.]

1. in botany, creeping and rooting.

2. in zoology, crawling; performing locomotion by moving on the belly; as, a worm is *reptant.*

Rep·tan'ti·ȧ (-shi-), *n.pl.* [LL., neut. pl. of L. *reptans* (*-antis*), ppr. of *reptare,* to crawl.]

1. the *Monotremata.*

2. the *Pectinibranchiata.*

rep·tā'tion, *n.* [L. *reptatio* (*-onis*), a creeping, a crawling, from *reptatus,* pp. of *reptare,* to crawl, creep.] the act of creeping or crawling.

rep·tȧ·tō'ri·ăl, *a.* moving by creeping, as a bird.

rep'tȧ·tō·ry, *a.* [L. *reptatus,* pp. of *reptare,* to creep, crawl.] crawling; creeping; repent; reptile.

rep'tile (*or* -tĭl), *a.* [Fr., from L. *reptilis,* creeping, crawling; LL. *reptile,* neut., a creeping, crawling animal, a reptile; from *reptus,* pp. of *repere,* to creep.]

1. of, characteristic of, or like a reptile or reptiles.

2. creeping or crawling.

3. sneaky, mean, groveling, malignant, etc.

rep'tile, *n.* 1. any of a group of cold-blooded vertebrates that move on their bellies, as snakes, or by means of small, short legs, as crocodiles, alligators, lizards, tortoises, turtles, and the like.

2. in zoology, an individual of the *Reptilia.*

3. a groveling, sneaky, malignant, or very mean person.

Rep·til'i·ȧ, *n.pl.* [LL., neut. pl. of *reptile,* a reptile.] a class of cold-blooded, egg-laying, air-breathing vertebrates, usually having a scaly or plated covering, and including snakes, lizards, turtles, and crocodiles.

rep·til'i·ăn, *a.* [LL. *reptile,* a reptile, and *-ian.*]

1. of or belonging to the *Reptilia,* or reptiles.

2. like or characteristic of a reptile.

3. sneaky, mean, groveling, malignant, etc.

rep·til'i·ăn, *n.* an animal of the class *Reptilia;* a reptile.

reptilian age; the Mesozoic Era, in which reptiles attained a high state of development.

rep·ti·liv'ō·rous, *a.* [LL. *reptile,* a reptile, and L. *vorare,* to devour.] devouring and using reptiles for food.

rep'ti·loid, *a.* [LL. *reptile,* a reptile, and Gr. *eidos,* form.] having the appearance and characteristics of a reptile.

rē·pub'liç, *n.* [Fr. *république;* L. *respublica; res,* an affair, interest, and *publica,* f. of *publicus,* public.]

1. (a) a state or nation in which the supreme power rests in all the citizens entitled to vote (the electorate) and is exercised by representatives elected, directly or indirectly, by them and responsible to them; (b) the form of government of such a state or nation.

> The founders of the Constitution laid the cornerstone of our national *republic.*
> —Joseph Story.

2. any group whose members are regarded as having a certain equality, common aims, etc.; as, the *republic* of letters.

3. a state or nation with a president as its titular head: distinguished from *monarchy.*

4. common interest; the public. [Obs.]

Grand Army of the Republic: see under *grand.*

rē·pub'liç·ăn, *a.* 1. of, characteristic of, or having the nature of, a republic.

2. favoring, or in accord with the nature of, a republic.

3. [R-] having to do with the Republican Party.

Liberal Republican Party; in the United States, a party led by Horace Greeley as a candidate for the presidency in 1872, advocating general amnesty to men who had taken part in rebellion, universal suffrage, and civil service reform.

rē·pub'liç·ăn, *n.* 1. one who favors or prefers a republican form of government.

2. [R-] one who belongs to and promotes the doctrines of the Republican Party.

3. in zoology, either of two birds, (a) the cliff swallow, *Petrochelidon lunifrons,* of North America; (b) the sociable weaverbird, *Philetærus socius,* of South Africa.

Red Republican; an extreme republican; one ready to fight for republican opinions. The term originated during the first French Revolution in the habit of the extreme republicans of wearing a red cap.

rē·pub'liç·ăn·iṣm, *n.* 1. republican form of government.

2. republican principles, doctrines, etc.

3. adherence to these.

4. [R-] the principles, policies, etc. of the Republican Party.

rē·pub'liç·ăn·īze, *v.t.;* republicanized, *pt., pp.;* republicanizing, *ppr.* to convert to republican principles; to change to a republican form of government; as, France was *republicanized.*

Rē·pub'liç·ăn Pär'ty, 1. one of the two major political parties in the United States, organized in 1854 to oppose the extension of slavery.

2. a former political party in the United States, organized by Thomas Jefferson.

rē″pub·li·çā'tion, *n.* 1. publication anew.

2. a book, pamphlet, etc. published again.

rē·pub'liç of let'tẽrṣ, 1. literary or learned people as a group.

2. the sphere of literature.

rē·pub'lish·ẽr, *n.* one who republishes.

rē·pū'di·ȧ·ble, *a.* that may be rejected; fit or proper to be repudiated.

rē·pū'di·āte, *v.t.;* repudiated, *pt., pp.;* repudiating, *ppr.* [L. *repudiatus,* pp. of *repudiare,* to put away, to divorce, from *re-,* away, back, and *pudere,* to feel shame.]

1. to refuse to have anything to do with; to disown; to cast off publicly, as a son, or divorce, as a wife.

2. to refuse to accept or acknowledge; to deny the validity or authority of.

3. to refuse to acknowledge or pay, as a debt.

4. to refuse to recognize as due; to refuse to pay (an obligation): said of a government.

Syn.—disavow, disown, discard, abjure, renounce, disclaim, divorce.

rē·pū·di·ā'tion, *n.* [Fr., from L. *repudiatio* (*-onis*).] the act of repudiating; the state of being repudiated.

rē·pū·di·ā'tion·ist, an advocate of repudiation, especially of the repudiation of a public obligation.

rē·pū'di·ā·tŏr, *n.* one who repudiates.

rē·pūgn' (-pūn'), *v.t.* and *v.i.* to oppose; to resist. [Rare or Obs.]

rē·pug'nȧ·ble, *a.* liable or fit to be repugned. [Rare or Obs.]

rē·pug'nănce, *n.* [L. *repugnantia,* opposition, repugnance, from *repugnans* (*-antis*), ppr. of *repugnare,* to fight against.]

1. extreme dislike or distaste; reluctance; unwillingness; intense antipathy; aversion.

2. opposition of qualities or principles; contrariety; inconsistency; incongruity; contradictoriness.

Syn.—aversion, antipathy, disgust, distaste, dislike, hostility.

rē·pug'năn·cy, *n.* same as *repugnance.*

rē·pug'nănt, *a.* 1. offering resistance; antagonistic; disobedient; refractory; inclined to disobey or oppose; unwilling.

2. being at variance or in opposition; opposite; contrary; contradictory; inconsistent.

3. causing repugnance; disagreeable; highly distasteful or offensive; as, such a course is most *repugnant* to me.

Syn.—hostile, inimical, disgusting, antagonistic, antipathetic, disagreeable, distasteful.

rē·pug'nănt·ly, *adv.* in a repugnant manner.

rē·pug'nāte, *v.t.* to oppose; to fight against. [Rare.]

rē·pug'nȧ·tō·ri·ăl, *a.* repugnant; serving to repel.

repugnatorial pores; in certain myriapods, the ducts secreting prussic acid for purposes of protection.

rē·pul'lū·lāte, *v.i.;* repullulated, *pt., pp.;* repullulating, *ppr.* [L. *repullulatus,* pp. of *repullulare,* to sprout again; *re-,* again, and *pullulare,* to sprout.] to rebud; resprout; to take on a new growth. [Now Rare.]

rē·pul·lū·lā'tion, *n.* the act of budding again. [Now Rare.]

rē·pulse', *n.* [L. *repulsa,* from *repellere; re-,* and *pellere,* to drive.]

1. the act of repulsing or the state of being repulsed.

2. a rejection, rebuff, refusal, or denial.

rē·pulse', *v.t.;* repulsed (-pulst), *pt., pp.;* repulsing, *ppr.* [from L. *repulsus,* pp. of *repellere,* to drive back.]

1. to repel; to beat or drive back; as, to *repulse* an assailant or advancing enemy.

2. to repel with discourtesy, coldness, indifference, etc.; to repel by unfriendly look, expression, or attitude; to refuse, reject, or rebuff; as, to *repulse* a lover.

rē·pulse'less, *a.* that cannot be repulsed.

rē·puls'ẽr, *n.* one who repulses.

rē·pul'sion, *n.* 1. the act of repelling, or the state of being repelled; repulse.

2. strong dislike, distaste, or aversion; repugnance.

3. in physics, the mutual action by which bodies, particles, etc. tend to repel each other: opposed to *attraction.*

rē·pul'sive, *a.* 1. tending to repel.

2. causing strong dislike or aversion; disgusting; offensive.

3. characterized by, or having the nature of, repulsion.

Syn.—forbidding, deterrent, ungenial, unattractive, disagreeable, revolting, uninviting, repellent.

rē·pul'sive·ly, *adv.* in a repulsive manner.

rē·pul'sive·ness, *n.* the quality of being repulsive.

rē·pul'sō·ry, *a.* repulsive; driving back. [Rare.]

rē·pũr'chăse, *v.t.* to purchase again; to buy back.

rē·pũr'chăse, *n.* a repurchasing.

rep″ū·tȧ·bil'i·ty, *n.* the state or quality of being reputable.

rep'ū·tȧ·ble, *a.* 1. being in or worthy of good repute; held in esteem; having a good reputation; well thought of; respectable; as, a *reputable* man or character; *reputable* conduct.

> In the article of danger, it is as *reputable* to elude an enemy as to defeat one.
> —Broome.

2. in good usage; not substandard: said of words.

Syn.—respectable, creditable, honorable, estimable.

rep'ū·tȧ·ble·ness, *n.* the quality of being reputable.

rep'ū·tȧ·bly, *adv.* in a reputable manner; without disgrace or discredit; as, to fill an office *reputably.*

rep·ū·tā'tion, *n.* [L. *reputatio* (*-onis*), a reckoning, an estimation, from *reputatus,* pp. of *reputare,* to reckon, to count over.]

1. the estimation in which a person, thing, or action is held by others; character in public or popular opinion, whether favorable or unfavorable; character attributed or reputed; repute.

> *Reputation* and character are widely different things. Character lives in a man; *reputation* outside of him. —J. G. Holland.
> Character is what a person is; *reputation* is what he is supposed to be. —Abbott.

2. such estimation when favorable; good repute; good name; as, she has lost her *reputation.*

3. fame; distinction.

4. the estimation of doing something specified, having specified qualities, etc.; as, he has the *reputation* of being a thief.

5. in law, the character attributed or imputed to a man in the community in which he lives or in which he is best known. It is admissible in evidence when a man's character is put in issue in court, or when his reputation becomes in any way a part of the issue in a trial.

6. worth; value. [Obs.]

Syn.—credit, renown, repute, regard, estimation, character, esteem, honor, fame.

rē·pūt'ȧ·tive·ly, *adv.* by repute. [Now Rare.]

rē·pūte', *v.t.;* reputed; *pt., pp.;* reputing, *ppr.* [L. *reputare,* to count over, to compute, to think over; *re-,* again, and *putare,* to think.] to hold in general opinion or thought; to think; to account; to hold; to reckon; to estimate; to give a (specified) reputation to: usually in the passive.

> The king was *reputed* a prince most prudent.
> —Shak.

rē·pūte', *n.* 1. reputation; estimation; established public opinion; character, whether in a good or bad sense; as, a person of evil *repute.*

2. good character; public esteem; the credit or honor derived from common or public opinion: opposed to *disrepute.*

rē·pū'ted, *a.* [pp. of *repute.*] generally accounted or supposed to be such; as, the *reputed* owner of a house.

rē·pū'ted·ly, *adv.* supposedly; in common opinion or estimation.

rē·pūte'less, *a.* disreputable; disgraceful; not having good repute. [Rare.]

rē·quest', *n.* [OFr. *requeste;* Fr. *requête,* from L. *requisita,* a thing required, a want, a need, from *requirere, requisitum; re-,* again, and *quærere, quæsitum,* to seek, to look or search for.]

1. an asking for, or expressing a desire for, something; an expression of desire to some person for something to be granted or done; a prayer; an entreaty; a petition.

2. that which is asked or begged for; the object of a petition or entreaty.

What is thy *request?* and it shall be performed. —Esther vii. 2.

3. a question. [Obs.]

4. the state of being demanded, asked for, or sought after; demand; repute; as, enterprise and originality are always in *request.*

by request; in response to someone's requesting, or to a demand; as, he played an encore *by request.*

court of request; in English law, a court of equity for the relief of such persons as addressed the sovereign by supplication: now abolished.

rē·quest′, *v.t.*; requested, *pt., pp.*; requesting, *ppr.* 1. to solicit; to express a wish or desire for; to ask for, usually in a polite way; as, the prince *requested* his ship.

2. to express desire to; to ask (a person) to do something; as, we *requested* a friend to accompany us.

Syn.—beseech, entreat, beg, solicit.

rē·quest′ẽr, *n.* one who requests; a petitioner.

Rē′qui·em, rē′qui·em (*or* rek′), *n.* [L., acc. of *requies*, rest; *re-*, again, and *quies*, quiet, rest: first word of the Introit in the Latin Mass for the Dead.]

1. in the Roman Catholic Church, (a) a Mass for the repose of the soul or souls of the dead; (b) a celebration of this; (c) a musical setting for this.

2. any musical service, hymn, or dirge for the repose of the dead.

3. a dirgelike song, chant, or poem.

4. rest; quiet; peace. [Obs.]

re·qui·es′çat (rek-wi-), *n.* [L., for *requiescat in pace*; subj. of *requiescere.*] a prayer or wish for the repose of the dead.

re·qui·es′çat in pā′ce, [L.] may he (or she) rest in peace: abbreviated to R. I. P. and frequently inscribed on headstones, tombstones, and cemetery vaults.

rē·quī′e·tō·ry, *n.* [L. *requietorium.*] a sepulcher. [Obs.]

rē′quin, *n.* [Fr.] a shark, the man-eater.

rē·quīr′ȧ·ble, *a.* that can be required; fit or proper to be demanded.

rē·quīre′, *v.t.*; required, *pt., pp.*; requiring, *ppr.* [ME. *requiren*; OFr. *requirer, requerir*, from L. *requirere*, to seek again, to ask, or inquire; *re-*, again, and *quærere*, to ask.]

1. to demand; to ask or claim as by right or authority; to insist on having.

I will *require* my flock at their hand. —Ezek. xxxiv. 10.

2. to ask for; to beg; to solicit; to request. [Archaic.]

Requiring at her hand the greatest gift,
A woman's heart, the heart of her I loved. —Tennyson.

3. to order; to command; to call upon to do something.

4. to ask or request to do something; to beg. [Obs.]

5. to seek for; to try to find or discover. [Obs.]

6. to have need or necessity for; to call for; to demand; to render necessary or indispensable; to need; to want.

Just gave what life *required*, but gave no more. —Goldsmith.

7. to find it necessary to; to have to; to be obliged to: followed by an infinitive; as, you will *require to* go.

rē·quīre′, *v.i.* to compel or demand.

rē·quīre′ment, *n.* 1. a requiring.

2. something required; something obligatory or demanded, as a condition; as, the *requirements* for college entrance.

3. something needed; a necessity; a need.

rē·quīr′ẽr, *n.* one who requires.

req′ui·ṣite (rek′wi-zit), *a.* [L. *requisitus*, pp. of *requirere*, to seek or ask again; *re-*, again, and *quærere*, to seek.] required by the nature of things or by circumstances; necessary for some purpose; so needful that it cannot be dispensed with; as, air is *requisite* to support life.

It is *requisite* that you resist with care the spirit of innovation. —George Washington.

Syn.—necessary, needed, needful, indispensable, essential, required.

req′ui·ṣite, *n.* that which is necessary; something indispensable.

req′ui·ṣite·ly, *adv.* in a requisite manner.

req′ui·ṣite·ness, *n.* the state of being requisite.

req·ui·ṣi′tion (-zish′un), *n.* [L. *requisitio* (*-onis*), a searching, an examination, from *requisitus*, pp. of *requirere*, to search for, to require.]

1. the act of requiring; a demanding, as by right or authority; formal demand; specifically, (a) the demand made by one State upon another for the surrender of a fugitive from law; (b) a demand made with authority for a supply of necessaries; (c) a levying of necessaries by hostile troops from the people in whose country they are; (d) in law, the series of inquiries and requests arising on behalf of a proposed purchaser, and with which the vendor must comply, unless he be exempt by the conditions of sale; (e) in Scots law, a demand made by a creditor that a debt be paid or an obligation fulfilled.

2. a formal written order, request, or application, as for equipment, tools, etc.

3. the state of being demanded, desired, or put to service or use; as, horses were in *requisition.*

4. a requirement; an indispensable condition.

req·ui·ṣi′tion, *v.t.*; requisitioned, *pt., pp.*; requisitioning, *ppr.* 1. to make a requisition or demand upon; to demand from; as, to *requisition* a community for the support of troops.

2. to demand, as by authority for the use of an army or the public service.

3. to present a requisition or request to; as, to *requisition* a person to become a candidate.

req·ui·ṣi′tion·ist, *n.* one who requisitions.

rē·quiṣ′i·tive, *a.* expressing or implying demand. [Rare.]

rē·quiṣ′i·tive, *n.* a requisitionist. [Rare.]

rē·quiṣ′i·tŏr, *n.* one who makes a requisition. [Rare.]

rē·quiṣ′i·tō·ry, *a.* 1. sought for; demanded. [Rare.]

2. making a demand or requisition.

rē·quīt′ȧ·ble, *a.* capable of being requited.

rē·quīt′ăl, *n.* 1. a requiting or being requited.

2. something given or done in return; a repayment, reward, retaliation, or compensation.

Syn.—compensation, recompense, retaliation, punishment.

rē·quīte′, *v.t.*; requited, *pt., pp.*; requiting, *ppr.* [*re-* and *quite*, or more common *quit.*]

1. to make return or repayment for (a benefit, service, etc., or an injury, wrong, etc.).

2. to make return or repayment to for a benefit, injury, etc.; to reward or retaliate on.

3. to compensate for; to make up for.

4. to give or do in return.

rē·quīte′ment, *n.* requital.

rē·quīt′ẽr, *n.* one who requites.

rē″rā·di·ā′tion, *n.* in physics, radiation that results from a prior absorption of radiation.

rēre′brāce, *n.* [ME. *rerebrace*; OFr. *arierebras*; Fr. *arrièrebras.*] armor for the part of the arm above the elbow.

rēre·de·māin′, *n.* [ME., from OFr. *rere*, back, *de*, of, and *main*, hand.] a backhanded stroke. [Obs.]

rēre′dos, *n.* [ME. *reredoos*; OFr. *reredos*; *rere*, rear, and *dos, dors*, L. *dorsum*, back.]

1. in architecture, (a) the screen or decorated portion of the wall behind the altar in a church; (b) the screen in front of the choir, on which the rood was displayed; (c) [Obs.] the wall or screen at the back of a seat; (d) [Archaic.] a fireback; (e) [Archaic.] an open hearth under the louver of medieval halls.

2. a piece of armor for the back. [Obs.]

rēre′fīef, *n.* [OFr. *rerefief*, abbrev. for *arrierefief*; *arriere*, back, and *fief*, fief.] a fief held by an inferior feudatory; an under fief, held by an under tenant.

rēre′mouse, *n.* a bat. [Dial.]

rēre′sup″pẽr, *n.* a late supper that follows a regular supper. [Obs.]

rēre′wărd, *n.* a rearward; a rear guard. [Archaic.]

rē·rōute′ (*or* -rout′), *v.t.* to send by a new or different route.

rē·run′, *v.t.* to run again.

rē′run, *n.* a rerunning; especially, a showing of a motion picture after the first showing.

rēṣ, *n. sing.* and *pl.* [L., a thing, affair.] a thing; a matter; a point; a cause or action: used in sundry legal phrases; as, *res gestæ*, things done, material facts, as opposed to mere hearsay; *res judicata*, a matter already decided.

rē·sāl′ȧ·ble, *a.* that can be sold again.

rē·sāle′, *n.* a sale at second hand; a selling again; a second sale; a sale of what was before sold.

rē·sal′găr, *n.* realgar. [Obs.]

rē·sa̤w′, *v.t.*; resawed, *pt.,pp.*; resawing, *ppr.* to saw again, as a piece of timber into smaller pieces.

res′çate, *v.t.* to ransom; to rescue. [Obs.]

res′çate, *n.* ransom; release. [Obs.]

rē·scind′, *v.t.*; rescinded, *pt., pp.*; rescinding, *ppr.* [OFr. *rescinder*, from L. *rescindere*, to cut off, annul, from *re-*, back, and *scindere*, to cut.]

1. to abrogate; to revoke; to annul; to vacate (an act) by the enacting authority or by superior authority; as, to *rescind* a law, a resolution, or a vote; to *rescind* an edict, decree, or judgment.

2. to cut off. [Obs.]

Syn.—abrogate, revoke, annul, cancel, reverse, void.

rē·scind′ȧ·ble, *a.* that can be rescinded.

rē·scind′ment, *n.* rescission.

rē·scis′si·ble, *a.* that can be rescinded.

rē·scis′sion (*or* -sizh′un), *n.* [LL. *rescissio* (*-onis*), a making void, an annulling, from L. *rescissus*, pp. of *rescindere*, to cut off.]

1. the act of abrogating, annulling, or vacating; as, the *rescission* of a law, decree, or judgment.

2. a cutting off. [Obs.]

rē·scis′sō·ry, *a.* rescinding; having power to rescind.

rē·sçōre′, *v.t.*; rescored, *pt., pp.*; rescoring, *ppr.* in music, to rearrange the score of; to score again; to write a new score for.

res′çous, *n.* rescue. [Obs.]

rē·sçrībe′, *v.t.*; rescribed, *pt., pp.*; rescribing, *ppr.* [L. *rescribere*, write back or again, from *re-*, back, again, and *scribere*, to write.]

1. to write back. [Obs.]

2. to write over again. [Obs.]

rē′sçript, *n.* [L. *rescriptum*, from *rescriptus*, pp. of *rescribere*; *re-*, back, and *scribere*, to write.]

1. an order or decree issued by a Roman emperor or by the Pope in answer to some difficulty or point of law presented to him, and having the force of law.

2. any official decree or order.

3. (a) a rewriting; (b) something rewritten; a copy.

4. in law, an order, as from a court to its clerk, or from an appellate court to a trial court, giving the disposition of a case.

5. a facsimile or counterpart. [Rare.]

rē·sçrip′tion, *n.* a writing back; the answering of a letter; also, a new or second copy.

rē·sçrip′tive, *a.* pertaining to or having the character of a rescript; decisive; settling; conclusive; final. [Rare.]

rē·sçrip′tive·ly, *adv.* by rescript. [Rare.]

res′çū·ȧ·ble, *a.* that can be rescued.

res′çūe, *v.t.*; rescued, *pt., pp.*; rescuing, *ppr.* [ME. *rescouen, rescowen*; OFr. *rescourre, rescoure*, to redeem, to rescue, from L. *re-*, again, and *excussus*, pp. of *excutere*, to shake off, drive away; *ex-*, off, and *quatere*, to shake.]

1. to free or deliver from any confinement, violence, danger, or evil; to liberate from actual restraint; to remove or withdraw from a state of exposure to evil; as, to *rescue* seamen from shipwreck.

2. in law, to take (a person or thing) out of legal custody by force.

Syn.—retake, recover, recapture, liberate, extricate, save, deliver, preserve.

res′çūe, *n.* 1. deliverance from restraint, violence, or danger, by force or by the interference of an agent.

2. in law, removal by force from legal custody.

res′çūe grȧss, a tall, smooth, early spring grass, *Bromus unioloides*, introduced into the Gulf States from South America about 1860: also called *Schrader's grass.*

res′çūe·less, *a.* incapable of being rescued.

res′çū·ẽr, *n.* one who rescues or retakes.

res·çus·see′, *n.* in law, one in whose favor a rescue is made. [Rare.]

res·çus′sŏr, *n.* in law, one who rescues a person or thing from lawful custody; a rescuer. [Rare.]

rēṣe, *v.i.* to tremble; to quake; to shake. [Obs.]

rē·seal′, *v.t.* in law, to seal (a writ) a second time to continue it or divest it of some irregularity.

rē·sēarch′ (*or* rē′sũrch), *n.* [OFr. *recerche*; Fr. *recherche*, diligent search, from *re-*, again, and *chercher*, to seek.]

1. [*often in pl.*] careful, patient, systematic,

diligent inquiry or examination in some field of knowledge, undertaken to establish facts or principles; laborious or continued search after truth; as, *researches* of human wisdom.
2. in music, an extemporaneous prelude, used to introduce themes. [Rare.]
Syn.—investigation, inquiry, scrutiny, examination.
rē·sēarch′, *v.t.* [OFr. *recercher*; Fr. *rechercher*, to search diligently; from *re-*, again, and *chercher*, to seek.] to search or examine with continued care; to seek diligently for. [Rare.]
rē·sēarch′, *v.i.* to do research; to make researches; to study.
rē-sēarch′, *v.i.* to search again; to examine anew.
rē·sēarch′ẽr, *n.* one who researches.
rē·sēarch′fụl, *a.* characterized by research; inquisitive.
rē·sēat′, *v.t.*; reseated, *pt., pp.*; reseating, *ppr.* 1. to seat or set again; to place in a position or office again.
2. to put a new seat or seats in or on; as, to *reseat* a hall; to *reseat* a chair.
re·seau′, ré·seau′ (rā-zō′), *n.*; *pl.* **re·seaux′, ré·seaux′** (rā-zō′), [Fr., dim., from OFr. *roiz*, from L. *rete*, net.]
1. a network; specifically, in astronomy, a network of fine lines on a glass plate, forming little squares of a standard size: used in photographic telescopes to produce a similar network on photographs of stars, for aid in measurement.
2. a netted ground or meshed foundation in lace.
3. a filter screen used in making color films.
rē·sect′, *v.t.* [L. *resectus*, pp. of *resecare*, to cut off, to cut loose, from *re-*, again, and *secare*, to cut.]
1. to cut or pare off. [Obs.]
2. in surgery, to perform a resection of (some part).
rē·sec′tion, *n.* [LL. *resectio* (*-onis*), a cutting off, a trimming, from *resectus*, pp. of *resecare*, to cut off; *re-*, again, and *secare*, to cut.]
1. the act of cutting or paring off. [Obs.]
2. in surgery, the removal of part of a bone, nerve, etc.
Rē·sē′dȧ, *n.* [L. *reseda*, a plant, from *resedare*, to calm; *re-*, back, and *sedare*, to calm.]
1. the typical genus of the family *Resedaceæ*, the most common species of which are the dyer's-weed and the mignonette.
2. [r-] any plant of this genus, having dense, fragrant spikes of flowers.
3. [r-] a greenish-white color, so named because like the color of some of the flowers of the mignonette.
rē·sē′dȧ, *a.* of the greenish-white color of some of the flowers of the mignonette.
Res·ē·dā′cē·ae, *n.pl.* [*Reseda* and *-aceæ.*] a family of annual or perennial herbs or shrubby plants, having alternate leaves, glandular stipules, and terminal spikes of small asymmetrical flowers.
res·ē·dā′ceous, *a.* of or pertaining to the family *Resedaceæ*, the mignonette family of plants.
rē·sēize′ (-sēz′), *v.t.* 1. to seize again; to seize a second time.
2. in law, to take possession of, as lands and tenements which have been disseized.
3. to reinstate; to place in possession again.
rē·sēiz′ẽr, *n.* 1. one who seizes again.
2. in English law, the taking of lands into the possession of the crown after they have been illegally taken.
rē·ṣem′blȧ·ble, *a.* capable of being compared; like. [Obs.]
rē·ṣem′blănce, *n.* [ME.; Anglo-Fr.]
1. the state, fact, or quality of resembling; similarity of appearance, or, sometimes, of character; likeness.
2. a point, degree, or sort of likeness.
3. something that resembles; a likeness or semblance of someone or something.
4. characteristic appearance. [Obs.]
5. likelihood; probability. [Obs.]
6. a comparison; a simile; a metaphor. [Obs.]
Syn.—likeness, similitude, similarity.
rē·ṣem′blănt, *a.* bearing a resemblance [Rare.]
rē·ṣem′ble, *v.t.*; resembled (-bld), *pt., pp.*; resembling, *ppr.* [Fr. *ressembler*, from L. *re-*, again, and *simulare*, to simulate, imitate, from *similis*, like.]
1. to be like or similar to in appearance or nature.
2. to liken; to compare; to represent as like something else. [Archaic.]
3. to cause to be like or similar. [Obs.]
4. to counterfeit; to copy; to imitate. [Obs.]
rē·ṣem′blẽr, *n.* one who or that which resembles.
rē·ṣem′bling, *a.* like or similar.
rē·ṣem′bling·ly, *adv.* in a manner exhibiting resemblance or likeness.
rē·sem′i·nāte, *v.t.* to reproduce from the seed; to seminate again. [Rare.]
rē·send′, *v.t.*; resent, *pt., pp.*; resending, *ppr.* 1. to send again.
2. to send back; to return; as, to *resend* a gift.
rē·ṣent′, *v.t.*; resented, *pt., pp.*; resenting, *ppr.* [Fr. *ressentir*, from L. *re-*, again, and *sentire*, to feel, to perceive by the senses.]
1. to feel or show displeasure and indignation at (some act, remark, etc.) or toward (a person), from a sense of being injured or offended.
2. to perceive by the senses, especially by the sense of smell; as, the dog *resents* blood. [Obs.]
3. to have a perception of; to derive sensation, either pleasant or painful, from. [Obs.]
rē·ṣent′, *v.i.* 1. to feel resentment. [Rare.]
2. to smell; to have a flavor. [Obs.]
rē·ṣent′ẽr, *n.* one who resents.
rē·ṣent′fụl, *a.* feeling or showing resentment; inclined or disposed to resent; easily provoked to anger; of an irritable temper.
rē·ṣent′fụl·ly, *adv.* with resentment.
rē·ṣent′i·ment, *n.* resentment. [Obs.]
rē·ṣent′ing·ly, *adv.* 1. with a sense of wrong or affront; with a degree of anger.
2. with deep sense or strong perception. [Obs.]
rē·ṣent′ive, *a.* easily provoked or irritated; quick to feel an injury or affront. [Obs.]
rē·ṣent′ment, *n.* [OFr. and Fr. *ressentiment*, from L. *resentire*, to feel, to resent.]
1. a feeling of displeasure and indignation, from a sense of being injured or offended.
2. the state of feeling or perceiving; strong or clear sensation, feeling, or perception; conviction; impression. [Obs.]
3. the taking of a thing well or ill; often, a taking well; a strong perception of good. [Obs.]
Syn.—anger, wrath, ire, indignation.
res′ẽr·āte, *v.t.* [L. *reseratus*, pp. of *reserare*, to unlock; *re-*, back, and *serare*, to sew.] to unlock; to open. [Obs.]
rē·ṣẽrv′ănce, *n.* reservation. [Obs.]
reṣ·ẽr·vā′tion, *n.* [OFr. *reservation*; LL. *reservatio* (*-onis*), from L. *reservare*, to keep back; *re-*, back, and *servare*, to keep.]
1. a reserving; a withholding.
2. something reserved or withheld.
3. (a) a withholding of a right, interest, etc.; (b) that part of a deed or contract which provides for this.
4. a limiting condition or qualification, tacit or expressed, as in an agreement; as, she accepted the invitation, with mental *reservations.*
5. public land set aside for some special use; as, an Indian *reservation*, military *reservation.*
6. (a) an arrangement by which a hotel room, theater or train ticket, etc. is set aside and held until called for; (b) anything so reserved in advance; (c) the promise or record of such an arrangement.
rē·ṣẽrv′ȧ·tive, *a.* keeping; reserving. [Obs.]
rē·ṣẽrv′ȧ·tō·ry, *n.* a place in which things are reserved or kept. [Obs.]
rē-sẽrve′, *v.t.* to serve again or anew.
rē·ṣẽrve′, *v.t.*; reserved, *pt., pp.*; reserving, *ppr.* [ME. *reserven*; OFr. *reserver*; from L. *reservare*, to keep back; *re-* and *servare*, to keep.]
1. to keep back, store up, or set apart for later use or for some special purpose.
2. to hold over to a later time.
3. to set aside or have set aside for a special person, etc.; as, *reserve* a seat on a train.
4. to keep back or retain for oneself; as, I *reserve* the right to come and go freely.
5. to make an exception of; to except. [Obs.]
6. to guard; to keep safe; to preserve. [Obs.]
rē·ṣẽrve′, *n.* 1. something kept back or stored up, as for later use or for a special purpose.
2. a limitation; reservation; exception.
3. the practice of keeping one's thoughts, feelings, etc. to oneself; self-restraint or avoidance of intimacy in speech and manner.
4. reticence; silence.
5. restraint and control in artistic expression; freedom from exaggeration or extravagance.
6. [*pl.*] troops held out of action for use in an emergency, for following up an advantage, or for replacing active units.
7. [*pl.*] men or units in the armed forces not on active duty but subject to call; militia.
8. cash, or assets easily turned into cash, held out of use by a bank or company to meet expected or unexpected demands.
9. land set apart for a special purpose; as, a forest *reserve.*
10. in calico printing, resist.
11. a system according to which only that portion of the truth is set before the people which they are regarded as able to comprehend or to receive with benefit.
in reserve; reserved for later use or for some person.
without reserve; (a) subject to no limitation; (b) without any minimum or asking price: said of goods offered at auction.
Syn.—reservation, retention, coldness, shyness, modesty, restraint, backwardness.
rē·ṣẽrve′, *a.* being or having the nature of, a reserve; as, a *reserve* supply.
reserve air; same as *supplemental air.*
reserve bank; (a) any one of the twelve main Federal Reserve Banks, which form the Federal Reserve System of U. S. banking; a Federal Reserve Bank; (b) a bank which holds the reserves of banks chartered by a State: such a bank must meet certain qualifications as prescribed by the banking laws of the State: it is selected by the State banking department.
rē·ṣẽrved′, *a.* [pp. of *reserve.*]
1. kept in reserve; set apart or kept back for some purpose or use, or for some person, etc.
2. keeping one's thoughts, feelings, etc. to oneself; self-restrained and withdrawn in speech and manner; not effusive; reticent.
To all obliging, yet *reserved* to all.
—Walsh.
3. characterized by reticence, etc.
rē·ṣẽrv′ed·ly, *adv.* with reserve; with backwardness; not with openness or frankness; cautiously; coldly.
rē·ṣẽrv′ed·ness, *n.* the state or quality of being reserved.
reṣ·ẽr·vee′, *n.* in law, one to whom anything is reserved. [Rare.]
rē·ṣẽrv′ẽr, *n.* one who reserves.
rē·ṣẽrv′ist, *n.* a member of a country's military reserves, or militia.
reṣ′ẽr·voir (-vwor), *n.* [Fr. *réservoir*, a storehouse, a reservoir.]
1. a place where anything is collected and stored, generally in large quantity; especially, a natural or artificial lake or pond in which water is collected and stored for use, as to supply the needs of a community.
2. a receptacle or part (in an apparatus) for holding a fluid, as oil, ink, etc.
3. a part, sac, or cavity (in an animal or plant) in which a fluid collects or is secreted.
4. a large supply or store of something.
rē·ṣẽrv′ŏr, *n.* in law, one who reserves. [Rare.]
rē·set′, *v.t.*; reset, *pt., pp.*; resetting, *ppr.* to set again; as, to *reset* a diamond; to *reset* type.
rē′set, *n.* 1. the act of resetting.
2. something reset.
3. a plant that is planted again.
rē·set′, *v.t.*; resetted, *pt., pp.*; resetting, *ppr.* in Scots law, to receive (stolen goods); to shelter (an outlaw).
rē·set′, *n.* [OFr. *recete*, a receiving.] in Scots law, the receiving of stolen goods or the sheltering of an outlaw.
rē·set′tẽr, *n.* in Scots law, a receiver of stolen goods; also, one who harbors a criminal. [Obs.]
rē·set′tẽr, *n.* one who resets.
rē·set′tle, *v.t.* to settle again.
rē·set′tle, *v.i.* to settle a second time.
rē·set′tle·ment, *n.* the act of settling again; the state of being resettled.
rēṣ ġes′tae, [L.] 1. things done; deeds; exploits.
2. in law, attendant facts and circumstances.
reṣh, *n.* [Heb. *rēsh*, lit., the head.] the twentieth letter of the Hebrew alphabet, corresponding to English *R, r.*
rē·ship′, *v.t.*; reshipped, *pt., pp.*; reshipping, *ppr.* 1. to ship again.
2. to transfer to another ship.
rē·ship′, *v.i.* 1. to go on a ship again; to embark again.

2. to sign up or go to sea again (as a member of a ship's crew) for another voyage.

rē·ship′ment, *n.* 1. the act of shipping a second time.

2. that which is reshipped.

rē·ship′pēr, *n.* one who reships.

reṣ′i·ănce, *n.* residence; abode. [Obs.]

reṣ′i·ănt, *a.* resident; dwelling. [Obs.]

rē·ṣīde′, *v.i.*; resided, *pt., pp.*; residing, *ppr.* [Fr. *résider*, from L. *residere*, to remain behind, to reside, to dwell; *re-* and *sedere*, to sit.]

1. to dwell permanently or for a length of time; to have a settled abode for a time; to abide; to live (*in* or *at*); as, to *reside in* New York.

2. to abide or be inherent (*in*), as a quality or element; to inhere.

In such like acts, the duty and virtue of contentedness doth especially *reside*. —Barrow.

3. to be vested (*in*): said of rights, powers, etc.

Syn.—dwell, abide, live, inhabit, stay, sojourn, remain.

rē·ṣīde′, *v.i.* to sink to the bottom, as sediment; to settle. [Obs.]

reṣ′i·dence, *n.* [ME.; OFr.; ML. *residentia*, from L. *residens* (-*entis*), ppr. of *residere*, to reside, to dwell.]

1. the act or fact of residing or dwelling in a place for some continuance of time; as, the *residence* of an American in France or Italy for a year.

2. the fact or status of living or staying in a place while working, going to school, carrying out official duties, etc. (usually preceded by *in*); as, students are required to be *in residence* two years.

3. the place in which a person or thing resides; dwelling place; abode; especially, a house.

4. a large or imposing house; a mansion.

5. the time during which a person resides in a place.

6. in English ecclesiastical law, the abode of an incumbent in his benefice: opposed to *nonresidence*.

7. that in which anything permanently rests.

Against the highest court and *residence* of all his regal power. —Milton.

Syn.—dwelling, habitation, abode, domicile, home, sojourn.

reṣ′i·dence, *n.* that which falls to the bottom of liquors; sediment; subsidence. [Obs.]

reṣ′i·den·cy, *n.*; *pl.* **reṣ′i·den·cieṣ,** 1. residence.

2. the official residence of a diplomatic officer or representative of a governor general at a foreign court, as in the East Indian native states.

3. an administrative division of the Netherlands Indies.

reṣ′i·dent, *a.* [L. *residens* (-*entis*), ppr. of *residere*, to reside, to dwell.]

1. dwelling or having an abode in a place for a continuance of time; residing (*in*); as, he is now *resident in* the city.

2. living or staying in a place while working, carrying on official duties, etc.; as, a *resident* physician of a hospital.

3. present; inherent; intrinsic.

4. not migratory: said of birds, etc.

5. fixed; firm. [Obs.]

reṣ′i·dent, *n.* 1. one who lives in a place, as distinguished from a visitor or transient.

2. a diplomatic representative living at a foreign court or capital, as in a protectorate.

3. a bird or animal that is not migratory.

reṣ′i·dent·ēr, *n.* a resident. [Dial.]

reṣ·i·den′tiăl (-shăl), *a.* 1. of or connected with residence; as, a *residential* requirement for students.

2. of, characterized by, or suitable for residences, or homes; as, a *residential* neighborhood.

reṣ·i·den′ti·ăr·y (-shi-), *a.* [ML. *residentarius.*]

1. living in a place; resident.

2. required to live in a place; officially resident.

reṣ·i·den′ti·ăr·y, *n.*; *pl.* **reṣ·i·den′ti·ăr·ieṣ,** 1. a resident.

2. in ecclesiastical usage, a clergyman required to live for some time in his official residence.

reṣ·i·den′ti·ăr·y·ship, *n.* the position or office of a residentiary.

reṣ′i·dent·ship, *n.* the functions or dignity of a resident; the office or position of a resident.

rē·ṣīd′ēr, *n.* one who resides.

rē·ṣid′ū·ăl, *a.* [L. *residuum*, residue.] 1. pertaining to or of the nature of a residue or residuum; remaining; left over after a part has been taken away or dealt with.

2. in mathematics, (a) left by the subtraction of one number from another; as, a *residual* quantity; (b) designating the difference (called *error*) between observed results and results obtained by formular computation; (c) designating the deviation (called *error*) of any of a series of values from the mean of the series.

residual abscess; an abscess located near the residue of a former inflammation.

residual air; the air which remains in the lungs and cannot be expelled, variously estimated at from seventy-five to one hundred cubic inches.

residual atmosphere; the traces of air or other gas remaining in a space which has been nearly exhausted of its gaseous contents by a pump or other means.

residual charge; in electricity, the charge remaining in a Leyden jar after it has been discharged.

residual figure; in geometry, the figure remaining after subtracting a less from a greater.

residual magnetism; see *remanent magnetism* under *remanent.*

residual quantity; in algebra, a binomial having one negative term, as $a - b$, $a - \sqrt{6}$.

residual root; in algebra, the root of a residual quantity, as $\sqrt{a - b}$.

rē·ṣid′ū·ăl, *n.* 1. what is left at the end of a process; remainder.

2. in geology, an elevated rock mass remaining in an area, where erosion has leveled most of the surrounding territory; a monadnock.

3. in mathematics, (a) a residual quantity; (b) a residual error.

rē·ṣid′ū·ăr·y, *a.* [L. *residuum*, a residue.]

1. of, or having the nature of, a residue or residuum; remaining; left over.

2. in law, (a) receiving the residue of an estate; as, a *residuary* legatee; (b) giving the disposition of the residue of an estate; as, the *residuary* clause in a will.

reṣ′i·dūe, *n.* [OFr. *residu*, from L. *residuum*, a remainder, neut. of *residuus*, remaining, from *residere*, to remain.]

1. that which remains after a part is taken, separated, removed, or designated; remainder; rest.

2. in chemistry, (a) a residuum (sense 2); (b) the remainder of a molecule after a portion of its constituents has been removed: used frequently in the same sense as *radical.*

3. in law, that part of a testator's estate which is left after all claims, charges, and bequests have been satisfied.

4. in mathematics, any number differing from another given number by a quantity which is a multiple of a given modulus; thus, when 9 is the modulus and 29 the given number, the numbers 2, 11, 20, etc. are *residues.*

rē·ṣid′ū·ent, *n.* in chemistry, a product of any compound that may be regarded as a by-product or waste product remaining after the separation or removal of the principal constituents.

rē·ṣid′ū·ous, *a.* residual. [Rare.]

rē·ṣid′ū·um, *n.*; *pl.* **rē·ṣid′ū·ȧ,** [L.] 1. residue.

2. in chemistry, the matter remaining at the end of a process, as after evaporation, combustion, filtration, etc.; residual product.

rē·ṣīgn′ (-zīn′), *v.t.*; resigned, *pt., pp.*; resigning, *ppr.* [Fr. *résigner*; L. *resignare*, to annul, to assign back, to resign; *re-*, back, and *signare*, to sign.]

1. to give up possession of; to relinquish, as a claim.

2. to give up (an office, position, etc.).

3. to commit; to consign. [Obs.]

to resign oneself; to submit; to accept something passively.

rē·ṣīgn′, *v.i.* 1. to give up an office, position of employment, etc., especially by formal notice (often with *from*).

2. to submit; to yield.

Syn.—abandon, abdicate, desert, renounce, forsake, surrender, submit, leave, relinquish.

rē-sīgn′, *v.t.* to sign again.

rē·ṣīgn′, *n.* resignation. [Obs.]

reṣ·ig·nā′tion, *n.* [Fr. *résignation*, from L. *resignare*, to resign.]

1. the act of resigning or giving up, as a claim or possession; as, the *resignation* of a commission.

2. formal notice of this, especially in writing.

3. passive acceptance; patient submission; unresisting acquiescence; as, a blind *resignation* to the authority of other men's opinions.

4. in Christian theology, quiet submission to the will of Providence; submission without discontent and with entire acquiescence in the divine dispensations.

Syn.—abdication, abandonment, relinquishment, submission, renunciation, acquiescence, surrender, patience, endurance.

rē·ṣīgned′, *a.* feeling or showing resignation; yielding and uncomplaining; not disposed to murmur; submissive.

rē·ṣīgn′ed·ly, *adv.* in a resigned manner; with submission.

rē·ṣīgn·ee′, *n.* one who receives a resignation.

rē·ṣīgn′ēr, *n.* one who resigns.

rē·ṣīgn′ment, *n.* the act of resigning. [Rare.]

rē·ṣīle′, *v.i.*; resiled, *pt., pp.*; resiling, *ppr.* [L. *resilire*, to jump back, to recoil; *re-*, back, and *salire*, to jump.]

1. to draw back; to recede from a purpose.

2. to bounce or spring back; to rebound; specifically, to come back into shape or position after being pressed or stretched: said of elastic bodies.

rē·ṣil′i·ence, rē·ṣil′i·en·cy, *n.* 1. the act of leaping or springing back; a rebounding; as, the *resilience* of a deformed body after the removal of the deforming force.

2. the quality of being resilient; ability to bounce or spring back into shape, position, etc. after being pressed or stretched; elasticity.

3. the ability to recover strength, spirits, good humor, etc. quickly; buoyancy.

4. in mechanics, the work done by a body in springing back.

rē·ṣil′i·ent, *a.* [L. *resiliens* (-*entis*), ppr. of *resilire*, to leap back; *re-*, back, and *salire*, to jump, to leap.]

1. bouncing or springing back into shape, position, etc.; elastic.

2. recovering strength, spirits, good humor, etc. quickly; buoyant.

reṣ·i·li′tion (-lish′un), *n.* resilience. [Rare.]

reṣ′in, *n.* [OFr. *resine*; L. *resina*, from Gr. *rhētinē*, resin or gum of trees.]

1. any of various solid or semisolid organic substances exuded from various plants and trees or prepared synthetically: resins are soluble in ether, alcohol, etc., are nonconductors of electricity, and are used in medicines, varnish, etc.

2. a substance prepared by distilling the resin of certain pine trees; rosin.

fossil resin; a resin from decayed plants, as amber.

hard resin; a resin containing little or no volatile oil; a resin hardened by evaporation.

Highgate resin; same as *fossil copal* under *fossil.*

mineral resin; a hydrocarbon resin, as mineral pitch.

soft resin; a resin containing its original volatile oil; resin before it has been hardened by exposure or evaporation.

reṣ′in, *v.t.* to treat or rub with resin.

reṣ·in·ā′ceous, *a.* [*resin* and *-aceous.*] resembling or having resin. [Rare.]

reṣ′in ac′id, any acid found in a resin.

reṣ′in·āte, *n.* [*resin* and *-ate.*] any one of the salts of the acids obtained from turpentine, as the salts of sylvic and pimaric acids.

reṣ′in·āte, *v.t.*; resinated, *pt., pp.*; resinating, *ppr.* to impregnate with resin.

reṣ′in·bush, *n.* a South African composite plant, *Euryops speciosissimus*, akin to *Senecio*: it is named from a gummy exudation often seen on the stem and leaves.

reṣ′in cell, a vegetable cell secreting resin.

reṣ′in duct, in vegetable tissue, a passage containing resin.

reṣ·in′iç, *a.* in chemistry, pertaining to or derived from resin; as, *resinic* odor.

reṣ·in·if′ēr·ous, *a.* [L. *resina*, resin, and *ferre*, to bear, to produce.] yielding resin; as, a *resiniferous* tree or vessel.

reṣ′in·i·form, *a.* having the nature of resin.

reṣ′in·i·fȳ, *v.t.*; resinified, *pt., pp.*; resinifying, *ppr.* [Fr. *résinifier*, from L. *resina*, resin, and *ficare*, from *facere*, to make.] to change or convert into resin; to make resinous; to coat or saturate with resin.

reṣ′in·i·fȳ, *v.i.* to change into resin; to become resinous or like resin.

reṣ″in·ō·ē·lec′triç, *a.* containing or exhibiting negative electricity, or that kind which is produced by the friction of resinous substances.

reṣ′in·oid, *a.* [*resin* and *-oid.*] resinous; resembling resin.

reṣ′in·oid, *n.* 1. a resinoid substance, as a synthetic resin.
2. gum resin.

reṣ′in·ous, *a.* [*resin* and *-ous.*]
1. of, having the nature of, characteristic of, or like resin.
2. obtained from resin.
3. containing resin.
4. electronegative. [Now Rare.]
resinous electricity; see under *electricity.*

reṣ′in·ous·ly, *adv.* by means of resin; as, *resinously* electrified.

reṣ′in·ous·ness, *n.* the quality of being resinous.

reṣ′in·weed, *n.* same as *rosinweed.*

reṣ′in·y, *a.* resinous.

res·i·pis′cence, *n.* [L. *resipiscens* (*-entis*), ppr. of *resipiscere,* to come into one's senses, from *resipere,* to taste; *re-,* again, and *sapere,* to be wise.] wisdom derived from severe experience; hence, repentance.

rē·ṣist′, *v.t.*; resisted, *pt., pp.*; resisting, *ppr.* [OFr. *resister,* from L. *resistere,* to stand back, to resist; *re-,* back, and *sistere,* to set, to stand back.]
1. to stand against; to withstand; to oppose; to fend off; to withstand the action of.
2. to oppose actively; to strive, fight, argue or work against; to endeavor to counteract, defeat, or frustrate.
3. to keep from yielding to, being affected by, or enjoying; as, she tried to *resist* temptation.
4. to be disagreeable or distasteful to; to offend. [Obs.]
Syn.—withstand, oppose, hinder, check, thwart, baffle, disappoint, obstruct.

rē·ṣist′, *v.i.* to withstand something; to offer resistance; to make opposition.

rē·ṣist′, *n.* a substance that resists, as a protective coating on a fabric that makes it unaffected by a dye: also called *resist-paste* and *reserve.*

rē·ṣist′ănce, *n.* [OFr. *resistance*; LL. *resistantia,* from L. *resistens* (*-entis*), ppr. of *resistere,* to resist.]
1. a resisting; an opposing; a withstanding.
2. power or capacity to resist; specifically, the ability of an organism to ward off disease.
3. opposition of some force, thing, etc. to another or others.
4. in electricity, (a) the property of opposing the passage of a current, causing electric energy to be transformed into heat: also called *true* (or *ohmic*) *resistance*; (b) something, as a coil or length of wire, that offers such resistance; a resistor; (c) impedance: also called *apparent resistance.*
5. [*often* R—] the organized movement, often underground, of resistance to a government or occupying power regarded as oppressive and unjust, as in France during the Nazi occupation.
head resistance; the impeding force encountered by an airplane in flight due to the exposed surfaces which make up the struts, nose, landing gear, etc.

rē·ṣist′ănce box, a box in which are coils of standard resistance, so arranged as to measure any required resistance.

rē·ṣist′ănce çoil, a coil in an electric circuit which increases the resistance, as a coil in a resistance box.

rē·ṣist′ănt, *a.* [L. *resistens.*] offering resistance; resisting.

rē·ṣist′ănt, *n.* one who or that which resists.

rē·ṣist′ẽr, *n.* one who opposes or withstands.

rē·ṣist′ful, *a.* making much resistance; liable to resist.

rē·ṣist·i·bil′i·ty, *n.* 1. the state or quality of being resistible.
2. the capacity for resisting.

rē·ṣist′i·ble, *a.* that can be resisted; as, a *resistible* force; *resistible* grace.

rē·ṣist′i·ble·ness, *n.* resistibility.

rē·ṣist′i·bly, *adv.* in a resistible manner.

rē·ṣist′ing, *a.* withstanding; opposing.

rē·ṣist′ing·ly, *adv.* in a resisting manner; with resistance.

rē·ṣist′ive, *a.* resisting, tending to resist, or having the power to resist.

rē·ṣis·tiv′i·ty, *n.* 1. property of, capacity for, or tendency toward resistance.
2. in electricity, the resistance between opposite faces of a centimeter cube of a substance: also called *specific resistance.*

rē·ṣist′less, *a.* 1. that cannot be effectually opposed or withstood; irresistible.
2. that cannot resist; unresisting; helpless.

rē·ṣist′less·ly, *adv.* in a resistless manner.

rē·ṣist′less·ness, *n.* the state of being irresistible.

rē·ṣis′tŏr, *n.* in electricity, a device used in a circuit primarily to provide resistance.

rēṣ jū·di·cā′tȧ, [L., thing decided.] in law, a case already decided by judicial authority.

rē·sōle′, *v.t.*; resoled, *pt., pp.*; resoling, *ppr.* to put a new sole on (a shoe, etc.).

reṣ″ō·lū·bil′i·ty, *n.* the quality or state of being resoluble.

reṣ′ō·lū·ble, *a.* [OFr. *resoluble*; LL. *resolubilis,* from L. *resolvere,* to resolve.] that can be resolved (in various senses).

reṣ′ō·lū·ble·ness, *n.* the state of being resoluble.

reṣ′ō·lūte, *a.* [Fr. *résolu,* from L. *resolutus,* pp. of *resolvere,* to resolve.] having or showing a fixed, firm purpose; determined; bold; firm; steady; resolved; unwavering.
Syn.—determined, decided, fixed, steadfast, firm, steady, constant, persevering, bold, unshaken.

reṣ′ō·lūte, *n.* 1. one who is resolute; hence, a reckless person.
2. a second delivery; a repayment. [Obs.]

reṣ′ō·lūte, *v.i.*; resoluted, *pt., pp.*; resoluting, *ppr.* to pass resolutions. [Colloq.]

reṣ′ō·lūte·ly, *adv.* with fixed purpose; steadily; with steady perseverance; boldly; firmly.

reṣ′ō·lūte·ness, *n.* fixed purpose; firm determination; unshaken firmness.

reṣ·ō·lū′tion, *n.* [Late OFr. *résolution,* from L. *resolutio* (*-onis*), a loosening, an untying, a relaxation, from *resolutus,* pp. of *resolvere,* to loose, to resolve.]
1. (a) the act or process of resolving something or breaking it up into its constituent parts or elements; (b) the result of this.
2. (a) a resolving; determining; deciding; (b) the thing resolved or determined upon; decision as to future action; resolve.
3. a resolute quality of mind.
4. a formal statement of opinion or determination adopted by an assembly or other group of persons.
5. a solving, as of a puzzle; the answering, as of a question; solution.
6. in medicine, the subsidence or disappearance of an inflammation, swelling, or fever.
7. in music, (a) the passing of a dissonant tone (in a chord), as an appoggiatura, to a consonant tone; (b) the passing of a dissonant chord to a consonant chord or, sometimes, to another dissonant chord; (c) a tone or chord to which such passing occurs.
8. in mathematics, solution, as of a problem or an equation. [Obs.]
resolution of a nebula; the process of magnifying a nebula by means of a telescope so that it is seen to be an aggregation of stars.
resolution of forces; the process of finding the components of given forces.
Syn.—courage, decision, determination, firmness, fortitude, analysis, separation, disentanglement, dissolution, resolvedness, resoluteness, constancy, perseverance, steadfastness, boldness, purpose, resolve.

reṣ·ō·lū′tion·ẽr, *n.* one who joins in the declaration of others; specifically, [R—] in the Scottish church, one who supported the resolution conciliating the Royalists passed by a commission of the Assembly in the seventeenth century.

reṣ·ō·lū′tion·ist, *n.* one who makes a resolution.

reṣ′ō·lū·tive, *a.* having the power to dissolve or relax. [Obs.]

reṣ′ō·lū·tō·ry, *a.* having the effect of voiding or rescinding; conferring the right to rescind.

rē·ṣolv·ȧ·bil′i·ty, *n.* the quality or state of being resolvable.

rē·ṣolv′ȧ·ble, *a.* that can be resolved (in various senses).

rē·ṣolv′ȧ·ble·ness, *n.* the state of being resolvable.

rē-solve′, *v.t.* to solve again or anew.

rē·ṣolve′, *v.t.*; resolved, *pt., pp.*; resolving, *ppr.* [OFr. *resolver,* from L. *resolvere,* to loosen, to dissolve, to melt; *re-,* again, and *solvere,* to loosen.]
1. to break up into separate, constituent elements or parts; to analyze.
2. to change; to transform (with *into*): used reflexively; as, the discussion *resolved* itself *into* an argument.
3. to cause (a person) to decide or make up his mind; as, the flood *resolved* him to sell.
4. to determine; to reach as a decision or intention (often followed by an infinitive); as, we *resolved to go.*

> That we here highly *resolve* that these dead shall not have died in vain.
> —Abraham Lincoln.

5. (a) to solve or explain; to make clear, as a problem; (b) to remove (doubt, etc.).
6. to decide by vote; to make a formal decision about; to express by resolution: said of a legislative assembly, etc.
7. to cause to dissolve or melt. [Obs.]
8. in medicine, to cause (a swelling, inflammation, etc.) to subside without the formation of pus.
9. in music, to cause (a tone or chord) to undergo resolution.
10. in optics, to make visible the individual parts of (an image).
11. in mechanics, to break up (a force) into components.
12. to relax; to put at ease. [Obs.]

rē·ṣolve′, *v.i.* 1. to form a resolution; to come to a decision; to determine in mind; as, he *resolved* on a firm course of action.
2. to be resolved, as by analysis (with *into* or *to*).
3. in music, to undergo resolution.
4. to melt; to dissolve; to become fluid. [Obs.]
5. to be settled in opinion. [Obs.]

rē·ṣolve′, *n.* 1. a fixed intention; a firm determination; a settled purpose; a resolution; as, a *resolve* to do better.
2. the act of a legislative body; the declaration of any corporate body. [Now Rare.]

rē·ṣolved′, *a.* firm and fixed in purpose; determined; resolute.

rē·ṣolv′ed·ly, *adv.* in a resolved manner; with firmness of purpose.

rē·ṣolv′ed·ness, *n.* set determination; resolution; fortitude; firmness.

rē·ṣolv′end, *n.* a number which is formed by extending the remainder after subtraction in extracting the square or cube root.

rē·ṣolv′ent, *a.* having the power to resolve or dissolve; causing solution or resolution; solvent.

rē·ṣolv′ent, *n.* [L. *resolvens* (*-entis*), ppr. of *resolvere,* to resolve.]
1. that which has the power of resolving.
2. in medicine, that which has power to cause resolution of a swelling or inflammation; a discutient.
3. an equation upon whose solution depends the solution of a given equation; a resolvent equation.

rē·ṣolv′ẽr, *n.* 1. one who resolves or forms a firm purpose or resolution.
2. that which separates parts; that which dissolves or disperses.
3. that which solves or clears.

reṣ′ō·nănce, *n.* [L. *resonantia,* an echo.]
1. the state or quality of being resonant.
2. reinforcement and prolongation of a sound by reflection or by vibration of other bodies.
3. in chemistry, the property of certain molecules of having two or more structures in which only the positions of electrons differ.
4. in electricity, the condition of adjustment of a circuit that allows the greatest flow of current of a certain frequency.
5. in medicine, the sound produced in the percussion of some part of the body, especially of the chest.
6. in phonetics, relative audibility: it rises in inverse proportion to the amount of stricture during articulation.
7. in physics, the reinforced vibration of a body exposed to the vibration, at about the same frequency, of another body.
cough resonance; the sound made by a cough as heard in auscultation.
pulmonary resonance; the sound obtained by percussion over the lungs.
vocal resonance; the sound obtained when the chest is auscultated during the use of the vocal organs.

reṣ′ō·năn·cy, *n.* resonance. [Rare.]

reṣ′ō·nănt, *a.* [L. *resonans* (*-antis*), ppr. of *resonare,* to resound.]
1. resounding; re-echoing; as, a *resonant* sound.
2. increasing the intensity of sounds by sympathetic vibration; as, *resonant* walls.
3. full of, or intensified by, resonance; as, a *resonant* voice.
4. of resonance.

5. of, relating to, or designating an articulate sound which is produced by the nasal chambers acting as a resonant cavity.

reș′ō·nănt·ly, *adv.* in a resonant manner.

reș′ō·nāte, *v.i.*; resonated, *pt., pp.*; resonating, *ppr.* 1. to have resonance; to be resonant; to resound.

2. to produce resonance.

reș′ō·nā·tŏr, *n.* [Mod. L., from pp. of L. *resonare*, to resound.]

1. a device for producing resonance or increasing sound by resonance.

2. an instrument for detecting a specific frequency by the use of resonance.

3. in electricity, an open electric circuit of small dimensions having ends nearly in contact: when subjected to the influence of electric resonance, a spark produced by inductance passes across the gap.

4. in radio, the high-frequency circuits of a radio receiving apparatus.

reș·ō·pȳ′rin, *n.* a derivative of resorcinol and antipyrin, used in medicine as an antipyretic.

rē·șorb′, *v.t.*; resorbed, *pt., pp.*; resorbing, *ppr.* [L. *resorbere*, to suck back, to swallow again; *re-*, again, and *sorbere*, suck up.] to reabsorb.

rē·șorb′ent, *a.* reabsorbent.

re·șọr′cin, reș·ọr′cine, *n.* resorcinol.

reș·ọr′cin·ōl, *n.* [*resin* and *orcinol*.] a colorless, crystalline compound, $C_6H_4(OH)_2$, prepared synthetically or by fusing certain resins with caustic alkalis: it is used in the manufacture of dyes, celluloid, and hair tonics, and as a medicinal astringent.

reș·or·cyl′iç, *a.* relating to or containing resorcinol.

rē·șorp′tion, *n.* [L. *resorptus*, pp. of *resorbere*, to resorb.] the process of resorbing or the state of being resorbed; reabsorption.

rē·șorp′tive, *a.* relating to or causing reabsorption.

rē·șort′, *n.* [ME.; OFr., from the *v.*]

1. a place to which people go often, customarily, or generally; especially, a place to which people go for rest or relaxation, as on a vacation.

2. a frequent, customary, or general going, gathering together, or visiting; as, a place of general *resort*.

3. a person or thing that one goes or turns to for help, support, etc.

4. a going or turning for help, support, etc.; recourse; as, he had *resort* to his brother.

5. the act of visiting; company. [Obs.]

Join with me to forbid him her *resort*.
—Shak.

6. spring; active power or movement: a Gallicism. [Obs.]

last resort; ultimate means of relief; also, final tribunal; that from which there is no appeal.

rē·șort′, *v.i.*; resorted, *pt., pp.*; resorting, *ppr.* [ME. *resorten*; OFr. *resortir*, to go out again, formerly to seek refuge, to resort, from *re-*, again, and *sortir*, to go out.]

1. to have recourse; to go or turn for use, help, support, etc.; he *resorted* to harsh measures.

2. to go; especially, to go often, customarily, or generally; to repair; as, the people *resort* to parks and beaches in the summer.

3. to fall back. [Obs.]

rē-sort′, *v.t.* to sort again or anew.

rē·șort′ẽr, *n.* one who resorts or frequents.

rē·șound′, *v.i.* [ME. *resounen*; OFr. *resoner*; L. *resonare*, from *re-*, again, and *sonare*, to sound.]

1. to be filled with sound; to re-echo; to reverberate: said of places.

2. to make a loud, echoing, or prolonged sound; to sound loudly; as, his voice *resounded* far.

3. to be echoed; to be sent back; to be repeated or prolonged: said of sounds.

4. to be celebrated; to be extolled; as, a name to *resound* for ages.

rē·șound′, *v.t.* 1. to echo; to reverberate; to sound again; to return the sound of; to re-echo.

The rocks *resound* her lays. —Dryden.

2. to give forth, utter, or repeat loudly.

3. to celebrate or extol (someone's praises, etc.).

rē-sound′, *v.t.* and *v.i.* to sound again or anew; as, to *re-sound* a note or syllable.

rē·șound′, *n.* return of sound; echo.

rē·sōurce′, *n.* [Fr. *ressource*, from OFr. *resourdre*, to arise anew; *re-*, again, and *sourdre*, to spring up as water, from L. *surgere*, to arise, contr. for *surrigere*; *sub*, under, and *regere*, to direct.]

1. something that lies ready for use or can be drawn upon for aid; a supply of something to take care of a need.

2. [*pl.*] wealth; assets; available money or property: opposed to *liabilities*.

3. [*usually in pl.*] something that a country, state, etc. has and can use to its advantage; as, our natural *resources* include coal and petroleum.

4. a means of accomplishing something; a measure or action that can be resorted to, as in an emergency; an expedient; as, his only remaining *resource* was flight.

5. [*in pl.*] a means of spending one's leisure time; amusement; recreation.

6. ability to deal promptly and effectively with problems, difficulties, etc.; resourcefulness.

Syn.—expedient, resort, means, contrivance, device.

rē·sōurce′fụl, *a.* full of resource; able to deal promptly and effectively with problems, difficulties, etc.; clever in finding resources.

rē·sōurce′less, *a.* lacking resources.

rē·spēak′, *v.t.* to speak again; to repeat.

rē·speçt′, *v.t.*; respected, *pt., pp.*; respecting, *ppr.* [L. *respectare*, to look behind, look intently, respect, freq. of *respicere*, to look at, look back upon, respect; *re-*, back, and *specere*, to look at, see, spy.]

1. to notice with special attention; to regard; to heed; to consider. [Obs.]

I am armed so strong in honesty,
That they pass by me as the idle wind,
Which I *respect* not. —Shak.

2. to have reference or regard to; to concern; to relate to; as, the treaty particularly *respects* our commerce.

3. to view, treat, or consider with some degree of reverence, deference, or courtesy; to feel or show honor or esteem for.

I always loved and *respected* Sir William.
—Swift.

4. to show consideration for; to avoid intruding upon or molesting; as, *respect* his privacy.

5. to look toward; to front upon or in the direction of. [Obs.]

Syn.—regard, esteem, honor, revere, venerate.

rē·speçt′, *n.* [L. *respectus*, a looking at, respect, regard, from *respicere*, to look at.]

1. the act of respecting or noticing with attention; the looking toward; attention.

We pass by common objects or persons without noticing them, whereas we turn back to look again at those which deserve our admiration, our regard, our *respect*. This was the original meaning of *respect* and *respectable*.
—Max Müller.

2. the act of holding in high estimation, deference, or honor; a feeling of esteem; regard.

Out of the great *respect* they bear to beauty.
—Shak.

3. a state of being held in honor or esteem; as, he died without the *respect* of his countrymen.

4. consideration; courteous regard; as, one must have *respect* for the feelings of others.

5. [*pl.*] courteous expressions of respect; regards; as, he paid his *respects* to the mayor.

6. a particular point or detail; as, in this *respect* you are wrong.

7. partiality; undue bias to the prejudice of justice.

8. consideration; motive in reference to something. [Now Rare.]

9. relation; regard; reference; as, with *respect* to your problem.

They believed but one Supreme Deity, which, with *respect* to the benefits men received from him, had several titles.
—Tillotson.

in respect of; with reference to; as regards.

in respect that; because of the fact that; considering.

rē·speçt·ȧ·bil′i·ty, *n.*; *pl.* **rē·speçt·ȧ·bil′i·tieș,**

1. state or quality of being respectable.

2. respectable character, reputation, or social status.

3. respectable people as a group.

4. [*usually in pl.*] something accepted or regarded as respectable.

rē·speçt′ȧ·ble, *a.* [ML. *respectabilis*, worthy of respect, from L. *respectare*, to respect.]

1. capable of being respected; worthy of respect or esteem.

No government, any more than an individual, will long be respected, without being truly *respectable*. —Madison.

2. having, or appropriate to, good social status, reputation, etc.; decent, honest, proper, etc.; as, a *respectable* hotel, *respectable* behavior.

3. fairly good in quality; of moderate excellence; as, his work was *respectable* but not outstanding.

4. fairly large in size, number, or amount.

5. good enough to be seen, used, etc.; presentable; as, a *respectable* suit of clothes.

rē·speçt′ȧ·ble·ness, *n.* respectability.

rē·speçt′ȧ·bly, *adv.* 1. in a respectable manner.

2. to a respectable extent or degree.

rē·speçt′ănt, *a.* [L. *respectans* (*-antis*), ppr. of *respectare*, to look at, respect.] in heraldry, designating two animals borne face to face.

LIONS RESPECTANT

rē·speçt′ẽr, *n.* one who respects.

respecter of persons; one whose behavior toward people is influenced by their social status, prestige, etc.

rē·speçt′fụl, *a.* full of or characterized by respect; showing respect; as, *respectful* deportment.

Syn.—civil, dutiful, obedient, courteous, complaisant.

rē·speçt′fụl·ly, *adv.* with respect; in a manner showing respect.

rē·speçt′fụl·ness, *n.* the quality of being respectful.

rē·speçt′ing, *prep.* concerning; about; regarding; in regard to; relating to; as, he was at fault *respecting* the source of my information.

rē·speç′tion, *n.* the act of respecting; regard. [Obs.]

rē·speç′tive, *a.* [ML. *respectivus*, from L. *respectus*, pp. of *respicere*, to observe, respect.]

1. relating individually to each of two or more persons or things; severally connected or belonging; several; particular; as, let them retire to their *respective* places of abode.

The Constitution controls the constitutions of the *respective* states.—John Marshall.

2. relative; having relation to something else; not absolute. [Obs.]

3. worthy of respect; respectable. [Obs.]

4. rendering respect; respectful. [Obs.]

5. observing or noting with attention; regardful; hence, careful; circumspect; cautious; attentive to consequences. [Obs.]

6. favoring one over others; discriminative; partial. [Obs.]

rē·speç′tive·ly, *adv.* 1. with respect to each of two or more, in the order named or mentioned; as, the first, second, and third prizes went to John, Mary, and George, *respectively*.

2. respectfully. [Obs.]

3. relatively; not absolutely. [Obs.]

rē·speçt′less, *a.* having no respect; without regard. [Obs.]

rē·speçt′less·ness, *n.* the state of having no respect or regard. [Obs.]

rē·speç′tū·ous, *a.* inspiring respect; also, respectful. [Obs.]

rē·spell′, *v.t.* to spell again; specifically, to indicate a pronunciation of, as a word in a vocabulary, by means of phonetic spelling.

rē·spẽrse′, *v.t.* to sprinkle. [Obs.]

rē·spẽr′sion, *n.* [L. *respersio* (*-onis*), a sprinkling, from *respersus*, pp. of *respergere*, to sprinkle.] the act of sprinkling. [Obs.]

rē·spīr·ȧ·bil′i·ty, rē·spīr′ȧ·ble·ness, *n.* the quality of being respirable.

rē·spīr′ȧ·ble, *a.* [Fr.] 1. that can be breathed; fit for respiration; as, *respirable* air.

2. that can respire; capable of breathing.

res·pi·rā′tion, *n.* [L. *respiratio* (*-onis*), from *respiratus*, pp. of *respirare*, to respire.]

1. act or process of respiring; breathing; inhaling and exhaling air.

2. the processes by which a living organism or cell takes in oxygen from the air or water, distributes and utilizes it in oxidation, and gives off products of oxidation, especially carbon dioxide.

3. a breathing space; a respite. [Obs.]

res·pi·rā′tion·ăl, *a.* relating to respiration.

rē·spīr′ȧ·tive, *a.* pertaining to respiration. [Rare.]

res′pi·rā·tŏr, *n.* [L. *respiratus*, pp. of *respirare*, to respire.]

1. a device, as gauze, used to cover the mouth and nose for the purpose of purifying, warming, or otherwise affecting the air taken into the lungs.

2. an apparatus for giving artificial respiration.

3. a gas mask. [Brit.]

rē·spi·rȧ·tō′ri·um, *n.*; *pl.* **rē·spi·rȧ·tō′ri·ȧ,** [LL., neut. pl. of *respiratorius*, respiratory.] one of the organs resembling gills, borne by certain aquatic larvae, used in obtaining air from the water.

rē·spīr′ȧ·tō·ry, *a.* of or for respiration; as, *respiratory* organs.

rē·spīre′, *v.i.*; respired, *pt.*, *pp.*; respiring, *ppr.* [OFr. *respirer*; L. *respirare*, to breathe, respire; *re-*, back, and *spirare*, to breathe.]
 1. to breathe; to inhale air into the lungs and exhale it, for the purpose of maintaining animal life.
 2. to breathe freely or easily again, as after exertion or anxiety; to enjoy a breathing space.

rē·spīre′, *v.t.* 1. to breathe; to inhale and exhale.
 2. to breathe out; to exhale; to give off (an odor, etc.). [Rare.]

res·pi·rom′ē·tēr, *n.* an instrument for measuring respiration and determining its character.

res′pite, *n.* [OFr. *respit*; L. *respectus*, respect, regard.]
 1. a temporary period of relief or rest, as from pain, work, duty, etc.; interval of rest.
 2. in law, (a) reprieve; temporary suspension of the execution of a capital offender; (b) prolongation of time for the payment of a debt beyond the legal time; (c) the delay of appearance at court granted to a jury, beyond the proper term.
 3. a temporary delay, postponement, or putting off of something fixed, especially of something disagreeable.
 4. respect. [Obs.]
 Syn.—reprieve, suspension, commutation, pause, delay, postponement, stay.

res′pite, *v.t.*; respited, *pt.*, *pp.*; respiting, *ppr.*
 1. to allow a respite to; to suspend the execution of a sentence upon beyond the time limited; to reprieve.
 2. to delay; to suspend; to put off; to postpone.
 3. to relieve by an interval of rest. [Obs.]

res′pite·less, *a.* having no respite.

rē·splen′dence, *n.* the quality or state of being resplendent; brilliant luster; vivid brightness; splendor.

rē·splen′den·cy, *n.* same as *resplendence*.

rē·splen′dent, *a.* [L. *resplendens* (*-entis*), ppr. of *resplendere*, to shine brightly; *re-*, again, and *splendere*, to shine.] full of splendor; dazzling; splendid; very bright; shining with brilliant luster.

rē·splen′dent·ly, *adv.* with resplendence.

rē·splen′dish·ănt, *a.* resplendent. [Obs.]

rē·splen′dish·ing, *a.* resplendent. [Obs.]

rē·spond′, *v.i.*; responded, *pt.*, *pp.*; responding, *ppr.* [OFr. *respondre* (Fr. *répondre*); L. *respondere*, to respond.]
 1. to answer; to reply.
 2. to act in return, as if in answer; as, he *responded* to the insult with a blow.
 3. to correspond (*to*). [Rare or Obs.]
 4. in law, to be answerable or liable.
 5. in physiology and psychology, to react.

rē·spond′, *v.t.* 1. to answer; to say in reply.
 2. to correspond to. [Obs.]

rē·spond′, *n.* 1. in architecture, an engaged column, pilaster, etc. supporting an arch.
 2. in ecclesiastical usage, a response or responsory.
 3. an answer; a response. [Rare.]

rē·spond′ence, *n.* the state or quality of being respondent; an answering; a response.

rē·spond′en·cy, *n.* respondence.

rē·spond′ent, *a.* [L. *respondens* (*-entis*), ppr. of *respondere*, to respond.]
 1. responding; answering.
 2. that answers to demand or expectation; corresponding. [Obs.]

rē·spond′ent, *n.* 1. a person who responds.
 2. in law, a defendant, especially in equity, admiralty, appellate, and divorce proceedings.
 3. one who maintains a thesis in reply, and whose province is to refute objections, or overthrow arguments.

rē·spon·den′ti·ȧ (-shi-), *n.* a loan upon goods laden on board a ship, the repayment of which is made to depend upon the safe arrival of the goods at the destined port. It differs from bottomry, which is a loan on the ship itself.

rē·spon′săl, *a.* responsible. [Obs.]

rē·spon′săl, *n.* 1. a response; an answer. [Obs.]
 2. one who is responsible. [Obs.]

rē·sponse′, *n.* [L. *responsum*, an answer, neut. of *responsus*, pp. of *respondere*, to respond.]
 1. something said or done in answer to something else; an answer; reply.
 2. in ecclesiastical usage, (a) words, phrases, etc. sung or spoken by the congregation or choir in answer to the officiating clergyman or priest; (b) a responsory.
 3. in physiology and psychology, any behavior resulting from the application of a stimulus; a reaction.
 4. an oracular answer.
 5. reply to an objection in formal disputation.
 6. in a fugue, a repetition of the given subject by another part.
 7. the act of replying or responding.

rē·sponse′less, *a.* making no response.

rē·spon·si·bil′i·ty, *n.*; *pl.* **rē·spon·si·bil′i·tieș,** 1. the condition, quality, fact, or instance of being responsible, answerable, accountable, or liable, as for a person, trust, office, or debt.
 2. a person or thing for which one is responsible.

rē·spon′si·ble, *a.* [LL. *responsabilis*, requiring an answer, from L. *responsum*, response.]
 1. expected or obligated to account (*for* something, *to* someone); answerable; accountable; as, he is *responsible for* the car.
 2. involving accountability, obligation, or duties; as, he has a *responsible* position.
 3. answerable or accountable as being the cause, agent, or source of something (with *for*); as, who is *responsible for* this state of affairs?
 4. able to distinguish between right and wrong and to think and act rationally, and hence accountable for one's behavior.
 5. (a) trustworthy; dependable; reliable; as, she is a *responsible* person; (b) able to pay debts or meet business obligations.
 Syn.—accountable, answerable, amenable.

rē·spon′si·ble·ness, *n.* the quality or state of being responsible; responsibility.

rē·spon′si·bly, *adv.* in a responsible manner.

rē·spon′sion, *n.* [L. *responsio* (*-onis*), an answer, a reply, from *responsus*, pp. of *respondere*, to respond.]
 1. the act of answering; a responding.
 2. [*pl.*] at Oxford University, England, the first of three examinations of a candidate for the B.A. degree.

rē·spon′sive, *a.* [LL. *responsiva*, f., an answering; L. *responsus*, pp. of *respondere*, to respond.]
 1. answering; making reply; responding.
 2. reacting easily or readily to suggestion or appeal; as, a *responsive* audience.
 3. containing or consisting of responses; as, *responsive* reading in church.
 4. correspondent. [Obs.]
 5. responsible. [Obs.]

rē·spon′sive·ly, *adv.* in a responsive manner.

rē·spon′sive·ness, *n.* the quality or state of being responsive.

rē·spon·sō′ri·ăl, *a.* [LL. *responsoria*, a response.] pertaining to response or to a responsory; antiphonal.

rē·spon·sō′ri·ăl, *n.* a book of responsories.

rē·spon′sō·ry, *a.* containing answer.

rē·spon′sō·ry, *n.*; *pl.* **rē·spon′sō·rieș,** [ME. *responsorye*; ML. *responsorium*.] in ecclesiastical usage, an anthem or series of responses sung or said in alternation by a soloist and choir after a lection.

res·sä′lä, *n.* same as *risala*.

res·săl·där′, *n.* same as *risaldar*.

res·saut′, *n.* [OFr., from L. *resilire*, to leap back.] in architecture, the projection of a member from a surface, as a wall, so as to be out of line with it.

rest, *n.* [ME. *reste*; AS. *ræst*; Ice. *röst*; Sw. and Dan. *rast*; Goth. *rasta*; O.H.G. *rasta*, rest or quiet.]
 1. (a) peace, ease, and refreshment as produced by sleep; (b) sleep or repose.
 2. refreshing ease or inactivity after work or exertion.
 3. a period or occasion of inactivity, as during work or on a journey.
 4. (a) relief from anything distressing, disturbing, annoying, tiring, etc.; (b) peace of mind; mental and emotional calm; tranquillity.

Sweet indeed is the *rest* which Christ giveth.
—Wilberforce.

 5. the repose of death.
 6. absence of motion; state of being still; immobility.
 7. a resting or stopping place; shelter; lodging place, as for travelers, sailors, etc.
 8. a device for supporting something; that on which anything leans or lies for support; specifically, (a) a device for supporting the turning tool or the work in a lathe; (b) a support for the muzzle of a gun in aiming and firing; (c) a support for the upper end of a billiard cue, when the player cannot reach sufficiently far to support it with his hand.
 9. in music, (a) an interval of silence between tones; (b) any of various symbols indicating the length of such an interval.
 10. in prosody, a short pause in a line of verse; a caesura.

A B C D E F

RESTS (in music)
A, whole; B, half; C, quarter rests; D, eighth; E, sixteenth; F, thirty-second

 at rest; in a state of rest; specifically, (a) asleep; (b) immobile; (c) free from distress, care, etc.; (d) dead.
 to lay to rest; to bury (a dead person).
 Syn.—cessation, pause, intermission, stop, stay, repose, slumber, quiet, ease, quietness, stillness, tranquillity, peacefulness, peace.

rest, *v.i.*; rested, *pt.*, *pp.*; resting, *ppr.* [AS. *restan*, *hrestan*, to pause, cease, be quiet; G. *rasten*; Sw. *rasta*.]
 1. (a) to get peace, ease, and refreshment by sleeping, lying down, etc.; (b) to sleep.
 2. to get ease and refreshment by ceasing from work or exertion.
 3. to be at ease or peace; to be tranquil.
 4. to have the repose of death; to be dead.
 5. to be, become, or remain quiet, still, or inactive for a while.
 6. to remain without change or further action; as, let the matter *rest*.
 7. to be, or seem to be, supported; specifically, (a) to lie, sit, or lean; (b) to be placed, based, or founded (*in*, *on*, *upon*, etc.).
 8. to be placed or imposed as a burden or responsibility (*on* or *upon*).
 9. to be or lie (where specified); as, the fault *rests* with him.
 10. to be directed or fixed (*on* or *upon*); as, his eyes *rested on* the picture.
 11. to rely (*on* or *upon*); to depend.
 12. to remain; stay; abide.
 13. in agriculture, to remain unploughed or uncropped; to lie fallow: said of land.
 14. in law, to end voluntarily the introduction of evidence in a case.
 to rest on one's laurels; to be satisfied with what one has already achieved.

rest, *v.t.* 1. to give rest to; to refresh by rest.
 2. to place, put, or lay for ease, support, etc.; as, *rest* your head on the pillow.
 3. to base; to ground; as, he *rested* his argument on trivialities.
 4. to direct or fix (the eyes, etc.).
 5. to bring to rest; to stop.
 6. in law, to end voluntarily the introduction of evidence in (a case); as, the State *rests* its case.

rest, *n.* [Fr. *reste*, from *rester*, to rest, remain, from L. *restare*, to stop, stand, rest, remain; *re-*, back, and *stare*, to stand.]
 1. that which is left, or which remains after the withdrawal or separation of a part, either in fact or in contemplation; remainder.
 2. [*construed as pl.*] those that are left; the others; those not included in a proposition, category, or description: used with *the*; as, all *the rest* of us had finished.
 3. surplus or reserve funds. [Brit.]
 4. in court tennis, the rapid and continuous returning of the ball from player to player.
 5. in accounting, (a) the striking of a balance of an account; (b) the amount of the balance.
 for the rest; as regards all other matters or points.
 Syn.—remainder, residue, remnant, surplus, balance, difference, leavings.

rest, *v.i.* 1. to go on being; to continue to be; to remain (as specified); as, *rest* assured that we will go.
 2. to be left over. [Obs.]

rest, *v.t.* to cause to remain; to keep; as, God *rest* you merry, gentlemen.

rest, *n.* [ME. aphetic var. of *arest*, an arrest.]
 1. a support for the butt of a lance, projecting from the side of the breastplate in medieval armor.
 2. in heraldry, a bearing that represents, (a) a support for a lance; (b) a musical instrument.

rē·stag′nănt, *a.* stagnant. [Obs.]

rē·stag′nāte, *v.i.* to stagnate. [Obs.]

rē·stag·nā′tion, *n.* stagnation. [Obs.]

res′tănt, *a.* [L. *restans,* ppr. of *restare.*] in botany, remaining, as footstalks after the fructification has fallen off; persistent.

rē·stāte′, *v.t.* 1. to state again.

2. to state (something previously stated) in a new form.

rē·stāte′ment, *n.* 1. a restating or being restated.

2. a statement made again.

3. a statement (of something stated before) in a new form.

res·taur′, *n.* [Fr. *restaur;* OFr. *restour;* LL. *restaurum,* a restoring, from L. *restaurare,* to restore.] the recourse which insurers have against each other, according to the dates of their insurances; or against masters of vessels if the loss arises through their default; also, the recourse a person has against his guarantor or other person who is to indemnify him from any damage sustained.

res′tau·rănt (-tō-), *n.* [Fr., an eating house, from LL. *restaurans* (*-antis*), ppr. of *restaurare,* to restore, refresh.] a place where meals can be bought and eaten; an eating house.

res′tau·rāte (-tō-), *v.t.* to restore. [Obs.]

res″tau·rȧ·teūr′ (-tō-), *n.* [Fr. *restaurateur;* LL. *restaurator,* one who keeps a restaurant, from L. *restauratus,* pp. of *restaurare,* to restore, to refresh.] a person who owns or operates a restaurant.

res·tau·rā′tion (-tō-), *n.* [L. *restaurare.*] restoration. [Obs.]

rest çūre, a treatment of disease, as of nervous disorders, by prolonged rest, often with special diet, etc.

rest′fụl, *a.* 1. quiet; being at rest.

2. full of or bringing rest; freeing from labor or care.

rest′fụl·ly, *adv.* in a restful manner.

rest′fụl·ness, *n.* the state or quality of being restful.

rest′har″rōw, *n.* any of a number of plants of the genus *Ononis,* of the pea family, with long, tough roots: so called because its roots arrest or stop the harrow.

rest′house, *n.* in India, a dak bungalow.

Res·tī·ā′cē·ae, *n.pl.* [from L. *restis,* a cord, because their stems are used as cords at the Cape of Good Hope, and *-aceæ.*] a family of perennial dioecious plants of the Southern Hemisphere, the cordleaf family: they are herbs or undershrubs with a creeping rhizome, or grow in tufts, with narrow leaves, the sheaths of which are usually split, and with inconspicuous brown rushlike panicles of flowers. They abound at the Cape of Good Hope and in Australia, where they form a hard, wiry, rushlike herbage. The stems of some species are manufactured into baskets and brooms, and *Restio tectorum* is employed for thatching.

rest′iff, *a.* restive. [Obs.]

rest′iff·ness, *n.* restiveness. [Obs.]

res′ti·fọrm, *a.* [L. *restis,* a cord, a rope, and *forma,* form.] in the form of a rope or cord; specifically, designating either of two cordlike bundles of nerve fibers (*restiform bodies*) connecting the medulla oblongata with each hemisphere of the cerebellum.

rest′i·ly, *adv.* in a resty manner; stubbornly; unwillingly. [Obs.]

rest′i·ness, *n.* the state or quality of being resty; sluggishness; stubbornness. [Obs.]

rest′ing, *a.* [ppr. of *rest* (to sleep).] in botany, dormant: said of spores, etc.

rest′ing cell, a resting spore.

rest′ing spōre, a spore which germinates only after a period of dormancy, as at the end of a winter season.

rē·stin′guish (-gwish), *v.t.* to quench or extinguish. [Obs.]

Res′ti·ō, *n.* [LL., from L. *restis,* a cord; so called from its stringlike stems.] a genus of plants of the *Restiaceæ.* They are characterized by one-celled anthers and spikelets which have imbricated glumes and numerous flowers.

Res″ti·ō·nā′cē·ae, *n.pl.* same as *Restiaceæ.*

res′ti·tūte, *v.t.* to restore to a former state. [Now Rare.]

res·ti·tū′tion, *n.* [L. *restitutio* (*-onis*), a restoring, from *restitutus,* pp. of *restituere,* to set up again, to restore.]

1. the act of restoring to the rightful owner that which is lost or has been taken away; the act of restoring to a person some thing or right of which he has been unjustly deprived; as, the *restitution* of ancient rights to a family.

2. the act of making good, or of giving an equivalent, for any loss, damage, or injury; reimbursement; indemnification.

3. a return to a former condition or situation.

4. in physics, the recovery of its shape by an elastic body after pressure or strain is released.

5. in surgery, the rotation of the presenting part of the fetus outside of the vagina.

coefficient of restitution; in mechanics, the ratio of the force of restitution to that of compression.

force of restitution; in mechanics, the force causing the separation of bodies which have been brought together by the force of compression.

Syn.—restoration, compensation, amends, return, remuneration, indemnification, reparation, recompense.

res′ti·tū·tive, *a.* pertaining to or having the character of restitution.

res′ti·tū·tŏr, *n.* one who makes restitution. [Rare.]

rest′ive, *a.* [OFr. *restif,* drawing backward, refusing to go forward, from *rester,* L. *restare,* to stay back, to remain; *re-,* behind, and *stare,* to stand.]

1. refusing to go forward; balky: said of a horse, etc.

2. hard to control; unruly; refractory.

3. nervous or impatient under pressure or restraint; restless.

4. being at rest; being less in motion. [Obs.]

rest′ive·ly, *adv.* in a restive manner.

rest′ive·ness, *n.* the state or quality of being restive.

rest′less, *a.* [AS. *restleás; rest,* rest, and *-leás,* -less; Sw. and Dan. *rastlös.*]

1. characterized by inability to rest or relax; unquiet; uneasy; continually moving; as, a *restless* child.

2. without sleep or rest; having or giving no rest or relaxation; disturbed or disturbing; as, *restless* sleep.

Restless he passed the remnant of the night. —Dryden.

3. never or almost never quiet or still; always active or inclined to action.

4. not satisfied to be at rest or in peace; desiring change; discontented; as, *restless* ambition.

Syn.—disquieted, agitated, anxious, unsettled, sleepless, roving, disturbed, uneasy, wandering.

rest′less cā′vy, the wild guinea pig of South America.

rest′less·ly, *adv.* in a restless manner.

rest′less·ness, *n.* the state or quality of being restless.

rē·stock′, *v.t.* and *v.i.* to stock again or provide with a new stock, as a store or farm.

rē·stōr′ȧ·ble, *a.* that can be restored to a former good condition; as, *restorable* land.

rē·stōr′ȧ·ble·ness, *n.* the state of being restorable.

res·tō·rā′tion, *n.* [OFr. *restauration;* LL. *restauratio* (*-onis*), from L. *restauratus,* pp. of *restaurare,* to restore.]

1. a restoring or being restored; reinstatement.

2. a putting or bringing back into a former, normal, or unimpaired state or condition.

3. a representation of the original form or structure, as of a building, fossil, animal, etc.; reconstruction.

4. in theology, the doctrine of the final recovery of all men from sin and alienation from God to a state of happiness; universal salvation; Universalism.

5. that which is restored.

the Restoration; (a) the re-establishment of the monarchy in England in 1660 under Charles II; (b) the period of the reign of Charles II (1660–1685): sometimes taken as including the reign of James II (1685–1688).

Syn.—replacement, re-establishment, renovation, reinstatement, revival, renewal, recovery, restitution, redintegration, reparation, return.

res·tō·rā′tion·ẽr, *n.* a restorationist.

res·tō·rā′tion·ịsm, *n.* the doctrines, beliefs, etc. of the restorationists.

res·tō·rā′tion·ist, *n.* a believer in a temporary future punishment and a final restoration of all to the favor and presence of God.

rē·stōr′ȧ·tive, *a.* [LL. *restaurativus,* a restorative, from L. *restaurare,* to restore.]

1. of restoration.

2. tending to restore or capable of restoring; especially, capable of restoring health, strength, consciousness, etc.

rē·stōr′ȧ·tive, *n.* something that restores; especially, something that restores to consciousness, as smelling salts.

rē·stōr′ȧ·tive·ly, *adv.* in a manner or degree that tends to renew strength or vigor.

rē·stōr′ȧ·tō·ry, *a.* restorative. [Rare.]

rē-stōre′, *v.t.* to store again; as, the goods taken out were *re-stored.*

rē·stōre′, *v.t.;* restored, *pt., pp.;* restoring, *ppr.* [OFr. *restorer;* Fr. *restaurer,* to restore, to renew, to repair, to reinstall, from L. *restaurare,* to restore, to repair; *re-,* again, and the primitive *staurare,* to make strong.]

1. to give or bring back; to return to a person, as a specific thing which he has lost, or which has been taken from him and unjustly detained; to make restitution of; as, to *restore* lost or stolen goods to the owner.

2. to give in place of or as satisfaction for; hence, to make amends for; to compensate. [Obs.]

All losses are *restored* and sorrows end. —Shak.

3. to put (a person) back in a former position, place, rank, or condition; to replace; to return to a former place.

Release me and *restore* me to the ground. —Tennyson.

4. to bring back to a former or normal condition, as by repairing, rebuilding, altering, etc.; as, *restore* a building, painting, etc.

5. to bring back to health, strength, etc.

6. to re-establish something which has passed away, as a custom, system of government, etc.

7. to recover or renew, as passages of an author defective or corrupted; to emend.

8. in paleontology, to put together in their proper places the bones or other remains of (an extinct animal).

Syn.—repay, return, replace, renew, refund, repair, recover, heal.

rē·stōre′, *n.* restoration. [Obs.]

rē·stōre′ment, *n.* the act of restoring; restoration. [Obs.]

rē·stōr′ẽr, *n.* one who or that which restores.

rē-strāin′, *v.t.* and *v.i.* to strain again or anew.

rē·strāin′, *v.t.;* restrained, *pt., pp.;* restraining, *ppr.* [ME. *restreynen;* OFr. *restraindre,* from L. *restringere,* to draw back tightly; *re-,* and *stringere,* to draw tight.]

1. to hold back; to check; to hold from action, proceeding, or advancing, either by physical or moral force, or by any interposing obstacle; to repress; to curb; as, to *restrain* men from crimes; to *restrain* anger.

2. to keep under control.

3. to deprive of physical liberty, as by putting in prison or in an asylum.

4. to limit; to restrict.

5. to withhold. [Obs.]

6. to strain; to draw tight. [Obs.]

Syn.—check, prevent, repress, hinder, coerce, stop, curb, suppress.

rē·strāin′ȧ·ble, *a.* capable of being restrained.

rē·strāin′ed·ly, *adv.* in a restrained manner; with restraint.

rē·strāin′ẽr, *n.* one who or that which restrains; specifically, in photography, potassium bromide, etc. added to a developer to retard its action.

rē·strāin′ment, *n.* the act of restraining. [Obs.]

rē·strāint′, *n.* [OFr. *restrainte.*]

1. a restraining or being restrained.

2. something that restrains, as an influence or action.

3. a means or instrument of restraining.

4. a loss or limitation of liberty; confinement.

5. control of emotions, impulses, etc.; reserve; constraint.

rē·strāint′ of trāde, interruption of the free movement of goods in commerce; restriction or prevention of business competition.

rē·strict′, *v.t.;* restricted, *pt., pp.;* restricting, *ppr.* [L. *restrictus,* pp. of *restringere,* to restrict, to restrain.] to keep within limits; to hold down; to limit; to confine; to restrain within bounds; as, to *restrict* words to a particular meaning; to *restrict* a patient to a certain diet.

Syn.—limit, bound, confine, curb, restrain, coerce.

rē·strict′ed, *a.* [pp. of *restrict.*]

1. limited; confined.

2. limited to a certain group or groups; especially, limited to white Christians: racist euphemism; as, a *restricted* hotel.

rē·striç′tion, *n.* [Fr. *restriction;* LL. *restrictio* (*-onis*), a restriction, from L. *restrictus,* pp. of *restringere,* to restrain.]

1. the act of restricting, confining, or limiting; the state of being restricted, limited, or confined within bounds.

2. that which restricts or limits; a limitation.

rē·stric̦′tion·ā·ry, *a.* restrictive. [Rare.]

rē·stric̦′tion·ist, *n.* in United States history, one who held that slavery should be restricted to certain territory.

rē·stric̦t′ive, *a.* [Fr. *restrictif.*]

1. restricting or tending to restrict; having the quality of limiting or of imposing restraint; as, *restrictive* laws of trade.

2. in grammar, designating a subordinate clause, phrase, or term felt as limiting the application of the word or words that it modifies as a relative clause (usually not set off by commas) that identifies the person or thing designated by the antecedent (e.g., in "automobiles that have bad brakes are dangerous," *that have bad brakes* is a restrictive relative clause; in "go when the bell rings," *when the bell rings* is a restrictive adverbial clause; in "a man with money is needed," *with money* is a restrictive phrase): opposed to *nonrestrictive, descriptive.*

3. styptic. [Obs.]

rē·stric̦t′ive·ly, *adv.* with limitation.

rē·stric̦t′ive·ness, *n.* the quality or state of being restrictive.

rē·strinġe′, *v.t.* to confine; to contract; to astringe. [Obs.]

rē·strin′ġen·cy, *n.* the quality or power of contracting; astringency. [Obs.]

rē·strin′ġent, *a.* [L. *restringens* (*-entis*), ppr. of *restringere*, to restrain.] astringent; styptic. [Obs.]

rē·strin′ġent, *n.* an astringent or styptic medicine. [Obs.]

rest′-ro̤om″, *n.* 1. a room or rooms (in a public building) equipped with toilets, washbowls, couches, and the like, for the convenience of patrons, employees, etc.

2. a toilet or lavatory, as in a theater, etc.

rest′y, *a.* restive; restless. [Obs.]

rē·sub·li·mā′tion, *n.* a second sublimation.

rē·sub·līme′, *v.t.* to sublime again.

rē·sū·dā′tion, *n.* [L. *resudatus*, pp. of *resudare*, to sweat out, to sweat again; *re-*, and *sudare*, to sweat.] the act of sweating again. [Obs.]

rē·ṣult′, *v.i.*; resulted, *pt., pp.*; resulting, *ppr.* [OFr. *resulter*, to rebound or leap back, come out of, result, from L. *resultare*, to spring back, rebound, resound, a freq. of *resilire*, to leap back.]

1. to leap back; to rebound. [Obs.]

2. to happen or issue as a consequence or effect of some cause (often with *from*); as, learning *results from* study.

3. to come out or have an issue; to terminate; to end as a consequence (*in* something); as, this measure will *result in* good or *in* evil.

rē·ṣult′, *n.* 1. resilience; the act of flying back. [Obs.]

2. consequence; outcome; issue; effect; that which proceeds naturally or logically from facts, premises, or the state of things; as, the *result* of reasoning; the *result* of reflection.

3. the decision of a deliberative assembly; a resolution; a decree. [Obs.]

4. in mathematics, a number, quantity, etc. obtained by calculation; the answer to a problem.

Syn.—consequence, effect, issue, outcome, end, event, consummation, inference, conclusion.

rē·ṣult′ănce, *n.* the act of resulting; a result. [Obs.]

rē·ṣult′ănt, *a.* [L. *resultans.*] 1. existing, proceeding, or following as a result, consequence, or conclusion; resulting.

2. resulting from the combination of two or more agents or forces acting together.

rē·ṣult′ănt, *n.* 1. something that results; a result.

2. in mechanics, a single force which is equivalent in effect to two or more forces; the single force which represents the combined effect of several forces: these several forces are termed *components* or *component forces.* When two forces act on a particle in the same direction, their resultant is equal to their sum, and acts in the same direction. When two forces act on a particle in opposite directions, their resultant is equal to their difference, and acts in the direction of the greater force. If two concurrent forces acting upon a point are represented in magnitude and direction by the two sides of a parallelogram, then their resultant is represented in magnitude and direction by the diagonal drawn through the given point.

3. in mathematics, an eliminant.

rē·ṣult′āte, *n.* a result. [Obs.]

rē·ṣult′fu̇l, *a.* showing or producing results. [Rare.]

rē·ṣult′ing trust, in law, a trust raised by implication in favor of the author of the trust himself or his representatives.

rē·ṣult′ing ūse, in law, a use returning by way of implication to the grantor himself.

rē·ṣult′ive, *a.* resultant. [Obs.]

rē·ṣult′less, *a.* not productive of results.

rē·ṣūm′ȧ·ble, *a.* capable of being taken back or up again; that can be resumed.

rē·ṣūme′, *v.t.*; resumed, *pt., pp.*; resuming, *ppr.* [OFr. *resumer*, from L. *resumere*, to take again, resume, from *re-*, and *sumere*, to take.]

1. (a) to take, get, or occupy again; as, *resume* your seat; (b) to take back or take on again; as, *resume* a former name.

2. to begin again or go on with again after interruption; as, we *resumed* the conversation.

rē·ṣūme′, *v.i.* to begin again or go on again, as after interruption; as, I shall *resume* later.

ré·su·mé′ (rā-zū-mā′), *n.* [Fr., pp. of *résumer.*] a summing up; a summary.

rē·ṣump′tion, *n.* [LL. *resumptio* (*-onis*), a restoration, a recovery, from L. *resumptus*, pp. of *resumere*, to take again, resume.] the act of resuming, taking back, or taking again; as, the *resumption* of a grant; specifically, in law, the taking again by the state of such lands, tenements, or privileges, etc. as had been granted by letters patent, on false suggestion, or other error.

rē·ṣump′tive, *a.* and *n.* [LL. *resumptivus*, from L. *resumptus*, pp. of *resumere*, to resume.] taking back or again; resuming.

rē·ṣump′tive, *n.* a restoring medicine. [Obs.]

rē·sū′pi·nāte, *a.* [L. *resupinatus*, pp. of *resupinare*, to bend or turn back, overthrow; *re-*, and *supinare*, to bend or lay backward.]

1. inverted; reversed; appearing as if turned upside down.

2. in botany, so turned or twisted that the parts naturally the undermost become the uppermost, and vice versa; as, a *resupinate* corolla; a *resupinate* leaf.

rē·sū′pi·nā·ted, *a.* resupinate.

rē·sū·pi·nā′tion, *n.* the state of lying on the back; the state of being resupinate or reversed.

rē·sū·pīne′, *a.* lying on the back; supine.

rē·sûr′fāce, *v.t.*; resurfaced, *pt., pp.*; resurfacing, *ppr.* to put a new or different surface on.

rē·sûr′gam, [L.] I shall rise again.

rē·sûrġe′, *v.i.* [L. *resurgere*, to rise again; *re-*, and *surgere*, to rise.]

1. to rise again; to be resurrected; to revive.

2. to surge back again.

rē·sûr′ġence, *n.* resurrection; the act of resurging.

rē·sûr′ġent, *a.* [L. *resurgens* (*-entis*), ppr. of *resurgere*, to rise again.] rising or tending to rise again, as in resurrection; resurging.

rē·sûr′ġent, *n.* one who rises again; one who rises from the dead.

reṣ·ur·rec̦t′, *v.t.*; resurrected, *pt., pp.*; resurrecting, *ppr.* [back-formation from *resurrection.*]

1. to raise from the dead or the grave; to bring back to life.

2. to bring back into notice, practice, use, etc.

3. to disinter; to remove from the grave as a dead body.

reṣ·ur·rec̦t′, *v.i.* to rise from the dead; to come back to life.

reṣ·ur·rec̦′tion, *n.* [Fr., from LL. *resurrectio* (*-onis*), from L. *resurrectus*, pp. of *resurgere*, to rise again, to appear; *re-*, and *surgere*, to rise.]

1. a rising from the dead, or coming back to life.

2. a coming back into notice, practice, use, etc.; restoration or revival, as of old customs.

3. the state of having risen from the dead.

the Resurrection; in Christian theology, (a) the rising of Jesus from the dead after his death and burial; (b) the rising of all the dead at the Last Judgment.

reṣ·ur·rec̦′tion·ăl, *a.* of, or having the nature of, resurrection.

reṣ·ur·rec̦′tion·ăr·y, *a.* 1. resurrectional.

2. of resurrectionism.

reṣ·ur·rec̦′tion·iṣm, *n.* the stealing of bodies from graves, especially for dissection.

reṣ·ur·rec̦′tion·ist, *n.* 1. one who practices stealing bodies from the grave, especially for dissection.

2. a person who brings something back into use or notice again.

3. a person who believes in resurrection.

reṣ·ur·rec̦′tion·ize, *v.t.* to raise from the dead; to resurrect.

reṣ·ur·rec̦′tion man, a resurrectionist.

reṣ·ur·rec̦′tion plant, any one of several species of the flowerless plants of the genus *Selaginella*, which, when dry, close up in the form of a bird's nest, but on being wetted re-expand.

rē·sûr·vey′, *v.t.* 1. to survey again.

2. to make a new survey of.

rē·sûr′vey, *n.* a second or new survey.

rē·sus′ci·tȧ·ble, *a.* capable of being resuscitated.

rē·sus′ci·tănt, *n.* [L. *resuscitans* (*-antis*), ppr. of *resuscitare*, to revive.] one who or that which resuscitates. [Rare.]

rē·sus′ci·tănt, *a.* resuscitative. [Rare.]

rē·sus′ci·tāte, *v.t.*; resuscitated, *pt., pp.*; resuscitating, *ppr.* [L. *resuscitatus*, pp. of *resuscitare*, to revive.] to revivify; to revive; particularly, to recover from apparent death or unconsciousness; as, to *resuscitate* a drowned person; to *resuscitate* withered plants.

rē·sus′ci·tāte, *v.i.* to revive; to come back to life or consciousness.

rē·sus′ci·tāte, *a.* resuscitated; restored to life. [Obs.]

rē·sus·ci·tā′tion, *n.* [LL. *resuscitatio* (*-onis*), a reviving, from L. *resuscitatus*, pp. of *resuscitare*, to revive.] the act of resuscitating; the state of being resuscitated.

rē·sus′ci·tā·tive, *a.* serving or tending to resuscitate; reviving; revivifying; raising from apparent death.

rē·sus′ci·tā·tŏr, *n.* [LL.] one who or that which resuscitates.

ret, *v.t.* to impute; to reckon. [Obs.]

ret, *v.t.*; retted, *pt., pp.*; retting, *ppr.* [ME. *retten, reten*; O.D. *reten, reeten*, to break or heckle (flax); Sw. *röta*, prob. same as *rot.*] to steep or macerate, as flax, hemp, timber, etc., in water in order to soften and separate the fiber by incipient rotting.

rē·tā′ble, *n.* [Fr. *retable*; OFr. *retaule, restaule*, from L. *restare*, to rest.] in architecture, a raised shelf or ledge above and behind an altar for holding candles, vases, etc.

rē′tāil, *n.* [OFr. *retaylen*, lit., a cutting, from *retailler*, to cut up; *re-*, again, and *tailler*, to cut.] the sale of commodities, goods, articles, etc. individually or in small quantities or parcels directly to the consumer; a dealing out in small portions: opposed to *wholesale.*

rē′tāil, *a.* of, connected with, or engaged in the sale of goods at retail.

rē′tāil (*or* rē-tāl′), *v.t.*; retailed, *pt., pp.*; retailing, *ppr.* 1. to sell individually or in small quantities; to sell directly to the consumer: opposed to *wholesale*; as, to *retail* cloth or groceries.

2. to repeat or pass on to others; to tell in detail; to tell to many; to spread by report; as, to *retail* slander or idle reports.

rē′tāil, *v.i.* to be sold at retail; as, these books *retail* at a dollar.

rē′tāil·ēr, *n.* 1. a retail merchant or dealer; one who sells goods in small quantities or parcels; one who retails; as, a *retailer* of groceries.

2. a circulator, as of gossip, etc.; as, a *retailer* of false reports.

rē·tāil′ment, *n.* the act of retailing.

rē·tāin′, *v.t.* [OFr. *retenir, retanir*, from L. *retentus*, pp. of *retinere*, to hold back; *re-*, and *tenere*, to hold.]

1. to hold or keep in possession; to keep from departure or escape; to hold; to detain; to keep.

> An executor may *retain* a debt due to him from the testator. —Blackstone.

2. to keep in a fixed state or condition.

3. to continue to practice, use, etc.

4. to keep in mind.

5. to hire, or arrange in advance for the services of, by paying a fee; as, *retain* a lawyer.

6. to withhold; to restrain; to keep back. [Obs.]

Syn.—hold, keep, preserve, hire, employ, secure, engage, maintain.

rē·tāin′, *v.i.* 1. to belong; to depend; to pertain. [Obs.]

2. to continue. [Obs.]

rē·tāin′ȧ·ble, *a.* capable of being retained.

rē·tāin′ăl, *n.* retention; the act of retaining.

rē·tāined′ ob′jec̦t, in grammar, an object in

passive constructions that is the same as the direct or indirect object in the corresponding active constructions (e.g., *money* in "John was given the *money* by me"; corresponding active construction, "I gave John the money").

rē·tāin'ēr, *n.* 1. one who or that which retains; a keeper; as, a *retainer* of sound.

2. a person serving someone of rank, as in feudal times, and owing him occasional service; attendant or adherent, as of a lord.

3. a groove, frame, etc., within which roller bearings are held.

4. a person who is not a regular soldier though associated with an army and subject to its rules.

rē·tāin'ēr, *n.* [substantive use of OFr. *retenir.*]

1. a retaining or being retained in one's service.

2. in law, (a) the act of engaging the services of a lawyer, counselor, etc.; (b) a fee paid to get such services; (c) the authority granted by thus engaging services; (d) the keeping of something one has in his possession by virtue of some right.

rē·tāin'ing, *a.* serving to retain.

retaining fee; a retainer (sense 2b).

retaining wall; (a) a wall built to keep a bank of earth from sliding or water from flooding; (b) a revetment.

rē·tāin'ment, *n.* retention; the act of retaining or state of being retained.

rē·tāke', *v.t.*; retook, *pt.*; retaken, *pp.*; retaking, *ppr.* 1. to take again, take back, or recapture.

2. in motion pictures and photography, to photograph again.

rē'tāke, *n.* 1. a retaking.

2. a picture, scene, etc. rephotographed or to be rephotographed.

rē·tal'i·āte, *v.t.*; retaliated, *pt., pp.*; retaliating, *ppr.* [L. *retaliatus*, pp. of *retaliare*, to requite, retaliate; *re-*, and *talis*, such.] to repay or requite by an act of the same kind; to return an injury, wrong, etc. for (an injury, wrong, etc. given).

It is unlucky to be obliged to *retaliate* the injuries of authors. —Swift.

rē·tal'i·āte, *v.i.* to return like for like, especially, evil for evil; to pay back injury for injury; as, to *retaliate* upon an enemy.

rē·tal·i·ā'tion, *n.* the act of retaliating; the return of like for like; the doing of that to another which he has done to us; especially, the return of evil for evil; retribution; revenge.

Syn.—requital, reprisal, revenge, retribution, punishment.

rē·tal'i·ā·tive, *a.* same as *retaliatory.*

rē·tal'i·ā·tō·ry, *a.* 1. of, having the nature of, or involving retaliation.

2. retaliating or tending to retaliate.

Re·tä'mȧ, *n.* [Sp. *retama*; Ar. *retama.*]

1. a former genus of leguminous shrubs, now included in the genus *Genista*, found in the Mediterranean region.

2. [r-] a plant of this genus.

rē·tärd', *v.t.*; retarded, *pt., pp.*; retarding, *ppr.* [OFr. *retarder*, to impede, hinder; L. *retardare*, to delay; *re-*, and *tardare*, to make slow, hinder, from *tardus*, slow.]

1. to obstruct in swiftness of course; to slow the advance or progress of; to keep delaying; to impede; to clog; to hinder; as, to *retard* the march of an army; to *retard* the motion of a ship: opposed to *accelerate.*

2. to defer; to put off; to render more late. [Rare.]

Syn.—impede, clog, hinder, thwart, obstruct, detain, delay.

rē·tärd', *v.i.* to be delayed.

rē·tärd', *n.* a retarding; a delay.

retard of the tide; the interval between the transit of the moon at which a tide originates and the appearance of the tide itself.

rē·tär·dā'tion, *n.* [L. *retardatio* (*-onis*), from *ratardatus*, pp. of *retardare*, to make slow, from *tardus*, slow.]

1. the act of retarding or the state of being retarded; hindrance; the act of delaying; putting off or rendering more late; as, the *retardation* of the motion of a ship.

2. that which retards; a hindrance; an obstruction.

3. in music, (a) the slackening or retarding of the time; (b) a suspension, especially one that resolves upwards. [Rare.]

4. in electricity, a decrease in the speed of telegraphic signaling due to distributed electrostatic induction and resistance.

5. in physics, the act of hindering the free progress or velocity of a body, and ultimately therefore stopping it. It arises from the opposition of the medium in which the body moves, or from the friction of the surface upon which it moves, or from the action of gravity.

retardation of the tides; a certain deviation between the time of the actual occurrence of high water at any place and what it would be if it occurred after the lapse of a uniform mean interval. In the second and fourth quarters of the moon there is retardation or lagging of high water.

rē·tärd'ȧ·tive, *a.* retardatory; retarding.

rē·tärd'ȧ·tō·ry, *a.* 1. of, or having the nature of, retardation.

2. retarding or tending to retard.

rē·tärd'ed mō'tion, in physics, motion which suffers continual diminution of velocity, as the motion of a body projected upward. If the diminutions of velocity are equal in equal times the motion is said to be uniformly retarded. The laws of retarded motion are the same as those of accelerated motion, only the order is reversed.

rē·tärd'ēr, *n.* one who or that which retards, hinders, or delays.

rē·tärd'ment, *n.* retardation; the act of retarding or delaying.

retch, *v.i.*; retched, *pt., pp.*; retching, *ppr.* [AS. *hræcan*, to try to vomit, from *hraca*, a cough, spittle; Ice. *hrækja*, to retch, from *hrâki*, spittle. Allied to Gr. *krazein*, to croak.] to make a straining, involuntary effort to vomit; to heave, as the stomach; to strain, as in vomiting: also written *reach.*

retch, *v.t.* and *v.i.* [ME. *rechen*; AS. *ræcan*, to reach.] to reach. [Dial.]

retch'less, *a.* careless; reckless. [Obs.]

retch'less·ly, *adv.* recklessly. [Obs.]

retch'less·ness, *n.* recklessness; carelessness. [Obs.]

rē'tē, *n.*; *pl.* **rē'ti·ȧ** (-shi-), [L. *rete*, net.] in anatomy, a network or plexus, as of blood vessels or nerve fibers; a part resembling a network.

rete mirabile; in anatomy, a complex network formed by the breaking up of a vessel into many branches which constitute a plexus. When the plexus is made up of arteries only or of veins only, it is called *rete mirabile simplex*; when made up of both arteries and veins, *rete mirabile conjugatum* or *rete mirabile geminum.*

rete mucosum; the layer of the skin intermediate between the cutis and the cuticle, the principal seat of color in man.

rē·tē'cious, *a.* same as *retiform.*

rē'tem, *n.* [Ar. *ratam*, pl. of *ratamah.*] a desert shrub of the bean family, with small, white flowers: the juniper of the Old Testament.

rē'tēne, *n.* [Gr. *rhētinē*, resin.] a hydrocarbon, $C_{18}H_{18}$, found in the form of fatty scales on fossil pine wood and also produced by the dry distillation of very resinous fir.

rē·tent', *n.* [L. *retentus*, pp. of *retinere*, to retain.] that which is retained.

rē·ten'tion, *n.* [Fr., from L. *retentio* (*-onis*), a retaining, from *retentus*, pp. of *retinere*, to retain.]

1. the act of retaining or keeping; the state of being retained.

2. the power of or capacity for retaining.

3. (a) a remembering; the faculty of the mind by which it retains ideas; memory; (b) ability to remember.

No woman's heart so big, to hold so much;
they lack *retention.* —Shak.

4. in medicine, a morbid accumulation of solid or liquid matter in vessels of the body or cavities intended to contain it only for a time.

5. the act of withholding; reserve; restraint. [Obs.]

His life I gave him, and did thereto add
My love without *retention* or restraint.
—Shak.

6. the state of being confined; custody; confinement. [Obs.]

7. in Scots law, a lien; a right of withholding a debt or retaining property until a debt due to the person claiming this right is paid.

rē·ten'tive, *a.* [OFr. *retentif*, from L. *retentus*, pp. of *retinere*, to retain.]

1. having the power or capacity to retain; as, a *retentive* memory; the *retentive* faculty; the *retentive* force of the stomach; a body *retentive* of heat or moisture.

2. retaining or tending to retain.

3. (a) tenacious; as, a *retentive* memory; (b) having a good memory.

rē·ten'tive, *n.* that which restrains or confines; a restraint. [Obs.]

rē·ten'tive·ly, *adv.* in a retentive manner.

rē·ten'tive·ness, *n.* the quality of being retentive; as, *retentiveness* of memory.

rē·ten·tiv'i·ty, *n.* 1. the power of or capacity for retaining; retentiveness.

2. in a magnetizable body, the power of retaining magnetization or of resisting demagnetization after the force of magnetization has stopped.

rē·ten'tŏr, *n.* in zoology, a muscle which, by retraction, keeps an organ in place.

Rē·tep'ō·rȧ, *n.* [L. *rete*, a net, and *porus*, a pore.] a genus of zoophytes of the class *Polyzoa* that live in colonies, their skeletons fusing to form corallike masses in a flattened foliaceous expansion pierced like network. The typical species, *Retepora cellulosa*, found in the Indian and Mediterranean seas, is known by the name of Neptune's ruffles. Fossil species occur in all formations.

RETEPORE

rē'tē·pōre, *n.* one of the genus *Retepora.*

rē·tex'tūre, *n.* a second or new texture; the act of weaving or forming anew.

reth'ō·ricke, *n.* rhetoric. [Obs.]

rē·ti·ā'ri·us (-shi-), *n.*; *pl.* **rē·ti·ā'ri·ī,** [L., one who fights with a net, from *rete*, a net.] in ancient Rome, one of a class of gladiators who with a net and a trident fought his adversary.

rē'ti·ăr·y (-shi-), *n.*; *pl.* **rē'ti·ăr·ies,** [L., properly an adjective, pertaining to a net, from *retiarius*, one who fights with a net, from *rete*, a net.]

1. in entomology, any spider which spins webs to catch its prey.

2. a retiarius.

rē'ti·ăr·y, *a.* 1. pertaining to the spinning spiders; web-spinning.

2. of or like nets or netmaking; having meshes; netlike.

3. armed or furnished with a net; hence, expert or skillful in entangling.

ret'i·cence, *n.* [L. *reticentia.*] the quality, instance, or state of being reticent; a refraining from talking; a keeping of one's own counsel; silence; reserve.

ret'i·cen·cy, *n.* reticence.

ret'i·cent, *a.* [L. *reticens* (*-entis*), ppr. of *reticere*, to be silent, from *re-*, again, and *tacere*, to be silent.] habitually silent or uncommunicative; indisposed to talk; taciturn; silent; reserved.

Upon this he is naturally *reticent.*—Lamb.

ret'i·çle, *n.* [L. *reticulum*, double dim. from *rete*, a net.]

1. in optics, a network of very fine lines, wires, etc. in the focus of the eyepiece of an optical instrument.

2. a small net. [Obs.]

rē·tiç'ū·lăr, *a.* 1. having the form of a net or of network; formed with interstices; netlike; as, a *reticular* membrane.

2. intricate; entangled; complicated.

3. in anatomy, designating any netlike membrane or part.

reticular cartilage; any form of cartilage in which the matrix is mainly a network of yellow fibers: also called *yellow cartilage.*

reticular tissue; in anatomy, any netlike tissue, as adenoid, retiform, or glandular tissue.

Rē·tiç·ū·lā'ri·ȧ, *n.pl.* same as *Foraminifera.*

rē·tiç·ū·lăr'i·ăn, *a.* having a reticular shell; belonging to or resembling the *Reticularia.*

rē·tiç·ū·lăr'i·ăn, *n.* any rhizopod belonging to the *Reticularia*; a foraminifer.

rē·tiç'ū·lăr·ly, *adv.* in a reticular, or netlike, manner.

rē·tiç'ū·lāte, *a.* [L. *reticulatus*, made like a net, from *rete*, a net.]

1. formed of network; constructed like the meshes of a net; having distinct lines crossing each other like network: applied to lattice windows, the crossbars of a fence, etc.

2. in botany, netted; having the veins arranged like the threads of a net: said of leaves, venation, cells, vessels, etc.

rē·tiç'ū·lāte, *v.t.*; reticulated, *pt., pp.*; reticulating, *ppr.* to divide or mark so as to look like network.

rē·tiç'ū·lāte, *v.i.* to be divided or marked like network.

rē·tiç'ū·lā·ted, *a.* reticulate.

reticulated glass; a species of ornamental glassware produced by a network of white or colored lines enclosed in the glass and arranged in regular interlacing series.

reticulated micrometer; a kind of micrometer invented by Malvasia and used for measuring small celestial distances. It consists of an eyepiece of low power having stretched across it a number of wires at right angles to and at equal and known distances from each other.

reticulated molding; an ornamental molding composed of a fillet interlaced in various ways, like network. It is found chiefly in buildings in the Norman style.

RETICULATED MOLDING

reticulated work; a variety of masonry consisting of layers of square stones laid diagonally, giving an appearance of network. It was common among the Romans.

RETICULATED WORK

rē·tiç·ū·lā′tion, *n.* a reticulate arrangement, formation, or pattern; the state of being reticulate or reticulated; network.

ret′i·çūle, *n.* [Fr. *réticule*; L. *reticulum*, a little net, double dim. of *rete*, a net.]
1. a small handbag carried by women, originally made of network.
2. a reticle.

Rē·tiç·ū·lō′sȧ, *n.pl.* same as *Foraminifera*.

rē·tiç′ū·lōse, *a.* same as *reticulated*.

rē·tiç′ū·lum, *n.*; *pl.* **rē·tiç′ū·lȧ,** 1. network; netlike pattern or structure; especially, finely meshed network, as in a cell or a delicate tissue.
2. in zoology, the second division of the stomach, or second stomach, of ruminants, as cows: named from its folds forming hexagons, as seen in tripe: also called *honeycomb bag*: see *ruminant*, illus.
3. the supporting structure of nervous tissue; neuroglia.
4. [R–] a small southern constellation.
5. in botany, any one of various reticulated structures, especially the web at the base of a palm leaf.
6. in biology, a netlike structure found in the protoplasm of cells.

rē′ti·fọrm (*or* ret′i-), *a.* [LL. *retiformis*, from L. *rete*, net, and *forma*, form.] having the form of a net; having criss-crossed lines; reticulate; composed of crossing lines and interstices; as, the *retiform* coat of the eye.

ret′i·nȧ, *n.*; *pl.* **ret′i·nȧṣ, ret′i·nae,** [ML.; prob. from L. *rete*, *retis*, a net.] the innermost coat of the back part of the eyeball, a layer of cells sensitive to light, in part an expansion of the optic nerve fibers: the image formed by the lens on the retina is carried to the brain by the optic nerve: see *eye*, illus.

ret·i·naç′ū·lum, *n.*; *pl.* **ret·i·naç′ū·lȧ,** [L., that which holds back, a holdfast, from *retinere*, to hold back.]
1. in anatomy, a restraining band; a structure retaining an organ or tissue in place.
2. in surgery, an instrument formerly used in operations for hernia, etc.
3. in botany, a viscid gland connected with the stigma and holding fast the pollen masses in orchids.
4. in entomology, a plate restraining the sting when protruded.

ret′i·năl, *a.* of, on, or relating to the retina.

rē·tin′ȧ·līte, *n.* [Gr. *rhētinē*, resin, and *lithos*, stone.] in mineralogy, a massive serpentine with a resinous luster.

ret·in·as′phạlt, ret″in·as·phạl′tum, *n.* same as *retinite*.

ret′in·ēne, *n.* [from *retina* and *-ene*.] visual yellow.

ret′i·nẽrved, *a.* [L. *rete*, net, and *nervus*, nerve.] in botany, having netted veins.

ret·i·nē′um, *n.*; *pl.* **ret·i·nē′ȧ,** in zoology, that part of a compound eye analogous in its uses to the retina.

rē·tin′iç, *a.* [Gr. *rhētinē*, resin.] relating to or produced from any of several resinous materials.

ret′i·nīte, *n.* 1. any of several fossil resins, especially one derived from lignite.
2. same as *pitchstone*.

ret·i·nī′tis, *n.* [from *retina* and *-itis*.] inflammation of the retina.

ret′i·noid, *a.* [Gr. *rhētinē*, resin, and *eidos*, likeness.] resinlike, or resiniform.

ret′i·nōl, *n.* [Gr. *rhētinē*, resin, and *-ol*.] a yellowish liquid hydrocarbon, $C_{32}H_{16}$, obtained in the rectification of the products of the dry distillation of turpentine resins: it is used as a lubricant, a solvent, an antiseptic, etc.

ret·i·noph′ō·rȧ, *n.*; *pl.* **ret·i·noph′ō·rae,** [LL., from *retina*, retina, and Gr. *-phoros*, from *pherein*, to bear.] in the embryonic eye of arthropods, a cell which secretes the crystalline cone.

ret·i·noph′ō·răl, *a.* relating to retinophorae.

ret′in·ō·sçōpe, *n.* a skiascope.

ret″in·ō·sçop′iç, *a.* of or by retinoscopy.

ret·i·nos′çō·py, *n.* [LL. *retina*, retina, and Gr. *skopia*, from *skopein*, to see.] a method for determining the refraction of the eye: also called *skiascopy*.

ret′i·nūe, *n.* [ME. *retenue*; OFr. *retenue*, f. of *retenu*, pp. of *retenir*, L. *retinere*, to retain.] the servants or attendants of a prince or distinguished personage, as on a journey or an excursion; a train of persons; a body of retainers; an escort.

rē·tin′ū·lȧ, *n.*; *pl.* **rē·tin′ū·lae,** [LL., dim. of *retina*, retina.] in zoology, the group of cells making up the retina of a single eye.

rē·tin′ū·lāte, *a.* resembling or characterized by retinulae.

ret′i·ped, *n.* [L. *rete*, net, and *pes*, *pedis*, foot.] a bird having the skin of the tarsi divided into small polygonal scales.

rē·tīr′ȧ·cy, *n.* retirement, as of a person from active life.

ret·i·räde′, *n.* [Fr., from *retirer*, to withdraw; Sp. *retirada*, to retreat.] in fortification, a kind of retrenchment in the body of a bastion or other work: it usually consists of two faces, which make a re-entering angle. [Now Rare.]

rē·tīre′, *v.i.*; retired, *pt.*, *pp.*; retiring, *ppr.* [Fr. *retirer*; *re-*, back, and *tirer*, to draw; It. *ritirare*; Sp. *retirar*.]
1. to withdraw; to draw back; to go away to a private, sheltered, or secluded place; as, to *retire* into a convent.
2. to retreat from danger, action, or battle; to give ground or withdraw; as, wars with a *retiring* enemy.
3. to move back or away, or seem to do so; to recede; to be bent or curved back; as, the shore *retires* to form a bay.
4. to withdraw oneself from business, active service, or public life, especially because of advanced age.

Thus Atticus, and Trumbull thus, *retired*. —Pope.

5. to disappear; to depart gradually; as, *retiring* day. [Poet.]
6. to go to bed.

rē·tīre′, *v.t.* 1. to withdraw; to take or lead away; as, *retire* troops from an action.

He might have *retired* his power. —Shak.

2. to take out of circulation, as money; to take up or pay off (stocks, bonds, bills, etc.).
3. to remove from a position or office; as, they *retired* several generals.
4. in baseball, etc., to put out (a batter, side, etc.).

rē·tīre′, *n.* 1. retreat; recession; a withdrawing. [Obs.]
2. retirement; place of privacy. [Obs.]

rē·tīred′, *a.* 1. withdrawn or secluded from society or public notice; secluded; quiet; private; as, to live a *retired* life.
2. secret; private; difficult to be seen, known, or discovered.

Language springs out of the most *retired* and inmost parts of us. —Jonson.

3. withdrawn from business or active life or service; having given up business; as, a *retired* merchant; a *retired* captain.
4. of or for a person or persons so withdrawn; as, a *retired* list.
5. withdrawn in space; bent or drawn back.

retired flank; in fortification, a flank bent inward toward the rear of the work.

rē·tīre′ment, *n.* 1. the act of retiring or condition of being retired; withdrawal, removal, etc.

Retirement is as necessary to me as it will be welcome. —Washington.

2. privacy; seclusion.
3. a place of privacy or seclusion.

rē·tīr′ẽr, *n.* one who retires.

rē·tīr′ing, *a.* [ppr. of *retire*.]
1. that retires.
2. drawing back from contact with others, from publicity, etc.; reserved; modest; shy.
3. of, pertaining to, or causing retirement.

retiring board; a board of officers of the army or navy who investigate and recommend concerning the alleged incapacity of an officer for active service.

ret′i·stēne, *n.* same as *retene*.

Ret·i·tē′lae, *n.pl.* a division of spiders whose webs are irregular.

rē·tōld′, *v.* past tense and past participle of *retell*.

rē·took′, *v.* past tense of *retake*.

rē·tọol′, *v.t.* and *v.i.* to adapt the machinery of (a factory) to the manufacture of a different product by changing the tools and dies.

rē·tọr′sion, *n.* same as *retortion*, sense 2.

rē·tọrt′, *v.t.*; retorted, *pt.*, *pp.*; retorting, *ppr.* [OFr. *retort*, from L. *retortus*, pp. of *retorquere*, to twist back; *re-*, back, and *torquere*, to twist.]
1. to turn (an insult, epithet, deed, etc.) back upon the person from whom it came.
2. to answer (an argument, etc.) in kind.
3. to throw back; to reverberate. [Obs.]
4. to bend or curve back; as, a *retorted* line. [Obs.]

rē·tọrt′, *v.i.* to make a sharp or witty reply; to reply in kind or in the same terms as the previous speaker.

rē·tọrt′, *n.* 1. a quick, sharp, or witty reply, especially one that turns the words of the previous speaker back upon himself.
2. the act or practice of making such reply.

Syn.—repartee.—A *retort* is a short and pointed reply, turning back on an assailant the censures or derision he had thrown out; *repartee* is usually a good-natured return to some witty or sportive observation of another.

rē·tọrt′, *n.* [Fr. *retorte*, a bent or twisted body, a retort; LL. *retorta*, a band, a tie, from L. *retorta*, f. of *retortus*, pp. of *retorquere*, to twist back.] in chemistry, a spherical container, generally of glass and with a long neck, in which substances are distilled or decomposed by heat.

RETORT
A, retort; B, Bunsen burner; C, flask for receiving distilled liquids

tubulated retort; a retort having a tubulure, for the introduction or removal of the materials to be acted upon.

rē·tọrt′, *v.t.* to separate, as different metals, in a retort.

rē·tọrt′ẽr, *n.* one who retorts.

rē·tọr′tion, *n.* [ML. *retortio*, *retorsio*, from L. *retortus*, pp. of *retorquere*.]
1. a turning, bending, or twisting back or being turned, bent, or twisted back.
2. in law, a retaliation; reprisal; especially, in international law, mistreatment by one country of the citizens or subjects of another in retaliation for similar mistreatment received from the latter country: also spelled *retorsion*.

rē·tọrt′ive, *a.* of the nature of a retort.

rē·tŏuch′, *v.t.* [Fr. *retoucher*; see *re-* and *touch*.]
1. to touch up or change details in (a painting, piece of writing, etc.) in order to improve it.
2. in photography, to change (a negative or print) by adding details or removing blemishes, as with a pencil or knife.

rē·tŏuch′ (*or* rē′tuch″), *n.* 1. a retouching.
2. a detail added or removed in retouching.
3. a photograph, etc. that has been retouched.

rē·tŏuch′ẽr, *n.* one who retouches; especially, one who retouches prints or negatives of photographs.

rē·tŏuch′ment, *n.* the act or operation of retouching; the state of being retouched. [Rare.]

rē·tōur′, *n.* 1. return. [Obs.]

2. in Scots law, an extract of the return made to a court of chancery on a brieve of inquest.

rē·trāce′, *v.t.*; retraced (-trāst′), *pt., pp.*; retracing, *ppr.* [Fr. *retracer.*]

1. to trace back or again; to go back over again, especially in the reverse direction; as, to *retrace* one's steps; to *retrace* one's proceedings.

2. to trace back, as a line of descent.

Then if the line of Turnus you *retrace.*
—Dryden.

3. to trace again the story of, from the beginning.

4. to go over again with the eyes or in memory.

rē-trāce′, rē·trāce′, *v.t.* to trace over again, as a drawing.

rē·traçt′, *v.t.*; retracted, *pt., pp.*; retracting, *ppr.* [OFr. *retracter,* from L. *retractare,* to retract, freq. of *retrahere,* to draw back; *re-,* and *trahere,* to draw.]

1. to recall; to disavow or withdraw (a statement, promise, offer, charge, etc.); to recant; as, to *retract* an accusation, charge, or assertion.

2. to draw back or in; as, a cat *retracts* its claws.

Syn.—abjure, revoke, deny, recant, disown, recall, withdraw.

rē·traçt′, *v.i.* 1. to withdraw or disavow a statement, promise, offer, etc.

2. to draw back or in.

rē·traçt′, *n.* in farriery, the pricking of a horse's foot in nailing a shoe. [Obs.]

rē·traçt′ȧ·ble, *a.* capable of being retracted.

rē·traç′tāte, *v.t.* to retract; to recant. [Obs.]

rē·traç·tā′tion, *n.* [OFr. *retractation,* from L. *retractatio* (-*onis*), a consideration, a refusal; *retractatus,* pp. of *retractare,* to reconsider, to draw back, to retract.] a retraction; the recalling of what has been said; recantation.

rē·traçt′i·ble, *a.* retractable.

rē·traç′tile, *a.* 1. that can be retracted; capable of being drawn back or in; as, *retractile* claws.

2. of retraction; as, *retractile* power.

rē·traç·til′i·ty, *n.* the quality or state of being retractile.

rē·traç′tion, *n.* [ME. *retraccion*; prob. via OFr., from LL. *retractio.*]

1. a retracting or being retracted; specifically, (a) withdrawal, as of a statement, promise, charge, etc.; (b) a drawing or being drawn back or in.

2. power of retracting.

rē·traç′tive, *n.* that which withdraws. [Obs.]

rē·traç′tive, *a.* retracting; tending to retract. [Rare.]

rē·traç′tive·ly, *adv.* by retraction; in a retracting manner. [Rare.]

rē·traç′tŏr, *n.* 1. one who or that which retracts.

2. in breech-loading firearms, a device for extracting cartridge shells after firing.

3. in surgery, (a) a bandage used in retracting the soft parts so as to protect them during amputation; (b) an instrument for drawing back a part or organ, as the flesh at the edge of an incision.

4. in anatomy and zoology, a muscle that retracts an organ, protruded part, etc.

rē′trad, *adv.* [L. *retro,* backward, and *-ad.*] in anatomy, toward a posterior or dorsal part.

rē′trȧ·hens̹, *n.*; *pl.* **rē·trȧ·hen′tēs̹,** [L. *retrahens* (-*entis*), ppr. of *retrahere,* to draw back.] in anatomy, a retractive auricular muscle.

rē′trȧ·hent, *a.* in anatomy, tending to draw back; retracting; as, a *retrahent* muscle.

rē·trāict′ (-trāt′), *n.* retreat. [Obs.]

rē·trāit′, *n.* [It. *ritratto,* from *ritrarre,* to draw.] a drawing; a portrait. [Obs.]

rē′trăl, *a.* [L. *retro,* backward, and *-al.*]

1. at, near, or toward the back; posterior.

2. retrorse.

rē·trans·fēr′, *v.t.* to transfer again.

rē·trans·fọrm′, *v.t.* to transform anew; to transform back.

rē·trans·fọr·mā′tion, *n.* the act of retransforming.

rē·trans·lāte′, *v.t.* to translate anew; to translate back into the original language.

rē·trax′it, *n.* [L., from *retrahere,* to withdraw.] in law, the withdrawing or open renunciation of a suit in court, by which the plaintiff lost his action and right of action.

rē·tread′ (-tred′), *v.t.* to put a new tread on (a worn pneumatic tire), especially by cementing, molding, and vulcanizing a whole new rubber tread on the bare underlayer of fabric: cf. *recap.*

rē′tread″, *n.* a retreaded tire.

rē-tread′, *v.t.*; re-trod, *pt.*; re-trod *or* re-trodden, *pp*; re-treading, *ppr.* to tread again: also spelled *retread.*

rē·trēat′, *n.* [OFr. *retrete, retraite,* a place of refuge, from L. *retrahere,* to withdraw.]

1. a going back or backward; a withdrawal; a giving ground before opposition.

2. withdrawal to a safe or private place.

3. a safe, quiet, or secluded place; a hiding place.

4. a period of retirement or seclusion, especially one devoted to religious contemplation away from the pressures of ordinary life.

5. an asylum or sanitarium for the mentally ill, for alcoholics, etc.

6. in military usage, (a) the withdrawal of troops, ships, etc. from a position, especially when forced by enemy attack; (b) a signal for such a withdrawal; (c) a signal given by drum or bugle at sunset for lowering the national flag; (d) the ceremony at which this is done.

to beat a retreat; (a) in military usage, to signal for retreat by beating a drum; (b) to retreat.

Syn.—withdrawment, seclusion, solitude, retirement, shelter, refuge, asylum.

rē·trēat′, *v.i.*; retreated, *pt., pp.*; retreating, *ppr.* 1. to retire, withdraw, or move back; to go back; to recede, as from before an enemy, or from an advanced position.

2. to withdraw or recede, as from a course of action, a claim, or a dispute.

3. in fencing, to step back beyond reach of a thrust.

4. to go into retirement, as for rest or for devotion; as, to *retreat* from the city.

5. to have a backward slope or curve; to slope backward; as, a *retreating* chin.

rē·trēat′, *v.t.* 1. in chess, to move (a piece) back.

2. to retrace. [Obs.]

rē·trēat′, *v.t.* to treat again or anew.

rē·trēat′ăl, *a.* pertaining to retreat or to something that has retreated.

retreatal moraine; in geology, a moraine deposited during the withdrawal of a glacier.

rē·trēat′ănt, *n.* a retreater.

rē·trēat′ēr, *n.* one who retreats.

rē·trēat′fu̧l, *a.* affording or serving as a retreat. [Rare.]

rē·trēat′ment, *n.* retreat. [Rare.]

rē·tree′, *n.* paper imperfect in any way, as wrinkled, broken, or containing specks or blemishes.

rē·trench′, *v.t.*; retrenched (-trencht′), *pt., pp.*; retrenching, *ppr.* [Fr. *retrancher*; *re-,* again, and *trancher,* to cut.]

1. to cut off or out; to pare away; to omit; to delete, as a portion of a book.

2. to lessen; to abridge; to curtail; to cut down; to reduce; as, to *retrench* superfluities or expenses.

3. to confine; to limit. [Obs.]

4. in fortification, to furnish with a retrenchment; as, to *retrench* bastions.

Syn.—curtail, diminish, economize.

rē·trench′, *v.i.* 1. to live at less expense; to curtail expenses; to economize.

2. to encroach; to make an inroad. [Rare.]

rē·trench′ment, *n.* [OFr. and Fr. *retranchement.*]

1. a retrenching; specifically, (a) a cutting down, off, or out; (b) a reduction of expenses.

2. in military usage, (a) a rampart or breastwork within or behind the main fortifications, to which troops can retreat in case the outer line is breached; (b) entrenchment.

Syn.—abridgment, reduction.

rē·trib′ū·tăr·y, *a.* retributive; retributory.

rē·trib′ūte, *v.t.* to pay back; to make payment, compensation, or reward to; as, to *retribute* one for his kindness. [Obs.]

rē·trib′ūte, *v.i.* to make retribution. [Obs.]

ret·ri·bū′tion, *n.* [ME. *retribucioun*; OFr.; L. *retributio* (-*onis*), recompense, from *retributus,* pp. of *retribuere,* to repay.]

1. deserved punishment for evil done, or, sometimes, reward for good done; merited requital.

2. in theology, reward or punishment in another life for things done in this.

Syn.—repayment, recompense, retaliation.

rē·trib′ū·tive, *a.* of, having the nature of, characterized by, or involving retribution; repaying; rewarding for good deeds, and punishing for offenses; as, *retributive* justice.

rē·trib′ū·tŏr, *n.* one who administers rewards and punishments.

rē·trib′ū·tō·ry, *a.* retributive.

rē·triēv′ȧ·ble, *a.* capable of being retrieved.

rē·triēv′ȧ·ble·ness, *n.* the state or quality of being retrievable.

rē·triēv′ȧ·bly, *adv.* in a retrievable manner.

rē·triēv′ăl, *n.* 1. the act of retrieving; restoration.

2. possibility of recovery or restoration.

rē·triēve′, *v.t.*; retrieved, *pt., pp.*; retrieving, *ppr.* [Fr. *retrouver,* to find again; *re-,* again, and *trouver,* to find.]

1. to get back; to recover.

2. to restore; to revive; as, he *retrieved* his spirits.

3. to make good; to set right; to make amends for (a loss, error, etc.).

4. to recall to mind.

5. in hunting, to find and bring back (killed or wounded game): said of dogs.

Syn.—recover, recruit, restore.

rē·triēve′, *v.i.* in hunting, to find and bring back game.

rē·triēve′, *n.* retrieval.

rē·triēve′ment, *n.* same as *retrieval.*

rē·triev′ēr, *n.* 1. one who or that which retrieves.

2. a dog specially trained to go in quest of game which a sportsman has shot, or a dog that takes readily to such work; specifically, any of several breeds of dog developed for this purpose.

RETRIEVER

ret′rō- (*or* rē′trō-), [from L. *retro,* backward.] a combining form meaning *backward, back, behind,* as in *retro*act, *retro*flex.

ret·rō·açt′, *v.i.* 1. to act backward or in return; to act in opposition; to react.

2. to have reference or application to or influence on things done in the past.

ret·rō·aç′tion, *n.* 1. opposed, reverse, or reciprocal action.

2. effect, as of a law, on things done prior to its enactment or effectuation.

ret·rō·açt′ive, *a.* acting or designed to act in regard to things past; intended to retroact; having application to or effect on things prior to its enactment or effectuation; as a *retroactive* law.

retroactive law or *statute*; a law which operates to affect or to make criminal or punishable acts done prior to the passing of the law.

ret·rō·açt′ive·ly, *adv.* in a retroactive manner; so as to retroact.

ret·rō·cēde′, *v.i.*; retroceded, *pt., pp.*; retroceding, *ppr.* [L. *retrocedere*; *retro-,* back, and *cedere,* to go.] to go back; to recede.

ret·rō·cēde′, *v.t.* [*retro-* and *cede.*] to cede back; to give back; to restore.

ret·rō·cēd′ent, *a.* prone or inclined to retrocede or go back; specifically, in medicine, to move from one part of the body to another, as the gout.

ret·rō·ces′sion (-sesh′un), *n.* [*retro-,* and L. *cessus,* pp. of *cedere,* to go.]

1. the act of going back; a retroceding.

2. in medicine, translation or metastasis of a disease from the surface to an interior organ.

3. in geometry, inflection.

ret·rō·ces′sion, *n.* a retroceding, or giving back.

ret′rō·çhoir (-kwīr *or* rē′trō-), *n.* [*retro-* and *choir,* after ML. *retrochorus.*] that part of a church which lies behind the choir or the main altar.

rē·trō·çlū′s̹ion, *n.* [*retro-* and *occlusion.*] closure of an artery by means of a pin passed into the tissue over, behind, and back under the vessel.

rē·trō·çol′liç, *a.* [*retro-,* and L. *collum,* neck.] pertaining to the back of the neck.

rē·trō·çop′ū·lănt, *a.* [*retro-,* and L. *copulans* (-*antis*), ppr. of *copulare,* to copulate.] copulating from behind or backward.

rē·trō·çop·ū·lā′tion, *n.* the act or characteristic of copulating from behind.

rē″trō·dis·plāce′ment, *n.* a backward displacement.

rē·trō·duç′tion, *n.* a leading or bringing back.

ret′rō·fire, *v.t.*; retrofired, *pt.*, *pp.*; retrofiring, *ppr.* to ignite (a retrorocket).

ret′rō·fire, *v.i.* to become ignited: said of a retrorocket.

ret′rō·fire, *n.* the igniting of a retrorocket.

ret·rō·flec′tion, *n.* retroflexion; the act of bending; the state of being bent back.

ret′rō·flex, *a.* [LL. *retroflexus*, pp. of *retroflectere*, to bend back.]
1. bent or turned backward.
2. in phonetics, (a) having the tip raised and bent backward: said of the tongue; (b) formed with the tongue in this position: said of sounds.

ret′rō·flexed (-flekst), *a.* retroflex.

ret·rō·flex′iŏn (-flek′shun), *n.* 1. the condition of being retroflex; a bending backward; specifically, in medicine, the bending backward of an organ, especially of the body of the uterus, upon itself.
2. in phonetics, (a) retroflex articulation; (b) the acoustic quality produced by this: also called *r-color*.

ret′rō·fract, *a.* retrofracted.

ret′rō·fract·ed, *a.* [*retro-*, and L. *fractus*, pp. of *frangere*, to break.] in botany, bent back so as to look as if broken; as, a *retrofract* peduncle.

rē·trō·ġen′ĕr·ā·tive, *a.* retrocopulant.

ret″rō·grā·dā′tion (*or* rē″), *n.* 1. the act or result of retrograding, or going backward; retrogression; a moving backward.
2. deterioration; decline in excellence.
3. the act of moving backward from east to west, or contrary to the usual planetary motion.

ret′rō·grāde (*or* rē′), *a.* [OFr. *retrograder*; LL. *retrogradare*, from L. *retrogradi*, to go backward; *retro-*, and *gradi*, to go.]
1. moving or directed backward; retiring or retreating.
2. inverse or reverse: said of order.
3. going back or tending to go back to an earlier or worse condition; retrogressive.
4. in astronomy, (a) designating motion, real or apparent, in a direction contrary to the order of the signs of the zodiac, or from east to west; (b) moving in an orbit in a direction opposite to that of the earth as it revolves around the sun.
5. opposed; contrary. [Obs.]

ret′rō·grāde, *n.* a downward tendency; decline; as, to be on the *retrograde*.

ret′rō·grāde, *v.i.*; retrograded, *pt.*, *pp.*; retrograding, *ppr.* [L. *retrogradi.*]
1. to go, or seem to go, backward.
2. to become worse; to decline; to deteriorate; to degenerate.
3. in astronomy, to have a retrograde motion.

ret′rō·grāde, *v.t.* to turn back. [Obs.]

ret′rō·grā·ding·ly, *adv.* by retrograde movement.

ret′rō·gress, *n.* [L. *retrogressus*, a retrogression, pp. of *retrogradi*, to go backward.] a going backward; retrograde; retrogression. [Rare.]

ret′rō·gress, *v.i.* [L. *retrogressus*, pp. of *retrogradi.*] to move backward, especially into an earlier, less complex, or worse condition; to decline; to degenerate.

ret·rō·gres′sion (-gresh′un), *n.* 1. the act of going backward; retrogradation.
2. in biology, degeneration; a return to a lower, less complex stage or state; a term used of an animal or plant.
3. in astronomy, same as *retrogradation*.

ret·rō·gres′sion·ăl, *a.* pertaining to retrogression.

ret·rō·gres′sive, *a.* retrogressing or showing retrogression; going or moving backward.

ret·rō·gres′sive·ly, *adv.* in a retrogressive manner.

rē·trō·min′ġen·cy, *n.* [*retro-*, and L. *mingere*, to discharge urine.] the act or practice of discharging the urine backward. [Obs.]

rē·trō·min′ġent, *a.* discharging the urine backward.

rē·trō·min′ġent, *n.* in zoology, an animal that discharges its urine backward.

rē·trō·min′ġent·ly, *adv.* in a retromingent manner.

rē·trō·mor′phō·sis, *n.* degenerate metamorphosis.

rē·trō·oc′ū·lăr, *a.* [*retro-*, and L. *oculus*, eye.] located behind the ball of the eye.

ret·rō·op′ĕr·ā·tive, *a.* retroactive; operating backward.

rē·trō·per″i·tō·nē′ăl, *a.* [*retro-*, and L. *peritoneum*, peritoneum.] located behind the peritoneum.

rē″trō·phar·yn′ġē·ăl, *a.* [*retro-*, and LL. *pharynx*, pharynx.] situated behind the pharynx.

rē″trō·pō·si′tion (-zish′un), *n.* a position behind the normal: said of the uterus.

rē·trō·pul′sion, *n.* [*retro-*, and LL. *pulsio* (-*onis*), a beating.]
1. a driving backward.
2. in medicine, a tendency to walk backward, as in some cases of locomotor ataxia.

rē·trō·pul′sive, *a.* [*retro-*, and L. *pulsus*, pp. of *pellere*, to drive, to push.] driving back; repelling.

ret′rō·rock·et, ret′rō-rock·et, *n.* a small rocket on a larger rocket or spacecraft, that produces thrust in a direction opposite to the direction of flight in order to reduce speed, as for landing.

rē·trorse′, *a.* [L. *retrorsus*, contr. form of *retroversus*, bent or turned backward; *retro*, and *versus*, pp. of *vertere*, to turn.] bent or turned downward or backward.

rē·trorse′ly, *adv.* in a backward direction.

rē·trō·ser′rāte, *a.* [*retro-*, and L. *serratus*, saw-shaped.] barbed; provided with retrorse teeth.

rē·trō·ser′ru·lāte, *a.* [*retro-*, and LL. *serrulatus*, from *serrula*, a little saw.] in entomology, having teeth which are minutely retrorse.

Rē·trō·sī·phō·nā′tȧ, *n.pl.* [*retro-*, and L. *sipho* (-*onis*), a siphon.] in conchology, a group of cephalopods, having the partitions surrounding the siphon directed backward.

rē·trō·sī′phŏn·āte, *a.* pertaining to the *Retrosiphonata*.

ret′rō·spect (*or* rē′), *v.i.* [*retro-*, and L. *spectus*, pp. of *specere*, to look.]
1. to think about the past. [Rare.]
2. to refer back (*to*). [Rare.]

ret′rō·spect, *v.t.* to look back on or think about (persons or things past). [Rare.]

ret′rō·spect, *n.* a looking back on or thinking about things past; view or contemplation of something past.
in retrospect; in reviewing the past.

ret·rō·spec′tion, *n.* 1. act, instance, or faculty of looking back on or reviewing past events, experiences, etc.
2. (a) a looking back or referring (*to*); (b) reference or allusion to past events. [Rare.]

ret·rō·spec′tive, *a.* 1. looking back on or directed to the past, past events, etc.; taking a retrospect; as, a *retrospective* view.
2. looking or directed backward.
3. having reference to what is past; retroactive; as, a *retrospective* act or law.

ret·rō·spec′tive·ly, *adv.* by way of retrospect.

rē·trō·stēr′năl, *a.* situated behind the sternum.

rē·trō·tär′săl, *a.* [*retro-*, and LL. *tarsus*, the cartilage at the edges of the eyelids.] posterior to the tarsus of the eyelid; as, the *retrotarsal* fold.

rē·trō·trā′chē·ăl, *a.* situated behind the trachea.

rē·trōus·sāġe′ (-sȧzh′), *n.* [Fr., from *retrousser*, to turn up.] in etching, the process of wiping, with a soft cloth, a previously inked engraved plate before printing, to produce effective tone.

ret·rous·sé′ (ret-rö-sā′), *a.* [Fr., pp. of *retrousser*, to turn up.] turned up at the tip: said of a pug nose.

rē·trō·ū′tĕr·ine, *a.* being behind the uterus.

rē·trō·vac′ci·nāte, *v.t.* to vaccinate (a human being) with virus obtained from a cow that has been previously inoculated with smallpox virus.

rē·trō·vac·ci·nā′tion, *n.* the act of retrovaccinating.

rē·trō·vac′cine, *n.* the vaccine obtained from a cow inoculated with smallpox virus.

ret·rō·vēr′sion, *n.* [*retro-*, and L. *versus*, pp. of *vertere*, to turn.]
1. a looking or turning back.
2. a turning or tilting, or being turned or tilted, backward, as of an organ or part; as, *retroversion* of the uterus.

ret·rō·vērt′, *v.t.*; retroverted, *pt.*, *pp.*; retroverting, *ppr.* to turn back.

ret·rō·vērt′ed, *a.* turned back.

rē·trūde′, *v.t.*; retruded, *pt.*, *pp.*; retruding, *ppr.* [L. *retrudere*, to thrust back; *re-*, and *trudere*, to thrust.] to thrust back. [Rare.]

rē·trūse′, *a.* [L. *retrusus.*] hidden; abstruse. [Obs.]

rē·trū′sion, *n.* the act of retruding; also, the state of being retruded. [Rare.]

rē·trȳ′, *v.t.* to try a second time; as, to *retry* a case in court.

ret′tĕr·y, *n.* a place where flax is rotted or retted.

ret′ting, *n.* 1. the act or process of preparing flax for the separation of the woody part from the filamentous part by soaking it in water or by exposure to dew.
2. the place where this operation is carried on; a rettery.

rē·tund′, *v.t.* [L. *retundere*, to beat or pound back.] to blunt; to turn, as an edge; to dull; as, to *retund* the edge of a weapon. [Obs.]

rē·tūrn′ *v.i.*; returned, *pt.*, *pp.*; returning, *ppr.* [ME. *returnen*, *retournen*; OFr. *returner*, *retorner*, from L. *retornare*, to turn back; *re-*, and *tornare*, to turn.]
1. to come back; to come or go back, as to a former place, condition, etc.; as, to *return* to the city.

> Alexander died, Alexander was buried,
> Alexander *returneth* into dust. —Shak.

2. to revert to a former owner; to pass back.

> Now shall the kingdom *return* to the house
> of David. —1 Kings xii. 26.

3. to appear or begin again after a periodical revolution; as, spring has *returned*.
4. to go back in thought or speech; to speak again of a subject laid aside for a time.
5. to answer; to reply; to respond.
6. in fencing, to attack, as by a thrust, after parrying a sword thrust.

rē·tūrn′, *v.t.* 1. to bring, carry, put, or send back; to restore or replace; as, to *return* a borrowed book; to *return* a hired horse.
2. to repay; as, to *return* borrowed money.
3. to give, send, or do (something of the same sort as, or equivalent to, what has been given, sent, or done); to give, send, or do in requital or reciprocation; as, *return* a visit.
4. to produce, as a profit or revenue; to yield.
5. (a) to report or announce officially or formally; (b) to turn in (a writ, account, or statement) to a judge or other official.

> Moses *returned* the words of the people unto
> the Lord. —Ex. xix. 8.

6. to give back in reply; as, to *return* an answer.
7. to retort; to recriminate. [Obs.]
8. to reflect (sound, light, etc.).
9. to elect or re-elect; as, he was *returned* to Congress.
10. to replace (a weapon) in its holder.
11. to turn back; to turn in the opposite direction.
12. to turn away from, or cause to continue on at an angle to, the previous line of direction.
13. to render (a verdict, etc.).
14. in card games, to respond to (a partner's lead) by leading a card of the same suit.
15. in sports, to hit back or throw back (a ball).

Syn.—restore, repay, render, requite, remit.

rē·tūrn′, *n.* [ME. *retorn*, from the *v.*]
1. a coming or going back, as to a former place, condition, etc.
2. a bringing, sending, carrying, or putting back; restoration or replacement.
3. something returned; specifically, [*pl.*] unsold merchandise returned to the distributor by a retailer or merchandise returned to a retailer by a purchaser.
4. a coming back again; reappearance; recurrence; as, on his birthday they wished him many happy *returns* of the day.
5. something done or given as an equivalent for that received; repayment; requital; reciprocation.
6. (a) profit made on an exchange of goods; (b) [*often in pl.*] yield, profit, or revenue, as from labor, investments, etc.; (c) yield per unit as compared to cost per unit, as in the manufacture of a given product; rate of yield.
7. (a) a bend or turn, as in a line, wall, etc.; (b) the section between two such bends.
8. an answer; a reply; response.
9. a report; especially, (a) an official or formal report, as of the financial condition of a company; (b) [*usually in pl.*] a report on a count of votes at polling places; as, election *returns*.
10. in architecture, etc., the continuation, as of a molding, colonnade, etc., in a different direction, often at a right angle.
11. in card games, a lead in response to a partner's lead.
12. in law, (a) the bringing or sending back of a writ, subpoena, summons, etc. to the

proper court or official, usually with a short report endorsed on it; (b) a certified report by an election official, assessor, etc.; (c) a certificate or report endorsed on any such document.

13. in tennis, etc., (a) a batting or throwing back of a ball; (b) a ball so returned.

14. [*pl.*] a kind of light-colored and mild tobacco made from the young leaves of the plant.

15. in fortification, one of the turnings and windings of a gallery leading to a mine.

16. in military and naval usage, an official account, report, or statement rendered to the commander or other superior.

in return; as a return; as an equivalent, response, etc.

rē·tûrn′, *a.* 1. of or for a return or returning; as, a *return* ticket.

2. given, sent, done, etc. in return; as, a *return* visit.

3. returning.

4. returned.

5. changing or reversing direction or formed by a change or reversal in direction, as a bend in a road.

rē·tûrn′, *v.t.* and *v.i.* to turn again.

rē·tûrn·à·bil′i·ty, *n.* the quality of being returnable.

rē·tûrn′à·ble, *a.* 1. that can be returned.

2. in law, legally required to be returned, delivered, given, or rendered; as, a writ or precept *returnable* at a certain day; a verdict *returnable* to the court.

rē·tûrn′ ball, a child's toy consisting of a ball held by a piece of elastic, so as to make it return to the hand from which it is thrown.

rē·tûrn′ bend, a fitting shaped like the letter U, used for connecting the ends of two pipes that lie parallel to each other.

rē·tûrn′ chärge, in electricity, a charge produced by an oscillatory return or back stroke of lightning; also, a charge produced inductively by a lightning discharge.

rē·tûrn′ check, a ticket to readmit someone who temporarily leaves an entertainment or other performance while it is still in progress.

rē·tûrn′ çŏn·duçt′ŏr, a return wire.

rē·tûrn′ çur′rent, in telegraphy, the electrostatic discharge from a cable or underground wire; also, the discharge current from a telegraph line passing to the ground at the sending end.

rē·tûrn′ dāy, in law, the day when a defendant is to appear in court and the sheriff is to return the writ and his proceedings.

rē·tûrn′ẽr, *n.* one who returns.

rē·tûrn′ing bōard, a board of State officials who canvass and make known officially the election returns.

rē·tûrn′ing of′fi·cẽr, in England, the presiding officer at an election, who returns the persons duly elected.

rē·tûrn′less, *a.* admitting no return.

rē·tûrn′ match, a second match or game played by the same sets of players, to give the defeated player or players another opportunity to win.

rē·tûrn′ strōke, an electric discharge induced by the direct discharge of a lightning flash, as distinguished from the direct discharge itself.

rē·tûrn′ tick′et, 1. a transportation ticket for the trip back to the original starting point.

2. a round-trip ticket.

rē·tûrn′ valve, a valve that opens to allow reflux of a fluid under certain conditions. In some cases it is merely an overflow valve which allows excess liquid to return to a reservoir.

rē·tûrn′ wīre, the wire or conductor by means of which the current returns to the electric source after having passed through the electroreceptive devices.

rē·tūse′, *a.* [L. *retusus*, blunt, dull, pp. of *retundere*, to beat back, dull.] in botany and zoology, terminating in a round end, the center of which is depressed; as, a *retuse* leaf.

rē·tȳpe′, *v.t.* to type over again.

rē′tȳpe, *n.* something retyped.

Reu′ben, *n.* in the Bible, (a) the eldest son of Jacob: Gen. xxix; (b) the tribe of Israel descended from him: Num. xxxii.

reùl, *n.* rule. [Obs.]

reùle, *n.* and *v.* rule. [Obs.]

reùme, *n.* realm. [Obs.]

rē·ūn′iŏn (-yun), *n.* 1. a bringing or coming together again; a second union; union formed anew after separation or discord; as, a *reunion* of parts or particles of matter; a *reunion* of parties or sects.

2. a gathering of persons after separation; a meeting, assembly, or festive gathering, as of a family, familiar friends, associates, or members of a college class or society.

rē·ūn′iŏn·ist, *n.* an advocate of reunion; specifically, an advocate of the reunion of the Anglican Church with the Roman Catholic Church.

rē·ū·nīte′, *v.t.*; reunited, *pt.*, *pp.*; reuniting, *ppr.* 1. to unite again; to join after separation.

2. to reconcile after variance.

rē·ū·nīte′, *v.i.* to be united again; to join and cohere again.

rē·ū·nīt′ed·ly, *adv.* in a reunited manner.

rē·ū·ni′tion (-nish′un), *n.* a second uniting. [Rare.]

Reu′tẽrș (roi′), *n.* [after Baron Paul Julius von *Reuter* (1821–1899), the founder.] a private British agency for gathering and distributing news among member newspapers: also *Reuter's News Agency.*

rev, *n.* a revolution, as of an engine. [Colloq.]

rev, *v.t.*; revved, *pt.*, *pp.*; revving, *ppr.* to change the speed of (an engine, motor, etc.): usually in *rev up*, to accelerate. [Colloq.]

rev, *v.i.* to undergo revving. [Colloq.]

rev·à·les′cent, *a.* getting well; regaining strength. [Rare.]

rē·vamp′, *v.t.* to vamp, mend, or patch up again or anew; specifically, (a) to put a new vamp on (a shoe or boot); (b) to renovate; to redo; to rehabilitate; to reconstruct.

rēve, *v.t.* to reave. [Obs.]

rēve, *n.* a reeve. [Obs.]

rē·vēal′, *v.t.*; revealed, *pt.*, *pp.*; revealing, *ppr.* [OFr. *reveler*, from L. *revelare*, to unveil; *re-*, back, and *velare*, to veil.]

1. to disclose; to show; to make known, as something before unknown, kept secret, or concealed; as to *reveal* secrets.

2. to expose to view; to show; to exhibit; to display.

3. to disclose, discover, or make known (that which would be unknown without divine or supernatural instruction).

Syn.—divulge, unveil, disclose, show, impart.

rē·vēal′, *n.* a revealing; a disclosure. [Rare.]

rē·vēal′, *n.* [from ME. *revalen*, to bring down; OFr. *revaler*, from *re-*, back, and *valer*, to descend.]

1. that part of the side of an opening for a window or door which is between the outer edge of the opening and the frame of the window or door.

2. the entire side of such an opening; jamb.

rē·vēal·à·bil′i·ty, *n.* the state or quality of being revealable.

rē·vēal′à·ble, *a.* capable of being revealed.

rē·vēal′à·ble·ness, *n.* the state of being revealable.

rē·vēaled′ rē·liġ′iŏn (-lij′un), any religion based on the belief that a deity has revealed himself and his will to his creatures.

rē·vēal′ẽr, *n.* one who or that which reveals.

rē·vēal′ment, *n.* the act of revealing or the state of being revealed; disclosure; revelation.

rev′eil·lē (rev′el-ē), *n.* [Fr. *réveiller*, to awake; *re-*, and *veiller*; L. *vigilare*, to watch.]

1. a signal on a bugle, drum, etc. at some fixed time early in the morning to waken soldiers or sailors or call them to first assembly.

2. the first assembly of the day.

rev′el, *v.i.*; reveled *or* revelled, *pt.*, *pp.*; reveling *or* revelling, *ppr.* [ME. *revel*; OFr. *revel*, *rivel*, from *reveler*, L. *rebellare*, to rebel.]

1. to make merry; to be noisily festive.

2. to take much pleasure; to delight (with *in*); as, he *revels in* sports.

rev′el, *n.* 1. merrymaking; boisterous festivity; revelry.

2. [*often pl.*] an occasion of merrymaking or boisterous festivity; celebration.

3. an old annual festival commemorating the dedication of a church. [Obs.]

rē·vel′, *v.t.* [L. *revellere*, to draw away; *re-*, away, and *vellere*, to pluck.] to draw back; to retract. [Obs.]

rev·ē·lā′tion, *n.* [Fr., from LL. *revelatio* (*-onis*), from L. *revelatus*, pp. of *revelare*, to draw away.]

1. a revealing, or disclosing.

2. something disclosed; disclosure; especially, a striking disclosure, as of something not previously known or realized.

3. in Christian theology, (a) God's disclosure or manifestation to his creatures of himself and his will; (b) an instance of this; (c) what is so disclosed or manifested; (d) something, as the Bible, containing such disclosure or manifestation.

4. [R–] the last book of the New Testament, ascribed to John (in full, *The Revelation of Saint John the Divine*); Apocalypse: also *Revelations.*

rev·ē·lā′tion·ist, *n.* 1. a person who believes in divine revelation.

2. [*also* R–] the author of Revelation.

rev′ē·lā·tŏr, *n.* one who makes a revelation; a revealer.

rev′el·ẽr, **rev′el·lẽr**, *n.* a person who revels or takes part in a revel; one who carouses with noisy merriment.

rē·vel′lent, *a.* [L. *revellens* (*-entis*), ppr. of *revellere*, to pluck or draw away.] causing revulsion.

rev′el·ment, *n.* the act of reveling.

rev′el·ous, *a.* fond of revelry or merrymaking. [Obs.]

rev′el·rout, *n.* 1. tumultuous festivity. [Obs.]

2. a mob; a rabble tumultuously assembled. [Archaic.]

rev′el·ry, *n.*; *pl.* **rev′el·rieș**, a reveling; boisterous merrymaking; noisy festivity.

rev′e·nănt, *n.* [Fr., ppr. of *revenir*, to come back, from L. *re-*, back, and *venire*, to come.]

1. a person who returns, as after a long absence.

2. a person who returns as a spirit after death; a ghost.

rē·ven′di·çāte, *v.t.* same as *revindicate.*

rē·ven·di·çā′tion, *n.* same as *revindication.*

rē·venġe′, *v.t.*; revenged, *pt.*, *pp.*; revenging, *ppr.* [OFr. *revenger*, *revencher*; *re-*, again, and *venger*, older form *vengier*, to take vengeance, from L. *vindicare.*]

1. to inflict damage, injury, or punishment in return for (an injury, insult, etc.); to take vengeance for; to retaliate for.

2. to take vengeance in behalf of (a person, oneself, etc.); to avenge.

to be revenged; to get revenge; to take vengeance.

O Lord, visit me, and *revenge* me of my persecutors. —Jer. xv. 15.

Syn.—avenge, vindicate, requite.

rē·venġe′, *v.i.* to execute vengeance: used with *upon.* [Obs.]

rē·venġe′, *n.* 1. a revenging; vengeance.

2. what is done in revenging.

3. desire to take vengeance; vindictive spirit.

The indulgence of *revenge* tends to make men more savage and cruel. —Kames.

4. a chance to retaliate or get satisfaction, as by a return match after defeat in a previous one.

rē·venġe′à·ble, *a.* calling for revenge; capable of being revenged. [Obs.]

rē·venġe′ànce, *n.* revenge. [Obs.]

rē·venġe′ful, *a.* full of revenge or a desire to inflict pain or evil for injury received; spiteful; malicious; wreaking revenge.

Syn.—vindictive, vengeful, resentful, malicious, spiteful, unforgiving.

rē·venġe′ful·ly, *adv.* by way of revenge; vindictively; with the spirit of revenge.

rē·venġe′ful·ness, *n.* vindictiveness; the quality of being revengeful.

rē·venġe′less, *a.* unrevenged.

rē·venġe′ment, *n.* revenge; return of an injury. [Rare.]

rē·ven′ġẽr, *n.* one who revenges; one who inflicts pain on another spitefully in return for an injury; an avenger.

rē·ven′ġing·ly, *adv.* with revenge; with the spirit of revenge; vindictively.

rev′e·nūe, *n.* [Fr., f. of *revenu*, pp. of *revenir*, to return, come back; *re-*, back, and *venir*, L. *venire*, to come.]

1. the return from property or investment; income.

2. (a) an item or source of income; (b) [*pl.*] items or amounts of income collectively.

3. the income from taxes, duties, etc. of a unit of government, as a city, county, state, nation, etc.

4. the governmental department or bureau that handles the collection of such income.

internal revenue; see under *internal.*

revenue cutter; see *cutter*, n. 5.

revenue stamp; a stamp placed on an article to show that a tax has been paid on it.

Syn.—receipts, returns, income, proceeds.

rē·vẽrb′, *v.t.* to reverberate.

rē·vẽr′bẽr·ănt, *a.* [L. *reverberans* (*-antis*), ppr.

of *reverberare*, to repel, beat back.] returning sound; resounding; reverberating.

rē·vẽr′bẽr·āte, *v.t.*; reverberated, *pt., pp.*; reverberating, *ppr.* [L. *reverberatus*, pp. of *reverberare*, to beat back, repel, from *re-*, again, and *verberare*, to beat.]

1. to throw back (sound); to cause (a sound) to re-echo.

2. (a) to reflect (light, etc.); (b) to deflect (heat, flame, etc.), as in a reverberatory furnace.

3. to subject to treatment in a reverberatory furnace or the like.

rē·vẽr′bẽr·āte, *v.i.* 1. to re-echo; to resound.

2. (a) to be reflected, as light or sound waves; (b) to be deflected, as heat or flame in a reverberatory furnace.

3. to recoil; rebound.

rē·vẽr·bẽr·ā′tion, *n.* 1. a reverberating or being reverberated; specifically, (a) a re-echoing or being re-echoed; (b) reflection, as of light or sound waves; (c) deflection of heat or flame, as in a reverberatory furnace; (d) subjection to treatment in a reverberatory furnace, etc.

2. something reverberated; re-echoed sound, reflected light, etc.

3. in physics, multiple reflection of sound waves in a confined area so that the sound persists for some time after the source is cut off.

rē·vẽr′bẽr·ā·tive, *a.* 1. reverberating or tending to reverberate.

2. having the nature of reverberation.

rē·vẽr′bẽr·ā·tŏr, *n.* one who or that which reverberates or causes reverberation; specifically, a reflecting lamp.

rē·vẽr′bẽr·ȧ·tō·ry, *a.* 1. operating, characterized, or produced by reverberation.

2. deflected, as flame or heat.

REVERBERATORY

3. designating a furnace, kiln, or the like in which ore, metal, etc. is heated by a flame deflected downward from the roof.

rē·vẽr′bẽr·ȧ·tō·ry, *n.* a reverberatory furnace, kiln, etc.

rē·vēre′, *v.t.*; revered, *pt., pp.*; revering, *ppr.* [Fr. *révérer*, from L. *revereri*, to reverence, to stand in awe of; from *re-*, again, and *vereri*, to fear, to feel awe.] to regard with deep respect, love, awe, and affection; to venerate; to reverence; to honor in estimation.

And some there are who still *revere* all the dreams of their youth.
—George P. Bradford.

rē·vēre′, *n.* a revers.

rev′ẽr·ence, *n.* [OFr., from L. *reverentia*, reverence, from *reverens* (*-entis*), reverent.]

1. a feeling or attitude of deep respect, love, awe, and esteem, as for something sacred; veneration.

This seems to me a sacred phrase,
With *reverence* impassioned.—Eugene Field.

2. a manifestation of this; specifically, an act of respect or obeisance, as a bow or curtsy.

Now lies he there,
And none so poor to do him *reverence*.
—Shak.

3. the state of being revered.

4. [R–] a title used in speaking to or of a clergyman: preceded by *your* or *his*.

saving your reverence; with all respect to you: a phrase used to introduce an objectionable expression or contradiction. [Obs.]

Syn.—honor, veneration, awe, adoration.

rev′ẽr·ence, *v.t.*; reverenced (-enst), *pt., pp.*; reverencing, *ppr.* 1. to regard or treat with reverence; to revere; to venerate.

2. to treat with reverence; specifically, to salute, as with a reverence. [Obs.]

rev′ẽr·en·cẽr, *n.* one who regards with reverence.

rev′ẽr·end, *a.* [Fr., from L. *reverendus*.]

1. worthy of reverence; entitled to respect mingled with awe and affection; as, *reverend* and gracious senators.

A *reverend* sire among them came.—Milton.

2. [*usually* R–] designating, as a title of respect, a clergyman: often prefixed to the name; as, *Reverend* Henry Ward Beecher.

3. of, characteristic of, or pertaining to the clerical office or profession, or to ecclesiastics in general; as, the *reverend* profession.

4. reverent. [Obs.]

rev′ẽr·end, *n.* a clergyman. [Colloq.]

rev′ẽr·ent, *a.* [OFr., from L. *reverens* (*-entis*), ppr. of *revereri*, to revere.]

1. characterized by, feeling, showing, or expressive of reverence or veneration; marked by reverence; reverential; as, *reverent* behavior.

2. reverend. [Obs.]

rev·ẽr·en′tiăl (-shăl), *a.* proceeding from reverence, or expressing it; reverent; as, *reverential* fear.

rev·ẽr·en′tiăl·ly, *adv.* with reverence.

rev′ẽr·ent·ly, *adv.* with reverence.

rē·vẽr′ẽr, *n.* one who reveres or venerates.

rev′ẽr·ie, rev′ẽr·y, *n.*; *pl.* **rev′ẽr·ieṣ,** [Fr. *rêverie*, from *rêver*, to dream, to rave, to be lightheaded.]

1. dreamy thinking or imagining, especially of agreeable things; fanciful musing; daydreaming.

2. a dreamy, fanciful, or visionary notion or daydream.

3. an instrumental musical composition expressing a dreamy or musing mood.

rev′ẽr·ist, *n.* one who is given to reverie; a dreamer.

rē·vẽrs′ (-vẽr′ *or* -vâr′), *n.*; *pl.* **rē·vẽrṣ′** (-vẽrz′ *or* -vârz′), [Fr., from L. *reversus*, turned back.]

1. a part (of a garment) turned back to show the reverse side, lining, or facing, as a lapel.

2. a piece of trimming used in simulation of such a part.

Also *revere*.

rē·vẽr′săl, *a.* intended to reverse; implying reverse. [Rare.]

rē·vẽr′săl, *n.* 1. in law, annulment, change, or revocation; as, the *reversal* of a judgment or decision by a higher court.

2. the act of reversing or the state of being reversed; the changing to a contrary or former condition; as, the *reversal* of the motion of a lever; the *reversal* of lines in the spectrum from light to dark.

rē·vẽrse′, *v.t.*; reversed (-vẽrst′), *pt., pp.*; reversing, *ppr.* [Fr., from LL. *reversare*, to turn about, to turn back, freq. of L. *revertere*, to revert, to turn back.]

1. to turn backward, in an opposite position or direction, upside down, or inside out.

2. to change to the opposite; to alter completely.

3. to cause to go or move backward or in an opposite direction.

4. to exchange or transpose.

5. in law, to revoke or annul (a decision, judgment, etc.).

6. to overturn; to subvert. [Obs.]

7. to recall. [Obs.]

rē·vẽrse′, *v.i.* 1. to move, go, or turn backward or in the opposite direction; as, the dancers *reversed*.

2. to put a motor, engine, etc. in reverse; to reverse the action of the mechanism.

3. to return. [Obs.]

rē·vẽrse′, *n.* 1. the contrary; the opposite of something; as, it is the *reverse* of what was expected.

2. the back or rear of something; specifically, the side of a coin, medal, etc. that does not have the main design: opposed to *obverse*.

3. a reversing; a change to the opposite.

4. a change from good fortune to bad; a defeat, check, or misfortune.

5. a mechanism, etc. for reversing, as a gear or gear ratio that causes a machine to run backward or in the opposite direction; as, the car was in *reverse*.

6. a reversing movement.

7. a reverse stroke in fencing; a backhanded thrust or blow. [Obs.]

rē·vẽrse′, *a.* 1. turned backward; opposite or contrary, as in position, direction, order, etc.

2. acting in a way or direction opposite or contrary to the usual, as a machine.

3. causing movement backward or in the opposite direction; as, a *reverse* gear ratio.

4. in biology, reversed.

reverse bearing; in surveying, the bearing of a course taken from an advance point by sighting backward.

reverse curve; in a railroad, a double curve formed or two curves lying in opposite directions, like the letter S.

reverse operation; in mathematics, an operation in which the steps are the same as in a direct operation, but taken in a contrary order; as, obtaining the price from the cost is the *reverse operation* of obtaining the cost from the price; similarly, addition and subtraction are *reverse operations*.

rē·vẽrsed′ (-vẽrst′), *a.* 1. turned side for side or end for end; changed to the contrary.

2. in law, overthrown or annulled.

3. in botany, resupinate.

4. in conchology, having the aperture opening on the left side when placed in front of the spectator; having the volutions the reverse way of the common screw; sinistral.

5. in heraldry, renverse.

6. in geology, having the axial plane oblique; as, a *reversed* flexure.

REVERSED SHELL

rē·vẽrs′ed·ly, *adv.* in a reversed manner.

rē·vẽrse′less, *a.* irreversible. [Rare.]

rē·vẽrse′ly, *adv.* 1. in a reverse manner, position, order, or direction.

2. on the contrary; on the other hand; contrariwise.

rē·vẽrs′ẽr, *n.* 1. one who or that which reverses; as, a *reverser* in an electric circuit to alter the polarity or reverse the current.

2. in law, a reversioner.

rē·vẽrs·i·bil′i·ty, *n.* capability of being reversed.

rē·vẽrs′i·ble, *a.* 1. adapted to be or capable of being reversed; as, a *reversible* lock, which may be used on either side of a door; a *reversible* cloak, to be worn with either side out; a *reversible* judgment, that may be made void.

2. that can reverse; specifically, that can change and then go back to the original condition by a reversal of the change: said of a chemical reaction, etc.

rē·vẽrs′i·ble, *n.* a reversible coat, jacket, etc.

rē·vẽrs′i·bly, *adv.* in a reversible manner; so as to be reversible.

rē·vẽrs′ing, *a.* serving to reverse; reversible.

rē·vẽrs′ing en′gine, a steam engine with reversing gear.

rē·vẽrs′ing gēar, the apparatus for reversing the motion of a marine or locomotive engine, by changing the time of action of the slide valve: the eccentric being in advance of the crank for the forward motion will, if turned to an equal distance behind the crank, produce a backward motion.

rē·vẽr′ṣion, *n.* [L. *reversio* (*-onis*), from *revertere*, to revert, to turn back.]

1. a turning or being turned the opposite way; reversal.

2. a return, as to a former state, custom, or belief; a reverting.

3. in biology, (a) a return to a former or primitive type; atavism; (b) the return, or reappearance, of characteristics present in early ancestral generations but not in those that have intervened; (c) an individual or organism with such characteristics.

4. a residue; remainder. [Obs.]

5. in law, (a) the right of succession, future possession, or enjoyment; (b) the return of an estate to the grantor and his heirs after the period of grant is over; (c) an estate so returning.

6. in annuities, a reversionary or deferred annuity.

rē·vẽr′ṣion·ăl, *a.* reversionary.

rē·vẽr′ṣion·ăr·y, *a.* in law, of, involving, or having the nature of a reversion, to be enjoyed in succession, or after the determination of a particular estate.

reversionary interest; the right to enjoy in the future property at present in the possession of another.

rē·vẽr′ṣion·ẽr, *n.* in law, a person who has a reversion or a right to receive an estate in reversion; one who has a reversionary interest.

rē·vẽr′sis, *n.* [OFr.] an old card game in which the player taking the fewest tricks won the game.

rē·vẽrt′, *v.t.*; reverted, *pt., pp.*; reverting, *ppr.* [OFr. *revertir*, from L. *revertere*, to turn back, to turn about; *re-*, back, and *vertere*, to turn.]

1. to turn or direct back; to reverse; to turn to the contrary. [Obs.]

2. to drive or turn back; to repel. [Obs.]

rē·vẽrt′, *v.i.* 1. to go back in action, thought, speech, etc.; to return, as to a former practice, opinion, state, or subject.

2. in biology, to return to a former or

primitive type; to show ancestral characteristics no longer present in the species.

3. in law, to go back to a former owner or his heirs.

4. in chemistry, to change, as certain superphosphates, from a soluble to an insoluble condition.

rē·vẽrt′, *n.* 1. one who or that which reverts; especially, one who returns to his previous faith.

2. in music, return; recurrence. [Obs.]

rē·vẽrt′ănt, *a.* in heraldry, bent and rebent.

rē·vẽrt′ed, *a.* in heraldry, flexed and reflexed; bent to the shape S; revertant.

rē·vẽrt′ẽr, *n.* a revert.

rē·vẽrt′ẽr, *n.* in law, reversion.

rē·vẽrt′i·ble, *a.* that may revert or return.

rē·vẽrt′ive, *a.* reverting; returning.

rē·vẽrt′ive·ly, *adv.* by way of reversion.

rev′ẽr·y, *n.*; *pl.* **rev′ẽr·ies**, same as *reverie.*

rē·vest′, *v.t.*; revested, *pt.*, *pp.*; revesting, *ppr.* [OFr. *revestir*, from LL. *revestire*, to clothe again; from L. *re-*, again, and *vestire*, to clothe.]

1. to clothe again. [Obs.]

2. to vest again, as with possession, power, or office; to reinvest; reinstate.

3. to vest (office, powers, etc.) again.

rē·vest′, *v.i.* to become vested again (*in*); to take effect again, as a title; to return to a former owner or holder; as, the title or right *revests in* A, after alienation.

rē·ves′ti·ăr·y, *n.* [Fr. *revestiaire*, from L. *revestio*, vestry.] the place in a church where the vestments are put on; a vestry. [Obs.]

rē·ves′try, *n.* a revestiary. [Obs.]

rē·ves′tūre, *n.* vesture. [Rare.]

rē·vet′, *v.t.*; revetted, *pt.*, *pp.*; revetting, *ppr.* [Fr. *revêtir*, to clothe again, to face, to line, as a foss or fortification.] in military and civil engineering, to face (a wall, bank of earth, etc.) with a layer of stone, brick, etc.

rē·vet′ment, *n.* [Fr. *revêtement*, the lining of a ditch, from *revêtir*, to clothe or line.]

1. a facing of stone, cement, sandbags, etc., built to protect a wall or an embankment.

2. in architecture, any facing or sheathing, as of stone or metal, used to protect or to beautify a structure, as a wall or a column.

3. in civil engineering, a retaining wall; any device for retaining and protecting a bank or the slope of a cut.

rē·vī′brāte, *v.i.* to vibrate again or in return.

rē·vī·brā′tion, *n.* the act of vibrating again.

rē·vict′uăl (-vit′l), *v.t.* to furnish again with provisions.

rē·vīe′, *v.t.* to vie with again. [Obs.]

rē·vīe′, *v.i.* to return the challenge of a wager at cards; to make a retort. [Obs.]

rē·view′ (-vū′), *v.t.*; reviewed, *pt.*, *pp.*; reviewing, *ppr.* [MFr. *reveue*; Fr. *revue*, a review, from *revu*, pp. of *revoir*; L. *revidere*, to see again; *re-*, again, and *videre*, to see.]

1. to see again. [Obs.]

2. to view again; to look at, look over, or study again.

3. to look back on; to view in retrospect.

Let me *review* the scene,
And summon from the shadowy Past
The forms that once have been.
—Longfellow.

4. to survey in thought, speech, or writing; to make or give a survey of.

5. to examine or inspect; specifically, to inspect formally, as troops.

6. to give or write a critical discussion of (a book, play, etc.).

7. to re-examine; specifically, to re-examine judicially, as a lower court's decision.

8. to go over (lessons, etc.) again, as in recitation.

rē·view′, *v.i.* to review books, plays, etc., as for a newspaper.

rē·view′, *n.* 1. a viewing again; a looking at, looking over, or studying again.

2. a general survey, report, or account.

3. a looking back on; a retrospective view or survey, as of past events, experiences, etc.

4. re-examination; specifically, judicial re-examination, as of the decision of a lower court.

5. a critical discussion or article, as in a newspaper or magazine, dealing with a book, play, concert, etc., especially with a recent one.

6. a magazine containing articles of criticism and appraisal, often in a specific field; as, a scientific *review*, literary *review*.

7. the act or process of going over a lesson or subject again, as in recitation.

8. a revue.

9. an examination or inspection; specifically, a formal inspection, as of troops on parade, ships, etc., by a high-ranking officer.

10. revision; a second examination with a view to amendment or improvement; as, an author's *review* of his works. [Obs.]

bill of review; in law, a bill filed to procure an examination by a court of equity of a final decree with a view to obtaining a reversal or alteration.

Commission of review; a commission formerly granted by the British crown to revise the sentence of the Court of Delegates.

Syn.—notice, revision, survey.

rē·view′ȧ·ble, *a.* admitting of review; requiring review.

rē·view′ăl, *n.* a review; the act of reviewing.

rē·view′ẽr, *n.* one who reviews or re-examines; especially, one who critically examines new books, plays, etc. and publishes his opinions of them in a periodical.

rē·vig′ŏr·āte, *a.* having new vigor; strengthened. [Obs.]

rē·vig′ŏr·āte, *v.t.* to give new vigor to. [Obs.]

rē·vīle′, *v.t.*; reviled, *pt.*, *pp.*; reviling, *ppr.* [OFr. *reviler*, to regard or treat as vile.] to reproach; to treat with opprobrious and contemptuous language; to use abusive language in speaking to or about; as, to *revile* an enemy.

Syn.—defame, vilify, reproach, traduce, calumniate.

rē·vīle′, *v.i.* to be reproachful or abusive in speech.

rē·vīle′, *n.* reproach; contumely; contemptuous language. [Obs.]

rē·vīle′ment, *n.* 1. a reviling, or abusing in words.

2. an instance of this; abusive speech.

rē·vīl′ẽr, *n.* one who reviles; one who decries another with contemptuous language.

rē·vīl′ing, *n.* the act of treating with reproachful words; reproach; vilification.

rē·vīl′ing·ly, *adv.* with reproachful or contemptuous language; with opprobrium.

rē·vin′di·çāte, *v.t.* [L. *revindicatus*, pp. of *revindicare*, to lay claim to; *re-*, again, and *vindicare*, to claim.] to vindicate again; to reclaim; to demand the return of, as goods or property unjustly held.

rē″vin·di·çā′tion, *n.* the act of revindicating; demand for the restoration of goods or property unjustly held.

rev·i·res′cence, *n.* renewal of strength or of youth. [Obs.]

rē·viș′a·ble, *a.* admitting of revision.

rē·viș′ăl, *n.* 1. a revising or being revised.

2. a revision.

rē·vīșe′, *v.t.*; revised, *pt.*, *pp.*; revising, *ppr.* [OFr. and Fr. *reviser*, from L. *revisere*, to look back on, revisit; *re-*, back, and *visere*, to survey, freq. of *videre*, to see.]

1. to review; to re-examine; to look over with care, as a manuscript, published book, etc., in order to correct and improve; as, to *revise* a writing; to *revise* a proof sheet.

2. to review, alter, and amend; as, to *revise* statutes.

rē·vīșe′, *n.* 1. a revising or a revised form of something; revision; review.

2. in printing, a second proof sheet; a proof sheet taken after the first corrections have been made, for looking over or correcting again.

Rē·vīșed′ Stand′ărd Vẽr′șion, a revised translation of the Bible in contemporary English by a group of American scholars: the complete version was published in the United States in 1952.

Rē·vīșed′ Vẽr′șion, a revision, or recension, of the Authorized, or King James, Version of the Bible, made by a committee of American and British scholars: the New Testament was published in 1881, the Old Testament in 1885.

rē·vīș′ẽr, *n.* one who revises or re-examines for correction: also spelled *revisor.*

rē·vi′șion (-vizh′un), *n.* [OFr. *revision*; LL. *revisio* (*-onis*), a seeing again, from L. *revisus*, pp. of *revidere*, to see again.]

1. the act, process, or work of revising; review; re-examination for correction; as, the *revision* of a book or of a proof sheet; a *revision* of statutes.

2. the result of revising; a revised form or version, as of a book, manuscript, etc.

rē·vi′șion·ăl, *a.* of or involving revision.

rē·vi′șion·ăr·y, *a.* pertaining to revision.

rē·vi′șion·ișm, *n.* the policy or practice of revisionists.

rē·vi′șion·ist, *n.* 1. a person who revises, or favors the revision of, some accepted theory, doctrine, etc.

2. a reviser; especially, one who prepared the Revised Version of the King James Bible.

rē·vi′șion·ist, *a.* of revisionists or revisionism.

rē·viș′it, *v.t.* [Fr. *revisiter*; L. *revisitare*; *re-*, again, and *visitare*, to visit.]

1. to visit again.

2. to revise. [Obs.]

rē·viș·it·ā′tion, *n.* the act of revisiting.

rē·vī′șŏr, *n.* a reviser.

rē·vī′șō·ry, *a.* that revises; of, or having the nature or power of, revision.

rē·vī′tăl·īze, *v.t.* to bring to life again; to restore vitality to; to revive.

rē·vīv′ȧ·ble, *a.* capable of being revived.

rē·vīv′ăl, *n.* 1. the act of reviving or the condition of being revived.

2. a bringing or coming back into use, attention, or being, after a decline.

3. a new presentation of a play, motion picture, etc. some time after it has first been presented.

4. restoration to vigor or activity.

5. a bringing or coming back to life or consciousness.

6. a stirring up of religious faith among those who have been indifferent, usually by dramatic, fervid preaching and meetings.

7. (a) a meeting characterized by fervid preaching, public confession of sins, professions of renewed faith, etc., aimed at arousing religious belief; (b) a series of such meetings.

8. in law, renewal of validity, as of a judgment or contract.

revival meeting; a special religious meeting, often prolonged, and generally conducted by a revivalist or revivalists, for the purpose of quickening interest in religion.

Revival of Learning (or *Letters, Literature*); the Renaissance as related to learning and literature.

rē·vīv′ăl·ișm, *n.* 1. the fervid spirit or methods characteristic of religious revivals; evangelical enthusiasm.

2. the tendency or desire to revive former ways, customs, institutions, etc.

rē·vīv′ăl·ist, *n.* 1. a person who promotes or conducts religious revivals.

2. a person who revives former ways, customs, institutions, etc.

rē·vīv′ăl·ist, *a.* concerned or assisting in the promotion of revivals of religion; as, a *revivalist* preacher.

rē·vīv·ăl·is′tiç, *a.* pertaining to revivalism, revivalists, or revivals.

rē·vīve′, *v.i.*; revived, *pt.*, *pp.*; reviving, *ppr.* [Fr. *revivre*; L. *revivere*, to live again; *re-*, again, and *vivere*, to live.]

1. to come back to life; to live again after dying.

2. to come back to consciousness.

3. to come back to health and vigor.

4. to flourish again after a decline.

5. to come back into use or attention.

6. to become valid, effective, or operative again.

7. in old chemistry, to recover its natural state, as a metal.

rē·vīve′, *v.t.* 1. to bring back to life.

2. to bring back to consciousness.

3. to bring back to a healthy, vigorous, or flourishing condition after a decline.

4. to bring back into use or attention.

5. to make valid, effective, or operative again.

6. to bring to mind again.

7. to produce (a play, etc.) again after an interval.

8. to renew; to renovate, as clothes. [Rare.]

9. in old chemistry, to restore or reduce to its natural or metallic state; as, to *revive* a metal after calcination.

Syn.—refresh, renew, revivify, reanimate, reproduce, renovate, recall, reinforce.

rē·vīve′ment, *n.* revivification; revival. [Rare.]

rē·vīv′ẽr, *n.* one who or that which revives.

rē·viv′i·fi·çāte, *v.t.* to revive. [Rare.]

rē·viv″i·fi·çā′tion, *n.* [LL. *revivificatio* (*-onis*), from *revivificare*, to restore to life.]

1. a revivifying or being revivified; renewal of life; restoration to life; the act of recalling to life.

2. in old chemistry, the reduction of a metal from a state of combination to its metallic state.

rē·viv′i·fȳ, *v.t.*; revivified, *pt.*, *pp.*; revivifying, *ppr.* [Fr. *revivifier.*]

1. to recall to life; to give new life or vigor to; to cause to revive.

2. to reactivate again by purification, as charcoal used in refining.

rē·viv′i·fȳ, *v.i.* to revive.

rē·vīv′ing·ly, *adv.* in a reviving manner.

rev·i·vis′cence, *n.* [from *reviviscent.*] act of reviving or state of being revived; revival; renewal of life.

rev·i·vis′cen·cy, *n.* same as *reviviscence.*

rev·i·vis′cent, *a.* [L. *reviviscens* (*-entis*), ppr. of *reviviscere*, to revive, incept. of *revivere*, to revive.] reviving; regaining or restoring life or vigor.

rē·vīv′ŏr, *n.* in law, the reviving of a suit which is abated by the death of any of the parties, or other cause; as, a bill of *revivor.*

rev″ō·ca·bil′i·ty, *n.* the quality or state of being revocable.

rev′ō·ca·ble, *a.* capable of being revoked.

rev′ō·ca·ble·ness, *n.* the state or quality of being revocable.

rev′ō·ca·bly, *adv.* in a revocable manner; so as to be revocable.

rev′ō·cāte, *v.t.* to recall; to call back. [Obs.]

rev·ō·cā′tion, *n.* [L. *revocatio* (*-onis*), from *revocare*, to revoke.]

1. the act of recalling or calling back; recall. [Obs.]

2. the state of being recalled. [Obs.]

3. a revoking or being revoked; cancellation; repeal; annulment; specifically, in law, nullification of an offer to contract.

rev′ō·ca·tō·ry, *a.* [LL. *revocatorius*, from L. *revocare*, to revoke.] revoking or tending to revoke; containing or expressing a revocation.

rē·voice′, *v.t.*; revoiced, *pt., pp.*; revoicing, *ppr.* 1. to refurnish with a voice; to refit, as an organ pipe, so as to restore the proper quality of tone.

2. to voice again, or in answer; to re-echo; to repeat; as, to *revoice* an exclamation.

rē·vōk′á·ble, *a.* that can be revoked.

rē·vōke′, *v.t.*; revoked (-vōkt′), *pt., pp.*; revoking, *ppr.* [ME. *revoken*; OFr. *revocquer*; L. *revocare*, to call back, revoke; *re-*, back, and *vocare*, to call.]

1. to withdraw; to rescind; to repeal; to cancel; to annul; as, to *revoke* a law, will, license, charter, or grant.

2. to call back. [Obs.]

3. to check; to repress; as, to *revoke* rage. [Obs.]

4. to draw back; to withdraw. [Obs.]

5. to recollect; to recall (something past). [Rare.]

Syn.—abolish, repeal, reverse, countermand, rescind, annul, abrogate, cancel.

rē·vōke′, *v.i.* 1. in card playing, to fail to follow suit when the player can and is required by the rules to do so; to renege.

2. to abrogate, annul, or recall some right, favor, or the like.

rē·vōke′, *n.* in card playing, an erroneous failure to follow suit; a revoking.

rē·vōke′ment, *n.* revocation; reversal. [Rare.]

rē·vōk′ẽr, *n.* one who revokes.

rē·vōk′ing·ly, *adv.* in a revoking manner.

rē·vōlt′, *v.i.*; revolted, *pt., pp.*; revolting, *ppr.* [Fr. *révolter*; It. *rivoltare*; *ri-*, and *voltare*, to turn, from L. *revolvere*; *re-*, again, and *volvere*, to turn.]

1. to rise up against the government.

2. to refuse to submit to authority; to rebel; to mutiny.

3. to turn in revulsion from a group or opinion that one has adhered to.

4. to be disgusted or shocked; to feel repugnance (with *at, against*, or *from*).

rē·vōlt′, *v.t.* 1. to turn; to put to flight. [Obs.]

2. to disgust; to fill with revulsion; to cause to shrink or turn away with abhorrence; as, to *revolt* the mind or the feelings.

rē·vōlt′, *n.* 1. a rising up against the government; rebellion; insurrection.

2. any refusal to submit to or accept authority.

3. the state of a person or persons revolting; as, they are in *revolt.*

4. a revolter; a rebel. [Obs.]

rē·vōlt′ẽr, *n.* one who revolts.

rē·vōlt′ing, *a.* [ppr. of *revolt.*]

1. engaged in revolt; rebellious.

2. causing revulsion; disgusting; repulsive; offensive; loathsome.

rē·vōlt′ing·ly, *adv.* in a revolting manner.

rev′ō·lū·ble, *a.* [L. *revolubilis*, that may be rolled or revolved, from *revolvere*, to revolve.] capable of being rotated or revolved; rolling; rotatory. [Rare.]

rev′ō·lūte, *a.* curled or rolled backward or downward at the tips or margins, as some leaves.

rev·ō·lū′tion, *n.* [OFr.; LL. *revolutio* (*-onis*), a revolving, from *revolutus*, pp. of *revolvere*, to turn over, revolve.]

1. movement of a body, as a star or planet, in an orbit or circle: in this sense, distinguished from *rotation.*

2. apparent movement of the sun and stars around the earth.

3. the time taken for a body to go around an orbit and return to its original position.

4. a turning or spinning motion of a body around a center of axis; rotation.

5. a single turn of such a rotating body.

6. a complete cycle of events; as, the *revolution* of the seasons.

7. a complete or drastic change of any kind; as, a *revolution* in modern physics.

8. overthrow of a government, form of government, or social system, with another taking its place; as, the English *Revolution* (1688), the American *Revolution* (1775), the French *Revolution* (1789), the Chinese *Revolution* (1911), the Russian *Revolution* (1917).

the American Revolution; see under *American.*

the Chinese Revolution; see following *Chinese.*

the English Revolution; that revolution by which James II was driven from the throne in 1688.

the French Revolution; see under *French.*

the Russian Revolution; see following *Russian.*

Syn.—rotation.—*Rotation* of a body is the motion of all its parts around a point or axis within that body, each part retaining its relation to the center; *revolution* of a body is its motion as a whole around a point outside that body. The earth makes an annual *revolution* around the sun; it makes a daily *rotation* on its axis.

rev·ō·lū′tion·ãr·y, *a.* 1. of, having the nature of, characterized by, tending toward, or causing a revolution, or drastic change, especially in a government or social system.

2. revolving or rotating.

Revolutionary Calendar; the official calendar of the first French republic: see *French Revolutionary Calendar* under *French.*

Revolutionary War; the war (1775–1783), by which the American colonies won their independence from England; the American Revolution.

rev·ō·lū′tion·ãr·y, *n.*; *pl.* **rev·ō·lū′tion·ãr·ies**, a revolutionist.

rev·ō·lū′tion·ẽr, *n.* one who is engaged in effecting a revolution; a revolutionist.

rev·ō·lū′tion·işm, *n.* the state of revolution; revolutionary principles or motives.

rev·ō·lū′tion·ist, *n.* one who engages in or favors a revolution.

rev·ō·lū′tion·īze, *v.t.*; revolutionized, *pt., pp.*; revolutionizing, *ppr.* 1. to make a complete and basic change in; to alter drastically or radically; as, the automobile has *revolutionized* American life.

2. to bring about a political revolution in. [Rare.]

rev′ō·lū·tive, *a.* turning over in the mind; cogitating. [Obs.]

rē·volv′á·ble, *a.* capable of revolving or being revolved.

rē·volve′, *v.i.*; revolved, *pt., pp.*; revolving, *ppr.* [L. *revolvere*, to roll back, to revolve; *re-*, back, and *volvere*, to roll.]

1. to move in a circle or orbit around a point.

2. to spin or turn around a center or axis; to rotate.

3. to recur at intervals; to occur periodically.

4. to fall back; to return. [Obs.]

Syn.—turn, roll, spin, circle.

rē·volve′, *v.t.* 1. to turn over in the mind; to reflect on.

2. to cause to travel in a circle or orbit.

3. to cause to rotate, or spin around on axis.

rē·volve′ment, *n.* the act of revolving. [Rare.]

rē·volv′en·cy, *n.* [L. *revolvens* (*-entis*), ppr. of *revolvere*, to revolve.] the tendency to revolve; capacity for revolving.

rē·volv′ẽr, *n.* one who or that which revolves; specifically, a firearm (ordinarily a pistol) having a revolving cylinder provided with chambers in which cartridges may be placed so that it can be fired in quick succession without reloading.

rē·volv′ing, *a.* that revolves; specifically, designating or of a radial engine with cylinders revolving around a stationary crankshaft.

revolving door; a door consisting of four vanes hung on a central axle and so arranged in a wall that a person using it turns it around by pushing on one of the vanes: used to keep out drafts of air.

revolving fund; a sum of money kept for making loans and maintained by putting back into it the money that has been lent, as it is repaid.

revolving light; a light in a lighthouse which either revolves about an axis or has a screen revolving around it, causing it to appear and disappear at certain fixed intervals.

rē·vom′it, *v.t.* [Fr. *revomir.*] to vomit again.

rē·vūe′, *n.* [Fr.] a type of musical show consisting of several loosely connected skits, songs, and dances, often parodying recent events, plays, etc.: also spelled *review.*

rē·vulse′, *v.t.* [Fr. *révulser*, from L. *revulsus*, pp. of *revellere*, to pluck back.] to pull back violently or with force. [Obs.]

rē·vul′sion, *n.* [Fr. *révulsion*, from L. *revulsio* (*-onis*), a tearing off or away, from *revulsus*, pp. of *revellere*, to pluck back.]

1. a drawing or being drawn back or away; withdrawal.

The *revulsion* of capital from other trades of which the returns are more frequent.
—Adam Smith.

2. a sudden, complete, and violent change, particularly of feeling; an abrupt, strong reaction in sentiment.

3. in medicine, the act of lessening disease in, or drawing away blood from, one part of the body to another by counterirritation.

rē·vul′sive, *a.* of or having the power of revulsion; tending to cause revulsion.

rē·vul′sive, *n.* that which causes or tends to cause revulsion; especially, in medicine, an agent producing revulsion.

rew (rö), *n.* a row or line. [Obs.]

rē·wāke′, *v.t.* and *v.i.* to wake again or a second time.

rē·wãrd′, *n.* [ME.; O. Norm. Fr., for OFr. *regarde*; cf. *regard.*]

1. something given in return for good or, sometimes, evil done, for services, for merit, or the like; requital.

Great is your *reward* in heaven.
—Matt. v. 12.

2. money offered, as for the capture of a criminal, the return of something lost, etc.

3. compensation; profit; return.

4. regard; heed. [Obs.]

5. in law, remuneration or recompense for services performed; a sum of money paid or received for the performance or nonperformance of some act.

Syn.—remuneration, recompense, requital, retribution, compensation, repayment, wages.

rē·wãrd′, *v.t.*; rewarded, *pt., pp.*; rewarding, *ppr.* 1. to give a reward to.

2. to give a reward for (service, etc.).

rē·wãrd′á·ble, *a.* deserving reward.

rē·wãrd′á·ble·ness, *n.* the state, condition, or quality of being rewardable.

rē·wãrd′á·bly, *adv.* in a rewardable manner; so as to be rewarded.

rē·wãrd′ẽr, *n.* one who or that which rewards.

rē·wãrd′fụl, *a.* producing reward; given compensation.

rē·wãrd′less, *a.* without reward.

rewe (rö), *v.t.* and *v.i.* to repent or rue. [Obs.]

rew′el bōne (rö′), ivory (perhaps from the narwhale). [Obs.]

rew′et, *n.* a wheel; a wheel lock; a gun with a wheel lock. [Obs.]

rew′fụl, *a.* rueful. [Obs.]

rē·wīre′, *v.i.* and *v.t.*; rewired, *pt., pp.*; rewiring, *ppr.* to wire again or anew; specifically, (a) to put new wires or wiring in or on (a house, motor, etc.); (b) to telegraph again.

rewle, (rụl) *n.* and *v.* obsolete form of *rule.*

rewme (rụm), *n.* realm. [Obs.]

rē·wõrd′, *v.t.*; reworded, *pt., pp.*; rewording, *ppr.* 1. to state or express again in different words; to change the wording of.

2. to re-echo. [Obs.]

3. to repeat in the same words.

rē·wrīte′, *v.t.* and *v.i.*; rewrote, *pt.*; rewritten, *pp.*; rewriting, *ppr.* 1. to write again.

2. to write in different words or a different form; to revise.

3. in journalism, to write (news turned in by a reporter) in a form suitable for publication.

rē′wrīte, *n.* in journalism, an article, story, or other item that has been put into final form for publication by someone other than the reporter who collected the facts.

rewrite man; in journalism, one employed to write articles from news turned in by reporters.

Rex, *n.*; *pl.* **Rē′ġēs̤,** [L., a king.] [*also* r-] king: the official title of a reigning king; as, George *Rex.*

Reye′s̤ syn′drōme, [named after R.D. *Reye,* 20th-c. Australian pathologist who first described it.] a rare, acute, often fatal disease, usually of children, characterized by neurological disorders, swelling of the brain, and enlargement of the liver: the cause is unknown but it most frequently occurs after a viral illness, as influenza.

rey̨n, *n.* rain. [Obs.]

Reyn′ărd (ren′ *or* rān′), *n.* [OFr. *Renard, Renart,* from O.H.G. *Reginhart,* from Gmc. (hyp.) *ragina,* counsel, judgment, and *hard-,* bold, brave.] the fox in the medieval beast epic Reynard the Fox; hence, a proper name for the fox in fable and folklore: also *Renard.*

Rh, in chemistry, rhodium.

rhä, *n.* [Gr. *rha,* rhubarb, from *Rha,* the river now known as the Volga.] rhubarb. [Obs.]

rhȧ·bär′bȧ·rin, rhȧ·bär′bȧ·rine, *n.* chrysophanic acid.

rhab′dīte (rab′), *n.* [Gr. *rhabdos,* rod, and *-ite.*]

1. an integumentary rodlike body present in the ectoderm of many turbellarian worms.

2. one of the horny stylets composing the ovipositor of some insects.

Rhab·dō·coe′lȧ, *n.pl.* [LL., from Gr. *rhabdos,* rod, and *koilos,* hollow.] a group of unsegmented turbellarian worms, small freshwater and marine forms of which represent the beginnings of definite bilateral symmetry.

rhab·dō·coe′lous, *a.* pertaining to the *Rhabdocoela.*

rhab·doid′ăl, *a.* shaped like a rod; sagittal; belonging to the sagittal suture connecting the two parietal bones.

rhab′dō·lith, *n.* [LL., from Gr. *rhabdos,* rod, and *lithos,* a stone.] one of the elements of the calcareous armature covering a rhabdosphere.

rhab·dol′ō·ġy, *n.* the act or art of computing or numbering by Napier's rods.

rhab′dŏm, *n.* [Gr. *rhabdōma,* a bundle of rods, from *rhabdos,* rod.] a rodlike, tubular structure in the axis of a cluster of retinal cells in an ommatidium.

rhab′dō·man·cy, *n.* [Gr. *rhabdos,* a rod, and *manteia,* divination.] divination by a rod or wand; specifically, the supposed art of finding things concealed in the earth, as ores, metals, springs of water, and the like, by a divining rod; dowsing.

rhab′dōme, *n.* a rhabdom.

rhab′dō·mēre, *n.* [Gr. *rhabdos,* rod, and *meros,* part.] a component part of a rhabdom.

rhab″dō·my·ō′mȧ, *n.* [Mod. L., from Gr. *rhabdos,* rod, and Mod. L. *myoma,* myoma.] in medicine, a tumor composed of striated muscular fibers.

Rhab·doph′ō·rȧ, *n.pl.* [Gr. *rhabdos,* rod, and *pherein,* to bear.] a group of fossil hydroids which includes the graptolites: so called because they generally possess a chitinous rod or axis supporting the perisarc.

rhab·doph′ō·răn, *n.* a graptolite.

Rhab·dō·pleu′rȧ, *n.* [Gr. *rhabdos,* rod, and *pleuron,* rib.] a genus of marine polyzoans having the primitive bud enclosed between two fleshy lobes or valvelike plates, attached along their dorsal margin, and giving exit in front to the rudimentary lophophore or horseshoe-shaped disk which bears the tentacles.

rhab′dō·sphēre, *n.* [Gr. *rhabdos,* rod, and *sphaira,* a sphere.] a minute, spherical, organic body bristling with rods or rhabdoliths, occurring on the surface and in the depths of the ocean.

rhab′dus, *n.*; *pl.* **rhab′dī,** [LL., from Gr. *rhabdos,* rod.] a simple, straight, rod-shaped sponge spicule.

rhā·ċhi·al′ġi·ȧ, rhā′ċhis, etc. see *rachialgia, rachis,* etc.

Rhad·ȧ·man′thine, Rhad·ȧ·man′tine (rad-), *a.* pertaining to or characteristic of Rhadamanthus; inflexibly or rigorously just and final.

Rhad·ȧ·man′thus, *n.* in Greek mythology, the son of Zeus and Europa, rewarded for the exemplary justice that he showed during his life by being made one of the three judges in Hades, with Aeacus and Minos; hence, any scrupulously just judge.

Rhae′tiăn, Rhē′tiăn (rē′shăn), *a.* of or pertaining to the people or province of ancient Rhaetia, a district of the Alps, west of Noricum, east of Helvetia, and south of Vindelicia.

Rhae′tiăn, *n.* a native or inhabitant of ancient Rhaetia.

Rhae′tiç, Rhē′tiç, *a.* [L. *Rhaeticus,* Rhaetian.] in geology, designating or of a group of strata of the European Triassic system, prominent in the Rhaetian Alps.

rhae′ti·zīte, *n.* a white variety of cyanite.

Rhae″tō-Rō·man′iç, *a.* designating or of a group of several closely associated Romance dialects spoken in southern Switzerland, the Tyrol, and northern Italy.

Rhae″tō-Rō·man′iç, *n.* the Rhaeto-Romanic group of dialects as a distinct Romanic language.

-rhāġe, -rhā′ġi·ȧ, same as *-rrhagia.*

Rham·nā′cē·ae (ram-), *n.pl.* [*Rhamnus* and *-aceæ.*] an order of dicotyledonous plants, the buckthorn family, including some 475 species of wide distribution.

rham·nā′ceous, *a.* pertaining to the *Rhamnaceæ.*

rham·nox·an′thin, *n.* same as *frangulin.*

Rham′nus, *n.* [L. Gr. *rhamnos,* the buckthorn.]

1. a genus of shrubs and trees of the buckthorn family, native to north temperate regions. *Rhamnus catharticus, Rhamnus frangula,* and *Rhamnus purshianus* are used medicinally.

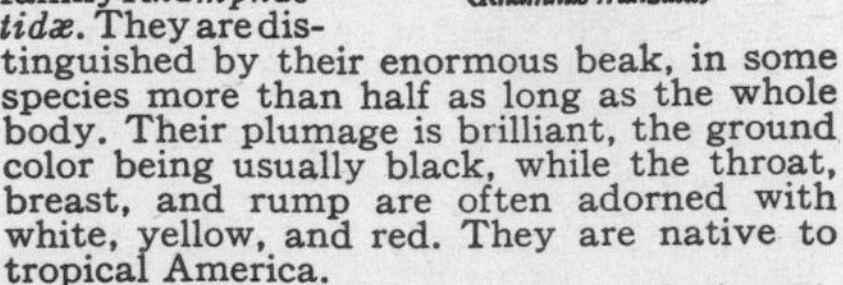

RHAMNUS (*Rhamnus frangula*)

2. [r-] a plant of this genus.

Rham·phas′tos, *n.* [Gr. *rhamphos,* a beak.] the true toucans, a genus of scansorial birds, and type of the family *Rhamphastidæ.* They are distinguished by their enormous beak, in some species more than half as long as the whole body. Their plumage is brilliant, the ground color being usually black, while the throat, breast, and rump are often adorned with white, yellow, and red. They are native to tropical America.

rham′phoid, *a.* [Gr. *rhamphōdēs,* beak-shaped, from *rhamphos,* a curved beak, and *-oid.*] resembling a beak, or formed like one.

Rham·phō·rhyn′ċhus, *n.* [Gr. *rhamphos,* a curved beak, and *rhynchos,* snout, beak.] a genus of pterodactyls in which the front part of both jaws was edentulous, teeth having been developed only in the hinder portion.

rham·phō·thē′ċȧ, *n.*; *pl.* **rham·phō·thē′cae,** [Gr. *rhamphos,* a curved beak, and *thēkē,* sheath.] the cornified outer integument of the bill of birds.

rhā′phē (rā′), *n.* same as *raphe.*

rhaph′i·dēs (raf′), *n.pl.* same as *raphides.*

rhȧ·phid′i·ăn (rȧ-), *a.* same as *raphidian.*

rhā′phis (rā′), *n.* same as *raphis.*

Rhap″i·dō·phyl′lum (rap″), *n.* [LL., from Gr. *rhapis, rhapidos,* rod, stick, and *phyllon,* a leaf.] a genus of fan palms, *Rhapidophyllum hystrix,* the blue palmetto of Florida being the only species.

Rhā′pis (rā′), *n.* [Gr., a rod.] a genus of dwarf palms of eastern Asia. *Rhapis flabelliformis* is the ground rattan.

rhȧ·pon′tiç (rȧ-), *n.* [L. *rhaponticum,* formerly *rha Ponticum,* rhubarb.] rhubarb; also, its root.

rhȧ·pon′ti·cin, *n.* a crystalline substance extracted from rhubarb.

rhap′sōde (rap′), *n.* [Gr. *rhapsōdos,* a writer of epic poetry.] a rhapsodist.

rhap′sō·dēr, *n.* a collector of literary pieces. [Obs.]

rhap·sod′iç, *a.* rhapsodical.

rhap·sod′iç·ăl, *a.* [Gr. *rhapsōdikos,* from *rhapsōdia,* a rhapsody.] of, characteristic of, or having the nature of, rhapsody; hence, extravagantly enthusiastic; ecstatic.

rhap·sod′iç·ăl·ly, *adv.* in a rhapsodic manner.

rhap′sō·dist, *n.* 1. in ancient Greece, a person who recited rhapsodies; especially, one who recited epic poems as a profession.

2. a person who rhapsodizes.

rhap′sō·dīze, *v.t.*; rhapsodized, *pt., pp.*; rhapsodizing, *ppr.* to utter or recite as a rhapsody; to recite or repeat in the manner of a rhapsody.

rhap′sō·dīze, *v.i.* 1. to write or recite rhapsodies.

2. to speak or write in an extravagantly enthusiastic manner.

rhap′sō·dō·man·cy, *n.* [Fr. *rhapsodomancie* from Gr. *rhapsōdos,* a rhapsodist, and *manteia,* divination.] divination by means of verses.

rhap′sō·dy, *n.*; *pl.* **rhap′sō·dies,** [Fr. *rapsodie*; L. *rhapsodia*; Gr. *rhapsōdia,* a tirade, a rhapsody, from *rhapsōdos,* one who stitches or strings songs together, a reciter of epic poetry, from *rhaps-,* the stem of fut. tense of *rhaptein,* to stitch together.]

1. (a) in ancient Greece, an epic poem, or a part of one, suitable for a single uninterrupted recitation; (b) a similar modern literary work.

2. any ecstatic or extravagantly enthusiastic utterance in speech or writing.

3. a miscellany. [Obs.]

4. in music, an instrumental composition of free, irregular form, suggesting improvisation.

rhat′ȧ·ny (rat′), *n.*; *pl.* **rhat′ȧ·nies,** [Sp. *ratania, rataña,* from Peruv. (Quechua) *rataña.*]

1. (a) a South American leguminous plant, *Krameria triandra* (*Peruvian,* or *knotty, rhatany*), with a thick, fleshy root used in medicine as an astringent and tonic, etc.; (b) a related plant; especially, *Brazilian rhatany.*

2. the dried root of any such plant.

-rhē′ȧ (rē′), same as *-rrhea.*

rhē′ȧ, *n.* [E. Ind.] the ramie.

Rhē′ȧ, *n.* [L.] 1. in Greek mythology, the daughter of Uranus and Gaea, wife and sister of Cronus, and mother of Zeus (Jupiter), Hestia (Vesta), Demeter (Ceres), Hera (Juno), Hades (Pluto), and Poseidon (Neptune): called *Mother of the gods* and identified with Cybele.

2. a genus of large nonflying birds, the three-toed ostriches of South America: they resemble the African ostriches, but are smaller and have a feathered head and neck. *Rhea americana* is the common American ostrich, which is found from Brazil to Patagonia. *Rhea macrorhyncha* is found in the northeastern part of Brazil.

3. [r-] a bird of the genus *Rhea.*

4. the fifth satellite of Saturn.

RHEA (*Rhea americana*)

Rhē′ae, *n.pl.* a suborder of birds including the rheas.

Rhē′ȧ Sil′vi·ȧ, in Roman legend, a vestal virgin who broke her vows and became by Mars the mother of Romulus and Remus.

rhee′bok, *n.* same as *reebok.*

rhē′iç, *a.* [LL. *rheum,* rhubarb.] pertaining to or obtained from rhubarb.

rheic acid; chrysophanic acid.

rhē′in, *n.* same as *chrysophanic acid.*

rhein′ber″ry (rīn′), *n.* [G. *Rheinbeere,* from *Rhein,* the Rhine, and *beere,* berry.] the fruit of the European buckthorn; also, the plant itself. [Obs.]

Rhein′gōld, *n.* [G., Rhine gold.] in Germanic mythology, the hoard of gold guarded by the Rhine maidens and afterward owned by the Nibelungs and Siegfried: the story is told in varying forms in the *Volsunga Saga, Nibelungenlied,* and Wagner's *Ring of the Nibelung*: also *Rhinegold*: see *Ring of the Nibelung.*

rhē·mat′iç (rē-), *a.* [Gr. *rhēmatikos,* belonging to a word or verb, from *rhēma,* a word, a verb, from *erein,* to speak.]

1. of word formation.

2. pertaining to a verb; derived from a verb.

rhē·mat′iç, *n.* the doctrine of propositions or sentences. [Rare.]

Rhē′mish, *a.* [*Rheims* and *-ish.*] pertaining to Rheims, or Reims, a city in the northeastern part of France.

Rhemish Version; the version of the New Testament of the Douay Bible.

Rhen′ish (ren′), *a.* [G. *rheinisch,* from *Rhein,* the Rhine.] of the river Rhine or the regions around it.

Rhen′ish, *n.* 1. Rhine wine.

2. the German dialects spoken along the Rhine.

rhē′ni·um (rē′), *n.* [Mod. L., from L. *Rhenus,* Rhine; and *-ium* as in *cadmium, radium.*] a rare metallic chemical element resembling manganese: it has the symbol *Re,* an atomic weight of 186.31, and the atomic number 75:

the sources of the element are the minerals columbite, tantalite, and wolframite.

rhē'ō-, [from Gr. *rheos*, current.] a combining form meaning *a flow, a current*, as in *rheo*scope.

rhē'ō·chord, *n.* [*rheo-*, and Gr. *chordē*, chord.] a metallic wire used as a means of measuring or varying the resistance of an electric current.

rhē·om'ē·tēr, *n.* [*rheo-*, and Gr. *metron*, a measure.]
1. an instrument to measure the intensity and direction of an electric current; a galvanometer.
2. an instrument which measures and records the velocity of flow of the blood in circulation.

rhē·ō·met'riç, *a.* of a rheometer or rheometry.

rhē·om'ē·try, *n.* the method of measuring velocity and force of electric and other currents.

rhē'ō·mō·tŏr, *n.* [*rheo-*, and L. *motor*, a mover.] any apparatus which generates an electric current. [Rare.]

rhē'ō·phōre, *n.* [*rheo-*, and Gr. *-phoros*, that which is brought in, from *pherein*, to bear, bring.] the connecting wire of a voltaic apparatus, which is the transmitter of the current.

rhē'ō·sçōpe, *n.* [*rheo-*, and Gr. *skopein*, to view.] a device for indicating the presence of an electric current.

rhē'ō·stat, *n.* [*rheo-*, and Gr. *statos*, standing still, from *histanai*, to stand.] a device for regulating strength of an electric current by varying the resistance without opening the circuit.

rhē·ō·stat'iç, *a.* of or by a rheostat.

rhē·ō·tax'is, *n.* [Mod. L., from *rheo-*, and Gr. *taxis*, an arranging.] the tendency of a living organism or cell to respond to the mechanical stimulus of a current of water by some movement.

rhē'ō·tōme, *n.* [*rheo-*, and Gr. *-tomos*, a cutting, from *temnein*, to cut.] an instrument for interrupting an electric current.

rhē'ō·tron, *n.* [*rheo-*and electron.] betatron.

rhē'ō·trōpe, *n.* [*rheo-*, and Gr. *-tropos*, a turn, from *trepein*, to turn.] an instrument used for changing the direction of an electric current.

rhē·ō·trop'iç, *a.* of or relating to rheotropism.

rhē·ot'rō·pişm, *n.* [*rheo-*, and Gr. *tropikos*, a turning, from *trepein*, to turn.] the tendency of a living organism, especially a plant, to respond to the mechanical stimulus of a current of water by growing with or against the current, the former being positive rheotropism, while the latter is negative rheotropism.

Rhē'sus, *n.* [L. *Rhesus*; Gr. *Rhēsos*.] in Greek legend, a king of Thrace and ally of Troy, whose horses were stolen by Diomedes and Odysseus: an oracle had said that Troy would not be captured if Rhesus' horses drank from the Xanthus River.

rhē'sus, *n.* [Mod. L.: arbitrary use of L. *Rhesus* (Gr. *Rhēsos*), proper name.] a small, short-tailed, brownish-yellow monkey, *Macacus rhesus*, of India.

Rhē'sus fac'tŏr, Rh factor.

Rhē'tiăn (-shăn), *a.* and *n.* same as *Rhaetian*.

Rhē'tiç, *a.* same as *Rhaetic*.

rhē'tŏr, *n.* [Fr. *rhéteur*; OFr. *retor*; L. *rhetor*; Gr. *rhētōr*, a speaker, an orator, from *erein*, to say, speak.] (a) an orator; (b) an instructor in or master of rhetoric.

rhet'ō·riç (ret'), *n.* [OFr. *rhetorique*; L. *rhetorica*; Gr. *rhētorikē*, the rhetorical art.]
1. the art or science of using words effectively in speaking or writing, so as to influence or persuade; especially, now, the art or science of literary composition, particularly in prose, including the use of figures of speech.
2. a treatise or book on this.
3. the art of oratory; the rules that govern the art of speaking with propriety, elegance, and force, or that regulate argumentative prose composition.
4. artificial eloquence; showiness and elaboration in language and literary style.
5. the power of persuading or influencing; as, the *rhetoric* of the heart or eyes.

rhe·tor'iç·ăl, *a.* 1. pertaining to, containing, or involving rhetoric; as, the *rhetorical* art.
2. using or characterized by mere rhetoric, or artificial eloquence; showy and elaborate in literary style.

rhe·tor'iç·ăl·ly, *adv.* 1. in a rhetorical manner.
2. according to, or from the standpoint of, rhetoric.

rhe·tor'iç·ăl·ness, *n.* the state or quality of being rhetorical.

rhe·tor'iç·ăl ques'tion (-chun), a question asked, as in oratory or writing, only for rhetorical effect, to emphasize a point, introduce a topic, etc., no answer being expected.

rhet·ō·ri'ciăn (-rish'ăn), *n.* [Fr. *rhétoricien*.]
1. one who teaches rhetoric.
2. one well versed in the rules and principles of rhetoric.
3. a person who writes or speaks in a rhetorical, or showy, elaborate manner.

rhet·ō·ri'ciăn, *a.* of or suiting a rhetorician.

rhet'ō·rīze, *v.i.* [LL. *rhetorissare*; Gr. *rhētōrizein*, to speak rhetorically.] to use rhetorical language. [Obs.]

rhet'ō·rīze, *v.t.* to represent by rhetorical devices or figures of speech. [Obs.]

Rhē'um, *n.* a genus of plants of the family *Polygonaceæ*, including the rhubarb.

rheum (röm), *n.* [OFr. *reume*, a catarrh; L. *rheuma*; Gr. *rheuma*, a flow.]
1. any watery or catarrhal discharge from the mucous membranes, as of the mouth, eyes, or nose.
2. a cold; rhinitis; catarrh.
salt rheum; any of various skin diseases, especially eczema.

rheu·mat'iç, *a.* 1. caused by or analogous to rheum; rheumic. [Obs.]
2. of or caused by rheumatism; also, affected with or causing rheumatism.

rheu·mat'iç, *n.* 1. a person suffering from or susceptible to rheumatism.
2. [*pl.*] rheumatism. [Dial.]

rheu·mat'iç fēv'ēr, an infectious disease associated with the presence of streptococci in the body: it most commonly attacks children, and is characterized by fever, pain and swelling of the joints, inflammation of the heart valves, etc.

rheu'mȧ·tişm, *n.* [L. *rheumatismus*; Gr. *rheumatismos*, liability to rheum.]
1. any of various painful conditions of the joints and muscles; especial y, a disease believed to be caused by a microorganism and characterized by inflammation and pain of the joints.
2. rheumatic fever.

rheu·mȧ·tiş'măl, *a.* of or relating to rheumatism.

rheu·mȧ·tiş'moid, *a.* resembling rheumatism.

rheu'mȧ·tişm rọọt, the twinleaf; also, the wild yam, *Dioscorea villosa*.

rheu'mȧ·toid, rheu·mȧ·toid'ăl, *a.* [Gr. *rheumatōdēs*, like a flux; *rheuma*, a flux, and *eidos*, form.]
1. of, resembling, or characteristic of rheumatism.
2. having rheumatism.

rheu'mȧ·toid är·thrī'tis, a chronic disease characterized by inflammation, stiffness, and often deformity, of the joints.

rheum'iç, *a.* of or pertaining to rheum.

rheum'y, *a.*; *comp.* rheumier; *superl.* rheumiest; affected with rheum; of, full of, or causing rheum.

Rhex'i·ȧ (rex'), *n.* a genus of plants of the family *Melastomaceæ*, common in the eastern part of the United States and known as deer grass: *Rhexia virginica* is called meadow beauty.

rhex'is, *n.* [Gr. *rhēxis*, a rupture, from *rhēgnynai*, to break.] in medicine, the rupture of an organ or a vessel.

Rh fac'tŏr, [from *rh*esus: from having been discovered first in the blood of rhesus monkeys.] an agglutinating factor, normally present in the blood of most people, which may cause hemolytic reactions during pregnancy or after transfusion with blood lacking this factor: individuals who have this factor are *Rh positive*; those who do not have it are *Rh negative*: also *Rhesus factor*.

rhig'ō·lēne (rig'), *n.* [Gr. *rhigos*, cold, and L. *oleum*, oil.] a colorless petroleum distillate composed of butane and certain hydrocarbons, very volatile and used as a local anaesthetic.

rhi·gō'sis, *n.* [Gr. *rhigos*, cold, and *-osis*.] the feeling or sensation of cold.

rhīn- (rīn), same as *rhino-*.

rhī'năl, *a.* of or relating to the nose; nasal.

rhīne, *n.* a ditch: also spelled *rine*. [Brit. Dial.]

Rhīne'gōld, *n.* same as *Rheingold*.

rhī''nen·cē·phal'iç, *a.* relating to the rhinencephalon.

rhī·nen·ceph'ȧ·lon, *n.*; *pl.* **rhī·nen·ceph'ȧ·lȧ**, the olfactory lobe of the brain.

rhīne'stōne, *n.* [named from the river *Rhine*, having been first made at Strasburg.] a colorless, bright, artificial gem made of glass or paste, often cut in imitation of a diamond.

Rhīne wīne, 1. any of various wines produced in the Rhine Valley, especially of the light, dry white wines.
2. a wine of this type produced elsewhere.

rhī·nī'tis, *n.* [*rhino-* and *-itis*.] inflammation of the mucous membrane of the nose.

rhī'nō-, [from Gr. *rhis*, *rhinos*, the nose.] a combining form meaning *nose*, as in *rhino*logy: also, before a vowel, *rhin-*.

rhī'nō, *n.*; *pl.* **rhī'nōş**, a rhinoceros. [Colloq.]

rhī'nō, *n.* money; cash. [Brit. Slang.]

> Drunker than any one you or I know.
> Who buys his Rhenish wine with ready *rhino*. —John G. Saxe.

rhī·nō·cē'ri·ăl, *a.* rhinocerotic.

rhī·nō·cer'iç·ăl, *a.* pug or turned up, as the nose. [Obs.]

rhī·noc'ēr·oid, *a.* [*rhinoceros*, and Gr. *eidos*, form.] rhinocerotoid.

rhī·noc'e·rŏs, *n.*; *pl.* **rhī·noc'e·rŏs·eş** or **rhī·noc'e·rŏs**, [L. *rhinoceros*; Gr. *rhinokerōs*, a rhinoceros; lit., nose-horned; *rhis*, *rhinos*, nose, and *keras*, horn.] a large, heavy, thick-skinned, plant-eating mammal belonging to the family *Rhinocerotidæ*, inhabiting the tropical regions of Asia and Africa: it has one or two upright horns on the snout.

INDIAN RHINOCEROS
(5—5 3/4 ft. high at shoulder)

rhī·noc'e·rŏs auk, an auk, *Ceratorhina monocerata*, of the family *Alcidæ*, characterized by a deciduous horny appendage at the base of the upper bill.

rhī·noc'e·rŏs bee'tle, any of various large beetles of the genus *Dynastes* and related genera; specifically, *Dynastes tityus*, the largest known North American beetle, the male being characterized by two strong horns projected forward, one from the thorax and one from the head.

rhī·noc'e·rŏs bird, 1. the African beef eater, *Bufaga africana*.
2. the rhinoceros hornbill.

rhī·noc'e·rŏs bush, a composite shrub, *Elytropappus rhinocerotis*, native to South Africa, said to be the chief food of the rhinoceros.

rhī·noc'e·rŏs horn'bill, see *hornbill*.

rhī·noc'e·rot, *n.* a rhinoceros. [Rare.]

rhī·noc·e·rot'iç, *a.* of, pertaining to, or resembling the rhinoceros.

rhī·noc'ēr·ō·toid, *a.* like a rhinoceros.

rhī·noc'ēr·ō·toid, *n.* one of the rhinoceros family.

rhī'nō·lith, rhī'nō·līte, *n.* [*rhino-*, and Gr. *lithos*, stone.] a concretion originating in the nasal cavities.

rhī·nō·log'iç·ăl, *a.* of or relating to rhinology.

rhī·nol'ō·gist, *n.* one skilled in rhinology.

rhī·nol'ō·gy, *n.* [*rhino-*, and Gr. *-logia*, from *legein*, to speak.] the branch of medicine which treats of the nose and its diseases.

rhī·nol'ō·phid, *n.* [*rhino-*, and Gr. *lophos*, crest.] any bat of the genus *Rhinolophus*, typical of the family *Rhinolophidæ*, characterized by cutaneous appendages on and over the nose; a horseshoe bat.

rhī·nol'ō·phine, *a.* of or designating the horseshoe bats.

rhī·nol'ō·phine, *n.* a rhinolophid.

rhī'nō·phōre, *n.* [*rhino-*, and Gr. *pherein*, to bear.] in mollusks, one of a pair of tentacles of certain of the *Gastropoda*, thought to be of use in smelling.

rhī·nō·plas'tiç, *a.* of or relating to rhinoplasty.

rhī'nō·plas·ty, *n.* [*rhino-*, and Gr. *plassein*, to form, to mold.] plastic surgery of the nose.

rhī''nō·sclē·rō'mȧ, *n.* [LL., from Gr. *rhis*, *rhinos*, nose, *sklēros*, hard, and *-oma*.] a hard nasal growth, supposed to be caused by a bacillus affecting the anterior nares, and spreading to the adjoining skin.

rhī'nō·sçōpe, *n.* [*rhino-*, and Gr. *skopein*, to view.] an instrument for the examination of the interior of the nose.

rhī·nō·sçop'iç, *a.* relating or pertaining to rhinoscopy.

rhī·nos'çō·py, *n.* examination of the internal structures of the nose, an exploration of the anterior nares being *anterior rhinoscopy*, that of the posterior nares, *posterior rhinoscopy*.

rhī·nō·thē′çȧ, *n.*; *pl.* **rhī·nō·thē′cae,** [LL., from Gr. *rhis, rhinos,* nose, and *thēkē,* sheath.] the corneous sheath of the upper mandible of a bird.

rhip′i·dāte, *a.* [Gr. *rhipis, rhipidos,* a fan, and *-ate.*] formed like a fan; flabelliform.

Rhip″i·dō·glos′sȧ, *n.pl.* [LL., from Gr. *rhipis* (*-idos*), a fan, and *glōssa,* a tongue.] a suborder of gastropods having a radula of which each transverse row is furnished with numerous lateral plates disposed in a fanlike manner.

Rhī·pip′tēr·ȧ, *n.pl.* [Gr. *rhipis,* a fan, and *pteron,* a wing.] an order of insects which have only one pair of wings fully developed, and these on the metathorax: also called *Strepsiptera.*

rhī·pip′tēr·ăn, *a.* of or pertaining to the *Rhipiptera.*

rhī·pip′tēr·ăn, *n.* one of the *Rhipiptera.*

Rhip′sȧ·lis, *n.* [LL., from Gr. *rhips, rhipos,* plaited work of rushes, a mat.] a genus of *Cactaceæ* consisting of a considerable number of small, fleshy, jointed-branched, leafless cacti growing in South and Central America, Mexico, and the West Indies.

rhī·zan′thous, *a.* [Gr. *rhiza,* root, and *anthous,* flower.] producing a flower or flowers (apparently) from a root.

rhī′zine, *n.* same as *rhizoid.*

rhī′zō-, [from Gr. *rhiza,* root.] a combining form meaning *root,* as in *rhizo*morphous, *rhizo*pod: also, before a vowel, *rhiz-.*

rhī·zō′bi·um, *n.*; *pl.* **rhī·zō′bi·ȧ,** [Mod. L., from *rhizo-,* and Gr. *bios,* life.] any of a genus of rod-shaped, nitrogen-fixing bacteria found in nodules on the roots of certain plants, as the bean and clover.

rhī·zō·çär′piç, *a.* same as *rhizocarpous.*

rhī·zō·çär′pous, *a.* [*rhizo-* and *-carpous.*] having perennial roots but annual stems and leaves: said of perennial plants.

rhī′zō·çaul, *n.* [LL. *rhizocaulus,* from Gr. *rhiza,* root, and *kaulos,* stalk.] the rootstock of a polyp.

Rhī·zō·ceph′ȧ·lȧ, *n.pl.* [LL., neut. pl. of *rhizocephalus*; Gr. *rhizokephalos,* having the flower growing straight from the root, from *rhiza,* root, and *kephalē,* head.] an order of hermaphroditic parasitic *Crustacea* living on crabs, etc.: they have a cephalic peduncle with rootlike filaments which pierce the body of the host and absorb nourishment.

rhī·zō·ceph′ȧ·lous, *a.* of the *Rhizocephala.*

rhī′zō·dont, *a.* [*rhizo-,* and Gr. *odous, odontos,* tooth.] having teeth rooted in sockets to the jaw, as in crocodiles and alligators.

rhī′zō·dont, *n.* a reptile having rhizodont teeth.

Rhī·zō·flaġ·el·lā′tȧ, *n.pl.* a group of active protozoans which have both pseudopods and flagella.

rhī′zō·ġen, *n.* [*rhizo-* and *-gen.*] one of a division of plants which are parasitic on the roots of other plants.

rhī·zō·ġen′iç, *a.* in botany, having the power to produce roots, as certain cells.

rhī·zoġ′e·nous, *a.* same as *rhizogenic.*

rhī′zoid, *a.* [*rhiz-* and *-oid.*] rootlike.

rhī′zoid, *n.* any of the rootlike filaments in a moss, fern, etc. that attach the plant to the substratum.

rhī·zoi′dăl, *a.* same as *rhizoid.*

rhī·zō′mȧ, *n.*; *pl.* **rhī·zō′mȧ·tȧ,** [Gr. *rhizoma* (*-atos*), a root.] a rhizome.

rhī·zō·mat′iç, *a.* rhizomatous.

rhī·zō′mȧ·tous, *a.* [Gr. *rhizoma* (*-atos*), a root, and *-ous.*] having, or having the nature or form of, a rhizome or rhizomes; like a rootstock.

rhī′zōme, *n.* [Mod. L. *rhizoma*; Gr. *rhizōma,* from *rhizousthai,* to take root, from *rhiza,* a root.] a rootlike stem under or along the ground, ordinarily in a horizontal position, which usually sends out roots from its lower surface and leafy shoots from its upper surface.

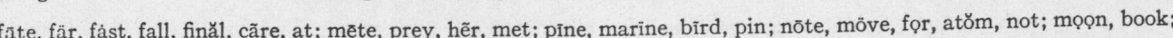

RHIZOME (of iris)

rhī′zō·morph, *n.* [*rhizo-* and *-morph.*] in botany, a form of mycelia attaching fungi to the roots of plants upon which they prey.

rhī·zō·mor′phous, *a.* [*rhizo-* and *-morphous.*] in botany, rootlike in form.

rhī·zoph′ȧ·gous, *a.* [*rhizo-* and *-phagous.*] feeding or subsisting on roots.

Rhī·zoph′ō·rȧ, *n.* a genus of trees belonging to the family *Rhizophoraceæ,* of which the mangrove is the principal representative.

Rhī″zō·phō·rā′cē·ae, *n.pl.* a family of trees of which the genus *Rhizophora* is typical, known as the mangrove family, noted for their seeds germinating while attached to the branches, and also for the numerous rootlike projections which support the stem. The wood of several species is hard and durable and the bark astringent. They are native to the tropics, where they root in the mud, and form a dense thicket down to the seacoast.

rhī·zoph′ō·rous, *a.* [LL. *rhizophorus*; Gr. *rhizophoros,* from *rhiza,* root, and *phoros,* from *pherein,* to bear.] root-bearing.

rhī′zō·pod, *n.* 1. in zoology, a member of the *Rhizopoda.*
2. in botany, the mycelium of a fungus.

rhī′zō·pod, *a.* [*rhizo-* and *-pod.*] having the characteristics of a rhizopod; root-footed.

Rhī·zop′ō·dȧ, *n.pl.* [*rhizo-* and *-poda.*] a division of protozoans having rootlike pseudopods.

rhī·zop′ō·dăn, *a.* of, like, or characteristic of the rhizopods.

rhī·zop′ō·dăn, *n.* same as *rhizopod.*

rhī·zop′ō·dous, *a.* same as *rhizopodan.*

Rhī′zō·pus, *n.* [*rhizo-,* and Gr. *pous, podos,* a foot.] a genus of fungi, the sporophores being produced from rhizoids: the most common species, *Rhizopus nigricans,* or bread mold, causes the disease of soft rot in the sweet potato; also, [r–] any plant of this genus.

Rhī·zō·stōm′ȧ·tȧ, *n.pl.* a division of jellyfishes having processes like rootlets around the mouth. They are covered with minute polyps interspersed with club-shaped tentacles suspended from the middle of the umbrella.

rhī′zō·stōme, *n.* any one of the *Rhizostomata.*

rhī·zō·tax′is, *n.* [LL., from Gr. *rhiza,* root, and *taxis,* order.] the arrangement or the order of arrangement of the roots of plants.

rhī′zō·tax·y, *n.* same as *rhizotaxis.*

rhī·zot′ō·my, *n.* [*rhizo-* and *-tomy.*] in surgery, a cutting of the spinal nerve roots, especially of the posterior nerves, for relieving pain or spastic paralysis.

Rh neg′ȧ·tive, see *Rh factor.*

rhō, *n.* [Gr. *rho.*] the seventeenth letter of the Greek alphabet corresponding to English *R, r.*

rhob, *n.* same as *rob* (juice).

rhō′dȧ·mine, rhō′dȧ·min, *n.* a synthetic rose-colored dye obtained by condensing an amino derivative of phenol with phthalic anhydride.

rhō·dan′iç, *a.* same as *sulfocyanic.*

Rhōde Is′lănd·ẽr (ī′), a native or inhabitant of Rhode Island.

Rhōde Is′lănd Red, any of a breed of American chickens with reddish-brown feathers, a black tail, and smooth legs.

rhō″dē·ō·rē′tin, *n.* [Gr. *rhodeos,* of roses, from *rhodon,* rose, and *rhētinē,* resin.] convolvulin.

Rhōdeş gràss, [after Cecil J. *Rhodes.*] a South African grass, cultivated as a forage crop in dry districts.

Rhō·dē′şi·ăn, *a.* of Rhodesia or its people.

Rhō·dē′şi·ăn, *n.* a native or inhabitant of Rhodesia.

Rhōdeş sçhol′ăr, one who holds, or has held, a Rhodes scholarship.

Rhōdeş sçhol′ăr·ship, one of a number of scholarships at Oxford University, England, under the will of Cecil J. Rhodes (1853–1902), English administrator in South Africa: these scholarships are tenable for three consecutive years and are open to selected students from certain British colonies and dominions and the United States.

Rhō′di·ăn, *a.* of the island of Rhodes, its people, or culture.

Rhō′di·ăn, *n.* a native or an inhabitant of Rhodes.

rhō′diç, *a.* of or containing rhodium.

rhō′di·um, *n.* [Gr. *rhodios,* roselike, from *rhodon,* a rose.] a hard, gray-white metallic chemical element of the platinum group, used as an alloy with platinum and gold to make the nibs of writing pens and in unalloyed form to electroplate silverware and jewelry: symbol, Rh; atomic weight, 102.91; atomic number, 45.

rhō·di·zon′iç, *a.* [Gr. *rhodizein,* to be rosy.] in chemistry, designating either of two acids whose salts are red.

rhō′dō-, [from Gr. *rhodon,* a rose.] a combining form meaning *rose, rose-red,* as in *rhodo*lite: also, before a vowel, *rhod-.*

rhō·dō·çhrō′site, *n.* [G. *rhodocrosit,* from Gr. *rhodochrōs,* rose-colored, and G. *-it,* -ite.] a mineral, carbonate of manganese, $MnCO_3$, of the group of anhydrous carbonates, of vitreous luster, and usually rose-red in color.

rhō·doç′ri·nīte, *n.* [*rhodo-,* and Gr. *krinon,* a lily.] a rose encrinite.

Rhō·dō·den′drŏn, *n.* [Gr. *rhododendron,* the oleander, from *rhodon,* rose, and *dendron,* tree.] a genus of evergreen trees or shrubs of the heath family, *Ericaceæ,* with showy flowers of pink, white, or purple: represented in the United States by a few species of hardy shrubs growing in the mountains of the Appalachian chain; also, [r–] any plant of this genus.

RHODODENDRON

rhō′dō·līte, *n.* [*rhodo-* and *-lite.*] a pink or rose-red variety of garnet, often used as a gem.

rhod″ō·mon·tāde′, *n.* same as *rodomontade.*

rhō′dō·nīte, *n.* [Gr. *rhodon,* rose, and *-ite.*] a glassy, crystalline mineral consisting chiefly of manganese silicate, $MnSiO_3$, mixed with silicates of iron, calcium, etc. It is generally found in rose-red masses and frequently used as an ornamental stone. Also called *manganese spar, red manganese.*

rhō′dō·phāne, *n.* [*rhodo-,* and Gr. *phanēs,* appearing, from *phainesthai,* to appear.] a red pigment found in the retinal cones of birds and fishes.

rhō′dō·phyll, rhō′dō·phyl, *n.* [*rhodo-,* and Gr. *phyllon,* leaf.] a pigment found in red seaweed.

rhō·dop′sin, *n.* [*rhodo-,* and Gr. *opsis,* view, and *-in.*] visual purple.

Rhō·dō′rȧ, *n.* [LL., from Gr. *rhodon,* rose.]
1. a genus of shrubs of the heath family, related to the *Rhododendron,* and having pink or rose-red flowers that appear before or with the leaves.
2. [r–] a shrub of this genus, *Rhodora canadensis.*

rhō′dō·spẽrm, *n.* one of the *Rhodospermeæ.*

Rhō·dō·spẽr′mē·ae, *n.pl.* [*rhodo-,* and Gr. *sperma,* seed.] the red algae.

-rhoe′ȧ, same as *-rrhea.*

rhoe′ȧ·din, rhoe′ȧ·dine, *n.* [LL., from Gr. *rhoias, rhoiados,* a kind of poppy.] an alkaloid, $C_{21}H_{21}NO_6$, obtained from opium.

rhomb (romb), *n.* same as *rhombus.*

rhom″ben·ceph′ȧ·lon, *n.* the part of the brain consisting of the cerebellum, pons, and medulla oblongata; hindbrain.

rhom′biç, rhom′biç·ăl, *a.* 1. of, or having the form, of a rhombus.
2. having a rhombus as the base or cross section: said of solid figures.
3. bounded by rhombuses.
4. in crystallography, orthorhombic.

rhom·bō·gan′oid, *n.* a fish having rhombic scales.

Rhom″bō·gȧ·noi′dē·ī, *n.pl.* same as *Ginglymodi.*

rhom′bō·ġen, *n.* a dicyemid worm producing infusoriform embryos.

rhom·bō·hē′drăl, *a.* relating to a rhombohedron; having the form of a rhombohedron.
rhombohedral system; in crystallography, a division of the hexagonal system comprising the rhombohedrons, scalenohedrons, etc.

rhom·bō·hē′drăl·ly, *adv.* as a rhombohedron.

rhom·bō·hē′driç, *a.* rhombohedral.

rhom·bō·hē′drŏn, *n.*; *pl.* **rhom·bō·hē′dronş, rhom·bō·hē′drȧ,** [Gr. *rhombos,* rhomb, and *hedra,* base.] in geometry and crystallography, a prism bounded by six rhombic planes.

rhom′boid, *n.* [L. *rhomboides*; Gr. *rhomboeidēs,* rhomboid - shaped; *rhombos,* rhomb, and *eidos,* form.]
1. in geometry, a parallelogram with oblique angles and only the opposite sides equal.
2. in crystallography, a solid having a rhomboidal form with three axes of unequal lengths, two of which are at right angles to each other, while the third is so inclined as to

RHOMBOIDS

be perpendicular to one of the two axes, and oblique to the other.

rhom′boid, rhom·boi′dăl, *a.* 1. having the shape of a rhomboid.

2. shaped somewhat like a rhombus.

rhom·boi′dēș, *n.* a rhomboid. [Obs.]

rhom″boid-ō′vāte, *a.* between rhomboid and oval in shape; partly rhomboid, partly oval.

rhomb spär, a rhombohedral variety of dolomite.

rhom′bus, *n.*; *pl.* **rhom′bus·eș, rhom′bī,** [L.; Gr. *rhombos*, object that can be turned; akin to *rhembein*, to turn, whirl.]

1. an equilateral parallelogram with oblique angles.

2. a rhombohedron.

RHOMBUS

rhoñ′çhăl, rhoñ′çhi·ăl, *a.* pertaining to, or having the nature of, a rhonchus.

rhonchal fremitus; in medicine, a vibration produced by the passage of air through a large bronchial tube filled with mucus.

rhoñ·çhis′ō·nănt, *a.* [LL. *rhonchisonus*, snorting; L. *rhonchus*, a snorting, and *sonare*, to sound.] snorting. [Obs.]

rhoñ′çhus, *n.*; *pl.* **rhoñ′çhī,** [L., from Gr. *rhonchos*, a snore.] a rattling in the chest; also, a dry course râle in the bronchial tubes, due to a partial obstruction.

rhō·pal′iç, *a.* [LL. *rhopalicus*; Gr. *rhopalikos*, lit., like a club, from *rhopalon*, club.] in ancient prosody, having each succeeding word containing one more syllable than the preceding word: said of a hexameter.

rhō·pā′li·um, *n.*; *pl.* **rhō·pā′li·ȧ,** a sensory body of a jellyfish.

Rhō·pȧ·loc′e·rȧ, *n.pl.* [LL., from Gr. *rhopalon*, a club, and *keras*, a horn.] that section of insects which comprises the diurnal *Lepidoptera*, or butterflies, as distinguished from moths.

rhō′tȧ·cișm, *n.* [LL. *rhotacismus*, from Gr. *rhotakizein*, to rhotacize.]

1. excessive use of the letter *r*.

2. faulty pronunciation of the letter *r*.

3. substitution of the sound of *r* for another sound, as that of *s*.

rhō′tȧ·cīze, *v.i.* to use the letter *r* incorrectly or too frequently.

Rh poș′i·tive, see *Rh factor*.

rhu̇′bärb *n.* [OFr. *rheubarbe*; LL. *rheubarbarum*; Gr. *rhēon barbaron*, the foreign rha or rhubarb; *rhēon*, a plant from the *Rha*, a river now called the Volga, and *barbaron*, foreign, barbarous.]

1. any species of the genus *Rheum*; especially, *Rheum rhaponticum*, the common pieplant, whose acid leafstalks are used for food.

MEDICINAL RHUBARB (*Rheum officinale*)

2. the leafstalks of one variety of rhubarb made into a sauce or baked in a pie.

3. the roots or rhizomes of one variety, *Rheum officinale*, used in medicine as a cathartic and tonic.

4. [perh. from the practice in radio broadcasts of repeating "rhubarb" in simulating crowd noises.] a heated discussion or argument, as in a baseball game. [Slang.]

rhu̇′bärb·y, *a.* like rhubarb.

rhumb, rumb (rumb *or* rum), *n.* [from Fr. *rumb* or Port. and Sp. *rumbo*; prob. from L. *rhombus*.]

1. a rhumb line.

2. any of the thirty-two points of a mariner's compass.

rhum′bȧ, *n.* a rumba.

rhumb līne, the course of a ship that keeps a constant compass direction, drawn as a line on a map, chart, or globe and cutting across all meridians at the same angle: also called *loxodromic curve*.

Rhus (rus), *n.* [L., from Gr. *rhous*, sumac.] a genus of deciduous trees and shrubs of the *Anacardiaceæ*; the sumacs. *Rhus toxicodendron* is the poison ivy, and *Rhus venenata*, the poison sumac. These cause severe skin eruptions, with violent itching, to some persons. The liquids from the bark of *Rhus vernicifera* yield the varnish used in Japanese and Chinese lacquer work. Many species are used for dyeing and tanning, as *Rhus coriaria*, the hide sumac of Europe, which is also known as tanning or tanners' sumac.

rhus′mȧ, *n.* a depilatory consisting of a mixture of lime and orpiment with water, used to remove superfluous hair or the hair from hides in tanning.

rhy·aç′ō·līte, *n.* [Gr. *rhyax*, *rhyakos*, a stream, and *-lite*.] a glassy variety of feldspar found in cavities in lavas.

rhȳme, *n.* [ME. *rime*; associated in ME. with AS. *rim*, a number, but from OFr. *rime*; prob. from L. *rhythmus*; Eng. sp. influenced by association with *rhythm*: in ML., *rithmus* meant "accentual verse," which was usually rhymed; hence the modern sense.]

1. a piece of verse, or poem, in which there is a regular recurrence of corresponding sounds, especially at the ends of lines.

2. such verse or poetry in general.

3. correspondence of end sounds in lines of verse or in words: cf. *assonance*, *consonance*.

4. a word that corresponds with another in end sound (e.g., *love* and *above*, *witty* and *pretty*).

Also spelled *rime*.

neither rhyme nor reason; neither order nor sense.

rhȳme, *v.i.*; rhymed, *pt.*, *pp.*; rhyming, *ppr.*

1. to make verse, especially rhyming verse.

2. to form a rhyme; as, "more" *rhymes* with "door."

3. to be composed in metrical form with rhymes: said of verses.

Also spelled *rime*.

rhȳme, *v.t.* 1. to put into or treat in rhyme.

2. to compose in metrical form with rhymes.

3. to use (a word or words) as a rhyme or rhymes.

Also spelled *rime*.

rhȳme′less, *a.* without rhyme.

rhȳm′ẽr, *n.* a maker of rhymes, or poems; especially, a rhymester.

rhȳme roy′ăl, a stanza of seven lines in iambic pentameter rhyming *ababbcc*, first used in English by Chaucer.

rhȳme sçhēme, the pattern of rhymes used in a piece of verse, usually indicated by letters, as in the above definition for *rhyme royal*.

rhȳme′stẽr, *n.* a maker of rhyme, or verse (in a derogatory sense); poetaster.

Rhyñ·çhob·del′lȧ, *n.pl.* [LL., from Gr. *rhynchos*, snout, and *bdella*, leech.] a group of leeches having a proboscis that can be protruded.

Rhyñ″çhō·ceph·ā′li·ȧ, *n.pl.* [LL., from Gr. *rhynchos*, snout, and *kephalē*, head.] a nearly extinct order of lizardlike reptiles of the *Reptilia* surviving in one species, *Hatteria punctata*, native to New Zealand.

rhyñ″çhō·cē·phā′li·ăn, *a.* of or like the *Rhynchocephalia*.

rhyñ″çhō·cē·phā′li·ăn, *n.* a member of the *Rhynchocephalia*.

Rhyñ·çhō·coe′lȧ, *n.pl.* same as *Nemertina*.

rhyñ·çhō·coe′lous, *a.* nemertean.

rhyñ′çhō·dont, *a.* [Gr. *rhynchos*, snout, and *odous*, *odontos*, tooth.] having the rim of the beak notched, as some birds of prey. [Obs.]

rhyñ′çhō·līte, *n.* [Gr. *rhynchos*, snout, and *-lite*.] the beaklike mandible of a fossil cephalopod.

Rhyñ·çhō·nel′lȧ, *n.* [LL. from Gr. *rhynchos*, snout.] a genus of brachiopods having a beaked shell.

Rhyñ·çhoph′ō·rȧ (-kof′), *n.pl.* [LL., from Gr. *rhynchos*, snout, and *phoros*, from *pherein*, to bear.] an extensive group of beetles in which the head is prolonged into a proboscis or snout: it includes the weevils or curculios.

rhyñ·çhoph′ō·răn, *n.* a beetle of the *Rhynchophora*.

rhyñ·çhoph′ō·răn, *a.* pertaining to the *Rhynchophora*.

rhyñ′çhō·phōre, *n.* a rhynchophoran.

rhyñ·çhoph′ō·rous (-kof′), *a.* rhynchophoran.

Rhyñ·çhō′si·ȧ, *n.* [LL., from Gr. *rhynchos*, snout.] a genus of plants of the bean family found chiefly in warm regions. *Rhynchosia phaseoloides* is sometimes called the Mexican rosary plant.

Rhyñ·çhō′tȧ, *n.pl.* [LL., from Gr. *rhynchos*, snout.] same as *Hemiptera*.

rhyñ′çhōte, rhyñ·çō′tous, *a.* of or relating to the *Rhynchota*; hemipterous.

rhȳ′ō·līte, *n.* [Gr. *rhyax*, a stream, and *-lite*.] a kind of volcanic rock containing much silica and resembling granite in composition but having a texture that shows flow.

rhȳ·ō·lit′iç, *a.* pertaining to rhyolite.

rhyp″ȧ·rō·graph′iç, *a.* pertaining to rhyparography.

rhyp·ȧ·rog′rȧ·phy, *n.* [Gr. *rhyparographos*, a painter of mean subjects; *rhyparos*, foul, mean, and *graphein*, to write.] literally, dirt painting: a contemptuous term applied by the ancients to genre or still-life pictures.

rhȳ·sim′ē·tẽr, *n.* [Gr. *rhysis*, a stream, and *-meter*.] an instrument for measuring the velocity of fluids or the speed of ships. It presents the open end of a tube to the impact of the current, which raises a column of mercury in a graduated tube.

rhythm (rith′m), *n.* [Fr. *rhythme*; L. *rhythmus*, from Gr. *rhythmos*, measure, measured motion, from *rhein*, to flow.]

1. (a) flow, movement, procedure, etc. characterized by basically regular recurrence of elements or features, as beat, or accent, in alternation with opposite or different elements or features; as, the *rhythm* of speech, of the heart, of an engine, of dancing, of the seasons, etc.; (b) such recurrence; pattern of flow or movement.

2. in art, aesthetic relation of part to part and of parts to the whole; pattern of arrangement; as, the *rhythm* of a picture, of a statue, of a building, etc.

3. in music, (a) regular (or, occasionally, somewhat irregular) recurrence of grouped strong and weak beats, or heavily and lightly accented tones, in alternation; arrangement of successive tones, usually in measures, according to their relative accentuation and duration; (b) form or pattern of this; as, rumba *rhythm*, triple *rhythm*.

4. in prosody, (a) basically regular recurrence of grouped, stressed and unstressed, long and short, or high-pitched and low-pitched syllables in alternation; arrangement of successive syllables, as in metrical units (*feet*) or cadences, according to their relative stress, quantity, and pitch: in English, rhythm depends on accent as composed of interconnected stress, quantity, pitch, and pause; (b) form or pattern of this; as, iambic *rhythm*.

rhyth′miç, *a.* rhythmical.

rhyth′miç, *n.* rhythmics.

rhyth′mi·çăl, *a.* of, having, or using rhythm.

rhyth·mi·çăl′i·ty, *n.* the property of being rhythmical.

rhyth′mi·çăl·ly, *adv.* 1. in a rhythmical manner.

2. as regards rhythm.

rhyth′miçs, *n. pl.* [*construed as sing.*] science or system of rhythm and rhythmical forms.

rhyth′mist, *n.* 1. a (specified) user of rhythm.

2. one who is versed in, or has a good sense of, rhythm.

rhyth′mīze, *v.t.* and *v.i.* to make rhythmical.

rhythm′less, *a.* having no rhythm.

rhythm meth′ŏd, a method of birth control involving abstinence from sexual intercourse during the woman's probable monthly ovulation period.

rhyth·mom′ē·tẽr, *n.* in music, a metronome.

rhyth′mō·phōne, *n.* [Gr. *rhythmos*, rhythm, and *phōnē*, voice.] an instrument for magnifying the sounds of the heart beat.

rhyth′mus, *n.* [L.] same as *rhythm*.

rhyt·i·dō′sis, *n.* [Gr., from *rhytis*, a wrinkle.] in pathology, a wrinkling of the cornea.

Rhy·tī′nȧ, *n.* [LL., from Gr. *rhytis*, a wrinkle, and *-ina*.] a genus of extinct aquatic mammals having no teeth, typical of the family *Rhytinidæ*. It contains the sea cows.

rī′ăl, *n.* a Spanish coin: also spelled *real*. [Obs.]

rī′ăl, *a.* royal. [Obs.]

rī′ăl, *n.* the ryal, a coin.

rī′ăl, *n.* [OFr. *rial*, *real*, lit., royal.] the monetary unit and a silver coin of Iran.

Rī·al′tō, *n.* 1. an island in Venice, formerly the business and trading center.

2. a bridge over the Grand Canal, connecting this island with San Marco island.

3. the theater district in New York City:

sometimes applied to theater districts in other cities.

4. [r–] a market or trading place.

rī′ănt, *a.* [Fr. *riant*, ppr. of *rire*, to laugh.]

1. laughing; gay; merry; cheerful.

2. cheerful; suggesting joy; inspiring a merry feeling; as, a *riant* landscape.

ri·ä′tȧ, *n.* [Sp. *reata*, from *reatar*, to tie again.] a lariat.

rib, *n.* [AS. *rib*, *ribb*; D. *rib*, *ribbe*; Dan. *ribbeen*; G. *rippe*, a rib; Ice. *rif*, a rib, also a reef of rocks.]

1. any of the arched bones attached posteriorly to the vertebral column and enclosing the chest cavity: in man there are twelve pairs of such bones, the upper seven pairs (*true ribs*) being attached by cartilage to the sternum, the next three pairs (*false ribs*) being attached each to the rib above, and the last two pairs (*floating ribs*) being unattached anteriorly.

2. a cut of meat having one or more ribs.

3. a wife: in humorous reference to the Biblical creation of Eve from Adam's rib (Gen. ii. 21–22).

4. a raised ridge in cloth, especially in knitted material.

5. any of the curved crosspieces extending from the keel to the top of the hull in a ship, forming its framework.

6. any of the short transverse pieces placed at intervals along the length of, and giving shape to, an airplane wing.

7. any narrow riblike piece used to form, strengthen, or shape something; as, a *rib* of an umbrella.

8. in architecture, (a) a long curved piece in an arch; (b) any of the transverse and intersecting arches of a vault.

9. in botany, any of the main veins in a leaf.

10. in bookbinding, one of the ridges on the back of a book which serve for covering the tapes and for ornament.

11. in machinery, an angle plate cast between two other plates to brace and strengthen them.

12. in mining, (a) a pillar of coal left as a support for the roof of a mine; (b) an irregular vertical table of metallic matter occurring in a vein of some other mineral.

false ribs; see sense 1 above.

floating ribs; see sense 1 above.

rib, *v.t.*; ribbed, *pt., pp.*; ribbing, *ppr.* 1. to provide, form, or strengthen with a rib or ribs.

2. to put ribs in; to mark with ribs.

3. to plow so as to leave riblike parallel ridges.

4. [prob. from *rib-tickle*.] to tease or make fun of. [Slang.]

rib′ăld, *a.* [ME. *ribault*; OFr. *ribaut*, *ribauld*, etc.; prob. specialized use of personal name *Ribaud*.] characterized by coarse joking or mocking; offensive, irreverent, or vulgar in language.

rib′ăld, *n.* a ribald person.

rib′ăld·ish, *a.* disposed to ribaldry.

rib′ăld·rous, *a.* of ribaldry; ribald. [Archaic.]

rib′ăld·ry, *n.* [ME. *ribawdrye*, *ribaudrye*; OFr. *ribauderie*.] ribald language or humor.

rib′ănd, *n.* a ribbon. [Archaic.]

rï·bät·tü′tȧ, *n.* [It.] in music, alternation of two adjacent tones which increases in rapidity till the effect is a trill or a shake.

ri·bau′dē·quin (-bō′dē-kin), *n.* [OFr.] a medieval cannon on wheels. [Obs.]

rib′au·dry, *n.* ribaldry. [Obs.]

rib′bănd″, *n.* a ribbon. [Archaic.]

rib′bănd, rib′band″, *n.* in shipbuilding, (a) one of the long, narrow, flexible pieces of wood or metal nailed temporarily on the outside of the frames lengthwise, so as to encompass the vessel and keep the framework in position while the outside planking or plating is being put on; (b) a piece of timber used in making gun platforms secure.

ribband line; in shipbuilding, one of the diagonal lines in a body plan by means of which the places for surmarks are found.

ribbed, *a.* 1. made with ribs; having parallel ridges; as, *ribbed* hose.

2. furnished with ribs or with something resembling ribs in form or use.

rib′bing, *n.* 1. ribs collectively; arrangement or collection of ribs, as in cloth, a ship, etc.

2. in agriculture, a method of plowing, formerly common, by which only alternate strips of land were turned over.

3. the cutting of a side of beef into fore and hind quarters, the division usually being made along a rib.

4. the act of teasing or joking. [Slang.]

rib′bing nāil, in shipbuilding, a nail with a large round head, used chiefly for fastening ribbands: also called *ribband nail*.

rib′bŏn, *n.* [Early Mod. Eng. var. of ME. *ribon(d)*, from OFr. *riban*, *ruban*.]

1. (a) a narrow strip of satin, silk, rayon, velvet, etc., finished at the edges and of various widths, used for decoration, tying things, etc.; (b) material in such strips.

2. anything like or suggesting such a strip; as, a *ribbon* of blue sky; specifically, a long, thin, flexible metal band, as for a measuring tape, band saw, etc.

3. [*pl.*] torn, ribbonlike strips or shreds; tatters; as, a garment torn to *ribbons*.

4. a narrow strip of cloth inked for use on a typewriter or similar device.

5. (a) a small strip of colored cloth worn as a badge or awarded as a symbol of honor, achievement, etc.; as, he won a blue *ribbon*; (b) in military usage, a similar strip worn on the left breast of the uniform to indicate an award of a decoration or medal.

6. [*pl.*] reins used in driving. [Colloq.]

7. a ribband.

8. a thin strip of lead for joining glasses in stained-glass work.

9. in heraldry, a diminutive bend.

10. a colored stripe on the hull of a ship from stem to stern in contrast with the color of the hull.

RIBBON

baby ribbon; very fine narrow ribbon.

blue ribbon; see under *blue*, a.

red ribbon; the badge of the Order of the Bath.

rib′bŏn, *v.t.*; ribboned, *pt., pp.*; ribboning, *ppr.* 1. to adorn, trim, or mark with or as with a ribbon or with ribbons.

2. to separate or split into ribbonlike strips or shreds.

rib′bŏn, *v.i.* to extend or form in a ribbonlike strip or strips.

rib′bŏn brāke, a friction brake having a band which nearly surrounds the wheel whose motion is to be checked.

rib′bŏn·fish, *n.*; *pl.* **rib′bŏn·fish** or **rib′bon·fish·eș,** one of various sea fishes with long compressed bodies covered with small scales, belonging to the genus *Trachipterus*.

rib′bŏn grȧss, canary grass, *Phalaris arundinacea*, a grass which is found in its wild state by the sides of rivers: also called *painted grass* and *gardener's-garters*.

Rib′bŏn·ișm, *n.* the doctrines of the members of the Ribbon Society.

rib′bŏn jas′pēr, jasper in which the colors are arranged in stripes like ribbons.

Rib′bŏn·măn, *n.*; *pl.* **Rib′bŏn·men,** a member of the Ribbon Society.

rib′bŏn map, a map printed on a long strip which winds on an axis within a case.

rib′bŏn saw, same as *band saw*.

Rib′bŏn Sō·cī′e·ty, an Irish secret society organized about 1808 to oppose the Orange organization in the north of Ireland, and named from the badge, a simple green ribbon, worn by all members of the society.

rib′bŏn tree, a malvaceous tree, *Plagianthus betulinus*, of New Zealand, the inner bark of which is a fine flaxlike fiber known by the name of New Zealand cotton.

rib′bŏn·wood, *n.* a malvaceous tree, *Hoheria populnea*, of New Zealand, whose ribbonlike bark is used for cordage.

rib′bŏn wŏrm, 1. a tapeworm.

2. any worm of the division *Nemertina*.

Rī′bēș, *n.* [from *Ribas*, a name given by the Arabian physicians of the eleventh and twelfth centuries to a species of rhubarb, and erroneously supposed to apply to the currant plant.] a genus of shrubs of the saxifrage family, among which are gooseberries and many varieties of currants.

rib grȧss, a plant, *Plantago lanceolata*, of the plantain family; the English ribwort.

rib′less, *a.* having no ribs; also, showing no ribs; fat.

rib′let, *n.* a little rib; also, a rudimentary rib.

rī·bō·flā′vin, *n.* [*ribose* and *flavin*.] a factor of the vitamin B complex, $C_{17}H_{20}O_6N_4$, found in milk, eggs, liver, kidney, grass, fruits, leafy vegetables, yeast, etc.; lack of riboflavin in the diet causes stunted growth, loss of hair, etc.: also called lactoflavin, vitamin B_2, vitamin G.

rī′bō·nū·clē′iç ac′id, [*ribose*, and *nucleic acid*.] an essential component of all living matter, present in the cytoplasm of all cells and composed of long chains of phosphate and sugar ribose along with several bases: one form is the carrier of genetic information from the nuclear DNA and is important in the synthesis of proteins in the cell.

rī′bōse, *n.* [G. *ribonsäure*, a tetrahydroxy acid; and *-ose* as in *pentose*.] a pentose sugar, $C_5H_{10}O_5$, derived from some nucleic acids.

rib piēce, a cut of meat containing one or more ribs or parts of ribs.

rib rōast, a cut of meat for roasting, containing one or more ribs or parts of ribs.

rib′rōast, *v.t.* to beat soundly. [Slang.]

rib′rōast″ēr, *n.* a body blow. [Slang.]

rib′rōast″ing, *n.* a beating. [Slang.]

rib′wŏrt, *n.* 1. a plantain with a long stem and ribbed, narrow leaves.

2. any of a number of similar plantains. Also *ribwort plantain*.

-riç, [ME. *-riche*, *-ricke*, realm, power, from AS. *rice*, reign, dominion.] a combining form meaning *jurisdiction*, *realm*, as in bisho*pric*.

Ri·çär′di·ăn, *a.* pertaining to David Ricardo, an English political economist of the early nineteenth century.

Ri·çär′di·ăn, *n.* a believer in the doctrine of David Ricardo.

rï·çäs′sō, *n.* [etym. unknown.] the part of the blade of a rapier between the cross guard and the outer guard for the hand.

Riç·ci·ā′cē·ae, *n.pl.* [named after P. Francisco *Riccio*, a Florentine botanist.] a family of liverworts, or *Hepaticæ*, mostly native to warm climates, consisting of delicate green membranous fronds.

riç·ci·ā′ceous, *a.* pertaining to the *Ricciaceæ*.

rīce, *n.* [Fr. *riz* or *ris*, from L. *oryza*, from Gr. *oryza*, *oryzon*, rice, from Ar. *ruz*, rice in the husk.]

1. a plant, *Oryza sativa*, of the grass family, of a single species, cultivated in all warm climates, especially in the Orient.

2. the starchy seeds or grains of this grass, used as food.

French rice; same as *amelcorn*.

Indian rice; see under *Indian*.

rice-grain decoration; a style of decoration seen in Chinese ceramics.

RICE

rīce, *v.t.*; riced (rīst), *pt., pp.*; ricing, *ppr.* to reduce potatoes, etc. to a ricelike consistency.

rīce′bīrd, *n.* 1. the Javanese sparrow, *Loxia oryzivora*.

2. in the southern United States, the bobolink: also called *rice bunting*.

RICEBIRD (*Loxia oryzivora*)

rīce hen, the gallinule, *Gallinula galeata*, of the United States.

rīce pā′pēr, 1. a light paper made from the straw of rice grass.

2. a thin white paper prepared by the Chinese from the pressed and dried pith of *Fatsia papyrifera*, a shrub. Rice paper is used in making artificial flowers and also in drawing and painting.

rīc′ēr, *n.* a utensil for ricing cooked potatoes, etc. by forcing them through small holes.

rīce sap′pēr, a bug, *Leptocorisa acuta*, of the East Indies that sucks the juice from rice kernels.

rīce shell, any small shell of the genus *Olivella*.

rīce tā′ble, in Java, the noonday meal, consisting mainly of rice with cooked meat, chicken, fish, eggs, pickles, and curries.

rīce trọọ′pi·ăl, the bobolink.

rīce wa′tēr, water in which rice has been boiled, often used as nourishment for invalids.

rice water discharge; a liquid having the appearance of rice water that is discharged from the bowels in Asiatic cholera.

rīce wee′vil, a destructive beetle, *Calandra*

oryzæ, that eats grain in the bin, as corn or rice.

rich, *a.*; *comp.* richer; *superl.* richest. [ME. *riche*; AS. *rice*, noble, powerful; influenced by OFr. *riche*, rich, from O.H.G. *richi*, powerful, rich.]

1. having wealth; owning much money or property; wealthy.

2. having abundant natural resources; as, a rich country.

3. well supplied; abounding (with *in* or *with*); as, *rich in* minerals.

4. valuable; as, a *rich* prize.

5. of valuable materials or fine, elaborate workmanship; costly and elegant; as, *rich* gifts.

6. elaborate; luxurious; sumptuous; as, a *rich* banquet.

7. having an abundance of good constituents or qualities; specifically, (a) full of nutritious or choice ingredients, as butter, sugar, cream, seasoning, etc.: often implying an excess of such ingredients; as, *rich* pastries; (b) full of strength and flavor; full-bodied; as, *rich* wine.

8. (a) full, deep, and mellow: said of sounds, the voice, etc.; (b) deep; intense; vivid: said of colors; (c) very fragrant: said of odors.

9. having a high proportion of gasoline to air; as, a *rich* carburetor mixture.

10. abundant; plentiful; ample; as, a *rich* fund of adventures.

11. yielding or producing in abundance, as soil, mines, ores, etc.

12. (a) abounding in humor; very amusing; (b) absurd; preposterous. [Colloq.]

the rich; the wealthy people collectively.

Syn.—affluent, opulent, wealthy, abundant, ample, copious, fruitful, plentiful, costly, sumptuous, precious, luscious, racy, spicy.

Ri·chär′di·ȧ, *n.* a genus of monocotyledonous araceous plants, of which the calla, *Richardia africana*, is the best-known.

Rich′ărd Rōe, [see *Doe.*] a name used in law courts, legal papers, etc. to refer to a person whose actual name is unknown, especially the second person when two names are unknown (the first being referred to as *John Doe*).

Rich·ărd·sō′ni·ȧ, *n.* [after Richard *Richardson* (1663–1741), an English botanist.] a genus of subtropical American herbs of the madder family.

rich′eṣ, *n.pl.* [*orig. sing.*] [Fr. *richesse.*] wealth; valuable possessions; land, goods, money, etc. in abundance.

> *Riches* do not consist in having more gold and silver, but in having more in proportion than our neighbors. —Locke.

Syn.—wealth, opulence, affluence.

rich′ly, *adv.* 1. in a rich manner.

> In Belmont is a lady *richly* left. —Shak.

2. abundantly; fully; as, a chastisement *richly* deserved.

rich′ness, *n.* the state or quality of being rich.

rich rhȳme, same as *perfect rhyme.*

rich′weed, *n.* (a) clearweed; (b) horse balm.

rī′cin, *n.* [L. *ricinus*, the castor-oil plant.] a toxin protein found in the castor bean and isolated in the form of a white powder: it agglutinates red blood corpuscles.

ric·in·el·ā·id′iç, *a.* of, pertaining to, or derived from ricinoleic and elaidic acids.

ric′i·nīne, ric′i·nin, *n.* an alkaloid derived from castor beans.

ric·in·ō′lē·āte, *n.* a salt of ricinoleic acid.

ric·in·ō·lē′iç, *a.* [from L. *ricinus*, castor-oil plant; and *oleic.*] designating or of an unsaturated organic acid, $C_{17}H_{34}O_3$, found as an ester of glycerin in castor oil.

ric·in·ō′lē·in, *n.* the glycerol ester of ricinoleic acid: it is the main constituent of castor oil.

Ric′i·nus, *n.* [L., a tick, from the shape of the seeds.] a genus of plants of the family *Euphorbiaceæ*: *Ricinus communis* is the castor-oil plant.

rick, *v.t.* and *v.i.* to wrench; to sprain. [Brit.]

rick, *n.* [AS. *hreâc*; akin to D. *rook.*]

1. a stack of hay, straw, etc. in a field, especially one covered or thatched for protection from rain.

2. a pile of firewood like a cord, but of less width.

3. a set of shelves for storing barrels or boxes.

rick, *v.t.*; ricked (rikt), *pt., pp.*; ricking, *ppr.* to make ricks of, as hay.

rick′ẽr, *n.* a pole used in building ricks, or for a spar, yard, or the like.

rick′et·i·ness, *n.* the quality or condition of being rickety.

rick′ets, *n.* [perhaps alteration of Gr. *rachitis*, rachitis.] a disease of the skeletal system, chiefly of children, resulting from a deficiency of calcium salts or vitamin D in the diet, or from lack of sunlight, and characterized by a softening and, often, bending of the bones: also called *rachitis.*

rick·ett′si·ȧ, *n.* [after Howard T. *Ricketts* (1871–1910), Am. pathologist.]

1. *pl.* **rick·ett′si·ae,** any of a genus of Gram-negative microorganisms that are the causative agents of certain diseases, as typhus or Rocky Mountain spotted fever: they are transmitted to animals and man by the bite of certain lice and ticks in whose bodies they live as parasites.

2. [R–] [*construed as pl.*] this genus of microorganisms.

rick·ett′si·ăl, *a.* of or caused by any rickettsia.

rick′et·y, *a.* 1. affected with rickets.

2. feeble in the joints; weak; tottering.

3. of or like rickets; as, *rickety* symptoms, *rickety* diseases.

4. liable to fall or break down because weak; shaky.

rick′ey, *n.* [said to be after a Col. *Rickey*; for discussion see H. L. Mencken, *Am. Lang., Suppl. I*, pp. 252–254.] a drink made of carbonated water, lime juice, and an alcoholic liquor, especially gin (*gin rickey*).

riç′kle, *n.* a loose heap; a little rick.

rick′rack, *n.* a trimming used on dresses, etc. made of flat, zigzag braid; also, the braid so used.

rick′shąw, rick′shą, *n.* a jinrikisha.

rick′stand, *n.* a basement of timber, iron, or masonry, on which ricks are built to keep the lower part of the stack dry and free from vermin.

riç·ō·çhet′ (-shā′ *or* -shet′), *n.* [Fr.] the motion made by an object that rebounds or skips one or more times in moving over a flat surface, as a pebble thrown along the surface of a body of water.

riç·ō·çhet′, *v.t.*; ricocheted *or* ricochetted, *pt., pp.*; ricocheting *or* ricochetting, *ppr.* to operate upon by ricochet firing.

riç·ō·çhet′, *v.i.* to rebound or skip along a surface, as a stone along the surface of water.

riç′tăl, *a.* pertaining to the rictus.

riç′tus, *n. sing.* and *pl.* [L. *rictus*, the opened mouth, pp. of *ringi*, to yawn.]

1. a gaping, as of the mouth of an animal or the beak of a bird.

2. a fixed, gaping grin.

rid, *v.t.*; rid *or* ridded, *pt., pp.*; ridding, *ppr.* [AS. *hreddan*, to take, whence *ahreddan*, *ariddan*, to rid, to set free, etc.; Ice. *rydja*, to clear, to empty, from *hrjóda*, to clear.]

1. to free; to clear; to disencumber, as from something undesirable (usually with *of*); as, to *rid* one *of* a burden or *of* a care.

2. to rescue; to save (with *from*, *out of*, etc.) as, to *rid* him *out of* bondage. [Obs.]

3. to dispatch; to accomplish. [Obs.]

to be rid of; to be freed from or relieved of (something undesirable).

to get rid of; (a) to free oneself or to become free from; as, *to get rid of* a burden; (b) to do away with; to destroy; to kill.

rid, *v.* archaic past tense and past participle of *ride.*

rīd′ȧ·ble, *a.* capable of being ridden upon, as a road or a horse.

rid′dănce, *n.* the act of ridding or the state of being rid; clearance or removal, as of something undesirable, or deliverance, as from something oppressive.

good riddance; welcome relief or deliverance: often used as an exclamation of approval at getting rid of someone or something.

rid′den, *v.* past participle of *ride.*

rid′den, *a.* dominated or obsessed (by the thing specified): used in hyphenated compounds, as hag-*ridden*, fear-*ridden.*

rid′dle, *n.* [AS. *hriddel*, a riddle or sieve; *hridder*, a fan; *hridrian*, to winnow; O.H.G. *hrîtarâ*, a sieve, *hrîtarôn*, to sift.]

1. a coarse-meshed sieve, particularly that used in foundry work or in mines for the sifting of coal.

2. a board with a zigzag row of pins, used to straighten wire.

rid′dle, *v.t.*; riddled, *pt., pp.*; riddling, *ppr.* 1. to separate or sift, as grain from the chaff, through a riddle.

2. to find and show flaws in; to criticize and disprove.

3. to perforate; to make many little holes in; as, a house *riddled* with shot.

rid′dle, *n.* [AS. *rædels*, a riddle, from *rædan*, to read, guess; D. *raadsel*, G. *räthsel.*]

1. a problem or puzzle in the form of a question, statement, etc. so formulated that some ingenuity is required to solve or answer it; a conundrum.

2. any puzzling, perplexing, or apparently inexplicable person or thing, as a difficult problem or enigmatic saying; an enigma.

rid′dle, *v.t.* to solve or explain (a riddle).

rid′dle, *v.i.* to speak obscurely or enigmatically; to propound riddles.

rid′dlẽr, *n.* one who sifts through a riddle.

rid′dlẽr, *n.* one who speaks obscurely or enigmatically.

rid′dling·ly, *adv.* in the manner of a riddle.

rid′dlings, *n.pl.* the coarse material left in a riddle after the firm grain has been sifted through.

rīde, *v.i.*; rode (rōd) *or archaic* rid, *pt.*; ridden *or archaic* rid or rode, *pp.*; riding, *ppr.* [ME. *riden*; AS. *ridan.*]

1. to sit on and be carried along by a horse or other animal; especially, to sit on and control a horse in motion.

2. to be carried along on or in a vehicle or conveyance.

3. to be carried on something as if on a horse, etc.

4. to move along; to be carried or supported in motion (*on* or *upon*); as, the automobile *rode on* the rims.

5. (a) to move or float on the water; (b) to lie at anchor; as, the ship *rode* close to shore.

6. to seem to be floating in space.

7. to be fit for riding or admit of being ridden; as, the car *rides* smoothly.

8. to overlap, as bones in a joint.

9. to move out of place (with *up*); as, his collar *rode up* constantly.

10. in jazz music, to improvise freely.

11. to continue undisturbed, with no action taken; as, I'll let the matter *ride* a few months. [Slang.]

to ride and tie; to alternate in riding and walking, as when two persons have but one horse, one rides to a point in advance, ties the horse and walks on, leaving the horse for the other to use in the same way.

to ride easy; to lie at anchor, as a ship, with no great strain on the cables.

to ride hard; to strain at the cables: said of a ship. [Obs.]

to ride out; (a) to ride on a military expedition; (b) to ride out of doors.

to ride to hounds; to ride close behind the hounds in fox hunting.

rīde, *v.t.* 1. to sit on or in and control so as to move along; as, *ride* a horse, a bicycle, etc.

2. (a) to move along on or be mounted, carried, or supported on; as, the ship rides the waters, the child *rode* the merry-go-round; (b) to rest on, as by overlapping.

3. to move over, along, or through (a road, area, etc.) by horse, automobile, etc.

4. to engage in or do by riding; as, he *rode* a race with me.

5. to cause to ride.

6. to carry (a person) on something as if riding on horseback; as, the mob *rode* him on a rail.

7. to keep (a ship) at anchor.

8. to control, dominate, tyrannize over, or oppress: often in the past participle, as *ridden* by doubts.

9. to torment, harass, or tease by making the butt of ridicule, criticism, etc.

10. in jazz music, to improvise freely on (a theme).

to ride a hobby; to discuss a subject to excess because of its especial interest to oneself.

to ride down; (a) to hit and knock down by riding against; (b) to overtake by riding; (c) to overcome; (d) to exhaust (a horse, etc.) by riding too long or hard.

to ride out; (a) to continue afloat during, and withstand the fury of, as a vessel does a gale; (b) to withstand or endure successfully.

rīde, *n.* 1. a riding; especially, a journey by horseback, automobile, bicycle, etc.

2. a saddle horse. [Colloq.]

3. a road, track, etc. for riding, especially for horseback riding.

4. a district established for excise purposes. [Brit.]

to take for a ride; to take somewhere, as in an automobile, and kill; also, to hoax; to deceive. [Slang.]

rï·deau′ (-dō′), *n.* [Fr.] a small mound of earth.

rid′en, *v.* obsolete past tense plural and past participle of *ride.*

rī′dent, *a.* laughing, smiling, or grinning. [Rare.]

rīd′ẽr, *n.* 1. one who or that which rides.

2. one who breaks or manages a horse.

3. a mounted robber. [Obs.]

4. formerly, one who traveled for a mercantile house to collect orders or money: now called a *commercial traveler.* [Brit.]

5. any addition to a manuscript, roll, record, or other document.

6. a clause, usually dealing with some unrelated matter, added to a legislative bill when it is being considered for passage.

7. any of various devices or pieces moving along, or resting or mounted on, something else, as the top of a rail fence or a sliding weight on the beam of a balance.

8. one of a series of interior ribs, sometimes used in a ship's hold, opposite to some of the principal timbers, to which they are bolted, and reaching from the keelson to the beams of the lower deck, to strengthen the frame.

9. a subsidiary problem in mathematics.

10. a second tier of casks in the hold of a ship.

rider's bone; an ossification of the muscles of the upper and inner part of the thigh caused by pressure upon the saddle when riding.

rīd′ẽr·less, *a.* having no rider.

rīd′ẽr·ship, *n.* the passengers using a particular system of public transportation over a period of time, or the estimated number of these.

ridġe (rij), *n.* [ME. *rigge*, etc.; AS. *hrycg, hricg,* a ridge, the back; Scot. *rig, rigg,* a ridge of land, *rigging,* the roof of a house; akin to Gr. *rhachis,* the spine.]

1. an animal's back.

2. the long, narrow top or crest of something, as of an animal's back.

3. a long, narrow elevation of land or range of hills or mountains.

4. any narrow raised strip on or in something, as on fabric.

5. the horizontal line formed by the meeting of two sloping surfaces; as, the *ridge* of a roof.

6. a narrow high-pressure area on a weather chart.

7. in fortification, the highest part of a glacis proceeding from a covered way at its breast height.

ridġe, *v.t.* and *v.i.*; ridged, *pt., pp.*; ridging, *ppr.* 1. to mark with or as with a ridge or ridges.

2. to form into or furnish with a ridge or ridges.

ridġe′band, *n.* the part of a harness that goes over the saddle and supports the shafts of a cart.

ridġe′bōne, *n.* the backbone. [Obs.]

ridġe′let, *n.* a small ridge.

ridġe′ling, ridġ′ling, *n.* [prob. from *ridge* and *-ling* (n. suffix): perh. after assumed location of the testicles.] a domestic animal in which one or both testicles have not descended into the scrotum.

ridġe′pōle, *n.* the timber which forms the ridge of a roof and onto which the rafters are fastened: also called *ridgepiece, ridgeplate.*

ridġ′y, *a.*; *comp.* ridgier; *superl.* ridgiest, having a ridge or ridges; rising in a ridge.

rid′i·cūle, *n.* [OFr., from L. *ridiculus,* laughable, comical, from *ridere,* to laugh.]

1. words or actions intended to express contempt and excite laughter; derision; banter; also, the act or practice of making someone or something the object of such words or actions.

2. any object which provokes contempt or mockery; an absurdity; as, turned into *ridicule.* [Rare or Obs.]

3. ridiculousness. [Rare.]

Syn.—satire, irony, sarcasm, derision.

rid′i·cūle, *v.t.*; ridiculed, *pt., pp.*; ridiculing, *ppr.* to laugh at with expressions of contempt; to deride; to treat with contemptuous laughter.

rid′i·cū·lẽr, *n.* one who ridicules.

ri·diç·ū·los′i·ty, *n.* 1. the state of being ridiculous; ridiculousness.

2. *pl.* **ri·diç·ū·los′i·tieṣ,** anything ridiculous.

Your pretty sayings and all your *ridiculosities.* —Bailey.

ri·diç′ū·lous, *a.* [L. *ridiculus,* from *ridere,* to laugh.] worthy of or calculated to excite ridicule; ludicrous; absurd.

Finding nothing *ridiculous* in national peculiarities. —Goldsmith.

ri·diç′ū·lous·ly, *adv.* in a ridiculous manner or degree; ludicrously; absurdly.

ri·diç′ū·lous·ness, *n.* the quality or state of being ridiculous; absurdity.

rīd′ing, *n.* [AS. *thrithing, trithing,* a third part, from *thri,* three. The initial *t* was easily lost in consequence of the difficulty of recognizing its sounds in the compounds *North-, East-,* and *West-trithing.*]

1. formerly, any of the three administrative divisions (*North Riding, East Riding,* and *West Riding*) of Yorkshire, England.

2. a similar division in the Commonwealth; specifically, a Canadian electoral district.

rīd′ing, *a.* 1. that rides.

2. used in or for riding or traveling; as, a *riding* costume, *riding* horses.

rīd′ing, *n.* 1. the act or state of one who or that which rides.

2. a road cut in a wood, etc. especially as a place for riding: also called a *ride.*

rīd′ing bitts, two strong upright timbers near the bow of a ship, to which the anchor cables are secured.

rīd′ing hab′it, any costume designed to be worn by horseback riders, especially such a one for women.

rīd′ing hood, a hood of varying style, formerly worn by women when riding; also, a cloak with a hood.

rīd′ing mȧs′tẽr, a teacher of horsemanship.

rīd′ing rhȳme, heroic verse: so called from its use in the Canterbury Tales.

rīd′ing sāil, a three-cornered sail bent to the mainmast and sheeted down aft: used to steady a vessel when head on to the wind.

rīd′ing sc̱hool, a school in which the art of riding and the nature and management of horses are taught.

ri·dot′tō, *n.*; *pl.* **ri·dot′tōṣ,** [It., from LL. *reductus.*]

1. a public entertainment or social gathering, often in masquerade, with music and dancing, popular in eighteenth-century England.

2. an abridged arrangement of a musical composition.

riē′beck·īte, *n.* [after E. *Riebeck,* German mineralogist.] an iron-sodium amphibole, which corresponds to the pyroxene aegirite and crystallizes in the monoclinic system.

riēf, *n.* robbery. [Scot.]

riēm, *n.* [D.] a thong cut from rawhide and rendered pliant: used in South Africa as a trace, and for hitching, tethering, etc.

riēt′bok, *n.* [D. *riet,* a reed, and *bok,* a buck.] an antelope of South Africa, *Redunca arundinum,* which lives in reedy marshes; the reedbuck.

rif, *n.* [reduction *i*n *f*orce.] the act of dismissing an employee, especially from a government job, as by eliminating the position. [Slang.]

rif, *v.t.*; riffed, *pt., pp.*; riffing, *ppr.* to dismiss from employment. [Slang.]

ri·fä″ci·men′tọ (-chē-, *or Eng.* ri-fä″chi-men′-tō), *n.*; *pl.* **ri·fä″ci·men′ti** (*or Eng.* -ti), [It., lit., a remaking, from *rifare,* to make over; *ri-,* re-, and *fare,* to make.] a remaking, recasting, or adaptation, as of a piece of writing or music.

rī·fam′pi·cin, *n.* same as *rifampin.*

rī·fam′pin, *n.* [from *rifamycin* (from *rifa-,* of unknown origin, and *-mycin,* from Gr. *mykēs,* fungus), an antibiotic derived from a fungus.] a derivative of an antibiotic prepared from a culture of a soil bacteria, *Streptomyces mediterranei,* used in treating tuberculosis, spinal meningitis, etc. by inhibiting the DNA synthesis of the virus or bacteria.

rīfe, *a.* [AS. *rife*: akin to M.D. *rȳf.*]

1. prevalent; frequently or commonly occurring; current.

2. abundant; plentiful.

3. filled; abounding: followed by *with.*

rīfe, *adv.* prevalently; abundantly.

rīfe′ly, *adv.* abundantly; prevalently.

rīfe′ness, *n.* the quality or state of being rife.

Riff, *n.* a member of a Berber people living in the Rif and near-by regions, along the Mediterranean coast of Morocco.

riff, *n.* in jazz music, a melodic phrase, repeated again and again, often used as the main theme, as in a final chorus, or as background.

riff, *n.* a rapid; a riffle. [Dial.]

Rif′fi·ăn, *a.* of the Rif or the Riffs.

Rif′fi·ăn, *n.* a Riff.

rif′fle, *n.* [from the v.]

1. a plank in a fish ladder so placed as to afford a rest for fish when ascending.

2. a polishing disk used by seal engravers.

3. (a) a shoal, reef, or rocky obstruction in a stream, producing a ripple or a stretch of shallow, rapid, or choppy water; (b) such a ripple or stretch of water.

4. in gold mining, (a) a contrivance, as of bars, slats, blocks, or stones, put across the bottom of a sluice, etc. to catch or hold the particles of gold in the grooves or channels left between the bars, slats, etc.; (b) any of the bars, slats, etc.; (c) any of the grooves or channels.

5. the act or method of riffling cards.

rif′fle, *v.t.* and *v.i.*; riffled, *pt., pp.*; riffling, *ppr.* [prob. var. of *ripple* merged with Canad. Fr. *riffler,* to scratch.]

1. to form, become, or flow over or through, a riffle.

2. to leaf rapidly through (a book, etc.), as by letting the edges or corners of the pages slip lightly across the thumb.

3. to shuffle (playing cards) by holding part of the deck in each hand, raising the corners or edges slightly, and letting the cards fall alternately together.

rif′flẽr, *n.* a kind of file with a somewhat curved end, suitable for working in small depressions.

riff′rȧff, *n.* [earlier *rif and raf,* every scrap.]

1. those people or that segment of society regarded as of no consequence or merit; mob.

2. trash. [Dial.]

rī′fle, *v.t.*; rifled, *pt., pp.*; rifling, *ppr.* [ME. *riflen*; OFr. *rifler*; Ice. *hrīfa, rīfa,* to seize, pull up, akin to *hrifsa,* to rob.]

1. to search and rob (a person).

2. to rob; to pillage; to plunder; as, to *rifle* a cash register.

3. to strip bare (usually with *of*); as, the thieves *rifled* the safe *of* valuables.

4. to take as plunder; to steal.

rī′fle, *v.t.* and *v.i.* to raffle.

rī′fle, *v.t.* [Fr. *rifler,* to scrape.]

1. to cut spiral grooves within (a gun barrel, etc.); as, to *rifle* a heavy gun.

2. to sharpen, as a scythe, with a rifle.

rī′fle, *v.i.* to use or fire a rifle. [Rare.]

rī′fle, *n.* [short for *rifled gun.*]

1. (a) a firearm the inside of whose barrel is rifled, that is, has spiral grooves cut into it, so that the ball may have a rotary motion on its own axis, and the accuracy and distance of the firearm be increased; especially, such a firearm to be fired from the shoulder: military rifles are distinguished from carbines in that they are longer and heavier and are designed to hold a bayonet; (b) one of the grooves in such a firearm.

2. an artillery piece or naval gun with such grooves.

3. [*pl.*] a body of troops armed with rifles; as, the Canadian Mounted *Rifles.*

4. a strop with a surface of emery for sharpening scythes, etc.

rī′fle·bird, *n.* an Australian bird, *Ptilorhis paradisea,* with a long curved bill, found only in the very thick bush. It is about the size of a large pigeon. The plumage in the upper parts is velvety black tinged with purple, in the under parts velvety black tinged with olive-green. The crown of the head and throat are covered with emerald-green specks.

rī′fle grē·nāde′, a grenade designed to be attached to the muzzle of a military rifle and fired by a special device: it explodes on contact.

rī′fle·măn, *n.*; *pl.* **rī′fle·men,** 1. a soldier, especially an infantryman, armed with a rifle.

2. a man who uses, or is skilled in using, a rifle.

rī′fle pit, a pit or short trench dug to protect riflemen firing at the enemy.

rī′flẽr, *n.* 1. one who rifles, plunders, or pillages.

2. in falconry, a hawk that does not return to the lure. [Archaic.]

rī′fle rānġe, 1. a place equipped with targets for practicing shooting with the rifle.

2. the range of a rifle; the distance covered by a bullet fired from a rifle.

rī′fle·ry, *n.* the skill or practice of shooting at targets with rifles.

rī′fle shot, a person who shoots with a rifle; also, a shot fired from a rifle.

rī′fling, *n.* the act of robbing or plundering.

rī′fling, *n.* 1. the system of grooves in a gun barrel.

2. the operation of making spiral grooves in a gun barrel.

rift, *n.* [ME. *rift*; Dan. *rift,* rift, rent; Ice. *ript,* a breach of contract; Sw. *ref,* from *rifva,* to tear.] a cleft; a fissure; an opening made by or as if by splitting.

rift, *v.t.* and *v.i.*; rifted, *pt., pp.*; rifting, *ppr.* to burst open; to crack; to split; as, to *rift* an oak or a rock.

rift, *v.i.* to belch. [Dial.]

rift, *n.* a shallow place in a stream; a riffle. [Brit. Dial.]

rig, *n.* a ridge. [Obs.]

rig, *v.t.*; rigged, *pt., pp.*; rigging, *ppr.* [ME. *rygge*; Sw. *rigga*, to rig (a ship), dial. *rigga pa*, to harness (a horse).]

1. (a) to fit (a ship, mast, etc.) with sails, shrouds, braces, etc.; (b) to fit (a ship's sails, shrouds, etc.) to the masts, yards, etc.

2. to assemble and adjust the wings, fuselage, etc. of (an aircraft).

3. to fit out; to equip (often with *out* or *up*).

4. to put together, prepare for use, or arrange, especially in a makeshift or hurried fashion (often with *up*).

5. to arrange in a dishonest way for selfish advantage; to manipulate fraudulently; as, speculators *rigged* the market.

6. to dress; clothe; attire (often with *out* or *up*). [Colloq.]

rig, *n.* 1. the distinctive manner of fitting the masts and rigging on a vessel.

2. any apparatus for a special purpose; equipment; gear; tackle.

3. equipment for drilling an oil well.

4. dress; costume, especially when odd or gay in style; as, decked out in a fantastic *rig*. [Colloq.]

5. (a) a carriage, cart, etc. with its horse or horses; (b) a combination of a tractor and a trailer used in trucking or, sometimes, the tractor alone.

gunter rig; a method of rigging in which the topmast is made to slide up and down alongside the lower mast.

rig, *n.* [origin doubtful; Wedgwood compares it with Manx *reagh*, ruttish, wanton, and *riggan*, to rut.] a wanton; a strumpet. [Brit. Dial.]

rig, *n.* same as *ridgel*.

rig, *n.* a ridge of land; a strip of land between two furrows. [Chiefly Scot.]

My blessings on that happy place.
Among the *rigs* of barley. —Burns.

rig·à·dōōn′, *n.* [Fr. *rigodon, rigaudon*, prob. from *Rigaud*, the inventor of the dance.]

1. a gay brisk dance for one couple, with a peculiar jumping step: it is no longer popular.

2. music for this dance, usually in duple time.

rī·gā′tion, *n.* [L. *rigatio* (*-onis*), a watering, wetting, from *rigare*, to water, wet.] irrigation. [Obs.]

Rī′gel (*or* -jel), *n.* a bluish star of the first magnitude, the brightest star in the constellation Orion.

rī·ġes′cent, *a.* [L. *rigescens* (*-entis*), ppr. of *rigescere*, to grow stiff or numb, from *rigere*, to stiffen.] becoming stiff or rigid.

rig′gẽr, *n.* 1. a person who rigs; specifically, (a) a person whose work is fitting the rigging of ships, or one who works with hoisting tackle and the like; (b) a person whose work is assembling and adjusting the fuselage, wings, etc. of aircraft.

2. a protective scaffold used, as on a building under construction, to catch tools or materials that might accidentally fall.

3. in machinery, a cylindrical pulley.

rig′ging, *n.* 1. the ropes, chains, etc., which support the masts, extend and contract the sails, etc., of a ship. It is of two kinds: standing rigging, as the shrouds and stays, and running rigging, consisting of all those ropes used in bracing the yards, making and shortening sail, etc., such as braces, sheets, halyards, clew lines, etc.

2. equipment; gear.

rig′ging, *n.* the top of anything; a roof. [Brit. Dial.]

rig′ging loft, 1. a room for preparing the rigging for a ship.

2. in a theater, that section above the stage and below the roof from which the scenery is raised and lowered.

rig′gish, *a.* having the qualities of a rig, or wanton.

The holy priests bless her when she is *riggish*. —Shak.

rig′gīte, *n.* a joker; one who jokes. [Rare.]

rig′gle, *v.i.* to wriggle. [Dial.]

Riggs′ diṣ·ēaṣe′, [after John M. *Riggs* (1810–1885), Am. dentist.] in dentistry, pyorrhea alveolaris.

rīght (rīt), *a.* [ME. and AS. *riht*, right, true, just, straight; akin to G. *recht*.]

1. not curved; straight; as, a *right* line.

2. (a) formed by, or with reference to, a straight line or plane perpendicular to a base; as, a *right* angle; (b) having the axis perpendicular to the base; as, a *right* cylinder.

3. in accordance with justice, law, morality, etc.; upright; virtuous; as, *right* conduct.

His conduct still *right*, with his argument wrong. —Goldsmith.

4. in accordance with fact, reason, some set standard, etc.; correct; as, the *right* answer.

If there be no prospect beyond the grave, the inference is certainly *right*, "Let us eat and drink, for tomorrow we die." —Locke.

5. correct in thought, statement, or action.

You are *right*, justice, and you weigh this well. —Shak.

6. (a) fitting; appropriate; suitable; (b) most convenient or favorable.

7. designating the side, surface, etc. meant to be seen; designating the finished, principal, or upper side or surface; as, the *right* side of cloth.

8. (a) sound; normal: said of the mind, etc.; (b) mentally sound or normal; sane: said of a person.

9. having sound health or good spirits.

10. in a satisfactory condition, or in good order; as, make things *right* again.

11. (a) designating or of that side of one's body which is toward the east when one faces north, usually the side of the more used hand; (b) designating or of the corresponding side of anything; (c) closer to the right side of a person directly before and facing the thing mentioned or understood; as, the top *right* drawer of a desk. Opposed to *left*.

12. of the political right; conservative or reactionary.

13. not spurious; genuine. [Archaic.]

at right angles; so as to form a right angle or right angles; perpendicular.

right bank of a river; the bank on the right hand of a person facing in the direction in which the water runs.

Right Center; those members of a legislative assembly, as in France, who belong to the Center and have sympathies with the Right.

right field; in baseball, the right-hand part of the outfield (as viewed from home plate).

right sailing; in nautical usage, sailing on one of the four cardinal points. [Rare.]

Syn.—lawful, true, correct, suitable.

rīght, *n.* 1. what is right, or just, lawful, morally good, proper, correct, etc.

With firmness in the *right* as God gives us to see the *right*. —Abraham Lincoln.

2. a just and fair claim to anything whatever; power, privilege, etc. that belongs to a person by law, nature, or tradition; also, that to which one has a just claim: often in the plural; as, the *rights* of the laborer; an inherent *right* to noninterference; the *right* to acquire property.

3. (a) all or part of the right side; (b) what is on the right side.

4. in boxing, (a) the right hand; (b) a blow delivered with the right hand.

5. in finance, (a) the privilege given to a company's stockholders of buying additional stock or shares in a new issue of stock, usually at par or a price below the current market price; (b) the negotiable certificate indicating this privilege; (c) [*often pl.*] a privilege of subscribing for some stock or bond.

6. [*often* R–] in politics, a conservative or reactionary position, party, or group: so called from the position of the seats occupied in some European legislatures.

by right, by rights; properly; fittingly.

by right of; by reason of.

in one's own right; through one's own authority, ability, etc.; without dependence on another or others.

in the right; right; correct.

to rights; in or into good or proper condition or order. [Colloq.]

rīght, *adv.* [ME. and AS. *rihte*.]

1. in a straight line; straight; directly (often with *to, into, through*, etc.); as, go *right* home.

2. (a) properly; fittingly; (b) favorable, conveniently, or well.

3. completely; thoroughly; as, the cold penetrated *right* through his clothes.

4. exactly; precisely; as, *right* here.

5. without pause or delay; immediately; as, come *right* now.

6. according to law, justice, etc.; in an upright way.

7. correctly or accurately.

8. on or toward the right hand or side.

9. very; extremely; as, he knows *right* well: dialectal or colloquial except in certain titles, as, the *right* honorable.

right along; continuously. [Colloq.]

right and left; in various directions. [Colloq.]

right away (or *off*); without delay or pause; at once.

right on! precisely! exactly! that's right!: an exclamation of approval or encouragement. [Slang.]

rīght, *v.t.* 1. to put in or restore to an upright or proper position; as, we *righted* the boat and started rowing.

2. to correct; to make conform with fact, etc.

3. to put in order; to set right; as, the maid *righted* the room.

4. to do justice to (a person); to make amends to.

5. to make amends for; to redress or avenge (a wrong, etc.).

rīght, *v.i.* to get into or resume an upright or proper condition or position.

rīght′à·bout, *n.* 1. a rightabout-face.

2. the direction directly opposite, as faced after turning completely about.

rīght′à·bout, *adv.* and *a.* with, in, or by a right-about-face.

rīght′à·bout-fāce′, *n.* 1. a turning directly about so as to face in the opposite direction.

2. a complete reversal of belief, conduct, etc.

rīght′à·bout-fāce′, *interj.* a military command to perform a rightabout-face.

rīght añ′gle, an angle of 90 degrees; angle made by the meeting of two straight lines perpendicular to each other.

RIGHT ANGLE

rīght′-añ′gled (-gld), *a.* rectangular; having or forming one or more right angles.

rīght as·cen′sion, in astronomy, (a) the rising of a star or point above the horizon on the celestial sphere; (b) the angular distance of a heavenly body from the vernal equinox, measured eastward along the celestial equator and expressed in degrees or hours, minutes, and seconds.

rīght′eous (rī′chus), *a.* [ME. and AS. *rihtwis*; *riht*, right, and *wise*, manner.]

1. upright; virtuous; acting in a just, upright manner; as, a *righteous* man.

2. morally right or justifiable.

And I thy *righteous* doom will bless. —Dryden.

3. good, excellent, satisfying, pleasant, authentic, etc.: a generalized term of approval. [Slang.]

Syn.—godly, just, upright, virtuous.

rīght′eous·ly, *adv.* justly; in accordance with the laws of justice; equitably; as, a criminal *righteously* condemned.

rīght′eous·ness, *n.* 1. the quality or condition of being righteous or just; rectitude.

2. a righteous act, quality, etc.

rīght′ẽr, *n.* one who sets right; one who does justice or redresses wrong.

rīght′ful, *a.* 1. having the right or just claim according to established laws; as, the *rightful* heir to a throne or an estate.

2. belonging or owned by right, or by just or lawful claim; as, *rightful* property.

3. just; right; fair; equitable.

4. righteous; virtuous. [Rare or Obs.]

rīght′ful·ly, *adv.* in a rightful manner.

rīght′ful·ness, *n.* the quality or state of being rightful.

rīght′-hand, *a.* 1. of, for, or with the right hand; as, a *right-hand* glove.

2. being on or directed toward the right; as, a *right-hand* movement.

3. most helpful or reliable; as, a *right-hand* man.

4. plain laid: said of a rope.

rīght′-hand′ed, *a.* 1. using the right hand more skillfully than and in preference to the left; as, a *right-handed* hitter.

2. turning left to right; clockwise.

3. done with the right hand; as, a quick, *right-handed* stroke.

4. made for use with the right hand.

5. spiraling from left to right, as most shells.

rīght′-hand′ed·ness, *n.* the condition or quality of being right-handed; by extension, dexterity.

rīght'-hand'ĕr, *n.* 1. one who is right-handed.
 2. a right-hand blow.

rīght'iṣm, *n.* in politics, conservative or reactionary ideas or actions.

rīght'ist, *n.* in politics, a person whose political position is conservative or reactionary.

rīght'ist, *a.* in politics, conservative or reactionary.

rīght'less, *a.* without rights.

rīght'-līned', *a.* having right lines; rectilineal; as, a *right-lined* angle.

rīght'ly, *adv.* 1. with justice; fairly; as, duty *rightly* performed.
 2. properly; fitly; suitably; as, a person *rightly* named.
 3. correctly; not erroneously; as, he has *rightly* conjectured.

rīght'-mīnd'ed, *a.* thinking or believing what is right; having correct views or principles.

rīght''-mīnd'ed·ness, *n.* the state of being right-minded.

rīght'ness, *n.* the state or quality of being right; conformity to rule, standard, or fact; correctness.

rīght'ō, *interj.* yes; all right; certainly: exclamation expressing affirmation or assent. [Brit. Colloq.]

rīght of sēarch, in maritime law, the right of a nation at war to stop the ships of neutral nations on the high seas and search them for contraband or the like, the finding of which makes the ship liable to seizure: also *right of visit* (or *visitation) and search.*

rīght'-of-wāy, *n.* right of way.

rīght of wāy, 1. the right, established by common or statutory law, of one ship, automobile, etc. to cross in front of another; precedence in moving, as at intersections.
 2. right of passage, as over another's property.
 3. a route that it is lawful to use.
 4. (a) a strip of land acquired or used by a railroad for its tracks; (b) land over which a public road, an electric power line, etc. passes.

rīght'-on, *a.* sophisticated, informed, current, etc. [Slang.]

rīght sphēre, a sphere so placed that the equator cuts the horizon at right angles.

rīght'-to-wŏrk', *a.* designating or of laws or legislation prohibiting the union shop.

rīght trī'aṅ·gle, a triangle with one right angle.

rīght'wărd, *adv.* toward the right; to the right.

rīght whāle, [perhaps "true (i.e., typical) whale" or "right whale to hunt for" (because valued for its oil).] a large-headed whalebone whale without teeth or dorsal fin.

rīght'-wing, *a.* in politics, of the right wing.

rīght wing, in politics, the more conservative or reactionary section of a party, etc.

rīght-wing'ĕr, *n.* a member of a right wing.

riġ'id, *a.* [L. *rigidus*, stiff, from *rigere*, to be stiff.]
 1. stiff; not pliant; not easily bent; inflexible; as, *rigid* in death.
 2. not moving; firmly fixed; set.
 3. severe; strict; as, a *rigid* taskmaster.
 4. not deviating or relaxing; rigorous; as, *rigid* regulations.
 5. in aeronautics, having a rigid framework that encloses containers for the gas: said of a dirigible or airship.

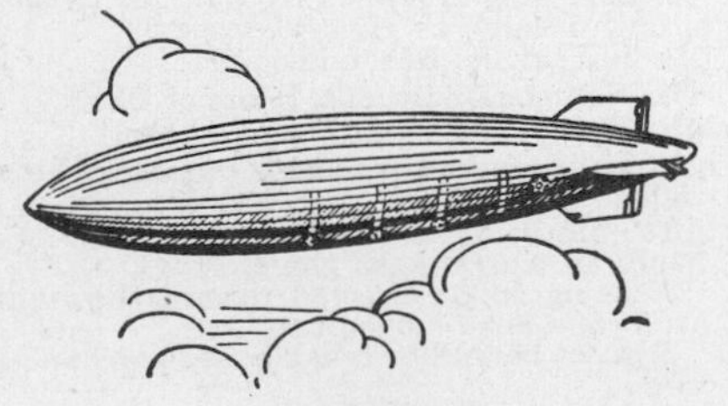

RIGID AIRSHIP

Syn.—stiff, unpliant, inflexible, unyielding, strict, severe, austere, stern, rigorous, unmitigated, hard, precise.

ri·ġid'i·ty, *n.*; *pl.* **riġ·id'i·tieṣ,** 1. quality, state, or instance of being rigid; stiffness; lack of pliability; rigidness.
 2. stiffness of appearance; lack of ease or grace.
 3. strictness; severity; austerity; sternness.

riġ'id·ly, *adv.* 1. in a rigid or stiff manner; stiffly; not flexibly or pliantly.
 2. with strictness or severity; strictly; inflexibly.

riġ'id·ness, *n.* 1. the quality or state of being rigid; stiffness; rigidity.
 2. strictness or austerity of temper; severity.

ri·ġid'ū·lous, *a.* slightly rigid. [Rare.]

rig'let, *n.* same as *reglet.*

rig'mȧ·rōle, *n.* [altered from *ragman roll.*] a long, unintelligible story; a succession of confused or disjointed statements; loose disjointed talk or writing; incoherent harangue; nonsense.

rig'mȧ·rōle, *a.* consisting of or characterized by rigmarole; unintelligible; nonsensical.

rig'ŏl, *n.* a circle; a crown. [Obs.]

rig'ŏr, *n.* [ME. *rigour*; OFr. *rigour*; L. *rigor*, stiffness, cold, from *rigere*, to be rigid.]
 1. extreme harshness or severity; specifically, (a) strictness or inflexibility; as, the *rigor* of martial law; (b) hardship or difficulty; as, the *rigors* of life; (c) inclemency, as of weather.
 2. a severe, harsh, or oppressive act, etc.
 3. stiffness; rigidity; specifically, a condition of rigidity in body tissues or organs, in which they are not responsive to stimuli.
 4. a shivering or trembling, as in the chill preceding a fever.
 Syn.—stiffness, rigidness, inflexibility, severity, austerity, sternness, harshness, strictness, exactness.

rig'ŏr·iṣm, *n.* 1. austerity in opinion or conduct; rigidity in style or living; strictness.
 2. strict conformity to form or to the letter.

rig'ŏr·ist, *n.* a person who believes in and practices rigorism.

rig'ŏr·ist, *a.* strict; also, of the doctrine of rigorism.

rī'gọr mọr'tis (*or* rig'ĕr), [L., stiffness of death.] the progressive stiffening of the muscles that occurs several hours after death as a result of the coagulation of the muscle protein.

rig'ŏr·ous, *a.* [OFr. *rigoureux*; LL. *rigorosus*, from L. *rigor*, rigor.]
 1. severe; allowing no abatement or mitigation; as, a *rigorous* officer of justice.
 2. severe; exact; strict; harsh; as, a *rigorous* execution of law; an enforcement of *rigorous* discipline.
 3. exact; strict; scrupulously accurate; precise; as, a *rigorous* definition or demonstration.
 4. very severe or sharp: said of climate or weather; as, a *rigorous* winter.
 Syn.—inflexible, unyielding, austere, inclement, harsh, stern.

rig'ŏr·ous·ly, *adv.* in a rigorous manner; strictly; exactly.

rig'ŏr·ous·ness, *n.* the quality or state of being rigorous; severity; strictness; rigor; exactness.

rig'oŭr, *n.* rigor: British spelling.

rig'oŭr·iṣm, *n.* rigorism: British spelling.

rig'oŭr·ist, *n.* rigorist: British spelling.

Rigs'dăg, *n.* the parliament of Denmark, consisting of an upper house, the *Landsting*, and a lower, the *Folkesting.*

rigṣ'dä''lĕr, *n.* an obsolete Danish silver coin; rix-dollar.

Rigs'mäal (-mäl), *n.* the ordinary literary language of Norway; the Dano-Norwegian "language of the realm."

Rig-Vē'dȧ, *n.* [Sans. *Rgveda*, from *ric*, praise, hymn, and *veda*, knowledge.] the Veda of Verses (Psalms), the oldest and most important of the Hindu sacred books, or Vedas.

Riks'dăg, *n.* the parliament of Sweden, composed of an upper and lower house.

rīle, *v.t.*; riled, *pt., pp.*; riling, *ppr.* [pronun. var. of *roil.*]
 1. to make (a liquid) thick and muddy by stirring the dregs. [Colloq. or Dial.]
 2. to make cross or angry; to vex; to irritate. [Colloq. or Dial.]

ri·lie'vō (-lye'), *n.*; *pl.* **ri·lie'vī,** [It.] in sculpture, architecture, etc., relief (sense 6).

rill, *n.* [cf. D. and Fris. *ril*, L.G. and G. *rille.*] a small brook; a rivulet; a streamlet.

rill, *v.i.* to run in a small stream or in streamlets.

rill, rille, *n.* [G. *rille*, a groove, furrow.] in astronomy, any of several long, narrow trenches or valleys seen on the moon's surface.

rill'et, *n.* [dim. of *rill.*] a little rill; a small stream; a rivulet.

rī'ly, *a.* easily irritated or angered; turbid; roily. [Colloq.]

rim, *n.* [ME. *rime*; AS. *rima*, an edge, border.]
 1. the edge, border, or margin, especially of something circular; often, a raised or projecting edge or border.
 2. (a) the outer, circular part of a wheel; (b) a circular strip of metal, often removable, on which the tire is mounted on the wheel of an automobile, etc.
 Syn.—brim, brink, verge, edge, margin, circumference, periphery, ring.

rim, *v.t.*; rimmed, *pt., pp.*; rimming, *ppr.*
 1. to put a rim or rims on or around.
 2. to roll around the rim of (the basket, in basketball, or the hole, in golf).
 3. to slit the sides of, as mackerel, to give the appearance of fatness. [Rare.]

rim, *n.* [AS. *reóma*, a ligament.] the membrane enclosing the intestines; the belly. [Obs.]

rī'mȧ, *n.*; *pl.* **rī'mae,** [L. *rima*, cleft, opening.] in anatomy, a fissure; an opening; a long aperture; as, the *rima* glottidis, the opening in the larynx through which the air passes in and out of the lungs.

rim'bāse, *n.* 1. the shoulder on the trunnion of a cannon.
 2. the shoulder on the stock of a musket against which the breech abuts.

rīme, *n.* [L. *rima*, a crack.] a chink; a fissure; a rent or long aperture.

rīme, *n.* [ME. *rim(e)*; AS. *hrim.*] a white, icy coating formed on grass, leaves, etc. from atmospheric moisture; hoarfrost.

rīme, *v.i.*; rimed, *pt., pp.*; riming, *ppr.* to freeze or congeal into hoarfrost.

rīme, *v.t.* to coat with rime.

rīme, *n.* a round of a ladder; a rung.

rīme, *n.* [sp. preferred by many for historical reasons, supposed association with AS. *rim*, number, reckoning, etc.; see *rhyme.*] same as *rhyme.*

rīme, *v.t.* and *v.i.*; rimed, *pt., pp.*; riming, *ppr.* to rhyme.

rīme'less, *a.* same as *rhymeless.*

rīm'ĕr, *n.* same as *rhymer.*

rīm'ĕr, *n.* a reamer. [Brit.]

rīme roy'ăl, same as *rhyme royal.*

rīme'stĕr, *n.* same as *rhymester.*

rīm'ey, *v.t.* to versify; to compose in rime. [Obs.]

rim'-fīre', *n.* 1. designating a cartridge which has the fulminating material in the rim of its base: opposed to *center-fire.*
 2. using such cartridges; as, a *rim-fire* gun.

rim'less, *a.* having no rim.

rim lock, a lock having an exterior metallic case that projects from the face of the door, thus differing from a mortise lock.

rim'mĕr, *n.* a device for cutting and ornamenting the edges of anything, as of pies, etc.

rī'mōse, *a.* [L. *rimosus*, full of chinks; from *rima*, chink, fissure.] full of chinks or fissures; having many clefts, cracks, or crevices, as the bark of trees.

rī'mōse·ly, *adv.* in a rimose manner.

ri·mos'i·ty, *n.* the state of being rimose.

rī'mous, *a.* same as *rimose.*

rim'ple, *n.* [ME. *rimpyl.*] a crease; a wrinkle; a rumple.

rim'ple, *v.t.* and *v.i.*; rimpled, *pt., pp.*; rimpling, *ppr.* to rumple; to wrinkle; to crease.

rim'rock, *n.* rock or rocks on the walls or edges of channels, cliffs, etc.

rī'mu, *n.* [Maori.] the imou pine.

rim'ū·lōse, *a.* [L. *rimula*, little crack.] in botany and zoology, having very small crevices or cracks.

rīm'y, *a.*; *comp.* rimier; *superl.* rimiest, covered with rime; frosty.

rin, *n.* [Japan.] a small copper coin of Japan, valued at one tenth of a sen.

rīnd, *n.* [ME. *rinde*; AS. *rind, rinde.*] a hard or firm outer layer or coating; as, the *rind* of cheese, of fruit, of a side of bacon, etc.; skin; husk; bark; peel.

rīnd, *v.t.* to remove the rind of; to decorticate.

rīnd'ed, *a.* having a (specified kind of) rind: usually in hyphenated compounds; as, soft-*rinded.*

rin'dĕr·pest, *n.* [G. *rinder*, pl. of *rind*, a horned beast, and *pest*, a plague.] an acute infectious disease of cattle and, often, sheep and goats, characterized by fever and inflammation of the mucous membrane of the intestines; cattle plague.

rin'dle, *n.* same as *runnel.*

rīnd'less, *a.* without a rind.

rīnd'y, *a.* with a rind or skin.

rīne, *n.* rind. [Obs.]

rin·fọr·zän'dō (-tsän'), *a.* [It.] in music, reinforcing or strengthening the power and emphasis of a musical sentence: a direction to the performer indicating that the sound is to be increased.

ring, *n.* [ME.; AS. *hring*; akin to G. *ring*.]
1. a small, circular band of metal, etc., especially of precious metal, often set with gems, to be worn on the finger as an ornament or a symbol of betrothal, marriage, etc.
2. any of various circular bands or objects, as of metal, plastic, etc., used for some special purpose; as, a key *ring*, napkin *ring*.
3. a circular line, mark, or figure.
4. the outer edge or border of something circular; a rim, as of a wheel.
5. a circular cut made, or a circle of bark cut from, around the trunk or a branch of a tree.
6. any of the concentric, roughly circular marks seen in cross sections, of the trunks of exogenous trees, resulting from the yearly addition of layers of wood: in full, *annual ring*.
7. any of the turns in a helix or spiral.
8. a circular course, as in dancing.
9. a number of people or things grouped in a circle.
Make a *ring* about the corpse of Caesar. —Shak.
10. a combination of persons for a selfish end, as for controlling the market in stocks, or for effecting some political purpose.
11. a commercial measure of staves, or wood prepared for casks, and containing four shocks, or 240 pieces.
12. an enclosed area, often circular, for contests, exhibitions, etc.; as, the *ring* of a circus.
13. an enclosure, now usually a square, canvas-covered area set off by stakes and ropes, in which boxing and wrestling matches are held.
14. the sport or profession of boxing; prize fighting (with *the*).
15. an enclosed space for betting at a race.
16. bookmakers collectively.
17. a contest or competition, especially a political one: now usually in *toss one's hat in the ring*, to announce publicly that one is a candidate, as for political nomination.
18. in chemistry, a closed chain of atoms; a number of atoms united in such a way that they can be represented graphically as a ring.
19. in geometry, the area or space between two concentric circles.
20. in architecture, the list, cincture, or annulet round a column.
21. an instrument formerly used for taking the sun's altitude, etc., consisting of a ring, usually of brass, suspended by a swivel, with a hole in one side, through which a solar ray entering indicated the altitude upon the inner graduated concave surface.
22. in botany, same as *annulus*.
abdominal ring; see under *abdominal*.
Müller's ring; a muscular ring surrounding the junction of the cervical canal and the body of the uterus at an advanced stage of pregnancy.
Newton's rings; the colored rings seen on the surface of thin transparent membranes, as soap bubbles, due to chromatic aberration.
Pacinotti's ring; in electricity, a ring-shaped armature core provided with projections, employed in his generator by Antonio Pacinotti, 19th-century Italian physicist, to receive the armature windings.

ring, *v.t.*; ringed, *pt.*, *pp.*; ringing, *ppr.* 1. to encircle; to surround with or as with a ring.
2. to cut out a ring of bark from (a tree, etc.); as, to *ring* branches or roots.
3. to exercise, as a horse, by causing it to run round in a ring while being held by a long rein; to lunge.
4. to form into a ring or rings.
5. to furnish with a ring or rings.
6. to put a ring in the nose of (an animal), as to prevent rooting or fighting.
7. to circle about (animals) so as to hem them in.
8. in some games, to toss a ring, horseshoe, quoit, etc. so that it encircles (a peg).

ring, *v.i.* 1. to form or gather in a ring or rings.
2. to move in a circular or curving course; to run, fly, etc. in circles or spirals; specifically, in falconry, to fly upward in spirals.

ring, *v.i.*; rang *or rarely* rung, *pt.*; rung, *pp.*; ringing, *ppr.* [ME. *ringen*; AS. *hringan*.]
1. to give forth a clear, resonant sound when struck or otherwise caused to vibrate, as a bell.
2. to produce, as by sounding, a specified impression on the hearer; as, her promises *rang* false.
3. to cause a bell or bells to sound.
4. to sound a bell as a summons (usually with *for*); as, she *rang for* the maid.
5. to sound loudly or be full of sound; to be resonant; to resound; as, the room *rang* with merriment: also used figuratively; as, the nation *rang* with praise for his deeds.
6. to have a sensation as of ringing, humming, etc.: said of the ears or head.
to ring in; to mark the time of one's arrival at work by means of a time clock.
to ring off; to end a telephone call.
to ring out; to mark the time of one's departure from work by means of a time clock.

ring, *v.t.* 1. to cause (a bell, etc.) to ring.
2. to sound (a peal, knell, etc.) by or as by ringing a bell or bells.
3. to signal, proclaim, announce, summon, usher (*in* or *out*), etc. by or as by ringing; as, the chimes *rang* the hours.
4. to test (coins, etc.).
5. to call by telephone (often with *up*).
to ring down the curtain; (a) to signal for a theater curtain to be lowered, as at the end of an act; (b) to end something.
to ring in; to bring in or put in by fraud or trickery. [Slang.]
to ring the bell; to achieve a success: in allusion to strength-testing devices, as at amusement parks, in which a bell rings to indicate a successful effort. [Colloq.]
to ring up; to record or enter (a specified amount) in a cash register.
to ring up the curtain; (a) to signal for a theater curtain to be raised, as at the beginning of an act; (b) to begin something.

ring, *n.* 1. the sound of a bell.
2. (a) any similar sound; as, the *ring* of laughter; (b) any loud sound, especially when repeated, continued, or reverberated.
3. a characteristic sound or quality; as, the *ring* of pride.
4. a set of bells.
5. the act of ringing a bell, etc.
6. a telephone call.

ring'-ȧ-liē'vi·ō, ring'-ȧ-lē'vi·ō, *n.* [from *ring*, and *relieve*.] a children's game in which members of one group try to find and capture hiding members of another group: a captured player is kept in a circle drawn on the ground and is set free by a free teammate.

ring är'mȧ·tūre, in electricity, an armature whose core is ring-shaped.

ring'bärk, *v.t.* to ring; to girdle, as a tree.

ring'bill, *n.* the necked scaup.

ring'-billed, *a.* having a color ring around the bill, as certain gulls.

ring'bīrd, *n.* the ring bunting.

ring black'bīrd, the ring ouzel.

ring'bōlt, *n.* an iron bolt having a ring at the head.

ring'bōne, *n.* a hard, callous, pathological growth in the hollow circle of the little pastern of a horse, just above the coronet; also, the lamed condition resulting from such growth.

ring bun'ting, the reed bunting.

ring çȧ·nal', in zoology, a circular water tube surrounding the esophagus of an echinoderm.

ring chuck, a chuck or appendage to a lathe, with a brass ring fitted over the end.

ring dī'ăl, a portable sundial in the form of a ring.

ring dot'tēr·el, a species of plover common in Britain, where it frequents the shores of bays and inlets of the sea and of rivers, feeding on worms, insects, small crustaceans, etc. It takes its name from a white ring round the neck.

ring'dŏve, *n.* 1. the European wood pigeon, with whitish markings on each side of the neck.
2. a European and Asiatic dove resembling the turtledove: also *ringed turtledove*.

ringed (ringd), *a.* 1. wearing or having a ring or rings; hence (with reference to a wedding or engagement ring), married or engaged.
2. decorated or marked with a ring or rings.
3. encircled or surrounded by a ring or rings.
4. formed like a ring or of rings.
ringed seal; a seal of the northern seas, marked with ringlike spots.
ringed snake; a harmless European snake, *Tropidonotus natrix*, having a yellow ring around its neck.
ringed worm; an annelid.

rin'gent, *a.* [L. *ringens* (*-entis*), ppr. of *ringi*, to gape openmouthed.]
1. gaping.
2. in botany, having the lips widely separated, as some corollas.

ring'ēr, *n.* a person or thing that rings, or encircles, etc.; specifically, (a) a horseshoe, quoit, etc. thrown so that it encircles the peg; (b) such a throw.

ring'ēr, *n.* 1. a person or thing that rings a bell, chime, etc.
2. [from *ring in*.] (a) a player, horse, etc. dishonestly entered in some competition by falsifying or concealing the facts of identity, status, age, record, etc.; (b) a person or thing that very much resembles another; as, he's a *ringer* for his father. [Slang.]

Ring'ēr's sō·lū'tion, [after Sydney *Ringer* (1835–1910), Eng. physiologist.] a solution used as a substitute for blood serum and also as a vehicle for local anesthetics.

ring fence, a fence encircling a whole estate within one enclosure.

ring fin'gēr, the third finger, especially of the left hand, on which the ring is placed in marriage.

ring frāme, a spinning machine in which the thread passes through a metal loop that revolves around each spindle.

ring gāuge, 1. a tapering rod bearing a graduated scale, used to determine the size of finger rings.
2. a circular steel gauge used in inspecting shot and shell.

ring'head (-hed), *n.* an instrument used for stretching woolen cloth.

ring'ing, *a.* having or giving the sound of a bell or other resonant metallic body; resounding; as, a *ringing* voice, *ringing* cheers.

ring'ing, *n.* 1. the act of sounding or of causing to sound, as sonorous metallic bodies; hence, the art or act of making music with bells.
2. a ringing sound; as, a *ringing* in the ear.

ring'ing, *n.* [ppr. and verbal noun of *ring*, to encircle.] the result or process of placing rings on or around something; the condition of being marked, encircled, or indicated by a ring or rings.

ring'ing, *n.* 1. in horticulture, the cutting out of a ring of bark from a tree.
2. the act of bedecking with rings.

ring'ing·ly, *adv.* in a ringing manner.

ring'lead, *v.t.*; ringled (-led), *pt.*, *pp.*; ringleading, *ppr.* to act as ringleader to.

ring'lēad″ēr, *n.* a person who leads others, especially in unlawful acts, opposition to authority, etc.

ring'let, *n.* [dim. of *ring*.]
1. a small ring or circle.
2. a curl; particularly, a curl of hair.

ring'let·ed, *a.* adorned with ringlets; wearing ringlets.

ring māil, defensive armor made by sewing strong rings of steel edgewise upon leather or strong quilted cloth; chain mail.

ring'mȧs″tēr, *n.* one who conducts the performances in a circus ring; hence, a leader.

ring mŏn'ey, a kind of money consisting of rings, in use at an early stage of society, before the invention of coining.

ring'neck, *n.* 1. any of the numerous species of small plovers that have rings around the neck.
2. the ring-necked duck.

ring'-necked (-nekt), *a.* having a distinct ring of color around the neck.
ring-necked duck; the scaup of North America, *Aythya collaris*, the male of which has a narrow red ring around the neck.

Ring of the Nï'be·lung, 1. in German legend, the ring made from the Rheingold by Alberich, leader of a race of dwarfs called the Nibelungs.
2. the tetralogy of music dramas by Richard Wagner, *Das Rheingold*, *Die Walküre*, *Siegfried*, and *Götterdämmerung*, telling the story of this ring.

ring ou'zel, a species of thrush, *Turdus torquatus*, resembling the blackbird, but having a white ring or bar on the breast.

ring par'rŏt, any Indian parrot of the genus *Palæornis* having a ringed neck.

ring plŏv'ēr, a ring dotterel; also, one of the small American plovers that have well-defined rings around the neck.

ring'sīde, *n.* 1. the space or place just outside the ring, as at a boxing match or circus.
2. any place that provides a close view of something.

ring snāke, a small, harmless, dark-colored snake of the genus *Diadophis*, having a white or yellow ring around the neck.

ring spin′nẽr, same as *ring frame.*

ring′stẽr, *n.* a member of a ring, particularly of a political ring. [Colloq.]

ring stop′pẽr, in nautical usage, a short length of chain used to secure an old type anchor at the ring.

ring′-strāked (-strākt), *a.* ring-streaked. [Archaic.]

ring′-strēaked (-strēkt), *a.* having circular streaks or lines on the body.

ring′tāil, *n.* 1. a bird having a bar or ring of color across the tail, as the female of the hen harrier, *Circus cyaneus.*

2. a light sail set abaft and beyond the spanker of a sailing vessel, to extend its area in light winds: also called *ringsail.*

ring′-tāiled, *a.* having a tail striped or otherwise marked by a series of rings or ringlike markings.

ring-tailed cat; the cacomistle.

ring-tailed eagle; a golden eagle in its immature stage.

ring thrush, the ring ouzel.

ring′toss, *n.* a game in which the object is to encircle an upright stick with rings of rope, etc. tossed by the players.

ring′wall, *n.* a wall surrounding a particular area.

ring′wŏrm, *n.* 1. any of various contagious skin diseases, as athlete's foot, caused by several related varieties of fungus and characterized by itching and the formation of ring-shaped, discolored patches covered with scales or vesicles.

2. a millepede of the genus *Julus.*

ring′wŏrm shrub, a shrub of the bean family found in tropical America, the leaves of which are applied externally as a remedy for ringworm.

rink, *n.* [Scot., earlier *renk,* from OFr. *renc,* rank.]

1. a smooth expanse of ice marked off for the game of curling.

2. a part of a bowling green large enough for a match to be played on it.

3. the players on one side in a game of curling, bowling, or quoits.

4. a smooth expanse of ice, often artificially prepared and enclosed, for skating.

5. a smooth floor, usually of wood, for roller skating.

6. a building or enclosure containing a surface for ice skating or roller skating.

rinse, *v.t.*; rinsed (rinst), *pt., pp.*; rinsing, *ppr.* [OFr. *rincer,* from LL. *recentiare,* to renew, from L. *recens,* fresh.]

1. to wash lightly, as by dipping into water or letting water run over, into, or through.

2. to remove soap, dirt, or impurities from by using clean water in this way as a last process in cleansing.

3. to remove (soap, dirt, etc.) in this way.

4. to flush (the mouth or teeth), as with clear water.

rinse, *n.* 1. a rinsing.

2. the water used in rinsing.

3. a substance mixed with water and used to rinse or tint hair.

rins′ẽr, *n.* one who or that which rinses.

rins′ing, *n.* 1. [*usually pl.*] (a) the liquid in or with which anything has been rinsed; (b) dregs.

2. the act of one that rinses; rinse.

rī′ō, *n.* [Sp.] a river.

rī′ŏt, *n.* [OFr. *riote,* disturbance, noise, combat, from *rioter,* to make a disturbance.]

1. wild or violent disorder, confusion, or disturbance; tumult; uproar.

2. a wild, violent public disturbance, or disturbance of the peace, by a number of persons (in law, three or more) assembled together.

3. an unrestrained outburst, as of laughter.

4. a brilliant, vivid display (*of* color).

5. (a) wild, loose living; debauchery; (b) unrestrained revelry; (c) a wild, noisy feast or revel.

Riot Act; an English law, passed in 1715, providing that if twelve or more persons are unlawfully assembled to the disturbance of the public peace they must disperse on proclamation (*reading the Riot Act*) or be held guilty of felony.

to read the riot act to; to command to stop doing something regarded as wrong, warning that disobedience will bring punishment.

to run riot; [orig. of dogs barking on the wrong scent.] (a) to run wild; act without restraint, control, or discipline; (b) to grow in luxuriance or profusion.

rī′ŏt, *v.i.*; rioted, *pt., pp.*; rioting, *ppr.* [OFr. *rioter.*]

1. to take part in a tumult or disturbance of the peace.

2. (a) to live in a wild, loose manner; (b) to engage in unrestrained revelry.

3. to indulge without restraint; to revel (*in* something).

rī′ŏt, *v.t.* to waste (money, time, etc.) in riotous living (usually with *away*).

rī′ŏt·ẽr, *n.* 1. one who lives in a wild, loose manner or engages in unrestrained revelry. [Archaic.]

2. in law, one who engages in a riot; one who disturbs the peace by rioting.

rī′ŏt gun, a short-barreled, repeating shotgun, as used to disperse rioters.

rī′ŏt·ous, *a.* 1. having the nature of a riot, or disturbance of the peace.

2. engaging in or inciting to riot.

3. loud and disorderly; boisterous; uproarious.

4. loose and wild; dissolute; profligate.

5. luxuriant, as growth.

rī′ŏt·ous·ly, *adv.* in a riotous manner.

rī′ŏt·ous·ness, *n.* the state or quality of being riotous.

rī′ŏt·ry, *n.* riot; the practice of rioting.

rip, *v.t.*; ripped (ript), *pt., pp.*; ripping, *ppr.* [Late ME.; prob. from M.D. or L.G.]

1. to cut or tear apart roughly or vigorously, often, as cloth, along a seam.

2. to remove by or as by cutting or tearing roughly or vigorously (with *off, out, away,* etc.).

He'll *rip* the fatal secret from her heart.
—Granville.

3. to produce a rip in; to tear.

4. to tear up for search or disclosure, or for alteration; to search to the bottom: with *up.* [Now Rare.]

They *ripped up* all that had been done from the beginning of the rebellion.
—Clarendon.

5. to saw (wood) in the direction of the grain instead of across it.

to rip off; (a) to steal or rob; (b) to cheat, exploit, or take advantage of. [Slang.]

to rip out; to utter violently or sharply, as in angry exclamation. [Colloq.]

rip, *v.i.* 1. to become torn or split apart, often, as in cloth, along a seam.

2. to move with speed or violence. [Colloq.]

to rip into; to attack violently or sharply, often with words. [Colloq.]

rip, *n.* 1. a torn place; a laceration; a rent; as, a *rip* in a coat.

2. a ripsaw. [Colloq.]

rip, *n.* [Ice. *hrip,* a carrying basket.] a wicker basket for carrying fish. [Dial.]

rip, *n.* [var. of *rep,* prob. abbrev. of *reprobate.*]

1. a dissolute, dissipated person. [Colloq.]

2. an old, worthless horse. [Colloq.]

3. a worthless thing. [Colloq.]

rip, *n.* [Early Mod. Eng.; prob. from *rip* (a torn place).] an extent of rough, broken water caused by the meeting of cross currents or tides.

rip, *n.* an implement for smoothing a scythe after whetting. [Dial.]

ri·pär′i·ăl, *a.* [L. *ripa,* a bank.]

1. riparian.

2. in zoology, riparious.

ri·pär′i·ăn, *a.* 1. of, designating, or situated on the banks of a river, lake, etc.

2. in anatomy, of or relating to a ripa.

riparian nations; nations possessing opposite banks or different parts of banks of the same river.

riparian rights; the legal rights regarding a waterway which belong to one who owns land bordering upon it.

ri·pär′i·ăn, *n.* one who dwells on the banks of a river.

ri·pär′i·ous, *a.* [L. *riparius,* of or belonging to the bank of a river.] in zoology and botany, growing or living along the bank of a stream.

rip çord, 1. a cord fastened to the gas bag of a balloon or dirigible so that pulling it will open the bag, releasing the gas and causing a rapid descent.

2. a cord, etc. for opening a parachute during descent.

rīpe, *a.*; *comp.* riper; *superl.* ripest, [AS. *ripe,* ripe; akin to G. *reif.*]

1. (a) ready for reaping; brought to perfection in growth or to the best state; mature, as grain or fruit; (b) fully grown or developed, as animals ready to be slaughtered for food.

2. advanced to the state of being fit for use; as, *ripe* cheese, *ripe* wine.

3. advanced to a full or high development; matured; finished; consummate; as, a *ripe* experience, *ripe* judgment.

4. in full readiness for action or effect; fully prepared.

I by letters will direct your course
When time is *ripe.* —Shak.

5. resembling ripe fruit, as in ruddiness, juiciness, or plumpness.

O, how *ripe* in show
Thy lips, those kissing cherries, tempting grow! —Shak.

6. ready to open or be lanced; maturated; suppurated; as, a *ripe* boil or abscess.

7. (a) characterized by full physical or mental development; as, a person of *ripe* years; (b) advanced in years; as, the *ripe* age of ninety.

8. ready for some operation, treatment, or process.

9. sufficiently advanced; far enough along (*for* some purpose): said of time.

10. under the influence of liquor; intoxicated. [Obs.]

Syn.—mature, mellow, complete, finished, perfect, prepared, ready.

rīpe, *v.i.* to ripen; to grow ripe; to be matured. [Rare or Poet.]

rīpe, *v.t.* to mature; to ripen. [Rare.]

rīpe′ly, *adv.* maturely; in a ripe manner.

rīp′en (rī′p'n), *v.i.*; ripened, *pt., pp.*; ripening, *ppr.* 1. to grow ripe; to become matured, as grain or fruit.

2. to approach or come to perfection; to be fitted or prepared; as, a project is *ripening* for execution.

rīp′en, *v.t.* 1. to make ripe or cause to mature, as grain or fruit.

2. to bring to maturity; to fit or prepare; to bring to perfection; as, to *ripen* a plan.

rīpe′ness, *n.* the state or quality of being ripe; maturity; full growth; high development; perfection; completeness; fitness; as, the *ripeness* of grain, the *ripeness* of experience.

Time, which made them their fame outlive,
To Cowley scarce did *ripeness* give.
—Denham.

ri·piç′ō·lous, *a.* [L. *ripa,* bank, and *colere,* to inhabit.] dwelling on or inhabiting river banks; riparian.

ri·pid′ō·līte, *n.* [Gr. *rhipis, rhipidos,* a fan, and *-lite.*] a green, translucent mineral of the chlorite family; a hydrous silicate of aluminum and magnesium: also called *clinochlore.*

ri·pi·ē′nist, *n.* a musician who plays in the ripieno, or supplementary, portion of an orchestra.

ri·pi·ē′nō, *a.* [It.] in music, supplementary; reinforcing: said of players or instruments used to swell the mass of an orchestra by merely doubling the parts of the leading instruments.

ri·pi·ē′nō, *n.*; *pl.* **ri·pi·ē′nï,** a ripieno instrument or performer; a supplementary part.

rip′-off, *n.* 1. a stealing, robbing, cheating, exploiting, etc. [Slang.]

2. a means of cheating, exploiting, etc. [Slang.]

ri·pōste′, ri·pōst′, *n.* [Fr. *riposte*; It. *risposta,* from *rispondere*; L. *respondere,* to respond.]

1. in fencing, a sharp, swift thrust made after parrying an opponent's lunge.

2. a sharp, swift return or retort.

ri·pōste′, ri·pōst′, *v.i.*; riposted, *pt., pp.*; riposting, *ppr.* to make a riposte.

rip′pẽr, *n.* 1. a person who rips.

2. a thing that rips; a device or tool for ripping.

3. a double-ripper.

4. some person or thing extraordinarily good or effective of its kind. [Chiefly Brit. Slang.]

rip′ping, *a.* 1. that rips.

2. excellent; fine. [Chiefly Brit. Slang.]

rip′ping saw, a ripsaw.

rip′ple, *v.t.*; rippled, *pt., pp.*; rippling, *ppr.* [ME. *ripplen*; D. *repelen.*] to clear or remove the seeds or capsules from (flax, etc.) with an instrument resembling a comb.

rip′ple, *n.* a large comb or hatchel for separating the seeds or capsules from flax, etc.

rip′ple, *v.i.*; rippled, *pt., pp.*; rippling, *ppr.* [Early Mod. Eng.; orig. of stormy, dangerous water; hence prob. from *rip, v.* and *-le,* freq. suffix.]

1. to form or have little waves or undulating movements on the surface, as water or grass stirred by a breeze.

2. to flow with such waves or movements on the surface.

3. (a) to make a sound like that of rippling water; (b) to proceed with an effect like that of rippling water: said of sound.

rip'ple, *v.t.* 1. to cause to ripple.

2. to give a wavy or undulating form or appearance to.

rip'ple, *n.* 1. a small wave or undulation, as on the surface of water.

2. a movement, appearance, or formation resembling or suggesting this.

3. a sound like that of rippling water.

4. a small rapid.

rip'ple gràss, [Scot. *ripple girse.*] a species of English plantain; rib grass, *Plantago lanceolata.*

rip'ple märk, any of the ripply lines on the surface of sand, mud, etc. caused by waves, wind, or both.

rip'ple-märked, *a.* having ripple marks.

rip'plẽr, *n.* one who or that which ripples flax; specifically, an implement for this.

rip'plet, *n.* a small ripple.

rip'pling·ly, *adv.* in a rippling manner; with ripples.

rip'ply, *a.*; *comp.* ripplier; *superl.* rippliest; characterized by or having ripples; rippling.

rip'rap, *n.* [redupl. echoism formed on *rap* with usual vowel dissimilation.]

1. a foundation or wall made of broken stones thrown together irregularly or loosely, as in water or on a soft bottom.

2. stones used for this.

rip'rap, *v.t.*; riprapped (-rapt), *pt., pp.*; riprapping, *ppr.* to construct a riprap in or on; to strengthen with riprap.

rip-rōar'ing, *a.* very lively and noisy; boisterous; uproarious. [Slang.]

rip'sack, *n.* the California gray whale, *Rachianectes glaucus.*

rip'saw, *n.* a saw with coarse teeth, for cutting wood along the grain.

rip'snort'ẽr, *n.* 1. a very noisy, violent person or thing, as a violent storm. [Slang.]

2. a very striking or remarkable person or thing. [Slang.]

rip'tīde, *n.* [from *rip* (rough water) and *tide.*] a tide opposing another tide or other tides, thus producing a violently disturbed area of water.

Rip·ū·är'i·ăn, *a.* [LL. *ripuarius,* from L. *ripa,* bank.] pertaining to or designating a group of Franks who in the fourth century settled along the Rhine, near Cologne.

Rip·ū·är'i·ăn, *n.* a Ripuarian Frank.

Rip van Wiñ'kle, the main character of a story of the same name by Washington Irving, published in the *Sketch Book* in 1819: Rip sleeps in the Catskill Mountains for twenty years and finds everything changed when he wakes.

rī·sä'lä, *n.* [Anglo-Ind.] in British India, a troop of native irregular horse soldiers.

ris·ăl·där', *n.* [Anglo-Ind.] the officer in command of a risala.

rīse, *v.i.*; rose, *pt.*; risen, *pp.*; rising, *ppr.* [AS. *risan,* to rise, G. *reisen* (of the sun).]

1. to stand or assume a vertical or more nearly vertical position, after sitting, kneeling, or lying.

2. to get up after sleeping or resting.

3. to return to life after dying; as, he *rose* from the grave.

4. to rebel; to revolt; as, the people *rose* against the king.

5. to end an official assembly or meeting; to adjourn; as, the legislature *rose* for vacation.

6. to go to a higher place or position; to ascend.

7. to appear above the horizon; as, the moon *rose.*

8. to attain greater height or a higher level; as, the river *rose* rapidly.

9. to ascend or advance in social status, rank, importance, etc.; to become rich, famous, successful, etc.

10. to become erect or rigid.

11. to make an elevation; to extend upward; as, the building *rose* high above the trees.

12. to have an upward incline or slant; as, the hills *rise* steeply.

13. to swim to the surface of the water in order to take a fly, bait, etc.: said of a fish.

14. to go up in pitch (of sound).

15. to increase in amount, degree, quantity, price, etc.

16. to increase in volume (of sound); to become louder.

17. to become stronger, more vivid, more buoyant, etc.; as, his spirits *rose.*

18. to become larger and puffier, as dough containing yeast.

19. to protrude; stick out; stand out.

20. to originate, begin, or spring up.

21. to have a source: said of a stream.

22. to happen; to occur.

23. to become apparent to the eye or mind; as, land *rose* ahead of the ship, doubts *rose* to disturb him.

24. to become apparent to the ear or nose.

25. to be built; as, a house is *rising* on the hill.

to rise to; to show oneself capable of coping with; as, he *rose to* the occasion.

Syn.—arise, ascend, climb, mount, scale.

rīse, *v.t.* 1. to cause to rise, as birds from cover or a fish to the surface of the water.

2. in nautical usage, to cause to appear above the horizon by coming nearer.

rīse, *n.* 1. the appearance of the sun, moon, etc. above the horizon.

2. upward motion; ascent.

3. an ascent or advance in social status, rank, importance, etc.

4. the appearance of a fish at the water's surface.

5. a return to life.

6. a piece of high or rising ground; a hill.

7. a slope upward.

8. the vertical height of something, as of a flight of stairs or a single step.

9. an increase in height, as of water level.

10. an increase in volume or pitch of a sound.

11. an increase in degree, amount, price, value, etc.

12. a beginning, origin, springing up, etc.

13. a raise (in wages, etc.). [Brit.]

to get a rise out of; to draw a desired response or retort from by teasing or provoking. [Slang.]

to give rise to; to cause to appear or come into existence.

riș'en, *v.* past participle of *rise.*

rīș'ẽr, *n.* 1. one who or that which rises; as, an early *riser.*

2. any of the vertical pieces between the steps in a stairway.

3. a mining shaft excavated upward.

4. in founding, an opening through a mold, into which metal rises as the mold fills.

rish, *n.* a plant, the rush. [Obs.]

riș·i·bil'i·ty, *n.*; *pl.* **riș·i·bil'i·tieș,** 1. the quality or state of being risible; ability or inclination to laugh.

2. [*usually pl.*] a sense of the ridiculous or amusing; appreciation of what is laughable.

riș'i·ble, *a.* [Fr. *risible;* L. *risibilis,* from *ridere,* to laugh.]

1. able or inclined to laugh.

2. of or connected with laughter.

3. causing laughter; laughable; funny; amusing; ludicrous.

Syn.—ludicrous, ridiculous, laughable.

riș'i·ble·ness, *n.* risibility.

riș'i·bly, *adv.* in a risible manner.

rīș'ing, *a.* 1. that rises; going up, ascending, mounting, advancing, sloping upward, etc.

2. advancing to adult years; growing; maturing; as, the *rising* generation.

rīș'ing, *prep.* 1. somewhat over, or more than. [Colloq.]

2. approaching; nearing; as, he was *rising* fifty. [Dial.]

rīș'ing, *n.* 1. the act or process of a person or thing that rises; especially, an uprising; a revolt; insurrection.

2. something that rises; specifically, (a) a projection or prominence; (b) [Dial.] a morbid swelling; a boil, abscess, etc.

3. in nautical usage, a narrow strake in a boat, beneath the thwarts.

4. [*pl.*] in shipbuilding, thick planking supporting the timbers of the decks.

rīș'ing līne, a curved line on the drafts of a ship, marking the height of the floor timbers throughout the length, and thereby fixing the sharpness and flatness of a vessel's bottom.

risk, *n.* [Fr. *risque;* It. *risco.*]

1. the chance of injury, damage, or loss; a dangerous chance; a hazard.

2. in insurance, (a) the chance of loss; (b) the degree of probability of loss; (c) the amount of possible loss to the insuring company: in full, *amount at risk;* (d) a person or thing with reference to the risk involved in insuring him or it; (e) the type of loss that a policy covers, as life, fire, etc.

to run (or *take*) *a risk;* to expose oneself to the chance of injury or loss; to endanger oneself; to take a chance.

Syn.—danger, peril, jeopardy, hazard.

risk, *v.t.*; risked, *pt., pp.*; risking, *ppr.* [Fr. *risquer,* from the *n.*]

1. to expose to the chance of injury, damage, or loss; to hazard; as, we *risked* our lives.

2. to incur the risk of; to take the chance of; as, he *risked* a fight.

risk'ẽr, *n.* one who risks.

risk'fụl, *a.* risky; full of risk.

risk'y, *a.*; *comp.* riskier, *superl.* riskiest, involving risk; dangerous; hazardous.

rī·sō·lụ'tō, *adv.* [It., resolute.] in music, with resolution: a direction to the performer.

Rī·sọr·ġi·men'tō, *n.* [It., lit., resurrection.] the period of or movement for liberation, reform, and unification of Italy from the latter part of the eighteenth century to c. 1870.

rī·sō'ri·ăl, *a.* [LL. *risorius,* laughing; L. *risor,* laughter, from *ridere,* to laugh.] pertaining to laughter; causing laughter; risible.

rī·sọt'tō, *n.* [It.] rice cooked with gravy, grated cheese, etc.

ris·qué' (ris-kā'), *a.* [Fr., pp. of *risquer,* to risk.] very close to being improper or indecent; daring; suggestive; as, a *risqué* anecdote.

ris'soid, *n.* [LL. *Rissoa,* from *Risso,* an Italian naturalist, and *-oid.*] a snail of the family *Rissoidæ,* found in fresh and salt water.

ris'sōle, *n.* [Fr.; ult. from LL. *russeolus,* reddish, from L. *russus,* red.] a small ball or roll of minced meat or fish mixed with bread crumbs, egg, etc., enclosed in a thin pastry and fried.

rī'sus, *n.* [L., from *ridere,* to laugh.] a laugh.

risus sardonicus or *caninus;* in medicine, a grinning expression produced by spasm of the facial muscles.

rī·tär·dän'dō, *a.* [It., gerund of *ritardare,* to retard.] in music, becoming gradually slower: a direction to the performer.

rīte, *n.* [Fr. *rite;* L. *ritus,* a rite.]

1. a ceremonial or formal, solemn act, observance, or procedure in accordance with prescribed rule or custom, as in religious use.

2. any formal, customary observance or procedure; as, the *rites* of courtship.

3. (a) a prescribed form or particular system of ceremonial procedure, religious or otherwise; ritual; as, the Scottish *rite;* (b) [*often* R–] liturgy; especially, any of the historical forms of the Eucharistic service; as, the Anglican *rite.*

4. [*often* R–] a division of (Eastern and Western) churches according to the liturgy used; specifically, a patriarchate.

Syn.—ceremony, ceremonial, form, ordinance.

rī·tẹ·nụ'tō, *a.* [It., pp. of *ritenere,* to retain.] in music, reducing the tempo by degrees; held back: a direction to the performer.

rī·tọr·nelle', rī·tọr·nel'lō, *n.* [It., dim. from *ritorno,* return, from *ritornare,* to return.] in music, (a) a repeat; the refrain of a song, or the repetition of a verse or strain; (b) an intermediate symphony or tutti instrumental passage; an interlude.

rī·trät'tō, *n.* [It.] a picture.

rit'tẽr, *n.* [G., rider, knight.] a knight.

rit'ting·ẽr·īte, *n.* [after Peter *Rittinger,* an Austrian mining official, and *-ite.*] a dark mineral containing arsenic, selenium, silver, and sulfur, occurring in monoclinic crystals.

ritt·màs'tẽr, *n.* [G. *rittmeister,* captain of cavalry.] a cavalry captain. [Rare.]

rit'ū·ăl, *a.* [L. *ritualis,* relating to rites.] of or pertaining to rites; consisting of rites; as, *ritual* law.

rit'ū·ăl, *n.* 1. a set form or system of rites, religious or otherwise.

2. the observance of set forms or rites, as in public worship.

3. a book containing rites or ceremonial forms.

4. a ritual service or procedure.

5. ritual acts or procedures collectively.

rit'ū·ăl·ișm, *n.* 1. the observance or use of, insistence on, or devotion to ritual.

2. the study of religious ritual.

3. the beliefs and practices of those in the Church of England who revived the use of the symbolic ornaments in church services.

rit'ū·ăl·ist, *n.* 1. one skilled or versed in ritual.

2. one who advocates or practices ritualism.

rit'u·ăl·ist, *a.* ritualistic.

rit″ū·ăl·is′tiç, *a.* 1. of ritual or ritualism.
2. devoted to or practicing ritual.

rit″ū·ăl·is′ti·çăl·ly, *adv.* in a ritualistic manner.

rit′ū·ăl·ly, *adv.* with, by, or according to ritual.

ritz′y, *a.*; *comp.* ritzier; *superl.* ritziest, [from any of the palatial hotels in London, Paris, or New York founded by César *Ritz.*] luxurious; fashionable; elegant. [Slang.]

riv′ăġe, *n.* [Fr., from L. *ripa,* bank.]
1. a bank, shore, or coast. [Archaic.]
2. in old English law, a duty or toll on river craft, assessed by the crown.

rī′văl, *n.* [Fr. *rival,* from L. *rivalis,* one who uses the same brook as another, neighbor, rival, associated in L. with *rivus,* brook, stream, but influenced from another (unknown) source.]
1. one who is in pursuit of the same object as another; one striving to reach or obtain something which another is attempting to obtain, and which only one can possess; a competitor; as, *rivals* in love.
2. a person or thing that can reasonably be said to equal or surpass another in some way; a person or thing that can bear comparison; as, plastics have become *rivals* of many metals.
3. an associate or companion in some duty. [Obs.]
Syn.—antagonist, competitor, emulator.

rī′văl, *a.* acting as a rival; competing.

rī′văl, *v.t.*; rivaled *or* rivalled, *pt., pp.*; rivaling *or* rivalling, *ppr.* 1. to try to equal or surpass.
2. to equal in some way; to be a match for; as, he *rivaled* his father in intelligence.

rī′văl, *v.i.* to be a rival or rivals; to compete (*with*). [Archaic.]

rī′văl·ess, *n.* a woman rival. [Rare.]

rī·val′i·ty, *n.* 1. rivalry. [Rare.]
2. equality of rank; partnership. [Obs.]

rī′văl·ry, *n.*; *pl.* **rī′văl·rieṣ,** act of rivaling or fact or condition of being a rival or rivals; competition; emulation.
Syn.—competition, contention, emulation, strife.

rī′văl·ship, *n.* the state or character of a rival; rivalry. [Rare.]

rīve, *v.t.*; rived, *pt.*; rived *or* riven, *pp.*; riving, *ppr.*; [ME. *riven*; ON. *rifa*; Sw. *rifva*; Dan. *rive,* to rive, tear; akin to *reave, rob, rip, reap.*]
1. to tear apart; to rend.
2. to split; to cleave.
3. to break or dismay (the heart, spirit, etc.).
4. to stab; to thrust. [Obs.]

rīve, *v.i.* to be or become rived.

rīve, *n.* 1. a rift; a tear. [Brit. Dial.]
2. something torn, as with the teeth. [Scot.]

rīve, *n.* a bank; a coast. [Obs.]

rīve, *v.i.* to arrive. [Obs.]

riv′el, *v.t.* to contract into wrinkles; to shrink; as, *riveled* flowers. [Obs.]

riv′el, *n.* a wrinkle [Obs.]

riv′en, *v.* alternative past participle of *rive.*

riv′en, *a.* torn apart or split.

rīv′ẽr, *n.* one who or that which rives, or splits.

riv′ẽr, *v.i.* to hunt with hawks beside a river. [Obs.]

riv′ẽr, *n.* [OFr. *riviere*; Fr. *rivière,* a river; It. *riviera,* a bank, shore, a river, from a LL. f. noun *riparia,* a river, from L. *riparius,* of, pertaining to, or frequenting the banks of a river, from *ripa,* a bank or shore.]
1. a natural stream of water larger than a creek and emptying into an ocean, a lake, or another river.
2. any similar or plentiful stream or flow; as, a *river* of lava.
River Brethren; a Mennonite sect that originated in the Susquehanna River Valley during the Revolutionary War: they reject infant baptism, baptize adults by threefold immersion, and practice foot washing.
to sell down the river; to betray, deceive, abuse, etc.: from the former selling of Negro slaves into harsh servitude on the plantations of the lower Mississippi.
up the river; (sent) to or confined in a penitentiary: from the sending of convicts up the Hudson River from New York to Sing Sing. [Slang.]

riv′ẽr·āin, *a.* pertaining to a river bank; riparian.

riv′ẽr bā′sin, the area or basin drained by a river and its tributaries.

riv′ẽr bȧss, the American smallmouthed black bass; any bass of the genus *Micropterus.*

riv′ẽr bed, the bed or bottom of a river.

riv′ẽr bĩrch, a species of the genus *Betula,* having reddish bark, growing along streams in the southeastern United States: also called *red birch.*

riv′ẽr bot′tŏm, the alluvial land through which a river runs; also, the bed of a river.

riv′ẽr chan′nel, the channel of a river.

riv′ẽr çot′tŏn·wood, a species of poplar, with downy leaves, found in the eastern United States: also called *swamp cottonwood.*

riv′ẽr çōurse, the course of a river.

riv′ẽr çrab, any fresh-water crab of the family *Thelphusidæ,* as the edible crab, *Thelphusa depressa,* of southern Europe.

riv′ẽr çrȧft, boats used only on rivers.

riv′ẽr dol′phin, any of various fresh-water dolphins of Asia and South America.

riv′ẽr drag′ŏn, a crocodile: applied figuratively to the king of Egypt.

> Pharaoh, king of Egypt, the great *dragon* that lieth in the midst of his rivers.
> —Ezek. xxix. 3.

riv′ẽr drīv′ẽr, a lumberman who drives logs or rafts down rivers.

riv′ẽr duck, a duck without a membranous lobe on its hind toe, as the mallard.

riv′ẽr·et, *n.* a rivulet. [Obs.]

riv′ẽr flat, an alluvial plain adjacent to or along a river; the area covered by the deposits of a river; a river bottom.

riv′ẽr gāuġe, a vertical post, stake, or column placed at the edge of a river and graduated so as to show the stages of water in the river at different times.

riv′ẽr-god, *n.* a deity supposed to preside over a river as its tutelary divinity.

riv′ẽr·head (-hed), *n.* the source of a river; the place where a river begins, as a spring or a lake.

riv′ẽr her′ring, a fish, the alewife.

riv′ẽr hog, 1. any African wild hog of the genus *Potamochœrus,* found along rivers and in marshes.
2. the capibara.

riv′ẽr·hood, *n.* the condition of being a river. [Rare.]

riv′ẽr hǫrse, the hippopotamus.

riv′ẽr·īne, *a.* 1. on or near the banks of a river; riparian.
2. of, like, or produced by a river or rivers.

riv′ẽr jack, (a) the common water snake of Europe; (b) a venomous African viper, *Clotho nasicornis,* having a spine on the nose.

riv′ẽr·ling, *n.* a small river or stream.

riv′ẽr·măn, *n.*; *pl.* **riv′ẽr·men,** one who earns a livelihood by odd jobs along a river. [Brit.]

riv′ẽr mead′ōw (med′), a meadow adjoining a river.

riv′ẽr mus′sel, a fresh-water bivalve mollusk.

riv′ẽr pẽrch, the common European perch, *Perca fluviatilis.*

riv′ẽr shrew, the otter shrew, *Potamogale velox,* of Africa, the only representative of its genus.

riv′ẽr·sīde, *n.* the bank of a river; the immediate environment of the side of a river.

riv′ẽr·sīde, *a.* on or near the bank of a river.

riv′ẽr sys′tem, a river and its tributaries.

riv′ẽr val′ley, in physical geography, the depression in the bottom of which a river flows, and the drainage of which the river receives.

riv′ẽr·weed, *n.* a plant, *Podostemon ceratophyllus,* growing attached to rocks in running water and having many leathery olive-green leaves.

riv′ẽr wolf (wụlf), the fur-bearing Brazilian otter.

riv′ẽr·y, *a.* full of rivers; abounding with rivers; also, riverlike.

riv′et, *n.* [OFr., from *river,* to clinch, from LL. (hyp.) *ripare,* to make firm (orig., to the shore), from *ripa,* a shore, bank.] a metal bolt or pin with a head on one end, used to fasten together two or more heavy plates or beams by being inserted through holes: the plain end is hammered into a head after insertion.

RIVET
A, rivet holding steel beams together; B, C, D, rivets

riv′et, *v.t.*; riveted, *pt., pp.*; riveting, *ppr.* 1. to fasten with a rivet or rivets.
2. to hammer or spread the end of (a bolt, etc.) into a head, for fastening something.
3. to fasten firmly.
4. to fix or hold (the eyes, attention, etc.) firmly.

riv′et·ẽr, *n.* one who or that which rivets.

riv′et·ing, *n.* 1. the act of fastening with a rivet or rivets.
2. an entire set of rivets and the work in which they are used.
double riveting; riveting in which two rows of rivets are used along a seam.
lap riveting; riveting in which the parts to be fastened by rivets overlap: distinguished from *butt riveting* where the parts jut against each other and are fastened by means of plates laid over the joint and riveted to each piece.
single riveting; riveting in which there is a single row of rivets.
staggered riveting; riveting in which the rivets in one row stand opposite the intervals in the next row: also called *cross-riveting.*
zigzag riveting; riveting in which the rivets are placed zigzag.

ri·vière′ (rē-vyer′), *n.* [Fr., lit., a stream, river.] a necklace, usually in several strands, of diamonds or other precious stones.

rī′vōse, *a.* in zoology, having sinuate and irregular furrows.

riv′ū·let, *n.* [L. *rivulus,* dim. of *rivus,* a stream.] a small stream or brook; a streamlet.

riv′ū·lōse, *a.* in botany, characterized by lines or marks resembling those of rivers on a map.

rix·ā′trix, *n.* [LL., f. of L. *rixator,* a brawler, from *rixatus,* pp. of *rixari,* to brawl.] a scolding woman. [Rare.]

rix′dä″lẽr, *n.* same as *rix-dollar.*

rix′-dol″lăr, *n.* [D. *ryksdaalder*; lit., the dollar of the realm.] formerly, in the Netherlands, Germany, Denmark, etc., any of several silver coins worth about a dollar.

rix′y, *n.*; *pl.* **rix′ieṣ,** a bird, the tern or sea swallow. [Brit. Dial.]

riz′zăr, *v.t.* to half-dry and salt, as fish. [Scot.]

Rn, in chemistry, radon.

RNA, ribonucleic acid.

rōach, *n.* [AS. *reohhe*; D. *roch*; G. *roche.*]
1. a European fish of the carp family, *Leuciscus rutilus,* of small size and gregarious in habits.
2. any of various American fishes resembling or supposed to resemble the roach, as (a) a sunfish of the genus *Lepomis* or *Pomotis*; (b) the lafayette; (c) a species of chub.

rōach, *n.* [Fr. *roche.*] a rock. [Obs.]

rōach, *n.* 1. in nautical usage, the curve or arch cut in the foot of some square sails, to keep the foot clear of stays and ropes.
2. a roll of the hair combed upward from the forehead. [Colloq.]

rōach, *v.t.*; roached (rōcht), *pt., pp.*; roaching, *ppr.* 1. to cause to project or be convex; as, to *roach* up the hair.
2. to trim (the mane of a horse) so as to stand erect.

rōach, *n.* a cockroach.

rōach′-backed (-bakt), *a.* having an arching back; as, a *roach-backed* horse. [Rare.]

rōad, *n.* [AS. *rad, rade,* a ride, a passing or traveling on horseback, a way, a road, from *ridan,* to ride.]
1. a way made for traveling between places, especially distant places, by automobile, horseback, etc.; a highway.
2. a way; path; course; as, the *road* to fortune.
3. a railroad.
4. [*often in pl.*] a protected place near shore, not so enclosed as a harbor, where ships can ride at anchor; a roadstead.
5. a journey on horseback. [Obs.]
6. an inroad; a raid. [Obs.]
on the road; (a) traveling, especially as a salesman; (b) on tour, as a troupe of actors.
the road; all the cities and towns generally visited by touring theatrical companies.
to take to the road; (a) to start traveling; (b) [Archaic.] to become a highwayman.

rōad, *v.t.*; roaded, *pt., pp.*; roading, *ppr.* to track on foot, following by scent: said of dogs.

rōad·ȧ·bil′i·ty, *n.* the degree of operating ease and riding comfort of a vehicle on the road.

rōad ā′ġent, a highwayman, especially as on former stagecoach routes in the western United States.

rōad′bed, *n.* 1. (a) the foundation laid to support the ties and rails of a railroad; (b) a layer of crushed rock, cinders, etc. immediately under the ties.
2. the foundation and surface of a road, or highway.

rōad′block, *n.* 1. in military usage, a blockade of logs, wire, cement, etc., for holding up enemy vehicles at a point covered by heavy fire.
2. any somewhat similar blockade, often of

squad cars, set up by police, as for cutting off the escape route of a fugitive from justice.
rōad′book, *n.* a guidebook.
rōad çärt, a light, two-wheeled conveyance.
rōad′ẽr, *n.* same as *roadster.*
rōad grād′ẽr, a machine used for leveling and grading roads, a common form of which has a suspended strip which may be adjusted to move dirt or gravel as desired.
rōad har′rōw, a machine for dragging over roads to replace the stones or gravel disturbed by the traffic.
rōad hog, a driver who keeps his car, truck, etc. in or near the middle of the road so that it is hard or impossible for others to pass.
rōad′house, *n.* a tavern, an inn, or, especially, a night club at the side of a road in the country.
rōad′iē, *n.* a person hired to travel with a group of rock musicians while they are on the road, for the purpose of handling their equipment, running errands, etc.
rōad′măn, *n.*; *pl.* **rōad′men,** a man who keeps roads in repair: also written *roadsman.*
rōad met′ăl, crushed rock, cinders, etc., used for making and repairing roads and roadbeds.
rōad rōll′ẽr, a heavy cylinder used for compacting the surfaces of roads, a common form consisting of a heavy engine mounted upon rollers instead of wheels.
rōad run′nẽr, a long-tailed desert bird of the southwestern United States, the chaparral cock, characterized by running swiftly instead of flying: related to the cuckoo.
rōad sçrāp′ẽr, a road grader.
rōad′sīde, *n.* the side of a road.
rōad′sīde, *a.* on or at the side of a road.
rōads′măn, *n.* see *roadman.*
rōad′stead (-sted), *n.* a protected place near shore, not so enclosed as a harbor, where ships can ride at anchor: also *road.*
rōad′stẽr, *n.* 1. an open automobile with a single seat for two or three persons: many roadsters have a rumble seat as well.
2. a horse for riding or driving on the road.
3. formerly, a bicycle or tricycle for road use.
rōad test, a manufacturer's test of a finished vehicle, conducted on a public highway.
rōad′wāy, *n.* 1. a road.
2. that part of a road used by cars, trucks, etc.; the traveled part of a road.
rōam, *v.i.*; roamed, *pt., pp.*; roaming, *ppr.* [ME. *romen, ramen,* to spread out; akin to AS. *aræman,* to rise.] to wander; to ramble; to rove; to go aimlessly; to walk or move about from place to place without any certain purpose or direction.
Daphne *roaming* through a thorny wood. —Shak.
Syn.—ramble, range, rove, stroll, wander.
rōam, *v.t.* to range; to wander over or through; as, to *roam* the woods.
rōam, *n.* a ramble; a roaming.
rōam′ẽr, *n.* one who roams.
rōan, *a.* [OFr. *roan*; Fr. *rouan*; It. *roano, rovano*; Sp. *ruano, roano,* the color of a horse having a mixture of bay and gray hairs; prob. ult. from L. *ravidus,* grayish, from *ravus,* grayish-yellow, tawny.] grayish-yellow or reddish-brown with spots of gray or white thickly interspersed: applied chiefly to a horse.
rōan, *n.* a roan color; also, an animal of a roan color.
rōan, *n.* [M. Scot.] in bookbinding, a kind of flexible sheepskin, often treated to look like morocco.
rōan, *a.* made of or bound in roan.
rō·ȧ·nōke′, *n.* [Am. Ind.] a kind of money made of small pieces of shells, formerly used by the American Indians in Virginia and other colonies.
rōar, *v.i.*; roared, *pt., pp.*; roaring, *ppr.* [ME. *roren*; AS. *rarian,* to lament, cry out. A reduplicated imitative form from the root *ra,* to bellow.]
1. to cry with a full, loud, rumbling sound; to bellow, as a beast; as, a *roaring* bull, a *roaring* lion.
2. to cry aloud, as in distress or anger.
3. to make a loud, continued, confused sound in moving, operating, etc., as a motor or gun.
4. to laugh or talk loudly and boisterously; as, the audience *roared* at his jokes.
5. to make a loud noise in breathing, as horses having the disease called *roaring.*
6. to resound with a noisy din.
rōar, *v.t.* 1. to cry aloud; to make known or proclaim loudly; to shout; as, they *roared* a welcome.
2. to make, put, force, etc. by roaring; as, the spectators *roared* themselves hoarse.
rōar, *n.* 1. a loud, deep sound, as of a bull, lion, person shouting, etc.; the sound of roaring.
2. a loud burst of laughter.
3. a loud noise, as of waves, a storm, a motor, etc.; a din.
rōar′ing, *n.* 1. the act of an animal, person, etc. that roars; also, the loud, deep sound so made.
I hear the *roaring* of the sea. —Tennyson.
2. a disease of the bronchial tubes in horses, which causes them to make a rasping noise in breathing under exertion.
rōar′ing, *a.* 1. characterized by or making a loud noise or roar.
2. disorderly; riotous.
3. going briskly; very active or successful; as, a *roaring* trade. [Colloq.]
roaring boy; a noisy, riotous ruffian. [Obs.]
rōar′ing for′ties, 1. the stormy areas of ocean, north and south, between the fortieth and fiftieth parallels of latitude.
2. the region between Fortieth and Fiftieth Streets along Broadway, in New York City.
rōar′ing·ly, *adv.* in a roaring manner.
rōast, *v.t.*; roasted, *pt., pp.*; roasting, *ppr.* [OFr. *rostir* (Fr. *rôtir*); O.H.G. *rosten,* from *rost,* gridiron, roast.]
1. originally, to cook (meat, etc.) over an open fire or in hot ashes, etc.
2. to cook (meat, etc.) by dry heat, as in an oven.
3. to dry and parch by exposure to heat; as, to *roast* coffee.
4. to heat to excess; to heat violently.
5. to heat, as ores, with access of air in a furnace in order to remove impurities or effect oxidation.
6. to warm (oneself), as at a fireplace.
7. to criticize severely; to ridicule unmercifully. [Colloq.]
rōast, *v.i.* 1. to cook meat, etc. by roasting.
2. to become roasted; to undergo roasting.
3. to become very hot.
rōast, *a.* roasted; as, *roast* beef.
roast-beef plant; the *Iris fœtidissima* of western Europe, the leaves of which, when bruised, have an odor similar to that of roast beef.
rōast, *n.* 1. that which is roasted, especially roasted meat or a piece of roasted meat.
2. a cut of meat for roasting.
3. a roasting or being roasted.
4. a picnic, or out-of-door entertainment, at which food is roasted and eaten; as, a steak *roast.* [Colloq.]
5. harsh criticism; severe chaffing. [Colloq.]
rōast′ẽr, *n.* 1. one who or that which roasts.
2. a special pan, oven, or apparatus for roasting meat, etc.
3. a young pig, chicken, etc. suitable for roasting.
4. a finishing furnace used in roasting certain ores.
rōast′ing ēar, an ear of corn fit for roasting, having fully developed milky grains in which the process of hardening has not begun.
rōast′ing jack, an old-fashioned device for turning the spit on which meat was roasted before an open fire.
rob, *n.* [Fr., Sp., from Ar. *rauba,* to be thick.] the thickened juice of ripe fruit, mixed with honey or sugar to the consistency of a sirup.
rob, *v.t.*; robbed, *pt., pp.*; robbing, *ppr.* [OFr. *rober*; O.H.G. *roubon.*]
1. to take property from unlawfully by using or threatening force and violence; to commit robbery upon.
2. to deprive of something legally belonging or due, or take or withhold something from unjustly or injuriously, as by stealth or fraud.
3. to plunder; to pillage; to rifle.
4. to ravish. [Rare.]
5. to steal; to seize unlawfully; as, to *rob* apples from an orchard. [Rare.]
Cf. *steal.*
to rob Peter to pay Paul; to satisfy one debt by incurring another.
rob, *v.i.* to commit robbery; to be a robber.
rob′ȧ·lō, *n.*; *pl.* **rob′ȧ·lōs,** *or* **rob′ȧ·lō,** [Sp. *róbalo* or Port. *robalo,* from Catal. *elobarro*; ult. from L. *lupus,* a wolf.] any of a family of tropical American sea fishes, especially the largest species, valued as a food fish.
rob′ănd, *n.* [earlier *raband* and *robbin*; ult. from ON. *rābenda,* to bend a sail on a yard; *rā,* sailyard, and *benda,* to bend, bind.] a short piece of spun yarn or rope, used to fasten the head of a sail to a yard, gaff, etc.
rob′bẽr, *n.* one who robs; one who commits a robbery.
Syn.—thief, depredator, despoiler, plunderer, pillager, rifler, brigand, freebooter, pirate.
rob′bẽr bar′ŏn, a nobleman of feudal times who robbed people traveling through his domain.
rob′bẽr çrab, a crab of the family *Paguridæ*; especially, *Birgus latro,* the purse crab; loosely, any hermit crab.
rob′bẽr flȳ, any of a group of flies, generally large, that prey on other insects.
rob′bẽr gull, a robber bird of the gull family; a jaeger.
rob′bẽr·y, *n.*; *pl.* **rob′bẽr·ies,** the act or practice of robbing; specifically, in law, the forcible and felonious taking of another's property from his person or in his immediate presence by the use of violence or intimidation.
Syn.—theft, depredation, spoliation, despoliation, despoilment, plunder, pillage, freebooting, piracy.
rob′bin, *n.* in commerce, a package in which pepper and other dry products are imported. [Rare.]
rob′bin, *n.* same as *roband.*
rōbe, *n.* [OFr. *robe,* from LL. *rauba,* spoil, the taking of a man's garments, from O.H.G. *raub,* a garment, spoil, which in primitive times consisted chiefly of articles of dress.]
1. a kind of gown or long loose garment worn over other dress, especially by persons in high position, or engaged in any ceremonial, ordinance, or rite; a gown of state or office, as of judges, priests, etc.
2. a bathrobe or dressing gown.
3. a woman's gown or dress, especially an elaborate or elegant one.
4. [*pl.*] clothes; apparel or dress in general; costume.
5. a covering or wrap, as of fur, cloth, etc.; as, a lap *robe.*
Master of the Robes; an officer in the English royal household who is in charge of the sovereign's robes.
Mistress of the Robes; a lady of high rank in the English royal household, charged with the care of the Queen's wardrobe.
rōbe, *v.t.*; robed, *pt., pp.*; robing, *ppr.* to invest with a robe or robes; to dress; to array.
rōbe, *v.i.* to put on robes; to array oneself in a robe or robes.
rōbe dē çhäm′bre, rōbe-dē-çhäm′bre (-shoṅ′br), *n.* [Fr.] a dressing gown.
rōbe-dē-nuit′ (-nü′y′), *n.* [Fr.] a nightgown.
rob′ẽrd, *n.* the chaffinch. [Brit.]
Rob′ẽrds·men, *n.* a class of marauding vagabonds in fourteenth-century England. [Obs.]
rob′ẽrt, *n.* same as *herb Robert.*
rob′in, *n.* [from OFr. *Robin,* dim. of *Robert.*]
1. a small European thrush, *Erythacus rubecula,* with a yellowish-red breast.
2. in North America, a thrush, *Merula migratoria* (or *Turdus migratorius*), with a dull-red breast and belly.
3. any of many other birds similar to either robin, as (a) in India, any of various chats of the genera *Pratincola* and *Thamnobia,* especially *Thamnobia fulicata*; (b) in Australia, any of various flycatchers of the genus *Petræca,* especially the scarlet-breasted robin, *Petræca multicolor.*
4. any of various fishes; especially, the sea robin.
5. any of various plants, as (a) the ragged robin, *Lychnis Flos-cuculi*; (b) the herb Robert; (c) the wake-robin.
blue-throated robin; the bluethroat.
Canada robin; the cedar bird.
ground robin; the chewink.
magpie robin; an East Indian thrushlike bird.
red robin; the scarlet tanager.
rob′in aç·cen′tŏr, a small Asiatic songster, *Accentor rubeculoides,* resembling the English robin in the color of its breast.
rob′in breast (brest), the robin snipe.
rob′in dip′pẽr, the buffle duck. [Dial.]
rob′i·net, *n.* 1. the European robin. [Brit. Dial.]
2. a chaffinch.
3. a faucet; a tap; a cock, as on an engine.
Rob′in Good′fel″lōw, in English folklore, a mischievous elf or fairy believed to play tricks on people: identified with Puck.

Rob′in Hood, in English legend, a traditional outlaw of the 12th century who lived with his followers in Sherwood Forest and robbed the rich to help the poor: he is the hero of many ballads and tales, celebrated for his courage, gaiety, courtesy, skill as an archer, etc.

Rō·bin′i·ȧ, *n.* [from Jean *Robin*, a Fr. botanist, who introduced the trees to Europe in 1635.] a small genus of the *Leguminosæ*, the locusts, comprising North American trees or shrubs, often with prickly spines for stipules, and odd-pinnate leaves. The best-known species is the *Robinia pseudacacia*, the false acacia, or black locust tree.

rob′in snīpe, the knot, or red-breasted sandpiper.

Rob′in·sŏn Çrū′sōe, the hero of Daniel Defoe's novel (1719) of the same name, an English sailor who, when shipwrecked on a tropical island, manages to live for years by various ingenious contrivances until he is rescued.

rō′blę, *n.* 1. the *Quercus lobata*, or white oak of California.

2. any of several other trees of the oak family, beech family, etc.

rō′bomb (-bom), *n.* a robot bomb.

rob′ō·rănt, *a.* strengthening.

rob′ō·rănt, *n.* a medicine that strengthens; a tonic.

rob′ō·rāte, *v.t.* to furnish strength to. [Obs.]

rob·ō·rā′tion, *n.* a strengthening. [Obs.]

rō′bŏt, *n.* 1. any of the manlike mechanical beings manufactured by Rossum in Karel Čapek's play R. U. R. (Rossum's Universal Robots), to do manual work for human beings.

2. (a) an automaton; (b) a person who acts or works mechanically and without thinking for himself.

rō′bŏt bomb (bom), a small, jet-propelled airplane steered by a gyropilot and loaded with high explosives: it falls as a bomb when its fuel is used up.

rō′bŏt pī′lŏt, a device that serves as an automatic pilot, as in an airplane.

rō′bŭr·īte, *n.* [L. *robur*, strength; and *-ite*.] a very powerful, flameless explosive containing chlorinated dinitrobenzene and ammonium nitrate: it is used especially in mining.

rō·bust′, *a.* [Fr., from L. *robustus*, from *robus*, an old form of *robur*, an oak, or strength.]

1. having or exhibiting sound health or great strength; strong; vigorous; also, strongly built; sturdy; muscular.

2. coarse; boisterous; rough; rude.

3. suited to or requiring physical strength or stamina; as, *robust* work.

Syn.—sound, lusty, vigorous, hale, hearty.

rō·bus′tious, *a.* 1. strong; sturdy; stout. [Archaic or Humorous.]

2. rough; rude; coarse; boisterous. [Archaic or Humorous.]

rō·bus′tious·ly, *adv.* in a robustious manner.

rō·bus′tious·ness, *n.* the state or quality of being robustious.

rō·bust′ly, *adv.* in a robust manner.

rō·bust′ness, *n.* the state or quality of being robust.

roç, *n.* [Fr., from the Per.] in Arabian and Persian legend, a fabulous bird of prey, so huge and strong that it could carry off the largest of animals.

rō·çaille′ (-kä′y′), *n.* [Fr., from *roche*, rock.] a conventional artistic representation of rockwork, in vogue in France as a decoration in the time of Louis XV; also, a kind of rococo or scroll ornament.

roç′ăm·bōle, *n.* [Fr., from G. *rockenbollen*; *rocken*, rye, and *bolle*, a bulb; so called because it grows among rye.] a European leek, the *Allium scorodoprasum*, a plant used like garlic for seasoning.

Roç·cel′lȧ, *n.* [LL. form of Fr. *orseille*, archil.] a genus of lichens, from a species of which, *Roccella tinctoria*, the dye archil is obtained.

roç·cel′liç, *a.* related to or derived from lichens of the genus *Roccella*.

roccellic acid; an acid obtained from the *Roccella tinctoria*, or archil weed.

roç·cel′lin, *n.* a coal-tar derivative used as a substitute for archil and cochineal in dyeing red.

roç·cel′line, *a.* of or pertaining to the genus *Roccella*.

Roch′dāle prin′ci·pleş, principles for the operation of a consumers' co-operative store, as formulated by the Rochdale Pioneers, one of the first co-operative groups in England: they include selling for cash at current market prices, distribution of profits among members, and democratic control.

rōche, *n.* [Fr.] a rock. [Obs.]

Rō′çhē·ȧ, *n.* [from Francis *Laroche*, a French naturalist.] a genus of South African plants belonging to the order *Crassulaceæ*, characterized by its showy varicolored flowers.

roche al′um, a pure form of alum occurring in natural crystalline fragments.

rōçhe′līme, *n.* [Fr. *roche*, rock.] quicklime, especially when in lumps.

Rō·çhelle′ pow′dẽr, Seidlitz powder.

Rō·çhelle′ sạlt, [after *Rochelle*, France: so named because discovered by Seignette, an apothecary in Rochelle.] a colorless, crystalline compound, potassium sodium tartrate, $KNaC_4H_4O_6 \cdot 4H_2O$, used as a laxative.

roche mou·ton·née′ (rōsh mö-tôn-nā′), [Fr., sheepback rock.] a rock worn into a smooth, rounded form by glacial action.

roch′et, *n.* [ME. *rochet*, from O.H.G. *roch*; Ice. *rokkr*, frock or coat; Ir. *rocan*, cloak; Gael. *rochall*, coverlet.] a sort of short linen surplice, with tight sleeves, and open at the sides, worn by bishops and some other church dignitaries.

roch′et, *n.* a kind of gurnard.

rock, *n.* [ME. *rokke*, from Ice. *rokkr*, a distaff.] a distaff used in spinning; the staff or frame about which flax is arranged and from which the thread is drawn in spinning.

rock, *v.t.*; rocked (rokt), *pt., pp.*; rocking, *ppr.* [ME. *rokken*; AS. *roccian*; prob. akin to G. *rücken*, to pull, push.]

1. to move or sway back and forth or from side to side, especially in a gentle, quieting manner, as a cradle, or a child in the arms.

2. to bring into a specified condition by moving or swaying in this way; as, she *rocked* the baby asleep: also used figuratively, as *rocked* into a false sense of security.

3. to move or sway strongly; to shake; to cause to tremble or vibrate; as, the explosion *rocked* the house.

4. in mezzotint engraving, to prepare the surface of (a plate) by roughening with a rocker (sense 5).

5. in mining, to wash (sand or gravel) in a rocker (sense 4).

rock, *v.i.* 1. to move or sway back and forth or from side to side in or as in a cradle.

2. to move or sway strongly; to shake; to vibrate.

3. to be rocked, as ore.

rock, *n.* 1. the act of rocking.

2. a rocking motion.

3. (a) same as *rock-and-roll;* (b) popular music evolved from rock-and-roll, variously containing elements of folk music, the blues, etc.

rock, *n.* [OFr. *roche*; cf. AS. *-rocc*, ML. *rocca*.]

1. a large mass of stone forming a peak or cliff.

2. (a) stone in the mass; (b) broken pieces of such stone.

3. (a) mineral matter variously composed, formed in masses or large quantities in the earth's crust by the action of heat, water, etc.; (b) a particular kind or mass of this.

4. anything like or suggesting a rock, as in strength or stability; especially, a firm support, basis, refuge, etc.

5. any cause of wreck or destruction; as, the *rock* upon which one breaks: in allusion to a ship.

6. a kind of hard, insoluble, soapy compound formed by the action of lime on fats.

7. the rockfish.

8. the rock dove.

9. a type of hard candy. [Chiefly Brit.]

10. a stone, whether large or small. [Colloq. or Dial.]

11. (a) [*usually in pl.*] a piece of money; as, a pocket full of *rocks*; (b) a diamond or other gem. [Slang.]

on the rocks; (a) out of money; (b) in or into a condition of ruin or catastrophe. [Colloq.]

rock al′um, the purest kind of alum.

rock′-ănd-rōll′, *n.* a form of popular music, characterized by a strong and regular rhythm, which evolved from jazz and the blues.

rock′ȧ·wāy, *n.* a light horse-drawn carriage with four wheels, open sides, and a standing top.

rock bär′nȧ·çle, a barnacle adhering to rocks along a shore, as *Balanus balanoides*.

rock bā′sin (-sn), a cavity or basin in solid rock.

rock bass, a fresh-water food fish of the sunfish family, found in eastern North America.

rock beaū′ty (bū′), a cruciferous alpine plant, *Draba pyrenaica*, noted for the beauty and fragrance of its flowers.

rock black′bīrd, the ring ouzel. [Brit.]

rock′-bot′tŏm, *a.* at rock bottom; lowest possible.

rock bot′tŏm, the very bottom; the lowest limit; as, prices have gone down to *rock bottom*.

rock′-bound, *a.* hemmed in by rocks.

rock brāke, any fern belonging to the genus *Pellæa*; especially, the parsley fern.

rock but′tẽr, a butterlike exudation from rocks, containing aluminum and iron.

rock can′dy, large, hard, clear crystals of sugar.

rock′cist, *n.* any plant of the genus *Helianthemum*; frostweed.

rock çod, 1. any one of several species of food fishes of the genus *Scorpæna*, native to Australian waters.

2. a small cod found around rocks; a kind of rockfish.

rock çork, a variety of asbestos resembling cork in its texture.

rock çrab, a crab living in rocky places, as the *Cancer borealis* of the New England coast.

rock çress, a plant of the genus *Arabis*.

rock çrys′tăl, a transparent quartz, especially when colorless.

rock dŏve, the common wild pigeon of Europe, living and nesting along rocky coasts.

rock drill, a drill for driving holes into rock, operated either by hand or by artificial power.

rock duck, same as *harlequin duck*.

rock eel, a smooth-bodied elongated fish, *Murænoides gunnellus*, inhabiting the North Atlantic and other northern waters.

rock′ē·lāy, rock′lāy, *n.* same as *roquelaure*.

rock′ẽr, *n.* 1. a person who rocks, as a cradle.

2. either of the curved pieces on the bottom of a cradle, rocking chair, etc.

3. a rocking chair.

4. a cradle for washing sand or gravel in gold mining.

5. a device consisting of a small steel plate with a toothed and curved edge, for roughening and thus preparing the surface of a plate to be engraved.

6. a skate with a curved blade.

rock′ẽr, *n.* same as *rock dove*.

rock′ẽr ärm, any one of the arms attached to a rock shaft.

rock′ẽred, *a.* having the shape of a rocker; as, a *rockered* keel of a ship.

rock′ẽr·y, *n.*; *pl.* **rock′ẽr·ieş,** a formation of fragments of rocks, soil, etc., about and among which plants are grown; a rock garden.

rock′et, *n.* [It. *rocchetta*, spool or bobbin, a rocket; dim. of *rocca*, a distaff; O.H.G. *roccho*, a distaff.]

1. a projectile consisting of a cylinder filled with a combustible substance which when ignited produces gases that escape through a vent in the rear and drive their container forward by the principle of reaction. Rockets are used as fireworks, signals, and weapons; in World War II rocket bombs proved to be effective military weapons.

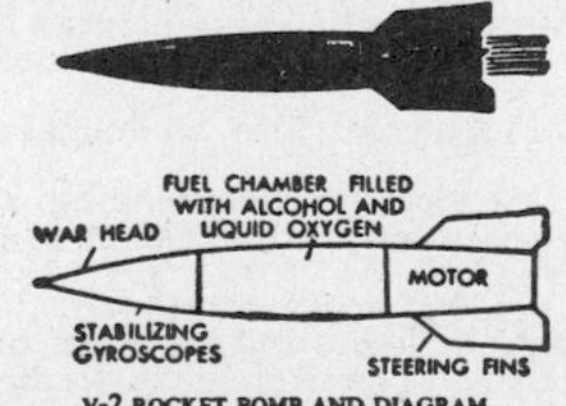

V-2 ROCKET BOMB AND DIAGRAM

2. a tilting spear having its point covered so as to prevent injury.

Congreve rocket; a destructive rocket, now no longer used, invented by Sir William Congreve. It was filled with highly inflammable materials, or with an explosive charge.

rock′et, *v.i.* 1. to go like a rocket; to dart ahead swiftly.

2. to fly swiftly and almost straight up when flushed: said of game birds.

rock′et, *n.* [Fr. *roquette*; It. *ruchetta*, dim. of *ruca*, a garden rocket, from L. *eruca*, a colewort.]

1. any of various plants of the genus *Hesperis* with white, pink, yellow, or purple flowers, as *Hesperis matronalis*, the dame's violet.

2. a European plant, *Eruca sativa*, grown like spinach and used in salads.

3. a weed found in some parts of the United States.

bastard rocket; *Brassica erucastrum*, a European weed.

dyer's rocket; dyer's-weed, *Reseda luteola*.

yellow rocket; the *Barbarea vulgaris*.

rock'et·ẽr, *n.* a bird that rockets.

rock'et gun, any weapon that launches a rocket projectile; especially, a bazooka.

rock'et lärk'spûr, a showy annual larkspur, *Delphinium ajacis*.

rock'et launch'ẽr, a device for launching rockets; specifically, in military usage, a bazooka.

rock fal'cŏn, same as *merlin*.

Rock fē'vẽr, [from *Rock* of Gibralter, where the disease is prevalent.] undulant fever.

rock'fish, *n.* any one of several fishes living in rocky places, as (a) the priestfish; (b) any of various food fishes of the North Pacific, as the rock cod; (c) any of several groupers of the waters around Bermuda, Florida, etc. (d) the striped bass; (e) a killifish; (f) the log perch.

rock flour, the pulverized rock formed by the grinding action of a glacier on its bed.

rock gär'den, a garden with flowers and plants growing on rocky ground or among rocks variously arranged.

rock gas, natural gas.

rock gōat, the ibex.

rock grouse, same as *rock ptarmigan*.

rock gûr'net, any Australian food fish of the genus *Centropogon*, particularly *Centropogon australis*.

rock'hâir, *n.* a delicate lichen, *Alectoria jubata*, which grows upon rocks in tufts.

rock'i·ness, *n.* the state or quality of being rocky.

rock'ing, *n.* the act of swinging or swaying backward and forward.

rock'ing châir, a chair mounted on rockers or springs, so as to allow a rocking movement.

rock'ing horse, a child's toy horse fitted with rockers or springs.

rock'ing shaft, same as *rock shaft*.

rock'ing stōne, a stone, often of great size and weight, so exactly poised on its foundation that it can be rocked, or slightly moved, with but little force.

rock kañ·gȧ·roo', a kangaroo living in rocky places.

rock kelp, a kind of seaweed; rockweed.

rock lärk, a kind of European pipit, *Anthus obscurus*.

rock'less, *a.* being without rocks.

rock lil'y, a fernlike plant of tropical America, *Selaginella convoluta*, growing in crowded bunches or tufts.

rock'ling, *n.* any small marine fish of either of the genera *Rhinonemus* or *Onos*, characterized by three or four barbels.

rock lob'stẽr, any of several large sea lobsters, distinguished by a spiny covering and the absence of the large claw.

rock man'ȧ·kin, same as *cock of the rock* under *cock*.

rock milk, a light, chalky variety of carbonate of lime deposited from water: also called *agaric mineral*.

rock moss, a lichen, *Lecanora tartarea*, abounding on rocks in the alpine districts of Europe.

rock oil, petroleum. [Chiefly Brit.]

rock par'ȧ·keet, a grass parakeet of Australia, *Euphema petrophila*, which builds its nest in a hole or crevice of a cliff.

rock pig'eŏn, a species of pigeon, *Columba livia*, found in Europe, Asia, and Africa: also called *rock dove*.

rock pip'it, the sea lark of Europe, *Anthus obscurus*.

rock plant, a plant distinguished by growing on or among rocks.

rock plant of St. Helena; same as *petrobium*.

rock plŏv'ẽr, any of the whistling plovers, *Squatarola helvetica*; also, the American sandpiper.

rock ptär'mi·găn (tär'), an arctic bird, *Lagopus rupestris*, which, in winter, changes its summer plumage, of a grayish-brown color, to white.

rock rab'bit, a small animal of the genus *Hyrax*; a hyrax.

rock'-ribbed, *a.* 1. having rocky ridges or elevations; as, *rock-ribbed* coasts.

2. firm; rigid; unyielding; as, a *rock-ribbed* policy.

rock'rōse, *n.* a plant of either of the genera *Helianthemum* or *Cistus*, bearing large roselike flowers of white, purple, or red; also, the flower of this plant.

Australian rockrose; a shrubby Australian plant bearing roselike flowers with thick and richly colored petals.

Cretan rockrose; a shrub, *Cistus creticus*, related to the rockrose and yielding labdanum.

rock rû'by, a fine reddish variety of garnet.

rock salm'ŏn (sam'), 1. any fish of the genus *Seriola* of the southern United States, as *Seriola carolinensis*.

2. in England, any fish of the genus *Pollock*, as *Pollock carbonarius*: also called *coalfish*.

rock salt, common salt (sodium chloride) occurring in solid form, especially in rocklike masses.

rock seal, same as *harbor seal*.

rock sẽr'pent, a rock snake.

rock shȧft, a shaft that rocks or oscillates on its journals rather than revolving, carrying arms or levers for reciprocating motion, as in a locomotive.

rock snāke, any one of many large snakes of the genus *Python*, especially *Python molurus*, of India.

rock snīpe, same as *rock plover*.

rock sōap, a kind of clay having the characteristics of soap: it is a hydrated silicate of aluminum.

rock spar'rōw, a sparrow of the genus *Petronia*, as *Petronia stulta*; also, a sparrow of the North American genus *Peucæa*, as *Peucæa ruficeps*.

rock staff, in machinery, a staff or lever that oscillates or has a rocking motion on a pivotal point.

rock suck'ẽr, a lamprey.

rock tär, petroleum.

rock thrush, any thrush belonging to the genus *Monticola* or *Petrocossyphus*.

rock trout, any species of marine trout belonging to the genus *Hexagrammus*.

rock war'blẽr, a singing bird of Australia, *Origma rubricata*, frequenting rocky ravines.

rock'weed, *n.* any of a number of seaweeds growing upon rocks.

rock'wood, *n.* ligniform asbestos; also, fossilized wood.

rock wool, mineral wool; a fibrous insulating material made by blowing steam through molten siliceous rock: it has the appearance of spun glass.

rock'wŏrk, *n.* 1. a wall formed of stones fixed in mortar and having a rough surface.

2. a rock garden.

rock wren (ren), 1. a South American songbird, *Hylactes tarni*.

2. a wren of the genus *Salpinctes*, inhabiting the dry regions of Mexico and the western parts of the United States.

rock'y, *a.*; *comp.* rockier; *superl.* rockiest, 1. inclined to rock, or sway; unsteady; shaky.

2. weak and dizzy, as from dissipation. [Slang.]

rock'y, *a.* 1. full of or containing rocks; as, a *rocky* mountain; a *rocky* shore.

2. consisting of rock.

3. like or suggesting a rock; specifically, (a) firm; stable; (b) hard; unfeeling; as, a *rocky* heart.

Rocky Mountain goat; a white, goatlike antelope of the mountains of northwestern North America, with a thick, shaggy coat and a pair of black horns.

Rocky Mountain grape; the Oregon grape.

Rocky Mountain locust; a predatory locust or grasshopper, *Caloptenus spretus*, abounding in the western part of the United States.

Rocky Mountain sheep; same as *bighorn*.

Rocky Mountain spotted fever; an acute, infectious disease caused by Rickettsia transmitted by ticks, peculiar to the territory in and around the Rocky Mountains; characterized by muscular and articular pain, fever, and spotty, red skin eruptions: it is also epidemic in other parts of the United States.

rō·çō'çō, *n.* [Fr., from *rocaille*, rockwork.]

1. a style of architecture and decoration developed in France from the baroque and characterized primarily by elaborate and profuse ornamentation imitating foliage, rockwork, shellwork, scrolls, etc., often done with much delicacy and refinement: it was popular especially in the first half of the 18th century.

2. a style of literature, etc. regarded, often disparagingly, as like this.

rō·çō'çō, *a.* 1. of or in rococo.

2. too profuse and elaborate in ornamentation; florid and tasteless.

roç'tȧ, *n.* [LL., from the Celtic *crot* or *cruit*, a fiddle.] a medieval musical instrument much like a violin.

rod, *n.* [ME. *rod*, from *rood*; AS. *rod*, a cross, beam, or rod; akin to L. *rudis*, a rod, staff.]

1. a shoot or slender stem of any woody plant, especially when cut off and stripped of leaves or twigs.

2. in Biblical use, an offshoot or branch of a family or tribe; stock or race; as, the *rod* of Isaiah.

3. any straight, or almost straight, stick, shaft, bar, staff, etc., of wood, metal, or other material.

4. (a) a stick or switch, or a bundle of sticks or switches, for whipping or beating as punishment; (b) punishment; chastisement.

5. a kind of scepter or badge of office; as, the usher's *rod*; hence, authority; power.

6. a long, slender pole for fishing or angling; a fishing rod.

7. a measure of length equal to $5\frac{1}{2}$ yards, or $16\frac{1}{2}$ feet: also called a *pole* or *perch*. A square rod is equal to $30\frac{1}{4}$ square yards.

8. a scale of wood or metal employed in measuring something.

9. a pistol or revolver. [Slang.]

10. in anatomy, any of the rod-shaped cells in the retina of the eye that are sensitive to dim light.

11. in bacteriology, any microorganism shaped like a rod.

rods of Corti; two sets of stiff rods, the inner and outer rods of Corti, within the epithelium of the organ of Corti covering the basilar membrane of the ear.

to spare the rod; to refrain from punishing.

rod'den, *n.* rowan. [Scot.]

rōde, *v.* past tense and archaic past participle of *ride*.

rō'dent, *a.* [L. *rodens* (*-entis*), gnawing.] gnawing; also, belonging or pertaining to the order *Rodentia*.

rodent ulcer; a carcinomatous ulcer, generally on the face, which gradually eats away the soft tissues and bones.

rō'dent, *n.* any mammal of the order *Rodentia*; especially, in popular usage, a rat or mouse.

Rō·den'ti·ȧ (-shi-), *n.pl.* [L. *rodens* (*-entis*), from *rodere*, to gnaw.] an order of mammals having two (rarely four) large incisor teeth in each jaw, adapted for gnawing or nibbling: they have no canine teeth, and the incisors grow continually from persistent pulps. The rat, mouse, squirrel, marmot, muskrat, beaver, etc. belong to this order. Also called *Glires*.

rō·den'tiăl, *a.* of or pertaining to the *Rodentia*. [Rare.]

rō'dē·ō (*or* rō-dā'ō), *n.*; *pl.* **rō'dē·ōs,** [Sp., a place for cattle at a market or fair.]

1. the driving together of cattle for branding, etc.; a roundup.

2. an enclosure for cattle that have been rounded up.

3. an exhibition or competition of the skills of cowboys, as horsemanship, lassoing, etc., for public entertainment.

rodġe, *n.* the gadwall. [Brit.]

rod'măn, *n.*; *pl.* **rod'men,** one who carries or works with a rod; specifically, one who carries a leveling rod for surveyors.

rod'ō·mont, *n.* a vain boaster; a braggart.

rod'ō·mont, *a.* bragging; vainly boasting.

rod″ō·mon·tāde', *n.* [Fr., from It. *rodomonte*, a bully, from *Rodomonte*, the boastful leader of the Saracens against Charlemagne, in Ariosto's *Orlando Furioso*.] vain boasting or bragging, arrogant boasting, or blusterous, ranting talk.

rod″ō·mon·tāde', *v.i.*; rodomontaded, *pt., pp.*; rodomontading, *ppr.* to boast; to brag; to bluster; to rant.

rod″ō·mon·tā'dist, *n.* a blustering boaster; one who brags.

rod″ō·mon·tā'dō, *n.* rodomontade. [Obs.]

rod″ō·mon·tā'dŏr, *n.* same as *rodomontadist*.

rodṣ'măn, *n.* same as *rodman*.

rod'stẽr, *n.* an angler. [Rare.]

rod'wood, *n.* any one of several shrubs or trees of the West Indies, as white rodwood, red rodwood, black rodwood.

rōe, *n.*; *pl.* **rōe** or **rōeṣ,** [AS. *ra*, *raha*.]

1. a small, agile, graceful European and Asiatic deer: also *roe deer*.

2. the female of the red deer.

rōe, *n.* [ME. *rowne*; Ice. *hrogn*; Dan. *rogn*, roe. The *n* was taken for a pl. termination and dropped in the sing. through error.]

1. the eggs or spawn of fishes: the roe of the male is called *soft roe* or *milt*; that of the female *hard roe* or *spawn*.

2. the spawn of various crustaceans, as the coral of the lobster.

3. a mottled appearance in wood, especially in mahogany, being the alternate streak of light and shade running with the grain.

rōe′buck, *n.*; *pl.* **rōe′bucks** or **rōe′buck,** [AS. *ra*, or *raa*, *ræge*, or *hræge*; Dan. *raa*, or *raabuk*; Sw. *rabock*.]

ROEBUCK (sense 1) (*Capreolus capræa*)

1. the male of the roe (deer).

2. any roe deer.

rōed (rōd), *a.* full of roe, as a fish.

rōe deer, a roe (sense 1).

roent′gen (rent′), *n.* [after Wilhelm Konrad Roentgen (1845–1923), German physicist.] in physics, a unit of X-ray radiation: it is the amount of radiation given off, after the secondary electrons have been fully utilized and the wall effect of the chamber avoided, to produce in 1 cc. of atmospheric air at zero degrees Centigrade and 76 millimeters of mercury pressure, a sufficient degree of conductivity so that one electrostatic unit of charge may be measured at saturation: also spelled *röntgen.*

Roent′gen, *a.* of or pertaining to the German physicist, Wilhelm Konrad Roentgen, or to his discoveries: also spelled *Röntgen.*

roent′gen·ism, *n.* in pathology, treatment with roentgen rays, or X rays; also, the effects or diseases caused by misuse of or overexposure to X rays: also spelled *röntgenism.*

roent′gen·ize, *v.t.*; roentgenized, *pt.*, *pp.*; roentgenizing, *ppr.* to subject to the action of X rays: also spelled *röntgenize.*

roent′gen·ō-, a combining form meaning *Roentgen rays, X rays,* as in *roentgenology*: also spelled *röntgeno-.*

roent′gen·ō·grȧm, *n.* an X-ray photograph: also spelled *röntgenogram.*

roent·gen·og′rȧ·phy, *n.* photography by the use of X rays: also spelled *röntgenography.*

roent·gen·ol′ō·gist, *n.* a physician who specializes in the use of X rays in the diagnosis and treatment of diseases; also, one who specializes exclusively in taking and interpreting X-ray pictures: also spelled *röntgenologist.*

roent·gen·ol′ō·gy, *n.* the study and use of X rays, especially in connection with the diagnosis and treatment of disease: also spelled *röntgenology.*

roent·gen·ō·ther′ȧ·py, *n.* the treatment of disease by means of X rays: also spelled *röntgenotherapy.*

Roent′gen rāy, [*also* r–] X rays: also spelled *Röntgen rays.*

rōe′stōne, *n.* same as *oölite.*

rof′fi·ȧ, rof′i·ȧ, *n.* same as *raffia.*

rog, *v.t.* to shake. [Obs.]

rō·gā′tion, *n.* [Fr., from L. *rogatio* (*-onis*), asking.]

1. [*usually in pl.*] a prayer or supplication, especially as chanted in church ceremonies during Rogation days.

2. in ancient Rome, (a) a consul's or tribune's proposal of a law to be passed or rejected by the people; (b) such a proposed law.

Rogation days; the three days immediately preceding Ascension Day, during which supplications are chanted.

Rogation Sunday; the fifth Sunday after Easter; the Sunday that precedes Rogation days.

Rogation week; the week in which the Rogation days occur.

rō·gā′tion flow′ẽr, the milkwort of Europe, *Polygala vulgaris.*

rog′ȧ·tō·ry, *a.* questioning or appointed to question for facts, as at law.

Roġ′ẽr, *interj.* [from conventional name of international signal flag for R.]

1. [*also* r–] received: term used in radiotelephony to indicate reception of a message.

2. [*also* r–] right! O.K.! [Slang.]

rōgue (rōg), *n.* [from 16th-c. thieves' slang; perh. from L. *rogare*, to ask.]

1. formerly, a wandering beggar or tramp; a vagabond.

2. a rascal; scoundrel.

3. a fun-loving, mischievous person: used affectionately.

4. an animal, as an elephant, that wanders apart from the herd and is fierce and wild.

5. in biology, an individual varying markedly from the standard, especially an inferior one.

rogue money; in Scotland, an assessment laid on each county for defraying the expense of apprehending, maintaining in jail, and prosecuting offenders.

rogues' gallery; a collection of photographs and personal data of criminals, as used by police in identification

rogue's march; (a) music played in a jeering manner when a soldier is dishonorably discharged from his regiment; (b) any jeering and noisy expulsion of a person from a community, group, etc.

rogue's yarn; a rope yarn twisted in a contrary manner to the other part of a rope.

rōgue, *v.t.*; rogued, *pt.*, *pp.*; roguing, *ppr.* 1. to denounce. [Obs.]

2. to cheat.

3. to destroy (plants, etc.) as biological rogues.

4. to remove such plants, etc. from (land, etc.).

rōgue, *v.i.* to live or act like a rogue.

rōgue house, a jail. [Brit. Dial.]

rō′guẽr·y (-gẽr-), *n.*; *pl.* **rō′guẽr·ieṣ,** 1. the life of a vagrant. [Obs.]

2. cheating; fraud; dishonest practices.

3. waggery; playful mischievousness; as, the child was full of *roguery.*

rōgue′ship, *n.* the quality or state of being a rogue; a rogue. [Rare.]

rō′guish (rō′gish), *a.* 1. vagrant; vagabond.

2. knavish; fraudulent; dishonest.

3. waggish; arch; playfully mischievous.

rō′guish·ly, *adv.* like a rogue; knavishly; archly.

rō′guish·ness, *n.* the state or quality of being a rogue.

rō′guy (-gē), *a.* roguish; vagrant; dishonest. [Obs.]

rō′hăn, *n.* [Hind.] an East Indian tree, *Soymida febrifuga*, having an astringent bark and wood like that of mahogany.

rō′hob, *n.* same as *rob*, n.

roi, *n.* [Maori.] the rootstock of the New Zealand brake, formerly roasted and eaten by the New Zealand aborigines.

roi′ăl, *a.* royal. [Obs.]

roil, *v.t.*; roiled, *pt.*, *pp.*; roiling, *ppr.* [OFr. *rouil, roille*, rust, mud; ult. from L. *robigo*, rust.]

1. to make turbid by stirring up the dregs or sediment; as, to *roil* wine, cider, or other liquor in casks or bottles.

2. to make angry or irritable; to displease; to vex.

roil′y, *a.*; *comp.* roilier; *superl.* roiliest, 1. muddy; turbid; as, a *roily* stream; *roily* water.

2. angry; irritable.

roin, *n.* a scab. [Obs.]

roin′ish, *a.* scabby. [Obs.]

roin′ous, *a.* scabby; worthless. [Obs.]

roint, *v.t.* to aroint. [Obs.]

roist, *v.i.* to roister. [Obs.]

roist′ẽr, *v.i.*; roistered, *pt.*, *pp.*; roistering, *ppr.* [Fr. *rustre, ruste*, a boor, from L. *rusticus*, rustic.]

1. to bluster; to swagger.

2. to be lively and noisy; to revel boisterously.

roist′ẽr-doist″ẽr, *n.* a roisterer.

roist′ẽr·ẽr, *n.* one who roisters.

roist′ẽr·ly, *a.* blustering; violent. [Obs.]

roist′ẽr·ly, *adv.* in a bullying, violent manner. [Obs.]

roist′ẽr·ous, *a.* roistering.

rok, *n.* same as *roc.*

rō′kȧ, *n.* a large tree, *Trichilia emetica*, of Africa, yielding an ointment and emetic.

rok′ăm·bōle, *n.* same as *rocambole.*

rōke, *n.* [a variant spelling of *reek*, smoke.] mist; smoke; damp. [Brit. Dial.]

rōke′āġe, rōk′ee, *n.* [Am. Ind.] Indian corn pounded after parching and mixed with sugar. [Dial.]

rōk′ē·lāy, *n.* same as *roquelaure.*

rō′kẽr, *n.* [prob. from *roach*, a fish.] a fish of the genus *Raia*; specifically, the thornback ray.

rōk′y, *a.* misty; foggy; cloudy. [Brit. Dial.]

Rō′lȧnd, *n.* a legendary hero of the *Chanson de Roland* and other stories of the Charlemagne cycle, famous for his strength, courage, and chivalrous spirit: he was killed while fighting the Saracens at Roncesvalles in 778 A.D.

a Roland for an Oliver; one thing in full return for another; tit for tat: in allusion to a legendary five-day fight between the hero Roland and his friend Oliver, which neither won.

Rō·lan′diç, *a.* pertaining to, described by, or named after L. Rolando (1773–1831), an Italian anatomist.

Rolandic area; the excitomotor region of the brain.

Rolandic fissure; the fissure between the parietal and frontal bones.

rōle, *n.* [Fr. *rôle.*] 1. a part, or character, represented by an actor.

2. a function or office assumed by someone, as a leading public character; as, the *role* of Romeo; in the *role* of a statesman.

rōll, *v.i.*; rolled, *pt.*, *pp.*; rolling, *ppr.* [OFr. *roler*; Fr. *rouler*; LL. *rotulare*, to roll, revolve, from L. *rotula*, dim. of *rota*, a wheel; Sp. *rollar, arrollar*; Port. *rolar*; It. *rotolare*; D. and G. *rollen*; Dan. *rulle*; Sw. *rulla*.]

1. to move by revolving; to rotate or revolve as on an axis; to turn over and over; as, a wheel *rolls* over the ground; a body *rolls* on an inclined plane.

2. to move or be moved on wheels.

3. to travel about; to wander.

4. to pass; elapse; as, the years *rolled* by.

5. to move in a periodical revolution: said of stars, planets, etc.; as, the moon *rolls* in its course.

6. to flow, as water, in a full swelling or sweeping motion; as, the waves *rolled* against the boat.

7. to extend in gentle swells.

8. to make a loud, continuous rising and falling sound; as, thunder *rolls.*

9. to rise and fall in a full mellow cadence, as sound, speech, etc.

10. to form a ball or cylinder by turning over and over on itself or something else; as, the string *rolled* into a tight ball.

11. to turn in a circular motion; as, her eyes *rolled.*

12. to move in a rocking, swaying motion; as, the ship *rolled.*

13. to walk by swaying.

14. to become flattened or spread under a roller.

15. to make progress; to advance; as, now we're *rolling.*

16. to tumble or fall over and over; as, the stone *rolled* over the hill.

17. to fluctuate; to move tumultuously.

What different sorrows did within thee *roll.*
—Prior.

18. to wallow; to tumble; as, a horse *rolls.*

19. to be enrolled. [Obs.]

20. to beat a drum with strokes so rapid that they can scarcely be distinguished by the ear.

to roll in; (a) to assemble or arrive, usually in large numbers; (b) [Colloq.] to have much of; to abound in.

to roll round; to recur, as in a cycle; as, winter *rolled round* again.

to roll up; to arrive in or as if in an automobile, carriage, etc. [Colloq.]

rōll, *v.t.* 1. to move by turning over and over; to move by turning on an axis.

2. to move or send on wheels or rollers.

3. to drive or impel forward with a sweeping, rolling motion; as, a river *rolls* its waters to the sea.

4. to beat (a drum) with blows in rapid, light succession.

5. to utter with full, flowing sound; as, he *rolled* his words.

6. to pronounce or say with a trill; as, he *rolls* his r's.

7. to give a swaying motion to; as, the waves *rolled* the ship along.

8. to move gently around and around or from side to side; as, she *rolled* her eyes.

9. to make into a ball or cylinder by winding over and over itself or something else; as, he *rolled* a cigarette.

10. to wrap or enfold, as in a covering; as, she *rolled* the child in a blanket.

11. to make flat, smooth, or spread out by using a roller, rolling pin, etc.

12. to throw (the dice) as in the game of craps.

13. to iron (sleeves, etc.) without forming a crease.

14. in printing, to spread ink on, as type, a form, etc., with a roller.

15. to revolve; to turn over and over in one's mind.

16. to utter in a prolonged, deep sound:

often with *out* or *forth*; as, to *roll out* the lines of a hymn.

to roll back; to reduce (prices) to a previous or standard level by government action and control.

to roll out; (a) to flatten into a sheet by rolling; (b) to spread out by unrolling.

to roll over: (a) to refinance (a maturing note, etc.); (b) to reinvest (funds) so as to defer the payment of taxes.

to roll up; (a) to make or put into the form of a roll; (b) to wrap up by turning over and over; (c) to accumulate; to increase.

rōll, *n.* [in some senses directly from the verb to *roll*; in others from OFr. *rolle, roule*; Fr. *rôle*, a roll, from LL. *rotulus*, a rol', from L. *rota*, a wheel; Sp. *rollo, rol, rolde*; Port. *rolo*; It. *rotolo, ruotolo, rullo*.]
1. a rolling.
2. a paper, parchment, etc. that is rolled up; a scroll.
3. a register; a catalogue.
4. a list of names for checking attendance; a muster roll; as, to call the *roll*.
5. a measure of something rolled into a cylinder; as, a *roll* of wallpaper.
6. a cylindrical mass of something; as, a sausage *roll*.
7. (a) any of variously shaped, small cakes of bread; (b) thin cake covered with fruit, nuts, etc. and rolled; as, a jelly *roll*; (c) beef, veal, rolled and cooked.
8. a roller.
9. a swaying or rolling motion.
10. a rapid succession of light blows on a drum.
11. a loud, reverberating sound; a peal, as of thunder.
12. a full, cadenced flow of words.
13. a slight swell or rise on the surface of something, as land.
14. money: especially, a wad of paper money. [Slang.]
15. in aeronautics, a maneuver in which an airplane in flight performs one complete rotation around its longitudinal axis.
16. in bookbinding, a revolving tool used in making an impression or pattern.
17. in building, a strip with a rounded top laid over a roof at the ridge to raise the sheet lead at those points.
18. in engraving, the cylindrical die in a transferring press.
19. in metallurgy, one of a pair, or series of rollers arranged in pairs, between which ores are crushed.
20. in metalworking, one of the pair of cylinders between which metal is passed to draw it into a bar or to flatten it out into a sheet.
21. in paper making, a cylinder mounted with blades for working paper pulp in the tub.
22. in organ playing, arpeggio.

master of the rolls; see under *master*.

to strike off the rolls; to expel from membership.

rōll'ȧ·ble, *a.* capable of being rolled.

rōll''-ănd-fil'let, *n.* a round molding with a square fillet on its face.

ROLL-AND-FILLET

rōll'ȧ·wāy, *a.* having rollers for easy moving and storing when not in use; as, a *rollaway* bed.

rōll'back, *n.* a reduction of prices to a previous level by government action and control.

rōll çall, the act of calling a list of names, as of students, soldiers, etc. to find out who is absent; also, the time the roll is called.

rōll'ēr, *n.* 1. one who or that which rolls.
2. any of various rolling cylinders or wheels; specifically, (a) a cylinder of metal, wood, etc. over which something is rolled for easier movement; (b) a cylinder on which something is rolled up or wound; as, the *roller* of a window blind; (c) a heavy cylinder of metal, stone, etc. used to crush or smooth something; (d) in printing, a cylinder, usually of hard rubber, for spreading ink on the form just before the paper is impressed.
3. a long bandage in a roll.
4. a heavy, swelling wave that breaks on the shoreline.
5. the studded barrel of a music box or chime-ringing machine.
6. in nautical usage, a cylindrical antifriction bar that revolves as a hawser or rope passes over it, and thus saves the rope from wear.
7. a cylinder of wood, used as a winch in mounting and dismounting guns.
8. a cylinder covered with a napped fabric, used for applying paint.
9. in saddlery, the broad, padded strap used as a girth to hold a blanket in place.
10. a thick-beaked bird of the genus *Coracias*, allied to the crows and jays, but wilder than either. It derives the name from its habit of tumbling in ascending flight. The common roller, *Coracias garrula*, is found in Europe, Asia, and Africa. The plumage of almost all the species is blue and green mixed with white, and heightened by the contrast of more somber colors. The name is also given to birds of the genus *Eurystomus*, as the oriental roller, *Eurystomus orientalis*, of India, Java, and Polynesia, and the Australian roller, *Eurystomus pacificus*.

COMMON ROLLER

11. a canary that rolls, or trills, its notes.
12. a tumbler pigeon.
13. a snake of the family *Tortricidæ*.

ground roller; a bird of the genus *Atelornis*, native of Madagascar. Its flight is very weak.

rōll'ēr beăr'ing, a bearing in which the shaft turns with rollers, generally of steel, arranged lengthwise in a ringlike track: used to reduce friction.

rōll'ēr çōast'ēr, an amusement device in which small, open cars move on tracks that dip sharply up and down, make sharp turns, etc., so as to thrill the riders.

rōll'ēr gin, a cotton gin in which dull knives and leather rollers separate the seeds from the cotton fiber.

rōll'ēr mill, 1. any mill that uses rollers, as (a) a mill for crushing or coarse grinding of grain for feed; (b) a mill in which wheat is made into flour by passing it between rollers.
2. a machine in which flaxseed is broken in preparing it for the press.

rōll'ēr-skāte, *v.i.* to move on roller skates.

rōll'ēr skāte, a skate with small wheels, usually four, instead of a runner, for use on a smooth surface.

rōll'ēr tow'el, a long towel with its ends sewed together and hung on a roller.

rōll'ey, *n.* in mining, a truck for carrying receptacles along underground ways. [Brit.]

rōll film, a strip of photographic film rolled on a spool for a series of consecutive exposures.

rol'li·chie, *n.* [D. *rolletje*, a little roll, from *rol*, a roll.] a favorite dish among the Dutch of New York, made by frying slices of chopped meat which has been stuffed into a bag of tripe.

rol'lick, *v.i.*; rollicked, *pt., pp.*; rollicking, *ppr.* [prob. *roll* and dim. *-ick*.] to be gay, carefree, and hilarious in play; to romp.

rol'lick·ing, *a.* carefree and gay; lively and hilarious.

rol'lick·sōme, *a.* rollicking.

rōll'ing, *a.* 1. moving by turning over and over.
2. moving on wheels or rollers.
3. recurring; as, the *rolling* seasons.
4. rotating or revolving on or as on an axis.
5. moving up and down or sideways; as, *rolling* eyes.
6. folded over or back; as, a *rolling* collar.
7. swaying; as, a *rolling* walk.
8. surging up or on in strong waves; as, *rolling* smoke, *rolling* waters.
9. resounding or reverberating; as, *rolling* thunder.
10. trilled; as, a *rolling* note.
11. dipping up and down in gentle slopes; as, *rolling* land.

rolling bridge; a bridge which is opened and closed by moving upon rollers.

rolling circle; in the paddle wheel of a vessel, the circle described by a point which moves with the same velocity as the vessel.

rolling fire; formerly, a fire, as of infantry, which begins at one end of a line or column and continues without interruption to the other.

rolling friction; the friction with which a body meets in rolling over a surface and which depends upon the character of the surfaces in contact.

rōll'ing, *n.* the action, motion, or sound of something that rolls or is rolled.

rōll'ing bar'rel, a barrel in which gunpowder is placed and rolled for the purpose of mixing.

rōll'ing hitch, a knot in which one or more turns are made between two hitches: see *knot*, illus.

rōll'ing kitch'en, a large metal vessel on wheels, with an undercompartment for fire: from it are served hot soup and other warm foods to soldiers on the march.

rōll'ing mill, 1. a plant where molten steel or iron is placed between heavy rolls and formed into sheets, rails, etc.
2. a machine used for such rolling.

ROLLING MILL

rōll'ing pin, a heavy, smooth cylinder of wood, glass, etc. used to roll out dough.

rōll'ing plant, same as *rolling stock*.

rōll'ing press, any machine which does pressing by means of rollers; specifically, (a) a press for printing from a copperplate by passing it under a roller; (b) a machine for pressing cloth by passing it between rollers; (c) a machine for calendering paper by passing it between smooth rollers; (d) a machine used by bookbinders, in which printed sheets are passed between hot rollers for the purpose of smoothing them; (e) a printing press with a cylinder that rolls back and forth.

rōll'ing stock, the locomotives, freight cars, box cars, passenger cars, etc., of a railroad; everything on wheels belonging to a railroad.

rōll'ing taç'kle, tackle for steadying the yards when a ship is rolling heavily: it is fastened to the mast and used in various ways.

rōll mōld'ing, in architecture, a round molding divided longitudinally along the middle, the upper half projecting over the lower. It occurs often in the early Gothic decorated style, where it is profusely used for dripstones, string courses, abacuses, etc.

ROLL MOLDING

rōll'mop, *n.* a salt herring, cleaned and stuffed with onion, pepper, and cucumber sliced, then rolled up and sewed or skewered.

rol'lŏck, *n.* same as *rowlock*.

rōll'out, *n.* in football, a play in which the quarterback moves laterally in preparing to throw a pass.

rōll'ō·vēr, *n.* 1. the refinancing of a mature note, etc.
2. the reinvesting of funds in such a way as to defer the payment of taxes.

rōll'-top, *a.* having a flexible top made of slats that rolls back, as a desk.

roll-top desk; a desk with a flexible top made of many narrow slats hinged together that rolls back.

rōll trāin, in a rolling mill, a train of two or three sets of rollers used for reducing and giving form to masses of highly heated iron or steel.

rōll'wāy, *n.* 1. any place or path along which round or cylindrical objects can be rolled; specifically, a natural or artificial chute down which logs can be rolled or slid into a river, etc. for transportation.
2. a pile of logs on the bank of a river awaiting removal.

rō'ly-pō'ly, *a.* [redupl. on *roll*.] resembling a roly-poly; fat; round; dumpy.

rō'ly-pō'ly, *n.*; *pl.* **rō'ly-pō'lieș,** 1. a short, plump, pudgy or dumpy person or thing; especially, such a child.
2. a kind of pudding made of rich pastry dough spread with fruit or jam, rolled up, and boiled, steamed, etc. [Chiefly Brit.]
3. a game formerly played by rolling a ball into a hole or a series of holes.

Rŏm, rŏm, *n.* a gypsy man or boy.

Rō·mā'iç, *a.* 1. of modern Greece.
2. designating or of the language of modern Greece.

Rō·mā'iç, *n.* the modern form of the ancient Greek language as spoken by the people generally, in distinction from Hellenic, the higher literary form.

rō·māine', *n.* [Fr., f. adj., Roman.] a kind of lettuce with leaves that form a long, slender head: also *romaine lettuce*.

rō·mal', *n.* same as *rumal*.

Rō'măn, *a.* [L. *Romanus*, from *Roma*, the principal city of the Romans, in Italy.]

1. of, characteristic of, or derived from ancient or modern Rome, its people, etc.
2. pertaining to the Roman Catholic Church, or the Latin rite.
3. [usually r–] designating or of the style of printing types most common in modern use, upright, light-faced, and with serifs.
Roman alphabet; the alphabet used by the ancient Romans, from which most modern European alphabets are derived: it consisted of twenty-three letters (*J*, *U*, and *W* were added later).
Roman alum; a kind of native alum found in volcanic rocks near Naples, free from iron but having a reddish color derived from the soil in which it is found.
Roman arch; a semicircular arch.
Roman architecture; the style of architecture used by the ancient Romans, characterized by the rounded arch and vault, thick, massive walls, and the use of much brick and concrete.
Roman calendar; the calendar used by the ancient Romans, from which the modern calendar is derived: it consisted originally of ten months but later was changed to twelve.
Roman candle; a kind of firework consisting of a tube which discharges upward a stream of white or colored stars or balls.
Roman Catholic; (a) pertaining to the Roman Catholic Church; (b) a member or adherent of the Roman Catholic Church.
Roman Catholic Church; the Christian church headed by the Pope (Bishop of Rome).
Roman Catholicism; the beliefs, practices, organization, etc. of the Roman Catholic Church.
Roman cement; a dark-colored hydraulic cement, which hardens quickly and is very durable.
Roman Curia; in the Roman Catholic Church, the papal court.
Roman Empire; the empire of ancient Rome, established by Augustus in 27 B.C.: it continued until 395 A.D.
Roman holiday; entertainment or gain acquired at the expense of others' suffering or loss: so called from the gladiatorial contests waged as entertainment in ancient Rome.
Roman law; the code of laws of the ancient Romans: it forms the basis for the modern legal system in many countries.
Roman nose; a nose with a high, prominent bridge.
Roman numerals; the Roman letters used as numerals until the 10th century A.D.: in Roman numerals I = 1, V = 5, X = 10, L = 50, C = 100, D = 500, and M = 1,000. Other numbers are formed from these by adding or subtracting: the value of a symbol following another of the same or greater value is added (e.g., III = 3, XV = 15); the value of a symbol preceding one of greater value is subtracted (e.g., IX = 9); and the value of a symbol standing between two of greater value is subtracted from that of the second, the remainder being added to that of the first (e.g., XIX = 19). Roman numerals are commonly written in capitals, though they may be written in lower-case letters. A bar over a letter indicates multiplication by 1,000 (e.g., $\overline{V}$ = 5,000).
Roman ocher; a pigment of a rich orange-yellow color; oxide of iron mixed with earthy matter.
Roman order; in architecture, the Composite order.
Roman punch; a frozen dessert made with lemon juice, rum, etc.
Roman rite; in the Roman Catholic Church, (a) the customary and authentic form or use of the Latin rite; (b) loosely, the Latin rite.

Rō′măn, *n.* 1. a native, inhabitant, or citizen of ancient or modern Rome.
2. the Italian spoken in Rome.
3. Latin.
4. loosely, a member of the Roman Catholic Church.
5. [usually r–] roman type or characters.

rō·män′, *n.* [Fr.; OFr. *Romain* (from L. *Romanus*), lit., of Rome.]
1. a type of metrical narrative developed in France in the Middle Ages.
2. popularly, any romantic novel.
roman à clef; [Fr., lit., novel with a key.] a novel in which real persons appear under fictitious names.
roman fleuve; [Fr., lit., river novel.] a long novel, usually in several volumes, dealing with a cross section of society, several generations of a family, etc.

rō·mance′ (*or* rō′mans), *n.* 1. originally, a long narrative in verse or prose, originally written in one of the Romance dialects, about the adventures of knights and other chivalric heroes.
2. a fictitious tale dealing not so much with everyday life as with extraordinary and often extravagant adventures or mysterious events; as, Washington Irving's *romance* of Rip Van Winkle.
3. a type of novel in which the emphasis is on love, adventure, etc.
4. the type of literature comprising such stories.
5. real happenings or adventures as exciting and unusual as those of such literature.
6. the quality or characteristic of excitement, love, and adventure found in such literature.
7. the tendency to derive great pleasure from romantic adventures.
8. an exaggeration or falsehood.
9. a love affair.
10. in music, a short, lyrical, usually sentimental piece, suggesting a love song.
11. [R–] the Romance languages collectively.

Rō·mance′, *a.* designating, of, or speaking any of the Romance languages.
Romance languages; the languages derived from Low Latin; Portuguese, Rhaeto-Romanic, Romanian, French, Italian, Spanish, Catalan, and Provençal.

rō·mance′, *v.i.*; romanced (-manst′), *pt.*, *pp.*; romancing, *ppr.* 1. to write or tell romances.
2. to be fanciful or imaginative in thinking or talking.
3. to make love; to court; to woo. [Colloq.]

rō·mance′, *v.t.* to make love to; to court. [Colloq.]

rō·man′cẽr, *n.* 1. one who invents fictitious stories.
2. a writer of romance.

rō·man′cist, *n.* a romancer; a writer of romance.

rō·man′cy, *a.* romantic. [Rare.]

Rō·măn·esque′ (-esk′), *a.* [Fr.; It. *romanesco*, *romanzesco*, a romance; OFr. *romanz*.]
1. of one of the Romance languages, especially Provençal.
2. designating or of a style of European architecture of the eleventh and twelfth centuries, based on the Roman and characterized by the use of the round arch and vault, thick, massive walls, interior bays, etc.
3. designating or of a style of painting, sculpture, etc. corresponding to this.
4. [r–] romantic.

Rō·măn·esque′, *n.* 1. the Romanesque style of architecture, painting, etc.
2. a Romance language.

Rō·mā′ni·ăn, *a.* of Romania, its people, their language, etc.: also *Rumanian*, *Roumanian*.

Rō·mā′ni·ăn, *n.* 1. a native or inhabitant of Romania.
2. the Romance language of the Romanians.
Also *Rumanian*, *Roumanian*.

Rō·man′iç, *a.* [L. *Romanicus*.] derived from ancient Rome or from vernacular Latin.

Rō·man′iç, *n.* in linguistics, Romance.

Rō′măn·ish, *a.* relating to or associated with the usages of the Roman Catholic Church: generally a contemptuous term.

Rō′măn·işm, *n.* 1. Roman Catholicism: hostile usage.
2. the spirit and influence of ancient Rome.

Rō′măn·ist, *n.* [Mod. L. *Romanista*.]
1. a Roman Catholic: hostile usage.
2. a person who studies or is expert in Roman law, antiquities, etc.

Rō″măn·i·zā′tion, *n.* a Romanizing or being Romanized.

Rō′măn·īze, *v.t.*; Romanized, *pt.*, *pp.*; Romanizing, *ppr.* 1. to make Roman in character, spirit, etc.
2. to make Roman Catholic.
3. to respell in the Roman alphabet.

Rō′măn·īze, *v.i.* 1. to follow or be influenced by Roman customs, law, etc.
2. to conform or become converted to Roman Catholicism.

Rō′măn·ī·zẽr, *n.* one who Romanizes.

Rō·mä′nō, *n.* [It., Roman.] a dry, sharp, very hard Italian cheese, usually grated for use as a flavoring.

Rō′măns, *n.pl.* [*construed as sing.*] the Epistle to the Romans, a book of the New Testament, which was a message from the Apostle Paul to the Christians of Rome.

Rō·mansh′, **Rō·mansch′** (-mänsh′), *n.* the language of the Grisons in Switzerland and of contiguous regions of the Tyrol and Italy: it is derived from vernacular Latin; Ladin; Rhaeto-Romanic.

rō·mänt′, **rō·mäunt′**, *n.* a romance. [Obs.]

rō·man′tiç, *a.* 1. of, having the nature of, characteristic of, or characterized by romance.
2. without a basis in fact; fanciful, fictitious, or fabulous.
3. not practical; visionary or quixotic; as, a *romantic* scheme.
4. full of or dominated by thoughts, feelings, and attitudes characteristic of or suitable for romance; as, a *romantic* youth.
5. (a) of, characteristic of, or preoccupied with idealized lovemaking or courting; (b) suited for romance, or lovemaking; as, a *romantic* night.
6. of, characteristic of, or supposedly characteristic of romanticism and the Romantic Movement: contrasted with *classical*, *realistic*, etc.

rō·man′tiç, *n.* 1. a romantic person.
2. a romanticist.
3. [*pl.*] romantic characteristics, thoughts, ways, etc.
Romantic Movement; the revolt in the 18th and early 19th centuries against the artistic, political, and religious principles that had become associated with neoclassicism: characterized in literature and in the arts by liberalism in form and subject matter, emphasis on feeling and originality, the use of imaginative suggestion, and sympathetic interest in primitive nature, medievalism, and the mystical.

rō·man′tiç·ăl, *a.* romantic.

rō·man′tiç·ăl·ly, *adv.* in a romantic manner.

rō·man′ti·cişm, *n.* 1. romantic spirit, outlook, tendency, etc.
2. (a) the Romantic Movement; (b) the spirit, attitudes, style, etc. of, or adherence to, the Romantic Movement or a similar movement: contrasted with *classicism*, *realism*, etc.

rō·man′ti·cist, *n.* an adherent of romanticism in literature, painting, music, etc.

rō·man′ti·cīze, *v.t.*; romanticized, *pt.*, *pp.*; romanticizing, *ppr.*; to treat or regard romantically; to give a romantic character to or interpretation of.

rō·man′ti·cīze, *v.i.* 1. to have or uphold romantic ideas, attitudes, etc.
2. to act in a romantic way.

Rom′ȧ·ny, *a.* of or pertaining to the gypsies or to their language: also spelled *Rommany*.

Rom′ȧ·ny, *n.* [gypsy *rom*, a man.]
1. *pl.* **Rom′ȧ·ny**, **Rom′ȧ·nieş**, a gypsy.
2. the Indic language of the gypsies, which occurs with many local modifications.
Also spelled *Rommany*.
Romany rye; a person not a gypsy who associates with the gypsies, speaks their language, etc.

rō·man′zȧ, *n.* a musical romance. [Obs.]

rō·mäunt′, *n.* same as *romant*.

rom·bōw′line, *n.* [etym. obscure.] canvas, rope, etc., so old and worn as to be useless except for chafing gear.

Rōme, *n.* [after *Rome*, Italy, the seat of the Vatican, or papal government.]
1. the Roman Catholic Church.
2. Roman Catholicism.

rō′mē·ine, **rō′mē·īte**, *n.* [after the Fr. mineralogist *Romé de L'Isle*.] a mineral consisting of antimoniate of calcium, of a hyacinth or honey-yellow color, occurring in octahedrons.

Rō′mē·ō, *n.* [It., from *Romolo*, from L. *Romulus*.]
1. the hero of Shakespeare's tragedy *Romeo and Juliet* (c. 1595), son of Montague and lover of Juliet, daughter of Capulet: at the death of the lovers their feuding families become reconciled.
2. *pl.* **Rō′mē·ōş**, a lover.

Rōme pen′ny, same as *Peter's pence*.

rō·me′rō, *n.* [Sp., pilgrim.] the pilot fish.

Rōme′sçot, **Rōme′shot**, *n.* same as *Peter's pence*.

Rōme′wȧrd, *a.* and *adv.* toward Rome or the Roman church.

Rō′miç, *n.* a method of phonetic notation formulated by Henry Sweet, so called because based on the original Roman values of the letters.

Rō′mish, *a.* Roman Catholic: hostile usage.

Rō′mist, *n.* a Roman Catholic. [Obs.]

Rom′mȧ·ny, *a.* and *n.* same as *Romany*.

romp, *n.* [from earlier *ramp*, vulgar woman, hussy, prob. from ME. *rampen*; OFr. *ramper*.]
1. one who romps, especially a girl.

2. noisy, hilarious play or frolic.
3. an easy, winning gait in a race; as, the horse won in a *romp*. [Slang.]

romp, *v.i.*; romped (rompt), *pt., pp.*; romping, *ppr.* 1. to play boisterously; to leap and frisk about in play.
2. to win with ease in a race, contest, etc.; as, the horse *romped* home. [Slang.]

romp'ẽr, *n.* 1. a person who romps.
2. [*pl.*] a type of loose-fitting outer garment worn by young children, combining a waist with bloomerlike pants.

romp'ing, *a.* fond of romps; indulging in romps.

romp'ing·ly, *adv.* in a romping manner.

romp'ish, *a.* inclined to romp; playful and lively.

romp'ish·ly, *adv.* in a rompish manner.

romp'ish·ness, *n.* the state or quality of being rompish; tendency to romp.

rom·pū', *a.* [Fr., broken.] in heraldry, broken; as, a chevron or bend *rompu*.

CHEVRON ROMPU

Rom'ū·lus, *n.* [L.] in Roman mythology, a son of Mars and founder and first king of Rome, deified as Quirinus: he and his twin brother Remus, left to die in the Tiber when they were babies, were reared by a shewolf; later Romulus killed Remus.

roñ·çȧ·dọr', *n.* [Sp., from LL. *rhonchare*, to snore.] any one of various species of fishes of the *Sciænidæ* found along the western coast of North America.

roñ'ĉhil, *n.* same as *ronquil*.

roñ'ĉhō, roñ'çō, *n.* a fish, the croaker.

ron·dȧche', *n.* [OFr., a round shield, from *rond*, round.] a small circular shield carried by medieval foot soldiers.

ronde, *n.* [Fr.] in printing, an angular script, having the upright strokes heavy; pen text.

This line is set in ronde

ron·deau' (-dō'), *n.* [Fr. *rondeau*, from *rond*, round.]
1. a short lyrical poem of thirteen (or sometimes ten) lines with only two rhymes, and an unrhymed refrain that consists of the opening words and is used in two places: also *roundel*.
2. in music, a rondo.

ron'del, *n.* 1. in fortification, a small, round tower, erected at the foot of a bastion. [Obs.]
2. a kind of rondeau, usually with fourteen lines, two rhymes, and the first two lines used as a refrain in the middle and at the end (the second line occasionally being omitted at the end): also *roundel*.

ron'de·let, *n.* [ME.; OFr., dim. of *rondel*.] a short rondel, usually of five or seven lines in one stanza and a refrain consisting of the opening words.

Ron·de·let'i·ȧ, *n.* [from G. *Rondelet*, Fr. naturalist.] a genus of shrubs of the *Rubiaceæ*, characterized by having a calyx with a subglobular tube. The various species are found largely in tropical America and the West Indies and are sometimes cultivated for their brilliant flowers.

ron·delle', *n.* 1. a small round buckler or shield; hence, any round disk or plate.
2. a plate of scale or crust formed on the top of molten metal as it cools.
3. a disk of colored glass used in making stained windows.
4. a rondel. [Obs.]

ron·dī'nō, *n.* a short rondo.

ron'dle, *n.* 1. any of various round things.
2. same as *rondelle*.
3. a round or step of a ladder. [Obs.]
4. a rondeau. [Obs.]

ron'dō, *n.* 1. a musical composition or movement, often the last movement of a sonata, having its principal theme stated three or more times in the same key, interposed with subordinate themes.
2. in poetry, same as *rondeau*.

ron·dō·let'tō, *n.* a rondino.

ron'dūre, *n.* 1. a round; a circle. [Poet.]
2. roundness; fullness; plumpness. [Poet.]

rong, *v.* obsolete past tense and past participle of *ring*.

rong, *n.* rung. [Brit. Dial.]

rọn·ġeur' (-zhẽr'), *n.* [Fr., a gnawer.] a kind of gouge forceps used in surgery for removing small portions of bone.

rŏn'iŏn, rŏn'yŏn (-yun), *n.* [Fr. *rogne*, itch, mange, scab, from L. *robigo* (*-inis*), rust.] a mangy, scabby animal; also, a scurvy person. [Obs.]

roñ'quil, *n.* [Sp. *ronquillo*, dim. of *ronco*, hoarse, from L. *raucus*, hoarse.]
1. a deep-water fish, *Bathymaster signatus*, of the northern Pacific coast of America.
2. any fish of the family *Icosteidæ*.

Ronș'dorf·ẽr, *n.* an Ellerian.

rŏnt, *n.* a runt. [Obs.]

Rönt'gen, Rönt'gen rāyș (rent'), [also r–] same as *Roentgen, Roentgen rays*.

rọọd, *n.* [ME. *rode*; AS. *rod*, a cross, measure; akin to G. *rute*, a rod, pole, Eng. *rod*.]
1. originally, the cross on which Jesus was crucified.
2. any cross representing this; a crucifix, especially a large one at the entrance to the chancel or choir of a medieval church, often supported on a rood beam or rood screen.
3. a cross as used in crucifixion.
4. in England, a measure of length varying from 5½ to 8 yards, according to locality; sometimes, 1 rod.
5. a measure of area usually equal to ¼ acre (40 square rods).
by the rood; by the cross: a former oath. [Archaic.]

rọọd bēam, a beam over the entrance to the chancel of a church, usually constituting the head of the rood screen and used to support the rood.

rọọ'de·bok, *n.* [D. *rood*, red, *bok*, a buck.] the Natal bushbuck, *Cephalophus natalensis*. It is reddish-brown, stands about two feet high, has large ears, and straight, pointed horns about three inches long.

rọọd gọọse, the brent, *Bernicla brenta*. [Scot. and Brit. Dial.]

rọọ'dle, *n.* [G. *rudel*, a crowd or hubbub.] in poker, a hand played with special rules, usually after an especially high hand has been held by a player.

rọọd lọft, a loft or gallery in a church over a rood screen.

rọọd sçreen, a screen or ornamental partition separating the choir of a church from the nave, often supporting the rood, or crucifix.

rọọd steē'ple, the tower or steeple built over the intersection of a cruciform church.

rọọd tow'ẽr, same as *rood steeple*.

rọọf, *n.* [AS. *hrōf*, a roof.]
1. the outside top covering of a building. Roofs are distinguished by the materials of which they are mainly formed, as stone, wood, slate, tile, thatch, etc., and by their form and mode of construction, as shed, curb, hip, gable, pavilion, ogee, and flat roofs.

SHED ROOF

GABLE ROOF

HIP ROOF CONICAL ROOF OGEE ROOF

The *span* of a roof is the width between the supports; the *rise* is the height in the center above the level of the supports; the *pitch* is the slope or angle at which it is inclined.
2. figuratively, a house or home.

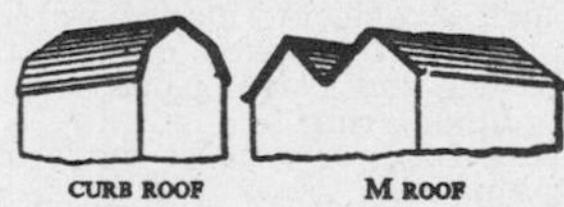
CURB ROOF M ROOF

3. the top or peak of anything; as, the *roof* of the world.
4. anything like a roof in position or use; as, the *roof* of the mouth.
false roof; in architecture, the ceiling of an upper apartment between which and the rafters of the outer roof a space is left.
to raise the roof; (a) to be very noisy, as in applause, anger, celebration, etc.; (b) to complain loudly. [Slang.]

rọọf, *v.t.*; roofed, *pt., pp.*; roofing, *ppr.* to provide or cover with or as with a roof.

rọọf'ẽr, *n.* one who builds or repairs roofs.

rọọf gär'den, 1. a garden on the flat roof of a building.
2. the roof or top floor of a high building, decorated as a garden and used as a restaurant, etc.

rọọf'ing, *n.* 1. the act of covering with a roof.
2. the materials of which a roof is composed; materials for a roof.
3. roofs in general; also, a roof.

rọọf'less, *a.* 1. having no roof; as, a *roofless* house.
2. having no house or home; unsheltered.

rọọf'let, *n.* a small covering or roof.

rọọf'tree, *n.* 1. the large horizontal beam extending along the top of a roof; ridgepole.
2. a roof.
3. a home or shelter.

rọọf'y, *a.* having roofs.

rook, *n.* [Fr. *roc*; It. *rocco*; Sp. *roque*, from Per. *rukh*, the rook or castle in chess.] in chess, either of the two corner pieces shaped like a castle tower: it can move in a vertical or horizontal direction over any number of consecutive, unoccupied squares.

rook, *n.* [ME. *roc*; AS. *hroc*; akin to G. *ruch*; prob. echoic.]
1. a gregarious European crow that builds its nest in trees around buildings.
2. a swindler; cheat, especially in gambling.

rook, *v.t.* and *v.i.* [prob. from the *rook's* thievishness.] to swindle; to cheat.

rook, *v.i.* to squat; to ruck.

rook'ẽr·y, *n.*; *pl.* **rook'ẽr·ieș,** 1. a breeding place or colony of rooks.
2. a breeding place or colony of other gregarious animals or birds, as seals, penguins, etc.
3. a building or group of buildings that are old and dilapidated and house many people; tenement house or tenement district.

rook'iē, *n.* [from *recruit*.]
1. an inexperienced recruit in the army.
2. any novice.

rook'y, *a.* full of or consisting of rooks; as, the *rooky* wood.

rọọl, *v.t.* to ruffle; to rumple. [Brit. Dial.]

rọọm, *n.* [AS. *rum*, room.]
1. a space that holds or can hold something; as, *room* for one more.
2. suitable scope or opportunity; as, *room* for doubt.
3. interior space enclosed by walls or separated from other similar spaces by walls or partitions.
4. [*pl.*] living quarters; lodgings; apartment.
5. the people gathered together in a room; as, the whole *room* was silent.
6. a position or office. [Obs.]
room and board; sleeping accommodations and meals.
room and space; the distance from any point in a ship's rib to the corresponding point in the adjoining rib.
to make room; to open a space or place for anything; to free from obstructions.
Syn.—apartment, chamber, compartment, scope, compass, latitude, space.

rọọm, *v.i.*; roomed, *pt., pp.*; rooming, *ppr.* to occupy a room in a house, hotel, etc.; to lodge; as, his friend *roomed* with him for five years.

rọọm, *v.t.* to provide with a room or lodgings.

rọọm, *a.* roomy; commodious. [Obs.]

rọọm'āġe, *n.* space; room. [Rare.]

rọọ'măl, *n.* see *rumal*.

rọọm'ẽr, *n.* one who rooms; a lodger.

rọọm'ẽr, *adv.* farther away; at a longer distance. [Obs.]

rọọm·ette', *n.* a small, private room in some railroad sleeping cars, furnished with a bed that folds into the wall, a toilet, washbasin, etc.

rọọm'fụl, *a.* having ample room; capacious. [Rare.]

rọọm'fụl, *n.*; *pl.* **rọọm'fụlș,** 1. as many or as much as a room will contain.
2. the people or objects in a room, collectively.

rọọm'i·ly, *adv.* spaciously; with plenty of room.

rọọm'i·ness, *n.* the quality or condition of being roomy; spaciousness; large extent of space.

rọọm'ing house, a house with furnished rooms for renting; a lodging house.

rọọm'less, *a.* without room; having no rooms.

rọọm'māte, *n.* the person, or any of the persons, with whom one shares a room or rooms.

rọọm'sōme, *a.* having ample room; roomy. [Obs.]

rọọmth, *n.* room; spaciousness; roominess. [Obs.]

rọọmth'y, *a.* roomy; spacious. [Obs.]

rọọm'y, *a.*; *comp.* roomier; *superl.* roomiest,

spacious; wide; large; having ample room; as, a *roomy* mansion; a *roomy* deck.
rọọp, *n.* roup. [Brit. Dial.]
rọọr'back, rọọr'bach, *n.* [after the supposed author of a group of alleged selections from a (non-existent) book, *Roorback's Tour through the Western and Southern States in 1836*, containing spurious charges against James K. Polk, then a presidential candidate.] a false or slanderous story devised for political effect, especially against a candidate for election.
rọọ'sȧ oil, see *rusa oil.*
rọọse, *n.*, *v.t.* and *v.i.*; roosed, *pt.*, *pp.*; roosing, *ppr.* praise. [Scot.]
rọọst, *n.* [AS. *hrost*, a roost.]
1. a perch on which birds, especially domestic fowls, can rest or sleep.
2. a place with perches for birds.
3. a place for resting, sleeping, etc.
at roost; on a roost; hence, in a state for rest and sleep.
to rule the roost; to be master.
rọọst, *v.i.*; roosted, *pt.*, *pp.*; roosting, *ppr.* 1. to sit, rest, or sleep, as birds on a pole, tree, or other perch at night.
2. to lodge; to stay or settle down for the night.
to come home to roost; to have repercussions, especially disagreeable ones; to boomerang.
rọọst, *n.* same as *roust.*
rọọst'çock, *n.* a rooster; the male of the domestic hen. [Rare.]
rọọst'ẽr, *n.* 1. a cock; the male of the domestic fowl.
2. any perching bird.
rọọt (*or* root), *n.* [ME. and late AS. *rote*; ON. *rot.*]
1. the part of a plant, usually below the ground, that holds the plant in position, draws water and nourishment from the soil, and stores food.
2. any underground part of a plant, as a rhizome.
3. the attached or embedded part of a bodily structure, as of the teeth, hair, nails, etc.
4. the source or origin of an action, quality, etc.

ROOT

5. a person or family that has many descendants; an ancestor.
6. a lower or supporting part; a base.
7. an essential part; a core; as, the *root* of the matter.
8. in mathematics, (a) a quantity that, multiplied by itself a specified number of times, produces a given quantity; as, 4 is the square *root* (4 × 4) of 16 and the cube *root* (4 × 4 × 4) of 64; (b) a quantity that, when substituted for an unknown quantity, will satisfy an equation.
9. in music, the basic tone of a chord, on which the chord is constructed; often, the fundamental.
10. in linguistics, a base; a morpheme to which prefixes, etc. are added.
aerial roots; (a) in botany, roots proceeding in the open air from the stem of a plant and serving to support it by attaching themselves to trees, other plants, etc.; (b) roots which proceed from the stem of a plant and grow downward into the ground.
crown of a root; see *root neck.*
multiple primary root; in botany, a fibrous root sprouting from the radicle: common to a large number of plants.
primary root; in botany, the root formed in the embryo, from which the rootlets sprout.
root and branch; as an entirety; entirely; completely; as, to demolish something *root and branch.*
secondary roots; in botany, roots proceeding from that part of a plant above the radicle.
to take or *strike root*; to root; to become planted and established in the soil, etc., by a root; hence, figuratively, to become established and fixed; to expand and increase.
rọọt (*or* root), *v.i.* 1. to begin to grow by putting out roots.
2. to become fixed, settled, etc.
rọọt (*or* root), *v.t.* 1. to fix the roots of in the ground.
2. to establish; settle.
to root up (or *out, away*); to pull out by the roots; to remove completely; to destroy entirely.
rọọt (*or* root), *v.t.* [from AS. *wrotan*, to root up, from *wrot*, snout.] to dig or turn up with the snout, as a pig.
rọọt (*or* root), *v.i.* 1. to search by rummaging (usually with *through*).
2. to work hard, as for a living; to plug. [Colloq.]
3. to support or encourage a contestant or team, as by applauding and cheering. [Slang.]
rọọt'āġe (*or* root'), *n.* 1. a taking root or being firmly fixed by means of roots.
2. the roots of a plant, collectively.
rọọt beer, a carbonated beverage made of root extracts from certain plants, as sassafras, etc.
rọọt bōr'ẽr, in zoology, (a) any beetle the larva of which bores into the roots of plants and trees; also, the larva itself, as the *Prionus laticollis* and *Mallodon melanopus* (oak root borer); (b) the larva of any of various species of moths.
rọọt'çap, *n.* in botany, a covering consisting of a mass of parenchymatous cells, for the growing cells at the extremity of a root.
rọọt çrop, a crop of plants with esculent roots, especially of plants having single roots, as turnips, beets, etc.
rọọt'ed, *a.* having its roots planted or fixed in the earth; hence, fixed; deep; radical; as, *rooted* sorrow; *rooted* aversion; *rooted* prejudices.
rọọt'ed·ly, *adv.* in a rooted manner.
rọọt'ed·ness, *n.* the state or condition of being rooted.
rọọt'ẽr, *n.* one who or that which roots; one who tears up by the roots.
rọọt'ẽr, *n.* one who applauds, as at outdoor games or sports, with the object of encouraging his own side. [Slang.]
rọọt'ẽr·y, *n.* a collection of roots and soil in which plants, etc. are set.
rọọt hāir, in botany, one of the thin-walled, hairlike tubular outgrowths from a growing root, which serve to absorb water and minerals from the soil.
rọọt'house, *n.* a house made of roots; also, a house for keeping roots.
rọọt'i·ness, *n.* the quality of being rooty.
rọọt knot (not), an outgrowth on a root resembling a knot.
rọọt lēaf, a leaf growing or apparently growing from the root; a radical leaf.
rọọt'less, *a.* having no roots.
rọọt'let, *n.* a radicel; a little root or small branch of a root.
rọọt neck, in botany, the collar of a plant.
rọọt par'ȧ·sīte, a plant which is parasitic upon or grows upon the root of another plant.
rọọt shēath, 1. in botany, (a) one of the epidermal sheaths surrounding some aerial roots; (b) same as *coleorhiza.*
2. in zoology, the sheath of the root of a hair, feather, or scale.
rọọt'stạlk (-stạk), *n.* a rhizome; rootstock.
rọọt'stock, *n.* 1. a rhizome.
2. an origin or source.
3. a root used as a stock in the propagation of plants.
rọọt vōle, a meadow mouse, *Arvicola æconomus*, of Siberia.
rọọt'y, *a.*; *comp.* rootier; *superl.* rootiest, 1. having many roots.
2. like a root or roots.
rō·pal'iç, *a.* same as *rhopalic.*
rōpe, *n.* [ME. *rop, rape*; AS. *rāp.*]
1. a thick, strong cord made of intertwisted strands of fiber, thin wires, leather strips, etc.
2. [*pl.*] such cords strung between posts to enclose a boxing ring.
3. such a cord, or a noose made of it, for hanging a person.
4. death by hanging.
5. a lasso.
6. a ropelike string of things put together by or as by twisting, twining, or braiding; as, a *rope* of pearls.
7. a ropelike, sticky formation in a liquid, as wine.
on the ropes; (a) in boxing, knocked against the ropes; (b) [Slang.] near collapse or ruin.
rope of sand; proverbially, a feeble union or tie; a band easily broken.
the end of one's rope; the end of one's actions, means, etc. in a desperate situation.
to give one rope; to allow one freedom of action in the expectation that he will overreach himself. [Colloq.]
to know the ropes; to be fully acquainted with the details of a business or procedure. [Colloq.]
rōpe, *v.t.*; roped, *pt.*, *pp.*; roping, *ppr.* 1. to fasten, tie, or confine with or as with a rope.
2. to connect or tie together by a rope, as mountain climbers.
3. to separate, mark off, or enclose with a rope (usually with *in, off,* or *out*).
4. to catch or throw with a lasso.
to rope in; to entice; persuade; lure; inveigle. [Slang.]
rōpe, *v.i.* to become ropelike and sticky; as, some candy is cooked until it *ropes.*
rōpe'band, *n.* in nautical usage, a short, flat plaited piece of rope, with an eye in one end, used in pairs to tie the upper edges of square sails to their yards: also written *robbin* and *roband.*
rōpe'bärk, *n.* a plant, leatherwood.
rōpe'dȧn"cẽr, *n.* a performer who dances, walks, or does tricks on a rope stretched between poles high above the ground.
rōpe'dȧn"cing, *n.* the art or practice of the ropedancer.
rōpe grȧss, any leafless rushlike grass of the family *Restiaceæ*, of Australia or South Africa.
rōpe'māk"ẽr, *n.* one who makes or manufactures ropes or cordage.
rōpe'māk"ing, *n.* the art or business of manufacturing ropes or cordage.
rōpe pump, a machine for raising water, consisting of a rope or ropes passing over a pulley above the water and under another pulley below the surface of the water.
rōp'ẽr, *n.* 1. a ropemaker.
2. one who ropes goods; a packer.
3. one who ropes cattle with a lasso.
4. one who decoys or ropes in. [Slang.]
rōpe'-rīpe", *a.* fit for hanging; deserving a rope. [Archaic.]
rōp'ẽr·y, *n.*; *pl.* **rōp'ẽr·ieṣ,** 1. a place where ropes are made.
2. a trick that deserves hanging; roguery. [Archaic.]
rōpe'ṣ'-end, *v.t.*; rope's-ended, *pt.*, *pp.*; rope's-ending, *ppr.* to punish with a rope's end.
rōpe trick, 1. a trick that deserves hanging. [Obs.]
2. a jugglers' trick with ropes.
rōpe'wạlk (-wạk), *n.* a long, covered walk or a long building where ropes are manufactured.
rōpe'wạlk"ẽr, *n.* a ropedancer.
rōpe'wāy", *n.* a rope or steel cable moved by revolving pulleys, used to convey coal, etc. in baskets or other receptacles suspended from it.
rōpe yärn, yarn for ropes, consisting of a single thread. The threads are twisted into strands, and the strands into ropes.
rōp'i·ly, *adv.* in a ropy, or viscous, manner.
rōp'i·ness, *n.* the quality or condition of being ropy.
rōp'ing, *n.* ropes collectively.
rōp'ing, *a.* ropy; viscous. [Rare.]
rōp'ish, *a.* ropy; becoming ropy.
rōp'y, *a*; *comp.* ropier; *superl.* ropiest, 1. stringy; adhesive; that may be drawn into a thread, as a glutinous substance; viscous; tenacious; glutinous; as, *ropy* wine; *ropy* lees.
2. ropelike; like a rope or ropes.
ropy lava; pahoehoe.
rōque (rōk), *n.* [from *croquet.*] a kind of croquet played on a hard court with special equipment, and requiring more skill than ordinary croquet.
Rōque'fôrt (rōk'), *n.* see *Roquefort cheese* under *cheese.*
roqu'e·lạure (rok'e-lạr), *n.* [named from the Duc de *Roquelaure* (1656–1738).] a heavy, knee-length cloak for men much used early in the eighteenth century.
rō·quet' (-kā'), *v.t.* and *v.i.*; roqueted (-kād'), *pt.*, *pp.*; roqueting, *ppr.* [from *croquet.*] in croquet and roque, to strike (the ball of another) with one's own ball: said of either a player or his ball.
rō·quet', *n.* a roqueting.
rō'răl, *a.* [L. *ros, roris*, dew.] of or pertaining to dew; dewy. [Rare.]
rō'riç, *a.* dewy; caused by dew.

ROQUELAURE

roric figures; figures exhibited by a polished

fāte, fär, fȧst, fạll, finăl, cāre, at; mēte, prẹy, hẽr, met; pīne, marïne, bïrd, pin; nōte, mōve, fọr, atŏm, not; mọọn, book;

surface when breathed upon under various conditions.

rō′rid, *a.* dewy. [Obs.]

rō·rif′ẽr·ous, *a.* generating or producing dew. [Rare.]

rō·rif′lū·ent, *a.* flowing with dew. [Obs.]

ror′quăl, *n.* [from Norw. *röyrkval*; ON. *reyðarhvalr*, lit., red whale: so called from its reddish color.] a finback; a whale of the genus *Balænoptera*, distinguished from the common whales by having a dorsal fin, with the throat and under parts wrinkled in deep longitudinal folds: some are very large.

Ror′sçhăçh test, [after Hermann *Rorschach* (1884–1922), Swiss psychiatrist.] in psychology, a test for the analysis of personality, in which the person being tested tells what is suggested to him by a series of ink-blot designs of various shapes: his responses are then analyzed and interpreted.

rō′rū·lent, *a.* [L. *rorulentus*, dewy, from *ros*, *roris*, dew.] full of dew; dewy. [Rare.]

rō′ry, *a.* dewy. [Obs.]

Rō′ṣȧ, *n.* [L., a rose.] a genus of plants of the family *Rosaceæ*, including all the true roses. It is characterized by a calyx with an urn-shaped fleshy tube, contracted at the mouth, enclosing the many pistils and achenes, and having five leafy lobes.

rōṣ·āce′, *n.* [Fr.] an ornamental piece of plaster work in the center of a ceiling or panel.

Rō·ṣā′cē·ae, *n.pl.* a large family of plants with alternate stipulate leaves and regular flowers with usually unconnected stamens inserted on the calyx, and commonly single seeds. In this family are included besides the rose, spiraea, hawthorn, and other flowering plants, the plum, cherry, peach, apricot, almond, pear, apple, quince, raspberry, blackberry, and strawberry.

rō·ṣā′ceous, *a.* [L. *rosaceus*, made of roses.]
1. of the rose family of plants, or *Rosaceæ*, including also the strawberry, blackberry, agrimony, etc.
2. having a corolla of five petals, like that of the rose.
3. like a rose.
4. rose-colored; rosy.

rō′ṣăl, *a.* 1. related to the *Rosaceæ*; belonging to the *Rosales*.
2. rosy; roseate. [Obs.]

Rō·ṣā′lēṣ, *n.pl.* an order of dicotyledons of which the *Rosaceæ* are typical, as the *Saxifragaceæ*, the *Crassulaceæ*, the *Leguminosæ*, and the *Hamamelideæ*.

rō·ṣä′li·ȧ, *n.* [It., from the first word of an old song in which such repetitions occur.] in music, a melody in which the phrases are repeated in ascending keys.

rōṣ·an′i·line, rōṣ·an′i·lin, *n.* [*rose* and *aniline*.] a crystalline base, $C_{20}H_{21}N_3O$, made by heating aniline and toluidine with nitrobenzene: many aniline dyes are derivatives of it.
rosaniline blue; spirit blue.

rō·ṣãr′i·ăn, *n.* one who grows roses.

rō′ṣȧ·ry, *n.*; *pl.* **rō′ṣȧ·rieṣ,** [LL. *rosarium*.]
1. a bed of roses or rose garden.
2. in the Roman Catholic Church, (a) a string of beads used to keep count in saying prayers: it contains sets, five or fifteen, of ten small beads and one large bead; each set (decade) is associated with a mystery of the Faith, or happening in the life of Jesus and the Virgin Mary; (b) [*also* R–] the prayers said with these beads: a paternoster (large bead), followed by ten Aves (small beads) and a Gloria Patri (large bead) for each set.
3. a string of beads used in a similar way among other religious groups.
4. a counterfeit coin of the reign of Edward I, worth about a halfpenny, coined abroad and brought surreptitiously into England. It was so called from bearing the figure of a rose.

rō′ṣȧ·ry shell, a gastropodous shell of the genus *Monodonta*, found in tropical seas.

ros′cid, *a.* [L. *roscidus*, from *ros*, dew.] dewy; containing dew; consisting of dew. [Rare.]

ros′çōe·līte, *n.* [from H. E. *Roscoe*, an English chemist, and *-lite*.] a pearly, dark-brown, soft, micaceous mineral containing vanadium and occurring in minute scales, sometimes arranged in fanlike or stellated groups.

rōṣe, *v.* past tense of *rise*.

rōṣe, *n.* [AS. *rose*, from L. *rosa*, a rose; Gr. *rhodon*; of Oriental origin.]
1. any of a number of related plants of the genus *Rosa*, characteristically with prickly stems and five-petaled, usually fragrant flowers of red, pink, white, yellow, etc. having many stamens.
2. the flower of any of these plants.
3. any of several similar or related plants.
4. rose color; pinkish red or purplish red.
5. erysipelas: with *the*.
6. a perfume made from or having the fragrance of roses.
7. a rosette.
8. a round, perforated nozzle for a hose, sprinkling can, etc.
9. a form in which gems are often cut so that the upper surface has many small facets.
10. a gem, especially a diamond, cut in this way.
11. a rose window.
12. in nautical usage, a compass card or a representation of this, as on maps.
13. in heraldry, a conventional representation of a five-leaved or five-lobed flower.
alpine rose; a hardy species of rose, *Rosa alpina*, found in the mountainous regions of Europe.
Australian rose; a shrub, *Beronia serrulata*, of the rue family, growing in Australia.
Ayrshire rose; *Rosa arvensis*, an English species of rose.
Banksian rose; *Rosa banksiæ*, a Chinese climbing species of rose.
bed of roses; a comfortable, easy state or position; luxury or idleness.
brier rose; the dogrose.
China rose; *Rosa indica*, a species of rose having very strong prickles.
Chinese rose; the China rose.
cinnamon rose; a European species of rose, *Rosa cinnamomea*.
evergreen rose; a climbing plant of southern Europe, *Rosa sempervirens*.
fairy rose; a small rose, *Rosa laurenciana*, probably a variety of the China rose.
Indian rose; the China rose.
Japan or *Japanese rose*; one of various Japanese roses, as *Rosa multiflora* and *Rosa rugosa*.
Michigan rose; see *prairie rose* under *rose*.
Nutka rose; a North American wild rose, *Rosa nutkana*.
prairie rose; a hardy American climbing plant, *Rosa setigera*: also called *Michigan rose*.
Provence rose, *Provins rose*; the cabbage rose.
red rose; the emblem of the House of Lancaster.
rose of China; the China rose.
Scotch rose; any variety of *Rosa spinosissima* or *Rosa pimpinellifolia*, an old-world plant with prickly stems.
South Sea rose; the oleander.
under the rose; [transl. of L. *sub rosa*.] secretly; privately; confidentially.
Wars of the Roses; in English history, the struggle for supremacy between the Houses of York and Lancaster (1455–1485): so called from the white and red roses, the badges respectively of the supporters of the York and Lancastrian families: the war ended with the establishment of the House of Tudor on the English throne.
white rose; (a) the badge worn by adherents of the House of York during the Wars of the Roses; (b) a much cultivated species of rose, *Rosa alba*, native to Europe.
yellow rose; (a) *Rosa lutea*, a summer rose of numerous varieties; (b) an Asiatic rose, *Rosa sulphurea*.

rōṣe, *v.t.*; rosed, *pt.*, *pp.*; rosing, *ppr.* 1. to make rose-colored; to cause to blush.
2. to perfume as with roses; to make rose-scented.

rōṣe, *a.* rose-colored.

rōṣe ȧ·cā′ciȧ (-shȧ), a North American shrub, *Robinia hispida*, of the pea family, with large rose-colored flowers: also called *bristly locust*.

rō′ṣē·ăl, *a.* like a rose in perfume or color.

rōṣe an′i·line, same as *rosaniline*.

rōṣe ā′phis, an aphid parasitic upon roses; specifically, *Siphonophora rosæ*.

rōṣe ap′ple, an oriental tree, *Eugenia jambos*, of the myrtle family or its fruit, which has a roselike perfume. The name is also given to certain other species of the same genus.

rō′ṣē·āte, *a.* [L. *roseus*, rosy.]
1. rose-colored; rosy.
2. made or consisting of roses.
3. bright, cheerful, or optimistic.
roseate tern; in zoology, a tern, *Sterna dougalli*, found in both hemispheres. Its under parts in the breeding season have a rosy tint.

rōṣe′bāy, *n.* any one of several plants, as (a) the oleander; (b) any species of *Rhododendron*; (c) [Brit.] the willow herb, *Epilobium angustifolium*.

rōṣe bee′tle, a beetle living in and destructive to rosebushes, as (a) the rose chafer of Europe; (b) the rose bug of America; (c) a beetle, *Aramigus fulleri*, of the family *Curculionidæ*.

rōṣe box, any plant of the rose family belonging to the genus *Cotoneaster*.

rōṣe′-breast″ed grōs′bēak, a North American bird of the finch family, the male of which has a rose-colored triangular patch on the breast.

rōṣe′bud, *n.* the bud of a rose.

rōṣe bug, a rose beetle: *Macrodactylus subspinosus* is the copper-colored, hard-shelled American species.

rōṣe bũrn′ẽr, a gas burner from which a flame is produces in the shape of a rose.

rōṣe′buṣh, *n.* the bush, vine, or shrub which produces the rose.

rōṣe cam′pi·ŏn, 1. a plant of the pink family, with white, woolly leaves and clusters of small, red or white flowers; mullein pink.
2. the corn cockle.

rōṣe çãr·nā′tion, a carnation striped with red, or the color of the typical rose.

rōṣe chāf′ẽr, any beetle injurious or destructive to the rose; specifically, the beetle *Cetonia aurata* of Europe, or the beetle *Macrodactylus subspinosus* of the United States.

rōṣe çōld (or **fē′vẽr**), a variety of hay fever most prevalent in the early months of summer and sometimes believed to be caused by the pollen of roses.

rōṣe çŏl′ŏr, pinkish red or purplish red.

rōṣe′-çŏl″ŏred, *a.* 1. having the color of a rose.
2. bright, cheerful, or optimistic.

rōṣe çrŏss, the combination of a rose and cross, the symbol of a religious sect, the Rosicrucians.

rōṣe′-çut, *a.* cut like a rose: said of a precious stone; as, a *rose-cut* diamond.

rōṣe′drop, *n.* a lozenge with rose flavor.

rōṣe ēar, a dog's ear turned so as to show the color of the skin on the inner side.

rōṣe el′dẽr, the guelder-rose.

rōṣe en′ġine, a kind of lathe used in engraving in fine curved lines, as on a watch case or on a plate for printing bank notes.

rōṣe′fāced (-fāst), *a.* having a rosy or red face; having a face shaped like a rose.

rōṣe′fish, *n.*; *pl.* **rōṣe′fish** or **rōṣe′fish·eṣ,** a North Atlantic food fish that is orange to red in color when grown: also called *Norway haddock*.

rōṣe ġē·rā′ni·um, any of several geraniums; especially, a pelargonium with small, pinkish flower clusters and lobed, fragrant leaves, much cultivated in South Africa.

rōṣe′head (-hed), *n.* 1. a head, as of a nail or bolt, bearing some resemblance to a rose.
2. same as *rose*, sense 8.

rōṣe hip, the fleshy, bright-colored fruit of the rose.

rōṣe′-hūed (-hūd), *a.* rose-colored.

rō′ṣē·ine, *n.* same as *fuchsin*.

rōṣe knot (not), an ornamental bunch of ribbon or the like in the form of a rose; a rosette.

rōṣe lāke, a bright red pigment.

rōṣe lash′ing, in nautical usage, a kind of lashing or seizing employed in woolding spars: so called from its shape.

rōṣe lāthe, same as *rose engine*.

rōṣe lēaf, the petal of a rose.

rōṣe lip, a lip of a rosy or ripe color.

Thy *rose lips* and full blue eyes.
—Tennyson.

rōṣe′līte, *n.* [from G. *Rose* (1798–1873), a German naturalist.] a reddish arsenate of cobalt occurring in small crystals.

rō·ṣel′lȧ, *n.* a native Australian parrot, sometimes called the *rose parakeet*, with head and back of the neck scarlet, breast yellow, and throat white.

rō·ṣel′lāte, *a.* [from L. *rosa*, a rose.] in botany, denoting leaves when they are arranged like the petals of a rose.

rō·ṣelle′ (-zel′), *n.* a species of rose mallow, *Hibiscus sabdariffa*, the acidulous calyxes of which are used in the East and West Indies for tarts, jellies, etc., and for beverages.

rōṣe mad′dẽr, rose lake.

rōṣe mal′lōw, 1. any of various related plants of the genus *Hibiscus*, with large, rose-colored flowers; hibiscus.
2. the hollyhock.

rōṣe′mal″ōeṣ, *n.* a species of liquid aromatic gum obtained from the *Liquidambar* of the East Indies. [Rare.]

rōṣe′mār·y, *n.* [L. *rosmarinus*; *ros*, dew, and *marinus*, sea.] a verticillate plant, *Rosmarinus officinalis*, of the mint family, native to the Mediterranean region, with clusters of small, light-blue flowers and leaves that yield a fragrant essential oil, used in making perfumes, in cookery, etc.: rosemary is conventionally a symbol of remembrance and constancy.

rōṣe′mār·y pīne, same as *loblolly pine*.

rōṣe moss, portulaca, especially the garden variety.

rō′ṣen, *a.* composed of roses; roseate. [Obs.]

Rō′ṣen·mūl·lẽr's ọr′găn, [after J. C. *Rosenmüller* (1771–1820), German anatomist.] in anatomy, the parovarium.

rō′ṣē·ō-, [from L. *roseus*, rosy.] a combining form applied in chemistry to certain reddish salts; as, a *roseo*-cobaltic compound.

rōṣe of heav′en (hev′), a plant of western Asia, *Lychnis cœli-rosa.*

rōṣe of Jer′i·chō, an Asiatic plant of the mustard family, with oval leaves and spikes of small, white flowers: it curls up when dry and expands again when moistened.

rōṣe of Ply′mouth (pli′muth), a gentianaceous plant of the eastern United States, *Sabbatica chloroides.*

rōṣe of Shăr′ŏn, 1. the althea, a tall shrub of the mallow family.

2. a St.-John's-wort, with evergreen leaves and large, yellow flowers.

3. a plant mentioned in the Bible: S. of Sol. (Cant.) ii. 1.

rō·ṣē′ō·lȧ, *n.* [Mod. L., dim. of L. *roseus*, rosy.] any rose-colored rash; especially, German measles, or rubella: also called *rose rash.*

rōṣe′-piṅk′, *a.* of a deep or crimson pink color; having a delicate bloom.

rōṣe piṅk, 1. a deep or crimson-pink color or pigment.

2. in botany, *Sabbatia angularis*, the American centaury.

rōṣe quartz, a variety of quartz which is rose-red.

rōṣe red, the color peculiar to the rose; the color rose.

rōṣe′-red′, *a.* of, pertaining to, or characterized by the red color characteristic of the rose.

rōṣe′rọọt, *n.* a plant, *Sedum rhodiola*, whose root has the odor of a rose.

rō′ṣẽr·y, *n.*; *pl.* **rō′ṣẽr·ieṣ,** a place for growing roses; a rosary.

rōṣe rȳ′ăl, ṛōṣe rī′ăl, [*rose* and *rial* for *royal*.] any of several British gold coins of various reigns and various values. The noble of the reign of Edward IV, of the value of 8s. 4d., was so called from the figure of a rose which was added to the reverse. There were rose ryals of James I of the value of 30s.

rōṣe sçāle, a scale insect, *Diaspis rosæ*, that feeds on and injures rosebushes.

rō′ṣet, *n.* [Fr., from *rose*.] a painters' red color. [Obs.]

Rō·ṣet′tȧ stōne, a tablet of black basalt found in 1799 at Rosetta, a town in Egypt at

ROSETTA STONE

one of the mouths of the Nile: because it bore parallel inscriptions in Greek and in ancient Egyptian demotic and hieroglyphic characters, it provided a key to the deciphering of ancient Egyptian writing.

rō·ṣet′tȧ wood, a furniture wood of an orange-red color, with very dark veins, imported from the East Indies.

rō·ṣette′, *n.* [Fr., a dim. of *rose*.]

1. an ornament made of ribbons, threads, etc. gathered or tufted in the shape of a rose.

2. any formation, arrangement, etc. resembling or suggesting a rose.

3. in architecture, a painted or sculptured ornament, usually circular, having petals and leaves radiating symmetrically from the center.

4. in botany, a circular cluster of leaves, petals, or other organs.

5. in zoology, anything having a flowerlike form or markings, as sea urchins and the spots on a leopard.

6. in metallurgy, a small thin plate resembling a rosette, formed by throwing water on molten metal.

rō·ṣē′tum, *n.* a garden or nursery of roses.

rōṣe wạ′tẽr, a preparation consisting of water and oil of roses, used as a perfume.

rōṣe′-wạ″tẽr, *a.* like, made with, or having the characteristics of rose water; hence, delicate, fine, etc. in an affected or sentimental way.

rōṣe win′dōw, in architecture, a circular window ornamented by radiating figures in such

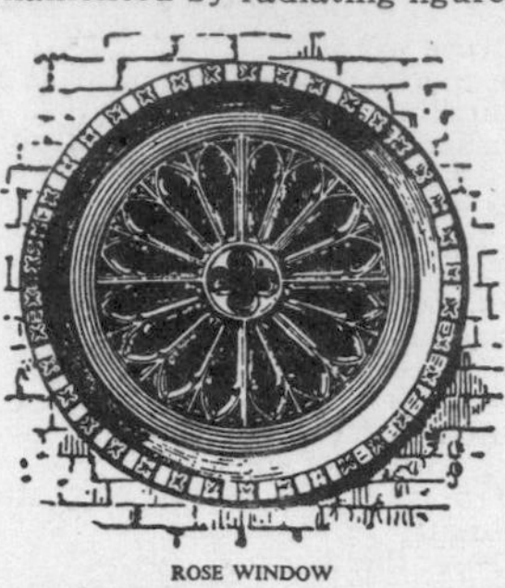
ROSE WINDOW

a way as to resemble a rose or by mullions arranged like the spokes of a wheel: also called *wheel window.*

rōṣe′wood, *n.* [so called from its odor.]

1. any of a number of valuable hard, reddish, black-streaked woods, sometimes with a roselike odor, obtained from certain tropical trees and used in making furniture, etc.

2. any tree producing rosewood, as *Dalbergia nigra.*

African rosewood; the molompi, *Pterocarpus erinaceus.*

rōṣe′wood oil, a volatile oil having an odor as of rosewood.

rōṣe′wọrm, *n.* the larva of a moth, *Cacæcia rosaceana*, subsisting upon the leaves of the rose, apple, peach, cotton, and other plants.

rōṣe′wọrt, *n.* 1. any plant of the rose family. [Obs.]

2. the roseroot.

Rōsh Hä·shä′nȧ, [Heb. *rōsh hashānāh*, lit., head (or first) of the year.] the Jewish New Year: also spelled *Rosh Hashona*, etc.

Rō·ṣi·çrụ′ciăn, *n.* [L. *rosa*, a rose, and *crux, crucis*, a cross. Popularized in the fifteenth century by one who bore the symbolical name of Christian Rosenkreuz (Christian of the Rosy Cross).]

1. any of a number of persons in the 17th and 18th centuries who professed to be members of a secret society said to have various sorts of occult lore and power, and holding esoteric religious doctrines: its symbol was a cross with a red rose in the center. The Rosicrucians have been known by various names, such as Brothers of the Rosy Cross, Rosy-Cross Knights, and Rosy-Cross Philosophers.

2. a member of any of several later groups with doctrines and practices said to be based on those of these persons; especially, the Rosicrucian Order, or the Ancient Mystic Order Rosae Crucis (AMORC). This order uses a golden cross with a red rose in its center as its symbol.

Rō·ṣi·çrụ′ciăn, *a.* of or pertaining to the Rosicrucians or Rosicrucianism.

Rō ṣi çrụ′ciăn·iṣm, *n.* the doctrines and practices of the Rosicrucians.

rō′ṣied, *a.* made rosy or to resemble a rose or roses.

rō′ṣiẽr (-zhẽr), *n.* a rosebush. [Obs.]

rō′ṣi·ly, *adv.* 1. in a rosy manner; cheerfully; optimistically.

2. with a rosy color.

roṣ′in, *n.* [ME.; OFr. *rosine*; var. of *resine*; see *resin*.] resin; specifically, the hard, brittle resin, light-yellow to almost black in color, remaining after oil of turpentine has been distilled from crude turpentine: it is rubbed on violin bows, used in making varnish, etc.

roṣ′in, *v.t.*; rosined, *pt., pp.*; rosining, *ppr.* to rub with rosin.

Roṣ·i·nan′te, *n.* [Sp. *rocinante*, from *rocin*, a jade, hack; ult. ML. *runcinus*, sturdy, low-grade horse.]

1. Don Quixote's old, bony, broken-down horse.

2. any old, broken-down horse; a jade.

rō′ṣi·ness, *n.* the quality or state of being rosy.

roṣ′in·weed, *n.* (a) the compass plant; (b) the prairie dock.

roṣ′in·y, *a.* full of, like, or covered with rosin.

ros′lănd, *n.* [W. *rhos*, peat, or a moor.] heathy land; moorish or watery land.

roṣ′mȧ·rīne, *n.* 1. rosemary. [Obs.]

2. sea dew. [Obs.]

roṣ′mȧ·rīne, *n.* [Dan. *rosmar*, a walrus.] a sea animal, similar to the walrus, reputed to feed upon sea dew, for which it climbed cliffs by its teeth.

Ros·mȧ·rī′nus, *n.* [L. *ros marinus*, sea dew.] a genus of plants of the mint family, of which the rosemary is the best-known species.

Ros·min′i·ăn, *a.* pertaining to Antonio Rosmini-Serbati, organizer of the Institute of Charity at Monte Calvario, Italy, in 1828, or his doctrines.

Ros·min′i·ăn, *n.* 1. a believer in the philosophy of Rosmini, which holds that all concepts can be traced objectively to the one first concept of divine origin.

2. a member of the Rosminian Institute of Charity.

rō·ṣō′liō, rō·ṣōg′liō (rō-zō′lyō), *n.* [Fr. and It., prob. from L. *rossolis*, sun dew.] a sweet cordial made from raisins, drunk especially in southern Europe: called also *rossolis.*

rō·sō′ri·ăl, *a.* [L. *rosus* (*-oris*), from *rodere*, to gnaw.] of or belonging to the stigma of the *Rodentia.*

ross, *n.* [Dan. *ros*, chips or peelings.]

1. the rough, scaly matter on the surface of the bark of certain trees.

2. refuse; rubbish. [Obs.]

ross, *v.t.*; rossed, *pt., pp.*; rossing, *ppr.* to strip of the ross.

ros′tel, *n.* same as *rostellum.*

ros·tel′lȧ, *n.* plural of *rostellum.*

Ros·tel·lā′ri·ȧ, *n.* a genus of marine univalve mollusks belonging to the family *Strombidæ*. It is found both recent and fossil. The shell is spindle-shaped, with an elevated pointed spire; the aperture is oval, canal projecting, and terminating in a pointed beak. The species are mostly found in the Asiatic seas.

ros′tel·lāte, *a.* having a rostellum or rostella.

ros·tel′li·fọrm, *a.* having the form of a rostellum.

ros·tel′lum, *n.*; *pl.* **ros·tel′lȧ,** [L., dim. of *rostrum*, a beak.] in botany, (a) an elevated and rather thickened portion of the stigma of orchids; (b) any small beak-shaped process or part, as in the stigma of many violets.

ros′tẽr, *n.* [D. *rooster*, a thing for roasting, a gridiron; hence, a grating, a table or list, a roster—the last meaning probably from perpendicular and horizontal lines of ruled paper giving a grated appearance.]

1. a list of military or naval personnel or groups showing the turn or rotation of service or duty of those who relieve or succeed each other; specifically, a register showing or fixing the rotation and assignments in which individuals, companies, regiments, etc. are called on to serve.

2. any list; roll.

ros′trȧ, *n.* alternative plural of *rostrum.*

ros′trăl, *a.* [LL. *rostralis*, from L. *rostrum*, beak.]

1. of, in, or on a rostrum.

2. decorated with rostrums, or beaks of ships; as, *rostral* pillars.

ros′trāte, ros′trā·ted, *a.* [L. *rostratus*, beaked.] beaked; having a process resembling a beak.

ros·trif′ẽr·ouṣ, *a.* having a beak.

ros′tri·fọrm, *a.* having the form of a beak.

ros′troid, *a.* resembling a beak.

ros′trụ·lăr, *a.* [L. *rostrular*, a little beak.] pertaining to a rostrulum.

ros′trụ·lum, *n.*; *pl.* **ros′trụ·lȧ,** [L., dim. of *rostrum*, a beak.] a small beak, as of an insect.

ros′trum, *n.*; *pl.* **ros′trumṣ, ros′trȧ,** [L., a beak, the prow of a ship, from *rodere, rosus*, to gnaw, to peck.]

1. in ancient Rome, a curved, beaklike projection at the prow of a ship; especially, such a projection on a war galley, used for ramming enemy vessels: also called *beak.*

2. in ancient Rome, a platform in the Forum at Rome, from which public speeches were delivered: called the *Rostra* by the Romans from the beaks of ships with which it was ornamented.

3. (a) a platform or elevated place from which a speaker addresses his audience; (b) a pulpit; (c) public speaking, or public speakers collectively.

4. in biology, a beaklike part or appendage.

5. in botany, any beaklike extension, as the stigma of some asclepiads.

6. in zoology, a snout or snout-shaped or-

gan, as the pointed part of the carapace of the *Macrura*.

7. the beak of a still.

8. in surgery, a crooked pair of forceps with beaklike jaws. [Obs.]

roṣ'ū·lăr, *a.* rosulate.

rōṣ'ū·lāte, *a.* arranged in little roselike clusters, as leaves.

rō'ṣy, *a.*; *comp.* rosier; *superl.* rosiest. 1. resembling a rose in color or qualities; blooming; red; often, blushing or flushed with a healthy, blooming red; as, *rosy* cheeks.

2. decorated with roses; made of roses; as, a *rosy* wreath.

3. bright, promising, cheerful, or optimistic; as, a *rosy* future, *rosy* expectations.

rot, *v.i.*; rotted, *pt.*, *pp.*; rotting, *ppr.* [AS. *rotian*; D. *rotten*, to rot; Ice. *rotna*, to rot, to decay, *rotinn*, rotten.]

1. to decay; to spoil; to decompose gradually.

What I loved, and long must love,
Like common earth can *rot*. —Byron.

2. to decay morally; to molder; to become corrupt; to degenerate.

3. to fall or pass (*off*, *away*, etc.) by decaying.

Syn.—decay; putrefy; decompose; corrupt.

rot, *v.t.* 1. to cause to be wholly or partially decomposed; as, to *rot* hay.

2. to ret; to soften the fibers of (flax, etc.) by soaking.

3. to cause to take rot; to affect with rot, as sheep.

rot, *n.* 1. the act, state, or process of rotting; putrefaction, decay, or decomposition.

2. something rotting or rotten.

3. any of various diseases, especially a parasitic disease of sheep and other domestic animals, characterized by decay, emaciation, etc.

4. a disease of plants, wood, etc. produced by fungi and bacteria and characterized by decay.

5. nonsense; rubbish; bosh. [Slang.]

bitter rot; a disease which the fungus *Glœosporium fructigenum*, produces in apples, grapes, etc.

black rot; a disease which the fungus *Læstadia bidwellii*, produces in fruits and vegetables; also, the fungus.

grinder's rot; same as *grinder's asthma*.

rot, *interj.* an exclamation expressing disgust, contempt, annoyance, etc.

Rō'tȧ, *n.* [L. *rota*, a wheel.]

1. in the Roman Catholic Church, a high tribunal consisting of ten prelates (called *auditors*) that serves especially as a court of appeal, as from diocesan courts in matrimonial cases or from the civil and criminal courts of the Vatican City: in full, *Sacra Romana Rota*, or *Sacred Roman Rota*.

2. in English history, a political club founded in 1659 by J. Harrington, who advocated the election of the officers of state by ballot, and the retirement of a certain number of members of parliament annually by rotation.

3. [r–] a round, as of duties; a routine. [Chiefly Brit.]

4. [r–] a roster.

rō'tȧ, *n.* [LL., from the Celtic; W. *erwth*; Gael. *cruit*, a fiddle.] a medieval stringed musical instrument shaped like a zither.

rō'tȧ·ciṣm, *n.* same as *rhotacism*.

rō'tăl, *a.* rotary; pertaining to circular or rotatory motion or to wheels. [Rare.]

rō'tȧ·līte, *n.* [L. *rota*, a wheel, and *-lite*.] a fossil foraminifer.

rō'tang, *n.* [Malay., rattan.] a rattan palm of the East Indies, *Calamus rotang*.

Rō·tār'i·ăn, *n.* a member of a Rotary Club.

Rō·tār'i·ăn, *a.* of Rotarians or Rotary Clubs.

Rō·tār'i·ăn·iṣm, *n.* the principles and practices of Rotarians.

rō'tȧ·ry, *a.* [L. *rota*, a wheel.]

1. turning around a central point or axis, as a wheel; rotating.

2. having a rotating part or parts; as, a *rotary* press.

3. occurring around an axis; as, *rotary* motion.

rotary drill; a rotating drill used for boring holes in rock.

rotary engine; (a) an engine in which rotary motion is produced directly, without reciprocating parts, as a steam turbine: distinguished from *reciprocating engine*; (b) an internal-combustion engine with radially arranged cylinders rotating around a stationary crankshaft, used in many airplanes.

rotary press; a printing press with one or more curved plates mounted on cylinders that rotate against and impress paper moving in a continuous sheet over rotating cylinders.

ROTARY PRESS

rotary pump; a pump in which the necessary action is produced by the revolution of pistons around their axes.

rotary valve; a valve which acts by continuous or partial rotation.

Rō'tȧ·ry Club, any local organization of Rotary International.

Rō'tȧ·ry In·tẽr·na'tion·ăl (-nash'un-), [from the fact that meetings were originally held in rotation at the members' offices.] an international association of business and professional men, founded in Chicago in 1905, with the aim of serving their communities and fostering understanding among nations: also *Rotary*.

rō'tȧ·sçōpe, *n.* [L. *rota*, a wheel, and *-scope*.] same as *gyroscope*.

rō'tā·tȧ·ble, *a.* that can be rotated.

rō'tā·tȧ·bly, *adv.* so as to be rotated.

rō'tāte, *a.* [L. *rotatus*, turned.] in botany, wheel-shaped, with radiating parts; as, a *rotate* corolla.

ROTATE COROLLA

rō'tāte, *v.i.*; rotated, *pt.*, *pp.*; rotating, *ppr.* 1. to revolve or turn round a center or axis.

2. to go in a regular and recurring succession of changes; to take turns.

rō'tāte, *v.t.* 1. to cause to turn round, as a wheel on its axis.

2. to cause to go in a regular and recurring succession of changes; to cause to take turns.

rō'tā·ted, *a.* [L. *rotatus*, turned.] rotate.

rō·tā'tion, *n.* [L. *rotatio* (*-onis*), from *rotare*, to turn; *rota*, a wheel.]

1. a rotating or being rotated; as, the daily *rotation* of the earth.

2. regular and recurring succession of changes; as, a *rotation* of duties.

3. same as *cyclosis*.

rō·tā'tion·ăl, *a.* pertaining to or caused by rotation; resembling or characterized by rotation.

rō·tā'tion of çrops, a system of rotating in a fixed order the kinds of crops, as grain, etc., grown in the same field, to maintain soil fertility.

rō'tȧ·tive, *a.* 1. rotating or occurring in rotation.

2. rotational; causing rotation.

rō'tā·tŏr, *n.* 1. a person or thing that rotates.

2. *pl.* **rō·tȧ·tō'rēṣ,** in anatomy, a muscle that serves to rotate a part of the body.

Rō·tȧ·tō'ri·ȧ, *n.pl.* same as *Rotifera*.

rō'tȧ·tō·ry, *a.* 1. rotary.

2. going or following in rotation, or in succession.

3. producing rotation.

4. of, or having the nature of, rotation.

rō'tȧ·tō·ry, *n.* a rotifer. [Rare.]

rotche, rotch (roch), *n.* [D. *rotje*, a petrel.] a small arctic auk, the dovekie.

rōte, *n.* a root. [Obs.]

rōte, *n.* a medieval stringed musical instrument, variously supposed to have been a kind of lyre or lute.

rōte, *n.* [OE. and Scot. *rowte*, *rout*; AS. *hrutan*; Ice. *rauta*, to roar.] the roar of surf upon a seashore.

rōte, *n.* [OFr. *rote*, a way, a route; hence, *rotine*, routine.] a fixed, mechanical way of doing something; a routine.

by rote; by memory alone, without understanding or thought; as, he repeated the lesson by *rote*.

rō'ten·ōne, *n.* a white, odorless, crystalline substance, $C_{23}H_{22}O_6$, obtained from the roots of certain tropical plants and used chiefly in insecticides.

rot grȧss, any of various plants thought to cause rot in sheep, as the butterwort.

rot'gut, *n.* raw, low-grade whisky. [Slang.]

roth'ẽr (-ẽr-), a bovine animal. [Brit. Dial.]

roth'ẽr, *n.* a rudder. [Obs.]

roth'ẽr·bēast, *n.* a rother. [Obs.]

roth'ẽr·muck, *n.* the barnacle goose. [Brit. Dial.]

roth'ẽr nāil, a nail with a very full head, used for fastening the rudder irons of ships.

rō'ti·fẽr, *n.* [L. *rota*, a wheel, and *ferre*, to bear.] one of the *Rotifera*.

Rō·tif'e·rȧ, *n.pl.* a group of microscopic, structurally complex water animals having ciliated appendages on the fore part of the body, which move in a rotary manner and look like rotating wheels.

rō·tif'ẽr·ăl, *a.* of a rotifer.

rō·tif'ẽr·ous, *a.* same as *rotiferal*.

rō'ti·fọrm, *a.* 1. having the shape of a wheel.

2. in botany, rotate.

rō·tis'se·riē, *n.* [Fr.] 1. a shop or restaurant where meats are roasted and sold.

2. a portable electric grill with a turning spit.

rot'l, *n.*; *pl.* **är'täl,** [Ar. *ratl*.]

1. a unit of weight used in Moslem regions, varying from about one to about five pounds, according to locality.

2. a varying unit of dry measure used in these regions.

rō'tō, *n.* short for *rotogravure*.

rō'tō·grȧph, *n.* a photograph produced by a process in which a sensitized strip of paper automatically rolls under the negative, making a series of prints.

rō″tō·grȧ·vūre' (*or* -grā'vūre), *n.* [from L. *rota*, a wheel, and *gravure*, Fr., a printing plate produced by hand, from OFr. *graver*, to impress or engrave.]

1. a process of printing pictures, letters, etc. on a rotary press using copper cylinders etched from photographic plates: clear, smooth reproductions are thus obtained.

2. a picture or print made by this process.

3. a newspaper pictorial section printed by this process: also called *roto section*.

rō'tŏr, *n.* 1. a mathematical quantity having magnitude, direction, and position.

2. the rotating part of a motor, dynamo, etc.; cf. *stator*.

3. a system of rotating airfoils, as of a helicopter.

4. one of the tall, revolving cylinders of a rotor ship.

rō'tŏr ship, a kind of sailing ship propelled by the action of the wind on one or more tall, vertical cylinders of sheet metal (*rotors*) that are rotated by a small electric motor: it is equipped with other means of propulsion for use when the wind fails.

ROTOR SHIP

rō'tō seç'tion, a rotogravure (sense 3).

rot'tȧ, rot'te, *n.* a rote (musical instrument).

rot'ten (rot'n), *a.* [ME. *roten*; ON. *rotinn*; cf. *rot*.]

1. decayed; decomposed; spoiled; putrefied; as, a *rotten* potato.

2. having a bad odor because of decomposition or decay; putrid; foul-smelling.

3. soft or easily broken because of decomposition; as, *rotten* rock, a *rotten* plank, *rotten* rope.

4. characterized by dishonesty; corrupt; as, *rotten* government.

5. unsound or weak, as if decayed within.

6. affected by rot, as an animal.

7. disagreeable, unsatisfactory, very bad, etc.; as, *rotten* weather. [Slang.]

Syn.—unsound, treacherous, deceitful, carious, decomposed, fetid, offensive, tainted.

rot'ten bŏr'ōugh (bũr'ō), see under *borough*.

rot'ten-egg', *v.t.* to throw rotten eggs at.

rot'ten·ly, *adv.* in a rotten manner.

rot'ten·ness, *n.* the state or condition of being rotten.

rot'ten·stōne, *n.* a siliceous limestone decomposed to a friable state, used for polishing metals.

rot'tẽr, *n.* a despicable or objectionable person. [Chiefly Brit. Slang.]

rott gọose, the brant. [Brit. Dial.]

rot'tlẽr·in (-lẽr-), *n.* [LL. *rottlera*, from Dr. *Rottler*, a Danish missionary.] a yellow crystalline compound present in the fruit of the kamala tree. It possesses purgative properties.

rot′ū·là, *n.* [L., dim. of *rota*, a wheel.]
1. in anatomy, the patella.
2. any disklike bony process.
3. a troche or lozenge.

rot′ū·lăr, *a.* pertaining to the rotula or patella.

rot′ū·li·fọrm, *a.* formed like a patella or kneepan; patelliform.

rō·tund′, *a.* [LL. *rotundus*, formed from *rota*, a wheel, on type of *jocundus*, from *jocus*. *Round* is a form of the same word passed through the French.]
1. round or rounded out; plump; as, a *rotund* short person.
2. full-toned; sonorous; as, *rotund* speech.
3. in botany, orbicular; circumscribed by one unbroken curve, or without angles; as, a *rotund* leaf.

rō·tund′, *n.* a rotunda. [Obs.]

rō·tun′dȧ, *n.* [It. *rotonda*, a round building, from L. *rotunda*, f. of *rotundus*, round.] a round building, hall, or room, especially one with a dome.

rō·tun′dāte, *a.* rounded off, especially at the ends or corners; also, in botany, rotund.

rō·tun·di·fō′li·ous, *a.* [L. *rotundus*, round, and *folium*, a leaf.] having round leaves.

rō·tun′di·ty, *n.* 1. the condition or quality of being rotund.
2. *pl.* **rō·tun′di·tieṣ**, something rotund.

rō·tund′ly, in a rotund form or manner.

rō·tund′ness, *n.* rotundity.

rō·tun′dō, *n.* a rotunda. [Rare.]

rō·tun″dō-ō′vāte, *a.* in botany, roundly egg-shaped.

rō·tụre′, *n.* [Fr., a piece of ground broken up, from L. *ruptura*, a breaking, from *rumpere*, to break.]
1. the state of being a roturier.
2. in French-Canadian law, a tenure of feudal lands subject to an annual rental or a ground rent, without any accompanying privilege.

rō·tụ·riẹr′ (-ryā′), *n.*; *pl.* **rō·tụ·riẹrs′** (-ryā′), [Fr.] 1. a person not of noble rank; a commoner.
2. in French-Canadian law, one who holds lands subject to a ground rent or annual charge.

röu′ble, *n.* same as *ruble.*

röuçhe, *n.* same as *ruche.*

röu·çōu′, *n.* [Fr.] same as *annatto* (sense 2).

rou·ē′ (rö-ā′), *n.* [Fr., from *rouer*, to break on the wheel, from L. *rota*, a wheel; lit., one worthy of suffering on the wheel.] a dissipated man; a debauchee; a rake.

röu·et′ (-ā′), *n.* same as *rewet.*

röuġe (rözh), *n.* [Fr., rouge, red.]
1. any of various red or reddish cosmetics, in powder, paste, or liquid form, used for coloring the cheeks and lips.
2. a reddish powder, mainly ferric oxide, used for polishing jewelry, metal, etc.

röuġe, *a.* red. [Rare.]
Rouge Croix; one of the pursuivants of the English heraldic establishment: so named from the red cross of St. George, England's patron saint.

röuġe, *v.i.*; rouged, *pt.*, *pp.*; rouging, *ppr.* to use cosmetic rouge.

röuġe, *v.t.* to color with rouge, as the cheeks.

röuġe′ber″ry, *n.* a shrub, *Rivina humilis*, of the pokeweed family, yielding berries of a bright red color.

röuġe′ ẹt noir′ (ā nwär′), [Fr., red and black.] a gambling card game played at a table having two red and two black diamond-shaped marks on which bets are placed.

röuġe plant, same as *rougeberry.*

rough (ruf), *a.*; *comp.* rougher; *superl.* roughest, [AS. *ruh*, rough, hairy; *ruw*, rough; cognate with D. *ruig*, hairy, rough, rude; O.D. *ru*; Dan. *ru*; O.H.G. *ruh*; L.G. *ruug*; G. *rauh.*]
1. not smooth; having prominences, bumps, etc.; not level; as, (a) not level or smooth; uneven; as, a *rough* road; (b) not polished or refined; unfinished; natural, crude, etc.; as, a *rough* diamond; (c) marked by coarseness; coarse; ragged; shaggy; as, a *rough* beard.
2. harsh to the senses; as, (a) harsh to the taste; sharp; astringent; sour; as, *rough* cider; (b) harsh to the ear; grating; jarring; discordant; as, a *rough* voice.
3. not mild or gentle in character, action, motion, disturbance, or irregularity; as, (a) wild; boisterous; untamed; as, a *rough* colt, *rough* play; (b) stormy; tempestuous; as, a *rough* gale; (c) harsh; not mild, gentle, or courteous; rude; unpolished; (d) harsh; severe; stern; cruel; unfeeling; as, *rough* men; (e) lacking refinements and luxuries or comforts and conveniences; as, the *rough* life of the pioneers.
4. coarse, as texture, cloth, food, etc.
5. vague; not exact or precise; approximate; as, a *rough* estimate.
6. not finished, elaborated, perfected, etc.; as, a *rough* sketch.
7. needing strength instead of skill, intelligence, etc.; as, *rough* labor.
8. difficult, severe, or disagreeable; as, they had a *rough* time of it. [Colloq.]
9. in phonetics, pronounced with an aspirate; having the sound of *h.*
rough diamond; a diamond that has not been cut; hence, colloquially, a person possessing many good qualities, but having a rude appearance or demeanor.
Syn.—coarse, rugged, ragged, harsh, rude, uneven, unpolished, shaggy, unfinished.

rough, *n.* 1. rough ground.
2. rough material or condition.
3. the rough part, aspect, etc. of something.
4. a rough person; a rowdy; tough; ruffian. [Chiefly Brit.]
5. in golf, any part of the course where grass, weeds, etc. are allowed to grow uncut, forming a hazard or obstacle.
6. a spike inserted in a horse's shoe to prevent slipping.
7. rough weather. [Obs.]
in the rough; (a) in a rough, or unrefined, crude, or unfinished, state; (b) [Colloq.] in a difficult situation: from the use in golf.

rough, *adv.* in a rough manner.

rough, *v.t.*; roughed (ruft), *pt.*, *pp.*; roughing, *ppr.* 1. to make rough; to roughen.
2. to handle or treat roughly; specifically, in football, etc., to subject (an opponent) to intentional and unnecessary roughness (often with *up*).
3. to make, fashion, sketch, shape, or cut roughly (usually with *in* or *out*); as, *rough out* a scheme.
4. to apply some preparatory or preliminary process or treatment to.
to rough a horse; in military usage, to break in a horse.
to rough it; to live under hardships; to travel in a rough manner.

rough, *v.i.* 1. to become rough.
2. to behave roughly.

rough′ȧġe, *n.* rough material; coarse substance; specifically, coarse food or fodder, as bran, straw, vegetable peel, etc., containing a relatively high proportion of cellulose and other indigestible constituents and serving in the diet as a stimulus to peristalsis.

rough″-ȧnd-read′y (-red′), *a.* 1. unpolished, rude, brusque, or unceremonious in manner, but reliable and effective enough.
2. characterized by rough vigor and prompt action rather than refinement, formality, or nicety; as, a *rough-and-ready* fellow.

rough″-ȧnd-tum′ble, *a.* violent and disorderly, without rules; as, a *rough-and-tumble* fight.

rough″-ȧnd-tum′ble, *n.* a rough-and-tumble fight or struggle; a scuffle; a brawl.

rough′-bōre′, *v.t.* to make a rough boring into or through, as in preparation for a finer finishing process.

rough brēath′ing, in Greek grammar, the mark (ʽ) placed over initial vowels or ρ (rho) to indicate a preceding *h* sound, or aspirate.

rough′ċast, *v.t.*; roughcast, *pt.*, *pp.*; roughcasting, *ppr.* 1. to form in its first rudiments, without revision, correction, and polish; to give rough shape to.
2. to plaster (walls, etc.) with a mixture of lime and gravel; as, to *roughcast* a building.

rough′ċȧst, *n.* 1. a crude, rough model; the form of a thing in its unfinished state.
2. a coarse plaster made of lime and gravel for covering outside surfaces, as walls.

rough′ċȧst″ēr, *n.* one who roughcasts.

rough′-ċut′, *a.* cut into small, chopped irregular pieces: said of tobacco and distinguished from *fine-cut.*

rough′drạw, *v.t.* to draw crudely.

rough-drȳ′, *v.t.*; rough-dried, *pt.*, *pp.*; rough-drying, *ppr.* to dry (washed laundry) without ironing: also *roughdry.*

rough-drȳ′, *a.* washed and dried but not ironed.

rough′en, *v.t.* and *v.i.*; roughened, *pt.*, *pp.*; roughening, *ppr.* to make or become rough.

rough′ēr, *n.* 1. one who prepares something roughly and handles it while in the rough.
2. a kind of hatchel.
3. woolen cloth in the rough before finishing.

rough′-foot′ed, *a.* having the feet feathered, as some birds.

rough′-grāined′, *a.* coarse-grained.

rough-hew′ (-hū′), *v.t.*; rough-hewed, *pt.*; rough-hewed *or* rough-hewn, *pp.*; roughhewing, *ppr.* 1. to hew coarsely without smoothing; as, to *rough-hew* timber, stone, etc.
2. to give a crude form or shape to.
Also *roughhew.*

rough-hew′ēr, *n.*; a person who rough-hews.

rough′house, *n.* rough, boisterous, or rowdy play, fighting, etc., especially indoors. [Slang.]

rough′house, *v.t.* to treat (a person) roughly and boisterously, usually in fun. [Slang.]

rough′house, *v.i.* to take part in roughhouse. [Slang.]

rough′ing-in′, *n.* the first of three coats of plastering, as on brickwork.

rough′ing rōllṣ, the first set of rolls in a rolling mill, which operate upon wrought iron and reduce it to bar form.

rough′ingṣ, *n.pl.* rowen. [Brit. Dial.]

rough′ish, *a.* somewhat rough.

rough′leg, *n.* a hawk of the genus *Archibuteo*, having feathered legs: also called *rough-legged hawk.*

rough′ly, *adv.* 1. in a rough manner.
2. approximately.

rough′neck, *n.* a person whose actions and manners are rough and crude; a rowdy. [Slang.]

rough′ness, *n.* 1. the state or quality of being rough.
2. rough fodder, as husks or cornstalks. [Dial.]

rough′rīd′ēr, *n.* 1. one who breaks horses to the saddle.
2. any horseman engaged in rough, hard work in the saddle, as a cowboy.
3. [R–] a member of a regiment of volunteer cavalry of the United States organized by Theodore Roosevelt and Leonard Wood for service during the Spanish-American War of 1898: also *Rough Rider.*

rough′sċuff, *n.* a rough; a rowdy; collectively, the rabble. [Colloq.]

rough′set″tēr, *n.* a mason who builds rough stonework.

rough′shod′, *a.* shod with horseshoes that have calks, or metal points, to prevent slipping; as, a *roughshod* horse.
to ride roughshod over; to treat in a harsh, arrogant, inconsiderate manner; to domineer over.

rough′string, *n.* one of the inclined rough timbers used in wooden stairs to support the steps.

rough′stuff, *n.* a coarse paint used for an undercoat.

rought (rạt), *v.* obsolete past tense of *reach.*

rought, *v.* obsolete past tense of *reck.*

rough′tāil (ruf′), *n.* a small, harmless snake of Ceylon and southern India, having a short, blunt tail with a rough plate or keeled scales.

rough tree, a rough, unfinished spar or mast.

rough·wŏrk′, *v.t.* to work over coarsely, without regard to nicety, smoothness, or finish.

rough·wrought′ (-rạt′), *a.* wrought or done coarsely.

röuke, *v.i.* to ruck (squat). [Obs.]

röu·lāde′, *n.* [Fr.] 1. a musical ornament consisting of a rapid succession of tones sung to one syllable.
2. a slice of meat rolled with a filling of minced meat and cooked.

röu·leau′ (-lō′), *n.*; *pl.* **röu·leaux′** or **röu·leauṣ′** (-lōz′), [Fr., a little roll.]
1. a little roll, as a roll of coins in a paper wrapper.
2. a roll or fold, as of ribbon, used for trimming millinery.

röu·lette′ (-let′), *n.* [Fr., a little ball or roller.]
1. a gambling game, in which a small ball is made to move rapidly around a shallow wheel with an inner disk (*roulette wheel*) revolving in the opposite direction: the circumference of the disk is usually divided into 38 compartments colored red and black alternately, and numbered from 1 to 36, with a zero and double zero. The ball finally drops into one of the compartments to determine the winning number or color.
2. a small toothed wheel or disk attached to a handle, for making rows of marks or dots,

as in engraving, or incisions, as between postage stamps.

3. in philately, small, consecutive incisions made in the paper between the stamps in a sheet of stamps, to facilitate their separation: it is unlike perforation in that no paper is removed.

4. in geometry, the locus of any point in the plane of a curve which rolls upon some other curve.

röu·lette′, *v.t.*; rouletted, *pt.*, *pp.*; rouletting, *ppr.* to make incisions or perforations in or on with a roulette; to separate by the use of such incisions.

Röu·mā′ni·ăn, *a.* and *n.* same as *Romanian.*

roun, *v.t.* and *v.i.* to whisper. [Obs.]

rounce, *n.* [etym. uncertain.] the handle on a hand printing press by which the bed, on which the form or matter to be printed is laid, is run in and under the platen: sometimes applied to the entire apparatus which moves the form.

rounce, *n.* [etym. uncertain.] a game of cards. [Dial.]

roun′cē·văl, *a.* [from *Roncesvalles*, a Spanish town at the foot of the Pyrenees.] strong; gigantic: from the human bones of great size dug up at Roncesvalles. [Obs.]

roun′cē·văl, *n.* 1. the marrowfat pea.

2. anything very large or stout. [Obs.]

roun′cy, *n.* [LL. *runcinus.*] a riding horse. [Archaic.]

round, *a.* [OFr. *roond*, round; Fr. *rond*, round, from L. *rotundus*, round, rotund, from *rota*, a wheel.]

1. shaped like a ball; spherical or globular.

2. shaped like a circle, ring, disk, or part of a circle; circular or curved.

3. shaped like a cylinder (in having a circular cross section); cylindrical.

4. curved in shape like part of a sphere.

5. not angular; plump; as, a *round* little person.

6. involving, or done in, by, or with, a circular motion; as, a *round* dance.

7. pronounced with the lips forming an approximately circular or oval opening; rounded; as, a *round* vowel.

8. (a) not lacking part; full; entire; complete; as, a *round* dozen; (b) completed; perfected.

9. completed or accomplished by progressing through a course which, as if circular, finally returns to the starting point; as, a *round* trip.

10. constituting, or expressed by, a whole number, or integer; not fractional.

11. expressed in tens, hundreds, thousands, etc.; as, 500 is a *round* number for 498, 503, etc.

12. approximately accurate; rough; as, a *round* guess.

13. not qualified or modified; as, a *round* oath.

14. full; large; not stinted; generous; as, a *round* sum or price.

15. full; smooth; flowing; finished; polished: said of style.

> In his satires, Horace is quick, *round*, and pleasant. —Peacham.

16. plain; open; candid; outspoken; straightforward.

> *Round* dealing is the honor of man's nature. —Bacon.

17. quick and vigorous; brisk; as, a *round* trot.

18. with a full tone; sonorous; as, a *round* note, a *round* voice.

at a round rate; with a rapid motion.

in round numbers; taken in units; not fractional; approximately; not exactly.

round clam; the quahog.

round dance; (a) originally, a dance with the dancers arranged or moving in a circle; (b) any of several dances, as the waltz, polka, fox trot, etc., performed by couples and characterized by revolving or circular movements. Distinguished from *square dance.*

round game; a game, as of cards, in which an indefinite number of players may take part, each playing on his own account.

round hand; careful handwriting in which the letters are rounded, distinct, full, and almost vertical: distinguished from *running hand.*

round robin; (a) a document, as a petition, protest, etc., with the signatures written in a circle to conceal the order of signing; (b) a contest or tournament, as in tennis, chess, etc., in which every entrant is matched with every other one.

round steak; a cut from a round of beef.

Round Table; (a) the large table around which, according to legend, King Arthur and his knights sat: it was made circular to avoid disputes about precedence; (b) King Arthur and his knights, collectively; (c) [r—t—] a group of persons gathered together for an informal discussion, conference, etc., at or as if at a circular table; also, such a discussion, conference, etc.

round tower; any of certain lofty towers, found chiefly in Ireland, that taper from the base to a conical cap or roof: they vary in height from 35 to 120 feet and were constructed in a period ranging from the ninth to the twelfth century, for use as strongholds into which, in times of danger, the people could seek refuge.

ROUND TOWER

round trip; a trip to a place and back to the starting point: also called *return trip.*

Syn.—circular, spherical, globular, globose, orbicular, orbed, cylindrical, full, plump, rotund.

round, *n.* 1. that which is round or rounded, as a circle, sphere, globe, or cylinder.

> With *rounds* of waxen tapers on their heads. —Shak.

2. rotation in office; established order of succession. [Rare.]

> Such new Utopians would have a *round* of government. —Holyday.

3. the step of a ladder, or a crossbar connecting the legs of a chair; a rung.

> All the *rounds* like Jacob's ladder rise. —Dryden.

4. the rounded part of the thigh of a beef animal, between the rump and the leg: in full, *round of beef.*

5. a kind of sculpture in which the figures are full and completely rounded, not projecting from a background (with *the*): distinguished from *relief.*

6. the state of being round.

7. an assembly or group of people.

8. movement in a circular course or about an axis.

9. a round dance.

10. a course, series, or succession of actions, events, operations, etc. that is complete or ends at a point corresponding to that where it began, as if circular; as, a *round* of parties.

11. the complete extent; whole range; as, the *round* of human beliefs.

12. [*often in pl.*] a regular, customary course or circuit; as, the watchman made his *rounds.*

13. a single distribution, as of drinks, to each of the members of a group.

14. a single shot from each of a number of rifles, artillery pieces, etc. fired together, or from a single gun.

15. ammunition for such a shot; cartridge, shell, etc.

16. a single outburst, as of applause, cheering, etc.; a salvo.

17. a slice (of bread). [Brit.]

18. in archery, a specified number of arrows shot at the target from a specified distance according to the rules.

19. in games and sports, a single period or division of action, usually one of a series; as, a *round* of poker; specifically, (a) in boxing, any of the timed periods of a fight: a round is now generally limited to three minutes, and the interval between rounds to one minute; (b) in golf, a number of holes or a period of play in a match.

20. in music, a short song to be repeated several times, the musical phrases of which are of equal length and harmonize with one another: one singer or group begins the song, and, when starting on the second phrase, is joined by another beginning the first phrase, etc.

21. a brewer's vessel for holding beer.

gentleman of the round; a gentleman soldier of low rank, who had to make the rounds. [Obs.]

round of beef; see *round, n.* (sense 4).

to go the round (or *rounds*); (a) to be circulated among a number of people, as a story, rumor, etc.; (b) to walk one's regular course or circuit, as a watchman.

round, *adv.* 1. on all sides; in every direction.

> Thine enemies shall compass thee *round*. —Luke xix. 43.

2. circularly; along or throughout a circular course or circumference; as, the dog ran *round* and *round.*

3. in a roundabout way; not in a direct line; by a course longer than the direct course.

4. in circumference; as, the tree measures forty inches *round.*

5. through a recurring period of time, or from beginning to end; as, the autumn came *round* once more, he worked the whole year *round.*

6. in or through a course or circuit, as from one person or place to another; as, the peddler went *round* with his goods.

7. for each of several; to include all in a group; as, not enough candy to go *round.*

8. so as to encircle, surround, or envelop, or be encircled, surrounded, or enveloped.

9. about; near; as, he visited all the people *round.*

10. in various places; here and there; as, the child played *round.*

11. with a rotating or revolving movement; as, the wheel spun *round.*

12. in or to the opposite direction; as, he turned *round.*

13. in or to an opposite belief, viewpoint, etc.

Round and *around* are used interchangeably in colloquial and informal usage; formal usage tends to prefer *round* for "in a circle," "with a rotating movement," etc. and *around* for "on all sides," "here and there."

round about; (a) in or to the opposite direction; (b) in every direction around.

round, *prep.* 1. on every side of; in every direction from; around; as, the people stood *round* him.

2. about; in various places in or on; as, to go *round* the city.

3. so as to encircle, surround, or envelop; about; as, the rope was tied *round* the tree.

4. on the circumference, border, or outer part of.

5. in the vicinity of; somewhat close to; as, farms *round* Cleveland.

6. to or through every part or various parts of; in a circuit or course through; as, we went *round* the museum.

7. from the beginning to the end of (a period of time); throughout; as, he worked *round* the day.

8. (a) so as to make a curve or partial circuit about, or turn to the other side of; as, the traffic flowed *round* the obstruction in the road; (b) located at a point reached by making such a circuit about; as, a store *round* the corner.

9. so as to rotate or revolve about (a center or axis); as, the wheel goes *round* an axle.

See also note following *round*, adv.

round, *v.t.*; rounded, *pt.*, *pp.*; rounding, *ppr.* 1. to make circular, spherical, or cylindrical; to make round; as, to *round* the edges of a board.

2. to surround; to encircle; to encompass.

3. to make full or complete; to finish.

> Our little life is *rounded* with a sleep. —Shak.

4. to give a circular form to; to give a round or convex figure to; to make plump.

> The figures on our modern medals are raised and *rounded* to very great perfection. —Addison.

5. to make a circuit of; to go, pass, or travel around; as, we *rounded* the island.

6. to pronounce with rounded lips; to labialize.

7. to make a turn about; as, he *rounded* the corner.

8. to cause to move in a circular course.

to round in; in nautical usage, to haul in, as a rope which passes through one or more blocks in a direction nearly horizontal.

to round off (or *out*); (a) to make or become round or rounded; (b) to complete; to finish.

to round up; (a) in nautical usage, to haul up (rope, tackle, etc.); (b) to drive (cattle, etc.) together; to collect in a herd, group, etc.; (c) [Colloq.] to gather, collect, or assemble.

round, *v.i.* 1. to become round.

> The queen your mother *rounds* apace. —Shak.

2. to go round; to make a complete or partial circuit.

They nightly *rounding* walk. —Milton.

3. to turn; to reverse direction.

4. to become complete or full; to develop (with *into*); as, the talk *rounded into* a plan.

5. to lose angularity or become plump.

to round to; to turn the prow of a ship toward the wind.

round, *v.t.* and *v.i.* [a form of *roun*, to whisper, with unhistoric *d*.] to whisper (to). [Obs.]

round′ȧ·bout, *a.* 1. indirect; circuitous; not straight or straightforward; as, a *roundabout* road.

2. encircling; encompassing; surrounding.

round′ȧ·bout, *n.* 1. a merry-go-round. [Chiefly Brit.]

2. something, as a path, speech, etc., that is indirect or circuitous.

3. a scene of incessant change or vicissitude.

4. an armchair with a rounded back.

5. a short, close-fitting jacket worn by boys and men.

6. a circular dance. [Obs.]

round′ȧ·bout″ly, *adv.* in a roundabout manner.

round′ȧ·bout″ness, *n.* the quality of being roundabout.

round′-ärched (-ärcht), *a.* in architecture, having semicircular arches.

round′-ärm, *a.* in cricket, designating a style of bowling in which the arm is swung round more or less horizontally.

round′-backed (-bakt), *a.* having a rounded back.

round′ed, *a.* 1. made round.

2. in phonetics, pronounced with the lips forming an approximately circular or oval opening; labialized.

roun′del, *n.* [OFr. *rondel*, from *rond*, round.]

1. anything having a round form or figure.

2. a round ornamental panel, plate, niche, etc.

3. a small, round window or pane.

4. (a) a rondel; (b) a rondeau; (c) an English modification of the rondeau, with three stanzas of three lines each and two refrains.

5. in heraldry, an ordinary in the form of a circle.

6. in ancient armor, a small round shield.

7. in fortification, a bastion of a semicircular form. [Obs.]

8. a round dance.

roun′de·lāy, *n.* [OFr. *rondelet*, dim. from *rond*, round.]

1. a song in which a short passage is continually repeated; also, music for such a song.

2. a dance in which the dancers move in a circle; a round dance.

roun·de·leer′, *n.* one who writes roundels or roundelays.

round′ẽr, *n.* 1. one who makes a round or frequent rounds, as a policeman, watchman, etc.

2. a person or thing that rounds; specifically, any of various tools for making round surfaces or edges.

3. [*pl.*] [*construed as sing.*] an old English game, similar to baseball, played with a soft ball and a bat, in which the player had to make the round of the bases after hitting the ball.

4. [R-] a Methodist preacher who travels a circuit among his congregations. [Brit.]

5. [from the idea of making the rounds of disreputable resorts.] a dissolute spendthrift, drunkard, or habitual criminal. [Colloq.]

round′fish, *n.* 1. a fish, *Coregonus quadrilateralis*, of the salmon family, found in the rivers of western North America.

2. any fish with a body cylindrical or nearly so.

Round′head (-hed), *n.* a member or supporter of the Parliamentary, or Puritan, party in England during the English civil war (1642–1652): originally a derisive term, with reference to the Puritans' close-cropped hair in contrast to the Cavaliers' long hair.

round′head″ed, *a.* 1. having a rounded top, as the head of a nail or bolt.

2. having a round head.

round′house, *n.* 1. a building, generally circular or semicircular, with a turntable in the center, used for storing, repairing, and switching locomotives.

2. in nautical usage, (a) a cabin or apartment in the after part of the quarter-deck having the poop for its roof: sometimes called *coach*; (b) a privy for officers near the fore part of the deck.

3. a constable's prison. [Obs.]

round′ing, *a.* having a curved edge or surface.

round′ing, *n.* 1. in nautical usage, small rope or spun yarn wound round a larger rope to keep it from chafing: also called *service*.

2. in phonetics, the action of the lips in producing a round vowel sound.

3. the act of turning; a going around; as, the rounding of a vessel in landing.

4. in bookbinding, the act of making the spine of a book rounded.

round′ish, *a.* somewhat round; nearly round; as, a *roundish* figure.

round′ish·ness, *n.* the state of being roundish.

round′let, *n.* a small circle or circular thing.

round′ly, *adv.* 1. in a round form or manner.

2. openly; boldly; peremptorily; severely; as, he was *roundly* rebuked.

3. plainly; fully; as, he gives them *roundly* to understand that their duty is submission.

4. briskly; with speed.

round′ness, *n.* 1. the state or quality of being round; rotundity.

2. fullness; as, the *roundness* of a period.

3. openness; plainness; boldness; positiveness; as, the *roundness* of an assertion.

Syn.—cylindricity, globosity, circularity, fullness, rotundity.

round′ridġe, *v.t.* to form into round ridges by plowing.

round′-shōul′dẽred, *a.* having the shoulders bent forward so that the upper back is rounded.

rounds′măn, *n.*; *pl.* **rounds′men,** a person who makes rounds of inspection or the like; especially, a police inspector in charge of a number of patrolmen.

round′-tā·ble, *a.* at or as if at a round table; as, a *round-table* discussion.

round′tāil, *n.* a fish, *Gila robusta*, that inhabits the Gila and Colorado rivers.

round′top, *n.* a platform, formerly round, at the masthead of a ship. [Rare.]

round′-trip′, *a.* of or for a round trip.

round′up, *n.* 1. the driving in of cattle, etc. from the outlying ranges and collecting them in herds ready to ship or drive to market, or for wintering, branding, etc.

2. the herd of cattle, etc. thus collected.

3. the men and horses engaged in a roundup.

4. any similar driving together, collecting, or gathering; as, a *roundup* of suspected persons.

5. in nautical usage, the upward turn of a deck.

round′wŏrm, *n.* 1. a nematode, *Ascaris lumbricoides*, parasitic in the intestines of man or other animals.

2. any of the round, unsegmented worms of the class *Nematelminthes*, as the pinworm, hookworm, etc.

round′y, *a.* round. [Obs.]

röup, *v.t.* and *v.i.* [ME. *roop*, *rope*, to cry, a cry, also hoarseness; AS. *hrōpan*, Ice. *hrōpa*, to cry. Akin to *croup*.] to cry or shout; hence, to expose to sale by auction. [Scot.]

röup, *n.* an outcry; a sale of goods by auction. [Scot.]

röup, *n.* [prob. from ME. *roupen*, to cry, shout, from ON.]

1. a poultry disease characterized by hoarseness and a catarrhal discharge from the eyes and nasal passages.

2. hoarseness; huskiness.

röup′y, *a.*; roupier, *pt.*, *pp.*; roupiest, *ppr.* 1. of, like, or having roup.

2. hoarse. [Chiefly Scot.]

rouș′ănt, *a.* in heraldry, designating a bird, rising as if preparing to fly.

SWAN ROUSANT

roușe, *v.t.*; roused, *pt.*, *pp.*; rousing, *ppr.* [ME. *rouzen*; Sw. *rusa*; Dan. *ruse*, to rush, go hastily.]

1. to cause (game) to rise from cover, come out of a lair, etc.; to stir up to flight or attack.

2. to stir up, as to anger or action; to excite.

3. to cause to come out of a state of sleep, repose, unconsciousness, etc.; to wake.

4. in nautical usage, to pull with force; to haul.

5. to erect; to rear. [Obs.]

roușe, *v.i.* 1. to awake from sleep or repose.

2. to rise from cover, etc.: said of game.

3. to become active.

roușe, *n.* 1. a rousing.

2. a signal for rousing; reveille.

roușe, *n.* [aphetic for *carouse* (from mistaking *drink carouse* as *drink a rouse*).]

1. a bumper of liquor, especially one drunk as a toast. [Archaic.]

2. a carouse. [Archaic.]

rouș′ẽr, *n.* 1. one who or that which rouses.

2. an exciting thing or event. [Colloq.]

3. in brewing, anything used as a stirrer for the boiling wort.

rouș′ing, *a.* 1. that rouses; stirring; as, a *rousing* speech.

2. very active or lively; vigorous; brisk; as, a *rousing* business.

3. astonishing, extraordinary, or outrageous, as a lie. [Colloq.]

rouș′ing·ly, *adv.* in a rousing manner.

röus·sette′, *n.* [Fr., from *rousse*, ruddy.]

1. a large fruit bat native to the islands of the Pacific.

2. a small shark of the genus *Scyllium*.

roust, *v.t.* [dial. form of *rouse* with unhistoric *-t*.]

1. to rouse or stir (someone or something): usually with *up*. [Colloq.]

2. to rout or drive out (someone or something): usually with *out*. [Colloq.]

röust, *n.* [Ice. *röst*, a current or stream in the sea.] a current caused by the tide. [Brit. Dial.]

roust′ȧ·bout, *n.* 1. a deck hand or waterfront laborer, as on the Mississippi.

2. a laborer in a circus.

3. an unskilled or transient laborer, especially one who does odd jobs, as a man of all work on a ranch.

rout, *v.i.* to snore. [Obs.]

rout, *n.* a clamor and tumult.

rout, *v.t.* 1. to dig up or turn over with the snout.

2. to find or get by turning up, poking about, etc.; to expose to view (with *out*).

3. to scoop, gouge, or hollow out.

4. to force out.

5. to make (a person) get out or up (with *out* or *up*).

rout, *v.i.* to turn up the ground with the snout, as swine do; to root or poke about.

rout, *n.* [OFr. *route*, a company, a band, a division; lit., a portion broken off or separated; from LL. *rupta*, *rutta*, *rotta*; L. *ruptus*, broken, from *rumpere*, to break.]

1. a disorderly crowd; a noisy mob.

2. the rabble.

3. a disorderly flight or retreat, as of defeated troops; as, the enemy was put to *rout*.

4. an overwhelming defeat.

5. (a) a group of people; company; band; (b) a band of followers; retinue; entourage. [Archaic or Poet.]

6. a large, fashionable social gathering or party, usually in the evening. [Archaic.]

7. in law, a disturbance of the peace by three or more persons with intent to create a riot.

rout, *v.t.*; routed, *pt.*, *pp.*; routing, *ppr.* 1. to put to disorderly flight.

2. to defeat overwhelmingly.

rout, *v.i.* [ME. *routen*, *ruten*, from Dan. *rotte*, Sw. *rota*, to assemble.] to bring together. [Obs.]

rout′ċāke, *n.* a sweet cake served at evening parties.

röute (*or* rout), *n.* [ME. and OFr. *rote*, a way, a path, from LL. *rupta*, a way, a path, properly *rupta via*, a way broken through forests or the like, a rough path, from L. *ruptus*, pp. of *rumpere*, to break.]

1. a road, way, or course traveled or to be traveled in going from one place to another or in delivering something, as mail, milk, or newspapers.

2. (a) a set of customers to whom one regularly delivers something, as newspapers or milk; (b) a job or business of delivering newspapers, etc.; as, the boy sold his newspaper *route*.

3. in military usage, an order specifying the course of travel to be followed by troops taking up a new position, the location of the new command posts, etc.

to go the route; in baseball, to pitch an entire game. [Colloq.]

röute, *v.t.*; routed, *pt.*, *pp.*; routing, *ppr.* 1. to prescribe a route for; to send by a certain route; as, to *route* a party over the Union Pacific.

2. to fix the order of procedure of (a series of operations, etc.); as, he *routed* the orders through the sales department.

röute märch, a military march for a long distance in easy fashion, without the observance of step, silence, or precision in carrying arms.

rout′ẽr, *n.* a person or thing that routs or a tool for routing; specifically, in carpentry, (a) a plane used in the work on circular edges; (b) a plane for working the bottom of a cavity.

röute step, an easy method of marching permitted on a route march.

röu·ti·er′ (-ā′), *n.* [Fr., from *route*, a road; lit., one who takes the road.] in French history, an adventurer of the twelfth century who took arms with the French kings against the feudal lords, and later engaged in brigandage; hence, a freebooter or brigand.

röu′ti·nãr·y, *a.* according to custom. [Rare.]

röu·tine′, *n.* [Fr., from *route*, a way, the customary way.]
1. a regular, more or less unvarying procedure, customary, prescribed, or habitual, as of business or daily life.
2. such procedure in general; as, he dislikes *routine*.

röu·tine′, *a.* having the nature of, using, or by routine.

röu·tin′iṣm, *n.* adherence to or prevalence of routine.

röu·tin′ist, *n.* one who follows a routine.

rout′ous·ly, *adv.* with that violation of common law called a rout.

röux (rö), *n.* [Fr. *roux beurre*, reddish-brown butter.] a mixture of browned flour with melted butter (or other fat), used to thicken sauces, soups, gravies, etc.

rōve, *v.i.*; roved, *pt.*, *pp.*; roving, *ppr.* [ME. *rove(n)*, orig. an archery term as *v.t.*; prob. from base of AS. *arafian*, to set free, unloose.]
1. to practice piracy. [Obs.]
2. to wander; to ramble; to range; to go from place to place, especially over an extensive area, with no particular course or destination; to roam.

For who has power to walk, has power to *rove*. —Arbuthnot.

3. in archery, to shoot at a chance mark. [Obs.]

rōve, *v.t.* 1. to wander over; to roam through; as, to *rove* the woods.
2. to plow (land) so as to turn the earth of two furrows together and form a ridge.

rōve, *n.* the act of roving; a ramble.

rōve, *v.t.*; roved, *pt.*, *pp.*; roving, *ppr.* [from same base as preceding.]
1. to put (fibers, etc.) through a small opening.
2. to card (wool).
3. to extend and twist (fibers) before spinning.

rōve, *n.* 1. an extended, twisted fiber of cotton, silk, wool, etc.
2. such fibers in cloth.
3. a metal washer used in boatbuilding in clinching the end of a nail.

rōve, *v.* alternative past tense and past participle of *reeve*.

rōve bee′tle, any of a group of swiftly moving beetles with a long, slender body, common in decomposing organic matter.

rōv′en, *v.* alternative past participle of *reeve*.

rōve′-ō″vẽr, *a.* [term coined by G. M. Hopkins.] in prosody, having a rhythm continued without final pause from one line to the next.

rōve′-ō″vẽr, *n.* rove-over verse.

rōv′ẽr, *n.* 1. a wanderer; one who roves.
2. a fickle or inconstant person.
3. a pirate; also, a pirate ship. [Archaic.]
4. in archery, (a) a random mark shot at; (b) any of several set marks for distance shooting; (c) an archer who starts from a distance; (d) a type of arrow.
5. in croquet, a ball that has made the entire play except the final hitting of the post but continues in play to help a partner; also the person playing with such a ball.

rōv′ẽr, *n.* 1. a person who operates a machine for roving fibers.
2. such a machine.

rō·ve′sciō (-vesh′ō), *n.* [It.] a reversal of motion.

rōv′ing, *n.* 1. the operation which gives the first twist to cotton thread by drawing it through an opening.
2. a sliver of slightly twisted wool or cotton.

rōv′ing, *n.* the act of rambling; in archery, the act of shooting at random marks.

rōv′ing frāme, a machine for drawing and twisting cotton or woolen slivers and winding them on bobbins.

rōv′ing·ly, *adv.* in a roving manner.

rōv′ing·ness, *n.* the state of roving.

rōw, *n.* [AS. *raw*, a row.]
1. a number of persons or things arranged in a continuous line, especially, a straight line.
2. any of the lines of seats in a theater or auditorium, usually numbered or lettered consecutively from front to rear.
3. a street with a line of buildings on either side.

rōw, *v.t.* to arrange or put in a row or rows (often with *up*).

row culture; a method of cultivating crops in drills or rows.

rōw, *v.t.*; rowed, *pt.*, *pp.*; rowing, *ppr.* [ME. *rowen*; AS. *rowan*, to row or sail; Ice. *roa*; Dan. *roe*, to row.]
1. to propel (a boat or vessel) on water by or as by using oars.
2. to carry in or on a boat, etc. propelled in this way.
3. to propel or carry in a way suggestive of using oars.
4. to use (a specified number of oars): said of a boat.
5. to use (a person or action) in rowing, especially in a race; as, the team *rowed* two new men; he *rowed* a powerful stroke.
6. to engage in (a race) by rowing.
7. to row against in a race.

rōw, *v.i.* 1. to use oars in propelling a boat.
2. to be propelled by means of oars: said of a boat.

rōw, *n.* 1. a rowing.
2. (a) a trip made by rowboat; (b) the distance of such a trip.

row, *n.* [prob. back-formation from *rouse*, with loss of *s*, as in *pea, cherry, sherry*.]
1. a noisy quarrel, dispute, or disturbance; a squabble, brawl, or commotion. [Colloq.]
2. noise; clamor. [Colloq.]

row, *v.i.* to make, or take part in, a noisy quarrel or disturbance. [Colloq.]

row, *v.t.* to scold or criticize severely. [Colloq.]

rōw′á·ble, *a.* capable of being rowed or rowed upon.

rōw′ăn, *n.* [properly *roun tree*, from Sw. *roun*; Dan. *ron*, the mountain ash.] the rowan tree or its berry.

rōw′ăn·ber·ry, *n.*; *pl.* **rōw′ăn·ber·rieṣ,** the reddish, berrylike fruit of the rowan.

rōw′ăn tree, 1. the European mountain ash, *Pyrus aucuparia*, which is related to the apple but produces small red berries.
2. two American trees, *Pyrus americana* and *Pyrus sambucifolia*: also called *roan tree*.
3. a rowanberry.

rōw′bōat, *n.* a boat designed to be rowed.

row′di·ly, *adv.* in a rowdy manner.

row′di·ness, *a.* the state or quality of being rowdy.

row′dy, *n.*; *pl.* **row′dieṣ,** [perh. from *row*, uproar.] a person whose behavior is rough, disorderly, and quarrelsome; a hoodlum.

row′dy, *a.* having the nature of or characteristic of a rowdy; rough; rowdyish; as, a *rowdy* assemblage.

row′dy·dow, *n.* [imitative.] a continuous noise; hubbub; uproar. [Colloq.]

row′dy-dow′dy, *a.* causing a rowdydow; uproarious. [Colloq.]

row′dy·ish, *a.* belonging to or characteristic of a rowdy; rough, quarrelsome, and disorderly; as, *rowdyish* conduct, *rowdyish* boys.

row′dy·iṣm, *n.* the conduct of a rough or rowdy; quarrelsome and disorderly behavior.

rōwed, *a.* arranged in or containing rows.

row′el, *n.* [OFr. *rouelle*, dim. of *roue*, a wheel, from L. *rota*, a wheel.]
1. a little wheel with sharp projecting points, forming the end of a spur.
2. something like or suggestive of a rowel; specifically, a hair, piece of leather, etc. inserted under the skin of a horse or other animal to produce or facilitate a discharge, as of pus.
3. formerly, a little flat ring or wheel of plate or iron on a horse's bit.

row′el, *v.t.*; roweled *or* rowelled, *pt.*, *pp.*; roweling *or* rowelling, *ppr.* 1. to spur or prick with or as with a rowel.
2. to insert a rowel in.

row′el spūr, a spur having a rowel.

row′en, *n.* [ME. *rewayn*.]
1. a stubble field not plowed until autumn, so that it may be cropped by cattle: usually in the plural. [Brit.]
2. the second growth of grass or hay in a season; aftermath.

rōw′ẽr, *n.* one who rows or manages an oar in rowing.

row′et, row′ett, *n.* rowen. [Brit. Dial.]

rōw′ing, *n.* the act, sport, or practice of propelling a boat by oars; as, a club for the encouragement of *rowing*.

rōw′lock, *n.* [properly *oarlock*, from AS. *ar loc*; *ar*, an oar, and *loc*, a hole.] a device, often U-shaped, for holding the oar in place in rowing or steering: also called *oarlock*.

ROWLOCKS (NOTCHED)

rōw′pōrt, *n.* a small square hole in the side of small vessels, near the surface of the water, for the purpose of rowing in a calm.

rōwṣ, *n.pl.* [ME. *row*, rough.] a coarse product from tin dressing: also called *roughs*. [Brit.]

rox′būrghe (-bũrg *or* -bur-ō), *n.* [from the third duke of *Roxburghe* (1740–1804).] a style of bookbinding consisting of plain leather back, paper or cloth sides, gilt-edged top, and front and bottom edges uncut.

Rox·bũr′ghi·á (-gi-), *n.* [from W. *Roxburgh*, a British botanist.] same as *Stemona*.

Rox·bũr·ghi·ā′cē·ae, *n.pl.* same as *Stemonaceæ*.

roy, *n.* [Fr. *roi*.] a king. [Obs.]

roy, *a.* royal. [Obs.]

roy′ăl, *a.* [OFr. *roial, real*; L. *regalis*, from *rex, regis*, king.]
1. of, from, or by a king or queen or kings and queens; as, the *royal* household, the *royal* family, a *royal* edict.
2. having the rank of a king or queen.
3. of a kingdom, its government, etc.; as, the *royal* fleet.
4. founded, chartered, or helped by, or under the patronage of, a king or queen; as, the *Royal* Society.
5. suitable for a king or queen; magnificent; splendid; princely; regal; as, *royal* robes.
6. like or characteristic of a king or queen; majestic; stately; noble; as, a *royal* bearing.
7. unusually large, fine, etc.

royal bay; the Indian bay, *Laurus indica*.
royal blue; a deep, vivid reddish blue.
royal eagle; see *golden eagle*.
royal fern; a fern with large, tall, upright fronds.
royal flush; the highest poker hand, consisting of the ace, king, queen, jack, and ten of the same suit.
royal mast; the small mast next above the topgallant mast.
royal moth; a large bombycid moth, *Citheronia regalis*.
royal palm; a tall West Indian palm tree, *Oreodoxa regia*.
royal pheasant; same as *curassow*.
royal purple; (a) a dark, bluish purple; (b) originally, crimson.
royal tern; a large crested tern, *Sterna maxima*, of the United States.
royal tiger; the common tiger, *Felis tigris*.

Syn.—kingly, kinglike, monarchical, imperial, august, superb, magnanimous.

roy′ăl, *n.* 1. a large size of paper, 20 by 25 inches (for printing) or 19 by 24 inches (for writing).
2. a small sail set on the royal mast and used only in light breezes: sometimes called the *topgallant royal*.
3. one of the tines of a stag's antlers.
4. in artillery, a small mortar. [Obs.]
5. a gold coin formerly current in England.
6. a stag having completely developed antlers.

the Royals; formerly, the first regiment of foot of the British Army: also called the *Royal Scots*.

Roy′ăl Āir Fōrce, the British organization for air defense, formed in 1918 by combining the Royal Flying Corps with the Royal Naval Air Service.

roy′ăl·et, *n.* a petty king; a king having no power. [Rare.]

roy′ăl·iṣm, *n.* 1. the principles of royal government; monarchism.
2. adherence to a monarch or monarchy.

roy′ăl·ist, *n.* an adherent of royalism; a person who supports a monarch or a monarchy, especially in times of revolution, civil war, etc.; specifically, [R–] (a) a supporter of Charles I of England; a Cavalier; (b) a supporter of the British in the American Revolution; a Tory; (c) a supporter of the Bourbons in France.

roy′ăl·ist, *a.* of royalists or royalism.

roy″ăl·i·zā′tion, *n.* the act of making royal.

roy′ăl·īze, *v.t.*; royalized, *pt., pp.*; royalizing, *ppr.* to make royal.

roy′ăl·ly, *adv.* in a royal manner; like a king; as becomes a king.

roy′ăl·ty, *n.*; *pl.* **roy′ăl·ties,** 1. kingship; the character, state, or office of a king or queen; sovereignty.

2. a royal person or, collectively, royal persons.

3. a royal domain or realm; a kingdom.

4. royal quality or character; kingliness; nobility, magnanimity, etc.

5. [*usually pl.*] a right, privilege, or prerogative of a monarch.

6. (a) a royal right, as over some natural resource, granted by a monarch to a person, corporation, etc.; (b) payment for such a right.

7. a share of the proceeds or product paid to the owner of a right, as a patent, for permission to use it or operate under it.

8. a share of the proceeds from his work, usually a specified percentage, paid to an author, composer, etc.

9. [*pl.*] emblems of royalty; regalia. [Obs.]

royne, *v.t.* to bite; to gnaw. [Obs.]

royn′ish, *a.* mean; paltry; as, the *roynish* clown. [Obs.]

roys′tĕr, *n.* same as *roister.*

roys′tĕr·ĕr, *n.* same as *roisterer.*

Roys′tŏn crōw, [from *Royston,* England.] the gray crow, *Corvus cornix*: also written *Roiston crow.*

roy′te·let, *n.* [Fr. *roitelet,* dim. of *roi,* king.] a little king. [Obs.]

-rrhā′ġi·ȧ (rā′), [Mod. L.; Gr. *-rrhagia,* from *rhēgnynai,* to burst.] a combining form meaning *abnormal discharge, excessive flow,* as in meno*rrhagia*: also *-rhagia, -rrhage, -rhage, -rrhagy.*

-rrhē′ȧ, -rrhoē′ȧ (rē′), [Mod. L.; Gr. *-rrhoia,* from *rhein,* to flow.] a combining form meaning *a flow, discharge,* as in gono*rrhea,* dia*rrhea*: also spelled *-rhea, -rhoea.*

Ru, in chemistry, ruthenium.

rub, *v.t.*; rubbed, *pt., pp.*; rubbing, *ppr.* [ME. *rubben*; prob. from M.L.G. or M.D.]

1. to move one's hand, a cloth, etc. over (a surface or object) with pressure and friction, in a circular or back-and-forth motion.

2. to move (one's hand, a cloth, etc.) over, or spread or apply (polish, etc.) on or over, a surface or object in this way.

3. to move (a thing) against something else, or move (things) over each other with pressure and friction (often followed by *together,* etc.).

4. to apply pressure and friction to, for cleaning, polishing, smoothing, etc.

5. to put into a specified condition by applying pressure and friction; as, he *rubbed* himself dry.

6. to make sore or chafed by rubbing.

7. to force, cause to go, etc. (*in, into,* etc.) by rubbing.

8. to remove by rubbing (with *out, off, away,* etc.).

to rub down; (a) to massage; (b) to smooth, polish, wear down, etc. by rubbing.

to rub it in; to keep on mentioning to someone his failure or mistake, often with some malice. [Slang.]

to rub off; to clean by or as if by rubbing; to separate by friction; as, to *rub off* rust.

to rub out; (a) to erase; to obliterate; as, *to rub out* marks or letters; (b) [Slang.] to kill.

to rub the wrong way; to be displeasing, irritating, etc. to; to annoy.

to rub up; (a) to burnish; to polish; to clean; (b) to excite; to awaken; to rouse to action; as, *to rub up* the memory.

rub, *v.i.* 1. to move with pressure and friction (*on, against,* etc. something); as, the tire *rubs against* the fender.

2. to rub something; to exert pressure and friction on something.

3. to admit of being rubbed or removed by rubbing (often with *off, out,* etc.).

4. to go, keep going, manage, etc. with exertion or difficulty, by or as if by rubbing (with *along, on, through,* etc.).

rub, *n.* 1. the act of rubbing; friction.

2. an obstacle, hindrance, or difficulty.

Now every *rub* is smoothed in our way.
—Shak.

3. a place or spot that has been rubbed until rough or sore.

4. something that irritates, annoys, hurts the feelings, etc., as a jeer or rebuke.

5. inequality of ground that hinders the motion of a bowl. [Obs.]

6. a whetstone or rubstone. [Brit. Dial.]

rub iron; the iron guard on a wagon body, to protect it from abrasion by the wheels.

rub′-ȧ-dub, *n.* [imitative.] the sound of a drum when beaten; hence, any clattering, clamorous, continuous noise.

Ru′bâi·yât, The (rū′bī-yät), [lit., the quatrains; Ar. *rubā'īyāt,* pl. of *rubā'īyah,* quatrain.] a long poem in quatrains (rhyming *aaba*), written by Omar Khayyám and known in English chiefly through the translation by Edward FitzGerald.

rū·bȧsse′, *n.* [from Fr. *rubace.*] a variety of crystalline quartz containing bits of iron oxide that produce a ruby-red color.

rū·bä′tō, *a.* [It., lit., stolen.] in music, having some notes arbitrarily lengthened (or shortened) in performance and, often, others correspondingly changed in length; intentionally and temporarily deviating from a strict tempo.

rū·bä′tō, *n.*; *pl.* **rū·bä′tōs,** 1. rubato modification or execution.

2. a rubato passage, phrase, etc.

rū·bä′tō, *adv.* with rubato; in a rubato manner.

rub′bāġe, *n.* rubbish. [Obs. or Dial.]

rub′bĕr, *n.* 1. (a) one who rubs, as in polishing something; (b) one who rubs down, or massages; a masseur.

2. any instrument or thing used in rubbing or cleaning.

3. a coarse file, or the rough part of it.

4. a whetstone; a rubstone.

5. [so named from use as an eraser.] an elastic substance produced from the milky sap (*latex*) of various tropical plants, or synthetically: in pure form it is a white, unsaturated hydrocarbon having the formula $(C_5H_8)n$: crude rubber is treated by vulcanization, etc., for use in making automobile tires, raincoats, electrical insulation, etc.: see also *India rubber.*

6. something made of this substance; specifically, (a) an elastic band for holding small objects together, etc.: in full, *rubber band*; (b) an eraser; (c) [*usually in pl.*] an overshoe; especially, a low-cut overshoe; (d) in baseball, an oblong piece of whitened rubber set in the pitcher's mound and serving as a mark that must not be overstepped in pitching; (e) a rubber condom.

antimony rubber; vulcanized rubber of a red color, containing antimony sulfide.

hard rubber; vulcanized rubber that is firm and comparatively inelastic.

Para rubber; a fine quality of South American rubber taking its name from Para, Brazil.

rub′bĕr, *a.* made of rubber; as, *rubber* boots.

rubber cloth; cloth covered with a preparation of rubber to make it impervious to water.

rubber dam; a piece of rubber used by dentists to stretch around a tooth to keep it dry.

rubber plant; (a) any plant yielding a milky sap (*latex*) from which crude rubber is formed; (b) a plant with large, glossy, leathery leaves, native to India, the East Indies, etc. and used as an ornamental house plant in America and Europe.

rubber stamp; (a) a stamp made of rubber, pressed on an inking pad and used for printing signatures, dates, etc.; (b) [Colloq.] a person, bureau, legislature, etc. that approves or endorses something in a routine manner, without thought.

rub′bĕr, *v.i.* to stretch one's neck or turn one's head to look at something. [Slang.]

rub′bĕr, *n.* [earlier *a rubbers* (applied to the deciding game at bowls).]

1. in bridge, whist, backgammon, etc., a series of games, usually three, sometimes five, the majority of which must be won to win the whole series.

2. the odd, or deciding, game in such a series.

rub′bĕr·īze, *v.t.*; rubberized, *pt., pp.*; rubberizing, *ppr.* to coat or impregnate with rubber or some preparation or solution of rubber.

rub′bĕr·neck, *n.* a person who stretches his neck or turns his head to look at things; one who gazes about in curiosity, as a sightseer. [Slang.]

rub′bĕr·neck, *a.* of or for sightseers; as, a rubberneck bus. [Slang.]

rub′bĕr·neck, *v.i.* to look at things or gaze about in curiosity, as a sightseer. [Slang.]

rub·bĕr-stamp′, *v.t.* 1. to put the impression of a rubber stamp on.

2. to approve or endorse (a plan, proposal, etc.) in a routine manner, without thought. [Colloq.]

rub′bĕr·y, *a.* like rubber in appearance, elasticity, toughness, etc.

rub′bidġe, *n.* rubbish. [Dial.]

rub′bing, *n.* the act of applying friction; a frictional movement.

rub′bish, *n.* [Anglo-Fr. *rubbous* (ML. *rubbosa*), rubble.]

1. fragments of buildings; broken or imperfect pieces of any structure; ruins.

He saw the towns one half in *rubbish* lie.
—Dryden.

2. waste or rejected matter; anything thrown away as worthless; trash; refuse: often distinguished from *garbage.*

3. worthless, foolish ideas, statements, etc.; nonsense.

rub′bish·y, *a.* trashy; consisting of or pertaining to rubbish.

rub′ble, *n.* [OFr. *robel,* from *robe,* rubbish.]

1. rough, irregularly broken pieces of stone, brick, etc.

2. masonry made of such pieces; rubblework.

3. crumbling stone fragments forming the top layer of rock deposits.

rub′ble·stōne, *n.* rubble.

rub′ble wall, in masonry, coarse walling constructed of rough stones of irregular size and shape.

rub′ble·wŏrk, *n.* coarse stonework.

rub′bly, *a.* pertaining to, resembling, or containing rubble.

rub′down, *n.* a brisk rubbing of the body; a massage.

rūbe, *n.* [from given name *Reuben.*] a person who lives in or comes from a rural region and lacks polish and sophistication; a rustic. [Slang.]

rū·bed′i·nous, *a.* reddish. [Rare.]

rū·bē·fā′cient (-shent), *a.* [L. *rubefacere,* to make red.] making red, as the skin.

rū·bē·fā′cient, *n.* in medicine, a substance or external application which produces redness of the skin.

rū·bē·faç′tion, *n.* the process of reddening, as with a rubefacient; also, redness of the skin, especially as caused by a rubefacient.

rū′be·let, *n.* a small ruby. [Obs.]

rū·bel′lȧ, *n.* [L. *rubellus,* dim. of *ruber,* red.] epidemic roseola, a disease of the skin resembling measles: also called *German measles.*

rū·belle′, *n.* [L. *rubellus,* reddish.] a red color, much used in enameling.

rū·bel′līte, *n.* a red variety of tourmaline, varying in color from a pale rose red to a deep ruby.

rū·bē′ō·lȧ, *n.* 1. measles.

2. German measles.

rū·bē′ō·loid, *a.* in medicine, like rubeola.

rū·bē·ryth′riç, *a.* [L. *rubia,* madder, and Gr. *erythros,* red.] derived from madder root; as, *ruberythric* acid.

rū·bes′cence, *n.* a growing rubescent or red; the state of becoming or being red; a blush.

rū·bes′cent, *a.* [L. *rubescens* (-*entis*), from *rubere,* to redden or be red.] growing or becoming red; specifically, blushing or flushing.

Rū′bi·ȧ, *n.* [L., madder, from *rubeus,* red; in allusion to the color obtained from the roots.] a genus of plants found both in Europe and Asia, belonging to the family *Rubiaceæ.* They are perennial herbs often woody below, with whorled entire leaves and small yellowish flowers.

Rū·bi·ā′cē·ae, *n.pl.* [LL., from L. *rubia,* madder.] a large family of exogenous plants, the madder family, containing many tropical shrubs, trees, and herbs, such as the coffee, ipecac, and cinchona plants, the gardenia, etc.

rū·bi·ā′ceous, *a.* of or pertaining to the *Rubiaceæ.*

rū′bi·ȧ·cin, *n.* a yellow crystalline coloring matter found in madder root.

Rū·bi·ā′lēs, *n.pl.* [LL., from L. *rubia,* madder.] a group of plants containing the families *Rubiaceæ, Adoxaceæ,* and *Caprifoliaceæ.*

rū′bi·ăn, *n.* [L. *rubia,* madder.] a glucoside found in madder root.

rū·bi·an′iç, *a.* contained in or derived from rubian.

rū′bi·āte, *n.* any pigment derived from madder root.

rū′bi·căn, *a.* [Fr., from L. *rubeus,* red.] of a bay, sorrel, or black color, with a light gray or white upon the flanks: said of a horse.

rū′bi·cel, rū′bi·celle, *n.* [Fr. *rubicelle,* from L. *rubeus,* red.] a variety of ruby of an orange-red color.

Rū′bi·çon, *n.* [L. *Rubico, Rubiconis.*] the small river in northern Italy, anciently forming the southern boundary of Cisalpine Gaul, which Caesar crossed at the head of his army in 49 B.C. to begin the civil war with Pompey.
to cross (or *pass*) *the Rubicon*; to start on a course of action from which there is no turning back; to take a final, irrevocable step.

rū′bi·çund, *a.* [L. *rubicundus.*] inclining to redness; reddish; ruddy.

rū·bi·çun′di·ty, *n.* the quality or state of being rubicund.

rū·bid′iç, *a.* pertaining to or containing rubidium.

rū′bi·dïne, rū′bi·din, *n.* an organic base of the pyridine series, obtained in liquid form from coal tar.

rū·bid′i·um, *n.* [Mod. L., from L. *rubidus,* red (from the red lines in its spectrum).] a soft, silvery-white metallic chemical element, resembling potassium: symbol, Rb; atomic weight, 85.48; atomic number, 37.

rū′bied, *a.* colored like a ruby; deep-red.

rū·bif′iç, *a.* [L. *ruber,* red, and *facere,* to make.] making red; as, *rubific* rays.

rū″bi·fi·çā′tion, *n.* the act of making red.

rū′bi·fȳ, *v.t.* [L. *ruber,* red, and *facere,* to make.] to make red. [Rare.]

rū·big′i·nōse, rū·big′i·nous, *a.* [LL. *rubiginosus,* rusty.]
1. rust-colored; reddish-brown; having a rusty appearance: in botany, usually used to denote a surface whose peculiar color is due to glandular hairs.
2. in medicine, having a rusty brownish color: said of sputum.

rū·bi·jẽr′vine, *n.* [L. *rubeus,* red, and E. *jervine.*] a poisonous alkaloid found in white hellebore, *Veratrum album.*

rū′bin, rū′bine, *n.* a ruby. [Obs.]

rū′bine, *n.* same as *fuchsin.*

rū·bin′ē·ous, *a.* of a ruby red; vivid red.

rū′bi·ous, *a.* [L. *rubeus,* red.] red; ruby-colored. [Rare.]

rū′ble, *n.* [Russ. *rubl′*; prob. from same source as Hind. *rūpiya,* rupee.] the monetary unit and a silver coin of the Soviet Union: one ruble is equivalent to 100 kopecks: also spelled *rouble.*

rū′briç, *n.* [Fr. *rubrique*; L., It., and Sp. *rubrica,* from L. *ruber,* red.]
1. in early books and manuscripts, a chapter heading, initial letter, specific sentence, etc. printed or written in red, decorative lettering etc.
2. a heading, title, etc., as of a chapter or section of a book.
3. a direction in a prayer book, etc. for conducting religious services, usually printed in red.
4. the title or a heading of a law or part of a legal code, originally written or printed in red.
5. red ocher. [Archaic.]

rū′briç, *v.t.* to adorn with red.

rū′briç, *a.* 1. inscribed in red.
2. red or reddish. [Archaic.]

rū′bri·căl, *a.* of, prescribed by, or according to rubrics, especially liturgical rubrics.

rū′bri·çāte, *v.t.*; rubricated, *pt., pp.*; rubricating, *ppr.* [L. *rubricatus,* pp. of *rubricare,* to redden.]
1. to mark, color, or illuminate (a book, etc.) with red; to write or print in red letters.
2. to provide with or regulate by rubrics.

rū′bri·çāte, *a.* marked with red.

rū·bri·çā′tion, *n.* 1. a rubricating or being rubricated.
2. something written or printed in red.

rū′bri·çā·tŏr, *n.* one who puts rubrics in books, etc.

rū·bri′ciăn (-brish′un), **rū′bri·cist,** *n.* one versed in or adhering to liturgical rubrics.

rū·bric′i·ty, *n.* redness.

rū′bri·çōse, *a.* reddish; rubricate.

rub′stōne, *n.* a stone, usually some kind of sandstone, used to sharpen instruments; a whetstone; a rub.

Rū′bus, *n.* [L., from *rubere,* to be red; in reference to the color of the fruit of some of the species.] a genus of plants, family *Rosaceæ,* including the blackberry and raspberry.

rū′by, *n.*; *pl.* **rū′bieṣ,** [ME. and OFr. *rubi*; ultimately from L. *rubeus,* red.]
1. a clear, deep-red variety of corundum, valued as a precious stone: also called *Oriental ruby, true ruby.*
2. something made of this stone, as a watch jewel.
3. deep red.
4. something deep red, as wine.
5. in printing, a size of type, 5½ point, corresponding to agate. [Brit.]
6. a blain; a blotch; a carbuncle.
7. the South American hummingbird, *Clytolæma rubineus,* the males being ruby-throated or ruby-breasted.
ruby of arsenic or *sulfur*; a red compound of arsenic and sulfur; realgar.
ruby of zinc; the sulfide of zinc, or red blende.

rū′by, *v.t.*; rubied, *pt., pp.*; rubying, *ppr.* to make red; to redden.

rū′by, *a.* of the color of the ruby; deep-red; as, *ruby* lips.
ruby glass; glass tinted a ruby color in the process of manufacture.

rū′by sil′vẽr, red silver ore; pyrargyrite.

rū′by·tāil, *n.* the gold wasp, *Chrysis ignita,* of Europe, which is red under the abdomen and elsewhere a metallic green-blue.

rū′by-tāiled, *a.* red-tailed.

rū′by thrōat, *n.* the hummingbird, *Trochilus colubris,* native to the eastern United States: the name is also applied to other hummingbirds which have patches of red on the feathers covering their throats.

rū′by wäsp, a brightly colored hymenopterous insect, of the family *Chrysididæ.*

rū′by wood, the wood of *Pterocarpus santalinus*; red sandalwood.

rū·cẽr′vine, *a.* [Malay *rusa,* a deer, and E. *cervine.*] of, relating to, or designating an Oriental genus of deer, *Rucervus,* in which is included the swamp deer of India.

rūçhe, *n.* [OFr. *rouche,* a beehive, from the resemblance of the quillings to honeycomb cells.] a frilling or pleating of lace, ribbon, muslin, net, etc. for trimming women's dresses: also spelled *rouche.*

rūçh′ing, *n.* 1. ruches collectively; trimming made of a ruche or ruches.
2. material used to make a ruche or ruches.

ruck, *n.* [ON. *hrukka,* a wrinkle or fold.] a wrinkle; a fold; a pucker.

ruck, *v.t.*; rucked, *pt., pp.*; rucking, *ppr.* to wrinkle, fold, or pucker: often with *up*; as, to *ruck up* a carpet.

ruck, *v.i.* to become wrinkled, folded, or puckered.

ruck, *n.* [ME. *ruke,* a heap, prob. from ON.]
1. originally, a heap or stack, as of fuel.
2. a large number or quantity; a multitude, mass, or crowd.
3. (a) the horses left behind by the leaders in a race; (b) the multitude or mass of undistinguished, ordinary people or things; the common run.

ruck, *v.t.* to gather into heaps. [Brit. Dial.]

ruck, *v.i.* [Dan. *ruge,* to brood.] to squat or sit, as a hen on eggs. [Dial.]

ruck′sack, *n.* [G., from dial. form of *rücken,* the back, and *sack.*] a knapsack carried on the back with the straps passing over the shoulders.

ruck′us, *n.* [prob. a merging of *rumpus* and *ruction.*] noisy confusion; uproar; row; disturbance. [Dial. or Colloq.]

ruç·tā′tion, *n.* [L. *ructare,* to belch.] the act of belching. [Rare.]

ruç′tion *n.* [altered, from *insurrection,* orig. with reference to the Irish Insurrection of 1798.] a riotous outbreak or uproar; a noisy disturbance or quarrel. [Colloq.]

rud, *n.* [AS. *rudu,* redness.]
1. redness; flush. [Obs.]
2. complexion. [Obs.]
3. reddle used in marking sheep. [Brit. Dial.]

rud, *v.t.* to make red. [Obs.]

rud, *v.i.* to redden. [Obs.]

Rud·beck′i·ȧ, *n.* [from Olaus *Rudbeck* (1630–1702), Swedish botanist.[a genus of composite North American plants with showy flowers. *Rudbeckia hirta,* the black-eyed Susan, is common along roadsides and in meadows of the United States.

rudd, *n.* [from the ruddy coloring.] a teleostean fish of Europe, of the genus *Cyprinus,* with a deep body like the bream, but thicker, a prominent back, and a small head. The back is of an olive color; the sides and belly yellow, marked with red; the ventral and anal fins and tail of a deep red color. Also called *red-eye.*

RUDD (*Cyprinus erythrophthalmus*)

rud′dẽr, *n.* [AS. *rother,* a paddle.]
1. a broad, flat, movable piece of wood or metal hinged vertically at the stern of a boat or ship, used for steering.
2. a piece like this in an aircraft, etc., used for steering to the left or right.
3. something serving to guide, direct, or control.

rud′dẽr chāin, one of the chains by which the rudder is fastened to the stern quarters.

rud′dẽr fish, 1. same as *pilot fish.*
2. any fish habitually following ships.

rud′dẽr·head (-hed), *n.* the upper end of the rudder into which the tiller is fitted.

rud′dẽr·hōle, *n.* a hole in the deck through which the head of the rudder passes.

rud′dẽr·less, *a.* having no rudder.

rud′dẽr·pōst, *n.* 1. a rudderstock.
2. in some ships, an added sternpost, to which the rudder is fastened.

rud′dẽr·stock, *n.* the main piece or broadest part of the rudder, attached to the sternpost by the rudder bands.

rud′died (-did), *a.* made ruddy or red.

rud′di·ly, *adv.* in a ruddy manner.

rud′di·ness, *n.* the state or quality of being ruddy; redness.

rud′dle, *n.* [AS. *rudu,* red.] red ocher.

rud′dle, *v.t.*; ruddled, *pt., pp.*; ruddling, *ppr.* to mark or color with red ocher.

rud′dle·măn, *n.*; *pl.* **rud′dle·men,** a person who sells ruddle.

rud′dŏck, *n.* [AS. *rudduc,* from *rudu,* red.]
1. the European robin.
2. a gold coin. [Obs.]

rud′dy, *v.t.*; ruddied, *pt., pp.*; ruddying, *ppr.* to make red or ruddy.

rud′dy, *a.*; *comp.* ruddier; *superl.* ruddiest, [AS. *rudig,* from *rudu,* red.]
1. of a red color; reddish; as, *ruddy* petals of a flower.
2. having a healthy red color; glowing; as, a *ruddy* complexion.
ruddy duck; an American duck, *Erismature rubida,* the male of which has a brownish-red neck and upper body, black crown, and white cheeks: also called *spoonbill, ruddy diver, stiff-tail, fool duck,* and *hardhead.*
ruddy plover; the sanderling.
Syn.—rubicund, rosy. —*Ruddy* denotes a healthlike color, as of the skin, and in an extended sense any similar red, as of an apple; *rubicund* suggests high color caused by drink or other excesses; *rosy* is descriptive of an attractive blooming red, as of the cheeks.

rūde, *a.*; *comp.* ruder; *superl.* rudest, [L. *rudis,* rough.]
1. coarse or rough in form or workmanship; crude.
2. barbarous or ignorant; as, *rude* savages.
3. lacking refinement, culture, or elegance; uncouth; boorish.
4. discourteous; unmannerly; as, a *rude* reply.
5. rough; violent; harsh; as, *rude* winds blew.
6. harsh in sound; discordant; not musical; as, *rude* tones.
7. having or showing little skill, accuracy, method, etc.; as, *rude* drawings.
8. not carefully worked out or finished; rough; as, a *rude* plan.
9. sturdy; robust; rugged.
Syn.—rough, uneven, shapeless, unfashioned, rugged, unpolished, uncouth, inelegant, rustic, coarse, vulgar, clownish, raw, unskillful, untaught, illiterate, ignorant, uncivil, impolite, impertinent, saucy, impudent, insolent, surly.

rūde′ly, *adv.* in a rude manner.

rūde′ness, *n.* the state or quality of being rude.

rụ·dent′ed, *a.* in architecture, cabled.

rụ·den′tūre, *n.* in architecture, cabling.

rụ′de·răl, *a.* [L. *rudus, ruderis,* rubbish.] in botany, growing in wastes or among rubbish.

Rụ′des·heim·ẽr, *n.* the white wine made near Rudesheim on the Rhine.

rụ′di·ment, *n.* [L. *rudimentum,* a first attempt.]
1. [*usually in pl.*] a first principle, element, or fundamental, as of a subject to be learned; as, the *rudiments* of art.
2. a first slight beginning or appearance, or undeveloped form or stage, of something.
3. in biology, an incompletely developed organ or part, as one in an embryonic condition; specifically, a vestigial organ or part with no functional activity; vestige.

rụ′di·ment, *v.t.*; rudimented, *pt., pp.*; rudimenting, *ppr.* to furnish with first principles; to ground; to instruct in first principles.

rụ·di·men′tăl, *a.* elementary; rudimentary.

rụ·di·men′tȧ·ri·ly, *adv.* 1. in a rudimentary manner.
2. so as to be rudimentary.

rụ·di·men′tȧ·ri·ness, *n.* the quality or condition of being rudimentary.

rụ·di·men′tȧ·ry, *a.* of, or having the nature of, a rudiment or rudiments; specifically, (a) elementary; (b) incompletely or imperfectly developed; (c) vestigial.

rūd′ish, *a.* [L. *rudis,* rough.] inclined to rudeness; rather rude.

Rụ·dis′tȧ, *n.pl.* an extinct order of bivalves: also called *Rudistes.*

Rụ·dolph′ine Tā′bleṣ, [after Rudolph II, Holy Roman Emperor.] a set of astronomical tables composed by Kepler on the observations of Tycho Brahe.

rūe, *v.t.*; rued, *pt., pp.*; ruing, *ppr.* [AS. *hreowan,* to be sorry for.]
1. to feel remorse or repentance for (a sin, fault, etc.).
2. to wish (an act, agreement, etc.) undone, unmade, etc.; to regret.
3. to make repentant or sorrowful; to afflict. [Obs.]

rūe, *v.i.* to be sorrowful or regretful.

rūe, *n.* 1. sorrow, repentance, or regret. [Archaic.]
2. pity; compassion. [Archaic.]

rūe, *n.* [OFr.; L. *ruta*; Gr. *rhytē,* rue.] any strong-scented plant of the genus *Ruta.* The species are woody herbaceous plants, with alternate exstipulated, pinnated, or decompound leaves. *Ruta graveolens,* or common rue, formerly called *herb of grace,* has been a traditional symbol of grief, regret, etc. (with punning allusion to *rue,* regret).
African or *Syrian rue*; the harmel.

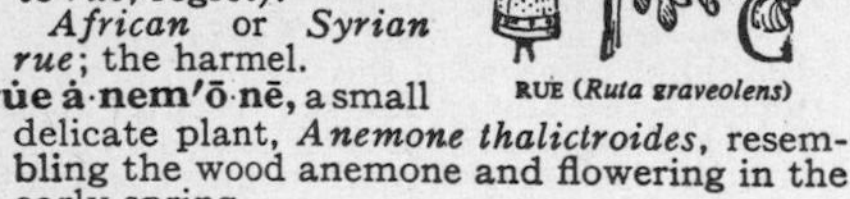

RUE (*Ruta graveolens*)

rūe ȧ·nem′ō·nē, a small delicate plant, *Anemone thalictroides,* resembling the wood anemone and flowering in the early spring.

rūe fẽrn, the wall rue.

rūe′fụl, *a.* 1. causing sorrow or pity; pitiable; lamentable.
2. feeling, expressing, or showing sorrow or pity; mournful.

rūe′fụl·ly, *adv.* in a rueful manner.

rūe′fụl·ness, *n.* the quality or state of being rueful.

rụ·elle′ (-el′), *n.* [Fr., dim. of *rue,* a street.]
1. a space or passage between a bed and the wall. [Obs.]
2. a bedchamber in which persons of rank in France during the seventeenth and eighteenth centuries held receptions in the morning; hence, a circle or coterie where the events of the day were discussed.

Rụ·el′li·ȧ, *n.* [after Jean *Ruel,* a 16th-c. French botanist.] a genus of tropical Asiatic and Australian plants of the *Acanthaceæ,* some species of which are cultivated in China and Assam for the indigo they yield, others on account of their flowers.

rụ′ẽr, *n.* one who rues.

rụ·fes′cence, *n.* reddishness; tendency to become red.

rụ·fes′cent, *a.* [L. *rufescere,* to grow red.] reddish; tinged with red.

ruff, *n.* [contr. of *ruffle.*]
1. a high, frilled or pleated collar of starched muslin, etc., worn by men and women in the sixteenth and seventeenth centuries.
2. something circular like this collar; specifically, a collar of prominent or colored feathers or fur on a bird or beast.
3. a European or Asiatic sandpiper, *Machetes pugnax,* the male of which grows a large ruff during the breeding season: the female is called a *reeve.*
4. a kind of pigeon with a ruff.
5. a display, as of pride, vanity, or hauteur. [Obs.]

RUFF (*Machetes pugnax*)

ruff, *v.t.* 1. to plait; to ruffle; to wrinkle.
2. to ruffle; to disorder.
3. in falconry, to hit without trussing.
4. to applaud by making noise with hands or feet. [Scot.]

ruff, ruffe, *n.* [prob. from *rough.*] a small spotted European fresh-water fish of the perch family.

ruff, *v.t.* 1. to nap, as a hat. [Obs.]
2. to hatchel, as flax.

ruff, *n.* a ruffle; a low rolling drumbeat.

ruff, *n.* [It. *ronfa,* a card game, from *trionfo,* trump.]
1. an old card game, somewhat like whist. [Obs.]
2. in card games, the act of trumping.

ruff, *v.t.* and *v.i.* in card playing, to trump when unable to follow suit.

ruffed (ruft), *a.* having a ruff or ruffs.
ruffed grouse; a grouse, *Bonasa umbellus,* having a ruff on each side of the neck. It is known as the *partridge* in the northern United States, as the *pheasant* in the southern United States, and as the *birch partridge* in Canada.
ruffed lemur; the black-and-white lemur, *Lemur varius.*

ruf′fi·ăn (*or* ruf′yăn), *n.* [Fr. *ruffian*; It. *ruffiano,* pander; Eng. sense influenced by *rough.*]
1. a brutal, violent, lawless person; a tough.
2. a pander; a pimp; a paramour. [Obs.]
3. the devil. [Obs.]

ruf′fi·ăn, *a.* brutal, violent, and lawless.

ruf′fi·ăn, *v.i.* to play the ruffian; to rage. [Rare.]

ruf′fi·ăn·ăġe, *n.* ruffians as a body; the state of being a ruffian.

ruf′fi·ăn·ish, *a.* having the qualities or manners of a ruffian.

ruf′fi·ăn·iṣm, *n.* the character or conduct of a ruffian.

ruf′fi·ăn·like, *a.* ruffianly.

ruf′fi·ăn·ly, *a.* like or characteristic of a ruffian; bold in crimes; brutal; violent; licentious.

ruf′fi·ăn·ous, *a.* violent; like a ruffian. [Obs.]

ruf′fle (-l), *v.t.*; ruffled, *pt., pp.*; ruffling, *ppr.* [ME. *ruffelen,* to entangle, from ON.]
1. to take away the smoothness or regularity of; to wrinkle; to ripple; as, the wind *ruffles* the surface of the water.
2. to fold or draw (cloth, etc.) into ruffles.
3. to put ruffles on as trimming.
4. to make (feathers, etc.) stand up in or as in a ruff, as a bird in fright.
5. to disturb, irritate, or annoy; as, nothing *ruffles* her.
6. (a) to turn over (the pages of a book, etc.) rapidly; (b) to shuffle (cards).
7. to throw together in a disorderly manner. [Rare.]

ruf′fle, *v.i.* 1. to become uneven, rough, wrinkled, etc.
2. to become disturbed, irritated, etc.

ruf′fle, *n.* 1. a narrow ornamental pleat or trimming of cloth, lace, etc.
2. something like this, as a bird's ruff.
3. a disturbance; irritation.
4. a break in surface smoothness; a ripple.
ruffle of a boot; the turned-down top hanging in a loose manner, like the ruffle of a shirt. [Archaic.]

ruf′fle, *n.* [echoic.] a low continuous beating of a drum, not so loud as a roll.

ruf′fle, *v.t.* and *v.i.*; ruffled, *pt., pp.*; ruffling, *ppr.* to beat (a drum, etc.) with a ruffle.

ruf′fle, *v.i.* [ME. *ruffelen*; prob. specialized use of prec.]
1. to make a noisy disturbance.
2. to be arrogant; to swagger.

ruf′fle, *n.* a noisy disturbance; a brawl.

ruf′fle·less, *a.* having no ruffles.

ruf′fle·ment, *n.* the act of ruffling. [Rare.]

ruf′flẽr, *n.* 1. a bully. [Obs.]
2. a swaggerer.
3. an attachment to a sewing machine, for making ruffles.

ruf′fling, *n.* manufactured ruffles; a length of ruffle; as, three yards of *ruffling.*

ruf′fly, *a.*; *comp.* rufflier; *superl.* ruffliest; of, in, or like a ruffle or ruffles.

rụ·fi·gal′liç, *a.* [from L. *rufus,* red, and E. *gallic.*] designating a brownish crystalline acid derived from anthracene.

rụ′fous, *a.* [L. *rufus,* red.] reddish; of a reddish or brownish-red color; rust-colored.

ruft, *n.* eructation. [Obs.]

ruf′tẽr·hood, *n.* [*ruff* and *hood,* the *ter* being merely connective.] in falconry, a hood to be worn by a hawk when first drawn.

rụ′fū·lous, *a.* in botany and zoology, inclined to be rufous.

rug, *n.* [of Scandinavian origin; akin to ON. *rögg,* rough fleece.]
1. a piece of thick, often napped fabric, woven strips of rag, an animal skin, etc. used as a floor covering: usually distinguished from *carpet* in being a single piece of definite shape, not intended to cover the entire floor.
2. a piece of heavy, warm cloth used as a lap robe, wrap, etc. [Chiefly Brit.]
3. a rough, woolly, or shaggy dog.
4. a coarse heavy frieze for garments. [Obs.]
made rug; a rug composed of more than one piece.

rug, *v.t.* [ME. *rogge,* to rend; ON. *rugga,* to rock.] to pull or haul roughly or hastily; to plunder; to tear. [Obs.]

rug, *n.* a pull; a tug. [Obs.]

rụ′gȧ, *n.*; *pl.* **rụ′gae,** [*usually in pl.*] [L. *ruga,* a wrinkle, fold.] in botany, zoology, etc., a ridge, wrinkle, or fold.
rugae of the stomach; wrinkles which appear on the surface of the mucous membrane of the stomach when the muscular coat contracts.

rụ′gāte, *a.* wrinkled; folded; creased; having alternate ridges and depressions.

Rug′by, *n.* [after the boys' school of the same name, founded in 1567 in Warwickshire, England.] a kind of football, first played at Rugby school, in which each team consists of 15 players and the oval ball may be passed, dribbled with the feet, or carried: the American game of football developed from this: in full, *Rugby football.*

rug′ged, *a.* [Sw. *rugga,* to roughen.]
1. having irregular surface projections and depressions; not smooth or regular in surface or contour; uneven; rough; wrinkled; as, *rugged* ground, *rugged* mountains.
2. (a) heavy, strong, and irregular, as facial features; (b) having such features; as, a *rugged* face.
3. stormy; tempestous; as, *rugged* weather.
4. sounding harsh; as, *rugged* tones.
5. severe; harsh; hard; stern; as, a *rugged* life, a *rugged* climate.
6. not polished, cultivated, refined, or elegant; rude; as, *rugged* manners.
7. strong; robust; sturdy; vigorous.
Syn.—rough, coarse, rude, uneven, stormy, harsh, austere, frowning, boisterous, hardy.

rug′ged·ly, *adv.* in a rugged manner.

rug′ged·ness, *n.* the quality or state of being rugged.

Rug′gẽr, *n.* Rugby football. [Brit. Slang.]

rug′ging, *n.* coarse woolen cloth used as a wrapping, blanket, rug, etc.

rug′-gowned, *a.* wearing a gown like a rug.

rug′gy, *a.* rough; shaggy. [Obs. or Dial.]

rug′head″ed (-hed″), *a.* shockheaded. [Obs.]

rụ′ġine, rụ′ġin, *n.* [Fr.] 1. a surgeon's rasp [Obs.]
2. a nappy cloth. [Obs.]

rụ′ġine, *v.t.* [Fr., from *ruginer,* to scrape.]
1. to scrape with a rugine. [Obs.]
2. to wipe with a nappy cloth. [Obs.]

Rụ·gō′sȧ, *n.pl.* [L. *rugosus,* wrinkled, from *ruga,* a wrinkle.] an order of extinct corals characteristic of the Paleozoic formations in which the septa were generally some multiple of four, but with one or three prominent, or with a small channel.

ru̇'gōse, *a.* [L. *rugosus*, from *ruga*, a wrinkle.] having or full of wrinkles; corrugated; ridged; as, a *rugose* leaf.

ru̇'gōse·ly, *adv.* in a rugose manner.

ru̇·gos'i·ty, *n.* 1. the condition or quality of being rugose.
2. *pl.* **ru̇·gos'i·ties,** a wrinkle or corrugation.

ru̇'gous, *a.* same as *rugose.*

ru̇'gū·lōse, *a.* minutely rugose.

Ru̇hm'korff çoil (ru̇m'), [named after H. D. *Ruhmkorff*, who invented it.] in electricity, an early form of induction coil.

ru̇'in, *n.* [Fr. *ruine*, from L. *ruina*, a downfall, from *ruere*, to fall.]
1. a falling down, as of a building, wall, etc. [Rare.]
2. [*pl.*] the remains of a fallen building, city, etc., or of something destroyed, devastated, decayed, etc.
3. (a) anything that has fallen to pieces, been destroyed, become decayed through age, etc.; as, the bombed city was a *ruin*; (b) a person regarded as being physically, mentally, or morally a wreck of what he was.
4. the state of having fallen to pieces or of being destroyed, devastated, decayed, etc.
5. downfall, complete destruction, overthrow, devastation, decay, etc., as of a thing or person, or in general; specifically, (a) complete loss of means, solvency, position, etc.; (b) moral downfall, or loss of chastity, of a woman.
6. anything that causes downfall, destruction, decay, etc.; as, gambling was his *ruin.*

Syn.—destruction, overthrow, bane, fall, downfall, subversion, mischief, perdition, pest, defeat.

ru̇'in, *v.t.*; ruined, *pt., pp.*; ruining, *ppr.* to bring or reduce to ruin; specifically, (a) to destroy, damage greatly or irreparably spoil, etc.; (b) to impoverish or make bankrupt; (c) to deprive (a woman) of chastity.

ru̇'in, *v.i.* to go or come to ruin.

ru̇'in·ȧ·ble, *a.* that can be ruined.

ru̇'in·āte, *v.t.* and *v.i.*; ruinated, *pt., pp.*; ruinating, *ppr.* to ruin. [Archaic.]

ru̇'in·āte, *a.* ruined; in ruins.

ru̇·in·ā'tion, *n.* 1. the act of ruining or the state of being ruined.
2. anything that ruins.

ru̇'in·ẽr, *n.* one who or that which ruins or destroys.

ru̇'in·i·fọrm, *a.* having the appearance of ruins, as certain minerals.

ru̇'in·ous, *a.* [OFr. *ruineux*; L. *ruinosus.*]
1. falling or fallen into ruin; entirely decayed; demolished; dilapidated; as, an edifice, bridge, or wall in a *ruinous* state.
2. destructive; harmful; disastrous; pernicious; bringing or tending to bring ruin; as, a *ruinous* practice.
3. composed of ruins; consisting of ruins; as, a *ruinous* heap.

ru̇'in·ous·ly, *adv.* in a ruinous manner; destructively.

ru̇'in·ous·ness, *n.* the state or quality of being ruinous.

ru̇kh, *n.* [Ar. *roc.*] the roc.

ru̇l'ȧ·ble, *a.* subject to rule; that can be ruled.

ru̇le, *n.* [ME. *reule, rewle*, from OFr. *reule, riule*; from L. *regula*, a straight piece of wood, a ruler, a rule.]
1. an established guide or regulation for action, conduct, method, arrangement, etc.
2. a complete set or code of regulations in a religious order; as, the Benedictine *rule.*
3. a fixed principle that determines conduct; habit; custom; as, morning prayer was a *rule* of the household.
4. a criterion or standard.
5. something that usually or normally happens or obtains; the customary or ordinary course of events; as, famine and disease are the *rule* following war.
6. government; reign; control; as, the *rule* of Elizabeth.
7. a ruler (sense 2).
8. way of acting; behavior. [Obs.]
9. in law, a decision, order, etc. made by a judge or court in regard to a specific question.
10. in mathematics, a method of procedure prescribed for computing or solving a problem.
11. in printing, a thin strip of metal, usually brass, as high as type, used to print lines between columns, make decorative borders, etc.

as a rule; usually; generally; for the most part.

joint rule; in parliamentary practice, a rule of conduct adopted by both branches of a legislative body.

rule of coss; algebra. [Obs.]

rule of three; in mathematics, the method of finding the fourth term of a proportion when three terms are given.

rule of thumb; a rule suggested by a practical rather than a scientific knowledge; hence, any way of doing things that is practical though crude.

Syn.—government, sway, empire, control, direction, regulation, law, canon, precept, maxim, guide, order, method.

ru̇le, *v.t.*; ruled, *pt., pp.*; ruling, *ppr.* 1. to have an influence over; to guide; as, he was *ruled* by his friends.
2. to lessen; restrain; as, reason *ruled* his fear.
3. to have authority over; to govern; to direct; as, the king *ruled* the country.
4. to be the most important element of; as, action *rules* the plot.
5. to settle by decree; to determine; as, the court *ruled* the validity of the point.
6. to mark lines on with or as with a ruler.
7. to mark (a line) with or as with a ruler.

ruled surface; in geometry, a surface that may be described by the motion of a line.

to rule out; to exclude by decision.

ru̇le, *v.i.* 1. to have or exercise supreme power, control, or authority; to govern: often with *over*; as, a king *rules over* that country.
2. to stand at or maintain a certain level; to prevail: said of prices, commodities, etc.; as, prices *ruled* high.
3. to issue a formal decree about a question; as, the court will *rule* on the matter.
4. to prevail; to control; as, peace should *rule.*

ru̇le joint, a movable joint in which a tongue on one piece enters a slot in the other, and is secured by a pin or rivet. When the two pieces are in line, their ends abut, so that movement is possible only in one direction. This arrangement is used for carpenters' rules and table leaves.

ru̇le'less, *a.* without rule; lawless.

ru̇le'less·ness, *n.* the quality or state of being without rule.

ru̇le'mŏñ"gẽr, an overstrict observer of rules; one who slavishly follows the letter of the rule.

ru̇l'ẽr, *n.* 1. a person or thing that rules or governs.
2. a thin strip of wood, metal, etc. with a straight edge and markings in inches or centimeters and their fractional parts, used in drawing straight lines, measuring length, etc.; a straightedge.
3. a person or device that rules lines on paper, etc.

ru̇l'ẽr·ship, *n.* the position, power, jurisdiction, or term of a ruler; sovereignty.

ru̇l'ing, *n.* 1. the act of governing; control.
2. a decision made by a court or judge.
3. the act of drawing or measuring with a ruler.
4. a line or lines so drawn.

ru̇l'ing, *a.* that rules; specifically, (a) governing; (b) predominating; (c) prevalent.

ru̇l'ing·ly, *adv.* in a ruling manner; controllingly.

ru̇l'ing pen, a pen for drawing lines of uniform thickness.

rul'li·chie, *n.* same as *rollichie.*

rul'liŏn (-yun), *n.* [from AS. *rifling*, a kind of shoe.]
1. a shoe made of untanned leather. [Scot.]
2. a rough, coarse-looking person or animal, especially a woman. [Scot.]

ru̇l'y, *a.* orderly; easily restrained. [Obs.]

rum, *n.* [short for *rumbullion*, name associated with the Fr. place name *Rambouillet* (with reference to peaches and gooseberries); cf. Fr. *rebouillir*, to boil again.]
1. an alcoholic liquor distilled from fermented molasses, sugar cane, etc.
2. any alcoholic liquor; intoxicating drink in general.

rum, *a.* [from obs. *rum*, good, great.]
1. old-fashioned; queer; odd. [Chiefly Brit. Slang.]
2. good; excellent. [Archaic Slang.]
3. bad, poor, etc.; as, a *rum* joke. [Slang.]

rum, *n.* rummy (card game).

ru̇·mäl', *n.* [Hind. *rūmāl*, a handkerchief.] a square cloth used variously as a veil, a shawl, or a kerchief.

Ru̇·mā'ni·ăn, *a.* and *n.* same as *Romanian.*

rumb, *n.* same as *rhumb.*

rum'bȧ, *n.* [Sp.; prob. of Afr. origin.]
1. a dance of Cuban Negro origin and complex rhythm.
2. a modern ballroom adaptation of this, characterized by emphasized rhythmic movements of the lower part of the body.
3. music for, or in the rhythm of, this dance. Also spelled *rhumba.*

rum'ble, *v.i.*; rumbled, *pt., pp.*; rumbling, *ppr.* [ME. *romblen, romlen.*]
1. to make a deep, heavy, continuous, rolling sound; as, thunder *rumbles* at a distance.
2. to move or go with such a sound; as, the truck *rumbled* down the street.
3. to make a murmuring sound; to ripple. [Archaic.]

rum'ble, *v.t.* 1. to cause to make or move with a low, heavy, continuous, rolling sound.
2. to utter or say with such a sound.
3. to polish, mix, etc. in a rumble, or tumbling box.

rum'ble, *n.* 1. a deep, heavy, continuous, rolling sound.
2. a space for luggage or a small extra seat, as for servants, in the rear of a carriage.
3. a rumble seat.
4. a tumbling box.

rum'blẽr, *n.* a person or thing that rumbles.

rum'ble sēat, in some automobiles, especially formerly, an extra open seat in the rear, behind the roofed seat: it can be folded shut when not in use.

rum'bling, *n.* a deep, heavy, continuous, rolling sound; a rumble; the act of making a rumble.

rum'bling·ly, *adv.* in a rumbling manner.

rum'bly, *a.*; *comp.* rumblier; *superl.* rumbliest; rumbling, or causing or characterized by a rumbling sound.

rum'bō, *n.* rum; grog. [Obs.]

rum·booze', *n.* a mixed alcoholic drink; formerly, any alcoholic drink. [Archaic.]

rum·bōw'līne, *n.* same as *rombowline.*

rum cher'ry, the North American wild black cherry, *Prunus serotina*, frequently steeped in rum to flavor the liquor.

ru̇'men, *n.* [L., the throat.]
1. the cud of a ruminant.
2. the first stomach of a ruminant; the paunch; the farding bag.

ru̇·men·ot'ō·my, *n.* in veterinary surgery, an incision made into the rumen to relieve from pressure, as from overfeeding.

Ru̇'mex, *n.* [L., lance, from the shape of the leaves.] a genus of coarse, bitter, perennial herbs or shrubs, the docks and sorrels, having stipulate leaves and small, greenish flowers in clusters: they are widely distributed in the North Temperate Zone.

ru̇'mi·cin, *n.* chrysophanic acid.

ru̇'mi·năl, *a.* [Fr., from L. *rumenalis*, ruminating.] ruminant. [Rare.]

ru̇'mi·nănt, *a.* [L. *ruminans*, ppr. of *ruminare*, to ruminate.]
1. chewing the cud; chewing again what has been swallowed.
2. of or pertaining to the *Ruminantia*, or cud-chewing animals.
3. meditative.

ru̇'mi·nănt, *n.* an animal that chews the cud; one of the *Ruminantia.*

Ru̇·mi·nan'ti·ȧ, *n.pl.* a division of four-footed, hoofed, even-toed, and cud-chewing mammals, as the cattle, buffalo, bison, goat, deer, antelope, camel, giraffe, llama, etc., which have a stomach consisting of four divisions or chambers, the rumen, reticulum, omasum (or manyplies, psalterium), and abomasum: the

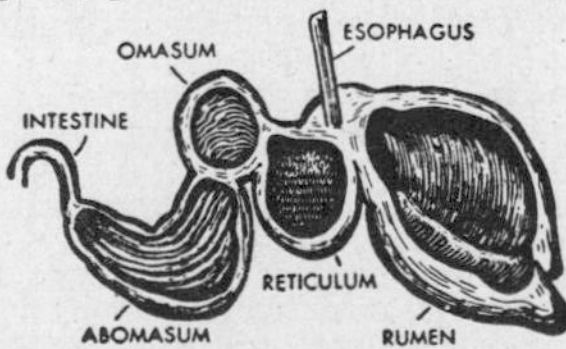

STOMACH OF A RUMINANT

grass, etc. that they eat is swallowed unchewed and passes into the rumen or reticulum, from which it is regurgitated, chewed and mixed with saliva, again swallowed, and then passed through the reticulum and omasum into the abomasum, where it is acted on by the gastric juice.

rū′mi·nănt·ly, *adv.* in a ruminant manner; by chewing the cud.

rū′mi·nāte, *v.i.*; ruminated, *pt., pp.*; ruminating, *ppr.* [Fr. *ruminer*; L. *ruminare*, to ruminate.]
 1. to chew the cud; to chew again what has been slightly chewed and swallowed.
 2. to muse; to meditate; to think again and again; to ponder.

rū′mi·nāte, *v.t.* 1. to chew over again.
 2. to muse on; to meditate upon.
 Mad with desire, she *ruminates* her sin.
 —Dryden.

rū′mi·nāte, rū′mi·nā·ted, *a.* in botany, having the appearance of having been chewed; pierced by numerous narrow cavities full of dry, cellular matter, like the albumen of a nutmeg.

rū·mi·nā′tion, *n.* [L. *ruminatio* (*-onis*).]
 1. the act, process, habit, or characteristic of chewing the cud.
 2. a musing or continued thinking on a subject; deliberate meditation or reflection.
 3. a condition in some diseases, in which the food after being swallowed is regurgitated.

rū′mi·nā·tive, *a.* inclined or given to rumination; reflective.

rū′mi·nā·tŏr, *n.* [LL.] one who ruminates.

rum′kin, *n.* a vessel for drinking. [Obs.]

rum′kin, *n.* a fowl without a tail. [Dial.]

rum′măġe, *n.* [MFr. *arrumage*, from *arrumere*, to stow cargo in the hold, from *aruner*, to arrange, from *run, rum*, ship's hold, from AS. *rum*, room.]
 1. miscellaneous articles; odds and ends.
 2. a rummaging, or thorough search.
 3. a rummage sale.
 4. (a) the arrangement of cargo in a ship's hold; (b) a stowage or storage place. [Obs.]

rum′măġe, *v.t.*; rummaged, *pt., pp.*; rummaging, *ppr.* 1. to search through (a place, receptacle, etc.) diligently and thoroughly, especially by moving the contents about, turning them over, etc.; to ransack.
 2. to get, turn up, or bring to light by or as by searching thoroughly (with *up* or *out*).
 3. in nautical usage, to prepare a place for stowing the cargo. [Obs.]

rum′măġe, *v.i.* 1. to search thoroughly and diligently, as through the contents of a receptacle.
 2. in nautical language, to stow the cargo. [Obs.]

rum′mă·ġẽr, *n.* 1. one who rummages.
 2. in nautical usage, one of a ship's crew who arranged or stowed the cargo. [Obs.]

rum′măġe sāle, 1. a sale of contributed miscellaneous articles, used or new, as clothing, household furnishings, etc., to raise money for charitable purposes or for some organization.
 2. a sale of miscellaneous merchandise at a shop, as for clearance before restocking, or of unclaimed articles at a warehouse, etc.

rum′mẽr, *n.* [D. *roemer, romer*, from *roemen*, to praise: hence, orig., a glass used for drinking toasts in praise of someone.] a large drinking glass or cup.

rum′my, *a.* of, pertaining to, resembling, or characteristic of rum; as, a *rummy* taste.

rum′my, *n.*; *pl.* **rum′mieș,** a drunkard. [Slang.]

rum′my, *a.*; *comp.* rummier; *superl.* rummiest, peculiar; unusual; strange: also *rum*. [Chiefly Brit. Slang.]

rum′my, *n.* [prob. from *rummy* (strange).] a card game, played in many variations, in which the object is to match cards into sets of the same denomination or sequences of the same suit: also *rum*.

rum′ney, rŏm′ney, *n.* a sweet, heavy Greek wine.

Rū·monsch′, *n.* same as *Romansh*.

rū′mŏr, *n.* [Fr. *rumeur*, from L. *rumor*, common talk.]
 1. general talk not based on definite knowledge; mere gossip; hearsay.
 2. an unconfirmed report, story, or statement in general circulation.
 3. loud disapproval, protest, clamor, or uproar. [Obs.]

rū′mŏr, *v.t.*; rumored, *pt., pp.*; rumoring, *ppr.* to tell, report, or spread by rumor or as a rumor.

rū′mŏr·ẽr, *n.* a teller of news; one who spreads rumors.

rū′mŏr·ous, *a.* circulated as a rumor. [Rare.]

rū′mŏur, *n.* and *v.t.* rumor: British spelling.

rump, *n.* [ON. *rumpr*; akin to G. *rumpf*, trunk (of the body).]
 1. the hind part of the body of an animal, where the legs and the back come together.
 2. a cut of meat, usually beef, from this part, behind the loin and above the round: see *beef*, illus.
 3. the buttocks.
 4. the last and unimportant or inferior part; fag end; mere remnant.
 5. a legislature, etc. having only a remnant of its former membership, as because of expulsions, and hence regarded as unrepresentative and without authority.

rump bōne, *n.* the sacrum.

Rum·pel·stilts′kin, *n.* in German folklore, a deformed dwarf who made an agreement with the young bride of a king to spin for her the large quantity of flax required by the king: in return she was to give the dwarf her first child unless she guessed his name within a month, but she succeeded and the dwarf disappeared.

Rump′ẽr, *n.* one who belonged to or supported the Rump Parliament. [Obs.]

rump′-fed, *a.* fattened in the rump; fat. [Archaic.]

rum′ple, *n.* [MD. *rompel*, from *rompe*, a wrinkle.] an uneven fold or crease; a wrinkle.

rum′ple, *v.t.* and *v.i.*; rumpled, *pt., pp.*; rumpling, *ppr.* to make rumples; to crumple; to muss.

rump′less, *a.* without a rump; as, a *rumpless* fowl.

rum′ply, *a.*; *comp.* rumplier; *superl.* rumpliest; rumpled.

Rump Pär′liȧ·ment, in English history, (a) the part of the Long Parliament remaining after the purge of 1648 until disbanded by Cromwell in 1653; (b) the same body recalled in 1659 and disbanded in 1660.

rump steāk, a beefsteak cut from or near the rump.

rum′pus, *n.* [said to be from Swiss G. student slang.] a disturbance; noise and confusion. [Colloq.]

rum′pus rọọm, a room, usually in the basement of a house, for games, dancing, etc.; a recreation room.

rum′run·nẽr, *n.* a person, ship, etc. engaged in the business of smuggling alcoholic liquor across a border.

rum′run·ning, *n.* the practice or business of a rumrunner.

run, *v.i.*; ran *or dial.* run, *pt.*; run, *pp.*; running, *ppr.* [AS. *rinnen*, from ON. *rinna, renna*, to run.]
 1. to go by moving the legs rapidly, faster than in walking, and (in a two-legged animal) in such a way that for an instant both feet are off the ground.
 2. to go rapidly; to move swiftly; as, we *ran* to her aid, the ship *ran* before the wind.
 3. to go, move, grow, etc. easily and freely, without hindrance or restraint; to be unchecked.
 4. to go away rapidly; to flee.
 5. to make a quick trip (*up to, down to, over to*, etc. a specified place) for a brief stay.
 6. (a) to take part in a contest or race; (b) to be a candidate in an election.
 7. to finish a contest or race in a specified numerical position; as, my horse *ran* last.
 8. to swim in migration, as upstream or inshore for spawning, etc.: said of fish; as, the salmon *run* every year.
 9. to go, as on a schedule; to ply between two points; as, the bus *runs* between Chicago and New York.
 10. to go or pass lightly and rapidly; as, a breeze *ran* through the trees.
 11. to be current; to circulate; as, the story *runs* that the bank will close.
 12. to climb or creep: said of plants; as, the vine *runs* over the porch.
 13. to extend in time; to extend through the years; as, his family line *runs* back to the Conquest.
 14. to move continuously; as, his tongue *ran* on and on.
 15. to become loosened and ravel; as, her stocking *ran*.
 16. to revolve or move with or as with parts that revolve, slide, etc.; to operate; as, the machine is *running*.
 17. to return constantly to the mind; to be remembered; as, thoughts *ran* in his head.
 18. to flow; as, blood *runs* in the veins.
 19. to melt and flow; as, the butter *ran*.
 20. (a) to spread when put on a surface, as a liquid; (b) to spread over or be diffused through cloth, etc. when moistened, as colors.
 21. to be wet or covered with a flow; as, the gutters *ran* with blood, her eyes *ran* with tears.
 22. to give passage to a fluid; specifically, (a) to discharge pus, mucus, etc.; (b) to leak, as a faucet.
 23. to elapse; as, the days *ran* into weeks.
 24. to appear or be presented continuously or in a continuing series; as, the play *ran* for a year.
 25. to continue in effect or force; as, the law *runs* for twenty years.
 26. to extend in or as in a continuous line; as, the fence *runs* through the woods.
 27. to proceed or pass into a specified condition, situation, etc.; as, he always *ran* into trouble.
 28. to sail or float (aground, etc.): said of a ship.
 29. to be written, expressed, played, etc. in a specified way; as, the proverb *runs* like this.
 30. to be or continue at a specified size, price, amount, etc.; as, the apples *run* large this year.
 to cut and run; see under *cut*, v.i.
 to run across; to encounter by chance.
 to run after; (a) to pursue or follow; (b) [Colloq.] to seek the company or companionship of.
 to run away; to flee; to escape.
 to run away with; (a) to deprive of self-control, balance, etc., as anger or enthusiasm; (b) to outdo greatly all other contestants or performers in; hence, to get (a prize, honors, etc.) in this way.
 to run down; (a) to cease to run, or stop operating, as a mechanical device, through lack of power; (b) to lessen or lower in worth, quality, etc., as a house through lack of repairs, or in health, strength, etc., as a person through overwork; to make or become run-down.
 to run for it; to run in order to escape or avoid something.
 to run in the blood; to be hereditary.
 to run into; (a) to encounter by chance; (b) to collide with.
 to run off; to run away; to flee.
 to run on; (a) to be continued; (b) to talk continuously.
 to run out; to come to an end; to expire or become used up, exhausted, etc.
 to run out of; to use up a supply of (something).
 to run over; (a) to overflow; (b) to ride or drive over.
 to run through; to use up, spend, etc. quickly or recklessly.
 to run up; to rise rapidly.

run, *v.t.* 1. to run along or follow (a specified course or route).
 2. to travel over; to cover by running, driving, etc.; as, wild horses *ran* the range.
 3. to do or perform by or as by running; as, he *ran* a race.
 4. to subject oneself to or be subjected to (a risk, etc.); to incur.
 5. to get past or escape by going through; as, the ship *ran* the blockade.
 6. to sew with a rapid, continuous succession of stitches.
 7. to pursue, or hunt (game, etc.).
 8. to compete with in or as in a race; to vie with.
 9. (a) to enter (a horse, etc.) in a race; (b) to put up as a candidate for election.
 10. to make run, move, operate, etc.
 11. to bring, lead, or force into a specified condition, situation, etc. by or as by running; as, he *ran* me breathless, his action *ran* us into difficulties.
 12. (a) to carry or convey, as in a ship or vehicle; to transport; (b) to carry (taxable or outlawed goods) in or out illegally; to smuggle.
 13. to drive, force, or thrust (an object) into or against (something).
 14. to allow to continue in force; as, he *ran* a bill at the store.
 15. to make move or pass rapidly, flow, etc. in a specified way, direction, place, etc.; as, *run* water into a glass.
 16. (a) to be in charge of; to manage; as, she *runs* the household; (b) to perform the steps of (an experiment, test, etc.).
 17. to mark, draw, or trace, as boundary lines on a map.
 18. to extend or trace in a specified way or direction; as, *run* the rope taut, *run* the story back to its source.
 19. to undergo or be affected by, as a fever, etc.

20. to flow with, discharge, or pour forth; as, the gutters *ran* blood.

21. to melt, fuse, or smelt (ore).

22. to cast or mold, as from molten metal; to found.

23. to publish (an advertisement or story) in a newspaper.

24. in billiards, etc., to complete successfully (a specified number of strokes, shots, etc.) in uninterrupted sequence.

to run down; (a) to run, ride, or drive against so as to knock down; (b) to pursue and capture or kill; (c) to speak of slightingly or injuriously; disparage; (d) to read through rapidly; (e) in baseball, to cause (a runner trapped between two bases) to be put out.

to run hard; (a) to press close upon in a race, etc.; (b) to urge importunately.

to run in; (a) to include or insert, as something additional; (b) [Slang.] to take into custody by the authority of the law; arrest; (c) in printing, to make continuous without a break or paragraph.

to run into the ground; to overdo; to perform (a work, an action, etc.) excessively.

to run off; (a) to print, typewrite, etc.; (b) to cause to be run, performed, played, etc.; (c) to decide the winner of (a race, etc.) by a runoff.

to run on; to continue; specifically, in printing, to continue without a break or new paragraph.

to run out; to force to leave; to drive out.

to run over; to examine, rehearse, etc. rapidly or casually.

to run through; (a) to pierce; (b) to run over.

to run up; to raise or make rapidly.

run, *n.* 1. (a) an act or period of running or moving rapidly; (b) a running pace; rapid gait; (c) capacity for running.

2. the distance covered or time spent in running.

3. a trip; journey; especially, (a) a single, customary, or regular trip, as of a train, ship, etc.; (b) a quick trip for a brief stay at a place; as, take a *run* up to Detroit.

4. a route; as, the milkman finished his *run*.

5. (a) movement onward, progression, or course, especially when quick, easy, or smooth; (b) the direction, as of the grain of wood, or tendency, as of events.

6. a continuous course or period of a specified condition, action, etc.; as, a *run* of good luck.

7. a continuous course of performances, etc.; as, the play had a *run* of a year.

8. continued demand, call, etc. or series of sudden, urgent demands, etc., as on a bank for payment of deposits.

9. a period of being in public demand or favor.

10. a continuous series or sequence, as of cards in one suit.

11. a continuous extent of something.

12. a flow or rush of water, etc., as of the tide.

13. a small, swift stream, as a brook, rivulet, etc.

14. (a) a period during which some fluid flows readily; (b) the amount of flow.

15. (a) a period of operation of a machine or machinery; (b) the amount of something produced during such a period; output.

16. (a) a kind, sort, or class, as of goods; (b) the ordinary, usual, or average kind.

17. something in, on, or along which something else runs or can run; specifically, (a) a way, track, channel, trough, pipe, runway, etc.; (b) an enclosed area in which domestic animals or fowls can move about freely; as, a chicken *run*.

18. freedom to move about at will through all the parts or to use all the facilities (*of* a place); as, we had the *run of* his grounds.

19. a number of animals in motion together.

20. a well-defined track made by some animals in migration, etc.; as, a buffalo *run*.

21. (a) a large number of fish migrating together, as upstream or inshore for spawning; (b) such migration of fish.

22. a ravel in something knitted, as in a stocking.

23. the bower of a bowerbird.

24. in aviation, the approach to the target made by a bombing plane: in full, *bombing run*.

25. in baseball, a scoring point, made by a successful circuit of the bases.

26. in billiards, etc., an uninterrupted sequence of successful strokes, shots, etc.

27. in cricket, a scoring point, made by a successful running of both batsmen from one wicket to the other.

28. in music, a rapid succession of tones, as a roulade.

29. in nautical usage, the extreme after part of a ship's bottom, from where it starts to curve up and in toward the stern.

a run for one's money; (a) powerful competition; (b) some satisfaction for what one has expended, as in betting on a near winner in a race.

end run; in football, a play in which one of the backfield men of the offensive team receives the ball and attempts to advance it by carrying it around one end of the defense.

in the long run; in the whole process or course of things taken together; in the final result; in the conclusion or end.

on the run; (a) running; (b) hurrying from place to place or task to task; (c) running away; in retreat.

the common run; the average of people or things; also, the ordinary course of events.

run, *a.* 1. melted; made liquid.

2. poured or molded while in a melted state; as, *run* metal.

3. drained or extracted, as honey.

4. illegally transported; smuggled; contraband. [Colloq.]

run'ȧ·bout, *n.* 1. a person who runs about from one place to another.

2. a light, one-seated, open carriage.

3. a light, one-seated, open automobile; a roadster.

4. a light motorboat.

run'ȧ·gāte, *n.* [ME. *renegat*, apostate or villain, from OFr. *renegat*, from LL. *renegatus*, pp. of *renegare*, to abjure, or deny again.]

1. a fugitive or deserter; a runaway. [Archaic.]

2. one who drifts or wanders about; a vagabond. [Archaic.]

run'-ȧ·round'', *n.* 1. a series of evasive excuses, equivocations, etc.: usually in *get* (or *give*) *the run-around*. [Slang.]

2. in printing, an arrangement of type in a column narrower than usual, as around an illustration.

3. a whitlow. [Colloq.]

run'ȧ·wāy, *n.* 1. a person, animal, etc. that runs away; specifically, (a) a fugitive or deserter; (b) a horse, team of horses, etc. that has broken loose from control of the rider or driver.

2. a running away.

3. a runaway race or victory.

run'ȧ·wāy, *a.* 1. running away or having run away; escaping, eloping, or breaking loose from control; as, *runaway* lovers, a *runaway* horse.

2. of or done by runaways or running away; as, a *runaway* marriage.

3. easily won, as a race, or decisive, as a victory.

4. (a) rising rapidly, as prices; (b) characterized by such prices; as, a *runaway* inflation.

run'back, *n.* in football, (a) a running back with the ball, as after receiving the kickoff; (b) the distance so run.

ruñ·çā'tion, *n.* [L. *runcatio*.] a weeding. [Obs.]

runch, *n.* in botany, (a) the wild radish; (b) charlock. [Scot. and Brit. Dial.]

run'ci·ble spoon, [prob. coined from *runc*inate and *-ible*; used by E. Lear in "The Owl and the Pussycat."] a kind of fork with two broad prongs and one sharp-edged, curved prong.

run'ci·nāte, *a.* [L. *runcina*, a plane.] in botany, pinnatifid, with the lobes convex before and straight behind, pointing backward, like the teeth of a double saw, as in the dandelion leaf.

RUNCINATE LEAF

rund, *n.* [variant of *rand*, a border or strip.] a remnant; selvage. [Scot.]

run'dāle, *n.* in Ireland and Scotland, a method of holding land in which the holdings are detached pieces separated by others' holdings.

run'dle, *n.* [a variant of *runnel*, a streamlet.] a runlet or small stream. [Dial.]

run'dle, *n.* [ME. *rundel*, var. of *roundel*.]

1. a rung, or round, as of a ladder.

2. one of the bars in a lantern pinion.

3. something that rotates, as a wheel or the drum of a capstan.

rund'let, run'let, *n.* [ME. *roundlet*; OFr. *rondelle*, a little tun or barrel, a round shield.]

1. a small barrel or cask of varying capacity. [Archaic.]

2. the amount of liquor contained in this: an old British liquid measure, usually taken as equal to about 18 wine gallons. [Archaic.]

run'-down', *a.* 1. not wound and therefore not running, as a spring-operated clock or watch.

2. in poor physical condition, as from overwork; weak and exhausted; debilitated.

3. fallen into disrepair; dilapidated; shabby.

run'-down, *n.* in baseball, the act of running down a base runner.

rụne, *n.* [ME., counsel; AS. *run*, a mystery, a secret.]

1. any of the characters of an alphabet used by the ancient Scandinavians and other ancient Germanic peoples.

2. something inscribed or written in such characters.

3. any similar character or mark having some mysterious meaning or magical powers attributed to it.

4. (a) a Finnish poem or canto; (b) loosely, any ancient Scandinavian poem; (c) [Poetic.] any poem, verse, or song.

RUNES

rụne'çrȧft, *n.* the ability to interpret runes; knowledge of runes.

rụned, *a.* inscribed with runic characters.

rụn'ẽr, *n.* a bard or learned man among the ancient Goths.

rụne'smith, *n.* one who makes or studies runes. [Rare.]

run'fish, *n.* a spent salmon.

rung, *v.* past participle of *ring* (to make the sound of a bell.)

rung, *n.* [ME. *rong*; AS. *hrung*, rod or bar.] any sturdy stick, bar, or rod, especially a rounded one, used as a crossbar, strengthening part, etc.; specifically, (a) any of the crosspieces constituting the steps of a ladder; (b) a supporting crosspiece between the legs of a chair, or across the back, etc.; (c) a spoke of a wheel; (d) [Scot. and Brit. Dial.] a stout timber cudgel.

rung, *a.* having a ring through the nose.

rung'head (-hed), *n.* the upper end of a floor in a ship.

rụ'niç, *a.* 1. of, consisting of, characterized by, or set down in runes.

2. like or suggestive of runes in decorative interlaced effect, as knots and other figures on the monuments, etc. of ancient peoples of northern Europe.

runic staff; same as *clog almanac*.

runic wand; a willow wand inscribed with runic characters and formerly supposed to have been used by the Teutons in magic incantations and rites.

rụ'niç, *n.* in printing, a style of decorative type having almost uniformly thick lines.

run'-in, *a.* in printing, that is run in.

run'-in, *n.* 1. run-in matter.

2. a quarrel, fight, etc. [Colloq.]

run'let, *n.* a runnel or rivulet.

run'let, *n.* a rundlet.

run'nel, *n.* [ME. *rinel*, from AS. *rinnan*, to run.]

1. a rivulet or small brook.

2. a small channel or watercourse.

run'nẽr, *n.* 1. a person, animal, or thing that runs, as a racer.

2. a person who runs errands, carries messages, etc., as for a bank or brokerage house.

3. an agent, collector, etc., as for a bank or broker.

4. a person whose work is to solicit patronage or business, as for a hotel or store.

5. (a) a smuggler; (b) a smuggling ship.

6. a person who operates or manages something, as a machine.

7. (a) a long, narrow, decorative cloth put across a table, chest of drawers, etc.; (b) a long, narrow rug, as for a hall or corridor.
8. a long ravel, as in hose; a run.
9. (a) a long, slender, trailing stem that puts out roots along the ground at its nodes or end, thus producing new plants; (b) any plant that spreads in this way, as the strawberry.
10. any of various twining plants; as, the scarlet *runner*.
11. (a) something on or in which something else moves, as a sliding part in machinery; (b) the moving stone of a grain mill.
12. either of the long, narrow pieces of metal or wood on which a sled or sleigh slides.
13. the blade of a skate.
14. a sharp, curved blade for opening a furrow in seeding.
15. in metallurgy, a channel through which molten metal is poured into a mold; a gate.
16. in zoology, the jurel, a food fish.
17. any bird that runs along the ground.
scarlet runner; see *scarlet bean* under *scarlet*.

run'nẽr bēan, a string bean. [Brit.]

run'nẽr-up', *n.* a person or team that finishes second in a race, contest, etc., especially in the final round of a tournament.

run'net, *n.* rennet. [Obs.]

run'ning, *n.* 1. the act of a person or thing that runs (in various senses); racing, management, etc.
2. power or ability to run.
3. (a) that which runs, or flows; (b) the amount or quantity that runs.
4. in a pipe organ, a leakage of air causing a pipe to sound when its digital is depressed.
in (or *out of*) *the running*; in (or out of) the competition; having (or having lost) a chance to win.

run'ning, *a.* 1. moving, passing, or advancing rapidly.
2. (a) run at a rapid gait; as, a *running* race; (b) trained to race at this gait: said of a horse.
3. flowing; as, *running* water.
4. cursive: said of handwriting.
5. melting; becoming liquid or fluid.
6. discharging liquid; especially, discharging pus, etc.; as, a *running* sore.
7. creeping or climbing: said of plants.
8. going, or in operation, as machinery.
9. in a straight line; linear: said of measurement; as, a *running* foot.
10. going on, extending, etc. without interruption; continuous; as, a *running* commentary, a *running* design.
11. in succession; successive: placed after the noun; as, for five days *running*.
12. prevalent.
13. in progress; current; as, a *running* account.
14. moving or going easily or smoothly.
15. slipping or sliding easily; as, a *running* knot.
16. moving when pulled, as a rope.
17. done in, with, or by a run; as, a *running* jump.
18. of the normal run (of a train, bus, etc.); as, the *running* time is two hours.
running block; a block in a system of pulleys that moves up or down, according to the tightening or slackening of the rope.
running board; especially formerly, a footboard, or step, extending along the lower part of the side of an automobile, etc.
running days; the consecutive days, including Sundays, that are allotted to a vessel to make a voyage for which it is chartered.
running fire; (a) a rapid succession of shots, as from soldiers in ranks; (b) any rapid succession, as of remarks, questions, etc.
running gear; the working parts of a machine; especially, the wheels, axles, transmission, etc. of a locomotive, automobile, or the like, together with their attachments, as distinguished from the body.
running hand; a style of handwriting in which the letters are slanted and close together and are formed by a continuous movement: distinguished from *round hand*.
running head (or *title*); a descriptive heading or title printed at the top of every page or, sometimes, every other page, usually the left-hand ones.
running knot; a knot so tied as to slide along the rope, thus forming a noose (*running noose*) that tightens as the rope is pulled.
running mate; (a) a horse that is a teammate for another horse, or a horse used to set the pace for another horse in a race; (b) a candidate for the lesser of two closely associated offices, as for the vice-presidency, regarded as running for election together with his party's candidate for the greater.
running part; that part of a rope in a pulley system that is hauled on.
running rigging; that part of a ship's rigging or ropes which passes through blocks, etc.: distinguished from *standing rigging*.
running string; a cord or tape passing through a hem, as at the top of a garment or bag, so as to contract it when pulled upon; a drawstring.
running title; in printing, the title of a book that is continued from page to page on the upper margin.

run'ning·ly, *adv.* in a running manner; continuously.

run'niŏn (-yun), *n.* a ronion. [Obs.]

run'-off, *n.* 1. something that runs off, as rain in excess of the amount absorbed by the ground.
2. waste products eliminated in manufacturing.
3. a deciding, final race, game, etc., as in case of a tie.

run'-of-the-mill, *a.* not selected or special; ordinary; average: also *mill-run*.

ru̇·nol'ō·gist, *n.* an expert in reading or interpreting runes.

ru̇·nol'ō·gy, *n.* the interpretation or knowledge of runes.

run'-on, *a.* in printing, that is run on.

run'-on, *n.* run-on matter.

run'-on sen'tence, two or more complete sentences faultily run together as one.

run'rig, *n.* a ridge of land so divided that the alternate rigs belong to different owners; also, in Scotland, the system by which different proprietors hold alternate ridges of land; rundale. [Scot.]
runrig lands; lands held by runrig.

run'round, *n.* a run-around (sense 2).

runt, *n.* [prob. akin to AS. *hrindan*, to thrust.]
1. (a) a stunted, undersized, or dwarfish animal, plant, thing, or (usually in a contemptuous sense) person; (b) the smallest animal of a litter.
2. an ox or cow of a small breed or size.
3. (a) an old cow or ox; (b) a withered old woman; (c) an old or decayed tree stump; (d) the hardened stem of a cabbage or other plant. [Scot. or Brit. Dial.]

run'-through (-thrö), *n.* a rehearsal, as of a dramatic or musical work or section, straight through from beginning to end.

runt'i·ness, *n.* a runty quality or state.

runt'y, *a.*; *comp.* runtier; *superl.* runtiest, resembling a runt; diminutive; stunted.

run'wāy, *n.* 1. a way, as a channel, track, chute, groove, trough, etc., in, on, or along which something runs, or moves; specifically, (a) the channel or bed of a stream; (b) a strip of leveled ground, often paved, for use by airplanes in taking off and landing; (c) a track or ramp for wheeled vehicles; (d) a beaten path made by deer or other animals; (e) in bowling, a track along which the bowls are returned to the bowlers.
2. an enclosed area in which chickens, etc. can move about freely: also *run*.

ru̇·pee', *n.* [Hind. *rūpiya*, from Sans. *rūpya*, silver.] the monetary unit of India, Pakistan, Ceylon, etc.

ru̇·pes'trine, *a.* [L. *rupes*, a rock.] found among rocks; living or growing in rocky places.

ru̇'pi·ȧ, *n.* [Gr. *rhupos*, filth.] a skin disease consisting of an eruption of small, flattened and distinct vesicles, surrounded by inflamed areolae, containing a serous, purulent, or dark bloody fluid, and thick, dark-colored scabs before healing.

ru̇·pī'ăh, *n.* [from Hind. *rūpiyah*, rupee.] the monetary unit of Indonesia.

ru̇'pi·ăl, *a.* pertaining to or characteristic of rupia.

Ru̇·pi·çap'rȧ, *n.* [L. *rupes*, a rock, and *capra*, she-goat.] a genus of antelopes, so named from their frequenting rocks and mountain cliffs. The chamois, *Rupicapra tragus*, is an example.

Ru̇″pi·çap·rī'nae, *n.pl.* a subfamily of *Bovidæ*; the chamois.

Ru̇·piç'ō·lȧ, *n.* [L. *rupes*, rock, and *colere*, to inhabit.] a genus of passerine birds, including the cock of the rock. They abound in South America.

Ru̇″pi·çō·lī'nae, *n.pl.* a subfamily of insessorial birds, allied to the manakins, generally arranged under the family *Pipridæ*. The genus *Rupicola* is the type.

ru̇·piç'ō·line, *a.* growing on or living among rocks.

ru̇·piç'ō·lous, *a.* rupicoline; rupestrine.

Rup'pi·ȧ, *n.* [from H. B. *Ruppius*, G. botanist.] a genus of monocotyledonous plants, distinguished by the absence of a perianth.

rup'tion, *n.* a breach; a break or bursting open.

rup'tive, *a.* causing or tending to cause rupture; bursting. [Rare.]

rup'tū·ăr·y, *n.* a plebeian; one of the common people. [Rare.]

rup'tūr·ȧ·ble, *a.* that can be ruptured.

rup'tūre, *n.* [Fr., from L. *ruptus*, broken, from *rumpere*, to break.]
1. the act of breaking apart or bursting, or the state of being broken apart or burst; a breach.
2. a breaking off of friendly or peaceful relations, as between countries or individuals.
3. in medicine, hernia; especially, abdominal or inguinal hernia.
Syn.—break, bursting, fracture, breach.

rup'tūre, *v.t.* and *v.i.*; ruptured, *pt., pp.*; rupturing, *ppr.* 1. to break apart or burst.
2. to affect with, undergo, or suffer a rupture.

rup'tūred, *a.* affected or suffering with a rupture, or hernia.

rup'tūre·wŏrt, *n.* a West Indian plant, *Alternanthera polygonoides*, resembling burstwort; also, the burstwort.

ru̇'răl, *a.* [Fr., from L. *ruralis*, from *rus*, the country.]
1. of or characteristic of the country (as distinguished from cities or towns), country life, or country people; rustic: opposed to *urban*.
2. living in the country.
3. having to do with farming; agricultural.
rural dean; see under *dean*.
rural free delivery; free delivery of mail by carriers on routes in rural areas.
Syn.—rustic, countrified, simple, artless, plain, unadorned.

ru̇'răl·ism, *n.* 1. a rural characteristic; the condition of being rural.
2. a rural idiom.

ru̇'răl·ist, *n.* one who leads or advocates a rural life.

ru̇·ral'i·ty, *n.*; *pl.* **ru̇·ral'i·ties,** 1. ruralism.
2. [*usually in plural*] a rural characteristic, feature, scene, etc.

ru̇·răl·ī·zā'tion, *n.* a ruralizing or being ruralized.

ru̇'răl·īze, *v.t.*; ruralized, *pt., pp.*; ruralizing, *ppr.* to make rural.

ru̇'răl·īze, *v.i.* to rusticate; to live or stay for a time in the country.

ru̇'răl·ly, *adv.* in a rural manner.

ru̇'răl·ness, *n.* the quality or state of being rural.

ru̇·ri·deç'ȧ·năl, *a.* of or pertaining to a rural dean or his office. [Rare.]

ru̇·rig'e·nous, *a.* [L. *rus*, the country, and *gignere*, to be born.] born in the country. [Rare.]

Ru̇″ri·tā'ni·ăn, *a.* [after *Ruritania*, imaginary kingdom in novels by A. Hope.] of, like, or characteristic of some quaint, romantic, unreal place.

Ru̇'sȧ, *n.* [Malay *rusa*, a deer.]
1. a genus of Oriental deer of large size, including the sambur.
2. [r-] any deer of this genus.

Rus'çus, *n.* [L. *ruscum*, butcher's broom.] a genus of erect, branching, evergreen herbs of the lily family, comprising three species common to Europe, including the butcher's broom.

ru̇şe, *n.* [Fr. *ruse*, from *ruser*, to dodge; OFr. *reüser*, to get out of the way; L. *recusare*, to refuse.] an artifice; trick; stratagem; wile.

rush, *n.* [AS. *risce*, akin to M.D. *risch*, G. *rusch*, a rush.]
1. any plant of the genus *Juncus*, family *Juncaceæ*. The species are numerous and found chiefly in moist, boggy areas of temperate regions.
2. one of various grassy plants with hollow or pithy stems, resembling the common rush.
3. a stem of such a plant, used for making baskets, mats, etc.
4. anything of little or no worth; the merest trifle; a straw, as, I do not care a *rush*.

rush, *v.i.*; rushed, *pt., pp.*; rushing, *ppr.* [ME. *ruschen*; OFr. *reüser*, to get out of the way.]

1. to move or go swiftly or impetuously; to dash.
2. to make a swift, sudden attack or assault (*on* or *upon*); to charge.
3. to dash recklessly or rashly (often with *into*).
4. to pass, come, go, come into view, act, etc. swiftly, suddenly, or hastily; as, the stars *rushed* out; a terrible thought *rushed* into her mind.

rush, *v.t.* 1. to move, send, push, drive, etc. swiftly, violently, or hastily; as, they *rushed* him out of the room; the resolution was *rushed* through the Senate.
2. to do, make, or cause to move, go, or act, with unusual or excessive speed or haste; to hurry; as, I don't like to *rush* my work; don't *rush* me.
3. (a) to make a swift, sudden attack or assault on; to charge; (b) to overcome or capture by such an attack or assault.
4. to lavish attentions on, as in courting. [Slang.]
5. in football, to advance (the ball) by a rush or series of rushes.

rush, *n.* 1. a rushing.
2. an eager movement of many people to get to a place, as to a new territory or a region where gold has recently been found.
3. busyness; haste; hurry; as, the *rush* of modern life.
4. a sudden, swift attack or assault; an onslaught.
5. in many American colleges, a kind of scrimmage between groups of students, as between freshmen and sophomores, held as a contest, often for the temporary possession of some trophy.
6. a press, as of business or traffic, necessitating unusual haste or effort.
7. in football, (a) an attempt to carry the ball through the opponent's line, as by plunging; (b) in former usage, any of certain players in the forward line (*rush line*); as, center *rush*.
8. [*usually in pl.*] in motion pictures, a first print, as of a scene photographed on the previous day, projected for inspection by the director, etc.
9. in Australia, a stampede, as of cattle.
10. the first, sudden euphoric effect of injecting a narcotic drug, as heroin, directly into a vein. [Slang.]
with a rush; suddenly and forcefully.

rush, *a.* 1. necessitating haste; as, *rush* orders.
2. characterized by a rush (sense 6); as, *rush* hours.

rush'beãr"ing, *n.* in England, the feast of dedication of a rural church, when the parishioners strew the church with rushes and sweet-smelling herbs.

rush brọọm, a leguminous Australian plant, *Viminaria denudata,* having long flexible branches.

rush çan'dle, a candle made with the pith of a rush as the wick; a rushlight.

rushed (rusht), *a.* abounding in or covered with rushes.

rush'ẽr, *n.* 1. one who or that which rushes.
2. in football, a player in the rush line.
3. an energetic person; a hustler.

rush gràss, any of certain wiry grasses of the genus *Sporobolus.*

rush hour, a time of the day when business, traffic, etc. are especially heavy.

rush'i·ness, *n.* the state of abounding with rushes.

rush'līght (-lit), *n.* a rush candle: also *rush light.*

rush'līke, *a.* resembling a rush or reed; weak.

rush līne, in football, the forward line, normally including the ends, tackles, guards, and center.

rush nut, a plant, *Cyperus esculentus,* having tubers used as food in southern Europe.

rush tōad, the natterjack, or running toad.

rush'y, *a.*; *comp.* rushier; *superl.* rushiest,
1. consisting or made of rushes (plants).
2. full of or covered with rushes.
3. rushlike.

rụ'sīne, *a.* [Malay *rusa,* a deer, and *-ine.*] of or belonging to a group of Asian deer typified by the genus *Rusa.*
rusine antler; a type of antler with a single tine at the brow and a simple, two-pronged fork at the tip.

rus in ūr'bē, [L.] the country in the city: said of a city, town, or city home characterized by trees, lawns, etc.

rusk, *n.* [Sp. *rosca,* a roll of bread.]
1. (a) sweet, raised bread or cake, toasted in an oven, or baked a second time, until browned and crisp; (b) a piece of this.
2. a light, soft, sweetened biscuit or bread.

rusk, *v.t.* to make into rusk; to convert (bread or cake) into rusk.

Russ, *a.* and *n.*; *pl.* **Russ,** Russian.

rus'sel, *n.* a ribbed or twilled woolen cloth: probably so named from its russet color. [Obs.]

rus'sel çord, a rep made of cotton and wool, or sometimes of wool alone.

Rus'sell·īte, *n.* a Jehovah's Witness: former name.

rus'set, *a.* [Fr. *rousset,* from L. *russus,* reddish, from *ruber,* red.]
1. of a reddish-brown or yellowish-brown color; as, a *russet* mantle.

Our summer such a *russet* livery wears.
—Dryden.

2. coarse; homespun; rustic. [Rare.]
3. made of russet (cloth).

rus'set, *n.* 1. reddish brown or yellowish brown.
2. a coarse homespun cloth, reddish-brown or brownish, formerly made and used for clothing by country people.
3. [*pl.*] clothes made of russet. [Obs.]
4. finished leather left unpolished and uncolored.
5. a kind of winter apple of a russet color and rough, mottled skin.

rus'set·ing, *n.* 1. a russet apple. [Obs.]
2. the act of dressing in russet. [Obs.]

rus'set·y, *a.* of a russet color.

rus'siȧ (rush'ȧ), *n.* Russia leather.

Rus'siȧ brāid, a kind of silk braid.

Rus'siȧ ī'rŏn (-ŭrn), a fine quality of sheet iron.

Rus'siȧ leath'ẽr (leth'), a fine, smooth leather originally made in Russia.

Rus'siăn (rush'ăn), *a.* of Russia, the people of Russia, or the language spoken by them.

Rus'siăn, *n.* 1. a native or inhabitant of Russia.
2. a member of the chief Slavic people of Russia.
3. the East Slavic language of the Russians, especially the form spoken by the Great Russians: the principal language of the Soviet Union.

Rus'siăn bȧth, a vapor bath in which the body is exposed to steam for a considerable time, then washed and massaged.

Rus'siăn dress'ing, mayonnaise mixed with chili sauce, chopped pickles, pimientos, etc.: used on salads.

Rus'siăn·ism, *n.* Russian characteristics, proclivities, or influence.

Rus'siăn·īze, *v.t.*; Russianized, *pt., pp.*; Russianizing, *ppr.* to make Russian in character.

Rus'siăn (Ọr'thō·dox) Chŭrch, a branch of the Orthodox Eastern Church: it was the national church of czarist Russia.

Rus'siăn Rev·ō·lū'tion, 1. the revolution of 1917 in which the government of the Czar was overthrown by Russian workers, peasants, soldiers, and sailors: it consisted of two distinct revolutions, the first (*February Revolution*) being the uprising of March (February, Old Style), in which a government headed by Kerensky came to power, the second (*October Revolution*) being the uprising of November (October, Old Style), in which this government was replaced by the Soviet government led by the Bolsheviks, or Communists, under Lenin.
2. the October Revolution.

Rus'siăn rou·lette' (-let'), 1. a deadly game of chance in which a person spins the cylinder of a revolver holding only one bullet, aims the gun at his head, and pulls the trigger.
2. any activity potentially destructive to its participants.

Rus'siăn this'tle (-l), see under *thistle.*

Rus'siăn wọlf'hound, any of a breed of large dog with a narrow head, long legs, and silky coat; borzoi: so called because of Russian origin.

RUSSIAN WOLFHOUND (32 in. high at shoulder)

Rus"si·fi·çā'tion, *n.* the act or operation of Russianizing; the state of being Russianized.

Rus'si·fȳ, *v.t.* to Russianize.

Rus'sō-, a combining form meaning: (a) *Russia* or *Russian,* as in *Russo*phobe; (b) *Russian and,* as in *Russo*-Japanese.

Rus'sō·phīle, *n.* one who admires or is extremely fond of Russia, its people, customs, etc.

Rus'sō·phīle, *a.* of Russophiles.

Rus'sō·phī·lism, *n.* the sentiments or principles of a Russophile.

Rus'sō·phī·list, *n.* a Russophile.

Rus'sō·phōbe, *n.* a person who has Russophobia.

Rus'sō·phōbe, *a.* of Russophobes.

Rus·sō·phō'bi·ȧ, *n.* [*Russo-* and *-phobia.*] hatred or fear of Russia, its people, customs, influence, etc.

Rus'sō·phō·bism, *n.* Russophobia.

Rus'sō·phō·bist, *n.* a Russophobe.

Rus'sū·lȧ, *n.* [LL. *russulus,* reddish, dim. of L. *russus,* red.] an extensive genus of fungi, most species of which are poisonous, only a few being edible.

rust, *n.* [AS. *rust*; Dan. *rust*; Sw. and G. *rost*; Ice. *ryth*; all from the same root as *red, ruddy.*]
1. the reddish-brown or reddish-yellow coating formed on iron or steel by oxidation, as during exposure to air and moisture: it consists mainly of ferric oxide, Fe_2O_3, and ferric hydroxide, $Fe(OH)_3$: also *iron rust.*
2. any coating or film formed on any other metal by oxidation or corrosion.
3. any stain or formation resembling iron rust.
4. any habit, influence, growth, etc. injurious to usefulness, to the mind or character, etc.
5. disuse of mental or moral powers; inactivity; idleness.
6. the color of iron rust; reddish brown or reddish yellow.
7. in botany, (a) any of a number of plant diseases caused by parasitic fungi and characterized by a spotted reddish or brownish discoloration of stems and leaves; (b) any fungus causing such a disease: also *rust fungus.*

rust, *v.i.* and *v.t.* 1. to have or cause to have rust (the fungous disease).
2. to become or cause to be coated with rust, as iron.
3. to deteriorate or spoil, as through disuse, inactivity, etc.; as, his mind had *rusted.*
4. to become or make rust-colored.

rust'-çŏl·ŏred, *a.* having the color of iron rust; reddish-brown or reddish-yellow.

rust'fụl, *a.* rusty; tending to produce rust; characterized by rust.

rus'tiç, *a.* [L. *rusticus,* from *rus,* the country.]
1. pertaining to or living in the country; rural; as, the *rustic* gods of antiquity.
2. lacking refinement, elegance, polish, or sophistication; specifically, (a) simple, plain, or artless; (b) rough, awkward, uncouth, or boorish.
3. made of rough, bark-covered branches or roots; as, *rustic* furniture.
4. in masonry, having a rough surface or irregular, deeply sunk, deliberately conspicuous joints; rusticated.
rustic moth; any noctuid moth.
rustic work; masonry made or finished in a rustic style.

Syn.—rural, rude, coarse, inelegant, simple, awkward, rough, unpolished, plain, unadorned, untaught, artless.

rus'tiç, *n.* 1. an inhabitant of the country, especially one regarded as unsophisticated, simple, awkward, uncouth, etc.
2. a person with a simple, unaffected character and manner.
3. rustic work.

rus'tiç·ăl, *a.* rustic. [Archaic or Rare.]

rus'tiç·ăl·ly, *adv.* in a rustic manner.

rus'tiç·ăl·ness, *n.* the quality or state of being rustical.

rus'ti·çāte, *v.i.*; rusticated, *pt., pp.*; rusticating, *ppr.* [L. *rusticari,* to rusticate.]
1. to dwell or reside in the country.
2. to go to the country.

rus'ti·çāte, *v.t.* 1. to send to the country; to compel to reside in the country.
2. to suspend from residence and studies at a university and send away for a time as a punishment. [Brit.]
3. to make (a person, etc.) rustic.
4. to make or finish (masonry, etc.) in the rustic style.

rus·ti·çā'tion, *n.* 1. the act of rusticating or

the state of being rusticated; also, a period of this.

2. in universities and colleges, the punishment of a student for some offense, by suspending him for a specified time. [Brit.]

3. in architecture, rustic work.

rus'ti·cā·tŏr, *n.* a person who rusticates.

rus·tic'i·ty, *n.*; *pl.* **rus·tic'i·ties,** 1. the quality or state of being rustic or rural; simplicity; artlessness; plainness.

2. rustic, or rural, life or character.

3. a rural characteristic.

rus'ti·cīze, *v.t.* to make rustic.

rus'tiç·ly, *adv.* in a rustic manner.

rust'i·ly, *adv.* in a rusty manner or state.

rust'i·ness, *n.* the state or quality of being rusty.

rust joint, a joint between iron or steel surfaces formed by a composition of iron filings, sal ammoniac, and a little sulfur, moistened with water to cause the formation of rust.

rus'tle (-l), *v.t.*; rustled, *pt., pp.*; rustling, *ppr.* to cause to rustle or make a rustling noise; as, the wind *rustled* the leaves.

rus'tle, *v.i.* and *v.t.* [AS. *hristlan*, to rustle, a dim. freq. form as if from *hristan*; Ice. *hrista*; Dan. *ryste*; Sw. *rysta*, to shake, to tremble.] to make, or move, stir, etc. so as to produce a quick, irregular succession of soft, rubbing sounds, like the rubbing of silk or dry leaves; as, *rustling* wings.

He is coming; I hear the straw *rustle*.
—Shak.

rus'tle, *n.* the noise made by one who or that which rustles; a rustling.

rus'tle, *v.t.* and *v.i.* [prob. from *rush*, v., and *hustle*.]

1. to work or proceed with, or move, bring, or get by, energetic or vigorous action. [Colloq.]

2. (a) originally, in the western United States, to round up (cattle, etc.), especially as a professional cowboy; (b) [Colloq.] to steal (cattle, etc.).

to rustle up; to collect or get together, as by foraging around. [Colloq.]

rus'tlẽr (-lẽr), *n.* one who or that which rustles; as, (a) a person who is pushing, energetic, smart, and successful; (b) a domestic animal capable of looking after itself under any conditions; (c) a cattle thief. [Colloq.]

rust'less, *a.* 1. free from rust.

2. rustproof.

rust mīte, a mite of the family *Phytoptidæ*, which makes a rustlike appearance on the leaves and fruit of certain plants. *Phytoptus oleivorus* is the rust mite of the orange.

rust'proof, *a.* resistant to rust.

rus'tre (-tẽr), *n.* [Fr.] in heraldry, a lozenge with a round opening in the center, through which the field appears.

RUSTRE

rust'y, *a.*; *comp.* rustier; *superl.* rustiest, 1. covered or affected with rust; as, a *rusty* knife or plant.

2. not working freely or easily because of, or as if because of, rust; stiff in operation.

3. (a) impaired by disuse, neglect, idleness, etc.; as, his geometry is *rusty*; (b) having lost facility through lack of practice; as, I'm a little *rusty* in chess.

4. having the color of rust; resembling rust.

5. consisting of rust; caused by rust; as, *rusty* stains.

6. having lost the original color; shabby; faded; as, a *rusty* coat.

7. in botany, rust-colored; light-brown, with a little mixture of red; rubiginose.

rut, *n.* [OFr., from L. *rugitus*, roaring, the noise of deer in rutting time.]

1. the periodic sexual excitement of male deer, camels, sheep, goats, etc., corresponding to *estrus* in the female; heat.

2. the period during which this occurs.

rut, *v.i.*; rutted, *pt., pp.*; rutting, *ppr.* to be in rut.

rut, *v.t.* to cover in copulation. [Rare.]

rut, *n.* [OFr. *route*, way, pass, road, etc.] a furrow or track worn in the ground by a wheel in passing over it or by the habitual passing of wheels; hence, a fixed routine procedure, line of conduct, thought, feeling, etc.

rut, *v.t.*; rutted, *pt., pp.*; rutting, *ppr.* to make a rut or ruts in.

Rụ'tȧ, *n.* [L. *ruta*, rue.] the typical genus of the *Rutaceæ*, the rue family.

rụ·tȧ·bā'gȧ, *n.* [Sw. dial. *rotabagge*.] a turnip with a large, yellow root; the Swedish turnip, *Brassica napobrassica*.

Ru·tā'cē·ae, *n.pl.* [L. *rutaceus*, of or belonging to rue.] a family of polypetalous shrubs, trees, and herbs, the simple or compound leaves dotted with glands, often having a strong heavy smell. About 800 species are known, including the rue, lemon, orange, lime, fraxinella, etc.

rụ·tā'ceous, *a.* 1. of or pertaining to the *Rutaceæ*.

2. of or like rue (the plant).

Rụth, *n.* [LL., from Heb. *rūth*, prob. contr. from *rĕ'ūth*, companion.] in the Bible, (a) the Moabite woman who left her own people to become the wife of Boaz of Bethlehem: she is celebrated for her devotion to her mother-in-law, Naomi; (b) a book of the Old Testament that tells the story of Ruth.

rụth, *n.* [ME. *reuthe*, from Ice. *hrygth*, sorrow.]

1. pity; tenderness. [Archaic.]

2. sorrow; grief; remorse. [Archaic.]

Rụ·thē'ni·ăn, *n.* 1. a member of a group of Ukrainians, or Little Russians, living in Ruthenia and eastern Czechoslovakia.

2. their East Slavic language, closely related to Ukrainian.

Rụ·thē'ni·ăn, *a.* 1. of Ruthenia or the Ruthenians.

2. of Ruthenian.

rụ·then'iç, *a.* pertaining to chemical compounds containing, or derived from ruthenium with a higher valence than in corresponding ruthenious compounds.

rụ·thē'ni·ous, *a.* pertaining to chemical compounds containing, or derived from ruthenium with a lower valence than in corresponding ruthenic compounds.

rụ·thē'ni·um, *n.* [from *Ruthenia*: so named because first found in ores from the Urals.] a hard, brittle, silvery-gray metallic element of the platinum group. symbol Ru; atomic weight, 101.7; atomic number, 44.

rụth'fụl, *a.* sorrowful; woeful, piteous. [Archaic.]

rụth'fụl·ly, *adv.* woefully; sadly. [Archaic.]

rụth'less, *a.* cruel; pitiless; without ruth.

rụth'less·ly, *adv.* without pity; cruelly; barbarously.

rụth'less·ness, *n.* the state or quality of being ruthless.

rụ'tiç, *a.* pertaining to or derived from rue; as, *rutic* acid. [Rare.]

rutic acid; same as *capric acid* under *capric*.

rụ'ti·lănt, *a.* [L. *rutians*, ppr. of *rutilare*, to have a reddish glow, from *rutilus*, red.] glowing, gleaming, or glittering. [Rare.]

rụ'ti·lāte, *v.i.* to shine. [Obs.]

rụ'ti·lāt·ed, *a.* containing rutile needles, as a kind of quartz.

rụ'tīle, *n.* [Fr., shining, from L. *rutilus*, red.] a lustrous, dark-red mineral, titanium dioxide, TiO_2, commonly found in prismatic crystals and usually containing some iron.

rụ·til'i·ăn, *n.* any beetle of the genus *Rutela*.

rụ'tin, *n.* a pale-yellow substance found in the garden rue, preserved capers, and other vegetables, as a glucoside.

rut'tẽr, *n.* anything that ruts.

rut'ti·ẽr, *n.* [OFr. *routier*, from *route*.] directions for finding one's course at sea. [Archaic.]

rut'ti·ness, *n.* a rutty quality or state.

rut'tish, *a.* in or inclined to rut (sexual heat); lustful; libidinous.

rut'tish·ness, *n.* the state or quality of being ruttish.

rut'ty, *a.*; *comp.* ruttier; *superl.* ruttiest, having or full of ruts; as, a *rutty* road.

rut'ty, *a.* ruttish.

RV (är'vē'), *n.*; *pl.* **RVs** [*R*ecreational *V*ehicle.] any of various vehicles, as campers, trailers, and motor homes, outfitted as a place to live, as when camping out.

Rx (är'eks), *n.* [altered from Rx, conventional symbol for L. *recipe* (see *recipe*), symbol for a medical prescription.] a remedy, cure, or the like suggested for any disorder or problem.

-ry, -ery: shortened form, as in dentis*try*, jewel*ry*.

rȳ'ăl, *n.* [a variant of *royal*.] an old English gold coin of varying value: in the reign of Henry VI, the gold ryal was worth 10s.; in the beginning of the reign of Queen Elizabeth I, ryals were current at 15s. each; in the reign of James I, the rose ryal of gold was current at 30s. and the spur ryal at 15s.

rȳ'dẽr, *n.* rider. [Obs.]

rȳe, *n.* [AS. *ryge*; Ice. *rúgr*; Dan. *rug*; Sw. *rog*; D. *rogge*.]

1. a hardy cereal plant, *Secale cereale*, widely grown for its grain and straw.

2. the grain or seeds of this plant, used for making flour and whisky, and as feed for livestock.

3. whisky made from the grain of rye; as, *rye* or Bourbon?

RYE (*Secale cereale*)

rȳe, *n.* [Gypsy *rei*, *rai*, a lord, from Sans. *rājan*, a king.] a gentleman; as, Romany *rye*.

rȳe grass, a quick-growing pasture grass, *Lolium perenne*.

Italian rye grass; a variety of the rye grass used for hay and for pasture.

rynd, *n.* [prob. AS. *hrindan*, to push.] an iron bar running across the under face of an upper millstone, giving it support on the spindle.

rȳ'ŏt, *n.* [Ar. *ra'iyat*, a peasant.] in India, a peasant or tenant farmer.

rȳ'ŏt·wär, rȳ'ŏt·wä·ri, *n.* a system under which a ryot pays his tax and land rent directly to the government without the intervention of middlemen.

rȳpe, *n.* [Dan., a ptarmigan.] a ptarmigan.

rȳ·sim'e·tẽr, *n.* same as *rhysimeter*.

ryt·i·dō'sis, *n.* [Gr. *rhytidōsis*, a wrinkling.] a wrinkling and shriveling of the cornea.

ryt'i·nȧ, *n.* same as *rhytina*.

S

S, s (es), *n.*; *pl.* **S's, s's, Ss, ss** (es'iz), 1. the nineteenth letter of the English alphabet: from the Greek *sigma*, a borrowing from the Phoenician.
2. a sound of S or s, usually a voiceless fricative.
3. a type or impression for S or s.
4. a symbol for the nineteenth in a sequence or group (or the eighteenth if J is omitted).

S, s, *a.* 1. of S or s.
2. the nineteenth (or eighteenth if J is omitted) in a sequence or group.

S, *n.* 1. an object shaped like S.
2. a medieval Roman numeral for 7 or 70: with a superior bar ($\bar{S}$), 70,000.
3. in chemistry, *the symbol for* sulfur.

S, *a.* shaped like S.

-s, 1. the inflectional ending by which the plural of most words is formed; as, books, tables, rooms, papers.
2. the inflectional ending by which the third person singular present indicative of English verbs is formed; as, writes, walks, talks.
3. a suffix used to form some adverbs; as, always, towards, etc.

-'s, the inflectional ending used to form the possessive singular of nouns (and some pronouns) and the possessive plural of nouns not ending in *s*; as, boy'*s*, one'*s*, women'*s*.

-'s, the unstressed and assimilated form of: (a) *is*, as in *he's here*; (b) *has*, as in *she's spoken*; (c) *us*, as in *let's go*.

Sa, in chemistry, samarium.

sab, *v.* and *n.* sob. [Scot.]

Sā'bȧ, *n.* same as *Sheba*.

sab·ȧ·dil'lȧ, *n.* [Sp. *cebadilla*, dim. of *cebada*, barley, from L. *cibare*, to feed.] a plant of the lily family, with dark, barleylike seeds used in medicine and insect poison; also, its seeds.

Sȧ·bae'ăn, *a.* [from L. *Sabaeus*; Gr. *Sabaios*.] of Saba (Biblical Sheba), its people, their language: also spelled *Sabean*.

Sȧ·bae'ăn, *n.* 1. a member of the Semitic people of Saba.
2. the South Arabic language of the Sabeans, known only from inscriptions.
Also spelled *Sabean*.

Sȧ·bae'ăn·iṣm, Sȧ·bae'iṣm, *n.* Sabaism; erroneous usage.

Sā'bȧ·iṣm, *n.* [from Heb. *tsābhā*, host (of heaven), army; and *ism*.] the worship of stars.

Sā'bȧ·ist, *n.* an adherent of Sabaism.

Sā'băl, *n.* [native name.] a genus of palmaceous trees, including the palmetto, *Sabal palmetto*.

sab'ȧ·lō, *n.* [Sp. *sábalo*, shad.]
1. the tarpon, *Megalops atlanticus*.
2. the milkfish.

Sab'ā·oth (*or* sȧ·bā'ōth), *n.pl.* [Heb. *tsebāōth*, pl. of *tsābā*, army.]
1. in the Bible, armies; hosts: chiefly in the Lord of *Sabaoth*: Rom. ix. 29, James v. 4.
2. the Sabbath. [Obs.]

Sab'băt, *n.* in demonology, a midnight assembly in which demons, witches, and sorcerers were supposed to celebrate their orgies; the witches' Sabbath.

Sab·bȧ·tār'i·ăn, *n.* [L. *sabbatarius*, of or belonging to the Sabbath, from *sabbatum*, Sabbath.]
1. one who regards the seventh day (Saturday) of the week as holy, in accordance with the letter of the fourth commandment in the decalogue. There were Christians in the early church who held this opinion, as the Seventh-day Baptists and Adventists do now.
2. a strict observer of Sunday as the Sabbath.

Sab·bȧ·tār'i·ăn, *a.* pertaining to the Sabbath; also, pertaining to the tenets of Sabbatarians.

Sab·bȧ·tār'i·ăn·iṣm, *n.* 1. observance of the Sabbath (Saturday).
2. rigid observance of Sunday as the Sabbath.

Sab'băth, *n.* [ME. *sabat*; L. *sabbatum*; Gr. *sabbaton*; Heb. *shabbāth*, rest, Sabbath, from Heb. *shābath*, to rest from labor.]
1. the day set apart in the fourth commandment of the decalogue to be observed as a day of rest from all secular labor or employment. This was originally the seventh day of the week (Saturday), as the day on which God rested from the work of creation; and this day is still observed by the Jews and some Christians as the Sabbath.
2. Sunday: name applied by most Protestant denominations.
3. [s-] the sabbatical year.
4. [s-] a time of rest.
Sabbath-day's journey; the distance which the Jews were permitted to travel on the Sabbath day. According to some authorities, it was $7^1/_2$ furlongs, or about 1,650 yards. The rabbis fix it at 2,000 cubits, which is about 1,350 yards.
Sabbath school; (a) Sunday school; (b) among Seventh Day Adventists, a similar school held on Saturday.

Sab'băth, *a.* of the Sabbath.

Sab·bȧ·thār'i·ăn, *n.* 1. a Sabbatarian. [Obs.]
2. a Southcottian.

Sab'băth·breāk"ēr, *n.* one who violates the Sabbath by breaking any law concerning its observance.

Sab'băth·breāk"ing, *n.* the act of violating any law concerning the observance of the Sabbath.

Sab·bā'thi·ăn, *n.* same as *Sabbatian*.

Sab'băth·less, *a.* having no Sabbath.

Sab·bā'ti·ȧ (*or* -shi-), *n.* [named after *Sabbati*, an Italian botanist.] a genus of North American plants of the gentian family, characterized by slender stems and cymose-panicled white or rose-purple flowers; also, [s-] a plant of this genus.

Sab·bā'tiăn (-shăn), *n.* in ecclesiastical history, a follower of Sabbatius, who contended that Easter and the Jewish Passover should be observed on the same day and in the same manner respecting fasting.

Sab·bat'i·căl, Sab·bat'iç, *a.* 1. pertaining to or resembling the Sabbath.
2. [s-] bringing a period of rest that recurs in regular cycles; as, a *sabbatical* leave.
sabbatical year; (a) among the ancient Jews, every seventh year, in which, according to Mosaic law, the land and vineyards were to remain fallow and debtors were to be released; (b) a year or half year of absence for study, rest, or travel, given every seven years to teachers, in some colleges and universities

sab·bat'i·căl, *n.* a sabbatical year.

Sab·bat'i·căl·ly, *adv.* in a Sabbatical manner.

sab'bȧ·tiṣm, *n.* rest; intermission of labor.

sab'bȧ·tŏn, *n.* [ME. *sabatoun*; LL. *sabbatum*, shoe.]. a round-toed armored shoe.

Sȧ·bē'ăn, *a.* and *n.* same as *Sabian*.

Sȧ·bē'iṣm, *n.* same as *Sabaism*.

sā'bel·ine, *n.* [OFr. *sabelin*; LL. *sabelinus*, of the sable, from L. *sabelum*, sable.] the skin or fur of the sable. [Obs.]

Sȧ·bel'lȧ, *n.* [LL., dim. of L. *sabulum*, sand, gravel.] a genus of tubicolous sea worms.

Sȧ·bel'li·ăn, *a.* pertaining to Sabellius or his doctrines.

Sȧ·bel'li·ăn, *n.* a follower of Sabellius, a presbyter of Ptolemais, in the third century, who maintained that there is but one divinity, and that the Son and Holy Spirit are only different powers, operations, or offices of the one God, the Father.

Sȧ·bel'li·ăn·iṣm, *n.* the doctrines or tenets of Sabellius.

sȧ·bel'loid, *a.* of, pertaining to, or resembling the *Sabella*.

sȧ·bel'loid, *n.* any worm of the genus *Sabella*.

sā'bēr, *n.* [Fr. *sabre*; Sp. *sable*; Sw. *sabel*; G. *säbel*. Origin uncertain.]
1. a cavalry sword with a broad and heavy blade, thick at the back, and a little curved toward the point.
2. in fencing, a type of weapon, heavier than a foil, used with a slashing as well as thrusting movement: a touch may be scored with the edge or point.
Also spelled *sabre*.

sā'bēr, *v.t.*; sabered, *pt., pp.*; sabering, *ppr.* to strike, cut, or kill with a saber: also spelled *sabre*.

sā'bēr·bill, *n.* the curlew.

sā'bēr rat'tling, a threatening of war, or a menacing show of armed force.

sā'bēr-tọọth, sā'bre-tọọth (-bēr-), *n.* a saber-toothed tiger.

sā'bēr-tọọthed, sā'bre-tọọthed (-tötht), *a.* having long, curved upper canine teeth.
saber-toothed tiger; any of a group of extinct animals of the cat family, closely resembling the tiger, but with a more massive body, shorter legs and tail, and long, curved upper canine teeth: found from the Oligocene to the Pleistocene, and of wide distribution.

sā'bēr·wing, *n.* a humming bird of the *Campylopterus* or allied genera, having long, curved wings.

Sā'bi·ȧ, *n.* [Hind. *sabjalat*.] the type genus of the *Sabiaceæ*.

Sā·bi·ā'cē·ae, *n.pl.* a family of tropical shrubs, trees, or woody climbers having a compressed or lobed ovary of two or three cells, alternate, simple, or pinnate exstipulate leaves, and panicles of small flowers.

sā·bi·ā'ceous, *a.* of, pertaining to, or resembling the *Sabiaceæ*.

Sā'bi·ăn, *a.* 1. of or pertaining to Sabaism.
2. of or pertaining to Sabianism.
3. of or pertaining to Saba, or Sheba, its people, their language, etc.

Sā'bi·ăn, *n.* [Heb. *tsābā*, army, host.]
1. a Sabaist.
2. a Mandean.

Sā'bi·ăn·iṣm, *n.* 1. the religion of the Sabians, or Sabaists.
2. same as Mandaeism, the religion of the Mandeans.

sab'i·cū, *n.* [Cuban name.] the very hard, dark-colored wood of the West Indian tree, *Lysiloma sabicu*.

sȧ·bī'nȧ, *n.* same as *savin*.

Sā'bīne, *a.* of or pertaining to the Sabines or their language.

Sā'bīne, *n.* [L. *Sabinus*, Sabine.]
1. a member of an ancient tribe living chiefly in the Apennines of central Italy, conquered by the Romans in the third century B.C.
2. the Italic language of the Sabines.

sab'ine, *n.* same as *savin*.

sȧ·bī'nō, *n.* [L. *Sabina herba*, a kind of juniper.] the swamp cypress, *Taxodium mucronatum*, found in Mexico.

sā'ble, *n.*; *pl.* **sā'bleṣ** or **sā'ble,** [Russ. *soboli*; G. *zobel*; Sw., Dan., and D. *sabel*; Fr. *zibeline*; It. *zibellino*; Sp. *cebellina*; L. *zoboia* or *zobola*, an ermine.]
1. a small, flesh-eating animal of the weasel family, *Mustela zibellina*, found in the northern latitudes of Europe and Asia. It resembles the marten, but has a longer head and ears. Its glossy, dark fur is exceedingly valuable.
2. a North American animal related to the sable.

3. the costly fur or pelt of the sable; also, [*pl.*] a coat, neckpiece, etc. made of this.

4. [*pl.*] a funeral garment; mourning clothes.

5. in heraldry, black; one of the tinctures used in engraving: it is represented by horizontal lines crossed by perpendicular ones producing a dark shading.

SABLE

sā′ble, *a.* 1. black; dark; as, night with her *sable* mantle.

2. made of or with the fur of the sable; as, a *sable* coat.

sable antelope; a large antelope, *Hippotragus niger*, with scimitar-shaped horns, found in the eastern and southern parts of Africa. The male is black and the female dark brown with streaks on the face and an under surface of white.

sable iron; a fine kind of Russian iron.

sable mouse; the lemming. [Obs.]

sā′ble, *v.t.*; sabled, *pt.*, *pp.*; sabling, *ppr.* to darken; to make black; to drape or clothe in black. [Archaic and Poet.]

sā′ble·fish, *n.*; *pl.* **sā′ble·fish** or **sā′ble·fishes**, an edible fish of the North Pacific, resembling the mackerel; beshow.

sa·bōt′ (-bō′), *n.* [Fr. *sabot*; Sp. *zapato*; LL. *sabbatum*, shoe.]

1. a wooden shoe worn by peasants in Europe.

2. a heavy leather shoe with a wooden sole.

3. a small sailing dinghy whose hull somewhat resembles such a shoe.

4. in military usage, a circular wooden disk or soft, metal clip formerly attached to a projectile to keep it in position; also, a metal cup or disk similarly attached to take the groove of the rifling.

SABOTS
A, wood; B, leather

sab′ō·tāge′ (-täzh′ *or Fr.* sȧ-bō-täzh′), *n.* [Fr., from *saboter*, to work badly, damage, from *sabot*, shoe, and *-age*.]

1. intentional destruction of machines, waste of materials, etc., as by employees during labor disputes.

2. intentional obstruction of or damage to some productive process, organized activity or effort, etc.

3. (a) destruction of railroads, bridges, machinery, etc. by enemy agents in time of war; (b) any deliberate obstruction of a nation's war work.

sab·ō·tāge′, *v.i.*; sabotaged, *pt.*, *pp.*; sabotaging, *ppr.* to engage in sabotage.

sab·ō·tāge′, *v.t.* to injure or destroy by sabotage.

sȧ·bō·teūr′, *n.* a person who engages in sabotage.

sā′bre (-bẽr), *n.* and *v.t.*; sabred, *pt.*, *pp.*; sabring, *ppr.* same as *saber.*

sā′bre·tache (-bẽr-tash), *n.* [Fr. *sabretache*; G. *säbeltasche*, a pouch hanging near the saber, worn by hussars, etc.; from *säbel*, sabre, and *tasche*, a pouch or pocket.] a square leather case worn at the left side suspended from the saber belt, sometimes worn by cavalrymen.

sā′bre-toothed (-tötht), *a.* same as *saber-toothed.*

sab′ū·line, *a.* same as *sabulous.*

sab′ū·lōse, *a.* same as *sabulous.*

sab·ū·los′i·ty, *n.* sandiness; grittiness.

sab′ū·lous, *a.* [L. *sabulosus*, from *sabulo*, sand.] sandy; gritty.

sab·ūr·rā′tion, *n.* [L. *saburra*, sand.] the application of hot sand enclosed in a bag to any part of the body; sand bathing.

Saç, *n.*; *pl.* **Saç**, any member of a tribe of North American Indians of Algonquian linguistic stock living originally in Michigan, Wisconsin, and Illinois, and now settled on reservations in Oklahoma and Iowa: also *Sauk.*

saç, *n.* [AS. *sac* or *sacu*, contention.] in English law, the privilege enjoyed by the lord of a manor of holding courts, trying cases, and imposing fines. [Obs.]

saç, *n.* [L. *saccus*, a bag.] a bag or cyst; a pouchlike part in a plant or animal, often filled with a liquid; as, the lachrymal *sac.*

lachrymal sac; the dilated upper end of the lachrymal duct.

saç′ȧ·lāit, *n.* a crappie.

saç·ȧ·tōn′, *n.* [Sp. *zacatón*, from *zacate*, *sacate*, from Nahuatl *çacatl*, kind of grass.] a coarse grass, used for hay or pasture in the southwestern United States.

saç′ȧ·trȧ, *n.* a person who is about seven-eighths Negro and one-eighth Caucasian.

saç·çāde′, *n.* [Fr., from an old verb *saquer*, *sacher*, to pull. Origin uncertain.]

1. a short, violent check of a horse by drawing or twitching the reins suddenly and with one pull.

2. in music, a pressure of the bow on the violin strings so as to play upon more than one at once.

saç′çāte, *a.* [LL. *saccatus*, from L. *saccus*, bag.]

1. having the form of a sac; pouchlike.

2. having a sac.

saç′çhar-, same as *saccharo-*.

saç′çhȧ·rāte, *n.* 1. a salt or ester derived from saccharic acid.

2. a compound of sugar with the oxide of calcium, strontium, or a similar metal.

saç·çhar′iç, *a.* [*sacchar*in and *-ic*.]

1. of, derived from, or relating to a saccharine compound.

2. designating or of a diacid, $(CHOH)_4(COOH)_2$, obtained by oxidizing dextrose and other hexoses.

saç′çhȧ·rīde (*or* -rid), *n.* [*sacchar*in and *-ide*.]

1. a compound of sugar with an organic base.

2. any of the carbohydrates; especially, a monosaccharide.

3. a saccharate.

saç·çhȧ·rif′ẽr·ous, *a.* [*sacchar*(*i*)- and *-ferous*.] containing or producing sugar; as, a *sacchariferous* tree.

saç·çhar″i·fi·çā′tion, *n.* the act or process of converting or of being converted into sugar; a saccharifying or being saccharified.

saç·çhar′i·fī·ẽr, *n.* a device used to change to sugar the starch contained in grain, potatoes, etc.

saç·çhar′i·fȳ, *v.t.*; saccharified, *pt.*, *pp.*; saccharifying, *ppr.* [LL. *saccharum*, sugar, and L. *-ficare*, *facere*, to make.] to convert (starch or dextrin) into sugar, as by chemical means; to saccharize.

saç·çhȧ·ril′lȧ, *n.* a variety of muslin.

saç·çhȧ·rim′e·tẽr, *n.* [LL. *saccharum*, sugar, and *-meter*.] an instrument for ascertaining the quantity of sugar in a solution, as a kind of polariscope.

saç″çhȧ·ri·met′ri·çăl, *a.* of, relating to, or effected by saccharimetry.

saç·çhȧ·rim′e·try, *n.* the operation or art of ascertaining the amount of sugar in a solution.

saç′çhȧ·rin, *n.* [from ML. *saccharum*, sugar; L. *saccharon*; Gr. *sakcharon*.]

1. an intensely sweet, white, crystalline substance, $C_7H_5O_3NS$, obtained from coal tar: it is about 400 times sweeter than cane sugar and is used as a sugar substitute in diabetic diets, etc.

2. a bitter, crystalline lactone of saccharic acid.

Also spelled *saccharine.*

saç′çhȧ·rine (*or* -rīn), *a.* [*sacchar-* and *-ine*.]

1. of or pertaining to sugar; having the qualities of or containing sugar.

2. overly sweet; as, a *saccharine* smile: used derisively.

saç′çhȧ·rine, *n.* same as *saccharin.*

saç·çhȧ·rin′iç, *a.* of, derived from, or relating to saccharin; saccharic.

saç·çhȧ·rin′i·ty, *n.* the quality or condition of being saccharine.

saç″çhȧ·ri·zā′tion, *n.* a saccharizing or being saccharized.

saç′çhȧ·rīze, *v.t.*; saccharized, *pt.*, *pp.*; saccharizing, *ppr.* to form or convert into sugar; to ferment; to saccharify.

saç′çhȧ·rō-, [from Gr. *sakcharon*, sugar.] a combining form meaning: (a) *sugar*, as in *saccharometer*; (b) *saccharine and*: also, before a vowel, *sacchar-*.

saç′çhȧ·roid, saç·çhȧ·roi′dăl, *a.* [Gr. *sakcharon*, sugar, and *-oid*.] having a texture resembling loaf sugar; crystalline and granular; as, *saccharoid* gypsum: said of stone.

saç·çhȧ·rom′e·tẽr, *n.* [*saccharo-* and *-meter*.] a form of hydrometer for finding out the amount of sugar in a solution.

Saç″çhȧ·rō·mȳ′çēs, *n.* [LL. *saccharum*, sugar, and Gr. *mykes*, mushroom.] a genus of sprouting fungi of the yeast family: they have the power of resolving sugar into alcohol and carbonic acid and of fermenting wine. *Saccharomyces cerevisiæ* is a common beer yeast.

Saç″çhȧ·rō·mȳ·cē·tā′cē·ae, *n.pl.* a family of sprout fungi including the yeast fungi, *Saccharomyces.*

Saç″çhȧ·rō·mȳ·cē·tā′lēs, *n.pl.* an order of fungi of which *Saccharomyces* is typical.

Saç·çhȧ·rō·mȳ·cē′tēs, *n.pl.* same as *Saccharomycetaceæ.*

saç′çhȧ·rō·nāte, *n.* a salt of saccharonic acid.

saç′çhȧ·rōne, *n.* [LL. *saccharum*, sugar, and E. *lactone*.] the lactone of saccharonic acid, $C_6H_8O_6$.

saç·çhȧ·ron′iç, *a.* of, derived from, or relating to saccharone.

saccharonic acid; a sour, crystalline substance, $C_6H_8O_6+H_2O$.

saç′çhȧ·rōse, *n.* [*sacchar-* and *-ose*.] sucrose; cane or beet sugar.

saç′çhȧ·rous, *a.* same as *saccharine*, sense 1.

saç′çhȧ·rum, *n.* [LL., from L. *saccharon*, Gr. *sakcharon*, sugar.]

1. sugar.

2. [S—] a genus of tropical grasses. *Saccharum officinarum*, or sugar cane, the best known species, is cultivated in tropical and semitropical countries and several varieties are known. It is a perennial, with a creeping root, sending up a number of stems which have many joints and are of various colors.

saç·çhō·laç′tāte, *n.* mucate. [Obs.]

saç·çhō·laç′tiç, *a.* mucic. [Obs.]

saç·çhul′miç, *a.* [*sacch*arin and *ulmic*.] of, relating to, or indicating an acid obtained by boiling sugar with dilute acids.

saç·çhul′min, *n.* a substance obtained in the production of sacchulmic acid.

saç·çif′ẽr·ous, *a.* [L. *saccus*, sack, and *ferre*, to bear.] having a sac.

saç′çi·fọrm, *a.* [L. *saccus*, sack, and *-form*.] having the shape of a sac.

saç·çō·bran′çhi·āte, *a.* [Gr. *sakkos*, sack, and *branchia*, gills.] having such saclike reticulated gills as characterize ascidians.

Saç·çō·lā′bi·um, *n.* [L. *saccus*, sack, and *labium*, lip.] a genus of plants, native to the Malay Archipelago and the East Indies, extensively cultivated in hothouses. It consists of caulescent epiphytes, with two-rowed coriaceous leaves and long, crowded, axillary spikes of small, usually white, purple-spotted flowers.

saç·çō·mȳ′i·ăn, *n.* [Gr. *sakkos*, sack, and *mys*, mouse.] a pouched mouse of the family *Saccomyidæ.*

saç·çō·mȳ′i·ăn, *a.* pertaining to the *Saccomyidæ.*

saç·çō·mȳ′id, *n.* a saccomyian.

Saç·çō·mȳ′i·dae, *n.pl.* a family of rodents; the pocket mice.

saç·çō·mȳ′oid, *a.* of, like, or relating to the saccomyians.

saç·çō·my′oid, *n.* a pocket gopher.

saç′ços, *n.* [Gr. *sakkos*, sack.] an alblike cross-ornamented vestment, usually of silk, worn by most bishops of the Greek Church.

saç′çū·lăr, *a.* like a sac; sacciform.

saç′çū·lāte, *a.* [LL. *sacculatus*, from L. *sacculus*, little sack.] formed of or divided into saccules or a series of saclike expansions.

saç′çū·lā·ted, *a.* sacculate.

saç′çūle, *n.* [L. *sacculus*, dim. of *saccus*, sack.] a small sac; especially, the smaller of the two divisions of the membranous labyrinth of the inner ear.

saç·çū·lō·ū·triç′ū·lăr, *a.* in anatomy, of or relating to the sacculus and the utriculus of the ear.

saç′çū·lus, *n.*; *pl.* **saç′çū·lī**, a saccule.

saç′çus, *n.*; *pl.* **saç′çī**, [L.] a sac.

sȧ·cel′lum, *n.*; *pl.* **sȧ·cel′lȧ**, [L., dim. from *sacrum*, a sacred place.]

1. in Roman architecture, a small, roofless enclosure containing an altar sacred to a deity.

2. in medieval architecture, a small, canopied, monumental chapel within a church, used as an altar.

sac·ẽr·dō′tăl, *a.* [L. *sacerdotalis*, from *sacerdos*, a priest.]

1. pertaining to priests or the priesthood; priestly; as, *sacerdotal* functions or garments.

2. characterized by belief in the divine authority of the priesthood.

sac·ẽr·dō′tăl·ism, *n.* the sacerdotal system or spirit; the character, system, method, or practices of the priesthood; priestcraft: often in a hostile sense.

sac·ẽr·dō′tăl·ly, *adv.* in a sacerdotal manner.

sā′chem, *n.* [Algonguian.]
1. a chief (of the tribe or of a confederation) among some North American Indian tribes.
2. any of the leading officials of the Tammany Society.

sā′chem·dŏm, *n.* the jurisdiction of a sachem.

sā′chem·ship, *n.* the office or position of a sachem.

sa·chet′ (-shā′), *n.* [Fr.]
1. a small bag, pad, etc. filled with perfumed powder, used to scent clothing.
2. powder for such a bag: also *sachet powder.*

sa·chet′pow′dẽr, perfume in the form of powder used in sachets.

sack, *n* [AS. *sacc*; Goth. *sakkus*, from L. *saccus*, Gr. *sakkos*, from Heb. *saq*, sackcloth, a grainsack; prob. from Coptic *sok*, Ethiopic *sak*, a sack.]
1. a bag, commonly of a large size, made of strong, coarse material, used for holding and carrying grain, foodstuffs, etc.
2. such a bag with its contents.
3. the capacity of a sack, considered as a measure or weight of varying amounts.
4. sackcloth. [Obs.]

SACK (sense 5)

5. a kind of loose gown or upper garment for women, introduced from France in the reign of Charles II. It hung loosely over the back and shoulders, the fullness of the back being gathered or plaited at the neck: also spelled *sacque.*
6. a short, loose-fitting coat or jacket, worn by women or babies; as, a dressing *sack*: also spelled *sacque.*
7. dismissal; discharge (with *the*). [Slang.]
8. (a) a sleeping bag; (b) a bed. [Slang.]
9. in baseball, a base.
to get the sack; to be dismissed or discharged. [Slang.]
to give the sack; to dismiss; to discharge. [Slang.]

sack, *v.t.*; sacked (sakt), *pt.*, *pp.*; sacking, *ppr.*
1. to put in a sack or sacks.
2. to give the sack to; to discharge. [Slang.]
3. to carry in or as in a sack. [Colloq.]

sack, *n.* [Fr. *sac*; It. *sacco*, plunder, pillage, from the use of sacks in removing plunder.]
1. the act of sacking or pillaging, especially by soldiers, of a captured town or city.
2. that which is obtained by sacking; booty; plunder; spoil.

sack, *v.t.* to pillage; to plunder; to devastate; as, to *sack* a town.

sack, *n.* [Fr. *sec*, dry, from L. *siccus*, dry.] any of various strong, light-colored dry wines, more especially those from Spain and the Canary Islands, popular in England in the sixteenth and seventeenth centuries.

sack′ăge, *n.* the act of sacking; sack. [Rare.]

sack beăr′ẽr, a basket worm.

sack′but, *n.* [formerly *sagbut*; Fr. *saquebute*; Sp. *sacabuche*, a sackbut or kind of trumpet; it has acquired its second meaning from somewhat resembling in form Heb. *sabbeca*, and being used to translate it.]
1. a medieval wind instrument, similar to the trombone.
2. in the Bible, a musical stringed instrument resembling a lyre: Dan. iii. 5.

sack′cloth, *n.* 1. sacking.
2. coarse, rough cloth worn as a symbol of penitence or mourning: it was originally made of goats' hair.
in sackcloth and ashes; (a) in the Bible, wearing sackcloth and sprinkling ashes on one's head to express mourning or penitence; (b) in a state of great mourning, penitence, or remorse.

sack′clothed (-klotht), *a.* clothed in sackcloth.

sack cōat, a man's short, loose-fitting, straight-backed, coat, usually part of a business suit.

sack′ẽr, *n.* one who sacks; a plunderer.

sack′ẽr, *n.* one who makes or fills sacks.

sack′ful, *n.*; *pl.* **sack′fuls,** the amount held by a sack; also, a large quantity.

sack′ful, *a.* prone to sack or to loot. [Obs.]

sack′ing, *n.* coarse cloth woven of flax, hemp, jute, etc., used for making sacks and bags, and for wrapping large bundles for shipment.

sack′less, *a.* [AS. *sacleas*, from *sacu*, contention, and *leas*, less.] quiet; peaceable; harmless. [Scot.]

sack moth, a moth that in its larval state was a sack bearer.

sack pos′set, a posset made of sack, milk, and other ingredients.

sack rāce, a race in which each contestant ties his legs in a sack and moves by jumping.

sack tree, the East Indian upas tree, from which bags are made by peeling the clothlike bark from sections of the branches, leaving a small portion of the wood to form the bottom of the sacks.

sacque (sak), *n.* a sack (senses 5 and 6).

sā′crăl, *a.* [from L. *sacrum*, neut. of *sacer*, sacred; and *-al.*] of or for religious rites and observances.

sā′crăl, *a.* [Mod. L. *sacralis.*] of or pertaining to the sacrum; situated near the sacrum.
sacral plexus; a nerve plexus situated in front of the sacrum.

sā·cral′gi·a, *a.* [LL., from *sacrum* and *-algia.*] pain in the sacrum.

sac′ra·ment, *n.* [L. *sacramentum*, a military oath of allegiance, an oath, from *sacer*, sacred.]
1. in ancient Rome; the military oath taken by every Roman soldier, pledging him to obey his commander, and not to desert his standard.
2. in Christianity, any of certain rites ordained by Jesus: in the Roman Catholic Church and the Orthodox Eastern Church it is held that there are seven sacraments, namely, baptism, confirmation, the Eucharist, penance, extreme unction, holy orders, and matrimony. Protestants in general acknowledge but two sacraments, baptism and the Lord's Supper.
3. [*sometimes* S–] the Eucharist: often with *the.*
4. (a) the consecrated bread and wine used in the Eucharist; (b) the bread alone. Often with *blessed* or *holy.*
5. something regarded as having a sacred character or mysterious meaning.
6. a symbol, sign, or token.
7. a solemn oath, promise, or pledge, as one ratified by a rite.

sac′ra·ment, *v.t.* to bind by an oath.

sac·ra·men′tăl, *a.* 1. of or pertaining to a sacrament or the sacraments; used in the sacrament; as, *sacramental* wine.
2. bound by a sacrament or oath.

sac·ra·men′tăl, *n.* 1. that which is used in or connected with the administration of a sacrament.
2. in the Roman Catholic Church, a ceremony or sacred object like a sacrament, but instituted by the Church, as the use of holy water.

sac·ra·men′tăl·ism, *n.* the doctrine that the sacraments are necessary to salvation.

sac·ra·men′tăl·ist, *n.* an adherent to the doctrine of sacramentalism.

sac·ra·men′tăl·ly, *adv.* in, by, or in the manner of a sacrament.

sac″ra·men·tār′i·ăn, *n.* 1. a sacramentalist.
2. [S–] a person who believes that the sacraments are the symbolic rather than corporeal manifestation of Christ: used by Luther in reference to Zwingli and his followers.

sac″ra·men·tār′i·ăn, *a.* 1. pertaining to a sacrament or sacraments; sacramental.
2. [S–] pertaining or relating to the Sacramentarians.

sac″ra·men·tār′i·ăn·ism, *n.* the principles, teachings, or practices of the sacramentarians.

Sac·ra·men′ta·ry, *n.*; *pl.* **Sac·ra·men′ta·ries,**
1. an ancient book of the Roman Catholic Church, in which were contained all the prayers and ceremonies practiced in the celebration of the sacraments.
2. [s–] same as *sacramentarian*, sense 2.

sac·ra·men′ta·ry, *a.* 1. pertaining or relating to a sacrament or the sacraments; sacramental. [Rare.]
2. pertaining or relating to the Sacramentarians. [Rare.]

sac′ra·ment·ize, *v.i.* to administer the sacraments.

sa·crār′i·um, *n.*; *pl.* **sa·crār′i·a,** [L.] 1. a sort of family chapel in the houses of the ancient Romans, in which sacred things are kept.
2. that part of a church where the altar or Communion table is situated; the sanctuary in a Christian Church.
3. in ancient Rome, the adytum of a temple.

sā′crāte, *v.t.* to consecrate. [Obs.]

sa·crā′tion, *n.* consecration. [Obs.]

sā′cre (-kẽr), *n.* a sacred service or ceremony. [Obs.]

sā′cre, *v.t.* to make sacred; to dedicate. [Obs.]

sā′cred, *a.* [pp. of old *sacre*, to set apart, consecrate; Fr. *sacré*, from L. *sacer*, sacred, from root seen also in *sanus*, sane, and in Gr. *saos*, safe.]
1. consecrated to or belonging to a god or deity; dedicated or appropriated to religious use; made holy; as, a *sacred* place; a *sacred* day.
2. relating to religion or religious rites and practices; as, *sacred* history; *sacred* music: opposed to *profane, secular.*
3. set apart for, and dedicated to, some person, place, purpose, sentiment, etc., rather than to a god; as, *sacred* to his memory.
4. entitled to the highest respect or reverence; venerable.

My heart has owned the magical tenderness
of the emotions first kindled amid these
sacred scenes. —Henry W. Grady.

5. not to be profaned, violated, or made common; inviolable; inviolate; as, to keep one's confidence *sacred.*
6. accursed; execrable.
sacred baboon; same as *hamadryas.*
sacred bean; the nut of the lotus, *Nelumbo speciosa*; also, the plant itself.
sacred beetle; a scarab, *Scarabæus sacer*, of Egypt.
sacred canon; the books of the Bible regarded as genuine Holy Scriptures.
Sacred College; see under *college.*
sacred cow; any person or thing regarded as above criticism or attack: used humorously.
sacred fish; any one of various fresh-water fishes of Africa: a large number of species, found in the river Nile, were venerated by the ancient Egyptians. *Mormyrus oxyrhynchus* is the best-known species.
sacred ibis; an ibis considered sacred by the ancient Egyptians.
sacred place; in civil law, the place where a person is buried.
Syn.—hallowed, holy, consecrated, religious, reverend, divine, devoted, dedicated.

sā′cred·ly, *adv.* in a sacred manner.

sā′cred·ness, *n.* the state or quality of being sacred.

sa·crif′ic, sa·crif′ic·ăl, *a.* sacrificial. [Obs.]

sa·crif′ic·a·ble, *a.* capable of being offered in sacrifice.

sa·crif′ic·ănt, *n.* one who offers a sacrifice. [Rare.]

Sac″ri·fi·cā′tī, *n.pl.* [L.] Christians of the early church who, to escape persecution, sacrificed to the gods.

sac′ri·fi·cā″tŏr, *n.* a sacrificer; one who offers a sacrifice.

sa·crif′ic·a·tō·ry, *a.* offering sacrifice.

sac′ri·fice, *n.* [OFr. and Fr. *sacrifice*; L. *sacrificium*, a rendering sacred, sacrifice, from *sacer*, sacred, and *facere*, to make.]
1. the offering of anything to a deity as propitiation or homage.
2. that which is sacrificed, offered, or consecrated to a deity as propitiation or homage.

My life if thou preserv'st, my life
Thy *sacrifice* shall be. —Addison.

3. (a) a giving up, destroying, permitting injury to, or foregoing of some valued thing for the sake of something of greater value or having a more pressing claim; (b) a thing so given up, etc.
4. (a) a selling or giving up of something at less than its supposed value; (b) goods sold at a loss; (c) the loss incurred.

5. in baseball, a sacrifice hit.
sacrifice hit; in baseball, a play in which the batter intentionally bunts the ball in such a manner that he can be put out but a base runner will be advanced.
the supreme sacrifice; the giving of one's life, as for a cause or an ideal.
Syn.—oblation, offering, atonement, expiation, surrender, propitiation, immolation.

saç′ri·fīce, *v.t.*; sacrificed, *pt., pp.*; sacrificing, *ppr.* 1. to offer to a god or deity in homage or propitiation.
2. to give up, destroy, permit injury to, or forego (a valued thing) for the sake of something of greater value or having a more pressing claim.
3. to sell or part with (something) at less than the supposed value; to incur a loss in selling.
4. in baseball, to advance (a base runner) by means of a sacrifice hit.

saç′ri·fīce, *v.i.* 1. to offer or make a sacrifice or sacrifices.
2. to make a sacrifice hit.

saç′ri·fī·cẽr, *n.* one who sacrifices.

saç·ri·fi′ciăl (-fish′ăl), *a.* pertaining to or connected with sacrifice; used in or offering sacrifice; as, *sacrificial* rites.

saç′ri·leġe (-lij), *n.* [Fr. *sacrilège*, from L. *sacrilegium*, the robbing of a temple, from *sacer*, sacred, and *legere*, to gather up, take away.]
1. the crime of appropriating to oneself, or to secular use, what is consecrated to God or religion; as, robbery of a church is a *sacrilege.*
2. the intentional desecration or disrespectful treatment of persons, places, things or ideas held sacred.

saç·ri·lē′ġious (*or* -lij′us), *a.* 1. injurious or disrespectful to sacred things; profane.
2. guilty of sacrilege.

saç·ri·lē′ġious·ly, *adv.* with sacrilege.

saç·ri·lē′ġious·ness, *n.* the state or quality of being sacrilegious.

sac′ri·lē·ġist, *n.* one who is guilty of sacrilege. [Rare.]

sā′çring, *n.* consecration of the bread and wine of the Eucharist. [Archaic.]

sā′çring bell, a bell rung during the Mass at the elevation of the bread and wine after consecration.

sā′çrist, *n.* [LL. *sacrista*, from L. *sacer*, sacred.] a sacristan.

saç′ris·tăn, *n.* [LL. *sacristanus*, from *sacrista*, a sacrist. *Sexton* is a contr. of this word.] an officer of the church who has charge of the sacristy of a church; also, a sexton.

saç′ris·ty, *n.*; *pl.* **saç′ris·tieṣ,** [Fr. *sacristie*; LL. *sacristia.*] an apartment or room in a church where the sacred utensils, vestments, etc., are kept; the vestry.

sā′çro- (*or* sak′rō), [from *sacrum.*] a combining form meaning (a) *the sacrum*; (b) *sacral* (of the sacrum) *and*, as in *sacro*iliac.

sā″crō·an·tē′ri·ŏr, *a.* [*sacro-* and *anterior.*] having the sacrum directed forward.

sā″crō·cox·ī′tis, *n.* [*sacro-*, and L. *coxa*, hip, and *-itis.*] inflammation of the sacroiliac joint.

sā·crō·il′i·aç, *a.* [*sacro-* and *ilium.*] pertaining to the sacrum and ilium; especially, designating the joint between them.

sā″crō·pos·tē′ri·ŏr, *a.* [*sacro-* and *posterior.*] having the sacrum directed backward.

saç′rō·sañçt, *a.* [L. *sacrosanctus*, from *sacer*, sacred, and *sanctus*, holy.] very holy or sacred; inviolable.

saç·rō·sañç′ti·ty, *n.* the state or quality of being sacrosanct.

sā″crō·scī·at′iç, *a.* [*sacro-*, and LL. *sciaticus*, sciatic.] of or pertaining to the sacrum and the ischium.

sā·crō·vẽr′tē·brăl, *a.* [*sacro-*, and L. *vertebra*, vertebra.] of or pertaining to the sacrum and the vertebrae.

sā′çrum, *n.*; *pl.* **sā′çrȧ, sā′çrumṣ,** [L., the sacred bone, sacrum: so called from being used formerly in sacrifices.] a thick, triangular bone situated at the lower end of the spinal column, where it joins both hipbones to form the dorsal part of the pelvis: it is formed in man of five fused sacral vertebrae.

sad, *a.*; *comp.* sadder; *superl.* saddest, [AS. *sæd*, sated, weary.]
1. having, expressing, or showing low spirits or sorrow; unhappy; mournful; sorrowful.
2. causing or characterized by dejection, melancholy, or sorrow.
3. dark-colored; dull.
4. very bad; deplorable: often used as an intensive. [Colloq.]
5. heavy, compact, or soggy: said of earth, pastry, etc. [Dial.]
6. sober; trustworthy; firm; constant. [Archaic.]
Syn.—dejected, gloomy, melancholy, heavy.

sad, *v.t.* to make sorrowful. [Now Dial.]

sad′den (-dn), *v.t.*; saddened, *pt., pp.*; saddening, *ppr.* 1. to make sad or sorrowful; to make melancholy or gloomy.
2. to make dark-colored.
3. to make heavy, firm, or cohesive. [Dial.]

sad′den, *v.i.* to become sad or to be made sad.

sad′dle, *n.* [AS. *sadel, sadol*; akin to G. *sattel*, a saddle.]
1. a padded leather seat for a rider on a horse, bicycle, etc.
2. the position of a person riding in such a seat.
3. a padded part of a harness worn over a horse's back to hold the shafts.
4. the part of an animal's back where a saddle is placed.
5. anything shaped like or suggestive of a saddle.
6. a ridge between two peaks or summits.
7. (a) a cut of mutton, etc. including part of the backbone and the two loins; (b) the rear part of the back of a fowl; (c) such a cut or part prepared for eating.
8. a block of wood bolted to a spar and hollowed out to receive the end of another spar.
9. in architecture, the separate piece forming the threshold of a door.
10. in worms, a clitellum.
11. in machinery, a flange for support or attachment.
12. in mining, a vein of quartz containing gold, formed along the crest of a ridge.
in the saddle; in a position of control.

sad′dle, *v.t.*; saddled, *pt., pp.*; saddling, *ppr.* 1. to put a saddle upon.
2. to load or encumber, as with a burden.
3. to impose as a burden, obligation, etc.

sad′dle·back, *a.* same as *saddle-backed.*
saddleback roof; same as *saddle roof.*

sad′dle·back, *n.* 1. anything that is saddle-backed; particularly, an elevation having a depression between two points.
2. in zoology, (a) a New Zealand bird much like the starling and having a band of brown feathers on its back and wings; (b) the larva of a moth with a saddle-shaped mark of bright green on its back; (c) the harp seal; (d) the great black-backed gull.

sad′dle-backed (-bakt), *a.* 1. having a low, hollow back curved like a saddle: said of an animal, especially a horse.
2. having a concave outline, as a ridge between two peaks.
3. having saddlelike markings on the back.

sad′dle·bag, *n.* a large bag, usually one of a pair, carried on either side of the back of a horse, etc., just behind the saddle.

sad′dle bär, a small iron bar securing the lead strips in a glazed window.

sad′dle·bōw, *n.* the arched front part, or bow, of a saddle, the top of which is the pommel.

sad′dle brack′et, a bracket in the shape of a saddle, used on telegraph poles to support the wires.

sad′dle·çloth, *n.* a thick cloth placed under a saddle on an animal's back.

sad′dled, *a.* marked by a saddle-shaped patch of color on the back; saddle-backed.

sad′dle feath′ẽr (feth′), one of the large tail feathers of the domestic cock.

sad′dle ġall, a sore on a horse's back, caused by the rubbing of the saddle.

sad′dle ġirth, the band that passes around a horse's body and secures the saddle in place.

sad′dle haç′kle, same as *saddle feather.*

sad′dle họrse, a horse trained or suitable for riding.

sad′dle joint, 1. in anatomy, an articulation in which the surfaces are saddle-shaped.
2. in roofing with sheet metal, a joint formed by bending the edge of one sheet over the turned-up edge of the other.

sad′dle·nōṣe, *n.* a nose with the bridge depressed.

sad′dle oys′tẽr, same as *saddle shell.*

sad′dlẽr, *n.* 1. one whose occupation is to make, repair, or sell saddles.
2. the harp seal.

sad′dle·rock, *n.* any large oyster. [Dial.]

sad′dle rọof, a roof that has two gables and one ridge.

sad′dlẽr·y, *n.*; *pl.* **sad′dlẽr·ieṣ,** 1. the materials for making saddles and harnesses; the articles usually offered for sale in a saddler's shop.
2. the trade, craft, or employment of a saddler.
3. a shop where saddles, bridles, etc. are sold.

sad′dle-shāped (-shāpt), *a.* having the shape of a saddle; specifically, (a) in botany, with the upper part rounded; (b) in geology, designating strata bent on each side of a mountain, without being broken on top.
saddle-shaped joint; same as *saddle joint.*

sad′dle shell, a shell having the shape of a saddle; a saddle oyster; any species of the genus *Anomia.*

sad′dle shōeṣ, flat-heeled sport shoes having a band of leather in a contrasting color across the instep: they are usually brown on white or black on white.

sad′dle sōap, a preparation for cleaning and softening leather, usually made of a mild soap and neat's-foot oil.

sad′dle stitch, a simple overcasting stitch, sometimes made with strips of leather.

sad′dle·tree, *n.* [ME. *sadeltre.*] 1. the frame of a saddle.
2. the North American tulip tree.

Sad·dū·çā′iç, *a.* pertaining to or characteristic of the Sadducees.

Sad·dū·cē′ăn, *a.* pertaining to or resembling the Sadducees or their doctrines.

Sad′dū·cee, *n.* any member of a strict sect of Jews at the time of Jesus that denied resurrection of the dead and the existence of angels and rejected those parts of the law handed down by oral tradition: opposed to the *Pharisees.*

Sad′dū·cee·iṣm, Sad′dū·ciṣm, *n.* the tenets of the Sadducees.

Sad′dū·cīze, *v.i.*; Sadducized, *pt., pp.*; Sadducizing, *ppr.* to become a Sadducee.

sädh (säd), *n.* [Anglo-Ind., from Sans. *sādhu*, pure.] of a Hindu holy man.

sä·dhḛ′ (sä-dā′ *or* tsä′di), *n.* [Heb. *tsādē.*] the eighteenth letter of the Hebrew alphabet.

sad′ī·ron (-ũrn), *n.* [*sad* (heavy) and *iron.*] a heavy flatiron.

sad′iṣm, *n.* [after Count Donatien de *Sade* (1740–1814), whose writings describe various sexual aberrations.]
1. the getting of sexual pleasure from dominating, mistreating, or hurting one's partner, physically or otherwise.
2. popularly, the getting of pleasure of any sort from mistreating or hurting another or others.
Distinguished from *masochism.*

sad′ist, *n.* a sadistic person.

sȧ·dist′iç, *a.* characterized by or pertaining to sadism.

sȧ·dist′iç·ăl·ly, *adv.* in a sadistic manner.

sad′ly, *adv.* 1. in a sad manner; sorrowfully; mournfully.
2. in ill health; poorly. [Dial.]
3. in a dark color; soberly. [Rare.]

sad′ness, *n.* 1. a sad state or condition.
2. a melancholy look; gloom of countenance. [Obs.]
3. seriousness; sedate gravity. [Obs.]
Syn.—sorrow, grief, distress, despondency.

sädr (säd′r), *n.* [Ar.] *Zizyphus lotus*, the lotus tree, whose berries are used as food by the Arabs of Barbary: also called *lote bush.*

sad sack, a soldier or other person who means well but is incompetent, ineffective, etc. and is consistently mistreated or in trouble. [Slang.]

sad tree, same as *night jasmine.*

saeç′ū·lăr, *a.* secular. [Rare.]

saeç′ū·lum, *n.*; *pl.* **saeç′ū·lȧ,** [L., a generation.] a long period of time; an age: also spelled *seculum.*

ṣaeng′ẽr·bụnd, *n.* [G.] an association of singers: also written *sängerbund.*

ṣaeng′ẽr·fest, *n.* [G.] a festival of German singers and singing societies.

sȧ·fä′ri, *n.*; *pl.* **sȧ·fä′riṣ,** [Swahili, from Ar. *safara*, to travel.]
1. a journey or hunting expedition, especially in eastern Africa.
2. the caravan of such an expedition.

sāfe, *a.*; *comp.* safer; *superl.* safest, [ME. *sauf,* from OFr. *sauf,* safe, from L. *salvus,* safe.]
 1. free from damage, danger, or injury; secure.
 2. having escaped danger or injury; unharmed.
 3. (a) giving protection; (b) involving no risk; (c) trustworthy.
 4. no longer dangerous; unable to cause trouble or damage; as, *safe* in jail.
 5. taking no risks; prudent; cautious: said of persons.
 6. in baseball, designating a batter or base runner who reaches a base without being put out.
 Syn.—secure, unendangered, sure, unharmful, protected, reliable.

sāfe, *n.* [earlier *save,* from *save,* v.]
 1. an air-cooled compartment for storing food; as, a meat *safe.*
 2. a locking container or box, usually of metal, in which to store valuables.
 3. any box in which articles are kept to protect them from dust, moths, water, etc.
 4. a piece of leather placed under a buckle, to prevent it from chafing.
 5. the smooth edge of a file.

sāfe, *v.t.* to render safe. [Obs.]

sāfe′-blōw″ẽr, *n.* a person who uses explosives to open and rob safes.

sāfe′-blōw″ing, *n.* the use of explosives to open safes for robbing them.

sāfe′-breāk″ẽr, *n.* a person who breaks open safes to rob them.

sāfe″-çon′duçt, *n.* [Fr. *sauf-conduit.*]
 1. permission to travel through foreign or enemy regions, protected against arrest or harm.
 2. a written pass giving such permission.
 3. a guard or convoy accompanying the holder of such a pass.

sāfe′-çŏn·duçt′, *v.t.* 1. to grant safe-conduct to.
 2. to escort or protect through hostile territory.

sāfe′-çrack″ẽr, *n.* a person who breaks open safes, as with a chisel, etc., and robs them.

sāfe′-çrack″iṅg, *n.* the breaking open and robbing of safes.

sāfe′-dē·poṣ′it box, a strong metal container for storing valuable papers, jewels, or keepsakes, as in a bank or safe-deposit company vault.

sāfe′-dē·poṣ′it cŏm′pȧ·ny, a business firm which provides a vault for the safekeeping of valuables.

sāfe′-edġed, *a.* having the edge blunt or otherwise fashioned for security against accident or injury; as, a *safe-edged* file.

sāfe′guärd (-gärd), *n.* [ME. and OFr. *sauvegarde.*] any person or thing that protects or guards against loss or injury; specifically, (a) a precaution or protective stipulation; (b) a permit or pass allowing safe passage; (c) a convoy or guard; (d) a mechanical contrivance for the prevention of accident.

sāfe′guärd, *v.t.* to guard; to protect.

safe hit, in baseball, a hit which enables the batter, unaided by fielding errors, to reach first base.

sāfe′keep′ing, *n.* the act of keeping or preserving in safety from injury or from escape; also, the state of being kept in safety.

sāfe′ly, *adv.* in a safe manner; securely.

sāfe′ness, *n.* the quality or condition of being safe; safety; as, the *safeness* of an undertaking.

safe pledġe, in law, surety for appearance at trial. [Obs.]

sāfe′ty, *n.*; *pl.* **sāfe′tieṣ,** [Fr. *sauveté,* from LL. *salvitas,* safety, from L. *salvus,* safe.]
 1. the quality or condition of being safe; freedom from danger, injury, or damage; security.
 2. any of certain devices for preventing accident.
 3. in baseball, a safe hit.
 4. in football, a play in which a player grounds the ball behind his own goal line when the ball was caused to pass the goal line by his own team: it scores as two points for the opponents: distinguished from *touchback.*

sāfe′ty, *a.* giving safety; reducing danger or harm.

sāfe′ty ärch, same as *discharging arch.*

sāfe′ty belt, 1. a life belt.
 2. a belt worn by telephone linesmen, window washers, etc. and attached, as to the telephone pole or window sill, to prevent falling.
 3. a belt securing a passenger, etc. in an airplane to his seat to protect against sudden bumps, as in landing.

sāfe′ty bī′cy·çle, the modern bicycle having wheels of equal diameter, as contrasted with the older form having one large and one small wheel.

sāfe′ty bōlt, a lock or bolt used to secure a door, gate, or window, and so situated and designed that it cannot be advantageously manipulated from the opposite side of the part to which it is fastened.

sāfe′ty buoy (boy), a life belt.

sāfe′ty çāġe, in mining, a hoisting cage provided with apparatus for preventing a fall when the rope or cable breaks.

sāfe′ty çatch, same as *safety bolt.*

sāfe′ty di·reçt′ŏr, a director of public safety, as in a city; also, a person in charge of the safety program of a factory.

sāfe′ty fūṣe, a long fuse that can be lighted at a distance from the explosive for increased safety.

sāfe′ty glȧss, 1. glass made by fastening together two sheets of glass with a transparent, plastic substance: it is shatterproof and is used for automobile windshields, etc.
 2. glass reinforced with wire.

sāfe′ty īs′lȧnd (ī′), a slightly raised concrete platform or a marked area in a street, where passengers may get on or off streetcars, buses, etc. in relative safety.

sāfe′ty lamp, 1. a miner's lamp in which a protective enclosure, as of wire gauze, surrounds the flame.
 2. any lamp constructed to avoid explosion, fire, etc.

WIRE GAUZE
GLASS
SAFETY LAMP

sāfe′ty lock, 1. a lock for a door, etc., which can be opened only by its own key, and which is designed to prevent picking.
 2. a safety catch on a firearm.

sāfe′ty match, a match which will ignite by friction on a specially prepared surface only.

sāfe′ty pin, a pin for fastening clothing, usually made of an elastic wire coiled and bent back upon itself, with the point at one end and a shield at the other to cover the point and prevent pricking or accidental unfastening when in use.

sāfe′ty plug, same as *fusible plug* under *fusible.*

sāfe′ty rā′zŏr, a razor with a detachable blade fitted into a holder provided with guards and fixed to the handle at an angle which minimizes the danger of cutting the skin.

sāfe′ty stop, any of several devices for stopping motion at some definite place or at a critical time, as (a) in an elevator or hoisting apparatus, a device which automatically prevents dropping when the cable or rope breaks; (b) in a firearm, a device for holding the hammer in a place where it cannot by accident explode the fulminate in the shell; (c) in a pulley, a latch or catch which prevents a sheave or a rope from moving in the wrong direction; (d) in a spinning machine and the like, a device for arresting motion in case of breakage of a sliver, yarn, or thread.

sāfe′ty valve, 1. an automatic valve for a steam boiler, etc., which opens and releases steam if the pressure becomes excessive. The form and construction of safety valves are

Fig. 1.

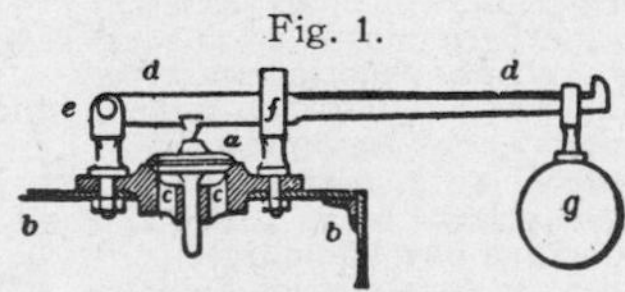

LEVER SAFETY VALVE

various, but their principle is the same: that of opposing the pressure within the boiler by such a force as will yield before it reaches the point of danger, and permit the steam to escape. The most simple kind of safety valve is that in which a weight is placed directly over a steam-tight plate, fitted to an aperture in the boiler. When, however, the pressure is high this form becomes inconvenient, and the lever safety valve is adopted. This form is represented in fig. 1, where *a* is the valve, fitted to move vertically, and guided by a stem passing through the seat; *b,* the boiler; *c,* the valve seat (the same letters indicate the corresponding parts in fig. 2); *d,* the lever, working upon a fixed center at *e,* and pressing upon the valve by a steel point; *f* is a guide for the lever, and *g* a weight which may be adjusted to any distance from the center, according to the pressure required. In locomotive engines, where the lever and weight would occupy too much space, it is usual to adopt the spring safety valve, one form of which is shown in fig. 2. A series of bent springs, *h h h,* are placed alternately in opposite directions, their extremities sliding upon the rods *i i,* and are forced down upon the valve *a* by means of a crossbar *k,* which may be adjusted by means of the nut so as to give the right pressure upon the valve.

Fig. 2.

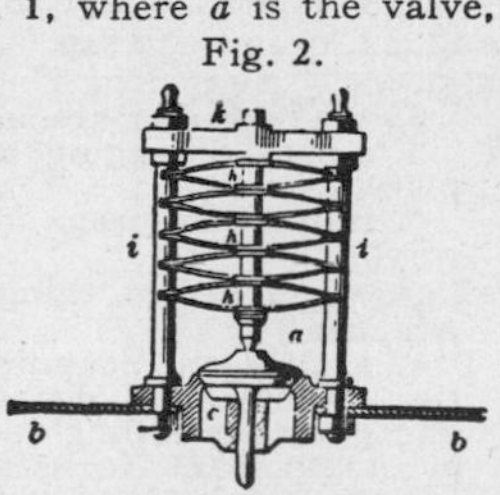

SPRING SAFETY VALVE

 2. anything which serves as an outlet for the release of strong emotion, excess energy, anxiety, etc.

sāfe′ty zōne, a safety island.

saf′fi·ăn, *n.* [Russ. *safĭyanŭ,* morocco, saffian.] a leather of Oriental origin, made from goatskins or sheepskins, and dyed in bright colors.

saf′flŏr·īte, *n.* [G. *safflor,* safflower, and *-ite.*] in mineralogy, a cobalt arsenide.

saf′flōw, *n.* the safflower. [Obs.]

saf′flow·ẽr, *n.* [D. *saffloer*; OFr. *saffleur*; It. *saffiore*; influenced in form by *flower.*] false saffron, a composite plant, *Carthamus tinctorius,* cultivated in China, India, Egypt, and also in the south of Europe, on account of its large, orange flowers which are dried for use as a drug and dyestuff; also, the dyestuff and drug prepared from the flowers.

SAFFLOWER (*Carthamus tinctorius*)

saf′frŏn, *n.* [Fr. *safran,* from Ar. *za'farân.*]
 1. a low ornamental plant, *Crocus sativus,* having large crocuslike flowers of a purple color.
 2. the dried orange-colored stigmas of the flowers of this plant, used as a dye, seasoning, and medicine.
 3. orange yellow.
 bastard (or *false*) *saffron*; the safflower.

saf′frŏn, *a.* orange-yellow.

saf′frŏn, *v.t.* to color or flavor with saffron. [Rare.]

saf′frŏn·wood, *n.* a tree, *Elæodendron croceum,* of South Africa, having a yellowish wood; also, this wood.

saf′frŏn·y, *a.* having the color of saffron.

saf′frŏn yel′lōw, a deep orange-yellow color.

saf′rȧ·nīne, saf′rȧ·nin, *n.* [Fr. *safran,* saffron, and *-ine.*]
 1. a yellowish-red aniline dye, $C_{20}H_{19}N_4Cl$, or any of several dyes closely related in structure to this.
 2. any mixture of the various salts of the safranine dyes, used in dyeing textiles and as a stain in microscopy.

SAFFRON (*Crocus sativus*)

saf′rōle, saf′rōl, *n.* [Fr. *safran,* saffron, and *-ol.*] a clear, colorless oil, $C_{10}H_{10}O_2$, found in sassafras oil, camphor wood, etc., and used in perfumes.

sag, *v.i.*; sagged, *pt., pp.*; sagging, *ppr.* [ME. *saggen*; prob. from ON. nautical language.]
 1. to sink, bend, or curve, especially in the middle, from weight or pressure.
 2. to hang down unevenly or loosely.

3. to lose firmness or strength; to weaken through weariness, age, etc.; to droop.
4. to decline in price or value.
5. in nautical usage, to drift.

sag, *v.t.* to cause to sag.

sag, *n.* 1. a sagging.
2. the degree or amount of sagging.
3. a place of sagging; a sunken or depressed place.
4. in nautical usage, drift to leeward; leeway.

sä′gȧ, *n.* [ON, *saga*, thing said, story; akin to AS. *sagu.*]
1. a medieval Scandinavian story of battles, customs, and legends, narrated in prose and generally telling the traditional history of an important Norse family.
2. any long story of adventure or heroic deeds.

sȧ·gā′cious, *a.* [L. *sagax, sagacis*, wise, foreseeing; akin to *sagire*, to perceive readily.]
1. keenly perceptive or discerning; shrewd; farsighted in judgment.
2. having a keen sense of smell. [Archaic.]
Syn.—acute, discerning, intelligent, judicious, wise.

sȧ·gā′cious·ly, *adv.* in a sagacious manner.

sȧ·gā′cious·ness, *n.* the quality of being sagacious.

sȧ·gac′i·ty, *n.*; *pl.* **sȧ·gac′i·tieṣ,** [Fr. *sagacité*; L. *sagacitas (-tatis)*, sagaciousness, from *sagax, sagacis*, sagacious.] quality or instance of being sagacious; quickness or acuteness of discernment or penetration and soundness of judgment; penetrating intelligence.

Sagacity finds out the intermediate ideas, to discover what connection there is in each link of the chain. —Locke.

Syn.—acumen, penetration, judgment, shrewdness.

sa·ga·mi·té′ (sȧ-gä-mē-tā′), *n.* [Algonguian.] a kind of gruel or mush made by boiling coarse hominy.

sag′ȧ·mōre, *n.* [Am. Ind.] a chief of second rank among some tribes of American Indians: sometimes equivalent to *sachem.*

sä′gȧ nov′el, a long rambling chronicle novel telling the story of several generations of a family.

sag′ȧ·pen, *n.* sagapenum. [Obs.]

sag·ȧ·pē′num, *n.* [L.Gr. *sagapenon*, a gum used as medicine.] a fetid gum resin obtained from the umbelliferous plant *Ferula persica.*

sag′ȧ·thy, *n.* [Fr. *sagatis.*] a lightweight serge fabric.

sāġe, *n.* [OFr. *sauge*, from L. *salvia*, sage, from *salvus*, safe, sound; on account of the reputed healing virtues of the plant.]
1. a perennial plant, *Salvia officinalis*, of the mint family, having gray-green leaves which are used for flavoring.
2. any related plant.
3. sagebrush.

sāġe, *a.*; *comp.* sager; *superl.* sagest, [OFr. *saige*, from hyp. LL. *sapius*, from L. *sapiens*, wise, orig. ppr. of *sapere*, to know, taste.]
1. wise, perceptive, and discerning.
2. based upon wisdom; showing judgment and discernment; as, a *sage* comment.
3. grave or solemn. [Obs.]
Syn.—sagacious, judicious, wise, prudent.

sāġe, *n.* 1. a very wise man.
2. a man, usually an old man, venerated and respected for his wisdom, experience, and judgment.

sāġe ap′ple, a gall or swelling on a species of sage, caused by the puncture of an insect, *Synips salviæ.*

sāġe′brush, *n.* 1. any low irregular shrub of the genus *Artemisia* such as that found in abundance on the western plains of the United States, with small white or yellow flowers and a sagelike odor.
2. a tract of land or section of country covered by a growth of sagebrush.

sāġe′bush, *n.* same as *sagebrush.*

sāġe çock, a male sage grouse.

sāġe green, a dull grayish green.

sāġe grouse, a large grouse, *Centrocercus urophasianus*, resembling the prairie fowl, but much larger. It is found on the western plains of the United States and feeds on the leaves of the sagebrush.

sāġe hãre, a sage rabbit.

sāġe hen, the female of the sage grouse.

sāġe′ly, *adv.* in a sage manner; with just discernment and prudence.

sä′ġen (-zhen), *n.* [Russ. *sazhenī.*] a Russian measure of about seven English feet.

sȧ·ġēne′, *n.* [L. *sagena.*] a fishnet; a seine.

sāġe′ness, *n.* the quality of being sage; sagacity.

saġ′en·īte, *n.* [Fr. *sagenite*; L. *sagena*; G. *sagēnē*, a large dragnet, and *-ite.*] acicular rutile, or red oxide of titanium. The acicular crystals cross each other, giving a reticulated appearance, hence the name.

saġ·e·nit′iç, *a.* containing acicular crystals of rutile, tourmaline, actinolite, and the like: applied to quartz.

sāġe rab′bit, a species of rabbit that lives among the sagebrush in the arid western regions of North America.

Saġ·e·rē′ti·ȧ, *n.* [named after Augustin *Sageret* (1763–1852), Fr. agriculturist.] a genus of shrubs of the buckthorn family consisting of about ten species, found in Asia and America. They bear an edible fruit, and the oblong leaves of some of the species are used as a substitute for tea.

sāġe′rōṣe, *n.* 1. the holly rose, *Turnera ulmifolia.*
2. any rockrose of the genus *Sistus.*

sāġe spar′rōw, any sparrow of the genus *Amphispiza* that lives among the sage brush on the arid plains of western North America.

sāġe thrash′ẽr, a songbird, *Oreoscoptes montanus*, that lives in the sagebrush of western North America.

sāġe tree, a rubiaceous shrub of Australia.

sāġe wil′lōw, a shrubby species of downy tufted willow found in dry and sandy plains in the northern and eastern United States.

sāġe′wood, *n.* same as *sagebrush.*

sag′gẽr, sag′gȧr, *n.* [contr. of *safeguard.*]
1. a cylindrical case of fire clay, in which fine stoneware is enclosed while being baked in the kiln: also called *saggard.*
2. the clay used in making these cases.

sag′gẽr, sag′gȧr, *v.t.* in ceramics, to bake in a sagger.

sag′ging, *n.* a bending or sinking in consequence of the weight.

Sȧ·ġī′nȧ, *n.* a genus of plants including the pearlwort.

saġ′i·nāte, *v.t.*; saginated, *pt., pp.*; saginating, *ppr.* to pamper; to glut; to fatten. [Rare.]

saġ·i·nā′tion, *n.* [L. *saginatio (-onis)*, a fattening, from *saginatus*, pp. of *saginare*, to stuff.] the act of fattening, or state of being fattened. [Rare.]

Sȧ·ġit′tȧ, *n.* [L., an arrow.]
1. in astronomy, the Arrow, one of the small northern constellations.
2. in zoology, a genus of annelids of transparent, marine form, the type of the *Chætognatha.*
3. [s–] in architecture, the keystone of an arch. [Rare.]
4. [s–] in zoology, one of the otoliths in the ear of a fish.

saġ′it·tăl, *a.* [Mod. L. *sagittalis*, from L. *sagitta*, an arrow.]
1. of or like an arrow or arrowhead.
2. in anatomy, (a) designating or of the suture between the two parietal bones along the length of the skull; (b) designating, of, or in the longitudinal plane of this suture, regarded as dividing the body into right and left halves; (c) of or in any plane parallel to this.

Saġ·it·tā′ri·ȧ, *n.* [from L. *sagitta*, an arrow, the leaves resembling an arrowhead.] a genus of plants, found in the warm and temperate parts of the globe: *Sagittaria sagittifolia* is the common arrowhead of England.

Saġ·it·tā′ri·us, *n.* [L., an archer.]
1. a southern constellation supposedly outlining a centaur shooting an arrow.
2. the ninth sign of the zodiac, which the sun enters about November 23.

saġ′it·tăr·y, *n.*; *pl.* **saġ′it·tăr·ieṣ,** 1. a centaur, a mythical being half man, half horse, armed with a bow and quiver.
2. [S–] the constellation Sagittarius.

saġ′it·tăr·y, *a.* 1. of an arrow or archery.
2. like an arrow.

saġ′it·tāte, *a.* in botany and zoology, shaped like the head of an arrow; triangular, hollowed at the base, with angles at the hinder part.

SAGITTATE LEAF

saġ′it·tā·ted, *a.* shaped like an arrow; sagittate.

sȧ·ġit′ti·fọrm, *a.* sagittate.

saġ′it·tō·cyst, *n.* [L. *sagitta*, an arrow, and Gr. *kystis*, bladder.] a defensive cell, found in certain *Turbellaria*, containing a small rodlike structure which can be extended.

saġ′it·toid, *a.* pertaining to or resembling *Sagitta* or allied genera.

sā′gō, *n.*; *pl.* **sā′gōṣ,** [Malay *sāgū.*]
1. a kind of starch prepared from the pith of certain palm trees, used in making puddings, etc.
2. any of the varieties of palm from which it is obtained.

sā′gō pälm, either of two palms of the East Indies belonging to the genus *Metroxylon*; the spineless sago palm, *Metroxylon læva* and the prickly sago palm *Metroxylon rumphii*; also, any of a number of other palm trees yielding sago.

SAGO PALM (*Metroxylon læva*)

sā′gō plant, the wake-robin, *Arum maculatum.*

sā′gō spleen, [from the corpuscles looking like grains of sago.] a diseased condition of the spleen characterized by an enlargement of the Malpighian corpuscles.

sā′gō tree, same as *coontie.*

sȧ·guä′rō, *n.*; *pl.* **sȧ·guä′rōṣ,** [Sp., from the Piman native name.] a giant cactus *Sereus giganteus*, with a thick, spiny stem and white flowers: it is found in Mexico and Central America.

sag′uin (-win), *n.* the marmoset: also written *sagoin* and *sogouin.*

sā′gum, *n.* [L.] the military cloak of the ancient Romans.

sā′ġy, *a.*; *comp.* sagier; *superl.* sagiest, full of sage; seasoned with sage.

sä′hib, sä′heb (sä′ib), *n.* [Hind., from Ar. *sāhib*, lord, master.] master; sir: the title used, until recently, in India by the natives, in speaking to or of Europeans.

sä′hi·bȧh, *n.* mistress; lady: feminine of *sahib.*

säh′līte, *n.* same as *salite.*

sä′ï, *n.* [Braz.] a long-tailed South American monkey; a capuchin.

sāi′bling, *n.* [Dial. G.] the European char, *Salvelinus alpinus*: also called *Bavarian char.*

sä′iç, *n.* [Fr. *saïque*; Turk. *shāïka.*] a kind of ketch, common in the Levant, without a topgallantsail or mizzen topsail.

said (sed), *a.* aforesaid; before mentioned: used chiefly in legal phraseology; as, the *said* defendant.

said, *v.* past tense and past participle of *say.*

sāi′gȧ, *n.* [Russ, *saïga*, antelope.] a species of antelope, *Colus* or *Antilope saiga*, found on the steppes of Russia and on the Russian borders of Asia. The nose is of peculiar structure, the openings being very large and covered by a soft cartilaginous arch.

sāil, *n.* [AS. *segel, segl*, a sail; akin to G. and Sw. *segel.*]
1. any of the shaped sheets of canvas or other strong material spread to catch or deflect the wind, by means of which some vessels and some land vehicles are driven forward.
2. sails collectively.
3. a sailing vessel or vessels.
4. a short or long trip in any vessel.
5. anything like a sail, as an arm of a windmill.
in sail; with sails set.
shoulder-of-mutton sail; a triangular sail used chiefly to set on a boat's mast.
to loose sails; to unfurl the sails.
to make sail; (a) to extend an additional quantity of sail; (b) to begin a trip by water.

to set sail; to hoist the sails in preparation for departure; hence, to begin a voyage.

to shorten sail; to reduce the extent of sail.

to strike sail; (a) to lower the sails suddenly, as in saluting, or in sudden gusts of wind; (b) to abate show or pomp.

SAILS ON A FULL-RIGGED SHIP

1. flying jib; 2. jib; 3. fore-topmast staysail; 4. foresail; 5. lower fore-topsail; 6. upper fore-topsail; 7. fore-topgallant sail; 8. foreroyal; 9. fore-skysail; 10. lower studding sail; 11. fore-topmast studding sail; 12. fore-topgallant studding sail; 13. foreroyal studding sail; 14. main staysail; 15. main-topmast staysail; 16. main-topgallant staysail; 17. main-royal staysail; 18. mainsail; 19. lower main topsail; 20. upper main topsail; 21. main-topgallant sail; 22. main royal; 23. main skysail; 24. main-topmast studding sail; 25. main-topgallant studding sail; 26. main-royal studding sail; 27. mizzen staysail; 28. mizzen-topmast staysail; 29. mizzen-topgallant staysail; 30. mizzen-royal staysail; 31. mizzen sail; 32. lower mizzen topsail; 33. upper mizzen topsail; 34. mizzen-topgallant sail; 35. mizzen royal; 36. mizzen skysail; 37. spanker

to take in sail; to lower sails, either at the end of a voyage or to reduce the area of sail set.

under sail; with the sails set; sailing.

sāil, *v.i.*; sailed, *pt.*, *pp.*; sailing, *ppr.* [ME. *seilen*; AS. *seglian*, from the noun.]

1. to be moved forward by means of a sail or sails, or by mechanical means such as a propeller.

2. to move upon or travel by water: said of a vessel or its passengers.

3. to begin a trip by water: said of a vessel or its passengers.

4. to glide, float, or move steadily through the air.

5. to move smoothly and with dignity, like a ship in full sail.

6. to pass quickly. [Colloq.]

7. to move vigorously into action (with *in*); as, he *sailed in* and finished the job. [Colloq.]

sāil, *v.t.* 1. to move through or upon (water or a body of water) in a boat or ship; as, he *sails* Lake Erie.

2. to handle, steer, or manage (a boat or ship).

3. to guide through water according to a compass, charts, etc.; to navigate.

sāil′ȧ·ble, *a.* navigable; that can be navigated.

sāil′bōat, *n.* a boat having a sail or sails by means of which it is propelled.

sāil bŭr′tŏn, a tackle for hoisting sails aloft for bending.

sāil′cloth, *n.* 1. long-fibered canvas or other cloth used in making sails.

2. heavy textile material like that used in making sails.

3. a piece of such material used as a covering, etc.

sāil′ẽr, *n.* 1. a sailor. [Obs.]

2. a ship or other vessel, with reference to its speed or manner of sailing; as, a heavy *sailer*, a fast *sailer*, a prime *sailer*.

sāil′fish, *n.*; *pl.* **sāil′fish** or **sāil′fish·eṣ**, 1. the basking shark, *Selache maximus*: so called from its habit of swimming on the surface of the water with its dorsal fin exposed, somewhat like the sail of a ship.

2. any of a group of large tropical marine fishes related to the swordfish, but with scales, teeth, and a large saillike dorsal fin in addition to the sword-shaped upper jaw.

sāil flūke, the whiff: a name used in the Orkney Islands.

sāil′ing, *n.* 1. the act of a thing or person that sails.

2. the art of navigation.

3. progression, in terms of speed or manner, of a vessel.

4. the start of a vessel or person on a trip by water.

sāil′ing, *a.* 1. driven forward by the action of wind on sails.

2. concerned with ships and shipping; as, *sailing* orders.

sāil′ing más′tẽr, the navigating officer of a vessel; in the United States Navy, formerly, a commissioned officer, usually with the rank of lieutenant, who has charge of the navigation of the vessel; a navigator.

sāil′less, *a.* without sails.

sāil loft, a loft or place where sails are cut out and made.

sāil′măk″ẽr, *n.* 1. one whose occupation is to make sails.

2. in the United States Navy, formerly, a warrant officer in charge of the repairing and altering of sails.

sāil′măk″ing, *n.* the art or work of making sails.

sāil′ŏr, *n.* 1. a person who makes his living by sailing; a mariner; seaman.

2. (a) an enlisted man in the navy; (b) any person in the navy.

3. a person sailing on a vessel, with reference to susceptibility to seasickness; as, he is a good *sailor*.

4. a straw hat with a shallow, flat crown and flat brim.

sāil′ŏr, *a.* like a sailor's; as, a boy's *sailor* suit.

sāil′ŏr fish, a sailfish of the genus *Histiophorus*.

sāil′ŏr·ing, *n.* the work and life of a sailor.

sāil′ŏr·ly, *a.* like, suited for, or characteristic of sailors.

sāil′ŏr·măn, *n.*; *pl.* **sāil′ŏr·men**, a seaman; a sailor.

sāil′ŏr plant, the strawberry geranium or beefsteak plant.

sāil′ŏr′ṣ-choice′, *n.*; *pl.* **sāil′ŏr′ṣ-choice′**, 1. a small porgy.

2. a pigfish.

sāil′ŏrṣ knot (not), any of a number of knots used by sailors.

sāil′y, *a.* like a sail. [Rare.]

sāil yärd, the yard or spar on which sails are extended.

sāim, *n.* lard; fat. [Dial.]

saī′mi·ri (sī′), *n.* [S. Am.] a squirrel monkey of the genus *Chrysothrix*.

sāin, *v.* obsolete past participle of *say*.

sāin, *v.t.* [ME. *sainen*, *signen*; AS. *segnian*; L. *signare*, to mark, to sign, from *signum*, sign.]

1. to make the sign of the cross on or over. [Archaic or Dial.]

2. to bless, as a protection against evil. [Archaic or Dial.]

3. to protect by prayer. [Archaic or Dial.]

sāin′foin, *n.* [Fr. *sainfoin*, from *sain*, wholesome, and *foin*, hay.]

1. cockshead, a perennial plant, *Onobrychis sativa*, cultivated in Europe as a forage plant: also written *saintfoin*.

2. a tick trefoil, *Desmodium canadense*, found in Canada.

sāint, *a.* holy; sacred; blessed; as, *Saint* Sepulchre.

sāint, *n.* [Fr., from L. *sanctus*, holy, consecrated.]

1. a holy person.

2. a person who is exceptionally meek, charitable, patient, etc.

3. [S-] a member of any of certain religious groups calling themselves *Saints*.

4. in certain churches, a person officially recognized as having lived an exceptionally holy life, and thus as being in heaven and capable of interceding for sinners; a canonized person.

Saint Agnes's Eve; the night of January 20, when a girl was supposed to have a revelation of her future husband if she performed certain superstitious rites.

Saint Anthony's cross; a cross shaped like the Greek letter *tau* (T).

Saint Bernard; a large, reddish-brown and white dog of a breed kept by the monks of the hospice of the Great St. Bernard Pass, in the Swiss Alps, trained to look for and rescue travelers in the snow.

Saint Patrick's Day; March 17, observed by the Irish in honor of the patron saint of Ireland.

Saint Valentine's Day; February 14, observed in honor of a martyr of the third century: the customary sending of valentines, candy, etc. to sweethearts on this day is not connected with the saint.

St.-Agnes's-flower; the snowflake, *Leucoium vernum*.

St. Andrew's cross; a cross having the shape of the letter X; hence, in botany, a shrub the petals of which resemble St. Andrew's cross.

St. Andrew's day; November 30, observed in honor of the patron saint of Scotland.

St. Anthony's fire; erysipelas.

St.-Anthony's-nut; the pignut, *Bunium flexuosum*.

St.-Anthony's-rape or-*turnip*; the bulbous crowfoot, a food for swine.

St. Augustine grass; a coarse creeping grass of Florida, *Stenotaphrum americanum*, used to bind drifting sand.

St.-Barnaby's-thistle; the *Centaurea solstitialis*, a plant found in cornfields in the south of England.

St.-Bruno's-lily; a lily, the *Paradisia liliastrum*, of the south of Europe.

St.-Catherine's-flower; ragged lady, *Nigella damascena*.

St.-Cuthbert's-duck; the eider duck, *Somateria mollissima*.

St.-Dabeoc's-heath; a heath, *Dabœcia polifolia*, found in Ireland, France, and Spain.

St. Elmo's fire; an electric discharge, resembling a flame, which is sometimes seen at prominent points of a mast, etc. on a ship at sea.

St. George's cross; the Greek cross, used on the flag of Great Britain.

St. George's day; April 23, observed in honor of St. George, the patron saint of England.

St.-Ignatius's-bean; the seed of a large climbing shrub, of the *Loganiaceæ*, having properties similar to nux vomica.

St. James's Court; see *Court of St. James* under *court*.

St.-James's-flower; a trefoil of the Cape Verde Islands, *Lotus jacobæus*.

St.-James's-lily; the jacobaea lily.

St. James's Palace; the Tudor palace in London where the kings and queens of England lived from the time of Henry VIII to Victoria's accession in 1837.

St.-James's-wort; the *Senecio jacobæa*, a kind of ragwort.

St.-John's-bread; the carob bean.

St. John's evil; epilepsy.

St.-John's-wort; any of a number of related plants of the genus Hypericum, as the rose of Sharon, having yellow flowers with many stamens.

St.-Joseph's-lily; the common white lily.

St. Marks; a cathedral in Venice, first built in the ninth century and rebuilt at various times until the fifteenth century: it combines Roman, Gothic, and Byzantine architecture.

St.-Martin's-flower; an ornamental plant, *Alstræmeria pulchra*, of the amaryllis family, cultivated for its flowers.

St.-Martin's-herb; a mucilaginous tropical plant, *Sauvagesia erecta*, used for medicinal purposes.

St. Martin's summer; the mild damp season which sometimes prevails in England and southern Europe from November till about Christmas, due to the prevalence of southwesterly winds.

St. Patrick's cross; a St. Andrew's cross.

St. Paul's; a cathedral in London, designed by Sir Christopher Wren.

St. Peter's; a cathedral in Rome whose dome was constructed chiefly under the guidance of Michelangelo.

St. Peter's fish; the dory, *Zeus faber*.

St.-Peter's-wort; (a) any plant of the genus *Ascyrum*; (b) the *Hypericum quadrangulum*; (c) the cowslip.

St.-Peter's-wreath; see *Italian May* under *May*.

St. Vitus's dance; chorea, especially of children: also *St. Vitus' dance*.

sāint, *v.t.*; sainted, *pt.*, *pp.*; sainting, *ppr.* to canonize; to make a saint of.

sāint, *v.i.* to act with a show of piety. [Rare.]

sāint′dŏm, *n.* saintly character; also, the realm of saints. [Rare.]

sāint′ed, *a.* 1. canonized; enrolled among the saints.

2. entered into bliss; gone to heaven: a euphemism for *dead;* as, his *sainted* father. [Rare.]

3. holy; pious; as, a *sainted* king.

4. of, like, or suitable for a saint; saintly.

sāint′ess, *n.* a female saint. [Rare.]

sāint′foin, *n.* sainfoin. [Obs.]

sāint′hood, *n.* the status or rank of a saint; also, saints collectively.

sāint′ish, *a.* somewhat like a saint: used in irony. [Rare.]

sāint′iṣm, *n.* the character or quality of saints; sanctimoniousness. [Rare.]

sāint′līke, *a.* resembling a saint; saintly.

sāint′li·ness, *n.* the state or quality of being saintly.

sāint′ly, *a.*; *comp.* saintlier; *superl.* saintliest, like or suitable for a saint.

sāint·ol′ō·ġist, *n.* one versed in the history of saints; one who writes of saints. [Rare.]

sāints′ bell, same as *sanctus bell* under *sanctus*.

sāint′ship, *n.* the character or qualities of a saint. [Rare.]

Sāint-Sī·mō′ni·ăn, a follower of the Count de St.-Simon (1760–1825), who maintained that the principle of joint stock property and just division of the fruits of common labor among the members of society is the true remedy for the social evils which exist.

Sāint-Sī·mō′ni·ăn·iṣm, the doctrine or principles of the Saint-Simonians.

Sāint-Sī′mōn·iṣm, the system of socialism advocated by Count de St.-Simon.

sāir, *a.* and *adv.* sore. [Scot.]

saith (seth), *v.* archaic third person singular, present indicative of *say*.

Saī′vȧ, *n.* [Hind.] a worshiper of Siva.

Saī′viṣm, *n.* devotion to or worship of Siva.

sȧ·jēne′, *n.* same as *sagene*.

sāke, *n.* [AS. *sacu*, contention, strife, a cause or suit at law; akin to G. *sache*, suit at law, cause, affair, thing.]

1. motive; purpose; end; cause; as, for the *sake* of money.

2. advantage; behalf; benefit; account; as, for my *sake*.

sä′kē, *n.* [Japan.] a Japanese alcoholic beverage made from fermented rice.

sȧ·keen′, *n.* [native name.] the ibex or wild goat, *Capra sibirica*, of the Himalayas.

sā′kẽr, *n.* [Fr. *sacre*; Sp. *sacro*; Ar. *sagr*.]

1. a large falcon of southern Europe, used in falconry.

2. a small piece of artillery. [Obs.]

sä′ki, *n.* [S. Am.] any of several platyrhine monkeys which constitute the genus *Pithecia*, inhabiting South America: they have a bushy, nonprehensile tail.

sak′i·ẹh, sak′i·yẹh (-yā), *n.* [Ar.] a form of water wheel used in Egypt for raising water, as from a well, for irrigation purposes.

Sak′tȧ, Sak′tï, *n.* [Sans.] Shakti.

Sak′tiṣm, *n.* Shaktism.

sal, *n.* [Hind. *sāl*.] a tree of the East Indies, *Shorea robusta*, valued for its close-grained and durable timber.

sal, *n.* [L., salt.] in pharmacy, etc., salt.

sal absinthii; an impure potassium carbonate obtained from the ashes of wormwood.

sal acetosella; salt of sorrel.

sal aeratus; saleratus.

sal alembroth; a compound of corrosive sublimate and sal ammoniac.

sal ammoniac; ammonium chloride: so called because said to have been prepared originally from camel dung near the shrine of Jupiter *Ammon*: also written *sal-ammoniac*.

sal catharticus; Epsom salts.

sal culinarius; common table salt; sodium chloride.

sal de duobus; potassium sulfate: also called *sal duplicatum*.

sal enixum; acid potassium sulfate.

sal gemmæ; common rock salt.

sal soda; crystallized sodium carbonate: also written *salsoda*.

sal volatile; a mixture of ammonium bicarbonate and ammonium carbonate, especially in aromatic solution for use as smelling salts.

sȧ·läam′, sȧ·läm′, *n.* [Ar. *salām*, health, peace.]

1. an Oriental greeting or ceremonial compliment, made by bowing low with the palm of the right hand placed on the forehead.

2. an obeisance or respectful greeting.

sȧ·läam′, sȧ·läm′, *v.i.* to make a salaam.

sȧ·läam′, sȧ·läm′, *v.t.* to greet with a salaam.

sāl·ȧ·bil′i·ty, sāle·ȧ·bil′i·ty, *n.* the quality or condition of being salable; salableness.

sāl′ȧ·ble, sāle′ȧ·ble, *a.* that can be sold; marketable.

sāl′ȧ·ble·ness, *n.* salability.

sāl′ȧ·bly, *adv.* in a salable manner.

sȧ·lā′cious, *a.* [L. *salax*, *salacis*, salacious, from *salire*, to leap.]

1. lustful; lecherous.

2. pornographic; obscene.

sȧ·lā′cious·ly, *adv.* in a salacious manner.

sȧ·lā′cious·ness, sȧ·lac′i·ty, *n.* the quality or condition of being salacious.

sal′ȧd, *n.* [OFr. *salade*; Pr. *salada*; L. *salata*, pp. of *salare*, to salt, from *sal*, salt.]

1. a dish, usually cold, of sea food, chicken, eggs, raw or cooked fruits or vegetables, especially lettuce, etc., in various combinations, prepared with a dressing of oil, vinegar, and spices or mayonnaise, etc.

2. any green plant or herb used for such a dish or eaten raw; especially, [Dial.], lettuce.

3. a finely chopped or ground food, as egg, ham, or chicken, mixed with mayonnaise and served on a bed of lettuce or in a sandwich.

sal′ȧd bûr′net, the common European burnet, eaten as a salad in Italy.

sal′ȧd dāyṣ, [after Shakespeare, *Antony and Cleopatra*, I, v.] time of youth and inexperience.

sal′ȧd dress′ing, a preparation similar to a sauce, usually some combination of oil, vinegar, spices, or vegetable products, served on a salad or mixed with it.

sal′ȧd·ing, *n.* herbs and vegetables used for salads. [Brit.]

sal′ȧ·gāne, *n.* same as *salangane*.

sal′ăl, *n.* [Am. Ind.] an evergreen shrub which bears the salal berry.

sal′ăl ber′ry, the fruit of *Gaultheria shallon*, the salal of California and Oregon, about the size of a common grape, of a dark color and sweet flavor.

sȧ·läm′, *n.* same as *salaam*.

sal′ȧ·man·dẽr, *n.* [OFr. *salamandre*; L. and Gr. *salamandra*, salamander.]

1. a mythological reptile resembling the lizard, supposed to be able to endure or live in fire.

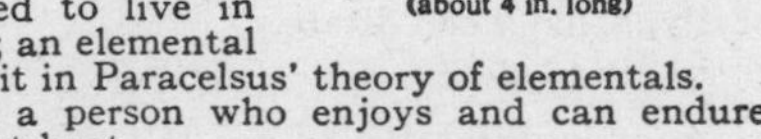
SALAMANDER (about 4 in. long)

2. a spirit supposed to live in fire; an elemental spirit in Paracelsus' theory of elementals.

3. a person who enjoys and can endure great heat.

4. any of various articles used in fire or able to withstand heat, as an iron poker, a plate for browning pastry, etc.

5. any of a group of scaleless, lizardlike animals related to the frogs and toads, with soft, moist skins and a tail.

Sal·ȧ·man′dri·dae, *n.pl.* a family of amphibians, comprising the salamanders.

Sal″ȧ·man·drī′nȧ, *n.* a genus of the *Salamandridæ*.

sal·ȧ·man′drine, *a.* pertaining to or resembling a salamander.

sal·ȧ·man′droid, *a.* pertaining to or having a resemblance to the salamanders.

sȧ·lä′mi, *n.* [It., pl., preserved meat, salt pork, from L. *sal*, salt.] a highly spiced, salted sausage, originally Italian.

sal am·mō′ni·aç, see *sal ammoniac* under *sal*.

sal′añ·gāne, *n.* [native name.] an Oriental swift or swallow whose nests are esteemed as a table delicacy by the Chinese.

sal′ȧ·ried (-rid), *a.* 1. receiving a salary; as, a *salaried* officer.

2. yielding a salary; as, a *salaried* office.

sal′ȧ·ry, *n.*; *pl.* **sal′ȧ·rieṣ,** [L. *salarium*, originally salt money, money given to buy salt, as part of the pay of Roman soldiers, hence, stipend, pay; from *sal*, salt.] a fixed payment at regular intervals for services, usually other than manual or mechanical: distinguished from *wages*, *fees*.

Syn.—recompense, compensation, pay, remuneration, stipend.

sal′ȧ·ry, *v.t.*; salaried, *pt.*, *pp.*; salarying, *ppr.* to pay a salary to; to put on a salary, as a clerk: chiefly in past participle.

sāle, *n.* [ME. *sale*; AS. *sala*; Ice. *sala*; Sw. *salu*, a sale, bargain.]

1. the act of selling; the exchange of property of any kind, or of some services, for an agreed sum of money or other valuable consideration; a contract made for the transfer of property.

2. opportunity or power of selling; market; demand; as, he went to market, but found no *sale* for his goods.

3. auction; public sale to the highest bidder.

4. a special offering of goods at prices lower than normal, or at bargain prices: such a sale is usually advertised, extending over a limited time only; as, a rummage *sale*.

bankruptcy sale; a sale caused by bankruptcy: see *sale*, sense 4.

bargain sale; a sale at which bargains are to be bought: same as *sale*, sense 4.

bill of sale; see under *bill*.

for sale or *on sale*; offered for purchase; to be sold.

liquidation sale; same as *bankruptcy sale*.

outlet sale; a bargain sale for the disposal of goods at the end of a season or a year, or before the close of a business.

regular sale; on the stock exchange, a sale of stock made for delivery on the following day.

removal sale; a bargain sale occasioned by the removal of the place of business, the manager or owner seeking to dispose of as much goods as possible before moving.

sāle·ȧ·bil′i·ty, sāle′ȧ·ble, etc., same as *salability*, etc.

sal′eb, *n.* in medicine, same as *salep*.

sal·ē·bros′i·ty, *n.* the quality or state of being salebrous. [Obs.]

sal′ē·brous, *a.* [L. *salebrosus*, rugged, rough, uneven, from *salire*, to jump, leap.] rugged; uneven. [Obs.]

sȧ·lee′tȧh, *n.* [E. Ind.] in India, a soldier's bag for carrying bedding, etc. during a march.

sal′ep, *n.* [Fr.; Sp.; Ar. *saḥlab*.]

1. a diet drink, formerly prepared from the powdered roots of *Orchis mascula*, and sold to the working classes of London.

2. the dried tubers of various orchids, ground up and used as food.

sal·e·rā′tus, *n.* [Mod. L. *sal aeratus*, aerated salt.] sodium (or sometimes potassium) bicarbonate; baking soda, as used in cooking.

sāle′rōom, *n.* same as *salesroom*.

sāleṣ ā′ġen·cy, the office or offices of a sales agent; also, the commission of a sales agent.

sāleṣ ā′ġent, a representative of a manufacturing company, who contacts prospective customers within a certain territory, or who distributes for sale the product or products of his company: a sales agent frequently works on a commission basis.

sāleṣ ap·pēal′, 1. the quality of attracting customers and sales; as, your window displays always have *sales appeal*.

2. of sales talk, the quality of convincing the customer to buy; as, your talk has good *sales appeal*.

sāleṣ book, a book kept by a salesclerk for recording sales.

sāleṣ′çlẽrk, *n.* a person employed to sell goods in a store.

sāles fōrce, the body of salesclerks or agents in a company.

sāleṣ′girl, *n.* a saleslady.

sāleṣ′lā″dy, *n.*; *pl.* **sāleṣ′lā″dieṣ,** a girl or woman employed to sell goods, especially in a store. [Colloq.]

sāleṣ′măn, *n.*; *pl.* **sāleṣ′men,** a man who is employed to sell goods, either in a store or as a traveling agent or representative.

sāleṣ man′ȧ·ġẽr, one whose work is managing the sales or the sales force of a business concern, or of a certain division of the concern; as, he is the *sales manager* for this floor only.

sāleṣ′măn·ship, *n.* 1. the work of a salesman.

2. the condition of being a salesman.

3. ability or skill at selling.

sāleṣ nōte, a reminder, in writing, of the terms of a contract involving a sale of goods.

sāleṣ′pēo″ple, *n.pl.* salespersons.

sāleṣ′pẽr″sŏn, *n.*; *pl.* **sāleṣ′pẽr″sŏnṣ,** a person employed to sell goods, especially in a store.

sāleṣ rē·ṣist′ănce, 1. resistance of potential customers to efforts and inducements aimed at getting them to buy.

2. the conditions or circumstances which have an adverse effect on buying, preventing or restricting sales.

sāleṣ′rōom, *n.* a room in which goods are offered for sale.

sāleṣ′tạlk, *n.* 1. the persuasive talk of a salesman; especially, the arguments which he presents to his prospective customer.

2. any argument aimed at persuading one to do something.

sāleṣ tax, a tax levied on sales or on receipts from sales, usually added to the price by the seller.

sāleṣ′wom″ăn (-woom″), *n.*; *pl.* **sāleṣ′wom″en** (-wim″), a saleslady.

sāle′yärd, *n.* a large enclosed space, as a yard, in which cattle and other live stock are sold.

sāle′wŏrk, *n.* work or things made for sale; hence, work carelessly done.

Sā′li·ăn, *a.* of or pertaining to a tribe of Franks who settled on the Ijssel River, in the Netherlands, from the third to the middle of the fourth century A.D.

Sā′li·ăn, *n.* a Salian Frank.

sal′i·ąunce, *n.* sally; onslaught. [Obs.]

Sal′iç (*or* sā′lik), *a.* [OFr. and Fr. *Salique*, from LL. *Salii*, a tribe of Franks.]
1. of the Salian Franks.
2. of the Salic law.
Also *Salique.*

Sal·i·çā′cē·ae, *n.pl.* [LL.] same as *Salicineæ.*

sal·i·çā′ceous, *a.* pertaining to the *Salicineæ*; of the willow family of trees and shrubs, including the willows and poplars.

sal·i·cē′tum, *n.*; *pl.* **sal·i·cē′tumṣ, sal·i·cē′tȧ,** [L., from *salix*, a willow.] a place where willows are grown; a collection of willows.

sal′i·cin, *n.* [L. *salix* (*-icis*), a willow, and *-in.*] a bitter glucoside, $C_{13}H_{18}O_7$, in white, powdery crystals, obtained from the bark of certain willows and poplars. It is used in medicine as a tonic and to reduce fever.

Sal·i·cin′ē·ae, *n.pl.* [LL.] a family of trees or shrubs native to the northern districts of Europe, Asia, and America. Only two genera are included in the family, *Salix*, or willow, and *Populus*, or poplar.

sȧ·li′ciŏn·ăl (-lish′un-), *n.* [L. *salix* (*-icis*), a willow.] in music, an organ stop of soft and delicate quality, supposed to be similar in character to the withy pipe.

Sal′iç law, 1. a code of laws of Germanic tribes, including the Salian Franks; especially, the provision of this code excluding women from inheriting land.
2. the law excluding women from succeeding to the throne in the French and Spanish monarchies.
3. any law of similar purport.

sal′i·cyl, *n.* [*salic*in and *-yl.*] the supposed radical, $C_7H_5O_2$, of salicylic acid.

sal′i·cyl·ăl, *n.* a thin, oily compound contained in the flowers of the meadowsweet, and also obtained by oxidation from saligenin, salicin, etc.

sal′i·cyl·āte, *n.* any salt or ester of salicylic acid.

sal′i·cyl·ā·ted, *a.* containing or impregnated with salicylic acid.

sal·i·cyl′iç, *a.* [L. *salix*, a willow, and Gr. *hylē*, matter.] pertaining to, designating, or obtained from salicylic acid.

sal·i·cyl′iç ac′id, a white, crystalline compound, $C_6H_4(OH)COOH$, prepared from salicin or phenol and used as a food preservative and mild antiseptic, and, in the form of its salts, to treat rheumatism, relieve pain, etc.

sal′i·cyl·īde, sal′i·cyl·id, *n.* a white substance, $C_7H_4O_2$, the anhydride of salicylic acid.

sal′i·cyl·iṣm, *n.* the toxic effects of excessive dosage with salicylic acid or its salts.

sal·i·cyl′ous, *a.* pertaining to or obtained from salicin.

sā′li·ence (*or* sāl′yuns), *n.* 1. the state or quality of being salient.
2. a salient part, feature, detail, etc.

sā′li·en·cy, *n.*; *pl.* **sā′li·en·cieṣ,** salience.

sā′li·ent (*or* sāl′yunt), *a.* [L. *saliens* (*-entis*), ppr. of *salire*, to spring forth, leap.]
1. (a) leaping; jumping; capering; (b) gushing; jetting forth.
2. pointing outward; jutting; projecting, as an angle.
3. standing out from the rest; noticeable; conspicuous; prominent.
4. in heraldry, designating a lion or other beast in a leaping posture, with its forepaws in the dexter point, and its hind legs in the sinister base of the escutcheon.

A LION SALIENT

sā′li·ent, *n.* 1. the part of a battle line, trench, fort, etc. which projects farthest toward the enemy.
2. a salient angle, part, etc.

Sal·i·en′ti·ȧ (-shi-), *n.pl.* [LL.] an order of amphibians including frogs, toads, and tree toads.

sāl·i·en′ti·ăn (-shi- *or* -shăn), *a.* of or pertaining to the *Salientia*, a group of animals that live both on land and in water, with a broad body, no tail, and hind legs which are helpful in jumping.

sāl·i·en′ti·ăn, *n.* a member of the *Salientia*; a salientian animal.

sā′li·ent·ly, *adv.* in a salient manner.

sȧ·lif′ẽr·ous, *a.* [L. *sal*, salt, and *ferre*, to produce.] producing or containing salt; as, *saliferous* rock.

sal′i·fī·ȧ·ble, *a.* capable of combining with an acid to form a salt.

sal″i·fi·çā′tion, *n.* the act of salifying; the state of being salified.

sal′i·fȳ, *v.t.*; salified, *pt., pp.*; salifying, *ppr.* [L. *sal*, salt, and *facere*, to make.] to make salty; specifically, (a) to impregnate with salt; (b) to form a salt with; to convert into a salt; (c) to combine with a salt.

sȧ·lig′e·nin, *n.* a crystalline compound, $C_7H_8O_2$, produced from salicin by the action of acids and of emulsin.

sal′i·got, *n.* [OFr. *saligots*, water nuts.] a plant, the water chestnut.

Sā′li·ī, *n.pl.* [L.] in ancient Rome, priests of Mars or Quirinus, whose duty it was to invoke the god of war.

sȧ·lim′e·tẽr, *n.* an instrument for measuring the amount of salt present in any given solution.

sȧ·lī′nȧ, *n.* [Sp.] 1. a salt marsh, pond, or lake, not connected with the sea.
2. a saltworks.

sal·i·nā′tion, *n.* 1. the act of washing with salt water.
2. the state or quality of being salty.

sā′līne, *a.* [Fr. *salin*, from L. *sal*, salt.]
1. of, characteristic of, or containing common salt, or sodium chloride; salty.
2. of or containing any of the salts of the alkali metals or magnesium.

sā′līne, *n.* 1. a salt spring, lick, marsh, mine, etc.
2. any of the metallic salts, especially a salt of magnesium or of an alkali metal, often used in medicine as cathartics.
3. a saline solution, especially one that is isotonic, used in medical treatment or for biological experiments.

sā′līne·ness, *n.* same as *salinity.*

sal·i·nif′ẽr·ous, *a.* [L. *sal*, salt, and *ferre*, to produce.] same as *saliferous.*

sȧ·lin′i·fôrm, *a.* [L. *sal*, salt, and *-form.*] having the form, nature, or quality of salt.

sȧ·lin′i·ty, *n.* the quality, state, or degree of being saline; saltiness.

sal·i·nom′ē·tẽr, *n.* an instrument for measuring the amount of salt in a solution: also called *salt gauge.*

sal·i·nom′ē·try, *n.* the science of the use of the salinometer.

sȧ·lī′nō·ter·rēne′, *a.* [L. *sal*, salt, and *terrenus*, from *terra*, earth.] of, pertaining to, or composed of a compound of salt and earth.

sȧ·līn′ous, *a.* saline. [Obs.]

sal·i·pȳ′rin, *n.* a substance, $C_{18}H_{18}N_2O_4$, composed of salicylic acid and antipyrin.

Sȧ·lïque′ (-lēk′ *or* sal′ik), *a.* same as *Salic.*

sal·i·rē′tin, *n.* [*sali*genin, and Gr. *rhētinē*, resin.] a whitish or yellowish resinous compound obtained from saligenin which has been acted on by diluted acids.

Sal·is·bū′ri·ȧ, *n.* [after Richard Anthony *Salisbury* (1761–1829), an English botanist.] a genus of trees having but one species, the maidenhair tree or gingko tree.

Salis′bur·y steāk (sǫlz′ber″y stāk), Hamburg steak.

Sā′lish·ăn, *a.* designating or of an American Indian linguistic family of the northwestern United States and southwestern Canada, including Flathead and Coeur d'Alêne.

Sā′lish·ăn, *n.* the Salishan linguistic family.

sā′līte, *v.t.* to salt. [Obs.]

sā′līte, *n.* [so called from *Sala*, a town in Sweden.] a massive variety of pyroxene, of a dingy green color, which crystallizes in the monoclinic system.

sal′i·trăl, *n.* [Sp., from L. *sal*, salt, and *nitrum*, niter.] a swampy place where saltpeter and occasionally other salts occur.

sȧ·lī′vȧ, *n.* [L., spittle, saliva, slime; Gr. *sialon*, spittle.] the thin, watery, slightly viscid fluid secreted by the salivary glands: it serves as an aid to digestion by moistening and softening food, and contains an enzyme, ptyalin, which converts starch to maltose.

sȧ·lī′văl, *a.* salivary. [Rare.]

sal′i·vănt, *a.* [L. *salivans* (*-antis*), ppr. of *salivare*, to spit out, from *saliva*, spittle.] producing salivation.

sal′i·vănt, *n.* that which produces salivation; especially, a medicine used to increase the flow of saliva.

sal′i·vār·y, *a.* of, pertaining to, secreting, or conveying saliva; as, *salivary* ducts or canals.

sal′i·vāte, *v.t.*; salivated, *pt., pp.*; salivating, *ppr.* [L. *salivatus*, pp. of *salivare*, to spit out, salivate, from *saliva*, spittle.] to produce an excessive flow of saliva in.

sal′i·vāte, *v.i.* to secrete saliva.

sal·i·vā′tion, *n.* 1. the act or process of salivating.
2. an excessive flow of saliva, as because of mercurial poisoning.

sal′i·vā·tŏr, *n.* in medicine, any sbustance that stimulates the flow of saliva.

sȧ·lī′vous, *a.* pertaining to saliva; partaking of the nature of saliva.

Sā′lix, *n.* [LL., from L. *salix*, a willow.] the type genus of the *Salicaceæ*, or willow family.

sȧlle, *n.* [Fr.] a hall or room.

salle à man·ger′ (sȧl ȧ mäṅ-zhā′), [Fr.] a room for eating; a dining room.

sal′lee, sal′ly, *n.* any one of several Australian acacias.

sal′lee·măn, *n.*; *pl.* **sal′lee·men,** 1. a Moorish pirate.
2. in zoology, a pelagic hydrozoan, as *Velella vulgaris.*

sal′len·dẽrṣ, *n.pl.* [Fr. *solandres*, pl. of *solandre.*] a dry eruption on the hock of a horse.

sal′let, *n.* [OFr. *salade*; It. *celata*, from L. *cælata*, (*cassis*, helmet understood), engraved, chiseled, from *cælare*, to engrave: so called from the figures cut on it.] a light, rounded helmet with a projecting neckguard and, often, a visor, worn in the fifteenth century.

sal′let, *n.* salad. [Archaic and Dial.]

sal′lōw, *n.* [ME. *salhe, salwe*; AS. *sealh*, from same base as *sallow*, a.]
1. any of certain trees or low shrubs of the willow family with large spikes of flowers which appear before the leaves; goat willow.
2. a willow twig; an osier.
3. same as *sallee.*

sal′lōw, *a.*; *comp.* sallower; *superl.* sallowest, [AS. *salu, salowig, sealwe*, sallow, dark; Ice. *sölr*; D. *saluwe*; O.H.G. *salo*, dusky.] having a yellowish color; of a pale, sickly color, tinged with a dark yellow: said especially of the human skin or complexion.

sal′lōw, *v.t.* to make sallow.

sal′lōw·ish, *a.* slightly sallow.

sal′lōw·ness, *n.* a yellowish color; paleness, tinged with a dark yellow; as, *sallowness* of complexion.

sal′lōw thọrn, a thorny European shrub, *Hippophaë rhamnoides*, having small flowers and bright orange-colored berries.

sal′lōw·y, *a.* full of sallows (willows).

sal′ly, *n.*; *pl.* **sal′lieṣ,** [Fr. *saillie*, from *saillir*, to rush out, from L. *salire*, to leap.]
1. a sudden rushing forth, as of troops to attack besieging forces.
2. any sudden start into activity.
3. a quick witticism; a bright retort; a quip.
4. an excursion or unusual side trip; a jaunt.
5. an act of levity or wild gaiety; as, a *sally* of youth. [Rare.]

sal′ly, *v.i.*; sallied (-lid), *pt., pp.*; sallying, *ppr.* 1. to rush out suddenly, as troops from a fortified place to attack besiegers; to make a sally.
2. (a) to start suddenly; (b) to come or go out of doors; (c) to set out on a trip.
Used with *forth* or *out.*

sal′ly, *n.* 1. in botany, a sallow.
2. same as *sallee.*

sal′ly, *n.* [Ir.] 1. a stone fly.
2. the wren of Europe.

Sal′ly Lunn, [from *Sally Lunn*, a woman who made and sold these in Bath, England, about the end of the eighteenth century.] a kind of sweet bun or teacake, larger than a muffin. It is toasted and eaten hot with butter. Also *sally lunn.*

sal′ly·măn, *n.* same as *salleeman*, sense 2.

sal′ly pōrt, 1. in fortification, a postern gate, or a passage under ground from the inner to the outer works, to afford free egress to troops in making a sally, closed by massive gates when not in use.
2. a large port on each quarter of a fire ship, for the escape of the men into boats when the train is fired; also, a large port in an ironclad.

säl′mä, sälm (säm), *n.* in Malta, a unit of weight equal to 490 pounds.

sal·mȧ·gun'di, *n.* [Fr. *salmigondis*; It. *salame*, salt meat (from L. *sal*, salt), and *conditi*, L. *conditus*, seasoned, savory, pp. of *condire*, to pickle.]
 1. a mixture of chopped meat, eggs, etc. flavored with oil, vinegar, pepper, anchovies, and onions.
 2. a mixture; an olio or medley.

sal'mi (*or Fr.* sȧl-mē'), *n.* [Fr.] a highly seasoned dish of partly roasted game or fowl, stewed in wine: also spelled *salmis*.

sal'mi·aç, *n.* sal ammoniac.

sal'min (sal'min *or* -mēn), *n.* [L. *salmo*, salmon, and *-in.*] a nitrogenous substance found in the spermatozoa of salmon.

sal'mis (-mi *or Fr.* sȧl-mē'), *n.* [Fr.] same as *salmi*.

sal'moid, *a.* and *n.* same as *salmonoid*.

salm'ŏn (sam'un), *n.*; *pl.* **salm'ŏn** or **salm-ŏns**, [L. *salmo*, *salmonis*, lit., leaper, from *salire*, to leap.]
 1. any of several varieties of game and food fishes of the genus *Salmo* and related genera, found in the North Atlantic, with silver scales and flesh that is yellowish-pink when cooked; they live in salt water and spawn in fresh water, though some varieties are landlocked in lakes.
 2. one of several other fishes resembling or thought to resemble the true salmon, as the pike perch or jack salmon, the California yellowtail, the spotted weakfish, etc.
 3. the color of cooked salmon flesh; yellowish pink or pale red.
 black or *lake salmon*; the namaycush.
 humpback salmon; same as *dog salmon*.
 king salmon; the quinnat or chinook salmon.
 landlocked salmon; a species of the common salmon found in some lakes, having been prevented from making its way to the sea by various obstructions.

salm'ŏn, *a.* having a color like the cooked flesh of a salmon; pinkish-orange.

salm'ŏn·ber''ry, *n.*; *pl.* **salm'ŏn·ber''ries**, 1. a bramble with purple or pinkish flowers and orange-pink berries found in western North America.
 2. the berry.

salm'ŏn çloud, same as *Noah's ark*, sense d, under *Noah*.

salm'ŏn dis·ēase', a disease of dogs, foxes, etc. caused by eating salmon infested with cysts of flukes.

sal·mŏ·nel'lȧ, *n.*; *pl.* **sal·mŏ·nel'laē, sal·mŏ·nel'lȧ, sal·mŏ·nel'lȧs**, [Mod. L.: named after D. E. *Salmon*, Am. veterinarian.] any of a genus (*Salmonella*) of Gram-negative, rod-shaped bacilli that cause various diseases in man and domestic animals, including typhoid fever, food poisoning, etc.

sal·mŏ·nel·lō'sis, *n.* a disease caused by various strains of salmonella and characterized by fever, malaise, and intestinal disorders.

salm'ŏn·et, *n.* a little salmon; a samlet.

salm'ŏn fly, an artificial fly hook used in catching salmon.

salm'ŏn fry, a smolt.

salm'ŏn hook, a fishing pole or gaff used by the Indians of the Columbia River for gaffing salmon and other large fish.

sal'mŏn·id, *a.* and *n.* same as *salmonoid*.

salm'ŏn kill'ẽr, *Gasterosteus cataphractus*, a fish found in the Pacific near North America and northern Asia: it destroys young salmon.

salm'ŏn lad'dẽr, a fish ladder.

salm'ŏn louse, in zoology, any species of crustacean, particularly *Caligus piscinus*, that is parasitic upon the gills of salmon.

sal'mŏn·oid, *a.* [L. *salmo*, *salmonis*, salmon, and *-oid.*]
 1. like a salmon.
 2. pertaining to or characteristic of the *Salmonidæ*, a family of fishes including the salmon and trout.

sal'mŏn·oid, *n.* any species of the *Salmonidæ*; a salmonoid fish.

salm'ŏn pēal, a young salmon.

salm'ŏn pink, yellowish pink or pale red.

salm'ŏn pīpe, a certain apparatus for catching salmon.

salm'ŏn spēar, any implement used in spearing salmon, particularly that used in Scotland, called a leister.

salm'ŏn stāir, same as *salmon ladder*.

salm'ŏn trout, 1. the European sea trout, *Salmo trutta*, somewhat resembling the salmon, though smaller.
 2. the namaycush of America; a Great Lakes trout.
 3. any large trout resembling a salmon; specifically, the steelhead, *Salmo gairdneri*.

sal'ōl, *n.* [*sal*icylic and *-ol.*] a crystalline compound, $C_{13}H_{10}O_3$, composed of phenol salicylate, and used in medicine as an internal antiseptic.

Sȧ·lō'me (*or G.* zä'lō-mā), *n.* 1. in the Bible, the daughter of Herodias: her dancing pleased Herod so much that he granted her request made at her mother's instigation, for the head of John the Baptist: Matt. xiv. 8.
 2. (a) a play (1894) written in French by Oscar Wilde, based on the story of Salome; (b) a one-act opera (1905) by Richard Strauss, based on this play.

sȧ·lom'e·tẽr, *n.* same as *salinometer*.

sȧ·lom'e·try, *n.* same as *salinometry*.

sȧ·lon' (*or Fr.* sȧ-lọṅ'), *n.*; *pl.* **sȧ·lons'** (*or Fr.* -lọṅ'), [Fr.]
 1. a large reception hall or room for receiving guests, especially a public room in a hotel or on a ship; a saloon.
 2. a drawing room of a private home in French-speaking countries.
 3. a regular gathering of distinguished guests such as might meet in a drawing room; especially, a meeting of literary or artistic people in a celebrity's home.
 4. a room or gallery for the exhibition of paintings or other works of art.
 5. an exhibition of works of art; especially, [S-] an annual art show of the work of living French artists, held in Paris.

sȧ·loon', *n.* [Fr. *salon*, from LL. *sala*, a hall.]
 1. any large room or hall designed for receptions, exhibitions, entertainments, etc.; specifically, the main social cabin of a passenger ship.
 2. any large public room used for some specific purpose; as, a dining *saloon*.
 3. a place where alcoholic drinks are sold to be drunk on the premises; a public bar.
 4. a sedan (automobile). [Brit.]

sȧ·loon'ist, *n.* 1. a saloon keeper.
 2. an advocate of saloons for drinking.

sȧ·loon'keep''ẽr, *n.* one who operates a saloon (sense 3).

sȧ·loop', *n.* a hot drink made from powdered salep or from sassafras.

sȧ·loop' bush, a shrub, *Rhagodia hastata*, found in Australia, belonging to the goosefoot family, used as a fodder plant for cattle.

Sȧ·lō'pi·ăn, *a.* of Shropshire or its people.

Sȧ·lō'pi·ăn, *n.* a native or inhabitant of Shropshire.

salp, *n.* [L. *salpa*, a kind of stockfish; Gr. *salpē.*] any tunicate of the genus *Salpa*.

Sal'pȧ, *n.* a genus of tunicate mollusks that float in the sea, protected by a transparent gelatinous coat. They have barrel-shaped bodies ringed with muscle and open at both ends.

sal'pi·ăn, sal'pid, *n.* in zoology, a tunicate of the genus *Salpa*.

sal'pi·çon, *n.* [Fr. and Sp., from *salpicar*, to besprinkle; Port., to corn, to powder; from *sal*, salt, and *picar*, to prick.] stuffing; chopped meat or bread, etc., used to stuff legs of veal.

sal'pi·fọrm, *a.* [L. *salpa*, salp, and *-form.*] in zoology, characteristic of or resembling the tunicates of the genus *Salpa*.

sal·pin·ġeç'tō·my, *n.*; *pl.* **sal·pin·ġeç'tō·mies**, [*salpingo-*, and *-ectomy.*] the severing or excising of a Fallopian tube, as in sterilizing a woman.

sal·pin'ġēs, *n.* plural of *salpinx*.

sal·pin'ġi·ăn, *a.* pertaining to a salpinx.

sal·pin·ġī'tis, *n.* in medicine, inflammation of the salpinx or syrinx.

sal·pin'gō-, [from Gr. *salpinx*, *salpingos*, a trumpet.] a combining form meaning: (a) *of a Fallopian tube*; (b) *of a Eustachian tube*: also, before a vowel, *salping-*.

sal'pinx, *n.*; *pl.* **sal·pin'ġēs**, [Gr., a trumpet.] in anatomy, a tube; particularly, the Eustachian tube or one of the Fallopian tubes.

sal'poid, *a.* [L. *salpa*, salp, and *-oid.*] relating to or characteristic of the genus *Salpa*.

sal'sȧ·fy̆, *n.* same as *salsify*.

sälse, *n.* [Fr., from L. *salsus*, pp. of *salire*, to salt, from *sal*, salt.] a mud volcano; an eruption of hot mud from a small hole, generally in volcanic regions and frequently accompanied by steam and gases at a high temperature.

sal'si·fy̆, *n.* [Fr. *salsifis*; It. *sassefrica.*] a plant with long, white, fleshy roots having an oysterlike flavor; an oyster plant.
 black salsify; same as *Viper's-grass*.

sal·sil'lȧ, *n.* [Sp., dim. of *salsa*, sauce.] any one of several plants producing edible tubers, and belonging to the genus *Bomarea*. One species, *Bomarea edulis*, is cultivated in the West Indies, its roots being eaten like the potato.

sal'sō-ac'id, *a.* [L. *salsus*, pp. of *salire*, to salt, and *acidus*, acid.] having a taste both acid and salt. [Rare.]

sal'sō'dȧ, *n.* sal soda.

sal sō'dȧ, crystallized sodium carbonate.

Sal'sō·lȧ, *n.* [LL., from L. *salsus*, pp. of *salire*, to salt down, from *sal*, salt.] a genus of plants of the goosefoot family, the saltworts, which grow on sandy seashores, the most widely known species of which is the prickly saltwort, *Salsola kali*.

sal·sō·lā'ceous, *a.* pertaining to or characteristic of the genus *Salsola*.

sal·sū'ġi·nōse, *a.* same as *salsuginous*.

sal·sū'ġi·nous, *a.* [L. *salsugo* (*-inis*), saltness.] growing in salty soil: said of plants.

sạlt, *n.* [AS. *sealt*, salt; a word found throughout the Indo-European languages, as Dan., Sw., Ice., and Goth. *salt*; D. *zout*; G. *salz*; W. *halen*; Gael. and Ir. *salann*; Russ. *soly*; L. *sal* (hence, Fr. *sel*; It. *sale*; Sp. *sal*); Gr. *hāls*; Sans. *sara.*]
 1. sodium chloride, NaCl, a white, crystalline substance with a characteristic taste, found in natural beds, in sea water, etc., and used for seasoning and preserving food, etc.
 2. a chemical compound derived from an acid by replacing hydrogen, wholly or partly, with a metal or an electropositive radical: the salt of an *-ous* acid is usually indicated by the suffix *-ite*, the salt of an *-ic* acid by the suffix *-ate*.
 3. [*pl.*] (a) mineral salts used in medicine, as for moving the bowels; (b) smelling salts.
 4. that which purifies, preserves, or corrects.
 5. that which gives a tang or piquancy to anything.
 6. sharp, pungent humor or wit.
 7. a veteran sailor; as, an old *salt*. [Colloq.]
 8. a saltcellar; as, an individual *salt*.
 9. taste; relish; smack. [Obs.]
 above (or *below*) *the salt*; according to an ancient custom, seated above (or below) the saltfoot at table.
 covenant of salt; a covenant or compact entered into at a sacrificial ceremony in which salt was used as a necessary element.
 ethereal salt; same as *compound ether* under *ether*.
 not worth one's salt; not worth one's wages, sustenance, etc.
 salt of Seignette; same as *Rochelle salt*.
 salt of the earth; [after Matt. v. 13.] any person or persons regarded as the finest, noblest, etc.
 salt of Venus; in old chemistry, copper sulfate.
 salt of wisdom; same as *sal alembroth* under *sal*.
 with a grain (or *pinch*) *of salt*; [Latinized as *cum grano salis.*] with allowance or reserve; skeptically.

sạlt, *a.* 1. containing salt.
 2. preserved with salt.
 3. tasting or smelling of salt.
 4. pungent; lively; witty.
 5. (a) flooded with salt water; (b) growing in salt water.
 salt bottom; a level piece of land covered with saline deposits. [Dial.]
 salt horse; salted beef.
 salt-water tailor; same as *bluefish*, sense 1.

sạlt, *v.t.*; salted, *pt.*, *pp.*; salting, *ppr.* 1. to sprinkle or season with salt; as, to *salt* fish, beef, or pork.
 2. to preserve with salt or in a salt solution.
 3. to treat with salt in chemical processes.
 4. to season or give tang to; as, he *salted* his conversation with wit.
 5. to give artificial value to; specifically, (a) to alter (books, prices, etc.) in order to give false value; (b) to scatter minerals or ores in (a mine), put oil in (a well), etc. in order to deceive prospective buyers.
 6. in photography, to treat (paper) for sensitizing with a solution of salt to cause decomposition of nitrate of silver.
 7. to give salt water to drink: a way of initiating formerly existing in English universities. [Old Slang.]
 to salt away (or *down*); (a) to preserve or

pack in salt or brine; (b) [Colloq.] to save or reserve (money, etc.).

to salt out; to separate (a dissolved substance) from a solution by adding salt.

sa̤lt, *v.i.* to deposit salt from a saline substance; as, the brine begins to *salt.*

sal'tănt, *a.* [L. *saltans* (*-antis*), ppr. of *saltare*, to leap.]

1. leaping; jumping; dancing.

2. in heraldry, springing forward; represented in a leaping position, as a cat, greyhound, or other small animal: distinguished from *salient*, which is applicable to large animals.

sal·tȧ·rel'lō, *n.* [It.] 1. a lively Italian dance with a hopping, skipping step.

2. the music for such a dance.

sal'tāte, *v.i.* to leap; to dance; to skip. [Rare.]

sal·tā'tion, *n.* [L. *saltatio* (*-onis*), a dancing, dance, from *saltatus*, pp. of *saltare*, to leap.]

1. a leaping, jumping, or dancing.

2. sudden change, movement, or development, as if by leaping.

3. a beating or palpitation; as, the *saltation* of the great artery.

4. in biology, mutation.

sȧl·tä'tō, *n.* [It.] in music, the act of making the bow rebound from the string, as in playing a violin.

Sal·tȧ·tō'ri·ȧ, *n.pl.* [LL., from L. *saltator*, a dancer.] a division of orthopterous insects, including grasshoppers, crickets, and locusts.

sal·tȧ·tō'ri·ăl, *a.* 1. of saltation.

2. in zoology, characterized by, given to, or formed for leaping.

3. of or pertaining to the *Saltatoria*.

sal·tȧ·tō'ri·ous, *a.* saltatory; adapted for or capable of leaping. [Rare.]

sal'tȧ·tō·ry, *a.* [L. *saltatorius*, pertaining to dancing.]

1. of, characterized by, adapted for, or pertaining to leaping or dancing.

2. proceeding by abrupt movements or changing by sudden variation.

saltatory evolution; a theory of evolution which holds that abrupt and marked variations occur with little change in intervening periods of reproduction.

saltatory spasm; a malady in which the patient makes, involuntarily, motions of jumping and hopping.

sa̤lt block, a saltern.

sa̤lt'bush, *n.* any one of various Australian plants, as *Atriplex nummularia*, of the goosefoot family.

sa̤lt ca̤ke, anhydrous sodium sulfate.

sa̤lt'ca̤t, *n.* a lump of salt; also, a mixture of gravel, salt, cumin seed, etc., used as food for pigeons.

sa̤lt'cel"lăr, *n.* [ME. *salt saler*; *salt*, salt, and Fr. *salière*, saltcellar, from L. *sal*, salt.] a small dish, or a container with a perforated top, for holding salt.

sa̤lt'ed, *a.* 1. sprinkled, seasoned, or preserved with salt.

2. experienced or proficient in some occupation, work, etc. [Colloq.]

3. rendered immune by previous attack; especially, immune from horse distemper by having had it previously. [Colloq.]

sa̤l'tee, *n.* [It. *soldi*, pl. of *soldo*, a small coin.] a penny. [Brit. Slang.]

sa̤lt'ẽr, *n.* 1. one who salts; especially, one who applies salt to cure fish, meat, etc.

2. one who sells or manufactures salt.

3. a salmon or trout ascending a stream from salt water. [Dial.]

säl·te̤·ret'tō, *n.* [It.] in music, a group of three notes with a dot after the first.

sa̤lt'ẽrn, *n.* [AS. *sealtærn*.] a salt works; a building or plot of ground in which salt is made by boiling or evaporation.

sa̤lt fish, a fish that has been salted.

sa̤lt'foot, *n.* a large saltcellar formerly placed midway on the dinner table to separate the noble guests from the inferior.

sa̤lt ga̤uġe, a salinometer.

sa̤lt'-green', *a.* green like the sea. [Rare.]

sal'tïer, *n.* same as *saltire.*

sal·tier'rȧ (-tyer'), *n.* [Mex. Sp., from Sp. *sal*, salt, and *tierra*, land, soil.] a salt basin formed by the evaporation of a salt lake.

sal'tïer·wīse, *adv.* same as *saltirewise.*

Sal·tig'rȧ·dae, *n.pl.* a division of leaping spiders with large eyes.

sal'ti·grāde, *a.* [L. *saltus*, a leap, and *gradi*, to walk.]

1. having legs adapted for leaping.

2. of or pertaining to the *Saltigradæ*.

sal'ti·grāde, *n.* one of the group of spiders *Saltigradae*, which leap to seize their prey.

sa̤lt'i·ly, *adv.* in a salty manner.

sal·tim·bañ'ço, *n.* [Fr. *saltimbanque*.] a mountebank; a quack. [Archaic.]

sa̤lt·ïne', *n.* [*salt*, and *-ine*.] a flat, crisp cracker sprinkled with salt.

sa̤lt'i·ness, *n.* salty quality or state.

sa̤lt'ing, *n.* 1. the act of sprinkling or impregnating with salt.

2. a salt marsh.

sa̤lt'ing box, a box with a perforated top, containing gunpowder meal for sprinkling upon the fuses of shells, that they may ignite readily after firing.

sal'tīre, *n.* [ME. *sawtire, sautire*; OFr. *sautoir*, stirrup loop; ML. *saltatorium*, from L. *saltatorius*, saltatory, from *saltare*, to leap.] in heraldry, a bearing in the form of a St. Andrew's cross, formed by a bend and a bend sinister crossing: also spelled *saltier.*

SALTIRE

sal'tīre·wīse, *adv.* in heraldry, in the manner of a saltire: also spelled *saltierwise.*

sa̤lt'ish, *a.* somewhat salty.

sa̤lt'ish·ly, *adv.* with a moderate degree of saltiness.

sa̤lt'ish·ness, *n.* a moderate degree of saltiness.

sa̤lt'less, *a.* without salt.

sa̤lt lick, an exposed natural deposit of mineral rock salt which animals come to lick.

sa̤lt'ly, *adv.* in a salty manner.

sa̤lt märsh, grassland subject to the overflow of salt water.

sa̤lt'ness, *n.* the quality of being impregnated with salt; as, the *saltness* of sea water or of provisions.

sal'tō, *n.* [It.] in music, a skip.

sa̤lt pan, a pan, basin, or pit in which salt is made.

sa̤lt·pē'tẽr, sa̤lt·pē'tre (-tẽr), *n.* [L. *sal*, salt, and *petra*, rock.] potassium nitrate, KNO_3; niter; also, sodium nitrate.

Chile saltpeter; sodium nitrate.

sa̤lt·pē'tẽr·ing, *n.* an efflorescence of saltpeter that forms in damp walls.

sa̤lt·pē'trous, *a.* pertaining to saltpeter or partaking of its qualities; impregnated with saltpeter.

sa̤lt pit, a pit where salt is obtained.

sa̤lt rheu̇m (röm), see under *rheum.*

Sa̤lt Riv'ẽr, in United States politics, the imaginary river up which defeated candidates are sent.

sa̤lt sha̤k'ẽr, a container for salt, with a perforated top.

sa̤lt tree, a small tree or shrub, *Halimodendron argenteum*, of the pea family, growing in dry salt fields on the Caspian Sea; also, a tamarisk of India, the twigs of which are incrusted with salt.

sal'tus, *n.* [L. *saltus*, a leap.]

1. a break in continuity.

2. in logic, a hasty conclusion or inference.

sa̤lt'-wa̤'tẽr, *a.* of, consisting of, or living in salt water.

sa̤lt wa̤'tẽr, water impregnated with salt; sea water.

sa̤lt'wŏrks, *n.*; *pl.* **sa̤lt'wŏrks,** a place where salt is made, as by evaporation, etc.

sa̤lt'wŏrt, *n.* [prob. after D. *zoutkruid*.]

1. any of a number of related plants used in making soda ash.

2. the glasswort.

sa̤lt'y, *a.*; *comp.* saltier; *superl.* saltiest. 1. of, tasting of, or containing salt.

2. smelling of the sea.

3. pungent; sharp; piquant; witty.

sȧ·lū'bri·ous, *a.* [L. *salubris*, healthful, healthy; from *salus, salutis*, health.] favorable to health; healthful; promoting health; as, *salubrious* air or water; a *salubrious* climate.

sȧ·lū'bri·ous·ly, *adv.* so as to promote health.

PRICKLY SALTWORT
(*Salsola kali*)

sȧ·lū'bri·ous·ness, *n.* healthfulness; salubrity.

sȧ·lū'bri·ty, *n.* [L. *salubritas*.] wholesomeness; healthfulness; the quality of being salubrious; as, the *salubrity* of the air, of a country, or of a climate.

sä·lu̇d', *interj.* [Sp., health.] to your health: a toast.

sȧ·lūe', *v.t.* to greet. [Obs.]

Sȧ·lu̇'ki, *n.* [Ar. *salūqi*, from *Salūq*, an ancient Arabian city.] any of a breed of dog of the greyhound family, with long ears and silky hair.

sal'ū·tăr·i·ly, *adv.* in a salutary manner.

sal'ū·tăr·i·ness, *n.* the quality of being salutary.

sal'u·tăr·y, *a.* [L. *salutaris*, healthful, from *salus, salutis*, health.]

1. wholesome; healthful; promoting health; as, a *salutary* diet.

2. promoting or contributing to some beneficial purpose; as, a *salutary* plan.

Syn.—wholesome, healthful, salubrious, beneficial, useful, advantageous, profitable.

sal·ū·tā'tion, *n.* [L. *salutatio* (*-onis*), salutation, from *salutatus*, pp. of *salutare*, to salute.]

1. the act of greeting, paying respect, addressing, or welcoming by gestures or words.

2. a form of words serving as a greeting or welcome; especially, the "Dear Sir," etc. of a letter.

sȧ·lū·tȧ·tō'ri·ăn, *n.* in some schools and colleges, the member of a class who gives the salutatory oration at the annual commencement, usually the student second in scholastic rank.

sȧ·lū'tȧ·tō·ri·ly, *adv.* by way of salutation.

sȧ·lū'tȧ·tō·ry, *a.* [L. *salutatorius*, pertaining to visiting or greeting, from *salutare*, to greet.] of or containing salutations.

sȧ·lū'tȧ·tō·ry, *n.*; *pl.* **sȧ·lū'tȧ·tō·rie§,** in schools and colleges, the salutatory address at a commencement.

sȧ·lūte', *v.t.*; saluted, *pt., pp.*; saluting, *ppr.* [L. *salutare*, to salute, wish health to, from *salus, salutis*, health, welfare, greeting, from *salvus*, safe, well.]

1. to greet or welcome in a friendly manner or by ceremonial gesture, such as bowing, tipping the hat, etc.; to welcome with customary actions or words.

2. to honor by performing a prescribed act or gesture, such as dipping the flag, firing cannon, raising the hand, etc., as a mark of military, naval, or official respect.

3. to present itself to, as if in greeting; as, laughter *saluted* us.

sȧ·lūte', *v.i.* to make a salute.

sȧ·lūte', *n.* 1. an act, words, or gesture made to express welcome, honor, respect, etc.; specifically, (a) a formal kiss as a gesture of greeting or respect; (b) a prescribed formal gesture such as raising the hand in a certain way to the head, in military and naval practice; (c) a firing of cannon; (d) a dipping of a flag or flags.

2. the position or attitude taken by a person in saluting; as, to stand at *salute.*

3. a gold coin struck by the House of Anjou. [Obs.]

sȧ·lūt'ẽr, *n.* one who salutes.

sal·ū·tif'ẽr·ous, *a.* [L. *salutifer*; *salus*, health, and *ferre*, to bring.] bringing health; healthy; as, *salutiferous* air. [Rare.]

sal·vȧ·bil'i·ty, *n.* the possibility of being saved. [Rare.]

sal'vȧ·ble, *a.* [L. *salvus*, safe, from *salvare*, to save.] that can be saved or salvaged.

sal'vȧ·ble·ness, *n.* the state of being salvable.

Sal·vȧ·dō'rȧ, *n.* [LL., named after Juan *Salvador*, a Spanish botanist.] the typical genus of the family *Salvadoraceæ*.

Sal"vȧ·dō·rā'cē·ae, *n.* a family of small trees or shrubs having opposite leaves and minute flowers, and comprising three genera, native to India, Syria, and northern Africa.

sal"vȧ·dō·rā'ceous, *a.* of, pertaining to, or designating the *Salvadoraceæ*.

Sal·vȧ·dō'răn, *a.* of El Salvador, its people, or their culture.

Sal·vȧ·dō'răn, *n.* a native or inhabitant of El Salvador.

Sal·vȧ·dō'ri·ăn, *a.* and *n.* same as *Salvadoran.*

sal'vāġe, *n.* [Fr., from LL. *salvagium*, from L. *salvus*, safe.]

1. the act of saving a ship, crew, and cargo from extraordinary danger, as from fire, shipwreck, capture, etc.

2. the compensation allowed to persons by whose assistance a ship or vessel, its cargo, or the crew are saved from danger in case of shipwreck, derelict, capture, etc.; also, the ship, cargo, or crew so saved.

3. the restoration of a sunken or wrecked ship and its cargo by divers and special apparatus.

4. in insurance, (a) the rescue of goods or property from damage by fire; (b) the property so rescued; (c) the amount paid for rescue; (d) the value of the goods; (e) proceeds from the sale of such goods.

5. utilization of any sort of damaged or waste material.

sal'văge, *v.t.*; salvaged, *pt., pp.*; salvaging, *ppr.* 1. to save from shipwreck, capture, fire, flood, etc.

2. to restore (sunken or wrecked ships) by divers and special apparatus.

3. to utilize (waste, damaged goods, etc.).

sal'vär·sȧn, *n.* arsphenamine, a compound of arsenic used in the treatment of syphilis, etc.: a trademark (*Salvarsan*): originally called 606.

sal·vā'tion, *n.* [L. *salvatio (-onis)*, deliverance, salvation, from *salvatus*, pp. of *salvare*, to save.]

1. the act of saving or being saved; preservation from destruction; rescue.

2. in theology, the redemption of man from the bondage of sin and liability to eternal death; the saving of the soul through the atonement of Jesus.

3. one who or that which saves; the cause of saving; as, his policy of delay proved the *salvation* of the state.

Salvation Army; an international organization on semi-military lines, founded in England by William Booth in 1865 for religious and philanthropic purposes among the very poor: name adopted in 1878.

sal·vā'tion·iṣm, *n.* 1. religious teaching which emphasizes salvation, especially the saving of the soul through the atonement of Jesus.

2. [S-] the tenets and practices of the Salvation Army.

sal·vā'tion·ist, *n.* 1. a religious teacher who emphasizes salvation.

2. [S-] a member of the Salvation Army.

sälve (säv or sav), *n.* [AS. *sealf*, a salve, an ointment; D. *zalve*; Dan. *salve*; G. *salbe*; O. H. G. *salba*, salve, ointment.]

1. any medicinal ointment applied to wounds, skin irritations, burns, etc. for purposes of soothing or healing.

2. something that soothes or heals; balm; as, her kind words were a *salve* for his tender conscience.

3. flattery.

sälve, *v.t.*; salved, *pt., pp.*; salving, *ppr.* [AS. *sealfian*, from the noun; Dan. *salve*; Goth. *salbôn*, from root *sal*, whence L. *salvus*, safe, etc.]

1. to apply salve to (wounds, etc.). [Archaic.]

2. to soothe; smooth over; palliate; assauge.

3. to flatter.

salve (salv), *v.t.* and *v.i.*; salved, *pt., pp.*; salving, *ppr.* [back-formation from noun *salvage*.] to salvage.

sal'vē, *interj.* [L.] hail!

sälve bug (säv), a large isopod crustacean, *Æga psora*, parasitic on the codfish: sometimes used by sailors in making a salve.

sal'vẽr, *n.* [Sp. *salva*, a salver; also, the previous tasting of a great man's food by a servant to see that it is wholesome, from L. *salvus*, safe.] a tray on which letters, visiting cards, refreshments, etc. are presented.

sal'vẽr, *n.* same as *salvor*.

sälv'ẽr (säv'), *n.* one who uses salve extensively as a remedy.

sal'vẽr·fọrm, *a.* same as *salver-shaped*.

sal'vẽr-shāped (-shāpt), *a.* in botany, having the tube short and the limb spreading out flat, as in the primrose: said of a gamopetalous corolla.

Sal'vi·ȧ, *n.* [LL., from L. *salvia*, sage.]

1. a genus of garden plants of the mint family.

2. [s-] any plant of this genus, especially the scarlet sage, grown for its brilliant red flowers.

SALVER-SHAPED COROLLA

sal·vif'iç, *a.* tending to save or to secure safety.

Sal·vin'i·ȧ, *n.* [LL., named after Antonio Maria *Salvini* (1653–1729), a Greek professor at Florence.] the typical genus of the order *Salviniaceæ*.

Sal·vin·i·ā'cē·ae, *n.pl.* a family of aquatic cryptogamous plants, found only in warm regions, characterized by small, simple, sessile fronds on the upper side of a slender floating stem, and by indehiscent, fluted, bladderlike fruit.

sal'vō, *n.*; *pl.* **sal'vōṣ,** [L. *salvo jure*, the right being intact; an expression used in reserving rights.]

1. a dishonest mental reservation; an excuse or quibbling evasion.

2. in law, a saving clause; a reservation.

sal'vō, *n.*; *pl.* **sal'vōṣ, sal'vōeṣ,** [Fr. *salve*; It. *salva*, a salvo, a salute, from L. *salve*, hail; *salvere*, to be safe.]

1. a discharge of a number of pieces of artillery or small arms, in regular succession, or at the same time, either as a salute or, especially in naval battles, as a hostile broadside.

2. a burst of shouts or cheers of applause, honor, or admiration.

sal vō·la'ti·lē, [Mod. L., volatile salt.] a mixture of ammonium bicarbonate and ammonium carbonate, especially in aromatic solution for use as smelling salts.

sal'vŏr, *n.* a person or ship that helps in the salvage of a ship, its cargo, etc.

sam, *adv.* same. [Obs.]

Sam·ȧ·dē'rȧ, *n.* same as *Samandura*.

sȧ·mädh', *n.* [Sans.] in India, a shrine erected over the burial place of a holy mendicant.

Sȧ·man'dū·rȧ, *n.* [E. Ind.] a genus of small smooth trees found in India and Africa, of the family *Simarubaceæ*, characterized by bisexual, polypetalous, umbellate flowers, by fruit of dry compressed drupes, and by dark green, alternate, undivided leaves.

sam'ȧ·rȧ, *n.* [L., the seed of the elm.] a dry, hard, winged fruit, as in the ash, maple, and elm; a key fruit.

SAMARA

Sȧ·mar'i·tăn, *n.* [LL. *Samaritanus*, Samaritan; Gr. *Samareitēs*, from *Samareia*, L. *Samaria*, Samaria.]

1. a native or inhabitant of Samaria.

2. a person who comes to the aid of another: also *good Samaritan*.

Sȧ·mar'i·tăn, *a.* of Samaria or its people.

Sȧ·mar'i·tăn·iṣm, *n.* the beliefs, idioms, and characteristics of the Samaritans.

sȧ·mā'ri·um, *n.* [Mod. L., from Eng. *samarskite*.] a rare, metallic chemical element of the rare-earth group, having a lustrous, pale-gray appearance: it is found in association with cerium, yttrium, and other elements: symbol, Sm; atomic weight, 150.35; atomic number, 62.

sam'ȧ·roid, *a.* [L. *samara*, the seed of an elm, and *-oid*.] resembling a samara.

sȧ·mär'skīte, *n.* [named after Col. *Samarski*.] an orthorhombic mineral having a velvet-black color and a hard, glasslike luster; it contains iron, thorium, uranium, and some of the rare-earth metals, as samarium, cerium, etc.

sam'bȧ (*or* säm'), *n.* [Port.; of Afr. origin.] a Brazilian dance of African origin.

sam'bȧ, *v.i.* to dance the samba.

sam'băr (*or* säm'), *n.*; *pl.* **sam'bărṣ** or **sam-băr,** [Hind. *sābar*; Sans. *śambara*.] a large Asiatic deer with a mane and three-pointed antlers.

Sam Browne belt, [after Gen. Sir *Samuel J. Browne* (1824–1901), Brit. army officer.] a military belt with one or two diagonal shoulder straps, usually one across the right shoulder: it is designed to carry the weight of a pistol or sword and is worn by officers.

Sam·bū'çus, *n.* [L., an elder tree.] a genus of shrubs and trees of the family *Caprifoliaceæ*, or honeysuckle family.

sam'būke, *n.* [L. *sambuka*; Gr. *sambykē*; Aram. *sabbĕkhā*.] an ancient Asiatic musical instrument similar to a harp.

sam'bul, *n.* [Ar.] muskroot.

sam'būr (or säm'), *n.*; *pl.* **sam'būrṣ** or **sam'būr,** a sambar.

sāme, *a.* [ME.; ON. *samr*, *sami*; akin to Goth. *sama*: seen also in Ice. *samr*; Dan. and Sw. *samme*; Goth. *sama*; L. *similis*, like, *simul*, together; Gr. *homos*, the same, *hama*, together; Sans. *sama*, like, equal, entire.]

1. identical; alike in every respect.

2. alike in degree, kind, character, or quality.

3. that was mentioned before; just spoken of.

A pound of that *same* merchant's flesh is thine. —Shak.

4. unchanged; not different; as, he looks the *same*.

Same is rarely used without *the*.

all the same; (a) nevertheless; (b) of no importance.

just the same; (a) in the same way; (b) nevertheless.

sāme, *pron.* the same person or thing (usually with *the, this*, or *that*).

sāme, *adv.* in the same way; in like manner (usually with *the*).

sä'mekh, sä'meçh (-mekh *or* -mek), *n.* the fifteenth letter of the Hebrew alphabet, corresponding to English *S, s*.

sāme'li·ness, *n.* sameness.

sāme'ly, *a.* dull; monotonous.

sāme'ness, *n.* 1. the state or quality of being the same; uniformity or identity; as, the *sameness* of an unchangeable being.

2. lack of change or variety; monotony; as, the *sameness* of objects in a landscape.

Sam Hill, hell: a euphemism. [Slang.]

Sā'mi·ăn, *a.* of or pertaining to the Greek island of Samos or its people.

Samian letter; same as *Pythagorean letter*.

Samian ware; an ancient kind of pottery made of fine earth, having a bright red or black color.

Sā'mi·ăn, *n.* a native or inhabitant of Samos, a Greek island off Asia Minor.

sam'iel (-yel), *n.* [Turk. *samyel*, a poisonous wind, from *samm*, *sem*, Ar. *samm*, poison, and *yel*, wind.] the simoom.

sä'mi·ri, *n.* same as *saimiri*.

sam'i·sen, *n.* [Japan.] a Japanese three-stringed musical instrument, somewhat like a banjo.

sam'īte (*or* sā'mīt), *n.* [OFr. *samit*; LL. *samitum*, from Gr. *hexamiton*; *hex*, six, and *mitos*, a thread.] a heavy silk material worn in the Middle Ages: it was sometimes interwoven with gold.

säm″iz·dät', *n.* [Russ., lit., self-published.] a system by which manuscripts denied official publication in the Soviet Union are circulated clandestinely in typescript or in mimeograph form, or are smuggled out for publication.

sam'let, *n.* a young or small salmon; a parr.

sam'mi·ẽr, *n.* in tanning, a machine for pressing the water out of skins.

sam'my, *v.t.* in leather manufacture, to moisten with water while dressing.

Sam'my, *n.*; *pl.* **Sam'mieṣ,** [from Uncle *Sam*.] a United States soldier in World War I: nickname used especially by Europeans. [Slang.]

Sam'nīte, *n.* a member of a pre-Roman people, descended from the Sabines, who lived in Samnium, an ancient country in south central Italy.

Sam'nīte, *a.* of Samnium or the Samnites.

Sȧ·mō'ăn, *n.* 1. an inhabitant or native of Samoa.

2. the Polynesian language of the Samoans.

Sȧ·mō'ăn, *a.* pertaining to Samoa or to its people, their language, etc.

Sam″ō·sȧ·tē'ni·ăn, *n.* same as *Paulian*.

Sam·ō·thrā'ciăn, *a.* pertaining to Samothrace, a Greek island in the Ægean Sea, its people, or culture.

Sam·ō·thrā'ciăn, *n.* a native of Samothrace.

sam'ō·vär, *n.* [Russ., lit., self-boiler.] a metal urn used throughout Russia and parts of China for boiling water for tea. It is heated by passing a tube filled with hot charcoal through the hollow center.

SAMOVAR

Sam″ō·yed', Sam″ō·yede', *n.* [Russ., lit., self-eater.]

1. any of a Uralic people living in Siberia.

2. their Uralic language, which has five distinct dialects.

3. any of a powerful breed of Siberian dog, with a thick, white coat.

Sam″ō·yed′, Sam″ō·yede′, *a.* of the Samoyeds (sense 1) or Samoyed.

Sam·ō·yed′iç, *a.* same as *Samoyed.*

samp, *n.* [Am. Ind. *sāpac, saupac,* made soft or thinned.]
1. coarse meal of Indian corn.
2. a porridge made of this.

sam′pan, *n.* [Chin. *san-pan,* from Port. *champão, champana;* Sp. *champán,* canoe; prob. of S. Am. Indian origin.] any of various small boats used in the harbors and rivers of China and Japan, rowed with a scull from the stern, and often having a sail and an awning.

SAMPAN

sam′phīre, *n.* [altered from Fr. (*herbe de*) *Saint Pierre,* St. Peter's (herb).]
1. a suffrutescent umbelliferous plant, *Crithmum maritimum,* the young leaves of which are used for salads, etc. It grows among rocks and on cliffs along the coast of southern Europe.
2. a kind of glasswort.

sam′ple, *n.* [OFr. *essample,* example.]
1. a part or piece taken or shown as representative of a whole group, species, etc.; a specimen; pattern.
2. an illustration; example; as, a *sample* of your singing ability.
Syn.—specimen, example, illustration.

sam′ple, *v.t.;* sampled, *pt., pp.;* sampling, *ppr.*
1. to compare with another thing; to match. [Obs.]
2. to take a sample of; to test by examining a portion of; as, to *sample* wine or sugar.

sam′ple cärd, a card to which samples are attached.

sam′ple çut′tẽr, a device used in cutting samples, as of cloth.

sam′plẽr, *n.* [from L. *exemplum,* a pattern; sense 1 from *sample* and *-er.*]
1. (a) a person who prepares samples for inspection; (b) any of various devices for extracting samples.
2. a piece of cloth embroidered with designs, mottoes, etc., formerly made by beginners to show skill in needlework.

sam′ple ro͝om, 1. a room for exhibition or test of samples.
2. a barroom. [Dial.]

sam′shu, sam′sho͝o, *n.* [Chin. *san-shao,* thrice fired or distilled; from *san,* three, and *shao,* to fire.] an alcoholic liquor distilled in China from boiled and fermented rice.

Sam′sŏn, *n.* [LL.; Gr. *Sampsōn;* Heb. *shimshōn,* from *Shemesh,* sun.]
1. in the Bible, an Israelite distinguished for his great strength: he was lured to his death at the hands of the Philistines by Delilah, his mistress: Jud. xiii.–xvi.
2. any very strong man.

Sam′sŏn fish, an Australian amber fish, *Seriola hippos.*

Sam′sŏn pōst, in a ship, (a) a strong pillar resting on the keelson and supporting a beam of the deck over the hold, thus helping to keep the cargo in its place: it is furnished with several notches that serve as steps to ascend or descend; (b) a temporary or movable spar supported in a vertical position by guys, used for the suspension of hoisting tackle, etc.

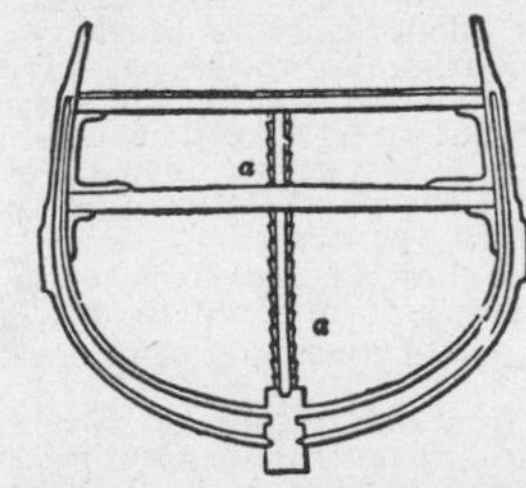

SECTION OF SHIP SHOWING SAMSON POST, *a, a*

Sam′ū·el, *n.* [LL.; Gr. *Samouēl;* Heb. *shĕmūēl,* lit., name of God.] in the Bible, (a) a Hebrew judge and prophet; (b) either of two books (1 Samuel, 2 Samuel) of the Old Testament.

sam′ū·raī, *n. sing.* and *pl.* [Japan.]
1. (a) a member of a military class in feudal Japan, consisting of the retainers of the daimios, or great nobles: a samurai wore two swords; (b) [*pl.*] this class.
2. (a) a Japanese army officer or member of the military caste; (b) [*pl.*] the Japanese military caste.

San (*or* sän), *n.* [Sp. and It.] Saint.

san·ȧ·bil′i·ty, *n.* the state of being curable. [Rare.]

san′ȧ·ble, *a.* [L. *sanabilis,* curable, from *sanare,* to cure, from *sanus,* sound.] that may be healed or cured; susceptible of remedy. [Rare.]

san′ȧ·ble·ness, *n.* sanability. [Rare.]

san′ȧ·tive, *a.* [LL. *sanativus,* serving to heal, from L. *sanatus,* pp. of *sanare,* to heal.] having the power to cure or heal; healing; sanatory. [Rare.]

san′ȧ·tive·ness, *n.* the power of healing. [Rare.]

san·ȧ·tō′ri·um, *n.; pl.* **san·ȧ·tō′ri·umṣ, san·ȧ·tō′ri·ȧ,** [LL., neut. of *sanatorius,* giving health.] a sanitarium.

san′ȧ·tō·ry, *a.* [LL. *sanatorius,* giving health.] healing; curative.

san·be·nï′tō, *n.* ; *pl.* **san·be·nï′tōṣ,** [Sp. *sambenito,* from *San Benito,* Saint Benedict: so named from resembling a Benedictine scapular.]
1. a yellow penitential garment resembling a scapular in shape, and having a red St. Andrew's cross in front and in back, worn by a confessed, penitent heretic.
2. a similar black garment painted with flames, devils, etc., worn by a condemned heretic at an auto-da-fé.

sañ′çhō, *n.* the nine of trumps in the game of sancho pedro.

Sañ′çhō Pan′zȧ (*or Sp.* sän′chọ pän′thä), the simple, credulous peasant acting as a squire to Don Quixote in Cervantes' romance, whose practical, rustic common sense serves as a contrast to the visionary idealism of his master.

sañ′çhō pē′drō, [Sp., proper names.] in card playing, a kind of auction pitch of eighteen points to a hand, the nine of trumps (sancho) and the five of trumps (pedro) being of face value, the ten of trumps counting game.

sanç·tȧ·nim′i·ty, *n.* [L. *sanctus,* holy, and *animus,* mind.] holiness of mind; purity. [Rare.]

sañç′ti·fi·çāte, *v.t.* to sanctify. [Rare.]

sañç″ti·fi·çā′tion, *n.* [LL. *santificatio* (*-onis*), a sanctification, from *sanctificatus,* pp. of *sanctificare,* to sanctify.] a sanctifying or being sanctified.

sañç′ti·fīed, *a.* 1. made holy; consecrated; set apart for sacred services.
2. affectedly holy; sanctimonious.

sañç′ti·fī·ẽr, *n.* a person or thing that sanctifies or makes holy; specifically, [S–] the Holy Spirit.

sañç′ti·fȳ, *v.t.;* sanctified, *pt., pp.;* sanctifying, *ppr.* [Fr. *sanctifier;* LL. *sanctificare,* to make holy, sanctify; from L. *sanctus,* holy, and *ficare,* from *facere,* to make.]
1. to make holy; specifically, (a) to make free from sin; to purify; (b) to set apart as holy; to consecrate; (c) to make (a person) holy.
2. to give sanction to; to cause to be respected; to make sacred, or inviolable.
3. to make productive of spiritual blessing.

sañç′ti·fȳ·ing·ly, *adv.* in a manner or degree tending to sanctify or make holy. [Rare.]

sanç·ti·mō′ni·ăl, *a.* sanctimonious. [Obs.]

sanç·ti·mō′ni·ous, *a.* [L. *sanctimonia,* holiness.]
1. saintly; having the appearance of sanctity; as, a *sanctimonious* observance. [Obs.]
2. pretending to be very holy or pious; affecting sanctity.

> The *sanctimonious* pirate that went to sea with the ten commandments. —Shak.

sanç·ti·mō′ni·ous·ly, *adv.* in a sanctimonious manner.

sanç·ti·mō′ni·ous·ness, *n.* the quality or state of being sanctimonious.

sañç′ti·mō·ny, *n.* [L. *sanctimonia,* from *sanctus,* holy.]
1. apparent sanctity; sanctimonious appearance.
2. sanctity. [Obs.]

sañç′tion, *n.* [L. *sanctio* (*-onis*), sanction, ordinance, from *sanctus,* pp. of *sancire,* to render sacred.]
1. the act of a recognized authority confirming or ratifying an action; authorization; authoritative permission.
2. support; encouragement; approval.
3. something that gives binding force to a law, as the penalty for breaking it, or a reward for carrying it out; a provision of law that secures obedience.
4. something, as a consideration, principle, or influence, which makes a rule of conduct, moral law, etc. binding.
5. a formal decree; law.
6. [*usually in pl.*] a coercive measure, usually taken by several nations together, for forcing a nation considered to have violated international law to stop the violation; as, *sanctions* may consist in withholding loans, limiting relations, imposing a blockade, etc.
punitive sanctions; in law, the inflicting of punishment upon a criminal offender.
remuneratory sanctions; punishment in the form of the withholding of a remuneration or reward from one who has failed to obey the law.

sañç′tion, *v.t.;* sanctioned, *pt., pp.;* sanctioning, *ppr.* to give sanction to; specifically, (a) to authorize; to ratify; to confirm; (b) to approve; to encourage; to support.
Syn.—confirm, approve, countenance, abet, allow.

sañç′tion·ăr·y, *a.* giving sanction. [Rare.]

sañç′ti·tūde, *n.* [L. *sanctitudo,* holiness, from *sanctus,* holy.] holiness; sacredness.

sañç′ti·ty, *n.; pl.* **sañç′ti·tieṣ,** [L. *sanctitas* (*-tatis*), holiness, from *sanctus,* holy.]
1. saintliness; holiness; purity.
2. the state of being consecrated to a deity; sacredness.
3. the quality of being regarded as sacred; binding force; inviolability.
4. anything held sacred.
Syn.—piety, godliness, holiness, devotion, purity.

sañç′tū·ȧ·rīze, *v.t.* [L. *sanctus,* holy.] to shelter by means of a sanctuary or sacred privileges. [Rare.]

sañç′tū·ăr·y, *n.; pl.* **sañç′tū·ăr·ieṣ,** [Fr. *sanctuaire;* LL. *sanctuarium,* a sacred place, shrine, from L. *sanctus,* sacred.]
1. a holy place; a building or place set aside for worship of a god or gods; specifically, (a) the Temple at Jerusalem; (b) a Christian church; (c) any church or temple; (d) a particularly holy place within a church or temple, as the part around the altar, the holy of holies in the Jewish Temple, etc.
2. a place of refuge or protection: originally fugitives from justice were immune from arrest in churches or other sacred places.
3. refuge or protection; immunity from punishment or the law, as by taking refuge in a church, etc.
4. a reservation where animals or birds are sheltered for breeding purposes and may not be hunted or otherwise molested.

sañç′tum, *n.; pl.* **sañç′tumṣ, sañç′tȧ,** [short for *sanctum sanctorum,* holy of holies; neut. of L. *sanctus,* pp. of *sancire,* to consecrate.]
1. a sacred or private place.
2. a study or private room where one is not to be disturbed.

sañç′tum sanç·tō′rum, [L., orig., transl. of Heb. *qodhesh haqqodhōshim,* holy of holies, via Gr.]
1. a most holy place.
2. in the Jewish Temple, the place where the Ark of the Covenant was placed; the holy of holies.
3. a place of utmost privacy: often used humorously.

Sañç′tus, *n.* [L., pp. of *sancire,* to consecrate.]
1. the hymn constituting the culmination of the preface of the Mass or Communion service, beginning *Sanctus, sanctus, sanctus* (Holy, holy, holy).
2. a musical setting for this.
Sanctus bell; a small bell rung during the most sacred parts of the Mass and at the singing of the Sanctus: also called *mass bell* and *sacring bell.*

sand, *n.* [AS. *sand*; akin to G. *sand*, ON. *sandr*.]
1. loose, gritty particles of worn or disintegrated rock, usually deposited along the shores of bodies of water, in river beds, or in deserts.
2. [*usually pl.*] a tract or area of sand; a beach, etc.
3. the sand in an hourglass.
4. [*pl.*] moments; particles of time; as, the *sands* of life.
5. grit; courage. [Slang.]
6. the reddish-yellow color characteristic of sand.

sand, *v.t.* 1. to sprinkle with sand.
2. to smooth or polish with sand or sandpaper.
3. to mix or adulterate with sand.
4. to beach on the sand.
5. to cover with sand.
6. to fill up with sand.

san'dăl, *n.* [Fr. *sandale*; L. *sandalium*, from Gr. *sandalion*, *sandalon*.]
1. a kind of shoe made of a sole fastened in various ways to the foot by straps over the instep, toes, or ankle.

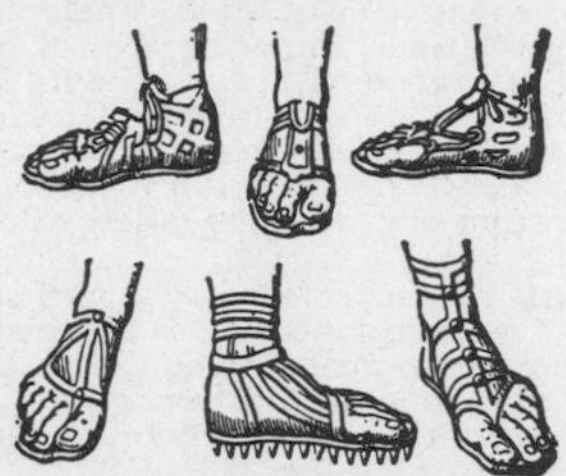
GRECIAN AND ROMAN SANDALS

2. a similar shoe for women, having the upper slashed with openwork or made of straps.
3. a low-cut rubber overshoe not covering much more than the sole of the shoe.
4. a strap for holding a low shoe or slipper on the foot.

san'dăl, *n.* a kind of narrow boat having two masts, used on the Nile and on the Barbary coast.

san'dăl, *n.* same as *sandalwood*.

san'dăl, *n.* same as *sendal*.

san'dăled, san'dălled, *a.* 1. wearing sandals.
2. fastened with a sandal, or strap.

san'dȧ·li·fọrm, *a.* shaped like a sandal or slipper.

san'dăl tree, an evergreen tree, *Sandoricum indicum*, of the East Indies, that bears an applelike fruit.

san'dăl·wood, *n.* 1. the wood of several species of trees of the genus *Santalum*, particularly of *Santalum album*, a low tree growing chiefly on the coast of Malabar and in the Indian archipelago, having a general resemblance to the privet. When the tree becomes old the harder central wood acquires a yellow color and great fragrance, while the softer exterior wood remains white and without fragrance.
2. any tree that yields sandalwood, particularly of the genus *Santalum*.

SANDALWOOD (*Santalum album*)

san'dȧ·raç, san'dȧ·rach, *n.* [L. *sandaraca*, from Gr. *sandarakē*, a word of Oriental origin.]
1. a resin in white drops, more transparent than those of mastic, which exudes from the bark of the sandarac tree, *Callitris quadrivalvis*. It is used as incense, and for making a pale varnish for light-colored woods: also called *juniper resin*.
2. the sandarac tree.
3. in mineralogy, arsenic sulfide; realgar.

san'dȧ·raç tree, *Callitris quadrivalvis*, a tree native to the mountains of Morocco, yielding the resin sandarac. The timber is fragrant, hard, durable, mahogany-colored, and is largely used in the construction of buildings.

sand badġ'ẽr, a badger, *Meles ankuma*, of Japan.

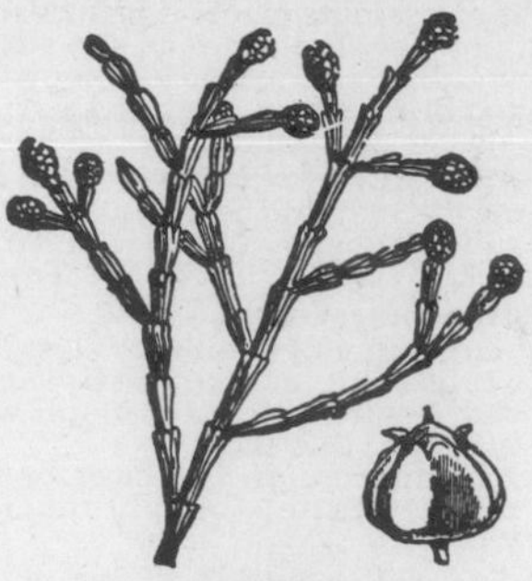
SANDARAC (*Callitris quadrivalvis*)

sand'bag, *n.* a bag filled with sand, as (a) a bag of sand or earth used in a fortification for repairing breaches, etc.; (b) a leather cushion, tightly filled with fine sand, used by engravers to prop their work at a convenient angle, or to give free motion to a plate or cut in engraving curved lines, etc.; (c) a form of ballast used in boats and balloons; (d) a bag of sand used in any of various ways as a weapon or club.

sand'bag, *v.t.*; sandbagged, *pt.*, *pp.*; sandbagging, *ppr.* 1. to place sandbags in or around.
2. to strike or stun with a sandbag.
3. to force into doing something. [Colloq.]

sand'bag″gẽr, *n.* one who assaults with a sandbag; a thug.

sand bär, a ridge or narrow shoal of sand formed in a river or along a shore by the action of currents or tides.

sand bȧth, 1. a vessel containing warm or hot sand, used as an equable heater for retorts, etc., in various chemical processes.
2. a form of therapeutic bath in which the body is covered with warm sea sand.

sand bĩrd, any shore bird, as a sandpiper.

sand'blȧst, *n.* 1. a current of air or steam carrying sand at a high velocity, used in etching glass and in cleaning the surfaces of metals, stone, buildings, etc.
2. the machine used to apply this blast.
3. any strong destructive force.

sand'blȧst, *v.t.* to engrave or clean with a sandblast.

sand'-blīnd, *a.* [from AS. (hyp.) *samblind*, from *sam*, half, and *blind*, blind.] weak-sighted; partially blind.

sand blīnd'ness, the condition of being sand-blind.

sand'bōard, *n.* in vehicles, a bar over and parallel to the hind axle. It rests upon the hind hounds where they cross the axle.

sand'box, *n.* 1. a box with a perforated top or cover formerly used for sprinkling sand on fresh ink.
2. a box filled with sand usually placed on top of the boiler of a locomotive, with a pipe to guide the sand to the rail when the wheels slip because of frost, wet, etc.
3. a box or similar receptacle filled with sand, as for children to play in.

sand'box tree, a tropical tree, *Hura crepitans*, with small, roundish, woody fruit that bursts with a loud noise when dry.

FRUIT OF THE SANDBOX TREE (*Hura crepitans*)

sand bug, a small crustacean of the family *Hippidæ* that burrows in sandy beaches.

sand'bũr, sand'bũrr, *n.* a plant, *Solanum rostratum*, that grows in sandy places. Its prickly calyx is closely filled by the fruit.

sand'-bũrned, *a.* in founding, designating a casting in which the heat of the melted metal has caused the silica of the sand to unite with the metal, resulting in a rough surface.

sand'-çȧst, *v.t.*; sand-cast, *pt.*, *pp.*; sand-casting, *ppr.* to make (a casting) by pouring metal in a mold of sand.

sand cher'ry, an American shrub, *Prunus pumila*.

sand çlam, the long clam, *Mya arenaria*.

sand çock, the redshank. [Brit. Dial.]

sand çol'lăr, same as *sand saucer*.

sand çrab, 1. the lady crab.
2. an ocypode.

sand çrack, a fissure or perpendicular crack occurring in the hoof of a horse, often causing lameness.

sand çrick'et, a large cricket of the genus *Stenopelmatus* found in the sandy portions of the western part of the United States.

sand çusk, any fish of the genus *Ophidium*.

sand dab, a dab, *Limanda ferruginea*, found in American waters: also called *rusty dab*.

sand därt'ẽr, an American fish of the Gulf Coast, as *Ammocrypta pellucida*.

sand dīv'ẽr, a sand darter.

sand dol'lăr, a small, flat sea urchin, as *Echinarachnius parma*, found on sandy bottoms.

sand dūne, same as *dune*.

sand'ed, *a.* 1. sprinkled with sand; as, a *sanded* floor.
2. covered, filled, or clogged with sand.
3. marked with small spots; variegated with spots; speckled; also, of a sandy color, as a hound.

sand eel, 1. a fish of the genus *Ammodytes*; a sand launce, *Ammodytes tobianus* is the common species.
2. a fish, *Gonorhynchus greyi*, of the Pacific Ocean.

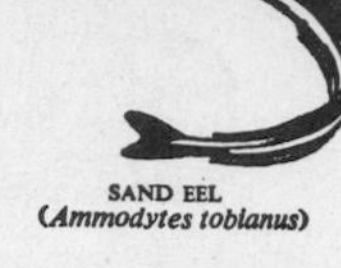
SAND EEL (*Ammodytes tobianus*)

San·dē·mā'ni·ăn, *n.* a follower of Robert Sandeman, an 18th-century Scottish theologian; one of the sect called Glassites.

San·dē·mā'ni·ăn·iṣm, *n.* the principles of the Sandemanians.

sand'ẽr, *n.* 1. a person who sands or sandpapers.
2. a device for sanding or sandpapering.

san'dẽr·ling, *n.* a small wading bird, *Calidris arenaria*. It attains a length of eight inches, and in winter is ashen-gray on the upper parts and white below. The plumage is a reddish-brown, mottled with black, in spring. It feeds on small marine insects and differs from the sandpipers only in having no hind toe.

san'dẽrṣ, *n.* sandalwood. [Obs.]

san'de·vẽr, *n.* same as *sandiver*.

sand'fish, *n.* a small fish, *Trichodon stelleri*, which buries itself in the sand. It is found on the Pacific coast of North America.

sand flag, sandstone of a lamellar or flaggy structure.

sand flēa, 1. any flea inhabiting sandy places.
2. the chigoe.
3. a small amphipodous crustacean; a beach flea.

sand floun'dẽr, in zoology, the windowpane or any other flounder found in shallow, sandy waters.

sand flụke, *n.* 1. the sandsucker.
2. the smear dab of Europe.

sand fly, any of the small pestilential flies of the genus *Simulium*, especially *Simulium nocivum*, found on sandy shores of the United States.

sand'glȧss, *n.* an instrument consisting of two glass globes with a connecting passage, used for measuring time by the flowing of sand from one globe to the other; hourglass.

sand grȧss, any grass that grows on sandy soil, especially *Triplasis purpurea*, a tufted grass of the United States.

sand grouse, a gallinaceous bird of the family *Tetraonidæ*, closely allied to the grouse. It is native chiefly to the warm parts of Asia and Africa, and lives in arid, sandy plains. Two species, the banded sand grouse, *Pterocles arenaria*, and the pintailed sand grouse, *Pterocles setarius*, are found in the south of Europe.

sand'hēat, *n.* the heat of warm sand used in chemical operations.

san'dhi (-di), *n.* [Sans., from *sandhi-*, a placing together.] in linguistics, (a) a context in which a word is phonetically modified by assimilation to contiguous words; as, *'s* is the form of *is* occurring in *sandhi*; (b) the assimilations, etc. shown by a word in such a context; as, in *won't*, *n't* occurs instead of *not* by *sandhi*; (c) the phonetic form assumed by a word in such a context.

san'dhi, *a.* showing the effects of sandhi; as, *'ll* is the *sandhi* form of *will* in *he'll*.

sand hill, a hill consisting of or covered with sand.
sand-hill crane; either of two American cranes, *Grus canadensis* or *Grus mexicanus*.

sand'-hill″ẽr, *n.* one of the poor white residents of the sand-hill regions of Georgia and South Carolina; a cracker. [Colloq.]

sand'hog, *n.* 1. a laborer who works or digs in sand.
2. a laborer employed in underground or underwater construction projects, working under compressed air, as in a caisson.
Also *sand hog.*

sand hop'pẽr, an amphipodous crustacean; a beach flea.

sand hor'net, a sand wasp. [Rare.]

san·dif'ẽr·ous, *a.* sand-bearing.

sand'i·ness, *n.* the state or quality of being sandy.

sand'ish, *a.* somewhat sandy. [Obs.]

san'di·vẽr, san'de·vẽr, *n.* [OFr. *suin de verre*, sweat or gall of glass; *suin*, grease or sweat, *de*, of, and *verre*, glass.] glass gall; anatron.

san'dix, *n.* [L., from Gr. *sandyx*, a bright red color.] a kind of red lead prepared by calcining carbonate of lead.

sand jack, the willow oak.

sand jet, a blast of sharp sand driven by steam or compressed air in a jet against a surface to be abraded.

sand lànce, a sand eel.

sand lärk, 1. any small wader of sandy shores, as the sandpiper, the sanderling, the dotterel, the dunlin, and the ringneck.
2. a small Asiatic lark of the genus *Ammomanes.*

sand launce, a sand eel.

sand lil'y, a plant of the lily family, with narrow grasslike leaves and clusters of white, star-shaped flowers.

sand liz'ărd, a small lizard of Europe, *Lacerta agilis*, living in sandy places.

sand lob, a lugworm.

sand'-lot, *a.* of or having to do with a sandy lot or field in or near a city: applied to games played in such lots; as, *sand-lot* baseball.

sand'man, *n.* a mythical person, as in fairy tales, supposed to make children sleepy by throwing sand in their eyes.

sand mär'tin, the bank swallow. [Brit.]

sand mā'sŏn, a tubeworm, *Terebella littoralis*, which builds and inhabits shell-like tubes of sand.

sand mōle, the coast rat.

sand mon'i·tŏr, a large lizard of Egypt, *Monitor* (or *Psammosaurus*) *arenarius.*

sand mouse, the dunlin. [Brit.]

sand myr'tle (mẽr'), a low evergreen shrub of the genus *Leiophyllum*, found in New Jersey and vicinity.

sand'nat″tẽr, *n.* any sand snake of the genus *Eryx.*

sand'neck″ẽr, *n.* the sandsucker.

sand'pā″pẽr, *n.* paper covered on one side with glue and then sprinkled with sand, for smoothing and polishing.

sand'pā″pẽr, *v.t.*; sandpapered, *pt., pp.*; sandpapering, *ppr.* to clean, polish, or smooth with sandpaper.

sand'pā″pẽr tree, any of various trees of the order *Dilleniaceæ*, having rough leaves resembling sandpaper.

sand pär'tridge, any Asiatic partridge of the genus *Ammoperdix.*

sand'peep, *n.* a small sandpiper.

sand piġ'eŏn, a sand grouse.

sand pīke, 1. the sauger.
2. a lizard fish.

sand pīpe, 1. a long, perpendicular, cylindrical cavity formed in some chalk deposits: so called from being filled with sand, gravel, or clay.
2. one of the pipes conveying sand from the sandbox of a locomotive.

sand'pī″pẽr, *n.*; *pl.* **sand'pī″pẽrṣ** or **sand'pī″pẽr,** 1. any of various gregarious shore birds resembling a snipe but distinguished by the length of the soft-tipped bill; specifically, a member of the *Tringeæ* or *Totaneæ*. The common spotted sandpiper of North America is *Actitis macularius*, closely allied to *Actitis hypoleucus*, which is the most common European species.
2. same as *sand pride.*

sand pit, a pit from which sand can be taken.

sand plŏv'ẽr, the ring dotterel.

sand prīde, a fresh-water European lamprey.

sand pump, a cylindrical metallic tube having at the bottom a valve opening inwardly, used for removing the sand that collects in the bore in drilling.

sand rat, a pocket gopher, *Thomomys talpoides.*

sand'rock, *n.* sandstone. [Rare.]

sand'run″nẽr, *n.* 1. the turnstone.
2. any sandpiper.

sand sau'cẽr, the saucerlike egg mass of *Lunatia heros*, or some closely allied gastropod.

sand screw, a burrowing amphipod, *Lepidactylis arenaria*, found in sandy beaches.

sand shärk, a shovelnose, *Odontaspis littoralis*, a shark of the Atlantic.

sand skink, any skink of the genus *Seps*, found in southern Europe.

sand skip'pẽr, a beach flea.

sand smelt, a silversides, as *Atherina presbyter.*

sand snāke, 1. any burrowing snake of the genus *Eryx.*
2. any snake of the genus *Psammophis.*

sand snīpe, a sandpiper.

sand stär, a starfish of the genus *Ophiura*, having five long slender arms attached to a circular disk; any starfish.

sand'stāy, *n.* an Australian shrub, *Leptospermum lævigatum*, used in binding the sand to prevent drifting.

sand'stōne, *n.* any stone that is an agglutination of grains of sand, whether calcareous, siliceous, or of any other mineral nature. Siliceous sandstones are the most common, varying in compactness from scarcely cemented sand to a hardness approaching that of quartz rock. The grains are cemented together by silica, lime, etc. The stones, which range in color from yellow to red and brown, are much used for buildings.
New Red Sandstone; in geology, a series of brick-red strata lying immediately above the Permian. Originally, the series included two groups of rocks, the one containing fossils belonging to the Paleozoic age, the other enclosing Mesozoic remains. These have been separated, and the name Permian given to the older and lower group, and that of Triassic, or New Red Sandstone, to the newer and upper.
Old Red Sandstone; a group of strata, chiefly sandstones and conglomerates, whose universally red color suggested their name. The lower strata pass into the upper Silurian and the upper beds pass into the Carboniferous. Fossils are few in comparison to the thickness of the strata.

sand'storm, *n.* a windstorm in which large quantities of sand are blown about in clouds.

sand'suck″ẽr, *n.* the sandnecker; the rough dab: also called *sand fluke.*

sand swäl'lōw, the bank swallow.

sand trap, a pit or trench filled with sand, serving as a hazard on a golf course.

sand tūbe, a tube made of sand; specifically, a vitrified tube of sand produced by lightning; a fulgurite.

sand vẽr·bē'nȧ, any of a number of related trailing plants with fragrant, pink, white, or yellow flowers.

sand vī'pẽr, 1. the horned viper.
2. the hognose snake.

sand wäsp, a hymenopterous insect of the genus *Ammophila.*

sand'weed, *n.* in botany, (a) the spurry; (b) the sandwort.

sand'wich, *n.* [after John Montagu, 4th Earl of *Sandwich* (1718–1792), said to have eaten these in order not to leave the gaming table for meals.]
1. two or more slices of bread with a filling of meat, fish, eggs, vegetables, etc. between them.
2. anything like a sandwich in arrangement.

sand'wich, *v.t.*; sandwiched (-wicht), *pt., pp.*; sandwiching, *ppr.* to make into a sandwich; to fit between two other persons, places, or things.

sand'wich man, 1. a man who makes or sells sandwiches.
2. a man who walks the street displaying two advertising boards hung from his shoulders, one in front and one behind.

sand'wood, *n.* a leguminous shrub of Mauritius, *Bremontiera ammoxylon*, having a purple flower.

sand'wŏrm, *n.* one of various species of annelids that burrow in sand.

sand'wŏrt, *n.* a small plant of the genus *Arenaria*, having white flowers and awl-shaped leaves and growing in sandy soil.

sand'y, *n.*; *pl.* **sand'ieṣ,** the sand lark; the laverock. [Brit. Dial. and Scot.]

sand'y, *a.*; *comp.* sandier; *superl.* sandiest, 1. full of sand; covered or sprinkled with sand; as, a *sandy* desert or plain; a *sandy* road or soil.
2. consisting of or like sand; not firm or solid; unstable; as, a *sandy* foundation.
3. of the color of sand; of a yellowish-red color; as, *sandy* hair.

San'dy, *n.* [Scot. abbrev. of *Alexander*.] a Scotsman. [Colloq.]

sāne, *a.*; *comp.* saner; *superl.* sanest, [L. *sanus*, sound, whole.]
1. mentally healthy; sound of mind; rational.
2. (of the mind) sound; not diseased.
3. showing good sense; sound; sensible; reasonable; as, a *sane* policy.

sāne'ly, *adv.* in a sane manner.

sāne'ness, *n.* the state of being sane or of sound mind.

San'fŏr·īze, *v.t.* and *v.i.*; Sanforized, *pt., pp.*; Sanforizing, *ppr.* [back-formation from *Sanforized*, a trademark applied to fabrics so treated; after *Sanford* L. Cluett, the inventor.] to preshrink (cotton or linen cloth) permanently by a patented process before making it into shirts, dresses, etc.

sang, *v.* past tense of *sing.*

sang, *n.* ginseng.

sañ'gȧ, sañ'gū, *n.* [Abyssinian.] the Galla ox of Abyssinia, *Gos africanus*, having a humped back and horns that grow to four feet in length.

sañ·gȧ·ree', *n.* [Sp. *sangría*, lit., bleeding; L. *sanguis*, blood.] a drink composed of wine and water sweetened, spiced, and iced.

sañ·gȧ·ree', *v.t.* to make sangaree of; as, to *sangaree* sherry.

säng″-froid' (säñ″frwȧ'), *n.* [Fr., cold blood.] coolness; freedom from agitation or excitement of mind; imperturbability.

sang'li·ẽr, *n.* [Fr., from LL. *singularis*, that is, *porcus singularis*, the wild boar.]
1. a wild boar of full size. [Obs.]
2. in heraldry, a wild boar.

Sañ·graal' (-grāl'), **Sañ'grē·ăl,** *n.* [from OFr. *Saint Graal.*] same as *Holy Grail* under *grail.*

sañ'gui-, [from L. *sanguis*, blood.] a combining form meaning *blood.*

sañ·guiç'ō·lous, *a.* [L. *sanguis*, blood, and *colere*, to inhabit.] living in the blood, as certain parasites; hematobic.

sañ·guif'ẽr·ous, *a.* [LL. *sanguifer*; L. *sanguis*, blood, and *ferre*, to bear.] conveying blood; as, the *sanguiferous* vessels, arteries, and veins.

sañ″gui·fi·çā'tion, *n.* [Fr., from L. *sanguis*, blood, and *facere*, to make.] the production of blood; the conversion of chyle into blood. [Rare.]

sañ'gui·fī·ẽr, *n.* a producer of blood.

sañ·guif'lu·ous, *a.* [L. *sanguis*, blood, and *fluere*, to flow.] flowing with blood. [Obs.]

sañ'gui·fy, *v.i.* [L. *sanguis*, blood, and *facere*, to make.] to produce blood. [Obs.]

sañ·guiġ'e·nous, *a.* producing blood. [Obs.]

sañ·gui·nā'ceous, *a.* [L. *sanguis, sanguinis*, blood, and *-aceous*.] of the color of blood.

Sañ·gui·nā'ri·ȧ, *n.* [LL., a plant so called because reputed to stanch blood, from L. *sanguinarius*, pertaining to blood.]
1. a genus of plants of the poppy family, of which the bloodroot is the only species.
2. [s–] any plant of this genus.
3. [s–] the root of the bloodroot, which has medicinal properties and is used as an emetic.

sañ'gui·nãr·i·ly, *adv.* in a sanguinary manner.

sañ'gui·nãr·i·ness, *n.* the state or quality of being sanguinary.

sañ'gui·nãr·y, *a.* [L. *sanguinarius*, pertaining to blood, from *sanguis, sanguinis*, blood.]
1. bloody; accompanied by much bloodshed; murderous; as, a *sanguinary* war, contest, or battle.
2. bloodthirsty; cruel; eager to shed blood.
3. consisting of blood; flowing with blood; bloodstained.

sañ'gui·nãr·y, *n.* 1. a plant of the genus *Sanguinaria*; bloodwort.
2. same as *yarrow.*

sañ'guine, *a.* [Fr. *sanguin*; L. *sanguineus*, from *sanguis, sanguinis*, blood.]
1. of the color of blood; ruddy: said especially of complexions.

2. in medieval physiology, having the warm, passionate, cheerful temperament and the healthy, ruddy complexion of one in whom the blood is the predominant humor of the four.
3. cheerful; confident; optimistic; hopeful.
4. sanguinary.
Syn.—warm, ardent, animated, lively, confident, hopeful.
sañ′guine, *n.* 1. blood red.
2. a drawing in red crayon, chalk, etc.
3. in heraldry, same as *murrey.*
4. bloodstone. [Obs.]
sañ′guine, *v.t.* to stain with or as with blood. [Obs.]
sañ′guine·less, *a.* without blood; pale. [Rare.]
sañ′guine·ly, *adv.* in a sanguine manner; optimistically; with confidence of success.
sañ′guine·ness, *n.* the state or quality of being sanguine.
sañ·guin′ē·ous, *a.* [L. *sanguineus,* of blood, bloody.]
1. of or containing blood.
2. having the color of blood; red.
3. of bloodshed; sanguinary.
4. sanguine; confident; hopeful.
sañ·guin′i·ty, *n.* sanguineness. [Rare.]
sañ·gui·niv′ō·rous, *a.* [L. *sanguis,* blood, and *vorare,* to eat.] eating or subsisting on blood.
sañ·guin′ō·lence, *n.* [L. *sanguinolentus,* bloody.] the condition of being sanguinolent.
sañ·guin′ō·lent, *a.* of, containing, or tinged with blood.
Sañ·gui·sor′bȧ, *n.* [L. *sanguis,* blood, and *sorbere,* to absorb.] a genus of plants of the order *Rosaceæ,* comprising several species, most of which possess astringent properties. The common burnet, *Sanguisorba officinalis,* is native to Britain, growing in moist pastures, and having smooth pinnate leaves and terminal ovate heads of small dark-purple flowers.
sañ′gui·sūġe, *n.* [L. *sanguisuga; sanguis,* blood, and *sugere,* to suck.] a bloodsucker; a leech. [Obs.]
sañ·gui·sū′ġent, *a.* [L. *sanguis,* blood, and *sugens (-entis),* ppr. of *sugere,* to suck.] living by sucking blood; as, a *sanguisugent* leech or bat. [Obs.]
sañ·guiv′ō·rous, *a.* [L. *sanguis,* blood, and *vorare,* to devour.] feeding on blood.
San′hē·drin, San′hē·drim, *n.* [Heb. *sanhedrīn;* Gr. *synedrion,* a sitting together, assembly, from *syn,* together, and *hedra,* seat.] the highest court and council of the ancient Jewish nation, consisting of seventy-one members. It decided the most important causes, both ecclesiastical and civil, and was abolished with the destruction of Jerusalem in 70 A.D.: also *Great Sanhedrin.*
San′hē·drist, *n.* a member of the Sanhedrin.
San′hi·tä, *n.* [Hind.] the portion of the Vedas, or sacred writings of the Brahmans, that contains the hymns.
san′i·çle, *n.* [LL. *saniculum,* sanicle, so called from its healing wounds, from L. *sanus,* sound, healthy.] any umbelliferous plant of the genus *Sanicula,* having long-stalked leaves and clusters of small, white or yellowish flowers: formerly regarded as having healing powers.
san′i·dine, *n.* [Gr. *sanis (-idos),* a board, a table, and *-ine.*] a very pure variety of orthoclase occurring in clear glassy crystals in certain volcanic rocks: also called *glassy feldspar.*
sā′ni·ēṣ, *n.* [L. *sanies,* bloody matter, diseased blood.] a thin, often greenish discharge from wounds or sores; a serous matter tinged with blood.
sā′ni·ous, *a.* [L. *saniosus,* full of bloody matter, from *sanies,* bloody matter, diseased blood.]
1. pertaining to sanies or having its nature and appearance; thin and serous, with a slight bloody tinge; as, the *sanious* matter of an ulcer.
2. excreting or effusing sanies; as, a *sanious* ulcer.
san·i·tãr′i·ăn, *a.* of the laws of health, sanitation, or hygiene; sanitary.
san·i·tãr′i·ăn, *n.* one who promotes or studies sanitation or sanitary measures.
san′i·tãr·i·ly, *adv.* in a sanitary manner.
san′i·tãr·i·ness, *n.* the quality or state of being sanitary.
san′i·tãr·ist, *n.* a sanitarian.
san·i·tãr′i·um, *n.; pl.* **san·i·tãr′i·umṣ, san·i·tãr′i·ȧ,** [Mod. L., from *sanitas,* health.]
1. a quiet, restful resort, as in the mountains, where people go to rest and regain health.
2. an insitution for the care of invalids or convalescents, especially one making use of local natural resources, as mineral springs, or one treating a specific disease, as tuberculosis.
Also *sanatorium.*
san′i·tãr·y, *a.* [L. *sanitas (-atis),* health.]
1. of health or the rules and conditions of health; especially, of absence of dirt and agents of infection or disease; tending to promote health and healthful conditions.
2. in a clean, healthy condition; hygienic.
sanitary belt; a narrow elastic belt for holding a sanitary napkin in place.
Sanitary Commission; see *United States Sanitary Commission* under *Commission.*
sanitary engineering; see under *engineering.*
sanitary napkin; an absorbent pad of cotton, etc. worn by women during menstruation.
san′i·tāte, *v.t.* to make hygienic or sanitary.
san·i·tā′tion, *n.* 1. the science and practice of effecting healthful and hygienic conditions; the study and use of hygienic measures such as drainage, ventilation, pure water supply, etc.
2. drainage and disposal of sewage.
san′i·tīze, *v.t.* to make sanitary.
san′i·ty, *n.* [L. *sanitas (-atis),* health.]
1. the condition of being sane; healthiness of mind.
2. soundness of judgment.
san′jak, *n.* [Turk. *sanjāq,* a banner.] formerly, a subdivision of a vilayet, or minor province, of Turkey: so called because its governor (called *sanjak bey*) was entitled to carry in war a standard of one horsetail.
san′jak·āte, *n.* a sanjak. [Rare.]
San Jō·ṣẹ′ sçāle (hō-zā′), see under *scale.*
sañk, *v.* alternative past tense of *sink.*
sañk′hȧ, *n.* [E. Ind.] a chank shell or an ornament made from chank shells.
Säñkh′yȧ, *n.* [Sans.] one of the six major systems of Hindu philosophy, dualistic in metaphysics, involving two ultimate principles of matter and spirit.
san′nup, *n.* [Am. Ind.] a male American Indian who is married.
san′pan, *n.* see *sampan.*
sanṣ, *prep.* [Fr., altered from L. *absentia,* absence (under influence of *sine,* without).] without. [Archaic or Poetic.]
San′sçrit, *n.* and *a.* see *Sanskrit.*
sanṣ-çū·lotte′ (*or Fr.* säṅ-kụ̈-lot′), *n.* [Fr., without breeches.]
1. a revolutionary: term of contempt applied by the aristocrats to the republicans of the poorly clad French Revolutionary army, who substituted pantaloons for knee breeches.
2. any radical or revolutionary.
sanṣ-çū·lot′tiç, *a.* pertaining to the sansculottes or sans-culottism; revolutionary.
sanṣ-çū·lot′tide (*or Fr.* säṅ-kụ̈-lọ-tēd′), *n.* [from *sans-culotte.*]
1. one of the five extra days (six in leap year) of the regular year in the French Revolutionary Calendar, added to the month Fructidor.
2. [*pl.*] the festivities held during these days.
Also *sans-culottid.*
sanṣ-çū·lot′tiṣm, *n.* the principles or teachings of the sans-culottes; extreme republicanism.
sans doute (säṅ dụ̈t), [Fr.] without doubt; certainly.
san′sẹi, *n.; pl.* **san′sẹi, san′sẹiṣ,** [Japan., third generation.] a native American citizen whose grandparents were Japanese immigrants to the United States; offspring of nisei parents.
San″sē·vi·ē′ri·ȧ, *n.* [named after the Prince of *Sanseviero* (1710–1771), a learned Neapolitan.] a genus of liliaceous plants native to the coasts of western Africa, Ceylon, and India: they have stiff, thick, sword-shaped sheathing leaves and simple spikes of small greenish flowers; also, [s-] a plant of this genus.
San′skrit, *n.* [from Sans. *saṃskṛta,* lit., made together, hence (with reference to its formalized literary and religious nature) well arranged, properly regulated: so called in distinction to *Prākrit,* lit., the common (spoken) language, dialect.]
1. the classical Old Indic literary language, as cultivated from the third century B.C. onward and still used in the ritual of the Northern Buddhist Church; because of the antiquity of its written expression and the detailed descriptive analysis in the *Sutras* of the Hindu grammarian Pānini (end of the fourth century B.C.), Sanskrit has provided the chief clue in the discovery of Indo-European and fostered the modern science of descriptive linguistics.
2. loosely, any written form of Old Indic, including Vedic.
Also spelled *Sanscrit.*

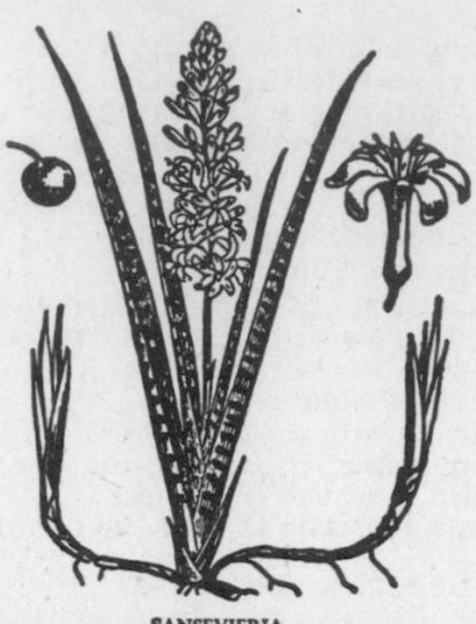

SANSEVIERIA
(*Sansevieria zeylanica*)

San′skrit, *a.* of or written in Sanskrit: also spelled *Sanscrit.*
San·skrit′iç, *a.* Sanskrit.
San′skrit·ist, *n.* a scholar of Sanskrit or the Sanskritic languages.
sanṣ·ser′if, *n.* [Fr. *sans* and Eng. *serif.*] a style of printing type with no serifs.
säṅs soụ̈·ci′ (säṅ sụ̈-sē′), [Fr.] without care or worry; gay.
San′tȧ, *n.* Santa Claus.
San′tȧ, *a.* [Sp. or It., fem. of *santo,* from L. *sanctus,* holy.] holy or saint; used in combinations, as *Santa Fé.*
San′tȧ Clauṣ, San′tȧ Klauṣ, [D.] in folklore, a fat, white-bearded, jolly old man in a red suit, who lives at the North Pole, makes toys for children, and distributes gifts at Christmas time: also called *Saint Nicholas, Saint Nick.*
San′tȧ Fẹ Trāil, a trade route between Santa Fe, New Mexico and Independence, Missouri: important from 1821 to 1880.
san′tăl, *n.* [LL. *santalum,* sandalwood.] sandalwood.
San·täl′ (sun-), *n.* a member of one of the chief tribes of India, living mainly in West Bengal: their language is Munda.
San·tȧ·lā′cē·ae, *n.pl.* [LL. *santalum,* sandalwood, and *-aceæ.*] sandalwood, an order of tropical herbs, shrubs, and trees, of which the genus *Santalum* is the type.
san·tȧ·lā′ceous, *a.* pertaining to the order *Santalaceæ.*
san·tal′iç, *a.* pertaining to or derived from sandalwood; as, *santalic* acid. [Rare.]
San″tȧ·lā′lēṣ, *n.pl.* an order of plants having two cotyledons and a unicellular, inferior ovary: some are either partly or wholly parasitic.
san′tȧ·lin, *n.* a red, crystalline, resinlike dye, $C_{15}H_{14}O_5$, contained in sandalwood: also called *santalic acid.*
San′tȧ·lum, *n.* [LL., sandal.] the typical genus of the order *Santalaceæ,* comprising eight species, native to Australia, the East Indies, and the islands of the Pacific.
Sän′tȧ Mȧ·rī′ȧ, the flagship that Columbus used in his voyage of 1492.
Sän′tȧ Mȧ·rī′ȧ tree, the calaba.
San·tee′, *n.* a North American Indian belonging to one of the seven tribes of the Dakotas.
san′tīr, *n.* [Ar. and Per.] an Oriental form of dulcimer.
san′tŏn, *n.* [Sp., from *santo,* holy.] a Moslem monk or hermit.
san·ton′i·çȧ, *n.* [LL.] a European wormwood tree, *Artemisia maritima;* also, a drug prepared from its dried flowers, containing santonin.
san′tō·nin, san′tō·nine, *n.* [Fr.] a colorless, crystalline, and poisonous compound, $C_{15}H_{18}O_3$, made from santonica: it is used in medicine for expelling intestinal worms.

san·tō·nin'iç, *a.* of, pertaining to, or obtained from santonin.

santoninic acid; an acid derived from santonin by the action of alkalis.

sap, *n.* [AS. *sæp*; akin to G. *saft.*]

1. the juice which circulates through a plant, especially a woody plant, bearing water, food, etc. to the tissues.
2. any fluid considered vital to the life or health of an organism.
3. vigor; energy; vitality.
4. sapwood.
5. [from dial. *sapskull* and *saphead.*] a stupid person; a fool. [Slang.]

sap, *v.t.*; sapped (sapt), *pt., pp.*; sapping, *ppr.* to drain of sap.

sap, *n.* [OFr. *sappe*, from the *v.*] an extended narrow trench for approaching or undermining an enemy position or a besieged place.

sap, *v.t.*; sapped (sapt), *pt., pp.*; sapping, *ppr.* [Fr. *sapper*, from *sappe*, a spade; It. *zappe*, from *zappa*, a goat: the handle resembled a goat's horns.]

1. to undermine by digging away foundations; to dig beneath.
2. to undermine in any way; weaken; exhaust; devitalize.

sap, *v.i.* 1. to dig saps.

2. to approach an enemy's position by saps.

sap·ȧ·dil'lō, *n.* same as *sapodilla.*

sap'ȧ·jöu, *n.* [Fr. *sapajou*, from Tupi name.] any of several species of South American platyrrhine, prehensile-tailed monkeys of the genus *Cebus*; a capuchin.

SAPAJOU (*Cebus capucinus*)

sȧ·pan'wood, sap·pan'wood, *n.* [Malay *sapang.*] a tree, *Cæsalpinia sappan*, whose wood yields a red dye: it is native to southern Asia and the neighboring islands. It resembles brazilwood in color and properties.

sap fag'ŏt, a bundle of fagots used to make a gabion tight and secure.

sap'ful, *a.* abounding in sap.

sap green, a dull-green pigment prepared from the juice of the ripe berries of the buckthorn.

sap'head (-hed), *n.* a simpleton; a stupid, silly person. [Colloq.]

sap'head''ed (-hed''ed), *a.* stupid; foolish. [Colloq.]

sȧ·phē'nȧ, *n.* [LL., from Ar. *ṣāfin.*] either of two large superficial veins of the leg.

sȧ·phē'nous, *a.* of, pertaining to, or associated with a saphena.

sap'id, *a.* [L. *sapidus*, having a taste, from *sapere*, to have a taste, to taste of.]

1. savory; having a pleasing taste.
2. having interest; engaging.

sȧ·pid'i·ty, sap'id·ness, *n.* savor; the quality of being sapid.

sā'pi·ence, sā'pi·en·cy, *n.* [L. *sapientia*, wisdom.] the state or quality of being sapient; sageness; knowledge.

sā'pi·ent, *a.* [L. *sapiens* (*-entis*), knowing, wise, ppr. of *sapere*, to taste, know.] wise; sage; discerning; knowing; sagacious: sometimes used in an ironical sense.

sā·pi·en'tiăl (-shăl), *a.* [LL. *sapientialis*, from L. *sapientia*, wisdom.] having, providing, or expounding wisdom.

sapiential books; the didactic books of ancient Hebrew literature, the Proverbs of Solomon and Ecclesiastes of the Old Testament, and the Book of Wisdom and Ecclesiasticus of the Apocrypha. [Obs.]

sā·pi·en'tiăl·ly, *adv.* in a sapiential manner.

sā·pi·ent·īze, *v.t.* to make sapient or wise. [Rare.]

sā'pi·ent·ly, *adv.* in a sapient manner; so as to be sapient.

Sap·in·dā'cē·ae, *n.pl.* a family of polypetalous plants, the soapberry family, consisting of trees or shrubs with erect or climbing stems and found especially in tropical South America and India: the leaves are usually alternate, simple, or compound, and the round fruit contains a soapy material.

sap·in·dā'ceous, *a.* of or pertaining to the *Sapindaceæ*.

Sȧ·pin'dus, *n.* [LL., from L. *sapo Indicus*, Indian soap.] the typical genus of the *Sapindaceæ*. Some of the species yield berries which are used as a soap.

sa'pi·ū'tan, sa'pi·oū'tan, *n.* [Malay, wild cow; from *sapi*, cow, and *ūtăn*, wild.] a ruminating animal of the subgenus *Anoa*.

sap'less, *a.* 1. without sap; dry; withered.

2. without vigor or energy; spiritless; lacking animation; as, a *sapless* voice.

sap'ling, *n.* 1. a young tree.

2. a young person; a youth.
3. a greyhound which has never followed the hares; a young greyhound.

sā'pō, *n.* [Sp.] the toadfish, *Batrachus tau*.

sap·ō·dil'lȧ, *n.* [Sp. *sapotilla*, dim. of *sapota*, the sapota tree, from Nahuatl *tzapotl.*]

1. a tall, evergreen, tropical American tree, *Achras sapota*, of the star-apple family; sapota: it yields chicle.
2. its edible apple-shaped fruit, brown and rough-skinned with a sweet, yellowish pulp: also *sapodilla plum.*

sap·ō·dil'lȧ plum, the fruit of the sapodilla.

sȧ·poġ'e·nin, *n.* a white, crystalline compound, $C_{14}H_{22}O_2$, obtained when saponin is decomposed with acids.

sap·ō·nā'ceous, *a.* [from L. *sapo* (*-onis*), soap.] soapy; resembling soap; having the qualities of soap.

sap·ō·nac'i·ty, *n.* the state or quality of being saponaceous: generally used humorously.

Sap·ō·nā'ri·ȧ, *n.* [LL., from L. *sapo*, *saponis*, soap.] a genus of herbs, chiefly native to Europe, including the soapwort.

sap'ō·năr'y, *a.* saponaceous. [Obs.]

sȧ·pon'i·fī·ȧ·ble, *a.* capable of being saponified, or converted into soap.

sȧ·pon''i·fi·çā'tion, *n.* chemical conversion of fats into soap; the process in which fatty substances, through combination with an alkali, form soap.

sȧ·pon'i·fī·ẽr, *n.* 1. a chemical agent used in saponification.

2. an apparatus for making glycerin and separating fatty substances.

sȧ·pon'i·fȳ, *v.t.*; saponified, *pt., pp.*; saponifying, *ppr.* [L. *sapo* (*-onis*), soap, and *facere*, to make.] to convert (a fat) into soap by reaction with an alkali.

sȧ·pon'i·fȳ, *v.i.* to undergo conversion into soap.

sap'ō·nin, *n.* [Fr. *saponine*, from L. *sapo*, *saponis*, soap.] any of a group of glucosides, found in soapwort, soapbark, etc., which form a soapy foam when dissolved in water.

sap'ō·nine (*or* -nēn), *n.* same as *saponin.*

sap'ō·nīte, *n.* [L. *sapo* (*-onis*), soap, and *-ite.*] a hydrous silicate of aluminum and magnesium, occurring in soft, soapy masses in veins and cavities of rock formations.

sap'ō·nul, *n.* [Fr. *saponule*, from L. *sapo*, *saponis*, soap.] an imperfect soap formed by the action of an alkali upon an essential oil. [Obs.]

sā'pŏr, *n.* [L., savor, from *sapere*, to taste.] that quality in a substance which produces taste or flavor; savor; relish: British spelling, *sapour.*

sap·ō·rif'iç, *n.* [Fr. *saporifique*, from L. *sapor*, savor, and *facere*, to make.] having the power to produce taste or savor; producing taste.

sap·ō·ros'i·ty, *n.* the quality of being saporous.

sap'ō·rous, *a.* of or having taste; yielding some kind of flavor.

Sȧ·pō'tȧ, *n.* [Sp. *zapote*; Mex. *zapotle.*]

1. in botany, the specific name of a tree or plant of the genus *Achras.*
2. [s–] the sapodilla.

Sap·ō·tā'cē·ae, *n.pl.* [*sapota* and *-aceæ.*] a family of plants belonging to the polycarpous group of monopetalous exogens, including trees and shrubs that yield a milky juice sometimes used for alimentary purposes. One of the most important species is *Isonandra gutta* that produces the gutta-percha of commerce.

sap·ō·tā'ceous, *a.* of or belonging to the *Sapotaceæ*.

sap·ō·til'lȧ, *n.* same as *sapodilla.*

sap·pȧ·dil'lō tree, same as *sapodilla.*

sap·pan'wood, *n.* same as *sapanwood.*

sap'pȧr, sap'pāre, *n.* same as *cyanite.*

sap'pẽr, *n.* 1. one who or that which saps.

2. a soldier who makes trenches, repairs fortifications, etc.

Sap'phiç (saf'ik), *a.* [L. *Sapphicus*; Gr. *Sapphikos*, from *Sapphō.*]

1. of Sappho, the Greek poet.
2. designating or of certain meters or a form of stanza or strophe used by or named after Sappho, especially a stanza of three five-stress lines followed by a short line.

Sap'phiç, *n.* a Sapphic verse.

Sap·phī'rȧ (sȧ-fī'rȧ), *n.* [Gr. *Sappheirē.*] in the Bible, the wife of Ananias, who was struck dead with her husband for lying. Acts v. 1–10.

sap'phīre (saf'īr), *n.* [L. *sapphirus*; Gr. *sappheiros*; Heb. *sappīr.*]

1. a hard, transparent precious stone of a clear, deep-blue corundum.
2. its color.
3. a hard, translucent or transparent variety of corundum, varying in color.
4. a gem made of this; as, white, yellow, or purple *sapphire.*
5. a hummingbird of South America, the sapphirewing: so called from the color of its wings.
6. in heraldic blazonry by precious stones, a tincture, the color blue.

sap'phīre, *a.* like sapphire; deep blue.

sap'phīre·wing, *n.* a South American hummingbird; the sapphire.

sap'phir·ine (saf'ẽr-), *a.* resembling sapphire; having the qualities of sapphire.

sap'phir·ine, *n.* 1. a blue or green silicate of magnesium and aluminum, $Mg_4Al_{12}Si_2O_{27}$.

2. a blue variety of spinel.

sap'phiṣm, *n.* [Gr. *Sapphō*, Sappho.] lesbianism: so called in allusion to the amorous verses of Sappho.

sap'phō (saf'ō), *n.* [Gr. *Sapphō*, Sappho.] a hummingbird, *Sappho sparganura*, of South America, with a brilliantly colored, long, forked tail.

sap pīne, the stiff-needled pine of the United States which yields a great quantity of pitch.

sap'pi·ness, *n.* a sappy state or quality.

sap'py, *a.*; *comp.* sappier; *superl.* sappiest, [AS. *sæpig*, sappy.]

1. full of sap; juicy; succulent.
2. energetic; vigorous.
3. foolish; silly; fatuous. [Slang.]

sapr-, see *sapro-.*

sap·rē'mi·ȧ, sap·rae'mi·ȧ, *n.* [*sapro-*, and Gr. *haima*, blood.] a form of blood poisoning caused by the products of putrefactive microorganisms in the blood.

sap'rin, *n.* [*sapro-* and *-in.*] a nonpoisonous ptomaine, $C_5H_{14}N_2$, from decaying visceral substances.

sap'rō-, [from Gr. *sapros*, rotten.] a combining form used in biology and medicine meaning *dead, putrefying, decaying*, as in *sapro*genic.

sap·rō·gen'iç, sap·roġ'e·nous, *a.* [*sapro-*, and Gr. *-genēs*, producing.] producing or produced by putrefaction.

Sap·rō·leg'ni·ȧ, *n.* a genus of fungi found on the bodies of both living and dead fishes. *Saprolegnia ferax* causes disease destructive to salmon and other fishes.

Sap·rō·leg·ni·ā'cē·ae, *n.pl.* [*sapro-*, and Gr. *legnon*, an edge, a border.] a family of fungi of which the genus *Saprolegnia* is a type.

Sap·rō·leg·ni·ā'lēṣ, *n.pl.* see *Saprolegniaceæ*.

sap'rō·līte, *n.* [*sapro-* and *-lite.*] decomposed rock.

sap rōll'ẽr, in military usage, a large bullet-proof gabion which the sapper rolls in front of him as a protection from the enemy's fire.

sȧ·proph'ȧ·găn, *n.* [*sapro-*, and Gr. *phagein*, to eat.] any of a group of lamellicorn beetles which feed on decaying animal and vegetable substances.

sȧ·proph'ȧ·gous, *a.* feeding on decaying organic matter.

sȧ·proph'i·lous, *a.* same as *saprophytic.*

sap'rō·phȳte, *n.* [*sapro-*, and Gr. *phyton*, a plant.] any organism that lives on decaying organic matter, as some fungi and bacteria.

sap·rō·phyt'iç, *a.* pertaining to, or having the nature of, saprophytes.

sap rot, same as *dry rot.*
sap′sȧ·gō, *n.* [altered from G. *schabzieger*; *schaben*, to scrape, and *zieger*, whey.] a kind of hard cheese, made in Switzerland, having a greenish color, and flavored with melilot.
sap shiēld, in military usage, a shield or plate, mounted on wheels, to protect a sapper, when the earthworks are not sufficient.
sap′skull, *n.* a saphead. [Dial.]
sap′suck″ẽr, *n.* any insect-eating woodpecker of the genus *Sphyrapicus*, especially *Sphyrapicus varius*, that drills holes in maples, apple trees, etc. and drinks the sap.
sap tūbe, a vessel for carrying sap.
sap·ụ·çā′iȧ (-yȧ), *n.* [Braz.] a Brazilian tree, *Lecythis zabucajo*, that bears an edible nut resembling the Brazil nut.
sap′wood, *n.* alburnum; the soft wood just beneath the bark of a tree.
Sar·ȧ·bā′īte, *n.* [LL. *Sarabaitæ.*] a member of a sect of Oriental monks who seceded from the ordinary monastic life of the Early Church.
sar′ȧ·band, *n.* [Fr. *sarabande*; Sp. *zarabanda*; ult. from Per. *sarband*, kind of dance and song.]
1. a graceful, stately, slow Spanish dance in triple time, developed from an earlier lively dance.
2. music for, or in the tempo of, this dance, with decided emphasis on the second beat of the measure, often constituting one of the movements of the classical suite.
Sar′ȧ·cen, *n.* [LL. *Saracenus*, from L.Gr. *Sarakēnos.*]
1. originally, any member of the nomadic tribes of Syria and near-by regions.
2. later, an Arab.
3. any Moslem, especially as opposed to the Crusaders.
Saracen's consound; the groundsel or ragwort, *Senecio saracenicus*, formerly used by the Saracens as an application for wounds.
Saracen stone; graywether.
Sar′ȧ·cen, *a.* of the Saracens.
Sar·ȧ·cen′iç, *a.* pertaining to the Saracens.
Sar·ȧ·cen′iç·ăl, *a.* same as *Saracenic.*
Sar′ăh, *n.* [Heb. *sārāh*, princess.] in the Bible, the wife of Abraham and the mother of Isaac.
Sā′raī, *n.* in the Bible, Sarah.
sȧ·ran′, *n.* any of various thermoplastic resins obtained by the polymerization or copolymerization of certain vinyl compounds: it is used in making various fabrics, acid-resistant pipes and fittings, wrapping film, etc.
Sä·räs·wä′tī, *n.* [Hind.] in Hindu mythology, the consort of Brahma, the first of the Hindu triad. She is the goddess of speech, music, arts, and letters.
Sar·ȧ·tō′gȧ truñk, [after *Saratoga* Springs, N. Y.] a large trunk, formerly much used by women.
sär′bȧ·çāne, sär′bȧ·çand, *n.* same as *sumpitan.*
särç-, see *sarco-.*
sär′çaṣm, *n.* [L. *sarcasmos*; Gr. *sarkasmos*, a bitter laugh, from *sarkazein*, to tear flesh like dogs, to speak bitterly, from *sarx, sarkos*, flesh.]
1. a taunting, sneering, cutting, or caustic remark; a gibe or jeer, generally ironical.
2. the making of such remarks.
3. the characteristic quality of such remarks.
Syn.—irony, banter, jeer, derision, satire.
sär·caṣ′mous, *a.* sarcastic. [Obs.]
sär·cas′tiç, *a.* 1. of, having the nature of, or characterized by sarcasm; sneering; caustic; taunting.
2. using, or fond of using, sarcasm.
sär·cas′tiç·ăl, *a.* sarcastic.
sär·cas′tiç·ăl·ly, *adv.* in a sarcastic manner.
sär′cel, *n.* [OFr. *cercel*; L. *circellus*, dim. of *circulus*, a circle, ring.] in falconry, any feather on the outer joint of a bird's wing. [Obs.]
sär′celed, sär′celled, *a.* in heraldry, cut or divided through the center, as an animal.
sär·celle′, *n.* [Fr.] a garganey or other species of teal.
särce′net, *n.* [Anglo-Fr. *sarzinett*, dim. from ME. *Sarsin, Sarasene*, Saracen.] a soft silk cloth, used for ribbons, linings, etc.
sär·cī′nȧ, *n.* [L. *sarcina*, bundle.] a genus of coccus in which the cell separates along all three dimensions, forming cuboidal packets.
sär′cine, *n.* same as *hypoxanthine.*
sär′çle, *v.t.* [Fr.] to take out, as weeds, with a hoe, harrow, or rake. [Obs.]

sär′çō-, [from Greek *sarx, sarkos*, flesh.] a combining form meaning *flesh*, as in *sarcology*: also, before a vowel, *sarc-.*
sär·çob′ȧ·sis, *n.*; *pl.* **sär·çob′ȧ·sēṣ,** [*sarco-*, and Gr. *basis*, a foot, base.] a dry fruit having many cells that do not burst open, clustered around an axis.
sär′çō·blast, *n.* [*sarco-* and *-blast.*] a granule in the cell tissue of certain protozoans.
sär′çō·çärp, *n.* [*sarco-*, and Gr. *karpos*, fruit.]
1. in botany, the fleshy part of a drupaceous pericarp, situated between the integument, or skin, and the endocarp, or stone.
2. loosely, any fleshy fruit.
sär′çō·cēle, *n.* [*sarco-*, and Gr. *kēlē*, tumor.] a fleshy tumor of a testicle.
sär′çō·çol, sär·çō·çol′lȧ, *n.* [*sarco-*, and Gr. *kolla*, glue.] the inspissated sap of a species of *Penæa*: so called from its supposed use in healing wounds and ulcers.
sär·çō·çol′lin, *n.* a bitter compound obtained from sarcocol by the action of solvents.
sär′çōde, *n.* [Gr. *sarkōdēs*, contr. of *sarkoeidēs*, fleshlike.] protoplasm, especially of the lower orders of animals: a term suggested by Du Jardin (1835).
sär′çō·dẽrm, sär·çō·dẽr′mȧ, *n.* that part of the covering of a seed that lies between the skin and the inner integument; a sarcocarp.
Sär·çō′dēṣ, *n.* [LL., so called because of the red, fleshy stem, from Gr. *sarkōdēs*, fleshlike.] a genus of plants of which *Sarcodes sanguinea*, the California snow plant, is the only known species.
sär·çod′iç, sär′çō·dous, *a.* relating to sarcode.
sär′çoid, *a.* like or consisting of flesh or sarcode.
sär·çō·laç′tiç, *a.* [*sarco-*, L. *lac, lactis*, milk, and *-ic.*] belonging to or obtained from flesh and milk; pertaining to an acid obtained from muscular tissue.
sär·çō·lem′mȧ, *n.* [*sarco-*, and Gr. *lemma*, skin.] the thin membrane that forms the covering of the fibers of striated muscle: also called *myolemma.*
sär′çō·line, *a.* [Gr. *sarx*, flesh.] in mineralogy, flesh-colored.
sär·çō·loġ′iç, sär·çō·loġ′i·çăl, *a.* relating to sarcology.
sär·çol′ō·ġy, *n.* [*sarco-* and *-logy.*]
1. the division of anatomy dealing with the soft tissues of the body.
2. an ancient science dealing with the effects of eating various animal organs, or using extracts made from them, as the use of the thyroid gland in treating cretinism.
sär·çō′mȧ, *n.*; *pl.* **sär·çō′maṣ** or **sär·çō′mȧ·tȧ,** [Gr. *sarkōma*, a fleshy excrescence.]
1. any of various malignant tumors that begin in connective tissue, or in tissue developed from the mesoblast and not epithelial.
2. in botany, a fleshy disk. [Obs.]
sär·çō′mȧ·toid, *a.* same as *sarcomatous.*
sär·çō·mȧtō′sis, *n.* a condition characterized by spread of sarcomas through the body.
sär·çom′ȧ·tous, *a.* of or like a sarcoma.
sär′çō·mēre, *n.* one of the sarcous disks of striped muscle fiber.
Sär·çoph′ȧ·gȧ, *n.pl.* [LL., neut. pl. of *sarcophagus*, flesh eating.] a marsupial suborder of carnivores, to which belong opossums.
Sär·çoph′ȧ·gȧ, *n.* the flesh flies, a genus of carnivorous dipterous insects.
sär·çoph′ȧ·găl, *a.* sarcophagous. [Rare.]
sär·çoph′ȧ·gous, *a.* [LL. *sarcophagus*; Gr. *sarkophagos*, flesh-eating, carnivorous.] carnivorous; flesh-eating.
sär·çoph′ȧ·gus, *n.*; *pl.* **sär·çoph′ȧ·gī, sär·çoph′ȧ·gus·eṣ,** [L., from Gr. *sarkophagos*; *sarx, sarkos*, flesh, and *phagein*, to eat.]

ROMAN SARCOPHAGUS

1. among the ancient Greeks and Romans, a limestone coffin or tomb, often inscribed and elaborately ornamented.
2. any stone coffin, especially one exposed to view in the open air or in a large or monumental tomb.
3. a species of stone used among the Greeks for making coffins: also called *lapis Assius.*
4. an eighteenth-century wine cooler, usually of mahogany with a lead lining, forming a part of a sideboard.
sär·çoph′ȧ·ġy, *n.* [Gr. *sarkophagia*, the eating of flesh.] the practice of eating flesh. [Rare.]
sär·çoph′i·lous, *a.* flesh-loving; carnivorous.
sär′çō·plaṣm, *n.* [*sarco-*, and Gr. *plasma*, anything formed.] the transparent intercolumnar substance of striped muscle fiber: also written *sarcoplasma.*
sär·çō·plaṣ′miç, *a.* of or relating to sarcoplasm.
Sär·çop′tēṣ, *n.* [*sarco-*, and Gr. *koptein*, to cut.] a genus of the *Acarida*, represented by the itch mites.
sär·çop′tiç, *a.* relating to or produced by sarcoptids.
sär·çop′tid, *n.* any individual of the *Sarcoptes.*
sär·çop′tid, *a.* of or pertaining to the itch mites.
Sär·çō·rham′phus, *n.* [*sarco-*, and Gr. *rhamphos*, beak.] a genus of birds of prey living chiefly on carrion, including the American vulture.
sär·çō·sep′tum, *n.* [*sarco-*, and LL. *septum*, septum.] a fleshy septum of a polyp.
sär′çō·sin, *n.* a derivative of creatine, formed by various methods of decomposition.
sär·çō′sis, *n.* [LL., from Gr. *sarkosis*, sarcoma, a fleshy excrescence.]
1. the development of sarcomas. [Now Rare.]
2. extraordinary development of flesh. [Now Rare.]
3. sarcomatosis. [Now Rare.]
sär′çō·spẽrm, *n.* [*sarco-*, and Gr. *sperma*, seed.] a sarcoderm.
sär·ços·tō′sis, *n.* [*sarco-*, and Gr. *osteon*, bone.] a sarcoma containing bony matter. [Obs.]
sär′çō·stȳle, *n.* [*sarco-*, and Gr. *stylos*, pillar.] a fibril or muscle column extending the entire length of a striped muscle fiber.
sär·çot′iç, *a.* in surgery, producing or generating flesh.
sär·çot′iç, *n.* a medicine which promotes the growth of flesh.
sär′çous, *a.* of or composed of flesh or muscle.
särd, *n.* [L. *sarda*; Gr. *sardios, sardion*, a sard, lit., Sardian stone, from *Sardeis*, Sardis, the capital of Lydia.]
1. a variety of chalcedony which has a rich brownish-red color: it is used in jewelry, etc
2. a piece of this.
Also *sardine.*
sär′dȧ·çhāte, *n.* [L. *sardachates*, from Gr. *sardios*, a sard, *achatēs*, an agate.] a kind of agate containing sard.
sär′del, *n.* [L. *sarda*, a sardine.]
1. same as *sardine.*
2. a clupeoid fish of the Mediterranean, similar to a sardine.
sär·dīne′, *n.*; *pl.* **sär·dīneṣ′** or **sär·dīne′,** [Fr. *sardine*, from L. *sardina*; Gr. *sardēnē*, dim. of *sarda*, a kind of tunny fish caught near Sardinia.]
1. any small fish of the herring family, suitable for eating when preserved in oil, particularly *Clupea pilchardus*, the pilchard of Europe. The West Indian or Spanish sardine is *Clupea pseudohispanica.* The California sardine is *Clupea sagax.*
2. any of several varieties of the genus *Stolephorus*, or anchovies.
3. young menhaden, herring, or other small food fishes, canned in salted oil, also with spices, mustard, etc.
sär′dine, *n.* same as *sard.*
Sär·din′i·ăn, *a.* pertaining to the island or people of Sardinia.
Sär·din′i·ăn, *n.* 1. a native or inhabitant of Sardinia.
2. the Romance dialect of Sardinia.
sär′di·us, *n.* [LL. *sardius*; Gr. *sardios, sardion*, a sard.]
1. a precious stone, one of twelve set in the breastplate of the Jewish high priest; a ruddy stone, perhaps a ruby. Ex. xxviii. 19.
2. a sard.
sär·dō′ni·ăn, *a.* sardonic. [Obs.]
sär·don′iç, *a.* [Fr. *sardonique*, from Gr. *sardanios*, bitter.] bitterly ironical; sarcastic; as, the *sardonic* grin of a ruffian.
sardonic laugh; a spasmodic action of the

muscles of the face, which often occurs in lockjaw.

sär·don'i·çăl·ly, *adv.* in a sardonic manner.

sär'dō·nyx, *n.* [L.; Gr. *sardonyx*, a sardonyx; from Gr. *sardios, sardion*, a sard, and *onyx*, an onyx] a kind of onyx composed of sard and a white chalcedony in alternating stripes or layers: it is used as a gem, especially in making cameos.

sä'ree, *n.* a sari.

sär·gas'sō, *n.* [Port. *sargaço, sargasso*, LL. *sargassum*, seaweed.] any of a number of related floating, brown seaweeds with berrylike air sacs; gulfweed: also *sargasso weed.*

sär·gas'sō çrab, a minute crustacean living upon plants of the genus *Sargassum*, and having all its varying colors.

sär·gas'sō pīpe'fish, a species of pipefish found in sargasso.

Sär·gas'sum, *n.* [Port. *sargaço, sargasso*, the gulfweed.] a genus of marine algae, the gulfweeds, found in the warmer seas; also, [s–] any plant of this genus.

sär'gō, *n.* [Sp.] a spinous-finned fish of the genus *Diplodus* or of related genera, especially *Diplodus sargus.*

sä'rï, *n.*; *pl.* **sä'rïş,** [Hind.] a long cotton or silk garment worn by Hindu women to wrap around the body with one end over the head: usually the chief garment.

sȧ·rïgue' (-rēg'), *n.* [Fr., from Braz. *sarigueya.*] *Didelphys opossum*, a marsupial mammal of South America.

sä'rin, *n.* [G.] a highly toxic nerve gas, C_4H_{10}-FPO, which attacks the central nervous system, bringing on convulsions and death.

särk, *n.* [ME. *sark*; AS. *serce*; Ice. *serkr*; Sw. *särk*, a shirt.] a shirt or chemise. [Scot. or Archaic.]

särk, *v.t.* to put sarking upon, as a roof. [Scot. and Brit. Dial.]

sär'kin, *n.* sarcine or hypoxanthine.

särk'ing, *n.* a sheathing of thin boards, usually as a support for roof slates or shingles. [Scot. and Brit. Dial.]

sär'lak, *n.* the yak: also spelled *sarlyk.*

Sär·mā'tiăn, *a.* [L. *Sarmata*; Gr. *Sarmatēs*, a Sarmatian.] pertaining to Sarmatia or its inhabitants.

Sär·mā'tiăn, *n.* any of an ancient people who lived in Sarmatia.

sär'ment, *n.* a sarmentum. [Obs.]

sär·men'tȧ, *n.* plural of *sarmentum.*

sär·men·tā'ceous, *a.* sarmentose.

sär·men'tōse, sär·men'tous, *a.* [L. *sarmentosus*, from *sarmentum*, twigs.] having sarmenta, or runners; having the form or character of a runner.

sär·men'tum, *n.*; *pl.* **sär·men'tȧ,** [L., twigs, from *sarpere*, to prune.] a long, slender running stem giving off leaves or roots at intervals, as that of the strawberry.

sä'rong, *n.* [Malay.] 1. the principal garment of men and women in the Malay Archipelago, the East Indies, etc., consisting of a long strip of cloth, often brightly colored and printed, worn around the lower part of the body like a skirt.

2. cotton fabric used for such garments.

sā'ros, *n.* [Gr., a Chaldean cycle.]

1. a cycle or astronomical period, the duration of which is 6,585 days and 8 hours, or 223 lunar months, at the expiration of which the lunar and solar eclipses are repeated in the same order as before at points 120° west of those in the preceding saros. This cycle is said to have been known to the Babylonian astronomers.

2. a Babylonian unit or numeral representing sixty sixties, 3,600.

Sär·pē'dŏn, *n.* [L.; Gr. *Sarpēdōn.*]

1. a son of Zeus and Europa, who became king of Lycia and was allowed to live three generations.

2. in one version, a son of Zeus and Laodamia, killed by Patroclus in the Trojan War.

sär'plăr, *n.* 1. a bale of wool weighing 2,240 pounds.

2. a coarse sacking or packing cloth. [Obs.]

sär'pō, *n.* same as *sapo.*

Sar·rȧ·cē'ni·ȧ, *n.* [named after Dr. *Sarrazin*, of Quebec.]

1. a genus of American plants, of the *Sarraceniaceæ*, with nodding flowers, yellow to purple, and mottled leaves. The leaves, which attract insects, are in the form of hollow tubes or pitchers winged down the inner side and open at the top, which has a curved hood. The style is expanded at the top into a broad, five-angled disk. *Sarracenia purpurea*, the pitcher plant, has a dark purple flower: also called *huntsman's cup.*

2. [s–] any plant of this genus.

Sar·rȧ·cē·ni·ā'cē·ae, *n.pl.* a family of herbaceous perennial bog plants having radical leaves with a hollow urnlike petiole. The family comprises *Sarracenia* of the eastern part of the United States, *Darlingtonia* of California, and *Heliamphora* of South America.

sar·rȧ·cē·ni·ā'ceous, *a.* belonging to the *Sarraceniaceæ.*

sär'rȧ·zin, *n.* [Fr.] buckwheat.

sär'sȧ, *n.* sarsaparilla.

sär"sȧ·pȧ·ril'lȧ, *n.* [Sp. *zarzaparrilla*, sarsaparilla, from Sp. *zarza*, a bramble, and *parrilla*, dim. of *parra*, a vine; or perhaps from *Parillo*, a physician, who first made use of it as a medicine.]

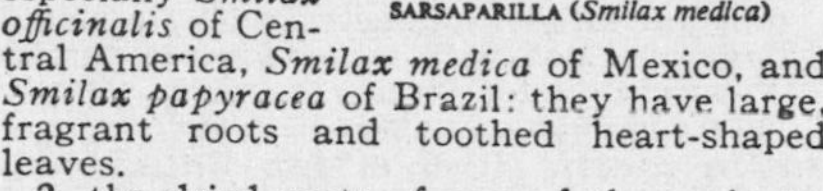

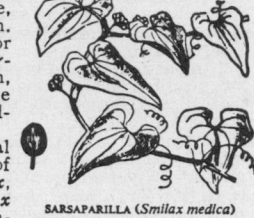

SARSAPARILLA (*Smilax medica*)

1. any tropical American plant of the genus *Smilax*, especially *Smilax officinalis* of Central America, *Smilax medica* of Mexico, and *Smilax papyracea* of Brazil: they have large, fragrant roots and toothed heart-shaped leaves.

2. the dried roots of any of these plants, used as a tonic and for flavoring.

3. an extract of this.

4. a carbonated drink flavored with sarsaparilla.

American sarsaparilla; a perennial herb, *Aralia nudicaulis*, whose roots are used as a substitute for sarsaparilla.

Australian sarsaparilla; an Australian climber, *Hardembergia monophylla*, of the *Leguminosæ*, used as a substitute for sarsaparilla.

sär"sȧ·pȧ·ril'lin, *n.* same as *parillin.*

sär'sen, *n.* [for *Saracen stone*, a heathen stone.] graywether: also *sarsen stone, Saracen stone.*

särse'net, *n.* same as *sarcenet.*

särt, *n.* [from *assart*; OFr. *essart*; LL. *exartum*, from L. *ex*, out, and *sarrire*, to hoe.] a piece of woodland turned into arable land. [Brit.]

sär'tŏr, *n.* [L.] a tailor: literary and humorous.

sär·tō'ri·ăl, *a.* [L. *sartor*, a tailor, from *sartus*, pp. of *sarcire*, to cut.]

1. of or pertaining to a tailor or to tailoring.

2. of clothing or dress, especially men's.

3. in anatomy, of or pertaining to the sartorius.

sär·tō'ri·us, *n.* [L. *sartor*, a tailor.] a narrow muscle of the thigh, the longest in the human body, that passes obliquely across the front of the thigh and assists in rotating the leg to the position assumed in sitting cross-legged.

Sā'rum ūse, [ML. *Sarum*; said to be from abbrev. of L. *Sarisburia*, from Late AS. *Searesburh.*] the form or order of divine service used in the churches of Sarum (Salisbury) before the Reformation.

sär'zȧ, *n.* sarsaparilla.

sȧ·san'quȧ, *n.* [Japan.] a camellia, *Camellia sasanqua*, of Japan and China.

sash, *n.* [Ar. *shāsh*, turban.]

1. a band or scarf worn round the waist or over the shoulder for ornament, as by women and children, or as a symbol of distinction by men.

2. in Oriental countries, a roll of silk, fine linen, or gauze, worn about the head; a turban.

sash, *v.t.*; sashed (sasht), *pt.*, *pp.*; sashing, *ppr.* to ornament with a sash or scarf.

sash, *n.* [Fr. *châsse, châssis*, a frame, a sash, from L. *capsa*, a box, a chest.]

1. a frame for holding the glass pane or panes of a window or door, especially a sliding frame. The side pieces are the stiles; the top and bottom pieces, rails; and the interior pieces, which hold the panes, bars.

2. the gate in which a mill saw is held.

French sash; a window sash or casement swung on hinges.

sash, *v.t.* to provide with a sash or sashes, as windows.

sa·shāy', *v.i.* [altered from *chassé* (dance).] to glide, move around, or go. [Colloq.]

sash bär, one of the vertical and transverse pieces within a window frame which hold the panes of glass in place.

sash çọrd (or **līne**), a cord attached to either side of a sliding sash, having balancing weights so that the window can be raised or lowered easily.

sȧ·shọọn', *n.* a kind of leather stuffing put into a boot for the wearer's ease. [Obs.]

sā'sin, *n.* [E. Ind.] the Indian antelope, *Antilope cervicapra*, or black buck.

SASIN

sā'sine, *n.* [Fr.] in Scots law, the act of giving legal possession of feudal property; also, the instrument by which the possession is acquired.

sas·kȧ·tọọn', *n.* [from Am. Ind. *misâskwatomin*, from *misâskwat*, shadbush, lit., tree with much wood, and *min*, berry.] a small bush of the rose family, with purple fruit; shadbush.

sas'quatch, *n.* [from Salishan *saskehavas*, wild men.] [*also* S-] a huge, hairy, manlike creature with long arms, reputed to live in the mountains of northwestern North America.

sass, *n.* [var. of *sauce.*] 1. (a) [Dial.] garden vegetables; (b) stewed fruit or preserves served as a desert.

2. impudent talk. [Colloq.]

sass, *v.t.* to talk impudently or disrespectfully to. [Colloq.]

sas'sȧ·by, *n.*; *pl.* **sas'sȧ·bieş,** [S. Afr.] any of a group of large South African antelopes, having strong crescentic horns with the points directed inward.

sas'sȧ·fras, *n.* [Fr. *sassafras*; Port. *sassafraz*, from L. *saxifraga*; *saxum*, a stone, and *frangere*, to break.]

1. any of a number of related trees of the laurel family, with yellow flowers and bluish fruit.

2. the dried root bark of any of these trees, used in medicine and for flavoring.

3. the flavor.

Australian sassafras; an Australian tree, *Doryphora sassafras*, the leaves and bark of which are used in medicine.

Brazilian sassafras; a tree, *Nectandra puchury*, of the laurel family, which yields pichurims.

California sassafras; the laurel of California.

Cayenne sassafras; a rosaceous tree, *Licania guianensis*, of South America.

Chilean sassafras; same as ***Peruvian nutmeg*** under ***nutmeg.***

Sas·sā'ni·ȧn, *n.* and *a.* same as *Sassanid.*

Sas'sȧ·nid, *a.* of the Sassanian Dynasty, ruling family of the Persian Empire (226–641 A.D.).

Sas'sȧ·nid, *n.*; *pl.* **Sas'sȧ·nidş, Sas·san'i·dae,** any member of the Sassanian Dynasty.

sasse, *n.* [D. *sas*, a sluice.] a sluice, canal, or lock on a navigable river. [Obs.]

Sas'sen·açh, *n.* [Gael. *Sasunnach*, Saxon.] a Saxon, Englishman, or Lowlander: term used by Irish and Scots.

sas'sō·lin, sas'sō·line, *n.* [Fr. *sassoline*, from It. *Sasso*, a town near Florence, Italy.] native boracic acid, found in saline incrustations on the borders of hot springs.

sas'sy, *a.*; *comp.* sassier; *superl.* sassiest, [dial. var. of *saucy.*] impudent; saucy. [Dial. or Colloq.]

sas'sy, *n.* [W. Afr.; prob. from Eng. *saucy.*] an African tree, *Erythrophlœum guineense*, with poisonous bark and wood: also *sassy bark.*

sas'sy bärk, *n.* same as *sassy.*

sas'sy·wood, *n.* a sassy.

säs'trȧ, *n.* same as *shaster.*

sȧs·trụ'gȧ, *n.*; *pl.* **sȧs·trụ'gi,** [Russ.] one of a series of long, parallel, and wavelike ridges of hard snow; *sastrugi* are caused by the action of the wind or snow and occur on the open plains: they often end in a perpendicular wall (of hard snow) having an overhanging crest: sometimes written *zastruga*.

sat, *v.* past tense and past participle of *sit*.

Sā'tăn, *n.* [Heb. *śāṭān*, enemy, from *sāṭan*, to be adverse.] in Christian theology, the great enemy of man and of goodness; the Devil: usually identified with Lucifer, the chief of the fallen angels, cast out of heaven by Michael, according to the Talmud.

sä·tang', *n.*; *pl.* **sä·tang',** [Siamese *satān*.] a bronze coin and money of account in Thailand, equal to 1/100 of a baht.

sā·tan'iç, sā·tan'i·çăl, *a.* of, having the qualities of, or resembling Satan; extremely malicious or wicked; devilish; infernal.

Detest the slander which, with a *satanic* smile, exults over the character it has ruined. —Dwight.

sā·tan'i·çăl·ly, *adv.* in a satanic manner.

sā·tan'i·çăl·ness, *n.* the quality or state of being satanical.

Sā'tăn·iṣm, *n.* worship of Satan; especially, the principles and rites of a cult which travesties Christian ceremonies.

sā'tăn·ist, *n.* 1. a very wicked person. [Rare].
2. [S-] one who worships Satan.

sā'tăn mŏñ'key, the couxia or black saki of South America.

Sā·tăn·oph'ȧ·ny, *n.* [Gr. *Satanas*, Satan, and *phainesthai*, to appear.] an appearance or incarnation of Satan; the state of being possessed by a devil. [Rare.]

Sā''tăn·ō·phō'bi·ȧ, *n.* [*Satan*, and Gr. *phobos*, fear.] fear of the devil. [Rare.]

sat'ȧ·rȧ, *n.* [origin doubtful.] a woolen cloth, ribbed, lustered, and highly dressed.

satch'el, *n.* [OFr. *sachel*; L. *saccellus*, dim. of *saccus*, a sack, bag.] a small bag for carrying clothes, books, etc., sometimes having a shoulder strap.

sāte, *v.t.*; sated, *pt.*, *pp.*; sating, *ppr.* [prob. shortened form from L. *satiatus*, pp. of *satiare*, to fill full, satisfy.]
1. to satiate; to gratify with more than enough, so as to weary or disgust; to glut.
Sate the hungry soul beyond an hour. —Lowell.
2. to satisfy (an appetite, desire, etc.) to the full; to gratify completely.

sāte, *v.* archaic past tense and past participle of *sit*.

sa·teen', [Fr. *satin*, satin.] a smooth, glossy, cotton fabric made in imitation of satin.

sāte'less, *a.* insatiable. [Rare.]

sat'el·līte, *n.* [OFr., from L. *satelles* (*-itis*), an attendant, guard.]
1. a follower or attendant attached to a prince or other person of importance.
2. a subordinate attendant; an obsequious or subservient follower.
That official and his *satellites* shot tumultuously down the stone stairway. —Gen. Charles King.
3. (a) a small planet revolving around a larger one; a moon; (b) a man-made object put into orbit around the earth, the moon, or some other heavenly body.
4. a small state that is economically dependent on, and hence adjusts its policies to, a larger, more powerful state.
5. a satellite sphinx.
6. in anatomy, (a) a vein that closely accompanies an artery; (b) a minor lesion situated near a larger one.

sat'el·līte sphinx, a large moth, *Philampelus satellitia*, the larva of which feeds on vines.

sat·el·li'tious (-lish'us), *a.* consisting of satellites.

Sath'ăn, Sath'ȧ·nas, *n.* Satan. [Obs.]

sā·ti·ȧ·bil'i·ty (-shi-), *n.* the quality of being satiable.

sā'ti·ȧ·ble, *a.* capable of being satiated.

sā'ti·ȧ·ble·ness, *n.* satiability.

sā'ti·āte (-shi-), *a.* [L. *satiatus*, pp. of *satiare*, to fill full, from *sat*, *satis*, sufficient.] having had enough or more than enough; sated.

sā'ti·āte, *v.t.*; satiated, *pt.*, *pp.*; satiating, *ppr.*
1. to fill; to satisfy the appetite or desire of completely; to feed to the full; as, to *satiate* appetite or sense. [Rare.]
2. to glut; to gratify with more than enough, so as to weary or disgust.
3. to saturate. [Obs.]
Syn.—content, satisfy, surfeit, cloy, glut.

sā·ti·ā'tion, *n.* the state of being satiated.

sȧ·tī'e·ty, *n.* [Fr. *satiété*; L. *satietas* (*-atis*), abundance, satiety.] the state of being satiated.
Syn.—fullness, satiation, surfeit, repletion.

sat'in, *n.* [ME.; OFr.; Sp. *setuni*; Ar. (*aṭlas*) *zaitūni*, (satin) of *Zaitūn*, Med. name of Chuanchow, China.] a silk, nylon, or rayon cloth having a smooth finish, glossy on the face, dull on the back.
Denmark satin; a kind of heavy worsted fabric woven with a twill and finished to resemble satin: used in the manufacture of women's shoes.

sat'in, *a.* made of satin; resembling satin; smooth, soft, and glossy.

sat'in bīrd, a bowerbird of Australia, *Ptilonorhynchus holosericeus*.

sat'in·bush, *n.* a leguminous shrub of South Africa, *Podalyria sericea*, having a glossy pubescence resembling satin.

sat·i·net', sat·i·nette', *n.* [Fr.] 1. a thin or inferior satin.
2. a particular kind of cloth made of cotton warp and woolen filling, made to resemble satin: used largely in the manufacture of trousers.

sat'in fin'ish, a finish resembling satin; specifically, a lustrous satinlike finish put on gold and silver with a scratchbrush.

sat'in flow'ẽr, a plant, *Lunaria biennis*, of the mustard family, characterized by a singular large oval pod with a broad white partition of satiny luster, which remains after the valves have fallen: also called *honesty*.

sat'in mọth, either of two British moths, *Leucoma salicis*, of the family *Arctiidæ*, or *Cymatophora duplaris*, a noctuid.

sat'in spär, a fine fibrous variety of carbonate or sulfate of calcium having a satiny luster.

sat'in spar'rōw, a sparrow of Australia and Tasmania, *Myiagra nitida*, having the dorsal parts covered with feathers of dark green with the luster of polished metal.

sat'in stōne, same as *satin spar*.

sat'in·wood, *n.* 1. any of several very smooth woods used in fine furniture.
2. any of a number of trees yielding such a wood; especially, an East Indian tree of the mahogany family, *Shloroxylon swietenia*.

sat'in·y, *a.* resembling satin; having the gloss of satin; lustrous; as, *satiny* fabrics.

sā'tion, *n.* [L. *satio* (*-onis*), a sowing, from *satus*, pp. of *serere*, to sow.] the planting or sowing of seed. [Obs.]

sat'īre, *n.* [Fr., from L. *satira* or *satura*, satire, *satura*, f. of *satur*, full.]
1. (a) a literary work in which vices, follies, stupidities, abuses, etc. are held up to ridicule and contempt; (b) such literary works collectively, or the art of writing them.
2. the use of ridicule, sarcasm, irony, etc. to expose, attack, or deride vices, follies, etc.

sȧ·tir'i·çăl, sȧ·tir'iç, *a.* [L. *satiricus*, satiric, from *satira*, a satire.]
1. of, having the nature of, or containing satire.
2. indulging in, or fond of indulging in, satire.

sȧ·tir'i·çăl·ly, *adv.* in a satirical manner.

sȧ·tir'i·çăl·ness, *n.* the quality of being satirical.

sat'i·rist, *n.* one who writes satire; also, one who indulges in satire.

sat'i·rīze, *v.t.*; satirized, *pt.*, *pp.*; satirizing, *ppr.* [Fr. *satiriser*.] to attack or criticize with satire.
It is as hard to *satirize* well a man of distinguished vices, as to praise well a man of distinguished virtues. —Swift.

sat·is·faç'tion, *n.* [OFr., from L. *satisfactio* (*-onis*), satisfaction, from *satisfactus*, pp. of *satisfacere*, to satisfy.]
1. a satisfying or being satisfied.
2. something which satisfies; specifically; (a) in theology, atonement for sin; (b) reparation for injury or insult; (c) settlement of debt; payment or discharge of obligation; (d) anything that brings gratification, pleasure, or contentment.
to give satisfaction; (a) to satisfy; (b) to accept a challenge to duel or fight.
Syn.—content, contentment, amends, relief, compensation, recompense, atonement.

sat·is·faç'tive, *a.* giving satisfaction. [Obs.]

sat·is·faç'tō·ri·ly, *adv.* in a manner to give satisfaction; in a satisfactory manner; as, the crime was *satisfactorily* proved.

sat·is·faç'tō·ri·ness, *n.* the state or quality of being satisfactory; as, the *satisfactoriness* of pleasure or enjoyment.

sat·is·faç'tō·ry, *a.* [Fr. *satisfactoire*, from L. *satisfactus*, pp. of *satisfacere*, to satisfy.]
1. satisfying; fulfilling all needs, expectations, wishes, desires, requirements, etc.
2. making amends, indemnification, or recompense; atoning; as, to make *satisfactory* compensation, or a *satisfactory* apology for.

sat'is·fī·ȧ·ble, *a.* having capacity for being satisfied.

sat'is·fī·ẽr, *n.* one who or that which satisfies.

sat'is·fȳ, *v.t.*; satisfied, *pt.*, *pp.*; satisfying, *ppr.* [Fr., from L. *satisfacere*, to satisfy.]
1. to gratify fully the wants, wishes, or desires of; to supply to the full extent with what is wished for; to make content; as, to *satisfy* hunger or thirst; to *satisfy* a hungry man.
2. (a) to give what is due to; (b) to answer or discharge, as a claim, debt, legal demand, or the like; to pay; to liquidate.
3. to fulfill the conditions of; to answer; as, an algebraical equation is said to be *satisfied* when, after the substitution of any expressions for the unknown quantities which enter it, the two members are equal.
4. (a) to free from doubt, suspense, or uncertainty; to give full assurance to; to set at rest the mind of; as, to *satisfy* oneself by inquiry; (b) to answer (a doubt, objection, etc.) adequately or convincingly; to solve.
5. to comply with (rules, standards, or obligations).
6. to make reparation to or for; to atone to or for.

sat'is·fȳ, *v.i.* 1. to give satisfaction.
2. to make amends; to atone. [Rare.]
Syn.—content, please, gratify, satiate, sate, recompense, compensate, remunerate, indemnify.

sat'is·fȳ·ing, *a.* giving satisfaction or enjoyment.

sat'is·fȳ·ing·ly, *adv.* in a manner tending to satisfy.

sat''is·pas'sion (-shun), *n.* [L. *satis pati*, to suffer enough.] in theology, suffering which gives satisfaction.

sā'tive, *a.* [L. *sativus*, that is sown, from *satus*, pp. of *serere*, to sow.] sown; raised from the seed. [Obs.]

Sā'trae, *n.pl.* [Gr. *Satrai*.] an ancient Thracian people inhabiting Mount Pangaeus: according to the historian Herodotus, they escaped the domination of other peoples.

sā'trap (*or* sat'răp), *n.* [Fr. *satrape*; L. *satrapes*; Gr. *satrapēs*, the title of a Persian governor; Zend *shōithra-paiti*, ruler of a religion.]
1. a governor of a province under the ancient Persian monarchy.
2. a ruler of a dependency, often a despotic, subordinate official; a petty tyrant.

sā'trap·ăl, *a.* pertaining to a satrap or a satrapy.

sā'trap·ess, *n.* a woman satrap. [Rare.]

sȧ·trap'i·çăl, *a.* satrapal. [Rare.]

sā'trap·y, *n.*; *pl.* **sā'trap·ieṣ,** 1. the government or jurisdiction of a satrap.
2. the province ruled by a satrap.

Sat'sụ·mȧ, *n.* 1. one of the four powerful southwestern Japanese clans which figured prominently in the revolution to restore the emperor's power between 1867 and 1868.
2. one of several varieties of the mandarin orange commercially produced in Alabama and Florida.
3. Satsuma ware.

Sat'sụ·mȧ an·thraç'nōse, in plant pathology, a disease peculiar to the Satsuma orange, attacking it only in Japan: it is characterized by spots on the leaves and fruit and twig blight: caused by *Gloeosporium foliicolum*.

Sat'sụ·mȧ ware, [Japan. name from province *Satsuma*, island of Kyushu, where it is manufactured.] a kind of pottery made at Satsuma, Japan, yellow to brown in color, of hard glaze, and crackled.

sat''ū·rȧ·bil'i·ty, *n.* the state or quality of being saturable.

sat'ū·rȧ·ble, *a.* [L., from *satur*, full.] capable of being saturated; admitting saturation.

sat'ū·rănt, *a.* [L. *saturans* (*-antis*), ppr. of *saturare*, to saturate.] saturating; impregnating to the full.

sat'ū·rănt, *n.* a substance that saturates.

sat'ū·rāte, *v.t.*; saturated, *pt.*, *pp.*; saturating, *ppr.* [L. *saturatus*, pp. of *saturare*, to fill full, saturate, from *satur*, full.]
1. to cause to become completely pene-

trated, impregnated, or soaked; to fill fully; to imbue thoroughly; to soak; as, to *saturate* a cloth with moisture; to *saturate* a mind with philosophy.

2. to cause (something) to be so completely filled, charged, or treated with something else that no more can be taken up.

3. in chemistry, to cause (a substance) to combine to the full extent of its combining capacity with another.

sat'ū·rāte, *a.* 1. saturated. [Chiefly Poetic.]

2. of a deep, intense color.

sat'ū·rā·ted, *a.* 1. filled to capacity; having absorbed all that can be taken up.

2. soaked through with moisture; wet.

3. undiluted with white: said of colors.

4. in geology, containing as much combined silica as is possible: said of rocks and minerals.

saturated compound; an organic compound containing no double or triple bonds and having no free valence.

saturated solution; a solution in equilibrium at a definite temperature with the undissolved solute; solution containing so much dissolved substance that no more can be dissolved at the given temperature.

sat'ū·rāt·ẽr, *n.* one who or that which saturates: also *saturator*.

sat·ū·rā'tion, *n.* [LL. *saturatio (-onis)*, filling, saturation, from L. *saturare*, to fill full.]

1. the act of saturating, or the state of being saturated.

2. the degree of intensity of a color, as measured by its freedom from mixture with white.

3. the condition of a magnetic substance that has been magnetized to the highest possible degree.

saturation bombing; the practice of dropping an intense concentration of bombs almost simultaneously from a number of bombers in close formation, in order to destroy virtually everything in a given target area.

saturation point; the point at which the greatest possible amount of a substance has been absorbed.

Sat'ūr·dāy, *n.* [AS. *Sæterdæg*, or *Sæternes-dæg*, *Sætern*, from L. *Saturnus*, Saturn.] the seventh or last day of the week; the day of the Jewish Sabbath.

Sat'ūr·dāy nīght spe'ciăl, [from their use in weekend crimes.] any small, cheap, short-barreled handgun that is readily available. [Slang.]

Sat'ūrn, *n.* [L. *Saturnus*, connected with *serere*, to sow.]

1. in Roman mythology, the god of agriculture and husband of Ops, the goddess of the harvest: identified with the Greek Cronos.

2. the second largest planet in the solar system, sixth in distance from the sun, notable for the three concentric rings which revolve around it in the plane of its equator: diameter, 72,000 mi.; diurnal rotation, 10 hrs., 14 min.; period of revolution, 29.5 years.

3. in alchemy, lead (the metal).

4. in heraldry, the tincture sable, in blazoning by the planets.

balsam of Saturn; see under *balsam*.

Sat·ūr·nā'li·à, *n.pl.* [L., neut. pl. of *Saturnalis*, of or belonging to Saturn.]

1. among the Romans, the festival of Saturn, held about December 17, as a period of unrestrained merriment in celebration of the winter solstice.

2. [s–] [*sometimes construed as sing.*] a period or occasion of noisy or unconstrained, often orgiastic, revelry.

Sat·ūr·nā'li·ăn, *a.* 1. pertaining to the Saturnalia.

2. [s–] riotously merry or orgiastic.

Sà·tūr'ni·à, *n.* [LL., from L. *Saturnius*, belonging to Saturn.] a genus of moths typical of the family *Saturniidæ*, which includes the silkworm moths.

Sà·tūr'ni·ăn, *a.* [Fr. *Saturnien*, from L. *Saturnius*, of Saturn.]

1. pertaining to the Roman god Saturn, whose reign was called "the golden age"; hence, prosperous, contented, happy, or peaceful: said of a period, age, etc.

2. of or pertaining to the planet Saturn.

sà·tūr'ni·ăn, *a.* pertaining to the genus *Saturnia*.

sà·tūr'ni·ăn, *n.* any bombycid moth of the genus *Saturnia*.

Sat"ūr·ni·cen'triç, *a.* [L. *Saturnus*, Saturn, and *centrum*, center.] in astronomy, pertaining to Saturn as a center; viewed from Saturn as a center.

sà·tūr'ni·id, *n.* any of a family, *Saturniidæ*, of large moths with a small head, broad wings, and hairy body.

Sat'ūr·nīne, *a.* [OFr. *saturnin*; Fr. *saturnien*, sad, sour, from L. *Saturnus*, Saturn.]

1. pertaining to the god or planet Saturn; also, [s–] in astrology, born under the supposed influence of the planet Saturn.

2. [s–] heavy; grave; gloomy; morose; phlegmatic; as, a *saturnine* person or temperament.

3. [s–] (a) pertaining to or like lead; as, *saturnine* compounds; (b) having lead poisoning.

saturnine colic; same as *painter's colic*.

sat'ūr·niṣm, *n.* chronic lead poisoning.

sat'ūr·nist, *n.* a saturnine person. [Obs.]

Sat'yà·gra·hà (sut'yà-gru-hà), *n.* [from Hind.; lit., a grasping for truth; Sans. *satya*, truth, and *grapha*, grasping.] the political doctrine of Mohandas K. Gandhi, which favored passive resistance and non-co-operation in opposing British rule in India.

sat'yr (-ẽr *or* sā'tẽr), *n.* [Fr. *satyre*; L. *satyrus*; Gr. *satyros*, a satyr, companion, sylvan god.]

1. in Greek mythology, a sylvan deity or demigod, usually represented as part man and part goat, usually having horns on his head, a hairy body, with the feet and tail of a goat; an attendant of Bacchus; it is thought of as fond of riotous merriment and lechery: see also *faun*.

2. a lascivious man.

3. a man having satyriasis.

4. an orangutan.

5. any butterfly of the subfamily *Satyrinæ*, with gray or brown wings often marked with eyelike spots.

sat·y·rī'à·sis, *n.* [Gr., from *satyros*, a satyr.]

1. uncontrollable and excessive sexual desire in a man: see also *nymphomania*.

2. leprosy. [Obs.]

sà·tyr'iç, sà·tyr'i·căl, *a.* 1. pertaining to satyrs.

2. designating or of a type of ancient Greek drama having a chorus of satyrs.

Sat·y·rī'nae, *n.pl.* [L., from Gr. *satyros*, satyr.] a subfamily of butterflies with only four legs adapted for walking.

sà·tyr'i·on, *n.* [Fr. *satyrion*; L. *satyrion*, also *satyrios*; Gr. *satyrion*, a plant supposed to excite lust.] a variety of orchid supposed to excite sexual desire. [Obs.]

sau'bà ȧnt, [S. Am. Ind. *sauba*, and Eng. *ant*.], a South American ant, *Œcodoma cephalotes*, living in colonies which contain individuals of five classes, three of which are workers and the remaining two males and queens. They destroy growing vegetation by stripping it of leaves.

sauce, *n.* [ME. *sause*; OFr. *sause*, *saulse*, from LL. *salsa*, sauce, from L. *salsus*, salted, from *salire*, to salt.]

1. (a) a liquid or soft dressing served with food to improve its taste; (b) a flavored syrup used as a topping, as on ice cream, custards, cakes, etc.

2. something that adds interest, zest, or flavor.

3. fruit stewed, sweetened, and often flavored; as, apple*sauce*.

4. any green vegetable. [Dial.]

5. insolence; impudence. [Colloq.]

6. a preparation consisting of various flavoring ingredients used in the tobacco and snuff manufacture.

7. alcoholic liquor: usually with *the*. [Colloq.]

sauce, *v.t.*; sauced, *pt.*, *pp.*; saucing, *ppr.* 1. to season or flavor with sauce.

2. to gratify; as, to *sauce* the palate.

3. to intermix or accompany with anything that acts as a relish; to give flavor or relish to; as, to *sauce* desire with threatening.

4. to treat with sauciness; to be impudent or flippant to; as, to *sauce* a superior. [Colloq.]

sauce'-à·lōne", *n.* garlic mustard.

sauce'bōat, *n.* a boatlike dish used for holding sauce or gravy.

sauce'box, *n.* a saucy person; especially, an impertinent child. [Colloq.]

sauce'dish, *n.* a dish for holding sauce (sense 3).

sauce'pan, *n.* 1. originally, a small pan for sauce.

2. a small metal pot with a long handle, used for cooking.

sau'cẽr, *n.* [Fr. *saucière*, from LL. *salsarium*, from L. *salsa*, salted things.]

1. a small dish in which sauce is served. [Obs.]

2. (a) a small, round, shallow dish designed to hold a cup and catch any spilled liquid; (b) any small, round, shallow dish.

3. anything round and shallow like a saucer.

4. a form of flat caisson for raising sunken ships.

5. a socket on which a capstan turns.

sau'ci·ly, *adv.* impudently; in a saucy or impudent manner.

sau'ci·ness, *n.* the quality of being saucy.

sau·cisse' (sō-sēs'), *n.* [Fr. *saucisse*, a sausage.]

1. in military usage, a long pipe or bag, made of cloth or leather, filled with gunpowder, used as a fuse.

2. a large fascine.

sau'cy, *a.*; *comp.* saucier; *superl.* sauciest, [*sauce* and *-y*.]

1. impudent; rude; transgressing the rules of decorum; as, a *saucy* boy.

2. pert; sprightly; as, a *saucy* pursing of the lips.

Syn.—impudent, impertinent, rude, insolent.

sau'ẽr·brä·ten (sou'), *n.* [G.; *sauer*, sour, and *braten*, roast.] a dish made of beef or pork marinated in vinegar before cooking.

sauer'kraut (sour'krout), *n.* [G. *sauer*, sour, and *kraut*, cabbage.] chopped cabbage preserved in a brine of its own juice with salt.

sauf, *a.* safe. [Obs.]

sauf, *prep.* and *conj.* save. [Obs.]

sauf'ly, *adv.* safely. [Obs.]

sau'gẽr, *n.* [prob. Am. Ind.] a small American pike perch related to the larger walleye but not valued as a game or food fish.

saugh, *v.* obsolete past tense of *see*.

Sauk, *n.* same as *Sac*.

saul, *n.* soul. [Obs.]

saul, *n.* same as *sal* (tree).

Saul, *n.* 1. in the Bible, the first king of Israel.

2. the original name of the Apostle Paul.

sau'lie, *n.* [etym. uncertain.] a person hired to mourn at a funeral. [Scot.]

sault (sö), *n.* [Fr. *saut*; OFr. *sault*; L. *saltus*, a leap, from *saltus*, pp. of *salire*, to leap.] a rapid in a river. [Dial.]

sau'nä (sou'), *n.* [Finn.] 1. a Finnish steam bath, accompanied by light beating of the skin with birch or cedar boughs.

2. the bathhouse.

säun'dẽrṣ (sän'), *n.* same as *sandalwood*.

saun'tẽr, *v.i.*; sauntered, *pt.*, *pp.*; sauntering, *ppr.* [Late ME. *santre(n)*, to muse, meditate; prob. via OFr., from some Romance form of *saint*.]

1. to wander about idly; as, *sauntering* from place to place.

2. to loiter; to linger over something.

säun'tẽr, *n.* 1. a leisurely and aimless walk.

2. a careless, slow gait.

säun'tẽr·ẽr, *n.* one who wanders about idly.

saur, *n.* soil; dirt. [Brit. Dial.]

-saur, [from Gr. *sauros*, lizard.] a combining form meaning *lizard*, as in dino*saur*.

sau'rel, *n.* [OFr., from *saur*, sorrel.] any salt-water food fish of the genus *Trachurus*, of Europe and America.

Sau'ri·à, *n.pl.* [LL., from Gr. *sauros*, a lizard.] a suborder of reptiles including the lizards: in former classifications, a division including crocodiles, dinosaurs, etc.

sau'ri·ăn, *a.* of, belonging to, a characteristic of the *Sauria*.

sau'ri·ăn, *n.* one of the *Sauria*.

sau'rō-, [from Gr. *saura*, *sauros*, a lizard.] a combining form meaning *lizard*, as in *sauro*pod: also, before a vowel, *saur-*.

sau'rō·dont, *a.* [Gr. *sauros*, lizard, and *odous*, *odontos*, tooth.] of the *Saurodontidæ*, an extinct family of large fishes which had teeth set in sockets in the jaws.

sau'rō·dont, *n.* a saurodont fish.

sau·rog'nà·thiṣm, *n.* the state of being saurognathous.

sau·rog'nà·thous, *a.* [Gr. *sauros*, lizard, and *gnathos*, jaw.] having a palate like a lizard; having a vomer of two lateral parts, as woodpeckers.

sau'roid, *n.* [Gr. *sauros*, lizard, and *-oid.*] an extinct ganoid fish believed to possess reptilian characteristics.
sau'roid, *a.* pertaining to or resembling the saurians.
sau·roph'a·gous, *a.* [Gr. *sauros*, lizard, and *phagein*, to eat.] subsisting on lizards.
sau'rō·pod, *n.* one of the *Sauropoda.*
sau'rō·pod, *a.* sauropodous.
Sau·rop'ō·da, *n.pl.* [Gr. *sauros*, lizard, and *pous*, *podos*, foot.] a group of herbivorous dinosaurs including three families: they had a long neck and tail, five-toed limbs, and a small head.
sau·rop'ō·dous, *a.* pertaining to the *Sauropoda.*
Sau·rop'si·da, *n.pl.* [Gr. *sauros*, lizard, *opsis*, appearance, and *-ida.*] in Huxley's classification, the second of his three primary sections of vertebrates, comprising birds and reptiles. The animals of this section are characterized by the absence of gills, by having the skull jointed to the vertebral column by a single occipital condyle, the lower jaw composed of several pieces, and united to the skull by means of a special (quadrate) bone, and by possessing nucleated red blood corpuscles, as well as by certain embryonic characters.
Sau''rop·tē·ryg'i·a, *n.pl.* an order of fossil reptiles including the *Plesiosauria.*
Sau·rū'rae, *n.pl.* [LL., fem. pl. of *saururus*, from Gr. *sauros*, lizard, and *oura*, tail.] an extinct order of lizard-tailed birds having two free claws on each wing.
sau·rū'răn, *n.* one of the *Saururæ.*
sau·rū'răn, *a.* saururous.
sau·rū'rous, *a.* pertaining to the *Saururæ.*
Sau·rū'rus, *n.* a genus of herbs containing but two species, *Saururus loureiri* and *Saururus cernuus*, found respectively in the eastern part of Asia and in North America.
-sau'rus, [from Gr. *sauros*, a lizard.] a combining form meaning *lizard*, used to form the genus names of certain reptiles, as in ichthyo*saurus.*
sau'ry, *n.*; *pl.* **sau'ries**, [prob. from Fr. *saur*, sorrel.] a long, slender sea fish of the genus *Scomberesox*, found in temperate Atlantic waters: it has a projecting beak.
sau'sāge, *n.* [OFr. *saulsage*, *saucisse*, *saulcisse*; LL. *salcicia*, sausage; L. *salsicium*, sausage, from *salsus*, salted.]
1. meat, usually pork, chopped fine, highly seasoned, and ordinarily stuffed into or enclosed in a tube of thin prepared intestine or other membranous tissue.
2. any object shaped like a sausage, as a captive observation balloon.
saus'sūr·īte, *n.* [named after H. B. de *Saussure*, its discoverer.] a mineral of a white, gray, or green color: it is an impure feldspar.
sau·té' (sō-tā'), *a.* [Fr., pp. of *sauter*, to leap.] fried quickly and turned frequently in a little fat.
sau·té', *v.t.*; sautéed, *pt.*, *pp.*; sautéing, *ppr.* to fry quickly and turn frequently in a little fat.
sau·té', *n.* a sautéed dish.
sau·ter' (sō-tā'), *v.t.* [Fr.] to sauté.
sau'tēr, *n.* psalter. [Obs.]
sau·te·relle' (sō-), *n.* [Fr., leapfrog, a grasshopper, from OFr. *sauterel*, a leaper.] a mason's implement, used in tracing and forming angles.
sau·tērne' (sō-), *n.* [from *Sauterne*, a place in France, department of Gironde.] a kind of white table wine, usually sweet, made of grapes grown in the neighborhood of Sauterne.
sau'trie, *n.* psaltery. [Obs.]
sauve'gärde, (sōv'), *n.* [Fr., safeguard.] a lizard of the genus *Monitor.*
sauve qui peut (sōv kē pē), [Fr., lit., save (himself) who can.] a disorganized retreat; a rout.
sāv'a·ble, *a.* capable of being saved.
sāv'a·ble·ness, *n.* capability of being saved.
sav'āge, *a.* [OFr. *savaige*, *salvage*, savage, wild; L. *silvaticus*, belonging to a wood, wild, from *silva*, a wood.]
1. pertaining to the forest; wild; remote from human residence and improvements; uncultivated; as, a *savage* wilderness.
2. wild; untamed; fierce; as, *savage* beasts of prey.
3. untaught; unpolished; rude; as, *savage* manners.
4. cruel; pitiless; inhuman; brutal; as, *savage* warfare.
5. without civilization; primitive; barbarous; as, a *savage* tribe.
6. furious; ill-tempered.
Syn.—ferocious, untaught, uncivilized, brutish, heathenish, barbarous, merciless, unmerciful, murderous.
sav'āge, *n.* 1. a human being living somewhat like an animal, in an uncivilized, primitive way.
2. a crude, boorish person.
3. a man of extreme, unfeeling, brutal cruelty; a barbarian.
sav'āge, *v.t.* to make wild, barbarous, or cruel.
sav'āge·ly, *adv.* in the manner of a savage.
sav'āge·ness, *n.* a state or condition of savagery; wildness; an untamed, uncultivated, or uncivilized state.
sav'āge·ry, *n.*; *pl.* **sav'āge·ries**, 1. the condition of being savage, wild, primitive, or uncultivated: said of men, animals, or nature.
2. cruelty; barbarity.
3. savages collectively.
4. wild growth, as of plants. [Obs.]
sav'āg·ism, *n.* savagery.
sav·a·nil'la, *n.* the tarpon. [Dial.]
sa·van'na, **sa·van'nah**, *n.* [Sp. *sabana*, from the Carib name.]
1. an extensive open plain in a tropical region of seasonal rains, destitute of trees, and covered with grass or reeds.
2. a grassland characterized by scattered trees, especially in tropical or subtropical regions.
sa·van'na flow'ēr, a West Indian species of *Echites.*
sa·van'na spar'rōw, one of several varieties of sparrow of the grassy regions of North America.
sa·van'na wät'tle, either of two West Indian fiddlewood trees of the genus *Citharexylum.*
sa·vänt', *n.* [Fr., a learned man, from *savant*, ppr. of *savoir*, to know.] a learned person; a scholar; a person of high literary or scientific attainments.
Sa·värt's' wheel (-värz' hwēl), in acoustics, an invention of Felix Savart, a French scientist, for measuring pitch in musical sounds.
sāve, *v.t.*; saved, *pt.*, *pp.*; saving, *ppr.* [ME. *saven*; Fr. *sauver*, to save; L. *salvare*, to secure, to make safe, from *salvus*, safe.]
1. to rescue or preserve from harm or danger; to keep or remove from damage or injury; to make or keep safe.
2. to keep in health and well-being: formerly used in greeting, as, *save* you, sir.
3. to preserve for future use; to lay by (often with *up*).
4. to prevent or guard against expense, loss, or waste of; to gain advantage of; as, this train *saves* hours.
5. to help (one) to avoid loss or waste of; as, it *saves* me time.
6. to avoid, prevent, lessen, or guard against; as to *save* expense.
7. to treat carefully in order to preserve, lessen wear, etc.
8. in theology, to deliver (a person, soul, etc.) from sin and punishment; to redeem from spiritual death.
Syn.—spare, preserve, protect.
sāve, *v.i.* 1. to avoid expense, loss, waste, etc.; to be economical.
2. to keep something or someone from danger, harm, etc.
3. to hoard; to put by money or goods.
4. to keep; to last.
5. in theology, to exercise power to redeem from evil and sin.
sāve, *prep.* [ME. *sauf*, *safe*; OFr. *sauf-*, safe, from L. *salvus.*] except; but.
sāve, *conj.* 1. except; but.
2. unless. [Archaic.]
sāve'a·ble, *a.* same as *savable.*
sāve'all, *n.* any device for saving time, preventing loss or waste, etc.; specifically, (a) a small pan inserted in a candlestick to hold the ends of candles so they may burn; (b) in nautical usage, a small sail sometimes set under the foot of another sail to catch the wind that would pass under it; (c) a trough in a papermaking machine which collects any pulp that may have slopped over the edge of the wire cloth; (d) overalls; (e) a pinafore; (f) a child's savings bank.
sav'e·loy, *n.* [Fr. *cervelas*, from *cervelle*, the brains; L. *cerebellum*, dim. of *cerebrum*, the brain.] a highly seasoned, dried sausage.
sāv'ēr, *n.* a person or thing that saves: usually in hyphenated compounds, as labor-*saver.*
sav'in, **sav'ine**, *n.* [Fr. *savinier*; L. and Sp. *sabina.*]
1. a bush or low tree, *Juniperus sabina*, with small, scalelike leaves, and light, bluish-green fruit: it is native to central Europe and parts of Asia.
2. an oily drug derived from the leaves and tops of the tree savin, used in medicine.
3. the red cedar.
sāv'ing, *a.* that saves; specifically, (a) rescuing; preserving; (b) economizing or economical; (c) containing an exception; making a reservation; as, a *saving* clause; (d) compensating; redeeming.
sāv'ing, *n.* 1. the act of one that saves.
2. any reduction in expense, time, labor, etc., or the result of such reduction; as, a *saving* of 10 per cent.
3. what is saved; especially, [*pl.*] sums of money saved.
4. in law, a reservation; an exception.
sāv'ing, *prep.* 1. with due respect for.
2. with the exception of; except; save.
sāv'ing, *conj.* save; except.
sāv'ing·ly, *adv.* in a saving manner.
sāv'ing·ness, *n.* the quality of being saving.
sāv'ings ac·count', an account in a bank, in which money is deposited for safekeeping, and on which interest is paid.
sāv'ings bank, a bank in which savings may be deposited; especially, a banking establishment whose business is to receive and invest depositors' savings, on which it pays interest.
sā'vior, **sā'viour**, *n.* [OFr. *salveor*, *sauveour*; LL. *salvator*, from L. *salvare*, to save.]
1. one who saves.
2. [S—; *usually* Saviour] Jesus Christ: with *the.*
sā'vior·ess, **sā'viour·ess**, *n.* a woman savior. [Rare.]
sav'oir-fāire (-wär-), *n.* [Fr., to know (how) to do.] ready knowledge of what to do or say, and of when or how to do or say it; tact.
sa·voir-vi'vre (-vwär-), *n.* [Fr., to know (how) to live.] good breeding; good manners.
sā'vŏr, **sā'vŏur**, *n.* [ME. *savour*; OFr. *savour*; Fr. *saveur*; L. *sapere*, to taste.]
1. the quality of something that perceptibly affects the organs of taste and smell; as, the *savor* of an orange or rose; also, a particular taste or smell.
2. characteristic quality; distinctive property.
3. perceptible trace; tinge.
4. power to excite interest, zest, etc.
5. character; reputation; repute. [Archaic.]
Syn.—flavor, relish, taste, fragrance, scent, smell, odor.
sā'vŏr, **sā'vŏur**, *v.i.*; savored, *pt.*, *pp.*; savoring, *ppr.* 1. to have a particular smell or taste.
2. to have, or to show traces or signs of, some particular characteristic or quality; to smack (*of*); as, his answer *savors of* insolence.
sā'vŏr, **sā'vŏur**, *v.t.* 1. to season or flavor; to give flavor or scent to.
2. to have the particular flavor or smell of.
3. to have the characteristic quality of.
4. to show traces or signs of.
5. to taste or smell, especially with relish.
6. to enjoy with appreciation; to relish.
sā'vŏr·i·ly, *adv.* in a savory manner.
sā'vŏr·i·ness, *n.* the quality of being savory; pleasing taste or smell; as, the *savoriness* of a peach.
sā'vŏr·less, *a.* without smell or taste; insipid.
sā'vŏr·ly, *a.* well-seasoned; of good taste. [Obs.]
sā'vŏr·ly, *adv.* with relish; keenly. [Obs.]
sā'vŏr·y, *a.*; *comp.* savorier; *superl.* savoriest, [OFr. *savouré*, pp. of *savourer*, to taste, from *savour*, savor.]
1. pleasing to the taste or smell; appetizing.
2. agreeable; pleasing.
3. morally pleasing; respectable.
4. salty or piquant, not sweet, as a relish.
Syn.—flavorous, piquant, pungent, rich, spicy, palatable, appetizing.
sā'vŏr·y, *n.*; *pl.* **sā'vŏr·ies**, a small, highly seasoned portion of food served at the end or beginning of dinner: also (British spelling) *savoury.* [Brit.]
sā'vŏr·y, *n.* [Fr. *savorée*; L. *satureia*, savory.]

an aromatic plant, *Satureia hortensis*, of the mint family, used in cooking.

sȧ·voy′, *n.* [after *Savoy*, France.] a variety of the common cabbage, *Brassica oleracea*, with crinkled leaves and a compact head.

Sȧ·voy′ärd (*or Fr.* sȧ-vo-yär′), *a.* [Fr., from *Savoie*, Savoy, and *-ard*.] pertaining to Savoy, its people, or culture.

Sȧ·voy′ärd, *n.* a native or inhabitant of Savoy.

Sȧ·voy′ärd, *n.* [from the *Savoy*, London theater where the operas were first produced.] an actor, producer, or enthusiastic admirer, of Gilbert and Sullivan operas.

sav′vy, sav′vey, *v.t.* and *v.i.*; savvied ,*pt.*, *pp.*; savvying, *ppr.* [Sp. *saber*, to know.] to know; to understand. [Slang.]

sav′vy, sav′vey, *n.* common sense; understanding. [Slang.]

sạw, *v.* past tense of *see*.

sạw, *n.* [AS. *saga*; akin to G. *säge*.]

1. (a) a cutting tool, of various shapes and sizes, consisting essentially of a thin blade of metal, usually steel, the edge of which is a series of sharp teeth, and which may be worked by hand or machinery; (b) any of various tools or devices somewhat like this but with a sharp edge, instead of teeth.

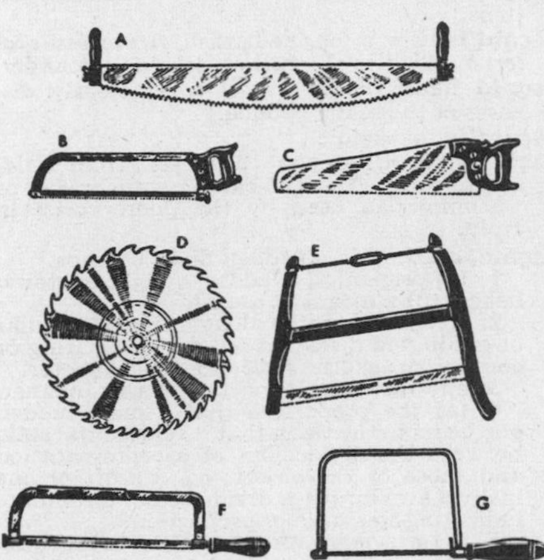

SAWS
A, crosscut saw; B, butcher's saw; C, handsaw; D, circular saw; E, bucksaw; F, hack saw; G, coping saw

2. a machine having such a tool or tools.

3. in zoology, any part of an animal which has an arrangement of spines resembling saw-teeth, as the snout of the sawfish.

circular saw; a saw in the form of a disk with a toothed edge, rotated at high speed by a motor.

crosscut saw; see following *crosscut*.

double saw; two saws mounted parallel and working so as to cut a board or strip of specific thickness.

endless saw; same as *band saw*.

sạw, *v.t.*; sawed, *pt.*; sawed *or* sawn, *pp.*; sawing, *ppr.* 1. to cut or divide with a saw.

2. to shape or form with a saw.

3. to make sawlike cutting motions through (the air, etc.).

4. to operate or produce with a to-and-fro motion suggestive of that used in working a saw; as, *saw* your knife through the meat; *saw* a tune out on the fiddle.

sạw, *v.i.* 1. to cut with or as with a saw.

2. to cut: said of a saw itself; as, the mill *saws* fast or well.

3. to be cut with a saw; as, the timber *saws* easily.

sạw, *n.* [ME. *sawe*; AS. *sagu*, a saying.]

1. a familiar saying; a proverb or maxim.

2. a speech; discourse. [Obs.]

sạw är′bŏr, the shaft on which a circular or rotating saw is mounted.

sạw′bel″ly, *n.* a fish, the alewife.

sạw′bill, *n.* in zoology, a bird having a rough or sawlike beak; specifically, a merganser or a motmot.

sạw′bōnẹs, *n.* a surgeon. [Slang.]

sạw′buck, *n.* [D. *zaagbuk*.]

1. a sawhorse, especially one with the legs projecting above the crossbar.

2. [from the resemblance of the crossed legs of a carpenter's sawbuck to an X (the Roman numeral for 10).] a ten-dollar bill. [Slang.]

sạw′dẽr, *n.* [corruption of *solder*.] flattery; gush: used principally in the phrase *soft sawder*. [Colloq.]

sạw′dust, *n.* minute particles of wood resulting as a by-product of sawing wood.

sạw′ẽr, *n.* one who saws; a sawyer.

sạw fīle, a file for sharpening saws; usually, a three-cornered file, but for large saws a flat file is used.

sạw′fish, *n.* an elasmobranch fish, *Pristis antiquorum*, related to the sharks and the rays. It attains a length of from twelve to eighteen feet, has a long beak or snout, with spines growing like teeth on both edges.

sạw′flȳ, *n.*; *pl.* **sạw′flīeṣ**, one of a genus of flies belonging to the family *Tenthredinidæ*, the females having ovipositors somewhat resembling a handsaw in shape, which cut into plants, the eggs being then deposited in the cuts.

sạw frāme, a frame in a sawmill for holding a saw or set of saws.

sạw gāte, same as *saw frame*.

sạw ġin, a cotton gin in which revolving circular saws are used in removing the seeds from the fiber.

sạw grȧss, a marsh grass, *Cladium effusum*, having linear leaves with sharp saw-toothed edges.

sạw′họrse, *n.* a kind of rack on which wood is placed for sawing.

sạw log, *n.* a log large enough for handling and sawing in a sawmill.

sạw′mill, *n.* 1. a factory or place where logs are sawed into boards.

2. a large sawing machine.

sạwn, *v.* alternative past participle of *saw*.

Sạw′ney, Sạw′ny, *n.* a nickname for a Scotsman: from Sandy, short for Alexander.

sạw pal·met′tō, a species of palmetto indigenous to the southeastern part of the United States.

sạw pit, a pit over which timber is sawed by two men, one standing below the timber and the other above.

sạw set, an instrument used to wrest or turn the teeth of saws alternately to the right and left so that they may make a kerf somewhat wider than the thickness of the blade: also called *saw wrest*.

sạw tọọth, a tooth of a saw or of any serrated series.

sạw′-tọọthed (-tọọtht), *a.* having teeth like those of a saw; serrate.

sạw′try, *n.* a psaltery. [Obs.]

sạw whet (hwet), in zoology, a small owl, *Nyctala acadica*, found in North America, noted for its shrill cry.

sạw′wŏrt, *n.* a plant of the genus *Serratula*, especially *Serratula tinctoria*, so named from its serrated leaves.

sạw wrest (rest), see *saw set*.

sạw′yẽr, *n.* [ME. *sawier*.]

1. one whose occupation is to saw timber, as into planks or boards.

2. a tree or log caught in a river so that its branches saw back and forth with the water.

3. any of a group of beetles whose larvae burrow in wood.

sax, *n.* a saxophone. [Colloq.]

sax, *n.* [AS. *seax*, a knife.]

1. a slatemaker's ax, for trimming slates to shape.

2. a short sword; a dagger. [Obs.]

sax′ȧ·fras, *n.* sassafras. [Obs.]

sax′ȧ·tile, *a.* [L. *saxatilis*, from *saxum*, a rock.] living or growing among rocks; saxicoline.

sax′ç̣or″net, *n.* a small saxhorn.

sax′họrn, *n.* [after A. J. *Sax* (1814–1894), Belgian inventor.] one of several valved brass-wind instruments with a wide mouthpiece. The tone is even and full. These horns comprise the very high small saxhorn, the soprano, the alto, the tenor, baritone, bass, and double bass.

Sax·iç′ȧ·vȧ, *n.* [LL., from L. *saxum*, a rock, and *cavare*, to hollow.] a genus of lamellibranch mollusks found in the hollows of rocks, among the roots of seaweed, etc.

sax·iç′ȧ·vous, *a.* hollowing out rocks, as some mollusks.

sax′i·çōle, *a.* saxicoline.

sax·iç′ō·līne, *a.* [LL. *saxicola*, from L. *saxum*, a rock, and *colere*, to inhabit.] living or growing among rocks.

sax·iç′ō·lous, *a.* saxicoline.

Sax·if′rȧ·gȧ, *n.* a genus of polypetalous plants, including about 180 species, native to cold and temperate regions.

Sax″i·frȧ·gā′cē·ae, *n.pl.* a family of plants typified by the genus *Saxifraga*; the saxifrage family.

sax″i·frȧ·gā′ceous, *a.* pertaining to the *Saxifragaceæ*.

sax·if′rȧ·găint, *a.* saxifragous. [Rare.]

sax′i·frăġe, *n.* [L. *saxifraga*; *saxum*, a stone, and *frangere*, to break.] any of a group of related plants with white, yellow, purple, or pinkish, small flowers, and leaves massed at the base of the plant: the saxifrages proper belong to the genus *Saxifraga* of the family *Saxifragaceæ*, the species are mostly inhabitants of alpine and subalpine regions of the colder and temperate parts of the northern zone.

sax·if′rȧ·gous, *a.* in medicine, breaking or dissolving calculi.

Sax′ŏn, *n.* [LL. *Saxo*, *Saxonis*, from a Teut. form akin to AS. *seaxan*, from *seax*, a short sword, hence lit., sword men.]

1. a member of an ancient Germanic people that lived in northern Germany: some Saxons invaded and conquered parts of England in the fifth and sixth centuries A.D.

2. an Anglo-Saxon (senses 1 and 3).

3. a native or inhabitant of modern Saxony.

4. the Low German dialect of the early Continental Saxons; Old Saxon.

5. the German dialect of modern Saxony.

Sax′ŏn, *a.* 1. of the early Continental Saxons, their language, etc.

2. English or Anglo-Saxon.

3. of modern Saxony.

Saxon blue; a deep-blue liquid used in dyeing, and obtained by dissolving indigo in concentrated sulfuric acid.

Saxon green; a color produced by dyeing yellow upon a Saxon-blue ground.

Sax·on′iç, Sax·on′iç·ăl, *a.* relating to Saxony or to the Anglo-Saxons or Saxons; Saxon.

Sax′ŏn·iṣm, *n.* a word, phrase, idiom, etc. of English or Anglo-Saxon origin.

Sax′ŏn·ist, *n.* one versed in the Saxon or Anglo-Saxon language.

sax′ŏn·īte, *n.* [*saxony* and *-ite*.] a kind of peridotite.

sax′ŏn·y, *n.* a fabric made from wool produced in Saxony.

sax′ō·phōne, *n.* [after A. J. *Sax*, the inventor, and Gr. *phōnē*, sound.] any of a group of single-reed, keyed wind instruments somewhat like the clarinet but having a curved metal body and a deeper, mellower tone.

SAXOPHONE

sax′ō·phōn·ist, *n.* a saxophone player.

sax·ō·trom′bȧ, *n.* an instrument similar to the saxhorn.

sax′tū′bȧ, *n.* [*sax-*, as in *saxhorn*, and *tuba*.] a bass saxhorn.

sāy, *v.t.*; said (sed), *pt.*, *pp.*; saying, *ppr.*; says (sez), *or archaic* saith (seth), *3rd pers. sing.*, *pres. indic.* [ME. *seggen*, *siggen*; AS. *secgan*, *secgean*, to say.]

1. to utter, pronounce, or speak.

2. to state; declare; tell; express in words.

3. to state positively, with assurance, or as an opinion; as, I wish I could *say* when it will happen.

4. to recite; repeat; as, *say* your prayers.

5. to estimate; assume; hypothesize; as, he is, *say*, forty.

6. to allege; report; as, people *say* he's angry.

it is said, they say; it is commonly reported; people assert or maintain.

that is to say; that means; in other words.

to go without saying; to be too obvious to need explanation; to be self-evident.

to say to; to think of; to judge of; to be of opinion regarding; as, what do you *say to* a vacation?

sāy, *v.i.* to speak; to express an opinion; to make a statement.

sāy, *n.* 1. what a person says; dictum.

2. a chance to speak; as, you've had your *say*.
3. power or authority, as to make a final decision: often with *the*.

sāy, *n.* [from *assay.*] 1. a sample. [Obs.]
2. trial by sample. [Obs.]

sāy, *n.* [from L. *sagum*, woolen mantle.] **1.** a thin silk or satin. [Obs.]
2. a kind of serge. [Obs.]

sāy'ẽr, *n.* one who says.

sāy·ette', *n.* a mixed fabric, used for linings and coverings; sagathy. [Rare.]

sä'yid, sāy'yid, *n.* [Ar. *sayyid.*] lord: a Moslem title applied to those who claim to be descendants of Mohammed through his daughter Fatima: also *said*.

sāy'ing, *n.* 1. the act of one who says.
2. something said; especially, an adage or a proverbial expression; as, many are the *sayings* of the wise.
Syn.—adage, apothegm, axiom, byword, maxim, proverb.

sāy'măn, *n.* one who makes assay. [Obs.]

sāy'mȧs''tẽr, *n.* an assay master. [Obs.]

says (sez), *v.* third person sing., pres. ind., of *say*.

sāy'-sō, *n.* 1. an unsupported statement or assertion. [Colloq.]
2. right of decision. [Colloq.]
3. a dictum. [Colloq.]

Sb, *stibium*, [L.] in chemistry, antimony.

sbir'rō, *n.*; *pl.* **sbir'rī,** [It.] a member of the police force in Italy.

'sblood (sblud), *interj.* God's blood: a euphemistic oath expressing surprise, anger, etc. [Archaic.]

Sc, in chemistry, scandium.

sçab, *n.* [AS. *scæb, sceb.*]
1. a crust which forms over a sore or wound during healing.
2. a skin disease of animals, especially sheep; mange.
3. (a) a plant disease caused by certain fungi; (b) one of the roundish, roughened spots marking this disease.
4. a low, contemptible fellow; a scoundrel. [Slang.]
5. in the labor movement, (a) a worker who refuses to join a union, or who works for less pay or under different conditions than those accepted by the union; (b) a worker who refuses to strike, or who takes the place of a striking worker.

sçab, *v.i.*; scabbed, *pt.*, *pp.*; scabbing, *ppr.* 1. to become covered with a scab; to form a scab.
2. to work or act as a scab.

sçab'bȧrd, *n.* [ME. *scauberd, scauberk*, prob. from O. H. G. *scar*, sword, and *bergan*, to hide, protect.] a sheath or case to hold the blade of a sword, dagger, or bayonet.

sçab'bȧrd, *v.t.*; scabbarded, *pt.*, *pp.*; scabbarding, *ppr.* to put into a scabbard; to sheathe.

sçab'bȧrd fish, a long, silvery, scabbard-shaped fish, *Lepidopus caudatus*.

sçabbed (skabd *or* skab'ed), *a.* 1. abounding with scabs; covered with scales; scabby.
2. affected with the scab, as a sheep.
3. paltry; mean; vile; dirty; impure; polluted. [Obs.]

sçab'bed·ness, *n.* the state of being scabbed.

sçab'bi·ly, *adv.* in a scabby manner.

sçab'bi·ness, *n.* the quality or state of being scabby.

sçab'ble, *v.t.*; scabbled, *pt.*, *pp.*; scabbling, *ppr.* [from OFr. *escapeler*, to dress timber.] to rough-dress; to dress, as a stone, with a fine ax or broad chisel, after pointing or broaching, and before the finer dressing.

sçab'blẽr, *n.* one who scabbles.

sçab'bling, *n.* a fragment broken or chipped from a stone.

sçab'by, *a.*; *comp.* scabbier; *superl.* scabbiest, 1. full of scabs; covered with or consisting of scabs.
2. diseased with the scab or mange; mangy.
3. low; base; mean; scurvy.

sçȧ·ber'ū·lous, *a.* slightly scabrous.

sçā'bi·ēṣ, *n.* [L., roughness, itch, from *scabere*, to scratch.] a contagious skin disease caused by certain mites that burrow under the skin and deposit eggs, causing intense itching; the itch.

sçā·bi·et'iç, *a.* of or having scabies.

Sçā·bi·ō'sȧ, *n.* [ML. *scabiosa* (*herba*): so called because considered a remedy for the itch.] a genus of plants of the teasel family, having showy, variously colored flowers with knobbed, protruding stamens.

sçā'bi·ous, *n.* any plant of the genus *Scabiosa*, as mourning bride or sweet scabious; also, the daisy fleabane, of the genus *Erigeron*.

sçā'bi·ous, *a.* [Fr. *scabieux*; L. *scabiosus*, rough, scabby, from *scabies*, itch, scale.]
1. scabby; consisting of scabs; rough.
2. of or like scabies.

sçā'brid, *a.* [L. *scabridus*, rough, from *scaber*, rough, scabby.] slightly roughened; scaberulous.

sçā'brous, *a.* [L. *scabrosus*, rough, from *scabere*, to scratch.]
1. rough with small points or knobs, like a file; scaly; scabby.
2. full of difficulties.
3. lacking in delicacy; risque; salacious; improper.

sçā'brous·ness, *n.* a scabrous quality or state.

sçab'wŏrt, *n.* elecampane.

sçad, *n.*; *pl.* **sçad** or **sçadṣ,** [variant of *shad.*] a fish, the saurel.

sçadṣ, *n.pl.* [prob. for *scat* (from AS. *sceat* and ON. *skattr*, a treasure, tribute, tax in money); the U.S. popularity of the term may be due to a dial. refashioning of the cognate G. *schatz*, a treasure.] a very large number or amount; as, *scads* of money. [Colloq.]

sçaff net, a small square dip net.

sçaf'fōld, *n.* [OFr. *escafalt, eschafault*; LL. *scadafaltum*; It. *catafalco*, a scaffold, a catafalque.]
1. a temporary wooden or metal framework for supporting workmen and materials during the erecting, repairing, or painting of a building, etc.
2. a raised platform on which criminals are executed, as by hanging, etc.
3. a temporary wooden stage or platform for exhibition purposes.
4. any raised framework.
5. scaffolding.
6. in metallurgy, ore or metal partly fused causing an obstruction in a blast furnace.

sçaf'fōld, *v.t.*; scaffolded, *pt.*, *pp.*; scaffolding, *ppr.* 1. to furnish or support with a scaffold.
2. to lay or put on a scaffold.

sçaf'fōld·āġe, *n.* scaffolding.

sçaf'fōld·ing, *n.* 1. a frame or structure for support in an elevated place; a scaffold or system of scaffolds.
2. materials for scaffolds.

sçagl'iȧ (skal'yȧ), *n.* [It., a shell.] a reddish variety of Italian limestone.

sçagl·iō'lȧ (skal-yō'lȧ), *n.* [It. *scagliuola*, dim. of *scaglia*, shell.] an imitation marble or granite, made of gypsum mixed with glue and colors, and finely polished.

sçā'lȧ, *n.*; *pl.* **sçā'lae,** [L., a ladder, flight of steps.] in anatomy, any one of the three canals of the cochlea; specifically, (a) the scala tympani; (b) the scala vestibuli; (c) the scala media.

sçāl'ȧ·ble, *a.* that can be scaled.

sçȧ·lāde', sçȧ·lä'dō, *n.* [It. *scalada*, from *scala*, ladder.] an escalade. [Obs.]

sçāl'āġe, *n.* [from *scale* and *-age.*]
1. the percentage by which anything is scaled down to allow for shrinkage, etc.
2. the estimate of lumber in a log being scaled.

sçā'lăr, *a.* [L. *scalaris*, of or pertaining to a ladder, flight of steps.] in mathematics, designating or of a quantity that has magnitude but no direction in space, as volume or temperature.

sçā'lăr, *n.* in mathematics, a scalar quantity: distinguished from *vector*.

Sçȧ·lā'ri·ȧ, *n.* [LL., from L. *scalaris*, of a ladder.] a genus of marine gastropods, commonly called wentletraps. There are about one hundred species known, mostly of tropical regions.

sçȧ·lar'i·fọrm, *a.* [L. *scalaris*, of a ladder, and *-form.*]
1. shaped like a ladder; having markings like the rungs of a ladder.
2. of or relating to the genus *Scalaria*.

sçā'lȧ·ry, *a.* resembling a ladder; formed with steps. [Obs.]

sçal'ȧ·wag, sçal'lȧ·wag, *n.* [perh. corruption of *Scalloway*, in the Shetland islands, origin of a small breed of ponies, yielding early sense of "undersized horse, runt."]
1. an inferior, undersized animal of little worth.
2. a tricky or worthless person; a scamp.
3. a white Southerner who was a Republican during the Reconstruction following the Civil War: an opprobrious term used by Southern Democrats.
Also *scallywag*.

sçald, *v.t.*; scalded, *pt.*,*pp.*; scalding, *ppr.* [OFr. *eschalder, eschauder*; Fr. *échauder*; It. *scaldare*, to heat, warm, scorch, scald, from L. *ex*, intens., and *caldus*, *calidus*, hot.]
1. to burn or injure with hot liquid or steam.
2. to heat almost to the boiling point.
3. to use boiling liquid on; specifically, (a) to sterilize by the use of boiling liquid; (b) to loosen the skins of (fruits, etc.) by the use of boiling water.

sçald, *v.i.* to be or become scalded.

sçald, *n.* 1. a burn or injury caused by scalding.
2. in botany, (a) a disease of cranberries; (b) a whitening or browning of plant tissues, caused by certain fungi or too much sun.

sçald, *a.* scurvy; scabby; paltry; poor; as, *scald* rhymers. [Obs.]

sçald, *n.* a skald (poet).

sçäld, sçäuld, *v.t.* to scold; to rate. [Scot.]

sçald'ber''ry, *n.* the blackberry, *Rubus fruticosus*, of Europe.

sçald çrōw, a hooded crow.

sçald'ẽr, *n.* a scald; a Scandinavian poet. [Obs.]

sçald'fish, *n.* a marine flatfish, *Arnoglossus laterna*, allied to the turbot, sole, and flounder.

sçald head (hed), any of several scaly diseases of the scalp. [Colloq.]

sçald'iç, *a.* skaldic.

sçȧl·dī'nō, *n.*; *pl.* **sçȧl·dī'nī,** [It., from *scaldare*, to warm, heat.] an earthenware brazier or warming pan used by the poorer class in Italy.

sçāle, *n.* [L. *scala*, a ladder, flight of steps.]
1. (a) originally, a ladder; a flight of stairs; hence, (b) a means of ascent.
2. a series of marks along a line, at regular or graduated distances, used in measuring or computing; as, the *scale* of a thermometer.
3. any instrument marked in this manner.
4. (a) the proportion that a map, model, etc. bears to the thing that it represents; ratio between the dimensions of a representation and those of the object; as, a *scale* of one inch to a mile; (b) a divided line, on a map, indicating this ratio or proportion.
5. (a) a system of grouping or classifying in a series of steps or degrees according to a standard of relative size, amount, importance, perfection, etc.; progressive graduated series; as, the social *scale*, wage *scale*; (b) any point, grade, level, or degree in such a series.
6. a system of numerical notation in which the value of a figure is determined by its place in the order according to the constant fixed as the basis of the system; basis for a numerical system; as, the decimal *scale*.
7. an escalade. [Obs.]
8. in music, a series of tones arranged in a sequence of rising or falling pitches in accordance with any of various systems of intervals; especially, all of such a series contained in one octave.
drawn to scale; drawn proportionally.
on a large (or *small*, etc.) *scale*; to a relatively large (or small, etc.) degree or extent.
scale of a series; in algebra, a succession of terms by the aid of which any term of a recurring series may be found when a sufficient number of the preceding ones are given.
scale of chords; in mathematics, a scale on which are given the numerical values of all chords of arcs from 0° to 90° in a circle whose radius is known.
scale of hardness; in mineralogy, a scale by which relative hardness of substances may be found, usually consisting of a series of minerals of uniformly increasing or decreasing hardness; as, talc, gypsum, calcite, fluorite, scapolite, feldspar, quartz, topaz, sapphire, diamond constitute a *scale of hardness* used in mineralogical tests.
scale of longitudes; a scale used for determining graphically the number of miles in a degree of longitude in any latitude.

sçāle, *v.t.*; scaled, *pt.*, *pp.*; scaling, *ppr.* **1.** to climb up or over; to go up by or as by a ladder or by clambering.
2. to regulate or make according to a scale.
3. to reduce according to a fixed ratio or proportion; as, prices were *scaled* down 5 per cent.
4. to measure by or as by a scale.

5. to measure (logs) or estimate the board feet of (timber).

sçāle, *v.i.* 1. to climb; to go up.
2. to go up in a graduated series.

sçāle, *n.* [from OFr. *escale* (Fr. *écale*), cup, husk, and OFr. *escaille*, fish scale, oyster shell.]
1. one of the thin, flat, overlapping, horny plates forming the outer protective covering of many fishes and reptiles.
2. one of the structurally similar thin plates on birds' legs or certain insects' wings.
3. any thin, flaky or platelike layer or piece, such as a thin flake of skin.
4. a flaky film of oxide which forms on metals when heated or rusted.
5. a coating which forms on the inside of boilers, kettles, or other metal containers when heated.
6. any scalelike leaf or bract; especially, such a leaf covering the bud of a seed plant.
7. any of a number of related sucking insects that attack plants.
black scale; a destructive scale which attacks such trees as the olive and orange.
San José scale; a scale insect, *Aspidiotus perniciosus*, which attacks fruit trees.

sçāle, *v.t.* 1. to strip or scrape scales from.
2. to remove in thin layers; to pare down.
3. to cause scales to form on; cover with scales.
4. to throw (a thin, flat object) so that its edge cuts the air, or so that it skips along the surface of water.

sçāle, *v.i.* 1. to flake or peel off in scales; to shed scales.
2. to form or become covered with scales.

sçāle, *n.* [ON. *skāl*, bowl, weighing balance, akin to O.H.G. *scala* and AS. *scealu*, a shell, cup.]
1. either of the shallow dishes or pans of a balance.
2. [*usually pl.*] (a) a balance itself; (b) any weighing machine.
3. a bowl or cup. [Obs.]
the Scales; Libra (constellation or sign of the zodiac).
to turn the scales; to determine; to decide.

sçāle, *v.t.*; scaled, *pt., pp.*; scaling, *ppr.* 1. to weigh in scales.
2. to have a weight of.
3. to balance; to compare.

sçāle, *v.i.* to be weighed.

sçāle är′mŏr, armor made up of small plates of metal partly overlapping each other, like the scales of a fish.

sçāle′back, *n.* in zoology, a sea annelid having along its back two rows of scales; a polynoid.

sçāle′bärk, *n.* *Carya ovata*, a hickory tree, the bark of which is shaggy and peels off in long strips: it yields the best variety of commercial hickory nuts.

sçāle bēam, 1. the lever of a scale, as one which holds the two pans for balancing.
2. a steelyard.

sçāle bee′tle, a tiger beetle.

sçāle′bōard (*often* skab′ŏrd), *n.* 1. a thin board or sheet of wood used for backing a framed picture or mirror, or for use as veneer.
2. in printing, a thin strip of wood used formerly in justifying.

sçāle′-brīght (-brīt), *a.* shining like or with the same brightness as fish scales.

sçāle bug, same as *scale insect.*

sçāle çärp, a carp with normal scales.

sçāle çat′ẽr·pil·lăr, the larva of *Laetilia coccidivora*, a small moth belonging to the family *Pyralididae*: so called because they feed on scale insects.

sçāled, *a.* 1. having the scales removed; as, *scaled* fish.
2. having scales.
3. in zoology, having feathers arranged or colored so as to imitate scales, as the *scaled* partridge.

sçāle dŏve, a gray dove, as *Scardafella inca* of America, having dark edging to its feathers resembling scales.

sçāle′-down, *a.* marked or characterized by scaling down.

sçāle′drāke, *n.* the sheldrake. [Brit. Dial.]

sçāle duck, a sheldrake: also a merganser. [Brit. Dial.]

sçāle ef·fect′, in aeronautics, the correction which must be made in the measurements of a model in a wind tunnel in order to arrive at equivalent values for the full-sized ship.

sçāle fẽrn, a small European fern of the genus *Ceterach*, so named from the imbricated tawny scales at the back of the fronds.

sçāle′fish, *n.* the pollack, torsk, hake, or haddock when dry-cured.

sçāle in′sect, any of a group of small insects destructive to plants, the females of which secrete a round scale under which they live and lay their eggs.

sçāle′less, *a.* without scales.

sçāle moss, the *Jungermanniaceæ*, plants resembling moss and belonging to the class *Hepaticæ*: so called from the small scalelike leaves.

SCALE MOSSES
1. *Jungermannia ciliaris*
2. *Jungermannia bidentata*

sçā·lēne′, *a.* [L. *scalenus*; Gr. *skalēnos*, uneven, odd.]
1. in anatomy, designating or of any of a group of deeply set muscles extending from the first two ribs to the cervical vertebrae, and serving to bend the neck.
2. in geometry, (a) having unequal sides and angles: said of a triangle; (b) having the axis not perpendicular to the base; oblique: said of a cone, etc.

sçā·lēne′, *n.* a scalene triangle.

sçā·lē·nō·hē′drăl, *a.* of or resembling a scalenohedron.

sçā·lē·nō·hē′drŏn, *n.* [LL., from Gr. *skalēnos*, uneven, and *hedra*, base.]
1. in crystallography, a pyramidal form under the rhombohedral system, in which the pyramids are six-sided and the bases are scalene triangles.
2. a hemihedral of the tetragonal system having eight faces, each a scalene triangle.

sçā·lē′nus, *n.* [LL.] a scalene muscle.

sçāle quāil, an American quail, as *Callipepla squamata*, with distinctive scalelike markings.

sçāl′ẽr, *n.* one who or that which scales; as, a dentist's *scaler.*

sçāle′tāil, *n.* a rodent of Africa, somewhat resembling a squirrel, having hard horny scales at the base of the tail.

sçāle′-winged (-wingd), *a.* having the wings covered with scales, as in lepidopterous insects.

sçāl′i·ness, *n.* the state or quality of being scaly; roughness.

sçāl′ing, *n.* the act or process of stripping scales off; also, the act or state of separating and coming off in scales or thin laminae.

sçāl′ing lad′dẽr, a ladder used in the assault of fortified places; also, a fireman's ladder for scaling buildings.

sçall, *n.* [ME.; ON. *skalli*, bald head.] any disease of the skin in which scurf or scabs are present.

sçal′là·wag, *n.* a scalawag.

sçalled, sçald, *a.* having scabs or scald; hence, mean; contemptible; base.

sçalled head, same as *scald head.*

sçal′liŏn (-yun), *n.* [O. Norm. Fr. *escalogne*, from L. *cæpa Ascalonia* or *allium Ascalonium*, the onion of Ascalon.] the shallot, *Allium ascalonicum*; also, the leek or any green onion with a long, thick stem and an almost bulbless root.

sçäl′lŏp, *n.* [OFr. *escalope*, lit., a shellfish.]
1. any of numerous related mollusks with two curved shells deeply grooved, ridged, and hinged together.
2. the large muscle of such a mollusk, used as food.
3. one of the two shells of the scallop; specifically, (a) one worn as a badge by pilgrims returning from the Holy Land; (b) one used as a baking dish.
4. a small dish in which fish or other food is baked and served.
5. one of a series of curves, circle segments, projections, etc. forming an ornamental edge on cloth, lace, etc.

sçäl′lŏp, *v.t.*; scalloped (-lupt), *pt., pp.*; scalloping, *ppr.* 1. to mark or cut the edge or border of in scallops.
2. to bake in a milk sauce with crumbs, seasoning, etc., until brown; to escallop: also *scollop.*

sçäl′lŏped (-lupt), *a.* 1. furnished with a scallop; made or done with or in a scallop.
2. cut at the edge or border into scallops.

sçäl′lŏp·ẽr, *n.* one who or that which scallops; also, one who gathers scallops.

sçal′ly·wag, *n.* a scalawag.

sçalp, *n.* a bed of shellfish. [Rare.]

sçalp, *n.* [ME. *scalp, scalpe*; ON. *skālpr*, a sheath.]
1. the skin on the top and back of the head, usually covered with hair.
2. a part of this, cut or torn off from the head of an enemy by North American Indians and preserved as a trophy.
3. a trophy.
4. the skin on the top of the head of a dog, wolf, etc.
5. a small profit made by scalping. [Colloq.]
6. the head or skull. [Obs.]
7. the upper part of the head of a whale.

sçalp, *v.t.*; scalped (skalpt), *pt., pp.*; scalping, *ppr.* 1. to cut or tear the scalp from.
2. to cheat, defeat, or rob.
3. to buy and sell in order to make small, quick profits. [Colloq.]
4. to buy and sell (theater tickets, etc.) as a scalper. [Colloq.]
5. in milling, to separate (the worthless parts) from the grain.
6. to lay bare by cutting away the upper part or covering, as grass or turf from a hilltop.

sçalp, *v.i.* to scalp bonds, tickets, etc. [Collog.]

sçal′pel, *n.* [L. *scalpellum*, a scalpel, dim. of *scalprum* or *scalper*, a knife, from *scalpere*, to cut.] a small, light, straight knife with a very sharp blade, used by surgeons and in anatomical dissections.

sçal·pel′lum, *n.*; *pl.* **sçal·pel′là,** one of four slender piercing organs in a hemipter's proboscis.

sçalp′ẽr, *n.* 1. one who or that which scalps.
2. a broker who makes small, quick profits as the market prices vary. [Colloq.]
3. a person who buys up quantities of theater tickets, etc. at relatively low prices and sells them at prices in excess of established rates. [Colloq.]

SCALPEL

sçalp lock, a lock or tuft of hair formerly left on the shaven crown of the head by North American Indians as a challenge to their enemies.

sçal′pri·form, *a.* [L. *scalprum*, knife, and *-form.*] in anatomy and zoology, chisel-shaped; as, the *scalpriform* incisors of rodents.

sçal′prum, *n.*; *pl.* **sçal′prà,** [L., a knife.] the front edge of an incisor tooth, or the edge that cuts.

sçāl′y, *a.*; *comp.* scalier; *superl.* scaliest, 1. covered with, composed of, or resembling scales; rough; as, a *scaly* fish; the *scaly* crocodile.
2. shedding or yielding scales or flakes.
3. mean; low; despicable; as, a *scaly* fellow. [Slang.]
4. in botany, composed of scales lying over each other; as, a *scaly* bulb; also, having scales scattered over it; as, a *scaly* stem.
5. infested with or full of scale insects.

sçāl′y ant′ēat·ẽr, a pangolin.

sçāl′y bärk, in plant pathology, a rough, scabby appearance of the bark, particularly the leprosis of Florida and the psorosis of California.

sçāl′y-winged (-wingd), *a.* having wings with scales.

sçam, *n.* [prob. altered from *scheme.*] same as *confidence game* under *confidence.* [Slang.]

sçam, *v.t.*; scammed, *pt., pp.*; scamming, *ppr.* to cheat or swindle, as in a confidence game. [Slang.]

sçam′ble, *v.i.*; scambled, *pt., pp.*; scambling, *ppr.* [from *shamble.*]
1. to stir about; to be busy; to scramble; to be bold or rude. [Obs.]
2. to shift awkwardly; to sprawl; to be awkward, unsteady, or irregular. [Dial.]

sçam′ble, *v.t.* 1. to mangle; to maul. [Obs.]
2. to scatter; to be careless of; to dissipate. [Obs.]

sçam′blẽr, *n.* 1. one who scambles. [Obs.]
2. an intruder upon the generosity or hospitality of others. [Scot.]

sçam′bling·ly, *adv.* with turbulence and noise; with bold intrusiveness; in a scambling manner. [Obs.]

sçȧ·mil'lus, *n.*; *pl.* **sçȧ·mil'lī,** [L., dim. of *scamnum*, a bench, a step, from *scandere*, to climb.] in Roman architecture, a sort of second plinth or block under a statue, column, etc., to raise it, but not ornamented with any kind of molding.

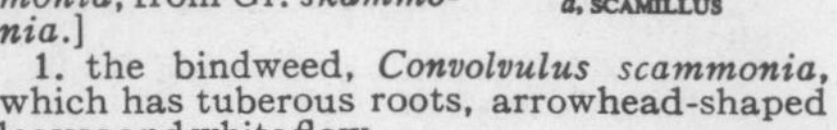
a, SCAMILLUS

sçam·mō'ni·āte, *a.* made with scammony.

sçam'mō·ny, *n.* [L. *scammonia*, from Gr. *skammōnia*.]

1. the bindweed, *Convolvulus scammonia*, which has tuberous roots, arrowhead-shaped leaves and white flowers.

2. a resin from the roots of this plant, used as a cathartic.

SCAMMONY (*Convolvulus scammonia*)

sçamp, *n.* [from *scamper*, signifying originally one who decamps without paying debts.]

1. a rascal; an unprincipled rogue: sometimes used good-naturedly of one who is mischievous and playful.

2. a vagabond; a fugitive from justice. [Obs.]

3. a subtropical American fish, *Mycteroperca falcata*.

sçamp, *v.t.* to perform in a hasty, slipshod, careless manner.

sçȧm·pȧ·vï'ȧ, *n.* [It.] a long, low, Neapolitan and Sicilian war boat moved by long oars and lateen sails: used in the nineteenth century.

sçam'pẽr, *v.i.*; scampered, *pt.*, *pp.*; scampering, *ppr.* [OFr. *escamper*; It. *scampare*, to save oneself, to escape; L. *ex*, out of, and *campus*, a plain, a field of battle; lit., to leave the field, to decamp.] to run or go hurriedly or quickly.

sçam'pẽr, *n.* the act of scampering; a hasty, impulsive flight.

sçam'pẽr·ẽr, *n.* one who scampers.

sçam'pi, *n.*; *pl.* **sçam'pieṣ,** [It. pl.], a large, greenish prawn, valued as food.

sçamp'ish, *a.* of, pertaining to, or resembling a scamp; knavish; rascally.

sçan, *v.t.*; scanned, *pt.*, *pp.*; scanning, *ppr.* [formerly written *scand*, from Fr. *scander*, to scan verse, from L. *scandere*, to climb, to mount, to scan.]

1. to analyze (verse) into its rhythmic components; to determine the rhythm of; to count accents and syllables, and determine metrical feet of.

2. to read or recite (verse) aloud in order to demonstrate its rhythmic structure.

3. to look at closely; to scrutinize.

4. to glance at quickly; to consider hastily.

5. in television, to traverse (a surface) rapidly with a beam of light or electrons in transmitting or reproducing a picture.

6. to mount; to climb step by step. [Obs.]

sçan, *v.i.* 1. to scan verse.

2. to conform to metrical principles: said of verse.

3. in television, to scan a surface.

sçan, *n.* 1. a scanning.

2. scope of vision.

sçan'dăl, *n.* [ME. *scandle*; OFr. *escandle*, scandal; LL. *scandalum*, from Gr. *skandalon*, a snare.]

1. any act, person, or thing that offends or shocks moral feelings and leads to disgrace; as, those slums are a *scandal*.

2. a reaction of shame, disgrace, outrage, etc. caused by such an act, person, or thing.

3. ignominy; disgrace.

4. malicious gossip; defamatory talk; backbiting; slanderous reports.

Syn.—discredit, disrepute, disgrace, detraction, slander.

sçan'dăl, *v.t.*; scandaled *or* scandalled, *pt.*, *pp.*; scandaling *or* scandalling, *ppr.* 1. to treat opprobriously; to defame; to slander. [Archaic or Dial.]

I do fawn on men, and hug them hard,
And after *scandal* them. —Shak.

2. to scandalize; to offend. [Obs.]

3. to disgrace. [Obs.]

sçan'dăl·īze, *v.t.*; scandalized, *pt.*, *pp.*; scandalizing, *ppr.* [Fr. *scandaliser*; LL. *scandalizare*, from Gr. *scandalizein*, to snare, from *scandalon*, a snare.]

1. to shock or outrage the moral feelings of; to offend by some improper or unconventional conduct; to shock.

2. to reproach; to disgrace; to defame; as, a *scandalizing* libeler.

sçan'dăl·mŏṅ·gẽr, *n.* a person who gossips maliciously and spreads scandal.

sçan'dăl·ous, *a.* 1. causing scandal; offensive and shocking to the moral feelings of the community; of such a nature as to outrage a sense of decency; shameful.

2. consisting of evil and malicious reports; libelous; defamatory; spreading slander.

3. fond of scandal.

sçan'dăl·ous·ly, *adv.* in a scandalous manner.

sçan'dăl·ous·ness, *n.* the quality or state of being scandalous.

sçan'dȧ·lum mag·nā'tum, [LL.] in law, a defamatory speech or writing made or published to the injury of a person holding a position of dignity: formerly treated as a more serious offense than mere slander.

sçan'dent, *a.* [L. *scandens* (*-entis*), from *scandere*, to climb.] in botany, climbing, either with spiral tendrils for its support, or by adhesive fibers, as a stalk; climbing; performing the office of a tendril, as a petiole.

sçan'di·ȧ, *n.* the oxide of scandium, Sc_2O_3, a white, amorphous powder.

Sçan'di·ăn, *a.* and *n.* same as *Scandinavian*.

sçan'diç, *a.* pertaining to or derived from scandium.

Sçan·di·nā'vi·ăn, *a.* relating to Scandinavia, its people, their languages, etc.

Sçan·di·nā'vi·ăn, *n.* 1. one of the people of Scandinavia.

2. the subbranch of the Germanic languages spoken by them; North Germanic; Norse.

3. Anglo-Norse.

sçan'di·um, *n.* [Mod. L., from ML. *Scandia*, Scandinavia.] a rare metallic chemical element found in combination with various elements of the rare-earth group: symbol, Sc; atomic weight, 45.10; atomic number, 21.

sçan'nȧ·ble, *a.* that can be scanned.

sçan'sion, *n.* [Fr., from L. *scansio* (*-onis*), a scanning, from *scandere*, to scan, climb.] the analysis of verse into its rhythmic components; the act of scanning: marks of scansion frequently used are: for an accented syllable, ′; for an unaccented syllable, ˘; for a foot division, |.

Sçan·sō'rēṣ, *n.pl.* [L. *scansus*, pp. of *scandere*, to climb.] an outmoded classification of birds having the toes in pairs, one pair directed backward, by which they are enabled to cling to and climb upon trees. The woodpeckers and parrots are examples of this order.

sçan·sō'ri·ăl, *a.* 1. of or adapted to climbing, as the feet of a bird.

2. that climbs or can climb.

3. of or belonging to the *Scansores*. [Obs.]

sçant, *a.*; *comp.* scanter; *superl.* scantest, [ME.; ON. *skant*, from *skammr*, short.]

1. inadequate in size or amount; not enough; meager.

2. lacking a small part of the whole; not quite up to full measure.

3. not entirely favorable for a ship's course; as, a *scant* wind.

scant of; short of; having an insufficient supply of.

sçant, *n.* scarcity; scantiness. [Dial.]

sçant, *v.t.*; scanted, *pt.*, *pp.*; scanting, *ppr.* 1. to limit in size or amount; to cut down; to stint.

2. to fail to give full measure of.

3. to treat in an inadequate manner.

sçant, *v.i.* to fail or become less; as, the wind *scants*. [Obs.]

sçant, *adv.* scarcely; hardly; not quite. [Dial.]

sçant'i·ly, *adv.* in a scanty manner.

sçant'i·ness, *n.* the state or quality of being scanty.

sçan'tle, *n.* a gauge by which slates are regulated to their proper length.

sçan'tle, *v.i.* to be deficient; to fail. [Obs.]

sçan'tle, *v.t.* to divide into thin or small pieces; to scant. [Obs.]

sçant'let, *n.* a small quantity. [Obs.]

sçant'ling, *n.* [from obs. *scantillon*; OFr. *eschantillon*, specimen, pattern, orig. corner piece, chip.]

1. a small quantity or amount.

2. dimensions of building material.

3. a small beam or timber, especially one of small cross section, as a 2 x 4.

4. a small, upright timber, as in the frame of a structure.

5. small beams or timbers collectively.

6. a rough draft; a rude sketch. [Obs.]

sçant'ling, *a.* not plentiful; small. [Obs.]

sçant'ly, *adv.* in a scant manner. [Rare.]

sçant'ness, *n.* the quality or state of being scant. [Rare.]

sçant'y, *a.*; *comp.* scantier; *superl.* scantiest, 1. narrow; small; lacking amplitude or extent.

His dominions were very narrow and *scanty*. —Locke.

2. barely sufficient; meager; as, a *scanty* supply of bread.

3. insufficient; not enough.

Syn.—scant, deficient, small, sparing, narrow, meager, poor, scarce, insufficient, limited.

sçāpe, *n.* [L. *scapus*, the shaft of a pillar, the stalk of a plant.]

1. in botany, a stem growing from the crown of the root, bearing the blossom without leaves, as in the narcissus and hyacinth.

s, SCAPE

2. in architecture, the shaft of a column; also, erroneously, the apophyge of a column.

3. in zoology, the shaft of a feather; also, the basal joint of an antenna of an insect.

sçāpe, *n.* [echoic.] the cry of a flushed snipe.

sçāpe, 'sçāpe, *v.t.* and *v.i.* to escape. [Obs.]

sçāpe, 'sçāpe, *n.* 1. an escape. [Obs.]

2. means of escape; evasion. [Obs.]

3. an escapade. [Obs.]

4. a moral transgression, such as a loss of chastity. [Obs.]

sçāpe'gal″lōwṣ, *n.* one who has narrowly escaped the gallows for his crimes.

sçāpe'gōat, *n.* [from *escape* and *goat*.]

1. a goat over the head of which the high priest of the ancient Jews confessed the sins of the people on the Day of Atonement, after which it was allowed to escape: Lev. xvi. 8–22.

2. a person, group, or thing that bears the blame for the mistakes or crimes of others or for some misfortune due to another agency.

sçāpe'grāce, *n.* a graceless, unprincipled fellow; a rogue; a rascal.

sçāpe'less, *a.* in botany, without a scape.

sçāpe'ment, *n.* same as *escapement*, sense 2.

sçāpe wheel (hwēl), in horology, the notched wheel in an escapement, whose teeth escape one at a time from the pallets.

sçȧ·phan'dẽr, *n.* [Gr. *skaphē*, *skaphos*, a boat, tub, bowl, and *anēr*, *andros*, man.] a device, as a cork belt, used as a support in swimming.

sçaph'iṣm, *n.* [Gr. *skaphē*, anything hollowed out, from *skaptein*, to dig or make hollow.] an ancient Persian punishment inflicted on criminals by confining them in a hollow tree or log in which holes were made for the head, legs, and arms. The exposed parts were smeared with honey to attract insects and the victims abandoned.

sçaph'īte, *n.* [LL., from Gr. *skaphē*, a boat, and *-ite*.] a boat-shaped fossil cephalopod, belonging to the family of ammonites.

sçaph″ō·cē·phal'iç, *a.* having a keeled or boat-shaped head; afflicted with scaphocephaly.

sçaph·ō·ceph'ȧ·ly, *n.* [Gr. *skaphē*, *skaphos*, boat, and *kephalē*, head.] a deformed condition of the skull, in which the vault is high and elongated, but narrow.

sçaph·ō·cē'rīte, *n.* [Gr. *skaphē*, *skaphos*, boat, and *keras* (*-atos*), horn.] a scalelike appendage on the second joint of the antennae of certain crustaceans.

sçȧ·phog′nȧ·thīte, *n.* [Gr. *skaphē*, *skaphos*, boat, *gnathos*, jaw, and *-ite*.] the boat-shaped appendage or epipodite of the second pair of maxilla in the lobster, the function of which is to spoon out the water from the branchial chamber.

sçaph′oid, *a.* resembling a boat in form.
scaphoid bone; in anatomy, (a) the outer bone of the first row of the carpal bones; (b) a bone on the inner side of the tarsus, before the astragalus and behind the cuneiform bone.

sçaph′oid, *n.* a scaphoid bone.

sçaph·ō·lū′năr, *a.* of or pertaining to the scaphoid and lunar bones of the wrist.
scapholunar bone; a bone in carnivores and other mammals formed by the coalescence of the scaphoid and lunar bones of the carpus.

sçaph·ō·lū′năr, *n.* the scapholunar bone.

Sçȧ·phop′ō·dȧ, *n.pl.* [Gr. *skaphē*, *skaphos*, boat, and *pous*, *podos*, foot.] a small class of mollusks having a body enclosed in a tubular shell, open at both ends and elongated, with a foot adapted for burrowing, and long cirri or tentacles.

sçȧ·phop′ō·dous, *a.* of or pertaining to the *Scaphopoda*.

sçap′i-, [from L. *scapus*, a stalk.] a combining form meaning *stalk, shaft*.

sçā′pi·fọrm, *a.* [L. *scapus*, a stem, and *-form*.] having a scapelike form; formed like a flower stem.

sçȧ·pig′ẽr·ous, *a.* scape-bearing or scapiform.

sçā′poid, *a.* [L. *scapus*, a stem, and *-oid*.] scapiform; formed like a scape.

sçap′ō·līte, *n.* [Gr. *skāpos*, rod, and *lithos*, stone.] one of a group of tetragonal silicates of aluminum, calcium, and sodium; wernerite.

sçā′pōse, *a.* scape-bearing; scapigerous; consisting of a scape.

sçap′ple, *v.t.* same as *scabble*.

sçap′ū·lȧ, *n.*; *pl.* **sçap′ū·lae, sçap′ū·lȧṣ,** [LL., the shoulder; L. *scapulæ*, the shoulder blades.]
1. the shoulder blade; the flat triangular bone in the back of the shoulder in man, or a similar bone on other vertebrates.
2. in zoology, same as *tegula*.

sçap′ū·lăr, *a.* [L. *scapularis*, from *scapulæ*, the shoulder blades.] pertaining to the shoulder or to the scapula or scapulae; as, the *scapular* region.
scapular arch; the pectoral arch.
scapular feathers; the shoulder feathers of a bird.
scapular index; the ratio of the length of the scapula to its breadth.
scapular region; the region of the back on each side and over the shoulders.

sçap′ū·lăr, *n.* 1. a sleeveless outer garment falling from the shoulders, worn as part of a monk's habit.
2. two small pieces of cloth joined by strings, worn on the chest and back, under the clothes, by some Roman Catholics as a token of religious devotion.
3. in anatomy and zoology, (a) a scapula; (b) a feather growing from a bird's scapular region.
4. in surgery, a bandage passed over the shoulder to support it or to keep another bandage in place.

sçap·ū·lā′rē, *n.* [LL., neut. of *scapularis*, of the shoulder.] the side of a bird's back; the part covered by the scapular feathers.

sçap′ū·lăr·y, *a.* same as *scapular*.

sçap′ū·lăr·y, *n.*; *pl.* **sçap′ū·lăr·ieṣ,** same as *scapular*.

sçap′ū·lā·ted, *a.* having prominent scapular feathers.

sçap′ū·let, *n.* [*scapula* and dim. *-et*.] a secondary fold of the oral cylinder; an appendage at the base of each of the armlike lobes of the manubrium in rhizostomous medusae.

sçap′ū·lō-, [from LL. *scapula*, shoulder, L. *scapulæ*, shoulder blades.] a combining form meaning *scapula* or *scapula and*: also *scapul-*.

sçap″ū·lō·çlȧ·viç′ū·lăr, *a.* pertaining to the scapula and the clavicle.

sçap″ū·lō·hū′mẽr·ăl, *a.* pertaining to the scapula and the humerus.

sçā′pus, *n.* [L., a shaft, stem.]
1. in architecture, a shaft; a scape.
2. the stem or trunk of a feather.
3. in botany, a scape.
4. in entomology, the second antennal joint.

sçär, *n.* [ME. *scarre*, *sker*; ON. *sker*.]
1. a precipitous rocky place or cliff. [Brit.]
2. a projecting or isolated rock, as in the sea. [Brit.]

sçär, *n.* [OFr. *escare*, a scar; L. *eschara*, a scar, especially one produced by a burn, from Gr. *eschara*, fireplace, brazier, scar of a burn.]
1. a mark left on the skin or other tissue after a wound, burn, ulcer, pustule, lesion, etc. has healed; cicatrix.
2. any blemish or mark resembling this, as on the stem of a plant where a leaf was attached.
3. (a) the result left on the mind by suffering or anguish; (b) the physical sign of suffering, such as a line on the face.
4. in founding, a fault in a casting.
5. the circular blemish seen on the nacreous lining of a bivalve shell, which marks the attachment of the adductor muscle.

sçär, *v.t.*; scarred, *pt.*, *pp.*; scarring, *ppr.* to mark with or as with a scar; to disfigure.

sçär, *v.i.* to form a scar; to cicatrize.

sçär, *n.* [L. *scarus*; Gr. *skaros*, a sea fish.] any fish of the genus *Scarus*; a parrot fish.

sçar′ăb, *n.* [Fr. *scarabée*; L. *scarabeus*.]
1. a beetle, especially the black, winged dung beetle, held sacred by the ancient Egyptians.
2. an image of this beetle, cut from a stone or gem, often engraved with symbols on the flat underside, and formerly worn as a charm.

EGYPTIAN SCARAB

sçar·ȧ·baē′ăn, *a.* and *n.* scarabaeid.

sçar·ȧ·bae′id, *n.* one of the *Scarabæidæ*.

sçar·ȧ·bae′id, *a.* pertaining to the *Scarabæidæ*: also written *scarabæidous*.

Sçar·ȧ·bae′i·dae, *n.pl.* [L. *scarabæus*, a beetle, and *-idæ*.] a very extensive group of beetles, forming the chief part of the section *Lamellicornia*, typified by the genus *Scarabæus*, having squat, stout bodies and antennae made up of small plates.

sçar·ȧ·bae′oid, *n.* in entomology, a scarabaeid; a scarab.

sçar·ȧ·bae′oid, *a.* pertaining to the *Scarabæidæ*; scaraboid.

Sçar·ȧ·bae′us, *n.* [L., a beetle.]
1. a large genus of coleopterous insects, formerly corresponding to the section *Lamellicornia*, but now restricted to about seventy species. *Scarabæus sacer* was the sacred beetle of Egypt.
2. [s–] a scarab.

sçar′ȧ·bee, *n.* a scarabaeus.

sçar′ȧ·boid, *a.* having the appearance or nature of a scarab.

sçar′ȧ·boid, *n.* 1. a scarabaeid.
2. a counterfeit scarab, of Phoenician or Greek origin, carved in imitation of the true Egyptian scarab.

Sçar′ȧ·mouch, *n.* [Fr. *scaramouche*; It. *scaramuccia*, a skirmish.]
1. a buffoon in motley dress: a stock character in Italian comedy, depicted as a braggart and a poltroon.
2. [s–] a boastful coward, poltroon, or rascal.

SCARAMOUCH

sçãrce, *a.* [OFr. *escars*, *eschars*, scarce, needy; LL. *scarpsus*, for L. *excerptus*, pp. of *excerpere*, to pick out, select; hence, that which is picked out and therefore scarce.]
1. not plentiful or abundant; being in small supply in proportion to the demand; deficient; wanting; as, water was *scarce*.
2. being few in number and scattered; seldom met with; rare; uncommon; infrequent; as, good horses are *scarce*.
3. scantily supplied; poorly provided; not having much (with *of*): as, *scarce of* money. [Rare.]
4. sparing; stingy; parsimonious; mean. [Obs.]
5. diminished; deficient; scant. [Obs.]
to make oneself scarce; to leave voluntarily; to go or stay away. [Colloq.]

sçãrce, *adv.* scarcely; as, *scarce* to believe one's eyes: a literary usage.

sçãrce′ly, *adv.* 1. hardly; barely; scantily; but just; with difficulty; as, I can *scarcely* speak.
2. probably not or certainly not; as, *scarcely* true.
3. with scantness; insufficiently. [Obs.]

sçãrce′ment, *n.* [ME.; *scarce* and *-ment*.]
1. a setback in the building of walls, or in raising banks of earth; a footing or ledge formed by the setting back of a wall.
2. in mining, a ledge of a stratum left projecting into a mine shaft as a footing for a ladder; a support for a pit cistern, etc.

sçãrce′ness, *n.* the quality or state of being scarce. [Rare.]

sçãr′ci·ty, *n.*; *pl.* **sçãr′ci·tieṣ,** [ME. *scarsite*; O.Norm. Fr. *escarseté*.] the state or condition of being scarce; (a) smallness of quantity or smallness in proportion to the wants or demands; deficiency; as, a *scarcity* of grain; (b) rareness; infrequency.
Syn.—deficiency, rarity, want, dearth, famine.

sçärd, *n.* a shard or fragment. [Brit. Dial.]

sçãre, *v.t.*; scared, *pt.*, *pp.*; scaring, *ppr.* [ME. *skerren*, from *sker*, afraid, from ON. *skiarr*, shy, timid.]
1. to startle; to fill with sudden terror; to strike fear into.
2. to drive (*away* or *off*) by frightening.
to scare up; (a) to drive from cover, as game; (b) to produce or gather quickly, as money. [Colloq.]

sçãre, *v.i.* to be frightened; to take sudden fright; as, nervous people *scare* easily.

sçãre, *n.* a sudden fear or panic; an attack of fright, often unreasonable.

sçãre, *a.* 1. showing timidity; shy. [Rare.]
2. intended or serving to scare, or frighten; as, a *scare* headline. [Colloq.]

sçãre′bābe, *n.* something to frighten a child; a bugbear. [Rare.]

sçãre′bug, *n.* anything terrifying; a bugaboo.

sçãre′çrow, *n.* 1. anything set up in a field to scare crows. etc, away from crops, usually a crude figure of a man roughly dressed.
2. anything that frightens one but is actually not harmful.
3. a person dressed in very old and ragged clothes.

sçãre′fīre, *n.* an alarming conflagration. [Obs.]

sçãre′head (-hed), *n.* in newspaper printing, an exceptionally large headline, for sensational news. [Colloq.]

sçãre′mŏn·gẽr, *n.* a person who circulates alarming rumors.

sçärf, *n.* [Ice. *skarfr*.] a cormorant; a shag. [Scot.]

sçärf, *n.*; *pl.* **sçärfs, sçärveṣ,** [O.Norm.Fr. *escarpe*, from OFr. *escreppe*, a purse suspended from the neck, wallet; ON. *skreppa*, wallet.]
1. a long, broad piece of silk or other cloth worn about the neck, head, or shoulders as an ornament or to give warmth and protection from the wind.
2. any neckerchief or necktie with hanging ends.
3. a long, narrow covering for a table, bureau top, etc.
4. in military usage, a sash.

sçärf, *v.t.* 1. to throw on loosely; to put on, as a scarf.
2. to dress in a loose wrap; to adorn with a scarf.

sçärf, *n.* [prob. from ON. *skarfr*, notch in a timber.]
1. a joint made by notching, grooving, or otherwise cutting the ends of two pieces and fastening them so that they lap over and join firmly into one continuous piece: also *scarf joint*.
2. the end of a piece cut in this fashion.
3. a groove along a whale's body.

sçärf, *v.t.* 1. to join by a scarf.
2. to make a scarf in the end of.
3. to cut scarfs in and remove the skin and blubber of (a whale).

sçärf joint, a scarf (joint made by notching, etc.).

sçärf′skin, *n.* the cuticle; the epidermis; the outermost integument of the body.

sçärf weld, a joint made by overlapping and welding two pieces of metal together.

sçärf′wīse, *adv.* in the manner of a scarf; across. [Rare.]

Sçar'i·dae, *n.pl.* a family of large oblong tropical food fishes having a compressed head and large scales: typified by the genus *Scarus.*

sçar"i·fi·çā'tion, *n.* [L. *scarificatio* (*-onis*), a scratching open, from *scarificare,* to scratch open.]
 1. the act of scarifying or the state of being scarified.
 2. scratches or cuts made by scarifying.

sçar'i·fi·çā·tŏr, *n.* [LL., from L. *scarificare,* to scratch open.] a surgical instrument containing movable lancets, used in scarifying the skin.

sçar'i·fī·ẽr, *n.* 1. a scarificator.
 2. in agriculture, an implement with prongs for loosening the soil without turning it over.

sçar'i·fȳ, *v.t.*; scarified, *pt., pp.*; scarifying, *ppr.* [Fr. *scarifier*; L. *scarificare*; Gr. *skariphasthai,* to scratch open or scrape up, from *skariphos,* a sharp-pointed instrument.]
 1. to make a series of small, superficial incisions or punctures in (the skin), as in surgery.
 2. to criticize sharply; to make cutting remarks about.
 3. in agriculture, (a) to loosen or stir (the topsoil); (b) to make incisions in the coats of (seeds) in order to hasten germination.

sçā'ri·ōse, *a.* same as *scarious.*

sçā'ri·ous, *a.* [LL. *scariosus,* rough.] in botany, tough, thin, dry, and semitransparent, as a perianth.

sçär·là·ti'nà, *n.* [Mod. L., from It. *scarlattina,* from *scarlatto,* scarlet.] scarlet fever: a term used popularly for a mild form of the disease.

sçär·là·ti'năl, *a.* pertaining to or due to scarlatina.

sçär·là·ti'ni·fọrm, *a.* resembling scarlatina.

sçär·là·ti'noid, *a.* resembling scarlatina or any of its symptoms.

sçär·là·ti'nous, *a.* pertaining to or of the nature of scarlatina.

sçär'less, *a.* without a scar or scars.

sçär'let, *n.* [OFr. *escarlate*; Fr. *écarlate,* from Per. *saqalāt, siqalāt, suqlāt,* scarlet cloth.]
 1. a bright-red color with a slightly orange tinge.
 2. cloth or clothing of a scarlet color.
 All her household are clothed with *scarlet.*
 —Prov. xxxi. 21.

sçär'let, *a.* 1. of the color scarlet; of a bright-red color; as, a *scarlet* cloth or thread; a *scarlet* lip.
 2. of sin; sinful; specifically, whorish.
 scarlet admiral; see *red admiral* under *red.*
 scarlet bean; a bean, *Phaseolus coccineus,* cultivated for its showy scarlet flowers: also called *Spanish bean* and *scarlet runner.*
 scarlet fever; an acute contagious disease, especially of children, caused by certain streptococci and characterized by sore throat, fever, and a scarlet rash.
 scarlet fish; a Chinese goldfish characterized by its scarlet color and its protuberant eyes: also called *telescope fish.*
 scarlet hat; in the Roman Catholic Church, the hat of a cardinal, especially as a symbol of rank.
 scarlet ibis; a bird, *Ibis rubra,* of South and Central America, with plumage of intense scarlet.
 scarlet letter; a scarlet letter A, which women condemned of adultery were formerly forced to wear.
 scarlet maple; the red maple, *Acer rubrum,* characterized by its scarlet flowers and reddish twigs: also called *swamp maple.*
 scarlet mite; a mite, *Trombidium holosericeum,* whose young are parasitic on the genus *Phalangium* of the *Arachnida.* The adult insect, which is bright scarlet, is found on the ground and in moss on the roots of trees.
 scarlet oak; a North American oak, *Quercus coccinea,* the leaves of which turn scarlet in the fall.
 scarlet rash; roseola.
 scarlet runner; same as *scarlet bean.*
 scarlet snake; a harmless snake, *Cemophora coccinea,* of the southern States, red with numerous pairs of black rings and a yellow ring between each pair.
 scarlet sumac; a plant, *Rhus glabra,* of the cashew family, with smooth stems and leaves, the leaflets being white beneath: sometimes cultivated for ornament.
 scarlet tanager; a redbird of the United States, with a scarlet body and black wings and tail; specifically, the *Piranga rubra,* or summer redbird, and the *Piranga erythromelas* of the northeastern States.
 Scarlet Woman; the Roman Catholic Church: an opprobrious term based on the reference in Rev. xvii. 1–6.

sçär'let, *v.t.* to color scarlet. [Rare.]

sçā'roid, *a.* relating to the *Scaridæ.*

sçärp, *n.* [Fr. *escarpe,* from It. *scarpa,* a scarp, a slope.]
 1. a steep slope; an abrupt declivity.
 2. ground formed into a steep slope as part of a fortification; a steep slope on the inner face of a ditch below the rampart.

sçärp, *v.t.*; scarped, *pt., pp.*; scarping, *ppr.* [Fr. *escarper,* to scarp.]
 1. to make or cut into a steep slope.
 2. to provide with a scarp.

sçärp, *n.* [OFr. *escarpe*; D. *sjerp*; Sw. *skärp,* a scarf, a belt.] in heraldry, a diminutive of the bend sinister, half its width and continued to the edges of the field.

SCARP

sçär'pines, *n.pl.* [Fr. *escarpins,* light shoes.] an instrument used during the Inquisition for torturing the legs and feet.

sçär'ring, *n.* a scar; a mark left by something that scars.

sçär'ry, *a.* having scars; full of scars; also, like a scar.

sçärt, *v.i.* and *v.t.* to make a mark; to scratch. [Scot.]

sçärt, *n.* a scratch; a mark, as by a pen. [Scot.]

sçär tis'sūe, the dense, fibrous, contracted connective tissue of which a scar is composed.

Sçā'rus, *n.* [L., from Gr. *skaros,* a kind of seafish.]
 1. a genus of fishes typical of the *Scaridæ* and remarkable for the structure and strength of their jaws.
 2. a fish of this genus: also called *parrot fish.*

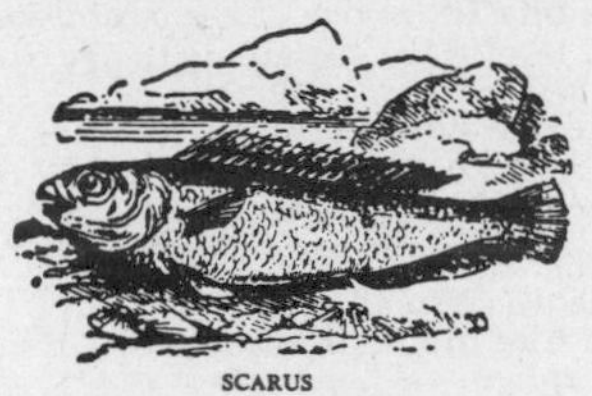

SCARUS

sçärves, *n.* alternative plural of *scarf* (cloth).

sçār'y, *a.* 1. easily alarmed; timid. [Colloq.]
 2. causing alarm; scaring. [Colloq.]

sçat, sçatt, *n.* [AS. *scætt,* money, tribute; Ice. *skattr*; Sw. *skatt,* tax; Goth. *skatts,* money.] a tax; tribute; especially, a land tax in the Shetland Islands.

sçat, *n.* a brisk shower of rain driven by the wind. [Brit. Dial.]

sçat, *n.* same as *skat.*

sçat, *n.* a blow; a spat; a hurt. [Brit. Dial.]

sçat, *v.i.*; scatted, *pt., pp.*; scatting, *ppr.* [perh. a hiss and *cat.*] to go away: usually in the imperative. [Colloq.]

sçat, *a.* [origin unknown.] in jazz, designating or of singing in which meaningless syllables are improvised, often in imitation of the sounds of a musical instrument.

sçat, *n.* scat singing.

sçat, *v.i.*; scatted, *pt., pp.*; scatting, *ppr.* to engage in scat singing.

sçatch, *n.* [Fr. *escache.*] a kind of bit for a bridle.

sçāth, *v.t.* and *n.* scathe. [Obs.]

sçāthe, *v.t.*; scathed, *pt., pp.*; scathing, *ppr.* [AS. *sceathan,* to harm, injure, from Teut. base *skath,* to harm.]
 1. (a) to injure or hurt; (b) to blast; wither; sear. [Archaic or Dial.]
 2. to denounce fiercely.

sçāthe, *n.* injury; harm; destruction. [Archaic or Dial.]

sçāthe'fụl, *a.* harmful; causing damage or destruction.

sçāthe'less, *a.* free from harm; escaping injury; without damage.

sçāth'ing, *a.* hurtful; damaging; burning; withering; as, *scathing* denunciation; a *scathing* fire.

sçāth'ing·ly, *adv.* with intense severity; so as to be felt keenly.

sçat'ō-, [from Gr. *skōr, skatos,* excrement.] a combining form meaning *feces, excrement,* as in *scatology.*

sçat·ō·loġ'i·căl, *a.* of, having the nature of, or concerned with scatology.

sçà·tol'ō·ġy, *n.* [Gr. *skōr, skatos,* dung, and *logia,* from *legein,* to speak.]
 1. the study of feces or of fossil excrement.
 2. the study of or obsession with excrement, excretion, etc. in literature.

sçat'ō·phāġe, *n.* [Gr. *skōr, skatos,* dung, and *phagein,* to eat.] an animal that eats dung, especially a fly or a beetle.

sçà·toph'à·gous, *a.* [Gr. *skatophagos,* dung-eating; from *skōr, skatos,* dung, and *phagein,* to eat.] subsisting on dung, as some flies.

sçà·tos'çō·py, *n.* [Gr. *skōr, skatos,* dung, and *skopein,* to view, examine.] examination of dung for diagnosis or divination.

sçatt, *n.* a scat.

sçat'tẽr, *v.t.*; scattered, *pt., pp.*; scattering, *ppr.* [ME. *scateren*; AS. *scateran,* from the base *scat*; Gr. *sked,* as in *skedasis,* a scattering; Sans. *skhad,* to cut.]
 1. to throw loosely about; to sprinkle; to strew; as, to *scatter* seed in sowing.
 2. to strew or besprinkle with something.
 3. to disperse; to separate and drive in several directions; to rout.
 4. to waste; to dissipate.
 5. in physics, (a) to reflect or refract in an irregular, diffuse manner; (b) to diffuse or deflect in an irregular manner.

sçat'tẽr, *v.i.* to separate and go in several directions; as, clouds *scatter* after a storm.

sçat'tẽr, *n.* 1. a scattering.
 2. what is scattered.

sçat'tẽr·brāin, *n.* one who is incapable of concentrated thought; a giddy, frivolous person.

sçat'tẽr·brāined, *a.* giddy; flighty.

sçat'tẽr·brāins, *n.* a scatterbrain.

sçat'tẽred, *a.* 1. dispersed; dissipated; thinly spread; sprinkled or thinly spread over.
 2. in botany, irregular in position; without any apparent regular order; as, *scattered* branches.

sçat'tẽred·ly, *adv.* in a scattered manner.

sçat'tẽred·ness, *n.* the state of being scattered.

sçat'tẽr·good, *n.* one who is wasteful; a spendthrift.

sçat'tẽr·ing, *a.* 1. distributed over a wide area; found or occurring at irregular intervals.
 2. cast so as to be distributed in small numbers among several or many candidates: said of votes.

sçat'tẽr·ing, *n.* the act of sprinkling about; also, anything scattered.

sçat'tẽr·ing·ly, *adv.* in a scattering manner.

sçat'tẽr·ling, *n.* a vagabond. [Archaic.]

sçat'tẽr rug, any of various types of small rug for covering only part of a floor.

sçat'tẽr·shot, *a.* 1. designating a shotgun shell that disperses the shot in a broad pattern.
 2. covering many points, but not thoroughly; random; as, *scattershot* criticism.

sçat'tẽr-sīte, *a.* designating or of inexpensive, publicly owned or financed housing units scattered throughout middle-class residential areas.

sçà·tū'ri·ent, *a.* gushing forth.

sçat·ū·riġ'i·nous, *a.* abounding in springs. [Obs.]

sçaup, *n.*; *pl.* **sçaups** or **sçaup,** [obs. var. of scalp.]
 1. a species of diving duck, *Nyroca collaris,* found in Europe and North America.
 2. a bed of shellfish. [Scot.]

sçaup duck, a scaup.

sçaup'ẽr, *n.* [prob. a variant of *scalper.*] a tool used by engravers for clearing out open spaces between lines.

sçaur, *n.* a scar; a cliff. [Scot.]

sçau'rie, *n.* [prob. Sw. *skiura.*] the herring gull of Europe. [Scot.]

sçav'āġe, *n.* [ME. *scavage,* from AS. *sceáwian,* to look at, inspect.] a toll or duty formerly exacted from merchant strangers.

sçav'enġe, *v.t.*; scavenged, *pt., pp.*; scavenging, *ppr.* 1. to clean up, as streets, alleys, etc.; to collect rubbish, dirt, or garbage from.
 2. to remove burned gases from (the cylinder of an internal-combustion engine).
 3. in metallurgy, to clean (molten metal) by using a substance that will combine chemically with the impurities present.

sçav'enġe, *v.i.* 1. to act as a scavenger.
 2. to look for food.

sçav'en·ġẽr, *n.* [ME. *scavager,* a scavenger, from AS. *sceáwian,* to inspect.]

1. a person whose employment is to clean streets and carry off the filth.
2. any animal that eats refuse; especially, the scavenger beetle.
3. anything that removes impurities, refuse, etc.
scavenger's daughter; an old instrument of torture said to have been invented by Sir W. Skevington. It compressed the body until blood flowed from the nose and ears.

sçav'en·ġẽr bee'tle, any beetle that eats refuse or carrion.

sçav'en·ġẽr çrab, any crab that feeds on carrion.

sçā'zon, *n.* [Gr. *skazōn*, limping.] a choliamb.

scel'i·dēṣ (sel'), *n.pl.* [Gr., pl. of *skelis*, a leg.] the hind, lower, or pelvic limbs of a mammal.

scel'i·dō·saur, *n.* a dinosaur of the genus *Scelidosaurus*.

scel''i·dō·sau'ri·ăn, *n.* [Gr. *skelis*, a leg, and *sauros*, a lizard.] any dinosaur of the *Scelidosauridæ*.

Scel''i·dō·sau'rus, *n.* the typical genus of *Scelidosauridæ*, a family of stegosaurian dinosaurs.

scē'nȧ, *n.*; *pl.* **scē'nae,** [L., a sheltered place, tent, stage, scene.]
1. a scene in an opera.
2. an elaborate solo, partly musical and partly recitative.

scē·när'i·ō (*or* -när'), *n.*; *pl.* **scē·när'i·ōṣ,** [It., from LL. *scenarius*, of stage scenes.]
1. an outline of the plot of a play or an opera, indicating the scenes and the stage directions.
2. in motion pictures, the outline of a photoplay: it includes the story of the play, specifications as to scenes, situations, cast of characters, and detailed directions as to acting.
3. an outline for any proposed or planned series of events, real or imagined.

scē·när'ist, *n.* the author of a motion-picture scenario.

scē·när'īze, *v.t.*; scenarized, *pt.*, *pp.*; scenarizing, *ppr.* to write a scenario based upon (a book, a novel, a short story); as, he has *scenarized Macbeth*.

scēn'ȧ·ry, *n.* scenery. [Obs.]

scend, *n.* the upward heaving of a ship: correlative of *pitch*: also spelled *send*.

scend, *v.i.* to be heaved upward, as by a wave: said of a ship: also spelled *send*.

scēne, *n.* [Fr. *scène*; L. *scena* or *scæna*; Gr. *skēnē*, a covered, sheltered place, from root of *skia*, a shadow, shade; Sans. *sku*, to cover.]
1. the place in which any event, real or imagined, occurs; as, London was the *scene* of his troubles.
2. the setting or locale of the action of a play, opera, story, etc.; as, the *scene* of Hamlet is Denmark.
3. a division of a play, usually part of an act, in which the action is continuous and there is no shift of place.
4. a part of a play, motion picture, story, etc. that constitutes a unit of development or action, as a passage between certain characters.
5. the painted screens, backdrops, and properties which represent the place of action in a play, motion picture, opera, or the like; as, change the *scenes*.
6. a view of people or places; a picture or spectacle.
7. a display of strong or excited feeling before others.
8. an episode, situation, or event, real or imaginary, especially as described or represented.
9. a theater stage. [Obs.]
behind the scenes; behind the scenery of a theater in the back of the stage; hence, in privacy or in secret.
to make the scene; (a) to be present; (b) to participate, especially in an effective or noticeable way. [Slang.]

scēne, *v.t.* to exhibit; to make a scene or exhibition of; to set out; to display. [Obs.]

scēne'măn, *n.*; *pl.* **scēne'men,** one who shifts the scenes in a theater; a sceneshifter. [Rare.]

scēn'ẽr·y, *n.*; *pl.* **scēn'ẽr·ieṣ,** [L. *scenarius*, of scenes, from *scena*, scene.]
1. dramatic action; an open display of feeling. [Obs.]
2. the representation of a place in a play, etc.; the painted screens, backdrops, flats, etc. representing the scenes on the stage.
3. the general appearance of a place; the features of a landscape; as, the *scenery* is beautiful.

scēne'shift''ẽr, *n.* one who moves the scenes in a theater.

scēn'iç, scēn'iç·ăl (*or* sen'), *a.* [L. *scenicus*; Gr. *skēnikos*, scenical, dramatical, from *skēnē*, scene.]
1. (a) of the stage; dramatic; theatrical; (b) relating to stage effects or stage scenery.
2. of natural scenery; affording many beautiful views; picturesque.
3. representing an action, event, situation, etc.

scēn'iç·ăl·ly, *adv.* in a scenic manner.

scēn'iç rāil'wāy, a roller coaster.

scēn'ō·grȧph, *n.* [Gr. *skēnē*, scene, and *graphein*, to write, describe.] a representation drawn in perspective.

scē·nog'rȧ·phẽr, *n.* one who makes drawings in perspective.

scēn·ō·graph'iç, scēn·ō·graph'iç·ăl, *a.* pertaining to scenography; drawn in perspective.

scēn·ō·graph'iç·ăl·ly, *adv.* in a scenographic manner.

scē·nog'rȧ·phy, *n.* [Gr. *skēnographia*, scene-painting, from *skēnē*, scene, and *graphein*, to write, describe.]
1. the art of drawing in perspective.
2. scene painting, especially in ancient Greece.

scent, *v.t.*; scented, *pt.*, *pp.*; scenting, *ppr.* [ME. *senten*; Fr. *sentir*, to feel, also to scent, smell, from L. *sentire*, to feel.]
1. to smell; to perceive by the olfactory organs; as, a hound *scents* game.
2. to have a suspicion of.
3. to perfume; to fill with odor, good or bad; as, aromatic plants *scent* the air.

scent, *v.i.* 1. to follow up or hunt by the sense of smell.
2. to smell. [Obs.]

scent, *n.* 1. odor; smell; the characteristic stimulation by a substance of the olfactory nerves; as, the *scent* of an orange or an apple; the *scent* of musk.
2. the power of smelling; the sense of smell; as, a hound of good *scent*.
3. a manufactured fluid preparation used to give fragrance; perfume.
4. an odor left by an animal, by which it is tracked in hunting.
5. a track followed in hunting.
6. any clue by which something is followed or detected.
7. an intuitive capacity for discovering or detecting; as, a *scent* for news.
8. in the game of hare and hounds, scraps of paper dropped on the ground by the hares to enable the hounds to follow.

scent'fụl, *a.* 1. odorous; emitting much smell.
2. of keen smell. [Obs.]

scent'ing·ly, *adv.* by scent or smell. [Obs.]

scent'less, *a.* having no smell.

scent'wood, *n.* in botany, *Alyxia buxifolia*, a fragrant evergreen shrub of Australia and Tasmania.

sçep'sis, *n.* skepticism. [Rare.]

sçep'tẽr, *n.* [Fr. *sceptre*, a royal scepter, from L. *sceptrum*, Gr. *skēptron*, a staff to lean on, from base of *skēptesthai*, to prop oneself, to lean on.]
1. a staff or rod held by sovereigns on solemn occasions, as a badge of authority; the appropriate ensign of sovereignty.
2. royal power or authority; as, to assume the *scepter*.

sçep'tẽr, *v.t.*; sceptered, *pt.*, *pp.*; sceptering, *ppr.* to furnish with a scepter; to invest with royal authority.

sçep·tẽr·el'lāte, *a.* in zoology, like a scepter with whorls of spines: applied to some sponge spicules.

sçep'tẽr·less, sçep'tre·less, *a.* having no scepter; having no authority; as, a *scepterless* ruler.

sçep'tiç, *n.* and *a.* same as *skeptic*.

sçep'tiç·ăl, *a.* same as *skeptical*.

sçep'ti·çiṣm, *n.* same as *skepticism*.

sçep'trăl, *a.* pertaining to or resembling a scepter.

sçep'tre (-tẽr), *n.* and *v.t.*; sceptred, *pt.*, *pp.*; sceptring, *ppr.* scepter: chiefly British spelling.

scẽrne, *v.t.* to discern. [Obs.]

sceū·ō·phō'ri·on, *n.*; *pl.* **sceū·ō·phō'ri·ȧ,** [Gr. *skeuos*, a vessel, and *pherein*, to bear.] in the Orthodox Eastern Church, a box that corresponds to the pyx.

sceū''ō·phy̆·lā'ci·um (-shi-um), *n.* [Gr. *skeuos*, a vessel, and *phylax*, *phylakos*, a guard.] in the Orthodox Eastern Church, a sacristy or vestry.

sceū·oph'y·lax, *n.* [Gr. *skeuos*, a vessel, and *phylax*, a guard.] in the Orthodox Eastern Church, a sacristan; one who keeps the sacred vessels.

sçhäb'ziē''gẽr (shäp'tsē''), *n.* same as *sapsago*.

Sçhaef·fē'ri·ȧ (shef-), *n.* [named after J. C. *Schäffer*, a German naturalist.] a genus of shrubs of the family *Celastraceæ*, of which there are two or three species found in the southern part of the United States and in tropical America. From *Schæfferia frutescens*, a species found in Florida, a valuable wood called yellowwood is obtained.

sçhäl, *n.* [prob. native name.] a catfish belonging to the genus *Synodontis*, found in the River Nile.

sçhät'chen (shät'khen), *n.* [Yid., from Heb. *shadhkhān*.] one who arranged marriages among European Jews; a marriage broker.

sçhed'ūle (*or Brit.* shed'ūl), *n.* [OFr. *schedule*, schedule, scroll, note, bill; LL. *schedula*, a small leaf of paper, from root *scid*, to cleave; Sans. *chhid*, to cut.]
1. a list, catalogue, or inventory of details, often as an explanatory supplement to a will, bill of sale, deed, etc.
2. a list of times of recurring events, projected operations, arriving and departing trains, etc.; timetable.
3. a timed plan for a procedure or project.

sçhed'ūle, *v.t.*; scheduled, *pt.*, *pp.*; scheduling, *ppr.* 1. to place or include in a schedule.
2. to make a schedule of.
3. to appoint or plan for a certain time or date.
to schedule out; to make a schedule of as required by law, in order to avoid the seizure of goods made exempt by statute.

Sçhed'ūled Çāstes, the groups of people in India formerly the class of untouchables.

Sçheele'ṣ green, a green coloring matter consisting of copper arsenite: also called *Swedish green*.

sçheel'īte, *n.* [after K.W. *Scheele* (1742–1786), Swed. chemist.] native calcium tungstate, $CaWO_4$, an important ore of tungsten, or wolfram.

sçhee'li·um, *n.* tungsten, or wolfram. [Obs.]

sçheff'ẽr·īte, *n.* [after H. G. *Scheffer*, a Swedish chemist.] a variety of pyroxene containing lime, magnesia, and manganese.

Sçhe·hẹ·rȧ·zä'de, *n.* in the Arabian Nights, the Sultan's bride, teller of the tales, who saves her life by keeping the Sultan interested in them.

Sçhel'ling·iṣm, *n.* [after F. W. J. von *Schelling*, German philosopher (1775–1854).] the philosophy of idealism.

sçhel'ly, *n.* a whitefish; the powan.

sçhelm, shelm, *n.* [OFr. *schelme*, a rogue.] a worthless fellow; a rogue. [Scot.]

sçhē'mȧ, *n.*; *pl.* **sçhē'mȧ·tȧ,** [L.; Gr. *schēma*, form, appearance.]
1. in Kantianism, a mediating factor making possible the application of the categories to phenomena.
2. in Leibnitz's monadology, the principle that is essential to each monad and constitutes its peculiar characteristics.
3. a diagrammatic representation of something; a summary; a scheme; an outline.
4. in logic, a syllogistic figure.

sçhē·mat'iç, *a.* pertaining to a scheme or schema.

sçhē·mat'i·căl·ly, *adv.* in a schematic manner.

sçhē'mȧ·tiṣm, *n.* [Gr. *schēmatismos*, from *schēma*, form, appearance.]
1. the particular form or disposition of a thing; an exhibition in outline of any systematic arrangement; outline; figure.
2. in astrology, the combination of the aspects of the heavenly bodies.
3. in logic, the character or figure of a syllogism.
4. the formation or use of schemata; also, a system of schemata.

sçhē'mȧ·tist, *n.* a projector; one given to forming schemes; a schemer; a promoter.

sçhē·mȧ·ti·zā'tion, *n.* a schematizing or being schematized.

sçhē'mȧ·tīze, *v.i.*; schematized, *pt.*, *pp.*;

schematizing, *ppr.* [Gr. *schēmatizein*, to give form, to fashion.]
 1. to form a scheme or schemes.
 2. to make an outline in the form of a schema.

sçhē'mȧ·tīze, *v.t.* to form into, or arrange according to. a scheme or schema.

sçhēme, *n.* [L. *schema*; Gr. *schēma*, form, appearance.]
 1. a carefully arranged and systematic program of action; a systematic plan for attaining some object.
 2. an orderly combination of things on a definite plan; system.
 3. a plot; underhand intrigue.
 4. a visionary plan or project.
 5. an outline or diagram showing different parts or elements of an object or system.
 6. an astrological diagram.
 7. in art, the plan of colors or tints in a picture; as, the color *scheme.*
 Syn.—plan, project, design, contrivance, purpose, device, plot.

sçhēme, *v.t.*; schemed, *pt., pp.*; scheming, *ppr.* 1. to make a scheme for; to plan as a scheme; to devise; to contrive.
 2. to plan in an underhand way; to plot.

sçhēme, *v.i.* 1. to make schemes; to form plans.
 2. to plot; to intrigue.

sçhēme ärch, in architecture, an arch that forms a portion of a circle less than a semicircle.

sçhēme'fụl, *a.* full of schemes, plans, or tricks.

sçhēm'ẽr, *n.* one who schemes, plots, or contrives; a projector; a contriver; a plotter.

sçhēm'ing, *a.* given to forming schemes; crafty; tricky.

sçhēm'ing, *n.* the act of forming a plan; planning; especially, crafty contriving.

sçhēm'ing·ly, *adv.* in the manner of a schemer; by or with scheming.

sçhēm'ist, *n.* a schemer; a projector. [Rare.]

sçhēm'y, *a.* resourceful in schemes; cunning. [Colloq.]

sçhēne, *n.* [L. *schœnus*; Gr. *schoinos*, a rush, rope, land measure.] an ancient Egyptian measure of length, equal to sixty stadia, or about seven miles.

sçheñk beer, [G. *schenkbier*, from *schenken*, to pour out, and *bier*, beer.] beer made with from four to six weeks' fermentation and designed for immediate use: also called *young beer.*

sçhe'pen, *n.* [D.] in Holland and the Dutch colonies, a magistrate.

sçhẽr'bet, *n.* sherbet. [Obs.]

sçher·zän'dō (-tsän'), *adv.* in music, in a playful, lively, or sportive manner: a direction to the performer.

sçher·zän'dō, *a.* in music, playful; sportive.

sçher'zō (-tsō), *n.*; *pl.* **sçher'zōṣ, sçher'zï,** a sportive, playful movement in ¾ time, usually following a slow one, and often constituting the third section of a sonata or symphony.

sçhē'sis, *n.* [Gr. *schesis*, condition, from *schein, echein*, to hold.]
 1. in rhetoric, a statement of what is considered to be the adversary's habitude of mind, by way of argument against him.
 2. condition; disposition; habitude. [Obs.]

sçhet'iç, sçhet'iç·ăl, *a.* of or pertaining to the state of the body; constitutional; habitual. [Obs.]

Sçhick test, [after Bela *Schick*, Am. pediatrician.] a test to determine immunity to diphtheria, made by injecting dilute diphtheria toxin under the skin: if an area of inflammation results, the patient is not immune.

Sçhie·dam', *n.* a type of gin, made at Schiedam, Holland.

sçhil'lẽr, *n.* [G., color play, from *schillern*, to change color.] a peculiar bronzelike luster in certain minerals, often iridescent, caused by internal reflection.

sçhil''lẽr·i·zā'tion, *n.* a change that takes place in the structure and chemical composition of certain minerals, giving rise to a glittering appearance upon certain crystallographic planes.

sçhil'lẽr·īze, *v.t.*; schillerized, *pt., pp.*; schillerizing, *ppr.* to give schiller to (a mineral) by the formation of minute cavities in the faces of crystals in parallel planes.

sçhil'lẽr spär, enstatite made iridescent by schillerization.

sçhil'ling, *n.* 1. the monetary unit and a coin of Austria.
 2. a former minor German coin.

sçhin·dy·lē'sis, *n.* [Gr. *schindylēsis*, a cleaving into fragments, from *schindylein*, *schizein*, to cleave.] in anatomy, an articulative form by which one bone fits into the groove of another.

Sçhī'nus, *n.* [LL., from Gr. *schinos*, the mastic tree.] a genus of tropical American and Australian trees or shrubs. *Schinus molle* yields a substance like mastic.

sçhip'pẽr·ke, *n.* [D. dial., little skipper.] any of a Belgian breed of small, black, shorthaired dog with a foxlike head, erect ears, a broad chest, and no tail, originally used as watchdogs on boats.

sçhir'rhus, *n.* same as *scirrhus*.

schiṣm (sizm), *n.* [ME. *schisme*; Fr. *schisme*, a schism, a division in or from the church; L.Gr. *schisma*, a rent, split, from Gr. *schizein*, to cleave, cut.]
 1. a split or division in an organized group or society, as the result of difference of opinion, of doctrine, etc.; especially, a formal split or division in the Christian church.
 2. the offense of causing or trying to cause a split or division in the church or in religion.
 3. a sect formed by such a split or division.
 Schism Act; an act of the British Parliament which required all teachers to conform to the Established Church and forbade them to be present at any dissenting place of worship. It took effect on Aug. 1, 1714, and in 1719 it was repealed.

sçhis'mȧ, *n.* [L. *schisma*; Gr. *schisma*, *schismatos*, a division of opinion, a rent, split.] in ancient music, an interval equal to half a comma.

schiṣ·mat'iç (siz-), *a.* 1. of, characteristic of, or having the nature of schism; as, *schismatic* opinions or proposals.
 2. tending to, causing, or guilty of schism.

schiṣ·mat'iç, *n.* one who separates or causes to separate from an established church or religious faith, because of a difference of opinions.

schiṣ·mat'iç·ăl, *a.* schismatic.

schiṣ·mat'iç·ăl·ly, *adv.* in a schismatic manner.

schiṣ·mat'iç·ăl·ness, *n.* the quality or condition of being schismatical.

schiṣ'mȧ·tīze, *v.i.* to commit or practice schism; especially, to make a breach of communion in the church.

schiṣm'less, *a.* free from or not affected by schism.

sçhist, *n.* [Gr. *schistos*, easily cleft, from *schizein*, to cleave.] a crystalline rock consisting of mineral ingredients so arranged as to impart a more or less laminar structure, that may be split easily into layers.

sçhis·tā'ceous, *a.* of a color like that of slate; bluish-gray.

sçhist'iç, *a.* schistose.

sçhis'tō- [from Gr. *schistos*, easily cleft, cloven, from *schizein*, to cleave.] a combining form meaning *cleft*: used chiefly in pathology.

sçhis·tō·ceph'ȧ·lus, *n.* [*schisto-*, and Gr. *kephalē*, head.] a fetus born with a cleft head.

sçhis·tō·coe'li·ȧ, *n.* [*schisto-*, and Gr. *koilia*, belly.] congenital fissure of the abdomen.

sçhis'tō·cȳte, *n.* [*schisto-*, and Gr. *kytos*, cell.]
 1. a blood corpuscle undergoing segmentation.
 2. a product of the division of a red blood corpuscle in malaria.

sçhis''tō·cȳ·tō'sis, *n.* [*schisto-*, and Gr. *kytos*, cell.] the accumulation of schistocytes in the blood.

sçhis·tō·glos'si·ȧ, *n.* [*schisto-*, and Gr. *glōssa*, tongue.] fissure of the tongue.

sçhis''tō·prō·sō'pi·ȧ, *n.* [*schisto-*, and Gr. *prosōpon*, face.] a fissure of the face due to defective development.

sçhis''tō·prō·sō'pus, *n.* a fetus born with a cleft face.

sçhis'tōse, sçhis'tous, *a.* having the structure of schist; pertaining to or of the nature of schist.

sçhis·tos'i·ty, *n.* the character or condition of being schistose.

sçhis'tō·sōme, *n.* [Mod. L. *Schistosoma*, from Gr. *schistos*, cleft, and *sōma*, body.] any of a group of flukes that live as parasites in the blood of mammals and birds, causing a disease that affects the intestines, liver, spleen, etc.

sçhis''tō·sō·mī'ȧ·sis, *n.* [from *schistosome* and *-iasis*.] the disease caused by schistosomes.

sçhis·tō·sō'mus, *n.*; *pl.* **sçhis·tō·sō'mī,** [*schisto-*, and Gr. *sōma*, body.] a fetus born with a fissured abdomen.

sçhis·tō·thō'rax, *n.* [*schisto-*, and Gr. *thōrax*, chest.] congenital fissure of the chest or sternum.

Sçhī'zae·ȧ, *n.* [Gr. *schizein*, to cleave.] the typical genus of the *Schizæaceæ*. One species only is found in North America, *Schizæa pusilla*, of New Jersey.

Sçhiz·ae·ā'cē·ae, *n.pl.* a family of ferns containing five genera, two of which are found in North America.

sçhiz·ae·ā'ceous, *a.* pertaining to the family *Schizæaceæ.*

sçhiz'ō- [from Gr. *schizein*, to cleave, split.] a combining form used in zoology, botany, etc., to mean *split, cleavage, division*, as in *schizocarp*.

sçhiz'ō·çärp, *n.* [*schizo-*, and Gr. *karpos*, fruit.] in botany, a dry fruit, as of the maple, that splits at maturity into two or more oneseeded carpels which remain closed.

sçhiz·ō·çär'pous, sçhiz·ō·çär'piç, *a.* pertaining to or like a schizocarp.

sçhiz'ō·coele, *n.* [*schizo-*, and Gr. *koilia*, a cavity, hollow.] in anatomy, a cavity in the body caused by the splitting of the mesoblast of the embryo.

sçhiz·ō·coe'lous, *a.* pertaining to or having a schizocoele.

sçhiz·ō·din'iç, *a.* [*schizo-*, and Gr. *ōdis*, *ōdinos*, the pangs of labor, birth pains.] expelling the genital products by rupture, as do certain worms.

sçhiz·ō·ġen'e·sis, *n.* [*schizo-*, and Gr. *genesis*, production, generation.] in biology, reproduction by fission.

sçhiz''ō·ġē·net'iç, *a.* schizogenic.

sçhiz·ō·ġen'iç, *a.* in botany, formed by splitting or separating: said of intercellular spaces in plants.

sçhī·zoġ'e·nous, *a.* schizogenic.

sçhiz'og·nath, *n.* [*schizo-*, and Gr. *gnathos*, jaw.] any bird with a cleft palate.

Sçhī·zog'nȧ·thae, *n.pl.* a division of carinate birds in which the maxillopalatine plates do not unite with the vomer or with each other.

sçhī·zog'nȧ·thiṣm, *n.* the condition of possessing a cleft palate.

sçhī·zog'nȧ·thous, *a.* belonging to, characteristic of, or resembling the *Schizognathæ.*

sçhī·zog'ō·ny, *n.* schizogenesis.

sçhiz'oid, *n.* a person who has schizophrenia.

sçhiz'oid, *a.* of, like, or having schizophrenia.

sçhiz''ō·mȳ·cēte', *n.* any one of the *Schizomycetes.*

Sçhiz''ō·mȳ·cē'tēṣ, *n.pl.* [*schizo-*, and Gr. *mykēs*, pl. *myketes*, mushroom.] a class of vegetable microorganisms comprising the bacteria.

sçhiz''ō·mȳ·cē'tous, *a.* pertaining to the *Schizomycetes.*

sçhiz''ō·mȳ·çō'sis, *n.* in medicine, any disease due to the presence of *Schizomycetes.*

Sçhiz''ō·nē·mẽr'tē·ȧ, *n.pl.* a suborder of worms characterized by deep, longitudinal, lateral, cephalic fissures.

sçhiz''ō·nē·mẽr'tē·ăn, *n.* [*schizo-*, and LL. *nemertes*, from Gr. *nēmertēs*, unerring.] one of the *Schizonemertea.*

Sçhiz·ō·neū'rȧ, *n.* [*schizo-*, and Gr. *neuron*, nerve.] a genus of plant lice of the subfamily *Pemphiginæ*, containing many species. *Schizoneura lanigera* is the woolly root louse of apple trees.

sçhiz·ō·pel'mous, *a.* same as **nomopelmous.**

sçhiz'ō·phrēne, *n.* a person who has schizophrenia.

sçhiz·ō·phrē'ni·ȧ, *n.* [Gr. *schizein*, to divide, and *phren*, the mind.] a mental disorder characterized by indifference, withdrawal, hallucinations, and delusions of persecution and omnipotence, often with unimpaired intelligence: a more inclusive term than *dementia praecox*, avoiding the implications of age and deterioration.

sçhiz·ō·phrē'ni·aç, *n.* same as **schizophrenic.**

sçhiz·ō·phren'iç, *a.* of or pertaining to schizophrenia; characterized by or having schizophrenia.

sçhiz·ō·phren'iç, *n.* a person having schizophrenia.

Sçhiz·ō·phȳ'cē·ae, *n.pl.* [*schizo-*, and Gr. *phykos*, a seaweed.] a group of unicellular algae which contain chlorophyll and reproduce asexually.

Schī·zoph′y·tȧ, *n.pl.* [*schizo-*, and Gr. *phyton*, a plant.] a group of plants, including the *Schizomycetes* and the *Schizophyceæ*, which consist of a single cell, or a chain or colony of cells, and reproduce only by simple fission or by asexual spores.

schiz′ō·phȳte, *n.* any plant of the *Schizophyta*.

schiz′ō·phȳte, *a.* pertaining to the *Schizophyta*.

schiz′ō·pod, *n.* [*schizo-*, and Gr. *pous, podos*, foot.] one of the *Schizopoda*.

schiz′ō·pod, *a.* resembling or pertaining to a schizopod.

Schī·zop′ō·dȧ, *n.pl.* a group of crustaceans resembling the shrimp but having a soft shell.

schī·zop′ō·dăl, *a.* schizopod.

schī·zop′ō·dous, *a.* schizopod.

schiz·ō·rhī′năl (-rī′), *a.* [*schizo-*, and Gr. *rhis, rhinos*, nose.] having the osseous external nares in the form of triangular openings, the apical angle of each of the triangles being situated between the inner and outer process of the nasal bone of the corresponding side, as in some birds.

schiz·ō·thē′căl, *a.* [*schizo-*, and Gr. *thēkē*, sheath, case, covering.] in ornithology, having the horny covering of the lower part of the leg divided as by scutella.

schiz′ō·thȳme, *n.* a person having schizothymia.

schiz·ō·thȳ′mi·ȧ, *n.* [Mod.L., from *schizo-*, and Gr. *thymos*, spirit.] a mild form of schizophrenia, characterized by introversion, withdrawal, etc.

schiz·ō·thy′miç, *a.* of or characterized by schizothymia.

schiz·ō·trich′i·ȧ, *n.* [*schizo-*, and Gr. *thrix, trichos*, a hair.] in medicine, splitting of the hair.

Schleī′chẽr·ȧ, *n.* [named after J. C. *Schleicher*, a Swiss botanist.] a genus of trees of the family *Sapindaceæ*. *Schleichera trijuga*, the only known species, has leaves abruptly pinnate, and small flowers disposed in spikelike racemes. It is native to tropical Asia and is valued for its timber, the oil of its seeds, and the shellac obtained from the young branches.

schle·mihl′, schle·miel′ (-mēl′), *n.* [Yid., from Heb. proper name *Shelumiēl*; current meaning prob. developed by metonymy and partly popularized after Peter *Schlemihl*, title character of a novel by Adelbert von Chamisso (1814).] an inefficient, bungling person who habitually fails or is easily victimized. [Slang.]

schlie′ren, *n.pl.*; *sing.* **schlie′re,** [G., lit., streaks.] small streaks or masses in igneous rocks, differing in composition from the main rock but blending gradually into it.

schmältz, *n.* [via Yid., from G. *schmalz*, lit., melted fat.]

1. anything very sentimental and unctuous, as certain music, literature, etc. [Slang.]

2. unctuous sentimentalism. [Slang.]

schmel′ze (-tse), *n.* [G. *schmelz*, enamel.] a decorative glass; specifically, a deep-red Bohemian glass used for flashing white glass.

schnap′pẽr, *n.* a spinous-finned Australian fish allied to the sea bream; a snapper.

schnäpps, *n.* [G., a dram, a nip.] Holland gin; hence, any strong alcoholic liquor: also spelled *schnaps*.

schnau′zẽr, *n.* [G., from *schnauzen*, to snarl, growl, from *schnauze*, snout.] any of three breeds of sturdy, active dog with a close, wiry coat and bushy eyebrows and beard, originally bred in Germany.

SCHNAUZER

Schneī·dē′ri·ăn, *a.* of or pertaining to Conrad Victor Schneider (1610–1680), German anatomist.

Schneiderian membrane; the pituitary membrane, first described in 1660 by Schneider.

schnit′zel, *n.* [G.] a cutlet of meat, usually of veal.

schnŏr′rẽr, *n.* [Yid.] a beggar.

schnoz′zle, *n.* [via Yid., from G. *schnauze*.] the nose. [Slang.]

Schō·har′ie, *n.* in geology, a formation found chiefly at Schoharie, N. Y., belonging to the Corniferous group of the Devonian system.

schol′ăr, *n.* [ME. *scolere*; AS. *scōlere*, a scholar, from LL. *scholaris*, pertaining to a school, from L. *schola*, a school.]

1. a learned person; one trained in a special branch of learning, as literature, arts, etc.; an advanced student.

2. a student who is given money or other aid, as by some institution, to continue his studies.

3. a student; a person attending a school.

4. a person who can read and write.

schol′ärch, *n.* [Gr. *scholē*, school, and *archein*, to rule.] the head of a school; specifically, the head of an ancient Athenian school of philosophy.

schō·lar′i·ty, *n.* scholarship. [Obs.]

schol′ăr·ly, *a.* 1. of or characteristic of scholars.

2. having or showing much knowledge, accuracy, and critical ability.

3. studious; devoted to learning.

4. orderly and thorough in methods of study.

schol′ăr′ly, *adv.* like a scholar.

schol′ăr·ship, *n.* 1. the quality of knowledge and learning shown by a student; standard of work done in school.

2. the systematized knowledge of a learned man, exhibiting accuracy, critical ability, and thoroughness; erudition.

3. a specific gift of money or other aid, as by an institution, to help a student continue his studies.

4. a foundation to supply such aid.

schō·las′tiç, *a.* [L. *scholasticus*; Gr. *scholastikos*, from *scholazein*, to devote one's leisure to study, to be at leisure, from *scholē*, school.]

1. of schools, colleges, universities, students, teachers, and studies; educational; academic.

2. of or characteristic of medieval schoolmen and their methods.

3. pedantic, dogmatic, formal, etc.

4. of secondary schools; as, *scholastic* football games.

schō·las′tiç, *n.* 1. a student; scholar.

2. a schoolman (sense 1).

3. a person who is devoted to logical subtleties and quibblings; a pedant.

4. a person who favors scholasticism.

schō·las′tiç·ăl, *a.* and *n.* same as *scholastic*.

schō·las′tiç·ăl·ly, *adv.* in a scholastic manner.

schō·las′ti·cism, *n.* 1. [*often* S–] the system of logic, philosophy, and theology of medieval university scholars, or schoolmen, from the tenth to the fifteenth century, based upon Aristotelian logic and the writings of the early Christian fathers.

2. an insistence upon traditional doctrines and methods.

schō′li·ȧ, *n.* pl. of *scholium*.

schō′li·ast, *n.* [Gr. *scholiastēs*, a commentator.] a commentator or annotator; especially, one who wrote on the margins of the manuscripts of the Greek and Latin classics.

schō·li·as′tiç, *a.* of or relating to a scholiast or scholiasts.

schō′li·āze, *v.i.* to write scholia. [Obs.]

schō′li·um, *n.*; *pl.* **schō′li·ȧ, schō′li·ums,** [LL. *scholium*; Gr. *scholion*, interpretation.]

1. a marginal note, annotation, or remark; an explanatory comment; specifically, an explanatory remark annexed to the text of a Latin or Greek writer.

2. in mathematics, a remark or comment tending to show use, connection, limitations, or manner of application, following a proof or demonstration.

schō′ly, *n.* a scholium. [Obs.]

schō′ly, *v.i.* to write comments. [Obs.]

Schom·bŭrgk′i·ȧ (-bŭrk′), *n.* a genus of tropical American orchids having extended flower stems enveloped by a dry sheath: named after R. H. Schomburgk (1804–1865).

school, *n.* [ME. *scole*; AS. *scolu*; OFr. *escole*; L. *schola*, school, from Gr. *scholē*, leisure, that in which leisure is employed, discussion, philosophy, a place where spare time is employed, a school.]

1. a place or institution in which persons are instructed in arts, science, languages, or any kind of learning; an educational establishment; specifically, (a) an institution for teaching children; (b) a place for training and instruction in some special field, skill, etc.; as, a dancing *school*; (c) a college or university.

2. the building or buildings, classrooms, laboratories, etc. of any such establishment.

3. the process of being educated; formal training and instruction; formal education; as, he never finished *school*.

4. the collective body of students and teachers in any place of instruction; as, the *school* was given a holiday.

5. one of the seminaries founded in the Middle Ages for teaching logic, metaphysics, and theology.

6. a session of an institution of instruction; exercises of instruction; school work.

7. a large room or hall in English universities where the examinations for degrees and honors take place.

8. the disciples or followers of a teacher, leader, or creed; those who hold a common doctrine or accept the same teachings or principles; a sect or denomination in philosophy, theology, science, art, etc.; as, the Socratic *school*.

9. a system or state of matters prevalent at a certain time; method or cast of thought; system of training generally.

10. any situation or means of discipline, improvement, instruction, or training; as, the *school* of hard knocks.

11. a particular division of an institution of learning; a special department of a college or university; as, the junior *school*, the *school* of liberal arts.

12. formerly, the regulations and drill instructions governing duties and training of any branch of the army or navy; as, the *school* of the soldier.

13. in music, a book of instructions in some particular line of study; as, a violin *school*.

intermediate school; a school between the primary and the high school; a junior high school.

national school; in Great Britain, a school maintained by the government for pupils of all religions.

school age; (a) the age at which a child may or must be sent to school; (b) the years during which attendance at school is required or customary.

school board; a body of people elected or appointed to have charge of local public schools.

school day; (a) a day on which school is in session; (b) the time, in any day, when school is in session.

school year; the part of a year when school is in session, usually from September to June.

school, *a.* 1. of or pertaining to a school or schools; as, a *school* custom.

2. of the schoolmen (sense 1). [Obs.]

school, *v.t.*; schooled, *pt., pp.*; schooling, *ppr.* 1. to instruct; to train; to educate; as, one *schooled* in diplomacy.

2. to reprimand; to chide and admonish; to reprove. [Archaic.]

3. to discipline; to control.

school, *n.* [D., a crowd, school of fish.] a large number of fish or water animals of the same kind swimming together.

school, *v.i.* to swim together in a school, as fish.

school′ȧ·ble, *a.* of the legal age for going to school.

school′book, *n.* a textbook; a book for school study.

school′boy, *n.* a boy attending school.

school′boy, *a.* characteristic of a boy attending school.

school′crȧft, *n.* learning. [Archaic.]

school′dāme, *n.* a woman teacher of a school.

school′ẽr·y, *n.* something taught in a school. [Rare.]

school′fel″lōw, *n.* a person educated at the same school and at the same time as another.

school′girl, *n.* a girl who attends a school.

school′girl, *a.* characteristic of a girl attending school.

school′house, *n.* 1. a building used as a school.

2. in England, the residence of the principal or master of a school.

sçhool′ing, *n.* 1. formal instruction in school; education.
2. cost of instruction and living at school; price paid to an instructor for teaching pupils.
3. reproof; reprimand. [Archaic.]

sçhool′mä′am, *n.* a schoolmarm. [Colloq.]

sçhool′măn (*for 2,* -man), *n.*; *pl.* **sçhool′men,** 1. [*often* S-] one of the medieval university teachers of philosophy, logic, and theology; scholastic.
2. a teacher, educator, or scholar.

sçhool′märm (-mäm *or* -märm), *n.* a woman schoolteacher, especially one who tends to be old-fashioned, prudish, and pedantic: often humorous or satirical. [Colloq.]

sçhool′mȧs″tẽr, *n.* 1. a man who teaches at a school.
2. a man who is manager, head, or principal of a school.
3. one who or that which disciplines, instructs, and teaches.
4. a kind of fish, the snapper, of the southern coasts of the United States and of the West Indies.

sçhool′māte, *n.* one who attends the same school at the same time as another.

sçhool′mis″tress, *n.* 1. a woman who teaches in a school.
2. a woman who is manager, head, or principal of a school.

sçhool′room, *n.* a room in which pupils are instructed, usually in a school.

sçhool ship, a ship on which boys and young men receive a free naval training.

sçhool′tēach″ẽr, *n.* one who teaches or instructs in a school.

sçhool′tēach″ing, *n.* the business of instructing in a school.

sçhool′yärd, *n.* the ground around or near a school, especially when used for games and sports.

sçhoon′ẽr, *n.* [origin from New England word *scoon,* to skim or skip upon the water.]
1. a vessel with two or more masts, rigged fore and aft.

TOPSAIL SCHOONER

2. a prairie schooner. [Colloq.]
3. a large glass or goblet, holding about a pint, for serving beer.

sçhoon′ẽr-rigged, *a.* rigged like a schooner, fore and aft.

Sçhō′pen·hau·ẽr·iṣm, *n.* the pessimistic philosophy of Arthur Schopenhauer, German philosopher (1788–1860), which holds that ultimate reality is "will," an all-impelling force expressing itself in the individual as the will to live, and that only by renouncing desire can the will be allayed.

sçhorl, shorl, *n.* [G. *schörl;* Sw. *skörl,* from *skör,* brittle.] black tourmaline.

sçhor·lā′ceous, shor·lā′ceous, *a.* like schorl; having the nature and character of schorl.

sçhorl′y, *a.* made of or containing schorl.

sçhot′tisçhe, sçhot′tish (-tish), *n.* [G. *schottisch,* Scottish.] a form of round dance in ²/₄ time, resembling the polka but with a slower tempo; also, the music for this dance.

sçhout, *n.* [D.] formerly, in the Dutch colonies of North America, a bailiff or municipal officer.

sçhreī′bẽrṣ·īte, *n.* [named after Carl von *Schreibers,* of Vienna.] a mineral found only in meteoric iron: it is a steel-gray, crystallized phosphide of iron and nickel.

schuss, *n.* [G., lit., shot, rush.] a straight run down a hill in skiing.

schuss, *v.i.* to ski straight down a slope at full speed.

schuss′boom·ẽr, *n.* [*schuss,* and *boom,* echoic of the sudden stop made by an expert skier, and *-er.*] a skier, especially one who schusses expertly.

Sçhutz′stäf·fel (shoots′shtäf-), *n.* [G., protective rank.] the personal bodyguard of Adolf Hitler; later, the Elite Guard of the Nazi militia, used to suppress opposition in Germany and conquered countries: also called *Black Shirts.*

sçhwä (*or G.* shvä), *n.* [G., from Heb. *sh'wa.*]
1. the unstressed, central vowel sound of most unstressed syllables in English; the neutralized sound of *a* in *ago, e* in *agent, i* in *sanity,* etc.
2. the symbol (ə) used to represent this sound, as in the International Phonetic Alphabet.

Sçhwänn′ṣ shēath, [named after Theodor *Schwann* (1810–1882), a German physiologist and anatomist.] the neurilemma.

schweit′zer·kä·se (shviti′sẽr-kā-zä), *n.* [G.] Swiss cheese.

Sçhweṅk′fel·di·ăn (shveṅk′), *n.* a member of a religious sect founded in the sixteenth century by Kaspar von Schwenkfeld, a Silesian reformer.

Scī·ȧ·dop′i·tys, *n.* [LL.; Gr. *skias, skiados,* anything serving as a shade, canopy, and *pitys,* a pine tree.] a genus of conifers consisting of a single species, *Sciadopitys verticillata,* the umbrella pine.

scī·ae′nid, *n.* a sciaenoid fish; any of the *Sciænidæ.*

Scī·aen′i·dae, *n.pl.* [Gr. *skiaina,* the maigre, and *-idæ.*] a family of spiny-finned fishes closely related to the perches, but having a large air bladder by means of which they produce various noises.

scī·ae′noid, *a.* relating to or resembling the *Sciænidæ.*

SCIAENOID (*Sciæna aquila*)

scī·ae′noid, *n.* any fish of the family *Sciænidæ,* as the weakfish, drumfish, kingfish, etc.

scī·am′ȧ·çhy, *n.* [from Gr. *skia,* a shadow, and *machein,* to fight.] a fighting with shadows or imaginary enemies: also *sciomachy.*

scī·ȧ·ther′iç, *a.* [Gr. *skiathēras,* a sundial, from *skia,* shade, shadow, and *thēran,* to chase, catch.] relating to a sundial; like a sundial. [Rare.]
sciatheric telescope; an instrument consisting of a horizontal dial with a telescope adjusted to it, for determining the time, whether of day or night, by means of shadows. [Rare.]

scī·ȧ·ther′iç·ăl, *a.* sciatheric.

scī·ȧ·ther′iç·ăl·ly, *adv.* after the manner of a sundial; by the use of a sundial.

scī·at′iç, *a.* [Fr. *sciatique;* ML. *sciaticus;* altered from L. *ischiadicus;* Gr. *ischiadikos,* from *ischion,* the hip, hip joint.]
1. pertaining to or in the region of the hip; as, the *sciatic* artery or nerve.
2. affecting the hip or the nerves about the hip; as, *sciatic* pains.

scī·at′iç, *n.* any part, organ, etc. connected with the hip.

scī·at′i·çȧ, *n.* [Mod.L., from ML. *sciaticus.*] any painful condition in the region of the hip and thighs; especially, neuritis of the long nerve (*sciatic nerve*) passing down the back of the thigh.

scī·at′iç·ăl, *a.* sciatic.

scī·at′iç·ăl·ly, *adv.* with, by, or in the nature of sciatica.

scī′ence, *n.* [Fr. *science,* from L. *scientia,* knowledge, from *sciens* (*-entis*), ppr. of *scire,* to know.]
1. originally, state or fact of knowing; knowledge, often as opposed to *intuition, belief,* etc.
2. systematized knowledge derived from observation, study, and experimentation carried on in order to determine the nature or principles of what is being studied.
3. a branch of knowledge or study, especially one concerned with establishing and systematizing facts, principles, and methods, as by experiments and hypotheses; as, the *science* of music.
4. (a) the systematized knowledge of nature and the physical world; (b) any branch of this.
5. skill, technique, or ability based upon training, discipline, and experience: often somewhat humorous, as, the *science* of boxing.
6. [S-] Christian Science.
mental science; mental philosophy.
moral science; ethics.
seven sciences; in the Middle Ages, the seven liberal arts constituting the trivium and quadrivium.
Syn.—literature, art, knowledge.

scī′ence fiç′tion, fiction of a highly imaginative or fantastic kind typically involving some actual or projected scientific phenomenon.

scī′ent, *a.* learned; skillful. [Rare.]

scī·en′tẽr, *adv.* [L.] in law, knowingly.

scī·en′tiăl (-shal), *a.* 1. of or producing science or knowledge.
2. having efficient knowledge.

scī·en·tif′iç, scī·en·tif′iç·ăl, *a.* [Fr. *scientifique;* L. *scientia,* knowledge, and *facere,* to make.]
1. pertaining to or used in natural science; as, a *scientific* instrument.
2. evincing or endowed with a knowledge of science; containing or treating of science; well versed in science; as, a *scientific* work.
3. according to, based on, or using the rules or principles of science; systematic and exact; as, a *scientific* arrangement of fossils.
4. trained in following or observing the principles and methods of science; as, a *scientific* thinker.
5. (a) played or done according to methods gained by training and experience; as, *scientific* boxing; (b) having or showing skill and training; highly trained; skillful.

scī·en·tif′iç·ăl·ly, *adv.* in a scientific manner; according to the rules or principles of science.

scī′en·tiṣm, *n.* 1. the techniques, beliefs, or attitudes characteristic of scientists.
2. the principle that scientific methods can and should be applied in all fields of investigation: often a disparaging usage.

scī′en·tist, *n.* 1. a person specializing in science, especially natural science.
2. [S-] a Christian Scientist.

scī′-fī′, *a.* and *n.* science fiction. [Colloq.]

scil′i·cet, *adv.* [L., contr. of *scire licet,* it is permitted to know.] to wit; namely; that is to say.

Scil′lȧ, *n.* [L. *scilla;* Gr. *skilla,* a squill.]
1. a genus of bulbous plants, mostly native to Europe, belonging to the family *Liliaceæ.*
2. [s-] in pharmacy, the sliced bulb of squill.

scil·li·piç′rin, *n.* [Gr. *skilla,* squill, and *pikros,* bitter.] a yellow, bitter, and amorphous active principle obtained from squill.

scim′i·tăr, scim′i·tẽr, *n.* [It. *scimitarra.*] a sword with a short, curved, one-edged blade, used by Turks, Persians Arabs, etc.

Sciñ′ci·dae, *n.pl.* [*scincus* and *-idæ.*] a large and widely distributed family of lizards, of which the genus *Scincus* is the type. Some species are without limbs, some have a single pair of limbs, and others have two pairs of well-developed limbs.

sciñ′ci·form, *a.* scincoid.

sciñ′çoid, *a.* of, pertaining to, or belonging to the *Scincidæ.*

sciñ′çoid, *n.* any of the *Scincidæ.*

sciñ·çoi′di·ăn, *a.* and *n.* same as *scincoid.*

Sciñ′çus, *n.* [LL., from L. *scincus,* Gr. *skinkos,* a kind of lizard.] the typical genus of the family *Scincidæ.*

sçiñk, *n.* same as *skink.*

scin·til′lȧ, *n.* [L.] 1. a spark.
2. the least particle; a trace; as, not a *scintilla* of evidence: used only figuratively.

scin′til·lănt, *a.* [L. *scintillans* (*-antis*), ppr. of *scintillare,* to sparkle.] emitting sparks; sparkling; glittering; scintillating.

scin·til·lăn′te (shēn-), *a.* [It.] in music, brilliant; sparkling: a direction to the performer.

scin′til·lāte, *v.i.*; scintillated, *pt., pp.*; scintillating, *ppr.* [L. *scintillatus,* pp. of *scintillare,* to sparkle.]
1. to emit sparks; to flash; to sparkle.
2. to sparkle, as the stars.
3. to sparkle intellectually; to be brilliant and witty.

scin′til·lāt·ing, *a.* that scintillates.

scin·til·lā′tion, *n.* [L. *scintillatio.*]
1. the act of scintillating; sparkling.
2. a spark; a flash.
3. a brilliant display of wit.
4. in astronomy, the twinkling of the stars.
5. in nuclear physics, the flash of light made by ionizing radiation upon striking certain detectors.
scintillation counter; an instrument for detecting and measuring the scintillations induced by ionizing radiation.

scin'til·lous, *a.* scintillant. [Rare.]

scin'til·lous·ly, *adv.* in a sparkling, or scintillant, manner. [Rare.]

scī'ō·graph, *n.* same as *skiagraph.*

scī·og'rȧ·phy, *n.* same as *skiagraphy.*

scī'ō·lism, *n.* [from L. *sciolus,* smatterer, dim. of *scius,* knowing, from *scire,* to know.] superficial knowledge; a smattering of knowledge on any subject combined with pretense to knowing more; quackery; charlatanism.

scī'ō·list, *n.* [L. *sciolus,* dim. formed on *scire,* to know.] one who knows little, or who knows many things superficially; a pretender to learning.

scī·ō·lis'tiç, *a.* of or pertaining to sciolism or sciolists.

scī'ō·lous, *a.* superficial; knowing imperfectly. [Rare.]

sciōl'tō (shōl'), *a.* and *adv.* [It., pp. of *sciogliere,* to loosen, dissolve; L. *exsolvere,* to loose.] in music, free; lively; quick; staccato; ad libitum.

scī·om'ȧ·çhy, *n.* same as *sciamachy.*

scī'ō·man·cy, *n.* [Gr. *skia,* a shade, shadow, and *-mancy.*] divination by communication with the dead.

scī'ŏn, *n.* [Fr. *scion,* a scion, shoot, twig, cutting, from *scier,* L. *secare,* to cut.]

1. a shoot or twig; especially, one taken for the purpose of being grafted upon another tree or for planting: also spelled *cion.*

2. a descendant; a child; an heir.

scī·op'tiç, *a.* [Gr. *skia,* shadow, and *optikos,* of seeing.] in optics, of or pertaining to the action or use of the camera obscura.

scioptic ball; an optical instrument that produces images in a darkened room: it consists of a convex lens that can be fixed in an opening in a window shutter and can be turned, like the eye, to different parts of the landscape.

scī·op'ti·çon, *n.* a modified form of magic lantern.

scī·op'tiçs, *n.* the art of exhibiting images of external objects, received through an arrangement of lenses into a darkened room.

scī·op'triç, *a.* same as *scioptic.*

Scī'ot, *a.* of or pertaining to the island Chios, or to its inhabitants.

Scī'ot, *n.* a native or inhabitant of Chios.

scī'ō·thē·iṣm, *n.* [Gr. *skia,* a shadow, and Eng. *theism.*] the worship of ghosts, particularly the spirits of departed ancestors.

scī·ō·ther'iç, *a.* same as *sciatheric.*

scī'ous, *a.* capable of knowing; having knowledge; cognizant. [Rare.]

scī'rē fā'ci·as (fā'shi-), [L., that you cause to know.] in law, a writ, founded on a record, requiring the person against whom it is issued to appear and show cause why the record should not be enforced or annulled; also, a proceeding begun by issuing such a writ.

sci·roç'çō, *n.* same as *sirocco.*

Scir'pus, *n.* [L., a rush.] an extensive genus of hardy plants, growing in moist places: it includes the bulrush, *Scirpus lacustris.*

sçir'rhoid, *a.* resembling scirrhus.

sçir·rhos'i·ty, *n.* the quality or condition of being scirrhous.

sçir'rhous (-rus), *a.* of, or having the nature of, a scirrhus; as, *scirrhous* affections; *scirrhous* disease.

sçir'rhus, *n.*; *pl.* **sçir'rhī, sçir'rhus·eṣ,** [L. *scirros;* Gr. *skirrhos,* a hardened swelling or tumor.] a hard cancer or cancerous tumor on any part of the body, usually proceeding from the induration of a gland, and made up of much fibrous connective tissue.

scis·ci·tā'tion, *n.* the act of inquiring; inquiry; demand. [Obs.]

scis'sel, *n.* [Fr. *cisaille,* from *ciseler,* to cut.]

1. the clippings of various metals, produced in several mechanical operations.

2. waste remnants of a metal plate from which circular blanks have been cut for coinage.

scis'si·ble, *a.* capable of being cut or divided by a sharp instrument. [Rare.]

scis'sil, *n.* same as *scissel.*

scis'sile, *a.* [L. *scissilis,* from *scissus,* pp. of *scindere,* to cut.] that can be cut or split smoothly and easily, as into plates or laminae.

sciṣ'ṣiŏn (sizh'un), *n.* [Fr., from L. *scissio* (*-onis*), a cutting, from *scissus,* pp. of *scindere,* to cut.] the act of cutting, dividing, or splitting, or the state of being cut, divided, or split; division; separation; fission.

scis·si·par'i·ty, *n.* same as *schizogenesis.*

sciṣ'ṣŏr, *v.t.* to cut, cut off, or cut out by means of scissors.

sciṣ'ṣŏr·bill, *n.* same as *skimmer* (bird).

sciṣ'ṣŏr·bird, *n.* same as *scissortail.*

sciṣ'ṣŏrṣ, *n.pl.* [ME. *sisoures;* OFr. *cisoires,* shears, scissors; Fr. *ciseaux,* little shears, pl. of *ciseau,* an older form for *cisel,* a chisel, cutting instrument; Eng. sp. altered by association with L. *scissor,* one who cuts, from *scissus,* pp. of *scindere,* to cut.]

1. a cutting instrument, smaller than shears, with two opposing blades, each having a looped handle, which are pivoted together in the middle so that they can slide over each other as the instrument is closed: also called *pair of scissors.*

2. [*construed as sing.*] (a) a gymnastic feat or exercise in which the legs are moved in a way suggestive of the opening and closing of scissors; (b) a scissors hold.

sciṣ'ṣŏrṣ-grīnd''ẽr, *n.* 1. one who sharpens scissors.

2. the European goatsucker.

sciṣ'ṣŏrṣ hōld, a wrestling hold in which one contestant clasps the other with his legs.

sciṣ'ṣŏrṣ kick, in swimming, a kick (used especially with a side stroke) imitating the action of scissors, in which one leg is swung forward from the hip, the other bent backward from the knee, then both brought together with a snap.

sciṣ'ṣŏr·tāil, *n.* variety of flycatcher, *Milvulus forficatus,* found in Mexico and in the southern part of the United States: so called from its deeply forked tail: also *scissor-tailed* (or *swallow-tailed*) *flycatcher.*

SCISSORTAIL (*Milvulus forficatus*)

sciṣ'ṣŏr tooth, a cutting tooth.

sciṣ'ṣūre, *n.* [OFr., from L. *scissura,* a cutting, from *scindere,* to cut.] a cleft or opening, natural or made by cutting.

scit·ȧ·min'ē·ous, *a.* [L. *scitamentum,* a delicacy.] of, belonging to, or pertaining to the *Scitamineæ,* an order of plants, mostly tropical herbs, as ginger, turmeric, etc.

Scī·ū'ri·dae, *n.pl.* a family of rodents, having *Sciurus* as the typical genus, consisting of squirrels, ground squirrels, marmots, etc.

scī'ū·rīne, *n.* [L. *sciurus,* a squirrel.] any of the *Sciuridæ.*

scī'ū·rīne, *a.* of or pertaining to the squirrel family.

scī'ū·roid, *a.* 1. like a squirrel.

2. in botany, resembling a squirrel's tail, as the spikes of barley and certain other grasses.

Scī·ū·rō·mor'phȧ, *n.pl.* [LL., from Gr. *skiouros,* squirrel, and *morphē,* form.] a division of rodents having a single pair of upper incisors: it includes the squirrels, gophers, marmots, beavers, woodchucks, etc.

Scī·ū·rop'tẽr·us, *n.* [Gr. *skiouros,* a squirrel, and *pteron,* wing.] a genus of flying squirrels.

Scī·ū'rus, *n.* [L. *sciurus,* from Gr. *skiouros,* squirrel, lit., the shade-tailed, from *skia,* shade, and *oura,* a tail.] a genus of squirrels, typical of the *Sciuridæ.*

sçlaff, *v.i.* [of echoic origin.]

1. to shuffle along; to move aimlessly or listlessly. [Scot.]

2. in golf, to strike the ground behind the ball before hitting it.

sçlaff, *v.t.* 1. in golf, to scrape (a club) along the ground before hitting the ball.

2. to make (a stroke) in this way.

3. to hit (the ball) in this way.

sçlaff, *n.* a sclaffing stroke.

sçlaun'dre (-dẽr), *n.* slander. [Obs.]

Sçläv, *n.* same as *Slav.*

Sçläv'iç, *a.* same as *Slavic.*

Sçläv'iṣm, *n.* same as *Slavism.*

Sçlȧ·vō'ni·ȧn, *a.* and *n.* same as *Slavonian.*

Sçlȧ·von'iç, *a.* same as *Slavonic.*

sçlen'dre (-dẽr), *a.* slender. [Obs.]

sçler-, see *sclero-.*

sçlē'rȧ, *n.* [Mod.L., from Gr. *sklēros,* hard.] a tough, white, fibrous membrane covering all of the eyeball except the area covered by the cornea.

sçler'ȧ·gō·ġy, *n.* [*sclera-,* and Gr. *agōgē,* training, education, from *agein,* to lead, conduct.] strict or rigid discipline. [Obs.]

sçlē'rȧl, *a.* same as *sclerotic.*

sçlēre, *n.* [Gr. *sklēros,* hard.] any of the spicules forming the body of a sponge.

sçlē·rē'mȧ, *n.* same as *scleroderma.*

sçle·reñ'çhy·mȧ, *n.* [*scler-,* and Gr. *enchyma,* an infusion, from *enchein,* to pour in.]

1. in botany, short-celled, thick-walled plant tissue, as in the shells of nuts, stems of palms, etc.

2. in zoology, the calcareous substance constituting the skeleton of stony corals.

sçlē·reñ·çhym'ȧ·tous, *a.* of, pertaining to, or composed of sclerenchyma.

sçlē·reñ'çhȳme, *n.* same as *sclerenchyma.*

sçlē·rī'ȧ·sis, *n.* 1. a hardening, or induration, of tissue.

2. a hardening of the edge of the eyeball.

sçlē'rīte, *n.* [*scler-* and *-ite.*] one of the hard plates or spicules forming the shell-like covering of certain invertebrates.

sçlē·rit'iç, *a.* of or having scleritis: also *sclerotitic.*

sçlē·rī'tis, *n.* inflammation of the sclera: also *sclerotitis.*

sçlē'rō-, [from Gr. *sklēros,* hard.] a combining form meaning: (a) *hard,* as in *sclero*meter; (b) of the sclera: also, before a vowel, *scler-.*

sçlẽr'ō·bāse, *n.* [*sclero-,* and Gr. *basis,* a base.] the calcareous axis of a coral.

sçlẽr·ō·bā'siç, *a.* of, pertaining to, or composed of sclerobase.

sçlẽr'ō·blast, *n.* [*sclero-,* and Gr. *blastos,* a germ.] a cell of a sponge which produces a sclere.

sçlẽr'ō·dẽrm, *n.* [*sclero-* and *-derm.*]

1. one of a family of plectognathic fishes, having the skin rough or covered with hard scales.

2. one of the *Sclerodermata.*

3. indurated integument, especially of coral.

sçlẽr·ō·dẽr'mȧ, *n.* [Mod. L.; *sclero-* and *derma.*] a chronic disease of the skin marked by rigid patches which cause a hidebound condition.

Sçlẽr·ō·dẽr'mȧ·tȧ, *n.pl.* the *Madreporaria.*

sçlẽr·ō·dẽr'mȧ·tous, *a.* 1. of or pertaining to the *Sclerodermata.*

2. in zoology, covered with a hard outer tissue, as of horny scales or plates.

3. in medicine, of or having scleroderma.

sçlẽr·ō·dẽr'mi·ȧ, *n.* same as *scleroderma.*

sçlẽr·ō·dẽr'miç, sçlẽr·ō·dẽr'mous, *a.* same as *sclerodermatous.*

sçlẽr·ō·dẽr'mīte, *n.* 1. the thick, hard integument of a crustacean.

2. sclerenchyma.

sçlẽr'ō·ġen, *n.* [*sclero-,* and Gr. *-genēs,* producing.] the thick, hard substance deposited in woody cells; lignin.

sçlē·roġ'ē·nous, *a.* 1. secreting a thick, hard substance; becoming hard.

2. in zoology, mail-cheeked.

sçlē'roid, *a.* [*scler-* and *-oid.*] in botany and zoology, hard and thick in texture, as nutshells; indurated.

sçlē·rō'mȧ, *n.*; *pl.* **sçlē·rō'mȧ·tȧ,** [Gr. *sklērōma,* a hardening, from *sklēros,* hard.] in medicine, hardening of the tissues; tumorlike induration.

sçlē·rom'e·tẽr, *n.* [*sclero-* and *-meter.*] an instrument by which the relative hardness of metals or minerals can be measured.

sçlē·rō·mū'cin, *n.* [*sclero-* and *mucin.*] a dark-colored, gummy, nitrogenous substance, an active principle in ergot.

sçlē·rō'sȧl, *a.* of, or having the nature of, sclerosis.

sçlē·rōsed' (-rōst'), *a.* hardened, or indurated, as by sclerosis.

sçlē·rō′sis, *n.*; *pl.* **sçlē·rō′sēs̹**, [LL., from Gr. *sklērōsis*, a hardening, from *sklēros*, hard.]
 1. in botany, a hardening of the cell wall of a plant, as by the formation of wood.
 2. in medicine, a hardening of body tissues or parts, as by an excessive growth of fibrous connective tissue.
 cerebrospinal sclerosis; multiple sclerosis: also called *disseminated* or *insular sclerosis*.

sçlē·rō·skel′e·tŏn, *n.* [*sclero-* and *skeleton*.] that part of a skeleton which is developed in tendons, ligaments, etc., as in a turkey's leg.

Sçlē·ros′tō·mȧ, *n.* [*sclero-*, and Gr. *stoma*, mouth.] a genus of parasitic worms belonging to the order *Nematoidea*, one species of which, *Sclerostoma duodenale*, inhabits the small intestine in the human body.

sçlē·rō′tăl, *a.* 1. of or pertaining to a sclerotal.
 2. same as *sclerotic*.

sçlē·rō′tăl, *n.* [*sclerotic* and *-al*.] the hard coat or tunic of the eye.

sçlē·rō′tiăl (-shăl), *a.* of sclerotium.

sçlē·rot′iç, *a.* [Gr. *sklērotēs*, hardness.]
 1. of, characterized by, or having sclerosis.
 2. of the sclera.
 3. in chemistry, pertaining to or derived from ergot.
 sclerotic parenchyma; thick-walled cells; sclerenchyma. The distinction is sometimes made that in *sclerotic parenchyma*, the cells are hardened but not thickened, and in *sclerenchyma*, they are hardened and thickened.

sçlē·rot′iç, *n.* the sclera: see *eye*, illus.

sçlē·rot′iç·ăl, *a.* sclerotic. [Rare.]

Sçlē·rō·tin′i·ȧ, *n.* [Gr. *sklērotēs*, hardness.] a large genus of fungi, very destructive to plants. They belong to the *Pezizales* and the sporocarps are developed from a sclerotium.

sçlē·rō′ti·oid (-shi-), *a.* of the nature of, or resembling, a sclerotium.

sçlēr·ō·tit′iç, *a.* scleritic.

sçlēr·ō·tī′tis, *n.* same as *scleritis*.

sçlē·rō′ti·um (-shi-), *n.*; *pl.* **sçlē·rō′ti·ȧ**, [LL., from Gr. *sklēros*, hard.]
 1. in certain fungi, a hardened, weblike, black or reddish-brown mass of threads in which food material is stored.
 2. the state of a plasmodium, when it has matured.

sçlēr′ō·tōme, *n.* [*sclero-*, and Gr. *temnein*, to cut.]
 1. one of the hard tissue partitions separating the myotomes.
 2. in surgery, a knife used in operating on the sclerotic coat of the eye.

sçlē·rot′ō·my, *n.*; *pl.* **sçlē·rot′ō·mieş**, [*sclero-* and *-tomy*.] surgical incision into the sclera.

sçlē′rous, *a.* indurated; hard; bony.

sçob′by, *n.* [origin unknown.] the chaffinch. [Brit. Dial.]

sçob′i·fọrm, *a.* [L. *scobis*, sawdust, and *-form*.] having the form of sawdust or raspings.

sçobş, *n.* [L. *scobis*, sawdust, from *scabere*, to scrape.] raspings of ivory, hartshorn, metals, or other hard substances; dross of metals, etc.

sçoff, *n.* [ME. *scof*; prob. via dial. from ON.]
 1. derision, ridicule, mockery, or reproach, expressed in language of contempt; expression of scorn or contempt.
 2. an object of contempt or derision; a butt.

sçoff, *v.t.* to mock at or deride.

sçoff, *v.i.*; scoffed (skọft), *pt.*, *pp.*; scoffing, *ppr.* to show mocking contempt, scorn, or derision, especially by language; to jeer (often with *at*).
 They shall *scoff at* the kings. —**Hab. i. 10.**

sçoff′ēr, *n.* one who scoffs; a scorner.

sçoff′ēr·y, *n.* the act of scoffing; mockery.

sçoff′ing·ly, *adv.* in a scoffing manner; with scoffs or derision.

sçōke, *n.* pokeweed, *Phytolacca decandra*.

sçō·lāie′, **sçō·lāy′**, *v.i.* scoley. [Obs.]

sçōld, *n.* [ME. *scolde*; prob. from ON. *skald*, poet.]
 1. a person, especially a woman, who habitually uses abusive language.
 2. a scolding. [Colloq.]

sçōld, *v.i.*; scolded, *pt.*, *pp.*; scolding, *ppr.* 1. to find fault angrily; to rebuke or chide severely.
 2. to use angry, abusive language.

sçōld, *v.t.* to chide or find fault with noisily and angrily; to rebuke severely.

sçōld′ēr, *n.* one who scolds or rails; a scold.

sçōld′ēr, *n.* in ornithology, (a) the oyster catcher; (b) the old squaw.

sçōld′ing, *a.* given to scolding.

sçōld′ing, *n.* the act of railing or finding fault noisily; noisy rebuke.

sçōld′ing·ly, *adv.* in a scolding manner; like a scold.

sçōle, *n.* school. [Obs.]

sçōl·e·çhī′ȧ·sis, *n.* [Gr. *skōlēx*, *skōlēkos*, a worm.] a disease caused by larvae of moths or butterflies in the body: also spelled *scholechiasis*.

sçō′le·cid, *a.* in zoology, of or relating to a scolex.

sçō·lec′i·fọrm, *a.* resembling a scolex in form and structure.

sçol′ē·cīte, *n.* a hydrous silicate of calcium and aluminum, $CaAl_2Si_3O_{10}{\cdot}3H_2O$.

sçō′lē·çoid, *a.* scalelike; resembling a worm.

sçō·lē·çoph′ȧ·gous, *a.* [Gr. *skōlēx*, *skōlēkos*, a worm, and *phagein*, to eat.] worm-eating: said of birds. [Rare.]

sçō′lex, *n.*; *pl.* **sçō·lē′cēş** or **sçō′li·cēş**, [Gr. *skōlēx*, *skōlēkos*, a worm, pl. *skōlēkes*.] the round segment forming the head of a tapeworm, provided with hooks or suckers.

sçō′ley, *v.i.* to study; to attend school or classes. [Obs.]

sçō·li·om′e·tēr, *n.* [Gr. *skolios*, curved, crooked, and *-meter*.] an apparatus for measuring curves, especially those of the spinal column.

sçō′li·ŏn, *n.* [Gr.] in ancient Greece, an impromptu lyric sung by guests in turn.

sçō·li·ō′sis, *n.* [Gr. *skoliōsis*, a curve, from *skolios*, bent, crooked.] in medicine, lateral curvature of the spine.
 scoliosis brace; a brace for treating lateral curvature of the spine.
 static scoliosis; spinal curvature due to unequal length of the legs.

sçō·li·ot′iç, *a.* of or relating to scoliosis.

sçol′i·thus, *n.* [Gr. *skolios*, curved.] a fossil in Potsdam sandstone which looks like a boring of a marine worm.

sçol′lŏp, *n.* and *v.* same as *scallop*.

sçol′ō·pac·ine, *a.* same as *scolopacoid*.

sçol′ō·pā̤ç·oid, *a.* [L. *scolopax*, a large snipelike bird, and *-oid*.] pertaining to or resembling snipes.

Sçol·ō·pen′drȧ, *n.* [L.Gr. *skolopendra*, milliped.] a genus of many-legged arthropods including the centipedes.

Sçol″ō·pen·drel′lȧ, *n.* [LL., dim. of *Scolopendra*.] in zoology, a genus of small myriapods, having sixteen dorsal scales: it is the type genus of *Scolopendrellidæ*.

sçol″ō·pen·drel′loid, *a.* [LL. *Scolopendrella* and *-oid*.] in zoology, of or resembling the *Scolopendrella*.

sçol·ō·pen′drid, *n.* one of the *Scolopendra*.

sçol·ō·pen′drine, *a.* of or resembling the *Scolopendra*.

Sçol·ō·pen′dri·um, *n.* a genus of ferns closely allied to the genus *Asplenium*.

sçol·ō·pen′droid, *a.* of or relating to centipedes.

Sçol′y·mus, *n.* [Gr. *skolymos*, a kind of thistle.] a genus of smooth, erect, thistlelike herbs, native to the Mediterranean region.

sçol′y·tid, *n.* any member of the genus *Scolytus* of the family *Xylophagi*, or wood eaters, which destroy immense numbers of trees, especially firs, pines, and elms, by piercing them and eating the inner bark.

Sçom′bēr, *n.* [L., from Gr. *skombros*, a mackerel.] the typical genus of the family *Scombridæ*.

sçom′bēr·oid, *a.* and *n.* same as *scombroid*.

sçom′brid, *n.* any member of the mackerel family of fishes.

Sçom′bri·dae, *n.pl.* a family of carnivorous fishes including the mackerel, tunny, etc.

Sçom·bri·fọr′mēş, *n.pl.* [LL.] a division of fishes of the family *Scombridæ* including the mackerels and allied fishes.

sçom′broid, *a.* 1. of the mackerel family or a larger group including it and related fishes.
 2. like a mackerel.

sçom′broid, *n.* a mackerel or related fish.

sçom′fish, *v.t.* and *v.i.* [corruption of *scomfit*.] to suffocate, as by noxious air or smoke. [Scot.]

sçom′fit, *n.* and *v.t.* discomfit. [Obs.]

sçonce, *n.* [O.D. *schantse*; D. *schans*; Sw. *skans*, a fortress or a sconce; OFr. *esconser*, *absconser*, to hide, from L. *absconsus*, pp. of *abscondere*, to hide.]
 1. a protection, cover, or shelter, as a hut or shed.
 2. a protection for the head, as a helmet.
 3. (a) the head or skull; (b) good sense; brains. [Colloq.]
 4. in military usage, a small fort; a detached bulwark or defense work.
 5. a fine; a penalty; a light fine, as in the universities of Cambridge and Oxford.
 6. a fragment of an ice floe.
 7. a fixed seat or shelf. [Chiefly Dial.]

sçonce, *n.* [OFr. *esconse*, a dark lantern, from L. *absconsus*, pp. of *abscondere*, to hide.]
 1. a hanging or projecting candlestick, generally with a mirror to reflect the light; a cover or protection for a light; a case or lantern for a candle; hence, also, the tube in an ordinary candlestick in which the candle is inserted.
 2. a lantern; a dark lantern; a lantern with a shade for protection. [Obs.]

SCONCE

sçonce, *v.t.*; sconced, *pt.*, *pp.*; sconcing, *ppr.* 1. to protect or provide with a sconce, or small fort.
 2. to fortify, shelter, or screen.

sçonce, *v.t.* to fine; especially, at Oxford University, to fine lightly for a breach of manners.

sçonce, *n.* a fine, such as one for a breach of manners.

sçonce, *v.t.* to ensconce. [Obs.]

sçon′çheŏn (-shun), *n.* in architecture, the portion of the side of an aperture from the back of the jamb or reveal to the interior of the wall. [Archaic.]

Sçōne, the Stōne of, the stone upon which the Scottish kings before 1296 were crowned at Scone, Scotland: stolen (1950) from under the coronation chair at Westminster Abbey; restored (1951).

sçōne, *n.* [Scot., contr. from M.D. *schoonbrot*, fine bread.] a kind of tea cake, often resembling a baking powder biscuit, usually baked over a hot fire on a griddle, and served with butter.

sçọọn, *v.i.* to skim or glide, as a vessel. [Dial.]

sçọọn, *v.t.* to skip (flat stones) on the surface of the water. [Dial.]

sçọọp, *n.* [ME. *scope*, from M.D. *schope*, bailing vessel, and *schoppe*, a shovel.]
 1. any of various ladles or other utensils like small, deep shovels; specifically, (a) one used for dipping or bailing liquids; (b) a kitchen utensil used to take up sugar or flour; (c) a small coal shovel; (d) a ladle; (e) a small, spoonlike, surgical instrument; (f) a small, hemispherical utensil for dishing up ice cream.
 2. the deep shovel of a dredge or steam shovel, which takes up sand, dirt, etc.
 3. the act of taking up with a scoop.
 4. the amount taken up at one time by a scoop.
 5. a hollowed-out place; a bowl-shaped depression.
 6. a motion as of scooping.
 7. a large profit made by speculation or by a business transaction. [Colloq.]
 8. a beat. [Newspaper Slang.]
 9. a tool for scooping out potato eyes from the tubers.
 10. the visor of a cap. [Scot.]

sçọọp, *v.t.*; scooped, *pt.*, *pp.*; scooping, *ppr.*
 1. to take up or out with or as with a scoop.
 2. to empty by bailing.
 3. to dig out; to hollow out.
 4. to make by digging or hollowing out.
 5. to gather (*in*) as if with a scoop. [Colloq.]
 6. to get and publish a piece of news before (a rival or rivals); to get a beat on. [Newspaper Slang.]

sçọọp, *v.i.* 1. to use a scoop; as, to *scoop* for fish with a net.
 2. to feed by swimming along with open mouth, as the whale and other animals.

sçọọp′ēr, *n.* 1. one who or that which scoops.
 2. the avoset, a water bird which scoops up mud and sand to find food.

sçọọp′fụl, *n.* as much as a scoop will hold.

sçọọp net, a hand net for catching bait; a net so formed as to sweep the bottom of a river.

sçọọp wheel (hwēl), a wheel with buckets on

its rim, used to raise water to a height equal to its diameter when the buckets, turning over, deposit the water in a trough or reservoir prepared to receive it.

sçoot, *v.i.*; scooted, *pt.*, *pp.*; scooting, *ppr.* [prob. via dial. from ON. *skiōta*, to shoot.]

1. to go quickly; to scurry off; to dart. [Colloq.]

2. to shoot or gush out suddenly and violently. [Scot and Brit. Dial.]

sçoot, *n.* a quick departure; a scurrying off; a darting. [Colloq.]

sçoot'ēr, *n.* [from *scoot*, v.]

1. a child's vehicle, consisting of a low, narrow footboard with a wheel at each end, the front one attached to a handlebar for steering: it is moved by a series of pushes made by one foot against the ground.

2. a somewhat similar vehicle equipped with a seat and propelled by a small internal-combustion engine: in full, *motor scooter*.

3. a flat-bottomed sailboat with runners, for use on water or ice.

4. a swift motorboat that skims over the water.

5. in the western U. S., a plow with one handle for laying out furrows.

sçoot'ēr, *n.* a scoter.

sçop, *n.* [AS. *scop*, a poet, from *sceapan*, *scapan*, to create, shape.] an Old English poet; a bard.

sçō'pȧ, *n.*; *pl.* **sçō'pae**, [L. *scopa*, twigs, shoots, a broom.] in entomology, a bunch of bristly hairs forming a brush, as on the legs or abdomen of certain bees, used for collecting pollen.

sçō'pȧ·rin, *n.* in chemistry, a yellowish substance obtained from the plant *Spartium scoparium*.

sçō'pāte, *a.* [L. *scopa*, twigs, a broom, brush.] having a covering of bristly hairs.

sçōpe, *n.* [It. *scopo*; L. *scopus*; Gr. *skopos*, a mark, spy, watcher, from *skopein*, to see.]

1. the area that the mind can cover; range of view; extent of perception or intellectual grasp; as, beyond the *scope* of a child's understanding.

2. the area or field within which any activity goes on; range or extent of action, observation, inquiry, etc.; as, the *scope* of a history book.

3. room for free outlook or liberty of action; opportunity.

4. the range of a missile.

5. length, extent, or sweep, as of a cable.

6. end; purpose. [Archaic.]

7. a mark shot at. [Obs.]

8. a liberty; a license enjoyed. [Obs.]

-sçōpe, [Mod. L. *-scopium*, from Gr. *-skopion*, from *scopein*, to see.] a combining form meaning (an instrument, etc. for) *seeing* or *observing*, as in tele*scope*.

sçō'pel·id, *n.* a fish belonging to the *Scopelidæ*.

Sçō·pel'i·dae, *n.pl.* [LL., from Gr. *skopelos*, a high rock.] a family of oceanic fishes typified by the genus *Scopelus*, most of which are small and marked by phosphorescent spots.

sçō'pē·līne, *a.* same as *scopeloid*.

sçō'pē·loid, *a.* [*scopelus* and *-oid*.] pertaining to or resembling the *Scopelidæ*.

sçō'pē·loid, *n.* a fish of the family *Scopelidæ*.

Sçop'e·lus, *n.* [LL., from Gr. *skopelos*, a cliff, headland.] the typical genus of the family *Scopelidæ*, with thirty species distributed over all temperate and tropical seas.

sçō·pif'ēr·ous, *a.* [L. *scopa*, a brush, and *ferre*, to bear.] having bunches or tufts of hair; scopiform.

sçō'pi·fọrm, *a.* [L. *scopa*, a broom, and *-form*.] having the form of a broom or brush; scopuliform.

sçō'pi·ped, *n.* [L. *scopa*, a broom, and *pes*, *pedis*, a foot.] same as *scopuliped*.

sçō·pol'ȧ·mīne, sçō·pol'ȧ·min, *n.* in chemistry, an alkaloid, $C_{17}H_{21}O_4N$, obtained from certain plants of the nightshade family and used in producing twilight sleep.

sçō'pō·līne, *n.* a colorless, crystalline compound, $C_8H_{13}NO_2$, derived from scopolamine and used as a narcotic.

sçō·poph'ō·rine, *a.* pertaining to a group of antelopes with lateral hoofs and tufts on the knees.

Sçops, *n.* [Gr., a small owl.]

1. a genus of small screech owls of the family *Strigidæ*.

2. [s—] a member of this genus.

sçops owl, a small owl of the genus *Scops*, having an ear tuft like the horned owl; the American screech owl; a scops.

sçop'tiç·ăl, *a.* scoffing; mocking. [Obs.]

sçop'ū·lȧ, *n.*; *pl* **sçop'ū·lae**, [LL., from L. *scopulæ*, a little broom, dim. of *scopa*, a broom.] in entomology, (a) a brushlike organ on the foot of a spider, used in the construction of its web; (b) the tuft of hairs on the hind tarsi of certain bees.

sçop·ū·lăr'i·ȧ, *n.*; *pl.* **sçop·ū·lăr'i·ae**, [LL., from L. *scopulæ*, a little broom.] a broom-shaped spicule having from two to eight knobbed or tylotate rays; a scopula.

sçop'ū·lāte, *a.* [L. *scopulæ*, a broom.] in zoology, brushlike.

sçop·ū·lif'ēr·ous, *a.* same as *scopiferous*.

sçop'ū·li·fọrm, *a.* broom-shaped; scopulate.

sçop'ū·li·ped, *a.* [L. *scopulæ*, broom, and *pes*, *pedis*, foot.] having a brushlike apparatus on the hind legs.

sçop'ū·li·ped, *n.* any bee having pollen brushes on the hind legs.

Sçop″ū·li·pē'dēṣ, *n.pl.* formerly, a group of solitary *Apidæ*, having on the hind legs a brush for carrying pollen.

-sçō'py, [from Gr. *skopein*, to see, view.] a combining form meaning *a seeing*, *observing*, *examination*, as in bio*scopy*.

sçọr·ȧ·crā'ti·ȧ (-shi-), *n.* involuntary discharge of feces.

sçọr'būte, *n.* scurvy. [Obs.]

sçọr·bū'tiç, *n.* a person with scurvy.

sçọr·bū'tiç, sçọr·bū'ti·çăl, *a.* [LL. *scorbutus*; LG. *schärbuuk*, from *scheren*, to tear, rupture, and *buuk*, belly.] of, like, or having scurvy.

sçọr·bū'ti·çăl·ly, *adv.* with scurvy or with a tendency to it.

sçọr·bū'tus, *n.* [LL.] in medicine, scurvy.

sçọrce, *n.* and *v.* scorse. [Obs.]

sçọrch, *v.t.*; scorched, *pt.*, *pp.*; scorching, *ppr.* [ME. *scorchen*; OFr. *escorcher*, *escorcer*, to flay or pluck off the skin; LL. *excorticare*, to take off the skin, from L. *ex*, off, and *cortex* (*-icis*), bark, rind.]

1. to burn slightly; to char and discolor the surface of.

2. to parch or shrivel by heat; to cause to wither.

3. to affect painfully; to wound the feelings of by verbal attack or sarcasm.

4. to burn and destroy everything in (a given area) before giving it up to the enemy.

sçọrch, *v.i.* 1. to be burned slightly; to be singed.

2. to go very fast, as on a bicycle; to ride or drive rapidly. [Colloq.]

sçọrch, *n.* a superficial mark or burn.

sçọrched'-ēarth' pol'i·cy (skọrcht'ũrth'), the policy of burning and destroying all property in a given area before giving it up to an advancing enemy.

sçọrch'ēr, *n.* a person or thing that scorches; specifically, [Colloq.] (a) an extremely hot day; (b) a severe or withering rebuke, sarcastic remark, etc.; (c) a person who drives at an excessive rate of speed.

sçọrch·ing·ly, *adv.* in a scorching manner.

sçọr·dä'tō, *a.* [It., pp. of *scordare*, to be out of tune.] in music, out of tune or discordant.

sçọr'di·um, *n.* [L.Gr. *scordion*, a plant smelling like garlic.] a plant, the water germander, a species of *Teucrium*. [Obs.]

sçōre, *n.* [AS. *scor*, twenty, from *sceran*, to cut; Ice. *skor*, *skora*; Sw. *skara*; Dan. *skaar*, a score, notch, incision.]

1. (a) a scratch, mark, incision, etc.; as, the *scores* made on ice by skates; (b) a line drawn or scratched, often to mark a starting point, etc.; (c) notches made in wood, chalk marks, or any marks made to keep tally or account.

2. an amount or sum due; an account; a debt.

3. figuratively, a grudge; grievance; as, pay off an old *score*.

4. anything offered as a reason or motive; as, on the *score* of poverty.

5. the number of points made in a game or contest by a player or team, or the record of these points; as, the *score* is 2 to 0.

6. grade or rating, as on a test or examination.

7. (a) twenty people or objects; a set of twenty; (b) [*pl.*] very many.

8. a successful move, stroke, remark, etc. [Colloq.]

9. the actual facts; realities of a situation or of life: often in *know the score*.

10. in music, (a) a written or printed copy of a composition, showing all the parts for the instruments or voices; (b) the music for a musical comedy or motion picture, usually when distinguished from the lyrics, dialogue, etc.

11. the number twenty, which was denoted on a tally by a longer and deeper cut.

12. in nautical usage, the groove around a block or a deadeye for the strapping, shroud, or backstay.

to go off at score; to start from the score or scratch, as a pedestrian in a foot race; to start off generally.

sçōre, *v.t.*; scored, *pt.*, *pp.*; scoring, *ppr.* 1. to mark with notches, scratches, cuts, etc.

2. to mark with lines, as with a pen or pencil; as, the page is *scored* with underlinings.

3. to cancel or mark out by lines drawn (with *out*).

4. to mark with lines or notches in keeping account.

5. to keep account of by or as by lines or notches; to reckon; to tally; to mark.

6. (a) to make (runs, hits, etc.) in a game and so add to the number of points made for oneself or one's team; as, he *scored* a hit; (b) to count toward the number of points; as, a safety *scores* two; (c) to record or enter the score of; (d) to record or add (points) to one's score; as, John *scores* five for that play.

7. (a) to scourge; (b) to criticize severely; to upbraid.

8. to grade (an examination, etc.); to rate or evaluate, as in testing.

9. to gain or achieve, as a success.

10. in cookery, to cut superficial gashes in (meat, etc.).

11. in music, to orchestrate, arrange, or write out in a score.

12. to set down, as a debt; to enter; to register; to charge.

13. to engrave; to cut; to striate. [Rare.]

sçōre, *v.i.* 1. to make a point or points, as in a game.

2. to run up a score.

3. to keep the score, as of a game.

4. (a) to gain an advantage; (b) to achieve credit or success.

5. to make notches, lines, gashes, etc.

sçōre'book, *n.* a book in which the scores of a game are written and preserved for reference.

sçōre cärd, 1. a blank form for entering the scores made at games, as in golf.

2. a rating card used at poultry and other such shows.

3. a card printed with players' names, weights, positions, etc. at a sports event.

sçōr'ēr, *n.* one who or that which scores; specifically, (a) one who keeps the score or tally at cricket, rifle matches, and the like; (b) an instrument used by woodmen in marking numbers, etc. on forest trees.

sçōre sheet, a sheet of paper ruled for scoring or recording the features of a game as it progresses.

sçō'ri·ȧ, *n.*; *pl.* **sçō'ri·ae**, [L., from Gr. *skoria*, that which is thrown off, refuse, dross, from *skōr*, *skatos*, dung.]

1. the slag or refuse left after the metal has been smelted from the ore.

2. loose, cinderlike lava.

sçō'ri·aç, *a.* scoriaceous. [Rare.]

sçō·ri·ā'ceous, *a.* having the nature of scoria.

sçō″ri·fi·çā'tion, *n.* in metallurgy, the process of scorifying.

sçō'ri·fī·ēr, *n.* one who or that which scorifies; specifically, a vessel shaped much like a cupel, used for the process of scorification in assaying silver.

sçō'ri·fọrm, *a.* [L. *scoria*, dross, refuse, and *-form*.] like scoria; in the form of dross.

sçō'ri·fȳ, *v.t.*; scorified, *pt.*, *pp.*; scorifying, *ppr.* [L. *scoria*, dross, refuse, and *facere*, to make.] to reduce to scoria, or slag.

sçō'ri·ous, *a.* drossy; cindery; of or containing scoria.

sçọrn, *n.* [ME. *scorn*, *schorn*, *scharn*; OFr. *escarn*, scorn, derision, from O.H.G. *skern*, mockery, scurrility.]

1. a feeling that a person or thing is mean and contemptible; disdain; extreme contempt.

2. the expression of this feeling in words or manners; contemptuous treatment or disdainful utterance.

3. an object of this feeling; person or thing held in contempt or disdain.
to laugh to scorn; to deride; to treat derisively.
to think scorn; to disdain; to despise.
Syn.—contempt, disdain, derision.

sçorn, *v.t.*; scorned, *pt., pp.*; scorning, *ppr.* 1. to hold in extreme contempt; to despise; to contemn; to disdain; as, to *scorn* a mean person: often with the infinitive; as, to *scorn* to take advantage of a person.
2. to treat with scorn; to refuse or reject as mean and contemptible.
Syn.—despise, contemn, detest, disdain, spurn.

sçorn, *v.i.* to scoff; to mock or jeer. [Obs.]

sçorn'ẽr, *n.* one who scorns; a despiser; one who scoffs at religion.

sçorn'fụl, *a.* 1. contemptuous; disdainful; full of scorn; insolent.
2. producing scorn. [Obs.]
Syn.—insolent, contemptuous, disdainful, reproachful, contumelious.

sçorn'fụl·ly, *adv.* in a scornful manner.

sçorn'fụl·ness, *n.* the quality of being scornful.

sçorn'y, *a.* scornful.

sçor'ō·dīte, *n.* [Gr. *skorodon*, garlic, from its smell under the blowpipe.] a native compound of arsenic acid and oxide of iron, having a leek-green or brownish color.

Sçor·pae'nȧ, *n.* [Gr. *skorpaina*, a kind of fish.] a genus of fishes to which belongs *Scorpæna scrofa*, found in European waters.

sçor·pae'nid, *n.* any scorpaenoid fish.

sçor·pae'noid, *a.* L. *scorpæna*; Gr. *skorpaina*, a fish, from *skorpios*, a scorpion.] pertaining to the *Scorpænidæ*, a family of spiny-finned sea fishes including the scorpene, rosefish, corsair, etc.

sçor·pae'noid, *n.* a scorpaenoid fish.

sçor'pēne, *n.* [It. *scorpina*; L. *scorpæna*, a fish.] a fish of the genus *Scorpæna*, as *Scorpæna guttata*, of California, or the European hogfish, *Scorpæna scrofa*.

sçor'pẽr, *n.* 1. same as *scauper*.
2. a jeweler's gouging tool for working in a depression, as in engraving or piercing metal.

Sçor'pi·ō, *n.* [L.] 1. a southern constellation between Libra and Sagittarius, supposedly resembling a scorpion in shape.
2. in astrology, the eighth sign of the zodiac, which the sun enters about October 24.
3. a genus of arachnidians; the scorpions.

Sçor·pi·ō'dē·ȧ, *n. pl.* same as *Scorpionida*.

sçor'pi·oid, *a.* [Gr. *skorpios*, a scorpion, and *-oid*.]
1. resembling a scorpion.
2. of the order consisting of the true scorpions.
3. rolled or curled like the tail of a scorpion.

sçor'pi·ŏn, *n.* [Fr., from L. *scorpio* (*-onis*), another form for *scorpius*, a scorpion; Gr. *skorpios*, a scorpion, a prickly sea fish, a prickly plant, literally, something sharp or stinging.]
1. any of an order of arachnids, *Scorpionida*, found in warm regions, with a front pair of nipping claws and a long, slender, jointed tail ending in a curved, poisonous sting.
2. in the Bible, a variety of whip or scourge, perhaps inset with spikes: 1 Kings xii. 11.
3. [S–] Scorpio.
4. any scorpene.
5. the gray lizard of the United States.
6. an ancient military engine used chiefly in the defense of the walls of a town.
7. an offensive person; one willfully annoying or perverse. [Colloq.]
false scorpion; any one of various scorpion-like arachnids, as the book scorpion.
the Scorpion's Heart; the bright star, Antares, which occurs in the constellation Scorpio.

SCORPION (1-8 in. long)

sçor'pi·ŏn brọọm, same as *scorpion plant*, sense 2.

sçor'pi·ŏn bug, the water scorpion.

Sçor·pi·ō'nēş, *n.pl.* same as *Scorpionida*.

sçor'pi·ŏn fish, a spiny fish of the family *Scorpænidæ*.

sçor'pi·ŏn flȳ, any insect of the genus *Panorpa* whose abdomen, in the male, curls up at the end and resembles a scorpion's sting.

sçor'pi·ŏn gràss, the forget-me-not.

Sçor·pi·on'i·dȧ, *n.pl.* an order of *Arachnida* the true scorpions, having approximately equal seven-jointed legs.

sçor'pi·ŏn lob'stẽr, any long-tailed slender crustacean of the family *Thalassinidæ*.

sçor'pi·ŏn plant, 1. a Javanese orchid, *Arachnanthe moschifera*, whose lemon-colored flowers have the scent of musk.
2. a thorny leguminous shrub, *Genista scorpius*, of southern Europe, bearing yellow flowers: also called *scorpion broom*.

sçor'pi·ŏn sen'nȧ, a shrub, *Coronilla emerus*, of southern Europe, bearing yellow flowers and producing slender jointed pods which suggest the tail of a scorpion.

sçor'pi·ŏn shell, a gastropod of the genus *Pteroceras*, having a shell with long channeled spines which give it the appearance in outline of a scorpion.

sçor'pi·ŏn spī'dẽr, any arachnid of the order *Pedipalpi*.

sçor'pi·ŏn'ş tāil, any plant of the genus *Scorpiurus*.

sçor'pi·ŏn thorn, same as *scorpion plant*, sense 2.

sçor'pi·ŏn·wŏrt, *n.* (a) *Ornithopus scorpioides*, a plant of southern Europe; (b) scorpion grass.

Sçor·pi·ū'rus, *n.* [Gr. *skorpiouros*, from *skorpios*, scorpion, and *oura*, tail.] a genus of small herbs, native to the Mediterranean region, with simple leaves and small, usually yellow, flowers, which are succeeded by long, jointed pods.

Sçor'pi·us, *n.* the constellation Scorpio.

sçorse, *n.* a trade or barter. [Obs.]

sçorse, *v.t.* 1. to chase. [Obs.]
2. to barter or exchange. [Obs.]

sçorse, *v.i.* to trade; to barter. [Obs.]

sçor'ta·tō·ry, *a.* [L. *scortator*, a fornicator, from *scortari*, to practice fornication.] lewd; vulgar; indecent.

sçor'zȧ, *n.* a mineral, a variety of epidote. [Obs.]

Sçor·zō·nē'rȧ, *n.* [It. *scorzonera*, black bark, from *scorza*, bark, and *nera*, black.]
1. a genus of composite plants, including the *Scorzonera hispanica*, or black salsify, which is cultivated in Europe for its parsnip-like root.
2. [s–] any plant of this genus.

sçot, *n.* [ME.; merging of ON. *skot* and OFr. *escot*: akin to *shot*.] money assessed or paid; tax; levy.
scot and lot; (a) an old parish tax in Great Britain, assessed according to ability to pay; (b) in full: in the phrase *pay scot and lot*.

Sçot, *n.* [AS. *Scotta*, *Scottas*, the Scots, originally the inhabitants of Ireland.]
1. a member of a Gaelic tribe of northern Ireland that migrated to Scotland in the fifth century A.D.
2 a native or inhabitant of Scotland: cf. *Scotsman*, *Scotchman*.

sçot, *n.* a horse. [Obs.]

sçot'āle, *n.* the keeping of an alehouse by the officer of a forest, where people would spend their money for liquor through fear of incurring his displeasure. [Obs.]

Sçotch, *a.* [from *Scottish*.] 1. pertaining to Scotland, its inhabitants, or its language; Scottish.
2. tight-fisted; stingy: opprobrious usage, from the vulgarized notion of the Scottish character.
Scotch bonnets; the fairy ring mushroom, *Marasmius oreades*.
Scotch broth; mutton broth thickened with barley.
Scotch heather; a heath, *Calluna vulgaris*, characteristic of Scotch moors.
Scotch mist; a heavy, dense mist, like fine rain.
Scotch tape; a thin, paperlike adhesive tape: a trade-mark.
Scotch terrier; same as *Scottish terrier*.
Scotch thistle; a variety of thistle, *Onopordon acanthium*: so named because it is the national emblem of Scotland.
Scotch whisky; whisky, often having a smoky flavor, distilled in Scotland from malted barley.
Scotch woodcock; eggs cooked and served on toast or crackers spread with anchovies or anchovy paste.

Sçotch, *n.* 1. any of the dialects spoken by the people of Scotland.
2. Scotch whisky.
the Scotch; the Scottish people.

sçotch, *v.t.* [ME. *scocchen*; prob. from Anglo-Fr. *escoche*, from OFr. etymon of Fr. *coche*, a notch, nick.]
1. to cut; scratch; score; notch.
2. [from Theobald's emendation of *scorch* in Shakespeare's *Macbeth*, III, iii, 13.] to wound without killing; to maim; to crush.
3. to put down; stifle; stamp out; as, he *scotched* the rumor.
scotched collops; hash or stew made of finely cut veal or beef seasoned with onion and other condiments.

sçotch, *v.t.* [prob. from preceding in specialized sense.] to block a wheel, log, etc. with a wedge, block, etc. to prevent movement.

sçotch, *n.* a block, wedge, etc. put under a wheel or log to prevent rolling, slipping, etc.

Sçotch çap, the wild raspberry. [Dial.]

sçotch'ing, *n.* in masonry, a method of dressing stone by means of a pick or pick-shaped chisel inserted into a socket formed in the head of a hammer: also written *scutching*.

Sçotch'-Ī'rish, *a.* 1. designating or of a group of people living in Northern Ireland who are descended from Scottish settlers.
2. of Scottish and Irish descent.

Sçotch'-Ī'rish, *n.* a person of Scottish and Irish descent.

Sçotch'măn, *n.*; *pl.* **Sçotch'men,** 1. a Scot; a Scotsman: often considered an opprobrious form.
2. [s–] among seamen, a shield of wood or hide used to protect shrouds, etc. from being rubbed.

sçōte, sçōat, *n.* something that blocks or stops; a prop or stay. [Brit. Dial.]

sçōte, *v.t.*; scoted, *pt., pp.*; scoting, *ppr.* to stop or block, as a wheel, by placing some obstacle, as a stone, to prevent its rolling; to scotch: also written *scoat*. [Brit. Dial.]

sçō'tẽr, *n.*; *pl.* **sçō'tẽrş** or **sçō'tẽr,** the black diver or sea duck, of the genus *Œdemia*, found along the Arctic coasts of Europe and America: also *scooter*.

sçot'-free', *a.* 1. free from payment of scot, or tax; untaxed.
2. unhurt; clear; safe.

sçō'tiȧ (-shȧ), *n.* [Gr. *skotia*, darkness.] in architecture, a deep concave molding, usually at the base of a column.

Sçō'tiȧ (-shȧ), *n.* Scotland. [Poet.]

Sçot'i·cē, *adv.* [L.] in the Scottish language, dialect, or manner.

Sçō'tişm, *n.* the scholastic philosophy of John Duns Scotus and his followers.

Sçō'tist, *n.* [from John Duns *Scotus*, a Scottish scholar and thinker who lived in the fourteenth century.] one of the followers of Scotus, a sect of school divines who maintained certain philosophical and theological doctrines in opposition to the Thomists, or followers of Thomas Aquinas.

Sçot'lănd yärd, (a) the headquarters of the London police, on the Thames embankment since 1890: in full, *New Scotland Yard*; (b) the London police, especially the detective bureau.

sçot'ō-, [from Gr. *skotos*, darkness.] a combining form meaning *darkness, dimness*.

sçot'ō·grȧph, *n.* [Gr. *skotos*, darkness, and *graphein*, to write.]
1. an instrument for writing without seeing.
2. a radiograph.

sçō·tō'mȧ, *n.*; *pl.* **sçō·tō'mȧ·tȧ,** [Gr. *skotōma*, darkness.]
1. a blind or partially blind area in the visual field; a blind spot.
2. vertigo.

sçot'ō·my, *n.* same as *scotoma*.

sçō"tō·phō'bin, *n.* [from Gr. *skotos*, darkness, and *phobos*, a fear, and *-in*.] a peptide which is produced in the brain of laboratory rats conditioned to fear darkness and which transmits this fear when injected into unconditioned rats: its discovery is thought to provide evidence that memory has a chemical basis.

Sçots, *n.* the Scottish dialect of English.

Sçots, *a.* Scottish.
Scots law; the system of jurisprudence in effect in Scotland, derived principally from the civil law.

Sçots'măn, *n.*, *pl.* **Sçots'men,** a Scot: the current term in Scotland.

sçot'tẽr·ing, *n.* the burning of a wad of pease straw at the end of harvest. [Brit. Dial.]

Sçot'ti·çişm, *n.* a Scottish idiom, expression, word, pronunciation, etc.

Sçot'ti·çīze, *v.t.*; Scotticized, *pt., pp.*; Scotticizing, *ppr.* to make like the Scotch or something Scottish.

Sçot'tish, *a.* pertaining to the people of Scotland, or to their country or language; as, a *Scottish* chief, the *Scottish* dialect.

Sçot'tish, *n.* the English spoken by the people of Scotland. *Scottish*, the original form, is preferred to *Scotch* and *Scots* in American and British formal and literary usage with reference to the people, the country, and its institutions and characteristics, and in Scotland has replaced *Scotch*, the colloquial form prevailing in the United States and England; but with some words, *Scotch* is almost invariably used (e.g., tweed, whisky), with others, *Scots* (e.g., law, mile).

the Scottish; the Scottish people.

Sçot'tish Gāel'iç, see *Gaelic*.

Sçot'tish ter'ri·ẽr, any of a breed of terrier with short legs, a squarish muzzle, rough, wiry hair, and pointed, erect ears.

sçoun'drel, *n.* [prob. a disparaging dim. from Anglo-Fr. *escoundre*, to abscond.] a mean, worthless fellow, without honor or virtue.

sçoun'drel, *a.* low; base; mean; unprincipled.

sçoun'drel·dŏm, *n.* rascaldom; scoundrelism.

sçoun'drel·işm, *n.* baseness; vileness; rascality.

sçoun'drel·ly, *a.* 1. having the character of a scoundrel.

2. of or like a scoundrel.

sçour, *v.t.*; scoured, *pt., pp.*; scouring, *ppr.* [ME. *scouren*; OFr. *escurer*, to scour; Sw. *skura*; L. *excurare*, to take great care of; *ex-*, intensive prefix, and *curare*, to take care of, from *cura*, care.]

1. to clean by vigorous rubbing, as with abrasives, soap, and water, etc.; to make clean or bright on the surface.

2. to remove grease or dirt from (wool, etc.) by pounding, washing, and the application of detergents; as, to *scour* cloth.

3. to remove as if by scouring or rubbing.

4. to cleanse or flush by a stream of water.

5. to purge violently; to clear the intestines of.

6. to clean (wheat).

7. to remove from as if by cleaning; to sweep away; to get rid of.

sçour, *v.i.* 1. to clean things by vigorous rubbing and polishing.

2. to become clean and bright by rubbing and polishing.

3. to take dirt or grease out of cloth.

4. to be purged to excess.

sçour, *n.* 1. the act of scouring.

2. a cleansing agent used in scouring.

3. a scoured place, as a part of a channel where mud has been washed away.

4. [*pl.*] dysentery in cattle, etc.

sçour, *v.t.* [ME. *scowen*; prob. from OFr. *escourre*, to run forth; L. *excurrere*, from *ex*, out, and *currere*, to run.] to pass over swiftly in search of something, or to drive something away; to overrun; to sweep; to search thoroughly; as, to *scour* the country for an escaped horse thief.

sçour, *v.i.* to run hastily or quickly; to scamper; also, to rove or range about, as in search or pursuit.

sçour'āġe, *n.* water left from scouring.

sçour'ẽr, *n.* one who or that which scours; specifically, (a) a machine for cleaning grain; (b) a strong cathartic.

sçour'ẽr, *n.* 1. one who runs with speed; a scout.

2. one who roams about the streets at night; a footpad; a highway robber; a roisterer.

sçoûrġe, *n.* [ME. *scourge*; OFr. *escorgie*, a scourge; L. *excoriatus*, lit., flayed off, hence, a shred of leather for a whip.]

1. an instrument for flogging; a whip.

2. any means of inflicting severe punishment, suffering, or vengeance.

3. the punishment or affliction itself.

4. any cause of serious trouble or affliction; as, the *scourge* of war.

sçoûrġe, *v.t.*; scourged, *pt., pp.*; scourging, *ppr.*

1. to whip severely; to lash.

2. to punish with severity; to chastise; to afflict.

sçoûrġ'ẽr, *n.* one who scourges.

sçoûrġe stick, a whip for a top (child's toy).

sçour'ing, *n.* the act of one who or that which scours.

sçour'ing, *a.* having an erosive, cleansing, or polishing action.

sçour'ing bar'rel, a tumbling barrel for freeing scrap iron or small articles of metal from dirt and rust by friction; a rumble.

sçour'ing rush, any of a number of plants of the genus *Equisetum*, especially *Equisetum hiemale*, or horsetail, with hollow, jointed stems and scalelike leaves, used to polish metal and wood.

sçour'ingş, *n.pl.* 1. dirt, refuse, or remains removed by or as if by scouring.

2. refuse removed from grain before milling.

sçour'ing stock, a machine used in cleansing and treating cloth after being woven.

sçōurse, *v.t.* and *v.i.* to scorse. [Obs.]

sçour'wāy, *n.* a furrow made by a strong current, as by a glacial river.

sçouse, *n.* [contr. from *lobscouse*.] a seaman's dish of vegetables and sea biscuit, with or without meat.

sçout, *n.* [OFr. *escoute*, a scout, from *escouter*, *escolter*, to hear, from L. *auscultare*, to listen.]

1. a person, ship, or plane sent out to gain and bring in information; specifically, one employed to observe and report the movements, number, etc. of an enemy.

2. a person who is a member of the Boy Scouts or Girl Scouts.

3. fellow; guy. [Slang.]

4. in sports, etc., a person sent out to observe the tactics of a competitor, to find new talent, etc.

5. at Oxford University, a college servant or waiter.

6. in cricket, a fielder. [Dial.]

7. the act of scouting; a reconnaissance; a lookout.

8. a scouting party. [Obs.]

9. a spy; a sneak. [Obs.]

sçout, *v.t.* 1. to spy upon; to follow closely.

2. to look for; to watch.

sçout, *v.i.* 1. to go in search of military or naval information about the enemy; to reconnoiter.

2. to go in search of something; to prowl; as, *scout* around for some firewood.

3. to be an active member of the Boy Scouts or Girl Scouts.

sçout, *v.t.* [Ice. *skúta*, *skúti*, a taunt, allied to *skota*, to shove.] to sneer at; to ridicule; to treat with contempt and disdain; to reject as absurd; to flout.

sçout, *n.* [Ice. *skuti*, a cave formed by jutting rocks; *skuta*, to jut out.] a high rock. [Brit. Dial.]

sçout, *n.* [Ice. *skúta*; D. *schuit*.] a swift Dutch sailboat.

sçout, *n.* 1. any of various auks.

2. the guillemot.

sçout'çraft, *n.* the art or practice of scouting; especially, the activities of the Boy Scouts or Girl Scouts.

sçout'ẽr, *n.* 1. one who scouts.

2. in stoneworking, a man who, by means of wedges, jumpers, etc., breaks off large pieces of stone.

sçōuth, *n.* room; scope. [Scot.]

sçōu'thẽr, *n.* 1. uproar; disorder. [Brit. Dial.]

2. a slight shower. [Scot.]

sçout'hood, *n.* 1. the state of being a Boy Scout or Girl Scout.

2. the character or characteristics of Boy Scouts or Girl Scouts.

sçout'ing, *n.* 1. the act or process of a person that scouts.

2. participation in, or the activities of, the Boy Scouts or Girl Scouts.

sçout'ing·ly, *adv.* in a scouting manner.

sçout'màs″tẽr, *n.* the adult leader of a troop of Boy Scouts.

sçōve, *v.t.* to enclose in a kiln, as brick.

sçōve, *n.* extra pure tin ore. [Cornwall.]

sçŏv'el, *n.* [W. *ysgubell*, from *ysgub*, a broom; L. *scopa*.] a mop for sweeping ovens. [Brit. Dial.]

sçō'vy, *a.* daubed; smeared. [Brit. Dial.]

sçow, *n.* [D. *schouw*, a scow.] a large, flat-bottomed boat with square ends, used for loading and unloading vessels, etc., now generally pulled by a tug.

sçow, *v.t.*; scowed, *pt., pp.*; scowing, *ppr.* to transport in a scow.

sçowl, *v.i.* [ME. *scoulen*; from Dan. *skule*, to scowl, from *skiule*, to hide.]

1. to wrinkle the forehead and lower the eyebrows in displeasure; to put on a frowning look; to look sour, sullen, irritated, or angry.

2. to look threatening; to lower; as, the *scowling* heavens.

sçowl, *v.t.* to affect, influence, or express with a scowl or scowls.

sçowl, *n.* 1. a wrinkling of the forehead and lowering of the eyebrows in displeasure; an angry frown.

2. gloom; threatening aspect, as of the heavens.

sçowl'ing·ly, *adv.* in a scowling manner.

sçrab, *v.t.*; scrabbed, *pt., pp.*; scrabbing, *ppr.* to scrape; to scratch. [Brit. Dial.]

sçrab'ble, *v.i.*; scrabbled, *pt., pp.*; scrabbling, *ppr.* [D. *schrabbelen*, from *schrablen*, to scrape.]

1. to scrape, paw, or scratch as though looking for something.

2. to make irregular, crooked, and unmeaning marks; to scribble.

3. to struggle.

sçrab'ble, *v.t.* 1. to scribble; to mark with irregular lines or letters; as, to *scrabble* paper.

2. to scrape together hastily.

sçrab'ble, *n.* 1. a scraping with the hands or paws.

2. a scramble.

3. a scribble; scrawl.

4. a struggle.

sçrā'bẽr, *n.* either of two birds; (a) *Puffinus anglorum*, the Manx shearwater; (b) the black guillemot.

sçraf'fle, *v.i.* to scramble; to struggle. [Brit. Dial.]

sçrag, *n.* [Sw. dial. *skrake*, a lean man; allied to Sw. *skrokig*, *krokig*, crooked.]

1. a lean, scrawny person or animal.

2. the neck, or back of the neck, of mutton, veal, etc.

3. the human neck. [Slang.]

4. a crooked or dwarfed tree or plant.

5. a scrag whale.

sçrag, *v.t.*; scragged, *pt., pp.*; scragging, *ppr.* to execute by hanging; also, to twist or wring the neck of. [Slang.]

sçrag'ged, *a.* rough with irregular points, or a broken surface; scraggy. [Obs.]

sçrag'ged·ness, *n.* the state or quality of being scragged.

sçrag'gi·ly, *adv.* in a scraggy shape or form.

sçrag'gi·ness, *n.* the condition or quality of being scraggy.

sçrag'gly, *a.*; *comp.* scragglier; *superl.* scraggliest; unkempt; rough, as a beard; jagged; irregular; splintered, as rocks.

sçrag'gy, *a.*; *comp.* scraggier; *superl.* scraggiest, 1. scraggly.

2. lean; bony; skinny.

sçrag whāle, a rough-backed whale of the North Atlantic, *Agaphelus gibbosus*.

sçram, *v.i.*; scrammed, *pt., pp.*; scramming, *ppr.* [contr. of *scramble*.] to go away or out: usually in the imperative. [Slang.]

sçram'ble, *v.i.*; scrambled, *pt., pp.*; scrambling, *ppr.* [perh. a fusion of *scamper* and *scrabble*.]

1. to climb, crawl, or clamber with the hands and feet.

2. to scuffle and fight for something, as for coins scattered on the ground; to struggle roughly with others.

3. to struggle to get something highly prized; as, they *scrambled* for office.

sçram'ble, *v.t.* 1. (a) to throw together haphazardly; to mix in a confused way; (b) in electronics, to modify (transmitted auditory or visual signals) so as to make unintelligible without special receiving equipment.

2. to gather haphazardly; to collect without method (often with *up*).

3. to cook (eggs) by mixing the white and yolk together, as with milk or butter.

sçram'ble, *n.* 1. a hard climb or advance, as over rough, difficult ground.

2. a disorderly struggle, as to get something prized.

sçram'blẽr, *n.* one who or that which scrambles.

sçram'bling, *a.* that scrambles; irregular; straggling; rambling.

sçram'bling·ly, *adv.* in a scrambling manner.

sçran, *n.* [Ice. *skran*, rubbish.] broken food; scraps. [Brit. Dial.]

bad scran to you; bad food (or luck) to you. [Irish.]

sçränch, *v.t.*; scranched (skräncht), *pt., pp.*; scranching, *ppr.* [prob. imitative; D. *schransen*, to scranch. The word is the same as *cranch, craunch*, with *s* prefixed.] to grind with the teeth, and with a crackling sound; to crunch. [Brit. Dial.]

sçrañk'y, *a.* [prob. a nasalized form of *scraggy*.] lean; thin; scraggy. [Scot.]

sçran'nel, *a.* 1. slight; lean; thin; scrawny. [Archaic.]
 2. harsh and feeble: said of sound. [Archaic.]

sçran'ny, *a.* scrawny; thin; scrannel. [Brit. Dial. and Scot.]

sçrap, *n.* [ME. *scrappe*; Ice. *skrap*, scraps, trifles, from *skrapa*, to scrape.]
 1. a small piece; a little bit; a fragment; as, *scraps* of meat.
 2. a part of anything written or printed; a brief extract; as, *scraps* of history or poetry.
 3. discarded metal in the form of machinery, auto parts, etc. suitable only for reprocessing.
 4. discarded articles or fragments of rubber, leather, cloth, paper, etc.
 5. [*pl.*] bits of food.
 6. [*pl.*] the remnants of animal fat after the oil has been removed by rendering.
 7. [*pl.*] souvenirs, pictures, clippings, etc. pasted as mementos into a book.
 8. refuse or fragments of animal waste, ground and used as fertilizer; as, fish *scrap*.

sçrap, *a.* 1. in the form of fragments, pieces, odds and ends, or leftovers.
 2. used and discarded.

sçrap, *v.t.*; scrapped, *pt., pp.*; scrapping, *ppr.* 1. to make into scrap; to break up.
 2. to treat as useless; to discard; to junk.

sçrap, *n.* [prob. from *scrape*, orig., nefarious scheme.] a fight or quarrel. [Slang.]

sçrap, *v.i.*; scrapped, *pt., pp.*; scrapping, *ppr.* to fight or quarrel. [Slang.]

sçrap'book, *n.* a blank book into which pictures, clippings from newspapers or books, souvenirs, etc. are pasted for preservation; a memory book.

sçrāpe, *v.t.*; scraped (skrāpt), *pt., pp.*; scraping, *ppr.* [ME. *scrapien, scrapen*; Ice. *skrapa*; Sw. *skrapa*, to scrape.]
 1. to rub the surface of with something rough or sharp; to mar the surface of by the abrading action of a sharp instrument; to grate; to abrade.
 2. to make smooth or clean by rubbing with something abrasive.
 3. to remove or take off by rubbing; to erase: with *out, off, from*, etc.
 4. to collect, gather, or accumulate by laborious effort; to gather slowly and with difficulty; as, he *scraped* together some money.
 5. to bring into contact with something rough so as to scratch or graze; as, I *scraped* my knee on the stone.
 6. to rub with a harsh sound; to draw along or over so as to cause a grating sound; as, the bow *scrapes* the fiddle.
 7. to dig, especially with the hands and nails.
 to scrape acquaintance; to insinuate oneself into acquaintance with a person.
 to scrape down; to express disapprobation of or attempt to drown the voice of at public meetings, by scraping the feet along the floor.

sçrāpe, *v.i.* 1. to rub the surface of anything so as to produce a harsh noise; also, to make a harsh, grating noise.
 2. to scrape something so as to remove dirt, etc.
 3. to collect or gather goods or money slowly and with difficulty.
 4. to manage to live; to exist with difficulty.
 5. to play awkwardly on a fiddle or similar instrument.
 6. to draw the foot back along the floor when bowing.

sçrāpe, *n.* 1. the act or noise of scraping.
 2. an awkward predicament; a difficulty; an embarrassing or perplexing situation, usually caused by one's own conduct.
 3. a scraped place; an abrasion or scratch on a surface.
 4. a shave. [Slang.]

sçrāpe'pen″ny, *n.* one who hoards his money; a miser.

sçrāp'ẽr, *n.* 1. one who or that which scrapes.
 2. any of various instruments used for scraping; specifically, (a) an iron plate at a door to remove mud from shoes; (b) an instrument, generally triangular, for scraping and cleaning the planks, masts, and decks of ships; (c) a large hoe for cleaning roads and streets; (d) a thin piece of wood shaped like a knife blade and provided with a handle, used to scrape the sweat from horses.

SCRAPER (sense 2b)

 3. a two-handled scoop, drawn by cattle, horses, etc., and used in making and leveling roads, excavating ditches, etc., and generally in raising and removing loosened soil or gravel.
 4. in engraving, a three-sided cutting tool, fluted, used in taking off the bur left by the etching needle or dry point.
 5. the board in an old form of lithographic press whose edge is lowered on to the tympan sheet, to bring the requisite pressure upon the paper, which lies upon the inked stone.
 6. a fiddler.
 7. one who scrapes money together by laborious parsimony; a scrapepenny.

sçrap·i·an'ȧ, *n.* a collection of literary scraps or fragments. [Obs.]

sçrāp'ing, *n.* 1. the act of one who or that which scrapes; also, the sound produced by such act.
 2. [*usually pl.*] that which is scraped off a surface, or collected by scraping, rubbing, or raking.

sçrāp'ing·ly, *adv.* in a scraping manner; by scraping.

sçrap ī'ron (-ūrn), iron cuttings, fragments, cast-off pieces, etc., collected for reworking or recasting.

sçrap'pẽr, *n.* a person or thing that scraps.

sçrap'pẽr, *n.* a person who engages in or is fond of scrapping or fighting, especially a plucky, hard boxer. [Slang.]

sçrap'pi·ly, *adv.* in a scrappy manner.

sçrap'ple, *n.* [dim. of *scrap*.] an article of food consisting of minced meats, usually scraps of pork, and herbs stewed with flour or corn meal, pressed into cakes, sliced, and fried.

sçrap'py, *a.*; *comp.* scrappier; *superl.* scrappiest, 1. composed of scraps; made up of odds and ends.
 2. disconnected; disjointed; as, *scrappy* thinking.

sçrap'py, *a.*; *comp.* scrappier; *superl.* scrappiest; fond of fighting. [Slang.]

sçrat, *v.t.* and *v.i.* to scratch. [Obs.]

sçrat, *n.* [etym. doubtful.] a hermaphrodite. [Now Dial.]

Sçratch, *n.* [ME. *skratte* (from ON. *skratti*, monster, devil, sorcerer), altered after *scratch*.] [*sometimes* s-] the Devil: usually *Old Scratch*.

sçratch, *v.t.*; scratched (skracht), *pt., pp.*; scratching, *ppr.* [ME. *scratten* (from ON.), fused with *cracchen*, to scratch, from M.D. *cratsen*, to scratch.]
 1. to tear, mark, or scrape the surface of slightly with something pointed or sharp.
 2. to dig or scrape with the nails or claws.
 3. to erase; to obliterate; to expunge; to strike out or cancel (writing, etc.).
 4. (a) to rub or scrape lightly, as with the fingernails, to relieve itching, etc.; (b) to chafe.
 5. to rub or scrape with a grating noise; as, he *scratched* a match on the wall.
 6. to write or draw hurriedly or carelessly.
 7. to gather or collect with difficulty; to scrape (with *up*).
 8. in politics, (a) to signify refusal to vote for (a candidate) by striking out his name; (b) to strike out a certain name or names on (the regular party ticket); (c) to divide (one's vote) or mark (one's ballot) so as to support mainly one party.
 9. in sports, to mark off (a competitor's name); especially, to withdraw (an entry) in horse racing.

sçratch, *v.i.* 1. to scrape or dig into by using the nails or claws; as, hens *scratch* in the ground.
 2. to scrape mildly, as with the fingernails, to relieve irritation of the skin.
 3. to get along with difficulty.
 4. to give out a harsh, scraping noise.
 5. to withdraw from a race or contest.
 6. in billiards, to score by chance or luck; also, in pool and billiards, to pocket the cue ball by error, to fail to hit a ball, etc.

sçratch, *n.* 1. the act of scratching; also, a slight incision, score, mark, or break made on a surface by something sharp or rough.
 2. a slight wound inflicted by nails, claws, or something pointed.
 3. a grating sound; a scraping.
 4. a hasty mark, as of a pen; a scribble.
 5. a mark or line from which contestants start, as in sprinting or, formerly, boxing.
 6. in billiards, an accidentally successful stroke; a fluke; also, in pool and billiards, an error made by pocketing the cue ball, by failure to hit a ball, etc.
 7. a kind of wig, covering only a part of the head; a scratch wig.
 8. in sports, (a) the starting point or time of a contestant who receives no handicap; (b) such a contestant.
 from (or *at, on*) *scratch*; (a) from the starting line, as in a race; (b) from nothing; without advantage.
 up to scratch; (a) toeing the mark in a prize fight or a race; ready to start a race, contest, etc.; (b) [Colloq.] ready to meet difficulties, start on an enterprise, etc.; (c) [Colloq.] up to a standard.

sçratch, *a.* 1. used for hasty notes, preliminary or tentative figuring, etc.; as, *scratch* paper.
 2. starting from scratch; having no handicap or allowance, as a contestant.
 3. done or made by chance, as a shot.
 4. put together in haste and without much selection; as, a *scratch* team.

sçratch'back, *n.* 1. a backscratcher.
 2. a toy which makes a noise like tearing cloth.

sçratch'brush, *n.* in metalworking, a brush made of fine wire or spun glass, used to clean or polish.

sçratch çōat, the first coating of plaster upon lath.

sçratch çrā'dle, the ribwort: also called *cat's-cradle*.

sçratch'ẽr, *n.* one who or that which scratches.

sçratch'eṣ, *n.pl.* [*often construed as sing.*] a skin disease of horses, characterized by the formation of dry scabs near the fetlock or behind the knee.

sçratch hit, in baseball, a chance hit credited to the batter, which normally would have been an out.

sçratch test, a test for determining the substances to which a person is allergic, made by rubbing allergens into small scratches or punctures in the skin.

sçratch'weed, *n.* same as *cleavers*.

sçratch wig, same as *scratch*, n. 7.

sçratch'wŏrk, *n.* a style of wall decoration made by scratching designs through the surface coat of plaster.

sçratch'y, *a.*; *comp.* scratchier; *superl.* scratchiest, 1. having the appearance of being drawn roughly, hurriedly, etc.; made with scratches.
 2. making a scraping, scratching noise.
 3. scratched together; haphazard.
 4. that scratches, scrapes, tears, chafes, etc.; irritating; itching; as, *scratchy* cloth.

sçrat'tle, *v.i.* [freq. of *scrat*.] to scramble; to scuttle. [Brit. Dial.]

sçraw, *n.* [Gael. and Ir. *scrath*, a turf.] sod; turf. [Brit. Dial.]

sçrawl, *v.t.* and *v.i.*; scrawled, *pt., pp.*; scrawling, *ppr.* [ME. *scrawlen*, to shamble.] to write, draw, or mark awkwardly, hastily, or carelessly; especially, to write with sprawling, shapeless handwriting.

sçrawl, *n.* 1. shapeless, sprawling, often illegible handwriting.
 2. something scrawled.

sçrawl'ẽr, *n.* one who scrawls.

sçrawl'y, *a.*; *comp.* scrawlier; *superl.* scrawliest; scrawling; irregular; not well formed.

sçraw'ni·ness, *n.* the quality or condition of being scrawny.

sçraw'ny, *a.*; *comp.* scrawnier; *superl.* scrawniest, [prob. from ON. (hyp.) *skrannig-*.] lean; thin; scraggy; scrubby.

sçrāy, sçrāye, *n.* [W. *ysgräen*, the sea swallow.] the sea swallow or tern. [Brit.]

sçrēak, *v.i.* [an older and northern form of *screech, shriek*; Sw. *skrika*; Ice. *skrækа*, to screak.] to utter suddenly a sharp, shrill sound or outcry; to scream, as in a sudden fright; also, to creak, as a door or wheel.

sçrēak, *n.* a creaking; also, a screech.

sçrēam, *v.i.*; screamed, *pt.*, *pp.*; screaming, *ppr.* [ME. *scremen, screamen*, to cry out, scream; Ice. *skræma*; Sw. *skrämma*, to scare, to terrify; Sw. *skrän*, a scream, from Teut. root *skri*, to cry aloud.]
1. (a) to utter a shrill, loud, piercing cry in anger, pain, or fright; (b) to make a shrill, piercing sound.
2. to laugh loudly or hysterically.
3. to have a startling effect; to leave a vivid impression.
4. to use heated, intense, or hysterical language.

sçrēam, *v.t.* 1. to utter with or as with a scream or screams.
2. to bring into a specified state by screaming: often reflexive.

sçrēam, *n.* 1. (a) a shriek, or sharp, shrill cry; (b) a shrill, piercing sound.
2. a hilariously funny person or thing. [Colloq.]

sçrēam'ẽr, *n.* 1. any one of a few species of long-toed South American birds of the genus *Palamedea*, usually ranked with the grallatorial or wading birds: so called from their loud, shrill cry.
2. a person who screams.
3. a person or thing of remarkable size, strength, excellence, etc. [Slang.]
4. a person or thing that makes one scream with laughter or thrills; especially, a very thrilling or funny story, etc. [Slang.]
5. an exclamation point: printer's term. [Slang.]
6. a sensational headline. [Slang.]

sçrēam'ing, *a.* 1. that screams.
2. having the nature of a scream; violent or startling in effect.
3. causing screams of laughter; very funny; hilarious.

sçree, *n.* [back-formation from pl. *screes*, from earlier *screethes*, from ON. *skritha*, a landslide, from *skritha*, to slide.]
1. a pebble; a stone. [Brit.]
2. an accumulation of small or broken stones, as at the foot of a steep slope. [Brit.]

sçreech, *v.i.*; screeched (skrēcht), *pt.*, *pp.*; screeching, *ppr.* [ME. *scriken, shryken*; Ice. *skrækja*; Sw. *skrika*; Dan. *skrige*, to shriek; Gael. *sgreach*.] to cry out with a sharp, shrill voice; to utter a sudden, shrill cry, as in terror or pain; to scream; to shriek.

sçreech, *v.t.* to utter with a shriek.

sçreech, *n.* a sharp, shrill, high-pitched cry or shriek.

sçreech bīrd, the fieldfare.

sçreech'ẽr, *n.* one who or that which screeches.

sçreech hawk, the goatsucker. [Brit. Dial.]

sçreech mär'tin, the swift. [Brit. Dial.]

sçreech owl, 1. any of a group of small owls with feathered ear tufts and an eerie, wailing screech instead of a hoot.
2. a barn owl.

sçreech'y, *a.*; *comp.* screechier; *superl.* screechiest; harsh; shrill; resembling a screech; screeching.

sçreed, *n.* [a variant of *shred*, from AS. *screade*, a shred.]
1. in plastering, (a) a strip of mortar about 6 or 8 inches wide, by which any surface about to be plastered is divided into bays or compartments. The screeds are 4, 5, or 6 feet apart, according to circumstances, and are accurately formed in the same plane by the plumb rule and straightedge. They thus form gauges for the rest of the work, the interspaces being latterly filled out flush with them; (b) a strip of wood similarly used.
2. a portion; a shred. [Scot.]
3. a harangue; an extended tirade.
4. the act of rending or tearing; a rent; a tear. [Scot.]
5. a long passage of prose, usually argumentative.

sçreen, *n.* [ME. *scren*; OFr. *escran*.]
1. (a) a light, movable, covered frame or series of frames hinged together, serving as a portable partition which separates, conceals, shelters, or protects; (b) any partition or curtain serving the same purpose.
2. that which shelters, protects, conceals, or shields in the manner of a curtain; as, a smoke *screen*, a *screen* of trees.
3. a kind of sieve; especially, (a) a sieve used by farmers for sifting earth or seeds; (b) a coarse mesh of wire for sifting sand, lime, gravel, etc.
4. in architecture, (a) a partition of wood, stone, or metal, usually so placed in a church as to shut out an aisle from the choir or the nave from the choir; (b) in medieval halls, a partition extending across the lower end, forming a lobby within the main entrance doors, and having often a gallery above; (c) an architecturally decorated wall, as for enclosing a courtyard in front of a building.
5. in electricity, a device placed over an electrical apparatus in order to protect or screen it from the effects of external electrostatic fields.
6. a frame covered with a fine mesh, as of wire, plastic, or cloth, used over doorways and windows for protection.
7. a large sheet, curtain, or surface upon which motion pictures or lantern slides may be projected.
8. the motion-picture industry or art; motion pictures collectively.
9. in color photography, a minutely patterned, tricolored mosaic used in the various screen processes in preparing negatives and examining the transparency.
10. in photoengraving, a pair of glass plates, cemented together, each plate being ruled with fine lines (from 60 to 150 to the square inch), one vertically and the other horizontally, so that minute squares are formed: used in the half-tone process.
11. in physics, part of an apparatus or instrument used to shield or protect another and more sensitive part from the effect of outside forces such as light, electricity, magnetism, etc.
12. in military usage, (a) a body of troops sent out to protect an area or cover troop movements; (b) a protective formation of light vessels, as destroyers, about heavier ones, as carriers.
13. in psychoanalysis, a form of concealment, as, in a dream, a person who stands for another or others with whom he has some characteristics in common.
the small screen; television. [Colloq.]

sçreen, *v.t.*; screened, *pt.*, *pp.*; screening, *ppr.* 1. to separate or cut off from view, or to shelter or protect, with or as with a screen.
2. to pass through a screen; to separate, as the coarse part of anything, from the fine, or as the worthless from the valuable.
3. (a) to interview or test in order to separate according to skills, personality, aptitudes, etc.; (b) to separate in this way (usually with *out*).
4. to show (a motion picture); to project (pictures, etc.) upon a screen, as with a motion-picture or slide projector.
5. to photograph with a motion-picture camera.
6. to adapt for motion pictures; to modify (a story, play, etc.) for reproduction as a movie.

sçreen, *v.i.* to be screened or suitable for screening, as in motion pictures; as, she *screens* well.

sçreen, *a.* 1. relating to the motion-picture screen, or to the motion-picture industry; as, the *screen* version of a play.
2. made of, or provided with, screen.

sçreen dōor, a door consisting of a frame to which netting, a metal screen, etc. is fastened.

sçreen'ẽr, *n.* one who or that which screens.

sçreen'ings, *n.pl.* the refuse left from the screenings of coal, ashes, sand, grain, etc.; also, the material that has been screened.

sçreen'plāy, *n.* a story written in a form suitable to production as a motion picture or adapted to this form from a novel, stage play, etc.

sçreen proc'ess, in color photography, a process making use of a minutely patterned, multicolored screen or filter which prevents the negative from recording all colors which are not complementary to the color of the finished block.

sçreeve, *v.t.* and *v.i.* to write on sidewalks; to write screeves. [Slang.]

sçreeve, *n.* a begging letter; also, a sidewalk drawing, writing, etc. used in panhandling. [Slang.]

sçrew (skrü), *n.* [OFr. *escroue*, the hole in which a screw turns; from L. *scrofa*, sow, influenced by *scrobis*, vulva.]
1. a mechanical device used for fastening things together, consisting of a naillike cylinder of metal grooved in an advancing spiral, and usually having a slotted head: it penetrates only by being turned: *male* (or *external*) *screw*.
2. anything like such a device.
3. a hollow cylinder equipped with a spiral groove on its inner surface into which the male screw fits: *female* (or *internal*) *screw*.
4. a steamer propelled by means of a screw propeller. [Rare.]

SCREWS

5. a screw propeller.
6. a twist or turn of a screw or resembling that of a screw.
7. a twist or turn to one side; as, to give a ball a *screw* in billiards.
8. one who makes a sharp bargain; also, a miser; a skinflint. [Chiefly Brit.]
9. a worn-out or broken-down horse; a jade. [Chiefly Brit.]
10. a small parcel of tobacco, etc. twisted up in a piece of paper. [Chiefly Brit.]
11. wages; salary; pay. [Brit. Slang.]
12. a teacher or professor who subjects students to rigid examinations or requires them to work hard. [Slang.]
13. in mathematics, a straight line in space, expressing the displacement of a rigid body, associated with a definite linear magnitude.
14. a prison guard. [Slang.]
Archimedean screw; see under *Archimedean*.
a screw loose; a defect; something lacking in the constitution or arrangement of a thing; as, there must be *a screw loose* somewhere.
Hindley's screw; a screw cut on a solid whose sides are arcs of the pitch circle of a wheel into which the screw is intended to work.
lag screw; a sharp-threaded screw with a square head, used for fastening lags in machinery.
to have a screw loose; to be eccentric, odd, etc. [Slang.]
to put the screws on or *to*; to subject to force; to exert pressure upon, as in exacting the payment of a debt.

HINDLEY'S SCREW

sçrew (skrü), *v.t.*; screwed, *pt.*, *pp.*; screwing, *ppr.* 1. to twist; turn; tighten.
2. to fasten, make secure, tighten, press, insert, etc. with or as with a screw or screws.
3. to contort; to squeeze; to twist out of natural shape; as, to *screw* one's face up.
4. to force to do something; to compel, as if by using screws.
5. to extort or practice extortion on; as, he *screwed* me out of money. [Slang.]
6. to have sexual intercourse with. [Slang.]

sçrew, *v.i.* 1. to come apart or go together by being turned or twisted in the manner of a screw; as, the lid *screws* on.
2. to be fitted for being put together or taken apart by a screw or screws.
3. to twist; to turn; to wind; to have a motion like that of a screw.
4. to practice extortion.

sçrew'à·ble, *a.* capable of being screwed; as, *screwable* timber.

sçrew'ball, *n.* 1. in baseball, a ball thrown by a right-handed pitcher that curves to the right, or one thrown by a left-handed pitcher that curves to the left.
2. anyone acting in an erratic, irrational, unconventional, or unbalanced manner. [Slang.]

sçrew'ball, *a.* peculiar; unbalanced; erratic. [Slang.]

sçrew bēan, 1. the spirally twisted pod growing on a mesquite tree of the southwestern United States and used for fodder.
2. this tree.

sçrew bōlt, a bolt with head at one end and thread at the other, for the purpose of binding together by means of a nut.

sçrew'drīv·ẽr, *n.* a tool resembling a blunt chisel, for tightening, loosening, or turning

screws, the narrow thin end fitting into the slot in the head of the screw: also *screw driver*.
screwed (skrüd), *a.* 1. having threads like a screw.
2. twisted.
3. drunk. [Chiefly Brit. Slang.]
screw'ẽr, *n.* one who or that which screws.
screw eȳe (ī), a screw the head of which is an eye or loop, used in picture frame backs, etc.; also, a similar screw of larger size used to secure stage scenery, etc.
screw hook, a screw with a hook for a head.
screw jack, a jackscrew; a lifting or hoisting jack operated by a screw.
screw kēy, a socket wrench for turning a nut or screw.
screw mȧ·chïne', a machine designed for making screws, etc., from wire or metal rods.
screw nāil, a wire nail with a thread or barbs, to prevent withdrawal.
screw peg, a small headless screw used in fastening the soles of shoes, etc.
screw pīle, a pile having a screw at the lower end.
screw pīne, any of the several species of trees and shrubs of the genus *Pandanus,* of the Malay Peninsula and tropical islands, with leaves arranged in spirals and aerial roots.

SCREW PINE (*Pandanus odoratissimus*)

screw plāte, a thin plate of iron having a series of holes of varying sizes with internal screws, used in forming small external screws; a kind of diestock.
screw pod, the screw bean.
screw prō·pel'lẽr, a propeller composed of a central hub upon which are symmetrically mounted two, three, or four identical blades, each having a twist so that a screwlike action is imparted to the device as it revolves on its axis: used for driving ships, airplanes, etc.

SCREW PROPELLER

screw shell, a gastropod of the genus *Turritella.*
screw spīke, a spike with the lower part barbed or threaded, so that it may retain its hold more securely.
screw'stem, *n.* any one of the several slender plants of the genus *Bartonia,* of North America: so named from their twisted stems.
screw'stock, *n.* a diestock or screw plate.
screw tap, a tool for cutting interior screw threads.
screw thread (thred), 1. the spiral ridge cut in a screw.
2. one turn of the thread or ridge of a screw; as, fifteen *screw threads* to the inch.
screw tree, a plant of the genus *Helicteres,* of several species, native to warm climates. They are evergreen, shrubby plants, with purple, brown, or yellow flowers, and twisted capsules. *Helicteres isora* is called *twisted horn* and *twisty.*
screw'wŏrm, *n.* the larva of an American blowfly, *Lucilia macellaria,* which deposits its eggs on sores on living animals, frequently with fatal effect.
screw wrench (rench), any wrench for turning screws.
screw'y, *a.*; *comp.* screwier; *superl.* screwiest. 1. with the motion of a screw.
2. unbalanced; irrational. [Slang.]
3. peculiar; eccentric. [Slang.]
4. impractical. [Slang.]
5. misleading. [Slang.]
6. broken-down; useless, as a horse. [Colloq.]
7. tipsy. [Slang.]
scrib, *n.* a stingy person. [Obs.]
scrīb'ȧ·ble, *a.* capable of being written upon or of being written.
scrī·bā'cious, *a.* skillful in or fond of writing. [Obs.]
scrī'băl, *a.* 1. pertaining to a scribe or copyist; clerical.
2. arising from the process of writing; as, a *scribal* error.
3. relating to the scribes of the Jews.
scrib'bet, *n.* the pencil of a painter. [Obs.]
scrib'ble, *v.t.*; scribbled, *pt., pp.*; scribbling, *ppr.* [ML. *scribillare,* from L. *scribere,* to write.]
1. to write carelessly or illegibly.
2. to cover with meaningless or illegible marks.
3. to compose hastily, without regard to style.
scrib'ble, *v.i.* 1. to write in a careless or illegible way.
2. to make meaningless or illegible marks.
scrib'ble, *n.* 1. illegible or careless writing; a scrawl.
2. a series of meaningless lines and marks.
3. an inferior literary work.
scrib'ble, *v.t.* to card, as wool, roughly; to run through a scribbler.
scrib'ble·ment, *n.* a scribble.
scrib'blẽr, *n.* a person who scribbles; specifically, (a) a person who writes illegibly or carelessly; (b) a hack writer; an inferior and unimportant author.
scrib'blẽr, *n.* 1. a scribbling machine for the coarse carding of wool.
2. one who operates a scribbling machine.
scrib'bling, *n.* the act of scribbling, or writing carelessly.
scrib'bling, *n.* the first course of treatment of wool, etc. by a scribbling machine.
scrib'bling·ly, *adv.* in a scribbling way.
scrībe, *n.* [L. *scriba,* a writer, from *scribere,* to write.]
1. a writer; an author.
2. a professional penman; a person who copied manuscripts before the invention of printing.
3. a clerk; a public writer or secretary.
4. a pointed instrument for marking a line on stone, brick, wood, etc. to show where it is to be cut.
5. in Scripture and Jewish history, (a) a teacher or doctor of the Jewish law; (b) a man of learning; one who read and explained the law to the people.
scrībe, *v.t.*; scribed, *pt., pp.*; scribing, *ppr.* 1. to mark (wood, bricks, etc.) with a scribe.
2. to mark (a line) with a scribe.
3. to fit the edge of (a board, etc.) to another edge or surface; as, to *scribe* a board to an irregular wall.
scrībe, *v.i.* to work as a scribe.
scrīb'ẽr, *n.* a scribe (sense 4).
scrīb'ism, *n.* the manner, character, or doctrines of the ancient Jewish scribes.
scrig'gle, *v.i.* to squirm; to wriggle. [Dial.]
scrim, *n.* [etym. uncertain.]
1. a loosely woven yet strong cloth of cotton or linen, made both plain and in openwork designs: used for upholstery, linings, curtains, etc.
2. [*pl.*] thin canvas fastened with glue on the backs of panels to prevent them from warping.
scrī'mẽr, *n.* a fencing master. [Obs.]
scrim'măġe, *n.* [a corruption of *skirmish.*]
1. a skirmish; a tussle or row; a rough-and-tumble fight.
2. in football, (a) the play that follows the pass from center when the two teams are lined up; (b) football practice in the form of actual play.
3. in Rugby, scrummage.
line of scrimmage; in football, an imaginary line on which the ball rests at the beginning of each play and along which the two teams line up.
scrim'măġe, *v.i.*; scrimmaged, *pt., pp.*; scrimmaging, *ppr.* to take part in a scrimmage.
scrim'măġ·ẽr, *n.* in Rugby, a forward.
scrimp, *v.t.*; scrimped (skrimpt), *pt., pp.*; scrimping, *ppr.* [Sw. *skrympa,* pp. of *skrumpen,* to shrink, shrivel, akin to AS. *scrimman,* to shrink.]
1. to make too small or short; to limit or straiten; to scant or make scanty; as, to *scrimp* the pattern of a coat.
2. to treat stingily; to stint.
scrimp, *v.i.* to be sparing and frugal; to try to make ends meet.
scrimp, *a.* scanty; curtailed.
scrimp, *n.* a pinching miser; a niggard. [Colloq.]
scrimp'i·ly, *adv.* in a scrimpy manner.
scrimp'i·ness, *n.* a scrimpy quality.
scrimp'ing bär, in a machine for printing cloth, a bar which serves to smooth the fabric for printing.
scrimp'ing·ly, *adv.* in a scrimping or scanty manner.
scrimp'ness, *n.* scantiness.
scrimp'tion, *n.* a pittance; a scant portion. [Brit. Dial.]
scrimp'y, *a.*; *comp.* scrimpier; *superl.* scrimpiest. 1. skimpy; scanty; meager.
2. stingy.
scrim'shaw, *n.* [earlier also *scrimshander*; the base is prob. a nautical adaptation of Fr. *escrimer,* to fight (with a sword), in the sense "to make flourishes."]
1. careful decoration and carving of shells, bone, ivory, etc. by sailors on long voyages.
2. a product of such handicraft.
3. any neat piece of mechanical work.
scrim'shaw, *v.t.* and *v.i.* to decorate (shells, etc.) by carving.
scrīne, *n.* [OFr. *escrin* (Fr. *écrin*); from L. *scrinium,* a box or case for papers.] a chest, bookcase, or other place where writings or curios are kept. [Obs.]
scringe, *v.i.* to cringe. [Dial.]
scrip, *n.* [ME. *scrippe*; Ice. *skreppa,* a scrip, bag; Norw. *skreppa,* a knapsack; Sw. *skräppa,* a scrip.] a small bag; a wallet; a satchel. [Archaic.]
scrip, *n.* [a corruption of *script.*]
1. a writing; a list, receipt, etc.
2. a small piece or scrap, especially of paper.
3. a certificate of a right to receive something; specifically, (a) a certificate representing fractions of shares of stock; (b) a temporary certificate given for part payment of a stock subscription or a bond, to be exchanged later when full payment is made; (c) a temporary paper to be exchanged for money, goods, land, etc.; (d) certificate of indebtedness, issued as currency.
4. paper money in amounts of less than a dollar, formerly issued in the United States; fractional currency.
scrip'ee, *n.* a holder of scrip issued by the government of the United States by which he is entitled to locate and possess a tract or tracts of the public land.
scrip'pāġe, *n.* what a script (wallet) contains. [Obs.]
script, *n.* [OFr. *escript,* from L. *scriptum,* a thing written, neut. of *scriptus,* pp. of *scribere,* to write.]
1. handwriting; written words, letters, or figures.
2. printing or printers' type which imitates handwriting.
3. a style of handwriting; manner or method of forming letters or figures.
4. a written document; an original manuscript: opposed to *copy.*
5. (a) a manuscript or typewritten copy of a play, radio show, role, or motion-picture screenplay; (b) the written part of a play, radio show, etc., excluding performance, music, scenery, etc.; as, the acting was poor, but I liked the *script.*
scrip'tion, *n.* a handwriting, especially when in the characteristic style of the writer or period. [Rare.]
scrip·tō'ri·um, *n.*; *pl.* **scrip·tō'ri·ȧ,** [L., from *scriptor,* a writer.] a room for writing; especially, a room in a monastery for the writing or copying of manuscripts.
scrip'tō·ry, *a.* expressed in writing; used for writing. [Rare.]
scrip'tūr·ăl, *a.* 1. [*often* S–] Biblical; of, contained in, or according to the Scriptures; Biblical; as, a *scriptural* phrase or account.
2. written; pertaining to writing.
scrip'tūr·ăl·ism, *n.* [*often* S–] the quality of being scriptural; hence, close adherence to the letter of the Scriptures.
scrip'tūr·ăl·ist, *n.* [*often* S–] one who adheres literally to the Scriptures.
scrip'tūr·ăl·ly, *adv.* [*often* S–] in a scriptural manner.
scrip'tūr·ăl·ness, *n.* [*often* S–] scriptural quality. [Rare.]
scrip'tūre, *n.* [OFr. *escripture,* from L. *scriptura,* a writing.]
1. a writing; anything written, as manuscripts, documents, etc. [Obs.]
2. [S–] [*usually in plural*] the books of the

Old and New Testaments; the Bible: also (*the*) *Holy Scriptures*, (*the*) *Holy Scripture*.
3. [S–] a passage or text of the Bible. [Rare.]
4. any sacred or religious writing or books.

Scrip·tū′ri·ăn, *n.* a Scripturist. [Obs.]

Scrip′tūr·ist, *n.* one well versed in the Scriptures; also, a Scripturalist.

sçrit, *n.* script; a writing; a scroll. [Obs.]

sçritch, *n.* a shrill cry; a screech. [Archaic.]

sçrīve, *v.t.*; scrived, *pt., pp.*; scriving, *ppr.* [a variant of *scribe.*] to scratch; to score; to scribe. [Chiefly Scot.]

sçri·vel′lō, *n.*; *pl.* **sçri·vel′lōeş,** [Port. *escrevelho.*] an elephant's tusk.

sçriv′en, *v.t.* and *v.i.* to write. [Obs.]

sçrive′nẽr, *n.* [OFr. *escrivain*; It. *scrivano*, from LL. *scribanus*, from L. *scribere*, to write.]
1. a public clerk, draftsman, or copyist; scribe. [Archaic.]
2. a notary. [Archaic.]
3. formerly, a moneylender; a broker.
scriveners' palsy; writers' cramp.

sçrōbe, *n.* [L. *scrobis*, a ditch.] in entomology, a groove, either on the outer side of the mandible or the inside of the rostrum.

sçrō·biç′ū·là, *n.*; *pl.* **sçrō·biç′ū·lae,** [L. *scrobiculus*, little ditch, dim. of *scrobis*, a ditch.] a smooth surface surrounding the tubercle of a sea urchin.

sçrō·biç′ū·lăr, *a.* of or relating to a scrobicula.

sçrō·biç′ū·lāte, sçrō·biç′ū·lā·ted, *a.* pitted; having numerous small, shallow depressions or hollows; furrowed.

sçrō·biç′ū·lus, *n.*; *pl.* **sçrō·biç′ū·lī,** [L., a little ditch.] a pit or fossa; a slight depression.
scrobiculus cordis; the pit of the stomach.

sçrod, *n.* [from M.D. *schrode*, strip.] a young codfish, split and prepared for cooking.

sçrof′ū·là, *n.* [L. *scrofula*, usually in pl. *scrofulæ*, little swellings.] tuberculosis of the lymphatic glands, especially of the neck, characterized by the enlargement and degeneration of the glands; king's evil.

sçrof′ū·lide, *n.* [*scrofula* and *-ide.*] any disorder of the skin or mucous membrane due to the presence of scrofula.

sçrof′ū·lous, *a.* 1. pertaining to scrofula, or partaking of its nature; as, *scrofulous* tumors.
2. diseased or affected with scrofula.
3. morally corrupt; degenerate.

sçrof′ū·lous·ly, *adv.* in a scrofulous manner.

sçrog, *n.* a stunted shrub, bush, or branch. [Scot. and Brit. Dial.]

sçrog′gy, *a.* stunted; shriveled; full of brushwood. [Scot. and Brit. Dial.]

sçrōll, *n.* [ME. *scrowe, scroue*; OFr. *escroue.*]
1. a roll of parchment or paper, usually with writing upon it.
2. an ancient book in the form of a rolled manuscript.
3. a list or schedule; as, the *scroll* of Fame.
4. anything resembling a partially unrolled sheet of paper, as (a) the volute of the Ionic and Corinthian capitals; (b) the curved head of instruments of the violin type, bearing the tuning pins; (c) a kind of volute at a ship's bow; a scrollhead; (d) a flourish added, as a seal, to a person's name in signing a paper; (e) in heraldry, the ribbonlike appendage to a crest or escutcheon on which the motto is inscribed; (f) a streamer or pennon; (g) a panel or tablet in the form of a parchment scroll, used for an inscription on stone or carved work; (h) the balloon or ribbon used to contain the words of a speaker in certain pictures; (i) a turbinate bone; (j) a spiral ornament on furniture, etc.

sçrōll, *v.t.*; scrolled, *pt., pp.*; scrolling, *ppr.* 1. to write, as on a scroll; to enroll; to record.
2. to make a scroll of; to ornament with scrolls.
3. to form into a scroll.

sçrōll, *v.i.* to roll or curl up into a spiral form.

sçrōll chuck, a spindle chuck for a lathe arranged to be adjusted by a plate with a spiral groove.

sçroll çreep′ẽr, in architecture, a curved ornament, sometimes resembling foliage; a crocket.

sçrōll′-çut, *a.* cut with a scroll saw or cut in the shape or form of a scroll.

sçrōlled, *a.* enclosed in a scroll or roll; formed into a scroll; ornamented with scrolls or scrollwork.

sçrōll′ẽr·y, *n.* scrollwork.

sçrōll frŏnt, in furniture making, a front with a compound curve.

sçrōll′head(-hed), *n.* an ornamental piece at the bow of a vessel, finished off with carved work in the form of a volute or scroll turning outward.

sçrōll saw, a very narrow blade or ribbon of steel with fine saw teeth on one edge, adjusted in a frame, adapted for sawing out intricate patterns in wood, involving short curves.

sçrōll′wŏrk, *n.* 1. ornamental work with a scroll or scrolls as the basic design.
2. ornamental work cut out with a scroll saw.

Sçrooġe, *n.* 1. the hard, miserly old man in Dickens' story *A Christmas Carol*, who is made kindly and gentle by the revelations of spirits that visit him on Christmas Eve.
2. any miserly, stingy person.

sçroop, *v.i.* [echoic.] 1. to produce a rustling or crisp crunching sound; said of silks.
2. to make a strident, grating sound. [Dial.]

sçroop, *v.t.* 1. to cause (a fabric, particularly silk) to produce a rustle, as by twisting or pressing it.
2. to treat (a fabric) so as to make (it) capable of producing a rustle; as, has this silk been *scrooped?*

sçroop, *n.* 1. a harsh tone or sound. [Dial.]
2. the rustle of silk; the rustling sound made by a silk fabric.

Sçroph·ū·lā′ri·à, *n.* [so called because supposed to cure scrofula.] a genus of plants, the species of which are commonly known as figwort.

Sçroph·ū·lā·ri·ā′cē·ae, *n.pl.* [from *Scrophularia*, one of the genera.] a large family of herbaceous or shrubby monopetalous exogens, inhabiting most parts of the world, and including about 160 genera and 2,000 species. Many of the genera, such as *Digitalis, Calceolaria, Veronica, Pentstemon*, etc., are valued for their flowers. Also written *Scrophularineæ*.

sçroph·ū·lā·ri·ā′ceous, *a.* of or relating to the *Scrophulariaceæ*, the figwort family.

sçrō′tăl, *a.* of or relating to the scrotum.

sçrō′ti·fọrm, *a.* [L. *scrotum*, scrotum, and *-form.*] pouch-shaped.

sçrō′tō·cēle, *n.* [L. *scrotum*, scrotum, and Gr. *kēlē*, a tumor.] a rupture or hernia in the scrotum.

sçrō′tum, *n.*; *pl.* **sçrō′tà, sçrō′tumş,** [L. *scrotum*, scrotum.] in anatomy, the pouch of skin containing the testes and related structures in the higher mammals.

sçrouġe, *v.t.*; scrouged, *pt., pp.*; scrouging, *ppr.* [earlier *scruze*, probably echoic.] to squeeze; to crowd. [Brit. Dial.]

sçrou′ġẽr, *n.* one who crowds. [Brit. Dial.]

sçrounġe, *v.t.* and *v.i.*; scrounged, *pt., pp.*; scrounging, *ppr.* [prob. echoic extension, suggested by *scrouge.*] to look around for and take (something) without permission; to pilfer. [Slang.]

sçrow, *n.* 1. clippings from hides used to make glue.
2. a scroll. [Obs.]

sçroyle (skroil), *n.* a mean fellow; a wretch. [Obs.]

sçrub, *v.t.*; scrubbed, *pt., pp.*; scrubbing, *ppr.* [ME. *scrobben*, probably from ON.]
1. to clean or wash by rubbing or brushing hard.
2. to remove by brushing or rubbing.
3. to rub hard.
4. to cleanse (a gas) of impurities.

sçrub, *v.i.* 1. to rub hard; to clean a thing by scrubbing.
2. to be diligent and penurious; as, to *scrub* hard for a living. [Dial.]

sçrub, *n.* 1. the act of scrubbing.
2. a person who works hard and lives meanly; a drudge.

sçrub, *n.* [dial. var. of *shrub*, influenced by ON.; collective senses, from Australia.]
1. (a) originally, a straggly, inferior tree or shrub; (b) short, stunted trees, bushes, or shrubs growing thickly together; (c) land covered with such growth.
2. any person or thing smaller than the usual, or inferior in quality, breed, etc.
3. in sports, (a) a player not on the varsity squad or regular team; (b) [*pl.*] a team made up of such players.

sçrub, *a.* 1. mean; poor; inferior.
2. undersized; undernourished; small.
3. of or for players not on the varsity squad or regular team.
4. impromptu; hastily got up; as, a *scrub* game.

sçrub′bẽr, *n.* 1. one who scrubs.
2. a scrubbing brush.
3. a washing device for illuminating gas.
4. a hide washer in a tannery.
5. in Australia, a domestic animal running wild in the scrub.

sçrub′bīrd, *n.* a brush bird of Australia, *Atrichornis clamosa*.

sçrub′bōard, *n.* a baseboard.

sçrub′by, *a.*; *comp.* scrubbier; *superl.* scrubbiest, 1. stunted in growth; undersized or inferior.
2. covered with or consisting of brushwood, or scrub.
3. paltry, shabby, etc.

sçrub grȧss, the scouring rush.

sçrub ōak, any of several small species of oak, as *Quercus ilicifolia*, a shrublike oak of the Eastern States, and *Quercus catesbæi*, of the Southern States.

sçrub pīne, in botany, any of several small species of pine, as the Jersey or New Jersey pine, the Hudson Bay pine, etc.

sçrub rob′in, a bird of the Australian scrub, of the genus *Drymodes*.

sçrub shrub, a gumwood shrub of St. Helena, of the aster family.

sçrub tũr′key, the lowan; a mound bird.

sçruff, *n.* [from earlier *scuff*, var. of *scurf.*] the back or nape of the neck; also, the loose skin covering it.

sçrum, *n.* a scrummage. [Brit. Colloq.]

sçrum′măġe, *n.* [dial. var. of *scrimmage.*] in Rugby, a formation around the ball in which the two sets of forwards compactly pressed together try to push their opponents away from the ball and restart the play by breaking away with it or kicking it out.

sçrum′măġe, *v.t.* and *v.i.*; scrummaged, *pt., pp.*; scrummaging, *ppr.* to play or place (the ball) in a scrummage.

sçrump′tious (-shus), *a.* [from *sumptuous.*] very fine; first-rate; splendid. [Slang.]

sçrunch, *v.t.* and *v.i.*; scrunched (skruncht), *pt., pp.*; scrunching, *ppr.* [from *crunch.*] to crunch; to crush; to chew noisily and with force.

sçrunch, *n.* a sound or act of crunching.

sçrṳ′ple, *n.* [Fr. *scrupule*, a scruple, from L. *scrupulum*, acc. of *scrupulus*, a small, sharp stone, hence, a small stone used as weight, a small weight; also a sharp stone, as in a man's shoe, an uneasiness, difficulty, small trouble, doubt.]
1. doubt; hesitation from the difficulty of determining what is right or expedient; reluctance to decide or to act because of questions of conscience; as, *scruples* of conscience.
2. an apothecary's weight of twenty grains, the third part of a dram, or 1/24 ounce.
3. a very small quantity or amount.
4. an ancient Roman weight, 1/288 of an as (1/24 of an ounce).

sçrṳ′ple, *v.t.* and *v.i.*; scrupled, *pt.; pp.*; scrupling, *ppr.* to hesitate (at) from doubt or uneasiness; to be unwilling because of conscientious motives; to have scruples (about): usually followed by an infinitive.

sçrṳ′plẽr, *n.* one who has scruples.

sçrṳ′pū·list, *n.* a scrupler.

sçrṳ′pū·līze, *v.t.* to scruple. [Obs.]

sçrṳ·pū·los′i·ty, *n.* [L. *scrupulositas* (*-atis*), from *scrupulosus*, scrupulous.]
1. the quality of being scrupulous.
2. *pl.* **sçrṳ·pū·los′i·tieş,** an instance of this.

sçrṳ′pū·lous, *a.* [L. *scrupulosus*, scrupulous.]
1. having or showing scruples; characterized by careful attention to what is right or proper; conscientiously honest and upright.
2. (a) careful of details; precise, accurate, and correct; exact; (b) demanding, or characterized by, precision, care, and exactness.
3. given to making objections; captious. [Obs.]
4. doubtful. [Obs.]

sçrṳ′pū·lous·ly, *adv.* in a scrupulous manner.

sçrṳ′pū·lous·ness, *n.* scrupulosity.

sçrṳ′tȧ·ble, *a.* discoverable by inquiry or critical examination; that can be scrutinized.

sçrṳ·tā′tion, *n.* search; scrutiny.

sçrṳ·tā′tŏr, *n.* [L., from *scrutari*, to examine.] one who scrutinizes; a close examiner or inquirer.

sçrṳ·tiṅ′(-taṅ′)d′ȧr·rọṅ·dïsse·ment′(-mäṅ′), see *scrutin de liste*.

scru·tin' (-tan') de liste, [Fr., voting by list.] in France, a method of voting for the Chamber of Deputies according to which the voter casts his ballot for the whole number of deputies apportioned to his department: distinguished from *scrutin d'arrondissement* in which the voter ballots only for the officers of his own arrondissement.

scru·ti·neer', *n.* one who scrutinizes; especially, one who makes an examination of votes.

scru'ti·nize, *v.t.*; scrutinized, *pt., pp.*; scrutinizing, *ppr.* [from *scrutiny* and *-ize.*] to observe closely; to examine or inquire into critically; as, to *scrutinize* the measures of administration.

Syn.—examine, investigate.

scru'ti·nize, *v.i.* to make close investigation.

scru'ti·ni·zer, *n.* one who scrutinizes.

scru'ti·nous, *a.* closely examining; captious.

scru'ti·nous·ly, *adv.* in a scrutinous manner.

scru'ti·ny, *n.*; *pl.* **scru'ti·nies,** [ME. *scruteny,* from LL. *scrutinium,* a careful inquiry; L. *scrutari,* to search into carefully.]

1. close observation; minute inquiry; critical examination; as, a *scrutiny* of votes.
2. formerly, an examination of catechumens in the last week of Lent, preparatory to baptism on Easter day.
3. in canon law, a ticket or little paper billet on which a vote is written.
4. in parliamentary language, an examination of the votes cast at an election, conducted by a committee.
5. one of the methods of electing a pope, consisting of a secret ballot.

scru·toire' (-twär'), *n.* an escritoire. [Archaic.]

scruze, *v.t.* to crowd; to squeeze. [Obs.]

scry, *v.t.* to descry. [Obs.]

scry, *v.i.* to cry out. [Obs.]

scry, *n.* a cry. [Obs.]

scu'ba, *n.* [self-contained *u*nderwater *b*reathing *a*pparatus.] an apparatus including tanks of compressed air, worn by divers for breathing underwater: also written **Scuba, SCUBA.**

scud, *v.i.*; scudded, *pt., pp.*; scudding, *ppr.* [prob. from dial, *scut,* a tail, especially of a hare; influenced by *scoot.*]

1. to run or move swiftly; to glide or skim along easily.
2. to be driven or run before the wind.

scud, *v.t.* to pass or skim rapidly over; as, to *scud* a plain.

scud, *n.* 1. the act of scudding; a driving along; a running or rushing with speed.

2. loose vapory clouds or spray driven swiftly by the wind.

Borne on the *scud* of the sea.—Longfellow.

3. a slight flying shower. [Brit. Dial.]
4. in school slang, a swift runner; a scudder.
5. a slap with the open hand. [Scot.]
6. a sand flea or any small crustacean.

scud'der, *n.* one who or that which scuds.

scud'dle, *v.i.* to scuttle. [Obs.]

scu'do, *n.*; *pl.* **scu'di,** [It., orig., a shield; L. *scutum,* a shield: so named from bearing a shield.] a former monetary unit and gold or silver coin of Italy and Sicily, valued at about one dollar.

scuff, *n.* [ON. *skopt,* hair.] the back part, or scruff, of the neck.

scuff, *v.t.*; scuffed (skuft), *pt., pp.*; scuffing, *ppr.* [from ON. *skūfa,* to shove, push.]

1. to scrape (the ground, floor, etc.) with the feet.
2. to wear a rough place or places on the surface of.
3. to touch or brush lightly in passing.
4. to move (the feet) with a dragging motion.

scuff, *v.i.* to walk without lifting the feet; to shuffle.

scuff, *n.* 1. a noise or act of scuffing.

2. a worn or rough spot.
3. a loose-fitting house slipper without a heel or counter.

scuf'fle, *v.i.*; scuffled (-fld), *pt., pp.*; scuffling, *ppr.* [from *scuff* and *-le,* freq. suffix.]

1. to struggle or fight in rough confusion.
2. to drag the feet; to shuffle; to scuff.

scuf'fle, *n.* 1. a rough, confused fight; a close, haphazard struggle.

2. a shuffling; as, the *scuffle* of feet.

scuf'fler, *n.* one who scuffles.

scug, *v.t.* and *n.* same as *skug.*

scul·dud'der·y, *n.* same as *skulduddery.*

scul·dug'ger·y, *n.* same as *skulduggery.*

sculk, *v.i.* same as *skulk.*

sculk'er, *n.* same as *skulker.*

scull, *n.* [Gael.] a large, wicker basket, usually shallow, used to carry fishing tackle or produce. [Scot.]

scull, *n.* [ME. *sculle;* prob. from ON.; akin to *skull.*]

1. an oar twisted from side to side over the stern of a boat to move it forward.
2. one of a pair of light oars with concave blades, used, one on each side of a boat, by a single rower.
3. a light, narrow racing boat for one or more rowers.

scull, *v.i.* and *v.t.* to use a scull or sculls; to propel, as a boat, with a scull or sculls.

scull'er, *n.* 1. a boat rowed by one man with two sculls or short oars.

2. one who sculls or rows with sculls; one who propels a boat by an oar over the stern.

scul'ler·y, *n.*; *pl.* **scul'ler·ies,** [OFr. *escueillier,* a place where bowls are kept; *escuelle,* a bowl, a platter, from L. *scutella,* a salver, tray.] a place where dishes, kettles, and other culinary utensils are kept and cleaned; a room back of the kitchen where the coarse work is done; a back kitchen.

scul'lion (-yun), *n.* [OFr. *escouillon,* a dishcloth.]

1. a servant who cleans pots and kettles and does other rough work in the kitchen.
2. a low, miserable fellow; a wretch.

sculp, *v.t.* 1. to carve; to engrave. [Obs.]

2. to remove the skin and blubber from; as, to *sculp* a seal.
3. to break scross the grain for splitting, as slate blocks.

sculp, *n.* the skin of a seal when removed from the animal and before the blubber has been detached.

scul'pin, *n.* [prob. from Fr. *scorpene,* from L. *scorpæna,* sea scorpion.]

1. any one of several marine fishes of the genus *Cottus,* generally scaleless, with a large head and wide mouth.
2. the bullhead, a related fresh-water fish.

sculp'sit, [L.] he (or she) carved (it): placed after the artist's name on a sculpture, etc.

sculpt, *v.t.* and *v.i.* [Fr. *sculpter,* altered (after *sculpture*) from *sculper,* from L. *sculpere,* to carve in stone.]

1. to carve or model as a sculptor.
2. to give sculpturelike form to (hair, fabric, etc.).

Also *sculp.*

sculp'tile, *a.* [L. *sculptilis,* formed by carving.] formed by carving; graven.

sculp'tor, *n.* [L., from *sculpere,* to carve in stone.] a person who models or carves figures of clay, stone, metal, wood, etc.; an artist who creates three-dimensional representations.

sculp'tress, *n.* a woman sculptor. [Rare.]

sculp'tur·al, *a.* of or like sculpture.

sculp'ture, *n.* [Fr.; L. *sculptura,* sculpture, from *sculptus,* pp. of *sculpere,* to carve in stone.]

1. the art of carving wood, chiseling stone, casting and welding metal, modeling clay or wax, etc. into three-dimensional representations, as statues, figures, forms, etc.
2. any work of sculpture, or such works collectively.
3. the shaping of the surface of the earth, as by weathering, especially by erosion by water or wind.
4. in zoology, the raised or incised markings or the manner of arrangement of such markings; as, the *sculpture* of a beetle's elytra.
5. an engraved illustration. [Obs.]

sculp'ture, *v.t.*; sculptured, *pt., pp.*; sculpturing, *ppr.* 1. to cut, carve, chisel, cast, or mold into statues, figures, etc.

2. to represent or portray by means of sculpture.
3. to make or form by means of sculpture.
4. to decorate with sculpture.
5. to change in form by erosion; as, the river has *sculptured* the rock.

sculp'tured, *a.* in zoology and botany, having raised or depressed surface markings.

sculptured tortoise; a land tortoise, *Glyptemys insculpta;* the wood tortoise.

sculp·tur·esque' (-esk'), *a.* having the appearance or characteristics of sculpture; pertaining to sculpture; statuelike; statuesque.

scum, *n.* [ME. *scume;* MD. *schum;* akin to G. *schaum,* foam, scum.]

1. a thin layer of impurities which forms on the top of liquids or bodies of water, often as the result of boiling or fermentation.
2. the dross or refuse on top of molten metals.
3. refuse; worthless parts of anything.
4. a low, despicable, worthless person, or such people collectively.

scum, *v.t.*; scummed, *pt., pp.*; scumming, *ppr.* to take the scum from; to clear off the impure matter from the surface of; to skim.

scum, *v.i.* to rise to the surface in the form of scum; to have or form a covering of scum.

scum'ber, *v.i.* to dung: said of foxes. [Obs. except Brit. Dial.]

scum'ber, *n.* dung, as of foxes. [Obs. except Brit. Dial.]

scum'ble, *v.t.*; scumbled, (-bld) *pt., pp.*; scumbling, *ppr.* [from *scum.*]

1. in painting, (a) to soften the outlines or color of by applying a thin coat of opaque color; (b) to apply (color) in this manner.
2. in drawing, to soften the outlines of by rubbing or blurring.
3. to make by either of these processes.

scum'ble, *n.* 1. a coat of color added in scumbling.

2. the softening of outline produced by scumbling.

scum'bling, *n.* 1. in painting and drawing, the toning down of a picture by one who scumbles it.

2. the color used in this process.

scum'mer, *v.i.* to scumber. [Obs.]

scum'mer, *n.* an instrument used for taking off scum; a skimmer.

scum'mings, *n.pl.* matter skimmed off.

scum'my, *a.*; *comp.* scummier; *superl.* scummiest, 1. covered with scum.

2. of or like scum.
3. despicable; low; worthless; mean.

scun'ner, *v.i.* 1. to loathe; to feel disgust. [Scot. and Brit. Dial.]

2. to shrink back from in disgust or fear. [Scot. and Brit. Dial.]

scun'ner, *n.* loathing; abhorrence. [Dial.]

scup, *n.* a swing. [Dial.]

scup, *n.*; *pl.* **scup** or **scups,** [Am.Ind.] any of a group of marine food fishes, as *Stenotomus argyrops,* related to the grunts and snappers, found on the Atlantic coast of the United States: also called *porgy.*

scup·paug', *n.* same as *scup* (the fish).

scup'per, *n.* [from OFr. *escope,* bailing scoop.] an opening in the sides of a ship for carrying off the water from the deck: also called *scupper-hole.*

scup'per, *v.t.* to disable; to put in great difficulty; to annihilate, as by a surprise attack. [Brit. Slang.]

scup'per·nong, *n.* [from the *Scuppernong* River in North Carolina.]

1. a yellowish-green grape with a plumlike flavor.
2. the wine made from this grape.

scur, *n.* and *v.* same as *skirr.*

scurf, *n.* [ME. *scurf, scorf, scrof;* AS. *scurf.*]

1. little, dry scales shed by the skin, as dandruff.
2. any scaly matter adhering to the surface.
3. in botany, scales on the leaves of some plants.
4. scum; refuse; offscouring.

scurf'i·ness, *n.* 1. the state of being scurfy.

2. scurf.

scurf'y, *a.*; *comp.* scurfier; *superl.* scurfiest, having scurf; covered with scurf; resembling scurf.

scur'ri·er, *n.* one who or that which scurries.

scur'rile, scur'ril, *a.* [L. *scurrilis,* buffoonlike, from *scurra,* a buffoon.] scurrilous; as, *scurrile* scoffing. [Archaic.]

scur·ril'i·ty, *n.* [L. *scurrilitas* (*-tatis*), from *scurrilis,* buffoonlike.]

1. the quality of being scurrilous; low, vile, or obscene jocularity.
2. *pl.* **scur·ril'i·ties,** that which is scurrilous; a scurrilous act or remark.

scur'ril·ous, *a.* 1. using low and indecent language; vulgar; as, a *scurrilous* fellow.

2. containing low indecency or abuse; mean; foul; vile; obscenely jocular; as, *scurrilous* language.

Syn.—low, foul, indecent, mean, opprobrious, gross, vulgar, ribald, coarse.

scur'ril·ous·ly, *adv.* in a scurrilous manner.

scur'ril·ous·ness, *n.* the state of being scurrilous; scurrility.

sçur'ry, *v.i.*; scurried, *pt., pp.*; scurrying, *ppr.* [from *hurry-scurry*; perhaps a fusion of *hurry* and *scour.*] to move rapidly; to hurry; to hasten; to scamper.

sçur'ry, *a.* scurrying.

sçur'ry, *n.* 1. a hasty running; scampering.
2. the sound of hasty running.
3. a short run or race.

sçũr'vi·ly, *adv.* in a scurvy manner; basely; meanly.

sçũr'vi·ness, *n.* the state or quality of being scurvy.

sçũr'vy, *a.*; *comp.* scurvier; *superl.* scurviest, [from *scurf.*]
1. originally, scurfy.
2. low; mean; vile; contemptible.

sçũr'vy, *n.* [from the adj.] a disease resulting from a deficiency of vitamin C in the body, characterized by weakness, anemia, spongy gums, bleeding from the mucous membranes, etc.

sçũr'vy gràss, *Cochlearia officinalis,* a plant of the mustard family with heart-shaped leaves, small white flowers, and a tarlike flavor, used in salads and as a medicine.

sçūse, *v.* and *n.* excuse. [Colloq.]

sçut, *n.* [ME., a tail, hare; prob. from ON.] a short, stumpy tail, as that of a hare or deer.

sçū'tȧ, *n.* plural of *scutum.*

sçū'tāġe, *n.* [LL. *scutagium,* from L. *scutum,* a shield.] in feudal law, a tax paid by the holder of a knight's fee, usually in lieu of military service.

sçū'tăl, *a.* of or pertaining to a scute or scutum.

sçū'tāte, *a.* [LL. *scutatus,* shield-shaped.]
1. in botany, formed like a shield: said especially of leaves joined to the stalk at about the center of the lower surface instead of at the base.
2. in zoology, protected or covered by bony or horny plates or scales.

sçutch, *v.t.*; scutched (skucht), *pt., pp.*; scutching, *ppr.* [LL. *excussare,* to shake much.]
1. to dress by beating; specifically, (a) to separate, as the individual fibers of cotton after they have been loosened and cleansed; (b) to beat off and separate, as the woody parts of the stalks of flax; (c) to disentangle, straighten, and cut into lengths, as floss and refuse silk.
2. to beat; to drub; to chastise. [Scot. and Brit. Dial.]

sçutch, *n.* 1. an instrument for dressing flax or hemp; a scutcher.
2. the tow or refuse of scutched flax.

sçutch'eŏn (-un), *n.* [ME. *scochoun*; contr. of *escutcheon.*]
1. an escutcheon.
2. in ancient architecture, the shield or plate on a door, from the center of which hung the door handle.
3. the ornamental cover or frame to a keyhole.
4. a metal plate, as for a name or initial, on a coffin, pocket knife, or other object.
5. a scute.

sçutch'eŏned (-und), *a.* emblazoned, as on a scutcheon.

sçutch'ẽr, *n.* one who or that which scutches; specifically, a machine in which cotton, flax, or silk is scutched.

sçutch gràss, same as *doob grass.*

sçūte, *n.* [L. *scutum,* a shield.]
1. an external bony or horny plate, as of a reptile; a scutum.
2. a small shield; a buckler. [Obs.]
3. an old French gold coin. [Obs.]

sçū·tel'lȧ, *n.* plural of *scutellum.*

sçū·tel'lȧ, *n.*; *pl.* **sçū·tel'lae,** [L., a tray.]
1. in zoology, a scutellum.
2. [S–] a genus of circular sea urchins, type of the family *Scutellidæ.*

sçū'tel·lăr, *a.* of or pertaining to a scutellum.

Sçū·tel·lā'ri·ȧ, *n.* [LL., from L. *scutella,* a tray.] a genus of perennial labiate plants, of the mint family, having toothed leaves and varicolored two-lipped flowers: also called *skullcap.*

sçū·tel'lā·rin, *n.* a crystalline resin, $C_{21}H_{18}O_{12}$, distilled from the *Scutellaria* and other labiate plants.

sçū'tel·lāte, *a.* [Mod. L. *scutellatus,* from *scutellum*; see *scutellum.*] covered or protected with scutella, or small scales or plates.

sçū'tel·lāte, *a.* [from L. *scutella,* a salver, dim. of *scutra,* a tray; and *-ate.*] in botany and zoology, shaped like a shield or platter; round.

sçū'tel·lā·ted, *a.* same as *scutellate.*

sçū·tel·lā'tion, *n.* the state of being covered with scutellae; the arrangement of scales on a tarsus.

sçū·tel'li·fọrm, *a.* having the form of a scutellum; scutellate, as the scales on a bird's leg.

sçū″tel·li·plan'tăr, *a.* [L. *scutellum,* dim. of *scutum,* shield, and *planta,* any flat surface, as the sole of the foot.] having scales on the back of the tarsus, as larks.

sçū·tel″li·plan·tā'tion, *n.* in zoology, the condition of having a scutelliplantar foot. [Rare.]

sçū·tel'lum, *n.*; *pl.* **sçū·tel'lȧ,** [L., dim. of *scutum,* a shield.]
1. in botany, any of various parts shaped like a shield; specifically, (a) the single large cotyledon enveloping the embryo in grasses; (b) in lichens, a shield with an elevated rim formed by the thallus.
2. in entomology, a part of the thorax, sometimes invisible, sometimes, as in some hemipters, large, and covering the elytra and abdomen.
3. in zoology, a small horny scale of plate.

sçū·tel'lum rot, a seedling disease of germinating corn, caused by fungi of the genera Penicillium, Rhizopus, and others.

sçū'ti·brañçh, *a.* of or pertaining to the *Scutibranchiata.*

sçū'ti·brañçh, *n.* a member of the *Scutibranchiata.*

Sçū·ti·brañ'çhi·ȧ, *n.pl.* same as *Scutibranchiata.*

sçū·ti·brañ'çhi·ăn, *a.* same as *scutibranch.*

Sçū″ti·brañ·çhi·ā'tȧ, *n.pl.* [LL., from L. *scutum,* shield, and *branchiæ,* gills.] in older classifications, an order of gastropods characterized by a shieldlike shell and a heart with two auricles and one ventricle.

sçū·ti·brañ'çhi·āte, *a.* same as *scutibranch.*

sçū·tif'ẽr·ous, *a.* [L. *scutum,* a shield, and *ferre,* to bear.] carrying a shield.

sçū'ti·fọrm, *a.* having the form of a shield; scutate.

sçū'ti·ġẽr, *n.* a centipede of the genus *Scutigera.*

Sçū·tiġ'ẽr·ȧ, *n.* [L. *scutum,* shield, and *gerere,* to carry.] in zoology, a genus of myriapod insects or centipedes; the typical genus of the family *Scutigeridæ,* characterized by numerous many-jointed legs and long, delicate, segmented antennae.

sçū·tiġ'ẽr·ous, *a.* characterized by bearing a scute or scutes.

sçū'ti·ped, *a.* [L. *scutum,* shield, and *pes, pedis,* foot.] designating birds which have the anterior part of the legs covered with segments of horny rings terminating on each side in a groove. [Rare.]

sçut'tẽr, *v.i.* [from *scuttle,* to run.] to scurry about; to bustle. [Brit. Colloq. or Dial.]

sçut'tẽr, *n.* a scurry; a hasty, rapid running. [Brit. Colloq. or Dial.]

sçut'tle, *n.* [ME. *scotille*; AS. *scutel,* a dish, bowl, from L. *scutella,* a salver, tray, dim. of *scutra,* a dish or platter.]
1. a broad, shallow basket with a narrow base and a wide mouth, used for carrying grain, vegetables, etc.
2. a bucketlike vessel of sheet metal, used for carrying or holding coal.

sçut'tle, *n.* [OFr. *escoutille,* the scuttle or hatch of a ship; Sp. *escotilla.*]
1. in ships, a small hatchway or opening in the deck, large enough to admit a man, and with a lid for covering it; also, a like hole in the side or bottom of a ship, or through the coverings of her hatchways.
2. a hole in a wall or roof, fitted with a lid or cover.
3. the lid or cover for such an opening.

sçut'tle, *v.t.*; scuttled, *pt., pp.*; scuttling, *ppr.* 1. to cut large holes through the bottom, deck, or sides of (a ship or boat).
2. to sink (a ship or boat) by making holes through the bottom; as, to *scuttle* a ship.

sçut'tle, *v.i.* [freq. of *scud,* and the same as *scuddle.*] to run or move quickly; to scurry, especially away from danger, trouble, etc.

sçut'tle, *n.* a scurry or scamper; a hasty flight or departure.

sçut'tle·butt, *n.* [from *scuttled butt,* a butt or cask on shipboard with fresh drinking water.]
1. a drinking fountain on shipboard. [Slang.]
2. rumor or gossip. [Slang.]

sçut'tle·çȧsk, *n.* same as *scuttlebutt.*

sçū'tū·lum, *n.* [L., dim. of *scutum,* shield.]
1. a little shield; specifically, in zoology, a scutellum.
2. in pathology, a scab; a crust of favus.

sçū'tum, *n.*; *pl.* **sçū'tȧ,** [L.] 1. the long, leather-covered, wooden shield carried by infantrymen in the Roman legions.

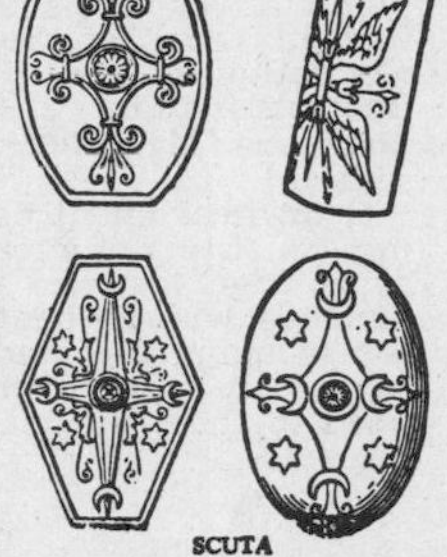
SCUTA

2. in zoology, (a) the second section of the upper surface of a thoracic segment of an insect; (b) a heavy horny scale or platelet, especially such as is developed in the integument of many reptiles.
3. [S–] in astronomy, a small constellation in the Milky Way, supposedly resembling a shield in shape.

sçuz'zy, *a.; comp.* scuzzier; *superl.* scuzziest, [origin unknown.] dirty, shabby, disreputable, etc. [Slang.]

scyb'ȧ·lȧ, *n.pl.* [LL., from Gr. *skybalon,* offal, dung.] in pathology, small indurated balls or fragments into which the feces become converted when too long retained in the colon.

scȳe (sī), *n.* the curve cut in the body piece of a garment before the sleeve is sewed in, to suit the contour of the arm.

Scyl'lȧ, *n.* [L. *Scylla*; Gr. *Skylla,* from *skylax,* dog, as *Scylla* is said to have barked like a dog.] a huge, dangerous rock on the coast of Italy, supposed to be the abode of the mythical monster, Scylla, which seized and wrecked passing vessels. Just across the narrow Straits of Messina, near Sicily, was a dangerous whirlpool, thought to be the home of another monster, Charybdis; for a vessel to avoid one meant the great risk of falling into the clutches of the other.
between Scylla and Charybdis; facing difficulty or danger on either hand; between two perils or evils, neither of which can be evaded without risking the other.

Scyl·lae'ȧ, *n.* [from L. *Scyllæus,* of Scylla.] a genus of nudibranchiate gastropods. The common species, *Scyllæa pelagica,* is found on gulfweed, wherever this appears.

scyl·lăr'i·ăn, *a.* of or pertaining to the *Scyllaridæ.*

scyl·lăr'i·ăn, *n.* one of the family *Scyllaridæ.*

Scyl·lar'i·dae, *n.pl.* [LL., Gr. *skyllaros,* a kind of crab.] a family of long-tailed decapod crabs, characterized by the wide, flat carapace, the large and leaflike outer antennae, and the partly flexible tail fan, by which they drive themselves through the water.

scy̆'phȧ, *n.*; *pl.* **scy̆'phae,** in botany, same as *scyphus,* sense 2 (b).

scy̆'phi-, [from L. *scyphus,* cup.] a combining form meaning *scyphus* or *cup,* as in *scyphiform.*

scy̆'phi·fọrm, *a.* [*scyphi-* and *-form.*] in botany, having the form of a cup or goblet.

scȳ·phis'tō·mȧ, *n.*; *pl.* **scȳ·phis·tō'mȧ·tȧ,** [LL., from Gr. *skyphos,* a cup, and *stoma,* mouth.] the larval form of *Discophora*; applied to it at the time when it is attached and resembles a hydroid.

scy̆'phis·tōme, *a.* of or pertaining to a scyphistoma.

Scȳ″phō·mē·dū'sae, *n.pl.* [LL., from Gr. *skyphos,* cup, and LL. *Medusa.*] a subclass of *Hydrozoa.*

Scȳ·phoph'ō·rī, *n.pl.* [LL., from Gr. *skyphos,* cup, and *pherein,* to bear.] an order of freshwater physostomous fishes found in the tropical waters of Africa.

scȳ·phoph'ō·rous, *a.* of or pertaining to the *Scyphophori.*

scȳ·phō·pol'yp, *n.* [Gr. *skyphos,* cup, and *polypous,* many-footed, from *poly,* many, and *pous,* foot.] in zoology, a coelenterate resembling the hydropolyp, but having the oral region modified into what is known as the esophageal tube.

scȳ'phōse, *a.* with or pertaining to scyphi.

scȳ'phō·stōme, *n.* same as *scyphistoma.*

scȳ·phō·zō'ăn, *n.* [from Gr. *skyphos,* cup, and *zōion,* an animal.] any of a number of sea coelenterates, chiefly jellyfishes.

scyph′ū·lus, *n.*; *pl.* **scyph′ū·lī,** [LL. *scyphulus*, dim. of L. *scyphus*, cup.] in botany, a cup-shaped false perianth, such as is found in lichens.

scȳ′phus, *n.*; *pl.* **scȳ′phī,** [Gr. *skyphos*, a cup or goblet.]
1. a form of ancient Greek drinking cup with two flat-topped handles and no foot.
2. in botany, (a) the coronet or cup of such plants as the narcissus; (b) in lichens, a cup-like dilatation of the podetium or stalklike elongation of the thallus, bearing shields upon its margin.

scȳthe, *n.* [ME. *sithe*; AS. *sithe*, for *sigthe*, a scythe.]
1. an instrument used in mowing or reaping, consisting of a long curving blade with a sharp edge, fastened at an angle to a handle, or snath, which is bent into a convenient form for swinging the blade to advantage. Most scythes have two small projecting handles, fixed to the principal handle, by which they are held.

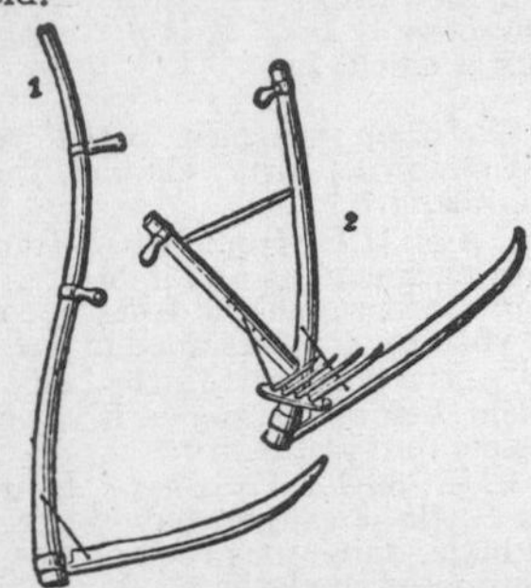

SCYTHE
1. common scythe; 2. cradle scythe

2. the sharp blade used in ancient times on the wheels or axles of war chariots.

scȳthe, *v.t.*; scythed, *pt.*, *pp.*; scything, *ppr.* to cut with a scythe.

scȳthed, *a.* armed with scythes, as a chariot.

scȳthe′măn, *n.*; *pl.* **scȳthe′men,** one who uses a scythe; a mower.

scȳthe′stōne, *n.* a whetstone used for sharpening scythes.

Scyth′i·ăn, *a.* pertaining to Scythia, an ancient region in southeastern Europe and Asia, its people, their language, etc.

Scyth′i·ăn, *n.* 1. one of a nomadic and warlike people who lived in ancient Scythia.
2. their Iranian language.

sdāin, *v.t.* and *n.* disdain. [Obs.]

'sdeath (zdeth), *interj.* God's death: a euphemistic. exclamation indicating anger, impatience, surprise, etc. [Archaic.]

sdeign (sdān), *v.t.* disdain. [Obs.]

Se, in chemistry, selenium.

sēa (sē), *n.* [ME. *see*; AS. *sæ*, sea, lake; Ice. *sær*; G. *see*; Goth. *saiws*; prob. connected with Gr. *huei*, it rains; Sans. *sava*, juice, water.]
1. the continuous body of salt water which covers the greater part of the earth's surface; the ocean.
2. a large body of salt water wholly or partly enclosed by land; as, the Red *Sea*, Irish *Sea*.
3. a large body of fresh water; as, *Sea* of Galilee.
4. something like or suggesting the sea in extent or vastness; very great amount or number; as, lost in a *sea* of debt.
5. a wave; a billow; as, to ship a *sea*.
6. the state of the surface of the ocean with regard to waves or swells; also, the direction of the waves; as, heavy *seas*; to head the *sea*.
at full sea; at high water.
at sea; (a) on the open sea; (b) in a vague uncertain condition; bewildered; as, he was quite *at sea* in his guess.
beyond the sea or *seas*; out of the realm or country.
cross sea or *chopping sea*; a sea in which waves are moving in different directions.
half seas over; half-drunk. [Slang.]
main sea; the open ocean. [Archaic.]
on the sea; (a) on the seacoast; as, a city *on the sea*; (b) on the ocean.
short sea; a sea in which the waves are irregular, broken, and interrupted.
the four seas; the seas bounding Great Britain, on the north, south, east, and west.
to follow the sea; to make one's living by serving on ocean-going ships.
to go to sea; (a) to become a sailor; (b) to sail away from land.

sēa ā′çorn, a barnacle.

sēa ad′dẽr, 1. the fifteen-spined stickleback.
2. any of various pipefishes of Europe.

sēa an̄′chŏr, a large, canvas-covered frame, usually conical, let out from a ship as a drag or float to reduce drifting or to keep the ship heading into the wind.

sēa ȧ·nem′ō·nē, any of various sea polyps of the *Actinozoa*, distinguished by the cylindrical form of the body, which is capable of dilatation and contraction. The mouth is furnished with numerous tentacles, by means of which the animal secures its food and which, when expanded, give the animal somewhat the appearance of a flower. They are often brightly colored and live attached to rocks.

sēa ān′ġel, the angel fish.

sēa āpe, 1. the sea otter.
2. the sea fox or fox shark.

sēa ap′ple, the fruit of *Manicaria plukenetii*, a palm of South and Central America, frequently found floating in the sea.

sēa ban̄k, 1. the seashore.
2. a bank built to defend against the sea.

sēa bȧs′ket, a basket fish.

sēa bȧss, 1. any serranoid fish, especially *Centropristis furvus* or *atrarius*, a food fish with large scales and a wide mouth, found along the Atlantic coast.
2. any of various similar marine fishes.
3. the sea salmon of the California coast, *Cynoscion nobilis*.

sēa bat, the batfish.

sēa′bēach, *n.* the beach of the sea, especially when sandy or shingly.

sēa bēan, a Florida bean.

sēa beãr, 1. a polar bear.
2. a fur seal.

sēa′bēard, *n.* a marine plant, *Cladophora rupestris*, growing in dense tufts.

sēa′bēast, *n.* a beast of the sea.

Sēa′bee, *n.* [from *Construction Battalion*.] a member of any of the construction battalions of the Civil Engineer Corps of the United States Navy: they build and defend harbor facilities, airfields, and the like.

sēa beet, a European wild beet, *Beta maritima*.

sēa bellṣ, a bindweed, *Convolvulus soldanella*, that grows on seacoasts.

sēa belt, a seaweed, *Laminnaria saccharina*, which grows upon stones and rocks by the seashore, the fronds of which resemble a belt or girdle.

sēa′ber″ry, *n.*; *pl.* **sēa′ber″rieṣ,** 1. the redberry.
2. an Australasian plant of the genus *Haloragis*.

sēa bīnd′weed, same as *sea bells*.

sēa bīrd, any bird living on or near the sea.

sēa bis′çuit (-kit), a type of hard biscuit formerly eaten by sailors; hardtack.

sēa blad′dẽr, the Portuguese man-of-war.

sēa blīte, any herb of the genus *Suæda*, found in salt marshes.

sēa blub′bẽr, a medusa or jellyfish.

sēa′bōard, *n.* the seashore.

sēa′bōard, *a.* bordering on the sea.

sēa bōat, 1. a vessel considered in reference to its capacity for withstanding a storm or the force of the sea; hence, a vessel adapted to heavy seas.
2. a mollusk of the genus *Chiton*.

sēa′-bọrn, *a.* 1. born in or of the sea.
2. produced by or originating in the sea.

sēa′-bọrne, sēa′bọrne (*or* -bōrn), *a.* 1. carried on or by the sea.
2. afloat: said of ships.

sēa′bound, *a.* bounded by the sea.

sēa boy, a boy employed on shipboard.

sēa brant, 1. the common brant. [Dial.]
2. the velvet scoter. [Dial.]

sēa brēach, irruption of the sea by breaking or overflowing the banks.

sēa bread (bred), hardtack; ship biscuit.

sēa brēam, 1. a marine fish, *Pagellus centrodontus*, of the family *Sparidæ*.
2. any fish of the family *Sparidæ*.

sēa breeze, a breeze blowing inland from the sea.

sēa brief, same as *sea letter*.

sēa buck′thorn, the sallow thorn.

sēa bū′gloss, the sea lungwort.

sēa but′tẽr·flȳ, a pteropod.

sēa çab′băġe, same as *sea kale*.

sēa çȧlf (kȧf), the harbor seal; the common seal.

sēa çam′pi·ŏn, a European. plant, *Silene maritima*.

sēa çȧ·nãr′y, same as *beluga* (sense 1).

sēa çap′tain (-tin), the chief officer of a seagoing vessel, especially in the merchant marine.

sēa çärd, the card of a mariner's compass.

sēa çat, [D. *zeekat*.] any one of several animals; (a) the wolf fish; (b) the fur seal; (c) the chimera; (d) the great weever; (e) the sea catfish.

sēa çat′fish, any one of many species of catfishes found on the eastern coast of America.

sēa çat′gut, a common seaweed, *Chorda filum*, the fronds of which are sometimes thirty or forty feet in length: also called *sea lace*.

sēa çau′li·flow·ẽr, a coral polyp, *Alcyonium multiflorum*.

sēa chick′weed, a plant that grows in large tufts in the seacoast sands of the North Atlantic: also called *sea purslane*.

sēa çlam, a large bivalve clam of the family *Mactridæ*, common in the United States on the sandy coasts of the Atlantic; the surf clam.

sēa çōal, coal dug from the earth; pit coal. [Archaic.]

sēa′çōast, *n.* the shore or border of the land adjacent to the sea or ocean; the seashore.

sēa′çōast, *a.* adjacent to the sea; as, a *seacoast* town.

sēa çob, a sea gull.

sēa çock, 1. either of two species of gurnard, *Trigla cuculus* and *Trigla hirax*.
2. a sea rover or viking.
3. any valve or cock in a vessel's hull that controls the pipe between the boiler and the water.

sēa çō′çō, a palm found in the Seychelles Islands that bears a large two-lobed fruit.

sēa çō′çō·nut, the double coconut, *Lodoicea seychellarum*.

sēa çŏl′ăn·dẽr, a brownish seaweed having fronds which are perforated with many small holes.

sēa çōle′wŏrt, sea cabbage.

sēa çŏm′pȧss, the mariners' compass.

sēa çọot, 1. a sea fowl, *Fulica americana*.
2. a black sea duck, the scoter.

sēa çọrn, a ribbon of egg capsules of certain species of whelk: also called *sea necklace*.

sēa çow, 1. any of several sea mammals, as the manatee and dugong.
2. the walrus.
3. the hippopotamus.

sēa′çrȧft, *n.* 1. ocean vessels.
2. naval skill.

sēa çrāy′fish, any edible crustacean of the genus *Palinurus*.

sēa çrōw, any seafowl of the gull kind, as the mire crow, cormorant, coot, razorbill, and chough.

sēa çū′çum·bẽr, any of a group of echinoderms with a cucumber-shaped body, leathery skin, and long, branched tentacles around the mouth; holothurian.

sēa daf′fō·dil, a perennial plant of the amaryllidaceous variety.

sēa dev′il, a large ray, especially *Manta birostris*; the devilfish; also, the angelfish (shark).

sēa dog, 1. the sea calf or harbor seal; also, the dogfish.
2. the fog dog.
3. a seaman, especially an experienced one.

sēa dot′tẽr·el, the turnstone.

sēa dōve, the dovekie or rotche.

sēa drag′ŏn, a teleostean fish, *Pegasus draco*, included among the *Lophobranchii*; a dragonet.

sēa drāke, 1. a cormorant.
2. a male eider duck.

sēa duck, any duck of the family *Anatidæ* inhabiting salt water; especially, the American eider duck.

sēa dust, fine powder or dust which has been blown out to sea from dry, arid lands: it is usually of a reddish color and when caught by falling rain drops, it becomes the so-called blood rain.

sēa ēa′gle, 1. the white-tailed eagle, *Haliaëtus albicilla*, found in all parts of Europe, generally on the seacoast, related to the bald

eagle, *Haliaëtus leucocephalus*; also, any fish-eating bird related to the bald eagle.
  2. the osprey.
  3. the eagle ray, a fish of the genus *Myliobatis*.

sēa′-ēar″, *n.* any mollusk of the genus *Haliotis*.

sēa eel, an eel living in salt water; especially, the conger eel.

sēa egg, *n.* a sea urchin.

sēa el′ē·phănt, any of several very large animals of the seal family, *Macrorhinus proboscideus*, that are hunted for oil: they sometimes attain a length of twenty feet. The nose of the adult male is elongated into a proboscis, somewhat like that of an elephant.

SEA ELEPHANT (*Macrorhinus proboscideus*)

sēa fan, *n.* a gorgonean coral that branches into the form of a fan.

sēa′fãr″ẽr, *n.* a traveler by sea; especially, a sailor or mariner.

sēa′fãr″ing, *a.* of or engaged in life at sea.

sēa′fãr″ing, *n.* 1. the business or profession of a sailor.
  2. travel by sea.

sēa feath′ẽr (feth′), *n.* 1. any plumelike gorgonean; a sea pen.
  2. a polyp, *Virgularia grandiflora*.

sēa fen′nel, same as *samphire*.

sēa fẽrn, a variety of coral resembling a fern.

sēa fīght (fīt), a battle fought between ships at sea; a naval action.

sēa fīr, any of certain polyps of the family *Sertulariidæ*.

sēa fīre, phosphorescence in the sea.

sēa flēa, any sand flea.

sēa′flow·ẽr, *n.* a sea anemone or a similar polyp.

sēa fōam, 1. the froth or foam of the sea.
  2. meerschaum.

sēa fo͝od, food prepared from or consisting of salt-water fish or shellfish.

sēa′fowl, *n.* a marine fowl; any bird that lives on or near the sea.

sēa fox, a kind of shark, *Alopias vulpes*, with a long tail fin: also called *fox shark*.

SEA FOX (*Alopias vulpes*)

sēa frŏnt, the part of a town or other built-up area facing on the sea.

sēa froth, same as *sea foam*.

sēa fũr′bē·lōw, any brown variety of seaweed, as of the genus *Laminaria*.

sēa′-gāte″, *n.* a long rolling wave or swell: also spelled *sea-gait*.

sēa gāte, 1. the entrance to a harbor from the sea.
  2. a gate to keep the water out of a dock, canal, basin, etc.

sēa gāuġe, 1. the draft, or depth, of water needed to float a ship.
  2. a gauge for ascertaining the depth of the sea.

sēa ghẽr′kin (gẽr′), any small holothurian that is formed like a gherkin or cucumber.

sēa gĩr′dle, a seaweed, *Laminaria digitata*: also called *tangle, sea wand*, etc.

sēa′gĩrt, *a.* surrounded by the sea or ocean; as, a *seagirt* island.

sēa′-god, *n.* a marine deity; a deity supposed to preside over the ocean or sea, as Neptune.

sēa′-god″dess, *n.* a female deity of the ocean; a marine goddess.

sēa′gō″ing, *a.* suitable for use on the open sea; as, a *seagoing* craft; also, seafaring.

sēa go͝ose, 1. a phalarope.
  2. a dolphin.

sēa go͝ose′foot, the sea blite, a marine plant.

sēa gown, a gown to be worn at sea. [Obs.]

sēa grāpe, 1. a plant of the genus *Ephedra*; especially, *Ephedra distachya*, closely allied to the conifers. The species consist of small trees or twiggy shrubs with jointed stems.
  2. the gulfweed.
  3. the eggs of cuttlefishes, which are agglutinated together in masses resembling bunches of grapes.

sēa gràss, 1. an aquatic plant of the genus *Ruppia*.
  2. eelgrass.

sēa′-green, *a.* having the color of sea water; a pale bluish-green.

sēa green, a sea-green color.

sēa gud′ġeŏn, the black goby, *Gobius niger*.

sēa gull, a bird with long wings and webbed feet, living near and feeding from the water; a gull.

sē′ăh, *n.* [Heb.] a Hebrew dry measure containing about twenty-four pints.

sēa hãre, a mollusk of the genus *Aplysia*.

sēa hawk, the jaeger.

sēa hēath, either of two species of British plants, *Frankenia lævis* and *Frankenia pulverulenta*.

sēa hedġe′hog, a sea urchin.

sēa hen, the guillemot.

sēa hog, the porpoise.

sēa hol′ly, a small plant of the genus *Eryngium*, with pale-blue flowers and spiny, bluish leaves.

sēa hōlm, sea holly.

sēa horse, 1. the walrus.
  2. the hippocampus, a small, semitropical fish with a slender tail, plated body, and a head and foreparts somewhat like those of a horse.
  3. a sea panther.
  4. a mythical sea creature depicted with fore parts like those of a horse, and with hinder parts like those of a fish.

SEA HORSE (3–10 in. long)

sēa′hound, *n.* a dogfish (shark).

sēa hul′vẽr, sea holly.

sēa′-īs″lănd (-ī′), *a.* of or from the Sea Islands, along the coast of Georgia, South Carolina, and Florida; as, *sea-island* cotton.

sēa′-īs″lănd çot′tŏn, a fine kind of longfibered cotton grown originally in the Sea Islands and now in other areas.

sēa jel′ly, a jellyfish.

sēa kāle, a fleshy mustard plant, *Crambe maritima*, whose young shoots are used like asparagus; sea cabbage.

sēa kid′ney, a polyp of the genus *Renilla*, resembling a kidney in shape.

sēa king, [Ice. *sækonungr*, a sea king, a viking.] a Norse pirate chief of the Middle Ages.

sēa kit′tie, the kittiwake. [Brit.]

sēal, *n.*; *pl.* **sēalṣ** or **sēal,** [ME. *sele*; AS. *seolh*, a seal; Ice. *selr*; Dan. *sæl*; Sw. *själ*; O.H.G. *selah*, a seal.]
  1. a sea mammal, of the family *Phocidæ*, the true seals, or *Otariidae*, the eared seals, with a torpedo-shaped body, a dog-like head, and four webbed feet or flippers: it lives in cold or temperate waters and eats fish: *fur seals* are hunted for the valuable fur.

FUR SEAL (5-6 ft. long)

  2. (a) the fur of the fur seal; sealskin; (b) a similar fur used as a substitute for this.
  3. leather made from sealskin.

sēal, *v.i.* to hunt seals.

sēal, *n.* [ME. *seel*; OFr. *seel*, a seal or signet, from L. *sigillum*, a seal, mark, lit., a little mark, from *signum*, a sign, mark.]
  1. a design, initial, or other device placed on a letter, document, etc. as a signature or proof of authenticity: letters were formerly closed with a wafer of molten wax into which was pressed the distinctive seal of the sender.
  2. a stamp, signet ring, etc. used for making such an impression.
  3. a wax wafer, piece of paper, etc. bearing the impression of some design recognized, usually by law, as official.
  4. something that seals, closes, or fastens tightly.
  5. something that confirms, authenticates, or guarantees; a pledge; as, his fear was a *seal* of secrecy.
  6. an indication; a sign; a token; as, their handshake was a *seal* of friendship.
  7. any device, as a looped trap filled with water, preventing the passage of gas through a pipe.
  8. an ornamental paper stamp; as, a Christmas *seal*.
  common seal; the official seal of a corporation, etc.

sēal, *v.t.*; sealed, *pt.*, *pp.*; sealing, *ppr.* [ME. *selen*; OFr. *seeler*; L. *sigillare*, to seal.]
  1. to fasten with a seal; to attach together with a wax wafer or with mucilage, tape, etc.; as, to *seal* a letter.
  2. to set or affix a seal to; as, to *seal* a deed.
  3. to confirm; to ratify; to establish.
  4. to shut; to close; to close completely; as, to *seal* one's lips.

> This is my alma mater; kind in the charity with which she *sealed* in sorrow my brief but stormy career within these walls.
> —Henry W. Grady.

  5. to mark with a stamp, as an evidence of standard exactness, of a given size, capacity, quality, etc.; as, to *seal* weights and measures.
  6. to attest to or confirm the truth or genuineness of (a promise, etc.).
  7. to grant, assign, or designate with a seal, pledge, etc.; as, he has *sealed* his estate to his son.
  8. to settle, determine, or decide finally or irrevocably.
  9. to fix, as a piece of wood or iron in a wall with cement, plaster, or other binding for staples, hinges, etc.
  10. in Mormonism, (a) to make formal and binding; to solemnize: said of a marriage, adoption, etc.; (b) to give (a woman) in marriage.
  11. in electricity, to bring into full, interlocking contact, as a plug and jack.
  Syn.—confirm, establish, ratify, close, fasten, shut.

sēal, *v.i.* to affix one's seal. [Obs.]

Sēa′lab, *n.* [*sea*, and *lab*oratory.] any of a series of experimental underwater laboratories developed by the United States Navy for undersea explorations and for research in oceanography, marine biology, etc.

sēa lāce, same as *sea catgut*.

sēa lam′prey, a common marine lamprey.

sēa lañ′guāġe, the slang, terms, and phraseology of seamen.

sēa lärk, a bird of the sandpiper kind, as the dunlin, turnstone, etc. [Brit. Dial.]

sēa lav′en dẽr, any of a number of related stiff plants with white, pink, lavender, or yellow flowers and many branches.

sēa law′yẽr, 1. a contentious sailor, who likes to argue points of sea law, usually on the basis of slight knowledge. [Colloq.]
  2. the gray snapper.
  3. a shark.

sēal′-brown, *a.* of a rich dark-brown color, like the dyed fur of a seal.

sēal brown, a seal-brown color.

sēaled or′dẽrṣ, written orders or instructions, as to the captain of a ship informing him of his destination, mission, etc., given in a sealed envelope not to be opened until a specified time or place is reached.

sēa legṣ, the ability to walk on a ship's deck without loss of balance, especially when it is pitching or rolling.

sēa lem′ŏn, a marine, nudibranchiate gastropod, of the genus *Doris*, having an oval body, convex, marked with numerous punctures, and of a lemon color.

sēa leop′ărd (lep′), an animal of the seal family near the antarctic circle: so named from being spotted like the leopard.

sēal′ẽr, *n.* 1. one who or that which seals.
  2. an officer appointed by proper authority, to inspect, test, and certify weights and measures, and set a stamp on such as are according to the standards established by the state.

sēal'ẽr, *n.* a hunter or ship engaged in sealing.
sēal'ẽr·y, *n.*; *pl.* **sēal'ẽr·ies,** a place where seals are hunted; also, the work of hunting seals.
sēa let'tẽr, a paper formerly issued by a customhouse, specifying the nature and quantity of the cargo on board a ship, its nationality, its destination, etc.
sēa let'tuce (-is), any of several seaweeds of the genus *Ulva*, with edible, leaflike parts.
sēa lev'el, the level of the surface of the sea, especially between high and low tides: used as a standard in measuring heights and depths.
sēal fish'ẽr·y, the occupation of hunting seals.
sealgh (selk), *n.* a seal. [Scot.]
sēa lil'y, a crinoid.
sēal'ing, *n.* the act of affixing a seal.
sēal'ing, *n.* the hunting of seals.
sēal'ing wax, a combination of resin and turpentine used for sealing letters, dry batteries, etc.: it is hard at normal temperatures but softens when heated.
sēa lī'ŏn, 1. any of several large, eared members of the seal family, *Otariidæ*, the best known of which is the *Otaria jubata*, or *Otaria stelleri*.

SEA LION (*Otaria jubata*)

2. in heraldry, a monster consisting of the upper part of a lion combined with the tail of a fish.
sēal lock, a lock in which the keyhole is covered by a seal, so arranged that the lock cannot be opened without breaking the seal.
sēa louse, any of various species of isopod crustaceans of the genus *Cymothoa*, parasitic on fishes; also, the Molucca crab.
sēal ring, a ring with an engraving or setting; a signet ring.
sēal'skin, *n.* 1. the skin or pelt of the seal, especially with the course outer hair removed and the soft undercoat dyed dark-brown or black.
2. a garment made of this.
sēal'skin, *a.* made of sealskin.
sēa lungs, any ctenophore.
sēa lung'wŏrt, a fleshy plant of the genus *Mertensia*, with egg-shaped, white-spotted leaves and white, purple, or blue flowers: it is found along northern seacoasts.
sēal'wŏrt, *n.* a plant, Solomon's seal.
Sēa'ly·ham ter'ri·ẽr, [so named from being bred at *Sealyham*, an estate in Pembrokeshire, Wales.] any of a small, long-bodied breed of terrier with short legs, a shaggy white coat, and a head like that of a Scottish terrier.
sēam, *n.* [AS. *seam*; G. *saum*, a sack of eight bushels, a horse load, from LL. *sauma*, *salma*, for L. *sagma*; Gr. *sagma*, a pack saddle.] a measure of eight bushels of grain, or the vessel that contains it. [Brit. Dial.]
sēam, *n.* tallow; grease; lard. [Obs.]
sēam, *n.* [ME. *seme*; AS. *seam*, a seam, suture.]
1. a line formed by sewing together two pieces of material.
2. any line formed by the joining together of separate pieces; a line marking adjoining edges, as of boards.
3. a mark, line, ridge, etc. like this, as a scar, wrinkle, mold line on glass, etc.
4. a thin layer or stratum of ore, coal, etc.
sēam, *v.t.*; seamed, *pt.*, *pp.*; seaming, *ppr.* 1. to join together so as to form a seam.
2. to mark with a seamlike line; as, *seamed* with wounds.
3. to give the appearance of a seam; to purl, as in knitting.
sēam, *v.i.* 1. to crack open; to become ridgy or fissured.
2. to sew. [Dial.]
3. in knitting, to purl.
sēa mag'pīe, same as *sea pie* (bird).
sēa māid, a mermaid; also, a sea nymph. [Obs. or Poetic.]
sēa mall, a sea gull.
sēa mal'lōw, the tree mallow, a plant of the genus *Lavatera*.
sēa'măn, *n.*; *pl.* **sēa'men,** 1. a sailor; a mariner.
2. an enlisted man ranking below a petty officer in the navy.
3. a merman. [Rare.]
sēa'măn·līke, *a.* like or characteristic of a good seaman; having or showing seamanship.
sēa'măn·ly, *a.* seamanlike.
sēa'măn·ship, *n.* the skill of a good seaman; skill in sailing or working a ship.
sēa man'tis, a squill.
sēa'märk, *n.* 1. any elevated object on shore, serving as a guide for a ship's course, as a beacon, lighthouse, mountain, etc.
2. a line marking the upper limit of the tide.
sēa mat, a bryozoan that forms a flat, frondlike coral.
sēa maw, a sea mew; a sea gull.
sēa mel'ŏn, a sea cucumber.
sēa mew, a sea gull.
sēa mīle, a nautical mile.
sēa milk'wŏrt, a fleshy, low, perennial herb of the primrose family, found in northern sea marshes.
sēam'ing, *n.* 1. the act of making seams.
2. the margin cords in a fish net to which the meshes are attached.
sēam'ing mȧ·chïne', a machine for forming seams or joints in the edges of sheet metal.
sēa mink, a kingfish, *Menticirrus saxatilis*.
sēam lāce, a lace used to cover seams and edges.
sēam'less, *a.* having no seam.
sēa mŏnk, the monk seal.
sēa mon'stẽr, 1. any huge marine animal.
2. a chimera.
sēa moss, 1. a mosslike marine bryozoan.
2. carrageen.
sēa mouse, 1. a segmented sea worm of the genus *Aphrodite*, with a flat, oval body covered with scales and iridescent bristles.
2. the dunlin. [Brit. Dial.]
sēam press'ẽr, 1. an implement consisting of two metal cylinders, which follows the plow to press down newly plowed furrows.
2. a tailors' pressing iron.
sēam set, a punch used by metalworkers to close seams in sheet metal, etc.
sēam'stẽr, *n.* one who sews well, or whose occupation is sewing; a tailor: now restricted to men.
sēam'stress, *n.* a woman who is expert at sewing, especially one who makes her living by sewing: also *sempstress*.
sēam'stress·y, *n.* the business of a seamstress. [Obs.]
sēa mud, a rich saline deposit from saltmarshes and seashores, sometimes used as a fertilizer: also called *sea ooze*.
sēam'y, *a.*; *comp.* seamier; *superl.* seamiest,
1. having a seam; containing seams or showing them.
2. having rough, unfinished edges, as the underside of a garment.
the seamy side; the least attractive aspect.
sean'ȧ·chie (sen'ȧ-ke), *n.* [Gael. *seannachaidh*, one skilled in history, a reciter of tales; *seannachar*, sagacious, *sean*, old.] a bard among the Scottish Highlanders who relates traditions of the clans.
Sean'äd Eir'eann (san'äd âr'ăn), [Ir.] the Senate, or upper house, of the legislature (*Oireachtas*) of Ireland.
sé'ance (sā'äns; *Fr.* sā-ons') *n.* [Fr. *séance*, from L. *sedens* (*-entis*), ppr. of *sedere*, to sit.]
1. a meeting or session, as of some public body.
2. a meeting of spiritualists at which they try to communicate with the spirits of the dead.
sēa neck'lăce, same as *sea corn*.
sēa nee'dle, the garfish, of the genus *Esox*.
sēa net'tle, any of certain *Medusæ* that sting when touched.
sēa nymph (nimf), a nymph or goddess of the sea.
sēa ŏn'iŏn (-yun), a plant, *Scilla maritima*, of the lily family, with wide leaves, dense clusters of small, whitish flowers, and a bulb used in medicine; squill.
sēa ooze, the soft mud on or near the seashore.
sēa or'ăch, an edible seacoast plant found in Europe.
sēa or'anġe (-enj), a red-tentacled holothurian having a globular body found in North America.
sēa orb, a globefish.
sēa ot'tẽr, a North Pacific web-footed sea mammal, *Enhydris marina*, of the family *Mustelidæ*, and closely related to the common otter. The fur is extremely soft, of a glossy dark-brown, and of great value.
sēa owl, the lumpfish.
sēa pad, a starfish.
sēa pan'thẽr, a fish like a lamprey.
sēa par'rŏt, the puffin.
sēa pär'tridġe (-trij), the English gilthead.
sēa pȧss, a passport carried by neutral merchant vessels in time of war to prove their nationality.
sēa pēach, an ascidian found in North America that resembles a ripe peach in appearance and size.
sēa peãr, a pear-shaped ascidian.
sēa pen, a kind of polyp that forms colonies having the shape of a feather.
sēa pẽrch, the European bass; also, various other fishes, especially the cunner and sea bass.
sēa pheas'ănt (fez'ănt), the pintail duck.
sēa pīe, a bird, the oyster catcher. [Brit.]
sēa pīe, a dish of food consisting of paste and meat boiled together.
sēa'pïēce, *n.* a picture representing the sea.
sēa pī'et, the sea pie (bird).
sēa pig, 1. the dugong.
2. a porpoise.
sēa pig'eŏn, the guillemot.
sēa pīke, 1. a fish of the perch family, *Centropomus undecimalis*, found on the coasts of tropical America: it resembles the pike in the elongation of its form.
2. the garfish.
3. the barracuda.
sēa pin'cush·iŏn, 1. a pentagonal starfish.
2. a sea purse.
sēa pink, a plant, *Armeria vulgaris*: also called *thrift*.

SEAPLANE

sēa'plāne, *n.* an airplane designed to land on and take off from water.
sēa pōach'ẽr, any small northern Atlantic fish of the family *Agonidæ*; especially, the lyrie and pogge: also called *sea poker*.
sēa pop'py, the horn poppy.
sēa por'cū·pīne, the *Diodon hystrix*, a fish having a body covered with spines; also, other similar fishes of the genus *Diodon*.
sēa'pōrt, *n.* 1. a port or harbor used for ocean ships.
2. a city or town having such a port or harbor.
sēa pow'ẽr, 1. naval strength.
2. a nation having great naval strength. Distinguished from *land power*.
sēa pump'kin, the sea cucumber.
sēa pũrse, a horny case or capsule in which the skate, ray, and certain sharks carry their eggs.
sēa pũrs'lāne, a plant of the genus *Atriplex*, as *Atriplex portulacoides* of Great Britain.
sēa pȳ'ŏt, same as *sea pie* (bird).
sēa quāil, the turnstone. [Dial.]
sēa'quāke, *n.* an earthquake on the floor of the sea.
sēar, *a.* [ME. *seer*; AS. *sear*, sere.] dry; withered.
sēar, *v.t.*; seared, *pt.*, *pp.*; searing, *ppr.* [ME. *seeren*; AS. *searian*, to dry up, to wither or pine away.]
1. to wither; to dry up.
2. to burn or scorch the surface of so as to make dry and hard.
3. to brand or cauterize with a hot iron.
4. to make callous or insensible; to harden; as, *seared* with wickedness.
to sear up; to close by searing or cauterizing; to stop.

sēar, *v.i.* to become sear; to wither.

sēar, *n.* any mark or condition produced by searing.

sēar, *n.* [Fr. *serre,* a lock, a bar, from L. *sera,* a bolt, a bar.] the catch in a gunlock by which the hammer is cocked or half-cocked.

sēa rag′wŏrt, same as *dusty miller* (sense 3).

sēa rat, a pirate. [Rare.]

sēa rā′ven, 1. an acanthopterygious fish of the sculpin or bullhead family, genus *Hemitripterus.*

2. a cormorant.

sēarce (sẽrs), *v.t.* to sift; to bolt. [Rare.]

sēarce, *n.* a sieve; a bolter. [Rare.]

sēar′cẽr, *n.* a searce, or sieve. [Rare.]

sēarch, *v.t.;* searched (sẽrcht), *pt., pp.;* searching, *ppr.* [ME. *serchen;* OFr. *cercher,* to seek, from L. *circare,* to go round, go about, explore; from *circus,* a ring, circle, *circum,* round about.]

1. to look over or through, for the purpose of finding something; to explore; to examine by inspection; as, to *search* the house for a book, to *search* the woods for a thief.

2. to examine (a person) for something concealed, by running one's hands over the clothing, through the pockets, etc.

3. to examine closely and carefully; to test and try; to probe; as, he *searched* his soul for the answer.

4. to pierce; to penetrate; to go through; as, the wind *searched* her ragged clothing.

to search out; (a) to seek by searching; (b) to find by searching.

Syn.—probe, examine, investigate, explore, hunt, pursue.

sēarch, *v.i.* to try to find something; to make a search.

sēarch, *n.* 1. an act of searching; scrutiny, inquiry, or examination in an attempt to find something, gain knowledge, etc.

2. a person or group that searches. [Rare.]

3. the act of a belligerent in stopping and searching a neutral ship for contraband: see *right of search.*

in search of; making a search for; trying to find, learn, etc. by searching.

sēarch′ȧ·ble, *a.* that can be searched or explored.

sēarch′ȧ·ble·ness, *n.* the state of being searchable.

sēarch′ẽr, *n.* 1. one who or that which searches.

2. an instrument used for examining the bore of a gun.

3. an instrument used in searching for calculi in the bladder.

sēarch′ing, *a.* 1. looking into or over; exploring; examining; inquiring; seeking; investigating; thorough; vigorous; as, a *searching* examination.

2. keen; sharp; piercing; penetrating; as, the *searching* wind.

sēarch′ing·ly, *adv.* in a searching manner.

sēarch′ing·ness, *n.* the quality of searching.

sēarch′less, *a.* inscrutable; eluding search or investigation.

sēarch′līght (-līt), *n.* 1. an apparatus so constructed that by means of reflectors, a powerful beam of light can be projected a great distance: it is usually mounted on a swivel so the beam may be directed.

2. the beam of light projected.

sēarch pär′ty, a group of people taking part in a search.

sēarch wạr′rănt, a legal document authorizing or directing a peace officer to search a specified person, premises, dwelling, etc., as for stolen or contraband articles, items to be used in evidence, suspected criminals, etc.

sēar′çloth, *n.* cerecloth.

sēared, *a.* scorched; hardened; also, insensible.

sēared′ness, *n.* the state of being seared.

sēa reed, a coarse grass, having roots that assist in binding shifting soil: also called *beach grass.*

sēa risk, risk or danger of injury or destruction involved in traveling or transporting by water.

sēa rob′bẽr, a pirate; one who robs on the sea.

sēa rob′in, any edible gurnard of the American genus *Prionotus,* having reddish coloring.

sēa rock′et, a cruciferous plant of the genus *Cakile,* growing on seashores.

sēa rod, a round-branched gorgonian.

sēa rọọm, space or distance from land, shoals, or rocks sufficient for maneuvering a ship.

sēa rōv′ẽr, 1. a pirate.

2. a pirate ship.

sēa′-rōv″ing, *a.* wandering on the ocean.

sēa ruf′fle, the sea corn.

sēa salm′ŏn (sam′), 1. a spotted squeteague or weakfish.

2. a young pollack.

sēa sạlt, salt obtained by evaporation of sea water.

sēa sand′pī·pẽr, the purple sandpiper.

sēa sand′wŏrt, a fleshy plant growing on the North Atlantic seacoast.

sēa′sçāpe, *n.* a view of the sea; also, a picture of this.

sēa sçor′pi·ŏn, a salt-water fish, *Cottus scorpius.*

sēa sẽr′pent, 1. any of various poisonous snakes of the family *Hydrophidæ,* of several genera, living in warm seas off the coast of Africa and in the Indian Archipelago: also called *sea snake.*

SEA SERPENT
(*Pelamis bicolor*)

2. a huge animal like a serpent living, or reported to live, in the sea.

sēa shell, the shell of any salt-water mollusk.

sēa′shōre, *n.* 1. the coast of the sea; the land that lies adjacent to the sea or ocean.

2. in law, the ground between the marks of ordinary high and low water.

sēa shrub, any gorgonian resembling a shrub.

sēa′sick, *a.* affected with seasickness.

sēa′sick″ness, *n.* the nausea, dizziness, etc. occasioned by the motion of a ship at sea.

sēa′sīde, *n.* the land bordering on the sea; the country adjacent to the sea; seashore; seacoast.

sēa′sīde, *a.* pertaining to or signifying the seaside.

seaside finch; a finch of the genus *Ammodromus,* common along the eastern coast of the United States. [Dial.]

seaside grape; the sea grape.

seaside pine; the pinaster.

sēa sleeve, a calamary.

sēa slug, 1. any of various gastropods lacking shells and belonging to the section *Nudibranchiata.*

2. a holothurian.

sēa snāil, a fish of the genus *Liparis;* also, any marine gastropod having a shell shaped like a helix.

sēa snāke, 1. any of a number of poisonous snakes living in tropical seas.

2. a sea serpent.

sēa snīpe, 1. the bellows fish.

2. the dunlin.

sēa′ṣŏn, *n.* [ME. *seson;* OFr. *seson, seison, saison;* Fr. *saison,* season, due time, from L. *sationem,* acc. of *satio,* a season, time of the year.]

1. a fit or suitable time; the convenient time; the usual or appointed time; as this is the topcoat *season.*

2. any one of the four arbitrary periods into which the year is divided, as marked by its characteristics of temperature, moisture, conditions of nature, and the like. In the temperate regions of the earth there are four distinct divisions or seasons—spring, summer, autumn, and winter. Spring lasts from March 21 to June 21, or 92 days; summer from June 21 to September 21, or 92 days; autumn from September 21 to December 21, or 91 days, and winter from December 21 to March 21, or 90 days, or 91 days in the case of leap year; that is, the interval from the autumnal to the vernal equinox is about three days shorter than the interval from the vernal to the autumnal equinox. This discrepancy is due to the form of the earth's orbit, the earth describing during the autumn and winter months that portion of its orbit nearest the sun, and therefore with the greatest velocity. Within the tropics the seasons are not greatly marked by the rise or fall of temperature, so much as by dryness and wetness, and they are usually distinguished as the *wet* and the *dry seasons.*

3. a time or part of the year during which a specified kind of agricultural work is done; as, the planting *season,* harvest *season,* etc.

4. the time when something specified flourishes, develops, takes place, is popular, permitted, or at its best; as, the opera *season,* orange *season,* fishing *season,* etc.

5. a period of time, especially a relatively short one.

6. the time of a specified festival; as, the Christmas *season.*

7. that which gives a relish; seasoning. [Obs.]

You lack the *season* of all nature, sleep.
—Shak.

for a season; for a while.

in good season; early enough.

in season; (a) available fresh for use as food: said of fruits, vegetables, sea food, etc., usually of a locality specified or understood; (b) at the legally established time for being hunted or caught: said of game, etc.; (c) in or at the suitable or proper time; (d) in good season; early enough; (e) ready to mate or breed: said of animals.

in season and out of season; at any time; at all times.

out of season; not in season.

sēa′ṣŏn, *v.t.;* seasoned, *pt., pp.;* seasoning, *ppr.* 1. to add to or change the flavor of (food); to flavor; as, to *season* meat with salt.

2. to give a relish, zest, or interest to.

The proper use of wit is to *season* conversation.
—Tillotson.

3. to imbue; to tinge or taint.

4. (a) to make more suitable for use; to improve the quality of, as by aging, exposure to air, etc.; to cure; to mature; (b) to give (an athlete) experience to improve his play.

5. to make used to; accustom; inure; acclimatize; as, he was *seasoned* to the hard life.

6. to make less harsh or severe; to temper; soften; as, *season* your remarks with discretion.

7. to impregnate or copulate with. [Obs.]

sēa′ṣŏn, *v.i.* 1. to become seasoned or more suitable for use.

2. to betoken; to savor. [Obs.]

sēa′ṣŏn·ȧ·ble, *a.* 1. opportune; that comes, happens, or is done at the right time; as, a *seasonable* supply of rain.

2. suitable to or usual for the time of year.

Syn.—opportune, timely, fit, convenient.

sēa′ṣŏn·ȧ·ble·ness, *n.* the state or quality of being seasonable, or in good time.

sēa′ṣŏn·ȧ·bly, *adv.* in a seasonable manner; at the right time or season; as, to sow or plant *seasonably.*

sēa′ṣŏn·ȧge, *n.* seasoning. [Obs.]

sēa′ṣŏn·ăl, *a.* 1. of or characteristic of the season or seasons.

2. affected by or depending on a season.

3. coming at regular intervals.

seasonal dimorphism; the quality possessed by certain insects of appearing in distinctly differing forms in different seasons.

sēa′ṣŏn·ăl·ly, *adv.* 1. with or at a given season.

2. in a seasonal manner; periodically.

sēa′ṣŏn·ẽr, *n.* one who seasons; that which seasons.

sēa′ṣŏn·ing, *n.* 1. that which is added to food as flavoring, as salt, spices, etc.

2. anything that adds zest, interest, or variety.

sēa′ṣŏn·less, *a.* without succession of the seasons.

sēa′ṣŏn tick′et, a ticket that entitles the holder to use or service, usually unlimited, for a given period or series of events: season tickets are sold for railroad travel, play on golf courses, entertainments, etc.

sēa spī′dẽr, 1. a marine crab of the genus *Maia.*

2. any pycnogonoid.

sēa squīrt, a small sea animal with a flabby body that contracts to shoot out jets of water; an ascidian; a tunicate.

sēa stär, a starfish.

sēa stär′wŏrt, a European maritime plant, *Aster tripolium.*

sēa sûr′ġeŏn, a surgeonfish.

sēa swäl′lōw, 1. any bird of the tern family; especially, the common tern.

2. the stormy petrel.

sēa swīne, 1. a dolphin or porpoise.

2. the ballan wrasse.

sēat, *n.* [ME. *sete;* ON. *sæti,* set; Sw. *säte,* a

seat, from base of *sit*; L.G. *sitt*, G. *sitz*. The AS. seems only to have had the dim. form *setl*.]

1. the manner of sitting, as on horseback.

2. the place or space where a person sits; a place to sit; as, I can't find a *seat*.

3. a thing to sit on; a chair, bench, stool, etc.

4. the buttocks.

5. the part of a garment covering the buttocks.

6. the part of a chair, bench, etc. that supports the buttocks.

7. the right to sit as a member; position of a member; membership; as, he has a *seat* on the commission.

8. a part or surface upon which the base of something rests.

9. the place where something is carried on, settled, or established; center; location; as, the *seat* of government, *seat* of learning.

10. the town where a king, bishop, etc. makes his home.

11. a home; residence; especially, a large house that is part of a country estate.

sēat, *v.t.*; seated, *pt., pp.*; seating, *ppr.* 1. to put or place in or on a seat; to cause to sit down.

2. to put, fix, or establish in a post of authority, in office, a place of distinction, etc.

3. to help or settle into a seat.

4. to have a seat or seats for; to accommodate with a seat or seats; as, the stadium *seats* 50,000 people.

5. to repair by making a new seat; to put a seat in or on; to reseat; as, to *seat* a garment or a chair.

6. to settle; to plant with inhabitants; as, to *seat* a country. [Obs.]

to be seated; (a) to take a seated position; to sit down; (b) to be in a seated position; to be sitting; (c) to be located, settled, or situated.

sēat, *v.i.* to rest; to lie down. [Archaic.]

sēa tan′gle, any of various seaweeds.

seat belt, a restraining device, usually consisting of anchored straps that buckle across the hips, to protect a seated passenger from abrupt jolts, as in a collision.

sēat′ẽr, *n.* something having (a specified number of) seats: used in hyphenated compounds, of automobiles, airplanes, etc., as in two-*seater*, four-*seater*.

sēa tẽrm, a word or term used by seamen; a nautical word or phrase.

sēa thiēf, a pirate. [Rare.]

sēa thọng, a kind of seaweed, *Himanthalia lorea*.

sēa thrift, the sea pink.

sēat′ing, *n.* 1. the act of furnishing with a seat or seats.

2. the material for making seats or seat covering, as horsehair, leather, etc.

3. the arrangement of seats or of persons seated.

4. (a) a seat (sense 8); (b) a part that rests on this.

sēa tit′ling, the rock pipit, *Anthus aquaticus*. [Brit. Dial.]

sēat′less, *a.* without a seat.

sēa tōad, 1. the angler, or sea frog, *Lophius piscatorius*.

2. the toadfish, *Batrachus tau*.

3. the sculpin.

sēa trout, 1. a rock trout, *Hexagrammus decagrammus*.

2. any of several species of weakfish.

3. any of the trout family that inhabit salt water before and after spawning: related to the salmon.

sea trum′pet, 1. a species of seaweed, *Ecklonia buccinalis*, found in the southern seas: a kind of trumpet is made from the hollow stem.

2. a gastropod of the genus *Triton*.

sēa tûrn, a wind or breeze from the sea, generally followed by inclement weather.

sēa tûr′tle, 1. a large marine turtle.

2. the black guillemot.

sēat wŏrm, the pinworm.

sēa ū′ni·cọrn, the narwhal.

sēa ûr′chin, any of several sea animals of the echinoderm family, having a flattened globular body of fused plates covered with a spiny skin.

sēa valve, a sea cock or valve communicating with the water through a ship's hull.

sēa vam′pīre, a devilfish.

sēave, *n.* [Sw. *säf*; Dan. *siv*.] a rush.

sēav′y, *a.* overgrown with rushes. [Brit. Dial.]

sēa wạll, a strong wall or embankment on the shore to prevent encroachments of the sea, to form a breakwater, etc.

sēa′-wạlled, *a.* surrounded or defended by a sea wall.

sēa′wăn, *n.* same as *sewan*.

sēa wänd, same as *sea girdle*.

sēa′wănt, *n.* same as *sewan*.

sēa′wărd, *n.* a direction or position away from the land and toward the sea.

sēa′wărd, *a.* 1. directed, going, or situated toward the sea.

2. from the sea: said of a wind.

sēa′wărd, *adv.* toward, or in the direction of, the sea.

sēa′wărdṣ, *adv.* same as *seaward*.

sēa′wāre, *n.* [via dial., from AS. *sæware*, seaweed; *sæ*, sea, and *ware*, alga.] seaweed; especially, large, coarse seaweed tossed up on shore.

sēa′wāy, *n.* 1. a way or route by sea; the sea as a means of travel.

2. the movement of a ship through the water.

3. the open sea.

4. a rough sea.

sēa′weed, *n.* 1. any sea plant or plants; especially, any marine alga, as kelp: in full, *marine seaweed*.

2. any similar freshwater plant: in full, *freshwater seaweed*.

sēa whip (hwip), a whiplike gorgonean coral.

sēa whip′cọrd, sēa whip′lash, same as *sea catgut*.

sēa whis′tle (hwis′l), a common seaweed with vesicles or bladders from which children make whistles.

sēa widġ′eŏn, the pintail duck; also, the scaup duck.

sēa′wīfe, *n.* a marine fish, *Labrus vetula*, allied to the wrasse.

sēa wil′lōw, a polyp of the genus *Gorgonia*.

sēa wind, a wind blowing from the sea over the land.

sēa wing, a bivalve mollusk allied to the mussels.

sēa with′wind, a species of bindweed, *Convolvulus soldanella*: also called *sea bells*.

sēa wolf (wulf), 1. any of several large ferocious sea fishes, as the sea bass, blenny, etc.: also called *wolf fish*.

2. a sea elephant, sea lion, etc. [Obs.]

3. a pirate.

sēa wood′çock, the bar-tailed godwit. [Brit. Dial.]

sēa wŏrm, any of the marine annelids.

sēa wŏrm′wood, a sort of wormwood, *Artemisia maritima*, growing by the sea.

sēa′wŏr″thi·ness, *n.* the quality or condition of being seaworthy.

sēa′wŏr″thy, *a.* fit to travel in on the open sea; safe in rough weather; sturdy: said of a ship.

sēa wrack (rak), seaweed, especially of the large kinds.

sēax, *n.* [AS., a knife.] a kind of weapon having a short curved blade, used by the early Celts and Germans. [Archaic.]

sē·bā′ceous, *a.* [L. *sebaceus*, of tallow, from *sebum*, tallow, grease.] of or like fat, tallow, or sebum; especially, designating certain glands in the skin that secrete sebum.

sē·bac′iç, *a.* [from L. *sebaceus*, tallow candle, from *sebum*, tallow; and *-ic*.] designating or of a white, crystalline acid, $C_{10}H_{18}O_4$, obtained by the distillation of oleic acid.

sē′-bap″tist, *n.* [L. *se*, oneself, and Eng. *baptist*.] one of a sect who baptize themselves, founded by John Smythe, who is said to have baptized himself on seceding from the Brownists in the seventeenth century.

Sē·bat′, *n.* same as *Shebat*.

sē′bāte, *n.* [L. *sebum*, tallow, and *-ate*.] in chemistry, a salt formed by sebacic acid and a base.

sē·bes′ten, *n.* either of two trees, *Cordia myxa* and *Cordia latifolia*, of the borage family, found in Egypt, India, and Australia, yielding very mucilaginous nuts, which are edible and also valued for medicinal properties.

sē′bi-, [from L. *sebum*, tallow.] a combining form meaning *tallow, wax*, as in *sebi*ferous.

sē′biç, *a.* sebacic. [Obs.]

sē·bif′ẽr·ous, *a.* [*sebi-* and *-ferous*.] secreting a fatty or waxlike substance; sebaceous.

sē·bip′ȧ·rous, *a.* producing tallow or fatty matter; sebaceous.

seb′kȧ, *n.* one of the salt marshes of northern Africa.

seb·ọr·rhē′ȧ, seb·ọr·rhoē′ȧ (-rē′), *n.* [L. *sebum*, tallow, and Gr. *rhoia*, a flow, from *rhein*, to flow.] a condition marked by an excessive discharge from the sebaceous glands, forming white or yellowish greasy scales on the skin.

sē′bum, *n.* [L., tallow.] a semiliquid, greasy matter secreted by the sebaceous glands.

sē·bun′dee, *n.* same as *sebundy*.

sē·bun′dy, *n.* [Anglo-Ind.] in India, formerly, an irregular native soldier, employed by the British chiefly on revenue and police service.

seç, *a.* [Fr.] dry; not sweet: said of wine.

Se·cā′lē, *n.* [L.] a genus of grasses including the cereal rye.

Seç·ȧ·mō′nē, *n.* a genus of plants belonging to the family *Asclepiadaceæ*, found in the warm parts of India, Africa, and Australia. The species form erect or climbing smooth shrubs with opposite leaves and lax cymes of small flowers.

sē′căn·cy, *n.* an intersection or cutting.

sē′çant, *a.* [L. *secans* (*-antis*), ppr. of *secare*, to cut.] cutting; intersecting.

sē′çant, *n.* 1. any straight line intersecting a curve at two or more points.

2. in trigonometry, (a) a straight line extending from the center of a circle through the end of an arc of its circumference to another straight line that is tangent to the radius at the other end of the arc; (b) the length of this; (c) the ratio of the length of this line to the length of the radius; hence, (d) the ratio of the length of the hypotenuse of any right-angled triangle to the length of either of the other two sides with reference to the enclosed angle.

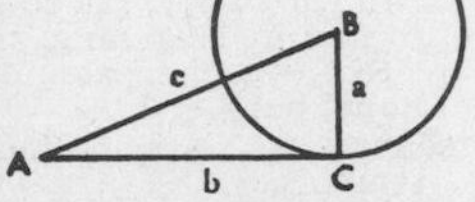

B c a A b C

SECANT

$\frac{c}{a}$, secant of angle ABC

$\frac{c}{b}$, secant of angle BAC

seç′cō, *a.* 1. in painting, dry.

2. in music, unaccompanied.

seç′cō, *n.* [It., from L. *siccus*, dry.] tempera painting done on dry plaster: distinguished from *fresco*.

sē·cēde′, *v.i.*; seceded, *pt., pp.*; seceding, *ppr.* [L. *secedere*, to go away; *se*, apart, and *cedere*, to go.]

1. to withdraw from fellowship; to go into retirement. [Obs.]

2. to withdraw formally from membership in a group, association, organization, etc.; to break off one's connection with others, as in a political or religious group.

sē·cēd′ẽr, *n.* 1. one who secedes.

2. [S–] in Scotland, one of a body of Presbyterians who seceded from the Church of Scotland in 1733.

sē·cẽrn′, *v.t.*; secerned, *pt., pp.*; secerning, *ppr.* [L. *secernere*, to sunder, separate; *se*, aside, and *cernere*, to separate.]

1. to discriminate, or distinguish.

2. in physiology, to secrete. [Rare.]

sē·cẽrn′ent, *a.* secreting.

sē·cẽrn′ent, *n.* any secreting organ.

sē·cẽrn′ment, *n.* the act of secerning or the state of being secerned.

sē·cesh′, *n.* a secessionist; also, secessionists collectively. [Colloq.]

sē·cess′, *n.* retirement; retreat. [Obs.]

sē·ces′sion (-sesh′un), *n.* [L. *secessio* (*-onis*), a going apart, separation, from *secessus*, pp. of *secedere*, to go away, withdraw.]

1. an act of seceding; formal withdrawal or separation.

2. [*often* S-] the withdrawal of a State from the Federal Union.

3. the act of withdrawing from fellowship and communion; retirement. [Obs.]

sē·ces′sion·ăl, *a.* of or constituting secession.

sē·ces′sion·iṣm, *n.* the doctrine or principles of secession.

sē·ces′sion·ist, *n.* 1. one who favors, takes part in, or upholds secession.

2. [often S–] in the history of the United States, one who believed in and advocated the right of a State to withdraw from the Federal Union; one who sympathized with or who aided in the secession of the Southern States at the start of the Civil War.

sē′chi·um, *n.* [Gr. *sēkos*, a pen or fold in which cattle are reared and fed.] a West Indian climbing plant, *Sechium edule*, of the gourd family: it yields an edible fruit, in size and form resembling a large pear, and has a large starchy root which is boiled and eaten by the natives.

Se·chuä′nä (-chwä′), *n.* any of a group of Bantu dialects spoken in the southern part of Northern Rhodesia.

seck, *a.* [Fr. *sec*, from L. *siccus*, dry.] barren; unprofitable.

Seck′el, *n.* a small, sweet, juicy, reddish-brown variety of pear. It ripens about the end of October, but keeps good for only a few days: first produced on the farm of Mr. Seckel, a Pennsylvania fruitgrower. Also *Seckel pear.*

sē′çle, *n.* a century. [Obs.]

sē·çlūde′, *v.t.*; secluded, *pt., pp.*; secluding, *ppr.* [L. *secludere*, to shut off; *se*, apart, and *claudere*, to shut.]

1. to keep away or apart from others; to bar or shut off from the view of or relations with others; to isolate.

2. to make private or hidden; to screen.

3. to shut out; to prevent from entering. [Obs.]

sē·çlūd′ed, *a.* shut off or kept apart from others; isolated; remote; withdrawn; as, a *secluded* meeting place.

sē·çlūd′ed·ly, *adv.* in a secluded manner.

sē·çlūd′ed·ness, *n.* the state of being secluded.

sē·çlūse′ness, *n.* the state of being secluded. [Obs.]

sē·çlū′ṣion, *n.* [ML. *seclusio* (*-onis*), from L. *secludere*, to shut off.]

1. a secluding or being secluded; retirement; as, to live in *seclusion*.

2. a secluded spot.

Syn.—privacy, solitude, retirement, separation, loneliness.

sē·çlū′sive, *a.* tending to seclude; also, fond of or seeking seclusion.

seç′ōhm, *n.* [*sec*ond, the unit of time, and *ohm*, the unit of resistance.] in electricity, a henry.

seç′ŏnd, *a.* [ME. *second, secounde*; Fr. *second*, second, from L. *secundus*, following, second, from *sequi*, to follow.]

1. next in order after the first in time or place; the ordinal of two; as, take the *second* apple in the row; the *second* day of the month.

2. in power, excellence, dignity, rank, etc., next after the first or highest; hence, inferior; secondary; subordinate; as, in accomplishments she is *second* to none; a city *second* in population.

3. like a preceding one in character; resembling a given original; as, a *second* Napoleon.

4. another; other; additional; supplementary; as, we all took a *second* helping.

5. in music, lower in pitch, or performing a part lower in pitch or secondary in importance; as, a *second* voice, a *second* flute.

at second hand; in the second place of order; not in the first place, or by or from the first; indirectly; not primarily; not originally; as, a report received *at second hand*.

Second Advent; in the theology of some Christian sects, the expected return of Christ to earth to sit in judgment of both the living and the dead; the millennium.

Second Adventist; a person who expects the Second Advent, especially a member of a sect having a belief in the millennium as part of its doctrine.

second base; in baseball, the base between first base and third base, located behind the pitcher.

second best; something next to the best.

second childhood; senility; dotage.

Second Coming; the Second Advent.

second cousin; the son or daughter of one's parent's first cousin.

second distance; in art, same as *middle distance*.

second estate; see *estate* (sense 2).

second fiddle; (a) the part played by the second violin section of an orchestra; also, any member of this section; (b) a person, part, or position of secondary importance.

second floor; (a) the floor above the ground floor of a building; (b) in Europe and Great Britain, the floor two stories above the ground floor: sometimes used in this sense in hotels, etc. in the United States.

second growth; tree growth on land stripped of virgin forest.

second hand; the hand (of a clock or watch) that indicates the seconds and moves around the dial once every minute.

Second International; an international organization of Socialist (Social-Democratic) parties, founded in Paris in 1889: it later became the Labor and Socialist International.

second lieutenant; a commissioned officer of the lowest rank in the United States Army, Air Force, or Marine Corps.

second mate; a ship's officer next in rank below the first mate.

second mortgage; an additional mortgage placed on property already mortgaged: the holder of a second mortgage may present his claim only after the conditions of the first mortgage have been fulfilled.

second nature; a habit, characteristic, etc. acquired and fixed so deeply as to seem part of a person's nature.

second papers; the final application of an alien for United States citizenship; petition for naturalization.

second person; the form of a pronoun or verb which refers to the person spoken to: in *you do*, *you* and *do* are said to be in the second person.

Second Republic; the republic established in France in 1848, when Louis Philippe was deposed and Louis Napoleon was elected president, lasting until 1852, when the Second Empire was established.

second self; a person so intimately associated with another as to have taken on many of his personality traits, attitudes, beliefs, etc.

second sight; the supposed ability to see that which cannot normally be seen, as future events, supernatural objects, etc.

second story; same as *second floor*.

second wind; see under *wind*.

Second World War; same as *World War II*.

seç′ŏnd, *n.* 1. a person or thing that is second.

2. the next after the first.

3. an article of merchandise that falls below the standard set for first quality.

4. [*pl.*] (a) a kind of coarse flour; (b) bread made from this.

5. a person who acts as an aid or official assistant to another, especially to one of the principals in a duel or boxing match.

6. in music, (a) the interval between consecutive diatonic tones; (b) a tone separated from another by this interval; (c) the combination of two such tones in harmony; (d) the second part in a harmonized composition; especially, the alto; (e) an instrument or voice taking this part.

seç′ŏnd, *v.t.*; seconded, *pt., pp.*; seconding, *ppr.* [Fr. *seconder*, from L. *secundare*, to favor, direct favorably, second, from *secundus*, favorable.]

1. to further; to reinforce; to encourage.

2. to express approval of (a motion, etc.) as a preliminary to further discussion or formal adoption.

3. to put into temporary retirement, as an officer of the Royal Artillery or Royal Engineers when he accepts civil employment. [Brit.]

4. to assist; to support; to act as an aid or second to; as, to *second* a prize fighter in the ring.

seç′ŏnd, *adv.* in the second place, rank, group, etc.

seç′ŏnd, *n.* [Fr. *seconde*; ML. *secunda minuta*, lit., second minute.]

1. $^1/_{60}$ of a minute of time.

2. a very short ti ıe; a moment; an instant.

3. $^1/_{60}$ of a minute of angular measurement; $^1/_{3600}$ of a degree of arc; symbol ″; as, 20°10′30″.

seç′ŏnd·ăr·i·ly, *adv.* so as to be secondary; in a secondary manner.

seç′ŏnd·ăr·i·ness, *n.* the state or quality of being secondary.

seç′ŏnd·ăr·y, *a.* [Fr. *secondaire*; L. *secundarius*, of the second class, inferior, from *secundus*, second.]

1. second, or below the first, in rank, importance, class, place, etc.; subordinate; minor; not primary.

2. derived or resulting from something considered primary or original; dependent; derivative.

3. coming after that which is first in a series of processes, events, stages, etc., as of growth or development.

4. coming next in sequence after the primary or elementary level; as, *secondary* school, *secondary* flight training.

5. in chemistry, (a) formed by the replacement of two atoms or radicals in the molecule; as, *secondary* sodium phosphate, Na_2HPO_4; (b) characterized by or designating a carbon atom that is directly attached to two other atoms or radicals in a closed or open chain.

6. in electricity, (a) designating or of an induced current or its circuit; (b) having current produced by induction; as, a *secondary* coil.

7. [S–] in geology, Mesozoic.

8. in zoology, designating or of the second joint or segment of a bird's wing or the quills attached to this.

secondary accent; see *accent*, n. 2.

secondary acids; acids derived from organic acids by the substitution of two equivalents of an alcohol radical for two of hydrogen.

secondary age; the Mesozoic age.

secondary alcohol; an alcohol in which the carbon atom, united to hydroxyl, is combined with only one atom of hydrogen.

secondary amides and *amines*; compounds derived from a single or multiple molecule of ammonia by replacing two thirds of the typical hydrogen by acid and basylous radicals respectively.

secondary amputation; amputation of a limb, etc., performed during suppuration.

secondary axis; in a lens, a line which does not intersect the center of curvature, but the optical center.

secondary bud; in botany, an additional bud formed after the primary one.

secondary circle; in geometry and astronomy, a great circle passing through the poles of another great circle perpendicular to its plane.

secondary circuit; a circuit produced by induction from a primary circuit.

secondary coil; the outer portion of an induction coil in which the secondary currents are induced: it is usually of fine wire and of great length.

secondary color; a color obtained by the mixture of any two primary colors in equal proportions, as purple from red and blue.

secondary crystal; a crystal derived from one of the primary forms.

secondary current; in electricity, (a) a momentary current induced in a closed circuit by a current of electricity passing through the same or a contiguous circuit at the beginning and also at the end of the passage of the primitive current; (b) the current produced in the secondary coil of a transformer.

secondary education; education, as in a high school, between the primary and collegiate levels.

secondary evidence; indirect evidence which may be admitted upon failure to obtain direct or primary evidence.

secondary fever; a fever which arises after the first fever has subsided.

secondary hemorrhage; a second flow of blood from a wound, after the first has been checked.

secondary impedance; in a secondary circuit, the impedance either of part or of all of the circuit.

secondary planet; a planet which revolves around a primary planet as a satellite.

secondary qualities; the qualities of bodies which are not inseparable from them, but which proceed from casual circumstances, such as color, taste, odor, etc.

secondary quills; the second row of quill feathers on the second joint or segment of a bird's wing.

secondary resistance; the resistance of a secondary coil or circuit.

secondary rocks or *strata*; in geology, the rocks or strata situated over or above the primary and below the tertiary. [Rare.]

secondary school; a school, especially a high school, giving a secondary education.

secondary syphilis; syphilis in the second of its three stages.

secondary tints; in painting, tints of a subdued kind, such as grays, etc.

secondary union; in surgery, the union of wounds by first intention.

Syn.—inferior, subsequent, subordinate.

seç′ŏnd·ăr·y, *n.*; *pl.* **seç′ŏnd·ăr·ieṣ,** 1. a delegate or deputy; one who acts in subordination to another; one next in rank to the chief officer; one who a:ts by delegated authority.

2. a thing of secondary or subordinate importance.

3. a secondary planet.

4. a secondary quill.

5. in electricity, a secondary circuit or coil.

seç′ŏnd-best′, *a.* of quality next below the first; next to the best.

seç′ŏnd-çlȧss′, *a.* 1. of the class, rank, excellence, etc. next below the highest; of secondary quality.
 2. designating or of accommodations next below the best; as, a *second-class* railway carriage.
 3. designating or of a class of mail consisting of newspapers, periodicals, etc.: such mail carries lower postage rates than first-class mail.
 4. inferior, inadequate, etc.

seç′ŏnd-çlȧss′, *adv.* 1. with accommodations next below the best; as, we traveled to Europe *second-class.*
 2. as or by second-class mail.

sē·conde′, *n.* [Fr., f. of *second,* second.] a parrying position in fencing.

seç′ŏnd·ẽr, *n.* one who supports what another attempts, affirms, moves, or proposes; as, the *seconder* of an enterprise or of a motion.

seç′ŏnd-fīrst, *a.* pertaining to or designating the second Sabbath in Passover week and the first Sabbath of Paschal week.

seç′ŏnd-foot′, *n.* the flow of a liquid, equal to one cubic foot per second, which is taken as a unit in indicating the discharge of a stream of water.

seç″ŏnd-guess′ (-ges′), *v.t.* and *v.i.* to use hindsight in criticizing or advising (someone), resolving (a past problem), remaking (a decision), etc. [Colloq.]

seç′ŏnd·hand′, *a.* [cf. Fr. *de seconde main.*]
 1. not direct from the original source; not original.
 2. used or worn previously by another; not new.
 3. of or dealing in merchandise that is not new.

seç′ŏnd·ly, *adv.* in the second place; second: used chiefly in enumerating topics.

sē·çon′dō, *n.*; *pl.* **sē·çon′dī,** [It.; L. *secundus,* second.] in music, (a) the second, usually the lower, part in a concerted piece, especially in a piano duet; (b) a person performing such a part.

seç′ŏnd-rāte′, *a.* 1. second in quality or other rating; second-class.
 2. inferior; mediocre.

seç′ŏnd-sīght′ed (-sīt′), *a.* having the power of second sight.

seç′ŏnd-stō′ry, *a.* of, on, or in the second story, or floor.

seç′ŏnd-stō′ry man, a burglar, especially one who enters a building through an upstairs window. [Slang.]

seç′pär, *n.* parsec, a unit of measure.

sē′çrē, *a.* secret; given to secrecy. [Obs.]

sē′çrē, *n.* a secret. [Obs.]

sē′çre·cy, *n.*; *pl.* **sē′çre·cies,** [from *secret.*]
 1. a state or quality of being secret; concealment from the observation of others, or from the notice of any persons not concerned; privacy.
 2. the ability to keep things from the knowledge of others; power to keep secrets.
 For *secrecy* no lady closer. —Shak.
 3. a tendency to keep things secret; quality or habit of being secretive.
 4. a secret or secrets. [Obs.]

sē′çret, *a.* [OFr. *secret,* from L. *secretus,* pp. of *secernere,* to set apart; *se-,* apart, and *cernere,* to sift, distinguish, discern, perceive.]
 1. kept from public knowledge or from the knowledge of certain persons.
 2. retired; remote; secluded.
 3. keeping one's affairs to oneself; secretive; close.
 4. beyond general knowledge or understanding; incomprehensible; deeply mysterious.
 5. concealed from sight or notice; hidden; as, a *secret* drawer.
 6. acting in secret; as, a *secret* society, a *secret* agent.
 secret agent; a person who carries on espionage or similar work of a secret nature, as for a government.
 secret service; see under *service.*
 secret society; any organized group that conceals some of its rituals and other activities from nonmembers.
 Syn.—concealed, private, hidden, obscure, secluded, clandestine, unseen, privy.

sē′çret, *n.* 1. something known only to a certain person or persons and purposely kept from the knowledge of others.
 2. something not revealed, understood, or explained; a mystery; as, the *secrets* of Egyptian embalming.
 3. the true cause or explanation, regarded as not obvious; as, *secrets* of success.
 4. [S–] a prayer said in a low voice after the Offertory in the Mass.
 5. secrecy. [Rare.]
 in secret; in privacy or secrecy; without the knowledge of others.

sē′çret, *v.t.* to secrete. [Obs.]

sē·çrē′tȧ, *n.pl.* [LL.] secretions.

sē′çret·āġe, *n.* [Fr. *secrétage.*] in furriery, a process in preparing or dressing furs, in which mercury or some of its salts are employed to impart to the fur the property of felting, which it did not previously possess.

se·çre·tāire′, *n.* [Fr.] a writing desk; a secretary.

seç·rē·tãr′i·ăl, *a.* pertaining to a secretary; appropriate to a secretary.

seç·rē·tãr′i·at, seç·rē·tãr′i·āte, *n.* [Fr. *secrétariat;* LL. *secretariatus,* from *secretarius,* a scribe, secretary.]
 1. the office or position of a secretary.
 2. the office or place where a secretary does his work.
 3. a staff or department headed by a secretary.
 4. a staff or group of secretaries.

seç′rē·tãr·y, *n.*; *pl.* **seç′rē·tãr·ies,** [ML. *secretarius,* one entrusted with secrets, from L. *secretum,* a secret.]
 1. a person employed to keep records, take care of correspondence and other writing tasks, etc. for an organization or individual.
 2. a general official in over-all charge of such work.
 3. an official in charge of a department of government.
 4. a writing desk, especially one topped with a small bookcase.
 5. one who keeps secrets; a confidential attendant. [Obs.]
 6. the secretary bird.
 recording secretary; see under *recording,* a.

seç′rē·tãr·y bīrd, *n.* [so named because the crest resembles pens stuck over the ear.] a large African bird of prey, *Serpentarius secretarius,* having long legs, a long neck, and an occipital crest of feathers, which can be raised or lowered: it feeds on insects, snakes, and other reptiles.

SECRETARY BIRD (*Serpentarius secretarius*)

seç′rē·tãr·y-ġen′ẽr·ăl, *n.*; *pl.* **seç′rē·tãr·ies-ġen′ẽr·ăl,** a secretary having authority over others; the head of a secretariat.

seç′rē·tãr·y·ship, *n.* the position or office of a secretary; also, a secretary's term of office.

sē·çrēte′, *v.t.*; secreted, *pt., pp.*; secreting, *ppr.* [from L. *secretus,* pp. of *secernere,* to separate, sift.]
 1. to hide; to conceal; to remove from observation or the knowledge of others; as, to *secrete* stolen goods; to *secrete* oneself.
 2. in biology and physiology, to separate (a substance) from the circulating fluid, as the blood, sap, etc., and elaborate into a new product to be used by the organism or excreted as waste.

sē·çrē′tin, *n.* [*secret*ion and *-in.*] a hormone, produced by the mucous membrane of the small intestine, which induces the secretion of pancreatic juice.

sē·çrē′tion, *n.* [OFr.; L. *secretio* (*-onis*), a separation, from *secretus,* pp. of *secernere,* to separate, sift.]
 1. a process in animal and plant physiology by which substances are separated from the blood or sap, elaborated, and then discharged as a new substance having some special function or excreted as waste.
 2. the substance so secreted by an animal or plant.
 3. the act of secreting or hiding; as, the *secretion* of stolen property.

sē·çrē·ti′tious (-tish′us), *a.* produced by secretion. [Rare.]

sē·çrē′tive (*for 1, often* sē′kre-tive), *a.* 1. tending to conceal one's thoughts, feelings, affairs, etc. from others; reticent; not frank or open.
 2. secretory.

sē·çrē′tive·ness, *n.* the quality or state of being secretive; tendency or disposition to conceal.

sē′çret·ly, *adv.* in a secret or hidden manner.

sē′çret·ness, *n.* the quality or state of being secret.

sē·çrē′tŏr, *n.* a duct, gland, etc. that secretes.

sē·çrē′tō·ry, *a.* of or relating to secretion; having the function of secretion; as, *secretory* vessels.

sē·çrē′tō·ry, *n.* a secretory gland, etc.

seçt, *n.* [from L. *sectus,* pp. of *secare,* to cut.] a part or section.

seçt, *n.* [ME. *secte;* Fr. *secte,* a sect or faction, a troop, a company of one opinion; L. *secta,* a set of people, a following, from *sequi,* to follow, thus, lit., a following.]
 1. a group of people having a common leadership, set of opinions, philosophical doctrine, etc.; a school; a following.
 2. any group holding certain views, political principles, etc. in common.
 3. a religious denomination, especially a small group that has broken away from an established church.

seç·tãr′i·ăl, *a.* same as *sectarian.*

seç·tãr′i·ăn, *a.* [from ML. *sectarius.*]
 1. of or characteristic of a sect.
 2. devoted to, or prejudiced in favor of, some sect.
 3. narrow-minded; bigoted.

seç·tãr′i·ăn, *n.* 1. originally, an apostate from an established church.
 2. a member of any religious sect.
 3. a person who is blindly and narrow-mindedly devoted to a sect.

seç·tãr′i·ăn·iṣm, *n.* the state or quality of being sectarian; adherence to or zeal for a particular sect.

seç·tãr′i·ăn·īze, *v.t.*; sectarianized, *pt., pp.*; sectarianizing, *ppr.* to imbue with sectarian principles, feelings, or ideas; to make sectarian in spirit.

seç′tȧ·riṣm, *n.* same as *sectarianism.*

seç′tȧ·rist, *n.* a sectary. [Rare.]

seç′tȧ·ry, *n.*; *pl.* **seç′tȧ·rieṣ,** 1. a sectarian.
 2. [*often* S–] a dissenter from an established church, especially a Protestant nonconformist.
 3. a follower; a pupil. [Rare.]

seç·tā′tŏr, *n.* an adherent; a follower. [Obs.]

seç′tile, *a.* [L. *sectilis,* divided, from *secare,* to cut.] capable of being cut; in mineralogy, designating minerals, as talc, mica, and steatite, which can be cut smoothly with a knife.

seç·til′i·ty, *n.* the condition of being sectile.

seç′tion, *n.* [Fr.; L. *sectio* (*-onis*), a cutting, from *sectus,* pp. of *secare,* to cut.]
 1. the act or process of cutting or separating by cutting.
 2. a part separated or removed by cutting; a slice; a division.
 3. a very thin slice of matter used for microscopic study.
 4. a part or division of something written.
 5. any distinct or separate part; as, a bookcase in five *sections,* various *sections* of society.
 6. a division of public lands constituting 640 acres, or 1/36 of a township.
 7. a loose subdivision of a biological genus, group, family, etc.
 8. a drawing, description, or remaining part of something as it would appear if cut straight through in a given plane.
 9. any of several subdivisions of military or naval forces.
 10. in railroading, (a) part of a sleeping car containing an upper and lower berth; (b) the smallest administrative division of the right of way, usually several miles of track under the care of a single maintenance crew; (c) any train running on the same schedule as another.

seç′tion, *v.t.* 1. to cut or divide into sections.
 2. to arrange by or represent in sections, as by shading in mechanical drawing.
 conic sections; see following *conic.*

seç′tion·ăl, *a.* 1. pertaining to or characteristic of a section or distinct part of a larger body or territory.
 2. composed of or made up in several separable sections; as, a *sectional* boat.

seç′tion·ăl·iṣm, *n.* undue concern for or devotion to the interest of a particular section of the country; sectional spirit, bias, etc.

seç·tion·al′i·ty, *n.* the quality of being sectional; sectionalism. [Rare.]

seç″tion·ăl·i·zā′tion, *n.* the act of sectionalizing or the state of being sectional.

seç′tion·ăl·īze, *v.t.*; sectionalized, *pt., pp.*; sectionalizing, *ppr.* 1. to make sectional.
 2. to divide into sections, especially geographical sections.

seç′tion·ăl·ly, *adv.* in a sectional manner; in or according to sections.

seç′tion gang, a crew of men who do the maintenance work on a railroad section.

seç′tion·īze, *v.t.*; sectionized, *pt., pp.*; sectionizing, *ppr.* to form or divide into sections.

seç′tion märk, the mark (§) used to indicate a section in a book, etc.

seç″ti·ō·plà·nog′rà·phy (-shi-), *n.* [L. *sectio*, a section, *planus*, a plane surface, and Gr. *graphein*, to describe.] a method of laying down the sections of engineering work, as railways and the like. It is performed by using the line of direction laid down on the plan as a datum line, the cuttings being plotted on the upper part, and the embankments upon the lower part of the line.

seçt′ism, *n.* sectarianism; devotion to a sect. [Rare.]

seçt′ist, *n.* a sectarian; one devoted to a sect. [Rare.]

seçt′i·uñ·çle, *n.* a petty sect. [Rare.]

seç′tive, *a.* sectile. [Rare.]

seç′tŏr, *n.* [L. *sector*, a cutter, from *sectus*, pp. of *secare*, to cut.]
 1. in geometry, a part of a circle bounded by any two radii and the arc included between them.
 2. a mathematical instrument consisting of two rulers jointed together at one end and so marked with lines of sines, tangents, secants, chords, etc., as to fit all radii and scales: used in making diagrams, laying down plans, etc.
 3. in astronomy, an instrument for determining with accuracy the zenith distances of stars passing within a few degrees of the zenith; a zenith sector.
 4. any of the districts into which an area is divided for military operations.
 dip sector; an instrument used for measuring the dip of the horizon.
 sector of a sphere; the solid generated by the revolution of the sector of a circle about one of its radii, which remains fixed; the conic solid whose vertex coincides with the center of the sphere, and whose base is a segment of the same sphere.

seç′tŏr, *v.t.* to divide into sectors.

seç′tŏr·ăl, *a.* of or pertaining to a sector; as, a *sectoral* circle.

seç·tō′ri·ăl, *a.* 1. in anatomy and zoology, adapted or intended for cutting; carnassial: said especially of the premolar teeth of carnivorous mammals.
 2. in mathematics, same as *sectoral*.

seç·tō′ri·ăl, *n.* a sectorial tooth.

seç′ū·lăr, *a.* [ME. *secular, seculer, seculere*; OFr. *seculier*, secular, temporal; LL. *sæcularis*, secular, wordly, L., belonging to an age, from *sæculum*, a generation, age.]
 1. coming or observed once in an age or century, or at long intervals; as, the *secular* games in ancient Rome.
 The *secular* year was kept but once in a century. —Addison.
 2. extending over, taking place in, or accomplished during a long period of time; as, the *secular* inequality in the motion of a heavenly body.
 3. living for an age or ages.
 A *secular* bird (the phoenix). —Milton.
 4. pertaining to the world or to things not spiritual or sacred; relating to or connected with worldly things; disassociated from religious teaching or principles; not devoted to sacred or religious use; temporal; nonecclesiastical; worldly; as, *secular* education, *secular* music.
 5. not bound by monastic vows or rules; not confined to a monastery or subject to the rules of a religious community; not regular; as, a *secular* priest.
 6. pertaining to the laity; nonclerical. [Rare.]
 7. secularistic.
 secular equation; the numerical expression of the secular inequalities of a planet's motion.
 secular games; in ancient Rome, games or festivals in honor of the gods, lasting three days and nights, held at irregular intervals and attended with sacrifices, combats, dramatic exhibitions, hymns, etc.

seç′ū·lăr, *n.* 1. an ecclesiastic not bound by monastic rules; a secular priest.
 2. a church officer whose functions are confined to the vocal department of the choir.
 3. a layman. [Obs.]

seç′ū·lăr·ism, *n.* 1. secular spirit, views, or the like; especially, a system of doctrines and practices that rejects any form of religious faith and worship.
 2. the belief that religion and ecclesiastical affairs should not enter into the functions of the state, especially into public education.

seç′ū·lăr·ist, *n.* an adherent of secularism.

seç′ū·lăr·ist, *a.* characterized by or adhering to the principles of secularism.

seç·ū·lăr·is′tiç, *a.* of or according to secularism.

seç·ū·lar′i·ty, *n.* 1. the state or quality of being secular.
 2. secularism.
 3. *pl.* **seç·ū·lar′i·t eş,** a secular concern, matter, etc.

seç″ū·lăr·i·zā′tion, *n.* the act of secularizing or the state of being rendered secular, as (a) the act of converting from religious or sacred to secular or lay possession, use, or purposes; as, the *secularization* of church property or of the Sabbath; (b) the transfer of civil jurisdiction of a district or country from ecclesiastics to laymen; (c) the act of converting a regular or monastic person, place, or benefice, into a secular one; as, the *secularization* of a monk; (d) the conversion, as of a class, to secularism; (e) the separation, as of civil and educational affairs, from religious or ecclesiastical influence or control.

seç′ū·lăr·īze, *v.t.*; secularized, *pt., pp.*; secularizing, *ppr.* 1. to convert from regular or monastic into secular; to free from monastic vows or rules; as, the abbey was *secularized*.
 2. to convert from religious or ecclesiastical to civil possession, use, or purpose.
 3. to make worldly or unspiritual; to deprive of any religious character, influence, or significance.
 4. to cause to believe in secularism.

seç′ū·lăr·ly, *adv.* in a secular manner.

seç′ū·lăr·ness, *n.* the state or quality of being secular.

seç′ū·lum, *n.*; *pl.* **seç′ū·là,** [L. *sæculum*, a generation, age.] a long period of time; an age; a saeculum.

sē′çund, *a.* [L. *secundus*, following.] in botany, arranged or growing on one side only, as the flowers in the lily of the valley.

sē·çun′dāte, *v.t.* to cause to prosper. [Rare.]

seç·un·dā′tion, *n.* prosperity. [Rare.]

sē·çun·di·flō′rous, *a.* [L. *secundus* following, second, and *flos, floris*, flower.] secund in the arrangement of flowers.

seç′un·dīne, *n.* [Fr. *secondine*; LL. *secundinæ*, afterbirth, from L. *secundus*, following.]
 1. in botany, the second, or inner, coat of an ovule.
 2. [*pl.*] the afterbirth.

sē·çun·dō·ġen′i·tūre, *n.* 1. a right of inheritance possessed by a second son.
 2. anything thus inherited.

sē·çun′dum, *prep.* [L.] according to: used in in Latin phrases, as in *secundum usum*, according to usage.
 secundum artem; according to art or professional rule.

sē·çūr′à·ble, *a.* that can be secured.

sē·çūre′, *a.* [L. *securus*, free from care; *se-*, free from, and *cura*, care.]
 1. free from fear, care, doubt, or anxiety; not worried, troubled, or apprehensive.
 2. free from danger; not exposed to damage, attack, etc.; safe.
 3. in safekeeping or custody.
 4. not likely to fail or give way; firm; strong; stable; as, make the knot *secure*.
 5. sure; certain; to be relied upon.
 6. overconfident; careless. [Archaic.]
 Syn.—safe, sure, certain, guarded, impregnable, protected, confident, undisturbed.

sē·çūre′, *v.t.*; secured, *pt., pp.*; securing, *ppr.* 1. to make safe or secure; to put into a state of safety or security against danger; to guard effectually; to protect.
 2. to make fast or secure; to fasten, as a door.
 3. to make sure or certain; to put beyond doubt or hazard; to assure; to insure.
 4. to shut up, enclose, or confine securely; to guard effectually against escape; to seize and confine; as, to *secure* a prisoner.
 5. to make certain of payment, as by a bond, surety, etc.; to warrant or insure against loss.
 6. to obtain; to gain possession of; to acquire.
 to secure arms; to hold a rifle or musket with the muzzle down, and the lock well up under the arm, the object being to guard the weapon from the weather.

sē·çūre′, *v.i.* to be or become secure, or safe; to have or give security; as, we must *secure* against possible obstacles.

sē·çūre′ly, *adv.* in a secure manner; so as to be secure.

sē·çūre′ment, *n* security; protection. [Obs.]

sē·çūre′ness, *n.* the state or quality of being secure.

sē·çūr′ẽr, *n.* one who or that which secures.

Seç·ū·rif′e·rà, *n.pl.* same as *Terebrantia*.

sē·çū′ri·fọrm, *a.* [L. *securis*, an ax, and *-form*.] in botany, having the form of an ax or hatchet.

sē·çū′ri·ty, *n.*; *pl.* **sē·çū′ri·ties,** [Fr. *sécurité*; L. *securitas* (*-atis*), freedom from care, from *securus*, free from care.]
 1. the state or feeling of being free from fear, care, danger, etc.; safety or a sense of safety.
 2. freedom from doubt; certainty.
 3. overconfidence; carelessness.
 4. something that gives or assures safety; protection; safeguard.
 5. something given as a pledge of repayment, fulfillment of a promise, etc.; a guarantee.
 6. a person who agrees to make good the failure of another to pay, perform a duty, etc.; surety.
 7. [*usually in pl.*] any evidence of debt or ownership of property, especially a bond or stock certificate.
 Syn.—protection, shelter, safety, certainty.

Sē·çū′ri·ty Coun′cil, the organ of the United Nations responsible for maintaining international peace and security.

sē·dan′, *n.* [earlier also *sidan*; prob. coined from L. *sedere*, to sit, by Sir S. Duncombe (1634); orig., a sedan chair.]
 1. a type of closed automobile having two or four doors, and two seats, front and rear.
 2. a sedan chair.

sē·dan′ chāir, an enclosed chair for one person, carried on poles by two men.

sē·dāte′, *a.* [L. *sedatus*, composed, calm, pp. of *sedare*, to settle, caus. of *sedere*, to sit.]
 1. composed; calm; quiet; serene.
 2. serious; sober; dignified; grave.

sē·dāte′ly, *adv.* in a sedate manner.

sē·dāte′ness, *n.* the quality or state of being sedate.

sē·dā′tion, *n.* in medicine, the act or process of reducing excitement, irritation, or pain, especially by means of a sedative.

sed′à·tive, *a.* [Fr. *sédatif*, from L. *sedatus*.] tending to calm, moderate, or tranquilize; specifically, in medicine, lessening excitement, irritation, and pain.

sed′à·tive, *n.* a sedative medicine or treatment.

sē′dent, *a.* sitting. [Rare.]

sed′en·tăr·i·ly, *adv.* in a sedentary manner.

sed′en·tăr·i·ness, *n.* the quality or state of being sedentary.

sed′en·tăr·y, *a.* [Fr. *sédentaire*, sedentary, ever-sitting; L. *sedentarius*, sedentary, from *sedens* (*-entis*), ppr. of *sedere*, to sit.]
 1. characterized by or involving sitting; as, a *sedentary* task.
 2. accustomed to sit much of the time.
 3. remaining in one locality; not migratory: said of birds, etc.
 4. in zoology, fixed to one spot, as a barnacle.

Sẹ′dẽr, *n.*; *pl.* **Sẹ′dăr·im,** [Heb. *sedher*, arrangement, service, lection.] in Judaism, the feast commemorating the exodus of the Jews from Egypt, observed in the home on the eve of the first day (and by orthodox Jews also the eve of the second day) of Passover.

sē·dē′runt, *n.* [L., lit., they sat.] a sitting or meeting of a court; by extension, a more or less formal meeting or sitting of any association, society, company, or body of men.

sē′dēş vā′çanş, [L.] a vacant see.

sē′dē vā·çan′tē, [L.] the see, or seat, being vacant.

sedġe, *n.* a brood or flock (of bitterns or herons).

sedġe, *n.* [ME. *segge*; AS. *secg*, sedge.] any of several grasslike plants of the genus *Carex*, found in the northern and temperate parts of the earth: they are distinguished from grasses by having no joints in the stems. They grow usually in clumps or tufts in marshes and swamps.

sedġed, *a.* composed of or edged by sedge.

sedġe hen, the clapper rail of North America.

sedġe wạr′blẽr, a species of insessorial birds, *Acrocephalus phragmitis,* of the warbler family, inhabiting the sedgy banks of European rivers and ponds.

SEDGE WARBLER (*Acrocephalus phragmitis*)

sedġ′y, *a.*; *comp.* sedgier; *superl.* sedgiest. 1. overgrown or bordered with sedge.
  2. like sedge.

sē·dil′i·ȧ, *n.pl.*; *sing.* **sē·dī′lē,** [L. *sedile,* a seat.] a set of stone seats for the priests in the south wall of the chancel of many churches and cathedrals. They are usually three in number, for the use of the priest, deacon, and sub-deacon when not officiating.

SEDILIA

sed′i·ment, *n.* [OFr. *sediment,* a sitting or settling of dregs; L. *sedimentum,* a settling, subsidence, from *sedere,* to sit.]
  1. any matter that settles to the bottom of water or other liquid; settlings; lees; dregs.
  2. in geology, any matter or mass deposited by water or wind.

sed·i·men′tăl, *a.* same as *sedimentary.*

sed″i·men·tā′ri·ly, *adv.* so as to be sedimentary.

sed·i·men′tȧ·ry, *a.* 1. of, having the nature of, or containing sediment.
  2. formed by the deposit of sediment, as rocks.

sed″i·men·tā′tion, *n.* the depositing of sediment; the accumulation of sediment to form strata.

sē·di′tion, *n.* [OFr. *sedition*; L. *seditio* (*-onis*), dissension, civil discord, sedition; from *sed-,* apart, and *itio,* a going, from *ire,* to go.]
  1. the stirring up of discontent, resistance, or rebellion against the government in power.
  2. rebellion; insurrection. [Rare.]

sē·di′tion·ăr·y, *a.* seditious.

sē·di′tion·ăr·y, *n.*; *pl.* **sē·di′tion·ăr·ieṣ,** a person charged with or convicted of sedition.

sē·di′tious (-dish′us), *a.* 1. pertaining to sedition; consisting of sedition; as, *seditious* writings.
  2. exciting or aiding in sedition; guilty of sedition; as, *seditious* persons.
  3. having a tendency to sedition.

sē·di′tious·ly, *adv.* in a seditious manner.

sē·di′tious·ness, *n.* the quality or state of being seditious.

Sed′litz, *a.* see *Seidlitz.*

sē·dūce′, *v.t.*; seduced, *pt., pp.*; seducing, *ppr.* [L. *seducere,* to lead apart; *se-,* apart, and *ducere,* to lead.]
  1. to persuade to do something disloyal, disobedient, etc.
  2. to persuade to do wrong, as by offering something; to tempt to evil or wrongdoing; to lead astray.
  3. to persuade to engage in unlawful sexual intercourse, especially for the first time; to induce to give up chastity.
  Syn.—lure, entice, mislead, corrupt, tempt, inveigle.

sē·dūce′ȧ·ble, *a.* seducible.

sē·dūce′ment, *n.* 1. the act of seducing; seduction.
  2. the means used to seduce.

sē·dū′cẽr, *n.* one who or that which seduces; especially, a man who seduces a woman.

sē·dū′ci·ble, *a.* that can be seduced.

sē·dū′cing, *a.* seductive. [Rare.]

sē·dū′cing·ly, *adv.* in a seducing manner. [Rare.]

sē·duc′tion, *n.* [L. *seductio* (*-onis*), a leading apart or astray, from *seductus,* pp. of *seducere,* to lead apart or astray.]
  1. the act of seducing or the state of being seduced.
  2. something that seduces.

sē·duc′tive, *a.* tending to seduce, or lead astray; tempting; strongly attractive; enticing.

sē·duc′tive·ly, *adv.* in a seductive manner.

sē·duc′tress, *n.* a woman who seduces.

sē·dū′li·ty, *n.* [L. *sedulitas,* sedulousness, from *sedulus,* diligent.] the quality or fact of being sedulous.

sed′ū·lous, *a.* [L. *sedulus,* diligent.] assiduous; diligent in application or pursuit; constant, steady, and persevering; steadily industrious.
  Syn.—industrious, unremitting, diligent, unwearied.

sed′ū·lous·ly, *adv.* in a sedulous manner; diligently.

sed′ū·lous·ness, *n.* sedulity.

Sē′dum, *n.* [L. *sedum,* houseleek.]
  1. a genus of plants of the houseleek family with opposite, alternate, or whorled leaves, thick, fleshy stalks, and cymose white, yellow, or pink flowers; stonecrop.
  2. [s-] a plant of this genus.

see, *n.* [ME. *se*; OFr. *sied, sie,* a seat, from L. *sedes,* a seat.]
  1. the official seat, or center of authority, of a bishop.
  2. the position, authority, or jurisdiction of a bishop.
  3. a seat of authority, especially a throne. [Obs.]
  Apostolic See; see under *Apostolic.*
  Holy See, See of Rome; same as *Apostolic See.*

see, *v.t.*; saw, *pt.*; seen, *pp.*; seeing, *ppr.* [AS. *seon,* to see.]
  1. to get knowledge or an impression of through the eyes and the sense of sight; to perceive visually; look at; to view.
  2. to get a clear mental impression of; to grasp by thinking; understand; as, I can't *see* your point.
  3. to learn; discover; find out; as, *see* what they want.
  4. to have personal knowledge of; to experience; live through; witness; as, she had *seen* better days, they have *seen* the results of three wars.
  5. to look over; inspect; examine; as, the doctor had better *see* your incision.
  6. to take care; make sure; as, *see* that he does the job properly.
  7. to escort; accompany; attend; as, I'll *see* you to the door, he will *see* her to her home.
  8. to encounter; meet; to come in contact with; as, have you *seen* her brother recently?
  9. to call on; to have an interview with; consult; as, you had better *see* a lawyer.
  10. to admit to one's presence; receive; as, he is too ill to *see* you.
  11. to be a spectator at; to visit; attend; as, have you *seen* the new musical?
  12. in card games, (a) to meet (a bet) by staking an equal sum; (b) to meet the bet of (another) in this way.
  to see off; to go with (another) to the place from which he is to leave, as on a journey.
  to see out; (a) to carry out; to finish; to go through with; (b) to wait till the end of.
  to see through; (a) to carry out to the end; to finish; (b) to help out or carry through a time of difficulty.
  Syn.—perceive, observe.

see, *v.i.* 1. to have the power of sight.
  2. to discern objects, colors, etc. by using the eyes; as, I can't *see* that far.
  3. to comprehend; to understand.
  4. to look for the purpose of finding out something.
  5. to think over a given matter; reflect; as, let me *see,* where did I put it?
  to see about; (a) to find out about; investigate; inquire into; (b) to attend to.
  to see after; to take care of; to look after.
  to see double; to see two of every object, through inability to focus the eyes, as from drunkenness.
  to see into; (a) to investigate; to look into; (b) to understand or perceive the true meaning, character, or nature of.
  to see through; to understand or perceive the true meaning, character, or nature of.
  to see to; to attend to; to look after.

see′-brīght (-brīt), *n.* same as *clary.*

see′ċatch, see′ċatch″ie, *n.* [Russ. *sekach.*] a full-grown male fur seal, *Callorhinus ursinus.*

seed, *n.* [ME. *sede*; AS. *sæd.*]
  1. the part of a flowering plant that contains the embryo and will develop into a new plant if sown; a fertilized and mature ovule.
  2. any part from which a new plant will grow; as, a potato *seed.*
  3. seeds collectively; as, we must buy *seed* for the lawn.
  4. the source, origin, or beginning of anything; as, oppression sows the *seeds* of revolt.
  5. family stock; ancestry.
  6. descendants; posterity.
  7. seed oysters.
  8. sperm; semen.
  to go to seed; (a) to shed seeds after the time of flowering or bearing has passed; (b) to deteriorate; to become weak, useless unprofitable, etc.

seed, *v.t.*; seeded, *pt., pp.*; seeding *ppr* 1. to plant with seed.
  2. to sow (seeds).
  3. to remove the seeds from.
  4. in sports, (a) to distribute the names of the ranking contestants in (the draw for position in a tournament) so that those with the greatest skill are not matched together in the early rounds; (b) to treat (a player) as a ranking contestant in this way.

seed, *v.i.* 1. to become ripe and produce seed.
  2. to go to seed; to shed seed.
  3. to sow seed.
  to seed down; to sow with grass seed.

seed′bed, *n.* a bed of soil, usually covered with glass, in which small plants are grown from seed for transplanting.

seed′box, *n.* 1. a mature seed vessel or capsule.
  2. same as *Ludwigia,* a North American marsh plant.

seed bud, any plant bud or ovule that develops into a seed.

seed′ċāke, *n.* a sweet cake or cookie containing spicy seeds.

seed′-ċāse, *n.* a seed vessel.

seed ċōat, the exterior coat of a seed.

seed ċor′ăl, fragments of coral used in ornaments.

seed ċọrn, corn for seed used in sowing a new crop.

seed drill, a machine for sowing seeds in rows.

seed′ẽr, *n.* 1. one who or that which sows or plants seeds.
  2. a device for removing seeds from fruit.
  3. a seed fish.

seed fish, a fish ready to spawn.

seed grāin, grain used for sowing or planting.

seed′i·ly, *adv.* in a seedy manner.

seed′i·ness, *n.* the state or quality of being seedy.

seed′ing mȧ·ċhīne′, a seeder.

seed′ing plow, a combined plow and seeder.

seed′-laç, *n.* same as *lac* (resinous substance).

seed lēaf, a cotyledon; an embryo leaf within a seed.

seed′less, *a.* having no seeds.

seed′ling, *n.* 1. a plant grown from a seed, as distinguished from one propagated by layers, buds, etc.
  2. a young tree under three feet in height.

seed′lip, seed′lop, *n.* a container in which a sower carries the seed to be sown. [Dial.]

seed′măn, *n.*; *pl.* **seed′men,** a seedsman.

seed′ness, *n.* seedtime. [Obs.]

seed oys′tẽrṣ, oyster spat; very young oysters, especially at the stage suitable for transplanting.

seed pēarl, a very small pearl, often imperfect.

seed plant, any seed-bearing plant.

seed plot, seed plat, a seedbed.

seedṣ′măn, *n.*; *pl.* **seedṣ′men,** 1. a sower.
  2. a person whose business is selling seeds.

seed stạlk, in botany, a funicle.

seed′stẽr, *n.* a sower. [Obs.]

seed tick, a small tick, as *Ixodes bovis,* or other mite of the same genus.

seed′tīme, *n.* the season for sowing seeds.

seed ves′sel, the pericarp; any dry, hollow fruit, as a pod, which contains the seeds: also called *seed capsule.*

seed wee′vil, a species of *Apion,* or other weevil infesting seeds.

 fate, fär, fȧst, fạll, finăl, cāre, at; mēte, prẹy, hẽr, met; pīne, marīne, bīrd, pin; nōte, mōve, fọr, atŏm, not; mọọn, book;

seed'y, *a.*; *comp.* seedier; *superl.* seediest. 1. containing much seed; as, this orange is too *seedy.*
2. gone to seed.
3. containing small bubbles: said of glass.
4. shabby, shabbily dressed, etc.
5. feeling or looking physically bad or low in spirits. [Colloq.]
6. full of spawn: said of a fish.

see'ing, *n.* 1. the sense or power of sight; vision.
2. the act of using the eyes to see.

see'ing, *a.* [ppr. of *see.*] having the sense of sight.

see'ing, *conj.* since; inasmuch as; considering.

See'ing Ēye (ī), an institution near Morristown, New Jersey, which breeds and trains dogs (*Seeing Eye dogs*) as guides and companions for blind people.

seek, *v.t.*; sought (sạt), *pt., pp.*; seeking, *ppr.* [AS. *secan, seccan,* to seek.]
1. to try to find; to search for; look for.
2. to go to; to resort to; as, he *sought* the woods for peace.
3. to search; to explore.
4. to ask or inquire for; to try to learn or discover; as, he *sought* the answer in many places.
5. to try to get or acquire; to aim at; pursue.
6. to try; to attempt: used with an infinitive; as, he *sought* to appease his enemies.

seek, *v.i.* 1. to try to find someone or something; to make a search or investigation.
2. to go; to resort; to pay a visit (*to*). [Obs.]
to seek after; to make pursuit; to attempt to find or take.

seek, *a.* sick. [Obs.]

seek'ẽr, *n.* 1. one who seeks; an inquirer; as, a *seeker* of truth.
2. [S–] a member of an English sect in the seventeenth century who claimed to be seeking the true church.

seek'-nō-fũr"thẽr, *n.* a winter apple of a reddish color having a slightly acid flavor.

seel, *v.t.*; seeled, *pt., pp.*; seeling, *ppr.* [OFr. *ciller, siller,* from *cil,* L. *cilium,* an eyelash.]
1. in falconry, to close the eyes of (a young hawk) by running a thread through the lids.
2. to close (the eyes).
3. to blind or hoodwink.

seel, *v.i.* to lean; to incline to one side; to roll, as a ship in a storm. [Obs.]

seel, *n.* the rolling or pitching of a ship in a storm. [Obs.]

seel, *n.* 1. time; opportunity; season, in respect to crops; as, hay *seel.* [Obs. or Brit. Dial.]
2. happiness; felicity. [Obs. or Brit. Dial.]

seel'i·ly, *adv.* in a silly manner. [Obs.]

seel'y, *a.* silly; foolish; simple. [Obs.]

seem, *v.i.*; seemed, *pt., pp.*; seeming, *ppr.* [ME. *semen*; AS. *seman,* to bring to agreement.]
1. to appear to be; to give the impression of being; appear; as, he *seems* glad to see us.
2. to appear to one's own mind; as, I *seem* to hear voices.
3. to appear to exist; as, there *seems* no point in going.
4. to be apparently true; as, it *seems* he was not there.
Syn.—appear, look.

seem, *v.t.* to become; to befit. [Obs.]

seem'ẽr, *n.* one who assumes an appearance or semblance.

seem'ing, *a.* apparent, especially as distinguished from *actual*; having the appearance or semblance of reality; specious; as, *seeming* friendship.

seem'ing, *n.* outward form or appearance; show; semblance; especially, a false appearance.

seem'ing·ly, *adv.* apparently; so far as can be observed.

seem'ing·ness, *n.* the quality or state of seeming. [Rare.]

seem'less, *a.* unseemly; unfit; indecorous. [Archaic.]

seem'li·head (-hed), *n.* seemliness. [Archaic.]

seem'li·ness, *n.* the quality of being seemly; fitness; propriety; decency; decorum.

seem'ly, *a.*; *comp.* seemlier; *superl.* seemliest. [ME. *semlich*; ON. *sæmiligr,* seemly, becoming, from *sæmr,* fitting.]
1. pleasing in appearance; fair; handsome. [Archaic or Dial.]
2. suitable, proper, fitting, or becoming, especially with reference to conventional standards of conduct or good taste; decent; decorous.
Syn.—becoming, fit, suitable, appropriate, congruous, meet, decorous.

seem'ly, *adv.* in a seemly manner; properly, fittingly, etc.

seen, *v.* past participle of *see.*

seen, *a.* 1. manifest; understood; evident.
2. versed; skilled. [Obs.]

seep, *v.i.*; seeped (sēpt), *pt., pp.*; seeping, *ppr.* [AS. *sipian,* to soak.] to flow through pores; to ooze gently.

seep, *n.* a place where water or petroleum oozes from the ground to form a pool.

seep'ăġe, *n.* the act or process of seeping; an oozing; also, the liquid that seeps.

seep'y, *a.* oozy; soggy: said especially of poorly drained land.

seer (*or* sē'ẽr), *n.* 1. one who sees; an onlooker.
2. a foreseer; a prophet; one who foretells; a soothsayer.

seer, *n.* a ser.

seer'ess, *n.* a prophetess.

seer'fish, *n.* a scombroid fish of the East Indian seas resembling the mackerel.

seer'hand, *n.* a kind of muslin.

seer'ship, *n.* the office, character, or quality of a seer.

seer'suck"ẽr, *n.* [Hind. *shirshaker,* from Per. *shir u shakar,* lit., milk and sugar, also a kind of striped linen cloth.] a light, crinkled fabric of linen or cotton, usually with a striped pattern.

see'sạw, *n.* [a reduplicated form of *saw,* from the action of sawing.]
1. a plank balanced on a support at the middle, used by children at play, one sitting at either end and causing his end to rise and fall alternately with the other.
2. the act of playing in this way.
3. any back-and-forth or up-and-down motion, action, or tendency, likened to that of a seesaw; as, the *seesaw* of pitched battle.
4. in whist, a crossruff.

see'sạw, *v.i.*; seesawed, *pt., pp.*; seesawing, *ppr.* to move with a reciprocating motion; to move back and forth or up and down; to teeter.

see'sạw, *v.t.* to cause to move in a seesaw manner.

see'sạw, *a.* having a motion like a seesaw; moving back and forth or up and down.

see'see, *n.* a small bird, *Ammoperdix bonhami,* the sand partridge of western Asia.

seet, *v.* obsolete past tense of *sit.*

seethe, *v.t.*; seethed *or obs.* sod, *pt.*; seethed *or obs.* sodden, *pp.*; seething, *ppr.* [ME. *sethen*; AS. *sēothan.*]
1. to cook by boiling.
2. to saturate, soak, or steep in liquid.

seethe, *v.i.* 1. to boil; to be boiling hot.
2. to surge, bubble, or foam, as boiling liquid.
3. to be violently agitated, excited, or disturbed.

seeth'ẽr, *n.* a boiler; a pot for boiling things. [Obs.]

seg, *n.* 1. sedge. [Brit. Dial.]
2. the yellow flower-de-luce. [Brit. Dial.]

seg, *n.* a castrated animal. [Scot.]

sē·gär', *n.* a cigar.

seg'găr, *n.* and *v.t.* same as *sagger.*

seg'grŏm, seg'gru n, *n.* the ragwort. [Brit. Dial.]

se·ghōl' (-gōl'), *n.* [Heb.] in Hebrew, a vowel point, or short vowel (∴), indicating the sound equivalent to English *e* in *men*: also written *segol.*

se'ghō·lāte, *a.* marked with a seghol: also written *segolate.*

seg'ment, *n.* [L. *segmentum,* a piece cut off, from *secare,* to cut.]
1. any of the parts into which a body is separated or divided; a division; a section.
2. in geometry, (a) a part cut off from a figure, especially of a circle or sphere, by a line or plane as the part of a circle contained between an arc and its chord; (b) any of the finite sections of a line.
3. in machinery, any working part in the shape of a segment of a circle.
4. in biology, any of the divisions formed by segmentation.
5. in zoology, (a) any of the sections that form the body of an arthropod; (b) a section of a limb between two joints.

C
A B
A B C,
SEGMENT OF A CIRCLE

seg'ment, *v.t.* and *v.i.*; segmented, *pt., pp.*; segmenting, *ppr.* to divide or become divided or split up into segments.

seg·men'tăl, *a.* 1. having the form of a segment of a circle.
2. of, or having the nature of, a segment or segments.
3. composed of segments.
segmental duct; in anatomy, the primitive duct in the excretory organs of the embryo.
segmental organs; certain organs placed at the sides of the body in annelids and connected with excretion; those organs from which the kidneys and genital ducts are developed in vertebrates.
segmental tube; a primitive tubule which develops into a urinary or a genital tube.

seg·men'tăl·ly, *adv.* in or by segments.

seg'men·tãr·y, *a.* segmented.

seg·men·tā'tion, *n.* 1. the act of dividing or the state of being divided into segments.
2. in biology, a progressive growth and cleavage of a single cell into many others to form a new organism.
segmentation of the ovum; the first process of germination of the ovum in higher plants and animals; that process by which the original cell becomes converted wholly or in part into a mass of smaller cells.
total segmentation; segmentation in which the entire ovum undergoes segmentation: also called *holoblastic segmentation.*

seg·men·tā'tion çav'i·ty, the central cavity of a blastula; the blastocoele.

seg·men·tā'tion nū'clē·us, the nucleus formed in an impregnated ovum by fusion of the male and female pronuclei.

seg·men·tā'tion sphēre, 1. the morula; the mass of cells formed by the segmentation of the nucleus of an ovum.
2. a blastomere; one of the cells formed by the segmentation of the ovum.

seg'ment·ed, *a.* arranged in segments or joints; articulated; jointed.

seg'ment gēar, in mechanics, a curved cogged surface or gear occupying but an arc of a circle.

se'gnō (-nyō), *n.*; *pl.* **se'gni** (-nyi), [It., a sign.] in music, a sign or mark used especially to indicate repetition: abbreviated *:S:.*

sē'gō, *n.* [Am. Ind.] a perennial bulb plant of the lily family, *Calochortus nuttalii,* which grows in the western part of North America and has an edible root and a trumpet-shaped flower: also *sego lily.*

seg'rē·gāte, *a.* [L. *segregatus,* pp. of *segregare,* to set apart, lit., to set apart from the flock; *se-,* apart, and *grex, gregis,* flock.] set apart from others; separate; segregated.
segregate polygamy; in botany, a mode of inflorescence, when several florets included within an anthodium or a common calyx are furnished also with proper perianths.

seg'rē·gāte, *v.t.*; segregated, *pt., pp.*; segregating, *ppr.* to set apart from others or from the main mass or group; to isolate.

seg'rē·gāte, *v.i.* 1. to separate from the main mass and collect together in a new body: said of crystals.
2. to separate from others; to be segregated.
3. in biology, to separate in accordance with Mendel's law; to undergo segregation.

seg'rē·gāt·ed, *adj.* conforming to a system that segregates racial groups.

seg·rē·gā'tion, *n.* 1. a segregating or being segregated.
2. a segregated part, group, number, etc.
3. in biology, the separation of allelomorphic genes or characters, as in meiosis.

seg'rē·gā·tive, *a.* 1. tending to segregate.
2. characterized by unsociability or disunity.

se'guē (-gwē), *v.i.* [It.] in music, to perform a part of a work in the manner of a preceding part.

seg·ui·dil'là (-i-dēl'yȧ), *n.* [Sp.] 1. a fast Spanish dance, danced and sung to the accompaniment of castanets.
2. the music for this dance, in $^3/_4$ time.
3. a stanza of four to seven short lines, partly assonant, with a distinctive rhythm, sung to this music.

sei·cen'tō (sā-chen'tō), *n.* [It.] the seventeenth century, with reference to the Italian art and literature produced then.

seiche (sāsh), *n.* [from Swiss Fr.] a movement back and forth of the water in a lake or other land-locked body of water, varying in duration and resulting in fluctuation of the water level.

se'id, *n.* same as *sayid.*

seī'del (zī'd'l *or* sī'd'l), *n.*; *pl.* **seī'del**, [G.] [*often* S–] a large beer mug, sometimes with a hinged lid.

Seid'litz (sed'), *a.* relating to the village of Seidlitz in Czechoslovakia, site of a famous mineral spring: also written *Sedlitz.*

Seid'litz pow'dẽrs, [so called (1815) because their properties are said to resemble those of natural waters from the spring at *Seidlitz,* Czechoslovakia.] a laxative composed of two powders, one of sodium bicarbonate and Rochelle salt, the other of tartaric acid: the two are separately dissolved in water, combined, and drunk while effervescing: also *Seidlitz powder.*

sei'gneur (sān'yēr), *n.* [Fr.; L. *senior*; see *senior.*] a feudal lord or noble; a seignior.

sei·gneū'ri·ăl (sān-yū'), *a.* same as *seignorial.*

sēign'iŏr (sēn'yẽr), *n.* [ME. *seignour*; OFr. *seigneur*, a lord, sir, seignior; from L. *senior*, elder, an elder or lord, from *senex*, old.]
1. originally, the lord of a fee or manor.
2. a lord; noble; gentleman.
3. a title of respect corresponding to *Sir.*

sēign'iŏr·āġe, *n.* 1. something claimed or taken by a sovereign or other superior as his just right or due.
2. any profits or charges arising from the minting of gold and silver coins from bullion, usually the difference between face value and intrinsic value.

sēign'iŏr·ăl, *a.* seignorial.

sēign'iŏr·ăl·ty, *n.* the domain or territory over which a seignior, or feudal lord, has jurisdiction.

sēi·gniōr'i·ăl (sēn-yōr'), *a.* same as *seignorial.*

sēign'iŏr·y (sēn'yẽr-), *n.*; *pl.* **sēign'iŏr·ieṣ**, [OFr. *seignorie*, from L. *senior*, an elder or lord.]
1. the dominion, rights, or authority of a seignior, or feudal lord; lordship.
2. the extent or territory covered by this.
3. a body of lords, especially those of a medieval Italian republic.
Also spelled *signory.*

sēi·gnō'ri·ăl (sēn-yō'), *a.* of or having to do with a seignior.

seine (sān), *n.* [Fr. *seine*, from L. *sagena*, Gr. *sagēnē*, a seine.] a large net for catching fish, buoyed along the top by corks and weighted along the bottom so as to float perpendicularly.

seine, *v.i.*; seined, *pt.*, *pp.*; seining, *ppr.* to use a seine in fishing.

seine, *v.t.* to catch with a seine; to use a seine in; as, to *seine* fish; to *seine* a stream.

sein'ẽr, *n.* one who or that which seines.

sein'tū·ăr·y, *n.* a sanctuary. [Obs.]

sēir'fish, *n.* same as *seerfish.*

seī'rō·spōre, *n.* [Gr. *seira*, a band, and *spora*, a spore.] in botany, a nonsexual organ of reproduction, several of which are arranged in the form of a chain in certain algae. [Obs.]

sēiṣe, *v.t.*; seised, *pt.*, *pp.*; seising, *ppr.* [var. of *seize.*] in law, to take possession of; to possess; to seize.

sēi'ṣin, *n.* same as *seizin.*

seīṣ'măl, *a.* same as *seismic.*

seīṣ'miç, *a.* [Gr. *seismos*, an earthquake, from *seiein*, to shake.]
1. of or having to do with an earthquake or earthquakes.
2. caused by an earthquake.
3. subject to earthquakes.
seismic vertical; the point upon the earth's surface vertically over the center of effort or focal point, whence the earthquake's impulse proceeds, or the vertical line connecting these two points.
the seismic area; the tract on the earth's surface within which an earthquake is felt.

seīṣ'mi·căl, *a.* same as *seismic.*

seīṣ'miṣm, *n.* [Gr. *seismos*, an earthquake.] the phenomena of earthquakes, collectively.

seīṣ'mō-, [from Gr. *seismos*, earthquake, from *seiein*, to shake.] a combining form meaning *earthquake*, as in *seismo*gram; also, rarely, *sismo-.*

seīs'mō·gram, *n.* [*seismo-* and *-gram.*] the record of an earthquake as made by a seismograph.

seīṣ'mō·grȧph, *n.* [*seismo-* and *-graph.*] an instrument for registering the direction, intensity, and time of earthquakes.

seīṣ·mō·graph'iç, *a.* 1. pertaining to seismography.
2. indicated or recorded by a seismograph.

seīṣ·mog'rȧ·phy, *n.* the study or observation of the phenomena of earthquakes; the science of recording such phenomena by means of the seismograph.

seīṣ·mō·loġ'i·căl, seīṣ·mō·loġ'iç, *a.* relating to seismology.

seīṣ·mō·loġ'i·căl·ly, *adv.* by means of or according to seismology.

seīṣ·mol'ō·ġy, *n.* [*seismo-* and *-logy.*] the science of earthquakes; that department of science which treats of earthquakes and all phenomena connected with them.

seīṣ·mom'ē·tẽr, *n.* [*seismo-* and *-meter.*] same as *seismograph.*

seīṣ·mō·met'riç, *a.* same as *seismographic.*

seīṣ·mom'ē·try, *n.* the use of a seismometer in measuring and recording the phenomena of earthquakes.

seīṣ'mō·sçōpe, *n.* [Gr. *seismos*, an earthquake, and *skopein*, to see.] an instrument which indicates only the occurrence and time of earthquakes.

seīs·mō·sçop'iç, *a.* of or recorded by a seismoscope.

seīṣ·mot'iç, *a.* same as *seismic.*

sē'i·ty, *n.* [L. *se*, oneself.] something peculiar to one's self; individuality.

sēiz'ȧ·ble, *a.* that can be seized.

sēize, *v.t.*; seized, *pt.*, *pp.*; seizing, *ppr.* [ME. *saysen*, *seysen*, OFr. *saisir*, *seisir*, to take possession of, from LL. *sacire.*]
1. originally, to put in legal possession of a feudal holding.
2. to take legal possession of.
3. to take possession of suddenly and by force.
4. to have a sudden and drastic effect upon; to attack; to strike; as, his mind was *seized* with a sudden paralysis.
5. to capture; to take prisoner; to catch; to arrest.
6. to grasp suddenly with the hand; to take hold of forcibly.
7. to grasp with the mind; to comprehend; to understand.
8. to take advantage of (an opportunity, etc.) quickly.
9. in nautical usage, to fasten together (ropes, etc.), as by lashings; to bind; to lash.
to seize on (or *upon*); (a) to take hold of suddenly and with force; (b) to take possession of.
Syn.—grasp, catch, apprehend, take.

sēiz'ẽr, *n.* one who or that which seizes.

sēi'zin, sēi'ṣin, *n.* [Fr. *saisine*, from *saisir*, to seize.]
1. in law, possession; specifically, possession of a freehold estate. Seizin in fact or deed is actual or corporal possession; seizin in law is constructive possession, as where there is no adverse claimant.
2. the act of taking possession.
3. the thing possessed; property so possessed.
livery of seizin; see under *livery.*

sēiz'ing, *n.* 1. seizure.
2. in nautical usage, (a) the act of binding or fastening together, as with lashings; (b) lashings or cordage used for this; (c) a fastening made in this way.

sēi'zŏr, *n.* in law, one who seizes or takes possession of a freehold estate.

sēi'zūre (-zhur), *n.* 1. the act of seizing; the act of laying hold on suddenly; as, the *seizure* of a thief.
2. the act of taking possession by force; as, the *seizure* of lands or goods; the *seizure* of a town by an enemy; the *seizure* of a throne by a usurper.
3. the act of taking by warrant; as, the *seizure* of contraband goods.
4. a sudden attack, as of a disease.
5. the thing taken or seized. [Obs.]
6. ownership; grasp; possession. [Obs.]

sē'jănt, sē'jeănt, *a.* [Fr. *séant*, ppr. of *seoir*, from L. *sedere*, to sit.] in heraldry, sitting with the forelegs straight and upright: applied to a lion, etc.
sejant affronté; sitting with the entire body facing the observer.

LION SEJANT

Sejm (sām), *n.* [Pol., assembly.]
1. formerly, the lower chamber of the Polish Parliament.
2. the Polish Parliament, now consisting of only one chamber.

sē·join', *v.t.* to separate. [Rare.]

sē·jū'gous, *a.* [L. *sejugis*; *sex*, six, and *jugum*, yoke.] in botany, having six pairs of leaflets.

sē·junc'tion, *n.* the act of disjointing; separation. [Obs.]

sēke, *a.* sick. [Obs.]

sēke, *v.t.* and *v.i.* to seek. [Obs.]

Sekh'et (sek'), *n.* [Egypt.] an Egyptian female deity portrayed as having the head of a cat or lioness.

sē'kŏs, *n.* [Gr., a pen, enclosure.] in ancient Greece, a shrine or sacred enclosure.

sel, *n.* self. [Scot. and Brit. Dial.]

sē·lā'çhi·ăn, *a.* of or belonging to the *Selachii.*

sē·lā'çhi·ăn, *n.* a member of the *Selachii.*

Sē·lā'çhi·ī, *n.pl.* [Gr. *selachos*, shark.] an order of fishes including the sharks, dogfishes, and rays: now sometimes restricted to the division of this order containing the sharks and dogfishes.

sel'ȧ·çhoid, *a.* like a shark.

Sel·ȧ·çhoi'dē·ī, *n.pl.* a group of fishes consisting of the sharks as contrasted with the rays.

sel·ȧ·çhol'ō·ġist, *n.* one who makes a study of selachians.

Sel·ȧ·çhos'tō·mī, *n.pl.* [Gr. *selachos*, shark, and *stoma*, mouth.] an order of ganoid fishes including the paddlefish.

Sel″a·ġi·nel'lȧ, *n.* [dim. of *Selago.*]
1. the typical genus of the *Selaginellaceæ*, consisting of evergreen herbs of mosslike appearance, resembling *Lycopodium.*
2. [s–] a member of this genus.

Sel·aġ″i·nel·lā'cē·ae, *n.pl.* an order or group of cryptogamous plants.

Sē·lā'gō, *n.* [L.] a South African genus of dwarf shrubs having narrow leaves and flowers sessile in slender spikes.

sē'lăh, *n.* [Heb., meaning not known, prob. connected with *sālāh*, rest.] in the Psalms, a Hebrew word found frequently at the end of a verse: its meaning is unknown, but it is often interpreted as an indication of a musical pause or rest.

sē·läm'lik, *n.* [Turk. *selāmliq*, from Ar. *salam* and Turk. suffix *-liq.*]
1. that part of a Turkish house set apart for men, in which guests are received.
2. formerly, the ceremonial visit of the Turkish sultan to a mosque every Friday.

sel'çouth, *a.* rare; unusual; uncommon. [Obs.]

seld, *a.* unusual; rare. [Obs.]

seld, *adv.* rarely; seldom. [Obs.]

sel'den, *adv.* seldom; rarely. [Obs.]

sel'dŏm, *adv.* [AS. *seldan*, *seldon*, *seldum.*] rarely; not often; not frequently.

sel'dŏm, *a.* rare; infrequent. [Obs.]

sel'dŏm·ness, *n.* rareness. [Rare.]

seld'seen, *a.* rarely seen. [Obs.]

sē·leçt', *a.* [L. *selectus*, pp. of *seligere*, to choose, from *se-*, apart, and *legere*, to choose.]
1. chosen in preference to another or others; picked out, especially for excellence or some special quality; picked.
2. choice; excellent; outstanding.
3. careful in choosing or selecting; fastidious.
4. exclusive; as, a *select* company of critics.

sē·leçt', *v.t.*; selected, *pt.*, *pp.*; selecting, *ppr.* to choose and take from a number; to pick out, as for excellence, desirability, etc.

sē·leçt', *v.i.* to make a selection; to choose.

sē·leçt'ed·ly, *adv.* with selection.

sē·leçt·ee', *n.* a person inducted into the armed forces under selective service.

sē·leç'tion, *n.* 1. a selecting or being selected.
2. that or those selected.
3. in biology, any process, whether natural or artificial, by which certain organisms or characteristics are permitted or favored to survive and reproduce in, or as if in, preference to others.

sē·leçt'ive, *a.* 1. of, having to do with, or characterized by selection.
2. having the power of selecting; tending to select.
3. in radio, excluding oscillations on all frequencies except the one desired.
selective absorption; that absorption manifested by a substance when it is impervious to certain rays of heat or light.
selective service; compulsory military training and service according to age, physical fitness, ability, etc.

sē·lect·iv'i·ty, *n.* 1. the state or quality of being selective.

2. the degree to which a radio receiver will reproduce the signals of a given transmitter while rejecting the signals of the others.

sē·lect'ive·ly, *adv.* by selection.

sē·lect'măn, *n.*; *pl.* **sē·lect'men,** in New England, a town officer chosen annually to manage the concerns of the town, provide for the poor, etc. The number is usually from three to seven in each town, and these, organized as a board, constitute a kind of executive authority.

sē·lect'ness, *n.* the state or quality of being select, or well chosen.

sē·lect'ŏr, *n.* one who or that which selects; specifically, in machinery, a device for separating and selecting.

sel'ē·nāte, *n.* a salt of selenic acid.

Sē·lē'nē, *n.* [Gr. *Selēnē*, from *selēnē*, the moon.] the Greek goddess of the moon: cf. *Luna, Artemis, Hecate.*

sē·len'iç, *a.* 1. designating or of compounds in which selenium has a higher valence than in corresponding selenious compounds.

2. designating or of a colorless, crystalline acid, H_2SeO_4.

sel'ē·nīde, sel'ē·nid, *n.* in chemistry, a compound of selenium with one other element or radical.

sel·ē·nif'ẽr·ous, *a.* containing selenium.

sē·lē'ni·ō-, [from *selenium.*] a combining form meaning *selenious.*

sē·lē'ni·ous, *a.* 1. designating or of compounds in which selenium has a lower valence than in corresponding selenic compounds.

2. designating or of a colorless, crystalline acid, H_2SeO_3.

Sē·lē·ni·pē'di·um, *n.* [Gr. *selēnē*, moon, and L. *pes, pedis*, foot.] a small genus of South American orchids containing but two species.

sel'ē·nīte, *n.* [from Gr. *selēnitēs* (*lithos*), moon (stone): so called because supposed to wax and wane with the moon.]

1. a kind of gypsum, occurring in transparent crystals or crystalline masses; specifically, a thin plate used to polarize light in the microscope.

2. in chemistry, a salt of selenium.

sel·ē·nit'iç, sel·ē·nit'iç·ăl, *a.* 1. pertaining to selenite, resembling it, or partaking of its nature and properties.

2. relating to the moon.

sē·lē'ni·um, *n.* [from Gr. *selēnē*, the moon, so named from its being associated with *tellurium*, from L. *tellus*, the earth.] a chemical element of the sulfur group: it is used in photoelectric devices because its electrical conductivity varies with the intensity of light: symbol, Se; atomic weight, 78.96; atomic number, 34.

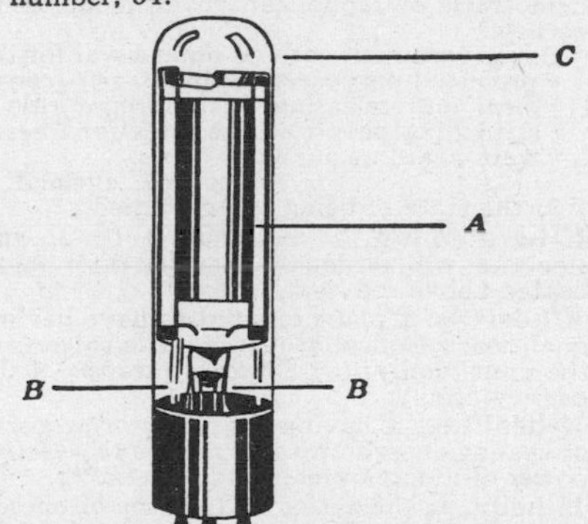

SELENIUM CELL
A. selenium—covered cathode; BB. electric connections; C. exhausted glass container

selenium cell; a photoelectric cell containing selenium plates.

sē·lē'niū·ret, *n.* a selenide. [Obs.]

sē·lē·nō·cen'triç, *a.* [Gr. *selēnē*, the moon, and *kentron*, center.] in astronomy, having relation to the center of the moon; observed or estimated as from that point.

sē·lē'nō·dont, *a.* [Gr. *selēnē*, the moon, and *odous, odontos*, tooth.] having the molars crescent-ridged.

sē·lē'nō·dont, *n.* a selenodont animal.

sē·lē'nō·grȧph, *n.* [Gr. *selēnē*, the moon, and *-graph.*] a picture or chart of the physical features of any part of the moon's surface.

sel·ē·nog'rȧ·phẽr, sel·ē·nog'rȧ·phist, *n.* one skilled in selenography.

sel·ē·nō·graph'iç, sel·ē·nō·graph'i·çăl, *a.* belonging or pertaining to selenography.

sel·ē·nog'rȧ·phy, *n.* [Mod. L. *selenographia*, from Gr. *selēnē*, the moon, and *-graphy.*] study of the surface and physical features of the moon: corresponding to *geography* in respect to the earth.

sel·ē·nō·loġ'i·çăl, *a.* relating to selenology.

sel·ē·nol'ō·ġy, *n.* [from Gr. *selēnē*, the moon; and *-logy.*] the branch of astronomy dealing with the moon.

Sē·leū'ci·ăn, *n.* same as *Seleucidan.*

Sē·leū'cid, *n.* any member of the Seleucidae.

Sē·leū'cid, *a.* same as *Seleucidan.*

Sē·leū'ci·dae, *n.pl.*; *sing.* **Sē·leū'cid,** the members of the dynasty founded by Seleucus Nicator, general of Alexander the Great, in 312 B.C.: they ruled most of Asia Minor, Syria, Persia, and Bactria till 64 B.C.

Sē·leū'cid·ăn, *a.* of, relating to, or having to do with a Seleucid or the dynasty of the Seleucidae.

self, *n.*; *pl.* **selveș,** [AS. *self, seolf.*]

1. the identity, character, or essential qualities of any person or thing.

2. the identity, personality, individuality, etc. of a given person; one's own person as distinct from all others.

3. myself, himself, herself, or yourself; as, tickets for *self* and wife: by some considered to be a pronoun. [Colloq.]

4. one's own welfare, interest, or advantage; selfishness; as, people concerned only with thought of *self.*

self, *a.* 1. being uniform or the same throughout.

2. of the same kind, nature, color, material, etc. as the rest; as, a *self* lining, *self* trim, etc.

self-, [ME.; AS. *self-, sylf-*, from *self*, n.] a prefix used in hyphenated compounds, meaning: (a) *of oneself* or *itself*: the object of the action, as *self*-appraisal, *self*-restraint; (b) *by oneself* or *itself*: the subject of the action, as in *self*-appointed, *self*-starting; (c) *in oneself* or *itself*, as in *self*-centered; (d) *to* or *with oneself* or *itself*, as in *self*-addressed, *self*-content. Many of those of which the meanings are self-evident are given in the list which follows.

self-abhorrence
self-abhorring
self-absorbed
self-accorded
self-accusation
self-accusatory
self-accused
self-admiration
self-admiring
self-advancement
self-affrighted
self-aggrandizement
self-amendment
self-annulling
self-applause
self-application
self-appreciation
self-approbation
self-approving
self-banished
self-baptizer
self-beguiled
self-betrayal
self-blinded
self-care
self-cognition
self-cognizance
self-commitment
self-communication
self-comprehending
self-concern
self-condemnation
self-condemning
self-conflict
self-congratulation
self-conquest
self-conservation
self-constituted
self-consumed
self-consuming
self-contemner
self-contemplation
self-contempt
self-correction
self-criticism
self-crucifixion
self-deceiving
self-dedicated
self-dedication
self-degradation
self-deluded
self-dependence
self-dependent
self-depending
self-depraved
self-depreciation
self-depreciative
self-despair
self-destroyer
self-destroying
self-development
self-devised
self-devouring
self-dialogue
self-diffidence
self-diffusive
self-discernment
self-disciplinarian
self-disparagement
self-display
self-dispraise
self-disserving
self-duplication
self-ease
self-enjoyment
self-evolution
self-exaggeration
self-exaltation
self-exalting
self-exertion
self-explication
self-exposure
self-exulting
self-fed
self-flattering
self-flattery
self-forgetfully
self-forgetfulness
self-generating
self-giving
self-gratulation
self-harming
self-humiliation
self-idolized
self-ignorance
self-ignorant
self-illustrative
self-immolate
self-immolating
self-immolation
self-immunity
self-impartation
self-imparting
self-indignation
self-indulging
self-infliction
self-inspection
self-introspection
self-invited
self-judging
self-killed
self-kindled
self-laudation
self-lauding
self-loathing
self-manifest
self-mortification
self-neglecting
self-oblivion
self-occupation
self-offering
self-originating
self-parade
self-partiality
self-perpetuating
self-planted
self-pleased
self-pleaser
self-pleasing
self-policy
self-power
self-praise
self-preference
self-preservative
self-preserving
self-pride
self-profit
self-propagating
self-reflection
self-reform
self-regardful
self-regarding
self-regulated
self-regulative
self-repression
self-reproof
self-reproved
self-reproving
self-reprovingly
self-repulsive
self-restriction
self-revealing
self-revelation
self-reverence
self-reverent
self-ruined
self-rule
self-sanctification
self-satisfying
self-scorn
self-security
self-sequestered
self-shining
self-similar
self-sold
self-sophistication
self-sought
self-spurring
self-starved
self-subdued
self-subjugation
self-subversive
self-suppression
self-suspended
self-suspicious
self-tormenting
self-tormentor
self-torturing
self-training
self-trust
self-upbraiding
self-valuing
self-worship
self-worshiper

self-ȧ·bāsed' (-bāst'), *a.* humbled by consciousness of guilt or shame.

self-ȧ·bāse'ment, *n.* 1. humiliation or abasement proceeding from consciousness of inferiority, guilt, or shame.

2. degradation of oneself by one's own act.

self-ȧ·bās'ing, *a.* abasing or humiliating oneself through consciousness of inferiority, guilt, or shame.

self-ab·nē·gā'tion, *n.* lack of consideration for oneself or one's own interests; self-denial.

self-ab·sorp'tion, *n.* absorption in one's own interests, affairs, etc.

self-ȧ·būse', *n.* 1. misuse of one's own abilities, talents, etc.

2. masturbation: a euphemism.

self-aç't'ing, *a.* acting of or by itself; working by itself; automatic.

self-aç'tion, *n.* action having its origin in or performed by oneself or itself.

self-aç'tive, *a.* acting of oneself or itself without influence from other agency.

self-aç·tiv'i·ty, *n.* self-motion, or the power of moving oneself or itself without aid.

self-ad·dressed' (-drest'), *a.* addressed to oneself; as, enclose a *self-addressed* envelope.

self-ăd·just'ing, *a.* adjusting by oneself or by itself; as, some machines are, in some respects, automatically *self-adjusting.*

self-adjusting bearing; in machinery, a bearing so supported as to tilt to accommodate itself to a shaft, the position of which changes within certain limits.

self-ăf·fāirș', *n.pl.* one's own private business.

self-ȧ·līgn'ing (-līn'), *a.* aligning by oneself or by itself; as, a *self-aligning* shaft.

self-ăn·nī·hi·lā'tion, *n.* 1. annihilation by one's own acts.

2. self-sacrifice.

self-ap·point'ed, *a.* appointed or chosen by oneself and not by others.

self-ăs·sẽrt'ing, *a.* forward in asserting oneself, or one's rights and claims; putting oneself forward confidently.

self-ăs·sẽr'tion, *n.* the act of demanding recognition for oneself or of asserting or insisting upon one's rights, claims, etc.

self-ăs·sẽrt'ive, *a.* characterized by self-assertion; forward; pushing.

self-ăs·sūmed', *a.* assumed by one's own act or without authority.

self-ăs·sūr'ance (-ă-shūr'), *n.* confidence in oneself; assurance in one's own ability, talent, etc.

self-ăs·sūred', *a.* having or showing self-assurance; self-confident.

self-ăt·traçt'ive, *a.* attractive by oneself.

self-bē·got'ten, *a.* begotten by one's own powers.

self-bīnd′ẽr, *n.* a harvesting machine equipped with an attachment for binding the cut grain into bundles, generally with twine; also, the attachment or device by which the operation of binding the bundles is performed.

self-bọrn′, *a.* born or produced by oneself.

self-cen′tẽred, *a.* 1. stationary or unmoving, as a center or point about which other things move.
2. occupied or concerned only with one's own affairs; egocentric; selfish.

self-cen′tẽr·ing, *a.* centering in oneself.

self-çŏl·leçt′ed, *a.* self-possessed.

self-çŏl′ŏr, *n.* a color without variegation or modification.

self-çŏl′ŏred, *a.* 1. having only one color.
2. having the natural color; with original color unchanged, as a fabric.

self-cŏm·månd′, *n.* self-control.

self-çŏm·mūne′, *n.* self-communion. [Rare.]

self-çŏm·mū′ni·çā·tive, *a.* imparted or communicated by its own powers.

self-çŏm·mūn′iŏn (-yun), *n.* communion with or thoughts of oneself.

self-çŏm·plā′cen·cy, *n.* the state or quality of being self-complacent; satisfaction with oneself or with one's own doings.

self-çŏm·plā′cent, *a.* pleased with oneself or one's own doings; self-satisfied.

self-çŏm·pōşed′ (-pōzd′), *a.* having or showing composure; calm; cool.

self-çŏn·cēit′, *n.* a high opinion of oneself; vanity.

self-çŏn·cēit′ed, *a.* vain; having a high or overweening opinion of one's own person or merits.

self-çŏn·cēit′ed·ness, *n.* vanity; an overweening opinion of one's own person or accomplishments.

self-çon′fi·dence, *n.* confidence in one's own judgment or ability; reliance on one's own opinion or powers, without other aid.

self-çon′fi·dent, *a.* confident of one's own strength or powers; relying on the correctness of one's own judgment, or the competence of one's own powers, without other aid.

self-çon′fi·dent·ly, *adv.* with self-confidence; in a self-confident manner.

self-çŏn·fīd′ing, *a.* confiding in one's own judgment or powers, without the aid of others.

self-çon′jụ·gāte, *a.* in geometry, describing a figure possessing the two elements that are conjugate to each other.

self-çon′scious, *a.* 1. unduly conscious of oneself as an object of notice; awkward or embarrassed in the presence of others; ill-at-ease; shy.
2. showing embarrassment, etc.; as, a *self-conscious* cough.
3. in philosophy and psychology, having or showing awareness of one's own existence, actions, etc., as distinguished from those of others; conscious of oneself or one's own ego.

self-çon′scious·ness, *n.* the quality or state of being self-conscious.

self-çŏn·sid′ẽr·ing, *a.* considering in one's own mind; deliberating.

self-çŏn·sist′en·cy, *n.* the state or character of being self-consistent.

self-çŏn·sist′ent, *a.* having each part consistent with all of the others; consistent with oneself; consistent with itself.

self-çŏn·tāined′, *a.* 1. keeping one's affairs to oneself; reserved; uncommunicative.
2. showing self-command or self-control.
3. having all working parts, complete with motive power, in an enclosed or covered unit: said of machinery.
4. having within oneself or itself all that is necessary; functioning independently; self-sufficient, as a community.
self-contained steam engine; an engine and a boiler connected, complete for operation; similar to a portable engine, but without the traveling gear.

self-çŏn·tent′, *a.* satisfied with what one has or is.

self-çŏn·tent′, *n.* self-satisfaction.

self-çŏn·tent′ment, *n.* self-satisfaction.

self-çŏn·trȧ·diç′tion, *n.* 1. the act of contradicting itself or oneself; as, to be and not to be at the same time is a *self-contradiction*.
2. a proposition consisting of elements that contradict each other.

self-çŏn·trȧ·diçt′ō·ry, *a.* contradicting itself or oneself; inconsistent.

self-çŏn·trōl′, *n.* control exercised over oneself or of one's own emotions, desires, actions, etc.

self-çŏn·viçt′ed, *a.* convicted by one's own consciousness, knowledge, or avowal.

self-çŏn·viç′tion, *n.* conviction proceeding from one's own consciousness, knowledge, or confession.

self-çrē·āt′ed, *a.* created by oneself; not formed or constituted by another.

self-çul′tūre, *n.* culture, training, or education of oneself without the aid of teachers.

self-dē·cēit′, *n.* a deceiving of oneself or being deceived by oneself; self-deception.

self-dē·cēived′, *a.* deceived or misled respecting oneself by one's own mistake or error.

self-dē·cep′tion, *n.* deception concerning oneself, proceeding from one's own mistake.

self-dē·fense′, *n.* 1. defense of oneself or of the things that are one's own, as property, security, rights, reputation, etc.
2. the art of boxing: usually in *manly art of self-defense.*
3. in law, the right to preserve oneself with whatever force is reasonably necessary against actual violence or the threat of violence.

self-dē·fens′ive, *a.* of or constituting self-defense.

self-def·i·ni′tion (-nish′un), *n.* the understanding or determination of one's own nature or basic qualities.

self-dē·lū′şion, *n.* self-deception.

self-dē·nī′ăl, *n.* the denial of oneself; the forbearing to gratify one's own appetites or desires, often for the sake of others.

self-dē·nȳ′ing, *a.* denying oneself; exercising self-denial.

self-dē·nȳ′ing·ly, *adv.* in a self-denying manner.

self-dē·struç′tion, *n.* the destruction of oneself or itself; voluntary destruction; specifically, suicide.

self-dē·struç′tive, *a.* tending to self-destruction.

self-dē·tẽr·mi·nā′tion, *n.* 1. determination or decision according to one's own mind or will, without outside influence; free will.
2. the right of a people to decide upon its own form of government, without coercion or outside influence.

self-dē·tẽr′mined, *a.* determined or decided by oneself or itself.

self-dē·tẽr′min·ing, *a.* determining by or of itself; characterized by, or having the power of, self-determination; as, the *self-determining* power of the will.

self-dē·vōt′ed, *a.* characterized by self-devotion.

self-dē·vō′tion, *n.* the devoting of one's person and services voluntarily to the interests of others; self-sacrifice; the state of being self-devoted.

self-di·ġes′tion (-chun), *n.* in medicine, autodigestion.

self-dis′ci·pline, *n.* planned control and training of oneself for the sake of development.

self-dis·çŏv′ẽr·y, *n.* a becoming aware of one's true potential, character, motives, etc.

self-dis·trust′, *n.* diffidence; lack of confidence in oneself or in one's abilities.

self-dọomed′, *a.* doomed by oneself.

self-driv′en, *a.* containing its own drive or motive power; automotive.

self-ef·fāce′ment, *n.* the practice of avoiding the notice or attention of others by keeping oneself in the background and minimizing one's own actions; modest, retiring behavior.

self-ē·leçt′ed, *a.* elected by oneself.

self-ē·leçt′ive, *a.* having the right to elect oneself, or, as a body, to elect its own members.

self-em·ployed′, *a.* working for oneself, with direct control over work, services, etc. undertaken and fees, charges, etc. set.

self-es·teem′, *n.* 1. belief in oneself; self-respect.
2. undue pride in oneself.

self-es·ti·mā′tion, *n.* 1. esteem or good opinion of oneself.
2. overestimation of oneself or powers.

self-ev′i·dence, *n.* evidence or certainty resulting from a proposition without proof; evidence that ideas offer to the mind upon bare statement.

self-ev′i·dent, *a.* evident without need of proof or discussion; that produces certainty or clear conviction upon mere presentation to the mind.

self-ev′i·dent·ly, *adv.* in a self-evident manner; so as to be self-evident.

self-ex·am·i·nā′tion, *n.* an examination or scrutiny into one's own state, conduct, and motives, particularly in regard to religious affections and duties; introspection.

self-ex·ci·tā′tion, *n.* in electromagnetism, the excitation of a field magnet, as in a dynamo, by means of its own or part of its own current, as distinguished from *separate excitation.*

self-ex·cīt′ed, *a.* excited by its own current, as a field magnet of a dynamo.

self-ex′ē·çū·ting, *a.* self-acting, as a treaty which by its own provisions becomes operative without legislative ratification; coming into effect automatically when specified, without further provision being made, as a death clause in a contract.

self-ex·ist′ence, *n.* the quality or state of being self-existent.

self-ex·ist′ent, *a.* existing by its own nature or essence, independent of any other cause; having independent existence; as, God is the only *self-existent* being.

self-ex·plāin′ing, *a.* self-explanatory.

self-ex·plan′ȧ·tō·ry, *a.* explaining itself; needing no explanation; obvious.

self-ex·pres′sion (-presh′un), *n.* the expression of one's own personality or emotions, especially through some art form.

self-feed′ing, *a.* capable of feeding oneself or itself; automatically supplying itself with material, fuel, work, etc.

self-fẽr′tile, *a.* designating a plant that fertilizes itself with its pollen: opposed to *self-impotent.*

self-fẽr″ti·li·zā′tion, *n.* fertilization by its own pollen or seed, as in some plants and animals.

self-fẽr′ti·līzed, *a.* fertilized by or as by its own pollen.

self-fọr·get′fụl, *a.* selfless; unselfish.

self-fụl·fill′ing, *a.* 1. bringing about self-fulfillment.
2. brought to fulfillment chiefly as an effect of having been expected or predicted; as, a *self-fulfilling* prophecy.

self-fụl·fill′ment, *n.* fulfillment of one's own aspirations, hopes, etc. through one's own efforts.

self-glō′ri·ous, *a.* springing from vainglory or vanity; vain; boastful.

self-gŏv′ẽrned, *a.* governed by oneself, or, as a body, by itself through officials chosen by it members.

self-gŏv′ẽrn·ment, *n.* 1. self-control. [Rare.]
2. a system of government by which the mass of a nation or people appoint the rulers; democratic or republican government; democracy.

> Our government entered upon a war for the professed purpose of aiding to *self-government* and releasing from foreign rule a struggling people whose cries for liberty were heard at our very doors.
> —Grover Cleveland.

3. the state of being self-governed.

self-härd′en·ing, *a.* designating or of any steel that will harden if air-cooled after being heated above red heat.

self′hēal″, *n.* a plant reputed to have healing qualities; specifically, (a) *Prunella vulgaris* of the mint family; (b) *Sanicula europæa* of the parsley family.

self-hēal′ing, *a.* having the power or property of healing oneself or itself; as, the *self-healing* power of living animals and vegetables.

self-help′, *n.* the act of taking care of oneself without outside help, as in improving the mind or abilities through study.

self′hood, *n.* 1. all the things that make a person what he is; personality; individuality.
2. the condition of being self-centered; selfishness.

self-ī·den′ti·ty, *n.* the identity of a thing with itself, or the awareness of this identity in the self.

self-im·pọr′tănce, *n.* an exaggerated opinion of one's own importance, expecially as shown in behavior; pompous or officious conceit.

self-im·pọr′tănt, *a.* important in one's own esteem; pompous.

self-im·pōşed′, *a.* imposed or inflicted on oneself by oneself, as a penalty.

self-im′pō·tent, *a.* not able to fertilize itself with its own pollen: opposite of *self-fertile.*

self-im·prōve′ment, *n.* improvement of one's condition, mind, abilities, etc. through one's own efforts.

self-in·clū′sive, *a.* including oneself or itself.

self-in·crim·i·nā′tion, *n.* incrimination of oneself by one's own statements or answers.

self-in·dūced′ (-dōōst′), *a.* 1. induced by oneself or itself.
2. produced by self-induction.

self-in·duc′tion, *n.* in electricity, induction produced in a circuit by the action of the current on itself at the moment of starting or stopping, or upon a variation in its strength.

self-in·dul′gence, *n.* the habit of indulging one's desires or passions with little thought of the cost to or effect upon others.

self-in·dul′gent, *a.* unduly indulgent of one's own tastes, desires, or passions.

self-in·fec′tion, *n.* in physiology, autointoxication.

self-in·flict′ed, *a.* inflicted on oneself by oneself.

self-in·i′ti·āt·ed (-i-nish′), *a.* initiated by oneself or itself.

self-in·sūr′ănce (-shūr′), *n.* insurance of oneself or one's property, usually by providing a fund out of current income.

self-in′tēr·est, *n.* 1. one's own interest or advantage.
2. an exaggerated regard for this, usually at the expense of others; selfishness.

self-in′tēr·est·ed, *a.* having self-interest; particularly concerned for oneself.

self-in·vō·lū′tion, *n.* reverie; mental abstraction.

self′ish, *a.* 1. caring only or chiefly for self; regarding one's own interest chiefly or solely; proceeding from love of self; influenced in actions solely by a view to private advantage; as, a *selfish* person; a *selfish* motive.
2. showing or caused by such regard, as an action.

self′ish·ly, *adv.* in a selfish way; with little or no regard for the rights of others.

self′ish·ness, *n.* the state or character of being selfish; the exclusive consideration by a person of his own interest or happiness.

self′ism, *n.* absolute selfishness. [Rare.]

self′ist, *n.* one whose conduct is ruled by selfism. [Rare.]

self-knōw′ing (-nō′), *a.* 1. knowing one's own character and mental and physical abilities and limitations.
2. knowing of oneself or without communication from another.

self-knowl′edge (-nol′ej), *n.* the knowledge of one's own real character, abilities, qualities, etc.

self′less, *a.* without regard for oneself or one's own interests; unselfish: the opposite of *selfish.*

self′less·ness, *n.* the state or character of being selfless or unselfish.

self-līfe′, *n.* an existence passed entirely for one's own pleasure or good; life for oneself.

self-lim′it·ed, *a.* limited by its own peculiarities, as diseases which run their course within self-determined periods, as measles, typhus fever, etc.

self-liq′ui·dāt·ing (-lik′wi-), *a.* providing profit in a short time; converting itself into cash in the normal course of business.

self-lōad′ing, *a.* loading again by its own action, as a gun.

self-lŏve′, *n.* the love of self; regard for or interest in oneself and one's happiness.
Syn.—selfishness, self-esteem.

self-lŏv′ing, *a.* having or showing self-love.

self-lū′bri·cāt·ing, *a.* lubricating by itself; as, a *self-lubricating* bearing.

self-lū′min·ous, *a.* possessing in itself the property of emitting light.

self-māde′, *a.* 1. made by oneself or itself.
2. successful, rich, etc. through one's own efforts.

self-mas′tēr·y, *n.* self-command; self-control.

self-med′i·cāte, *v.i.*; self-medicated, *pt., pp.*; self-medicating, *ppr.* to treat oneself with medicine without consulting a physician.

self-mō′tion, *n.* motion given by inherent powers without external impulse; spontaneous motion.

self-mŏved′, *a.* moved by inherent power without the aid of external impulse.

self-mŏv′ing, *a.* moving or able to move under its own power, or of itself.

self-mŭr′dēr, *n.* the murder of oneself; suicide.

self-mŭr′dēr·ēr, *n.* one who voluntarily takes his own life.

self′ness, *n.* 1. the quality or qualities which constitute individuality; identity of person.
2. egotism; absolute selfishness.

self-ō·pin′iŏn (-yun), *n.* 1. one's opinion of himself; especially, high opinion of oneself.
2. high regard for, or stubbornness in, one's own opinion.

self-ō·pin′iŏn·ā·ted, *a.* 1. without regard for the opinion of others; stubborn in holding to one's own opinions.
2. conceited.

self-ō·pin′iŏned, *a.* self-opinionated.

self-or·dāined′ (-dānd′), *a.* ordained or appointed by oneself and not by others.

self-pēr·plexed′ (-plext′), *a.* perplexed by one's own thoughts or misgivings.

self-pit′y, *n.* pity for oneself.

self-poised′, *a.* kept well-balanced by regard for oneself or by self-respect.

self-pol′li·nāt·ed, *a.* pollinated by the transfer of pollen from stamen to pistil in the same flower.

self-pol·li·nā′tion, *n.* pollination by its own pollen.

self-pol·lū′tion, *n.* masturbation: a euphemism.

self-pōr′trāit, *n.* a painting, drawing, etc. of oneself, done by oneself.

self-pos′it·ed, *a.* posited of or by itself.

self-pŏs·sessed′ (-zest′), *a.* not disturbed; calm; composed.

self-pŏs·ses′sion (-zesh′un), *n.* the possession of one's faculties or feelings; calmness; self-command.

self-pres·ēr·vā′tion, *n.* 1. preservation of oneself from danger, injury, or death.
2. the urge to preserve oneself, regarded as an instinct.

self-prō·dūced′ (-dūst′), *a.* produced by oneself or itself.

self-prō·nounc′ing, *a.* having diacritical marks or other aids to pronunciation directly applied to the original spelling instead of being rewritten in phonetic transcription; as, a Bible with *self-pronouncing* proper names.

self-prō·pelled′ (-peld′), *a.* producing its own power of movement or propulsion; propelled of itself.

self-prō·pel′ling, *a.* self-propelled.

self-prō·tec′tion, *n.* self-defense.

self-rē″ăl·i·zā′tion, *n.* the complete fulfillment or development of the self and all its possibilities.

self-rē·cord′ing, *a.* making an automatic record of its own functions or operations, as a machine; autographic.

self-rē·gärd′, *n.* regard or concern for oneself and one's interests.

self-reg′is·tēr·ing, *a.* registering automatically; applied to any instrument which records its own indications at stated times, or continuously, or at maximum or minimum points; as, a *self-registering* thermometer.

self-rē·lā′tion, *n.* self-identity.

self-rē·lī′ănce, *n.* reliance on one's own powers, judgment, ability, etc.

self-rē·lī′ănt, *a.* relying on oneself; trusting to one's own abilities.

self-rē·ly′ing, *a.* self-reliant.

self-rē·nun·ci·ā′tion, *n.* the act of renouncing one's own rights; self-abnegation.

self-rē·pel′len·cy, *n.* the inherent power of repulsion in a body.

self-rē·pel′ling, *a.* repelling by its own inherent power.

self-rep·ē·ti′tion (-tish′un), *n.* the act of repeating one's own words or deeds.

self-rē·prōach′, *n.* the act of condemning oneself; reproach by one's own conscience.

self-rē·prōached′ (-prōcht′), *a.* reproached by one's own conscience.

self-rē·prōach′ful, *a.* reproachful of oneself.

self-rēprōach′ing, *a.* reproaching oneself.

self-rē·prōach′ing·ly, *adv.* in a self-reproachful manner.

self-rē·pug′nănt, *a.* repugnant to itself; inconsistent; self-contradictory.

self-rē·spect′, *n.* respect for oneself or for one's own character and reputation.

self-rē·spect′ing, *a.* having or showing self-respect.

self-rē·strāined′, *a.* restrained by itself or by one's own power or will; not controlled by external force or authority.

self-rē·strāint′, *n.* a restraint over oneself; self-control.

self-rīght′eous (-rī′chus), *a.* 1. righteous, proper, moral, etc. in one's own opinion; pharisaical.
2. characteristic of a self-righteous person.

self-rīght′eous·ness, *n.* the quality or state of being self-righteous.

self-rīght′ing (-rīt′), *a.* that regains its position when overturned; as, a *self-righting* boat.

self-rīs′ing, *a.* rising by itself, as dough, without the use of a leavening agent.
self-rising flour; flour to which baking powder and salt have been added: used in making griddlecakes, biscuits, etc.

self-sac′ri·fīce, *n.* sacrifice of oneself or of self-interest for the supposed good of another; self-denial.

self-sac′ri·fī·cing, *a.* yielding up one's own interest, feelings, etc.; sacrificing oneself.

self′sāme, *a.* the very same; identical.

self-sat·is·fac′tion, *n.* the quality or state of being self-satisfied.

self-sat′is·fīed, *a.* feeling or showing satisfaction with oneself or one's accomplishments; self-complacent.

self-sēal′ing, *a.* made with a substance that automatically seals bullet holes, punctures, etc.; as, a *self-sealing* gas tank or pneumatic tire.

self-seek′ēr, *n.* one who seeks only his own selfish interest.

self-seek′ing, *a.* selfish; characteristic of a self-seeker.

self-seek′ing, *n.* selfishness; the behavior or traits of a self-seeker.

self-sērve′, *a.* designating a restaurant or store in which the customer serves himself with food or goods.

self-sēr′vice, *n.* the act or practice of serving oneself in a cafeteria, store, etc.

self-sēr′vice, *a.* designating an establishment characterized by self-service.

self-sērv′ing, *a.* serving one's own selfish interests, especially at the expense of others.

self-slaugh′tēr (-slą′), *n.* suicide.

self-sōwn′, *a.* sown by such means as wind, water, or other natural agency, as some weeds, rather than by man or animal.

self-stärt′ēr, *n.* a mechanism for automatically starting an internal-combustion engine.

self-stȳled′ (-stīld′), *a.* named (as such) by oneself; as, a *self-styled* guardian of democracy.

self-suf·fi′cien·cy (-fish′en-), *n.* the state or quality of being self-sufficient.

self-suf·fi′cient, *a.* 1. having undue confidence in one's own abilities or endowments; hence, haughty; overbearing; conceited.
2. capable of effecting one's own ends or fulfilling one's own desires without the aid of others.

self-suf·fī′cing, *a.* sufficient for itself or oneself.

self-sug·gest′ed, *a.* excited or produced by causes inherent in its own nature or organism; not produced by external influence.

self-sup·port′, *n.* support of oneself or itself without external aid or reinforcement.

self-sup·port′ed, *a.* supported by oneself or itself.

self-sup·port′ing, *a.* supporting oneself or itself.

self-sur·ren′dēr, *n.* the yielding up of one's person, tastes, affections, or will to another.

self-sus·tāined′, *a.* sustained by one's own power or efforts; upheld by one's strength of will.

self-sus·tāin′ing, *a.* supporting or able to support oneself or itself.

self-sus′tē·nănce, *n.* self-support.

self-taught′ (-tąt′), *a.* taught through one's own efforts without help from others; self-educated.

self-tor′tūre, *n.* any mental or physical distress inflicted upon oneself.

self-view′ (-vū′), *n.* a view of one's own character or actions.

self-vī′ō·lence, *n.* violence to oneself.

self-will′, *n.* one's own will; obstinacy.

self-willed′, *a.* governed by one's own will; not yielding to the wishes of others; obstinate.

self-willed′ness, *n.* obstinacy; self-will.

self-wīnd′ing, *a.* wound automatically, as some wrist watches, clocks, etc.

self-wrọng′ (-rọng′), *n.* wrong done by a person to himself.

sel′iŏn (-yun), *n.* a ridge of land between two furrows; also, a piece of land broken up into ridges. [Obs.]

Sel·jụk′, *n.* [Turk.] a member of any of several Turkish dynasties from the eleventh to the thirteenth centuries.

Sel·jụk′, *a.* 1. of the Seljuk dynasties.
2. of the Seljuk Turks.

Sel·jụk′i·ăn, *a.* of or characteristic of the Seljuks.

Sel·jụk′i·ăn, *n.* a Seljuk.

Sel·jụk′ Tŭrks, a branch of Turkic peoples that expanded westward from Turkestan in the 11th century.

sell, *n.* self. [Scot.]

sell, *n.* a sill. [Obs.]

sell, *n.* a seat; a high seat; also, a saddle. [Obs.]

sell, *v.t.*; sold, *pt., pp.*; selling, *ppr.* [AS. *sellan, syllan,* to give, deliver up.]
1. to give up, deliver, or exchange (goods, services, etc.) for money or its equivalent; to part with for a price.
2. to make a practice of offering or stocking for sale; to have or offer regularly for sale; to deal in; as, a department store *sells* many things.
3. (a) to give up or deliver (a person) to his enemies or into slavery, bondage, etc.; (b) to betray (a country, cause, etc.).
4. to give up (one's honor, trust, etc.) for profit.
5. to bring about, help in, or promote the sale of; to cause to be sold; as, radio *sells* many products.
6. to establish faith, confidence, or belief in; as, he couldn't *sell* the scheme even to his friends. [Colloq.]
7. to persuade (a person) of the value of; to convince (with *on*); as, he was *sold on* the idea.
8. to cheat; dupe; hoax. [Slang.]
to sell off; to get rid of by selling, especially at low prices.
to sell oneself; (a) to exchange one's services for a price, especially for a dishonorable or sexual purpose; (b) [Colloq.] to convince another of one's worth.
to sell out; (a) to get rid of completely by selling; (b) [Colloq.] to sell or betray (someone, one's trust, etc.).
to sell up; (a) to sell all of; (b) [Brit.] to sell all of, as land or household goods, to satisfy debts, as in bankruptcy; (c) [Brit.] to sell all the goods of (a person).

sell, *v.i.* 1. to exchange goods or services for money, etc.; to engage in selling.
2. to be a popular item on the market; to attract buyers.
3. to be widely approved or accepted; as, do you think the idea will *sell?* [Colloq.]

sell, *n.* a trick or hoax. [Slang.]
to sell out; (a) to dispose of all one's belongings, goods, shares, etc.; (b) in the English army, to sell one's commission in the army and retire from the service.

sel′lăn·dẽrṣ, *n.pl.* same as *sallenders.*

sell′ẽr, *n.* 1. one who sells; a vendor.
2. something that sells, usually with reference to its rate of sale; as, a good *seller.*

sell′ẽr, *n.* a saltcellar. [Obs.]

sell′ing, *a.* 1. of sale; as, *selling* price.
2. engaged in the business of offering something for sale.
3. easily salable; in great demand.

sell′ing rāce, a claiming race immediately after which the winning horse is offered for sale at auction.

sell′out, sell′-out, *n.* 1. a selling out. [Colloq.]
2. an entertainment for which all the seats or tickets are sold. [Colloq.]

Selt′zẽr, *n.* [from *Neider Selters,* a town near Wiesbaden, Germany.]
1. natural spring water of high mineral content and effervescent quality.
2. [*often* s–] any similar water prepared artifically.
Also *Seltzer water.*

sel′vāġe, sel′vedġe, *n.* [*self* and *edge*; lit., an edge formed of the stuff itself, in opposition to one sewed on.]
1. the edge of a piece of cloth so woven as not to unravel, and finished so as to require no hem.
2. the plate of a lock through which the bolt passes.
3. in mining, a layer of soft matter between lode and wall rock, composed of clay, gouge, etc.

sel′vāġe, sel′vedġe, *v.t.* to form a selvage on.

sel′vāġed, sel′vedġed, *a.* having a selvage.

sel·vȧ·ġee′, *n.* in nautical usage, a skein of parallel rope yarns, wound round with yarns or marline, and used for stoppers, straps, etc.

selveṣ, *n.* pl. of *self.*

Sē·mae·ō·stom′ȧ·tȧ, *n.pl.* in zoology, same as *Semostomæ.*

sē·man′tiç, *a.* [Gr. *sēmantikos,* significant meaning.]
1. of meaning, especially meaning in language; as, syllable stress is a *semantic* factor.
2. of or according to the science of semantics.

sē·man′ti·cist, *n.* a specialist in semantics.

sē·man′tiçs, *n.pl.* [*construed as sing.*] [from *semantic,* after Fr. *sémantique* as adopted by Bréal (1887), of the same origin.]
1. the branch of linguistics concerned with the nature, structure, and, especially, the development and changes, of the meanings of speech forms; semasiology.
2. the scientific study of the relations between signs, or symbols, and what they mean, or denote, and of behavior in its psychological and sociological aspects as it is influenced by signs.

sem′ȧ·phōre, *n.* [Gr. *sēma,* a sign, and *-phora,* a carrying, from *pherein,* to bear.]
1. any apparatus for signaling, as by an arrangement of lights, flags, and mechanical arms on railroads.
2. a system of signaling by the use of two flags, one held in each hand: the letters of the alphabet are represented by the various positions of the arms.
3. any system of signaling by semaphore.

sem′ȧ·phōre, *v.t.* and *v.i.*; semaphored, *pt., pp.*; semaphoring, *ppr.* to signal by or as by semaphore.

sem′ȧ·phōre plant, in botany, the telegraph plant of the East Indies, *Desmodium gyrans.*

sem·ȧ·phor′iç, sem·ȧ·phor′iç·ăl, *a.* pertaining to or like a semaphore; telegraphic.

sem·ȧ·phor′iç·ăl·ly, *adv.* with the aid or by means of a semaphore.

sem′ȧ·phōr·ist, *n.* one who signals by a semaphore.

sē·mā″si·ō·loġ′i·çăl, *a.* semantic.

sē·mā·si·ol′ō·ġy, *n.* [Gr. *sēmasia,* the signification of a word, and *logos,* discourse.] in linguistics, semantics.

sē·mat′iç, *a.* [Gr. *sēma, sēmatos,* a sign.] in biology, serving as a warning or sign of danger, as the color of some poisonous snakes.

sem·ȧ·tol′ō·ġy, *n.* [Gr. *sēma, sēmatos,* a sign, and *-logy.*] the study of the use of signs for the expression of ideas. [Rare.]

sem′ȧ·trōpe, *n.* [Gr. *sēma,* a sign, and *-tropos,* from *trepein,* to turn.] a kind of heliograph used for signaling.

sem′blȧ·ble, *a.* [OFr. *sembler,* to seem.]
1. similar; like.
2. suitable.
3. apparent or seeming but not real.

sem′blȧ·ble, *n.* 1. something similar. [Archaic.]
2. resemblance; likeness. [Archaic.]

sem′blănce, *n.* [Fr. *semblance,* from *sembler,* to seem, to appear, from L. *similare, simulare,* to make like, from *similis,* like.]
1. outward form or appearance; aspect.
2. the look or appearance of something else; resemblance.
3. a likeness, image, representation, or copy.
4. false, assumed, or deceiving form or appearance.
5. mere empty show; pretense.

sem′blănt, *n.* show; figure; resemblance. [Obs.]

sem′blănt, *a.* like; resembling. [Obs.]

sem′blȧ·tive, *a.* resembling.

sem′ble (-bl), *v.i.* 1. to seem; to appear; to make a likeness. [Obs.]
Where *sembling* art may carve the fair effect. —Prior.
2. in law, it seems: used impersonally and commonly prefixed to a point of law not necessary to be decided in the case, which has not been directly settled, but on which the court indicates its opinion.

sem′ble, *a.* resembling. [Obs.]

se·mé′ (se-mā′), *a.* [Fr., sown.] in heraldry, a sprinkling, strewing, or sowing, as of ornamental figures.

SEMÉ OF FLEURS-DE-LIS

sē·meī·og′rȧ·phy, *n.* same as *semiography.*

sē″meī·ō·loġ′iç·ăl, *a.* same as *semiological.*

sē·meī·ol′ō·ġy, *n.* same as *semiology.*

sē·meī·ot′iç, *a.* same as *semiotic.*

sē·meī·ot′içs, *n.* same as *symptomatology.*

Sem′e·lē, *n.* in Greek mythology, the daughter of Cadmus and mother of Zeus's son Dionysus: when she desired to see Zeus as he appeared to the gods, she was destroyed by his lightning.

sē′men, *n.*; *pl.* **sem′i·nȧ,** [L., seed.]
1 seed of plants.
2. the fluid secreted by the testes of male animals. It is whitish and viscid and contains the spermatozoa.

sem·e·nif′ẽr·ous, *a.* seminiferous.

sē·mes′tẽr, *n.* [Fr. *semestre*; L. *semestris,* half-yearly; *sex,* six, and *mensis,* month.]
1. a six-month period; a half year.
2. one of the two (or three) terms, of fifteen to eighteen weeks each, which make up a school or college year in most American educational institutions.

sem′ī, *n.* a detachable trailer and the tractor to which it is attached and by which it is partly supported: in full, *semitrailer.*

sem′i- (*or* sem′ī-), [L.; akin to Gr. *hemi-,* Sans. *sami-,* AS. *sam-.*] a prefix meaning: (a) *half,* as in *semi*diameter; (b) *partly, not fully, imperfectly,* as in *semi*civilized; (c) *twice in a* (specified period), as in *semi*annually.

sem·i·ac′id, *a.* partly acid.

sem″i·ad·hẽr′ent, *a.* partly adherent.

sem″i·ā·ē′ri·ăl, *a.* in botany, developed partly in the air instead of in soil or water.

sem″i·am·plex′i·çaul, *a.* in botany, partially amplexicaul; embracing half the stem, as some leaves.

sem·i·añ′gle, *n.* half of a given angle.

sem·i·an′nū·ăl, *a.* 1. happening, prepared, presented, etc. every half year.
2. lasting half a year, as some plants.

sem·i·an′nū·ăl·ly, *adv.* every half year.

sem·i·an′nū·lăr, *a.* having the figure of a half circle.

sem′i·āpe, *n.* a lemur.

Sem·i-Ā′ri·ăn, *n.* in ecclesiastical history, a member of a fourth-century sect which held that the Son was of a like substance but not of the same substance with the Father.

Sem·i-Ā′ri·ăn, *a.* pertaining to Semi-Arianism.

Sem·i-Ā′ri·ăn·iṣm, *n.* the doctrines or tenets of the Semi-Arians.

sem·i·ar′id, *a.* partially arid.

sem″i·ạu·tō·mat′iç, *a.* 1. partly automatic and partly hand-controlled: said of machinery.
2. having an automatic chambering mechanism but requiring a trigger pull for each round fired: said of repeating firearms.

sem″i·ạu·ton′ō·mous, *a.* granted autonomy with regard to internal affairs only, by a controlling nation, organization, etc.

sem·i·ax′is, *n.* one-half the axis, as of an ellipse.

sem″i·bär·bãr′i·ăn, *a.* partially civilized.

sem″i·bär·bãr′i·ăn, *n.* a partially civilized person.

sem″i·bär·bar′iç, *a.* partially civilized.

sem·i·bär′bȧ·riṣm, *n.* the quality or state of being partially civilized.

sem·i·bär′bȧ·rous, *a.* partially civilized.

sem·i·bas′tion (-chun), *n.* either of the halves which compose a bastion.

sem′i·brēve, *n.* [It.] in music, a note of half the duration or time of the breve; a whole note.

sem′i·brief, *n.* a semibreve. [Rare.]

sem′i·bụll, *n.* a papal bull issued between the election of a pope and his coronation.

sem″i·cal·cā′rē·ous, *a.* partly calcareous.

sem·i·cal′cīned, *a.* half-calcined; as, *semicalcined* iron.

sem″i·cȧ·nal′, *n.* a duct with one side open.

sem·i·cär·ti·laġ′i·nous, *a.* consisting partly of cartilage.

sem·i·çạu′dāte, *a.* possessing a rudimentary or short tail.

sem′i·cell, *n.* in biology, either half of a cell constricted in the middle.

sem″i·cen·ten′ni·ăl, *a.* 1. happening once in a period of 50 years.
2. lasting for 50 years.

sem″i·cen·ten′ni·ăl, *n.* 1. a 50th year of existence or duration; 50th anniversary.
2. the celebration of this.

sem″i·chā·ot′iç, *a.* partially chaotic.

sem′i·chō·rus, *n.* a part of a chorus performed by only a few of the singers.

sem′i·cîr·cle (-kl), *n.* 1. a half circle; the part of a circle included between its diameter and half of its circumference; also, a semicircumference.
2. any body in the form of a half circle.
3. an instrument used in surveying for taking angles.

sem′i·cîr·cled (-kld), *a.* semicircular.

sem·i·cîr′cū·lăr, *a.* having the form of a half circle.
semicircular canals; three bony tubes of the inner ear that serve to maintain balance in the organism.

sem″i·cîr·çum′fēr·ence, *n.* half a circumference.

sem′i·cīrque (-sērk), *n.* an opening among trees or hills in the form of a semicircle.

sem·i·civ′i·līzed (-līzd), *a.* partly civilized.

sem′i·cō·lŏn, *n.* a mark of punctuation (;) used to denote a degree of separation greater than that marked by the comma and less than that marked by the period, etc.: conventionally used chiefly to separate units that contain elements separated by commas, and to separate co-ordinate clauses having a relationship in meaning not explicitly stated.

sem′i·cō·lŏn but′tēr·flȳ, a butterfly, *Polygonia interrogationis*, marked on the under part of the wings with a silvery mark like a semicolon.

sem′i·çol·umn (-um), *n.* a half column.

sem″i·cō·lum′năr, *a.* like a half column; flat on one side and round on the other.

sem″i·cŏm·paçt′, *a.* half compact; imperfectly indurated.

sem″i·cŏn·duçt′ŏr, *n.* a substance, as germanium or silicon, whose conductivity is poor at low temperatures but is improved by minute additions of certain substances or by the application of heat, light, or voltage: used in transistors, rectifiers, etc.

sem·i·çon′scious (-shus), *a.* not fully conscious or awake; partially conscious.

sem′i·çōpe, *n.* an ancient clerical garment, being a short cloak. [Obs.]

sem″i·çrus·tā′ceous, *a.* half crustaceous.

sem·i·çrys′tăl·line, *a.* imperfectly crystallized, as certain rocks.

sem·i·çū′biç·ăl, *a.* in conic sections, designating a species of parabola of which the cubes of the ordinates are proportional to the squares of the corresponding abscissas.

sem″i·cy·lin′driç, *a.* semicylindrical.

sem″i·cy·lin′driç·ăl, *a.* half cylindrical.

sem·i·dāi′ly, *a.* twice daily.

sem″i·dē·is′tiç·ăl, *a.* half deistical; bordering on deism.

sem·i·dem·i·sem·i·quā′vēr (-kwā′), *n.* in music, a sixty-fourth note.

sem″i·dē·tached′ (-tacht′), *a.* partly separated, as a pair of houses which are detached from other buildings and joined together by a single wall; as, a *semidetached* villa.

sem″i·dē·vel′ŏped (-ŏpt), *a.* partly developed.

sem·i·dī·am′ē·tēr, *n.* half the diameter; a radius.

sem·i·dī·ȧ·pā′ṣŏn, *n.* in music, an imperfect octave; a diminished octave.

sem·i·dī·ȧ·pen′tē, *n.* in music, an imperfect fifth.

sem·i·dī·aph′ȧ·nous, *a.* imperfectly transparent.

sem·i·dī·ȧ·tes′sȧ·ron, *n.* in music, an imperfect or defective fourth. [Rare.]

sem·i·dī′tōne, *n.* in music, a lesser third, having its terms as 6 to 5; a hemiditone. [Rare.]

sem″i·dī·ūr′năl, *a.* 1. pertaining to or accomplished in half a day or twelve hours; continuing half a day.
2. coming twice a day, or about every twelve hours, as the tides.
semidiurnal arc; in astronomy, half the arc described by a heavenly body between its rising and setting.

sem″i·di·vīne′, *a.* in theology, not having full divinity.

sem′i·dōme, *n.* half a dome, especially as formed by a vertical section.

sem·i·dŏu′ble (-dub′l), *n.* an ecclesiastical office or feast celebrated with less solemnity than the double ones.

sem·i·dŏu′ble, *a.* in botany, having the outermost stamens converted into petals, while the inner ones remain perfect: said of a flower.

sem″i·el·lip′ti·căl, *a.* 1. having the form of a half ellipse.
2. nearly, or not perfectly, elliptical.

sem·i·eq′ui·tant (-ek′wi-), *a.* in botany, partially equitant, as some leaves.

sem·i·fā′ble, *n.* a narrative or tale that is part fable and part truth. [Rare.]

sem·i·fī′năl, *a.* 1. half final.
2. in sports, relating to the round in a game or contest which precedes the finals.

sem·i·fī′năl, *n.* in sports, a semifinal contest or, [*pl.*] a semifinal round.

sem·i·fī′năl·ist, *n.* in sports, any one of the contestants who compete in the semifinal round of an elimination match.

sem′i·flexed (-flekst), *a.* bent part way, as a limb.

sem·i·flex′iŏn (-flek′shun), *n.* the position of a limb midway between flexion and extension.

sem·i·flō′ret, *n.* same as *semifloscule.*

sem·i·flos′çū·lăr, *a.* semiflosculous.

sem·i·flos′çūle, *n.* a floscule whose corolla consists of a single strap-shaped petal.

sem·i·flos′çū·lous, sem·i·flos′çū·lōse, *a.* [*semi-*, and L. *flosculus*, a little flower.] in botany, having the corolla split and turned to one side, as in the ligule of composites.

sem·i·flụ′id, *a.* neither liquid nor solid; heavy or thick but capable of flowing; viscous but fluid.

sem·i·flụ′id, *n.* a viscous but fluid substance.

sem′i·fọrm, *n.* a half or imperfect form.

sem′i·fọrmed, *a.* half-formed; imperfectly formed; as, *semiformed* crystals.

sem·i·frā′tēr, *n.* [*semi-*, and L. *frater*, brother.] formerly, a layman who, for his gifts and services to some religious order, was looked upon as connected with it.

sem·i·glāzed′, *a.* partially but not fully glazed.

sem″i·his·tor′iç·ăl, *a.* half historical; partly historical.

sem·i·hō′răl, *a.* half-hourly.

sem·i·in′dū·rā·ted, *a.* incompletely hardened.

sem″i·lȧ·pid′i·fīed, *a.* imperfectly changed into stone; partially petrified.

sem′i·lenṣ, *n.* the half of a lens divided in the plane of its axis.

sem″i·len·tiç′ū·lăr, *a.* half lenticular or convex; imperfectly resembling a lens.

sem·i·lig′nē·ous, *a.* half or partially ligneous or woody: applied to a stem that is woody at the base and herbaceous at the top, as of the common rue, sage, and thyme.

sem·i·liq′uid (-lik′wid), *a.* semifluid; half liquid.

sem″i·li·quid′i·ty, *n.* the condition of being semiliquid or semifluid.

sem·i·loġ′iç·ăl, *a.* half or partly logical.

sem′i·lọr, *n.* same as *similor.*

sem·i·lū′năr, *n.* [*semi-*, and L. *luna*, the moon.] the semilunar bone of the wrist.

sem·i·lū′năr, *a.* shaped like a half moon.
semilunar bone; a crescent-shaped bone of the carpus, or wrist.
semilunar valve; either of the two crescent-shaped valves, one at the junction of the right ventricle and pulmonary artery (*pulmonary valve*), the other at the junction of the left ventricle and aorta (*aortic valve*), which function to prevent blood from flowing back into the ventricles.

sem·i·lū′nȧ·ry, *a.* semilunar.

sem·i·lū′nāte, *a.* semilunar.

sem′i·lūne, *n.* [*semi-*, and L. *luna*, the moon.] in geometry, half a lune.

sem·i·mem′brȧ·nous, *a.* made up in part of membrane or fascia.

sem′i·met·ăl, *n.* in old chemistry, a nonmalleable element possessing some metallic properties, as bismuth, arsenic, etc.

sem″i·mē·tal′liç, *a.* pertaining to a semimetal or partaking of its nature and qualities.

sem·i·mŏnth′ly, *a.* occurring twice in a month.

sem·i·mŏnth′ly, *n.* something made or completed every half month, as a semimonthly periodical.

sem·i·mŏnth′ly, *adv.* twice monthly; every half month.

sem·i·mūte′, *a.* having the faculty of speech imperfectly developed or partially lost.

sem′i·mūte, *n.* a person who is partly mute.

sem′i·năl, *a.* [Fr., from L. *seminalis*, relating to seed, from *semen*, seed.]
1. of or containing seed or semen.
2. of reproduction; as, *seminal* power.
3. like seed in being a source or a first stage in development; germinal; originative; as, a *seminal* book.
4. being an early and influential example; as, a *seminal* jazz band.
seminal leaf; same as *seed leaf.*
seminal vesicle; a vessel connected with the seminal duct; a spermatocyst.

sem′i·năl, *n.* the seminal state; a seed. [Obs.]

sem·i·nal′i·ty, *n.* the quality of being seminal or germinal.

sem′i·när, *n.* [G. *seminar*; L. *seminarium*, a seed plot.]
1. a group of supervised students doing research or advanced study.
2. (a) a course for such a group; (b) the room where it meets.

sem·i·nār′i·ăn, *n.* a member of a seminary; specifically, a student in a seminary for Roman Catholic priests.

sem′i·nȧr·ist, *n.* a seminarian. [Chiefly Brit.]

sem′i·nār·y, *n.*; *pl.* **sem′i·nār·ieṣ,** [L. *seminarium*, a seed plot, a nursery garden, neut. of *seminarius*, belonging to seed.]
1. a place where something develops, grows, or is cultivated; as, slums are *seminaries* of crime.
2. a school, especially a private school for young women.
3. a school or college where priests, ministers, etc. are trained.
4. a seminar.
5. a seminarist; especially, a seminary priest. [Obs.]
6. the seminal state; seminality. [Obs.]

sem′i·nār·y, *a.* 1. of or pertaining to seed; seminal. [Obs.]
2. of or pertaining to a seminary.

sem′i·nāte, *v.t.*; seminated, *pt.*, *pp.*; seminating, *ppr.* [L. *seminatus*, pp. of *seminare*, to sow.] to sow; to spread; to propagate; to disseminate. [Archaic.]

sem·i·nā′tion, *n.* [L. *seminatio* (*-onis*), a sowing, from *seminatus*, pp. of *seminare*, to sow.]
1. a spreading or propagation; dissemination.
2. in botany, the act or process of sowing seeds.

sem·i·nif′ēr·ous, *a.* [L. *semen*, seed, and *ferre*, to produce.]
1. seed-bearing; producing seed.
2. producing, containing, or conveying seminal fluid; as, *seminiferous* vesicles.

sem·i·nif′iç, *a.* [L. *semen*, seed, and *facere*, to make.] forming or producing seed or semen.

sem·i·nif′iç·ăl, *a.* same as *seminific.*

sem′i·nist, *n.* in biology, one who believed in the early theory that the embryo is formed by admixture of the semen of the male with the supposed seed of the female.

sem·i·niv′ō·rous, *a.* [from L. *semen*, *seminis*, a seed; and *-vorous.*] seed-eating.

Sem′i·nōle, *n.*; *pl.* **Sem′i·nōle, Sem′i·nōleṣ,** [Am. Ind.] a member of a tribe of American Indians who settled in Florida: a branch of the Creek tribe.

Sem′i·nōle, *a.* of or pertaining to the Seminoles.

sem·i·nọr′măl, *a.* in chemistry, having half the normal or standard strength.

sem·i·nūde′, *a.* partially nude; half-naked.

sem·in·ū′ri·ȧ, *n.* [L. *semen*, seed, and Gr. *ouron*, urine.] the discharge of semen in the urine.

sem·in·vār′i·ănt, *n.* a function of the coefficients of a rational homogeneous function of two variables, which does not change when one variable is increased by a constant, but does change if a similar increase occurs in the other variable.

sem′i·nymph (-nimf), *n.* the nymph or pupa of insects which undergo only a slight change in passing to a perfect state; a propupa.

sem″i·ŏç·çā′ṣion·ăl·ly, *adv.* once in a while; seldom. [Colloq.]

sem″i·of·fi′ciăl (-fish′ăl), *a.* having some, but not full, official authority; partly official.

sē·mi·og′rȧ·phy, sē·mei·og′rȧ·phy, *n.* [Gr. *sēmeion*, a mark, and *graphein*, to write.] the doctrine of signs in general; specifically, in pathology, a description of the symptoms of disease.

sē″mi·ō·loġ′iç·ăl, sē″meī·ō·loġ′iç·ăl, *a.* pertaining to semiology.

sē·mi·ol′ō·ġy, sē·meī·ol′ō·ġy, *n.* 1. the science of signs or sign language.

2. the branch of medicine having to do with symptoms; symptomatology.

sem″i·ō·pā′çous, *a.* same as *semiopaque.*

sem·i·ō′păl, *a.* a variety of opal not possessing opalescence.

sem″i·ō·pāque′ (-pāk′), *a.* half transparent only; half opaque.

sem″i·or·biç′ū·lăr, *a.* having the shape of a half orb or sphere.

sem·i·or′di·nāte, *n.* in geometry, a half chord divided by the transverse diameter of a conic.

sē·mi·ot′iç, sē·meī·ot′iç, *a.* 1. of signs or sign language.

2. in medicine, (a) of symptoms; (b) symptomatic.

sē·mi·ot′i·căl, sē·meī·ot′i·çal, *a.* semiotic.

sem·i·ō′văl, *a.* half oval.

sem·i·ō′vāte, *a.* half ovate.

sem″i·ō·vip′ȧ·rous, *a.* producing young whose natal development is incomplete, as marsupials.

sem·i·ox′y·ġen·ā·ted, *a.* combined with oxygen only in part.

sem·i·pā′găn, *a.* half-pagan.

sem·i·pal′māte, sem·i·pal′mā·ted, *a.* in zoology, partly palmated or webbed; having a half web connecting the anterior toes; not fully palmate.

sem″i·pal·mā′tion, *n.* the state of being semipalmate.

sem″i·pȧ·rab′ō·lȧ, *n.* in mathematics, a curve of such a nature that the powers of its ordinates are to each other as the next lower powers of its abscissas.

sem″i·par·ȧ·sit′iç, *a.* 1. in biology, ordinarily parasitic but capable of a saprophytic life.

2. in botany, taking part of its food from the host and making the rest by itself, as the mistletoe; both parasitic and photosynthetic.

sem′i·ped, *n.* [*semi-*, and L. *pes, pedis*, a foot.] a half foot in poetry.

sem′i·ped·ăl, *a.* containing a half foot.

Sem″i-Pē·lā′ġi·ăn, *a.* of or pertaining to the Semi-Pelagians or their beliefs.

Sem″i-Pē·lā′ġi·ăn, *n.* a believer in Semi-Pelagianism.

Sem″i-Pē·lā′ġi·ăn·işm, *n.* the doctrines of John Cassianus, a French monk, who, in the fifth century, modified the doctrines of Pelagius, by denying human merit, and maintaining the necessity of the Spirit's influences, while he rejected the doctrine of unconditional election, the inability of man to do good, irresistible grace, and the certain perseverance of the saints.

sem″i·pel·lū′cid, *a.* half clear, or imperfectly transparent; as, a *semipellucid* gem.

sem·i·pel·lū·cid′i·ty, *n.* the quality or state of being imperfectly transparent.

sem·i·pen′ni·form, *a.* in anatomy, partially penniform; penniform on one side only; as, a *semipenniform* muscle.

sem″i·pēr′mē·ȧ·ble, *a.* allowing some substances to pass; permeable to smaller molecules but not to larger ones, as a membrane in osmosis.

sem″i·pēr·spiç′ū·ous, *a.* imperfectly clear; half transparent.

sem″i·phlō·gis′ti·cā·ted (-flō-), *a.* partially impregnated with phlogiston. [Obs.]

sem·i·plas′tiç, *a.* partly plastic.

sem′i·plūme, *n.* a feather which has a downy web and a stem like an ordinary feather.

sem″i·pō·lit′i·căl, *a.* political in some respects only.

sem″i·pōr′ce·lain (-lin), *n.* an opaque porcelain with a finish like that of earthenware.

sem·i·pre′cious (-presh′us), *a.* designating gems of lower value than those classified as precious: said of the garnet, turquoise, etc.

sem·i·prī′văte, *a.* partly but not completely private; specifically, designating or of a hospital room having two, or sometimes three or four, beds.

sem′i·prō, *n.* a person who engages in a sport for pay but not as a regular occupation. [Colloq.]

sem·i·prōne′, *a.* in surgery, neither erect nor prostrate; half prone.

sem′i·proof, *n.* partial proof.

sem·i·pub′liç, *a.* partly but not completely public.

sem·i·pū′pȧ, *n.* [*semi-*, and LL. *pupa*, pupa.] the young of an insect in the developmental stage intermediate between the larva and pupa.

sem·i·quȧd′rāte (-kwod′), *n.* [*semi-*, and L. *quadratus*, or *quartus*, fourth.] an aspect of two planets when they are forty-five degrees apart.

sem·i·quar′tile, *n.* same as *semiquadrate.*

sem′i·quā·vēr, *n.* in music, a note of half the duration of the quaver; a sixteenth note.

sem′i·quā·vēr, *v.t.* to sound or sing in semiquavers.

SEMIQUAVERS

sem·i·quin′tile, *n.* an aspect of two planets when they are thirty-six degrees apart.

Se·mir′ȧ·mis, *n.* an Assyrian queen, the legendary founder of Babylon, noted for her beauty, wisdom, and sexual excesses.

sem·i·reç′ŏn·dīte, *a.* in zoology, half hidden, as an insect's head when partially concealed by the shield of the thorax.

sem·i·reg′ū·lăr, *a.* relating to or designating a quadrilateral having four equal sides and equal angles in pairs.

sem″i·riġ′id, *a.* 1. partly rigid; not wholly rigid.

2. designating an airship having a rigid internal keel but no other supporting framework.

sem′i·ring, *n.* in zoology, a bronchial or tracheal ring when incomplete.

sem·i·round′, *a.* generally round but with one flat surface.

sem·i·round′, *n.* anything having a semiround shape.

sem·i·saġ′it·tāte, *a.* resembling half of a barbed arrowhead.

sem·i·sav′ăġe, *a.* half savage; half barbarian.

sem·i·sav′ăġe, *n.* one who is half savage or imperfectly civilized.

Sem″i-Sax′ŏn, *a.* and *n.* Early Middle English: formerly applied to the period from (approximately) 1150 to 1250.

sem·i·sex′tile, *n.* an aspect of two planets when they are thirty degrees apart.

sem·i·skilled′, *a.* 1. partly skilled.

2. of or doing manual work that requires some but not extensive training.

sem′i·smīle, *n.* a half laugh; a forced grin.

sem·i·sol′id, *a.* not fluid but capable of changing shape, as gelatin; partly solid.

sem·i·sol′id, *n.* a semisolid substance.

sem′i·sound, *n.* a half sound; a low or broken tone. [Rare.]

sem·i·spā′tȧ, *n.* [*semi-*, and L. *spatha*, a broad two-edged sword.] a long Frankish dagger, with one edge and a grooved back.

sem·i·spher′iç, sem·i·spher′iç·ăl, *a.* having the figure of a half sphere.

sem″i·sphē·roid′ăl, *a.* formed like a half spheroid.

sem″i·spī·nā′lis, *n.*; *pl.* **sem″i·spī·nā′lēş,** in anatomy, a muscle extending from transverse processes to spines of the vertebrae.

sem′i·steel, *n.* puddled steel.

sem·i·sū·pēr·nat′ū·răl, *a.* designating the classic heroes or demigods held to be half human and half divine.

sem′i·tȧ, *n.*; *pl.* **sem′i·tae,** [LL., from L. *semita*, a path.] a spine of an echinoderm.

sem·i·tan′ġent, *n.* in mathematics, the tangent of half an arc.

Sem′īte, Shem′īte, *a.* [LL. *Sem*; Gr. *Sēm*, Shem.] of, belonging to, or characteristic of the Semites.

Sem′īte, Shem′īte, *n.* a member of any of the peoples whose language is Semitic, including the Hebrews, Arabs, Assyrians, Phoenicians, Babylonians, etc.; not, specifically, a Jew.

sem″i·tē·rēte′, *a.* half-round.

sem·i·tēr′tiăn (-shăn), *a.* in medicine, designating a fever possessing the characters of both the tertian and quotidian intermittent.

sem·i·tēr′tiăn, *n.* a semitertian fever.

Sē·mit′iç, *a.* 1. of, characteristic of, or like a Semite or the Semites.

2. designating or of a major group of languages of southwestern Asia and northern Africa, related to the Hamitic languages and divided into *East Semitic* (Akkadian), *North West Semitic* (Phoenician, Punic, Aramaic, Hebrew, Modern Hebrew, etc.), and *South West Semitic* (Arabic, Ethiopic, Ambaric).

Sē·mit′iç, *n.* the Semitic family of languages.

Sē·mit′içs, *n.pl.* [*construed as sing.*] the study of Semitic culture, languages, literature, etc.

Sem′i·tişm, Shem′i·tişm, *n.* 1. a Semitic idiom or word.

2. characteristics of the Semites; especially, the ideas, cultural qualities, etc. originating with the Jews.

sem′i·tōne, *n.* 1. in music, a tone at an interval of a half step from another in a diatonic scale; a half tone.

2. such an interval.

sem·i·ton′iç, *a.* pertaining to a semitone; consisting of a semitone or of semitones.

sem·i·tran′sept, *n.* the half of a transept or cross aisle.

sem″i·trans·lū′cent, *a.* transmitting light in a slight degree.

sem″i·trans·păr′en·cy, *n.* imperfect transparency; partial opaqueness.

sem″i·trans·păr′ent, *a.* half or imperfectly transparent.

sem·i·trop′iç·ăl, *a.* having some of the characteristics of the tropics; partly tropical.

sem·i·tū′bū·lăr, *a.* resembling half a tube, or a tube divided longitudinally in half.

sem″i·vēr·tic′il·lāte, *a.* partially verticillate.

sem·i·vit′rē·ous, *a.* partially vitreous.

sem·i·vit″ri·fi·cā′tion, *n.* 1. the state of being imperfectly vitrified.

2. a substance imperfectly vitrified.

sem·i·vit′ri·fīed, *a.* half or imperfectly vitrified; partially converted into glass.

sem′i·vīve, sem′i·vif, *a.* half-alive. [Obs.]

sem·i·vō′căl, *a.* pertaining to a semivowel: half-vocal; imperfectly sounding.

sem·i·vow′el, *n.* a vowel used as a consonant: the English *w, y* are phonetically vowels (o͞o; ē) used as consonants, as in *wall, yoke.*

sem·i·week′ly, *a.* occurring, coming, done, etc. twice a week or every half week.

sem·i·week′ly, *n.* something that comes, happens, is done, etc. twice weekly or every half week, as a newspaper published twice a week.

sem·i·yēar′ly, *a.* coming, happening, done, etc. twice a year or every half year.

sem·i·yēar′ly, *n.* something that comes, happens, is done, etc. twice yearly or every half year.

sem·i·yēar′ly, *adv.* twice yearly; every half year.

sem·nō·pith′ē·cine, *a.* [Gr. *semnos*, sacred, and *pithēkos*, ape.] of or pertaining to the genus *Semnopithecus.*

sem·nō·pith′ē·cine, *n.* a monkey of the genus *Semnopithecus.*

Sem″nō·pi·thē′çus, *n.* a genus of catarrhine old-world monkeys having long slender tails.

sem·ō·li′nȧ, *n.* [It., small seed, dim. of *semola*, bran.] the large hard grains left in the bolting machine after the fine flour has been passed through it: used in making macaroni, puddings, etc.: also written *semolino.*

Sē·mos′tō·mae, *n.pl.* [Gr. *sēma*, sign, and *stoma*, mouth.] a group of discophorous jellyfish.

sē·mos′tō·mous, *a.* of or pertaining to the *Semostomæ.*

se·möule′, *n.* same as *semolina.*

sem′pēr ē′ȧ·dem, [L.] always the same: Queen Elizabeth I's motto.

sem′pēr fi·dē′lis (*or* -dā′), [L.] always faithful: the motto of the United States Marine Corps.

sem′pēr ī′dem, [L.] always the same.

sem′pēr pȧ·rā′tus, [L.] always prepared: the motto of the United States Coast Guard.

sem·pēr·vī′rent, *a.* [L. *semper*, always, and *virens* (*-entis*), ppr. of *virere*, to be green or verdant.] always fresh; evergreen. [Rare.]

sem′pēr·vīve, *n.* the houseleek.

Sem·pēr·vī′vum, *n.* a genus of plants including the houseleek.

sem·pi·tēr′năl, *a.* [Fr. *sempiternel*; L. *sempiternus*; *semper*, always, and *eternus*, eternal.]

1. eternal in futurity; everlasting, endless; having beginning, but no end.

2. eternal; having neither beginning nor end.

sem·pi·tēr′ni·ty, *n.* the state or quality of being sempiternal; eternity.

sem′pre, *adv.* in music, throughout.

semp′stēr, *n.* a seamster.

semp′stress, *n.* a seamstress.

sem′stēr, *n.* a seamster. [Obs.]

sē·mun′ci·ȧ (-shi-), *n.* an old Roman coin equal to one twenty-fourth of a Roman pound.

sen, *n.* [Jap.] a copper or bronze coin of Japan equal to $^{1}/_{100}$ of a yen.

se·ñal′, (-nyal′), *n.* [Sp.] a landmark.

sē·nā′ri·us, *n.*; *pl.* **sē·nā′ri·ī,** [L., consisting of six each.] in prosody, any verse which consists of six feet.

sen·är·mont′īte, *n.* [named after H. H. de *Sénarmont* (1808–1862), a French mineralogist and physicist.] an oxide of antimony, Sb_2O_3, of resinous luster and grayish to white color.

sen′ȧ·ry, *a.* [L. *seni, senarius,* consisting of six each.] of six; on the basis of six; six; containing six units.

sen′ăte, *n.* [Fr. *sénat,* from L. *senatus,* from *senex, senis,* old, aged; Gr. *henos*; Sans. *sana,* old.]

1. literally, an assembly or council of elders.

2. in ancient Rome, a council of elders appointed or elected from among citizens of free birth and entrusted with the supreme legislative power: it was composed originally only of patricians but later included the plebeians.

3. a law-making assembly; a state council.

4. [S–] a legislative group, generally the smaller, and called the *upper,* of the two houses forming certain national and State legislatures: in the United States Senate there are two senators from each State, regardless of its size.

5. a governing body or advisory council in a college or university.

courtesy of the senate; the custom in the United States Senate of overlooking certain parliamentary rules in order to facilitate business, especially the confirmation of nominations; the punctilious courtesy usually extended by one senator to another.

sen′ăte chām′bẽr, a chamber or hall in which a senate holds its sessions.

sen′ăte house, a house in which a senate meets; a place of public council.

sen′ȧ·tŏr, *n.* 1. a member of a senate; as, a United States *senator.*

2. in Scotland, a lord of session; as, a *senator* of the College of Justice.

3. in old English law, a king's councilor.

sen·ȧ·tō′ri·ăl, *a.* 1. of or suitable for a senator or a senate.

2. composed of senators.

3. entitled to elect a senator: said of an electoral district.

sen·ȧ·tō′ri·ăl·ly, *adv.* in the manner of a senate or senator; with dignity or solemnity.

sen·ȧ·tō′ri·ăn, *a.* senatorial. [Rare.]

sen·ȧ·tō′ri·ous, *a.* senatorial. [Obs.]

sen′ȧ·tŏr·ship, *n.* the position, term of office, etc. of a senator.

sē·nā′tus, *n.* [L.] a senate; a governing body.

senatus academicus; a governing body in a Scottish university, composed of the faculty and charged with general superintendence.

senatus consultum; a decree of the senate of ancient Rome.

sē·nā″tus·cŏn·sult′, *n.* same as *senatus consultum* under *senatus.*

send, *v.t.*; sent, *pt., pp.*; sending, *ppr.* [AS. *sendan,* to send, pt. *ic sende,* I sent; Ice. *senda*; Dan. *sende*; D. *zenden*; G. *senden*; Goth. *sandjan,* to send, lit., to make to go; Goth. *sinthan,* to go, from *sinth,* AS. *sīth,* a path.]

1. (a) to cause to go or be carried; to dispatch; to transmit; as, food, medicine, and doctors were *sent* by plane; (b) to dispatch (a letter, telegram, etc.) by mail, messenger, etc.

2. to cause (a person) to go from one place to another, especially by asking, directing, or commanding; as, *send* the man to me, the storm *sent* them hurrying to their homes.

3. to arrange for the going of; to enable to go or attend; as, his father *sent* him to college.

4. to cause to move, as by releasing, hitting, discharging, throwing, etc.; as, the explosion *sent* a cloud of smoke high in the air, he *sent* the ball over the trees.

5. to bring or drive into some state or condition; as, the noise will *send* him out of his mind.

6. to cause to happen, come, etc.; to give; as, a crop *sent* to reward our toil.

7. to perform jazz music in such a way as to cause great excitement or exhilaration in (the listener or performer). [Slang.]

8. to appoint to go with authority to represent; as, to *send* an ambassador to a foreign court; to *send* an agent to negotiate business.

to send away; to dismiss; to cause to depart.

to send flying; (a) to dismiss or cause to depart hurriedly; (b) to stagger or repel, as with a blow; (c) to put to flight; to rout; (d) to scatter abruptly in all directions.

to send forth; (a) to cause to depart; as, Noah *sent forth* a dove; (b) to put out or cause to appear; as, trees *send forth* leaves in the spring.

to send in; to dispatch, hand in, or send to a central point.

to send off; (a) to mail, dispatch, or send away, as a letter, gift, etc.; (b) to dismiss; (c) to give a send-off to.

to send out; (a) to dispatch, distribute, issue, mail, etc. from a central point; (b) to send forth.

to send packing; to dismiss abruptly; drive (another) away, as in disgrace.

to send to Coventry; to banish; to ostracize; to cut off from customary privileges; to cut.

to send up; (a) to cause to rise, climb, or go up; (b) [Colloq.] to sentence to imprisonment.

send, *v.i.* to send a message or messenger.

to send for; to request or require by message to come or be brought; as, *to send for* a physician; *to send for* a coach.

send, *n.* [prob. from *send* (to dispatch.)] 1. the driving motion of a wave or the sea.

2. a scend.

send, *v.i.* 1. to be plunged forward, as by the force of a wave.

2. to scend.

sen′dăl, *n.* [Sp.] 1. a light thin fabric of silk or thread.

2. anything made of this material.

send′ẽr, *n.* one who or that which sends; specifically, in telegraphing, etc., the transmitting device, as distinguished from the *receiver.*

send′-ŏff, *n.* 1. an expression or demonstration of friendly feeling toward someone starting out on a trip, career, etc. [Colloq.]

2. a start or beginning given to someone or something. [Colloq.]

Sen′ē·çȧ, *n.*; *pl.* **Sen′ē·çȧs,** [Am. Ind.] a member of a tribe of Iroquoian Indians who lived in the area of the Genesee River, New York.

Sen′ē·çȧ, *a.* of the Senecas.

Seneca root or *Seneca snakeroot*; the rootstock of an American variety of milkwort, *Polygala senega.* The drug prepared from it is said to have been used as an antidote for the bite of the rattlesnake. It is now used in cough mixtures.

Sen′ē·çȧ oil, petroleum: so called because it was first used by the Senecas as a liniment.

Sē·ne′ci·ō, *n.* [L., groundsel; lit., an old man, from *senex,* old; so called because of the naked receptacle, resembling a bald head.] a large genus of composite plants, widely distributed in temperate climates, and including the groundsel and ragwort.

sē·neç′ti·tūde, *n.* old age.

sen′ē·gȧ, *n.* [from *Senega,* var. of *Seneca.*]

1. a North American plant of the milkwort family.

2. its dried root, used as an expectorant: also called *Seneca root.*

Sen″ē·gạl·ēṣe′, *a.* of Senegal or its people.

Sen″ē·gạl·ēṣe′, *n.*; *pl.* **Sen″ē·gạl·ēṣe′,** 1. one of the native Moors or Negroes of Senegal, French West Africa.

2. their language.

sen′ē·ġin, *n.* same as *saponin.*

sē·nes′cence, *n.* the process or state of growing old; the onset of old age.

sē·nes′cent, *a.* [L. *senescens* (-*entis*), ppr. of *senescere,* to grow old, from *senex,* old.] growing old; aging.

sen′es·çhăl, *n.* [OFr. *seneschal,* prob. from Goth. *sins,* old, and *skalks,* a servant.] a powerful official in the household of a medieval noble: he was in charge of administering justice and managing the domestic affairs of the estate, and he represented his lord in court.

sen′es·çhăl·ship, *n.* the position or jurisdiction of a seneschal.

senġe, *v.t.* to singe. [Obs.]

sen′green, *n.* [G. *singrün,* a plant, as periwinkle; *sin,* a root signifying strength, force, duration, and *grün,* green.] the houseleek, a plant of the genus *Sempervivum.*

se·nhōr′ (-nyōr′), *n.* [Port.] a man; gentleman: Portuguese title equivalent to *Mr.* or *Sir.*

se·nhō′rä, *n.* [Port.] a married woman; lady; Portuguese title equivalent to *Mrs.* or *Madam.*

se·nhō·rī′tä, *n.* [Port.] an unmarried woman or girl; young lady: Portuguese title equivalent to *Miss.*

sē′nīle, *a.* [L. *senilis,* of or pertaining to an old man, or to old age.]

1. of old age.

2. showing signs of old age; elderly; weak in mind and body.

3. resulting from old age.

4. in physical geography, nearing the end of an erosion cycle.

senile atrophy; the emaciation of old age which is brought about by a waste of tissue.

senile gangrene; that form of dry gangrene in people of advanced age brought about by an insufficient supply of blood, as because of arteriosclerosis.

sē·nil′i·ty, *n.* 1. the condition or quality of being senile; old age.

2. the characteristics of old age; weakness; infirmity of mind and body.

sēn′iŏr (-yẽr), *a.* [L. *senior,* comp. of *senex,* old.]

1. of the greater age; older: often indicating the older of two having the same name, as a father and son.

2. of higher rank or standing, or longer in service.

3. of or belonging to the graduating class in a high school or college.

sēn′iŏr, *n.* 1. a person older than another or others.

2. a person of greater rank, standing, or length of service.

3. a person in the graduating class of a high school or college.

sēn′iŏr hīgh sçhọọl, high school: usually the tenth, eleventh, and twelfth grades: distinguished from *junior high school.*

sēn·ior′i·ty (-yor′), *n.*; *pl.* **sēn·ior′i·ties,** 1. the state or quality of being senior; precedence in birth, rank, etc.

2. status, priority, or precedence achieved by length of service in a given job, as in determining an employee's eligibility for promotion.

sēn′iŏr·y, *n.* seniority. [Obs.]

sen′nȧ, *n.* [Fr. *séné*; It. *sena,* from Ar. *sanā,* senna.]

1. a drug consisting of the dried leaves of various species of *Cassia,* the best of which are natives of the East. *Cassia acutifolia* is known as Alexandrian senna and *Cassia angustifolia* as Indian senna. Senna possesses valuable cathartic properties.

2. any plant of the genus *Cassia,* with pods and yellow or pinkish flowers.

SENNA (*Cassia acutifolia*)

American senna; an herb, *Cassia marilandica,* growing in the eastern part of the United States: the leaves are used medicinally: also called *wild senna.*

sen′nȧ·çhie, sen′nȧ·çhy, *n.* same as *seanachie.*

sen′net, *n.* [OFr. *senet, sinet, signet,* dim. of *signe,* a sign.] a trumpet call used as a signal for ceremonial entrances and exits: a stage direction in Elizabethan drama. [Archaic.]

sen′net, *n.* the barracuda.

sen′nīght (-nit), *n.* [*seven* and *night.*] the space of seven nights and days; a week. [Archaic.]

sen′nit, *n.* [prob. from *seven* and *knit.*] a flat, braided cord, formed by plaiting strands of rope yarn; also, plaited grass or palm leaves for making hats.

sē·noç′ū·lăr, *a.* [L. *seni,* six each, and *oculus,* eye.] having six eyes.

Sē·nō′ni·ăn, *n.* [named from the district *Sénonais,* in France.] in geology, a division of the Upper Cretaceous formation of Europe.

se·ñor′ (se-nyōr′), *n.*; *pl.* **se·ñor′es,** [Sp.] a man; a gentleman: Spanish title corresponding to the English *Mr.* or *Sir.*

se·ño′ra (se-nyō′rä), *n.* [Sp.] a married woman; a lady: Spanish title given to a lady, corresponding to the English *Mrs.* or *Madam.*

se·ño·ri′ta (se-nyō-rē′tä), *n.* [Sp.] an unmarried woman or girl; a young lady: Spanish title given to a young lady, corresponding to the English *Miss.*

sen′sāte, *v.t.*; sensated, *pt., pp.*; sensating, *ppr.* to have perception of through a sense or the senses. [Rare.]

sen′sāte, *a.* [LL. *sensatus,* intelligent, from L. *sensus,* sense.]

1. having the power of physical sensation.

2. registering on the senses; felt by the senses.

sen·sā′tion, *n.* [Fr., from LL. *sensatio* (*-onis*), from L. *sentire*, to feel, perceive.]
1. the power or process of receiving conscious sense impressions through direct stimulation of the bodily organism or of the sense organs; as, hearing, seeing, touching, tasting, and smelling are *sensations*.
2. an immediate reaction to external stimulation of a sense organ; a conscious feeling or sense impression; as, a *sensation* of cold.
3. a generalized feeling or reaction, often vague and without reference to immediate stimulus; as, a *sensation* of happiness.
4. a state or feeling of excitement and interest caused in a group, community, etc.; as, the play caused a *sensation*.
The *sensation* caused by the appearance of that work is still remembered by many. —Brougham.
5. that which produces such a feeling.

sen·sā′tion·ăl, *a.* 1. of the senses or sensation.
2. of, or in accordance with, philosophical sensationalism.
3. arousing intense interest and excitement; startling; exciting.
4. using or having effects intended to startle, shock, thrill, or arouse interest and intense excitement.

sen·sā′tion·ăl·iṣm, *n.* 1. the use of subject matter, style, language, or artistic expression that is intended to shock, startle, excite, or arouse intense interest; addiction to what is sensational (sense 4) in literature, art, public speaking, etc.; sensational methods.
2. in ethics, sensualism.
3. in philosophy, the theory or doctrine that all knowledge is derived solely through the use of the senses.

sen·sā′tion·ăl·ist, *n.* 1. one who advocates or believes in philosophical sensationalism.
2. a person who indulges in sensationalism.

sen·sā″tion·ăl·is′tiç, *a.* of sensationalists or sensationalism.

sen·sā′tion·ăl·īze, *v.t.*; sensationalized, *pt.*, *pp.*; sensationalizing, *ppr.* to make sensational; treat in a sensational way.

sense, *n.* [Fr. *sens*, from L. *sensus*, feeling, sense, from *sensus*, pp. of *sentire*, to feel, perceive.]
1. the ability of the nerves and the brain to receive and react to stimuli, as light, sound, impact, constriction, etc.: formerly confined to denoting any of five faculties of receiving impressions through specific bodily organs and the nerves associated with them (sight, touch, taste, smell, and hearing); as, not perceptible to the *senses*: see also *sixth sense*.
2. the senses considered as a total function of the bodily organism, as distinguished from intellect, movement, etc.
3. feeling, impression, perception, or recognition, either through the senses or through the intellect; awareness; as, a *sense* of warmth, an uneasy *sense* of guilt.
4. an ability to judge, distinguish, or estimate external conditions, sounds, etc.; as, a *sense* of direction, pitch, etc.
5. an ability to feel, appreciate, understand, or comprehend some quality, as humor, honor, etc.
6. the ability to think or reason soundly; normal intelligence and judgment, often as reflected in behavior.
7. meaning; especially, any of several meanings conveyed by or attributed to the same word or phrase.
8. essential signification; gist; as, few people grasped the *sense* of his remarks.
9. soundness of judgment or reasoning; evidence of normal intelligence or understanding; as, there is some *sense* in what he says.
10. something wise, sound, or reasonable; as, there's no *sense* in going.
11. the general opinion, sentiment, or attitude of a group.
12. direction; tendency.
13. in geometry, one of two opposite directions in which that which has length, breadth, or thickness may be described.
good sense; sound judgment.
in a sense; from one aspect; to some extent or degree.
senses; normal ability to think or reason soundly; as, come to your *senses*.
to make sense; to be intelligible or logical.

sense, *v.t.*; sensed (senst), *pt.*, *pp.*; sensing, *ppr.* 1. to be or become aware of; to perceive; as, he *sensed* our hostility.
2. to understand; to comprehend; to grasp; as, to *sense* a suggestion. [Colloq.]

sense′fụl, *a.* full of sense; reasonable; judicious.

sense′less, *a.* 1. destitute of sense; having no power of sensation or perception; incapable of sensation or feeling; unconscious.
The ears are *senseless* that should give us hearing. —Shak.
2. lacking feeling, sympathy, or appreciation; without sensibility. [Now Rare.]
3. contrary to reason or sound judgment; unreasonable; meaningless.
4. acting without sense or judgment; foolish; stupid.

sense′less·ly, *adv.* in a senseless manner; as, a man *senselessly* arrogant.

sense′less·ness, *n.* the quality or state of being senseless.

sense ọr′găn, an organ or structure which receives specific stimuli and transmits them as sensations to the brain; any organ of sense, as the ear, eye, or nose; a receptor.

sense pẽr·cep′tion, 1. perception or the knowing of facts from stimuli received and responded to by the senses.
2. the process of obtaining such knowledge.
3. the ability to gain such knowledge.

sen·si·bil′i·ty, *n.*; *pl.* **sen·si·bil′i·tieṣ**, [OFr. *sensibilité*; LL. *sensibilitas*, from L. *sensibilis*, sensible.]
1. the state or quality of being sensible or capable of physical sensation; the power of responding to stimuli.
2. [*often pl.*] the capacity for being affected emotionally or intellectually, whether pleasantly or unpleasantly; receptiveness to impression; mental or emotional responsiveness.
3. [*often pl.*] the capacity to respond intelligently and perceptively to intellectual, moral, or aesthetic events or values, especially those which are considered higher or refined; delicate, sensitive awareness or responsiveness; keen intellectual perception.
4. responsiveness, as of a plant, thermometer, etc., to changing conditions. [Rare.]
5. readiness to respond to suffering or to the pathetic. [Archaic.]
Syn.—sensitiveness, susceptibility, feeling, taste.

sen′si·ble, *a.* [L. *sensibilis*, sensible, from *sensus*, pp. of *sentire*, to feel, perceive.]
1. capable of being perceived by the senses; capable of exciting physical sensation.
2. perceptible to the intellect.
3. capable of sensation; having senses; sensitive; as, the eye is *sensible* to light.
4. very liable to impression from without; easily affected. [Archaic.]
5. easily perceived; marked; striking; appreciable.
6. having appreciation or understanding; cognizant; aware; emotionally or intellectually conscious; as, he was *sensible* of their grief.
7. easily or readily moved or affected by natural agents; capable of indicating slight changes of condition; sensitive; as, a *sensible* thermometer or balance. [Now Rare.]
8. possessing or containing sense, judgment, or reason; endowed with or characterized by good or common sense; intelligent; reasonable; wise; as, a *sensible* man, a *sensible* proposal.
sensible note or *tone*; in music, the seventh note of any diatonic scale: so termed because, being but a semitone below the octave or keynote, and naturally leading up to that, it makes the ear *sensible* of its approaching sound.

sen′si·ble, *n.* 1. that which produces sensation; something perceptible.
2. that which possesses sensibility. [Rare.]

sen′si·ble·ness, *n.* the quality or state of being sensible.

sen′si·bly, *adv.* 1. in a sensible manner; intelligently; wisely.
2. so as to be sensible or noticeable; appreciably.

sen·si·fā′cient (-shent), *a.* [L. *sensus*, sense, and *faciens* (*-entis*), *ppr.* of *facere*, to make.] producing sensation.

sen·sif′ẽr·ous, *a.* [L. *sensus*, sense, and *ferre*, to bear.] carrying sensation.

sen·sif′iç, *a.* [L. *sensus*, sense, and *facere*, to make.] producing sensation.

sen·sif′i·çā·tō·ry, *a.* producing sensation.

sen′sile, *a.* 1. capable of sensation; sentient.
2. in meteorology, sensed or felt but not recorded by the usual dry-bulb thermometer: said of temperature.

sen·sil′lȧ, *n.*; *pl.* **sen·sil′lae**, [L. *sensus*, sense.] in zoology, a primary form of epithelial sense organ: it is composed of one or more cells having a nerve connection.

sens′ist, *n.* a sensationalist (sense 1).

sen′si·tive, *a.* [OFr. *sensitif*; ML. *sensitivus*, from L. *sensus*, pp. of *sentire*, to feel, perceive.]
1. of the senses or sensation; especially, connected with the reception or transmission of sense impressions; sensory.
2. receiving and responding to stimuli from outside objects or agencies; having sensation.
3. responding or feeling readily and acutely; very keenly susceptible to stimuli; as, a *sensitive* ear.
4. tender; raw; easily hurt, as a healing wound.
5. having or showing keen sensibilities.
6. easily offended, disturbed, shocked, irritated, etc., as by the actions of others; high-strung, tense, and touchy.
7. changing easily or quickly in the presence of some force or agency; very responsive to external conditions, as to light, heat, etc.; as, photographic film is *sensitive* to light.
8. showing, or liable to show, unusual variation; fluctuating; as, a *sensitive* stock market.
9. serving to affect the senses; perceptible by the senses. [Obs.]
sensitive fern; see under *fern*.

sen′si·tive·ly, *adv.* in a sensitive manner.

sen′si·tive·ness, *n.* the state or quality of being sensitive.

sen′si·tive plant, a tropical American plant, *Mimosa pudica*, with a spiny stem and purplish flowers, whose leaflets fold and leafstalks droop at the slightest touch: it is often cultivated in hothouses.
bastard sensitive plant; a plant of the genus *Æschynomene*.

SENSITIVE PLANT (*Mimosa pudica*)

sen·si·tiv′i·ty, *n.* the condition or quality of being sensitive.

sen·si·tiv′i·ty trāin′ing, a kind of group therapy in which the members of the group, under the guidance of a leader, seek a deeper understanding of themselves and others, as by the exchange of intimate feelings and experiences, physical contacts, etc.

sen″si·ti·zā′tion, *n.* the act of sensitizing.

sen′si·tīze, *v.t.*; sensitized, *pt.*, *pp.*; sensitizing, *ppr.* to make sensitive or susceptible; specifically, (a) in photography, to make (a film or plate) sensitive to light, etc.; (b) in immunology, to make sensitive or hypersensitive to a serum by repeated injection.

sen′si·tī·zẽr, *n.* a sensitizing agent.

sen·si·tom′ē·tẽr, *n.* [*sensitive* and *-meter.*] an instrument by which the degree of sensitiveness, as of a photographic film or the eyes, may be tested.

sen′si·tō·ry, *n.*; *pl.* **sen′si·tō·rieṣ**, same as *sensorium*.

sen′sive, *a.* sensitive. [Obs.]

sen·sō′ri·ȧ, *n.* alternative pl. of *sensorium*.

sen·sō′ri·ăl, *a.* sensory.

sen′sō·ri·mō″tŏr, *a.* both sensory and motor.

sen·sō′ri·um, *n.*; *pl.* **sen·sō′ri·umṣ**, **sen·sō′ri·ȧ**, [LL., from L. *sensus*, sense.]
1. the whole sensory apparatus of the body.
2. the supposed seat of physical sensation in the gray matter of the brain.

sen′sō·ry, *n.*; *pl.* **sen′sō·rieṣ**, same as *sensorium*.

sen′sō·ry, *a.* 1. of the senses or sensation.
2. connected with the reception and transmission of sense impressions.

sen′sụ·ăl (-shoo-), *a.* [L. *sensualis*, from L. *sensus*, sense, feeling.]
1. sensory or sensuous. [Rare.]
2. of the body and the senses as distinguished from the intellect; as, *sensual* pleasures.
3. (a) connected or preoccupied with bodily or sexual pleasures; voluptuous; (b) lustful; licentious; lewd.
4. resulting from, or showing preoccupation with, bodily or sexual pleasure; as, a *sensual* expression.
5. of the doctrine of sensationalism.

sen'sū·ăl·ism (-shoo), *n.* 1. frequent or excessive indulgence in sensual pleasures.
2. the belief that the pleasures of the senses constitute the greatest good.
3. the expression of this belief, as in art; emphasis on what is sensuous.
4. in philosophy, sensationalism.

sen'sū·ăl·ist, *n.* 1. a person given to excessive indulgence in sensual pleasures.
2. one who believes in sensualism.

sen"sū·ăl·is'tic, *a.* sensual.

sen·sū·al'i·ty, *n.* [Fr. *sensualité*; LL. *sensualitas (-atis)*, capacity for feeling, sensuality, from L. *sensus*, sense.]
1. the state or quality of being sensual; fondness for or indulgence in sensual pleasures.
2. lasciviousness; lewdness.

sen"sū·ăl·i·zā'tion, *n.* the act of sensualizing or the state of being sensualized.

sen'sū·ăl·īze, *v.t.*; sensualized, *pt., pp.*; sensualizing, *ppr.* to make sensual; to instill with sensualism; as, *sensualized* by pleasure.

sen'sū·ăl·ly, *adv.* in a sensual manner.

sen'sū·ăl·ness, *n.* sensuality.

sen'sū·ism, *n.* in philosophy, sensationalism.

sen·sū·os'i·ty, *n.* sensuousness.

sen'sū·ous, *a.* [L. *sensus*, sense, and *-ous.*]
1. of, derived from, based on, affecting, appealing to, or perceived by the senses.
2. easily affected through the senses; enjoying the pleasures of sensation.

sen'sū·ous·ly, *adv.* in a sensuous manner.

sen'sū·ous·ness, *n.* the state or quality of being sensuous.

sent, *v.* past tense and past participle of *send.*

sen'tence, *n.* [ME.; OFr.; L. *sententia*, a way of thinking, opinion, sentiment, prob. for *sentientia*, from the stem of *sentiens (-entis)*, ppr. of *sentire*, to feel, perceive.]
1. a decision, opinion, or judgment, as of a court.
2. the determination or declaration by a court of the punishment of a convicted person; also, the punishment itself.
3. a word or group of words stating, asking, commanding, requesting, or exclaiming something; the conventional unit of connected speech or writing, usually containing a subject and predicate, beginning with a capital letter, and ending with an end mark (period, question mark, exclamation point, or points of suspension); linguistically, as much of a speaker's expression as he places between definite final pitches and pauses.
4. a maxim; an axiom; a meaningful saying. [Archaic.]
5. an expressed or pronounced opinion. [Obs.]
6. sense; meaning. [Obs.]
7. in music, a complete idea; a period.

sen'tence, *v.t.*; sentenced, *pt., pp.*; sentencing, *ppr.* 1. to pronounce judgment or punishment upon (a convicted person).
2. to decree. [Obs.]
3. to express energetically. [Obs.]

sen'ten·cēr, *n.* one who pronounces a sentence

sen'tence stress, the voice stress given to certain words in a sentence to emphasize the meaning: in English it normally falls on the noun elements in the subject and on the object or complement.

sen·ten'tiăl (-shăl), *a.* [L. *sententialis*, in the form of a sentence.]
1. comprising sentences. [Archaic.]
2. of a grammatical sentence.
3. of, or having the nature of, a decision, judgment, or judicial sentence.

sen·ten'tiăl·ly, *adv.* in a sentential manner.

sen·ten'ti·ȧ·rist (-shi-), *n.* same as *sententiary.*

sen·ten'ti·ăr·y, *n.*; *pl.* **sen·ten'ti·ăr·ies,** [LL. *sententiarius*, one who passes sentence, from L. *sententia*, sentence.] formerly, one who read lectures or commented on the *Sentences* of Peter Lombard (c. 1100–c. 1160), Italian theologian and archbishop of Paris.

sen·ten·ti·os'i·ty, *n.* sententiousness.

sen·ten'tious, *a.* [OFr. *sententieux*; L. *sententiosus*, full of meaning, sententious.]
1. expressing much in words; pointed, compact, and terse; short and pithy.
2. full of, or fond of using, maxims, proverbs, and axioms; aphoristic; often, ponderously trite and moralizing.
3. comprising sentences. [Obs.]

sen·ten'tious·ly, *adv.* in a sententious manner.

sen·ten'tious·ness, *n.* the quality or state of being sententious.

sen'ti·ence (-shi-), *n.* 1. a sentient state or quality; capacity for feeling or perceiving; consciousness.
2. mere awareness or sensation that does not involve thought or perception.

sen'ti·en·cy, *n.* same as *sentience.*

sen'ti·ent, *a.* [L. *sentiens (-entis)*, ppr. of *sentire*, to perceive by the senses.] of, having, or capable of feeling or perception; conscious; as man is a *sentient* being.

sen'ti·ent, *n.* 1. one who or that which is sentient.
2. the mind.

sen'ti·ent·ly, *adv.* in a sentient manner.

sen'ti·ment, *n.* [ME. *sentement*; OFr. *sentement*; ML. *sentimentum*, feeling, affection, from L. *sentire*, to feel, perceive.]
1. a complex combination of feelings and opinions as a basis for action or judgment; general emotionalized attitude; as, patriotism has been called a noble *sentiment.*
2. a thought, opinion, judgment, or attitude, usually a result of deliberation, but often colored with emotion; as, what are his *sentiments* about prohibition?
3. sensibility; delicacy of feeling; susceptibility to feeling or to emotional appeal; tendency to be influenced by emotions, not reason.
4. appeal to the emotions in literature or art; expression of delicate, sensitive feeling.
5. sentimentality; maudlin emotion.
6. a short sentence expressing some trite thought, as in a toast.
7. the thought or meaning behind something said, as distinct from the words used.
8. [*pl.*] in phrenology, those faculties which not only produce a desire to act, but are combined with some emotion.

sen·ti·men'tăl, *a.* 1. having or showing tenderness, emotion, delicate feeling, etc., as music, poetry, etc.
2. affectedly or superficially emotional; pretending but lacking true depth of feeling; maudlin; mawkish.
3. influenced more by emotion than reason; acting from feeling rather than from practical and utilitarian motives; moved by emotional factors.
4. of or caused by sentiment; as, a *sentimental* reason.

sen·ti·men'tăl·ism, *n.* 1. the habit, quality, or condition of being sentimental.
2. any expression of this.

sen·ti·men'tăl·ist, *n.* a person showing or indulging in sentimentalism; a sentimental person.

sen"ti·men·tal'i·ty, *n.* 1. the quality, character, or condition of being sentimental.
2. *pl.* **sen"ti·men·tal'i·ties,** any expression of this.

sen·ti·men'tăl·īze, *v.i.*; sentimentalized, *pt., pp.*; sentimentalizing, *ppr.* to be sentimental; to think or behave in a sentimental manner.

sen·ti·men'tăl·īze, *v.t.* 1. to treat or consider in a sentimental manner.
2. to make sentimental.

sen·ti·men'tăl·ly, *adv.* in a sentimental way.

sen'ti·nel, *n.* [Fr. *sentinelle*; It. *sentinella*, a watch, a sentinel.]
1. a person or animal that guards a group against surprise; a sentry.
2. guard; watch. [Obs.]
to stand sentinel; to serve as a sentinel.

sen'ti·nel, *a.* acting as a sentinel or sentinels.
The *sentinel* stars set their watch in the sky. —Campbell.

sen'ti·nel, *v.t.*; sentineled *or* sentinelled, *pt., pp.*; sentineling *or* sentinelling, *ppr.* 1. to guard with sentinels; to provide sentinels for, as, a camp.
2. to watch over or guard as a sentinel.
3. to post as a sentinel.

sen'ti·nel crab, a sea crab, *Podophthalmus vigil*, of the Pacific and Indian oceans, characterized by its very lengthy eyestalks.

sen·ti·sec'tion, *n.* vivisection with pain.

sen'try, *n.*; *pl.* **sen'tries,** [corruption of *sentinel.*]
1. a sentinel, especially each of the men of a military guard who are posted to guard against, and give warning of, danger.
2. guard; watch; as, to keep *sentry.*

sen'try box, a small boxlike structure to cover a sentry at his post and shelter him from the weather.

Se·nū'si, Se·nus'si, *n.* a religious brotherhood of North African Moslems: during and after World War I their tribes were attacked and finally subjugated by French, British, and Italian forces.

Se·nū'si·ăn, *a.* of or like the Senusi.

sen'zȧ, *prep.* [It.; Fr. *sans.*] in music, without.

sē'păl (*or* sep'ăl), *n.* [Fr. *sépale*; Mod. L. *sepalum*, coined (1790) by H. J. de Necker from L. *separatus*, separate, and *petalum*, petal.] in botany, any of the leaf divisions of the calyx. When a calyx consists of but one part, it is said to be *monosepalous*; when of two parts, it is said to be *disepalous*; when of a variable and indefinite number of parts, it is said to be *polysepalous*; and when the parts are more or less united, it is said to be *gamosepalous.*

sē'păled, *a.* having sepals.

sep'ăl·ine, *a.* of, pertaining to, or like sepals.

sep'ăl·ō·dy, *n.* the change of other floral parts to sepals or sepaloid members.

sep'ăl·oid, *a.* like a sepal.

-sep'ăl·ous, [*sepal* and *-ous.*] a combining form meaning *having* (a specified number or kind of) *sepals*, as in tri*sepalous.*

sep"ȧ·rȧ·bil'i·ty, *n.* the state or quality of being separable.

sep'ȧ·rȧ·ble, *a.* [L. *separabilis*, that can be separated, from *separare*, to separate.] capable of being separated.

sep'ȧ·rȧ·ble·ness, *n.* the state or quality of being separable.

sep'ȧ·rȧ·bly, *adv.* in a separable manner; so as to be separable.

sep'ȧ·rāte, *v.t.*; separated, *pt., pp.*; separating, *ppr.* [L. *separatus*, pp. of *separare*, to separate; *se-*, apart, and *parare*, to arrange, provide.]
1. to set or put apart (two or more things) into parts, groups, sets, etc.; to disunite; to divide; to sever; to part in any manner; to disconnect; to disjoin.
2. to be between; to make a boundary, barrier, or space between; to divide; as, a wall *separated* the two fields.
3. to see the differences between; to distinguish or discriminate between.
4. to cause (two people) to cease associating or living together, as through legal action; as, how long have the Parkers been *separated?*
5. to single out or set apart from others for a special purpose; to sort; segregate.
6. to take away (a part or ingredient) from a combination or mixture.
7. to discharge or release from active duty in the armed forces.
Syn. detach, disengage, disjoin, part, sunder, dissolve.

sep'ȧ·rāte, *v.i.* 1. to withdraw or secede (with *from*); as, he has *separated from* the party.
2. to part, come to draw apart, or become disconnected.
3. to part company; to go in different directions; to cease to associated.
4. to stop being together as man and wife.
5. to become distinct or disengaged; as, cream *separates* from milk.

sep'ȧ·rāte, *a.* 1. divided from the rest; being parted from another; disjoined; disconnected.
2. unconnected; not united; distinct; individual; alone; as, *separate* reasons, *separate* farms.
3. thought of or regarded as having its own individual form or function; as, the *separate* parts of the body.
4. withdrawn from the company or association of others; solitary; isolated; secluded.
5. of or peculiar to one; not shared or held in common; as, they wanted *separate* rooms.
separate estate; the property of a married woman, which she holds independently of her husband's interference and control.
separate maintenence; a provision made by a husband for the sustenence of his wife, where they live in separation.

sep'ȧ·rāte, *n.* 1. anything separate.
2. a separate publication, as a single article from a book.

sep'ȧ·rāte·ly, *adv.* in a separate state; singly; distinctly; apart.

sep'ȧ·rāte·ness, *n.* the state of being separate.

sep·ȧ·rat'ic·ăl, *a.* of separation in religion. [Rare.]

sep·ȧ·rā'tion, *n.* [OFr., from L. *separatio (-onis)*, a separating, from *separatus*, pp. of *separare*, to separate.]
1. the act of separating or the state of being separated.
2. the place where a separating occurs; a break; division.
3. something that separates.

4. a divorce.
5. an arrangement by which a man and wife live apart by agreement or by court decree.
6. the process of chemical analysis. [Obs.]

sep·ȧ·rā′tion cen′tẽr, a center where men and women in the armed forces are discharged or released from active duty, or where their records are processed.

sep·ȧ·rā′tion·ist, *n.* same as *separatist.*

sep′ȧ·rȧ·tiṣm, *n.* the act of separating; disposition to withdraw or practice of withdrawing from a church or other association.

sep′ȧ·rȧ·tist, *n.* 1. a person who withdraws or secedes, especially one who is a member of a group that has seceded from a larger group; a dissenter; nonconformer.
2. a person who advocates political or religious separation.

sep″ȧ·rȧ·tis′tiç, *a.* relating to separatists.

sep′ȧ·rȧ·tive, *a.* [LL. *separativus,* from L. *separare,* to separate.] tending to separate or causing separation.

sep′ȧ·rȧ·tŏr, *n.* [LL., one who separates.]
1. one who or that which separates.
2. any of several devices for separating one substance from another; as, (a) a mechanism for purifying exhaust steam; (b) a machine for separating the cream from milk; (c) a device on a threshing machine for separating the grain from the chaff.

sep′ȧ·rȧ·tō·ry, *a.* causing or effecting separation; separative.

sep′ȧ·rȧ·trix, *n.* [LL., f. of *separator,* one who separates.]
1. in printing, a slanting line; a virgule.
2. in mathematics, a decimal point. [Obs.]

sē·pa̧wn′, *n.* same as *supawn.*

sep·ē·li′tion (-lish′un), *n.* burial; interment. [Obs.]

Sē·phär′diç, *a.* of the Sephardim, their characteristics, or culture.

Sē·phär′dim, *n.pl.; sing.* **Sē·phärd′,** [Heb. *sĕphārādhīm,* from *Sĕphāradh,* a region mentioned in Obadiah iii.20, often identified with Spain.]
1. the Jews of Spain and Portugal before the Inquisition.
2. their descendants.
Distinguished from *Ashkenazim.*

seph′en, *n.* [Ar.] a sting ray belonging to the genus *Trygon,* found chiefly in Arabian waters: its skin is of commercial value.

Seph′i·roth, *n.pl.; sing.* **Seph′i·rȧ,** [Heb.] in the cabala, the ten emanations or attributes of God.

sē′pi·ȧ, *n.* [L., from Gr. *sēpia,* a cuttlefish.]
1. any of several cuttlefishes with an internal shell.
2. a dark-brown pigment prepared from the inky fluid secreted by cuttlefish.
3. a dark reddish-brown color.
4. a photographic print in this color.
5. [S–] a genus typical of the family *Sepiidæ.*

sē′pi·ȧ, *a.* [L., from Gr. *sepia,* the cuttlefish.]
1. dark reddish-brown.
2. of sepia.

Sē·pi·ā′cē·ȧ *n.pl.* same as *Sepiidæ.*

sē·pi·ā′cē·ăn, *a.* of or pertaining to the *Sepiacea.*

sē·pi·ā′ceous, *a.* of or relating to the sepia or to the genus *Sepia.*

sē·pi·ãr′i·ăn, *a.* and *n.* same as *sepiary.*

sē′pi·ãr·y, *a.* of or pertaining to the genus *Sepiidæ.* [Rare.]

sē′pi·ãr·y, *n.* one of the genus *Sepiidæ.* [Rare.]

sē′piç *a.* of, pertaining to, or done in sepia, as as drawing.

sē·piç′ō·lous, *a.* [L. *sepes,* a hedge, and *colere,* to inhabit.] growing in hedges.

Sē·pī′i·dae, *n.pl.* the family of cuttlefishes, typified by the genus *Sepia.*

sep′i·ment, *n.* [L. *sepimentum,* a hedge, from *sepire,* to hedge, to fence.] something that separates or defends; a hedge; a fence.

sē′pi·ō·lite, *n.* [Gr. *sēpion,* the bone of the cuttlefish, and *-lite.*] same as *meerschaum.*

sē′pi·ost, *n.* [Gr. *sēpia,* cuttlefish, and *osteon,* bone.] the shell or bone of a cuttlefish.

sē″pi·ō·stâire′, *n.* same as *sepiost.*

sē·pon′, *n.* same as *supawn.*

sē·pōṣe′, *v.t.* to set apart or aside. [Obs.]

sē·poṣ′it, *v.t.* to sepose. [Obs.]

sep·ō·ṣi′tion (-zish′un), *n.* the act of putting aside or relinquishing. [Obs.]

sē′poy, *n.* [corruption of Hind. *sipāhī,* soldier; Per. *sipāhī,* from *sipāh,* army.] a native of India, employed as a soldier in a European army, especially the British army.

sep·pụk′ụ, *n.* [Japan.] same as *hara-kiri.*

Seps, *n.* [Gr. *sēps,* a small lizard, the bite of which causes putrefaction, from *sēpein,* to make putrid.]
1. a genus of scincoid reptiles, sometimes called serpent lizards.
2. [s–] a lizard of this genus.
3. [s–] a poisonous snake mentioned frequently in classical literature.

sep′sine, *n.* [*sepsis* and *-ine.*] a soluble poison formed in the putrefaction of blood and other protein matter.

sep′sis, *n.* [Gr. *sēpsis,* putrefaction, from *sēpein,* to make putrid.] poisoning caused by the absorption into the blood of pathogenic microorganisms, as from putrefying material; blood poisoning.

sept-, same as *septi-.*

sept, *n.* [OFr. *septe,* var. of *secte,* sect.]
1. an old Irish clan or tribe ruled by a patriarch.
2. any similar group, especially one localized and based on common descent in both male and female lines: properly distinguished from *sib.*

sep′tȧ, *n.* plural of *septum.*

sep′tăl, *a.* 1. of or forming a septum or septa.
2. of or pertaining to a sept.

sep′tăn, *a.* recurring on the seventh day.

sep′tāne, *n.* heptane. [Rare.]

sep′tañ·gle, *n.* a heptagon.

sep·tañ′gū·lăr, *a.* [*sept-,* and L. *angulus,* angle.] having seven angles.

sep·tãr′i·ăn, *a.* of or like septarium.

sep·tãr′i·um, *n.; pl.* **sep·tãr′i·ȧ,** [L. *septa,* partitions.] a cementlike mass, as of limestone, shot through with fissures filled with some other material, as calcite.

sep′tāte, *a.* [L. *septatus,* surrounded with a fence, from *septum,* fence.] having or divided by a septum or septa.

sep′tȧ·vā·lent, *a.* heptavalent. [Rare.]

sep·teç′tō·my, *n.* the surgical removal of part of the nasal septum.

sep′tem-, [from L. *septem,* seven.] a combining form meaning *seven* or *seventh,* as in *septempartite:* also *sept-.*

Sep·tem′bẽr, *n.* [ME. *Septembre,* from L. *September,* the name of the seventh month of the Roman year, from *septem,* seven.] the ninth month of the year, having thirty days.

Sep·tem′bẽr mas′sȧ·çre (-kẽr), the massacre of the Royalists in Paris, September 2 to 6, 1792, during the Revolution.

Sep·tem′brist, *n.* a person who took part in the September massacre; hence, one who is bloodthirsty.

sep·tem′flū·ous, *a.* flowing in seven streams.

sep·tē′mi·ȧ, sep·tae′mi·ȧ, *n.* same as *septicemia.*

sep·tem·pär′tīte, *a.* divided into seven parts.

sep·tem′vīr, *n.* [*septem-,* and L. *vir,* man.] one of a group of seven men, especially in ancient Rome, associated in some office or work.

sep·tem′vi·rāte, *n.* government under septemvirs; also, the office or rank of a septemvir.

sep′ten·ăr·y, *a.* [L. *septenarius,* consisting of seven, from *septem,* seven.]
1. of the number seven.
2. consisting of or forming a group of seven.
3. septennial.

sep′ten·ăr·y, *n.; pl.* **sep′ten·ăr·ieṣ,** 1. the number seven.
2. a group or set of seven, especially seven years.
3. a line of verse of seven feet.

sep′ten·āte, *a.* [L. *septeni,* seven each.] having a group or groups, each of seven parts; as, a *septenate* leaf, a leaf with seven leaflets.

sep·ten′nāte, *n.* a period of seven years, usually a term of office lasting seven years; any seven-year tenure.

sep·ten′ni·ăl, *a.* [L. *septennium; septem,* seven, and *annus,* year.]
1. lasting or continuing seven years; as, *septennial* parliaments.
2. happening, returning, etc. every seven years; as, a *septennial* election.

sep·ten′ni·ăl·ly, *adv.* once in seven years.

sep·ten′ni·um, *n.* [L.] a period of seven years.

Sep·ten′tri·ō, *n.* [L.] the constellation Ursa Major, or Great Bear.

sep·ten′tri·ŏn, *n.* [Fr., from L. *septentrio* (*-onis*), the north.] the north or northern regions. [Obs.]

sep·ten′tri·ŏn, *a.* [L. *septentrionalis.*] septentrional. [Rare.]

sep·ten′tri·ŏn·ăl, *a.* [OFr.; L. *septentrionalis,* from *septentriones,* the seven stars near the north pole, lit. seven plowing oxen, from *septem,* seven, and *triones,* plowing oxen.] northern; pertaining to the north; boreal. [Archaic.]

sep·ten″tri·ŏn·al′i·ty, *n.* northerliness.

sep·ten′tri·ŏn·ăl·ly, *adv.* northerly; toward the north.

sep·ten′tri·ŏn·āte, *v.i.* to tend northerly. [Rare.]

sep·tet′, sep·tette′, *n.* a group of seven persons or things; especially, in music, a musical composition arranged for seven parts, either vocal or instrumental; also, the seven performers of such a composition.

sept′foil, *n.* [L. *septem,* seven, and E. *foil.*]
1. a plant having a leaf with seven leaflets, as in some species of the *Potentilla.*
2. any object, such as a flower or an architectural ornament, having seven parts.

sep′ti-, a combining form of various origins and meanings: (a) [from L. *septem,* seven.] *seven* or *seventh,* as in *septilateral;* (b) [from Gr. *septos,* putrid.] *decomposed, vitiated,* as in *septicemia;* (c) [from L. *septum,* partition, fence.] *a dividing wall,* as in *septifragal.* Also, before a vowel, *sept-.*

sep′tiç, *a.* [Gr. *sēptikos,* from *sēpein,* to make putrid.]
1. causing sepsis or putrefaction; infective.
2. produced by or due to sepsis or putrefaction.

sep′tiç, *n.* a septic substance or agent.

sep′tiç·ăl, *a.* septic.

sep′tiç·ăl·ly, *adv.* in a septic manner.

sep·ti·cē′mi·ȧ, sep·ti·cae′mi·ȧ, *n.* [Mod. L., from Gr. *sēptikos,* putrefactive, and *haima,* blood.] blood poisoning caused by the presence of pathogenic microorganisms and their toxic products in the blood.

sep·ti·cē′miç, sep·ti·cae′miç, *a.* of or having septicemia.

sep′ti·cī·dăl, *a.* [L. *septum,* a partition, and *cædere,* to cut or divide.] in botany, dividing at the septa or partitions; breaking open at a natural dividing line: said of a form of dehiscence.

sep·tic′i·ty, *n.* 1. a septic quality.
2. a tendency to be or become septic or to cause infection.

sep′tiç sōre thrōat, an acute, severe infection of the throat, caused by certain hemolytic streptococci and characterized by fever, inflammation of the tonsils, etc.

sep′tiç tañk, a tank in which waste matter is putrefied and decomposed through bacterial action.

sep·tif′ẽr·ous, *a.* [L. *septum,* fence, and *ferre,* to bear.] bearing a septum or septa.

sep·tif′lụ·ous, *a.* flowing in seven streams.

sep·ti·fō′li·ous, *a.* having seven leaves.

sep′ti·fọrm, *a.* having the form of a septum.

sep·tif′rȧ·găl, *a.* [L. *septum,* a partition, and *frangere,* to break.] in botany, breaking away from a natural dividing line: said of a method of dehiscence.

sep·ti·lat′ẽr·ăl, *a.* [L. *septem,* seven, and *latus, lateris,* side.] having seven sides; as, a *septilateral* figure.

sep·til′liŏn, *n.* 1. in the United States and France, the number represented by 1 followed by 24 zeros.
2. in Great Britain and Germany, the number represented by 1 followed by 42 zeros.

sep·til′liŏn, *a.* amounting to one septillion in number.

sep′ti·măl, *a.* [from L. *septimus,* seventh; and *-al.*] of the number seven.

sep′tīme, *n.* [from L. *septimus,* seventh.] parry, the seventh position in fencing.

sep′ti·mōle, *n.* in music, a group of seven notes to be played in the time of four or six of the same value.

sep·tin′sū·lăr, *a.* [L. *septem,* seven, and *insula,* isle.] consisting of seven islands.

sep′ti·syl·lȧ·ble, *n.* a word of seven syllables.

sep′tō-, [from L. *septum,* a partition or fence.] a combining form meaning *a dividing wall.*

sep′tō-, [from Gr. *sēptos,* putrid.] a combining form meaning *decomposed, vitiated.*

sep·tō′iç, *a.* heptoic. [Rare.]

sep·tō·max'il·lăr·y, *a.* related to a maxillary bone and a septum of the nose.

sep·tō·max'il·lăr·y, *n.* in reptiles, amphibians, and some birds, a bone forming a septum of the nose.

sep·tom'ē·tĕr, *n.* an instrument for measuring the thickness of the nasal septum.

sep·tō·nā'ṣăl, *a.* pertaining to the nasal septum.

Sep·tō'ri·ȧ, *n.* [L. *septum*, a partition.] a genus of fungi parasitic on leaves of certain cultivated plants.

sep·tū·aġ·e·nār'i·ăn, *a.* [from L. *septuagenarius*, from *septuageni*, seventy each, from *septuaginta*, seventy.] seventy years old or between seventy and eighty.

sep·tū·aġ·e·nār'i·ăn, *n.* a person seventy or between seventy and eighty years of age.

sep·tū·aġ'e·nār·y, *a.* and *n.*; *pl.* **sep·tū·aġ'e·nār·ieṣ,** septuagenarian. [Rare.]

Sep″tū·ȧ·ġes'i·mȧ, *n.* [L. *septuagesimus*, seventieth.]

1. the third Sunday before Lent: supposedly so called because it is about seventy days before Easter: also called *Septuagesima Sunday*.

2. [s–] a period of seventy days. [Obs.]

sep″tū·ȧ·ġes'i·măl, *a.* septuagenarian. [Obs.]

Sep'tū·ȧ·ġint, *n.* [L. *septuaginta*, seventy.]

1. a Greek translation of the Old Testament: so called because it was said to be the work of seventy-two Palestinian Jews in the third century B.C., who completed the work in seventy days.

2. the group of seventy-two persons who are believed to have made this translation. [Obs.]

sep'tū·ăr·y, *n.* [L. *septem*, seven.] something composed of seven; a week. [Obs.]

sep'tū·lāte, *a.* [dim., L. *septum*.] designating fruits with imperfect septa.

sep'tū·lum, *n.*; *pl.* **sep'tū·lȧ,** a small septum.

sep'tum, *n.*; *pl.* **sep'tȧ,** [L., a partition.] a partition; a part that separates; a dividing wall; as, the *septum* between the two auricles of the heart; specifically, (a) in botany, a partition that separates the cells of some fruits; (b) in zoology, a calcareous plate or partition in the shell of an invertebrate; also, the partition in the body cavity of an annelid worm.

sep'tū·or, *n.* same as *septet*.

sep'tū·ple, *a.* [LL. *septuplus*, from L. *septem*, seven, and *plicare*, to fold.]

1. sevenfold; seven times as much or as many.

2. consisting of or including seven.

sep'tū·ple, *n.* a group or set of seven.

sep'tū·ple, *v.t.*; septupled, *pt., pp.*; septupling, *ppr.* to make sevenfold; to multiply by seven.

sep'tū·plet, *n.* same as *septimole*.

sep'ul·chĕr, *n.* [Fr. *sépulcre*, from L. *sepulcrum*, from *sepelire*, to bury.]

1. a grave; a tomb; a vault for burial.

He rolled a great stone to the door of the *sepulchre*, and departed.
—Matt. xxvii. 60.

2. a place for the safekeeping of relics, as in an altar.

3. in early church architecture, a recess for the reception of the holy elements consecrated on Maundy Thursday until Easter.

sep'ul·chĕr, *v.t.*; sepulchered, *pt. pp.*; sepulchering, *ppr.* to place in a sepulcher; to bury.

sē·pul'chrăl, *a.* [L. *sepulcralis*, from *sepulcrum*, a sepulcher.]

1. pertaining to sepulchers, burial, the grave, etc.

2. suggestive of a sepulcher; tomblike; dismal; gloomy.

3. deep and melancholy: said of sound.

sep'ul·chre(-kĕr), *n.* and *v.t.*; sepulchred, *pt., pp.*; sepulchring, *ppr.* sepulcher: British spelling.

sep'ul·tūre, *n.* [Fr., from L. *sepultura*, from *sepelire*, to bury.]

1. burial; interment.

2. a grave; a burial place; a sepulcher. [Archaic.]

sep'ul·tūre, *v.t.* to bury; to entomb; to sepulcher.

sē·quā'cious, *a.* [L. *sequax*, from *sequi*, to follow.]

1. tending to follow any leader; lacking individuality, as in thought; dependent; servile; compliant.

2. ductile; pliant; malleable.

3. having or following logical sequence.

sē·quā'cious·ly, *adv.* in a sequacious manner.

sē·quā'cious·ness, *n.* the state of being sequacious.

sē·quac'i·ty, *n.* a following, or disposition to follow; sequaciousness.

sē'quel, *n.* [OFr. *sequelle*, from L. *sequi*, to follow.]

1. something that follows; anything subsequent or succeeding; continuation.

2. something that comes as a result of something else; aftermath; effect; consequence.

3. any literary work complete in itself but continuing a story started in an earlier work.

4. sequence; succession; also, successors. [Obs.]

sē·quē'lȧ, *n.*; *pl.* **sē·quē'lae,** [L., from *sequi*, to follow.] one who or that which follows; specifically, (a) an adherent; a follower; a band of adherents or followers; (b) an inference; a conclusion; (c) in medicine, a diseased condition resulting from a previous disease.

sē'quence, *n.* [Fr. *séquence*, from L. *sequens*, ppr. of *sequi*, to follow.]

1. the state of being sequent or following; a following or coming of one thing after another; succession.

2. a particular order of succession or following; an arrangement; order.

3. a continuous or related series of things following in a certain order or succession; specifically, a set of three or more playing cards inmediately following each other in value in the same suit, as two, three, four, five, and six; a run.

4. result; consequence; sequel.

5. in motion pictures, a part of a film story treating an episode without any interruptions of continuity.

6. in music, the recurrence of a harmonic progression or melodic figure at a different pitch or, sometimes, in a different key to that in which it was first given.

7. in the Roman Catholic Church, a hymn coming between the gradual and the gospel; a prose.

sē'quent, *a.* 1. following; succeeding; coming after in time or order.

2. following as a result or effect; consequent.

sē'quent, *n.* 1. a follower. [Obs.]

2. something that follows, especially as a result; a sequence.

sē·quen'tiăl (-shăl) *a.* 1. being in succession; succeeding; following.

2. characterized by a graduated sequence of parts; forming a regular series.

sē·quen'tiăl·ly, *adv.* by sequence or succession.

sē·ques'tĕr, *v.t.*; sequestered, *pt., pp.*; sequestering, *ppr.* [OFr. *sequestrer*, from LL. *sequestrare*, to remove, lay aside, separate.]

1. to set off or apart; to separate; segregate.

2. to take possession of (property) as security for a debt, claim, etc.

3. to take over; confiscate; to seize, especially by authority.

4. to withdraw; to seclude: sometimes used reflexively. [Rare.]

sē·ques'tĕr, *v.i.* 1. in law, to decline, as a widow, any concern with the estate of her husband.

2. to withdraw; to retire. [Obs.]

sē·ques'tĕr, *n.* 1. the act of sequestering; sequestration; separation. [Rare.]

2. in law, a person with whom two or more parties to a suit or controversy deposit the subject of controversy; a mediator or referee between two parties; an umpire. [Obs.]

sē·ques'tĕred, *a.* secluded; retired; as, a *sequestered* nook.

sē·ques'trȧ·ble, *a.* capable of being sequestered; subject or liable to sequestration.

sē·ques'trāte, *v.t.*; sequestrated, *pt., pp.*; sequestrating, *ppr.* 1. to sequester. [Archaic.]

2. to confiscate.

sē·ques·trā'tion, *n.* 1. in law, (a) the separation of a thing in controversy from th possession of those who contend for it; (b) the setting apart of the goods or property of a deceased person to whom no one was willing to take out administration; (c) a writ directed by the court to commissioners allowing them to enter the lands and seize the goods of the person against whom it is directed, as a defendant who is in contempt by reason of neglect or refusal to appear or answer or to obey a decree of court; (d) the act of taking property from the owner for a time till the rents, issues, and profits satisfy a demand; (e) in ecclesiastical law, the gathering of the profits of a vacant benefice for the use of the next incumbent; (f) in international law, the seizure of the property of an individual for the use of the state: applied especially to the seizure by a belligerent power of debts due by its subjects to the enemy; (g) in Scots law, the seizing of a bankrupt's estate by decree of a competent court, for the benefit of the creditors.

2. the act of sequestering or the state of being sequestered or set aside; separation; retirement; seclusion.

3. disjunction; division.

sē'ques·trā·tŏr, *n.* 1. one who sequestrates.

2. one to whom the administration of sequestrated property is appointed.

sē·ques·treç'tō·my, *n.*; *pl.* **sē·ques·treç'tō·mieṣ,** [LL. *sequestrum*, something put aside, and Gr. *temnein*, to cut.] the surgical removal of a sequestrum or sequestra.

sē·ques'trum, *n.*; *pl.* **sē·ques'trȧ,** [LL., from *sequestrare*, to surrender.] in medicine, a piece of dead tissue, especially bone, which has become separated from the surrounding healthy tissue.

sē'quin, *n.* [Fr., from It. *zecchino*, from *zecca*, a mint, from Ar. *sikkah*, *sekkah*, a stamp, die.]

1. an obsolete Italian gold coin first struck at Venice about the end of the thirteenth century: it was equivalent to about $2.25.

2. a small, shiny ornament or spangle, as a metal disk, especially one of many sewn on fabric for decoration.

Sē·quoi'ȧ, *n.* [from *Sikwâyi*, Cherokee who invented the Cherokee syllabary.]

1. a genus of giant conifers, consisting of two species only, *Sequoia sempervirens*, the redwood, and *Sequoia gigantea*, the big tree of California. Both attain heights upward of 300 feet: they are characterized by small oval cones and hard wood.

2. [s–] any tree of this genus.

sēr, *n.* [Hind.] in India, a unit of weight of a little over two pounds, equal to about 1/40 of a maund: also *seer*.

ser-, see *sero-*.

sē'rȧ, *n.* alternative plural of *serum*.

sé·rac' (sā-rak'), *n.* [Swiss Fr., a kind of cheese put up in cubic form.] a pointed mass or pinnacle of ice left standing among the crevasses of a glacier.

sē·ragl'iō (-ral'yō), *n.*; *pl.* **sē·ragl'iōṣ,** [LL. *seracula*, dim. of L. *sera*, a lock.]

1. the palace of a Turkish sultan or noble; formerly, [S–] the palace of the sultan of Turkey at Constantinople.

2. a harem; a place where a Moslem keeps his wives or concubines.

3. a place of licentious pleasure.

4. an enclosure; a place of confinement.

sē·rä'i, *n.* [Per. *sarāī*, a palace.] in the Orient, a place for the accommodation of travelers; a caravansary; a khan.

sēr·al·bū'min, *n.* [*serum* and *albumin*.] an albumin present in the blood stream.

sē·rang', *n.* [E. Ind., from Per. *sarhang*, a captain.] in the East Indies, the boatswain of a lascar crew; also, the captain of a small native vessel.

sē·rä'pē, *n.* [Mex. Sp.] a woolen blanket or shawl, often brightly colored, worn as an outer garment in Spanish American countries.

ser'ăph (-ăf), *n.*; *pl.* **ser'ăphs, ser'ȧ·phim,** [Heb.] in theology, a member of the highest of the nine orders of angels, represented in the Bible as the celestial beings with three pairs of wings.

sē·raph'iç, *a.* pertaining to, like, or suitable for a seraph; angelic; sublime; as, *seraphic* purity.

sē·raph'iç, *n.* a zealot [Obs.]

sē·raph'iç·ăl, *a.* same as *seraphic*.

sē·raph'iç·ăl·ly, *adv.* in a seraphic manner; angelically.

sē·raph'iç·ăl·ness, *n.* the state or quality of being seraphic. [Rare.]

sē·raph'i·ciṣm, *n.* seraphicalness. [Rare.]

ser'ȧ·phim, *n.* alternative plural and, formerly, alternative singular of *seraph*.

ser″ȧ·phï'nȧ, *n.* same as *seraphine*.

ser'ȧ·phïne, *n.* an obsolete keyed reed instrument resembling the harmonium, invented about 1830.

Sē·rā'pis, *n.* [L. and Gr.] in Egyptian, Greek, and Roman mythology, a god of the lower world.

sē·ras'kïer (-kēr), *n.* [Fr. *sérasquier*, from Per. *serasker*; *ser*, *seri*, head, chief, and *'asker*, an army.] a Turkish general or commander of land forces.

se·ras′kïer·āte, *n.* the office or authority of a seraskier; also, formerly, the ministry of war at Constantinople.

Sẽrb, *n.* 1. one of a Slavic people of the Balkans.

2. their language.

Sẽrb, *a.* Serbian.

Sẽr′bi·ăn, *n.* a native or inhabitant of Serbia; especially, one of the Slavic people of Serbia; a Serb.

Sẽr′bi·ăn, *a.* pertaining to Serbia, the inhabitants of Serbia, or their language.

Sẽr′bō-, a combining form meaning *Serbian*: also *Servo-*.

Sẽr′bō-Çrō·ā′tiăn, *n.* the South Slavic language spoken in Yugoslavia: it is generally written with Roman characters in Croatia but with Cyrillic characters in Serbia.

Sẽr′bō-Çrō·ā′tiăn, *a.* of the South Slavic language spoken in Yugoslavia or the people who speak it.

Sẽr·bō′ni·ăn, *a.* of or designating Lake Serbonis in ancient Egypt, a bog, now dry, in which whole armies were said to have sunk.

sēre, *n.* [back-formation from *series*.] in ecology, the complete series of changes occurring in the cycle of a plant formation.

sēre, *a.* [var. of *sear*.] dried up; withered. [Poetic.]

sē·reiṅ′ (-raṅ′), *n.* [Fr., from L. *serenus*, clear.] a mist or excessively fine rain which falls from a clear sky just after sunset: a phenomenon of tropical climates.

ser·ē·nāde′, *n.* [Fr. *sérénade*; It. *serenata*.]

1. a vocal or instrumental performance of music outdoors at night, especially by a lover under the window of his sweetheart.

2. a piece of music suitable for this.

ser·ē·nāde′, *v.t.* and *v.i.*; serenaded, *pt.*, *pp.*; serenading, *ppr.* to play or sing a serenade (to).

ser·ē·nād′ẽr, *n.* one who serenades.

ser·ē·nä′tȧ, *n.*; *pl.* **ser·ē·nä′tȧṣ**, **ser·ē·nä′tẹ**, [It.] 1. a type of dramatic or pastoral secular cantata.

2. an orchestral composition having several movements, intermediate between the suite and the symphony.

ser·en·dip′i·ty, *n.* [coined by Horace Walpole (c. 1754) after his tale *The Three Princes of Serendip* (i.e., Ceylon), who made such discoveries.] an apparent aptitude for making fortunate discoveries accidentally.

sē·rēne′, *a.* [L. *serenus*, clear, calm.]

1. fair; clear; undimmed; as, a *serene* sky.

2. calm; undisturbed; as, a *serene* soul.

3. [S-] exalted; honorable; high-ranking: used in the titles of certain European royal families; as, His *Serene* Highness.

sē·rēne′, *n.* 1. clearness; calm expanse, as of sky or water. [Poetic or Rare.]

2. serenity; tranquillity; calmness.

sē·rēne′, *v.t.*; serened, *pt.*, *pp.*; serening, *ppr* 1. to make clear and calm; to tranquilize.

2. to clear; to brighten. [Rare.]

sē·rēne′ly, *adv.* in a serene manner; deliberately; quietly.

sē·rēne′ness, *n.* the state of being serene.

sē·ren′i·tūde, *n.* serenity; calmness. [Obs.]

sē·ren′i·ty, *n.*; *pl.* **sē·ren′i·tieṣ**, [Fr. *sérénité*; L. *serenitas*.]

1. the quality or state of being serene; calmness; quietness; peace.

2. calmness of mind; evenness of temper; undisturbed state; coolness.

3. clearness; brightness.

4. [S-] a title of honor used in speaking to or of members of certain royal families, etc.: preceded by *His*, *Her*, or *Your*.

Sē·rē′nō·ȧ, *n.* [from Dr. *Sereno* Watson of Harvard.] a genus of palms of which the only species is *Serenoa serrulata*, the saw palmetto, found in the southeastern United States.

sẽrf, *n.* [Fr., from L. *servus*, a slave, from *servire*, to be a slave.]

1. originally, a slave.

2. a person in feudal servitude, bound to his master's land and transferred with it when it passed to another owner.

3. any person who is oppressed or without freedom.

sẽrf′ăġe, *n.* serfdom.

sẽrf′dŏm, *n.* the condition or status of a serf.

sẽrf′hood, *n.* serfs collectively.

sẽrf′iṣm, *n.* serfdom.

sẽrġe, *n.* [Fr. *serge*; L. *serica (lana)*, (wool of the) *Seres*, an Oriental people, prob. the Chinese.]

1. a kind of twilled worsted cloth used for suits, etc.

2. a twilled silk, rayon, etc., used for linings.

ser′ġeăn·cy (sär′), *n.*; *pl.* **ser′ġeăn·cieṣ**, the position or rank of a sergeant.

ser′ġeănt (sär′), *n.* [from Fr. *sergent*; OFr. *serjent*, originally a servant, a servitor, from L. *serviens*, serving, from *servire*, to serve.]

1. formerly, a feudal servant who attended his master in battle.

2. a sergeant-at-arms.

3. a sergeant-at-law: also spelled *serjeant*.

4. a police officer ranking next below a captain or a lieutenant.

5. in the United States armed forces, a noncommissioned officer ranking just above a corporal: in the Army, formerly the fourth grade of enlisted man (now *corporal*) and now the third grade (formerly *staff sergeant*); in the Marine Corps and Air Force, the fourth grade.

6. a sergeant fish.

ser′ġeănt-at-ärmṣ, *n.*; *pl.* **ser′ġeănts-at-ärmṣ**, an officer appointed to keep order in a legislature, court, social club, etc.

ser′ġeănt-at-lạw, *n.*; *pl.* **ser′ġeănts-at-lạw**, a member of a former group of high-ranking British barristers (lawyers) having certain special privileges in the king's courts: also spelled *serjeant-at-law*.

ser′ġeănt băk′ẽr, an Australian fish, *Aulopus purpurissatus*.

ser′ġeănt·cy, *n.* same as *sergeantship*.

ser′ġeănt fīrst çlȧss, in the United States Army, the second grade of enlisted man (formerly *technical sergeant*) ranking just below master sergeant.

ser′ġeănt fish, 1. a large, striped, marine fish, *Elacate canada*: also called *cobia*.

2. the robalo.

ser′ġeănt mā′jŏr, *pl.* **ser′ġeănts mā′jŏr**, 1. in the United States Army, an enlisted man, usually a master sergeant, who is assistant to an adjutant, as of a regiment: an occupational title and not a rank.

2. in the United States Marine Corps, the highest ranking noncommissioned officer.

ser′ġeănt·ry, **ser′jeănt·ry**, *n.* sergeanty. [Archaic.]

ser′ġeănt·ship, **ser′jeănt·ship**, *n.* the rank, position, or duties of a sergeant.

ser′ġeănt·y, **ser′jeănt·y**, *n.* in feudal law, a tenure of knightly or honorable distinction, under which the holder had to perform some service directly for the king.

grand sergeanty; a tenure requiring the personal service of the holder, in battle or at court, as carrying the king's sword or banner, or the like.

petty sergeanty; the annual presentation of a sword, banner, etc.

sẽrġe′dụ·soy, *n.* [Fr. *serge de soie*, silk serge.] a fabric made of silk, or sometimes of silk and wool: used in the eighteenth century for men's coats, etc.

sē′ri·ăl, *a.* [ML. *serialis*, from L. *series*, a row, order, or sequence.]

1. of, arranged in, or forming a series; as, *serial* numbers.

2. appearing, published, etc. in a series or succession of continuous parts at regular intervals.

3. of a serial or serials; as the magazine has the *serial* rights to the story.

sē′ri·ăl, *n.* 1. any novel, story, etc. published or presented in serial form.

2. a periodical.

sē·ri·al′i·ty, *n.* the state or condition of following in successive order; sequence.

sē′ri·ăl·īze, *v.t.*; serialized *pt.*, *pp.*; serializing, *ppr.* to put or publish in serial form, as a story.

sē′ri·ăl·ly, *adv.* 1. in a series; in regular order.

2. in a succession of parts; as a serial.

sē′ri·ăl num′bẽr, a number, usually one of a series, used to identify; as, *serial numbers* are given to soldiers at enlistment, to engines at the time of manufacture, etc.

Sē′ri·ăn, *a.* same as *Seric*.

sē′ri·āte, *a.* arranged or occurring in a series or succession.

sē′ri·āte·ly, *adv.* in a regular series. [Obs.]

sē·ri·ā′tim, *adv.* [L.] in regular order; point by point; serially.

sē·ri·ā′tion, *n.* arrangement in a series; position according to some law of a series.

Ser′iç, *a.* [L. *sericus*; Gr. *sērikos*, silken.] of or pertaining to the Seres, a people now usually identified with the Chinese. They were mentioned by the Greeks and Romans as producing the first silk.

sē·ri′ceous (-rish′us), *a.* [L. *sericus*, from *sericum*, silk.]

1. pertaining to or like silk; downy; consisting of silk; silky.

2. in botany, covered with short, straight, silky hairs.

3. in zoology, having fine close hairs which give a silklike luster. [Rare.]

ser′i·ci·çul″tūre, *n.* same as *sericulture*.

ser′i·cin, *n.* [L. *sericum*, silk.] a gelatinous compound obtained from crude silk: also called *silk gelatin*.

ser′i·cīte, *n.* a silky, scaly variety of muscovite, ch racteristic of sericite schist.

ser·iç·tē′ri·um, *n.*; *pl.* **ser·iç·tē′ri·ȧ**, [LL., from Gr. *sērikon*, silk.] a gland secreting silk, as in a silkworm. [Rare.]

ser′i·çul·tūre, *n.* the art or process of keeping and breeding silkworms for the production of raw silk.

ser·i·ẹ′mȧ, *n.* [Mod. L., from Tupi *seriema*, lit., crested.]

1. a crested Brazilian bird of the crane family, with gray and umber coloring and long legs and neck.

2. an Argentinian bird similar to this bird but smaller.

sē′rieṣ (-rēz), *n.* [L., a row, order, succession, from *serere*, to join or weave together; Gr. *seira*, a rope; Sans. *serat*, a thread.]

1. a continued succession of similar things, or of things bearing a similar relation to each other; an extended order, line, or course; sequence; succession; as, a *series* of presidents; a *series* of calamitous events.

2. a number of things produced as a related group; a set, as of novels by one author dealing with the same characters.

3. in mathematics, an infinite number of terms following one another, each of which is derived from one or more of the preceding ones, by a fixed law, called the law of the series; especially, the indicated sum of such a set of terms.

4. in botanical classification, one of the grand divisions of plant life; a subkingdom.

5. in chemistry, a group of compounds, each containing the same radical. Thus the hydrocarbon, CH_4, methane, may take up any number of the molecules of the radical CH_2, thereby giving rise to the series, C_2H_6, ethane, C_3H_8, propane, C_4H_{10}, quartane, etc.

6. in geology, a division of a system.

Within the systems smaller aggregates of formations may be recognized, which shall be called *series*.—Nomenclature and Classification for the Geologic Atlas of the United States.

7. in numismatics or philately, a set of coins or stamps having some characteristic in common, as those issued by one government.

8. in rhetoric, a group of successive co-ordinate elements of a sentence.

9. in biology, any comprehensive group of organisms: a term loosely applied.

10. in electricity, an arrangement as of cells in which the positive electrode of one is in connection with the negative electrode of another.

in series; in electricity, connected in a series circuit.

sē′rieṣ cir′çuit (-kit), an electrical circuit in which the parts are connected end to end, positive pole to negative pole, so that current flows from part to part in succession: opposed to *parallel circuit*.

sē′rieṣ-wound, *a.* in electricity, designating a dynamo or motor in which the armature and the field magnet coil are connected in series with the outer circuit: opposed to *shunt-wound*.

ser′if, *n.* [D. *schreef*, a stroke, line, from *schrijve*, to write, from L. *scribere*.] in printing, one of the fine lines of a letter, especially one of the fine cross lines at the top or bottom, as of I.

ser′i·grȧph, *n.* [from L. *sericum*, silk, and *-graph*.] a color print made by the silkscreen process and printed by the artist himself.

sē·rig′rȧ·phẽr, *n.* a person who makes serigraphs.

sē·rig′rȧ·phy, *n.* the art of making serigraphs.

ser'in, *n.* [Fr.] a song bird of the finch family, closely related to the canary, found in the central parts of Europe.

ser'in, *n.* serine.

ser'ïne, *n.* [from L. *sericus*, silken, and *-ine.*] a colorless crystalline compound, $C_3H_7NO_3$ present in many proteins.

se·rin'gȧ, *n.* [Port., a syringe, rubber having been first used for making syringes.] any one of the Brazilian trees of the genus *Hevea*, yielding rubber.

sē"ri·ō·çom'iç, sē"ri·ō·çom'i·çăl, *a.* partly serious and partly comic.

Sē·rī'ō·lȧ, *n.* a genus of carangoid food fishes including the medregal, amber fish, etc.

sē'ri·ous, *a.* [Fr. *sérieux*; L. *serius*, grave.]
1. of, showing, having, or caused by earnestness or deep thought; earnest, grave, sober, or solemn; as, a *serious* man.
2. of a grave or solemn aspect; as, a frivolous mind behind a *serious* face.
3. (a) meaning what one says or does; not joking or trifling; sincere; (b) not thought, said, or done in play.
4. concerned or dealing with grave or important matters, problems, etc.; weighty; important.
5. requiring careful consideration or thought; involving difficulty, effort, or considered action.
6. giving cause for anxiety; critical; dangerous; alarming; as, a *serious* wound.
Syn.—grave, solemn, important, weighty.

sē'ri·ous·ly, *adv.* in a serious manner; gravely; solemnly; in earnest; without levity; in an important degree.

sē'ri·ous-mind'ed, *a.* of, having, or showing earnestness or seriousness of purpose, method, etc.; characterized by preoccupation with serious matters and not by levity, joking, etc.

sē'ri·ous·ness, *n.* the quality or state of being serious.

ser'iph, *n.* same as *serif.*

Ser·jā'ni·ȧ, *n.* [LL., from Philippe *Sergeant*, a French botanist.] a genus of South American shrubs, some of which are narcotic and poisonous.

ser'jeȧnt (sär'jent), *n.* sergeant. [Especially Brit.]

sẽr·moc·i·nā'tion, *n.* speechmaking. [Obs.]

sẽr·moc'i·nā·tŏr, *n.* one who makes sermons or speeches. [Obs.]

sẽr'mŏn, *n.* [OFr. and Fr., from L. *sermo* (*-onis*), speech.]
1. a speech, discourse, or writing. [Obs.]
2. a discourse delivered in public, especially by a clergyman or preacher in a pulpit using a text from Scripture, for the purpose of religious instruction or the inculcation of morality; a similar discourse written or printed, whether delivered or not; a homily.
3. a serious exhortation, rebuke, or reproof; an address on one's conduct or duty, especially a long, tedious, annoying one.

sẽr'mŏn, *v.t.* 1. to discourse as in a sermon. [Rare.]
2. to tutor; to lesson; to teach. [Obs.]

sẽr'mŏn, *v.i.* to compose or deliver a sermon. [Obs.]

sẽr·mŏn·eer', *n.* one who sermonizes. [Rare.]

sẽr'mŏn·ẽr, *n.* a sermonizer.

sẽr·mŏn·et', *n.* a brief sermon: also written *sermonette.*

sẽr·mon'iç, sẽr·mon'i·çăl, *a.* pertaining to or resembling a sermon; didactic; solemn.

sẽr'mŏn·ish, *a.* resembling a sermon.

sẽr'mŏn·ist, *n.* a sermonizer.

sẽr'mŏn·ïze, *v.i.*; sermonized, *pt., pp.*; sermonizing, *ppr.* 1. to preach, especially in a dogmatic, moralizing way.
2. to inculcate rigid rules.
3. to compose, deliver, or write a sermon or sermons.

sẽr'mŏn·ïze, *v.t.* to preach to; to exhort; to lecture; to influence by a sermon.

sẽr'mŏn·ī·zẽr, *n.* one who sermonizes.

Sẽr'mŏn on the Mount, the sermon delivered by Jesus to his disciples: Matt. v.–vii., Luke vi. 20–49: it contains the essentials of Christian belief.

sē'rō-, [from *serum*] a combining form meaning *serum*, as in *serology*: also, before a vowel, *ser-.*

sē'rō·cyst, *n.* a cyst which holds serum.

sē·rō·en·te·rī'tis, *n.* inflammation of the serous coat of the intestines.

ser'ō·lin, *n.* a substance consisting of several fats, extracted from dried blood serum.

sē·rō·loġ'i·çăl, *a.* pertaining to serology.

sē·rol'ō·ġy, *n.* [*sero-* and *-logy.*] the science concerned with the preparation, use, and properties of serums.

sē·rō·mū'çous, *a.* consisting of serum and mucus.

sē·roon', *n.* [Sp. *seron*, a basket.] a kind of hamper or crate for carrying figs, almonds, and the like, used in Spain and the Mediterranean region and varying in capacity.

sē·rō·pū'rŭ·lent, *a.* composed of serum containing pus.

sē'rōse, *a.* watery; serous. [Obs.]

sē·ros'i·ty, *n.*; *pl.* **sē·ros'i·ties,** [Fr. *sérosité*, from L. *serum*, whey.]
1. the state or quality of being serous.
2. a thin, watery fluid, as that found in the joints of the body.

sē·rō·thēr'ȧ·py, *n.* in medicine, a method of treatment by the use of serum from inoculated animals.

ser'ō·tine, *n.* [Fr., from L. *serotinus*, late.] a species of European bat, *Vesperugo serotinus*, somewhat rare in England but common in France, of a chestnut color, solitary in its habits, frequenting forests, and of slow flight.

ser'ō·tine, *a.* [Fr. *sérotine*, from L. *serus*, late.] late or delayed in development: said especially of late-flowering plants.

sē·rot'i·nous, *a.* same as *serotine.*

sē'rous, *a.* [Fr. *séreux*; LL. *serosus*, from L. *serum*, whey.]
1. thin; watery; like serum.
2. pertaining to or containing serum.
serous cavity; a cavity which has a lining of serous membrane.
serous fluid; any of several serumlike fluids in the body cavities, especially those lined with serous membrane.
serous gland; a gland that secretes a watery fluid, as a salivary gland.
serous membrane; a thin membrane that lines most of the closed cavities of the body: the peritoneum is the serous membrane lining the abdominal cavity.

ser'ōw, sur'rōw, *n.* [native (Tibet or Sikkim) name.] any of a group of goat antelopes of eastern Asia, especially *Nemorhædus bubalinus*, of the Himalayas, whitish below with reddish-brown back and sides.

sẽr·ped'i·nous, *a.* serpiginous. [Rare.]

Sẽr'pens, *n.* a northern constellation supposedly like a snake in shape.

sẽr'pent, *n.* [L. *serpens, serpentis*, from *serpere*, to creep.]
1. a snake, expecially a large or poisonous one.
2. a sly, sneaking, treacherous person.
3. a firework which, as it burns, lengthens out and writhes like a snake.
4. in the Bible, Satan; the Devil, in the form he assumed to tempt Eve: Gen. iii. 1–5.
5. in music, an obsolete, coiled, bass wind instrument of wood covered with leather.
pharaoh's serpent; a chemical phenomenon produced by burning a cone of mercuric thiocyanate, by which is produced a long strip or roll of brownish ash with serpentine twists and folds.

sẽr'pent, *v.i.* to twist about; to curve like a serpent. [Rare.]

sẽr'pent, *v.t.* to wind around; to entwine. [Rare.]

sẽr·pen·tā'ri·ȧ, *n.* in medicine, the rhizome and roots of *Aristolochia serpentaria* and *Aristolochia reticulata*: used as aromatic medicines.

Sẽr·pen·tā'ri·us, *n.* [L.] a constellation in the northern hemisphere: also called *Ophiuchus.*

sẽr'pen·tār·y, *n.* the Virginia snakeroot, *Aristolochia serpentaria.*

sẽr'pent çū'çum·bẽr, a plant, *Trichosanthes colubrina*, so called from the serpentlike appearance of its fruit; the snake melon.

sẽr'pent ēa'gle, one of several birds which prey upon serpents, as *Circaetus gallicus* of Europe and *Spilornis cheela* of India.

sẽr'pent ēat'ẽr, the secretary bird.

sẽr'pent fish, a fish with a body of a ribbonlike and compressed form, and a band of red running lengthwise; the red bandfish, *Sepola tænia* or *rubescens.*

sẽr·pen'ti·form, *a.* having the form of a serpent.

sẽr'pen·tïne (*or* -tīn), *a.* [LL. *serpentinus*, from L. *serpens*, a serpent.]
1. resembling a serpent; winding or turning one way and the other, like a moving serpent; spiral; coiled or twisted.
2. evilly cunning or subtle; treacherous.
3. having the color or properties of a serpent.
serpentine verse; a verse which begins and ends with the same word.

sẽr'pen·tïne, *n.* [from resemblance to a serpent's skin.] a mineral, magnesium silicate, $Mg_3Si_2O_7 \cdot 2H_2O$, usually green or brownish red and often mottled.

sẽr'pen·tïne, *v.i.* to meander.

sẽr'pen·tïne·ly, *adv.* in a serpentine manner.

Sẽr·pen·tin'i·ăn, *n.* one of an ancient sect of serpent worshipers; an Ophite.

sẽr·pen·tin'iç, *a.* serpentinous.

sẽr·pen·tin·i·zā'tion, *n.* the act or process of changing into serpentine, a species of metamorphism.

sẽr'pen·tin·ïze, *v.t.*; serpentinized, *pt., pp.*; serpentinizing, *ppr.* to change into serpentine.

sẽr'pen·tin·oid, *a.* resembling serpentine in structure or in composition.

sẽr'pen·tin·ous, *a.* of the nature or character of serpentine.

sẽr'pent·ïze, *v.i.*; serpentized, *pt., pp.*; serpentizing, *ppr.* to wind; to turn or bend, first in one direction and then in the opposite; to meander, as a river in its course.

sẽr'pent·līke, *a.* like a serpent.

sẽr'pent·ry, *n.* 1. serpents collectively.
2. a place where serpents abound.

sẽr'pent stär, a brittle star.

sẽr'pent's tŏngue (tung), 1. a plant of the genus *Ophioglossum*; adder's tongue.
2. the fossil teeth of a species of shark: so called because they resemble tongues with their roots.

sẽr'pent-tŏngued (-tungd), *a.* having a forked tongue.

sẽr'pent·wood, *n.* an East Indian shrub, the root of which is used in India for medicinal purposes.

sẽr·pette', *n.* [Fr., dim. of *serpe*, a pruning knife.] a curved knife used in pruning.

sẽr·piġ'i·nous, *a.* 1. affected with serpigo.
2. in medicine, like a serpigo.

sẽr·pī'gō, *n.* [LL., from L. *serpere*, to creep.] any spreading skin disease, as ringworm.

sẽr'pō·let, *n.* the wild thyme, *Thymus serpyllum.*

Sẽr'pū·lȧ, *n.* [LL., from L. *serpere*, to creep.]
1. a genus of annelids inhabiting cylindrical and tortuous calcareous tubes attached to rocks, shells, etc., in the sea.
2. [s–] any individual member of this genus.

SERPULA

sẽr·pū'li·ăn, *n.* one of the *Serpulidæ.*

Sẽr·pū'li·dae, *n.pl.* a family of annelids, typified by the genus *Serpula.*

sẽr'pū·line, *a.* pertaining to or composed of the remains of serpulas.

sẽr'pū·līte, *n.* a petrified shell or fossil of the genus *Serpula.*

sẽr'pū·loid, *a.* having the characteristics of the family *Serpulidæ.*

ser'rȧ, *n.*; *pl.* **ser'rae,** [L., a saw.]
1. in anatomy, a dentation, or toothlike articulating process of certain bones, as those of the cranium.
2. a kind of sawfish found in California.

ser·rȧ·del'lȧ, *n.* [Port., dim. of *serrado*, sawlike.] a leguminous plant, *Ornithopus sativus*, grown in Europe for forage.

ser'rȧ·nid, *n.* any fish belonging to the family *Serranidæ.*

Ser·ran'i·dae, *n.pl.* a family of fishes of which *Serranus* is the typical genus.

ser'rȧ·noid, *a.* pertaining to the *Serranidæ*, a family of carnivorous fishes including the sea bass and related types.

ser'rȧ·noid, *n.* one of the *Serranidæ.*

Ser·rā'nus, *n.* [L. *serra*, a saw; from the sawlike form of the dorsal fin.] a genus of teleostean fishes, included in the family *Serranidæ* or perches, but readily distinguished by their possessing only one dorsal fin and seven branchiostegous rays. *Serranus cabrilla* is found off the British coast, where it is known under the name of *comber*. *Serranus scriba* inhabits the Mediterranean.

ser′rāte, *a.* [L. *serratus*, pp. of *serrare*, to saw.] notched on the edge like a saw; toothed; specifically, in botany, having sharp notches along the edge, pointing toward the apex; as, a *serrate* leaf. When a serrate leaf has small serratures upon the large ones, it is said to be *doubly serrate*, as in the elm. A *serrate-ciliate* leaf is one having fine hairs, like eyelashes, on the serratures. A *serrate-dentate* leaf has the serratures toothed.

SERRATE LEAF

ser′rāte, *v.t.*; serrated, *pt., pp.*; serrating, *ppr.* to form into teeth along the edge, as a saw.

ser′rā·ted, *a.* same as *serrate*.

ser·rā′tion, *n.* 1. the condition of being serrate.

2. a single tooth or notch in a serrate edge.

3. a formation or set of these.

ser″rā·ti·ros′trăl, *a.* having a notched or toothed bill, as the toucan.

ser′rā·tūre, *n.* same as *serration*.

ser′ri-, [from L. *serra*, a saw.] a combining form used in entomology, zoology, etc., and meaning *a saw*.

ser′ri·çorn, *a.* having the antennae serrated.

ser′ried, *a.* [Fr. *serrer*, to crowd, from LL. *serare*, to bolt, lock.] crowded; compact, as soldiers in ranks; placed close together; as, *serried* files.

Ser·rif′e·rȧ, *n.pl.* [*serri-*, and L. *ferre*, to bear.] a division of hymenopterous insects, including the sawflies and horntails.

ser·rif′ẽr·ous, *a.* serrate; having a serra or serrate organ.

ser′ri·fọrm, *a.* toothed like a saw; serrate: applied to insects.

ser′ri·ped, *a.* having serrate feet, as insects.

ser·ri·ros′trāte, *a.* [*serri-*, and L. *rostrum*, a beak.] having a serrated beak or bill.

ser′ru̇·lāte, ser′ru̇·lā·ted, *a.* finely serrate; having very minute notches or small, fine teeth along the edge.

ser·ru̇·lā′tion, *n.* 1. the condition of being serrulate.

2. a single tooth or notch in a serrulate edge.

3. a formation or set of these.

ser·ru̇·rē·rïe′, *n.* [Fr., ironwork, from *serrure*, a lock; LL. *serare*, to join or bind together.] artistic and ornamental wrought-metal work.

ser′ry, *v.t.*; serried, *pt., pp.*; serrying, *ppr.* [Fr. *serrer*.] to crowd; to press together: used chiefly in the past participle.

Sẽr·tū·lā′ri·ȧ, *n.* [LL., from L. *serta*, garlands.]

1. a genus of hydroids made up of doublerowed branches of cupped polyps; the sea firs.

2. [s—] a polyp of this genus.

sẽr·tū·lãr′i·ăn, *n.* a member of the *Sertularia*.

sẽr·tū·lãr′i·ăn, *a.* pertaining to the *Sertularia*.

sẽr·tū·lãr′i·oid, sẽr·tū·lãr′oid, *a.* resembling or pertaining to the sertularians.

sē′rum, *n.*; *pl.* **sē′rumṣ, sē′rȧ,** [L., whey.]

1. any watery animal fluid, especially blood serum, the clear, yellowish fluid which separates from the clot when blood coagulates.

2. blood serum containing agents of immunity, taken from an animal made immune to a specific disease by inoculation: it is used as an antitoxin.

3. the whey of milk.

4. watery vegetable fluid.

blood serum; the clear liquid part of the blood, freed from its fibrin and corpuscles.

muscle serum; muscle plasma deprived of its myosin.

serum albumin; same as *seralbumin*.

serum anaphylaxis; anaphylaxis produced by the injection of a serum to which the patient shows sensitivity.

sẽrv′ȧ·ble, *a.* that can be served.

sẽrv′ăġe, *n.* servitude; slavery; serfdom. [Obs.]

sẽr′văl, *n.* [Fr., from L. *cervus*, a stag.] a digitigrade carnivorous mammal, *Felis serval*, of southern Africa. It has a long ringed tail, long legs, and black spots on a tawny body.

sẽr′văl·ine, *a.* related to or like the serval.

sẽrv′ănt, *n.* [Fr., from L. *serviens*, ppr. of *servire*, to serve.]

1. a person employed to perform services, especially household duties, for another or others.

2. a slave.

3. a person employed by a government; a public servant; a civil servant.

4. a person ardently devoted to another or to a cause, creed, etc.

servant of servants; one debased to the lowest condition of servitude.

servant of the servants of God; a title (*Servus Servorum Dei*) assumed by the popes since the time of Gregory the Great.

servants' hall; the room in a house set apart for the use of the servants in common, in which they take their meals together, etc. [Brit.]

your humble servant, your obedient servant; phrases of civility used formerly, especially in closing a letter, and expressing or understood to express the willingness of the speaker or writer to do service to the person addressed.

Our betters tell us they are our *humble servants*, but understand us to be their slaves.
—Swift.

sẽrv′ănt, *v.t.* to subject. [Obs.]

sẽrv′ănt·ess, *n.* a maidservant. [Obs.]

sẽrv′ănt·ry, *n.* a corps or body of servants; the servants of a household or institution, collectively.

sẽrve, *v.t.*; served, *pt., pp.*; serving, *ppr.* [Fr. *servir*, from L. *servire*, to serve, from *servus*, a servant, a slave or serf.]

1. to work for; to be a servant to.

2. (a) to do services or duties for; to give service to; to aid; to assist; to help; as, he *served* his country as a great statesman; (b) to give obedience and reverent honor to as God.

3. to fight for; to do military or naval service for.

4. to go through or spend (a term of imprisonment, service, etc.); as, he *served* four years in the navy.

5. to carry out the duties connected with (a position, office, etc.).

6. to wait on (customers), as in a store.

7. to provide (customers or users) with goods or services.

8. to provide (goods) for customers; to supply.

9. to prepare and offer (food, etc.) in a certain way to others, etc.; as, she *served* cocktails to us; he *served* the chicken with chestnut dressing.

10. to offer or set food, etc. before (a person); to help (a person) to food, etc.

11. to meet the needs or satisfy the requirements of; to be sufficient for; as, one nail will *serve* my purpose.

12. to be used by; as, one hospital *serves* the entire city.

13. to function or perform for; as, my memory *serves* me well.

14. to behave toward; to treat; as, she was cruelly *served*.

15. to deliver (a legal instrument), as a summons.

16. to deliver a legal instrument to; to present with a writ, etc.

17. to hit (a ball, etc.) to one's opponent in order to start play, as in tennis, badminton, etc.

18. to operate or tend (a large gun).

19. in animal husbandry, to copulate with (a female).

20. in nautical usage, to put a binding around in order to protect or strengthen (rope, etc.).

to serve an attachment or *writ of attachment*; in law, to levy an attachment on the person or goods by seizure, or to seize.

to serve an execution; to levy an execution on lands, goods, or person, by seizure or taking possession.

to serve an office; to discharge the duties incident to an office.

to serve a person heir to a property; in Scots law, to take the necessary legal steps for putting an heir in possession of the property.

to serve a process; in general, to read a process to the party concerned to give due notice, or to leave an attested copy with him or his attorney, or at his usual place of abode.

to serve a warrant; to read a warrant, and to seize the person against whom it is issued.

to serve a writ; to read a writ to the defendant, or to leave an attested copy at his usual place of abode.

to serve one right; to bring evil or misfortune to one deservedly; to give one his just deserts.

to serve out; to deal out or distribute in portions; as, *to serve out* provisions or ammunition to soldiers; *to serve out* grog to the sailors.

to serve the turn; to be equal to the emergency; to be sufficient for the purpose or occasion; to answer the purpose.

sẽrve, *v.i.* 1. to work as or be a servant.

2. to be in service; to do service; as, he *served* in the navy.

3. to carry out the duties connected with an office or position.

4. to be used or usable; to be of service; to function.

5. to meet needs; to satisfy requirements; to be adequate or sufficient; as, this nail is too short to *serve*.

6. to provide guests with something to eat, drink, or smoke; to wait on table.

7. to be suitable or favorable; as, the weather hardly *serves* for strolling.

8. to start play by hitting the ball, etc. to one's opponent, as in tennis.

9. to act as server at Mass.

sẽrve, *n.* in tennis, badminton, etc., (a) the act or manner of serving the ball, etc.; (b) the flight of the ball, etc. in service; (c) a turn at serving the ball, etc.

sẽrv′ẽr, *n.* 1. one who serves, as a waiter, etc.

2. one who assists the priest at the celebration of the Eucharist, by lighting the altar tapers, arranging the books, bringing in the bread, wine, water, etc., and by making the appointed responses for the congregation.

3. a salver or small tray; a thing used in serving.

Sẽr·vē′tiăn (-shăn), *n.* a follower of Servetus, a Spanish theologian who was burned at the stake in 1553 for his doctrines, afterward known as *Socinianism*.

Sẽr′vi·ăn, *a.* and *n.* same as *Serbian*.

sẽr′vice, *n.* [Fr., from L. *servitium*, from *servus*, slave.]

1. the occupation or condition of a servant.

2. employment, especially public employment.

3. a branch or department of this, including the people working in it.

4. the United States armed forces; Army, Navy, Air Force, or Marine Corps; as, he was in the *service* for three years.

5. work done for a master or superior.

6. work done or duty performed for another or others; a serving; as, professional *services*, repair *service*, a life devoted to public *service*.

7. respect; attention; devotion, as of a lover to his lady. [Rare or Archaic.]

8. the serving of God, as through good works, prayer, etc.

9. any religious ceremony, usually public worship; as, church *service*, marriage *service*, etc.

10. a musical setting for such a ceremony, as a canticle.

11. helpful, beneficial, or friendly action or conduct; act giving assistance or advantage to another.

12. the result of this; benefit; advantage.

13. the act or manner of serving food; as, the food was of even worse quality than the *service*.

14. a set of utensils or articles used in serving; as, silver tea *service*, breakfast *service*, etc.

15. an activity carried on to provide people with the use of something, as electric power, water, transportation, mail delivery, telephones, etc.

16. the act or method of providing these.

17. the quality of that which is provided; as, our electric *service* is poor.

18. anything useful, as maintenance, supplies, installation, repairs, etc., provided by a dealer or manufacturer for people who have bought things from him.

19. (a) an act, manner, or turn of serving in tennis, badminton, etc.; (b) the ball, etc. as served.

20. in animal husbandry, the covering of a female by the male

21. in law, notification of legal action, especially through the serving of a writ, etc.

22. in nautical usage, any material as wire, used in serving (ropes, etc.).

at one's service; (a) ready to serve or cooperate with one; (b) ready for one's use.

civil service; see under *civil*.

divine service; (a) the worship of God according to some established form; (b) formerly, in law, a kind of tenure by which the

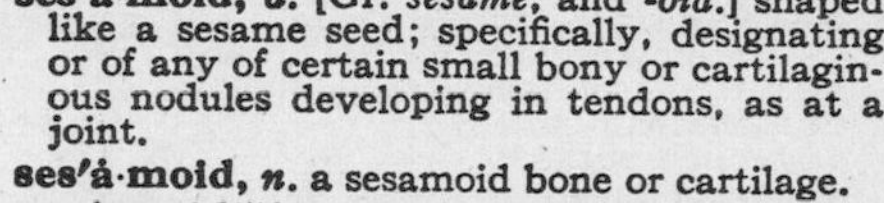

tenant held his lands on condition of the due performance of certain religious services, as masses, alms, etc.

of service; giving aid or assistance; helpful.

personal service; delivery of an original writ, notice, or other paper, or a copy thereof, with oral information as to the contents, to the person who is to be affected by the service.

public service; employment in some governmental office, especially in an office of a civil department.

secret service; (a) a government service organized to carry on secret investigation and the like; specifically, [S– S–] a division of the United States Treasury Department concerned with the discovery and arrest of counterfeiters, the protection of the President, etc.; (b) espionage service, as conducted by the armed forces.

service by publication; notice given to a person by publishing, as a writ, an order, and the like, in a newspaper, and, if required, by mailing a copy to the party's last address: used in cases of nonresidents whose whereabouts is not known and who are presumed to be evading legal process.

to take service; to accept service as a servant or employee.

service of an attachment; the seizing of the person or goods according to the direction.

service of a writ, process, etc.; the reading of a writ, etc. to the person to whom notice is intended to be given, or the leaving of an attested copy with the person or his attorney, or at his usual place of abode.

sẽrv'ice, *v.t.*; serviced (-ist), *pt., pp.*; servicing, *ppr.* 1. to furnish with a service; as, one power company *services* the entire valley.

2. to make fit for service, as by inspecting, adjusting, repairing, refueling, etc.

sẽr'vice, *n.* [AS. *syrfe*, from LL. *sorbea*, from L. *sorbus*, service tree.]

1. a European tree of the rose family, resembling the mountain ash and having small, edible fruit: also *service tree*.

2. a small tree or bush similar to this: also *wild service tree*.

sẽrv″ice·ȧ·bil'i·ty, *n.* the quality or degree of being serviceable.

sẽrv'ice·ȧ·ble, *a.* 1. that can be of service; ready for use; useful; usable.

2. that will give good service, especially in long, hard use; durable; as, a *serviceable* fabric.

3. beneficial; profitable; helpful.

4. willing to serve; attentive and obliging. [Archaic.]

sẽrv'ice·ȧ·ble·ness, *n.* the state or quality of being serviceable.

sẽrv'ice·ȧ·bly, *adv.* in a serviceable manner.

sẽrv'ice·ăge, *n.* servitude. [Obs.]

sẽr'vice·ber″ry, *n.*; *pl.* **sẽr'vice·ber″ries**, 1. the fruit of any service tree.

2. the shadbush or Juneberry.

sẽrv'ice book, a prayer book or missal.

sẽrv'ice çap, a military cap with a round, flat top and a visor.

sẽrv'ice çlub, any of various clubs, as Rotary, Kiwanis, etc., organized to provide various services for its own members, and to promote the community welfare.

sẽrv'ice el'ē·vā·tŏr, an elevator used by servants and tradespeople and for carrying goods, baggage, etc.

sẽrv'ice en'trănce, an entrance used by tradespeople, employees, etc. rather than by the general public.

sẽrv'ice flag, see under *flag*.

sẽrv'ice līne, in lawn tennis, one of two lines parallel with and twenty-one feet from the net.

sẽrv'ice măg·ȧ·zīne', a magazine for storing ammunition intended for immediate use.

sẽrv'ice·man, *n.*; *pl.* **sẽrv'ice·men**, a member of the armed forces: also written *service man.*

sẽrv'ice pīpe, a pipe for conducting gas or water from a main to a building.

sẽrv'ice stā'tion, 1. a place providing maintenance service, parts, supplies, etc. for mechanical or electrical equipment; as, a radio *service station.*

2. a place providing such service for automobiles, trucks, etc.; a gas station.

sẽrv'ice strīpe, a stripe, or one of a number of stripes, worn on the lower sleeve of a uniform to indicate the number of years spent as a soldier, policeman, etc.

sẽr'vice tree, same as second *service*, n.

sẽr'vi·ent, *a.* [L. *serviens.*] subordinate.

servient tenement or *estate*; in Scots law, a tenement on which there is a burden of servitude to a dominant tenement.

ser·vi·ette', *n.* [Fr., from *servir*, to serve.] a table napkin.

sẽr'vile, *a.* [Fr., from L. *servilis*, from *servire*, to serve.]

1. of a slave or slaves.

2. like that of slaves or servants; as, *servile* employment.

3. like or characteristic of a slave, especially in behavior; humbly yielding or submissive; slavish; cringing.

4. held in slavery; not free. [Archaic.]

5. in linguistics, (a) not belonging to the original root; as, a *servile* letter; (b) not itself sounded; silent, as the final *e* in *time*, etc.

sẽr'vile, *n.* 1. in linguistics, a letter which forms no part of the original root; also, a silent letter.

2. a menial; a servant or hired worker.

sẽr'vile·ly, *adv.* in a servile manner.

sẽr'vile·ness, *n.* servility.

sẽr·vil'i·ty, *n.*; *pl.* **sẽr·vil'i·tieṣ**, 1. slavery; the condition of a slave or bondman.

2. mean submission; baseness; slavishness.

3. mean obsequiousness; slavish deference; as, the common *servility* to custom.

sẽrv'ing·māid, *n.* a woman servant.

sẽrv'ing·man, *n.*; *pl.* **sẽrv'ing·men**, a man servant. [Archaic.]

Sẽrv'īte, *n.* a member of a mendicant order known as the Religious Servants of the Holy Virgin, which was founded in Florence in 1233.

sẽrv'i·tŏr, *n.* [OFr. *servitour*; LL. *servitor.*]

1. one who serves; a servant; an attendant.

2. a follower; an adherent.

3. formerly, (a) a soldier; (b) a student at Oxford who paid part of the tuition by waiting upon the table.

sẽrv'i·tŏr·ship, *n.* the state of being a servitor.

sẽrv'i·tūde, *n.* [Fr., from L. *servitudo*, slavery.]

1. the state of involuntary subjection to a master; slavery; bondage.

2. a state of mental submission or subordination; a slavish dependence; servility.

3. compulsory service or labor, such as a prisoner has to undergo as a punishment.

4. in law, a charge upon one estate for the benefit of another; an easement; as, the *servitude* of way or of water draining.

5. servants collectively. [Obs.]

personal servitude; a real right granted over a subject without regard to possession or ownership.

predial servitude; the easement which one estate or tenement owes to another; (a) *urban servitude*, or right in a party wall, common drain, etc.; (b) *rural servitude* or right in a road, pasture, etc.

sẽrv'i·tūre, *n.* servitude. [Obs.]

sẽrv'i·tūte, *n.* servitude. [Obs.]

Sẽr'vō-, same as *Serbo-*.

sẽr″vō·mech'ȧ·niṣm, *n.* [*servo*motor, and *mechanism.*] an automatic control system in which the output is constantly or intermittently compared with the input through feedback so that the error or difference between the two quantities can be used to bring about the desired amount or control.

sẽr'vō·mō·tŏr, *n.* [from Fr. *servo-moteur*, from L. *servus*, a slave, and *moteur*, motor.] a device, as an electric motor, hydraulic piston, etc., that is controlled by an amplified signal from a command device of low power, as in a servomechanism.

ses'ȧ·mē, *n.* [OFr., from L. *sesamum*; Gr. *sēsamē.*] 1. a plant of the genus *Sesamum*. The species, though now cultivated in many countries, are native to India. They have alternate leaves and axillary yellow or pinkish solitary flowers. *Sesamum indicum* is cultivated in various countries, especially in India, Egypt, and Syria. *Sesamum orientale* is the benne plant.

2. the seeds of this plant: they are flat, yield an oil, and are used for food.

SESAME
(*Sesamum indicum*)

ses'ȧ·mine, *a.* possessing the qualities of sesame; derived from sesame. [Obs.]

ses'ȧ·moid, *a.* [Gr. *sēsamē*, and *-oid.*] shaped like a sesame seed; specifically, designating of or any of certain small bony or cartilaginous nodules developing in tendons, as at a joint.

ses'ȧ·moid, *n.* a sesamoid bone or cartilage.

ses·ȧ·moid'ăl, *a.* same as *sesamoid*.

ses'ban, *n.* any one of several leguminous plants of the genus *Sesbania*; (a) *Sesbania ægyptiaca*, the jyntee, having pinnate leaves and yellowish flowers; (b) *Sesbania aculeata*, which yields a fiber used in ropemaking.

Ses·bā'ni·ȧ, *n.* [Fr., from Ar. *seiseban*; Per. *sīsabān.*] a genus of plants of the order *Leguminosæ*, comprising about thirty species of shrubs or herbs found in the warmer parts of the world.

Ses'e·li, *n.pl.* [L. *seselis*, from Gr. *seseli.*] a genus of umbelliferous plants, including meadow saxifrage, hartwort, cicely, stone parsley, and horse fennel.

ses'qui- (-kwi), [from Latin, more by a half, from *semis*, half, and *que*, and.] a combining form meaning *one and a half*, as in *sesquicentennial.*

ses·qui·al'tẽr, *n.* [L.] in music, same as *sesquialtera.*

ses·qui·al'tẽr·ȧ, *n.* in music, (a) a perfect fifth, being an interval with a ratio of 2 to 3; (b) a rhythm which makes 3 minims equal to the 2 preceding minims; (c) a compound stop on the organ, consisting of several ranks of pipes sounding high harmonics, for the purpose of strengthening the ground tone.

ses·qui·al'tẽr·ăl, *a.* having the ratio of one and a half to one; as, the ratio of 9 to 6 is *sesquialteral.*

ses·qui·al'tẽr·āte, *a.* same as *sesquialteral.*

ses·qui·al'tẽr·ous, *a.* same as *sesquialteral.*

ses·qui·bā'siç, *a.* relating to a compound in which three acid elements or radicals are joined with two basic ones.

ses″qui·cen·ten'ni·ăl, *a.* [*sesqui-* and *centennial.*] of or ending a period of one hundred and fifty years.

ses″qui·cen·ten'ni·ăl, *n.* the anniversary or celebration of the anniversary of an event which occurred 150 years before.

ses·qui·dū'pli·çāte, *a.* [*sesqui-*, and L. *duplicatus*, double.] in the ratio of two and one-half to one, or where the greater term contains the lesser twice and a half, as that of 50 to 20.

ses·qui·ox'īde, *n.* an oxide in which three atoms or equivalents of oxygen are combined with two of some other element or radical.

ses'qui·ped·ăl, *n.* and *a.* same as *sesquipedalian.*

ses″qui·pē·dā'li·ăn, *a.* [*sesqui-*, and L. *pedalis*, from *pes*, *pedis*, a foot.]

1. measuring a foot and a half.

2. very long: said of words.

3. using long words.

ses″qui·pē·dā'li·ăn, *n.* a long word.

ses″qui·pē·dā'li·ăn·ism, *n.* 1. the condition or state of being sesquipedalian.

2. addiction to the use of long words; sesquipedalism.

ses·qui·ped'ăl·iṣm, *n.* sesquipedalianism; sesquipedality.

ses″qui·pē·dal'i·ty, *n.* 1. the quality of being sesquipedal.

2. the use of long words or a sesquipedalian style.

ses·quip'li·çāte, *a.* having or denoting the ratio of the cube of a number to its square. [Rare.]

ses·qui·sul'fīde, ses·qui·sul'fid, *n.* a basic compound of sulfur with some other element, in the proportion of three to two.

ses·qui·tẽr'tiăl (-shăl), *a.* same as *sesquitertian.*

ses·qui·tẽr'tiăn, ses·qui·tẽr'tiăn·ăl, *a.* having the ratio of four to three.

ses'qui·tōne, *n.* in music, a minor third; an interval of three semitones. [Obs.]

sess, *v.t.* to assess; to tax. [Obs.]

sess, *n.* a tax. [Obs.]

sess, *n.* a frame in which soap is solidified.

ses'sȧ, *interj.* hurry: a cry used by way of exhorting to swift running. [Obs.]

Let the world slide, *sessa!* —Shak.

ses'sile, *a.* [L. *sessilis*, from *sessus*, pp. of *sedere*, to sit.]

1. in botany, attached by a base; as, a *sessile* leaf, one issuing directly from the main stem or branch without a petiole or footstalk; a *sessile* flower, one having no peduncle or pedicel; a *sessile* stigma, one without a style, as in the poppy. The first figure shows the sessile flower of chicory, and the second the sessile leaves of American snakeroot.

SESSILE FLOWER SESSILE LEAVES

2. in zoology and anatomy, (a) attached directly by its base; (b) permanently fixed; immobile.

ses'sile-eȳed (-īd), *a.* having eyes attached by the base, as distinguished from those having a stalk.

ses'sion, (sesh'un), *n.* [Fr., from L. *sessio* (*-onis*), act of sitting, from *sedere*, to sit.]

1. the sitting together or meeting of a group; assembly, as of a court, legislature, council, etc.

2. a continuous, day-to-day series of such sittings.

3. the term or period of either of these.

4. a school term or period of study, classes, etc.

5. a period of activity of any kind, especially one that is trying or burdensome; as, he had quite a *session* with the policeman. [Colloq.]

6. the lowest court or governing committee in the Presbyterian Church, consisting of the pastor of a congregation and elders chosen by the members.

Court of Session; the supreme civil court of Scotland.

in session; meeting; assembled.

session of the peace; a court, in England, consisting of justices of the peace, held in each county, for inquiring into trespasses, larcenies, etc.

ses'siŏn·ăl, *a.* 1. of or pertaining to a session or sessions.

2. taking place each session.

ses'tẽrce, *n.* [L. *sestertius* (*nummus*), for *semis tertius*, two and a half, because equal in value to two and a half asses.] an old Roman coin, originally of silver, later of brass or copper, equal to 1/4 denarius or about five cents.

ses·tẽr'ti·um (-shi-), *n.*; *pl.* **ses·tẽr'ti·ȧ,** an old Roman monetary unit, equal to 1,000 sesterces.

ses·tẽr'ti·us, *n.*; *pl.* **ses·tẽr'ti·ī,** same as *sesterce*.

ses'tet, *n.* [It. *sestetto*, dim. of *sesto*, sixth; L. *sextus*, sixth; *sex*, six.]

1. a musical composition for six instruments or voices; a sextet.

2. in a sonnet, the last six lines, usually separated into two three-line stanzas.

ses·tet'tō, *n.* [It.] a sextet.

ses·tī'nȧ, *n.*; *pl.* **ses·tī'nȧs, ses·tī'ne,** [It.] a kind of poem having six six-line stanzas and a three-line envoy: the end words of the first stanza are repeated with progressively changed order in the other five stanzas and are included, medially and finally, in the envoy.

ses'tine, *n.* same as *sestina*.

Set, Seth, *n.* an Egyptian god represented as having the head of a beast and a pointed snout. He was brother to Osiris and the personification of physical evil and darkness, the adversary of good. Called *Typhon* by the Greeks.

set, *v.t.*; set, *pt.*, *pp.*; setting, *ppr.* [ME. *setten*; AS. *settan*, to set.]

1. to place in a sitting position; to cause to sit; to seat.

2. (a) to cause (a fowl) to sit on eggs in order to hatch them; (b) to put (eggs) under a fowl or in an incubator to hatch them.

3. to put in some place or position; to cause to be, lie, stand, etc. in a place; as, *set* the book on the table.

4. to put in the place designed or meant to receive or hold it; to put in the right place; as, he *set* the wheel on the axle.

5. to put or move (a part of the body) into or on a specified place; as, he *set* his hand on my shoulder.

6. to bring (something) into contact with something else; to cause to be next or applied to something; as, she *set* a match to the paper.

7. (a) to put down on paper, in a record book, etc.; to write down; to record; (b) to put or affix (one's signature, seal, etc.) on a document.

8. to cause to be in a condition or relation specified by a following adverbial expression; specifically, (a) to cause to be or become: as, he *set* the house on fire; (b) to cause to take a certain physical position; as, he *set* the book on end.

9. to cause to be in working or proper condition; to put in order; arrange; fix; adjust; specifically, (a) to fix (a net, trap, etc.) in a position to catch animals; (b) to fix (a sail) in a position to catch the wind; (c) to put (a movable part of an instrument or machine) in position to work, as a chuck on a lathe; (d) to adjust so as to be in a desired position for use; to regulate; as, *set* a radio dial, clock, etc.; (e) to put an edge on (a knife, razor, etc.); (f) to adjust (teeth of a saw); (g) to arrange (a table) with knives, forks, plates, etc. for a meal; (h) to put (a joint or bone) into normal position for healing, mending, etc. when dislocated or fractured.

10. to cause to be in a settled or rigid position; specifically, (a) to put or press into a fixed or rigid position: as, he *set* his jaw; (b) to cause (one's mind, purpose, etc.) to be fixed, unyielding, determined, etc.; (c) to cause to become firm or hard in consistency; as, pectin *sets* jelly; (d) to make (a color) fast in dyeing; (e) to mount, embed, or fix (gems) in rings, bracelets, etc.; (f) to cover, encrust, or decorate (gold, watches, etc.) with gems; to fix gems in; (g) to fix firmly in a frame; as, *set* the glass in the window.

11. to cause to take a particular direction; specifically, (a) to cause to move in a certain direction; to propel; as, the current *set* them northward; (b) to point, direct, or face in a certain direction; as, he *set* his face toward home; (c) to direct (one's desires, hopes, heart, etc.) with serious attention *in* or *on* someone or something.

12. to appoint; institute; establish; ordain; specifically, (a) to post or station (a person) for certain duties; as, we *set* sentries at all the gates; (b) to place in a position of authority; (c) to fix (limits or boundaries); (d) to fix or appoint (a time) for something to happen; as, he *set* September 30 as the deadline; (e) to fix a time for (an event); (f) to establish (a regulation, law, etc.); to prescribe (a form, order, etc.); (g) to give or furnish (an example, pattern, etc.) for others; (h) to introduce (a fashion, style, etc.); (i) to allot or assign (a task, lesson, etc.) for work or study; (j) to fix (an amount of work, quota, etc.) for a given period; (k) to begin to apply (oneself) to a task, etc.

13. to estimate or fix; to place mentally; specifically, (a) to fix (the amount of a price, fine, rent ceiling, etc.); as, the judge *set* fifty dollars as the fine; (b) to fix the amount of (a price, fine, rent ceiling, etc.); as, the judge *set* the fine at fifty dollars; (c) to estimate or value (a person or thing) in some specified way; as, I *set* at nothing what once I loved; (d) to have (a certain estimate of a person or thing); as, I *set* little store by him.

14. in baking, to put aside (leavened dough) to rise.

15. in hunting, to point toward the position of (game): said of dogs.

16. in music, (a) to write or fit (words) to music; (b) to write or fit (music) to words.

17. in printing, (a) to compose (type); (b) to put (manuscript) into type.

18. in the theater, (a) to place (a scene) in a given locale; as, Shakespeare *set* the scene in Venice; (b) to make up or put together (scenery) on the stage; to arrange (items of scenery) in a certain way; (c) to arrange the scenery and properties on (the stage).

to set against; (a) to balance; (b) to compare; (c) to make hostile toward; to make an enemy of.

to set apart; to separate and keep for a purpose; to reserve.

to set aside; (a) to set apart; (b) to discard; dismiss; reject; (c) to annul; to declare void.

to set back; (a) to put (a clock or its hands) to an earlier time, especially to standard time; (b) to reverse or hinder the progress of.

to set down; (a) to place so as to rest upon a surface; to put down; to let alight; (b) to put in writing or print; to record; (c) to consider; estimate; ascribe; attribute.

to set flying; to secure (a sail) by sheets and halyards.

to set forth; (a) to manifest; to show; (b) to set forth in words; to state; (c) to publish; to promulgate.

to set forward; to help in the advancement of.

to set in order; to arrange systematically.

to set milk; (a) to put milk in a vessel and let it stand until the cream rises to the surface; (b) to curdle milk, as by rennet.

to set off; (a) to start (a person) doing something; (b) to set in relief; to make prominent by contrast; (c) to show to advantage; to enhance; (d) to cause to explode.

to set on; to incite; to urge on to do something.

to set out; (a) to limit; define; mark out; (b) to plan; to lay out (a town, garden, etc.); (c) to display, as for sale; to exhibit; (d) to plant.

to set over; to appoint or constitute as supervisor, inspector, ruler, or commander of.

to set right; to correct; to put in order.

to set sail; see under *sail*.

to set store by; to appreciate highly.

to set the watch; on board ship, to call to duty the starboard or port watch.

to set up; (a) to place in an upright or high position; hence, to raise or raise to power; (b) to put together or erect (a tent, machine, etc.); (c) to establish; to found; (d) to begin; (e) to provide with money, etc., as for a business; to fit out; (f) to cause to feel stimulated, exhilarated, etc.; (g) to advance or propose (a theory, etc.); (h) to cause; (i) to put (drinks, etc.) before customers; hence, to treat.

set, *v.i.* 1. to sit on eggs: said of a fowl.

2. to become firm or hard in consistency; as, the cement *set* after several hours.

3. to become fast: said of a dye, color, etc.

4. to begin to move, travel, etc. (with *out*, *forth*, *on*, *off*, or *forward*).

5. to have a certain direction; to tend; as, the wind *sets* to the south.

6. to make an apparent descent toward and below the horizon; to go down.

7. to wane; to decline.

8. to hang, fit, or suit in a certain way; as, the jacket *sets* well.

9. to sit. [Now Dial.]

10. in botany, to begin to develop after pollination; to form fruit in the blossom.

11. in hunting, to point toward the position of game: said of a dog.

to set about; to begin; to take the first steps in; as, *to set about* one's work.

to set forth or *forward*; to start a journey, etc. (often with *on*, *against*, *for*, etc.).

to set in; (a) to begin; as, winter in England usually *sets in* about December; (b) to become settled in a particular state; (c) to flow or blow toward the shore; as, the tide *sets in*.

to set off; (a) in printing, to deface or soil the next sheet: said of the ink on a newly printed sheet when another sheet comes in contact with it before it has had time to dry; (b) to start; to enter on a journey.

to set on or *upon*; (a) to begin a journey or an enterprise; (b) to assault; to attack; as, they all *set upon* him at once.

to set out; to begin a journey or course; as, *to set out* for London; *to set out* in business; *to set out* in life or the world.

to set to; (a) to make a beginning; to get to work; (b) to begin fighting.

to set up; (a) to begin business or a scheme of life; as, *to set up* in trade; (b) to profess openly; to make pretensions; as, he *sets up* as a man of wit.

set, *a.* 1. fixed or appointed in advance; as, a *set* time.

2. established; prescribed, as by authority.

3. deliberate; intentional; purposeful.

4. conventional; stereotyped; not spontaneous; as, a *set* speech.

5. fixed; motionless; rigid; immovable.

6. resolute; obstinate; unyielding.

7. firm or hard in consistency.

8. ready; as, get *set*.

9. formed; put together; built: often used in composition, as thick*set*, well-*set*.

all set; prepared; ready. [Colloq.]

Syn.—fixed, established, firm, determined, regular, formal.

set, *n.* 1. a setting or being set; specifically, (a) the act of a dog in setting game; (b) a becoming hard or firm in consistency.

2. the way or position in which a thing is set; specifically, (a) direction; course, as of a

current; (b) tendency; inclination; (c) change of form resulting from pressure, twisting, strain, etc.; warp; bend; also, sidewise deflection of saw teeth; (d) the way in which an article of clothing fits or hangs; (e) the position or attitude of a limb or part of the body; as, the *set* of her head; (f) in psychology, an adjustment of an organism in preparation for a certain definite kind of activity.

3. something which is set; specifically, (a) a twig or slip for planting or grafting; (b) a number of backdrops, flats, properties, etc. constructed and assembled for a scene in a play or motion picture; formal, constructed scenery; (c) [Obs.] a wager; a stake; a venture.

4. a group of persons; specifically, (a) a company or group with common habits, occupations, interests, etc.; as, a *set* of smugglers; (b) an exclusive or select group; a clique; coterie; (c) the number of couples needed for a country or square dance.

5. a collection of things belonging, issued, used, or growing together; specifically, (a) a number of tools or instruments used for the same purpose; as, a carpentry *set*; (b) the collection of objects necessary for playing a game, especially a parlor game; (c) a collection or group of books, magazines, etc. by one author, in one series, on one subject, etc.; (d) a matching collection of china, silverware, etc.; (e) the complement of natural or artificial teeth of a person or animal; (f) a clutch of eggs; (g) the figures that make up a country or square dance; (h) receiving equipment for radio or television assembled, as in a cabinet, for use; (i) in tennis, a group of six or more games won before the other side wins five or by a margin of two if the score is tied at more than four games each; (j) in squash, etc., a similar group of games; (k) in mathematics, a prescribed collection of points, numbers, or other objects that satisfy a given condition.

sē'tȧ, *n.*; *pl.* **sē'tae,** [L. *seta*, a bristle.] in botany and zoology, a bristle or bristlelike part or organ, as a slender straight prickle, the stalk that supports the theca, capsule, or sporangium of mosses, the stiff short hairs that cover many caterpillars and insects, the bristles or processes that cover the limbs and mandibles of many crustaceans, etc.

sē·tā'ceous, *a.* [L. *seta*, a bristle.]

1. bristly; set with bristles; consisting of or having bristles.

2. like a bristle; bristle-shaped; having the thickness and length of a bristle; as, a *setaceous* leaf or leaflet.

sē·tā'ceous·ly, *adv.* in a setaceous manner; so as to be setaceous.

sē'tăl, *a.* pertaining to setae.

Sē·tā'ri·ȧ, *n.* a genus of grasses, the flower spikes of which have long bristles. *Setaria glauca* and *Setaria viridis* are common weeds.

sē·tā'ri·ous, *a.* resembling a bristle; terminating in a bristle; aristate.

set'back, *n.* 1. a reversal, check, or interruption in progress; a relapse; an upset.

2. a steplike indentation or recessed section, as in a wall or the upper parts of a building; an offset.

3. a current running opposite to the main flow of water; an eddy.

set chis'el, a broad-pointed chisel used in cutting the heads from rivets, bolts, etc.

set'down, *n.* a humiliating rebuke or reprehension; a crushing retort or reply.

set·ee', *n.* same as *settee*.

Seth, *n.* [LL.; Gr. *Sēth*; Heb. *Shēth*, lit., appointed.] in the Bible, the third son of Adam: Gen. iv. 25.

Seth (sāt), *n.* Set, an Egyptian god.

set ham'mẽr, a form of smith's hammer, the face of which is rectangular and the edges square: it is laid upon the work and struck with a heavier hammer or sledge in order to form a shoulder.

Seth'i·ăn, *n.* a Sethite.

Seth'īte, *n.* one of an obscure Gnostic sect in the second century, who are said to have regarded Seth, the son of Adam, as the Messiah.

sē'ti-, [from L. *seta*, bristle.] a combining form meaning *bristle*, as in *set*iferous.

Sē·tif'ẽr·ȧ, *n.pl.* in zoology, a superfamily of hoofed animals, the swine.

sē·tif'ẽr·ous, *a.* [L. *seta*, a bristle, and *ferre*, to bear.] producing or having bristles.

sē'ti·form, *a.* [L. *seta*, a bristle, and *-form*.] having the form of a bristle.

sē'ti·ġẽr, *n.* [L., bristle-bearing, from *seta*, a bristle.] an annelid with setae.

sē·tiġ'ẽr·ous, *a.* setiferous.

set'-in, *n.* time of an occurrence; a beginning.

set'-in, *a.* fixed, built, or placed, usually as part of something already existing, as a *set-in* bookcase.

sē·tip'ȧ·rous, *a.* [L. *seta*, bristle, and *parere*, to bring forth.] generating setae; as, *setiparous* glands.

set'līne, *n.* in fishing, a strong line reaching across a stream and having shorter, hooked lines hanging from it into the water; a trotline.

set'ness, *n.* the state or quality of being set.

set nut, in mechanics, any nut set against another to hold it secure.

set'off, *n.* 1. that which is set off against another thing; an offset.

2. that which is used to improve the appearance of anything; a decoration; an ornament.

3. a counterclaim or demand; a cross-debt; a counterbalance; an equivalent.

4. in law, the merging, wholly or partially, of a claim of one person against another in a counterclaim by the latter against the former. Thus, a plea of setoff is a plea whereby a defendant acknowledges the justice of the plaintiff's demand, but sets up another claim of his own, to counterbalance that of the plaintiff either in whole or in part.

5. the part of a wall, etc. which is exposed horizontally when the portion above it is reduced in thickness: also called *offset*.

6. in printing, an offset.

sē'tŏn, *n.* [Fr., from L. *seta*, a bristle.]

1. a twist of silk or similar material passed under the skin and the cellular tissue beneath, in order to cause or maintain a discharge.

2. the discharge so produced.

sē'tose, *a.* setaceous.

set'out, *n.* 1. preparations, as for beginning a journey, etc.

2. (a) company; set; clique; (b) a display, as of plate, etc.; (c) dress and accessories; (d) equipage; turn-out. [Colloq.]

set piece, 1. an artistic composition, in literature, music, sculpture, etc., designed to give an impressive effect, often in a conventional style.

2. a scenic display of fireworks.

3. a piece of stage scenery.

4. any situation carefully planned beforehand, as in a military or diplomatic maneuver.

set'screw, *n.* 1. a machine screw passing through one part and against or into another to prevent movement, as of a ring around a shaft.

2. a screw used in regulating or adjusting the tension of a spring, etc.

set'-stitched (-sticht), *a.* stitched in accordance with a regular pattern.

sett, *n.* same as *set*.

set''te·cen'tō (-chen'), *n.* [It.] the eighteenth century, with reference to the Italian art and literature produced then.

set·tee', *n.* [from *set*; regarded as dim. of *seat*.]

1. a seat or bench with a back, usually for two or three people.

2. a small or medium-sized sofa.

set'tee, *n.* [Fr. *scétie*, *sétie*; It. *saettia*, a long-prowed vessel.] a vessel with one deck and a very long sharp prow, carrying two or three masts with lateen sails: used on the Mediterranean.

set'tẽr, *n.* 1. one who or that which sets; as, a *setter* of precious stones, a *setter* of rules: often used in composition; as, type*setter*, *setter*-off, *setter*-on, etc.

2. one who acts as a decoy for sharpers or swindlers.

3. in gunnery, a round stick for driving fuses into paper cases.

4. in ceramics, a sagger adapted and shaped to receive an article of porcelain biscuit, for firing in the kiln.

5. any of a breed of long-haired bird dog of which there are three varieties (*English*, *Irish*, and *Gordon setters*): they are trained to find the game and point out its position by standing rigid (formerly by crouching).

set'tẽr''grȧss, *n.* same as *setterwort*.

set'tẽr-on, *n.* an inciter.

set'tẽr-up, *n.* one who sets up, establishes, makes, or appoints.

set'tẽr·wŏrt, *n.* a perennial plant, *Helleborus fœtidus*; bear's-foot.

set'ting, *n.* 1. the act of a person or thing that sets.

2. a thing in or upon which something, especially a gem, is set.

3. time and place, environment, background, or surroundings, as of a story, poem, person's life, etc.

4. actual physical surroundings or scenery whether real, as of a garden, or artificial, as on a stage.

5. the music or the composing of music for a set of words, as a poem.

6. the eggs in the nest of a setting hen.

set'ting çoat, a finishing coat of fine plaster laid by a trowel over the floating coat, which is of coarse plaster.

set'ting dog, a setter. [Obs.]

set'ting pōle, a long pole, often iron-pointed, used for pushing boats, etc. along in shallow water.

set'ting rule, in printing, same as *composing rule*.

set'ting stick, in printing, a composing stick.

set'tle, *n.* [AS. *setl*, a seat, a stool.] a long seat or bench with arms, a high back, and sometimes a chest beneath the seat.

set'tle, *v.t.*; settled, *pt.*, *pp.*; settling, *ppr.* [AS. *setlan*, from *setl*, a seat.]

1. to put in order; to arrange or adjust as desired, as clothing, a room, one's affairs, etc.

2. to put, plant, or set in place so as to be firmly or comfortably situated.

3. to establish as a resident or residents; as, the firm has *settled* its employees in near-by houses.

4. to migrate to and set up residence or a community in; to colonize; as, New York was *settled* by the Dutch.

5. to cause to sink and become more dense and compact; as, he *settled* the ashes by shaking them; the rain will *settle* the dust.

6. to clarify (a liquid) by settling the sediment.

7. to free from disturbance, as the mind, nerves, stomach, etc.

8. to prevent from creating a disturbance or interfering, as by a reprimand or a blow. [Colloq.]

9. to make stable or permanent; to establish; as, experience has *settled* the system by which they work.

10. to establish in business, office, work, marriage, etc.

11. to fix definitely; to determine; decide (something in doubt or question).

12. to end (a dispute).

13. to pay (a bill, debt, account, etc.).

14. to decide (a legal dispute) by agreement without court action.

to settle upon (or *on*); to make over (property, etc.) to by legal action.

set'tle, *v.i.* 1. to stop moving and stay in one place; to come to rest; as, the bird *settled* on the wire; his gaze *settled* on the latest arrival.

2. to cast itself over the landscape, as darkness, fog, etc., or over a person or group, as gloom or silence; to descend.

3. to become localized or fixed in a given part of the body: said of pain or disease.

4. to take up permanent residence; to make one's home; as, they *settled* in Canada.

5. to move downward; to sink, especially gradually, as by its own weight; as, the car *settled* in the soft ground; the bridge *settled* at one end.

6. to become more dense or compact by sinking, as sediment or loose soil when shaken.

7. to become clearer by the settling of sediment or dregs: said of liquid.

8. to become more stable or composed; to stop fluctuating or changing; to settle down.

9. to reach an agreement or decision (usually with *with*, *on*, or *upon*).

10. to pay what is owing; as, he won't *settle* without court action.

to settle down; (a) to take up permanent residence, a regular job, etc.; to lead a more routine, settled life, as after marriage; (b) to become less nervous, restless, or erratic; (c) to apply oneself steadily or attentively.

to settle up; to determine what is owed and make the necessary adjustments.

to settle upon (or *on*); to make up one's mind about; to decide; to resolve.

set'tle bed, a bed constructed so as to form a seat when not in use; a folding bed; also, a half-canopy bed.

set'tled·ness, *n.* the state or quality of being settled; confirmed state.

set'tle·ment, *n.* 1. a settling or being settled.
2. establishment in life, business, marriage, etc.
3. an inhabiting or colonizing, as of a new land.
4. a group of people or a place concerned in this; a colony.
5. a small or isolated community; a village.
6. an agreement, arrangement, or understanding.
7. payment or adjustment, as of a claim.
8. the conveyance or disposition of property for the benefit of a person.
9. the amount of property thus conveyed.
10. a community center offering social and educational activities: the services are usually free and directed at the underprivileged element of the population.
11. the gradual subsidence of all or part of a structure.
12. dregs; lees; settlings. [Obs.]
13. formerly, a sum of money or other property granted to a clergyman on his ordination, exclusive of his salary.
Act of Settlement; in English history, the act passed in 1701, by which the crown was settled (on the death of Queen Anne) upon Sophia, electress of Hanover, and the Protestant heirs of her body (the present royal line).
settlement house; a settlement (sense 10).
settlement worker; a social welfare worker associated with a settlement house.
social settlement; a settlement (sense 10).

set'tlēr, *n.* 1. one who or that which settles.
2. a person who settles in a new country or colony.

set'tling, *n.* 1. the act of one who or that which settles.
2. [*pl.*] lees; dregs; sediment.

set'tling dāy, a day set apart for the settling of accounts; specifically, in the British stock exchange, the half-monthly account day for shares and stocks.

set'tlŏr, *n.* in law, the person who makes a settlement of property.

set'-tö', *n.*; *pl.* **set'-tös',** [from the phrase *set to.*] 1. a fight or struggle, especially a fist fight. [Colloq.]
2. any sharp contest or argument; a bout. [Colloq.]

set'ū·lȧ, *n.*; *pl.* **set'ū·lae,** [LL., dim. of L. *seta*, a bristle.] in botany, a small bristle or hair; also, the stipe of certain fungi.

set'ūle, *n.* a small, short bristle or hair; a setula.

set'ū·lōse, *a.* bearing or provided with setules.

set'up, *n.* 1. the way in which something is set up; plan, make-up, or arrangement, as of equipment, an organization, etc.
2. bodily posture; carriage.
3. soda water, ice, etc. for mixing with alcoholic liquor.
4. (a) a contest in which the contestants are so unevenly matched that the outcome is certain; a contest deliberately arranged to result in an easy victory; hence, (b) any undertaking that is, or is purposely made, very easy. [Slang.]

set'wall, *n.* a species of *Valeriana.*

sev'en (sev'n), *a.* [AS. *seofon, seofan*; akin to G. *sieben.*] totaling one more than six.
seven deadly sins; see under *deadly sins.*
Seven Hills of Rome; the seven hills on and about which the city of Rome was built; the Palatine, Capitoline, Quirinal, Caelian, Aventine, Esquiline, and Viminal.
seven seas; all the oceans of the world.
seven stars; same as *pleiades.*
seven wonders of the world; see under *wonder.*
seven-year apple; a West Indian plant, *Genipa clusiifolia*; also, its fruit, which is edible.
Seven Years' War; a war lasting from 1756 to 1763 in which England and Prussia defeated Austria, France, Russia, Sweden, and Saxony: Prussia established her power in Europe and England seized French colonies in America and India.
seven-year vine; a plant, *Ipomœa tuberosa*, growing in warm regions.

sev'en, *n.* 1. the cardinal number following six and preceding eight; a group of things amounting to this number.
2. a symbol representing this number, as 7 or VII.
3. a person or thing numbered seven, as a contestant, playing card, etc.
4. a form of versification.
Seven against Thebes; in Greek legend, the story of the expedition of seven heroes to help Polynices recover the throne of Thebes from his brother Eteocles, who had agreed to share it with him but refused to give it up after his turn: subject of a tragedy by Aeschylus.

sev'en·eyes (-īz), *n.* same as *sevenholes.*

sev'en·fōld, *a.* repeated seven times; multiplied seven times; increased to seven times the size or amount; having seven parts or folds; composed of seven.

sev'en·fōld, *adv.* seven times as much or as many; in the proportion of seven to one.

sev'en·hōles, *n.* the river lamprey: so named from the seven gill apertures on each side. [Brit. Dial.]

sev'en·nīght (-nīt *or* sen'nit), *n.* a week. [Archaic.]

sev'en·scōre, *n.* and *a.* seven times twenty, that is, one hundred and forty.

sev'en·teen', *a.* consisting of one more than sixteen, or one less than eighteen; seven and ten added; as, *seventeen* pounds.

sev'en·teen', *n.* 1. the cardinal number between sixteen and eighteen; a group of things amounting to this number.
2. a symbol representing this number, as 17 or XVII.

sev'en·teenth', *a.* [AS. *seofon-teōtha* or *seofonteogetha.*]
1. next in order after the sixteenth; the ordinal of seventeen; as, the *seventeenth* letter of the alphabet.
2. being or constituting one of seventeen equal parts into which a thing is or may be divided.

sev'en·teenth', *n.* 1. the next in order after the sixteenth; the seventh after the tenth.
2. one of seventeen equal parts into which a thing is or may be divided; the quotient of unity divided by seventeen.
3. in music, an interval consisting of two octaves and a third.

sev'en·teen'-yēar lō'cust, a cicada which lives underground as a larva for from thirteen to seventeen years before emerging as an adult to live in the open for a brief period.

sev'enth, *a.* [ME. *seventhe*, from AS. *seofande, seofotha.*] 1. coming or being next after the sixth; the ordinal of seven.
2. being or constituting one of seven equal parts into which a thing is or may be divided.

sev'enth, *n.* 1. the one next in order after the sixth.
2. one of seven equal parts into which a thing is or may be divided; the quotient of unity divided by seven.
3. in music, (a) a note seven degrees above or below another in the diatonic scale; (b) the interval between these; (c) the seventh note of the diatonic scale; the leading note; the subtonic; (d) the chord formed by any tone and the third, fifth, and seventh of which it is the fundamental: also *seventh chord.*

sev'enth dāy, Saturday, the seventh day of the week.

sev'enth-dāy, *a.* 1. of the seventh day of the week (Saturday).
2. [*often* S–] observing the Sabbath on Saturday; as, *Seventh-day* Adventists.

sev'enth heav'en (hev'), 1. the seventh, usually highest, of the concentric spheres in which the stars are supposed to be fixed, according to various ancient systems of astronomy, or in which God and his angels are, according to certain theologies.
2. a condition of perfect happiness.

sev'en-thir'ty, *a.* yielding interest at 7.30 per cent, as, formerly, certain United States government notes.

sev'en-thir'ties, certain United States government notes issued in 1861, 1864, and 1865, bearing interest at 7.30 per cent, and redeemable in three years.

sev'enth·ly, *adv.* in the seventh place.

sev'en·ti·eth, *a.* 1. coming next after the sixty-ninth; as, a man in his *seventieth* year.
2. constituting or being one of seventy equal parts into which a thing is or may be divided.

sev'en·ti·eth, *n.* 1. the one next in order after the sixty-ninth.
2. one of the seventy equal parts into which a thing is or may be divided; the quotient of unity divided by seventy.

sev'en·ty, *a.* [AS. *hund-seofontig* (*hund-* being dropped later), from *seofon*, seven, and *-tig*, ten.] seven times ten.

sev'en·ty, *n.*; *pl.* **sev'en·ties,** 1. the cardinal number between sixty-nine and seventy-one.
2. a symbol which represents this number, as 70 or LXX.
the seventies; the years from seventy through seventy-nine (of a century or a person's age).
the Seventy; the seventy (or more) translators of the Old Testament into the Greek language.

sev'en·ty-five', *n.* a rapid-fire 75 millimeter field gun which fires thirty shells per minute: used especially by the French in World War I.

sev'en·ty-fōur', *n.* a ship of war equipped with seventy-four guns. [Archaic.]

sev'en-up', *n.* a card game for two, three, or four persons in which seven points constitute a game.

sev'ēr, *v.t.*; severed, *pt., pp.*; severing, *ppr.* [OFr. *sevrer, severer*, to separate; Fr. *sevrer*, to wean, from L. *separare*, to separate.]
1. to part or divide in two, especially by violence; to separate, as by cutting or rending; as, he *severed* the cable at a single stroke.
2. to part from the rest by violence, cutting, or the like; as, to *sever* the head from the body.
3. to separate; to disjoin, as things distinct but united by some tie.
4. to keep distinct or apart; to separate.
5. in law, to disunite; to disconnect; to part possession of; as, to *sever* an estate in joint tenancy.

sev'ēr, *v.i.* 1. to make a separation or distinction; to distinguish.
2. to suffer disjunction; to be parted or rent asunder; to become divided or separated.

sev'ēr·ȧ·ble, *a.* that can be severed or divided; specifically, in law, separable into distinct, independent obligations: said of a contract.

sev'ēr·ăl, *a.* [OFr., from LL. *separalis*, from L. *separ*, separate.]
1. separate; distinct.
2. single; individual; particular.
Each *several* ship a victory did gain.
—Dryden.
3. different; diverse; various; respective; as, the *several* opinions of the people present.
4. consisting of a number more than two, but not many; of an indefinite but small number; few; as, *several* persons were present when the event took place.

sev'ēr·ăl, *adv.* separately; severally; diversely. [Obs.]

sev'ēr·ăl, *n.* 1. a particular person or thing; an item; an individual: used chiefly in plural. [Obs.]
2. an enclosed or separate place; a piece of enclosed ground. [Obs.]
3. several persons or things; a few; a small number; as, *several* of them came.
in several; in a state of separation. [Rare.]

sev·ēr·al'i·ty, *n.* each particular taken singly. [Rare.]

sev'ēr·ăl·īze, *v.t.* to distinguish. [Obs.]

sev'ēr·ăl·ly, *adv.* 1. separately; distinctly.
2. respectively; as, the proposals which the parties have *severally* made.

sev'ēr·ăl·ty, *n.*; *pl.* **sev'ēr·ăl·ties,** [Anglo-Fr. *severauté*, from OFr. *several.*]
1. the condition or character of being several or distinct.
2. property owned by individual right.
3. the condition of property so owned.
estate in severalty; an estate which the tenant holds in his own right, without being joined in interest with any other person: distinguished from *joint tenancy, coparcenary*, and *estate in common.*

sev'ēr·ănce, *n.* [ME., from OFr. *sevrance.*] the act of severing or the state of being severed; separation; the act of dividing or disuniting; partition.
severance of a jointure; in law, a severance made by destroying the unity of interest, as when there are two joint tenants for life and the inheritance is purchased by or descends upon either.

sē·vēre', *a.*; *comp.* severer; *superl.* severest, [Fr. *sévère*, from L. *severus*, serious, severe.]
1. harsh or strict, as in treatment; unsparing; stern.
2. serious; grave; forbidding, as in expression or manner.
3. conforming strictly to a rule, method, standard, etc.; rigidly accurate.
4. extremely plain or simple; unornamented; restrained: said of style, as, a dress with *severe* lines.

5. keen; violent; extreme; intense, as pain, heat, etc.
6. difficult; rigorous; trying, as a rule, test, etc.
Syn.—austere, harsh, rigid, grave, rigorous, rough, strict, stern, exacting, acrimonious, cruel, keen, unrelenting.

sē·vēre′ly, *adv.* in a severe manner; so as to be severe.

sē·vēre′ness, *n.* severity.

sev′ẽr·ẽr, *n.* one who or that which severs.

Sē·vē′ri·ăn, *n.* 1. one of a party of Monophysites, who followed the teaching of Severus, patriarch of Antioch in the sixth century, who asserted that the body of Jesus Christ, prior to his resurrection, was corruptible.
2. one of a sect of Gnostics of the second century; also, an Encratite.

sē·ver′i·ty, *n.*; *pl.* **sē·ver′i·tieṣ,** [L. *severitas.*]
1. the quality or state of being severe, as (a) gravity or austerity; extreme strictness; rigor; harshness; as, the *severity* of a reprimand or reproof; *severity* of discipline or training; *severity* of penalties; (b) the quality or power of afflicting, distressing, or paining; extreme degree; extremity; keenness; as, the *severity* of pain or anguish; the *severity* of cold or heat; (c) extreme coldness or inclemency; as, the *severity* of the winter; (d) harshness; cruel treatment; sharpness of punishment; as, *severity* practiced on prisoners of war; (e) exactness; rigor; niceness; as, the *severity* of a test; (f) strictness; rigid accuracy; (g) in art and literature, strict conformity to an ideal rule or standard; austerity of style.
2. something severe, as a punishment.

sev′ẽr·y, *n.* [a corruption of *ciborium.*] in architecture, a bay or compartment in a vaulted roof; also, a compartment or division of scaffolding: also written *civery.*

Sev′in, [from the groups of *seven* atoms in its molecular structure.] an insecticide, $C_{12}H_{11}O_2N$, derived from a salt of carbamic acid, that is highly toxic when first applied but that breaks down and becomes harmless: a trade-mark.

Sè′vres (se′vr), *a.* of or belonging to the town of Sèvres, France; specifically, pertaining to the national porcelain works for which the town is famous.

Sè′vres, *n.* a fine procelain manufactured at Sèvres, France: also called *Sèvres procelain* and *Sèvres ware.*

sē′vum, *n.* [L., suet.] fat or tallow, as used in the preparation of ointments.

sew, *n.* gravy; broth; juice. [Obs.]

sew, *v.t.* to drain dry, as land; to drain off, as water. [Brit. Dial.]

sew (sō), *v.t.*; sewed, *pt.*; sewed or sewn, *pp.*; sewing, *ppr.* [AS. *siwian, seowian, suwan*; akin to Goth. *siujan*; L. *suere,* to sew.]
1. to join together by stitches, as by means of a needle and thread; as, to *sew* a piece of cloth on a coat.
2. to close up, make, mend, etc. by sewing.
to sew up; (a) to close or bring together the edges of with stitches; (b) to enclose in something by sewing; (c) [Colloq.] to get or have absolute control of or right to; to monopolize.

sew (sō), *v.i.* to do sewing; to work with a needle and thread or at a sewing machine.

sew′äge, *n.* [from *sew,* to drain.]
1. the refuse matter carried off in a drain or sewer.
2. same as *sewerage,* senses 1, 2.

sē′wăn, *n.* [Am. Indian.] shells used as money by the Algonquian Indians.

sew′el, sew′ell, *n.* a shewel. [Obs.]

sē·wel′lel, *n.* [Am. Ind.] a small rodent, *Aplodontia rufa,* inhabiting the Pacific coast of America. It is about a foot long, and has a very short tail. It is brownish above and lighter below. Also called *boomer, mountain beaver.*

sew′en, *n.* same as *sewin.*

sew′ẽr, *n.* [from OFr. *seuwiere,* a drain, a conduit.] an underground pipe or drain used to carry off water and waste matter.

sew′ẽr, *n.* [from OFr. *asseoir,* to seat, to cause to sit.] a servant of high rank in medieval times who served up a feast and arranged the dishes, and who also provided water for the hands of the guests.

sew′ẽr (sō′), *n.* 1. one who or that which sews, as with a needle.
2. the larva of a moth, which fastens together the edges of leaves with silk, as the apple-leaf sewer, *Phoxopteris nubeculana.*

sew′ẽr·äge, *n.* 1. the process of receiving and carrying off the superfluous water and filth of a city by sewers.
2. sewage; the matter carried off by sewers.
3. a system of sewers, as in a city; as, the *sewerage* of Chicago.

sew′in, sew′en, *n.* a species of salmon trout, *Salmo trutta,* found in the British Isles.

sew′ing (sō′), *n.* 1. the act or occupation of one who sews, as with the needle, a sewing machine, a wire stitcher, etc.
2. that which is or is to be sewed; needlework.

sew′ing cĩr′cle, a number of women who regularly assemble together to sew.

sew′ing mȧ·chïne′, a machine with a mechanically driven needle used for sewing and stitching.

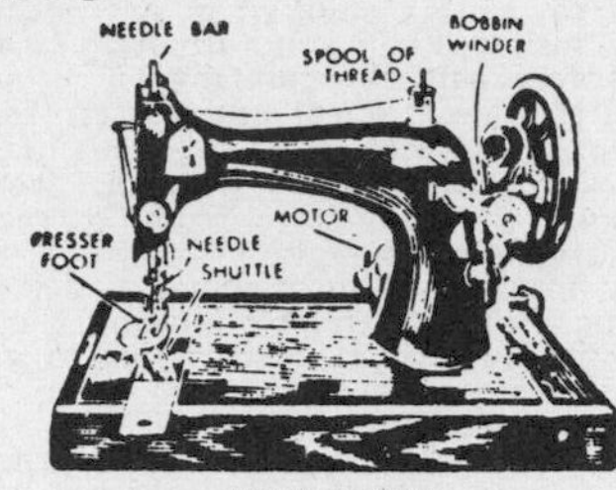

SEWING MACHINE

sew′ing press, a device consisting of a frame, etc., for holding the cords to which the back edges of books are stitched.

sewn, *v.* alternative past tense and past participle of *sew.*

sew′stẽr, *n.* a seamstress. [Obs.]

sex, *n.* [ME. *sexe*; OFr. *sexe*; L. *sexus,* earlier *secus,* from *secare,* to cut, divide.]
1. either of the two divisions of organisms distinguished as male or female; males or females (especially men or women) collectively.
2. the character of being male or female; all of the things which distinguish a male from a female.
3. anything connected with sexual gratification or reproduction or the urge for these, especially the attraction of individuals of one sex for those of the other.
4. the female sex; women: with the article *the.*
sex appeal; sex attraction, or the quality or qualities of an individual that are attractive to a member of the opposite sex.
the fair (or *gentle, weaker*) *sex*; women.
the sterner (or *stronger*) *sex*; men.

sex-, [from Latin *sex,* six.] a combining form meaning *six.*

sex″ȧ·gē·nãr′i·ăn, *a.* [from L. *sexagenarius,* of sixty, from *sexageni,* sixty each; and *-an.*] sixty years old or between sixty and seventy.

sex″ȧ·gē·nãr′i·ăn, *n.* a person who is between sixty and seventy years old.

sex·ag′ē·nãr·y, *a.* [Fr. *sexagénaire*; L. *sexagenarius,* belonging to sixty.]
1. designating or composed of the number sixty.
2. proceeding by sixties.
3. sexagenarian.

sex·ag′ē·nãr·y, *n.*; *pl.* **sex·ag′ē·nãr·ieṣ,** a sexagenarian.

Sex·ȧ·ġes′i·mȧ, *n.* [L. *sexagesimus,* sixtieth.] the second Sunday before Lent: also *Sexagesima Sunday.*

sex·ȧ·ġes′i·măl, *a.* sixtieth; pertaining to the number sixty.
sexagesimal arithmetic; a method of computation by sixties, as that which is used in dividing degrees into minutes, minutes into seconds, etc.

sex·ȧ·ġes′i·măl, *n.* a fraction whose denominator is sixty or a power of sixty.

sex′añ·gled (-gld), *a.* [*sex,* six, and L. *angulus,* angle.] having six angles; hexagonal.

sex·añ′gū·lăr, *a.* same as *sexangled.*

sex·añ′gū·lăr·ly, *adv.* with six angles; hexagonally.

sex·cen′tē·nãr·y, *a.* consisting of or pertaining to six hundred, especially six hundred years.

sex·cen′tē·nãr·y, *n.*; *pl.* **sex·cen′tē·nãr·ieṣ,** a six-hundredth anniversary.

sex ċhrō′mō·sōme, a sex-determining chromosome in the germ cells of most plants and animals: fertilized eggs containing two X chromosomes (one from each parent germ cell) develop into females, those containing one X and one Y chromosome (male germ cells carry either one or the other) develop into males.

sex·diġ′i·tāte, *a.* [*sex-,* and L. *digitus,* finger or toe.] six-toed or six-fingered.

sex·diġ′i·tiṣm, *n.* the state or condition of having six fingers or six toes.

sex·diġ′i·tist, *n.* a person having six fingers or six toes.

sexed (sext), *a.* 1. of or having sex or sexual differentiation.
2. having (a specified degree of) sexuality.

sex·en′ni·ăl, *a.* [*sex-,* six, and L. *annus,* year.]
1. lasting six years.
2. coming, happening, etc. every six years.

sex·en′ni·ăl, *n.* a sexennial event.

sex·en′ni·ăl·ly, *adv.* once every six years.

sex′foil, *n.* [*sex-,* and L. *folium,* a leaf.] in architecture, any surface, panel, or opening, bounded by six arcs, six lobes, etc.

sex hȳ′ġiēne, the branch of hygiene dealing with sex and sexual behavior as they relate to the welfare of both the individual and the community.

sex′i-, same as *sex-.*

sex′i·ly, *adv.* in a sexy manner.

sex′i·ness, *n.* the state or quality of being sexy.

sex′iṣm, *n.* [*sex,* and rac*ism.*] the economic exploitation and social domination of members of one sex by the other, specifically of women by men.

sex′ist, *a.* of or characterized by sexism.

sex′ist, *n.* a person who believes in, advocates, or practices sexism.

sex′i·vā·lent, *a.* [*sexi-,* and L. *valens* (*-entis*), from *valere,* to have power.]
1. having a valence of six.
2. having six valences.

sex kit′ten, a young woman who has much sex appeal. [Slang.]

sex′less, *a.* 1. lacking the characteristics of sex; asexual.
2. apparently lacking in normal sexual passion or drive; without love; sexually cold.

sex′-liñked (-linkt), *a.* in genetics, designating or of any factor linked to the sex chromosomes of either parent, or any character dependent on such a factor.

sex·ol′ō·ġy, *n.* the science dealing with human sexual behavior.

sex·pär′tīte, *a.* [*sex-,* and L. *partitus,* pp. of *partire,* to divide.] consisting of or divided into six parts.

sex·ploi·tā′tion, *n.* [*sex,* and ex*ploitation.*] the use of explicit sexual material, especially in a motion picture, for promotional purposes.

sext, *n.* [Fr. *sexte*; LL. *sexta,* f. of *sextus,* sixth.] in ecclesiastical usage, the fourth of the seven canonical hours; it falls at or shortly before noon, the sixth hour of the day; also, the service held daily at this hour.

sex′tăin, [L. *sextans,* a sixth, from *sex,* six.] a stanza of six lines.

sex′tăn, *a.* recurring every sixth day, counting from the first day of occurrence.

sex′tăṇs, *n.* 1. a bronze coin of ancient Rome valued at the sixth part of an as.
2. [S-] a small southern constellation near the equator, between Leo and Hydra: also called *Sextant.*

sex′tănt, *n.* [L. *sextans,* a sixth.]
1. in mathematics, the sixth part of a circle. [Rare.]

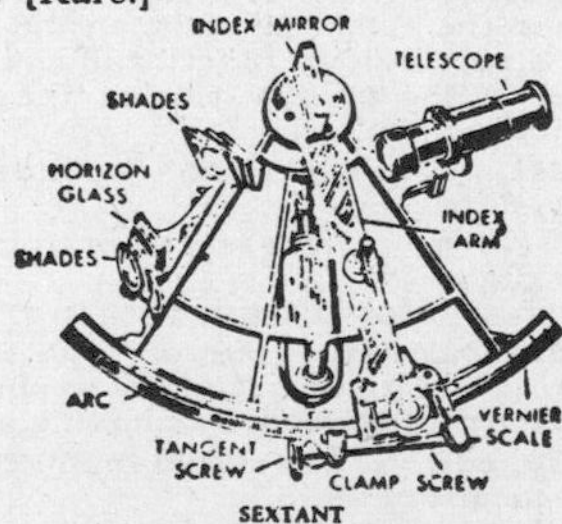

SEXTANT

2. an instrument capable of measuring angles of 120 degrees and more. It consists of a frame of metal, ebony, etc., stiffened by cross braces, and having an arc of usually sixty degrees. It is employed chiefly by navigators for measuring the altitudes of a heavenly body and its angle with the horizon or another heavenly body, thereby determining the latitude and longitude at sea.

sex′tȧ·ry, *n.* a sextarius.

sex·tet′, sex·tette′, *n.* 1. in music, (a) a group of six players; (b) a choir of six singers; (c) a composition for six voices or six instruments.
2. any group of six.

sex′tiç, *a.* of the sixth order or degree.

sex′tiç, *n.* an equation or quantic of the sixth degree.

sex′tile, *a.* in astrology, designating the aspect of two heavenly bodies which have a difference of longitude of sixty degrees or two signs.

sex′tile, *n.* [L. *sextilis*, from *sex*, six.] the aspect or position of two planets when distant from each other sixty degrees or two signs.

sex·til′liŏn (-yun), *n.* [Fr., from L. *sex*, six, and Fr. sep*tillion*.]
1. in the United States and France, the number represented by 1 followed by 21 zeros.
2. in Great Britain and Germany, the number represented by 1 followed by 36 zeros.

sex·til′liŏn, *a.* amounting to one sextillion in number.

sex′tō, *n.*; *pl.* **sex′tōṣ,** a volume composed of sheets each of which, when folded, makes six leaves.

sex·tō·dec′i·mō, *n.*; *pl.* **sex·tō·dec′i·mōṣ,** [L., abl. of *sextusdecimus*, sixteenth.]
1. the page size of a book made up of printer's sheets folded into sixteen leaves, each sheet being approximately 4½ by 6¾ inches.
2. a book consisting of pages of this size: usually written *16mo* or *16°* and called *sixteenmo.*

sex·tō·dec′i·mō, *a.* consisting of printer's sheets folded into sixteen leaves.

sex′tō·let, *n.* in music, a group of six notes of equal length played in the time usually given to four of the same value.

sex′tŏn, *n.* [contracted from *sacristan.*] an officer of a church whose business is to take care of the building, vessels, vestments, etc., to ring the bell, to attend on the officiating clergyman or minister, and, sometimes, to dig the graves in the churchyard.

sex′tŏn·ess, *n.* a woman sexton.

sex′tŏn·ship, *n.* the office of a sexton.

sex′tū·ple, *a.* [LL. *sextuplus*; L. *sex*, six, and *duplus*, double.]
1. sixfold; six times as much or as many.
2. consisting of or including six.
3. in music, having six beats to the measure.

sex′tū·ple, *n.* an amount six times as much or as many.

sex′tū·ple, *v.t.* and *v.i.*; sextupled, *pt.*,*pp.*; sextupling, *ppr.* to make or become six times larger in amount; to multiply by six.

sex′tū·plet, *n.* 1. (a) one of six offspring born at a single birth; (b) [*pl.*] six offspring born at a single birth.
2. a collection or group of six, usually of one kind.
3. in music, a sextolet.

sex′tū·plex, *a.* capable of transmitting six telegraphic messages simultaneously.

sex′ū·ăl, *a.* [L. *sexualis*, from *sexus*, sex.]
1. of, characteristic of, or affecting sex, the sexes, the organs of sex and their functions, or sex instincts or drives.
2. in biology, (a) having sex; (b) designating or of reproduction by the union of male and female germ cells.
sexual selection; the selection of mates, especially in the higher animals, on the basis of certain structural or functional characters, resulting in the preservation of these characters in the population.

sex′ū·ăl·ist, *n.* one who classifies plants by the sexual system.

sex·ū·al′i·ty, *n.* 1. the state or quality of being sexual.
2. interest in or concern with sex.

sex′ū·ăl·īze, *v.t.*; sexualized, *pt.*, *pp.*; sexualizing, *ppr.* (a) to give sex to; (b) to characterize as sexed; (c) to regard as having sex.

sex′ū·ăl·ly, *adv.* 1. in a sexual manner.
2. by means of sex.
3. with reference to sex.

sex′y, *a.*; *comp.* sexier; *superl.* sexiest; (a) exciting or intended to excite sexual desire; erotic; lascivious; (b) concerned to a large extent with sex; as, a *sexy* movie. [Colloq.]

sey′bērt·īte, *n.* [after H. *Seybert* (1802–1883), Am. mineralogist.] an orthorhombic mineral occurring mostly in tabular crystals with a thin foliated micaceous structure; a hydrated silicate of alumina, magnesia, and lime.

seye, seyn, *v.* obsolete past participles of *see.*

Sēy′fērt gal′ax·y, [after Carl K. *Seyfert*, American astronomer who discovered them in the 1940's.] any of a number of spiral galaxies with a small, intensely bright nucleus emitting strong, broad spectral lines which indicate a high state of excitation in the atoms.

seynt, *n.* a girdle. [Obs.]

sfer′içs, *n.pl.* [*construed as sing.*] [altered and shortened from *atmospherics.*]
1. same as *atmospherics.*
2. the study of atmospherics.
3. the locating, tracking, and evaluating of natural electrical discharges.

sfor·zän′dō (-tsän′), **sfor·zä′tō** (-tsä′), *a.* and *adv.* [It., forced.] in music, with force or emphasis: a direction to the performer.

sfū·mä′tō, *a.* [It., smoky.] in art, indicating vague outlines and a generally hazy or smoky appearance: said of a painting.

sgraf·fi′tō (skra-), *n.*; *pl.* **sgraf·fi′tī,** [It. from *sgraffiare*, to scratch, from *s-*, intens. (from L. *ex-*), and *graffiare*, to scratch, from L. *graphium*, a writing style, from Gr. *graphion* from *graphein*, to write.]
1. a method of producing a design on ceramics, murals, etc. by incising the outer coating of slip or glaze to reveal a ground of a different color.
2. such a design.
3. an object bearing such a design.

sh, *interj.* be still! hush!

shab′bed, *a.* mean: shabby. [Dial.]

shab′bi·ly, *adv.* in a shabby manner.

shab′bi·ness, *n.* 1. shabby quality or state; as, the *shabbiness* of a garment.
2. shabby conduct or treatment.

shab′ble, *n.* a crooked sword; especially, a rusty one. [Obs.]

shab′by, *a.*; *comp.* shabbier; *superl.* shabbiest, [variant of *scabby.*]
1. broken down; worn out; unkempt; deteriorated; as, *shabby* surroundings.
2. showing much wear; old; ragged; threadbare: said of clothing.
3. wearing such clothing; seedy.
4. beggarly; mean; unworthy; as, a *shabby* offering.
5. disgraceful; shameful; as, *shabby* treatment of one's parents.
Syn.—beggarly, contemptible, paltry, ragged, threadbare.

shab′by-ġen·teel′, *a.* shabby but trying to give an appearance of dignity and self-respect.

shab′rack, *n.* [G. *schabracke.*] a cavalry saddle-cloth.

Shä·bū′ōth (-vū′ōth), *n.pl.* [*construed as sing.*] [Heb. *shebuōth*, lit., weeks.] a Jewish holiday, the Feast of Weeks, or Pentecost, originally celebrating the spring harvest, but now also associated with the revelation of the Law at Mount Sinai.

shack, *n.* [variant of *shake.*]
1. grain shaken from the ripe ear and eaten by hogs, etc., after harvest; also, fallen acorns. [Brit. Dial.]
2. the right of pasturage on such shack. [Brit. Dial.]
3. a shiftless fellow; an itinerant beggar; a vagabond. [Dial.]

shack, *n.* [said to be contr. from Mex. *jacal*, from Aztec, *xacalli*, wooden hut, but influenced by and perh. from *ramshack*, contr. from *ramshackle.*] a small house or cabin that is crudely built and furnished; a hut; shanty.
to shack up; (a) to spend the night; (b) to cohabit (*with*). [Slang.]

shack′le, *n.* stubble. [Brit. Dial.]

shack′le, *n.* [AS. *scacul*, *sceacul*, a shackle, from *scacan*, *sceacan*, to shake; D. *schakel*, a link of a chain.]
1. a metal fastening, usually one of a linked pair, for the wrists or ankles of a person kept prisoner; a fetter; manacle.
2. that which obstructs freedom of expression or action; a hindrance; a restraint.

SHACKLES

3. any of several kinds of fasteners; (a) a link in a chain cable fitted with a movable pin, so that the chain can be separated; a clevis; (b) a ring through which the port bar is passed to close the porthole; (c) a coupling link for railway cars; (d) a padlock bow; (e) a strong form of insulator used in places of high tension.
4. an ornamental chain or band used as an arm or leg decoration. [Obs.]
5. in heraldry, a bearing representing part of a manacle.
6. the wrist. [Brit. Dial.]

shack′le, *v.t.*; shackled, *pt.*, *pp.*; shackling, *ppr.* 1. to put shackles on; to fetter.
2. to fasten or connect with a shackle or shackles.
3. to restrain in freedom of expression or action.

shack′le bär, a coupling bar; a link to fasten railroad cars together. [Colloq.]

shack′le bōlt, 1. a shackle.
2. the movable bolt in a clevis, or shackle.
3. a bolt with a shackle at one end.

shack′le joint, 1. a joint made by a shackle, or clevis, with its bolt.
2. a joint in certain fishes in which the spine has a bony loop linked into a ringlike process of the exoskeleton.

shack′ly, *a.* weak; rickety; shaky. [Dial.]

shad, *n.*; *pl.* **shad** or **shadṣ,** [AS. *sceadda*, a kind of fish; Ir. and Gael. *sgadan*, a herring.]
1. any of several salt-water fishes of the genus *Alosa*, related to the herring but having a deeper body and spawning in rivers: the common shad, *Alosa sapidissima*, found along the North Atlantic coast, is a valuable food fish.
2. any of various similar fishes; as the gold shad, *Alosa chrysochloris*; the gizzard-shad, a kind of herring; the yellow-tailed shad, or menhaden; the long-boned shad of the West Indies and Bermuda, a fish of the genus *Gerres.*

shad′-bel″lied, *a.* without a protruding belly; lank. [Colloq.]

shad′ber″ry, *n.*; *pl.* **shad′ber″rieṣ,** a shadbush; also, its fruit.

shad′bïrd, *n.* 1. the snipe. [Dial.]
2. the sandpiper. [Brit. Dial.]

shad′-blōw, *n.* a shadbush.

shad′bush, *n.* [so named from flowering when the shad appear in U. S. rivers.] any of a number of related plants of the rose family, genus *Amelanchier*, with white flowers and purple-black berries; shad-blow; Juneberry.

shad′dŏck, *n.* [from Capt. *Shaddock*, who first carried this fruit (1696) from the East to the West Indies.]
1. a large, yellow, coarse-grained, pear-shaped fruit, *Citrus maxima*, resembling a grapefruit. The pompelmous is a large variety.
2. the tree it grows on.

SHADDOCK (*Citrus maxima*)

shāde, *n.* [AS. *sceadu*, shade, shadow.]
1. comparative darkness caused by the interception or interruption of rays of light by a more or less opaque object.
2. an area less brightly lighted than its surroundings.
3. a shadow. [Archaic or Poet.]
4. [*chiefly pl.*] a retired or secluded place.
5. an indication or representation of darkness in painting, drawing, photography, etc.
6. degree of darkness of a color; gradation of a color with reference to its mixture with black; as, various *shades* of blue.
7. (a) a small difference or variation; as, *shades* of opinion; (b) a slight amount or de-

gree; a trace; touch; suggestion; as, a *shade* of humor in his voice.

8. (a) anything lacking substance or reality; a phantom; (b) a ghost; specter; spirit. [Poetic.]

9. a screen; something that protects or screens from light; as, (a) a curtain or screen, usually of some opaque material, as specially treated oilcloth, paper, linen, or the like, generally fastened to a spring roller upon which it may be rolled as desired; (b) a colored glass in a sextant or other optical instrument for solar observations; (c) a hollow conic frustum of paper, metal, ground glass, etc., surrounding the light of a lamp, to diffuse the light or confine it within a given area; (d) a hollow glass covering for protecting ornaments, etc., from dust; (e) a device for protecting the eyes from the direct rays of the sun or artificial light.

10. a swell-box shutter in a pipe organ.

in (or *into*) *the shade*; (a) in darkness or shadow; (b) in comparative obscurity; as, an author put in the *shade* by brilliant, new writers.

the shades; (a) the increasing darkness, as of evening; (b) the world of the dead; the nether world; Hades; also, the disembodied spirits of the dead, collectively.

shāde, *v.t.*; shaded, *pt.*, *pp.*; shading, *ppr.* 1. to shelter or screen from light or heat; as, a tree *shades* the plants under its branches.

2. to overspread with darkness; to obscure; to dim.

3. to shelter, hide, or screen with or as with a shadow.

4. (a) to represent the effects of shade in (a painting, photograph, etc.); to add shading to; (b) to depict in, or mark with, gradations of light or color.

5. to alter by a slight degree or gradation, as the pitch of a note, string, pipe, etc.

6. to reduce in quantity or quality by a slight gradation; as, to *shade* a price.

7. to typify beforehand; to prefigure; to foreshadow. [Obs.]

shāde, *v.i.* to become altered very slightly or by degrees; as, one meaning *shades* into another.

shāde′ful, *a.* shady; giving shade.

shāde′-grōwn″, *a.* grown in the shade: applied particularly to those plants grown under artificial shade, as tobacco.

shāde′less, *a.* unshaded; without shade.

shāde plȧnt, any plant grown solely to provide shade for other plants.

shāde′tāil, *n.* a squirrel. [Dial.]

shād′ẽr, *n.* one who or that which shades.

shad′flow″ẽr, *n.* the trailing arbutus.

shad flȳ, any of various May flies seen in the shad-spawning season.

shad frog, an American species of frog, *Rana virescens*, seen in spring at the season of shad-spawning.

shād′i·ly, *adv.* in a shady manner.

shad′ïne, *n.* small menhaden prepared like sardines.

shād′i·ness, *n.* the state or quality of being shady.

shād′ing, *n.* 1. protection or shielding against light or heat.

2. the representation of light or shade in a picture.

3. any small difference or variation, as in quality, kind, etc.

4. in music, an effect obtained by subtle changes and variations in dynamics, which are not indicated on the score.

shād′ing ç̧oil, in electricity, a coil employed to make single-phase motors self-starting: it consists of a short-circuited coil placed around part of the pole of an alternating-current magnet; the currents thus induced in the coil have the effect of reducing the magnetic flux in that part of the pole surrounded by the coil.

shȧ·dọọf′, shȧ·dụ́f′, *n.* [Ar. *shādūf.*] a contrivance employed in the East to raise water for irrigation. It consists of a long stout rod suspended on a frame at about one-fifth of its length from the end. The short end is weighted as a counterpoise, and from the long end a bucket is suspended by a rope.

shad′ōw, *n.* [AS. *scadu, sceadu*, a shadow; akin to Goth. *skadus*, D. *schaduw*, O.H.G. *scato*, G. *schatten*, shade, shadow.]

1. shade within defined limits cast upon a surface by a body that intercepts the rays of light; as, the *shadow* of a man or a tower.

2. the dark image made by such a body.

3. [*pl.*] the growing darkness after sunset.

4. a vague indication; symbol; omen; prefiguration; as, coming events cast their *shadows* before.

5. the shaded part of a picture; hence, the darker phases of life; unhappiness; gloom; as, the *shadow* of life's evening.

6. (a) a faint suggestion or representation; a trace; (b) a remnant; a vestige.

7. (a) a spirit; a ghost; (b) something without reality or substance; an imaginary vision.

8. anything having any of the characteristics of a shadow, as (a) a mirrored image; a reflection, as in a stream or in a glass; (b) one who follows closely, as a detective or a spy; (c) a close or constant companion.

9. protection; shelter; as, within the king's *shadow*. [Rare.]

in the shadow of; very close to; verging upon.

shadow dance; a dance in which the performers are not visible, their movements being shown in shadow on a screen.

under the shadow of; (a) very close to; verging upon; (b) in danger of; apparently fated for.

shad′ōw, *v.t.*; shadowed, *pt.*, *pp.*; shadowing, *ppr.* 1. to throw a shadow upon; hence, to make dark or gloomy; to cloud.

2. to represent faintly, mystically, or prophetically; to prefigure (often with *forth*).

Augustus is *shadowed* in the person of Aeneas. —Dryden.

3. to mark with slight gradations of color or light; to shade in painting, drawing, etc.

4. (a) to conceal; to hide; to screen; to protect; (b) to shelter from light or heat. [Archaic.]

5. to follow secretly and observe closely; as, to *shadow* a suspect.

shad′ōw, *v.i.* 1. to become clouded; to be darkened by a shadow.

2. to shade away by slight degrees; to blend.

shad′ōw bīrd, the umber (bird).

shad′ōw box, a frame of polished wood with a glass cover placed over a framed painting to protect it.

shad′ōw·box·ing, *n.* sparring with an imaginary opponent: an exercise used by boxers.

shad′ōw·gràph, *n.* 1. an image or silhouette produced by throwing a shadow upon a lighted surface.

2. an X-ray photograph; a radiograph.

shad′ōw·i·ness, *n.* the state or quality of being shadowy.

shad′ōw·ing, *n.* 1. a shading; gradation of light and color.

2. the act of watching closely; surveillance.

shad′ōw·ish, *a.* obscure; shadowy; vague. [Rare.]

shad′ōw·less, *a.* 1. having no shadow.

2. without shade or shadow, as a lighted surface.

shad′ōw·y, *a.* [AS. *sceadwig.*]

1. resembling, or of the nature of, a shadow; specifically, (a) without reality or substance; fleeting or illusory; (b) dim; indistinct.

2. covered with or producing shade or shadow; shaded.

3. vaguely indicative; symbolic. [Obs.]

Shā′drach, *n.* [Heb. *shadhrakh*; of Bab. origin.]

1. in the Bible, one of the three Jewish captives in Babylonia who were cast into a blazing furnace by Nebuchadnezzar and came out miraculously unharmed: Dan. iii. 12.

2. [s-] a mass of unfused material at the bottom of a blast furnace.

shad spir′it, the American snipe.

shad wāit′ẽr, the roundfish.

shād′y, *a.*; *comp.* shadier; *superl.* shadiest, 1. giving shade.

2. shaded, as from the sun; full of shade.

3. of darkness, secrecy, or concealment.

4. of questionable character or honesty. [Colloq.]

on the shady side of; beyond (a given age); older than.

to keep shady; to keep concealed; to stay out of sight. [Slang.]

shaf′fle, *v.i.* to shamble. [Brit. Dial.]

shaf′flẽr, *n.* one who shambles. [Brit. Dial.]

Shaf′i·ïte, *n.* [from the founder, *Shāfiī.*] a member of one of the four Sunnite sects.

shȧft, *n.* [AS. *sceaft*, a dart, an arrow, a spear, a pole; akin to Ice. *skaft*, *skapt*, an arrow or dart, a handle; Dan. *skaft*, a handle or haft, a column; D. and G. *schaft*, a shaft, pole, handle.]

1. the stem of an arrow or spear; also, an arrow or spear.

2. a missile or something compared to a missile; bolt; as, *shafts* of lightning, derision, etc.

3. a cone or column of light; a ray; a beam.

4. a long slender part or object; specifically, (a) [Rare.] the trunk of a tree or stem of a plant; (b) the mid section of a long bone; (c) the supporting stem of a branched candlestick; (d) a flagpole; (e) a tall, slender building or part of a building; a spire; (f) a bar supporting, or transmitting motion to, a mechanical part; as, the drive *shaft* of an engine.

5. a vertical opening passing through the floors of a building, as for an elevator.

6. a pit or long narrow opening or entrance into the earth: it may be perpendicular or slightly inclined; as, a mine *shaft*.

7. in architecture, (a) the body of a column, or the pillar between the base and the capital; also, a column or obelisk; (b) that part of a chimney which rises above the roof.

8. the stem or stock of a feather or quill.

9. either of the two thills of a carriage.

10. a handle; the long, slender handle of a tool or implement.

11. a narrow passage through which air may be admitted or forced out; an air shaft, as used in heating or ventilating.

12. the interior cone of a blast furnace.

line shaft; the principal shaft in a factory, bearing pulleys which drive the machines.

shȧft al′ley, a passage in a screw steamer between the after bulkhead of the engine-room and the shaft pipe.

shȧft ç̧oup′ling (kup′), a device for connecting two or more lengths of shafting.

shȧft′ed, *a.* 1. having shafts; ornamented with shafts or small clustering pillars.

2. having a handle: a term used in heraldry of a spearhead with a handle.

shȧft fūr′nāce, a furnace with a vertical body or stack.

shȧft họrse, the horse that goes in the shafts of a vehicle.

shȧft house, a structure built at the opening of a mining shaft for the safekeeping of machinery and tools.

shȧft′ing, *n.* 1. a system or group of shafts, as for transmitting motion, conveying air, etc.

2. material for making shafts.

shag, *n.* a dance step, popular in the late 1930's, consisting of a fast hopping step first with one foot and then the other.

shag, *v.i.*; shagged, *pt.*, *pp.*; shagging, *ppr.* to dance the shag.

shag, *n.* [AS. *sceacga*, a brush of coarse hair; probably allied to Ice. *skegg*, a beard.]

1. heavily matted wool or hair. [Rare.]

2. a heavy, rough nap, as on some woolen cloth.

3. cloth with such a nap.

4. any disordered or tangled mass.

5. coarsely shredded tobacco.

shag, *n.* [specialized use of prec. word with reference to the rough crest.] a small cormorant, a sea bird having a crest during the breeding season.

shag, *a.* 1. coarse; shaggy; hairy.

2. made of shag, as a garment.

shag, *v.t.* 1. to make rough or hairy.

2. in baseball, to chase after and catch (balls) in batting practice. [Slang.]

shag·ȧ·nap′py, *n.* rawhide that is cut into strips.

shag·ȧ·nap′py, *a.* tough.

shag′bärk, *n.* 1. a kind of hickory, the *Carya alba*; shellbark; also, its wood or nut.

2. a leguminous tree of the West Indies, the *Pithecolobium micradenium*.

shag′ged, *a.* unkempt; rough; tangled; covered with a coarse growth of hair or brushwood.

shag′gi·ly, *adv.* in a shaggy manner.

shag′gi·ness, shag′ged·ness, *n.* 1. the state of being shaggy; roughness with long, loose hair or wool.

2. roughness produced by scrubby growths.

shag′gy, *a.* 1. covered with or having long, coarse hair or wool.

2. carelessly groomed; unkempt: said of a person.

3. of tangled, coarse growth; straggly; scrubby.

4. having a rough nap or surface.

shag′gy dog, [from such an anecdote involving a shaggy dog.] a humorous anecdote with a surprise ending involving ludicrously unreal or irrational behavior.

shag′-hāired, *a.* having thick, rough hair.

shag′rag, *n.* the rabble. [Obs.]

shȧ·green′, *n.* [Fr. *chagrin,* Venetian *sagrin,* from Turk. *sagri,* the back of a horse, from which part the leather was made.]
 1. rawhide with a rough, granular surface, made from the skin of the horse, camel, seal, etc.
 2. the hard, rough skin of the shark or dogfish, sometimes used as a polisher.
 shagreen ray; the skate; a variety of ray found off the British coasts, covered with shagreen.

shȧ·greened′, shȧ·green′, *a.* having a covering of shagreen or a surface rough like sharkskin.

shäh, *n.* [Per., a king, a prince.] the title given to the ruler of Iran and to the rulers of certain other Eastern countries.

Shä·hap′ti·ăn, *n.* a member of a subgroup of the Oregonian family of American Indians, formerly living in the upper Columbia River Valley.

Shä·hap′ti·ăn, *a.* designating or of the Shahaptians.

shȧ·heen′, *n.* [Per. *shāhīn,* a falcon.] a falcon of Asia, *Falco peregrinator.*

shāik, *n.* same as *sheik.*

shaī′tän, sheī′tän, *n.* [Ar.] 1. [*often* S–] in Moslem usage, the Devil; Satan.
 2. an evil being; fiend.

shāke, *v.t.*; shook, *pt.*; shaken, *pp.*; shaking, *ppr.* [ME. *schaken*; AS. *sceacan, scacan*; Ice. *skaka*; Dan. *skaga,* to veer, shift, shake.]
 1. to cause to move up and down, back and forth, or from side to side with short, quick movements.
 2. to bring, force, throw, stir up, dislodge, etc. by or as by abrupt, brisk movements.
 3. to cause to quiver or tremble; to vibrate; as, the wind *shook* the building.
 4. (a) to cause to totter or become unsteady; (b) to unnerve; to weaken; as, he was visibly *shaken* by the news.
 5. to brandish; to flourish; to wave.
 6. to clasp (another's hand), as in greeting.
 7. to get away from or rid of; as, he *shook* his pursuers. [Slang.]
 8. in dice, to rattle (the dice) just before casting them.
 9. in music, to trill.
 to shake a loose leg; to live an unsettled life.
 to shake down; (a) to bring down or cause to fall by shaking, as an apple from a tree; (b) to cause to settle or become lower by shaking; (c) to condition (new equipment, etc.); (d) [Slang.] to extort money from, as by blackmail.
 to shake hands; (a) to salute or greet by clasping hands; (b) to indicate agreement by shaking hands, as at the close of a compact.
 to shake off; to get away from or rid of (an undesirable person or thing).
 to shake (off) the dust from one's feet; to renounce all dealings with a person or place.
 to shake out; (a) to cause to fall out by shaking, as salt from a shaker; (b) to clean or empty by shaking, as a shoe with gravel in it, a rug, etc.; (c) to straighten out by shaking, as a folded or wrinkled cloth.
 to shake out a reef; to let out a reef and thereby enlarge the sail area.
 to shake the sails; to cause the sails to flap by bringing the bow of the ship to the wind.
 to shake up; (a) to shake, especially so as to mix or blend; (b) to disturb or rouse by or as by shaking; (c) to jar or shock; (d) to redistribute by or as by shaking.

shāke, *v.i.* 1. to move or be moved quickly and irregularly up and down, back and forth, or from side to side; to vibrate.
 2. to tremble; to shiver; to quake, as from cold or fear.
 3. to become unsteady; to totter; reel.
 4. to shake hands, as in greeting.
 5. in music, to trill.

shāke, *n.* 1. an act of shaking; back-and-forth movement.
 2. an unsteady or trembling movement; a tremor.
 3. a natural split or fissure in rock or timber.
 4. an earthquake. [Colloq.]
 5. a very short time; a moment; as, I'll be there in two *shakes.* [Slang.]
 6. in music, a rapid alternation between two notes; a trill.
 7. a motion of hands clasped.

Our salutations were very hearty on both sides, consisting of many kind *shakes* of the hand. —Addison.

 8. one of the staves of a cask; a shingle.
 9. in coopering, a shook.
 10. the redshank. [Ir. Dial.]
 11. in printing, a blur resulting from the moving of the sheet while it is being printed.
 no great shakes; of no account; not unusual; ordinary. [Colloq.]
 the shakes; a convulsive trembling, often accompanying intermittent fever, alcoholism, etc. [Colloq.]

shāke′down, *a.* for testing the performance or operational characteristics or acclimating the personnel; as, the *shakedown* cruise of a new battleship. [Colloq.]

shāke′down, *n.* 1. a makeshift bunk on the floor or on chairs, etc.
 2. an extortion of money, as by blackmail. [Slang.]

shāke′fork, *n.* 1. a pitchfork. [Obs.]
 2. in heraldry, a Y-shaped bearing having bluntly pointed ends.

SHAKEFORK

shāk′en, *v.* past participle of *shake.*

shāk′ẽr, *n.* 1. one who or that which shakes: specifically, any device used for shaking, mixing, or blending; as, the *shaker* of the sieves of a threshing machine.
 2. [S–] [so called by others from movements of a dance constituting a part of their ritual.] any member of a religious sect observing a doctrine of celibacy, common ownership of property, and community living.
 3. a species of pigeon.

Shāk′ẽr·ess, *n.* a woman Shaker.

Shāk′ẽr·iṣm, *n.* the belief and practices of the Shakers.

Shāke·spēar′ē·ăn, Shāke·spēar′i·ăn, *a.* of or relating to Shakespeare, his time, character, and work.
 Shakespearean sonnet; a sonnet composed of three groups of four lines each (*quatrains*) typically with the rhyme scheme *abab cdcd efef,* and a final couplet with the rhyme *gg:* also called *Elizabethan sonnet.*

Shāke·spēar′ē·ăn, Shāke·spēar′i·ăn, *n.* a scholar specializing in Shakespeare and his works.

Shāke·spēar′ē·ăn·iṣm, Shāke·spēar′i·ăn·iṣm, *n.* 1. Shakespearean style.
 2. a Shakespearean expression.

shāke′-up, *n.* a shaking up; specifically, a reorganization of a drastic or extensive nature, as in policy or personnel.

shāk′i·ly, *adv.* in a shaky manner; insecurely; weakly; tremblingly.

shāk′i·ness, *n.* the condition of being shaky.

shāk′ing, *n.* 1. the act of shaking or agitating.
 2. successive shocks; a concussion.
 3. a trembling or shivering; the ague or a chill.
 4. [*pl.*] in nautical usage, refuse scraps of cordage and rope yarn which accumulate on shipboard.

shāk′ing piēce (pēs), a piece of beef taken from the underside of the neck.

shak′ō, *n.*; *pl.* **shak′ōṣ,** [Fr. *schako,* from Hung. *csákó,* a cap, shako.]
 1. a stiff, cylindrical military dress hat, usually with a flat top and a plume.
 2. a large military dress hat made of fur.

SHAKO

Shāk·spēr′i·ăn, *a.* Shakespearean.

Shak′ti (shuk′), *n.* in Hinduism, (a) [s–] power; (b) the female principle or generative power; (c) Devi. Also *Sakti.*

Shak′tiṣm (shuk′), *n.* Shakti worship: also *Saktism.*

shak′ụ·dō, *n.* [Japan.] a dark-blue alloy of copper and gold, used in Japanese decorative metalwork.

shāk′y, *a.*; *comp.* shakier; *superl.* shakiest. 1. inclined to shake or tremble; unsteady; shaking; as, a *shaky* hand; a *shaky* building.
 2. full of shakes or clefts; as, a *shaky* tree.
 3. not dependable or reliable; questionable, as a person or his word.

shāle, *n.* [a form of *scale* or *shell*; G. *schale,* a skin or bark, a shell, a thin layer.]
 1. a shell or husk. [Obs.]
 2. in geology, a fine-grained rock formed by the hardening of clay: it splits into thin layers when broken.

shāle oil, a dark mineral oil derived from bituminous shale or brown coal.

shall, *v.*; should, *pt.*; shalt, *archaic 2d pers. sing., pres. tense*; shouldest *or* shouldst, *archaic 2d pers. sing., pt.* [ME. *shal, schal,* often with the sense of *is to*; AS. *sceal,* an old past tense used as a present.] an auxiliary used in formal speech: (a) to express futurity in the first person, and determination, compulsion, obligation, or necessity in the second and third persons; (b) in a question expecting *shall* in the answer; (c) in laws and resolutions; as, the fine *shall* not exceed $100; (d) in subordinate clauses introduced by *if, when,* etc. These formal conventions, however, do not reflect prevailing usage, in which *shall* and *will* are used interchangeably with *will* predominating in all persons. See also *will, should,* and *would.*

shall, *n.* the catfish of the Nile, of the genus *Synodontis.*

shal′lŏn, *n.* the salal.

shal·lọon′, *n.* a twilled woolen fabric used for dresses and coat linings.

shal′lŏp, *n.* [Fr. *chaloupe*; D. *sloep,* sloop.] a small light boat fitted with oars or sails or both; a dinghy.

shal·lot′, *n.* [OFr. *eschalotte,* a kind of onion, from L. *Ascalonicus,* belonging to Askalon, from Gr. *Askalon,* a city of the Philistines.]
 1. a vegetable, *Allium ascalonicum,* native to Syria and resembling the garlic.
 2. a small onion.

shal′lōw, *a.* [ME. *schalowe*; prob. from AS. *scealu,* from the base of *sceald,* shallow.]
 1. not deep; having little depth; as, *shallow* water; a *shallow* trench; a *shallow* basket.
 2. not intellectually deep; not profound; superficial; empty; as, a *shallow* mind or understanding; *shallow* skill.
 3. thin and weak of sound; not deep, full, or round.
 Syn.—shoaly, slight, flimsy, trifling, simple, superficial, unprofound.

shal′lōw, *n.* 1. a bar or shoal; a shelf; a flat; a sandbank; any shallow place in a body of water.
 2. a fish, the rudd. [Brit. Dial.]

shal′lōw, *v.t.* to make shallow.

shal′lōw, *v.i.* to become shallow.

shal′lōw-bod″ied, *a.* having a shallow hold: applied to ships.

shal′lōw·brāined, *a.* not intellectually deep; mentally weak.

shal′lōw-heärt″ed, *a.* having no depth of feeling.

shal′lōw·ly, *adv.* 1. with little depth.
 2. superficially; simply; without depth of thought or judgment.

shal′lōw·ness, *n.* a lack of depth; superficiality.

shal′lōw-pāt″ed, *a.* mentally weak.

shal′lōw-wāist″ed, *a.* having a flush deck: applied to ships.

shạlm (shạm), *n.* same as *shawm.*

shal′ōte, *n.* shallot. [Obs.]

shalt, *v.* archaic second person singular, present indicative, of *shall.*

shāl′y, *a.*; *comp.* shalier; *superl.* shaliest; of, like, or containing shale.

sham, *n.* [prob. from a northern dial. var. of *shame.*]
 1. formerly, a trick or fraud.
 2. an imitation that is meant to deceive; a counterfeit; a deception; a fake.
 3. a person who falsely affects a certain character.
 4. an ornamental cover simulating some piece of personal or household linen; as, a pillow *sham.*

sham, *a.* false; counterfeit; mock; make-believe; pretended; as, a *sham* fight.

How *sham* is the article, so it but shines. —Moore.

sham, *v.t.*; shammed, *pt., pp.*; shamming, *ppr.*
 1. to cheat or trick. [Rare.]
 2. to be or make an imitation or false show of; to counterfeit; to feign.
 to sham Abraham; see under *Abraham-man.*

sham, *v.i.* to pretend to be what one is not; to make false pretenses.

shä'mȧ, *n.* [Hind. *shāmā.*] an East Indian bird, *Kittacincla macrura*, noted for its ability to imitate the notes of various birds and animals.

shä'măn, *n.* [Hind. and Per., an idolater.] a professor or priest of shamanism; a wizard or conjurer among those who profess shamanism.

shȧ·man'iç, *a.* of a shaman or shamanism.

shä'măn·ism, *n.* 1. the religion of certain peoples of northeast Asia, based on the doctrine that the workings of good and evil spirits can be influenced only by the shamans.
2. any similar religion, as of some American Indians.

shä'măn·ist, *n.* a believer in shamanism.

shä·măn·is'tiç, *a.* of or like shamanism.

Shä'măsh, *n.* [Assyr.] in Assyro-Babylonian religion, the sun god, responsible for summer warmth and the success of crops, and a symbol for justice.

shä'măsh, *n.* [Heb.] the secretary of a synagogue.

sham'ble, *v.i.*; shambled, *pt., pp.*; shambling, *ppr.* [from obs. *shamble, a.*, in *shamble legs*; prob. from *shamble, n.*, in obs. sense of stool, bench.] to walk in a lazy or clumsy manner, barely lifting the feet.

sham'ble, *n.* a shambling walk or gait.

sham'bleṣ, *n.pl.* [*construed as sing.*] [ME. *schamel*, a bench; AS. *scamel, sceamul*, a bench or stool.]
1. (a) a place where meat is sold; a butcher's shop; (b) [Brit.] [*in sing.*] a bench or stall for the sale of meat.
2. a slaughterhouse.
3. a place where much killing has been done; scene of bloodshed or carnage: sometimes extended to mean any scene or condition of great destruction or disorder, as, the children left the house a *shambles*.

sham'bling, *a.* moving with an awkward, irregular, clumsy pace; as, a *shambling* trot; *shambling* legs.

sham'bling, *n.* an awkward, clumsy, irregular pace or gait.

shāme, *n.* [AS. *sceamu, scamu*; Ice. *skamm, skömm*; Dan. and Sw. *skam.*]
1. a disturbed or painful feeling of guilt, incompetence, indecency, or blameworthiness.
2. a tendency to have feelings of this kind.
3. dishonor; disgrace; as, he brings *shame* upon his name.
4. a person or thing that brings shame, dishonor, or disgrace.
5. something regrettable, unfortunate, or outrageous; as, it's a *shame* that they were cheated.
for shame!; you ought to be ashamed!; here is cause for shame!
to put to shame; (a) to cause to feel shame; (b) to do much better than; to surpass; to outshine.
shame on; shame should be felt by; this is shameful of.

shāme, *v.t.*; shamed, *pt., pp.*; shaming, *ppr.* 1. to make ashamed; to cause to feel shame.
2. to dishonor; to disgrace.
3. to drive, force, or impel by a sense of shame; as, he was *shamed* out of his prejudice.
to shame it out; to face disgrace brazenly.

shāme, *v.i.* to experience shame. [Archaic and Dial.]

shāme'fāced (-fāst), *a.* [AS. *scam-fæst*, shamefast, held or restrained by shame.]
1. extremely bashful or diffident.
2. showing a feeling of shame or guilt; ashamed.

shāme'fāced·ly, *adv.* in a shamefaced manner.

shāme'fāced·ness, *n.* the state of being shamefaced.

shāme'fụl, *a.* 1. shamefaced. [Obs.]
2. bringing or causing shame or disgrace; disgraceful.
3. violating what is considered to be just, moral, or decent; offensive.
Syn.—scandalous, outrageous, disgraceful, dishonorable.

shāme'fụl·ly, *adv.* in a shameful manner; with indecency; disgracefully.

shāme'fụl·ness, *n.* 1. bashfulness. [Obs.]
2. the state or quality of being shameful.

shāme'less, *a.* 1. having no feeling of shame, modesty, or decency; brazen; impudent.
2. done without shame; indicating lack of shame; as, a *shameless* disregard of honesty.

shāme'less·ly, *adv.* without shame; brazenly.

shāme'less·ness, *n.* the state or quality of being shameless.

shāme'-prọọf, *a.* callous or insensible to shame.

shām'ẽr, *n.* one who or that which makes ashamed.

sham'i·sen, *n.* same as *samisen.*

sham·mä'thȧ, *n.* [Heb.] final excommunication by the Jewish synagogue.

sham'mel, *n.* in mining, a set of shelves left at suitable distances to receive the ore, which is thrown from one to another and thus raised to the top. [Brit. Dial.]

sham'mẽr, *n.* one who shams; an impostor.

sham'my, *n.*; *pl.* **sham'mieṣ**, same as *chamois.*

sham'ois (sham'i), *n.* chamois.

sham'oy, *v.t.*; shamoyed, *pt., pp.*; shamoying, *ppr.* [from *chamois.*] to dress (skin) with oil instead of an astringent; to treat in the way chamois leather is dressed.

sham·pọọ', *v.t.*; shampooed, *pt., pp.*; shampooing, *ppr.* [Hind. *chāmpnā*, to press or rub.]
1. to massage.
2. to wash (the hair and scalp), usually with a specially prepared soap, etc.
3. to wash the hair and scalp of.
4. to cleanse (rugs, tapestries, etc.) with soap and water, or with the aid of special preparations designed to remove dirt.

sham·pọọ', *n.* 1. the process or act of shampooing.
2. a preparation, as of soap, used for shampooing.

sham·pọọ'ẽr, *n.* a person who shampoos.

sham'rock, *n.* [Ir. *seamrog*; Gael. *seamrag*, trefoil or white clover.] any one of various clovers or cloverlike plants with leaflets in groups of three, used as the emblem of Ireland.

SHAMROCK

sham'rock pēa, a leguminous plant, *Parochetus communis*, with trifoliate leaves, found in Asia and Africa.

Shän, *n.* 1. a member of a group of Mongoloid tribes who live in Indo-China.
2. their Thai language.

shan'dry·dan, *n.* [from North West Brit. dial. *shandry*, a cart.]
1. a two-wheeled chaise or cart. [Dial.]
2. any decrepit vehicle. [Dial.]

shan'dy·gaff, *n.* a mixture of ale and ginger beer, or of lager beer and ginger ale, etc.

shang·haī', *v.t.*; shanghaied, *pt., pp.*; shanghaiing, *ppr.* [from *Shanghai*, China.]
1. [orig. said of sailors thus kidnapped for crew duty on the China run.] to kidnap, usually by drugging, for service aboard ship.
2. to induce (another) to do something through force or underhand methods. [Slang.]

Shang'haī, *n.* [from *Shanghai*, China.] a kind of chicken with long, feathered legs: ancestor of the Cochin and Brahma.

Shañ'gri·Lä', *n.* [from the scene of James Hilton's novel, *Lost Horizon.*]
1. any imaginary, idyllic utopia or hidden paradise.
2. (a) the mythical starting place of the bombing raid over Tokyo and other cities, April 18, 1942; (b) any secret starting place of bombing raids or other military operations: the term was first used in this sense by Franklin Roosevelt.

shañk, *n.* [AS. *scanc, sceanc, scanca, sceanca*, bone of leg, the leg; *earm-scanca*, arm bone.]
1. the whole leg.
2. the lower part of the leg; the part of the leg from the knee to the ankle.
3. a cut of beef from the upper foreleg or hind leg.
4. the part, usually straight or stemlike, between the top or handle and the working part; shaft: said of instruments, tools, etc.
5. the whole of a piece of type exclusive of the printing surface; body.
6. (a) the narrow part of a shoe sole in front of the heel; (b) the piece of metal, etc. that gives it form.
7. the end or latter part of anything; as, the *shank* of the journey. [Colloq.]
8. in botany, a footstalk.
9. in founding, a large ladle to contain molten metals, managed by a straight bar at one end and a crossbar with handles at the other.
10. a long-legged wading bird.
11. [*pl.*] opticians' flat-nosed pliers for chipping off the edges of and rounding a lens.
the shank of the evening; (a) originally, the end or latter part of the evening (afternoon); twilight; (b) the beginning or early part of the evening (night). [Colloq.]
to ride (or *go*) *on shanks' mare*; to walk.

shañk, *v.i.* in botany, to fall off by decay of the footstalk, as a flower: usually with *off*.

shañk, *v.t.* [AS. *sceacan*, to escape, flee.]
1. to dismiss unceremoniously. [Scot.]
2. to trim and round a lens with an optician's pliers, or shanks.

shañked (shañkt), *a.* 1. having a shank.
2. affected with disease of the shank or footstalk.

shañk'ẽr, *n.* [Fr. *chancre.*] chancre.

shañk pāint'ẽr, a short rope and chain which holds the shank and flukes of an anchor against the ship's side.

shan'ny, *n.*; *pl.* **shan'nieṣ**, the smooth blenny, *Blennius pholis*, of Europe, a mottled green salt-water fish.

shan'ny, *a.* silly. [Brit. Dial.]

shȧn't, shall not.

shant'ey, *n.*; *pl.* **shant'ieṣ**, a chantey, a sailor's work song: also *shanty.*

Shan'tung', *n.* [from *Shantung*, a province of China.]
1. [*sometimes* s–] a silk fabric made from the silk of wild silkworms: it is usually undyed.
2. [*sometimes* s–] a somewhat similar rayon or cotton fabric.

shan'ty, *a.* gaudy; flashy. [Brit. Dial.]

shan'ty, *n.*; *pl.* **shan'tieṣ**, [Ir. *sean*, old, and *tig*, a house.]
1. a hut or shabby dwelling; a temporary building.
2. in Australia, a public house. [Slang.]

shan'ty, *v.i.* to live in a shanty.

shāpe, *n.* [AS. (*ge*)*sceap*, created thing, from *scieppan*, to create.]
1. the quality of a thing that depends on the relative position of all points composing its outline or external surface; physical or spatial form.
2. the form characteristic of a particular person or thing.
3. the contour of the body, exclusive of the face; figure.
4. assumed or feigned appearance; guise; as, an enemy in the *shape* of a friend.
5. an imaginary or spectral form; a phantom.
6. something having a particular shape, used as a mold or basis for shaping or fashioning; a form, as for making hats, molding gelatin, etc.
7. any of the forms, structures, etc. in which a thing may exist or be embodied; as, dangers of every *shape*.
8. definite, regular, or suitable form; orderly arrangement; as, his story began to take *shape*.
9. condition; state, especially of health; as, the injured man was in bad *shape*. [Colloq.]
10. a portion of gelatin, etc. prepared in a shape, or mold.
to shape up; (a) to develop to a definite form, condition, etc.; (b) to develop satisfactorily or favorably. [Colloq.]
to take shape; to come to have definite condition, etc.; to show distinct development.

shāpe, *v.t.*; shaped (shāpt), *pt., pp.*; shaping, *ppr.* [AS. *sceapan, scapan*; Goth. *skapjan*; Ice. *skapa*; Dan. *skabe*; O.H.G. *scaffan*, to shape, form, create.]
1. to give definite shape to; to make, as by cutting or molding material.
2. to arrange, fashion, express, or devise in definite form, as a plan, answer, etc.
3. to adapt or adjust; as, shape your *plans* to your abilities.
4. to direct or conduct, as one's life, the course of events, etc.
5. to appoint; decree; ordain. [Obs.]
6. to image; to conceive.
Syn.—form, mold, figure, delineate, contrive, create, execute, make.

shāpe, *v.i.* 1. to become suited; to conform. [Rare.]
2. to come about; to happen. [Rare.]
3. to take shape or form (often with *into*). [Colloq.]

shāpe'less, *a.* 1. without distinct or regular shape or form.
2. not pleasing to the eye; without symmetry; unshapely.
shāpe'less·ness, *n.* shapeless condition.
shāpe'li·ness, *n.* the state or quality of being shapely.
shāpe'ly, *a.*; *comp.* shapelier; *superl.* shapeliest. 1. well-formed; having a regular shape; symmetrical; pleasing to the eye.
2. likely; suitable. [Obs.]
shāp'ẽr, *n.* 1. one who molds, shapes, or adjusts.
2. a combination planer and lathe for metalwork.
3. in woodworking, a machine for cutting moldings.
4. a stamping press for sheet metal.
shä'pọọ, *n.* a wild sheep of Northern India.
shaps, *n.pl.* [contraction of Sp. *chaparejos.*] leather leggings or riding overalls. [Dial.]
Shä'rȧ, *n.* Sharra.
shärd, *n.* [AS. *sceard,* from *scearan,* to shear, separate.]
1. a piece or fragment of an earthen vessel, or of any brittle substance; a potsherd.
2. the shell of an egg or a snail; a scale.
3. the thin, hard wing cover of a beetle or weevil.
4. a gap, as a gap in a fence; an opening in a wood. [Obs.]
5. chard. [Obs.]
6. a boundary or division. [Obs.]
7. dung. [Obs.]
shärd'-bōrne, *a.* borne on sharded wings, as a beetle. [Obs.]
shärd'ed, *a.* having wings sheathed with a hard covering; as, the *sharded* beetle.
shärd'y, *a.* having shards.
shāre, *n.* [AS. *scearu,* a portion, a sharing, a division, from *scear, scær,* that which divides, the share of a plow, both from *sceran,* to cut.]
1. a part; a portion; a quantity. [Obs.]
2. a part or portion which is allotted or belongs to an individual; part contributed by one.
3. a just, due, reasonable, or full share; as, everyone has done his *share* of work, we had our *share* of laughs.
4. any of the parts or portions into which the ownership of a piece of property is divided; especially, any one of the equal parts into which the capital stock of a corporation is divided.
5. the sharebone.
on shares; with each person concerned taking a (usually equal) share of the profit or loss.
share and share alike; in equal shares.
to go shares; to partake; to be equally concerned; to take part jointly, as in an enterprise.
shāre, *v.t.*; shared, *pt., pp.*; sharing, *ppr.* [AS. *sceran,* to divide, cut.]
1. to divide in portions; to distribute in shares.
2. to partake or enjoy with others; to seize and possess jointly or in common.
shāre, *v.i.* to have or take a share or part; to participate (often with *in*).
shāre, *n.* [ME. *schar*; AS. *scear,* from *sceran,* to cut.] the part of a plow or other agricultural tool that cuts the soil; a plowshare.
shāre'ȧ·ble, shār'ȧ·ble, *a.* that can be shared.
shāre'bēam, *n.* that part of a plow to which the share is attached.
shāre'bōne, *n.* the pubis, a bone located at the upper and fore part of the pelvis.
shāre'brō"kẽr, *n.* a dealer or broker in stocks and bonds. [Brit.]
shāre'çrop, *v.t.* and *v.i.*; sharecropped, *pt., pp.*; sharecropping, *ppr.* to work (land) as a sharecropper.
shāre'çrop"pẽr, *n.* a tenant farmer who obtains on credit land, a house, and tools and seeds for farming, from a landowner with whom he shares the crop.
shāre'hōld"ẽr, *n.* one who holds or owns a share or shares.
shār'ẽr, *n.* one who shares.
shāre'wŏrt, *n.* a composite plant, *Pallenis spinosa,* native to southern Europe. [Obs.]
shärk, *n.* [prob. from G. *schurke,* scoundrel, rogue, sharper.]
1. a viciously dishonest person; a swindler; a cheat.
2. a person having great ability in a given activity; an adept; an expert. [Slang.]
3. a trick; a fraud. [Obs.]
shärk, *v.t.* to get by fraud or strategems. [Archaic.]
shärk, *v.i.* to live by the methods of a shark, or swindler.
shärk, *n.* [prob. same word as prec.] one of a group of elasmobranch fishes mostly marine, with a slender, rounded body, separate lateral gill openings, and a thick, fleshy tail. The mouth is large and located on the underside

WHITE SHARK (*Carcharodon carchiaras*)

of the body. The slate-gray skin is usually very rough, covered with a multitude of little osseous tubercles or placoid scales. The sharks are divided into several families, as the *Carchariidæ,* or sand sharks, *Lamnidæ,*

HAMMERHEAD SHARK (*Sphyrna zygæna*)

or mackerel sharks, *Carcharhinidae,* or requiem sharks, *Squalidae,* or dogfishes, and many others. Most sharks are fish-eaters and the larger ones will attack man.
shärk, *v.i.* to fish for sharks.
shärk'ẽr, *n.* one who lives by sharking; an artful fellow. [Obs.]
shärk'ing, *n.* the act of one who sharks.
shärk'skin, *n.* 1. leather made from the skin of a shark.
2. a cloth of cotton or rayon, with a smooth, silky surface used for summer suits, etc.
3. (a) a small, pebbly pattern woven into fabric; (b) fabric woven with such a pattern.
shärn, *n.* cattle dung. [Scot.]
shärp, *a.*; *comp.* sharper; *superl.* sharpest. [ME. *scharp*; AS. *scearp*; Ice. *skarpr*; D. *scherp,* sharp.]
1. having a very thin edge or fine point; keen; suitable for use in cutting or piercing; as, a *sharp* knife; a *sharp* needle.
2. terminating in a point or edge; not obtuse or rounded; peaked; as, a hill terminates in a *sharp* peak or a *sharp* ridge.
3. clearly defined; distinct; clear; as, a *sharp* difference.
4. made up of hard, angular particles, as sand.
5. quick, acute, or penetrating in perception or intellect; clever; shrewd.
6. showing or having a keen awareness; attentive; vigilant; as, *sharp* eyes, *sharp* lookout.
7. crafty; designing; underhanded.
8. severe; harsh; biting; sarcastic; as, *sharp* words; a *sharp* rebuke.
9. fierce; ardent; fiery; violent; as, a *sharp* contest.
10. not gradual; acute; abrupt; as, a *sharp* descent; a *sharp* turn.
11. brisk; active; vigorous; as, a *sharp* run, encounter, etc.
12. having a keen effect on the senses or emotions; specifically, (a) cold; cutting, as the wind; (b) severe; intense; acute; keen, as pain, grief, appetite, etc.; (c) strong; biting; pungent, as in taste or smell; (d) high-pitched; shrill; piercing: said of sound; (e) brilliant; intense; as, a *sharp* flash of light.
13. attractively dressed or groomed; good-looking; handsome; beautiful. [Slang.]
14. in phonetics, voiceless; surd; as, the *sharp* mutes *p, t, k.*
15. in music, (a) raised a semitone or half step, as a note; (b) too high; so high as to be out of tune or above true pitch; (c) with the signature in sharps.
sharp practice; the taking of an unfair advantage.
Syn.—biting, keen, acute, penetrating, shrewd.
shärp, *adv.* 1. in a sharp manner; specifically, (a) abruptly or briskly; (b) attentively or alertly; (c) so as to have a sharp point or edge; (d) keenly; piercingly; (e) in music, above the true pitch.
2. exactly; precisely; promptly; to the moment; not a minute behind.
shärp, *n.* 1. in music, (a) a note or tone one half step above another; (b) the sign (♯) which, when placed on a line or space of the staff at the commencement of a movement, raises all the notes on that line or space or their octaves a semitone in pitch. When, in the course of the movement, it precedes a note, it has the same effect on it or its repetition, but only within the same bar.
2. a pointed weapon. [Archaic.]
3. [*usually in pl.*] a long sewing needle with a very fine point, the finest of the three grades, sharps, betweens, and blunts.
4. the part of a stream where the water runs swiftly. [Rare.]
5. [*pl.*] middlings. [Brit.]
6. a long, flat-bottomed boat carrying one or more triangular sails, used by oystermen on the Connecticut coast. [Rare.]
7. one who is an expert in his business or profession; an expert or adept. [Colloq.]
8. a sharper. [Colloq.]
shärp, *v.t.*; sharped, *pt., pp.*; sharping, *ppr.* 1. to make keen or acute; to sharpen. [Dial.]
2. in musical composition, to make sharp; to raise (a note) a semitone.
shärp, *v.i.* 1. to engage in sharp practice; to swindle.
2. in music, to sing or play above the true pitch.
shärp'-çut, *a.* 1. cut so as to be sharp.
2. clearly outlined or defined; clear; distinct.
shärp'-ēared', *a.* 1. having pointed ears.
2. having keenly sensitive hearing.
shärp'-edġed, *a.* having a fine edge or edges; cutting; sharp.
shärp'en, *v.t.* and *v.i.*; sharpened, *pt., pp.*; sharpening, *ppr.* to make or become sharp or sharper.
shärp'en·ẽr, *n.* one who or that which sharpens.
shärp'ẽr, *n.* 1. a person, usually a gambler, dishonest in dealing with others; a trickster; a rogue; a swindler; a rascal.
2. a large oyster, native to the Gulf coast. [Dial.]
shärp'-eȳed' (-īd'), *a.* seeing things that are hard to see; having keen sight or perception.
shärp'ie, *n.* [from *sharp,* with reference to the sharp lines and fast sailing qualities.] a long, narrow, flat-bottomed, New England fishing boat: it has a centerboard and one or two masts, each rigged with a triangular sail.
shärp'ly, *adv.* in a sharp manner.
shärp'ness, *n.* the state or quality of being sharp.
shärp'-nōṣed', *a.* 1. having a thin, pointed nose.
2. having a sharp, projecting front.
3. having a keen sense of smell.
shärp'-set, *a.* 1. intensely desirous; affected by a keen appetite, as for food.
2. set so as to be sharp or at an acute angle.
shärp'-shinned' hạwk, a small, North American hawk, *Accipiter velox,* with a dark-blue back and a barred, reddish and white breast, feeding mainly on small birds.
shärp'shọọt"ẽr, *n.* 1. a person who shoots with great accuracy; a good marksman.
2. in the United States Army, (a) a rating of proficiency of a rifleman, ranking above a marksman and below an expert; (b) a soldier with this rating.
shärp'shọọt"ing, *n.* a shooting with great precision and effect.
shärp'-sīght"ed (-sīt"), *a.* 1. having keen sight; sharp-eyed.
2. sharp-witted; keenly observant.
shärp'tāil, *n.* the sharp-tailed grouse.
shärp'-tŏngued' (-tungd'), *a.* using or characterized by severe, sharp, or harshly critical language.
shärp'-wit"ted, *a.* having or showing keen intelligence or discernment; thinking quickly and effectively.
Shär'rȧ, *n.* 1. *pl.* **Shär'rȧ,** one of a Mongoloid people living in Outer Mongolia.
2. the East Mongolic language of the Sharra.
Also spelled *Shara.*

shar′rag, *n.* same as *shearhog.*

Shas′tȧ dāi′ṣy, [after Mt. *Shasta,* a mountain in northern California.] a kind of daisylike chrysanthemum; also, its flower.

shas′tēr, shas′trȧ, *n.* [Sans. *shastra,* from *shas,* to teach.] any one of the scriptures of the Hindus.

shath′mŏnt, *n.* a shaftment. [Scot.]

shat′tēr, *v.t.*; shattered, *pt., pp.*; shattering, *ppr.* [ME. *schateren,* to dash or scatter, a weakened form of *scatter.*]

1. to break at once into many pieces; to dash, burst, or part by violence into fragments; to rend, split, or rive into splinters; as, an explosion of gunpowder *shatters* a rock.

2. to damage severely, as a structure, one's health or nerves, etc.; to give a destructive shock to; as, his constitution was *shattered* by dissipation.

3. to scatter; to disperse. [Obs.]

shat′tēr, *v.i.* to be broken into fragments; to fall or crumble to pieces; to smash.

Syn.—split, dissipate, disrupt, derange, break in pieces, rend, demolish, shiver, dismember, disintegrate.

shat′tēr, *n.* one part of many into which anything is broken; a fragment: used in the plural, and chiefly in the phrases *in* or *into shatters.*

shat′tēr·brāined, *a.* mentally disordered; intellectually weak.

shat′tēr·pāt″ed, *a.* shatterbrained.

shat′tēr·prọọf, *a.* that will not shatter.

shat′tēr·y, *a.* brittle; easily falling into many pieces; also, [Brit. Dial.] not compact; loose of texture.

shāve, *v.t.*; shaved, *pt.*; shaved *or* shaven, *pp.*; shaving, *ppr.* [ME. *schaven*; AS. *sceafan*; Ice. *skafa*; Dan. *skave,* to scrape.]

1. to cut or scrape away a thin slice or slices from, as the edge of a plank.

2. to cut or scrape into thin sections, as ice.

3. to cut off (hair, especially the beard) at the surface of the skin (often with *off* or *away*).

4. to cut the hair to the surface of (an area of the body); to cut the beard of (a person).

5. to pass close to or skim the surface of; to graze.

6. to cut short or trim closely, as grass.

7. to lower by a slight margin, as a price. [Colloq.]

8. in commerce, to purchase (a note, draft, etc.) at a discount greater than the legal rate of interest. [Colloq.]

9. to strip; to cheat; to fleece. [Colloq.]

shāve, *v.i.* 1. to remove hair from the skin with a razor or other shaving implement; to shave oneself.

2. to make close, hard bargains; to cheat; to practice extortion.

shāve, *n.* 1. a tool used for shaving, paring, slicing, etc.

2. something shaved or sliced off; a shaving.

3. the act of shaving the beard or the result of this; as, a sharp razor means a good *shave.*

4. in the stock market, a premium paid for extending payment or delivery, or a consideration given for the right to modify a contract; also, a high discount for cashing a note or draft.

5. the act of nearly scraping or grazing; a bare miss; a narrow escape. [Colloq.]

6. a long blade with a handle at each end for shaving wood; a drawing knife.

shāve grȧss, the scouring rush.

shāve hook, a triangular plate of steel, with sharpened edges, used in scraping the surfaces of metal which are to be soldered, so that the solder may adhere.

shāve′ling, *n.* 1. a person whose head is entirely or partly shaved, especially a priest or monk: used contemptuously.

2. a youth.

shāv′en, *v.* alternative past participle of *shave.*

shāv′en, *a.* 1. shaved or tonsured.

2. closely trimmed.

shāv′ēr, *n.* 1. one who shaves; specifically, one whose occupation is to shave.

2. an instrument used in shaving; as, an electric *shaver.*

3. a sharp driver of bargains; one who fleeces by usury and extortion.

4. a youngster; a lad; a boy. [Colloq.]

shāve′-tāil″, *n.* [orig., an unbroken mule.] a second lieutenant, especially one recently appointed. [Slang.]

Shā′vi·ăn, *a.* [from Mod. L. *Shavius,* Latinized from *Shaw.*] of or characteristic of George Bernard Shaw or his work.

Shā′vi·ăn, *n.* an admirer of Shaw or his work.

shāv′ing, *n.* 1. the action of a person or thing that shaves.

2. something shaved off with a shave, a knife, a plane, or other cutting instrument.

shāv′ing brush, a short, cylindrical brush used in shaving to spread lather over the part to be shaved.

shāv′ing çrēam, a creamy salve used to moisten and soften the beard in shaving.

shāv′ing çup, a cup in which the lather for shaving is made.

shaw, *n.* [Ice. *skogr*; Sw. *skugga*; Dan. *skove,* a thicket, and *skygge,* a shade.]

1. a thicket; a clump of bushes or trees. [Archaic or Dial.]

2. a stem with the leaves, as of a potato or turnip. [Scot.]

shaw′fowl, *n.* a target made to represent some fowl. [Obs.]

shawl, *n.* [Per. *shāl.*] an article of dress, usually of wool, of a square or oblong shape, worn principally by women, as a covering for the head or shoulders.

shawl, *v.t.* to cover with a shawl.

shawl gōat, the Kashmir goat.

shawl strap, a device consisting of straps, a handle, buckles, etc., for carrying a package.

shawm, *n.* [OFr. *chaume* or *chalemie,* from L. *calamus,* a reed.] a wind instrument, resembling the oboe, having a globular mouthpiece enclosing a double reed. [Obs.]

Shaw·nee′, *n.*; *pl.* **Shaw·nee′, Shaw·nees′,** [from Am. Ind. (Algonquian).] a member of a tribe of Algonquian Indians that migrated from the Savannah River Valley into Ohio and Indiana and now live in Oklahoma.

shāy, *n.* [back-formation from *chaise,* assumed as pl.] a light carriage; a chaise.

shāy′ȧ·rọọt, *n.* same as *chay.*

shē, *pron.* [ME. *sche, sheo,* from AS. *seó,* f. of *se,* that, but afterward used as a definite article. Though now used as the feminine corresponding to *he,* it is not strictly so, having taken the place of *heó,* the proper feminine, in the twelfth century. It was first used in the northern dialects as a pronoun in the forms of *sco, sho.* The possessive *her* and the later *hers* are from the old feminine pronoun *heó,* genit. *hire*; whereas, *seó* had genit. *thære.*] the girl, woman, or female animal (or, sometimes, the object regarded as female) previously mentioned; *she* is the nominative case form, *her* the objective, *her* or *hers* the possessive, and *herself* the intensive and reflexive of the feminine third personal pronoun.

shē, *n.* a girl, woman, or female animal; as, our dog is a *she.*

shē-, a combining form meaning *female,* used in hyphenated compounds, as *she*-bear.

shē′ȧ, *n.* [Mandingo *si, se.*] an African tree, *Bassia parkii,* whose seeds yield shea butter.

shē′ȧ but′tēr, a thick, white fat, used as a food, etc., obtained by crushing, boiling, and straining the seed of the shea tree.

shēad′ing, *n.* [AS. *sceâdan*; Goth. *skaidan*; D. and G. *scheiden,* to divide; akin to *shed,* as in *watershed.*] any one of the six districts into which the Isle of Man is divided.

shēaf, *n.*; *pl.* **shēaveṣ,** [AS. *sceaf,* a sheaf, a bundle, as of arrows; D. *schoof*; Ice. *skauf.* The root is that of *shove,* seen in AS. *scûfan,* to shove, thrust, push.]

1. a bunch of cut stalks of wheat, rye, oats, barley, etc. bound together.

2. any bundle or collection of things set or bound together; as, a *sheaf* of arrows.

3. a sheave.

4. a quiverful of arrows, usually twenty-four in number.

shēaf, *v.t.*; sheafed, *pt., pp.*; sheafing, *ppr.* to collect and bind in a sheaf or sheaves.

shēaf, *v.i.* to make sheaves.

shēaf′y, *a.* pertaining to, consisting of, or resembling a sheaf or sheaves.

shēal, *n.* [Ice. *skáli, skaale,* a hut or shed, from root of *shelter, shield.*] a temporary shelter; a hut or small cottage used by hunters, fishermen, shepherds, etc. [Scot.]

shēal, *v.t.* to shelter. [Scot.]

shēal, *v.t.* to shell or husk. [Brit. Dial.]

shēal′ing, *n.* a pod, shell, or husk. [Scot.]

shēar, *v.t.*; sheared, *pt.*; sheared *or* shorn, *pp.*; shearing, *ppr.* [AS. *sceran,* to shear, shave, share, divide; Ice. *skera,* to cut.]

1. to cut with shears or a similar sharp-edged instrument.

2. to remove (the hair, wool, etc.) by cutting or clipping; as, to *shear* a fleece.

3. to cut or clip the hair, wool, etc. from.

4. to strip or divest (*of* a power, right, etc.).

5. to fleece; to swindle by extortion or sharp practice.

6. to reap with a sickle. [Dial.]

shēar, *v.i.* 1. (a) to use a cutting tool, as shears, in trimming or cutting wool, shrubbery, metal, etc.; (b) [Dial.] to use a sickle in reaping.

2. to come apart or break under the action of shearing stress.

3. to move by or as if by cutting; as, the airplane *sheared* through the clouds.

4. in mining, to make vertical cuts in a coal seam.

shēar, *n.* [AS. *scear.*]

1. (a) [Rare.] a pair of large scissors; shears; (b) a single blade of such a pair.

2. any machine used in cutting metal, especially sheet metal.

3. the action, process, or result of shearing.

4. something shorn or removed by shearing, as a sheep or its wool.

5. a shearing: used in designating a sheep's age; as, a sheep of three *shears.*

6. (a) shearing stress; (b) any strain or distortion in shape resulting from the action of shearing stress.

7. a sheer.

shēar′bill, *n.* the black skimmer.

shēar′ēr, *n.* one who or that which shears; as, a *shearer* of sheep.

shēar′hog, *n.* a sheep after the first shearing. [Brit. Dial.]

shēar hulk, a sheer hulk.

shēar′ing, *n.* 1. the act or operation of clipping with or as with shears; as, the *shearing* of metallic plates and bars.

2. something cut off with shears; as, the whole *shearing* of a flock; the *shearings* from cloth.

3. a shearling.

4. the act or operation of reaping. [Scot.]

5. in mining, the making of vertical cuts at the ends of a portion of a seam of coal.

6. tilting; the process of making shear steel.

shēar′ing dīeṣ, in machinery, those cutting dies which consist of a shearing punch and matrix designed for shearing or cutting off certain parts, as work, from the main body or stock.

shēar′ing mȧ·chïne′, 1. a machine used for cutting plates and bars of iron and other metals.

2. a machine for shearing cloth.

shēar′ing stress, the action or force causing two contacting parts or layers to slide upon each other, moving apart in opposite directions parallel to the plane of their contact.

shēar legṣ, same as *shears,* sense 3: also *sheer legs.*

shēar′ling, *n.* a sheep that has been sheared once, usually a yearling.

shēar′măn, *n.*; *pl.* **shear′men,** one whose work it is to shear cloth, metal, etc.

shēarṣ, *n.pl.* 1. large scissors.

2. any of several large tools or machines used to cut metal, etc. by the action of two opposed cutting edges working against each other upon the material being cut.

3. a device used in hoisting, consisting of two or more guyed poles or legs spread at the base and joined at the top to hold hoisting tackle: also *shear* (or *sheer*) *legs.*

4. the bed or track of a lathe, upon which the lathe head, puppet head, and rest are placed.

rotary shears; a machine consisting of two revolving circular disks or knives with overlapping edges, used for cutting sheet metal.

shēar steel, blistered steel treated by a process of drawing.

shēar struç′tūre, in geology, any rock structure resulting either entirely or partially from faulting.

shēar′tāil, *n.* 1. a hummingbird of the genus *Thaumastura,* having a forked tail.

2. a tern.

shēar′wa″tēr, *n.* 1. any of several black-and-white marine birds of the genus *Puffinus,* having the tip of the lower mandible curved downward and the nostrils having separate openings: they usually skim the water in flight; they are the size of a pigeon and are related to the petrels and albatrosses. *Puffinus cinereus*, the greater shearwater, is found on the southwest coasts of England and Wales. The Manx shearwater, *Puffinus anglorum*, is common on the British coasts and occurs also in more northern regions.

MANX SHEARWATER (*Puffinus anglorum*)

2. the skimmer.

shēar zōne, in geology, a section of shear structure dividing masses of rock.

shēat′fish, *n.*; *pl.* **shēat′fish** or **shēat′fish·eṣ,** [prob. from AS. *sceota*, recorded as "trout," from base of *sceotan*, to shoot.] any of various fishes of the family *Siluridæ*; specifically, an extremely large fresh-water catfish, *Silurus glanis*, of eastern and central Europe: some specimens weigh over 300 pounds.

sheath, *n.* [AS. *scæth*, *sceāth*; Dan. *skede*; Ice. *skīthi*, a sheath; generally referred to same root as *shed*; AS. *sceādan*, to divide.]

1. a case for the blade of a knife, sword, etc.

2. any somewhat similar covering; as, (a) in botany, a leaf base which wraps round the stem on which it grows, as in the scape of many endogenous plants; (b) the wing case of an insect; (c) the membrane around a muscle.

3. a structure of loose stones for confining a river within its banks.

sheath of Henle; a connective tissue envelope of a nerve fiber outside of the neurilemma.

shēath, *v.t.* to sheathe.

shēath′bill, *n.* either of two antarctic, snow-white sea birds having the base of the bill covered with a horny, saddlelike sheath.

shēath′clạw, *n.* a gecko of the genus *Thecodactylus*.

shēathe, *v.t.*; sheathed, *pt., pp.*; sheathing, *ppr.* [ME. *schethen*, from *schethe*.]

1. to put into a sheath or scabbard; as, to *sheathe* a sword or dagger.

2. to enclose in or protect with a casing or covering; to case or cover, as with boards, metal, or cloth.

3. to thrust or sink into flesh, as a sword.

4. to retract (claws).

5. to cover up; to hide. [Rare.]

6. (a) [Obs.] to take away sharpness or acridity from; (b) to blunt; to obtund.

to sheathe the sword; to cease war and to make peace.

shēathed, *a.* encased in, provided with, or covered with a sheath or sheathing; vaginate.

shēath′ẽr, *n.* one who or that which sheathes.

shēath′fish, *n.* same as *sheatfish*.

shēath′ing, *a.* covering or enclosing with a sheath; as, the *sheathing* stipules.

shēath′ing, *n.* 1. the act of placing in or encasing with a sheath.

2. something that sheathes or encases; covering; casing; specifically, (a) the inner covering of boards or waterproof material on the roof or outside wall of a frame house; (b) the protective covering of a ship's bottom or hull; (c) the material for either of these.

shēath knīfe (nīf), a knife carried in a sheath.

shēath′less, *a.* without a sheath; unsheathed.

shēath′-winged, *a.* sharded.

shēath′y, *a.* like a sheath. [Obs.]

shē′ȧ tree, same as *shea*.

shēave, *n.* [a variant of *shive*.]

1. a grooved wheel in a pulley block, mast, yard, etc. on which a rope works; the wheel of a pulley or any similarly grooved wheel.

2. a sliding scutcheon for covering a keyhole.

3. a cut; a slice. [Dial.]

shēave, *v.t.*; sheaved, *pt., pp.*; sheaving, *ppr.* to gather or bring together into a sheaf or into sheaves.

shēave, *v.i.* to stop or reverse a rowboat by action of the oars.

shēaved, *a.* 1. made of straw. [Obs.]

2. spreading or flaring at the top like a sheaf.

shēaveṣ, *n.* 1. plural of *sheaf*.

2. plural of *sheave*.

Shē′bȧ, Queen of, in the Bible, the queen who visited King Solomon to investigate his reputed wisdom and greatness: 1 Kings. x. 1–13.

shē′-bal″săm, *n.* the balsam fir, *Abies balsamea*.

sheb′ăn·dẽr, *n.* in the East Indies, a commercial officer.

shē·bang′, *n.* [a variant of *shebeen*.]

1. a rough dwelling; a shanty. [Slang.]

2. a particular matter of concern; an affair, business, establishment, contrivance, thing, etc. [Slang.]

She·bät′, *n.* [Heb.] the fifth month of the Jewish calendar.

shē·been′, *n.* [Ir. *seapa*, a shop.] an unlicensed house or establishment where liquor is sold illegally. [Chiefly Ir. and Scot.]

Shē·chī′nȧh, *n.* same as *Shekinah*.

shech′i·tȧ, *n.* the method of slaughtering animales for food in accordance with the Jewish dietary law.

sheck′lȧ·ton, *n.* ciclatoun.

shed, *v.t.*; shed, *pt., pp.*; shedding, *ppr.* [ME. *scheden*; AS. *sceādan*, *scādan*, to separate, distinguish, hence to scatter.]

1. to separate or part; as, to *shed* the hair. [Brit. Dial.]

2. to cause to flow in a stream or fall in drops; as, to *shed* tears; to *shed* blood.

3. to repel; to throw off; to cause to flow off without penetrating; as, a roof or a covering of oiled cloth, or the like, is said to *shed* water.

4. to send forth or spread about; to diffuse; as, flowers *shed* their fragrance; books *shed* light on the subject.

5. to pour out; to give off; to emit.

6. to cast off or lose (a natural growth or covering, as leaves, skin, hair, etc.).

7. to sprinkle; to intersperse; as, hair *shed* with gray. [Rare.]

8. in weaving, to separate warp threads for the shuttle.

shed, *v.i.* 1. to shed a natural growth or covering; as, our dog is *shedding* badly.

2. to drop off or fall out, as leaves, seeds, etc.

3. to be poured out; to be spilled. [Dial.]

shed, *n.* [ME. *schede*, a division.]

1. a line or ridge from which water flows in two directions; a watershed.

2. a separation or division; as, the *shed* of the hair. [Obs.]

3. in weaving, the interstice between the different parts of the warp of a loom, through which the shuttle passes.

shed, *n.* [earlier *shad*, var. of *shade*, from AS. *scead*, in sense "protection."]

1. a small, roughly built shelter, storage place, or workshop, built either as a separate structure or as a lean-to.

2. a large, strongly built, barnlike or hangarlike structure, as for storage, often with open front or sides.

shē′d, a contraction of (a) she had; (b) she would.

shed′dẽr, *n.* 1. one who or that which sheds.

2. in zoology, that which is shedding or has shed its shell, as a crab, lobster, etc.

3. a female salmon after spawning.

shed′ding, *n.* 1. the act of one who or that which sheds.

2. that which is shed.

shed′ding, *n.* a collection of sheds.

Shẹ′dụ, *n.*; *pl.* **Shẹ′dim,** [Assyrian-Babylonian *shēdū*.] in Babylonian religion, one of the semidivine beings depicted as enormous bulls or lions with human heads.

sheel′fȧ, *n.* the chaffinch.

sheel′ing, *n.* a shelter; a sheal.

sheel′y, *n.* the sheelfa, or chaffinch.

sheen, *a.* [AS. *scēne*, bright, the old orthography of *shine*.] bright; shining; glittering. [Poetic.]

sheen, *n.* 1. luster; splendor; brightness.

2. bright or shining attire.

sheen, *v.i.* to shine. [Dial. or Poetic.]

sheen′ly, *adv.* radiantly; brightly. [Rare.]

sheen′y, *a.*; *comp.* sheenier; *superl.* sheeniest, bright; shining.

sheep, *n.*; *pl.* **sheep,** [ME. *schep*; AS. *sceāp*, *scēp*, and D. *schaap*; G. *schaf*, a sheep.]

BROAD-TAILED SHEEP (*Ovis laticauda*)

1. any of a wide variety of ruminant animals of the genus *Ovis*, related to the goats, with heavy wool, edible flesh called mutton, and skin used in making leather, parchment, etc.: they are found wild in the higher mountains of Asia, Europe, Africa, and North America. The principal English varieties of the domesticated sheep are the large Leicester, the Cotswold, the Southdown, the Cheviot, and the black-faced breeds. The broad-tailed sheep, *Ovis laticauda*, is common in Asia and Egypt and is noted for its large, heavy tail.

2. a person who is silly, stupid, meek, timid, defenseless, etc.

3. leather made from the skin of sheep; specifically, leather used in bookbinding.

4. mankind regarded as being under the government and protection of God; also, a congregation considered as under a pastor.

to make sheep's eyes at; to look at with great or exaggerated tenderness; to look shyly and lovingly at.

sheep′back, *n.* roche moutonnée.

sheep′ber″ry, *n.*; *pl.* **sheep′ber″rieṣ,** a shrub or small tree, *Viburnum lentago*, native to North America, with white flowers and blue-black berries.

sheep′bīt″ẽr, *n.* a shepherd dog that bites sheep; hence, a petty thief. [Obs.]

sheep bot, a larva of the botfly, *Œstrus ovis*, common to Europe and America, and very destructive to sheep.

sheep′çot, *n.* same as *sheepcote*.

sheep′çōte, *n.* an enclosure for sheep; a sheepfold.

sheep′-dip, *n.* any chemical preparation used as a bath to free sheep from vermin and sheep scab or to clean the fleece and skin before shearing.

sheep dog, a dog trained to herd and protect sheep; specifically, (a) a collie; (b) a large, gentle dog with a short tail and long, rough hair covering the face and eyes: also called *old English sheep dog*.

sheep′fāced (-fāst), *a.* sheepish.

sheep′fōld, *n.* a place where sheep are penned or confined.

sheep′head″ed (-hed″), *a.* dull; feeble-minded; silly.

sheep′hẽrd·ẽr, *n.* a person who herds or tends a large flock of sheep grazing in open pasture.

sheep′hook, *n.* a shepherds' crook.

sheep′ish, *a.* 1. like a sheep; shy; bashful or embarrassed in manner.

2. resembling a sheep in meekness, timidity, etc.

sheep′ish·ly, *adv.* in a sheepish manner.

sheep′ish·ness, *n.* the character of being sheepish.

sheep′kill, *n.* same as *sheep laurel*.

sheep lạu′rel, a small North American shrub, *Kalmia angustifolia*, with pinkish flowers, the leaves of which are considered poisonous to sheep.

sheep′man, *n.*; *pl.* **sheep′men,** 1. a person who makes a business of raising sheep.

2. a sheepherder or shepherd.

sheep′mȧs″tẽr, *n.* an owner of sheep.

sheep pest, an Australian weed, *Acæna ovina*, the barbed fruit of which sticks to the wool of sheep.

sheep pox, a contagious disease among sheep, characterized by a skin eruption resembling that of smallpox.

sheep rack, 1. the starling.

2. a portable rack holding food for feeding sheep.

sheep run, same as *sheepwalk*.

sheep's′-bēard, *n.* an ornamental herb of the genus *Urospermum*, found in the Mediterranean region.

sheep's eȳe (ī), a bashful, amorous glance: usually in the plural; as, he was casting *sheep's eyes* at her.

sheep's′-foot, *n.* in printing, a tool having a hammer at one end and a claw at the other.

sheep'shank, *n.* 1. the shank of a sheep.
2. a kind of knot used for shortening a rope: see *knot*, illus.
3. something thin, scrawny, or weak.

sheeps'head (-hed), *n.* 1. a sheep's head prepared as food.
2. a foolish or stupid person.
3. *pl.* **sheeps'head** or **sheeps'heads**, a large, salt-water food fish, *Archosargus probatocephalus*, with massive head and forepart, two sets of teeth, and a striped body: it is common along the Atlantic coast of the United States; also, any one of several other fishes, as the drum, porgy, moonfish, etc.

sheep'shēar″ēr, *n.* 1. one who shears sheep.
2. any tool or machine used in shearing sheep.

sheep'shēar″ing, *n.* 1. the act of shearing sheep.
2. the time of shearing sheep; also, a feast held on that occasion.

sheep sil'vēr, a sum of money formerly paid tenants in substitution of the ancient right of keeping a few sheep. [Brit.]

sheep'skin, *n.* 1. the skin of a sheep; especially, a skin dressed with the fleece on it.
2. the parchment or leather prepared from it: diplomas and other documents are sometimes written on parchment.
3. a diploma. [Colloq.]

sheep sor'rel, a weed, *Rumex acetosella*, with fleshy, acid-tasting leaves, that grows in dry places.

sheep'split, *n.* split sheepskin leather.

sheeps'-wool, *n.* a sponge, *Spongia equina*, found among the Florida Keys.

sheep tick, the *Melophagus ovinus*, a dipterous insect of the family *Hippoboscidæ*, that lives as a parasite on sheep.

SHEEP TICK (natural size and magnified)

sheep'wạlk (-wạk), *n.* a pasture for sheep; a place where sheep feed.

sheep'y, *a.* having the appearance of sheep; sheepish.

sheer, *a.* [ME. *schere*, *skere*; Ice. *skær*, bright, clear; Dan. *skær*, pure, clear, bright.]
1. pure; not mixed with anything foreign; unmingled; as, *sheer* ale.
2. thin; transparent; diaphanous: said of textiles; as, *sheer* muslin.
3. absolute; unqualified; downright; as, *sheer* falsehood.
4. straight up and down; perpendicular; precipitous, as the face of a cliff.
Syn.—pure, mere, unmixed, unqualified, unmitigated, absolute, unadulerated.

sheer, *adv.* 1. completely; utterly; outright.
2. perpendicularly or very steeply.

sheer, *n.* thin, fine material, or a garment made of it.

sheer, *v.t.* to shear. [Obs.]

sheer, *v.i.*; sheered, *pt.*, *pp.*; sheering, *ppr.* [D. *scheren*, to shear, withdraw, stretch.] to deviate from a course, as a ship; to turn aside; to swerve.
to sheer off; to turn or move aside to a distance.
to sheer up; to turn and approach to a place or ship obliquely.

sheer, *v.t.* to cause to turn or sheer.

sheer, *n.* 1. the upward curve or bend of a ship's hull or deck lines as seen from the side.
2. the oblique position in which a ship is sometimes kept at single bow anchor, to keep her clear of it.
3. a swerving course; an abrupt change in a course.
4. the paint strake of a vessel's hull.
to break sheer; to deviate from the position called sheer and risk fouling the anchor.

sheer bat'ten, 1. in shipbuilding, a long strip of wood nailed to the ribs to show the position of the wales or bends before bolting the planks on.
2. same as *sheer pole*.

sheer bo͝om, a boom fixed in a slanting manner across a stream to direct floating logs.

sheer hook, a combination of hooks having the concave curves sharpened: used formerly in naval engagements in order to entangle or cut the enemy's rigging.

SHEER HOOKS

sheer hulk, an old ship cut down to the lower deck, and fitted with shears or other apparatus for hoisting purposes.

sheer legs, a kind of hoisting apparatus; shears.

SHEER HULK

sheer'ly, *adv.* thoroughly; quite; absolutely.

sheer pōle, an iron rod lashed to the shrouds just above the deadeyes to prevent the shrouds from turning.

sheer strāke, in shipbuilding, the uppermost strake under the gunwale: also called *paint strake*.

Sheer Thurs'dāy, [Ice. *skīri-thorsdagr*, from *skīra*, to cleanse, purify.] Maundy Thursday, the day that precedes Good Friday.

sheer'wạ·tēr, *n.* same as *shearwater*.

sheet, *n.* [ME. *schete*; AS. *scete*, a sheet, the fold of a garment, closely allied to AS. *sceat*, a nook, a projecting corner.]
1. a large, rectangular piece of cotton, linen, etc., used in pairs as bedding, one above and one below the body.
2. a sail. [Poetic.]
3. (a) a rectangular piece of paper, especially one of a number of pieces cut to a definite, uniform size, as for use in writing, printing, etc.; (b) [*pl.*] the leaves of a book, magazine, etc., especially when unbound; (c) a newspaper.
4. a broad continuous surface, layer, or expanse, as of flame, water, ice, etc.
5. a broad, thin, usually rectangular piece of any material, as glass, plywood, tin, etc.
6. in geology, any layer or deposit of rock, gravel, soil, ice, etc. that is broad in extent and comparatively thin.
7. in philately, the unseparated block of stamps printed by a single impression of a plate.
8. [*pl.*] a book or pamphlet. [Rare.]
9. in anatomy, a layer of tissue.
10. in geometry, a portion of any surface.
advance sheets; sheets of a book or periodical sent out before the day of publication.
in sheets; not bound: said of printed matter as delivered from the press, either flat or folded.

sheet, *v.t.*; sheeted, *pt.*, *pp.*; sheeting, *ppr.* 1. to cover or furnish with a sheet or sheets.
2. to make into sheets.
to sheet home; to tighten the sheets of (a square sail) so as to extend it against the wind.

sheet, *n.* [from AS. *sceatline*, a line attached to the lower corner of a sail.]
1. a rope or chain attached to a lower corner of a sail: it is shortened or slackened to control the set of the sail.
2. [*pl.*] the spaces not occupied by thwarts, or cross seats, at the bow and stern of an open boat.
a sheet in (or *to*) *the wind*; slightly drunk. [Slang.]
both sheets or *three sheets in* (or *to*) *the wind*; very drunk. [Slang.]

sheet an̄'ch̤ŏr, [formerly, *shoot anchor*; lit., one that can be shot out suddenly in case of danger.]
1. a large anchor carried amidships and used only in emergencies.
2. a person or thing to be relied upon in danger or emergency.

sheet bend, in nautical usage, a knot used in fastening a rope to the bight of another rope or to an eye.

sheet çā'ble, the cable attached to a sheet anchor.

sheet chāin, a chain used as a cable for a sheet anchor.

sheet'fụl, *n.* as much as a sheet contains; sufficient to fill a sheet.

sheet'ing, *n.* 1. cloth for sheets; specifically, a wide cotton or linen cloth.
2. material used in covering or lining a surface; as, copper *sheeting*.
3. the process of covering with or forming into sheets.

sheet ī'ron (-ūrn), iron rolled thin to the form of a sheet.

sheet līght'ning (līt'), a sheetlike illumination caused by lightning whose path of discharge is hidden by clouds, etc.

sheet met'ăl, metal rolled thin to the form of a sheet.

sheet mū'ṣiç, music printed on unbound sheets of paper.

sheet pīle, a pile, generally formed of thick plank, shot or jointed on the edge, and sometimes grooved and tongued, driven between the main or gauge piles of a cofferdam.

sheet rub'bēr, latex, freshly coagulated and pressed for drying into thin sheets.

shēik (*or* shāk), *n.* [Ar. *sheikh*, lit., old man, from *shakha*, to grow old.]
1. among Arabs, an old man; hence, the head of a family, clan, or tribe: used as a title of respect; also, one of the higher order of religious persons who preach in Moslem mosques.
2. [from E. M. Hull's novel, *The Sheik*.] a masterful man to whom women are irresistibly attracted. [Slang.]
Also spelled *sheikh*.
sheik ul Islam; the highest Moslem ecclesiastical functionary in Turkey.

shēik'dŏm, *n.* the territory ruled by a sheik: also spelled *sheikhdom*.

shēil'ing, *n.* same as *shealing*.

shei·tän', *n.* same as *shaitan*.

shek'el, *n.* [Heb. *shaqal*, to weigh.]
1. an ancient weight unit used by the Hebrews, Babylonians, etc., equal to about half an ounce.
2. a half-ounce gold or silver coin of the ancient Hebrews.
3. the monetary unit of Israel.
4. [*pl.*] money, especially coins. [Slang.]

Shē·kī'nȧh, *n.* [Heb. *shekhinah*, from *shakhan*, to dwell.] in Hebrew theology, the manifestation of the presence of God; Divine Presence.

sheld, *a.* piebald; variegated; spotted. [Brit. Dial.]

sheld'ap″ple, *n.* 1. the chaffinch. [Brit. Dial.]
2. the crossbill, *Loxia curvirostra*. [Brit. Dial.]

sheld'fowl, *n.* the sheldrake. [Brit. Dial.]

shel'drāke, *n.*; *pl.* **shel'drākes** or **shel'drāke**, [ME. *sheldedrake*, either from *sheld*, a shield, hence, emblazoned, varicolored, and *drake*, or from a ME. cognate of M.D. *schillede*, variegated.]
1. any of several large European wild ducks, especially the common sheldrake, *Tadorna vulpanser*, or the ruddy sheldrake, *Casarca rutila*, that feed on fish, shellfish, etc. and nest in burrows: the plumage is variegated and often brightly colored.
2. any of several other ducks, especially the merganser.
Also written *shelldrake*, *shieldrake*, *shielddrake*.

shel'duck, *n.* the sheldrake.

shelf, *n.*; *pl.* **shelves** (shelvz), [ME. *schelfe*; M.L.G. *schelf*, set of shelves; AS. *scylfe*, a plank or shelf.]
1. a thin, flat length of wood or other material set horizontally at right angles to a wall and used for holding things.
2. a similar support built into a frame, as in a bookcase or cupboard: usually one of a set.
3. the contents or capacity of a shelf.
4. something like a shelf, as a flat ledge jutting out from a cliff.
5. a sandbar or reef.
6. in mining, bedrock, as under deposits of soil, gravel, etc.
7. in shipbuilding, an inner timber following the sheer of the vessel and bolted to the inner side of the ribs, to strengthen the frame and support the deck beams.
to put or *lay on the shelf*; to put aside or out of use; to lay aside, as from duty or active service.

shelf'y, *a.* full of shelves; abounding with sandbars or reefs.

shell, *n.* [ME. *schelle*; AS. *scyll*; Ice. *skel*, a tile, from a Teut. root *skal*, to peel off or separate.]

1. the hard outside covering of anything, especially of certain fruits and animals, as (a) the outside covering of a nut; (b) the calcareous or chitinous covering for the soft bodies of various animals; specifically, the outer covering of the *Mollusca*: also applied to the carapace and plastron of the tortoise, the elytrum of insects, the covering or outside layer of an egg, the integument or crust of a lobster, crab, or the like, or of an echinoderm, and the calcareous or siliceous case of various protozoans.

2. material of or like animal shell, used in manufacturing, decorating, etc.

3. anything resembling or likened to a shell in use or structure, as (a) a hollow, explosive missile of the kind fired from a large gun: the more common kinds of shell contain high explosives, shrapnel, or chemicals producing gas, smoke, fire, etc.; (b) a small arms cartridge consisting of a metal or paper case holding the primer, the powder charge, and the bullet or shot; (c) a pyrotechnic cartridge which explodes high in the air; (d) the exterior plates of a steam boiler; (e) a long, thin-hulled racing boat rowed usually by a team of oarsmen; (f) the wooden outer portion or casing of a block; (g) a kind of thimble deadeye block employed in joining the ends of two ropes; (h) the thin coating of copper deposited by the current in electrotyping, which is backed with type metal for use; (i) a thin engraved copper roller used in calico printing; (j) a plate forming part of the guard of a sword hilt; (k) a coarse kind of coffin, or a thin, interior coffin enclosed by the more substantial one; (l) a concave-faced tool of cast iron, in which convex lenses are ground; (m) [Poet.] the lyre; (n) the outer ear; (o) a shell jacket; (p) a gouge bit; (q) in chemistry, one of the spherical layers of electrons contained in an atom; also, the space taken up by such a layer.

4. a mollusk.

5. outward show or a hollow semblance without real substance, content, or meaning.

6. in English public schools, an intermediate form or class.

blind shell; in gunnery, a shell containing no charge, or one that does not explode on impact.

tear shell; a shell containing tear gas.

to come out of one's shell; to become more sociable and less shy or reserved.

to retire into one's shell; to become less sociable and more shy or reserved.

shell, *v.t.*; shelled, *pt.*, *pp.*; shelling, *ppr.* 1. to strip or break off the shell of; to take out of the shell; as, to *shell* nuts.

2. to separate from the cob or ear; as, to *shell* corn.

3. to fire shells at from a large gun or guns; to bombard.

to shell out; to hand over; to pay out (money). [Slang.]

shell, *v.i.* 1. to fall, slough, or peel off, as a shell, crust, or exterior coat.

2. to separate or become freed from the shell or exterior covering; as, nuts *shell* in falling.

shē'll, a contraction of (a) she shall; (b) she will.

shel·laç', shel·lack', shell-laç', *n.* [*shell* and *lac*, used as transl. of Fr. *laque en écailles*, lac in fine sheets.]

1. refined lac, a resin usually produced in thin, flaky layers or shells and used in making varnish, phonograph records, insulating materials, etc.

2. a thin, usually clear kind of varnish containing shellac resin and alcohol.

shel·laç', *v.t.*; shellacked *or* shell-lacked, *pt.*, *pp.*; shellacking *or* shell-lacking, *ppr.* 1. to apply shellac to; to cover or treat with shellac.

2. (a) to beat; (b) to defeat decisively. [Slang.]

shel·lack'ing, *n.* 1. a whipping; a flogging; a beating.

2. a thorough defeat.

shell'ap″ple, *n.* same as *sheldapple*.

shell'back, *n.* [*shell* and *back*; prob. with reference to the shell of the sea turtle.]

1. an old, experienced sailor.

2. anyone who has crossed the equator by ship.

shell'bärk, *n.* the shagbark.

shell bēan, any bean, as the lima, of which only the seeds are used as food: distinguished from *string bean*.

shell bit, a gouge-shaped tool for boring wood.

shell but'tŏn, a button formed of two convex disks, as of metal, usually covered with cloth.

shell'çrack″ẽr, *n.* a sunfish inhabiting the fresh waters of Florida and other southern States.

shell çrest, a crest in the shape of a half circle on the heads of some pigeons: distinguished from *peak crest*.

shell dŏve, same as *scale dove*.

shell'drāke, *n.* same as *sheldrake*.

shell'duck, *n.* same as *shelduck*.

shell'ēat″ẽr, *n.* same as *openbill*.

-shelled (-sheld), a combining form meaning: *having a* (specified kind of) *shell*, as in *soft-shelled*.

shell'ẽr, *n.* one who or that which shells; as, a corn*sheller*.

shell'fīre, *n.* bombardment with shells; artillery attack.

shell'fish, *n.*; *pl.* **shell'fish** or **shell'fish·eṣ**, any aquatic animal whose external covering consists of a shell, as the lobster, oyster, clam, etc.

shell flow'ẽr, small shells so arranged as to imitate a flower.

shell'flow″ẽr, *n.* the turtlehead, *Chelone glabra*.

shell gāme, 1. a swindling game in which a small ball is placed under one of three nutshells or cones, the spectators being challenged to place a bet on the location of the ball, and being deceived by the sleight of hand of the operator.

2. any game or scheme in which the customers are victimized.

shell gland, 1. a gland containing the imperfectly developed shell found in the early stages of certain mollusks.

2. a gland that secretes the embryonic shells of certain invertebrates.

3. an excretory organ in some of the lower crustaceans.

shell grīnd'ẽr, a shark of the genus *Cestracion*.

shell'head (-hed), *n.* a hellgrammite. [Dial.]

shell ī'bis, the openbill.

shell īce, ice from which the water beneath has been withdrawn.

shell'ing, *n.* 1. the act of removing a shell or shells.

2. the act of bombarding; bombardment.

3. groats.

shell jack'et, a close-fitting semi-formal jacket; a mess jacket.

shell-laç', *n.* same as *shellac*.

shell'-less, *a.* not having a shell.

shell līme, lime made by burning the shells of oysters or other shellfish.

shell'măn, *n.*; *pl.* **shell'men**, a man who swindles people by means of the shell game.

shell mēat, food consisting of shellfish. [Obs.]

shell mound, same as *kitchen midden*.

shell par'ȧ·keet, the Australian grass parakeet, *Melopsittacus undulatus*; the zebra parakeet.

shell'prọọf, *a.* strong enough to resist damage from shells or bombs.

shell quāil, an American quail of the genus *Callipepla*; a scale quail.

shell rōad, a road having its surface laid with oyster or other shells.

shell saç, same as *shell gland* (sense 2).

shell shock, combat fatigue: formerly so called because thought to be a direct result of the continued concussion of artillery fire.

shell'-shocked (-shokt), *a.* suffering from shell shock.

shell'wŏrk, *n.* work composed of or adorned with shells.

shell'wŏrm, *n.* (a) any tubicolous annelid; (b) a tooth shell.

shell'y, *a.*; *comp.* shellier; *superl.* shelliest. 1. covered with or having many shells; as, a *shelly* patch of sea bottom.

2. of, like, or having a shell or shells.

shel'tȧ, *n.* [earlier *sheldru*, *shelter*, prob. a repatterning of OIr. *bēlre*, speech.] an esoteric jargon based in part on the systematic alteration of Irish and Gaelic and still spoken in some parts of England and Ireland by tinkers, vagrants, etc.

shel'tẽr, *n.* [altered from ME. *sheltrum*, a bodyguard, squadron, from AS. *sceld-truma*, shield troop.]

1. something that covers, protects, or defends; protection, or place affording protection, as from the elements, danger, etc.; a place of refuge.

2. the state of being covered, protected, or defended; protection; refuge.

shel'tẽr, *v.t.*; sheltered, *pt.*, *pp.*; sheltering, *ppr.* 1. to cover from violence, injury, annoyance, or attack; as, the valley is *sheltered* from the north wind by a mountain.

2. to defend; to protect from danger; to secure or render safe; to harbor.

3. to betake to cover or to a safe place: used with a reflexive pronoun; as, they *sheltered* themselves under a rock.

shel'tẽr, *v.i.* to take shelter; to find protection or refuge.

shel'tẽred wŏrk'shop, a workshop and training center for handicapped persons, where they can earn wages but are free from the competitive stress of the usual job.

shel'tẽr·less, *a.* without shelter.

shel'tẽr tent, a small, portable tent large enough to shelter two men: it consists of two sections (*shelter halves*), each of which is carried by a soldier as part of his field equipment: also called *pup tent*.

shel'tẽr·y, *a.* affording shelter. [Rare.]

shel'tie, *n.* [a dim. formed from the word *Shetland*.] a Shetland pony or Shetland sheep dog: so called from Shetland where they were originally bred: also written *shelty*.

shelve, *v.t.* shelved, *pt.*, *pp.*; shelving, *ppr.* 1. to equip with shelves; as, to *shelve* a bookstore or library.

2. to place on a shelf or on shelves; hence, to put aside out of active employment, or out of use; to dismiss; as, to *shelve* a question, a person, or claim.

shelve, *v.i.* [from Ice. *skjālgr*, sloping.] to incline; to slope gradually.

shelv'ẽr, *n.* a person or thing that shelves.

shelveṣ, *n.* pl. of *shelf*.

shelv'ing, *n.* 1. material for shelves; also, shelves collectively.

2. a framework for a cart or wagon to increase its carrying capacity.

3. the act of placing or putting on a shelf or shelves; the act of putting away or neglecting; as, the *shelving* of an order.

4. a place that shelves or slopes.

shelv'ing, *a.* inclining; sloping; as, a *shelving* rock.

shelv'y, *a.* having a gradual slope; as, the *shelvy* beach.

Shem, *n.* [Heb. *shēm*.] in the Bible, the eldest of the three sons of Noah and traditional ancestor of the Semitic people.

She·mä', *n.* [Heb., hear: the first word of one of the verses.] a number of verses from the books of Deuteronomy and Numbers, recited daily as part of the Jewish liturgy.

Shem'īte, *a.* and *n.* same as *Semite*.

Shem·it'iç, *a.* same as *Semitic*.

Shem'i·tish, *a.* Semitic.

Shem'i·tiṣm, *n.* same as *Semitism*.

shē·nan'i·găn, *n.* [perh. altered from Ir. *sionnachuighim*, I play the fox.] [*now usually pl.*] nonsense; trickery; mischief; often, a treacherous or deceitful trick. [Colloq.]

shend, *v.t.* [AS. *scendan*, to bring to shame.]

1. to injure; to mar; to spoil. [Obs.]

2. to blame; to revile; to disgrace. [Obs.]

shent, *a.* [ME. *schent*, from pp. of *schenden*, to put to shame.]

1. disgraced.

2. lost, ruined, or defeated, as a cause.

3. injured; damaged.

4. reproached.

[Archaic or Dial. in all senses.]

shē'-ōak, *n.* an Australian tree of the genus *Casuarina*, of the beefwood family. Its wood, which is very hard, is used for various purposes.

Shē'ōl, *n.* [Heb.] 1. in the Old Testament, a place in the depths of the earth where the dead are supposed to go; underworld.

2. [s–] hell. [Colloq.]

shep'hẽrd (-ẽrd), *n.* [AS. *sceaphyrde*, *scephyrde*; *sceap*, sheep, and *hyrde*, a herd, protection.]

1. a person who herds and takes care of sheep.

2. a religious leader; a minister; pastor.

3. a sheep dog.

shepherd kings; see *Hyksos*.

shepherd's crook; a long staff having its upper end curved so as to form a hook, used by shepherds.

shepherd's dog; a sheep dog.

shepherd's plaid or *tartan*; a woolen material with a check pattern of black and white.

shepherd's weatherglass; the pimpernel.

shep'hẽrd, *v.t.*; shepherded, *pt., pp.*; shepherding, *ppr.* 1. to tend or guide as a shepherd.

2. to attend on or escort, as a lady. [Humorous.]

3. in Australia, to hold, as a mining claim, by doing only the amount of work on it required by law. [Slang.]

shep'hẽrd dog, a sheep dog.

shep'hẽrd·ess, *n.* a woman who tends sheep: a stock character in pastoral poetry.

shep'hẽrd god, in Greek mythology, Pan.

Shep·hẽr'di·ȧ (-ẽr'), *n.* [after John *Shepherd*, an English botanist.] a genus of small North American shrubs, of the order *Elæagnaceæ*, having opposite deciduous leaves and small flowers. *Shepherdia argentea* is the buffalo berry.

shep'hẽrd·ish, *a.* of or like a shepherd; pastoral; rustic.

shep'hẽrd·iṣm, *n.* pastoral life or occupation.

shep'hẽrd·ling, *n.* a little shepherd. [Rare.]

shep'hẽrd·ly, *a.* pastoral; rustic. [Rare.]

shep'hẽrd'ṣ-bag, *n.* same as *shepherd's-purse*.

shep'hẽrd'ṣ-çlub, *n.* the common mullein.

shep'hẽrd'ṣ-çress, *n.* a European plant, *Teesdalia nudicaulis*, of the mustard family.

shep'hẽrd'ṣ-knot (-not), *n.* a plant, the tormentil, *Potentilla tormentilla*.

shep'hẽrd'ṣ-nee'dle, *n.* same as *Venus's-comb*.

shep'hẽrd spī'dẽr, any species of the *Phalangoidea*; a harvestman.

shep'hẽrd'ṣ-pouch, *n.* same as *shepherd's-purse*.

shep'hẽrd'ṣ-pūrṣe, *n.* a weed, *Capsella bursa-pastoris*, of the mustard family, having small, white flowers and triangular, pouchlike pods.

shep'hẽrd'ṣ-rod, *n.* a teazel, *Dipsacus pilosus*, found in Europe.

shep'hẽrd'ṣ-stȧff, *n.* same as *shepherd's-rod*.

shē'-pīne, *n.* a coniferous tree of Australia, *Podocarpus elata*.

sher'ȧrd·ize, *v.t.*; sherardized, *pt., pp.*; sherardizing, *ppr.* [after the inventor, *Sherard* Cowper-Coles.] to coat a metal surface with zinc by vapor galvanizing.

Sher'ȧ·tŏn, *a.* designating or of furniture made by, or in the style of, Thomas Sheraton (1751–1806), an English cabinetmaker: it is characterized by simplicity and lightness of form, straight lines, and classically chaste decoration.

shẽr'bet, *n.* [Ar. *sherbet, shorbet, sharbat*, from Ar. *sharaba*, to drink.]

1. a beverage made of watered fruit juice and sugar: it is served cold. [Brit.]

2. a frozen dessert of fruit juice, sugar, and water, milk, or egg white.

shẽr'bet·lee, *n.* in the Near East, an itinerant sherbet seller.

shẽrd, *n.* a shard; a fragment: used only in composition; as, pot*sherd*.

sher·eef', *n.* same as *sherif*.

shēre'wa''tẽr, *n.* shearwater. [Obs.]

sher'i·at, *n.* [Turk. *sherī'at*.] the sacred code of the Moslems, embracing the Koran and the teachings of Mohammed.

sher·if', sher·eef', *n.* [Ar. *sharīf*, lofty, noble.]

1. a descendant of Mohammed through his daughter Fatima: a title of nobility inheritable through either parent.

2. an Arab prince or ruler.

3. the chief magistrate of Mecca.

sher'iff, *n.* [AS. *scīr-gerēfa*; *scīr*, a shire, and *gerēfa*, a reeve.]

1. the chief law-enforcement officer of a county, charged in general with the keeping of the peace and the execution of court orders.

2. in England before the Norman Conquest, the chief administrative and judicial officer of a shire.

sheriff's sale; a sale of property by a sheriff or his deputy, in execution of the mandate of legal process.

sher'iff·ăl·ty, *n.* 1. the office or jurisdiction of a sheriff; shrievalty.

2. the length of time a sheriff holds office.

sher'iff·dŏm, *n.* 1. the district over which a sheriff has jurisdiction.

2. the office of sheriff.

sher'iff·ry, *n.* same as *sheriffship*.

sher'iff·ship, *n.* the position or jurisdiction of a sheriff.

sher'iff·wick, *n.* a sheriffdom.

sher'ris, *n.* sherry. [Archaic.]

sher'ry, *n.*; *pl.* **sher'rieṣ,** [taken as sing. of earlier *sherris*, from *Xeres* (now Jerez), Spain, where first obtained.]

1. a strong, nonsparkling Spanish wine: its color varies from light yellow to dark brown.

2. any similar wine.

sherry cobbler; a beverage made of sherry, citrus juice, water, sugar, etc., and cooled with ice.

sher'ry·val''lieṣ, *n.pl.* [Sp. *zaragüelles*, ill-made breeches, or overalls.] overalls of some heavy material, as leather or thick cloth, buttoned on the outside of the legs and worn for protection against mud, dust, etc. [Dial.]

shē'ṣ, a contraction of (a) she is; (b) she has.

shet, *v.t.* to shut. [Dial.]

shete, *v.t.* to shoot. [Obs.]

sheth, *n.* the part of a plow projected downward from the beam, to which are attached the moldboard and other parts.

shēthe, *n.* a sheath. [Rare.]

Shet'lănd, *n.* 1. a Shetland pony.

2. Shetland wool.

Shetland lace; a kind of ornamental openwork woolen lace made with a needle and used for wraps.

Shetland pony; any of a breed of small, hardy shaggy ponies, originally bred in the Shetland Islands.

Shetland sheep dog; any of a breed of dogs closely resembling collies but only 12 to 15 inches high: originally from the Shetland Islands.

Shetland wool; a kind of soft, fine, loosely twisted wool yarn.

She·vū'ōth, *n.* same as *Shabuoth*.

shew (-shō), *v.* and *n.* same as *show*.

shew'bread (shō'bred), *n.* [*shew*, older var. of *show*, and *bread*, after G. *schaubrot*.] the twelve loaves of unleavened bread placed at the altar before Jehovah every Sabbath by the ancient Hebrew priests and eaten by them alone at the end of the week: also spelled *showbread*.

shew'el (shō'), *n.* a scarecrow. [Obs.]

shew'ẽr (shō'), *n.* same as *shower*.

Shī'ăh, *n.* a Shiite.

shib'bō·leth, *n.* [Heb., a stream, or flood, from *shabal*, to flow.]

1. in the Bible, the test word used by the Gileadites to distinguish the escaping Ephraimites, who could not pronounce the initial *sh*: Jud. xii. 6.

2. any test word or password.

3. any phrase, formula, custom, etc. considered distinctive, as of a party, class, faction, etc.

shī'cẽr, *n.* [from G. *scheisser*, defecator.] in mining, a claim yielding no returns. [Australia.]

Shick'shack dāy, May 29: also called *Royal Oak* day. [Brit. Dial.]

shīde, *n.* [AS. *sceadan*, to divide.] a piece split off; a billet of wood; a splinter. [Brit. Dial.]

shīed, *v.* past tense and past participle of *shy*.

shiēld, *n.* [AS. *scild, scyld, sceld*, a shield, refuge, protection.]

1. a broad piece of defensive armor carried in the hand or worn on the forearm; a buckler formerly used in war for protection of the body.

2. any person or thing that guards, protects, or defends.

3. in heraldry, the escutcheon on which are depicted heraldic bearings.

4. anything shaped like a shield, as a plaque or trophy.

5. a movable canopy protecting workers from caveins in mines, tunnels, etc.

6. a heavy metal screen attached to an artillery piece for the protection of the gunners.

7. a guard or safety screen, as over the moving parts of machinery.

8. a device worn inside a part of a garment, as at the armpits, to prevent the fabric from being soiled by perspiration.

SHIELDS
1. lozenge shield 2. and 3. fanciful forms 4. spade shield

9. in zoology, a hard surface covering or shell; a protective plate, as on a turtle.

10. in botany, a little cup with a hard disk, surrounded by a rim and containing the fruit of lichens.

shiēld, *v.t.*; shielded, *pt., pp.*; shielding, *ppr.* 1. to cover as with a shield; to defend; to protect; to guard with care, so as to prevent injury.

2. to prevent or forbid; as, heaven *shield* that it should happen. [Archaic.]

shiēld, *v.i.* to act as a shield; to serve as protection.

shiēld'-beăr'ẽr, *n.* 1. an attendant who carried the shield of a knight.

2. a moth whose larva envelops itself in a covering of leaves.

shiēld'drāke, shiēl'drāke, *n.* a sheldrake.

shiēld'less, *a.* having no shield or protection.

shiēld'less·ly, *adv.* without protection.

shiēld'less·ness, *n.* the state or condition of being shieldless.

shiēld'-shāped (-shāpt), *a.* having the shape of a shield; in botany, peltate; in zoology, scutate.

shiēld'tāil, *n.* a snake with a rough tail; one of the *Uropeltidæ*.

shī'ẽr, *n.* a horse that shies easily.

shift, *v.t.*; shifted, *pt., pp.*; shifting, *ppr.* [AS. *scyftan*, to divide, to order, to drive away; Dan. *skifte*, to change, to shift, to divide; Ice. *skipta*, to divide, distribute, also to change.]

1. to move or transfer from one person, place, or position to another; as, don't *shift* the responsibility.

2. to put another or others in place of; to replace by another of the kind; to change.

3. to change (gears) from one arrangement to another.

4. to change phonetically, as by Grimm's law.

5. to change (clothes). [Archaic or Dial.]

6. to alter the character of; to change; as, observing men may *shift* their policy.

7. to put out of the way. [Obs.]

8. to distribute; to apportion. [Obs. or Brit. Dial.]

to shift a berth; to move a vessel from one place to another in a harbor.

to shift off; (a) to delay; to defer; as, to *shift off* the duties of religion; (b) to get rid of.

to shift the scene; in dramatic presentation, to make a change in scenery; to change the setting.

shift, *v.i.* 1. to change position, direction, form, character, etc.

2. to get along; to manage; as, you must *shift* for yourself now.

3. to use tricky or fraudulent methods; to practice evasion.

4. to change from one gear to another; as, this car *shifts* automatically.

5. to change one's clothing. [Archaic or Dial.]

6. to digress. [Obs.]

7. to make a livelihood by fraud or temporary expedients.

8. in playing an instrument, as a violin, to change the position of the fingering hand.

to shift about; to turn around and proceed in an opposite direction, as in a course or in an argument or a narration.

to shift for oneself; to make one's own way, as in life or in an emergency; to take care of oneself.

Syn.—change, alter, transfer, displace, remove, reverse.

shift, *n.* 1. a means or plan of conduct, especially one followed in an emergency or difficulty; an expedient; a stratagem.

2. a fraudulent scheme or method; fraud; artifice; an evasion; a trick to escape detection or evil.

3. the act of shifting from one person, place, position, etc. to another; a change; transfer; substitution.

4. a set or group of employees working in relay with another or others; as, three members of the night *shift* were absent.

5. the daily working period of such a group.

6. a change in direction, as of the wind.

7. a change of clothing. [Archaic or Dial.]

8. a chemise. [Now Rare.]

9. in football, a lateral movement or regrouping of the offensive backfield just before the ball is put in play.

10. in geology, a fault or displacement, as in a vein.

11. in linguistics, a phonetic change: see *Great Vowel Shift* under *great*.

12. in music, a change in the position of the hand, as on the finger board of a violin.
13. in building, the overlapping of materials to separate joints.
shift of crops; in agriculture, a change of crops raised on the same ground; as, a *shift* from wheat to grass.
to make shift; (a) to do as well as one can under unsatisfactory or difficult conditions; to use the means, however inadequate, at one's disposal; (b) to do one's best (*with*).

shift'a·ble, *a.* capable of being changed or shifted.

shift'ẽr, *n.* 1. one who shifts; a person who plays tricks or practices artifice.
2. in mechanics, (a) a device for changing a belt from one pulley to another; (b) a device in a knitting machine that shifts the yarn on the needles; (c) a locomotive used for making up trains; a switch engine.

shift'i·ly, *adv.* in a shifty manner.

shift'i·ness, *n.* a shifty quality.

shift'ing, *a.* 1. changing place or position.
2. resorting from one expedient to another; shifty.
3. capable of being shifted; as, a *shifting* bar.
shifting backstay; a stay requiring release when tacking or jibing.
shifting center; same as *metacenter*.

shift'ing bōards, plank bulkheads in a ship's hold to prevent the ballast from shifting.

shift'ing·ly, *adv.* in a shifting manner.

shift'less, *a.* 1. lacking the will or ability to do or accomplish; incapable, inefficient, lazy, etc.
2. showing such lack or incapacity.

shift'less·ly, *adv.* in a shiftless manner.

shift'less·ness, *n.* the state of being shiftless.

shift'y, *a.*; *comp.* shiftier; *superl.* shiftiest, 1. full of shifts or expedients; resourceful.
2. tricky; evasive.

Shi'gȧ's bȧ·cil'lus, a bacillus, *Shigella dysenteriae*, that causes dysentery: named after Shiga, a Japanese physician.

Shih' Tzu' (shē' dzu'), *n.*; *pl.* **Shih Tzus, Shih Tzu** [from Chin. *shih*, lion, and *tzu*, son.] any of a Chinese breed of small dog with long, silky hair and short legs.

Shi'ism, *n.* the doctrine of the Shiites.

Shi'ite, *n.* [Ar. *shī'i*, a follower, partisan; and *-ite*.] a member of one of the two great sects of Moslems: Shiites consider Ali, Mohammed's son-in-law and the fourth of the caliphs, as the first Imam and the rightful successor of Mohammed and do not accept the Sunna as authoritative: opposed to *Sunnite*: also called *Shiah*.

Shi·it'ic, *a.* of the Shiites or their doctrine.

shi·kär', *n.* [Hind., hunting.] in India, hunting.

shi·kär', *v.t.* and *v.i.* in India, to hunt.

shi·kä'ree, shi·kä'ri, *n.* [Hind., a hunter.] in India, a hunter, especially a native hunter who serves as a guide.

shik'ō, *n.* [Hind.] bowing of the body to show respect.

shik'rȧ, *n.* [Hind.] a small trained East Indian falcon, *Accipiter badius*.

shilf, *n.* [G. *schilf*, sedge.] straw. [Brit. Dial.]

shil'fȧ, *n.* the chaffinch. [Brit. Dial.]

shill, *v.t.* to shell. [Brit. Dial.]

shill, *v.t.* to put under cover; to sheal. [Brit. Dial.]

shill, *n.* [perh. from *shillibeer* (from G. *Shillibeer*, 19th-c. Eng. coach owner), a combined hearse and mourning coach.] the confederate of a gambler, barker, or peddler, as at a carnival, who pretends to buy something, make a bet, etc. in order to lure onlookers into participating. [Slang.]

shil·le'lȧgh (-lȧ), **shil·lā'lȧh,** *n.* [from *Shillelagh*, in County Wicklow, Ireland.] an oak or blackthorn sapling made into a cudgel; hence, any club or cudgel.

shil'ling, *n.* [ME. *schilling*; AS. *scylling*; akin to G. *schilling*; prob. basic sense "what is cut off (from a piece of metal) to serve as money."]
1. a British money of account and silver coin, equal to 5 (new) pennies or 1/20 of a pound; symbol, /.
2. any of several coins or moneys of account of different values used in other countries.
3. a coin of colonial America, varying in value from about 12 to 16 cents.
to cut off with a shilling; to disinherit.
to take the shilling; formerly, in Great Britain, to accept a shilling upon enlistment as a soldier.

shil'ly-shal''ly, *n.* [a reduplication of *shall I?* meaning shall I or shall I not?] foolish trifling; irresolution; indecision; vacillation.

shil'ly-shal''ly, *v.i.* to hesitate; to act in an undecided or irresolute manner; hence, to occupy oneself with silly or trifling things.

shil'ly-shal''ly, *adv.* in an irresolute manner.

shil'ly-shal''ly, *a.* vacillating; hesitant; irresolute.

shī'ly, *adv.* shyly.

shim, *n.* 1. a tool used to break land or to clear it of weeds: also called a *shim plow*.
2. a thin, usually wedge-shaped piece of metal, wood, etc., used for filling space, leveling, etc., as in masonry.

shim, *v.t.*; shimmed, *pt.*, *pp.*; shimming, *ppr.* to fill out with a shim; to make full or even by means of a shim.

shim'mẽr, *v.i.*; shimmered, *pt.*, *pp.*; shimmering, *ppr.* [AS. *scymrian*, freq. of *scīmrian*, to gleam, from *scīma*, a gleam, brightness, splendor; Dan. *skimre*; G. *schimmern*, to gleam.] to shine with an unsteady light; to glimmer.

shim'mẽr, *n.* a shimmering light; a glimmer.

shim'mẽr, *n.* one who shims.

shim'mẽr·ing, *n.* a gleam of light.

shim'mẽr·y, *a.* shimmering.

shim'mey, *n.*; *pl.* **shim'mieṣ,** a shimmy.

shim'ming, *n.* the insertion of shims into cracks or spaces; also, the shims themselves.

shim'my, *n.* 1. a marked shaking, vibration, or wobble, as in automobile wheels.
2. a jazz dance, popular in the 1920's, characterized by much shaking of the body.
3. a chemise. [Dial. or Colloq.]

shim'my, *v.i.*; shimmied, *pt.*, *pp.*; shimmying, *ppr.* 1. to dance the shimmy, or make movements suggesting this dance.
2. to vibrate, shake, or wobble.

shin, *n.* [ME. *shine*; AS. *scina*, shin, *scin-ban*, shin bone.]
1. the front part of the leg between the ankle and the knee.
2. the lower part of the foreleg in beef cattle: distinguished from *shank*, the upper foreleg.
3. the fish plate of a railroad.

shin, *v.t.* and *v.i.*; shinned, *pt.*, *pp.*; shinning, *ppr.* 1. to climb, as a mast, pole, etc., by embracing it successively with the arms and legs.
2. to kick (another) in the shins.
3. to trudge about; to walk; as, to *shin* down a hill.

shin'bōne, *n.* the tibia.

shin'dig, *n.* [folk-etym. form of *shindy*, understood as shin-dig, jovial kick in the shin.]
1. a dance. [Colloq.]
2. any social affair; a party. [Colloq.]

shin'dle, *n.* a shingle; also, a roofing slate. [Obs.]

shin'dle, *v.t.* to cover with shindles. [Obs.]

shin'dy, *n.*; *pl.* **shin'dieṣ,** [origin doubtful.]
1. a row; a rumpus; a disturbance; as, to kick up a *shindy*. [Colloq.]
2. a shindig. [Colloq.]
3. the game of shinny. [Brit. Dial.]
4. a fancy; a liking. [Dial.]

shīne, *v.i.*; shone, *pt.*, *pp.*; shining, *ppr.* [AS. *scīnan*; akin to D. *schijnen*, Ice. *skīna*, Dan. *skinne*, Goth. *skeinan*, G. *scheinen*, to shine.]
1. to emit rays of light; to give or reflect light; to beam with steady radiance; to exhibit brightness; to gleam; to glow; as, the sun *shines* by day; the moon *shines* by night.
2. to stand out; to excel; to be eminent, conspicuous, or brilliant.
3. to exhibit itself clearly or brightly; to appear conspicuously; as, happiness *shone* from her face.
4. to be radiant with splendor or beauty.
to shine up to; to try to become friendly with. [Slang.]
Syn.—radiate, beam, sparkle, glare, coruscate, glitter, glisten.

shīne, *v.t.* 1. to cause to shine; as, *shine* your flashlight over here.
2. to make shiny or bright by polishing, as shoes.
3. in night hunting, to cause (the eyes of an animal) to shine by using a light, so that the hunter may take good aim.

shīne, *n.* 1. brightness; radiance.
2. luster; polish; gloss.
3. a shoeshine.
4. splendor; brilliance; show.
5. a disturbance; commotion. [Slang.]
6. a trick or prank. [Slang.]
rain or shine; regardless of whether it is raining or fair weather.
to cut up shines; to play pranks. [Slang.]
to take a shine to; to develop a liking for. [Slang.]
to take the shine out of; to outshine; to eclipse. [Slang.]

shīne, *a.* shining. [Obs.]

shīn'ẽr, *n.* 1. one who or that which shines.
2. a coin, especially a bright one; a gold coin. [Slang.]
3. *pl.* **shīn'ẽrṣ** or **shīn'ẽr,** one of various fresh-water fishes with shining scales, as (a) the red fin; (b) a cyprinoid fish, *Notemigonus chrysoleucas*, the golden shiner; (c) the menhaden; (d) the dollarfish; (e) the moonfish.
4. a black eye resulting from a bruise. [Slang.]

shiṅ'gle (-gl), *n.* [formerly also *shindle*, which was corrupted to *shingle*, the word (like G. *schindel*) being borrowed from L. *scindula*, a shingle, from *scindere*, to split, divide.]
1. a thin, wedge-shaped slat or board laid with others in a series of overlapping rows as a covering for roofs and the sides of houses.
2. a piece of any kind of material, as asbestos, used in the same way.
3. a woman's short haircut in which the hair in back is cropped close.
4. a small signboard, especially that of a physician or lawyer. [Colloq.]
to hang out one's shingle; to open an office for professional consultation: used especially of physicians and lawyers. [Colloq.]

shiṅ'gle, *v.t.*; shingled, *pt.*, *pp.*; shingling, *ppr.*
1. to cover with shingles; as, to *shingle* a roof.
2. to perform the process of shingling on; as, to *shingle* iron.
3. to cut (the hair) in shingle style.

shiṅ'gle, *n.* [Norw. *singel*, coarse gravel; of echoic origin.]
1. coarse round gravel on the seashore; the accumulation of small rounded stones found on the shores of rivers or of the sea.
2. an area, as a beach, covered with coarse gravel.

shiṅ'gle mill, a sawmill for cutting logs into shingles.

shiṅ'gle nāil, a cut nail of proper size for fastening shingles on a roof.

shiṅ'gle ōak, an oak tree, *Quercus imbricaria*, of the United States. Its wood was formerly used for shingles.

shiṅ'glẽr, *n.* one who or that which shingles.

shiṅ'gleṣ, *n.* [L. *cingulum*, a belt, from *cingere*, to gird.] herpes zoster; an acute virus disease marked by the eruption of small blisters on the skin along the course of a nerve, usually about the waist.

shiṅ'gle·wood, *n.* a tree of the West Indies, *Nectandra leucantha*, often used for making shingles.

shiṅ'gling, *n.* 1. the act of covering with shingles, or a covering of shingles.
2. in ironworking, the process of removing impurities from the metal in its conversion from the cast to the malleable state.

shiṅ'gly, *a.*; *comp.* shinglier; *superl.* shingliest; of, like, or covered with shingle, or gravel.

shin guärd, a heavily padded or stiffened guard worn to protect the shins in certain games, as hockey, baseball, etc.

shīn'i·ness, *n.* the state or quality of being shiny; luster; polish.

shīn'ing, *a.* 1. emitting or reflecting light; beaming; gleaming; radiant; bright; as, a *shining* sun, *shining* armor.
2. brilliant; remarkable; eminent; as, a *shining* example of charity.
Syn.—brilliant, sparkling, radiant, glistening, bright, splendid, illustrious.—*Shining* describes the emission of a strong light from a radiant or polished surface; *brilliant* denotes a shining of great brightness, but with gleams or flashes; *sparkling* implies a shining intensely from radiant points or sparks by which the eye is dazzled.

shīn'ing, *n.* brightness; emission or reflection of light.

shīn'ing·ly, *adv.* in a shining manner.

shīn'ing·ness, *n.* brightness; splendor. [Rare.]

shin'lēaf, *n.* a plant, *Pyrola elliptica*, of the heath family: so called because its leaves were used for shinplasters.

shin'ny, *n.*; *pl.* **shin'nieṣ,** [prob. from cry *shin ye*, used in game; origin obscure.]

1. a simple form of hockey, popular especially with children.
 2. the crooked stick or club used in this game.
 Also spelled *shinney.*

shin′ny, *v.i.*; shinnied, *pt., pp.*; shinnying, *ppr.* to play shinny: also spelled *shinney.*

shin′ny, *v.i.*; shinnied, *pt., pp.*; shinnying, *ppr.* to climb by using the shins for gripping (usually with *up*). [Colloq.]

shin′plȧs″tẽr, *n.* 1. any of several kinds of plasters and poultices used on sore shins.
 2. a piece of paper money made almost worthless, as by inflation or inadequate security.
 3. a piece of paper money of small face value, usually less than a dollar.

shin′splints, *n.pl.* [*construed as sing.*] (compare *shin*, and *splint* (*n.* 3b).] painful strain of extensor muscles in the lower leg, caused as by running on a hard surface.

Shin′tō, *n.* [Japan., from Chin. *shin*, god or spirit, and *tao*, way or law.] a principal religion of Japan: its chief emphasis is upon the worship of ancestors and ancient heroes and upon the divinity of the emperor: prior to 1945, the state religion.

Shin′tō·iṣm, *n.* 1. the principles of Shinto.
 2. a belief in Shinto.

Shin′tō·ist, *n.* a believer in Shinto.

shīn′y, *a.*; *comp.* shinier; *superl.* shiniest. 1. bright; shining; luminous; clear; unclouded; as, a *shiny* day.
 2. having a glittering appearance; smoothly polished; glossy.

-ship, [ME. *-schipe*; AS. *-scipe*, from base of *sceppan*, to create, make.] a suffix added to nouns (or, rarely, adjectives) to form nouns meaning: (a) *the quality, condition*, or *state of*, as in fellow*ship*, friend*ship*; (b) *the rank, status*, or *office of*, as in king*ship*, governor*ship*; also, *a person having the rank* or *status of*, as in lord*ship*; (c) *ability* or *skill in*, as in penman*ship*, leader*ship*.

ship, *n.* [AS. *scip, scyp*, a ship; akin to D. *schip*, Ice. and Goth. *skip*, Dan. *skib*, O.H.G. *scif*, G. *schiff*.]
 1. any vessel of considerable size navigating deep water and not propelled by oars, paddles, or the like: distinguished from *boat*.
 2. a sailing vessel with a bowsprit and at least three square-rigged masts, each composed of lower, top, and topgallant members.
 3. a ship's officers and crew.
 4. any aircraft; as, a B-29 is a large *ship*.
 5. a dish or utensil formed like the hull of a ship for holding incense. [Obs.]
 about ship; see under *about, adv.*
 armed ship; a private ship taken into the service of the government in time of war, and armed and equipped like a ship of war. [Brit.]
 capital ship; see following *capital*.
 general ship; a ship engaged in carrying cargo generally, as distinguished from one under charter to a particular person.
 ship of the desert; the camel.
 ship of the line; formerly, a man-of-war large and strong enough to take its place in the line of battle: it carried at least seventy-four guns.
 ship's carpenter; a carpenter whose duty is to do repair work about a vessel.
 ship's company; the crew of a vessel.
 ship's days; the days allowed a ship for loading or unloading cargo.
 ship's papers; all the documents that a merchant ship must carry to meet the requirements of port authorities, international law, etc.
 to pump ship; to pump the water from the hold of a ship.
 to take ship; to embark.
 when one's ship comes home (or *in*); when one's fortune has been made or one's expectations have been realized.

ship, *v.t.*; shipped (shipt), *pt., pp.*; shipping, *ppr.* 1. to put or take on board a ship.
 2. to transport or send by any carrier; as, we *shipped* the cattle by rail.
 3. to take in (water) over the gunwale or side, as in a heavy sea.
 4. to put or fix (an object) in its proper place on a ship or boat; as, *ship* the oars.
 5. to engage for service on board a ship or other vessel; as, to *ship* a sailor.
 6. to get rid of; to dismiss; frequently with *off* or *away*. [Colloq.]

ship, *v.i.* 1. to engage for service on board a ship.
 2. to go aboard ship; to embark; as, to *ship* for Boston.

ship bis′cuit (-kit), a kind of hard, coarse biscuit that will not spoil easily; hardtack: it is used on long voyages.

ship′bōard, *n.* 1. a ship.
 2. the side of a ship. [Obs.]
 on shipboard; on or in a ship.

ship bŏr′ẽr, same as *shipworm*.

ship′-bōrne, *a.* carried by a ship.

ship′boy, *n.* a boy who serves on board a ship: also called *ship's boy*.

ship breāk′ẽr, one who makes a business of breaking up vessels unfit for sea.

ship brō′kẽr, see under *broker*.

ship′build″ẽr (-bild″), *n.* one engaged in shipbuilding; a shipwright.

ship′build″ing, *n.* the construction of ships.

ship′build″ing, *a.* of or used in ship construction.

ship cȧ·nal′, a canal large enough to allow the passage of ships.

ship cärv′ẽr, formerly, one who carved figureheads and other ornamental work for ships.

ship chan′dlẽr, one who deals in ship supplies.

ship chan′dlẽr·y, the business and commodities of a ship chandler.

ship fē′vẽr, a form of typhus fever, formerly very prevalent on ships.

ship′ful, *n.* as much or as many as can be carried in a ship; enough to fill a ship.

ship′hōld″ẽr, *n.* the owner of a ship. [Rare.]

ship′keep″ẽr, *n.* 1. a watchman on board a vessel lying in dock.
 2. one who manages a whaling vessel while the boats are chasing a whale.

ship′less, *a.* having no ships; unoccupied by ships.

ship let′tẽr, a letter carried by a ship not engaged in the mail service.

ship′lōad, *n.* a ship's cargo; a full load for a ship.

ship′măn, *n.*; *pl.* **ship′men,** 1. a seaman or sailor. [Archaic.]
 2. a shipmaster.

ship′mȧs″tẽr, *n.* the captain, master, or commander of a ship.

ship′māte, *n.* one who serves in the same ship with another; a fellow sailor.

ship′ment, *n.* 1. the shipping or transporting of goods; consignment for transportation; as, he was engaged in the *shipment* of coal for London.
 2. goods or things shipped, either by land or water; as, a *shipment* of flour.

ship mŏn′ey, a tax levied on English ports, maritime counties, etc. to provide money for the construction of warships: it was abolished in 1640.

ship′ōwn″ẽr, *n.* the owner of a ship or ships.

ship′pȧ·ble, *a.* that can be shipped.

ship′pen, *n.* a stable; a stall. [Scot. and Brit. Dial.]

ship′pẽr, *n.* 1. a seaman. [Obs.]
 2. one who or that which ships.
 3. one who consigns for shipment, goods, merchandise, or the like, to any common carrier or transportation company, as to a railroad or express company.
 4. any goods that are shipped or suitable for shipping; as, wheat is a good *shipper*.

ship′ping, *n.* 1. ships collectively, as of a nation, port, industry, etc., especially with reference to tonnage.
 2. the act or business of sending or transporting goods.

ship′ping ā′ġent, an agent whose duties pertain to the receiving and forwarding of goods.

ship′ping är′ti·cleṣ, articles of agreement between the captain of a vessel and the seamen on board, in respect to the amount of wages, length of time for which they are shipped, etc.

ship′ping bill, an invoice of merchandise or goods shipped.

ship′ping çlērk, an employee who prepares and enters goods for shipment.

ship′ping rōom, a room or department, as in a factory, from which goods are taken by a carrier for shipment.

ship′pō′, *n.* [Japan., lit., the seven precious things.] Japanese cloisonné.

ship′pŏn, *n.* same as *shippen*.

ship rāil′wāy, a railway constructed for the transportation of ships.

ship′-rigged, *a.* having three masts and square sails on each mast; also, square-rigged.

ship′shāpe, *a.* in order; snug; trim.

ship′shāpe, *adv.* in a shipshape manner.

ship′wāy, *n.* 1. the supporting structure or track on which a ship is built and from which it is launched.
 2. a ship canal or channel.

ship′wŏrm, *n.* the teredo, a slender bivalve mollusk, like a worm, which bores into ship bottoms, wharves, and other wood under water.

ship′wreck (-rek), *n.* 1. the loss or destruction of a ship through storm, collision, going aground, etc.
 2. ruin; destruction; as, made *shipwreck* on a sea of promises.
 3. the remains of a wrecked ship; wreckage.

ship′wreck, *v.t.* 1. to cause to suffer or experience shipwreck (sense 1).
 2. to ruin, wreck, or destroy; as, to *shipwreck* one's prospects.

ship′wrīght (-rit), *n.* one whose occupation is to construct or repair ships.

ship′yärd, *n.* a place where ships are built and repaired.

shīre, *n.* [AS. *scire*, office, charge, administration.]
 1. formerly, a district or region in Great Britain, generally coinciding with the modern county.
 2. any of the counties of Great Britain with the name containing the terminal combining form *-shire*.
 3. [S–] a breed of large, heavy draft horses; a shire horse.

shīre hōrse, any of a breed of large, powerful draft horses, originally raised in the shires, or midland counties, of England.

shīre′măn, *n.*; *pl.* **shīre′men,** 1. a sheriff. [Obs.]
 2. a man who comes from or belongs to the shires of England.

shīre mōot, in old English times, a court held periodically in a shire by the sheriff: also written *shire mote* and *shire gemote*.

shīre town, the chief town of a shire.

shīrk, *v.t.*; shirked (shẽrkt), *pt., pp.*; shirking, *ppr.* [a variant of *shark*.]
 1. to neglect or evade doing (something that should be done); as, to *shirk* one's duty.
 2. to procure by fraud and trickery. [Obs.]

shīrk, *v.i.* 1. to evade an obligation or duty.
 2. to live by fraud or trickery; to shark. [Obs.]

shīrk, *n.* 1. one who evades a duty or obligation.
 2. one who lives by shifts and tricks. [Obs.]

shīrk′ẽr, *n.* one who evades a duty or obligation.

shīrk′y, *a.* having the disposition or inclination to shirk.

shīrl, *a.* shrill. [Brit. Dial.]

shīrl, *n.* schorl.

shīrr, *n.* in sewing, a series of parallel rows of short, running stitches with gatherings between rows.

shīrr, *v.t.*; shirred, *pt., pp.*; shirring, *ppr.* 1. to make a shirr or shirrs in cloth; as, to *shirr* a skirt.
 2. to bake (eggs) with crumbs in small buttered dishes.

shīrr′ing, *n.* a shirr or shirrs.

shīrt, *n.* [ME. *schurte*; AS. *scyrte*.]
 1. any of various cloth garments worn by men on the upper part of the body, often under a coat or jacket.
 2. an undershirt.
 3. a woman's shirtwaist.
 boiled shirt; a white shirt having a stiffened front. [Slang.]
 in one's shirt sleeves; not wearing a coat or jacket over one's shirt.
 to keep one's shirt on; to be patient or calm. [Slang.]
 to lose one's shirt; to lose all of one's possessions. [Slang.]

shīrt, *v.t.*; shirted, *pt., pp.*; shirting, *ppr.* to cover or clothe, as with a shirt; to clothe.

shīrt′band, *n.* a strip of cloth sewn into a shirt, as on the collar, for stiffening.

shīrt′dress, *n.* a dress having trim, simple lines, with the waist styled like a shirt.

shīrt frāme, a machine for knitting shirts.

shīrt frŏnt, the front of a man's shirt; especially, a heavily starched panel sewn into the front of a dress shirt.

shīrt′ing, *n.* material used for making shirts.

shīrt′less, *a.* without a shirt; not wearing a shirt.

shirt'less·ness, *n.* the state of being shirtless.
shirt'-sleeve, *a.* 1. simple; plain; informal.
2. homespun; unpolished; plebeian; as, *shirt-sleeve* philosophy.
shirt'waist, *n.* a woman's tailored blouse, usually worn with a separate, unmatching skirt.
shist, *n.* same as *schist.*
shite'pōke, *n.* a small green American heron, *Ardea virescens.*
shit'tah, shit'tah tree, [Heb. *shittāh,* pl. *shittīm.*] a tree generally recognized as a species of *Acacia,* probably *Acacia vera* or *Acacia seyal,* having close-grained, yellowish-brown wood.
shit'tim, shit'tim wood, [Heb.] 1. the wood of the shittah, from which the boards, altars, tables, and ark of the Jewish tabernacle were made.
2. the weak, soft, yellow wood of *Bumelia lanuginosa* of southern United States, or the tree itself.
3. *Rhamnus purshiana* or cascara buckthorn of the Pacific coast.
4. the wood of *Halesia carolina* or silverbell tree of southeastern United States.
shiv·à·ree', *n.* [altered from *charivari.*] a noisy demonstration or celebration; especially, a mock serenade with kettles, horns, etc. to a couple on their wedding night; a charivari.
shiv·à·ree', *v.t.*; shivareed, *pt., pp.*; shivareeing, *ppr.* to serenade with a shivaree.
shīve, *n.* [ME. *schive*; AS. (hyp.) *scife*; akin to G. *scheibe,* anything round and flat.]
1. a slice, fragment, or splinter.
2. an external scale of a cornstalk or a piece of the bark of flax removed in breaking.
3. refuse consisting of such pieces.
4. a small, flat cork used to close wide-mouthed bottles; also, a small bung for barrels.
5. in papermaking, a group of raw fiber splinters not completely reduced in cooking and bleaching.
shiv'ēr, *n.* [dim. of *shive,* a slice.]
1. a variety of blue slate; schist; shale.
2. in nautical usage, a little wheel; a sheave. [Obs.]
3. a small piece or fragment into which a thing breaks by any sudden violence.
shiv'ēr, *v.t.* and *v.i.*; shivered, *pt., pp.*; shivering, *ppr.* to break into many small pieces or splinters; to shatter; to dash to pieces by a blow.
shiver my timbers; a mild form of oath formerly used by sailors.
shiv'ēr, *v.i.* [ME. *cheveren,* probably from AS. *ceafl,* a jaw; probable basic sense "to have chattering teeth."] to quake; to tremble; to shudder; to shake, as from fear or cold.
shiv'ēr, *v.t.* to cause (a sail) to flutter by presenting the edge to the wind.
shiv'ēr, *n.* a shaking, quivering, or trembling, as from fear or cold.
the shivers; the ague; chills. [Colloq.]
shiv'ēred, *a.* shattered; broken, as a lance. [Archaic.]
shiv'ēr·ing, *n.* the act of breaking or dashing to pieces; division; severance.
shiv'ēr·ing, *n.* a trembling; a shaking with cold or fear.
shiv'ēr·ing·ly, *adv.* with shivering, or slight trembling.
shiv'ēr spär, [G. *schiefer-spath.*] a variety of calcite: so called from its slaty structure: also called *slate spar.*
shiv'ēr·y, *a.* easily falling into many pieces; brittle and easily broken into shivers; as, *shivery* stone.
shiv'ēr·y, *a.* 1. shivering or inclined to shiver; suffering from cold, fear, etc.
2. causing or likely to cause shivering; chilly; chilling; terrifying.
shi'zō·kū, *n.* [Japan.] formerly in Japan, the samurai and their descendants.
shle·mihl', *n.* same as *schlemihl.*
shōad, *n.* same as *shode.*
shōal, *n.* [AS. *scolu,* a company; akin to D. *school,* a school, a shoal.] a large number assembled; a great quantity; a throng; a crowd; specifically, a large school of fish.
shōal, *v.i.* to come together in or move about as a shoal or school.
shōal, *a.* shallow; of little depth.
shōal, *n.* [ME. *scholde, scheald*; AS. *sceald,* shallow.]
1. a shallow place in a lake, river, or sea.
2. a sandbar; particularly, one visible at ebb tide.
shōal, *v.i.* to become shallow; as, water *shoals.*
shōal, *v.t.*; shoaled, *pt., pp.*; shoaling, *ppr.* 1. to make or cause to become shallow.
2. to sail (a ship) into a shallow or shallower part of (water).
shōal duck, the American eider duck.
shōal'ing, *a.* gradually becoming shallow; filling up with shoals.
shōal'ness, shōal'i·ness, *n.* the state of abounding with shoals; shallowness.
shōal'y, *a.*; *comp.* shoalier; *superl.* shoaliest, full of shoals or shallow places.
shōat, *n.* [ME. *schote,* probably from L.G.] a young hog, especially when able to feed alone: also written *shote.*
shock, *n.* [Fr. *choc,* a shock, from *choquer,* to shock.]
1. the impact of persons or forces in combat.
2. (a) a sudden, powerful concussion; a violent blow, shake, or jar; as, the *shock* of an earthquake; (b) the result or effect of such concussion.
3. (a) any sudden disturbance or agitation of the mind or emotions, as through great loss or surprise; (b) something causing this.
4. an extreme stimulation of the nerves and convulsion of the muscles accompanying the passage of electric current through the body: also *electric shock.*
5. a paralytic stroke. [Colloq.]
6. in medicine, a condition of disorder of the circulatory system, resulting from injury or a sudden psychic disturbance, and characterized by a decrease in blood pressure, a weak and rapid pulse, and, often, unconsciousness.
shock, *v.t.* [Fr. *choquer,* from M.D. *schokken,* to collide.]
1. to disturb the mind or emotions of; to affect with great surprise, distress, disgust, etc.
2. to affect with physical shock.
3. to produce electrical shock in (a body).
shock, *v.i.* to come together violently; to collide. [Archaic or Poet.]
shock, *n.* [ME. *shockke*; prob. from M.D. or M.L.G.]
1. a bunch or pile of grain sheaves stacked together in a field to cure and dry; a collection of cut cornstalks.
2. in commerce, a lot consisting of sixty pieces. [Obs.]
shock, *v.t.*; shocked (shokt), *pt., pp.*; shocking, *ppr.* to pile or make up into a shock or shocks; as, to *shock* corn.
shock, *v.i.* to make shocks, as of wheat in a field.
shock, *n.* [prob. back-formation from *shock dog.*]
1. a mass of thick, shaggy hair.
2. a shock dog. [Obs.]
shock, *a.* bushy; shaggy; woolly.
shock ab·sorb'ēr, a mechanical device for lessening, by absorbing, the force of shocks and jarring, as on the springs of an automobile.
shock dog, [from *shough,* lap dog from Iceland.] any dog with long, bushy hair, as a poodle. [Obs.]
shock'ēr, *n.* 1. a person or thing that shocks.
2. a sensational piece of writing. [Brit.]
shock'-head (-hed), *n.* a head with a bushy covering of hair.
shock'-head, *a.* shockheaded.
shock'head'ed, *a.* having the hair of the head thick and bushy.
shock'ing, *a.* 1. having an effect like that of a heavy blow or shock; staggering; as, the *shocking* news of his death.
2. highly offensive or revolting; disgusting, as to good taste, propriety, etc.: sometimes used as a mere intensive meaning "very bad."
Syn.—horrible, disgraceful, loathsome, hateful, revolting, abominable, foul.
shock'ing·ly, *adv.* in a shocking manner.
shock'ing·ness, *n.* the state or quality of being shocking.
shock prō·bā'tion, [from the theory that the shock of even a brief confinement may have a deterrent effect.] the release on probation of a criminal after brief imprisonment.
shock tac'tics, in military science, an attack procedure, usually of a surprise nature, carried out by a heavy concentration of forces.
shock ther'à·py, in psychiatry, a method of treating certain psychotic conditions by injecting such drugs as insulin or metrazol or by applying electric current to the brain, in order to induce shock artificially: also *shock treatment.*
shock troops, troops especially chosen, trained, and equipped to lead an attack.
shock wŏrk'ēr, a worker who has excelled in voluntary increase of production, usually under an efficiency system: see *Stakhanovism.*
shod, *v.* past tense and past participle of *shoe.*
shod'dy, *n.*; *pl.* **shod'dies,** [from Yorkshire dial., orig., inferior quarry stone or coal; prob. from *shode,* loose pieces, from AS. *sceādan,* to shed, divide.]
1 an inferior woolen yarn made from fibers taken from used fabrics and reprocessed.
2. cheap woolen cloth made from this.
3. anything of less worth or quality than it appears or is claimed to have; sham.
shod'dy, *a.*; *comp.* shoddier; *superl.* shoddiest, 1. made of shoddy; inferior in quality.
2. lacking the quality or worth that it appears or is claimed to have; sham.
shōde, *n.* in mining, a loose collection of mineral separated by some natural agency from its original position in a vein. [Brit. Dial.]
shōd'ēr, *n.* [AS. *scead,* separation.] the package of goldbeater's skin employed in the second stage of gold-leaf making.
shōe, *n.*; *pl.* **shōes,** *archaic* or *dial.* **shoon,** [ME. *sho, scho,* from AS. *scōh, scēoh.*]
1. an outer covering for the human foot, having a light upper part and a stiff or thick sole and heel: sometimes restricted to footwear that does not cover the ankle, as distinguished from a boot.
2. a metal plate nailed to the hoof of a horse, mule, or ox, to protect the hoof from wear and to prevent it from becoming sore; a horseshoe.
3. anything resembling a shoe in form or use, as (a) in a harvester, the metallic block on the inner end of a finger bar: it runs on the ground next to the standing grain; (b) the shaking portion of a winnowing machine or grain separator; (c) a block or base piece for the reception of a pillar, a truss, or girder, as in a bridge; (d) the short, horizontal section at the foot of a rain-water pipe to give direction to the issuing water; (e) in a machine, a bottom piece on which a body is supported; (f) a piece on which an object is placed while moving, to prevent its being worn; (g) the iron point of a pile; (h) the spout beneath the feeding hopper in a mill; (i) an inclined trough used in an ore-crushing mill; (j) a removable piece of iron at the bottom of a stamp or muller; (k) a wooden piece secured to an anchor during the operation of fishing: it holds the point as the anchor rises and keeps it from tearing the ship's side; also, a board lashed to the fluke of an anchor to extend its area and consequent bearing surface when in the ground; (l) a footboard on which a spar is erected to act as a jib in hoisting; (m) that part of a brake which is brought in contact with the wheel to create friction and retard or stop motion; (n) the step of a mast; (o) a strip of wood or steel fastened beneath the runner of a sled or sleigh; (p) in an electric railway, a metal piece attached to the motorcar to receive current from the third rail; (q) in a printing office, a box or pocket attached to the composing stand as a receptacle for imperfect type; (r) the claw of a stork resembling a shoe; (s) a metal cap or ferrule fitted over the end of a cane, pole, staff, etc.; (t) the outer covering or casing of a pneumatic rubber tire.
dead men's shoes; vacancies created by death, especially of offices or places of distinction.
in another's shoes; in another's position.
the shoe is on the other foot; the situation is completely reversed.
to fill one's shoes; to take one's place.
where the shoe pinches; the source of trouble, grief, difficulty, etc.
shōe, *v.t.*; shod, *pt., pp.*; shoeing, *ppr.* 1. to furnish or fit with a shoe or shoes; to put shoes on; as, to *shoe* a horse or an ox.
2. to cover, tip, or sheathe (a stick, wearing surface, etc.) with a metal plate, ferrule, etc.
shōe'bill, *n.* a large wading bird with long legs and a heavy shoelike bill, related to the storks and herons: found along the White Nile in central Africa.
shōe'black, *n.* a person who cleans and polishes shoes; a bootblack.
shōe'black plant, a tree of the mallow family, *Hibiscus rosa-sinensis,* of East India, the large flowers of which yield an astringent juice used for blacking shoes.

shöe block, in nautical usage, a block having two sheaves at right angles to each other and placed one above the other.

shöe bōlt, a bolt used for fastening runners on sleighs.

shöe'horn, *n.* 1. an implement made of horn, metal, etc. with a troughlike blade curved to fit the heel, inserted at the back of a shoe to aid in slipping it on.
2. anything by which a transaction is facilitated; anything used as a medium.

shöe'ing horn, same as *shoehorn*.

shöe'lāce, *n.* a length of cord, leather, etc. used for lacing and fastening a shoe.

shöe'less, *a.* without shoes.

shöe'māk″ẽr, *n.* 1. one whose occupation or trade is to make or repair shoes and boots.
2. a fish; (a) the threadfish; (b) the runner.

shöe'māk″ing, *n.* the occupation of a shoemaker.

shöe'pack, *n.* a moccasin of tanned leather.

shō'ẽr, *n.* a person who shoes horses.

shöe'shīne, *n.* 1. the cleaning and polishing of a pair of shoes.
2. the polished surface resulting from this.

shöe stōne, a whetstone used by a shoemaker.

shöe'string, *n.* a shoelace.
on a shoestring; with little capital and resources, as in starting a business.

shöe tree, a shoe-shaped form inserted in a shoe to stretch it or preserve its shape.

shō'fär, *n.* a shophar.

shog, *n.* a sudden shake; a shock. [Archaic.]

shog, *v.t.* to shake; to agitate. [Archaic.]

shog'gle, *v.t.* to shake; to joggle. [Brit. Dial.]

shō'gun', *n.* [Japan., from Chinese *chiang-chun*, leader of an army.] any of the military governors of Japan who, until 1868, constituted a quasi-dynasty exercising absolute rule and relegating the emperors to a nominal position.

shō'gun·āte, *n.* the office, jurisdiction, and government of a shogun; government by a shogun or the shoguns.

shō'ji, *n.*; *pl.* **shō'ji, shō'jis,** [Japan. *shōji.*]
1. a translucent sliding panel of rice paper on a wooden frame, used in Japanese homes as a partition or door.
2. any panel, screen, etc. like this.
Also *shoji screen.*

shōle, *n.* a plank used to increase the surface under one of the shores or props supporting a ship in the dry dock so as to prevent its sinking into soft ground.

shōne (*or* shon), *v.* alternative past tense and past participle of *shine.*

shoo, *interj.* [a natural cry.]
1. an exclamation used in scaring away chickens and other animals.
2. go away! get out!

shoo, *v.i.*; shooed, *pt., pp.*; shooing, *ppr.* to cry "shoo."

shoo, *v.t.* to drive away abruptly, as by crying "shoo."

shood, *n.* 1. the husks of rice used in adulterating linseed cake.
2. chaff, as of oats, etc. [Brit. Dial.]

shoo'flȳ, *n.* 1. [from the phr. *shoo fly, don't bother me*, in a Civil War nonsense song.] originally, a kind of shuffling dance.
2. a child's rocker with a seat mounted between supports typically designed in the form of horses, swans, etc.
3. [said to be so named from attracting flies which must be shooed away.] an open pie with a filling of molasses and brown sugar: in full *shoofly pie.*

shook, *v.* past tense of *shake.*

shook, *n.* [a variant of *shock*, a pile of sheaves.]
1. a set of staves, boards, etc. for one hogshead, barrel, box, and the like, prepared for use and bound up in a compact form for convenience of transportation.
2. furniture made in parts and not set up, but shipped in packs.
3. a shock of grain sheaves.

shook, *v.t.* to pack in shooks.

shoon, *n.pl.* shoes. [Archaic or Dial.]

shoot, *n.* a shoat.

shoot, *v.t.*; shot, *pt.*; shot *or obs.* shotten, *pp.*; shooting, *ppr.* [ME. *schoten*; AS. *sceotan*, akin to G. *schiessen*, to shoot, dart.]
1. to pass swiftly over, by, across, etc.; as, he *shot* the rapids in his canoe.
2. to pour or empty out; to dump, as down a chute.
3. to throw or hurl out or forth; to cast (an anchor, fish net, etc.).
4. to slide (a door bolt) into or out of its fastening.
5. to variegate, streak, fleck, etc. with another color or substance; as, a blue sky *shot* with white clouds.
6. to put or thrust out or forth, as a branch, leaves, etc.
7. (a) to send forth (a missile or projectile); to discharge or fire (a bullet, arrow, etc.); (b) to discharge or emit (rays) with force.
8. to send forth swiftly, dartingly, or with force or feeling, as a question, reply, glance, fist, etc.
9. to discharge or fire (a gun, bow, charge of explosive, etc.).
10. to hunt game in or on (a tract of land).
11. to take the altitude of, as a star, with a transit, sextant, etc.
12. (a) to hit, wound, or kill with a missile discharged from a weapon; (b) to make by firing a bullet; as, to *shoot* a hole in a door.
13. to take a picture of with a camera; to photograph; to film.
14. to send; hand; give; as, *shoot* the salt to me. [Slang.]
15. in games and sports, (a) to throw, drive, or propel (a ball, marble, etc.) toward the objective; (b) to make or score (a goal, points, total strokes, etc.); (c) to play, as golf, pool, craps, etc.
shot through with; having too much or too many; filled with (something unwanted, dangerous, etc.).
to shoot down; to bring down by hitting with a shot or shots.
to shoot up; (a) to hit with several or many shots; (b) [Colloq.] to spread terror and destruction throughout by lawless and wanton shooting.

shoot, *v.i.* 1. to move swiftly, as an arrow from a bow; to rush; to dart.
2. to be felt suddenly and keenly, as heat, pain, etc.
3. to grow or sprout, especially rapidly.
4. to jut out; to project.
5. to send forth a missile or projectile, especially from a gun.
6. to discharge bullets, arrows, etc.; to go off; to fire; as, the gun won't *shoot* until it is cocked.
7. (a) to photograph a scene or subject; (b) to start the camera working in photographing a motion-picture scene.
8. to hunt game with a gun; as, he fishes but he doesn't *shoot.*
9. in sports, (a) to propel a ball, etc. toward the objective; (b) to play golf, pool, etc.; as, he's been *shooting* poorly for some time.
to shoot at; to try to reach, gain, or accomplish; to strive for. [Colloq.]
to shoot off one's (or *at the*) *mouth*; to speak without caution or discretion; to blab.
to shoot up; to grow or rise rapidly.

shoot, *n.* 1. the act of shooting; the discharge of a missile; a shot. [Archaic.]
2. a shooting party; a shooting contest.
3. a young branch which shoots out from the main stock; hence, an annual growth, as the annual layer of growth on the shell of an oyster, a deer's antler, etc.
4. shooting distance; range. [Obs.]
5. the thrust of an arch.
6. in weaving, the thread put into place by the movement of the shuttle through the shed; a pick; also, a single such movement of the shuttle.
7. in mining, a vein running parallel to the strata in which it occurs; also, a passage down which the coal or ore mined is dropped or shot.
8. a kind of sloping trough; chute.
9. a receptacle into which rubbish is shot.
10. in a stream, a place through which the water rushes swiftly; a river fall; a rapid; also, in dam construction, a passage for boats, logs, or the discharge of superfluous water.
11. action or motion like that of something shot, as of water from a hose.
12. a twinge or spasm of pain.
13. in rowing, the interval between strokes.

shoot, *interj.* an exclamation expressing disgust, disappointment, etc. [Slang.]

shoot'bōard, *n.* a shooting board.

shoot'ẽr, *n.* 1. one who shoots; a rifleman; a gunner.
2. an implement for shooting; a gun: used in hyphenated compounds, as six-*shooter.*
3. a shooting star. [Rare.]
4. one who acts as guard of a coach. [Obs.]

shoot'ing, *n.* 1. the act of a person or thing that shoots; the act or practice of discharging firearms; especially, the act or practice of killing game with firearms; as, to be fond of *shooting* and fishing.
2. a right to shoot game over a certain district.
3. a district or defined tract of ground over which game is shot.

shoot'ing, *a.* 1. pertaining to one who or that which shoots; especially, pertaining to or connected with the killing of game by firearms; as, the *shooting* season.
2. darting or piercing, as pains.
shooting star; a meteor in a state of incandescence seen suddenly darting along some part of the sky.

shoot'ing bōard, a board or planed metallic slab with a race on which an object is held while its edge is squared or reduced by a side plane.

shoot'ing box, a small house or cabin used by sportsmen during the shooting season.

shoot'ing gal'lẽr·y, a place, as at an amusement park, for practice shooting at enclosed targets.

shoot'ing ī'ron (-ũrn), a firearm. [Slang.]

shoot'ing stär, 1. a meteor.
2. any of a number of related plants with oblong leaves and clusters of rose, white, and purple flowers whose petals are turned back.

shoot'ing stick, an implement used by printers for tightening or loosening the quoins that lock up the forms in a chase.

shoot'-out, shoot'out, *n.* a battle with handguns, etc., as between police and criminals. [Slang.]

shop, *n.* [ME. *schoppe*; AS. *sceoppa*, a stall, a booth at a fair.]
1. a place where goods are sold at retail.
2. a building or room in which workmen carry on their trades or occupation; as, a carpenter's *shop.*
3. figuratively, the source or origin; the place where anything is made.
to set up shop; to open or start a business.
to shut up shop; (a) to go out of business; (b) to close a place of business, as for the night.
to talk shop; to discuss one's work or things related to one's work.

shop, *v.i.*; shopped, *pt., pp.*; shopping, *ppr.* to visit shops for the purpose of examining or purchasing goods.

shop'bōard, *n.* a bench or board on which work is performed.

shop'book, *n.* a book in which a tradesman keeps his accounts.

shop'girl, *n.* a girl who works as a clerk in a store.

shō'phär, *n.* [Heb. *shōphār.*] a ram's horn formerly used as a signaling trumpet by the Jews in battle and still blown in synagogues on the New Year and the Day of Atonement: also spelled *shofar.*

shop'keep″ẽr, *n.* a trader who sells goods in a shop or by retail; a storekeeper.

shop'lift″ẽr, *n.* a person who steals articles exposed for sale in a shop.

shop'lift″ing, *n.* the stealing of articles exposed for sale in a shop.

shop'līke, *a.* vulgar; calculating.

shop'măn, *n.*; *pl.* **shop'men,** 1. a shopkeeper.
2. a salesman in a shop; a clerk.
3. one who works in a shop or factory.

shop'pẽr, *n.* 1. one who shops.
2. a person hired by a store to shop for others.
3. a person hired by a store to compare competitors' merchandise and prices.

shop'ping, *n.* the act of visiting a shop or store to look at, price, or buy goods offered for sale.

shop'ping cen'tẽr, a complex of stores, restaurants, etc. grouped together and having a common parking area.

shop stew'ărd, a person elected by his fellow workers in the local branch of a labor union to represent them in dealing with the employer and to see that union rules are enforced.

shop'talk″, *n.* 1. the specialized or technical vocabulary and idioms of those in the same work, way of life, etc.: see *slang.*
2. conversation about one's work or business, especially after hours.

shop′wạlk″ẽr (-wạk″), *n.* a person hired by a store to supervise clerks and direct customers; a floorwalker.

shop′win″dōw, *n.* a show window.

shop′wọrn, *a.* damaged, soiled, wrinkled, or otherwise deteriorated by being kept or displayed in a shop.

Shōr′an, shōr′an, *n.* [from *Sho*rt *R*ange *N*avigation.] a radar system by which positions on the earth's surface are located by means of high-frequency radio waves transmitted from a plane to ground stations.

shōre, *v.* archaic or dialectal past tense and past participle of *shear.*

shōre, *n.* [ME. *schore,* from M.L.G. *schore,* point of division.]
1. land at or near the edge of a body of water, especially a large body.
2. land as opposed to water.
3. in law, the land area between the marks of high and low water.
in shore; close to the shore.
off shore; (a) away from the shore and toward the water; (b) close to shore.
on shore; on land or on land near the water.

shōre, *v.t.*; shored, *pt., pp.*; shoring, *ppr.* to set ashore; to land.

shōre, *n.* [ME. *schore,* from M.L.G. *schore,* probably from base of *shear.*] a prop or timber placed as a brace or support on the side of a building, boat, etc.

SHORES

shōre, *v.t.*; shored, *pt., pp.*; shoring, *ppr.* to prop; to support with a shore or shores: usually with *up*; as, to *shore up* a building.

Shō′rē·ȧ, *n.* [after John *Shore* (1751–1834), governor of India.] a small genus of Indian plants of the order *Dipteraceæ.* One species, *Shorea robusta,* is a large tree, with entire leaves and fruit shaped like a shuttlecock. The wood is of a uniform light-brown color, close-grained, and strong. The tree exudes a resin called by the natives *ral* or *dhoona.*

shōre′-bāsed (-bāst), *a.* designating aircraft that operate from bases on shore rather than from aircraft carriers.

shōre bĩrd, any limicoline bird nesting on the shore: the group includes the curlews, snipes, sandpipers, ruffs, etc.

shōre din′nẽr, a meal consisting of freshly caught sea food.

shōre grȧss, same as *shoreweed.*

shōre lärk, the American lark, *Otocoris alpestris,* which in winter inhabits the Atlantic and Pacific coasts and the prairies of the West: also called *horned lark.*

shōre lēave, leave granted to a ship's crew members for going ashore.

shōre′less, *a.* having no shore or coast; of indefinite or unlimited extent; as, a *shoreless* ocean.

shōre līne, a line marking the edge of a body of water.

shōre′ling, *n.* same as *shorling.*

shōre pȧ·trōl′, a detail of the United States Navy, Coast Guard, or Marine Corps acting as military police on shore.

shōre plŏv′ẽr, the large-billed plover, *Eascus magnirostris,* of Australia.

shōr′ẽr, *n.* one who shores or props; a device to prop or shore.

shōre′wărd, *adv.* toward the shore.

shōre′wărd, *a.* moving toward the shore.

shōre′weed, *n.* a European plant, *Littorella lacustris,* growing in muddy and sandy places.

shōr′ing, *n.* 1. the act of supporting with or as with props or shores.
2. a number or set of props or shores, taken collectively.

shorl, *n.* same as *schorl.*

shor·lā′ceous, *a.* same as *schorlaceous.*

shōr′ling, *n.* 1. a newly shorn sheep; a shearling. [Brit. Dial.]
2. the skin of a sheep shorn while living, as distinguished from a *morling.* [Obs.]

shōrn, *v.* alternative past participle of *shear.*

shọrt, *a.*; *comp.* shorter; *superl.* shortest. [AS. *sceort, scort,* short; O.H.G. *scurz,* short, cut off; ON. *skort,* short piece of clothing.]
1. not extending far from end to end; not long.
2. not great in span, range, or scope, as a distance, journey, throw, view, etc.
3. low in height; not tall.
4. lasting but a little time; brief.
5. not retentive for long: said of memory.
6. condensed; concise; brief, as a literary style, story, speech, etc.
7. brief or abrupt to the point of rudeness; curt.
8. short-tempered.
9. less than or lacking a sufficient or correct amount; as, a *short* measure; the loss of my laundry has left me *short*; we are *short* ten dollars.
10. not far enough to reach the mark, objective, etc.; as, a shot that fell *short.*
11. having a tendency to break or crumble; friable, as clay, pastry, etc.
12. in commerce, (a) not having in possession at the time of sale the commodities or securities one is selling; (b) of or designating a sale of commodities or securities not in the possession of the seller.
13. in phonetics and prosody, comparatively brief in duration: said of sounds, syllables, etc.
short account; (a) the account of a person who sells securities or commodities short; (b) the total short sales in a particular commodity or in the market as a whole.
short and; same as *ampersand.*
short and sweet; brief, usually unexpectedly so.
short cause; in law, a cause which may be advanced on the docket if shown to need but a short time for disposal.
short clothes; clothes of a length to permit the free use of the limbs; the first change from the long clothes of infancy.
short commons; insufficient fare; scanty rations.
short covering; the buying of securities or commodities to close out a short sale.
short cut; (a) a shorter way to get to the same place; (b) any way of saving time, effort, expense, etc.
short division; division, usually by any number up to twelve, without written indication of the process used.
short entry; in banking, the entry made in a customer's bankbook when a bill or note not yet due has been sent to the bank for collection.
short for; being a shortened form of; being an abbreviation or nickname for.
short of; (a) not equaling; less than; (b) without a sufficient or correct amount of; lacking; (c) not far enough to reach (the mark, objective, etc.).
short rib; a false rib.
short sale; a sale of securities or commodities which the seller does not yet have but expects to buy at a lower price before the date of delivery as contracted.
short short story; a story so short that it can usually be printed complete on one page of a magazine: characteristically it conveys a single mood, is concise, fastmoving, and has a surprise ending.
short shrift; (a) originally, a very brief period of confession and absolution before death; (b) very little care or attention, as from lack of patience or sympathy; (c) little or no mercy or respite.
short snort; a quick drink of liquor. [Slang.]
short snorter; a member of an informal organization composed of passengers or pilots who have made transoceanic flights, and who carry, as a token of membership, a dollar bill or pound note autographed by three or more other members.
short story; a kind of story varying widely in length but shorter than the novel or novelette: characteristically it develops a single central theme or impression and is limited in scope and number of characters.
short subject; any short presentation shown along with the featured picture in a motion-picture program: animated cartoons and travelogues are *short subjects.*
short suit; in whist, any suit having no more than three cards.
short time; in manufacturing, etc., less than the usual number of working hours.
short ton; a unit of weight equal to two thousand pounds avoirdupois.
to fall (or *come*) *short*; to be lacking or insufficient.
to make short shrift of; to make short work of; to dismiss summarily: also, *to give short shrift.*
to make short work of; to deal with, handle, or dispose of quickly.

shọrt, *n.* 1. something that is short; specifically, (a) a short sound or syllable contrasted with one that is long, as in prosody; (b) a motion-picture short subject; (c) a fish, etc. that is below the size that may be legally taken; (d) a shot that falls short of the target or objective.
2. (a) a person making a short sale with the intention of profiting from a future decline in price; (b) a short sale or something sold in one.
3. [*pl.*] (a) knee breeches; smallclothes; (b) short, loose trousers reaching part way to the knee, worn in sports, etc.; (c) a man's undergarment of similar form.
4. [*pl.*] a by-product of wheat milling that consists of bran, germ, and coarse meal.
5. [*pl.*] trimmings, clippings, etc. left over in the manufacture of various products.
6. in baseball, shortstop.
7. in electricity, a short circuit.
for short; by way of abbreviation or contraction.
in short; (a) in summing up; (b) in a few words; briefly.

shọrt, *adv.* 1. abruptly; suddenly.
2. rudely; curtly.
3. briefly; concisely.
4. so as to be short; as, he cut the board off too *short.*
5. on the near side of a given point; so as not to reach a given condition, etc.; as, we were stopped just *short* of disaster.
6. without having possession (of that which is sold).
to fall (or *come*) *short*; to fail to reach or attain.
to run short; to have less than enough.

shọrt, *v.t.* to shorten. [Obs.]

shọrt, *v.t.* and *v.i.* in electricity, to short-circuit.

shọrt′ăġe, *n.* [*short* and *-age.*] a deficiency in the quantity or amount needed; deficit; insufficiency.

shọrt′-ärmed, *a.* 1. having disproportionately short arms.
2. having a short reach.
3. struck with the arm bent, as a blow.

shọrt′bread (-bred), *n.* a rich, crumbly cake or cooky made with shortening.

shọrt′-breathed (-bretht), *a.* having short breath or quick respiration.

shọrt′çāke, *n.* 1. a crisp, light biscuit served with fruit, whipped cream, etc. as a dessert.
2. any sweet cake, as spongecake, served in this way.
3. a dessert made with either of these; as, strawberry *shortcake.*

shọrt″chānġe′, *v.t.*; shortchanged, *pt., pp.*; shortchanging, *ppr.* to give less than the correct change to in changing money; by extension, to cheat in any manner.

shọrt″chānġe′, *v.i.* to give less than the correct change; to cheat.

shọrt″-cĩr′çuit (-kit), *v.t.* and *v.i.* to make a short circuit (in).

shọrt cĩr′çuit, 1. a side circuit of very low relative resistance connecting two points in an electric circuit of higher resistance so as to deflect most of the current.
2. loosely, a disrupted electric circuit resulting from this.

shọrt′çŏm″ing, *n.* a coming short of what is expected or required; a fault; a deficiency; an inadequacy; a defect, as in character.

shọrt′-dāt″ed, *a.* having little time to run.

shọrt′-drąwn, *a.* drawn in without filling the lungs; imperfectly inspired; as, *short-drawn* breath.

shọrt′en, *v.t.* 1. to make short in measure, extent, or time; as, to *shorten* distance; to *shorten* a road; to *shorten* days of calamity.
2. to abridge; to lessen; to make to appear short; as, to *shorten* labor or work.
3. to curtail; as, to *shorten* the hair by clipping.
4. to contract; to lessen; to diminish in extent or amount; as, to *shorten* an allowance of provisions.
5. to confine; to restrain; to hinder.
6. to take something from; to lop; to deprive.

7. to make short or friable, as pastry, with butter or lard.
8. to furl or reef (a sail) so that less canvas is exposed to the breeze.

short'en, *v.i.* 1. to become short or shorter.
2. to contract; as, a cord *shortens* by being wet; a metallic rod *shortens* by cold.

short'en·ẽr, *n.* one who or that which shortens.

short'en·ing, *n.* 1. the act of making or becoming short or shorter.
2. fat used in baked goods to make them crisp or flaky.

Short'ẽr Cat'ē·chism, a catechism adopted by the Westminster Assembly in 1647: used chiefly by the Presbyterians.

short'-hāired, *a.* having short hair or fur.

short'hand, *n.* any system of speed writing using symbols that can be made quickly to represent letters, words, and phrases.

short'hand, *a.* 1. using shorthand.
2. written in shorthand.

short'hand'ed, *a.* not having the necessary number of hands, servants, or assistants.

short'head (-hed), *n.* 1. a sucking whale under twelve months old.
2. a head with a cephalic index of 80 or more.
3. a person having such a head; a brachycephalic person.

short'-head'ed, short'head'ed, *a.* having a shorthead.

short'horn, *n.* any one of a certain breed of heavy domestic cattle having short horns: they are raised both for beef and for milk and vary widely in color.

Shor'ti·ȧ, *n.* [named after Dr. C. W. *Short* (1794–1863), an American botanist.]
1. a genus of related evergreen plants with nodding bell-shaped white flowers on long stalks.
2. [s–] a plant of this genus.

short'ish, *a.* rather short.

short'-joint''ed, *a.* having short spaces between articulations; as, a horse is said to be *short-jointed* when the pastern is too short.

short'-leg''ged (*or* short'-legd''), *a.* having short legs.

short'-līved', *a.* not living or lasting long; being of short continuance; as, a *short-lived* race of beings; *short-lived* pleasure.

short'ly, *adv.* 1. in a few words; briefly.
2. in a short time; soon.
3. abruptly.
4. rudely; curtly.

short'ness, *n.* the quality or state of being short in space or time; little length or little duration; brevity; conciseness; lack of reach or the power of retention; deficiency; imperfection; limited extent.

short'-or'dẽr, *a.* [from *in short order.*] offering or cooking short orders.

short or'dẽr, any food quickly prepared after it has been ordered in a restaurant.
in short order; quickly.

short'-rānge', *a.* limited in range; carrying or reaching only a short distance.

short'sīght'ed (-sīt'), *a.* 1. not able to see far; having limited vision; nearsighted; myopic.
2. not able to look far into futurity; not able to understand things deep or remote; of limited foresight.
3. having little forethought; heedless of the future.

short''sīght'ed·ly, *adv.* in a heedless manner; with lack of penetration.

short''sīght'ed·ness, *n.* 1. a defect in vision, consisting in the inability to see things at a distance, or at the distance to which the sight ordinarily extends.
2. defective or limited intellectual sight; inability to see far into futurity or into things deep or abstruse.
3. heedlessness.

short'-spō'ken, *a.* 1. using only a few words to express one's thoughts; laconic.
2. brief to the point of rudeness; curt.

short'stop'', *n.* in baseball, (a) the infield player whose place is between second base and third base; (b) the position of this player.

short'tāil'', *n.* a snake with a short tail; a roller.

short'-tem'pẽred, *a.* easily disturbed; quick to be offended; having a tendency to lose one's temper.

short'-tẽrm', *a.* requiring payment or coming due in a short time, as a loan.

short'-wāist'ed, *a.* 1. having a short waist or body between the shoulders and hips; with a high waistline.
2. applying to costumes of this character; as, a *short-waisted* gown.

short'-wāve', *a.* in radio, of, by, or using short wave.

short wāve, a radio wave sixty meters or less in length.

short'-wind'ed, *a.* 1. easily put out of breath by exercise.
2. breathing with quick, labored breaths.

short'-winged', *a.* having short wings; as, a *short-winged* hawk.

short'-wit'ted, *a.* having little wit; not wise; of scanty intellect or judgment.

short'y, *n.*; *pl.* **short'ies,** a person or thing of less than average height or size. [Colloq.]

Shō·shō'nē, *n.* 1. a member of a group of Shoshonean Indians originally scattered over Montana, Wyoming, and Oregon: also spelled *Shoshoni.*
2. an American Indian language spoken by this group.

Shō·shō'nē·ăn, *a.* designating or of a subbranch of the Uto-Aztecan linguistic family of North American Indians: it includes the Shoshone, Comanche, Ute, Paiute, Hopi, etc.

shot, *n.* [ME. *schot*; AS. *gesceot*, from *sceotan*, to shoot.]
1. the act of shooting; discharge of a missile, especially from a gun.
2. (a) the distance over which a missile travels; (b) figuratively, range; reach; scope.
3. an attempt to hit with a missile.
4. (a) any attempt; a try; (b) a guess; conjecture.
5. a pointed, critical remark.
6. a stroke, throw, drive, etc. in any of several games.
7. (a) a projectile designed to be discharged from a firearm or cannon, especially a solid ball or bullet as distinguished from an explosive shell; (b) such projectiles collectively.
8. (a) lead in small pellets, of which a quantity is used for a single charge of a shotgun; (b) a single pellet of this kind.
9. a heavy metal ball cast for distance by contestants.
10. a blast or the amount of explosive used for a blast, as in mining.
11. a marksman; as, he's a fair *shot.*
12. a photographic record; a single photograph, or a sequence in motion-picture film.
13. an amount due, especially for drinks or entertainment, or one's share of payment. [Colloq.]
14. a dose, as of morphine, given by hypodermic injection. [Slang.]
15. a drink of liquor; specifically, a jigger. [Slang.]
16. something to bet on, considered from the standpoint of odds or chances of winning; as, that horse is a twenty-to-one *shot.* [Colloq.]
a long shot; (a) an attempt not likely to succeed; (b) [Colloq.] a bet against heavy odds; (c) [Colloq.] someone or something considered to have little chance of winning or succeeding.
chilled shot; shot formed from casehardened steel, used to pierce the armor of ships, etc.
like a shot; (a) quickly; rapidly; (b) suddenly.
not by a long shot; not at all; not by any means. [Slang.]
to have (or *take*) *a shot at*; to make a try at. [Colloq.]
to put the shot; to heave or throw a heavy metal ball with an overhand pushing motion in a field contest for distance.

shot, *v.t.*; shotted, *pt., pp.*; shotting, *ppr.* to load or weight with shot.

shot, *v.* past tense and past participle of *shoot.*

shot, *a.* [pt. and pp. of *shoot.*]
1. variegated, streaked, flecked, etc. with another color or substance.
2. woven with threads of different colors so as to appear iridescent.
3. no longer usable; ruined; worn out. [Colloq.]
4. destined for, or having met with, failure, defeat, frustration, etc.; as, his chances are *shot.* [Colloq.]

shot cär'tridge (-trij), a cartridge loaded with shot instead of a single ball, used in a breech-loading gun.

shot'-clog, *n.* a tedious person who is received solely because he pays the shot. [Obs.]

shot cross'bōw, a combined crossbow and firearm.

shōte, *n.* a young pig: also spelled *shoat.*

shot ef·fect', an irregularity in the emission of thermions from the electron tube filament, resulting in popping noises upon amplification.

shot'-free, *a.* scot-free. [Rare.]

shot gär'lănd, a stand for the shot and shell used in land batteries to keep them from depreciation. [Obs.]

shot glàss, a small drinking glass designed to hold a single jigger, as of whisky.

shot'gun'', *n.* a gun having a smooth bore and used for firing a charge of small shot at short range, as distinguished from a rifled gun firing a single ball.

shot hōle, 1. a hole made by a shot or shots.
2. a drill hole charged for firing.

shot līne, the cord or light line attached to the projectile fired over a vessel it is designed to reach: a device used in the life-saving service.

shot lock'ẽr, a compartment for shot or projectiles, as on a ship.

shot met'ăl, an alloy of lead and arsenic from which shot is made.

shot plug, a plug for stopping shot holes, formerly used on wooden men-of-war.

shot pouch, a pouch, generally of leather, to hold the shot for hunting, rarely used except with a muzzle-loading gun.

shot'proof', *a.* proof against shot.

shot prop, on a ship, a device for filling a shot hole below the water line. [Archaic.]

shot'put'', *n.* 1. a contest in which athletes put the shot.
2. a single throw of the shot.

shott, *n.* [Ar.] in north Africa, a lake bed left bare by evaporation, except for precipitated salt and drifted sand.

shot'ted, *a.* 1. designating a cannon loaded with ball as well as powder.
2. weighted with or having a shot attached.

shot'ten, *v.* obsolete past participle of *shoot.*

shot'ten, *a.* 1. having ejected the spawn and become of inferior food value: said of a fish, especially herrings.
2. undesirable; worthless. [Archaic.]
3. shot out of its socket; dislocated, as a bone.

shot tow'ẽr, a high tower from the summit of which molten lead is dropped into a liquid, thereby forming hard globules, or shot.

shot'ty, *a.* like shot.

shot win'dōw, a casement. [Archaic.]

shough (shok), *n.* a kind of shaggy dog. [Obs.]

should (shood), *v.* [ME. *scholde, shold*; AS. *sceolde, scolde*, pt. of *sceal, scal*, I am obliged.]
1. past tense of *shall.*
2. an auxiliary used to express (a) obligation, duty, propriety, necessity: e.g., children *should* get hot lunches; (b) expectation or probability: e.g., since they left Saturday they *should* be here by Monday: equivalent to *ought to* and not replaceable by *would*; (c) futurity from the standpoint of the past in indirect quotations where *shall* and *will* were used in the direct quotations: replaceable by *would*: e.g., I said I *should* (or *would*) be home by nine; (d) futurity in polite or unemphatic requests or in statements with implications of uncertainty or doubt: replaceable by *would*: e.g., *should* (or *would*) you like some tea? I *should* (or *would*) think he'd like it; (e) a future condition: e.g., if I *should* go, would you be there?: in this sense *would* is considered colloquial or, by some, substandard; (f) a past condition, real or unreal: replaceable by *would*: e.g., I *should* (or *would*) have gone, but you never asked me.
N.B. In formal speech the distinctions between *should* and *would* are the same as those between *shall* and *will.*

shōul'dẽr, *n.* [ME. *shulder*; AS. *sculdor*; akin to G. *schulter*, the shoulder, the shoulder blade.]
1. (a) the joint connecting the arm or forelimb with the body; (b) the part of the body including this joint and extending along the top (in quadrupeds, the side) of the trunk to the base of the neck.
2. [*pl.*] the two shoulders and the part of the back between them: often used figuratively with reference to this region of the body as a place where burdens are often carried.
3. a cut of meat consisting of the upper foreleg and attached parts.

4. the part of a garment that covers the shoulders.
5. the part of a hide anterior to the butt, corresponding to the animal's shoulders.
6. something like a shoulder in shape or position; a shoulderlike projection.
7. the angle between the face and flank of a bastion in a fortification.
8. the part of the top of a piece of type which extends beyond the base of the raised letter or character.
9. either edge of a road or highway.
shoulder to shoulder; (a) side by side and close together; (b) working together; with common or united effort.
straight from the shoulder; (a) moving straight forward from the shoulder: said of a blow; (b) without reserve or evasion; frankly.
to cry on someone's shoulder; to seek comfort or sympathy in someone; to tell one's troubles to someone.
to put one's shoulder to the wheel; to set to work vigorously; to put forth vigorous effort.
to rub shoulders with; to associate or mingle with (famous or prominent people, etc.).
to turn (or *give*) *a cold shoulder to*; (a) to treat with coldness or disdain; to show dislike for; (b) to avoid; to shun.

shoul'dẽr, *v.t.*; shouldered, *pt., pp.*; shouldering, *ppr.* 1. to push or thrust along or through, with or as with the shoulder; to push with violence.
2. to take or carry upon the shoulder.
3. to assume the burden of; as, to *shoulder* another's responsibilities.
4. to form a shoulder upon; as, to *shoulder* a spoke.
to shoulder arms; to rest a rifle against the (right or left) shoulder, supporting the butt with the hand on the same side while holding the arm bent and close to the side.

shoul'dẽr, *v.i.* to press forward with or as with the shoulder or shoulders.

shoul'dẽr belt, a belt that passes across the shoulder.

shoul'dẽr blāde, either of the two flat bones in the upper back articulated with the humerus; the scapula.

shoul'dẽr block, in nautical usage, a large single block having a projection on the shell to prevent the rope that is roved through it from becoming jammed between the block and the yard.

SHOULDER BLOCK

shoul'dẽr'-çlap pẽr, *n.* one who claps another on the shoulder, or uses great familiarity; also, a bailiff. [Rare.]

shoul'dẽred, *a.* having a shoulder or shoulders; as, a *shouldered* type; frequently in compounds; as, stoop-*shouldered*; narrow-*shouldered*; broad-*shouldered.*

shoul'dẽr gĩr'dle, the girdle of bones or cartilage surrounding the articulation at the shoulder, consisting of the scapula, coracoid, and clavicle, and minor attachments; the pectoral arch.

shoul'dẽr knot (not), a knot of ribbon or lace or a gold wire cord worn on the shoulder as an insigne, decoration, etc.

shoul'dẽr pad, in tailoring, a pad made of layers of cloth or cloth and cotton quilted together and placed in the shoulder of a garment, as a coat or a jacket, to give it symmetry and to preserve its shape.

shoul'dẽr-shot''ten, *a.* strained in the shoulder, as a horse.

shoul'dẽr slip, dislocation of the shoulder or of the humerus.

shoul'dẽr strap, 1. a strap worn over the shoulder to hold up the dress or to carry a package, etc.
2. a piece of cloth fixed to the shoulder of a uniform to hold insignia.

should'n't (shood'nt), should not.

shouldst (shoodst), *v.* archaic second person singular, present indicative, of *should*: used with *thou.*

shout, *n.* [ME. *schoute.*]
1. a loud sound made with the voice; a loud, sudden cry or call.
2. any sudden, loud outburst or uproar.

shout, *v.t.* to utter in a loud voice; to say or express in a shout.
to shout (*someone*) *down*; to silence or overwhelm (someone) by loud shouting; to shout louder than (another).

shout, *v.i.* to utter a shout; to cry out loudly.

shout, *n.* a flat-bottomed skiff. [Brit. Dial.]

shout'ẽr, *n.* one who shouts.

shȯve, *v.t.*; shoved, *pt., pp.*; shoving, *ppr.* [ME. *shouen*; AS. *scofian* or *scufan*, to push or thrust.]
1. to push; to propel; to drive along by the direct application of strength; to push by sliding or causing to move along a surface either by the hand or by an instrument; as, to *shove* a bottle along a table; to *shove* a table along the floor; to *shove* a boat on the water
2. to thrust or push away. [Archaic.]
3. to bring into prominence. [Obs.]
4. to jostle; to push without ceremony.
to shove off; to push (a boat) away from shore, as in departing.

shȯve, *v.i.* 1. to push or drive forward, as along a surface.
2. to push roughly.
3. to push off; to move in a boat by pushing a pole; as, he *shoved* from shore.
to shove off; to start off; to leave; to depart. [Colloq.]

shȯve, *n.* 1. the act of pushing or pressing against by strength; a push or thrust.
2. the forward movement of piled broken pieces of ice.

shȯve'bōard, *n.* same as *shovelboard.*

shȯve'grōat, *n.* same as *shovelboard.*

shŏv·el, *n.* [ME. *schovele*, from AS. *sceofol*, from *scufan*, to shove.]
1. a tool with a broad, deep scoop or blade and a long handle: used in lifting and moving loose material, as earth, snow, gravel, etc.
2. a shovelful.
3. a shovel hat.

shŏv'el, *v.t.*; shoveled *or* shovelled, *pt., pp.*; shoveling *or* shovelling, *ppr.* 1. to lift and move with a shovel.
2. to clean or dig out with a shovel, as a path.
3. to put or throw in large quantities; as, he *shoveled* sugar into his coffee.

shŏv'el·ärd, *n.* same as *shoveler*, n. 2.

shŏv'el·bill, *n.* a river duck; a shoveler.

shŏv'el·bōard, *n.* same as *shuffleboard.*

shŏv'el·ẽr, *n.* 1. one who or that which shovels.
2. a species of duck, *Spatula* or *Rhynchaspis clypeata*, with a very long, broad, flattened bill: it is native to Europe and America, is about 20 inches in length, and has brightly marked plumage.
Also spelled *shoveller.*

shŏv'el·fish, *n.* same as *shovelhead.*

shŏv'el·fu̇l, *n.*; *pl.* **shŏv'el·fu̇ls,** the contents of a shovel; as much as a shovel will hold.

shŏv'el hat, a stiff, low-crowned hat with a broad brim turned up at the sides: worn by some English clergymen.

shŏv'el·head (-hed), *n.* 1. a small shark related to the hammerhead: its head resembles the blade of a shovel.
2. the shovel-nosed sturgeon.

shŏv'el·lẽr, *n.* same as *shoveler.*

shŏv'el·nōṣe, *n.* any of several shovel-nosed animals.

shŏv'el-nōṣed, *a.* having a nose broad and flat like a shovel.

shŏv'el-nōṣed shärk, either of two flat-headed sharks found along the California coast.

shŏv'el-nōṣed stũr'ġeŏn, a kind of freshwater sturgeon of the Mississippi Valley, valued as a food fish.

shŏv'el plow, a simple plow with a triangular metal share, used for cultivating ground between rows of plants and for drawing furrows before planting.
double shovel plow; a shovel plow with two shares, one set behind and to one side of the other, so as to make two adjacent furrows when used in cultivating.

shŏv'ẽr, *n.* 1. one who or that which pushes or shoves.
2. one who propels a boat in shallow water by means of a pole or oar.

shōw, *v.t.*; showed, *pt.*; shown *or* showed, *pp.*; showing, *ppr.* [ME. *schewen*; AS. *sceawian*, to look, see, behold, akin to G. *schauen*, to behold.]
1. to bring or put in sight or view; to cause or allow to appear or be seen; to make visible; to exhibit; to display.
2. to enter (animals, flowers, paintings, etc.) in a show or exhibition.
3. to guide; to conduct; as, the bellboy *showed* him to his room.
4. to direct a person's observation or attention to; to point out; as, we *showed* him the sights.
5. to reveal, manifest, or make evident (an emotion, condition, quality, etc.) by behavior or outward sign; as, he *showed* his anger without meaning to, the judge *showed* mercy to the prisoners.
6. to exhibit or manifest (oneself or itself) in a given character, condition, etc.; as, the group has *shown* itself to be reliable.
7. to make known, manifest, or clear; to reveal; explain; as, he has *shown* the difference between them.
8. to make evident by logical procedure; to prove; demonstrate; as, scientists have *shown* that it is possible.
9. to register; to indicate; as, a barometer *shows* the air pressure.
10. to grant or bestow (favor, grace, etc.).
11. in law, to allege; to plead; as, *show* cause.
to show forth; to manifest; to publish; to proclaim.
to show in; to usher or conduct into a given place.
to show off; to make a display of; to exhibit in a showy manner.
to show out; to usher or conduct out of a given place.
to show up; (a) to bring to light; to expose, as faults; (b) [Colloq.] to be far superior to.
Syn.—exhibit, present, demonstrate, unfold, reveal, explain, teach, inform, conduct, manifest, evince, evidence, prove.

shōw, *v.i.* 1. to be or become seen or visible; to appear.
2. to be apparent or noticeable; as, the scratch won't *show.*
3. to have a given appearance; to appear; as, it *shows* poorly in this light.
4. to finish third or better in a horse or dog race; as, this horse *showed* in five of the last seven races.
5. in the theater, to give a performance; to appear.
to show off; to behave in a manner intended to attract attention; to make a vain display.
to show up; (a) to come to light; to be exposed, as faults; (b) to be clearly seen; to be prominent or apparent; (c) to come; to arrive; to make an appearance.

shōw, *n.* 1. a showing, demonstration, or manifestation; as, a *show* of passion.
2. a display or appearance, specifically a colorful or striking one; as, the costumed dancers made quite a *show.*
3. spectacular, pompous display; ostentation.
4. an indication of the presence of metal, coal, oil, etc. in the earth; a trace.
5. something false or superficial; semblance; pretense; as, her sympathy was mere *show.*
6. a person or thing looked upon as peculiar, ridiculous, laughable, etc.; spectacle; sight.
7. a public display or exhibition, as of art, animals, flowers, etc.
8. a presentation of entertainment, especially of a theatrical nature; as, the *show* begins at eight o'clock, who sponsors this radio *show?*
9. any undertaking, matter, or affair; as, his political career was a disgraceful *show.* [Colloq.]
10. an engagement, battle, campaign, etc.; as, our casualties were high in the last *show.* [Military Slang.]
for show; in order to attract notice or attention.
show of hands; a display or raising of hands, as in voting, volunteering, etc.
to stand (or *have*) *a show*; to have a chance, especially a remote one. [Colloq.]

shōw bill, a placard, poster, or large billboard advertisement, usually printed, containing announcements of goods for sale, a theatrical performance, etc.

shōw'bōat, *n.* a boat containing a theater and carrying a troupe of actors who play river towns.

shōw box, a box holding something odd or curious which is used for exhibition purposes.

shōw'bread, *n.* same as *shewbread.*

shōw buṣi'ness (biz'nes), the theater, vaudeville, motion pictures, circuses, etc. as a business or industry.

shōw çärd, a show bill.

shōw'çāse, *n.* a case with glass top and sides, used to display articles and protect them from dust and injury, as in a store or exhibition.

shōw'down, *n.* 1. in poker, a laying down and exhibition of the cards face up. [Colloq.]

2. a revelation or disclosure, as of the true nature of a situation. [Colloq.]

shōw′ẽr, *n.* 1. one who or that which shows or exhibits.

2. that which shows, as a mirror. [Obs.]

show′ẽr, *n.* [ME. *shoure, schowre;* AS. *scur;* akin to Ice. *skūr;* Sw. *skur;* O.H.G. *scūr,* a shower, a tempest; G. *schauer,* a shower.]

1. a brief fall of rain, hail, or sleet.

2. a sudden, abundant fall or discharge, as of tears, meteors, rays, sparks, etc.

3. an abundant flow; a rush; as, a *shower* of complaints.

4. a party during which a number of gifts are presented to the guest of honor; as, a bridal *shower.*

5. a shower bath.

show′ẽr, *v.t.;* showered, *pt., pp.;* showering, *ppr.* 1. to make wet with water or other liquid; to sprinkle; to spray.

2. to pour down copiously and rapidly; to bestow liberally; to distribute or scatter in abundance.

show′ẽr, *v.i.* 1. to come in a shower; to fall as a shower; as, tears *showered* down his cheeks.

2. to take a shower bath.

show′ẽr bȧth, 1. a bath in which the body is sprayed with fine streams of water from small jets.

2. an apparatus or room used for such a bath.

show′ẽr·fụl, *a.* full of showers.

show′ẽr·i·ness, *n.* the quality or state of being showery.

show′ẽr·less, *a.* without showers.

show′ẽr·y, *a.* 1. raining in showers; raining briefly and frequently.

2. of or resembling a shower.

shōw′girl, *n.* a woman in show business; especially, a chorus girl in a musical show or night-club entertainment.

shōw glȧss, 1. a mirror used for display; especially, a magic mirror.

2. a showcase.

shōw′i·ly, *adv.* in a showy manner; pompously.

shōw′i·ness, *n.* the condition or quality of being showy.

shōw′ing, *n.* 1. the act of exhibiting or bringing to notice.

2. an exposition; formal display.

3. a performance, appearance, etc.; as, a good *showing* in the contest.

shōw′ish, *a.* rather showy. [Rare.]

shōw′măn, *n.; pl.* **shōw′men,** 1. a person who makes a business of producing or managing shows.

2. a person who is skilled at this or at presenting anything in an interesting or dramatic manner.

shōw′măn·ship, *n.* the art of being a showman; skill as a showman.

shōwn, *v.* alternative past participle of *show.*

shōw′-ọff, *n.* 1. the act of showing off; vain or showy display.

2. one who shows off. [Colloq.]

shōw′piēce, *n.* 1. something displayed or exhibited.

2. something that is a fine example of its kind.

shōw plāce, 1. a place that is displayed or exhibited to the public for its beauty, etc.

2. any place that is beautiful, lavishly furnished, etc.

3. a gymnasium. [Obs.]

shōw′rọom, *n.* a room in which goods are displayed to attract purchasers; a sample room.

shōw stōne, a crystal used in divination.

shōw win′dōw, a shop window used to display goods.

shōw′y, *a.; comp.* showier; *superl.* showiest, 1. of striking or attractive appearance; making a show.

2. attracting attention in a cheap or artificial way; flashy; ostentatious.

Syn.—magnificent, flashy, glaring, garish, pompous, sumptuous, gorgeous, dressy.

shōw′yärd, *n.* an enclosure for the exhibition of cattle, machinery, etc. at a fair.

shrag, *n.* a twig of a tree cut off. [Obs.]

shrag, *v.t.* to clip; to lop off; to shred; to trim, as a tree. [Obs.]

shrag′gẽr, *n.* one who trims trees. [Obs.]

shram, *v.t.* to cause to shrink or shrivel; to make numb, as with cold. [Brit. Dial.]

shrañk, *v.* alternative past tense of *shrink.*

shrap′nel, *n.* [after Gen. H. *Shrapnel* (1761–1842), of the British Army, who invented it.]

1. an artillery shell filled with an explosive charge and many small metal balls, set to explode in the air over the objective.

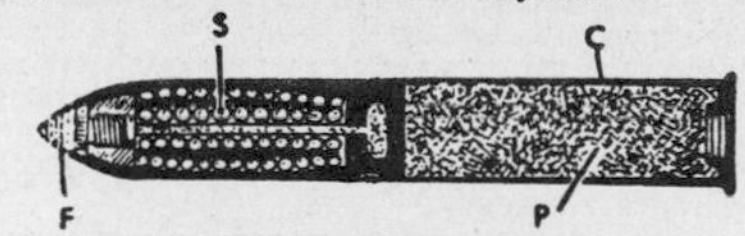

DIAGRAM OF SHRAPNEL SHELL
C, cartridge; F, fuse; P, powder charge; S, shrapnel

2. such shells collectively, or the metal balls scattered by the explosion of such shells.

3. shell fragments scattered by any exploding shell.

shred, *n.* [ME. *schrede;* AS. *screada,* a piece, strip.]

1. an irregular strip or long, narrow piece cut or torn off; as, *shreds* of cloth.

2. a very small piece or amount; a fragment; a particle; as, *shreds* of wit.

shred, *v.t.;* shredded *or* shred, *pt., pp.;* shredding, *ppr.* [AS. *screadan,* to cut off.]

1. to tear or cut into small strips, especially long, narrow pieces, as cloth or leather.

2. to trim; to tear; to prune. [Obs.]

shred′çock, *n.* the fieldfare. [Brit. Dial.]

shred′dẽr, *n.* a person or thing that shreds.

shred′ding, *n.* 1. a cutting or tearing into shreds.

2. that which is shredded off; a shred.

3. in architecture, furring.

shred′dy, *a.; comp.* shreddier; *superl.* shreddiest; having or consisting of shreds; shredlike; shredded.

shred′less, *a.* having no shreds.

shrew, *n.* [sense 2 only in ME. *schrewe,* malicious person; AS. *screawa;* sense 1 may be a special application of this in view of the malignant reputation of the mammal.]

1. a small, mouselike mammal of the family *Soricidae,* that has soft, brown fur and a long snout: it feeds on insects and worms and was once thought venomous.

2. a scolding, nagging, evil-tempered woman.

3. originally, any wicked or evil person; a malignant or spiteful person.

4. a danger; an evil; also, an evil planet. [Obs.]

shrew, *v.t.* to beshrew; to curse. [Obs.]

shrew, *a.* malign; evil. [Obs.]

shrewd, *a.; comp.* shrewder; *superl.* shrewdest, [ME. *shrewed, schrewed,* accursed, wicked, pp. of *schrewen,* to curse.]

1. keen-witted, clever, or sharp in practical affairs; astute.

2. (a) keen; sharp; (b) artful; cunning. [Archaic.]

3. (a) evil; bad; wicked; (b) sly; mischievous; (c) shrewish. [Obs.]

shrewd′ly, *adv.* in a shrewd manner; astutely.

shrewd′ness, *n.* the state or quality of being shrewd.

shrew′ish, *a.* having the qualities, disposition, or manners of a shrew; evil-tempered.

shrew′ish·ly, *adv.* in a shrewish manner.

shrew′ish·ness, *n.* the quality or state of being shrewish.

shrew mōle, an insectivorous mole, *Neurotrichus gibbsi,* of North America, having a long muzzle that is cartilaginous at its tip, long, powerful claws on the forefeet, and fine, thick, gray fur.

shrew′mouse, *n.; pl.* **shrew′mīce,** a shrew.

shrew′-struck, *a.* poisoned or otherwise harmed by the bite or contact of a shrew, formerly believed to be venomous.

shriēk, *v.i.;* shrieked (shrēkt), *pt., pp.;* shrieking, *ppr.* [ME. *schriken,* prob. from hyp. ON. *skrika,* to cry.] to make a loud, sharp, piercing cry or sound, as certain birds and beasts, persons in terror, anger, pain, or laughter, or inanimate things that produce sound; to screech; to scream.

shriēk, *v.t.* to utter with a shriek, or shrill cry.

shriēk, *n.* a sharp, shrill cry or scream, as of one in anguish or extreme terror; a loud, shrill noise.

shriēk′ẽr, *n.* 1. one who shrieks.

2. the bar-tailed godwit.

shriēk owl, 1. the screech owl. [Obs.]

2. the swift. [Brit. Dial.]

shriēv′ăl, *a.* of or pertaining to a sheriff.

shriēv′ăl·ty, *n.; pl.* **shriēv′ăl·ties,** 1. the office of a sheriff; the period during which a sheriff holds office.

2. the district served by a sheriff.

shriēve, *n.* a sheriff. [Obs.]

shriēve, *v.t.* to shrive. [Obs.]

shrift, *n.* [AS. *scrift,* from *scrifan,* to receive confession, from L. *scribere,* to write, or draw up a law.]

1. confession to and absolution by a priest. [Archaic.]

2. the act of shriving; absolution. [Archaic.]

short shrift; see under *short, a.*

shrift, *v.t.* to shrive. [Rare.]

shrift fä′thẽr, a father confessor. [Archaic.]

shrīght (shrīt), *v.i.* and *v.t.* to shriek. [Obs.]

shrīght, *n.* a shriek; screaming. [Obs.]

shrīke, *n.* [AS. *scric,* a shrike, a thrush; Ice. *skrikja,* a shrike.]

1. an insessorial bird of the family *Laniidæ,* having a shrill voice, a hooked beak, gray, black, and white plumage, and a long tail; a butcherbird. The species are numerous and are very widely distributed; most types feed on insects, some on frogs, small birds, etc. *Lanius excubitor* is the European great gray shrike. *Lanius borealis* is the northern butcherbird of North America.

GREAT GRAY SHRIKE (*Lanius excubitor*)

2. any of various other birds resembling the true shrikes, as the crow shrike, bush shrike, drongo, etc. The fork-tailed crested shrike is a drongo of India.

FORK-TAILED CRESTED SHRIKE
(*Dicrurus cristatus*)

shrīke thrush, 1. a bird of the genus *Gampsorhyncus,* resembling a thrush.

2. an Australian bird of the genus *Colluricincla,* resembling a shrike.

shrīke tit, 1. an Australian shrike of the genus *Falcunculus.*

2. a hill tit.

shrill, *a.; comp.* shriller; *superl.* shrillest, [ME. *shirl, shril;* akin to G. *schrill.*]

1. having or producing a high, thin, piercing tone; high-pitched.

2. characterized or accompanied by shrill sounds.

3. keen; sharp; biting; poignant. [Archaic or Poetic.]

shrill, *v.i.;* shrilled, *pt., pp.;* shrilling, *ppr.* to make a shrill noise or sound.

Break we our pipes, that *shrilled* as loud as lark. —Spenser.

shrill, *v.t.* to make a shrill sound; to utter with a shrill sound.

shrill, *n.* a sharp, piercing sound.

shrill, *adv.* shrilly.

shrill′-gọrġed, *a.* having a gorge, or throat, that gives a shrill or acute sound; having a clear or high-pitched voice or note.

shrill′ing, *n.* a shrill noise or cry.

shrill′ness, *n.* the quality or state of being shrill; acuteness of sound; sharpness of voice.

shrill′-tŏngued (-tungd), *a.* having a shrill voice; speaking in a shrill tone.

shrill′-voiced (-voist), *a.* shrill-tongued.

shril′ly, *adv.* in or with a shrill tone, sound, or voice.

shril′y, *a.* shrill. [Poetic.]

shrimp, *v.t.* [from AS. *scrimman,* to wither.] to contract; to shrink. [Dial.]

shrimp, *n.*; *pl.* **shrimps** or **shrimp,** [ME. *schrimpe*, shrimp, puny person, from base of AS. *scrimman*, to shrink, dry up.]

1. a small, slender, long-tailed crustacean of the family *Crangonidæ*, related to the lobster, crayfish, and prawn: many species are valued as food.

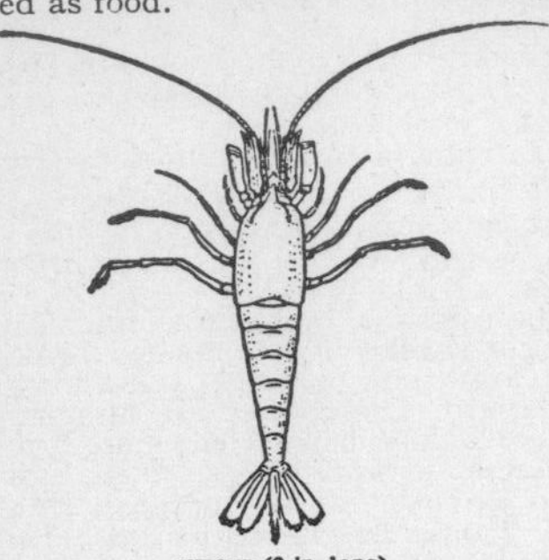

SHRIMP (2 in. long)

2. a small or insignificant person. [Colloq.]

shrimp, *v.i.* to fish for shrimps; to catch shrimps.

shrimp çatch'ẽr, the small tern.

shrīne, *n.* [ME. *schrin*; AS. *scrin*, the ark of the covenant; L. *scrinium*, a chest or box.]

1. a case or other container holding sacred relics, as the bones of a saint.

2. the tomb of a saint or other person held sacred.

3. a place of worship, usually one centered around some sacred object or scene.

4. a place or thing endowed with a sacred character because of its history or associations.

shrīne, *v.t.*; shrined; *pt., pp.*; shrining, *ppr.* to enshrine.

shrin̄k, *v.i.*; shrank *or* shrunk, *pt.*; shrunk *or* shrunken, *pp.*; shrinking, *ppr.* [ME. *shrinken*, to draw together, from AS. *scrincan*, to shrivel up.]

1. to contract, as from heat, cold, moisture, etc.

2. to lessen, as in amount, worth, etc.

3. to draw back; turn away; cower, as from fear.

4. to avoid or wish to avoid taking action; to be reluctant; withdraw; as, I *shrink* from going to the city.

shrin̄k, *v.t.* 1. to cause to shrink or contract.

2. to withdraw. [Obs.]

to shrink on; to fix firmly by causing to shrink; thus, a tire is *shrunk on* a wheel by making it slightly smaller than the part it is to fit, expanding by heat till it can be slipped into place, and then allowing it to cool.

shrin̄k, *n.* the act of shrinking; shrinkage; also, a withdrawing, from fear or horror; recoil.

shrin̄k'à·ble, *a.* that can shrink or be shrunk.

shrin̄k'āġe, *n.* 1. the act or process of shrinking; contraction in size, as of a fabric in washing.

2. decrease in value; depreciation.

3. the total loss in weight of livestock from the time of shipment to the final processing as meat.

4. the amount of such contraction, decrease, or loss.

shrin̄k'ẽr, *n.* one who shrinks; one who withdraws from danger.

shrin̄k'ing·ly, *adv.* in a shrinking manner.

shrin̄k'-wrap, *v.t.*; shrink-wrapped (-rapt), *pt., pp.*; shrink-wrapping, *ppr.* to wrap (a commodity) in a tough, transparent plastic material which is then shrunk by heating to form a sealed, tight-fitting package.

shrin̄k'-wrap, *n.* a wrapping of a material used in shrink-wrapping.

shrīte, *n.* the misselthrush. [Brit. Dial.]

shrīve, *v.t.*; shrived *or* shrove, *pt.*; shriven *or* shrived, *pp.*; shriving, *ppr.* [ME. *shriven*; AS. *scrifan*, to shrive, from L. *scribere*, to write or draw up a law; by extension, to impose a penalty.]

1. to hear or receive the confession of and, usually after penance, administer absolution to. [Archaic.]

2. to get absolution for (oneself) by confessing and doing penance. [Archaic or Rare.]

shrīve, *v.i.* 1. to receive confession and grant absolution. [Archaic.]

2. to make or go to confession. [Archaic.]

shriv'el, *v.t.* and *v.i.*; shriveled *or* shrivelled, *pt., pp.*; shriveling *or* shrivelling, *ppr.* [Early Mod. Eng. dial.; the form suggests an etymon either from AS. or from L.G.; akin to Sw. dial. *skryvla*, to wrinkle.]

1. to curl up or wrinkle; to wither.

2. to make or become helpless, useless, or inefficient.

Syn.—contract, dry up, wither, wrinkle, corrugate, decrease.

shriv'en, *v.* alternative past participle of *shrive.*

shrīv'ẽr, *n.* a confessor. [Archaic.]

shrīv'ing, *n.* shrift; the act of a confessor. [Archaic.]

shroff, *n.* [Anglo-Ind. *sharaf*, from Ar. *sarrāf*, a moneychanger.] in the Orient, a banker or moneychanger; also, an expert in testing coins.

shroff, *v.t.*; shroffed (shroft), *pt., pp.*; shroffing, *ppr.* in the Orient, to inspect (money) for the purpose of detecting and rejecting spurious and imperfect coins.

Shrop'shīre, *n.* a kind of large, black-faced, hornless sheep originally developed in Shropshire, England.

shroud, *n.* [ME. *schroud*; AS. *scrūd*, a garment; akin to ON. *skrud*, a dress, ornament.]

1. a cloth used to wrap a corpse for burial; a winding sheet.

2. something that covers, protects, or screens; a veil; shelter.

3. one of a set of ropes stretched from a ship's side to a masthead to offset lateral strain on the mast.

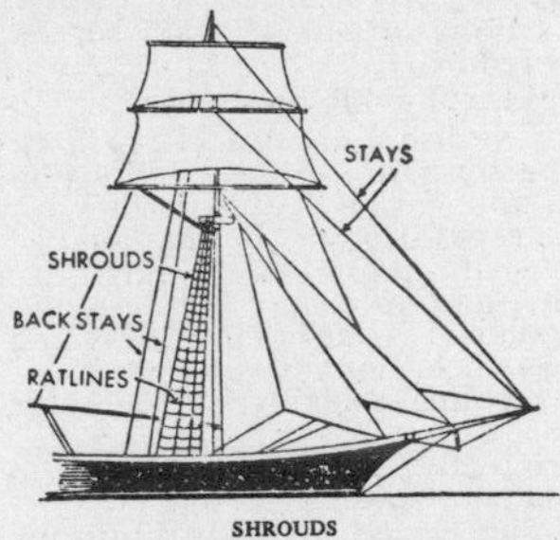

SHROUDS

4. an annular plate that strengthens the edge and forms the sides of the buckets on a water wheel, or strengthens the teeth in a gearwheel; a shroud plate.

5. a branch of a tree. [Obs.]

shroud, *v.t.*; shrouded, *pt., pp.*; shrouding, *ppr.* 1. to hide; to cover; to screen.

2. to wrap (a corpse) in a shroud.

3. to shelter and protect. [Archaic.]

4. to trim; to lop. [Brit. Dial.]

shroud, *v.i.* to take shelter or harbor. [Archaic.]

shroud'ing, *n.* the shrouds on a water wheel, collectively.

shroud knot (not), an overhand knot: see *knot*, illus.

shroud'-lāid, *a.* made by twisting four strands around a core: said of rope.

shroud'less, *a.* without a shroud.

shroud plāte, a shroud (sense 4).

shroud'y, *a.* affording shelter. [Rare.]

shrōve, *v.i.* to join in the festivities of Shrovetide. [Obs.]

shrōve, *v.* alternative past tense of *shrive.*

Shrōve'tīde, *n.* [ME. *schroffetide*; prob. a 15th-c. formation in which the 1st element (from *shrive*) replaces earlier *fast-, fasten-.*] the three days before Ash Wednesday (*Shrove Sunday, Monday,* and *Tuesday*), formerly set aside as a special period for going to confession and a season of festivity just before Lent.

shrōw, *n.* a shrew or scold. [Obs.]

shrub, *n.* [ME. *shrob*; AS. *scrybb*, brushwood.] a bushy, woody plant with several permanent stems instead of a single trunk; a bush.

shrub, *v.t.* to clear of shrubs; to lop. [Obs.]

shrub, *n.* [Ar. *sharab*, drink.] a beverage made of the juice of an acid fruit, sugar, and, usually, rum or brandy.

shrub'bẽr·y, *n.*; *pl.* **shrub'ber·ies,** 1. shrubs in general.

2. a place where many shrubs are grown.

shrub'bi·ness, *n.* the state or quality of being shrubby.

shrub'by, *a.*; *comp.* shrubbier; *superl.* shrubbiest, 1. full of or covered with shrubs; as, a *shrubby* plain.

2. resembling a shrub; as, plants *shrubby* and curled.

shrub'less, *a.* having no shrubs.

shruff, *n.* [a form of *scurf* or *scruff.*] refuse; rubbish; dross of metals; also, [Brit. Dial.] light dry wood used as fuel.

shrug, *v.t.* and *v.i.* shrugged, *pt., pp.*; shrugging, *ppr.* [Dan. *skrugge*, to stoop; Sw. *skrukka*, to huddle oneself up; allied to *skrinka*, to shrink.] to draw up (the shoulders), as in expressing dislike, dissatisfaction, doubt, etc.

shrug, *n.* the act of shrugging the shoulders; a drawing up or raising of the shoulders, as to express dislike, dissatisfaction, contempt, doubt, etc.

> Then casting away, with loathful *shrug*, the unclean waif. —Moore.

shrun̄k, *v.* alternative past tense and past participle of *shrink.*

shrun̄k'en, *v.* alternative past participle of *shrink.*

shrun̄k'en, *a.* shrunk; atrophied; shriveled up; withered; contracted; diminished; as, *shrunken* values; *shrunken* limbs.

shtiçk, *n.* [Yid., a prank, caprice.]

1. a comic scene or piece of business, as in a vaudeville act. [Slang.]

2. an attention-getting device. [Slang.]

3. a special trait, talent, etc. [Slang.]

shuck, *n.* [perhaps a metathesis of *husk.*]

1. a shell or covering; a husk or pod; especially, the shell or covering of a nut, or the husk of corn.

2. the case or covering of the larva of certain insects, as the caddis fly.

3. the shell of an oyster or clam.

4. [*pl.*] something valueless; as, not worth *shucks.* [Colloq.]

5. a shock; a stook. [Brit. Dial.]

6. (a) a hoax or fraud; (b) a fraudulent person or thing; a phony. [Slang.]

shuck, *v.t.*; shucked (shukt), *pt., pp.*; shucking, *ppr.* 1. to shell; to remove the shucks or husks of; as, to *shuck* corn.

2. to remove like a shuck; as, to *shuck* off one's coat for a fight.

3. to fool or hoax. [Slang.]

shuck'-bot''tŏm, *a.* provided with a bottom or seat made of shucks; as, a *shuck-bottom* chair. [Dial.]

shuck'ẽr, *n.* one who or that which shucks; specifically, one who shucks oysters or clams.

shuck'ing, *n.* a husking bee. [Dial.]

shucks, *interj.* an exclamation denoting disgust or disappointment. [Colloq.]

shud'dẽr, *v.i.*; shuddered, *pt., pp.*; shuddering, *ppr.* [ME. *shoderen*; D. *schudderen*; G. *schüttern*, to shake, to shiver, freq. forms from D. *schudden*; G. *schütten*; O.H.G. *scuttan*, to shake, allied to E. *shed*, to cast.] to tremble or shake suddenly and violently, as in fear, horror, or extreme disgust.

shud'dẽr, *n.* the act of shuddering; a trembling or shaking, as in fear, horror, etc.

shud'dẽr·ing·ly, *adv.* in a shuddering manner; with shudders.

shūde, *n.* same as *shood.*

shuf'fle, *v.t.*; shuffled, *pt., pp.*; shuffling, *ppr.* [prob. from L.G. *schuffeln*, to walk clumsily, to shuffle cards.]

1. (a) to move (the feet) along the ground or floor with a dragging or shoving gait; (b) to perform (a dance) with such steps.

2. to mix (playing cards) so as to change their order or arrangement.

3. to push or mix together in a jumbled or disordered mass.

4. to shift from one place to another.

5. to bring, put, or thrust (*into* or *out of*) clumsily or trickily.

to shuffle off; to get rid of; to rid oneself of; to shake off.

shuf'fle, *v.i.* 1. to move with a dragging gait without lifting the feet, as in walking or dancing.

2. to get into or out of a situation or condition by trickery, evasion, lies, etc.; as, he has *shuffled* out of responsibility time and again.

3. to act in a shifty, dishonest manner; to practice deceit, trickery, evasion, etc.

4. to change or shift repeatedly from one position or place to another.

5. to shuffle cards.

6. to make clumsy, fumbling motions in getting into or out of clothing.

Syn.—confuse, interchange, shift, intershift, intermix, evade, prevaricate, equivocate, quibble.

shuf'fle, *n.* 1. the act of shuffling.

2. a tricky or deceptive action; an evasion or inconsistency; a trick.

3. a shuffling of the feet.
4. a gait, dance, motion, etc. characterized by this.
5. (a) the act of rearranging the order of a pack of playing cards; (b) the right of, or one's turn at, shuffling the cards.

shuf′fle·bōard, *n.* [prob. for *shovel board*: so named because of the shape of the cues.]
1. a game in which disks are slid, or pushed with a cue, along a flat surface toward numbered squares.
2. the board or surface on which it is played.
Also *shovelboard.*

shuf′fle·ça̧p, *n.* a game in which money is shaken in a cap or hat.

shuf′flẽr, *n.* 1. one who or that which shuffles.
2. (a) a scaup duck; (b) the coot, *Fulica americana.*

shuf′fle sçāle, a measure used by tailors, graduated at both ends, each end being independently adjustable.

shuf′fle·wing, *n.* the hedge sparrow, *Accentor modularis.* [Brit. Dial.]

shuf′fling, *a.* 1. characterized by a shuffle, as a walk.
2. evasive; deceitful; shifty; as, a *shuffling* answer.

shuf′fling·ly, *adv.* in a shuffling manner.

shug, *n.* and *v.* shrug. [Brit. Dial.]

Shụ′lăm·īte, *n.* an epithet applied to the maiden in the Song of Solomon: vi. 13.

shụ′maç, *n.* same as *sumac.*

shun, *v.t.*; shunned, *pt., pp.*; shunning, *ppr.* [ME. *shunien*; AS. *scunian,* to flee away; Ice. *skunda,* to hurry away.] to avoid scrupulously or consistently; to keep clear of; as, to *shun* evil associates.
Syn.—avoid, elude, eschew.

shun, *v.i.* to refrain; to shrink back. [Obs.]

shun′less, *a.* not to be avoided; inevitable; unavoidable; as, *shunless* destiny.

shun′nẽr, *n.* a person who shuns.

shun′-pīke, *n.* a byway; a lane. [Dial.]

shunt, *v.t.* and *v.i.*; shunted, *pt., pp.*; shunting, *ppr.* [ME. *shunten*; prob. a blending of AS. *scyndan,* to hasten, with a L.G. cognate of O.H.G. *scunten.*]
1. to shun. [Obs.]
2. to give a start to; to shove.
3. to shift or switch, as a train, car, etc., from one track to another.
4. in electricity, to divert or be diverted by a shunt: said of a current.
5. to provide or connect with a shunt.
6. to turn away, as from a topic; to turn off or out of the way.

shunt, *n.* 1. the act of shunting.
2. a railroad switch.
3. in electricity, a conductor connecting two points in a circuit and serving to divert part of the current from the main circuit.
shunt dynamo; a shunt wound dynamo.

shunt′ẽr, *n.* one who or that which shunts; specifically, a man employed to shunt cars from one track to another.

shunt gun, a rifled cannon with two sets of grooves, down one of which the shell passes in loading, passing out by the other when fired, having been shunted from one set to the other by turning on its axis.

shunt′-wound, *a.* in electricity, designating a dynamo or motor wound in such a way that a shunt from the armature circuit passes through the coils of the field magnets: opposed to *series-wound.*

shush, *interj.* [echoic.] hush! be quiet!

shush, *v.t.* to say "shush" to; to tell (another) to be quiet; to hush.

shut, *v.t.*; shut, *pt., pp.*; shutting, *ppr.* [ME. *shutte, shitte, shette*; AS. *scyttan, scittan,* to bolt, to lock, to shoot the bolt, from *sceōtan,* to shoot; hence, also, *scyttel,* a bolt.]
1. to move (a door, window, curtain, lid, etc.) into a position that closes the opening to which it is fitted.
2. to fasten (a door, etc.) securely, as with a bolt or catch.
3. to close (an opening, passage, container, etc.).
4. to prevent or forbid entrance to or exit from; to close; to bar.
5. to fold up or bring together the parts of, as an umbrella, the hand, lips, etc.
to shut in; (a) to enclose; to confine; (b) to bring one point, as of land, to cover or intercept the view of another, so that one point of land shuts in the other point.
to shut off; (a) to exclude; (b) to stop from flowing or escaping; as, *to shut off* steam or gas; (c) to prevent passage through (a road, faucet, etc.).
to shut out; (a) to deny admission to; to exclude; as, *to shut out* rain by a tight roof; (b) to prevent (an opposing side or team) from scoring.
to shut up; (a) to close; to make fast all the entrances to; as, *to shut up* a house; (b) to obstruct; (c) to confine; to imprison; to lock or fasten in; as, *to shut up* a prisoner; (d) to end; to terminate; to conclude; (e) to weld together; (f) [Colloq.] to cause to become silent.

shut, *v.i.* to close itself; to be or become closed; as, the door *shuts* of itself; it *shuts* hard.
to shut down; to cease operations; to close, usually temporarily, as a factory.
to shut down on or *upon*; to suppress; to cause to cease. [Colloq.]
to shut in; to collect so as to close in; as, darkness *shuts in* the day.
to shut up; to stop talking; as, *shut up* and let me sleep. [Colloq.]

shut, *a.* 1. closed, fastened, or secured.
2. rid; clear; free: with *of*; as, to get *shut of* an unpleasant thing. [Dial.]
3. in phonetics, checked; also, with the oral and nasal passages closed, as in the utterance of the consonants *p, t, k, b, d,* and hard *g.*

shut, *n.* 1. the close; the act or time of closing; as, the *shut* of a door; the *shut* of evening.
2. a shutter. [Obs.]
3. the line where two metallic pieces are joined by welding.

shut′down″, *n.* a discontinuance of work, especially the temporary closing of a mine, factory, etc.

shụte, *n.* same as *chute.*

shut′-eȳe, *n.* sleep. [Slang.]

shut′-in″, *n.* an invalid who is unable to go out.

shut′-in″, *a.* 1. unable to go out; confined, as by illness, etc.
2. in psychiatry, inclined to shun others; abnormally introverted.

shut′ọff, *n.* 1. something that shuts off a flow or movement, as of a liquid.
2. a condition of being shut off; stoppage.

shut′out, *n.* 1. a lockout of employees.
2. in sports, (a) a preventing of the opposing team from scoring; (b) a game in which one team is shut out.

shut′tẽr, *n.* 1. a person or thing that shuts or closes.
2. a movable screen or cover for a window, usually hinged and fitted with louvers.
3. anything used to cover an opening, as a slide or door on a lantern.
4. a device for opening and closing the aperture of a lens in a camera to expose the film or plate.
5. a removable cover or gate for cutting off the supply of metal from a mold.

shut′tẽr, *v.t.* to close or furnish with a shutter or shutters.

shut′tẽred, *a.* equipped with shutters.

shut′tle, *n.* [AS. *sceātel, scytel,* a shuttle, from *sceōtan,* to shoot: so called because shot to and fro with the thread in weaving; Ice. *skutul*; Dan. *skyttel,* shuttle.]
1. an instrument used by weavers for passing or shooting the thread of the woof from one side of the cloth to the other between the threads of the warp; also, a smaller but similar thread holder used in tatting, etc.
2. in sewing machines, the sliding thread holder which carries the lower thread between the needle and the upper thread to make a lock stitch.
3. any of several devices having a similar to-and-fro action.
4. a shuttle train or shuttle bus.

shut′tle, *v.t.* and *v.i.*; shuttled, *pt., pp.*; shuttling, *ppr.* to move rapidly to and fro, like a shuttle.

shut′tle box, a case at the end of a weavers' lay for holding shuttles so as to facilitate the weaving of cloth composed of yarns of more than one color.

shut′tle bus, a motorbus making short, regular trips between an outlying district and some point on a main transportation line.

shut′tle·çock, *n.* [ME. *shyttelcocke,* not *shuttlecork,* as sometimes given, because first made of wood and stuck with feathers like a cock.]
1. a rounded piece of cork having a flat end stuck with feathers: it is struck back and forth across a net by players with rackets in badminton or with paddles in battledore and shuttlecock: also called *bird.*
2. the game of battledore and shuttlecock.
3. a crimson flowering shrub, *Periptera punicea,* growing in Mexico.

SHUTTLECOCK

shut′tle·çock, *v.t.* to throw or bandy back and forth like a shuttlecock; as, to *shuttlecock* words.

shut′tle·çọrk, *n.* shuttlecock. [Obs.]

shut′tle çrab, same as *paddle crab.*

shut′tle·head (-hed), *n.* a flighty person. [Obs.]

shut′tle·head·ed, *a.* flighty. [Obs.]

shut′tle rāce, a sort of smooth shelf in a weavers' lay, along which the shuttle runs in passing the weft.

shut′tle shell, a shell of the genus *Radius,* so named from its longitudinally produced lips.

shut′tle trāin, a train making regular and frequent trips back and forth over a short route.

shut′tle·wīse, *adv.* like the motion of a shuttle.

shut′tle-wit″ted, *a.* flighty. [Scot.]

shwän′pan, swän′pan, *n.* [Chinese.] the abacus as used by the Chinese.

shȳ, *a.*; *comp.* shyer *or* shier; *superl.* shyest *or* shiest, [Dan. *sky,* shy, skittish, *skye,* to shun, avoid; Ice. *skjarr*; G. *scheu,* shy, timid.]
1. timid; readily frightened or startled; as, a *shy* bird; a *shy* horse.
2. uncomfortable in the presence of, and avoiding contact with, others; extremely self-conscious; bashful.
Shy she was, and I thought her cold.
—Tennyson.
3. cautious; wary; showing distrust; as, *shy* of hard labor; *shy* about speaking.
4. not bearing prolifically, as trees.
5. lacking; short (often with *on*). [Slang.]
6. not having contributed a certain or required portion; specifically, in poker, not having made good an announced ante or bet; as, to be *shy* in a jackpot. [Slang.]
to fight shy of; to keep from; to avoid; to evade.
Syn.—timid, reserved, modest, bashful, suspicious, shrinking, chary.

shȳ, *v.i.*; shied, *pt., pp.*; shying, *ppr.* 1. to move suddenly as though startled; to jump; to start; to recoil; as, the horse *shied* at the white stone.
2. to react negatively; to be or become cautious, doubtful, or unwilling (often with *at*).

shȳ, *n.*; *pl.* **shīeṣ,** an act of shying; a start, as of a horse.

shȳ, *v.t.* and *v.i.* [prob. from *cockshy,* to throw at a cock, from *shy cock,* a cock that will not fight unless tormented into doing so.] to throw or fling, especially sidewise with a jerk; as, he *shied* a stone over the wall.

shȳ, *n.* 1. a shying throw or fling.
2. a try or attempt. [Colloq.]
3. a verbal fling; a gibe. [Colloq.]

Shȳ′lock, *n.* 1. the relentless moneylender in Shakespeare's *Merchant of Venice.*
2. a person without sentiment in business matters; an exacting creditor.

shȳ′ly, *adv.* in a shy manner.

shȳ′ness, *n.* the state or quality of being shy.

shȳ′stẽr, *n.* [also earlier *shuyster*; understood as *shy* (in earlier sense of "disreputable"), and *-ster.*] a person, especially a lawyer, who uses unethical or tricky methods; a pettifogger. [Slang.]

Si, in chemistry, silicon.

sī, *adv.* [It. and Sp.] yes.

sī, *n.* in music, a syllable denoting the seventh tone in the diatonic scale, *do* being the first.

sī″ȧ·lȧ·gog′iç, *a.* stimulating the flow of saliva.

sī″ȧ·lȧ·gog′iç, *n.* same as *sialagogue.*

sī·al′ȧ·gogue (-gog), *n.* [from Gr. *sialon,* saliva; and *-agogue.*] anything, especially a medicine, that stimulates the flow of saliva.

sī′ȧ·lid, *a.* pertaining to the *Sialidæ*.

sī′ȧ·lid, *n.* an insect belonging to the *Sialidæ*.

Sī·al′i·dae, *n.pl.* a family of neuropterous insects, with prothorax enlarged, reticulate wings, and aquatic larvae: it includes the dobson fly.

sī·al′i·dăn, *a.* and *n.* same as *sialid*.

Sī′ȧ·lis, *n.* the typical genus of the *Sialidæ*.

sī′ȧ·lō-, sī′al-, [from Greek *sialon*, saliva.] combining forms meaning *saliva*.

sī″ȧ·lō·gog′iç, *a.* and *n.* same as *sialagogic*.

sī·al′ō·gogue (-gog), *n.* same as *sialagogue*.

sī′ȧ·loid, *a.* like saliva.

sī″ȧ·lor·rhē′ȧ, sī″ȧ·lor·rhoe′ȧ (-rē′), *n.* salivation.

sī′ȧ·mang, *n.*; *pl.* **sī′ȧ·mangs,** [Malay.] a large gibbon of Sumatra, with long black hair: it is the largest of all gibbons.

Sī·ȧ·mēṣe′, *a.* pertaining to Siam, its people, their language, etc.

Sī·ȧ·mēṣe′, *n.* 1. *pl.* **Sī·ȧ·mēṣe′,** a native of Siam: the Siamese are of Thai stock.

2. the Sino-Tibetan language of the Siamese; Thai.

Sī·ȧ·mēṣe′ çat, a breed of short-haired cat characterized by a fawn-colored coat shading to brown at the face, paws, and tail.

Sī·ȧ·mēṣe′ twins, [from a set of twin Siamese boys, Chang and Eng (1811–1874), born with chests joined by a thick band of cartilage and flesh.] any pair of twins, animal or human, born joined at similar points of the body.

sib, *n.* [ME. *sibb*, kinship; AS. *sib*(*b*).]

1. a person's blood relatives; kin.

2. a blood relative; kinsman or kinswoman; especially, a brother or sister.

3. in anthropology, a unilinear, usually exogamous kin group based on traditional common descent, whether patrilineal or matrilineal, and often having a common totem: usually distinguished from *clan*, *sept*.

sib, *a.* 1. related by blood.

2. closely related; akin. [Rare.]

sib′benṣ, *n.* [Gael. *subhag*, raspberry, from the appearance of the eruptions.] a disease formerly prevalent in Scotland, resembling syphilis or yaws. [Obs.]

sib′bō·leth, *n.* same as *shibboleth*.

Sī·bē′ri·ăn, *a.* of Siberia, the region of the Soviet Union in northern Asia, or its people.

Siberian dog; a dog similar to the Eskimo dog and, like it, used as a beast of burden.

SIBERIAN DOG

Sī·bē′ri·ăn, *n.* a native or inhabitant of Siberia.

sib′i·lănce, *n.* 1. the condition or quality of being sibilant.

2. a sibilant sound; a hissing.

sib′i·lăn·cy, *n.*; *pl.* **sib′i·lăn·cieṣ,** a sibilance.

sib′i·lănt, *a.* [L. *sibilans* (*-antis*), from L. *sibilare*, to hiss.] hissing; making a hissing sound; as, *s* and *z* are *sibilant* letters.

sib′i·lănt, *n.* a sound that is uttered with a hissing or the symbol for it, as *s* or *z*.

sib′i·lāte, *v.t.* and *v.i.*; sibilated, *pt.*, *pp.*; sibilating, *ppr.* to hiss; to pronounce with a hissing sound.

sib·i·lā′tion, *n.* the act of sibilating or hissing; also, a hissing sound; a hiss.

sib′i·lȧ·tō·ry, *a.* hissing; sibilous.

sib′i·lous, *a.* sibilant.

sib′ling, *n.* [*sib*, from AS. *sib*(*b*); and *-ling*.] [*often in pl.*] one of two or more persons born at different times of the same parents; brother or sister.

sib′yl, *n.* [ME. *sibil*; L. *sibylla*; Gr. *sibylla*.]

1. any of certain women consulted as prophetesses or oracles by the ancient Greeks and Romans. They resided in various parts of Persia, Greece, and Italy, the most celebrated being the Cumaean sibyl, of Cumae, Italy.

2. a witch; a sorceress; a fortuneteller.

si·byl′liç, si·byl′liç, *a.* same as *sibylline*.

sib′yl·line (*or* -lin), *a.* [L. *sibyllinus*.]

1. of or like the sibyls or their prophecies.

2. prophetic; oracular; mysterious.

Sibylline Books; (a) books or documents of prophecy and wisdom supposed to contain the history of the Roman empire, and said to have been purchased by Tarquin the Proud from the sibyl of Cumae; (b) a collection of books written at different times from about a century before to the third century after Christ, containing a mixture of ecclesiastical literature, both Jewish and Christian: also called *Sibylline Oracles*.

sib′yl·list, *n.* a devotee of the sibyls; a believer in the sibylline prophecies.

siç, *a.* such. [Dial.]

siç, *adv.* [L.] thus; it is so: in a quotation, used within brackets in order to call attention to the fact that the quotation is literally given, though containing an error or a misstatement; as, whom [*sic*] do men say that I am?

siç, *v.t.*; sicked, *pt.*, *pp.*; sicking, *ppr.* to sick; to attack.

siç′ȧ·mōre, *n.* same as *sycamore*.

Si·cā′ni·ăn, *a.* same as *Sicilian*.

siç′çȧ, *n.* [Hind.] 1. an Indian jeweler's weight of about 180 grains troy.

2. a freshly coined rupee.

siç′çȧ rū·pee′, a rupee formerly current in India, which contained about 176 grains of pure silver.

siç′çȧ·tive, *a.* [L. *siccare*, to dry.] drying; causing to dry.

siç′çȧ·tive, *n.* a substance that promotes the process of drying, especially one used in painting; a drier.

sīce *n.* [Fr. *six*.] the number six at dice.

sīce, *n.* same as *syce*.

sī′cẽr, *n.* strong drink. [Obs.]

sich, *a.* such. [Obs.]

Si·cil′i·ăn, *a.* pertaining to Sicily, its people, their dialect, etc.

Sicilian Vespers; the massacre of the French in Sicily in 1282 on Easter Monday, which began in Palermo at the hour of vespers: it was a popular uprising of the Sicilian people against French oppression under Charles of Anjou.

Si·cil′i·ăn, *n.* 1. a native or inhabitant of Sicily.

2. the Italian dialect of the Sicilians.

si·cil·i·ä′nȧ, *n.* [It.] in music, a composition in measures of $\frac{6}{8}$ and $\frac{12}{8}$ time, to be performed in a gay and graceful manner; also, a dance to such music by the peasantry of Sicily.

si·cil·i·enne′, *n.* a dress material resembling a rich poplin.

sick, *a.*; *comp.* sicker; *superl.* sickest, [ME. *sik*, *sek*; AS. *seoc*; Dan. *syg*; Ice. *sjūkr*, to be ill.]

1. suffering from disease or illness; unwell; ill: this sense is rare or literary in England.

2. having nausea; vomiting or ready to vomit: the predominant sense in England.

3. characteristic of or accompanying sickness; as, a *sick* expression, *sick* headache.

4. of or for sick people; as, *sick* bay, *sick* leave.

5. deeply disturbed or distressed; extremely upset, as by grief, disappointment, disgust, failure, etc.

6. impaired; unsound.

7. of sickly color; pale.

8. mentally ill.

9. disgusted; having a strong dislike from satiety; as, *sick* of flattery.

10. corrupted. [Obs.]

11. lying-in; confined.

12. languishing; having a great longing (with *for*); as, *sick for* friends.

13. in nautical usage, in need of repairs, as a ship or boat.

14. in agriculture, (a) incapable of producing an adequate yield of a certain crop; as, wheat-*sick* soil; (b) infested with harmful microorganisms; as, a *sick* field.

15. spawning, as an oyster; poor and watery, as an oyster after spawning.

Syn.—diseased, ill, disordered, distempered, indisposed, weak, ailing, feeble, morbid, nauseated, disgusted, impaired, valetudinarian.

sick, *n.* 1. illness. [Rare.]

2. sick people (with *the*).

sick, *v.i.* to become sick. [Rare.]

sick, *v.t.* to make sick. [Rare.]

sick, *v.t.* [a variant of *seek*.] 1. to urge or incite to attack; as, to *sick* a dog on a suspicious-looking stranger.

2. to set on; to pursue and attack: said especially of or to a dog.

sick bāy, a ship's hospital and dispensary.

sick′bed, *n.* the bed used by a sick person.

sick bẽrth, a sick bay.

sick çall, 1. in military usage, (a) a daily formation made up of those men who wish to receive medical attention; (b) a signal for or the time of such a formation.

2. a message calling a clergyman to visit a sick person.

sick′en, *v.t.* and *v.i.* sickened, *pt.*, *pp.*; sickening, *ppr.* to make or become sick.

sick′en·ẽr, *n.* something that sickens; something very painful or unpleasant experienced.

sick′en·ing, *a.* 1. making sick; causing sickness or nausea.

2. completely disgusting or revolting.

sick′en·ing·ly, *adv.* in a sickening manner.

sick′ẽr, sik′ẽr, *a.* [L. *securus*, sure.] sure; certain. [Scot.]

sick′ẽr, sik′ẽr, *adv.* surely; certainly. [Obs.]

sick′ẽr, *v.t.* to assure; to secure. [Obs.]

sick′ẽr, *v.i.* to seep, ooze, or percolate, as water into a mine. [Rare.]

sick head′āçhe (hed′), 1. a headache caused by or resulting from nausea.

2. migraine.

sick′ish, *a.* 1. somewhat sick or nauseated.

2. somewhat sickening or nauseating; as, a *sickish* taste.

sick′ish·ly, *adv.* in a sickish manner.

sick′ish·ness, *n.* the quality of being sickish.

siç′kle *n.* [ME. *sikel*; AS. *sicol*, from L. *secula*, a sickle, from *secare*, to cut.]

1. a cutting tool consisting of a crescent-shaped blade with a short handle: used for cutting down tall grasses and weeds.

2. a gaff or spur shaped like a sickle formerly used for a fighting cock.

3. [S—] a group of six stars in the constellation Leo, resembling a sickle in form.

SICKLE

sick lēave, leave of absence granted because of sickness or injury: often a fixed number of days.

siç′kle·bill, *n.* any bird with a sharply curved bill resembling a sickle; specifically, (a) any hummingbird of the genus *Eutoxeres*, with three species, from Central America; (b) the long-billed curlew; (c) a bird of paradise of the genus *Epimachus*; (d) any bird of the genera *Drepanornis*, *Drepanis*, and *Campylorhamphus*.

sick′le-cell ȧ·nē′mi·ȧ, an inherited chronic anemia found chiefly among Negroes, characterized by an abnormal red blood cell containing a defective form of hemoglobin that causes the cell to become sickle-shaped when deprived of oxygen: also called *sickle cell disease*.

siç′kle-cell trāit, sicklemia without accompanying anemia.

siç′kled, *a.* furnished with a sickle.

siç′kle feath′ẽr (feth′), any long curving feather, as in the tail feather of a rooster.

siç′kle·măn, *n.*; *pl.* **siç′kle·men,** one who uses a sickle.

sick·lē′mi·ȧ, *n.* [*sickle* cell, and *-emia*.] the presence of sickle cells in the blood, with or without accompanying anemia.

siç′kle·pod, *n.* a rock cress, *Arabis canadensis*, having long, flat, scythe-shaped pods.

siç′klẽr, *n.* one who uses a sickle; a reaper.

siçk′le-shāped (-shāpt), *a.* having the shape of a sickle.

sic′kle·wŏrt, *n.* the heal-all, *Prunella vulgaris*.

sick′li·ness, *n.* the quality or state of being sickly.

sick list, a list containing the names of the sick.

sick′ly, *a.*; *comp.* sicklier; *superl.* sickliest, 1. in poor health; chronically sick or prone to sickness; not strong or robust.

2. of or produced by sickness; as, a *sickly* pallor.

3. characterized by the prevalence of disease or sickness; producing illness; unhealthy.

4. sickening; nauseating, as an odor.
5. faint; feeble; pale, as light or color.
6. weak; mawkish; insipid.

Syn.—weak, diseased, disordered, ailing, feeble, pining, drooping, morbid, unhealthy, vitiated, delicate, tainted, valetudinary.

sick'ly, *adv.* in a sick manner.

sick'ly, *v.t.*; sicklied, *pt., pp.*; sicklying, *ppr.* to make sickly, as in color, vigor, etc.

sick'ness, *n.* 1. the state or quality of being sick or suffering from some disease; illness; ill health.
2. a disease; a malady.
3. nausea.
4. a weakened and disordered state of anything, as of a fortune, etc.

serum sickness; in medicine, a reaction following the injection of some substance to which an individual is allergic or hypersensitive, symptomatized by skin eruptions, swelling, fever, and pain: also called *serum disease.*

sick'out, *n.* a joint action by a group of employees claiming illness and not reporting for work in order to force the granting of certain demands; especially, such an action by a group forbidden by law to strike.

sick'room, *n.* a room in which a sick person is confined.

sī'çle, *n.* a shekel. [Obs.]

siç pas'sim, [L., lit., so everywhere.] thus throughout (the book, passage, etc.).

siç'saç, *n.* [prob. imitative.] the crocodile bird of Egypt.

siç sem'pēr tȳ·ran'nis, [L.] thus ever to tyrants.

siç trans'it glō'ri·ȧ mun'dī, [L.] thus passes away the glory of the world; thus vanishes earthly fame.

Sī'dȧ, *n.* [Gr. *sidē*, the pomegranate.] an extensive genus of herbs and shrubs of the *Malvaceæ.* The species are extensively distributed throughout the warm parts of the world. They abound in mucilage, like all malvaceous plants, and have tough fibers, which are used for cordage.

Sid·dhär'thȧ, (-där'tȧ), see *Buddha.*

sid'dōw, *a.* [etym. obscure.] soft; pulpy. [Obs.]

sid'dūr, *n.* [Heb. *siddūr*, arrangement, order.] the Jewish prayer book containing prayers for weekdays and the Sabbath.

sīde, *n.* [ME. *side*; AS. *side*; Ice. *sidha*; Dan. *side*; O.H.G. *sita*, side. Original sense was prob. "long"; AS. *sid*, long.]
1. the right or left half of a human or animal body, especially either half of the trunk.
2. a position or space beside one.
3. (a) any of the lines or surfaces that bound or limit something; as, a square has four *sides*, a cube six; (b) any bounding line or surface of an object other than the ends or top and bottom; (c) either of the two bounding surfaces of an object that are distinguished from the front, back, top, and bottom.
4. either of the two surfaces of a thing having no appreciable thickness, as paper, cloth, etc.
5. a surface or part of a surface having a specified aspect; as, the inner *side* of a vase, the visible *side* of the moon.
6. any aspect or phase as contrasted with another or others; as, the cruel *side* of him.
7. either of the two lateral surfaces of a ship from stem to stern above the water line.
8. the slope of a hill, bank, or other incline.
9. the shore of a river or other body of water.
10. any location, area, space, direction, etc. considered with reference to its position in relation to an observer or to a point or line thought of as central.
11. the action, position, or attitude of one person or faction opposing another; as, explain your *side* of the argument.
12. one of the parties in a contest, conflict, etc.; a faction.
13. line of descent through either parent; maternal or paternal lineage.
14. assumed superiority; arrogance. [Brit. Slang.]
15. in billiards, English. [Brit.]

exterior side; see under *exterior.*

interior side; in fortification, the line drawn from the center of one bastion to that of the next, or the line of the curtain produced to the two oblique radii in front.

on the side; (a) as a secondary or part-time occupation; (b) in addition to the primary issue. [Colloq.]

side by side; beside each other; together.

to choose sides; to select parties for competition in exercises of any kind.

to take sides; to embrace the opinions or attach oneself to the interest of a party when in opposition to another.

Syn.—margin, edge, verge, border, face, aspect, plane, party, interest, cause, policy, behalf.

sīde, *a.* 1. of, at, or on a side or sides.
2. being from or toward the side; oblique; indirect; as, a *side* view; a *side* glance.
3. not of primary importance; minor; secondary, as an interest or consideration.
4. ordered separately, along with the main dish; as, a *side* order of cole slaw.
5. long; large; extensive. [Obs.]

side issue; an issue of a trivial or subordinate character.

side partner; any partner who works alongside another.

sīde, *v.i.*; sided, *pt., pp.*; siding, *ppr.* 1. to lean on one side.
2. to embrace the opinions of one party, or engage in its interest, when opposed to another party: followed by *with*; as, to *side with* the ministerial party.

sīde, *v.t.* 1. to furnish with sides or siding.
2. to stand at the side of. [Obs.]
3. to suit; to pair. [Obs.]
4. to flatten or even the side or sides of, as with a plane; as, to *side* timber.
5. to cut into sides; as, to *side* a carcass of mutton. [Obs.]
6. to thrust aside; to set aside. [Colloq.]

sīde'ärm, *a.* and *adv.* with a sweeping forward motion of the arm from the side of the body at or below shoulder level; as, a *sidearm* pitch.

sīde ärms, arms or weapons that may be worn at the side or at the waist, as sword, bayonet, etc.

sīde ax, an ax with the handle bent somewhat to one side.

sīde bär, 1. in Scots law, a former bar in the Outer Parliament House; also, in English law, a former bar in Westminster Hall.
2. in saddlery, one of two plates which unite the pommel and cantle of a saddle.
3. one of the longitudinal sidepieces of a vehicle, supporting the body.

side-bar rule; in English law, a rule obtained at chambers, without counsel's signature, on a note of instructions from an attorney.

sīde'bōard, *n.* 1. a piece of dining-room furniture with drawers or shelves, used to hold linen, silver, china, etc.
2. a board that forms or is part of a side; as, the *sideboards* of a wagon.

sīde'bōne, *n.* 1. an abnormal ossification about the pasterns of a horse.
2. the hip bone.

sīde box, a box or enclosed seat on the side of the stage of a theater.

sīde'bŭrns, *n.pl.* [reversed from *burnsides*, after Gen. A. E. *Burnside*, who wore them.]
1. short whiskers grown only on the cheeks.
2. the hair growing on the sides of a man's face, near the ears, when the rest of the beard is cut off.

sīde'çär", *n.* 1. a small car attached to the side of a motorcycle, usually accommodating only one passenger.
2. a car attached to an airship.
3. a cocktail made of brandy, orange liqueur, and lemon juice.

sīde'-çut, *n.* a canal, road, etc. branching out from the main one

sīd'ed, *a.* having sides: usually in combination; as, one-*sided*, six-*sided.*

sīde dish, 1. any food served in addition to the chief course, and usually in a separate dish.
2. a small dish used for this.

sīde drum, a snare drum.

sīde'head (-hed), *n.* 1. an auxiliary slide rest on a planing machine.
2. in printing, a subhead set as a part of the first line of the matter, instead of as a separate line above it.

sīde'-kick, *n.* 1. a close friend; a companion. [Slang.]
2. a partner; a confederate. [Slang.]

sīde'less, *a.* lacking a side or sides; open at the side or sides.

sīde lev'ēr (*or* lē'vēr), in steam engines, a heavy lever, working alongside the steam cylinder; a working beam.

side-lever engine; a marine engine having a working beam.

sīde līght (līt), 1. a light coming from the side.
2. an additional item of interest; incidental information; as, a *side light* on history.
3. a window or opening in or at the side of a wall, door, etc.
4. a lamp or light carried on the side: a ship carries a red *side light* on the port side and a green one on the starboard.

sīde līne, 1. a line attached to the side of anything; specifically, a hobble connecting the fore and hind foot on the same side of an animal, especially a horse.
2. an auxiliary or subordinate line of business or merchandise as stockings sold by an agent for a shoe company.
3. a small line branching off the main line, as of a railroad, pipeline, etc.
4. either of two lines marking the side limits of a playing field, court, etc., as in hockey or tennis.
5. [*pl.*] the space immediately outside the lines marking off a playing field, etc., usually occupied by those not participating in the contest or game.

sīde'līne, *v.t.* and *v.i.*; sidelined, *pt., pp.*; sidelining, *ppr.* to hobble with a side line, as an animal. [Dial.]

sīde'līn·ēr, *n.* a sidewiper; a massasauga.

sīde'ling, *adv.* sidewise; sidelong; obliquely; as, to go *sideling* through a crowd.

sīde'ling, *a.* 1. inclined; sloping; oblique; as, *sideling* ground.
2. directed or moving to the side; as, a stealthy *sideling* approach.

sīde'lọng, *a.* 1. inclined; slanting; sloping.
2. directed to the side, as a glance.
3. indirect; subtle, as a remark.

sīde'lọng, *adv.* 1. laterally; obliquely, in the direction of the side.
2. on the side; side downward; as, to lay a thing *sidelong.*

sīde mēat, meat from the side of a pig; bacon or salt pork. [Dial.]

sīde'piēce (-pēs), *n.* a piece forming or attached to the side of something.

sīde plāne, a plane whose bit is on the side: used to trim the edges of objects.

sīd'ēr, *n.* one who takes a side.

sī'dēr, *n.* cider. [Obs.]

sīde rāil, a rail at or on the side of something.

sid'ēr·ăl, *a.* [L. *sideralis*, of a star.]
1. pertaining to the stars; sidereal. [Rare.]
2. in astrology, influenced by the stars; baleful; as, a *sideral* blast. [Rare.]

sī·dē'rē·ăl, *a.* [L. *sideralis*, from *sidus*, a star.]
1. pertaining to the stars or constellations; starry; astral; as, *sidereal* light.
2. measured or marked out by the apparent motions of the fixed stars; as, *sidereal* calculations.

sidereal day; the interval between two successive transits of a star over the meridian: it equals 23 hours, 56 minutes, 4.09 seconds of mean solar time.

sidereal hour; one twenty-fourth of a sidereal day.

sidereal time; time as reckoned by sidereal days, or as measured by the apparent diurnal motion of the stars.

sidereal year; the period in which the earth makes one revolution in its orbit with respect to the stars; the exact period in which the earth completes one revolution round the sun.

sī·dē'rē·ăl·īze, *v.t.*; siderealized, *pt., pp.*; siderealizing, *ppr.* to raise or exalt, as to the stars; to etherealize.

sid'ēr·īte, *n.* [L. *sideritis*; Gr. *sidēritēs*, from *sidēros*, iron.]
1. in mineralogy, (a) formerly, magnetic iron ore or loadstone; (b) a valuable ore of iron, $FeCO_3$, consisting chiefly of iron carbonate and usually yellowish to light-brown in color; (c) [Obs.] cube ore; (d) a blue variety of quartz.
2. a plant of the genus *Sideritis.*
3. a meteorite consisting chiefly of iron.

sid·ēr·it'iç, *a.* of siderite.

Sid·ēr·ī'tis, *n.* [Gr. *sidēros*, iron.] a genus of shrubs and herbs of the family *Labiatæ*, found in Europe and Asia: known as ironworts.

sid'ēr·ō- [from Gr. *sidēros.*] a combining form meaning *iron*, as in *sidero*lite: also, before a vowel, *sider-.*

sid'ēr·ō-, [from L. *sidus, sideris*, a star.] a combining form meaning *star*, as in *sidero*stat: also, before a vowel, *sider-.*

sīde rod, one of the rods of a side beam engine; also, a locomotive coupling rod.

sid′ẽr·ō·grȧph, *n.* [*sidero-* (iron) and *-graph.*] an engraving produced by siderography.

sid″ẽr·ō·graph′iç, *a.* pertaining to siderography; produced from engraved plates of steel.

sid″ẽr·ō·graph′iç·ăl, *a.* same as *siderographic.*

sid·ẽr·og′rȧ·phist, *n.* one who engraves steel plates; one skilled in siderography.

sid·ẽr·og′rȧ·phy, *n.* the art or practice of engraving on steel; especially, the system by means of which impressions may be transferred from a steel plate to a steel cylinder.

sid′ẽr·ō·līte, *n.* [*sidero-* (iron) and *-lite.*] any meteorite containing large proportions of both iron and silicates.

sid′ẽr·ō·man·cy, *n.* [*sidero-* (iron) and *-mancy.*] a kind of divination by burning straws, etc. upon red-hot iron and observing their figures, bendings, sparkling, and burning.

sid′ẽr·ō·sçōpe, *n.* [*sidero-* (iron) and *-scope.*] an instrument for detecting small quantities of iron in any substance by means of a delicate combination of magnetic needles.

sid·ē·rō′sis, *n.* [Mod. L., from *sider-* and *-osis.*]

1. any disease of the lungs caused by the inhaling of particles of iron or other metal.

2. an abnormal deposit of iron in the body tissues.

sid′ẽr·ō·stat, *n.* [*sidero-* (star) and *-stat.*] a mirror which turns with the apparent motion of a star so as to keep the star constantly within the field of a fixed telescope or similar instrument.

sid′ẽr·ō·tech·ny, *n.* [*sidero-* (iron), and Gr. *technē*, art.] the metallurgy of iron and steel. [Rare.]

Sid·ē·rox′y·lon, *n.* [*sidero-* (iron), and Gr. *xylon*, wood.] a genus of trees of the family *Sapotaceæ*, including about sixty species, with very hard wood: also called *ironwood.*

sid·ẽr·ũr′ġiç·ăl, *a.* pertaining to siderurgy.

sid·ẽr·ũr′ġy, *n.* [Gr. *sidēros*, iron, and *ergon*, work.] the metallurgy of iron and steel.

sīde′sad″dle, *n.* a saddle in which the rider sits with both legs on the same side of the animal: designed for women wearing skirts while riding.

sīde′sad″dle flow′ẽr, an aquatic plant of the genus *Sarracenia*: so called because the stigma of the flower resembles a sidesaddle.

sīde′shōw, *n.* 1. a small show run in connection with the main show or attraction, as of a circus.

2. something of minor or secondary importance; a subordinate event.

sīde′slip, *n.* 1. the act of skidding or slipping to the side.

2. in aeronautics, a maneuver in which an airplane is made to fall sideways and slightly forward by holding the control stick forward and to one side while depressing the rudder control on the opposite side: a standard method of reducing altitude.

3. in skiing, a deviation from a set course by skidding or slipping.

sīde′slip, *v.i.*; sideslipped, *pt.,p p.*; sideslipping, *ppr.* 1. to skid or slip to the side.

2. in aeronautics, to perform a sideslip.

sīde′slip, *v.t.* to cause to sideslip.

sīdeş′măn, *n.*; *pl.* **sīdeş′men,** 1. an assistant to a churchwarden.

2. a party man; a partisan. [Obs.]

sīde′split″ting, *a.* 1. very hearty; convulsive: said of laughter.

2. causing hearty laughter; as, a *sidesplitting* account of the evening.

sīde step, 1. a step to one side, as to avoid something.

2. a step or stair at the side of anything.

sīde′-step, *v.i.* side-stepped (-stept), *pt., pp.*; side-stepping, *ppr.* to step to one side; to take a side step.

sīde′-step, *v.t.* to avoid by or as by stepping aside; to dodge; as, he *side-stepped* the issue of taxation.

sīde′stick, *n.* in printing, one of a pair of sticks placed at the side of type in locking up.

sīde strōke, a swimming stroke performed, while lying sideways in the water, by working the arms alternately backward and forward while executing a scissors kick with the legs.

sīde′swīpe, *v.t.* and *v.i.*; sideswiped, *pt., pp.*; sideswiping, *ppr.* to hit along the side in passing.

sīde′swīpe, *n.* a glancing blow along the side.

sīde tā′ble, in a dining room, a small table placed beside a main table or against a wall.

sīde′-tāk″ing, *n.* a taking sides, as with a party or a faction.

sīde tọọl, a tool whose cutting edge is at the end and side, used for working in wood or metal.

sīde′track, *n.* a track at the side of the main line; a railroad siding.

sīde′track, *v.t.*; sidetracked (-trakt), *pt., pp.*; sidetracking, *ppr.* 1. to shunt; to shift, as a train, from the main line to a siding.

2. to divert from the main course or issue; as, he *sidetracked* the measure in the Senate.

sīde′track, *v.i.* 1. to shift a train to a siding.

2. to turn away from the main course or issue.

sīde′wạlk (-wąk), *n.* a path or area, usually paved, at the side of a street, for pedestrians.

sīde′wărd, *a.* and *adv.* directed or moving to one side.

sīde′wărdş, *adv.* same as *sideward.*

sīde′wāy, *a.* and *adv.* same as *sideways.*

sīde′wāy, *n.* a byway: also *side way.*

sīde′wāyş, *adv.* 1. from the side.

2. so as to present a side; with one side forward.

3. toward one side; laterally; obliquely.

sīde′wāyş, *a.* turned or moving toward or from one side.

sīde′-wheel (-hwēl), *a.* designating a steamboat having a paddle wheel on each side.

sīde′-wheel″ẽr, *n.* a side-wheel steamboat.

sīde whisk′ẽrş, whiskers growing at the side of the face.

sīde wind, 1. a wind blowing from or against the side; a cross-wind.

2. an indirect manner, source, influence, etc.; as, the announcement reached us by a *side wind.*

sīde′wīnd″ẽr, *n.* 1. the horned rattlesnake.

2. a powerful swinging blow of the fist, delivered from the side. [Colloq.]

sīde′wip″ẽr, *n.* a massasauga.

sīde′wīşe, *a.* and *adv.* same as *sideways.*

sīd′ing, *n.* 1. on a railroad, a short track to one side of the main track and joined to it at one or both ends by a switch: used for unloading, bypassing, etc.: also called *sidetrack.*

2. material of any kind used for the covering of the outside of a frame building.

3. the thickness of the timbers of a ship.

4. the act of joining oneself to one side in a controversy, or of becoming an advocate of a special party or cause.

sī′dle, *v.i.*; sidled, *pt., pp.*; sidling, *ppr.* [prob. back-formation from *sideling.*] 1. to go or move side foremost; to move sideways, especially in a shy, fearful, or stealthy manner.

2. to saunter idly about. [Brit. Dial.]

sī′dle, *n.* a sidling movement.

Sī·dō′ni·ăn, *a.* of Sidon (the capital of ancient Phoenicia), its people, or culture.

Sī·dō′ni·ăn, *n.* a native of inhabitant of Sidon.

siè′cle (sye′kl), *n.*; *pl.* **siè′cles** (-kl), [Fr.] a century; a period; an age.

siè′cle d'or (dọr), [Fr.] (the) golden age: said of the reign of Louis XIV of France.

siēġe, *n.* [OFr. *siege*, a seat or sitting, a siege; hyp. LL. *sedium, sidium*, seen in *obsidium*, the sitting down before a town, a siege, from *sedere*, to sit.]

1. the encirclement of a fortified place by an opposing armed force intending to take it, usually by blockade and bombardment.

2. any continued endeavor to gain possession, overcome opposition, etc.

3. seat; throne. [Obs.]

4. position; rank. [Obs.]

5. a long, distressing or wearying period; as, a *siege* of illness. [Colloq.]

6. excrement; fecal matter. [Obs.]

7. the floor of a glass furnace.

8. a workman's table or bench.

to lay siege to; to subject to a siege; to attempt to win, gain, overcome, etc.

siēġe, *v.t.*; sieged, *pt., pp.*; sieging, *ppr.* to lay siege to; to besiege.

siēġe gun, a heavy gun used in attacking fortified places.

Siēġe Per′il·ous, a seat at King Arthur's Round Table, fatal to all occupants except the knight destined to find the Holy Grail.

siēġe trāin, artillery which is carried with an army for the purpose of attacking fortified places.

siēġe′wŏrks, *n.pl.* the offensive works of a besieging force.

Siēg′frīed, *n.* [G., from Gmc. (hyp.) *segu-*, power, victory, and (hyp.) *frith-*, peace, protection.] the hero of a Germanic legend having several versions: in the Nibelungenlied, he wins the treasure of the Nibelungs, kills a dragon, rescues and betroths Brunhild only to secure her as wife for Gunther, whose sister Kriemhild he then marries.

Siēg′frīed līne, a heavily fortified defense line built along the French border in Germany between 1933 and 1938: also called *Westwall.*

Şiēg heil, (zēk hīl), [G.] hail to victory: a salute used in Germany under the Nazis.

Siē′menş Mär′tin proc′ess, see *open hearth process* under *open.*

sī·en·it′iç, *a.* same as *syenitic.*

si·en′nȧ, *n.* [from *Sienna*, in Italy.]

1. an earth pigment containing iron and manganese, yellowish-brown in the natural state; raw sienna.

2. a reddish-brown pigment made by burning this; burnt sienna.

3. the color of either of these.

si·er′rȧ, *n.* [Sp., from L. *serra*, a saw.]

1. a range of hills or mountains with jagged or sawlike ridges; as, the *Sierra* Nevada.

2. same as *chromosphere.*

3. any of several salt-water game and food fishes resembling the mackerel: also called *pintado, kingfish.*

si·es′tȧ, *n.* [Sp., from L. *sexta hora*, the sixth hour, or noon, the hottest part of the day.] a brief nap or rest, especially as taken at midday or after the noon meal in Spain, some Latin American countries, etc.

sieũr (syũr), *n.* [Fr., from L. *senior*, elder.] sir: a title of respect formerly used by the French.

Siē′vȧ bēan, Siē′vȧ, *n.* a variety of the Lima bean, *Phaseolus lunata*, a twining plant with small greenish-white flowers and broad simitar-shaped pods containing a few large and flat seeds; also, any of these seeds.

sieve (siv), *n.* [ME. *sive*; AS. *sife.*]

1. a utensil having many small meshed or perforated openings of a size allowing passage only to liquids or to the finer particles of loose or pulverized matter; a sifter; a strainer.

2. a kind of basket used in England as a measure and holding about a bushel.

3. in calico printing, a cloth extending over the vat containing the coloring.

4. a person who cannot keep a secret; one who tells everything he knows; a garrulous person.

sieve and shears; same as *coscinomancy.*

sieve of Eratosthenes; a device for ascertaining all prime numbers between any specified limits by first writing down all numbers between those limits and then cutting mats that will cover, first all the numbers divisible by two, then all that are divisible by three, and so on until only prime numbers remain visible.

sieve, *v.t.* and *v.i.*; sieved, *pt., pp.*; sieving, *ppr.* to pass through a sieve; to sift.

sieve cell, in botany, a cell of a sieve tube.

sieve disk, in botany, a sieve plate.

sieve plāte, in botany, a thin, perforated area in the wall of a sieve tube.

sieve tūbe, in botany, one of the tubes made of thin-walled cells in the inner bark of a tree or shrub, serving to conduct food substances.

sif′fle, *n.* [ME. *siflen*, from OFr. *syflen*, to whistle.] in medicine, a hissing sound accompanying respiration; a sibilant râle.

sif′fle·ment, *n.* a sibilant; a hissing or a whistling sound. [Rare.]

sift, *v.t.*; sifted, *pt., pp.*; sifting, *ppr.* [AS. *siftan*, to sift, from *sife*, a sieve.]

1. to pass through a sieve so as to separate the coarse from the fine particles.

2. to scatter (a pulverized substance) by or as by the use of a sieve.

3. to separate; screen; distinguish; as, he sifted fact from fable.

4. to examine minutely or critically; to scrutinize; to weigh (evidence, etc.); as, let the principles of the party be thoroughly *sifted.*

sift, *v.i.* 1. to sift something.

2. to pass through or as through a sieve.

sift′ẽr, *n.* one who sifts; also, that which sifts; a sieve.

sift′ingş, *n.pl.* 1. something sifted; as, *siftings* of snow beside the door.

2. something removed by sifting; residue.

sig, *n.* [AS. *sihan*, to strain, filter.] urine. [Brit. Dial.]

Si·gaul'ti·ăn, *a.* of, by, or pertaining to Sigault, a French surgeon.
Sigaultian section; delivery of the fetus by symphyseotomy in cases of contracted pelvic outlet.

sig'gēr, *v.i.* to leak through a crevice, as into a mine. [Brit. Dial.]

sīgh (sī), *v.i.*; sighed, *pt., pp.*; sighing, *ppr.* [AS. *sīcan*, to sigh; prob. imitative in origin, or allied perhaps to *suck*, a drawing in of the breath.]
1. to take in and let out a long, deep, audible breath, especially in expressing sorrow, relief, fatigue, longing, etc.
2. to make a sound like that of a sigh; as, trees *sighing* in the wind.
3. to feel longing or grief; to yearn or lament (often with *for*).

sīgh, *v.t.* 1. to express with a sigh.
2. to spend (time) in sighing; as, he *sighed* his youth away.
3. to lament with sighing. [Rare.]

sīgh, *n.* the act or sound of sighing.

sīgh'-bọrn, *a.* indicative of grief or sorrow; sad; miserable. [Rare.]

sīgh'ing, *a.* grieving; heaving sighs.

sīgh'ing·ly, *adv.* with sighing.

sīght (sīt), *n.* [AS. *siht, gesiht*, from *segen, gesegen*, pp. of *seon*, to see.]
1. the act of seeing; perception by the eyes.
2. the faculty of vision; the power to see; eyesight.
3. range or field of vision.
4. [*pl.*] the eyes. [Brit. Dial.]
5. (a) something seen; view; (b) a remarkable or spectacular view; spectacle; as, the dawn was a *sight* to behold; (c) [*chiefly pl.*] a thing worth seeing; as, the *sights* of the city.
6. a view; look; glimpse.
7. aim or an observation taken with mechanical aid, as on a sextant, gun, etc.
8. mental vision or perception.
9. any of various devices used to aid the eyes in lining up a gun, optical instrument, etc. on its objective.
10. inspection; as, a document prepared for the *sight* of but one man.
11. mental view; judgment; opinion.
12. that portion of a picture inside the border or the frame.
13. a large amount or number; as, it'll need a *sight* of fixing. [Colloq.]
14. anything having a strikingly unpleasant or unusual appearance; as, our house was a *sight* after the party; she's a *sight* without her make-up. [Colloq.]
a sight for sore eyes; a person or thing that is pleasant to see; a welcome sight. [Colloq.]
at first sight; when seen for the first time; without further study or deliberation.
at (or *on*) *sight*; (a) as soon as seen, without further study or deliberation; as, to read music *at sight*; (b) upon demand or presentation; as, to pay *at sight*.
by sight; by appearance; not through being acquainted.
not by a long sight; (a) not nearly; (b) not at all.
out of sight; (a) not in the range of vision; (b) far off; remote; (c) [Colloq.] beyond reach; unattainable; extremely high, as in standards, price, etc.; (d) [Slang] excellent; wonderful.
out of sight of; (a) not in sight of; (b) not close or near to; remote from.
out of sight, out of mind; persons or things not seen or present are forgotten or neglected.
sight unseen; without seeing (the thing mentioned) beforehand.
telescopic sight; a small breech sight with telescopic lens or lenses attached, used for taking more accurate aim at long range.
to catch sight of; (a) to make out by means of the eyes; to discern; to see; (b) to see briefly; to glimpse.
to lose sight of; (a) to fail to keep in sight; to see no longer; (b) to let escape from memory; to forget.
to take sight; to adjust a gun by means of sights; to get the range of an object, with a view to definite aim in shooting.
Syn.—seeing, perception, view, vision, visibility, spectacle, show, inspection, examination, representation, appearance.

sīght, *v.t.*; sighted, *pt., pp.*; sighting, *ppr.* 1. to observe or examine by taking a sight; as, he *sighted* their movements carefully.
2. to catch sight of; to see.
3. to bring into the sights of a rifle, etc.; to aim at.
4. to furnish with sights or a sighting device.
5. to adjust the sights of (a gun, etc.).

sīght, *v. i.* 1. to take aim or an observation with a sight.
2. to look carefully in a specified direction; as, *sight* along the line.

sīght drȧft, a draft payable on presentation.

sīght'ed, *a.* having the power of vision; having (a) sight: usually in combination; as, far-*sighted*, keen-*sighted*, etc.

sīght'fụl, *a.* easily seen; perspicuous. [Obs.]

sīght'fụl·ness, *n.* clearness of sight. [Obs.]

sīght'hōle, *n.* a hole for seeing or sighting through, as on a quadrant.

sīght'less, *a.* 1. without sight; blind.
2. offensive or unpleasing to the eye; as, *sightless* stains. [Obs.]
3. invisible.

sīght'less·ly, *adv.* in a sightless manner.

sīght'less·ness, *n.* the state of being without sight.

sīght'li·ness, *n.* the condition of being sightly.

sīght'ly, *a.*; *comp.* sightlier; *superl.* sightliest. 1. pleasant to the sight; comely.
2. providing a fine view.

sīght'prọọf, *a.* not discoverable to sight; well concealed.

sīght rēad'ing, the act or art of reading, singing, or playing music at first sight of the score.

sīght sāv'ing, the means or measures employed for the treatment of those whose vision is already impaired, the purpose being to check the progress of the deterioration.

sīght'-sāv"ing, *a.* pertaining to the means or measures used in sight saving; of or for sight saving.
sight-saving class; a class of pupils having impaired vision: the classroom, the textbooks, and supplies for such a group are especially designed for sight saving.

sīght'see"ing, *a.* for or engaged in seeing sights.

sīght'-see"ing, *n.* the act of seeing sights; particularly, a going about to see interesting places and things for pleasure, education, etc.

sīght'-sē"ēr, *n.* one who is engaged in sight-seeing.

sīght shot, the distance to which the vision can be projected. [Rare.]

sīghts'măn, *n.* 1. in music, one who reads readily at sight.
2. one who shows the sights to visitors, etc.; a guide.

sīght'wŏr"thy, *a.* worth seeing.

siġ'il, *n.* [L. *sigillum*, dim. of *signum*, a sign.]
1. a seal; a signet.
2. in astrology and magic, an image or sign supposed to exercise occult powers.

Siġ·il·lā'ri·ȧ, *n.* [L. *sigillum*, dim. of *signum*, a sign.]
1. a genus of fossil trees of the Paleozoic age, principally found in the older coal formations: so named from the seallike leaf scars found on them.
2. [*construed as pl.*] in ancient Rome, minute facsimiles of pottery and earthenware made for sale or to be given as presents during the latter part of the Saturnalia.

siġ·il·lār'i·ăn, *a.* relating to the *Sigillaria* (sense 2).

siġ·il·lār'i·ăn, *n.* one of the *Sigillaria* (sense 1).

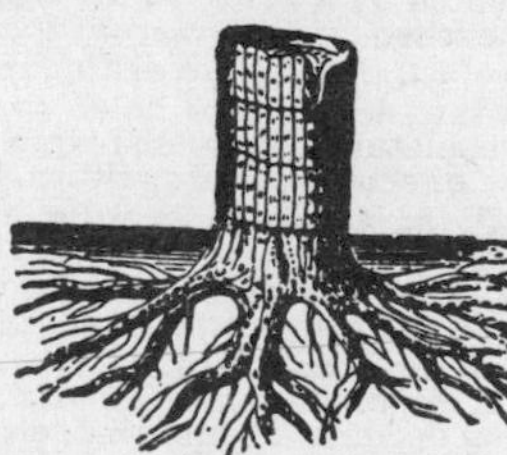

SIGILLARIAN

siġ'il·lȧ·roid, siġ·il·lā'ri·oid, *a.* same as *sigillarian.*

siġ'il·lȧ·ry, *a.* 1. of or pertaining to occult signs or sigils.
2. of the nature of a seal.

siġ'il·lāte, *a.* 1. having a pressed-in pattern, as earthenware, pottery, etc.
2. in botany, marked with seallike scars, as in *Sigillaria.*

siġ·il·lā'tion, *n.* 1. the art of pressing patterns in pottery, earthenware, etc.
2. formation of new flesh in a wound; a cicatrix.

siġ'il·lȧ·tive, *a.* [OFr. *sigillatif*; L. *sigillum*, a seal.] fit to seal; belonging to a seal; composed of wax. [Obs.]

siġ·il·log'rȧ·phy, *n.* the science or study of seals.

si·ġil'lum, *n.*; *pl.* **si·ġil'lȧ,** [L., dim. of *signum*, a sign.] a sigil; a seal.

sig'lȧ, *n.pl.* [LL., contr. of *sigilla*, signs or marks.] abbreviations of names, words, etc., in ancient manuscripts, or on medallions, coins, etc.

sig'los, *n.*; *pl.* **sig'lī,** [Gr.] one of the coins of ancient Persia.

sig'mȧ, *n.* [Gr.] 1. the eighteenth letter of the Greek alphabet, corresponding to the English *S, s.*
2. a sponge spicule having the shape of the letter C.

sig'mȧ·spīre, *n.* a sponge spicule having the shape of the letter S.

sig'māte, *a.* shaped like a sigma or an S.

sig'māte, *v.t.*; sigmated, *pt., pp.*; sigmating, *ppr.* to add sigma, or *s*, to the end of, as a word or stem.

sig'mȧ·tịṣm, *n.* the use or repetition of the letter *s.*

sig'mō·dont, *n.* any one of the *Sigmodontes.*

sig'mō·dont, *a.* relating to the *Sigmodontes.*

Sig·mō·don'tēṣ, *n.pl.* a group of American rodents including most of the murine rodents.

sig'moid, *a.* 1. curved like the letter S.
2. of the sigmoid flexure of the colon.
sigmoid flexure; (a) in anatomy, the last curve of the colon before it terminates in the rectum; (b) in zoology, an S-shaped curve.
sigmoid valve; same as *semilunar valve.*

sig'moid, *n.* a sigmoid curve; also, the sigmoid flexure.

sig·moid'ăl, *a.* same as *sigmoid.*

sig·moid'ăl·ly, *adv.* in the manner of a double curve.

sīgn (sīn), *n.* [ME. *signe*; OFr. *signe*, a sign or mark, from L. *signum*, a mark.]
1. that by which anything is shown, made known, or represented; something that indicates a fact, quality, etc.; a mark; a token; an indication; as, a black arm band is a *sign* of mourning.

The first faint *signs* of a change of public feeling. —Macaulay.

2. a motion, action, or gesture by which a thought is expressed, a wish made known, or a command given; hence, one of the gestures by which information is communicated or conversation carried on, as by deaf mutes.
3. any symbol or emblem which prefigures, typifies, or represents an idea; as, the *sign* of the cross.
4. (a) an act or happening regarded as a miraculous demonstration of divine power; (b) an omen; a portent.
5. a publicly displayed board, placard, etc. bearing some information or advertisement.
6. anything marking the trail of an animal, as droppings, a track, etc.; as, deer *signs* were plentiful.
7. any visible trace or indication; vestige; as, he showed no *sign* of friendship.
8. a mark of distinction; a standard. [Obs.]
9. in theology, that which, being external, represents or signifies something internal or spiritual; as, an outward and visible *sign.*
10. in astrology, any division or house of the ecliptic or zodiac containing 30 degrees, or a twelfth part of the complete circle. The signs are reckoned from the point of intersection of the ecliptic and equator, and are counted onward, proceeding from west to east, according to the annual course of the sun, all round the ecliptic. Each of the divisions is represented by a symbol. See *zodiac.*
11. in medicine, an objective indication of a disease, apparent to someone other than the patient.
12. a mark or symbol having an accepted and specific meaning; as, the *sign* ? indicates a question; specifically, (a) in mathematics, a symbol denoting an operation to be performed, to show the nature of a result of some previous operation, or to indicate the sense in which an indicated quantity is to be considered. Thus the sign + (plus) prefixed to a quantity indicates that that quantity is to be added, while the sign − (minus) indicates

that the quantity to which it is prefixed is to be subtracted. Other signs are: × (multiplied by), indicating multiplication; ÷ (divided by), indicating division; √ for the square root; ∛ for the cube root; ⁿ√ for the *nth* root, etc. The signs indicating relation are > (greater than), < (less than), = (equal to), etc.; (b) in music, any character that is used in notation, as a flat, sharp, dot, etc.

sign language; communication of thoughts or ideas by means of manual signs and gestures.

sign manual; a personal signature; specifically, a royal signature on an official document.

sign of the cross; in the Roman Catholic Church, the motion of the right hand making the outline of a cross.

sign of the zodiac; any of the twelve divisions or houses of the zodiac, each represented by a symbol.

Syn.—symbol, indication, token, mark, omen, presage, emblem, manifestation, symptom, note, index, signal, prognostic.

sīgn, *v.t.*, signed, *pt., pp.*; signing, *ppr.* 1. to mark with a sign, especially with the sign of the cross, as in blessing or consecrating.

2. to write one's name on, as in acknowledging authorship, authorizing action, etc.

3. to write (one's name) as a signature.

4. to hire or engage by written contract; to sign on.

5. to express, indicate, or signify with a sign; as, he *signed* his approval with a nod.

to sign away (or *over*); to abandon or transfer title to (something) by or as by signing a document; to convey.

to sign on; to engage (oneself or others) for employment; to hire or be hired, especially by a signed agreement.

to sign up; (a) to sign on; specifically, (b) to enlist in some branch of military service.

sīgn, *v.i.* 1. to be a sign or omen. [Obs.]

2. to make a sign or signal.

3. to write one's signature, as in attesting or confirming something.

to sign off; (a) in radio, to stop broadcasting after making station identification; (b) [Slang.] to cease speaking or writing; to abandon or leave, usually temporarily, some duty or task.

sīgn'ȧ·ble, *a.* capable of being signed; that may be signed, as a deed.

sig'năl, *n.* [ME. and Fr. *signal*, from LL. *signale*, from L. *signum*, a sign.]

1. an indication; sign; token.

2. a sign or event fixed or understood as the occasion for prearranged combined action; as, a *signal* for a fire drill.

3. anything which incites to action.

4. a sign given by gesture, mechanical device, etc. to convey command, warning, or other information; as, a red light is a stop *signal*.

5. in card games, a bid or play designed to give information to one's partner.

6. in telegraphy, radio, television, etc., the electrical impulses, sound or picture elements, etc. received or transmitted.

7. in surveying, any structure or appliance employed to designate to the observer the position of a station work.

sig'năl, *a.* eminent; remarkable; memorable; not ordinary; as, a *signal* exploit, a *signal* act of benevolence.

2. used as a signal or in signaling.

Syn.—conspicuous, extraordinary, notable, illustrious, important, salient, distinguished.

sig'năl, *v.t.*; signaled *or* signalled, *pt., pp.*; signaling *or* signalling, *ppr.* 1. to make a signal or signals to; as, the vessel *signaled* the harbor master.

2. to make known or communicate (information) by signals; as, the vessel *signaled* its arrival.

sig'năl, *v.i.* to make or use a signal or signals.

sig'năl box, 1. a small house in which railway signals are worked.

2. a fire-alarm box.

sig'năl cōde, a code of signals used at sea, in which differently colored flags or lights are employed.

Sig'năl Cōrps (cōr), in the United States Army, the combat arm in charge of most forms of communication and many meteorological, photographic, and range-finding services.

sig'năl·ẽr, sig'năl·lẽr, *n.* one who or that which signals.

sig·nȧ·let'iç, *a.* [Fr. *signalétique.*] pertaining to the algebraic signs plus and minus.

sig'năl fīre, a fire intended for a signal.

sig'năl flag, a flag used in signaling and belonging to a series used for that purpose.

sig'năl gun, a gun used for signaling; also, its report.

sig'năl·ist, *n.* one who makes or uses signals.

sig'năl·īze, *v.t.*; signalized, *pt., pp.*; signalizing, *ppr.* 1. to make remarkable or eminent; to distinguish; as, he *signalized* his term of office by many good deeds.

2. to make signals to; to indicate by a signal; to signal.

3. to call attention to; to point out distinctly.

sig'năl·ly, *adv.* eminently; remarkably; memorably.

sig'năl·măn, *n.*; *pl.* **sig'năl·men,** a signaler; one responsible for operating, sending, or receiving signals.

sig'năl·ment, *n.* a description giving distinguishing or identifying marks, as of someone wanted by the police.

sig'năl of'fi·cẽr, a signal-service officer; an officer belonging to the Signal Corps.

sig'năl sẽrv'ice, the system or work of conveying information by means of a series of signals; also, a body of persons organized for that purpose.

Signal Service Bureau; formerly, a bureau of the United States government, connected with the War Department. Since 1891, the duties have been assumed by the Signal Corps and the Weather Bureau.

sig'năl tow'ẽr, a tower from which signals are sent or controlled, often in connection with the opening and closing of a railroad switch or switches.

sig'nȧ·tā·ry, *a.* same as *signatory.*

sig'nāte, *a.* 1. determinate.

2. in zoology, marked as if with letters.

sig·nā'tion, *n.* the act of signing with a cross or marking with a seal.

sig'nȧ·tō·ry, *a.* 1. relating to a seal; used in sealing. [Rare.]

2. joining or taking part in the signing of something.

sig'nȧ·tō·ry, *n.*; *pl.* **sig'nȧ·tō·rieş,** a person, agency, government, etc., usually one of several, whose signature is attached to a document.

sig'nȧ·tūre, *n.* [OFr.; ML. *signatura*, from L. *signare*, to sign.]

1. a person's name written by himself, or a representation of this in a mark, stamp, deputy's handwriting, etc.

2. the act of signing one's name.

3. that part of a doctor's prescription telling the patient how to use the medicine prescribed: usually marked *S.* or *Sig.*

4. a musical number or sound effect which opens or closes a radio program.

5. in music, a sign or signs placed at the beginning of a staff to show key or time.

6. in printing, (a) a large sheet upon which are printed four, or some multiple of four, pages and which, when folded and bound, forms one section of a book or pamphlet; (b) a letter or number at the bottom of the first page in such a sheet showing in what order the sheet is to be bound.

7. in old medicine, an external mark on a plant, etc., which was supposed to indicate its suitableness to cure particular diseases, or diseases of particular parts.

8. in Scots law, a writing formerly prepared and presented by a writer to the signet to the baron of exchequer as a warrant for a grant.

sig'nȧ·tūre, *v.t.* to mark; to distinguish. [Obs.]

sig'nȧ·tūr·ist, *n.* one who holds to the doctrine of signatures impressed upon objects, indicative of character or qualities. [Rare.]

sīgn'bōard, *n.* a board, bearing a sign or notice, especially one advertising a business.

sīgn'ẽr, *n.* one who signs or subscribes his name; as, a petition with a hundred *signers.*

sig'net, *n.* [OFr. *signet*, dim. of *signe*, a sign.]

1. a seal, especially one used as a signature in marking documents as official, etc.

2. an impression made by or as by a signet.

sig'net, *v.t.* to stamp or make official with a signet.

sig'net·ed, *a.* marked with a signet.

sig'net ring, a finger ring containing a signet, often in the form of an initial.

sig'ni·fẽr, *n.* [L. *signum*, sign, and *ferre*, to bear.] the zodiac. [Obs.]

sig'ni·fi·ȧ·ble, *a.* that can be signified.

sig·nif'i·ănce, *n.* significance. [Obs.]

sig·nif'i·çănce, *n.* [from L. *significans* (*-antis*), significant.]

1. that which is signified; meaning.

2. the quality of being significant; suggestiveness; expressiveness.

3. importance; consequence; moment.

sig·nif'i·çăn·cy, *n.* same as *significance.*

sig·nif'i·çănt, *a.* 1. (a) having or expressing a meaning; (b) full of meaning.

2. important; momentous.

3. having or conveying a special or hidden meaning; suggestive.

4. representative of something; standing as a sign of something.

5. in mathematics, denoting figures standing for numbers.

sig·nif'i·çănt, *n.* a thing which is of significance; a symbol or token. [Archaic.]

sig·nif'i·çănt·ly, *adv.* in a significant manner; meaningly.

sig·nif'i·çāte, *n.* in logic, one of several things signified by a common term.

sig″ni·fi·çā'tion, *n.* [OFr. *significacium*, from L. *significatio* (*-onis*), a meaning.]

1. significance; meaning.

2. the act of signifying; indication.

sig·nif'i·çȧ·tive, *a.* significant.

sig·nif'i·çȧ·tive·ly, *adv.* in a significative manner.

sig·nif'i·çȧ·tive·ness, *n.* the quality of being significative.

sig·nif'i·çā·tŏr, *n.* one who or that which signifies or makes known by words or symbols.

sig·nif'i·çȧ·tō·ry, *a.* significant; significative.

sig·nif'i·çȧ·tō·ry, *n.*; *pl.* **sig·nif'i·çȧ·tō·rieş,** that which signifies or represents.

sig″ni·fi·çā'vit, *n.* in ecclesiastical law, a writ of imprisonment for six months for contempt of an order of the ecclesiastical court. [Obs.]

sig'ni·fī·ẽr, *n.* a person or thing that signifies.

sig'ni·fȳ, *v.t.*; signified, *pt., pp.*; signifying, *ppr.* [Late OFr. *signifier*, from L. *significare*; *signum*, a sign, and *facere*, to make.]

1. to be a sign or indication of; to mean; as, his rags *signify* his poverty.

2. to show or make known, as by a sign, words, etc.; as, *signify* "yes" by raising your hand.

Syn.—express, manifest, declare, utter, intimate, betoken, denote, imply, mean.

sig'ni·fȳ, *v.i.* to be of consequence; to have meaning; to matter.

sīgn'iọr (sēn'yọr), *n.* same as *signor.*

si'gnọr (sē'nyọr), *n.* [It.] 1. an Italian lord or gentleman; by extension, any gentleman.

2. [S—] Mr.: Italian title of respect, used before the name.

si·gnō'rȧ (-nyō'), *n.* [It.] a woman; a lady: an Italian title equivalent to *Madam, Mrs.*

si·gnō're, *n.*; *pl.* **si·gnō'rï,** [It.] 1. a gentleman; man.

2. sir: Italian title of respect, used in direct address but not before the name: cf. *signor.*

si·gnō·rï'nä, *n.* [It.] an unmarried woman or girl; a young lady: an Italian title equivalent to the English *Miss* and the French *Mademoiselle.*

si·gnō·rï'nō, *n.*; *pl.* **si·gnō·rï'nï,** [It.] a young man; young gentleman: Italian title equivalent to *Master.*

si'gnō·ry, *n.*; *pl.* **si'gnō·rieş,** seigniory.

sīgn'pōst (sīn'), *n.* 1. a post which holds a sign; a guidepost.

2. a clear indication; an obvious clue, symptom, etc.

Si'gŭrd, *n.* in Norse legend, the hero of the Volsunga Saga: identified with the German Siegfried.

sīke, *a.* such. [Obs.]

sīke, *n.* [Ice. *sīk.*] a small stream of water; a rill. [Scot. and Brit. Dial.]

sīke, *v.i.* to sigh. [Now Dial.]

sīke, *n.* a sigh. [Now Dial.]

sīke, *n.* a person who is sick. [Brit. Dial.]

Sïkh (sēk), *n.* [Hind. *Sikh*, a disciple.] a believer in Sikhism.

Sïkh, *a.* of or belonging to the Sikhs.

Sïkh'işm, *n.* the doctrines of a Hindu religious sect founded in northern India about 1500: belief in one god and rejection of the caste system are the main principles.

sī'lăġe, *n.* green fodder preserved in a silo.

sī'lăġe, *v.t.*; silaged, *pt., pp.*; silaging, *ppr.* to ensile.

sīle, *v.t.* to strain, as fresh milk from a cow. [Brit. Dial.]

sīle, *v.i.* to flow down; to fall. [Brit. Dial.]

sīle, *n.* 1. a sieve; a strainer. [Brit. Dial.]
2. dirt; dregs. [Brit. Dial.]

sīle, *n.* [etym. doubtful.] a small herring. [Brit. Dial.]

sī·lē·nā′ceous, *a.* [from Mod.L. *Silene.*] in botany, caryophyllaceous.

sī′lence, *n.* [ME. and OFr.; L. *silentium,* silence.]
1. the state or fact of being silent; a refraining from speech or the making of noise.
2. stillness; absence of any sound or noise.
3. a withholding of knowledge; omission of mention; as, we noted the author's *silence* on that point.
4. failure to communicate, write, keep in touch, etc.
5. oblivion; obscurity; absence of mention.
Syn.—taciturnity, stillness, calm, peace, hush, muteness, secrecy, oblivion.

sī′lence, *v.t.*; silenced (-lenst), *pt., pp.*; silencing, *ppr.* 1. to make silent; to cause to be silent.
2. to oppose or refute with arguments which are unanswerable.
3. to put (enemy guns) out of action.
4. to restrain in reference to liberty of speech; especially, to restrain or interdict from preaching by revoking a license to preach.
5. to still; to quiet; to appease; to restrain; as, to *silence* opposition, to *silence* complaints.

sī′lence, *interj.* be silent!

sī′lenc·ẽr, *n.* 1. one who or that which silences.
2. any device to reduce the buzzing of telephone and telegraph wires.
3. a device for deadening the sound of a gun.
4. a muffler for an internal-combustion engine. [Chiefly Brit.]
Maxim silencer; a device for the muzzle of a rifle that makes the discharge almost noiseless.

Sī·lē′nē, *n.* [from L. *Silenus,* Silenus.] an extensive genus of plants belonging to the family *Caryophyllaceæ.* They exude a viscid substance at the joints of the stems, in which insects are frequently caught; hence the common name, *catchfly.*

sī′lent, *a.* [L. *silens (-entis),* from *silere,* to be silent.]
1. making no vocal sound; not speaking; speechless; mute.
2. seldom speaking; saying little; not talkative.
3. free from or making no sound or noise; quiet; still; noiseless.
4. not spoken, uttered, or expressed; tacit; as, *silent* longing.
5. withholding knowledge; omitting mention; uncommunicative; as, the report was *silent* on this matter.
6. inactive; as, the machines had been *silent* for six months.
7. designating or of motion pictures that do not have an accompanying synchronized speech and sound recording: printed captions are used to present dialogue in silent films.
8. in phonetics, not pronounced or expressed; not sounded in pronunciation; as, the *e* in fable is *silent.*
9. having no effect. [Obs.]
silent butler; an ornamental dish with a hinged cover and handle, in which to empty ash trays, etc.
silent partner; a partner who shares in financing but not in managing a business, firm, etc.

sī′lent, *n.* 1. a silent film.
2. in electricity, a switch device for preventing the action of an electric alarm by short-circuiting it.

sī·len′ti·ā·ry (-shi-), *n.* 1. one appointed to keep silence and order in court.
2. one sworn not to divulge secrets of state.

sī·len′tious (-shus), *a.* of a silent nature; reserved; taciturn. [Rare.]

sī′lent·ly, *adv.* in a silent manner.

sī′lent·ness, *n.* the state of being silent; stillness; silence.

Sī·lē′nus, *n.* [Gr. *Seilēnos,* Silenus.]
1. in Greek mythology, (a) the foster father and tutor of Bacchus and leader of the satyrs, traditionally pictured as a fat, drunken, jovial old man with pointed ears and goat's legs; (b) [s-] any of a group of woodland deities resembling the satyrs.
2. [s-] in zoology, the wanderoo.

si·lē′si·ȧ (-shi-ȧ), *n.* a strong, lightweight linen or twilled cotton cloth used for linings: the linen was originally made in Silesia.

Sī·lē′siăn, *a.* of Silesia, its people, or culture.

Sī·lē′siăn, *n.* a native or inhabitant of Silesia.

sī′lex, *n.* 1. silica, especially in the form of flint or quartz.
2. heat-resistant glass made of fused quartz.
3. a device of such glass used for making coffee: a trade-mark (*Silex*).

sil·hou·ette′ (-ö-et′), *n.* [from Étienne de *Silhouette,* French minister of finance in 1759.]
1. an outline drawing, especially a profile portrait, filled in with a solid color: silhouettes are usually cut from black paper and fixed on a light background.
2. any dark shape or outline seen against a light background.

SILHOUETTE

sil·hou·ette′, *v.t.*; silhouetted, *pt., pp.*; silhouetting, *ppr.* to show or project in a silhouette.

sil′iç-, see *silico-.*

sil′i·çȧ, *n.* [L. *silex, silicis,* flint.] silicon dioxide, SiO_2, a hard, glassy mineral found in a variety of forms, as in quartz, sand, opal, etc.

sil′i·çȧ ġel, a colloidal form of silica used as a drying agent in air-conditioning equipment, as a carrier of catalysts in chemical reactions, etc.

sil′i·çāte, *n.* a salt or ester derived from silica or a silicic acid.

sil′i·çā·ted, *a.* combined with silica.
silicated soap; a hard soap containing sodium silicate.

sil·i·çā·ti·zā′tion, *n.* silicification.

Si·liç′ē·ȧ, *n.pl.* a class or subclass of sponges including those having a skeleton chiefly composed of siliceous fibers.

si·li′ceous, *a.* 1. of, containing, or like silica.
2. growing in soil that has a large proportion of silica in it.

sil′i·ci-, [from L. *silex, silicis,* flint.] a combining form used in mineralogy, chemistry, etc., to signify *containing* or *relating to silica.*

si·lic′iç, *a.* like, pertaining to, or derived from silica or silicon.
silicic acid; any of several hypothetical acids of which the different mineral silicates may be regarded as salts.

sil″i·ci·cal·çā′rē·ous, *a.* [L. *silex, silicis,* flint, and *calcarius,* pertaining to lime.] consisting of silica and calcareous matter.

sil″i·ci·cer′ȧ·tous, *a.* [*silici-,* and Gr. *keras,* horn.] both siliceous and horny: applied to certain sponges.

Sil″i·ci·çoi′dē·ȧ, *n.pl.* same as *Silicea.*

sil′i·cīde, *n.* a binary compound of silicon.

sil·i·cif′ẽr·ous, *a.* [*silici-,* and L. *ferre,* to bear.] producing, containing, or united with silica.

si·lic″i·fi·çā′tion, *n.* conversion into silica.

si·lic′i·fȳ, *v.t.*; silicified, *pt., pp.*; silicifying, *ppr.* [L. *silex,* flint, and *facere,* to make.] to convert into or impregnate with silica.

si·lic′i·fȳ, *v.i.* to become silicified, as wood.

si·li′cious, *a.* same as *siliceous.*

Sil″i·ci·spon′gi·ae, *n.pl.* same as *Silicea.*

si·li′ci·um, *n.* same as *silicon.*

si·li′ciū·ret·ed, *a.* united with silicon.

sil′i·çle, *n.* [L. *silicula,* dim. of *siliqua,* a pod.] in botany, a short, broad silique.

sil′i·çō-, [from *silicon.*] a combining form meaning *silicon, silica,* as in *silicosis*: also, before a vowel, *silic-.*

sil″i·çō·cal·çā′rē·ous, *a.* same as *silicicalcareous.*

sil″i·çō·flū·or′iç, *a.* containing silicon and fluorine; as, *silicofluoric* acid.

sil″i·çō·flū′ŏr·ide, *n.* a salt or silicofluoric acid.

Sil·i·çoi′dē·ȧ, *n.pl.* the *Silicea.*

sil′i·çon, *n.* [L. *silex, silicis,* flint.] a nonmetallic chemical element found always in combination and more abundant in nature than any other element except oxygen, with which it combines to form silica: symbol, Si; atomic weight, 28.06; atomic number, 14.

sil′i·çōne, *n.* [from *silicon.*] any of a group of synthetic resins, oils, greases, plastics, etc. in which the carbon has been replaced by silicon: such compounds are characterized by relatively high resistance to temperature changes, to water, etc. and are used in lubricants, synthetic rubber, polishes, and the like.

sil′i·çŏn·īze, *v.t.*; siliconized, *pt., pp.*; siliconizing, *ppr.* to combine or cause to combine with silicon, as in some processes of metallurgy.

sil·i·çō′sis, *n.* [LL.] a chronic lung disease due to continued inhalation of silica dust, as in quarrying stone.

sil″i·çō·tung′stiç, *a.* pertaining to acids of silicon and tungsten.

si·liç′ū·lȧ, *n.*; *pl.* **si·liç′ū·lae,** [LL.] same as *silicle.*

si·liç′u·lăr, *a.* having the shape or appearance of a silicle.

sil′i·çūle, *n.* a silicle.

si·liç′ū·lōse, *a.* 1. having silicles.
2. having the form of a silicle.

si·liç′ū·lous, *a.* same as *siliculose.*

si·liġ′i·nōse, si·liġ′i·nous, *a.* made of white wheat. [Obs.]

sīl′ing dish, a colander; a sile. [Brit. Dial.]

sil′i·quȧ, *n.*; *pl.* **sil′i·quae,** [L. *siliqua,* a pod; also, a very small weight.]
1. in botany, same as *silique.*
2. a weight of 4 grains, used in weighing gold and precious stones; a carat.
3. an ancient Roman unit of weight.

Sil·i·quā′ri·ȧ, *n.* a genus of marine gastropodous mollusks, having a tubular shell that is formed into chambers by entire septa.

si·lique′ (-lēk′), *n.* [L. *siliqua,* a pod.] the long, narrow pod of plants of the mustard family, *Cruciferæ,* with two valves which fall away from a frame bearing the seeds.

sil′i·qui·fọrm, *a.* having the form of a silique.

Sil·i·quō′sȧ, *n.pl.* a family of plants in the Linnean system, comprising those bearing siliques.

sil′i·quōse, *a.* [L. *siliquosus,* having pods, from *siliqua,* a pod.]
1. having siliques; as, *siliquose* plants.
2. having the form of a silique.

sil′i·quous, *a.* same as *siliquose.*

silk, *n.* [AS. *seoloc,* silk, for *seric,* from L. *sericus,* fabric of the *Seres,* the Chinese.]
1. the fine, soft, shiny fiber produced by silkworms to form their cocoons. The silkworm draws the fiber from two large glands, containing a viscid substance, which extend along the sides of the body and end in two spinnerets at the mouth. With this substance the silkworm envelops itself, forming a cocoon.
2. thread or fabric made from silk.
3. a garment made of silk.
4. [*pl.*] the distinctive silk uniform of a jockey, prize fighter, acrobat, etc.
5. the silk gown worn by a king's (or queen's) counsel in British law courts.
6. any silklike filament or substance, as that within a milkweed pod, on the end of an ear of corn, etc.
artificial silk; collodion made into fine threads resembling silk fibers, by being forced through a tiny opening.
spun silk; a cheap yarn made from waste silk, pierced cocoons, floss, etc., dressed, combed, formed into rovings, and spun.
thrown silk; silk formed of one, two, three, or more reeled threads (called *singles*), twisted together in a contrary direction to that in which the singles are twisted. The silk so twisted is called *organzine.*
to hit the silk; to leave an aircraft by means of a parachute. [Slang.]
Virginia silk; see *silk vine.*

silk, *a.* pertaining to silk; consisting of silk.

silk, *v.i.* to bloom: said of Indian corn.

silk·ȧ·līne′, silk·ȧ·lēne′, *n.* a soft, thin, cotton cloth with a finish resembling that of silk, much used for draperies, etc.

silk bunt′ing, a bird of the genus *Spiza,* having silky plumage.

silk cot′tŏn (kot′n), a short, silky, elastic fiber surrounding the seeds of the silk-cotton tree, used for stuffing mattresses, cushions, etc.: also called *kapok.*

silk′-cot′tŏn tree, a tree of the genus *Bombax,* especially one from which silk cotton is obtained, as the ceiba, or kapok tree.

silk dress'ẽr, one employed in dressing or stiffening and smoothing silk.

silk'en, *a.* [AS. *seolcen.*]
1. made of silk.
2. dressed in silk.
3. like silk; soft to the touch; smooth, glossy.
4. (a) smooth and ingratiating; as, *silken* flattery; (b) elegant; luxurious; as, *silken* ease; (c) soft; gentle; delicate; as, a *silken* caress.

silk'en, *v.t.* to make soft or smooth. [Rare.]

silk' flow"ẽr, *n.* 1. a leguminous tree of Peru, *Calliandra trinervia,* whose stamens are long and silky.
2. the silk tree.

silk fowl, a variety of the domestic fowl with silky plumage.

silk ġel'ȧ·tin, same as *sericin.*

silk gland, a sericterium.

silk glūe, same as *sericin.*

silk gown, in England, the canonical robe of a king's or queen's counsel, differing from that of an ordinary barrister in being made of silk; hence, the counsel himself.

silk grȧss, 1. a plant of the genus *Yucca,* or *Agave.*
2. any of various grasses having silky awns, as *Stipa comata.*

silk'grōw·ẽr, *n.* one who grows silkworms for their silk.

silk hat, a tall, cylindrical hat covered with silk or satin, worn by men in dress clothes.

silk hen, the female of the silk fowl.

silk'i·ness, *n.* 1. the state or quality of being silky; softness and smoothness.
2. softness; effeminacy; pusillanimity. [Rare.]

silk'līke, *a.* having the nature of silk; similar to silk.

silk'mă̆n, *n.*; *pl.* **silk'men,** a dealer in silks; a manufacturer of silks; the director of a silk mill.

silk mẽr'cẽr, a silkman.

silk mill, a mill or factory in which silk is spun into thread or fabric.

silk mọth, any moth whose larva is a silkworm.

silk'-sçreen' print, a print made by the silk-screen process.

silk'-sçreen' proc'ess, a stencil method of printing a flat color design through a piece of silk or other fine cloth on which all parts of the design not to be printed have been stopped out by an impermeable substance.

silk spī'dẽr, any spider that produces a silky web, as *Nephila plumipes.*

silk'-stock'ing, *a.* 1. fashionably or richly dressed; elegant.
2. wealthy; aristocratic; as, the *silk-stocking* trade.

silk'-stock'ing, *n.* 1. a member of the wealthy, aristocratic class.
2. a Federalist or Whig. [Colloq.]

silk thrōw'ẽr, silk thrōw'stẽr, one who winds, twists, spins, or throws silk, to prepare it for weaving.

silk tree, an ornamental deciduous tree, *Albizzia julibrissin,* native to the Levant.

silk vīne, a climbing vine, *Periploca græca,* whose seeds have tufts of long silky hairs like those of the milkweed, of the same family: also called *Virginia silk.*

silk'weed, *n.* 1. milkweed.
2. any of several seaweeds of the *Confervaceæ.*

silk'wood, *n.* the calabur tree.

silk'wŏrm, *n.* a worm that produces silk; especially, the larva of the lepidopterous insect *Bombyx mori,* and of other related in-

SILKWORM (larva, chrysalis, and cocoon)

sects. The common silkworm feeds upon the leaves of the mulberry, and when full-grown is about three inches long. The cocoon, or case of silky fiber which it spins round its body, is the receptacle in which it changes to the chrysalis state, and from which it finally emerges as the adult insect.
silkworm gut; a substance prepared from the secretions of the silkworm glands, used in making lines for angling.

silk'y, *a.* 1. of or like silk; soft; smooth; lustrous.
2. having fine, soft, silklike hairs, as some leaves.
3. pliant; yielding. [Rare.]

sill, *n.* [AS. *syl, syll,* a base, foundation, sill; akin to Ice. *syll* (also *svill*), a sill of a door or window; O.H.G. *suelli*; G. *schwelle,* a threshold.]
1. a block forming a basis or foundation; a stone or a piece of timber on which a structure rests; as, the *sills* of a house.
2. the horizontal piece of timber or stone forming the bottom frame of a door or window.
3. a timber at the base of a canal lock against which gates close.
4. the floor of a passage in a mine.
5. in geology, a sheet of igneous rock that has been forced between existing strata.

sill, *n.* the shaft of a carriage. [Brit. Dial.]

sill, *n.* a herring that has not attained full size. [Brit.]

sil'lȧ·bub, *n.* [prob. a var. of dial. *sillibouk,* lit., silly (i.e., happy) stomach.] a dessert or beverage made of sweetened milk or cream mixed with wine or cider and beaten to a froth: also spelled *syllabub, sillibub.*

sil'lȧ·där, *n.* [Hind.] a soldier of an irregular troop of Hindu cavalry.

sill çourse, a course of brick, stone, etc., in line with a door or window sill.

sil'lẽr, *n.* and *a.* silver. [Scot.]

sil'li·bub, *n.* same as *sillabub.*

sil'li·ly, *adv.* in a silly manner; foolishly.

sil'li·mă̆n·īte, *n.* [named after Benjamin *Silliman* of Yale University.] a mineral, fibrolite.

sil'li·ness, *n.* 1. the quality or state of being silly.
2. something silly; silly behavior.

sil'lŏck, *n.* [dim. of *sill,* a young herring.] the coalfish. [Scot.]

sil'lŏn, *n.* in fortification, a defense built in a wide ditch.

sil'ly, *a.*; *comp.* sillier; *superl.* silliest, [ME. *seely, sely*; AS. *sælig,* happy, prosperous, blessed, from *sæl,* innocent.]
1. feeble-minded; imbecile.
2. having or showing little sense, judgment, or sobriety; foolish, stupid, absurd, ludicrous, etc.
3. dazed; senseless, as from a blow. [Colloq.]
4. helpless; weak. [Dial.]
5. feeble; infirm. [Archaic.]
6. simple; plain; innocent. [Archaic.]
Syn.—witless, foolish, brainless, simple.

sil'ly, *n.*; *pl.* **sil'lieṣ,** a silly person. [Colloq.]

sil'ly·how, *n.* a caul. [Scot. and Brit. Dial.]

sī'lō, *n.*; *pl.* **sī'lōṣ,** [Fr., from Sp. *silo,* from L. *sirus*; Gr. *siros,* a corn pit.]
1. an airtight pit or tower in which green fodder is prepared and kept.
2. a large, underground structure for the storage and launching of a long-range ballistic missile.

sī'lō, *v.t.* to store in a silo.

Sī·lō'ăm, *n.* [Heb. *shiloah,* lit., sending forth.] in the Bible, a spring and pool outside Jerusalem. John ix. 7.

Sil'phi·um, *n.* [L., from Gr. *silphion,* a resinous plant.] a genus of plants, native to the United States, comprising about thirty species, including the prairie dock and compass plant.

silt, *n.* [ME. *silte,* sand, prob. from ON.] any earthy material composed of fine particles, as soil or sand, suspended in or deposited by water.

silt, *v.t.*; silted, *pt., pp.*; silting, *ppr.* to choke, fill, or obstruct with silt or mud: often with *up*; as, the channel became *silted up.*

silt, *v.i.* 1. to ooze through crevices.
2. to become choked with silt: often with *up.*

silt grȧss, joint grass.

silt'y, *a.*; *comp.* siltier; *superl.* siltiest, 1. consisting of or resembling silt.
2. full of silt.

Si·lun'dum, *n.* [from *silicon* and *carborundum.*] silicon carbide, SiC, produced in an electric furnace and used as an abrasive for electric resistors, etc.: a trade-mark.

Sil'ū·rēṣ, *n.pl.* an ancient, warlike tribe of southeastern Wales, conquered by the Romans about 80 A.D.

Si·lū'ri·ă̆n, *a.* 1. of the Silures or the territory held by them.
2. designating or of the geological period after the Ordovician and before the Devonian in the Paleozoic Era, characterized by the appearance of scorpions (the first land animals) and extensive coral reefs: so called because its rocks were first found in an area occupied by the Welsh, assumed to be descendants of the Silures.
the Silurian; the Silurian Period or its rocks.

Si·lū'riç, *a.* of the Silures; Silurian.

si·lū'rid, *n.* any fish of the family *Siluridæ.*

Sī·lū'ri·dae, *n.pl.* [L. *silurus*; Gr. *silouros,* the sheatfish.] a family of fishes, between the *Esocidæ,* or pikes, and the *Salmonidæ,* or salmon; the catfishes. They are found mainly in the fresh waters of warm climates.

sī·lū'ri·dă̆n, *n.* a fish of the family *Siluridæ.*

si·lū'roid, *a.* of, or pertaining to the *Siluridæ.*

si·lū'roid, *n.* a silurid.

Si·lū'rus, *n.* 1. a genus of malacopterygious fishes, the type of the family *Siluridæ.*

SILURUS (*Silurus glanis*)

2. [s–] any fish of this genus.

sil'vȧ, *n.*; *pl.* **sil'vȧṣ, sil'vae,** [L., a forest.]
1. the forest trees of a certain area.
2. a book or treatise describing the trees of a certain area.
Also spelled *sylva.*

sil'vă̆n, *a.* and *n.* sylvan.

Sil·vā'nus, *n.* [L., from *silva,* forest.] a Roman god of the woods and farming.

sil'vāte, *n.* same as *sylvate.*

sil'vẽr, *n.* [AS. *seolfer, sylfer*; akin to Ice. *silfr*; D. *zilver*; Dan. *sölv*; G. *silber,* silver.]
1. a white, precious, metallic chemical element that is extremely ductile and malleable, capable of a high polish, and an excellent conductor of heat and electricity: symbol, Ag; atomic weight, 107.880; atomic number, 47.
2. the metal regarded as a commodity or medium of exchange, as in the form of ingots, coins, etc.
3. money of any kind.
4. something, especially tableware, made of or plated with silver; silverware.
5. a lustrous, grayish-white color; a silvery color.
6. something having this color, as the material used in coating the back of a mirror.
7. a salt of silver, as used in photography, etc.
black silver; the mineral stephanite.
fulminating silver; a very explosive powder formed by heating aqueous nitrate of silver with strong nitric acid and alcohol.
German silver; see under **German, a.**
gray silver; same as ***Freieslebenite.***
horn silver; same as *cerargyrite.*
mock silver; Britannia metal; also, pewter.
mosaic silver; a mixture of bismuth, mercury, and tin, used to give the color of silver.
old silver; silver to which the appearance of age has been given by treatment with graphite and grease.
red silver; same as ***proustite.***
ruby silver; same as ***pyrargyrite.***
vitreous silver; same as *argentite.*

sil'vẽr, *a.* 1. made of, containing, or plated with silver; as, *silver* thread.
2. of, based on, or having to do with silver; as, the *silver* standard.
3. of or advocating the adoption of silver as a standard of currency; as, the *silver* bloc.
4. having the color or luster of silver; silvery.
5. having a silvery tone or sound.
6. eloquent; as, a *silver* tongue.
7. marking or celebrating the twenty-fifth year; as, a *silver* wedding anniversary.
Silver Age; (a) in classical mythology, the

second age of the world succeeding and inferior to the Golden Age, and characterized by voluptuousness; (b) the period of Latin literature coming between 14 and 180 A.D., distinguished by the writings of Martial, Juvenal, Tacitus, etc.

silver bass; see *bass* (fish).

silver bath; a solution of silver nitrate for sensitizing photographic plates and printing paper.

silver bell; any of a number of related trees of the genus *Halesia*, with drooping, bell-shaped, white flowers: also called *silver-bell tree*.

silver birch; the white birch.

silver bromide; a yellow-white crystalline compound, AgBr, which becomes dark when exposed to light: used in photography.

silver cedar; a species of red cedar, *Juniperus virginiana*.

silver certificate; a piece of paper money issued on the basis of a government's possession of silver in the amount of the face value of the certificate, payable to the bearer on demand: a United States silver certificate is legal tender for all debts, public and private.

silver chain; the common locust tree, *Robinia pseudacacia*.

silver chickweed; a small herb of the southeastern United States.

silver chloride; a white crystalline compound, AgCl, which becomes dark when exposed to light: used in photography.

silver chub; same as *fallfish*.

silver eel; (a) the hairtail; (b) the cutlass fish.

silver fern; same as *Gymnogramme*.

silver fir; the balsam fir.

silver foil; silver beaten into thin sheets.

silver fox; (a) a fox with black fur in which the individual hairs are banded with white near the tips; (b) the fur.

silver gar; the American garfish, *Tylosurus marinus*.

silver gilt; (a) silver with a thin coating of gold; (b) an imitation of this made with silver leaf coated with yellow lacquer.

silver glance; same as *argentite*.

silver grain; the lines or surfaces formed by the medullary rays in the wood of trees.

silver king; the tarpon, *Megalops atlanticus*.

silver leaf; very thin silver foil.

silver lining; some basis for hope in the midst of despair, misfortune, etc.

silver mill; a mill for reducing silver ore.

silver moth; a silverfish (sense 2).

silver nitrate; a colorless crystalline salt, $AgNO_3$, prepared by dissolving silver in dilute nitric acid and used in silver plating, photography, as an antiseptic, etc.

silver owl; the common barn owl.

silver paper; sensitized paper; also, paper having a surface like silver.

silver plate; tableware made of silver.

silver printing; the process of producing photographic prints on paper sensitized with a silver salt.

silver sand; a fine, silver-colored sand used in grinding lithographic stones.

silver screen; (a) a screen on which motion pictures are projected in theaters; (b) motion pictures collectively: with *the*.

silver solder; any of various solders used in soldering silver objects.

silver standard; a monetary standard in which the basic currency unit is equal to a specified quantity of silver.

Silver Star Medal; a United States military decoration in the form of a bronze star with a small silver star at the center, awarded for gallantry in action.

silver thistle; the acanthus.

silver tree; a South African evergreen shrub or small tree of the genus *Leucadendron*.

silver wedding; a twenty-fifth wedding anniversary.

silver white; the color silver; also, a whitish hue like silver.

silver whiting; a sciaenoid fish, *Menticirrus littoralis*.

sil′vẽr, *v.t.*; silvered, *pt., pp.*; silvering, *ppr.* 1. to cover or coat with silver or something like silver.

2. to cover with tin foil amalgamated with quicksilver; as, to *silver* glass.

3. to cause to resemble silver; to give a silvery sheen to.

4. to make hoary; to tinge with gray.

sil′vẽr, *v.i.* to acquire the color of silver; to become silvery in appearance.

sil′vẽr·back, *n.* a bird, the knot, *Tringa canutus*.

sil′vẽr·bēat″ẽr, *n.* one who beats silver or forms it into a thin leaf or foil.

sil′vẽr-bell tree, same as *silver bell*.

sil′vẽr·bel″ly, *n.* a Tasmanian fish, a species of the silversides.

sil′vẽr·ber″ry, *n.*; *pl.* **sil′vẽr·ber″ries,** an American oleaster, *Elæagnus argentea*, with fragrant flowers and silvery foliage and fruit.

sil′vẽr·bill, *n.* any of several Indian and African birds of the genus *Munia*; a finch; a waxbill.

sil′vẽr·bil″ly, *n.* an Australian fish, *Gerres ovatus*.

sil′vẽr-black, *a.* black having a silvery luster.

sil′vẽr·bush, *n.* Jupiter's-beard, an evergreen plant.

sil′vẽr·ẽr, *n.* one who silvers; especially, one who silvers glass.

sil′vẽr·eȳe (-ī), *n.* an insectivorous bird, *Zosterops cærulescens*: also called *blightbird*.

sil′vẽr·fin, *n.* a small cyprinoid North American fish, *Notropis whipplei*.

sil′vẽr·fish, *n.* 1. *pl.* **sil′vẽr·fish, sil′vẽr·fish·es,** any of various fishes of silvery color, as the tarpon, silversides, etc.

2. a wingless insect with silvery scales, long feelers, and a bristly tail: it thrives in dampness and darkness and lives chiefly on starches and sugars.

sil′vẽr-grāy, *a.* gray with a silvery luster; as, a *silver-gray* fur.

sil′vẽr grāy, a silver-gray color.

sil′vẽr-hāired, *a.* having silvery-white or gray hair.

sil′vẽr-head″ed (-hed″), *a.* having a head of silver; as, a *silver-headed* stick.

sil′vẽr·i·ness, *n.* the quality or state of being silvery.

sil′vẽr·ing, *n.* 1. the art, operation, or practice of covering the surface of anything with silver; as, the *silvering* of copper or brass.

2. silver applied to a surface, as by plating.

3. a silvery sheen or appearance.

4. in photography, the act of sensitizing paper with silver salt.

sil′vẽr·īte, *n.* one who favors the use of silver as a coin metal equally with gold; a bimetallist. [Colloq.]

sil′vẽr·īze, *v.t.*; silverized, *pt., pp.*; silverizing, *ppr.* to coat with silver; to dip into a silver solution.

sil′vẽr·lēaf, *n.* any one of a variety of trees having a silvery leaf.

sil′vẽr·less, *a.* without silver.

sil′vẽr·ling, *n.* an ancient silver coin of small value. [Archaic.]

sil′vẽr·ly, *adv.* with a silvery appearance or sound; as, raindrops ringing in water *silverly*.

sil′vẽrn, *a.* [ME. *silveren*, from AS. *seolfren*.] of or like silver; as, a *silvern* image.

sil′vẽr-plāt″ed, *a.* coated with silver.

sil′vẽr·point, *n.* a drawing pencil having a silver point for use on prepared paper.

sil′vẽr·rod, *n.* a plant, *Asphodelus ramosus*, of southern Europe.

sil′vẽr·sīdes, *n.*; *pl.* **sil′vẽr·sīdes,** any fish of the family *Atherinidæ*, marked by a silvery stripe along the side. *Menidia notata* and *Labidesthes sicculus* are common varieties: also called *silverside*.

sil′vẽr·smith, *n.* one who makes or repairs silver articles.

sil′vẽr·spot, *n.* any silver-spotted butterfly.

sil′vẽr-spot″ted, *a.* having spots of the color of silver, as the under side of the wings of certain butterflies.

sil′vẽr·tip, *n.* a grizzly bear having the ends of the hair white.

sil′vẽr-tŏngue (-tung), *n.* the song sparrow.

sil′vẽr-tŏngued, *a.* eloquent; persuasive; as, a *silver-tongued* orator.

sil′vẽr·top, *n.* a disease of grasses in which the upper part of the stalk whitens and withers.

sil′vẽr·vīne, *n.* a climbing plant, *Scindapsus argyræa*, native to the Philippine Islands.

sil′vẽr·wāre, *n.* articles, especially tableware, made of or plated with silver.

sil′vẽr·weed, *n.* in botany, (a) a yellow flowering plant, *Potentilla anserina*, growing in low lands of the north temperate zone; (b) a plant of the genus *Argyreia*.

sil′vẽr·wŏrk, *n.* ornamental work in silver.

sil′vẽr·y, *a.* 1. having the appearance of silver; like silver in color or luster.

2. softly and clearly ringing; as, a *silvery* tone.

3. covered with or containing silver.

silvery iron; iron showing silvery fracture.

silvery thistle; see *silver thistle* under *silver*.

sil′vi·cul·tūre, *n.* the art of cultivating a forest; forestry.

s'il vous plaît (sēl vö plā′), [Fr., lit., if it pleases you.] if you please; please.

sī′mȧ, *n.* same as *cyma*.

sim′ȧ·gre (-gẽr), *n.* [Fr. *simagrée*.] a grimace. [Obs.]

si·mär′, *n.* [Fr. *simarre*.] a woman's robe; a loose, light garment: also spelled *cimar*, *cymar*, *samare*, *simarre*.

sim·ȧ·röu′bȧ, *n.* [Mod. L.; from the Carib. name.]

1. any of a number of related tropical American trees with bitter bark, large-disked flowers, and pulpy fruit.

2. the bark, used in pharmacy.

Sim″ȧ·röu·bā′cē·ae, *n.pl.* in botany, an order of usually bitter trees or shrubs, with simple or compound leaves and regular unisexual flowers, native chiefly to the torrid zones.

sim″ȧ·röu·bā′ceous, *a.* of or pertaining to the *Simaroubaceæ*.

sim′bil, *n.* a stork, *Sphenorhynchus abdimi*, native to Africa.

sim′blin, sim′bling, *n.* same as *simlin*.

sim′blot, *n.* the harness of a weavers' drawloom.

Sim·chath′ To·rah′ (sim-khäth′ tō-rȧ′), [Heb. *simhath torah*, lit., rejoicing in the Torah, or Law.] a Jewish holiday, the Rejoicing in the Law: also spelled *Simhath Torah*.

Sim′ē·ōn, [LL.; Gr. *Symeōn*; Heb. *shim'ōn*, lit., heard.] in the Bible, (a) a son of Jacob; (b) a tribe of Israel descended from him; (c) a pious man who, on seeing the infant Jesus in the Temple, spoke the words later set to the canticle "Nunc Dimittis": Luke ii. 25.

Sim′i·ȧ, *n.* [L., an ape, from *simus*, flat-nosed.] the Linnaean genus including all the quadrumanous mammals (monkeys) except the lemurs.

sim′i·ăn, *a.* of or pertaining to an ape; resembling an ape; having the character of an ape; apelike.

sim′i·ăn, *n.* an ape or monkey, especially an anthropoid ape.

sim′i·lăr, *a.* [Fr. *similaire*, from a hypothetical L. form *similaris*, from L. *similis*, like.]

1. like; resembling; having a general resemblance but not exactly the same.

2. homogeneous; of like structure or character throughout. [Obs.]

3. in geometry, having the same shape but not the same size or position.

similar curves; curves whose equations are of the same form, and the ratio of the constants in those equations equal.

similar rectilinear figures; in geometry, such figures as have their several angles equal each to each, and the sides about the equal angles proportional. Such figures are to one another as the squares of their homologous sides.

similar segments; of circles, those segments which contain equal angles.

similar solids; such solids as are contained by the same number of similar planes, similarly situated, and having like inclinations to one another. Such solids are to one another as the cubes of their homologous sides.

Syn.—correspondent, resembling, alike, common, homogeneous, concordant, harmonious, congruous.

sim′i·lăr, *n.* that which is similar; one who or that which resembles something else in form, appearance, quality, or the like.

sim·i·lar′i·ty, *n.* 1. the state of being similar; close likeness; resemblance; as, a *similarity* of features.

2. *pl.* **sim·i·lar′i·ties,** a point or instance in which things are similar.

sim′i·lăr·ly, *adv.* in like manner; so as to be similar.

sim′i·lăr·y, *a.* similar. [Obs.]

sim′i·lā·tive, *a.* denoting resemblance. [Rare.]

sim′i·lē, *n.* [L., a like thing, from *similis*, like.] a figure of speech in which one thing is likened to another, dissimilar thing by the use of *like*, *as*, etc. (e.g., a heart as big as a whale, her tears flowed like wine): distinguished from *metaphor*, in that the comparison is made explicit.

sim′i·lē, *adv.* in music, similarly: a direction to the performer.

si·mil′i·ȧ, *n.pl.* [LL.] like things.

si·mil′i·tẽr, *n.* [L., in like manner.] in law, the form by which either party, in pleading, accepts the issue tendered by his opponent.

si·mil′i·tūde, *n.* [Fr., from L. *similitudo*, likeness.]

1. a person or thing resembling another; a counterpart; facsimile.

2. form; image.

3. (a) [Rare.] a simile; (b) a parable or allegory.

4. similarity; likeness; resemblance.

si·mil·i·tū′di·năr·y, *a.* denoting resemblance or comparison. [Obs.]

sim′i·līze, *v.t.*; similized, *pt., pp.*; similizing, *ppr.* to compare; to liken.

sim′i·lọr, *n.* an alloy of copper and zinc, resembling gold and used in making jewelry.

sim′i·oid, *a.* same as *simian*.

sim′i·ous, *a.* same as *simian*.

sim′i·tăr, *n.* same as *scimitar*.

sim′kin, *n.* [*Sim*, Simon, and *-kin*.] a simpleton; a dullard. [Rare.]

sim′kin, simp′kin, *n.* [Hind.] champagne.

sim′lin, *n.* 1. a species of summer squash: also spelled *cymlin, cymling, simblin,* and *simbling*.

2. same as *simnel*.

sim′mẽr, *v.i.*; simmered, *pt., pp.*; simmering, *ppr.* [earlier *simper*; of echoic origin.]

1. to boil gently with a low, murmuring sound; to be or stay at or just below the boiling point.

2. to be about to break out, as in anger, revolt, etc.

to simmer down; (a) to simmer, as a liquid, until the volume is reduced or condensed; (b) to cease simmering; to subside; to cool off; to abate.

sim′mẽr, *v.t.* to keep at or just below the boiling point.

sim′mẽr, *n.* the state of simmering; as, keep the water at a *simmer*.

sim′nel, *n.* [ME. *simenal*, from OFr. *simenel, siminel*, a cake of fine flour; LL. *simenellus, siminellus* (for *similellus*), from L. *simila*, the finest wheat flour.]

1. a rich fruitcake prepared at Christmas, Easter, etc. [Archaic or Dial.]

2. a crisp bread or biscuit made of fine flour, and often boiled before baking. [Archaic or Dial.]

si·mō′lē·ŏn, *n.* a dollar. [Slang.]

Sī′mŏn, *n.* [L.; Gr. *Simōn, Seimōn*; Heb. *shim'ōn*, lit., heard.]

1. in the Bible, one of the twelve apostles (called Peter): see *Peter*.

2. a brother or relative of Jesus: Mark vi. 3.

si·mō′ni·aç, *n.* [Fr. *simoniaque*, from ML. *simoniacus*.] one who buys or sells preferment in the church; one who practices simony.

sim·ō·nī′ȧ·căl, *a.* 1. guilty of simony.

2. of or constituting simony; as, a *simoniacal* presentation.

sim·ō·nī′ȧ·căl·ly, *adv.* with the guilt or offense of simony; so as to be simoniacal.

si·mō′ni·ăl, *n.* a simoniac. [Obs.]

Sī·mō′ni·ăn, *a.* relating to Simon Magus or to his followers.

Sī·mō′ni·ăn, *n.* one of the Gnostic sect founded by Simon Magus.

Sī·mō′ni·ăn·iṣm, *n.* the teachings of the Simonians.

si·mō′ni·ous, *a.* partaking of simony; simoniacal. [Rare.]

sim′ō·nist, *n.* one who practises simony.

Sī′mŏn·īze, *v.t.*; Simonized, *pt., pp.*; Simonizing, *ppr.* [from *Simoniz*, trade-mark for a preparation used for this purpose.] to clean and wax the enameled surface of (an automobile body, etc.).

Sī′mŏn Le·grēe′, [from the villainous slave overseer in Harriet Beecher Stowe's *Uncle Tom's Cabin*.] any relentless taskmaster.

Sī′mŏn Mā′gus, in the Bible, a Samaritan magician who offered money for instruction in the rite of imparting the Holy Ghost by the laying on of hands: Acts viii. 9–24.

Sī′mŏn Pē′tẽr, see *Peter* (apostle).

sī′mŏn-pūre′, *a.* [after *Simon Pure*, a Quaker in Susanna Centlivre's play *A Bold Stroke for a Wife* (1718), who must prove his identity against an impostor's claims.] genuine; real; authentic.

sim′ō·ny (*or* sī′mō-), *n.* [ME. *symonye*; Fr. *simonie*; LL. *simonia*, from *Simon* Magus, who wished to purchase the gift of the Holy Ghost.] the act of buying or selling ecclesiastical preferment, ecclesiastical pardons, or other things regarded as sacred or spiritual.

si·mọol′, *n.* the silk-cotton tree, *Bombax malabarica*, of the East and West Indies.

si·mọọm′, *n.* [Ar. *samūm*, from *samma*, he poisoned.] a hot, violent, sand-laden wind that blows in Arabia, Syria, and the neighboring countries, characterized by its suffocating effects upon travelers: also called *samiel*.

si·mọọn′, *n.* same as *simoom*.

sī′mous, *a.* [L. *simus*; Gr. *simos*, flat-nosed.]

1. having a very flat or snub nose with the end turned up.

2. concave; as, the *simous* part of the liver. [Obs.]

simp, *n.* a simpleton. [Slang.]

sim′paī (-pī), *n.* [native name.] a small monkey of Sumatra, *Presbytes melalophus*, characterized by a black crest on the crown of its head.

sim′pẽr, *v.i.*; simpered, *pt., pp.*; simpering, *ppr.* [ME., prob. akin to M.D. *simperlije*, affected.]

1. to smile in a silly or self-conscious manner; to smirk.

2. to twinkle or flicker. [Obs.]

sim′pẽr, *v.t.* to say or express with a simper.

sim′pẽr, *n.* a smile with an air of silliness; an affected or self-conscious smile or smirk.

sim′pẽr·ẽr, *n.* one who simpers.

sim′pẽr·ing, *a.* smiling foolishly.

sim′pẽr·ing·ly, *adv.* in a simpering manner.

simp′kin, *n.* same as *simkin*.

sim′ple, *a.*; *comp.* simpler; *superl.* simplest, [Fr. *simple*, from L. *simplex*, simple.]

1. having or consisting of only one part, feature, substance, etc.; not compounded or complex; single.

2. having few parts or features; not complicated or involved; as, a *simple* pattern.

3. easy to do, solve, or understand, as a task, question, etc.

4. without additions or qualifications; mere; bare; as, here are the *simple* facts.

5. (a) not ornate; unembellished; unadorned; as, *simple* clothes; (b) not luxurious or elegant; plain; as, *simple* tastes.

6. without guile or deceit; innocent; artless.

7. without ostentation or affectation; unpretending; natural.

8. of low rank or position; specifically, (a) humble; lowly; (b) common; ordinary.

9. lacking significance; unimportant.

10. having or showing little sense or reasoning ability; easily misled or deceived; foolish; stupid.

11. feeble-minded. [Dial.]

12. in chemistry, (a) elementary; (b) unmixed.

13. in law, unconditional; absolute; as, a fee *simple*.

14. in music, (a) not compound: said of time or measure; (b) not having overtones; as, a *simple* tone; (c) not elaborated; as, *simple* harmony.

15. in zoology, not divided into or made up of parts; not compounded; as, a *simple* tunicate.

16. in mineralogy, homogenous; as, *simple* quartz.

fee simple; in law, an absolute inheritance, clear of any condition, limitation, or restriction to particular heirs, but descendible to the heirs general, whether male or female, lineal or collateral.

simple contract; a contract, verbal or written, not formally recorded and attested; an agreement.

simple equation; an equation in which the expressions of the unknown are stated in the first power only: $x + y = z$ is a simple equation, $x^2 + y^3 = 31$ is not.

simple fraction; a fraction in which both the numerator and denominator are whole numbers, as $^1/_2$.

simple fruit; any fruit developing from a single pistil.

simple harmonic curve; in electricity, the curve which results when a simple harmonic motion in one line is compounded with uniform motion in a straight line at right angles thereto.

simple honors; in auction bridge, three honor cards in trump held by the same side.

simple idea; in philosophy, an idea not associated with any other idea, as the idea presented by a color as distinct from the notion of form, odor, or any other quality or characteristic possessed by an object having the color; a simple, abstract idea.

simple interest; interest paid only on the principal lent and not on previously accumulated interest.

simple machine; any one of the simple devices, including the lever, wheel and axle, pulley, wedge, screw, and inclined plane, once believed to constitute the basic features of all machines.

simple sentence; a sentence having one main clause and no subordinate clauses (e.g., "The boy ran.").

Simple Simon; (a) a foolish character in a nursery rhyme of the same name; (b) [Colloq.] any simpleton.

Syn.—single, incomplex, uncompounded, unblended, isolated, pure, unmixed, mere, absolute, plain, unadorned, artless, sincere, undesigning, unaffected, silly, humble, homely, lowly, elementary.

sim′ple, *n.* 1. something not mixed or compounded; something having only one part, substance, etc.

2. a medicinal herb or medicine obtained from an herb: so called because each vegetable was supposed to possess its particular virtue and, therefore, to constitute a simple remedy.

3. in the Roman Catholic Church, a feast of the lowest rank.

4. in weaving, (a) [Rare.] a drawloom employed in fancy weaving; (b) a cord hanging from the tail of a harness cord in a drawloom, having at its end a bob by which it is pulled, to work a certain portion of the harness.

5. [*pl.*] foolish or silly behavior; as, to have a fit of the *simples*.

6. a person who is ignorant or easily misled.

7. a person of humble parentage or position. [Archaic.]

sim′ple, *v.i.* to gather simples, or plants.

sim′ple-heärt″ed, *a.* having a simple heart. frank; openhearted; unsophisticated.

sim′ple-mīnd″ed, *a.* 1. simple-hearted; unsophisticated.

2. having little sense; foolish; stupid.

3. feeble-minded.

sim′ple-mīnd″ed·ness, *n.* the quality or state of being simple-minded.

sim′ple·ness, *n.* 1. the state or quality of being simple, single, or uncompounded; as, the *simpleness* of the elements.

2. artlessness; simplicity.

3. weakness of intellect.

sim′plẽr, *n.* one who collects simples; a herbalist; a simplist. [Obs.]

sim′plẽr's-joy, *n.* a plant, the vervain.

sim·plesse′, sim′pless, *n.* simplicity; silliness. [Obs.]

sim′ple·tŏn, *n.* a person of weak intellect; someone who is easily fooled; a fool.

sim′plex, *a.* [L., simple.]

1. having only one part; not complex or compounded.

2. relating to simplex telegraphy.

sim′plex tē·leg′rȧ·phy, a system of telegraphy in which only one message may be sent over a wire at one time.

sim·pli′ciăn (-plish′ăn), *n.* a simpleton. [Obs.]

sim·plic′i·dent, *a.* having but one pair of upper incisors.

sim·plic′i·dent, *n.* one of the *Simplicidentata*.

Sim″pli·ci·den·tā′tȧ, *n.pl.* an order of simplicident rodents including the rats, mice, squirrels, beavers, etc.

sim″pli·ci·den′tāte, *a.* simplicident.

sim·plic′i·ty, *n.*; *pl.* **sim·plic′i·tieṣ,** [Fr. *simplicité*, from L. *simplicitas*, simplicity.]

1. singleness; the state or quality of being unmixed or uncompounded; as, the *simplicity* of metals or of earths.

2. the state of being not complex, or of consisting of few parts; as, the *simplicity* of a machine.

3. artlessness of mind; freedom from subtlety or cunning; freedom from duplicity; sincerity.

4. plainness; freedom from artificial ornament or affectation; as, the *simplicity* of dress, of style, of language, etc.

5. plainness; freedom from complexity or abstruseness.

6. weakness of intellect; silliness; foolishness.

Syn.—artlessness, plainness, ingenuousness.

sim″pli·fi·çā′tion, *n.* [Fr.] 1. a simplifying or being simplified.

2. any result of this, as a simpler form, process, or device.

sim′pli·fī·ẽr, *n.* a person or thing that simplifies.

sim′pli·fȳ, *v.t.*; simplified, *pt., pp.*; simplifying, *ppr.* [Fr. *simplifier*, from L. *simplex*, simple, and *facere*, to make.] to make simple; to reduce to greater simplicity; to make plain or easy; to divest of complexity.

sim′plist, *n.* one skilled in simples, or medicinal plants. [Obs.]

sim·plis′tiç, *a.* 1. of or pertaining to simples; also, pertaining to a simplist. [Rare.]

2. depending too much upon simplicity, as in explaining what is really very complex.

sim′plō·cē, *n.* same as *symploce.*

sim′ply, *adv.* 1. in a simple manner; so as to be simple.

2. of itself; without addition; alone.

3. merely; solely; as, his answer was *simply* this.

4. weakly; foolishly.

5. absolutely; quite; as, this is *simply* ridiculous.

sim′ū·lā·çre (-kẽr), *n.* a simulacrum. [Obs.]

sim·ū·lā′çrum, *n.*; *pl.* **sim·ū·lā′çrȧ,** [L., likeness, image.]

1. an image.

2. a mere pretence or semblance; vague representation; counterfeit; travesty; sham.

sim′ū·lănt, *a.* [L., *simulans*, ppr.] having a false resemblance or appearance; also, in biology, exhibiting simulation.

sim′ū·lănt, *n.* one who or that which simulates.

sim′ū·lăr, *n.* one who simulates.

sim′ū·lăr, *a.* 1. simulated; feigned.

2. simulative (of something).

sim′ū·lāte, *v.t.*; simulated, *pt., pp.*; simulating, *ppr.* [L. *simulare*, to feign.]

1. to give a false indication or appearance of; to pretend; to feign; as, *simulate* an interest.

2. to have the external characteristics of; to look or act like; as, the insect *simulated* a twig.

sim′ū·lāte, *a.* feigned; pretended.

sim·ū·lā′tion, *n.* [Fr., from L. *simulatio* (*-onis*), a feigning.]

1. the act of feigning; pretense.

2. false resemblance, as through imitation.

Syn.—pretense, counterfeiting.

sim′ū·lā·tive, *a.* practicing or characterized by simulation.

sim′ū·lā·tŏr, *n.* one who or that which simulates; specifically, a training device that duplicates artificially the conditions likely to be encountered in some operation, as in a spacecraft; as, a flight *simulator.*

sim′ū·lȧ·tō·ry, *a.* consisting in or characterized by simulation.

sī′mul·çȧst, *v.t.*; simulcast, *pt., pp.*; simulcasting, *ppr.* [from *simul*taneous and broad*cast.*] to transmit (a program, event, etc.) simultaneously by radio and television.

sī′mul·çȧst, *n.* a program, event, etc. transmitted simultaneously by radio and television.

si·mū′li·id, *a.* pertaining to the family *Simuliidæ.*

si·mū′li·id, *n.* any one of the species of the *Simuliidæ.*

Sim·ū·lī′i·dae, *n.pl.* a family of nemocerous dipters with well-developed oral organs. Its only genus is *Simulium.*

Si·mū′li·um, *n.* [L. *simulare*, to feign.] a genus of biting gnats including the black fly, the buffalo gnats, etc. They resemble mosquitos, and their bite often produces very painful swellings. The larva is subaquatic.

sī″mul·tȧ·nē′i·ty (*or* sim″ul-), *n.* the state or quality of being simultaneous.

sī·mul·tā′nē·ous (*or* sim-ul-), *a.* [Fr. *simultané*, from L. *simul*, at the same time.] existing, done, or happening at the same time; as, *simultaneous* events.

simultaneous equations; two or more equations used together in the same problem and having unknowns of the same value.

Syn.—synchronous, concomitant, concurrent.

sī·mul·tā′nē·ous·ly, *adv.* at the same time; so as to be simultaneous.

sī·mul·tā′nē·ous·ness, *n.* the state or quality of being or happening at the same time; as, the *simultaneousness* of transactions in two different places.

si·múrg′, si·múrgh′ (-múrg′), [Per. *sīmurgh.*] *n.* a fabulous gigantic bird in Persian mythology.

sin, *adv., prep.,* and *conj.* since. [Obs.]

sin, *n.* [Heb.] the twenty-first letter of the Hebrew alphabet, corresponding to English S.

sin, *n.* [AS. *synn, sin*, sin, evil, wickedness; akin to G. *sünde*, sin.]

1. any voluntary transgression of a religious law or moral principle; moral depravity; wickedness; iniquity. Sin may consist in commission, when a known divine law or moral principle is violated, or in omission, when a positive divine command or a rule of duty is voluntarily and willfully neglected.

2. an offense in general; a transgression; a breach; as, a *sin* against good taste.

actual, canonical, original, venial sin; see under *actual, canonical*, etc.

deadly or *mortal sin*; see following *deadly.*

like sin; with strenuous endeavor; very hard; as, he ran *like sin.* [Colloq.]

the unpardonable sin; in Christian theology, blasphemy against the Holy Ghost: Matt. xii. 31.

Syn.—transgression, iniquity, unrighteousness, ungodliness, wickedness.

sin, *v.i.*; sinned, *pt., pp.*; sinning, *ppr.* 1. to break a religious law or moral principle; to commit sin.

2. to commit an offense or fault of any kind; to do wrong.

sin, *v.t.* 1. to commit sinfully.

2. to spend, bring about, etc. by sinning.

sin, same as *sine.*

Sī·nae′ăn, *a.* pertaining to the Sinae, the people of ancient China.

Sī′naī, Mount, in the Bible, the mountain (probably in the southern part of the Sinai peninsula but not identified) where Moses received the law from God: Ex. xix.

Sī·nā′iç, *a.* same as *Sinaitic.*

Sī·nā·it′iç, *a.* [from *Sinai*, the mountain.] of or from Mount Sinai; given or made at Sinai.

sin·al′bin, *n.* [L. *sinapis*, mustard, and *alba*, white.] a pale-yellow crystalline glucoside, $C_{30}H_{42}O_{15}N_2S_2$, obtained from white mustard seed.

sin′ȧ·mīne, *n.* a crystalline compound, $CN·NHC_3H_5$, obtained from the oil of mustard.

sin′ȧ·pāte, *n.* a salt of sinapic acid.

si·nap′iç, *a.* [L. *sinapis*, mustard.] of sinapine.

sinapic acid; a crystalline compound derived from sinapine or one of its salts.

sin′ȧ·pīne, sin′ȧ·pin, *n.* [Fr., from L. *sinapis*, mustard.] an alkaloid derivative of sinalbin, $C_{16}H_{25}O_6N$, known only in the form of its salts.

Si·nā′pis, *n.* a former genus of the *Cruciferæ*, including mustard: now referred to *Brassica.*

sin′ȧ·pişm, *n.* [from L. *sinapis*, mustard.] a mustard plaster.

si·nap′ō·līne, *n.* [L. *sinapis*, mustard, and *oleum*, oil.] a white crystalline, nitrogenous base, $CO(NHC_3H_5)_2$, originally extracted from oil of mustard.

sin·är′çhişm, sin·är′quişm (-kizm), *n.* [from Sp. *sin-, syn-* and Eng. *anarchism*, Sp. *anarquismo.*] an armed fascist movement in Mexico, formed in 1937 to fight for the establishment of a totalitarian clerical state.

sin·är′çhist, *n.* a follower of sinarchism.

sĭn·är·quis′tȧ (-kēs′), *n.* a sinarchist.

Sin′bad the Sāil′ŏr, a merchant in The Arabian Nights who made seven adventurous voyages: also *Sindbad.*

sin′-bred, *a.* produced or bred by sin.

sin′çȧ·līne, *n.* [L. *sinapis*, mustard, and *alkaline.*] choline.

since, *adv.* [ME. *sins, sinnes, sithens, sithence*, all genitive forms from AS. *siththan*; *sith*, after, since, and *than*, that time, a dative form of *thæt*, the, that, demonstrative article.]

1. from then until now; as, he came last Tuesday and has been here ever *since.*

2. at some or any time between then and now; as, he was injured a year ago but has *since* fully recovered.

3. before the present time; before now; ago; as, he disappeared many years *since.*

long since; long before now; a long time ago.

since, *prep.* 1. continuously or without exception or interruption from (the time given) until now; as, we have been walking *since* one o'clock.

2. during the period between (the time given) and now; subsequently to; as, he's written twice *since* his departure.

since, *conj.* 1. during the period following the time when; as, they've seen each other often *since* they met.

2. continuously or without exception or interruption from the time when; as, she has been unhappy *since* she left home.

3. inasmuch as; because; as, *since* he was king he could do no wrong.

sin·cēre′, *a.*; *comp.* sincerer; *superl.* sincerest, [Fr., from L. *sincerus*, from *sine*, without, and base of *caries*, decay; hence, orig., undecayed.]

1. without deceit, pretense, or hypocrisy; truthful; faithful; straightforward; honest; as, he gave a *sincere* statement of his feelings.

2. being the same in actual character as in outward appearance; genuine; real; as, *sincere* grief; a life of *sincere* devotion.

3. not mixed or adulterated; as, *sincere* wine. [Archaic.]

4. uninjured; whole. [Obs.]

Syn.—honest, true, plain, frank, incorruptible, upright.

sin·cēre′ly, *adv.* in a sincere manner.

sin·cēre′ness, *n.* sincerity.

sin·cer′i·ty, *n.* [Fr. *sincérité*; L. *sinceritas.*] the state or quality of being sincere; honesty of mind or intention; freedom from simulation or hypocrisy; truthfulness; genuineness; earnestness.

sinch, *n.* and *v.* same as *cinch.*

sin·cip′i·tăl, *a.* of or pertaining to the sinciput.

sin′ci·put, *n.* [L., half a head; *semi*, half, and *caput*, head.] the forepart of the head from the forehead to the coronal suture: distinguished from the *occiput.*

Sind′bad, *n.* same as *Sinbad the Sailor.*

Sind′ī, *n.* a native of Sind, India, especially one of Hindu stock.

sin′doç, *n.* same as *sintoc.*

sin′dŏn, *n.* [L., from Gr. *sindōn*, prob. from *Sindos*, the Indus.] in surgery, a small piece of rag or fine cloth used to fill a wound; a tampon.

sīne, *n.* [L. *sinus*, a bending, curve.]

1. originally, the length of a perpendicular dropped from one end of an arc of a circle to the diameter passing through the other end of the arc.

2. the ratio of this line to the radius of the circle.

3. the ratio of the side opposite an acute angle of a right triangle to the hypotenuse.

SINE

$\frac{DC}{DB}$, sine of angle X;

$\frac{CB}{DB}$, sine of angle Y

artificial sines; logarithms of the natural sines or logarithmic sines.

coversed sine; the versed sine of the complement of an angle.

curve of sines; same as *sinusoid.*

logarithmic sine; the logarithm of a sine.

natural sines; sines expressed by natural numbers.

sine complement; the cosine.

sine curve; a sinusoid.

sine law; a law of magnitude defined by the sines of angles.

subversed sine; same as *supplemental versed sine.*

supplemental versed sine; the difference between unity minus the cosine and the diameter.

versed sine; unity minus the cosine.

sī′nē, *prep.* [L.] without: used in Latin phrases.

sin ēat′ẽr, formerly, in some parts of England, a person at a funeral, who, for a small compensation, ate a piece of bread and drank some water, thereby assuming the sins of the deceased.

sī′nē·çū·răl, *a.* of or pertaining to a sinecure; of the nature of a sinecure.

sī′nē·çūre (*or* sin′ē-), *n.* [L. *sine*, without, and *cura*, cure, care.]

1. an office which has revenue without employment; any office or post which gives remuneration without requiring much work, responsibility, etc.

2. an ecclesiastical benefice without cure (care) of souls.

sī′nē·çūre, *v.t.*; sinecured, *pt., pp.*; sinecuring, *ppr.* to place in a sinecure.

sī′nē·çūre, *a.* pertaining to a sinecure; that has a sinecure.

sī′nē·çū·rişm, *n.* 1. a system in which sinecures are available.

2. the policy or principle of giving or taking sinecures.

sī′nē-çū·rist, *n.* one who has or seeks a sinecure.

sī′nē dī′ē, [L.] without (a) day (being set for meeting again); for an indefinite period; as, the assembly adjourned *sine die.*

sī′nē prō′lē, [L.] in law, without offspring; childless.

sī′nē quā (kwā) **non,** [L.] an essential condition, qualification, etc.; an indispensable thing; an absolute prerequisite.

sin′ew (-ū), *n.* [ME. *sinewe*; AS. *sionu.*]
1. in anatomy, a tendon; the tough fibrous tissue which unites a muscle to a bone.
2. that which supplies power or strength; as, the *sinews* of war.
3. muscular power; strength; force.

sin′ew, *v.t.*; sinewed, *pt., pp.*; sinewing, *ppr.*
1. to knit strongly together, as with sinews.
2. to strengthen; to supply with or as with sinews; to make robust.

sin′ew·i·ness, *n.* the state or quality of being sinewy.

sin′ew·ish, *a.* sinewy. [Obs.]

sin′ew·less, *a.* without sinews; having no strength or vigor.

sin′ew·ous, *a.* sinewy.

sin′ew-shrunk, *a.* having the sinews under the belly shrunk by excess of fatigue, as a horse.

sin′ew·y, *a.* 1. pertaining to, consisting of, or resembling a sinew; tough; strong.

The *sinewy* thread my brain lets fall.
—Donne.

2. having many or large sinews, as a cut of meat.
3. having good muscular development; as, *sinewy* shoulders.
4. vigorous; powerful; robust; as, a *sinewy* style of writing.

sin·fō·nī′ȧ, *n.*; *pl.* **sin·fō·nī′e,** [It.] in music, same as *symphony.*

sin′fųl, *a.* full of or characterized by sin; wicked; iniquitous; as, *sinful* men; *sinful* actions.

sin′fųl·ly, *adv.* in a sinful manner; so as to be sinful.

sin′fųl·ness, *n.* the quality or state of being sinful.

sing, *v.i.*; sang *or now rarely* sung, *pt.*; sung, *pp.*; singing, *ppr.* [AS. *singan*; akin to G. *singen,* to sing.]
1. (a) to produce musical sounds or notes with the voice, especially in a connected series, as in voicing a song; (b) to deliver musical selections vocally, especially as a professional.
2. to use song or verse in description, praise, etc.; as, of thee I *sing.*
3. to sound somewhat like the singing of a human voice; to produce a musical note or notes, as a songbird, steaming teakettle, wind, etc.
4. to buzz, hum, ring, etc., as the ears, an insect, flying missile, etc.
5. to admit of being sung.
6. to be exultant; to rejoice; as, a sight to make one's heart *sing.*
7. to confess to a crime, especially so as to implicate others. [Slang.]
to sing out; to speak or call out loudly; to shout. [Colloq.]

sing, *v.t.* 1. to render or deliver (a song, musical role, etc.) by singing; to utter with musical inflections.
2. to chant or intone (part of a church service, etc.).
3. to describe, proclaim, extol, celebrate, etc. in or as in song or verse; as, they all *sing* his praises.
4. to bring to a given state, as sleep, by singing.
5. to accompany, escort, etc. with singing.

sing, *n.* 1. a shrill buzzing, whistling, or humming sound; as, the *sing* of arrows overhead.
2. (a) group singing; (b) a gathering for this purpose. [Colloq.]

sing′ȧ·ble, *a.* 1. that can be sung.
2. easy to sing; tuneful; lyrical; melodic.

singe, *v.t.*; singed, *pt., pp.*; singeing, *ppr.* [AS. *sengan,* to singe, causative of *singan,* to sing; akin to G. *sengen,* to singe.]
1. to burn superficially or slightly.
2. to expose (an animal carcass) to flame in removing bristles or feathers.
3. to burn the nap from (cloth) as a process of manufacture.
4. to burn the ends of (hair) after cutting.

singe, *n.* 1. a singeing.
2. a superficial or slight burn.

sing′ẽr, *n.* 1. one who sings; one versed in music; one whose occupation is to sing; as, a chorus of *singers.*
2. a bird that sings.
3. one who composes verse; a poet.

sin′ġẽr, *n.* 1. one who or that which singes; one who singes the nap of cloth.
2. a machine for singeing cloth.

sing′ẽr·ess, *n.* a songstress. [Obs.]

Siñ·ghȧ·lēşe′ (-gȧ-), *a.* [from Sans. *Siṅhala,* Ceylon; and *-ese.*] of Ceylon, its principal race, their language, etc.

Siñ·ghȧ·lēşe′, *n.* 1. *pl.* **Siñ·ghȧ·lēşe′,** a member of the Singhalese people.
2. their Indic language.
Also *Sinhalese.*

sing·hä′rȧ nut, same as *water chestnut.*

sing′ing, *n.* 1. the act of uttering sounds with musical inflection.
2. the act of narrating in verse.
3. the sensation of a continual ringing noise in the ears; as, I have a *singing* in my head.

sing′ing, *a.* producing or that can produce musical tones or sounds.
singing bird; any bird that sings; specifically, an oscine.
singing fish; a toadfish of the genus *Porichthys,* native to California.
singing flame; in physics, a flame, generally enclosed in a tube, which emits a musical sound.

sing′ing·ly, *adv.* in a singing manner.

siñ′gle (-gl), *a.* [L. *singulus,* single.]
1. one only; one and no more; individual.
2. without another or others; alone; solitary.
3. of or for one person, as a bed, room, etc., or one family, as a house.
4. weak in quality: said of beer, ale, etc. [Brit.]
5. between two persons only; with only one on each side; as, *single* combat.
6. (a) unmarried; (b) of or characteristic of the unmarried state.
7. having only one part; not double, compound, multiple, etc.
8. having only one row or set of petals: said of flowers and plants.
9. honest; sincere.
10. seeing justly; as, judge with *a single* eye.
11. in telegraphy, simplex.
single bill; a note of hand or other written agreement to pay money without conditions.
single file; (a) a single column of persons or things placed or moving one directly behind another; (b) in such a column; as, the men are marching *single file.*
single standard; (a) a moral code establishing one code of behavior for men and women alike, especially in matters of sex; (b) a standard of monetary values based on a single metal, as either gold or silver: opposed to *double standard.*
single whip; in nautical usage, one rope only running through a block.
Syn.—one, only, sole, solitary, individual, separate, uncombined, unmarried, uncompounded.

siñ′gle, *v.t.*; singled, *pt., pp.*; singling, *ppr.*
1. to select, as an individual person or thing, from among a number; to choose from others: usually with *out*; as, he could not understand why he was *singled out.*
2. to sequester; to withdraw; to retire. [Obs.]

siñ′gle, *v.i.* 1. to separate from others, as a hunted deer when it leaves the herd.
2. to move with a single-footed gait, as horses.
3. in baseball, to make a single.

siñ′gle, *n.* 1. a single person or thing; specifically, (a) a hotel room, travel space, etc. for one person; (b) [*pl.*] unmarried persons collectively; (c) a one-dollar bill [Colloq.]; (d) a small phonograph record, usually recorded at 45 r.p.m., with a single, short performance on each side. [Colloq.]
2. in baseball, a hit by which the batter reaches no farther than first base.
3. in cricket, a hit by which one run is scored.
4. in golf, a match between two persons; a twosome: distinguished from *foursome.*
5. [*pl.*] in tennis, etc., a game with only one player on each side.
6. the tail of a deer or buck. [Brit.]

siñ′gle-aç′ting, *a.* acting in or impelled from one direction only; not reciprocating.
single-acting engine; an engine in which the steam acts only against the under side of the piston, the weight of the atmosphere pressing it down again, against the vacuum produced by the condensation of the spent steam. Such engines are now out of date.
single-acting piston; a piston which is in contact with the fluid upon which it acts on one side only.
single-acting pump; a pump which delivers liquid at each alternate stroke only, one stroke being spent in drawing or lifting the liquid into the pump, the other in delivering it.

siñ′gle-aç′tion, *a.* designating a firearm whose hammer must be cocked by hand before the weapon can be fired.

siñ′gle-bañked (-bañkt), *a.* 1. having one oarsman to a thwart.
2. having one bank or tier of oars, as some vessels of former times.
3. having one row of keys, as an organ.

siñ′gle·bär, *n.* a singletree.

siñ′gle-breast′ed (-brest′), *a.* covering the front of the body with only one thickness, overlapping just enough to fasten: said of coats, vests, etc.: opposed to *double-breasted.*

siñ′gle-en′try, *a.* having to do with bookkeeping by single entry.

siñ′gle en′try, *n.* a system of bookkeeping in which the only account kept is a single one consisting of debts owed to and by the concern in question.

siñ′gle-fīre, *a.* not intended to be loaded a second time after firing; having the fulminating material inside the head or base, as a breech-loading cartridge.

siñ′gle-foot, *n.* the gait of a horse in which the legs move in lateral pairs, each foot falling singly and the body being supported alternately upon one foot and two feet: also called *rack.*

siñ′gle-foot, *v.i.* to go with a single-foot gait, as horses: also called *rack.*

siñ′gle-hand′ed, *a.* 1. having one hand or workman only.
2. unassisted; by oneself alone; alone.
3. worked or managed by one hand only; as, a *single-handed* sword.

siñ′gle-heärt′ed, *a.* having a single or honest heart; without duplicity.

siñ′gle-heärt′ed·ly, *adv.* in a single-hearted manner.

siñ′gle-mīnd′ed, *a.* 1. having a single or honest mind or heart.
2. having but one purpose in view.

siñ′gle·ness, *n.* the state or quality of being single.

siñ′gle-phāşe′, *a.* in electricity, denoting a phase present in ordinary alternating currents in a simple alternating current system.

siñ′gle-phāş′ẽr, *n.* in electricity, a machine that produces a single-pressure wave.

siñ′gle-seed′ed, *a.* containing one seed only.

siñ′gle-stick, *n.* 1. a swordlike stick used for fencing and fitted with a basket hilt to protect the hand.
2. the sport of fencing with such sticks.
3. a wooden sword used in practice in place of the cutlass.

siñ′gle-stick′ẽr, *n.* a sailboat, especially a sloop, having but a single mast. [Colloq.]

siñ′glet, *n.* 1. an unlined waistcoat, the opposite of a *doublet,* which is lined. [Archaic.]
2. a man's undershirt or jersey. [Brit.]

siñ′gle-tax, *a.* advocating or having to do with single tax.

siñ′gle tax, 1. a system of taxation in which all revenue is from a tax on a single object, specifically on land.
2. a tax of this kind.

siñ′gle·tŏn, *n.* [from *single,* after proper names ending in *-ton*].
1. a playing card that is the only one of its suit held by a given player.
2. a single thing, as distinguished from one of a pair, several, etc.

siñ′gle-track′, *a.* 1. having only one set of rails; as, a *single-track* trolley or railroad.
2. having a limited scope; narrow; as, a *single-track* mind.
Also *one-track.*

siñ′gle·tree, *n.* [a corrupted form of ME. *swingle-tre,* from *swingle,* a swinger, and *tre,* a piece of wood.] the swinging horizontal crossbar to which the traces or tugs of a harnessed horse are fastened: also called *swingletree, whippletree, whiffletree.*

sin'gle-valved, *a.* having one valve only.
sin'glings, *n.* in distilling, the crude spirit which is the first to appear.
sin'gly, *adv.* 1. as a single, separate person or thing; alone.
2. individually; particularly; separately; one by one.
3. alone; without companions or associates; unaided.
4. in an honest, sincere manner. [Obs.]
5. uniquely; singularly. [Obs.]
sing'sing, *n.* [African.] a species of African antelope, *Kobus defassus.*
sing'song, *n.* 1. a rising and falling tone in a monotonous cadence.
2. verse, sound, voice, etc. characterized by such tone or cadence.
sing'song, *a.* drawing; chanting; monotonous, as sound; as, a *singsong* tone of voice.
sing'song, *v.t.* and *v.i.* to speak, sing, etc. in a singsong manner; hence, to compose monotonous, dreary poetry.
Sing'spiēl (*or G.* zing'shpēl), *n.* [G.] a play in which dialogue and song are combined; a kind of dramatic peformance of which singing is the principal feature. It was the forerunner in Germany of opera.
sing'stēr, *n.* a singer. [Obs.]
sin'gū·lăr, *a.* [ME. *singuler*; OFr. *singuler, singulaire*; L. *singularis,* from *singulus,* single.]
1. (a) individual; separate; (b) [Obs.] of or having to do with an individual; (c) [Obs.] peculiar to one; private.
2. in grammar, of or denoting only one: opposed to *plural.*
3. remarkable; eminent; extraordinary; as, a man of *singular* gravity or *singular* attainments.
4. not common; odd; unusual; queer; implying something censurable or not approved.

His zeal
None seconded, as *singular* and rash.
—Milton.

5. being alone; having no duplicate or parallel; unique; sole; single.
6. in logic, not general; of an individual or particular thing considered by itself.
singular proposition; in logic, a proposition which has for its subject either a singular term or a common term limited to one individual.
singular successor; in Scots law, a purchaser of feudal property by single title, in contradistinction to the heir, who succeeds by a general title.
singular term; a term which stands for one individual.
Syn.—unexampled, unprecedented, eminent, extraordinary, remarkable, uncommon, rare, unusual, peculiar, strange, odd, eccentric.
sin'gū·lăr, *n.* 1. in logic, that which stands by itself.
2. in grammar, (a) the number denoting one person or thing; (b) the singular form of a word: opposed to *plural.*
sin'gū·lăr·ist, *n.* one who affects singularity. [Obs.]
sin·gū·lar'i·ty, *n.*; *pl.* **sin·gū·lar'i·ties,** [Fr. *singularité.*]
1. peculiarity; some character or quality of a person or thing by which it is distinguished from all others; peculiar feature or characteristic.
2. th condition or quality of being singular.
3. a singular person or thing.
4. particular privilege, prerogative, or distinction. [Obs.]
sin'gū·lăr·īze, *v.t.*; singularized, *pt., pp.*; singularizing, *ppr.* 1. to make singular.
2. to make prominent.
sin'gū·lăr·ly, *adv.* 1. unusually; in a manner or degree not common to others; as, to be *singularly* good.
2. oddly; strangely.
3. so as to express one, or the singular number.
sin'gult, *n.* [L. *singultus,* a sob.] a sob. [Obs.]
sin·gul'tous, *a.* in medicine, affected with hiccups.
sin·gul'tus, *n.* [L.] a hiccup or hiccups.
Sin·hȧ·lēse', *a.* and *n.* same as *Singhalese.*
Sin'iç, *a.* [LL. *Sinicus,* from L. *Sina,* China.] Chinese; Sinitic.
sin'iç·ăl, *a.* pertaining to or making use of sines; as, a *sinical* quadrant.
Sin'i·cism, *n.* any peculiarity or characteristic, as a custom or language trait, of the Chinese race.
sin'i·grin, *n.* a glucoside salt, $C_{10}H_{16}KNO_9S_2$, found in the seeds of black mustard, resembling sinalbin.
sin'is·tēr, *a.* [ME. and OFr. *sinistre*; L., on the left hand.]
1. originally, on, to, or toward the left-hand side; left.
2. forming, or placed on, the left half of a coa of arms, regarded from the bearer's point of view (the right, from the observer's).
3. suggesting the approach of disaster, misfortune, etc.; threatening harm or evil; ominous; portentous.
4. wicked, evil, or dishonest, especially in some dark, mysterious way; as, it is somehow to their own *sinister* interest.
5. disastrous; unfortunate (often with *to*).
sinister base point, sinister chief point; the lower and upper left-hand corners respectively of a shield or escutcheon.
sin'is·tēr-hand"ed, *a.* left-handed.
sin'is·tēr·ly, *adv.* in a sinister manner.
si·nis'trä, *adv.* [It., left hand.] in music, with the left hand: used as an instruction for the playing of notes with the left hand.
sin'is·trad, *adv.* toward the left side of the body; sinistrally.
sin'is·trăl, *a.* 1. pertaining to or situated on the left side.
2. having whorls that rise to the apex in clockwise spirals: said of sea shells.
3. left-handed.
sin·is·tral'i·ty, *n.* the condition of being sinistral.
sin'is·trăl·ly, *adv.* in a sinistral manner; toward the left.
sin·is·trā'tion, *n.* the state of being sinistral.
sin'is·trin, *n.* a carbohydrate, $C_6H_{10}O_5$, found in squill.
sin'is·trō-, [from L. *sinister,* left.] a combining form meaning *of, at, toward,* or *using the left,* as in *sinistro*dextral: also, before a vowel, *sinistr-.*
sin"is·trō·cer'ē·brăl, *a.* pertaining to or situated in the left cerebral hemisphere.
sin"is·trō·dex'trăl, *a.* going or directed from left to right, as the movement of the hand in writing.
sin·is·tror'săl, *a.* same as *sinistrorse.*
sin'is·trorse, *a.* [L. *sinistrorsus,* contr. of *sinistrovorsus,* from *sinister,* to the left, and *versus, vorsus,* pp. of *vertere,* to turn.] in botany, twining upward to the left, as the stems of some vines: opposed to *dextrorse.*
sin'is·trous, *a.* 1. threatening or accompanied by misfortune or disaster; unfortunate.
2. sinistral.
3. wrong; absurd. [Obs.]
sin'is·trous·ly, *adv.* in a sinistrous manner.
Si·nit'iç, *n.* a branch of the Sino-Tibetan languages, including Chinese and its dialects.
Si·nit'iç, *a.* of China, the Chinese, or their language.
sink, *v.i.*; sank *or* sunk, *pt.*; sunk *or obs.* sunken, *pp.*; sinking, *ppr.* [ME. *sinken*; AS. *sincan*; Dan. *synke*; D. *zinken*; G. *sinken*; Goth. *siggkwan,* to sink; nasalized forms corresponding to AS. and O.H.G. *sîgan,* to sink.]
1. to go beneath the surface of water, deep snow, soft ground, etc. so as to be partly or completely covered.
2. to fall gradually; to go down slowly; as, she *sank* into a chair.
3. to enter or penetrate into any body.

The stone *sunk* into his forehead.
—1 Sam. xvii. 49.

4. to fall; to become lower in level; to subside or settle to a level; to diminish in height or depth; as, the lake *sank* two feet.
5. to be overwhelmed or depressed; to lose position, prestige, etc.

Our country *sinks* beneath the yoke.
—Shak.

6. to enter deeply; to be impressed; to enter and have a lasting effect, as upon the mind or heart.

Let these sayings *sink* down into your ears.
—Luke ix. 44.

7. to seem or become deep or hollow, as the eyes or cheeks.
8. to lessen; to become lower in value or amount, as the price of stock, etc.
9. to appear to fall or descend; as, the moon *sank* behind a cloud.
10. to become less intense; to diminish or decrease in degree or volume; to subside, as wind, flames, sound of a voice, etc.
11. to pass gradually (*into* a given condition), as sleep, despair, lethargy, etc.
12. to become increasingly and dangerously ill; to approach death; to fail; as, he is *sinking* rapidly.
13. to fall in pitch, as the voice or sounds of a musical instrument.
Syn.—fall, decline, droop, descend, subside, drop, enter, penetrate, lower, decay, lessen.
sink, *v.t.* 1. to cause to sink; to put beneath the surface; as, to *sink* a ship.
2. to make by digging, drilling, or cutting; as, to *sink* a shaft or a well.
3. to lower; to degrade; as, his vices *sink* him in public estimation.
4. to plunge into destruction; to ruin; to defeat: now usually in the passive.

If I have a conscience, let it *sink* me.
—Shak.

5. to reduce in quantity, degree, or intensity.

You *sunk* the river with repeated draughts.
—Addison.

6. to depress; to overbear; to crush; as, to *sink* the spirit of a hero.
7. to cause or allow to fall or go down; to lower; as, she *sank* her head in her hands.
8. to suppress; to conceal; to hold back (evidence, identity, etc.).
9. to lose by investing or speculation; as, to *sink* a fortune in mining.
10. to lose sight of, as oneself or one's own interest.
11. to pay up (a debt).
12. to invest, as money.
sink, *n.* [ME. *sinke,* from the v.]
1. a sewer or cesspool.
2. any of various basins or receptacles, as in a kitchen, connected with a drainpipe and, usually, a water supply.
3. any place or thing considered morally filthy or corrupt.
4. in geology, (a) same as *sinkhole,* sense 2; (b) an area of sunken land, especially one in which water collects without a natural outlet, often forming a salt lake.
sink'ēr, *n.* 1. a worker whose job is to sink something; as, a die *sinker.*
2. a thing that sinks, especially a lead weight used in fishing.
3. in a knitting machine, one of the devices that work in conjunction to loop the thread between the needles.
4. a doughnut. [Colloq.]
dividing sinker; a sinker that acts alternately between two jacks in a knitting machine.
sink'ēr bär, 1. the bar in a knitting machine to which the sinkers are attached.
2. a heavy bar above the jars of a rope-drilling apparatus to add force to the blow.
sink'hōle, *n.* 1. an opening, as the down pipe to a sewer, made for the drainage of water, sewage, etc.
2. a hollow or hole into which surface water drains, especially such a hole worn through rock and leading to an underground channel: also *sink.*
sink'ing, *n.* 1. a falling, subsiding, or depressing; a declining.
2. that which is depressed; a hole.
sink'ing fund, a fund created by gradual accumulations of money, usually invested at interest, for paying a debt, meeting depreciation expenses, etc.
sink'ing head (hed), in founding, same as *deadhead.*
sink'ing pump, an adjustable vertical pump used in mining.
sink'stōne, *n.* 1. a stone used as a sinker in fishing. [Archaic.]
2. a perforated stone used as a trough or sink. [Brit. Dial.]
sin'less, *a.* free from sin; pure; innocent; as, a *sinless* soul.
sin'less·ly, *adv.* in a sinless manner; innocently.
sin'less·ness, *n.* freedom from sin and guilt.
sin'nēr, *n.* one who sins; a wrongdoer.
sin'nēr, *v.i.* to act as a sinner.
sin'nēr·ess, *n.* a woman sinner.
sin'net, *n.* same as *sennit.*
Sinn Fein (shin fān), *n.* [Ir., we ourselves.] a revolutionary society and movement founded in Ireland about 1905 to establish political and economic independence and to revive Irish culture.
Sī'nō- (*or* sin'ō-), [Gr. *Sina,* China, from *Sinai,* the Orient or an Oriental people.]

1. a combining form which signifies *pertaining to the Chinese people* or *language*; as, *Sinology*.
2. a combining form which means *Chinese and*; as, *Sino*-Japanese.

Sī″nō-Jap·ȧ·nēṣe′, *a.* having to do with both China and Japan.

Sin·ō·loġ′iç·ăl, *a.* pertaining to Sinology.

Si·nol′ō·ġist, *n.* a Sinologue.

Sin′ō·lo̤gue (-lo̤g), *n.* [Fr. *sinologue*, from Gr. *Sina*, China, and *logos*, discourse.] one who is an expert in or makes a study of Sinology.

Si·nol′ō·ġy, *n.* the study of Chinese culture, including language, literature, characteristics, etc.

sin′ō·pēr, *n.* sinople, the quartz. [Obs.]

si·nō′pi·ȧ, si·nō′pis, *n.* a pigment of a red color obtained from sinopite.

sin′ō·pīte, *n.* [L. *Sinopis*, a town on the Black Sea.] a ferruginous clay from which a red pigment is obtained.

sin′ō·ple, *n.* [Fr. *sinople*, from LL. *sinopis*, a red color, also a green color; L. *sinopis*, Gr. *sinōpis*, earth of Sinope, red ocher, from *Sinope*, a town on the Black Sea, near which it occurs.]
1. red ferruginous quartz, of a blood or brownish red color, sometimes with a tinge of yellow.
2. in heraldry, green; vert. [Obs.]

Sī″nō-Ti·bet′ăn, *a.* designating or of a family of Eastern Asiatic languages spoken in Tibet, China, Burma, and Thailand: it comprises Tibeto-Burman, Chinese, Thai, etc.

sinque (sin̄k), *n.* cinque. [Obs.]

sins′ring, *n.* same as *banxring*.

sin′tēr, *n.* [AS. *sinder*; Ice. *sindr*; G. *sinter*, dross.]
1. a crust or deposit of silica or calcium carbonate formed by water from some mineral springs, geysers, etc.
2. dross of iron.
calcareous sinter; a variety of calcium carbonate composed of a series of successive layers, concentric, plane, or undulated, and nearly parallel.

Sin′tō, Sin′tu̇, *n.* same as *Shinto*.

sin′toç, sin′doç, *n.* the bark of a species of *Cinnamomum*: also written *syndoc*.

Sin′tō·iṣm, Sin′tu̇·iṣm, *n.* same as *Shintoism*.

sin′ū·āte, sin′ū·ā·ted, *a.* [L. *sinuatus*, pp. of *sinuare*, to bend.]
1. bending; winding; sinuous.
2. in botany, having a wavy margin, as some leaves.

SINUATE LEAF

sin′ū·āte, *v.i.*; sinuated, *pt., pp.*; sinuating, *ppr.* to wind; to turn; to bend in and out; to be sinuous or wavy.

sin·ū·ā′tion, *n.* a winding or bending in and out; also, sinuosity.

sin′ū·ōse, *a.* sinuous.

sin·ū·os′i·ty, *n.* 1. *pl.* **sin·ū·os′i·tieṣ,** a series of bends and turns in arches or other irregular figures.
2. the state or quality of being sinuous.

sin′ū·ous, *a.* [Fr. *sinueux*, from L. *sinus*, bent, curved.]
1. winding; crooked; bending in and out; of a serpentine or undulating form; as, a *sinuous* pipe.
2. devious; crooked; not straightforward or honest.
3. in botany, sinuate.

sin′ū·ous·ly, *adv.* in a sinuous manner; windingly; crookedly.

sī·nū·pal′li·āte, *a.* having a pallial sinus.

sī′nus, *n.*; *pl.* **sī′nus·eṣ, sī′nus,** [L., a bent surface, a curve, a fold or hollow, a bosom, a bay.]
1. a bend or curve.
2. any cavity or hollow formed by a bending or curving.
3. in anatomy and zoology, any of various cavities, hollows, or passages; especially, (a) any of the air cavities in the skull opening into the nasal cavities; (b) a large channel for venous blood; (c) a dilated part in a blood vessel, etc.
4. in botany, the rounded depression between two consecutive lobes, as of a leaf.
5. in medicine, a narrow channel leading from a pus-filled cavity.
6. popularly, sinusitis.
7. a bay of the sea; a recess in the coast. [Obs.]
8. in conchology, a groove or cavity.

sinus venosus; (a) the main part of the cavity of either auricle of the heart: it is the portion into which the veins empty their blood: also called *atrium*; (b) the common venous receptacle in the embryo attached to the posterior wall of the auricle.

sī·nus·ī′tis, *n.* inflammation of a sinus or sinuses, especially of the skull.

sī′nus·oid, *n.* a curve, which, to rectangular coordinates, has an ordinate at each point proportionate to the sine of an angle proportionate to the abscissa: also called *curve of sines*.

sī·nus·oid′ăl, *a.* pertaining to a sinusoid.
sinusoidal current; an alternating electric current whose strength can be correctly represented by a sinusoid.

siō′go̤on (shyō′), *n.* same as *shogun*.

siō′go̤on·āte, *n.* same as *shogunate*.

-sion (-shăn), [L. *-sio, -sionis.*] a suffix meaning *the act, quality, condition,* or *result of*, as in revul*sion*, confu*sion*.

Sī′ŏn, *n.* same as *Zion*.

Sī′ŏn·īte, *n.* 1. same as *Ellerian*.
2. same as *Zionite*.

Siōu′ăn (sö′), *a.* designating or of a linguistic family of North American Indians formerly inhabiting the west central United States, central Canada, and parts of Virginia and Carolina: it includes Catawba, Iowa, Winnebago, Omaha-Osage, Dakota, Crow, etc.

Siōux (sö), *n.*; *pl.* **Siōux** (sö *or* söz), [Am. Ind.] a member of a confederation of Siouan Indian tribes that lived in the northern plains of the United States: Indian name, *Dakota*.

sip, *v.t.*; sipped (sipt), *pt., pp.*; sipping, *ppr.* [prob. from AS. *sypian*, to drink in.]
1. to drink only a little at a time; to drink in small quantities; as, to *sip* wine; to *sip* tea or coffee.
2. to draw into the mouth; to extract; as, a bee *sips* nectar from the flowers.

sip, *v.i.* to drink a small quantity; to take a sip.

sip, *n.* 1. the act of sipping.
2. a small quantity sipped.

sip′ăġe, *n.* seepage. [Scot. and North Eng. Dial.]

sīpe, *v.* and *n.* seep. [Scot. and North Eng. Dial.]

siph′i·lis, *n.* syphilis.

sī′phoid, *n.* a siphon bottle.

sī′phon-, sī′phon·ō-, sī′phon·i-, [from Gr. *siphōn*, a hollow tube.] combining forms meaning *siphon, tube, pipe*.

sī′phŏn, sȳ′phon, *n.* [Fr.; L. *sipho, siphonis*; Gr. *siphōn*, a hollow tube, a reed.]
1. a bent pipe or tube whose legs are of unequal length, used for drawing liquid out of a vessel by causing it to rise in the tube over the rim or top through the force of atmospheric pressure upon the surface of the liquid. For this purpose the shorter leg is inserted in the liquid, and the air is exhausted by being drawn through the longer leg. The liquid then rises by the weight of the atmosphere till it reaches the top of the tube, and then descends in the lower leg of the siphon, and continues to flow till the liquid in the vessel reaches the level of the end of the shorter leg. Sometimes an exhausting tube is placed on the longer leg for exhausting the air by suction and causing the flow to begin.

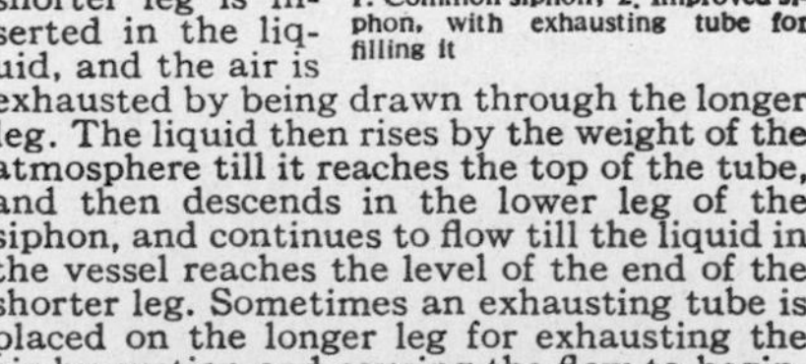

SIPHONS
1. Common siphon; 2. Improved siphon, with exhausting tube for filling it

2. in zoology, (a) one of the membranous and calcareous tubes which connects the chambers of certain shells; (b) a tubelike organ in some animals, as cuttlefishes, used for drawing in or ejecting liquids; (c) the sucking tube of some insects and parasites; (d) a prolongation along the margin of a gastropod shell to protect the soft siphon; (e) a sproutlike prolongation in the front of the mouth of certain gephyrean worms; (f) the siphuncle or funnel of cephalopods.
3. a siphon bottle.
inverted siphon; a siphon with both legs equal and turned up at the extremities.
siphon barometer; a barometer in which the lower end of the tube is bent upward, in the form of a siphon.
siphon condenser; a condenser used in some steam engines, operating upon the principle of the siphon.
siphon recorder; a contrivance consisting of a siphon made to oscillate by an electric current transmitting signals in a cable: ink is conveyed by this siphon to a moving strip of paper, producing a continuous wavy line from which the message may be deciphered.

sī′phŏn, sȳ′phŏn, *v.t.*; siphoned, *pt., pp.*; siphoning, *ppr.* to convey, transmit, or remove by or as by a siphon.

sī′phŏn, sȳ′phŏn, *v.i.* to pass through a siphon.

sī′phŏn·ăġe, *n.* the work of a siphon; the operation of emptying by means of a siphon.

sī′phŏn·ăl, *a.* pertaining to or formed like a siphon.

Sī·phō·nap′tēr·ȧ, *n.pl.* [*siphon-*, and Gr. *apteros*, wingless.] an order of insects, including fleas and other wingless insects, supplied with sucking tubes.

Sī·phō·nā′ri·ȧ, *n.* a genus typical of the *Siphonariidæ*.

sī·phō·nā′rid, *a.* of or relating to the *Siphonariidæ*.

sī·phō·nā′rid, *n.* a gastropod belonging to the family *Siphonariidæ*.

Sī″phō·nȧ·rī′i·dae, *n.pl.* a family of gastropods characterized by a patelliform shell with a deep siphonal groove on the right side.

Sī·phō·nā′tȧ, *n.pl.* a division of bivalve mollusks including all those which have one or two siphons, as clams.

sī′phŏn·āte, *a.* furnished with a siphon or siphons.

sī′phŏn bot′tle, a heavy, sealed bottle with a tube on the inside connected at the top with a nozzle and valve which, when opened, allows the flow of pressurized, carbonated water contained within.

sī′phŏn çup, in machinery, a cup containing oil which is supplied to the part to be lubricated by means of a capillary wick carrying it over the brim.

sī′phŏn·et, *n.* a honey tube of an insect.

sī′phŏn gāuġe (gāj), a pressure gauge consisting of a U-shaped glass tube sealed at one end, the sealed end containing a column of mercury.

Sī″phō·ni·ā′tȧ, *n.pl.* same as *Siphonata*.

sī·phon′iç, *a.* same as *siphonal*.

Sī·phō·nif′ēr·ȧ, *n.pl.* a division of cephalopods, equivalent to the *Tetrabranchiata*.

sī·phō·nif′ēr·ous, *a.* relating to the *Siphonifera*.

sī·phō′ni·um, *n.* in certain birds, a bony tube connecting the tympanum with a cavity in the mandible.

Sī″phō·nō·bran̄·çhi·ā′tȧ, *n.pl.* a former division of gastropods with a siphonal prolongation of the mantle, as a spout to convey water to the gill cavities.

sī″phō·nō·bran̄′çhi·āte, *a.* of or pertaining to the *Siphonobranchiata*.

sī″phō·nō·bran̄′çhi·āte, *n.* one of the *Siphonobranchiata*.

sī′phō·nō·glyph, *n.* [*siphono-*, and Gr. *glyphē*, a carving.] the gonidial groove of an actinian.

Sī·phō·noph′ō·rȧ, *n.pl.* [*siphono-*, and Gr. *phorein*, to bear.] an order of small swimming or floating sea hydrozoans, some adapted for nutrition, some for reproduction, budding into colonies of many different shapes and forms.

sī·phō·noph′ō·răn, *a.* and *n.* same as *siphonophore*.

sī′phō·nō·phōre″, *n.* any one of the *Siphonophora*.

sī′phō·nō·phōre″, *a.* of or pertaining to the *Siphonophora*.

Sī·phon′ō·plax, *n.* [*siphono-*, and Gr. *plax*, tablet.] one of the plates which combine to form a tube around the siphon of a pholad.

sī·phon′ō·rhīne (-rīn), *a.* having tubelike nostrils, as a bird of the petrel family.

sī′phō·nō·stē″lē (*or* -stēl″), *n.* [from Gr. *siphon*, a tube, siphon; and *-stele*.] in botany, a hollow tube of vascular tissue in certain stems, as that of a fern.

Sī·phō·nos′tō·mȧ, *n.pl.* same as *Siphonostomata*.

Sī″phō·nō·stō′mȧ·tȧ, *n.pl.* [*siphono-*, and Gr. *stoma*, mouth.]
1. a tribe of crustaceans with mouth parts adapted for piercing and sucking.

2. a division of gastropods having a shell with a notched lip, and provided with a kind of tube for the protrusion of a respiratory siphon.

sī″phō·nō·stom′ȧ·tous, *a.* 1. of or related to the *Siphonostomata.*

2. having a channel in the shell as a protection to the siphon.

sī′phō·nō·stōme, *n.* any one of the *Siphonostomata.*

SIPHONOSTOME (gastropod)
Neptunea antiqua (red whelk)
a, branchial siphon. b, proboscis. c, operculum. d d, tentacles. f, foot.

sī′phŏn slīde, a slide for a microscope, with a cell through which water circulates by means of a siphon.

sī·phō·rhī′năl (-rī′), *a.* [*siphon-*, and Gr. *rhis, rhinos*, nose.] with nostrils like a tube or siphon, as a petrel; siphonorhine.

sī·phō·rhin′i·ăn (-rin′), *a.* of or pertaining to a bird with tubelike nostrils, as those of the petrel family.

sī′phuñ·cle, *n.* [L. *siphunculus*, a little tube, dim. of *siphon*.] in conchology, the opening which runs through the partitions of chambered or nautiloid shells.

sī′phuñ·cled (-kld) *a.* having a siphuncle.

sī·phuñ′cū·lăr, *a.* pertaining to a siphuncle.

sī·phuñ′cū·lāte, *a.* having a siphuncle.

sī·phuñ′cū·lā·ted, *a.* siphunculate.

sip′id, *a.* having a fine flavor or taste; savory. [Rare.]

sip′pẽr, *n.* one who sips.

sip′pet, *n.* [prob. dim. of *sop*.]

1. a small piece of toast soaked in soup, gravy, etc.

2. a small piece of toasted or fried bread used as a garnish.

3. any small piece; a fragment.

sip′ple, *v.i.*; sippled (-pld), *pt., pp.*; sippling, *ppr.* to sip frequently; to tipple. [Scot.]

Sī·puñ·cū·lā′cē·ȧ (-shē-), *n.pl.* [LL. *sipunculus*, a little tube or siphon.] same as *Gephyrea.*

Sī·puñ·cū′li·dae, *n.pl.* a family of gephyrean worms.

sī·puñ′cū·loid, *a.* of or related to the *Sipunculoidea.*

sī·puñ′cū·loid, *n.* one of the *Sipunculoidea.*

Sī·puñ·cū·loi′dē·ȧ, *n.pl. Gephyrea*, a class of worms comprising the spoonworms.

sip′y·līte, *n.* [from *Sipylos*, a child of Niobe.] a rare mineral; erbium columbate.

sī quis, [L., if any one.] in the Church of England, a notification by a candidate for orders of his intention to inquire whether any impediment may be alleged against him.

sir, *n.* [ME. *sir*; OFr. *sire, seure*, master, a Norman form of L. *senior*, lit., an elder.]

1. [sometimes S-] a respectful term of address used to a man: not followed by the given name or surname.

2. [S-] the title used before the given name or full name of a knight or baronet; as, *Sir* Walter Raleigh.

3. a term of address used with the title of a man's office, rank, or profession; as, *sir* priest, *sir* judge, *sir* knight. [Archaic.]

4. a man of rank. [Obs.]

5. a title used humorously or derisively; as, *sir* grouch.

Sir·bō′ni·ăn, *a.* same as *Serbonian.*

sir·çär′, *n.* [Hind. *sarkār*, from Per. *sarkār*, chief or head, from *sar*, the head, and *kār*, work.]

1. a Hindu clerk or writer.

2. in India, the government; also, a master.

sir·där′, *n.* [Hind. *sardār*, from Per. *sardār*, leader; *sar*, the head and *dār*, holding.]

1. in India, (a) a native chief or noble; (b) a high military officer; (c) a head servant, especially a litter bearer.

2. formerly, in Egypt, the British commander in chief of the army.

sir·där′ beãr′ẽr, in India, the chief of the palanquin bearers, who is generally a head servant: also *sirdar.*

sīre, *n.* [ME., from OFr. *sire*, master.]

1. formerly, a person of authority; a man of high rank: now used only as a title of respect in addressing a king, equivalent to "your majesty."

2. a father or a progenitor. [Poet.]

3. the male parent of a quadruped: particularly used of horses; as, the horse had a good *sire.*

sīre, *v.t.*; sired, *pt., pp.*; siring, *ppr.* to beget; to procreate: used now chiefly of quadrupeds.

Sī·rē′dŏn, *n.* [Gr. *seirēdon*, a siren.] the axolotl, a larval salamander.

sī′ren, *n.* [Gr. *seirēn*, a siren, supposed to mean lit. an entangler, from *seira*, a cord.]

1. in Greek and Roman mythology, one of several sea nymphs, who by their seductive singing fascinated those who sailed by their island, and then destroyed them: they are represented as having partly the form of birds.

2. a mermaid.

3. a charming or enticing woman; a woman who makes obvious use of her charms to entice or allure.

4. something insidious or deceptive.

5. [S-] a genus of perennibranchiate, slime-coated, lizard-shaped amphibians which have only one pair of feet, and are supplied both with internal lungs and external gills: they live in water or moist mud; also, [s-] any animal of this genus.

6. (a) an acoustical instrument in which steam or air is driven against a rotating, perforated disk so as to generate sound; (b) a similar device used as a warning signal, foghorn, factory whistle, etc.

sī′ren, *a.* pertaining to or like a siren; seductive; bewitching; fascinating; as, a *siren* song.

sī·rēne′, *n.* same as *siren* (sense 6).

Sī·rē′ni·ȧ, *n.pl.* an order of large, vegetarian sea mammals, including the dugong and the manatee, or sea cow, with a cigar-shaped body, a blunt snout, large, mobile lips, flipperlike forelimbs, and a large tail fluke.

sī·rē′ni·ăn, *n.* any one of the *Sirenia.*

sī·rē′ni·ăn, *a.* of or belonging to the order *Sirenia.*

sī·ren′iç·ăl, *a.* relating to or characteristic of a siren.

sī′ren·īze, *v.i.* to use the enticements of a siren; to charm. [Rare.]

sir′gang, *n.* [E. Ind.] the crested green jackdaw or magpie of Asia.

si·rī′ȧ·sis, *n.* 1. a sunstroke.

2. a sun bath; exposure to the sun for the cure of a disease. [Obs.]

sī′ris, *n.* [E. Ind.] a tree of the genus *Albizzia*, native to tropical Asia and Africa.

Sir′i·us, *n.* [ME; L., from Gr. *Seirios*, lit., scorching.] the brightest star in the heavens, located in the constellation Canis Major: also called *Dog Star.*

sir′kär, *n.* same as *sircar.*

sir′keer, *n.* an Asiatic cuckoo of the genus *Taccocua.*

sir′loin, *n.* [OFr. hyp. *surloigne*, from *sur*, over, and *longe*, loin: sp. after *sir* from legend that the cut was knighted for its excellence.] a choice cut of beef from the loin end between the rump and the porterhouse.

Sir′mi·ăn, *a.* relating to Sirmium, a Roman city in what is now Yugoslavia, especially to the religious councils which met there in the fourth century and set forth a modified form of the Nicene creed.

si·roç′çō, *n.*; *pl.* **si·roç′çōs,** [It., from Ar. *sharq*, the east, which meant in this case, from the direction of the desert.]

1. a hot, steady, oppressive wind blowing from the Libyan deserts across the Mediterranean into southern Europe, where it is sometimes accompanied by rain.

2. any hot, oppressive wind, especially one blowing toward a center of low barometric pressure.

sir′răh, *n.* [from *sir*.] a contemptuous word of address used to a man. [Archaic.]

sir·rev′ẽr·ence, *interj.* [confused from *sa'-reverence*, shortened from *save reverence*, saving your reverence.] begging your pardon: an expression of apology formerly used before a word or expression regarded as indelicate or coarse. [Obs.]

sir′up, *n.* [ME. *sirupe*; OFr. *sirop*; ML. *sirupuum*; Ar. *sharāb*, from *shariba*, to drink.] any sweet, thick liquid; specifically, (a) a solution made by boiling sugar with water and, often, fruit juices, artificial flavoring, etc.; (b) any solution of sugar used in pharmacy as a vehicle for medicines; (c) the sweet, thick liquid obtained in the process of manufacturing cane sugar or glucose; (d) maple sirup, corn sirup, etc.: also spelled *syrup.*

sir′up·y, *a.* 1. of sirup.

2. like sirup in sweetness or thickness.

sir·vente′ (-voṅt′), *n.* [Fr.] a kind of poetry, usually satirical, often used by the troubadours of the middle ages.

sis, siss, *n.* sister. [Colloq.]

sī′săl (*or* sis′ăl), *n.* [from *Sisal*, a port in Yucatán.]

1. a strong fiber obtained from the leaves of an agave of Yucatan, used for making rope.

2. the plant yielding this fiber.

Also *sisal hemp.*

sis′çō·wet, sis′kō·wet, *n.* [Am. Ind.] a Mackinaw trout.

sis′el, *n.* [Russ.] the suslik.

Sis′ẽr·ȧ, *n.* [Heb. *shīsherā'*; prob. of Hittite origin.] in the Bible, a military leader of the Canaanites against the Israelites, murdered by Jael, who drove a nail through his head while he slept: Judges iv. 5.

sis·ẽr·ãr′y, *n.* [popular corruption of L. *certiorari*, a legal writ.] a severe blow. [Brit. Dial.]

sis′kin, *n.* [via Fl., from G. *sisschen*, dial. var. of *zeischen*, dim. of *zeizig*, from Czech *čížek*, dim. of *číž*: of echoic origin.]

1. a European and Asiatic finch with green plumage and black and yellow markings.

2. a North American finch with a gray breast, yellow back, and brown markings.

siss, *v.i.* [ME. *sissen*; Dan. *sissen*, to hiss; imitative.] to hiss. [Brit. Dial.]

siss, *n.* a hissing sound. [Brit. Dial.]

sis′si·fȳ, *v.t.*; sissified, *pt., pp.*; sissifying, *ppr.* to cause (a boy or man) to be a sissy. [Colloq.]

sis′sọọ, *n.* [E. Ind.] a valuable timber tree of India, *Dalbergia sissoo*, the wood of which somewhat resembles the finer species of teak, but is tougher and more elastic.

sis′sy, *n.*; *pl.* **sis′sieṣ,** [dim. of *sis*.]

1. a boy or man whose behavior, tastes, interests, etc. seem more feminine than masculine. [Colloq.]

2. a timid person or coward. [Colloq.]

3. a homosexual. [Slang.]

sis′sy bär, a metal bar shaped like an inverted U, attached behind the seat of a motorcycle or bicycle, as to prevent a rider from sliding backward.

sis′sy·ish, *a.* of, like, or like that of a sissy. [Colloq.]

sist, *v.t.* [L. *sistere*, to cause to stand.] in Scots law, (a) to stay; (b) to cite or summons.

sist, *n.* in Scots law, the act of legally staying proceedings.

sis′tẽr, *n.* [ME. *suster*, from Scand. *systir*, a sister; AS. *sweostor*. Origin uncertain.]

1. (a) a woman or girl related to one by having the same parents; sometimes also used of animals; (b) a woman or girl related to one by having one parent in common; a half sister; (c) a stepsister; (d) a foster sister.

2. (a) a friend thought of as a sister; (b) a female fellow member of the same race, creed, profession, or organization.

3. a member of a female religious order; a nun; as, *Sisters* of Mercy nurse the sick and give aid to the poor.

4. a thing thought of as feminine and associated with some kindred thing; one of the same kind, model, etc.

5. a nurse, especially a head nurse. [Brit.]

6. any woman: often used as a familiar term of address. [Colloq.]

sis′tẽr, *a.* related or seeming to be related as sisters; sisterly.

sis′tẽr, *v.t.* to treat as a sister.

sis′tẽr block, a turned cylindrical block having two sheave holes, one above the other, used on ships.

sis′tẽr·hood, *n.* 1. the state or fact of being a sister; relationship of sisters.

2. a group of women having some interest, belief, etc. in common, as the women's auxiliary of an organization.

3. an association of women forming a religious order.

sis′tẽr hook, one of a pair of hooks fitted together and so mounted that they face and overlap each other.

sis′tẽr·ing, *a.* contiguous; allied.

sis′tẽr-in-lạw, *n.*; *pl.* **sis′tẽrṣ-in-lạw,** 1. a husband's or wife's sister.

2. the wife of one's brother.

3. occasionally, the wife of one's husband's or wife's brother.

sis′tẽr·less, *a.* having no sister.

sis′tẽr·li·ness, *n.* the act of bestowing sisterly attentions.

sis′tẽr·ly, *a.* like a sister; of or befitting a sister; as, *sisterly* kindness.

sis′tẽr·ly, *adv.* as a sister should.

Sis′tïne (*or* -tin), *a.* [It. *Sistino*, of Sisto or Sixtus.] belonging or relating to any pope of the name Sixtus.

Sistine Chapel; the principal chapel in the Vatican at Rome, famous for its frescoes by Michelangelo and other artists: built by order of Sixtus IV.

Sistine Madonna; the Madonna painted by Raphael in 1515 for the Church of St. Sixtus at Piacenza, Italy.

sis′tren, *n.* obsolete plural of *sister*.

sis′troid, *a.* in mathematics, designating the angle formed by the convex sides of two intersecting curves: opposed to *cissoid*.

sis′trum, *n.*; *pl.* **sis′trums, sis′trȧ,** [L., from Gr. *seistron*, from *seiein*, to shake.] a metal rattle or noisemaker which the Egyptian priests of Isis used to shake at the festivals of that goddess. It consisted of a thin lyre-shaped metal frame, through which passed a number of loosely held metal rods.

SISTRUM

Si·sym′bri·um, *n.* [LL., from Gr. *sisymbrion*.] a genus of plants of the family *Cruciferæ*. The species are mostly perennial or annual herbs with yellow or white flowers, variable leaves, and pods having numerous seeds with one row in each cell.

Sis·y·phē′ăn, *a.* pertaining to or like that of Sisyphus; hence, endless and difficult; incessantly recurring; as, *Sisyphean* labors.

Sis′y·phus, *n.* [L.; Gr. *Sisyphōs*.] in Greek mythology, the shrewd and greedy king of Corinth who was doomed forever in Hades to roll uphill a heavy stone which always rolled down again.

Sis·y·riñ′chi·um, *n.* [LL., from Gr. *sisyrinchion*.] a genus of North American grasslike plants belonging to the iris family. They have narrow, erect, chiefly basal leaves and flowers with three undivided style branches.

sit, *v.i.*; sat *or archaic* sate, *pt.*; sat *or obs.* sitten, *pp.*; sitting, *ppr.* [AS. *sittan*, for older *sitian*, pt. *sæt*, pp. *geseten*; akin to G. *sitzen*; Goth. *sitan*, to sit, from widely spread root *sad*, seen also in L. *sedere*, to sit; *sedes*, a seat. *Set* is the causative of this verb.]

1. to rest the weight of the body upon the buttocks and the backs of the thighs, as on a chair, rock, etc.; to be seated; also, to rest on the haunches with the forelegs braced: said of quadrupeds.

2. to perch or roost; as, a bird *sits* on a tree.

3. to incubate; to cover and keep eggs warm for hatching; to set; to brood.

4. to occupy a place or seat in an official capacity, as a judge, legislator, etc.; as, to *sit* in the House of Representatives.

5. to meet, or be convened, as an assembly; to be in session; to meet for business; to be officially engaged in public business; as, the city council *sat* last night.

6. to be inactive or out of use.

7. to remain; to dwell; to abide. [Archaic.]

8. to have a seat or position; to be placed or located.

> Is there no pity *sitting* in the clouds?
> —Shak.

9. to rest, lie, or bear in any position or condition; as, the burden *sits* heavily upon him.

10. to pose; to assume a position for a certain purpose, as having one's picture taken.

11. to have position or direction.

12. to fit; as, the coat *sits* well.

13. to take a formal examination, as for an academic degree, scholarship, etc. (usually with *for*). [Brit.]

14. to baby-sit.

to sit down; (a) to place oneself on a chair or other seat; as, *to sit down* at a meal; (b) to take up a place or position; to begin a siege; as, the enemy *sat down* before the town; (c) to settle; to fix a permanent abode; (d) to rest; to cease as satisfied; to pause.

to sit on or *upon*; (a) to hold a meeting or session concerning; to investigate; as, three judges *sat on* the case; (b) to be a member of; to be on (a jury, etc.); (c) [Colloq.] to check; to snub; to repress; (d) [Colloq.] to reprimand or rebuke severely.

to sit out; (a) to take no part in; as, to *sit out* a performance or a dance; (b) to remain longer than (another); (c) to stay until the end of.

to sit under; to be under the instruction or ministrations of; to be a member of the congregation of.

to sit up; (a) to rise to a sitting position; (b) to sit erect; (c) to sit on the haunches with the forelegs drawn up before the chest: said of animals; (d) to postpone the time of going to bed until a late hour; (e) [Colloq.] to become suddenly alert.

sit, *v.t.* 1. to keep one's seat on; as, he *sits* a horse well.

2. to place on a seat; to seat; to cause to sit: often used reflexively; as, *sit* yourself down.

si·tär′, *n.* [Hindi *sitār*.] a lutelike instrument of India with a long, fretted neck, a resonating gourd or gourds, and usually six playing strings and a number of strings that vibrate sympathetically.

sit′çom, *n.* a situation comedy.

sit′-down, *n.* 1. a strike in which the strikers stay inside a factory, etc. refusing to work or leave until agreement is reached: in full, *sit-down strike*.

2. a form of civil disobedience in which demonstrators sit down, as in public streets or places, in resistance to being moved away.

sīte, *n.* [L. *situs*, position, situation, seat, from the root of L. *sedere*, to sit.]

1. a piece of land considered from the standpoint of its use for some specified purpose; as, a good *site* for a picnic.

2. the place where something is, is to be, or was located; as, we stood on the *site* of an ancient city.

sīt′ed, *a.* placed; situated. [Obs.]

sit′fȧst, *a.* fixed; steadfast. [Scot.]

sit′fȧst, *n.* an ulcerated horny sore or tumor on a horse's back, under the saddle.

sith, *adv.*, *prep.*, and *conj.* [AS. *sith*, *siththan*.] since. [Archaic.]

sīthe, *v.i.* to sigh. [Now Dial.]

sīthe, *n.* a scythe. [Obs.]

sīthe, *v.t.* to scythe. [Obs.]

sith′en, *adv.*, *prep.*, and *conj.* since. [Obs.]

sith′ence, *adv.*, *prep.*, and *conj.* since. [Archaic.]

sit′-in, *n.* a sit-down inside a public place by a group demonstrating for civil rights, against war, etc.

sit′i·ō-, [from Gr. *sition*, food, grain.] a combining form meaning *food* or *eating*: also *sito-*.

sit·i·ol′ō·ġy, *n.* same as *sitology*.

sit″i·ō·mā′ni·ȧ, *n.* same as *sitomania*.

sit″i·ō·phō′bi·ȧ, *n.* same as *sitophobia*.

sī′tō-, [from Gr. *sitos*, food, grain.] a combining form meaning *food* or *eating*: also *sitio-*.

sī·tol′ō·ġy, *n.* [*sito-* and *-logy*.] the study of foods, food values, nutrition, diet, etc.; dietetics.

sī·tō·mā′ni·ȧ, *n.* an abnormally great desire for food: also *sitiomania*.

sī·tō·phō′bi·ȧ, *n.* [Gr. *sitos*, food, and *phobos*, fear.] fear of food.

sī·tos′tẽr·in, *n.* same as *sitosterol*.

sī·tos′tẽr·ōl, *n.* [*sito-*, and chole*sterol*.] a crystalline alcohol, $C_{27}H_{46}OH$, found in wheat, corn, Calabar beans, etc.

Sit·tel′lȧ, *n.* [Gr. *sittē*, woodpecker.]

1. a genus of small running or creeping birds of Australia and New Guinea.

2. [s-] any bird of this genus.

sit′ten, *v.* obsolete past participle of *sit*.

sit′tẽr, *n.* one who or that which sits; (a) one who sits for his portrait, bust, or the like; (b) a person hired to sit with a child or children when the parents are out, as for the evening: also *baby sitter*; (c) a brooding hen.

Sit·tī′nae, *n.pl.* formerly, a subfamily of insessorial birds consisting of the nuthatches.

sit′tine, *a.* of or resembling the *Sittinæ*.

sit′ting, *a.* 1. having a seat; that sits.

2. in botany, sessile. [Obs.]

3. becoming; befitting. [Obs.]

sit′ting, *n.* 1. the act or position of one who sits; the posture of being on a seat.

2. the time during which one sits, as for his portrait, bust, or the like.

3. a seat in a church, especially one for which rent is paid.

4. a session; a meeting; the meeting or presence of any body for the transaction of business.

5. a set of eggs placed under a hen for a single hatching; also, a brooding upon eggs, as by a hen.

sit′ting rọọm, 1. same as *living room*.

2. any room, especially a small one next to a bedroom, used as a living room.

sit′ū·āte, *a.* [ML. *situatus*, pp. of *situare*, to place, for L. *situs*, position.] situated. [Rare or Archaic.]

sit′ū·āte, *v.t.*; situated, *pt.*, *pp.*; situating, *ppr.*

1. to locate; to put in a given place or position; as, a town *situated* on a hill.

> For thousands of years everybody supposed the earth to be *situated* in the center of the universe, and that all the heavenly bodies revolved around it as a center.
> —Lewis Swift, F.R.A.S.

2. to place in certain relations or circumstances; to put in a particular condition.

sit′ū·āt·ed, *a.* 1. having a given site or location; placed; located.

2. subject to certain circumstances or conditions.

sit·ū·ā′tion, *n.* [Fr.; ML. *situatio*, from L. *situare*, to place, from *situs*, a place.]

1. manner in which a thing is situated in relation to its surroundings; location.

2. a place; locality.

3. position or condition with regard to circumstances.

4. (a) the combination of circumstances at any given moment; state of affairs; (b) any significant combination of circumstances developing in the course of a novel, play, etc.

5. a position of employment.

sit·ū·ā′tion çom′e·dy, a comedy, especially a comic television series, with a story line made up of contrived episodes involving stock characters.

sit·ū·ā′tion eth′içs, a system of ethics according to which moral rules are not absolutely binding but may be modified in the light of specific situations.

sī′tus, *n.* [L.] position or location; especially, the normal position, as of an organ of the body or a plant part.

sitz bȧth (sits), [partial transl. of G. *sitzbad*; *sitz*, a seat, and *bad*, a bath.]

1. a bath in which only the hip area is immersed, usually as a medical treatment.

2. a tub or basin used for such a bath.

Sī′vȧ, *n.* [Hind., from Sans., *çiva*, auspicious.] the third god of the Hindu triad, representing the principle of destruction and reproduction: also *Shiva*. His emblem is the lingam, symbolical of creation which follows destruction.

Sī′vȧ·işm, *n.* the worship of Siva.

Sī·vȧ·is′tiç, *a.* of Sivaism.

Sī′vȧ·īte, *n.* a member of the Hindu sect which worships Siva.

Sī·vän′, *n.* [Heb.] the ninth month of the Jewish year.

sī′vȧ snāke, a poisonous East Indian snake resembling the cobra.

Siv·ȧ·thē′ri·um, *n.* [*Siva*, the Hind. god, and Gr. *thērion*, a wild beast.] an extinct ruminant found fossil in the Tertiary strata of the Siwalik Sub-Himalayan range. It surpassed all known ruminants in size. It had four horns and a protruding upper lip, and must have resembled an immense antelope or gnu.

SIVATHERIUM (restored)

Sī′wȧsh, *n.* [Chinook from Fr. *sauvage*, savage.]

1. an Alaskan breed of dog.

2. [s-] a north Pacific coast Indian.

sī′wȧsh, *v.i.* to live outdoors like an Indian. [Dial.]

six, *a.* [ME.; AS.] twice three; one more than five.

Six Nations; a confederation of Indian tribes consisting of the Five Nations and the Tuscaroras.

six, *n.* 1. the cardinal number between five and seven.
2. a symbol representing this number, as 6 or VI.
3. a person or thing numbered six or something having six units as its essential characteristic, as a playing card with six pips.
to be at six and seven or *at sixes and sevens*; (a) to be in disorder or confusion; (b) to be at odds; to disagree. [Colloq.]

six'āin, *n.* [Fr., from LL. *sexanus*, sixth, from L. *sex*, six.] a six-line stanza.

six'fōld, *a.* 1. six times repeated; having six times as much or as many.
2. having six parts.

six'fōld, *adv.* six times as much or as many.

six'-foot'ēr, *n.* a person six feet tall. [Colloq.]

six'-pack, *n.* a package containing six units of a product, especially one with six cans of beer.

six'pence, *n.* 1. an English silver coin of the value of six pennies; half a shilling.
2. the sum of six pence (pennies).

six'pen·ny, *a.* 1. worth sixpence; costing sixpence; hence, of small worth; cheap; as, a *sixpenny* loaf.
2. designating a size of nails, usually two inches.

six'scōre, *a.* and *n.* six times twenty; one hundred and twenty.

six'-shoot'ēr, *n.* a six-chambered revolver; a revolver that can be fired six times without reloading. [Colloq.]

six'teen', *a.* [AS. *sixtēne, sixtȳne.*] being the sum of six and ten; consisting of six and ten; twice eight; one more than fifteen.

six'teen', *n.* 1. the sum of six and ten; the cardinal number between fifteen and seventeen.
2. a symbol representing this sum, as 16 or XVI.

six·teen'mō, *n.*; *pl.* **six·teen'mōs,** sextodecimo; 16 mo: a size of book.

six'teenth', *a.* [AS. *sixteótha.*]
1. the sixth after the tenth; preceded by fifteen others in a series.
2. being one of sixteen equal parts into which a whole is divided.

six'teenth', *n.* 1. one of sixteen equal parts.
2. anything next in order after the fifteenth.
3. in music, an interval consisting of two octaves and a second; also, a sixteenth note.

six'teenth' nōte, in music, a note having the duration of one sixteenth of a whole note: called also a *semiquaver.*

sixth, *a.* [AS. *sixta.*]
1. being the first after the fifth; preceded by five others in a series.
2. being one of six equal parts into which a whole is divided.

sixth, *n.* 1. any one of the six equal parts of something.
2. that which follows the fifth in order.
3. in music, (a) an interval of six degrees in a diatonic scale; (b) a tone six degrees above or below a given tone; (c) the combination of two tones separated by this interval; (d) the sixth note of a diatonic scale; submediant; superdominant.

sixth chord, in music, an inverted triad, as e-g-c.

sixth'ly, *adv.* in the sixth place.

sixth sense, a power of perception which seems as strong as any of the five senses; intuition.

six'ti·eth, *a.* 1. next in order after the fifty-ninth in a series.
2. being one of sixty equal parts into which anything is divided.

six'ti·eth, *n.* 1. any one of sixty equal parts of something.
2. the one following the fifty-ninth.

Six'tine, *a.* same as *Sistine.*

six'ty, *a.* consisting or made up of six times ten.

six'ty, *n.*; *pl.* **six'ties,** 1. the cardinal number between fifty-nine and sixty-one.
2. a symbol representing sixty units, as 60 or LX.
the sixties; the years from sixty through sixty-nine (of a century or a person's age).

six'ty-fōur dol'lăr ques'tion (-chun), the most important, or principal, question: so called from the award given for answering correctly the final one of a series of questions on a radio quiz program.

six'ty-fōurth' nōte, in music, a note having the duration of one sixty-fourth of a whole note: also called a *hemidemisemiquaver.*

six'ty-six', *n.* a game of cards commonly played by two persons with twenty-four cards, each player endeavoring to secure as many marriages, that is the possession of a king and queen of the same suit, as possible, sixty-six scoring one point.

sīz'ȧ·ble, *a.* of considerable size or bulk; large; as, *sizable* timber: also spelled *sizeable.*

sīz'ȧ·bly, *adv.* so as to be sizable.

sī'zăr, *n.* [from *size.*] in the University of Cambridge, England, and at Trinity College, Dublin, Ireland, a student, who, being of limited means, receives a scholarship allowance from the college: also spelled *sizer.*

sī'zăr·ship, *n.* the rank or station of a sizar.

sīze, *n.* [ME.; OFr. *sise*, contr. of *assise.*]
1. that quality of a thing which determines how much space it occupies; dimensions or magnitude of a thing.
2. (a) extent, magnitude, amount, etc.; as, the *size* of this undertaking is incredible; (b) sizable amount, dimensions, etc.
3. character with regard to ability to meet requirements; as, the governorship is too big for the *size* of him.
4. any classification applied to a series of manufactured articles, usually indicated by a number, letter, etc., marking either its place in a graduated scale or its measure.

I am sorry that these shoes are a full *size* too large. —Dickens.

5. actual condition; true state of affairs; as, that's the *size* of it. [Colloq.]
6. standard ration or allowance, as of food. [Obs.]
7. [*pl.*] assize or assizes. [Dial.]
8. an instrument consisting of thin leaves fastened together at one end by a rivet, used to measure pearls.
of a size; of one or the same size.
Syn.—dimensions, bigness, largeness, greatness, magnitude, bulk.

sīze, *v.t.*; sized, *pt., pp.*; sizing, *ppr.* 1. to adjust or arrange according to a given size.
2. to arrange or grade according to size; as, to *size* weights and measures.
3. in military usage, to take the size of (soldiers) with the view of placing them in the ranks according to their sizes; to arrange according to sizes or statures.
to size up; (a) to make an estimate concerning; (b) to meet requirements or specifications. [Colloq.]

sīze, *v.i.* 1. at Cambridge and other universities, to order food or drink from the buttery.
2. to increase in size.

sīze, *n.* [contr. of Fr. *assise*, layer.]
1. any thin, pasty substance used as a glaze or filler on porous materials, as on plaster, paper, or cloth.
2. the buffy coat which appears on the surface of coagulated blood in certain conditions.

sīze, *v.t.* to cover with size; to fill, stiffen, or glaze with size.

size, *n.* same as *sice* (dice).

-sīze, same as *-sized.*

sīze'ȧ·ble, *a.* same as *sizable.*

-sīzed, a combining form, usually in hyphenated compounds, meaning *having* (a specified) *size*, as in small-*sized*: also *-size*, as in life-*size.*

sī'zel, *n.* same as *scissel.*

sīz'ēr, *n.* a sizar.

sīz'ēr, *n.* an instrument or contrivance of perforated plates, wirework, etc. having holes through which articles of varying sizes fall; a kind of gauge; as, a coffee *sizer*; a bullet *sizer.*

sīze rōll, a small piece of parchment added to some part of a roll or record.

sīze stick, a measuring stick, used by shoemakers to determine the length of the foot.

sīz'i·ness, *n.* the state or quality of being sizy; glutinousness; viscousness.

sīz'ing, *n.* 1. the act of covering with size.
2. size (glaze or filler).

sīz'ing, *n.* 1. the act of arranging according to size.
2. at Cambridge and other universities, food or drink ordered by a student from the buttery; a size.

sīz'y, *a.* containing, consisting of, or resembling size; glutinous; viscous.

siz'zle, *v.i.*; sizzled, *pt., pp.*; sizzling, *ppr.* [imitative.] to make a hissing sound when in contact with heat, as a drop of water on hot metal.

siz'zle, *v.t.* to burn: with *up.*

siz'zle, *n.* a hissing sound.

siz'zlēr, *n.* something hot, as a hot day. [Colloq.]

sjam'bok (sham'), *n.* a heavy whip used in South Africa.

skag, *n.* same as *skeg.*

skāin, *n.* same as *skean.*

skāin, *n.* same as *skein.*

skāins'māte, *n.* a messmate; a companion. [Obs.]

skāit'bīrd, *n.* a skua, *Megalestris skua.* [Scot.]

skāith, *n.* injury; harm; scathe. [Dial.]

skald, *n.* [ME.; ON. *skāld*; akin to Eng. *scold.*] any ancient Scandinavian poet, specifically one of the Viking period, writing in the complex late Old Norse style: also spelled *scald.*

skald'ic, *a.* of the skalds or their poetry: also spelled *scaldic.*

skāll, *v.t.* to climb; to scale. [Obs.]

skat, *n.* [G.; from It. *scartare*, to discard.] a card game played by three persons with thirty-two cards, the odd two forming the skat, which is laid separately, but may be taken into his hand by one of the players.

skāte, *n.* 1. a worthless fellow; a pretender; an impostor; as, a cheap *skate.* [Slang.]
2. a worn-out old horse. [Slang.]

skāte, *n.* [from D. *schaats*, a shake; OFr. *escache.*]
1. (a) a bladelike metal runner mounted in a frame having clamps and straps for fastening it to the sole of a shoe and used for gliding on ice; (b) a shoe with such a runner permently attached: also *ice skate.*
2. a similar frame or shoe with a pair of small wheels near the toe and another pair at the heel, for gliding on a hardwood floor or other smooth surface: also *roller skate.*

skāte, *v.i.*; skated, *pt., pp.*; skating, *ppr.* to move along or glide on or as on skates.

skāte, *n.*; *pl.* **skāte, skātes,** [ME. *scate*; ON. *skata*; said to be from L. *squatus*, flat fish.] any of several salt-water food fishes of the genus *Raia*, with a broad, flat body. *Raia batis*, the common skate of Europe, often attains a weight of 200 pounds. *Raia lævis*, the barn-door skate of the United States, is about four feet long.

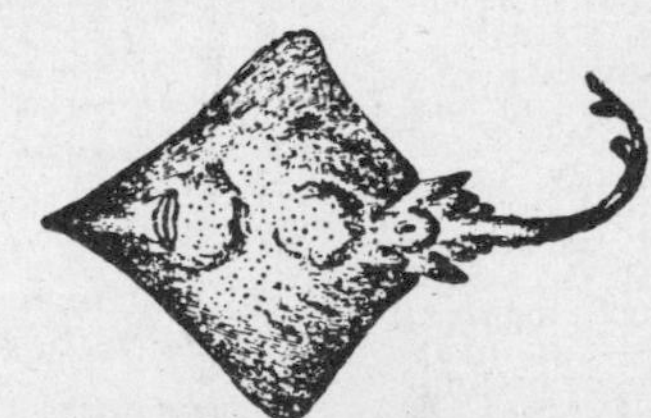

GRAY SKATE (*Raia batis*)

skāt'ēr, *n.* 1. one who skates.
2. a long-limbed aquatic insect which runs about on the surface of water as if skating.

skāt'ing, *n.* the act or art of moving on skates.

skāt'ing rink, a surface or area specially prepared or set aside for skating.

skat'ōl, *n.* skatole.

skat'ōle, *n.* [Gr. *skōr, skatos*, dung, and *-ole.*] a foul-smelling crystalline substance, C_9H_9N, produced by the decomposition of proteins, as in the intestine.

skȧ·tox'yl, *n.* an oxidation product of skatole, C_9H_9NO, found in some cases of intestinal disease.

skāyles, *n.* a game like skittles. [Obs.]

skēan, *n.* [Gael. and Ir. *sgian*, a knife.] a two-edged, bronze dagger formerly used in Ireland and Scotland.

skē·dad'dle, *v.i.*; skedaddled, *pt., pp.*; skedaddling, *ppr.* [etym. unknown.] to leave in a hurry; to go or run away. [Colloq.]

skē·dad'dle, *n.* a running or scurrying away. [Colloq.]

skee, *n.* and *v.i.*; skeed, *pt., pp.*; skeeing, *ppr.* ski.

skeed, *n.* same as *skid.*

skeel, *n.* [ME. *skele*, from ON. *skjōla*, a pail.] a shallow wooden vessel for holding milk or cream. [Obs.]

skeel duck, same as *sheldrake.*

skeel goose, same as *shelduck.*

skeel'ing, *n.* [Ice., *skyling*, a screen or cover.]
1. an outhouse; a shed. [Brit.]
2. a bay of a barn. [Obs.]
3. the side of an attic under a slope of a roof. [Brit. Dial.]

skeen, *n.* a skean. [Scot.]

skeet, *n.* a long scoop formerly used to wet the sails of sailing vessels.

skeet, *n.* a form of trapshooting in which the shooter fires from eight different angles at clay targets thrown from traps to simulate birds in flight.

skeg, *n.* a wild plum. [Brit. Dial.]

skeg, *n.* [D. *schegge,* from ON. *skegg,* a beard.] in nautical usage, the afterpart of the keel, or an extension of this upon which the rudder post is mounted.

skeg, *n.* a kind of oats. [Brit. Dial.]

skeg′gẽr, *n.* a young salmon; a parr.

skein, *n.* [ME. *skeyn;* OFr. *esca(i)gne.*]
1. a quantity of thread, silk, or yarn wound in a coil.
2. something like this, as a coil of hair.
3. a flock of wild birds, as geese or ducks, in flight.

skel′dẽr, *n.* a vagrant; a swindler. [Obs.]

skel′dẽr, *v.t.* and *v.i.* to swindle; to trick; to play the swindler. [Obs.]

skel′drāke, *n.* 1. same as *sheldrake.* [Brit. Dial.]
2. a bird, the oyster catcher. [Brit. Dial.]

skel′et, *n.* a mummy; also, a skeleton. [Obs.]

skel′ē·tăl, *a.* relating to or having the nature of a skeleton; forming part of a skeleton.

skel′ē·tin, *n.* any one of a number of gelatinous nitrogenous substances occurring in invertebrate tissue, and including chitin, sericin, spongin, etc.

skel·ē·tog′ē·nous, *a.* producing or forming a skeleton or parts of a skeleton.

skel′ē·tŏn, *n.* [Gr., a mummy or dried body.]
1. the hard framework of an animal body for supporting the tissues and protecting the organs; specifically, all the bones collectively, or the bony framework, of a human being or other vertebrate animal.
2. anything like a skeleton in any of various ways; specifically, (a) a very lean or emaciated person or animal; (b) a supporting framework, as of a ship; (c) an outline or preliminary sketch, as of a novel; (d) the meager or devitalized remains of something.

HUMAN SKELETON

skeleton at the feast; a person or event that brings gloom or sadness to an occasion of joy or celebration.
skeleton in the closet; some fact about a member of a family, etc. kept secret because of shame or fear of disgrace.

skel′ē·tŏn, *a.* consisting of or having the character of a skeleton; as, a *skeleton* sermon.
skeleton key; a key having a large part of the bit filed away so that it can be used to open a number of locks as a master key.
skeleton leaf; the fibrous part of a leaf which remains when the pulpy substance is removed.
skeleton proof; in engraving, a proof of a print or engraving with the inscription outlined in hair strokes only, such proofs being earlier than others.
skeleton regiment; a regiment in which the officers are retained after the men are disbanded, with a view to future service.
skeleton shrimp; a slender crustacean of the family *Caprellidae;* a specter shrimp.
skeleton suit; a suit of clothes consisting of a tight-fitting jacket and pair of trousers, the trousers being buttoned to the jacket.

skel′ē·tŏn·īze, *v.t.;* skeletonized, *pt., pp.;* skeletonizing, *ppr.* 1. to reduce (a body) to a skeleton.
2. to outline; sketch briefly.
3. to reduce greatly in number or size, as an office force.

skel′ē·tŏn·ī·zẽr, *n.* an insect that skeletonizes leaves by eating the parenchyma.

skel′lọch, *n.* [ON. *skella,* to clash, rattle.] a shrill cry. [Scot.]

skel′lọch, *n.* [Gael. *sgeallag,* wild mustard.] wild mustard or wild radish; charlock: also spelled *skeldock.* [Scot.]

skel′lum, *n.* [G. *schelm.*] a scoundrel; a rogue; a scamp. [Archaic or Brit. Dial.]

skel′ly, *v.i.* to squint. [Dial.]

skel′ly, *n.* a squint. [Dial.]

skel′ly, *n.* 1. a chaffinch.
2. a fish, the chub. [Brit. Dial.]

skelp, *v.t.* to thrash; to strike, especially with the open hand. [Scot.]

skelp, *n.* [echoic.]
1. a blow; a smart stroke. [Brit. Dial.]
2. a heavy rainstorm; a squall. [Scot.]

skelp, *n.* a thin bar of steel or iron, which is bent, welded, and drawn to form tubing.

skel′tẽr, *v.i.* to hasten; to run pellmell. [Dial.]

sken, *v.i.* to squint. [Brit. Dial.]

skēne, *n.* a short sword or knife; a skean.

skep, *n.* [AS. *scep,* from ON. *skeppa,* a bushel.]
1. a sort of wicker or wood basket, narrow at the bottom and wide at the top.
2. the amount held by such a basket.
3. a straw beehive.
4. a ladle or dipper.

skep′tiç, sçep′tiç, *a.* [OFr. *sceptique,* from Gr. *skeptikos,* thoughtful, inquiring.] skeptical: used especially in philosophy.

skep′tiç, sçep′tiç, *n.* 1. [S-] a member of any of the ancient Greek philosophical schools which denied the possibility of real knowledge of any kind.
2. a person who believes in or practices philosophical skepticism.
3. a person who habitually doubts, questions, or suspends judgment upon matters generally accepted.
4. a person who doubts religious doctrines, especially those of Christianity.

skep′ti·çăl, sçep′ti·çăl, *a.* 1. of or characteristic of skeptics or skepticism.
2. not easily persuaded or convinced; doubting; questioning.
3. doubting the fundamental doctrines of religion.

skep′ti·çăl·ly, sçep′ti·çăl·ly, *adv.* in a skeptical manner.

skep′ti·çăl·ness, sçep′ti·çăl·ness, *n.* a skeptical quality or state; doubt.

skep′ti·cişm, sçep′ti·cişm, *n.* [Fr. *scepticisme.*]
1. the philosophical doctrine that the truth of all knowledge must always be in question and that inquiry must be a process of doubting.
2. a skeptical or doubting attitude or state of mind.
3. doubt or disbelief with regard to the doctrines of Christianity.

skep′ti·cīze, sçep′ti·cīze, *v.i.* to act the skeptic; to doubt; to practice skepticism.

skẽrl′ing, *n.* a young salmon. [Brit. Dial.]

sker′ry, *n.; pl.* **sker′ries,** [O.N. *sker.*] a rocky island; a reef. [Scot.]

sketch, *n.* [D. *schets,* from It. *schizzo,* a sketch, from L. *schedius,* Gr. *schedios,* offhand, sudden.]
1. a simple, rough drawing or design, done rapidly and without much detail.
2. a brief plan or description of major parts or points; an outline.
3. a short, light, informal story, description, play, or piece of music.
4. in painting, a copy from nature only sufficiently finished for the artist to secure materials for a picture; an outline of a building or street view; a transcript of the human figure in pencil or chalk, with simple shades only, or a rough draft of the same in colors.

sketch, *v.t.;* sketched (sketcht), *pt., pp.;* sketching, *ppr.* 1. to draw the outline or general figure of; to make a rough draft of; to describe quickly.
2. to describe by giving the principal points or ideas of; to delineate; to depict.

sketch, *v.i.* to make a sketch or sketches; to draw in outline.

sketch′book, *n.* 1. a book of drawing paper for making sketches.
2. a book of literary sketches.
Also *sketch book.*

sketch′ẽr, *n.* one who sketches.

sketch′i·ly, *adv.* in a sketchy manner.

sketch′i·ness, *n.* the state or quality of being sketchy.

sketch′y, *a.; comp.* sketchier; *superl.* sketchiest, 1. having the form of a sketch; presenting only major parts or points; not detailed.
2. lacking completeness or thoroughness; rough; inadequate.

skēte, *n.* [Gr. *skētē,* from *skētis,* lower Egyptian desert renowned for its hermits.] a community of monks or hermits of the Greek Church.

skew (skū), *adv.* awry; obliquely; askew. [Rare.]

skew, *v.t.;* skewed, *pt., pp.;* skewing, *ppr.* [O. Norm. Fr. *escuer,* varied, from OFr. *eschiuver.*]
1. to move obliquely.
2. to turn suddenly aside; to shy.
3. to squint; to glance sideways (with *at*). [Dial.]
4. to escape; to slip away. [Obs.]

skew, *v.t.* 1. to make slanting or oblique.
2. to bias, distort, or pervert.

skew, *a.* 1. oblique; turned to one side; twisted.
2. having such a part, as gearing.
3. not symmetrical.
skew arch; an arch with jambs not at right angles with the face, as in a vault or tunnel which narrows or widens from its opening.
skew corbel; in architecture, a stone built into the bottom of a gable to support the skews or coping above.
skew curve; a curve of which no two consecutive portions lie in the same plane.
skew determinant; a determinant, each element of which in any column is equal to the corresponding element of the corresponding row with the reverse sign.
skew gearing; a form of bevel gearing for shafts lying at an angle to each other and in different planes.
skew surface; a surface generated by a straight line moving in such a manner that no two successive positions intersect.

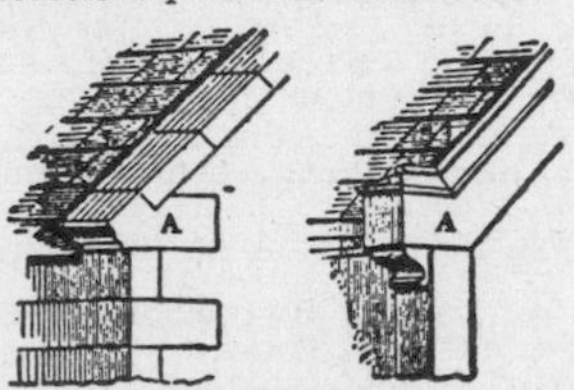

A A. SKEW CORBELS

skew, *n.* 1. a skew corbel.
2. the sloping top of a buttress where it slants off into a wall; the coping of a gable.
3. a slanting part or movement.
4. a skew motion, glance, or idea; a perversion or twist.

skew′back, *n.* 1. the slanting surface which slopes to receive the end of a segmental arch.
2. a supporting piece, as a stone, with such a surface.

skew′bạld, *a.* [from ME. *skewed,* piebald.] irregularly marked with white and a color other than black, as a horse.

skew′ẽr, *n.* [formerly written *skiver,* from O.N. *skifa,* a slice.]
1. a pin of wood or iron for fastening meat to a spit, or for holding it together while roasting.
2. any of several things shaped or used like a meat skewer.

skew′ẽr, *v.t.* to fasten with or as with skewers; to pierce.

skew′ẽr·wood, *n.* the European dogwood, *Cornus sanguinea,* and the European spindle tree or prickwood, *Euonymus europæus,* from each of which skewers are made. [Brit. Dial.]

skew′ness, *n.* 1. the fact or condition of being skew, or unsymmetrical.
2. in statistics, deviation of the curve for a frequency distribution from the symmetrical curve for such a distribution.

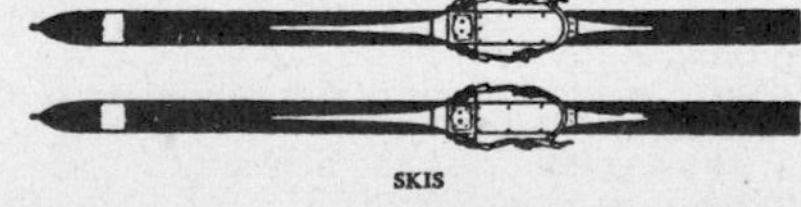
SKIS

skī (*also Norw.* shē), *n.; pl.* **skis** (*or* shēs), **skī,** [Norw.; O.N. *skith,* snowshoe.] one of a pair of long, thin, wooden runners that can be fastened to the feet for traveling on snow: also *skee.*

skī, *v.i.;* skied (skēd), *pt., pp.,* skiing, *ppr.* 1. to travel on skis by gliding over the snow.
2. to engage in the sport of gliding down snow-covered inclines on skis.
Also *skee.*

skī′a-, [from Greek *skia,* a shadow] a combining form meaning *shadow, image, form.*

skī′ȧ·gram, *n.* [*skia-* and *-gram.*] a skiagraph: also spelled *sciagram, skiogram.*

skī′ȧ·gràph, *n.* [Gr. *skia,* a shadow, and *graphein,* to write.] a picture made of shadows, especially those cast on a sensitized surface by X rays: also spelled *sciagraph, sciograph, skiograph.*

skī'ȧ·grȧph, *v.t.* to make a skiagraph of: also spelled *sciagraph, sciograph, skiograph.*

skī·ag'rȧ·phy, *n.* 1. the art or practice of making skiagraphs, especially by X ray.

2. in architecture, the profile or vertical section of a building to exhibit its interior structure. [Obs.]

3. in astronomy, the art of finding the hour of the day or night by the shadows of objects caused by the sun, moon, or stars; the art of dialing.

skī'ȧ·sçōpe, *n.* the instrument used in skiascopy; a retinoscope.

skī·as'çō·py, *n.* [*skia-*, and Gr. *skopein*, to view.] a method for refracting an eye by illuminating the retina with a skiascope and observing the movements of light and shadow on the pupil; retinoscopy.

skid, *n.* [ME. *schide*; AS. *scid*; O.N. *skith*, a billet of wood.]

1. a plank, log, etc., often one of a pair or set, used as a support or as a track upon which to slide or roll a heavy object.

2. a low, wooden platform for holding loads or stacks.

3. [*pl.*] a wooden structure placed against the side of a ship to protect it from damage, as when unloading.

4. the brake of a crane.

5. a shoe or drag used for preventing the wheels of a wagon or carriage from revolving when descending a hill; a skidpan.

6. a runner used in place of a wheel on an aircraft landing gear.

7. the act of skidding.

on the skids; about to meet with some misfortune; falling from power; losing prestige, etc. [Slang.]

skid, *v.t.*; skidded, *pt., pp.*; skidding, *ppr.* 1. to brake or lock (a wheel) with a skid.

2. to support with or slide on a skid or skids.

3. to cause (a wheel, vehicle, etc.) to slide or skid, as on ice.

skid, *v.i.* 1. to slide without turning, as a wheel when skids or brakes are applied on a slippery surface.

2. to slide or slip sideways, as a vehicle when not gripping the road on ice or in a fast turn.

3. in aeronautics, to move sideways and outward while turning, as a result of failing to bank sufficiently.

skid chāin, a chain or arrangement of chains attached to the tire of an automobile to increase the traction and reduce skidding.

skid·dọọ', *v.i.* [from *skedaddle*.] to go away: used imperatively. [Slang.]

skid fin, in aeronautics, a longitudinal fin placed edge upright, usually along the top wing of a biplane, to reduce skidding.

skid'pan, *n.* same as *skid*, n. 5.

skid'prọọf, *a.* that prevents skidding, as an automobile tire, a road surface, etc.

skid rōw, a section of a city frequented by hobos, vagrants, derelicts, etc. [Slang.]

skid'wāy, *n.* a line of parallel skids.

skīed (skīd), *v.* past tense of *sky*; also (skēd), past tense of *ski*.

skī'ẽr, *n.* a person who skis.

skī'ey, *a.* same as *skyey*.

skiff, *n.* [OFr. *esquif*, a skiff, from It. *schifo*, skiff.]

1. any light rowboat.

2. a long, narrow rowboat, especially one with a centerboard, outrigger, and a small sail.

skiff, *v.t.* and *v.i.* to travel or navigate in a skiff.

skif'fling, *n.* in a quarry, knocking off the larger knobs or corners as a rough first shaping; knobbing.

skī'ing, *n.* the act or sport of traveling or gliding on skis.

skī·jōr'ing, *n.* a winter sport in which a person on skis is drawn over the ice or snow, usually by a horse or automobile.

skī jump, 1. a jump made by a person wearing skis.

2. an incline or track used for such jumping, especially as a competitive sport.

skil'dẽr, *v.i.* to live by begging or pilfering; to skelder. [Scot. and Brit. Dial.]

skil'fụl, *a.* same as *skillful*.

skil'fụl·ly, *adv.* same as *skillfully*.

skil'fụl·ness, *n.* same as *skillfulness*.

skill, *n.* [O.N. *skil*, discernment, knowledge, a distinction; akin to *skilja*, to separate, to divide.]

1. great ability or proficiency; expertness; as, his *skill* in mathematics is well known.

2. an art, craft, or science, especially one involving the use of the hands or body.

3. ability in such an art, craft, or science.

4. knowledge; understanding; judgment. [Obs.]

Syn.—dexterity, adroitness, expertness, art, aptitude, ability, ingenuity, wisdom.

skill, *v.t.* to know; to understand. [Dial.]

skill, *v.i.* 1. to be knowing; to be dexterous in performance. [Obs.]

2. to differ; to make a difference; to matter or be of interest. [Archaic.]

skilled, *a.* 1. having skill; skillful.

2. having or requiring an ability, as in a particular industrial occupation, machine operation, etc., gained by special experience or a regular program of training or apprenticeship; as, a toolmaker is a *skilled* workman.

skil'less, *a.* without skill; inexpert; inexperienced.

skil'let, *n.* [OFr. *escuellette*, dim. of *escuelle*; Fr. *écuelle*, a porringer, basin, from L. *scutella*, dim. of *scutra*, a dish.]

1. a round, shallow cooking utensil; a frying pan.

2. a small, heavy, deep kettle of iron or other metal for culinary use, having a long handle and sometimes legs; a stew pan.

skill'fụl, *a.* 1. knowing; well-versed in any art; expert; able in management; able to perform dexterously any manual operation in the arts or professions; as, a *skillful* mechanic; a *skillful* operator in surgery.

2. exhibiting or due to skill; revealing dexterity and intelligence; as, a *skillful* operation.

skill'fụl·ly, *adv.* in a skillful manner.

skill'fụl·ness, *n.* the state or quality of being skillful.

skil''li·gȧ·lee', *n.* a thin, watery gruel, usually of oatmeal. [Brit. Slang.]

skil'ling, *n.* same as *skeeling*.

skil'ling, *n.* [Sw. and Dan., shilling.] formerly, a Scandinavian and North German copper coin or money of account, ranging in value from three-fourths of a cent in Norway to a little over two cents in Hamburg.

skilts, *n.pl.* [prob. variant of *kilt*.] a kind of wide, coarse, short trousers formerly worn in New England. [Dial.]

skim, *v.t.*; skimmed, *pt., pp.*; skimming, *ppr.* [OFr. *escumer*, lit., to scum, from O.H.G. *scum*.]

1. to clear (a liquid) of floating matter; as, he *skimmed* the milk of its cream.

2. to remove (floating matter) from a liquid; as, *skim* cream from the milk.

3. to coat or cover with a thin layer; as, a pond *skimmed* with ice.

4. to look at hastily or carelessly; to glance through a book, etc. without reading word for word.

5. to glide or pass swiftly and lightly over.

6. to cause to move in this way; as, he *skimmed* a flat stone across the creek.

skim, *v.i.* 1. to glide along over the surface; to pass lightly through space; to sail.

2. to apply the finishing coat of plaster.

3. to make a rapid or careless examination, as of a book (usually with *over* or *through*).

4. to become thinly coated, as with scum.

skim'ble-sçam''ble, *a.* [a reduplication of *scamble*.] wandering; disorderly; incoherent.

skim'ble-sçam''ble, *n.* incoherent talk; nonsense; rigmarole.

skim çōat, the thin coat of plaster put on as a finish.

skim çōl'tẽr, a colter for paring off the surface of land.

skīme, *v.i.* to scowl or leer. [Scot.]

skim'mẽr, *n.* 1. one who or that which skims.

2. a utensil for skimming liquids.

BLACK SKIMMER (*Rhynchops nigra*)

3. any of several long-winged sea birds that skim over the water in search of food, as the American black skimmer, *Rhynchops nigra*: also called *cutwater, scissorbill, shearwater.*

skim'mẽr·tŏn, *n.* same as *skimmington*.

Skim'mi·ȧ, *n.* [Japan. *skimmi*.] a genus of Oriental evergreen shrubs of a polypetalous character.

skim milk, milk from which the cream has been removed.

skim'ming, *n.* 1. the act of taking from the surface, as cream from milk.

2. the act of gliding lightly along near the surface.

3. [*usually pl.*] anything that has been skimmed from the surface of a liquid; scum.

skim'ming dish, a flat-bottomed yacht built for speed.

skim'ming·ly, *adv.* with a skimming motion.

skim'ming·tŏn, *n.* a public ridicule of a henpecked husband or a shrewish wife, as in the phrase *to ride skimmington*, to be derided in this way by being forced to ride on a horse, followed by a procession playing rough music, with frying pans, bulls' horns, marrow bones, cleavers, etc.: also written *skimington, skimmerton, skimmily*. [Archaic.]

skimp, *a.* [prob. altered from *scrimp*.] scanty. [Colloq.]

skimp, *v.t.*; skimped (skimt), *pt., pp.*; skimping, *ppr.* 1. to give scant, insufficient, or illiberal measure or allowance to; to curtail the expenses of unduly.

2. to do poorly or carelessly.

skimp, *v.i.* 1. to give or allow too little; to be stingy; to scrimp. [Colloq.]

2. to keep expenses very low; as, we *skimped* to save money. [Colloq.]

skimp'i·ly, *adv.* in a skimpy manner; so as to be skimpy.

skimp'i·ness, *n.* the quality or condition of being skimpy.

skimp'y, *a.*; *comp.* skimpier; *superl.* skimpiest. 1. barely or not quite enough; somewhat less in size, fullness, etc. than is needed; scanty.

2. stingy.

skin, *n.* [ME. *skynn*; ON. *skinn*, akin to G. *schinden*, to peel.]

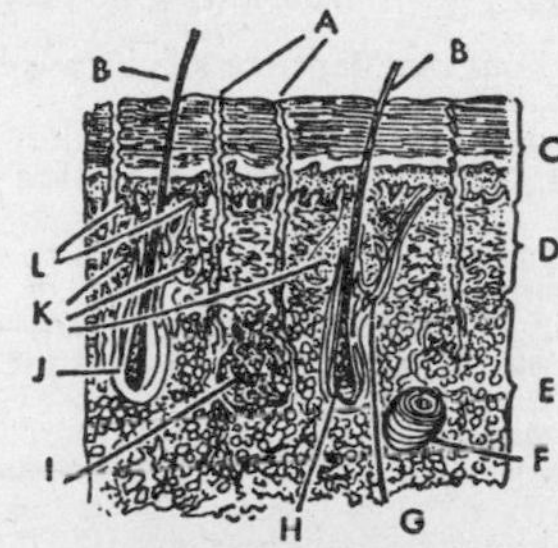

CROSS SECTION OF SKIN

A, ducts of sweat glands; B, B, hairs; C, epidermis; D, corium; E, subcutaneous fatty tissue; F, oblique section through a Pacinian corpuscle; G, erector muscle of hair; H, papilla of hair; I, glomerulus of sweat gland; J, hair follicle; K, sebaceous glands; L, papillae of corium

1. the external covering or integument of most animals, in all vertebrates consisting of two layers, an outer and an inner. The outer layer, called the *epidermis, cuticle*, or *scarfskin*, is without nerves and blood vessels, and is nonsensitive; the inner layer, called the *dermis, corium*, or *true skin*, is highly vascular and sensitive.

2. a hide; a pelt; the skin of an animal, especially of a small animal, separated from the body; a hide or pelt, whether green, dry, or tanned.

3. (a) a piece of parchment consisting of the skin of an animal; (b) an animal hide used as a vessel for holding liquids; as, a wine *skin*.

4. the bark or husk of a plant; the exterior rind of fruit or plants; as, the *skin* of an apple.

5. the outside of a furled sail that forms its cover.

6. the shell or plating of a ship.

7. a dishonest person; a sharper; one who cheats; also, anything unfair. [Slang.]

8. a miserly person; a skinflint. [Slang.]

9. the thin film of hard metal on the surface of a casting or forging, owing to the chilling or hardening of such surfaces against the sand, in contact with the air, etc.

10. a film or scum, as that which forms on boiling milk.

11. the outermost nacreous layer in a pearl.

by the skin of one's teeth; by the least possible margin; by merest chance.

in (or *with*) *a whole skin*; without injury. [Colloq.]

skin friction; the friction between a fluid and the surface of a solid in motion through it.

skin game; (a) a crooked or fraudulent game of chance; (b) any cheating, swindling trick. [Colloq.]

skin grafting; the surgical transplanting of skin from another part of the body or from another person to replace skin destroyed, as by burning.

skin resistance; the resistance caused by skin friction, as that to a ship in motion through the water.

skin wool; wool pulled from the dead skin.

to be no skin off one's back; to affect one not at all; to be of no concern to one. [Slang.]

to get under one's skin; to anger, irritate, or annoy one. [Slang.]

to have a thick skin; to be undisturbed by criticism, insults, etc.; to be callous or insensitive.

to have a thin skin; to be acutely sensitive to blame, criticism, insults, etc.

to save one's skin; to avoid death or injury. [Colloq.]

to skin alive; (a) to remove the skin from (a living person or animal); (b) [Colloq.] to scold or punish severely; (c) [Colloq.] to overcome or defeat decisively.

skin, *v.t.*; skinned, *pt., pp.*; skinning, *ppr.* 1. to cover with or as with skin; to grow skin on.
2. to remove skin from.
3. to strip or peel off, as or like skin.
4. to defraud or cheat; to swindle. [Colloq.]

skin, *v.i.* 1. to be or become covered with skin; as, a wound *skins* over.
2. to do any fraudulent act. [Slang.]
3. to lose the skin; to shed.
4. to run away; to depart quickly: used with *out*; as, the absconder *skinned out.* [Slang.]

skin'bound, *a.* with skin drawn tight over the flesh.

skinch, *v.t.* [akin to *skimp, scant.*] to stint; to scrimp; to give short allowance. [Brit. Dial.]

skin'-deep', *a.* 1. penetrating no deeper than the skin.
2. without real depth or significance; superficial; shallow.

skin'-deep', *adv.* so as to be only skin-deep.

skin'flick, *n.* a pornographic motion picture. [Slang.]

skin'flint, *n.* [from thieves' slang; lit., one who would skin a flint for the sake of gain or economy.] a niggardly person; a miser.

skin'ful, *n.*; *pl.* **skin'fuls,** 1. as much liquid as a skin container can hold.
2. as much as the stomach can hold; a bellyful. [Colloq.]

skin'head, *n.* 1. a person who is bald or has his hair shaved off or closely cropped. [Slang.]
2. any of a group of working-class British youth of the late 1960's and the 1970's with closely cropped hair, often engaging in rowdyism. [Slang.]

skink, *n.* drink; pottage. [Archaic.]

skink, *v.i.* to draw or serve drink. [Archaic.]

skink, *v.t.* to serve out or draw, as liquor; to pour out for drinking. [Archaic.]

skink, *n.* [L. *scincus*, from Gr. *skinkos*, a kind of lizard.] any of several lizards belonging to the genus *Scincus*. They have a long body entirely covered with rounded imbricate scales, and are native to warm climates. One species, the adda, *Scincus officinalis*, was formerly reputed throughout the East to be efficacious in the cure of various cutaneous diseases. It is about six inches long, has a cylindrical body and tail, and burrows in the sand.

ADDA OR COMMON SKINK (*Scincus officinalis*)

skin'less, *a.* without a skin; as, *skinless* fruit.

skinned (skind), *a.* having a (specified kind of) skin: usually in hyphenated compounds, as *dark-skinned.*

skin'nẽr, *n.* 1. one who skins.
2. one who deals in or processes skins, pelts, or hides.
3. one who cheats; a swindler.
4. a driver of mules or horses. [Colloq.]
5. [S–] one of a roaming band of adventurers active during the American Revolution.

Skin'nẽr box, [after B. F. *Skinner* (1904–), American psychologist who invented it.] an enclosure in which small animals, as rats or pigeons, are conditioned by rewards and punishments to perform certain acts in response to specific stimuli.

skin'ni·ness, *n.* the quality or state of being skinny.

skin'ny, *a.*; *comp.* skinnier; *superl.* skinniest, 1. of or like skin.
2. without much flesh; emaciated; thin.

skin'-pop, *v.t.*; skin-popped, *pt., pp.*; skin-popping, *ppr.* to inject (a narcotic drug) subcutaneously: cf. *mainline.* [Slang.]

skin'-pop·pẽr, *n.* one who skin-pops. [Slang.]

skin'-tight' (-tīt'), *a.* clinging closely to the skin; tight-fitting, as a garment.

skip, *v.i.*; skipped (skipt), *pt., pp.*; skipping, *ppr.* [ME. *skippen* (prob. from ON.); cf. earlier Sw. *scuppa, scoppa*, in the same sense.]
1. to leap, jump, or spring lightly; to move along with quick steps and jumps; as, the girls *skipped* gaily by.
2. to be deflected from a surface; to ricochet.
3. to pass, or direct the attention, from one point to another, omitting what lies between.
4. to be promoted in school beyond the next regular grade.
5. to leave hurriedly, especially under questionable circumstances; to abscond. [Colloq.]

skip, *v.t.* 1. to jump or leap lightly over.
2. to pass over without noticing, reading, mentioning, doing, etc.
3. to cause to skip or ricochet.
4. to leave (a place) hurriedly. [Colloq.]
skip it!; never mind! it doesn't matter!

skip, *n.* 1. (a) an act of skipping; a leap; a spring; (b) a skipping gait in which hops and steps are alternated.
2. a passing over or omitting.
3. in music, a passing from one note to another at an interval greater than a second.

skip, *n.* in the games of bowling and curling, an experienced player chosen by each of the rival parties or sides as their leader or captain, and who usually plays the last bowl or stone which his team has to play: also called *skipper.*

skï pants, loose-cut slack trousers that fit tightly around the ankle: used in skiing and other winter sports.

skip'-bomb (-bom), *v.t.* and *v.i.* to fly low and drop bombs so that they explode under water against the side of (a ship or other target).

skip dis'tănce, in radio, the distance along the surface of the earth between the farthest point reached by the ground wave of a transmitting station and the nearest point at which the radio wave is reflected back to the earth from the ionosphere.

skip'jack, *n.*; *pl.* **skip'jacks** or **skip'jack,** 1. an upstart. [Archaic.]
2. any of several beetles of the family *Elateridæ*: so called from their being able to spring into the air and regain their feet when laid on their backs.
3. any of the numerous species of fish that leap out of, or play at the surface of, the water, as the saury, bluefish, bonito, runner, threadfish, etc.
4. a variety of sailboat with broad bows, used on the Atlantic coast.

skip'ken·nel, *n.* a lackey; a footboy. [Obs.]

skip'pẽr, *n.* [M.D. *schipper*, from *schip*, a ship.]
1. the captain of a ship, especially of a small ship.
2. any person who leads or directs.

skip'pẽr, *n.* 1. one who or that which skips.
2. the saury, *Scomberesox saurus.*
3. a young, thoughtless person; a skipjack. [Archaic.]
4. a cheese maggot.
5. any butterfly of the family *Hesperiidæ.*
6. any of various skipping insects.

skip'pet, *n.* a skiff, or small boat. [Obs.]

skip'pet, *n.* [dim. of *skep.*] a small box or envelope used to protect a seal tied to a document.

skip'ping·ly, *adv.* in a skipping manner.

skirl, *n.* [variant of *shrill.*] a shrill sound, specifically that of a bagpipe. [Scot. and Dial.]

skirl, *v.t.* and *v.i.* to sound out in shrill, piercing tones: said especially of a bagpipe. [Scot. and Brit. Dial.]

skir'mish, *n.* [ME. *scarmishe, skrymishe*; OFr. *escarmuche*; It. *scaramuccia.*]
1. a brief fight or encounter carried on between small groups, usually part of a battle or war.
2. any slight conflict; a contention.

They never meet but there's a *skirmish* of wit. —Shak.

skir'mish, *v.i.*; skirmished (-misht), *pt., pp.*; skirmishing, *ppr.* to engage in a skirmish.

skir'mish·ẽr, *n.* 1. one who skirmishes.
2. any of a group of soldiers taking part in a skirmish or spread out in extended order for attack.

skirr, *v.i.* [echoic.] to scurry; to move, fly, or run quickly, especially with a whirring sound.

skirr, *v.t.* 1. to cover or pass through in searching; to scour. [Dial.]
2. to cause to skim or glide, as by throwing. [Dial.]

skirr, *n.* a whirring sound.

skir'ret, *n.* [ME. *skirwhit*, from OFr. *eschervis*; from Ar. *karawya.*] a plant, the water parsnip, *Sium sisarum*, native to China, Korea, Japan, etc., and cultivated in Europe for its esculent tuberous root, which somewhat resembles the parsnip in flavor.

SKIRRET (*Sium sisarum*)

skir'rhus (-rus), *n.* same as *scirrhus.*

skirt, *n.* [ME.; ON. *skyrt*, shirt, *kirtle*, cognate with AS. *scyrte.*]
1. that part of a garment, as of a robe, dress, etc., that hangs below the waist.
2. a woman's garment that hangs from the waist to cover the lower part of the body.
3. something like a skirt, as a flap hanging from the side of a saddle.
4. [*pl.*] the outer parts; border; edge; fringe; outskirts, as of a city.
5. a girl or woman. [Slang.]
6. in butchering, the diaphragm or midriff of animals.

skirt, *v.t.*; skirted, *pt., pp.*; skirting, *ppr.* 1. to lie along or form the border or edge of.
2. to move along the border or edge of; to pass around instead of across or through, as a woods.
3. to border or edge (*with* something).

skirt, *v.i.* to be on, or move along, the edge or border; as, the path *skirts* along the edge of the pond.

skirt dance, a form of ballet dancing characterized by the wavy movements of the dancer's long, flowing skirts.

skirt dan·cẽr, one who performs a skirt dance.

skirt'ing, *n.* 1. the narrow board placed round the margin of a floor.
2. skirts collectively.
3. material from which skirts are made.
4. wool of an inferior quality.

skï run, a slope or course used for skiing.

skit, *n.* [Ice. *skūti*, a taunt, scoff.]
1. a verbal slap; a gibe.
2. a short piece of satirical or humorous writing.
3. a comic theatrical sketch, as in a revue.
4. a silly or wanton girl. [Dial.]

skit, *v.i.*; skitted, *pt., pp.*; skitting, *ppr.* to spring aside; to shy.

skit, *v.t.* to cast aspersions on.

skï tour'ing, *n.* the sport of cross-country skiing.

skï tōw, a motor-driven endless cable which skiers can grasp and be towed up the ski slope on their skis.

skit'tẽr, *v.i.* [freq. of *skit.*]
1. to skip or move along quickly and lightly, especially over water.
2. to draw a fish bait or lure over the surface of the water with a skipping motion.

skit'tẽr, *v.t.* to cause to skitter.

skit'tish, *a.* [from *skit* and *-ish.*]
1. shy; easily frightened; timorous; as, a *skittish* colt, a *skittish* girl.

2. spirited; volatile; playful, especially in a coy manner.

3. changeable; fickle; as, *skittish* fortune.

skit'tish·ly, *adv.* in a skittish manner; shyly; spiritedly; changeably.

skit'tish·ness, *n.* the quality or state of being skittish.

skit'tle, *n.* [prob. from the ON. cognate of *shuttle* with reference to the ball or projectile: cf. Dan. *skyttel*, a shuttle, marble, etc.]

1. [*pl.*; *construed as sing.*] the game of ninepins.

2. any of the pins used in this game.

(*not*) *all beer and skittles*; (not) pure pleasure and enjoyment.

skit'tle al'ley, an oblong court in which the game of skittles is played.

skit'ty, *n.* the water rail, or skitty cock; the spotted rail. [Brit. Dial.]

skīve, *v.t.*; skived, *pt.*, *pp.*; skiving, *ppr.* [ON. *skifa*, akin to Eng. *shive.*]

1. to slice or cut off (leather, rubber, etc.) in thin layers; to shave or pare.

2. to grind away the surface of (a gem).

skīve, *n.* the revolving table or lap used by diamond and other gem polishers in finishing the facets of a gem.

skī'vẽr, *v.t.* [variant of *skewer.*] to impale; to run through; to skewer.

skī'vẽr, *n.* a skewer. [Dial.]

skiv'ẽr, *v.i.* to scatter in a confused manner; to disperse. [Rare.]

skī'vẽr, *n.* [freq. of *skive*, to shave.]

1. a soft, thin leather made from the outer half of split sheepskin, tanned by immersion in sumac and dyed: used for hat linings, pocketbooks, bookbinding, etc.

2. the knife, cutting tool, or machine used in splitting sheepskins.

3. a person who skives leather.

skī'vẽr·wood, *n.* skewerwood.

skī'ving, *n.* 1. the act of one who or that which skives.

2. a shaving from a piece of leather.

skiv'vy, *n.*; *pl.* **skiv'vies,** [from Scot. Gaelic *skaivie*, askew; ON. *skeifr*, crooked.] a man's, especially a sailor's, undershirt or [*pl.*] underwear. [Slang.]

sklent, *n.* and *v.* same as *slant.* [Scot. and Brit. Dial.]

skōal, *interj.* [Dan. and Nor.] to your health!: a toast.

skol'ē·cīte, *n.* same as *scolecite.*

skō'li·on, *n.*; *pl.* **skō'li·ȧ,** [Gr., a song, prob. from *skolios*, curved, winding.] an ancient Greek drinking song sung successively by the guests and accompanied by the lyre.

skonce, *n.* same as *sconce.*

skor'ō·dīte, *n.* same as *scorodite.*

skot'ō·graph, *n.* same as *scotograph.*

skout, *n.* [Am. Ind.] the guillemot.

skrael'ling (skrel'), *n.* an American Indian or Eskimo: a name given by early Norse explorers.

skrīke, *v.t.* and *v.i.* to shriek. [Obs.]

skrike, *n.* [variant of *shriek.*] a mistlethrush. [Brit. Dial.]

skrimp, *v.t.* same as *scrimp.*

skringe, *v.i.* same as *scringe.*

skū'ȧ, *n.* [adapted (c. 1604) from Faroese *skūgver*, from ON. *skūfr*; prob. so called from the dark color.] any of several large, brown, northern sea birds related to the gulls; a jaeger: they rob other birds of their food: also *skua gull.*

skūe, *v.i.* to skew. [Obs.]

skug, *v.t.* to protect; to shelter; to hide. [Scot.]

skug, *n.* the declivity of a hill; a place of shelter. [Scot.]

skul·dud'dẽr·y, *n.* grossness; obscenity. [Scot.]

skul·dug'gẽr·y, *n.* [Early Mod. Scot. *sculduddrie*; OFr. (hyp.) *escoulourgie*, a slipping, from *escoulourgier*, to slip.] mean, contemptible actions; plotting; trickery. [Colloq.]

skulk, *v.i.*; skulked (skulkt), *pt.*, *pp.*; skulking, *ppr.* [ME. *sculken* (prob. from ON.); cf. Dan. *skulke*, to sneak, to skulk.]

1. to move or lurk about in a stealthy, craven manner; to slink.

2. to avoid work or responsibility; to shirk; malinger.

skulk, *n.* a skulker.

skulk'ẽr, *n.* a person who skulks or avoids performing duties.

skulk'ing·ly, *adv.* in a skulking manner.

skull, *n.* [ME. *scolle*, of Scand. origin.]

1. the bony framework of the head, enclosing and protecting the brain.

2. the head regarded as the seat of thought or intelligence: usually with derogatory allusion; as, thick *skull*, empty *skull.*

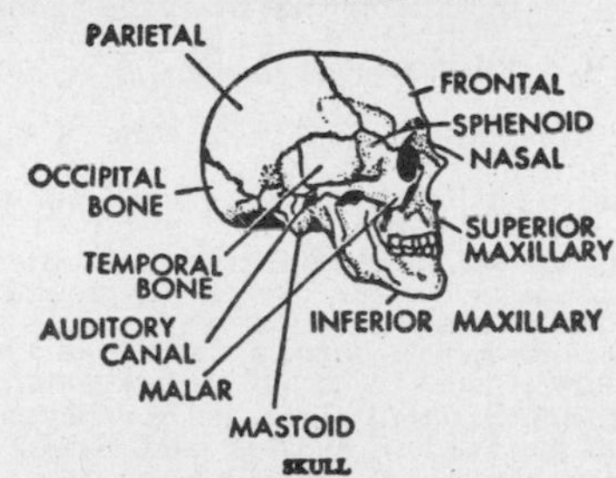

SKULL

skull and çross'bōnes, a human skull facing forward with two long bones crossed beneath it, as formerly pictured on pirates' flags: now used as a warning sign, as in labeling poisons.

skull'çap, *n.* 1. a light, brimless cap fitting closely to the head or skull, especially for indoor wear.

2. in anatomy, the sinciput.

3. a plant of the genus *Scutellaria.*

skull'fish, *n.* a whale more than two years of age.

skull praç'tice (or **ses'sion**), a class session, as of a football team, at which plays are studied and discussed. [Slang.]

skuñk, *n.*; *pl.* **skuñks** or **skuñk,** [contr. from Am.Ind. *segonku.*]

1. a digitigrade carnivorous quadruped of genus *Mephitis*, family *Mustelidæ*, having a bushy tail and glossy black fur, usually with white stripes down its back: it has two glands near the inferior extremity of the alimentary canal, which secrete an extremely offensive-smelling fluid, which the animal ejects when molested.

SKUNK (about 2 ft. long)

2. a despicable, offensive person. [Colloq.]

skuñk, *v.t.*; skunked, *pt.*, *pp.*; skunking, *ppr.* to defeat overwhelmingly and prevent from scoring in a game or contest. [Slang.]

skuñk beär, the wolverine.

skuñk'bill, *n.* the surf duck.

skuñk bird, the bobolink or ricebird: so called from its colors: also called *skunk blackbird.*

skuñk çab'bāge, a North American perennial herb, *Symplocarpus fœtidus*, with thick roots and wide leaves, and a disagreeable smell.

skuñk'ish, *a.* 1. having an offensive odor, like that of the skunk.

2. like or pertaining to a skunk.

skuñk pọr'poise (-pus), a North Atlantic porpoise, *Lagenorhynchus acutus*, having stripes of white and yellow on its sides.

skuñk'weed, *n.* skunk cabbage.

skūr'ry, *n.* and *v.* same as *scurry.*

skut'tẽr·ud·īte, *n.* [from *Skutterud*, Norway, where the crystals are found, and *-ite.*] a pale-gray lustrous mineral composed of arsenic and cobalt, $CoAs_3$.

skȳ, *n.*; *pl.* **skīes,** [ME. *sky, skye*; ON. *sky*, cloud; akin to AS. *scūa*, a shade or shadow.]

1. [*often pl.*] the upper atmosphere, especially with reference to its appearance; as, blue *skies*, a cloudy *sky.*

2. the expanse of the heavens, apparently arching over the earth; the firmament.

3. heaven; celestial regions.

4. climate; weather; as, the balmy southern *sky.*

out of a clear sky; without warning; suddenly.
to the skies; without reserve; extravagantly.

skȳ, *v.t.*; skied, *pt.*, *pp.*; skying, *ppr.* 1. to hit, throw, shoot, etc. high in the air. [Colloq.]

2. to hang (a picture) high up on the wall, especially in an exhibition. [Colloq.]

skȳ'-blūe', *a.* of the color sky blue.

skȳ blūe, a blue color like that of the sky on a clear day.

skȳ'-bọrn, *a.* born or produced in the sky; of heavenly origin.

skȳ'çap, *n.* a porter, or redcap, at an air terminal.

skȳ çŏl'ŏr, same as *sky blue.*

skȳ dīv'ing, the sport of jumping from an airplane and executing free-fall maneuvers before opening the parachute, often at the last possible moment.

Skȳe ter'ri·ẽr, [after the Isle of *Skye*, Scotland.] a small dog of the terrier breed, with shaggy hair, a long body, and short legs.

SKYE TERRIER
(9 in. high at shoulder)

skȳ'ey, *a.* 1. of or like the sky, as a shade of blue. [Poet.]

2. of great height; lofty. [Poet.]

skȳ'-gāz"ẽr, *n.* 1. a skysail. [Rare.]

2. a fish of the family *Uranoscopidæ*; a stargazer.

skȳ'-hīgh' (-hī), *a.* and *adv.* of or to a great height; very high.

skȳ'ish, *a.* like the sky; skyey. [Rare.]

skȳ'jack, *v.t.*; skyjacked, *pt.*, *pp.*; skyjacking, *ppr.* to hijack (an aircraft). [Colloq.]

skȳ'jack·ẽr, *n.* a person who skyjacks. [Colloq.]

Skȳ'lab, *n.* [*sky*, and *lab*oratory.] an American space station (May 14, 1973 – July 11, 1979) orbiting the earth and carrying alternating crews of astronauts, who conducted scientific experiments and made astronomical and meteorological observations.

skȳ'lärk, *n.* the Old World lark, famous for the song it utters as it soars toward the sky.

Australian skylark; an Australian oscine bird resembling the European skylark.

Missouri skylark; an American bird, *Anthus spraguei*, whose flight and note suggest the skylark.

skȳ'lärk, *v.i.* to play about boisterously; to frolic.

skȳ'lärk"ing, *n.* [*sky* and *lark*, to play.] the act of running or gamboling about in the rigging of a vessel in sport; hence, frolicking; tricks or games of any kind.

skȳ'līght (-līt), *n.* a window in a roof or ceiling.

skȳ'līne, *n.* 1. the line along which the sky seems to touch the earth; the visible horizon.

2. the outline, as of a city, seen against the sky.

Also *sky line.*

skȳ mär'shăl, a Federal officer assigned to prevent the hijacking of commercial airliners.

skȳ pär'lŏr, a room next to the roof; an attic.

skȳ pī'lŏt, a missionary, chaplain, or clergyman; also, a licenced aviator. [Slang.]

skȳ pip'it, same as *Missouri skylark* under *skylark.*

skȳ'rock"et, *n.* a firework rocket that explodes in mid-air, giving off a display of colored flame, sparks, etc.

skȳ'rock"et, *v.i.* to rise rapidly, as a driven ball, prices, etc. [Colloq.]

skȳ'sāil, *n.* the sail set next above the royal at the top of a square-rigged mast.

skȳ'scrāp"ẽr, *n.* a very tall building.

skȳ'wärd, *a.* moving or leading toward the sky.

skȳ'wärd, *adv.* toward the sky.

skȳ'wärds, *adv.* skyward.

skȳ wāve, a radio wave that is reflected back to earth from one of the layers of the ionosphere.

skȳ'wāys, *n.pl.* routes of air travel; air lanes.

skȳ'wrīt"ẽr (-rīt"), *n.* an aviator skilled in skywriting.

skȳ'wrīt·ing, *n.* the formation of words, letters, or designs in the sky by trailing smoke from an airplane in flight.

slab, *n.* [ME. *sclabbe.*]

1. a piece that is flat, broad, and fairly thick; as, a *slab* of concrete.

2. an outside, half-curved piece taken from a log or timber in sawing it into boards, planks, etc.

3. in baseball, the pitcher's plate. [Slang.]

slab, *a.* [from ON. *slabb*, mud.] thick; viscous; slimy. [Archaic.]

slab, *n.* moist earth; slime. [Archaic.]

slab′bẽr, *v.t.* and *v.i.*; slabbered, *pt., pp.*; slabbering, *ppr.* to slobber.

slab′bẽr, *n.* slobber.

slab′bẽr, *n.* 1. in metalworking, a machine for dressing the sides of nuts or heads of bolts.

2. in woodworking, a saw for removing a portion from the outside of a log so as to square it.

slab′bẽr·ẽr, *n.* one who slabbers; a slobberer.

slab′bẽr·i·ness, *n.* the quality or state of being slabbery; slobberiness.

slab′bẽr·ing·ly, *adv.* in a slabbering manner.

slab′bẽr·y, *a.* covered with or resembling slabber.

slab′bi·ness, *n.* the state of being slabby; sloppiness.

slab′bing mȧ·ȼhïne′, a machine for milling connecting rods, nuts, etc.

slab′by, *a.*; *comp.* slabbier; *superl.* slabbiest, 1. thick; viscous.

2. wet; slimy.

slab līne, in nautical usage, a line running through a block on the lower yard and used in taking up the slack of the sail.

slab′-sīd″ed, *a.* having long, flat sides; hence, thin and tall. [Colloq.]

slab′stōne, *n.* stone which separates naturally into slabs; flagstone.

slack, *a.*; *comp.* slacker; *superl.* slackest, [AS. *slæc.*]

1. slow; idle; sluggish.

2. barely moving: said of a current, as of air or water.

3. characterized by little work, trade, or business; not busy or active; dull; as, a *slack* period.

4. loose; relaxed; not tight, taut, or firm.

5. easily changed or influenced; weak; lax.

6. careless; neglectful; indifferent; as, a *slack* workman, *slack* bookkeeping.

slack in stays; in nautical usage, slow in going about, as a ship.

slack water; (a) the time when the tide runs slowly or the water is at rest; the interval between the flux and reflux of the tide; (b) water arrested in its course and retained, as in a dam or reservoir.

Syn.—loose, relaxed, weak, remiss, backward, abated, inactive, tardy, slow, diminished, dull.

slack, *n.* 1. a part that is slack or hangs loose.

2. a lack of tension or tautness; looseness; as, there was *slack* in the rope.

3. a stoppage of movement in a current.

4. a time of little activity; a dull period; a lull.

5. in prosody, the unstressed syllable or syllables within a foot, especially in sprung rhythm.

slack, *v.t.* 1. to make slack; to slacken.

2. to slake.

slack, *v.i.* to be or become slack; to slacken.

to slack off; to slacken.

to slack up; to go more slowly.

slack, *adv.* in a slack manner; so as to be slack.

slack, *n.* [ME. *sleck, slacke,* from M.L.G. or M.D.] a mixture of small pieces of coal, coal dust, and dirt left from the screening of coal.

slack, *n.* [ON. *slakki,* a slope on a mountain.]

1. (a) a small valley or dell; (b) a hollow in the ground or in a hillside. [Scot. and Brit. Dial.]

2. a boggy hollow; a morass. [Scot. and Brit. Dial.]

slack′en, *v.i.*; slacked (slakt), slackened, *pt., pp.*; slacking, slackening, *ppr.* [from *slack,* a.]

1. to become less tense, firm, or rigid; to decrease in tension; as, a wet cord *slackens* in dry weather.

2. to be remiss or backward; to be negligent.

3. to abate; to become less active, intense, etc.

4. to become slower or less brisk; as, business *slackened*; the tide *slackens.*

slack′en, *v.t.* 1. to lessen the tension of; to relax; to loosen; as, to *slacken* a rope or a bandage.

2. to neglect; to remit; as, to *slacken* exertion or labor.

3. to mitigate; to diminish in severity; as, to *slacken* pain.

4. to cause to become more slow; to lessen the rapidity of; as, to *slacken* one's pace.

5. to abate; to lower; as, to *slacken* the heat of a fire.

6. to relieve; to unbend; as, to *slacken* cares.

7. to withhold; to use less liberally.

slack′en, *n.* in smelting, slag mixed with the ores of metals to prevent their fusion.

slack′ẽr, *n.* one who attempts to evade a responsibility or duty, especially one who shirks an obligation to his country in time of war, as by attempting to evade military service.

slack′ly, *adv.* in a slack manner; so as to be slack.

slack′ness, *n.* the quality or state of being slack.

slacks, *n.pl.* full-cut trousers for casual wear by men and women.

slack′-wạ″tẽr, *a.* pertaining to slack water.

slack-water haul; in fishing, the ground for seining when the tide is turning.

slack-water navigation; navigation in small, shallow streams by means of slack water.

slāde, *n.* [AS. *slaed.*] a little dell or valley; also, a flat piece of low, moist ground. [Dial.]

slāde, *n.* the sole of a plow.

slag, *n.* [M.L.G. *slagge*; akin to G. *schlacke* and var. of *slack,* n.]

1. the fused refuse or dross separated from a metal in the process of smelting.

2. lava resembling this.

slag, *v.t.* and *v.i.*; slagged, *pt., pp.*; slagging, *ppr.* in smelting, to change or form into slag.

slag brick, a kind of brick made by molding molten slag.

slag bug′gy, in smelting, a carriage on which a slag pot is moved.

slag ȼär, same as *slag buggy.*

slag dump, a place for dumping slag from a slag buggy.

slag fũr′nāce, in smelting, a furnace or hearth for separating lead from slag or inferior ore.

slag′gy, *a.*; *comp.* slaggier; *superl.* slaggiest, pertaining to or resembling slag.

slag heärth, same as *slag furnace.*

slag pot, in smelting, a movable vessel into which slag is run from a furnace.

slag wool, same as *mineral wool* under *wool.*

slāie, *n.* slay. [Obs.]

slāin, *v.* past participle of *slay.*

slāke, *v.t.*; slaked (slākt), *pt., pp.*; slaking, *ppr.* [ME. *slakien*; AS. *slacian,* from *slaec,* slack.]

1. to allay or make less active or intense by satisfying, as thirst, desire, etc.; to assuage; satisfy.

2. to cause (a fire) to die down or go out.

3. to produce a chemical change in (lime) by combination with water: slaked lime is calcium hydroxide.

4. to lessen, reduce, or relieve. [Obs.]

5. to lessen the tension of. [Obs.]

slāke, *v.i.* 1. to go out; to become extinct; to desist; to fail. [Obs.]

2. to abate; to become less active or intense; to decrease. [Now Rare.]

3. to become slaked or undergo slaking, as lime, thirst, etc.

slāke′less, *a.* that cannot be slaked.

slāke trough (trọf), a blacksmith's cooling trough filled with water, into which he thrusts hot iron to cool or to temper it.

slak′in, *n.* same as *slacken,* n.

slä′lōm, *n.* [Norw.] a downhill skiing race over a zigzag course marked by posts, etc.

slä′lōm, *v.i.* to ski in or as in a slalom.

slam, *v.t.*; slammed, *pt., pp.*; slamming, *ppr.* [prob. from ON. via. Brit. dial.]

1. to close or allow to close with force and noise; to shut or to push to with violence; as, to *slam* a door.

2. to strike down; to beat or cuff. [Brit. Dial.]

3. to hit, throw, or put in place with force and noise; as, he *slammed* the box into the cupboard.

4. to criticize severely. [Colloq.]

slam, *v.i.* to shut or go into place violently or noisily, as a door or a moving part of a machine, etc.

slam, *n.* 1. a heavy, driving impact or shutting, as of a door when violently closed by the wind.

2. the noise made by this.

3. severe criticism. [Colloq.]

slam, *n.* [from preceding *slam,* n. with reference to its finality in the game.]

1. the winning of all the tricks in one deal, as in whist: in bridge, called *grand slam,* or when one trick short of this, *little slam.*

2. an old card game resembling ruff.

slam′-baṅg′, *adv.* swiftly or abruptly and with loud noise. [Colloq.]

slam′mẽr, *n.* a prison or jail. [Slang.]

slan′dẽr, *n.* [ME. *sclaunder,* from OFr. *esclandre,* from LL. *scandalum.*]

1. the utterance or spreading of a false statement or statements, harmful to another's character or reputation: legally, *slander* is spoken, as distinguished from *libel,* which is written.

2. such a statement.

3. disgrace; reproach; ill name. [Obs.]

slan′dẽr, *v.t.*; slandered *pt., pp.*; slandering, *ppr.* 1. to make a slanderous statement about.

2. to detract from; to disparage.

3. to disgrace; to dishonor; to discredit. [Obs.]

Syn.—defame, asperse, calumniate, vilify, malign, brand, traduce, blacken.

slan′dẽr·ẽr, *n.* a defamer; one who slanders.

slan′dẽr·ous, *a.* 1. uttering or spreading slander; disposed to slandering others.

2. characterized by or constituting slander.

3. scandalous; reproachful. [Obs.]

slan′dẽr·ous·ly, *adv.* in a slanderous manner.

slan′dẽr·ous·ness, *n.* the quality of being slanderous or defamatory.

slang, *v.* dialectal and archaic past tense of *sling.*

slang, *n.* a promontory. [Brit. Dial.]

slang, *n.* [prob. from D. *slang,* a snake.] 1. [*pl.*] fetters worn by convicts.

2. a watch chain; any kind of chain.

slang, *n.* [perh. akin to Eng. *sling* (cf. Norw. *slengjenamn,* nickname); perh. a cant clipped form from sling *lang*uage.]

1. originally, the specialized vocabulary and idioms of criminals, tramps, etc., the purpose of which was to disguise from outsiders the meaning of what was said: now usually called *cant.*

2. the specialized vocabulary and idioms of those in the same work, way of life, etc.: now usually called *shoptalk, argot, jargon.*

3. colloquial language that is outside of conventional or standard usage and consists of both coined words (*blurb, whoopee*) and those with new or extended meanings (*rubberneck, sap*): slang develops from the attempt to find fresh and vigorous, colorful, pungent, or humorous expression, and generally either passes into disuse or comes to have a more formal status.

slang, *v.t.* to address with slang or abusive talk.

slang, *v.i.* to use slang or abusive talk.

slang, *a.* of the nature of or resembling slang; as, a *slang* expression.

slang′i·ly, *adv.* in a slangy manner; with slang.

slang′i·ness, *n.* the quality of being slangy.

slang′iṣm, *n.* a slang expression; the use of slang.

slang′-whang′ẽr, *n.* a noisy or abusive talker or writer. [Slang.]

slang′y, *a.*; *comp.* slangier; *superl.* slangiest, 1. of or containing slang; having the characteristics of slang.

2. inclined to the use of slang.

slaṅk, *n.* low land inundated when the water is high in an adjoining stream. [Scot.]

slaṅk, *a.* slim; lank. [Dial.]

slaṅk, *v.* archaic past tense of *slink.*

slȧnt, *v.t.* and *v.i.*; slanted, *pt., pp.*; slanting, *ppr.* [ME. *slenten,* to glide, slope; prob. from ON.; cf. Norw. *slenta,* to fall sideways.]

1. to incline or turn from a direct line or course, especially one that is perpendicular or level; to slope.

2. to write or tell so as to express a particular bias or attitude. [Colloq.]

slȧnt, *n.* 1. an oblique or inclined surface, line, direction, etc.; a slope; an incline.

2. a point of view; an attitude; opinion; bias. [Colloq.]

3. a glance; a quick look. [Colloq.]

slȧnt, *a.* [prob. short for *on slante,* aslant, hence of same origin as the v.] oblique; sloping; inclined.

slȧnt′ing·ly, *adv.* in a slanting manner.

slȧnt′ly, *adv.* obliquely; slantingly.

slȧnt′wāyṣ, *adv.* same as *slantwise.*

slȧnt′wīṣe, *adv.* so as to slant or slope; slantingly; obliquely.

slȧnt′wīṣe, *a.* slanting; oblique.

slap, *n.* [L.G. *sklapp*; of echoic origin.]

1. a blow or smack, especially with something flat, as the palm of the hand.

2. an injury to pride, self-respect, etc.; an insult; a rebuff.

slap, *v.t.*; slapped (slapt), *pt., pp.*; slapping, *ppr.* 1. to strike with the open hand, or with something broad or flat.
2. to put, throw, hit, etc. carelessly or with force; as, she *slapped* the butter into the pan.
slap, *adv.* 1. suddenly; abruptly. [Colloq.]
2. straight; directly; as, he ran *slap* into the wall. [Colloq.]
slap, *n.* a gap in a wall or dike. [Scot.]
slap, *a.* first-rate; of the finest kind. [Old Slang.]
slap'-bang', *a.* and *adv.* slapdash. [Colloq.]
slap'dash, *adv.* in a careless, rash manner; haphazardly.
slap'dash, *v.t.* 1. to do in a rough or careless manner.
2. to roughcast (a wall) with mortar.
slap'dash, *n.* 1. material for roughcasting.
2. carelessness; abruptness.
3. something done carelessly and hastily; as, his book is mere *slapdash.*
slap'dash, *a.* hasty and careless; rash; offhand.
slāpe, *a.* slippery; smooth. [Brit. Dial.]
slāpe'fāce, *n.* a smooth, crafty, hypocritical fellow. [Brit. Dial.]
slap'-hap''py, *a.* 1. dazed or mentally impaired by or as by blows on the head; punch-drunk. [Slang.]
2. foolish; silly. [Slang.]
slap'jack, *n.* 1. a pancake; a flapjack.
2. a simple card game.
slap'pēr, *n.* 1. one who or that which slaps.
2. a person or thing of large size; a whopper. [Dial.]
slap'ping, *a.* very large; great. [Colloq.]
slap'stick, *n.* 1. an implement made of two flat pieces of wood that slap together loudly when hit against something: formerly used by stage comedians to increase the sound of a blow.
2. crude comedy in which the humor depends upon violent activity, horseplay, etc.
slap'stick, *a.* characterized by such comedy.
slap'-up', *a.* excellent; first-rate. [Old Slang.]
slär·gän'dō, *a.* same as *rallentando.*
slash, *v.t.*; slashed (slasht), *pt., pp.*; slashing, *ppr.* [OFr. *esclechier,* to dismember, sever, from *escleche,* a portion, part.]
1. to cut or wound with sweeping strokes or blows, as of a knife.
2. to gash; as, he fell on the broken glass and *slashed* his arm.
3. to whip viciously; to lash; to scourge.
4. to cut slits in (a fabric, dress, etc.), especially so as to expose underlying material, usually of another color.
5. to reduce drastically; as, our budget has been *slashed.*
6. to criticize severely.
slash, *v.i.* to strike violently and at random with or as with a sword, knife, or other edged instrument; also, to cut or criticize violently.
Hewing and *slashing* at their idle shades.
—Spenser.
slash, *n.* 1. a sweeping stroke made with a knife, etc.
2. a cut made by or as by such a stroke; a gash; a slit.
3. an ornamental slit in a fabric, dress, etc.
4. (a) an open place in a forest, cluttered with branches, chips, or other debris, as from the cutting of timber; (b) such debris or trimmings.
5. a piece of lace or tape worn on the sleeve of a noncommissioned officer to distinguish him from a private. [Obs.]
slash, *n.* [from Brit. dial. *slash,* boggy hollow, and *slashy,* swampy; prob. from AS. *slæc,* slack, with palatalized final consonant, but associated with *slosh* and *slush* via echoism.] a low, swampy area, usually covered with brush.
slashed (slasht), *a.* 1. in botany, divided by deep, taper-pointed incisions; multifid; laciniate: said of a leaf.
2. in a garment, having narrow slashes showing an interlining.
slash'ēr, *n.* 1. one who or that which slashes.
2. a machine for sizing warp yarns.
shash'ing, *n.* a slash.
slash'ing, *a.* 1. severe; merciless; violent.
2. dashing; spirited.
3. immense; tremendous; as, a slashing success. [Colloq.]
slash pine, 1. a pine, *Pinus caribaea,* growing in slashes, or swamps, along the southern United States coastal region, parts of Cuba, and the Bahamas; also, its wood.
2. the loblolly pine.

slash'y, *a.* [Sw. *slaska,* to play in water.] wet; slushy. [Dial.]
slat, *n.* [ME. *sclat*; OFr. *esclat,* a fragment, from *esclater,* to splinter.]
1. a thin, narrow strip of wood or metal; a lath; as, the *slats* of a bedstead.
2. a thin slab of stone, as for roofing. [Dial.]
slat, *v.t.*; slatted, *pt., pp.*; slatting, *ppr.* to provide or make with slats.
slat, *n.* a spent salmon. [Brit.]
slat, *v.i.*; slatted, *pt., pp.*; slatting, *ppr.* [ME. *sclatten,* as if from *sclat,* a thin strip of wood, slat; prob. partly echoic.] to flap or beat vigorously, as clothes blowing on a line.
slat, *v.t.* 1. to jerk; to throw down violently. [Dial.]
2. to crack; to split. [Brit. Dial.]
3. to beat; to strike. [Dial.]
slat, *n.* a sharp blow. [Dial.]
slatch, *n.* [variant of *slack.*] in nautical usage, (a) the period of a transitory breeze; (b) an interval of fair weather; (c) the slack of a rope. [Rare.]
slāte, *n.* [ME. and Scot. *sclate*; OFr. *esclat,* a splinter.]
1. a kind of hard, fine-grained rock that cleaves naturally into thin, smooth-surfaced layers.
2. a thin piece of slate or slatelike material, especially one used as a roofing tile or as a tablet for writing on with chalk.
3. the bluish-gray color of most slate.
4. a list of candidates proposed for nomination or election.
a clean slate; a record showing no marks of discredit, dishonor, etc.; a clean record.
adhesive slate; see under *adhesive.*
aluminous slate; a kind of slate containing alumina.
bituminous slate; slate impregnated with bitumen.
hornblende slate; a tough, slaty rock consisting principally of hornblende and feldspar.
slāte, *v.t.*; slated, *pt., pp.*; slating, *ppr.* 1. to cover with slate; as, to *slate* a roof.
2. to put on a list or designate, as for candidacy, appointment, theatrical engagement, etc.; as, he is *slated* for governor.
slāte, *v.t.*; slated, *pt., pp.*; slating, *ppr.* [Anglo-Ir., from the notion of hurling slate, or rocks.]
1. to punish severely; to abuse. [Colloq.]
2. to scold or criticize harshly. [Colloq.]
slāte ax, a mattock with an ax end: used in slating.
slāte çlāy, shale.
slāte'-çol''ōr, *n.* a dark bluish-gray color.
slāte'-grāy, *a.* gray with a bluish tinge.
slāte pen'cil, a pencil of soft slate, used for writing on slates in schools, etc.
slāt'ēr, *n.* 1. one who lays slate roofs, etc.
2. an isopod of the genus *Porcellio* and related genera, as the sow bug.
slāte spär, a variety of calcareous spar: also called *shiver spar.*
slath'ēr, *n.* [dial., to slither; var. of north Brit. dial. *slither,* large quantity of loose stones, from *slither,* to slip.] [*usually in pl.*] a large quantity; lot. [Dial. or Colloq.]
slath'ēr, *v.t.* to use a lot of. [Dial. or Colloq.]
slāt'ing, *n.* 1. the act or craft of laying slates.
2. slates collectively, as a material for roofing, etc.
slat sign, a sign having thin plates fixed perpendicularly to a flat surface; both the flat surface and the sides of the plates are painted in such a manner as to cause letters, pictures, or both to appear when viewed at different angles.
slat'tēr, *v.i.* [akin to *slat,* to throw about.]
1. to be careless of dress; to be slatternly. [Dial.]
2. to be careless, negligent, or awkward; to be wasteful. [Dial.]
slat'tērn, *n.* a woman who is careless and untidy in her dress, appearance, work, etc.; a slut.
slat'tērn, *a.* having the characteristics of a slattern; slatternly.
slat'tērn·li·ness, *n.* the state or quality of being slatternly.
slat'tērn·ly, *a.* 1. having the habits of a slattern; dirty; slovenly; untidy.
2. characteristic of or fit for a slattern.
slat'tērn·ly, *adv.* in a slatternly manner.
slat'ting, *n.* 1. slats collectively.
2. material for making slats.
slāt'y, *a.*; *comp.* slatier; *superl.* slatiest, 1. resembling slate; having the nature or properties of slate; composed of thin, parallel plates, capable of being separated by splitting.
2. slate-colored.
slaty cleavage; cleavage into thin plates or laminae, like those of slate: applied especially to those rocks in which the planes of cleavage are often oblique to the true stratification and perfectly symmetrical and parallel even when the strata are contorted.
slaty gneiss; a variety of gneiss in which the scales of mica or crystals of hornblende, which are usually minute, form thin layers, making the rock easily cleavable.
slaugh'tēr (slą'), *n.* [ME. *slahter*; ON. *slātr,* lit., slain flesh.]
1. the killing of an animal or animals for food; a butchering.
2. the killing of a human being, especially in a brutal manner.
3. the killing of people in large numbers, as in battle.
Syn.—butchery, carnage, murder, massacre.
slaugh'tēr, *v.t.*; slaughtered, *pt., pp.*; slaughtering, *ppr.* 1. to butcher; to kill (an animal or animals) for food.
2. to kill (people), especially brutally or in great numbers; as, to *slaughter* men in battle.
slaugh'tēr·ēr, *n.* a person employed in slaughtering; a butcher.
slaugh'tēr·house, *n.* a place where animals are butchered for food; an abattoir.
slaugh'tēr·măn, *n.* one employed in slaughtering; a butcher.
slaugh'tēr·ous, *a.* brutally destructive; murderous; bent on killing.
slaugh'tēr·ous·ly, *adv.* destructively; murderously.
Släv, *n.* [G. *Slave,* Fr. *slave,* ML. *Slavus.*] a member of any of a group of peoples of eastern, southeastern, and central Europe, generally divided into Eastern Slavs (Great Russians, Ukrainians, and Byelorussians), Southern Slavs (Serbs, Croats, Bulgars, Slovenes, Slavonians, etc.), and Western Slavs (Czechs, Poles, Slovaks, Moravians, etc.).
Släv, *a.* Slavic.
Släv'dŏm, *n.* Slavs collectively.
slāve, *n.* [OFr. *esclave,* from ML. *Slavus,* Slav, from L.Gr. *Sklabos,* slave, ultimately from O.Slav. *Slovēne, slovo,* a word: first applied to captives of Slavic origin in southeastern Europe.]
1. a bond servant divested of all freedom and personal rights; a human being who is owned by and wholly subject to the will of another, as by capture, purchase, or birth.
2. one who has lost the power of resistance, or one who surrenders himself to any power whatever; as, a *slave* to passion, lust, ambition, etc.
3. a mean person; an abject wretch. [Archaic.]
4. a drudge; one who labors like a slave.
5. a slave ant.
Syn.—bond servant, bondman, bond slave, captive, vassal, dependent, drudge.
slāve, *v.i.*; slaved, *pt., pp.*; slaving, *ppr.* to drudge; to toil; to labor like a slave.
slāve, *v.t.* to enslave. [Rare.]
slāve ȧnt, an ant held captive and made to work for ants of another species.
slāve'born, *a.* born in bondage.
Slāve Çōast, the west African coast between the Volta and Benin rivers, on the Gulf of Guinea: former center of the African slave trade.
slāve drīv'ēr, an overseer of slaves; hence, any cruel taskmaster.
slāve fork, a forked piece of wood placed around a slave's neck by slave catchers to prevent escape.
slāve'hōld''ēr, *n.* an owner of slaves.
slāve'hōld''ing, *a.* owning or having slaves.
slāve'hōld''ing, *n.* possession or ownership of slaves.
slāve'-māk''ing ant, an ant belonging to a species that enslaves other ants: also *slave maker.*
slāv'ēr, *n.* 1. a slave ship.
2. a person engaged in slave trade.
slav'ēr, *v.i.*; slavered, *pt., pp.*; slavering, *ppr.* [ON. *slafra,* to slaver.] to let saliva, etc. dribble or run from the mouth; to drool.
slav'ēr, *v.t.* to smear with saliva issuing from the mouth; to cover with saliva.
slav'ēr, *n.* 1. saliva driveling from the mouth.
2. nonsense; drivel.

slav'ẽr·ẽr, *n.* a driveler; one who slavers.

slav'ẽr·ing·ly, *adv.* in a slavering manner.

slāv'ẽr·y, *n.* 1. the owning or keeping of slaves as a practice or institution; slaveholding.
2. the condition of a slave; bondage; servitude.
3. a condition of submission to or domination by some influence, habit, etc.
4. hard, continuous work like that done by slaves; drudgery.

slāve ship, a ship for carrying people to a place where they are to be sold as slaves.

Slāve Stātes, Alabama, Arkansas, Delaware, Florida, Georgia, Kentucky, Louisiana, Maryland, Mississippi, Missouri, North Carolina, South Carolina, Tennessee, Texas, and Virginia: in these fifteen States slavery was legal before the Civil War.

slāve trāde, traffic in slaves; specifically, the former transportation of African Negroes to America for sale as slaves.

slāve trād'ẽr, one who deals or traffics in slaves.

slāv'ey, *n.*; *pl.* **slāv'eyṣ,** a maidservant, especially a woman or girl who does hard, menial work. [Brit. Colloq.]

Slāv'iç, *a.* of the Slavs, their languages, etc.; Slavonic.

Slāv'iç, *n.* a major subbranch of the Indo-European family of languages, generally divided into West Slavic (Polish, Sorbian, Czech, and Slovak), South Slavic (Old Church Slavonic, Bulgarian, Serbo-Croatian, and Slovene), and East Slavic (Russian, or Great Russian; Ukrainian, or Little Russian; and Byelorussian, or White Russian).

Slāv'i·cism, *n.* Slavism.

slāv'ish, *a.* 1. of or characteristic of a slave or slaves; hopelessly submissive; servile.
2. of or characteristic of slavery; oppressive; despotic.
3. blindly dependent or imitative; as, *slavish* adherence to a model.

slāv'ish·ly, *adv.* in a slavish manner.

slāv'ish·ness, *n.* the state or quality of being slavish; servility; meanness.

Slāv'iṣm, *n.* the characteristics, interests, culture, etc. common to all Slavs.

Slä'vō-, a combining form meaning *Slav.*

slāv·oç'rà·cy, *n.*; *pl.* **slāv·oç'rà·cieṣ,** [from *slave* and *-cracy.*] in the United States before 1865, slaveholders and pro-slavery forces as a dominant or powerful class.

Slä·vō'ni·ăn, *a.* 1. of or relating to Slavonia or its people.
2. Slavic.

Slä·vō'ni·ăn, *n.* 1. a native or inhabitant of Slavonia.
2. a Slav.
3. the Slavic language group.

Slä·von'iç, *a.* 1. Slavonian.
2. Slavic.

Slä·von'iç, *n.* the Slavic language group.

Slä·von'i·cīze, *v.t.*; Slavonicized, *pt., pp.*; Slavonicizing, *ppr.* to cause to become Slavonic in character, etc.

Släv'ō·phīle, Släv'ō·phil, *n.* [*Slavo-* and *-phile.*] a person interested in or very fond of the Slavs, their culture, influence, etc.

Släv'ō·phīle, *a.* of Slavophiles.

Släv'ō·phōbe, *n.* a person who has Slavophobia.

Släv'ō·phōbe, *a.* of Slavophobes.

Släv·ō·phō'bi·ȧ, *n.* [*Slavo-* and *-phobia.*] hatred or fear of the Slavs, their culture, influence, etc.

Slä·vŏph'ō·bist, *n.* a Slavophobe.

slaw, *n.* [D. *sla, slaa,* contr. of Fr. *salade,* salad.] shredded cabbage served as a salad or relish.

slāy, *v.t.*; slew, *pt.*; slain, *pp.*; slaying, *ppr.* [AS. *slahan, sleahan, slagan,* or contr. *slean,* to strike, to beat, to slay.]
1. to kill by violence; to bring death upon; to destroy; as, he *slew* his enemy with a sword.
2. to strike or hit. [Obs.]

slāy, slęy, *n.* [AS. *slæ,* a weavers' tool, from *slean,* to strike, smite.]
1. the reed of a loom.
2. one of the guideways of a knitting machine.

slāy, slęy, *v.t.* to prepare (threads, etc.) for the slay, or reed of a loom.

slāy'ẽr, *n.* one who slays; a killer; a murderer; an assassin; a destroyer of life.

slēave, *n.* [AS. *-slæfan,* to separate.]
1. (a) a fine silk thread separated from a larger thread; (b) untwisted silk that tends to mat or tangle; floss.
2. any tangle, as of ravelings.

slēave, *v.t.*; sleaved, *pt., pp.*; sleaving, *ppr.* to separate or pull apart, as twisted or tangled threads; to divide a collection of (threads).

slēaze, *n.* [from *sleazy.*]
1. the quality or condition of being sleazy; sleaziness. [Slang.]
2. anything cheap, vulgar, shoddy, etc. [Slang.]

slēa'zi·ness (*or* slā-), *n.* the condition or quality of being sleazy.

slēa'zy (*or* slā-), *a.*; *comp.* sleazier; *superl.* sleaziest, [from obs. *Sleasie,* cloth made in Silesia, Germany.] flimsy or thin in texture or substance; lacking firmness; as, a *sleazy* rayon fabric.

sled, *n.* [ME. *sledde*; M.L.G. *sledde*; akin to G. *schlitten.*]
1. any of several kinds of vehicle mounted on runners; specifically, (a) a sledge or sleigh; (b) a light seat or platform on a pair of runners, used for coasting or carrying light burdens on the snow or ice; (c) a low platform on runners used to haul heavy loads.
2. a piece of metal that forms a sliding contact with an underground wire to operate an electric railway car.

sled, *v.t.*; sledded, *pt., pp.*; sledding, *ppr.* to convey or transport on a sled.

sled, *v.i.* to ride on a sled; to be conveyed on a sled.

sled'dẽr, *n.* 1. a person who rides or drives a sled.
2. an animal used for drawing a sled.

sled'ding, *n.* 1. a riding or carrying on a sled.
2. the condition of the ground with reference to the use of sleds: often used figuratively; as, the work was hard *sledding.*

sledġe (slej), *n.* [AS. *slecge,* from *slahan, slagan,* to strike, to slay.] a large, heavy hammer, usually used with both hands.

sledġe, *v.t.* and *v.i.*; sledged, *pt., pp.*; sledging, *ppr.* to strike with or as with a sledge.

sledġe, *n.* [MD. *sleedse*; akin to D. *slede.*]
1. a vehicle moved on runners or on low wheels, for the conveyance of loads or passengers over snow or ice; a sled; a sleigh.

RUSSIAN SLEDGE

2. the hurdle used as a conveyance for persons about to be executed. [Obs.]
3. a card game; old sledge.

sledġe, *v.i.* and *v.t.*; sledged, *pt., pp.*; sledging, *ppr.* to go or take by sledge.

sledġe'-ham"mẽr, *v.t.* 1. to hit with a sledge hammer.
2. to attack with force so as to have an overpowering effect upon.

sledġe'-ham"mẽr, *a.* crushingly destructive; forceful; powerful.

sledġe ham'mẽr, a sledge (heavy hammer).

sleek, *a.* [var. of *slick.*]
1. smooth and shiny; glossy, as a highly polished surface, well-kept hair or fur, etc.
2. of well-fed or well-groomed appearance; as, fat, *sleek* pigeons.
3. polished in speech and behavior, especially in a way that does not seem genuine; unctuous; oily.

sleek, *n.* a smooth, shining place; a slick.

sleek, *v.t.*; sleeked (sleekt), *pt., pp.*; sleeking, *ppr.*
1. to make even and smooth; to make soft and glossy; to polish; as, to *sleek* the hair.
2. to remove roughness from; to calm.

sleek, *adv.* with ease and dexterity; sleekly.

sleek'ẽr, *n.* 1. a kind of smoother and polisher used in the manufacture of leather.
2. in founding, a tool used for smoothing the curved surfaces of molds.

sleek'it, *a.* sleek; also, sly. [Scot.]

sleek'ly, *adv.* in a sleek manner; so as to be sleek.

sleek'ness, *n.* the quality or state of being sleek.

sleek'y, *a.*; *comp.* sleekier; *superl.* sleekiest.
1. of a sleek or smooth appearance or character.
2. sly; obsequious. [Scot.]

sleep, *n.* [ME. *slep*; AS. *slæp,* sleep; akin to G. *schlaf,* sleep, *schlaff,* loose, lax.]
1. (a) a natural, regularly recurring condition of rest for the body and mind, during which there is little or no conscious thought, sensation, or movement; (b) a period or occasion of sleeping.
2. any condition resembling sleep, as death, unconsciousness, hibernation, etc.
3. in botany, the tendency, as of petals or leaves, to assume a different position at night; nyctitropism.
last sleep; death.

sleep, *v.i.*; slept, *pt., pp.*; sleeping, *ppr.* [AS. *slæpan*; akin to G. *schlafen.*]
1. to be in the state of sleep; to slumber.
2. to be in a condition resembling sleep, as that of death, quiescence, hibernation, etc.
3. in botany, to assume a different position at night, as petals or leaves.
to sleep in; to sleep at the place where one is employed as a household servant.

sleep, *v.t.* 1. to slumber in (a specified kind of sleep); as, he *slept* a peaceful sleep.
2. to furnish lodging for; as, this inn *sleeps* thirty people. [Colloq.]
to sleep away; (a) to spend in sleeping; to sleep during; (b) to get rid of by sleeping.
to sleep off; to rid oneself of by sleeping.
Syn.—slumber, doze, drowse, nap.

sleep'-ăt-nọọn", *n.* a plant, *Tragopogon pratensis*: also called *goatsbeard.*

sleep'ẽr, *n.* 1. a person or animal that sleeps, especially in a specified way; as, the man is a sound *sleeper.*
2. a timber or beam laid horizontally, as on the ground, to support something above it.
3. a tie supporting a railroad track. [Brit.]
4. a railroad sleeping car.
5. a race horse, book, etc. that unexpectedly achieves a striking success.
6. an animal that lies dormant in winter or summer, as the bear, the marmot, certain mollusks, etc.
7. a large West Indian gobioid fish.
8. the European dormouse, which usually hiberates.
9. the sleeper shark, *Somniosus microcephalus.*
10. anything dormant, as a law not executed.
11. a drone or lazy person.
12. in faro, stakes won by a player who fails to claim them and which hence remain for the winner of another play.

sleep'fụl, *a.* sleepy.

sleep'fụl·ness, *n.* sleepiness.

sleep'i·ly, *adv.* in a sleepy or drowsy manner.

sleep'i·ness, *n.* the quality or state of being sleepy.

sleep'ing, *a.* 1. reposing in sleep.
2. occupied in or used for sleep; as, *sleeping* hours.
3. used for sleeping in; as, a *sleeping* room.
4. tending to produce sleep; as, a *sleeping* pill.

sleep'ing bag, a large, warmly lined bag made to sleep in, especially out of doors.

sleep'ing çär, a railway car furnished with berths, compartments, etc. in which passengers may sleep.

sleep'ing pärt'nẽr, a silent partner. [Brit.]

sleep'ing rent, a fixed rent, as distinguished from rent varying with the amount of profits.

sleep'ing sick'ness, 1. an infectious disease, especially common in tropical Africa, caused by certain species of trypanosome that are transmitted by the bite of certain flies, especially the tsetse fly: it is characterized by fever, weakness, tremors, lethargy, and finally prolonged coma ending in death.
2. inflammation of the brain, caused by a virus and characterized by apathy, drowsiness, and lethargy: also called *encephalitis lethargica, epidemic encephalitis.*

sleep'ing tā'ble, a fixed sloping table used in washing ore.

sleep'less, *a.* 1. with little or no sleep; wakeful; restless; unquiet.
2. alert at all times; constantly watchful.
3. constantly in action or motion; never at rest; as, the *sleepless* wind.

sleep'less·ly, *adv.* in a sleepless manner.

sleep'less·ness, *n.* the quality or state of being sleepless.

sleep'wāk"ẽr, *n.* one who has been hypnotized.

sleep'wāk"ing, *n.* the state of being hypnotized.

sleep′wạlk″ẽr (-wạk″), *n.* a somnambulist; one who walks in his sleep.
sleep′wạlk″ing, *n.* the act or practice of walking while asleep; somnambulism.
sleep′wŏrt, *n.* lettuce, especially the European wild variety, *Lactuca virosa,* from which lactucarium, a narcotic, is obtained.
sleep′y, *a.*; *comp.* sleepier; *superl.* sleepiest, 1. ready or inclined to sleep; needing sleep; drowsy.
2. characterized by an absence of activity; dull; idle; lethargic; as, a *sleepy* river town.
3. causing drowsiness; inducing sleep.
4. of or exhibiting drowsiness.
sleepy duck; the ruddy duck. [Dial.]
sleep′y·head (-hed), *n.* 1. one who is dull or sleepy.
2. the ruddy duck. [Dial.]
sleet, *n.* [ME. *slete*; hyp. AS. *sliete*; akin to G. *schlosse,* hail.]
1. partly frozen rain, or rain that freezes as it falls.
2. a mixture of rain with snow or hail.
3. the icy coating formed when rain freezes on trees, streets, etc.
sleet, *v.i.* to shower in the form of sleet.
sleet′i·ness, *n.* the quality or condition of being sleety.
sleet′y, *a.*; *comp.* sleetier; *superl.* sleetiest; characterized by, consisting of, or like sleet.
sleeve, *n.* [ME. *sleeve, sleve*; AS. *slefe, slyf,* from *slipan,* to slip.]
1. the part of a garment that is fitted to cover the arm or part of the arm; as, the *sleeve* of a coat.
2. in mechanics, a tube into which a rod or another tube is inserted.
3. a sleeve nut.
4. a short tube connection, usually with right and left threads.
5. a long, tubular cloth bag towed on a long line by an airplane, used as a target for antiaircraft gunnery practice: also *sleeve target.*
to laugh in one's sleeve; see under *laugh.*
up one's sleeve; hidden or secret but ready at hand.
sleeve, *v.t.*; sleeved, *pt., pp.*; sleeving, *ppr.* to furnish with sleeves; to put sleeves in.
sleeve but′tŏn, a button or stud to fasten the sleeve or wristband.
sleeved, *a.* fitted with sleeves: often in hyphenated compounds, as short-*sleeved.*
sleeve′fish, *n.* the penfish or squid.
sleeve′less, *a.* 1. having no sleeves.
2. futile; feeble; without pretext. [Dial.]
sleeve nut, a coupling with the threads cut in opposition, for connecting and tightening pipes or rods.
sleeve valve, a rotating, reciprocating sleeve between the piston and cylinder wall of some internal-combustion engines: the sleeve has two slots which open and close the fuel intake and exhaust ports in the cylinder wall.
sleigh (slā), *n.* [D. *slee,* a contr. form of *sleede,* a sled or sledge.] a light passenger vehicle mounted on runners, used for travel on snow or ice.
sleigh, *v.i.* to ride in or drive a sleigh.
sleigh bell, any of a number of small bells attached to a sleigh or to the harness of the animal drawing it.
sleigh′ing, *n.* 1. a riding or carrying in a sleigh.
2. the condition of the snow or ice in winter that makes this possible; as, good *sleighing.*
sleight (slīt), *n.* [ME. *slehthe*; Ice. *slægth,* slyness, cunning, from *slægr,* sly.]
1. cunning or craft used in deceiving. [Rare or Archaic.]
2. a clever act of deception; a skillful trick or stratagem.
3. skill; deftness; dexterity.
sleight′ful, *a.* artful; cunningly dexterous.
sleight′i·ly, *adv.* craftily. [Obs.]
sleight of hand, 1. skill with the hands, especially in confusing or deceiving onlookers, as in magic; legerdemain.
2. a trick or series of tricks thus performed.
sleight′y, *a.* crafty; tricky. [Rare.]
Sleip′nẽr, *n.* in Norse mythology, the eight-legged steed on which Odin rode to the lower world.
slen′dẽr, *a.* [ME. *slendre, sclendre,* prob. from Anglo-Fr. *esclendre.*]
1. small in width or girth for the length or height; long and thin; slim.
2. small or limited in amount, size, extent, etc.; meager; as, *slender* earnings.
3. of little force or validity; having slight foundation; feeble; as, *slender* hope.
Mighty hearts are held in *slender* chains. —Pope.
4. lacking volume or fullness, as sound.
5. in phonetics, thin; close; narrow.
Syn.—fragile, slight, slim, thin.
slen′dẽr gràss, any grass with slender spikes, belonging to the genus *Leptochloa.*
slen′dẽr·īze, *v.t.* and *v.i.*; slenderized, *pt., pp.*; slenderizing, *ppr.* to make or become slender.
slen′dẽr·ly, *adv.* in a slender manner; so as to be slender.
slen′dẽr·ness, *n.* the quality or condition of being slender.
slent, *v.i.* to jest. [Obs.]
slep, *v.* obsolete past tense and past participle of *sleep.*
slē·pez′ (-pets′), *n.* [Russ. *slyepets,* blind.] a molelike rodent, *Spalax typhlus,* of Europe.
slept, *v.* past tense and past participle of *sleep.*
sleůth, *n.* [ME. *sloth* (mod. sp. from northern dial.), from Ice. *sloth,* a track or trail.]
1. a sleuthhound.
2. a detective. [Colloq.]
sleůth, *v.i.* to act as a detective.
sleůth′hound, *n.* 1. a dog, especially a bloodhound, that can follow a trail by scent.
2. a detective. [Colloq.]
slew, *n., v.t.* and *v.i.* same as *slue* (turn).
slew, *n.* a slough; wet place.
slew, *v.* past tense of *slay.*
slew, *n.* a large number, group, or quantity; a lot: also spelled *slue.* [Colloq.]
slęy, *v.* and *n.* in weaving, same as *slay.*
slīce, *n.* [OFr. *esclice*; O.H.G. *slizan,* to break, split.]
1. a relatively thin, broad piece cut from an object having some bulk or volume; as, a *slice* of apple.
2. a part, portion, or share; as, he spent a large *slice* of his winnings.
3. any of various implements with a flat, broad blade, used for turning food in a skillet, serving fish, etc.
4. a spatula for spreading printing ink.
5. in golf, a sliced stroke.
6. in shipbuilding, a wedge to be driven between the timbers before planking.
slīce, *v.t.*; sliced (slīst), *pt., pp.*; slicing, *ppr.* 1. to cut into slices.
2. (a) to cut as a slice or slices (with *off, from, away,* or *out*); (b) to cut across or through like a knife; as, the plow *sliced* the land.
3. to separate into parts or shares.
4. to use a slice (implement) or slice bar to work at, spread, remove, etc.
5. in golf, to cause (a ball) to curve to the right (for a right-handed player) or to the left (for a left-handed player) by hitting it with a glancing stroke.
slīce, *v.i.* in golf, to slice a ball.
slīce bär, an iron tool with a broad, thin end, used in a coal furnace for breaking clinkers and clearing out ashes, etc.
slīce gal′ley, in printing, a galley, usually of wood, with a sliding bottom which facilitated the removal of composed types to and from the stone. [Obs.]
slī′cẽr, *n.* 1. one who or that which slices.
2. a slightly concave circular saw used in gem cutting.
slick, *v.t.* [ME. *slikien,* prob. from AS. *-slician,* lit., to smooth by hammering, from *slic,* a mallet, hammer.]
1. to make sleek, glossy, or smooth.
2. to make smart, neat, or tidy (usually with *up*). [Colloq.]
slick, *a.* 1. sleek; glossy; smooth.
2. slippery; oily, as a surface.
3. accomplished; adept; clever; smart; ingenious.
4. clever in deception or trickery; deceptively plausible; smooth; as, a *slick* alibi. [Colloq.]
5. having or showing skill in composition or technique but little depth or literary significance; as, a *slick* book, a *slick* style of writing. [Colloq.]
6. excellent; fine; enjoyable; as, it was a *slick* meal. [Slang.]
7. having a pleasing appearance; attractive. [Slang.]
slick, *n.* 1. a smooth area on the surface of water, as resulting from a film of oil.
2. something used for smoothing and polishing, as a kind of broad, flat chisel.
3. a magazine printed on paper with a glossy finish: distinguished from *pulp.* [Slang.]
slick, *adv.* smoothly, cleverly, deftly, easily, etc.
slick′en, *a.* sleek; smooth. [Brit. Dial.]
slick′enş, *n.pl.* in mining, the dust made by a quartz mill; also, the light soil from a hydraulic mine. [Rare.]
slick′en·sīde, *n.* [*often in pl.*] a smooth, polished rock surface produced by friction, pressure, or cleavage.
slick′ẽr, *n.* 1. a loose, waterproof coat made of oil-treated cloth.
2. a tricky, cleverly deceptive person. [Colloq.]
slid, *v.* past tense and alternative past participle of *slide.*
slid′den, *v.* alternative past participle of *slide.*
slid′dẽr·y, *a.* slippery. [Dial.]
slīde, *v.i.*; slid, *pt.*; slid *or* slidden, *pp.*; sliding, *ppr.* [ME. *sliden, slyden,* from AS. *slidan,* to slide.]
1. to move along in constant frictional contact with some surface or substance; as, the boxes *slide* across the deck, the car *slid* to a stop.
2. to move in this manner on a sled, the feet, etc. in contact with a smooth surface, as ice.
3. to move quietly and smoothly; to glide.
4. to move stealthily or secretly; as, the cat *slid* around the corner.
5. to slip; as, the sword *slid* from his hand.
6. to slip or pass gradually into or out of some condition, habit, situation, etc.
7. in baseball, to drop down and slide along the ground toward a base to avoid being tagged out by the baseman.
8. in music, to pass from one tone to another without breaking the sound.
slīde, *v.t.* 1. to cause to slide; to make move with a smooth, gliding motion.
2. to move, place, or introduce quietly or dexterously (usually with *in* or *into*).
slīde, *n.* 1. an act of sliding.
2. a smooth, usually inclined track, surface, or trough used for sliding; a chute; as, the children made a *slide* on the snow bank.
3. something that operates by sliding; a sliding part.
4. a transparent plate bearing a picture for projection on a screen, as by a magic lantern.
5. a small glass plate used as a mounting for objects to be examined under a microscope.
6. (a) the fall of a mass of rock, snow, earth, etc. down a slope; (b) the mass that falls.
7. in music, (a) a portamento; (b) a U-shaped section of tubing which is moved to change the pitch of certain brass-wind instruments, especially the trombone; (c) a grace or ornamentation made up of two or more notes leading to a main note.
8. a brooch or clasp, as for a belt or chain.
9. the lower part of a ship's carronade or howitzer carriage, on which the top carriage rested and was run in and out. [Obs.]
10. the guide bars of a box or crosshead in a steam engine.
slīde box, in electricity, a resistance box that uses a slide wire instead of a coil.
slīde bridġe, in electricity, a style of Wheatstone's bridge, a device for measuring resistances.
slīde çar′ri·ẽr, a device used in a stereopticon for inserting the slides and carrying them in front of the light.
slīde fȧs′ten·ẽr (fȧs′n-), a device used to fasten together or unfasten two adjoining edges of material, as on the fly of a sweater, the placket of a dress, etc.: it consists of two rows of small interlocking tabs which are joined or separated by the action of a part that slides up and down: also called *zipper.*
slīde′grōat, *n.* shuffleboard. [Obs.]
slīde knot (not), a slipknot.
slīde lāthe, a metalworker's lathe in which the tool rest slides on the bed from end to end.
slīd′ẽr, *n.* 1. one who slides.
2. the part of an instrument or machine that slides.
3. the potter or red-bellied terrapin, *Pseudemys rugosa,* of the United States.
slī′dẽr, *a.* slidder. [Obs.]
slīde rāil, 1. a switch rail.
2. a contrivance for transferring cars from

one track to another by carrying the rails on which they stand to the desired line of rails, as a turntable or a transverse movable platform.

slīde rest, in a lathe, a tool holder admitting of a sliding movement either longitudinally or transversely, so as to facilitate accurate and quick adjustment of the tool to the material to be cut.

slīd′ẽr pump, a variety of rotary pump having a sliding valve.

slīde rule, an instrument consisting of a ruler with a central sliding piece, both being marked with logarithmic scales: used in making rapid mathematical calculations.

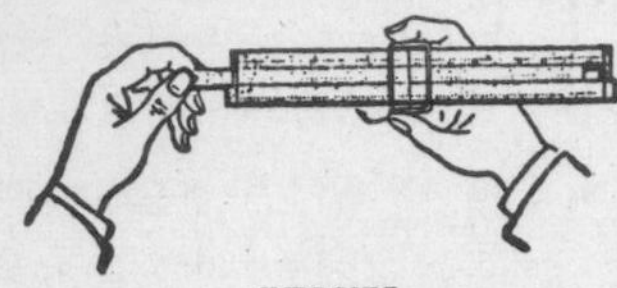

SLIDE RULE

slīde trom′bōne, a long brass-wind instrument having, instead of valves, a U-shaped tube which slides in and out, so that the length of the air column can be adjusted to vary the tone.

slīde valve, a valve which opens or closes a passageway by sliding over the port or ports.
circular slide valve; a cylindrical valve with ports which are opened and closed by turning, as in a faucet.

slīde′wāy, *n.* an inclined ramp, chute, etc. used as a slide.

slīd′ing, *n.* 1. the act of moving with a slide.
2. the act of coasting.
3. a backsliding. [Obs.]

slīd′ing, *a.* 1. varying in accordance with given conditions; adjustable; as, a *sliding* rate of liability.
2. operating or moving on the principle of a slide, as a door or panel.
3. slippery; uncertain; also, sloping. [Obs.]

slīd′ing bạlk (bąk), in shipbuilding, one of the bottom timbers on a launching runway.

slīd′ing bōw (bō), a metal, transverse, horizontal bow mounted on top of electric locomotives or other electric cars to connect with an overhead electric wire.

slīd′ing çon′taçt, an electrical contact which is connected with one part of a circuit and closes that circuit by being slid over a conductor connected with another part of the circuit.

slīd′ing gun′tẽr, in boats, a rig on a sliding topmast for extending a triangular sail.

slīd′ing keel, same as *centerboard.*

slīd′ing sçāle, 1. a standard or schedule, as of rates, wages, etc., which varies with other conditions or standards.
2. a slide rule.

slī·dom′e·tẽr, *n.* a device used in determining and recording the strains or shocks to railway cars caused by sudden stopping.

slīght (slīt), *a.*; *comp.* slighter; *superl.* slightest. [ME. *slight*, not in AS., from O.D. *slicht*, even or plain, *slecht*, vile, of little account; Ice. *slēttr*, smooth, trivial, common.]
1. light in form or build; not stout or heavy; slender.
2. frail; fragile.
3. lacking weight, strength, substance, or significance.
4. small in amount or extent; not great or intense; as, a *slight* fever.
5. cursory; superficial; not thorough; as, *slight* examination.
6. foolish; silly; weak in intellect.
7. contemptuous; slighting; as, a *slight* reply. [Rare.]
Syn.—cursory, fragile, insignificant, little, shallow, small, slender.

slīght, *v.t.*; slighted, *pt., pp.*; slighting, *ppr.* 1. to neglect; to disregard intentionally; to do carelessly or poorly.
2. to treat with disrespect or indifference; to be discourteous toward.
3. to treat as unimportant.
4. to overthrow; to demolish. [Obs.]
to slight off; to dismiss hastily or slightingly, as of no importance. [Rare.]
to slight over; to run over in haste; to perform superficially; to treat carelessly; as, *to slight over* a theme. [Rare.]

slīght, *n.* 1. a slighting or being slighted by pointedly indifferent, disrespectful, or supercilious treatment.
2. an insignificant amount, quantity, etc. [Obs.]

slīght′ẽr, *n.* one who slights.

slīght′ing, *a.* constituting or imparting a slight; discourteous; contemptuous.

slīght′ing·ly, *adv.* in a slighting manner.

slīght′ly, *adv.* 1. in a slight manner.
2. to a slight degree.

slīght′ness, *n.* the quality or state of being slight.

slī′ly, *adv.* same as *slyly.*

slim, *a.*; *comp.* slimmer; *superl.* slimmest. [Ir. *slīm*, thin, lank; Gael. *slīom*, slender, smooth; Ice. *slæmr*, bad, vile.]
1. slender; of small diameter or thickness in proportion to the height or length; as, a *slim* person; a *slim* tree.
2. small in amount, degree, or extent; slight; scant; meager; as, *slim* pickings, a *slim* possibility.
3. sly; crafty. [Dial.]
4. worthless. [Brit. Dial.]

slim, *v.t.* and *v.i.* slimmed, *pt., pp.*; slimming, *ppr.* to make or become slim.

slīme, *n.* [ME. *slyme*, from AS. *slīm*; Ice. *slīm*; Dan. *sliim*, mucus.]
1. soft, moist earth, having an adhesive quality; viscous mud.
2. any soft, ropy, glutinous, or viscous substance.
3. asphalt or bitumen. [Obs.]
4. a mucous, viscous substance exuded from the bodies of certain animals.
5. any moist or sticky substance that is considered filthy or disgusting.
6. [*pl.*] in mining, ore reduced to a fine powder, forming a kind of ore mud: also called *slums.*

slīme, *v.t.*; slimed, *pt., pp.*; sliming, *ppr.* 1. to cover or smear with or as with slime.
2. to clean slime from.

slīme eel, an eellike marine marsipobranch; a hag.

slīme flux (fluks), a liquid given off from the wood or bark of some deciduous trees, usually signifying a diseased condition.

slīme fuñ′gus, same as *slime mold.*

slīme gland, a gland, as in a snail, secreting a slimy mucus.

slīme′man, *n.* one who works with slime (sense 6).

slīme mōld, any organism of the order *Myxomycetes*: also called *slime fungus.*

slīme pit, a pit of slime or adhesive mire.

slīm′ẽr, *n.* the toadfish.

slīme spŏnġe, a myxospongian.

slīme tā′ble (-bl), in mining, a table used as a buddle.

slīm′i·ly, *adv.* in a slimy manner.

slīm′i·ness, *n.* the quality or state of being slimy; viscosity.

slim′ly, *adv.* in a slim state or manner; slenderly.

slim′ness, *n.* the state or quality of being slim.

slimp′sy, *a.*; *comp.* slimpsier; *superl.* slimpsiest, slimsy.

slim′sy, *a.*; *comp.* slimsier; *superl.* slimsiest, [from *slim*, weak, slender.] flimsy. [Colloq.]

slīm′y, *a.*; *comp.* slimier; *superl.* slimiest, 1. of or like slime.
2. covered with or composed of slime.
3. disgusting; repulsive; filthy.

slīne, *n.* a natural transverse rock cleavage, making a sharply defined surface. [Brit.]

slī′ness, *n.* same as *slyness.*

sling, *n.* 1. an instrument for throwing stones, consisting of a strap and two cords: the stone, which is placed in the strap, is thrown by whirling the sling and releasing one of the cords.
2. a slingshot.
3. the act of throwing with or as with a sling; a cast; a throw; a fling.
4. a device, usually a supporting band or strap, used in raising and lowering a heavy object or for carrying something, as a rifle, from the shoulder.
5. a wide piece of cloth looped under an injured arm for support.
6. a chain or rope for fastening a yard to a mast.

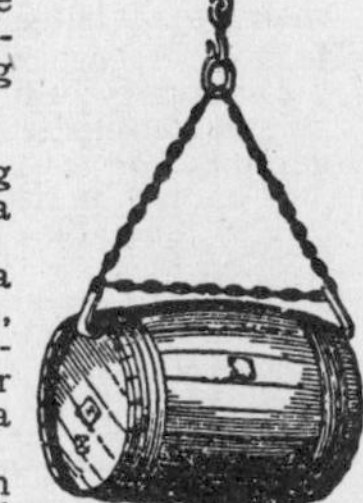

SLING USED IN UNLOADING VESSELS

sling, *v.t.*; slung, *pt., pp.*; slinging, *ppr.* [ME. *slyngen*, from AS. *slingan*; Ice. *slyngva*; Dan. *slynge*; Sw. *slunga*, to sling.]
1. to throw with a sling; as, to *sling* a stone.
2. to throw; to hurl; to cast; to fling.
3. to raise, lower, or carry in a sling.
4. to hang loosely or in a sling; to suspend, especially by several attachments, as a hammock.

sling, *v.i.* to move with long, swinging, elastic steps. [Colloq.]

sling, *n.* [L.G. *slingen*, to swallow.] an iced drink made with alcoholic liquor, water, sugar, and, usually, lemon juice.

sling çärt, a cart for transporting cannon and their carriages, etc. short distances.

sling dog, an iron hook for a sling, with a fang at one end and an eye at the other for a rope, used in pairs with connecting tackle.

sling′ẽr, *n.* 1. a man using a sling for throwing missiles, as in ancient warfare.
2. a person who throws or slings.
3. a person operating, or supervising the use of, a sling, as in loading.

sling psȳ·chrom′e·tẽr (sī-), *n.* a psychrometer that can be whirled about in the air until the reading remains unchanged, thus closely indicating the temperature of the air.

sling′shot″, *n.* a forked stick having an elastic band attached to the forks: used to sling stones.

sling′stōne″, *n.* a stone shot from a sling.

sliñk, *v.i.*; slunk, *pt., pp.*; slinking, *ppr.*; slank, *archaic pt.* [AS. *slincan*, to slink, to crawl, to creep; Sw. *slinka*, to go away secretly and stealthily.] to move in a quiet, furtive, or sneaking manner, as from fear, guilt, etc.; to sneak.

sliñk, *v.t.*; slinked *or* slunk, *pt., pp.*; slinking, *ppr.* to give birth to before the normal time; to expel (a fetus) prematurely: said of animals.

sliñk, *a.* 1. produced prematurely; unfit for food; as, a *slink* calf.
2. thin; slender; lean; starved and hungry. [Dial.]
3. contemptible; sneaky.

sliñk, *n.* 1. a sneaking fellow; a cheat. [Dial.]
2. a calf or other animal born prematurely; also, the flesh of an animal born prematurely.

sliñk′y, *a.* 1. sneaking; stealthy; furtive.
2. sinuous and graceful in movement, line, etc. [Slang.]

slip, *v.i.*; slipped (slipt) *or archaic or poet.* slippt, *pt., pp.*; slipping, *ppr.* [AS. *slipan*, to slip, to glide; D. *slippen*; Dan. *slippe*; Ice. *sleppa*, to slip, slide, glide away.]
1. to go quietly or secretly; to move without attracting notice; as, he *slipped* out of the house.
2. (a) to go imperceptibly; to pass unmarked; as, time *slipped* by; (b) to go, move, pass, etc. smoothly, quickly, or easily.
3. to pass gradually into or out of some condition, activity, habit, opinion, etc.
4. to escape or pass from a person's memory, mind, power, grasp, etc.; as, here is a chance you mustn't allow to *slip.*
5. to move out of place by sliding; to shift or slide from position; as, the plate *slipped* from his hand, the child *slipped* off my knee.
6. to slide accidentally on a slippery surface, lose footing, etc.
7. to make a mistake; to fall into error; to err.
8. to become worse; to lose strength, abilty, mental keenness, etc.; as, he has been *slipping* for several years.
9. to decline slightly; to fall off; as, the market has *slipped.* [Colloq.]
to let slip; to say or tell without intending to.
to slip a cog; (a) to make a mistake; (b) to undergo a mishap; to go wrong; miscarry. [Colloq.]
to slip off; to depart unnoticed.
to slip up; (a) to make a mistake; to be in error; (b) to undergo a mishap; to miscarry. [Colloq.]

slip, *v.t.* 1. to cause to slip or move with a smooth, sliding motion; as, he *slipped* the bolt through the hole.
2. to put (*on*) or take (*off*) quickly or easily, as an article of clothing.
3. to put, pass, insert, etc. quickly, deftly, or stealthily; as, she *slipped* a pill into her mouth; he *slipped* in a cutting remark.
4. (a) to escape or pass from (the mind or memory); (b) to let pass unheeded; to overlook; to miss.
5. to get loose from; to become free of (some

restraining device); as, the prisoner has *slipped* his bonds.

6. to let loose: said of hounds freed for the pursuit of game.

7. to transfer (a stitch) from one needle to another without knitting it, as in forming patterns in, or decreasing the width of, a knitted piece.

8. to slink (a fetus).

to slip one over on; to trick; to hoodwink; to cheat. [Colloq.]

to slip over; to pass over (a matter, etc.) superficially or without adequate attention.

to slip the leash (or *collar*); to disengage oneself from a leash or collar, as a dog; hence, to free oneself from all restraining influences.

slip, *n.* 1. (a) a pier or platform sloping into the water to serve as a landing place; (b) an inclined plane leading down to water, on which ships are built or repaired; (c) a space between piers or wharves, used for the docking of ships.

2. the difference between the actual speed of a vessel and the speed at which it would move if the propeller were acting against a solid.

3. a leash for a dog or other animal.

4. a woman's undergarment, generally about the length of a dress.

5. a child's dress or pinafore.

6. a covering, as for a pillow, that can be easily put on or taken off.

7. an act of slipping, sliding, or falling down.

8. a deviation or turning aside, especially from a practice, course of conduct, etc. considered beneficial or proper.

9. an error or mistake, especially one made inadvertently in speaking, writing, etc.

10. an accident or mishap.

11. the amount or degree of operative inefficiency of a mechanical device, expressed in terms of the difference between theoretical and actual output.

12. movement of one part upon another where no movement is meant to exist; play; slippage.

13. a cleavage and displacement in a rock mass or strata.

14. in cricket, a fielder placed behind the wickets on the off side of the batter.

15. matter found in troughs of grindstones after the grinding of edge tools. [Brit. Dial.]

16. a brass counterfeit piece of money covered with silver. [Obs.]

17. a narrow passage between buildings. [Brit. Dial.]

to give one the slip; to evade or escape from one.

slip, *n.* [ME. *slippe*; M.D. *slippe*, from *slippen*, to cut.]

1. a stem, root, twig, etc. cut or broken off a plant and used for planting or grafting; a cutting; scion.

2. a young person, especially one who is small or slender.

3. any slender person; as, she's a mere *slip* of a woman.

4. a long, thin piece or strip, as of wood.

5. a small piece of paper, especially one prepared for a specific use; as, an order *slip*.

6. a narrow church pew.

7. a particular quantity of yarn. [Brit. Dial.]

8. in insurance, a note of a contract made out before a policy is effected, for the purpose of asking the acceptance of underwriters of the proposed risk.

9. in printing, a proof from a galley.

slip, *v.t.*; slipped (slipt), *pt., pp.*; slipping, *ppr.* to take a slip from (a plant) for grafting.

slip, *n.* [ME.; AS. *slypa*, a paste, slime.] in ceramics, clay thinned to the consistency of cream for use in decorating or casting, or as a cement or coating.

slip'bōard, *n.* a board sliding in grooves.

slip clutch, in machinery, a form of coupling belonging to the class of friction couplings. On the shaft B is fixed a pulley which is tightly surrounded by a friction band *a*. This band is provided with projecting ears, with which the prongs *bb* of a fixed cross *d* on the driving shaft A can be shifted into contact. This cross is free to slide endlong on its shaft, but is connected to it by a sunk feather, so that when it is thrown forward into gear with the gears of the friction band while the shaft is in motion, the band slips round on its pulley until the friction becomes equal to the resistance, and the pulley gradually attains the same motion as the clutch. The arms and sockets *c c*, which are keyed fast on the shaft A, are intended to steady and support the prongs, and to remove the strain from the shifting part.

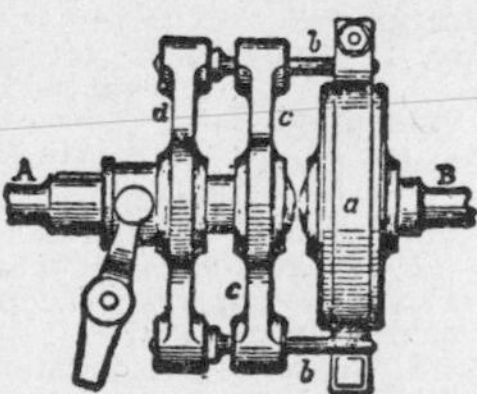

SLIP CLUTCH

slip cŏv'ēr, a removable, fitted cloth cover for an armchair, sofa, etc.

slip'dock, a dock whose floor slopes toward the water, so that its lower end is in deep water and its upper end above high-water mark.

slīpes, *n.pl.* in mining, sledge runners used to drag a skip in a mine.

slip'knot (-not), *n.* a knot made so that it will slip along the rope, etc. around which it is tied; a running knot: also *slip knot*: see *knot*, illus.

slip noose, a noose made with a slipknot.

slip'-on, *a.* 1. easily put on or taken off.

2. to be put on and taken off over the head: said of garments.

slip'-on, *n.* a slip-on garment, as a sweater.

slip'ō″vēr, *a.* and *n.* same as *slip-on*.

slip'pāge, *n.* 1. a slipping, as of one gear past another.

2. the amount of this.

3. the resulting loss of motion or power, as in a chain drive.

slip'pēr, *n.* 1. any person or thing that slips.

2. a kind of light shoe, which may be slipped on with ease; as, bedroom *slippers*.

3. a kind of apron for children.

4. a kind of iron slide or drag for easing heavily loaded wagons down hills.

5. in machinery, a shoe or gib, usually made of a flat piece of iron, attached to a sliding part as a means of adjustment and as a protection against friction.

slip'pēr, *a.* slippery. [Obs.]

slip'pēr an·i·mal'çūle, in zoology, an infusorian of the genus *Paramæcium*.

slip'pēred (-pērd), *a.* wearing slippers.

slip'pēr·flow″ēr, *n.* the slipper plant; also, the slipperwort.

slip'pēr·i·ly, *adv.* in a slippery manner.

slip'pēr·i·ness, *n.* the state or quality of being slippery.

slip'pēr lim'pet, the slipper shell.

slip'pēr·ness, *n.* slipperiness. [Obs.]

slip'pēr plant, in botany, any one of the tropical American plants of the genus *Pedilanthus*; also, the lady's-slipper plant.

slip'pēr shell, a gastropodous mollusk of the genus *Crepidula*.

slip'pēr·wŏrt, *n.* in botany, a plant of the genus *Calceolaria*: so called from the form of the lower lip of the corolla.

slip'pēr·y, *a.*; *comp.* slipperier; *superl.* slipperiest. 1. causing or liable to cause sliding or slipping, as wet, waxed, or greasy surfaces.

2. tending to slip away, as from a grasp or hold.

3. evasive; shifty; deceitful; not reliable or trustworthy.

4. immoral. [Obs.]

slip'pēr·y elm, 1. an American tree, *Ulmus fulva*, with a fragrant, sticky inner bark which is used as a demulcent: also, the bark.

2. a shrub of the Pacific coast, *Fremontia californica*, of the mallow family.

slip'pi·ness, *n.* slipperiness. [Obs.]

slip'py, *a.* slippery. [Dial. or Colloq.]

slip rāils, a series of removable fence rails, used as a gate.

slip ring, one of two or more continuous rings by means of which current is conducted to or from the brushes in a motor or dynamo.

slip rōpe, in nautical usage, a line used to hold a cable about to be slipped.

slip'sheet, *n.* a blank sheet of paper inserted between freshly printed sheets to prevent offset.

slip'sheet, *v.t.* and *v.i.* to insert slipsheets between (printed sheets).

slip'shod, *a.* 1. wearing shoes with worn-down heels.

2. careless or slovenly in manners, actions, and the like; as, a *slipshod* style of writing.

slip'shöe, *n.* a slipper. [Brit. Dial.]

slip'skin, *a.* slippery; elusive. [Obs.]

slip'slop, slip'slap, *n.* 1. cheap, weak liquor; slops. [Colloq.]

2. shallow, pointless talk or writing; twaddle. [Colloq.]

slip stop'pēr, in nautical usage, a device for suddenly releasing an anchor or a chain cable.

slip strēam, the current of air thrust backward by the spinning propeller of an aircraft; propeller wash.

slip'string, *n.* one who has shaken off restraint; a prodigal. [Obs.]

slipt, *v.* archaic and poetic past tense of *slip*.

slip'thrift, *n.* a slipstring. [Obs.]

slip'-up, *n.* an error; an oversight. [Colloq.]

slip'wāy, *n.* a slope or incline leading into the water, as in a shipyard.

slish, *n.* [a variant spelling of *slash*.] a cut; a slit. [Rare.]

slit, *v.t.*, slit *or obs.* slitted, *pt., pp.*, slitting, *ppr.* [AS. *slitan*, to tear, to rend, to break through; Ice. *slita*; Dan. *slide*; Sw. *slita*, to tear, to separate by force.]

1. to cut lengthwise into long pieces or strips, as, to *slit* iron bars into nail rods.

2. to cut or split a long incision or fissure in; as, to *slit* the ear, tongue, or nose.

3. to cut in general.

4. to sever. [Obs.]

slit, *n.* 1. a long, straight cut or tear; as, a *slit* in the ear.

2. a narrow opening, as under a door.

3. a cleft or crack in the breast of cattle. [Brit. Dial.]

slith'ēr, *v.i.* [Ice. *slytha*, to slide.]

1. to slip or slide on or as on a gravelly slope or a similar loose, broken surface.

2. (a) to move along by sliding, slipping, or gliding, as a snake; (b) to walk with a sliding motion.

slith'ēr, *v.t.* to cause to slide or slither.

slith'ēr, *n.* a sliding, slithering motion.

slith'ēr·y, *a.* 1. slippery.

2. like or characterized by a slither; as, a *slithery* walk.

slit shell, a gastropodous shell of the family *Pleurotomariidæ*, distinguished by a deep slit in the outer lip of the aperture.

slit'tēr, *n.* one who or that which slits.

slit'ting mill, 1. a mill where iron bars or plates are slit into nail rods, etc.

2. a machine for slitting or cutting gems, stones, etc. before grinding and polishing.

slit trench, a narrow, relatively shallow trench for protecting the individual soldier from shellfire, etc.

slīve, *v.i.* to sneak. [Brit. Dial.]

sliv'ēr, *n.* [from dial. *slive*, to cut; ME. *sliven*; AS. *slifan*.]

1. a thin, often pointed piece that has been cut, split, or broken off; a splinter.

2. a loose, thin, continuous fiber, as of wool or flax, ready to be drawn and twisted.

sliv'ēr, *v.t.* and *v.i.*; slivered, *pt., pp.*; slivering, *ppr.* to form, cut, split, or break into slivers.

sli'vō·vitz, *n.* [Russ., from *sliva*, a plum.] a kind of plum brandy drunk especially in Slavic countries.

slōat, *n.* same as *slot* (a bar or bolt).

slob, *n.* [Gael. *slaib*, mud.]

1. mud; muddy land. [Dial.]

2. any soft, sloppy surface.

3. a sloppy, stupid, clumsy person. [Colloq.]

slob'bēr, *n.* 1. slaver; slabber.

2. a jellyfish.

3. [*pl.*] in veterinary medicine, salivation.

4. extreme sentimentality in talk, etc.

slob'bēr, *v.t.*; slobbered, *pt., pp.*; slobbering, *ppr.* to slaver or drivel upon.

slob'bēr, *v.i.* 1. to slaver; to drivel saliva upon.

2. to indulge in extreme sentimentality.

slob'bēr·ēr, *n.* 1. one who slobbers; a driveler.

2. a slovenly farmer; also, a jobbing tailor. [Brit. Dial.]

slob'bēr·y, *a.* 1. unpleasantly wet; sloppy; slimy.

2. characterized by slobber or slobbering.

slock, slock'en, *v.t.* to quench; to slake; to allay. [Brit. Dial.]

slock'ing stōne, a piece of rich ore used to lure investors into a worthless mining enterprise. [Brit. Dial.]

slōe, *n.* [AS. *slâ*; Scot. *slae*.]

1. a small, bitter, blue-black wild plum, the fruit of the blackthorn, *Prunus spinosa*; also, the tree bearing it, having black bark, finely serrulate leaves, and white flowers.

2. any of various wild plums.

slōe'-eyed (-īd), *a.* having large, dark eyes.

slōe gin, alcoholic liquor distilled from grain and flavored with fresh sloes.

slog, *v.t.* and *v.i.*; slogged, *pt., pp.*; slogging, *ppr.* to slug; to hit hard.

slog, *v.t.* and *v.i.* [ME. *sloggen.*] to make (one's way) heavily and with great effort; to plod; to toil.

slō'găn, *n.* [Gael. *sluaghgairm*, the signal for battle among the Highland clans; *sluagh*, a host, and *gairm*, a call.]
1. the war cry or gathering signal of a Highland clan in Scotland.
2. a catchword or rallying motto distinctly associated with a political party or other group.
3. a catch phrase used to advertise a product.

slog'gẽr, *n.* one who slogs.

sloid, slojd (sloid), *n.* a sloyd.

slōke, *n.* [Ir. *sleabhac.*] 1. an edible seaweed; laver.
2. the vegetable ooze in river beds.

slo͞o, *n.* a slough. [Brit. Dial.]

slo͞op, *n.* [D. *sloep*, *sloepschip*; L.G. *sluup*, from *slupen*, to glide.] a small, one-masted vessel originally rigged fore-and-aft with a jib, mainsail, and often topsails and staysails: the modern sloop usually has a jib-headed mainsail and is distinguished from the cutter in having the mast further forward and only a single headsail.

SLOOP

slo͞op of war, 1. originally, a sailing vessel rigged in any of several ways and mounting from 10 to 32 guns.
2. later, any war vessel larger than a gunboat, having guns mounted on one deck only.

slo͞op'-rigged (-rigd), *a.* having rigging like that of a sloop.

slop, *n.* [Ice. *slabb*, dirt from sleet and rain.]
1. watery snow or mud; slush.
2. a splash or puddle of spilled liquid.
3. any liquid or semiliquid food that is unappetizing or of poor quality.
4. [*often pl.*] (a) liquid waste of any kind; (b) kitchen waste or swill, used for feeding animals.
5. [*pl.*] distillery mash after the alcohol has been removed.
6. a sloppy, careless, or slovenly person. [Slang.]

slop, *v.t.*; slopped (slopt), *pt., pp.*; slopping, *ppr.* 1. to spill or cause to overflow, as a liquid.
2. to drink grossly and greedily.
3. to spill liquid upon; to soil by spilling liquid upon.

slop, *v.i.* 1. to spill or splash.
2. to walk or splash through slush or mud.
to slop over; (a) to overflow or spill, as a liquid when its container is tilted; (b) [Colloq.] to make a display of sentimentality; to gush.

slop, *n.* [AS. *slop*, a frock or overgarment; Ice. *sloppr*, a wide outer dress, a gown; D. *slobbe*, a pair of slops, or loose, bagging trousers.]
1. a smock frock; any kind of outer garment made of linen, as a nightgown, cloak, or mantle.
2. [*pl.*] a loose lower garment; wide breeches.
3. [*pl.*] cheap, ready-made clothing.
4. [*pl.*] in the navy, the clothes and bedding of a sailor.

slop bā'sin (-sn), a vessel into which the dregs from tea or coffee cups are emptied at the table.

slop book, in the British navy, a register of clothing, soap, tobacco, and religious books supplied to the men.

slōpe, *n.* [from AS. *slopen*, pp. of *slūpan*, to slip, to glide; Ice. *slapa*, to hang loosely.]
1. a piece of ground that is not flat or level; rising or falling ground.
2. any inclined line, surface, position, etc.; slant.
3. deviation from the horizontal or vertical.
4. the amount or degree of this.
5. the land area that drains into a given ocean.
6. in mathematics, the rate of change in a vector function when at the maximum rate of decrease.

slōpe, *a.* sloping. [Poetic.]

slōpe, *v.t.*; sloped (slōpt), *pt., pp.*; sloping, *ppr.* to cause to slope.

slōpe, *v.i.* to have an upward or downward inclination; to take an oblique direction; to incline; to slant.

slōpe'ness, *n.* slant; obliquity.

slōp'ing, *a.* that slopes or slants; inclined.

slōp'ing·ly, *adv.* in a sloping manner; obliquely.

slop mōld'ing, a process in brickmaking in which the mold is made wet to prevent the adhesion of clay.

slop pāil, a pail or bucket for slops.

slop'pi·ly, *adv.* in a sloppy manner.

slop'pi·ness, *n.* the state or quality of being sloppy.

slop'py, *a.* 1. consisting of or covered with slop; wet and splashy; muddy, slushy.
2. splashed or spotted with liquids.
3. (a) very untidy; showing lack of care; slovenly; messy; (b) careless; slipshod. [Colloq.]
4. gushingly sentimental. [Colloq.]

slop'sell″ẽr, *n.* one who sells cheap, ready-made clothes.

slop'shop, *n.* a shop where cheap, ready-made clothes are sold.

slop'wŏrk, *n.* 1. the manufacture of cheap, ready-made clothing.
2. careless, untidy work of any kind.

slōp'y, *a.* sloping; having many inclines.

slosh, *n.* slush.

slosh, *v.i.*, sloshed (slosht), *pt., pp.*; sloshing, *ppr.* 1. to splash or flounder in slush.
2. to go about carelessly. [Colloq.]

slosh, *v.t.* to shake or agitate (a liquid or something in a liquid).

slosh wheel (hwēl), a trammel wheel.

slosh'y, *a.* slushy.

slot, *n.* [ME. *slotte*; D. *sluiten*, to shut; Sw. *sluta*, to shut, *slöt*, closed.]
1. the fastening of a door; a bar; a bolt. [Brit. Dial.]
2. a piece of timber that connects or holds together larger pieces; a slat.

slot, *n.* [ME. *sleuth*, a path; Ice. *slóth*, a track or trail, as in snow; Scot. *sleuth*, a track, whence *sleuth* hound.]
1. a track or trail of an animal, especially a deer.
2. any track, trace, or trail.

slot, *v.t.*; slotted, *pt., pp.*; slotting, *ppr.* to follow the slot, or trail, of.

slot, *n.* [from OFr. *esclot*, the hollow between the breasts.]
1. a hollow in a hill or between two ridges. [Scot.]
2. a narrow notch, groove, or opening, as a keyway in a piece of machinery, a slit for a coin in a vending machine, etc.
3. a nozzle-shaped passage through a wing of an airplane near the leading edge, formed by a main and an auxiliary airfoil and designed to minimize wind drag.
4. the narrow opening which accommodates the shank of the grip of a cable car.
5. a trapdoor in the stage of a theater. [Rare.]

slot, *v.t.*; slotted, *pt., pp.*; slotting, *ppr.* 1. to shut with violence; to slam.
2. to make a slot or slots in.

slōth (*or* sloth), *n.* [AS. *slæwth*, from *slāw*, slow.]

SLOTH (24 in. long)

1. disinclination to action or labor; sluggishness; habitual indolence; laziness; idleness.
2. slowness; delay.
3. any of certain edentate, tree-dwelling mammals, of which only two species are known; *Bradypus tridactylus*, native to South America, about the size of a common cat, of a gray color, though frequently spotted with brown and white, especially when young; and *Bradypus* or *Cholopus didactylus*, native to the West Indies, about half the size of the former. These animals are so called from the slowness of their motions.
4. one of the extinct edentates; a mylodon or megathere.
Australian or *native sloth*; a koala.

slōth, *v.i.* to be idle. [Obs.]

slōth, *v.t.* to hinder; to delay. [Obs.]

slōth an·i·mal'cūle, a tardigrade.

slōth beăr, a bear with shaggy black fur, a flexible snout, and long white claws: it is found in India and Ceylon.

slōth'fụl, *a.* inactive; sluggish; lazy; indolent; idle.

slōth'fụl·ly, *adv.* in a slothful manner; lazily; sluggishly; idly.

slōth'fụl·ness, *n.* the state or quality of being slothful; inactivity; laziness.

slōth mŏn'key, a slow lemur.

slot'hound, *n.* a sleuthhound. [Scot.]

slot mȧ·chīne', a vending machine, gambling device, etc. fitted with a slot in which a coin must be inserted before the mechanism will work.

slot'ted, *a.* having a slot.

slot'tẽr, *n.* a slotting machine.

slot'tẽr·y, *a.* 1. sluggish; slothful. [Obs.]
2. foul; wet. [Brit. Dial.]

slot'ting, *n.* the act or process of making slots; the operation of a slotting machine.

slot'ting mȧ·chīne', a variety of planing machine for making slots in machinery.

slouch, *n.* [akin to Ice. *slókr*, a slouch, or dull, inactive person; Sw. *sloka*, to droop.]
1. a person who is awkward, lazy, or (in colloquial usage and usually with a negative) incompetent; as, he's no *slouch* at tennis.
2. (a) a drooping or bending forward of the head and shoulders; (b) slovenly posture in general.
3. a drooping or hanging down, as of the brim of a hat.

slouch, *v.i.*; slouched (sloucht), *pt., pp.*; slouching, *ppr.* 1. to have, or move with, a slovenly, drooping gait or posture.
2. to hang down; to droop, as a hat brim.

slouch, *v.t.* to cause to hang down; as, to *slouch* one's hat.

slouch hat, a soft hat with a broad, flexible brim.

slouch'i·ly, *adv.* in a slouchy manner.

slouch'i·ness, *n.* the state or quality of being slouchy.

slouch'ing, *a.* 1. hanging limply.
2. slow, lazy, or awkward, as in gait or carriage.

slouch'y, *a.* slouching, especially in posture.

slough (sluf), *n.* 1. the skin of a snake, especially the outer layer that is periodically cast off.
2. any castoff layer or covering: often used figuratively.
3. in medicine, a mass of dead tissue that separates from the surrounding tissue.
4. a shell, pod, or husk. [Brit. Dial.]

slough, *v.i.*; sloughed, *pt., pp.*; sloughing, *ppr.*
1. to be shed, as the skin of a snake; to come off; to fall away.
2. to shed skin or other covering: often used figuratively.
3. in medicine, to separate from the surrounding tissue: said of dead tissue.
Often with *off* or *away*.

slough, *v.t.* 1. to throw off; to shed; to discard; to get rid of (often with *off*).
2. in bridge, to get rid of (a card considered valueless).

slough (slou; *for* 4, slö), *n.* [AS. *slōh*, a slough.]
1. a place of deep mud or mire; a hole full of mire; a deep quagmire.
2. [from *slough of despond*, in Bunyan's *Pilgrim's Progress*.] deep, hopeless dejection or discouragement.
3. moral degradation.
4. a swamp, bog, or marsh, especially one that is part of an inlet or backwater: also spelled *slew*, *slue*.

slough grȧss (slou), an American grass, sometimes called *nimble Will.*

slough′ing (sluf′), *n.* the act of casting off a skin or shell, as in certain reptiles and insects.

slough′y (sluf′), *a.* of or resembling slough, or dead tissue.

slough′y (slou′), *a.* of, like, or full of sloughs; miry.

Slō′vak, *n.* 1. any of a Slavic people living chiefly in Slovakia.
 2. the West Slavic language of the Slovaks, closely related to Czech.

Slō′vak, *a.* of Slovakia, the Slovaks, their language, etc.

Slō·vä′ki·ăn, *n.* and *a.* Slovak.

slŏv′en, *n.* [M.D. *slof,* a careless person, from *sloffen,* to neglect.]
 1. a slovenly person; one who is careless in his habits, behavior, appearance, or methods of work; a dirty or untidy person.
 2. a rascal; a rogue. [Obs.]

Slō·vēne′, *n.* 1. any of a Slavic people living chiefly in Slovenia.
 2. their South Slavic language.

Slō·vēne′, *a.* of Slovenia, the Slovenes, their language: also *Slovenian.*

Slō·vē′ni·ăn, *a.* and *n.* Slovene.

Slō·vē′nish, *a.* and *n.* slovenian.

slŏv′en·li·ness, *n.* the state or quality of being slovenly.

slŏv′en·ly, *a.* 1. characteristic of a sloven.
 2. careless in habits, behavior, appearance, or methods of work; untidy; slipshod.

slŏv′en·ly, *adv.* in a slovenly manner; negligently; carelessly.

slŏv′en·ness, *n.* slovenliness. [Obs.]

slŏv′en·ry, *n.* slovenliness. [Obs.]

slōw, *v.* obsolete past tense of *slay.*

slōw, *a.*; *comp.* slower; *superl.* slowest, [AS. *slāw,* slow, lazy; Dan. *slöv*; Sw. *slö,* Ice. *sljór,* blunt, dull, slow; O.H.G. *slēo,* slow; akin to Goth. *slavan,* to be still or silent.]
 1. not quick or clever in understanding; dull; obtuse.
 2. (a) taking a longer time than is expected or usual to act, move, go, happen, etc.; (b) not quick, ready, or prompt; as, a *slow* retort; *slow* to appreciate.
 3. making relatively little progress for the time spent; marked by low speed, rate of rhythm, etc.; not fast or rapid.
 4. holding back fast progress, development, etc.; making speed difficult or impossible; as, a *slow* growing season; a *slow* track.
 5. showing a time that is behind the correct time: said of a timepiece.
 6. passing slowly or tediously; dull; not interesting; as, a *slow* afternoon.
 7. characterized by little activity; slack; as, *slow* trading.
 8. lacking in energy; sluggish.
 9. behind the times; out of fashion.
 10. burning so as to give off a low or moderate heat; as, a *slow* fire.
 11. gradual, as growth.
 slow lemur or *loris*; a nocturnal, slow-moving species of lemur, *Nycticebus tardigradus* or *Loris stenops*. It is a small animal of the East Indies.

slōw, *adv.* slowly.

slōw, *v.t.*; slowed, *pt., pp.*; slowing, *ppr.* 1. to make slow or slower.
 2. to retard; to delay.
 Often with *up* or *down.*

slōw, *v.i.* to go or become slow or slower (often with *up* or *down*).

slōw, *n.* in zoology, (a) a slow-moving skink; (b) a newt or eft that moves slowly.

slōw′back, *n.* a lubber; a loiterer. [Obs.]

slōw çōach, one who moves or acts slowly. [Slang.]

slōw′down, *n.* a slowing down or being slowed down; specifically, a planned slowing down of industrial production on the part of labor or management.

slōw′-gāit″ed, *a.* having a slow gait or pace.

slōwh (slō), *v.* obsolete past tense of *slay.*

slōw′hound, *n.* a bloodhound. [Archaic.]

slōw′ly, *adv.* in a slow manner; not rapidly.

slōw match, a match, or fuse, that burns slowly, used for setting off blasting charges.

slōw′-mō′tion, *a.* 1. moving or operating below usual or normal speed.
 2. denoting a motion picture photographed by exposing more pictures per minute than is usual, so that the action on the screen, when the film is projected at the normal speed, appears much slower than the original action.

slōw′-mōv′ing, *a.* 1. moving slowly; showing little progress or activity.
 2. selling in a relatively small quantity, as merchandise, stocks, etc.

slōw′ness, *n.* the state or quality of being slow in any sense.

slōw′pōke, *n.* a person who acts or moves slowly. [Slang.]

slōw tīme, standard time, as distinguished from daylight-saving time, war time, etc. [Colloq.]

slōw′-wit″ted, *a.* having a mind that works slowly and ineffectively; not bright or alert; dull.

slōw′wŏrm, *n.* [AS. *slāwyrm,* slay worm, from its supposed deadly sting.] the blindworm, a legless lizard.

sloyd, *n.* [Sw. *slöjd,* skill.] a Swedish system of manual training devised for use in elementary schools, and intended to teach the use of tools and materials while giving mental and physical development.

slub, *n.* [perh. from M.D. *slubbe,* thick mud, ooze.]
 1. a roll of fiber, as of wool or cotton, twisted slightly for use in spinning.
 2. yarn with fibers that are untwisted at intervals.

slub, *v.t.*; slubbed, *pt., pp.*; slubbing, *ppr.* to draw out and twist slightly for use in spinning, as wool; to form into slubs.

slub′bẽr, *n.* 1. one who slubs or who manages a slubbing machine.
 2. a slubbing machine.

slub′bẽr, *v.t.*; slubbered, *pt., pp.*; slubbering, *ppr.* [a form of *slabber, slobber.*]
 1. to daub; to stain; to smear over. [Dial.]
 2. to do carelessly or awkwardly; to botch. [Dial.]

slub″bẽr·dē·gul′liŏn (-yun), *n.* a mean, dirty, base wretch. [Archaic.]

slub′bẽr·ing·ly, *adv.* in a slovenly manner.

slub′bing bil′ly, a slubbing machine as formerly made.

slub′bing mȧ·ȼhïne′, a machine used in spinning factories for drawing out the rolls of wool and slightly twisting them.

slud, *n.* wet mud. [Brit. Dial.]

sludġe (sluj), *n.* [a variant of *slutch.*]
 1. mud, mire, or ooze covering the ground or forming a deposit at the bottom of bodies of water.
 2. finely broken drift ice.
 3. any heavy, slimy deposit, sediment, or mass, as the waste resulting from oil refining, the mud brought up by a mining drill, the precipitate in a sewage tank, the sediment in a steam boiler, etc.
 sludge acid; the waste acid from refining petroleum.

sludġe dōor, the door in a boiler used in removing sediment.

sludġ′ẽr, *n.* a device for removing the sludge from a bore hole.

sludġ′y, *a.*; *comp.* sludgier; *superl.* sludgiest, of or like sludge; muddy; oozy; miry; slushy.

slūe, *v.t.* and *v.i.*; slued, *pt., pp.*; sluing, *ppr.* [Early Mod. Eng. from nautical use.] to turn or swing around a pivot or fixed point: also spelled *slew.*

slūe, *n.* 1. the act of sluing.
 2. the position to which a thing has been slued.
 Also spelled *slew.*

slūe, *n.* same as *slough* (swamp).

slūe, *n.* a slew (large number).

slug, *v.t.*; slugged, *pt., pp.*; slugging, *ppr.* [AS. *slean,* to strike.] to hit hard, as with the fist or with a blackjack. [Colloq.]

slug, *n.* a hard hit; a blow. [Colloq.]

slug, *n.* [ME. *slugge,* slow, clumsy person or thing.]
 1. a small mollusk of the family *Limacidæ,* resembling and moving like a land snail, but having only a rudimentary internal shell or none at all.
 2. any of several caterpillars that resemble slugs.
 3. an animal, vehicle, etc. that moves sluggishly.
 4. a sea slug.
 5. an obstruction. [Obs.]

slug, *v.i.* to be slow or lazy, dull or inert.

slug, *v.t.* to make sluggish; also, to hinder; to retard.

slug, *a.* slow. [Obs.]

slug, *n.* 1. a small piece of metal, generally approaching a rounded form, as a bullet.
 2. anything used as a projectile, as a scrap of iron.
 3. in printing, (a) a strip of metal less than type high used to separate lines of type or fill in the top or bottom of a column; (b) an indicator bearing a word or number cast on a strip of metal, used for identification; (c) a line of type made in one piece or strip, as by a linotype machine.
 4. a piece of metal shaped like and used in place of a coin in automatic coin machines.
 5. formerly, a heating iron used by hatters.
 6. a gold coin issued privately in California in 1849; also, the $50 commemorative piece issued in 1915 for the Panama Exposition.
 7. in metallurgy, partially roasted ore.
 8. a stunted horn or stump.

slug, *v.t.* to load, as a gun, with slugs.

slug, *v.i.* to become changed so as to fit the bore of a gun: said of a bullet. [Rare.]

slug, *n.* [D. *sluck,* a swallow.] a single drink, especially of straight alcoholic liquor. [Slang.]

slug′ȧ·bed, *n.* [from ME. *slugge,* a lazy person or thing.] a lazy person who stays in bed after others are up.

slug çat′ẽr·pil·lăr, same as *slug worm.*

slug flȳ, a fly, the larva of which is a slug worm.

slug′gȧrd, *n.* [*slug,* to be lazy, and *-ard.*] one habitually lazy and inactive; an indolent or slothful person.

slug′gȧrd, *a.* sluggish; lazy.

slug′gȧrd·ïze, *v.t.* to make sluggard. [Rare.]

slug′gȧrd·y, *n.* the condition or quality of indolence; sluggishness.

slug′gẽr, *n.* one who hits or strikes hard; specifically, (a) a prize fighter; (b) a baseball player with a high percentage of extra base hits. [Colloq.]

slug′gish, *a.* [from *slug* (mollusk), and *-ish.*]
 1. lacking in energy, alertness, or vigor; indisposed to exertion; lazy; slothful.
 2. slow or slow-moving; not active; dull.
 3. not functioning with normal vigor; as, a *sluggish* disgestive system.

slug′gish·ly, *adv.* in a sluggish manner; lazily; slothfully; slowly.

slug′gish·ness, *n.* 1. natural or habitual indolence; sloth; dullness.
 2. inertness; lack of power to move.
 3. slowness; as, the *sluggishness* of a stream.

slug′gy, *a.* sluggish. [Obs.]

slug hôrn, 1. a horn, as of an ox, short and ill-formed, as if stunted in its growth.
 2. a slogan. [Obs.]

slug wŏrm, any legless insect larva whose outward appearance and movements resemble a slug.

slūice, *n.* [D. *sluys, sluis,* from OFr. *escluse*; Fr. *écluse*; LL. *exclusa,* f. pp. from L. *excludere,* to shut out, exclude, *ex,* out, and *claudere,* to shut.]
 1. any natural or artificial body of water controlled by a floodgate.
 2. an artificial water channel or passage which is regulated at its head by gates or valves, as in canals.
 3. the water held back by or passing through such a gate.
 4. a gate or valve used in opening or closing a sluice; a floodgate: also *sluice gate.*
 5. any channel, especially one for excess water.
 6. a sloping trough or flume through which water is run, as in washing gold ore, carrying logs, etc.

slūice, *v.t.*; sluiced (slöst), *pt., pp.*; sluicing, *ppr.* 1. to draw off by or as by means of a sluice.
 2. (a) to wash with water flowing in or from a sluice; (b) to wash off with a rush of water; as, the sailors *sluiced* the deck with hoses.
 3. to carry (logs, etc.) in a sluice.

slūice, *v.i.* to run or flow in or as in a sluice.

slūice gāte, the gate closing a sluice; a floodgate or water gate.

slūice valve, 1. a sluice gate.
 2. a gate valve which regulates the discharge of a water main or pipe.

slūice′wāy, *n.* a sluice; an artificial channel for water, with or without a floodgate.

slūi′cy (slū′), *a.* 1. falling in streams; descending copiously, as a drenching rain.
 2. of or like a sluice. [Rare.]

slūit, *n.* [D.] in South Africa, a channel made by a temporary stream.

slum, *n.* [c. 1800, from *cant*; orig. sense, a room.] a heavily populated area in which housing and other living conditions are extremely poor.

slum, *v.i.*; slummed, *pt., pp.*; slumming, *ppr.*
1. to frequent or live in slums.
2. to visit or make a tour of slums.

slum, *n.* in mining, slime.

slum'bẽr, *v.i.*; slumbered, *pt., pp.*; slumbering, *ppr.* [AS. *slumerian*, from *sluma*, slumber; Dan. *slumre*; D. *sluimeren*; G. *schlummern*, to sleep or slumber. As to insertion of *b*, compare *number, humble.*]
1. to sleep.
2. to be in an inactive state or one of negligence or dormancy.

slum'bẽr, *v.t.* 1. to put or lay to sleep.
2. to stupefy or stun.
3. to spend in sleeping.

slum'bẽr, *n.* 1. sleep.
2. an inactive or quiescent state.

slum'bẽr·ẽr, *n.* one who slumbers.

slum'bẽr·ing·ly, *adv.* in a sleepy or slumbering manner.

slum'bẽr·less, *a.* deprived of or denied slumber; sleepless.

slum'bẽr·ous, *a.* 1. inclined to slumber; sleepy; drowsy.
2. suggestive of or characterized by slumber.
3. causing sleep or drowsiness; soporific.
4. tranquil; calm; quiet; as, a *slumberous* little desert town.

slum'bẽr·y, *a.* given to sleep; disposed to slumber; slumberous.

slum'brous, *a.* same as *slumberous.*

slum·gul'liŏn (-yun), *n.* 1. the refuse draining from the cutting-up of a whale for its blubber; also, the offal of any fish.
2. a drink of weak tea or coffee; also, a meat stew with vegetables. [Slang.]
3. a low, worthless fellow: used in derision.

slum'mẽr, *n.* 1. one who slums.
2. one who lives in a slum.

slum'ming, *n.* the act or the practice of visiting slums.

slump, *v.i.* [prob. from L.G. *slumpen*, to come about by accident.]
1. to fall, sink, or collapse, especially suddenly or heavily.
2. to fall or sink into a bog or through a crust of ice or snow.
3. to decline suddenly, as in value, activity, etc.
4. to have a drooping posture or gait.

slump, *n.* 1. the act of slumping; a sudden or sharp fall.
2. a sudden falling in prices, business activity, etc.; as, a *slump* in corn.

slump, *n.* a lump; the whole; a lump sum or gross amount. [Scot.]

slump, *v.t.*; slumped (slumpt), *pt., pp.*; slumping, *ppr.* to bring together in a heap; to lump. [Scot.]

slump'y, *a.* yielding; not firm; marshy; swampy. [Brit. Dial.]

slung, *v.* past tense and past participle of *sling.*

slung shot, a small, heavy weight attached to a strap or thong, for use as a weapon.

slun̄k, *v.* alternative past tense and past participle of *slink* (to give birth).

slun̄k, *v.* past tense and past participle of *slink* (to move).

slũr, *v.t.*; slurred, *pt., pp.*; slurring, *ppr.* [prob. from M.D. *slooren, sleuren*, to drag along the ground, to do negligently or carelessly.]
1. to soil; to sully; to stain; to tarnish. [Dial.]
2. to disparage or discredit; to depreciate; to calumniate; to traduce; to asperse; to speak slightingly of.
3. to pass over quickly and carelessly; to make little of (often with *over*).
4. to cheat, originally by slipping or sliding a die in a particular way: an old gambling term. [Obs.]
5. to pronounce in an indistinct, rapid manner.
6. in music, (a) to sing or play (different and successive notes) by gliding from one to another without a break; (b) to mark (notes) with a slur.
7. in printing, to blur or smear, as an impression from type; to mackle.

slũr, *v.i.* 1. to cheat; especially, to cheat by slipping a die out of a box so that it will not turn. [Obs.]
2. to walk or move in a slovenly, shuffling manner. [Brit. Dial.]

slũr, *n.* 1. the act or process of slurring.
2. something slurred, as a pronunciation.
3. a blot, stain, or smear.
4. anything harmful or intended to be harmful to a person's reputation; aspersion, reproach, stigma, etc.
5. a trick; an imposition. [Obs.]
6. in music, the smooth blending of slurred notes; also, a curved mark (⌒) connecting several notes of different degree, indicating that they are to be played or sung in a smooth, gliding manner.
7. in printing, a blurred spot.
8. in a knitting machine, a device for depressing the jack sinkers.

slũr'ry, *n.*; *pl.* **slũr'rieṣ,** [from ME. *sloor.*] a thin mixture of water and any of several fine, insoluble materials, as clay, cement, soil, etc.

slush, *n.* [prob. via dial. from O.N.]
1. sludge or watery mire; soft mud; slosh.
2. wet, half-melted snow or ice.
3. in nautical usage, the refuse fat or grease, especially of salt meat, skimmed off in cooking.
4. overly sentimental talk or writing; drivel.
5. any of several greasy compounds used as lubricants or rust preventitives for machinery; especially, a mixture of white lead and lime with which the bright parts of machinery are covered to prevent their rusting.

slush, *v.t.*; slushed (slusht), *pt., pp.*; slushing, *ppr.* 1. to splash or cover with slush, especially in lubrication or protecting.
2. to patch with mortar or cement.
3. in nautical usage, to grease with slush, as a mast.
4. to wash roughly; as, to *slush* a floor with water. [Colloq.]

slush fund, 1. money used for bribery, political pressure, or other corrupt purposes.
2. a fund established aboard ship from the sale of slush, refuse, and the like and used to purchase minor luxuries.

slush'y, *a.*; *comp.* slushier; *superl.* slushiest,
1. covered with or full of slush.
2. of or like slush.

slut, *n.* [Ice. *slöttr*, a heavy, loglike fellow; Sw. *slata*, an idle woman; Dan. *slatte*, a slut.]
1. a woman who is negligent of her appearance; a dirty, slovenly woman.
2. a woman of loose character.
3. a bold or impudent girl: a humorous usage.
4. a female dog; a bitch.

slutch, *n.* sludge; mire; slush. [Brit. Dial.]

slut'tẽr·y, *n.* the character and practices of a slut. [Obs.]

slut'tish, *a.* 1. like a slut; not neat or cleanly; dirty; careless of dress and neatness.
2. having the morals of a slut; meretricious.

slut'tish·ly, *adv.* negligently; dirtily.

slut'tish·ness, *n.* the practice of a slut.

slȳ, *a.*; *comp.* slier *or* slyer; *superl.* sliest *or* slyest, [ME. *slye, slie*; O.N. *slægr*, sly.]
1. skillful or clever. [Dial.]
2. skillful at trickery or deceit; crafty; wily.
3. showing a secretive, crafty, or wily nature; cunningly underhanded.
4. mischievous in a playful or waggish way; roguish.
5. secret; concealed; illicit.
on the sly; secretly; stealthily.
Syn.—cunning, subtle, crafty, artful, wily, underhanded, astute, stealthy.

slȳ'boots, *n.* a sly, cunning, or waggish person. [Colloq.]

slȳ'ly, *adv.* stealthily; cunningly; in a sly way: also spelled *slily.*

slȳ'ness, *n.* the condition of being sly; sly conduct.

slȳpe, *n.* [prob. from L.G.] in a cathedral or monastic church, a covered passage leading from the transept to the chapter house.

smack, *n.* [ME. *smac, smak*; AS. *smæc.*]
1. a distinctive taste or flavor, especially one that is faint or slight.
2. a small amount; a touch; a trace; a suggestion.
3. a taste, bit, or mouthful.
4. a slight or superficial knowledge; a smattering. [Rare.]

smack, *v.i.* to have a smack (usually with *of*); as, diction that *smacks of* the stage.

smack, *n.* [of Gmc. echoic origin.]
1. a sharp noise made by pressing the lips together and parting them suddenly, as in gusto.
2. a loud kiss.
3. a sharp blow with the hand or any flat object; a slap; a crack.
4. the sound of such a blow.

smack, *v.t.* 1. to press (the lips) together and part them suddenly so as to make a smack.
2. to kiss or slap loudly.

smack, *v.i.* to make a loud, sharp noise, as on impact; as, the snowball *smacked* against the wall.

smack, *adv.* 1. with or as with a smack; violently; sharply.
2. directly; fully; as, he ran *smack* into trouble.

smack, *n.* [D. *smak*, Dan. *smakke*, a smack; AS. *snacc*, Ice. *snekkja*, a ship, so called from its snakelike appearance.]
1. a small sailboat, commonly rigged as a sloop, used chiefly in the coasting and fishing trade.
2. a fishing vessel fitted with a well for keeping fish alive.

smack'ẽr, *n.* 1. one who or that which smacks; especially, a loud or emphatic kiss.
2. a hard punch or blow. [Slang.]
3. a dollar. [Slang.]

smack'ing, *a.* sharp; brisk; lively; vigorous.

smack'ing, *n.* an explosive sound; a smack.

small, *a.* [ME. *smal*, narrow; AS. *smal, smæl*; L.G. and D. *smal*; Goth. *smals*; Dan. and Sw. *smal*; Ice. *smár*. Probably from root *mal*, with strengthening *s*.]
1. little in size, especially when compared with others of the same kind; not great or large; as, a *small* house.
2. (a) little in quantity, extent, numbers, value, duration, etc.; as, a *small* income; (b) of slight intensity; of limited degree or scope; (c) consisting of relatively few units; numerically low.
3. being of little moment, weight, or importance; trivial; insignificant; petty; trifling; as, it is a *small* matter or thing; a *small* subject.
4. containing little of the principal quality, or little strength; weak; diluted; light; as, *small* beer.
5. (a) fine; clear; (b) gentle; soft; faint; not loud: said of sound or the voice.
6. characterized by littleness of mind or character; narrow-minded; sordid; selfish; ungenerous; mean; base; unworthy.
7. carrying on business on a small scale; having only a little investment, capital, etc.; as, a *small* farmer.
8. of low or inferior rank; obscure; not notable.
small coal; coal which has been screened.
small fry; (a) young or small fish; (b) people or things regarded as of little or no importance; (c) small children; youngsters.
small letter; a lower-case letter, as distinguished from a capital.
small pica; a size of type, about 11 point.
small potatoes; (a) a person or thing of little or no importance; (b) petty or insignificant people or things. [Colloq.]
small stuff; in nautical usage, small ropes and cordage, etc.
small talk; light conversation about common, everyday things; chitchat.
to feel small; to feel shame or humiliation.

small, *n.* 1. something small; small part; as, the *small* of the back.
2. [*pl.*] small things or articles collectively.
3. [*pl.*] knee breeches; smallclothes.

small, *adv.* 1. in small pieces.
2. in a low, faint tone; softly.
3. in a small manner.
to sing small; to become humble or timid after having been arrogant, boastful, etc.

small, *v.t.* to make smaller; to lessen; to minify.

small'ăġe, *n.* a kind of wild celery, *Apium graveolens.*

small çal'ō·rie, see *calorie*, sense 1.

small chanġe, 1. coins, especially those of low denomination.
2. something of little value or importance.

small'çlōtheṣ, *n.pl.* close-fitting knee breeches of the kind worn during the eighteenth century. [Archaic.]

small hourṣ (ourz), the first few hours following midnight.

small in·tes'tine, the narrow, convoluted upper part of the intestines, extending from the pyloric end of the stomach to the large intestine.

small'ish, *a.* somewhat small.

small'-mīnd'ed, *a.* blindly selfish, prejudiced, vindictive, etc.; petty; mean; narrow.

small'ness, *n.* the condition or quality of being small.

small of the back, the concave part of the back just above the hips.

small'pox, *n.* an acute, infectious virus disease characterized by vomiting, and an eruption which is first papular, then vesicular, and finally pustular; also, by fever which is marked by a distinct remission, beginning with the eruption and continuing until the latter becomes pustular. The period of incubation is about twelve days, the eruption beginning about the third or fourth day after incubation with the formation of small red spots on the forehead, face, and wrists. This eruption spreads over the body. The pustules finally dry up and break, forming soft yellow crusts. After a week the scabs fall off, often leaving pitted scars or pockmarks.

smalls, *n.pl.* 1. smallclothes.
2. responsion (sense 2).

small stōres, small miscellaneous articles, as tobacco, soap, etc., stocked by a ship's store for sale to the crew.

small'swōrd (-sōrd), *n.* a light, tapering, straight sword, used especially in fencing.

small tīme, the inferior vaudeville circuits.

small'-tīme', *a.* limited, minor, or petty; not large-scale, extensive, or significant: opposed to *big-time.* [Slang.]

small'-town', *a.* of or characteristic of a small town as opposed to a city.

smal'ly, *adv.* in a small manner, quantity, or degree. [Obs.]

smalt, *n.* [It. *smalto,* a name given to different bodies which are used as coatings in a melted or liquefied state and subsequently harden, from O.H.G. *smalzjan,* to smelt.]
1. deep-blue glass prepared from silica, potash, and oxide of cobalt: used, when pulverized, as a pigment.
2. pigment made in this way.
3. the deep-blue color of this pigment.

smalt'ine, *n.* same as *smaltite.*

smalt'īte, *n.* [*smalt* and *-ite.*] a white to gray native cobalt arsenide, $CoAs_2$, crystalline or granular in form and used as a blue pigment in coloring glass and ceramics.

smäl'tō, *n.*; *pl.* **smäl'tï,** [It., from Gmc. base seen also in Eng. *smelt,* M.D. *smalt,* melted fat].
1. a kind of colored glass or enamel used in mosaics.
2. a piece of this.

smär'agd, *n.* [Gr. *smaragdos,* a bright green stone.] an emerald.

smȧ·rag'dine, *a.* [L. *smaragdinus,* from Gr. *smaragdos,* emerald.]
1. pertaining to emerald; consisting of emerald.
2. emerald in color.

smȧ·rag'dīte, *n.* an emerald-green mineral, a variety of amphibole or hornblende.

smärt, *v.t.*; smarted, *pt., pp.*; smarting, *ppr.* [ME. *smerten*; AS. *smeortan.*]
1. (a) to cause sharp, stinging pain, as a slap; (b) to be the source of such pain, as a wound; (c) to feel such pain.
2. to feel mental distress or irritation, as in grief, resentment, remorse, etc.; to suffer.
3. to be punished; to bear penalties or the evil consequences of anything.

smärt, *v.t.* to cause to smart.

smärt, *n.* 1. a smarting sensation; sharp pain or distress whether physical or mental.
2. [pl.] shrewdness, intelligence, or acumen. [Slang.]

smärt, *a.*; *comp.* smarter; *superl.* smartest. 1. causing a keen pain; as, a *smart* lash.
2. severe; sharp; intense; as, *smart* pain.
3. quick; vigorous; lively; as, a *smart* skirmish.
4. (a) alert; clever; capable; quick; witty; (b) shrewd or sharp, as in one's dealings.
5. neat; clean; fresh.
6. in keeping with the current fashion; stylish.
7. quite strong, intense, numerous, etc.; considerable; as, that's a right *smart* rain. [Dial.]
8. dressed in a showy manner; pretentious. [Rare.]
9. impertinent; impudent; pert. [Obs.]
smart set; sophisticated, fashionable people, collectively.
Syn.—keen, pungent, piercing, quick, vigorous, sharp, severe, active, clever, brilliant, vivacious, witty, ready, spruce, brisk, fresh, dressy, showy.

smärt al'eck (-ik), [*smart* and *Aleck,* nickname for *Alexander.*] a person who is offensively conceited and self-assertive; a cocky, bumptious person. [Colloq.]

smärt bomb, a bomb directed to its target by a self-contained guidance system which responds to a laser beam or television signals, as from an aircraft.

smärt'en, *v.t.* and *v.i.* 1. to make or become smart; to improve in appearance or style; to spruce up.
2. to make or become brisk, bright, or alert.

smärt'ly, *adv.* in a smart manner.

smärt mŏn'ey, [from *smart,* n.]
1. money paid as compensation for injuries, wounds, etc. received in the line of duty.
2. money paid to cancel, or compensate for failure to keep the terms of, a contract, agreement, etc.
3. money paid over and above usual damages as an extra penalty for gross negligence, cruelty, etc.
4. [from *smart,* a. 4.] money bet by those thought to have the best chance of picking a winner.

smärt'ness, *n.* 1. the state or quality of being smart; as, the *smartness* of pain.
2. liveliness; briskness; vivacity; wittiness; as, the *smartness* of a reply or of a phrase.
3. fashionableness.

smärt'weed, *n.* any of several plants, especially *Persicaria hydropiper,* growing in wet places, with spikes of tiny flowers and leaves which cause the skin to smart on contact.

smash, *n.* [prob. from *mash,* with intens. *s-.*]
1. a hard, heavy hit or blow; specifically, a hard, overhand tennis stroke that is difficult to return.
2. (a) a violent, noisy breaking or shattering; (b) the sound of this.
3. (a) a violent collision; (b) a wreck.
4. complete ruin or defeat; total failure, especially in business; smashup.
5. a drink made of mint, sugar, water, and some kind of alcoholic liquor.
6. an overwhelming popular success.
to go (or *come*) *to smash*; (a) to become smashed or broken; (b) to fail utterly; to be ruined. [Colloq.]

smash, *a.* that is a smash (*n.* 6).

smash, *v.t.* 1. to break or shatter into pieces with noise or violence.
2. to hit (a tennis ball) with a hard, overhand stroke.
3. to hit with a hard, heavy blow or impact.
4. to ruin completely; to defeat utterly; to destroy; to wreck.

smash, *v.i.* 1. to break into pieces.
2. to be destroyed; to come to ruin.
3. to collide with crushing force.
4. to move by smashing or with force.

smash'ẽr, *n.* 1. one who or that which smashes.
2. anything out of the ordinary in any way. [Slang.]
3. one who passes counterfeit coin. [Slang.]

smash'up, *n.* 1. a wreck or collision, especially one that does great damage.
2. complete defeat or failure; ruin.
3. any disaster or catastrophe.

smatch, *n.* taste; smack. [Obs.]

smat'tẽr, *v.t.*; smattered, *pt., pp.*; smattering, *ppr.* [ME. *smateren,* to chatter, from O.N.]
1. to talk or utter with only slight or superficial knowledge.
2. to dabble in; to study or learn superficially.

smat'tẽr, *v.i.* 1. to talk superficially.
2. to have a slight or superficial knowledge of anything. [Now Rare.]

smat'tẽr, *n.* a smattering.

smat'tẽr·ẽr, *n.* one who has only a slight, superficial knowledge of any subject.

smat'tẽr·ing, *n.* 1. slight, superficial knowledge (usually with *of*).
2. a small number.

smēar, *v.t.*; smeared, *pt., pp.*; smearing, *ppr.* [ME. *smerien*; AS. *smerian,* from *smeru,* grease; Ice. *smyrjan,* from *smör,* grease.]
1. to cover, daub, or soil with something greasy, sticky, or dirty.
2. to apply or daub (something greasy, sticky, or dirty) so as to leave a coating, mark, etc.
3. to make a smear with; as, he *smeared* his hand across the wet paint.
4. to harm the reputation of; to malign; to defame; to slander.
5. to overwhelm, defeat, stop, thwart, etc. completely and decisively. [Slang.]

smēar, *v.i.* to be or become smeared.

smēar, *n.* 1. a spot or mark made by smearing.
2. a small quantity of some substance, as blood, smeared on a slide for microscopic study, etc.
3. a smearing or slandering of a reputation.
4. (a) [Obs.] ointment; oily substance; (b) a substance to be smeared on something.

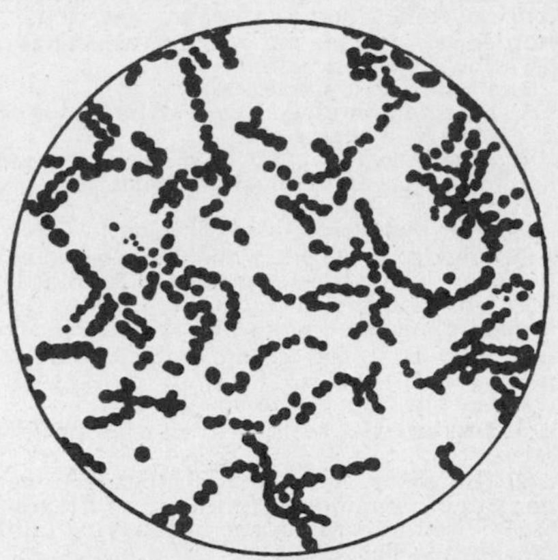

SMEAR CULTURE
Streptococcus from pus; agar culture

smear culture; in bacteriology, a culture or bacterial growth obtained by spreading the substance used for inoculation on the material in which the culture is grown.

smēar'çāse, *n.* [from G. *schmierkäse,* from *schmieren,* to spread, and *käse,* cheese.] same as *cottage cheese.*

smēar dab, a flounder of Europe, *Microstomus kitt.*

smēar'i·ness, *n.* the quality or condition of being smeary.

smēar'y, *a.*; *comp.* smearier; *superl.* smeariest.
1. covered with or having smears; smeared.
2. tending to smear, as wet ink.

smēath, *n.* the smew. [Brit. Dial.]

smeç'tīte, *n.* [from Gr. *smēktis,* fuller's earth, from *smēchein,* to wipe off, to cleanse.] an argillaceous earth: so called from its property of taking grease out of cloth, etc.

smed'dum, *n.* 1. ground malt flour; powder. [Scot.]
2. mettle; spirit; liveliness. [Scot.]
3. fine particles of ore left after sifting; slack; also, the shale or clay between beds of coal. [Scot.]

smee, *n.* 1. the smew. [Brit. Dial.]
2. a pochard.
3. the widgeon or baldpate.
4. the pintail duck, *Dafila acuta.* [Dial.]

smeeth, *v.t.* to smooth. [Obs.]

smeg'mȧ, *n.* [Gr. *smēgma,* soap.] in physiology, a thick, cheesy secretion found under the prepuce in males and around the clitoris and labia minora in females.

smeg·mat'iç, *a.* being of the nature of soap.

smell, *v.t.*; smelled *or* smelt, *pt., pp.*; smelling, *ppr.* [ME. *smellen, smillen, smullen,* allied to L.G. *smellen, smelen,* to burn slow with a strong smoke, to smoke; D. *smeulen,* to smoulder; Dan. *smul,* dust, powder.]
1. to perceive by the nose, or by the olfactory nerves; to perceive the scent or odor of; as, to *smell* a rose; to *smell* perfumes.
2. to perceive as though by the smell or scent; to sense the presence or existence of.
3. to test by the scent or odor; to sniff; as, *smell* the milk and tell me if it's sour.
to smell out; to look for or find by or as by smelling.
to smell up; to fill with a disagreeable odor; to cause to smell bad.

smell, *v.i.* 1. to affect the olfactory nerves; to have an odor or suggestion of something specified: followed by *of*; as, to *smell of* smoke; to *smell of* musk.
2. to have a particular smell or odor; also, to have or emit an unpleasant odor.
3. to use the sense of smell; to sniff (often with *at* or *of*).
4. to lack ability, worth, merit, etc.; to be of poor quality. [Slang.]

smell, *n.* 1. that one of the five senses of the body by which a substance is perceived through the chemical stimulation of nerves (olfactory nerves) in the nasal cavity by particles given off by that substance.
2. scent; odor; the characteristic stimulation of any specific substance upon the olfactory nerves.
The sweetest *smell* in the air is the violet. —Bacon.
3. an act of smelling.
4. that which suggests the presence or existence of something; a trace; a suggestion.

smell'ẽr, *n.* 1. a person or animal that has or uses the sense of smell.
2. a thing that smells.
3. a person employed to test by the sense of smell; as, a cheese *smeller*.
4. a sensitive hair, bristle, antenna, etc. used as an organ of touch; a feeler.
5. the nose. [Slang.]
6. a prying person; a spy. [Slang.]

smell'-fēast, *n.* 1. one who is apt to find and frequent good tables; a parasite. [Archaic.]
2. a feast at which the guests are supposed to feed upon the odors of the viands. [Rare.]

smell'ing, *n.* 1. the sense by which odors are perceived.
2. the act of one who smells.

smell'ing bot'tle, a bottle filled with smelling salts.

smell'ing salts, an aromatic mixture of carbonate of ammonium with some fragrant scent, used as an inhalant in relieving faintness, headaches, etc.

smell'-less, *a.* without smell; not having the sense of smell.

smell'y, *a.*; *comp.* smellier; *superl.* smelliest, having or giving off a bad or disagreeable odor.

smelt, *v.* alternative past tense and past participle of *smell.*

smelt, *n.*; *pl.* **smelts or smelt,** [AS. and Dan.]
1. a small, troutlike food fish of the genus *Osmerus*, inhabiting northern seas. It is of a silvery-white color, the head and body being semitransparent. They spawn in tidal rivers. The American smelt, *Osmerus mordax*, inhabits the coast of New England.
2. a gull; a simpleton. [Obs.]

SMELT
(*Osmerus mordax*)

smelt, *v.t.*; smelted, *pt., pp.*; smelting, *ppr.* [M.D. or M.L.G *smelten.*]
1. to melt or fuse, as ore, for the purpose of separating the pure metal from extraneous substances; to scorify.
2. to refine or extract (metal) in this way.

smelt, *v.i.* to undergo fusing or smelting.

smelt'ẽr, *n.* 1. one who smelts or is engaged in the work or business of smelting.
2. an apparatus for smelting; a smeltery.
3. one who is occupied in smelting a particular thing; as, an ore *smelter.*

smelt'ẽr, *n.* a fisherman who fishes for smelts.

smelt'ẽr·y, *n.*; *pl.* **smelt'ẽr·ies,** a place, business, etc. for smelting.

smelt'ing fũr'năce, a furnace used for the reducing or fusing of ore; a blast furnace.

smelt'ing wŏrks, an establishment in which smelting is carried on.

smẽrk, smẽrk'y, same as *smirk, smirky.*

smẽr'lin, *n.* a loach. [Obs.]

smethe, *n.* 1. the pintail duck. [Dial.]
2. the smew. [Brit. Dial.]

SMEW
(*Mergus albellus*)

smew (smū), *n.* [etym. doubtful.] a small duck of the merganser family, *Mergus albellus*, of Europe and Asia. The hooded merganser, *Lophodytes cucullatus*, is sometimes called the hooded smew.

smick'ẽr, *v.i.* [Sw. *smickra*; Dan. *smigre*, to flatter.] to look amorously or wantonly. [Obs.]

smick'et, *n.* a woman's undergarment; a chemise. [Brit. Dial.]

smid'dum tāils, *pl.* in mining, the sludge or slime of ore.

smid'dy, *n.* a smithy. [Brit. Dial.]

smidg'en (-in), *n.* a small particle; an insignificant part or piece. [Dial.]

smift, *n.* in mining, a match of paper saturated with niter or other combustible substance, for igniting a charge of powder; a fuse.

smig'gins, *n.* a thick soup prepared from barley. [Old Slang.]

smī·lȧ·çā'ceous, *a.* of or belonging to a family of woody vines (*Smilacaceæ*) with parallel-veined leaves, one-sexed flowers, and round berries.

Smī·lā'cē·ae, *n.pl.* an order of climbing plants of which smilax is typical: now included in the order *Liliaceæ.*

Smī''lȧ·cī'nȧ, *n.* in botany, a genus of plants, family *Convallariaceae*, native to America and Asia and characterized by panicles of small, white flowers which give way to variously colored berries, and alternate leaves.

smī'lax, *n.* [L.; Gr. *smilax*, bindweed.]
1. a twining greenhouse vine of the lily family, having small soft, bright-green leaves: much used in forming festoons and garlands in decorations.
2. any of a number of related, usually prickly, woody vines of the order *Smilaceæ*, including the sarsaparilla.

smīle, *v.i.*; smiled, *pt., pp.*; smiling, *ppr.* [ME. *smilen*, from a L.G. source.]
1. to have or take on a facial expression showing pleasure, amusement, affection, friendliness, irony, derision, etc. and characterized by an upward curving of the corners of the mouth and a sparkling of the eyes.
2. to look (*at, on,* or *upon* someone) with a pleasant expression of this kind.
3. to have a favorable, pleasing, or agreeable appearance; as, hillsides *smiling* in the sunlight.

smīle, *v.t.* 1. to express by or with a smile; as, to *smile* a welcome.
2. to change or affect by smiling.

smīle, *n.* 1. the act of smiling.
2. the facial expression made in smiling.
3. a favorable, pleasing, or agreeable appearance; bright, pleasant aspect.

smīle'äġe book, a folder of coupons exchangeable by United States soldiers for tickets of admittance to the theatres maintained at army camps during World War I. [Slang.]

smīle'fụl, *a.* smiling; full of smiles.

smīle'less, *a.* not having a smile.

smīl'ẽr, *n.* one who smiles.

smīl'et, *n.* a half-smile. [Rare.]

smīl'ing·ly, *adv.* in a smiling manner.

smīl'ing·ness, *n.* the state of being smiling.

smin·thū'rid, *n.* a member of the *Sminthuridæ.*

Smin·thū'ri·dae, *n.pl.* [Gr. *sminthos*, a mouse, and *oura*, a tail.] a family of insects, typified by the genus *Sminthurus*, having an oviform body and four-jointed antennae with a long terminal joint.

smīrch, *v.t.*; smirched (smīrcht), *pt., pp.*; smirching, *ppr.* [ME. *smorchen*; prob. from OFr. *esmorcher*, to hurt.]
1. to make dirty or discolor, as by smearing or staining with grime.
2. to sully; to dishonor (a reputation, good name, etc.).

smīrch, *n.* 1. a smudge; smear; stain.
2. a stain on reputation, etc.

smīrk, *v.i.*; smirked, *pt., pp.*; smirking, *ppr.* [AS. *smercian*, to smile.] to smile in a conceited, knowing or annoying, complacent way.

smīrk, *n.* a conceited, complacent smile.

smīrk, *a.* spruce; neat. [Brit. Dial.]

smīrk'ing·ly, *adv.* in a smirking manner.

smīrk'y, *a.* smirking. [Dial.]

smit, *v.* past participle of *smite*; also, obsolete third person present indicative of *smite.*

smit, *n.* a fine clay used for marking sheep. [Scot. and Dial.]

smitch, *n.* a bit; a particle.

smīte, *v.t.*; smote *or obs.* smit, *pt.*; smitten, smit, *or* smote, *pp.*; smiting, *ppr.* [ME. *smiten*; AS. *smittan*, to smite, dash, pt. *smat*; also *be-smitan*, to defile, pollute, infect; D. *smijten*, to beat, kick, cast, or throw; Dan. *smide*, to fling, pitch.]
1. (a) to hit or strike hard; (b) to bring into a specified condition by or as by a blow; as, the Lord will *smite* him dead.
2. to defeat, punish, destroy, or kill.
3. to strike or attack with powerful or disastrous effect.
4. to affect strongly and suddenly (*with* some feeling); as, *smitten with* dread.
5. to disquiet mentally; to distress; as, *smitten* by conscience.
6. to strike or impress favorably; to inspire with love; to enamor; as, she has *smitten* him with her charms.

smīte, *v.i.* 1. to strike hard; to deal a heavy blow or blows; as, he *smote* upon the door with his sword.
2. to fall, dash, come, pass, etc. with sudden force.

smīte, *n.* a blow.

smīt'ẽr, *n.* one who smites or strikes; also, [Obs.] a weapon, as a sword, used in smiting.

smith, *n.* [ME.; AS. *smith*, a craftsman, a carpenter, a smith; Ice. *smidhr*; Goth. *smitha*, an artificer; D. *smid*; G. *schmied*, a smith. From the root of *smooth* rather than that of *smite.*]
1. a person who makes or repairs metal objects, especially by shaping the metal while it is hot and soft; metalworker: usually in combination, as silver*smith.*
2. a blacksmith.

smith'ăm, *n.* same as *smeddum.*

smith'çrȧft, *n.* the art or occupation of a smith.

smith·ẽr·eens', *n.pl.* [Ir. *smidirin.*] small fragments or broken pieces; bits. [Colloq.]

smith'ẽrs, *n.pl.* smithereens. [Colloq.]

smith'ẽr·y, *n.*; *pl.* **smith'ẽr·ies,** 1. the workshop of a smith.
2. the work or craft of a smith.

smith'ing, *n.* the act or art of working metal into the intended shape.

Smith·sō'ni·ăn, *a.* of or pertaining to James Smithson (1765–1829), a British mineralogist and chemist, who gave a large sum of money to the United States for the foundation of an educational institution (the *Smithsonian Institution*) which was founded at Washington, D. C. in 1846.

Smith·sō'ni·ăn, *n.* the Smithsonian Institution.

smith'sŏn·īte, *n.* [after James *Smithson* and *-ite.*]
1. native zinc carbonate, $ZnCO_3$.
2. a native silicate of zinc; calamine.

smith'y, *n.*; *pl.* **smith'ies,** [AS. *smiththe.*] the shop of a smith, especially a blacksmith; a forge.

smī'ting līne, a line by which a stoppered sail may be loosened without sending a man aloft. [Brit.]

smitt, *n.* same as *smit* (clay).

smit'ten, *v.* alternative past participle of *smite.*

smit'ten, *a.* 1. struck with great force.
2. disastrously or deeply affected; afflicted.
3. deeply in love. [Colloq.]

smit'tle, *v.t.* to infect. [Brit. Dial.]

smit'tle, *a.* infectious. [Brit. Dial.]

smock, *n.* [from AS. *smoc* or O.N. *smokkr*, a smock. It may mean properly a garment one creeps into or slips over one's head; compare Ice. *smjugan*, to creep through or into; Ice. *smokka*, to put on a shirt, sleeve, loop, or the like.]
1. a chemise; a woman's undergarment. [Archaic.]
2. a loose, shirtlike, outer garment worn to protect the clothes.

smock, *v.t.*; smocked (smokt), *pt., pp.*; smocking, *ppr.* 1. to furnish with or dress in a smock.
2. to decorate with smocking.

smock, *a.* relating to a smock; hence, pertaining to a woman. [Archaic.]

smock frock, *n.* a coarse linen frock or shirt, especially of the kind worn over the coat by European farm laborers.

smock'ing, *n.* decorative stitching used in gathering cloth to make it hang in even folds.

smock'less, *a.* lacking a smock; naked.

smock mill, a windmill whose top is the only part which turns to meet the wind.

smock rāce, a race formerly run by women for the prize of a fine smock.

smog, *n.* a mixture of smoke and fog.
smōk'ȧ·ble, *a.* capable of being smoked; suitable for smoking.
smōke, *n.* [AS. *smoca*; D. and L.G. *smook*; Dan. *smög*; G. *smauch*, smoke.]
1. the vaporous matter arising from something burning and made visible by minute particles of carbon suspended in it.
2. any vapor, fume, mist, etc. resembling smoke.
3. an act or period of smoking tobacco, etc.; as, do we have time for a *smoke?*
4. something without substance, significance, or lasting reality; fruitless or insubstantial result; as, our plans went up in *smoke*.
5. something that is beclouding or obscuring.
6. something to smoke, as a cigarette or pipeful of tobacco.
7. in physical chemistry, a suspension of solid particles in a gas.
a dry smoke; the holding of an unlighted cigar in the lips. [Colloq.]
London smoke; a dark gray or lead color.
smōke, *v.i.*; smoked (smōkt), *pt.*, *pp.*; smoking, *ppr.* 1. to give off smoke or a smokelike substance.
2. to discharge smoke in the wrong place, especially into a room, as a furnace, fireplace, etc.
3. to give off too much smoke, as a lamp, type of fuel, etc.
4. to move very rapidly, especially so as to raise dust.
5. to draw the smoke of tobacco, etc. into the mouth, and often lungs, and blow it out again.
6. to suffer; to be punished. [Obs.]
smōke, *v.t.* 1. to stain or color with smoke.
2. to treat with smoke, as in flavoring or curing some meats, controlling insects, etc.
3. to drive or force out with or as with smoke; as, we *smoked* the woodchuck from his hole.
4. to draw the smoke of or from (tobacco, a pipe, cigar, etc.) into the mouth, and often lungs, and blow it out again.
5. to detect or be suspicious of; as, he smoked the *trick* at once. [Archaic.]
6. to tease or mock. [Obs.]
to smoke out; to drive or force into the open with or as with smoke; to force out of hiding, secrecy, etc.
smōke ärch, the smokebox of a locomotive.
smōke ball, 1. a spherical case of pasteboard or canvas filled with a composition, which, while burning, emits a great quantity of thick smoke.
2. a puffball.
3. a ball used in trapshooting, which on being hit emits a puff of smoke.
smōke black, lampblack.
smōke bōard, a sliding or suspended board or metal plate placed before the upper part of a fireplace to cause an increased draft, and prevent the smoke from coming out into the room.
smōke bomb (bom), a kind of bomb containing chemicals which when ignited give off dense clouds of smoke: used in military operations to make a smoke screen.
smōke'box, *n.* a compartment in a steam boiler between the flues and the smokestack.
smōke çloud, a cloud of smoke.
smōke'-drȳ, *v.t.*; smoke-dried, *pt.*, *pp.*; smoke-drying, *ppr.* to cure or dry by smoke, as beef, hams, etc.
smōke'house, *n.* 1. a place in which meats or fish are flavored and cured by smoke.
2. a room in which hair is removed from hides subjected to the smoke, heat, and gases of burning tan.
smōke'jack, *n.* a device for turning a fireplace roasting spit by means of a fly or wheel rotated by the current of ascending air in a chimney.
smōke'less, *a.* having or making little or no smoke; as, *smokeless* chimneys.
smokeless powder; a kind of gunpowder exploding with little or no smoke.
smōke'less·ly, *adv.* without smoke.
smōk'ẽr, *n.* 1. a person or thing that smokes; as, that chimney is a bad *smoker*.
2. a person who habitually smokes tobacco.
3. a railroad car or compartment in which smoking is allowed, especially on a train on which smoking is not elsewhere allowed.
4. a social gathering for men only: so called because at one time etiquette forbade smoking in mixed gatherings.
5. a contrivance used to blow smoke among bees to prevent them from leaving the hive or swarming.
smōke sāil, a small sail hoisted before the funnel of a vessel's galley, to allow the smoke to rise before it is blown aft by the wind.
smōke sçreen, a cloud of artificial smoke spread to screen the movements of troops, ships, etc.
smōke'stack, *n.* a chimney or pipe for the discharge of smoke from a steamship, locomotive, factory, etc.
smōke'stōne, *n.* same as *cairngorm*.
smōke'tīght (-tīt), *a.* so close as not to allow the passage of smoke.
smōke tree, a small ornamental tree, *Rhus cotinus*, which bears long feathery fruit stalks, and when in full bloom appears as if covered with a cloud of smoke or mist: also called *smoke plant*.
smōke wash'ẽr, a device to remove from smoke the particles of unconsumed carbon which it contains.
smōke'wood, *n.* the *Clematis vitalba*, or virgin's-bower, whose stems are sometimes smoked by boys.
smōk'i·ly, *adv.* in a smoky manner
smōk'i·ness, *n.* the quality or condition of being smoky.
smōk'ing, *n.* 1. the act of emitting smoke.
2. the act or practice of smoking tobacco.
smōk'ing bēan, the pod of the catalpa tree, sometimes used by boys for smoking.
smōk'ing çär, a railroad car in which smoking is permitted: also called *smoker*.
smōk'ing jack'et, a loose, heavy jacket, usually trimmed with braid and worn for smoking indoors to protect other clothing from the smell of tobacco.
smōk'ing room, a room set apart in a residence, hotel, etc. for smoking.
smōk'y, *a.*; *comp.* smokier; *superl.* smokiest, 1. giving off smoke, especially more than is usual or desirable.
2. having the appearance or nature of smoke; as, a *smoky* fog.
3. filled with smoke; as, a *smoky* atmosphere.
4. having the color of smoke.
5. colored, soiled, or tarnished with smoke; as, *smoky* rafters.
6. doubtful; suspicious.
smoky quartz; cairngorm, a variety of quartz.
smōl'dẽr, *v.i.*; smoldered, *pt.*, *pp.*; smoldering, *ppr.* [Late ME. *smoldren*, from hyp. Gmc. *smul-* (cf. *smell*).]
1. to be consumed by slow combustion; to burn and smoke without flame.
2. to exist in a suppressed state or with activity stifled.
3. to show suppressed signs of anger or hate; as, his glance *smoldered*.
Also spelled *smoulder*.
smōl'dẽr, *v.t.* to suffocate; to smother. [Obs.]
smōl'dẽr, *n.* a smoldering.
smōl'dẽr·ing·ness, *n.* the state or condition of smoldering.
smōl'dẽr·y, *a.* suffocating; smothering. [Obs.]
smōlt, *n.* [Gael. *smal*, a spot.] a salmon when it has acquired its silvery scales, and first leaves fresh water to descend to the sea.
smooch, *v.t.* and *n.* same as *smutch*.
smoor, *v.t.* to smother. [Scot.]
smooth, *a.*; *comp.* smoother; *superl.* smoothest, [ME. *smothe*; AS. *smōthe*.]
1. (a) having an even or level surface; having no roughness or projections that can be seen or felt; (b) having its projections leveled by wear; as, a *smooth* tire.
2. having an even consistency; without lumps; as, a *smooth* paste.
3. even, calm, or gentle in flow or movement; untroubled by storm or roughness; as, *smooth* seas, a *smooth* voyage, etc.
4. free from interruptions, irregularities, obstacles, difficulties, etc.; as, *smooth* progress.
5. calm; serene; not easily agitated or ruffled, as a temper, disposition, etc.
6. free from hair, beard, etc.; as, a *smooth* cheek.
7. pleasing to the taste; not harsh or irritating; bland.
8. having an easy, gentle, flowing rhythm or sound.
9. suave, polished, or ingratiating, especially in a flattering, insincere way; as, *smooth* words, a *smooth* manner.
This *smooth* discourse and mild behavior oft conceal a traitor. —Addison.
10. very pleasant, attractive, or enjoyable; as, a *smooth* time. [Slang.]
11. polished; competent; charming; as, a *smooth* dancer. [Slang.]
12. in mechanics, frictionless.
13. in phonetics, not aspirated.
14. in botany, void of roughness or pubescence.
Syn.—glossy, even, plain, flat, level, unruffled, bland, sleek, calm.
smooth, *n.* 1. that which is smooth; the smooth part of anything; as, the *smooth* of the neck.
2. the act of smoothing.
smooth, *v.t.*; smoothed, *pt.*, *pp.*; smoothing, *ppr.* 1. to make level or even.
2. to remove the lumps from.
3. to free from interruptions, difficulties, etc.; to make easy.
4. to make calm or serene; to soothe.
5. to make less crude; to polish; to refine.
to smooth away; to remove (difficulties, obstacles, etc.).
to smooth down; to make smooth or calm; to soothe.
to smooth over; to cause to seem unimportant; to make light of; to palliate; to minimize, as faults.
smooth, *v.i.* 1. to use flattering or soothing words. [Obs.]
2. to become smooth.
smooth, *adv.* smoothly.
smooth'bōre, *a.* having no grooves or ridges on the inner surface of the barrel: said of guns: opposed to *rifled*.
smooth'bōre, *n.* a smoothbore gun.
smooth'bōred, *a.* smoothbore.
smooth brēath'ing, in Greek, (a) the sound of a vowel beginning a word when it is pronounced without an aspiration, or the sound of *h*, preceding it; (b) the symbol (') placed before such a vowel in writing. Distinguished from *rough breathing*.
smooth'-chinned, *a.* beardless.
smooth'en, *v.t.* and *v.i.* to make or become smooth.
smooth'ẽr, *n.* one who or that which smooths.
smooth'-fāced' (-fāst'), *a.* 1. having no beard or mustache; smooth-shaven.
2. having a smooth face, or surface; as, a *smooth-faced* tile.
3. having a false semblance of sincerity; plausibly ingratiating.
smooth'ing ī'ron (-ũrn), an iron instrument with a polished face for smoothing clothes; a flatiron.
smooth'ing plāne, a small, fine plane, used for smoothing and finishing work.
smooth'ly, *adv.* in a smooth manner.
smooth mus'cle, muscle controlled by the involuntary nervous system, as that in the uterus, intestines, etc.: also called *nonstriated muscle*.
smooth'ness, *n.* the condition or quality of being smooth; as, the *smoothness* of a floor, *smoothness* of speech.
smooth'-shāv'en, *a.* wearing no beard or mustache.
smooth'-spō'ken, *a.* speaking in a pleasing, persuasive, or polished manner.
smooth'-tŏngued' (-tungd'), *a.* smooth-spoken, especially in a plausible or flattering way.
smör'gås·bord, smor'gas·bord (smor'gȧs-bōrd, smũr'gȧs-bōrd; *Sw.* smẽr'gōs-bōrd), *n.* [Sw.] 1. hors d'oeuvres or appetizers, especially as served buffet style at a long table.
2. a meal composed of these.
3. a restaurant serving smörgåsbord.
smor·zän'dō (-tsän'), **smor·zä'tō** (-tsä'), *a.* and *adv.* [It.] in music, dying away.
smōte, *v.* alternative past tense and past participle of *smite*.
smŏth'ẽr, *v.t.*; smothered, *pt.*, *pp.*; smothering, *ppr.* [ME. *smortheren*, from AS. *smorian*, to stifle, preserved in Scot. *smoor*.]
1. to stifle; to suffocate; to prevent (a person) from breathing or getting air; also, to kill by smothering.
2. to cover (a fire), excluding air from it and causing it to smolder or die down.
3. to suppress; to stifle; to conceal; to hide by or as by covering; as, he *smothered* a yawn.
4. to cook thickly covered with another substance; as, liver *smothered* in onions.

smŏth′ẽr, *v.i.* 1. to be suffocated; to be stifled.
2. to be suppressed or concealed.
3. to smolder. [Dial.]

smŏth′ẽr, *n.* 1. dense, suffocating smoke, dust, steam, etc.
2. a smoldering fire. [Archaic.]
3. a smoldering state or condition.
4. a confused turmoil; a welter.

smŏth′ẽr flȳ, any of the various species of *Aphis.* [Brit.]

smŏth′ẽr·i·ness, *n.* the state of being smothery.

smŏth′ẽr·ing·ly, *adv.* suffocatingly; suppressingly.

smŏth′ẽr·y, *a.* tending to smother or stifle; suffocating.

smouch, *v.t.* to kiss. [Now Dial.]

smouch, *n.* a noisy kiss. [Now Dial.]

smöuch, *v.t.* [closely allied to *smut,* but perhaps directly from the Scandinavian; Sw. *smuts*; Dan. *smuds,* filth, dirt.] to soil or smut.

smöuch, *n.* a dirty spot; a smutch.

smouch, *v.t.* [AS. *smeogan,* to creep.] to acquire by pilfering; to filch.

smōul′dẽr, *n.* and *v.* same as *smolder.*

smōul′dry, *a.* smoldery. [Obs.]

smudġe, *n.* [variant of *smutch.*]
1. a suffocating smoke.
2. a fire burning in such a way as to produce a dense smoke, as for the purpose of driving away insects or protecting plants from frost.
3. a smutch; a dirty streak; a stain, blur, or smear.

smudġe, *v.t.*; smudged, *pt., pp.*; smudging, *ppr.* 1. to subject to smoke to cure or preserve, as herring. [Obs.]
2. to smutch; to stain; to streak with dirt.
3. to smoke (an orchard, etc.) to drive away insects or protect against frost.

smudġ′ẽr, *n.* one who or that which smudges.

smudġ′i·ly, *adv.* in a smudgy manner.

smudġ′i·ness, *n.* the quality or condition of being smudgy.

smudġ′y, *a. comp.* smudgier; *superl.* smudgiest, covered with smudges, stained, smeared, etc.

smudġ′y, *a.* smoldering; making a dense smoke. [Brit. Dial.]

smug, *a.*; *comp.* smugger; *superl.* smuggest, [prob. from L.G. *smuk,* trim, neat.]
1. originally, neat; spruce; trim; smart.
2. narrowly contented with one's own accomplishments, beliefs, morality, etc.; self-satisfied; complacent.

smug, *n.* 1. a recluse student who studies very hard. [Brit. Slang.]
2. a smug person. [Obs.]

smug, *v.t.*; smuged, *pt., pp.*; smugging, *ppr.* to make spruce; to cause to be smug.

smug′gle, *v.t.*; smuggled, *pt., pp.*; smuggling, *ppr.* [from D. *smuckeln* or L.G. *smuggeln*; akin to AS. *smûgan*; Ice. *smjûga,* to creep.]
1. to import or export secretly, as goods which are forbidden by a government to be imported or exported; secretly to import or export (dutiable goods) without paying the duties imposed by law.
2. to bring, take, carry, introduce, etc. secretly or stealthily.

smug′gle, *v.i.* to export or import goods contrary to law; to be a smuggler.

smug′glẽr, *n.* 1. one who smuggles.
2. a ship employed in smuggling.

smug′gling, *n.* the act, practice, or offense of clandestinely importing or exporting prohibited goods or dutiable goods without paying the customs.

smug′ly, *adv.* in a smug manner.

smug′ness, *n.* the quality or condition of being smug.

smut, *n.* [from L.G. *smutt*; akin to G. *schmutz,* dirt.]
1. (a) sooty matter; (b) a particle of this.
2. a spot made by something dirty.
3. obscene language.
4. any of various parasitic fungi, as *Ustilago segetum,* or black smut, which forms on grain, converting all parts affected into a black powdery mass; also, the disease caused by this fungi.
5. very soft coal so mixed with earth as to make it practically worthless: usually found at an outcrop or in the region of a fault. [Brit.]

smut, *v.t.*; smutted, *pt., pp.*; smutting, *ppr.* 1. to stain or mark with smut; to blacken with coal, soot, or other dirty substance.
2. to taint or affect with smut or mildew, as grain.
3. to blacken; to tarnish; to defile.
4. to cleanse of smut, as grain.

smut, *v.i.* to be marked or affected by smut; to become smutty.

smut ball, (a) a puffball; (b) one of various species of smut, as *Tilletia caries.*

smutch, *v.t.*; smutched (smutcht), *pt., pp.*; smutching, *ppr.* [from ME. (hyp.) *smuchchen,* (hyp.) *smochchen.*] to make a dirty spot on; to smudge; to blacken; to stain.

smutch, *n.* 1. a dirty spot or mark; a smudge.
2. soot, smut, grime, or dirt.

smutch′in, *n.* snuff. [Rare.]

smutch′y, *a.*; *comp.* smutchier; *superl.* smutchiest, same as *smudgy.*

smut mill, a mill for removing smut from grain.

smut′ti·ly, *adv.* in a smutty manner.

smut′ti·ness, *n.* the quality or condition of being smutty.

smut′ty, *a.*; *comp.* smuttier; *superl.* smuttiest,
1. soiled with smut; dirty.
2. affected with plant smut, as corn or wheat.
3. foul in word or thought; obscene; as, *smutty* talk.

Smyr′nē·ăn (smĭr′), *a.* of Smyrna, in Turkey.

Smyr′nē·ăn, *n.* an inhabitant or native of Smyrna.

Smyr′ni·ot, Smyr′ni·ōte (smĭr′), *a.* and *n.* same as *Smyrnean.*

Sn, *stannum,* [L.] in chemistry, tin.

snack, *n.* [ME. *snake,* a bite, from *snaken,* to bite, snap.]
1. a share; a portion: used in the phrase *to go snacks*; that is, to take equal shares, as in an investment.
2. a light meal, usually one taken between regular meals; a bite to eat.

snack, *v.t.* snacked (snakt), *pt., pp.*; snacking, *ppr.* to snap; to bite; also, to go snacks in. [Brit. Dial.]

snack, *v.i.* 1. to snap or bite (*at*). [Brit. Dial.]
2. to eat a snack; to lunch; to go snacks; to share mutually; to take equal shares and chances.

snack′et, *n.* snecket. [Obs.]

snaç′ŏt, *n.* a pipefish. [Obs.]

snaf′fle, *n.* [short for *snaffle piece,* from D. *snavel,* a horse's muzzle; O.D. *snabel, snavel,* dim. of *snabbe, snebbe,* the bill of a bird; G. *schnabel,* bill, snout.] a bridle bit with a joint in the middle, rings at the ends for the attachment of the reins, without curbs, but in some cases having cheeks (side bars) to keep the rings from getting inside the mouth of a horse: also called *snaffle bit.*

snaf′fle, *v.t.*; snaffled (-fld), *pt., pp.*; snaffling, *ppr.* to fit with or control by a snaffle.

sna·fū′, *a.* [from *s*ituation *n*ormal, *a*ll *f*ouled (euphemism) *u*p.] in characteristic disorder or confusion; mixed up as usual. [Military Slang.]

sna·fū′, *v.t.*; snafued, *pt., pp.*; snafuing, *ppr.* to throw into confusion; to entangle. [Military Slang.]

snag, *n.* [via North. dial., from ON.]
1. a piece, part, or point that sticks out, especially one that is sharp or rough, as the broken end of a tree limb.
2. an underwater tree stump or branch that is dangerous to the navigation of a river, lake, etc.
3. a broken or irregular tooth; a snaggle-tooth.
4. a break or tear, as in cloth, made by a splinter, snag, etc.
5. an obstacle, difficulty, etc. which is unexpected or hidden.
6. a small branch of an antler; a point.

snag, *v.t.*; snagged, *pt., pp.*; snagging, *ppr.*
1. to catch, tear, or damage in any way on a snag.
2. to impede with or as with a snag.
3. to clear (a body of water) of snags.

snag bōat, a steamboat specially constructed for removing snags and other obstructions to navigation in rivers.

snag′ged, *a.* snaggy; full of snags.

snag′gle·tọọth, *n.*; *pl.* **snag′gle·teeth,** [from *snag.*] 1. a tooth that sticks out beyond the others.
2. a crooked or broken tooth.

snag′gle·tọọthed (-tọọth), *a.* having snaggleteeth.

snag′gy, *a.*; *comp.* snaggier, *superl.* snaggiest,
1. of, or having the nature of, a snag.
2. full of snags, as a body of water.
3. having snags.
4. petulant; cross. [Brit. Dial.]

snāil, *n.* [AS. *snægel, snægl*; akin to Ice. *snigill*; Dan. *snegl,* dim. forms from root of *snake, sneak,* the name signifying the creeping animal.]
1. a slow-creeping, gastropod mollusk belonging to the genus *Helix,* family *Helicidæ,* and differing from the slugs chiefly in being covered with a protective spiral shell. The head is furnished with four retractile horns or tentacula, and on the pair at the extremity, the eyes are placed. The common garden snail, *Helix hortensis,* is the most familiar species of the typical genus. The edible snail, *Helix pomatia,* is largely found in France, and cultivated there and elsewhere for food purposes.
2. any lazy, slow-moving person or animal.
3. a piece of spiral machinery somewhat resembling a snail; specifically, the piece of metal forming part of the striking work of a clock.
4. [*pl.*] snail clover.
5. any gastropod resembling a true snail.

snāil bōre, a univalve mollusk that bores into the shells of oysters. [Dial.]

snāil bōr′ẽr, a snail bore.

snāil çlō′vẽr, a plant of the genus *Medicago,* as *Medicago scutellata.*

snāil′fish, *n.* a fish of the genus *Liparis,* which has the habit of adhering to rocks by means of a sucker; a sea snail.

snāil′flow″ẽr, *n.* a plant of the genus *Phaseolus,* allied to the kidney bean.

snāil′līke, *a.* resembling a snail; moving very slowly.

snāil′līke, *adv.* in the manner of a snail; slowly.

snāil′-pāced (-pāst), *a.* having the pace or slow movement of a snail; very slow-moving.

snāil plant, snail clover.

′ṣnāilṣ, *interj.* an oath abbreviated from *his* (Christ's) *nails* (those fastening him to the cross). [Obs.]

snāil shell, the shell of a snail.

snāil trē′foil, snail clover.

snāke, *n.* [AS. *snaca,* from *snīcan,* to creep, sneak; akin to Ice. *snákr, snókr,* Sw. *snok,* Dan. *snog.* See *snail.*] any of various limbless reptiles of the group *Ophidia,* with an elongated, scaly body and a tapering tail. They may be broadly classified as *tree snakes,* usually green in color, slender in body, and active in motion; *water snakes,* found both in fresh and salt water; *burrowing snakes,* with rigid cylindrical bodies and narrow mouths; and *ground snakes,* to which class the majority of species belong. They are covered with scales, which ventrally are developed into strong shields. To each of these shields is attached a pair of ribs and by their grip on the ground the animal moves. Some snakes are poisonous, the poison being conveyed through a fang to the blood of the victim.
2. a person or thing resembling a snake in any of various ways; specifically, (a) a treacherous or deceitful person; (b) a plumber's tool consisting of a long, flexible metal rod for removing obstructions from pipes, etc.
a snake in the grass; a person or thing that is evil or dangerous and hidden or seemingly harmless.
to have snakes, to have snakes in the boots, to see snakes; to have delirium tremens. [Slang.]

snāke, *v.t.*; snaked (snākt), *pt., pp.*; snaking, *ppr.* 1. in nautical usage, to wind, as a small rope round a large one spirally, the small rope lying in the spaces between the strands of the large one.
2. to drag or haul, especially lengthwise and with force. [Colloq.]
3. to pull quickly; to jerk. [Colloq.]

snāke, *v.i.* to move like a snake.

snāke′bīrd, *n.* 1. a tropical, fish-eating bird of the genus *Plotus,* with a long, snakelike neck, slender head, and sharp-pointed bill.
2. the wryneck. [Brit. Dial.]

snāke buz′zărd, an eagle, *Sircaëtus gallicus.*

snāke çāne, a South American reedlike palm, found in mountainous regions.

snāke chärm′ẽr, a person, especially an Oriental, who charms or hypnotizes snakes by means of music or movements of the hands.

snāke çrāne, the seriema, *Cariama cristata.*
snāke çū'çum·bĕr, viper gourd.
snāke dȧnce, 1. a dance forming part of a religious ceremony performed every two years by the Hopi Indians: the participants handle live rattlesnakes as part of the ritual.
2. a kind of informal parade in which the celebrants join hands in a long line, winding back and forth as they progress.
snāke doç'tŏr, any dragonfly; also, a hellgrammite. [Dial.]
snāke'-ēat'ẽr, *n.* same as *serpent eater.*
snāke eel, any of various eels which constitute the family *Ophichthyidæ,* natives of warm seas.
snāke feed'ẽr, a snake doctor.
snāke fence, a zigzag fence of rails that cross each other at an angle.
snāke fish, *n.* 1. the bandfish.
2. a lizard fish.
3. the oarfish.
snāke flȳ, any of several neuropterous insects of the family *Raphidiidæ*: so called from the elongated form of the head and neck.
snāke gōurd, viper gourd.
snāke'head (-hed), *n.* 1. the end of a flat rail formerly used on railroads, which was sometimes loosened and thrown up by the carwheels, and frequently penetrated the cars.
2. a kind of American figwort with spikes of white or purple flowers; the turtlehead, *Chelone glabra.*
snāke kill'ẽr, 1. the secretary bird.
2. the chaparral cock.
snāke liz'ărd, a lizard having the form of a snake.
snāke moss, the common club moss, *Lycopodium clavatum.*
snāke'mouth, *n.* an orchid, *Pogonia ophioglossoides,* of the eastern part of the United States, with pink flowers and lance-shaped leaves.
snāke'neck, *n.* a snakebird (sense 1).
snāke nut, the fruit of the tree, *Ophiocaryon paradoxum,* the large embryo of which resembles a snake.
snāke'rọọt, *n.* 1. any of a number of plants of different species and genera, most of which are or formerly were reputed to be remedies for snake bites. Among the best known is *Aristolochia serpentaria,* Virginia snakeroot.
2. the roots of any of these plants.
Canada snakeroot; the wild ginger, *Asarum canadense.*
Sampson's snakeroot; a plant, *Psoralea meliloloides,* of the southern part of the United States.
Texas snakeroot; a plant, *Aristolochia reticulata,* of the southwestern part of the United States.
snāke's'-bēard, *n.* an herb of the genus *Ophiopogon,* native to China and Japan.
snāke's'-head (-hed), *n.* the guinea-hen flower of the genus *Fritillaria.*
snake's-head iris; an herb, *Hermodactylus tuberosus,* of southern Europe.
snāke'skin, *n.* 1. a snake's skin.
2. leather made from this.
snāke's'-mouth, *n.* the snakemouth.
snāke'stōne, *n.* 1. an ammonite. [Now Dial.]
2. a small rounded piece of stone, or other porous material believed to cure snake bites.
3. a kind of hone or whetstone occurring in Scotland.
snāke's'-tŏngue(-tung), *n.* the adder's-tongue.
snāke'weed, *n.* 1. a plant of the genus *Polygonum*; the bistort.
2. the Virginia snakeroot.
snāke'wood, *n.* 1. the wood of *Strychnos colubrina,* a loganiaceous tree growing in the Isle of Timor and other parts of the East, having a bitter taste, and supposed to be a remedy for snake bites.
2. the leopardwood, *Brosimum aubletii*: so called from its hard wood being mottled with irregularly shaped dark spots.
3. any of various plants of the genus *Ophioxylon,* from their twisted roots and stems.
4. the trumpet tree.
5. the serpentwood.
snāk'ish, *a.* snaky.
snāk'y, *a.*; *comp.* snakier; *superl.* snakiest, 1. of or like a snake or snakes.
2. having a snakelike form; serpentine; winding; twisting.
3. cunningly treacherous or evil.
4. full of or infested with snakes.
5. formed of or entwined with snakes, as the caduceus.
snap, *v.t.*; snapped (snapt), *pt., pp.*; snapping, *ppr.* [M.L.G. and M.D. *snappen*; akin to Dan. *snappe,* G. *schnappen,* to snap.]
1. to break or sever suddenly or with a snapping sound.
2. to bite or seize suddenly, as with the teeth; to take eagerly; to snatch (often with *up*).
3. to speak or utter sharply or harshly, as in anger (often with *out*).
4. to cause to make a snapping sound.
5. to close, fasten, put into place, etc. with a snapping sound; as, he *snapped* the safety before putting the gun away.
6. to strike sharply by releasing one end of something held under tension; as, he *snapped* her with a rubber band.
7. to cause to move suddenly and smartly; as, he *snapped* the ball to first base.
8. to take a snapshot of.
9. in football, to put (the ball) into play by sending it back to a receiver: said of a center.
to snap (a person's) head off; to speak sharply or harshly to, as in anger or impatience.
to snap one's fingers at; to show lack of concern for; to be careless of or indifferent toward.
snap, *v.i.* 1. to bring the jaws together sharply; to bite suddenly (often with *at*); as, the animal *snapped at* the meat.
2. to snatch or grasp quickly or eagerly (with *at*); as, we *snapped at* the invitation.
3. to speak sharply, abruptly, or irritably (often with *at*).
4. to break or part suddenly, especially with a sharp, cracking sound.
5. to give way suddenly under strain, as nerves, resistance, etc.
6. to make a sudden, sharp cracking or clicking sound; as, the fire is *snapping*; the whip *snapped* loudly.
7. to close, fasten, go into place, etc. with a snapping sound; as, the lock *snapped* shut.
8. to move or act suddenly and smartly; as, the soldiers *snapped* to attention.
9. to open and shut rapidly so as to appear to flash, as in anger: said of the eyes.
to snap out of it; to change suddenly from a bad condition to a better one; to improve or recover quickly.
10. to miss fire: said of a firearm; as, the gun *snapped.*
snap, *n.* 1. a sudden breaking or parting.
2. a sudden bite, grasp, snatch, catch, etc.; a sudden seizing, or attempt to seize, as with the teeth; as, the *snap* of a dog.
3. a sudden, sharp, cracking or clicking sound; as, the *snap* of a whip.
4. a short, angry utterance or manner of speaking.
5. a snapshot.
6. the spring catch of a bracelet, book clasp, purse, reticule, etc.
7. a sudden and severe interval or spell: applied to cold weather; as, a cold *snap.*
8. a crisp kind of ginger cooky.
9. a scrap; a fragment; a morsel. [Dial.]
10. a snack; a slight repast. [Dial.]
11. an earring furnished with a snap to prevent its coming out of the lobe of the ear. [Obs.]
12. a children's game of cards, played by three or more players.
13. an easy situation, job, problem, etc. [Slang.]
14. an implement used in making glassware.
15. a tool used for giving the head of a rivet a round and symmetrical form before it cools but after it has been closed.
16. briskness; vigor; alertness; as, he is all *snap.* [Colloq.]
17. a person who is easy to influence, persuade, control, etc.; a tractable person. [Slang.]
not a snap; not a bit; not at all.
snap, *a.* 1. made or done quickly or on the spur of the moment without deliberation; impulsive; as, a *snap* decision.
2. that fastens with a snap.
3. simple; easy; as, a *snap* assignment. [Slang.]
snap, *adv.* with a snap.
snap'back, *n.* in football, the act of the center in passing the ball back to a receiver.
snap bee'tle, a click beetle.
snap block, same as *snatch block.*
snap bug, a click beetle.
snap'drag''ŏn, *n.* [from *snap,* and *dragon*; from the mouth-shaped flowers.]
1. any of various related plants of the genus *Antirrhinum,* with white, yellow, red, or purplish, saclike, two-lipped flowers.
2. (a) a game in which raisins, etc. are snatched from a bowl of burning brandy; flapdragon; (b) that which is so snapped.
3. a glassmaker's tongs.
Jamaica snapdragon; a blue-flowered plant, *Ruellia tuberosa.*
snāpe, *v.t.*; snaped (snāpt), *pt., pp.*; snaping, *ppr.* [etym. doubtful.] in nautical usage, to bevel the end of (a piece of timber), so as to make it fit against a surface which it meets obliquely.
snāpe, *n.* the act or process of snaping. [Rare.]
snap flȧsk, in founding, a two-part flask having its halves joined together by a butt hinge at one corner and a latch at the diagonally opposite corner.
snap'hance, *n.* [D. *snaphaan*; *snap,* snap, and *haan,* the cock of a gun.]
1. a spring lock to a gun or pistol; also, the gun itself, a Dutch firelock in general use in the seventeenth century. [Obs.]
2. a snappish retort; a curt, sharp answer. [Obs.]
snap'head (-hed), *n.* 1. a round head to a pin, bolt, or rivet.
2. a swaging tool with a hollow corresponding to the required form of a rivet.
snap hook, a hook with a spring snap by which it is prevented from accidental disengagement from the object to which it is attached.
snap liñk, an open link with a spring, for the purpose of connecting parts of harness, chains, etc.
snap lock, a lock with a spring latch which fastens by snapping.
snap'pẽr, *n.*; *pl.* **snap'pẽrṣ** or **snap'pẽr,** one who or that which snaps or snatches, as (a) a snapping beetle; (b) the cracker on the end of a whip; (c) a cracker bonbon; (d) a snapping turtle; (e) [*pl.*] castanets; (f) the green woodpecker; (g) any of a group of tropical food fishes resembling the bass; especially, the red snapper.
snap'pẽr-back, *n.* in football, the center.
snap'pi·ly, *adv.* in a snappy manner.
snap'pi·ness, *n.* the quality or condition of being snappy.
snap'ping bee'tle, any of several beetles of the family *Elateridæ,* which jerk their bodies, making a snapping sound, when held in the fingers or turned on their backs.
snap'ping tọọl, a stamping tool used to force a plate into holes in a die.
snap'ping tũr'tle, a large, fresh-water turtle, *Chelydra serpentina,* of the eastern and southern United States, having powerful jaws which snap with great force: it feeds largely on fish and is widely used as food.
snap'pish, *a.* 1. ready or apt to snap at or bite.
2. cross; irritable; uncivil; sharp-tongued.
snap'pish·ly, *adv.* in a snappish manner.
snap'pish·ness, *n.* the quality or state of being snappish.
snap'py, *a.*; *comp.* snappier; *superl.* snappiest, 1. snappish; cross.
2. that snaps; snapping.
3. full of life or vigor; brisk; strong; sharp; as, a *snappy* reply, pace, etc. [Colloq.]
4. stylish; smart. [Colloq.]
to make it snappy; to be quick; to hurry. [Slang.]
snap rōll, a maneuver in which an airplane makes one complete fast roll about its longitudinal axis while keeping its horizontal direction.
snap'sack, *n.* a knapsack. [Obs.]
snap'shot, *n.* 1. a hurried shot fired with little or no aim; a quick, offhand shot.
2. a small photograph taken in an instant by snapping the shutter of a hand camera.
snap tọọl, a snaphead.
snap'weed, *n.* a plant of the genus *Impatiens.*
snär, *v.i.* to snarl; to growl fiercely. [Obs.]
snāre, *n.* [AS. *sneare,* a snare, a noose; Ice. *snara*; Dan. *snare,* a snare, a gin; D. *snaar*; O.H.G. *snare,* a string; Ice. *snara,* to turn quickly, to twist.]
1. a kind of trap for small animals, usually consisting of a noose which jerks tight upon the release of a spring trigger.
2. anything dangerous, risky, etc. that tempts or attracts; a thing by which a person is entangled; a trap.

3. a length of gut stretched across the bottom of a snare drum; hence, [*pl.*] a set of snare drums.

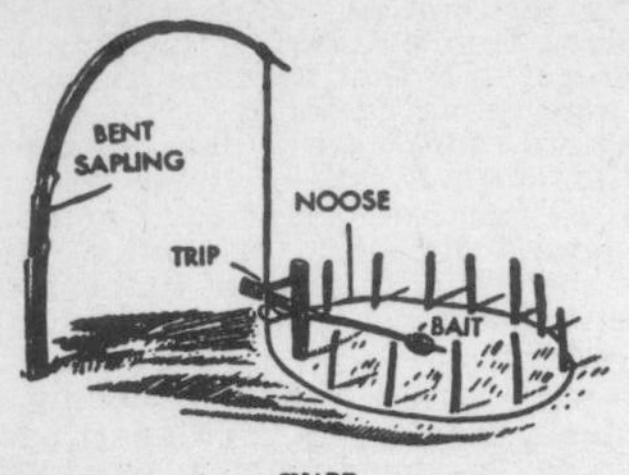

SNARE

4. in surgery, a wire loop for cutting out tumors, etc.

snâre, *v.t.*; snared, *pt., pp.*; snaring, *ppr.* 1. to catch in or with a snare.
2. to tempt or attract into unexpected evil, danger, perplexity, etc.

snâre drum, a small, double-headed drum with snares, or lengths of gut, strung across the bottom to increase the resonance.

snâr'ẽr, *n.* one who lays snares or traps.

snärk, *n.* [prob. from *sn*ake and sh*ark*.] an imaginary animal created by Lewis Carroll in his poem *The Hunting of the Snark.*

snärl, *v.i.* [extended from earlier *snar*, to growl.]
1. to growl fiercely or harshly, baring the teeth, as a threatening dog.
2. to speak harshly and sharply, as in anger, impatience, etc.

snärl, *v.t.* to utter or give vent to with a snarl; as, he *snarled* his contempt.

snärl, *n.* 1. a snarling; a fierce, angry growl.
2. a harsh utterance expressing anger, impatience, etc.

snärl, *v.t.* [ME. *snarlen*, from *snare.*]
1. to make knotted or tangled, as thread.
2. to make disordered or confused; to complicate; as, traffic is *snarled.*
3. to ornament (metalwork) with a raised design, as by hammering.

snärl, *v.i.* to become knotted or tangled.

snärl, *n.* 1. a knotted or tangled mass or tuft; a tangle; as, his hair is full of *snarls.*
2. a confused, disordered state or situation; complication; confusion.

snärl'ẽr, *n.* one who snarls or growls; a growling, surly, quarrelsome person.

snärl'ẽr, *n.* one who uses a snarling iron.

snärl'ing, *a.* growling; surly; quarrelsome.

snärl'ing, *n.* the act of one who or that which snarls.

snärl'ing ī''ron (-ŭrn), a tool used for fluting or embossing metal: also called *snarling tool.*

snärl'y, *a.*; *comp.* snarlier; *superl.* snarliest, snarling; cross; bad-tempered.

snärl'y, *a.*; *comp.* snarlier; *superl.* snarliest, snarled; tangled; confused.

snash, *v.i.* [Sw. *snaska*, to chide.] to speak insolently or abusively. [Scot.]

snash, *n.* impertinent or abusive language. [Scot.]

snast, *n.* the charred wick of a candle. [Obs.]

snatch, *v.t.*; snatched (snacht), *pt., pp.*; snatching, *ppr.* [ME. *snacchen, snecchen*; prob. var. of *snakken*, to seize.]
1. to seize hastily, abruptly, or without permission, warning, etc. as, he *snatched* the letter from her hand; to *snatch* a kiss.
2. to remove abruptly or hastily.
3. to take, get, or avail oneself of hastily or while there is a chance; as, he *snatched* a few hours of rest.
4. to kidnap. [Slang.]
5. to place (a rope) in a snatch block.
to snatch at; (a) to attempt to grasp or seize with a sudden movement; to grab at; (b) to accept or take advantage of (a chance, etc.) with great eagerness.

snatch, *n.* 1. a hasty catch or seizing; a catching at suddenly.
2. a short period; a brief time; as, a *snatch* of sleep.
3. a small portion, especially one that is incomplete or disconnected; a fragment; a bit; as, *snatches* of gossip.
4. a kidnaping. [Slang.]
5. a hasty repast; a snack.
6. in weight lifting, a lift in which the barbell is raised in one continuous motion from the floor to a position directly overhead with the arms completely extended.

snatch block, a kind of block having an opening in one side to receive the bight of a rope: also called *snap block.*
dumb snatch; a sheaveless snatch block.

SNATCH BLOCK

snatch'ẽr, *n.* one who snatches.

snatch'ing·ly, *adv.* by snatching; hastily.

snatch'y, *a.*; *comp.* snatchier; *superl.* snatchiest, done in snatches; irregular; disconnected; not complete or continuous.

snath, snāthe, *n.* [AS. *snæd.*] the curved handle of a scythe.

snat'tŏck, *n.* a chip; a slice; a fragment. [Obs.]

snaw, *n.* snow. [Scot.]

snaz'zy, *a.*; *comp.* snazzier; *superl.* snazziest, [perhaps from *sn*appy, and j*azzy.*] stylishly and showily attractive; flashy. [Slang.]

snēad, *n.* the handle of a scythe; a snath. [Now Dial.]

snēak, *v.i.*; sneaked (snēkt), *pt., pp.*; sneaking, *ppr.* [ME. *sniken*; AS. *snican*, to creep, sneak.]
1. to move quietly and stealthily so as to avoid being seen or heard; to go furtively.
2. to be a sneak; to behave in a stealthy, underhand, or cowardly manner.
to sneak out of; to avoid or escape (duty, a task, etc.) by sneaking or stealth.

snēak, *v.t.* 1. to give, put, conduct, transfer, etc. secretly or in a stealthy, sneaking manner; as, he *sneaked* the jewels across the border.
2. to take stealthily; to steal. [Colloq.]

snēak, *n.* 1. a person who sneaks; a stealthy, underhand, contemptible person.
2. an act of sneaking.
3. a petty thief.
4. in cricket, a ball bowled so as to roll along on the ground.

snēak bōat, snēak box, a small boat used by sportsmen, adapted for concealment while hunting ducks, etc.

snēak'-çup, *n.* one who sneaks from his cup. [Obs.]

snēak'ẽr, *n.* 1. a person or animal that sneaks.
2. [*pl.*] [so named from their noiseless tread.] canvas shoes with continuous sole and heel of one piece of soft rubber, used for indoor sports, etc.: also called *tennis shoes.*
3. a vessel to hold drink; a kind of punch bowl. [Rare.]

snēak'i·ness, *n.* the quality or fact of being sneaky.

snēak'ing, *a.* 1. pertaining to a sneak; acting like a sneak; cowardly, stealthy; underhand.
2. secret or clandestine; not admitted or made known to others; as, a *sneaking* fondness for jazz.
sneaking suspicion; a slight or increasing suspicion.

snēak'ing·ly, *adv.* in a sneaking manner.

snēak'ing·ness, *n.* the quality of being sneaky.

snēak prē'view (-vū), an advance, usually unpublicized, showing of a motion picture, as for evaluating audience reaction prior to the regular showing. [Colloq.]

snēaks, *n.pl.* sneaker (sense 2). [Slang.]

snēaks'by, *n.* a paltry fellow; one who is sneaky. [Obs.]

snēak thiēf, a person who commits thefts in a sneaking way, without the use of force or violence.

snēak'y, *a.*; *comp.* sneakier; *superl.* sneakiest, of or like a sneak; sneaking; cowardly.

snēap, *v.t.* 1. to check; to reprove abruptly; to reprimand. [Dial or Archaic.]
2. to nip; to pinch. [Dial. or Archaic.]

snēap, *n.* a rebuke. [Archaic.]

snēath, snēathe, *n.* same as *snath.*

sneb, *v.t.* to snib. [Scot.]

sneck, *v.t.* [ME. *snecke*, variant of *snack*, in the sense of catch quickly with the jaws.] to put the door latch or catch on; as, to *sneck* a door. [Scot. and Brit. Dial.]

sneck, *n.* the latch of a door. [Scot. and Brit. Dial.]

sneck draw'ẽr, a sly person; a thief. [Scot. and Brit. Dial.]

sned, *n.* snead. [Brit. Dial.]

sneer, *v.i.*; sneered, *pt., pp.*; sneering, *ppr.* [ME. *sneren*, to deride; akin to Dan. *snærre*, to grin like a dog.]
1. to smile derisively; to show scorn or contempt by a smiling grimace.
2. to express derision, scorn, or contempt in speech or writing.

sneer, *v.t.* 1. to utter with a sneer or in a sneering manner.
2. to affect in a particualr way by sneering; as, the proposal was *sneered* down.

sneer, *n.* 1. an act of sneering.
2. a sneering expression, insinuation, etc.
Syn.—scoff, gibe, jeer, taunt.

sneer'ẽr, *n.* one who sneers.

sneer'ful, *a.* given to sneering.

sneer'ing, *a.* characterized by a sneer; derisive; scornful.

sneer'ing·ly, *adv.* with a look of contempt or scorn.

sneeze, *v.i.*; sneezed, *pt., pp.*; sneezing, *ppr.* [ME. *snesen*, altered from *fnesen* (AS. *fneosan*).] to exhale breath through the nose and mouth in a sudden, involuntary, explosive action as a result of an irritation of the mucous membrane of the nose.
not to be sneezed at; not to be considered lightly.

sneeze, *n.* an act of sneezing.

sneeze'weed, *n.* any of a number of related coarse plants, especially *Helenium autumnale*, of the composite family, with bronze or yellow flowers said to cause sneezing.

sneeze'wood, *n.* a South African tree, *Ptæroxylon utile*, of the soapberry family, yielding a solid, strong, durable timber.

sneeze'wŏrt, *n.* 1. a European composite plant, *Achillea ptarmica*, closely allied to yarrow, with long, narrow, serrate leaves and strong-smelling white flowers: the leaves are used in snuff.
2. same as *sneezeweed.*

sneez'ing, *n.* a sneeze or the act of one who sneezes; sternutation.

snell, *a.* [ME.; AS. *snel.*]
1. active; brisk; nimble. [Dial.]
2. keen; sharp. [Dial.]
3. clever; smart; acute. [Dial.]
4. severe; extreme; harsh. [Dial.]

snell, *n.* [etym. obscure.] a short length of gut or horsehair for fastening a fishhook to a fishline; a leader.

snell, *v.t.*; snelled, *pt., pp.*; snelling, *ppr.* to furnish, as a fishhook, with a snell; as, a *snelled* hook.

snet, *n.* fat. [Obs.]

snew, *v.* obsolete past tense of *snow.*

snib, *v.t.* to snub; to reprove. [Obs.]

snib, *n.* a snub; a reproof. [Obs.]

snick, *n.* [prob. back-formation from *snick and snee*; see *snickersnee.*]
1. a small cut or mark; a nick.
2. an irregularity or a kink in thread or yarn.
3. in cricket, a stroke in which the ball glances from the bat.

snick, *v.t.*; snicked (snikt), *pt., pp.*; snicking, *ppr.* 1. to snip; to cut slightly.
2. to hit sharply.
3. in cricket, to hit lightly or glancingly, as a ball.

snick, *n., v.t.* and *v.i.* [echoic.] click.

snick'ẽr, *v.i.*; snickered, *pt., pp.*; snickering, *ppr.* [imitative.]
1. to laugh in a sly, partly stifled manner; to giggle; to titter; as, the class *snickered* at the teacher's mistake.
2. to neigh; nicker.

snick'ẽr, *v.t.* to utter with a snicker.

snick'ẽr, *n.* a sly, partly stifled laugh; a giggle.

snick'ẽr·snee, *n.* [from *snick and snee*, a combat with knives.] a sheath knife; a bowie knife; a knife used as a thrusting and cutting weapon.

snīde, *a.* [orig., counterfeit, bogus, from thieves' slang.] sly and malicious; as, a *snide* remark. [Slang.]

snīde, *n.* a sly and malicious person or thing. [Slang.]

Snī'dẽr rī'fle, a form of breech-loading rifle formerly used in the British service: also called *Snider*, from the inventor's name.

sniff, *v.i.*; sniffed (snift), *pt., pp.*; sniffing, *ppr.* [ME. *sniffen.*]
1. to draw in air through the nose with enough force to be heard, as in clearing the nose or smelling something.
2. to express contempt, skepticism, etc. by sniffing.

sniff, *v.t.* 1. to breathe in forcibly through the nose.
2. to perceive, detect, or get an understanding of by sniffing; to smell; to scent; as, to *sniff* danger.
3. to test the smell of by sniffing.

sniff, *n.* 1. the act of sniffing.
2. that which is taken by sniffing; as, a *sniff* of fresh air.
3. the sound produced by sniffing.

snif'fle, *v.i.*; sniffled (-fld), *pt.*, *pp.*; sniffling, *ppr.* to sniff repeatedly so as to check mucus running from the nose.

snif'fle, *n.* an act or sound of sniffling.
the sniffles; (a) a head cold; (b) the sniffling that accompanies a crying spell. [Colloq.]

snif'flẽr, *n.* a light breeze or wind.

snif'fy, *a.*; *comp.* sniffier; *superl.* sniffiest, characterized by or having a tendency to sniff, especially as a sign of contempt; scornful; contemptuous; disdainful. [Colloq.]

snift, *v.i.*; snifted, *pt.*, *pp.*; snifting, *ppr.* to snort; to sniff. [Dial.]

snif'tẽr, *v.i.* to sniff.

snif'tẽr, *n.* 1. a sniff.
2. [*pl.*] a catarrhal stoppage of the nostrils.
3. a small drink of liquor. [Slang.]
4. a blizzard. [Dial.]
5. a liquor glass that tapers to a small opening to concentrate the aroma.

snift'ing valve, a valve in the cylinder of a steam engine, for the escape of air: so called from the noise it makes.

snift'y, *a.* smelling inviting; as, the *snifty* odors of dinner. [Slang.]

snig, *v.t.* to chop. [Brit. Dial.]

snig, *n.* a kind of eel. [Brit. Dial.]

snig'gẽr, *n.*, *v.t.* and *v.i.* [echoic.] snicker.

snig'gẽr·ẽr, *n.* one who sniggers.

snig'gle, *v.i.*; sniggled, *pt.*, *pp.*; sniggling, *ppr.* to fish for eels by thrusting the bait into their burrows.

snig'gle, *v.t.* [from Prov. E. *snig*, eel.] to catch (eels) by thrusting bait into their burrows.

snigs, *interj.* an oath. [Obs.]

snip, *v.t.*; snipped (snipt), *pt.*, *pp.*; snipping, *ppr.* [D. *snippen*, to nip.]
1. to clip; to cut with shears or scissors in a short, quick stroke or strokes.
2. to snap; to snatch. [Rare.]
3. to remove by or as by a quick shearing cut; as, to *snip* a hole in a garment.

snip, *v.i.* to make a short, quick shearing cut or cuts, as with the point of a pair of scissors; to clip.

snip, *n.* 1. a clip; a small cut with shears or scissors.
2. the sound of this.
3. (a) a small piece cut off; (b) any small piece; a bit.
4. [*pl.*] heavy hand shears used for cutting sheet metal, etc.
5. a young, small, or insignificant person, especially one regarded with contempt. [Colloq.]
6. share; a snack. [Old Slang.]
to go snips; to share. [Obs.]

WILSON'S SNIPE
(*Gallinago wilsoni*)

snīpe, *n.*; *pl.* **snīpes** or **snīpe**, [ME. *snype*; O.N. *snipa*].
1. any of several wading birds belonging to the *Gallinago*, *Macrorhamphus*, or related genera, having a slender, comparatively long bill used in digging for worms, etc., no feathers on the lower part of the legs, and frequenting streams or marshy places. The common snipe of the United States is *Gallinago wilsoni*, being known by various names, as jacksnipe, Wilson's snipe, etc.
2. any snipelike bird, as certain sandpipers, the dunlin, etc.
3. a blockhead or simpleton.
4. a discarded, partly-smoked cigar or cigarette. [Slang.]
5. a shot from a hidden position.
English snipe; the common American snipe.
winter snipe; a sandpiper, *Tringa maritima*.

snīpe, *v.i.*; sniped (snīpt), *pt.*, *pp.*; sniping, *ppr.* 1. to hunt or shoot snipe.
2. to shoot from a hidden position at separate individuals of an enemy force.

snīpe'bill, *n.* 1. in carpentry, a plane with a sharp arris for forming the grooves of moldings.
2. a bolt for attaching the body of a cart to the axle.

snīpe eel, any fish of the family *Nemichthyidæ*, as *Nemichthys scolopaceus*, found in deep waters of the Atlantic.

snīpe'fish, *n.* 1. the bellows fish.
2. a snipe eel.

snīpe'-nōsed, *a.* having a long, slender, pointed nose: said of dogs.

snī'pẽr, *n.* in military usage, a sharpshooter concealed to harass the enemy by picking off individual members, usually at long range with a telescopic rifle.

snip'pẽr, *n.* one who or that which snips or clips.

snip'pẽr·snap·pẽr, *n.* a whippersnapper.

snip'pet, *n.* [dim. of *snip*.]
1. a small part or fragment, especially one snipped or cut off.
2. a young, small, or insignificant person; a snip. [Colloq.]

snip'pet·i·ness, *n.* the state or condition of being snippety.

snip'pet·y, *a.* 1. made up of scraps or snippets.
2. snippy. [Colloq.]

snip'pi·ly, *adv.* in a snippy manner.

snip'pi·ness, *n.* a snippy state or quality.

snip'ping, *n.* a clipping.

snip'py, *a.*; *comp.* snippier; *superl.* snippiest, 1. made up of small scraps or snips; fragmentary.
2. curt, sharp, or snappish, especially in an insolent manner. [Colloq.]
3. stingy. [Brit. Dial.]

snip'-snap, *n.* a clever dialogue with quick replies.

snīp'y, *a.* resembling a snipe; snipelike.

snitch, *v.t.* [from 18th-c. thieves' slang; orig. sense "a nose".] to steal (usually something of little value). [Slang.]

snitch, *v.i.* 1. to be a petty thief; to steal. [Slang.]
2. to be an informer; to tell; to peach (usually with *on*). [Slang.]

snitch, *n.* an informer. [Slang.]

snīte, *n.* a snipe. [Obs.]

snīte, *v.t.* [Scand., to wipe the nose.]
1. to blow (the nose). [Scot.]
2. to snuff (a candle). [Scot.]

snīthe, snith'y, *a.* [AS. *snithan*, to cut.] sharp; piercing: applied to the wind. [Brit. Dial.]

sniv'el, *v.i.*; sniveled *or* snivelled, *pt.*, *pp.*; sniveling *or* snivelling, *ppr.* [ME. *snivelen*; AS. hyp. *snyflan*, from base seen in *snofk* and *snyflung*, mucus.]
1. to have mucus running from the nose.
2. to sniff repeatedly, as from a head cold, crying, etc.; to sniffle; to snuffle.
3. to cry and sniffle.
4. to fret or complain in a whining, tearful manner.
5. to make a whining, tearful, often false display of grief, sympathy, disappointment, etc.

sniv'el, *n.* 1. nasal mucus.
2. the act of sniveling or sniffling.
3. a sniveling, whining display of grief, etc.

sniv'el·ẽr, sniv'el·lẽr, *n.* one who snivels.

sniv'el·ing, sniv'el·ling, *a.* running at the nose; whining.

sniv'el·y, sniv'el·ly, *a.* running at the nose; whining.

snob, *n.* [Ice. *snāpr*, a dolt, idiot; Sw. dial. *snopp*, anything stumpy, from *snoppa*, to cut off, make stumpy, hence, to snub.]
1. a shoemaker. [Brit. Dial.]
2. in certain English universities, a townsman as opposed to a gownsman. [Old Slang.]
3. a person having no wealth or social rank; one of the common people. [Obs.]
4. a person who attaches great importance to wealth, social position, etc., having contempt for and keeping aloof from those whom he considers his inferiors, often one admiring, imitating, and seeking to associate with those whom he considers his superiors.
5. a person who regards himself as better than others in some (specified) way and behaves undemocratically; as, an intellectual *snob*.

> A *snob* is that man or woman who is always pretending to be something better—especially richer or more fashionable—than they are. —Thackeray.

6. a scab (sense 5). [Brit. Dial.]

snob, *v.i.* to weep or sob violently. [Obs.]

snob'bẽr·y, *n.*; *pl.* **snob'bẽr·ies**, snobbish behavior or character, or an instance of this.

snob'bish, *a.* of, like, or having the character or ways of a snob or snobs.

snob'bish·ly, *adv.* in a snobbish manner.

snob'bish·ness, *n.* the state or quality of being a snob; the conduct of a snob.

snob'bism, *n.* snobbishness.

snob'by, *a.* snobbish.

snob'ling, *n.* a little snob.

snob·oc'ra·cy, *n.* snobs as a class or social factor.

snock, *n.* the Australian barracuda.

snod, *n.* snood. [Obs.]

snod, *a.* neat; trim; smooth. [Scot.]

snoff, *n.* [prob. variant of *snuff*, of a candle.] in mining, a candle end with which to light a fuse.

snood, *n.* [AS. *snod*, from Ice. *snuthr*, a twist or twirl; Sw. *sno*, a twist, string.]
1. a tie or ribbon formerly worn around the hair, especially by young unmarried women.
2. a netlike bag worn at the back of a woman's head to hold the hair.
3. a hat or part of a hat resembling this.
4. in fishing, a snell.

snood, *v.t.* to bind or hold up (the hair) with a snood.

snood'ed, *a.* wearing or having a snood.

snood'ing, *n.* the gut or cord of which a snood is made; a snood.

snook, *v.i.*; snooked (snökt), *pt.*, *pp.*; snooking, *ppr.* [ME. *snoke*, to smell, to search out, to pry into; Sw. *snoka*, to lurk, to dog a person.] to smell; to nose around; to pry about; to search out. [Scot.]

snook, *n.* 1. a fish of the genus *Centropomus*.
2. the sergeant fish, *Elacate canada*.
3. a garfish.
4. the barracuda of Australia.

snoop, *v.i.* to look about in a sneaking, prying manner. [Colloq.]

snoop, *n.* 1. a person who snoops. [Colloq.]
2. a snooping. [Colloq.]

snoot, *n.* [ME. *snute*.] (a) the nose; (b) the face; (c) a grimace. [Colloq.]

snoot'i·ly, *adv.* in a snooty manner. [Colloq.]

snoot'i·ness, *n.* the quality or state of being snooty. [Colloq.]

snoot'y, *a.*; *comp.* snootier; *superl.* snootiest, haughty; snobbish. [Colloq.]

snooze, *n.* [probably imitative of the sound made in drawing the breath while asleep, and allied to *snore*; compare *sneeze*; Dan. *snuse*, to snuff or sniff.] a nap or short sleep. [Colloq.]

snooze, *v.i.*; snoozed, *pt.*, *pp.*; snoozing, *ppr.* to take a short sleep; to nap; to doze; to drowse. [Colloq.]

snōre, *v.i.*; snored, *pt.*, *pp.*; snoring, *ppr.* [AS. *snora*, a snoring; Dan. *snorke*, to snore; akin to *snar*, *snarl*, *snort*.] to breathe with a rough, hoarse, vibrating sound while sleeping, usually with the mouth open.

snōre, *v.t.* to spend or pass (time) in snoring (with *away*, etc.)

snōre, *n.* the act or sound of snoring.

snōre hōle, the hole in the wind bore or lower stock of a mining pump, to admit the water.

snōre pièce, in mining, the suction pipe which dips into the sump.

snōr'ẽr, *n.* one who snores.

snōr'ing, *n.* the act of one who snores.

snor'kel, *n.* [G. *schnörkel*, spiral.]
1. a device for submarines, consisting of air intake and exhaust tubes: it permits submergence for long periods.
2. a breathing tube extending above the surface of the water, used in swimming just below the surface.
3. a hydraulic crane with a bucketlike aerial platform, mounted on a truck for firefighting, etc.

snor'kel, *v.i.*; snorkeled, *pt.*, *pp.*; snorkeling, *ppr.* to move or swim underwater using a snorkel.

snort, *v.i.*; snorted, *pt.*, *pp.*; snorting, *ppr.* [ME. *snorten*, *snurten*; prob. from *snoren*, to snore.]
1. to force breath suddenly and violently through the nostrils so as to make a harsh sound; as, the horse *snorted* at our approach.
2. to express anger, contempt, or the like by a snort.
3. to make a noise like a snort; as, the outboard motor *snorted* and stopped.
4. to laugh with a loud outburst or boisterously. [Colloq.]
5. to snore. [Obs.]

snōrt, *v.t.* 1. to express or utter with a snort.
2. to expel or emit by or as by a snort.

snōrt, *n.* 1. the act or sound of snorting.
2. a small drink of liquor.

snort'ẽr, *n.* 1. one who snorts; a snorer.
2. anything of unusual fierceness, as a gale. [Slang.]

3. a stonechat. [Brit. Dial.]

snort'ing, *n.* a snort.

snot, *n.* [AS. (*ge*)*snot*, mucus.]
1. mucus discharged from or secreted in the nose. [Vulgar.]
2. an offensive or contemptible person. [Slang.]
3. the snuff of a candle. [Dial.]

snot, *v.t.* to free from snot; to blow or wipe, as the nose. [Dial.]

snot'tẽr, *v.i.* to snivel; to sob. [Dial.]

snot'tẽr, *n.* [freq. form of *snood*, a twist or tie.] in nautical usage, a rope going over a yard-arm with an eye forming a becket to bend a tripping line to in sending down topgallant and royal yards; also, a piece of rope fitted round a boat's mast, having a bight to fit the lower end of the sprit, which it confines to the mast.

snot'tẽr·y, *n.* filth. [Obs.]

snot'ti·ly, *adv.* in a snotty manner.

snot'ti·ness, *n.* the quality or condition of being snotty.

snot'ty, *a.*; *comp.* snottier; *superl.* snottiest, 1. of, like, or dirtied with snot.
2. (a) offensive; contemptible; (b) impudent; haughty. [Slang.]

snout, *n.* [ME. *snoute*; prob. from M.D. *snute, snuite*.]
1. (a) the projecting nose and jaws, or muzzle, of an animal; (b) some anterior prolongation of the head resembling this, as in a weevil; rostrum.
2. something like an animal's snout, as a nozzle or spout.
3. a human nose, especially one that is large, prominent, etc. [Colloq.]

snout, *v.t.* to furnish with a nozzle or point.

snout bee'tle, a small, scaly weevil with a long beak or snout, living chiefly on grains, fruits, and nuts.

snout mo̧th, any one of several families of moths having snoutlike palpi, as the *Pyralidæ*.

snout'y, *a.* resembling a beast's snout.

snōw, *n.* [ME.; AS. *snāw*; D. *sneeuw*; Dan. *snee*; Sw. *snö*; Ice. *snjór*; Goth. *snaivs*; L. *nix*; Gr. *niphas* (without initial *s*); probably from root seen in Sans. *snu*, to flow, to drop, to trickle, to distil.]
1. particles of water vapor which when frozen in the upper air fall to earth as soft, white, crystalline flakes.
2. a falling of snow.
3. a mass or accumulation of fallen snow.
4. whiteness. [Poetic.]
5. something like snow in whiteness, texture, etc.
6. cocaine or heroin. [Slang.]
7. the season of snows; winter. [Poet.]

snōw, *v.i.*; snowed, *pt., pp.*; snowing, *ppr.* [AS. *sniwian*.] to fall as or like snow.

snōw, *v.t.* 1. to shower or let fall as or like snow; as, it *snowed* fine crystals.
2. to surround, overwhelm, etc. with or as with snow (with *in, up, under*, etc.); as, the herd was *snowed in* by a blizzard.

snōw, *n.* [contr. of *snout*.] a ship equipped with two masts, resembling the main and fore masts of a ship, and a third small mast just abaft the mainmast, carrying a trysail. [Rare.]

snōw ap'ple, an autumn apple, the Fameuse.

snōw'ba̧ll, *n.* 1. a mass of snow, pressed or rolled together into a ball.
2. a variety of cranberry bush of the genus *Viburnum*, bearing large balls of white flowers; the guelder-rose.
3. in cookery, any one of various dishes resembling a snowball in appearance.
wild snowball; the redroot.

snōw'ba̧ll, *v.t.*; snowballed, *pt., pp.*; snowballing, *ppr.* to fling snowballs at.

snōw'ba̧ll, *v.i.* 1. to fling snowballs.
2. to increase or accumulate rapidly like a rolling ball of snow.

snōw'bañk, *n.* a large mass of snow, especially a drift on a hillside, in a gully, etc.

snōw'ber"ry, *n.*; *pl.* **snōw'ber"rieş,** 1. any of a number of plants with round, white berries; as, (a) *Chiococca racemosa*, a shrub of the West Indies; (b) *Symphoricarpus racemosus*, a shrub native to the United States; (c) *Chiogenes hispidula*, an evergreen creeper resembling the evergreen in flavor: usually called the *creeping snowberry*.
2. the fruit of any of these plants.

snōw'bird, *n.* 1. an American bird of the finch family, with a gray back and white breast; junco.
2. the snow bunting.
3. in England, (a) the fieldfare; (b) the ivory gull.
4. a person addicted to the use of cocaine or heroin. [Slang.]

snōw'-blīnd, *a.* having snow blindness.

snōw blīnd'ness, temporary blindness caused by the glare of sunlight reflected from snow.

snōw blōw'ẽr, a motorized, hand-guided machine on wheels, for removing snow as from walks: also *snow thrower*.

snōw'-bound, *a.* enclosed or confined by snow; snowed in.

snōw'-bro̧th, *n.* snow and water mixed.

snōw bun'ting, a finch of the cold regions of the Northern Hemisphere of the genus *Plectrophenax*, which often descends in winter into Europe and the northern part of the United States; a snowbird: also *snowflake*.

snōw'bu̧sh, *n.* any of a number of related California shrubs with many small, white flowers.

snōw'çap, *n.* 1. a tropical American hummingbird having snow-white head feathers, as *Microchæra albocoronata*, or *Microchæra parvirostris*.
2. a cap of snow, as on a mountain.

snōw'-çapped (-kapt), *a.* capped or crowned with snow, as a mountain, tree, etc.

snōw'-çlad, *a.* covered with snow. [Poet.]

snōw çock, a snow partridge.

snōw'drift, *n.* 1. a mass or pile of snow formed by the action of the wind.
2. snow carried along with the wind.

snōw'drop, *n.* 1. a bulbous plant, *Galanthus nivalis*, bearing drooping white flowers which appear in early spring; also, its flower.
2. the common anemone.

snōw'drop tree, the silverbell tree.
African snowdrop tree; a tree of South Africa, *Royena lucida*, with white flowers.

snōw ēat'ẽr, a chinook, or warm wind, rapidly melting the snow. [Dial.]

snōw'fa̧ll, *n.* 1. a fall of snow.
2. the quantity of snow that falls during a specified time or in a given area; as, a *snowfall* of six inches in a week.

snōw'finch, *n.* the brambling. [Brit.]

snōw'flāke, *n.* 1. a single feathery crystal of snow.
2. the snow bunting.
3. any plant resembling the snowdrop.

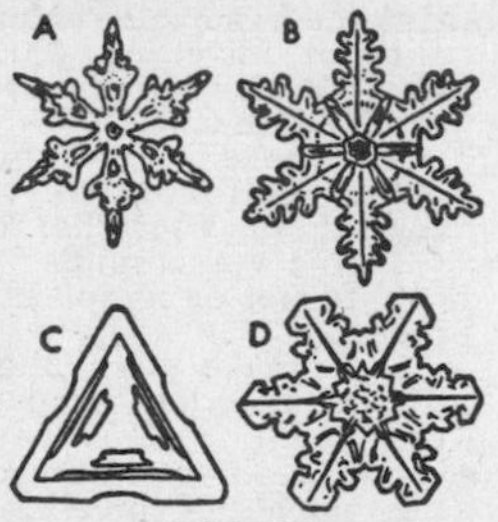

snōw flēa, a leaping insect or springtail, especially *Achoreutes nivicola*, found on the snow in large numbers in some parts of the United States.

snōw'fleck, *n.* a snow bunting, *Plectrophenax nivalis*.

SNOWFLAKES
A, star form; B, composite form; C, triangular form; D, tabular form

snōw'flight (-flīt), *n.* a snow bunting. [Brit. Dial.]

snōw'flow"ẽr, *n.* 1. the fringe tree.
2. the snowdrop.

snōw flȳ, (a) a scorpion fly of the genus *Boreus*, found upon the snow; (b) the snow flea; (c) the snow gnat.

snōw'fowl, *n.* a snow bunting. [Brit. Dial.]

snōw ġem, the snow glory.

snōw glō'ry, one of various bulbous plants of the genus *Chionodoxa*: also called *glory of the snow*.

snōw gnat (nat), any gnat of the genus *Chironomus*; a snow fly.

snōw go̧ose, any goose of the genus *Chen*, native to the arctic regions, but descending in winter to the northern part of the United States, as the white brant, *Chen hyperboreus*.

snōw grouse, a ptarmigan.

snōw īce, white, opaque ice consisting of frozen slush.

snōw'i·ly, *adv.* in a snowy manner.

snōw'i·ness, *n.* the quality or condition of being snowy.

snōw'-in-här"vest, *n.* a white-flowered plant blooming profusely in harvest or late summer, as the mouse-ear chickweed, *Cerastium tomentosum*. [Brit. Dial.]

snōw in'seçt, a snow fly.

snōw'-in-sum"mẽr, *n.* snow-in-harvest. [Brit. Dial.]

snowl, *n.* the merganser. [Dial.]

snōw leop'ärd (lep'), the ounce.

snōw'less, *a.* without snow.

snōw'līke, *a.* resembling snow.

snōw lil'y, a white dogtooth violet of the Rocky Mountains.

snōw līne (or **lim'it**), the line of a high region above which is perpetual snow.

snōw'man, *n.* a figure of snow made to represent a man.

snōw'mō·bīle, *n.* any of various motor vehicles for traveling over snow, usually with steerable runners at the front and tractor treads at the rear.

snōw'mō·bīle, *v.i.*; snowmobiled, *pt., pp.*; snowmobiling, *ppr.* to travel by snowmobile.

snōw mouse, a rodent of European mountains

snōw'-on-the-moun"tain (-tin), *n.* a species of spurge, *Euphorbia marginata*, having leaves with white margins.

snōw pär'tridġe (-trij), 1. any partridge of the genus *Tetraogallus*, of the Himalayas.
2. a snow grouse or ptarmigan.

snōw peār, a European variety of pear whose hard fruit is mellowed by exposure to snow.

snōw pheaş'ănt (fez'), 1. a Chinese mountain pheasant of the genus *Crossoptilon*.
2. the snow partridge, especially one of the genus *Tetraogullus*.

snōw pig'eŏn, an Asiatic pigeon, *Columba leuconota*.

snōw plant, 1. a red, fleshy, parasitic plant, *Sarcodes sanguinea*, with hanging red flowers and no leaves, growing in the pine forests of the Sierra Nevada, and often found in early spring before the snow has melted.
2. the red snow, *Protococcus nivalis*.

snōw'plow, *n.* a machine or device operating like a plow for clearing away the snow from roads, railways, etc.

snōw pu̧d'ding, a kind of pudding made white and fluffy by beaten egg whites and often containing sugar and flavored gelatin.

snōw'shed, *n.* a shed, roof, etc. used to protect places on a railroad likely to be filled with snow, as narrow passes.

snōw'shōe, *n.* a racket-shaped frame of wood fitted with crosspieces and crisscrossed with strips of leather, etc., worn on the feet to prevent sinking in deep snow.

snōw'shōe, *v.i.* snowshoed, *pt., pp.*; snowshoeing, *ppr.* to use snowshoes in walking.

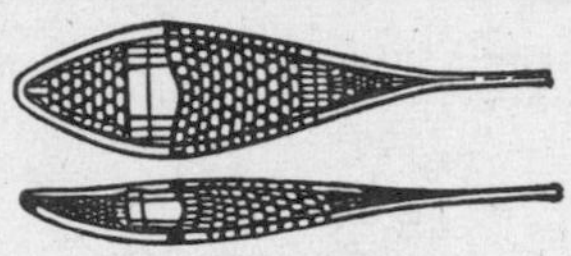

SNOWSHOES

snōw'shōe"ing, *n.* the use of snowshoes; also, the sport of using snowshoes.

snōw'shō"ẽr, *n.* one who uses snowshoes.

snōw spar'rōw, a snowbird, especially of the genus *Junco*.

snōw'sto̧rm, *n.* a snow accompanied by a strong wind.

snōw'-whīte' (-hwīt'), *a.* white as snow.

snōw'y, *a.*; *comp.* snowier; *superl.* snowiest, 1. characterized by snow.
2. covered or filled with snow; as, a *snowy* valley.
3. like or suggestive of snow; specifically, (a) pure; unsoiled; spotless; (b) white.
4. of or consisting of snow.
snowy egret or *heron*; a white egret or heron, *Ardea candidissima*, of both Americas.
snowy owl; an owl, *Nyctea nyctea*, seen in the northern part of the United States in winter.
snowy plover; a small species of ring plover.

snub, *v.t.*; snubbed, *pt., pp.*; snubbing, *ppr.* [ME. *snubben*; O.N. *snubba*, to snub, chide, check.]
1. to nip; to clip or break off the end of; to check in growth. [Dial.]
2. originally, to check or interrupt with sharp or slighting words.
3. to treat with scorn, contempt, disdain, etc.; to behave coldly toward; to slight.
4. to stop or check the movement of suddenly: said of a rope, cable, etc., or of something, as a boat, to which this is attached.
Syn.—mortify, check, rebuke, reprimand.

snub, *n.* 1. a knot or protuberance. [Obs.]
2. a deliberate discourtesy; an affront; scornful, slighting action or treatment.
3. a snubbing, or checking.
4. a short, turned up nose.

snub, *a.* short and turned up: said of the nose.

snub'bẽr, *n.* 1. a person who snubs.

2. a thing used for checking motion by snubbing.

3. a kind of automobile shock absorber which operates by restricting the action of the body springs.

snub'by, *a.*; *comp.* snubbier; *superl.* snubbiest, 1. turned up; snub.

2. tending to snub or slight.

snub'-nōṣed', *a.* having a snub nose.

snub-nosed cachalot; a pygmy sperm whale.

snub pōst, a short post on a dock or landing to which a line may be fastened to check a vessel's motion: also called *snubbing post.*

snudġe (snuj), *v.i.* to lie close; to snug. [Obs.]

snudġe, *n.* a miser or a sneaking fellow. [Obs.]

snuff, *v.t.*; snuffed (snuft), *pt., pp.*; snuffing, *ppr.* [MD. *snuffen*; base as in *snout.*]

1. to draw in (the breath) forcibly through the nose; to inhale; as, to *snuff* the wind.

2. to scent; to smell; to perceive by the smell.

3. to smell of; to nose: said of dogs and other animals.

snuff, *v.i.* 1. to sniff or snort.

2. to smell or sniff doubtfully, as dogs do: generally with *at.*

3. to turn up the nose and inhale air in contempt; hence, to take offense.

4. to take or use powdered tobacco or snuff. [Rare.]

snuff, *n.* 1. the act or sound of snuffing; a sniff.

2. (a) a preparation of powdered tobacco taken up into the nose by sniffing or applied to the gums with a snuff stick; (b) a pinch of this.

3. any powder taken by inhaling.

4. smell; scent; odor.

up to snuff; (a) up to the usual standard, as in health, quality, etc.; (b) not easily cheated or deceived; knowing; alert. [Colloq.]

snuff, *n.* [ME.; prob. akin to M.H.G. *snipfen,* to snip.] 1. the burning or charred end of a candlewick.

2. a candle almost burnt out. [Rare.]

snuff, *v.t.* 1. to trim off the charred end of (a candlewick).

2. to put out (a candle) with snuffers or by pinching.

to snuff out; (a) to put out (a candle, etc.); to extinguish; (b) to bring to an end suddenly or violently; to destroy.

snuff'box, *n.* a small, usually ornamental box for carrying snuff.

devil's snuffbox; same as *puffball.*

snuff dip'ping, the act or habit of dipping snuff.

snuff'ẽr, *n.* 1. one who snuffs.

2. a porpoise. [Dial.]

snuff'ẽrṣ, *n.pl.* an instrument for cropping the snuff of a candle: also *pair of snuffers.*

snuf'fi·ness, *n.* a snuffy quality or state.

snuff'ing, *n.* the act or habit of using or taking snuff.

snuff'ing·ly, *adv.* in a snuffing manner.

snuff'ing pig, the porpoise.

snuf'fle, *v.i.*; snuffled, (-fld) *pt., pp.*; snuffling, *ppr.* [freq. of *snuff.*]

1. to breathe audibly and with difficulty or by constant sniffing, as a dog in trailing; to sniff or sniffle.

2. to speak or sing in a nasal tone.

3. to speak in a whining, hypocritical manner. [Rare.]

snuf'fle, *v.t.* to utter by snuffling.

snuf'fle, *n.* 1. the act or sound of snuffling.

2. a nasal tone or twang.

3. whining, hypocritical speech. [Rare.]

the snuffles; a condition in which the nostrils are obstructed by mucus, as in a cold, causing snuffling.

snuf'flẽr, *n.* 1. one who snuffles.

2. one who uses cant; a hypocrite. [Rare.]

snuff stick, a soft stick chewed at one end and used for dipping snuff and applying it to the gums.

snuff'y, *a.*; *comp.* snuffier; *superl.* snuffiest, 1. resembling snuff, as in color or texture.

2. having the habit of taking snuff.

3. soiled with snuff.

4. disagreeable; unattractive.

snuff'y, *a.*; *comp.* snuffier; *superl.* snuffiest, [*snuff* (to sniff) and *-y.*] sulky; displeased; annoyed.

snug, *n.* a small lug or ridge on a plate acting as a lateral support to keep an attached object in place.

snug, *a.* [Early Mod. Eng., from nautical language; prob. from L.G.]

1. protected from the weather or the cold; comfortable; secure; warm; cozy.

2. small but well arranged; compact and convenient; neat; trim; as, a *snug* cottage.

3. large enough to provide ease and comfort: said of an income.

4. tight or close in fit; as, is the coat too *snug?*

5. trim and well-built; seaworthy.

6. hidden; as, the thief kept *snug* behind the door.

snug, *adv.* so as to be snug.

snug, *v.i.*; snugged, *pt., pp.*; snugging, *ppr.* to move close; to snuggle: generally with *up* or *up to*; as, a child *snugs up to* its mother or nurse. [Dial.]

snug, *v.t.* 1. to make smooth, as a rope, by rubbing.

2. to put in a snug position; to make secure.

to snug down; in nautical usage, to make ready for a storm by reducing sail, lashing movable gear, etc.

snug'gẽr·y, *n.*; *pl.* **snug'gẽr·ieṣ,** a snug comfortable place, room, position, etc.

snug'gle, *v.i.*; snuggled, *pt., pp.*; snuggling, *ppr.* [freq. of *snug,* to lie close.] to lie close for convenience or warmth; to nestle.

snug'gle, *v.t.* to hold or draw close or in a comfortable position; to cuddle; to nestle.

snug'ly, *adv.* in a snug manner.

snug'ness, *n.* the state or quality of being snug.

snȳ, *n.* [Ice. *snua*; Sw. and Dan. *sno,* a turn, *twist.*] in shipbuilding, (a) a gentle bend in timber curving upward; (b) the upward bend of the lines of a ship.

snȳ'ing, *n.* a curved planking set edgewise in the frame of a vessel at the bow or stern. [Rare.]

sō, *adv.* [ME. *so, swo*; AS. *swā,* so, as; akin to Goth. *sva, svē*; L.G. and G. *so*; D. *zoo.*]

1. in the way or manner shown, expressed, indicated, understood, etc.; as stated or described; in such a manner; as, hold your golf club *so.*

2. (a) to the degree expressed or understood; to such an extent; as, why are you *so* late?; (b) to a very high degree; very; as, they are *so* happy together; (c) [Colloq.] very much; as, she *so* wants to go.

3. for the reason specified; therefore; as a result; consequently; as, they were late, and *so* didn't go.

4. more or less; approximately that number, amount, etc.; as, he won fifty dollars or *so*: in this sense, *so* is often regarded as a pronoun.

5. also; likewise; as, she enjoys music, and *so* does he: also used colloquially in contradicting a negative statement; as, I did *so* tell the truth!

6. then; as, *so* you really don't like my hat.

7. very well; elliptical for *sobeit*; as, read, and if it please you, *so.*

8. do you mean it? elliptical for *is it so?* as, is that all? *So?*

9. after that; as, an hour to read and *so* to work. [Archaic.]

10. in like manner with the oath or statement; as, *so* help me God!

and so forth or *on*; and others; and the rest; and in like manner; et cetera (etc.).

quite so; yes, indeed; exactly.

so as; (a) in such a manner; to such a degree; with such a purpose or result (followed by an infinitive); (b) provided that; so long as; if only.

so far; thus far; to this or that extent; in that point.

so far forth; as far. [Obs.]

so much; (a) such a quantity, not specified; as, *so much* flour and *so much* sugar; (b) as much as is stated or determined; as, we owe just *so much.*

so what? even if so, what then?: used to express disregard, challenge, contempt, etc. [Colloq.]

sō, *conj.* 1. in order that; with the purpose that: usually followed by *that,* as, he died *so* (that) we might live.

2. with the result that. [Colloq.]

3. if only; as long as; provided that (often followed by *that*). As a conjunction, *so* is sometimes used colloquially as a superfluous element connecting clauses in narration. Example: *So* I told him we would go. *So* he said we shouldn't bother. *So* we didn't.

4. as. [Obs.]

sō, *pron.* 1. that which has been specified or named; as, he was a poor man, but he did not remain *so.*

2. see *adv.,* sense 4.

sō, *interj.* an exclamation expressing surprise, approval or disapproval, triumph, etc., or a command to stop.

sō, *n.* in music, sol.

sōak, *v.t.*; soaked (sōkt), *pt., pp.*; soaking, *ppr.* [AS. *socian,* to soak; prob. from Celtic, the root being that of L. *sugere,* to suck.]

1. to saturate or make thoroughly wet, as by placing in liquid for a long period.

2. to take in (liquid) by sucking or absorbing (usually with *up*).

3. to take in mentally, especially with little effort (usually with *up*).

4. to drink (liquor), especially to excess. [Colloq.]

5. to give a heavy blow to. [Slang.]

6. to charge excessively; to make pay too dearly. [Slang.]

7. to make (one) drunk. [Slang.]

8. to pawn. [Slang.]

to soak out; to draw out by or as by soaking.

sōak, *v.i.* 1. to remain in long contact with moisture so as to become thoroughly wet or saturated.

2. to pass or penetrate; as, water *soaks* into the earth or other porous matter.

3. to drink to excess. [Colloq.]

sōak'aġe, *n.* the act of soaking or the state of being soaked; also, the amount of liquid that soaks in or through a substance.

sōak'ẽr, *n.* one who or that which soaks.

sōak'ẽrṣ, *n.pl.* short knitted pants of absorbent material, especially wool, put on over a baby's diaper for added protection.

sōak'ing·ly, *adv.* in a soaking manner.

sōak'y, *a.* soppy; wet.

sōal, *n.* a dirty pool [Brit. Dial.]

sōam, *n.* a chain or rope used in pulling anything, as a plow. [Scot. and Brit. Dial.]

sō'-ănd-sō, *n.*; *pl.* **sō'-ănd-sōṣ,** a person or thing not clearly named or determined: often used euphemistically in place of a stronger epithet. [Colloq.]

sōap, *n.* [AS. *sāpe*; Ice. *sapa*; Sw. *sapa,* from L. *sapo (-onis),* soap.]

1. a substance mixed with water to produce suds for washing or cleaning: soaps are usually produced by the action of an alkali, as caustic soda or potash, on a fat or oil.

2. any metallic salt of a fatty acid.

3. money, especially as used for bribery. [Slang.]

4. flattery. [Slang.]

5. a soap opera. [Slang.]

arsenical soap; a soap containing arsenic: used in taxidermy to preserve skins.

carbolic soap; a disinfectant soap containing ten per cent of carbolic acid.

Castile soap; see under *Castile.*

hard soap; a soap made from soda and the harder fats, or their acids, and hardened into a solid.

lead soap; an insoluble white soap made from lead oxide and olive oil: also called *lead plaster, diachylon,* etc.

milled soap; a soap that has been pressed into cakes after being subjected to milling.

mineral soap; a plastic clay found in Wyoming, possessing cleansing properties, but not forming a lather with water.

no soap; the offer, suggestion, etc. is not acceptable. [Slang.]

soap chips; soap flakes.

soap flakes; soap that has been finely flaked or chipped so that it dissolves almost immediately in warm or hot water.

soap liniment; a household remedy made of alcohol, camphor, and soap.

soap powder; dried soap in powder form, commercially prepared with sodium carbonate or sodium silicate.

soft soap; see under *soft.*

zinc soap; a soap containing zinc oxide or zinc sulfate: used as a plaster or ointment.

sōap, *v.t.*; soaped (sōpt), *pt., pp.*; soaping, *ppr.* 1. to rub or wash over with soap.

2. to flatter. [Slang.]

sōap'bärk, *n.* 1. a tree of the rose family, with leathery leaves, white flower clusters, and soaplike inner bark used in cleansing preparations: also *soapbark tree.*

2. any of several shrubs of the mimosa family with such bark: also *soapbark tree.*

3. the bark of any of these trees.

sōap'ber″ry, *n.*; *pl.* **sōap'ber″ries,** 1. any tree of the genus *Sapindus,* as *Sapindus saponaria,* with white or yellowish flowers and round fruit containing a soapy material: also *soapberry tree.*

2. the fruit of these trees.

sōap'box, *n.* 1. a box or carton for soap.

2. any box used as the platform of a street or stump orator.

sōap'box, *a.* pertaining to a soapbox; carried on from a soapbox (used as a platform); as, a *soapbox* orator.

sōap'box, *v.i.* to speak informally to a street audience.

sōap bub'ble, 1. a bubble of soapy water.
 2. figuratively, anything short-lived, unsubstantial, or ephemeral.

sōap cē'rāte, an ointment of soap, olive oil, white wax, and subacetate of lead, used to alleviate inflammation.

sōap ẽarth, same as *steatite.*

sōap'ẽr, *n.* a soap opera. [Slang.]

sōap'fish, *n.* a serranoid fish of the genus *Rhypticus,* found along the Atlantic coast of the United States: so called from its soapy skin.

sōap flākes, soap in the form of thin flakes or chips: also *soap chips.*

sōap'i·ness, *n.* the quality or condition of being soapy.

sōap'nut, *n.* 1. the legume of *Acacia concinna;* also, the plant.
 2. same as *soapberry.*

sōap op'ẽr·ȧ, a daytime radio or television serial drama of a highly melodramatic, sentimental nature: so called since many original sponsors were soap companies. [Colloq.]

sōap plant, any plant, as *Chlorogalum pomeridianum,* whose bulbs may be used as soap.

sōap'rọọt, *n.* a perennial of the pink family, *Gypsophila struthium,* growing in Spain, the root of which is used as soap.

sōap'stōne, *n.* steatite, a soft talc in rock form, used for griddles, bed warmers, etc.

sōap'sudṣ, *n.pl.* soapy water, especially when stirred into a foam.

sōap'weed, *n.* same as *amole.*

sōap'wŏrt, *n.* a plant of the genus *Saponaria,* with white, pink, or red flowers and thick juice which produces a lather in water. Common soapwort is *Saponaria officinalis.*

sōap'y, *a.; comp.* soapier; *superl.* soapiest, 1. resembling soap; having the qualities of soap; soft and smooth.
 2. smeared with or containing soap.
 3. suave; unctuous; oily. [Slang.]

sōar, *v.i.;* soared, *pt., pp.;* soaring, *ppr.* [Fr. *essorer,* to expose to the air, hence, to soar into the air, as a falcon; from LL. *exaurare,* to take to the air; L. *ex,* out and *aura,* air.]
 1. to rise or fly high into the air.
 2. to fly, sail, or glide along high in the air.
 3. to glide without loss of altitude, as an airplane.
 4. to rise above the usual or ordinary level; to be elevated.

sōar, *v.t.* to reach by soaring. [Poet.]

sōar, *n.* 1. soaring range or scope.
 2. the act of soaring; upward flight.

sōar'ănt, *a.* in heraldry, poised aloft on wings; volant.

sōar'ing·ly, *adv.* in a soaring manner.

sō·ä've, *adv.* [It.] with tenderness; softly; sweetly.

sō·ä·ve·men'te, *adv.* same as *soave.*

sob, *v.i.;* sobbed, *pt., pp.;* sobbing, *ppr.* [ME. *sobben;* AS. *sobbian,* from base of *supan,* to swallow, suck in.]
 1. to weep aloud with a catch or break in the voice and short, gasping breaths.
 2. to make a sound like a sob, as the wind, an animal in pain, etc.

sob, *v.t.* 1. to bring (oneself) into a given state, especially sleep, by sobbing.
 2. to utter amid sobs; to relate while sobbing; as, to *sob* one's woe.
 3. to cause to make a subdued sound, as by dampening a lute string.
 4. to soak. [Dial.]

sob, *n.* 1. a convulsive sigh accompanied with weeping.
 2. any mournful sound or cry of distress.

sob'bing, *n.* the act of one who sobs; a series of sobs or similar sounds.

sob'bing·ly, *adv.* with sobs or sobbing.

sō·bē'it, *conj.* provided; if it should be that. [Archaic.]

sō'bẽr, *a.* [Fr. *sobre,* from L. *sobrius,* sober; *so-* priv., and *ebrius,* drunken.]
 1. temperate in the use of alcoholic liquor; habitually temperate; as, a *sober* man.
 2. not intoxicated, or drunk; as, he is *sober* at times.
 3. temperate in any way; not extreme or extravagant.
 4. serious; solemn; grave; as, the *sober* livery of autumn.
 5. quiet; plain; not bright or garish: said of color, clothes, etc.
 6. not exaggerated or distorted; as, the *sober* truth.
 7. characterized by reason, sanity, or self-control; showing mental and emotional balance.

sō'bẽr, *v.t.* and *v.i.;* sobered, *pt., pp.;* sobering, *ppr.* to make or become sober (often with *up* or *down*).

sō'bẽr·īze, *v.t.* to make sober. [Rare.]

sō'bẽr·ly, *adv.* in a sober manner; with sobriety.

sō'bẽr-mīnd'ed, *a.* of a sober mind.

sō'bẽr-mīnd'ed·ness, *n.* the state or condition of being sober-minded.

sō'bẽr·ness, *n.* the state or quality of being sober.

sob'ō·lēṣ, *n.* [L., from *sub,* under, and *olere,* to grow.] in botany, a shoot or sucker borne at or near the ground.

sob·ō·lif'ẽr·ous, *a.* having shoots near the ground.

Sō·brän'je (-ye), *n.* the national assembly or legislature of Bulgaria.

sō·brī'e·ty, *n.* [Fr. *sobriété;* L. *sobrietas,* from *sobrius,* sober.] the state or quality of being sober; specifically, (a) temperance or moderation, especially in the use of drink; (b) seriousness, solemnity, gravity, or sedateness of manner or appearance.
 Syn.—temperance, abstemiousness, soberness, gravity, steadiness, sedateness.

sō'brï·quet (-kā), *n.* [Fr., from *sous,* under, and *briquet,* brisket; of Celtic origin; lit., a chuck under the chin, a mock or flout, a nickname.]
 1. a nickname.
 2. an assumed name.
 Also spelled *soubriquet.*

sob sis'tẽr, in journalism, a woman who writes sentimental news stories. [Slang.]

sob stō'ry, a sentimental account or story intended to arouse pity or compassion.

sob stuff, a sob story or stories. [Slang.]

soc, *n.* [AS. *sac,* from *sacan,* to contend.] same as *soke.*
 sac and soc; in old English law, the unrestricted right to hold court and dispense justice in a manor or district.

soç'āġe, soç'çāġe, *n.* [LL. *socagium,* socage; lit., the tenure of one over whom his lord had a certain jurisdiction, from *soc.*] a medieval English system of land tenure in which a tenant held land in return for a fixed payment or for certain stated nonmilitary services to his lord.

soç'ȧ·ġẽr, *n.* a tenant by socage; a socman.

sō'-cạlled, *a.* so named; known or called by this term, but usually inaccurately or improperly; as, he is a *so-called* liberal.

soç'çẽr, sock'ẽr, *n.* [altered from *association.*] a game played with a round ball by two teams of eleven men on a field with a goal at either end: the ball is moved chiefly by kicking or by bunting with the head, the use of the hands and arms being prohibited: also called *association football.*

sō·ciȧ·bil'i·ty (-shȧ-), *n.; pl.* **sō·ciȧ·bil'i·tieṣ,** [Fr. *sociabilité.*] the quality, fact, or instance of being sociable.

sō'ciȧ·ble, *a.* [Fr. *sociable;* L. *sociabilis,* from *socius,* a companion, prob. from *sequi,* to follow.]
 1. enjoying the company of others; fond of companionship; companionable.
 2. friendly; agreeable, especially in an easy, informal way; affable.
 3. characterized by pleasant, informal conversation and companionship; as, a *sociable* evening.
 sociable weaver; same as *weaverbird.*

sō'ciȧ·ble, *n.* 1. a social, especially a church social.
 2. a kind of carriage in which the seats face each other.
 3. a sofa in the shape of the letter S, for two persons to sit side by side but facing in opposite directions: also called *tete-à-tete.*
 4. a tricycle for two riders seated side by side.

sō'ciȧ·ble·ness, *n.* disposition to be sociable.

sō'ciȧ·bly, *adv.* in a sociable manner.

sō'ciăl (-shăl), *a.* [L. *socialis,* from *socius,* companion.]
 1. of or having to do with human beings living together as a group in a situation requiring that they have dealings with one another; as, *social* consciousness, *social* reform, *social* problems.
 2. living in this way; as, modern man is *social,* the family is a *social* unit.
 3. of or having to do with the ranks or activities of society, especially the more exclusive or fashionable of these; as, a *social* climber, *social* notes.
 4. sociable; getting along well with others; as, a *social* nature.
 5. of, for, or fond of friends, companionship, etc.; as, a *social* club.
 6. offering material aid, vocational advice, etc. to those who need it; of or engaged in welfare work; as, a *social* worker or agency.
 7. living or associating in groups or communities; as, the ant is a *social* creature.
 8. socialist.
 9. in botany, growing in clumps or masses.
 10. in history, of or between allies or confederates, as a war.
 social climber; a person who tries to get acquainted with distinguished or wealthy people.
 social contract (or *compact*); the theory, put forward by Hobbes, Locke, and Rousseau, that society had its origin in loose associations of individuals for mutual protection, and that since out of these grew the concepts of law and sovereignty, government cannot be by force alone but must rest upon the consent of the governed.
 Social Credit; the theory that the profits of industry are not true earnings and should be returned to their source, the community as a whole, together with all interest, in the form of dividends to consumers: put forward by Major C. H. Douglas (1879–), English economist and engineer.
 social dancing; ballroom dancing.
 Social Democracy; (a) Social Democratic parties collectively; (b) their doctrines, methods, etc.
 Social Democrat; a member or adherent of a Social Democratic party.
 Social Democratic Party; (a) a German Marxist political party formed in 1875 by the merger of the General German Workers' Association, founded in 1863 by F. Lassalle, with the Social Democratic Workers' Party, founded in 1869 by A. Bebel and W. Liebknecht; (b) any of various similar political parties in other countries, often called *Socialist* parties.
 social disease; venereal disease.
 social evil; (a) anything that threatens the welfare of the people, as illicit trade in narcotics, slum housing, etc.; (b) prostitution: a euphemism.
 social insurance; any government insurance intended to protect people in low-income groups against economic and industrial hazards: it includes accident insurance, unemployment insurance, health insurance, old-age pensions (for wage earners), and maternity insurance.
 social lion; any person who is considered a social celebrity or anyone whose society is much sought.
 social register; a book containing the names of socially prominent people.
 social science; (a) the study of people and how they live together as families, tribes, communities, races, etc.; sociology; (b) any of several studies, as history, economics, civics, etc., dealing with the structure of society and the activity of its members.
 social security; any system by which a group provides for those of its members who may be in need; specifically, in the United States, a Federal system of old-age, unemployment, or disability insurance for various categories of employed and dependent persons, financed by a fund maintained jointly by employees, employers, and the government.
 social weaver; a species of weaverfish.
 social whale; the caaing whale: named from its habit of herding.

sō'ciăl, *n.* a social gathering of an informal character; a party.

Sō'ciăl-Dem·ō·çrat'iç, *a.* of, characteristic of, or like Social Democracy or Social Democrats.

sō'ciăl·iṣm, *n.* 1. the theory or system of the ownership and operation of the means of production and distribution by society or the community rather than by private individuals, with all members of society or the community sharing in the work and the products.
 2. [*often* S–] (a) political movement for establishing such a system; (b) the doctrines, methods, etc. of the Socialist parties.
 3. in Communist doctrine, the stage of

society coming between the capitalist stage and the communist stage, in which private ownership of the means of production and distribution has been eliminated, as in the Soviet Union, and the production of goods is sufficient to permit realization of the slogan *from each according to his ability, to each according to his work*.

sō′ciăl·ist, *n.* 1. an advocate or supporter of socialism.

2. [S–] a member of a Socialist party.

sō′ciăl·ist, *a.* 1. of, characteristic of, or like socialism or socialists.

2. advocating or supporting socialism.

sō·ciăl·is′tiç, *a.* socialist.

sō·ciăl·is′ti·çăl·ly, *adv.* in a socialistic manner.

Sō′ciăl·ist Pär′ty, a political party based on the principles of socialism advocated by Marx and Engels but later extensively modified by various revisionists.

sō′ciăl·īte, *n.* a person prominent in high society; especially, one who is entered in the social register. [Colloq.]

sō·ci·al′i·ty (-shi-), *n.* 1. the quality of being social; sociability.

2. *pl.* **sō·ci·al′i·ties,** the trait or tendency in individuals to join together in groups and associate with one another.

sō″ciăl·i·zā′tion, *n.* a socializing or being socialized.

sō′ciăl·īze (-shăl-), *v.t.*; socialized, *pt., pp.*; socializing, *ppr.* 1. to make social; adjust or make fit for co-operative group living.

2. to adapt, as oneself or others, to the common needs of a social group.

3. to subject to governmental ownership and control; to nationalize.

4. to cause to become socialist.

sō′ciăl·īze, *v.i.* to take part in social activity. [Colloq.]

sō′ciăl·īzed med′i·cine, 1. complete medical care, made available through public funds, for all the people in a community, district, or nation.

2. group medicine.

sō′ciăl·ly, *adv.* in a social manner or way.

sō′ciăl·mīnd′ed, *a.* having an active interest in society or in social welfare.

sō′ciăl·ness, *n.* the quality or character of being social.

sō′ciăl-sẽrv′ice, *a.* of or having to do with social work.

sō′ciăl sẽrv′ice, social work.

sō′ciăl set′tle·ment, same as *settlement*, sense 10.

sō′ciăl wŏrk, any service or activity designed to promote the welfare of the community and the individual, as through health and psychology clinics, recreation halls and playgrounds, aid for the needy, the aged, the physically handicapped, etc.

sō′ciăl wŏrk′ẽr, one who does social work.

sō′ci·āte (-shi-), *v.i.* to associate; to mix with company. [Obs.]

sō·cī′e·tăl, *a.* of society or a society.

sō·cī·ē·târ′i·ăn, *a.* relating or belonging to society; of a social nature.

sō·cī′e·târ·y, *a.* societarian. [Rare.]

sō·cī′e·ty, *n.*; *pl.* **sō·cī′e·ties,** [Fr. *société*; L. *societas*, from *socius*, a companion.]

1. partnership; participation; connection. [Obs.]

2. a group of animals or plants living together under the same environment and regarded as constituting a homogeneous unit or entity; especially, a group of persons regarded as forming a single community.

3. all people, collectively, regarded as constituting a community of related, interdependent individuals.

4. the system or condition of living together as a community; as, a primitive *society*.

5. company or companionship; as, I do not seek his *society*.

6. one's friends or associates; as, for *society* he had two old aunts.

7. any organized group of people joined together because of some interest in common; as, a medical *society*.

8. the members of the wealthy, fashionable class; as, all *society* attended the concert.

9. the conduct, standards, activities, etc. of this class.

society column; a newspaper column that reports the social affairs of the wealthy, fashionable class.

Society of Friends; a Christian religious sect founded in England in 1650 by George Fox: the Friends have no formal creed, rites, liturgy, or priesthood, and reject violence, including war: see *Quakers*.

Society of Jesus; a Roman Catholic religious order: see *Jesuit*.

society verse; poetry of a light, entertaining, polished character.

Sō·cin′i·ăn, *a.* of or pertaining to Faustus Socinus or his theological teachings.

Sō·cin′i·ăn, *n.* one who believes in the doctrines of Socinianism.

Sō·cin′i·ăn·ism, *n.* the theological doctrines of Faustus Socinus, denying the divinity of Jesus, the Trinity, the natural immortality of man, etc., and explaining sin and salvation rationalistically.

Sō·cin′i·ăn·īze, *v.t.*; Socinianized, *pt., pp.*; Socinianizing, *ppr.* to cause to conform to Socinianism.

sō′ci·ō-, [from L. *socius*, a companion.] a combining form meaning *society, societal*.

sō″ci·ō·bī″ō·log′iç·al, *a.* of or having to do with sociobiology.

sō″ci·ō·bī·ol′ō·gist, *n.* one who treats of or specializes in the study of sociobiology.

sō″ci·ō·bī·ol′ō·gy, *n.* the scientific study of the biological basis for animal and human behavior: it is based on the theory that some or much of such behavior is genetically determined.

sō·ci·oç′rȧ·cy (-shi-), *n.* [L. *socius*, companion, and Gr. *kratein*, to rule, to be strong.] government by society as a whole.

sō″ci·ō·lin·guis′tiçs, *n.pl.* [*construed as sing.*] the branch of linguistics that analyzes the effects of social and cultural differences within a speech community upon its language patterns.

sō″ci·ō·log′iç, *a.* sociological.

sō″ci·ō·log′iç·ăl, *a.* 1. of or having to do with human society, its organization, needs, development, etc.

2. of sociology.

sō″ci·ō·log′iç·ăl·ly, *adv.* from the standpoint of sociology; by means of sociology.

sō·ci·ol′ō·gist, *n.* one who treats of or makes a specialty of the study of sociology.

sō·ci·ol′ō·gy, *n.* [L. *socius*, companion, and *-logy*.] the study of the history, development, organization, and problems of people living together as social groups; social science.

sō·ci·om′e·try, *n.* [*socio-*, and *-metry*.]

1. the quantitative study of group relationships.

2. a technique for measuring what members of a group perceive, think, and feel about other members of the group.

sō′ci·ō·path, *n.* [*socio-*, and psycho*path*.] a psychopathic personality whose behavior is aggressively antisocial.

sō′ci·us (-shi-), *n.*; *pl.* **sō′ci·ī,** [L.] a companion; an associate; a member.

socius criminis; an accomplice in crime.

sock, *n.* [OFr. *soc*, plowshare.] a plowshare. [Scot. and Brit. Dial.]

sock, *n.* [ME. *sok, socke*; AS. *socc*, from L. *soccus*, a kind of light, low-heeled shoe.]

1. the light shoe worn by ancient Greek and Roman comic actors; hence, comedy.

2. the muse of comedy.

3. a stocking reaching only a short distance up the leg.

4. a warm inner sole for a shoe.

sock, *v.t.* 1. to hit or strike with force, especially with the fist. [Slang.]

2. to put or place; as, he *socked* all his money in the bank. [Slang.]

sock, *n.* a blow. [Slang.]

sock, *adv.* directly, squarely. [Slang.]

sock·dol′o·gẽr, sock·dol′ȧ·gẽr, *n.* [from *sock* and *doxology*, used in the sense of final.]

1. something so effective or forceful as to be final or decisive, as a heavy blow; a finisher. [Slang.]

2. something very large for its kind. [Slang.]

sock′et, *n.* [Anglo-Fr. *soket*, spearhead, from OFr. *soc*, plowshare.]

1. an opening, or tubular recess, in which anything is fitted; any hollow thing or place which receives and holds something else; as, the *sockets* of the eyes.

2. a hollow tube or opening into which a candle is fitted in a candlestick or chandelier.

sock′et chis′el, a chisel used for heavy mortising, having a hollow tang to receive the handle: it is used with a mallet.

sock′et·ed, *a.* placed in or having a socket.

sock′et wrench (rench), a wrench supplied with a socket, for turning nuts, boltheads, etc.

sock′eȳe (-ī), *n.* [altered from Salishan *sukkegh*.] a red salmon of the north Pacific, used for canning.

sock′less, *a.* without socks.

sō′çle, *n.* [Fr., from L. *socculus*, dim. of *soccus*, a shoe.] in architecture, a plain block or plinth, forming a low pedestal for a statue, column, etc.; also, a plain face or plinth at the lower part of a wall.

soç′măn, *n.* one who holds lands or tenements by socage.

soç′măn·ry, *n.* tenure by socage.

Sō·çō′trăn, *a.* of or pertaining to Socotra, an island situated in the Indian Ocean, near the east coast of Africa.

Sō·çō′trăn, *n.* a native or inhabitant of Socotra.

Sō·çō′trine, *a.* and *n.* same as *Socotran*.

Sō·crat′iç, *a.* pertaining to Socrates, the Athenian idealist philosopher and teacher, or to his philosophy or manner of teaching.

Sō·crat′iç, *n.* 1. a follower of Socrates.

2. any Greek philosopher directly influenced by Socrates.

Sō·crat′iç·ăl, *a.* Socratic.

Sō·crat′iç·ăl·ly, *adv.* in a Socratic manner.

Sō·crat′iç ī′rŏn·y, pretense of ignorance in a discussion to expose the fallacies in the opponent's logic.

Sō·crat′i·cism, *n.* any Socratic characteristic.

Sō·crat′iç meth′ŏd, a method of teaching or discussion, as used by Socrates, in which one asks a series of easily answered questions that inevitably lead the answerer to a logical conclusion foreseen by the questioner.

Soç′rȧ·tism, *n.* the doctrines or philosophy of Socrates.

Soç′rȧ·tist, *n.* a disciple of Socrates; a Socratic.

sod, *n.* [ME.; prob. from M.D. *sode*; akin to Eng. *seethe, sodden*: the name prob. refers to the wet ground from which fuel turf was cut.]

1. a surface layer of earth containing grass plants with their matted roots; turf; sward.

2. a piece of this layer.

the old sod; one's native land; specifically, Ireland.

under the sod; dead and buried.

sod, *a.* consisting of sod; as, a *sod* seat.

sod house; a house whose walls consist of layers of sod.

sod kiln; a limekiln consisting of an excavation lined and covered with sod.

sod, *v.t.*; sodded, *pt., pp.*; sodding, *ppr.* to cover with sod; to turf.

sod, *n.* the rock dove. [Scot.]

sod, *v.* obsolete past tense of *seethe*.

sō′dȧ, *n.* [ML. *soda*; It. *sodo*, firm, from L. *solidus*, solid; first used of ash in glassmaking.]

1. sodium carbonate.

2. sodium bicarbonate.

3. sodium hydroxide.

4. sodium oxide.

5. soda water (sense 1).

6. a beverage made of soda water flavored with sirup, fruit, etc., often mixed with ice cream.

7. in faro, the card turned face up in the dealing box before the start of play.

salt of soda; same as *sodium carbonate*.

sō′dȧ al′um, a crystalline mineral, a hydrated double sulfate of aluminum and sodium, $NaAl(SO_4)_2 \cdot 12H_2O$, found on the island of Milo, at Solfatara, and near Mendoza, east of the Andes.

sō′dȧ ash, crude sodium carbonate.

sō′dȧ ball, black ash.

sō′dȧ bis′çuit (-kit), 1. a bread or biscuit made with baking soda and sour milk or buttermilk.

2. a soda cracker.

sō′dȧ çrack′ẽr, a light, crisp cracker usually salted, prepared from dough made of flour, water, soda, and cream of tartar.

sō′dȧ foun′tăin, 1. a counter fitted with equipment for making and serving soft drinks, sodas, milkshakes, sundaes, sandwiches, etc.

2. a container for soda water, with faucets by which it is drawn off.

sō·dā′iç, *a.* of, pertaining to, or containing soda; as, *sodaic* powders.

sō′dȧ jẽrk, a person who works at a soda fountain. [Slang.]

sō′dȧ līme, a white, powdery mixture of sodium hydroxide and calcium oxide, used as a chemical reagent and as an absorbent for moisture and acid gases.

sō′dăl·ist, *n.* a member of a sodality.
sō′da·līte, *n.* a silicate of sodium and aluminum with some chlorine, $Na_4Al_3Si_3O_{12}Cl$: it resembles marble when polished and is used as an ornamental stone.
sō·dal′i·ty, *n.*; *pl.* **sō·dal′i·ties,** [L. *sodalitas,* from *sodalis,* a companion.]
1. fellowship.
2. an association or brotherhood.
3. in the Roman Catholic Church, a lay association formed to carry on devotional or charitable activity.
sō′dȧ lȳe, a lye consisting of a solution of sodium hydrate in water.
sōd·am′ide (*or* -īd), a crystalline fusible substance, $NaNH_2$, produced by heating sodium in ammonia.
sō′dȧ pop, a soft drink made of carbonated water with various, often artificial flavorings, sold in tightly capped bottles or cans.
sō′dȧ wa′tẽr, 1. water charged under pressure with carbon dioxide gas, used in making ice-cream sodas, mixed drinks, etc.
2. a solution of water, acid, and sodium bicarbonate, used for the same purposes.
sod′den, *a.* [obs. past participle of *seethe.*]
1. filled with moisture; soaked through.
2. moist or heavy as a result of improper baking or cooking; soggy, as bread.
3. dull; stupid; not lively or alert, as from fatigue or overindulgence.
4. boiled or steeped. [Rare.]
5. having a boiled, soaked, or bloated look.
sod′den, *v.i.* to become sodden.
sod′den, *v.t.* to make sodden.
sod′dy, *a.*; *comp.* soddier; *superl.* soddiest, consisting of sod; covered with sod; turfy.
sō′diç, *a.* relating to or containing sodium.
sō′di·um, *n.* [Mod.L., from *soda.*] a waxy, unstable, silver-white metal which is found in nature only in combined form and is extremely active chemically: symbol, Na (for *natrium*); atomic weight, 22.997; atomic number, 11.
sō′di·um ben′zō·āte, a sweet, odorless, white powder, $NaC_7H_5O_2$, the sodium salt of benzoic acid, used as a food preservative, antiseptic, etc.
sō′di·um bī·cär′bŏn·āte, a white, crystalline compound, $NaHCO_3$, used in baking powder, as an antacid, etc.: also called *baking soda.*
sō′di·um brō′mīde, a white, crystalline compound, NaBr, used in medicine as a sedative and in photography to produce silver bromide.
sō′di·um cär′bŏn·āte, 1. the anhydrous sodium salt of carbonic acid, Na_2CO_3: also called *soda ash.*
2. any of the hydrated carbonates of sodium; especially, the colorless, crystalline compound $Na_2CO_3 \cdot 10H_2O$, commonly called *sal soda* or *washing soda.*
sō′di·um çhlō′rāte, a colorless, crystalline salt, $NaClO_3$, used as an oxidizing agent in matches, explosives, etc.
sō′di·um çhlō′rīde, common salt, NaCl.
sō′di·um cȳ′ȧ·nīde, a white, highly poisonous salt, NaCN, used in electroplating, as an insecticide, etc.
sō′di·um dī·çhrōm′āte, a red, crystalline salt, $Na_2Cr_2O_7$, used as an oxidizing agent, antiseptic, etc.
sō′di·um hȳ·drox′īde, a white substance, NaOH, in the form of powder, flakes, sticks, etc., widely used in chemistry, oil refining, paper and rayon manufacture, etc.: also called *caustic soda, lye, sodium hydrate.*
sō′di·um hȳ·pō·çhlō′rīte, a greenish, unstable salt, NaOCl, usually stored in solution, used especially as a bleaching agent and disinfectant.
sō′di·um hȳ·pō·sul′fīte, 1. a clear, crystalline salt, $Na_2S_2O_4$, used as a chemical reagent.
2. sodium thiosulfate.
sō′di·um līght (līt), the yellow light of burning sodium vapor.
sō′di·um nī′trāte, a clear, odorless, crystalline salt, $NaNO_3$, used in manufacturing nitric acid, explosives, fertilizers, etc., and as a reagent and oxidizing agent in chemistry: also called *Chile saltpeter.*
sō′di·um pen′tō·thal, see *pentothal sodium.*
sō′di·um pẽr·ox′īde, a yellowish-white powder, Na_2O_2, used as a bleaching agent, air and water purifier, and oxidizing agent.
sō′di·um phos′phāte, any of three clear, crystalline sodium salts of phosphoric acid widely used in industry.
sō′di·um sul′fāte, a white, crystalline salt, Na_2SO_4, used in medicine and in the making of dyes, glass, etc.
sō′di·um sul′fīte, a white salt, Na_2SO_3, in the form of crystals or powder, used in dyeing, engraving, and photography, and as a bleaching agent, etc.
sō′di·um thī·ō·sul′fāte, a white, crystalline salt, $Na_2S_2O_3$, used as an antichlor, as a fixing agent in photography, etc.: popularly but incorrectly called (*sodium*) *hyposulfite* or *hypo.*
sō′di·um-vā′pŏr lamp, a globe fitted with two electrodes and filled with sodium vapor, which sheds a yellow, glareless light when electric current is passed through it: also *sodium lamp.*
sod oil, oil obtained from sheepskin.
Sod′ŏm, in the Bible, a city destroyed by fire together with a neighboring city, Gomorrah, because of the sinfulness of the people: Gen. xviii–xix.
Sod′ŏm·īte, *n.* 1. an inhabitant of Sodom.
2. [s–] a person who practices sodomy.
sod·ŏm·it′iç·ăl, *a.* pertaining to sodomy.
sod′ŏm·īze, *v.t.*; sodomized, *pt., pp.*; sodomizing, *ppr.* to engage in sodomy with; specifically, to forcibly subject to sodomy.
sod′ŏm·y, *n.* any sexual intercourse regarded as abnormal, as between persons of the same sex, especially males, or between a person and an animal.
sōe, *n.* [AS. *saa*; Fr. *seau,* a bucket.] a large wooden vessel for holding water; a cowl. [Dial.]
sō·ev′ẽr, *adv.* [*so* and *ever.*]
1. in any way; to any extent or degree (usually following *how* and an adjective); as, how dark *soever* the night may be.
2. of any kind; at all; whatever; as, no rest *soever.*
-sō·ev′ẽr, a combining form added for emphasis or generalization to *who, what, when, where, how,* etc., and meaning *any* (person, thing, time, place, or manner) *of all those possible.*
sō′fȧ, *n.* [Fr. and Sp. *sofa,* a sofa, from Ar. *soffah,* cushion on a saddle for a camel.] an upholstered couch, usually of spring construction, with fixed back and arms.
sō′fȧ bed, a sofa adapted for use as a bed.
sō′fär, *n.* [*so*und *f*ixing *a*nd *r*anging.] a system for determining the location of underwater sounds as far as 2000 miles from shore, which facilitates the rescue of survivors of sea disasters.

S S, SOFFITS

sof′fit, *n.* [Fr. *soffite*; It. *soffitta,* from L. *suffixus.*] in architecture, (a) the lower surface of a vault or arch; (b) the under horizontal face of an architrave between columns; (c) the ceiling of an apartment divided by crossbeams into compartments; (d) the under part of an overhanging cornice, eave, etc.
sǫft, *a.*; *comp.* softer; *superl.* softest, [AS. *softe,* gentle, quiet; akin to G. *sanft.*]
1. giving way easily under pressure, as a feather pillow or moist clay; easily shaped or worked.
2. easily cut, marked, or worn away, as pine wood or pure gold.
3. not hard for its kind; not as hard as is normal, desirable, etc.; as, *soft* butter.
4. smooth or fine to the touch; not rough, harsh, or coarse.
5. bland; not acid, sour, or sharp.
6. nonalcoholic: said of drinks.
7. having in solution few or none of the mineral salts that interfere with the lathering and cleansing properties of soap: said of water.
8. mild, gentle, or temperate, as a breeze, the weather, climate, etc.
9. weak; delicate; not strong or vigorous; not able to endure hardship, privation, etc.
10. requiring little effort; not difficult; easy; as, he has a very *soft* job.
11. (a) kind or gentle, especially to the point of weakness; not severe; lenient or compassionate; (b) easily impressed, influenced, or imposed upon.
12. subdued; not bright or intense: said of color.
13. showing little contrast or distinctness; not sharp; as, a *soft* etching, a *soft* line or border.
14. gentle; low; not loud or harsh: said of sound.
15. in phonetics, (a) sibilant: said of *c* and *g,* as in *citrus,* and *German*; (b) lenis, or lenis and voiced; (c) palatalized, as certain consonants in Slavic languages.
Syn.—mild, gentle, pliant, yielding, impressible, smooth, plastic, pliable, bland, compliant, irresolute, submissive, mellifluous.
sǫft, *n.* something soft; a soft part.
sǫft, *adv.* softly; gently; quietly.
sǫft, *interj.* 1. be quiet! hush! [Archaic.]
2. slow up! stop! [Archaic.]
sof′tȧ, *n.* [Turk.] in Turkey, a pupil of a secondary school engaged in professional studies, especially in theological studies.
sǫft′ball, *n.* 1. a kind of baseball played with a ball larger and softer than the ordinary baseball, and sometimes without gloves.
2. the ball used.
sǫft′-boiled′, *a.* boiled only a short time so that the yolk is soft: said of eggs.
sǫft çlam, the common clam, *Mya arenaria.*
sǫft çōal, coal that yields pitch and tar when it is burned and makes more smoke and ashes than hard coal: also called *bituminous coal.*
sǫft çrab, a soft-shelled crab.
sǫft driñk, a nonalcoholic drink, especially a carbonated drink.
sǫf′ten (sǫf′n), *v.t.*; softened, *pt., pp.*; softening, *ppr.* to make soft or softer as (a) to make less hard in substance; (b) to mollify; to make less fierce or intractable; to make more susceptible of humane or fine feelings; as, to *soften* a hard heart; (c) to make less harsh or severe, less rude, less offensive or violent; as, to *soften* an expression; (d) to palliate; to represent as less enormous; as, to *soften* a fault; (e) to make easy; to compose; to mitigate; to alleviate; (f) to make calm and placid; (g) to make less glaring; to tone down; as, to *soften* the coloring of a picture; (h) to make tender; to make effeminate; to enervate; as, troops *softened* by luxury; (i) to make less strong or intense in sound; to make less loud; to make smooth to the ear; as, to *soften* the voice.
Syn.—mollify, palliate, mitigate, moderate.
sǫf′ten (sǫf′n), *v.i.* to become soft or softer, as (a) to become more pliable and yielding to pressure; (b) to become less rude, harsh, or cruel; (c) to become less obstinate or obdurate; to become more susceptible of humane feelings and tenderness; to relent; (d) to pass by soft imperceptible degrees; to melt; to blend.
sǫf′ten·ẽr, *n.* something that softens, as a positively charged compound added to water in treating fabrics to make them softer and fluffier (in full, *fabric softener*).
sǫf′ten·ing, *n.* the act of making less hard, less cruel or obdurate, less violent, less glaring, etc.
softening of the brain; (a) degeneration of the brain tissues into a soft, fatty substance; (b) in popular usage, progressive dementia.
sǫft′-finned′, *a.* having fins without spines; malacopterygian.
sǫft′goods, *n.pl.* goods that last a relatively short time, especially textile products: also *soft goods.*
sǫft grȧss, a perennial grass, *Holcus lanatus,* of the Old World, introduced from Europe as a meadow grass into the United States, characterized by its pale color and its velvety softness: also called *velvet grass.*
sǫft′head (-hed), *n.* a stupid or feeble-minded person; a simpleton.
sǫft′head″ed (-hed″), *a.* stupid or foolish.
sǫft′heärt″ed, *a.* 1. full of compassion or tenderness.
2. not strict or severe, as in discipline.
sǫft′heärt″ed·ness, *n.* the quality or state of being softhearted.
sǫft′ie, *n.*; *pl.* **sǫft′ies,** a softy. [Colloq.]
sǫft′ish, *a.* somewhat soft.
sǫft land′ing, a safe landing, as of a spacecraft on the moon, in which the craft and its contents remain unharmed.
sǫft′ling, *n.* an effeminate person.
sǫft′ly, *adv.* without hardness; in a soft manner; without noise; gently; mildly; tenderly.
sǫft′nẽr, *n.* same as *softener.*
sǫft′ness, *n.* the quality or state of being soft.

soft pal′ăte, the soft, fleshy part at the rear of the roof of the mouth; velum.

soft-ped′ăl, *v.t.*; soft-pedalled, *pt.*, *pp.*; soft-pedalling, *ppr.* 1. to soften or dampen the tone of (a musical instrument) by use of a pedal made for this purpose.

2. to tone down; to play down; to make less emphatic, less obstrusive, less conspicuous, etc. [Colloq.]

soft ped′ăl, a pedal used to soften or dampen the tone of a musical instrument, as a piano.

soft′-rāyed′, *a.* having soft or jointed fin rays; soft-finned; not spiny-rayed.

soft sell, selling that relies on subtle inducement or suggestion rather than high-pressure salesmanship.

soft′-shell, *n.* an animal having a soft shell, as a crab or a turtle.

soft′-shell′, *a.* same as *soft-shelled.*

soft′-shelled′, *a.* 1. having a soft covering, as a crab or lobster after molting.

2. having a leathery carapace, as a turtle.

soft′-shelled′ crab, a crab at the stage between the shedding of its old shell and the hardening of the new.

soft′-shelled′ tûr′tle, a mud turtle with a soft leatherlike shell.

soft′-shoe′ (-shọọ′), *a.* designating a kind of tap dancing done without metal taps on the shoes.

soft shōul′dẽr, a soft strip of ground along the edge of a highway.

soft′-sōap′, *v.t.* 1. to apply soft soap to.

2. to flatter. [Colloq.]

soft sōap, 1. soap in liquid or semifluid form.

2. flattery. [Colloq.]

soft′-spō″ken, *a.* 1. having a soft voice; speaking softly.

2. smooth; ingratiating; suave.

soft′tack, *n.* leavened bread: cf. *hardtack.*

soft′wãre, *n.* the programs, data, routines, etc. for use in a digital computer, as distinguished from the physical components (*hardware*).

soft′wood, *n.* 1. any light, easily cut wood.

2. the wood of any tree with true cones.

3. any tree with soft wood.

soft′y, *n.*; *pl.* **soft′ies,** 1. a person who is overly sentimental or trusting. [Colloq.]

2. a person who lacks physical stamina or vigor. [Colloq.]

Sog′di·ăn, *n.* 1. one of an Iranian people who lived in Sogdiana, an ancient land in the region of modern Uzbekistan.

2. their extinct Iranian language.

sō′gẽr, sō′jẽr, *n.* a soldier. [Dial.]

sog′gi·ly, *adv.* in a soggy manner.

sog′gi·ness, *n.* the state or quality of being soggy.

sog′gy, *a.*; *comp.* soggier; *superl.* soggiest, [from obs. *sog*, a damp place, from ON. *sog*, lit., a sucking.] wet; filled with water; soft and heavy with moisture; as, *soggy* land; *soggy* timber: also used figuratively.

sō·hō′, *interj.* hello: a word used in calling from a distant place; a sportsmen's halloo.

soi′-di·sant′ (swä′dē-zäṅ′), *a.* [Fr.] so-called by oneself; self-styled.

soi·gné′ (swä-nyā′), *a.* [Fr.] 1. well-cared for or attended to.

2. neat; tidy; well-groomed.

soi·gnée′ (swä-nyā′), *a.* feminine of *soigné.*

soil, *v.t.*; soiled, *pt.*, *pp.*; soiling, *ppr.* [OFr. *saouler*, from L. *satullare*, to satiate.]

1. to stall-feed with green grass instead of pasturing, as horses and cattle.

2. to purge (animals) by means of green food.

soil, *v.t.* [OFr. *soillier*, to soil; ultimately from L. *suculus*, dim. of *sus*, a pig.]

1. to make dirty, especially on the surface.

2. to smirch or stain.

3. to bring disgrace upon.

4. to corrupt or defile; to sully.

5. to treat with manure; to manure. [Obs.]

soil, *v.i.* to become soiled.

soil, *n.* 1. any soiled spot; stain; smirch.

Free from touch or *soil.* —**Shak.**

2. manure used for fertilizing.

3. a soiling or being soiled.

4. filth; excrement.

soil, *n.* [OFr. *soil, soile*; Fr. *sol*, from L. *solum*, the soil.]

1. the surface layer of earth, supporting plant life.

2. figuratively, a place for growth or development of any kind.

3. land; country; territory; as, native *soil.*

4. ground or earth; as, barren *soil.*

soil′ăge, *n.* [*soil-* and *-age.*] green crops, cultivated for fodder.

soil çap, in geology, the accumulated mass of disintegrated rock material lying immediately upon the bedrock from which it is formed: also called *soil in place.*

soil′i·ness, *n.* stain; foulness. [Obs.]

soil′ing, *n.* the act or practice of feeding cattle or horses with fresh grass or green food, cut daily for them, instead of pasturing them.

soil′less, *a.* without soil.

soil pīpe, an iron pipe connected with a house for carrying off sewage or night soil.

soil′ūre, *n.* [Fr. *souillure.*]

1. a soiling, dirtying, or sullying.

2. the result of this; a stain; blot.

soil′y, *a.* stained; dirty; foul. [Rare.]

soi·rée′ (swä-rā′), *n.* [Fr.] an evening party or gathering.

Sō′jȧ (*or* -yȧ), *n.* [Japan., from *soy.*]

1. a genus of leguminous plants, the soy beans, having trifoliolate leaves and axillary racemose flowers.

2. [s–] (a) the soy bean: also *soja bean*; (b) a sauce made from it.

sō′journ (*or* sō-jŭrn′), *v.i.*; sojourned, *pt.*, *pp.*; sojourning, *ppr.* [OFr. *sojorner, sojourner*; It. *soggiornare*, from LL. (hyp.) *subdiurnare*; *sub*, under, and *diurnus*, pertaining to a day, from *dies*, a day.] to dwell for a time; to dwell or live in a place as a temporary resident; as, Abraham *sojourned* in Egypt.

Syn.—abide, tarry, dwell, stay, live.

sō′journ, *n.* a temporary residence or visit, as that of a traveler in a foreign land.

sō′journ·ẽr, *n.* a temporary resident; a stranger or traveler who dwells in or visits a place for a time.

sō′journ·ing, *n.* the act of dwelling in or visiting a place for a time; also, the time spent.

sō′journ·ment, *n.* a sojourn.

sōke, *n.* [variant of *soc.*]

1. in old English law, the power or privilege of holding a court in a given district, as in a manor.

2. the territorial jurisdiction of a court.

sōke′măn, *n.* same as *socman.*

sōke′măn·ry, *n.* same as *socmanry.*

sō′ken, *n.* 1. a toll formerly taken by millers for grinding grain in a certain district. [Obs.]

2. a district held by tenure of socage. [Obs.]

sōke reeve, a bailiff and tax gatherer of a soke.

Sol, *n.* [L.] 1. the sun.

2. [s–] in alchemy, gold.

3. the sun god of the ancient Romans.

sol, *n.* [OFr.] an old French coin, equal to twelve deniers, now superseded by the sou.

sōl, *n.*; *pl.* **sōls,** Sp. **sō′les,** [Sp.] 1. the monetary unit of Peru.

2. a silver coin of this value.

sōl, *n.* [It., abbreviation of word *solve*, in a L. hymn from which the names of the notes were taken.] in music, (a) the syllable representing the fifth tone of the diatonic scale; (b) the tone itself.

sol (*or* sōl), *n.* [from hydro*sol.*] a colloidal dispersion in a liquid.

sō′lȧ, *n.* [E. Ind.] 1. a small, partly submerged bush, *Æschynomene aspera*, growing in marshes in Bengal.

2. a light hat made of the pith of the sola.

sō′lȧ, *a.* [L.] feminine of *solus.*

sol′ăce, *v.t.*; solaced, *pt.*, *pp.*; solacing, *ppr.* [OFr. *solace, solas*, from L. *solatium*, from *solatus*, pp. of *solari*, to solace, to comfort.]

1. to cheer in grief or under calamity; to comfort; to relieve in affliction; to console.

2. to allay; to assuage or lessen; as, to *solace* grief.

3. to amuse or delight: sometimes used reflexively; as, to *solace* oneself with study.

sol′ăce, *v.i.* 1. to be amused; to take enjoyment or pleasure. [Rare.]

2. to take comfort; to be cheered or relieved in grief. [Rare.]

sol′ăce, *n.* 1. an easing of grief, loneliness, discomfort, etc.

2. something that eases or relieves; comfort; consolation; relief.

sol′ăce·ment, *n.* 1. a solacing.

2. that which solaces.

sō′lăn, *n.* the solan goose.

Sol·ȧ·nā′cē·ae, *n.pl.* a family of monopetalous exogenous plants, composed of herbs or, rarely, shrubs, native to most parts of the world, and especially to the tropics. The nightshade, potato, capsicum, tomato, eggplant, and tobacco are all found in this order.

sol·ȧ·nā′ceous, *a.* of or belonging to the *Solanaceæ.*

sō′lănd, *n.* the solan goose.

sō·land′ẽr, *n.* same as *sellanders.*

sō′lăn goose, [ON. *sūla.*] the gannet.

sō·lā′ni·ȧ, *n.* same as *solanine.*

sō·lan′i·dine, sō·lan′i·din, *n.* a base produced together with glucose by the action of dilute, boiling hydrochloric acid on solanine.

sol′ȧ·nine, *n.* [LL. *solanum*, nightshade.] a complex glycosidic alkaloid, $C_{45}H_{73}NO_{15}$, found in potato sprouts and various plants of the nightshade family.

sō·lä′nō, *n.* [Sp., from L. *solanus* (*ventus*), easterly wind, from *sol*, the sun.] a hot, oppressive wind in the Mediterranean, particularly on the eastern coast of Spain.

Sō·lā′num, *n.* a genus of gamopetalous plants, the typical genus of the *Solanaceæ.*

sō′lăr, *a.* [Fr. *solaire*; L. *solaris*, from *sol*, the sun.]

1. of or having to do with the sun.

2. produced by or coming from the sun; as, *solar* energy.

3. depending upon the sun's light or energy; as, *solar* heating, *solar* telegraphy.

4. fixed or measured by the earth's motion with relation to the sun; as, *solar* time.

5. in astrology, under the influence of the sun.

solar apex; see *apex of the sun's way* under *apex.*

solar battery; an assembly of one or more photovoltaic cells (*solar cells*) used to convert the radiant energy of sunlight into electric power.

solar constant; the constant expressing the amount of solar heat received by the earth, estimated at 1.95 calories a minute for each square centimeter of the earth's surface.

solar day; (a) the period of the rotation of the earth with relation to the sun; twenty-four hours, measured from noon to noon or from midnight to midnight; (b) in law, the period from sunrise to sunset.

solar eyepiece; a device by which the light and heat are reduced in solar observations by observing only a very minute portion of the solar surface.

solar flare; a sudden, short-lived increase of intensity in the light of the sun, usually near sunspots, often accompanied by a large increase in cosmic rays, X rays, etc. and by resultant magnetic storms.

solar lamp; an Argand lamp.

solar myth; a nature myth that is regarded as a primitive explanation of solar phenomena.

solar phosphori; substances that become luminous in the dark, after having been exposed to solar rays.

solar plexus; (a) a network of nerves in the abdominal cavity behind the stomach and in front of the uppermost part of the aorta, containing ganglia that send nerve impulses to the abdominal viscera; (b) [Colloq.] the upper middle part of the abdomen.

solar prominences; the visibly extended portions of the body of burning gas which surrounds the sun: also *solar protuberances.*

solar spots; sun spots.

solar system; the sun and all the heavenly bodies that revolve around it.

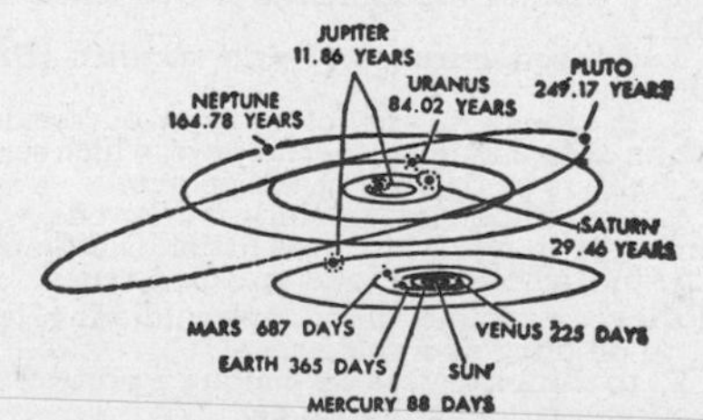

SOLAR SYSTEM

The diagram shows the approximate orbits and lengths of the solar years of the nine planets, with the satellites of each. The orbit of Jupiter, shown as the smallest innermost ring in the upper figure, is also reproduced as the outermost ring in the lower figure in order to show the orbits of Mars, Earth, Venus, and Mercury. The broken line in the orbit of Pluto indicates where it lies south of the plane of the ecliptic.

solar telegraph; a heliograph.

solar time; see *apparent time* under *time.*

solar year; a period during which any planet makes one complete revolution around the sun: 365 days, 5 hours, 48 minutes, and 46 seconds is the length of the earth's solar year.

sō′lăr, *n.* same as *sollar.*

sō′lăr·ism, *n.* the explanation of myths and folklore by reference to the sun or the personification of the sun.

sō·lăr′i·um, *n.*; *pl.* **sō·lăr′i·ȧ,** 1. a sundial.
2. a glassed-in room to which the sun has free access, as the sun rooms of hospitals; also, an apartment built on a roof or a space railed off on a roof.
3. [S–] a genus of depressed shells resembling a stairway in form.

sō″lăr·i·zā′tion, *n.* a solarizing or the state of being solarized.

sō′lăr·īze, *v.t.*; solarized, *pt., pp.*; solarizing, *ppr.* 1. to affect by exposing to the sun's rays.
2. to overexpose (a photographic film or plate).

sō′lăr·īze, *v.i.* in photography, to become injured by overexposure.

sō·lā′ti·um (-shi-), *n.*; *pl.* **sō·lā′ti·ȧ,** [L., consolation, solace.] anything that compensates for mental suffering or financial loss; specifically, in Scots law, a sum of money paid, over and above actual damages, to an injured party by the person who inflicted the injury, as a solace for wounded feelings.

sōld, *v.* past tense and past participle of *sell*.

sol′dăn, *n.* a sultan; any Moslem ruler or prince.

sol′dȧ·nel, *n.* [from It. *soldanella*.] a plant of the genus *Soldanella*, natural order *Primulaceæ*. The species are small herbs, native to alpine districts of Europe.

sol′dăn·rie, *n.* the functions or dignity of a sultan. [Archaic.]

sold′ẽr (sod′), *n.* [OFr. *soudure, souldure*, from L. *solidare*, to make firm.]
1. a metal or metallic composition used when melted for joining or patching metal parts or surfaces; a metallic cement.
2. figuratively, that which unites in any way.
hard solder; a solder that requires a red heat to melt it: it is used for joining brass, iron, and the more refractory metals.
soft solder; a solder that melts at a comparatively low temperature and is used for fusing lead and tin.

sold′ẽr, *v.t.*; soldered, *pt., pp.*; soldering, *ppr.* 1. to unite (the surfaces of metals) with solder.
2. figuratively, to unite or fuse in general; to hold together.

sold′ẽr·ẽr, *n.* one who or that which solders; a machine for soldering.

sold′ẽr·ing, *n.* the process of uniting the surfaces of metals by means of solder.

sold′ẽr·ing ī′ron (-ūrn), a pointed metal tool used for melting and applying solder: it must be heated, as in a flame or electrically.

sold′ẽr·ing pāste, a greaselike flux used in soldering.

sōl′diẽr (-jẽr), *n.* [ME. *soudiour*; OFr. *soldier*, from LL. *solidarius*, a soldier, from *solidare*, to pay; *solidus*, a piece of money, from L. *solidus*, firm, solid.]
1. a man engaged in military service; specifically, a man enlisted for service in an army.
2. an enlisted man, as distinguished from one holding a warrant or commission.
3. a man of much military experience and skill.
4. the red gurnard, *Trigla cuculus*. [Brit. Dial.]
5. in zoology, any of a type of asexual white ants, having powerful jaws, which serve as fighters in defense of the colony.
6. one who tries to shirk work; one who pretends to work but does little. [Old Slang.]
7. one who works for a specified cause.

sōl′diẽr, *v.i.*; soldiered, *pt., pp.*; soldiering, *ppr.* 1. to do duty as a soldier.
2. to shirk duty, as by making a pretense of working, feigning illness, etc.

sōl′diẽr bee′tle, a carabid beetle of America, *Chauliognathus pennsylvanicus*, which subsists on the larvae of other insects.

sōl′diẽr bug, in zoology, any hemipterous insect of *Podisus, Perillus*, or allied genera, which has a powerful beak with which it pierces the larvae of other insects and penetrates the bodies of insects to suck their blood.

sōl′diẽr·bụsh, *n.* soldierwood.

sōl′diẽr çrab, the hermit crab; also, the fiddler crab.

sōl′diẽr·ess, *n.* a woman soldier. [Rare.]

sōl′diẽr·fish, *n.* the blue darter or rainbow darter, *Etheostoma cœruleum*, found in rivers of the Mississippi valley.

sōl′diẽr flȳ, any one of many species of flies of the family *Stratiomyidæ*.

sōl′diẽr·ing, *n.* the state of being a soldier; the occupation of a soldier.

sōl′diẽr·līke, *a.* soldierly.

sōl′diẽr·ly, *a.* like or characteristic of a good soldier; brave; martial; heroic; honorable.

sōl′diẽr mọth, a large moth, *Euschema militaris*, of the East Indies.

sōl′diẽr of fọr′tūne, a military adventurer, willing to serve wherever he can get pay, pleasure, etc.

sōl′diẽr ọr′çhis, an orchid, *Orchis militaris*, of Europe, which bears flowers the sepals of which have a helmetlike formation.

sōl′diẽr·ship, *n.* 1. skill or ability in military matters.
2. military science.

Sōl′diẽr‧ş Med′ăl, a United States military decoration given for deeds of heroism outside of combat.

sōl′diẽr·wood, *n.* a West Indian shrub, *Calliandra purpurea*, of the bean family, with long, tasseled, purple stamens.

sōl′diẽr·y, *n.*; *pl.* **sōl′diẽr·ieş,** 1. soldiers collectively.
2. a group of soldiers.
3. military science; soldiership.

sol′dō, *n.*; *pl.* **sol′di,** [It., from L. *solidus*, firm.] an Italian coin and unit of money, equal to $^1/_{20}$ of a lira.

sōle, *n.* [Fr. *sole*, the sole of the foot, of a shoe, etc., from L. *solea*, a sandal, a sole, of same origin as *solum*, the ground, soil.]
1. the underside of the foot; the planta.
2. the foot itself. [Rare or Poetic.]
3. the under part of a boot, shoe, sock, etc.
4. the bottom frame of a wagon.
5. in agriculture, (a) the lower part of the plow, which runs in contact with the bottom of the furrow: it generally consists of the lower surfaces of the share and landside; (b) the bottom of the furrow.
6. the horny substance under a horse's foot which protects the more tender parts.
7. in fortification, the bottom of an embrasure.
8. the lower edge of the barrel of a turbine or water wheel.
9. in carpentry, the lower surface of a plane.
10. in machinery, (a) the top or floor of a bracket on which a plumber block rests; (b) the plate which constitutes the foundation of a marine steam engine, and which is bolted to the keelsons.
11. the floor or hearth of the metal chamber in a reverberatory, puddling, or boiling furnace.
12. the seat or bottom of a passage in a mine.
13. in shipbuilding, (a) the bottom plank of the cradle, resting on the bilgeways and sustaining the lower ends of the poppets, which are mortised into the sole and support the vessel; (b) an additional piece on the lower end of a rudder, to make it level with the false keel.
14. a strip of metal or wood fastened beneath the runner of a sled or sleigh to take the wear.
15. the bottom surface of a golf club.

sōle, *n.* [Fr. *sole*, from L. *solea*, the sole: so named from its flatness.] a marine flatfish belonging to the family *Soleidæ*, of an oblong form, with a rounded muzzle. *Solea vulgaris* is the common sole of Europe. The American sole is *Achirus lineatus*. The name is also given to various flounders, resembling the true soles.

sōle, *v.t.*; soled, *pt., pp.*; soling, *ppr.* 1. to furnish with a sole, especially a new one; as, to *sole* a shoe.
2. in golf, to put the sole of (a club) on the ground, as in getting ready to hit the ball.

sōle, *a.* [ME. *sole*, from OFr. *sol*, from L. *solus*, alone.]
1. without another or others; single; one and only.
2. of or having to do with only one (specified) person or group.
3. acting, working, etc. automatically or without help.
4. alone; solitary. [Archaic.]
5. in law, unmarried: only in *feme sole* and *woman sole*.

sol′ē·çişm, *n.* [Gr. *soloikismos*, from *soloikos*, speaking incorrectly, from corrupt Attic dialect used by colonists in *Soloi*, in Cilicia.]
1. a violation of the conventional usage, grammar, etc. of a language; substandard use of words (e.g., "I seen him" for "I saw him"): see also *barbarism*.
2. a violation of good manners; breach of etiquette.
3. a mistake or impropriety.
Syn.—barbarism.

sol′ē·cist, *n.* a person who habitually commits solecisms.

sol·ē·cis′tiç, sol·ē·cis′ti·çăl, *a.* 1. incorrect; incongruous; involving or of the nature of a solecism.
2. characteristic of a solecist.

sol·ē·cis′ti·çăl·ly, *adv.* in a solecistic manner.

sol′ē·cīze, *v.i.* to commit a solecism.

sōle leath′ẽr (leth′), thick, strong leather, used for the soles of shoes.

sōle′ly, *adv.* 1. alone; without another or others; as, we are *solely* to blame.
2. only, exclusively, merely, or altogether; as, he reads *solely* for enjoyment.

sol′emn (-em), *a.* [L. *sollemnis, sollennis*, that occurs every year, hence, from the stated occurrence of religious festivals, religious, festal, solemn, from *sollus*, all, entire, and *annus*, a year.]
1. set aside according to ritual or tradition: said especially of religious ceremonies, festivals, etc.
2. sacred.
3. according to strict form; formal, as a ceremony.
4. serious; grave; deeply earnest.
5. arousing feelings of awe; very impressive; as, a *solemn* occasion.
6. somber because dark in color.
7. festive. [Obs.]
Syn.—grave, serious, formal, ceremonial, sober, devout.

sol′em·ness, *n.* the state or quality of being solemn; reverential manner; seriousness; solemnity; gravity of manner. [Rare.]

sol·em′ni·fy, *v.t.*; solemnified, *pt., pp.*; solemnifying, *ppr.* to make solemn.

sō·lem′ni·ty, *n.*; *pl.* **sō·lem′ni·tieş,** [Fr. *solennité*, from L. *solemnitas*.]
1. a religious ceremony; a ritual performance attended with religious reverence; as, the *solemnity* of a funeral or a sacrament.
2. solemn feeling, character, or appearance; serious or awesome quality; impressiveness; gravity.
3. festivity. [Obs.]
4. a proceeding adapted to impress awe or reverence.
5. in law, a solemn or formal observance; the formality requisite to render a thing done valid.
6. the state or quality of being solemn; seriousness; gravity; ceremoniousness.

sō·lem′ni·zāte, *v.t.* to solemnize. [Obs.]

sol″em·ni·zā′tion, *n.* a solemnizing or being solemnized; as, the *solemnization* of a marriage.

sol′em·nīze, *v.t.*; solemnized, *pt., pp.*; solemnizing, *ppr.* 1. to dignify or honor by ceremonies; to celebrate; as, to *solemnize* the birth of Christ.
2. to perform with ritual ceremonies and respect, or according to legal forms; as, to *solemnize* a marriage.
3. to make grave, serious, and reverential; as, to *solemnize* the mind for the duties of the sanctuary.

sol′em·nīze, *n.* solemnization. [Rare.]

sol′em·nī·zẽr, *n.* one who solemnizes.

sol′emn·ly (-em-), *adv.* in a solemn manner; gravely; seriously; formally; reverentially.

sol′emn·ness, *n.* same as *solemness*.

sō·lemp′ne, *a.* solemn. [Obs.]

Sō′len, *n.* [Gr. *sōlēn*, tube, a shellfish.]
1. a genus of mollusks, the type of the family *Solenidæ*; the razor shells.
2. [s–] any member of the genus *Solen*; a razor shell or razor clam.

sol·ē·nā′cē·ăn, *n.* any species of the family *Solenidæ*.

sol·ē·nā′ceous, *a.* relating to the solens or the family *Solenidæ*.

sōle′ness, *n.* singleness; the state or quality of being sole or unconnected with others.

sōle·nette′, *n.* [Fr., dim. of *sole*, a kind of fish.] a small sole, *Solea minuta*, of Europe.

Sō·len′i·dae, *n.pl.* a family of lamellibranchiate mollusks, including the genus *Solen* and several others.

sō·lē′nō-, sō′len-, [from Gr. *sōlēn*, a pipe.] combining forms used in zoology, etc., to signify *channel* or *pipe*.

Sō·lē·nō·çon′chae, *n.pl.* [*soleno-*, and Gr. *konchē*, a shell.] a class of mollusks; the tooth shells.

Sō·lē′nō·don, *n.* [*solen-*, and Gr. *odous, odontos*, tooth.]
1. a genus of insectivorous mammals, closely resembling opossums, of which the agouta of Haiti is a species. *Solenodon cubanus* is a Cuban species.
2. [s-] a species of this genus.

sō·lē′nō·dont, *a.* pertaining to the genus *Solenodon*.

sō·lē′nō·dont, *n.* a species of the genus *Solenodon*.

Sō·lē·nō·gas′trēs, *n.pl.* [*soleno-*, and Gr. *gastēr*, the belly.] an order of worms; the *Isopleura*.

sō·lē′nō·glyph, *a.* pertaining to the *Solenoglypha*.

sō·lē′nō·glyph, *n.* a member of the *Solenoglypha*.

Sō·lē·nog′ly·phȧ, Sō·lē·nō·glyph′i·ȧ, *n.pl.* [*soleno-*, and Gr. *glyphein*, to engrave.] a group of snakes characterized by tubular fangs, as the rattlesnakes and vipers.

sō″lē·nō·glyph′iç, *a.* solenoglyph.

sō′len·oid, *n.* [*solen-* and *-oid*.] a coil of wire carrying an electric current and having the properties of a magnet: solenoids regulate the timing of aircraft machine guns fired through the propeller arc.
solenoid core; a core consisting ordinarily of soft iron introduced into a solenoid, in which position the magnetic flux of the magnetizing current magnetizes it.

sō·lē·noi′dăl, *a.* acting like or pertaining to a solenoid.

Sō·lē·nos′tō·mus, *n.* [*soleno-*, and Gr. *stoma*, mouth.] a genus of fishes, of the suborder *Lophobranchii*, characterized by a fistulous snout, as the pipefish.

sōle′plāte, *n.* in machinery, (a) a bedplate; (b) in a water wheel, the back plate of a bucket.

sō′lēr, sō′lēre, *n.* solar. [Obs.]

sō·lēr′tious·ness, *n.* craftiness. [Obs.]

sōle′ship, *n.* single state; soleness. [Obs.]

sō·lē′us, *n.* [L., from *solea*, a sole.] a muscle of the leg shaped like a sole. It serves to extend the foot.

sōl″-fä′, *n.* [It. *solfa*; *sol* and *fa*, two of the notes of the gamut.]
1. the syllables *do* (formerly *ut*), *re, mi, fa, sol, la, ti* (formerly *si*), *do* (or *ut*), used to represent the tones of a scale, regardless of its key.
2. the use of these syllables, as in vocal exercises.

sōl″-fä′, *v.t.* and *v.i.*; sol-faed (-fäd′), *pt., pp.*; sol-faing, *ppr.* to sing (a scale, phrase, or song) to the sol-fa syllables.

sōl″fä′ist, *n.* a person who uses sol-fa.

sōl·fä·tä′rä, *n.* [It. *solfo*, sulfur.] a vent or fissure of a dormant volcano, from which vapors, especially sulfurous gases, are emitted.

sōl·feġ′ġi·ō, *n.*; *pl.* **sōl·feġ′ġi·ōs, sōl·feġ′ġi,** [It., from *solfa*.]
1. voice practice in which scales are sung to the sol-fa syllables; solmization.
2. the use of these syllables in singing, especially in reading a song, etc. at sight.

sōl·fe·rī′nō, *n.* [from *Solferino*, in Italy.]
1. fuchsin, a red dye.
2. a bright purplish red.

sō′lī, *n.* plural of *solo*.

sō·lic′it, *v.t.*; solicited, *pt., pp.*; soliciting, *ppr.* [Fr. *solliciter*, from L. *sollicitare*, from *sollicitus*, agitated, anxious, solicitous, from *sollus*, whole, and *ciere*, to move, stir, agitate.]
1. to ask or seek earnestly or pleadingly; to beg; to entreat; as, we *solicit* your support, he *solicited* them for help.
2. to tempt or entice (another) to do wrong.
3. to accost (another) for some immoral purpose, as a prostitute does.
4. to disturb; to disquiet. [Rare.]
Syn.—ask, request, beseech, beg, implore. entreat, importune, crave.

sō·lic′it, *v.i.* to make request or solicitation.

sō·lic′it·ănt, *a.* begging; solicitous.

sō·lic′it·ănt, *n.* one who solicits.

sō·liç′it·āte, *a.* solicitous. [Obs.]

sō·lic·i·tā′tion, *n.* 1. earnest request; a seeking to obtain something from another.
2. temptation or enticement to wrongdoing.

sō·lic′it·ŏr, *n.* [Fr. *solliciteur*, from L. *sollicitare*, to solicit.]
1. a person who solicits; especially, one who seeks trade, asks for contributions, etc.
2. in England, any lawyer other than a barrister: solicitors are not members of the bar and may not plead cases in superior courts.
3. a lawyer serving as official law officer for a city, department, or other division of government.

sō·lic′it·ŏr ġen′ẽr·ăl, *n.*; *pl.* **sō·lic′it·ŏrṣ ġen′ẽr·ăl, sō·lic′i·tŏr ġen′ẽr·ălṣ,** 1. in the United States, an officer associated with the attorney general; also, in some States having no attorney general, the chief law officer.
2. in Great Britain, an officer of the crown, who is associated with the attorney general in managing the legal business of the crown.

sō·lic′it·ŏr·ship, *n.* the office, rank, or condition of a solicitor.

sō·lic′it·ous, *a.* [L. *sollicitus*.]
1. showing care, attention, or concern; as, he was *solicitous* for his employees' welfare.
2. showing anxious desire; eager; as, he was *solicitous* to make friends.
3. full of anxiety or apprehension; troubled.

sō·lic′it·ous·ly, *adv.* in a solicitous manner.

sō·lic′it·ous·ness, *n.* the quality or state of being solicitous.

sō·lic′it·ress, *n.* a woman solicitor.

sō·lic′i·tūde, *n.* [L. *sollicitudo*.]
1. the state of being solicitous; care, concern, etc.; sometimes, excessive care or concern.
2. [*pl.*] causes of care or concern.
Syn.—anxiety, care, concern, fear, apprehension, foreboding.

sol′id, *a.* [Fr. *solide*, from L. *solidus*, solid, firm, compact.]
1. offering some resistance to pressure; not easily changed in shape; relatively firm or compact: distinguished from *liquid, gaseous*.
2. filled with matter beneath the surface; not hollow.
3. in or of length, breadth, and thickness; cubic; as, a *solid* yard of concrete.
4. substantial; firm; strong; sound; as, a *solid* structure, *solid* reasoning, a *solid* citizen.
5. serious; not superficial or trivial; as, a *solid* problem.
6. complete; thoroughgoing; as, *solid* satisfaction.
7. having no breaks or divisions; as, a *solid* line of fortifications, a *solid* word.
8. characterized by no pauses or interruptions; as, he talked for two *solid* hours.
9. (a) of one or the same color, material, or consistency throughout; (b) containing no more alloy than is specified by law to insure hardness: said of gold, etc.
10. characterized by or showing complete unity; unanimous; as, a *solid* vote for world government.
11. thick or dense in appearance or texture, as fog, etc.
12. real; genuine.
13. firm or dependable in views, sympathy, partisanship, etc. [Colloq.]
14. having a firmly favorable or good relationship. [Colloq.]
15. very good; excellent; as, a *solid* dance band. [Slang.]
16. in printing, having no lead separators between the lines of type: opposed to *open*.
17. in trade, without extraneous matter, as fluids; as, a *solid* pint of oysters.
Syn.—hard, firm, stable, stout, strong.

sol′id, *n.* 1. a substance that offers some resistance to pressure and is not easily changed in shape: distinguished from *gas, liquid*.
2. a body or magnitude which has three dimensions, length, breadth, and thickness: distinguished from a *surface*, which has two dimensions, and from a *line*, which has one.

Sol·i·dā′gō, *n.* [L. *solidare*, to strengthen: in reference to its supposed healing powers.]
1. the large American genus of composite perennial plants with plumelike clusters of tiny, usually yellow flowers: it includes the goldenrod.
2. [s-] a member of this genus.

sol′id aṅ′gle, an angle formed at a point where three or more planes meet, as at any corner of a square box.

sol·i·dar′i·ty, *n.*; *pl.* **sol·i·dar′i·tieṣ,** [Fr. *solidarité*.] combination or agreement of all elements or individuals, as of a group; complete unity, as of opinion, purpose, interest, feeling, etc.

sol′i·dãr·y, *a.* [Fr. *solidaire*.] having or showing solidarity; completely united.

sol′i·dāte, *v.t.* [L. *solidare*, to unite, solidify.] to make solid or firm. [Rare.]

sol′id fū′el, any of various rocket fuels neither liquid nor gaseous, consisting of a homogeneous base that acts as both fuel and oxidizer or of a composite mixture of fuel and oxidizer: also *solid propellant*.

sol′id ġē·om′e·try, the geometry of solid figures.

sō·lid′i·fī·ȧ·ble, *a.* capable of being solidified.

sō·lid″i·fi·çā′tion, *n.* a solidifying or being solidified.

sō·lid′i·fȳ, *v.t.* and *v.i.*; solidified, *pt., pp.*; solidifying, *ppr.* [L. *solidus*, solid, and *facere*, to make.]
1. to make or become solid, complete, or compact; as, to *solidify* a gas or liquid.
2. to crystallize.

sol′id·iṣm, *n.* [L. *solidus*, solid.] the obsolete doctrine that changes in the solids of the body are the causes of disease.

sol′id·ist, *n.* one who advocates or believes in the theory of solidism.

sol·id·ist′iç, *a.* pertaining to solidists or to solidism.

sō·lid′i·ty, *n.* [Fr. *solidité*; L. *soliditas*.] the quality or condition of being solid; firmness, hardness, soundness, etc.

sol′id·ly, *adv.* with solidity; firmly; compactly; so as to be solid.

sol′id·ness, *n.* solidity.

Solid South, those Southern States traditionally regarded as solidly supporting the Democratic Party.

sol′id squãre (skwãr), a square body of troops; a body in which the ranks and file are equal.

sol′id-stāte′, *a.* 1. designating or of the branch of physics dealing with solids, such as metals or crystals, and their properties with regard to heat, light, electricity, atomic arrangement, electronic movement, etc.
2. designating, of, or equipped with semiconductors, such as transistors.

sol′i·dum, *n.* 1. in architecture, the dado of a pedestal.
2. in law, the entire amount or sum.
to be bound in solidum; to be bound for the entire debt, though but one of the obligors.

Sol·id·uṅ′gū·lȧ, *n.pl.* [L. *solidus*, solid, and *ungula*, hoof.] the group of hoofed quadrupeds, comprising the horses, asses, and zebras, characterized by the feet having only a single perfect toe, each enclosed in a single broad hoof, without supplementary hoofs.

sol·id·uṅ′gū·lăr, *a.* having single hoofs.

Sol·id·uṅ·gū·lā′tȧ, *n.pl.* same as *Solidungula*.

sol·id·uṅ′gū·lāte, *n.* one of a group of mammals having a single hoof on each foot.

sol·id·uṅ′gū·lāte, *a.* solid-hoofed; solipedous.

sol·id·uṅ′gū·lous, *a.* [L. *solidus*, solid, and *ungula*, hoof.] same as *solidungulate*.

sol′i·dus, *n.*; *pl.* **sol′i·dī,** [LL.] 1. a gold coin of the Late Roman Empire, valued at about three dollars: later called *bezant*.
2. a medieval money of account worth twelve denarii.
3. the slant line (/), originally the old long s (ſ), used to separate shillings from pence, as 7/6, or as a dividing line in fractions, dates, etc.

sol·i·fid′i·ăn, *n.* [L. *solus*, alone, and *fides*, faith.] in theology, one who maintains that faith alone, without works, insures salvation.

sol·i·fid′i·ăn·iṣm, *n.* the tenets of the solifidians.

sol′i·fọrm, *a.* [L. *sol*, the sun.] having the character or form of the sun; like the sun.

Sō·lif′ū·ġae, *n.pl.* an order of the *Arachnida*, characterized by the segmented abdomen, the articulation of the cephalothorax with the abdomen, and a spiderlike appearance.

sō·lil′ō·quist, *n.* a person who soliloquizes.

sō·lil′ō·quīze, *v.i.*; soliloquized, *pt., pp.*; soliloquizing, *ppr.* to utter a soliloquy; to talk to oneself.

sō·lil′ō·quīze, *v.t.* to utter in or as a soliloquy.

sō·lil′ō·quy, *n.*; *pl.* **sō·lil′ō·quieṣ,** [Fr. *soliloque*; L. *solus*, alone, and *loqui*, to speak.]
1. an act or instance of talking to oneself.
2. lines in a drama, in which a character reveals his thoughts to the audience but not to the other characters by speaking as if to himself.

sol′i·ped, *n.* [L. *solus*, single, and *pes, pedis*, a foot.] a solidungulate.

sol′i·ped·ăl, *a.* solidungulate.

sō·lip′e·dous, *a.* solidungulate.

sol′ip·sism, *n.* [from L. *solus*, alone, and *ipse*, self; and *-ism.*] in philosophy, (a) the theory that the self can be aware of nothing but its own experiences and states; (b) the theory that nothing exists or is real but the self.

sol′ip·sist, *n.* a believer in solipsism.

sol·i·sē′qui·ous, *a.* [L. *sol, solis*, the sun, and *sequi*, to follow.] following the sun's course as the sunflower. [Obs.]

sol·i·tāire′, *n.* [Fr. *solitaire*, from L. *solitarius.*]
1. originally one who lives in solitude; a recluse; a hermit.
2. a precious stone, especially a diamond, set by itself, as in a ring.
3. any of several games, especially card games which one person can play alone.
4. any of various birds, as (a) *Pezophaps solitarius*, a bird of large size, now extinct, formerly found in certain islands in the Indian Ocean; (b) an American fly-catching thrush, *Myiadestes armillatus*; (c) the rock thrush, *Monticola solitaria.*

sol·i·tăr·i·ăn, *n.* a hermit. [Obs.]

sol′i·tăr·i·ly, *adv.* in solitude; so as to be solitary.

sol′i·tăr·i·ness, *n.* the state or quality of being solitary.

sol′i·tăr·y, *a.* [Fr. *solitaire*; L. *solitarius*, from *solus*, alone.]
1. living or being alone.
2. without others; single; only; as, a *solitary* case of measles.
3. characterized by loneliness or lack of companions.
4. lonely; remote; unfrequented; as, a *solitary* place.
5. done in solitude.
6. in biology, separate; one only in a place; simple; not clustered; as, a *solitary* stipule.
Syn.—sole, only, alone, lonely, retired, separate, single, individual, desolate, desert.

sol′i·tăr·y, *n.*; *pl.* **sol′i·tăr·ies,** 1. one who lives alone or in solitude; a hermit; a recluse.
2. solitary confinement. [Colloq.]

sol′i·tăr·y cŏn·fīne′ment, confinement of a prisoner in a place separate from all other prisoners so that he has contact with no human being other than his jailers: usually a form of extra punishment for misconduct.

sol′i·tūde, *n.* [Fr., from L. *solitudo*, from *solus*, alone.]
1. the state of being solitary, or alone; seclusion; isolation; remoteness.
2. a lonely or secluded place.

sol′lăr, *n.* [L. *solarium*, a gallery or balcony exposed to the sun, from *sol*, the sun.]
1. a garret or upper room. [Obs.]
2. in mining, a platform in a shaft; a brattice in a passage.
3. in a church, an elevated chamber from which the burning of the altar lamps may be watched. [Rare.]

sol·lĕr·et′, *n.* [Fr. *soleret*, dim. of OFr. *soller*, a slipper.] one of the overlapping plates that formed the iron shoe of an armed knight; hence, the iron shoe itself.

SOLLERETS (*a*)

sol·mi·zā′tion, sol·mi·sā′tion, *n.* [Fr.] the act or practice of singing certain syllables, especially the sol-fa syllables, to the notes of the musical scale, as opposed to the use of a vowel sound, such as *ah.* The basis of our present system is to be found in the gamut of Guido d'Arezzo, in the eleventh century, who named his six notes *ut, re, mi, fa, sol, la*, after the initial syllables of a Latin hymn. The name *ut* was gradually rejected in favor of *do*, and *si* was the name given to the seventh degree, making the seven recurring syllables, *do, re, mi, fa, sol, la, si* (now *ti*).

sō′lō, *n.*; *pl.* **sō′lōs,** *or rarely* **sō′lī,** [It., from L. *solus*, alone.]
1. a musical piece or passage to be played by a single instrument or sung by a single voice with or without accompaniment.
2. in aviation, a flight accomplished by a pilot without passengers or instructor; as, he did his first *solo* today.
3. any of various games of cards in which there are no partners.
4. any performance by one person alone.
5. in solo whist, a bid to win five tricks, playing alone against the other players.
solo whist; a game in which the full pack of fifty-two cards is used, the players bidding on any one of seven distinct modes of play, the highest bid superseding all lower ones.

sō′lō, *v.i.*; soloed, *pt., pp.*; soloing, *ppr.* in aviation, to make a solo flight, especially one's first.

sō′lō, *adv.* alone.

sō′lō·ist, *n.* one who performs a solo.

Sol′ō·mŏn, *n.* [LL. *Solomon, Salomon*; Gr. *Solomōn, Salōmōn*; Heb. *shĕlōmōh*, lit., peaceful, from *shalom*, peace.]
1. the son of David and king of Israel in the tenth century B.C.: he built the first Temple and was noted for his wisdom.
2. a very wise man; a sage.

Sol·ō·mon′iç, *a.* 1. wise.
2. relating to Solomon, king of Israel.

Sol′ō·mŏn's-sēal, *n.* [ML. *sigillum Salomonis*: so called prob. from markings on the rootstock.] any of various perennial plants with bell-shaped flowers and black or blue fruit, belonging to the genus *Polygonatum.*
false Solomon's-seal; any species of the genus *Smilacina* allied to *Polygonatum.*

SOLOMON'S-SEAL (*Polygonatum vulgare*)

Sol′ō·mŏn's sēal, 1. a ring having a jewel in which it was supposed King Solomon could view distant places.
2. a mystic symbol in the form of a six-pointed star: same as *Star of David.*

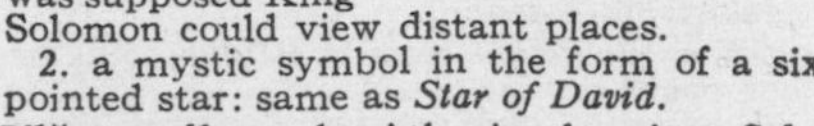

Sō′lŏn, *n.* [from the Athenian lawgiver *Solon* (638–559 B.C.)] [*sometimes* s-] a legislator or sage.

sō long, [said to be folk etym. from *salaam.*] good-by. [Colloq.]

Sol·pū′gi·dȧ, *n.pl.* same as *Solifugæ.*

Sol·pū·gi·dē′ȧ, *n.pl.* same as *Solpugida.*

sol′stice, *n.* [Fr., from L. *solstitium*; *sol*, the sun, and *stitium*, from *statum*, pp. of *sistere*, to make to stand still, from *stare*, to stand.]
1. in astronomy, (a) the point in the ecliptic at the greatest distance from the equator, at which the sun appears to stop or cease to recede from the equator; the summer solstice of the Northern Hemisphere is on June 21, the winter on December 22; the summer solstice in the Southern Hemisphere is on December 22, the winter on June 21; (b) the time at which the sun is at its greatest distance from the equator, and when its diurnal motion in declination ceases.
2. a furthest point, turning point, or point of culmination.
3. a standing still of the sun. [Obs.]

sol·sti′tiăl (-stish′ăl), *a.* 1. pertaining to or characteristic of a solstice, especially the summer solstice.
2. occurring at the time of a solstice.
solstitial point; one of the two points in the ecliptic which mark the place of the sun when it is farthest from the equator.

sol·ū·bil′i·ty, *n.*; *pl.* **sol·ū·bil′i·ties,** 1. the property or quality of being soluble or solvable; as, the *solubility* of an element; the *solubility* of an equation.
2. the amount of a substance that can be dissolved in a given solvent under specified conditions.

sol′ū·ble, *a.* [L. *solubilis*, from *solvere*, to melt.]
1. capable of entering into solution or of being dissolved; as, a *soluble* substance.
2. capable of being solved; susceptible of being resolved into ultimate constituents, unraveled, or disentangled; as, a *soluble* example; a *soluble* tangle.
3. not obstructed; relaxed. [Rare.]
soluble glass; water glass (sodium silicate, etc.).
soluble starch; same as *amylodextrin.*

sol′ū·ble·ness, *n.* the property or quality of being soluble; solubility.

sol′ū·bly, *adv.* so as to be soluble.

sō′lum, *n.* [L., the ground.] in law, ground; a piece of ground.

sō′lus, *a.* [L.] alone, single: a stage direction; as, enter the prince *solus*: see also *sola.*

sō′lūte, *a.* [L. *solutus*, from *solvere*, to loose.]
1. free; liberal; loose. [Obs.]
2. dissolved; in solution.
3. soluble; dissolvable; as, a *solute* substance. [Rare.]
4. in botany, free or separate; not adhering: opposed to *adnate*; as, a *solute* tendril.

sō′lūte, *n.* the substance dissolved in a solution: distinguished from *solvent.*

sō·lūte′, *v.t.* 1. to resolve; to dissolve. [Obs.]
2. to absolve; as, to *solute* crime. [Obs.]

sō·lū′tion, *n.* [OFr., from L. *solutio* (*-onis*), a loosening.]
1. the act, method, or process of solving a problem.
2. an explanation, clarification, answer, etc.; as, the *solution* of a mystery.
3. the act or process of dispersing one or more substances in another, usually a liquid, so as to form a homogeneous mixture; a dissolving.
4. the state or fact of being dissolved.
5. a homogeneous molecular mixture, usually a liquid, so produced; as, a *solution* of sugar and water.
6. a separation or breaking up, as into component parts; dissolution; a break; a breach.
7. in medicine, (a) the termination of a disease; (b) the crisis of a disease; (c) a drug in watery solution; medicine in liquid form.
8. discharge; deliverance; release. [Obs.]
chemical solution; a perfect chemical union of a solid with a liquid, in accordance with the laws of definite proportions, as a solution made by the union of zinc with dilute sulfuric acid.
mechanical solution; the union of a solid with a liquid in such a manner that its aggregate form is changed without any alteration of the chemical properties of either the solid or its solvent, as a union of sugar and water or of salt and water.
saturated solution; see under *saturated.*
standardized solution; a solution of known strength or composition, used as a standard of comparison.

sō·lū′tion plāne, a plane or planes in a crystal which offers least resistance to chemical erosion.

sol′ū·tive, *a.* laxative; loosening; tending to dissolve. [Obs.]

solv·ȧ·bil′i·ty, *n.* 1. the condition or quality of being solvable.
2. ability to meet financial obligations; solvency; as, the *solvability* of a state. [Obs.]

solv′ȧ·ble, *a.* 1. capable of being solved; as, a *solvable* problem.
2. that can be dissolved.
3. solvent. [Obs.]
4. payable; as, a *solvable* note. [Rare.]

solv′ȧ·ble·ness, *n.* the state or quality of being solvable.

Sol′vāy proc′ess, a process developed by Ernest Solvay, Belgian chemist (1838–1922), for making soda (sodium carbonate) by treating common salt (sodium chloride) with ammonia and carbon dioxide.

solve, *v.t.*; solved, *pt., pp.*; solving, *ppr.* [L. *solvere*, to loosen, release, free; for *se-luere, se*, apart, and *luere*, to let go, to set free.]
1. to clear up; to find or provide a satisfactory answer or solution for; to explain or resolve; as, to *solve* a quarrel, he *solved* the mystery.
2. to find a satisfactory answer or solution for (a problem); as, to *solve* an equation, to *solve* a riddle.
Syn.—decipher, interpret, elucidate, understand.

sol′ven·cy, *n.* the state or quality of being solvent.

sol′vend, *n.* a substance to be dissolved. [Rare.]

sol′vent, *a.* 1. having the power of dissolving; used for dissolving; as, a *solvent* body.
2. able to pay all one's debts; meeting all financial responsibilities; as, the merchant is *solvent.*

sol′vent, *n.* [L. *solvens* (*-entis*), ppr. of *solvere*, to loosen.]
1. a substance that dissolves or makes a solution of another substance.
2. anything that solves, clears up, or makes plain; a solution; as, the *solvent* of an intricacy.

solv′ẽr, *n.* one who or that which solves or explains.

solv′i·ble, *a.* solvable. [Obs.]

sō′mȧ, *n.* [Sans. *soma*, juice.] a plant, *Asclepias acida*, of the milkweed family, growing in northern India, from which in Vedic times was manufactured an intoxicating liquor said

fāte, fär, fȧst, fạll, finăl, cãre, at; mēte, prey, hẽr, met; pīne, marīne, bīrd, pin; nōte, mŏve, fọr, atŏm, not; mọọn, book;

to be acceptable not merely to men but to the gods; also, the liquor made from the milky juice of the plant taken from its leafless stems.

sō′mȧ, *n.*; *pl.* **sō′mȧ·tȧ,** [Gr., a dead body, the body as opposed to the spirit.]

1. the body or trunk of an animal, from the top of the head to the tip of the tail, excluding the limbs.

2. the entire body of an animal or plant, with the exception of the germ cells.

sō′mā·çūle, *n.* in biology, a small particle of protoplasm.

Sō·mäj′, *n.* same as *Brahmo Somaj.*

Sō′mä·lĭ, *n.*; *pl.* **Sō′mä·lĭ, Sō′mä·lĭş,** 1. a member of a group of Hamitic tribes living in and near Somaliland.

2. their Cushitic language.

Sō·mas′chi·ăn, *n.* in the Roman Catholic Church, one of a religious order founded in the sixteenth century at Somascha, Italy, to take charge of and educate orphans and foundlings.

sō·mat′iç, *a.* [Gr. *sōmatikos*, from *sōma*, body.]

1. corporeal; pertaining to the body as distinct from the soul, mind, or psyche.

2. pertaining to the soma.

3. in anatomy and zoology, of the framework or outer walls of the body, as distinguished from the viscera; parietal.

somatic cell; any of the cells of an organism that become differentiated into the tissues, organs, etc. of the body: opposed to *germ cell.*

somatic death; cessation of the functions of the vital organs.

sō·mat′iç·ăl, *a.* somatic.

sō·mat′içs, *n.* same as *somatology.*

sō′mȧ·tişm, *n.* in philosophy, materialism.

sō′mȧ·tist, *n.* a believer in somatism; a materialist.

sō′mȧ·tō-, [from Greek *sōma*, body.] a combining form meaning *body*, as in *somato*logy; also, before a vowel, *somat-*.

sō′mȧ·tō·cyst, *n.* an inflatable bag in the body of certain siphonophores, which serves to buoy them.

sō″mȧ·tō·cys′tiç, *a.* pertaining to a somatocyst.

sō″mȧ·tō·ġen′iç, *a.* originating in the soma by reason of its environment.

sō″mȧ·tō·loġ′iç, *a.* of somatology.

sō″mȧ·tō·loġ′i·căl, *a.* somatologic.

sō·mȧ·tol′ō·ġy, *n.* 1. the science concerned with the properties of organic bodies.

2. a treatise or teaching regarding the human body.

3. that part of anthropology which considers the various races of man from the purely physical standpoint, making comparative study of their physical nature and characteristics.

sō′mȧ·tōme, *n.* [Gr. *sōma*, body, and *tomē*, a cutting.] one of the sections into which certain animal bodies are structurally divided.

sō′mȧ·tō·plaşm, *n.* the protoplasm of a body cell as distinguished from that of a germ cell.

sō″mȧ·tō·pleū′răl, *a.* derived from or constituting the somatopleure; somatopleuric.

sō′mȧ·tō·pleūre (-plūr), *n.* [*somato-*, and Gr. *pleura*, the side.] in embryology, the outer of the two layers of the mesoblast of vertebrates, from which the body wall is developed.

sō″mȧ·tō·pleū′riç, *a.* of or pertaining to the somatopleure.

som′bẽr, som′bre, *a.* [Fr. *sombre*; ult. from L. *sub*, under, and *umbra*, a shade.]

1. dark; dull; dusky; gloomy; as, a *somber* hue; *somber* clouds.

2. dismal; melancholy; mentally depressed or depressing; sad.

som′bẽr, *v.t.*; sombered, *pt., pp.*; sombering, *ppr.* to make somber, dark, or gloomy.

som′bẽr, *n.* gloom; obscurity; somberness. [Rare.]

som′bẽr·ly, *adv.* in a somber manner; darkly; gloomily.

som′bẽr·ness, *n.* the state or quality of being somber; darkness; gloominess.

som·bre̤′rīte, *n.* an earthy mineral consisting mainly of calcic and aluminic phosphates, found on the island of Sombrero in the West Indies.

som·bre̤′rō, *n.*; *pl.* **som·bre̤′rōş,** [Sp., from *sombra*, a shade.] a wide-brimmed hat, usually of felt, worn in Spain, Latin America, etc.

som′brous, *a.* somber. [Archaic.]

som′brous·ly, *adv.* gloomily. [Archaic.]

som′brous·ness, *n.* the state of being sombrous. [Archaic.]

-sŏme, [AS. *-sum*, from base of *same.*] a suffix meaning *like, apt* or *tending to (be)*, as in lone*some*, tire*some.*

-sŏme, [AS. *sum.*] a suffix meaning *in* (a specified) *number*, as in three*some.*

-sōme, [from Gr. *sōma*, body.] a combining form meaning *body*, as in chromo*some.*

sŏme, *a.* [ME. *som, some*; AS. *sum, som*, some, one, a certain, also about, as *sume tēn geār*, about ten years; Goth. *sums*, some one; Ice. *sumr*, some, a certain; Dan. *somme* (pl.), some; Dan. and Sw. *som*, who, which; perhaps of same origin as *same.*]

1. being a certain one or ones not specified or known; as, *some* people never change their minds.

2. being of a certain unspecified (but often considerable) number, quantity, degree, etc.; as, *some* guests are here already, won't you have *some* butter?

3. about; as, *some* twenty of us were injured.

4. remarkable, striking, etc.; as, that was *some* fight. [Colloq.]

sŏme, *pron.* 1. a certain one or ones not specified or known; some one or ones; as, *some* will agree, others will not.

2. a certain indefinite or unspecified number, quantity, etc., as distinguished from the rest.

sŏme, *adv.* 1. somewhat; a little; as, I am *some* better. [Colloq.]

2. about or near; as, a village of *some* eighty houses.

3. to a great extent or at a great rate; as, you'll have to travel *some* to get there on time. [Colloq.]

sŏme′bod″y, *pron.* a person unknown or uncertain; some person; someone.

> *Somebody* hath touched me.
> —Luke viii. 46.

sŏme′bod″y, *n.*; *pl.* **sŏme′bod″ieş,** a person of importance.

sŏme′dāy, *adv.* at some future day or time.

sŏme′dēal, *adv.* in some degree. [Archaic.]

sŏme′gāte, *adv.* somewhere; somehow. [Scot.]

sŏme′how, *adv.* one way or another; in some way not yet known or indicated; as, the thing happened *somehow.*

somehow or other; somehow.

sŏme′one (-wun), *pron.* a person unknown or unidentified; somebody.

> . . . suddenly there came a tapping, as of *someone* gently rapping—rapping at my chamber door.
> —Poe.

sŏm′ẽr·sa̤ult, *n.* [altered from OFr. *soubresault*; It. *soprasalto*, lit., an overleap; from L. *supra*, over, and *salere*, to leap.] an acrobatic stunt performed by turning the body one full revolution forward or backward, heels over head: often used figuratively, as of a complete reversal of opinion, sympathies, etc.: also *summersault, somerset, summerset, sommerset.*

sŏm′ẽr·sa̤ult, *v.i.* to perform a somersault: also *summersault, somerset, summerset, sommerset.*

sŏm′ẽr·set, *n.* and *v.i.* same as *somersault.*

sŏme′thing, *n.* 1. a thing not definitely known, understood, or identified; some undetermined thing; as, there's *something* sinister in his laugh.

2. some thing or things, definite but unspecified; as, he has *something* to show for his efforts.

3. a person or thing meriting consideration; a person or thing of importance.

there's something doing; something is afoot; the unusual is happening; times are lively. [Slang.]

sŏme′thing, *adv.* in some degree or measure; somewhat; rather; a little; as, the patient is *something* peevish today.

sŏme′tīme, *a.* having been formerly (as specified); being or existing formerly; former; late; whilom.

sŏme′tīme, *adv.* 1. at a time in the past; once; formerly. [Archaic.]

2. at one time or other; at some time not known or specified.

3. at some unspecified time in the future.

4. sometimes. [Rare.]

sŏme′tīmeş′, *adv.* 1. now and then; at times; occasionally.

2. formerly; at some time in the past. [Obs.]

sŏme′wāy, *adv.* in some manner; somehow: also *some way.*

sŏme′wāyş, *adv.* same as *someway.*

sŏme′whăt, *n.* 1. some portion, part, thing, quantity, or degree; as, *somewhat* of a nuisance.

2. some person or thing of importance.

sŏme′whăt, *adv.* in some degree; to some extent; a little; rather; as, *somewhat* changed.

sŏme′when, *adv.* at some indefinite time.

sŏme′where (-hwâr), *adv.* 1. in, to, or at some place, unknown or not specified; in one place or another.

2. at some unspecified point in amount, degree, time, etc. (with *about* or *in*); as, *somewhere* about eight o'clock.

sŏme′where, *n.* an unspecified or undetermined place.

sŏme′whereş, *adv.* somewhere: in general use, considered solecistic. [Chiefly Dial.]

sŏme′whīle, *adv.* at some time; for a period. [Rare.]

sŏme′whith″ẽr, *adv.* to some place; somewhere; also, in some direction. [Archaic.]

sŏme′wīşe, *adv.* in some way or to some degree (usually preceded by *in*). [Archaic.]

sō′mi·tăl, *a.* of or characterized by a somite or somites.

sō′mīte, *n.* [from Gr. *sōma*, body; and *-ite.*]

1. any of the longitudinal series of segments into which the body of certain organisms, as the arthropods, is divided.

2. a similar segment in the human embryo.

sō·mit′iç, *a.* same as *somital.*

sŏm′mẽr·set, *n.* and *v.i.* same as *somersault.*

som·nam′bū·lănce, *n.* somnambulism.

som·nam′bū·lănt, *a.* characterized by somnambulism; walking while sleeping.

som·nam′bū·lăr, *a.* of or relating to somnambulism.

som·nam′bū·lāte, *v.i.*; somnambulated, *pt., pp.*; somnambulating, *ppr.* [L. *somnus*, sleep, and *ambulatus, ambulare*, to walk.] to walk in sleep; to wander in a trancelike state while asleep.

som·nam′bū·lāte, *v.t.* to walk across or through while sleeping.

som·nam·bū·lā′tion, *n.* [L. *somnus*, sleep, and *ambulatio (-onis)*, a walking, from *ambulare*, to walk.] the act of walking in sleep; somnambulism.

som·nam′bū·lā·tŏr, *n.* same as *somnambulist.*

som·nam′būle, *n.* same as *somnambulist.*

som·nam′bū·liç, *a.* walking in sleep; pertaining to or practicing somnambulism; somnambulistic.

som·nam′bū·lişm, *n.* 1. the habit or act of somnambulating.

2. the characteristic actions of a person who somnambulates.

som·nam′bū·list, *n.* one who is subject to somnambulism; a person who walks in his sleep; a sleepwalker.

som·nam·bū·lis′tiç, *a.* pertaining to or characteristic of somnambulism or somnambulists.

som·nam′bū·līze, *v.t.* to cause to become somnambulic.

som·nam′bū·līze, *v.i.* to become somnambulistic.

som·nam′bū·lous, *a.* somnambular.

sŏm′ne, *v.t.* to call; to summon. [Obs.]

sŏm′nẽr, *n.* a summoner. [Obs.]

sŏm′ni-, [from L. *somnus*, sleep.] a combining form meaning *sleep.*

som′ni·ăl, *a.* [L. *somnium*, a dream.] pertaining to or involving dreams; relating to dreams. [Rare.]

som′ni·ȧ·tive, *a.* pertaining to dreaming; relating to or producing dreams. [Rare.]

som′ni·ȧ·tō·ry, *a.* somniative. [Rare.]

som·niç′ū·lous, *a.* [L. *somniculosus*, drowsy, from *somnus*, sleep.] inclined to sleep; drowsy. [Obs.]

som·ni·fā′cient (-shent), *a.* [*somni-*, and L. *facere*, to make.] inducing sleep; somnific.

som·ni·fā′cient, *n.* a medicine which induces sleep.

som·nif′ẽr·ous, *a.* [*somni-*, and L. *ferre*, to bear, bring.] causing or inducing sleep; soporific; as, a *somniferous* potion.

som·nif′iç, *a.* [L. *somnus*, sleep, and *facere*, to make.] same as *somniferous.*

som·nif′ū·gous, *a.* [*somni-*, and L. *fugare*, to put to flight.] driving away sleep; preventing sleep. [Obs.]

som·nil′ō·quence, *n.* [*somni-*, and L. *loquens*, from *loqui*, to speak.] the act or custom of talking in sleep; somniloquy.

som·nil′ō·quişm, *n.* somniloquence; sleep-talking.

som·nil′ō·quist, *n.* one who talks in his sleep.

som·nil′ō·quous, *a.* apt to talk in sleep.

som·nil′ō·quy, *n.* [from L. *somnus*, sleep, and *loqui*, to speak.]
1. the habit or act of talking while asleep.
2. the words spoken by a person while asleep.

som·nip′ȧ·thist, *n.* a person in a state of somnipathy.

som·nip′ȧ·thy, *n.* [*somni-*, and Gr. *pathos*, suffering.] sleep induced by hypnosis or mesmerism.

som′nō·lence, *n.* sleepiness; drowsiness; inclination to sleep.

som′nō·len·cy, *n.* somnolence.

som′nō·lent, *a.* 1. sleepy; drowsy.
2. inducing drowsiness.

som′nō·lent·ly, *adv.* drowsily.

som·nō·les′cent, *a.* becoming somnolent; drowsy.

som′nō·lişm, *n.* the state of being in hypnotic sleep.

som·nop′ȧ·thy, *n.* same as *somnipathy.*

Som′nus, *n.* in Roman mythology, the god of sleep, described as a brother of Death, and as a son of Night.

sŏn, *n.* [AS. *sunu*; Ice. *sonr, sunr*; Sw. *son*; Dan. *son*; Goth. *sunus*; O.H.G. *sunu*, son. The word is widely spread, and the Sanskrit form of it is not very different from the English, viz., *sūnu*, son. The root meaning is seen in Sans. *su*, to beget.]
1. a male child in relation to his parents or parent.
2. any male descendant.
3. (a) a son-in-law; (b) an adopted male child.
4. any male person considered as the product of a given school, cause, native land, etc. as, *sons* of Oxford.
5. the produce of anything.
Earth's tall *sons*, the cedar, oak, and pine.
—Sir R. Blackmore.
6. a person whose character partakes so strongly of some quality or characteristic as to suggest the relationship of son and parent; as, *sons* of light, *sons* of pride.
7. [S-] the second person of the Trinity, Jesus Christ, the Saviour, called *the Son of God*: with *the*.
8. an affectionate or familiar form of address to a boy or man, as used by an older person.
favorite son; (a) a famous man honored and praised in his native city, district, etc. because of his achievements; (b) a candidate favored by the political leaders of his own State, city, etc. for nomination to a high office, especially the presidency.
son of Adam; any man or boy.
son of a gun; (a) a person or thing regarded angrily, contemptuously, indulgently, familiarly; (b) an interjection expressing surprise, annoyance, etc. [Slang.]
Son of God; Jesus Christ.
Son of Heaven; the emperor of Japan.
Sons of Liberty; any of various secret, subversive societies, formed prior to the American Revolution.
Son of Man; Jesus Christ.
sons of the prophets; see *school of the prophets* under *prophet*.

sō′nănce, *n.* [L. *sonans*, sounding.]
1. a sound; also, a tune. [Obs.]
2. the state or quality of being sonant.

sō′nănt, *a.* [L. *sonans*, sounding, ppr. of *sonare*, to sound.]
1. of sound.
2. having sound; sounding.
3. in phonetics, voiced: opposed to *surd, voiceless*.

sō′nănt, *n.* in linguistics, (a) a voiced speech sound; (b) a speech sound used in any given language as a syllabic: opposed to *consonant*; (c) in Indo-European, a sonorant.

sō′när, *n.* [*so*und *na*vigation *r*anging.] an apparatus that transmits high-frequency sound waves in water and registers the vibrations reflected back from an object, used in detecting submarines, locating schools of fish, finding depths of oceans, etc.

sō·nä′tȧ, *n.* [It., from L. *sonare*, to sound.] in music, an extended instrumental composition for piano or for some other solo instrument or instruments, in contradistinction to vocal compositions, called *cantatas*. Sonatas are of a certain form, consisting, at first, of three movements, the allegro, adagio, and rondo, to which afterward a fourth was added, the minuetto or scherzo, which differ from one another in tempo, rhythm, and melody but are held together by a unity of subject and style.

sō·nä′tȧ fọrm, a complex form of musical composition, typically used for the first movement of a sonata, symphony, concerto, etc., and consisting basically of an exposition (or statement), development, and recapitulation (or restatement), usually followed by a coda.

sō·nä·tī′nȧ, *n.* [It.] a brief or simplified sonata.

Son′chus, *n.* [L., from Gr. *sonchus*, the sow thistle.] a genus of plants, family *Compositæ*. The most common species is *Sonchus oleraceus*, the common sow thistle, having downy subumbellate flower stalks, small yellow flowers, and a conical involucre when in seed.

son′cy, *a.* same as *sonsy.*

sond, sonde, *n.* a message or messenger; also, a sending. [Obs.]

son′de·li, *n.* [E. Ind.] the muskshrew, *Sorex indicus, Crocidura myosura*, or *Crocidura cœrulea*.

ṣon′dẽr·çlass, *n.* [from G. *sonder*, separate, special.] any of a class of small, narrow racing yachts of extremely light displacement, limited in dimensions, sail area, etc.

sọng, *n.* [ME. *songe*; AS. *song*; D. *zang*; Sw. *siong*; Dan. *sang*.]
1. the act or art of singing; as, he broke into *song*.
2. a piece of music sung or as if for singing.
3. (a) poetry; verse; (b) a relatively short metrical composition for, or suitable for, singing, usually having rhymed stanzas, as a ballad or simple lyric.
4. a musical sound like singing; as, the *song* of the lark.
5. a laughingstock. [Archaic.]
an old song; a trifle; an insignificant sum.
for a song; for very little money; cheaply.
song and dance; (a) singing and dancing; (b) a performance having singing and dancing, as in vaudeville; (c) [Colloq.] talk, especially an explanation, that is pointless or evasive.
song of ascents or *song of degrees*; any one of the fifteen psalms, cxx to cxxxiv inclusive, sung by Hebrew pilgrims while journeying to Jerusalem.
Song of Solomon or *Song of Songs*; a book of the Old Testament consisting of a love poem, dramatic and lyrical in character, traditionally supposed to have been composed by Solomon: also called *Canticles*.

sọng′bīrd, *n.* 1. a bird that makes vocal sounds resembling music.
2. a woman singer.

sọng′çrȧft, *n.* the art of composing songs; skill in versification. [Poet.]

sọng′ful, *a.* inclined or able to sing; full of song.

sọng′ish, *a.* consisting of songs. [Rare.]

sọng′less, *a.* not having the power of song; also, without song.

sọng spar′rōw, a sparrow, *Melospiza fasciata*, common in North America, noted for its singing.

sọng′stẽr, *n.* 1. one who sings.
2. a bird that sings.
3. one who writes songs or poems.

sọng′stress, *n.* 1. a woman singer; also, a woman who writes songs or poems.
2. a female singing bird.

sọng thrush, the mavis; a European thrush, *Turdus musicus*, noted for its singing.

son′iç, *a.* [from L. *sonus*, sound; and *-ic*.]
1. of or having to do with sound.
2. designating or of a speed equal to the speed of sound (about 1,088 feet per second or 738 miles per hour).
sonic barrier; the large increase of aerodynamic resistance encountered by some aircraft when flying near the speed of sound.
sonic boom; an explosive sound generated by the accumulation of pressure in a wave preceding an aircraft or other object traveling at or above the speed of sound: where the wave touches the ground, the variation in pressure is experienced as a loud report.

son·i·faç′tion, son″i·fi·çā′tion, *n.* [L. *sonus*, sound, and *facere*, to make.] the act of producing sound, as the stridulation of insects.

sō·nif′ẽr·ous, *a.* producing sound; conveying sound.

sŏn′-in-lạw″, *n.*; *pl.* **sŏnṣ′-in-lạw″,** the husband of one's daughter.

sŏn′less, *a.* having no son.

Son·nē·rā′ti·ȧ (-shi-), *n.* [named after P. *Sonnerat* (1745–1814), a French naturalist.] a genus of polypetalous plants, native to Australia, Asia, and Africa. *Sonneratia apetala* is the kambala.

son′net, *n.* [Fr., from It. *sonnetto*, from L. *sonus*, a sound.]
1. a poem normally of fourteen lines in any of several fixed verse and rhyme schemes, typically in rhymed iambic pentameter: sonnets characteristically express a single theme or idea: see *Petrarchan sonnet, Shakespearean sonnet.*
2. a short poem, usually a love poem. [Obs.]

son′net, *v.t.* and *v.i.* to compose sonnets (about).

son·net·eer′, son·net·teer′, *n.* [Fr. *sonnetier*.]
1. a composer of sonnets.
2. any minor or inferior poet: usually in contempt.

son·net·eer′, son·net·teer′, *v.t.* and *v.i.* to sonnet.

son′net·ist, *n.* a sonneteer. [Rare.]

son′net·īze, *v.t.* and *v.i.* to sonnet.

Sŏn′nīte, *n.* same as *Sunnite*.

sŏn′ny, *n.*; *pl.* **sŏn′nieṣ,** little son: used in addressing any young boy in a familiar way.

Sō·nō′mȧ ōak, [named after *Sonoma* County, California.] an oak, *Quercus kelloggii*, found in the mountains of Oregon and California.

sō·nom′e·tẽr, *n.* [L. *sonus*, sound, and *-meter*.] an instrument for testing the hearing of a person; an audiometer.

Sō·nō′rȧ gum, [from *Sonora*, a state in northwestern Mexico.] an acidulous substance obtained from the creosote bush.

sō·nō′rănt, *n.* in phonetics, a voiced consonant that is sufficiently sonorous to be used, like a vowel, as a syllabic sound: *l, m, n*, and *r* are often so used in the final unstressed syllables of English words.

son·ō·res′cence, *n.* [L. *sonus*, sound, and *-escence*.] the property of certain substances, as hard rubber, of emitting sounds, when acted upon by radiation.

son·ō·res′cent, *a.* having the property of sonorescence.

son·ō·rif′iç, *a.* [L. *sonus*, sound, and *facere*, to make.] producing sound; as, the *sonorific* quality of a body. [Rare.]

sō·nor′i·ty, *n.*; *pl.* **sō·nor′i·tieṣ,** [from Fr. or LL.; Fr. *sonorité*; LL. *sonoritas*.] quality, state, or instance of being sonorous; resonance.

sō·nō′rous, *a.* [L. *sonorus*, from *sonus*, sound.]
1. producing or capable of producing sound, especially sound of full, deep, or rich quality; resonant.
2. full, deep, or rich: said of sound.
3. high-sounding; having a powerful, impressive sound; as, *sonorous* music.
4. in phonetics, having a degree of resonant tonality: said of vowels, nasals, etc.
sonorous figures; those figures which are formed by the vibrations produced by sound, as the figures formed when some fine sand is strewed on a disk of glass or metal, and a violin bow drawn down on its edge, producing a musical note.

sō·nō′rous·ly, *adv.* in a sonorous manner.

sō·nō′rous·ness, *n.* the quality of being sonorous.

sŏn′ship, *n.* the state of being a son, or of having the relation of a son; filiation.

son′sy, son′sie, *a.* [from dial. *sonse*, prosperity, plenty, from Scot. Gael. *sonas*, good fortune; and *-y*.]
1. lucky.
2. buxom; handsome; pleasing.
3. comfortable.
4. good-natured.
[Scot., Irish, and N. Eng. Dial. in all senses.]

son′tăg, *n.* [named after Madame *Sontag*, a famous singer.] a jacket or cape of knitted worsted worn by women.

son′tieṣ, *n.pl.* sanctity: used in the oath *God's sonties* [Obs.]

sọọ·çhong′, *n.* same as *souchong*.

Sọọ′drȧ, Sọọ′dẽr, *n.* same as *Sudra*.

Sọọ′fee, *n.* same as *Sufi*.

sọọ′jee, *n.* same as *sujee*.

sọọ′lȧ çlō′vẽr, a leguminous herb of Europe of the genus *Hedysarum*.

sọọm, *v.* and *n.* swim. [Scot.]

sọọn, *adv.*; *comp.* sooner; *superl.* soonest, [ME. *sone, sune*; AS. *sōna*, at once.]
1. in a short time (after a time specified or understood); shortly; before long; as, do come to see us *soon*.
2. promptly; quickly; as, I'll come as *soon* as possible.
3. ahead of time; early; as, but you came so *soon*!
4. readily; willingly; as, I would just as *soon* stay home as go.
5. at once; immediately. [Obs.]
as soon as, so soon as; immediately at or after another event.

had sooner; would rather; would prefer to.
no sooner than; as soon as.
sooner or later; inevitably; eventually.
soon, *a.* speedy; quick; prompt; early. [Dial.]
Soo'nee, *n.* same as *Sunni*.
soon'ẽr, *n.* 1. any person who occupies homestead land, as in the western United States, before the authorized time for doing so, thus gaining an unfair advantage in choice of location. [Slang.]
2. anyone who gains an unfair advantage over others by doing something before the proper time. [Slang.]
3. [S–] a native or inhabitant of Oklahoma. [Slang.]
soon'ly, *adv.* quickly; speedily; promptly. [Rare.]
soop, *v.t.* to sweep. [Scot.]
soord, *n.* sward. [Obs.]
soor'ma, *n.* a powder of antimony; kohl; surma.
soo'soo, *n.* same as *susu*.
soot (*or less often* soot), *n.* [AS. *sōt*; akin to M.D. *soet*.] a black substance, consisting chiefly of carbon particles formed by incomplete combustion of burning matter.
soot, *v.t.*; sooted, *pt., pp.*; sooting, *ppr.* to cover, soil, or treat with soot.
soot, *a.* sweet. [Obs.]
soot'ẽr·kin, *n.* a kind of false birth reputed to be produced by Dutch women from sitting over their stoves; hence, an abortive project. [Obs.]
sooth, *n.* [AS. *sōth*, true, truth.]
1. truth; reality. [Archaic.]
2. prognostication; soothsaying. [Rare.]
3. sweetness; kindness; cajolery. [Obs.]
sooth, *a.* 1. soothing; smooth. [Poetic.]
2. true; faithful; trustworthy; reliable. [Archaic.]
soothe, *v.t.*; soothed, *pt., pp.*; soothing, *ppr.* [AS. *sōthian*, to confirm, from *sōth*, truth.]
1. to flatter; to please with blandishments or soft words.
2. to soften; to assuage; to mollify; to calm; to comfort; as, to *soothe* one in pain or passion; to *soothe* pain.
3. to gratify; to please.
4. to maintain. [Obs.]
Syn.—appease, assuage, allay, soften, pacify, compose, calm.
soothe, *v.i.* to have a soothing effect; to give calm, relief, etc.
sooth'ẽr, *n.* a flatterer; one who or that which soothes.
sooth'fȧst, *a.* [AS. *sothfæst*.]
1. truthful, honest, or loyal. [Archaic.]
2. true or real. [Archaic.]
sooth'fȧst, *adv.* soothly. [Obs.]
sooth'fȧst″ness, *n.* the quality of being soothfast. [Obs.]
sooth'ing, *n.* the act of comforting or assuaging.
sooth'ing, *a.* [ppr. of *soothe*.] tending or intended to soothe; calming; giving ease or relief.
sooth'ing·ly, *adv.* in a soothing manner; so as to be soothing.
sooth'ly, *adv.* in truth; really. [Archaic.]
sooth'ness, *n.* reality; fact; truth. [Obs.]
sooth'sāy, *n.* 1. a prognostication; a prediction; a forecast.
2. an omen; a sign. [Rare.]
sooth'sāy, *v.i.*; soothsaid (-sed), *pt., pp.*; soothsaying, *ppr.* to foretell; to predict.
sooth'sāy″ẽr, *n.* [ME. *sothseyere*, one who speaks the truth.]
1. a prognosticator; one who predicts or pretends to foretell the future.
2. a mantis.
sooth'sāy″ing, *n.* 1. a predicting, or foretelling.
2. a prediction, or prophecy.
soot'i·ness, *n.* the quality or state of being sooty or foul with soot.
soot'ish, *a.* partaking of soot; like soot.
soot'y, *a.*; *comp.* sootier; *superl.* sootiest, 1. of or like soot.
2. covered or soiled with soot.
3. dark-brown or black; dark; dusky.
sooty albatross; a South Pacific albatross, *Diomedea fuliginosa*, having grayish wings and tail and black feet and beak.
sooty shearwater; a shearwater, *Puffinus fuliginosus*, of the northern Atlantic waters of America, having uniformly sooty plumage.
sooty tern; a tern, *Sterna fuliginosa*, sooty-black above and snowy-white below, common on the seacoasts of warm countries and found as far north as the Carolinas.
sop, *n.* [ME. *soppe*; AS. *sopp*.]
1. a piece of food, as bread, soaked in milk, gravy, etc.
2. (a) something given as a reward, concession, or appeasement; (b) a bribe.
3. a milksop.
a sop in the pan; a piece of bread dipped into a pan and soaked with gravy from roasting or frying meat; hence, a tidbit.
Sops of Wine; a yellow-red variety of apple.
to throw a sop to Cerberus; to satisfy the demands of an opponent or a troublesome person by giving him a bribe of some kind: an allusion to the fabled guardian of the infernal regions and the manner of pacifying him.
sop, *v.t.*; sopped (sopt), *pt., pp.*; sopping, *ppr.*
1. to soak, steep, or saturate in or with liquid.
2. to take up, as water, by absorption (usually with *up*).
sop, *v.i.* 1. to soak or ooze (with *in*, etc.): said of a liquid.
2. to be or become thoroughly wet.
soph, *n.* 1. a sophomore. [Colloq.]
2. a sophister. [Brit.]
Sō'phẽr·iç, *a.* relating to the Sopherim.
Sō'phẽr·im, *n.pl.* Hebrew scribes and expounders of Jewish laws.
soph'iṣm, *n.* [Fr. *sophisme*, from Gr. *sophisma*, a clever or cunning contrivance, a trick, a quibble such as the sophists used, a sophism, from *sophizesthai*, to play the sophist, from *sophos*, clever, skillful, wise.] a fallacious argument; an argument that is not supported by sound reasoning or in which the inference is not justly deduced from the premises; a fallacy, whether or not intended to deceive; also, an ingenious statement and arrangement of propositions devised for the purpose of misleading.
soph'ist, *n.* [Fr. *sophiste*; It. *sofista*; L. *sophista*; Gr. *sophistēs*, a wise man.]
1. [*often* S–] in ancient Greece, any of a group of teachers of rhetoric, politics, philosophy, etc., some of whom were notorious for their clever, specious arguments.
2. a learned person.
3. any person practicing clever, specious reasoning.
soph'ist·ẽr, *n.* 1. a sophist.
2. a student in his second year (*junior sophister*) or third year (*senior sophister*) at certain British universities.
sō·phis'tiç, *a.* same as *sophistical*.
sō·phis'tiç, *n.* sophistry; the methods of the Greek sophists.
sō·phis'ti·çăl, *a.* [from L. *sophisticus*; Gr. *sophistikos*, from *sophistēs*, sophist.]
1. of or characteristic of sophists or sophistry.
2. clever or plausible but unsound and tending to mislead; as, a *sophistical* argument.
3. using sophistry.
sō·phis'ti·çăl·ly, *adv.* in a sophistical manner.
sō·phis'ti·çăl·ness, *n.* the state or quality of being sophistical.
sō·phis'ti·çāte, *v.t.*; sophisticated, *pt., pp.*; sophisticating, *ppr.* [L. *sophisticus*, sophistical.]
1. to make sophistical; to involve or obscure in sophistry.
2. to mislead by fallacious arguments; to delude.
3. to adulterate; to render spurious by admixture; as, to *sophisticate* liquors.
4. to change the meaning of, as a document, by interpolation or elimination; to falsify.
5. to deprive of naturalness; to render artificial.
6. to make worldly, as a person, or to deprive of simplicity, as a novel or play.
sō·phis'ti·çāte, *v.i.* to practice sophistry; to be sophistical.
sō·phis'ti·çāte, *n.* one who is sophisticated.
sō·phis'ti·çā·ted, *a.* 1. not simple, artless, naive, etc.; urbane, worldly-wise, etc. or knowledgeable, perceptive, subtle, etc.
2. designed for or appealing to sophisticated people.
3. highly complex, refined, or developed; characterized by advanced form, technique, etc.; as, *sophisticated* equipment.
sō·phis·ti·çā'tion, *n.* 1. the act or process of sophisticating.
2. the act of quibbling or arguing sophistically; sophistry.
3. the state, quality, or character of being sophisticated.
sō·phis'ti·çā·tŏr, *n.* one who sophisticates, in any sense.
soph'is·tress, *n.* a woman sophist. [Rare.]
soph'ist·ry, *n.*; *pl.* **soph'ist·ries**, 1. fallacious reasoning; reasoning sound in appearance only.
2. the methods and teachings of the Greek sophists.
Soph·ō·çlē'ăn, *a.* pertaining to or in the style of Sophocles, the Athenian dramatic poet.
soph'ō·mōre, *n.* [Gr. *sophos*, wise, and *mōros*, foolish.]
1. a student in the second year of college or high school.
2. a sophomoric person; a know-it-all whose thinking is really immature or foolish.
3. a person in his second year of any enterprise; as, Senator Brown is a *sophomore* in Congress.
soph'ō·mōre, *a.* pertaining to or characteristic of a sophomore or sophomores; as, *sophomore* oratory.
soph·ō·mor'iç, *a.* 1. of or pertaining to, like, or characteristic of a sophomore or sophomores, aften regarded as self-assured, opinionated, etc., though immature and inexperienced.
2. inflated in style or manner; affected; bombastic.
soph·ō·mor'i·çăl, *a.* same as *sophomoric*.
soph·ō·mor'i·çăl·ly, *adv.* in a sophomoric manner.
Sō·phō'rȧ, *n.* [altered from *sophāra*, the Arabic name of a papilionaceous tree.] a genus of the *Leguminosæ*, having many species. *Sophora japonica*, the pagoda tree, is an ornamental flowering tree introduced into the United States from Japan and China.
sō·phros'y·nē, *n.* [Gr. *sōs*, safe, and *phrēn*, mind.] the quality of being wise, moderate, or discreet; mental equipoise; common sense.
soph'tȧ, *n.* same as *softa*.
-so·phy, [from Gr. *sophia*, skill, wisdom.] a combining form meaning *knowledge* or *thought*, as in philo*sophy*.
sō'pīte, *v.t.*; sopited, *pt., pp.*; sopiting, *ppr.* [L. *sopire*, to lay at rest.]
1. to quiet; to put to sleep or rest; to lull. [Rare.]
2. in Scots law, to set at rest; to quash.
sō·pi'tion (-pish'un), *n.* the act of putting to sleep; also, sleep. [Obs.]
sō'pọr, *n.* [L., sleep.] unnatural or prolonged sleep from which a person can with difficulty be aroused; stupor.
sop'ō·rāte, *v.t.* [L. *soporare*.] to stupefy. [Obs.]
sop·ō·rif'ẽr·ous, *a.* [L. *soporifer*; *sopor*, sleep, and *ferere*, to bring.] soporific; somniferous.
sop·ō·rif'ẽr·ous·ly, *adv.* in a soporiferous manner; so as to produce sleep.
sop·ō·rif'ẽr·ous·ness, *n.* the quality of causing sleep.
sop·ō·rif'iç, *a.* [from L. *sopor*, sleep; and *-fic*.]
1. causing or tending to cause sleep.
2. of or characterized by sleep or sleepiness.
sop·ō·rif'iç, *n.* a medicine, drug, plant, or other thing that has the quality of inducing sleep.
Syn.—opiate, anodyne, narcotic.
sop'ō·rōse, *a.* same as *soporous*.
sop'ō·rous, *a.* [L. *soporus*, from *sopor*, sleep.] causing sleep; affected with coma.
sop'pẽr, *n.* one who sops.
sop'ping, *a.* [ppr. of *sop*.] thoroughly wet; drenched; soaking.
sop'py, *a.*; *comp.* soppier; *superl.* soppiest.
1. sopping.
2. rainy.
3. too sentimental. [Brit. Slang.]
sō'prȧ, *a.* [It.] in music, above; over; before: a direction to the performer.
sō·prä'nist, *n.* a treble singer.
sō·prä'nō, *n.*; *pl.* **sō·prä'nōṣ**, **sō·prä'nï**, [It., from *sopra* (L. *supra*), above.]
1. the highest singing voice, of women and boys, usually ranging two octaves or more up from middle C.
2. a singer with such a range.
3. a part for such a voice.
sō·prä'nō, *a.* of, for, or having the range of, a soprano.
sops'ȧ·vīne, *n.* same as *Sops of Wine* under *sop*.
sō'rȧ, *n.* a small, short-billed wading bird of eastern North America, *Porzana carolina*: also called *ortolan* and *Carolina crake*.
king sora; the Florida gallinule.
sor'āġe, *n.* the period previous to a hawk's molting after first being taken from the nest.
sor'ănce, *n.* soreness; a sore feeling. [Obs.]
sō'rȧ rāil, same as *sora*.
sorb, *n.* [Fr. *sorbe*; It. *sorba*, *sorbo*; L. *sorbum*, *sorbus*, the service tree.]
1. any of a number of European trees of the apple family; especially, the service tree or rowan tree.
2. the fruit of any of these trees.

Sorb, *n.* [G. *Sorbe.*] one of an old Slavic people, ancestors of the Wends.

sor′bāte, *n.* a compound of sorbic acid with a base.

sor·bē·fā′cient (-shent), *n.* [L. *sorbere*, to absorb, and *facere*, to make.] a medicine which produces absorption.

sor·bē·fā′cient, *a.* producing absorption.

sorb′ent, *n.* an absorbent. [Rare.]

sor′bet, *n.* a sherbet.

Sorb′i·ăn, *n.* 1. the West Slavic language of the Sorbs; Wendish.
2. a Sorb.

sor′biç, *a.* pertaining to the sorb; as, *sorbic* acid.
sorbic acid; an acid, $C_6H_8O_2$, derived from the green berries of the mountain ash or rowan tree.

sor′bin, sor′bine, *n.* a crystalline, nonfermentable sugar, $C_6H_{12}O_6$, isomeric with grape and milk sugar, existing in the ripe juice of the mountain-ash berries.

sor′bi·tol, *n.* [*sorb*, and *-ite*, and *-ol.*] a white, sweet, odorless, crystalline alcohol, $C_6H_8(OH)_6$, found in certain berries and fruits, used as a moistening agent in lotions, creams, etc., as a sugar substitute, etc.

Sor′bŏn·ist, *n.* a doctor of the Sorbonne, a (formerly, theological) college, in the University of Paris, founded by Robert de Sorbon, A.D. 1250.

sor′bōse, *n.* [*sorb*itol, and *-ose.*] a white crystalline carbohydrate, $C_6H_{12}O_6$, obtained by fermenting sorbitol: it is used in the manufacture of vitamin C.

Sor′bus, *n.* a Linnaean genus of plants, comprising the mountain ash, rowan tree, and service tree.

sor′cēr·ēr, *n.* [Fr. *sorcier*, a sorcerer, from LL. *sortiarius*, one who throws or declares a lot, from L. *sors, sortis*, a lot.] one who practices sorcery; an enchanter; a magician; a wizard.

sor′cēr·ess, *n.* a woman sorcerer; a witch; an enchantress.

sor′cēr·ous, *a.* of, having the nature of, characterized by, or practicing sorcery.

sor′cēr·y, *n.*; *pl.* **sor′cēr·ieṣ**, the supposed use of an evil supernatural power over people and their affairs; witchcraft; black magic.

sor′dēṣ, *n.* [L.] foul matter; excretions; dregs; especially, in medicine, the dark-brown matter that gathers on the tongue and teeth in low fevers, consisting of epithelial tissue and microorganisms.

sor′did, *a.* [Fr. *sordide*; L. *sordidus*, from *sordes*, filth.]
1. filthy; foul; dirty.
2. vile; base; mean.
3. squalid; depressingly wretched.
4. mercenary; avaracious; grasping or meanly selfish.
5. in botany, of a dirty color.

sor′did·ly, *adv.* in a sordid manner.

sor′did·ness, *n.* the state or quality of being sordid.

sor′dīne, *n.* same as *sordino*.

sor·dī′nō, *n.*; *pl.* **sor·dī′nī**, [It.] in music, (a) a mute; a damper; (b) a small-sized violin.

sore, *a.*; *comp.* sorer; *superl.* sorest, [AS. *sar*, sore, painful, also a sore, sorrow, pain; akin to G. *sehr*, very, lit. sore.]
1. (a) giving physical pain; painful; tender; as, a *sore* tooth; (b) feeling physical pain, as from wounds, bruises, etc.
2. easily irritated or angered; touchy; temperamental; oversensitive.
3. filled with sadness, grief, or sorrow; distressed; as, our hearts are *sore* for them.
4. causing sadness, grief, misery, or distress; as, a *sore* hardship.
5. provocative of irritation or disagreeable feelings.
6. angry; offended; feeling hurt or resentful. [Colloq.]
Syn.—painful, irritated, excoriated, raw, scarified, ulcerous, grievous, afflictive, heavy, burdensome.

sore, *n.* 1. a place in an animal body where the skin and flesh are ruptured or bruised, so as to be tender or painful; a spot on the surface of the body where there is pain; a boil; an ulcer; a wound.
2. any source of pain, irritation, grief, distress, etc.

sore, *adv.* sorely. [Archaic.]

sore, *v.t.*; sored, *pt.*, *pp.*; soring, *ppr.* to inflict soring on (a horse).

sore, *n.* [Fr. *saure, sor*, sorrel, reddish.] a buck of the fourth year. [Obs.]

sō·rē′di·ăl, *a.* like or pertaining to a soredium.

sō·rē′di·āte, *a.* sorediferous.

sor·ē·dif′ēr·ous, *a.* bearing soredia.

sō·rē′di·um, *n.*; *pl.* **sō·rē′di·ȧ**, [Gr. *sōros*, a heap, and LL. *-edium*, for Gr. *-idion*, a diminutive suffix.] one of the little mealy patches scattered over the surface of the thallus in lichens.

sō′ree, *n.* same as *sora*.

sore′fal″çon (-fa″kn), *n.* a falcon of the first year.

sore′head (-hed), *n.* one who is discontented and easily irritated, as by defeat. [Colloq.]

sore′head″ed (-hed″), *a.* discontented; disgruntled; angry. [Colloq.]

sore′ly, *adv.* [ME. *sorelie*; AS. *sarlice.*]
1. grievously; painfully; severely; as, his patience was *sorely* tried.
2. urgently; greatly; extremely; as, help was *sorely* needed.

sō·rē′mȧ, *n.* [LL., from Gr. *sōros*, a heap.] a mass of carpels in a single flower.

sōre′ness, *n.* the state or quality of being sore.

sore skin, a plant disease that dries the lower part of the stalk of a tobacco plant and stops the continuous flow of sap.

Sō′rex, *n.* [LL., from Gr. *hyrax*, a shrewmouse.]
1. a genus of insectivorous mammals, the type of the family *Soricidæ*, including the shrewmice.
2. [s-] any mammal of this genus.

Sor′ghum (-gum), *n.* [It. *sorgo*, from L. *syricus*, Syrian.]
1. a genus of grasses, the species of which are known by the general name millet. They are tall grasses with succulent stems, and are found in the warmer parts of Europe, Asia, and America: now commonly classed as a subgenus of the genus *Andropogon*.
2. [s-] a plant of this genus; especially, *Sorghum vulgare*, extensively grown in the United States for its juice, which is used in making molasses.
3. [s-] a sirup made from sorghum juice.

sor′gō, *n.* any plant of the genus *Sorghum*, grown for sirup or fodder.

sō′rī, *n.* plural of *sorus*.

sō′ri·cid, *n.* any sorex.

sō′ri·cid, *a.* pertaining to the genus *Sorex* or the family *Soricidæ*.

Sō·ric′i·dae, *n.pl.* a family of small mammals of which *Sorex* is the typical genus.

sō′ri·cine, *a.* of or resembling a shrew or shrewmouse.

sō·rif′ēr·ous, *a.* in botany, bearing sori.

sor′ing, *n.* the practice of making the front feet of a show horse sore, as by bruising or blistering, so as to force it to take high, exaggerated steps in exhibitions.

sō·rī′tēṣ, *n.* [LL., from Gr. *sōros*, a heap.] in logic, a series of premises followed by a conclusion, arranged so that the predicate of the first premise is the subject of the next and so forth, the conclusion uniting the subject of the first with the predicate of the last in an elliptical series of syllogisms.

sō·rit′iç·ăl, *a.* pertaining to or characteristic of sorites.

sorn, *v.t.* [perhaps from OFr. *sorner*, to play tricks, to jest, to cheat.] to impose an another for food and lodging or entertainment. [Scot.]

sorn′ēr, *n.* one who obtrudes himself on another for bed and board. [Scot.]

sō·rō′răl, *a.* [L. *soror*, sister.] sisterly. [Rare.]

sō·ror′i·cīde, *n.* [L. *soror*, sister, and *cædere*, to strike, to kill.]
1. one who kills his own sister.
2. the act of killing one's sister.

sō·ror′i·ty, *n.*; *pl.* **sō·ror′i·tieṣ**, [L. *soror, sororis*, sister, and *-ity.*]
1. a group of women or girls joined together by common interests, for fellowship, etc., as in a social club.
2. a club or other organization composed of women or girls, as at many colleges.

sō′rŏr·ize, *v.i.* [L. *soror*, sister; on type of *fraternize.*] to associate as sisters; to be in communion or sympathy as sisters. [Rare.]

sō′rōse, *a.* having sori.

sō·rō′sis, *n.*; *pl.* **sō·rō′sēṣ**, [LL., from Gr. *sōros*, a heap.]
1. a kind of collective fruit, consisting of a spike or raceme converted into a fleshy fruit by the cohesion in a single mass of the ovaria and the floral envelopes.
2. a women's club or society.

sor′rănce, *n.* same as *sorance*.

sor′rel, *n.* [OFr. *sorel*, from *sor*, a hawk with red plumage.]
1. reddish brown.
2. a horse or other animal of a sorrel color.
3. a buck of the third year.

sor′rel, *a.* reddish-brown.

sor′rel, *n.* [Fr. *surelle*, a species of sorrel, from O.H.G. *sûr*, sour.]
1. a plant of the genus *Rumex*, the common sorrel of the Old World being *Rumex acetosa*, and used, as is *Rumex scutatus*, the French sorrel, in salads and soups or cooked as a spinach. *Rumex acetosella*, the common sheep sorrel of America, is sometimes eaten but is not commonly prepared for the table.
2. any of various other similar plants, as the wood sorrel.
salt of sorrel; acid potassium oxalate.

sor′rel tree, a North American tree, *Oxydendrum arboreum*, having white flowers, thick bark, grayish fruit, and sour evergreen leaves.

Sor·ren′tō wŏrk, ornamental work, either carved or inlaid, named from Sorrento, Italy, where made; also, any similar work.

sor′ri·ly, *adv.* in a sorry manner.

sor′ri·ness, *n.* the state or quality of being sorry; wretchedness.

sor′rōw, *n.* [ME. *sorwe*; AS. *sorg*; akin to G. *sorge.*]
1. mental suffering caused by loss, disappointment, etc.; sadness, grief, or regret.
2. that which produces such suffering; trouble, loss, affliction, etc.
3. the outward expression of such suffering; mourning; lamentation.
4. the devil. [Scot. and Ir.]
Syn.—grief, sadness.

sor′rōw, *v.i.*; sorrowed, *pt.*, *pp.*; sorrowing, *ppr.* to feel sorrow; to grieve; to be sad.

sor′rōw·fụl, *a.* 1. full of sorrow; feeling or exhibiting sorrow; sad; dejected; depressed.
2. producing or causing sorrow; sad; mournful; pitiable; as, a *sorrowful* accident.
3. expressive of grief; accompanied with grief.
Syn.—sad, mournful, dreary, lamentable, distressing.

sor′rōw·fụl·ly, *adv.* in a sorrowful manner.

sor′rōw·fụl·ness, *n.* the state or quality of being sorrowful; grief.

sor′rōw·less, *a.* without sorrow.

sor′ry, *a.*; *comp.* sorrier; *superl.* sorriest, [AS. *sarig, sari*, from *sar*, sore.]
1. full of sorrow, pity, sympathy, or regret; as, we were *sorry* to hear of his death, we were *sorry* to have missed you: often used as an expression of apology.
2. inferior in worth or quality; poor; as, a *sorry* exhibition of acting.
3. wretched; miserable; dismal; pitiful; as, a slum is a *sorry* place.

sorṣ, *n.*; *pl.* **sor′tēṣ**, [L.] divination or prophecy by the chance selection of an author's writings.

sort, *n.* [Fr. *sorte*, sort, kind, species, from L. *sors, sortis*, a lot, condition.]
1. a kind or species; any number or collection of individual persons or things characterized by the same or like qualities; a class or order; as, a *sort* of men; a *sort* of horses; a *sort* of trees; a *sort* of poems or writings.
2. quality; type; nature; character; as, remarks of that *sort*.
3. manner; fashion; way; as, he spoke in a queer *sort*. [Archaic.]
4. a number or collection of things which are of the same kind or suited to each other, or which are used together; a set; a class; as, he is of that *sort*.
5. [*usually in plural*] in printing, any of the kinds of characters in a font of type.
6. lot; chance; fate; destiny. [Obs.]
of sorts; (a) of various kinds; (b) of a poor or inferior kind; also, *of a sort*.
out of sorts; (a) in printing, lacking certain sorts of type; (b) [Colloq.] not in a good humor; cross; (c) [Colloq.] not feeling well; slightly ill.
sort of; somewhat. [Colloq.]
Syn.—rank, species, kind, class, character, degree, denomination, description.

sort, *v.t.*; sorted, *pt.*, *pp.*; sorting, *ppr.* 1. to distribute by lot. [Obs.]
2. to separate, as things having like qualities, from other things, and arrange them according to class or kind (often with *out*).
3. to select from a number. [Obs.]
4. to adapt; to fit; to make conformable; to accommodate. [Rare.]
I pray thee, *sort* thy heart to patience.
—Shak.
5. to correct by whipping; to punish. [Scot.]

sort, *v.i.* 1. to be joined with others of the same kind. [Archaic.]

2. to consort; to associate. [Archaic.]
3. to suit; to fit; to harmonize; to agree. [Archaic.]
4. to cast lots; to soothsay. [Obs.]

sort'à·ble, *a.* 1. that can be sorted.
2. suitable; befitting. [Obs.]

sort'à·bly, *adv.* suitably; fitly. [Obs.]

sort'ăl, *a.* pertaining to or designating a sort.

sort'ănce, *n.* suitableness; agreement. [Obs.]

sor·tā'tion, *n.* the act of separating or sorting.

sort'ẽr, *n.* one who or that which sorts or culls; as, a wool-*sorter*.

sor'tēs, *n.* plural of *sors.*

sort'ful·ly, *adv.* suitably. [Obs.]

sor'tiē, *n.* [Fr., from *sortir*, to issue, to go out.]
1. a sudden attack by forces of a besieged place upon the besiegers; raid.
2. the forces making such an attack.
3. one mission or attack by a single military airplane.

sor'ti·lēge, *n.* [Fr., from LL. *sortilegium*; L. *sors*, lot, and *legere*, to read.] the act or practice of drawing lots; divination by drawing lots; hence, sorcery.

sor·ti·lē'gious, *a.* pertaining to sortilege.

sor·til'e·gy, *n.* same as *sortilege.*

sort'ing, *n.* the act of separating into sorts or kinds.

sor·ti'tà, *n.* [It., from *sortire*, to go out.] in music, (a) the first selection sung by a principal singer in an opera; (b) a postlude.

sor·ti'tion, *n.* [L. *sortitio.*] selection or appointment by lot.

sort'ment, *n.* an assortment. [Obs.]

sō'rus, *n.*; *pl.* **sō'rī,** [Gr. *sōros*, a heap.] a cluster of spore cases on the under surface of a fern frond, or a similar cluster or spot, as of fungus spores.

sor'we, *n.* and *v.* sorrow. [Obs.]

sor'we·ful, *a.* sorrowful. [Obs.]

sō'ry, *n.* an earth, black in color, impregnated with vitriol. [Obs.]

S O S (es'ō-es'), 1. the standard signal of distress (...---...) used internationally in wireless telegraphy, as by ships, aircraft, etc.
2. any call or appeal for help. [Colloq.]

sō'-sō, *adv.* indifferently; just tolerably or passably: also *so so.*

sō'-sō, *a.* not very good or well; rather poor, bad, or unwell: also *so so.*

soss, *n.* [ME. *sosse*, a mess of food.] a mess; also, a dirty puddle. [Brit. Dial.]

soss, *v.t.* to make dirty or foul. [Brit. Dial.]

soss, *v.i.* to prepare messes or meals. [Scot.]

sos'sle, *v.t.* and *v.i.* to splash; to make a slop. [Brit. Dial.]

sos·te·nū'tō, *a.* [It.] in music, held for the full indicated time value, or somewhat prolonged in the time value of the tones.

sos·te·nū'tō, *n.*; *pl.* **sos·te·nū'tōs, sos·te·nū'tī,** in music, a sostenuto movement or passage.

sot, *n.* [Fr. *sot*, a fool, from LL. *sottus*, stupid.]
1. a stupid person; a blockhead; a dull fellow; a dolt. [Obs.]
2. a person stupefied by excessive drinking; a habitual drunkard.

sot, *v.t.*; sotted, *pt.*, *pp.*; sotting, *ppr.* to stupefy; to infatuate; to besot.

sot, *v.i.* to be a sot or tippler.

sot, *v.* 1. obsolete or dialectal past tense and past participle of *sit.*
2. obsolete or dialectal past tense and past participle of *set.*

Sō·tà·dē'ăn, Sō·tad'iç, *a.* pertaining to or resembling the scurrilous verses of the Greek poet Sotades, who lived in the third century B.C.

Sō·tad'iç, *n.* a Sotadean verse or poem.

sōte, *a.* sweet. [Obs.]

sō·tē"ri·ō·log'iç·ăl, *a.* of or relating to soteriology.

sō·tē·ri·ol'ō·gy, *n.* [Gr. *sōtērios*, salubrious, and *-logy.*]
1. a treatise on health, or the science of promoting and preserving health.
2. in theology, the doctrine of salvation through Jesus Christ.

sōth, *a.* and *n.* sooth. [Obs.]

Sō'thi·aç, *a.* same as *Sothic.*

Sō'thiç, *a.* [from Gr. *Sōthis*, the dog star, from Egypt. *Septit.*] of or pertaining to the dog star, *Sirius.*
Sothic cycle; a period of 1,460 Sothic years (1,461 years) in the ancient Egyptian calendar: also *Sothic period.*
Sothic year; the ancient Egyptian year, having 365¼ days.

sot'ni·à, *n.* [Russ. *sotniya*, a hundred.] a company or squadron of a Cossack regiment.

sō'tōl, *n.* [Sp. *sotol, zotol*, from Nahuatl *tzotolli.*] any of a number of related treelike desert plants with dense clusters of whitish, lilylike flowers, growing in the southwestern United States and northern Mexico.

sot'ted, *a.* besotted.

sot'tẽr·y, *n.* foolishness. [Obs.]

sot'tish, *a.* 1. of or like a sot.
2. stupid or foolish from or as from too much drinking.

sot'tish·ly, *adv.* in a sottish manner; so as to be sottish.

sot'tish·ness, *n.* the quality or state of being sottish.

sot'tō vō'ce (-chē), [It., lit., under the voice.] in an undertone, so as not to be overheard.

sōu, *n.* [Fr., from L. *solidus*, a coin.]
1. a small French coin equal to $^1/_{20}$ of a franc; a 5-centime piece.
2. a French 10-centime piece.
3. a former French coin of varying value and composition.
sou marqué; (a) a former French copper coin worth 15 deniers, or a little over one cent; (b) a mere trifle: also *sou marquee.*

sōu·ä'ri, *n.* [native name.] any of several trees of the genus *Caryocar*, native to British Guiana.

sōu·ä'ri nut, the butternut of any of a number of tall South American trees of the genus *Caryocar.*

sōu'bȧh, *n.* same as *subah.*

sōu'bäh·där, *n.* same as *subahdar.*

sōu·bïse', *n.* [Fr., after Marshal *Soubise* (1715–1787).] a sauce containing onions and melted butter.

sōu·brette' (-bret'), *n.* [Fr., from OFr. *soubret*, sly, cunning.] in the theater, (a) a lady's maid or maidservant, especially one involved in intrigue; (b) any pretty, flirtatious, or frivolous young woman character; (c) an actress who plays such characters.

sōu·bri·quet' (-kā'), *n.* same as *sobriquet.*

sou·cär', *n.* [Hind. *sāhūkār*, from Sans. *sādhu*, straight.] in India, a Hindu banker: also spelled *sowcar.*

souce, *n.* and *v.* souse. [Obs.]

sōu·çhet' (-shā'), *n.* the pendulous mucilaginous tubers of *Cyperus esculentus*, cultivated as food in southern Europe.

sōu·çhong', *n.* [Chin. *hsiao*, small or young, and *chung*, kind.] a kind of black tea, grown especially in China.

sōu·dän', *n.* [Fr. *soldan.*] a sultan. [Obs.]

Sōu·dăn·ēse', *a.* and *n.* same as *Sudanese.*

souf·flé' (sö-flā'), *a.* [Fr., a puff of wind, from *souffler*, to blow.]
1. in ceramics, decorated with drops of color, which has the appearance of having been blown on by air pressure.
2. in cooking, light and frothy; as, cheese *soufflé.*

souf·flé (sö-flā'), *n.* any of several baked foods made light and puffy by the addition of beaten egg whites before baking.

sōuf'fle' (-fl), *n.* in medicine, a soft, blowing sound heard on auscultation.
electric souffle; the slight current of electrified air that comes from a static electric machine while it is in action.
fetal souffle; a blowing sound sometimes heard in pregnancy, supposed to be caused by compression of the umbilical vessels.

souf·flēed' (sö-flād'), *a.* soufflé.

sou·frière'bird (sö-fryãr'), [after La *Soufrière*, volcano in the West Indies where found.] a flycatcher of the West Indies, *Myadestes sibilans.*

sough (suf), *n.* a small drain; an adit. [Brit.]

sough (sow), *n.* a sow. [Obs.]

sough (suf), *n.* [ME. *swough*, from AS. *swogan*, to sound.]
1. a murmuring, sighing sound; a rustling or whistling sound, as of the wind; a deep sigh.
2. a current rumor; a report. [Scot.]
3. a whining way of speaking, especially in preaching or praying. [Scot.]

sough, *v.i.* to make a sough.

sough, *v.t.* to utter with a sough; to utter in a whining, monotonous tone. [Scot.]

sought (sot), *v.* past tense and past participle of *seek.*

sōul, *v.t.* to endow with a soul. [Obs.]

sōul, *n.* [ME. *saul*; AS. *sawōl*; akin to Goth. *saivala*; G. *seele*, the soul.]
1. an entity which is regarded as being the immortal or spiritual part of the person and, though having no physical or material reality, is credited with the functions of thinking and willing, and hence determining all behavior.
2. the moral or emotional nature of man.
3. spiritual or emotional warmth, force, etc., or evidence of this; as, the painting, like the artist, lacks *soul.*
4. vital or essential part, quality, or principle; as, "brevity is the *soul* of wit."
5. the person who leads or dominates; the central figure; as, Cromwell, *soul* of the Commonwealth.
6. embodiment; personification; as, she is the *soul* of kindness.
7. a person; as, I didn't see a *soul* about.
8. the spirit of a dead person, thought of as separate from the body and leading an existence of its own.
upon my soul!; (a) originally, "I shall risk eternal damnation if this is not so!"; (b) an exclamation of surprise.
Syn.—life, ardor, spirit, courage, force, mind, intellect.

sōul bell, the passing bell.

sōuled, *a.* having a soul or feeling: usually in hyphenated compounds; as, noble-*souled*, mean-*souled.*

sōul'ful, *a.* full of or expressive of emotion or deep feeling.

sōul'less, *a.* without soul, sensitivity, or deepness of feeling; spiritless; without inspiration.

sōul'less·ly, *adv.* in a soulless way.

sōul sçot, a funeral duty, or money paid for a requiem for the soul. [Obs.]

sōul shot, same as *soul scot.*

sōul sleep'ẽr, a psychopannychist.

soum, sowm, *n.* [variant of *sum*, amount.]
1. the number of cattle or sheep for which any given piece of land will provide grazing. [Scot.]
2. the area of land that will provide pasturage for a given number of sheep or cattle. [Scot.]

sōun, *n.* and *v.* sound. [Obs.]

sound, *a.*; *comp.* sounder; *superl.* soundest, [AS. *sund, gesund*, sound, healthy; akin to Dan. *sund*, G. *gesund*, etc.]
1. whole; unimpaired; unhurt; unmutilated; not weak, diseased, or damaged; as, of *sound* mind and body.
2. free from imperfection, defect, or decay; whole and in good condition; undecayed; as, *sound* timber.
3. firm; safe; stable; secure, especially financially; as, only *sound* banks withstood the crash.
4. founded on truth; strong; valid; reliable; sensible; as, a *sound* argument.

Under the guidance of *sound* moral principles. —Morse.

5. founded on right or law; valid; legal; not defective; indisputable; as, a *sound* title.
6. orthodox; conservative.
7. morally strong; honest, honorable, upright, virtuous, etc.
8. thorough; complete; as, a *sound* investigation.
9. deep; profound; unbroken; undisturbed; heavy; said of sleep.
10. heavy; lusty; laid on with force; severe; as, a *sound* thrashing.
Syn.—healthy, whole, unimpaired, hearty, hale, vigorous, entire, undecayed, sensible, rational.

sound, *adv.* soundly.

sound, *n.* [AS. *sund*, a swimming, from *swimman*, to swim.]
1. a wide channel or strait linking two large bodies of water or separating an island from the mainland.
2. a long inlet or arm of the sea.
3. the air sac, or swimming bladder, of a fish.

sound, *n.* [from ME. *soun*; OFr. *son*; L. *sonus.*]
1. that which is or can be heard; the sensation of hearing, resulting from the stimulation of the auditory nerves by vibrations carried in the air, water, etc.
2. such vibrations (*sound waves*).
3. any auditory effect that is distinctive or characteristic of its source; an identifiable noise; as, the *sound* of aircraft overhead.
4. a noise made by the organs of speech.
5. the distance within which a given sound may be heard; earshot; as, within *sound* of the guns.
6. mental impression or effect; meaning; suggestion; implication; as, we liked the *sound* of his report.
7. mere meaningless noise.
8. report; rumor. [Archaic.]

sound, *v.i.* 1. to make a sound.
2. to give a specified mental impression as through sound; to be heard or understood; seem; appear; as, her voice *sounds* troubled, the plan *sounds* feasible.
3. in law, to be concerned only; to have effect or significance; as, an action *sounding* in damages.
to sound off; (a) to speak in turn, as in counting off for a military formation; (b) [Slang.] to start speaking, especially when silence is in order; (c) [Slang.] to speak in a loud or offensive way, as in boasting.

sound, *v.t.* 1. to cause to sound, or to produce the sound of.
2. to utter audibly; to pronounce; as, he doesn't *sound* his *r*'s.
3. to order or direct by a sound; to express, indicate, announce, or signal; as, to *sound* a retreat, the clock *sounds* the hour.
4. to celebrate or honor by sounds; to spread abroad; to proclaim; to publish; as, to *sound* one's praise.
5. to examine, as the chest, by auscultation and percussion.
6. to import; to indicate. [Obs.]

sound, *v.t.* [OFr. *sonder*, from LL. *subundare*, to submerge, from L. *sub*, under, and *unda*, a wave.]
1. to measure the depth of various depths of (water or a body of water), especially with a weighted line; as, the bay was *sounded* and found navigable.
2. to measure (depth) in this way.
3. to investigate or examine (the bottom of the sea, etc.) with a weighted line that brings up adhering particles.
4. to investigate, examine, or try to find out, as a person's opinions.
5. to try to find out, or to find out, the opinions or feelings of (another or others) on a given matter, as by roundabout questioning or allusive remarks (often with *out*).
6. in medicine, to examine with a sound, or probe.

sound, *v.i.* 1. to sound water or a body of water.
2. to move downward through water; to dive.
3. to try to find out something, as by roundabout questioning, etc.

sound, *n.* 1. a sounding.
2. in medicine, a long probe used in examining body cavities.

sound'a·ble, *a.* that can be sounded.

sound'bōard, *n.* same as *sounding board.*

sound bōard'ing, short boards placed transversely between the joists or under flooring, to hold the pugging which deadens sounds.

sound bōne, the bone of a fish forming part of the backbone, situated near the sound, or air sac.

sound bōw, the thickest part of a bell on which the clapper strikes.

sound ef·fects', sounds, as of thunder, blows, animals, traffic, etc., artificially produced to simulate sounds called for in the script of a radio, stage, motion-picture, or television production.

sound'ẽr, *n.* 1. one who or that which makes a sound or sounds.
2. a telegraphic device that converts electric code impulses into sound.

sound'ẽr, *n.* a person or thing that sounds the depth of water, etc.

sound'ẽr, *n.* 1. a herd of wild swine. [Obs.]
2. a young wild boar. [Obs.]

sound fig'ūres, same as *sonorous figures* under *sonorous.*

sound film, a motion-picture film with a sound track.

sound'ing, *a.* 1. making or giving forth sound.
2. resonant or sonorous.
3. imposing in sound; high-sounding; bombastic.

sound'ing, *n.* 1. the act of measuring the depth or examining the bottom of a body of water, etc., with or as with a weighted line.
2. depth so measured.
3. [*pl.*] a place, usually less than 600 feet in depth, where such measurements can be taken.
in or *on soundings*; in nautical usage, in a place where the bottom of a body of water can be reached by a plummet and line: said of a vessel.
off soundings; in nautical usage, in such a depth of water that it is not possible to reach the bottom with a plummet and line: said of a vessel.

sound'ing bal·loon', a small balloon to which a small radio apparatus is attached and sent into the upper atmosphere: also called *radiosonde.*

sound'ing bōard, 1. a canopy, as over a pulpit, to reflect the sound of a speaker's voice toward the audience.
2. a board used in the deadening of floors, partitions, etc.
3. a thin plate, as of wood, built into a musical instrument to increase its resonance.

sound'ing lead (led), the weight used at the end of a sounding line.

sound'ing līne, a line or cable weighted at one end and used for measuring the depth of water.

sound lens, in acoustics, a lens for focusing sound waves.

sound'less, *a.* incapable of being sounded or fathomed; unfathomable. [Rare.]

sound'less, *a.* having no sound; noiseless; silent; dumb.

sound'less·ly, *adv.* in a soundless manner.

sound'less·ness, *n.* the quality or state of being soundless.

sound'ly, *adv.* 1. in a sound manner; without weakness or error; as, he reasons *soundly.*
2. so as to be not easily awakened.
3. thoroughly; completely; forcefully; as, they were *soundly* defeated.

sound'man, *n.*; *pl.* **sound'men,** a man in charge of sound effects.

sound'ness, *n.* the quality or state of being sound.

sound'-on-disk', *n.* a flat phonograph disk on which the sound for a motion picture is recorded: it is played to synchronize with the action of the motion picture as it is projected on a screen.

sound'-on-film', *n.* in motion pictures, a film or part of a film on which sound has been recorded; a sound film.

sound pic'tūre, a motion picture accompanied by sound, as dialogue, music, etc.

sound'pōst, *n.* a post set beneath the bridge of a violin, violoncello, etc., for transmitting sound vibrations to the body of the instrument.

sound prō·jec'tŏr, an apparatus designed to project motion pictures on a screen in synchronization with the sound that has been recorded for them.

sound'proof, *a.* impervious to sound.

sound'proof, *v.t.*; soundproofed, *pt.*, *pp.*; soundproofing, *ppr.* to make soundproof.

sound'proof''ing, *n.* a building material that makes anything impervious to sound, or insulates against sound.

sound screen, a motion-picture screen used with sound pictures: usually made of a porous material through which sound from the loudspeaker may filter.

sound shad'ōw, 1. in acoustics, the obstruction of sound, as by a hill or building.
2. an area behind a screen through which sound waves cannot pass.

sound track, the area along one side of a motion-picture film, carrying the sound record of the film.

sound wāve, a wave by which sound is transmitted in a medium, as the atmosphere.

sōune, *v.t.* and *v.i.* to sound. [Obs.]

sōup, *n.* [Fr. *soupe*, a word of Germanic origin.]
1. a liquid food made by cooking meat, vegetables, fish, etc., in water, milk, etc.
2. nitroglycerin. [Slang.]
3. a heavy overcast, often with rain, that makes aerial navigation difficult. [Slang.]
4. capacity for speed; as, his new car has plenty of *soup.* [Slang.]
in the soup; in a difficult, disappointing, or hopeless situation. [Slang.]

sōup, *v.t.* to feed soup to. [Colloq.]
to soup up; to increase in capacity for speed, as an engine, by enriching the fuel mixture, supercharging, etc. [Slang.]

sōup'-and-fish', *n.* clothes worn on a formal occasion; full dress: from the variety and abundance of food served at formal dinners. [Slang.]

sōup'bōne, *n.* a large bone of meat, especially beef, with its cartilage, ligaments, and marrow, used in making soup.

soup·çon' (söp-s'ọn), *n.* [Fr., a suspicion.] literally, a suspicion; hence, a very small quantity; a suggestion or trace, especially of a given flavor, as onion.

sōup house, same as *soup kitchen.*

sōup kitch'en, 1. a place where free food is given to people unable to provide their own.
2. a mobile kitchen, as used by an army in the field.

sōu'ple, *n.* the striking part of a flail; a swiple. [Scot.]

sōup māi'gre (-gẽr), [Fr. *soupe maigre.*] a very thin soup, as of seasoned vegetables. [Obs.]

sōup'spọọn, *n.* a spoon with a large bowl, used in eating soup.

sōup'y, *a.*; *comp.* soupier; *superl.* soupiest, of or like soup.

sour, *a.*; *comp.* sourer; *superl.* sourest. [AS. *sūr*, sour, acid; akin to G. *sauer.*]
1. having a sharp, acid taste; tart, as lime or lemon juice, vinegar, green fruit, etc.
2. made acid by fermentation; rank; rancid; spoiled; as, this milk smells *sour.*
3. cross; disagreeable; bad-tempered; peevish; morose; bitter; as, failure made him *sour.*
4. below the usual or desired standard or quality; not satisfactory; poor; as, his game has gone *sour.*
5. distasteful or unpleasant.
6. excessively acid: said of soil.
7. tainted with sulfur compounds: said of gasoline, etc.
8. coarse, as grass. [Brit. Dial.]
sour grapes; see under *grape.*
Syn.—tart, acid, coagulated, crabbed, austere, crusty.

sour, *n.* 1. that which is sour; a sour or acid substance.
2. an acid liquid used in bleaching or dyeing.
3. an acid drink; as, a whisky *sour.*

sour, *v.t.*; soured, *pt.*, *pp.*; souring, *ppr.* 1. to make sour; to cause to have a sharp taste.
2. to make acid, as soil.
3. to make harsh in temper; to make cross, crabbed, peevish, or discontented.
4. to make uneasy or unhappy.
5. to macerate, as lime, and make fit for plaster or mortar.
6. to treat with an acid liquid in bleaching or dyeing.

sour, *v.i.* 1. to become sour; to acquire the quality of tartness or pungency to the taste; as, cider *sours* rapidly in the rays of the sun.
2. to become peevish or crabbed.
to sour on; to tire of; to stop favoring; to go back on. [Colloq.]

sōurce, *n.* [Fr. *source*; OFr. *sourse*, from L. *surgere*, to rise.]
1. first cause; place of origin from which something comes or develops; that which gives rise to anything.

> As a very important *source* of strength and security, cherish public credit.
> —George Washington.

2. the spring, fountain, etc. from which a stream of water proceeds; as, the *source* of a river.
3. a person or thing from which information is or may be gotten; as, the author's *sources* were all recognized authorities.
4. the person or business firm that makes payment of dividends, interest, etc.
5. the act of soaring or rising. [Obs.]
Syn.—origin, fountain, cause, spring, beginning, primogenitor.

sōurce, *v.i.* to spring up; to take origin. [Obs.]

sōurce mȧ·tē'ri·ăl, original or primary sources of information on any given study or subject.

sōurd, sōurde, *v.i.* to spring; to rise. [Obs.]

sōur·dīne', *n.* [Fr.; It. *sordina*, from L. *surdus*, deaf.]
1. originally, any of several musical instruments of low or soft tone.
2. a mute, especially one for a trumpet.

sour dock, *Rumex acetosa*, the sorrel; also, *Rumex acetosella*, the sheep sorrel.

sour'dōugh (-dō), *n.* 1. leaven; especially, fermented dough saved from one baking so that it can be used in the next, thus avoiding the need for fresh yeast. [Dial.]
2. a prospector or settler in the western United States, Canada, or Alaska, especially one living alone: so called from his using sourdough.

sour gōurd, an Australian or African evergreen tree, *Adansonia gregorii*, which yields a fruit with woody, acid pulp and many large seeds; the cream-of-tartar tree; also, the fruit of this tree.

sour gum, any of a number of tall related trees with crooked branches and leaves that turn bright red in the fall; the tupelo.

sour'ing, *n.* 1. that which causes sourness.
2. any apple having a sour taste. [Brit. Dial.]

sour'ish, *a.* somewhat sour; not sweet.

sour'krout, sour'çrout, *n.* same as *sauerkraut.*

sour'ly, *adv.* in a sour manner.

sour'ness, *n.* the state of being sour; the quality that renders sour.

sour'pu̦ss, *n.* a person who has a gloomy or disagreeable expression or nature. [Slang.]

sour'sop, *n.* a small evergreen tree of the West Indies, *Anona muricata*, which bears a large succulent fruit; also, the fruit of this tree.

sour'wood, *n.* same as *sorrel tree.*

söus (sö), *n.* plural of *sou.*

sou'sȧ·phōne, *n.* [after John Philip *Sousa*, who suggested it.] a brass-wind instrument of the tuba class: it was developed from the helicon and is used especially in military bands.

souse, *n.* [OFr. *souz, soult*; O.H.G. *sulza*, brine.]
1. a pickled food, especially the feet, ears, and head of a pig.
2. liquid used for pickling; brine.
3. the act of plunging into a liquid, especially into brine for pickling.
4. a drunkard. [Slang.]

souse, *v.t.* and *v.i.*; soused (soust), *pt., pp.*; sousing, *ppr.* 1. to pickle.
2. to plunge or steep in a liquid.
3. to make or become soaking wet.
4. to make or become intoxicated. [Slang.]

souse, *n.* [altered from ME. *source*, from OFr. *sors, source*, in the same sense.]
1. the act of rising in flight: said of a hunted bird.
2. the act of swooping down on a hunted bird: said of a hawk, falcon, etc.

souse, *v.i.* [Sw. *susa*, to rush, rustle.] to fall suddenly; to rush with speed, as a hawk on its prey: followed by *on* or *upon*; as, a hawk *souses upon* a chicken.

souse, *v.t.* to strike with sudden violence; to pounce upon.

souse, *adv.* with a swoop or plunge; suddenly; with a thump or a splash; as, *souse* he went into the lake.

souse, *n.* [prob. echoic.] a pounding blow.

soused (soust), *a.* [pp. of *souse* (to pickle).] drunk; intoxicated. [Slang.]

söu'shum·bẽr, *n.* a tropical plant, *Solanum mammosum*, of the West Indies: also called *nipple nightshade*, from its yellow nipple-shaped fruit.

söus'lik, *n.* same as *suslik.*

söu'söu, *n.* same as *susu.*

söu·tȧche', *n.* [Fr.] a narrow flat braid, used to sew upon garments in ornamental designs.

sout'ăge, *n.* [etym. unknown.] a kind of coarse cloth; particularly, the material from which hop bags are made. [Obs.]

söu·tāne', *n.* [Fr.] a cassock or tunic worn by Roman Catholic priests.

söu'tẽr, *n.* [AS. *sūtere*, from L. *sutor*, a shoemaker.] a shoemaker; a cobbler. [Scot. and Brit. Dial.]

söu'tẽr·ly, *adv.* like a cobbler; lowly. [Obs.]

söu'tẽr·rāin, *n.* [Fr.] a grotto or cavern under ground; a cellar.

south, *n.* [AS. *sūth*, probably for *sunth*, from *sunne*, the sun; akin to Ice. *suthr, sunnr*, Dan. *syd, sönden*, O.H.G. *sund*, south.]
1. that cardinal point which is directly opposite the north and on the right hand of a person facing east.
2. the point on a compass at 180°, directly opposite north.
3. that region or country that lies in a southern direction from the point of reckoning.
4. [*often* S–] the southern part of the earth, especially the antarctic regions.
Solid South; see following *solid.*
the South; (a) that part of the United States which is bounded on the north by the southern border of Pennsylvania, the Ohio River, and the eastern and northern borders of Missouri; (b) the Confederacy.

south, *a.* 1. in, of, to, toward, or facing the south.
2. blowing from the south; as, a *south* wind.
3. [S–] designating the southern part of a continent, country, etc.; as, *South* America, *South* India.

south, *adv.* in or toward the south; in a southerly direction; as, the stream flows *south.*

south, *v.i.*; southed (southt), *pt., pp.*; southing, *ppr.* 1. to move toward or to approach the south.
2. in astronomy, to cross the meridian, as the moon, a star, or a planet.

South Af'ri·çăn, 1. of southern Africa.
2. of the Union of South Africa.
3. a native or inhabitant of the Union of South Africa, especially one of European ancestry.

South Af'ri·çăn Dutch, 1. the Boers.
2. their language; Afrikaans.

South Ȧ·mer'i·çăn, 1. of South America or its people.
2. a native or inhabitant of South America.

south'bound, *a.* going southward.

south bȳ ēast, the direction, or the point on a mariner's compass, halfway between due south and south-southeast; 11°15′ east of due south.

south bȳ west, the direction, or the point on a mariner's compass, halfway between due south and south-southwest; 11°15′ west of due south.

South Çar·ō·lin'i·ăn, 1. of South Carolina or its people.
2. a native or inhabitant of South Carolina.

South·çot'ti·ăn, *n.* one of the followers of Joanna Southcott (1750–1814), a religious zealot who claimed she was the woman spoken of in the book of Revelation.

South Dȧ·kō'tăn, 1. of South Dakota or its people.
2. a native or inhabitant of South Dakota.

South'down, *a.* of or pertaining to the South Downs of Sussex, England; as, a *Southdown* sheep, *Southdown* mutton.

South'down, *n.* one of a breed of small, hornless English sheep having short wool and bred chiefly for food; also, mutton from such sheep.

south·ēast', *n.* 1. the direction, or the point on a mariner's compass, halfway between south and east; 45° east of due south.
2. a region or district in or toward this direction.
the Southeast; the southeastern part of the United States.

south·ēast', *a.* 1. in, of, to, toward, or facing the southeast.
2. from the southeast; as, a *southeast* wind.

south·ēast', *adv.* toward, in, or from the southeast; as, the wind veered *southeast.*

south·ēast' bȳ ēast, the direction, or the point on a mariner's compass, halfway between southeast and east-southeast; 11°15′ east of southeast.

south·ēast bȳ south, the direction, or the point on a mariner's compass, halfway between southeast and south-southeast; 11°15′ south of southeast.

south·ēast'ẽr, *n.* a wind or gale from the southeast.

south·ēast'ẽr·ly, *a.* and *adv.* 1. in or toward the southeast.
2. from the southeast; as, a *southeasterly* wind.

south·ēast'ẽrn, *a.* 1. in, of, or toward the southeast.
2. from the southeast; as, a *southeastern* wind.
3. [S–] of or characteristic of the Southeast.

south·ēast'wărd, *adv.* and *a.* toward the southeast.

south·ēast'wărd, *n.* a southeastward direction, point, or region.

south·ēast'wărd·ly, *adv.* and *a.* 1. toward the southeast.
2. from the southeast; as, a *southeastwardly* wind.

south·ēast'wărds̤, *adv.* southeastward.

south'ẽr, *n.* a wind, gale, or storm from the south.

south'ẽr, *v.i.* to shift or veer to the southern quarter, as a vane.

south'ẽr·li·ness (suth'), *n.* the state of being southerly.

south'ẽr·ly, *n.* a long-tailed arctic sea duck: also called *old wife.*

south'ẽr·ly, *a.* 1. in, of, or toward the south.
2. from the south; as, a *southerly* wind.

south'ẽr·ly, *adv.* 1. toward the south.
2. from the south; as, the wind blew *southerly.*

south'ẽr·mōst, *adv.* same as *southernmost.*

south'ẽrn, *a.* [AS. *suthern*, from *suther, suth*, south.]
1. in, of, toward, or facing the south.
2. from the south; as, a *southern* wind.
3. [S–] of or characteristic of the South.
southern buckthorn; a species of *Bumelia.*
southern cattle fever; same as *Texas fever.*
Southern Confederacy; see *the Confederacy* under *Confederacy.*
Southern Cross; Crux, a southern constellation containing eighteen stars so grouped as to resemble a cross.
Southern Crown; the southern constellation Corona Australis.

south'ẽrn, *n.* a southerner.

south'ẽrn·ẽr, *n.* 1. an inhabitant or native of the south.
2. [S–] a native or inhabitant of a Southern State.

south'ẽrn·iṣm, *n.* an idiom of southerners.

south'ẽrn·īze, *v.t.*; southernized, *pt., pp.*; southernizing, *ppr.* to cause to become southern in characteristics, ideas, or sentiments.

south'ẽrn·īze, *v.i.* to become southern in character, tendencies, or feelings.

south'ẽrn·li·ness, *n.* the state of being southerly.

south'ẽrn·ly, *a.* and *adv.* same as *southerly.*

south'ẽrn·mōst, *adv.* farthest south.

south'ẽrn·wood, *n.* same as *abrotanum.*
Tatarian southernwood; same as *santonica.*

south'ing (south'), *n.* 1. inclination or motion to or toward the south.
2. in astronomy, the distance in degrees that a heavenly body is south of the celestial equator; southern declination.
3. in navigation, the variation in latitude toward the south from the last reckoning of position.
to make southing; in surveying, said of a course when its second extremity is farther south than the first extremity.

south'land, *a.* of or pertaining to the south.

south'land, *n.* 1. land lying in the south.
2. the southern part of a country, etc.

south'ly, *a.* toward, in, or from the south. [Obs.]

south'mōst, *adv.* farthest south.

south'ness, *n.* the tendency of a magnetic needle to point south.

south'pa̦w, *n.* in baseball, a left-handed pitcher; hence, any left-handed person, especially one who throws with his left hand. [Slang.]

south'pa̦w, *a.* left-handed. [Slang.]

south'rŏn (suth'), *a.* living in or coming from the south; southern.

south'rŏn, *n.* a southerner: applied specifically in Scottish dialect to an Englishman.

söuth'sāy, söuth'sāy·ẽr, etc. *soothsay, soothsayer*, etc. [Obs.]

South Sēa Īs'lănd·ẽr (ī'), a native or inhabitant of the South Sea Islands.

south'-south·ēast', *n.* the direction, or the point on a mariner's compass, halfway between due south and southeast; 22°30′ east of due south.

south'-south·ēast', *a.* and *adv.* 1. in or toward the south-southeast.
2. from this direction; as, a *south-southeast* wind.

south'-south'ẽr·ly (-suth'), *n.* same as *southerly.*

south'-south·west', *n.* the direction, or the point on a mariner's compass, halfway between due south and southwest; 22°30′ west of due south.

south'-south·west', *a.* and *adv.* 1. in or toward the south-southwest.
2. from this direction; as, a *south-southwest* wind.

south'wărd, *n.* a southern direction, point, or region.

south'wărd, *a.* lying toward the south; directed toward the south.

south'wărd, *adv.* toward the south; in a southerly direction.

south'wărd·ly, *a.* and *adv.* 1. toward the south.
2. from the south; as, a *southwardly* wind.

south'wărds̤, *adv.* southward.

south·west' *n.* 1. the direction, or the point on a mariner's compass, halfway between south and west; 45° west of due south.
2. a district or region toward this direction.
the Southwest; the southwestern part of the United States, especially Oklahoma, Texas, New Mexico, Arizona, and southern California.

south·west', *a.* 1. in, of, to, toward, or facing the southwest.
2. from the southwest; as, a *southwest* wind.

south·west', *adv.* in, toward, or from the southwest.

south·west' bȳ south, the direction, or the point on a mariner's compass, halfway between southwest and south-southwest; 11°15′ south of southwest.

south·west' bȳ west, the direction, or the point on a mariner's compass, halfway between southwest and west-southwest; 11°15′ west of southwest.

south·west'ẽr, *n.* 1. a strong southwest wind or storm.

2. a sailor's waterproof hat with a flap hanging over the neck, worn in bad weather.
south·west'ẽr·ly, *a.* and *adv.* 1. in or toward the southwest.
2. from the southwest; as, a *southwesterly* wind.
south·west'ẽrn, *a.* 1. in, of, or toward the southwest.
2. from the southwest; as, a *southwestern* wind.
3. [S–] of or characteristic of the Southwest.
south·west'wărd, *adv.* and *a.* toward the southwest.
south·west'wărd, *n.* a southwestward direction, point, or region.
south·west'wărd·ly, *a.* and *adv.* 1. toward the southwest.
2. from the southwest; as, a *southwestwardly* wind.
south·west'wărds, *adv.* southwestward.
söu·vē·nïr', *n.* [Fr.] something kept or serving as a reminder of a place, a person, or an occasion; a keepsake; a memento.
söu·vlä'kï, *n.* same as *souvlakia.*
söu·vlä'kï·ȧ, *n.* [from Mod. Gr. *soubla*, skewer, from Gr., awl.] a Greek dish consisting of small chunks of meat, especially lamb, placed on skewers alternately with tomatoes, onions, greenpeppers, etc., marinated and then broiled.
sou'·west'ẽr, *n.* same as *southwester.*
sov, *n.* a coin, the sovereign. [Brit. Slang.]
sov'ẽr·eign (sov'ẽr·ăn *or* sov'răn), *a.* [ME. *soveraine, sovereyn,* from OFr. *soverain,* from LL. *superanus,* from L. *super,* above, over.]
1. above or superior to all others; chief; greatest; supreme.
2. supreme in power, rank, or authority.
3. of or holding the position of ruler; royal; reigning.
4. independent of all others; as, a *sovereign* state.
5. excellent; very effectual, as a cure or remedy.
sov'ẽr·eign, *n.* 1. one who exercises supreme power; a supreme ruler; the person having the highest authority in a state, as a king, emperor, queen, etc.; a monarch.
2. a group of persons or a state that possesses sovereign authority.
3. any of several gold coins; (a) a British gold coin, 123.274 grains troy in weight, of the value of 20 shillings; (b) a gold coin current at 22s. 6d. from the reign of Henry VII to that of James I.; (c) a gold coin formerly used in Austria.
sov'ẽr·eign·ly, *adv.* 1. as a sovereign; royally.
2. in the highest degree; supremely.
sov'ẽr·eign·ty, *n.*; *pl.* **sov'ẽr·eign·ties,** 1. the state or quality of being sovereign.
2. the status, dominion, rule, or authority of a sovereign.
3. supreme and independent political authority; as, state *sovereignty.*
4. a sovereign state or governmental unit.
sō'vi·et, *n.* [Russ., literally, a council.]
1. a council or body of delegates.
2. in the Soviet Union, any of the various governing councils, local, intermediate, and national, elected by and representing the people: they constitute a pyramidal governmental structure, with the village and town soviets as its base and the Supreme Soviet as its apex.
3. any similar council in various socialist governing systems elsewhere.
sō'vi·et, *a.* 1. of a soviet or soviets.
2. of or connected with government by soviets.
3. [S–] of or connected with the Soviet Union.
sō'vi·et·iṣm, *n.* government by soviets; soviet system.
sō"vi·et·i·zā'tion, *n.* a sovietizing or being sovietized.
sō'vi·et·īze, *v.t.*; sovietized, *pt., pp.*; sovietizing, *ppr.* to change to a soviet form of government.
sŏv'răn, *a.* and *n.* [old sp., under influence of It. *sovrano* (from OFr.).] sovereign.
sow, *n.* [AS. *sugu*; O.D. *sowe, sogh*; D. *zeug*; O.H.G. *su*; Dan. and Sw. *so,* sow, cognate with L. *sus,* Gr. *hys,* sow.]
1. an adult female pig.
2. the sow bug. [Dial.]
3. (a) a channel or sluice carrying molten metal from a blast furnace to the molds in which pig bars are cast; (b) metal solidified in this channel.
4. a movable covered shed anciently used in sieges to cover and protect men who were employed in sapping and mining operations.
sōw, *v.t.*; sowed, *pt.*; sown *or* sowed, *pp.*; sowing, *ppr.* [AS. *sāwan,* pt. *seōw, pp. sāwen*; Ice. *sá*; Dan. *saae*; Goth. *saian.*]
1. to scatter or plant, as seed upon the earth, for growing.
2. to plant (a field, ground, earth, etc.) with seed; to plant seed on or in.
3. to spread abroad; to disseminate; to propagate; as, to *sow* discord.
4. to implant; to inculcate.
sōw, *v.i.* to sow seed for growing.
sow'ăns, *n.pl.* same as *sowens.*
sō·wär', *n.* [Anglo-Ind.] in India, a native horseman or an orderly of cavalry.
sow'bāne, *n.* the maple-leaved goosefoot, *Chenopodium hybridum,* thought to poison swine.
sow'bel·ly, *n.* salt pork. [Colloq.]
sow'bread (-bred), *n.* same as *Cyclamen.*
sow bug, a small terrestrial isopod living in damp places, as under rocks or logs.
sow·çär', *n.* a soucar.
sow'ens, *n.pl.* in Scotland, a kind of porridge made from the husk of oats.
sōw'ẽr, *n.* one who or that which sows.
sōwn, *v.* alternative past participle of *sow.*
sow this'tle (this'l), any plant of the genus *Sonchus,* especially *Sonchus oleraceus,* having yellow flowers and spiny leaves.
sox, *n.pl.* socks (hose).
soy, *n.* [Japan.] 1. a dark, salty sauce made from soybeans fermented and steeped in brine, used especially as a flavoring in Chinese and Japanese dishes: also *soy sauce.*
2. the soybean (plant or seed).
soy'ȧ, *n.* soy. [Chiefly Brit.]
soy'ȧ, *n.* [Hind.] dill.
soy'bēan, *n.* 1. an annual crop plant, *Soja* or *Glycine max,* of the legume family, native to China and Japan but widely grown for its seeds, which contain much protein and oil, and as a forage and cover crop.
2. its seed.

SOYBEAN

soyned, *a.* alarmed; anxious. [Obs.]
sō'zăl, *n.* [Gr. *sōzein,* to save.] a chemical antiseptic compound, obtained from aluminum in the form of an astringent crystalline salt.
sō'zin, *n.* [Gr. *sōzein,* to save.] any of several defensive proteins found in the animal body, which destroy invading bacteria or counteract their toxins.
sō·zō·ī'ō·dōl, *n.* an antiseptic derived from iodine and phenosulfonic acid.
soz'zle, *n.* 1. a sluttish woman. [Dial.]
2. a condition of slovenly disorder. [Dial.]
soz'zle, *v.t.*; sozzled, *pt., pp.*; sozzling, *ppr.* [a variant of *sossle.*]
1. to mingle confusedly. [Dial.]
2. to spill or wet through carelessness; to move about confusedly or carelessly. [Dial.]
spä, *n.* [from *Spa,* a celebrated watering place in Belgium.]
1. a mineral spring.
2. any place, especially a resort, having a mineral spring.
späad, *n.* a kind of mineral; spar. [Obs.]
spāce, *n.* [OFr. *espace*; L. *spatium,* space, from *spatiari,* to wander.]
1. distance extending without limit in all directions; that which is thought of as a boundless, continuous expanse extending in all directions or in three dimensions, within which all material things are contained.
2. distance, interval, or area between or within things; extent; room; as, leave a wide *space* between the rows.
3. (enough) area or room for some purpose; as, we couldn't find a parking *space,* put your answers in these *spaces.*
4. reserved accommodations, as on a train or ship.
5. interval or length of time; as, too short a *space* between arrival and departure.
6. the universe outside the earth's atmosphere: in full, *outer space.*
7. in mathematics, a set of points or elements assumed to satisfy a given set of postulates; as, four-dimensional *space.*
8. in music, an open place between the lines of a staff.
9. in printing, any blank piece of type metal used to separate characters, etc.
10. in telegraphy, an interval when the key is open, or not in contact, during the sending of a message.
11. time available for something. [Obs.]
12. a short time; a while. [Rare.]
spāce, *v.i.* to rove; to roam about. [Obs.]
spāce, *v.t.*; spaced (spāst), *pt., pp.*; spacing, *ppr.* to arrange at proper intervals; to arrange the spaces in or between; specifically, in printing, typewriting, etc., to arrange the spaces between (words, letters, or lines).
Spāce Āge, [also s- a-] the period characterized by the launching of artificial satellites and manned space vehicles: regarded as beginning with the launching of the first sputnik on October 4, 1957.
spāce band, in a linotype or similar typesetting machine, the device for spacing out the line of matrices to the proper width.
spāce bär, the bar on a typewriter that is used for inserting spaces between letters.
spāce'çrȧft, *n. sing. & pl.* any spaceship(s) or other vehicle(s) designed for travel, exploration, etc. in space outside the earth's atmosphere.
spāced'-out', *a.* under the influence of a drug, marijuana, etc.: also *spaced.* [Slang.]
spāce fiç'tion, novels and stories about interplanetary travel in the future.
spāce'flīght, *n.* a flight through outer space.
spāce hēat'ẽr, a small heating unit for warming the air of a single confined area, as a room.
spāce'less, *a.* 1. having no spatial limits.
2. occupying no space.
spāce līne, in printing, a lead.
spāce'măn, *n.*; *pl.* **spāce'men,** an astronaut or, as in space fiction, any of the crew of a spaceship.
spāce'pōrt, *n.* a center where spacecraft are assembled, tested, and launched.
spā'cẽr, *n.* 1. a device used for making spaces, as in printing.
2. a device used to increase the speed of telegraphic transmission by reversing the current.
3. a person or thing that spaces.
spāce rūle, in printing, a fine line of brass type-high, used for printing the lines in tabular matter.
spāce'-sāv"ing, *a.* that saves space.
spāce'-sāv"ing, *n.* the act or practice of saving space.
spāce'ship, *n.* a rocket-propelled vehicle for travel in outer space.
spāce shut'tle, a spacecraft designed to transport persons and equipment between earth and an orbiting space station.
spāce stā'tion (or **plat'fọrm**), a structure designed to orbit in space as a satellite from which to launch other spacecraft, or as an experimentation or observation center.
spāce tīme, space-time continuum.
spāce'-tīme' çon·tin'ū·um, the four-dimensional continuum involving the three dimensions of space and that of time, in which all things exist.
spāce wrīt'ẽr, a writer, especially a journalist, whose pay is based upon the amount of space occupied by his copy.
spāce'y, *a.* same as *spaced-out.* [Slang.]
spā'ciăl (-shăl), *a.* same as *spatial.*
spāc'ing, *n.* 1. the arrangement of spaces.
2. space or spaces, as between printed words.
3. the act of a person or thing that spaces.
spā'cious, *a.* [OFr. *spacieux*; L. *spatiosus.*]
1. having large or ample room; vast; extensive; as, a *spacious* church.
2. great; large; not confined or limited.

Syn.—ample, capacious.—*Ample* implies largeness in quantity or amount; *spacious* denotes wide physical extent or space; *capacious* denotes wide or comprehensive power of holding.

spā'cious·ly, *adv.* in a spacious manner.

spā'cious·ness, *n.* the state or quality of being spacious.

spȧ·dȧs·siǹ' (-saǹ'), *n.* [Fr., from It. *spada*, a sword, from L. *spatha*, a broad flat instrument, a broad pointless sword.] a swordsman; a bravo.

spad'dle, *n.* [dim. of *spade.*] a little spade. [Obs.]

spāde, *n.* [Gr. *spadōn*, a eunuch.] an emasculated man or animal; a eunuch; a gelding.

spāde, *n.* [AS. *spadu*; akin to G. *spaten.*]
1. a heavy, flat-bladed, long-handled tool used for digging: the metal blade is pressed into the ground with the foot.
2. any of several tools resembling a spade, as (a) a sharp instrument for flensing whales; (b) a tool used by cameo-cutters for applying diamond powder.
3. a part of the trail of a gun carriage which digs into the ground to take up recoil.
4. same as *spay*.
to call a spade a spade; to call a thing by its simplest and best-understood name; to use plain, blunt words.

spāde, *v.t.* and *v.i.*; spaded, *pt., pp.*; spading, *ppr.* to dig or cut with a spade.

spāde, *n.* [Sp. *espada*, sword (the sign used on Spanish cards), from L. *spatha*, spatula.]
1. the black figure ♠ marking one of the four suits of playing cards.
2. [*pl.*] the suit of cards so marked.
3. a card of this suit.

spāde bāy'ō·net, a broad-bladed bayonet which may be used for digging shelter holes or rifle pits.

spāde'bōne, *n.* the shoulder blade. [Brit. Dial.]

spāde'fish, *n.*; *pl.* **spāde'fish** or **spāde'fish"eṣ**
1. a fish, *Chætodipterus faber*, which is found along the southern coasts of America and is valued as food: it is disk-shaped and has sharp-spined fins: also called *angel fish, moonfish*, and *porgy*.
2. the paddlefish.

spāde'foot, *n.*; *pl.* **spāde'foots,** a toad with a hornlike projection on the hind foot which is used in digging: also called *spadefoot toad.*

spāde'fụl, *n.* as much as a spade will hold.

spāde han'dle, the handle of a spade; also, in machinery, a pin held at both ends by the forked ends of a connecting rod.

spād'ẽr, *n.* one who or that which spades; a machine used in digging.

spāde'wŏrk, *n.* any difficult or tiresome work necessary to make a beginning.

spȧ·di'ceous (-dish'us), *a.* [L. *spadiceus*, from *spadix*, a date-brown color.]
1. of a bright-brown color.
2. in botany, having a spadix.
3. of the nature of a spadix.

spā·dī·ci·flō'răl, *a.* producing flowers on a spadix.

spā'di·çōse, *a.* [L. *spadix*, a palm branch.] spadiceous.

spȧ·dil'lȧ, *n.* in the old game of solo, the queen of spades, the highest trump.

spȧ·dille', *n.* [Fr., from Sp. *espadilla*, dim. of *espada*, a spade.] the ace of spades at ombre and quadrille.

spā'dix, *n.*; *pl.* **spā'dix·eṣ, spā·dī'sēṣ,** [L., a palm branch.]
1. a fleshy spike of tiny flowers, usually enclosed in a spathe.
2. in zoology, the reproductive arm of a male cephalopod.

spā'dō, *n.* [L.] 1. a castrated man or animal.
2. in law, one who from any cause has not the power of procreation; an impotent person.

spȧ·drọọn', *n.* [Fr. *espadron*, from Sp. *espadon*, a broadsword, from L. *spath*, a broad flat instrument.] a cut-and-thrust sword; a broadsword.

spāe, *v.i.*; spaed, *pt., pp.*; spaeing, *ppr.* [Ice. *spa*; Dan. *spaae*, to foretell.] to foretell; to divine; to forebode; as, to *spae* one's fortune. [Scot.]

spāe'măn, *n.* a diviner; a soothsayer. [Scot.]

spāe'wīfe, *n.*; *pl.* **spāe'wīveṣ,** a woman who tells fortunes. [Scot.]

spȧ·ghet'ti (-get'), *n.* [It., pl. of *spaghetto*, dim. of *spago*, a small cord.]
1. a food consisting of long strings of flour paste, cooked by boiling or steaming and served with a sauce: it resembles macaroni except that the strings are solid, not tubular.
2. in electricity, an insulating tubing somewhat resembling macaroni, used for sheathing bare wire.

spȧ·ġir'iç, *a.* iatrochemical. [Obs.]

spaġ'i·rist, *n.* an iatrochemist. [Obs.]

spȧ·ġyr'iç, *a.* spagiric. [Obs.]

spȧ·ġyr'iç, *n.* a spagirist. [Obs.]

spaġ'y·rist, *n.* a spagirist. [Obs.]

spä'hï, spä'hee, *n.* [Turk. *sipāhī*; Pers. *sipāhee*, soldier.]
1. formerly, one of the Turkish organizations of cavalry, disbanded in 1826.
2. a native Algerian cavalry soldier in the French army.

spāid, *n.* spayed. [Obs.]

spāke, *v.* archaic past tense of *speak.*

spāke'net, *n.* a net used in catching crabs.

spạld'ing knīfe (nīf), a knife used in splitting codfish: also called *spalting knife.*

spāle, *n.* [ME. *spale*; Ice. *spölr*, a rail, bar, or short piece.]
1. a chip or splinter of wood; a lath. [Scot.]
2. in shipbuilding, a cross timber used as a temporary brace.

spāle, *v.t.*; spaled, *pt., pp.*; spaling, *ppr.* [from *spall*, to splinter; possibly connected with *spill.*]
1. to fine for breach of some rule of a mine. [Brit. Dial.]
2. in mining, to spall.
3. in shipbuilding, to brace with spales.

spạll, *n.* 1. in anatomy, the shoulder. [Obs.]
2. a flake or chip, especially of stone.

spạll, *v.t.*; spalled, *pt., pp.*; spalling, *ppr.* [D. *spell*, a chip; Old and Prov. G. *spellen*, to split.]
1. in mining, to break, as ore, with a hammer, previous to cobbing.
2. in masonry, to reduce irregular blocks of stone to an approximately level surface.

spạll, *v.i.* to give off spalls; to chip, as a stone.

spạll'ing ham"mẽr, a heavy ax-shaped hammer used in rough-dressing stones.

spạl·peen', *n.* [Ir. *spailpīn*, a rascal, from *spailp*, a beau, also conceit.] a mean fellow; a scamp; a good-for-nothing. [Irish.]

spạlt, *a.* brittle; liable to break or split. [Brit. Dial.]

spạlt, *v.t.* and *v.i.* [Dan. *spalte*, to split.] to split off, as chips from timber. [Brit. Dial.]

span, *v.* archaic past tense of *spin.*

span, *n.* [AS. *span, sponn*; Ice. *spönn*; Dan. *spand*; D. *span*, the measure of a span.]
1. the space from the end of the thumb to the end of the little finger when extended; nine inches.
2. the full amount or extent between any two limits; as, the *span* of life; also, the distance between two ends or supports; as, the *span* of an arch.
3. a part between two supports; as, a bridge of four *spans.*
4. a pair of horses; a yoke of animals; a team of two animals used together.
5. a short space of time.
6. in nautical usage, (a) a rope secured at both ends to an object, the purchase being hooked into the bight; (b) a leader for running rigging, conducted through a thimble at each end of the span, which is secured to the stay.
7. in aeronautics, the length or spread of a wing; the distance between the wing tips.
8. in psychology, breadth of comprehension, when referring to the amount of material dealt with in a single psychological reaction; as, the *span* of memory.

span, *v.t.*; spanned, *pt., pp.*; spanning, *ppr.*
1. to measure with the hand, having the thumb and little finger extended; also, to measure with the hand or hands encompassing the object; as, to *span* a wrist.
2. to extend, reach, pass, or stretch across or over, as a bridge.
3. to furnish with something that extends or stretches over; as, we *spanned* the aisle with an arch.
4. in nautical usage, to confine with ropes; as, to *span* the booms.
5. to shackle the legs of, as a horse; to hobble. [Brit. Dial.]
6. to measure in any way.
7. to cock with a spanner. [Rare.]
8. in South Africa, to attach, as horses or oxen, to a carriage, cart, etc.

span, *v.i.* 1. to travel by regular stages; to measure distances from point to point.
2. to agree in color or in size; as, the horses *span* well.

span, *adv.* entirely; wholly; as, *span*-new clothes.

spȧ·nae'mi·ȧ, *n.* same as *spanemia.*

span bēam, in mining, the horizontal beam into which the upper pivot of the axis of the whim is journaled.

span block, in nautical usage, a block attached to each end of a span or length of rope which lies across a cap and hangs down at each side.

span'cel, *n.* [AS. *spannan*, to join, and *sâl*, a rope, a fastening.] a rope used to hobble a horse or to tie a cow's hind legs while milking; a tether.

span'cel, *v.t.*; spanceled *or* spancelled, *pt., pp.*; spanceling *or* spancelling, *ppr.* 1. to tie the legs of, as a horse or cow, with a rope; to hobble.
2. to place a peg, etc., in the claws of, as a crab, to prevent pinching.

span'-çoun"tẽr, *n.* an old game consisting in the tossing of a coin so that it will rest upon one previously thrown or come within spanning distance of it: also called *span farthing.*

span'doġṣ, *n.pl.* a pair of iron hooks with sharp claws at one end, linked together, and used to grapple timber, the fangs of the extended ends being driven into the log.

span'drel, *n.* [OFr. *esplanader*, to level, plane, lay even.]
1. in architecture, the triangular space between the outer curve of an arch and a rectangular frame or mold enclosing it.

S S, SPANDRELS

2. one of the spaces between a series of arches and a straight cornice running above them.

span'drel wạll, a wall built on the extrados of an arch.

spāne, *v.t.*; spaned, *pt., pp.*; spaning, *ppr.* [AS. *spanu, spana*, a teat.] to wean. [Brit. Dial.]

spȧ·nē'mi·ȧ, *n.* [Gr. *spanis*, scarcity, and *haima*, blood.] anemia.

spȧ·nē'miç, *a.* relating to spanemia; anemic.

spȧ·nē'my, *n.* same as *spanemia.*

spang, *v.t.* to decorate with spangles. [Obs.]

spang, *n.* a spangle. [Obs.]

spang, *v.i.* to spring; to jump. [Scot.]

spang, *v.t.* to cause to spring; also, to throw violently. [Scot.]

spang, *n.* a spring; a leap; also, a violent blow. [Scot.]

spang, *n.* a span. [Scot.]

spang, *adv.* directly; exactly; entirely; wholly; as, he went *spang* into the wall. [Colloq.]

spañ'gle, *n.* [dim. of *spang*, a spangle; AS. *spange*, a buckle, a clasp; D. *spang*; Ice. *spong*, a spangle, a stud.]
1. a small plate or boss of shining metal, especially one of many sewn on fabric as an ornament.
2. any little thing sparkling and brilliant.
3. a spongy excrescence on the leaves and branches of an oak.

spañ'gle, *v.t.*; spangled, *pt., pp.*; spangling, *ppr.* to set, sprinkle, or adorn with spangles or other small, brilliant objects; as, a *spangled* breastplate.

spañ'gle, *v.i.* to glitter with or as with spangles.

spañ'gled (-gld), *a.* adorned with spangles.
spangled coquette; a hummingbird, *Lophornis reginæ*, with crest and brilliant neck plumage.

spañ'glẽr, *n.* one who or that which spangles.

spañ'gly, *a.*; *comp.* spanglier; *superl.* spangliest; of, like, or made up of spangles; glittering; glistening.

spañ'gō·līte, *n.* [after Norman *Spang*, of Pittsburgh, Pa.] a hydrous aluminum-copper sulfate occurring in hexagonal crystals of a dark-green color.

Span'iărd (-yărd), *n.* a native or inhabitant of Spain.

span'iel (-yel), *n.* [OFr. *espagneul*; Fr. *épagneul*; lit., a little Spanish dog, from LL. *Hispaniolus*, Spanish, from L. *Hispania*, Spain.]
1. any of several breeds of small and medium-sized dogs characterized by a rather broad muzzle, long, drooping ears, thick hair waved or tightly curled, a small tail, and short legs: spaniels are divided into three main

classes, *field spaniels* (used for hunting), *water spaniels*, and *toy spaniels* (chiefly pets).

SPANIEL

2. a cringing, fawning person; a sycophant.

span'iel, *a.* like a spaniel; fawning.

span'iel, *v.i.*; spanieled, *pt., pp.*; spanieling, *ppr.* to fawn; to cringe; to be obsequious. [Rare.]

span'iel, *v.t.* to follow like a spaniel. [Rare.]

Span'i·ō·līze, *v.t.* and *v.i.* to become or cause to become Spanish in character, sentiments, etc. [Rare.]

Span'ish, *a.* of or belonging to Spain, its people, their language, etc.; as, the *Spanish* customs.

Spanish arbor vine; same as *arbor vine*.
Spanish Armada; same as *armada*, sense 2.
Spanish bayonet; a species of yucca, *Yucca aloifolia*, growing in deserts, having sword-shaped, sharp-pointed rigid leaves: also *Spanish dagger*.
Spanish bean; same as *scarlet bean* under *scarlet*.
Spanish berry; same as *Persian berry* under *Persian*.
Spanish black; a pigment obtained from burnt cork.
Spanish broom; a shrub, *Spartium junceum*, of the Mediterranean region, having green, flexible rushlike twigs.
Spanish brown; earth used in pigments, its color depending upon the iron oxide which it contains.
Spanish buckeye; a small tree, *Ungnadia speciosa*, of the southwestern United States and Mexico, having pinnate leaves and a three-seeded fruit.
Spanish bugloss; same as *alkanet* (sense 1).
Spanish burton; same as *burton*.
Spanish cedar; a tree, *Cedrela australis*, of South and Central America yielding a light, aromatic wood used in making cigar boxes, etc.; also, its wood.
Spanish chalk; a variety of steatite or soapstone, obtained from Aragon, in Spain.
Spanish chesinut; the common chestnut of southern Europe.
Spanish cockle; a large bivalve of the West Indies, *Codakia tigrina*.
Spanish cress; a species of pepperwort, *Lepidium cardamines*.
Spanish curlew; (a) the long-billed curlew; (b) [Dial.] the white ibis.
Spanish dagger; same as *Spanish bayonet*.
Spanish elm; same as *princewood*.
Spanish fly; a bright-green beetle of southern Europe: it is finely ground and used in medicine as a blistering agent, diuretic, or genito-urinary stimulant; cantharides.
Spanish grass; same as *esparto*.
Spanish juice; the extract of the root of the licorice, *Glycyrrhiza glabra*.
Spanish Inquisition; the Inquisition as reorganized in Spain in 1478 under the control of the Spanish sovereigns: notorious for its cruel and extreme practices: see *inquisition*.
Spanish lace; any lace made in Spain, especially one of black silk in a floral pattern.
Spanish ladyfish; same as *ladyfish*, sense 2.
Spanish leather; same as cordovan, sense 1.
Spanish mackerel; any of various edible sea fishes related to the mackerel.
Spanish Main; (a) formerly, the mainland of America adjacent to the Caribbean Sea; especially, the northern coast of South America, from the Isthmus of Panama to the mouth of the Orinoco River; (b) later, the Caribbean Sea, or that part of it adjacent to the northern coast of South America, formerly traveled by Spanish merchant ships sailing between the Eastern and Western Hemispheres.
Spanish moss; a mosslike plant having small flowers and slender, gray stems with tiny leaves: it usually hangs in long, graceful strands from the branches of trees: also called *Florida moss*.
Spanish n; in printing, the letter *n* with a tilde over it, ñ.
Spanish needles; a plant of the genus *Bidens*, with small, spiny, hard, dry fruit; also, the fruit itself.
Spanish nut; a bulbous plant of southern Europe, *Moræa sisyrinchium*.
Spanish oak; same as *pin oak*.
Spanish onion; a large, mild-flavored kind of onion, often eaten raw.
Spanish oyster plant; see under *oyster plant*.
Spanish pack; in card playing, a pack of cards with the eights, nines, and tens left out.
Spanish paprika; (a) a mild red pepper of Spanish origin; (b) the plant on which it grows.
Spanish porgy; a brilliantly colored West Indian fish, of the genus *Scarus*.
Spanish potato; the sweet potato, *Ipomœa batatas*.
Spanish red; a color resembling Venetian red.
Spanish reef; a knot tied in the head of the jib.
Spanish rider; a herisson. [Rare.]
Spanish sheep; the merino.
Spanish soap; soap made with olive oil; Castile soap.
Spanish sword; a long rapier.
Spanish white; a pigment prepared from chalk which has been separated by washing.
Spanish windlass; an apparatus for setting up rigging, etc.: it consists of a wooden roller, about which a rope is wound, having an iron bolt inserted in its bight for heaving the roller around.
to walk Spanish; to walk or act as under compulsion. [Dial.]

Span'ish, *n.* the Romance language of Spain and of Spanish America: its dialects include Aragonese, Asturian, Andalusian (the basis of the Spanish spoken in Spanish America), and Castilian (the standard language of Spain).
the Spanish; the Spanish people.

Span"ish-Ȧ·mer'i·çăn, *a.* 1. of both Spain and America.
2. of Spanish America or its people.
Spanish-American war; the war between the United States and Spain (1898).

Span"ish-Ȧ·mer'i·çăn, *n.* a native or inhabitant of Spanish America, especially one of Spanish descent.

Span'ish flag, a fish, *Sebastes rubrivinctus*, of the California coast, having bright crimson crossbars on a pale rose red.

spank, *v.t.*; spanked (spankt), *pt., pp.*; spanking, *ppr.* [echoic.] to strike with the open hand; especially, to slap with something flat, as with the open hand, upon the buttocks.

spank, *v.i.* to move with a quick, lively step between a trot and a gallop.

spank, *n.* a smart slap with the open hand.

spank'ẽr, *n.* 1. one who or that which spanks.
2. a fleet horse. [Colloq.]
3. anything big, dashing, or mettlesome; a stunner; a whopper. [Colloq.]
4. a gold coin. [Obs.]
5. in nautical usage, (a) a fore-and-aft sail, usually hoisted on a gaff, on the aftermast of a square-rigged vessel: also called *driver*; (b) the aftermast and its sail on a schooner-rigged vessel of more than three masts.

S S SPANKER, sense 5 (a)

spank'ẽr boom, the boom which serves to extend the foot of a spanker.

spank'ing, *a.* 1. moving with a quick, lively pace; rapid.
2. brisk; strong: said of a wind, breeze, etc.
3. large; dashing; stunning. [Colloq.]

span'less, *a.* not to be spanned; not to be measured.

span'nẽr, *n.* 1. one who or that which spans.
2. the lock of a fusee or carbine. [Obs.]
3. a fusee or carbine. [Obs.]
4. [G., from *spannen*, to stretch.] a tool for tightening up or loosening the nuts upon screws; a wrench. [Brit.]
5. a fireman's wrench by which are fastened or unfastened the couplings of a hose.
6. a bar used in parallel motion of the side-lever marine engine; also, in some earlier engines, the handbar or lever by which the valves were moved to admit or shut off steam.
7. a cross brace.

span'-new, *a.* [ME. *spannewe*; Ice. *spān-nȳr*, entirely new; *spānn*, a chip, shaving, and *nȳr*, new.] perfectly new. [Dial.]

span'pïēce, *n.* the collar beam of a framed roof.

span'wŏrm, *n.* the larva of a geometrid moth; a measuring worm.

Spar, SPAR (spär), *n.* [from *semper paratus* (always prepared), L. motto of the U. S. Coast Guard.] a member of the United States Coast Guard Women's Reserve (SPARS).

spär, *n.* [AS. *spær*, *spærstan*, a kind of stone.] any of various crystalline minerals which easily break into rhomboidal, cubical, or laminated fragments with polished surfaces, but without metallic luster; as, blue *spar*, lazulite; calcareous *spar*, calcite; cube *spar*, anhydrite; adamantine *spar*, corundum; heavy *spar*, barite; tabular *spar*, wollastonite; Iceland *spar*, a transparent, doubly refracting calcite, etc.

spär, *n.* [ME. *sparre*; Ice. *sparri*, *sperra*, a spar, a rafter; Dan. *sparre*, a rafter; O.H.G. *sparro*, a beam, a bar.] any pole; specifically, (a) a long, wooden beam, generally rounded, and used for supporting or extending the sails of a ship, as a mast, yard, boom, gaff, or sprit; (b) [Archaic] a rafter of a roof; (c) [Obs.] the bar of a gate or door; (e) in aviation, a structural member of an airplane wing, running the length of the wing and supporting the ribs.

spär, *v.t.*; sparred, *pt., pp.*; sparring, *ppr.* 1. to bar; to shut close; to fasten with a bar. [Obs.]
2. to rig or supply with spars.

spär, *v.i.*; sparred, *pt., pp.*; sparring, *ppr.* [OFr. *esparer*; It. *sparare*, to fling out the hind legs, to kick.]
1. to strike with the feet and spurs: said of gamecocks.
2. to box, especially with skill and some caution, landing few heavy blows.
3. to quarrel; to wrangle.

spär, *v.t.* to engage in a boxing match with.

spär, *n.* 1. in boxing, a maneuver of offense or defense; also, the boxing contest itself.
2. a debate or argument.
3. a cockfight.

spar'ȧ·ble, *n.* [altered from *sparrow bill*: from the shape.] a small, headless nail used by shoemakers.

spā·rä'dȧ, *n.* a marine fish, *Micrometrus aggregatus*, found along the Pacific coast of North America.

spar'ȧ·drap, *n.* [Fr.] a cerecloth. [Obs.]

spar'ăge, *n.* asparagus. [Obs.]

spar'ȧ·gràss, spar'ȧ·gus, *n.* asparagus. [Obs.]

Spȧ·rax'is, *n.* a genus of the *Iridaceæ*, native to the Cape of Good Hope, having brightly colored flowers and sword-shaped leaves.

spär'ble, *v.t.* to cause to scatter; to disperse. [Obs.]

spär buoy (boy), a buoy in the shape of a spar with the free end rising above the water.

spär'çle, *n.* and *v.* sparkle. [Obs.]

spär deck, the upper deck running the full length of a ship.

spär dust, the wood dust made by the boring of insects.

spāre, *v.t.*; spared, *pt., pp.*; sparing, *ppr.* [ME.; *sparien*; AS. *sparian*; Ice. and Sw. *spara*; Dan. *spare*; G. and D. *sparen*, to spare.]
1. to treat with mercy or lenience; to save; to refrain from killing, injuring, troubling, or distressing.
2. to save or free (a person) from (something); as, she was *spared* the agony of seeing the accident, we have *spared* you the trouble.
3. to refrain from, omit, avoid using, or use frugally; as, don't *spare* your efforts.
4. to give up the use or possession of; to get along without; to dispense with; as, I can't *spare* the money or the time.
5. to part with or give up conveniently.

spāre, *v.i.* 1. to live frugally; to be parsimonious.
2. to use mercy or forbearance; to be restrained, as in punishing.

spāre, *a.* 1. scanty; frugal; not abundant; as, a *spare* diet.
2. not taken up with regular duties; free: said of time.
3. held in reserve; not in regular use or immediately needed; extra; as, a *spare* anchor.
4. lean; not fleshy; thin.
5. slow. [Brit. Dial.]

Syn.—scanty, unplentiful, reserved, meager, economical, frugal, stinted, restricted, parsimonious, niggardly, chary, superfluous, disposable, available, lean, thin, ill-conditioned.

spâre, *n.* 1. parsimony; frugality; economy. [Obs.]
 2. in bowling, the act of knocking down ten pins with two consecutive rolls of the ball; also, a score so made.
 3. a placket in a woman's skirt. [Obs.]
 4. a spare, or extra, part, thing, etc.; as, a *spare* tire.

spâre'-built (-bilt), *a.* not robust; of a slight build; slender.

spâre'fụl, *a.* chary; sparing. [Obs.]

spâre'fụl·ness, *n.* the state of being spareful. [Obs.]

spâre'less, *a.* unsparing. [Rare.]

spâre'ly, *adv.* so as to be spare; sparingly; scantily.

spâre'ness, *n.* the state of being spare.

spâre pärt, an extra part or a duplicate of anything, to be used in emergencies.

spâr'ẽr, *n.* one who or that which spares.

spâre'rib, *n.* [prob. altered (after *spare, a.*) from M.L.G. *ribbespēr.*] a cut of pork consisting of the thin end of the rib with most of the meat cut away.

spâre rọọm, an extra bedroom, not ordinarily used: called also a *guest room.*

spâre'sǒme, *a.* economical; frugal.

spär·gȧ·nō'sis, *n.* spargosis. [Obs.]

spärġe, *v.t.* and *v.i.*; sparged, *pt., pp.*; sparging, *ppr.* [L. *spargere,* to sprinkle.] to splash or sprinkle.

spär·ġē·fac'tion, *n.* the act of sprinkling. [Obs.]

spär'ġẽr, *n.* a sprinkler; specifically, a container with a perforated lid, used for dampening clothes, etc.

spär·gō'sis, *n.* [Gr. *spargōsis,* a swelling.] abnormal distention of the breasts with milk.

spär'hawk, *n.* a sparrow hawk. [Brit. Dial.]

spar'id, *n.* any fish of the family *Sparidæ.*

Spar'i·dae, *n.pl.* [L. *sparus,* the gilthead, and Gr. *eidos,* likeness.] a family of spiny-finned, teleostean fishes, of which the genus *Sparus* is the type. They somewhat resemble the perches in form, the body being generally ovate and covered with large scales. The *Sparidæ* are mostly inhabitants of warm climates. *Sparus aurata* is the European gilthead.

SPARID
(*Sparus aurata*)

spâr'ing, *a.* 1. that spares.
 2. careful; frugal.
 3. scanty, meager, or limited.

spâr'ing·ly, *adv.* in a sparing manner.

spâr'ing·ness, *n.* the quality of being sparing.

spärk, *n.* [ME. *sparke, sperke, spearke;* AS. *spearca;* D. *spark, sperk,* from the same root as L. *spargere,* to scatter, sprinkle.]
 1. a small, glowing piece of matter, especially one thrown off by a fire.
 2. any flash or sparkle of light like this.
 3. a particle or trace; as, a *spark* of interest.
 4. a trace of life or animation; a particle of vitality.
 5. (a) the small, brief flash of light accompanying the discharge, or arcing, of an electric current from one point to another, as between the points of a spark plug; (b) such a discharge; (c) a device controlling such a discharge, as in an internal-combustion engine.

spärk, *v.i.* 1. to produce or give off sparks.
 2. to come forth as or like sparks.
 3. to form the sparks properly: said of the ignition in an internal-combustion engine.

spärk, *v.t.* to serve as the activating or animating influence of or in; to kindle or fire into activity, especially of a vigorous and sustained kind.

spärk, *n.* [Ice. *sparkr,* lively.]
 1. a gay, dashing, gallant young man.
 2. a lover; a beau. [Colloq.]

spärk, *v.i.* and *v.t.*; sparked (spärkt), *pt., pp.*; sparking, *ppr.* to court; to woo. [Colloq.]

spärk är·res'tẽr, 1. a device used on a locomotive to keep the sparks from escaping the smokestack; also, any similar device.
 2. in electricity, a device used to prevent sparking.

spärk çoil, an electric induction coil producing a spark, as in an internal-combustion engine.

spärk çŏn·dens'ẽr, in electricity, an instrument having a glass cage, in which a spark may be passed between the battery connections: it is used for burning metals or obtaining the spectra of gases, and is designed to isolate the atmosphere in which the experiment is conducted.

spärk'ẽr, *n.* 1. a spark arrester (sense 2).
 2. a person or thing that sparks.
 3. in the British navy, a wireless operator. [Slang.]
 4. a lady's man; a lover or gallant. [Slang.]
 5. a means for igniting fuel in certain internal-combustion engines.

spärk'fụl, *a.* smart. [Obs.]

spärk gap, in electricity, (a) the air space or gap through which a disruptive discharge passes; (b) a gap forming part of a circuit between two opposing terminals across which sparks pass.

spärk'ish, *a.* of or like a gay, dashing, gallant young man.

spär'kle, *v.i.*; sparkled, *pt., pp.*; sparkling, *ppr.* [ME. *sparklen,* freq. of *sparken,* to spark.]
 1. to give off sparks.
 2. to gleam or shine intermittently; to glitter; to glisten, as jewels, wet grass in the sun, etc.
 3. to be brilliant and lively; as, her wit *sparkled.*
 4. to effervesce.

spär'kle, *v.t.* to cause to sparkle.

spär'kle, *n.* 1. a spark; a glowing particle.
 2. a sparkling, or glittering.
 3. brilliance; liveliness; vivacity.

spär'kle, *v.t.* and *v.i.* 1. to disperse; to scatter. [Dial.]
 2. to sprinkle. [Obs.]

spär'klẽr, *n.* 1. one who or that which sparkles; specifically, (a) a noiseless, sparkling, pencil-shaped firework; (b) [*pl.*] [Colloq.] eyes that are clear and brilliant; (c) a diamond or other sparkling gem.
 2. a tiger beetle.

spärk'less, *a.* free from sparks; not giving off sparks.

spärk'let, *n.* a small spark.

spärk'li·ness, *n.* vivacity. [Obs.]

spär'kling, *a.* 1. that sparkles or sparks; glittering, brilliant, or lively.
 2. effervescent.

spär'kling·ly, *adv.* with twinkling or vivid brilliancy.

spär'kling·ness, *n.* vivid or twinkling luster.

spär'kling wạ'tẽr, soda water.

spärk mi·crom'ē·tẽr, in electricity, a device for the adjustment of a spark gap.

spärk plug, a piece fitted into the cylinder of an internal-combustion engine to ignite the fuel mixture within: it carries an electric current into the cylinder, which sparks between two terminals in the presence of the mixture.

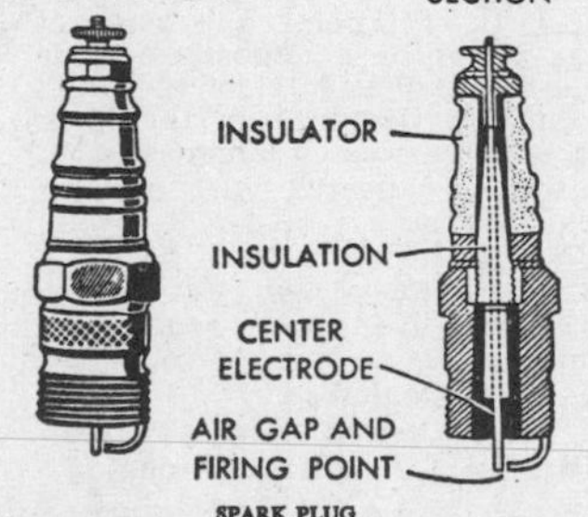

SPARK PLUG

spär'ling, *n.* [ME. *sparlyng;* OFr. *esperlanc;* LL. *sperlingus,* a smelt.]
 1. the European smelt.
 2. a young herring.
 3. a tern. [Brit. Dial.]

spär'ling fowl, the merganser of Europe. [Brit. Dial.]

spăr'oid, *a.* [L. *sparus,* gilthead, and *-oid.*] like the gilthead; belonging to the *Sparidæ,* a family of fishes which includes the gilthead, sea bream, porgy, scup, sheepshead, etc.

spăr'oid, *n.* any of the *Sparidæ.*

spär'rẽr, *n.* a boxer; one who spars.

spär'ring, *n.* in boxing, maneuvering for advantage; also, practice or training for a boxing contest.
 2. verbal disputation.
 sparring partner; any person with whom a prize fighter boxes for practice.

spar'rōw, *n.* [ME. *sparwe;* AS. *spearwa;* Goth. *sparwa;* Dan. *spurv;* Ice. *sporr,* sparrow; lit., a flutterer.] any of several small weaverbirds or birds of the finch family, *Fringillidae,* especially the common small bird, *Passer domesticus* (*house sparrow*), usually known in America as the *English sparrow:* others are the European or American *tree sparrow,* the American *song sparrow, chipping sparrow, sage sparrow,* etc.

spar'rōw·bill, *n.* a small, headless nail; a sparable.

spar'rōw·gràss, *n.* asparagus. [Colloq.]

spar'rōw hạwk, 1. a small European hawk with short wings, *Accipiter nisus.*
 2. a small falcon, *Falco sparverius,* of North America, that feeds on insects and small birds and game.
 3. any of several hawks or falcons resembling either of these.

SPARROW HAWK
(*Accipiter nisus*)

spar'rōw owl, any of the small owls of the genus *Glaucidium.*

spar'rōw tŏngue (tung), the knotgrass.

spar'rōw·wŏrt, *n.* any plant of the genus *Passerina.*

spär'ry, *a.*; *comp.* sparrier; *superl.* sparriest,
 1. of or like spar.
 2. rich in spar, as land.
 sparry iron; carbonate of iron.

spärse, *a.* [L. *sparsus,* pp. of *spargere,* to scatter.]
 1. thinly scattered or distributed; not dense or crowded; as, a *sparse* population.
 2. in botany, not opposite, nor alternate, nor in any apparent regular order: applied to branches, leaves, and peduncles.

spärse, *v.t.* to disperse. [Obs.]

spärs'ed·ly, *adv.* sparsely; thinly.

spärse'ly, *adv.* in a sparse manner.

spär'sile, *a.* in astronomy, scattered. [Rare.]

spär'si·ty, *n.* the condition of being sparse.

Spär'tȧ·çăn, *a.* of or relating to the most extreme of the German radicals after the fall of the Hohenzollerns.

Spär'tȧ·çăn, *n.* a member of the Spartacan group of German radicals.

Spär'tăn, *a.* 1. of ancient Sparta, its people, or their culture.
 2. like or characteristic of the Spartans; warlike, brave, hardy, stoical, severe, frugal, highly disciplined, etc.
 Spartan dog; a bloodhound.

Spär'tăn, *n.* 1. a citizen or native of Sparta.
 2. a person with Spartan traits.

Spär'tăn·ịsm, *n.* 1. the folkways, strict standards of discipline and fortitude, attitudes, etc. of the ancient Spartans.
 2. any similar standards, etc.

spär'tē·in, *n.* same as *sparteine.*

spär'tē·ine, *n.* [L. *spartum,* Spanish broom.] an oily liquid, $C_{15}H_{26}N_2$, derived from broom and used in medicine as a heart stimulant.

spär'tẽr·ie, *n.* [Sp. *esparto,* from L. *spartum,* broom.] the various articles made from esparto grass, as mats, nets, cordage, ropes, etc.

spärth, *n.* a battle ax, halberd, or mace. [Obs.]

spâr'y, *a.* parsimonious; penurious. [Rare.]

spaşm, *n.* [OFr. *spasme;* L. *spasmus,* from Gr. *spasmos,* from *spān,* to draw, to pull, to wrench.]
 1. an abnormal, sudden, and involuntary contraction of one or more muscles or muscular fibers. Spasm is either clonic or tonic. In clonic spasm, the muscles or muscular fibers contract and relax alternately in very quick succession, producing the appearance of agitation, as in epilepsy. In tonic spasm the muscles or muscular fibers contract in a steady and uniform manner, and remain contracted for a comparatively long time, as in tetanus.
 2. any sudden, violent, temporary effort, emotion, action, etc.; as, a *spasm* of remorse.

spaş·mat'iç·ăl, *a.* spasmodic. [Rare.]

spaş·mod'iç, spaş·mod'iç·ăl, *a.* [Fr. *spasmodique;* Gr. *spasmos,* spasm, and *eidos,* likeness.]

1. relating to, consisting in, or characterized by a spasm or spasms; sudden, violent, and temporary; fitful; intermittent; as, *spasmodic* stricture.
2. characterized by emotional outbursts or excitability.
spasmodic croup; a spasm of the muscles of the glottis, with general symptoms of croup but without the secretions.

spaș·mod′iç·ăl·ly, *adv.* in a spasmodic manner.

spaș·mō′tin, *n.* a poisonous acid principle, $C_{20}H_{21}O_9$, from ergot.

spaș·mō·tox′in, *n.* [Gr. *spasmos*, spasm, and E. *toxin*.] a poison secreted by the tetanus bacillus.

spas′tiç, *a.* [L. *spasticus*; Gr. *spastikos*, drawing, pulling, from *spān*, to draw.] of or characterized by spasm; specifically, designating a form of paralysis in which certain muscles are in a state of continuous contraction, causing rigidity of a normally movable part.

spas′tiç, *n.* a person with spastic paralysis.

spas′tiç·ăl·ly, *adv.* in a spastic manner.

spas·tic′i·ty, *n.* 1. a state of spasm.
2. the tendency to or capability of suffering spasm.

spat, *v.* alternative past tense and past participle of *spit*.

spat, *n.* [imitative, like *pat*.]
1. a light blow or slap; also, the sound of such a slap. [Colloq.]
2. a brief, petty quarrel or dispute. [Colloq.]

spat, *v.i.*; spatted, *pt.*, *pp.*; spatting, *ppr.* 1. to have a trivial quarrel. [Colloq.]
2. to slap.

spat, *v.t.* to slap.

spat, *n.* a small splash or spatter; as, *spats* of paint.

spat, *n.* [contr. from *spatterdash*.] [*usually in pl.*] a covering for the instep and ankle, usually of heavy cloth; a short gaiter.

spat, *n.* [ME.; Anglo-Fr.; prob. akin to *spit*.]
1. the spawn of the oyster or other bivalve shellfish.
2. (a) young of oysters collectively; (b) a young oyster.

spat, *v.i.*; spatted, *pt.*, *pp.*; spatting, *ppr.* to spawn: said of oysters.

Spȧ·tan′ġi·dȧ, *n.pl.* same as *Spatangoida*.

spȧ·tañ′goid, *a.* relating to the order *Spatangoida*.

spȧ·tañ′goid, *n.* any one of the *Spatangoida*.

Spat·añ·goi′dȧ, *n.pl.* an order of sea urchins of which the genus *Spatangus* is the type.

Spat·añ·goi′dē·ȧ, *n.pl.* same as *Spatangoida*.

Spȧ·tañ′gus, *n.* [L., from Gr. *spatangēs*, a sea urchin.] a genus of *Echinoidea*, or sea urchins, order *Spatangoida*, consisting of the heart urchins.

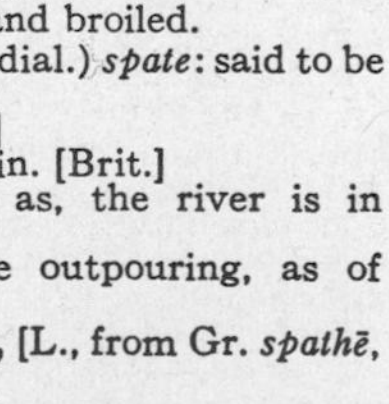
SPATANGOID (*Spatangus purpureus*) one half shown with its spines removed

spatch′çock, *n.* [possibly from *dispatch*.] a fowl killed and immediately dressed and broiled.

spāte, *n.* [ME. (northern dial.) *spate*: said to be from OFr. *espoit*.]
1. a flash flood. [Brit.]
2. a sudden, heavy rain. [Brit.]
3. flooded condition; as, the river is in *spate*. [Brit.]
4. an unusually large outpouring, as of words.

spā′thȧ, *n.*; *pl.* **spā′thae,** [L., from Gr. *spathē*, a broad, flat blade.]
1. a heavy two-edged broadsword.
2. a spathe.

spȧ·thā′ceous, *a.* 1. having a spathe.
2. of, or having the nature of, a spathe.

spā′thăl, *a.* having a spathe.

spāthe, *n.* [Fr.; L. *spatha*; Gr. *spathē*, flat blade.] a large, leaflike part or pair of such parts enclosing a flower cluster (especially a spadix).

spāthed, *a.* having a spathe.

SPATHE

spath′iç, *a.* of or like spar; foliated or lamellar.
spathic iron; siderite.

spath′i·fọrm, *a.* resembling spar in form.

spȧ·thil′lȧ, *n.* a minor or secondary spathe, as in the spadix of certain palms. [Rare.]

spath′ōse, *a.* spathic.

spā′thōse, *a.* spathaceous.

spā′thous, *a.* spathaceous.

spath′ū·lāte, *a.* in botany, spatulate.

spā′tiăl (-shăl), *a.* [L. *spatium*, space.]
1. of or relating to space.
2. happening or existing in space.

spā′tiăl·ly, *adv.* with relation to space; also, in or by means of space.

spā′ti·āte (-shi-), *v.i.* [L. *spatiari*.] to rove; to ramble.

spā″ti·ō·tem′pō·răl (spā″shi-), *a.* existing in both space and time.

spat′tēr, *v.t.*; spattered, *pt.*, *pp.*; spattering, *ppr.* [from L.G.; cf. Fris. *spateren*, freq. of *spatten*, to splash, spurt.]
1. to scatter in drops or small blobs: said of soft or liquid substances; as, she *spattered* white paint over the red.
2. to splash or spot with such drops or blobs.
3. to injure the name or reputation of; to defame.

spat′tēr, *v.i.* 1. to splutter in speaking; to sputter.
2. to emit or spurt out in drops or small blobs, as a boiling liquid.
3. to fall or strike in or as in a shower, as raindrops or pellets.

spat′tēr, *n.* 1. the sound of spattering or a succession of spats; as, the *spatter* of raindrops on a roof.
2. a mark or wet spot caused by spattering; also, the thing spattered; as, a *spatter* of mud.
3. the act of spattering.

spat′tēr·dash, *n.* [*usually in pl.*] a long legging worn to protect the stocking or trouser leg from water and mud.

spat′tēr·dashed (-dasht), *a.* protected with spatterdashes.

spat′tēr·dock, *n.* 1. a common pond lily, *Nymphæa advena*, with thick roots, flat, heart-shaped leaves, and yellow, cup-shaped flowers.
2. any pond lily of the same or a related genus, especially one with yellow flowers.

spat′tēr·wŏrk, *n.* a method employed, as in pen-and-ink drawing, to produce a softly shaded surface.

spat′tle, *n.* 1. a spatula.
2. a mottling tool in ceramics.

spat′tling pop′py, [from *spat*, pt. of *spit*.] a plant, *Silene inflata*, of the pink family: also called *bladder campion*.

spat′ū·lȧ (spach′), *n.* [L., dim. of *spatha*; Gr. *spathē*, a broad, flat instrument.] a knifelike implement with a broad, flat, flexible blade, used for spreading or blending foods, paints, etc.

spat′ū·lăr, *a.* of or like a spatula.

spat′ū·lāte, *a.* shaped like a spatula or a spoon; resembling a spatula in shape, as some leaves.

SPATULATE LEAF

spauld, spawld, *n.* shoulder. [Obs.]

spav′in, *n.* [ME. *spaveyne*; OFr. *esparvain*; O.It. *spavano*.] a disease of horses in which a deposit of bone (*bone spavin*) or an infusion of lymph (*bog spavin*) develops in the hock joint, usually causing lameness.

spav′ined, *a.* affected with spavin; lame.

spaw, *n.* spa. [Obs.]

spawl, *v.i.*; spawled, *pt.*, *pp.*; spawling, *ppr.* [contr. from AS. *spadl*, *spatl*, spittle, from *spætan*, *spatan*, to spit.] to spit. [Archaic.]

spawl, *n.* spittle. [Obs.]

spawl, *n.* a fragment of stone; a spall.

spawl′ing, *n.* [*pl.*] spittle. [Archaic.]

spawn, *v.t.* and *v.i.* [ME. *spaunnen*; Anglo-Fr. *espaundre*; OFr. *espandre*, to shed, from L. *expandere*, to expand.]
1. to produce or deposit (spawn or eggs).
2. to bring forth or be the source of (especially something regarded with contempt and produced prolifically or in great quantity).
3. in horticulture, to plant with spawn, or mycelium.

spawn, *n.* 1. the mass of eggs emitted by fishes, mollusks, crustaceans, amphibians, etc.
2. something produced, especially in great quantity, or some person or thing regarded as a product or offspring: usually contemptuous.
3. the mycelium of fungi, especially of mushrooms grown to be eaten, used for propagation.

spawn′ēat″ēr, *n.* any fish feeding on spawn, as the carp.

spawn′ēr, *n.* 1. the female fish after maturity.
2. any producer of spawn.

spawn fuñ′gus, any fungus whose propagation is carried on by means of spawn, as the mushroom.

spāy, *v.t.*; spayed, *pt.*, *pp.*; spaying, *ppr.* [Anglo-Fr. *espeier*, from OFr. *espeer*, to cut with a sword, from *espee*, sword; L. *spatha*, broad, flat instrument.] to remove the ovaries of (a living animal); to sterilize (a female).

spāy, *n.* [etym. unknown.] a male red deer in his third year.

spēak, *v.i.*; spoke *or archaic* spake, *pt.*; spoken *or archaic* spoke, *pp.*; speaking, *ppr.* [ME. *speken*; AS. *specan*, *sprecan*, to speak.]
1. to utter words or articulate sounds in the ordinary voice; to talk.
2. to make a speech; to deliver an address or lecture; to discourse.
3. to express or communicate opinions, feelings, ideas, etc. by or as by talking; as, he would not *speak* on our behalf; actions *speak* louder than words.
4. to make mention; to tell by speech or writing.

> Lucan *speaks* of a part of Caesar's army
> that came to him from the Leman lake.
> —Addison.

5. to make or emit sound; to sound; as, the guns *spoke* sharply; they taught their dog to *speak* for food.
6. to communicate orally with another or others; to converse; as, they no longer *speak* to each other.
so to speak; in a manner of speaking; that is to say.
to speak for; (a) to speak in behalf of; (b) to evidence; to be a sign of; (c) to engage; to establish a claim to; (d) to ask for; to ask to have kept for onself.
to speak of; to talk about; to be worth mentioning; as, he has no money *to speak of*.
to speak out (or *up*); to declare openly, without reservation; also, to speak audibly or clearly.
to speak to; to admonish; to rebuke. [Colloq.]
to speak well for; to be a commendatory or favorable indication or sign.
to speak with; to converse with.

spēak, *v.t.* 1. to utter with the mouth; to pronounce; to utter articulately, as human beings; as, not to *speak* a word.
2. to tell; to say; to make known by or as by speaking; to declare; to announce; as, to *speak* the truth; to *speak* one's mind.
3. to proclaim; to celebrate; declare or show to be; as, his record *speaks* him a blackguard. [Archaic.]

> It is my father's music
> To *speak* your deeds. —Shak.

4. to use or be able to use (a given language) in speaking.
5. to address; to speak to.
6. in nautical usage, to hail (a ship).
Syn.—talk, discourse, utter, tell, say.

spēak′ȧ·ble, *a.* 1. that can, or can with propriety, be spoken.
2. having the power of speech. [Rare.]

spēak′ēaṣy, *n.*; *pl.* **spēak′ēaṣ·ies,** an establishment in which intoxicating liquor is sold illegally. [Slang.]

spēak′ēr, *n.* 1. a person who speaks; especially, (a) a person who makes a speech or speeches in public; (b) a person who speaks effectively in public; (c) the officer presiding over any of various lawmaking bodies; specifically, [S–] the presiding officer of the United States House of Representatives: in full, *Speaker of the House*.
2. a book of selections for use as exercises in declamation.
3. a loud-speaker.

spēak′ēr·ship, *n.* the office or position of speaker, or presiding officer.

spēak′house, *n.* a reception room in convents. [Obs.]

spēak′ing, *a.* 1. that speaks or seems to speak; expressive; eloquent; vivid; as, a *speaking* appearance of grief, a *speaking* likeness.
2. used in or for speech.
3. allowing or admitting of speech; as, he approached within *speaking* range; she had a *speaking* acquaintance with him.

on speaking terms; (a) making a practice of speaking or conversing (with another or each other); (b) having a relationship friendly enough to allow of speech or conversation, as in greeting.

spēak′ing, *n.* 1. the act or art of a person who speaks.
2. that which is spoken; utterance; discourse.

spēak′ing·ly, *adv.* in a speaking manner.

spēak′ing trump′et, a conical, flaring-mouthed tube employed for intensifying the sound of the human voice.

spēak′ing tūbe, a tube for communicating orally from one room to another.

spēar, *n.* [AS. *spere*; akin to D. *speer*, Dan. *sper*, Ice. *spjör*, L. *sparus*, a hunting spear. Probably akin to *spar*, a beam or rafter, and to *spire.*]

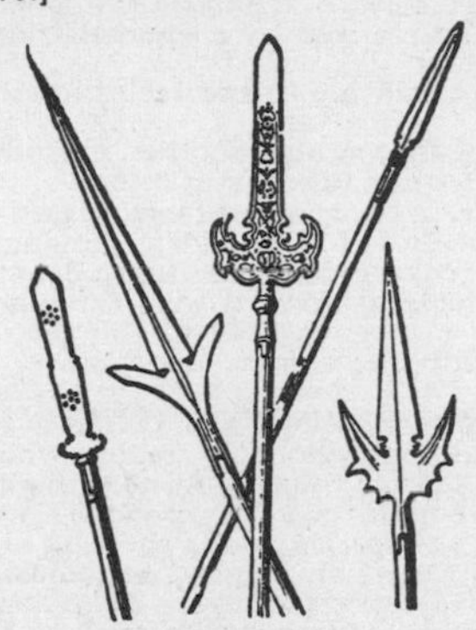

ANCIENT SPEARS

1. a weapon consisting of a long wooden shaft with a sharp point, usually of metal or stone, for thrusting or throwing; also, its point.
2. a sharp-pointed, often forked, instrument with barbs, used for thrusting, as in fishing.
3. a long blade or shoot, as of grass; a spire.
4. the feather of a horse.
5. a pump rod. [Brit.]
6. a spearman.
spear side; the paternal side or male line of a family.

spēar, *v.t.*; speared, *pt.*, *pp.*; spearing, *ppr.* 1. to pierce or stab with something pointed, as a spear.
2. to catch, as fish, with a spear.

spēar, *v.i.* 1. to shoot into a long stem: said of certain plants.
2. to pierce, penetrate, or shoot like a spear.

spēar′ẽr, *n.* one who spears; a spearman.

spēar′fish, *n.*; *pl.* **spēar′fish** or **spēar′fish·eṣ,** a large marine fish of the genus *Tetrapturus*, with a long, spearlike growth on its upper jaw, related to the swordfish and sailfish.

spēar foot, the off hind foot of a horse.

spēar gráss, any of various kinds of grass having long, spearlike leaves.

spēar hand, a horseman's right hand, in which the spear is held: the left hand is called the *shield hand.* [Archaic.]

spēar′head (-hed), *n.* 1. the head or point of a spear.
2. the leading person, part, or group in an endeavor, especially in a military attack.

spēar′head, *v.t.* to be the leading person, part, or group in (an attack, etc.); as, the Third Army *spearheaded* the invasion.

spēar′măn, *n.*; *pl.* **spēar′men,** one who is armed with a spear.

spēar′mint, *n.* [prob. so named from the appearance of the flowers on the stem.] a fragrant plant, *Mentha spicata*, of the mint family, used for flavoring.

spēar pȳ·ri′tēṣ, same as *marcasite.*

spēar this′tle (this′l), the common thistle.

spēar′wood, *n.* a tree, *Eucalyptus doratoxylon*, of southwest Australia; also, *Acacia doratoxylon*: the wood is used by the natives for spears.

spēar′wŏrt, *n.* any of a number of related plants of the crowfoot family, with spear-shaped leaves: the great spearwort is *Ranunculus lingua*, and the lesser spearwort, *Ranunculus flammula.*

spēar′y, *a.* shaped like a spear.

spe′ciăl (spesh′ăl), *a.* [OFr. *especial*; L. *specialis*, from *species*, kind, sort.]
1. unusual; uncommon; exceptional; extraordinary.
2. differing from others; distinctive, peculiar, or unique; as, the play requires a *special* stage.
3. designed for a particular purpose, occasion, person, etc.; as, a *special* edition, a *special* correspondent.
4. specified; definite; as, do you want any *special* kind?
5. especial; chief; as, her *special* friend, my *special* hate.
6. not general or regular; specific; limited; as, *special* legislation, a *special* tax.
special agent; an agent authorized to transact only a particular business for his principal: distinguished from a *general agent.*
special bail; see under *bail, n.* (surety).
special case; a statement of facts agreed to on behalf of two or more litigant parties, and submitted for the opinion of a court of justice as to the law bearing on the facts so stated.
special court-martial; a military court for judging offenses less grave than those judged by a general court-martial: it consists of three or more officers or (since 1948) enlisted men.
special damages; damages in addition to the act complained of or the loss or injury incurred.
special delivery; a postal service involving special handling and special messenger service, the purpose of which is to have a letter or package arrive at its destination before the regular mail delivery: the sender pays an extra fee for such service.
special demurrer; a demurrer in which the case is particularly stated.
special deposit; a bank deposit in which the depositor retains title to the thing delivered and the bank becomes a bailee under obligation to take ordinary care of the deposit and to return it to the owner on demand.
special endorsement; an endorsement of a note that restrains negotiability to a particular person, or for a special purpose.
special injunction; a prohibitory writ or interdict against acts of parties such as waste, nuisance, etc.
special issue; an issue which denies some one substantial point as decisive of the whole case.
special jury; see under *jury.*
special orders; in military usage, orders which concern only a particular corps, detail of officers, etc.
special partner; in law, a partner with restricted responsibility.
special plea; in law, a plea in bar in a criminal matter, not being a plea of the general issue.
special pleader; in law, a counsel whose professional occupation it is to give verbal or written opinions on matters submitted to him, and to draw pleadings, civil and criminal, and such practical proceedings as may be out of the usual course.
special pleading; (a) in law, the allegation that special or new matter exists that will offset matter presented by the other side; (b) an argument or presentation that leaves out what is unfavorable and develops only what is favorable to the case.
special property; in law, a right of a bailee in the thing bailed.
special session; a session, as of a legislature, called for the transaction of urgent or special business, or at an unusual time.
special student; a college student who does not pursue a regular course and who is not a candidate for a degree.
special term; in reference to courts having two or more judges, a term in which only one judge is in attendance; also, a term held for a special purpose.
special verdict; a verdict in which the jury state the bare facts as they find them to be and ask the advice of the court thereon.
Syn.—particular, specific, peculiar, appropriate, proper, distinctive, extraordinary, especial, exceptional.

spe′ciăl (spesh′ăl), *n.* a special or particular thing or person, as a special train, edition, etc.

spe′ciăl·iṣm (spesh′ăl-), *n.* 1. the following of a special field or branch of a profession or subject, as science or art; the distinctive work or study of a specialist; limitation to a specialty.
2. such a branch or field.

spe′ciăl·ist, *n.* a person who devotes himself to a particular branch of a profession, art, or science; a person who has studied and acquired specific knowledge on some particular subject; as, oculists and aurists are *specialists* as regards surgery.

spe′ciăl·ist, *a.* same as *specialistic.*

spe·ciăl·is′tiç, *a.* of a specialist or specialism.

spe·ci·al′i·ty (spe-shi-), *n.*; *pl.* **spe·ci·al′i·tieṣ,** [ME. *specialte*; OFr. *specialité.*]
1. a special or distinctive mark, quality, or characteristic.
2. [*pl.*] special points or details; particulars.
3. a specialty (in various senses).

spe″ciăl·i·zā′tion (spesh″ăl-), *n.* 1. the act of specializing or the state or quality of being specialized.
2. in biology, the process whereby organs or parts of common nature become differentiated in shape or function.

spe′ciăl·īze, *v.t.*; specialized, *pt.*, *pp.*; specializing, *ppr.* [Fr. *spécialiser.*]
1. to make special, specific, or particular; to specify; as, *specialize* your accusation.
2. to direct toward or concentrate on a specific end.
3. to adapt to a special condition, use, or requirement; as, a rooster's spurs are toes *specialized* for fighting.
4. to specify the payee in endorsing (a check, etc.).

spe′ciăl·īze, *v.i.* 1. to follow a special profession, study, or subject; to do a distinctive work; to take a specific turn.

The scholar should *specialize*; he should be an authority on one particular subject.
—George L. Scherger.

2. to become adapted to meet a special condition, use, etc., as parts of an organism.

spe′ciăl·ly, *adv.* 1. in a special manner; particularly; especially.
2. for a special or particular purpose; as, a meeting *specially* summoned.

spe′ciăl·ty, *n.*; *pl.* **spe′ciăl·tieṣ,** [ME. *specialte*; OFr. *especialte.*]
1. a special quality, feature, point, characteristic, etc.
2. a thing specialized in; special interest, field of study or professional work, etc.
3. the state of being special.
4. an article or product which is distinctive; something peculiar to the place of manufacture or characteristic of the producer and for which he claims special merit; as, boys' clothing a *specialty.*
5. in law, a special contract; an obligation or bond; the evidence of a debt by deed or instrument under seal.

spē′ciē (-shē), *n.* [the ablative form of L. *species*, and so used as an English word probably from its occurrence in the frequent phrase *paid in specie.*] gold, silver, and other coin, as distinguished from paper money; hard money.
in specie; (a) in kind; (b) in coin.

spē′cieṣ (-shēz), *n.*; *pl.* **spē′cieṣ,** [L., a seeing, that which is seen, appearance, shape, a peculiar sort, kind, or quality, from L. *specere*, to look at, to behold.]
1. outward appearance or form; mental image. [Obs.]
2. a public spectacle or exhibition; a show. [Obs.]
3. a single, distinct kind of plant or animal, having certain distinguishing characteristics: a category of biological classification: cf. *genus.*
4. in logic, a group of individuals or objects agreeing in common attributes and designated by a common name; a conception subordinated to another conception, called a genus or generic conception, from which it differs in containing or comprehending more attributes, and extending to fewer individuals; thus "man" is a *species* under "animal" as a *genus*, and "man" in its turn may be regarded as a *genus* with respect to European, Asiatic, and the like.

Man alone of the animal creation preys upon his own *species.*—Charles Sumner.

5. a distinct kind; sort; variety; description; as, a coarse *species* of wit; a *species* of low cunning; a fine *species* of cloth; a rare *species* of generosity.
6. specie. [Obs.]
7. (a) a component part of a compound medicine; a simple; (b) a compound powder of any kind.
8. in the Roman Catholic Church, (a) the outward form, or appearance of bread or wine, of the respective transubstantiated elements of the Eucharist; (b) either of these elements.
the species; the human race.

spec′i·fī·ȧ·ble, *a.* allowing specification; capable of being specified.

spē·cif′iç, *a.* [ML. *specificus*, from L. *species*, and *facere*, to make.]

1. pertaining to, characterizing, or constituting a species; possessing the peculiar property or properties which constitute a species and distinguish it from other things; as, the *specific* form of an animal or a plant; the *specific* qualities of a plant or a drug.

2. limiting or limited; tending to specify or particularize; definite; precise; as, a *specific* statement.

I could give you *specific* instances where he [President Roosevelt] has stood between rash men in Congress. —Elihu Root.

3. peculiar to or characteristic of something, as traits, etc.

4. of a special, or particular, sort or kind.

5. in medicine, (a) specially indicated as a cure of a particular disease: said of a remedy; (b) produced by a single kind of microorganism: said of a disease.

specific character; in biology, a character distinguishing one species from every other species of the same genus.

specific conductivity; the particular conductivity of a substance for electricity.

specific duty; a tariff impost of specified amount upon a special article, or upon an indicated quantity of a commodity.

specific gravity; the ratio of the weight or mass of a given volume of a substance to that of an equal volume of another substance (water for liquids and solids, air or hydrogen for gases) used as a standard.

specific heat; (a) the ratio of the amount of heat required to raise the temperature of a unit mass of a substance one degree to the amount of heat required to raise the temperature of the same mass of water one degree; (b) the number of calories needed to raise the temperature of one gram of a given substance 1° C.

specific inductive capacity; the ability of a dielectric to permit induction to take place through its mass as compared with the ability possessed by a vacuous space of the same dimensions under the same conditions.

specific legacy; in law, a bequest of a particular thing, as of a particular piece of furniture, specified and distinguished from all others.

specific name; the name which, appended to the name of the genus, constitutes the distinctive name of the species.

specific performance; the performance, decreed by a court of equity, of the precise terms of a contract.

specific resistance; in electricity, resistivity.

specific rotatory power; the power of a substance to turn the plane of polarization of light.

specific stain; in microscopy, a pigment having an affinity for certain chemical compounds.

spē·cif′iç, *n.* 1. in medicine, a specific cure or remedy.

2. something specially suited for a given use or purpose.

spē·cif′i·căl, *a.* specific.

spē·cif′i·căl·ly, *adv.* 1. in a specific manner; definitely; particularly.

2. as regards a specific difference or species.

spē·cif′i·căl·ness, *n.* the state of being specific.

spē·cif′i·cāte, *v.t.* to specify. [Rare.]

spec″i·fi·cā′tion, *n.* 1. the act of determining by a mark or limit; notation of limits.

2. the designation of particulars; particular mention; as, the *specification* of a charge against a military or naval officer.

3. [*usually pl.*] a particular and detailed account or description of a thing; specifically, a statement of particulars, describing the dimensions, details, or peculiarities of any work about to be undertaken, as in architecture, building, engineering, etc.

4. an article, item, or particular specified.

5. in law, the formation of a new property from materials belonging to another.

spec·i·fic′i·ty, *n.* the quality or state of being specific.

spē·cif′iç·ness, *n.* the state or character of being specific.

spec′i·fȳ, *v.t.*; specified, *pt., pp.*; specifying, *ppr.* [Fr. *spécifier*, as if from LL. *specificare*, from L. *species*, and *facere*, to make.]

1. to mention, describe, or define in detail; to state definitely; as, he *specified* the reasons for their failure.

2. to include as an item in a set of specifications.

3. to state explicitly as a condition.

spē·cil′lum, *n.*; *pl.* **spē·cil′lȧ,** a probe; a stylet.

spec′i·men, *n.* [L. *specimen*, lit., that by which a thing is seen and recognized, a mark or token, an example or specimen, from *specere*, to see, to behold.]

1. a part of a whole, or one individual of a class or group, used as a sample or example of the whole, class, or group; typical part, organism, etc.

2. a (specified kind of) individual or person; as, an unsavory *specimen*. [Colloq.]

3. a sample of urine for analysis. [Colloq.]

spē·ci·os′i·ty (-shi-), *n.* 1. *pl.* **spē·ci·os′i·tieș,** something specious.

2. the state or quality of being specious.

spē′cious, *a.* [Fr. *spécieux*; L. *speciosus*, showy, beautiful, plausible, from *species*, look, show, appearance.]

1. resembling, simulating, or apparently corresponding with right or truth; appearing just, fair, or proper without really being so; plausible but not genuine; as, a *specious* argument; *specious* promises.

Resist with care the spirit of innovation upon its principles, however *specious* the pretexts. —George Washington.

2. of pleasant or inviting aspect; agreeable to the eye; showy. [Obs.]

Syn.—ostensible, colorable, plausible.

spē′cious·ly, *adv.* in a specious manner.

spē′cious·ness, *n.* the condition or quality of being specious.

speck, *n.* [AS. *spic*, bacon; D. *spek*, fat.]

1. the fat or blubber of whales and other marine mammals.

2. fat pork or bacon. [Dial.]

speck, *n.* [AS. *specca*; L.G. *spaak*, a speck; perhaps from root of *spew*.]

1. a small spot, splotch, or stain; as, a *speck* in linen.

2. a very small thing or a minute fragment; a mite; an atom; as, a *speck* of dust.

3. a small fish, *Ulocentra stigmæa*, native to the streams of the southeastern United States.

speck, *v.t.*; specked (spekt), *pt., pp.*; specking, *ppr.* to make specks upon or cause them to appear in; to speckle; to spot; as, rust *specks* textiles.

speck block, a block used in stripping the blubber of a whale, through which the speckfall is rove.

speck′fąll, *n.* the rope of the speck block by means of which the whale blubber is hoisted on board.

speç′kle, *n.* [dim. of *speck*, spot.] a diminutive spot or speck of contrasting color; a fleck.

speç′kle, *v.t.*; speckled, *pt., pp.*; speckling, *ppr.* to mark with speckles; as, to *speckle* calicoes.

speç′kle·bel″ly, *n.* gadwall. [Dial.]

speç′kled, *a.* exhibiting speckles; dotted with spots; variegated with specks; as, a *speckled* hen.

speckled hind; same as *John Paw*.

speckled Indians; same as *Pintos*.

speckled trout; (a) the brook trout, *Salvelinus fontinalis*; (b) the rainbow trout, *Salmo irideus*.

speckled wood; palmyra wood quarter-sawed to produce a mottled effect.

speç′kled·bill″, *n.* an American goose, *Anser albifrons*. [Dial.]

speç′kled·ness, *n.* the property or quality of being speckled.

speck·sion·eer′, *n.* in whale fishing, the chief harpooner.

speck′y, *a.* full of specks; made up of specks; somewhat spotted.

speçs, specks, *n.pl.* spectacles; eyeglasses. [Colloq.]

speç′tȧ·çle, *n.* [Fr., from L. *spectaculum*, from *spectare*, to behold, freq. of *specere*, to see.]

1. something; to look at usually, something presented to view as extraordinary, or something that is beheld as unusual and worthy of special notice.

2. a pageant; a public show or exhibition on a grand scale, which is mainly attractive to the eye; as, a dramatic *spectacle*.

3. anything seen; a sight.

4. [*pl.*] a pair of lenses, or two sets of lenses, provided with a suitable frame, worn in front of the eyes to improve the sight or correct errors of refraction, or more rarely to protect the eyes from wind, dust, glare, etc.: often called *a pair of spectacles*.

5. [*pl.*] something through which one views things, or something that influences, colors, or biases one's views or ideas.

6. [*usually pl.*] something like a pair of spectacles, or eyeglasses, in shape, use, etc., as the frame with one red and one green glass in a semaphore.

7. [*pl.*] in zoology, marks or markings having the appearance of spectacles.

compound spectacles; pantoscopic spectacles, or bifocals.

speç′tȧ·çled (-kld), *a.* 1. having or wearing spectacles.

2. having markings simulating spectacles in form: said of animals.

spectacled bear; a bear, *Ursus ornatus*, of the Andes.

spectacled duck or *coot*; the surf duck, *Œdemia perspicillata*. [Dial.]

spectacled eider; a sea duck, *Arctonetta fischeri*.

spectacled goose; the gannet, *Sula bassana*. [Brit.]

speç·taç′ū·lăr, *a.* [from L. *spectaculum*, a show, sight, and *-ar*.]

1. of or pertaining to a spectacle or show.

2. unusual to a striking or wonderful degree; characterized by a great display, as of daring.

3. of or relating to spectacles for the eyes. [Rare.]

speç·taç′ū·lăr, *n.* an elaborate, extended television program, usually in color.

speç′tănt, *a.* [L. *spectans* (*-antis*), ppr. of *spectare*, to behold.] in heraldry, designating an animal looking forward; also, denoting an animal looking upward with the nose bent wise.

speç·tā′tion, *n.* aspect; appearance; regard. [Obs.]

speç′tā·tŏr (*or* spek-tā′), *n.* [L., from *spectare*, to behold.] one who looks on; one who sees or beholds a given thing or event without taking an active part; as, the *spectators* were numerous; the *spectators* of a show.

the Spectator; an English periodical (1711–1712; 1714), successor to the *Tatler*, published and written by Joseph Addison and Richard Steele: it was composed chiefly of short essays professedly edited by the members of the imaginary Spectator Club, representative types in the social life of the times.

Syn.—looker-on, observer, witness.

speç·tȧ·tō′ri·ăl, *a.* of or relating to a spectator.

speç·tā′tŏr·ship, *n.* the state or condition of being a spectator.

speç·tā′tress, speç·tā′trix, *n.* a woman spectator.

speç′tẽr, *n.* [Fr. *spectre*, from L. *spectrum*, an appearance, an apparition, from *spectare*, to behold.]

1. an apparition; the appearance of a person who is dead; a ghost.

2. any object of fear or dread.

3. in zoology, any of various animals, as the specter bat, specter insect, etc.

specter of the Brocken; an optical phenomenon peculiar to high mountains or aircraft in which a greatly magnified image of the spectator appears upon a background of clouds: named from a mountain of the Harz range.

speç′tẽr bat, a bat, *Phyllostoma spectrum*, native to South America.

speç′tẽr çan′dle, a belemnite.

speç′tẽr çrab, same as *glass crab*.

speç′tẽr in′seçt, any insect of the genus *Phasma*.

speç′tẽr lē′mŭr, same as *tarsier*.

speç′tẽr shrimp, a small marine crustacean, *Caprella tuberculata*.

speç′trȧ, *n.* alternative plural of *spectrum*.

speç′trăl, *a.* 1. resembling or of the nature of a specter; ghostly; as, a *spectral* hue.

2. of or pertaining to the spectrum; caused by the spectrum; as, *spectral* phenomena.

speç·tral′i·ty, *n.* the quality or state of being spectral.

speç′trăl·ly, *adv.* in a spectral manner or form.

speç′tre (-tẽr), *n.* a specter: British spelling.

speç′trō-, [from Latin *spectrum*, an appearance, apparition.] a combining form meaning (a) *of radiant energy as exhibited in a spectrum*, as in *spectro*gram; (b) *of* or *by a spectroscope*, as in *spectroheliogram*.

speç″trō·bō·lom′e·tẽr, *n.* a spectroscope to which a bolometer is attached to measure the amount of heat in any region of the spectrum.

speç′trō·gram, *n.* a photograph of a spectrum.

speç′trō·grȧph, *n.* [*spectro-*, and Gr. *graphein*, to write.]

1. an instrument for dispersing light radiation into a spectrum and recording the spectrum photographically.

2. a photograph of a spectrum.

speç·trō·graph′iç, *a.* of or pertaining to the spectrograph or to spectrography.

spec·trog′rȧ·phy, *n.* the art of using the spectrograph.

spec·trō·hē′li·ō·gram, *n.* [*spectro-* and *helio-* and *-gram.*] a photograph of the sun made by monochromatic light, usually showing streaks or prominences on the sun's surface.

spec·trō·hē′li·ō·gràph, *n.* an instrument used to make spectroheliograms.

spec·trō·log′ic·ăl, *a.* of or pertaining to spectrology.

spec·trō·log′ic·ăl·ly, *adv.* in a spectrological manner.

spec·trol′ō·gy, *n.* [*spectro-*, and Gr. *logos*, a discourse.] the scientific study of spectra.

spec·trom′e·tēr, *n.* 1. an instrument used for measuring spectral wave lengths.
2. an instrument used for determining the index of refraction.

spec·trō·met′ric, *a.* of or made by a spectrometer.

spec·trō·mī·crō·scop′ic·ăl, *a.* of or pertaining to combined observations made by the spectroscope and the microscope.

spec′trō·phōne, *n.* a modification of the spectroscope, by which a spectrum causes a medium sensitive to sound to vibrate audibly.

spec·trō·phon′ic, *a.* of or relating to the spectrophone.

spec″trō·phō·tom′e·tēr, *n.* an instrument in which two spectra may be brought into visual comparison, to determine their relative intensity, etc.

spec·trō·phō·tō·met′ric, *a.* of or relating to the spectrophotometer.

spec″trō·phō·tom′e·try, *n.* the science of using the spectrophotometer.

spec″trō·pō·lar′i·scōpe, *n.* an instrument consisting of a combined spectroscope and polariscope.

spec″trō·py̆·rom′e·tēr, *n.* a form of spectrophotometer used for the determination of high temperatures.

spec′trō·scōpe, *n.* [*spectro-*, and Gr. *skopein*, to view.] an optical instrument used for forming spectra for study. It usually consists of a tube with a slit in one end, and a convex lens called a collimator at the other, from which parallel rays of light proceed; a prism, or train of prisms, to separate the differently refrangible rays; and a telescope to view a magnified image of the spectrum produced.

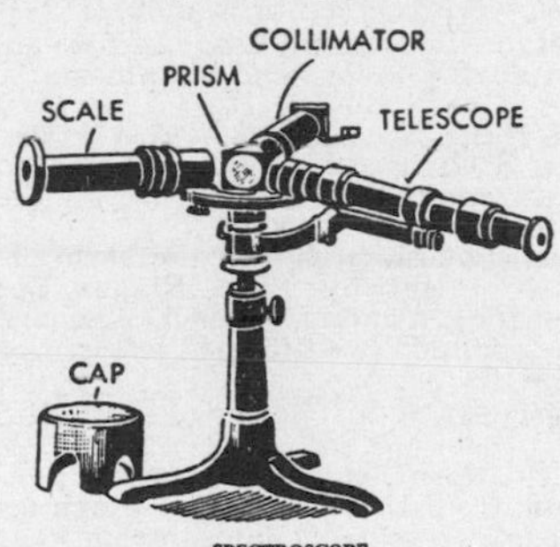

SPECTROSCOPE

analyzing spectroscope; a spectroscope in which different parts of the slit receive light from different parts of a luminous object.
diffraction spectroscope; a spectroscope in which the spectrum is produced by a fine grating ruled on metal, instead of a prism.
direct-vision spectroscope; a small spectroscope which contains the essential parts in a single tube.
integrating spectroscope; a spectroscope in which the slit receives light from all parts of a luminous object.
prismatic spectroscope; a spectroscope in which the spectrum is produced by a prism.

spec′trō·scōpe, *v.t.* and *v.i.* to observe by means of a spectrocope.

spec·trō·scop′ic, spec·trō·scop′ic·ăl, *a.* of, relating to, or obtained by means of the spectroscope or spectroscopy; as, *spectroscopic* data.

spec·trō·scop′ic·ăl·ly, *adv.* in a spectroscopic manner.

spec′trō·scō·pist, *n.* a student of or expert in spectroscopy.

spec′trō·scō·py, *n.* the study of spectra through the use of the spectroscope.

spec′trum, *n.*; *pl.* **spec′trȧ, spec′trums,** [L., an appearance, image, or specter.]
1. the series of colored bands diffracted and arranged in the order of their respective wave lengths by the passage of white light through a prism or other diffracting medium and shading continuously from red (produced by the longest wave visible) to violet (produced by the shortest).

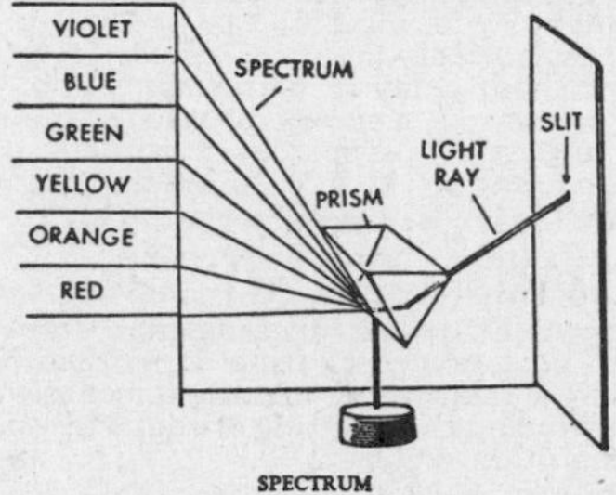

SPECTRUM

2. any of various arrangements of colored bands or lines, together with invisible components at both ends of the spectrum, similarly formed by light from incandescent gases or other sources of radiant energy, which can be studied by a spectrograph.
3. an afterimage.
4. in radio, the range of wave lengths of radio waves, from 3 centimeters to 30,000 meters, or of frequencies of radio waves, from 10 to 10,000,000 kilocycles: also *radio spectrum.*
5. an apparition; a specter.
chromatic spectrum; the region of the spectrum occupied by the visible rays.
diffraction spectrum; the spectrum of light produced by a grating.
fluted spectrum; a discontinuous spectrum having bands of fluted form.
gaseous spectrum; the spectrum of an incandescent gas or vapor.
heat spectrum or *thermal spectrum*; the spectrum composed of dark infrared rays.
line spectrum; a spectrum of light consisting of distinct and separated lines.
normal spectrum; the spectrum produced by means of a diffraction grating, the colors being so spaced as to agree with their wave lengths.
prismatic spectrum; a spectrum produced by means of a prism.
solar spectrum; the spectrum produced by a ray of solar light. Its characteristic feature is the presence of extremely numerous dark lines.
spectrum analysis; analysis of substances or bodies through study of their spectra.

spec′ū·lăr, *a.* [L. *specularis*, belonging to a mirror, from L. *speculum*, mirror.]
1. of, like, or by means of a speculum.
2. assisting sight by means of optical properties. [Obs.]
3. affording view. [Obs.]
specular iron ore; same as *hematite.*

spec′ū·lāte, *v.i.*; speculated, *pt., pp.*; speculating, *ppr.* [L. *speculari* (*-latus*), to view, from *specere*, to see.]
1. to meditate; to contemplate; to consider a subject by turning it in the mind and viewing it in its different aspects and relations; as, to *speculate* on political events; to *speculate* on the origin of life.
2. to think about or theorize on any subject; to reason from assumed premises; to conjecture.
3. to buy or sell stocks, commodities, land, etc., hoping to take advantage of an expected rise or fall in price; to take part in any risky business venture or enterprise on the chance of making huge profits.

spec′ū·lāte, *v.t.* to consider earnestly or with considerable attention. [Rare.]

spec·ū·lā′tion, *n.* [LL. *speculatio* (*-onis*), a viewing, from *speculari*, to view.]
1. the act, process, or result of speculating; as, the *speculations* of a metaphysician.
2. mental view of anything in its various aspects and relations; contemplation; intellectual examination.
3. the act of speculating in stocks, land, etc.
4. a speculative business venture.
5. an old card game, the leading principle of which is the buying and selling of cards in an attempt to secure the highest trump.
6. view; power of sight. [Obs.]
Syn.—contemplation, consideration, weighing, thought, theory, scheme, hypothesis, view, conjecture.

spec′ū·lā·tist, *n.* one who speculates or forms theories; a speculator.

spec′ū·lā·tive, *a.* 1. of, characterized by, or having the nature of, speculation, or meditation, contemplation, conjecture, etc.
2. theoretical, not practical.
3. of or characterized by financial speculation.
4. risky.
5. indulging in or fond of speculation.
6. prying; inquisitive. [Obs.]

spec′ū·lā·tive·ly, *adv.* in a speculative manner.

spec′ū·lā·tive·ness, *n.* the state, condition, or quality of being speculative.

spec′ū·lā·tiv·ism, *n.* the indulgence or cultivation of theoretical investigation, as opposed to experimentation. [Rare.]

spec′ū·lā·tŏr, *n.* 1. one who forms theories; also, an observer, contemplator, or watcher.
2. one devoted to or engaged in commercial or financial speculation.

spec′ū·lȧ·tō·ry, *a.* speculative.

spec′ū·lum, *n.*; *pl.* **spec′ū·lȧ, spec′ū·lums,** [L., a mirror.]
1. a mirror, especially one of polished metal used as a reflector in a telescope, etc.
2. in medicine and surgery, an instrument for dilating a passage or cavity to facilitate its examination.
3. in zoology, a distinctive, usually iridescent patch of color on the wings of certain birds, especially ducks.

spec′ū·lum met′ăl, a metal used for making the specula of reflecting telescopes. It is an alloy of two parts copper, and one of tin, often whitened by the addition of arsenic.

sped, *v.* alternative past tense and past participle of *speed.*

speece, *n.* species; kind. [Obs.]

speech, *n.* [AS. *spæc*, from *sprecan*, to speak.]
1. the act of speaking; the expression or communication of thoughts and feelings by spoken words, vocal sounds, and gestures.
2. the power or ability to speak.
3. the manner of speaking; as, Southern *speech.*
4. that which is spoken; utterance, remark, statement, talk, conversation, etc.
5. a talk or address given in public.
6. the language used by a certain group of people; dialect or tongue.
7. the study of the theory and practice of oral expression and communication; as, a college course in *speech.*
8. rumor; report. [Archaic.]
9. the sounding of a musical instrument; especially, the sound of a pipe in a pipe organ.
figure of speech; see under *figure*, n.
Syn.—oration, address, harangue, dissertation, discourse, disquisition.

speech, *v.i.* to make a speech. [Rare.]

speech cen′tēr, the nerve center in the cortex of the brain which controls the power of speech.

speech clin′ic, a school or clinic for correcting speech disorders.

speech cŏm·mū′ni·ty, all the people speaking a particular language or dialect, whether in a single geographical area or dispersed throughout various regions.

speech′craft, *n.* the art or science of language; also, the art or science of speaking.

speech dāy, in England, the periodical examination day of a public school.

speech dis·or′dēr, any conspicuous speech imperfection, or variation from the accepted speech standards, caused either by a physical defect in the speech organs or by a mental disorder, as aphasia, stuttering, etc.

speech′ful, *a.* loquacious; talkative; voluble.

speech″i·fi·cā′tion, *n.* the act of making a speech, or of haranguing: used humorously or contemptuously.

speech′i·fī·ēr, *n.* one who speechifies.

speech′i·fy̆, *v.i.*; speechified, *pt., pp.*; speechifying, *ppr.* to make a speech; to harangue: used humorously or contemptuously.

speech′ing, *n.* the act of making a speech.

speech′less, *a.* 1. incapable of speech; unable to speak.
2. not speaking at or for a given time; silent, as from shock.
3. not expressed or expressible in words; as, *speechless* terror.

speech′less·ly, *adv.* in a speechless manner; mutely; without speaking.

speech′less·ness, *n.* the state or quality of being speechless; muteness.

speech′māk″ēr, *n.* one who makes speeches;

an orator; one who speaks much in public: often derisive.

speech'-rēad"ing, *n.* same as *lip reading.*

speed, *n.* [AS. *spēd,* success, wealth, from *spōwan,* to succeed.]
1. the act or state of moving rapidly; swiftness; quick motion.
2. (a) the rate of movement or motion; velocity; as, the *speed* of sound; (b) the rate or rapidity of any action; as, reading *speed.*
3. a gear or arrangement of gears for the drive of an engine; as, this truck has five forward *speeds.*
4. one's kind or level of taste, capability, etc. [Colloq.]
5. any of various amphetamine compounds, especially Methedrine. [Slang.]
6. luck; success; prosperity; as, she wished him good *speed.* [Archaic.]
7. a protecting and assisting power. [Obs.]
St. Nicholas be thy *speed.* —Shak.
8. in photography, (a) the sensitivity to light of film as measured by the rate of exposure it requires; (b) the widest effective aperture of a camera lens: see also *F number;* (c) the length of time the shutter is opened for an exposure.
good speed, God speed; see under *good,* a.
Syn.—swiftness, celerity, quickness, haste, dispatch, expedition, hurry, acceleration, quickness, rapidity, precipitance.

speed, *v.i.;* sped *or* speeded, *pt., pp.;* speeding, *ppr.* 1. to move rapidly, especially more rapidly than is safe or allowed by law.
2. (a) to get along; to fare; (b) to have fortune, good or bad; (c) to have good fortune; to prosper; succeed. [Archaic.]

speed, *v.t.* 1. to help (a project) to succeed; to aid; to promote.
2. to wish Godspeed to; as, *speed* the parting guest.
3. to send, convey, or cause to move, go, etc. swiftly; as, he *sped* the ball on its way.
4. to increase the speed of; to make go or work faster.
5. to cause or design (a machine, etc.) to operate at a certain speed or speeds.
6. to cause to succeed or prosper. [Archaic.]
to speed up; to increase in speed; to accelerate.
Syn.—dispatch, expedite, accelerate, urge, hasten, hurry, press.

speed'bōat, *n.* a small motorboat designed for speed.

speed çōne, in mechanics, a contrivance that regulates by means of a belt the ratio of velocity communicated between parallel shafts.

speed'ẽr, *n.* 1. one who makes rapid progress; one who succeeds. [Obs.]
2. one who or that which is characterized by unusual speed; specifically, one who drives an automobile at a higher speed than is safe or legal.
3. one who or that which accelerates or promotes speed; specifically, in mechanics, a contrivance that increases speed.
4. in cotton manufacturing, a machine that twists slivers from the carders into rovings.

speed'i·ly, *adv.* quickly; with haste; in a short time.

speed in'di·çā·tŏr, a device for showing the rate of speed of any mechanism.

speed'i·ness, *n.* the quality of being speedy; promptness; dispatch.

speed'ing, *n.* the act of driving a motor vehicle at a higher speed than is safe or legal.

speed·om'e·tẽr, *n.* [from *speed* and *-meter.*]
1. a device attached to an automobile or other vehicle to indicate speed, as in miles per hour; tachometer.
2. a similar device for indicating the distance traveled as well as the speed; odometer.

speed'stẽr, *n.* 1. a speeder.
2. an open automobile, usually a two-seater, built for speed.

speed trap, a region, municipality, etc. where traffic police are especially on the alert for violations of the speed laws, and where even minor violations are dealt with severely.

speed'-up, *n.* 1. acceleration; the act of speeding up.
2. an increase in, or system for increasing, production rate, output, etc.

speed'wāy, *n.* 1. a track for racing automobiles.
2. a road built to accommodate high-speed traffic safely.

speed'well, *n.* any of several plants of the genus *Veronica.* The species consist of herbs or shrubs with opposite, alternate or verticillate leaves. The flowers are of a blue, white, or red color, having two stamens, and are arranged in axillary or terminal spikes or racemes. The common speedwell, *Veronica officinalis,* was once extensively used as a substitute for tea, and also as a tonic and diuretic.

speed'y, *adj.; comp.* speedier; *superl.* speediest. 1. quick; swift; nimble; hasty; rapid in motion; as, a *speedy* flight; on *speedy* foot.
2. without delay in performance; not dilatory or slow; as, a *speedy* dispatch of business.
3. successful; prosperous; fortunate. [Obs.]

speer, *v.t.* and *v.i.* to ask; to inquire. [Scot.]

spe̤ight (spāt), *n.* a woodpecker. [Obs.]

spēir, *v.t.* and *v.i.* same as *speer.*

speis·kō'bält (-bolt), *n.* [G.] same as *smaltine.*

speīss, *n.* [G. *speise,* an amalgam, from LL. *spesa,* cost, expense, from L. *expendere,* to spend.] a mixture of metallic arsenides produced during the smelting of copper, iron, and certain other ores.

spek'bo̤om, *n.* [S. Afr. D., from *spek,* fat, and *boom,* tree.] a plant native to South Africa.

spē·lae'ăn, spē·lē'ăn, *a.* [L. *spelæum;* Gr. *spēlaion,* a cave.] of, like, or pertaining to a cave or caves; also, dwelling in a cave or caves.

spel'ding, *n.* [from archaic *speld,* to split, and *-ing.*] a small fish split and dried in the sun: also written *spelden, speldring, speldrin, speldron.* [Scot.]

spē·lē·ol'ō·ġy, *n.* [from L. *spelæum,* Gr. *spēlaion,* a cave.] the science of exploring caves.

spelk, *n.* [AS. *spelc,* a splinter.]
1. a splinter; a small stick or rod used in thatching. [Brit. Dial.]
2. a splint used in setting a broken bone; a rod by which a thing is kept straight. [Brit. Dial.]

spell, *n.* [AS. *spel,* a saying, tale, charm; akin to Goth. *spill,* recital, tale.]
1. a word, formula, or form of words supposed to have some magic power.
2. magical power or irresistible influence; charm; fascination.
3. a story; a tale. [Obs.]
to cast a spell on; to enchant; to win the complete affection of.
under a spell; held in a spell or trance; enchanted.

spell, *v.t.* 1. to charm; to act upon with or as with a spell or charm.
2. to endow with magical properties.

spell, *v.t.;* spelled *or* spelt, *pt., pp.;* spelling, *ppr.* [ME. *spellen;* OFr. *espeler;* Fr. *épeler,* to spell, from the Germanic.]
1. to name, write, print, or signal the letters which make up (a word, syllable, etc.), especially the right letters in the right order.
2. to make up (a word, etc.): said of specified letters.
3. to signify; mean; as, this chance *spelled* success for him.
to spell out; (a) to read letter by letter or with difficulty; (b) to make out, or discern, as if by close reading.

spell, *v.i.* 1. to spell a word or words, etc.; especially, to do so correctly.
2. to study deeply; to contemplate carefully. [Obs.]

spell, *v.t.* to tell; to relate. [Obs.]

spell, *v.t.* [AS. *spelian,* to substitute for.]
1. to serve or work in place of (another), especially so as to give a period of rest to; to relieve. [Colloq.]
2. to relieve, as a horse, by giving a period of rest to. [Chiefly Australian.]

spell, *v.i.* to take a period of rest or relief. [Chiefly Australian.]

spell, *n.* 1. a turn of serving or working in place of another.
2. a period or turn of work, duty, etc.; as, his *spell* as guard was a short one.
3. a turn, period, or fit of something; as, a *spell* of brooding.
4. a period of a specified sort of weather; as, a cold *spell.*
5. a period of time that is indefinite, short, or of a specified character. [Colloq.]
6. a short distance. [Colloq.]
7. a period or fit of some illness, indisposition, etc. [Colloq.]
8. a period of rest or relief from activity. [Chiefly Australian.]

spell'ȧ·ble, *a.* capable of being spelled or expressed in letters.

spell'bīnd, *v.t.;* spellbound, *pt., pp.;* spellbinding, *ppr.* to bind or hold by or as by a spell; to fascinate; to control mentally.

spell'bīnd"ẽr, *n.* one who holds or binds others to him or his cause by or as by a spell: used especially of political orators. [Colloq.]

spell'bound, *a.* bound or held by or as by a spell or charm.

spell'down, *n.* a spelling bee, especially one in which a contestant is eliminated from further competition by a specified number of misspellings.

spell'ẽr, *n.* 1. one who spells; one skilled in spelling.
2. a book containing exercises or instructions in spelling; a spelling book.

spell'ẽr, *n.* a small shoot projecting from the upper part of the antler of a deer.

spell'fu̱l, *a.* full of charms; fascinating; calculated to cast a spell. [Rare.]

spell'ing, *n.* 1. the act of forming words, etc. by putting letters together.
2. the study of this.
3. the way in which a word is spelled; orthography.
spelling reform; any of various proposed plans for changing the orthography of English, either by a simplified spelling of certain words or by the phonetic spelling of the entire vocabulary.

spell'ing bee, a competition in which the person or team spelling the most words correctly is the winner.

spell'ing book, an exercise book used to teach spelling.

spell'ing match, a spelling bee.

spell'ken, *n.* a playhouse; a theater. [Obs.]

spell'wŏrk, *n.* that which is worked by spells or charms; power of magic; enchantment.

spelt, *n.* [AS.; LL. *spelta.*] a hard-grained kind of wheat, or any of its varieties.

spelt, *v.* alternative past tense and past participle of *spell.*

spelt, *v.t.* to split. [Obs.]

spel'tẽr, *n.* [OFr. *espeautre;* probably akin to Eng. *pewter.*] zinc cast into the ingots of commerce.

spē·luñç', spē·luñk', *n.* [L. *spelunca;* Gr. *spēlunx,* a cave.] a cave; a vault. [Obs.]

spē·luñ'kẽr, *n.* a person whose hobby is exploring caves.

spence, *n.* [OFr. *despense.*] a larder or pantry: also spelled *spense.* [Archaic or Dial.]

spen'cẽr, *n.* [named after the second Earl of *Spencer* (1758–1834).] a short jacket, usually of wool, worn by men or women.

spen'cẽr, *n.* in nautical usage, a fore-and-aft sail set abaft the fore and mainmasts; a trysail.

Spen·cē'ri·ăn, *a.* 1. of or having to do with Herbert Spencer or his system of philosophy, which attempted to systematize all the sciences into a coherent whole.
2. of or characteristic of the style of penmanship taught by Platt Rogers Spencer (1800–1864), American teacher, characterized by rounded, well-formed letters slanting to the right.

Spen·cē'ri·ăn, *n.* a follower of Herbert Spencer.

spend, *v.t.;* spent, *pt., pp.;* spending, *ppr.* [AS. *spendan,* from L. *expendere,* to weigh out.]
1. to use up, exhaust, consume, or wear out; as, he *spends* his energy quickly, his fury was *spent.*
2. to pay out (money); to disburse.
3. to give or devote, as time, labor, thought, or effort, to some enterprise or for some purpose.
4. to pass (a period of time); as, they *spent* an hour together.
5. to waste; to squander.
6. in nautical usage, to lose; as, they *spent* their rudder.

spend, *v.i.* 1. to pay out or use up money, etc.; as, he *spends* like a prudent man.
2. to be lost or wasted; to vanish; to be dissipated; to be consumed; to dissipate or spread; as, candles *spend* fast in a current of air. [Obs.]
3. to be employed to any use; to be diffused. [Obs.]

spend'ȧ·ble, *a.* that can be spent.

spend'-all, *n.* a spendthrift.

spend'ẽr, *n.* one who or that which spends; specifically, a prodigal; one who spends freely or lavishly.

spend'ing, *n.* the act of laying out, expending, consuming, or wasting.

spend'ing mŏn'ey, money for miscellaneous personal expenses.

spend'thrift, *n.* one who spends money carelessly or wastefully; a squanderer.

spend'thrift, *a.* wasteful; lavish; extravagant.
spend'thrift"y, *a.* spendthrift.
spense, *n.* same as *spence.*
Spen·sē'ri·ăn, *a.* of or pertaining to Edmund Spenser, the English poet, or his writing.
Spen·sē'ri·ăn, *n.* 1. a follower or imitator of Spenser.
2. a Spenserian stanza, or a poem in such stanzas.
Spen·sē'ri·ăn stan'zȧ, a stanza consisting of eight lines of iambic pentameter and a final line of iambic hexameter (an alexandrine), with a rhyme scheme *ababbcbcc,* used by Spenser in the *Faerie Queene* and by other English poets afterward.
spent, *a.* [past participle of *spend.*] 1. tired out; physically exhausted; without energy.
2. used up; worn out; without power or force.
spē'rȧ·ble, *a.* [L. *sperabilis,* from *sperare,* to hope.] that may be hoped. [Rare.]
sper'ȧ·ble, *n.* sparable. [Obs.]
spē'rāte, *a.* [L. *speratus,* pp. of *sperare,* to hope.] hoped for. [Rare.]
spēre, *v.t.* and *v.i.* same as *speer.*
spēre, *n.* a sphere. [Obs.]
spẽr'ling, *n.* [a variant of *sparling,* a smelt.]
1. a smelt. [Brit. Dial.]
2. a young herring.
spẽrm, *n.* [Fr. *sperme;* L. *sperma;* Gr. *sperma,* a seed.]
1. the male generative fluid; semen.
2. one of the germ cells contained in this fluid; spermatozoon.
spẽrm, *n.* 1. spermaceti.
2. sperm oil.
3. a sperm whale.
-spẽrm, a combining form meaning *seed,* as in gymno*sperm.*
spẽr'mȧ-, spẽr'mȧ·tō-, spẽr'mō-, [from Gr. *sperma,* a seed.] combining forms meaning *seed, germ,* or *beginning.*
spẽr·mȧ·cē'ti, *n.* [L. *sperma,* sperm, and *cetus,* a whale.] a white, waxlike substance taken from the oil in the head of a sperm whale, dolphin, etc., used in making cosmetics, ointments, candles, etc.
spẽr·mȧ·cē'ti whāle (hwāl), *n.* the sperm whale.

SPERMACETI WHALE (*Physeter macrocephalus*)

spẽr'mȧ·duct, *n.* a seminal passage serving to convey or hold the sperm.
spẽr'mȧ·gōne, *n.* same as *spermogonium.*
-spẽr'măl, -spermous.
spẽr'măl·ist, *n.* same as *spermist.*
spẽr'mȧ·phōre, *n.* [*sperma-,* and Gr. *pherein,* to bear.] in botany, that part of the ovary from which the ovules arise; a placenta. [Rare.]
spẽr'mȧ·ry, *n.*; *pl.* **spẽr'mȧ·ries,** the organ in male animals in which spermatozoa are produced; the spermatic gland or glands of the male.
spẽr·mȧ·thē'çȧ, *n.*; *pl.* **spẽr·mȧ·thē'cae,** [*sperma-,* and Gr. *thēkē,* case.] a cavity in certain female insects, as queen bees, in which the sperm of the male is received.
spẽr·mā'ti·ȧ (-shi-), *n.* pl. of *spermatium.*
spẽr·mat'iç, spẽr·mat'iç·ăl, *a.* 1. of or having to do with sperm or sperm cells; generative.
2. of or having to do with a spermary.
spẽr·mat'iç çord, the cordlike structure suspending a testicle within the scrotum and containing the vas deferens, blood vessels and nerves supplying the testicle, etc.
spẽr'mȧ·tid, *n.* a cell derived from a secondary spermatocyte by fission, developing into a spermatozoon: also called *spermatoblast.*
spẽr'mȧ·tin, *n.* an albuminoid substance found in semen, related to mucin and to alkali albumin.
spẽr·mȧ·ti·oġ'e·nous, *a.* bearing spermatia.
spẽr'mȧ·tişm, *n.* the emission or discharge of semen.
spẽr'mȧ·tist, *n.* a spermist.

spẽr·mȧ·tī'tis, *n.* inflammation of a vas deferens or spermatic cord.
spẽr·mā'ti·um (-shi-), *n.*; *pl.* **spẽr·mā'ti·ȧ,** [Gr. *spermation,* dim. of *sperma,* a seed.]
1. a nonmotile male gamete in red algae.
2. a very small cell thought to be a male gamete, found in some lichens and fungi.
spẽr'mȧ·tīze, *v.t.* and *v.i.* to discharge, or fertilize with, seed.
spẽr'mȧ·tō-, see *sperma-.*
spẽr'mȧ·tō·blȧst, *n.* the germ of a spermatozoon; a spermatid: also called *spermatocyte* and *nematoblast.*
spẽr'mȧ·tō·cēle, *n.* [*spermato-,* and Gr. *kēlē,* a tumor.] a swelling of the spermatic vessels; cystic distention of the epididymis.
spẽr'mȧ·tō·cyst, *n.* same as *seminal vesicle* under *seminal.*
spẽr"mȧ·tō·cys·tī'tis, *n.* inflammation of the seminal vesicles.
spẽr'mȧ·tō·cȳte, *n.* [*spermato-* and *-cyte.*] a cell that develops through several stages to form spermatozoa or spermatozoids.
spẽr"mȧ·tō·ġem'mȧ, *n.*; *pl.* **spẽr"mȧ·tō·ġem'mae,** [*spermato-,* and Gr. *gemma,* a bud.] an aggregation of spermatocytes; a spermatic cyst of many nuclei which project into the seminal tubules and develop into spermatoblasts. [Obs.]
spẽr"mȧ·tō·ġen'e·sis, *n.* the production and development of spermatozoa.
spẽr"mȧ·tō·ġē·net'iç, *a.* pertaining to, exhibiting, or characterized by spermatogenesis.
spẽr·mȧ·toġ'e·nous, *a.* producing spermatozoa or sperm.
spẽr·mȧ·toġ'e·ny, *n.* spermatogenesis. [Rare.]
spẽr"mȧ·tō·gō'ni·ăl, *a.* of or having to do with a spermatogonium.
spẽr"mȧ·tō·gō'ni·um, *n.*; *pl.* **spẽr"mȧ·tō·gō'ni·ȧ,** [*spermato-,* and Gr. *gonē,* generation.]
1. a primitive male germ cell.
2. a spermogonium.
spẽr'mȧ·toid, *a.* resembling sperm; spermlike.
spẽr"mȧ·tō·loġ'iç·ăl, *a.* pertaining to spermatology.
spẽr·mȧ·tol'ō·ġist, *n.* one versed in spermatology; a spermologist.
spẽr·mȧ·tol'ō·ġy, *n.* [*spermato-,* and Gr. *logos,* discourse.] the branch of science dealing with semen, sperm, etc.
spẽr·mȧ·toph'ō·răl, *a.* pertaining to a spermatophore.
spẽr'mȧ·tō·phōre", *n.* [*spermato-,* and Gr. *pherein,* to bear.] a case or capsule containing a number of spermatozoa, expelled whole by the male of certain animals, as the segmented worms and mollusks.
spẽr·mȧ·toph'ō·rous, *a.* bearing or producing sperm or seed; seminiferous.
spẽr'mȧ·tō·phȳte", *n.* [*spermato-,* and Gr. *phyton,* plant.] any seed-bearing plant.
spẽr"mȧ·tō·phyt'iç, *a.* of or having to do with a spermatophyte.
spẽr"mȧ·tor·rhē'ȧ, spẽr"mȧ·tor·rhoe'ȧ (-rē'), *n.* [*spermato-,* and Gr. *rhein,* to flow.] involuntary, abnormal, or excessive discharge of semen without an orgasm.
spẽr'mȧ·tō·spōre", *n.* a spermatogonium.
spẽr"mȧ·tō·thē'çȧ, *n.* same as *spermatheca.*
spẽr·mȧt·ō'vum, *n.*; *pl.* **spẽr·mȧt·ō'vȧ,** a fecundated ovum. [Rare.]
spẽr"mȧ·tō·zō'ȧ, *n.* pl. of *spermatozoon.*
spẽr"mȧ·tō·zō'ăl, *a.* spermatozoan.
spẽr"mȧ·tō·zō'ăn, *a.* pertaining to or resembling spermatozoa.
spẽr"mȧ·tō·zō'ăn, *n.* a spermatozoon.
spẽr"mȧ·tō·zō'iç, *a.* spermatozoan.
spẽr"mȧ·tō·zō'id, *n.* [*spermato-,* and Gr. *zōon,* a living creature, and *-oid.*]
1. in certain mosses, ferns, etc., a male sex cell, or gamete, that moves by means of cilia: it is usually produced in an antheridium.
2. a spermatozoon. [Rare.]
spẽr"mȧ·tō·zō'oid, *n.* a spermatozoid.
spẽr"mȧ·tō·zō'on, *n.*; *pl.* **spẽr"mȧ·tō·zō'ȧ,** [*spermato-,* and Gr. *zōon,* a living being.] the male germ cell, found in semen, which penetrates the ovum, or egg, of the female to fertilize it: it has a well-defined head, mid-section, and tail, and moves with a swimming action: also *sperm.*
spẽrm cell, 1. a spermatozoon.
2. a spermatoblast or spermatocyte.
spẽr'miç, *a.* of or having to do with sperm.
spẽr'min, *n.* spermine.

spẽr'mīne, *n.* [*sperm* and *-ine.*] a basic substance, $C_{10}H_{26}N_4$, found in semen, yeast, and some animal tissue.
spẽrm'işm, *n.* a former theory that the spermatozoon is the whole germ of the future animal.
spẽrm'ist, *n.* a believer in the theory of spermism.
spẽrm nū'çlē·us, a nucleus, as of a spermatozoon.
spẽr'mō-, see *sperma-.*
spẽr'mō·blȧst, *n.* a spermatoblast.
spẽr'mō·çärp, *n.* the fruit of the *Characeæ.* [Rare.]
spẽr'mō·dẽrm, *n.* [*spermo-,* and Gr. *derma,* skin.] in botany, the whole integument of a seed in the aggregate; the testa.
spẽr'mō·gōne, *n.* same as *spermogonium.*
spẽr·mō·gō'ni·um, *n.*; *pl.* **spẽr·mō·gō'ni·ȧ,** [*spermo-,* and Gr. *gonē,* offspring.] in certain lichens, a cup-shaped cyst in which spermatia are produced.
spẽrm oil, a valuable lubricating oil obtained from the head of the sperm whale.
spẽr·mol'ō·ġist, *n.* one who studies seeds; a collector of seeds.
spẽr·mol'ō·ġy, *n.* that branch of botany which investigates the seeds of plants.
spẽr'mō·phile, *n.* [*spermo-,* and Gr. *philein,* to love.] any rodent of the genus *Spermophilus,* including the chipmunk, ground squirrel, suslik, and gopher: they can do much damage to crops.
spẽr'mō·phōre, *n.* [*spermo-,* and Gr. *pherein,* to bear.] same as *spermophorum.*
spẽr·moph'ō·rum, *n.*; *pl.* **spẽr·moph'ō·rȧ,** the placenta of a plant.
Spẽr·moph'y·tȧ, *n.pl.* a phylum of plants including the higher flowering plants and those that bear true seeds; the *Phanerogamia.*
spẽr'mō·phȳte, *n.* [*spermo-,* and Gr. *phyton,* plant.] one of the *Spermophyta;* any plant producing true seeds.
spẽr·mō·phyt'iç, *a.* in botany, capable of producing seeds.
spẽr'mō·plaşm, *n.* [*spermo-,* and Gr. *plasma,* anything molded.] the protoplasm of a spermatozoon.
spẽr'mō·sphēre, *n.* a group or mass of spermatids formed by the segmentation of a secondary spermatocyte. [Obs.]
spẽr'mō·spōre, *n.* same as *spermatospore.*
spẽr'mous (-mus), *a.* of or like sperm.
-spẽr'mous, a combining form meaning *having* (a specified number or kind of) *seed,* as in mono*spermous.*
spẽr'mūle, *n.* a sperm cell or spermatozoon. [Obs.]
spẽrm whāle (hwāl), the cachalot or physeter, *Physeter macrocephalus,* a large, toothed whale inhabiting warm seas: a closed cavity in its square head contains spermaceti and sperm oil: also called *spermaceti whale.*
porpoise or *pygmy sperm whale;* a tropical whale not over twenty feet long, occasionally found in American waters: also called *snub-nosed cachalot.*
sperm-whale porpoise; a bottle-nosed whale of the genus *Hyperoodon* found in both Europe and America.
sper'ry·līte, *n.* [named after F. L. *Sperry,* its discoverer.] a silvery-white granular or crystalline native compound of platinum and arsenic, $PtAs_2$.
spẽrse, *v.t.* to disperse. [Obs.]
spes'särt·īte, spes'särt·ine, *n.* [from *Spessart,* in Germany.] a manganesian garnet.
spet, *v.t.* to spit; to throw out. [Dial.]
spet, *n.* spittle; a flow. [Dial.]
spetch'eş, *n.pl.* the trimmings of skins and hides, used for making glue.
spew (spū), *v.t.*; spewed, *pt., pp.*; spewing, *ppr.* [AS. *spiwan,* to spit; akin to G. *speien.*]
1. to vomit; to eject from or as from the stomach.
2. to eject; to cast forth violently or with abhorrence.
spew, *v.i.* 1. to vomit; to discharge the contents of the stomach.
2. to cast up seed, as wet land swollen with frost.
spew, *n.* that which is spewed; vomit.
spew'ẽr, *n.* one who or that which spews.
spew'i·ness, *n.* the state of being spewy, moist, or damp. [Brit. Dial.]
spew'y, *a.*; *comp.* spewier; *superl.* spewiest, wet; boggy; moist; damp. [Brit. Dial.]
sphac'el, *n.* same as *sphacelus.*

sphac′ē·lāte, *v.i.*; sphacelated, *pt., pp.*; sphacelating, *ppr.* 1. to mortify; to become gangrenous, as flesh.
2. to decay or become carious, as a bone.
sphac′ē·lāte, *v.t.* to make gangrenous.
sphac′ē·lāte, *a.* 1. in botany, decayed, withered, or dead.
2. affected with gangrene.
sphac′ē·lā·ted, *a.* sphacelate.
sphac·ē·lā′tion, *n.* the process of becoming or making gangrenous; mortification.
sphac′ē·lism, *n.* sphacelation; a sphacelate condition.
sphac′ē·lous, *a.* affected with or pertaining to gangrene.
sphac′ē·lus, *n.* [Gr. *sphakelos*, from *sphazein*, to kill.] a slough or mass of gangrenous tissue.
sphae·raph′i·dēs, *n.pl.* [Gr. *sphaira*, a sphere, and *rhaphis*, needle.] in botany, the round crystal masses occurring in some plant cells: also called *sphere crystals*.
Sphae·rel′lȧ, *n.* [LL., dim. from Gr. *sphaira*, a sphere.] a large genus of parasitic plant fungi, comprising 150 North American species.
sphae·rĕn′chy·mȧ, *n.* [*sphaer-*, and Gr. *enchyma*, anything poured out.] spherical or spheroidal cellular tissue, such as is found in the pulp of fruits.
sphae·rid′i·um, *n.*; *pl.* **sphae·rid′i·ȧ,** [Gr. *sphaira*, a sphere, and *eidos*, resemblance.] one of numerous stalked appendages with buttonlike heads, covered with cilia, found in almost all sea urchins.
sphae′rō-, [from Gr. *sphaira*, a ball, a sphere.] a combining form meaning *a sphere* or *like a sphere*: also, before a vowel, *sphaer-*.
sphae′rō·spōre, *n.* same as *spherospore*.
Sphae·rō·thē′cȧ, *n.* [*sphaero-*, and Gr. *thēkē*, a case.] a genus of fungi, some of which cause a destructive, whitish mildew on plants, especially the hop vine and gooseberry.
sphaer′ū·līte, *n.* same as *spherulite*.
Sphag·nā′cē·ae, *n.pl.* a family of caulescent bog plants typified by the genus *Sphagnum*; the peat mosses.
sphag·nā′ceous, *a.* relating to the *Sphagnaceæ*.
Sphag·nā′lēs, *n.pl.* the peat mosses.
sphag·nic′ō·lous, *a.* growing among or in sphagnum mosses.
sphag′nous, *a.* of, consisting of, or covered with mosses of the genus *Sphagnum*.
Sphag′num, *n.* [Gr. *sphagnos*, a kind of moss.]
1. the typical and only genus of the family *Sphagnaceæ*. The mosses of this genus are widely diffused over the surface of the earth in temperate climates, readily recognized by their pale grayish tint, fasciculate branchlets, and apparently sessile globose capsules. They are aquatic plants, and constitute the great mass of the bogs in swampy and moory districts. The formation of the peat in such situations is often owing, in a great measure, to these plants.
2. [s-] a moss of the genus *Sphagnum*; also, a mass of such mosses, used to make fertilizer, to pack and pot plants, to make surgical dressings, etc.
sphal′ĕr·īte, *n.* [Gr. *sphaleros*, deceptive, uncertain; and *-ite*.] a transparent, cleavable resinous zinc sulfide, ZnS, the principal ore of zinc: also called *zinc blende, black jack, false galena*, etc.
Sphe̤′i·dae, *n.pl.* a family of fossorial hymenopters or digger wasps which burrow in sandbanks for nidification.
sphen-, same as *spheno-*.
sphēne, *n.* [Fr. *sphène*, from Gr. *sphēn*, a wedge.] same as *titanite*.
sphē·neth′moid, *a.* designating the curved plate in front of the lesser wing of the ethmoid bone.
sphē·neth′moid, *n.* the sphenethmoid bone, as in the skull of a frog.
sphenethmoid bone; a cranial bone of a frog in front of the parasphenoid and circling the front of the brain: also called *girdle bone*.
sphē·neth·moid′ăl, *a.* same as *sphenethmoid*.
sphē′niç, *a.* 1. wedge-shaped.
2. designating or of a number having three unequal prime factors.
sphē·nis′căn, *n.* [Gr. *sphēniskos*, dim. of *sphēn*, a wedge.] a penguin.
sphē′nō-, [from Gr. *sphēn*, a wedge.] a combining form meaning, (a) *shaped like a wedge*, as in *spheno*gram; (b) *of the sphenoid bone*: also, before a vowel, *sphen-*.
sphen·oç·cip′i·tăl, *a.* relating to the sphenoid and the occipital bones.
sphenoccipital bone; the hindmost bone of the skull, formed by the union of the sphenoid and occipital bones in adults.

Sphē′nō·don, *n.* same as *Hatteria*.
sphē″nō·eth·moid′ăl, *a.* same as *sphenethmoid*.
sphē′nō·gram, *n.* [*spheno-* and *-gram*.] a cuneiform or wedge-shaped character or symbol, as on a monolith.
sphē·nog′rȧ·phẽr, *n.* one versed in sphenography or in deciphering cuneiform inscriptions.
sphē·nō·graph′iç, *a.* pertaining to sphenography.
sphē·nog′rȧ·phist, *n.* same as *sphenographer*.
sphē·nog′rȧ·phy, *n.* [*spheno-*, and Gr. *graphein*, to write.] writing done in wedge-shaped and arrow-headed characters; also, the art of deciphering cuneiform writings; that branch of philological science which concerns itself with such writings.
sphē′noid, sphē·noid′ăl, *a.* [*spheno-*, and Gr. *eidos*, form.]
1. wedge-shaped.
2. in anatomy, designating or of the wedge-shaped compound bone at the base of the skull.
sphē′noid, *n.* 1. a wedge-shaped crystal contained under four equal isosceles triangles.
2. the sphenoid bone.
sphē·nō·pal′ȧ·tine, *a.* related to or in the region of the sphenoid and palatal bones.
sphenopalatine ganglion; a ganglion of the sympathetic, facial, and other nerves situated near the right auricle of the heart: also called *Meckel's ganglion*.
sphē·not′iç, *a.* relating to the sphenoid bone and the hard parts of the ear, or otic capsule.
sphenotic bone; in a fish, a bone situated back of the frontal bone.
sphē′nō·trībe, *n.* [*spheno-*, and Gr. *tribein*, to bruise.] an obstetrical instrument to crush the head of the fetus to facilitate delivery when normal delivery is not possible.
sphēr′ăl, *a.* 1. of or like a sphere.
2. rounded in form; spherical.
3. symmetrical.
sphēre, *n.* [Fr., from L. *sphæra*, Gr. *sphaira*, a ball, globe.]
1. any round body or figure having the surface equally distant from the center at all points; a globe; a ball.
2. a star or planet.
3. the visible heavens; sky.
4. the apparent globe (*celestial sphere*) formed by the heavens and visible only as a dome extending from horizon to horizon.
5. any of a series of hypothetical spherical shells, transparent, concentric, and postulated as revolving one within another, in which the stars, planets, sun, moon, etc. were were supposedly set: a concept of ancient astronomy.
6. the place or range of action or existence; field or extent of knowledge, experience, influence, etc.; province; compass; domain.
7. social stratum; place in society; walk of life.
8. a circuit, as of a heavenly body. [Obs.]
9. in logic, whatever comes within the scope of a general concept; the entire content of a concept, as including individuals, species, and genera. [Rare.]
armillary sphere; see under *armillary*.
axis of a sphere; any diameter of a sphere; specifically, the diameter about which it rotates, as the axis of a planet.
circle of a sphere; see *circles of the sphere* under *circle*.
music of the spheres; see under *music*.
oblique sphere; see under *oblique*, a.
parallel sphere; see under *parallel*, a.
right sphere; see under *right*, a.
terrestrial sphere; (a) the earth; (b) anything representing the earth as an illustrative globe with the earth's features marked upon it.
Syn.—ball, globe, orb.
sphēre, *v.t.*; sphered, *pt., pp.*; sphering, *ppr.*
1. to place in or as in a sphere.
2. to form into a sphere; as, light *sphered* in a radiant cloud.
3. to put among the heavenly spheres.
-sphēre, combining form meaning *a sphere* or *like a sphere*, as in blasto*sphere*, strato*sphere*.
sphēre çrys′tăls, same as *sphaeraphides*.
sphēre′less, *a.* without a sphere or spheres; having no place of action; wandering; errant; as, a *sphereless* star.
spher′iç, *a.* same as *spherical*.
spher′i·căl, *a.* 1. shaped like a sphere; globular.
2. of a sphere or spheres.
3. of the heavenly spheres (sometimes with astrological reference).
spherical aberration; optical distortion resulting from spherical form, as in a lens or mirror.
spherical angle (or *triangle*, etc.); an angle (or triangle, etc.) formed by intersecting arcs of great circles of a sphere.
spherical excess; see under *excess*.
spherical geometry; that branch of geometry which treats of spherical magnitudes; the doctrine of the sphere, particularly of the circles described on its surface.
spherical lune; the part of the surface of a sphere included between the semicircumferences of two great circles having a common diameter.
spherical polygon; a portion of the surface of a sphere bounded by the arcs of three or more great circles.
spherical sector; same as *sector of a sphere* under *sector*.
spherical segment; a portion of a sphere included between a zone and a secant plane or between two parallel secant planes.
spherical trigonometry; that branch of trigonometry concerned with spherical triangles and polygons.
spherical ungula; a portion of a sphere bounded by a lune and two semicircles meeting in a diameter of the sphere: also called *spherical wedge*.
spher′i·căl·ly, *adv.* 1. in the form of a sphere or spherical section.
2. so as to be spherical.
spher′i·căl·ness, *n.* the condition or quality of being spherical. [Rare.]
sphē·riç′i·ty, *n.* the state or quality of being orbicular or spherical; roundness; as, the *sphericity* of a drop of water.
spher′i·çle, *n.* a small sphere.
spher′içs, *n.pl.* [*construed as sing.*] the geometry and trigonometry of figures formed on the surface of a sphere.
sphē′rō-, same as *sphaero-*.
sphē·rō·çon′iç, *n.* in mathematics, the nonplane curve of intersection formed by a sphere and a quadric cone whose vertex is the center of the sphere.
sphē′rō·grȧph, *n.* a nautical instrument for the determination of the angular position of a ship, and distance sailed.
sphē′roid, *n.* [*sphero-*, and Gr. *eidos*, form.]
1. a body or figure that is almost but not quite a perfect sphere: the earth is a *spheroid*.
2. same as *ellipsoid of revolution* under *ellipsoid*.
sphē′roid, *a.* same as *spheroidal*.
sphē·roid′ăl, *a.* having the form of a spheroid; almost spherical.
spheroidal state; the form taken by a drop of liquid, as water, when placed on the level surface of a very hot metal, being held aloof from the metal by a layer of its own vapor and assuming a more or less flattened spheroidal shape: also called *calorific paradox*.
sphē·roid′iç, *a.* spheroidal.
sphē·roid′iç·ăl, *a.* spheroidal.
sphē·roi·diç′i·ty, *n.* the character or condition of being spheroidal.
sphē·roid′i·ty, *n.* same as *spheroidicity*.
sphē·rom′e·tẽr, *n.* [Fr. *sphéromètre*.] an instrument used for measuring the surface curvature of bodies that are spherical, cylindrical, etc., as lenses, by means of a scale and a micrometer screw.
sphē·rō·sid′ẽr·īte, *n.* carbonate of iron siderite in spheroidal masses.
sphē′rō·spōre, *n.* the quadruple spore peculiar to some of the *Algæ*.
spher′ū·lȧ, *n.*; *pl.* **spher′ū·lae,** [L. *sphærula*, dim. of *sphæra*, a sphere.] a small sphere; specifically, (a) a globose peridium of a fungus; (b) a globose siliceous part of the skeleton of a sponge.
spher′ū·lăr, *a.* spherical.
spher′ū·lāte, *a.* in zoology, provided or covered with spherules or tubercles.
spher′ūle, *n.* [L. *sphærula*, a little sphere.] a little sphere or spherical body, as of quicksilver when poured upon a plane; a globule.
spher′ū·līte, *n.* a group of crystals arranged in the shape of a sphere, as in certain volcanic rocks.
spher·ū·lit′iç, *a.* referring to, containing, or composed of spherulites.
sphēr′y, *a.*; *comp.* spherier; *superl.* spheriest, 1. of or like a sphere, especially a heavenly body. [Poet.]
2. celestial; starlike. [Poet.]

Sphex, *n.* [Gr. *sphēx*, a wasp.]
1. a genus, mostly tropical, of digger wasps, typical of the family *Sphegidæ*.
2. [s–] any wasp of the genus *Sphex*.

sphinc′tēr, *n.* [Gr. *sphinktēr*, from *sphingein*, to draw close.] in anatomy, a ring-shaped muscle that surrounds a natural opening in the body and can open or close it by expanding or contracting.
sphincter ani; the muscle that closes the anus.

sphinc′tēr, *a.* relating to, performing as, or designating a sphincter.

sphinc′tēr·ăl, *a.* of, or having the nature of, a sphincter.

sphinc′tēr·āte, *a.* 1. provided with a sphincter.
2. moved or controlled by a sphincter.

sphinc·tē′ri·ăl, *a.* same as *sphincteral*.

sphin′ġid, *a.* of, pertaining to, or related to the *Sphingidæ*.

sphin′ġid, *n.* one of the *Sphingidæ*.

Sphin′ġi·dae, *n.pl.* a family of lepidopterous insects of the section *Crepuscularia*. This family embraces some of the largest European *Lepidoptera*, as the hawk moths.

sphin′ġi·form, *a.* resembling a sphingid.

sphin̄′goid, *a.* sphingiform.

sphin̄x, *n.*; *pl.* **sphin̄x′eș, sphin′ġēș,** [Gr., lit., the strangler.]
1. any Egyptian statue or figure having, typically, the body of a lion and the head of a man, ram, or hawk.
2. [S–] a huge statue of this kind with the head of a man, at Gîza, near Cairo, Egypt.
3. in Greek mythology, (a) a winged monster with a lion's body and the head and breasts of a woman; specifically, (b) [S–] a monster of this kind that perched on a rock near Thebes and asked a riddle of every passer-by, strangling all who could not answer: Oedipus solved the riddle, and the Sphinx killed herself.

GREEK SPHINX

EGYPTIAN SPHINX

4. a person whose manner or expression suggests that his character is deep and mysterious.
5. in zoology, a hawk moth.

sphin̄x moth, any insect of the family *Sphingidæ*.

sphraġ′ide, *n.* [Fr. *sphragide*, from L. *sphragis* (*-idis*), a kind of stone used for seals, Lemnian earth, from Gr. *sphragis* (*-idos*), a seal. The earth is said to have been so called because sold in sealed packets.] same as *Lemnian earth* under *Lemnian*.

sphrȧ·ġis′tics, *n.pl.* [*construed as sing.*] [Gr. *sphragis*, a seal.] the science of engraved seals, their history, age, and distinctions.

sphyġ′mic, *a.* [Gr. *sphygmos*, the pulse.] of or pertaining to the pulse.

sphyġ′mō-, [from Gr. *sphygmos*, the pulse.] a combining form meaning *the pulse*, as in *sphygmo*graph.

sphyġ′mō·gram, *n.* the record made by the sphygmograph; a series of tracings showing the force and extent of the undulations of the pulse.

sphyġ′mō·grȧph, *n.* an instrument which, when applied over an artery, indicates the rate, force, and variations of the pulse.

sphyġ·mō·graph′ic, *a.* of, pertaining to, or registered by the sphygmograph.

sphyġ·mog′rȧ·phy, *n.* the recording of the pulse by means of a sphygmograph.

sphyġ′moid, *a.* pulselike.

sphyġ·mol′ō·ġy, *n.* the scientific study of the pulse.

sphyġ″mō·mȧ·nom′e·ter, *n.* an instrument for measuring arterial blood pressure.

sphyġ·mom′e·tēr, *n.* an instrument for measuring the force and rate of the pulse.

sphyġ′mō·phōne, *n.* [*sphygmo-*, and Gr. *phōnē*, a sound.] an instrument for determining the character of pulse undulations by means of the hearing.

sphyġ′mō·scōpe, *n.* [*sphygmo-*, and Gr. *skopein*, to view.] sphygmograph.

sphyġ′mus, *n.* [Gr. *sphygmos*, the pulse.] the pulse.

Sphȳ·rae′nȧ, *n.* the type genus of the *Sphyrænidæ*. Of the twenty known species, including the barracuda, all are closely related and are rapacious and savage. They are found in temperate and tropical seas.

Sphȳ·raen′i·dae, *n.pl.* [LL., from Gr. *sphyraina*, the hammer fish.] a family of acanthopterygious teleostean fishes, closely allied to the perches. The species are elongated, active, predaceous fishes, having the jaws armed with formidable teeth. They live principally in tropical seas, although one or two species are found in the Mediterranean and along the coast of New England. The barracuda of the West Indies, *Sphyræna picuda*, is a large and powerful fish of this family.

sphȳ·rae′noid, *a.* of or pertaining to the *Sphyrænidæ*.

spī′ăl, *n.* a spy; a scout. [Obs.]

spī′cȧ, *n.*; *pl.* **spī′cae,** [L., an ear of grain.]
1. in surgery, a spiral bandage: so called because wound with reverse turns in such a way as to resemble a spike of barley.
2. in botany, a spike, as of a flower.
3. [S–] in astronomy, a bright star in the constellation Virgo.

spī′cāte, *a.* [L. *spicatus*, pp. of *spicare*, to furnish with spikes.]
1. having the form of a spike.
2. arranged in a spike or spikes.

spī′cā·ted, *a.* same as *spicate*.

spic·cä′tō, *a.* [It.] in music, detached; played with the bow wrist relaxed so that the bow rebounds between notes: a direction to the violinist, etc.

spīce, *n.* [OFr. *espice*; L. *species*, appearance, species, kind, sort, in late Latin, goods, wares, assorted goods, especially spices and drugs.]
1. (a) any of several vegetable substances, as clove, cinnamon, nutmeg, pepper, etc., used to season food: spices are usually dried for use and have distinctive flavors and aromas; (b) such substances collectively or as a material.
2. a spicy fragrance or aroma.
3. that which gives zest or piquancy; interesting or flavorful part.
4. a small bit; trace; suggestion; as, a *spice* of envy in her tone.
5. a sample, specimen, sort, or kind. [Obs.]

spīce, *v.t.*; spiced (spīst), *pt.*, *pp.*; spicing, *ppr.*
1. to season or flavor with spice; to mix aromatic substances with; as, to *spice* wine.
2. to add zest or piquancy to; to make entertaining or piquant; as, he *spiced* his speech with witty stories.

spīce′ber″ry, *n.*; *pl.* **spīce′ber″ries,** 1. the checkerberry or wintergreen, *Gaultheria procumbens*.
2. a Florida tree of the myrtle family, having orange or black fruit.
3. the fruit of this tree.

spīce′bush, *n.* a North American shrub, *Lindera benzoin*: also called *spicewood*, *wild allspice*, and *feverbush*. The bark and leaves have a spicy odor, the flowers are small and yellowish, and the fruit is red.

spīce nut, a small sweet spiced cake.

spī′cēr, *n.* 1. one who seasons with spice.
2. one who deals in spice. [Obs.]

spī′cēr·y, *n.*; *pl.* **spī′cēr·ieș,** [Fr. *épicerie*.]
1. spices.
2. something spicy; spicy quality, flavor, or aroma.
3. a place where spices are kept. [Obs.]

spīce tree, a fragrant evergreen tree, *Umbellularia californica*, of the western part of the United States, having aromatic leaves. Its hard wood takes a high polish.

spīce′wood, *n.* same as *spicebush*.

spī·cif′ēr·ous, *a.* [L. *spicifer*, bearing spikes or ears, from *spica*, an ear, and *ferre*, to bear.] in botany, bearing ears, as corn; producing spikes; spicate; eared.

spī′ci·form, *a.* in botany, having the form of a spike.

spī′ci·ly, *adv.* in a spicy manner; so as to be or make spicy.

spī′ci·ness, *n.* the quality of being spicy.

spick, *n.* a titmouse. [Brit. Dial.]

spick′-ănd-span′, *a.* [short for *spick-and-span-new*; *spick*, var. of *spike*, a nail, and *span-new*, from ME. *spon-neowe*; O.N. *spān-nȳr*, from *spānn*, a chip, shaving, and *nyr*, new.]
1. new; fresh.
2. neat and clean.

spick′-ănd-span′-new′, *a.* brand new; quite new; as, a *spick-and-span-new* sail.

spick′nel, spig′nel, *n.* the herb baldmoney, *Meum athamanticum*.

spick′-span-new′, *a.* spick-and-span-new. [Rare.]

spī′cōse, *a.* spicous.

spī·cos′i·ty, *n.* the state or quality of having or being full of ears, like corn.

spī′cous, *a.* [L. *spica*, a spike.] having ears or spikes, like corn.

spic′ū·lȧ, *n.*; *pl.* **spic′ū·lae,** [LL., dim. of L. *spica*, a spike or ear.] in botany, a small spike or spikelet; also, a pointed, fleshy, superficial appendage.

spic′ū·lăr, *a.* [L. *spiculum*, a dart.] spiculate.

spic′ū·lāte, *v.t.* [L. *spiculare*, to sharpen, from *spiculum*, a dart.] to sharpen to a point. [Rare.]

spic′ū·lāte, *a.* 1. shaped like a spicule.
2. covered with or consisting of spicules.

spic′ūle, *n.* 1. a small, hard, sharp-pointed, needlelike piece or process, especially of bony or calcareous material, as in the skeleton of the sponge.
2. a small spike of flowers.

spic·ū·lif′ēr·ous, *a.* [L. *spiculum*, a spicule, and *ferre*, to bear.] bearing spicules.

spic′ū·li·form, *a.* having the form of a spicule.

spic·ū·liġ′e·nous, *a.* containing spicules; producing spicules.

spic·ū·liġ′ēr·ous, *a.* spiculiferous.

spic′ū·lōse, *a.* spiculous.

spic′ū·lous, *a.* having spicules.

spic′ū·lum, *n.*; *pl.* **spic′ū·lȧ,** a spicule; especially, any of several spinelike organs found in lower animals, as the starfish.

spī′cy, *a.*; *comp.* spicier; *superl.* spiciest, 1. containing or abounding in spices.
2. having the flavor or aroma of a spice or spices; fragrant; aromatic.
3. piquant; pungent.
4. risqué; racy.
Syn.—fragrant, tart, keen, piquant, lively, smart, aromatic, pungent.

spī′dēr, *n.* [ME. *spithre*; AS. *spithra*, from *spinnan*, to spin.]
1. any of a number of small, eight-legged animals having a body composed of two divisions, a cephalothorax bearing the legs and an abdomen bearing two or more pairs of spinnerets, whose function is to spin the silk threads from which they make nests, cocoons, or webs for trapping insects: the spider is an arachnid and not an insect.
2. a person thought of as spiderlike in nature or appearance.
3. a trivet.
4. a frying pan, originally one with attached legs for use over an open fire.
5. a device for pulverizing the ground, used with a cultivator.
6. in machinery, (a) a skeleton of radiating spokes, as a rag wheel; (b) the internal frame or skeleton of a gear wheel, for instance, on which a cogged rim may be bolted, shrunk, or cast; (c) the solid interior portion of a piston to which the packing is attached and to whose axis the piston rod is secured.
7. in nautical usage, (a) an iron outrigger to keep a block clear of the ship's side; (b) an iron hoop round the mast for the attachment of the futtock shrouds; also, a hoop round a mast provided with belaying pins.
8. any one of certain arachnids resembling the true spider.

spī′dēr ȧnt, an insect of the family *Mutillidæ*.

spī′dēr band, same as *spider*, 7 (b).

spī′dēr bug, a hemipterous insect, *Emesa longipes*, with long legs.

spī′dēr catch′ēr, 1. one who or that which catches spiders; specifically, a bird, the wall-creeper, *Tichodroma muraria*, found in southern Europe.
2. a spider hunter.

spī′dēr cellș, neuroglia cells.

spī′dēr crab, any marine crab of the genus *Maia*. The body is triangular, the legs slender and long. The Japanese species occasionally measures more than twelve feet across the extended legs.

spī′dẽr dī′vẽr, the dabchick. [Brit. Dial.]

spī′dẽr ēat′ẽr, the spider hunter.

spī′dẽred (-dẽrd), *a.* infested with spiders; cobwebbed.

spī′dẽr·flow″ẽr, *n.* any plant of the genus *Cleome* which has long stamens, suggestive of a spider.

spī′dẽr flȳ, a dipterous insect of the family *Pupipara,* many species of which are found parasitic on birds and quadrupeds.

spī′dẽr hunt′ẽr, any one of a genus of birds, the *Arachnothera,* inhabiting the Indian archipelago and feeding on spiders.

spī′dẽr·līke, *a.* resembling a spider.

spī′dẽr līne, one of the threads of a spider's web used in optical instruments as a reticle.

spī′dẽr mīte, one of a family of mites, *Gamasidæ,* found upon plants.

spī′dẽr mŏn′key, a name given to many species of platyrrhine monkeys of South and Central America having long, spidery limbs and long, prehensile tails.

SPIDER MONKEY

spī′dẽr or′chis, a European plant of the genus *Ophrys* which has a spiderlike flower.

spī′dẽr shell, any shell of the genus *Pteroceras,* found in tropical waters.

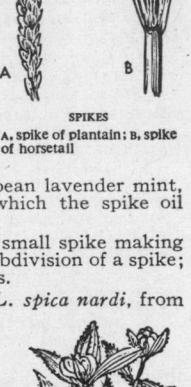

spī′dẽr wäsp, any one of numerous species of wasps that catch spiders and other insects and store them in their nests as food for their young.

spī′dẽr web, the netlike web spun by a spider to catch insects.

spī′dẽr·wŏrt, *n.* a plant of the genus *Tradescantia*; specifically, *Tradescantia virginica,* an American garden plant, having grasslike leaves and blue or purplish flowers. The name is also given to various other plants, as the liliaceous plant, *Lloydia serotina,* known as the mountain spiderwort.

spī′dẽr·y, *a.* 1. like a spider or spiders.
2. long and thin like a spider's legs.
3. infested with spiders.

spīed, *v.* past tense and past participle of *spy.*

spiē′gel, *n.* spiegeleisen: also *spiegel iron.*

spiē′gel·eī″sen, *n.* [G. *spiegel,* a mirror, and *eisen,* iron, named from its fracture showing large, smooth, shining surfaces.] a kind of hard, white pig iron made from specular iron ore, or hematite, containing manganese.

spiē′gel ī′ron (-ũrn), same as *spiegeleisen.*

spiēl, *n.* [G. *spiel,* play, game.] a speech or talk, as of an actor or street-vender. [Slang.]

spiēl, *v.i.*; spieled, *pt., pp.*; spieling, *ppr.* to talk, speak, or orate. [Slang.]

spiēl′ẽr, *n.* one who spiels; specifically, one who by spieling or talking calls attention to a show, exhibit, or the like; a barker. [Slang.]

spī′ẽr, *n.* a person who spies; a spy.

spif′fy, *a.*; *comp.* spiffier; *superl.* spiffiest, [from dial. *spiff,* a well-dressed person.] attractive to the eye; smart; neat; fine; spruce. [Slang.]

spif′li·cā·ted, *a.* very drunk; intoxicated. [Slang.]

Spī·gē′li·ȧ, *n.* [from A. *Spiegel* (1558–1625), a Dutch botanist.] a genus of plants of the *Loganiaceæ,* native to the warmer parts of America; the pinkroots.

spīght (spīt), *n.* and *v.* spite. [Obs.]

spīght, *n.* speight. [Obs.]

spig′nel, *n.* same as *spicknel.*

spig′net, *n.* the American spikenard.

spig′ŏt, *n.* [ME. *spigotte,* prob. via OFr., from base of *spike.*]
1. a plug or peg used to stop the vent in a barrel, etc.
2. (a) a faucet; (b) the valve or plug in a faucet.
3. the end of a pipe that is inserted into an enlarged end of another pipe so as to form a joint.

spig′ŏt joint, an expansion joint for uniting two parts of a straight metallic pipe, which is exposed to great variations of temperature.

spīke, *n.* [probably from ON. *spikr,* a nail; ultimately from L. *spica,* ear of corn.]
1. a sharp-pointed part or projection, usually slender and of metal, as along the top of an iron fence, etc.
2. a long, heavy nail.
3. any long, slender, pointed object, as the single antler of a young deer.
4. [*pl.*] sharp or pointed metal projections on the soles, and often on the heels, of shoes used for baseball, golf, track, etc., to prevent slipping.
5. a young mackerel not more than six inches long.

spīke, *v.t.*; spiked, *pt., pp.*; spiking, *ppr.* 1. to fasten or fit with or as with a spike or spikes.
2. to mark, pierce, cut, etc. with a spike or spikes, or impale on a spike.
3. to make (a cannon) unusable by driving a spike into the touchhole.
4. to thwart, frustrate, or block, as a scheme.
5. to add alcohol or strong alcoholic liquor to (a drink).
6. in baseball, etc., to injure (an opponent, another player, etc.) with the spikes on one's shoes.

spīke, *n.* [ME. *spik*; L. *spica.*]
1. an ear of grain.
2. a long flower cluster with flowers attached directly to the stalk.

SPIKES
A, spike of plantain; B, spike of horsetail

spīke′bill, *n.* 1. the hooded merganser. [Dial.]
2. the marbled godwit. [Dial.]

spīke′fish, *n.* same as *sailfish.*

spīke gráss, one of several perennial grasses found in America, characterized by broad leaves, and flowers in spikelets, as *Uniola paniculata.*

spīke′hòrn, *n.* 1. the unbranched or simple antler of a young deer.
2. a deer having a simple antler.

spīke lav′en·dẽr, a European lavender mint, *Lavandula spica,* from which the spike oil used in art is obtained.

spīke′let, *n.* in botany, a small spike making a part of a large one; a subdivision of a spike; as, the *spikelets* of grasses.

spīke′nȧrd, *n.* [ME.; ML. *spica nardi,* from L. *spica,* a spike, and *nardus,* an aromatic root.]
1. a fragrant oil or ointment used by the ancients, believed to be derived from the roots of *Nardostachys jatamansi,* of the valerian family, or from some closely allied plant; also, the plant itself; nard.
2. an American plant, *Aralia racemosa,* with whitish flowers, purplish berries, and fragrant roots, allied to the ginseng: sometimes called *spignet.*
3. any one of various other plants, as *Lavandula spica,* and *Valeriana celtica,* the Celtic spikenard.
4. any one of various fragrant essential oils.
Cretan spikenard; a species of valerian, *Valeriana phu,* of western Asia.
false spikenard; a plant, *Smilacina racemosa,* of America.
West Indian spikenard; a kind of mint, *Hyptis suaveolens.*

SPIKENARD
(*Nardostachys jatamansi*)

spīke′nȧrd tree, same as *angelica tree* under *angelica.*

spīke oil, a volatile oil obtained by distilling *Lavandula spica* with water. It has a less agreeable odor than true lavender oil, and is specifically heavier.

spīke rush, any of several plants of the genus *Eleocharis.*

spīke shell, a slender conical shell of the genus *Styliola.*

spīke′tāil, *n.* a duck, the pintail. [Dial.]

spīke tēam, a team of three horses, or other draft animals, hitched two abreast and the third a leader. [Dial.]

spīk′y, *a.*; *comp.* spikier; *superl.* spikiest, 1. shaped like a spike; long and pointed.
2. having or set with spikes.

spīle, *n.* [M.D., a splinter or spindle.]
1. a small peg or wooden pin used as a spigot to stop a hole.
2. a tap or spout driven into a sugar-maple tree to conduct the sap into a receptacle below.
3. a stake driven into the ground to protect a bank, form wharfs, abutments, etc.; a pile.
4. a stick or timber used in casing a mine shaft.

spīle, *v.t.*; spiled, *pt., pp.*; spiling, *ppr.* 1. to furnish or support with spiles, or stakes.
2. to set a spile into (a tree, barrel, etc.).
3. to draw off (liquid) through a spile.
4. to stop up (a hole) with a spile, or plug.

spīle hōle, a small aperture made in a cask when placed on tap, usually near the bunghole, to admit air, in order to permit the contained liquid to flow freely.

spīle′wŏrm, *n.* the teredo, or shipworm.

spil′i·kin, *n.* [from M.D. *spilleken,* dim. of *spille,* a splinter, a pin.]
1. one of a set of pegs or strips, as of bone, used in playing certain games, as jackstraws, cribbage, etc.
2. [*pl.*] [*construed as sing.*] a game in which these are used.
Also spelled *spillikin.*

spīl′ing, *n.* [from *spill,* dial. var. of *spile.*] spiles or timbers collectively; piling.

spill, *n.* [var. of *spile.*]
1. a small peg or pin for stopping a hole; a spile.
2. a small bar or pin of metal.
3. a spindle, as in a spinning machine.
4. a slender piece of any substance, especially a thin roll or fold of paper, to be lighted in a fire and used as a match.
5. in mining, a spile.
6. a splinter.

spill, *v.t.*; spilled *or* spilt, *pt., pp.*; spilling, *ppr.* [AS. *spillan,* to spill, ruin, waste, destroy.]
1. to allow or cause, especially in an unintentional or accidental manner, to run, fall, or flow over from a receptacle or container, usually with resulting loss or waste: said of a liquid or a loose or granular substance.
2. to shed (blood).
3. to empty the wind from (a sail).
4. to scatter, especially by emptying from a receptacle or container.
5. [Obs.] (a) to kill; (b) to destroy or ruin; (c) to squander; waste.
6. to make known (something secret or unknown); divulge. [Colloq.]
7. to cause or allow to fall; to throw off (a rider, load, etc.). [Colloq.]

spill, *v.i.,* 1. to waste; to be prodigal. [Obs.]
2. to be spilled from a receptacle or container; to overflow; to run out; to fall out.

spill, *n.* 1. a spilling.
2. the amount spilled.
3. a spillway.
4. a fall or tumble, as from a horse, bicycle, etc. [Colloq.]
5. a downpour, as of rain. [Colloq.]

spill′ẽr, *n.* 1. one who or that which spills or sheds.
2. a kind of fishing line; a trawl; a bultow; also, a small seine used to remove the fish from a larger one, as in mackerel fishing when the larger seine cannot be used because of the rocky bottom, etc. Also called *spillet.*

spil′let fish′ing, fishing with a spiller.

spill′li·kin, *n.* same as *spilikin.*

spill′ing line, a line to spill a sail for furling.

spill′wāy, *n.* a channel or passageway used to carry off the excess of water, as from a reservoir.

spilt, *v.* alternative past tense and past participle of *spill.*

spilth, *n.* [from *spill, v.*]
1. a spilling.
2. that which is spilled; especially, anything spilled profusely.

spin, *v.t.*; spun *or archaic* span, *pt.* spun *pp.*; spinning, *ppr.* [AS. *spinnan*; akin to G. *spinnen.*]
1. to draw out and twist fibers of (wool, cotton, etc.) into thread.
2. to make (thread, yarn, etc.) by this process.

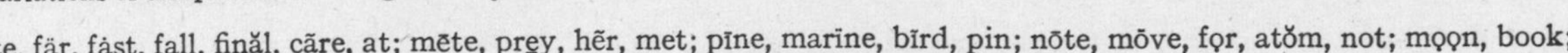
fāte, fär, fȧst, fạll, finăl, cãre, at; mēte, prẹy, hẽr, met; pīne, marīne, bïrd, pin; nōte, mōve, fọr, atŏm, not; mọọn, book;

3. to make (a web, cocoon, etc.) from a filament of a viscous fluid that is extruded from the body and hardens on exposure to the air: said of spiders, silkworms, etc.
4. to make or produce in a way suggestive of spinning.
5. to carry out to a great length; to prolong; to protract (a story, etc.): usually with *out.*
6. to tell (a story, yarn, etc.).
7. to cause to whirl or rotate swiftly; as, the boy *spun* the top.
8. to troll for fish.

spin, *v.i.* 1. to spin thread or yarn.
2. to form a thread, web, etc.: said of spiders, etc.
3. to fish with a spoon or spinner.
4. to whirl or rotate swiftly.
5. to seem to be spinning from dizziness.
6. to move along swiftly and smoothly.

spin, *n.* 1. a whirling or rotating action or movement.
2. the act of causing such an action or movement.
3. a moving along swiftly and smoothly.
4. a ride or short trip in a vehicle.
5. any of various maneuvers in which an airplane comes down nose first along a spiral path of large pitch and small radius.

spī′nȧ, *n.*; *pl.* **spī′nae,** [L., spine, or prickle.]
1. a spine.
2. in ancient Rome, a ridge or wall dividing the race course of a circus into two sides.

spī′nȧ bif′i·dȧ, [L. *spina,* spine, prickle; *bifida,* f. of *bifidus,* forked; from *bis,* twice, and *findere,* to cleave, divide.] a congenital defect characterized by imperfect closure of the spinal column exposing some of the nervous system and often resulting in hydrocephalus, paralysis, etc.

spī·nā′ceous, *a.* of or having the appearance or the characteristics of spinach or other plants of the goosefoot family.

spin′ach (-ij), *n.* [OFr. *espinoche, espinace*; It. *spinace*; Sp. *espinaca,* from Ar. *isbānah*].
1. a plant of the goosefoot family with dark-green, juicy, edible leaves, usually eaten cooked; also, its leaves.
2. one of several plants used as a spinach, as lamb's-quarters, watercress, mustard, dandelion, etc.
Australian spinach; a species of goosefoot, *Chenopodium auricomum,* found in central Australia.

spī′năl, *a.* [LL. *spinalis.*]
1. of or having to do with the spine or spinal cord.
2. of a spine or needle-shaped process.
spinal accessory nerves; the eleventh pair of cranial nerves, having motor function.
spinal anesthesia; in surgery, local anesthesia of the lower half of the body by the injection of an anesthetic into the lumbar portion of the spinal cord.
spinal canal; the canal, tube, formed by the vertebral arches, which contains the spinal cord.
spinal column; the backbone; the spine; the column composed of the vertebrae with their fibrocartilages and ligaments and enclosing the spinal canal.
spinal cord; the cordlike structure of nerve tissue contained in the spinal canal and extending from the medulla oblongata to the second lumbar vertebra.
spinal ganglion; a ganglion on the posterior root of a spinal nerve.
spinal marrow; the spinal cord; the myelon.

spī′năl, *n.* spinal anesthesia.

spī′nāte, *a.* having spines; shaped like a spine.

spin′dle, *n.* [AS. *spinel,* from *spinnan,* to spin.]
1. a slender rod or pin used in spinning; specifically, (a) in hand spinning, a rounded rod, usually wooden, tapering toward each end, for twisting into thread the fibers pulled from the material on the distaff and notched at one end so as to hold the thread; (b) on a spinning wheel, the rod by which the thread is twisted and on which it is then wound; (c) in a spinning machine, one of the rods holding the bobbins on which the thread is wound as it is spun.
2. a measure for yarn, equal to 14,400 yards in linen or 15,120 yards in cotton.
3. something having the long, slender shape of a spindle, as the bundle of nuclear fibers formed during one stage of mitosis, or a short turned piece in a baluster.
4. any rod, pin, or shaft that revolves or serves as an axis for a revolving part.
5. a small axis, axle, arbor, mandrel, or shaft.
6. in a lathe, a shaftlike part (*live spindle*) that rotates while holding the thing to be turned, or a similar part (*dead spindle*) that does not rotate.
7. a hydrometer.
8. a metal rod, pipe, etc., usually with a lantern, ball, or other easily visible object at its top, fastened to a rock, shoal, or the like as a warning to vessels.
9. in architecture, same as *newel.*
10. any of several shells of certain mollusks: so called from their resemblance to a spindle, as in species of the genera *Fusus* and *Rostellaria*: also called *spindle shell.*
dead spindle; the arbor of a machine tool which does not revolve.
live spindle; the revolving arbor of a machine tool.

spin′dle, *a.* 1. of or like a spindle or spindles.
2. designating or of the maternal side or female line of a family.

spin′dle, *v.i.*; spindled, *pt., pp.*; spindling, *ppr* 1. to grow in a long, slender shape.
2. to grow into a long, slender stalk or stem.

spin′dle, *v.t.* 1. to form into a spindle.
2. to fit or equip with a spindle.

spin′dle-leg·ged, *a.* having long, thin, spindle-like legs.

spin′dle·legs̹, *n.pl.* 1. long, thin legs.
2. [*construed as sing.*] a person with thin legs. [Colloq.]

spin′dle-shan̄ked (-shan̄kt), *a.* same as *spindle-legged.*

spin′dle·shan̄ks, *n.pl.* same as *spindlelegs.*

spin′dle-shāped (-shāpt), *a.* having the shape of a spindle.

spin′dle shell, same as *spindle,* sense 10.

spin′dle·tail, *n.* a duck, the pintail. [Dial.]

spin′dle tree, a shrub of the genus *Euonymus.* The fine, hard-grained wood of *Euonymus europæus* was used for spindles and skewers.

spin′dle whŏrl (hwũrl), a small perforated disk forming a rude flywheel, formerly fixed on the spindle to maintain its rotatory motion before the introduction of the spinning wheel.

spin′dle wŏrm, the caterpillar of an American moth, *Achatodes zeæ,* which is destructive to corn.

spin′dling, *a.* tall and slender; shooting into a tall, slender stalk.

spin′dling, *n.* a spindling person or thing.

spin′dly, *a.*; *comp.* spindlier; *superl.* spindliest, spindling.

spin′drift, *n.* [altered from *spoondrift,* from earlier *spoom drift.*] spray blown from a rough sea or surf.

> The mountainous seas crashed down upon our decks and the stinging, wind-driven *spindrift* burned its way into our flesh.
> —Vaughn.

spīne, *n.* [L. *spina,* a thorn.]
1. any of the short, sharp, woody processes projecting from certain plants, as the cactus.
2. any of the sharp, stiff projections on the bodies of certain animals, as the quill of a porcupine or a ray of a fish's fin.
3. anything resembling either of these projections.
4. the spinal column; backbone.
5. anything regarded as resembling a backbone; specifically, (a) a ridge of ground, etc.; (b) the back of a bound book, usually bearing the title and author's name.

spīne′bill, *n.* an Australian bird of the genus *Acanthorhynchus*; a honey eater.

spīned, *a.* having a spine or spines; spiny.

spi·nel′ (*or* spin′el), *n.* [Fr. *spinelle*; It. *spinella,* from L. *spina,* a spine.] a hard, crystalline mineral composed chiefly of oxide of aluminum, magnesium, and iron, and found in various colors: a red variety (*spinel ruby*) is used as a gem.

spīne′less, *a.* 1. invertebrate; having no spine.
2. having a weak or flexible backbone.
3. without spines, or thorny processes.
4. lacking moral fiber; without courage or will power.

spi·nelle′, *n.* same as *spinel.*

spī·nes′cent, *a.* [LL. *spinescens,* ppr. of *spinescere,* to grow spiny, from L. *spina,* spine.]
1. spiny; having spines.
2. becoming spiny or spinelike.

spin′et, *n.* [OFr. *espinete*; It. *spinetta*; prob. from Giovanni *Spinetti* (c. 1500), of Venice, said to be the inventor.]
1. an obsolete, small variety of harpsichord with a single keyboard.
2. a small upright piano, either of an early oblong form or of modern design.

spī′net (*or* spin′et), *n.* a small wood or place where briers and thorns grow. [Obs.]

spīne′tāil, *n.* 1. an American passerine bird of the family *Dendrocolaptidæ.*
2. a swift of the subfamily *Chæturinæ* having the shafts of the tail feathers ending in spines.
3. the ruddy duck. [Dial.]

spīne′-tāiled, *a.* having the tail ending in a spine or the tail feathers in sharp points.

spin house, a house in which spinning is done.

spī·nif′ẽr·ous, *a.* [L. *spina,* spine, and *ferre,* to bear.] producing spines; bearing thorns.

spīn′i·fex, *n.* [L. *spina,* spine, and *facere,* to make.] any one of various Australian grasses of the genus *Triodia,* especially *Triodia irritans,* which has stiff and sharp-pointed leaves and seeds with an elastic spine.

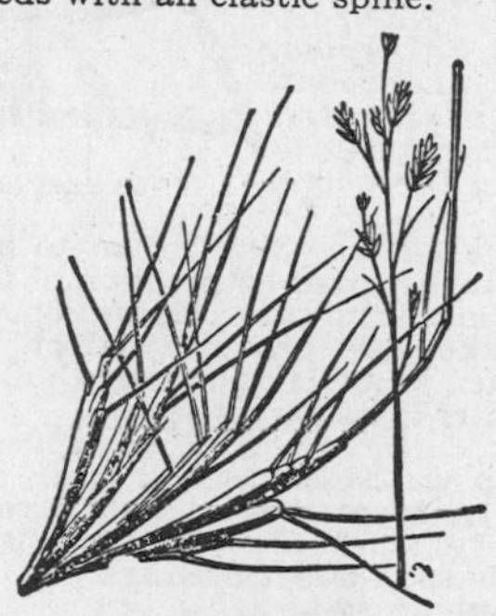

SPINIFEX (*Triodia irritans*)

spīn′i·fọrm, *a.* having the shape of, or resembling, a spine.

spī·nig′ẽr·ous, *a.* bearing a spine or spines.

spīn′i·ness, *n.* the state or quality of being spiny; thorniness.

spin̄k, *n.* [Sw.; allied to *finch.*] the chaffinch. [Brit. Dial.]

spin̄k, *n.* [origin obscure.] the primrose, *Primula veris*; also, the cuckooflower. [Scot. or Brit. Dial.]

spin′nȧ·kẽr, *n.* [said to be formed from *spinx,* altered from *Sphinx,* name of a yacht which carried the sail; prob. an altered form of *spanker.*] a large, triangular sail on racing yachts, set from a boom that swings out on the side opposite the main boom and used especially when running before the wind.

spin′nel, *n.* a spindle. [Scot. and Brit. Dial.]

spin′nẽr, *n.* a person or thing that spins; specifically, (a) a person who spins yarn, etc. for a living; (b) a shiny fish lure than spins like a propeller when drawn through the water; (c) a domelike cap that fits over the hub of an airplane propeller; (d) a football play in which the ball carrier whirls around to prevent the opposing team from knowing in which direction he will run; (e) [Dial.] a garden spider or spinning spider; (f) [Rare.] a spinneret; (g) a goatsucker.

spin′nẽr·et, *n.* [dim. of *spinner.*] in entomology, one of the nipplelike organs with which spiders, caterpillars, etc. spin threads of silk.

spin′nẽr·ūle, *n.* one of the numerous minute tubes with which each spinneret of the spider is studded, every one of which emits a thread of fine silk.

spin′nẽr·y, *n.*; *pl.* **spin′nẽr·ies̹,** a factory where yarn is spun; a spinning mill.

spin′ney, *n.*; *pl.* **spin′neys̹,** [OFr. *espinaye,* a place full of briers, from *espine,* a brier or bramble, from L. *spina,* a thorn, a spine.] a small clump of trees; a thicket or grove. [Brit.]

spin′ning, *n.* the act of making thread or yarn from fibers or filaments.

spin′ning, *a.* that spins.

spin′ning frāme, a machine used for twisting thread hard for use as warp.

spin′ning gland, in zoology, any one of the glands, as in silkworms and kindred larvae, that spins a silky substance.

spin′ning head (hed), an early form of spinning machine, which combined the drawing and twisting mechanisms in one head.

spin′ning house, same as *spin house.*

spin′ning jack, in cotton manufacturing, a contrivance for receiving a sliver after passing through rollers, and for winding it on spools.

spin′ning jen′ny, the first spinning machine on which a number of threads could be spun at once. It was invented about 1767 by James Hargreaves, a Lancashire weaver, and consisted of a number of spindles turned by a common wheel or cylinder worked by hand.

spin′ning mȧ·chïne′, any machine for spinning, especially one which spins continuously.

spin′ning mill, a factory where thread is spun.

spin′ning mīte, a red spider of the family *Tetraonychidæ*.

spin′ning wheel, a primitive spinning machine fitted with a single spindle driven by rotation of a large wheel spun by a foot treadle or by hand.

SPINNING WHEEL

spin′ny, *a.* thin; slender. [Obs.]

spin′ny, *n.* a spinney. [Brit.]

spī′nōde, *n.* [L. *spina*, a thorn, and *nodus*, a knot.] in geometry, a stationary point or cusp on a curve. [Obs.]

spin′off, *n.* 1. the distribution to its shareholders by a parent corporation of the stock it holds in a subsidiary corporation.
2. a secondary benefit, product, development, etc., as a television series built around a character in an earlier series.

spī′nōse, *a.* [L. *spinosus*, from *spina*, spine.] full of spines; covered with thorns; thorny.

spī′nōse·ly, *adv.* in a spinose manner.

spī·nos′i·ty, *n.* 1. the state of being spinose.
2. a sharp or cutting remark.
3. anything spinose.

spī′nous, *a.* 1. same as *spinose*.
2. like a spine or thorn in form.
spinous process; a neural spine.

Spi·nō′zişm, *n.* the philosophy of Spinoza, who maintained that there is but one substance, God, having two aspects, thought and extension.

Spi·nō′zist, *n.* a believer in Spinozism, or the doctrines of Spinoza.

spin′stẽr, *n.* 1. a woman who spins, or whose occupation is to spin.
2. an unmarried woman; especially, an elderly woman who has never married; an old maid.

spin′stẽr·hood, *n.* the state of being a spinster.

spin′stress, *n.* a woman or girl who spins.

spin′stry, *n.* the business of spinning. [Obs.]

spin·thar′i·scōpe, *n.* [Gr. *spinthēr*, a spark, and *skopein*, to see.] a small device with a fluorescent screen, for observing the scintillations of the alpha rays given off by a radioactive substance.

spī′nūle (*or* spin′ūl), *n.* a small spine.

spin·ū·les′cent, *a.* in botany, producing little spines; having small spines.

spin′ū·lōse, spin′ū·lous, *a.* 1. having or covered with spinules.
2. having the shape of a spinule.

spīn′y, *a.*; *comp.* spinier; *superl.* spiniest, 1. full of spines; thorny; as, a *spiny* tree.
2. troublesome; thorny; difficult.
3. spine-shaped.
spiny anteater; the echidna, an egg-laying mammal resembling a porcupine.
spiny crab; a spider crab having a spiny carapace.
spiny lobster; any of a group of sea crustaceans, related and similar to the common lobster, but lacking the large pincers.

spīn′y-finned, *a.* having fins in which the membrane is supported by stiff, unbranched, and unsegmented rays.

spīn′y-head·ed wŏrm, an acanthocephalan.

Spī·ō′dē·ȧ, *n.pl.* same as *Spionidæ*.

Spī·on′i·dae, *n.pl.* a family of annelids forming a kind of tube and having gills near the head.

spī′rȧ, *n.*; *pl.* **spī′rae,** [L.] in architecture, the base of a column.

spī′rȧ·ble, *a.* capable of being breathed; respirable. [Obs.]

spir′ȧ·çle (*or* spīr′), *n.* [L. *spiraculum*, from *spirare*, to breathe.]
1. a small opening allowing the outer air to come through into a confined space; air hole.
2. in zoology, (a) an opening through which air or water is taken in and expelled in respiration, as in the whale; a blowhole; (b) any of the small openings of the tracheal respiratory system of certain arthropods, etc., ordinarily along the sides of the body.

spī·raç′ū·lȧ, *n.* plural of *spiraculum*.

spī·raç′ū·lăr, *a.* of or consisting of a spiracle.

spī·raç′ū·lāte, *a.* having a spiracle.

spī·raç·ū·lif′ẽr·ous, *a.* bearing a spiracle.

spī·raç′ū·li·fọrm, *a.* formed like or resembling a spiracle.

spī·raç′ū·lum, *n.*; *pl.* **spī·raç′ū·lȧ,** 1. a spiracle.
2. a hole in a helmet, through which to breathe.

spī′rae, *n.* plural of *spira*.

Spī·rae′ȧ, *n.* [L. *spiræa*, from Gr. *speira*, a coil.]
1. a genus of plants of the family *Rosaceæ*, having dense clusters of small pink or white flowers, as the meadowsweet. Several North American, Indian, and Japanese shrubby species are in cultivation.
2. [s–] a plant of this genus: also spelled *spirea*.

spī·rae′iç, *a.* 1. of, pertaining to, or derived from a species of *Spiræa*.
2. salicylic. [Obs.]

spī′răl, *a.* [ML. *spiralis*, from L. *spira*, a coil.]
1. winding round a fixed point or center, and continually receding from it, like a watch spring; coiled or coiling in one plane.
2. winding round a cylinder or other round body and at the some time rising or advancing forward, like a corkscrew; helical.
3. pointed or shaped like a spire.
spiral axis; see under *axis*.
spiral balance; a balance in which the weight of an object is determined by the stretching of a spiral to which the object is suspended.
spiral duct; a spiral vessel.
spiral gear; a gear in which the teeth are cut at an angle to the axis: so called from the action of the teeth, which act as a portion of a screw or spiral.

SPIRAL WHEELS

spiral gearing; a train of spiral gears.
spiral nebula; a distant galaxy having the visible form of a spiral: also *spiral galaxy*.
spiral screw; a screw formed upon a conical or conoidal core.
spiral spring; a spring in the shape of a coil whose rounds have the same diameter.
spiral vessel; in botany, one of various forms of fine transparent membranous tubes, with one or more spiral fibers coiled up in their interior. The fiber coils either from right to left, or the reverse, somewhat in the manner of a corkscrew. The illustration shows (1) a compound spiral vessel; (2) three simple spiral vessels.

1 2
SPIRAL VESSELS

spī′răl, *n.* 1. a spiral curve occurring in a single plane.
2. a spiral curve occurring in a series of planes, as the thread of a screw; helix.
3. something having a spiral form, as a coiled snake or a bedspring.
4. a spiral path or flight; as, the descending *spiral* of a falling leaf.
5. a section or segment of a spiral.
6. a continuous, widening decrease or increase; as, an inflationary *spiral* is an economic condition in which an increase in prices, etc. results in a series of further increases, to the point of financial collapse.
7. in football, a kick or pass in which the ball rotates on its longer axis as it moves through the air.
equiangular spiral; a logarithmic spiral.
hyperbolic or *reciprocal spiral*; a spiral in which the length of a radius vector is in inverse ratio to the angle through which it turns. Like the logarithmic spiral, it has an infinite number of convolutions about the pole which it never reaches.
logarithmic spiral; see under *logarithmic*.
loxodromic spiral; see under *loxodromic*.
parabolic spiral; a helicoid.
spiral of Archimedes; a curve generated by a point having a uniform motion around a fixed point or pole, combined with uniform motion toward or from it. It is formed in the right section of an oblique helicoid.

spī′răl, *v.i.*; spiraled or spiralled, *pt.*, *pp.*; spiraling *or* spiralling, *ppr.* to move in or form a spiral.

spī′răl, *v.t.* to cause to move in or form into a spiral.

spī·ral′i·ty, *n.* the state or character of being spiral.

spī′răl·ly, *adv.* in a spiral form or direction.

spī′ral·tāil, *n.* the king bird of paradise.

spī′rănt, *n.* [L. *spirans* (*-antis*), ppr. of *spirare*, to breathe.] a consonantal sound, as (sh) or (v), produced by the passage of breath through the partially closed oral cavity; fricative.

spī′rănt, *a.* having the nature of a spirant; fricative.

Spī·ran′thēş, *n.* [LL., from Gr. *speira*, a coil, and *anthos*, flower.] a genus of orchids including about eighty species: also called *lady's tresses*.

spī·ran′thiç, *a.* of, relating to, or affected with spiranthy.

spī·ran′thy, *n.* in botany, the occasional twisted growth of the parts of a flower.

spī·ras′tẽr, *n.* [LL., from Gr. *speira*, coil, and *astēr*, star.] in zoology, a sponge spicule with spirally arranged rays.

spī·rā′tion, *n.* a breathing. [Obs.]

spīre, *v.i.* to breathe. [Obs.]

spīre, *n.* [ME., a young shoot or blade of grass; AS. *spir*: akin to ON. *spīra*.]
1. a sprout, spike, or stalk of a plant, a blade of grass, etc.
2. the top part of a pointed, tapering object or structure, as a mountain peak; a summit.
3. anything that tapers to a point, as a pointed tower or steeple.
4. in mining, the tube carrying the train to the charge in the blast hole: so called from the spires of grass or rushes used for the purpose.

spīre, *v.i.*; spired, *pt.*, *pp.*; spiring, *ppr.* 1. to extend upward, tapering to a point; to shoot up, rise in, or put forth a spire or spires.
2. to sprout, as grain in malting.

spīre, *v.t.* to furnish with a spire or spires.

spīre, *n.* [L. *spira*, a coil.]
1. a winding line like the thread of a screw; a spiral; a coil; a wreath.
2. the convolutions of a spiral or coil.
3. in zoology, the upper part of a spiral shell.
4. in geometry, that portion of a spiral which is generated during one revolution of the straight line revolving about the pole.

spīre, *n.* a male red deer in its third year.

spī·rē′ȧ, *n.* same as *spiraea*.

spīre′-beâr″ẽr, *n.* in paleontology, a spirifer.

spīred, *a.* having a spire or spires.

spī′rēme, spī′rem, *n.* [Gr. *speirēma*, a coil, from *speira*, a spiral, coil.] in biology, the nuclear chromatin of a cell, a threadlike form seen in an early stage of mitosis.

spī′ri·çle, *n.* [L. *spira*, a coil.] in botany, one of various coiled threads on the surface of certain seeds. These threads uncoil when wet and assist in the germination of a small seed.

Spī′ri·fẽr, *n.* 1. a fossil genus of brachiopoda, having a shell with two spiral appendages.
2. [s–] a member of this genus.

spī·rif′ẽr·ous, *a.* 1. having a spire, or spiral structure, as some shells, or spiral appendages, as a brachiopod.
2. yielding fossil spirifers: applied to strata.

spir′ig·nath, *n.* [Gr. *speira*, a coil, and *gnathos*, a jaw.] in zoology, the spiral proboscis of a lepidopter.

Spī·ril′lum, *n.* [dim. of L. *spira*, a coil.]
1. a genus of bacteria the cells of which have the form of a spiral thread and are characterized by flagella.
2. [s–] *pl.* **spī·ril′lȧ,** any bacterium of this genus.
3. any of various other microorganisms having a similar form.

spir′it, *n.* [L. *spiritus*, breath, courage, vigor, the soul, life, from *spirare*, to blow, to breathe.]
1. (a) the life principle, especially in man, originally regarded as an animating vapor infused by the breath, or as bestowed by a deity; (b) the soul.
2. the thinking, motivating, feeling part of man, often as distinguished from the body; mind; intelligence.
3. [*also* S–] life, will, consciousness, thought, etc., regarded as separate from matter.
4. a supernatural being, especially one thought of as haunting or possessing a person, house, etc., as a ghost, or as inhabiting a certain region, being of a certain (good or evil) character, etc., as an angel, demon, fairy, or elf.
5. an individual person or personality

thought of as showing or having some specific quality; as, she was a brave *spirit*.

6. [*often pl.*] frame of mind; disposition; mood; temper; as, in high *spirits*.

7. vivacity, courage, vigor, enthusiasm, etc.; as, answer with *spirit*.

8. enthusiastic loyalty; as, school *spirit*.

9. real meaning; true intention: opposed to *letter*, as, he followed the *spirit* if not the letter of the law.

10. a pervading animating principle, essential or characteristic quality, or prevailing tendency or attitude; as, the *spirit* of the Renaissance.

11. a divine animating influence or inspiration.

12. [*often pl.*] a strong alcoholic liquor produced by distillation.

13. (a) any of certain substances or fluids thought of as permeating organs of the body; (b) in alchemy, sulfur, sal ammoniac, mercury, or orpiment. [Obs.]

14. [*also pl.*] in chemistry, (a) any liquid produced by the distillation of certain materials, as wood fermentation mixtures, etc.; as, *spirits* of turpentine; (b) ethanol.

15. in dyeing, a solution of a tin salt, etc., used as a mordant.

16. in pharmacy, an alcoholic solution of a volatile or essential substance; as, *spirits* of camphor.

17. a breath of air; air; wind. [Obs.]

18. an aspirate; a breathing, as the letter *h*. [Obs.]

animal spirits; vivacity; liveliness.

aromatic spirit; a liquid solution of alcohol and spirit of orange.

astral spirit; a spirit formerly thought to inhabit the aerial regions, as a fallen angel.

familiar spirit; see under *familiar*, a.

Holy Spirit; see under *holy*.

out of spirits; sad; depressed.

poor in spirit; see under *poor*, a.

public spirit; see under *public*, a.

spirit of ammonia; an alcoholic solution of ammonia used in medicine.

spirit of camphor; a liquid solution of camphor, alcohol, and water.

spirit of Mindererus; an aqueous solution of acetate of ammonia.

spirit of nitrous ether; a yellowish liquid consisting of alcohol and nitrous ether: also called *sweet spirit of niter*.

spirit of orange; alcohol flavored with oil of orange.

spirit of salt; hydrochloric acid. [Obs.]

spirit of sense; an extreme nicety of sensation. [Obs.]

spirit of vitriol; sulfuric acid. [Obs.]

spirits of hartshorn; a solution of liquid ammonia, as for household use: also *spirit of hartshorn*.

spirits of turpentine; volatile oil of turpentine: also *spirit of turpentine*.

spirits of wine; alcohol: also *spirit of wine*.

sweet spirit of niter; same as *spirit of nitrous ether*.

the Spirit; (a) the Holy Ghost; (b) God.

spir′it, *v.t.*; spirited, *pt.*, *pp.*; spiriting, *ppr.* 1. to animate or actuate; to excite; to encourage; to rouse: often with *up*.

2. to carry (*away* or *off*) secretly and swiftly, as though in a supernatural manner.

The ministry had him *spirited away*, and carried abroad, as a dangerous person.
—Arbuthnot and Pope.

3. to use spirits in the treatment of.

spir′it, *a.* 1. of spirits or spirtualism.

2. operating by the burning of alcohol; as, a *spirit* lamp.

spir′it·ăl·ly, *adv.* by means of the breath. [Obs.]

spir′it blūe, either of two aniline dyestuffs, a derivative of diphenyl amine or a derivative of rosaniline.

spir′it but′tẽr·fly, any butterfly of the genus *Ithomia*.

spir′it duck, the buffle duck; also, any duck that dives quickly when pursued as game.

spir′it·ed, *a.* 1. having a (specified) character, mood, or disposition: used in hyphenated compounds, as evil-*spirited*, fine-*spirited*, low-*spirited*, etc.

2. full of spirit; lively; vigorous; energetic; animated.

3. possessed by a spirit. [Rare.]

spir′it·ed·ly, *adv.* in a lively manner; with spirit; with animation.

spir′it·ed·ness, *n.* life; animation.

spir′it·fu̧l, *a.* lively; full of spirit. [Obs.]

spir′it·fu̧l·ly, *adv.* in a lively amnner. [Obs.]

spir′it·fu̧l·ness, *n.* liveliness; sprightliness. [Obs.]

spir′it·ing, *n.* behavior or activity of a spirit.

spir′it·iṣm, *n.* same as *spiritualism*.

spir′it·ist, *n.* same as *spiritualist*.

spir′it lamp, a lamp in which alcohol or methylated spirit is burned.

spir′it·lēaf, *n.* the manyroot.

spir′it·less, *a.* 1. lacking spirit, energy, or vigor; not lively or animated; listless; depressed.

2. having no breath; extinct; dead.

spir′it·less·ly, *adv.* without spirit; without exertion.

spir′it·less·ness, *n.* dullness; lack of life or vigor.

spir′it lev′el, a glass tube held in a frame and containing a liquid, usually alcohol, with a bubble in it: when the bubble rests at the center of the tube, the frame, or a surface upon which it is placed, is known to be level, or horizontal.

spï·rï·tō′sō, *a.* [It.] in music, lively; spirited.

spir′it·ous, *a.* 1. like spirit; refined; pure. [Obs.]

2. fine; ardent; active. [Obs.]

spir′it·ous·ness, *n.* the state or quality of being spiritous. [Obs.]

spir′i·trompe, *n.* [L. *spira*, a coil, and Fr. *trompe*, a trump.] same as *spirignath*.

spir′it·ū·ăl, *a.* [Fr. *spirituel*, from L. *spiritualis*.]

1. of the spirit or the soul, often in a religious or moral aspect, as distinguished from the body.

2. of, from, or concerned with the intellect, or what is often thought of as the better or higher part of the mind.

3. of or consisting of spirit; not corporeal.

4. characterized by the ascendancy of the spirit; showing much refinement of thought and feeling.

5. of religion or the church; sacred, devotional, or ecclesiastical; not lay or temporal.

6. spiritualistic or supernatural.

spiritual coadjutor; a Jesuit teacher.

spiritual court; an ecclesiastical court; a court held by a bishop or other ecclesiastic.

spiritual incest; see under *incest*.

spiritual man; the spiritual nature: distinguished from *physical man*, *psychical man*.

spir′it·ū·ăl, *n.* 1. a religious folk song of American Negro origin, often treating Biblical matter in a way suggestive of the folk ballad, with the use of refrain and vigorous rhythm.

2. a spiritual thing or concern; especially, [*pl.*] church matters.

spir′it·ū·ăl·iṣm, *n.* 1. the belief that the dead survive as spirits which can communicate with the living, especially with the help of a third party, called a medium.

2. any practice arising from this belief.

3. the philosophical doctrine that all reality is in essence spiritual; idealism.

4. spirituality; spiritual quality, etc.

Also *spiritism*.

spir′it·ū·ăl·ist, *n.* 1. one who believes in or practices spiritualism (senses 1 and 2).

2. one who believes in the doctrine of philosophical spiritualism.

3. a person concerned with or devoted to spiritual things.

spir″it·ū·ăl·is′tiç, *a.* pertaining to spiritualism or spiritualists.

spir″it·ū·al′i·ty, *n.*; *pl.* **spir″it·ū·al′i·tieṣ,** 1. spiritual nature, character, or quality; spiritual-mindedness: opposed to *worldliness*, *sensuality*.

2. [*often pl.*] the rights, jurisdiction, tithes, or reverence due to the church, or to an ecclesiastic; respect: distinguished from *temporality*.

3. the fact or state of being incorporeal.

4. an ecclesiastical body. [Obs.]

spir″it·ū·ăl·i·zā′tion, *n.* the act of spiritualizing or the state of being spiritualized.

spir′it·ū·ăl·ize, *v.i.*; spiritualized, *pt.*, *pp.*; spiritualizing, *ppr.* 1. to make spiritual; to refine intellectually or morally; to deprive of materiality or worldliness.

2. in old chemistry, to extract spirit from natural bodies.

3. to give a spiritual sense or meaning to; to derive a spiritual sense or meaning from.

spir′it·ū·ăl·ī·zẽr, *n.* one who spiritualizes.

spir′it·ū·ăl·ly, *adv.* in a spiritual manner.

spir′it·ū·ăl-mīnd″ed, *a.* having the mind inclined or devoted to spiritual things; spiritual; pious.

spir′it·ū·ăl-mīnd″ed·ness, *n.* the state of being spiritual-minded; spirituality.

spir′it·ū·ăl·ness, *n.* the state or quality of being spiritual.

spir′it·ū·ăl·ty, *n.* 1. the clergy.

2. [*often pl.*] spiritual or ecclesiastical things, as ecclesiastical property, rights, etc.

3. the quality of being spiritual [Obs.]

spï·rï·tū·el′, spï·rï·tū·elle′, *a.* [Fr.] 1. having or showing a refined, ethereal nature.

2. having or showing a quick, graceful wit or mind.

spir″it·ū·os′i·ty, *n.* spirituousness.

spir′it·ū·ous, *a.* [Fr. *spiritueux*.]

1. of, like, or containing alcohol: said especially of distilled as opposed to fermented beverages.

2. having the quality of spirit; fine; pure; active. [Obs.]

3. lively; gay; vivid; airy. [Obs.]

spir′it·ū·ous·ness, *n.* the quality or condition of being spirituous.

spir′i·tus, *n.* [L., a breath.]

1. a breathing.

2. in pharmacy, spirit.

spiritus asper; in Greek grammar, the rough breathing.

spiritus frumenti; whisky.

spiritus lenis; in Greek grammar, the smooth breathing.

spir′it·weed, *n.* same as *manyroot*.

spī′ri·valve, *a.* having a shell of spiral form, as a mollusk.

spïrl′ing, *n.* a fish, the smelt. [Scot.]

spī′rō-, [from L. *spirare*, to breathe.] a combining form meaning *respiration*, as in *spirograph*.

spī′rō-, [from Gr. *speira*, a coil.] a combining form used to indicate *a spiral* or *coil*, as in *spiro*chete.

spī″rō·baç·tē′ri·um, *n.*; *pl.* **spī″rō·baç·tē′ri·ȧ,** any of a class of spiral bacteria containing the genera *Spirillum*, *Spirochæta*, and *Vibrio*.

Spī″rō·çhae′tȧ, Spī″rō·çhae′te, *n.* [Gr. *spiro*, coil, and Gr. *chaeta*, hair.] a genus of *Spirochætales* having slender flexible bodies: found usually in water.

Spī″rō·çhae·tā′cē·ae, *n.* in bacteriology, a group of microscopic organisms comprising the order *Spirochætales*: they are related to the protozoic trypanosomes.

Spī″rō·çhae·tā′lēṣ, *n.* a family of the class *Schizomycetes*, characterized by their slender, spiral forms: they reproduce by dividing either laterally or transversely.

spī′rō·çhēte, spī′rō·çhaete, *n.* any member of the order *Spirochætales*, several of which cause disease.

SPIROCHETES

spī″rō·çhē·tō′sis, spī″rō·çhae·tō′sis, *n.* an infectious disease of chickens, etc., caused by a spirochete and usually fatal.

spī′rō·grȧph, *n.* an instrument for registering respiratory movements.

Spī·rō·ġȳ′rȧ, *n.* [*spiro-*, and Gr. *gyros*, a ring.] a genus of fresh-water algae of a bright-green color: they form dense, slimy masses and have chlorophyll bands winding spirally to the right.

spī′roid, *a.* like a spiral; having a spiral form.

spī·rō·loç′ū·line, *a.* having loculi, or chambers, arranged in a spiral form, as in some species of foraminifera.

spī·rom′ē·tẽr, *n.* an instrument for measuring the breathing capacity of the lungs, consisting usually of an inverted chamber submerged in a water bath. The breath is conducted by a flexible pipe and internal tube so as to collect in the chamber, which rises in the water. A graduated index is attached to the chamber, indicating the cubic inches of air expired.

spī·rom′ē·try, *n.* the measurement of the capacity of the lungs by means of a spirometer.

spī′rō·phōre, *n.* [*spiro-*, and Gr. *pherein*, to bear.] an instrument for producing artificial respiration.

Spī·rọr′bis, *n.* [L. *spira*, coil, and *orbis*, globe.] a genus of parasitic annelids of the family *Serpulidæ*, having a shell coiled into a spiral, disklike form: it is commonly found on the shells of lobsters.

spī′rō·sçōpe, *n.* a spirometer.

spīrt, *v.* and *n.* same as *spurt.*

spīr′tle, *v.* and *n.* same as *spurtle.*

Spir′ū·lȧ, *n.* [LL., dim. of L. *spira*, a spire.] a genus of two-gilled cephalopods related to the squid and cuttlefish, with a flat spiral shell that is partitioned into a series of chambers and is largely internal.

spir′ū·lȧ, *n.*; *pl.* **spir′ū·lae,** any mollusk of the genus *Spirula.*

spir′ū·lāte, *a.* in zoology, spirally arranged or marked.

spīr′y, *a.*; *comp.* spirier; *superl.* spiriest, of a spiral form; wreathed; curled; coiled.

spīr′y, *a.*; *comp.* spirier; *superl.* spiriest, 1. having the form of a spire, or pyramid; tapering like a spire, slender stalk, steeple, etc.; as, *spiry* turrets.

2. having many spires or steeples; as, *spiry* towns.

spiss, *a.* thick; close; dense. [Obs.]

spis′sā·ted, *a.* inspissated; thickened.

spis′si·tūde, *n.* [L. *spissitudo*, from *spissus*, thick.] a thickened state or quality; viscosity; density; as, the *spissitude* of coagulated blood.

spit, *n.* [AS. *spitu*, a spit; D. *spit*, *spet*, a spit; Ice. *spȳta*, a spit, a wooden peg; from a root *spi*, to be pointed.]

1. a thin, pointed rod or bar on which meat is impaled and held to be broiled or roasted over a fire.

2. a small point of land running into a body of water.

3. a long, narrow shoal, reef, or sandbank extending from the shore; as, a *spit* of sand.

4. a spade; hence, such a depth of earth as is pierced by the spade at one time; also, a spadeful. [Brit. Dial.]

spit, *v.t.*; spitted, *pt.*, *pp.*; spitting, *ppr.* 1. to thrust a spit through; to fix or impale on or as on a spit; as, to *spit* a loin of veal.

2. to spade; to dig. [Brit. Dial.]

spit, *v.i.*; spat *or* spit, *pt.*, *pp.*; spitting, *ppr.* [AS. *spittan*; Dan. *spytte*; Ice. *spȳta*, to spit out; same root as *spew.*]

1. to eject saliva from the mouth; to expectorate.

2. to fall in light scattered drops, as rain or snow.

3. to make an explosive hissing noise, as an angry cat.

to spit on or *at*; to insult; to treat with the utmost contempt; to abuse shamefully.

spit, *v.t.* 1. to eject from within the mouth.

2. to eject, throw out, emit, or utter explosively; as, the man *spat* an oath.

3. to light (a fuse).

to spit cotton; to have a dry mouth, as after a long thirst: also *to spit sixpences.* [Slang.]

spit, *n.* 1. saliva.

2. the act of spitting.

3. something like saliva, as the frothy secretion of certain insects; also, the insect itself.

4. a slight, brief shower of rain or snow.

5. the likeness or counterpart, as of a person. [Colloq.]

spit and image; perfect likeness; exact image. [Colloq.]

spit′ăl, *n.* [respelling (after *hospital*) of earlier *spittle*; ME. *spital.*]

1. a hospital, especially one for the very poor and for those having leprosy or other diseases regarded as loathsome. [Obs.]

2. a loathsome place. [Obs.]

3. a shelter for the use of travelers on a road. [Obs.]

spit′ball, *n.* 1. a piece of chewed paper fashioned into a ball for throwing.

2. in baseball, a pitch, now illegal, made to curve by moistening one side of the ball with saliva.

spit′box, *n.* a spittoon; a cuspidor.

spit bug, any insect or larva that secretes spume or froth; a spittle insect.

spitch′çock, *n.* [perh. from *spit* and *cock*; earlier *spechcoke.*] an eel split open or cut up in pieces and broiled or fried.

spitch′çock, *v.t.* to prepare (an eel) by splitting open or cutting up in pieces and broiling or frying.

spit çũrl, a small curl of hair dampened, as with spit, and pressed flat upon the temple or forehead.

spīte, *n.* [a contr. of *despite.*]

1. a mean or evil feeling toward another characterized by a desire to annoy, vex, disappoint, etc.; ill will; malice; malevolence; malignity.

2. that which is done to thwart, annoy, vex, disappoint, etc.; any manifestation of ill will, malice, or malevolence; a spiteful action; a grudge.

3. chagrin; disappointment; vexation. [Archaic.]

in spite of; in defiance of; notwithstanding; as, to succeed *in spite of* all opposition.

Syn.—grudge, malice, pique, malignity, malevolence, rancor.

spīte, *v.t.*; spited, *pt.*, *pp.*; spiting, *ppr.* 1. to behave in a spiteful manner toward; to vent one's spite upon by hurting, annoying, frustrating, etc.

2. to annoy or offend. [Archaic.]

to cut off one's nose to spite one's face; to injure or inconvenience oneself in an attempt to injure or annoy another. [Colloq.]

spīte fence, an unsightly fence or fencelike structure erected by a person for the purpose of venting his spite against a neighbor by injuring his property.

spīte′fụl, *a.* filled with spite; purposely annoying; malignant; malicious.

spīte′fụl·ly, *adv.* in a spiteful manner; with spite.

spīte′fụl·ness, *n.* the quality or state of being spiteful.

spit′fīre, *n.* a person who is easily aroused to violent outbursts of anger; especially, such a woman or girl.

spit′frog, *n.* a small sword. [Obs.]

spit′fụl, *n.* a spadeful.

spit′ous, *a.* spiteful; malicious. [Obs.]

spit′ous·ly, *adv.* in a spiteful or malicious manner. [Obs.]

spit′poi″ṣŏn, *n.* a venomous person; a slanderer and mischief-maker.

spit′ted, *a.* 1. pierced with a spit; skewered.

2. long and tapering to a sharp point without branches: said of the antlers of a deer.

spit′tẽr, *n.* 1. one who puts meat on a spit and turns it over a fire.

2. a young deer whose antlers are beginning to sprout and become sharp.

spit′tẽr, *n.* 1. a person or animal that spits saliva, etc.

2. in baseball, a spitball. [Colloq.]

spit′ting, *n.* 1. the action of a person or thing that spits.

2. the condition that occurs during the cooling of molten platinum or silver, in which drops of liquid metal are thrown through openings made in the crust by gases bursting out from within: also called *sprouting.*

spit′ting im′ăġe, spit and image; perfect likeness. [Colloq.]

spit′ting snāke, a venomous South African snake, *Sepedon hæmachates*, that spits its venom.

spit′tle, *n.* a hospital. [Archaic.]

spit′tle, *n.* [altered from *spattle*, after *spit* (to eject).]

1. saliva; spit.

2. the frothy secretion of larval spittle insects.

spit′tle, *n.* a small spade. [Brit. Dial.]

spit′tle, *v.t.* [dim. of *spit*, spade.] to dig with a small spade. [Brit. Dial.]

spit′tle flȳ, same as *spittle insect.*

spit′tle in′sect, any of a number of leaping insects whose larvae surround themselves with a frothy secretion.

spit′tle-of-the-stärṣ′, *n.* same as *fallen star* (sense 1).

spit·tọọn′, *n.* a jarlike container to spit into; a cuspidor; a spitbox.

spitz (spits), *n.* [G. *spitze*, point.] a variety of small Pomeranian dog having a pointed muzzle, erect ears, and silky hair, usually white and long.

SPITZ DOG (14 in. high at shoulder)

spitz′en·bũrg, spitz′en·bẽrg, *n.* [also *Esopus Spitzenberg*, from D. *spits*, a point, pointed, and *berg*, hill, mountain: so called because the seedling was found on a hillside near Esopus, New York.] [*sometimes* S–] any of several kinds of winter apples having red and yellow skin and a fine flavor.

spitz′flūte, *n.* an organ stop producing a thin, reedy sound.

spiv, *n.* [prob. dial. var. of 19th-c. slang *spiff*, person who dresses flashily.] a person who lives by his wits, without doing any regular work. [Brit. Slang.]

splanch-, see *splanchno-.*

splanch″nap′ō·phyṣ′i·ăl, *a.* relating to a splanchnapophysis.

splanch·nȧ·poph′y·sis, *n.* [*splanchno-*, and Gr. *apophysis*, an offshoot.] any skeletal element, as the lower jaw, connected with the alimentary canal.

splanch′niç, *a.* of or pertaining to the viscera.

splanch′niç, *n.* a splanchnic nerve.

splanch′nō-, [from Gr. *splanchnon*, viscera.] a combining form meaning *the viscera*, as in *splanchno*logy: also, before a vowel, *splanchn-.*

splanch′nō·coele (-sēl), *n.* [*splanchno-*, and Gr. *koilos*, hollow.] that portion of the embryonic body cavity, or coelum, from which are developed the abdominal, pericardial, and pleural cavities.

splanch·nog′rȧ·phy, *n.* splanchnology.

splanch·nol′ō·ġy, *n.* that branch of medical study which deals with the structure, functions, and diseases of the viscera.

splanch″nō·mē·gā′li·ȧ, *n.* [*splanchno-*, and Gr. *megas*, *megalos*, large.] enlargement of the viscera.

splanch′nō·pleūre, *n.* [*splanchno-*, and Gr. *pleura*, the side.] the visceral layer developed from the mesoderm of an embryo, from which the alimentary canal and the umbilical vesicle are formed.

splanch·nō·skel′e·tŏn, *n.* those parts of the skeleton that have special relations to the viscera, as the teeth, tracheal rings, etc.

splanch·not′ō·my, *n.* [*splanchno-*, and Gr. *tomē*, a cutting.] dissection of the viscera.

splash, *v.t.*; splashed (splasht), *pt.*, *pp.*; splashing, *ppr.* [intens. extension of *plash*, to bespatter.]

1. to cause (a liquid substance) to fly or scatter.

2. to dash or scatter a liquid substance, mud, etc. on, so as to wet or soil.

3. to cause to splash a liquid; as, stop *splashing* your feet in the puddles.

4. to make (one's way) by splashing.

5. to mark or spot by or as by splashing; as, a street *splashed* with sunlight.

splash, *v.i.* 1. to cause a liquid substance to fly or scatter.

2. to fall, strike, or scatter with a splash or splashes; as, rain *splashed* against the door.

3. to move with splashes; as, the dog *splashed* eagerly into the water.

splash, *n.* 1. the act or sound of splashing.

2. a mass of flying water, mud, etc.

3. a spot or mark made by or as by splashing.

to make a splash; to attract great, often brief, attention by doing something striking, spectacular, or ostentatious. [Colloq.]

splash′bōard, *n.* 1. any screen or board protecting riders on a vehicle from being splashed in wet weather; a dashboard or mudguard.

2. a screen to keep water from splashing onto the deck of a boat.

3. a trap for closing a sluice or spillway.

splash′down, *n.* the landing of a spacecraft on water.

splash′ẽr, *n.* 1. one who or that which splashes.

2. anything giving protection from splashes; specifically, a curtain or screen to prevent a wall being splashed by water from a washbowl.

splash'y, *a.*; *comp.* splashier; *superl.* splashiest. 1. splashing; making splashes.
2. liable to splash; wet, muddy, etc.
3. covered or marked with splashes.
4. attracting much notice or attention; spectacular; striking. [Colloq.]

splat, *n.* [via dial. from base of *split.*] a thin, flat piece of wood, especially as used in the back of a chair.

splat'tẽr, *n.* and *v.* [variant of *spatter.*] spatter; splash.

splat'tẽr·dash, *n.* same as *spatterdash.*

splat'tẽr·fācèd (-fāst), *a.* same as *platter-faced.*

splāy, *n.* [contr. of *display.*]
1. a sloped or beveled surface, or a surface that forms an oblique angle with another, as when the opening through a wall for a door, window, etc., widens toward one face; a large chamfer.

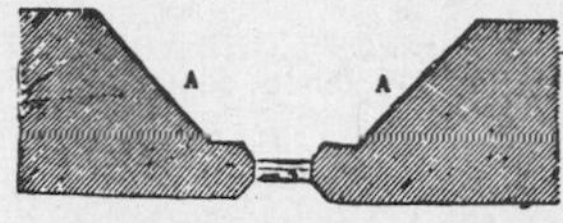

SPLAY
(Cross section of window) A A, internal splay

2. a spreading; expansion; enlargement.

splāy, *a.* 1. sloping or spreading out.
2. broad and flat.
3. awkward.
4. awry.

splāy, *v.t.* [ME. *splaien.*]
1. to spread, enlarge, or expand.
2. to make beveled or sloping.
3. to dislocate (a bone): said of animals.

splāy, *v.i.* to spread out, especially so as to slant or slope.

splāyed, *a.* same as *splay,* a. (senses 1 and 2).

splāy'ẽr, *n.* a segment of a cylinder on which a molded tile is pressed to give it the desired curve.

splāy'foot, *n.*; *pl.* **splāy'feet,** 1. a flat foot turning outward.
2. the physical abnormality characterized by feet of this kind.

splāy'foot, *a.* same as *splayfooted.*

splāy'foot″ed, *a.* having splayfoot.

splāy'mouth, *n.* an unusually wide mouth.

splāy'mouthed (-mouthd), *a.* having a very wide mouth.

spleen, *n.* [from OFr. or L.; OFr. *esplen*; L. *splen*; Gr. *splēn*, the spleen.]
1. a large, vascular, ductless organ in the upper left part of the abdominal cavity near the stomach: it has various functions in modifying the structure of the blood, and was formerly regarded as the seat of certain emotions.
2. anger; spite; ill humor; as, to vent one's *spleen.*
3. a fit of anger.
4. melancholy; low spirits. [Archaic.]
5. a sudden fancy; a caprice; a whim. [Obs.]
6. a fit of laughter. [Obs.]

spleen, *v.t.* 1. to take the spleen from.
2. to dislike. [Obs.]

spleen, *v.i.* to have a loathing; to feel anger.

spleen'fụl, *a.* full of spleen; angry; peevish; ill-tempered.

spleen'ish, *a.* same as *spleenful.*

spleen'ish·ly, *adv.* in a spleenish manner.

spleen'ish·ness, *n.* the state of being spleenish.

spleen'less, *a.* without a spleen; hence, kind; gentle; mild.

spleen'wŏrt, *n.* [L. *splenium.*] any fern of the genus *Asplenium,* with simple or compound fronds and linear or oblique sori on the upper surface of an oblique veinlet.

spleen'y, *a.*; *comp.* spleenier; *superl.* spleeniest, spleenful.

splēn-, same as *spleno-.*

splē·nal'ġi·ȧ, *n.* [*splen-* and *-algia.*] pain around or in the spleen.

splen̄'cū·lus, *n.*; *pl.* **splen̄'cū·lī,** [LL., dim. of L. *splen,* spleen.] in anatomy, a small supplementary spleen.

splen'dent, *a.* [L. *splendens* (*-entis*), from *splendere,* to shine.]
1. shining; glossy; beaming with light; as, *splendent* planets; *splendent* metals.
2. very conspicuous; illustrious.
3. brilliant; splendid; magnificent.

splen'did, *a.* [L. *splendidus,* from *splendere,* to shine.]
1. shining; very bright; glittering; brilliant; as, a *splendid* sun.
2. showy; magnificent; sumptuous; pompous; as, a *splendid* palace; a *splendid* procession.
3. illustrious; heroic; brilliant; famous; celebrated; as, a *splendid* victory.
4. fine; excellent; very good. [Colloq.]

splen·did'i·ous, *a.* splendid. [Obs.]

splen'did·ly, *adv.* in a splendid manner; magnificently; sumptuously; gorgeously; grandly; brilliantly.

splen'did·ness, *n.* the quality or state of being splendid; splendor.

splen·dif'ẽr·ous, *a.* showing splendor; gorgeous: used humorously. [Colloq.]

splen'dŏr, *n.* [OFr. *splendeur,* from L. *splendor,* brightness.]
1. great brightness; brilliant luster; as, the *splendor* of the sun.
2. great show of richness and elegance; magnificence; impressiveness; pomp; grandeur; as, the *splendor* of equipage or of royal robes; the *splendor* of a victory.

Enduring in heart and in brain, the exhaustless *splendor* of those early days.
—Henry W. Grady.

in splendor; in heraldry, said of the sun when represented with a human face and environed with rays.

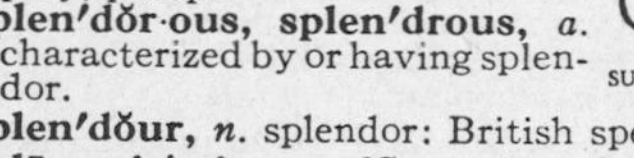

SUN IN SPLENDOR

Syn.—showiness, renown, display, pomp.

splen'dŏr·ous, splen'drous, *a.* characterized by or having splendor.

splen'dŏur, *n.* splendor: British spelling.

splē·neç'tȧ·sis, *n.* [Gr. *splēn,* spleen, and *ectasis,* a stretching out.] an enlarged condition of the spleen.

splē·neç'tō·my, *n.* [*splen-* and *-ectomy.*] excision or removal of the spleen.

splē·net'iç, *a.* [Fr. *splénétique*; LL. *spleneticus,* full of spleen.]
1. of the spleen; splenic.
2. bad-tempered; irritable; peevish; spiteful; spleenful.
3. melancholy. [Obs.]

splē·net'iç, *n.* a spleenful person.

splē·net'i·çăl, *a.* splenetic.

splē·net'i·çăl·ly, *adv.* in a splenetic manner.

splē'ni·ăl, *a.* [Gr. *splēnion,* a bandage.] pertaining to the splenius.
splenial bone; the splenial.

splē'ni·ăl, *n.* an element of the lower jaw between the mandible and the dentary of many vertebrates.

splen'iç, *a.* [Fr. *splénique*; L. *splenicus*; Gr. *splēnikos.*]
1. of or having to do with the spleen.
2. located in or near the spleen.
splenic fever; same as *anthrax,* sense 3.

splen'iç·ăl, *a.* splenic.

splen″i·fi·çā'tion, *n.* splenization.

splēn'ish, *a.* spleenish. [Obs.]

splē·nī'tis, *n.* [*splen-* and *-itis.*] inflammation of the spleen.

splen'i·tive, *a.* splenetic.

splē'ni·um, *n.*; *pl.* **splē'ni·ȧ,** [LL., from Gr. *splēnion,* a compress.] the posterior rounded end of the corpus callosum.

splē'ni·us, *n.* [Mod. L., from Gr. *splēnion,* a bandage.] a large, flat muscle on either side of the back of the neck, serving to rotate the neck and head.

splen·i·zā'tion, *n.* that condition of a part, especially the lung, in which it has the appearance of the tissue of the spleen, due to congestion and lack of air.

splē'nō-, [from Gr. *splēn,* spleen.] a combining form meaning *the spleen*: also, before a vowel, *splen-.*

splē'nō·cēle, *n.* [*spleno-,* and Gr. *kēlē,* a tumor.] hernia of the spleen.

splē·nog'rȧ·phy, *n.* a treatise on the spleen.

splē'noid, *a.* having the form or appearance of a spleen.

splē·nol'ō·ġy, *n.* the branch of anatomy treating of the spleen.

splē″nō·mȧ·lā'ci·ȧ, *n.* [*spleno-,* and Gr. *malakia,* softness.] abnormal softness of the spleen.

splē″nō·mē·gā'li·ȧ, splē·nō·meg'ȧ·ly, *n.* enlargement of the spleen.

splē·not'ō·my, *n.* [*spleno-,* and Gr. *tomē,* a cutting.] surgical incision of the spleen.

splent, *n.* same as *splint.*

spleu'ċhăn, spleu'ghăn (-găn), *n.* [Ir. *spliuchan,* a pouch.] a pouch; especially, a tobacco or money pouch. [Scot. and Irish.]

splīce, *v.t.*; spliced (splīst), *pt., pp.*; splicing, *ppr.* [Dan. *splisse, splidse*; D. *splitsen*; Sw. *splissa,* to splice. Closely akin to *split.* The ends of the rope are *split* in splicing.]
1. to unite or join together, as two ropes or the parts of a rope, by interweaving the strands of the ends.
2. to unite or join together pieces, as of wood by overlapping and binding, especially at the ends.
3. to join in marriage. [Slang.]
to splice the main brace; to take a drink of liquor. [Slang.]

splīce, *n.* 1. the union or joining together of two ropes or parts of a rope by a particular manner of interweaving part of the untwisted strands. The long splice occupies a great extent of rope, but by the three joinings being fixed at a distance from one another, the increase of bulk is diminished; hence it is adapted to run through the sheave hole of a block. The short splice is used upon cables, slings, and all ropes in general which are not intended to run through blocks. The eye splice forms a sort of eye or circle at the end of a rope, and is used for splicing in thimbles.

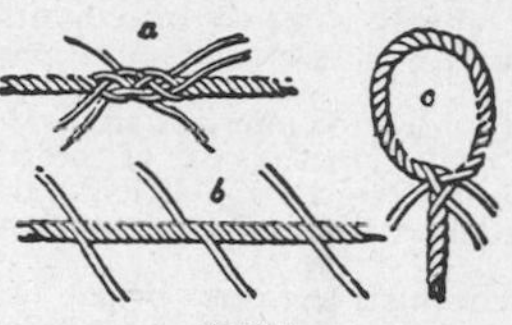

SPLICES
a, short splice; *b,* long splice; *c,* eye splice

2. the junction of two pieces of wood, metal, etc. by overlapping and bolting or otherwise fastening the ends.

splice gráft'ing, grafting performed by cutting the ends of the scion and stock completely across in an oblique direction, in such a way that the sections are of the same shape, then laying the oblique surfaces together so that one exactly fits the other, and securing them by tying or otherwise.

splīne, *n.* [from East Anglian dial. *splind,* from the base of *split.*]
1. a long, flat, pliable piece, as of wood or metal, especially one used in drawing curves.
2. a flat key or strip that fits into a groove or slot between parts, as between a shaft and a pulley, so as to allow only relative lengthwise motion of the parts.
3. the groove or slot into which it fits.

splīne, *v.t.*; splined, *pt., pp.*; splining, *ppr.* 1. to provide with a spline.
2. to cut a groove or slot in for a spline.

splī'ning mȧ·chine', a machine tool for cutting grooves and key beds.

splint, *n.* [ME. *splent*; M.D. *splinte.*]
1. a piece of wood or other substance split off; a splinter. [Brit. Dial.]
2. a thin piece of wood or other substance, used to hold or confine a broken bone when set, or to maintain any part of the body in a fixed position.

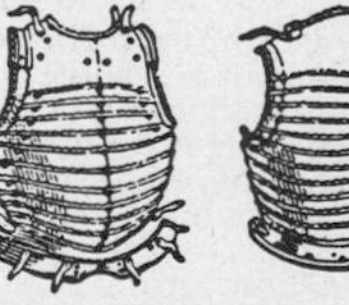

SPLINT ARMOR

3. in farriery, (a) the splint bone; (b) a bony growth or tumor on the cannon bone of a horse, mule, etc.
4. one of the overlapping plates used in the manufacture of splint armor, particularly at the joints, in order to allow freedom of motion: used in medieval armor.
5. a thin strip of wood or cane woven together with others to make baskets, chair seats, etc.

splint, *v.t.*; splinted, *pt., pp.*; splinting, *ppr.* 1. to splinter; to shiver. [Obs.]
2. to join together, confine, or support by means of a splint or splints, as a broken limb.

splint är'mŏr, armor which is made of several overlapping plates.

splint bōne, in horses and related animals, either of the two small bones extending from the hock to the fetlock, one on each side of the cannon bone.

splint çōal, a splintery coal which is non-caking, owing to the high percentage of carbon and the low amount of bituminous substance it contains.

splin'tẽr, *v.t.*; splintered, *pt., pp.*; splintering, *ppr.* [Dan. *splintre*, to splinter.]
1. to split or break into thin, sharp pieces; to shiver; as, the lightning *splintered* the tree.
2. to splint; to support by a splint, as a broken limb.

splin'tẽr, *v.i.* to split or break into long, sharp pieces.

splin'tẽr, *n.* a fragment of anything split or shivered off; a thin, sharp piece of wood or other solid substance split or broken from the main body; as, *splinters* of a ship's mast rent off by a shot.

splin'tẽr bär, a crossbar in front of a vehicle to which the traces of the horses are attached; also, the crossbar which supports the springs.

splin'tẽr-proof, *a.* proof against the splinters of bursting shells.

splin'tẽr·y, *a.* 1. easily splintered.
2. of or like a splinter.
3. resulting in splinters, as a fracture.
4. full of splinters; splintered; jagged; rough.

split, *v.t.*; split *or obs.* splitted, *pt., pp.*; splitting, *ppr.* [ME. *splitten*; akin to M.H.G. *splizen.*]
1. to separate, cut, or divide into two or more parts; to cause to separate along the grain or length; to break into layers.
2. to break or tear apart by force; to burst; to rend.
3. to divide into parts or shares; to portion out; as, they *split* the cost of the trip.
4. to cause (a group, political party, etc.) to separate into divisions or factions; to disunite.
5. in chemistry, (a) to break (a molecule) into atoms; to separate the components of; (b) to produce nuclear fission in (an atom or atoms).
to split off; (a) to break off by splitting; (b) to separate or divide by or as by splitting.
to split one's sides; to burst with laughter.
to split one's vote; to vote for candidates of different parties on the same ballot.

split, *v.i.* 1. to separate or divide lengthwise into two or more parts; to separate along the grain or length.
2. to break or tear apart; to burst; to rend.
3. to separate or break up through failure to agree, etc.
4. to divide something with another or others, each taking a share; as, winners *split*. [Colloq.]
5. to burst with laughter. [Colloq.]

Each had a gravity would make you *split*.
—Pope.

6. to betray confidence; to inform on an accomplice; as, he *split* on his associate. [19th-c. Slang.]
7. to move rapidly; as, he *split* across the lot. [Colloq.]

split, *n.* 1. the act or process of splitting.
2. a crack, rent, or fissure.
3. a division or separation, as in a political party; a breach; as, there is a *split* in the cabinet.
4. a splinter; a fragment.
5. one of the short flat strips of steel, cane, etc., placed in vertical parallel order at small distances from each other in a frame to form the reed of a loom.
6. a flexible strip of wood used in basket weaving.
7. a confection made of a split banana or other fruit with ice cream, nuts, sauces, whipped cream, etc.
8. [*often pl.*] the feat of spreading the legs apart until they lie flat on the floor, the body remaining upright.
9. (a) a small bottle of carbonated water, wine, etc., half the usual size, often about six ounces; (b) a drink or portion half the usual size; (c) a half pint. [Colloq.]
10. a share, as of loot or booty. [Slang.]
11. in bowling, an arrangement of pins after the first bowl, so separated as to make a spare almost impossible.
12. in leather manufacturing, any part of divided skins which have been separated into two sections by the cutting machine.
13. in the game of faro, a division of a stake occurring when two cards of the same value turn up together, the person making the bet losing half of his stake.

split, *a.* 1. divided; rent; separated.
2. divided or separated along the length or grain; broken into parts.
3. in the stock market, given in sixteenths, and not in eighths: said of a quotation smaller than the normal trading unit.
4. in botany, cleft; deeply divided into segments.
split dynamometer; a dynamometer employed in connection with alternating currents provided with two coils, so arranged that separate currents of the same frequency can be passed independently through each other.
split infinitive; in grammar, an infinitive with the verbal and the *to* separated by an adverb. Example: he decided *to gradually change* his procedure. Despite the objections of some people to this construction, many writers use split infinitives where ambiguity or awkwardness would otherwise result.
split moss; a moss of the family *Andreæaceæ*: so named from the way in which its capsules split.
split peas; peas husked and split for making soup, pudding, etc.
split phase; in electricity, a difference produced between the phases of two or more alternating currents into which a single-phase alternating current has divided.
split-phase motor; a multiphase motor operated from a single-phase alternating-current circuit by the introduction of a phase-splitting device.
split pin; a pin or cotter with a head at one end and a split at the other. The split ends diverging after passing through an object prevent the accidental retraction of the pin.
split ring; a ring which practically consists of two turns of a spiral, thus admitting of other rings being threaded upon it: the split key ring is an example.
split ticket; see under *ticket*.

split'bēak, *n.* the plantain eater.

split'mouth, *n.* a sucker found in the Mississippi River, *Lagochila lacera*.

split'tāil, *n.* 1. a fish found in California, *Pogonichthys macrolepidotus*.
2. the pintail duck.

split'tẽr, *n.* one who or that which splits.

split'ting, *a.* 1. that splits.
2. (a) aching severely: said of the head; (b) severe or sharp, as a headache.
3. very quick; as, a *splitting* pace. [Colloq.]

splōre, *n.* [etym. unknown.] a frolic; also, a carouse. [Scot.]

splotch, *n.* [prob. a fusion of *spot* and *blotch*.] a spot; a stain; a daub; a smear, especially one that is irregular.

splotch, *v.t.* to mark or soil with a splotch or splotches.

splotch'y, *a.*; *comp.* splotchier; *superl* splotchiest, having splotches; marked with splotches.

splũrġe, *n.* [imitative.] any very showy display or effort; an ostentatious demonstration. [Colloq.]

splũrġe, *v.i.*; splurged, *pt., pp.*; splurging, *ppr.* to make a showy display, for the purpose of attracting attention; to show off. [Colloq.]

splut'tẽr, *v.i.*; spluttered, *pt., pp.*; spluttering, *ppr.* [variant of *sputter*.]
1. to speak hastily and confusedly, as when excited or embarrassed.

A huge Cyclops that hissed and *spluttered*.
—W. A. Fraser.

2. to make hissing or spitting sounds, or to give off or scatter particles or drops in an explosive way; to sputter.

splut'tẽr, *v.t.* 1. to utter hurriedly and confusedly; to sputter.
2. to spatter or bespatter.

splut'tẽr, *n.* 1. a spluttering sound or utterance; confused noise or talk; fuss.
2. a loud sputtering or splash.

splut'tẽr·ẽr, *n.* one who splutters.

Spōde, *n.* a fine porcelain or chinaware originated by Josiah Spode at Staffordshire, England, about 1799: also *spode*.

spō'di·um, *n.* [L., from Gr. *spodos*, ashes.] a residue of vegetable or animal matter which is the result of slow oxidation. [Rare.]

spō·doġ'e·nous, *a.* in medicine, having the character of waste matter.

spod'ō·man·cy, *n.* [Gr. *spodos*, ashes, and *-mancy*.] divination by means of ashes.

spod·ō·man'tiç, *a.* pertaining to spodomancy.

spod'ū·mēne, *n.* [Fr. *spodumene*; Gr. *spodoumenos*; part. passive of *spodoūn*, to reduce to ashes, from *spodos*, ashes.] a light-green or yellow, crystalline mineral, $LiAl(SiO_3)_2$: it is a silicate of lithium and aluminum: it is sometimes used as a gem.

spof'fish, *a.* zealous and active in matters of little or no importance. [Slang.]

spof'fle, *v.i.* to fret and worry about trifles. [Brit. Dial.]

spoil, *v.t.*; spoiled *or* spoilt, *pt., pp.*; spoiling, *ppr.* [ME. *spoilen*; OFr. *espoillier*, from L. *spoliare*, to plunder, from *spolium*, hide stripped from an animal.]
1. to damage or injure in such a way as to make useless, valueless, etc.; to destroy.
2. to mar or impair the enjoyment, quality, or functioning of; as, the rain *spoiled* our picnic.
3. to cause to demand or expect too much by overindulgence.
4. (a) to strip (a person) of goods, money, etc. by force; (b) to rob; pillage; plunder; (c) to seize (goods) by force. [Archaic.]

spoil, *v.i.* 1. to plunder; to pillage. [Archaic.]

Outlaws, which, lurking in woods, used to break forth to rob and *spoil*.
—Spenser.

2. to be damaged or injured in such a way as to become useless, valueless, etc.; to decay, as food.

spoil, *n.* 1. [*usually pl.*] that which is taken from others by violence; especially, the plunder taken from an enemy; pillage; booty; loot.
2. an object of plunder; prey.
3. waste material removed in making excavations, etc.
4. that which is gained by strength or effort.

Each science and each art his *spoil*.
—Bentley.

5. the art or practice of plundering; robbery; waste. [Archaic.]
6. corruption; damage; impairment. [Obs.]
7. the slough, or cast skin, of a serpent or other animal. [Obs.]
8. [*usually pl.*] the emoluments of public offices and the offices themselves, regarded as a reward for service rendered in a political contest.
spoils system; the system or practice of regarding and treating appointive public offices as the booty of the successful party in an election, to be distributed, with their opportunities for profit, among political henchmen and party workers.

spoil'ȧ·ble, *a.* capable of being spoiled.

spoil'āġe, *n.* 1. a spoiling or being spoiled.
2. something spoiled, or the amount lost through spoiling.

spoil bank, a place for depositing refuse or excavated material.

spoil'ẽr, *n.* 1. a plunderer; a pillager; a robber.
2. one who corrupts, mars, or renders useless.

spoil'fīve, *n.* a game of cards played with the whole pack, and by any number of persons up to ten, each player receiving five cards. Three tricks make the game, and when no one can take so many the game is said to be *spoiled*.

spoil'fụl, *a.* destructive; rapacious. [Obs.]

spoils'măn, *n.*; *pl.* **spoils'men,** a person who advocates the spoils system; one who supports a political party for private gain or to obtain office for himself or his friends.

An overwhelming majority carried the reform measure through the senate and the *spoilsmen* were routed. —Elliot.

spoils'mŏn″gẽr, *n.* a distributor of political spoils.

spoil'spōrt′, *n.* one who spoils another's sport or pleasure.

spoilt, *v.* alternative past tense and past participle of *spoil*.

spōke, *v.* past tense and archaic past participle of *speak*.

spōke, *n.* [AS. *spāca*; Ice. *spóki*, a spoke. Same root as *spike*.]
1. the radius or ray of a wheel; any of the small bars which are inserted in the hub and which serve to support the rim.
2. a rung of a ladder.
3. any of the handles jutting from the circumference of the steering wheel of a ship.
4. a contrivance for fastening the wheel of a vehicle in order to prevent its turning, as when going down a hill.
to put a spoke in one's wheel; to put an impediment in one's way; to thwart one's purpose or design.

spōke, *v.t.*; spoked, *pt., pp.*; spoking, *ppr.* 1. to fit or furnish with spokes, as a wheel.
2. to thrust a spoke, or bar, into (a wheel) to prevent movement.

spōke au′gẽr, a hollow auger for making the round tenons on the outer ends of spokes.

spō′ken, *a.* 1. oral; uttered: opposed to *written.*

2. having a manner of speaking: used in hyphenated compounds; as, civil-*spoken.*

spō′ken, *v.* past participle of *speak.*

spōke′shāve, *n.* a cutting or planing tool consisting of a blade with a handle at either end: so called because originally used to shape spokes, but now used for trimming and smoothing rounded surfaces.

spōkes′măn, *n.*; *pl.* **spōkes′men,** one who speaks for or in behalf of another or others.

spōkes′pẽr″sŏn, *n.* same as *spokesman*: used to avoid the masculine implication of *spokesman.*

spōkes′wom″ăn (-woom″) *n.*; *pl.* **spokes′-wom″en** (-wim″), a woman who speaks for or in behalf of another or others.

spōke′wīṣe, *a.* radiating out from a center, as the spokes of a wheel.

spōke′wīṣe, *adv.* so as to be spokewise.

spō′li·ȧ, *n.* plural of *spolium.*

spō′li·ăr·y, *n.*; *pl.* **spō′li·ăr·ieṣ,** in ancient Rome, the place in the amphitheaters where the slain gladiators were dragged to be stripped of their clothes.

spō′li·āte, *v.t.* and *v.i.*; spoliated, *pt.*, *pp.*; spoliating, *ppr.* [L. *spoliatus,* pp. of *spoliare,* to plunder.] to plunder; to pillage; to rob; to despoil.

spō·li·ā′tion, *n.* 1. the act of plundering; robbery; plunder; particularly, the act of plundering an enemy in time of war.

2. the act or practice of seizing neutral ships in wartime under authority.

3. in ecclesiastical law, the act of an incumbent who has resigned, in taking the fruits of his benefice without right.

4. in law, intentional destruction, mutilation, or alteration of a document by an unauthorized person.

spō′li·ȧ·tive, *a.* having a reducing or diminishing effect; specifically, in medicine, having this effect on the blood.

spō′li·ā·tŏr, *n.* one who robs or plunders.

spō′li·ȧ·tō·ry, *a.* of spoliation; causing spoliation; destructive.

spon·dā′iç, spon·dā′i·căl, *a.* 1. of, pertaining to, or characterized by a spondee or spondees.

2. composed of spondees; constituting a spondee.

spon′dee, *n.* [Fr. *spondée,* from L. *spondeus;* Gr. *spondeios,* from *spondē,* a solemn libation, because such libations were accompanied by a slow and solemn melody.] a metrical foot consisting of two long syllables or, in English poetry, two heavily accented syllables: most alleged spondees in English really have one secondary accent.

Spon′di·as, *n.* [Gr., the bullace tree.] the typical genus of the family *Anacardiaceæ.* The leaves are alternate, without dots, and the five carpels surrounded by a cup-shaped disk. The fruit of various West Indian and South American species are edible.

spon·dū′liçs, *n.* money; coin; wealth: also written *spondulix.* [Slang.]

spon′dyl, spon′dyle, *n.* [L. *spondylus;* Gr. *spondylos,* a joint, a vertebra.]

1. a joint of the backbone; a vertebra.

2. a joint, as of a wheel, etc. [Obs.]

spon′dy·lid, *a.* of or pertaining to the *Spondylidæ,* a family of mollusks.

spon′dy·lid, *n.* one of the *Spondylidæ.*

Spon·dyl′i·dae, *n.pl.* a family of marine mollusks named from the genus *Spondylus.*

spon·dyl·ī′tis, *n.* [*spondyl-* and *-itis.*] inflammation of the vertebrae.

spon′dy·lō-, [from Gr. *spondylos,* joint of the back, a vertebra.] a combining form meaning *vertebra,* as in *spondylitis*: also, before a vowel, *spondyl-.*

spon′dy·loid, *a.* of, pertaining to, or like the genus *Spondylus.*

Spon′dy·lus, *n.* [L., a joint of the backbone.]

1. a genus of inequivalve lamellibranchiate mollusks with unequal beaks, the hinge with two recurved teeth, separated by a small hollow. They are noted for their spines. It is the type of the family *Spondylidæ.*

2. [s-] any member of this genus.

spŏnġe, *n.* [from OFr. *esponde;* L. *sponda,* frame (of a bed).] the heel of a horseshoe. [Obs.]

spŏnġe, *n.* [ME.; Late AS.; L. *spongia;* Gr. *spongia,* a sponge.]

1. a plantlike sea animal having a porous structure and a tough, fibrous skeleton, and growing fixed (except in the larval stage), in large colonies.

2. the skeleton, or a piece of the skeleton, of such animals, which is light in weight, remains somewhat tough while becoming soft when wet, has a characteristic elastic compressibility, and can absorb many times its own weight in water: it is used in washing surfaces, in bathing, etc.

3. any substance like this; specifically, (a) a pad of gauze or cotton, as used in surgery; (b) any of several light, porous cakes or puddings; (c) bread dough; (d) any of several metals, as platinum, found in a porous mass; (e) a spongy substance made of rubber, plastic, etc. and used in washing, bathing, etc.

4. (a) a person having a spongelike capacity, as for drink, knowledge, etc.; (b) [Colloq.] a person who, though able to work, depends on others for food, money, etc.

5. a sponge bath.

6. in gunnery, an instrument for cleaning cannon after a discharge. It consists of a cylinder of wood, covered with lambskin or wool, and having a handle or staff.

sheepswool sponge; same as *sheepswool.*

to throw, toss, etc. *up* (or *in*) *the sponge*; to admit defeat; to submit; to give up: from the practice by a boxer's second of throwing a sponge into the ring to concede defeat. [Colloq.]

vegetable sponge; same as *sponge gourd.*

velvet sponge; a variety of soft sponge, *Spongia equina meandriformis.*

vitreous sponge; same as *glass sponge.*

yellow sponge; an American and West Indian sponge, valuable commercially.

spŏnġe, *v.t.*; sponged, *pt., pp.*; sponging, *ppr.*

1. to use a sponge on so as to dampen, wipe clean, etc.

2. to remove or obliterate with or as with a damp sponge (with *out, off, away,* etc.).

3. to absorb with, as with, or like a sponge (often with *up*).

4. to drain; to deprive by extortion; to squeeze; to plunder. [Obs.]

5. to get without cost, as by begging, imposition, etc. [Colloq.]

To *sponge* a breakfast once a week.
—Swift.

6. to set a sponge for, as bread.

spŏnġe, *v.i.* 1. to suck in or imbibe liquid like a sponge.

2. to depend on others for food, money, etc.; as, an idler who *sponges* on his neighbor. [Colloq.]

3. to gather sponges from the sea.

spŏnġe bȧth, a bath taken by using a wet sponge or cloth without getting into water.

spŏnġe′çāke, *n.* a light, porous kind of cake made of flour, beaten eggs, sugar, etc., but no shortening: also *sponge cake.*

spŏnġe çū′çum·bẽr, same as *sponge gourd.*

spŏnġe glȧss, a glass-bottomed vessel used in fishing for sponges.

spŏnġe gōurd, a gourd, *Luffa cylindrica* or *Ægyptiaca,* native to India. Its inner, netted fiber is used as a sponge.

spŏnġe grȧft, in medicine, a bit of sponge inserted in an ulcer or wound to promote granulation.

spŏnġe′let, *n.* 1. in botany, same as *spongiole.*

2. a small sponge.

spŏnġe moth, the gypsy moth.

spŏn′ġeŏus, *a.* spongy.

spŏn′ġẽr, *n.* 1. one who cleans, etc. with a sponge.

2. one who or that which gathers or fishes for sponges; a vessel employed in sponge gathering; a person who dives for sponges.

3. one who obtains by sponging; a parasite. [Colloq.]

4. a machine which dampens, by means of steam, cloth which is to be ironed.

spŏnġe tree, a tropical American evergreen shrub, *Acacia farnesiana,* the flowers of which yield a fragrant perfume.

spŏnġe′wood, *n.* 1. a plant of the *Æschynomene.*

2. an erect pinnate-leaved araliaceous shrub, *Gastonia cutispongia,* having a spongy bark, native to Africa.

Spon′ġi·ȧ, *n.* the typical genus of the family *Spongidæ.*

Spon′ġi·ae, *n.pl.* same as *Porifera.*

spon′ġi·ăn, *a.* of or pertaining to the sponges.

spon′ġi·ăn, *n.* any sponge.

spon·ġiç′ō·lous, *a.* existing within sponges.

Spon′ġi·dae, *n.pl.* a family of sponges of which *Spongia* is the type genus.

spŏn′ġi·fọrm, *a.* resembling a sponge; soft and porous; elastic; spongy.

Spon·ġil′lȧ, *n.* a genus of fresh-water sponges that contain silica, typical of the family *Spongillidæ.*

spon·ġil′lid, *n.* any sponge of the genus *Spongilla.*

Spon·ġil′li·dae, *n.pl.* a family of sponges inhabiting fresh water.

spon′ġil·line, *a.* belonging or pertaining to the *Spongillidæ.*

spŏn′ġin, *n.* a horny substance that forms the skeletons of certain sponges.

spŏn′ġin·blȧst, *n.* [*spongin,* and Gr. *blastos,* a germ.] a cell which produces spongin; a spongoblast.

spŏn′ġi·ness, *n.* the quality or state of being spongy.

spŏn′ġing house, formerly, in England, a place where persons arrested for debt were kept by a bailiff for twenty-four hours until they either paid their debts or were put in prison for nonpayment. The charge for such keeping was extortionate.

spŏn′ġi·ōle, *n.* [Fr., from L. *spongiola,* dim. of *spongia,* a sponge.] in botany, an expansion of the termination of a radicle, resembling a sponge, for absorbing the nutriment of plants; a spongelet. [Obs.]

SPONGIOLE

spon′ġi·ō·pī′line, spon″ġi·ō·pī′lin, *n.* [Gr. *spongion,* a sponge, and *pilos,* felt.] in surgery, a substitute for a poultice, made of an absorbent layer of sponge and fiber on rubber backing.

spon′ġi·ō·plaṣm, *n.* [Gr. *spongion,* a sponge, and *plasma,* anything formed or molded.] the reticulum of a cell.

spon″ġi·ō·plaṣ′miç, *a.* pertaining to spongioplasm.

spŏn′ġi·ōse, *a.* spongelike; full of small cavities, like a sponge; as, *spongiose* bones.

spŏn′ġi·ous, *a.* same as *spongiose.*

Spon″ġi·ō·zō′ȧ, *n.pl.* the sponges.

spon″ġi·ō·zō′on, *n.*; *pl.* **spon″ġi·ō·zō′ȧ,** a sponge.

spon′ġīte, *n.* a fossil sponge.

spoñ′gō·blȧst, *n.* same as *sponginblast.*

spoñ′goid, *a.* [Gr. *spongos,* a sponge, and *eidos,* form.] resembling sponge; spongy.

spoñ·gol′ō·ġist, *n.* one versed in the science of sponges.

spoñ·gol′ō·ġy, *n.* the science or study of sponges.

spŏn′ġy, *a.*; *comp.* spongier; *superl.* spongiest, 1. like a sponge; specifically, (a) light, soft, and elastic; (b) full of holes; porous; (c) absorbent.

2. of or characteristic of a sponge.

spŏñk, *n.* spunk. [Obs.]

spon′săl, *a.* [L. *sponsalis,* from *spondere,* to betroth.] pertaining or relating to marriage.

spon′si·ble, *a.* [contraction of *responsible.*] worthy of credit; reliable. [Brit. Dial.]

spon′sing, *n.* same as *sponson.*

spon′sion, *n.* [L. *sponsio* (-*onis*), from *spondere,* to engage solemnly.]

1. the act of becoming surety for another.

2. a formal promise, pledge, or engagement, especially one made on behalf of another person.

3. in international law, an act or engagement on behalf of a state, by an agent not specially authorized.

spon′sŏn, *n.* [said to be seaman's alteration of *expansion;* orig. applied to the platforms on each side of a steamer's paddlewheels.]

1. a structure that projects over the side of a ship or boat; specifically, (a) a projecting gun platform; (b) an air chamber built into the gunwale of a canoe.

2. a short, winglike piece attached to the hull of a seaplane just above water level to give stability in the water.

spon′sŏn bēam, a lateral beam which supports a paddle box. [Obs.]

spon′sŏn rim, the wale connecting the paddle beam with the ship's side.

spon′sŏr, *n.* [L., a surety.]

1. one who binds himself to answer for another by agreement, and is responsible for his default; a surety.

2. one who, at the baptism of an infant, professes the faith in its name, and makes

the prescribed promises; a godfather or godmother.

3. a person or agency that gives endorsement to or vouches for some person or thing.

4. a business firm or other agency that pays the costs of a radio or television program (usually a program that combines entertainment with advertising for the benefit of the firm or agency).

spon'sŏr, *v.t.* to act as sponsor for.

spon·sō'ri·ăl, *a.* of or pertaining to a sponsor.

spon'sŏr·ship, *n.* 1. a sponsoring.

2. the position, policies, etc. of a sponsor.

spon·tȧ·nē'i·ty, *n.* [Fr. *spontanéité.*]

1. the state or quality of being spontaneous.

2. *pl.* **spon·tȧ·nē'i·ties,** spontaneous behavior, movement, action, etc.; specifically, (a) in biology, the tendency to changes in animal and plant life, uninfluenced by environment; (b) in physiology, the tendency toward activity of muscular tissue, without apparent stimulus.

spon·tā'nē·ous, *a.* [L. *spontaneus*, from *sponte*, of free will.]

1. acting in accordance with or resulting from natural feeling, temperament, or disposition, or from a native internal proneness, readiness, or tendency, without compulsion, constraint, or premeditation; as, a *spontaneous* gift or proposition.

2. acting by its own impulse, energy, or natural law, without external cause or influence; as, *spontaneous* motion; *spontaneous* growth; *spontaneous* combustion.

3. growing without being planted; indigenous; wild; as, a *spontaneous* growth of wood.

spontaneous combustion; see under *combustion.*

spontaneous generation; see under *generation.*

spon·tā'nē·ous·ly, *adv.* in a spontaneous manner.

spon·tā'nē·ous·ness, *n.* the quality or state of being spontaneous; spontaneity.

spon·to͞on', *n.* [Fr. *sponton, esponton*; It. *spontone, spuntone*, spontoon, from *punto*; L. *punctum*, a point.] a short pike or halberd carried by eighteenth century officers of infantry: used for signaling orders to the regiment.

spo͞of, *n.* [orig. a game involving hoaxing and nonsense.] a hoax, joke, or deception. [Slang.]

spo͞of, *v.t.* and *v.i.* to fool; to deceive; to trick. [Slang.]

spo͞ok, *n.* [D. *spook*; Sw. *spöke*; Dan. *spögelse*, a ghost. Perhaps connected with Celtic forms *puck, pug.*] a spirit; a ghost. [Colloq.]

Never did I succeed in capturing a *spook* of any sort. —René Bache.

spo͞ok, *v.t.* and *v.i.* to haunt or affright, as a spook; to play the spook. [Colloq.]

spo͞ok'ish, *a.* having the appearance of a spook; ghostly; spooky. [Colloq.]

spo͞ok'y, *a.*; *comp.* spookier; *superl.* spookiest; of, like, or suggesting a spook or spooks; ghostly; weird; eerie.

spo͞ol, *n.* [ME. *spole*; M.D. *spoele*; akin to G. *spul.*] 1. a rod or cylinder, usually having a hole running from end to end and a rim at either end, upon which thread, wire, etc. is wound.

2. something like a spool.

spo͞ol, *v.t.*; spooled, *pt., pp.*; spooling, *ppr.* to wind on spools.

spo͞ol çot'tŏn, cotton thread wound upon spools.

spo͞ol'ẽr, *n.* one who or that which winds thread or yarn on spools.

spo͞om, *v.i.* [prob. variant of *spume*, to foam.] to be driven swiftly before the wind: said of a ship. [Archaic.]

spo͞on, *n.* [ME. *spon*, a spoon, chip, splinter; AS. *spôn*; Ice. *spónn, spánn*; Dan. and D. *spaan*, a chip, a splinter, the meaning being originally a chip of wood for supping up liquids.]

1. a utensil consisting of a small, shallow, usually oval-shaped bowl and a handle, used in eating and cooking for picking up or stirring food or drink.

2. something shaped like a spoon; specifically, (a) a shiny, curved fishing bait, usually made of metal, set above a hook or hooks so as to revolve when drawn through the water, as in casting: also *spoon bait*; (b) an oar or paddle having a curved blade; (c) a curved projecting part at the top of a torpedo tube, for keeping the torpedo on a horizontal course.

3. a golf club with a wooden head and more loft than a driver or brassie: see *golf club*, illus.

4. a foolish person; a simpleton; especially, one given to exuberant demonstrations of affection. [Slang.]

5. a chip; a splinter. [Obs.]

apostle spoon; see under *apostle.*

bag and spoon; a kind of dredge having a bag or receptacle attached to the cutting lip.

deflagrating spoon; a spoon-shaped vessel upon which substances are deflagrated.

to be born with a silver spoon in one's mouth; to be born to good fortune; to be born rich.

to be spoons on; to be in love with. [Slang.]

wooden spoon; (a) at Cambridge University, the student having lowest mathematical honors; (b) at Yale University, the most popular student in a class; also, formerly, one who took the last junior appointment.

spo͞on, *v.t.*; spooned, *pt., pp.*; spooning, *ppr.* 1. to take up with or as with a spoon.

2. to push, lift, or hit with a scooping motion, as the ball in some games.

3. to shape or hollow out like a spoon bowl.

spo͞on, *v.i.* 1. to fish with a spoon bait.

2. to spoon or scoop a ball, etc.

3. to lie or sleep spoon fashion. [Colloq.]

4. to make love, as by kissing and caressing. [Colloq.]

spo͞on, *v.i.*, to be driven by the wind; to spoom. [Archaic.]

spo͞on'ăġe, *n.* feeding with a spoon. [Obs.]

spo͞on bāit, same as *spoon*, sense 2a.

spo͞on'bill, *n.* 1 any wading bird of the genus *Platalea*; specifically, *Platalea leucorodia*, the white spoonbill, found over the greater part of Europe and Asia, and the north of Africa. The adult male has white plumage with a pale-pink tinge; at the junction of the neck with the breast there is a band of buffy yellow. The legs and feet are black, and the bill is very much flattened and grooved at the base and spoon-shaped at the tip. There is a white occipital crest in both sexes.

WHITE SPOONBILL (*Platalea leucorodia*)

2. any of a number of other birds with a bill like this.

3. the paddlefish.

4. a spoon-shaped bill.

spo͞on'-billed, *a.* having a broad, flattened, spoonlike bill.

spoon-billed sandpiper; the sandpiper, *Eurynorhynchus pygmæus*, of Siberia.

spo͞on bit, a bit with a spoonlike point for boring wood.

spo͞on bread (bred), a kind of bread, usually of corn meal, that remains doughy after baking and must be served with a spoon.

spo͞on'drift, *n.* same as *spindrift.*

spo͞on'ẽr·ism, *n.* [after Rev. W. A. *Spooner* (1844–1930), of New College, Oxford.] an unintentional interchange of sounds, usually initial sounds, in two or more words. Example: It is kistumary to cuss the bride.

spo͞on'ey, *a.*; *comp.* spoonier; *superl.* spooniest, same as *spoony.*

spo͞on'ey, *n.*; *pl.* **spo͞on'ies,** same as *spoony.*

spo͞on'-fash''iŏn (-un), *adv.* after the manner of packed spoons; with the face of one toward the back of another. [Colloq.]

spo͞on'fed, *a.* 1. fed with a spoon.

2. (a) treated with too much indulgence or solicitude; pampered; coddled; (b) given no chance to develop initiative or independence in action and thought.

spo͞on'flow''ẽr, *n.* an aquatic perennial West Indian plant, *Peltandra sagittæfolio*, having a spathe resembling a spoon.

spo͞on'fụl, *n.*; *pl.* **spo͞on'fụls,** as much as a spoon will hold.

spo͞on mēat, food that is or must be taken with a spoon; liquid food.

spo͞on net, a net used in landing fish.

spo͞on'wood, *n.* same as *mountain laurel*, sense 1.

spo͞on'wŏrm, *n.* a gephyrean of the genus *Thalassema*: so called because of its spoonlike proboscis.

spo͞on'wŏrt, *n.* any plant of the genus *Cochlearia*, as *Cochlearia officinalis*; scurvy grass.

spo͞on'y, *a.*; *comp.* spoonier; *superl.* spooniest, 1. foolishly fond or sentimental; amorous in a silly way. [Colloq.]

2. silly; foolish. [Chiefly Brit. Colloq.]

Also spelled *spooney.*

spo͞on'y, *n.*; *pl.* **spo͞on'ies,** 1. a person who spoons, or is amorous in a silly, sentimental way. [Colloq.]

2. a silly, foolish, or simple-minded person. [Chiefly Brit. Colloq.]

Also spelled *spooney.*

spo͞or, *n.* [AS. and Ice. *spor*; D. *spoor*, a track.] the footprints or track of an animal, especially of a wild animal hunted as game.

spo͞or, *v.t.* and *v.i.* to track, trail, or trace by a spoor.

spo͞or'ẽr, *n.* one who tracks game by spoors.

spo͞orn, *n.* in English folklore, a hobgoblin. [Obs.]

spō·rā'ceous, *a.* of or relating to spores.

spor'ȧ·dēs, *n.pl.* [Gr., from *sporas*, scattered.] formerly, in astronomy, stars not included within any constellation.

spō·rā'di·ăl, *a.* sporadic. [Rare.]

spō·rad'iç, *a.* [Fr. *sporadique*; Gr. *sporadikos*, separate, scattered.]

1. occurring singly or apart from other things of the same kind; separate; single; scattered.

2. happening from time to time; not constant or regular; occasional.

sporadic disease; a disease which attacks only a person here and there, without spreading extensively.

spō·rad'i·çăl, *a.* sporadic. [Rare.]

spō·rad'i·çăl·ly, *adv.* in a sporadic manner.

spō·rad'i·çăl·ness, *n.* the quality of being sporadic.

spō'răl, *a.* resembling or pertaining to spores.

spō·ran'ġi·ȧ, *n.* plural of *sporangium.*

spō·ran'ġi·ăl, *a.* 1. of, or having the nature of, a sporangium.

2. characterized by sporangia.

spō·ran·ġif'ẽr·ous, *a.* producing or bearing sporangia.

spō·ran'ġi·oid, *a.* having the appearance of a sporangium.

spō·ran'ġi·ōle, *n.* a sporangium of small size.

spō·ran·ġi'ō·lum, *n.*; *pl.* **spō·ran·ġi'ō·lȧ,** a sporangiole.

spō·ran'ġi·ō·phōre, *n.* [*sporangium*, and Gr. *phoros*, bearing.] the axis or columella on which sporangia are borne.

spō·ran'ġi·um, *n.*; *pl.* **spō·ran'ġi·ȧ,** [Gr. *spora*, a seed, and *angeion*, a vessel.] in botany, a spore case or single cell in which spores are formed. The illustration shows; (1) a sporangium of the male fern; (2) a sporangium burst and the spores escaping.

SPORANGIA

spō·rā'tion, *n.* same as *sporulation.*

spōre, *n.* [Gr. *sporos, spora*, seed.]

1. in biology, any of various small reproductive bodies, often consisting of a single cell, produced by mosses, ferns, certain protozoans, etc. asexually (*asexual spore*) or by the union of gametes (*sexual spore*): they are highly resistant and are capable of giving rise to a new adult individual, either immediately or after an interval of dormancy. The illustration shows (a) spores of *Agaricus grammocephalus*; (b) sporophores or stalks supporting the spores; (c) sterigmata or spicules; (d) trama (network) of spawn.

SPORES

2. any small organism or cell that can develop into a new individual; seed, germ, etc.

spōre, *v.i.*; spored, *pt., pp.*; sporing, *ppr.* to bear or develop spores.

spōre çāse, a case which contains spores; a sporangium.

spōred, *a.* having spores.

spōre fruit, any specialized structure in which spores are formed.

spōre saç, the sac which lines the cavity of a sporangium.

spō'rid, *n.* same as *sporidium.*

spō'ri·desm, *n.* [Gr. *spora*, seed, and *desmē*, a bundle.] a cellular body made up of numerous cells, each capable of germination.

spō·rid'i·ȧ, *n.* plural of *sporidium.*

spō·ri·dif'ẽr·ous, *a.* bearing sporidia.

spō·rid'i·um, *n.*; *pl.* **spō·rid'i·ȧ,** [Gr. *spora*, a seed, and dim. *-idion.*] in botany, a small spore; also, a case containing small spores.

spō·rif′ẽr·ous, *a.* [Gr. *spora,* a seed, and L. *ferre,* to bear.] producing or bearing spores.

spō″ri·fi·cā′tion, *n.* the production of spores; spore formation.

spō·ri·par′i·ty, *n.* reproduction by means of spores.

spō·rip′ȧ·rous, *a.* [Gr. *spora,* a seed or spore, and L. *parere,* to produce.] reproducing by spores.

spō′rō-, [from Greek *spora,* a seed, from *speirein,* to sow or scatter.] a combining form meaning *spore,* as in *sporo*carp: also, before a vowel, *spor-.*

Spō·rob′ō·lus, *n.* [LL., from Gr. *spora,* seed, and *ballein,* to cast forth.] a genus of coarse grasses the grain of which separates easily.

spō′rō·çärp, *n.* [*sporo-* and *-carp.*] a many-celled body produced from a fertilized archicarp, serving for the development of spores in red algae, lichens, and certain fungi.

spō·rō·çär′pi·um, *n.*; *pl.* **spō·rō·çär′pi·ȧ,** same as *sporocarp.*

spō′rō·cyst, *n.* [*sporo-* and-*cyst.*]
1. in botany, a resting cell giving rise to asexual spores.
2. in zoology, (a) a saclike stage in the development of some trematodes which produces daughter sporocysts by asexual means; (b) a cyst produced by some protozoans before sporulation, or a protozoan in encystment.

spō′rō·dẽrm, *n.* [*sporo-,* and Gr. *derma,* skin.] the skin or wall of a spore. [Obs.]

spō′rō·ġen, *n.* [*sporo-,* and Gr. *-genēs,* producing.] a spore-producing plant. [Obs.]

spō·rō·ġen′e·sis, *n.* reproduction by means of spores; also, the formation of spores.

spō·roġ′e·nous, *a.* producing spores; also, reproducing by means of spores.

spō·rō·gō′ni·um, *n.*; *pl.* **spō·rō·gō′ni·ȧ,** the sporophyte in mosses and liverworts, usually a spore-bearing capsule on a stalk.

spō·rog′ō·ny, *n.* [*sporo-* and *-gony.*] the process by which sporozoites are produced from a zygote in the sexual phase of certain sporozoans.

spōr′oid, *a.* [*sporo-,* and Gr. *eidos,* form.] having the appearance of a spore; sporelike.

spō′rō·phōre, *n.* [*sporo-* and *-phore.*] an organ or branch which bears spores.

spō·rō·phor′iç, *a.* of the nature of a sporophore.

spō·roph′ō·rous, *a.* in botany, (a) pertaining to a sporophore; (b) bearing spores.

spō′rō·phyll, spō′rō·phyl, *n.* [*sporo-* and *-phyll.*] a leaf or leaflike part producing spores or sporangia.

spō·rō·phyl′lum, *n.*; *pl.* **spō·rō·phyl′lȧ,** same as *sporophyll.*

spō′rō·phȳte, *n.* [*sporo-* and *-phyte.*] the form bearing asexual spores, in plants having alternation of generations.

spō·rō·phyt′iç, *a.* relating to or characteristic of a sporophyte.

spō′rō·saç, *n.* [*sporo-,* and L. *saccus,* a bag.]
1. one of the simple generative buds of certain hydrozoa in which the medusoid structure is not developed.
2. a sporocyst.

-spōr′ous, [from *spore,* and *-ous.*] a combining form meaning *having* (a specified number or kind of) *spores,* as in mono*sporous.*

spōr′ous, *a.* resembling or relating to a spore.

Spō·rō·zō′ȧ, *n.pl.* [*sporo-,* and Gr. *zōon,* an animal.] a group of one-celled parasites which pass through phases of both sexual generation and asexual generation, during which sporogenesis takes place: the organisms of malaria and Texas fever belong to this group.

spō·rō·zō′ăn, *n.* any one of the *Sporozoa.*

spō·rō·zō′ăn, *a.* of or relating to the *Sporozoa.*

spō·rō·zō′iç, *a.* sporozoan.

spō·rō·zō′īte, *n.* an active spore that is the offspring of the passive spores formed by the division of a zygote, in sporozoans.

spō·rō·zō′oid, *n.* a zoospore. [Obs.]

spō·rō·zō′on, *n.* any one of the *Sporozoa.* [Rare.]

spor′răn, *n.* [Gael. *sporan,* a purse, from LL. *bursa,* a purse or pouch.] a pouch or large purse worn by Scottish Highlanders in full dress, usually covered with fur or long hair and often ornamented with silver and stones. It is worn hanging from the front of the belt.

SPORRANS
1. fancy-dress sporran; 2. sporran as worn in the British Army

spōrt, *n.* [ME. *sporte;* contr. of *disport.*]
1. any activity or experience that gives enjoyment or recreation; pastime; diversion.
2. such an activity requiring more or less vigorous bodily exertion and carried on according to some traditional form or set of rules, whether outdoors, as football, hunting, golf, racing, etc., or indoors, as basketball, bowling, squash, etc.
3. fun; play; as, it was great *sport* to play in the surf.
4. (a) a thing joked about; object of ridicule; laughingstock; (b) a thing played with; plaything.
5. a gambler. [Colloq.]
6. (a) a person who has sportsmanlike or sporting characteristics; as, be a *sport!*; (b) a person judged according to his ability to take loss, defeat, teasing, etc.; as, is he a good or a poor *sport?* [Colloq.]
7. a gay, fast, showy person; a flashy fellow. [Colloq.]
8. amorous trifling or play. [Obs.]
9. in biology, a plant or animal showing some marked variation from the normal type.
10. in botany, a bud variation.
in (or *for*) *sport;* in joke or jest; not in earnest.
to make sport of; to mock or ridicule; to poke fun at.
Syn.—play, game, diversion, amusement, frolic, mock, mockery, mirth, jest, joke.

spōrt, *v.i.* 1. to play or frolic.
2. to engage in a sport or sports (senses 1 and 2).
3. (a) to joke or jest; (b) to make sport; to trifle.
4. to engage in amorous trifling or play. [Archaic.]
5. in biology, to vary markedly from the normal type; to mutate.
6. in botany, to show bud variation.

spōrt, *v.t.* 1. to divert or amuse (oneself, etc.). [Obs.]
2. to represent by any kind of play. [Obs.]
3. to wear or display, especially with unnecessary show; as, to *sport* a new equipage; to *sport* a new hat. [Colloq.]
to sport one's oak; see under *oak.*

spōrt, spōrts, *a.* 1. of or for sports; as, the *sport* page of a newspaper, a *sport* academy.
2. suitable for informal, casual wear, as when engaged in outdoor activities; not dressy: said of clothes; as, a *sport* coat, a *sports* skirt.

spōrt·ȧ·bil′i·ty, *n.* frolicsomeness; sportiveness.

spōrt′ăl, *a.* pertaining to or employed in sports. [Obs.]

spōrt′ẽr, *n.* one who sports.

spōrt′fụl, *a.* 1. full of sport; frolicsome; full of jesting; playful; as, a *sportful* companion.
2. sportive; done in jest or for mere play.
3. amorous; wanton. [Obs.]

spōrt′fụl·ly, *adv.* in a sportful manner.

spōrt′fụl·ness, *n.* the state of being sportful or playful; as, the *sportfulness* of kids and lambs.

spōrt′i·ly, *adv.* in a sporty manner.

spōrt′i·ness, *n.* the quality of being sporty.

spōrt′ing, *a.* 1. of or having to do with sports, or athletic games, etc.
2. interested in or taking part in sports, or athletic games, etc.
3. sportsmanlike; fair.
4. interested in or having to do with games, races, etc. characterized by gambling or betting.
5. in botany and zoology, assuming the character of a sport.
sporting chance; a fair chance, involving loss in case of failure. [Colloq.]
sporting man; one who is interested in sports, especially in games, races, etc. characterized by gambling or betting.

spōrt′ing book, a book in which bets are recorded.

spōrt′ing goods, equipment, clothing, and the like for participating in sports, athletic games, etc.

spōrt′ing house, 1. a gambling house. [Colloq.]
2. a house of prostitution. [Colloq.]

spōrt′ing·ly, *adv.* in a sportive manner.

spōrt′ing plant, in botany, a sport.

spōrt′ive, *a.* 1. tending to or engaging in sport; gay; merry; frolicsome; playful.
2. of, or having the nature of, sport, especially outdoor sport.
3. done in fun or playfully, not in earnest.
4. amorous; wanton; sportful. [Obs.]
Syn.—gay, merry, sprightly, jocund, jesting.

spōrt′ive·ly, *adv.* in a sportive manner.

spōrt′ive·ness, *n.* the state of being sportive; playfulness; gaiety; frolicsomeness; as, the *sportiveness* of one's humor.

spōrt′less, *a.* without sport or mirth; joyless.

spōrt′ling, *n.* a small person or creature that sports or plays about. [Rare.]

spōrts, *a.* same as *sport,* a.

spōrts′măn, *n.*; *pl.* **spōrts′men,** 1. a man who is interested in or takes part in sports, especially hunting, fishing, horse racing, etc.
2. a person who can take loss or defeat without complaint, or victory without gloating, and who treats his opponents with fairness, generosity, courtesy, etc.

spōrts′măn·līke, *a.* characteristic of or befitting a sportsman.

spōrts′măn·ly, *a.* sportsmanlike.

spōrts′măn·ship, *n.* 1. skill in or fondness for sports.
2. qualities and behavior befitting a sportsman.

spōrts′weãr, *n.* sport clothes.

spōrts′wom″ăn (-woom″), *n.*; *pl.* **spōrts′wom″en** (-wim″), a woman who is interested in or engages in sports.

spōr′tū·lăr·y, *a.* subsisting on alms or charitable contributions. [Obs.]

spōr′tūle, *n.* [L. *sportula,* a little basket.] an alms; a dole; a charitable gift. [Obs.]

spōrt′y, *a.*; comp. *sportier;* superl. *sportiest,* 1. sporting or sportsmanlike. [Colloq.]
2. characteristic of a sport or sporting man. [Colloq.]
3. loud, flashy, or showy, as clothes. [Colloq.]

spor′ū·lāte, *v.i.*; sporulated, *pt., pp.*; sporulating, *ppr.* to undergo sporulation.

spor·ū·lā′tion, *n.* [LL. *sporula,* dim. of *spora,* a spore.] spore formation, especially by multiple fission after encystment; sporation.

spor′ūle, *n.* a spore or, especially, a small spore.

spor·ū·lif′ẽr·ous, *a.* bearing sporules.

spot, *n.* [D. *spat,* a spot, a speckle; Dan. *spætte,* a spot, a fleck; Ice. *spotti, spottr,* a bit, a small piece.]
1. a small area that is different, as in color or texture, from the background or main area of which it is a part; often, a mark made by some foreign matter; a stain; mark; blot; speck; patch.
2. a flaw or defect, as in character or reputation; something blameworthy; a fault.
3. a locality; place; as, there's a good fishing *spot* in the middle of the lake.
4. a salt-water food fish, *Liostomus xanthurus,* having a black spot behind the shoulders and dark stripes on the sides.
5. a small quantity; a bit; as, let's have a *spot* of lunch. [Brit. Colloq.]
6. a spotlight. [Slang.]
7. position; situation; as, he's got a good *spot* with that firm. [Slang.]
8. position or place in a schedule or listing; as, he has one of the best *spots* in radio. [Slang.]
9. a variety of the common domestic pigeon: so called from a spot on its head just above its beak.
10. the redfish, *Sciæna ocellata,* which has a black spot at the base of the tail fin.
11. a circular patch of black cloth pasted on a billiard or pool table at each of two points equally distant from each end and the sides.
12. [*pl.*] commodities sold for immediate payment and actual or legal delivery. [Slang.]
13. a dollar bill: usually used with higher denominations; as, a five *spot,* a ten *spot.* [Slang.]
baby spot; a small, portable spotlight. [Slang.]
in a spot; in an uncomfortable or bad situation; in trouble; as, the bookkeeper's false entry put him *in a spot.* [Slang.]
on the spot; (a) on or at the locality or place mentioned; (b) at once; immediately; without delay; (c) [Slang.] in a bad situation; in trouble or difficulty; (d) [Slang.] in a position where something, as a reply, is expected of one; (e) [Slang.] in danger, especially in danger of death by murder.
to hit the high spots; to treat only the main points or outstanding features of a topic, as in a rapid or cursory discussion. [Colloq.]
to hit the spot; to satisfy a particular desire or yearning; as, this coffee *hits the spot.* [Colloq.]

to touch a (or *one's*) *sore spot*; to touch upon a point or subject about which one is sensitive. [Colloq.]

Syn.—blot, blemish, flaw, speck, stain, place, location, situation.

spot, *v.t.*; spotted, *pt., pp.*; spotting, *ppr.* 1. to mark with spots; as, to *spot* a garment; to *spot* paper.
2. to patch by way of ornament; to put a patch upon. [Obs.]
3. to stain; to blemish; to disgrace; to tarnish, as reputation.
4. to mark for future consideration.
5. to place in or on a given spot or spots; to locate; as, the officer *spotted* his men at strategic points.
6. to remove (individual spots, marks, etc.), as in dry cleaning.
7. to detect; to see; to recognize; to pick out; as, I couldn't *spot* her in the crowd. [Colloq.]
8. to allow as an advantage or handicap; as, I *spotted* him two points. [Colloq.]
9. to cut or chip in preparation for hewing, as timber.
10. in photography, to put spots of pigment on, as on a negative or print to remedy a defect.

spot, *v.i.* 1. to become marked with spots; as, this fabric will not *spot* in the rain.
2. to cause a spot or stain.

spot, *a.* 1. (a) that can be paid out or delivered immediately; ready; as, *spot* cash; (b) involving immediate payment of cash; (c) engaged in cash transactions only.
2. made at random; as, a *spot* check.
3. (a) broadcast from a local radio or television station; (b) inserted between regular radio or television programs: said of advertisements or announcements.

spot lens, a condensing lens in a microscope in which the light is confined to an annular opening by a round spot in the middle.

spot'less, *a.* free from spots; clear of stain; free from reproach or impurity; pure; untainted; innocent; as, a *spotless* mind; *spotless* behavior.

spot'less·ly, *adv.* in a spotless manner.

spot'less·ness, *n.* the condition of being spotless; freedom from spot or stain.

spot'līght (-līt), *n.* 1. a strong beam of light used to illuminate prominently a particular person, thing, or group, as on the stage of a theater.
2. a lamp used to project such a beam of light.
3. public notice or prominence.
4. an accessory light with a strong focused beam, attached to an automobile, usually at the side of the windshield, so that the driver can direct the beam in any direction by moving an inward-projecting shaft or handle.

spot'neck, *n.* the Hudsonian curlew.

spot'rump, *n.* the Hudsonian godwit.

spot'tȧ·ble, *a.* that can be spotted.

spot'ted, *a.* 1. marked with spots; as, a *spotted* beast.
2. stained; blemished; sullied.
spotted adder; the milk snake.
spotted crake; a small European bird of the rail family, resembling the American sora.
spotted crane's-bill; the wild geranium.
spotted fever; any of various febrile diseases accompanied with skin eruptions; especially, typhus, cerebrospinal meningitis, or Rocky Mountain spotted fever.
spotted sickness; a Mexican skin disease; the pinta.

spot'ted·ness, *n.* the state or quality of being spotted.

spot'ted tree, an Australian species of mahogany, *Flindersia maculosa*, spotted by the falling off of its outer bark in patches.

spot'tẽr, *n.* a person or thing that spots; specifically, (a) a detective or any person hired to watch for dishonesty among employees, as in a bank; (b) a person whose duty is to keep a lookout for, and report the position of, the enemy; as, an aircraft *spotter*; (c) a device used on railroads to mark automatically irregularities in the roadbed; (d) a person whose duty is to determine for a gunner or gun crew the position of a target and the relative closeness to it of the projectiles fired; (e) a person whose work is removing spots, etc. in dry cleaning.

spot'ti·ly, *adv.* in a spotty manner.

spot'ti·ness, *n.* the state or quality of being spotty.

spot'ty, *a.*; *comp.* spottier; *superl.* spottiest, 1. having, occurring in, or marked with spots.
2. not uniform or consistent; irregular, as in quality; uneven.

spouș'āġe, *n.* the act of espousing. [Obs.]

spouș'ăl, *a.* pertaining to marriage; nuptial; matrimonial; connubial; as, *spousal* rites.

spouș'ăl, *n.* [OFr. *espousailles*; Sp. *esponsales*; L. *sponsalia.*]
1. wedlock. [Obs.]
2. [*often pl.*] marriage; nuptials. [Archaic.]

spouse, *n.* [OFr. *espouse*, from L. *sponsus*, betrothed, pp. of *spondere*, to promise solemnly, to engage oneself.] a husband or wife; either member of a married couple spoken of in relation to the other.

spouse, *v.t.* 1. to wed; to espouse. [Archaic.]
2. to give in marriage. [Archaic.]

spouse brēach, adultery. [Obs.]

spouse'less, *a.* without a husband or a wife; as, a *spouseless* king or queen.

spouș'ess, *n.* a wife. [Obs.]

spout, *n.* [ME. *spute*, *spoute*, from the v.]
1. a nozzle, pipe, or projection (as on a teapot, sprinkling can, or pitcher) by which a liquid is poured or discharged.
2. the stream, as of grain, water, etc., issuing from a spout; as, a *spout* of water from a fountain; *spout* of spray cast up by a whale.
3. a waterspout.
4. a small elevator formerly used by pawnbrokers to carry up pawned articles for storage.
5. a pawnbroker's establishment. [Slang.]
6. a narrow channel in a river.
7. the spouthole of a whale.
up the spout; originally, up the spout at a pawnbroker's; hence, lost; in straits; ruined. [Slang.]

spout, *v.t.*; spouted, *pt., pp.*; spouting, *ppr.* [ME. *sputen*, *spouten*, to spout, vomit, from MD. *spuiten*, to spout.]
1. to shoot out (liquid, etc.) from or as from a spout; as, a whale *spouted* water high in the air.
2. to furnish with spouts, as a grain elevator.
3. to speak or utter in a loud, pompous, oratorical manner.
4. to pawn. [Slang.]

spout, *v.i.* 1. to flow or shoot out with force in a jet; as, water *spouts* from a cask or a spring; blood *spouts* from an artery.
2. to throw out liquid in a jet, as a whale.
3. to spout words or speeches.
4. to put an article in pawn. [Slang.]

spout'ẽr, *n.* 1. a declaimer. [Slang.]
2. something that spouts, as an oil well or a geyser.
3. a whale or a whaleman. [Sailors' slang.]

spout'fish, *n.* any marine animal that spouts water; a mollusk that squirts water, as the soft clam.

spout hōle, the opening through which a jet of water flows; specifically, the blowhole of a whale; the nostril of a seal or walrus.

spout'less, *a.* having no spout.

spout'shell, *n.* a marine shell whose outer lip is elongated like a siphon.

sprack, *a.* [Ice. *sprækr*, brisk, sprightly, also *sparkr*, brisk, lively; Ir. and Gael. *spraic*, strength, vigor; *spraiceach*, vigorous, strong.] vigorous; alert; sprightly. [Scot. and Brit. Dial.]

spradde, sprad, *v.* obsolete past tense and past participle of *spread*.

sprad'dle, *v.t.* and *v.i.*; spraddled, *pt., pp.*; spraddling, *ppr.* [from a merging of *spread* and *straddle.*] to spread (the legs) so as to span or straddle. [Dial. or Colloq.]

sprag, *n.* [Gael. and Ir. *spraic*, vigor, strength.]
1. a young salmon; a smolt. [Dial.]
2. a half-grown cod. [Dial.]

sprag, *n.* [Dan. dial., Sw. dial. *spragg*, a billet of wood.]
1. a roof prop used in a coal mine.
2. a piece of wood, etc. used to block the wheel of a vehicle or to prevent a vehicle from rolling backward on a grade.

sprag, *v.t.*; spragged, *pt., pp.*; spragging, *ppr.* 1. to stop or check the motion of (a wheel) by placing a block of wood under it or between the spokes.
2. to prop or support by means of a sprag.

sprag, *a.* same as *sprack*.

sprag rōad, in mining, a grade so steep that it is necessary to sprag the ore cars in descending it.

sprāin, *v.t.*; sprained, *pt., pp.*; spraining, *ppr.* [OFr. *espreindre*, to force out, to strain, from L. *exprimere*, to press out.] to wrench or twist a ligament or muscle of (a joint, as the ankle) without dislocating the bones.

sprāin, *n.* 1. an act of spraining.
2. an injury resulting from this, characterized by swelling, pain, and disablement of the joint.
sprain fracture; the separation of a tendon or ligament from its insertion, taking with it a piece of bone.

sprāints, *n.pl.* [OFr. *espraintes*; Fr. *épreintes*, lit., outpressings, from OFr. *espreindre.*] the dung of an otter.

sprang, *v.* alternative past tense of *spring*.

sprañ'gle, *v.i.*; sprangled, *pt., pp.*; sprangling, *ppr.* [nasalized form of Ice. *sprökla*, to straggle, clamber, get on with difficulty.] to grow in a straggling manner, with no uniformity; to straggle. [Dial.]

sprat, *n.* [formerly also *sprot*, from D. and L.G. *sprot*, sprat, from root of verb to *sprout*.]
1. a small European fish, *Clupea sprattus*, of the herring family, closely related to the pilchard.
2. any one of several other fishes of the herring family.

sprat, *n.* 1. one of various kinds of rushes, as *Juncus articulatus*, used for thatching and for fodder. [Scot.]
2. [*pl.*] small wood. [Brit. Dial.]

sprat bōr'ẽr, the red-throated loon, *Colymbus septentrionalis*: so called from its feeding on sprats.

sprat mew, the kittiwake.

sprawl, *v.i.*; sprawled, *pt., pp.*; sprawling, *ppr.* [ME. *spraulen*; AS. *spreawlian*, to move convulsively.]
1. to spread the limbs in a relaxed, awkward, or unnatural position.
2. to sit or lie in such a position; as, the wounded man *sprawled* in his chair.
3. to crawl in an awkward, ungainly way.
4. to spread awkwardly or without a regular pattern; to take up more space than is necessary, as handwriting, a line of men, etc.

sprawl, *v.t.* to cause to sprawl; as, certain trees *sprawl* their branches.

sprawl, *n.* the act or state of sprawling.

sprawl'ẽr, *n.* 1. one who or that which sprawls.
2. a noctuid moth, *Asteroscopus sphinx*, or its larva; also, any one of other noctuid moths.
3. the hellgrammite. [Dial.]

sprawl'y, *a.*; *comp.* sprawlier; *superl.* sprawliest, sprawling or tending to sprawl.

sprāy, *n.* [ME. *sprag*, sprig.]
1. a small shoot or branch; a leafy branch of a plant; a twig.
2. a collective body of small branches; as, the tree has a beautiful *spray*.
3. a design or ornament like a spray.
4. a set of castings attached by their individual sprues to the main stem.

sprāy, *n.* [prob. from L.G.; cf. *sprei*, spray, drizzle.]
1. a cloud or mist of fine liquid particles, as of water from breaking waves.
2. (a) a jet of fine liquid particles, as from an atomizer or spray gun; (b) liquid, as perfume or insecticide, used in such a device.
3. a device for shooting out such a jet or jets.
4. something likened to a spray (senses 1 and 2a); as, a *spray* of gunfire.

sprāy, *v.t.*, sprayed, *pt., pp.*; spraying, *ppr.* [Ice. *spræna*, a jet of water.]
1. to direct a spray upon; to treat with a spray.
2. to shoot out in a spray; as, he sprayed paint on the wall.

sprāy'bōard, *n.* a board fastened on the upper edge of a ship's gunwale to keep out spray.

sprāy çŏn·dens'ẽr, in a steam engine, an injection condenser in which a spray of water is introduced to condense the steam.

sprāy çūre, a variety of water cure in which water is applied in the form of spray.

sprāy drāin, in agriculture, a drain constructed by laying twigs or small branches in a trench and placing a loose covering of earth over them.

sprāy'ẽr, *n.* one who or that which sprays; specifically, an apparatus, variously constructed, for spraying; an atomizer.

sprāy'ey, *a.* consisting of or resembling sprays, as a tree; branching; bushy.

sprāy'ey, *a.* consisting of or resembling liquid spray, as a wave.

sprāy gun, a device that shoots out a spray of liquid, as paint or insecticide, by air pressure.

sprāy noz'zle, a nozzle fastened on the end

of a garden hose, which throws the water out in the form of spray.

spread (spred), *v.t.*; spread, *pt.*, *pp.*; spreading, *ppr.* [AS. *sprædan*; D. *spreiden*; Sw. *sprida*; Dan. *sprede*, to spread; Ice. *sprita*, to sprawl.]

1. to draw out so as to display more fully; to open out or expand so as to cover more space; to unfold; unfurl.

Reverently, piously, in hopeful patriotism, we *spread* this banner on the sky. —Henry Ward Beecher.

2. to lay out in display; to exhibit.

3. to stretch out (the fingers, arms, legs, wings, etc.); to extend.

4. to distribute over a surface or area; to scatter; disperse.

5. (a) to distribute in a thin layer; to smear; as, she *spread* butter on the toast; (b) to cover by smearing with a thin layer of something; as, *spread* this slice with jelly.

6. to extend over a certain period of time; to prolong; as, the bank *spread* the payments on the loan over eighteen months.

7. to cause to be widely or more widely known, felt, existent, etc.; to disseminate; propagate; diffuse; as, radio *spreads* news quickly; unsanitary conditions *spread* disease.

8. to cover, overlay, or deck with something.

9. (a) to set (a table) for a meal; (b) to set (food) on a table.

10. to push apart or farther apart.

11. to record in full; to recount.

12. to flatten out, as the end of a rivet by hammering.

13. to emit; to diffuse; as, plants *spread* their fragrance.

to spread oneself; (a) to put forth great effort in order to make a good impression; (b) to show off; to brag. [Colloq.]

to spread oneself thin; to try to do too many things at once.

Syn.—dispense, expand, circulate, extend; disseminate, prepare, lay, cover.

spread, *v.i.* 1. to extend itself; to expand; to be outstretched.

2. to become distributed or dispersed.

3. to be made widely or more widely known, felt, existent, etc.; to be disseminated, propagated, or diffused.

4. to be pushed apart or farther apart.

5. to be of such consistency that it can be distributed in a thin layer, as butter; to admit of being smeared.

6. to be extended by drawing or beating, as a metal.

spread, *n.* 1. the act of spreading or the state of being spread; extent; compass.

2. the extent to which something is spread or can be spread.

3. an expanse; extent; stretch; compass.

4. (a) two facing pages of a newspaper, magazine, etc., treated as a single continuous sheet, as in advertising; (b) printed matter set across the page of a newspaper, magazine, etc., or across several columns.

5. a cloth cover for a table, bed, etc.

6. any soft substance, as jam, butter, etc., used for spreading on bread.

7. a meal, especially one with a wide variety of food. [Colloq.]

8. a pretentious display. [Colloq.]

9. in aeronautics, wing span.

10. in rummy, etc., a set of three or four cards of the same suit and consecutive denominations.

11. the privilege of demanding shares of stock at a certain price, or of delivering shares of stock at another price, within a certain time agreed on.

12. a gem that is thin in proportion to its face.

13. in mathematics, a continuous number of related points.

14. in nautical usage, a sprit for extending a sail.

spread, *a.* 1. covering a large surface; broad.

2. thinner or more shallow than the standard: said of gems.

spread ēa′gle (-gl), 1. in heraldry, a figure of an eagle with outspread wings and legs: used as an emblem of the United States.

2. formerly on shipboard, a sailor or other person lashed for punishment to some part of the rigging, with outspread limbs.

3. in cooking, a fowl that has been broiled after being split open down the back.

SPREAD EAGLE

4. in stockbrokers' language, same as *straddle*.

5. an acrobatic figure in fancy skating.

spread′-ēa″gle, *a.* 1. resembling a spread eagle.

2. bombastic; boastful; ostentatious: said especially of a type of patriotism; as, his oratory is of the *spread-eagle* variety. [Colloq.]

spread-eagle orchid; a showy orchid, *Oncidium carthaginense*, found in the West Indies.

spread′-ēa″gle, *v.t.*; spread-eagled, *pt.*, *pp.*, spread-eagling, *ppr.* 1. to extend out in the position of a spread eagle, as for a flogging.

2. to spread out; to disperse; to scatter.

spread′-ēa″gle, *v.i.* to perform a spread eagle, as in figure skating, etc.

spread′-ēa″gle·ism, *n.* ostentation; bombast; pompousness. [Colloq.]

spread′ẽr, *n.* 1. one who or that which spreads; specifically, (a) a knifelike utensil for spreading butter, etc.; (b) a contrivance for scattering something; as, a manure *spreader*; (c) a device, as a bar, for keeping apart wires, stays, or the like.

2. in the manufacture of textiles, (a) same as *lapper*, sense 2; (b) a machine that draws fibers of flax into slivers.

3. in wagons, plows, etc., a stick that stretches apart the ends of a chain to which the singletrees are attached.

4. a device for flattening and spreading the jet from a hose pipe.

spread′ing ad′dẽr, same as *puff adder*, sense 2.

spread′ing·ly, *adv.* in a spreading manner.

spread′ing mȧ·chine′, a machine that cleans loose cotton and puts it in condition for carding.

spreagh′ẽr·y (sprākh′), *n.* [Ir. and Gael. *spreidhk* cattle, and *-ery.*] cattle stealing; also, small spoil; paltry booty of small articles: also written *spreacherie* or *sprechery*. [Scot.]

sprech′stim·me (shprekh′shtim-), *n.* [G.] a form of vocal expression partly like speech and partly like song.

spreç′kled (-ld), *a.* speckled. [Scot. and Brit. Dial.]

spree, *n.* [Ir. *spre*, spark, spirit.]

1. a merry, noisy frolic.

2. a drinking bout; a period of drunkenness.

3. a period of uninhibited activity; as, a shopping *spree*.

Sprē·ke′li·ȧ, *n.* [after J. H. von *Sprekelsen*, G. botanist.] a genus of bulbous plants of the order *Amaryllideæ*. The only species, *Sprekelia formosissima*, is very ornamental, and in cultivation is known as the jacobaea lily.

Spreng′el ex·plō′sive, one of a group of explosives, formed by combining oxidizing and combustible agents which are nonexplosive in themselves.

Spreng′el pump, a device having no piston, but producing a vacuum by means of the flow of mercury through a narrow tube, which acts as an aspirator, and causes a higher degree of exhaustion than could be obtained by the ordinary air pump: sometimes called *mercury pump*.

sprent, *v.* obsolete past tense and past participle of *spreng*.

sprew, *n.* same as *sprue* (the disease).

sprig, *n.* [ME. *sprigge*; prob. from base seen in *spray* (sprig), *spark*, etc.]

1. a small shoot or twig of a tree or other plant; a spray; as, a *sprig* of laurel or of parsley.

2. a design or ornament like this.

3. a small brad without a head.

4. a small, three-cornered piece of tin or zinc used to hold a pane of glass in the sash.

5. a young fellow; stripling.

6. a person as the offspring or scion of a family, institution, class, etc.: used humorously.

7. a small eyebolt ragged at the point.

8. in lacemaking, one of the separate pieces of lace, usually in the form of flowers or leaves, which are fastened upon net to fashion appliqué.

sprig, *v.t.*; sprigged, *pt.*, *pp.*; sprigging, *ppr.* 1. to remove a sprig or sprigs from (a bush, tree, etc.).

2. to mark or adorn with a design of small branches; to work with sprigs; as, to *sprig* muslin.

3. to nail or fasten with small, headless brads.

sprig, *a.* spruce; neat; stylish. [Obs.]

sprig çrys′tăl, a cluster of pointed, prismatic crystals of quartz, adhering by one extremity to the rock.

sprig′gẽr, *n.* 1. one who sprigs, as a worker in embroidery or a cobbler.

2. that which sprigs; specifically, a device for driving sprigs.

sprig′gy, *a.* 1. full of sprigs or small branches.

2. suggestive of a sprig or sprigs.

sprīght (sprīt), *v.* and *n.* sprite. [Obs.]

sprīght′fụl, *a.* [from *sprite*, a spirit.] lively; brisk; nimble; vigorous; gay. [Obs.]

Spoke like a *sprightful* noble gentleman. —Shak.

sprīght′fụl·ly, *adv.* briskly; vigorously. [Obs.]

sprīght′fụl·ness, *n.* briskness; liveliness; vivacity. [Obs.]

sprīght′less, *a.* having no life; dull; sluggish. [Obs.]

sprīght′li·ness, *n.* the condition or state of being sprightly; liveliness; vigor; gaiety; vivacity.

sprīght′ly, *a.*; *comp.* sprightlier; *superl.* sprightliest, [a modern spelling of *spritely*.] lively; brisk; animated; vigorous; airy; gay; as, a *sprightly* youth; a *sprightly* air; a *sprightly* dance.

Syn.—cheerful, animated, brisk, nimble, vivacious, spry.

sprīght′ly, *adv.* in a sprightly manner.

sprig′tāil, *n.* 1. the pintail, *Dafila acuta*.

2. the sharp-tailed grouse.

spring, *v.i.*; sprang *or* sprung, *pt.*; sprung, *pp.* springing, *ppr.* [AS. *sprincan*; akin to G. *springen*.]

1. to move suddenly and rapidly; specifically, (a) to move upward or forward from the ground by suddenly contracting the muscles; to leap; to bound; (b) to rise suddenly and quickly from or as from a sitting or lying position; as, he *sprang* to his feet; (c) to move, appear, come, etc. suddenly and quickly; to dart: often used figuratively; as, a curse *sprang* to his lips; (d) to move as a result of resilience; to be elastic.

2. to come or arise as from some source; specifically, (a) to grow or develop; as, the plant *springs* from a seed; (b) to come as a result; as, this error *springs* from faulty reasoning; (c) to come into existence; as, cities and towns *sprang* up; (d) to be descended; as, he *springs* from a famous stock; (e) [Archaic.] to begin to appear, as day; to dawn.

3. to explode or discharge: said of a military mine.

4. to become warped, bent, split, cracked, etc.; as, two boards of the siding have *sprung*.

5. to rise up above surrounding objects; to tower; as, the church steeple *springs* high above the town.

6. in architecture, to rise from the impost with an outward curve.

7. to thrive; to grow; to prosper. [Obs.]

In many senses of the v.i., *spring* is often followed by *up*.

to spring at; to leap toward; to attempt to reach by a leap.

to spring forth; to leap out; to rush.

to spring in; to rush in; to enter with a leap or in haste.

to spring on or *upon*; to leap on; to rush on with haste or violence; to assault.

Syn.—issue, arise, leap, jump, flow, bound.

spring, *v.t.* 1. to cause to start or rise suddenly; to start or rouse, as game; to cause to rise from the earth or from cover; as, to *spring* a pheasant.

2. to cause to explode or burst; to discharge.

Several of the enemies' mines, who have *sprung* divers others. —Tatler.

3. to crack; to bend or strain, so as to crack or split; as, to *spring* a mast.

4. to cause to close suddenly, or come together violently, as the parts of an instrument which are acted upon by a spring; as, to *spring* a trap.

5. to bend by force, as something stiff or strong; to insert, as a beam in a place too short for it, by bending it so as to bring the ends nearer together and allowing it to straighten when in place: usually with *in*; as, to *spring in* a slat or bar.

6. to leap over; to jump; to pass by leaping; as, to *spring* a wall.

7. in architecture, to start from an abutment or pier; as, to *spring* an arch.

8. to produce or announce quickly or unexpectedly; as, to *spring* a new scheme; to *spring* a joke on one.

9. to haul, as a vessel, by means of springs or cables.

10. to get (someone) released from jail or custody, as by paying bail. [Slang.]

to spring a butt; to loosen the end of a plank in a ship's bottom.

to spring a leak; to begin to leak suddenly.

to spring the luff; to yield to the helm and sail nearer to the wind than before: said of a ship.

spring, *n.* 1. the act, the ability, an instance, etc. of springing; specifically, (a) a jump or leap forward or upward, or the distance covered by this; (b) a sudden darting or flying back; (c) the ability to do this; resilience; elasticity.

2. a device, as a coil of wire, that returns to its original form after being forced out of shape: springs are used to absorb shock in beds, automobiles, etc., and as the motive power in clocks and similar mechanisms.

3. a flow of water from the ground, the source of a stream.

4. any source, origin, or motive.

5. that session of the year in which plants begin to grow after lying dormant all winter: in the North Temperate Zone, regarded as including the months of March, April, and May: in the astronomical year, that period between the vernal equinox and the summer solstice.

6. any period of beginning or newness; as, the *spring* of his life.

7. a warping, bending, crack, break, etc., as of the mast of a ship.

8. the dawn or dawning, as of day or light. [Archaic.]

9. in architecture, the line or plane in which an arch rises from its impost.

10. a gay, lively song or dance. [Scot.]

11. a young shoot; a bud. [Obs.]

12. a plant or a young tree; also, a grove of trees or a small shrubbery. [Obs.]

13. a youth; a springal. [Obs.]

14. in nautical usage, (a) a leak; an opening in a seam; (b) a crack in a mast or yard, running obliquely or transversely; (c) a rope or hawser passed from the stern of a ship and made fast to the cable on the anchor from the bow, by which she is riding, the object being to bring the broadside to bear in any direction; (d) a check on a cable while unshackling it; (e) a rope extending diagonally from the stern of one ship to the head of another, to make one ship sheer off to a greater distance.

spring balance; a contrivance for determining the weight of any article by observing the amount of deflection or compression which it produces upon a helical steel spring properly adjusted and fitted with an index working against a graduated scale.

spring, *a.* 1. of, for, appearing in, or planted in the spring.

2. of or acting like a spring; elastic; resilient.

3. having, or supported on, a spring or springs; as, a *spring* mattress.

4. coming from a spring; as, *spring* water.

spring'ăl, *n.* [Scot. *springel, springald*; prob. from *spring*, v.] an active young man; a youth. [Archaic.]

spring'ăld, *n.* a springal. [Archaic.]

spring back, in bookbinding, a curved or semicircular false back, made of thin sheet iron or of stiff pasteboard fastened to the under side of the true back, and causing the leaves of a book thus bound to lie flat when open: commonly used in binding ledgers and other blank books.

spring bēam, in shipbuilding, the fore-and-aft timber uniting the outer ends of the paddle-box beams.

spring beaū'ty (bū'), a spring-blooming wild flower belonging to the genus *Claytonia*, found in the eastern part of the United States and bearing white or pinkish flowers.

spring bed, a bed with elastic metal springs in the mattress or mattress frame.

spring bee'tle (-tl), an insect of the family *Elateridæ*; a click beetle.

spring bell, an American flowering plant, *Sisyrinchium grandiflorum*.

spring'bōard, *n.* 1. a flexible, springy board used by acrobats, gymnasts, etc. as a take-off in performing various feats of leaping.

2. a somewhat flexible board projecting over water, used as a take-off in diving: usually called *diving board*.

spring'bok, *n.*; *pl.* **spring'boks** or **spring'bok,** [D., lit., the springing buck.] a species of South African gazelle, *Gazella euchore*. It is brown on the upper parts, pure white beneath, with a broad band of deep vinous red where the colors meet on the flanks. It receives its name from its habit of leaping high in the air when alarmed.

SPRINGBOK (*Gazella euchore*)

Also written *springboc, springbuck*, etc.

spring box, 1. the box that contains the spring of any mechanism.

2. the frame of a sofa or the like, containing the springs.

3. a box that opens and shuts with a spring.

spring'buck, *n.*; *pl.* **spring'bucks** or **spring'buck,** same as *springbok*.

spring chick'en, 1. a young chicken, especially one only a few months old, used for broiling or frying.

2. a person, especially a woman, who is young, inexperienced, naive, etc. [Slang.]

spring çlēan'ing, a thorough house cleaning undertaken in the springtime.

spring çress, an American plant, *Cardamine rhomboidea*, of the mustard family, bearing white flowers in early spring.

spring çot'tēr, a metal split pin used in holding together parts of a mechanism or structure.

springe, *n.* a noose fastened to something under tension, as a bent tree, used for catching birds or the like; a snare.

springe, *v.t.*; springed (sprinjd), *pt., pp.*; springeing, *ppr.* to catch in a springe.

springe, *v.i.* to set springes.

sprin'gēr, *n.* one who catches birds or the like in a springe.

spring'ēr, *n.* 1. one who or that which springs.

2. a grampus.

3. in architecture, (a) the impost, or point at which an arch unites with its support; (b) the bottom stone of an arch, which lies on the impost; (c) the rib of a groined roof.

4. a species of antelope of South Africa; the springbok.

5. a springer spaniel.

6. a spring chicken.

spring'ēr·le (shpring'ēr-le), *n.* [G.] a German cooky made with an embossed design, eaten particularly during the Christmas season.

spring'ēr span'iel (-yel), a breed of large field spaniel, used for flushing, or springing, game.

spring fē'vēr, the feeling of laziness and listlessness or restlessness that many people have during the first warm, sunny days of spring.

Spring'fiēld rī'fle (-fl), [from *Springfield*, Mass., location of a U. S. armory.] a .30-caliber, breech-loading, magazine-fed rifle, operated by a bolt, adopted for use by the United States Army in 1903 and replaced as the standard infantry weapon by the Garand rifle in World War II.

spring'fin·gēr, *n.* a condition of the finger in which flexion and extension beyond certain points are difficult because of accumulated scar tissue.

spring flȳ, same as *caddis fly*.

spring grȧss, same as *vernal grass* under *vernal*.

spring gun, a concealed gun which is arranged to be discharged by a spring when connecting cords are disturbed, as by a trespasser.

spring'häas, *n.* [S. Afr. D.] a species of jerboa found in South Africa; the jumping hare, *Pedetes caffer*.

spring'halt, *n.* same as *stringhalt*.

spring'head (-hed) *n.* a source or fountainhead.

spring hook, 1. a hook for fastening a driving wheel spring to the frame of a locomotive.

2. a kind of door hook with a spring for keeping it in place.

3. a fishhook that is set like a spring trap; a snap hook.

spring'house, *n.* a small building enclosing a spring or brook, used for cooling milk, etc.

spring'i·ly, *adv.* in a springy manner.

spring'i·ness, *n.* the quality, state, or power of being springy.

spring'ing, *n.* 1. the act or process of leaping, arising, issuing, or proceeding.

2. growth; increase.

3. in architecture, the point of an arch contiguous to the part on which it rests.

spring latch, a latch that closes by means of a spring.

sprin̄'gle, *n.* a springe; a noose.

spring'let, *n.* a small spring of water.

spring lock, a lock in which the bolt is shot automatically by a spring.

spring pin, in a locomotive, a rod between the springs and axle boxes, to regulate the pressure on the axles.

spring pōle, a pole used, because of its elasticity, (a) for suspending a well drill; (b) in a pole lathe; (c) for binding a load of hay and the like; (d) for attaching a trolley to the trolley wire; a trolley pole.

spring rȳe, rye that is sown in the spring.

spring stāy, in nautical usage, a preventer stay, used to assist a principal stay.

spring'tāil, *n.* a wingless insect that moves, hops, or jumps by means of an elastic appendage of the hind part of its body, as the bristletail.

spring'tīde, *n.* springtime.

spring tīde, 1. the tide that occurs at or soon after the new moon and the full moon: it is normally the highest tide of the month.

2. any great flow, rush, or flood.

spring'tīme, *n.* 1. the season of spring; the spring of the year; springtide.

2. the period or time resembling or suggesting spring; earliest period.

spring tool, the light tongs used by a glass blower to grasp handles and light objects.

spring'trap, *n.* 1. a trap with a falling bar or door that is operated by a spring as soon as the detent is released.

2. a form of steam trap.

spring valve, a valve that is closed by a spring; especially, a kind of safety valve in which a spring balance secures automatic closing and opening as pressure upon it decreases or increases.

spring wa̤'tēr, water that flows from a natural spring.

spring wēir, a weir so arranged as to allow fish to pass over it as the tide comes in and to retain them when the tide goes out.

spring whēat (hwēt), any species or variety of wheat that is planted in the spring and harvested in the summer or fall: distinguished from *winter wheat*.

spring'wŏrm, *n.* a pinworm.

spring'wŏrt, *n.* a plant, *Euphorbia lathyris*, of the spurge family; caper spurge.

spring'y, *a.*; *comp.* springier; *superl.* springiest, 1. having elasticity like a spring; elastic; flexible; resilient; as, a *springy* board.

2. having many springs of water; wet; spongy; as, a *springy* meadow.

sprin̄'kle, *v.t.*; sprinkled(-kld), *pt., pp.*; sprinkling, *ppr.* [ME. *sprengen*, to scatter, from AS. *sprengan*, to spring.]

1. to scatter in small drops or particles, as water or salt.

2. to scatter drops or particles upon; to cover or strew with a sprinkling.

3. to baptize by sprinkling.

4. to place or to distribute here and there; as, to *sprinkle* humor throughout a book.

sprin̄'kle, *v.i.* 1. to scatter something in drops or particles.

2. to fall in drops or particles.

3. to rain lightly or infrequently.

sprin̄'kle, *n.* 1. the act of sprinkling.

2. a sprinkling; a small or scattered number or amount.

3. a light rain.

sprin̄'klēr, *n.* 1. one who or that which sprinkles.

2. any of various sprinkling devices as (a) a container with a perforated disk at the end of a spout, used for watering plants, etc.; (b) a brush for scattering holy water in a church; (c) a nozzle, or a device with several attached nozzles, in a sprinkler system; (d) a wheeled tank for sprinkling water on streets to settle dust.

sprin̄'klēr sys'tem, 1. a system of pipes and attached nozzles or sprinklers carrying water or other extinguishing fluid to the various parts of a building, etc.: the system is usually made to operate automatically in the presence of great heat.

2. a system of pipes and nozzles used for watering a lawn, garden, greenhouse, golf course, etc.

sprin̄'kling, *n.* 1. the act of a person or thing that sprinkles.

2. a small quantity or number, especially one that is sprinkled, scattered, or thinly distributed; as, a forest with a *sprinkling* of dead trees.

3. in bookbinding, the process of mottling the edges of a book.

sprint, *v.i.*; sprinted, *pt., pp.*; sprinting, *ppr.* [ME. *sprenten*, from hyp. Anglo-N. *sprenta.*] to run, usually for a short distance, at full speed.

sprint, *v.t.* to traverse by sprinting.

sprint, *n.* 1. the act of sprinting.

2. a short race at full speed.

3. a brief period of intense activity.

sprint'ẽr, *n.* a fast runner for short distances; one who runs in a sprint.

sprint rāce, a short foot race.

sprit, *v.i.* to sprout; to germinate.

sprit, *n.* [AS. *sprēot*, a sprout or a pole.]

1. a shoot; a sprout.

2. a boom, pole, or spar extended diagonally upward from a mast to the topmost corner of a fore-and-aft sail, serving to extend the sail.

sprīte, *n.* [Fr. *esprit*; OFr. *espirit*; L. *spiritus*, spirit.]

1. a spirit; a shade; an apparition or ghost. [Archaic.]

2. an elf, pixie, fairy, or goblin.

3. the faculty of thought; the mind. [Obs.]

4. the breath; the life principle; the soul. [Obs.]

sprīte'li·ness, *n.* sprightliness. [Obs.]

sprīte'ly, *a.* sprightly. [Obs.]

sprit'sāil (*in nautical usage*, sprit'sl), *n.* 1. a sail extended by a sprit.

2. formerly, a sail attached to a yard under the bowsprit of large vessels: it was equipped with a large hole at each of the lower corners, to let out water that filled the cavity of the sail: also formerly called *spritsail topsail, spritsail topgallant-sail.*

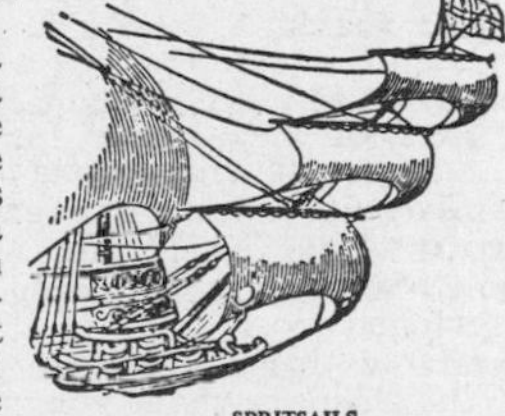

SPRITSAILS

sprit'sāil yärd, formerly, a yard placed across the bowsprit on which a spritsail was rigged.

sprit'tāil, *n.* the pintail duck, *Dafila acuta.* [Dial.]

spritz (sprits; *G.* shprits) *v.t.* and *v.i.*; spritzed, *pt., pp.*; spritzing, *ppr.* [via Pennsylvania Dutch and Yid.; G. *spritze*; M.H.G. *sprütze*, from *sprützen*, to spray.] to squirt or spray.

spritz, *n.* a squirt or spray.

spritz'er, *n.* [G., a splash; see *spritz.*] a drink of wine, usually white wine, and soda water.

sprock'et, *n.* [Early Mod. Eng.; prob. from a L.G. source.]

1. any of a number of toothlike projections, as on the rim of a wheel, to engage with the links of a chain.

2. a sprocket wheel.

sprock'et wheel (hwēl), a wheel with projecting teeth, or sprockets, on its outer rim, used in a chain drive.

SPROCKET WHEEL

sprod, *n.* a salmon in its second year. [Brit. Dial.]

sprọng, *v.* obsolete past tense of *spring.*

sprọng, *n.* a prong. [Brit. Dial.]

sprọng, *n.* the house sparrow, *Passer domesticus.* [Brit. Dial.]

sprout, *v.i.*; sprouted, *pt., pp.*; sprouting, *ppr.* [ME. *sprouten, spruten*, from AS. *sprutan*, to sprout.]

1. to begin to grow or germinate; to give off shoots.

2. to spread into ramifications. [Obs.]

3. to grow or develop rapidly, like shoots of plants; to spring up.

sprout, *v.t.* 1. to cause to sprout or grow; as, the warm rains *sprouted* the bushes.

2. to remove the sprouts from.

sprout, *n.* 1. a young growth on a plant, as a stem or branch; a shoot.

2. a new growth from a bud, rootstock, germinating seed, etc.

3. something like or suggestive of a sprout, as an offshoot or scion.

4. [*pl.*] Brussels sprouts.

sprout cell, in botany, a cell sprouting from another cell: a common method of reproduction.

sprout'ing, *n.* 1. same as *gemmation.*

2. in metallurgy, same as *spitting* (sense 2).

sprụ̂ce, *a.* [ME. *Spruce*, for *Pruce*, Prussia, *Pruce* leather being regarded as particularly fine and elegant.]

1. neat; smart in appearance; dapper.

2. too fastidious; finical. [Rare.]

Syn.—trim, smart, dapper, fastidious, immaculate.

sprụ̂ce, *v.t.*; spruced (sprụ̂st), *pt., pp.*; sprucing, *ppr.* to make spruce; to dress neatly: usually with *up.*

sprụ̂ce, *v.i.* to become spruce or neat: usually with *up.*

sprụ̂ce, *n.* a fine leather first made in Prussia: also called *Pruce, Prussian leather, spruce leather.* [Obs.]

sprụ̂ce, *n.* [from ME. *Spruce, Pruce*, Prussian, because the tree was first known as native to Prussia.]

1. any species of coniferous tree of the genus *Picea.* They are evergreens with needle-shaped leaves and drooping cones or berrylike fruit

2. the wood of any of these trees.

NORWAY SPRUCE
(*Picea excelsa*)

black spruce; a species of spruce, *Picea nigra*, native to the northern United States and Canada: the wood is used in shipbuilding, and from the branches is obtained essence of spruce which is used as an antiscorbutic.

blue spruce; *Picea pungens*, a variety of white spruce.

double spruce; same as *black spruce.*

Engelmann's spruce; a large tree, *Picea engelmanni*, found throughout the Rocky Mountain region, having coarsely grained wood.

Himalayan or *Indian spruce*; a tall tree, *Picea morinda*, found in the warmer parts of the Himalayas and yielding a light wood of straight grain.

Norway spruce; a tall, hardy tree, *Picea excelsa*, found in northern Europe and Asia, which yields a tough, white, elastic wood.

red spruce, a stunted variety of black spruce, *Picea rubra*, that grows in swamps in various parts of the United States: it has large, dark leaves and reddish cones.

silver spruce; *Picea pungens*, a variety of white spruce.

single spruce; *Picea alba*, a variety of white spruce.

tideland spruce or *Sitka spruce*; a tree, *Picea sitchensis*, found along the Pacific coast from Alaska to California: it grows to a height of 180 feet and is valued for its wood.

white spruce; (a) a tree, *Picea alba*, found in North America, having wood similar to that of the black spruce: also called *single spruce*; (b) a large tree, *Picea pungens*, found in the mountainous regions of the western United States: also called *blue spruce, silver spruce*; (c) same as *Engelmann's spruce.*

sprụ̂ce beer, a fermented liquor made with an extract of spruce leaves and twigs.

sprụ̂ce bud'wõrm, the larva of any of several tortricid moths which eat the end buds of spruce and other evergreen trees.

sprụ̂ce fīr, any spruce tree; especially, the Norway spruce.

sprụ̂ce grouse, the spotted or Canada grouse, *Dendragapus canadensis*, native to the spruce forests of northeastern North America.

sprụ̂ce gum, a hard, resinous substance exuded by various spruces, used as a chewing gum.

sprụ̂ce'ly, *adv.* in a spruce manner; with extreme neatness.

sprụ̂ce'ness, *n.* the state or quality of being spruce; neatness of appearance.

sprụ̂ce pär'tridġe (-trij), same as *spruce grouse.*

sprụ̂ce pīne, any of a number of pine trees, especially *Pinus glabra*, a medium-sized tree native to the swamps of the southern United States.

sprụ̂ce sa̤w'flȳ, a common sawfly, *Lophyrus abietis*, found in the United States on the spruce, fir, pine, and cedar.

sprụ̂'ci·fȳ, *v.t.* to make or be spruce or neat. [Obs.]

sprụ̂e, *n.* [D. *spruw, sprouw.*] a chronic tropical disease characterized by anemia, gastrointestinal disorders, sore throat, etc.; psilosis.

sprụ̂e, *n.* in casting metal, (a) the ingate, or hole, through which melted metal is poured into the mold; (b) the waste piece of metal cast in the ingate; hence, dross; scoria; (c) a piece of metal or wood used by a molder in making the ingate through the sand.

sprụ̂'it, *n.* [S. Afr. D.] a small stream or creek that is often dry.

sprung, *v.* past participle and alternative past tense of *spring.*

sprung, *a.* tipsy; slightly intoxicated. [Colloq.]

sprung rhythm (rithm), in prosody, a kind of rhythm characterized by different types of feet of equal time length, stressed always on the first syllable: the feet may differ in number of syllables.

sprunt, *v.i.* 1. to spring up; to start. [Brit. Dial.]

2. to spring forward. [Brit. Dial.]

sprunt, *n.* 1. anything short and not easily bent. [Obs.]

2. a leap; a spring. [Obs.]

3. a steep ascent in a road. [Brit. Dial.]

sprunt, *a.* active; vigorous; strong. [Obs.]

sprunt'ly, *adv.* 1. vigorously; youthfully; like a young man. [Obs.]

2. smartly; gaily; neatly. [Obs.]

sprȳ, *a.*; *comp.* sprier *or* spryer; *superl.* spriest *or* spryest, [from Brit. Dial. *sprey, spree, spry*, etc.; of O.N. origin.] full of life; nimble; active; vigorous.

spud, *n.* [ME. *spudde*; prob. from ON.]

1. a dagger. [Obs.]

2. a small spade, somewhat like a chisel with a long handle, used in cutting the roots of weeds without stooping.

3. a spudder.

4. a spade-shaped tool used in recovering tools from a bored well.

5. a short, dwarfish person. [Brit. Dial.]

6. a potato. [Colloq.]

7. a baby's hand. [Dial.]

8. [*pl.*] money. [Slang.]

spud, *v.t.*; spudded, *pt., pp.*; spudding, *ppr.* 1. to dig up, remove, or handle with a spud.

2. to begin sinking (an oil well) with a windlass called a bull wheel.

spud'dẽr, *n.* [from *spud* and *-er.*] a heavy bar with a chisel point, used for removing bark from trees.

spud'dy, *a.* short and stout; fat. [Dial.]

spūe, *v.t.* and *v.i.*; spued, *pt., pp.*; spuing, *ppr.* same as *spew.*

spụ̂il'zie, spụ̂l'zie (*or* -yi), *n.* [Fr. *spolier*, from L. *spoliare*, to strip, to plunder.]

1. spoil; booty. [Scot.]

2. the unlawful taking away of a person's movable goods. [Scot.]

spūke, *n.* same as *spook.*

spul'lẽr, *n.* same as *spooler.*

spụ̂l'zie (*or* -yi), *n.* spuilzie. [Scot.]

spūme, *n.* [L. *spuma*, from *spuere*, to spit out.] froth; foam; scum.

spūme, *v.i.* and *v.t.* spumed, *pt., pp.*; spuming, *ppr.* to froth; to foam.

spū'mē·ous, *a.* consisting of froth or scum; foamy; spumous. [Obs.]

spū·mes'cence, *n.* frothiness; the state of being foamy.

spū·mes'cent, *a.* 1. resembling froth or foam.

2. frothing or foaming.

spū·mif'ẽr·ous, *a.* producing foam or froth.

spūm'i·ness, *n.* the quality or condition of being spumy.

spu·mō'nē (*or It.* spụ̂-mō'ne), *n.* spumoni.

spu·mō'ni, *n.* [It., pl. of *spumone.*] an Italian frozen dessert made of various layers of smooth ice cream, often containing candied fruits and pistachio nuts.

spūm'ous, *a.* of, consisting of, or covered with froth or foam; foamy; frothy.

spūm'y, *a.*; *comp.* spumier; *superl.* spumiest, frothy; spumous; covered with foam.

spun, *v.* past tense and past participle of *spin.*

spun, *a.* formed by or as if by spinning.

spun glass; fine glass fiber, made by forming liquid glass into a thread.

spun gold; silk thread wound with flattened gold or silver gilt wire.

spun silk; see under *silk.*

spun silver; silk thread wound with flattened silver wire.

spun sugar; melted sugar, usually with coloring added, that is drawn out into threadlike form and gathered into fluffy balls to be eaten as a confection.

spun yarn; in nautical usage, a line made of several rope yarns twisted together.

spuñk, *n.* [Ir. *sponc*, tinder, touchwood, sponge; Gael. *sponc*, from L. *spongia*, a sponge.]

1. touchwood; tinder; a kind of wood or fungus that takes fire easily; amadou; punk.

2. mettle; spirit; courage; pluck. [Colloq.]

3. a very small fire; a fiery spark or small flame. [Brit. Dial.]

spuñk, *v.i.* to flare up; to kindle.

spuñk'ie, *n.* [Scot.] 1. a small fire; a spark.

2. the will-o'-the-wisp; ignis fatuus.

3. a person of a fiery or irritable temper. [Rare.]

4. liquor.

spuñk'i·ly, *adv.* in a spunky manner. [Colloq.]

spuñk'i·ness, *n.* the quality or state of being spunky. [Colloq.]

spuñk'y, *a.*; *comp.* spunkier; *superl.* spunkiest, spirited; having spunk; plucky. [Colloq.]

spun'ny, *n.* in mining, an automatic or self-acting, short incline. [Brit. Dial.]

spun'-out, *a.* protracted; lengthened.

spŭr, *n.* [AS. *spura*, *spora*, a spur.]

1. any of several kinds of pointed devices worn by a horseman on the heel of a riding boot, having a rowel or wheel of points to prick a horse's side, used to urge the animal forward.

HORSEMAN'S SPUR

2. anything that serves to goad, spur, or impel to action; a goad; an incitement; an incentive; a stimulus.

His ferocious temper needed no *spur*; yet a *spur* was applied. —Macaulay.

3. something that projects; a snag.

4. a spinelike process on a bird's wing or leg, especially that on the leg of a cock, which serves for defense and attack.

5. a climbing iron, as used by lumberjacks.

6. a sharp metal device attached to the leg of a gamecock, for injuring the other bird in a cockfight.

7. a short, stunted, or projecting branch or shoot of a tree, etc.

8. a ridge, range, or lesser elevation projecting in a lateral direction from the main mass of a mountain or mountain range.

9. in architecture, (a) a griffe; (b) a buttress.

10. in botany, a slender, tubelike structure formed by an extension of one or more petals or sepals, as in columbine or larkspur.

11. ergot of rye.

12. in carpentry, a strut or brace strengthening a rafter or stiffening a post.

13. in fortification, (a) a tower or blockhouse in the outworks before the port; (b) a wall across part of a rampart and connected to the interior work. [Obs.]

14. a projection built out from the bank of a river to deflect the current and protect the bank.

15. in nautical usage, (a) a sole with spikes, to enable a seaman to stand on a whale while flensing it; (b) a prong on the arm of some forms of anchor, to assist in turning the lower arm from the shank.

16. in shipbuilding, (a) a shore extending from the bilgeways, and bolted to the ship's side; (b) a curved piece of timber, serving as a half beam to support the deck where a whole beam cannot be placed.

17. in mining, a branch of a vein.

18. a spur track.

19. a projection on the edge of an auger.

on the spur of the moment; hastily and abruptly; without forethought or preparation.

to win one's spurs; to attain distinction or honor, especially for the first time; to establish one's reputation.

spŭr, *v.t.*; spurred, *pt.*, *pp.*; spurring, *ppr.* 1. to prick or strike with a spur or spurs; as, to *spur* a horse.

2. to incite; to instigate; to urge or encourage to action, or to a more vigorous pursuit of an object; to impel; to drive.

Love will not be *spurred* to what it loathes. —Shak.

3. to put a spur or spurs on; as, to *spur* a horseman's boot.

4. to strike or injure with or as with a spur (sense 6).

spŭr, *v.i.* 1. to spur a horse.

2. to hurry; to hasten.

spŭr bun'ting, same as *lark bunting*.

spŭr fowl, an Asiatic bird of the genus *Galloperdix*.

spŭr'gall, *v.t.* to gall or wound with a spur.

spŭr'gall, *n.* a gall or wound caused by much use of the spur.

spŭrġe, *v.i.* [OFr. *espurger*, to purge.] to froth, as ale while fermenting. [Obs.]

spŭrġe, *n.* [OFr. *espurger*, to purge, from L. *expurgare*, to cleanse thoroughly.] any plant of the genus *Euphorbia*, having a milky juice and shrubby, herblike growth.

Allegheny-mountain spurge; a low herb, *Pachysandra procumbens*, related to the true spurge.

spŭr ġēar, 1. a gear wheel having radial teeth parallel to the axle.

2. a system of gearing having this kind of gear wheel: also *spur gearing*.

SPUR GEAR

spŭr ġēar'ing, same as *spur gear*.

spŭrġe flax, an evergreen shrub, *Daphne gnidium*, native to southern Europe.

spŭrġe lau'rel, an evergreen shrub, *Daphne laureola*, with yellowish-green flowers, oblong leaves, and poisonous berries, found in Europe and Asia.

spŭrġe net'tle, an American shrub, *Jatropha urens*, with stinging spines.

spŭrġe ol'ive, the mezereon.

spŭrġe'wŏrt, *n.* any plant of the order *Euphorbiaceæ*.

spŭr'-heeled, *a.* having a long, straight hind claw, as a lark.

spū'ri·ous, *a.* [L. *spurius*, bastard.]

1. illegitimate; bastard.

2. false; counterfeit; not genuine.

3. in botany, false; like in appearance but unlike in structure or function.

spurious primary or *quill*; the outer primary quill when rudimentary or very short, as in certain singing birds.

Syn.—counterfeit, fictitious, apocryphal, false, adulterate, bastard.

spū'ri·ous·ly, *adv.* in a spurious manner; so as to be spurious; falsely.

spū'ri·ous·ness, *n.* the state or quality of being spurious.

spŭr'less, *a.* without a spur or spurs (in any sense).

spŭr'ling, *n.* a sparling. [Obs.]

spŭr'ling līne, in nautical usage, the line that forms the communication between the wheel and the telltale.

spŭrn, *v.t.*; spurned, *pt.*, *pp.*; spurning, ppr. [AS. *spurnan*, to spurn, to kick.]

1. to drive back or away contemptuously with or as with the foot; to kick against.

2. to push or strike against. [Obs.]

3. to reject with disdain; to scorn to receive or associate with; to treat with contempt.

spŭrn, *v.i.* 1. to kick. [Obs.]

2. to stumble; to rush. [Obs.]

3. to manifest a disdainful contempt in rejecting or refusing anything; to make contemptuous opposition.

spŭrn, *n.* 1. a blow with the foot; a kick.

2. disdainful rejection; contemptuous refusal or treatment.

3. a stumble. [Obs.]

4. in mining, a narrow mass of coal left as a temporary support in a vein.

spŭrn'ēr, *n.* one who or that which spurns.

spŭrn'wa"tēr, *n.* in nautical usage, a V-shaped breakwater on a ship's deck, forward of the foremast, to check and turn aside water that washes over the bows.

spŭrred, *a.* 1. wearing spurs; having or fitted with spurs; as, a *spurred* horseman.

2. having prolongations or spurlike parts; calcarate.

spurred corolla; a corolla having a hollow, hornlike prolongation at its base.

spurred rye; ergot of rye.

spŭr'rēr, *n.* one who or that which spurs.

spŭr'rey, *n.* same as *spurry*.

spŭr'ri·ēr, *n.* one who makes spurs.

spŭr roy'ăl, a gold coin issued by James I of England, worth about fifteen shillings: so named from the design on its reverse side resembling the rowel of a spur. Also *spur ryal*.

spŭr'ry, *n.* 1. a plant of the genus *Spergula*, of the chickweed family, *Caryophyllaceæ*.

2. *Spergula arvensis*, a weed with white flowers and threadlike leaves.

Also spelled *spurrey*.

spŭr shell, a trochoid shell having spinelike projections on the margin, resembling the rowel of a spur.

spŭrt, *v.t.*; spurted, *pt.*, *pp.*; spurting, *ppr.*; [prob. from ME. *sprutten*, *spritten*, to sprout or spring out, from AS. *spryttan*.] to shoot forth suddenly or eject in a stream or jet, as water; to force out with violence, as from a narrow opening; to squirt: also spelled *spirt*.

spŭrt, spĭrt, *v.i.* 1. to sprout. [Obs.]

2. to gush out suddenly and forcibly, in a stream or jet.

3. to show a sudden, brief burst of energy or spell of activity; as, the runners *spurted* in the last lap.

spŭrt, spĭrt, *n.* 1. a sudden gushing or shooting forth; a jet.

2. a shoot; a sprout. [Obs.]

3. a sudden, brief burst of energy or spell of activity.

A sudden *spurt* of woman's jealousy. —Tennyson.

spŭr'tle, *v.t.* and *v.i.* to flow in jets; to spurt.

spŭr'tle, *n.* a stream, jet, or spurt.

spŭr'tle, *n.* a stick for stirring porridge. [Brit. Dial. and Scot.]

spŭr'tle·blāde, *n.* a broadsword. [Scot.]

spŭr track, a short side track that connects with the main track of a railroad: also *spur*.

spŭr vȧ·lē'ri·ăn, a plant of the genus *Sentranthus*, of the valerian family (*Valerianaceæ*), having a spurred corolla tube.

spŭr'wāy, *n.* a narrow road; a bridle path.

spŭr wheel (hwēl), same as *spur gear*.

spŭr'wing, *n.* a spur-winged bird, as the spur-winged goose.

spŭr'-winged, *a.* in zoology, having spurs on the shoulder of the wing.

spur-winged goose; a long-legged bird, *Plectropterus gambensis*, resembling the goose. It is native to Africa, and has two strong spurs on the shoulder of the wing.

spur-winged plover; a plover, *Hoplopterus spinosus*, having spurs on the shoulder of the wing, found in the lands bordering on the Mediterranean and the Red Sea.

spŭr'wŏrt, *n.* a plant, *Sherardia arvensis*, the field madder: so called from its leaves bearing a resemblance to the rowel of a spur.

sput, *n.* a thimble or the like used to reinforce a hole in a boiler.

spū'tȧ, *n.* plural of *sputum*.

spū·tā'tion, *n.* the act of expectorating; that which is spit up or out. [Obs.]

spū'tȧ·tive, *a.* inclined to spit; relating to spitting.

spūte, *v.i.* [from *dispute*.] to discuss; to wrangle. [Obs.]

sput'nik, *n.* [Russ.; lit., co-traveler.] an artificial satellite of the earth, especially [often S-] any of those put into orbit by the U.S.S.R. beginning in 1957.

sput'tēr, *v.i.*; sputtered, *pt. pp.*; sputtering, *ppr.* [from *spout* and *-er*, freq. suffix.]

1. to spit or to emit saliva, food, etc. from the mouth in small or scattered portions, as in rapid or excited speech; to splutter.

2. to speak hastily in a confused, explosive manner.

3. to throw off in small particles with sharp sizzling sounds, as burning wood, frying fat, etc.

When sparkling lamps their *sputtering* lights advance. —Dryden.

sput'tēr, *v.t.* 1. to spit or throw out (bits or drops) in an explosive manner.

2. to utter by sputtering.

sput'tēr, *n.* 1. a sputtering.

2. the noise of sputtering.

3. bits or drops thrown out in sputtering.

4. hasty, confused, explosive utterance.

sput'tēr·ēr, *n.* one who or that which sputters.

spū'tum, *n.*; *pl.* **spū'tȧ,** [L., that which is spit out, from *sputus*, pp. of *spuere*, to spit.]

1. spit; saliva.

2. mucus together with saliva, etc., spat out from the mouth.

spȳ, *v.t.*; spied, *pt.*, *pp.*; spying, *ppr.* [OFr. *espier*, to spy or espy, from O.H.G. *spehon*, *spiohon*, to search out, examine, investigate.]

1. to watch or observe closely and secretly, with unfriendly purpose (usually with *out*).
2. to catch sight of; to make out; to perceive; to see.
3. to examine closely; to inspect carefully; to scrutinize.
4. to discover by close examination, careful inspection, etc. (with *out*).

spȳ, *v.i.* 1. to watch or observe closely and secretly; to act as a spy.
2. to keep watch.
3. to make a close examination or careful inspection.

spȳ, *n.*; *pl.* **spīes**, 1. a person who keeps close and secret watch on another or others.
2. a person employed by a government to get secret information about the affairs of another or other governments, especially about the armed forces, armaments, war plans, etc., or one who, in time of war, acts as a secret agent to get information for the enemy.
3. a spying.
Spy Wednesday; the Wednesday preceding Easter, from the preparations Judas Iscariot made on that day to betray Christ.

spy'bōat, *n.* a boat sent to make discoveries and bring intelligence.

spy'glȧss, *n.* a small telescope.

spy'ism, *n.* the act or business of spying or of employing spies. [Rare.]

squäb, *n.* [prob. from O.N.; cf. Sw. *squabb*, loose flesh.]
1. a nestling pigeon, still unfledged.
2. a short, stout person.
3. a cushion.
4. a sofa or couch.

squäb, *a.* 1. fat; short and stout; plump; as, a *squab* person.
2. unfledged; unfeathered; as, a *squab* pigeon.

squäb, *adv.* so as to strike heavily; with a heavy fall; plump. [Colloq. and Dial.]

squäb, *v.i.* to fall plump; to strike at one dash or with a heavy stroke. [Obs.]

squȧ·bash', *v.t.* to crush, quash, or squash. [Colloq. Scot.]

squäb'bish, *a.* thick; fat; heavy.

squäb'ble, *v.i.*; squabbled, *pt.*, *pp.*; squabbling, *ppr.* [from Sw. *skvabbel*, a squabble.] to engage in a low, noisy quarrel or row; to quarrel and fight noisily over a small matter; to brawl; to scuffle; to wrangle.

squäb'ble, *v.t.* in printing, to put awry; to disarrange or knock off the straight line, as types that have been set up.

squäb'ble, *n.* a scuffle; a wrangle; a brawl; a noisy, petty quarrel.

squäb'blẽr, *n.* one who squabbles; a contentious person; a brawler; a noisy disputant.

squäb'by, *a.*; *comp.* squabbier; *superl.* squabbiest, squabbish; squat.

squäb pīe, a pie made of squabs or young pigeons; also, a pie made of meat, apples, and onions.

squaç'cō, *n.* a species of heron, *Ardea comata.*

squäd, *n.* [Fr. *escouade*; Sp. *escuadra*, a square.]
1. a small group of soldiers assembled for inspection, duty, etc.; the smallest military tactical unit, a subdivision of a platoon, normally led by a sergeant (formerly staff sergeant).
2. any small group of people acting together: an athletic team is often called a *squad.*

squäd, *v.t.*; squadded, *pt.*, *pp.*; squadding, *ppr.* 1. to form into a squad or squads.
2. to assign to a squad.

squäd çär, a police patrol car, now usually equipped with short-wave radio telephone facilities for communicating with headquarters.

squäd'rŏn, *n.* [Fr. *escadron*; It. *squadra*, a squadron, a square, from L. *quadra*, a square.]
1. a square or square form, and hence, a square body of troops; a body of men drawn up in a square. [Obs.]
2. a group of warships assigned to some special duty; a unit or subdivision of a fleet.
3. a unit of cavalry consisting of from two to four troops, a headquarters troop, and certain auxiliary units.
4. a unit of military aviation consisting of two or more flights.
5. any organized body or group.

squäd'rŏn, *v.t.* to form into a squadron or squadrons.

squāil, *n.* [variant of *scale*, a flat disk.]
1. one of the rings or disks with which the game of squails is played. [Archaic.]
2. [*pl.*] a game in which small rings or disks are snapped from the edge of a board at a mark in the center; also, ninepins. [Rare.]

squāil, *v.i.* to throw a missile at a mark. [Obs.]

Squā'lī, *n.pl.* [L. *squalus*, a shark.] a division of fishes; the true sharks.

squäl'id, *a.* [L. *squalidus*, stiff with dirt, filthy, squalid, from *squalere*, to be foul or filthy.]
1. foul; filthy; extremely dirty; as, a *squalid* beggar; a *squalid* house.
2. wretched; miserable; sordid.

Squal'i·dae, *n.pl.* [L. *squalus*, a fish of the shark or dogfish family, and *-idæ*.] a family of elasmobranch fishes, which includes the various species of sharks. The type of this family is the Linnaean genus *Squalus.*

squȧ·lid'i·ty, *n.* the quality or state of being squalid; foulness; filthiness.

squäl'id·ly, *adv.* in a squalid, filthy manner.

squäl'id·ness, *n.* the quality or condition of being squalid; squalidity.

squā'li·fọrm, *a.* resembling a shark.

squạll, *v.t* and *v.i.*; squalled, *pt.*, *pp.*; squalling, *ppr.* [prob. of echoic origin.] to cry out; to scream or cry violently or harshly; as, the infant *squalled.*

squạll, *n.* a loud scream; a harsh cry.

squạll, *n.* [prob. of Scand. origin.]
1. a brief, violent windstorm, usually with rain or snow.
2. trouble or disturbance. [Colloq.]
arched squall; a tropical squall of a violent nature in which masses of black clouds form a vast arch.
line squall; a squall which sweeps across the country broadside on, following the trough of a barometric depression.

squạll, *v.i.* to storm briefly; to blow a squall.

squạll çloud, a silvery cloud underneath the black mass of a storm.

squạll'ẽr, *n.* one who or that which squalls or cries aloud.

squạll'y, *a.*; *comp.* squallier; *superl.* squalliest, 1. abounding with squalls; disturbed often with sudden and violent gusts of wind; as, *squally* weather.
2. having an ominous outlook; threatening; stormy.

squạll'y, *a.* 1. having unproductive spots interspersed throughout: said of a field of turnips or corn. [Dial.]
2. in weaving, faulty or uneven, as cloth. [Dial.]

Squā'lō·don, *n.* [L. *squalus*, a shark, and Gr. *odous, odontis*, tooth.]
1. a genus of extinct cetaceans or fossil whales peculiar for having serrated teeth.
2. [s-] any individual of this genus.

squā'lō·dont, *a.* belonging to the genus *Squalodon.*

squā'loid, *a.* [L. *squalus*, a shark, and Gr. *eidos*, likeness.] resembling a shark of the genus *Squalus.*

squäl'ŏr (*or occas.* skwā'lọr), *n.* [L.] the quality or condition of being squalid; foulness; filthiness; coarseness.

squäm, *n.* [from *Annisquam*, Mass.] a waterproof hat, made of oilskin, worn by fishermen and sailors. [Dial.]

squā'mȧ, *n.*; *pl.* **squā'mae**, [L., a scale.]
1. in botany, one of the bracts of an ament or catkin; one of those parts which are arranged upon a plant in the same manner as the scales of fishes and other animals, as the undeveloped external leaves of the buds of most plants.
2. in anatomy, an opaque and thickened lamina of the cuticle; a horny scale.
3. a feather resembling a scale, as those on the wing of a penguin.
4. the false wing of an insect.

squȧ·mā'ceous, *a.* same as *squamous.*

Squȧ·mā'tȧ, *n.pl.* 1. an order of reptiles comprising the *Ophidia* and *Lacertilia*, in which the integument develops horny scales, but in which there are no dermal ossifications.
2. a suborder of insectivorous edentates, the pangolins. The body is covered with horny, overlapping scales.

squā'māte, squā'mā·ted, *a.* scaly; having or covered with small scalelike bodies.

squȧ·mā'tion, *n.* 1. the condition of being squamate.
2. epidermal scale arrangement.

squäm duck, the eider duck. [Dial.]

squāme, *n.* [L. *squama*, a scale.]
1. a squama.
2. a scale. [Obs.]

squȧ·mel'lȧ, *n.*; *pl.* **squȧ·mel'lae**, [LL., dim of L. *squama*, a scale.] a squamula.

squȧ·mel'lāte, *a.* scaly; squamulate.

squam·el·lif'ẽr·ous, *a.* having or bearing squamellae.

squȧ·mel'li·fọrm, *a.* squamiform.

squā'mi-, [from L. *squama*, a scale.] a combining form meaning *a scale* or *scales.*

squȧ·mif'ẽr·ous, *a.* squamate.

squā'mi·fọrm, *a.* having the form or shape of scales.

squȧ·miġ'ẽr·ous, *a.* [*squami-*, and L. *gerere*, to bear.] bearing or having scales.

squā'mi·pen, *n.* [*squami-*, and L. *penna*, a wing.] one of the *Squamipinnes.*

squā·mi·pen'nāte, *a.* 1. having scaly feathers.
2. belonging to or resembling the *Squamipinnes.*

Squā·mi·pen'nēs, *n.pl.* 1. the *Squamipinnes.*
2. the penguins.

squā·mi·pin'nāte, *a.* relating to the *Squamipinnes.*

Squā·mi·pin'nēs, *n.pl.* a suborder of acanthopterygian fishes, so named on account of their fins being covered with scales, not only on the parts which have soft rays, but frequently also on those that have spinous ones.

squā'mō-, [from L. *squama*, a scale.] a combining form meaning *squama.*

squā·mō·cel'lū·lăr, *a.* [L. *squama*, a scale, and *cellula*, a cell.] having squamous cells.

squā'moid, *a.* [*squamo-*, and Gr. *eidos*, form.] resembling a scale or scales; also, covered with scales or scalelike integuments; scaly.

squā·mō·mas'toid, *a.* pertaining to the squamous and mastoid portions of the temporal bone.

squā″mō·pȧ·rī'e·tăl, *a.* pertaining to the squamous and parietal bones.

squȧ·mō'sȧ, *n.* [L.] the squamous bone or squamous portion of the temporal bone.

squȧ·mō'săl, *a.* 1. squamous.
2. in zoology, designating or of a bone in the skull of lower vertebrates analogous to the squamous portion of the temporal bone in man.

squȧ·mō'săl, *n.* a squamosal bone.

squā'mōse, *a.* same as *squamous.*

squā·mō·sphē'noid, *a.* pertaining to the squamosa and to the sphenoid bone.

squā'mous, *a.* [L. *squamosus*, covered with scales.]
1. formed of, like, or covered with scales.
2. in anatomy, designating or of the thin, scalelike, upper anterior portion of the temporal bone.

squā·mō·zyg·ō·mat'iç, *a.* pertaining to the squamous and zygomatic portions of the temporal bone.

squam'ū·lȧ, *n.*; *pl.* **squam'ū·lae**, [L., a little scale.]
1. a small scale found on the stamens of grass flowers; a lodicule.
2. in entomology; a tegula; also, any small organ or attachment resembling a scale.

squam'ū·lāte, *a.* same as *squamulose.*

squam'ūle, *n.* same as *squamula.*

squam'ū·li·fọrm, *a.* of the nature of or resembling a squamule.

squam'ū·lōse, *a.* having, covered with, or consisting of small scales.

squän'dẽr, *v.t.*; squandered, *pt.*, *pp.*; squandering, *ppr.* [prob. from dial. *squander*, to scatter.]
1. to spend lavishly or profusely; to spend or use prodigally; to dissipate; to waste without economy or judgment; as, to *squander* an estate.
2. to scatter; to disperse; as, to *squander* troops. [Obs.]
Syn.—waste, lavish, expend, dissipate, scatter.

squän'dẽr, *v.i.* 1. to be wasteful or extravagant; to spend heedlessly.
2. to roam about; to scatter. [Obs.]

squän'dẽr, *n.* the act of spending lavishly; prodigality.

squän'dẽr·ẽr, *n.* one who squanders; a spendthrift; a prodigal; a waster.

squän'dẽr·ing·ly, *adv.* by squandering; prodigally.

squän'tum, *n.* [from *Squantum*, Mass.] a picnic. [Dial.]

squāre, *a.*; *comp.* squarer; *superl.* squarest, [OFr. *esquarre*, a square; It. *squadra*, from L. *ex* and *quadra*, a square, from *quadrus*, square, *quattuor*, four.]

1. (a) having four equal sides and four right angles; (b) more or less cubical; rectangular and three-dimensional, as a box.

2. forming a right angle, or having a rectangular part or parts.

3. correctly adjusted or positioned; straight, level, even, etc.

4. leaving no balance; balanced; even.

5. just; fair; honest; not crooked.

6. clear; direct; straightforward; unequivocal; as, a *square* refusal.

7. (a) designating or of a unit of surface measure in the form of a square having sides of a specified length; (b) given or stated in terms of such surface measure.

8. having a shape broad for its length or height, with a solid, sturdy appearance, and somewhat rectangular.

9. having a square or rectangular section, as some files.

10. designating a number that is the product of another number multiplied by itself.

11. satisfying; solid; substantial; as, a *square* meal. [Colloq.]

12. not conversant with the current fads, styles, slang, etc.; old-fashioned or unsophisticated. [Slang.]

13. in nautical usage, at right angles to the keel and mast, as the yards of a square-rigged ship.

all square; all arranged; all right.

fair and square; see under first *fair*.

square peg in a round hole; a person poorly suited to his job, environment, etc.; a misfit.

to get square with; to be or get even with. [Colloq.]

squãre, *n.* [ME.; OFr. *esquarre*; ult. from L. *ex*, out, and *quadrare*, to square, from *quadrus*, a square.]

1. a four-sided plane rectilineal figure, having all its sides equal, and all its angles right angles; a rectangular figure formed from any given line as the side.

2. anything which nearly approaches this shape; a square piece or square surface.

3. a square block of houses on the streets of a town; the area occupied or intended to be occupied by such a block, bounded by streets on four sides; also, the distance along a street from one intersection to another; as, two *squares* north of our house.

4. (a) an open area bounded by, or at the intersection of, several streets; (b) buildings surrounding such an area.

5. a square body of troops; a squadron.

6. a pane of glass.

7. an implement used by artificers, draftsmen, etc., for laying off or testing right angles. It consists essentially of two rules at right angles to each other, one of which is sometimes pivoted, so that other angles than a right angle may be measured.

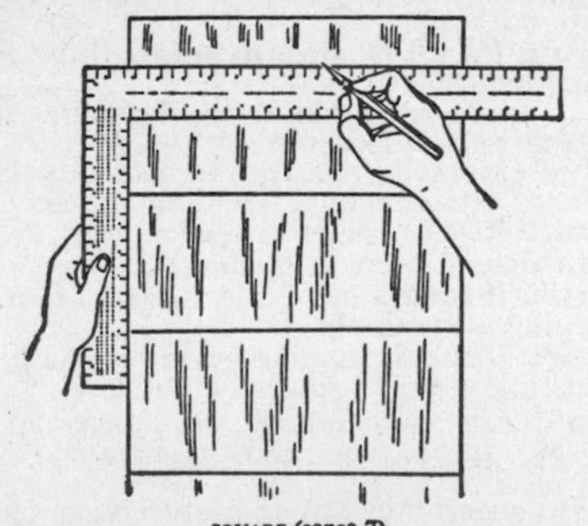

SQUARE (sense 7)

8. a measure, standard, pattern, or model.

9. rule; regularity; exact proportion; justness of workmanship and conduct. [Obs.]

I have not kept my *square*. —Shak.

10. a quarrel. [Rare.]

11. the front part of a woman's dress near the bosom, generally worked or embroidered.

12. the product of a number or quantity multiplied by itself; as, 9 is the *square* of 3.

13. in astrology, quartile; the position of planets 90 degrees distant from each other. [Obs.]

14. in bookbinding, the projection of a cover beyond the leaves.

15. in carpentry, one hundred square feet: a unit of measurement used in boarding and roofing.

16. in horology, that portion of the arbor on which the winding key is placed, or a similar part on the arbor of the hands of a watch, whereby they are set.

17. in nautical usage, that part of the shank of an anchor to which the stock and shackle are attached.

18. a person who is square (*a.* 12). [Slang.]

on the square; (a) at right angles (to something specified); (b) [Colloq.] honest; fair; genuine; (c) [Colloq.] honestly, fairly, genuinely; as, he deals *on the square*.

out of square; (a) not at right angles (with something specified); (b) [Colloq.] not in harmony, order, or agreement; (c) [Colloq.] incorrectly.

to be all square; to be entirely settled. [Colloq.]

squãre, *v.t.*; squared, *pt.*, *pp.*; squaring, *ppr.* [ME. *squaren*; OFr. *esquarrer*: see the n.]

1. to make into a form having four equal sides and four right angles; to make square.

2. to make into a form having straight sides and right angles.

3. to make or check with regard to straightness or evenness; as, he *squared* the surface with a straightedge.

4. to bring to or near to the form of a right angle or straight line; as, *square* your shoulders.

5. to settle; to adjust; to make right or even; as, we have *squared* accounts.

6. to adjust or settle the accounts of; as, this money will *square* him.

7. to make equal; as, his touchdown *squared* the score.

8. to adapt; to regulate; to reconcile; to make conform; as, *square* these figures with the latest information.

9. to mark off (a surface) in a series of connected squares.

10. to bring into the correct position, as with reference to a line, course, etc.

11. to multiply (a number or quantity) by itself.

12. to find the number of square units in (an area).

13. to bribe. [Slang.]

to square oneself; to compensate for a wrong, damage, hurt, etc. done by oneself to another or others; to make amends. [Colloq.]

to square the circle; (a) to construct or find a square equal in area to a circle: an insoluble problem; (b) to do or attempt something that seems impossible.

squãre, *v.i.* 1. to suit; to fit; to accord or agree; as, his opinions do not *square* with the doctrines of philosophers.

2. to be or fit at right angles.

3. to quarrel; to go to opposite sides; to take an attitude of offense or defense, or of defiance. [Obs.]

4. in golf, to even the scores.

to square away; (a) to bring a ship's yards around so as to sail directly before the wind; (b) to square off.

to square off; to assume a posture of attack or self-defense, as in boxing.

to square up; (a) to make a settlement, as by paying, balancing accounts, etc.; (b) to assume a posture of opposition (*to* an adversary).

squãre, *adv.* 1. honestly; fairly; justly.

2. so as to be or form a square; in square shape; at right angles.

3. directly; exactly.

4. so as to face.

5. firmly; solidly.

squãre brack′et, in printing, a bracket; either of the paired parenthetical marks [].

squãre dȧnce, a dance, as a quadrille, in which the couples are grouped in a given form, as a square.

squãred cĩr′çle, the boxing ring; the prize ring: also *squared ring*. [Colloq.]

squãre dēal, any treatment or dealing that is honest, fair, and just. [Colloq.]

squãre′-fāced (-fāst), *a.* having a face that is somewhat rectangular in outline.

squãre′flip″pẽr, *n.* the bearded seal, *Erignathus barbatus*.

squãre′-frāmed, *a.* in joinery, framed squarely without molding or beveling, as a door.

squãre′head (-hed), *n.* 1. a Scandinavian. [Slang.]

2. a German. [Slang.]

A vulgar term of contempt.

squãre knot (not), a double knot in which the free ends run parallel to the standing parts; reef knot: see *knot*, illus.

squãre′ly, *adv.* in a square manner; so as to square or be square in any sense of the word.

squãre mēal, a complete and satisfying meal.

squãre meaṣ′ūre (mezh′), a system of measuring area, in which 144 square inches = 1 square foot, 9 square feet = 1 square yard, 30¼ square yards = 1 square rod, 160 square rods = 1 acre, 640 acres = 1 square mile.

squãre′ness, *n.* the quality or the condition of being square; uprightness.

squãr′ẽr, *n.* 1. one who or that which squares.

2. a quarrelsome person. [Obs.]

squãre′-rigged, *a.* rigged with square sails extended by yards suspended by the middle, and not by stays, gaffs, booms, and lateen yards; as, a brig is a *square-rigged* vessel.

squãre′-rig′gẽr, *n.* a square-rigged ship.

squãre rọọt, the number or quantity which when squared will produce a given number or quantity; as, 3 is the *square root* of 9.

squãre sāil, a four-sided sail extended to a yard suspended by the middle.

squãre shọọt′ẽr, a person who is honest and just. [Colloq.]

squãre′-shōul″dẽred, *a.* having an erect posture with the shoulders held level and back: opposed to *round-shouldered*.

squãre′-tōed′, *a.* 1. having the toe or toes broad and square: said of a shoe.

2. prim; narrowly conservative or formal.

squãre′-tōeṣ, *n.* a formal, conventional, old-fashioned person.

squãr′ish, *a.* approaching squareness; somewhat square.

squar′rōse, *a.* [L. *squarrosus*.]

1. in botany and zoology, rough or scaly.

2. in botany, stiff and crowded together, as some leaves.

squar′rous, *a.* squarrose.

squar′rụ·lōse, *a.* in botany, somewhat squarrose; minutely squarrose.

squäsh, *n.* [Am. Ind. *asquash*.]

1. a vine of the gourd family, of the genus *Cucurbita*, resembling the pumpkin in its edible, fleshy fruit: in cultivation there are three species, varying greatly both in shape and in size; *Cucurbita pepo* includes the pumpkin and many of the ordinary squashes.

2. the edible fruit.

squäsh, *n.* a musquash. [Obs.]

squäsh, *v.t.*; squashed, *pt.*, *pp.*; squashing, *ppr.* [OFr. *esquasser*; LL. *exquassare*, from L. *ex-* intens., and *quassus*, pp. of *quatere*, to shake.]

1. to beat, press, or squeeze into or as into a soft, flat mass or pulp; to crush.

2. to quash; to suppress; to bring to an abrupt end; as, he tried to *squash* his son's ambition.

3. to silence or disconcert (another) in a crushing manner. [Colloq.]

squäsh, *v.i.* 1. to be squashed, as by a heavy fall, pressure, etc.

2. to make a sound of squashing or splashing.

3. to force one's way; to crowd; to squeeze.

squäsh, *n.* 1. something easily squashed or crushed.

2. a soft, pulpy mass.

3. a squashing or the fact of being squashed.

4. the sound of squashing.

5. a drink made of fruit juice and other ingredients; as, lemon *squash*. [Brit.]

6. either of two similar games combining elements of both tennis and handball; specifically, (a) *squash rackets*, played in a walled court with a small racket and a rubber ball; (*b*) *squash tennis*, played in a larger court with a larger racket and a livelier ball.

squäsh, *adv.* 1. so as to squash.

2. with a squashing sound.

squäsh bee′tle, same as *cucumber beetle*.

squäsh bōr′ẽr, the larva of a moth, *Trochilium cucurbitæ*, which by boring injures or kills squash vines.

squäsh bug, a large, dark-colored insect, characterized by an offensive odor, that attacks squash vines and similar plants.

squäsh çourt, a walled court used for playing squash.

squäsh′ẽr, *n.* one who or that which squashes. [Colloq.]

squäsh′i·ly, *adv.* 1. so as to be squashy.

2. with a squashing sound.

squäsh′i·ness, *n.* the state or quality of being squashy; soft; yielding.

squäsh′y, *a.*; *comp.* squashier; *superl.* squashiest, 1. soft and wet; mushy.

2. easily squashed or crushed.

3. characterized by a squashed appearance.

squät, *v.i.*; squatted *or* squat, *pt.*, *pp.*; squatting, *ppr.* [ME. *squatten*, to squat or cower down; OFr. *esquatir*, to duck, to bend; from L. *coactus*, pp. of *cogere*, to compress.]

1. to sit on the heels with the knees bent.
2. to crouch with the feet drawn in close to the body.
3. to crouch or cower close to the ground, as an animal.
4. to settle on land, especially public or unoccupied land, without right or title.
5. to settle on public land under regulation by the government, in order to get title to it.

squät, *v.t.* to cause to squat: usually reflexive.

squät, *a.* 1. sitting or seated in a squatting position.
2. short and thick, like the figure of an animal squatting; as, a *squat* woman.

squät, *n.* 1. the posture of one who squats.
2. the act of squatting.
3. a small separate vein of ore.
4. a mineral consisting of tin ore and spar. [Brit. Dial.]

squät, *n.* the angelfish.

squat'à·rōle, squat'e·rōle, *n.* the gray plover or sandpiper, *Squatarola helvetica.*

Squat'i·nà, *n.* the typical genus of the *Squatinidæ*, a family of cartilaginous fishes somewhat akin to the rays, including *Squatina angelus*, the angelfish or monkfish.

squat'i·noid, *a.* like or pertaining to the genus *Squatina.*

squat'i·noid, *n.* a fish of the genus *Squatina.*

squät'tăge, *n.* in Australia, land leased from the government. [Colloq.]

squät'tẽr, *n.* 1. a person or animal that squats, or crouches.
2. one who settles on public or unclaimed land without a title.
3. one who occupies an unsettled tract of land under regulation of the government, in order to get title to it.

squät'tẽr, *v.i.* to plunge and splash along through water; to wade with a splashing noise. [Scot. and Brit. Dial.]

squät'ty, *a.*; *comp.* squattier; *superl.* squattiest, dumpy; short and stout.

squaw, *n.* [Am. Ind.]
1. an American Indian woman or wife.
2. any woman: chiefly humorous.

squäw'ber"ry, *n.*; *pl.* **squäw'ber"ries,** the squaw huckleberry.

squäw'fish, *n.*; *pl.* **squäw'fish** or **squäw'fish·es,** a long, slender fish of the carp family, found in rivers of the northern Pacific coast of the United States and Canada.

squaw huç'kle·ber"ry, the deerberry, a low shrub of the heath family, growing in the eastern part of the United States.

squawk, *v.i.* [echoic.]
1. to utter a loud, harsh cry, as a parrot or chicken.
2. to complain or protest, especially in a loud or raucous voice. [Slang.]

squäwk, *v.t.* to utter in a squawk.

squäwk, *n.* 1. a loud, harsh cry.
2. a loud, raucous complaint or protest. [Slang.]
3. the black-crowned night heron.

squawk duck, a duck of the genus *Anas*, having patches of reddish-brown about the eyes: also called the *bimaculate duck*. [Brit. Dial.]

squäwk'ẽr, *n.* one who or that which squawks; especially, a decoy used in hunting ducks.

squäwk'ing thrush, the mistlethrush. [Brit. Dial.]

squäwl, *v.i.* to squall.

squäw man, a white man married to or living with an American Indian woman.

squäw'root, *n.* 1. an American leafless parasitic herb, *Conopholis americana*, found growing in clusters on the roots of some trees, especially of oaks.
2. the blue cohosh.

squäw'weed, *n.* the golden ragwort, *Senecio aureus.*

squēak, *v.i.*; squeaked (skwēkt), *pt.*, *pp.*; squeaking, *ppr.* [Sw. *sqväka*, to cry like a frog.]
1. to utter or make a thin, sharp, high-pitched cry or sound.
2. to act as an informer; to squeal. [Slang.]

squēak, *v.t.* 1. to utter or produce in a squeak.
2. to cause (a door, etc.) to squeak.

squēak, *n.* 1. a squeaking.
2. a thin, sharp cry or sound, usually short.
narrow squeak; a narrow escape: also *close* (or *near*) *squeak*. [Colloq.]

squēak'ẽr, *n.* 1. one who or that which squeaks.
2. an Australian crow shrike of the genus *Strepera.*

squēak'i·ly, *adv.* with a squeaky sound.

squēak'i·ness, *n.* the quality or state of being squeaky.

squēak'ing·ly, *adv.* in a squeaking manner.

squēak'y, *a.*; *comp.* squeakier; *superl.* squeakiest, making squeaks; squeaking.

squēal, *v.i.*; squealed, *pt.*, *pp.*; squealing, *ppr.* [ME. *squelen*; prob. echoic.]
1. to utter or make a loud, sharp, high-pitched cry or sound.
2. to act as an informer; to betray a secret. [Slang.]

squēal, *v.t.* to utter in a squeal.

squēal, *n.* 1. a squealing.
2. a loud, sharp, high-pitched cry or sound, somewhat prolonged.

squēal'ẽr, *n.* 1. one who or that which squeals.
2. the American golden plover.
3. the European swift; the screecher.
4. the harlequin duck.
5. an informer. [Slang.]

squēam'ish, *a.* [ME. *squaimous*, from Anglo-Fr. *escoimous*, orig., disdainful, shy.]
1. having a digestive system that is easily upset; easily nauseated; queasy.
2. easily shocked or offended; prudish.
3. excessively fastidious; oversensitive.

squēam'ish·ly, *adv.* in a squeamish manner.

squēam'ish·ness, *n.* the quality or state of being squeamish.

squēam'ous, *a.* squeamish. [Obs.]

squēa'si·ness, *n.* nausea; queasiness. [Obs.]

squēa'sy, *a.* queasy; nice; squeamish. [Obs.]

squee'ġee, *n.* [prob. from *squeege*, intens. form of *squeeze.*]
1. a T-shaped tool having the crossbar edged with a strip of rubber or the like, used to scrape water from a flat surface, as in washing windows.
2. a rubber roller used for this purpose in photographic development, lithography, etc. Also *squilgee.*

squee'ġee, *v.t.*; squeegeed, *pt.*, *pp.*; squeegeeing, *ppr.* to scrape, press, or treat with a squeegee: also *squilgee.*

squeez'à·ble, *a.* 1. that can be squeezed, pressed, compressed, etc.
2. capable of being constrained or forced to yield something.

squeeze, *v.t.*; squeezed, *pt.*, *pp.*; squeezing, *ppr.* [ME. *squise*, from AS. *cwīsan*, to squeeze.]
1. to press hard or closely; to exert pressure on, especially from two or more sides, often in order to extract liquid, as juice, or the like; to compress.
2. to get, bring forth, or extract by pressure; as, she *squeezed* water from the clothes.
3. to get, extract, or extort by force or unfair means.
4. to force or cause to pass by pressing; as, he *squeezed* his hand through the opening.
5. to oppress with exactions, burdensome taxes, or the like.
6. to embrace closely; to hug.
7. to make a fascimile impression, or squeeze, of.
8. to put pressure or bring influence to bear upon (a person or persons) to do a certain thing, as to pay money, etc. [Colloq.]
9. in bridge, to force (an opponent) to play a potentially winning card in a trick that he cannot win.

Syn.—hug, compress, crowd, pinch.

squeeze, *v.i.* 1. to yield or give way to pressure.
2. to exert pressure.
3. to force one's way by pushing or pressing (with *in*, *out*, *through*, etc.).

squeeze, *n.* 1. a squeezing or being squeezed; hard or close pressure.
2. (a) a close embrace; a hug; (b) a firm pressing or grasping of another's hand in one's own.
3. the state of being closely pressed or packed; crush.
4. a facsimile impression made by pressing a soft substance onto something, as a coin or inscription.
5. a small quantity of something extracted by squeezing.
6. pressure or influence brought to bear, as in extortion. [Colloq.]
7. in bridge, a play in which one player is squeezed by another.

squeeze plāy, 1. in bridge, a play in which an opponent's discard forces him to reveal a possible taking card in one suit or to relinquish control of another suit.
2. in baseball, a play in which the batter tries to bunt, permitting a runner on third base to try for home on the pitch.

squeez'ẽr, *n.* 1. one who or that which squeezes.
2. in metallurgy, a machine used to squeeze the balls of puddled iron.
3. [*pl.*] playing cards, having the number of spots and the suit indicated in the upper left-hand corner.

squeez'ing, *n.* 1. the act of one who or that which squeezes.
2. [*pl.*] that which is forced out by pressure; dregs.
3. same as *squeeze*, n. 4.

squelch, *n.* [from earlier *quelch* (fusion of *quell* and *crush*) with *s-* intens.]
1. the sound of liquid, mud, slush, etc. moving under pressure or suction, as in wet shoes.
2. a crushed mass of something.
3. a crushing retort, answer, rebuke, etc. [Colloq.]

squelch, *v.t.*; squelched, *pt.*, *pp.*; squelching, *ppr.* 1. to crush or smash by or as by falling or stamping upon; to squash.
2. to suppress, subdue, or silence completely and with a crushing effect.

squelch, *v.i.* 1. to make a squelch (sense 1).
2. to walk heavily, as through mud or slush, or in wet shoes, making such a sound.

squench, *v.t.* to quench. [Obs.]

squē·tēague' (-tēg'), *n.*; *pl.* **squē·tēague',** [Am. Ind.] any of several food fishes of the genus *Cynoscion* found off the Atlantic coast of eastern North America: also called *weakfish* and *sea trout.*

squib, *n.* [prob. echoic.]
1. a little pipe or hollow cylinder of paper, filled with powder, or combustible matter, sent into the air burning, and bursting with a crack; a firecracker which hisses and spurts, ending in an explosion; also, in England, any firecracker.
2. a broken firecracker that burns without exploding, making a hissing noise.
3. a sarcastic speech or attack; a lampoon.
4. one who writes squibs; a petty fellow. [Obs.]

squib, *v.t.* and *v.i.*; squibbed, *pt.*, *pp.*; squibbing, *ppr.* 1. to burn or shoot off (a squib).
2. to write or utter a squib or squibs (against).
3. to fire or explode with the sound of a squib.

squid, *n.*; *pl.* **squids** or **squid,** [prob. from dial. *squit*, squirt.]
1. a cephalopod with ten arms, two being much longer than the others, and a long slender body: small squid are used as bait and for food.
2. an artificial bait, made in imitation of a squid, used in fishing.
giant squid; a very large cephalopod.

squid, *v.i.* to fish with squids.

squid'ding, *n.* fishing with squids.

squid hound, a fish; the striped bass.

squid'-jig"gẽr, *n.* a device consisting of a number of fishhooks fastened together by their shanks, the points standing out in different directions, used in trolling for squids.

squig'gle, *v.t.* [dial. for *swiggle.*] to shake a fluid about in the mouth with the lips closed. [Brit. Dial.]

squig'gle, *v.i.* to move about like an eel; to squirm. [Slang.]

squil'ġee, *n.* same as *squeegee.*

squil'ġee, *v.t.*; squilgeed, *pt.*, *pp.*; squilgeeing, *ppr.* same as *squeegee.*

squill, *n.* [Fr. *squille*; from L. *squilla*, *scilla*; Gr. *skilla*, a quill.]
1. a liliaceous plant, *Scilla maritima* (*Urginea scilla*), found in southern Europe and northern Africa: it is nearly allied to the hyacinths, onions, etc., having a spreading perianth, stamens shorter than the perianth, smooth filaments, a three-parted ovary, and a three-cornered capsule with three many-seeded cells: also called *sea onion.*
2. the dried bulb of this plant, sliced and used in medicine as an expectorant, diuretic, etc.
3. any of a number of related plants of the lily family, with blue, white, or purple flowers.

SQUILL (*Scilla maritima*)

squill, *n.* [L. *squilla, scilla,* a small fish of the lobster kind.] same as *squilla.*

Squil'là, *n.* 1. a genus of crustaceans that burrow along the seashore, typical of the *Squillidæ,* having the body long and semicylindrical.

2. [s–] *pl.* **squil'làṣ** or **squil'lae,** a member of this genus; a mantis crab.

squil'là·ġee, squill'ġee, *n.* and *v.t.* same as *squilgee, squeegee.*

squil'li·ăn, *a.* relating to or characteristic of the genus *Squilla,* or the family *Squillidæ.*

squil'li·ăn, *n.* any species of *Squilla.*

Squil'li·dae, *n.pl.* a family of crustaceans of which *Squilla* is the typical genus.

squin'ăn·cy, *n.* [Fr. *squinancie,* quinsy.]

1. quinsywort. [Obs.]

2. quinsy. [Obs.]

squinch, *n.* [contr. of *scoucheon;* OFr. *escoisson,* from LL. *excussio,* a striking out.] an interior corner support, as a small arch, corbeling, or lintel, supporting a weight, as of a spire, resting upon it.

SQUINCH

squin'ny, *v.i.* to squint. [Obs.]

squin'sy, *n.* the quincy. [Obs.]

squint, *v.i.;* squinted, *pt. pp.;* squinting, *ppr.* [contr. of *asquint.*]

1. to look or peer with the eyes partly closed.

2. to look with the eyes turned to the side; to look obliquely or askance.

3. to be cross-eyed.

4. to incline or have a tendency (*toward* a given direction, belief, etc.).

5. to deviate from a given line, tendency, etc.

squint, *v.t.* 1. to cause to squint.

2. to keep (the eyes) partly closed in looking at something, as when the light is too strong.

squint, *n.* 1. a squinting.

2. an inclination or tendency.

3. an oblique or perverse tendency or bent.

4. the condition of being cross-eyed; strabismus.

5. a look or glance, often sidelong, quick, or casual. [Colloq.]

6. in architecture, a hagioscope.

squint, *a.* 1. squinting; looking obliquely, askance, or sidelong.

2. characterized by strabismus; as, *squint* eyes.

3. regarding with suspicion.

squint'ẽr, *n.* one who or that which squints.

squint'-ēye (-ī), *n.* a person or animal that squints.

squint'-ēyed, (-īd), *a.* 1. having eyes that squint; affected with strabismus.

2. oblique; indirect; malignant; as, *squint-eyed* praise.

3. looking obliquely or by side glances; as, *squint-eyed* jealousy or envy.

squint'ing, *a.* affected with strabismus.

squint'ing, *n.* the act or habit or looking asquint.

squint'ing·ly, *adv.* in a squinting way; with sidelong glances.

squin'y, *v.i.* same as *squinny.*

squīr, squirr, *v.t.* and *v.i.* to throw with a jerk. [Brit. Dial.]

squīr'ärch, *n.* a squirearch.

squīr'ärch·y, *n.* same as *squirearchy.*

squīre, *n.* a square. [Obs.]

squīre, *n.* [contr. of *esquire.*]

1. a young man of high birth who served a knight as an attendant or armor bearer.

2. an attendant or escort; especially, a man escorting a woman; a gallant.

3. in England, the title of a gentleman next in rank to a knight.

4. in England, a title of respect given to a country gentleman or landed proprietor.

5. a title of respect applied commonly to a justice of the peace or similar local dignitary, as in a rural district.

squīre, *v.i.* and *v.t.;* squired, *pt., pp.;* squiring *ppr.* to act as a squire (to).

squīre'ärch, *n.* a member of the squirearchy.

squīre'ärch·ăl, squīre·ärch'iç·ăl, *a.* of or pertaining to the squirearchy; fit for a squire.

squīre'ärch·y, *n.* [*squire* and Gr. *archē,* rule.]

1. country gentry or large landowners collectively; the power or influence of the squires considered as a body.

2. government by squires.

Also spelled *squirarchy.*

squīr·een', *n.* [*squire* and Ir. dim. suffix *-een.*] a small landowner; a petty squire.

squīre'hood, *n.* the state, rank, or office of a squire.

squīre'ling, *n.* a squirelet.

squīre'ly, *a.* befitting a squire; like a squire.

squīre'ship, *n.* squirehood.

squīrm, *v.i.;* squirmed, *pt., pp.;* squirming, *ppr.* [prob. dial. echoism, influenced by *worm.*]

1. to twist and turn the body in a snakelike movement; to wriggle; to writhe.

2. to show or feel distress, as from painful embarrassment, humiliation, etc.

squīrm'y, *a.; comp.* squirmier; *superl.* squirmiest, squirming.

squīrr, *v.t.* and *v.i.* same as *squir.*

squīr'rel, *n.; pl.* **squīr'relṣ** or **squīr'rel,** [OFr. *esquirel, escurel;* Fr. *écureuil,* from LL. *sciuriolus,* dim. of L. *sciurus;* Gr. *skiouros,* a squirrel, *skia,* a shadow, and *oura,* a tail.]

COMMON GRAY SQUIRREL (1 1/2 ft. long)

1. a small, tree-dwelling rodent of various species of the genus *Sciurus* and family *Sciuridæ,* characterized by a slender body, heavy fur, a long, bushy tail, and large, prominent eyes: common species are the *gray squirrel,* the *red squirrel,* the *fox squirrel,* and the *European squirrel.*

2. any of various other rodents related to these, as the chipmunks, certain flying phalangers of Australia, woodchucks, etc.

3. the fur of some of these animals.

4. one of the small rollers in a carding machine.

barking squirrel; same as *prairie dog.*

Java squirrel; the jelerang, *Sciurus javanensis.*

squīr'rel, *v.t.;* squirreled or squirrelled, *pt., pp.;* squirreling or squirrelling, *ppr.* to store, hide, or hoard (usually with *away*): squirrels store up nuts and seeds for winter.

squīr'rel çāge, a cage for a squirrel, hamster, etc. containing a drum that revolves when the animal runs inside it: often used figuratively of an existence, repetitive task, etc. that seems endless and without purpose.

squīr'rel çorn, a plant, *Dicentra canadensis,* of the fumitory family, bearing a raceme of cream-colored, heart-shaped flowers and having roots with yellow, grainlike buds.

squīr'rel çup, 1. a plant, *Hepatica triloba,* of the crowfoot family, with delicate cup-shaped flowers appearing in early spring.

2. the flower of this plant.

squīr'rel fish, 1. a fish, *Diplectrum fasciculare,* of the West Indies: also called *serrano.*

2. a fish, *Holocentrus ascensionis,* of Florida and the West Indies.

3. the pinfish, *Lagodon rhomboides.*

squīr'rel hāke, same as *hake* (sense 3).

squīr'rel hąwk, the roughleg, *Archibuteo ferrugineus,* a large hawk of California.

squīr'rel mŏn'key, any of various small, bushy-tailed South American monkeys, as the marmosets.

squīr'rel shrew, a tree shrew, as the banxring or pentail.

squīr'rel·tāil, *n.* any of various species of wild barley of the genus *Hordeum,* as *Hordeum jubatum,* of the northern United States, and *Hordeum murinum,* of California, with long, barbed awns: also *squirrel grass.*

squīrt, *v.t.;* squirted, *pt., pp.;* squirting, *ppr.* [L.G. *swirljen,* squirt.]

1. to eject or shoot out, as liquid, in a jet or thin stream; as, to *squirt* water.

2. to wet (a person or thing) with liquid so shot out.

squīrt, *v.i.* to spurt; to issue in a jet or thin stream, as from a small opening.

squīrt, *n.* 1. something used to squirt liquid, as a syringe.

2. the act of squirting.

3. a small amount of squirted liquid; a jet or thin stream.

4. a small or insignificant person, especially one who is impudent. [Colloq.]

squīrt'ẽr, *n.* one who or that which squirts.

squīrt gun, 1. a toy gun that shoots a stream of liquid.

2. a spray gun.

squīrt'ing çū'çum·bẽr, a trailing plant with cucumber-shaped fruit which bursts when ripe, ejecting the seeds.

squish, *v.i.;* squished, *pt., pp.;* squishing, *ppr.* to make a soft, splashing sound when walked on, squeezed, etc.

squish, *v.t.* to squeeze into a soft mass; squash. [Colloq.]

squish, *n.* 1. a squishing sound.

2. the act of squashing; squash. [Colloq.]

squish'y, *a.; comp.* squishier; *superl.* squishiest,

1. soft and pliable; yielding to pressure.

2. making a squishing sound.

squitch gràss, same as *couch grass.*

squoosh, *v.t.;* squooshed, *pt., pp.;* squooshing, *ppr.* [altered from *squash.*]

1. to squeeze or crush into a soft, liquid mass.

2. same as *slosh.*

squoosh'y, *a.; comp.* squooshier; *superl.* squooshiest, soft and wet; squashy.

Sr, in chemistry, strontium.

sri (shrē), *n.* [Hind., lit., glorious, reverent, from Sans. *śrī.*] a Hindu title of address, equivalent to English *mister.*

St., St-, Saint: terms beginning *St.* or *St-* are entered in this dictionary under *Saint.*

-st, see *-est* (suffix used to form verbs).

stab, *v.t.;* stabbed, *pt., pp.;* stabbing, *ppr.* [from ME. *stob,* a stake, a stump.]

1. to pierce or wound with or as with a pointed weapon; as, to be *stabbed* by a dagger.

2. to go into in a sharp, thrusting way.

3. to thrust or plunge a pointed weapon, as into a thing.

4. to make rough with a pick, as a brick wall, for plastering.

stab, *v.i.* 1. to make a thrust or cause a wound with or as with a knife, dagger, etc.

2. to give the sensation of a knife wound: said of pain.

stab, *n.* 1. a thrust with a pointed weapon.

2. a wound made by stabbing.

3. a sudden sensation of anguish or pain.

4. an attempt; a try. [Colloq.]

Stä'băt Mä'tẽr, [L., the mother stood.]

1. a Latin hymn about the sorrows of the Virgin Mary at the crucifixion of Jesus.

2. any musical setting of this hymn.

stab'bẽr, *n.* 1. one who stabs.

2. any instrument used for stabbing; as, (a) a three-cornered awl used in making sails; (b) an awl for opening eyelets.

stab'bing·ly, *adv.* in a stabbing manner.

stā'bile, *a.* [L. *stabilis.*]

1. stable; stationary; fixed in position.

2. in medicine, (a) designating or of a method of applying electricity for therapeutic purposes, in which the active electrode remains fixed over the diseased part: opposed to *labile;* (b) somewhat resistant to heat.

stȧ·bil'i·tāte, *v.t.* to establish.

stȧ·bil'i·ty, *n.; pl.* **stȧ·bil'i·tieṣ,** [L. *stabilitas,* from *stabilis,* firm.]

1. the state or quality of being stable, or fixed; steadiness.

2. firmness of character, purpose, etc.

3. resistance to change; permanence.

4. the capacity of an object to return to equilibrium or to its original position after having been displaced.

5. in the Roman Catholic Church, a monk's vow to remain for life in the same monastery.

stā″bi·li·zā'tion, *n.* a stabilizing or being stabilized.

stā'bil·īze, *v.t.;* stabilized, *pt., pp.;* stabilizing, *ppr.* 1. to cause to be steady or secure.

2. to equip (an airplane, ship, etc.) with a stabilizer.

3. to keep from changing or fluctuating, as in price.

stā'bil·ī·zẽr, *n.* a person or thing that stabilizes; specifically, (a) any of various parts or devices used to make an airplane steady in flight; (b) a substance added to an explosive to prevent it from exploding spontaneously.

stā′ble, *a.* [L. *stabilis*, stable, standing firmly, from *stare*, to stand.]
1. not easily moved or thrown off balance; not likely to break down, fall apart, or give way; firm; steady; fixed.
2. firm in character, purpose, or resolution; steadfast.
3. resisting change; permanent; enduring.
4. capable of returning to equilibrium or original position after having been displaced.
5. in chemistry, not easily decomposing.

stā′ble, *n.* [L. *stabulum*, a standing place for animals, from *stare*, to stand.]
1. a building in which horses or cattle are sheltered and fed.
2. a group of animals kept or belonging in such a building.
3. all the race horses belonging to one owner.
4. the people employed to take care of and train such a group of race horses.

stā′ble, *v.t.* and *v.i.*; stabled, *pt.*, *pp.*; stabling, *ppr.* to lodge, keep, or be kept in or as in a stable.

stā′ble·boy, *n.* a boy employed in a stable.

stā′ble fly̆, a fly, *Stomoxys calcitrans*, that lives in stables and bites horses and cattle.

stā′ble·man, *n.*; *pl.* **stā′ble·men,** a man employed in a stable.

stā′ble·ness, *n.* the state or quality of being stable; stability.

stā′blẽr, *n.* the keeper of a stable; one who stables horses or other domestic animals.

stā′bling, *n.* 1. the act or practice of keeping cattle in a stable.
2. a stable or stables.
3. accommodations in a stable or stables, for horses, etc.

stab′lish, *v.t.* to fix; to establish. [Archaic.]

stȧç·cȧ·tis′si·mō, *a.* [It.] in music, extremely staccato.

stȧç·cä′tō, *a.* [It., detached.]
1. in music, with distinct breaks between successive tones; abrupt; detached; as, a series of *staccato* notes, a *staccato* passage: opposed to *legato*.
2. made up of abrupt, distinct elements or sounds; as, a *staccato* outburst of rage, gunfire, etc.

stȧç·cä′tō, *adv.* so as to be staccato.

stȧç·cä′tō, *n.*; *pl.* **stȧç·cä′tōs,** something, as a speech pattern, that is staccato.

Stā′çhys (-kis), *n.* [Gr., an ear of corn, from the mode of flowering.] a genus of labiate plants, the woundworts.

stack, *n.* [ME. stack; ON. *stakkr*.]
1. a large pile of straw, hay, etc., especially one symmetrically arranged with a smooth outer surface for outdoor storage.
2. any somewhat orderly pile or heap, as of boxes, poker chips, etc.
3. a number of arms, especially three rifles, leaning against each other on end so as to form a cone.
4. in Great Britain, a unit of solid measure equal to 108 cubic feet, used for cut wood, coal, etc.
5. a chimney; specifically, (a) a number of flues or pipes arranged together; (b) a single smoke pipe or chimney, especially one of metal, as on a ship, locomotive, etc.
6. a set of book shelves.
7. [*pl.*] the section where the books are kept in a library.
8. (a) the part of a computer memory used to store data temporarily; (b) the data so stored.
9. a large number or quantity. [Colloq.]
10. an isolated columnar rock in the sea. [Scot.]

stack, *v.t.*; stacked (stakt), *pt.*, *pp.*; stacking, *ppr.* 1. to pile or arrange in a stack.
2. to load or furnish with stacks of something.
3. to assign (aircraft) to various altitudes for circling while awaiting a turn to land.
4. to arrange in advance underhandedly so as to predetermine the outcome; as, to *stack* a jury.
to stack the cards; (a) to arrange the order of playing cards secretly so that certain cards are dealt to certain players; (b) to prearrange circumstances, usually secretly and unfairly. Also *to stack the deck*.
to stack up; (a) to amount (*to* a specified sum); (b) to stand in comparison (*with* or *against*); to measure up.

stack, *v.* obsolete and dialectal past tense of *stick*.

stack′āġe, *n.* 1. stacks or their contents collectively. [Rare.]
2. a tax on things stacked. [Rare.]

stack′ẽr, *v.i.* to stagger. [Brit. Dial.]

stack′ẽr, *n.* a device for removing threshed straw from a threshing machine, consisting of an endless band or a suction tube to deposit the straw in stacks.

Stack·hou′sī·ȧ, *n.* [named after John *Stackhouse*, an English botanist.] a genus of Australasian plants with yellow or white flowers.

stack′ing band, stack′ing belt, a band or rope used in binding thatch or straw upon a stack.

stack′ing swiv′el (-l), a swivel on a rifle which enables it to be stacked without a bayonet.

stack′stand, *n.* a structure of timber, masonry, or, sometimes, iron, raised on props and placed in a stackyard, on which to build a stack, as of hay.

stack′up, *n.* an arrangement of circling aircraft at various altitudes awaiting their turn to land.

stack′yärd, *n.* a yard or enclosure for stacks of hay or grain.

staç′tē, *n.* [L., from Gr. *staktē*, f. of *staktos*, dropping, from *stazein*, to drop.] one of the sweet spices which the ancient Jews used to make incense: Ex. xxx. 34.

staç·tom′ē·tẽr, *n.* [Gr. *staktos*, dropping, and *-meter*.] a tube used for measuring liquid in drops.

städ (stät), *n.* [D.] in South Africa, a city or town.

stad′dle, *n.* [AS. *stathol*, *stathel*, a foundation, a basis, firm seat, from root of *stand*.]
1. a staff; a crutch. [Obs.]
2. a lower part or structure; a support; specifically, the base or supporting framework of a stack, as of hay.
3. a small tree of any kind, especially a forest tree.

stad′dle, *v.t.* 1. to leave staddles, or small trees, in, as when a forest is cut. [Rare.]
2. to put (hay) in staddles.

stāde, *n.* [L. *stadium*.] a stadium (sense 1). [Obs.]

Stā′dẽr splint, [after Otto *Stader* (1894—), Am. veterinary surgeon.] a metal splint consisting of two pins driven through the bone above and below a fracture and held in place by two rods extending between them on the outside of the limb: the splint allows freedom of movement of the fractured limb.

stad′hōld″ẽr, stadt′hōld″ẽr (stat′), *n.* [D. *stadhouder*; *stad*, a city, and *houder*, holder.]
1. the chief magistrate of the United Provinces of the Netherlands.
2. formerly, the governor or viceroy of a province of the Netherlands.

stad′hōld″ẽr·āte, stad′hōld″ẽr·ship (stat′), *n.* the office of a stadholder.

stā′di·ȧ, *n.* [LL., from L. *stadium*, stage, station, stadium.]
1. a temporary station for surveying purposes.
2. a device used in calculating distance through measurement of angles; specifically, (a) a surveyor's transit used together with a graduated rod (*stadia rod*); (b) the rod; (c) any of several military range finders, as a stick with graduations, used in judging distance by measuring the apparent height of a man viewed from a distance.
3. a method of surveying using a stadia.

stā′di·ȧ, *n.* pl. of *stadium* (senses 1 and 3).

stā′di·ȧ rod, a graduated rod used in making stadia measurements.

stā′di·ȧ wīreṣ, the two cross hairs of a transit used in making stadia measurements.

stā·di·om′ē·tẽr, *n.* [Gr. *stadion*, fixed standard of length, and *-meter*.]
1. an instrument for measuring angles and making a graphic record of their bearings.
2. a device for measuring the length of a curve, broken line, etc., consisting of a toothed wheel that traverses the curve, line, etc., and an index.

stā′di·um, *n.*; *pl.* **stā′di·ȧ,** [L., from Gr. *stadion*, a fixed standard of length, from *histanai*, to stand.]
1. in ancient Greece, (a) a track for foot races, usually semicircular, with tiers of seats for spectators; (b) any of several measures of linear distance, based on the length of such tracks (at Athens, 607 ft.; but the Olympic stadium was slightly over 630 ft., and others varied considerably).
2. *pl.* **stā′di·umṣ,** a place used for outdoor games, meetings, etc., partly or completely surrounded by tiers of seats, usually for thousands of spectators.
3. a stage, as of a disease.
4. a stadia or stadia rod.

stad′le, *n.* a staddle.

stadt′hōld″ẽr (stat′), *n.* a stadholder.

stȧff, *n.* [from G. *staffieren*, to fill out, from OFr. *estoffe*, stuff.] a building material of plaster and a fibrous material, used for temporary decorative structures, statues, etc.

stȧff, *n.*; *pl.* **stāveṣ** or **stȧffs,** [AS. *stæf*, a stick, a staff, a support; akin to G. *stab*.]
1. a stick, rod, or pole; specifically, (a) a stick used as a support in walking; (b) a pole or club used as a weapon; (c) a pole for supporting a banner or flag; (d) a rod, wand, etc. used as a symbol of authority; (e) [Archaic.] a shaft, as of a lance; (f) any of several graduated sticks or rules used for measuring, as in surveying.
2. figuratively, a support; as, he was a *staff* to the whole group.
3. *pl.* **stȧffs,** a group of people assisting a chief, manager, president, or other leader.
4. *pl.* **stȧffs,** a group of officers serving a military or naval commanding officer in an advisory and administrative capacity without combat duties or command.
5. *pl.* **stȧffs,** a specific group of workers or employees; as, a teaching *staff*, office *staff*, maintenance *staff*.
6. in music, the five horizontal lines and four intermediate spaces on which music is written or printed.
7. the round of a ladder.
8. a stanza; a series of verses so disposed that, when it is concluded, the same order begins again. [Obs.]
9. in surgery, a grooved steel instrument having a curvature, used to guide the knife or gorget through the urethra into the bladder in the operation of lithotomy.
general staff; see under *general*, a.
personal staff; a body of officers attached to commanding general officers as military secretaries and aides-de-camp.
staff of life; bread, regarded as the basic food.
Syn.—stay, prop, support.

stȧff, *a.* of or having to do with a staff (senses 3, 4, 5).

stȧff, *v.t.*; staffed (staft), *pt.*, *pp.*; staffing, *ppr.* to provide with a staff, as of workers or employees.

stȧff an′gle, in architecture, a square rod of wood standing flush with the wall on each of its sides, at the external angles of plastering, to prevent their being damaged.

stȧff çap′tain (-tin), formerly, in the British navy, a captain of the navigating staff.

stȧff çŏm·mȧnd′ẽr, formerly, a commander of the navigating branch in the British navy.

stȧf′fi·ẽr, *n.* an attendant bearing a staff. [Obs.]

stȧff′ish, *a.* stiff; unwieldy. [Obs.]

stȧff′măn, *n.*; *pl.* **stȧff′men,** a man who throws silk or spins the filaments into thread.

stȧff of′fi·cẽr, an officer serving on a staff.

stȧff ser′ġeănt (sär′), 1. in the United States Army, formerly, the third grade of enlisted man (now *sergeant*).
2. in the United States Marine Corps and Air Force, the third grade of enlisted man, ranking just below technical sergeant.

stȧff sūr′ġeŏn, formerly, a senior officer in the medical branch of the navy.

stȧff tree, any of several plants of the genus *Selastrus*. *Selastrus scandens* is the American bittersweet.

stag, *n.*; *pl.* **stagṣ** or **stag,** [AS. *stagga*; akin to ON. *steggr*, male bird.]
1. (a) a full-grown male deer; said specifically of the European red deer; (b) the male of some other animals, as the caribou.
2. a male animal castrated in maturity.
3. (a) a man who attends a social gathering unaccompanied by a woman; (b) a social gathering attended by men only.
4. a colt or filly. [Scot. and Brit. Dial.]
5. in commercial slang, (a) an outside irregular dealer in stocks, not a member of the exchange; (b) a person who applies for the allotment of shares in a joint-stock company, not because he wishes to hold the shares, but because he hopes to sell the allotment at a premium.
6. the wren. [Brit. Dial.]

stag, *v.i.*; stagged, *pt.*, *pp.*; stagging, *ppr.* 1. in commercial slang, to act as a stag on the stock exchange.

2. to attend a social gathering unaccompanied by a woman: said of a man.

stag, *v.t.* to watch or follow secretly; to spy on. [Slang.]

stag, *a.* for men only; as, a *stag* party.

to go stag; to go as a stag (sense 3a). [Colloq.]

stag bee′tle, a lamellicorn, coleopterous insect of the family *Lucanidæ*, characterized by branched antlerlike mandibles in the males. *Lucanus cervus* is the common European stag beetle. *Lucanus dama* is the American species.

STAG BEETLE
(*Lucanus cervus*)

stāġe, *n.* [OFr. *estage*; LL. *staticum*, from *status*, pp. of *stare*, to stand.]

1. a platform or dock.
2. a scaffold.
3. a level, floor, or story.
4. a shelf attached to a microscope for holding the object to be viewed.
5. a raised floor or platform upon which plays, speeches, etc. are presented before an audience.
6. the whole area back of the footlights in a theater.
7. the theater, drama, or acting as a profession; as, she left the *stage* after her husband's death.
8. the scene of an event or series of events; as, Central Europe has been the *stage* of many wars.
9. a place where a stop is made on a journey, especially a regular stopping point with accommodations for travelers.
10. the distance or a part of a route between stopping places; leg of a journey.
11. (a) a stagecoach; (b) a motor bus.
12. a period, level, or degree in a process of development, growth, or change; as, an advanced *stage* of an insect.
13. in geology, a division of stratified rocks ranking just below *series*, corresponding to *age* in the scale of chronology.
14. in radio, an element or part in some complex arrangement of parts; specifically, a tube with its accessory apparatus in an amplifier made up of a number of tubes.

by easy stages; (a) traveling only a short distance at a time; (b) working or acting gradually, not hurriedly, with plenty of stops, as for rest.

to be in the center of the stage; to occupy any conspicuous position; to be in the public eye.

stāġe, *v.t.*; staged, *pt., pp.*; staging, *ppr.* 1. to present, represent, or exhibit on or as on a stage.

2. to plan, arrange, and carry out; as, the enemy *staged* a counteroffensive.

stāġe, *v.i.* 1. to be suitable for presentation on the stage; as, the play *stages* well.

2. to travel by stagecoach.

stāġe′ċōach, *n.* a horse-drawn coach carrying passengers, parcels, and mail on scheduled trips over a regular route.

stāġe ċōach′măn, *pl.* **stāġe ċōach′men,** a man who drives a stagecoach.

stāġe′ċrȧft, *n.* skill in, or the art of, composing and staging plays.

stāġe di·reċ′tion, 1. an instruction, written into the text of a play, directing the movements, actions, etc. of the performers.

2. the art or practice of directing the production of a play.

stāġe dōor, the entrance at the back of the theater used by the actors and the workmen in general.

stāġe′-dōor John′ny, a man who associates with, or seeks the company of, actresses or chorus girls. [Slang.]

stāġe ef·feċt′, theatrical effect; effect produced on or as on the stage by action, lighting, scenery, etc.

stāġe frīght (frīt), nervousness felt when appearing before an audience, as by an inexperienced performer.

stāġe′hand, *n.* a person who does manual work connected with producing a play, as the arrangement of scenery, operation of lights, etc.

stāġe′house, *n.* a house that serves as a station for a coach en route.

stāġe man′ȧ·ġẽr, one who superintends the production and performance of a play, and regulates all matters behind the scenes.

stāġe mī·ċrom′ē·tẽr, a micrometer adapted to the stage of a microscope, to measure an object within the the field of view.

stāġe plāy, 1. a theatrical entertainment.

2. a play adapted for representation on the stage.

stāġe plāy′ẽr, an actor on the stage; one whose occupation is to represent characters on the stage.

stā′ġẽr, *n.* 1. an actor. [Archaic.]

2. a person or animal of experience or of skill derived from long experience; an old hand; a veteran: usually with *old*.

3. a horse employed in drawing a stagecoach. [Colloq.]

stā′ġẽr·y, *n.* exhibition on the stage.

stāġe set′tẽr, one who arranges the scenery on a stage.

stāġe′-struck, *a.* smitten with a love for the stage; possessed by a passion for the drama, or to become an actor or actress.

stag′-ē″vil, *n.* a disease in horses, tetanus or lockjaw.

stāġe wag′ŏn, a stagecoach. [Obs.]

stāġe whis′pẽr (hwis′), 1. a loud whisper by actor on the stage, intended to be heard by the audience.

2. any similar whisper intended to be heard by others than the person to whom it is addressed.

stāġe′wrīght (-rīt), *n.* a playwright. [Rare.]

stā′ġey, *a.*; *comp.* stagier; *superl.* stagiest, same as *stagy*.

stag′gȧrd, stag′gȧrt, *n.* a stag four years old.

stag′gẽr, *v.i.*; staggered, *pt., pp.*; staggering, *ppr.* [ME. *stakeren*; ON. *stakra*, to cause to stumble.]

1. to reel, totter, or sway, as from a blow, fatigue, drunkenness, etc.; to vacillate; to move to one side and the other in standing or walking.

2. to hesitate; to begin to doubt and waver in purpose; to become less confident or determined.

stag′gẽr, *v.t.* 1. to cause to stagger, as with a blow.

2. to affect strongly with astonishment, horror, grief, etc.; to overwhelm.

3. to set or incline alternately, as on either side of a line; to make zigzag in arrangement; as, the teeth of most saws are *staggered*.

4. to arrange (periods of activity, duties, etc.) so as to eliminate crowding or overconcentration; as, employees' vacation periods have been *staggered*.

5. in aeronautics, to set in a stagger.

stag′gẽr, *n.* 1. the act of staggering; a sudden, tottering motion, as if one were about to fall.

2. [*pl.*] [*construed as sing.*] a nervous disease of horses and cattle, causing the animals to stagger or fall when walking: also called *blind staggers*.

3. a staggered or zigzag arrangement.

4. in aeronautics, (a) the setting of one wing of an airplane forward of another wing above or below it so that there is a difference in the projection of their leading edges; (b) the amount of this difference.

5. an attempt, usually without great success; as, he made a *stagger* at doing it. [Old Slang.]

stag′gẽr·bush, *n.* a shrub, *Andromeda mariana*, found in low, sandy parts of the middle and southern parts of the United States. It bears red or white flowers poisonous to livestock.

stag′gẽr·ẽr, *n.* 1. one who or that which staggers.

2. a statement, argument, or question which staggers one; a poser. [Colloq.]

stag′gẽr grȧss, the atamasco lily, *Zephyranthes atamasco*: so called because it is supposed to produce the staggers in horses.

stag′gẽr·ing·ly, *adv.* in a reeling manner; with hesitation or doubt.

stag′gẽr·wŏrt, *n.* same as *staverwort*.

stag′-head″ed (-hed″), *a.* being dead at the top; having the upper branches dead: said of a tree.

stag′hǫrn, *n.* 1. a club moss, *Lycopodium clavatum*: also called *staghorn moss* and *stag's-horn*.

2. a large, ornamental coral, *Madrepora cervicornis*, or related species: so called because it radiates in such a way as to resemble the antlers of a stag.

staghorn fern; any fern of the small but widely scattered genus, *Platycerium*, but especially *Platycerium alcicorne*: so called because the fertile fronds fork in such a way as to resemble the antlers of a stag.

stag′-hǫrned, *a.* having long, branching horns, mandibles, or antennae, somewhat resembling the antlers of a stag, as the longicorn beetle.

stag′hound, *n.* a hunting dog; specifically, (a) the Scotch deerhound or wolf dog, of great size, strength, and speed, used in running down game; (b) a large foxhound, trained to track down deer.

stā′ġi·ly, *adv.* in a stagy manner.

stā′ġi·ness, *n.* the quality or condition of being stagy or affected; a theatrical manner or style.

stā′ġing, *n.* 1. a temporary structure used for support; scaffolding.

2. the business of operating stagecoaches.

3. travel by stagecoach.

4. the act or process of presenting a play on the stage.

stā′ġing ā′rē·ȧ, in military usage, the place of embarkation of troops leaving for a combat zone.

Stag′i·rīte, *n.* [L. *Stagirites*; Gr. *Stageiritēs*, a native of *Stageira*, Stagira.] a native or inhabitant of the ancient Macedonian city, Stagira; specifically, Aristotle, "the Stagirite," who was born there.

stag′năn·cy, *n.*; *pl.* **stag′năn·cieṣ,** 1. the state or condition of being stagnant or without motion, flow, or circulation, as a fluid.

2. anything stagnant; a stagnant pool.

Stagnancies left by the flood. —Cotton.

stag′nănt, *a.* [L. *stagnans* (*-antis*), ppr. of *stagnare*, to cause to stand, stagnate.]

1. without motion or current; not flowing or moving.

2. foul from lack of movement: said of water, etc.

3. lacking in activity, interest, etc.; dull; sluggish; as, a *stagnant* mind.

stag′nănt·ly, *adv.* in a stagnant or motionless, inactive manner.

stag′nāte, *v.i.*; stagnated, *pt., pp.*; stagnating, *ppr.* [L. *stagnatus*, pp. of *stagnare*, to stagnate.]

1. to cease to flow; to be motionless; as, blood *stagnates* in the veins of a dead animal.

2. to cease to be brisk or active; to become dull; as, business *stagnates*.

stag′nāte, *v.t.* to make stagnant.

stag′nāte, *a.* stagnant. [Obs.]

stag·nā′tion, *n.* 1. a stagnating or being stagnated.

2. a stagnant condition.

stag·niċ′ō·lous, *a.* living in stagnant water or swamps.

stag pär′ty, a party or entertainment given for men only.

stag′ṣ′-hǫrn, *n.* same as *staghorn*, sense 1.

stag tick, a dipterous insect, *Leptoptena cervi*, parasitic on the stag and other animals.

stag′wŏrm, *n.* the larva of any one of twelve varieties of botflies, parasitic on the stag. Those of the genus *Hypoderma* are found in the tissue beneath the skin of the back and loins, while those of the genera *Cephenomyia* and *Pharyngomyia* infest the nose and throat.

stā′ġy, *a.*; *comp.* stagier; *superl.* stagiest, 1. of or characteristic of the stage; theatrical (usually in an unfavorable sense).

2. affected; not real or genuine; as, a *stagy* type of diction.

Also spelled *stagey*.

Stag′y·rīte, *n.* same as *Stagirite*.

Stähl′helm (shtäl′helm), *n.* [G., literally, steel helmet.] a military body composed of German war veterans and organized after World War I with the purpose of restoring the German monarchy and re-establishing the territories lost at the end of World War I.

Stähl′helm·ist, *n.* a member of the Stahlhelm; also, one who believes in the views of the Stahlhelm; loosely, a German monarchist.

Stähl′iăn (-yăn), *a.* of or pertaining to G. E. Stahl (1660–1734), a German scientist, or his theories.

Stähl′iăn, *n.* a believer in animism or the theories of Stahl.

Stähl′iăn·iṣm, *n.* same as *animism*.

 fāte, fär, fȧst, fạll, finăl, cãre, at; mēte, prey, hẽr, met; pīne, marïne, bīrd, pin; nōte, mȯve, fọr, atŏm, not; mọọn, book;

Stähl'ism, *n.* same as *animism.*

stähl'spiēl, *n.* [G., from *stahl*, steel, and *spiel*, play, from *spielen*, to play.] a musical instrument of steel bars, resembling a lyre, and used chiefly for military music.

stāid, *v.* archaic past tense and past participle of *stay* (to remain).

stāid, *a.* 1. resisting change; fixed; settled. [Rare.]

2. sober; sedate; settled and steady.

Syn.—grave, demure, steady, sober, sedate.

stāid'ly, *adv.* in a staid manner.

stāid'ness, *n.* the state or quality of being staid; sobriety; gravity; steadiness; regularity.

stāig, *n.* a stag. [Dial.]

stāin, *v.t.*; stained, *pt.*, *pp.*; staining, *ppr.* [contr. of *distain*; OFr. *desteindre*, to discolor, from L. *dis-*, from, and *tingere*, to color.]

1. to discolor by the application of foreign matter; to make foul; to spot; as, to *stain* the hand with dye; to *stain* clothes with vegetable juice.

2. to color by some other means than painting or covering the surface; specifically, (a) to color, as wood, fabrics, paper, glass, etc., by the use of something which combines chemically with the substance to be colored, or penetrates it; (b) in microscopy, to treat (material for microscopic study) with a coloring matter that facilitates study, as by making transparent parts visible or by producing a different effect upon different structures or tissues.

3. to impress with figures, in colors different from the ground; as, to *stain* paper for hangings.

4. to blot; to soil; to spot with guilt or infamy; to tarnish; to bring reproach on; as, to *stain* the character.

5. to darken; to dim; to obscure. [Obs.]

6. to excel; to surpass; to eclipse. [Obs.]

Syn.—soil, sully, tarnish, blot, foul, spot, color, discolor, dye, tinge.

stain, *v.i.* to receive or impart a stain or color.

stāin, *n.* 1. a color, discoloration, or spot resulting from or as from staining.

2. a moral blemish; dishonor; guilt; taint.

3. a substance used to impart color in staining; specifically, (a) a dye or pigment in solution, for staining wood, cloth, etc.; (b) a dye used to stain material for microscopic study.

4. a tincture; a tinge.

diffuse stains; those pigments which stain all parts uniformly.

general stains; in microscopy, those stains which take effect on all the elements of a preparation.

nuclear stains; those selective stains which exhibit great affinity for the nuclear material, particularly the chromatin.

oyster-shell stains; in photography, an imperfection on a plate sensitized with collodion and salt of silver. It is caused by impurities in the bath.

plasma stains; those pigments which do not permanently stain the chromatin material, but show affinity for the cytoplasm.

selective stains; those stains which affect different elements of a tissue in different ways, staining some more deeply or more quickly than others: also called *specific stains* and *elective stains.*

stāin'ȧ·ble, *a.* capable of being stained.

stāined glȧss, glass colored in any of various ways, as by fusing metallic oxides into it, by enameling, by burning pigments into its surface, etc.: it is used especially for church windows.

stāin'ẽr, *n.* 1. one who or that which stains, blots, or tarnishes.

2. a workman who stains; as, a paper *stainer.*

3. any of several insects which stain the material upon which they feed.

stāin'less, *a.* 1. without a mark or stain.

2. free from reproach of guilt; free from sin.

3. that will not become stained or discolored.

stāin'less·ly, *adv.* in a stainless manner.

stāin'less steel, steel alloyed with chromium, etc., virtually immune to rust and corrosion.

stāir, *n.* [AS. *stæger*, from *stigan*, to climb.]

1. a step; a stone or a frame of boards or planks by which a person rises one step.

2. a series of steps, arranged one behind and above the other, in such a way as to permit ascent or descent from one level to another: usually in the plural.

below stairs; in the lower part or basement of a house; hence, in the servants' quarters.

flight of stairs; the stairs which make the whole ascent of a story; in winding stairs, the stairs from the floor to a turn, or from one turn to another.

pair of stairs; a flight of stairs.

spiral stairs; a flight of stairs winding around a solid newel, in spiral fashion: also called *corkscrew stairs* and *winding stairs.*

stāir'bēak, *n.* a bird of the genus *Xenops*: so called from the shape of its beak.

stāir cär'pet, a carpet having a complete pattern woven in a single width so that it is suitable for covering stairs.

stāir'çāse, *n.* the part of a building which contains the stairs; especially, a flight of stairs with the supporting framework and a handrail or balustrade.

stāir'çāse shell, a shell of the genus *Solarium.*

stāir'foot, *n.* the bottom of a staircase.

stāir'head (-hed), *n.* the top of a staircase.

stāir rod, a metallic rod for holding a stair carpet in its place against the bottom of each riser.

stāir'wāy, *n.* a staircase.

stāir'well, *n.* the vertical shaft (in a building) containing a staircase: also *stair well.*

stāith, *n.* [ME. *stathe*, from AS. *stæth*, shore.]

1. a stage or wharf with equipment for loading and unloading. [Brit. Dial.]

2. (a) an embankment; (b) a path or narrow road along an embankment. [Brit. Dial.]

stāith'măn, *n.*; *pl.* **stāith'men,** one who works at a staith and is engaged in shipping coal, etc. [Brit. Dial.]

stāke, *n.* [ME.; AS. *staca*, a stake; Ice. *stjaki*, a stake; Sw. *stake*, a stake, candlestick.]

1. a piece of wood, etc. sharpened at one end for driving into the ground as a support for a fence, vine, hedge, tent, net, etc.

2. an upright pole or post fixed in a socket at the side or end of a car, cart, etc. to confine the load.

3. the post to which one condemned to die by fire was fastened; as, to suffer at the *stake*; hence, execution by burning.

4. a small anvil used by blacksmiths and sheet-metal workers. It usually has a tang, by which it is stuck in a square socket of a bench.

5. a post on which a skin is stretched for currying or graining.

6. a truck having a stake body.

7. [*often pl.*] something, especially money, risked or hazarded, as in a wager, game, or contest; as, the gamblers were playing for high *stakes.*

8. [*often pl.*] a reward given a winner, as in a race; a prize.

9. a race in which a prize is offered.

10. a share or interest, especially a financial one, in property, a person, a business venture, or the like.

11. a grubstake. [Colloq.]

12. in the Mormon Church, a territorial division for ecclesiastical purposes, presided over by three high priests.

at stake; being risked or hazarded, or dependent upon the outcome (of something specified or implied).

to pull up stakes; to change one's place of residence, business, etc. [Colloq.]

stāke, *v.t.*; staked (stākt), *pt.*, *pp.*; staking, *ppr.* 1. to fasten, support, or protect with a stake or stakes; as, to *stake* vines or plants.

2. to mark the limits or boundaries of by or as by stakes, specifically so as to establish a claim: with *out* or *off*; as, to *stake out* a new road; to *stake off* house lots.

3. to hitch or tether to a stake.

4. to close (*up* or *in*), shut (*out*), etc. by stakes in the form of a fence or barrier.

5. to risk or hazard; to gamble; to bet; as, he *staked* his winnings on the next hand.

6. to furnish with money or resources, as for a business venture. [Colloq.]

7. to grubstake. [Colloq.]

8. to soften and stretch (skins), formerly by rubbing the skins by hand against a blunt semicircular knife fixed on the top of an upright post: now done by machine.

stāke bōat, a boat anchored as a mark in aquatic races.

stāke bod'y, a flat truck body having sockets into which stakes may be fitted, as to support railings.

stāke drīv'ẽr, the American bittern: so named because its note resembles the sound produced in driving a stake into the ground.

stāke'head (-hed), *n.* in ropemaking, a horizontal bar supported by posts, stationed at intervals in the length of the ropewalk, to support the yarns while spinning. The upper edge of the bar has pegs to separate the yarns.

stāke'hōld''ẽr, *n.* one who holds stakes when a wager is made by others and pays it to the winner.

Stȧ·khä'nō·vism, *n.* [after Aleksei G. *Stakhanov*, Soviet miner who initiated it in 1935.] in the Soviet Union, an efficiency system in which workers voluntarily increase their production by improvement of techniques, etc., and are rewarded with bonuses and privileges.

Stȧ·khä'nō·vīte, *n.* in the Soviet Union, a worker officially declared to have excelled in Stakhanovism.

Stȧ·khä'nō·vīte, *a.* of Stakhanovism or Stakhanovites.

stak·tom'e·tẽr, *n.* same as *stactometer.*

stăl, *v.* obsolete past tense of *steal.*

stȧ·laç'tiç, stȧ·laç'tiç·ăl, *a.* stalactitic.

stȧ·laç'ti·fọrm, *a.* having the form or position of a stalactite; like a stalactite; stalactitic.

stȧ·laç'tīte, *n.* [Mod. L. *stalactites*, from Gr. *stalaktos*, trickling or dropping, from *stalassein* or *stalazein*, to let fall drop by drop.]

1. a pendent cone or cylinder of carbonate of lime, attached, like an icicle, to the roof or side of a cavern and formed by the evaporation of dripping water from the rock above holding carbonate of lime in solution.

2. anything of similar form or position.

STALACTITES AND STALAGMITES

stal·aç·tī'tēs, *n.* a stalactite. [Rare.]

stal·aç·tit'iç, stal·aç·tit'iç·ăl, *a.* 1. stalactiform.

2. of or covered with stalactites.

stal·aç·tit'i·fọrm, *a.* same as *stalactiform.*

stä'läg (shtä'läk, *or Eng.* stal'ag), *n.* [G. contr. from *stammlager*; *stamm*, a base, lit. stem, and *lager*, a camp.] a German prisoner-of-war camp for captured privates and noncommissioned officers.

stȧ·lag'mīte, *n.* [Mod. L. *stalagmites*, from Gr. *stalagmos*, dropping, from *stalazein*, to drop or drip.] a cone-shaped deposit of carbonate of lime extending vertically from the floor of a cave, often forming beneath, and becoming continuous with, a stalactite above: see *stalactite.*

stȧ·lag'mīte mär'ble, onyx marble: so called because it is often a stalagmitic deposit.

stal·ag·mit'iç, stal·ag·mit'iç·ăl, *a.* 1. having the form or position of a stalagmite.

2. of or covered with stalagmites.

stal·ag·mit'iç·ăl·ly, *adv.* in the form or manner of a stalagmite.

stal·ag·mom'e·tẽr, *n.* same as *stactometer.*

stal'dẽr, *n.* a wooden frame to set casks on. [Brit. Dial.]

stāle, *n.* [AS. *stæl*, *stel*; D. *steel*; G. *stiel*, a stalk, stem, handle.]

1. a stalk; a stem; a shaft. [Obs.]

2. a rung of a ladder. [Obs.]

3. the handle of anything; a long handle; as, the *stale* of a rake. [Obs.]

stāle, *a.* [ME. *stel*, stale; perh. akin to Sw. *stalla*, to put into a stall, to stall feed; Dan. *stalde*, to stall, from Sw. *stall*, a stable.]

1. having lost freshness; worsened by having been kept too long; specifically, (a) flat; vapid; tasteless; as, *stale* beer; (b) hard and dry: said of bread, etc.; (c) low in oxygen content; stagnant; as, *stale* water or air; (d) in an early stage of decay, as meat or eggs.

2. having lost originality or newness; lacking in interest through familiarity or overuse; hackneyed; trite; as, a *stale* joke, *stale* gossip.

3. past the peak of mental or physical vigor and keenness; out of condition as a result of either too much or too little activity.

4. in law, having lost legal force or effect through lack of use or action, as a claim or lien.

5. having lost the vigor or charm of youth. [Obs.]

stāle, *v.t.* and *v.i.*; staled, *pt.*, *pp.*; staling, *ppr.* to make or become stale (in any sense).

stāle, *v.i.* [G. *stallen*, to urinate, from *stall*, stable.] to discharge urine: said of horses and cattle.

stāle, *n.* urine of horses or cattle.

stāle, *n.* [AS. *stalu*, theft, from *stelan*, to steal.]
1. something set or offered as an allurement to draw others to any place or purpose; a decoy; a bait; a trap. [Obs.]
2. a butt for ridicule; a victim. [Obs.]

stāle′ly, *adv.* in a stale manner. [Rare.]

stāle′māte, *n.* 1. in chess, the position of the king when so situated that, though not in check, he cannot move without being placed in check, there being no other available move: it results in a draw.
2. any situation making further action impossible; a deadlock; draw.

stāle′māte, *v.t.*; stalemated, *pt., pp.*; stalemating, *ppr.* 1. to subject to or bring into a stalemate.
2. to bring to a standstill.

stāle′ness, *n.* the state or quality of being stale.

Stä′lin·iṣm, *n.* the political theories and practices of Josef Stalin (1879–1953), premier and marshall of the Soviet Union.

Stä′lin·ist, *n.* one who believes in the political views and practices of Josef Stalin; a follower of Stalinism.

Stä′lin·īte, *n.* same as *Stalinist*.

stalk (stąk), *n.* [probably from Dan. *stilk*; Sw. *stjelk*; Ice. *stilkr*, a stalk.]
1. the stem or main axis of a plant, which supports the leaves, flowers, and fruit; as, a *stalk* of wheat, rye, or oats; the *stalks* of hemp.
2. in botany, any lengthened support on which an organ grows, as the petiole of a leaf or the peduncle of a flower.
3. anything resembling the stalk or stem of a plant; as, the *stalk* of a spoon; the *stalk* of a tobacco pipe, etc.
4. in architecture, an ornament in the Corinthian capital that resembles the stalk of a plant and is sometimes fluted: the volutes and helixes spring from it.
5. in zoology, any supporting part, stem, or peduncle, as of certain invertebrate animals.
6. in founding, a spiked rod or bar forming the center of a core.
7. one of the upright pieces of a ladder in which the rungs or steps are placed. [Obs.]

stąlk, *v.i.*; stalked, *pt., pp.*; stalking, *ppr.* [AS. *stælcan*, to go softly or warily; Dan. *stalke*, to stalk, from stem of *steal*, meaning, lit., to walk in a stealthy manner.]
1. to walk softly and warily; to walk in a sly or stealthy manner. [Obs.]
2. to walk screened from view; to pursue game, an enemy, etc. by approaching softly and warily, as from cover.
3. to walk in a stiff, haughty manner; as, he *stalked* out of the room in anger: sometimes used figuratively; as, plague *stalks* across the land.

stąlk, *v.t.* 1. to pursue stealthily and behind cover; to watch and follow warily for the purpose of killing, as game.
2. to stalk through; as, terror *stalked* the streets.

stąlk, *n.* 1. the act of hunting game, an enemy, etc. stealthily and under cover.
2. a slow, stiff, haughty step or walk.
With martial *stalk*. —Shak.

stąlk bōr′ēr, in zoology, the larva of a moth, *Gortyna nitela*, that bores into the stalks of garden plants, particularly tomatoes, asters, strawberries, raspberries, etc.

stalked (stąkt), *a.* having a stalk or stalks.

stąlk′ēr, *n.* 1. one who stalks.
2. a kind of fish net. [Obs.]

stąlk′-eȳed, *a.* having the eyes elevated on peduncles, as some of the crustaceans: the opposite of *sessile-eyed*.

stąlk′ing họrse, 1. a horse, or a figure of a horse, used as cover by a hunter stalking game.
2. anything used to disguise or conceal intentions, schemes, or activities; a blind; a pretext.
3. in politics, a candidate whose candidacy is a mere maneuver to conceal that of someone more important or to divide and thus defeat the opposition.

stąlk′less, *a.* having no stalk.

stąlk′let, *n.* a little stalk; in botany, a subordinate stalk or stem.

stąlk′y, *a.*; *comp.* stalkier; *superl.* stalkiest, 1. like a stalk; long and slender.
2. having or consisting of stalks.

stąll, *n.* [ME. *stal*; AS. *steall*, *stall*, place, station, stall, stable; akin to Ice. *stallr*, a shelf or other support, a stall; D. *stal*; G. *stall*; Sw. *stall*; Dan. *stald*, a stall, a stable, etc.; O.H.G. *stallan*; G. *stellen*, to place.]
1. the stand or place where an animal is kept and fed; the division of a stable, or the compartment for one animal; as, the stable contains eight or ten *stalls*.
2. a stable; a place for horses or cattle.
3. a small compartment or booth; specifically, (a) any of a number of booths, tables, or counters, as at a market or fair, at which goods are sold; (b) a pew or enclosed seat in the main part of a church or in the choir; (c) [Brit.] a seat near the stage in a theater, especially one in the front part of the orchestra, separated from adjacent seats by railings or the like.

STALLS IN A CHURCH

4. a protective sheath, as of rubber, for a finger or thumb; a cot.
5. any of various sheaths or marked-off or enclosed areas.
6. in aeronautics, the condition that is the result of stalling.
7. a seat of dignity. [Obs.]
8. in mining, an opening made between pillars, in the direction that the work is progressing.
9. a room in which ores are roasted.

stąll, *v.t.*; stalled, *pt., pp.*; stalling, *ppr.* 1. to put into a stall or stable, or to keep in a stall, sometimes so as to fatten.
2. to cause to stick fast, as in mud.
3. to check or stop the motion or progress of; to bring to a standstill, especially unintentionally.
4. to cause (an airplane, motor, etc.) to stall.
5. to install; to place in an office with the customary formalities. [Obs.]
6. to forestall. [Obs.]
7. to satiate; to fatten. [Brit. Dial.]
8. to arrange for payment of (a debt) by installments. [Obs.]

stąll, *v.i.* 1. to be kept in, or occupy, a stall.
2. to kennel, as dogs.
3. to stick fast, as in mud.
4. to be brought to a standstill, especially unintentionally.
5. to stop operating because of overloading or insufficient fuel supply: said of a motor or engine.
6. in aeronautics, to lose the amount of forward speed necessary to maintain altitude and be controlled, as, the plane *stalls* at forty-three miles per hour.

stąll, *v.i.* [from *stall*, a decoy, var. of obs. *stale*, a person who lures or snares.] to act or speak evasively or hesitantly so as to deceive or delay; as, stop *stalling* and tell us the rest. [Colloq.]

stąll, *v.t.* to put off or delay by stalling (usually with *off*); as, he could no longer *stall off* his creditors. [Colloq.]

stąll, *n.* 1. any action, device, story, etc. used to deceive or delay; evasive trick. [Colloq.]
2. a pickpocket's assistant who walks before or behind the pickpocket and the intended victim, so as to conceal the crime, make off with the booty, etc. [Obs.]

stąll′āġe, *n.* 1. the right of erecting a stall or stalls at fairs; also, rent paid for such a stall. [Brit.]
2. manure. [Obs.]

stąl·lā′tion, *n.* installation. [Obs.]

stąlled, *a.* 1. kept in a stall; fattened.
2. stopped and unable to move, as an automobile.

stąll′-fed, *a.* kept and fed in a stall to fatten.

stąll′-feed, *v.t.*; stall-fed, *pt., pp*; stall-feeding, *ppr.* to feed and fatten in a stall or stable; also, to feed with dry fodder; as, to *stall-feed* an ox.

stąll′ing, *n.* stabling.

stal′liŏn (-yun), *n.* [OE. *stalon*, *stallant*; OFr. *estalon*; Fr. *étalon*, a stallion; It. *stallone*, from O.H.G. *stal*; lit., the horse kept in the stall.] a male horse not castrated, especially one kept for breeding purposes.

stąll′măn, *n.*; *pl.* **stąll′men,** a man who keeps a stall at a market or fair.

stąll rēad′ēr, one who reads books at the stall where they are sold.

stąl′wărt, *a.* [ME. *stalworthe*; AS. *stælwyrthe*, short for AS. *statholwyrthe*, firm; from *stathol*, foundation, and *wyrthe*, worth.]
1. strong; stout; big and strong in frame; sturdy.
2. brave; bold; redoubted; daring.
3. resolute; firm; unyielding.

stąl′wărt, *n.* 1. a stalwart person.
2. a person who supports any given cause, especially that of a political party, with firm partisanship; specifically, [S–] in 1880, one of a faction in the Republican party who wished to bring about the nomination of Grant for a third term.

stąl′wărt·ly, *adv.* in a stalwart manner; stoutly; bravely.

stąl′wărt·ness, *n.* the quality or state of being stalwart.

stąl′wŏrth, *a.* stalwart. [Archaic.]

stąl′wŏrth·ness, *n.* stalwartness. [Archaic.]

stā′men, *n.*; *pl.* **stā′menṣ** *rare* **stam′i·nȧ,** [L., a warp in an upright loom, a thread; lit., that which stands up, from *stare*, to stand.]
1. a warp thread, especially in the ancient upright loom at which the weaver stood upright instead of sitting. [Obs.]
2. in botany, the male reprodutive organ in flowers, formed principally of cellular tissue: it is situated immediately within the petals, and is composed, in most cases, of two parts, the filament and the anther, which is filled with pollen; the microsporophyll of a seedplant.

a a, STAMENS

stā′mened, *a.* furnished with stamens.

stā′min, *n.* a variety of coarse woolen cloth. [Obs.]

stam′i·nȧ, *n.* alternative pl. of *stamen*.

stam′i·nȧ, *n.* [L., plural of *stamen*.]
1. resistance to fatigue, illness, hardship, etc.; endurance; staying power.
2. the fixed, firm part of a body, which supports it or gives it strength and solidity. [Obs.]

stam′i·năl, *a.* 1. of, showing, or having to do with stamina.
2. in botany, of or relating to a stamen or stamens.

stam′i·nāte, *a.* 1. furnished with stamens but lacking pistils; producing stamens, as male flowers.
2. having or bearing a stamen or stamens.

stam′i·nāte, *v.t.* to endue with stamina; to invigorate. [Rare.]

stȧ·min′ē·ăl, *a.* in botany, staminal.

stȧ·min′ē·ous, *a.* consisting of, producing, or pertaining to stamens.

stam′i·ni-, [from L. *stamen*, *staminis*.] a combining form meaning *stamen*, as in *staminiferous*: also *stamin-*.

stam·i·nif′ēr·ous, *a.* [L. *stamen* (*-inis*), a thread, stamen, and *ferre*, to bear.] having or bearing a stamen or stamens.

stam·i·niġ′ēr·ous, *a.* same as *staminiferous*.

stam′i·nōde, *n.* same as *staminodium*.

stam·i·nō′di·um, *n.*; *pl.* **stam·i·nō′di·ȧ,** [LL., from L. *stamen* (*-inis*), a thread, stamen, and Gr. *eidos*, form.] a sterile stamen or an organ resembling one.

stam′i·nō·dy, *n.* the changing of various parts of a flower, as bracts, pistils, etc., into stamens.

stam′mel, *n.* [OFr. *estamel*, from *estame*, woolen thread, from L. *stamen*, a warp, thread.]
1. a coarse, red cloth of wool, or wool mixed with linen or cotton, used for undergarments.
2. the red color of this cloth.

stam′mel, *a.* made of or pertaining to stammel; also, of a red color like stammel. [Obs.]

stam′mel, *n.* a large, clumsy horse. [Obs.]

stam′mẽr, *v.t.* and *v.i.*; stammered, *pt.*, *pp.*; stammering, *ppr.* [a freq. form; ME. *stameren, stamber*, to stammer; AS. *stamor, stamer*; L.G. *stammern*; D. *stameren, stamelen*; G. *stammeln*; Ice. *stamma*, to stammer, from *stamr, stammr*, stammering, speaking with difficulty.] to speak or say with involuntary pauses and rapid repetitions of syllables and sounds, as from excitement, confusion, embarrassment, etc.

stam′mẽr, *n.* act, instance, or habit of stammering.

stam′mẽr·ẽr, *n.* one who stammers.

stam′mẽr·ing, *a.* that stammers.

stam′mẽr·ing, *n.* the act of one who stammers.

stam′mẽr·ing·ly, *adv.* in a stammering manner.

stam′nos, *n.* [Gr.] a short-necked earthenware jar used by the Greeks to hold oil, wine, etc.

stamp, *v.t.* [Early ME. *stampen*; akin to Ice. *stampa*; Dan. *stampe*; Sw. *stampa*; D. *stampen*; G. *stampfen*, to stamp with the feet; nasalized forms from *stap*, stem of D. *stappen*, Ice. *stappa*, G. *stapfen*, to step, to set down the feet, to stamp.]

1. to bring (the foot) down forcibly upon something.

2. (a) to strike down on forcibly with the foot; as, he *stamped* the floor in anger; (b) to beat, press, force, crush, drive, etc. with or as with a forcible downward thrust or thrusts of the foot; as, to *stamp* out a cigarette; to *stamp* out a revolt.

3. to imprint or cut out (a mark, form, device, etc.) by bringing a form forcibly against a material; as, he *stamped* his initials into the leather; these ashtrays are *stamped* from metal sheets.

4. to impress, mark, or imprint with some design, device, characters, etc., as to decorate or show authenticity, ownership, sanction, or the like.

5. to impress or mark distinctly, deeply, or indelibly; as, a face *stamped* with greed; the incident was *stamped* in her memory.

6. to put an official seal or a stamp on (a document, letter, etc.).

7. to characterize or reveal distinctly, as if by imprinting.

8. to pulverize (ore, etc.) by grinding or crushing. [Dial.]

to stamp out; to extinguish, as fire, by stamping on with the foot; hence, to eradicate; to exterminate; to suppress; as, *to stamp out* a social evil.

stamp, *v.i.* 1. to strike the foot forcibly downward, as in showing anger or removing mud from the shoes.

But starts, exclaims, and *stamps*, and raves, and dies. —Dennis.

2. to walk with loud, heavy steps, as in anger, etc.

stamp, *n.* 1. the act of stamping; as, a *stamp* of the foot.

2. an instrument for making impressions or marks on other bodies; an engraved block by which a mark may be delivered by pressure.

3. a mark or figure impressed or imprinted; an impression.

4. a distinguishing mark, sign, or impression.

5. a character or reputation, good or bad, attached to anything.

A peculiar *stamp* of impiety. —South.

6. kind; class; type; character.

7. that which is stamped or marked; a medal. [Obs.]

8. a picture cut in wood or metal, or made by impression; an engraving; a plate. [Obs.]

9. a mark, seal, impression, etc. used to show officially that a tax has been paid, authority given, service performed, etc.

10. (a) a small piece of paper, imprinted on the face with a distinctive design or picture, and usually gummed on the back, issued by a government for a specified price and required to be affixed to a letter, parcel, document, commodity subject to duty, etc., as evidence that the prescribed fee, as for carrying mail, has been paid; (b) any more or less similar piece of paper, issued by an organization, business firm, etc.; as, trading *stamps*.

11. authority or currency, as that given by a stamp

12. [*pl.*] money, especially paper money. [Slang.]

13. in the manufacture of leather, a machine for softening hides by pounding them in a vat.

14. in metallurgy, a kind of pestle raised by water or steam power, for beating ores to powder; also, anything like a pestle used for pounding or beating.

Stamp Act; an act passed by the British Parliament in 1765, imposing a duty on all paper, parchment, etc. used in the American colonies, and declaring all writings on unstamped materials to be null and void: it aroused so much opposition that it was repealed in March, 1766.

stamp bat′tẽr·y, a series of stamps in a machine for comminuting ores.

stamp çŏl·leçt′ŏr, 1. a philatelist.

2. a collector or receiver of stamp duties.

stamp çop′pẽr, in mining, copper contained in rock, which has been, or must be, stamped and washed preparatory to being smelted.

stamp dū′ty, a duty or tax imposed on the paper, parchment, etc. used for legal instruments, the evidence of the payment of which is a stamp.

stam·pēde′, *n.* [Am. Sp. *estampida*, a crash, from Sp. *estampar*, to stamp.]

1. a sudden, headlong running away of a group of frightened animals, especially horses or cattle.

2. a sudden, confused rush or flight of a large number of persons.

3. any sudden, impulsive, spontaneous mass movement; as, there developed a *stampede* to support the new candidate.

stam·pēde′, *v.i.*; stampeded, *pt.*, *pp.*; stampeding, *ppr.* to move, or take part, in a stampede.

stam·pēde′, *v.t.* to cause to stampede; to cause to take flight in panic.

stamp′ẽr, *n.* a person or thing that stamps; specifically, (a) a person who cancels stamps, etc. in a post office; (b) a person who stamps (something specified), as in a factory; as, a metal *stamper*; (c) any of various machines or tools for stamping, as for pulverizing stone or cleaning textiles in a rotating vessel.

stamp ham′mẽr, a direct-acting hammer where the hammer block is lifted vertically, either by cams or friction rollers, or, usually, by steam or water pressure acting on a piston in a closed cylinder.

stamp′head (-hed), *n.* the heavy metal block forming the head or lower end of a bar that is lifted and let fall vertically, as in a stamp mill.

stamp′ing ground, a place much frequented by certain specified persons or animals; a habitual resort. [Colloq.]

stamp′ing mill, a stamp mill.

stamp mill, a mill or machine consisting of pestles, moved by water or steam power, for breaking or crushing ore.

stamp nōte, a list of goods to be shipped submitted by the shipper to the customhouse officer, stamped by him as correct, and sent with the goods to the ship. [Brit.]

stamp of′fice, an office where stamps are issued and stamp duties collected

stamp rock, ore that must be stamped or crushed before going to the smelting furnace.

stance, *n.* [OFr. *estance*, a standing, a position.] manner of standing; posture, especially with reference to the position of the feet, as in certain sports.

stȧnch, *v.t.*; stanched (stȧncht), *pt.*, *pp.*; stanching, *ppr.* [OFr. *estancher*; Fr. *étancher*, to stop from running, to stanch, from LL. *stancare*, for L. *stagnare*, to make or be stagnant.]

1. to stop or check the flow of (blood or other body fluid); as, cold applications to the neck will often *stanch* nose-bleed.

2. to stop or check the flow of blood from (a cut or wound).

3. to quench or stop, as thirst; to allay, appease, or quell. [Archaic or Dial.]

Also written *staunch*.

stȧnch, *v.i.* to stop flowing, as blood; to cease to flow: also written *staunch*.

stȧnch, *n.* 1. anything that stanches. [Obs.]

2. a dam or weir for accumulating a body of water to flood a shallow place so as to float a vessel over it.

Also written *staunch*.

stȧnch, *a.* [OFr. *estanche*, f. of *estanc*; akin to *v.*]

1. sound; strong and watertight; seaworthy; as, a *stanch* ship.

2. firm in principle; steady; constant and zealous; loyal; as, a *stanch* churchman, a *stanch* friend or adherent.

3. strong; firm; substantial; solidly made.

4. in hunting, pursuing without fault or wavering, as a hound.

Also written *staunch*.

stan′chel, *n.* staniel. [Scot.]

stan′chel, *n.* stanchion. [Scot.]

stȧnch′ẽr, *n.* one who or that which stanches.

stan′çhiŏn (-shun), *n.* [OFr. *estanson, estancon*, from *estance*, that which supports, from LL. *stantia*, from L. *stare*, to stand.]

1. an upright prop or support; a piece of timber in the form of a stake or post, used for a support.

2. in shipbuilding, any of various pieces of wood or iron of different forms used to support the deck, the quarter rails, the nettings, awnings, etc.

3. one of a pair of linked, upright bars that fit behind an animal's head to confine it in a stall.

stan′çhiŏn, *v.t.* 1. to provide or support with stanchions.

2. to confine (cattle, etc.) with stanchions.

stan′çhiŏn gun, a pivot gun, especially a gun mounted in a boat, used in hunting ducks.

stȧnch′less, *a.* that cannot be stanched or stopped.

stȧnch′ly, *adv.* in a stanch manner; stoutly; firmly.

stȧnch′ness, *n.* the quality or condition of being stanch.

stand, *v.i.*; stood, *pt.*, *pp.*; standing, *ppr.* [ME. *standen*; AS. *standan*; akin to Ice. *standa*, O.H.G. *standan, stantan*, Goth. *standan*, D. *staan*, G. *stehen*; from a root common to the Indo-European languages, being seen also in L. *stare*, Gr. (*hi*)*stanai*, Sans. *sthâ*.]

1. to be or remain in an upright position, supported on the feet (or foot): distinguished from *kneel, crouch, lie, sit*, etc.: said of human beings and some animals.

And all the congregation of Israel *stood*. —1 Kings viii. 14.

2. to be or remain in an upright position, supported on its base, bottom, pedestal, etc.: said of physical objects.

3. to grow upright or erect: said of plants.

4. to take a standing position.

5. (a) to take, move into, or be in a (specified) standing position; as, he *stood* aloof, *stand* back!; (b) to take or maintain a (specified) position, attitude, or course, as of support, antagonism, responsibility, sponsorship, etc.; as, I *stand* opposed to this act.

6. to be as regards position or situation; to occupy a site or situation; to be situated or located; as, London *stands* on the Thames.

7. to cease from progress; not to proceed; to come to a state of rest; to cease moving in any direction; to stop action or movement; to stop; to pause; to halt; also, to be stationary.

8. to maintain one's ground; to remain resolute or firm; to be pertinacious, unyielding, or obstinate; to insist; as, to *stand* on ceremonies.

Stand not upon the order of your going,
But go at once. —Shak.

9. to make resistance, as to hostile action; to take up a fixed position, as of opposition, resistance, or defense.

10. to be placed with regard to relative position, rank, or order; as, among gems, the diamond *stands* first.

11. to be in any particular condition, relation, or circumstance; as, they *stood* in awe.

12. to continue unchanged or valid; not to fail or become void; as, the government still *stands*.

13. to hold a course at sea; as, to *stand* from the shore; to *stand* for the harbor.

14. to be consistent; to agree; as, it *stands* with his station in life.

15. to become a candidate for an office or the like; to run; as, he *stood* for Parliament at election. [Chiefly Brit.]

How many *stand* for consulships?—Shak.

16. to have a (specified) height when standing.

He *stood* four feet six inches and three-quarters in his socks. —Dickens.

17. to gather and remain; to stagnate; not to flow.

Or the black water of Pomptina *stands*. —Dryden.

18. to point: said of a dog.

19. to hesitate, as at doing something; to scruple.

20. to show the (specified) relative position of those involved: said of a score, account, reckoning, etc.

to stand against; to oppose with firmness; as, *to stand against* monopolization.

to stand by; (a) to be near and ready to act if or when needed; (b) to aid or support; (c) to make good (a promise, etc.); to keep to; to maintain, as a policy; (d) to be near or present, especially in a passive manner or as a mere onlooker; (e) in radio, to remain tuned in, as for continuance of a program, or to remain ready to transmit without actually doing so.

to stand down; in law, to leave the witness stand, as after testifying.

to stand fast; to be fixed; to be unshaken or immovable.

to stand for; (a) to be a symbol for or sign of; to represent; to mean; (b) [Colloq.] to tolerate or endure.

to stand from under; to avoid anything about to fall. [Slang.]

to stand high; (a) to be in good repute; to have an exalted position, as in society or public office; (b) in printing, to be a little higher than standard; said of type, engravings, etc.

to stand in; (a) to cost; as, the suit *stands* me *in* forty dollars; (b) to be on good terms; to be in a position of favor and influence, as *with* an important person. [Colloq.]

to stand in one's own light; to assume an attitude or to pursue a course of action which is injurious to oneself or one's reputation.

to stand in the gap; see under *gap*.

to stand off; (a) to fail or refuse to agree or comply; (b) in nautical usage, to take or hold a course away from shore.

to stand on; (a) to be based or founded upon; to depend on; (b) to insist upon; to demand due observance of (ceremony, one's dignity or rights, etc.); (c) in nautical usage, to hold the same course or tack.

to stand out; (a) to project; (b) to be prominent, notable, or outstanding; (c) to hold out; to be firm in maintaining a position; as, one juror *stood out* for acquittal; (d) to show up clearly; to be distinct in appearance; (e) in nautical usage, to take or hold a course away from shore.

to stand over; to postpone or be postponed; to hold over.

to stand to; (a) to keep working at without pause; (b) to stand by; to be ready; (c) to abide by; to adhere to, as to a contract, promise, etc.; (d) to support; to refuse to yield; to maintain one's ground.

to stand together; (a) to be consistent; to agree; (b) to make common cause; not to desert one another.

to stand to it; (a) to stand one's ground; to refuse to give up; to be unflinching; (b) to persist; to maintain unflinchingly, as a principle or belief.

to stand to reason; to be consistent with reason; to follow as a legitimate conclusion; as, it *stands to reason* that the whole is equal to the sum of its parts.

to stand under; to undergo; to sustain; as, *to stand under* heavy obligations.

to stand up; (a) to rise from sitting; to be on the feet; (b) to prove valid, satisfactory, durable, etc.; (c) [Slang.] to fail to keep an engagement with.

to stand up for; to rise in defense of; to support; to defend; as, *to stand up* for equal rights.

to stand up to; to face boldly or bravely, as a danger or an obligation; to confront fearlessly.

to stand up with; (a) to take as a partner in dancing; (b) to act in the capacity of a groomsman or bridesmaid; as, *to stand up with* the groom at a marriage ceremony. [Colloq.]

Syn.—stop, rest, stagnate, remain, be, exist, insist, depend, await, consist, hold, continue, endure, pause, halt.

stand, *v.t.* 1. to make stand; to set or place upright.

2. to endure; tolerate; bear.

3. to remain uninjured or unaffected by; to withstand; resist.

4. to be subjected to; to undergo; as, they *stood* trial.

5. to bear the cost of (a dinner, etc.), as when treating. [Colloq.]

6. in military usage, to stand in formation at (reveille, retreat, etc.).

to stand a chance (or *show*); to have a chance, as of victory or survival.

to stand fire; to receive the fire of arms from an enemy without giving way.

to stand off; (a) to keep at a distance; (b) to put off, stave off, or evade, as a creditor or assailant.

to stand one's ground; to keep the ground or station one has taken; to maintain one's position, as against attack.

to stand out; to endure to the end; to contend to the last; to refuse to yield.

stand, *n.* [AS. *stand*, from *standan*, to stand.]

1. a standing (in various senses); especially, a stopping; a halt or stop; specifically, (a) a stopping to counterattack, resist, etc., as in a retreat; (b) a halt made by a touring theatrical company to give a performance, or the place stopped at.

2. the place where a person stands or is supposed to stand; a position; station; as, he took his *stand* at the rear.

3. a view, opinion, or position, as on an issue; as, I have made my *stand* clear.

4. a structure for a person or persons to stand or sit on; specifically, (a) a raised platform, as for a band or for spectators along the line of march of a parade; as, a reviewing *stand*; (b) a set of steplike tiers of benches, as for the spectators at an athletic field or stadium; (c) the place where a witness testifies in a courtroom.

5. a place of business; specifically, (a) a booth, stall, etc. where goods are sold; (b) a parking space along the side of a street, reserved for taxicabs, etc.; (c) a business site or location.

6. a rack, small table, etc. for holding certain things; as, a music *stand*.

7. a standing growth of trees or plants.

8. a group, set, etc. [Obs. or Dial.]

9. rank; post; station; standing. [Rare.]

10. a young tree reserved for timber when the other trees are cut.

11. in commerce, a unit of weight used in weighing pitch, from two hundred and fifty to three hundred pounds.

stand of arms; a set of arms for one soldier, consisting of a rifle, bayonet, cartridge box, and belt; also, the rifle and bayonet alone. [Rare.]

stand of colors; in military usage, a set of flags, as of a regiment, battalion, or company. [Rare.]

to be at a stand; to stop on account of some doubt or difficulty; to be perplexed.

to make a stand; (a) to take a position for defense or resistance; (b) to come to a stop; (c) to support a definite position, opinion, etc.

to take the stand; to sit (or stand) in the designated place in a courtroom and give testimony.

stand'ăġe, *n.* 1. in mining, a place sunk in the bottom of a shaft where water is allowed to accumulate to be pumped out later. [Brit.]

2. a stall. [Obs.]

stand'ărd, *n.* [ME.; OFr. *estandart, estendart*; prob. from Gmc. (hyp.) *standan*, to stand, and *ort*, a place; hence, a standing place.]

1. any figure or object, especially a flag or banner, used as an emblem or symbol of a people, military unit, etc.; specifically, (a) in heraldry, a long, tapering flag used as an ensign, as by a king; (b) in military usage, the colors of a cavalry unit.

2. something established for use as a rule or basis of comparison in measuring or judging capacity, quantity, content, extent, value, quality, etc.; as, *standards* of weight and measure are fixed by the government.

3. the proportion of pure gold or silver and base metal prescribed for use in coinage.

4. the commodity or commodities used as the basis of a given monetary system, as gold (the *gold standard*).

5. anything recognized as correct by common consent, by approved custom, or by those most competent to decide; a model; a type; a pattern; a criterion.

> Traditions shall above all things be inviolably preserved as guides to our national activity and *standards* for the measurement of every national achievement.
> —Grover Cleveland.

6. a level or grade of excellence, attainment, etc., regarded as a goal or measure of adequacy.

7. in horticulture, a standing tree or shrub, especially one not grafted on another stock, nor supported or attached to a wall, trellis, etc.

8. in botany, the upper petal or banner of a butterfly-shaped flower; a vexillum.

9. any upright timber, post, beam, or rigid support; a supporting piece; specifically, (a) one of the supports of a scaffold; (b) an inverted knee placed on the deck of a ship; (c) the bar attaching the moldboard to the beam of a plow; (d) any of the upright supports in various machines; (e) the upright part of a table lamp or of a candelabrum; (f) in a frame building, an upright timber, as in a partition or door frame; a stud.

10. a large drinking cup.

11. the bearer of a standard (sense 1). [Rare.]

12. in education, a grade or class (in an elementary school). [Brit.]

double standard; see under *double*.

gold standard; see under *gold*.

silver standard; see under *silver*.

standard of living; a level of subsistence, as of a nation, social class, or person, with reference to the adequacy of necessities and comforts in daily life.

stand'ărd, *a.* 1. having the quality or qualities of a model, gauge, pattern, or type; serving as a standard; hence, generally recognized as excellent and authoritative.

2. having no special or unusual features; ordinary; regular; typical; as, the *standard* model of an automobile.

3. generally used, and regarded as proper for use, in books, periodicals, lectures, speeches, documents, literary compositions of various sorts, and the conduct of public affairs; of a level of linguistic usage that excludes locutions, constructions, pronunciation, etc. considered too informal, vulgar, provincial, mistaken, or otherwise likely to detract from the dignity or prestige of the user; as, *standard* English.

4. in printing, of ordinary height, width, or face weight: said of type.

5. in horticulture, standing alone, without support of any kind; as, a *standard* tree or rose.

standard candle; a unit of light equal to the light given off by a candle of a specified material, size, and burning rate, as a $^{7}/_{8}$-inch candle of spermaceti burning at the rate of 120 grains per hour.

standard dollar; (a) since January 31, 1934, a United States dollar of 15 $^{5}/_{21}$ grains of gold, 0.900 fine; (b) prior to 1934, a United States dollar of 25.8 grains of gold, 0.900 fine.

standard solution; see *standardized solution* under *solution*.

standard star; see under *star*.

standard time; see under *time*.

stand'ărd-beăr"ēr, *n.* 1. the man assigned to carry the standard, or flag, of a group, especially of a military organization.

2. the leader or chief representative of a movement, political party, etc.

3. a species of African goatsucker, *Macrodipteryx longipennis*, bearing a long graceful pennant on each wing.

stand'ărd·bred', stand'ărd-bred', *a.* bred in accordance with the requirements of an established standard; specifically, designating or of a breed of horses used for harness racing.

stand'ărd-gāuġe', *a.* of, for, or having the standard gauge.

stand'ărd gāuġe, 1. a width of 4 feet, 8 $^{1}/_{2}$ inches between the rails of a railroad track, established as standard.

2. a railroad having such a gauge.

3. a locomotive or car for a standard-gauge railroad.

stand"ărd·i·zā'tion, *n.* the act of standardizing or the state of being standardized.

stand'ărd·īze, *v.t.*; standardized, *pt., pp.*; standardizing, *ppr.* 1. to cause to conform to a given standard; to make standard or uniform; to cause to be without variations or irregularities.

2. to compare with or test by a standard.

stand'ărd·wing, *n.* a bird of paradise, *Semioptera wallacei*, of which the male has two long white plumes on each wing.

stand'-bȳ, *n.*; *pl.* **stand'-bȳs,** something that one can rely or depend upon; something always at hand when required; a trustworthy aid or supporter.

stand·ee', *n.* a person who stands, usually because there are no vacant seats, as at a concert or play. [Colloq.]

stand'el, *n.* a young tree, left standing for timber. [Archaic.]

stand'ēr, *n.* 1. one who or that which stands.

2. a standel. [Obs.]

3. [*pl.*] consistentes.

stand'ẽr-bȳ', *n.* a bystander; a mere spectator.
stand'ẽr·gràss, *n.* the long-purples, *Orchis mascula.* [Brit.]
stand'ẽr·wŏrt, *n.* same as *standergrass.*
stand'fàst, *n.* 1. a stable, reliable person or thing.
2. a firm, fixed position.
stand'gāle, *n.* the staniel, or kestrel.
stand'-in, *n.* 1. a person who serves as a substitute for a motion-picture actor or actress while lights and cameras are being adjusted, etc.
2. any substitute for another.
3. a position of favor or influence, as with an important person.
stand'ing, *a.* 1. erect; in an upright position; not sitting, kneeling, or lying.
2. fixed; not movable.
3. established either by law or custom; continuously existing; not temporary.
4. lasting; permanent; not transitory; as, a *standing* color.
5. stagnant; not flowing; as, *standing* water.
6. relatively stationary, as a portion of an object which has several parts, one or more of them moving; as, the *standing* leaf of a hinge, that attached to the post.
7. not in operation, use, activity, etc., as a machine.
8. composed, as type; set up and not yet distributed.
9. made or done in or from a standing position; as, a *standing* jump.
standing army; see under *army.*
standing order; (a) in military usage, formerly, a general order always in force in a particular command, establishing a standard or uniform procedure: now called *standard operating procedure*; (b) [*pl.*] in parliamentary procedure, the rules for procedure which continue in force through all sessions until changed or repealed.
standing rigging; the heavy ropes and stays that support the masts and spars of a ship.
standing room; room in which to stand, especially where there are no vacant seats, as in a theater.
stand'ing, *n.* 1. the act, state, or position of a person or thing that stands.
2. a place to stand; standing room.
3. status, position, rank, or reputation; as, he has lost his *standing* as an authority.
4. duration or length of service, existence, membership, etc.; as, a record of long *standing.*
stand'ing press, a form of press in which printed sheets of paper are subjected to pressure.
stand'ish, *n.* a receptacle for pens and ink; an inkstand. [Archaic.]
stand'ǫff, *n.* 1. a standing off or being stood off.
2. a counterbalancing or equalizing effect.
3. a tie or draw in a game or contest.
stand"ǫff'ish, *a.* withdrawn; aloof; reserved.
stand oil, linseed oil thickened by heat treatment, as for use in paint.
stand'-out, *n.* a person who steadfastly refuses to concur in the otherwise unanimous opinion, decision, etc. of the group. [Colloq.]
stand'pat, *a.* of or characterized by a tendency to stand pat, or resist change; conservative. [Colloq.]
stand"pat'tẽr, *n.* a person who follows a standpat policy; a conservative. [Colloq.]
stand'pīpe, *n.* 1. a vertical pipe or cylindrical tank into which water is forced by mechanical means, in order to obtain a head of pressure sufficient to convey it to a distance, to lift it to a required height, or to force it into a boiler against the pressure of steam.
2. a portable water pipe supported by a truck and capable of being controlled mechanically: used for fighting fires in tall buildings.
3. a pipe connected with a water main.
stand'point, *n.* [composed on the form of G. *standpunkt.*]
1. a fixed point or station; a position from which things are seen or viewed.
2. figuratively, mental position from which things are viewed and judged; point of view.
stand rest, a kind of stool which supports a person behind while sanding almost in an upright position, as at an easel.
stand'still, *n.* a stop, halt, or cessation; as, to come to a *standstill.*
stand'-up, 1. standing upright or erect.
2. done or taken while standing; as, a *stand-up* drink.
3. high, stiff, and without folds: said of a collar.
stāne, *n., a., v.t.* stone. [Scot. and Brit. Dial.]
stang, *n.* [AS. *stæng, steng*, a pole.] a rod; a pole; a wooden bar. [Scot. and Brit. Dial.]
to ride the stang; to be carried on a pole on men's shoulders: a form of punishment. [Obs.]
stang, *n., v.t.* and *v.i.* [from ME. *stangen*, from ON. *stanga*, to prick, goad.] sting; pain. [Scot. and Brit. Dial.]
stang, *v.* archaic past tense and past participle of *sting.*
stan'hōpe, *n.* [after Fitzroy *Stanhope* (1787–1864), Eng. clergyman for whom the first was built.] a light, open carriage with two or four wheels and, usually, a single seat.
Stan'hōpe lenş, a lens of small diameter with two convex faces of different radii enclosed in a metallic tube.
stan'iel (-yel), *n.* [AS. *stāngella*, a kestrel; *stān*, stone, and *gellan*, yell, scream.] the windhover, or kestrel: also called *stannel, stanchel, standgale,* and *stonegall.*
stañk, *v.* alternative past tense of *stink.*
stañk, *n.* a stagnant pool; a pond; a tank. [Scot. and Brit. Dial.]
stañk, *v.t.* to dam up. [Scot. and Brit. Dial.]
stañk, *a.* exhausted; worn-out; weak. [Obs.]
stañk hen, the moor hen, *Gallinula chloropus.* [Scot.]
stañk'ie, *n.* same as *stank hen.*
stan'nȧ·ry, *a.* [LL. *stannaria*, a tin mine; L. *stannum*, tin.] pertaining to tin or to stannaries. [Brit.]
stannary courts; courts in Devonshire and Cornwall, England, for the administration of justice among those connected with the tin mines.
stan'nȧ·ry, *n.*; *pl.* **stan'nȧ·rieş**, a tin mine or place where tin is smelted. [Brit.]
stan'nāte, *n.* a salt of stannic acid.
stan'nel, *n.* same as *staniel.*
stan'niç, *a.* [L. *stannum*, tin, and *-ic.*] of or containing tin, specifically with a valence of four.
stannic acid; an acid, H_2SnO_3, obtained by adding barium or calcium carbonate, not in excess, to a solution of stannic chloride. It unites with bases forming stannates.
stannic chloride; a volatile liquid, $SnCl_4$, forming crystals with fine molecules of water.
stannic oxide; the common ore of tin, SnO_2. It may be prepared by heating tin in the air: used for polishing glass, etc.
stan·nif'ẽr·ous, *a.* [L. *stannum*, tin, and *ferre*, to bear.] bearing or yielding tin; as, a *stanniferous* formation.
stan'nīte, *n.* [from LL. *stannum*, tin; and *-ite.*]
1. a gray or black mineral with metallic luster, a native sulfide of tin, copper, and iron: also called *tin pyrites.*
2. a salt formed by the reaction of stannous hydroxide (stannous acid) or stannous oxide with alkali hydroxides.
stan'nō·tȳpe, *n.* a tintype. [Rare.]
stan'nous, *a.* of or containing tin, specifically with a valence of two.
stannous chloride; a gray resinous-looking compound, SnCl, volatile at a high temperature, used in solution as a deoxidizing agent.
stan'num, *n.* [L. *stannum, stagnum*, an alloy of silver and lead (in LL., tin).] tin: symbol, Sn (no period).
stan'zȧ, *n.* [It., lit., stopping place, room, from LL. (hyp.) *stantia*, abode.]
1. a group of lines of verse forming one of the divisions of a poem: it is usually recurrent, made up of four or more lines, and characterized by a regular pattern with respect to the number of lines and the arrangement of meter and rhyme.
2. *pl.* **stän'zę** (-tsā), in architecture, an apartment or room.
stan·zā'iç, *a.* of, or in the form of, a stanza or stanzas.
stan'ziç, *a.* stanzaic. [Rare.]
stan'zō, *n.* a stanza. [Obs.]
stā·pē·deç'tō·my, *n.* [LL. *stapes, stapedis*, stirrup, and Gr. *ektomia*, from *ektomē*, an excision; *ek*, out of, from, and *temnein*, to cut.] removal of the stapes by excision.
stȧ·pē'di·ăl, *a.* of or pertaining to the stapes.
stȧ·pē'di·us, *n.*; *pl.* **stȧ·pē'di·ī**, [L.] in anatomy, the muscle attached to the stapes.
Stȧ·pē'li·ȧ, *n.* [named after J. B. van *Stapel* (died 1636), a Dutch botanist and physician.]

STAPELIA
(Stapelia variegata)

1. a genus of cactuslike plants of the milkweed family, embracing more than a hundred species, having a fleshy rotate corolla, containing a double staminal corona of leaves or lobes and large, star-shaped, yellowish or purple flowers with an odor like that of carrion.
2. [s-] a plant of this genus.
stā'pēş, *n.* [LL., a stirrup.] a small, stirrup-shaped bone, the innermost of a chain of three bones in the middle ear of mammals: it is joined to the fenestra ovalis, and corresponds to the columella in *Sauropsida.*
Staph·y·lē'ȧ, *n.* [abridged from Gr. *staphyle dendron*, the bladder nut.] the type genus of the *Staphyleaceæ.*
Staph"y·lē·ā'cē·ae, *n.pl.* a small family of plants, the bladdernut family, native to the warmer and temperate parts of the earth.
staph"y·lē·ā'ceous, *a.* of or pertaining to the *Staphyleaceæ.*
staph'y·line, *a.* [Gr. *staphylē*, bunch of grapes.]
1. in mineralogy, having the form of a bunch of grapes; botryoidal.
2. in anatomy, belonging to the uvula.
staph·y·lin'id, *a.* of or relating to the family *Staphylinidæ.*
staph·y·lin'id, *n.* a rove beetle of the genus *Staphylinus.*
Staph·y·lin'i·dae, *n.pl.* a family of coleopterous insects of which the genus *Staphylinus* is the type.
Staph·y·lī'nus, *n.* [LL., from Gr. *staphylinos*, a kind of insect.] a genus of coleopterous insects, with short wing sheaths, the type of the family *Staphylinidæ*; the rove beetles: they are usually found in decomposing organic matter.

STAPHYLINID
(*Staphylinus olens*)

staph'y·lō-, [from Gr. *staphylē*, bunch of grapes.] a combining form meaning: (a) *uvula*, as in *staphylor*rhaphy; (b) *staphylococcus.* Also, before a vowel, *staphyl-.*
staph"y·lō·coç'ciç, *a.* of or caused by staphylococci.
staph"y·lō·coç'çus, *n.*; *pl.* **staph"y·lō·coç'cī**, any of a group of spherical, Gram-positive bacteria that generally occur in irregular clusters or short chains and are the cause of pus formation in boils, abscesses, etc.
staph"y·loe·dē'mȧ, *n.* swelling of the uvula.
staph·y·lō'mȧ, *n.*; *pl.* **staph·y·lō'mȧ·tȧ**, [LL., from Gr. *staphylōma*, a disease of the eye, from *staphylē*, a bunch of grapes.] an inflammatory condition of the cornea or sclera of the eye marked by bulging or protrusion.
staph·y·lō'mȧ·tous, *a.* of, pertaining to, or affected with staphyloma.
staph'y·lō·plas"tiç, *a.* of or relating to staphyloplasty.
staph'y·lō·plas"ty, *n.* [Gr. *staphylē*, the uvula, and *plassein*, to shape.] in plastic surgery, an operation for repairing defects of the soft palate.
staph'y·lor·rhaph"iç(-raf"),**staph'y·lō·raph"iç**, *a.* of or pertaining to staphylorrhaphy.
staph·y·lor'rhȧ·phy, staph·y·lor'ȧ·phy, *n.* [Gr. *staphylē*, the uvula, and *rhaphē*, a swelling.] in plastic surgery, the operation of uniting a cleft palate.
staph·y·lō'sis, *n.* same as *staphyloma.*
staph'y·lō·tōme", *n.* in surgery, a knife for operating upon the uvula or palate.
staph·y·lot'ō·my, *n.* [Gr. *staphylē*, the uvula, and *tomē*, a cutting, from *temnein*, to cut.] in surgery, removal of the uvula.
stā'ple, *n.* [ME. *stapel*; OFr. *estaple*; M.D. *stapel*, mart, emporium, post, orig. support.]
1. the chief commodity, or one of several important commodities, made, grown, or sold in a particular place, region, country, etc.
2. a chief item, part, material, or element in anything.
3. raw material.

4. any chief item of trade, regularly stocked and in constant demand; as, flour, sugar, and salt are *staples*.

5. (a) the fiber of cotton, wool, flax, etc., with reference to length and fineness; (b) a particular length and degree of fineness of such fiber.

6. a principal market, trading center, etc. [Archaic.]

7. a district, especially one granted to an abbey. [Obs.]

stā′ple, *a.* 1. regularly found on the market or in stock as a result of a constant demand.

2. produced, consumed, or exported regularly and in quantity.

3. most important; leading; principal; as, *staple* industries, *staple* topics for gossip.

4. pertaining to or being a staple or market for commodities; as, a *staple* town. [Obs.]

5. marketable; fit to be sold. [Rare.]

stā′ple, *v.t.*; stapled, *pt., pp.*; stapling, *ppr.* to sort, as wool, cotton, etc., according to the nature of its staple.

stā′ple, *n.* [ME. *stapel*; AS. *stapol*, a post, pillar; akin to G. *stapel*, stake, beam.]

1. a U-shaped piece of metal with sharp-pointed ends, driven into a surface to hold a hook, hasp, wire, etc. against it.

2. a similar piece of thin wire driven through papers and clinched over as a binding.

3. a prop; a foundation; a support. [Obs.]

4. in founding, a short iron nail with a flat disk of thin sheet iron riveted to one end, used to hold a core steady.

5. in mining, a shaft between different levels of a mine. [Brit. Dial.]

stā′ple, *v.t.*; stapled, *pt., pp.*; stapling, *ppr.* to provide with a metal staple; to attach, fasten, or bind by means of a staple.

stā′plẽr, *n.* 1. a person who deals in staple goods.

2. a person who staples (wool, etc.).

stā′plẽr, *n.* a machine used for driving wire staples into a material, especially for the purpose of binding papers, pamphlets, booklets, magazines, etc.

stär, *n.* [ME. *sterre*; AS. *steorra*; akin to Sw. *stjerna*, Ice. *stjarna*, Goth. *stairno*, D. *ster*, O.D. *sterne*, G. *stern*, L. *stella*, Gr. *astēr*; Corn. *steren*; Per. *satarah*.]

TABLE OF STARS

Name	Designation in Constellation	Position R. A.*		Dec.†	
		h	*m*	°	′
Achernar	α Eridani	1	36.0	−57	28
Alcor	80 Ursae Majoris	13	21.9	+55	11
Alcyone	η Tauri	3	44.8	+23	58
Aldebaran	α Tauri	4	33.3	+16	25
Algenib	γ Pegasi	0	10.9	+14	56
Algol	β Persei	3	5.2	+40	48
Alioth	ε Ursae Majoris	12	52.0	+56	13
Altair	α Aquilae	19	48.5	+ 8	45
Antares	α Scorpii	16	26.6	−26	20
Arcturus	α Boötis	14	13.6	+19	25
Bellatrix	γ Orionis	5	22.7	+ 6	19
Betelgeuse	α Orionis	5	52.7	+ 7	24
Canopus	α Argus (Carinae)	6	22.9	−52	40
Capella	α Aurigae	5	13.3	+45	57
Caph	β Cassiopeiae	0	6.7	+58	54
Castor	α Geminorum	7	31.7	+32	0
Cor Caroli	α Canum Venaticorum	12	53.7	+38	35
Deneb	α Cygni	20	39.9	+45	7
Denebola	β Leonis	11	46.7	+14	50
Dubhe	α Ursae Majoris	11	0.9	+62	0
Fomalhaut	α Piscis Australis	22	55.1	−29	52
Markab	α Pegasi	23	2.3	+14	56
Mira	σ Ceti	2	16.8	− 3	12
Mizar	ζ Ursae Majoris	13	22.1	+55	10
Polaris	α Ursae Minoris	1	51.5	+89	3
Pollux	β Geminorum	7	42.5	+28	8
Procyon	α Canis Minoris	7	36.9	+ 5	21
Regulus	α Leonis	10	5.9	+12	12
Rigel	β Orionis	5	12.3	− 8	15
Sirius	α Canis Majoris	6	43.1	−16	39
Spica	α Virginis	13	22.8	−10	55
Vega	α Lyrae	18	35.4	+38	44

* right ascension † declination

1. any of the heavenly bodies seen as small fixed points of light in the night sky.

2. any one of these bodies that is a distant sun: distinguished from *moon, planet, meteor, comet*, etc.

3. a conventionalized flat figure having (usually five or six) symmetrical projecting points, regarded as a representation of a star of the sky.

4. any mark, shape, emblem, or the like resembling such a figure.

5. an asterisk (*).

6. any heavenly body, as a planet, meteor, the moon, etc.

7. (a) in astrology, a planet, zodiacal constellation, etc. regarded as influencing human fate or destiny; (b) [*often pl.*] fate; destiny; fortune.

8. a person who excels or performs brilliantly in a given activity, especially a sport.

9. a prominent actor or actress, especially one playing a leading role in a given production.

10. an ornamental figure having rays like a star, and worn upon the breast to indicate rank or honor.

11. a radiating crack or flaw, as in ice or glass.

12. in pyrotechny, a piece having the appearance of a star when burning at a considerable distance in the air.

13. a spot on the forehead of an animal lighter than the surrounding part.

14. in zoology, a starfish or aster.

15. in heraldry, an estoile.

16. in fortification, a small fort having five or more points, or salient and re-entering angles flanking one another.

binary star; see under *binary*.
circumpolar star; see *circumpolar*.
double star; see under *double*.
falling star; a meteor.
fixed star; see under *fixed*.
multiple star; a group of stars appearing as one star to the eye unaided by the telescope.
nebulous star; a star, the light of which is similar to that emitted by nebulae.
North Star; the northern polestar.
periodic star; see under *periodic*.
standard star; a star having a determined position so that it may be used in astronomical calculations and locations.
to see stars; to experience the sensation of lights brightly flashing before the eyes, as from a blow on the head. [Colloq.]
to thank one's (*lucky*) *stars*; to be thankful for what appears to be good luck.
variable star; a fixed star varying in brightness from time to time. There are four classes: (a) stars or systems appearing to us as a single star, of which the apparent variability arises solely or mainly from the rotation of the system as a whole, or from the revolution of its components around each other; (b) those stars in which the changes of light arise from some cycle of change going on in the star, but which may be due to the action of an external body; (c) stars subject to small and irregular but frequently recurring fluctuations of light; (d) new stars, or novas.

stär, *a.* 1. resembling a star in shape, arrangement, brilliance, etc.

2. marked with a star, or asterisk.

3. of a star of stars.

4. brilliant or outstanding for skill and talent; excelling others; leading; as, a *star* performer.

stär, *v.t.*; starred, *pt., pp.*; starring, *ppr.* 1. to mark or set with stars as a decoration.

2. to mark with one or more stars as a grade of quality.

3. to mark with an asterisk.

4. to present or feature (an actor or actress, etc.) in a leading role.

stär, *v.i.* 1. to perform brilliantly; to excel.

2. to play a leading role, as in a theatrical production.

stär an′i·măl, a radiate or starfish.

stär an′ise, the fruit of *Illicium anisatum* (*verum*), a plant native to China.

stär ap′ple, a tropical evergreen tree, *Chrysophyllum cainito*, with shining leaves, whitish flowers, and applelike fruit showing a starlike figure inside when cut across.

2. the fruit itself.

STAR APPLE (*Chrysophyllum cainito*)

stär′bēam, *n.* a ray of light from a star.

stär′blīnd, *a.* purblind; seeing obscurely.

stär′bōard (*or* -bẽrd), *n.* [AS. *steôrbord*, that is *steerboard*, from *steôran*, to steer, the old rudder being a kind of large oar used on the right side of the ship.] the right-hand side of a ship, boat, airplane, etc. when one faces forward, toward the bow: opposed to *port, larboard*.

stär′bōard, *a.* of or on the starboard; being or lying on the right side; as, the *starboard* shrouds, *starboard* quarter.

stär′bōard, *v.t.* and *v.i.*; starboarded, *pt., pp.*; starboarding, *ppr.* to put to the starboard side; to turn (the helm) to the right.

stär′bōard, *adv.* to or toward the starboard side.

stär bōard′ẽr, a boarder receiving privileges not commonly granted; a favored boarder.

stär′bōw″lines, *n.pl.* in nautical usage, the men on the starboard watch. [Obs.]

stär buz′zărd, a goshawk of America, of the genus *Asturina*, with starlike markings.

stär çap′si·çum, a shrub, *Solanum capsicastrum*, of South America, with red berries.

stär çat′ȧ·logue (-log), in astronomy, a list of stars, with astronomical data.

stärch, *a.* stiff; precise; rigid. [Rare.]

stärch, *n.* [ME. *starche*, from *sterchen*, to stiffen; AS. *stercan*, from *stearc*, rigid, stiff.]

1. a white, tasteless, odorless food substance found in potatoes, cereals, yams, peas, and many other foods: it is a granular solid, chemically a complex carbohydrate, $(C_6H_{10}O_5)_n$.

2. a powdered form of this, used in water solution for stiffening cloth fabrics, etc.

3. [*pl.*] starchy foods.

4. formal, unbending manner or behavior; stiffness.

5. energy; vigor. [Colloq.]

stärch, *v.t.*; starched (stärcht), *pt., pp.*; starching, *ppr.* to stiffen with or as if with starch.

Stär Chăm′bẽr, [ME. *Sterred Chambre*; Anglo-Fr. *chambre d'estoiles*; Anglo-L. *camera stellata*: so called because the roof was ornamented with stars.]

1. formerly, an English court made up of councilors appointed by royal authority, which met in secret session without a jury, used torture to force confessions, and handed down arbitrary judgments that were extremely severe: abolished in 1641.

2. any tribunal, investigating body, etc. similarly unjust, arbitrary, and inquisitorial.

stärched, (stärcht), *a.* 1. stiff; precise; formal.

2. made stiff with starch.

stärch′ed·ness, *n.* stiffness in manners; formality.

stärch′ẽr, *n.* one who starches, or whose occupation is to starch.

stärch gum, same as *dextrin*.

stärch hȳ′ȧ·cinth, a plant, *Muscari racemosum*, bearing a flower with the smell of starch: also called *musk hyacinth* and *grape hyacinth*.

stärch′i·ly, stärch′ly, *adv.* in a starchy manner; so as to be starchy.

stärch′i·ness, stärch′ness, *n.* the quality or condition of being starchy.

stärch stär, a bulblet of the *Characeæ*, used for propagation.

stärch sụg′ăr (shụg′), same as *glucose*.

stärch′wŏrt, *n.* in botany, the cuckoopint.

stärch′y, *a.*; *comp.* starchier; *superl.* starchiest, 1. of, having the nature of, or like starch.

2. containing starch.

3. stiffened with starch.

4. stiff; formal; unbending.

stär′çrȧft, *n.* astrology. [Rare.]

stär′-çrossed (-krost), *a.* hindered or obstructed by the stars; ill-fated.

stär çū′çum·bẽr, a climbing plant, *Sicyos angulatus*, bearing prickly fruit and white flowers.

stär′dŏm, *n.* 1. the status of a star; as, the young actress finally attained *stardom*.

2. stars of the theater, motion pictures, etc., collectively.

stär dust, 1. a patch or cluster of stars too distant to be seen separately with the naked eye.

2. an enchanting, dreamlike quality, tone, or mood. [Colloq.]

stâre, *n.* a bird, the starling. [Archaic and Dial.]

stâre, *v.i.*; stared, *pt., pp.*; staring, *ppr.* [AS. *starian*, to stare, to gaze; akin to D. and L.G. *staren*, G. *starren*, Ice. *stara*.]

1. to look with eyes fixed and wide open; to gaze earnestly, as in admiration, wonder, surprise, stupidity, horror, fright, impudence, or the like; to fix an earnest gaze upon some object.

2. to stand on end; to bristle, as hair, etc.

3. to stand out with undue prominence; to be glaring or conspicuous: said especially of color.

stãre, *v.t.* 1. to stare at; as, he *stared* the stranger up and down.

2. to affect in a given way by staring; as, we *stared* her into confusion.

to stare down; to meet the gaze of (another), causing him to look away by continued staring.

to stare one in the face; (a) to look at one steadily and intently; (b) to be imminent, pressing, or inescapable.

to stare out of countenance; to stare at (another) until he becomes annoyed, embarrassed, etc.

stãre, *n.* the act of one who stares; a fixed look with the eyes wide open.

stãr′ẽr, *n.* one who or that which stares.

stärf, *v.* obsolete past tense of *starve*.

stär finch, *n.* the redstart.

stär′fish, *n.*; *pl.* **stär′fish** or **stär′fish·eṣ,** 1. a small sea animal of the *Echinodermata*, with a hard, spiny outer covering and five or more arms or rays arranged like the points of a star; an asteroid. In the middle of the under surface of the center is situated the mouth, opening into a digestive system which sends prolongations into each ray. Starfishes are found in almost all tropical and European seas, and some species are found as far north as Greenland.

2. the dollarfish, or butterfish. [Dial.]

STARFISHES

stär′flow″ẽr, *n.* 1. any of a group of related plants of the primrose family, with white or pink, five-petaled, star-shaped flowers.

2. any of various other plants with star-shaped flowers, as the star-of-Bethlehem.

stär fōrt, in fortification, a fort having five or more points, or salient and re-entering angles flanking one another.

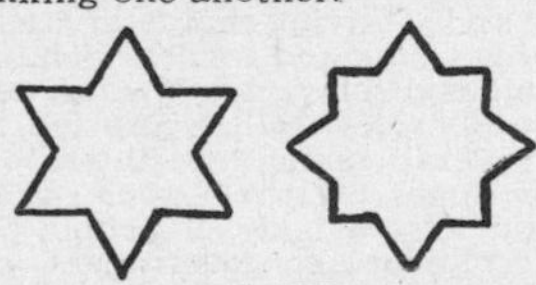

STAR FORTS

hexagonal star fort octagonal star fort

stär′fru̇it, *n.* an aquatic plant of Europe, *Damasonium stellatum*.

stär gāuġe, a gauge with starlike points for measuring the bore of a gun.

stär′gāze, *v.i.*, stargazed; *pt.*, *pp.*; stargazing, *ppr.* [back-formation from *stargazer*.]

1. to gaze at the stars.

2. to indulge in dreamy, absent-minded thoughts.

stär′gāz″ẽr, *n.* 1. one who gazes at the stars; specifically, (a) an astrologer; (b) an astronomer: used humorously.

2. any of several marine fishes having eyes in the top of the head; especially, a fish of the family *Uranoscopidæ*. A common American stargazer is *Astroscopus guttatus*.

stär′gāz″ing, *n.* 1. the act or practice of a person who gazes at the stars.

2. absent-mindedness.

3. dreaminess; impracticality.

stär grȧss, any grasslike plant having its flowers or leaves so disposed as to resemble a star, as *Hypoxis erecta*.

stär hąwk, a goshawk. [Obs.]

stär hȳ′ȧ·cinth, a plant, *Scilla amœna*, of Europe, bearing blue flowers.

stãr′ing, *a.* 1. gazing fixedly and earnestly with widely opened eyes.

2. standing stiffly up; standing on end; bristling.

3. very bright; glaring; dazzling; as, *staring* colors.

stãr′ing·ly, *adv.* in a staring manner.

stär jel′ly, one of various algae of the genus *Nostoc*.

stärk, *a.* [AS. *stearc*, stiff, hard, rough; akin to G. and Sw. *stark*, D. *sterk*, Ice. *sterkr*. The root is that of G. *starr*, stiff.]

1. stiff; rigid, as in death.

Many a nobleman lies *stark* and stiff.—Shak.

2. standing out in sharp outline; as, a tree *stark* in the snow.

3. bleak; desolate; barren; unadorned.

4. stark-naked.

5. sheer; utter; downright; as, *stark* terror.

6. (a) hard, harsh, or severe; (b) strong; powerful. [Archaic.]

stärk, *adv.* 1. in a stark manner; severely; vigorously.

2. wholly; entirely; absolutely; downright; quite; as, *stark* mad, *stark* blind.

stärk, *v.t.* to make stark or rigid. [Archaic.]

stärk′en, *v.t.* to render rigid or inflexible. [Now Dial.]

stärk′ly, *adv.* in a stark manner.

stärk′-nāk′ed, *a.* [altered (by association with *stark*), from ME. *stertnaked*, lit., tail-naked; *stert-*, from AS. *steort*, tail, rump.] absolutely naked.

stärk′ness, *n.* the quality or condition of being stark.

stär′less, *a.* having no visible stars; without stars.

stär′let, *n.* 1. a small star.

2. a small starfish.

3. a young motion-picture actress being prepared for starring roles.

stär′līght (-līt), *n.* the light given by the stars; as, to skate by *starlight*.

stär′līght, *a.* 1. of starlight.

2. lighted by the stars, or by the stars only; as, a *starlight* evening.

stär′līke, *a.* 1. resembling a star in shape; stellated; radiated like a star; as, *starlike* flowers.

2. bright; luminous; as, *starlike* eyes.

stär′ling, *n.* [dim. of *stare*, a starling.]

1. any bird of the genus *Sturnus*, sometimes extended to the whole family *Sturnidæ*, but specifically applied to *Sturnus vulgaris*, the common starling. Starlings have a characteristic iridescent plumage and are native to Europe, but some have been introduced into the United States.

STARLING (*Sturnus vulgaris*)

2. the rock trout of California.

3. an enclosure consisting of piles driven closely together into the bed of a river, and secured by horizontal pieces at the top. The space between the rows of piling, being filled with gravel or stone, forms an effectual protection for the foundation of a pier.

stär′lit, *a.* lighted by stars; as, a *starlit* night.

stär mōld′ing, in architecture, a Norman molding ornamented with rayed or pointed starlike figures.

STAR MOLDING

stär′mŏṅ″ġẽr, *n.* an astrologer: used contemptuously. [Rare.]

stärn, *n.* the starling. [Brit. Dial.]

stärn, *n.* a star. [Scot.]

stär′nel, *n.* a starling; a starn. [Brit. Dial.]

stär′nōṣe, *n.* a star-nosed mole.

stär′-nōṣed mōle, a North American long-tailed mole of the genus *Condylura*, distinguished by bearing at the extremity of its muzzle a structure of fleshy and somewhat cartilaginous rays.

stär′-of-Beth′lē·hem, *n.* any of a number of related plants, especially *Ornithogalum umbellatum*, of the lily family, having white, starlike flowers and long, narrow leaves.

stär of Beth′lē·hem, the bright star which is supposed to have hung low over Bethlehem at the birth of Jesus of Nazareth, guiding the Magi to the manger. Matt. ii. 2, 9, 10.

Stär of Dā′vid, [transl. from Heb. *mogēn dovid*, lit., shield of David.] a six-pointed star formed of two (often interlaced) equilateral triangles: a symbol of Judaism and now of the Republic of Israel: as a mystic symbol in the Middle Ages, called *Solomon's Seal*.

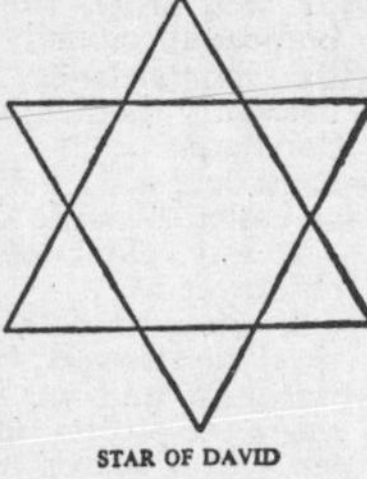

STAR OF DAVID

stär′-of-Jē·ru̇′sȧ·lem, *n.* the goat's-beard, or salsify.

stär′-of-nīght′ (-nīt′), *n.* a tree of the American tropics, *Clusia rosea*, with large bright flowers.

stär′-of-the-ẽarth′, *n.* a European plant of the genus *Plantago*.

star′ost, *n.* [Pol. *starosta*, elder, from *stary*, old.]

1. formerly, in Poland, a nobleman possessed of a castle and domain called a starosty.

2. formerly, in Russia, the head of a mir or commune.

star′os·ty, *n.* [Pol. *starostwo*.] formerly, in Poland, castles and domains conferred on noblemen for life by the crown.

stär′pro͝of, *a.* impervious to the light of the stars.

stär′-rēad, *n.* astronomy; astrology. [Obs.]

stärred, *a.* 1. studded, decorated, or adorned with or as with a star or stars.

2. thought to be influenced or affected by the stars: often in composition; as, an ill-*starred* enterprise.

3. cracked, with many rays proceeding from a central point; as, a *starred* pane of glass, a *starred* mirror.

4. marked with a star, or asterisk.

5. presented as a star, or leading performer.

stär reed, a Peruvian plant, *Aristolochia fragrantissima*, the root of which is used in Peru as a remedy against dysentery, malignant inflammatory fevers, colds, rheumatic pains, etc.

stär′ri·ness, *n.* the quality or state of being starry.

stär röute, a mail route in a not easily accessible, thinly settled region, over which service has been contracted for by the post office department.

stär ru̇′by, a ruby exhibiting asterism.

stär′ry, *a.*; *comp.* starrier; *superl.* starriest, 1. set or marked with stars.

2. shining like stars; bright.

3. star-shaped.

4. lighted by or full of stars.

5. of or coming from the stars.

6. consisting of, or having the nature of, stars.

starry campion; a plant, *Silene stellata*, native to the eastern part of the United States.

starry puffball; the earthstar.

starry ray; a fish, *Raia radiata*, one of the varieties of the European skate.

Stärṣ and Bärṣ, the flag first used by the American Confederacy: it had three horizontal bars—one of white between two of red—and in the upper left corner a blue field marked with a circle of white stars, one for each seceded State.

Stärṣ and Strīpes, the flag of the United States, consisting of a rectangle with seven red, horizontal stripes alternating with six white ones, and, in the upper left corner, a blue field with 48 white stars, one for each State.

stär sap′phīre (saf′īr), a sapphire cut with a convex surface and seeming, by reflected light, to have a star-shaped figure in it.

stär sax′i·frāġe, a saxifrage, *Saxifraga stellaris*, of northern climates, bearing white stellate flowers.

stär shāke, *n.* a defect in timber, consisting in clefts radiating from the pith to the circumference.

stär shell, in military usage, a shell timed to burst in mid-air in a shower of bright particles that momentarily light up the surrounding terrain.

stär′shīne, *n.* the shine or light of a star or stars; starlight.

stär′sho͝ot, *n.* same as *star jelly*.

stär′shot, *n.* same as *star jelly*.

stär slough (sluf), same as *star jelly*.

stär′-spaṅ″gled (-gld), *a.* studded or spangled with stars.

Stär′-Spaṅ″gled Ban′nẽr, 1. the flag of the United States.

2. the national anthem of the United States: the words were written by Francis Scott Key during the bombardment of Fort McHenry (1814) in the War of 1812.

stär′stōne, *n.* same as *star sapphire*.

stär sys′tem, a group of stars constituting a system of their own.

stärt, *v.i.*; started, *pt.*, *pp.*; starting, *ppr.* [ME. *sterten* (orig. Kentish and Northern), from AS. *styrtan* and cognate ON. *sterta*; akin to G. *stürzen*, to overthrow.]

1. to move suddenly, usually involuntarily, as from rest, a given position, etc.; to jump, leap, jerk, etc.; as, the backfire made her *start*; the cat *started* back.

2. to be displaced; to become loose, warped, etc.

3. to stick out or seem to stick out, as the eyes in fear, surprise, etc.

4. (a) to begin to do something or go somewhere; to go into action or motion; (b) to make or have a beginning; to commence.

5. to be among the beginning entrants in a race; to be a starter; as, since two of the horses were scratched, only six *started*.

6. to spring into being, activity, view, or the like.

to start after; to set out in pursuit of; to follow.

to start in; to begin a task, activity, etc.

to start out; (a) to start a journey; (b) to make a start on some course of action or procedure, as a career.

to start up; (a) to rise up or stand suddenly, as in fright; (b) to come into being suddenly; to spring up.

stärt, *v.t.* 1. to cause to jump or move suddenly; to rouse; to flush; as, we *started* three birds at one time.

2. to displace, loosen, warp, etc.; as, the collision *started* a seam.

3. to cause or enable to begin; to set into motion or action.

4. to introduce (a subject, topic, or discussion).

5. to open and make the contents flow from (a receptacle); to tap.

6. to give the starting signal for (a race) or to (the contestants in a race).

7. to cause to be an entrant in a race, etc.

8. to startle; to cause to start, or move involuntarily. [Archaic or Dial.]

to start up; to cause (a motor, etc.) to begin running.

stärt, *n.* 1. a sudden, brief shock or fright; a startled reaction.

2. a sudden, startled movement; a jump, leap, jerk, etc.

3. [*pl.*] sudden, usually brief bursts of activity: usually in the phrase *by fits and starts*.

4. (a) a part that is loosened, warped, etc.; (b) a break or gap resulting from this.

5. a starting, or beginning; a getting into action or motion; commencement.

6. a place where, or a time when, a beginning is made, as in a race; starting point.

7. a factor or position giving an advantage, as in a race or contest; lead; edge.

8. a signal to begin, as in a race.

9. an opportunity of beginning or entering upon a career, etc.

10. an outburst or fit, as of emotion, or a sally, as of wit. [Archaic.]

a flying start; in racing, a start in which the contestants get off at full speed before crossing the official starting line.

to get or *have the start*; to gain the advantage; to get ahead.

stärt, *n.* 1. the tail of an animal: now only in combination, as in red*start*.

2. something like a tail; a plowtail; a handle. [Brit. Dial.]

3. in mining, the lever of a crab or gin, to which the horse is attached.

4. one of the sides of a bucket in an overshot water wheel.

5. the point of a young stag's horn. [Obs.]

stärt'ẽr, *n.* a person or thing that starts; specifically, (a) one who sets out on a journey, a pursuit, or the like; (b) a dog that rouses game; (c) the first in a series; (d) a person or animal that starts in a race; as, of the ten *starters* only six finished; (e) a person who gives the signal to start, as in a race; (f) a person who supervises the departure of busses, commercial aircraft, etc.; (g) a self-starter.

stärt'fụl, *a.* apt to start; skittish. [Rare.]

stärt'fụl·ness, *n.* the quality or state of being startful. [Rare.]

stär this'tle (this'l), 1. a European weed, *Centaurea calcitrapa*, which grows in gravelly, sandy, and waste places, especially near the sea, and has long, spreading, spiny bracts and heads of purple flowers.

2. a related weed with yellow flowers; caltrop.

stär'thrōat, *n.* in zoology, a hummingbird of the genus *Heliomaster*, native to South America.

stärt'ing, *n.* the act of making a start.

stärt'ing bär, a hand lever for moving the valves so as to start a steam engine.

stärt'ing hōle, a loophole; an evasion; a subterfuge. [Obs.]

stärt'ing·ly, *adv.* by sudden fits or starts.

stärt'ing point, the point from which a person or thing starts; the point of departure.

stärt'ing pōst, the place where a horse race starts, usually marked by a post.

stärt'ish, *a.* apt to start; skittish: said of horses. [Colloq.]

stär'tle, *v.t.*; startled (-tld), *pt., pp.*; startling, *ppr.* [ME. *stertlen*, to rush, stumble along, freq. of *sterten*, to start.]

1. to frighten or alarm suddenly or unexpectedly; to cause to start, or move involuntarily, as from sudden fright.

2. to cause to feel a shock of surprise; as, he was *startled* at the extent of the uprising.

stär'tle, *v.i.* to be startled.

stär'tle, *n.* 1. a start or shock, as of surprise or fright.

2. something that startles.

stärt'ling, *a.* [ppr. of *startle*.] impressing suddenly with fear or surprise; strongly exciting or surprising; shocking; as, a *startling* discovery.

stärt'ling·ly, *adv.* in a startling manner.

stärt'lish, *a.* apt to start; skittish. [Colloq.]

stärt'-up, *n.* a kind of rustic shoe with a high top or half gaiter. [Obs.]

stärt'-up, *n.* one that comes suddenly into notice; an upstart. [Obs.]

stärt'-up, *a.* suddenly coming into notice or importance; upstart. [Obs.]

stär·vā'tion, *n.* the act of starving or state of being starved; a suffering extremely from lack of food; hence, any suffering resulting from depravation experienced by the senses; as, mental or spiritual *starvation*.

stär·vā'tion, *a.* tending to cause hunger or privation; as, *starvation* wages.

stärve, *v.i.*; starved, *pt., pp.*; starving, *ppr.* [AS. *steorfan*, to die, perish; akin to L.G. *starven*, D. *sterven*, G. *sterben*, to die.]

1. to perish with hunger; to die from lack of food.

2. to suffer or become weak from hunger.

3. to suffer extreme hunger or want; to be very indigent.

4. to suffer from the lack of anything, whether mental, spiritual, or aesthetic; as, I am *starving* for good music.

5. to suffer or die from cold. [Dial.]

6. to be very hungry. [Colloq.]

7. to die. [Obs.]

to starve for; to be in great need of; to have a strong desire for (affection, etc.).

stärve, *v.t.* 1. to cause to starve; to deprive of food.

2. to force or compel by starvation; as, they *starved* the city into submission.

3. to kill with cold. [Dial.]

4. to deprive of force or vigor.

stärve'ā″çre (-kẽr), *n.* a crowfoot or buttercup, *Ranunculus arvensis*: so called because believed to be a sign or a cause of a poor soil or crop. [Brit.]

stärved, *a.* in heraldry, stripped of leaves; blasted: said of a branch in a bearing.

stärv'ed·ly, *adv.* in a state of starvation; stingily.

stärve'ling, *a.* [from *starve*.]

1. starving; weak and hungry.

2. poverty-stricken.

3. characterized by or suggestive of starvation or poverty.

4. of poor quality or inadequate quantity.

stärve'ling, *n.* a person, animal, or plant that is made thin and weak through lack of nutriment.

stärv'en, *v.* obsolete past participle of *starve*.

stärv'ẽr, *n.* one who starves or causes starvation.

stär'wărd, *adv.* toward the stars.

stär wheel (hwēl), a disk or wheel having radial projections or teeth, used chiefly in clock mechanisms.

stär'wŏrm, *n.* any worm of the species *Gephyrea*.

stär wŏr'ship, the worship of the heavenly bodies; specifically, Sabaism.

stär wŏr'ship·ẽr, one who worships the heavenly bodies; specifically, a believer in Sabaism.

stär'wŏrt, *n.* 1. any plant of the genus *Aster*: so called because of the shape of the rays.

2. any plant of the genus *Stellaria*; the chickweed.

3. same as *water starwort*.

yellow starwort; the elecampane.

stash, *v.t.* and *v.i.* [prob. a blend of *store* and *cache*.] to put or hide away (money, valuables, etc.) in a secret or safe place, as for future use. [Slang.]

stȧ·sid'i·on, *n.*; *pl.* **stȧ·sid'i·ȧ,** [Gr. *stasis*, a standing place.] in the Orthodox Eastern Church, a stall in a church for a monk or patriarch: so called because originally they were arranged without seats, for standing only.

stas'i·mon, *n.*; *pl.* **stas'i·mȧ,** [Gr.] in ancient Greek tragedy, a song, or an ode, sung by the chorus after the opening ode.

stā'sis, *n.*; *pl.* **stā'sēṣ,** [Mod. L.; Gr. *stasis*, a standing, from *histanai*, to stand.] a stoppage of the flow of some fluid in the body, as of blood in a blood vessel or feces in the intestines.

-stat, [Gr. *-statēs*.] a combining form meaning *stationary, making stationary*, as in gyro*stat*, thermo*stat*.

stāt'ȧ·ble, *a.* capable of being stated.

Stā'tăl, *a.* in the United States, of or relating to a State, as distinguished from *federal* or *national*. [Rare.]

stā'tănt, *a.* [OFr. *estant*, standing, from L. *stare*, to stand.] in heraldry, in a standing position with all four legs on the ground.

LION STATANT

stȧ·tăr'i·ăn, *a.* fixed; steady. [Rare.]

stȧ·tăr'i·ăn·ly, *adv.* in a statarian manner. [Rare.]

stā'tȧ·ry, *a.* fixed; settled [Obs.]

stāte, *n.* [OFr. *estat*, state, case, condition, circumstances, etc.; L. *status*, state, position, standing, from *stare*, to stand.]

1. a set of circumstances or attributes characterizing a person or thing at a given time; way or form of being; condition; as, his affairs are in a bad *state*, what is his mental *state?*

2. a particular mental or emotional condition; as, a *state* of melancholy.

3. condition as regards physical structure, constitution, internal form, stage or phase of existence, etc.

4. (a) condition or position in life; social status, rank, or degree; (b) high rank or position. [Obs. or Rare.]

5. the style of living characteristic of people having high rank and wealth; rich, imposing, ceremonious display; dignity and pomp.

6. [*sometimes* S-] [*pl.*] legislative bodies in any of several countries; estates.

7. [*sometimes* S-] the power or authority represented by a body of people politically organized under one government, especially an independent government, within a territory or territories having definite boundaries.

8. [*sometimes* S-] such a body of people; body politic.

9. [*usually* S-] one of the territorial and political units constituting a federal government, as in the United States.

10. the territory of a state (senses 8 and 9).

11. the political organization constituting the basis of civil government; as, church and *state*.

12. the sphere of highest governmental authority and administration; as, matters of *state*.

13. crisis; height; point from which the next movement is regression. [Obs.]

14. estate; possession. [Obs.]

15. a person of high rank or distinction; a noble; one of the ruling class. [Obs.]

16. a seat of dignity or honor; a chair of honor, usually elevated on a platform and covered with a canopy; sometimes, the canopy itself. [Obs.]

17. stability; permanence. [Obs.]

18. one of several stages or phases in engraving or etching; also, an engraving from a plate still in process of completion.

19. that which is stated or expressed in writing or in words or figures; a statement; a document containing a statement. [Obs.]

Border States; see under *border*, a.

chair of state; the seat or office of a chief executive.

free state; (a) any body politic which does not depend on any other for law and control; (b) [F- S-] see under *free*.

in (or *into*) *a state*; (a) in (or into) a bad condition, as of disorder or difficulty; (b) in (or into) a condition of agitation or excitement.

Papal States; same as *States of the Church*.

the States; the United States: often so called abroad. [Colloq.]

to lie in state; to lie, surrounded with pomp and solemnity, in some public place for public view: said of the dead before burial.

stāte, *a.* 1. [*sometimes* S-] of or pertaining to the body politic, government, or state; public; as, *state* affairs.
2. of, for, or characteristic of ceremonious occasions; formal; as, a *state* carriage.
3. [*usually* S-] of or pertaining to one of the commonwealths or states which make up a federal republic; as, a *State* institution.
4. stately. [Obs.]

stāte, *v.t.*; stated, *pt., pp.*; stating, *ppr.* 1. to set; to settle; to establish by specifying.
2. to express the particulars of in writing or verbally; to represent in words, especially in a specific, formal, or definite way; to narrate; to recite; as, the witnesses *stated* all the circumstances.
3. in law, to aver; to allege.
Syn.—say, declare, propound, aver, set forth, narrate, specify, particularize, avow, recite.

stāte bank, a bank controlled or chartered by a state.

stāte cap′i·tăl·ism, a form of capitalism in which much of the capital, industry, etc. is state-owned.

stāte chām′bẽr, a room used on formal or ceremonial occasions.

stāte chŭrch, the established church of a country.

stāte′craft, *n.* the art of, or skill in, conducting state affairs; state management; statesmanship.

stāt′ed, *a.* [pp. of *state*.]
1. established; fixed; regular.
2. declared; alleged.
3. formulated.

Stāte Dē·pärt′ment, the department of the executive branch of the United States government in charge of relations with foreign countries.

stāt′ed·ly, *adv.* regularly; at certain times.

Stāte flow′ẽr, the floral emblem selected for or adopted by a State, often by action of the legislature.

stāte′fụl, *a.* stately. [Obs.]

stāte′hood, *n.* the condition of existence and recognition as a state rather than as a territory, dominion, etc.

Stāte′house, *n.* the official meeting place of the legislature of a State of the United States; State Capitol: also *State house.*

stāte lands, territory granted to or held by a state.

stāte′less, *a.* 1. having no state or nationality.
2. without pomp.

stāte′li·ly, *adv.* in a stately manner. [Rare.]

stāte′li·ness, *n.* the state or quality of being stately; loftiness of mien or manner; majestic appearance; dignity.

stāte′ly, *a.*; *comp.* statelier; *superl.* stateliest,
1. lofty; dignified; majestic; magnificent; grand; as, a *stately* edifice, a *stately* manner.
2. slow, dignified, and deliberate.
Syn.—imposing, elevated, lordly, proud, pompous.

stāte′ly, *adv.* in a stately manner; majestically; loftily.

stāte′ment, *n.* 1. the act of stating, reciting, or presenting verbally or on paper.
2. that which is stated, specified, or said; an account or declaration; a formal embodiment in language of facts or opinions; a narrative; a recital; the expression of a fact or of an opinion; as, a verbal *statement.*
3. an abstract of a financial account, especially of money due.

stāte′mŏn″gẽr, *n.* one versed in politics or one who dabbles in state affairs.

stāte of facts, in law, a statement of facts made by a party to a suit.

stāte pā′pẽr, 1. a document relating to the political interests or government of a state.
2. a newspaper in which official notices and reports of a state are published.

Stāte priṣ′ŏn, 1. a prison maintained by a State.
2. [s-] a prison where political prisoners are confined.

Stāte priṣ′ŏn·ẽr, 1. a prisoner confined in a State prison.
2. [s-] a political prisoner.

stāt′ẽr, *n.* one who states.

stā′tẽr, *n.* [ME.; L.; Gr. *statēr*, orig., a weight.] any of various gold and silver coins of ancient Greece and Persia.

Stāte rīghts (rīts), States' rights.

stāte′rọom, *n.* 1. a magnificent room in a palace or mansion, used on state occasions.
2. a cabin on board ship.
3. a private sleeping room in a railway car.
4. in the navy, the sleeping apartment or cabin of an officer.

Stāte's at·tŏr′ney, a lawyer appointed or elected to prepare cases for the State and represent it in court.

stāte's ev′i·dence, in law, evidence given by or for the prosecution in a criminal case, usually evidence given by a criminal against his associates.
to turn state's evidence; to give evidence for the prosecution in a criminal case.

Stātes′-Ġen′ẽr·ăl, *n.* [transl. of Fr. *états généraux*, D. *staaten generaal*.]
1. the legislative body in France before the Revolution of 1789, made up of representatives of the clergy, the nobility, and the third estate.
2. the legislative assembly of the Netherlands.

stāte′sīde, *a.* of or characteristic of the United States; as, *stateside* newspapers. [Colloq.]

stāte′sīde, *adv.* in, to, or toward the United States; as, I haven't been *stateside* for three years.

stātes′măn, *n.*; *pl.* **stātes′men,** 1. a person who shows wisdom and skill in conducting state affairs and treating public issues, or one experienced or engaged in the business of government.
2. a small landholder. [Brit. Dial.]

stātes′măn·līke, *a.* 1. of or befitting a statesman.
2. having the manner or wisdom of statesmen; having the qualities considered typical of a statesman.

stātes′măn·ly, *a.* relating to or befitting a statesman; statesmanlike.

stātes′măn·ship, *n.* the ability, character, or methods of a statesman; skill in managing public affairs.

stāte sō′ciăl·iṣm, the theory, doctrine, or practice of an economy planned and controlled by the state, based on state ownership of public utilities, basic industries, etc.

Stātes of the Chŭrch, the Papal States; the lands in central and north central Italy formerly ruled by the Church.

Stātes' rīghts (rīts), all the rights and powers which the Constitution neither grants to the federal government nor denies to the various State governments; sometimes, all the rights and powers claimed for the States, including the right of secession from the United States: also *State rights.*

stātes′wom″ăn (-woom″), *n.*; *pl.* **stātes′ wom″en** (-wim″), a woman with statesmanlike ability.

stāte trī′ăl, a prosecution by the state, especially for a political offense.

Stāte ū·ni·vẽr′si·ty, a university kept up by a State government as part of its public educational system.

stāte′-wīde′, *a.* extending throughout a state; over all the state.

stāthe, *n.* same as *staith.*

stath′mō·graph, *n.* [Gr. *stathman*, measure, and *-graph*.] a device for registering the velocity of a railroad train.

stat′iç, *a.* [Mod. L. *staticus*; Gr. *statikos*, causing to stand, from *histanai*, to cause to stand.]
1. acting through weight only: said of the pressure exerted by a motionless body or mass.
2. of bodies, masses, or forces at rest or in equilibrium: opposed to *dynamic.*
3. not moving or progressing; at rest; inactive; stationary.
4. in electricity, designating, of, or producing stationary electrical charges, as those resulting from friction.
5. in radio, of or having to do with static.

stat′iç, *n.* 1. electrical discharges in the atmosphere that interfere with radio reception, etc.
2. interference or noises produced by such discharges.
static ataxia; in medicine, lack of muscular co-ordination during states of rest.
static electricity; see *electricity, n.* 4.
static gangrene; gangrene that results from stasis.
static induction; electrostatic induction.
static voltmeter; in electricity, (a) a voltmeter operated by electrostatic action, as opposed to a voltmeter operating electromagnetically; (b) a voltmeter in which the moving system is displaced by electrostatic forces; (c) a voltmeter of the electroscope or electrometer type.

stat′iç·ăl, *a.* static.
statical moment; see under *moment.*

stat′iç·ăl·ly, *adv.* in a static manner.

Stat′i·cē, *n.* [from Gr. *statikos*, making to stop: in allusion to the powerful astringency of some of the species.]
1. a genus of herbaceous or subshrubby plants, family *Plumbagineæ*, characterized by the flowers being spiked or panicled, the calyx funnel-shaped, the petals slightly connate, the stamens attached to the base of the petals, and the nut one-seeded, enclosed in the calyx. *Statice latifolia*, a Siberian species, bears blue flowers. The root of one species, *Statice caroliniana*, is a very powerful astringent.
2. [s-] a plant of this genus.

stat′içs, *n.pl.* [*construed as sing.*] [Gr. *statikos*, at a standstill, from *statos*, standing.] that department of mechanics which treats of bodies, masses, or forces in a state of rest or equilibrium, and of the properties and relations of forces in equilibrium.
social statics; that branch of sociology which treats of the forces which constitute or regulate society as its exists for the time being.

stā′tion, *n.* [ME. *stacioun*; Late OFr.; L. *statis*, a standing, post, station, from *status*, pp. of *stare*, to stand.]
1. the act or manner of standing; attitude; posture; pose. [Rare.]
2. the place where a person or thing stands or is located, especially an assigned post, position, or location; specifically, (a) the place where a person, as a guard, stands while on duty; (b) the post, building, base, or headquarters assigned to a group of people working together; as, a police *station*, first-aid *station*, postal *station*, military-government *station*; (c) in Australasia, a sheep or cattle ranch; (d) a place or region to which a naval fleet, ship, etc. is assigned for duty; (e) in India, formerly, the place of residence of British officials or military officers of a district.
3. (a) a regular stopping place, as on a bus line or railroad; (b) the building or buildings at such a place, for passengers, etc.
4. condition of life; social standing or position; rank; state; status.

He went his humble way, at peace with the world and himself; a man completely satisfied with his *station* in life.—King.

5. Employment; occupation; business; sphere or department of duty. [Obs. or Rare.]
6. in ecclesiastical usage and church history, (a) formerly, in the Roman Catholic Church, the devotional fast on Wednesdays and Fridays; (b) a church in which a procession of the clergy halts on stated days to say any stated prayers; (c) a stopping place in a monastic procession; (d) any one of the series of stopping places in the devotion of the stations of the cross; (e) in Ireland, the visitation of a priest, as on circuit, to places having no regular church or pastor.
7. a place equipped to transmit or receive radio waves; especially, the studios, offices, and technical installations collectively of an establishment for radio or television transmission.
8. a fixed point from which measurements are made in surveying.
9. in biology, a habitat, especially the characteristic habitat of a given plant or animal.
10. the fact or condition of being stationary. [Archaic.]
11. in mining, an enlargement in a shaft or gangway, as one in which to place machinery.

stā′tion, *v.t.*; stationed, *pt., pp.*; stationing, *ppr.* to assign to a station; to post; to place; to set; as, to *station* troops at the border.

stā′tion ā′ġent, a person who manages a railroad station.

stā′tion·ăl, *a.* pertaining to a station.

stā′tion·ãr·i·ness, *n.* the condition or quality of being stationary.

stā′tion·ãr·y, *a.* 1. fixed; at rest; not moving; not appearing to move.
2. remaining or continuing in the same state or condition; neither progressing nor receding; neither improving nor getting worse; not increasing or decreasing.
3. not migratory or itinerant.
4. in astronomy, not changing its relative place in the heavens for some days: said of a planet at the beginning and ending of the planet's retrogradation.
stationary air; air which remains in the lungs during normal respiration.

stationary engine; an engine fixed on a foundation, as distinguished from a portable engine, a locomotive, etc.

stationary engineer; a person who operates and maintains stationary engines and mechanical equipment, such as steam boilers, ventilating equipment, etc.

stā'tion·ăr·y, *n.*; *pl.* **stā'tion·ăr·ieṣ,** a person or thing that is stationary.

stā'tion bill, in nautical usage, a list containing the appointed posts of the ship's company when navigating the ship; a quarter bill.

stā'tion·ẽr, *n.* [ME *stacionere*; ML. *stationarius*, tradesman with a fixed station or shop (by contrast with a peddler), from L. *stationarius*, stationary.]
1. originally, a bookseller or publisher.
2. a person who sells paper, ink, pens, and other writing materials.

stā'tion·er·y, *n.* [from *stationer*.] writing materials; specifically, paper and envelopes used for writing letters.

stā'tion·er·y, *a.* belonging to a stationer; pertaining to writing materials.

stā'tion house, 1. a building used as a station, especially by a company of police or firemen.
2. a railway station, especially a small country station.

stā'tion·mȧs''tẽr, *n.* the person in charge of a railway station; a station agent.

stā'tion point'ẽr, in surveying, a circular plotting instrument, having a standard radius and two movable ones, by which the position of the observer can be indicated on a chart.

stā'tion pōle, stā'tion stȧff, in surveying, an instrument for marking a station; a range pole or leveling rod.

stā'tionṣ of the çross, [*sometimes* S- C-] a series of fourteen images or pictures, as in a church or along a path leading to a shrine, representing the stages of Jesus' sufferings, visited in succession by worshipers.

stā'tion wag'ŏn, an automobile with folding or removable rear seats and a back end that opens for easy loading of luggage, etc., having a body of wood or metal panels.

stāt'iṣm, *n.* 1. the doctrine of state sovereignty, as in a republic, or adherence to this.
2. the doctrine or practice of vesting economic control, economic planning, etc. in a centralized state government: the current sense.
3. statecraft or politics. [Obs.]

stāt'ist, *n.* 1. a statesman; a politician; one skilled in government. [Obs.]
2. a statistician.
3. a person who believes in or advocates statism.

stāt'ist, *a.* of, characteristic of, or advocating statism.

stȧ·tis'tiç, *a.* statistical.

stȧ·tis'tiç, *n.* 1. a statistical item or element.
2. statistics (sense 2). [Rare.]

stȧ·tis'tiç·ăl, *a.* [from ML. *statisticus*, from (hyp.) *statista*, statesman, from L. *status*, state.] of, having to do with, consisting of, or based on statistics; as, *statistical* reports.

stȧ·tis'tiç·ăl·ly, *adv.* 1. in the form of statistics.
2. according to statistics.
3. by means of statistics.

stat·is·ti'ciăn (-tish'ăn), *n.* an expert or specialist in statistics, or a person who assembles, classifies, and tabulates statistical data.

stȧ·tis'tiçs, *n.pl.* 1. facts or data of a numerical kind, assembled, classified, and tabulated so as to present significant information about a given subject.
2. [*construed as sing.*] the science of assembling, classifying, and tabulating such facts or data.

stat·is·tol'ō·ġy, *n.* a discourse or treatise on statistics.

stā'tive, *a.* pertaining to a fixed camp or military post or quarters. [Obs.]

stat'ō·blast, *n* [Gr. *statos*, standing, and *-blast*.] any of a number of internal buds developed in some of the *Polyzoa*, and liberated after the death of the parent organism. After a time the statoblast is ruptured, and there emerges a young polyzoon.

stat·ō·blas'tiç, *a.* pertaining to or of the nature of a statoblast.

stȧ·toç'rȧ·cy, *n.* state government as distinguished from government by ecclesiastical power. [Rare.]

stat'ō·cyst, *n.* [from Gr. *statos*, standing, stationary; and *-cyst*.] a sense organ found in many invertebrate animals, consisting typically of a sac filled with fluid and containing small sensory hairs and particles of lime, etc.: it functions as an organ of balance or equilibrium.

stā'tŏr, *n.* [Mod. L.; L., a supporter, from pp. of *stare*, to stand.] a fixed part forming the pivot or housing for a revolving part (*rotor*), as in a motor, dynamo, etc.

stat'ō·sçōpe, *n.* [Gr. *statos*, standing, and *skopein*, to view.]
1. an aneroid barometer that indicates very slight changes in pressure.
2. such a barometer adapted for use as an altitude indicator for an aircraft.

stat'ū·ȧ, *n.* a statue. [Obs.]

stat'ū·ăr·y (stach'), *n.*; *pl.* **stat'ū·ăr·ieṣ,** [Fr. *statuaire*, from L. *statuarius*, of statues, from *statu a*, astatue.]
1. statues considered as a whole; a group of statues.
2. the art of making statues.
3. a sculptor.

stat'ū·ăr·y, *a.* of or suitable for a statue or statues.

stat'ūe (stach'u), *n.* [Fr. *statue*; L. *statua*, from *statuere*, to set, place, from stem of *stare*, to stand.]
1. the form of a person or animal carved in wood, stone, etc., modeled in a plastic substance, or cast in plaster, bronze, etc., especially when done in the round rather than in relief.
2. a picture. [Obs.]

Statue of Liberty; a copper statue, over 150 feet high, of a crowned woman, the Goddess of Liberty, holding a torch in her upraised hand: it was given to the United States by France and is located on Liberty Island in New York harbor.

stat'ūe, *v.t.*; statued, *pt.*, *pp.*; statuing, *ppr.* to form a statue of.

stat'ūed, *a.* 1. adorned with statues.
2. sculptured.

stat'ūe·less, *a.* without a statue.

stat'ūe·līke, *a.* without motion; like a statue.

stat·ū·esque' (-esk'), *a.* of or like a statue; specifically, (a) tall and well-proportioned; as, a *statuesque* figure; (b) stately; graceful; showing poise and dignity.

stat·ū·esque'ly, *adv.* in a statuesque manner.

stat·ū·esque'ness, *n.* the quality of being statuesque.

stat·ū·ette', *n.* [Fr., dim. of *statue*, a statue.] a small statue.

stȧ·tū'mi·nāte, *v.t.* to prop or support. [Obs.]

stat'ūre (stach'), *n.* [OFr.; L. *statura*, height or size of body, from *statuere*, to cause to stand.]
1. the height of the body (of an animal, especially of man) in a natural standing position.
2. the height of an object. [Rare.]
3. development, growth, or elevation reached: used figuratively, as, moral *stature*.

stat'ūred, *a.* arrived at full stature. [Rare.]

stā'tus, *n.*; *pl.* **stā'tus·eṣ,** [L.] 1. condition or position with regard to law; as, her *status* is that of a married woman.
2. position; rank; standing; as, no one can question his *status* as a scholar.
3. state, or condition, as of affairs.

status quo; the existing state of affairs (at any specified time), or the existing condition (of anything specified): also *status in quo*.

status quo ante; the previous state of affairs, or the previous condition (of anything specified).

stat'ū·tȧ·ble, *a.* statutory.

stat'ū·tȧ·bly, *adv.* in a statutable manner.

stat'ūte (stach'), *n.* [OFr. *statut*; L. *statutum*, a statute, neut. of *statutus*, pp. of *statuere*, to set, establish.]
1. an established rule or law; as, the *statutes* of a university.
2. (a) a law passed by a legislative body and set forth in a formal document; (b) such a document.
3. a statute fair. [Brit. Dial.]

statute merchant; in law, a bond of record, now obsolete, acknowledged before the chief magistrate of some trading town, on which, if not paid at the day, an execution might be awarded against the body, lands, and goods of the obligor.

statute staple; in law, a bond of record, now obsolete, acknowledged before the mayor of the staple, by virtue of which the creditor might forthwith have execution against the body, lands, and goods of the debtor on nonpayment.

stat'ūte book, a register of statutes, laws, or legislative acts.

stat'ūte çap, a woolen cap enjoined to be worn in England by a statute passed in 1571 in the interest of the capmakers. [Obs.]

stat'ūte fāir, a fair held by regular legal appointment, in contradistinction to one authorized only by use and wont; especially, one at which servants are hired. [Brit.]

stat'ūte law, law established by a legislative body.

stat'ūte mīle, 5,280 feet.

stat'ūte of lim·i·tā'tionṣ, a statute limiting the period within which legal action can be taken in a given matter.

stat'ū·tō·ry, *a.* 1. of, or having the nature of, a statute or statutes.
2. fixed, authorized, or established by statute.
3. declared by statute to be such, and hence punishable legally: said of an offense.
4. conforming to the provisions of a statute.

staum'rel, *a.* stupid; half-witted. [Scot.]

stäunch, *n.*, *a.*, and *v.* same as *stanch*.

stau'rȧ·cin, *n.* a silken cloth with a pattern containing many small crosses, used in medieval ecclesiastical vestments and in the Byzantine court.

stau'rō·līte, *n.* [Gr. *stauros*, a cross, and *-lite*.] an orthorhombic mineral occurring in crystals which are often found twinned in the form of a cross. It is a reddish-brown silicate of iron and aluminum.

stau·rō·lit'iç, *a.* pertaining to or resembling staurolite.

stau'rō·sçōpe, *n.* [Gr. *stauros*, a cross, and *skopein*, to view.] an instrument for finding the position of planes of polarized light vibration in crystals.

stau'rō·tide, *n.* same as *staurolite*.

stau·rō·ty̆·pous, *a.* [Gr. *stauros*, a cross, and *typos*, form.] in mineralogy, having markings in the form of a cross.

stāve, *n.* [ME. *stave*, taken as sing. of *staves*, pl. of *staff*.]
1. one of the thin, shaped strips of wood set edge to edge to form the wall of a barrel, wooden bucket, etc.
2. a stick or staff.
3. a rung, as of a ladder.
4. a set of verses, or lines, of a poem or song; a stanza.
5. in music, a staff.
6. one of the boards joined laterally to form a hollow cylinder, a curb for a well or shaft, the curved bed for the intrados of an arch, or the like.

stāve, *v.t.*; staved *or* stove, *pt.*, *pp.*; staving, *ppr.* 1. to break a hole in; to break; to burst; to break in staves of; as, to *stave* a cask.
2. to push, as with a staff; hence, to put off, ward off, or hold off, as by force, guile, or evasion: usually with *off*.
3. to furnish with staves.
4. to suffer to be lost or poured out by staving a cask. [Rare.]
5. to make firm by compression; to shorten or compact, as a heated rod or bar by endwise blows, or as lead in the socket joints of pipes.

to stave and tail; in bear baiting, to check the bear with a staff, and to hold back the dog by the tail; hence, to cause to cease or stop.

to stave in; to break a hole in; to crush inward.

stāve, *v.i.* 1. to fight with staves. [Obs.]
2. to be or become stove in, as a boat; to break up or in.
3. to move or act vigorously or roughly; as, to *stave* out of the room. [Dial.]

stāve joint'ẽr, a device for truing the edges of staves.

stā'vẽr, *n.* 1. a quick, energetic person; one who rushes work through. [Colloq.]
2. something very large; a whopper. [Colloq.]

stāve rhȳme (rīm), in old Germanic poetry, alliteration; an alliterative word.

stā'vẽrṣ, *n.pl.* the staggers in horses. [Rare.]

stā'vẽr·wŏrt, *n.* staggerwort; ragwort, *Senecio jacobæa*, regarded as a remedy for stavers.

stāveṣ, *n.* 1. alternative plural of *staff*.
2. plural of *stave*.

stāveṣ'ā''çre (-kẽr), *n.* 1. a European larkspur, *Delphinium staphisagria*, with poisonous seeds having strongly emetic and cathartic properties.
2. the seeds of this plant.

stāve set′tẽr, a contrivance for holding the staves in place while a barrel, tub, or the like is made.
stāve′wood, *n.* a West Indian tree, *Simarouba amara*, allied to the quassia, and known also as the *bitter damson*.
stāv′ing, *n.* 1. staves collectively.
2. a casing of staves or planks which forms a curb around a turbine or similar water wheel.
3. the act of shortening or compacting a heated rod or bar by endwise blows.
stāv′ing, *adv.* in a marked degree; very; as, a *staving* big boy. [Slang.]
staw, *v.i.* to be fixed, set, or stalled. [Scot. and Brit. Dial.]
staw, *v.t.* to stall; to clog; to surfeit. [Scot. and Brit. Dial.]
staw, *v.* Scottish past tense of *steal*.
stāy, *n.* [AS. *stæg*; akin to Ice., Dan., Sw., D., and G. *stag*, a stay.]
1. a strong rope or cable, usually of wire, used to support a mast, and leading from the head of one mast down to some other, or to some part of the vessel. Those stays leading forward are called *fore-and-aft stays*, and those leading down to the vessel's sides, *backstays*.
2. a rope used for similar purposes; a guy supporting the mast of a derrick, etc.
in stays or *hove in stays*; in the process of tacking: said of a ship.
to miss stays; to fail in the attempt to tack about.
stāy, *v.t.* 1. to brace or support with a stay or stays.
2. to change the angle of (a mast) by shifting the stays.
3. to put (a ship) on the other tack.
stāy, *v.i.* to tack: said of a ship.
stāy, *n.* [OFr. *estai*, from base of *stay* (rope).]
1. a support; prop; brace.
2. a strip of stiffening material used in a corset, the collar of a shirt, etc.
3. [*pl.*] a corset, especially one stiffened with whalebone.
stāy, *v.t.* 1. to support; to hold up or prop up.
2. to strengthen, comfort, or sustain in mind or spirit.
3. to cause to rest (*on, upon*, or *in*) for support; to base.
4. to support or strengthen with stays.
stāy, *v.i.*; stayed *or archaic* staid, *pt., pp.*; staying, *ppr.* [ME. *staien*; Anglo-Fr. *estaier*; OFr. *ester*; L. *stare*, to stand.]
1. to remain; to continue in a specified place; as, you *stay* here while I go to the next house.
2. to remain in a state or condition; as, these clothes won't *stay* white.
3. to be located for a while, especially as a guest or resident; to live, dwell, or reside (for the time specified).
4. to stop; to stand still.
5. to pause; tarry; wait; delay; as, *stay* a little before going on with your labors.
6. to be able to continue or endure; to hold out; to last; as, he doesn't *stay* well in the mile run. [Colloq.]
7. to keep up, as with another contestant in a race. [Colloq.]
8. to cease. [Archaic.]
9. to make a stand; to stand one's ground. [Archaic.]
10. in poker, to remain in a hand by seeing, or meeting, a bet, ante, or raise.
11. to rest; to rely; to confide; to trust. [Now Rare.]

Because ye despise this word, and trust in oppression, and *stay* thereon.
—Isa. xxx. 12.

12. to wait; to give ceremonious or submissive attendance: with *on* or *upon*. [Archaic.]

I have a servant comes with me along,
That *stays upon* me. —Shak.

to stay put; to remain as placed; not to be disturbed. [Colloq.]
stāy, *v.t.* 1. to stop; to halt; to check.
2. to hinder, impede, restrain, or detain.
3. to delay; to put off; to postpone; as, to *stay* a legal proceeding.
4. to quell or allay (strife, etc.). [Rare.]
5. to satisfy or appease for a time the pangs or cravings of (thirst, appetite, etc.).
6. to remain through, during, for, or (with *out*) to the end of; as, *stay* the week (out).
7. to await; to wait for. [Archaic.]
8. to endure. [Obs.]
to stay the stomach; to eat something to appease hunger temporarily.
stāy, *n.* 1. (a) a stopping or being stopped; (b) a stop, halt, check, or pause.
2. a postponement or delay in legal action or proceedings; as, the man was given a *stay* of execution.
3. (a) the action of remaining or continuing in a place for a time; (b) time spent in a place; as, she had a long *stay* in the hospital.

Looking forward beyond my *stay* on earth.
—Peabody.

4. staying power. [Colloq.]
5. a standstill. [Archaic.]
6. (a) a hindrance; (b) restraint or control; (c) delay. [Obs.]
7. restraint; moderation; caution; sobriety. [Obs.]
8. a station or fixed anchorage for vessels. [Obs.]
stay of proceedings; in law, an interruption, arrest, or suspension of proceedings.
stāy′-ăt-hōme″, *n.* a person who stays much at home; one not given to traveling or roaming about: also used adjectively; as, a *stay-at-home* person.
stāy bär, 1. in architecture, the horizontal iron bar which extends in one piece along the top of the mullions of a traceried window.
2. same as *stay rod*.
stāy bōlt, in machinery, a bolt or rod binding together opposite plates.
stāy busk, same as first *busk*, sense 1.
stāy chāin, in a vehicle, one of two chains attaching the doubletree to the front axle and serving to limit the horizontal movement of the doubletree.
stāyed, *a.* staid. [Obs.]
stāyed′ly, *adv.* staidly. [Obs.]
stāyed′ness, *n.* staidness. [Obs.]
stāy′ẽr, *n.* 1. one who stops or restrains.
2. one who upholds or supports; that which props.
3. a person of endurance and pluck; one who will not abandon an undertaking or violate an agreement: opposed to *quitter*. [Colloq.]
4. one who remains; a stay-at-home.
stāy′hōle, *n.* one of the holes in a staysail through which it is fastened to the stay. [Obs.]
stāy′ing pow′ẽr, ability to last or endure; endurance.
stāy′lāce, *n.* a lace for fastening stays.
stāy′less, *a.* without stop or delay. [Rare.]
stāy′māk″ẽr, *n.* one who makes stays
stāy′nil, *n.* the starling. [Brit. Dial.]
stāy plow, same as *restharrow*.
stāy rod, one of various rods, as, in architecture, a tie rod in a building, which prevents spreading of the parts connected, or, in a steam engine, (a) a tension rod in a marine steam engine; (b) one of the rods supporting a boiler plate that forms the top of a firebox, to keep the top from being bulged down by the pressure of steam; (c) a rod in a boiler that supports plates by connecting parts exposed to rupture in contrary directions; (d) one of the sling rods connecting a locomotive boiler to its frame; (e) a rod beneath the boiler supporting the inside bearings of the crank axle of a locomotive
stāy′sāil (*or* stā′sl), *n.* a sail, especially a triangular sail, fastened on a stay.
stāy′ship, *n.* a sucking fish, the remora: so called on account of the belief that it stayed the progress of a ship.
stāy taç′kle, a large tackle attached to the mainstay by means of a pendant, and used to hoist heavy objects.
stāy wedġe, in a locomotive, a wedge fitted to the inside bearings of the driving axles to keep them in their proper position.
stead (sted), *n.* [AS. *stede, styde*; akin to D. and L.G. *stede*, Dan. *sted*, Ice. *stadr*, Goth. *staths*, G. *statt*, place, stead; from root of *stand*.]
1. the place or position of a person or thing as filled by a replacement, substitute, or successor; as, if you can't come, send her in your *stead*.
2. advantage, service, or avail.
3. a place, site, or locality. [Archaic or Dial. except in combination.]
4. the frame on which a bed is laid: more commonly called *bedstead*. [Rare.]
5. a place of abode; a homestead. [Obs. or Dial.]
to stand (one) in good stead; (a) to give (one) good use or service; (b) to give (one) an advantage.
stead, *v.t.* 1. to help; to support; to be helpful to; as, it nothing *steads* us. [Archaic.]
2. to fill the place of. [Obs.]
stead′fȧst (sted′), *a.* [ME. *stedefast*; AS. *stedefæste*, from *stede*, a place, and *fæst*, fast.]
1. fast fixed; firm; firmly fixed or established.
2. constant; firm; resolute; not fickle or wavering.
3. steady; as, *steadfast* sight.
Also spelled *stedfast*.
stead′fȧst·ly, *adv.* in a steadfast manner.
stead′fȧst·ness, *n.* the quality or the condition of being steadfast.
stead′i·ly, *adv.* in a steady manner.
stead′i·ness, *n.* the state or quality of being steady.
stead′ing (sted′), *n.* 1. the house and other buildings connected with a farm. [Scot. and Brit. Dial.]
2. a site for a building. [Scot and Brit. Dial.]
stead′y (sted′), *a.*; *comp.* steadier; *superl.* steadiest. [AS. *stedig*, from *stede*, place.]
1. firm in standing or position; fixed; stable; not tottering or shaking.
2. constant, regular, uniform, or continuous; not changing, wavering, faltering, etc.; as, a *steady* gaze, a *steady* rise in prices.
3. not given to sudden changes in behavior, loyalty, disposition, etc.
4. not easily agitated, excited, or upset; calm and controlled; as, *steady* nerves.
5. grave; sober; staid; reliable; not frivolous or dissipated.
6. keeping almost upright, as in a rough sea, or keeping headed as it is: said of a ship.
to go steady; to be sweethearts. [Colloq.]
steady, *v.t.* and *v.i.*; steadied, *pt., pp.*; steadying, *ppr.* to make or become steady.
stead′y, *n.* 1. any device for steadying, as (a) a support for the hand in button making; (b) a support for holding a stone in dressing.
2. a combmakers' handsaw: also called *stadda*.
3. one's regular sweetheart. [Slang.]
stead′y, *interj.* 1. be steady! remain calm and controlled!
2. keep the ship headed as it is: a command to the helmsman.
stead′y-gō″ing, *a* steady in habit; pursuing a steady course; as, a *steady-going* young man.
stead′y pin, a dowel.
steāk (stāk), *n.* [ME. *steike*; ON. *steik*, from base of *steikja*, to roast on a spit.]
1. a slice of meat, especially beef, cut thick for broiling or frying.
2. ground beef or other meat cooked in this way; as, Salisbury *steak*.
stēal, *v.t.*; stole, *pt.*; stolen, *pp.*; stealing, *ppr.* [AS. *stælan, stelan*, pt. *stæl*, pp. *stolen*, to steal, to move in a stealthy manner; akin to D. *stelen*, Ice. *stela*, Goth. *stilan*, G. *stehlen*, to steal.]
1. to take or appropriate (another's property, ideas, etc.) without permission, dishonestly, or unlawfully, especially in a secret or surreptitious manner.
2. to get or take slyly, surreptitiously, or without permission; as, he *stole* a look.
3. to take or gain insidiously or artfully; as, the costs of lobbying *stole* his profits, he *stole* her heart.
4. to move, put, carry, or convey surreptitiously or stealthily (with *in, into, from*, etc.).
5. in baseball, to gain (a base or bases) safely without the help of a hit or an error: said of a base runner.
to steal a march; to march secretly; hence, to gain an advantage stealthily (with *on* or *upon*.)
Syn.—pilfer, purloin, plunder, rob, filch, thieve, swindle, rifle.
stēal, *v.i.* 1. to practice or be guilty of theft; to be a thief.
2. to move secretly or stealthily; to slip along or away unperceived; to go or come furtively; as, to *steal* into the house.
stēal, *n.* 1. any act of stealing. [Colloq.]
2. something stolen. [Colloq.]
3. something obtained at a ludicrously low cost. [Colloq.]
stēal′ẽr, *n.* 1. a thief; one who steals.
2. in shipbuilding, the plank at the end of a strake.
stēal′ing, *n.* 1. the act of one who steals; theft.
2. that which is stolen; stolen property: used chiefly in the plural; as, his *stealings* amounted to $500.
stēal′ing, *a.* that steals.
stēal′ing·ly, *adv.* by stealing; slyly; stealthily; imperceptibly. [Rare.]

stealth (stelth), *n.* [ME. *stalthe, stelthe,* from base of *stelen,* to steal; and *-th.*]
1. the act of stealing. [Obs.]
2. the thing stolen. [Obs.]
3. a surreptitious or clandestine method of procedure; secret or furtive action or behavior.
4. a going secretly. [Obs.]

stealth'fụl, *a.* given to stealth; stealthy. [Archaic or Poet.]

stealth'fụl·ly, *adv.* stealthily. [Archaic or Poet.]

stealth'fụl·ness, *n.* stealthiness. [Archaic or Poet.]

stealth'i·ly, *adv.* in a stealthy manner.

stealth'i·ness, *n.* the quality of being stealthy.

stealth'y, *a.*; *comp.* stealthier; *superl.* stealthiest, characterized by stealth; done or acting in a secret, furtive manner; as, a *stealthy* movement, a *stealthy* glance.

stēam, *n.* [ME. *steme*; AS.; akin to D. *stoom*; W. Fris. *steam*; only in W. Gmc.] 1. originally, a vapor, fume, or exhalation.

A *steam* of rich, distilled perfumes. —Milton.

2. water as converted into an invisible vapor or gas by being heated to the boiling point; vaporized water: it is used for heating and cooking and, under pressure, as a source of power.
3. condensed water vapor, seen as a mist on windows, rising from boiling water, etc.
4. steam power; as, many sailing vessels were converted to *steam.*
5. power; force; energy. [Colloq.]
to let (or *blow*) *off steam*; to express strong feeling; to release pent-up emotions.

stēam, *a.* 1. using steam, as for heating or propulsion, or heated, operated, propelled, etc. by steam.
2. containing or conducting steam, as a pipe.
3. treated with, or exposed to the action of, steam.
steam fire engine; a fire engine whose power is furnished by steam.

stēam, *v.i.*; steamed, *pt., pp.*; steaming, *ppr.* 1. to give off steam or vapor; to give off any fume or exhalation.
2. to rise or be given off as steam.
3. to become covered with steam, or condensed water vapor, as a window, etc.
4. to produce or generate steam.
5. to move or travel by steam power.

stēam, *v.t.* 1. to treat with, or expose to the action of, steam, as in cooking, cleaning, etc.
2. to give off (vapor) or emit as steam.

stēam blōw'ēr, 1. a blower for producing a draft by means of discharging steam.
2. a fan blower that has steam for its motive power.

stēam'bōat, *n.* a steamship.

stēam'bōat çōal, a large-sized coal prepared in the Pennsylvania collieries for special uses.

stēam'bōat·ing, *n.* 1. the business of running steamboats.
2. rush and carelessness in work. [Colloq.]
3. in bookbinding, the cutting of many boards for book covers at a single operation.

stēam boil'ēr, a tank in which water is heated to produce steam and hold it under pressure.

stēam çär, a car driven by steam power.

stēam çās'ing, a steam jacket.

stēam chest, 1. a compartment in a steam engine through which steam passes from the boiler to the cylinder: also *steam box.*
2. in calico printing, a form of steam apparatus in which steam is applied to cloth in order to fix the colors.
3. a chamber heated by steam, and used for softening timber which is to be bent to a curved form, as ships' planking.

stēam chim'ney, an annular chamber around the chimney of a boiler-furnace for superheating steam.

stēam çōal, steamboat coal; also, coal used to heat steam boilers.

stēam çock, a faucet or valve in a steam pipe.

stēam çoil, a steam pipe shaped like a coil.

stēam çŏl'ŏr, any dye that is fixed in a print by a chemical reaction caused by steam.

stēam cyl'in·dēr, the cylinder of a steam engine.

stēam dōme, a division or compartment in the boiler of a steam engine above the water, from which steam is conducted to the engine.

stēam en'ġine, an engine using steam under pressure to supply mechanical energy, usually through the action of a piston sliding in a cylinder. Steam engines are classified in various ways, as portable, marine, locomotive, pumping, blowing, winding, etc. According to the arrangement of the chief parts they

SINGLE-CYLINDER HORIZONTAL STEAM ENGINE

are classed as beam, oscillating cylinder, horizontal, vertical, etc. The mechanical energy of a steam engine is usually estimated in horsepower.
portable steam engine; a steam engine in which the boiler and engine are joined and mounted on wheels, in order that it may readily be transported.
rotary steam engine; a steam engine in which the cylinder revolves upon the piston or the piston revolves in the cylinder.
semiportable steam engine; a steam engine of the portable type which, instead of being mounted on wheels, is movable with its foundation plate.

stēam'ēr, *n.* 1. something operated by steam power; specifically, (a) a steamship; (b) a truck or automobile driven by steam power; (c) a steam engine; (d) a steam fire engine.
2. a person or thing that steams.
3. a container in which articles are subjected to the action of steam, as in washing or cookery.
4. an apparatus for steaming grain preparatory to grinding.
5. a steamer duck.

stēam'ēr duck, a large duck of the genus *Tachyeres,* native to South America, distinguished by its small, short wings, and the swiftness with which it paddles over the water.

stēam'ēr rug, a coarse woolen blanket of the kind used by passengers in deck chairs on shipboard.

stēam'ēr truñk, a broad, low, rectangular trunk, originally designed to fit under a bunk on shipboard.

stēam fit'tēr, a mechanic who specializes in the installation and maintenance of the boilers, pipes, etc. in steam pressure systems.

stēam fit'ting, the business, trade, or occupation of a steam fitter.

stēam gas, superheated steam.

stēam gāuġe, an attachment to a boiler to indicate the pressure of steam; a pressure gauge.

stēam gun, a gun the projectile force of which is derived from the expansion of steam issuing through a tube.

stēam ham'mēr, a form of heavy forge hammer operated by steam, consisting usually of a steam cylinder and piston, with metal striker attached, placed vertically over the anvil. There are two principal varieties: in one the cylinder is fixed, and the hammer is attached to the piston rod and is operated by the direct action of the steam in the cylinder; in the other the piston is fixed, and the hammer is attached to the lower end of the cylinder, which similarly rises and falls by the action of the steam in the cylinder.

stēam hēat, heat obtained from a steam boiler by a closed system of conducting pipes, coils, radiators, etc.

stēam'-hēat″ed, *a.* warmed or heated by means of steam heat; as, a *steam-heated* flat.

stēam hēat'ēr, 1. a plant for heating any building by means of steam.
2. the part of a steam-heating plant which radiates the heat: a radiator.

stēam'i·ly, *adv.* in a steamy manner.

stēam'i·ness, *n.* the state or quality of being steamy or vaporous; vaporousness; mistiness.

stēam jack'et, a cavity for steam surrounding a cylinder or vessel, for maintaining the required temperature.

stēam joint, any packed joint in a steam pipe.

stēam lo͝op, an arrangement of pipes for returning water of condensation to the boiler.

stēam nav'vy, a digging machine or dredge having steam for its motive power; a steam shovel. [Brit.]

stēam pack'ing, packing which is used in the stuffing boxes of engine cylinders, steam chests, etc. to make them steam tight without interfering with the free movement of the rods.

stēam pīpe, any pipe which conducts steam.

stēam pōrt, in a slide-valve steam engine, one of two oblong passages from the steam chest to the inside of the cylinder, by which the steam enters and returns, above and below the piston.

stēam pow'ēr, the power furnished by a steam engine.

stēam pump, any pump or pumping engine using steam as its motive power.

STEAM ROLLER

steam rōll'ēr, 1. a heavy roller driven by steam and used in paving and repairing roads, streets, etc.
2. figuratively, an overwhelming power or influence, especially when used relentlessly to force acceptance of a policy, override opposition, etc.

stēam'-rōll″ēr, *v.t.* 1. to crush by use of a steam roller.
2. to bring overwhelming force to bear upon; to crush or override as if with a steam roller; as, he *steam-rollered* the opposition.
3. to cause the passage or defeat of (a legislative bill, etc.), or make (one's way, etc.), by crushing the opposition or overriding obstacles.

stēam'-rōll″ēr, *v.i.* to move with overwhelming, crushing force, or use steam-roller tactics.

stēam'-rōll″ēr, *a.* suggestive of a steam roller.

stēam ro͝om, in a steam boiler, the space occupied by steam.

stēam'ship, *n.* a ship propelled by steam power.

stēam shŏv'el, a large, mechanically operated digger, powered by steam.

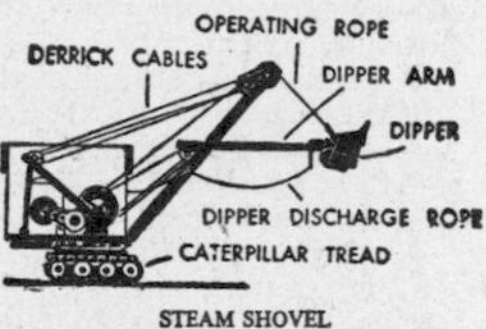

STEAM SHOVEL

stēam tā'ble, a type of table or counter, as in restaurants, having a metal top with steam-heated compartments in which food may be kept warm.

stēam'tīght (-tīt), *a.* that will prevent the passage or leakage of steam; as, a *steamtight* valve.

stēam trap, an automatic device for discharging the accumulated water of a steam pipe or vessel.

stēam tug, a small powerfully-built vessel used to tow ships in and out of a port.

stēam tūr'bine, a turbine turned by steam moving under great pressure.

stēam ves'sel, a steamship.

stēam whis'tle (hwis'l), a sounding device worked by a jet of steam, usually from the boiler of a steam engine, and used for signaling. Steam whistles are made to give musical tones varying in pitch by graduating the length of their pipes or cups, and a series of whistles tuned to different notes and operated by keys forms the musical instrument called the *calliope.*

stēam'y, *a.*; *comp.* steamier; *superl.* steamiest, 1. of or like steam.
2. covered or filled with steam.
3. giving off steam or steamlike vapor.

stēan, *n.* and *v.t.* same as *steen.*

stēan'ing, *n.* same as *steening.*

stēap'sin, *n.* [G., from *stea*rin, and pe*psin.*] an enzyme found in the pancreatic secretion: it converts oils and fats into glycerol and free acids.

stē'ȧ·rāte, *n.* a salt or ester of stearic acid.

stē·ar'iç, *a.* [Fr. *stéarique,* from Gr. *stear,* tallow.] of, derived from, or like stearin or fat.
stearic acid; a colorless, waxlike fatty acid, $C_{18}H_{36}O_2$, found in many animal and vege-

table fats, and used in making candles, stearates, soaps, etc.

stē·ar′i·fọrm, *a.* of or pertaining to stearin.

stē′ȧ·rin, *n.* [Gr. *stear, steatos,* stiff fat, tallow, suet.]
  1. a white, crystalline substance, glyceryl stearate, $(C_{18}H_{35}O_2)_3C_3H_5$, found in the solid portion of most animal and vegetable fats.
  2. stearic acid (as used in commerce).

stē′ȧ·rine, *n.* same as *stearin.*

stē·ȧ·rol′iç ac′id, an acid of the acetylene series, derived from oleic acid.

stē′ȧ·rōne, *n.* a ketone, $C_{35}H_{70}O$, obtained by the partial decomposition of stearic acid.

stē·ȧ·rop′tēne, *n.* [Gr. *stear,* fat, tallow, and *ptēnos,* winged.] the oxygenated, chiefly solid part of an essential oil: distinguished from *elaeoptene.*

stē·ar·rhē′ȧ (-rē′), *n.* same as *seborrhea.*

stē′ȧ·ryl, *n.* the radical of stearic acid.

stē′ȧ·tīte, *n.* [L. *steatitis;* Gr. *steatitēs,* of dough made of flour of spelt, from *stear,* tallow, also dough made of flour of spelt.] talc occurring in the form of a mass; soapstone.

stē·ȧ·tit′iç, *a.* of or pertaining to steatite.

stē′ȧtō-, stē′at-, [from Gr. *stear, steatos,* stiff fat, tallow, suet.] a combining form used to denote fatty substances or the quality of fattiness.

stē·ȧ·toġ′ē nous, *a.* [*steato-,* and *genēs,* producing.] causing steatosis.

stē·ȧ·tol′y·sis, *n.* [*steato-,* and Gr. *lysis,* a loosing, setting free.] the emulsifying process which fats undergo preparatory to absorption.

stē·ȧ·tō′mȧ, *n.* [Gr. *steatōma,* a kind of fatty tumor, from *stear, steatos,* stiff fat, tallow, suet.] a tumor arising from a diseased sebaceous gland or glands; a lipoma.

stē·ȧ·tom′ȧ·tous, *a.* of or relating to a steatoma.

stē″ȧ·tō·path′iç, *a.* [*steato-,* and Gr. *pathikos,* passive, from *paschein,* to suffer.] pertaining to or designating disorders of the sebaceous glands.

stē″ȧ·tō·pȳ′ġi·ȧ, *n.* [Gr. *stear, steatos,* fat, tallow, suet, and *pygē,* the rump.] excessive fatness of the hips and buttocks, expecially as found among the Hottentots and certain other African tribes, particularly in the women.

stē″ȧ·tō·pyġ′iç, *a.* of or characterized by steatopygia.

stē″ȧ·tō·pȳ′gous, *a.* same as *steatopygic.*

stē·ȧ·top′y·ġy, *n.* same as *steatopygia.*

stē″ȧ·tọr·rhē′ȧ, stē″ȧ·tọr·rhoe′ȧ (-rē′), *n.* [*steato-,* and Gr. *rhein,* to flow.]
  1. seborrhea.
  2. an excessive amount of fat in the feces.

stē·ȧ·tō′sis, *n.; pl.* **stē·ȧ·tō′sēş,** 1. fatty degeneration.
  2. a diseased condition of the sebaceous glands.

sted, *n.* stead. [Obs.]

sted′fȧst, *a.* same as *steadfast.*

stee, *n.* [AS. *stīgan,* to mount.] a ladder. [Brit. Dial.]

steed, *n.* [ME. *stede;* AS. *stēda,* a stud horse, stallion, war horse, from *stōd,* a stud.]
  1. a horse, especially a riding horse: literary term.
  2. a high-spirited horse. [Archaic.]

steed′less, *a.* having no steed.

steek, *v.t.* 1. to pierce with a sharp-pointed instrument; also, to stitch or sew with a needle. [Brit. Dial.]
  2. to shut; to close; to fasten. [Scot.]

steel, *n.* [AS. *stel;* akin to L.G., D., and Dan. *staal,* Ice. *stål,* G. *stahl,* O.H.G. *stahal.*]
  1. a hard, tough metal composed of iron alloyed with various small percentages of carbon: steel may be alloyed with other metals, as nickel, chromium, etc., to produce specific properties, as hardness, resistance to rusting, etc.
  2. a particular kind of steel: *hard* (or *high*) *steel* has a relatively high carbon content, as distinguished from *soft* (or *mild* or *low*) *steel,* which has a relatively low carbon content, and *medium steel,* which has a medium carbon content.
  3. anything made of steel; specifically, (a) [Poet.] a weapon made of steel, as a sword; (b) a piece of steel used for striking sparks from flint; (c) a round rod of steel, having longitudinal striations, used for sharpening knives; (d) a narrow slip of steel used for stiffening or expanding women's dresses, corsets, etc.; (e) formerly, a plate of polished steel used as a mirror.
  4. great strength or hardness; as, sinews of *steel,* a heart of *steel.*
  5. [*often in pl.*] the market price of shares in a steel-making company; as, *steels* fell during the week.
  alloy steel; an alloy of iron with another metal, such as nickel, chromium, manganese, etc.
  basic steel; steel formed by the basic process.
  Bessemer steel; see under *Bessemer process.*
  blister steel; steel of blistered appearance, formed by heating bar iron in contact with carbon in a cementing furnace.
  carbon steel; steel the properties of which have been derived principally from carbon: opposed to *alloy steel.*
  cast steel; steel formed by casting, as distinguished from rolling or forging.
  damask steel; see under *damask.*
  German steel; steel made from crude iron.
  tungsten steel; a hard, malleable, heat-resistant steel containing tungsten.

steel, *a.* composed of or containing steel; of the nature of steel.

steel, *v.t.;* steeled, *pt.; pp.;* steeling, *ppr.* 1. to overlay, point, or edge with steel; as to *steel* the point of a sword; to *steel* an ax.
  2. to make hard, tough, relentless, unfeeling, etc.
  3. to cause to resemble steel in qualities.
  4. to put a thin electrolytic deposit of iron, as on the surface of an electrotype, for the purpose of hardening it.

steel blūe, a metallic blue color which steel takes on in the tempering process.

steel′-blūe′, *a.* of the color steel blue.

steel′bow goodş, in Scots law, corn, cattle, straw, implements of husbandry, etc. delivered by the landlord to his tenant, by means of which the tenant is enabled to stock and work the farm, and in consideration of which he becomes bound to return articles equal in value and quality at the expiration of the lease. [Obs.]

steel en·grāv′ing, 1. an engraving made on a steel plate.
  2. a print from such a plate.
  3. the process used in making such engravings.

steel′ēr, *n.* one who steels or overlays with steel.

steel′ēr, *n.* in shipbuilding, a stealer.

steel grāy, a dark, somewhat bluish gray.

steel′-grāy′, *a.* of the color steel gray.

steel gui·tär′ (gi-), a type of guitar, now especially an electric guitar, with raised metal strings, held on the lap or mounted on legs and played by plucking while sliding a steel bar across the strings to change the pitch.

steel′head (-hed), *n.; pl.* **steel′head** or **steel′headş,** 1. the ruddy duck. [Dial.]
  2. a large rainbow trout found along the Pacific coast of North America.

steel′i·ness, *n.* the condition or quality of being steely.

steel′ing, *n.* the process of facing or edging with steel or making steellike.

steel mill, a mill where steel is made, processed, and shaped in various forms.

steel-plāt′ed, *a.* plated with steel.

steel wool, long, fine steel shavings matted together and used for cleaning, smoothing, and polishing.

steel′wŏrk, *n.* 1. articles or parts made of steel.
  2. a frame or structure made of steel.
  3. [*pl.*] [*often construed as sing.*] a steel mill.

steel′wŏrk″ēr, *n.* a worker in a steel mill.

steel′y, *a.; comp.* steelier, *superl.* steeliest, 1. made of steel; consisting of steel.
  2. hard; firm; of the nature or color of steel.

steel′yärd, *n.* [*steel,* and *yard* (in obs. sense of rod, bar).] a balance or scale consisting of a metal arm suspended off center from above: the object to be weighed is hung from the shorter end, and a sliding weight is moved along the graduated longer end until the whole arm balances.

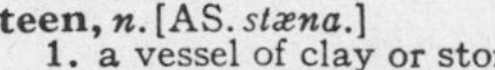

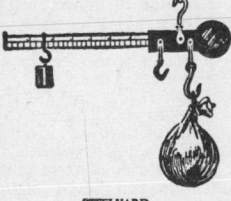

STEELYARD

steen, *n.* [AS. *stæna.*]
  1. a vessel of clay or stone. [Brit. Dial.]
  2. a steening. [Brit. Dial.]

steen, *v.t.* [AS. *stænan,* to set with stones.] to line with stone or brick, as a well, cesspool, etc.; also, [Brit. Dial.] to mend with stones, as a road.

steen′bok, *n.; pl.* **steen′bok** or **steen′boks,** [D., from *steen,* stone, and *bok,* buck.] a small African antelope of the genus *Raphicerus,* of which *Raphicerus campestris* is the common species: also *steinbok.*

steen′ing, *n.* the brick or stone wall or lining of a well or cesspool.

steen′kīrk, steīn′kirk, *n.* [D., lit., stone church.] a large lace necktie, worn casually, which came into fashion after the battle of Steenkirk (1692), where, supposedly, the French nobles were called into battle so hastily as to leave them no time to straighten their dress.

steep, *a.; comp.* steeper; *superl.* steepest, [ME. *step, steep;* AS. *steāp,* steep, high, lofty.]
  1. having a relatively sharp rise or slope; precipitous; as, a *steep* incline.
  2. (a) unreasonably high or great; exorbitant; excessive; as, his demands seem rather *steep;* a *steep* price; (b) extreme; as, a *steep* statement. [Colloq.]
  3. lofty; towering; high. [Obs.]
  4. glittering; bright; fiery. [Obs.]

steep, *n.* a steep slope or incline; a precipitous place, hill, mountain, rock, ascent, or descent; a precipice.

steep, *v.t.;* steeped (stēpt), *pt., pp.;* steeping, *ppr.* [Ice. *steypa,* to overturn, to pour out liquids, to cast metals; Sw. *stöpa,* to steep, *stöpa korn,* to steep barley.]
  1. to soak in a liquid, in order to soften, clean, or extract the essence of; as, to *steep* corn; to *steep* tea.
  2. to drench; to soak thoroughly; to immerse or saturate.
  3. to imbue or impregnate thoroughly with some influence; as, *steeped* in crime.

steep, *v.i.* to be steeped or soaked in a liquid.

steep, *n.* 1. the act or process of steeping; also, the state of being steeped.
  2. something steeped or used in steeping; specifically, a fertilizing liquid in which seeds are steeped to quicken germination.
  3. rennet. [Brit.]

steep′down, *a.* descending abruptly; precipitous. [Rare.]

steep′en, *v.t.* and *v.i.;* steepened, *pt., pp.;* steepening, *ppr.* to make or become steep or steeper.

steep′ēr, *n.* a vessel, vat, or cistern in which things are steeped.

steep′grȧss, *n.* butterwort, *Pinguicula vulgaris:* so called because it is used as rennet: also called *steepweed, steepwort.*

steep′i·ness, *n.* the state or quality of being steep. [Obs.]

steep′ish, *a.* slightly steep.

stee′ple, *n.* [ME. *stepel;* AS. *stypel,* a lofty tower, from AS. *steāp,* lofty, high.]
  1. a tower rising above the main structure of a building, especially of a church, usually capped with a spire.
  2. a church tower with a spire.
  3. a spire, as on a church tower.

stee′ple·bush, *n.* same as *hardhack.*

stee′ple·chāse, *n.* so called because the race usually had as its goal a steeple visible from a considerable distance.]
  1. originally, a horse run across country.
  2. a horse race run over a prepared course obstructed with artificial ditches, hedges, walls, etc.
  3. a foot race run across country or over a prepared course obstructed with ditches and other obstacles.

stee′ple·chās″ēr, *n.* a horse or person taking part in steeplechases.

stee′ple·chās″ing, *n.* the act or sport of riding or running in steeplechases.

stee′ple-ċrowned, *a.* 1. surmounted or crowned by a steeple.
  2. designating a hat or a crown of a hat shaped like a steeple.

stee′pled (-pld), *a.* furnished with a steeple or steeples.

stee′ple house, a church. [Obs.]

stee′ple·jack, *n.* a man who climbs steeples, tall chimneys, etc. to make repairs, paint, erect scaffolding, etc.: also *steeple jack.*

steep′ly, *adv.* in a steep manner; with steepness; precipitously.

steep′ness, *n.* the quality or state of being steep; precipitousness; as, the *steepness* of a river bank.

steep′-up, *a.* ascending steeply; sheer; lofty.

steep′weed, steep′wŏrt, *n.* same as *steepgrass.*

steep'y, *a.* steep; precipitous; as, *steepy* crags. [Poet.]

steer, *n.* [ME. *ster*; AS. *steōr*; akin to D. and G. *stier*, Ice. *stjórr*, a steer, a bull.]
 1. a young castrated male of the cattle family; a young ox.
 2. any male of beef cattle.

steer, *v.t.* to castrate; to make a steer of; as, to *steer* male calves.

steer, *v.t.*; steered, *pt.*, *pp.*; steering, *ppr.* [ME. *steren*; AS. *stieran*, *stȳran*, to rule, govern, direct, steer.]
 1. to guide (a ship or boat) by means of a rudder.
 2. to direct the course or movement of; as, he *steered* the automobile, she *steered* herself around the corner.
 3. to oversee, direct; control; as, she *steered* our efforts in the right direction.
 4. to set and follow (a course).

steer, *v.i.* 1. to steer a ship, automobile, etc.
 2. to be steered or guided; as, the car *steers* easily.
 3. to conduct oneself; to take or pursue a certain course.
 to steer clear of; to keep clear of or away from; to avoid.

steer, *n.* advice or suggestion as to how to proceed; a tip. [Slang.]

steer, *n.* a steersman; a helmsman. [Obs.]

steer'à·ble, *a.* capable of being directed or steered.

steer'ăġe, *n.* 1. the act or practice of steering, directing, governing, or controlling in a course; as, the *steerage* of a ship.
 He left the city, and, in a most tempestuous season, forsook the helm and *steerage* of the commonwealth. —Milton.
 2. the effect of a helm on a ship; the manner in which a ship is affected by the movement of the helm.
 3. that by which a course is steered or directed. [Rare.]
 Here he hung on high
 The *steerage* of his wings, and cut the sky. —Dryden.
 4. the stern of a ship. [Rare.]
 5. steering apparatus.
 6. way; course; conduct.
 7. direction; regulation; control; management.
 But He that hath the *steerage* of my course
 Direct my sail. —Shak.
 8. in passenger ships, the quarters allotted to the passengers paying the lowest rate of fare: originally, the part of the ship containing the steering mechanism; on warships, the quarters assigned to the junior officers, situated just forward of the wardroom.

steer'ăġe pas'sen·ġẽr, a passenger who travels in the steerage.

steer'ăġe·wāy, *n.* the minimum forward movement of a ship which renders her governable by the helm.

steer'ẽr, *n.* 1. one who or that which steers; a steersman; a guide.
 2. the rod and wheel (the latter usually small) which guide or turn a tricycle.

steer'ing cŏm·mit'tee, a committee, as of a legislative body, appointed to arrange the order of business.

steer'ing gēar, any mechanism used for steering, as in a ship, automobile, airplane, etc.

steer'ing wheel (hwēl), a wheel that is turned to operate a steering gear.

steer'less, *a.* having no steer or rudder. [Obs.]

steer'ling, *n.* a young steer or bullock.

steers'măn, *n.*; *pl.* **steers'men,** one who steers; the helmsman of a ship.

steers'māte, *n.* a steersman. [Obs.]

steeve, *v.t.* and *v.i.*; steeved, *pt.*, *pp.*; steeving *ppr.* [prob. from OFr. *estive*, tail of a plough.] to set or be set at an angle above the line of the horizon or of the keel: said of a bowsprit.

steeve, *n.* the angle at which the bowsprit is set.

steeve, *v.t.* and *v.i.* to stiffen [Scot. and Brit. Dial.]

steeve, *a.* stiff; rigid; firm; unyielding. [Scot. and Brit. Dial.]

steeve'ly, *adv.* firmly; stoutly. [Scot. and Brit. Dial.]

steeve, *v.t.* [Fr. *estiver*; L. *stipare*, to cram.] to stow (cargo), as in the hold of a ship, by means of a spar or derrick having a block at one end.

steeve, *n.* a long derrick with a block at one end for stowing cargo firmly in the hold.

steev'ing, *n.* the angle of elevation which a ship's bowsprit makes with the horizon.

steg, *n.* a stag. [Scot. and Brit. Dial.]

steg·à·nog'rà·phist, *n.* one who practices the art of writing in cipher; one skilled in steganography.

steg·à·nog'rà·phy, *n.* [Gr. *steganos*, covered, secret, and *-graphy*.] the art of writing in cipher; cryptography.

Steg"à·noph·thal'mà·tà, *n. pl.* [Gr. *steganos*, covered, and *ophthalmos*, eye.] same as *Lucernarida*.

steg"à·noph·thal'māte, *a.* having the eyes hidden: also written *steganophthalmatous*, *steganophthalmic*, *steganophthalmous*. [Rare.]

steg'à·nō·pod, *a.* having all four toes webbed; totipalmate, as the pelican and gannet.

steg'à·nō·pod, *n.* any one of the *Steganopodes*.

steg·à·nop'ō·dăn, *a.* totipalmate; steganopod.

Steg·à·nop'ō·dēs, *n. pl.* [Gr. *steganos*, covered, and *pous*, *podos*, foot.] a group of swimming birds with all four toes connected by a broad web. It includes the pelicans, gannets, cormorants, darters, frigate birds, and tropic birds.

steg·à·nop'ō·dous, *a.* same as *steganopod*.

steg·nō'sis, *n.* [LL., from Gr. *stegnōsis*; *steganos*, covered, closed.] in pathology, a stoppage of the functions of the pores and organs of evacuation.

steg·not'iç, *a.* tending to render costive, or to diminish excretions or discharges generally.

steg·not'iç, *n.* a medicine which tends to produce costiveness; one that diminishes excretions or discharges generally.

steg·ō·cär'pous, *a.* having a capsule which opens by a deciduous lid or cap. said of mosses.

steg·ō·mȳ'ià, *n.* [ML., from Gr. *stegos*, a roof, and *myia*, a fly.] the yellow-fever mosquito, *Aēdes aegypti*: the former name.

Steg·ō·sau'ri·à, *n.pl.* [Gr. *stegein*, to cover, and *sauros*, a lizard.] a group of dinosaurs, including two families, the *Scelidosauridæ* and *Stegosauridæ*.

steg·ō·sau'ri·ăn, *a.* of, pertaining to, or resembling the *Stegosauria*.

steg·ō·sau'ri·ăn, *n.* any dinosaur of the order *Stegosauria*.

Steg·ō·sau'ri·dae, *n.pl.* a family of herbivorous dinosaurs having a small head and heavy bony plates with sharp spines down the backbone. Some remains have been found in the Jurassic beds of the Rocky Mountains.

steg·ō·sau'roid, *a.* and *n.* same as *stegosaurian*.

Steg·ō·sau'rus, *n.* 1. the type of genus of the *Stegosauridæ*.
 2. [s–] any dinosaur of this genus.

stēik, *v.t.* same as *steek*.

stein, *n.* [G.] a drinking mug, as of stone or earthenware, often with a cover and decorated with figures either painted or in bas relief: used for serving beer; also, any similar mug, as of glass, etc.

stein'bok, *n.* same as *steenbok*.

Stei·nē'ri·ăn, *a.* of, pertaining to, or advanced by Jacob Steiner (1796–1863), a German mathematician.

stein'kirk, *n.* same as *steenkirk*.

stē'là, *n.* same as *stele*.

stē'lē, *n.*; *pl.* **stē'lēs, stē'lae,** or **stē'lai,** [L., from Gr. *stēle*, a post or slab, an upright stone, from stem *sta*, to stand.]
 1. an upright stone slab or pillar engraved with an inscription or design and used as a monument, grave marker, etc.
 2. in architecture, a prepared surface, as on a façade, having an inscription, carved design, etc.
 3. in botany, a central tube of tissue in the roots and stems of plants which grow by the addition of layers on the outside.

stēle, *n.* same as *stale*.

stell, *n.* [allied to *stall*.] a fenced enclosure forming a shelter for cattle or sheep. [Scot. and Brit. Dial.]

stell, *v.t.* [D. and G. *stellen*, to set, to place; akin to *stall*.] to fix; to set; to place in a permanent manner. [Scot.]

stel'là, *n.*; *pl.* **stel'lae,** [L., a star.] in spongology, a star-shaped spicule; a stellate.

stel'lăr, *a.* [LL. *stellaris*, from L. *stella*, a star.]
 1. of the stars or a star.
 2. like a star, as in shape.
 3. by or as by a star performer; excellent.
 4. leading; chief; as, the *stellar* role in a play.

Stel·lā'ri·à, *n.* [LL., from L. *stella*, a star, from the shape of the flowers.] a genus of plants of the family *Caryophyllaceæ*: also called *Alsine*; stitchwort. Most of the species are weeds, which are distributed over the temperate and cold regions of the world. They are slender, usually smooth herbs, with broad or grassy leaves and white flowers in dichotomous cymes.

stel'là·ry, *a.* same as *stellar*.

stel'lāte, *a.* [L. *stellatus*, pp. of *stellare*, to cover with stars, from *stella*, a star.] resembling a star; arranged in the form of a star; coming out in rays or points from a center.

STELLATE LEAVES

stel'lāte, *n.* a stellate sponge spicule.

stel'lā·ted, *a.* same as *stellate*.

stel'lāte·ly, *adv.* in a stellate manner; starlike; radiately.

stel·lā'tion, *n.* 1. radiation of light. [Obs.]
 2. adornment with stars. [Obs.]
 3. a constellation. [Obs.]

stel'lā·tūre, *n.* same as *stellionate*.

stelled, *a.* studded, as with stars. [Obs.]

stel'lẽr·id, *n.* one of the *Stellerida* or *Asteridea*; a starfish.

Stel·ler'i·dà, *n.pl.* [LL., from *stellaris*, starry.] same as *Asteridea*.

stel·ler'i·dăn, *a.* of or pertaining to the *Stellerida*.

stel·ler'i·dăn, *n.* one of the *Stellerida*.

stel·lẽr·id'ē·ăn, *n.* same as *stelleridan*.

stel·lif'ẽr·ous, *a.* having or full of stars. [Rare.]

stel'li·form, *a.* stellate; star-shaped.

stel'li·fȳ, *v.t.*; stellified, *pt.*, *pp.*; stellifying, *ppr.* to turn into or make to resemble a star; to make glorious; to glorify.
 Methought I saw him *stellified* in heaven. —Rowley.

Stel'li·ō, *n.* [L., a lizard.] a genus of old-world lizards having the tail surrounded by rings composed of great scales which are often spiny.

stel'liŏn (-yun), *n.* [LL., from L. *stellio* (*-onis*), lizard.] a lizard of the genus *Stellio*; a star lizard.

stel'liŏn·āte, *n.* [LL. *stellionatus*, cozenage, from L. *stellio* (*-onis*), a lizard; fig., a crafty, knavish person.] in Scots and Roman law, any fraud that has no special name to distinguish it, as when one sells the same thing to two purchasers or when a debtor pledges what does not belong to him.

stel'lū·lăr, *a.* [LL. *stellula*, a little star, dim. of *stella*, a star.]
 1. stellate.
 2. covered with small stars or starlike spots of color.

stel'lū·lāte, *a.* resembling or having little stars; stellular.

stē·log'rà·phy, *n.* [Gr. *stelographia*, from *stēle*, a stele, and *graphein*, to write.] inscriptions on steles. [Rare.]

stem, *n.* [AS. *stemn*; akin to G. *stamm*, tree trunk.]
 1. (a) the main upward-growing axis of a plant, usually extending in a direction opposite to that of the root and above the ground; (b) the main stalk or trunk of a tree, shrub, or other plant; the main body of the aboveground part of a plant, from which leaves, flowers, and fruit develop.
 2. (a) any stalk or part supporting leaves, flowers, or fruit; (b) a pedicel, petiole, or peduncle; (c) a stalk of bananas.
 3. a stemlike piece or part; as, the *stem* of a goblet, the *stem* of a tobacco pipe; specifically, (a) the cylindrical shaft projecting from a watch, with a knurled knob at its end for winding the spring; (b) the rounded rod in some locks, about which the key fits and is turned; (c) the main or thick stroke of a letter, as in printing; (d) the vertical line constituting part of a musical note (other than a whole note or breve).
 4. the upright piece to which the side timbers or plates are attached to form the prow of a ship.
 5. the forward part of a ship; prow; bow.
 6. the part of a word to which inflectional endings are added or in which phonetic changes are made for inflection.
 7. (a) a branch of a family; (b) lineage; ancestry; stock.

from stem to stern; (a) from one end of a ship to the other; (b) through the entire length of anything.

stem, *v.t.*; stemmed, *pt.*, *pp.*; stemming, *ppr.*
 1. to remove the stem or stems from (a fruit, etc.)
 2. to provide (artificial flowers, etc.) with stems.
 3. [from *n.* 4 and 5.] to make headway or progress against; as, the small boat could not *stem* the incoming tide.

stem, *v.i.* to originate, derive, or be descended.

stem, *v.t.*; stemmed, *pt.*, *pp.*; stemming, *ppr.* [ON. *stemma*, to stop.]
 1. to stop or check; especially, to dam up (a river, etc.), or to stop or check as if by damming up.
 2. to close or stop by tamping or by using a lute, as a pipe joint.

stem, *v.i.*to stop or slow down in skiing by turning one ski (*single stemming*) or both skis (*double stemming*) with the heel more or less outward.

stem, *n.* in skiing, an act or manner of stemming.

stem, *n.* steam. [Obs.]

stem'-clasp"ing, *a.* embracing the stem with its base; amplexicaul, as a leaf or petiole.

stem'less, *a.* having no stem.

stem'let, *n.* a small or young stem.

stem'ma, *n.*; *pl.* **stem'ma·ta,** [L., from Gr. *stemma*, a wreath.]
 1. an ocellus, or simple eye of an insect.
 2. a corneal facet of an ocellus or of a compound eye.
 3. a tubercle bearing an antenna.
 4. a family tree or pedigree; line of descent.

stemmed, *a.* 1. having a stem, usually of a specified kind; as, a thin-*stemmed* goblet.
 2. with the stem or stems removed.

stem'mẽr, *n.* one who or that which stems, as (a) a tamping rod; (b) one who stems fruits, tobacco leaves, etc.

stem'mẽr·y, *n.* a place where the stems are removed from leaf tobacco.

stem'my, *a.*; *comp.* stemmier; *superl.* stemmiest, having or containing stems.

Stē'mō·na, *n.* a genus of the *Stemonaceæ*.

Stē·mō·nā'cē·ae, *n.pl.* [Gr. *stēmōn*, thread, warp, lit., that which stands up, from *histanai*, to stand, and *-aceæ*.] a family of herbaceous plants, native to the tropical countries of the western Pacific Ocean, one species being also found in Florida.

stem'ple, stem'pel, *n.* [G. *stempel*, a stamp.] a crossbar of wood in a mine shaft, as (a) a step of a fixed ladder; (b) a supporting timber of a stull, set into the rock at each end.

stem'sŏn, *n.* [from *stem*, after *keelson*.] in shipbuilding, a piece of curved timber fixed on the afterpart of the apron inside. The lower end is scarfed into the keelson, and receives the scarf of the stem, through which it is bolted.

stem'-wīnd"ẽr, *n.* 1. a stem-winding watch.
 2. something very excellent. [Old Slang.]

stem'-wīnd"ing, *a.* wound by turning a knurled knob at the other end of the stem.

stench, *n.* [AS. *stenc*, a strong smell, from *stanc*, pt. of *stincan*, to smell, stink.] an offensive odor; a stink.

stench, *v.t.* to cause to emit a stench. [Obs.]

stench, *v.t.* to stanch; to stop. [Obs.]

stench trap, a device to keep foul air from passing out of a sewer or the like.

stench'y, *a.*; *comp.* stenchier; *superl.* stenchiest, having an offensive smell; stinking.

sten'cil, *v.t.*; stenciled *or* stencilled, *pt.*, *pp.*; stenciling *or* stencilling, *ppr.* [from OFr. *estenceler*, to ornament with spangles, from *estencele*, a spark; L. *scintilla*, a spark.] to mark or paint with a stencil.

sten'cil, *n.* 1. a thin sheet, as of paper or metal, perforated or cut through in such a way that when ink, paint, etc. is applied to the sheet, patterns, designs, letters, etc. form on the surface beneath the sheet.
 2. a pattern, design, letters, etc. made by stenciling.

STENCIL

sten'cil·ẽr, sten'cil·lẽr, *n.* a person or thing that makes stencils.

stend, *n.* a leap; a long stride. [Scot.]

Sten gun, [after *S*heppard and *T*urpin, the inventors, and *En*gland.] a British light machine gun that can be held when fired: it is capable of firing at the rate of 550 rounds per minute and weighs a little less than 8 pounds.

steno-, sten-, [from Gr. *stenos*, narrow.] combining forms meaning *small, thin, narrow, abbreviated*, etc., as in *steno*graphy.

sten'ō·dẽrm, *n.* [*steno-*, and Gr. *derma*, skin, hide.] any tropical American stenodermine bat.

sten·ō·dẽr'mine, *a.* of or relating to a genus of bats, *Stenoderma*, having a short muzzle, characteristic nose leaves, and a tail rudimentary or lacking.

sten'ō·gràph, *v.t.*; stenographed (-gràft), *pt.*, *pp.*; stenographing, *ppr.* [back-formation from *stenographer*.] to write in shorthand.

sten'ō·gràph, *n.* 1. something written in shorthand.
 2. a symbol used in shorthand.
 3. a keyboard machine that prints shorthand symbols.

stē·nog'rà·phẽr, *n.* one skilled in stenography.

sten·ō·graph'iç, *a.* 1. of or having to do with stenography.
 2. written in shorthand and, usually, transcribed in typewriting.

sten·ō·graph'iç·ăl, *a.* same as *stenographic*.

sten·ō·graph'iç·al·ly, *adv.* by means of stenography.

stē·nog'rà·phist, *n.* a stenographer.

stē·nog'rà·phy, *n.* [*steno-* and *-graphy*.] shorthand writing or, often, the process of taking down dictation in shorthand and later transcribing it in typewriting.

sten·ō·pae'iç, *a.* same as *stenopaic*.

sten·ō·pā'iç, *a.* [*steno-*, and Gr. *opē*, an opening.] containing a narrow slit or opening.
 stenopaic slit; a narrow slit in a plate of some opaque substance, used in testing the eye for astigmatism.
 stenopaic spectacles; spectacles with opaque plates having small central openings.

sten·ō·pet'ăl·ous, *a.* [*steno-*, and Gr. *petalon*, a petal.] having narrow petals.

sten·ō·phyl'lous, *a.* [*steno-*, and Gr. *phyllon*, a leaf.] having narrow leaves.

stē·nōsed' (-nōst'), *a.* in medicine, affected with stenosis or constriction.

sten·ō·sep'ăl·ous, *a.* having narrow sepals.

stē·nō'sis, *n.* [Gr. *stenōsis*, a straitening, from *stenos*, strait, narrow.] in medicine, the narrowing or stricture of a passage, duct, or opening; as, *stenosis* of the pylorus.

sten·ō·stom'à·tous, *a.* having a small mouth.

sten'ō·stōme, *a.* same as *stenostomatous*.

stē·not'iç, *a.* in medicine, affected with stenosis or abnormal narrowness.

sten'ō·tȳpe, *n.* 1. a symbol or symbols representing a sound, word, or phrase in stenotypy.
 2. a keyboard machine that prints such symbols: a trademark (*Stenotype*).

sten'ō·tȳ·py, *n.* [from *steno-* and Gr. *typē*, impression.] a kind of shorthand using ordinary letters as symbols for sounds, words, and phrases.

stent, *n.* and *v.* obsolete or dialectal form of *stint*.

stent, *v.t.* to stretch or straighten; also, to limit or restrain. [Scot.]

stent, *v.t.* in Scots law, to assess for taxation; to tax.

stent, *n.* in Scots law, an assessment; a tax.

stent, *n.* in mining, refuse; rubbish. [Brit. Dial.]

sten'tẽr, *v.t.*; stentered, *pt.*, *pp.*; stentering, *ppr.* to subject (light cotton fabrics) to a special process that produces an elastic finish.

sten'tẽr, *n.* a machine with which fabric is stretched by means of hooks and rollers and subjected to a current of heated air to make it elastic.

Sten'tŏr, *n.* [Gr. *Stentōr*, from *stenein*, to groan, make noise.]
 1. a Greek herald of the Trojan war who, according to Homer, had a voice as loud as fifty men.
 2. [s—] a person with a loud or powerful voice.
 3. [s—] in zoology, (a) a howling monkey; (b) a protozoan, genus *Stentor*, that is trumpet-shaped.

sten·tō'ri·ăn, *a.* 1. extremely loud or powerful; as, a *stentorian* voice.
 2. able to utter a very loud sound or sounds.

sten'tō·rine, *a.* of or relating to the genus *Stentor*.

sten·tō'ri·ous, *a.* [L. *Stentoreus*.] stentorian.

sten"tō·rō·phon'iç, *a.* speaking or sounding very loud; stentorian.

step, *n.* [AS. *stepe*; akin to (rare) G. *stapf*.]
 1. the action of moving the foot once and bringing it to rest again, as in walking or running.
 2. the distance covered by such a movement.
 3. a short distance; as, the tavern is just a *step* from here.
 4. a manner of stepping; gait.
 5. the sound of stepping; tread; footfall.
 6. a mark or impression made by stepping; footprint.
 7. a rest for the foot in climbing, as a stair or the rung of a ladder.
 8. [*pl.*] (a) a flight of stairs; (b) [Brit.] a stepladder.
 9. something resembling a stair step; specifically, (a) an offset in a piece of machinery; (b) a shelf or ledge cut in mining or quarrying; (c) a raised frame or platform supporting the butt end of a mast.
 10. a degree; rank; level; stage; as, they were one *step* nearer defeat.
 11. any of a series of acts, processes, etc.; as, let me explain the next *step*.
 12. a sequence of movements in dancing, usually repeated in a set pattern.
 13. in music, (a) a degree of the staff or scale; (b) the interval between two such consecutive degrees.
 14. in kinematics, a change of position unaccompanied by rotation.
 15. in machinery, the distance from one of the belt faces on a speed pulley to the belt face of its contiguous step measured radially.
 in step; (a) conforming to a rythym or cadence in marching, dancing, etc.; especially, conforming to the cadence of another marcher or other marchers; (b) in conformity or agreement.
 out of step; not in step.
 step by step; by degrees; gradually.
 to break step; to stop marching in cadence.
 to keep step; to stay in step.
 to watch one's step; (a) to exercise care in walking or stepping; (b) [Colloq.] to be careful or cautious.

step, *v.i.*; stepped (stept), *pt.*, *pp.*; stepping, *ppr.* [AS. *steppan*, *stapan*, to step.]
 1. to move forward or backward by executing a step or steps.
 2. to walk, especially a short distance; as, *step* here a moment.
 3. to move with measured steps, as in dancing.
 4. to move quickly or briskly: often with *along*; as, he *stepped* along at a fast clip.
 5. to come or enter (*into* a situation, condition, etc.); as, he *stepped into* a small fortune.
 6. (a) to put the foot down (*on* something); as, he accidentally *stepped on* my foot; (b) to press down with the foot (*on* something); as, he *stepped on* the accelerator.
 to step down; to resign or abdicate (*from* an office, position, etc.).
 to step in; to start to participate; to intervene.
 to step on it; to go faster; hurry; hasten. [Colloq.]
 to step out; (a) to leave a room, building, etc., especially for a short time; (b) [Colloq.] to go out for a good time; to go on a date; (c) to start to walk briskly, especially with long strides.
 to step up; (a) to go or come near; approach; (b) to advance or progress.

step, *v.t.* 1. to take (a stride, pace, etc.).
 2. to set down (the foot).
 3. to execute the steps of (a dance); as, to *step* a gavotte.
 4. to measure by taking steps: usually with *off*; as, he *stepped off* twenty paces.
 5. to provide with steps; specifically, (a) to cut steps in; as, he *stepped* the hill leading to his house; (b) to arrange in a series of degrees or grades.
 6. in nautical usage, to set and fix (a mast) in its step, or supporting structure.
 to step down; to decrease or reduce, as in rate, by or as by one or more steps, or degrees.
 to step it; to dance.
 to step up; to increase or raise, as in rate, by or as by one or more steps, or degrees.

step'brŏth"ẽr, *n.* the son of one's stepparent by a previous marriage.

step'child, *n.*; *pl.* **step'chil·dren,** [ME. *steop*, from AS. *astepan*, to bereave: originally applied to orphan children, but later to those related by remarriage, of a parent.] a child of one's husband or wife by a previous marriage.

step'dāme, *n.* a stepmother. [Archaic.]

step'daugh"tẽr (-dą"), *n.* a daughter of one's husband or wife by a previous marriage.

step'-down, *a.* that steps down, or decreases; specifically, (a) designating a transformer that converts an electric current from a higher to a lower voltage; (b) designating a gear that reduces the ratio. Opposed to *step-up*.

step'fä"thẽr, *n.* a male stepparent.

steph'ȧ·nē, *n.* [Gr. *stephanē*, the brim of a helmet.] an ornamental headdress resembling a coronet, wide in front and narrowing toward the back, worn by the ancient Greeks.

stē·phā'ni·on, n. [LL., from Gr. *stephanion*, dim. of *stephanos*, a wreath.] in anatomy, the point at the intersection of the temporal ridge and the cranial suture.

steph'ăn·īte, *n.* [named after *Stephan*, Archduke of Austria.] a sulfide of silver and antimony, crystallizing in the orthorhombic system.

steph'ȧ·nōme, *n.* [Gr. *stephanos*, crown, and *nomos*, law.] a graduated instrument for ascertaining the angular dimensions of indistinct objects, as fog bows, etc.

steph'ȧ·nos, *n.* [Gr., a wreath, crown, from *stephein*, to wreathe, crown.] an antique headdress similar to a stephane, but having a uniform width.

Steph·ȧ·nō'tis, *n.* [Gr. *stephanos*, a crown, and *ous, ōtos*, an ear.]

1. a genus of plants of the milkweed family, embracing fourteen species, ten of which are native to the Eastern Hemisphere. *Stephanotis floribunda* is the waxflower.

2. [s–] any plant of the genus *Stephanotis*.

step'-inṣ, *n.pl.* 1. women's short, loose-fitting underpants.

2. open-heeled shoes or slippers.

step'lad"dẽr, *n.* a four-legged ladder, usually hinged at the top for easy storage, and having broad, flat rungs or steps.

step'mŏth"ẽr, *n.* a female stepparent.

step'-off, *n.* a drop to a lower level or plane; a drop-off, as from an underwater ledge or shelf.

step'pãr"ent, *n.* the person who has married one's parent after the death or divorce of the other parent; stepfather or stepmother.

steppe, *n.* [Fr., from Russ. *step'*.]

1. one of the great plains of southeastern Europe and Asia, having few or no trees.

2. any extensive, relatively treeless plain.

steppe murrain; same as *rinderpest*.

stepped (stept), *a.* furnished with steps or something resembling steps.

stepped cone; same as *cone pulley*.

stepped gable; a gable constructed like a set of steps.

stepped gearing; gearing in which the teeth are arranged as though cut into successive slices in their breadth, and these slices placed at a definite and constant distance behind one another in their plane of rotation. The arrangement is made to obtain continuous bearing contact between wheels gearing with one another, and consequent steady motion.

step'pẽr, *n.* a person or animal that steps, usually in a specified manner, as a horse or a dancer.

step'ping·stōne, step'ping stōne, *n.* 1. a raised stone in a stream or in a swampy place to save the feet in walking.

2. an aid or means by which an end may be accomplished or an object gained; an assistance to progress.

These obstacles his genius had turned into *stepping stones*. —Macaulay.

step'sis"tẽr, *n.* a stepfather's or stepmother's daughter by a former wife or husband.

step'sŏn, *n.* a male stepchild.

step'stōne, *n.* a stone laid before a door as a stair to rise on in entering the house.

step'-up, *a.* that steps up, or increases: said of a transformer, gear, etc.: cf. *step-down*.

step'wīṣe, *adv.* like a series of steps.

-stẽr, [AS. *-estre*, f. suffix.] a suffix meaning *a person who is, does,* or *creates* (something specified), as in old*ster*, pun*ster*: often derogatory, as in rhyme*ster*, trick*ster*.

stẽr·ço·bi'lin, *n.* [L. *stercus, stercoris*, dung, and *bilis*, bile.] a brownish-red pigment occurring in the feces and derived from the bile.

stẽr·çō·rā'ceous, *a.* [L. *stercus, stercoris*, dung, and *-aceous*.] pertaining to, containing, like, or having the nature of feces, or dung.

stẽr'çō·răl, *a.* stercoraceous.

Stẽr'çō·rȧ·niṣm, *n.* the doctrine or belief of the Stercoranists.

Stẽr'çō·rȧ·nist, *n.* [L. *stercus, stercoris*, dung.] in ecclesiastical history, one of a party in the fifth and sixth centuries who held that the consecrated elements in the Eucharist undergo the process of digestion, so that the divine body, if materially present, must be changed into the fecal substance: so called in contempt.

Stẽr·çō·rãr'i·ăn, *n.* a stercoranist.

Stẽr·çō·rãr'i·ăn·ism, *n.* Stercoranism.

stẽr'çō·rãr·y, *n.* [L. *stercorarius*, pertaining to dung, from *stercus, stercoris*, dung.] a place, properly secured from the weather, for containing dung.

stẽr·çō·rā'tion, *n.* the act of manuring with dung. [Rare.]

stẽr·çō·rē'mi·ȧ, stẽr·çō·rae'mi·ȧ, *n.* [L. *stercus*, dung, and Gr. *haima*, blood.] a toxic state occasioned by poisons absorbed into the blood from unexpelled feces.

Stẽr·çō'ri·ăn·iṣm, Stẽr·çō'ri·ăn·ist, same as *Stercoranism*, etc.

stẽr·çō·riç'ō·lous, *a.* [L. *stercus*, dung, and *colere*, to inhabit.] inhabiting or existing in dung.

stẽr'çō·rin, *n.* a crystallizable substance resembling cholesterin, extracted from the feces.

Stẽr'çō·rist, *n.* a Stercoranist.

stẽr'çō·rīte, *n.* [L. *stercus*, dung, and *-ite*.] a mineral, $HNaNH_4PO_4 4H_2O$, found in crystalline masses and nodules in guano on the island Ichaboe, off the west coast of Africa.

stẽr'çō·rous, *a.* same as *stercoraceous*.

stẽr'çō·ry, *n.* dung; excrement. [Obs.]

Stẽr·çū'li·ȧ, *n.* [from L. *Sterculius*, a deity presiding over manure, from *stercus*, dung. The flowers and leaves of some of the species have a fetid odor.] a genus of tropical plants of the order *Sterculiaceæ*. The species consist of various-sized trees with soft timber, with simple or compound leaves and axillary panicles or racemes of flowers.

Stẽr·çū·li·ā'cē·ae, *n.pl.* a family of mainly tropical trees and shrubs, as the cacao and the kola, with alternate, stipulate, simple, and often toothed leaves, with a variable inflorescence and a stellate pubescence. *Sterculia* is the typical genus.

stẽr·çū·li·ā'ceous, *a.* pertaining or belonging to the order *Sterculiaceæ*.

stēre, *n.* [Fr. *stère*, from Gr. *stereos*, solid, cubic.] a cubic meter, or 35.3156 cubic feet.

stēre, *v.t.* and *v.i.* to move or stir. [Obs.]

Ster·el·min'thȧ, *n.pl.* [Gr. *stereos*, solid, and *helmins, helminthos*, an intestinal worm.] a primary division of *Entozoa*, comprising those intestinal worms which have no true abdominal cavity, as the tapeworm and trematode worms.

ster·el·min'thiç, ster·el·min'thous, *a.* pertaining or belonging to the *Sterelmintha*.

ster'ē·ō-, (*or* stẽr'), [from Gr. *stereos*, hard, firm, solid.] a combining form meaning *solid, firm, three-dimensional*, as in *stereo*scope, *stereo*graphy; also, before some vowels, *stere-*.

ster'ē·ō·bāte", *n.* [*stereo-*, and Gr. *basis*, a base.] in architecture, the lower part or basement of a building; a kind of continuous pedestal under a plain wall: distinguished from a *stylobate*, under a series of columns or pilasters.

ster"ē·ō·blas'tū·lȧ, *n.* a solid blastula, or one having no cavity.

ster"ē·ō·çhem'iç, ster"ē·ō·çhem'i·çăl, *a.* pertaining to stereochemistry, or the space relations of the atoms of a molecule.

stereochemical isomerism; isomerism in which the atoms are the same and are connected in the same way, but are arranged differently in the molecule.

ster"ē·ō·çhem'is·try, *n.* the branch of chemistry dealing with the spatial arrangement of atoms or groups of atoms that make up molecules.

ster'ē·ō·çhrōme, *n.* a picture produced by stereochromy.

ster"ē·ō·çhrō'miç, *a.* pertaining to or produced by stereochromy.

ster"ē·ō·çhrō'miç·ăl·ly, *adv.* by a stereochromic method.

ster'ē·ō·çhrō·my, *n.* [*stereo-*, and Gr. *chrōma*, color.] a process of mural painting using water glass as a fixative, either mixed with the pigment or laid over the finished painting.

ster"ē·ō·ē·leç'triç, *a.* designating the electric current generated when two solids, especially two metals, as bismuth and antimony, are brought together at different temperatures.

ster"ē·ō·gas'trū·lȧ, *n.* [*stereo-*, and LL. *gastrula*, from Gr. *gastēr*, the stomach.] a solid gastrula, or one without a cavity.

ster"ē·og·nō'sis, *n.* [*stereo-*, and Gr. *gnōsis*, knowledge.]

1. the faculty of recognizing the nature of objects by handling them.

2. perception by the senses of the solidity of objects.

ster'ē·ō·gram, *n.* a stereographic diagram or picture, or a stereograph.

ster'ē·ō·grȧph, *n.* a picture or a pair of pictures prepared for use with a stereoscope.

ster"ē·ō·graph'iç, ster"ē·ō·graph'i·çăl, *a.* of or produced by stereography; delineated on a plane; as, a *stereographic* chart of the earth.

stereographic projection; that projection of the sphere which is represented upon the plane of one of its great circles, the eye being situated at the pole of that great circle.

ster"ē·ō·graph'i·çăl·ly, *adv.* by stereography.

ster·ē·og'rȧ·phy, *n.* the art of delineating the forms of solid bodies on a plane; a branch of solid geometry which shows the construction of all solids which are regularly defined.

ster"ē·ō·ī·som'ẽr·iṣm, *n.* [*stereo-* and *isomerism*.] isomerism of optically active compounds, the atoms or atomic groups of which have different spatial arrangements.

ster'ē·ōme, *n.* [Gr. *stereōma*, a solid body, from *stereos*, hard, firm, solid.] the tissue of plants which gives them strength and solidity.

ster·ē·om'ē·tẽr, *n.* 1. an instrument for determining the specific gravity of liquid bodies, porous bodies, and powders.

2. an instrument for measuring the solid or liquid contents or the capacity of a vessel.

ster"ē·ō·met'riç, ster"ē·ō·met'ri·căl, *a.* pertaining to or produced by stereometry.

ster"ē·ō·met'riç·ăl·ly, *adv.* by stereometry.

ster·ē·om'ē·try, *n.* 1. the art of determining the dimensions and volume of solids.

2. the art or process of determining the specific gravity of liquids, porous bodies, etc.

ster"ē·ō·phon'iç, *a.* [*stereo-* and *-phonic*.] designating sound reproduction as from a motion-picture sound track, employing a number of loudspeakers placed variously in the theater to reproduce the sounds from the directions in which they were originally recorded.

ster'ē·ō·plaṣm, *n.* [*stereo-*, and Gr. *plasma*, anything formed.]

1. in biology, the firm or solid part of protoplasm.

2. the fine endothecal structure of corals varying somewhat in structure and greatly in position, often connecting septa or filling the corallum on its inner and under side.

ster"ē·ō·plaṣ'mȧ, *n.* stereoplasm. [Rare.]

ster"ē·ō·plaṣ'miç, *a.* resembling, formed by, or of the nature of stereoplasm.

ster·ē·op'sis, *n.* stereoscopic vision.

ster·ē·op'ti·çon, *n.* [*stereo-*, and Gr. *optikos*, denoting sight.] a magic lantern having a powerful projection light, especially one using double pictures, each with a separate lens, for producing dissolving views.

ster'ē·ō·sçōpe, *n.* [*stereo-* and *-scope*.] an instrument that gives a three-dimensional effect to photographs viewed through it: it has two eyepieces, through which two slightly different views of the same scene are viewed side by side.

STEREOSCOPE

ster"ē·ō·sçop'iç, ster"ē·ō·sçop'i·çăl, *a.* of, like, or used in a stereoscope; as, *stereoscopic* pictures; *stereoscopic* views.

ster"ē·ō·sçop'i·çăl·ly, *adv.* 1. by means of the stereoscope.

2. so as to appear three-dimensional.

ster′ē·ō·sçō·pist, *n.* a specialist in the use or manufacture of stereoscopes.

ster′ē·ō·sçō·py, *n.* 1. the science of stereoscopic effects and techniques.
2. the viewing of things as in three dimensions.

ster·ē·ō·tax′is, *n.* [*stereo-* and *taxis.*] a movement of an organism for which the stimulus is contact with a solid body.

ster″ē·ō·tom′iç, ster″ē·ō·tom′i·căl, *a.* pertaining to or performed by stereotomy.

ster·ē·ot′ō·my, *n.* [*stereo-*, and Gr. *-tomia*, from *temnein*, to cut.] the science or art of cutting solids into certain figures or sections.

ster′ē·ō·tȳpe, *n.* [Fr. *stéréotype*, *a.*; see *stereo-* and *-type.*]
1. a one-piece printing plate cast in type metal from a mold taken of a printing surface, as a page of set type.
2. stereotypy.
3. an unvarying form or pattern; fixed or conventional expression, notion, character, mental pattern, etc., having no individuality, as though cast from a mold; as, the Negro is too often portrayed as a *stereotype.*

ster′ē·ō·tȳpe, *a.* of or pertaining to a stereotype or a process of making or using stereotypes; as, a *stereotype* plate.

ster′ē·ō·tȳpe, *v.t.*; stereotyped (-tīpt), *pt.*, *pp.*; stereotyping, *ppr.* 1. to make a stereotype of; as, to *stereotype* a cut.
2. to print from stereotype plates; as, to *stereotype* an edition of books.
3. to arrange in a permanent or unalterable form.

ster′ē·ō·tȳped (-tīpt), *a.* 1. printed from or made of stereotype plates.
2. formed in a fixed, unchangeable manner; hackneyed; trite; not original or individualized; as, *stereotyped* opinions.

ster′ē·ō·tȳ·pẽr, *n.* a person or thing that stereotypes.

ster″ē·ō·tȳ′pẽr·y, *n.*; *pl.* **ster″ē·ō·tȳ′pẽr·ieṣ,**
1. the process of making stereotype plates.
2. an establishment where stereotype plates are made.

ster′ē·ō·tȳp′iç, *a.* 1. of or produced by stereotypy.
2. stereotyped; hackneyed.

ster′ē·ō·tȳ·ping, *n.* the art or process of making stereotype plates, and of producing printed work from such plates.

ster′ē·ō·tȳ·pist, *n.* same as *stereotyper.*

ster″ē·ō·tȳ·pog′rȧ·phẽr, *n.* a stereotype printer.

ster″ē·ō·tȳ·pog′rȧ·phy, *n.* the art, act, or practice of printing from stereotypes.

ster′ē·ō·tȳ·py, *n.* [Fr. *stéréotypie.*]
1. the process of making or printing from stereotype plates.
2. (a) abnormal repetition of an action, phrase, etc., especially as seen in one phase of dementia praecox; (b) the abnormal maintenance of a single position, or posture, over an extended period of time, as in some phases of schizophrenia.

stẽr·hȳ·drau′liç, *a.* [Gr. *stereos*, hard, firm, and E. *hydraulic.*] pertaining to or designating a form of hydraulic press in which a powerful hydrostatic pressure is obtained by introducing, by a steady, uninterrupted movement, a solid substance into the cylinder of a hydraulic press already filled with liquid.

ster′iç, *a.* of or pertaining to the spatial arrangement of the atoms in a molecule.

ster′i·căl, *a.* same as *steric.*

stē·rig′mȧ, *n.*; *pl.* **stē·rig′mȧ·tȧ,** [LL., from Gr. *stērigma*, a prop, from *sterizein*, to prop.] in botany, (a) one of certain filiform or pointed protuberances on special cells which develop into spores in fungi, the filaments forming the pedicels of the spermatia in fungi; (b) one of the elevated lines on the stems of various thistles, etc., produced by decurrent leaves.

ster·ig·mat′iç, *a.* pertaining to or like a sterigma.

ster′ile, *a.* [Fr. *stérile*, from L. *sterilis*, barren, unfruitful, unproductive.]
1. incapable of producing others of its kind; barren.
2. producing little or nothing; unfruitful; as, *sterile* soil, a *sterile* policy.
3. lacking in interest or vitality; not stimulating or effective; as, a *sterile* style or presentation.
4. deprived of its usual power or function; ineffective: said of gold (in monetary usage).
5. free from living microorganisms.
6. in botany, (a) unable or failing to bear fruit or spores, as a plant, or to germinate, as a seed; (b) having stamens only, as a male flower, or having neither pistils nor stamens.

stē·ril′i·ty, *n.*; *pl.* **stē·ril′i·tieṣ,** the state or quality of being sterile.

ster″il·i·zā′tion, *n.* 1. a sterilizing or being sterilized.
2. the state or condition of being sterile.

ster′il·īze, *v.t.*; sterilized, *pt.*, *pp.*; sterilizing, *ppr.* to make sterile; specifically, (a) to make incapable of producing others of its kind, as by removing the organs of reproduction or preventing them from functioning effectively: usually with reference to surgical operations; (b) to free from living microorganisms, as by subjecting to great heat or chemical action. Also spelled *sterilise.*

ster′il·ī·zẽr, *n.* a person or thing that sterilizes, especially a device used to destroy living microorganisms by heat or chemical action.

stẽr′let, *n.* [Fr. or G., from Russ. *sterlyadi.*] a small sturgeon of the Caspian Sea and of the rivers in Russia, the *Acipenser ruthenus* of Linnaeus, valued as a food fish and as a source of fine caviar.

stẽr′ling, *n.* [ME. *sterlinge*, Norman silver penny.]
1. originally, an early English silver penny: a pound weight of these pennies was later standardized as a money of account.
2. English money having the fineness of quality of the standard silver penny.
3. sterling silver or articles made of it.
4. the standard of fineness of legal British coinage: for silver, 0.500 (0.925 before 1920); for gold, 0.91666 (0.995 formerly).
5. British money.

stẽr′ling, *a.* 1. of standard quality: said of silver that is at least 92.5 per cent pure; originally said of silver having the quality of that in the sterling (sense 1).
2. of or payable in British money.
3. made of sterling silver.
4. having genuinely high quality or value; excellent; as, a man of *sterling* principles.

stẽrn, *a.*; *comp.* sterner; *superl.* sternest, [AS. *sterne, styrne*, stern, severe.]
1. severe; forbidding; grim; austere; gloomy; rigid; fixed with an aspect of severity and authority; as, a *stern* look, a *stern* countenance, a *stern* frown.
2. severe; hard; unyielding; strict; as, *stern* measures.
3. rigidly steadfast; immovable; relentless; inexorable; as, *stern* virtue, *stern* honesty.
Syn.—severe, austere, rigid, rigorous, harsh, unrelenting.

stẽrn, *n.* [ME. *steorne*; prob. from O.N. *styra*, to steer.]
1. the rear end of a ship or boat; the part opposite the stem or prow.
2. the helm of a vessel; hence, the post of management; direction. [Obs.]
3. the buttocks or tail part of an animal; the tail itself. [Colloq.]
4. the rear end of anything.

stẽr′nȧ, *n.* alternative plural of *sternum.*

stẽrn′āġe, *n.* sterns collectively. [Rare.]

stẽr′năl, *a.* 1. pertaining to the sternum.
2. ventral; near or on the same side with the sternum.

stẽrn′bẽrg·īte, *n.* [after Count Kaspar Maria von *Sternberg* (1761–1838), of Prague.] a soft, brown mineral, $AgFe_2S_3$, occurring in orthorhombic laminae.

stẽrn bōard, a backward motion of a vessel; hence, a loss of way in making a tack.
to make a stern board; in nautical usage, to fall back from the point gained in the last tack; also, to set the sails so that the vessel may be impelled sternforemost.

stẽrn chāse, a chase in which two vessels sail on one and the same course, one following in the wake of the other; as, a *stern chase* is a long chase.

stẽrn chās′ẽr, a gun placed in a ship's stern, used for firing to the rear.

stẽr′nē·bẽr, *n.* same as *sternebra.*

stẽr′nē·brȧ, *n.*; *pl.* **stẽr′nē·brae,** [LL., from *sternum* and *vertebra.*] a bony segment or element of the sternum of a vertebrate.

stẽr′nē·brăl, *a.* of or pertaining to a sternebra.

stẽrned, *a.* having a stern of a particular kind; as, square-*sterned.*

stẽrn′ẽr, *n.* a director. [Obs.]

stẽrn fȧst, a rope, chain, or cable used to confine the stern of a ship or other vessel to a wharf.

stẽrn·fōre′mōst, *adv.* with the stern in front; hence, awkwardly; clumsily.

stẽrn frāme, the several pieces of timber, iron, or steel which form the stern of a ship.

stẽr′nīte, *n.* [LL. *sternum*, the breastbone, and *-ite.*] a ventral sclerite, or the ventral portion of any somite or segment of an arthropod.

stẽrn knee (nē), same as *sternson.*

stẽrn′ly, *adv.* in a stern manner.

stẽrn′mōst, *a.* 1. nearest the stern.
2. farthest astern; rearmost; as, the *sternmost* ship in the fleet.

stẽrn′ness, *n.* the state or quality of being stern.

stẽr′nō-, [from LL. *sternum*, the breastbone.] a combining form meaning *of the sternum and*: also, before a vowel, *stern-.*

stẽr″nō·clȧ·viç′ū·lăr, *a.* [*sterno-*, and LL. *clavicula*, the clavicle.] belonging to the sternum and the clavicle.

stẽr·nō·çor′ȧ·çoid, *a.* belonging to the sternum and the coracoid.

stẽr·nō·ços′tăl, *a.* of or pertaining to the sternum and the ribs.

stẽr·nō·glos′săl, *a.* belonging to the sternum and the tongue.

stẽr·nō·hȳ′oid, *a.* pertaining or attached to the sternum and the hyoid bone.

stẽr·nō·mas′toid, *a.* belonging to the sternum and the mastoid process.

stẽr·nō·thȳ′roid, *a.* of, pertaining to, or attached to the sternum and the thyroid cartilage.

stẽrn′pōst, *n.* the principal piece of timber or iron in a vessel's stern frame. Its lower end is tenoned into the keel, and to it the rudder is hung and the transoms are bolted.

stẽrn sheets, the space at the rear of an open boat, usually furnished with seats for passengers.

stẽrn′sŏn, *n.* [from *stern* (of a ship), after *keelson.*] in nautical usage, a heavy curved piece connecting the keelson to the sternpost: also *sternson* (or *stern*) *knee.*

stẽr′num, *n.*; *pl.* **stẽr′nȧ, stẽr′numṣ,** [Mod. L., from Gr. *sternon*, the breastbone.]
1. the breastbone; a thin, flat structure of bone and cartilage to which most of the ribs are attached in front of the chest in most vertebrates. It is flattened and presents a slight vertical curve with the convexity in front. All mammals and birds possess a sternum, and the presence or absence of a ridge on that bone in birds is used as a means of classification. Fishes, amphibians, and ophidians have no sternum, and in saurians the broad portion is generally expanded.
2. the ventral portion of a somite of an arthropod.

stẽr·nū·tā′tion, *n.* [LL. *sternutatio* (*-onis*), a sneezing, from L. *sternutare*, to sneeze.] a sneeze or sneezing.

stẽr·nū′tȧ·tive, *a.* sternutatory.

stẽr·nū′tȧ·tō·ry, *a.* of or causing sternutation.

stẽr·nū′tȧ·tō·ry, *n.*; *pl.* **stẽr·nū·tȧ·tō·rieṣ,** a substance that provokes sneezing, as snuff, etc.

stẽrn′wărd, *adv.* toward the stern; astern.

stẽrn′wāy, *n.* the backward movement of a ship.

stẽrn wheel′, a large paddle wheel, mounted astern, for propelling a steam vessel: used especially on river steamers of light draft.

stẽrn′-wheel″ẽr, a steam vessel propelled by a stern wheel.

STERN-WHEELER

ster′oid, *n.* [*ster*ol and *-oid.*] any of a group of compounds including the sterols, bile acids, sex hormones, etc., characteristically having the carbon ring structure of the sterols.

ster′ōl, *n.* [contr. of *cholesterol.*] any of a group of solid cyclic alcohols found in plant and animal tissues, as cholesterol.

stẽr·quil′i·nous, *a.* pertaining to a dunghill; mean; dirty; paltry. [Obs.]

stẽrre, *n.* a star. [Obs.]

ster′riñck, *n.* the saw-toothed or crab-eating seal, *Lobodon carcinophagus*, found in the southern seas.

ster·rō·met′ăl, *n.* [Gr. *sterrhos*, solid, and E. *metal.*] an alloy of copper and zinc with a small proportion of tin and iron.

stẽrt, *v.* obsolete past tense and past participle of *start.*

stẽr'tŏr, *n.* a deep snoring accompanying breathing, as in certain diseases, as apoplexy.

stẽr'tō·rous, stẽr·tō'ri·ous, *a.* [L. *stertere,* to snore.] characterized by a deep snoring sound, such as frequently accompanies certain diseases, as apoplexy.

The *stertorous,* unquiet slumber of sick life. —Carlyle.

stẽrve, *v.t.* and *v.i.* to starve. [Obs.]

stet, [L., third pers. sing. pres. subj. of *stare,* to stand.] let it stand: a printer's term used to indicate that matter previously struck out is to remain.

stet, *v.t.*; stetted, *pt., pp.*; stetting, *ppr.* to mark with the word *stet*; to order anything previously deleted to be left as before, by placing the word *stet* in the margin and a series of dots under the line in question.

steth'ăl, *n.* [*st*earic and *ethal.*] a higher alcohol of the paraffin series, $C_{18}H_{37}OH$, corresponding to stearic acid. [Obs.]

steth'ō-, [Gr. *stēthos, stēth-,* from *stethos.* the chest, breast.] a combining form meaning *chest, breast,* as in *stetho*scope: also, before a vowel, *steth-.*

steth'ō·grȧph, *n.* [*stetho-* and *-graph.*] an instrument for recording the movements of the chest in respiration.

stē·thom'ē·tẽr, *n.* [*stetho-* and *-meter.*] an instrument for measuring the expansion of the chest or abdomen during respiration.

steth'ō·sçōpe, *n.* [*stetho-* and *-scope.*] in medicine, a hearing instrument used in auscultation, for examining the heart, lungs, etc. by listening to the sounds they make.

binaural stethoscope; a form of stethoscope with two adjustable branches designed for use with both ears.

differential stethoscope; a stethoscope by which sounds at two different portions of the body may be compared.

steth'ō·sçōpe, *v.t.*; stethoscoped, *pt., pp.*; stethoscoping, *ppr.* to examine by means of a stethoscope.

steth·ō·sçop'iç, steth·ō·sçop'i·căl, *a.* 1. of or pertaining to the stethoscope or to stethoscopy.

2. made or obtained by use of the stethoscope.

steth·ō·sçop'i·căl·ly, *adv.* by means of a stethoscope.

ste·thos'cō·pist, *n.* an expert in the use of the stethoscope.

ste·thos'cō·py, *n.* [Gr. *stēthos,* the breast, and *skopein,* to view.] the use of the stethoscope.

stē've·dōre, *n.* [Sp. *estivador,* from *estivar,* to stow, to ram tight; L. *stipare,* to cram, to stuff.] one whose occupation is to stow goods in a ship's hold; one who loads or unloads vessels.

stē've·dōre, *v.t.* and *v.i.*; stevedored, *pt., pp.*; stevedoring, *ppr.* to load or unload the cargo of (a ship).

stē've·dōre's knot (not), a kind of knot: see *knot,* illus.

stē'ven, *n.* 1. a voice; also, clamor; noise. [Obs.]

2. an appointment. [Obs.]

stew, *n.* [ME. *stuwe*; OFr. *estui,* a sheath, fish tub, from *estuier,* to enclose.]

1. a pool, tank, or small pond in which live fish or oysters are kept ready for the table.

2. an artificial oyster bed. [Dial.]

3. a place where tame pheasants are kept for breeding. [Brit. Dial.]

stew, *v.t.*; stewed, *pt., pp.*; stewing, *ppr.* [ME. *stuen, stuwen,* from OFr. *estuver,* to stew, bathe.]

1. to immerse or lave, as in a vapor bath. [Obs.]

2. to steep.

3. to boil slowly with a simmering heat; to cook or prepare, as meat or fruit, by bringing very gradually to a low boiling point; as, to *stew* meat, to *stew* prunes.

4. to worry. [Colloq.]

stew, *v.i.* 1. to simmer; to be boiled in a slow gentle manner, or in heat and moisture.

2. to worry. [Colloq.]

stew, *n.* 1. a room heated for bathing, or drying purposes; a hothouse; also, a stove. [Obs.]

2. [*usually in pl.*] a house of prostitution; a brothel.

In a tavern or a *stews* he and his associates spend their hours. —B. Jonson.

3. a prostitute. [Obs.]

4. a room; a closet. [Obs.]

5. a dish, especially a mixture of meat and several vegetables, cooked by slow boiling.

6. a stewpan. [Obs.]

7. a state of agitation, confusion, or excitement. [Colloq.]

stew'ărd, *n.* [AS. *stīweard, stigeweard,* a steward, lit., a *styward,* from *stigu,* a sty, a pen for cattle, and *weard,* a ward, a keeper.]

1. a man intrusted with the management of the household or estate of another; one employed to manage the domestic affairs, superintend the servants, collect the rents or income, keep the accounts, etc.

2. one who acts as a supervisor or administrator, as of finances and property, for another or others.

3. an officer or employee who has charge of the table supplies, as (a) an officer on a vessel who distributes provisions to the officers and crew; (b) in passenger ships, a man who superintends the provisions, etc., or one of his assistants who waits at table, etc.; (c) in colleges, a purveyor for the commons; (d) in hotels and restaurants, one who selects, buys, and superintends the preparation of food; (e) one in general charge of a club house.

4. a person, usually one of a group, in charge of arrangements for a ball, race, meeting, etc.

5. in Scotland, an officer appointed by the king over special lands belonging to the crown.

6. in labor unions, a worker who is elected as a representative of his department; a shop steward.

Lord High Steward; in England, one of the ancient officers of state, the greatest under the crown. The office was abolished at the close of the reign of Henry III., and is now revived only for particular occasions, as a coronation or the trial of a peer, the office to cease when the business requiring it is ended.

stew'ărd·ess, *n.* a woman steward; specifically, a woman who attends to the wants of various passengers on a ship, airplane, etc.

stew'ărd·ly, *a.* provident; attentive; economical. [Rare.]

stew'ărd·ly, *adv.* with the care or in the manner of a steward. [Rare.]

stew'ărd·ship, *n.* the position, duties, or service of a steward.

Stew·ăr'ti·ȧ, *n.* same as *Stuartia.*

stew'ărt·ry, *n.* 1. stewardship; the rank and condition of a steward. [Scot.]

2. in Scotland, the authority of a steward, as well as the real estate under his supervision. [Obs.]

stewed, *a.* 1. cooked by stewing, as food.

2. drunk; inebriated. [Slang.]

stew'ish, *a.* suiting or pertaining to a brothel or stew. [Obs.]

stew'pan, *n.* a pan used for stewing.

stew'pot, *n.* a covered pot used for stewing.

stey̆, *n.* sty. [Obs.]

sthē·nī'ȧ, *n.* [Gr. *sthenos,* strength.] health; strength; virility; specifically, in medicine, unusual vigor: opposed to *asthenia.*

sthen'iç, *a.* 1. active; strong; vigorous.

2. in pathology, of or pertaining to sthenia; attended with morbid increase of vital action, especially of the heart; as, *sthenic* diseases are opposed to *asthenic* diseases.

sthen'ō·chīre, *n.* [Gr. *sthenos,* strength, and *cheir,* the hand.] a device for strengthening the hands and fingers for piano playing.

stiäc·ciä'tō (styä-chä'tō), *n.* [It., crushed, flat, from *stiacciare,* to crush; *stiacciato,* a cake.]

1. the act or process of carving or modeling in very low relief.

2. an object, as the head on a coin, produced in this way.

stiäc·ciä'tō, *a.* in very low relief.

stī'ăn, *n.* styan. [Obs.]

stib'i·ăl, *a.* [LL. *stibium,* antimony, and *-al.*] like or having the qualities of antimony; antimonial.

stib'i·ăl·ism, *n.* a poisoning or intoxication by antimony.

stib'i·ā·ted, *a.* impregnated with antimony. *stibiated tartar*; tartar emetic.

stib'iç, *a.* same as *antimonic.*

stib'i·cō·nīte, *n.* a native compact yellow oxide of antimony, $H_2Sb_2O_6$, occurring massive.

stib'īne, stib'in, *n.* [*stib*ium and *-ine.*] the hydride of trivalent antimony, SbH_3, a colorless, poisonous gas.

stib'i·ous, *a.* same as *antimonious.*

stib'i·um, *n.* [L.] antimony: symbol, Sb (no period).

stib'nīte, *n.* an important ore of antimony, Sb_2S_3, occurring in lead-gray, orthorhombic crystals.

sti·bō'ni·um, *n.* the hypothetical compound, SbH_4, which resembles ammonium: also called *antimonium.*

stiç·çä'dō, *n.* [It.] a kind of xylophone.

stiçh, *n.* [Gr. *stichos,* a line, verse.] in prosody, a line or verse.

sti·çhā'ri·on, *n.*; *pl.* **sti·çhā'ri·ȧ,** [Gr., vestment.] in the Orthodox Eastern Church, a clerical robe, made usually of white linen, sometimes richly ornamented: in the Western church, a similar robe is called an *alb.*

sti·çhē'ron, *n.*; *pl.* **sti·çhē'rȧ,** [Gr. *stichēron,* neut. of *stichēros,* of a verse, from *stichos,* a line, verse.] in the Orthodox Eastern Church, a brief hymn sung after a verse from one of the Psalms.

stiçh'iç, *a.* 1. of or made up of stichs.

2. made up of lines having the same metrical form.

stiçh'id, *n.* stichidium.

sti·çhid'i·um, *n.*; *pl.* **sti·çhid'i·ȧ,** [Gr. *stichos,* a rank, a line, and *eidos,* appearance, resemblance.] one of the podlike processes containing tetraspores in some rose-spored algae.

stiçh'ō·man·cy, *n.* [Gr. *stichos,* a line, verse, and *-mancy.*] divination by lines or passages of books taken at hazard.

stiçh·ō·met'riç, stiçh·ō·met'ri·çăl, *a.* of or characterized by stichometry; of or relating to stichs or lines.

sti·çhom'e·try, *n.* [Gr. *stichos,* a line, verse, and *metron,* measure.]

1. the measurement or length of books as ascertained by the number of verses or lines contained in each book.

2. a division of the text of books into lines accommodated to the sense: a practice followed before punctuation was adopted.

stiçh·ō·myth'i·ȧ, *n.* [Gr. *stichomythia,* from *stichos,* a line, and *mythos,* speech, talk.] dialogue in single alternate lines, as in ancient Greek drama.

stiçh·ō·myth'iç, *a.* of, or having the form of, stichomythia.

sti·çhom'y·thy, *n.* same as *stichomythia.*

stiçh'os, *n.*; *pl.* **stiçh'oi,** [Gr.] 1. in the Orthodox Eastern Church, a verse, usually of the psalter or of one of the nine odes included in the service.

2. a line settled upon as a unit of measurement in estimating the length of a manuscript; a stich.

-stiçh'ous, [from Gr. *stichos,* a line, row; and *-ous.*] a combining form meaning *having* (a specified number or kind of) *rows,* as in tri*stichous.*

stich'wŏrt, *n.* same as *stitchwort.*

stick, *n.* [ME. *stikke,* from AS. *sticca,* a stick, peg, or nail.]

1. a long, usually slender piece of wood; specifically, (a) a twig or small branch broken off or cut off, especially a dead and dry one; (b) a tree branch of any size, used for fuel, etc.; (c) a long, slender, and usually tapering piece of wood shaped for a specific purpose, as a wand, staff, club, baton, cane, rod, etc.

2. a stalk, as of celery.

3. something shaped like a stick.

4. an individual, sticklike piece; as, a *stick* of chewing gum.

5. a sticklike playing implement; as, a hockey *stick.*

6. something made of sticks, as a racing hurdle.

7. a sticking, as with a pointed weapon; a stab.

8. the power of adhering or making adhere.

9. an amount of rum, brandy, etc. added to a beverage.

10. a number of bombs dropped from the air in such a way as to fall in a line across a target.

11. a stoppage, delay, or obstacle. [Archaic.]

12. a dull, stupid, or spiritless person. [Colloq.]

13. in aeronautics, a lever for operating the elevators and ailerons of an airplane, thus controlling its movements lengthwise and sideways: also *joy stick.*

14. in nautical usage, a mast or a part of a mast.

15. in printing, (a) a composing stick; (b) its contents.

the sticks; the rural districts; the country. [Colloq.]

to go to sticks and staves; to go to pieces; to be ruined.

stick, *v.t.*; stuck, *pt.*, *pp.*; sticking, *ppr.* [ME. *steken*, strong verb, to pierce, fix, pt. *stak*, from a hypothetical AS. verb *stecan*.]

1. to pierce or puncture as with a pointed instrument.
2. to kill by piercing; to stab.
3. to thrust, push, or press (a knife, pin, etc.) so as to pierce.
4. to fasten by making pierce or penetrate; as, *stick* a thumbtack in the board.
5. to decorate with things fastened in this way; as, a coat *stuck* with medals.
6. to set with piercing objects; as, a cushion *stuck* with pins.
7. to thrust or poke; as, *stick* your nose out the door.
8. to fasten or attach as by gluing, pinning, etc.; as, *stick* the poster on the wall.
9. (a) to transfix or impale; (b) to impale (insect specimens, etc.), as on a pin, and mount for exhibit.
10. (a) to obstruct, entangle, bog down, etc.; (b) to detain, delay, etc. Usually used in the passive; as, the wheels were *stuck*, I was *stuck* in town.
11. sticked (stikt), *pt.*, *pp.*; sticking, *ppr.* [from the *n.*] (a) to prop (a vine, etc.) with a stick or sticks; (b) in printing, to set in a composing stick.
12. to place; put; set. [Colloq.]
13. to make sticky by smearing. [Colloq.]
14. to puzzle; baffle; as, I'm *stuck* by this question. [Colloq.]
15. (a) to make pay, often exorbitantly; (b) to impose a disagreeable task, burden, etc. upon; (c) to cheat or defraud. [Slang.]
16. to endure or tolerate. [Slang.]

to stick up; to commit armed robbery upon. [Slang.]

stick, *v.i.* 1. to be or remain fixed or embedded by a pointed end, as a nail, etc.

2. to be or remain attached by adhesion; to adhere; to cleave.
3. to remain in the same place; to stay; to abide; as, they *stick* at home.
4. to remain in close association; to be fixed; to cling; as, friends *stick* together, the nickname *stuck*.
5. to keep close; as, he *stuck* to the trail.
6. to persevere; persist; as, she *stuck* at (or to) her work.
7. to remain firm and resolute; to endure; as, she *stuck* through thick and thin.
8. to become fixed, blocked, lodged, etc., as by an obstacle; specifically, (a) to become embedded and immovable; as, my shoe *stuck* in the mud; (b) to become unworkable; to jam; as, the gears *stuck*; (c) to become stopped or delayed; to come to a standstill; as, the bill *stuck* in committee; (d) to remain unsold.
9. to be puzzled.
10. to be reluctant; to hesitate; to scruple; as, he'll *stick* at nothing.
11. to protrude, project, or extend (with *out*, *up*, *down*, etc.).

to stick around; to stay near at hand; not go away. [Slang.]

to stick by; to remain faithful or loyal to.

to stick to or *in one's fingers*; to be retained unlawfully: used euphemistically of one who pilfers; as, things are apt *to stick to her fingers*.

to stick up for; to support; uphold; defend. [Colloq.]

stick′ȧ·dōre, stick′ȧ·dŏve, *n.* a species of lavender, *Lavandula stœchas*.

stick bug, 1. a stick insect.

2. any bug of the genus *Emesa*, as *Emesa longipes*; the spider bug.

stick chim′ney, a chimney made with sticks laid crosswise and plastered with clay inside and out, built on the outside of a log cabin.

sticked (stikt), *v.* past tense and past participle of *stick*, v.t. 11.

stick′ẽr, *n.* 1. a person or thing that sticks; specifically, (a) a bur, barb, or thorn; (b) a gummed patch or label; (c) a tenacious or persistent person; (d) [Colloq.] something puzzling or difficult to solve.

2. an article of merchandise which does not meet with a ready sale, and thus sticks to the shelves.
3. a rod connecting the far end of the key of an organ manual with the lever by which the valve is opened to allow the wind to pass from the chest to the appropriate reed or pipe of the organ.
4. [*pl.*] the arms of a crank axle employed to change the plane and direction of a reciprocating motion.
5. a machine used to cut out moldings.

stick′ful (-ful,) *n.* in printing, the contents or capacity of a printing stick.

stick′i·ly, *adv.* in a sticky manner.

stick′i·ness, *n.* the quality or condition of being sticky.

stick′ing piēce, a cut of coarse beef from the neck. [Brit.]

stick′ing plāce, the place where anything holds tight or sticks; a point of determination.

stick′ing plȧs′tẽr, adhesive material for covering a slight wound, usually made of a thin cloth gummed on one side; court plaster.

stick′ing point, sticking place.

stick in′sect, any of several insects, of the family *Phasmidæ*, whose bodies resemble a small stick: also called *walking stick*.

stick′-in-the-mud, *n.* 1. a vehicle that moves at a very slow pace.

2. a person who is slow in moving, who lingers or loiters. [Colloq.]
3. figuratively and by extension, an individual who is stubbornly unprogressive; an ultraconservative; a reactionary. [Colloq.]

stick′it, *a.* stuck. [Scot.]

stick′laç, *n.* lac in its natural state, encrusting small twigs.

stiç′kle, *v.i.*; stickled, *pt.*, *pp.*; stickling, *ppr.* [ME. *stightlen*, to rule, direct, hold sway, or govern, from AS. *stihtan*, to order, dispose, govern.]

1. to interpose between combatants and separate them; to arbitrate. [Obs.]
2. to take part actively. [Obs.]
3. to raise objections, haggle, or make difficulties, especially in a stubborn, narrow manner, usually about trifles.
4. to have scruples or objections; to scruple; to demur.

stiç′kle, *v.t.* to intervene in; to part the combatants in; to arbitrate between or in. [Obs.]

stiç′kle, *n.* a rapid shallow in a stream; also, the current below a waterfall. [Archaic and Brit. Dial.]

stiç′kle·back, *n.* [ME. *stykylbak*, from AS. *sticel*, from *stician*, to stick.] one of various small, scaleless salt-water and fresh-water fishes, of the genus *Gasterosteus* and related genera, named from the spines on the back, ventral fins, and other parts. The male builds a nest for the female's eggs.

stick′lẽr, *n.* 1. formerly, a person who attended upon combatants in a trial of skill to part them when they had fought enough, and to see fair play; a second to a duelist; one who stands to judge a combat, an arbitrator or umpire, as of a duel. [Obs.]

2. one who insists uncompromisingly on the observance of something specified; as, a *stickler* for etiquette.
3. an obstinate, tenacious, or persistent person. [Colloq.]

stick′pin″, *n.* a pin worn as an ornament in a cravat or necktie.

stick′seed, *n.* a weed, any species of *Echinospermum*, of the borage family, the ripened seeds of which have prickly barbs.

stick′tāil, *n.* the ruddy duck, *Erismatura rubida*. [Dial.]

stick′tight″ (-tīt″), *n.* an herb of the aster family with flat, needlelike seeds that stick to clothing, fur, etc.: also called *bur marigold*.

stick″-tö′-it-ive·ness, *n.* the state or quality of unusual determination or doggedness. [Colloq.]

stick′-up″, *n.* a holdup. [Slang.]

stick′weed″, *n.* ragweed.

stick′y, *a.*; *comp.* stickier; *superl.* stickiest, 1. that sticks; adhesive; tending to cling to anything touched.

2. covered with an adhesive substance; as, *sticky* fingers.
3. humid; as, *sticky* heat. [Colloq.]

Stiç′tȧ, *n.* [from Gr. *stiktos*, dotted, in allusion to the little pits on the under surface of the fronds.] a genus of lichens found growing upon trees.

stiff, *a.*; *comp.* stiffer; *superl.* stiffest, [AS. *stif*; akin to G. *steif*.]

1. hard to bend or stretch; rigid; firm; not flexible or pliant.
2. hard to move or operate; not free or limber; as, the steering gear is *stiff*.
3. stretched tight; taut; tense.
4. sore or limited in movement: said of joints and muscles.
5. having such joints or muscles, as from exertion, cold, etc.
6. not fluid or loose; thick; dense; firm; as, beat the egg whites until *stiff*, this soil is too *stiff* for easy digging.
7. strong; specifically, (a) moving swiftly, as a breeze or current; (b) containing much alcohol: said of a drink; (c) of high potency; as, a *stiff* dose of medicine.
8. harsh; as, *stiff* punishment.
9. difficult; as, a *stiff* assignment, a *stiff* climb.
10. excessively formal, constrained, or awkward; not easy, natural, or graceful.
11. resolute, stubborn, or uncompromising, as a person, a fight, etc.
12. [Colloq.] (a) resistant to lowering influences; maintaining a firm level; (b) high. Said of prices, etc.
13. in nautical usage, not careening or heeling over much despite the amount of sail carried or the strength of the wind.
14. sturdy; stalwart; robust. [Scot. and Brit. Dial.]

to keep a stiff upper lip; see under first *keep*.

Syn.—unbending, inflexible, rigid, unyielding, unpliant, strong, stubborn, obstinate, pertinacious, constrained, affected, formal, ceremonious, difficult.

stiff, *n.* 1. a corpse. [Slang.]

2. an excessively formal or constrained person. [Slang.]
3. an awkward or rough person; as, you big *stiff*. [Slang.]
4. a hobo. [Slang.]
5. a man: in *working stiff*. [Slang.]

stiff′-backed (-bakt), *a.* having a stiff back; obstinate; determined.

stiff′en (stif′n), *v.t.*; stiffened, *pt.*, *pp.*, stiffening, *ppr.* [Sw. *styfna*; D. *styven*; G. *steifen*; Dan. *stivner*, to stiffen.]

1. to make stiff; to make less pliant or flexible; as, to *stiffen* cloth with starch.
2. to make torpid; as, grief that *stiffens*.
3. to inspissate; to make more thick or viscous; as, to *stiffen* paste.

stiff′en, *v.i.* 1. to become stiff; to become more rigid or less flexible.

2. to become more thick or less soft; to be inspissated; to approach to hardness; as, melted substances *stiffen* as they cool.
3. to become less susceptible of impression; to become less tender or yielding; to grow more obstinate.

Some souls, we see,
Grow hard and *stiffen* with adversity.
—Dryden.

stiff′en·ẽr, *n.* one who or that which stiffens, as stiff materials used as interlinings.

stiff′en·ing, *n.* 1. the act of making stiff; the state of becoming stiff or stiffer.

2. something used to make a substance, garment, etc. stiff.

stiff′en·ing or′dẽr, a customhouse warrant by which ballast or heavy goods may be taken on board before the whole inward cargo is discharged, to prevent a vessel becoming too light.

stiff′ish, *a.* somewhat stiff. [Rare.]

stiff′ly, *adv.* in a stiff manner.

stiff′-necked′ (-nekt′), *a.* stubborn; inflexibly obstinate; as, a *stiff-necked* people.

stiff″neck′ed·ness, *n.* stubbornness.

stiff′ness, *n.* the state or quality of being stiff.

stiff′tāil, *n.* the ruddy duck. [Dial.]

stī′fle, *v.t.*; stifled, *pt.*, *pp.*; stifling, *ppr.* [ME. *stufflen*, from OFr. *estouffer*, to smother.]

1. to block the passage of; to arrest the free action or passage of; to stop.
2. to suppress; to keep from any active manifestation; to keep back from public notice or knowledge; to conceal; to repress; to put down.
3. to kill by impeding the respiration of, as by covering the mouth or nose, or by other means; to suffocate or greatly oppress by foul air or otherwise; to smother.

stī′fle, *v.i.* 1. to die from lack of air.

2. to suffer from lack of fresh, cool air.

stī′fle, *n.* [ME. *stifle*.] the joint of a horse or other animal next to the buttock, and corresponding to the knee in man: also called *stifle joint*.

stī′fle bōne, a bone in the leg of a horse, corresponding to the kneepan in man.

stī′fled (-fld), *a.* choked; suffocated.

stī′fle joint, the stifle: corresponding in a horse to the knee in man.

stī′flẽr, *n.* 1. one who or that which stifles.

2. a camouflet.

stī′fling, *a.* that stifles; choking; suffocating.

stig′mȧ, *n.*; *pl.* **stig′mȧs** or, and for senses 5, 6, and 7 usually, **stig′mȧ·tȧ,** [L., from Gr. *stigma*, lit., a prick with a pointed instrument, from *stizein*, to prick.]
1. a distinguishing mark burned or cut into the flesh, as of a slave or criminal.
2. something that detracts from the character or reputation of a person, group, etc.; mark of disgrace or reproach.
3. a mark, sign, etc. indicating that something is not considered normal or standard.
4. in botany, the upper tip of the pistil of a flower, receiving the pollen. It is generally situated at the upper extremity of the style.
5. a spot; a mark; a pore; as, (a) one of the apertures in the body of insects and arachnids communicating with the tracheae, or air vessels; (b) a small red speck on the human skin, causing no elevation of the cuticle; a natural mark or spot on the skin, a nevus; (c) the projecting part of a Graafian follicle at which rupture occurs; (d) a pigmented spot in certain infusorians; (e) a pore in the segmental organs of leeches; (f) one of the openings by which the pneumatocyst communicates with the exterior in some of the *Physophoræ*.
6. in medicine, (a) a spot on the skin, especially one that bleeds as the result of certain nervous tensions; (b) any sign characteristic of a specific disease.
7. [*pl.*] marks said to have been supernaturally impressed upon the bodies of certain persons in imitation of the wounds on the crucified body of Christ.

stig′mȧ disk, the disk which forms the seat of the stigma of certain plants, as the milkweed.

stig′măl, *a.* stigmatic.

Stig·mā′ri·ȧ, *n.* [LL., from L. *stigma*, a mark.]
1. a former genus of fossil plants, actually the roots chiefly of *Sigillaria*, but in some cases of *Lepidodendron*.
2. [s—] one of such roots. These plants have cylindrical, trunklike bodies, often more or less compressed, the external surface of which is covered with shallow pits, sometimes with a rootlet projecting.

stig·măr′i·ăn, *a.* pertaining to or composed of stigmarias.

stig·măr′i·oid, *a.* resembling *Stigmaria*.

stig′mȧ·tȧ, *n.* alternative plural of *stigma*.

stig′mȧ·tăl, *a.* pertaining to a stigma.

stig·mat′iç, *n.* 1. a person marked with stigmata.
2. one on whom nature has set a mark of deformity. [Obs.]
3. a branded criminal. [Rare.]

stig·mat′iç, *a.* 1. of, like, having, or characterized by a stigma, stigmas, or stigmata.
2. anastigmatic.

stig·mat′i·căl, *a.* same as *stigmatic*.

stig·mat′i·căl·ly, *adv.* in a stigmatic manner.

stig·mȧ·tif′ẽr·ous, *a.* [L. *stigma*, mark, brand, and *ferre*, to bear.] stigma-bearing.

stig′mȧ·ti·fọrm, *a.* having the form of a stigma.

stig′mȧ·tiṣm, *n.* 1. the condition characterized by the presence of stigmata.
2. the condition of a lens, and the normal condition of the eye, in which rays of light from a single point are focused upon a single point: opposed to *astigmatism*.

stig′mȧ·tist, *n.* one on whom the stigmata, or the marks of Christ's wounds, are said to have been supernaturally impressed.

stig″mȧ·ti·zā′tion, *n.* a stigmatizing or being stigmatized.

stig′mȧ·tīze, *v.t.*; stigmatized, *pt.*, *pp.*; stigmatizing, *ppr.* [Fr. *stigmatiser*; Gr. *stigmatizein*, to mark, from *stigma*, mark, brand.]
1. to mark with a stigma or stigmas; to brand.
2. to characterize or mark as disgraceful.
3. to cause stigmata to appear on.

stig′mȧ·tōse, *a.* stigmatic.

stig′ō·nō·man″cy, *n.* [Gr. *stigōn*, from *stizein*, to mark with points, tattoo, and *manteia*, divination.] divination by writing on the bark of a tree.

stī′lăr, *a.* same as *stylar*.

stil′bēne, *n.* a crystalline hydrocarbon, $C_6H_5CH:CHC_6H_5$, used in the manufacture of dyes.

stil·bes′trōl, *n.* [*stilb*ene and *estr*in and *-ol.*] a synthetic hormone, $C_{18}H_{20}O_2$, a source of various estrogens, some of which have greater potency than the natural estrogens.

stil′bīte, *n.* [Gr. *stilbein*, to shine.] a mineral, $Na_2CaAl_2Si_6O_{16}·6H_2O$, of a pearly luster, shaded with gray, yellow, or red. It is a hydrous silicate of calcium and aluminum, often found in the form of sheaf-like crystalline aggregates.

stīle, *n.* same as *style*.

stīle, *n.* [AS. *stigel*, a step, a ladder, from *stīgan*, to mount.]
1. a step or a set of steps for ascending and descending, in passing a fence or a wall.
2. a turnstile.

stīle, *n.* [D. *stijl*, doorpost.] a vertical piece in a panel or frame, as of a door or window.

sti·let′, *n.* a stiletto. [Rare.]

stī′let, *n.* a surgical instrument for probing; a stylet.

sti·let′tō, *n.*; *pl.* **sti·let′tōṣ** or **sti·let′tōeṣ,** [It., dim. of *stilo*, a dagger, from L. *stilus*, a pointed instrument, a style.]
1. a small dagger with a thin, tapering blade.
2. a pointed instrument for making eyelet holes.
3. a beard trimmed to a sharp point. [Obs.]

sti·let′tō, *v.t.*; stilettoed, *pt.*, *pp.*; stilettoing, *ppr.* to pierce, or kill by stabbing with a stiletto.

still, *a.* [ME. *stille*; AS. *stille*, still; akin to G. *still*.]
1. without sound; quiet; silent.
2. hushed, soft, or low in sound.
3. stationary; at rest; motionless.
4. characterized by little or no commotion or agitation; tranquil; calm; serene; as, the *still* water of the lake.
5. not effervescent or bubbling; without sparkle: said of wine.
6. in photography, (a) designating or of an individual, usually posed photograph; (b) having to do with a single photograph taken from a reel of motion-picture film.

Syn.—quiet, calm, noiseless, hushed, silent, pacific, serene, motionless, stagnant, peaceful, quiescent, tranquil, stationary.

still, *n.* 1. silence; quiet. [Poetic.]
2. a still photograph.
3. (a) a still-life picture; (b) a still alarm. [Colloq.]

still, *adv.* 1. at or up to the time indicated, whether past, present, or future.
2. even; yet: used as an intensifier with a comparative form, etc., as, it was cold yesterday, but today it is *still* colder.
3. nevertheless; even then; yet; as, he is old and *still* he is able.
4. ever; constantly; continually. [Poetic.]
still and anon; at intervals and repeatedly; continually.

still, *conj.* nevertheless; yet.

still, *v.t.*; stilled, *pt.*, *pp.*; stilling, *ppr.* to make still; to quiet; specifically, (a) to make silent; (b) to make motionless; (c) to calm; relieve; allay.

Syn.—silence, quiet, calm, allay, lull, pacify, appease, suppress, stop, check, restrain.

still, *v.i.* to be or become still.

still, *n.* [from obs. *still*, to distill, from L. *stillare*, to drip, trickle, from *stilla*, a drop.]
1. an apparatus for distilling liquids, especially alcoholic liquors. It assumes many forms according to its uses, but consists essentially of a vessel in which the substance is heated, and one in which the vapor is cooled. In the illustration, A is the boiler which contains the substance to be distilled; B the head in which the vapor is collected, and from which it is conveyed to the worm, a coiled tube which is packed in the refrigerator E, the cold water in which exercises a condensing action upon the vapor.

STILL

2. the house or works in which liquors are distilled; a distillery.

still, *v.t.* and *v.i.* to distill. [Obs.]

stil′lăġe, *n.* [etym. unknown.] a low stool to keep something off the floor, as textiles in a bleachery.

still ȧ·lärm′, a fire alarm given by telephone or by any means other than the regular signal apparatus.

stil·lȧ·ti′tious (-tish′us), *a.* falling in drops, drawn by a still. [Rare.]

stil′lȧ·tō·ry, *n.*; *pl.* **stil′lȧ·tō·rieṣ,** 1. an alembic, a vessel for distillation. [Rare.]
2. a laboratory; a place or room in which distillation is performed. [Rare.]

still′bīrth, *n.* 1. the birth of a stillborn fetus.
2. a stillborn fetus.

still′bọrn, *a.* born lifeless; dead at birth.

still′-bũrn, *v.t.* to burn during distillation.

still′ẽr, *n.* one who or that which stills, or quiets.

still′-fish, *v.i.* to fish from a motionless boat with the line resting still in the water.

still′house, *n.* a distillery.

still hunt, 1. a stealthy hunt for game, as by stalking or using cover.
2. a stealthy or quiet, cautious pursuit of anything; specifically, a political canvass carried on in secret or unfairly; as, a *still hunt* for delegates. [Colloq.]

still′-hunt, *v.i.* and *v.t.* to hunt or pursue stealthily.

still′-hunt″ẽr, *n.* one who still-hunts.

stil′li·cīde, *n.* [L. *stillicidium*, a dropping, from *stilla*, a drop, and *cadere*, to fall.]
1. a continual falling or succession of drops. [Rare.]
2. in Scots law, the right to have the rain from one's roof drop on another's land or roof.

stil·li·cid′i·ous, *a.* falling in drops. [Rare.]

stil′li·fọrm, *a.* [L. *stilla*, a drop, and *-form.*] formed like a drop; drop-shaped.

still′ing, *n.* [L.G. *stelling*, from G. *stellen*, to set, place.] a stand for casks, etc.

Stil·lin′ġi·ȧ, *n.* [named after Benjamin *Stillingfleet* (1702-1771), an English botanist.] a genus of shrubs of the *Euphorbiaceæ*, one of the species being the tallow tree of China.

stil′liŏn (-yun), *n.* same as *stilling*.

still′-līfe″, *a.* of or having to do with still life.

still līfe, 1. small inanimate objects, as fruit, bottles, flowers, books, etc., used as subjects for a picture.
2. a picture having such a subject.

still′ness, *n.* the quality or condition of being still.

still′rọọm, *n.* 1. a room for distilling.
2. a room connected with the pantry, in which wines, preserves, etc. are kept. [Brit.]

Still′sŏn wrench, a wrench having a jaw which moves through a collar pivoted loosely to the shaft, used for turning pipes, etc.: the jaw tightens as pressure is applied to the handle: a trade-mark: see *wrench*, illus.

still′stand, *n.* a standstill; a halt. [Rare.]

still′y, *a.*; *comp.* stillier; *superl.* stilliest, [ME. *stillich*; AS. *stillic.*] still; silent; quiet; calm. [Poet.]

still′y, *adv.* [ME. *stilleli*, etc.; AS. *stillice.*] in a still manner; silently; quietly; calmly.

stilp·nom′ē·lāne, *n.* [Gr. *stilpnos*, shining, and *melas*, *melanos*, black.] a black or greenish-black hydrous silicate of iron and aluminum, having a luster in parts pearly, sometimes submetallic.

stilp·nō·sid′ẽr·īte, *n.* same as *limonite*.

stilt, *n.* [ME. *stilte*; akin to Dan. *stylte*; Sw. *stylta*; L.G. and D. *stelt*; G. *stelze*, a stilt.]
1. a long piece of wood with a rest for the foot, used in pairs for walking with the feet raised above the ground, as through water or for amusement.
2. the handle of a plow. [Obs.]
3. a long post or pole used to hold something above ground or out of the water; as, the henhouse is placed on *stilts*.
4. one of a set of piles forming the back for the sheet piling of a starling.
5. a small piece of pottery placed between two pieces of biscuit or china in the kiln to prevent the adherence of the pieces.
6. *pl.* **stilts** or **stilt,** any species of the genus *Himantopus* of the plover family, comprising wading birds living in marshes and characterized by slender bills and three-toed legs. The common stilt of Europe, the stilt plover, is *Himantopus melanopterus* or *candidus*; the American black-necked stilt is *Himantopus mexicanus*.

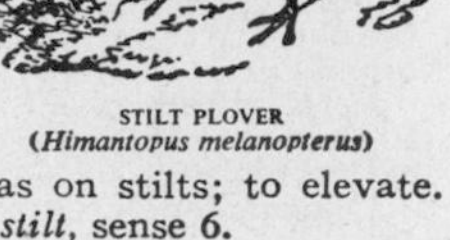
STILT PLOVER (*Himantopus melanopterus*)

stilt, *v.t.*; stilted, *pt.*, *pp.*; stilting, *ppr.* to raise on or as on stilts; to elevate.

stilt′bīrd, *n.* same as *stilt*, sense 6.

stilt′ed, *a.* raised on or as on stilts; hence, artificially formal or dignified; pompous.
stilted arch; in architecture, a form of the arch which does not spring immediately from the imposts, but from a vertical piece of masonry resting on them so as to give to the arch an appearance of being on stilts.
stilt′i·fȳ, *v.t.* to raise on or as on stilts.
Stil′tŏn cheese, Stil′tŏn, *n.* see under *cheese.*
stilt plŏv′ẽr, same as *stilt,* sense 6.
stilt sand′pī·pẽr, a North American long-legged sandpiper, *Micropalama himantopus.*
stilt′y, *a.* unnaturally elevated; stilted.
stī′lus, *n.* same as *stylus.*
stīme, *n.* a glimpse; a glimmer. [Scot.]
stim′ū·lănt, *a.* [L. *stimulans (-antis),* ppr. of *stimulare,* to goad, prick, stimulate.] stimulating; serving to stimulate.
stim′ū·lănt, *n.* anything which stimulates, incites, or provokes; a stimulus; a spur; specifically, (a) an alcoholic drink; (b) in medicine and physiology, any drug, etc. that temporarily increases the activity of some vital process or of some organ.
stim′ū·lāte, *v.t.*; stimulated, *pt., pp.*; stimulating, *ppr.* [L. *stimulare,* to prick, goad, excite, from *stimulus,* a goad.]
1. to excite, rouse, or animate to action or more vigorous action, as by goading; to spur on; as, to *stimulate* one by the hope of reward, or by the prospect of glory.
2. to invigorate by an alcoholic drink.
3. in medicine and physiology, to excite (an organ, part, etc.) to activity or increased activity.
Syn.—encourage, animate, incite, impel, urge, instigate.
stim′ū·lāt·ẽr, *n.* one who or that which stimulates.
stim·ū·lā′tion, *n.* the act of stimulating or the condition of being stimulated.
stim′ū·lā·tive, *a.* stimulating or tending to stimulate.
stim′ū·lā·tive, *n.* that which stimulates.
stim′ū·lā·tŏr, *n.* one who or that which stimulates.
stim′ū·lā·tress, *n.* a woman who stimulates.
stim′ū·lōse, *a.* in botany, having stings. [Rare.]
stim′ū·lus, *n.*; *pl.* **stim′ū·lī,** [L., a goad, sting, torment, pang, spur, incentive.]
1. that which stimulates, excites, or animates to action or increased action; anything that rouses or excites the spirits, mind, or body; an incitement; a spur; a stimulant.
2. in physiology and psychology, any action or agent that causes or changes an activity in an organism, organ, or part, as something that excites an end organ, starts a nerve impulse, activates a muscle, etc.
3. in botany, a sting.
stī′my, *n.*; *pl.* **stī′mieṣ,** a stymie.
stī′my, *v.t.*; stimied, *pt., pp.*; stimying, *ppr.* to stymie.
sting, *v.t.*; stung, *or archaic* stang, *pt., pp.*; stinging, *ppr.* [ME. *stingen*; AS. *stingan,* to thrust, stab, pierce, sting; Ice. *stinga;* Sw. *stinga;* Dan. *stinge.*]
1. to prick or wound with a sting: said of plants and insects.
2. to cause sharp, sudden, smarting pain to, by or as by pricking with a sharp point; as, the nettles *stung* her legs, salt will *sting* raw flesh.
3. to pain, or cause to suffer, in the mind; as, his conscience *stung* him sharply.
4. to stir up or stimulate suddenly and sharply; as, her words *stung* him into action.
5. to get the better of; to cheat; to dupe: usually in the passive or past participle, as, he got *stung* on that deal. [Slang.]
sting, *v.i.* 1. to use a sting; to prick or wound with a sting.
2. to cause or feel sharp, smarting pain, either physical or mental; as, iodine *stings,* his legs *stung* from the nettles.
sting, *n.* [AS. *sting.*]
1. the act of stinging.
2. a pain or wound resulting from or as from stinging.
3. a thing that urges or stimulates; a goad.
4. the ability or power to sting.
5. a sharp-pointed organ in insects and certain other animals, used to prick, wound, or inject poison.
6. in botany, any of a number of stinging, hollow hairs on some plants, as nettles.
7. the biting, sarcastic or cutting effect of sharp words; the point, as of an epigram.
sting′à·ree, *n.* [altered from *sting ray.*] a sting ray.
sting′bụll, *n.* a fish, the greater weever.
sting′ẽr, *n.* 1. a person or thing that stings; specifically, (a) an animal or plant that stings; (b) a sharp-pointed organ used for stinging; (c) [Colloq.] a blow, reply, etc. that stings.
2. an alcoholic drink made with white crème de menthe, brandy, and ice.
3. a highball of whisky and soda. [Brit. Slang.]
sting′fish, *n.* same as *stingbull.*
stin′ġi·ly, *adv.* miserly; niggardly; in a stingy manner.
stin′ġi·ness, *n.* the state or quality of being stingy, or miserly.
sting′ing, *a.* piercing with or as with a sting; also, causing acute pain; sharp; keen; biting; as, a *stinging* remark.
sting′ing bụsh, same as *tread-softly.*
sting′ing hāir, in botany, a sting.
sting′ing·ly, *adv.* with stinging.
sting′less, *a.* having no sting.
sting mọth, an Australian moth, *Doratifera vulnerans,* whose lạrva is provided with stinging organs.
stiñ′gō, *n.* [from the sharpness of the taste.]
1. strong beer or ale. [Slang.]
2. energy; vim; zest. [Slang.]
sting rāy, any ray of the family *Trygonidæ;* specifically, *Trygon pastinaca,* from tropical seas. The whiplike tail is armed with sharp, flattened bony spines, serrated on both sides, and capable of inflicting very severe wounds: also *stingaree.*
sting′rāy, *n.* same as *sting ray.*
sting′tāil, *n.* same as *sting ray.*
sting wiñ′kle, a gastropod of the genus *Murex:* so named from its boring holes in other shellfish.
sting′y, *a.* having the power to sting; stinging.
stin′ġy, *a.*; *comp.* stingier; *superl.* stingiest, [from *stinge,* dial. form of *sting.*]
1. extremely close and covetous; meanly avaricious; niggardly; miserly; as, a *stingy* churl.
2. less than needed or expected; scanty; not full or abundant.
Syn.—close, avaricious, mean, niggardly, closefisted, parsimonious, sparing, sordid, penurious.
stiñk, *v.i.*; stank *or* stunk, *pt.*; stunk, *pp.*; stinking, *ppr.* [AS. *stincan,* to give out an odor good or bad; akin to G. *stinken;* Dan. *stinke;* Sw. *stinka,* to stink.]
1. to have a strong, offensive smell.
2. to be offensive; to be hateful or abhorrent.
3. to be no good; to be of low standard or quality.
stiñk, *v.t.* to cause to stink (usually with *up*).
stiñk, *n.* a strong, offensive smell; a stench.
fire stink; the odor arising in a mine from the decomposition of iron pyrites.
stink bomb; a device that emits a foul odor upon being exploded or burned.
stiñk′ărd, *n.* a stinker. [Obs. or Rare.]
stiñk′bạll, *n.* in nautical usage, a preparation of offensive and suffocating ingredients placed in earthen jars, formerly used for throwing on an enemy's decks at close quarters.
stiñk′bīrd, *n.* same as *hoatzin.*
stiñk′bug, *n.* a bug that stinks; any one of various species of bugs emitting an offensive odor, many of which have a broad, flat body.
stiñk′ẽr, *n.* 1. a person or thing that stinks.
2. any large malodorous petrel of the antarctic region; especially, the giant fulmar.
3. a stinkpot.
4. a person regarded with disgust. [Slang.]
stiñk′họrn, *n.* any one of several fungi belonging to the genus *Phallus:* so called from their foul odor.
stiñk′ing, *a.* that stinks; bad-smelling; in vulgar colloquial usage often a general term of condemnation or disapproval, or a mere intensive.
stinking badger; the teledu.
stinking cedar; a small tree of Florida of the genus *Torreya,* the leaves of which emit a fetid odor; also, the California nutmeg.
stinking smut; bunt, a variety of wheat smut.
stiñk′ing·ly, *adv.* with an offensive smell.
stiñk′ing weed, a tropical weed of the genus *Cassia,* having fetid leaves.
stiñk′ing wood, 1. same as *stinking weed.*
2. a shrub, *Anagyris fœtida,* growing in southern Europe.
stiñk′pot, *n.* 1. a vessel containing a disinfectant. [Obs.]
2. a musk tortoise.
3. a kind of stink bomb formerly used in naval warfare.
stiñk rat, a musk tortoise.
stiñk shad, the gizzard shad.
stiñk′stōne, *n.* any stone, as some limestones, which gives off a foul smell when rubbed or struck, as from decayed organic matter contained in it.
stiñk trap, same as *stench trap.*
stiñk tũr′tle, same as *musk tortoise.*
stiñk′weed, *n.* any of several plants, as the jimson weed, having a foul or strong smell.
stiñk′wood, *n.* 1. any of several trees with wood of a disagreeable odor, as (a) a South African tree, *Ocotea bullata;* (b) the sand-fly bush of Australia and Tasmania, *Cieria smithii;* (c) a tree, *Fœtidia mauritiana,* growing on the island of Mauritius.
2. the wood of any of these trees.
stint, *v.t.*; stinted, *pt., pp.*; stinting, *ppr.* [ME. *stynten, stinten, stenten,* to stint, cease, stop; AS. *styntan, stintan,* to blunt or dull, from *stunt,* blunt, dull, stupid; O.Sw. *stunta;* Ice. *stytta,* to shorten, *stuttr,* short.]
1. to restrain within certain limits, often small or scanty; to bound; to confine; to limit; as, to *stint* the body in growth, to *stint* the mind in knowledge.
2. to assign a certain task or quantity of work to.
3. to put an end to; to stop. [Archaic.]
4. to serve (a mare) successfully; to get with foal.
stint, *v.i.* 1. to stop; to cease. [Archaic and Dial.]
2. to be sparing or grudging in giving or using.
stint, *n.* 1. limit; bound; restraint.
2. an assigned task or quantity of work.
3. a limited or fixed quantity, allotment, share, etc.
4. cessation or pause. [Obs.]
stint, *n.* any sandpiper of the genus *Actodromas;* the dunlin.
stint′ed, *a.* restrained to a certain limit or quantity; limited.
stint′ed·ness, *n.* the state of being stinted.
stint′ẽr, *n.* one who or that which stints.
stint′less, *a.* 1. without stint; unstinted; bountiful.
2. ceaseless. [Obs.]
Stī′pà, *n.* [L. *stipa, stupa,* tow.] a genus of tall tufted grasses, the species of which are generally known as *feather grass.*
stīpe, *n.* [Fr.; L. *stipes,* a log, stock, trunk of a tree.]
1. a stem; a stalk; a support of some sort; specifically, in botany, (a) the petiole of a fern; (b) the stalk supporting the pileus or cap of a fungus; (c) the caudex or stem of a tree fern.
2. in zoology, a stipes.
stī′pel, *n.* in botany, a small or secondary stipule at the base of a leaflet.
sti·pel′lāte, *a.* in botany, having a stipel or stipels.
stī′pend, *n.* [L. *stipendium,* a tax, impost, tribute; contr. for *stipipendium,* from *stips,* a small coin, or a contribution in small coin, and *pendere,* to weigh out, pay.] any periodical payment for services, as a salary or allowance.
Syn.—allowance, wages, salary, pay, remuneration, compensation.
stī′pend, *v.t.* to pay by settled wages. [Rare.]
stī·pen·di·ăr′i·ăn, *a.* mercenary; also, stipendiary.
sti·pen′di·ăr·y, *a.* 1. receiving wages or salary; performing services for a stated price or compensation.
2. paid for by a stipend: said of services.
3. of, or having the nature of, a stipend.
4. paying taxes or rendering services, as to a feudal lord.
stī·pen′di·ăr·y, *n.*; *pl.* **stī·pen′di·ăr·ieṣ,** 1. one who performs services for a settled stipend, payment, or allowance; one who receives a stipend.
2. a tenant paying tribute to a feudal lord.
stī·pen′di·āte, *v.t.* to give a stipend to; to remunerate; to compensate. [Obs.]
stī′pend·less, *a.* without a stipend.
stī′pēṣ, *n.*; *pl.* **stip′i·tēṣ,** [L., a stock, trunk.] a stalk; a stipe; particularly, in zoology, (a) the second subbasal joint of the maxilla of an insect or crustacean; (b) the stalk of the halter of a dipterous insect.
stī′pi·fọrm, *a.* [L. *stipes,* a stock, trunk, and *-form.*] in botany, having the form of a stipe.
stip′i·tāte, *a.* having, or growing on, a stipe.

stip′i·ti·fọrm, *a.* [L. *stipes* (*-itis*), a stock, and *-form.*] same as *stipiform.*

stip′ple, *v.t.*; stippled, *pt., pp.*; stippling, *ppr.* [D. *stippelen,* to speckle, cover with dots, from *stippel,* a speckle, dim. of *stip,* a point.] to engrave, paint, or draw by using small points or dots instead of lines or solid areas.

stip′ple, stip′pling, *n.* 1. the art or method of painting, drawing, or engraving in dots.
2. the effect produced by this, or an effect, as in nature, resembling it.
3. stippled work.

stip′plẽr, *n.* 1. a person who works in stipple.
2. a brush, sponge, etc. used in stippling.

stip′pling, *n.* same as *stipple.*

stip′tiç, *a.* and *n.* same as *styptic.*

stip′ū·lȧ, *n.*; *pl.* **stip′ū·lae,** [L., a stalk.] same as *stipule.*

stip·ū·lā′ceous, *a.* same as *stipular.*

stip′ū·lăr, *a.* 1. of or like a stipule or stipules.
2. growing on stipules or close to them; as, *stipular* glands.

stip′ū·lăr·y, *a.* of or relating to stipules; stipular.

stip′ū·lāte, *a.* [L. *stipula,* a stalk.] having stipules; as, a *stipulate* stalk.

stip′ū·lāte, *v.t.*; stipulated, *pt., pp.*; stipulating, *ppr.* [L. *stipulatus,* pp. of *stipulari,* to settle an agreement, bargain; lit., to make fast, from Old L. *stipulus,* firm.]
1. to include specifically in the terms of an agreement, contract, etc.; to arrange definitely.
2. to specify as an essential condition of or requisite in an agreement.

stip′ū·lāte, *v.i.* to make a specific demand or arrangement (*for* something) as a condition of or requisite in an agreement.

stip′ū·lāt·ed, *a.* same as *stipulate.*

stip·ū·lā′ti·ō (-shi-), *n.* [L., a contract, bargain.] in law, a verbal contract witnessed by a public officer.

stip·ū·lā′tion, *n.* [Fr.; L. *stipulatio* (*-onis*), a covenant, bargain, from *stipulari,* to settle an agreement, bargain.]
1. the act of stipulating, bargaining, agreeing, or covenanting; a bargaining, contracting, or agreeing.
2. that which is stipulated or agreed on; a contract or bargain; a particular article, item, or condition in a contract or covenant.
3. an undertaking, in the nature of bail, taken in the admiralty courts.
Syn.—covenant, contract, agreement, compact, bargain, arrangement.

stip·ū·lā′tion, *n.* in botany, the situation and structure of the stipules. [Rare.]

stip′ū·lā·tŏr, *n.* [L.] one who stipulates.

stip′ū·lȧ·tō″ry, *a.* of, having the nature of, or characterized by stipulation.

stip′ūle, *n.* [L. *stipula,* a stalk, a straw, dim. of *stipes,* trunk.]
1. in botany, a small leaflike appendage situated at the base of a leafstalk or leaf petiole in pairs, either adhering to it or standing separate.
2. a newly sprouted feather; a pinfeather. [Rare.]

STIPULES, *s s*

stip′ūled, *a.* furnished with stipules.

stip·ū·li·fọrm, *a.* formed like a stipule.

stĩr, *v.t.*; stirred, *pt., pp.*; stirring, *ppr.* [ME. *stirien, styrien*; AS. *styrian, stirian,* to stir, to move, to agitate.]
1. to move; to cause to move; to cause to change place or position in any way, especially slightly.
2. (a) to agitate; to cause the particles of, as of a liquid, to change their relative places by passing some implement through it; to disturb; as, to *stir* your coffee; to *stir* paint; (b) to impart a similar motion to (something consisting of separate particles).
3. to change the position of slightly; to displace; as, he *stirred* the log.
4. to rouse from dormancy, lethargy, indifference, etc.
5. to put (oneself, one's limbs, etc.) into motion or activity, often briskly.
6. to excite the feelings of; to move strongly.
7. to incite or provoke (often with *up*).
Syn.—move, agitate, excite, disturb, stimulate, rouse, provoke, enliven.

stĩr, *v.i.* 1. to move or change position, especially only slightly; as, the patient hasn't *stirred* for an hour.
2. to be up and about; to be busy and active.
3. to be taking place, going on, happening, etc.; as, things are *stirring* in the office.
4. to begin to show signs of activity; to begin to come to life; as, a grass-roots movement was *stirring.*
5. to be stirred; as, the mixture *stirs* easily.

stĩr, *n.* 1. a stirring, as with a spoon.
2. movement; activity; agitation.
3. a state of excitement; commotion; tumult; as, the crowd was in a *stir.*
4. a poke; jog; shove.
5. a public disturbance or revolt. [Archaic.]

stĩr, *n.* [19th-c. thieves' slang.] a prison. [Slang.]

stĩr′ȧ·bout″, *n.* 1. a porridge of oatmeal or corn meal stirred in boiling water or milk.
2. a pudding of oatmeal and drippings of bacon.

stir′i·ous, *a.* resembling icicles. [Obs.]

stĩrk, *n.* [AS. *styrc, styric,* a dim. from *steór,* a steer.] a bullock or heifer, especially one between one and two years old.

stĩr′less, *a.* still; motionless.

Stĩr′ling en′gine, [after R. *Stirling* (1790–1878), Scot. engineer who developed the operating principle.] an engine in which the heat released from the burning fuel is transferred to a confined gas, as hydrogen, which activates the pistons.

stĩrp, *n.* stock; race; family. [Rare.]

stĩr·pi·çul′tūr·ăl, *a.* pertaining to stirpiculture.

stĩr′pi·çul·tūre, *n.* [L. *stirps,* a stock, and *cultura,* culture.] selective breeding for the development of strains with certain characteristics.

stĩrps, *n.*; *pl.* **stĩr′pēṣ,** [L., stock.]
1. stock; race, family, or branch of a family.
2. in law, the person from whom a family or branch of a family is descended.
3. in biology, the total number of determinant factors present in a fertilized ovum.

stĩr′rẽr, *n.* 1. one who stirs or is very active and industrious.
2. one who or that which puts in motion; especially, an instrument to keep a solution or the like from settling, or to mix more completely the components of a mixture.
3. an inciter or exciter; an instigator: often with *up*; as, a *stirrer up* of mischief. [Obs.]

stĩr′ring, *a.* 1. active; busy; bustling.
2. animating; rousing; awakening; stimulating; exciting; as, a *stirring* oration.
Syn.—exciting, arousing, animating, quickening.

stĩr′ring, *n.* 1. the act of moving or putting in motion; activity.
2. in agriculture, the second plowing.
3. a riot; a tumult. [Obs.]

stir′rup (*or* stẽr′), *n.* [ME. *stirop*; AS. *stigerāp, stigrāp, stirāp,* a stirrup, from *stigan,* to mount or ascend, and *rap,* a rope; Ice. *stigreip.*]
1. a kind of ring, or bent piece of metal, horizontal on one side for receiving the foot of the rider, and attached to a strap which is fastened to the saddle: used to assist persons in mounting a horse, and to enable them to sit steadily in riding, as well as to support a part of the weight of the body.
2. any of various supports, clamps, etc. resembling or suggesting such a ring.
3. in nautical usage, a rope secured to a yard, with an eye in its lower end, for reeving a footrope.
4. in anatomy, the stapes, or stirrup bone.

stir′rup bär, that part of a saddle to which the strap of the stirrup is fastened.

stir′rup bōne, in anatomy, the stapes: see *ear,* illus.

stir′rup çup, 1. a farewell drink presented to a rider on having mounted his horse to depart.
2. any farewell drink.

stir′rup hōṣe, heavy hose or leggings formerly worn by horsemen over their other garments. [Obs.]

stir′rup ī′ron (-ŭrn), the metal part of the stirrup hung by the strap to the saddle.

stir′rup lan′tẽrn, a lantern attached to the stirrup.

stir′rup leath′ẽr (leth′), the leather strap by which the stirrup is attached to the saddle: also *stirrup strap.*

stir′rup oil, a sound beating; a thrashing: humorous term.

stir′rup pump, a hand pump for putting out fires, set in a bucket and held firm by a stirrup, or bracket, for one foot.

stĩrt, *v.* obsolete past tense and past participle of *start.*

stitch, *n.* [ME. *stiche*; AS. *stice,* a puncture, stab.]
1. a single in-and-out movement of a threaded needle in sewing, etc.
2. a single turn of the thread round a needle in knitting, crocheting, etc.; as, to let down a *stitch*; to take up a *stitch.*
3. a loop, knot, etc. made by stitching.
4. a particular kind of stitch or style of stitching; as, cross-*stitch*; hem*stitch*; lock *stitch,* etc.
5. a sudden, sharp pain; a sharp spasmodic pain in the intercostal muscles, like the piercing of a needle; as, a *stitch* in the side.
6. in agriculture, a ridge.
7. a contortion or twist of the face. [Obs.]
8. the least portion of clothing; as, he hadn't a *stitch* on his back; hence, a bit; as, he hasn't done a *stitch* of work. [Colloq.]
false stitch; see *false pinhole* under *pinhole.*
in stitches; in a state of uproarious laughter.

stitch, *v.i.* to make stitches; to sew.

stitch, *v.t.* 1. to fasten, join, repair, adorn, or operate upon with or as with stitches; to sew.
2. to fasten or unite (cartons, etc.) with staples.
3. in agriculture, to form into ridges.
to stitch up; (a) to mend or make to hold together with or as with a needle and thread; as, *to stitch up* a rent; *to stitch up* an artery; (b) to fasten or put together by sewing.

stitch′el, *n.* a kind of hairy wool. [Obs.]

stitch′ẽr, *n.* one who or that which stitches.

stitch′ẽr·y, *n.* 1. the art of ornamental needlework, as embroidery, crewelwork, etc.
2. *pl.* **stitch′ẽr·ieṣ,** something made or decorated in this way.

stitch′ing, *n.* the act of stitching; also, stitches collectively, especially of an ornamental nature.

stitch′ing hợrse, a harness maker's frame in which the work is fastened while being stitched.

stitch′wheel (-hwēl), *n.* a pricking wheel.

stitch′wŏrk, *n.* embroidery.

stitch′wŏrt, *n.* any one of several plants of the genus *Stellaria*; the chickweed or starwort.

stith, *n.* an anvil; a stithy. [Obs.]

stith′ly, *adv.* strongly; greatly; stiffly. [Obs.]

stith′y, *n.*; *pl.* **stith′ieṣ,** [O.N. *stethi,* anvil.]
1. an anvil.
2. a smithy; a forge.

stith′y, *v.t.*; stithied, *pt., pp.*; stithying, *ppr.* to make on a forge. [Archaic.]

stīve, *n.* a stew. [Obs.]

stīve, *v.t.*; stived, *pt., pp.*; stiving, *ppr.* 1. to stuff up close. [Obs.]
2. to make hot, sultry, and close. [Obs.]

stīve, *v.i.* to be stifled; to stew, as in a close atmosphere. [Obs.]

stīve, *n.* [M.D. *stuyve*; G. *staub*; Dan. *støv,* dust.] the dust that fills the atmosphere of flour mills during the operation of grinding. [Brit. Dial.]

stī′vẽr, *n.* [D. *stuiver*; Sw. *styfver,* a stiver.]
1. a Dutch coin and money of account equal to $^1/_{20}$ of a guilder.
2. anything of small value, or a small quantity.

stī′vẽr, *n.* an inhabitant of the stews; a harlot. [Obs.]

stī′vy, *n.* and *v.t.* same as *stymie.*

stō′ȧ, *n.*; *pl.* **stō′ae, stō′ȧṣ,** [Gr., a porch.] a portico or covered colonnade having a wall on one side and pillars on the other, especially one of considerable extent and near a public place.

stōat, *n.*; *pl.* **stōats** or **stōat,** [ME. *stote.*] an ermine, especially when in its brown summer coat.

stob, *n.* 1. a gad or wedge used in bringing down coal from a vein which has been holed. [Brit. Dial.]
2. a post; a stump. [Scot.]
3. a thorn; a splinter. [Brit. Dial.]

stoç·çāde′, *n.* [It. *stoccata,* a thrust; from G. *stock,* a stick, staff.]
1. a stab; a thrust with a rapier, as taught in the sixteenth and seventeenth centuries; a stoccado. [Obs.]
2. a stockade. [Obs.]

stoç·çāde′, *v.t.* to stockade. [Obs.]

stoç·çä′dō (*or* -kā′), *n.* [from Fr. and It.; Fr. *estocade*; It. *stoccata,* from *stocca,* a dagger, sword point, from Fr. *estoc,* from OFr. *estoquier,* to strike with the edge or point, from L.G. *stoken,* to stick, prick.] a stab or thrust with a pointed weapon. [Archaic.]

stoç·çä′tȧ (*or* -kā′), *n.* a stoccado. [Archaic.]

stō·chas′tiç, *a.* conjectural; able to conjecture. [Obs.]

stock, *n.* [AS. *stoc, stocc,* a stem, stick, block; D. and Dan. *stok*; Ice. *stokkr*; G. *stock,* stick, stock, block, etc., in the plural, stocks, of a vessel.]

1. the trunk of a tree.
2. (a) a tree stump; (b) a wooden block or log. [Archaic.]
3. anything lacking life, motion, or feeling.
4. one who is lacking in life, motion, or feeling; a blockhead.
5. (a) a plant stem into which a graft is inserted; (b) a plant from which cuttings are taken.
6. an underground plant stem; a rhizome.
7. any of a number of plants of the mustard family, as the evening stock, the gillyflower, or the Virginia stock.
8. (a) the first of a line of descent; original progenitor, as of a human line, or type, as of a group of animals or plants; (b) lineage; descent; ancestry; (c) a strain, race, or other related group of animals or plants; (d) an ethnic group or major division of the human race; (e) a group of related languages or families of languages.
9. a supporting block, as for an anvil.
10. the body, main part, or handle of an implement, weapon, etc., to which the working parts are attached; specifically, (a) a bitstock or brace; (b) the butt or handle of a whip, fishing rod, etc.; (c) the block of a plane, in which the cutting blade is inserted; (d) the frame of a plow, to which the share, handles, etc. are attached; (e) the wooden or metal piece of a rifle, carbine, or similar firearm, or the corresponding part of a machine gun or other rapid-fire weapon, holding the barrel, etc.; (f) the long beam forming the base part of the body of a field-gun carriage; (g) a kind of wrench for holding thread-cutting dies; (h) in nautical usage, the crossbar at the upper end of the shank of an anchor, which cants the anchor and turns a fluke down; (i) the wooden frame which supports the wheel and post of a spinning wheel.
11. [*pl.*] a former instrument of punishment consisting of a heavy wooden frame with holes for confining an offender's feet and, sometimes, his hands.

STOCKS

12. [*pl.*] a frame of timbers supporting a ship during construction.
13. [*pl.*] a frame in which an animal is held for shoeing, etc.
14. something out of which other things are made; specifically, (a) raw material; as, paper *stock*; (b) water in which meat, fish, etc. has been boiled, used as a base for soup or gravy.
15. a store or supply; specifically, (a) all the animals, equipment, etc. kept and used on a farm; (b) livestock; (c) the total amount of goods on hand in a store, etc.; (d) the portion of a pack of playing cards or dominoes not dealt out but left to be drawn from.
16. (a) formerly, the part of a tally given to the creditor; (b) a debt represented by a tally or tallies; (c) a debt owed to persons who have lent their money for interest, or the certificates representing this; (d) the capital, or fund of invested money, used by a business firm in making its transactions; (e) shares of corporate capital, or the certificates of ownership representing them; (f) [Colloq.] a part interest in something.
17. (a) a stock company (sense 2); (b) its repertoire.
18. a large, wide, stiff cravat, worn formerly.
19. a stocking. [Obs.]
20. in zoology, a colony of connected zooids, forming a compound organism.
21. portion; also, evidence. [Obs.]
22. a good grade of red and gray brick, used for the exterior of walls and the front of buildings. [Brit.]
23. in heraldry, the stump of a tree as a bearing.
24. in ecclesiastical use, a holy water vessel or the pillar by which it is supported.
25. the net proceeds of a catch of fish. [Dial.]
26. in mining, a mass of ore thick and irregular in form.

in stock; available for sale or use; on hand.
on the stocks; being built: said of a ship, etc.
out of stock; not immediately available for sale or use; not in stock.
to accept stock; in early feudal custom, to receive a vassal: said of the lord.
to take stock; (a) to inventory the amount of stock on hand; (b) to make an estimate or appraisal, as of available resources, probabilities, etc.
to take stock in; (a) to buy a share or shares of stock in (a company, etc.); (b) [Colloq.] to have faith in, give credence to, or attribute real significance to.
to take stock of; to set a value upon.

stock, *v.t.* 1. to provide with or attach to a stock, as a firearm, plow, etc.
2. to furnish with stock, as a farm, or a stock, as a shop, etc.
3. to keep or put in a supply of for sale or for future use.
4. to sow (land) with grass, clover, etc.
5. to put in the stocks. [Obs.]
6. to allow to retain their milk, as cows, for some considerable time previous to sale.
7. to stack, as cards.

stock, *v.i.* 1. to put forth new shoots: said of a plant.
2. to put in a stock, or supply (often with *up*).

stock, *a.* 1. continually kept in stock; as, *stock* sizes.
2. of the nature of something kept in stock; common, ordinary, hackneyed, or trite; as, a *stock* joke.
3. that deals with stock; as, a *stock* checker.
4. relating to stock or a stock company.
5. for breeding; as, a *stock* mare.
6. of, or for the raising of, livestock; as, *stock* farming.

stock, *n.* a thrust with a rapier. [Obs.]

stock ac·count′, the account in a ledger showing on one side the amount of the original stock with accumulations, and on the other the amount withdrawn. [Brit.]

stock·āde′, *n.* [Fr. *estacade* (also *estocade*, by association with OFr. *estoc*, a trunk, log; of Gmc. origin); Pr. *estacado*, from *estaca*, a post, stake, from Gmc. base akin to Eng. *stake*.]
1. a barrier of stakes driven into the ground side by side, for defense against attack.
2. any similar enclosure.

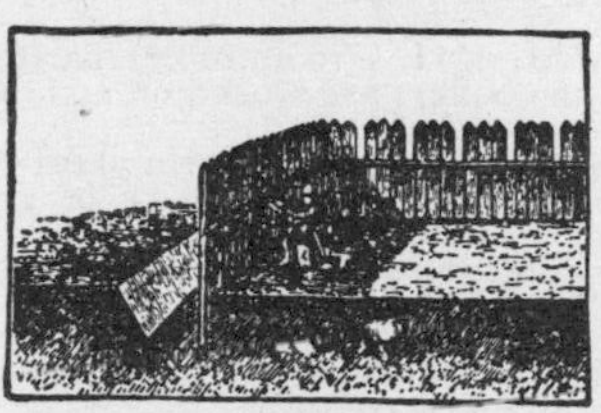
STOCKADE

stock′āde, *v.t.*; stockaded, *pt., pp.*; stockading, *ppr.* to surround, protect, or fortify with a stockade.

stock′-blīnd″, *a.* entirely blind.

stock bōard, 1. the board above the arrangement of register slides by which is regulated the access of air to the respective systems of pipes or reeds which form the stops of an organ.
2. the board over which the brick mold slips, and which forms the bottom of the latter while the brick is molding.

stock′breed″ēr, *n.* one whose work is the breeding of livestock or domestic animals, as horses or cattle.

stock′brō″kēr, *n.* a person who acts as an agent for others in buying and selling stocks and bonds.

stock′brō″kēr·āġe, *n.* a stockbroker's work or business.

stock′brō″king, *n.* stockbrokerage.

stock çär, 1. a railway car built to carry livestock.
2. any passenger automobile of standard make, but with a supercharged engine, used in professional races with similar automobiles.

stock cēr·tif′i·çāte, a certificate that is evidence of ownership of a specified number of shares in a specified corporation: also *certificate of stock*.

stock çŏm′pȧ·ny, 1. a company or corporation whose capital is divided into shares.
2. a theatrical company established to present a repertoire of plays, usually at one theater.

stock dŏve, the wild pigeon of Europe, *Columba œnas*: so called because it nests in hollow trees.

stock duck, the mallard.

stock′ēr, *n.* one whose business it is to make gunstocks.

stock ex·chānġe′, 1. a place where stocks and bonds are regularly bought and sold.
2. an association of stockbrokers who meet together for the business of buying and selling stocks and bonds according to fixed regulations.

stock färm, a farm devoted mainly to the raising of livestock.

stock färm′ēr, a farmer who devotes himself to the breeding and rearing of different kinds of livestock, especially horses and cattle.

stock′fish, *n.*; *pl.* **stock′fish** or **stock′fish″eṣ,** [ME. *stokfysshe.*] any fish, as cod, ling, hake, or torsk, cured by being split open and dried in the sun without salting.

stock ġil′ly·flow″ēr, a plant of the genus *Matthiola*; the common stock, *Matthiola incana*.

stock gōld, gold hoarded or accumulated so as to form a stock. [Rare.]

stock′hōld″ēr, *n.* 1. a person owning stock, especially a share or shares of stock in a given company.
2. in Australia, a stockman (sense 1).

stock′hǫrse, *n.* a trained horse used for driving, cutting out, and mustering on an Australian stock station.

stock′i·ly, *adv.* so as to be stocky.

stock′i·ness, *n.* the quality of being stocky.

stock·i·net′, *n.* an elastic, machine-knitted fabric, of which stockings, undergarments, etc. are made.

stock′ing, *n.* [from *stock*, in obsolete sense of stocking or leg covering.]
1. a close-fitting garment made to cover the foot and leg. Stockings were formerly made of cloth or milled stuff, sewed together, but they are now usually knitted by hand or woven in a frame, the material being wool, cotton, silk, nylon, etc.
2. something resembling a stocking, as a bandage, patch of color, the feathers on the leg of a cock, etc.
in one's stocking feet; without one's shoes on but wearing stockings or socks.

stock′ing, *v.t.* to dress in stockings; to cover as with stockings.

stock′ing·ēr, *n.* 1. one who knits or weaves stockings.
2. a dealer in stockings and small wares.

stock′ing frāme, a machine for weaving or knitting stockings or other hosiery goods; a knitting machine.

stock′ing lo͝om, a stocking frame.

stock in trāde, 1. goods kept available for sale at a store or shop.
2. tools, materials, etc. used in carrying on a trade or a business.
3. any resources, practices, or devices characteristically employed by a given person or group.

stock′ish, *a.* like a stock or block of wood; stupid; blockish; dull; thick-headed.

stock′job″bēr, *n.* 1. an operator in the stock exchange who deals only with brokers, not with the public. [Brit.]
2. a stockbroker or stock salesman: often contemptuous.

stock′job″bing, *n.* the practice or business of dealing in stocks or shares: often used in a disparaging sense.

stock′keep″ēr, *n.* 1. in a mercantile house, one who has charge of stock.
2. in Australia, the head herdsman or manager of a stock station.

stock list, a list published daily or periodically in connection with a stock exchange, enumerating the leading stocks dealt in, the prices current, and the actual transactions; also, any schedule of stocks.

stock lock, a lock adapted to be placed on an outer door. It is enclosed in an outer wooden case, and is opened and locked from the outside by the key, and bolted only inside.

stock′măn, *n.*; *pl.* **stock′men,** 1. a man who owns or raises livestock.
2. a man who works in a stockroom or warehouse where goods, materials, etc. are kept.
3. a man who has charge of livestock or works on a stock farm.

stock mär′ket, 1. a stock exchange.
2. business carried on at a stock exchange; as, the *stock market* was active today.
3. the prices quoted on stocks and bonds.
4. a cattle market.

stock′owl, *n.* the eagle owl, *Bubo maximus,* of Europe. [Brit.]

stock pig̀′eŏn, same as *stock dove.*

stock′pīle, *n.* a reserve supply of raw materials or goods; the total of available materials not yet being used: also *stock pile.*

stock′pīle, *v.t.* and *v.i.*; stockpiled, *pt., pp.*; stockpiling, *ppr.* to accumulate a stockpile or stockpiles (of).

stock′pot, *n.* 1. a pot used for boiling down stock for soup.
 2. a pot, etc. containing a mixture of any kind.

stock pump, a pump operated by the weight of the livestock watering at it.

stock pũrse, a common purse.

stock rāiṣ′ing, the raising of livestock.

stock′rīd″ẽr, *n.* in Australia, a mounted drover or herdsman.

stock′ro͝om, *n.* a room in which a store of goods, materials, etc. is kept: also *stock room.*

stock röute, in Australia, a route mapped out by government survey, not necessarily fenced off, over which livestock may be driven.

stocks, *n.pl.* see *stock, n.* 11, 12, 13.

stock stā′tion, in Australia, a stock farm or ranch.

stock′-still, *a.* as still as a stock, or log; perfectly still.

stock taç′kle, a tackle used in hoisting an anchor.

stock′tāk″ing, *n.* a periodical examination, inventory, and valuation of the stock or goods in a business house or factory.

stock′whip (-hwip), *n.* a short-handled whip with a long plaited lash used by stockriders in Australia.

stock′wŏrk, *n.* 1. in mining, a method of working ore where, instead of lying in veins or strata, it is found in solid masses, so that it is worked in chambers and stories.
 2. a condition in which the ore is deposited regularly throughout a mass of rock.

stock′y, *a.*; *comp.* stockier; *superl.* stockiest, [*stock* (block) and *-y.*]
 1. heavily built; sturdy; thickset and relatively short.
 2. thick; stout; stumpy; as, a *stocky* stem.
 3. headstrong. [Brit. Dial.]

stock′yärd, *n.* a yard for livestock; especially, an enclosure, usually with pens, etc., in which cattle, hogs, sheep, or horses are kept temporarily before being slaughtered or sent to market.

stodġe (stoj), *v.t.* to stuff or crowd together. [Dial.]

stodġ′i·ly, *adv.* in a stodgy manner.

stodġ′i·ness, *n.* the quality or condition of being stodgy.

stodġ′y, *a.*; *comp.* stodgier; *superl.* stodgiest, [from dial. *stodge,* heavy food, and *-y.*]
 1. heavy and uninteresting: said of food.
 2. heavily built; bulky.
 3. crammed full; packed.
 4. dull; tedious; uninteresting; philistine; as, a *stodgy* person or book.

stoe·çhī·ol′ō·ġy, *n.* same as *stoichiology.*

stoe·çhī·om′ē·try, *n.* same as *stoichiometry.*

stöep, *n.* in South Africa, a porch or stoop.

stō′gie, stō′gy, *n.*; *pl.* **stō′gieṣ,** [for earlier *stoga,* aphetic for Conestoga, town in Pennsylvania: said to be so named because favored by drivers of Conestoga wagons.]
 1. a long, thin, inexpensive cigar.
 2. a heavy, roughly made shoe or boot.
 Also spelled *stogey.*

stō′gy, *a.* crude; rough; uncouth. [Colloq.]

Stō′iç, *n.* [L. *Stoicus*; Gr. *Stōikos,* a Stoic, lit., belonging to a colonnade, because Zeno taught under a colonnade, the Poecile at Athens, from *stoa,* a place enclosed by pillars, a colonnade.]
 1. a disciple of the philosopher Zeno, who founded a sect about 308 B.C. He taught that men should be free from passion, unmoved by joy or grief, and submit without complaint to the divine will and unavoidable necessity by which all things are governed.
 2. [s–] a person not easily excited; an apathetic or stoical person, or one who appears or professes to be indifferent to pleasure or pain.

Stō′iç, *a.* 1. of or pertaining to the Stoics or to their philosophy.
 2. [s–] stoical.

Stō′i·çăl, *a.* 1. Stoic.
 2. [s–] not affected by passion; able completely to repress feeling; manifesting or maintaining austere indifference to joy, grief, pleasure, or pain.

stō′i·çăl·ly, *adv.* in a stoical manner; like a stoic; with real or assumed indifference to pleasure or pain.

stō′i·çăl·ness, *n.* the state of being stoical; indifference to pleasure or pain.

stoi″çheī·ō·loġ′i·çăl, *a.* stoichiological.

stoi·çheī·ol′ō·ġy, *n.* stoichiology.

stoi″çheī·ō·met′ri·çăl, *a.* stoichiometric.

stoi·çheī·om′ē·try, *n.* stoichiometry.

stoi″çhi·ō·loġ′i·çăl, *a.* of or having to do with stoichiology.

stoi·çhi·ol′ō·ġy, *n.* [from Gr. *stoicheion,* a first principle; and *-logy.*]
 1. the physiological study of the component elements of animal tissues.
 2. the doctrine of the elementary requisites of thought.
 3. the study of fundamental principles.

stoi″çhi·ō·met′riç, *a.* of or having to do with stoichiometry.

stoi″çhi·ō·met′ri·çăl, *a.* stoichiometric.

stoi″çhi·om′ē·try, *n.* [from Gr. *stoicheion,* a first principle, element, base; and *-metry.*]
 1. the determination of the atomic weights of elements, the proportions in which they combine, and the weight relations in any chemical reaction.
 2. the branch of chemistry dealing with the relationships of elements in combination, especially with quantitative relationships.

Stō′i·çiṣm, *n.* 1. the philosophical system of the Stoics.
 2. [s–] a real or pretended indifference to pleasure or pain; the bearing of pain without betraying feeling; stoical behavior; impassivity.

stō·iç′i·ty, *n.* stoicalness. [Obs.]

stoit, *v.i.* 1. to walk in a staggering way; to totter; to stumble on any object. [Scot.]
 2. to jump from the water, as certain fish. [Brit. Dial.]

stoit′ẽr, *v.i.* to stoit.

stōke, *v.t.*; stoked (stōkt), *pt., pp.*; stoking, *ppr.* [D. *stoken,* to make or kindle a fire, to instigate, stir up.]
 1. to jab; to thrust. [Obs.]
 2. to stir up and feed fuel to (a fire, furnace, etc.).
 3. to tend (a furnace, boiler, etc.).

stōke, *v.i.* to attend to and supply a fire, furnace, boiler, etc. with fuel; to act as a stoker.

stōke′hōld, *n.* 1. a room or compartment in which the boilers are stoked on a ship.
 2. a stokehole (sense 2).

stōke′hōle, *n.* [*stoke* and *hole*; in part transl. of D. *stookgat,* from *stoken,* to stoke, and *gat,* a hole.]
 1. the opening in a furnace or boiler through which the fuel is put.
 2. a space in front of a furnace or boiler from which the fire is tended, as on a ship.
 3. a stokehold (sense 1).

stōk′ẽr, *n.* [D. *stoker,* a setter or kindler of fire, from *stoken,* to make or kindle a fire.]
 1. one who feeds and trims a furnace or large fire; especially, one employed to tend the furnace of a steam boiler, as on a locomotive or marine engine.
 2. a mechanical device that feeds coal, etc. into a furnace.
 3. a poker. [Rare.]

stōkes′īte, *n.* in mineralogy, a silicate occurring in orthorhombic, colorless crystals and composed of calcium and tin.

stō′key, *a.* oppressively warm; sultry. [Brit. Dial.]

stō′lȧ, *n.* [L., a robe, from Gr. *stolē,* a long robe.] a long garment, descending to the ankles, worn by Roman matrons over the tunic: it was fastened around the body by a girdle, leaving broad folds above the breast, and had a flounce sewed to the bottom. It was the characteristic dress of the Roman matrons, as the toga was of the men, and was not allowed to be worn by women divorced from their husbands, or by courtesans.

STOLA

stōle, *v.* past tense of *steal.*

stōle, *n.* stolon. [Rare.]

stōle, *n.* 1. a long, narrow, decorated scarf, with fringed extremities, worn by officiating clergymen of various churches: by deacons over the left shoulder and fastened under the right arm; by bishops around the neck, with both ends pendent in front to the knees; and by priests similarly, but with the ends crossed over the breast at Mass.
 2. a stola; a long robe or garment worn by women, reaching to the ankles or heels.
 3. a woman's long scarf of cloth or fur worn with the ends hanging in front.
 groom of the stole; the first lord of the bedchamber in the household of the English kings.

stōle, *n.* a stool. [Obs.]

stōled, *a.* wearing a stole or long robe; robed like an antique statue.

stōle fee, a remuneration paid to a priest for religious service.

stōle mesh, a double mesh in a fisherman's net.

stō′len, *v.* past participle of *steal.*

stol′id, *a.* [L. *stolidus,* firm, slow, stupid.] having or showing little or no emotion or awareness; unexcitable; dull; impassive; expressionless.

stō·lid′i·ty, *n.*; *pl.* **stō·lid′i·tieṣ,** [L. *stoliditas.*] dullness; the quality or condition of being stolid.

stol′id·ly, *adv.* in a stolid manner.

stol′id·ness, *n.* stolidity.

stō′lon, *n.* [LL., from L. *stolo, stolonis,* a twig, shoot.]
 1. in botany, a shoot which proceeds from a stem above the ground, takes root at the tip, and develops a new plant; a runner or rhizome.
 2. in zoology, a stemlike part in certain compound organisms, as the coral, giving rise to buds from which new individuals grow.

stol·ō·nif′ẽr·ous, *a.* [L. *stolo, stolonis,* a shoot, sucker, and *ferre,* to bear.] producing or putting forth stolons.

stolz′īte, *n.* [named after Dr. *Stolz,* of Bohemia.] tungstate of lead, occurring as a mineral in tetragonal crystals.

stō′mȧ, *n.*; *pl.* **stō′mȧ·tȧ** (*or* stom′ȧ-), [Gr., a mouth, any outlet or entrance, a chasm or cleft, an opening.]
 1. in anatomy, an intercellular pore or aperture in serous tissues and blood vessels.
 2. in botany, (a) a minute orifice or pore in the epidermis of leaves, etc., which opens directly into the air cavities pervading the parenchyma, and through which exhalation takes place; a breathing pore; a stomatium; (b) the opening on the side of the spore case of ferns, through which dehiscence takes place; (c) the orifice through which the spores of certain fungi are discharged.
 3. in zoology, a mouth or mouthlike opening, especially an ingestive opening in lower animals; specifically, (a) one of the breathing holes of insects; a stigma; a spiracle; (b) a small inhalant opening in a sponge; an ostiole; (c) a gill aperture in an ascidian.

stō·maç′ȧ·cē, *n.* [Gr. *stomakakē*; *stoma,* the mouth, and *kakos,* evil, bad.] ulcerative stomatitis.

stŏm′ȧçh, *n.* [ME. *stomak*; Fr. *estomac*; L. *stomachus,* the gullet, esophagus, stomach, from Gr. *stomachos,* the throat, the gullet, from *stoma,* a mouth.]
 1. (a) the large, saclike organ into which food passes from the esophagus or gullet for storage while undergoing the early processes of digestion; (b) any of the separate sections of such a digestive organ, as in ruminants, or all these sections collectively.
 2. any digestive cavity, as in invertebrates.
 3. appetite; the desire for food caused by hunger; as, a good *stomach* for roast beef.
 4. inclination; liking; fondness; desire.
 5. character or disposition. [Archaic.]
 6. anger; resentment. [Obs.]
 7. willful obstinacy. [Obs.]
 8. pride; haughtiness. [Obs.]
 9. the throat; the gorge; the gullet. [Obs.]
 10. the belly; the abdomen.
 pit of the stomach; the hollow or depression below the lower end of the sternum.
 sour stomach; a condition of the stomach which produces acid eructations.

stŏm′ȧçh, *v.t.*; stomached (-ăkt), *pt., pp.*; stomaching, *ppr.* 1. to resent; to remember with anger. [Obs.]
 2. to brook; to bear without open resentment; to put up with; to tolerate; to endure.
 3. to be able to eat or digest.

stŏm'ăch, *v.i.* to be angry. [Obs.]
stŏm'ăch-āche, *n.* pain in the stomach, abdomen, or bowels.
stŏm'ăch·ăl, *a.* 1. cordial; helping the stomach; stomachic.
2. relating to the stomach; gastric; abdominal.
stŏm'ăch·ăl, *n.* a stomachic.
stŏm'ăch·ēr, *n.* 1. a part of the dress of both men and women from the fifteenth to the seventeenth centuries. It was usually an ornamented, triangular piece of cloth of rich material and covered the front of the body extending from the breast to the waist or below it.
2. one who stomachs. [Obs.]
stŏm'ăch·fụl, *a.* willfully obstinate. [Obs.]
stŏm'ăch·fụl·ly, *adv.* stubbornly. [Obs.]
stŏm'ăch·fụl·ness, *n.* stubbornness. [Obs.]
stō·măch'iç, stō·măch'i·căl, *a.* 1. of or pertaining to the stomach; as, *stomachic* vessels.
2. strengthening to the stomach; acting as a digestive tonic; stimulating the action of the stomach; cordial.
stō·măch'iç, *n.* a digestive tonic.
stŏm'ăch·ing, *n.* resentment. [Obs.]
stŏm'ăch·less, *a.* 1. without a stomach.
2. without an appetite. [Rare.]
stŏm'ăch·ous, *a.* sullen; obstinate. [Obs.]
stŏm'ăch pump, an apparatus, consisting usually of a flexible rubber tube that is introduced into the stomach through the mouth (or nose) and esophagus, used, as in the case of poisoning, to remove the contents of the stomach by suction.
stŏm'ăch stag'gẽrş, a variety of staggers characterized by swelling of the stomach.
stŏm'ăch tọọth, either of the lower canine teeth of infants: so named because of the gastric disorders often accompanying its appearance.
stŏm'ăch tūbe, a tube to be introduced into the stomach for introducing or removing substances.
stŏm'ăch wŏrm, a common roundworm, *Ascaris lumbricoides*, sometimes found in the human stomach.
stŏm'ăch·y, *a.* obstinate; sullen; proud. [Brit. Dial.]
stō'mȧ·pod, *a* and *n.* same as *stomatopod*.
Stō·map'ō·dȧ, *n.pl.* same as *stomatopoda*.
stō·mȧ·pod'i·fọrm, *a.* [Gr. *stoma*, a mouth, *pous, podos*, foot, and *-form*.] formed like a stomatopod, as certain larvae.
stō·map'ō·dous, *a.* stomatopod.
stō'mȧ·tȧ, *n.* plural of *stoma*.
stom'ȧ·tăl, *a.* in botany and zoology, of, like, or having a stoma or stomata.
stom·ȧ·tal'ġi·ȧ, *n.* [Gr. *stoma* (*-atos*), mouth, and *-algia*.] pain in the mouth.
stō'māte, *n.* in botany, a stoma.
stō'māte, *a.* having a stoma or stomata.
stō·mat'iç, *a.* 1. of, like, or relating to a stoma; as, a *stomatic* cell, one of the guard cells surrounding a stoma.
2. of the mouth.
stō·mat'iç, *n.* a medicine for disorders of the mouth.
stō·mȧ·tif'ẽr·ous, *a.* in botany, bearing stomata.
stō·mȧ·tī'tis, *n.* inflammation of the mouth.
stō·mā'ti·um (-shi-), *n.* same as *stoma*.
stom'ȧ·tō- (*or* stō'ma-), [from Gr. *stoma, stomatos*, mouth.] a combining form used in medicine, physiology, botany, etc., to mean *like* or *relating to a mouth*: also *stomat-*.
Stō·mȧ·tō'dȧ, *n.pl.* [*stomat-*, and Gr. *eidos*, form.] a former division of the *Protozoa*, including those forms which possess a mouth.
stom"ȧ·tō·dae'um, *n.* a stomodaeum.
stom'ȧ·tōde, *a.* of the *Stomatoda*.
stom'ȧ·tōde, *n.* any one of the *Stomatoda*.
stom"ȧ·tō·gas'triç, *a.* [*stomato-*, and Gr. *gastēr*, stomach.] relating to both the mouth and the stomach.
stō·mȧ·tol'ō·ġy, *n.* the branch of medicine dealing with the mouth and its diseases.
stom"ȧ·tō·mȧ·lā'ci·ȧ, *n.* a softening of the structures of the mouth.
stom·ȧ·top'ȧ·thy, *n.* any disorder of the mouth.
Stō·mȧ·toph'ō·rȧ, *n.pl.* the *Stomatoda*.
stō·mȧ·toph'ō·rous, *a.* [*stomato-*, and Gr. *pherein*, to bear.] relating to the *Stomatophora*.
stom"ȧ·tō·plas'tiç, *a.* relating to plastic surgery of the mouth.
stom'ȧ·tō·plas"ty, *n.* [*stomato-*, and Gr. *plastos*, formed, shaped, from *plassein*, to form, shape.] plastic surgery of the mouth or of the os uteri.
stom'ȧ·tō·pod, *a.* of or belonging to the *Stomatopoda*.
stom'ȧ·tō·pod, *n.* one of the *Stomatopoda*.
Stō·mȧ·top'ō·dȧ, *n.pl.* an order of malacostracous crustaceans, including the squilla, having gills on appendages attached to the abdomen: also known as *Stomapoda*.

STOMATOPOD
Squilla stylifera

stō·mȧ·top'ō·dous, *a.* same as *stomatopod*.
stom"ȧ·tor·rhā'ġi·ȧ, *n.* hemorrhage from the mouth.
stom'ȧ·tō·sçōpe, *n.* an instrument for examining the inside of the mouth.
stom'ȧ·tōse, *a.* stomatous.
stom"ȧ·tō·tȳ'phus, *n.* typhus fever with severe lesions of the mouth.
-stom'ȧ·tous, same as *-stomous*.
stom'ȧ·tous, *a.* having a stoma or stomata.
-stōme, [from Gr. *stoma*, a mouth.] a combining form meaning *mouth*, as in cyclo*stome*.
stō·mō·dae'ăl, stō·mō·dē'ăl, *a.* pertaining to the stomodaeum.
stō·mō·dae'um, stō·mō·dē'um, *n.*; *pl.* **stō·mō·dae'ȧ, stō·mō·dē'ȧ,** [Mod. L., from Gr. *stoma*, mouth, and *hodios*, on the way, from *hodos*, way, road.]
1. in embryology, an invagination of the ectoderm from which is formed the mouth and upper part of the pharynx.
2. in zoology, the pharynx or esophagus of certain coelenterates.
-stō·mous, [from Gr. *stoma*, a mouth; and *-ous*.] a combining form meaning *having a* (specified kind of) *mouth*.
stomp, *n.* and *v.* dialectal form of *stamp*.
-stō·my, [Gr. *-stomia*, from *stomos*, the mouth.] a suffix meaning *a surgical opening into* (a specified part or organ).
stond, *n.* and *v.* stand. [Obs.]
stōne, *n.* [ME. *ston, stoon*; AS. *stān*, stone; akin to D. *steen*; Ice. *steinn*; Dan. and Sw. *sten*; G. *stein*; Goth. *stains*; the base *sti* also appears in Russ. *stiena*, a wall, and Gr. *stia*, a stone, pebble.]
1. the hard, solid, nonmetallic mineral matter of which rock is composed.
2. a piece of rock of relatively small size.
3. a piece of rock shaped or finished for some purpose; specifically, (a) a building block; (b) a paving block; (c) a gravestone or memorial; (d) a boundary mark or milestone; (e) a grindstone or whetstone.
4. something that resembles a small stone; specifically, (a) a hailstone; (b) a testicle; (c) the stonelike seed of certain fruits; specifically, the hard endocarp of a drupe, as of the peach; (d) [Obs.] a gunflint.
5. a precious stone or gem.
6. *pl.* **stōne,** in Great Britain, 14 pounds avoirdupois.
7. in medicine, (a) a small stony mass abnormally formed in the kidney, bladder, or gall bladder; calculus; (b) a disease characterized by such formations.
8. in printing, a table with a smooth top, originally of stone, on which page forms are composed.
Arkansas stone; a fine-grained stone used for making hones; novaculite.
Caen stone; a kind of cream-colored limestone used for building: so called because found near Caen, France.
meteoric stones; meteorites.
to cast the first stone; to be the first to censure, criticize, or attack.
to leave no stone unturned; to do everything that can be done.
stōne, *a.* of stone or stoneware; as, a *stone* jar.
stōne, *v.t.*; stoned, *pt., pp.*; stoning, *ppr.* 1. to throw stones at; to pelt, beat, or kill with stones.
And they *stoned* Stephen. —Acts vii. 59.
2. to harden; to make like stone. [Obs.]
3. to free from stones; as, to *stone* raisins.
4. to wall or face with stones; to line or pave with stones; as, to *stone* a well, to *stone* a cellar.
5. to polish, sharpen, etc. with a stone; as, to *stone* leather.
stōne-, [from *stone*, *n.* with the sense of "like, or as is, a stone."] a combining form used as an intensive in hyphenated compounds, meaning *very, completely*, as in *stone*-broke, *stone*-blind.
Stōne Āġe, the period in human culture during which stone implements were used: it is divided into the Eolithic, Paleolithic, and Neolithic Periods.
stōne ax, 1. an ax used by a stonecutter.
2. a kind of ax made of stone.
stōne baş'il, basilweed.
stōne băss, one of various marine food fishes with serrated dorsal spines, especially *Polyprion cernium* or *Polyprion oxygenius*.
stōne'bīrd, *n.* either of two birds: (a) the moro; (b) the stone snipe.
stōne'bīt"ẽr, *n.* a fish of the genus *Anarrhichas*.
stōne'-blīnd', *a.* totally blind.
stōne'bōat, *n.* a flat-bottomed sled for hauling stones or other heavy objects; also, a wagon bed hung under the axles. [Dial.]
stōne boil'ing, the act of boiling water, etc., by dropping hot stones into it.
stōne bōr'ẽr, any of certain lamellibranch mollusks which bore into rocks by means of rasplike imbrications with which their shell is armed; a species of *Lithodomus*.
stōne'bōw, *n.* a crossbow for shooting stones. [Obs.]
stōne bram'ble, same as *roebuck berry*.
stōne'brash, *n.* in agriculture, a subsoil composed of shattered rock or stone.
stōne breāk'ẽr, a machine constructed for breaking or crushing stone.
stōne'-brōke', *a.* having no money at all; penniless. [Slang.]
stōne brụ̈iṣe, a bruise on the sole of the foot, caused by walking on stones.
stōne'buck, *n.* the steenbok.
stōne çȧ·nal', the tube by which water is conveyed from the exterior to the locomotive system of an echinoderm.
stōne'çȧst, *n.* a stone's throw; the distance that a stone may be thrown by hand.
stōne'çat, *n.* a fresh-water catfish of the genus *Noturus*, of North America, armed with a sharp pectoral spine, which causes a painful wound.
stōne'chat, stōne'chat"tẽr, *n.* 1. a small bird of Europe. *Pratincola rubicola*, of the thrush family: its note resembles the sound of pebbles being knocked together.
2. any one of various species of the genera *Saxicola* and *Pratincola*.
stōne chī'nȧ, a kind of stoneware containing a variety of feldspar found in England.
stōne çlō'vẽr, same as *hare's-foot* (sense 1).
stōne çōal, hard coal; also, mineral coal.
stōne'-çōld, *a.* cold as a stone.
stōne çol'lăr, in archaeology, one of a kind of large, circular stones of the size and shape of a horse collar, found mainly in Puerto Rico: though their use is unknown, they usually have symbolic decoration.
stōne çor'ăl, a calcareous coral, especially when hard and massive.
stōne çrab, 1. an edible crab of the genus *Menippe*, found along the southern Atlantic coast of the United States.
2. a spiny crab of Europe.
stōne çraw'fish, a crawfish, *Astacus torrentium*, of Europe.
stōne çrick'et, a cricket, especially of the genus *Ceuthophilus*: it is wingless and is usually found beneath stones.
stōne'crop, *n.* 1. a sort of tree. [Obs.]
2. any of various related plants of the genus *Sedum*, with fleshy leaves and usually yellow or white flowers, found on rocks and walls; the wall pepper.
Virginia stonecrop; a plant of the genus *Penthorum*, found in ditches in the United States and Canada.
stōne çrush'ẽr, a machine for grinding or crushing stones, as for road construction.
stōne çūr'lew, 1. a large species of plover, *Œdicnemus crepitans*, of Europe: also called *thick-knee*.
2. the whimbrel. [Brit. Dial.]
3. the willet. [Dial.]
stōne'çut"tẽr, *n.* one whose occupation is cutting and dressing stones; also, a machine for trimming stones.
stōne'çut"ting, *n.* the work of cutting and dressing stones for walls, steps, cornices, monuments, etc.

stōne′-dead′(-ded′), *a.* as lifeless as a stone.
stōne′-deaf′(-def′), *a.* totally deaf.
stōne ēat′ẽr, a stone borer.
stōne fąl′çŏn, a merlin.
stone fence, 1. an alcoholic mixed drink, particularly one of cider and applejack. [Slang.]
2. a wall or fence made of stone.
stōne fẽrn, a fern of the genus *Asplenium*, common in Europe, growing on walls and in rocky places.
stōne′fish, *n.* the shanny.
stōne flȳ, a pseudoneuropterous insect of the genus *Perla*, used by anglers as bait.
stōne fruit, a fruit whose seeds are covered with a hard shell enveloped in the pulp, as peaches, cherries, plums, etc.; a drupe.
stōne′gąll, *n.* same as *staniel*.
stōne grig, a lamprey. [Brit. Dial.]
stōne ham′mẽr, a hammer for breaking or roughdressing stones.
stōne′hatch, *n.* a ring plover. [Brit. Dial.]
stōne hąwk, the stone falcon.
stōne′heärt′ed, *a.* hardhearted; cruel; pitiless; unfeeling.
Stōne′henġe, *n.* a prehistoric structure of upright and horizontal stones on Salisbury Plain, England.
stōne′-horse, *n.* a horse not castrated; a stallion. [Obs.]
stōne leek, the cibol, a species of onion.
stōne lift′ẽr, a fish of Tasmania, *Kathetostoma læve*.
stōne lil′y, a fossil crinoid.
stōne lug′gẽr, same as *stone roller*.
stōne mär′ten, a marten, genus *Mustela*, of central and southern Europe and Asia, having a white patch on its throat and breast; also, its fur.
stōne′mā·sŏn, *n.* a person who cuts stone to shape and uses it in making walls, buildings, etc.: also *stone mason*.
stōne ōak, a tree of Java, *Quercus javanensis*, named from the extreme hardness of its acorns.
stōne oil, petroleum.
stōne pärs′ley, any of a number of plants of the parsley family, genus *Seseli*, with cream-colored flowers and fragrant seeds.
stōne′peck″ẽr, *n.* 1. the turnstone.
2. the purple sandpiper.
stōne pīne, one of several trees of the genus *Pinus*, as the Swiss pine.
stōne pit, a pit or quarry where stones are dug.
stōne pitch, hard, thickened pitch.
stōne plŏv′ẽr, 1. the stone curlew of Europe, *Œdicnemus crepitans*.
2. any one of certain plovers of the genus *Esacus*; also, any of various shore birds, as the ring plover, the gray plover, the bartailed godwit, etc.

STONE PLOVER (*Œdicnemus crepitans*)

stōn′ẽr, *n.* one who or that which stones; specifically, (a) a person who cuts stones; (b) an implement used in removing stones from fruit.
stōne rag, a lichen of the genus *Parmelia*. [Rare.]
stōne rōll′ẽr, 1. one of a group of fresh-water carp, *Campostoma nigricans*.
2. a fish of the sucker family, *Hypentelium nigricans*.
stōne′rọọt, *n.* same as *horse balm*.
stōne run′nẽr, a stone plover.
stōne sạw, an instrument or machine for cutting building stone into blocks or slabs.
stōne′ṣ ċast, a stone cast.
stōne′seed, *n.* the stoneweed.
stōne′smiċ″kle, *n.* the stonechat.
stōne snīpe, the greater yellowlegs of North America.
stōne′ṣ thrōw, 1. the distance that a stone can be thrown.
2. a relatively short distance.
stōne′-still′, *a.* still as a stone; perfectly still or motionless.

stōne suck′ẽr, a lamprey.
stōne tōt′ẽr, 1. an American cyprinoid fish of the genus *Exoglossum*; the cutlips.
2. a stone roller.
stōne·wall′, *v.i.* in cricket, to play only a defensive game in order to gain a draw: said of a batsman.
stōne′wąll″ing, *n.* in Australia, obstruction or delay of parliamentary proceedings by needless debate, trifling objections, etc.; filibustering.
stōne′wãre, *n.* a coarse, dense, heavily glazed kind of pottery containing much silica or sand and flint.
stōne′weed, *n.* a weed of the genus *Lithospermum*: so named from the hardness of the seeds.
stōne′wŏrk, *n.* 1. the art or process of working in stone, as in masonry or jewelry.
2. something made or built in stone; specifically, masonry; as, the first story is *stonework*.
3. [*pl.*] a place where masonry stone is cut and dressed.
stōne′wŏrt, *n.* any of a number of related green algae of the genus *Chara*, with jointed stems and curved branches, usually covered with lime.
stōn′i·ly, *adv.* in a stony manner.
stōn′i·ness, *n.* the quality or condition of being stony.
stōn′y, *a.*; *comp.* stonier; *superl.* stoniest, [ME. *stoony*; AS. *stænig*; akin to G. *steinig*; Sw. *stenig*.]
1. pertaining to, abounding in, or resembling stone; as, a *stony* tower, *stony* ground.
2. petrifying; converting to stone.
3. cruel; unrelenting; pitiless.
4. obdurate; cold; rigid.
5. hard like stone.
6. stone-broke. [Slang.]
7. made or consisting of stone. [Poet.]
stōn′y-brōke′, *a.* stone-broke. [Slang.]
stōn′y·heärt′ed (-härt′), *a.* hard; unfeeling; pitiless; cruel.
stood, *v.* past tense and past participle of *stand*.
stọọġe, *n.* 1. (a) an actor stationed in the audience to assist a comedian by heckling him; (b) an actor who assists a comedian by feeding him lines, being the victim of pranks, etc. [Colloq.]
2. any person who acts as a foil, underling, etc. to another: term of contempt. [Colloq.]
stọọġe, *v.i.* to be a stooge (*for* someone). [Colloq.]
stọọk, *n.* [ME. *stouke*; prob. from a L.G. source.] a bundle of sheaves of cut grain; a shock. [Brit.]
stọọl, *n.* [ME. *stool*; AS. *stol*, a seat, throne.]
1. a single seat without a back or arms, supported on three or four legs.
2. a kind of low bench on which to kneel or put the feet; a footstool.
3. a toilet; a water closet; a privy; hence, a bowel movement; also, feces.
4. in shipbuilding, (a) [*pl.*] chocks or supports, beneath the transoms, for the attachment of the fashion pieces; (b) a piece of plank fastened to a ship's side to receive the bolting of the gallery; (c) a small channel on a ship's side for containing the deadeyes of the backstays.
5. a bishop's seat or see.
6. an artificial oyster bed. [Dial.]
7. a plant from which young plants are propagated by layering. [Rare.]
8. the root or stump of a timber tree, which throws up shoots; also, the set or cluster of shoots thus produced.
9. a portable perch to which a bird, as a pigeon, is fastened to lure other birds.
10. a bird or other object used as a lure or decoy; hence, a stool pigeon.
stool of a window; the flat part of a window frame on which the sash shuts down.
stool of repentance; formerly, in Scotland, the cutty stool.
stọọl, *v.i.* 1. to put out shoots in the form of a stool.
2. to evacuate the bowels.
3. to act as a stool pigeon, or informer. [Colloq.]
stọọl′ball, *n.* an outdoor game of ball, containing some of the elements of cricket, and at one time used as a substitute for it, especially among young women.
stọọl pig′eŏn, 1. a pigeon or other bird used as a decoy.
2. a person serving as a decoy.
3. a spy or informer. [Colloq.]

stọọp, *v.i.*; stooped (stọọpt), *pt., pp.*; stooping, *ppr.* [ME. *stoupen*; AS. *stupian*; akin to O.D. *stuypen*, to bow; Sw. *stupa*, to fall, to tilt, *stupande*, sloping, *stupning*, a leaning forward.]
1. to bend the body downward and forward; to bend or lean forward or in a crouch.
2. to be bent; specifically, to have the head and shoulders habitually bent forward.
3. to yield; to submit; to bend by compulsion; as, Carthage at length *stooped* to Rome. [Rare.]
4. to descend from rank or dignity; to condescend; to deign; to belittle oneself; as to *stoop* to his level; to *stoop* to answer the insult.
5. to descend; specifically, to swoop down on prey, as a hawk.
Syn.—bend, condescend, submit, bow, yield, descend.
stọọp, *v.t.* 1. to bend or bow downward and forward; to bow down.
2. to cause to incline downward; to tilt; as, to *stoop* a cask of liquor. [Brit. Dial.]
3. to overcome; to prostrate. [Rare.]
4. to debase or humble. [Archaic.]
5. to swoop down upon, as a hawk on prey. [Obs.]
stọọp, *n.* 1. the act of stooping or bending the body forward; especially, a habitual bend of the back or shoulders; as, to walk with a *stoop*.
2. descent from dignity or superiority; condescension.
3. the swoop of a bird on its prey.
stọọp, *n.* [D. *stoep*, stoop.] originally, a raised platform at the entrance of a house with steps and, usually, seats; hence, any small porch at the entrance of a house.
stọọp, *n.* same as *stoup*.
stọọp, *n.* 1. the stock or stump of a tree.
2. a post or pillar.
3. in mining, a prop or pillar, especially one of coal left to support the roof of the mine.
4. a sustainer or supporter; a patron.
[Brit. Dial. in all senses.]
stoop and roop; completely; every bit; altogether. [Scot.]
stọọp′ẽr, *n.* one who or that which stoops.
stọọp′ing·ly, *adv.* in a stooping position; with the head and shoulders bent forward.
stọọr, *n.* and *v.* same as *stour*.
stọọr, *a.* [AS. *stor*; Sw. *stor*, large.] strong; bold; inflexible; mighty; harsh; powerful. [Archaic and Dial.]
stop, *v.t.*; stopped *or poetic* stopt, *pt., pp.*; stopping, *ppr.* [ME. *stoppen*; AS. *stoppian*, *forstoppian*, to stop up, from LL. *stuppare*, to stop up with tow, from L. *stuppa*, tow.]
1. to close up by filling, stuffing, or otherwise obstructing; also, to fill in, plug up, or cover (a hole, cavity, opening, etc.); as, to *stop* a vent; to *stop* the ears.
2. to stanch (a wound, cut, etc.).
3. to obstruct; to make impassable; as, to *stop* a way, road, or passage.
4. to close (a bottle, jug, or other container) with a cork, plug, etc.
5. (a) to close (a finger hole of a wind instrument) so as to produce a desired tone; (b) to produce (a tone) in this way.
6. to cause to cease motion, activity, etc.
7. to prevent the passage or further passage of (water, light, etc.); to block; obstruct; intercept.
8. to prevent the movement or further movement of; specifically, (a) to halt the progress of (a person, animal, vehicle, etc.); (b) to check (a blow, stroke, or thrust of an opponent); to parry; to counter; (c) to defeat (an opponent); (d) to intercept (a letter, etc.) in transit.
9. to cease; to desist from (with a gerund); as, he *stopped* talking.
10. to cause to cease or end; as, *stop* that racket.
11. to cause (an engine, machine, etc.) to cease operation.
12. to press down (a violin string, etc.) against the finger board to produce a desired pitch.
13. to place a stop order on (a stock or other security).
14. in bridge, to block future play of (a suit) by holding key cards.
15. in rhetoric, to punctuate.
16. in nautical usage, to make fast; to bring to anchor.
17. in horticulture, to top.
18. to keep from beginning, acting, happening, etc.; to prevent.

19. to keep (a person) from doing something contemplated.

20. to prevent the starting, advent, etc. of; to preclude.

21. to notify one's bank to withhold payment on (one's check).

to stop off; in founding, to fill (a portion of a mold) with sand to prevent the molten metal from running into that portion.

to stop one's mouth; to silence one.

to stop out; (a) to cover (a surface) with some preparation that can resist chemical or other action, as in photography or etching; (b) in the theater, to cover (a tooth) with some black preparation, to make it invisible.

Syn.—obstruct, stay, impede, hinder, delay, repress, keep back, end.

stop, *v.i.* 1. to cease moving, walking, proceeding, etc.; to halt.

2. to leave off doing something, either temporarily or permanently; to desist from continuing.

3. to cease operating, as from mechanical failure or lack of fuel.

4. to be able to go no further; as, his arguments *stop* there.

5. to become clogged or choked.

6. to tarry; to stay.

to stop off; to stop for a short, temporary, or incidental stay en route to a place.

to stop out; to spend the night away from one's usual lodgings. [Colloq.]

to stop over; (a) to stay for a while; (b) to break a journey, as for a rest.

stop, *n.* 1. the act of stopping or the state of being stopped; cessation; arrest; halt; termination; as, a *stop* in speaking, writing, or walking.

2. a coming to an end; a finish; an end.

3. a stay or sojourn.

4. a place stopped at, as on a bus route, streetcar line, etc.

5. something that stops; an obstruction; obstacle; specifically, (a) a plug or stopper; (b) a stop order; (c) an order to withhold payment on a check; (d) a mechanical part that stops, limits, or regulates motion, as the pawl in a watch or clock; (e) a punctuation mark, especially a period.

6. (a) pressure, as of a finger, on a string of a violin, etc. to produce a desired pitch; (b) a fret on a guitar, etc.

7. (a) the closing of a finger hole of a wind instrument to change tone; (b) a hole in a wind instrument closed by a finger or key.

8. (a) a tuned set of organ pipes or reeds of the same specific type and tone quality; (b) a pull, lever, or key for putting such a set or sets into or out of operation.

9. in phonetics, (a) the act of completely stopping the outgoing breath, as with the velum, lips, or tongue; (b) a consonant formed in this way, as *p, b, k, g, t,* and *d.*

10. in photography, (a) the aperture, usually adjustable, of a lens; hence, (b) the F number.

11. in joinery, one of the pieces of wood nailed on the frame of a door to form the recess or rebate into which the door shuts.

12. in nautical usage, a projection at the upper part of a mast, outside of the cheeks; also, a piece of line used to secure something.

13. in optics, a perforated diaphragm between two lenses, to intercept the extreme rays that might disturb the perfection of the image.

14. the depression between the cranial and nasal bones in the face of a dog, especially prominent in the bulldog and pug.

15. in lacemaking, a point at which the warp threads come together, taken as a basis of measurement.

complete stop; in musical instruments, a stop having at least one pipe or reed to each key.

compound stop; in musical instruments, a stop having two or more pipes or reeds to each key.

Geneva stop; a stop, common in Swiss watches, which serves to prevent overwinding.

string stop; in an organ, a stop which produces a sound resembling that of a stringed instrument.

to hunt upon the stop; to hunt after the manner of a stophound, without speed or great effort. [Obs.]

to put a stop to; to cause to stop; to end.

Syn.—cessation, impediment, obstruction.

stop, *n.* a bucket; a pail. [Obs.]

stop bēad, a narrow molding used in making a groove for a window sash.

stop'çock, *n.* a cock or valve for stopping or controlling the movement of a fluid, as through a pipe; a faucet.

stōpe, *n.* in mining, a horizontal excavation forming one of a series of steps from which ore has been excavated.

stōpe, *v.t.* and *v.i.*; stoped, *pt., pp.*; stoping, *ppr.* in mining, to remove the contents of (a vein) in stopes.

stōpe, stō'pen, *v.* obsolete past participle of *step.*

stop'gap, *n.* 1. that which fills a gap or crevice.

2. a person or thing serving as a temporary substitute for another; a makeshift.

stop'gap, *a.* that is a stopgap.

stop gāte, in canals, a gate separating one section from another and used to shut it off, in case of a break in the embankment.

stop'hound, *n.* a hound trained to stop at every signal from the hunter.

stōp'ing, *n.* the act of forming into stopes.

stop knob (nob), in an organ, a knob by which a particular stop is controlled.

stop'less, *a.* not to be stopped.

stop līght (līt), 1. a traffic light, usually red, signaling vehicles to stop.

2. a light at the rear of a vehicle, that lights up when the brakes are applied.

stop mō'tion, in mechanics, an automatic contrivance for stopping motion suddenly.

stop'-off, *n.* the act of making a brief stop en route to a place; also, the stop made.

stop ọr'dẽr, an order to a broker given by a buyer, ordering purchase or sale when a specified stock reaches a certain figure.

stop'ō″vẽr, *n.* 1. a brief stop or stay at a place in the course of a journey.

2. a train ticket, etc. permitting such a stop.

stop'păġe, *n.* 1. the act of stopping or the state of being stopped; as, the *stoppage* of the circulation of the blood; the *stoppage* of commerce.

2. an obstructed condition; a block.

3. a deduction made from pay or allowances to repay advances, etc.

stoppage in transit or *in transitu*; in law, the right which an unpaid vendor of goods has, on hearing that the vendee is insolvent, to stop and reclaim the goods while in their transit and not yet delivered to the vendee.

stopped (stopt), *a.* 1. in music, produced by stopping.

2. in phonetics, produced with a stop.

stop'pẽr, *n.* 1. one who or that which stops, closes, shuts, hinders, etc.

2. something inserted to close an opening; a plug.

3. in nautical usage, a short piece of rope used for making something fast, as the anchor or cables.

4. any of various small trees of the genus *Eugenia,* found in Florida and the West Indies.

5. the upper pad or principal callosity of the sole of a greyhound's foot.

stop'pẽr, *v.t.*; stoppered, *pt., pp.*; stoppering, *ppr.* to close or secure with a plug or stopper.

stop'pẽr bōlt, in nautical usage, a large ringbolt, driven into the deck before the main hatch, etc., for securing the stoppers.

stop'pẽr hōle, in iron puddling, a hole in the door of the furnace through which the iron is stirred and the operation observed.

stop'pẽr knot (not), a knot in a rope, used as a stopper.

stop'ping, *n.* 1. the act of one who or that which stops; specifically, the process of filling cracks.

2. something that stops, as (a) in mining, a door or screen in a gallery, that stops the passage of air at a certain point; (b) in dental surgery, material for filling hollow teeth; (c) in farriery, a ball or pad for stuffing the space on a horse's foot within the inner edge of the shoe.

stop plañk, in some hydraulic works, a vertical plank used with others to form a dam.

stop'ple, *n.* [ME. *stoppel,* dim. from *stoppen,* to stop.]

1. that which stops or closes the mouth of a vessel; a stopper; as, a glass *stopple*; a cork *stopple.*

2. a plug to be inserted in the hole of a flute or flageolet, to regulate and change its scale.

stop'ple, *v.t.*; stoppled (-pld), *pt., pp.*; stoppling, *ppr.* to stopper.

stop'ple, *n.* stubble. [Obs.]

stop rod, in weaving, a rod extending lengthwise under the batten of the loom and constituting part of the stop motion.

stop street, a street intersection at which vehicles must come to a complete stop before continuing.

stopt, *v.* poetic past tense and past participle of *stop.*

stop thrust, in fencing, a slight thrust, intended not to disarm the opponent, but to counter his advance.

stop valve, a valve to regulate flow, as of a liquid through a pipe; specifically, in steam engines, a valve fitted to the steam pipes where they leave the several boilers, in such a way that any boiler may be shut off from the others and from the engines.

stop wätch, a watch used for timing races, etc., in which one of the hands can be stopped and started instantly so as to indicate fractions of seconds.

stọr, *a.* stoor. [Obs.]

stōr'āġe, *n.* 1. the act of storing or the state of being stored; specifically, the act of depositing in a store or warehouse for safekeeping.

2. the price charged or paid for storing goods.

3. the space used for storing goods.

4. the charging of a storage battery so as to make possible the subsequent generation of electricity.

cold storage; the storage in refrigerating rooms of perishable merchandise for preservation by artificial cold.

storage battery; a battery of electrochemical cells for generating electric current: the cells can be recharged by passing a current through them in the direction opposite to the discharging flow of current.

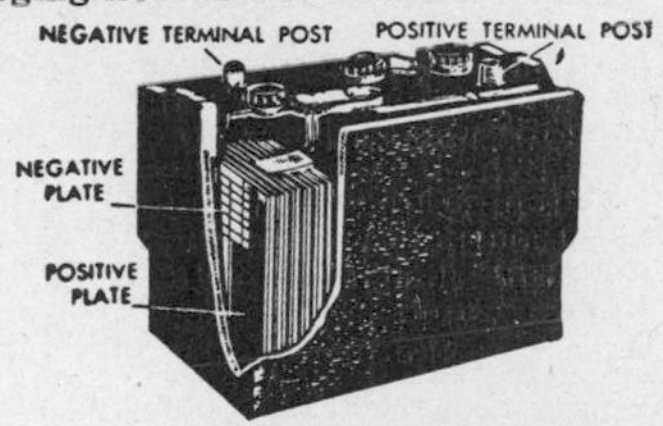

STORAGE BATTERY

storage bellows; a horizontal bellows of a pipe organ in which, through the operation of weights, the air is maintained at a uniform pressure.

storage cell; a cell which can give no current until it has been acted upon electrolytically by a current from some outside source. It consists, in its ordinary form, of two lead electrodes, made in the form of a grid to increase the effective surface and immersed in a ten per cent solution of sulfuric acid. While the charging current is passing, the water is broken up into hydrogen and oxygen; the hydrogen passes to the cathode and thence off into the air, while the oxygen goes to the anode and attacks the lead, changing it first to the oxide of lead, then to the peroxide. The cathode remains pure lead. In charging, electrical energy has been transformed into chemical energy. When the charging current is interrupted and the electrodes of the cell are metallically connected, a current passes in a direction opposite to that of the charging current, and the lead peroxide of the anode is reduced to lead oxide, while the pure lead cathode is oxidized to lead oxide. Energy of chemical combination is thus transformed back into electrical energy. When the electrodes are both lead oxide, the cell is discharged.

stō'rax, *n.* [ME.; L. *storax, styrax*; Gr. *styrax,* a sweet-smelling gum from the styrax tree.]

1. the balsam of the Asiatic liquidambar tree, used in medicine and perfumery.

2. a gum resin obtained from certain styracaceous trees.

3. a tree yielding storax, or any tree of the same genus.

stōre, *n.* [ME. *stoor, store,* store, farm stock, from OFr. *estore,* store, provisions, from *estorer,* to erect, furnish, equip, store, from a verb, *staurare,* seen in L. *instaurare,* to repair, to restore, erect, from the root of *stare,* to stand.]

1. that which is collected and stored against future use; a stock accumulated; a supply; a hoard; specifically, [*pl.*] articles, especially of food, provided for some special purpose; supplies, as of provisions, arms, ammunition, clothing, etc.; as, army *stores*; ship's *stores,* or the like.

2. a great quantity; plenty; abundance; a large number.

3. a place where supplies are stored for future use; a storehouse; a warehouse; a magazine.

4. an establishment where goods are regularly offered for sale; a shop; as, a book*store*; a dry-goods *store*.

appraiser's store; a government warehouse where goods are kept until appraised.

general store; see under *general*.

in store; set aside for the future; in reserve.

marine stores; old ropes, sails, anchors, etc.

to set store by; to have regard or esteem for; to value.

to tell no store of; to hold of small account; to set no store by. [Obs.]

Syn.—supply, provision, accumulation, fund, abundance.

stōre, *a.* 1. hoarded; laid up; as, *store* treasure. [Obs.]

2. containing stores; set apart for receiving stores.

All the *store* cities that Solomon had.
—2 Chron. viii. 4.

3. obtained at a store or shop; purchased or purchasable at a shop or store; as, *store* clothes. [Dial.]

store cattle; stock cattle; also, cattle bought lean to be fattened.

store pay; payment for produce or labor taken in goods from a store, as provisions, clothing, etc., instead of in money.

stōre, *v.t.*; stored, *pt., pp.*; storing, *ppr.* **1.** to stock; to furnish; to supply; to equip.

2. to stock or supply with stores, provisions, etc. against a future time; as, a city well *stored*.

3. to deposit in a store or warehouse for safekeeping; as, to *store* goods.

4. to store or lay up against future need; to hoard.

stōre′house, *n.* 1. a place for storing things; especially, a warehouse.

2. a great mass, quantity, or supply.

stōre′keep″ēr, *n.* 1. one who owns or is in charge of a store; a shopkeeper; a merchant; a retail dealer in merchandise.

2. a person charged with the care and distribution of stores or supplies, as in government service.

stōr′ēr, *n.* one who lays up or forms a store.

stōre′rọom, *n.* a room in which things are stored.

stōre′ship, *n.* a ship used to carry supplies.

stō′rey, *n.*; *pl.* **stō′reys,** a story (of a building). [Brit.]

stọr′gē, *n.* [Gr.] parental affection; the strong affection which animals have for their young.

stō′ri·ăl, *a.* historical. [Obs.]

stō′ried, *a.* 1. connected with actual or imaginary events of the past; having historical or legendary associations.

2. painted with scenes from stories or history; adorned with historical paintings.

stō′ried, *a.* having, consisting of, or comprising (a specified number of) stories: usually in hyphenated compounds; as, a twelve-*storied* structure.

stō′ri·ēr, *n.* a relater of stories; also, [Obs.] a historian.

stō·ri·ette′ (-et′), *n.* a very short story.

stō′ri·fȳ, *v.t.*; storified, *pt., pp.*; storifying, *ppr.* to make up or tell stories about.

stọrk, *n.*; *pl.* **stọrks** or **stọrk,** [ME.; AS. *storc*; akin to D., Dan., and Sw. *stork*, stork; origin uncertain.] any large, long-legged wading bird of the genus *Ciconia*, or of the family *Ciconiinæ*: it resembles the heron, but has a larger bill and shorter toes, with a nonserrated claw on the middle toe. It inhabits marshes and rivers, where it feeds on frogs, lizards, fishes, young birds, etc. Storks are migratory, arriving from the south at their breeding haunts in the early spring, and departing again in the autumn. The white or house stork, *Ciconia alba*, of central Europe, is the most common, and constructs its nest frequently on the chimneys of cottages, the tops of tall trees, spires, walls of ruined buildings, etc. The plumage is pure white, the quills and longest feathers on the wing covers black, the beak and feet red. The black stork, *Ciconia nigra*, from central and eastern Europe, Asia, and Africa, has the upper surface black, the lower parts white.

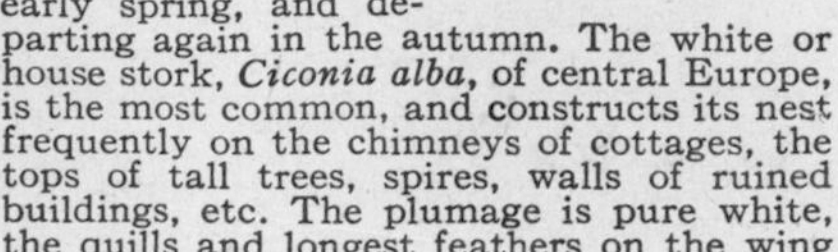

WHITE STORK (*Ciconia alba*)

saddle-billed stork; a species of jabiru, native to Africa.

stọrk′-billed, *a.* having a straight stout bill, like a heron or a stork.

stọrk's′-bill, *n.* any of a number of plants of the genus *Erodium*; also, any species of the genus *Pelargonium*, family *Geraniaceæ*: so called from the beak of the fruit resembling in form the bill of the stork.

stọrm, *n.* [AS. *storm*; Ice. *stormr*, storm.]

1. a disturbance of the atmosphere, characterized by a strong wind, usually accompanied by rain, snow, hail, or thunder and lightning; also, any heavy fall of rain, snow, etc.

2. a wind with a velocity of from 64 to 75 miles per hour.

3. a disturbance or agitation of a political or social nature; a tumult; a clamor; a commotion.

4. a violent or vehement outbreak of emotion, passion, or excitement; as, a *storm* of rage, a *storm* of applause.

5. a heavy shower or fall of anything, especially missiles; as, a *storm* of bullets.

6. in military usage, a sudden, violent assault on a fortified place or strong position.

cyclonic storm; a cyclone.

storm and stress; see *Sturm und Drang*.

Syn.—agitation, disturbance, riot, tempest, bluster, rage; hurricane, typhoon, tornado.

stọrm, *v.t.*; stormed, *pt., pp.*; storming, *ppr.* 1. to attack or assault violently and unceasingly; as, they *stormed* him with questions.

2. in military usage, to capture or attempt to capture (a fortified place) with a sudden, strong attack.

stọrm, *v.i.* 1. to blow with violence; to be stormy; to rain, hail, snow, etc., especially with violence.

2. to rage; to be in a violent agitation or passion; to fume.

Wherefore *storm* you so? —Shak.

3. to rush or move violently or tumultuously; as, he *stormed* into the office.

stọrm ā′rē·ȧ, the region over which a storm extends.

stọrm ax′is, the shifting axis or perpendicular line about which a cyclone spirals.

stọrm′-bēat, stọrm′-bēat″en, *a.* beaten or damaged by storms; weather-beaten.

stọrm belt, a zone of the earth's surface over which storms prevailingly move.

stọrm′bīrd, *n.* any bird whose presence is believed to presage storms; especially, the stormy petrel.

stọrm′bound, *a.* held, detained, or cut off by storms; as, they were *stormbound* for three days.

stọrm cel′lăr, an underground shelter used during hurricanes, tornadoes, etc.

stọrm cen′tēr, 1. the shifting center about which a cyclone spirals, an area of lowest barometric pressure and comparative calm.

2. a center of trouble, turmoil, or disturbance.

stọrm çloud, any cloud threatening a storm; also, the indications of any impending trouble or event.

stọrm′çock, *n.* 1. the missel. [Brit. Dial.]

2. the green woodpecker. [Brit. Dial.]

3. the fieldfare. [Brit. Dial.]

stọrm çōne, a cone-shaped device used as a storm signal.

stọrm çur′rent, a current caused by a storm.

stọrm dōor, an outer, additional door for protection against storms or winter weather.

stọrm drum, a drum-shaped device used as a storm signal.

stọrm′ēr, *n.* one who storms.

stọrm finch, a stormy petrel. [Brit. Dial.]

stọrm′fụl, *a.* having many storms.

stọrm′fụl·ness, *n.* the quality or condition of being stormy.

stọrm glȧss, a tube containing a liquid holding a solution which is supposed to be sensitive to atmospheric changes. In clear weather the substance settles near the bottom of the tube, the liquid remaining comparatively clear; preceding a storm the substance rises, causing the liquid to become cloudy.

stọrm′i·ly, *adv.* in a stormy manner.

stọrm′i·ness, *n.* the quality or condition of being stormy.

stọrm′ing pär′ty, in military usage, the party assigned to storm a fortress.

stọrm kīte, a contrivance for sending a rope from a stranded ship to the shore.

stọrm lāne, a path over which storm centers pass frequently and more or less regularly.

stọrm′less, *a.* free from storms.

stọrm pȧth, same as *storm track*.

stọrm pāve′ment, the sloping stone paving that lines the sea face of piers and breakwaters.

stọrm pet′rel, same as *stormy petrel* under *stormy*.

stọrm′prọof, *a.* 1. that can withstand a storm.

2. giving protection against storms.

stọrm sāil, in nautical usage, a sail made of very stout canvas, smaller in size than an ordinary sail.

stọrm sig′năl, a signal for indicating the probable approach of a storm.

stọrm stāy, a stay on which a storm sail is bent.

stọrm track, the path traveled by a cyclone.

stọrm trọọp′ēr, a member of the Sturmabteilung.

stọrm wāve, a very high rolling wave caused by a violent storm.

stọrm′wind, *n.* the wind or blast of a storm.

stọrm win′dōw, a window placed outside of a regular window as added protection against winter weather; also, a protected window raised above a roof.

stọrm′y, *a.*; *comp.* stormier; *superl.* stormiest, 1. of, characteristic of, or affected by storms.

2. having or characterized by storms.

3. violent; raging; passionate.

stormy petrel; (a) any of several small, black-and-white sea birds thought to presage storms; (b) a person thought to presage or bring trouble.

Stọr′ting, Stọr′thing (-ting), *n.* [Norw. *stor*, great, and *thing*, meeting.] the parliament of Norway.

stọr′ven, *v.* obsolete past tense plural and past participle of *starve*.

stō′ry, *n.*; *pl.* **stō′ries,** [ME. *storie*; OFr. *estoire*; L. *historia*, history.]

1. the telling of a happening or connected series of happenings, whether true or fictitious; an account; narration.

2. a fictitious literary composition in prose or poetry, shorter than a novel; narrative; tale.

3. such tales, collectively, as a form of literature.

4. the plot of a novel, play, etc.

5. a report or rumor.

6. a falsehood; a fib. [Colloq.]

7. history. [Archaic.]

8. in journalism, (a) a news article; (b) a person or event considered newsworthy.

short story; see under *short*.

short short story; see under *short*.

Syn.—anecdote, incident, memoir, narrative, tale, romance, parable, legend, yarn.

stō′ry, *v.t.*; storied, *pt. pp.*; storying, *ppr.* **1.** to describe in a story; to tell the story of; to narrate; to relate. [Archaic.]

2. to ornament with paintings or sculptures of scenes from legend or history.

stō′ry, *n.*; *pl.* **stō′ries,** [prob. of same origin as *story* (narrative).]

1. a section or horizontal division of a building extending from the floor to the ceiling or roof lying directly above it; as, a house having only one *story*, a building of many *stories*.

2. all the rooms on the same level of a building.

3. any horizontal section or division.

Also spelled *storey*.

stō′ry·book, *n.* a book containing one or more stories or tales.

stō′ry pōst, a vertical post used to support a floor or superincumbent wall.

stō′ry-tell″ēr, *n.* 1. one who tells stories.

2. one who tells falsehoods; a fibber; a liar. [Colloq.]

stō′ry-tell″ing, *n.* **1.** the art or act of telling stories.

2. the act or practice of telling falsehoods. [Colloq.]

stō′ry·wrīt″ēr (-rīt″), *n.* **1.** a historian. [Obs.]

2. one who writes stories.

stoss, *a.* [G. *stoss*, blow, push.] in geology, facing the iceward side of a rock, ledge, or hill rising above a land surface overridden by a glacier: opposed to *lee*.

stot, *n.* [Ice. *stûtr*; Sw. *stut*, a bull.] a young bull or steer. [Scot.]

stọ·tin̄′kȧ, *n.*; *pl.* **stọ·tin̄′ki,** [Bulg.] a unit of currency in Bulgaria, equal to 1/100 lev.

stound, *n.* [ME.; AS. *stund.*]
1. a time; moment. [Archaic or Dial.]
2. a pain or pang; a shock. [Obs. or Dial.]

stound, *v.i.* to ache, pain, or smart. [Scot. or Brit. Dial.]

stound, *n.* a vessel to put small beer in. [Obs.]

stöup, *n.* [ME. *stowpe*, bucket, from ON. *staup*; sense of "drinking vessel" prob. from M.D. *stoop.*]
1. (a) a drinking cup; tankard; (b) as much as such a cup will hold. [Archaic or Brit. Dial.]
2. a pail, or bucket. [Scot.]
3. a basin for holy water in a church.
Also spelled *stoop.*

STOUP

stöur, *n.* [ME. *stowre, sture*; OFr. *estour, estorn*, from the base seen in *storm.*]
1. combat or conflict.
2. turmoil.
3. a storm.
4. wind-blown dust.
[Archaic or Dial. in all senses.]

stöur, *v.i.* 1. to rise in clouds, as dust, smoke, etc. [Obs. or Scot. and Brit. Dial.]
2. to move actively; to stir quickly. [Obs. or Scot. and Brit. Dial.]

stout, *a.*; *comp.* stouter; *superl.* stoutest, [ME. *stoute, stowte*, from OFr. *estout, estot*, bold; L.G. *stolt*; D. *stout*; G. *stolz*, bold, stout, haughty.]
1. courageous; brave; undaunted.
2. (a) strong in body; sturdy; (b) strong in construction; firm; substantial; as, a *stout* wall.
3. powerful; forceful.
4. fat; thickset; fleshy; corpulent.
5. proud; arrogant. [Archaic.]
Syn.—corpulent, strong, lusty, vigorous, robust, sturdy, brawny, resolute, brave, valiant.

stout, *n.* 1. a stout person.
2. a garment for a stout person.
3. strong, dark-brown beer, ale, or porter.

stout′heärt″ed, *a.* having a stout heart; courageous; brave.

stout·heärt′ed·ness, *n.* courage; the quality of being stouthearted.

stouth′rief, *n.* [Scot. *stouth*, that which is stowed or laid up, and *rief*, the carrying off by force.] in Scottish law, theft, accompanied by violence; robbery.

stout′ish, *a.* inclined to be stout.

stout′ly, *adv.* in a stout manner; as, he *stoutly* defended himself.

stout′ness, *n.* the quality or condition of being stout.

stō·vā′ine, stō·vā′in, *n.* [from *stove* (trans. of Fr. *Fourneau*, name of the discoverer); and *-aine*, after *cocaine*, etc.] a local anesthetic, $C_6H_5OCO{\cdot}(CH_3)C(C_2H_5){\cdot}CH_2{\cdot}N(CH_3)_2HCl$, having small, lustrous scales, readily soluble in water: it is usually injected spinally: a trade-mark (*Stovaine*).

stōve, *v.* alternative past tense and past participle of *stave.*

stōve, *n.* [AS. *stofa, stofe*, a hot air bath; Ice. *stofa*, older *stufa*, a bathroom with a stove, a chamber; D. *stoof*, a stove, a furnace; L.G. *stove, stave*; G. *stube*, a room.]
1. an apparatus, made usually of iron or steel, of various sizes and designs, using fuel or electricity in producing heat for warming, cooking, etc.
2. any heated chamber or room, as a kiln, used for drying manufactured articles, raising plants, etc.
3. a simple, boxlike apparatus furnished with a pan for holding coal or jets for burning gas, used in warming the feet. [Brit.]
cannon stove; a long, upright, cylindrical stove.

stōve, *v.t.*; stoved, *pt., pp.*; stoving, *ppr.* 1. to keep warm in a house or room by artificial heat; as, to *stove* orange trees.
2. to heat as in a stove.
3. to stew. [Scot.]

stōve′house, *n.* a hothouse or drying room.

stōve′pipe, *n.* 1. a metal pipe used for conducting smoke and gases from a stove, as into a chimney flue.
2. a stovepipe hat. [Colloq.]
stovepipe hat; a man's tall silk hat. [Colloq.]

stōve plant, a plant kept or cultivated in a hothouse.

stō′vēr, *n.* [ME. *stauer*; OFr. *estover, estovoir*, necessaries, provisions.]
1. corn stalks, excluding the grain, used as fodder for animals.
2. fodder of any kind. [Brit. Dial.]

stōw, *v.t.*; stowed, *pt., pp.*; stowing, *ppr.* [ME. *stowen*, from AS. *stōw*, a place; O.D. *sto.*]
1. to pack or store away; especially, to pack in an orderly, compact manner.
2. to fill by packing in an orderly manner.
3. to hold or receive: said of a room, container, etc.
4. to provide lodging for. [Obs.]
5. to stop; to cease; as, *stow* the chatter. [Slang.]
to stow away; (a) to put or hide away, as in a safe place; (b) to be a stowaway.
to stow down; (a) to put into the hold of a ship; (b) to furnish or yield for stowing.

stōw′āġe, *n.* 1. the act or operation of stowing.
2. a place or room for things to be stowed.
3. the state of being stowed.
4. money paid for stowing.
5. that which is stowed; something stowed.

stōw′ȧ·wāy, *n.* a person who hides aboard a ship, train, etc. so as to obtain free passage or evade port officials, etc.

stōw′bōard, *n.* in mining, a place for rubbish.

stowce, *n.* 1. a small windlass. [Brit.]
2. [*pl.*] pieces of wood of particular forms and constructions placed together, by which the possession of mines is marked. [Brit.]

stōw′ing, *n.* in mining, the method of filling old workings with rubbish either from the mine or from above; also, the rubbish so used.

stowre (stör), *n.* and *v.* stour. [Obs.]

STP, [prob. arbitrary use of *STP*, a commercial motor oil additive (from *S*cientifically *T*reated *P*etroleum), said to "make your motor run better."] a hallucinogenic drug similar to mescaline and amphetamine.

strā′bişm, *n.* strabismus.

strȧ·biş′măl, *a.* strabismic.

strȧ·biş′miç, *a.* 1. of or relating to strabismus; affected with strabismus.
2. cross-eyed.

strȧ·biş′miç·ăl, *a.* strabismic.

strā·biş·mom′ē·tēr, *n.* an instrument for measuring strabismus.

strȧ·biş′mus, *n.* [LL., from Gr. *strabismos*; *strabizein*, to squint; *strabos*, twisted.] a disorder of the eyes, as cross-eye, in which both eyes cannot be focused on the same point at the same time; squint.

strad′dle, *v.t.*; straddled, *pt., pp.*; straddling, *ppr.* [freq. of *stride.*] 1. to place oneself with a leg on either side of; to sit or stand astride of.
2. to spread (the legs) wide apart.
3. to take or appear to take both sides of (an issue). [Colloq.]
4. in poker, to double (whatever is staked before the deal).

strad′dle, *v.i.* 1. to sit, stand, or walk with the legs wide apart; to be astride.
2. to straddle an issue, argument, etc.; to refuse to commit oneself; to hedge. [Colloq.]

strad′dle, *n.* 1. the act or position of straddling.
2. the distance between the legs or feet of one who straddles.
3. in the stock exchange, an option giving the holder the right to buy from the seller, or sell to him, a specified number of shares at a specified price within the stated time.
4. in poker, the act of doubling what is staked before the deal.
5. the assumption of an equivocal position regarding any matter of controversy. [Colloq.]

strad′dle·bug, *n.* a long-legged scarabaeid, especially of the genus *Canthon.*

Strad·i·vär′i·us, *n.* a string instrument, especially a violin, made by Antonio Stradivari (1644–1737), a violin maker of Cremona, Italy.

strad·ō·met′riç·ăl, *a.* pertaining to the measuring of roads, streets, etc. [Rare.]

strāfe, *v.t.*; strafed, *pt., pp.*; strafing, *ppr.* [from G. phr. *Gott strafe England* (God punish England) used in World War I.] to attack with gunfire; especially, to attack (ground positions, troops, etc.) with machine-gun fire from low-flying aircraft.

strag′gle, *v.i.*; straggled, *pt., pp.*; straggling, *ppr.* [for *strackle*, freq. of ME. *straken*, to go, roam.]
1. to wander from the direct course or way; to stray from the main group.
2. to wander at large without any certain direction or object; to ramble.
3. to leave, arrive, or occur at scattered, irregular intervals.

strag′gle, *n.* the act of straggling. [Rare.]

strag′glēr, *n.* 1. one who straggles; one who has deserted or has been left behind by his companions; one who departs from the direct or proper course; one who rambles without any settled direction; as, *stragglers* from the army.
2. a vagabond; a wandering, shiftless fellow. [Obs.]
3. something that grows or proceeds irregularly beyond the rest or too far.
4. something that stands apart from others.

strag′gling·ly, *adv.* in a straggling manner.

strag′gly, *a.*; *comp.* stragglier; *superl.* straggliest; straggling.

strag′ū·lum, *n.* the back, scapulars, and folded wings of a bird.

strāight (strāt), *a.* [ME. *streght*, pp. of *strecchen*, to stretch, from AS. *streht*, pp. of *streccan*, to stretch.]
1. having the same direction throughout its length; having no curvature or angularity; as, a *straight* line.
2. not crooked, bent, bowed, wavy, curly, etc.; upright; erect; as, a *straight* back, *straight* hair.
3. with all cylinders in a direct line: said of some internal-combustion engines.
4. direct; undeviating; continuous; uninterrupted, etc.; as, a *straight* course.
5. following strictly the principles, slate of candidates, etc. of a political party; as, he votes a *straight* ticket.
6. following a direct or systematic course of reasoning, etc.; methodical; accurate.
7. in order; properly arranged, etc.; as, put your room *straight.*
8. (a) honest; sincere; upright; (b) [Colloq.] reliable, as information.
9. outspoken; frank.
10. unmixed; undiluted; as, *straight* whisky.
11. unqualified; unmodified; as, a *straight* answer.
12. at a fixed price per unit regardless of the quantity bought or sold; as, the apples are ten cents *straight.*
13. in card games, consisting of cards in sequence; as, a *straight* flush.
straight angle; an angle of 180 degrees.
straight arch; same as *flat arch.*
straight man; in the theater, an actor who serves as a foil for a comedian.
Syn.—direct, rectilinear, undeviating, unswerving, right.

strāight, *n.* 1. the state or quality of being straight.
2. something straight; specifically, (a) the straight part of a racecourse between the last turn and the winning post; (b) in poker, a series of five cards in sequence.

strāight, *adv.* 1. in a straight line; unswervingly.
2. directly; without deviation, delay, or circumlocution.
3. upright; erectly.
straight away (or *off*); at once; without delay.

strāight′-ärm, *v.t.* in football, to push away (a tackler) with the arm outstretched.

strāight′-ärm, *n.* the act of straight-arming.

strāight′-ar″rōw, *a.* proper, righteous, conscientious, etc.: often used with connotations of conservatism, stodginess, dullness, or the like. [Slang.]

strāight ar′rōw, a person who is straight-arrow. [Slang.]

strāight′ȧ·wāy, *a.* continuing in a straight line, as a race track.

strāight′ȧ·wāy, *n.* a track, or part of a track, that extends in a straight line.

strāight′-çut, *a.* having the leaf cut lengthwise; as, *straight-cut* tobacco.

strāight′edġe, *n.* a piece or strip of wood, etc. having one edge perfectly straight, used to ascertain whether a surface or edge is true.

strāight′en, *v.t.*; straightened, *pt., pp.*; straightening, *ppr.* to make straight; to reduce from a crooked to a straight form.

strāight′en, *v.i.* to become straight.

strāight′en·ēr, *n.* one who or that which straightens.

strāight fāce, a face showing no amusement or other emotion.

strāight′-fāced (-fāst), *a.* showing no amusement or other emotion.

strāight′fōrth, *adv.* directly; henceforth. [Obs.]

straight″for′wărd, *a.* 1. proceeding in a straight or direct line; not deviating.
2. upright; honest; open; frank; as, a *straightforward* man.

straight″for′wărd, *adv.* directly forward; straight on.

straight″for′wărd·ly, *adv.* in a straightforward manner.

straight″for′wărd·ness, *n.* the quality or state of being straightforward; undeviating rectitude.

straight″for′wărds, *adv.* straightforward.

straight′-joint, *a.* having the boards so laid that their joints at the ends form continuous transverse lines: said of a floor.

straight′-līne′, *a.* 1. composed of straight lines.
2. having the parts arranged in a straight line or lines.
3. designating a linkage or similar device (*straight-line motion*) used to produce or copy motion in straight lines.

straight′ly, *adv.* in a straight line; not crookedly.

straight′ness, *n.* the quality or state of being straight.

straight′-out, *a.* 1. straightforward; direct. [Colloq.]
2. unrestrained; outright. [Colloq.]
3. thoroughgoing; unqualified. [Colloq.]

straight′-pīght (-pīt), *a.* erect. [Obs.]

straight′-spō″ken, *a.* speaking plainly and to the point; plain-spoken.

straight′wāy, *adv.* immediately; without delay.

straight′wāys, *adv.* straightway. [Rare.]

strāik, *n.* same as *strake.*

strāin, *v.t.*; strained, *pt., pp.*; straining, *ppr.* [ME. *streinen*; OFr. *estraindre,* to strain, wring hard, from L. *stringere,* to draw tight.]
1. to draw or stretch tight.
2. to exert, use, or tax to the utmost; as, he *strained* every nerve to get there.
3. to overtax; to injure by exertion; to sprain; as, he *strained* a muscle climbing.
4. to injure or weaken by force, pressure, etc.; as, the wind *strained* the roof.
5. to stretch or force beyond the normal, customary, or legitimate limits; as, he *strained* the rule to his own advantage.
6. to change the form or size of, by applying external force.
7. (a) to pass through a screen, sieve, filter, etc.; to filter; (b) to remove or free by filtration, etc.
8. to hug; to embrace: now only in *to strain to one's bosom* (or *heart,* etc.).
9. to force; to constrain. [Obs.]

strāin, *v.i.* 1. to make violent or continual efforts; to strive hard; as, she *strained* to win.
2. to be or become strained.
3. to be subjected to great stress or pressure.
4. to pull with force.
5. to filter, ooze, or trickle.
to strain at; (a) to use great effort in trying to move (an object); to push or pull hard at; (b) to have unusually great difficulty accepting; to balk at.

strāin, *n.* 1. a straining or being strained.
2. great effort, exertion, or tension.
3. a strain or wrench.
4. change in form or size, or both, resulting from stress or force.
5. stress; force.
6. a great or excessive demand on one's emotions, resources, etc.; as, a *strain* on my imagination.

strāin, *n.* [ME. *strene, streen, stren*; AS. *streon,* gain, procreation, stock, race, from base of *strynan, streonan,* to produce.]
1. originally, (a) a begetting; (b) offspring.
2. ancestry; lineage; descent.
3. the descendants of a common ancestor; race; stock; line; breed; variety.
4. a line of individuals of a certain species or race, differentiated from the main group by certain, generally superior, qualities, especially as the result of artificial breeding.
5. an inherited or natural character or tendency.
6. a trace; a streak.
7. the manner, style, or mood of a speech, book, action, etc.; as, he wrote in an angry *strain.*
8. [*often pl.*] a passage of music; a tune; an air.
9. a flight or outburst of eloquence, profanity, etc.

strāin′ȧ·ble, *a.* 1. capable of being strained.
2. violent; compelling. [Obs.]

strāin′ȧ·bly, *adv.* violently. [Obs.]

strāined, *a.* stretched; tense; forced; perverted; distorted; unnatural; also, weakened; ready to part; as, *strained* courtesy.

strāin′ẽr, *n.* 1. a device for straining, sifting, or filtering; a sieve, filter, colander, etc.
2. a device for tightening or stretching something.
3. in carriage building, a stretcher.

strāin′ẽr vīne, the sponge gourd, *Luffa cylindrica.*

strāin′ing piēce, a horizontal beam placed between two opposite rafters in a roof truss: also called *straining beam.*

strāin nor′măl, in mechanics, a line perpendicular to the direction of any homogeneous strain.

strāin sheet, an outline drawing of the whole or part of a truss, bridge, etc., on which is indicated the amount of stress to be borne by each member.

strāint, *n.* a violent stretching or tension. [Rare.]

strāit, *a.* [ME. *streit*; OFr. *estreit, estroict,* strait, narrow, close, contracted, strict, from L. *strictus,* pp. of *stringere,* to draw tight.]
1. narrow; close; not broad; tight; confined; as, a *strait* path; a *strait* sleeve. [Archaic.]
2. close; intimate. [Obs.]
3. strict; rigorous; exacting. [Archaic.]
4. difficult; distressing; straitened.
5. mean; close; stingy. [Obs.]

strāit, *adv.* rigidly; exactly; closely. [Obs.]

strāit, *n.* 1. a narrow pass or passage. [Rare.]
2. a narrow strip of land with water on both sides; an isthmus. [Rare.]
3. [*often in pl.*] a narrow waterway connecting two large bodies of water.
4. [*often in pl.*] distress; difficulty; distressing necessity; as, in sad *straits.*

strāit, *v.t.* to put to difficulties. [Obs.]

strāit′en, *v.t.*; straitened, *pt., pp.*; straitening, *ppr.* 1. to make strait or narrow; to contract; to hem in.
2. to make tense or tight; as, to *straiten* a cord. [Obs.]
3. to restrict or confine; to hamper. [Rare.]
4. to bring into difficulties, especially financial hardships; to distress: usually in the past participle, especially in the phrase *in straitened circumstances,* lacking sufficient money.

strāit′hand′ed, *a.* parsimonious; sparing. [Obs.]

strāit·hand′ed·ness, *n.* niggardliness. [Obs.]

strāit jack′et, a coatlike device that binds the arms tight against the body: used to restrain mentally deranged persons, criminals, etc. who are violent.

strāit′-lāced′ (-lāst′), *a.* 1. (a) tightly laced, as a corset; (b) wearing tightly laced garments. [Archaic.]
2. stiff; constrained. [Rare.]
3. narrowly strict or severe in behavior, opinions, etc.

strāit′ly, *adv.* in a strait manner; narrowly; tightly; strictly; intimately; grievously. [Archaic.]

strāit′ness, *n.* the state or quality of being strait. [Archaic.]

strāit′-wāist″ċōat, *n.* same as *strait jacket.*

strāke, *v.* obsolete past tense of *strike.*

strāke, *n.* [variant of *streak* and *stroke.*]
1. a streak. [Obs.]
2. a continuous line of planking or metal plating extending from one end of a ship to the other.
3. a metal band on the fellies of a wheel, in sections, and not continuous like a tire.
4. in mining, an inclined trough for washing ore; a launder. [Brit. Dial.]
5. a rut; also, a crack in a floor.

stram, *v.i.*; strammed, *pt., pp.*; stramming, *ppr.* [prob. echoic.] to rebound with great force. [Brit. Dial.]

stram·ash′, *v.t.* to strike, beat, or bang; to break; to destroy. [Scot. and Brit. Dial.]

stram′ash, *n.* a tumult; a struggle; a conflict. [Scot. and Brit. Dial.]

stram′ȧ·zōne, *n.* [It. *stramazzone,* a cut, slash.] a descending blow or cut with a sword in contrast to a stockade or thrust. [Obs.]

strȧ·min′ē·ous, *a.* [L. *stramineus,* from *stramen,* straw.]
1. of or like straw.
2. straw-colored.

strȧ·mō′ni·um, *n.* [Mod. L.; ML. *stramonia,* thought by some to be altered from a Tartar word.]
1. a poisonous weed of the nightshade family, with toothed leaves, white flowers, and prickly fruit; jimson weed; thorn apple; stinkweed.
2. its dried leaves used in medicine as a narcotic, etc.

stram′ō·ny, *n.* stramonium.

strand, *n.* a small brook; also, a passage for water; a gutter. [Scot.]

strand, *n.* [AS. *strand*; D. *strand*; Ice. *strond,* margin, edge.] land at the edge of a body of water; shore, especially ocean shore.

strand, *v.t.* and *v.i.*; stranded, *pt., pp.*; stranding, *ppr.* 1. to drive or run aground, as a ship.
2. to put or come into a difficult, helpless position: used especially in the passive, as, *stranded* in a strange city with no money.

strand, *n.* [OFr. *estran*; prob. of Gmc. origin.]
1. any of the bundles of thread, fiber, wire, etc. that are twisted together to form a length of string, rope, or cable.
2. a string, thread, or other ropelike filament; as, a *strand* of beads.

strand, *v.t.* 1. to break one or more of the strands of (a rope).
2. to make (rope, etc.) by uniting or twisting together strands.

strand līne, a shore line, especially a former one from which the water has receded.

strand′lo͝op″ẽr, *n.* a South African shore bird, *Ægialitis tricollaris.*

strand plöv′ẽr, the black-bellied plover.

strand rat, a South African mole rat, *Bathyergus maritimus.*

strand wolf (wụlf), a South African brown hyena, *Hyæna villosa.*

strang, *a.* strong. [Obs. or Dial.]

strānġe, *a.*; *comp.* stranger; *superl.* strangest, [OFr. *estrange*; Fr. *étrange,* from L. *extraneus,* that is without, from *extra,* on the outside.]
1. (a) [Archaic.] foreign; alien; (b) of another place or locality.
One of the *strange* queen's lords.—Shak.
2. not one's own; not pertaining to oneself or one's belongings; belonging to others. [Obs.]
3. new; unused; not previously known, heard, seen, or experienced; as, a *strange* custom.
4. wonderful; causing surprise; exciting curiosity; extraordinary; remarkable; singular.
'Tis *strange,* but true; for truth is always *strange,*—
Stranger than fiction. —Byron.
5. odd; unusual; irregular; not according to the common way.
He's *strange* and peevish. —Shak.
6. reserved; distant; estranged; not familiar.
7. unaccustomed; lacking experience; as, he was *strange* to the job.
strange woman; in the Bible, a harlot.

strānġe, *adv.* strangely; in a strange manner.

strānġe, *v.t.* to alienate; to estrange. [Obs.]

strānġe, *v.i.* 1. to wonder; to be astonished. [Obs.]
2. to be estranged or alienated. [Obs.]

strānġe′ly, *adv.* in a strange manner.

strānġe′ness, *n.* the state or quality of being strange.

strān′ġẽr, *n.* 1. a foreigner; one who belongs to another country or place.
2. one unknown or not familiar; as, the gentleman is a *stranger* to me.
3. one unaccustomed (*to* something specified); a novice; as, he is a *stranger* to hate.
4. a guest or a visitor.
5. (a) a marine fish, *Odax richardsoni,* of Australia; (b) a noctuid moth.
6. in law, one not privy or party (*to* an act, agreement, title, etc.).

strān′ġẽr, *v.t.* to estrange; to alienate. [Obs.]

strañ′gle, *v.t.*; strangled, *pt., pp.*; strangling, *ppr.* [ME. *strangelen*; OFr. *estrangler*; L. *strangulare,* to throttle, choke, from Gr. *strangalan,* to strangle, from *strangalē,* a halter, from *strangos,* twisted.]
1. to kill by squeezing the throat so as to shut off the breath, as with the hands, a noose, etc.; to throttle; to choke.
2. to suffocate or choke in any manner.
3. to suppress; to stifle; to repress.

strañ′gle, *v.i.* to be strangled; to choke; to suffocate.

strañ′gle·ȧ·ble, *a.* capable of being strangled.

strañ′gle hōld, 1. a wrestling hold that chokes off an opponent's breath.
2. figuratively, any force or action that restricts or suppresses freedom.

strañ′glẽr, *n.* one who or that which strangles or destroys.

strañ′gles, *n.* an infectious disease of horses, characterized by a catarrhal inflammation of the mucous membrane of the respiratory tract.

straṅ′gū·lāte, *v.t.*; strangulated, *pt., pp.*; strangulating, *ppr.* 1. to strangle.

2. in medicine, to constrict or obstruct (a tube, duct, etc.) so as to arrest or obstruct a function; as, to *strangulate* a hernia.

straṅ′gū·lā·ted, *a.* 1. in medicine, congested by constriction or hernial stricture.

2. in biology, contracted and expanded in an irregular manner.

strangulated hernia; see under *hernia*.

straṅ·gū·lā′tion, *n.* a strangulating or being strangulated.

straṅ·gū′ri·ous, *a.* laboring under strangury; of the nature of strangury; denoting the pain of strangury.

straṅ′gū·ry, *n.* [L. *stranguria*; Gr. *strangouria*, retention of urine when it falls by drops; *stranx, strangos*, a drop, and *ouron*, urine.]

1. in medicine, a difficult and painful passage of urine, due to spasm of the urethra and bladder.

2. in botany, a disease in plants produced by tight ligatures.

strā′ny, *n.* the common guillemot, *Uria troile*. [Brit. Dial.]

strap, *n.* [ME. *strope*, a noose, loop; AS. *stropp*, from L. *struppus*, a strap, thong, fillet.]

1. a narrow strip or band of leather or other flexible material, often with a buckle or similar fastener at one end, for binding or securing things.

2. any flat, narrow piece, as of metal, used as a fastening.

3. any of several straplike objects, as a shoulder strap, a loop for pulling on boots, etc.

4. a razor strop.

5. in botany, (a) the flat part of the corollet in ligulate florets; (b) the leaf of certain grasses exclusive of its sheath.

6. in carpentry, an iron plate for connecting two or more timbers, to which it is bolted or screwed.

7. in machinery, a band or strip of metal, usually curved, to clasp and hold other parts.

8. in nautical usage, a circular piece of rope or hoop of iron, used to surround the body of a block so that the latter may be hung to any particular station about the masts, yards, or rigging.

strap, *v.t.*; strapped (strapt), *pt., pp.*; strapping, *ppr.* 1. to beat or chastise with a strap.

2. to fasten or bind with a strap.

3. to strop (a razor).

4. to hang (a criminal). [Scot.]

strap bōlt, a lug bolt.

strap′hang·ẽr, *n.* a standing passenger, as on a crowded bus or streetcar, who supports himself by holding onto a strap, etc. suspended from above.

strap hinge, a hinge with long flaps, by which it is secured on both sides.

strap oil, a flogging with a strap. [Old Slang.]

strap·pā′dō, *n.*; *pl.* **strap·pā′dōes,** [It. *strappata*, a pulling, wringing, from *strappare*, to pull, wring.]

1. a form of torture in which the victim was tied by his wrists to a long rope, lifted in the air, and suddenly dropped part way to the ground.

2. the instrument used in this torture.

strap·pā′dō, *v.t.* to torture by the strappado.

strapped (strapt), *a.* without funds. [Slang.]

strap′pẽr, *n.* 1. a person or thing that straps.

2. a strapping person. [Colloq.]

strap′ping, *a.* [ppr. of *strap*, used (like *thumping, whopping*, expressing violent action) to denote something of large size.] tall and well-built; strong; robust. [Colloq.]

strap′ple, *v.t.* to bind with a strap; to entangle; to strap. [Obs.]

strap′-shāped (-shāpt), *a.* ligulate; shaped like a strap.

strap′wŏrk, *n.* a style of architectural ornamentation consisting of a narrow fillet or band folded, crossed, and occasionally interlaced with another.

strap′wŏrt, *n.* a trailing herb, *Carrigiola littoralis*, found on the coast of western and southern Europe.

strass, *n.* [G., after the inventor, Josef *Strasser*, G. jeweler.] a lustrous lead glass used in making artificial jewels; paste.

strā′tà, *n.* alternative plural of *stratum*.

strat′à·ġem, *n.* [OFr. *stratageme*; L. *strategema*; Gr. *stratēgēma*, the device or act of a general, from *stratēgos*, a general; *stratos*, an army, and *agein*, to lead.]

1. an artifice, plan, or scheme for deceiving an enemy in war.

2. any artifice; a trick or deception.

Syn.—artifice, ruse, blind, trick, subterfuge, chicanery, plot, snare.

strat·à·ġem′iç·ăl, *a.* containing stratagem or artifice.

strā′tăl, *a.* characteristic of or pertaining to a stratum or strata.

strat·ē·ġet′iç, strat·ē·ġet′iç·ăl, *a.* strategic.

strà·teġ′iç, strà·teġ′iç·ăl, *a.* 1. of or having to do with strategy.

2. characterized by sound strategy; favorable; advantageous.

3. essential to effective military strategy; as, *strategic* materials.

strategic point; any position in the field of war that one side may use to particular advantage against a foe.

strà·teġ′iç·ăl·ly, *adv.* 1. in a strategic manner.

2. with reference to strategy.

strà·teġ′içs, *n.pl.* [*construed as sing.*] strategy.

strat′ē·ġist, *n.* one skilled in strategy.

strà·tē′gus, *n.*; *pl.* **strà·tē′gī,** [L., from Gr. *stratēgos*, a general.] in ancient Greece, a military commander.

strat′ē·ġy, *n.*; *pl.* **strat′ē·ġies,** [Gr. *stratēgia*, generalship, from *stratēgos*, general.]

1. the science of planning and directing large-scale military operations, specifically (as distinguished from *tactics*), of maneuvering forces into the most advantageous position prior to actual engagement with the enemy.

2. a plan or action based on this.

3. skill in managing or planning, especially by using stratagem.

strath, *n.* [Gael. *srath.*] a wide river valley.

strath′spey, *n.* [from *Strathspey*, a district in Scotland.]

1. a Scottish dance in duple time, resembling the reel but in slower tempo.

2. the music for this dance.

strà·tiç′ū·lāte, *a.* [dim. of L. *stratum*, and *-ate.*] in geology, arranged in thin layers or strata.

strat″i·fi·çā′tion, *n.* 1. a stratifying; the process by which substances are formed into strata or layers.

2. the state of being stratified; the arrangement of substances in strata or layers, one upon another, like the leaves of a book.

3. in physiology, the thickening of a cell wall by the deposit of successive layers of thin membrane; also, the arrangement of the layers so deposited.

4. in electricity, the banded appearance of an electric discharge in a rarefied medium.

5. in geology, (a) formation in strata; (b) a stratum.

strat″i·fi·çā′tion·ăl gram′măr, a grammar that attempts to analyze language and its functions on the basis of certain underlying but limited phenomena (called *impulses*), that appear in contrasting pairs.

strat′i·fīed, *a.* formed or arranged in strata or layers.

strat′i·fọrm, *a.* having the form of a stratum; showing stratification; specifically, (a) designating or of clouds arranged in a stratus; (b) in anatomy, designating cartilage occurring in a bone in layers, as a support for tendons.

strat′i·fȳ, *v.t.*; stratified, *pt., pp.*; stratifying, *ppr.* [L. *stratum*, a layer, pavement, and *facere*, to make.]

1. to form or arrange in layers or strata.

2. in horticulture, to preserve (seeds) by placing them between layers of soil, peat moss, etc.

strat·i·graph′iç, strat·i·graph′iç·ăl, *a.* of or relating to stratigraphy.

strat·i·graph′iç·ăl·ly, *adv.* in a stratigraphical manner.

strà·tig′rà·phy, *n.* [L. *stratum*, a stratum, and *-graphy.*]

1. the arrangement of rocks in layers or strata.

2. the branch of geology dealing with such stratification.

strā″tō-cir′rus, *n.* a low thick layer of clouds, resembling cirro-stratus.

strà·toç′rà·cy, *n.* [Gr. *stratos*, an army, and *kratein*, to hold.] a military government.

strā″tō-çū′mū·lus, *n.*; *pl.* **strā′tō-çū′mū·lī,** a dark cloud formation having the appearance of mounds piled one on top of the other, usually seen in winter.

strat·ō·graph′iç, strat·ō·graph′iç·ăl, *a.* of or relating to stratography.

strà·tog′rà·phy, *n.* [Gr. *stratos*, an army, and *-graphy.*] a study or description of the handling of an army.

strā′tō·sphēre, *n.* [Fr. *stratosphère*, from L. *stratum*, stratum, and Fr. *atmosphère*, atmosphere.] the upper part of the earth's atmosphere, beginning at an altitude of about seven miles and continuing to the ionosphere: it is characterized by an almost constant temperature at all altitudes.

strā′tum, *n.*; *pl.* **strā′tà, strā′tums,** [L., a covering, quilt, blanket, pavement, from *stratus*, pp. of *sternere*, to spread.]

1. a horizontal layer or section of material, especially any of several lying one upon another; specifically, (a) in biology, a layer of tissue; (b) in geology, a single layer of sedimentary rock representing the deposition of a single geological period.

2. a section, level, or division regarded as like a stratum; as, the highest *stratum* of society.

stratum granulosum; in anatomy, one of the layers of the epidermis, consisting of granular cells.

strā′tus, *n.* [L., a strewing, covering, a coverlet, pp. of *sternere*, to spread, stretch out, extend.] a cloud formation at a low level spreading out in a long layer.

STRATUS CLOUDS

strąught (strąt), *a.* distraught. [Obs.

strąught, *v.t.* to make straight. [Obs.]

strąw, *n.* [AS. *streaw, streow, strea*, straw; D. *stroo*, Ice. *strā*, Dan. *straa*, Sw. *strā*, G. *stroh*, straw.]

1. hollow stalks or stems of grain after threshing: used for fodder, as a stuffing for mattresses, etc.

2. a single one of such stalks.

3. such a stalk or, now especially, a tube of waxed paper, glass, etc. used for sucking beverages.

4. something of little or no value; worthless trifle.

a straw in the wind; an indication of what may happen.

straw boss; a person having subordinate authority, as a foreman's assistant. [Colloq.]

straw vote; an unofficial vote or poll taken to determine general group opinion on a given issue.

to catch (or *clutch, grasp*) *at a straw*; to try anything that offers even the least hope.

strąw, *a.* 1. straw-colored; yellowish.

2. made of straw.

3. of little or no value or significance; worthless; meaningless.

strąw, *v.t.* to cover or provide with straw.

strąw, *v.t.* to spread or scatter. [Obs.]

strąw′ber″ry, *n.*; *pl.* **strąw′ber″ries,** the small, red, cone-shaped, fleshy fruit of any species of the genus *Fragaria*, of the family *Rosaceæ*, or the plant itself. The species are perennial plants, with trifoliate leaves and long runners. All are native to temperate or cold climates, and are found in Europe, America, and the mountains of Asia. *Fragaria virginiana* is the common strawberry of America. The common European species is *Fragaria vesca*. *Fragaria chilensis* is the Chilean strawberry.

barren strawberry; (a) in England, *Potentilla fragariastrum*, a plant resembling the strawberry; (b) in America, *Waldsteinia fragarioides*, an herb resembling the strawberry but bearing yellow flowers.

Indian strawberry; an Indian plant, *Duchesnea indica*, bearing yellow flowers and tasteless fruit.

scarlet strawberry; the common American strawberry, *Fragaria virginiana*.

strawberry bass; see *calico bass* under *calico*.

strąw′ber″ry blīte, an herb, the goosefoot, *Chenopodium* or *Blitum capitatum*, having a fruit that resembles the strawberry, native to Europe and North America.

strąw′ber″ry blonde, reddish blonde.

strąw′ber″ry bŏr′ẽr, an insect whose larvae burrow in the strawberry plant. *Tyloderma fragariæ*, a small weevil, is an example.

strąw′ber″ry bụsh, a low shrub of North America, *Euonymus americana*, having rough, red pods, and seeds with a red covering.

strąw′ber″ry çlō′vẽr, a species of clover, *Trifolium fragiferum*, of the Old World, having pinkish heads of flowers resembling strawberries.

straw'ber"ry crab, a European spider crab, *Eurynome aspera,* having its back covered with reddish tubercles.

straw'ber"ry finch, the amadavat.

straw'ber"ry gē·rā'ni·um, a variety of saxifrage, having runners that resemble those of the strawberry.

straw'ber"ry lēaf, 1. the leaf of the strawberry vine.

2. in England, a symbol for a dukedom, the coronet of a duke being ornamented with eight strawberry leaves.

straw'ber"ry märk, a small, red birthmark.

straw'ber"ry peär, 1. a kind of cactus, *Hylocereus undatus,* growing in the West Indies, and bearing slightly acid fruit.

2. the fruit of this plant.

STRAWBERRY PEAR (*Hylocereus undatus*)

straw'ber"ry pērch, the calico bass.

straw'ber"ry rōan, reddish roan.

straw'ber"ry saw'flȳ, a sawfly, *Emphytus maculatus,* whose larvae eat the leaves of the strawberry.

straw'ber"ry shrub, any of several species of *Calycanthus,* having dark-red flowers of a strawberry fragrance.

straw'ber"ry tō·mā'tō, any of a number of related plants with white or yellowish flowers, large bright calyxes, and small, yellow fruit.

straw'ber"ry tŏngue (tung), a tongue with enlarged, red, fungiform papillae, as in scarlet fever.

straw'ber"ry tree, 1. a European evergreen tree, *Arbutus unedo,* having clusters of small, white flowers and edible fruit resembling strawberries in shape and color.

2. any of various other species of this genus.

straw'ber"ry vīne, the strawberry; any species of the genus *Fragaria.*

straw'ber"ry wee'vil, a small weevil whose larva feeds on the strawberry.

straw'bōard, *n.* thick paperboard made of straw: used in the manufacture of packing materials, cartons, etc.

straw çat, the pampas cat.

straw çŏl'ŏr, a pale-yellow color.

straw'-çŏl"ŏred, *a.* pale-yellow.

straw'flow"ēr, *n.* a tall plant with variously colored, paperlike flowers dried for winter bouquets.

straw'-hat', *a.* [from the practice, especially formerly, of wearing straw hats in summer.] designating, of, or having to do with a summer theater or summer theaters.

straw man, 1. a bundle of straw made to look like a man, as for a scarecrow.

2. a person of little importance; a nonentity.

3. a weak argument or opposing view set up by a politician, debater, etc. so that he may attack it and gain an easy, showy victory.

4. a person used to disguise another's intentions, activities, etc.; blind.

straw'small, *n.* the strawsmear. [Brit. Dial.]

straw'smēar, *n.* 1. the whitethroat of Europe, which builds its nest of straw. [Brit. Dial.]

2. the garden warbler. [Brit. Dial.]

3. the willow warbler. [Brit. Dial.]

straw wīne, a sweet, rich wine made from grapes that have been spread out on straw and dried in the sun.

straw'wŏrm, *n.* 1. the caddis worm.

2. any of several insect larvae which damage the stalks of wheat, etc.

straw'y, *a.*; *comp.* strawier; *superl.* strawiest, 1. of or like straw.

2. covered or thatched with straw.

strāy, *v.i.*; strayed, *pt., pp.*; straying, *ppr.* [ME. *straien*; OFr. *estraier,* to stray.]

1. to wander from a given place, limited area, direct course, etc., especially aimlessly; to roam; to rove.

2. to go wrong; to be in error; to deviate (*from* what is right).

3. to turn aside from the matter at hand; to fail to concentrate; to be inattentive or digress; as, their thoughts *strayed* as she entered the room.

Syn.—deviate, wander, err, rove, roam.

strāy, *v.t.* to cause to stray. [Obs.]

strāy, *a.* 1. having strayed or wandered; lost.

2. isolated; occasional; incidental; as, we caught only a few *stray* words.

strāy, *n.* 1. a person or thing that strays; especially, a domestic animal wandering at large.

2 the act of wandering. [Rare.]

3. a truant; a runaway; a lost child.

4. [*usually in pl.*] an electrical disturbance interfering with radio reception; static.

strāy'ēr, *n.* one who or that which strays.

strāy līne, in nautical usage, that part of a log line run off from the reel before the fly of the log begins to revolve: used to insure accuracy in measurement.

strē, *n.* straw. [Obs.]

strēak, *n.* [AS. *strica,* a line, a stroke.]

1. a line or long, thin mark; a stripe or smear, generally differing in color or texture from the surrounding area.

2. a vein or stratum of a mineral.

3. a layer, as of fat in meat.

4. a strain, element, or tendency in behavior, temperament, etc.; trait; as, a nervous *streak.*

5. a period or spell; as, a long *streak* of bad luck. [Colloq.]

6. in mineralogy, a colored line of powder produced by rubbing a mineral over a hard, white surface: it serves as a distinguishing character.

7. in shipbuilding, a strake.

like a streak; at high speed; swiftly. [Colloq.]

strēak, *v.t.*; streaked (strēkt), *pt., pp.*; streaking, *ppr.* to form streaks or stripes on or in; to stripe; to variegate with lines of a different color or colors.

Now *streaked* and glowing with the morning red. —Prior.

strēak, *v.i.* 1. to form streaks; to become streaked.

2. to move at high speed; to go fast; to hurry.

3. to engage in the prank of dashing naked for a short distance in a public place.

strēak, *v.t.* to stretch; to extend; to lay out as a dead body. [Obs.]

strēaked (strēkt), *a.* 1. marked or variegated with stripes.

2. agitated; uneasy; uncomfortable. [Dial.]

strēak'ēr, *n.* a person or thing that streaks.

strēak'i·ly, *adv.* in a streaky manner.

strēak'i·ness, *n.* the quality or condition of being streaky.

strēak'y, *a.*; *comp.* streakier; *superl.* streakiest, 1. marked with or showing streaks; streaked.

2. occurring in streaks.

3. uneven or variable, as in quality.

strēam, *n.* [AS. *strēam,* a stream, a river; D. *stroom*; Ice. *straumr*; Dan. and Sw. *ström*; G. *strom.*]

1. any current or flow of running water, especially one running along the surface of the earth; specifically, a small river.

2. a flow of any fluid or liquid substance; a gush; an outflow.

3. a steady flow or movement of any fluid (a *stream* of cold air) or of rays of energy (a *stream* of light).

4. a steady current in the sea or in a river; especially, the middle or most rapid part of a tide or current; as, the Gulf *Stream.*

5. anything issuing from a source and moving in a continuous series or succession of parts; as, a *stream* of words, a *stream* of sand.

6. a trend or course; the course or current of affairs or events; current; drift.

Syn.—current, eddy, tide, course.

strēam, *v.i.*; streamed, *pt., pp.*; streaming, *ppr.* 1. to flow in or as in a stream.

2. to give off a stream; to flow (*with*); as, eyes *streaming with* tears.

3. to move steadily or continuously.

4. to move swiftly; to rush; as, fire *streamed* up the side of the wall.

5. to extend or stretch out; to float; to fly, as a flag in the breeze.

strēam, *v.t.* 1. to mark with colors or embroidery in long stripes. [Obs.]

2. to cause to flow.

3. to extend (a flag, etc.) out to its length.

strēam aṅ'çhŏr, an anchor having one-fourth the weight of a bower anchor, used for warping and similar purposes.

strēam çā'ble, the cable used with a stream anchor.

strēam'ēr, *n.* 1. a long, narrow, ribbonlike flag or banner.

2. any long, narrow strip of material or ribbon hanging loose at one end.

3. a ray or stream of light extending up from the horizon.

4. a newspaper headline that extends across the full page.

5. a miner who washes deposits for stream tin.

strēam'ing, *a.* 1. flowing; running in a current.

2. emitting; pouring out in abundance; as, *streaming* eyes.

strēam'ing, *n.* 1. the action of that which streams.

2. the act of washing for stream tin; also, the separation of stream tin from the dirt with which it is found.

3. in biology, the streamlike motion of protoplasmic particles when changes in form are taking place, as in an amoeba.

strēam'less, *a.* having no streams.

strēam'let, *n.* a small stream; a rivulet; a rill.

strēam'līne, *n.* 1. the movement or flow of a small portion of a fluid, especially in relation to a solid body which lies in the path of this flow.

2. a shape or contour with reference to its resistance in moving through air, etc.

strēam'līne, *a.* 1. pertaining to, or similar to, a streamline; moving freely and swiftly.

2. designating, of, or having a contour designed to offer the least resistance in moving through air, water, etc. by permitting an unbroken flow of the fluid about it.

strēam'līne, *v.t.*; streamlined, *pt., pp.*; streamlining, *ppr.* to build, design, or construct with a streamline shape or contour.

strēam'līned, *a.* 1. having a streamline form.

2. so arranged or fashioned as to secure the greatest progress and efficiency with the least delay and obstruction; as, a *streamlined* office.

strēam-of-çon'scious·ness (-shus-), *a.* designating or of a form of novel in which the story is developed through recording the thoughts of one or more of the characters.

strēam of çon'scious·ness, [term originated by William James (1842–1910).] in psychology, individual conscious experience regarded as a continuous series of occurrences rather than as separate, disconnected events.

strēam tin, in mining, small masses of tin ore found in alluvial ground in rounded particles mixed with alluvial matter.

strēam'y, *a.*; *comp.* streamier; *superl.* streamiest, 1. full of streams or currents.

2. like a stream; flowing; running.

streek, *v.t.* to stretch. [Obs.]

streel, *v.i.*; streeled, *pt., pp.*; streeling, *ppr.* to trail; to drag. [Rare.]

streen, *n.* a strain. [Obs.]

street, *n.* [ME. *strete*; AS. *stræt*; L. *strata,* for *strata via,* a paved road; *strata,* f. of *stratus,* pp. of *sternere,* to strew, scatter, pave.]

1. a paved way or road. [Obs.]

2. a public road in a town or city; especially, a paved thoroughfare with the sidewalks and buildings along one or both sides.

3. such a road apart from its sidewalks; as, don't play in the *street.*

4. the people living, working, etc. in the buildings along a given street; as, the whole *street* contributed.

street Arab; a homeless or neglected child left to roam the streets; a gamin.

street broker; see *curbstone broker* under *broker.*

street railway; a railway that runs along the public streets; a streetcar line.

street sweeper; one who or that which sweeps a street.

street urchin; same as *street arab.*

the man in the street; the average citizen.

the street; the section of a city where stock and other exchanges are located and where business in stocks and securities is carried on; also, the aggregate of persons engaged in such business.

street, *a.* 1. of, in, on, or near the street.

2. suitable for everyday wear in public; as, *street* clothes.

street'çär, *n.* a large coach or car for public transportation, that follows a regular route along certain streets, usually on rails.

street pēo'ple, young people who, in their alienation from conventional society, have become homeless transients, gathering on streets, malls, and other public places, often near a university.

street thē'ȧ·tēr, street thē'ȧ·tre, an amateur theatrical production performed in a street, park, etc. or indoors, usually for a nonpaying audience, with an improvised script generally on a social or political theme.

street'walk"ēr (-wak"), *n.* one who walks in

the streets; specifically, a prostitute who seeks trade along the street.

street'wărd, *a.* facing the street.

street'wīse', *a.* experienced or knowledgeable in dealing with the people in poverty areas of a city, especially in those areas where vice and crime are prevalent. [Colloq.]

streight(strāt), *a.*, *n.*, and *adv.* obsolete spelling of *straight.*

Strē·litz'i·ȧ, *n.* [Mod.L., after Charlotte of Mecklenburg-*Strelitz,* queen of George III of England.] a genus of South African plants of the banana family, having rigid glaucous leaves and irregular flowers of a yellow, blue, or white color.

strength, *n.* [ME. *strengthe;* AS. *strengthu,* from *strang,* strong.]

1. the state or quality of being strong; force; power; vigor.

2. the power to resist strain, stress, etc.; toughness; durability.

3. the power to resist attack; impregnability.

4. legal, moral, or intellectual force or effectiveness.

5. (a) capacity for producing a reaction or effect; potency, as of drugs, liquors, etc.; (b) great capacity for producing such effect.

6. intensity, as of sound, color, odor, etc.

7. force, as measured in numbers; as, the battalion is at full *strength.*

8. a source of strength; that which makes strong; support.

9. in the stock exchange, a tendency to rise or remain firm in prices.

on the strength of; based or relying on.

strength of an electric current; the amount of electricity passing in a circuit in a given time; amperage.

strength of a magnetic field; the intensity of a magnetic field at any point as shown by the force with which it acts on a unit magnet pole at that point.

ultimate strength (of a material, etc. ; in mechanics, the result found by dividing the maximum load by the original area of cross section; the greatest inherent force which the particles of a material can exert in opposition to a stress.

Syn.—force, power, robustness, toughness, lustiness, firmness, solidity, puissance, efficiency, energy, vehemence, potency, vigor.

strength'en, *v.t.;* strengthened, *pt., pp.;* strengthening, *ppr.* 1. to make strong or stronger; to add strength to, either physical, legal, or moral; as, to *strengthen* a limb; to *strengthen* an obligation.

2. to animate; to encourage; to fix in resolution.

strength'en, *v.i.* to grow strong or stronger.

strength'en·ẽr, *n.* one who or that which strengthens.

strength'en·ing, *a.* increasing strength; giving strength.

strength'en·ing·ly, *adv.* in a strengthening manner.

strength'fụl, *a.* full of strength; strong. [Rare.]

strength'fụl·ness, *n.* the quality or state of being strengthful. [Rare.]

strength'less, *a.* lacking strength; without strength.

strength'y, *a.* strong. [Rare.]

stren·ū'i·ty, *n.* strenuousness.

stren·ū·os'i·ty, *n.* the quality of being strenuous.

stren'ū·ous, *a.* [L. *strenuus,* vigorous, active; allied to Gr. *strēnēs,* strong.]

1. zealous; ardent; eagerly pressing or urgent; earnest; enthusiastic; active; vigorous; energetic; as, a *strenuous* supporter of a cause.

2. strong; bold; vigorous; as, *strenuous* services.

3. necessitating vigor or energy; accompanied by labor or exertion.

Syn.—strong, resolute, determined, earnest, vigorous, ardent, bold, energetic, vehement.

stren'ū·ous·ly, *adv.* in a strenuous manner.

stren'ū·ous·ness, *n.* the quality or state of being strenuous.

strep'ent, *a.* noisy; loud.

strep'ẽr·ous, *a.* loud; boisterous. [Rare.]

strep'i·tănt, *a.* [L. *strepitans* (*-antis*), ppr. of *strepitare,* to make a continuous noise.] noisy; loud; clamorous.

strep'i·tous, *a.* [L. *strepitus,* a noise, din.] noisy.

Strep·sip'tẽr·ȧ, *n.pl.* [Gr. *strephein,* to twist, and *pteron,* a wing.] a small order of parasitic insects, having the front pair of wings in the form of twisted filaments, the posterior pair fan-shaped. The females are apterous, and never leave the abdomen of the wasp or bee to which they are attached.

strep·sip'tẽr·ăn, *a.* of or pertaining to the *Strepsiptera.*

strep·sip'tẽr·ăn, *n.* one of the *Strepsiptera.*

strep·sip'tẽr·ous, *a.* relating to the *Strepsiptera.*

strep thrōat, a sore throat caused by a streptococcus and characterized by inflammation and fever. [Colloq.]

strep·tō·çoc'çăl, *a.* of or caused by streptococci.

strep·tō·çoc'çic (-sik), *a.* same as *streptococcal.*

strep·tō·çoc'çus, *n.;* *pl.* **strep·tō·çoc'çī** (-sī), [LL., from Gr. *streptos,* bent, twisted, and *kŏkos,* a grain, seed, berry.] any of a group of spherical, Gram-positive bacteria that divide in only one plane, occurring generally in chains: some species cause various serious diseases.

hemolytic streptococcus; in biochemistry, any streptococcic organism capable of dissolving red blood corpuscles.

strep·tō·mȳ'cin, *n.* [from Gr. *streptos,* twisted, and *mykēs,* fungus; and *-in.*] an antibiotic drug similar to penicillin, obtained from certain molds and used in the treatment of various diseases.

Strep·tō·neū'rȧ, *n.pl.* [Gr. *streptos,* bent, twisted, and *neuron,* a nerve.] a subclass of the *Gasteropoda* in which the visceral nerves form a loop twisted in the shape of the figure 8.

strep·tō·thrī'cin, *n.* [from Mod. L. *Streptothrix,* name of the fungus (from Gr. *streptos,* twisted, and *thrix,* hair); and *-in.*] an antibiotic drug derived from a certain species of fungus.

Strep'tō·thrix, *n.* [Gr. *streptos,* bent, twisted, and *thrix,* hair, bristles.]

1. a genus of *Schizomycetes* occurring in the form of long, slender, sheathed filaments.

2. [s–] a member of this genus.

stress, *n.* [OFr. *estrece;* LL. *estrictia,* from L. *strictus,* strict; also, in some senses, contr. of *distress.*]

1. strain; pressure; especially, (a) force exerted upon a body, that tends to strain or deform its shape; (b) the intensity of such force, usually measured in pounds per square inch; (c) the resistance or cohesiveness of a body resisting such force.

2. urgency; importance; significance.

3. tension; strained exertion; as, the *stress* of war affected all the people.

4. in music, accent.

5. in phonetics, (a) the relative force with which a syllable is uttered; in English, there are normally *primary* (or *strong*) *stress, secondary* (or *light*) *stress,* and *zero stress* (lack or reduction of stress); (b) primary stress.

6. in prosody, (a) the relative force of utterance given a syllable or word according to the meter; (b) an accented syllable.

7. distress. [Obs.]

8. in Scots law, the act of distraining; distress.

to lay stress upon; to make emphatic.

stress, *v.t.;* stressed, *pt., pp.;* stressing, *ppr.* [OFr. *estrecer, estrecier;* L. *strictus,* pp. of *stringere,* to draw tight, compress.]

1. to distress. [Obs.]

2. to subject to force or stress; to put pressure or strain upon.

3. to emphasize.

4. to give stress or accent to.

-stress, [from *-ster* and *-ess.*] a feminine suffix corresponding to *-ster,* as in song*stress.*

stress dī'ȧ·gram, a diagram representing the deformation for various stresses in structural material.

stress'fụl, *a.* possessing great stress. [Rare.]

stretch, *v.t.;* stretched (strecht), *pt., pp.;* stretching, *ppr.* [ME. *strecchen,* from AS. *streccan;* akin to G. *strecken.*]

1 to hold or reach out; to extend (an arm, hand, etc.).

2. to cause (the body or limbs) to reach out to full length, as in yawning, relaxing, etc.

3. to pull or spread out to full extent or to greater size; as, *stretch* the carpet out to dry, she *stretched* the sweater to make it fit.

4. to cause to reach or extend over a given space or distance; to extend.

5. (a) to cause to reach or extend farther, especially too far; to force beyond normal limits; strain; as, don't *stretch* the material or you'll rip it, they have *stretched* the law; (b) to exaggerate.

6. to make tense or tight with effort; to strain (a muscle, etc.).

7. to knock down, especially so as to cause to lie at full length. [Slang.]

8. to execute by hanging. [Archaic or Dial.]

9. to lay out for burial. [Slang or Dial.]

stretch, *v.i.* 1. (a) to spread or be spread out to full extent or beyond normal limits; (b) to extend or continue over a given space or distance.

2. to extend the body or limbs to full length, as in yawning or reaching for something.

3. to become stretched or be capable of being stretched to greater size, as any elastic substance.

4. to lie down at full length (usually with *out*).

5. to be executed by hanging; to hang. [Slang.]

6. to strain beyond the truth; to exaggerate; as, a man who is apt to *stretch* has less credit than others. [Colloq.]

7. in nautical usage, to direct a course; to sail under a great spread of canvas close-hauled. [Rare.]

8. to make violent efforts; to exert oneself vigorously.

Syn.—lengthen, extend, draw out, reach, spread, tighten, exaggerate.

stretch, *n.* 1. a stretching or being stretched.

2. an unbroken period; a continuous space (*of* time); as, over a *stretch of* three months.

3. a prison sentence. [Slang.]

4. the extent to which something can be stretched.

5. an unbroken length, tract, or space; a continuous extent or distance; as, a long *stretch* of white beach.

6. one of the sections of a course or track for racing, especially the straight length of track before the finish line in horse racing.

7. a course or direction.

8. in sailing, a tack; the reach or extent of progress on one tack.

stretch'ẽr, *n.* 1. one who or that which stretches or expands; specifically, (a) an instrument for expanding gloves, boots, or shoes; (b) a frame for expanding a canvas for painting; (c) one of the rods of an umbrella attached at one end to one of the ribs, and at the other to the tube sliding upon the handle; (d) in a vehicle, a jointed piece that can be extended in such a way as to spread the hood or cover; (e) a strip of wood placed across the strings of a hammock to spread it open.

2. in masonry, a brick or stone laid horizontally with its length in the direction of the face of the wall: distinguished from a *header,* which is laid lengthwise across the thickness of the wall, so that its head, or end, is seen in the face of the wall.

3. in carpentry, a tie timber in a frame.

4. in nautical usage, a narrow piece of plank placed across a boat for the rowers to set their feet against; also, a crosspiece placed between a boat's sides to keep them apart.

5. a litter or frame, usually covered with canvas, etc., for carrying sick, wounded, or dead persons.

6. a rail connecting the legs of a chair; a round or rung.

7. in angling, (a) the leader at the extreme end of a casting line; (b) the tail fly: also called *stretcher fly.*

8. in carriage building, a piece of canvas, a button, etc., that serves as a strengthener of a panel: also called *strainer.*

9. a statement that overstretches the truth; a lie. [Old Slang.]

stretch'ẽr-beăr"ẽr, *n.* a person who helps carry a stretcher (sense 5).

stretch'ẽr bond, in building, a form of bond in which the bricks are laid lengthwise in courses, the joints of each course coming in the middle of the bricks above or below it.

stretch'-hạl"tẽr, *n.* one who ought to be hanged, a villain; a scoundrel. [Obs.]

stretch'i·ness, *n.* the quality of being stretchy.

stretch'ing çōurse, in masonry, a course of stretchers.

stretch'-out, *n.* a system of industrial operation in which workers are required to do more work with little or no increase in pay. [Colloq.]

stretch'-out, *a.* of or having the nature of a stretch-out. [Colloq.]

stretch'y, *a.;* *comp.* stretchier; *superl.* stretchiest, 1. that can be stretched; elastic.

2. liable to stretch too far.

3. inclined to stretch oneself, as from sleepiness.

stret'tȧ, *n.;* *pl.* **stret'te, stret'tȧş,** same as *stretto* (especially sense 2).

stret'tō, *n.;* *pl.* **stret'tī, stret'tōş,** [It., from L. *strictus,* tight, narrow, strait, pp. of *stringere,* to draw tight.]

1. in a fugue, the following of the voices in close succession, especially in the closing section.

2. any concluding passage performed with a climactic increase in speed: in this sense, usually *stretta.*

strew (strů), *v.t.*; strewed, *pt.*; strewed *or* strewn, *pp.*; strewing, *ppr.*; [AS. *streówian, streáwian, strewian*; to strew, scatter.]

1. to scatter; to spread by or as by sprinkling; as, to *strew* sand on or over a floor; to *strew* flowers over a grave.

2. to cover irregularly by or as by sprinkling or scattering loosely about; as, to *strew* the aisle with flowers.

3. to spread abroad; to diffuse; to give currency to.

4. to be scattered or dispersed over (a surface).

strew′ing, *n.* 1. the act of scattering or spreading over.

2. [*usually in pl.*] anything strewed or that may be strewed. [Rare.]

strew′ment, *n.* the act of strewing or that which is strewn. [Obs.]

strewn, *v.* alternative past participle of *strew.*

strī′ȧ, *n.*; *pl.* **strī′ae,** [L., a furrow, groove, channel.]

1. in anatomy, zoology, and botany, a slight superficial furrow or channel, longitudinal, transverse, or oblique.

2. in architecture, a fillet or ridge between the channels or flutes of columns, pilasters, etc.

3. a fine streak or line; especially, one of a number of parallel lines.

4. [*pl.*] in electricity, parallel streaked bands, consisting of alternate light and dark spaces, produced in low vacuum tubes by an electrical discharge through them.

strī′ăl, *a.* of the nature of, resembling, or marked by striae. [Rare.]

strī′āte, *v.t.*; striated, *pt., pp.*; striating, *ppr.* [L. *striatus*, grooved, furrowed, pp. of *striare*, to groove, channel.] to mark with striae.

strī′ā·ted, strī′āte, *a.* 1. marked with striae; marked or scored with superficial or very slender lines; marked with fine parallel lines.

2. in the fine arts, disposed in ornamental lines, parallel or wavy.

strī′āte·ly, *adv.* in a striate manner; with striae.

strī·ā′tion, *n.* 1. the state of being striated or marked with fine parallel lines; a striated pattern or appearance.

2. in geology, the grooving or channeling of rock surfaces by the passage over them of masses of ice having stones frozen into their under surfaces.

3. in mineralogy, one of a series of fine parallel lines on a crystalline face.

4. a stria.

strī·ā′tum, *n.*; *pl.* **strī·ā′tȧ,** same as *corpus striatum.*

strī′ȧ·tūre, *n.* disposition of striae; striation; also, a stria.

strich, *n.* a screech owl. [Obs.]

strick, *n.* [variant of *strike.*]

1. a flat piece of wood used in leveling grain in a measure. [Dial.]

2. a handful of flax or other fiber, hatcheled or ready to be hatcheled.

strick′en, *a.* [occasional past participle of *strike.*]

1. struck or wounded, as by a missile.

2. afflicted or affected, as by something disagreeable, painful, or overwhelming.

3. having the contents level with the top: said of a measure or container.

stricken hour; a full hour, as denoted by the striking of the clock.

stric′kle, *n.* [ME. *strikile*; AS. *stricel*, from *strican*, to hit.]

1. a strike; an instrument for leveling grain in a measure.

2. an instrument for whetting scythes.

3. a wooden flax-dressing instrument.

4. a template or pattern used by masons and carpenters.

5. in founding, (a) a template or pattern used in sweeping sand or loam into a core; (b) a straightedge of wood with which to remove superfluous sand from a flask after ramming it.

strick′le, *v.t.*; strickled, *pt., pp.*; strickling, *ppr.* to use a strickle on.

strict, *a.*; *comp.* stricter; *superl.* strictest, [L. *strictus*, pp. of *stringere*, to draw tight, compress.]

1. strained; drawn close; tight; as, a *strict* ligature. [Archaic.]

2. exact; accurate; precise; not loose or vague.

3. perfect; absolute; entire.

4. (a) allowing no difference or deviation; following or enforcing a rule or rules with great care; punctilious; (b) closely enforced; rigorous.

5. close; intimate; as, a *strict* friendship. [Rare.]

6. in zoology, constricted; not diffuse; narrow or close.

7. in botany, upright and close: said of a stem or cluster of flowers.

strict observance; in the Roman Catholic Church, the principle or practice of the Observantines.

strict settlement; in law, a settlement by which land is settled to the parent for life, and after his death to his first son and other children in tail, trustees being interposed to preserve the contingent remainders.

Syn.—severe, precise, accurate, austere, rigorous, exact, strained, tense.

stric′tion, *n.* constriction.

line of striction; a straight or curved line containing the shortest distance between consecutive elements of a warped surface.

strict′ly, *adv.* in a strict manner.

strict′ness, *n.* the quality or state of being strict.

stric′tūre, *n.* [L. *strictura*, f. of fut. part. of *stringere*, to draw tight, compress.]

1. a stroke; a glance; a touch. [Obs.]

2. adverse criticism; censure.

3. in medicine, stenosis, or the abnormal narrowing of a canal, duct, or passage.

4. strictness. [Obs.]

5. a binding, closing, or contraction. [Rare.]

stric′tūred, *a.* in medicine, having a stricture.

strid, *v.* obsolete past tense and past participle of *stride.*

strid, *n.* a very narrow passage between steep rocks or walls, through which a stream flows: a ravine.

strīde, *v.i.*; strode *or obs.* strid, *pt.*; stridden *or obs.* strid, *pp.*; striding, *ppr.* [ME. *striden*; AS. *stridan*, to strive, also to stride.]

1. to walk with long steps, especially in a vigorous or pompous manner.

2. to take a single, long step, as in passing over something.

3. to sit or stand astride. [Rare.]

strīde, *v.t.* 1. to take a single, long step in passing over (an obstacle, etc.).

2. to stride along or through; as, they *strode* the street.

3. to sit or stand astride of; to straddle.

strīde, *n.* 1. the act of striding.

2. a long step.

3. a forward movement by a four-legged animal, completed when the legs return to their original relative positions.

4. the distance covered in such a step.

5. [*usually pl.*] progress; advancement.

to hit one's stride; to reach one's normal speed or level of efficiency.

to take in one's stride; to do or cope with easily and without undue effort or hesitation.

strī′dence, *n.* the quality of being strident or the degree of this.

strī′den·cy, *n.* stridence.

strī′dent, *a.* [L. *stridens* (*-entis*), ppr. of *stridere*, to make a grating or hissing noise, to rattle, creak, rasp.] creaking; harsh; grating.

strī′dent·ly, *adv.* in a strident manner; so as to be strident.

strīd′ẽr, *n.* one who or that which strides.

strī′dŏr, *n.* [L.] 1. a strident sound.

2. in medicine, a harsh, high-pitched whistling sound produced in breathing by an obstruction in the bronchi, trachea, or larynx.

strid′ū·lănt, *a.* stridulating.

strid′ū·lāte, *v.i.*; stridulated, *pt., pp.*; stridulating, *ppr.* [L. *stridulus*, creaking, rattling.] to make a harsh grating, creaking, or chirping sound by rubbing parts of the body together, as the males of certain insect species; to chirr.

strid·ū·lā′tion, *n.* the act, process, or function of stridulating; especially, the ability possessed by certain male insects to produce a shrill, grating noise by friction between a serrated part of the body and a hard part; also, the sound so produced.

strid′ū·lā·tŏr, *n.* an insect that stridulates; that which stridulates.

strid′ū·lȧ·tō·ry, *a.* pertaining to stridulators or stridulation; shrill.

strid′ū·lous, *a.* [L. *stridulus*, creaking, rattling, hissing.] making a shrill grating or chirping sound.

strīfe, *n.* [OFr. *estrif*, strife, debate, from Ice. *strīth*, strife, contention, by the common change of *th* for *f*; D. *strijd*; Dan. and Sw. *strid*; G. *streit*, strife.]

1. exertion or contention with another; competition.

2. contest; struggle; quarrel.

3. earnest attempt; the act of doing one's best. [Archaic.]

strīfe′fụl, *a.* contentious.

strī′gȧ, *n.*; *pl.* **strī′gae,** [L. *striga*, a furrow, channel, groove.]

1. in zoology, a stripe.

2. in botany, a straight, hairlike scale or bristle.

3. in architecture, the fluting of a column.

strī′gāte, *a.* in zoology, strigose.

Strī′gēṣ, *n.pl.* [L. *strix*, *strigis*, an owl.] a suborder of nocturnal birds, including the owls.

strig′il, *n.* [L. *strigilis*, a flesh scraper.]

1. among the ancient Greeks and Romans, an instrument of metal, ivory, or bone, used for scraping the skin after the bath.

2. in Roman architecture, one of a series of wavelike decorative flutings.

strig′i·lāte, *a.* having a strigilis, as a bee.

strig′i·lis, *n.*; *pl.* **strig′i·lēṣ,** an organ having a fringe of rigid hairs, borne on a bee's foreleg and used in cleaning the antennae.

strig′i·lōse, strig′il·lōse, *a.* [dim. of *strigose.*] in botany, provided with small, firm, and slender bristles.

strig′ine, *a.* of, pertaining to, or designating an owl or the owls.

strig′ment, *n.* scraping; that which is scraped off with a strigil. [Obs.]

strī′gōse, strī′gous, *a.* [Mod.L. *strigosus*, from L. *striga*, a furrow.]

1. in botany, having stiff hairs or bristles, as some leaves.

2. in zoology, having fine, close-set grooves or streaks.

strīke, *v.t.*; struck, *pt.*; struck *or occas.* stricken *or obs.* strook, strucken, *pp.*; striking, *ppr.* [ME. *striken*, originally, to proceed, especially with a smooth motion, as to strike with rod or sword; AS. *strican*, to go, proceed, advance; akin to D. *strijken*, G. *streichen*, to smooth, stroke; L. *striga*, a furrow.]

1. to touch or hit with some force, either with the hand or an instrument; to smite; to give a blow to, as with the hand, a stick, a whip, etc.; as, an arrow *struck* the shield; a shot *strikes* a ship.

2. to give, deal, or inflict (a blow, etc.).

Who would be free, themselves must *strike*
the blow. —Byron.

3. to give a blow to; to hit with force; as, he *struck* the nail with a hammer.

4. to separate, take off, take away, etc. by or as by a blow; as, they *struck* the gun from his hand.

5. to cause to come into violent or forceful contact; specifically, (a) to cause to hit something; to dash; to cast; as, she *struck* her elbow against the door; (b) to bring forcefully into contact; as, he *strikes* the cymbals together; (c) to cause to ignite by friction; as, he *struck* a match.

6. to produce (a light, etc.) by friction.

7. to come into violent or forceful contact with; to crash into; to hit; as, the stone *struck* his head; the lightning *struck* the chimney.

8. to wound with the fangs: said of snakes.

9. to attack.

10. to come into contact with; specifically, (a) to fall on; to shine on; as, the light *struck* the windows; (b) to catch or reach (the ear): said of a sound; (c) to come upon; to arrive at; as, we *struck* the main road; (d) to notice, find, or hit upon suddenly or unexpectedly; (e) to discover; to find after drilling or prospecting; as, they *struck* oil; (f) to appear to; as, what a sight *struck* my eyes.

11. to affect as if by contact, a blow, etc.; specifically, (a) to come into the mind of; to occur to; as, the idea just *struck* me; (b) to be attractive to; to impress (one's fancy, sense of humor, etc.); (c) to seem to; as, that *strikes* me as rather silly; (d) to cause to become suddenly; as, he was *struck* dumb; (e) to influence, inspire, or overcome suddenly with strong feeling; as, they were *struck* with amazement; (f) to cause (a feeling, emotion, etc.) to come suddenly; to arouse; as, the scream *struck* terror to my heart.

12. (a) to make and ratify (a bargain, agreement, truce, etc.); (b) to arrive at by figuring, estimating, etc.; as, they *struck* a balance.

13. to lower or haul down (a sail, flag, etc.): sailors formerly *struck* sails in protest of grievances, to prevent a ship from sailing.

14. to refuse to continue to work at (a factory, etc.) until certain demands have been met.

15. to produce (a tone, etc.) by hitting a key on a musical instrument; hence, to play, as a song or tune.

Strike up the drums. —Shak.

16. to announce (time), as by causing a hammer to hit a bell: said of clocks, etc.

17. to fight (a battle). [Obs.]

18. to level, as a measure of grain, salt, or the like, by scraping off with a straight instrument what is above the level of the top.

19. (a) to send down or put forth (roots): said of plants, etc.; (b) to cause (cuttings, etc.) to take root.

20. to take forcibly or fraudulently; as, to *strike* money. [Old Slang.]

21. to lade into a cooler, as the cane juice in sugar making.

22. to stroke; to pass lightly over, as with the hand. [Obs.]

23. in masonry, to remove the surplus mortar from (a joint).

24. to assume; as, to *strike* an attitude or pose.

25. to draw liquor from (a cask or vessel). [Obs.]

26. in founding, to remove the surplus sand from; as, to *strike* a mold.

27. to provide with lines; to line, as by means of a chalked string. [Obs.]

28. to make (a molding or moldings) with a plane.

29. to hit (a whale) with the harpoon.

30. to borrow from or make an urgent request of: now usually *hit, touch.* [Slang.]

31. in the theater, (a) to dismantle and remove (a scene); (b) to remove the scenery of (a play); (c) to turn (a light) down or off.

32. in angling, to hook (a free fish risen to the bait) by manipulation of the line.

33. to make or impress by stamping, punching, printing, etc.; as, a mint *strikes* coins.

34. in electroplating, to form the first deposit on.

35. in chemistry, to cause (a precipitate) to form in a solution.

36. in electricity, to separate the carbons of (an arc light), so producing the arc.

to be struck with; to be attracted to or impressed by.

to strike a balance; see under *balance*.

to strike a jury; to select a struck jury.

to strike camp; to break up or abandon a camp by taking down tents, etc.

to strike down; (a) to prostrate by a blow or blows; to fell; (b) to have a disastrous or disabling effect upon: said of illness, etc.

to strike dumb; to amaze; astound; astonish.

to strike hands with; (a) to shake hands with in token of agreement; (b) to make a compact or agreement with; to agree with.

to strike it rich; (a) to discover a rich deposit of ore, oil, etc.; (b) to become rich or successful suddenly.

to strike off; (a) to erase or expunge, as from a record; (b) to impress; to print; as, to *strike off* a thousand copies of a book; (c) to separate by a blow or any sudden action.

to strike out; (a) to make by hitting or striking; (b) to originate; to produce; to devise; (c) to remove from a record, etc.; to erase; to expunge; (d) in baseball, to put (a batter) out by pitching three strikes.

to strike soundings; in nautical usage, to ascertain the depth of water with the hand, lead, etc.

to strike up; (a) to begin (a friendship, etc.); (b) to begin to play or sing; as, *to strike up* a merry air; (c) to emboss (metal, decorative figures, etc.).

strīke, *v.i.* 1. to pierce; to penetrate; as, till a dart *strike* through his liver.

2. to glance; to graze; as, a ray of light *strikes* and reflects. [Rare.]

3. to make a quick blow or blows; to hit.

Willing to wound, and yet afraid to *strike*. —Pope.

4. to aim a blow or blows; as, I *struck* at the ball, but missed.

5. to attack; to fight; as, the enemy *struck* at dawn.

6. to hit; to collide; to clash (with *against, on,* or *upon*); as, the hammer *strikes against* the bell of a clock.

7. to run, dash, or be driven upon the shore a rock, or a bank; to be stranded; as, the vessel *struck*.

8. to make a sound or sounds, with or as with blows; as, a clock *strikes*.

9. to be announced by the striking of a bell, etc.; as, three o'clock had *struck*.

10. to give out a sound, as a musical instrument.

Let our drums *strike*. —Shak.

11. to ignite or be capable of igniting; as, this match won't *strike*.

12. to seize or snatch at a bait: said of a fish.

13. to make a darting movement in an attempt to inflict a wound: said of a snake, tiger, etc.

14. to come suddenly or unexpectedly; to fall, light, etc. (with *on* or *upon*); as, we *struck on* the right combination.

15. to refuse to continue to work until certain demands are met; to go on strike.

16. to move or pass quickly; to dart.

17. to lower a flag, or colors, in token of respect, or of surrender to an enemy; also, to lower sail.

18. to take root; to grow, as a slip of a plant.

19. to take a course or line; to turn, especially in a new direction; as, hounds *striking* to the right.

20. to steal money. [Old Slang.]

21. to row: from the oar striking the water.

22. to become fixed or set: said of young oysters.

23. in the United States Army, to act as an officer's servant: said of an enlisted man.

24. to become salty, as fish in curing.

25. to fade or run: said of colors when goods are cleaned.

to strike home; (a) to give an effective or crippling blow; (b) to achieve a desired or significant effect.

to strike in; to put in one's word suddenly; to interpose; to interrupt.

to strike into; (a) to break forth into; to commence suddenly; as, *to strike into* a run; (b) to turn into quickly or abruptly.

to strike in with; to conform to; to join with.

to strike out; (a) to aim or strike a blow; to hit out; (b) to begin moving or acting; to start out; (c) in baseball, to be put out as the result of three strikes.

to strike up; to begin playing or singing.

strīke, *n.* 1. a striking; a blow.

2. a strickle.

3. a unit of dry measure varying from two pecks to four bushels. [Brit. Dial.]

4. excellence of quality.

Three hogsheads of ale of the first *strike*. —Scott.

5. (a) a concerted refusal by employees to go on working in an attempt to force an employer to grant certain demands, as for higher wages, better working conditions, collective bargaining, etc.; (b) any similar refusal by a group of people to do something; as, a buyers' *strike*.

6. a finding of a rich deposit of oil, coal, minerals, etc.

7. a sudden success, especially one bringing large financial return.

8. the act or evidence of a fish's seizing or snatching at bait; as, I just got a *strike*!

9. the metal piece on a doorjamb into which the latch fits when the door is shut.

10. in baseball, a pitched ball which is (a) struck at but missed; (b) fairly delivered but not struck at; (c) hit as a foul tip (and, if there are already two strikes, caught by the catcher); (d) hit foul (unless there are already two strikes): three strikes put the batter out.

11. in geology and mining, the trace of a rock bed, fault, or vein on the horizontal.

12. in bowling, the knocking down of all the pins with the first ball; also, the score made in this way.

13. a bunch or handful, as of flax, after hatcheling.

14. the output of one complete process of coining or medal making.

15. in sugar manufacturing, the quantity of sirup used at one time.

16. in type founding, that bar or piece of metal bearing in reverse the character to be cast, inserted in the mold to make the complete matrix.

17. in founding, a puddler's paddle.

18 in politics, an attempt to obtain money, a concession, etc., as by introducing a bill or measure in a legislature with the idea of being bought off. [Slang.]

19. an iron pale or standard in a gate or fence. [Obs.]

(*out*) *on strike*; striking: see *strike*, v.i. 15.

to have two strikes against one; to be at a decided disadvantage: from the three strikes permitted a batter in baseball. [Colloq.]

strīke'-à-līght'' (-līt''), *n.* a device, as of flint and steel, from which sparks may be obtained by striking.

strīke block, a plane shorter than a jointer.

strīke'breāk''ẽr, *n.* a person who engages in strikebreaking, as by working as a scab, supplying scabs for the employer, intimidating strikers, etc.

strīke' breāk''ing, *n.* the act of trying to break up or frustrate a workers' strike.

strīke fault, a fault in which the strike lies parallel to the strike of the faulted strata.

strīke'-or-sī''lent, *n.* the part of the mechanism of a clock which controls the striking device.

strīke'-out, *n.* in baseball, the act of striking out.

strīke pāy, the pay allowed a striking workman, as by his own or an affiliated union.

strīke plāte, a fastener for a beveled latch bolt.

strīk'ẽr, *n.* 1. one who or that which strikes.

2. a blacksmith's helper, so called because he wields a sledge.

3. a male associate of lewd women. [Obs.]

4. a worker who goes on strike.

5. a thing that strikes, as the clapper in a bell, the striking device in a clock, the firing pin in a gun, etc.

6. in the United States Army, an enlisted man employed as an officer's servant or orderly.

7. in politics, one who attempts a strike (see *strike*, n. 18). [Slang.]

8. one who wields a lance or harpoon on a whaling ship; also rarely, the instrument itself.

strīk'ẽr plāte, the metal plate securing a door latch.

strīk'ing, *a.* 1. prominent; remarkable; notable; standing out conspicuously; as, a *striking* feature; a *striking* resemblance.

2. that strikes or is on strike.

striking distance; the distance through which a given effort or force will be effective.

strīk'ing, *n.* the act of one who or that which strikes; specifically, the removal of a center upon which an arch has been built.

strīk'ing·ly, *adv.* in a striking manner.

strīk'ing·ness, *n.* the quality of being striking.

strīk'ing plāte, in carpentry, the device by which the wooden centering of an arch is lowered when the arch is completed.

strik'le, *n.* same as *strickle*.

string, *n.* [ME. *string, streng*; AS. *strenge*, from its being strongly twisted, from *strang*, strong.]

1. (a) a thin line of twisted fiber, or a very thin strip or length of wire, leather, etc., used for tying, pulling, fastening, etc.; small cord; thick thread; very thin rope; twine; (b) a narrow strip of leather or cloth for fastening shoes, clothing, etc.; a lace; as, an apron *string*, boot *string*.

2. a number of objects threaded, strung, or hung on a string; as, a *string* of pearls.

3. a number of things arranged as though on a string; a line of things in succession; as, a *string* of houses.

4. a group of players or athletes arranged according to ability; as, the players of the second *string* will play the varsity.

5. (a) a slender cord of wire, gut, nylon, etc. stretched on a musical instrument, as a violin, harp, piano, etc., and bowed, plucked, or struck to make a musical sound; (b) [*pl.*] all the stringed instruments of an orchestra, especially those played with a bow; (c) [*pl.*] the players of such instruments.

6. a strong, slender organ, formation, etc. resembling a string; specifically, a fiber of a plant, especially one connecting the two halves of a pod.

7. a nerve or tendon of an animal body. [Obs.]

Heart with *strings* of steel. —Shak.

8. the line or cord of a bow.

9. a strip of leather or the like, by which the covers of a book are held together.

10. [*usually in pl.*] a condition, limitation, or proviso attached to a plan, offer, donation, etc. [Colloq.]

11. in architecture, (a) any of the notched sides of a stair, supporting the treads; (b) a stringcourse.

12. in billiards, (a) a line across the table at one end, from behind which the cue ball must be played after being out of play: in full, *string line*; (b) the act of stroking the cue ball so that it rebounds from the far cushion to stop as close as possible to the string line, for determining the order of play; (c) the number of points made in a game by a single player.

13. in horse racing, a number of horses belonging to one owner.

14. in shipbuilding, the highest range of planks in a ship's ceiling, or that between the gunwale and the upper edge of the upper-deck ports.
15. in mining, a small filamentous ramification of a vein.
16. in printing, a number of proofs pasted together as representative of a compositor's work for a given time.
to harp upon one string; see under *harp*.
to have one on a string; to have a person under one's influence; to have one under control.
to pull strings; (a) to get someone to use influence in one's behalf, often secretly; (b) to direct action of others, often secretly.

string, *v.t.*; strung, *pt.*; strung *or rare* stringed, *pp.*; stringing, *ppr.* 1. to provide with strings.
2. to put on a string; to thread or bead on a string.
3. to tie, pull, fasten, hang, lace, etc. with a string or strings.
4. to adjust or tune the strings of (a musical instrument) by tightening, etc.
5. to tighten; brace; strengthen.
6. to make excited, tense, or nervous.
7. to remove the strings (sense 6) from (beans, etc.).
8. to arrange in a row.
9. to stretch like a string; to extend; as, *string* a cable.
10. to fool; hoax; josh (often with *along*). [Colloq.]
11. to hang: with *up*; as, the bandit was *strung up*. [Colloq.]

string, *v.i.* 1. to form into a string or strings.
2. to stretch out in a line; to extend; to stretch; to move or progress in a string.
3. to become stringy or assume a stringy appearance; as, the gum *strings*.
4. in billiards, to determine who shall lead off, each player striking his ball so that it shall hit the far cushion and come back toward the string line: he whose ball stops nearest the string line is entitled to choice of playing first.
to string along with; to follow faithfully; to adhere to; to be faithful to; to have confidence in.

string band, a band of musicians who play only or principally on stringed instruments.

string bärk, same as *stringy bark*.

string bēan, 1. any of a number of varieties of bean having thick, meaty pods eaten as a vegetable when still unripe.
2. the pod of any of these plants.

string'bōard, *n.* a board which supports the ends of the steps in a staircase.

string'çōurse, *n.* in architecture, a narrow molding or projecting band continued horizontally along the face of a building, frequently under windows. It is sometimes merely a flat band, but often ornamented.

stringed, *v.* rare past participle of *string*.

stringed, *a.* 1. having strings; as, a *stringed* instrument.
2. produced by strings.
3. tied or fastened with a string.

strin'ġen·cy, *n.*; *pl.* **strin'ġen·cieṣ,** the quality or state of being stringent; specifically, (a) strictness; severity; (b) scarcity: said of money, as in the market; (c) a convincing quality, as in debate.

strïn·ġen'dō, *n.* [It.] in music, accelerating the tempo, as toward a climax: a direction to the performer.

strin'ġent, *a.* [L. *stringens* (*-entis*), ppr. of *stringere*, to draw tight, compress.]
1. binding tightly; drawing tight. [Obs.]
2. making strict claims or requirements; strict; rigid; binding strongly; as, to make *stringent* regulations against some practice.
3. short in loan or investment money: said of a market.
4. compelling; convincing.

strin'ġent·ly, *adv.* in a stringent manner.

strin'ġent·ness, *n.* the quality or state of being stringent.

string'ẽr, *n.* 1. one who or that which strings; as, a *stringer* of pearls; a piano-*stringer*.
2. a horizontal timber connecting upright posts in a frame.
3. a stringpiece.
4. in railroad engineering, a longitudinal timber upon which the rail is spiked down.
5. in shipbuilding, an inside strake of plank or of plates, secured to the ribs and supporting the ends of the beams; a shelf.
6. a fornicator. [Obs.]

string'hạlt, *n.* [altered from *springhalt*.] a condition in horses causing the hind legs to jerk spasmodically in walking: also *springhalt*.

string'i·ness, *n.* the state or quality of being stringy.

string'less, *a.* having no strings.

string or'ches·trȧ, an orchestra composed only of players of stringed instruments.

string'piēce, *n.* a long, horizontal timber for supporting a framework, especially at the edge of a floor.

string quar·tet', 1. a quartet of players on stringed instruments, usually comprising first and second violins, a viola, and a violoncello.
2. a composition to be performed by such a group.

string tīe, a narrow necktie, usually tied in a bow.

string'y, *a.*; *comp.* stringier; *superl.* stringiest,
1. like a string or strings; long, thin, wiry, etc.
2. consisting of strings or fibers.
3. having tough fibers, as meat, celery, etc.; fibrous.
4. forming strings; viscous; ropy; as, *stringy* molasses.

string'y bärk, any of a number of Australian trees of the genus *Eucalyptus*, so called from the character of their bark, as *Eucalyptus robusta*, of which the natives make cordage and canvas.

strī'ō·lȧ, *n.*; *pl.* **strī'ō·lae,** [dim. of L. *stria*, furrow, groove, channel.] same as *striolet*.

strī'ō·lāte, *a.* same as *striolated*.

strī'ō·lā·ted, *a.* in botany, minutely striate.

strī'ō·let, *n.* a short or minute stria.

strip, *v.t.*; stripped *or rare* stript, *pt.*, *pp.*; stripping, *ppr.* [ME. *stripen*, *strepen*; AS. *strypan*, in the comp. *bestrypan*, to plunder; D. *stroopen*, to plunder, strip, from base *strup*, to strip off.]
1. (a) to remove the clothing or covering of (a person); to make naked; to undress; (b) to remove (the clothing, covering, etc.) from a person; as, he *stripped* the shirt from his back.
2. (a) to deprive or dispossess (a person or thing) of honors, titles, attributes, etc.; (b) to remove or take (honors, attributes, etc.) from a person or thing; (c) to plunder; to spoil; to make destitute; to rob.
3. (a) to pull, tear, or take off (a covering, skin, etc.); (b) to pull, tear, or take off the covering, skin, etc. of.
4. to press out the last milk of (a cow) with a stroking movement of the thumb and forefinger.
5. to deprive of; to make bare; to take away from; to remove; as, (a) to remove the large central rib from (tobacco leaves); also, to remove the leaf from (the stalk); (b) to remove the husk from (corn); (c) to remove the roe or milt from (a fish), by pressure; (d) to pull off the thread from (a nut or screw); as, to *strip* a screw; also, to pull off (the thread) from a nut or screw; as, to *strip* a thread; (e) to clean out the fibers, etc., from (card teeth); (f) to tear off the surface of (a shot) without giving a rotary motion: said of a rifled gun; (g) to shape and smooth (a blank for a file) ready to be ground and cut; (h) to take off the earth or detritus from (a mineral vein or bed); (i) to unrig; to dismantle; as, to *strip* a ship; (j) to break off the teeth of (a gear).
6. to take apart (a firearm, etc.) piece by piece, as for cleaning; to dismantle.
7. to outrun; to outstrip. [Obs.]

strip, *v.i.* 1. to take off all clothing; to undress.
2. to have the spiral thread tear off; as, a screw *strips*.
3. to peel off or come apart in strips, as bark.
4. to leave a rifled gun without rotating, as a shot.

strip, *n.* [a variation of *stripe*.]
1. a narrow piece, comparatively long; as, a *strip* of cloth, of land, of timber, etc.
2. any of several ore-washing troughs in a series. [Brit.]
3. [*pl.*] stripped tobacco leaves.
4. a comic strip.
5. a long narrow runway for the take-off and landing of airplanes, usually laid out in the direction of the prevailing wind: also *airstrip*, *landing strip*.
6. in philately, a vertical or horizontal row of three or more attached stamps.

strip, *v.t.* to cut or tear into strips.

strip crop'ping, crop planting in which strips of heavy-rooted and loose-rooted plants are alternated to lessen erosion, as on a hillside.

strīpe, *n.* [from a L.G. source: cf. M.L.G. and M.D. stripe; akin to Eng. *strip*.]
1. a long, narrow band, mark, or streak of anything, of a different color, texture, or material from the adjoining surface; as, a *stripe* of red on a green ground.
2. the welt or discoloration made on the flesh by a lash or rod.
3. a stroke made with a lash, whip, rod, strap, or scourge.
4. any of various strips of cloth or braid worn on the sleeve of a military uniform or the like to indicate rank, length of service, wounds, etc.
5. a distinctive mark or color.
6. type; kind; sort.
7. cloth woven or printed in stripes.

strīpe, *v.t.*; striped (strīpt), *pt.*, *pp.*; striping, *ppr.* to mark with a stripe or stripes.

strīpe, *v.i.* to make stripes, as in painting, etc.

strīped (strīpt), *a.* having a stripe or stripes.

strīped squir'rel (skwīr'), a chipmunk.

strīp'ẽr, *n.* any enlisted man, or a naval officer, who wears a stripe or stripes (sense 4): usually in hyphenated compounds, meaning *one wearing* (a specified number of) *stripes*, as a four-*striper*. [Military Slang.]

strip'ling, *n.* [ME. *strypling*, lit., one as thin as a strip.] a youth just passing from boyhood to manhood; a grown boy.

strip'pẽr, *n.* 1. one who or that which strips; specifically, [Slang.] a woman who does a strip tease.
2. a cow whose milk must be stripped; a cow nearly dry.

strip'pingṣ, *n.pl.* the last milk drawn from a cow at a milking.

strip plant'ing, strip cropping.

stript, *v.* rare past tense and past participle of *strip*.

strip tēaṣe, in the burlesque theater, an act performed by one or more women in which they remove their clothing, article by article, usually while moving about the stage in time to music.

strī'py, *a.*; *comp.* stripier; *superl.* stripiest, striped.

strīve, *v.i.*; strove *or less often* strived, *pt.*; striven *or* strived, *pp.*; striving, *ppr.* [ME. *striven*; OFr. *estriver*, from *estrif*, strife.]
1. to make great efforts to do one's best; to try very hard.

> With malice toward none, with charity for
> all, . . . let us *strive* on to finish the work
> we are in. —Abraham Lincoln.

2. to contend; to struggle in opposition; to battle; to fight; to be in conflict; as, to *strive* against temptation; to *strive* for mastery.
3. to compete; to vie. [Obs.]
4. to oppose by contrariety of qualities: followed by *with*.

> Now private pity *strove with* public hate.
> —Derham.

Syn.—labor, endeavor, aim, dispute, quarrel, wrangle, contest.

strīved, *v.* alternative past tense and past participle of *strive*.

striv'en, *v.* past participle of *strive*.

strīv'ẽr, *n.* one who strives or contends.

strīv'ing, *n.* strenuous exertion; earnest effort; struggle.

strīv'ing·ly, *adv.* in a striving manner; with earnest efforts; with struggles.

strix, *n.* [L., a channel, groove.] a channel in a fluted column or pillar.

Strix, *n.* [L., an owl.] the typical genus of *Strigidæ*, the owl family.

strōam, *v.i.* 1. to wander about idly and vacantly. [Obs.]
2. to stride. [Brit. Dial.]

strob, *n.* [Gr. *strobos*, a twisting or whirling round, from *strephein*, to twist, whirl.] in physics, a velocity of one radian per second, taken as a unit of measure for angular velocity.

strob'iç, *a.* in physics, spinning or appearing to spin.
strobic disks; disks with rings drawn concentrically upon them, that seem to spin around when the disks are moved about.

strob'il, *n.* a strobile.

strō·bī'lȧ, *n.*; *pl.* **strō·bī'lae,** [Gr. *strobilos*, anything twisted, a pine cone, from *strephein*, to twist.]
1. a stage in the development of the larva of a discophoran, when the body elongates and subdivides, the subdivisions being arranged somewhat like a pine cone.
2. a mature tapeworm, with its generative segments.

strob·i·lā′ceous, *a.* 1. resembling or relating to strobiles.
2. producing or bearing strobiles.

strob′i·lāte, *v.i.*; strobilated, *pt., pp.*; strobilating, *ppr.* to produce a strobila; to become, or divide metamerically, as a strobila.

strob·i·lā′tion, *n.* the process of dividing metamerically.

strob′ile, *n.* [LL. *strobilus,* a pine cone, from Gr. *strobilos,* anything twisted, a pine cone, from *strephein,* to twist.]
1. a conelike mass of closely packed, scalelike, spore-bearing leaves, as of the horsetail.
2. a seed-bearing cone, as of the pine.
3. in zoology, a strobila.

STROBILE SECTION OF STROBILE

strob·i·lif′ēr·ous, *a.* bearing strobiles.

strō·bil′i·fọrm, *a.* shaped like a strobile.

strob′i·line, *a.* strobilaceous; of, pertaining to, or resembling a strobile.

strob″i·lī·zā′tion, *n.* same as *strobilation.*

strob′i·loid, *a.* resembling or pertaining to a strobile.

strob·i·loph′ȧ·gous, *a.* [LL. *strobilus,* a pine cone, and Gr. *phagein,* to eat, devour.] living on pine cones.

strō·bī′lus, *n.*; *pl.* **strō·bī′lī,** same as *strobile.*

strob′ō·sçōpe, *n.* [Gr. *strobos,* a twisting round, and *skopein,* to view.]
1. an instrument for studying periodic or varying motion by illuminating a moving body at frequent, rapid intervals. It enables a movement that really takes place in a hundredth or thousandth of a second to be seen drawn out to a quarter of a minute or more.
2. a form of phenakistoscope.

strob·ō·sçop′iç, *a.* pertaining to or characteristic of the stroboscope.

strob·ō·sçop′i·çăl, *a.* same as *stroboscopic.*

strō′çăl, stroç′kle, strō′çle, *n.* same as *strokle.*

strōde, *v.* past tense of *stride.*

strōke, *v.* obsolete past tense of *strike.*

strōke, *n.* [ME. *strok, strook,* from AS. *strac,* a stroke, from *strican,* to strike.]
1. a blow; a knock; the striking of one thing against another; as, a piece of timber falling may kill a man by its *stroke*; more specifically, a blow struck by the human arm; a hostile blow; a blow with a weapon; as, a man, when whipped, can hardly fail to wince at every *stroke.*
2. (a) a sudden action resulting in a powerful or destructive effect, as if from a blow; as, a *stroke* of lightning; (b) any action having an immediate effect, often a pleasant one; as, a *stroke* of luck.
3. any sudden attack of disease or illness, especially of apoplexy or paralysis.
4. (a) a single effort to do, produce, or accomplish something, especially a successful effort; (b) something accomplished by such an effort.
5. (a) the sound of striking, as of a clock; (b) the time indicated by this; as, he arrived at the *stroke* of nine.
6. (a) a single movement of the arms, hands, etc. or of an instrument in the hands, especially such a movement as for striking the ball in tennis, golf, billiards, etc.; (b) any of a series of repeated rhythmic motions made against water, air, etc.; as, the *stroke* of a swimmer, rower, etc.; (c) a type, manner, or rate of such movement; as, a slow *stroke*; (d) a single movement of a pen or similar marking tool.
7. a mark made by or as by a pen or similar marking tool.
8. a beat of the heart.
9. a gentle, caressing motion with the hand.
10. in mechanics. any of a series of continuous, often reciprocating, movements; specifically, a single movement of a piston from one end of its range to the other, constituting a half revolution of the engine.
11. in rowing, (a) the rower who sits nearest the stern and sets the rate of rowing for the others; (b) the position occupied by this rower.
12. a series of operations; as, to carry on a great *stroke* in business.
13. power; efficacy. [Obs.]
to keep stroke; to make strokes in rhythm.

strōke, *v.t.*; stroked (strōkt), *pt., pp.*; stroking, *ppr.* [ME. *stroken*; AS. *strācian,* to stroke, a causal verb, from *strāc,* pt. of *strican,* to go, pass swiftly over.]
1. to draw one's hand, a tool, etc. gently over the surface of, as in caressing.
2. to soothe; to flatter.
3. to make smooth.
4. in masonry, to produce a sort of fluted surface upon, as a stone.
5. to pull the stroke oar for; to set the rate of rowing for (a crew); as, to *stroke* a college crew.

strōke ōar, 1. the oar set nearest the stern.
2. the oarsmen who operates this oar, usually setting the pace for the other oarsmen.

strōk′ēr, *n.* 1. one who strokes.
2. one who professes to cure by stroking. [Obs.]
3. a flat instrument of wood, bone, etc., used by press feeders to advance the sheets of paper to a printing press. [Brit.]

strōkes′măn, *n.*; *pl.* **strōkes′men,** a stroke oar, or stroke.

strōk′ing, *n.* 1. the act of making strokes.
2. the act of laying flutes or gathers in cloth by strokes of the needle.
3. [*pl.*] strippings; the last milk drawn at a milking.

strō′kle, *n.* an instrument used by glassmakers to empty the metal from one pot to another.

strōll, *v.i.*; strolled, *pt., pp.*; strolling, *ppr.* [ME. *stroyl, stroul*; Dan. *stryge*; Sw. *stryka,* to stroll about; Sw. dial. *strykel,* one who strolls about.]
1. to walk in an idle, leisurely manner; to saunter.
2. to go idly from place to place; to wander.
Syn.—ramble, range, roam, rove, saunter, stray, wander.

strōll, *v.t.* to stroll along or through (the countryside, etc.).

strōll, *n.* the act of strolling; a leisurely walk.

strōll′ēr, *n.* 1. one who strolls, or saunters.
2. a vagabond; a vagrant.
3. a strolling player.
4. a small cart with openings for the legs, in which an infant can stand supported while learning to walk.
5. a light baby carriage.

strō′mȧ, *n.*; *pl.* **strō′mȧ·tȧ,** [Gr. *strōma,* anything spread out for lying or sitting upon, a mattress, bed, from *strōnnynai,* to spread out.]
1. in anatomy, the tissue which forms the ground substance, framework, or matrix of an organ; also, the colorless framework of a red blood corpuscle or other cell.
2. in botany, the fleshy substance of some fungous plants, in which the perithecia are embedded.

strō·mat′iç, *a.* pertaining to or resembling a stroma.

strō·mat′i·fọrm, *a.* having the form of a stroma.

strō·mȧ·tol′ō·ġy, *n.* [Gr. *strōma, strōmatos,* a bed, and *-logy.*] that branch of geology which treats of the formation of stratified rocks, their succession, and their organic remains. [Rare.]

stromb (strom), *n.* any mollusk of the genus *Strombus.*

strom′bi·fọrm, *a.* shaped like a stromb.

strom′bīte, *n.* a fossil shell of the genus *Strombus.*

strom·bū·lif′ēr·ous, *a.* in botany, producing strombuliform pods.

strom·bū′li·fọrm, *a.* [LL. *strombulus,* dim. of L. *strombus,* a spiral shell, and *-form.*]
1. in geology, formed like a top.
2. in botany, spirally coiled or twisted like a screw.

Strom′bus, *n.* [L., a spiral shell; Gr. *strombos,* anything twisted or turned, a top, spiral shell, from *strephein,* to turn.] a genus of marine gastropodous mollusks, having the external border or lip of the shell dilated into a wing.

WINGED STROMBS (*Strombus tricornis*)

strō′meȳ·ēr·īte, *n.* [after Friedrich *Stromeyer,* 19th-c. German chemist.] a lustrous, steel-gray mineral, $(Ag, Cu)_2S$, sulfide of silver and copper.

strond, *n.* strand. [Obs.]

strọng, *a.*; *comp.* stronger; *superl.* strongest, [AS. *strang, strong*; akin to O.N. *strangr,* strong, severe.]
1. (a) physically powerful; having great muscular strength; robust; (b) in a healthy and sound condition; hale; hearty; as, I feel *stronger* today.
2. morally powerful; having strength of character or will.
3. (a) intellectually powerful; able to think vigorously and clearly; (b) having special competency or ability (*in* a specified subject or field); as, he's *strong in* chemistry.
4. powerfully made or built; tough; firm; durable; as, a *strong* wall.
5. hard to capture; easily defended; able to resist and endure attack; as, a *strong* fort.
6. having many resources; powerful in wealth, numbers, supplies, etc.; as, a *strong* army.
7. having a specified number or amount; reaching a certain degree in number or strength; as, a task force 6,000 *strong.*
8. having a powerful effect; vigorously effective; drastic; as, *strong* measures.
9. having a large amount of its essential quality; not weak or diluted; as, *strong* coffee.
10. affecting the senses powerfully; intense in taste, flavor, etc.; as, a *strong* light, *strong* smell, etc.
11. having an offensive taste or smell; rank; as, *strong* butter.
12. firm and loud; as, a *strong* voice.
13. intense in degree or quality; not mild; specifically, (a) ardent; passionate; warm; as, *strong* affection; (b) forceful; persuasive; cogent; (c) felt deeply; pronounced; decided; as, a *strong* opinion; (d) zealous; vigorously active; as, a *strong* Democrat; (e) vigorous, forthright, and unambiguous, often offensively so; as, *strong* language; (f) clear; distinct; marked; as, a *strong* resemblance.
14. moving rapidly and with force; as, a *strong* wind.
15. characterized by rapidly rising prices; as, a *strong* market.
16. in English and other Germanic languages, designating or of those verbs expressing variation in tense by internal change of vowel rather than by the addition of inflectional endings, as *swim, swam, swum*: also called irregular: opposed to *weak.*
17. substantial; solid; nourishing.
Strong is used as an element in many self-explanatory compounds; as, *strong*-backed, *strong*-fisted, *strong*-bodied, *strong*-smelling, *strong*-voiced, and the like.
strong conjugation; the conjugation of irregular verbs.
strong drink; drink containing a high percentage of alcohol.
strong water; (a) [Obs.] any corrosive acid; (b) [*pl.*] [Archaic.] formerly, any distilled spirits or liquor.
Syn.—vigorous, powerful, stout, robust, hardy, muscular, forcible, cogent.

strọng, *adv.* in a strong manner; greatly; severely; with force.

strọng′-ärm, *a.* using physical force. [Colloq.]

strọng′-ärm, *v.t.* to use physical force upon. [Colloq.]

strọng′back, *n.* 1. in a ship, a beam above the windlass, used to trice up the chain.
2. a spar connecting the davits, used for securing a ship's boat at sea.

strọng′bärk, *n.* a small tree of Florida and the West Indies, with strong, hard, orange-streaked, brown wood.

strọng′box, *n.* a heavily made box or safe for storing valuables.

strọng′hōld, *n.* a place having strong defenses; a fort; a fortified place; a place of security.

strọng′ish, *a.* having a tendency toward strength; somewhat strong.

strọng′ly, *adv.* in a strong manner.

strọng măn′ṣ weed, a plant, *Petiveria alliacea,* native to the American tropics.

strọng′-mīnd′ed, *a.* 1. having a strong or vigorous mind or will; determined.
2. not according to the female character or manners; unfeminine: applied ironically to women claiming the privileges of men.

strọng′-mīnd′ed·ness, *n.* the state or quality of being strong-minded.

strọng′room, *n.* a strongly built room used for the safekeeping of valuables.

strọng′-willed′, *a.* strong-minded.

stron′ġy·lāte, *a.* in zoology, belonging to, resembling, or having strongyles.

stron′ġyle, stron′ġyl, *n.* [LL., from Gr. *strongylos,* round, circular.]
1. any of various roundworms of the genus *Strongylus.*
2. a spicule with blunt ends.

stron′ġy·lid, *a.* and *n.* strongyloid.

stron'ġy·loid, *a.* belonging or related to the genus *Strongylus*; resembling a strongyle.
stron'ġy·loid, *n.* a strongyle.
stron'ġy·lon, *n.*; *pl.* **stron'ġy·la,** same as *strongyle*, sense 2.
stron·ġy·lō'sis, *n.* [Mod. L.] the condition of being infested by strongyles.
stron·ġy·lox'ē·a, *n.*; *pl.* **stron·ġy·lox'ē·ae,** [Gr. *strongylos*, round, circular, and *oxys*, sharp, keen.] a strongyle with one end blunt, the other pointed.
stron·ġy·lox'ē·āte, *a.* belonging to or resembling a strongyloxea.
Stron'ġy·lus, *n.* [Gr. *strongylos*, round, circular.] a genus of intestinal worms having a cylindrical body; *Strongylus armatus* infests arteries of the horse and ass; *Strongylus gigas* infests man as well as animals and measures from ten inches to three feet in length: both cause severe damage or death.
stron'ti·a (-shi-), *n.* 1. the oxide of strontium, SrO, a white powder somewhat like lime.
2. loosely, strontium hydroxide, $Sr(OH)_2$.
stron'ti·ăn, *n.* strontium, especially in the form of a compound.
stron'ti·ăn, *a.* of or containing strontia.
strontian yellow; a solution of strontia added to chromate of potash. It is a pale canary-yellow, and is a permanent color.
stron"ti·ăn·if'ēr·ous, *a.* containing or giving out some form of strontian.
stron'ti·ăn·īte, *n.* native carbonate of strontia, $SrCO_3$, a white, greenish, or yellowish mineral that occurs massive, fibrous, and crystallized in the form of a hexahedral prism.
stron'tiç, *a.* of strontium.
stron·tit'iç, *a.* same as *strontic*.
stron'ti·um, *n.* [named from *Strontian*, in Argyllshire, Scotland.] a pale-yellow, metallic chemical element resembling calcium in properties and found only in combination: strontium compounds burn with a red flame and are used in fireworks: symbol, Sr; atomic weight, 87.63; atomic number, 38.
strook, *v.* obsolete past participle of *strike*.
stroot, *v.i.* to strut. [Obs.]
strop, *n.* [ME. *stroppe*; AS., from L. *struppus*, a strap, thong.]
1. a strip of leather; a strap.
2. a device used for putting a fine edge on razors: strops are made of leather, leather-covered wood, or specially treated cloth.
3. in ropemaking, a rope with an eye at each end, used in twisting strands.
strop, *v.t.*; stropped (stropt), *pt., pp.*; stropping, *ppr.* to sharpen on a strop.
strō·phan'thin, *n.* [from Mod. L. *Strophanthus*, type genus.] a white or pale-yellow poisonous crystalline compound, $C_{31}H_{48}O_{12}$, used as a heart stimulant.
Strō·phan'thus, *n.* [Gr. *strophos*, a twisted cord, and *anthos*, flower.] a genus of tropical plants of the family *Apocynaceæ*, bearing showy flowers.
strō'phē, *n.* [Gr. *strophē*, a turning, twist, from *strephein*, to turn.]
1. in the Greek drama, (a) the movement of the chorus in turning from right to left of the stage; (b) that part of a choric song performed while making this movement.
2. in a Pindaric ode, the stanza which is answered by the antistrophe.
3. a stanza; especially, any of the irregular divisions of an ode, etc.
4. in botany, a spiral formed in the development of leaves.
stroph'iç, *a.* of or like a strophe.
stroph'i·căl, *a.* same as *strophic*.
strō'phi·ō·lāte, strō'phi·ō·lā·ted, *a.* in botany, having strophioles or caruncles, as seeds.
strō'phi·ōle, *n.* [L. *strophiolum*, a garland.] in botany, a little tubercular part near the base or hilum of some seeds; also, a caruncle.
stroph'ū·lus, *n.* any of various mild forms of milaria, especially common in children.
stroud, *n.* [etym. obscure.]
1. a kind of coarse blanket or garment made of strouding, worn by North American Indians.
2. strouding.
stroud'ing, *n.* a kind of coarse cloth used by North American Indians for strouds.
strout, *v.* to strut. [Obs.]
strōve, *v.* alternative past tense of *strive*.
strōw, *v.t.*; strowed, *pt.*; strowed *or* strown, *pp.*; strowing, *ppr.* to strew. [Archaic.]
stroy, *v.t.* to destroy. [Obs.]
strub, *v.t.* to strip; to rob. [Obs.]

struck, *v.* past tense and past participle of *strike*.
struck, *a.* closed or affected by a labor strike.
struck jū'ry, in law, a jury of twelve drawn from the panel of twenty-four names remaining after each side has been permitted to strike out twelve of the original list of forty-eight names.
struck'en, *v.* obsolete past participle of *strike*.
struç'tūr·ăl, *a.* 1. pertaining to structure; having or characterized by structure.
2. of or resulting from changes in the structure of the earth's crust; tectonic.
3. used in construction or building.
structural botany; see under *botany*.
structural disease; an organic disease.
structural formula; see under *formula*.
structural linguistics; language study based on the assumptions that a language is a coherent system of formal signs and that the task of linguistic study is to inquire into the nature of those signs and their peculiar systematic arrangement, without reference to historical antecedents or comparison with other languages.
structural steel; steel prepared and shaped for constructing buildings, bridges, etc.
struç'tūr·ăl·iṣm, *n.* 1. a movement for determining and analyzing the basic, relatively stable structural elements of a system, especially in the behavioral sciences.
2. same as *structural linguistics*.
struç'tūr·ăl·ist, *n.* a follower or advocate of structural principles, as in the analysis or application of social, economic, or linguistic theory.
struç'tūr·ăl·ist, *a.* of or relating to structuralists or their theories.
struç"tūr·ăl·i·zā'tion, *n.* 1. the act of structuralizing.
2. the development of parts, patterns, etc. into a unified structure.
struç'tūr·ăl·ize, *v.t.*; structuralized, *pt., pp.*; structuralizing, *ppr.* to form or organize into a structure.
struç'tūr·ăl·ly, *adv.* with reference to structure.
struç'tūre, *n.* [Fr. *structure*; L. *structura*, a building, from *structus*, pp. of *struere*, to heap together, arrange.]
1. the act of building; construction. [Obs.]
2. manner of building or constructing; form; make; construction.
3. something built or constructed, as a building or dam.
4. the arrangement or interrelation of all the parts of a whole; manner of organization or construction; as, they studied the *structure* of the atom, the *structure* of society.

> In proportion as the *structure* of a government gives force to public opinion, it is essential that public opinion should be enlightened. —George Washington.

5. something composed of parts; as, a plant is a complex *structure*.
columnar structure; see under *columnar*.
struç'tūre, *v.t.*; structured, *pt., pp.*; structuring, *ppr.* to put together systematically; to construct; to organize.
struç'tūre·less, *a.* having no regular organic structure; homogeneous.
strū'del (*or* G. shtrọ̈'del), *n.* [G., lit., whirlpool, eddy, pancake.] a kind of pastry made of a very thin sheet of dough filled with apples, cherries, cheese, etc. and rolled.
strug'gle, *v.i.*; struggled, *pt., pp.*; struggling, *ppr.* [ME. *strogelen*, a freq. formation, prob. partly echoic.]
1. to contend or fight violently with an opponent.
2. to make great efforts or attempts; to strive; to labor; as, she *struggled* to overcome her prejudice.
3. to make one's way with difficulty; as, he *struggled* through the thicket.
strug'gle, *v.t.* to bring about, make, dispute, etc. by struggling. [Rare.]
strug'gle, *n.* 1. great effort or series of efforts; violent exertion.
2. contest; contention; strife.
struggle for existence; the competition among living organisms to survive in a given environment, especially as a factor in natural selection.
strug'glēr, *n.* one who struggles.
strum, *v.t.* and *v.i.*; strummed, *pt., pp.*; strumming, *ppr.* [echoic.]
1. to pluck (a stringed musical instrument) carelessly, idly, or unskillfully.
2. to play (a tune) in this way.

strum, *n.* the act or sound of strumming.
strū'ma, *n.*; *pl.* **strū'mae,** [L., a scrofulous tumor.]
1. in botany, a swelling at the base of an organ, as in *Mimosa sensitiva*.
2. in medicine, scrofula; also, goiter.
strū·mif'ēr·ous, *a.* [L. *struma*, a tumor, and *-ferous*.] in botany, bearing strumae.
strum'mēr, *n.* a person who strums.
strū'mōse, *a.* 1. strumous.
2. in botany, having a struma.
strū'mous, *a.* [L. *strumosus*.] in medicine, of, characteristic of, or having a struma.
strum'pet, *n.* [ME.; ? connected with OFr. *strupe* (L. *stuprum*), dishonor.] a prostitute; a harlot.
strum'pet, *a.* like or pertaining to a strumpet.
strum'pet, *v.t.* 1. to debauch. [Obs.]
2. to call a strumpet, or give the reputation of a strumpet to; hence, to slander.
strung, *v.* past tense and alternative past participle of *string*.
strung out; suffering from the physical or mental effects of addiction to a narcotic drug. [Slang.]
strunt, *v.i.* to strut. [Scot.]
strunt, *n.* 1. spirituous liquor. [Scot.]
2. a pet; a sullen fit. [Scot.]
strūse, *n.* [Russ. *strug'*.] a long, flat-bottomed boat used on the inland waters of Russia. [Obs.]
strut, *v.i.*; strutted, *pt., pp.*; strutting, *ppr.* [ME. *strouten*, to spread out, to swell out; AS. *strutian*, to stand rigid.]
1. to walk with a lofty, proud gait; to walk in a vain, stiff, swaggering manner.
2. to swell; to protuberate. [Rare.]
strut, *n.* 1. the act of strutting; a vain, swaggering walk or gait.
2. a brace fitted into a framework to resist pressure in the direction of its length.
strut, *v.t.* to brace or hold in place with a strut or struts.
strut, *a.* swelling out; protuberant. [Obs.]
strū'thi·ăn, *a.* struthious.
strū'thi·form, *a.* same as *struthioniform*.
Strū'thi·ō, *n.* [L.; Gr. *strouthiōn*, the ostrich, from *strouthos*, a sparrow.] a genus of birds of the order *Struthiones*. *Struthio camelus*, the African ostrich, is the only species.
strū'thi·oid, *a.* like an ostrich; struthious.
Strū·thi·oi'dē·a, *n.pl.* same as *Struthiones*.
Strū·thi·ō'nēṣ, *n.pl.* [LL.] an order of birds; the ostriches.
Strū·thi·on'i·dae, *n.pl.* a family of birds incapable of flight, the wings being, in most cases, merely rudimentary, but having long and strong legs which enable them to run with great rapidity. This family includes the ostrich, and, formerly, the cassowary, emu, etc.
strū·thi·on'i·form, *a.* of the form of an ostrich.
strū'thi·ō·nine, *a.* struthious.
strū'thi·ous, *a.* [from L. *struthio* (from Gr. *strouthion*, sparrow, ostrich); and *-ous*.] designating or of any of a group of large, flightless birds including the ostriches, rheas, emus, etc.; specifically, of or like the African ostrich.
strut'tēr, *n.* one who struts.
strut'ting, *n.* struts, collectively.
strut'ting·ly, *adv.* with a proud, lofty step; boastingly; defiantly.
strū'vīte, *n.* [after F. G. W. von *Struve*, a Russian diplomat.] a vitreous, yellowish to brown, orthorhombic mineral occurring only in isolated crystals. It is a hydrous phosphate of ammonium and magnesium, and is found in guano in various localities.
stryçh'ni·a, *n.* strychnine. [Obs.]
stryçh'niç, *a.* of, pertaining to, obtained from, or resulting from strychnine; as, *strychnic* acid.
stryçh'nine, stryçh'nin, *n.* [LL., from Gr. *strychnos*, nightshade.] a highly poisonous vegetable alkaloid, $C_{21}H_{22}N_2O_2$, obtained from *Strychnos tieuté*, *Strychnos ignatii*, *Strychnos nux vomica*, *Strychnos colubrina*, etc. It is usually obtained from the seeds of the nux vomica. It is colorless, odorless crystalline, unalterable by exposure to the air, and extremely bitter. Strychnine and its salts, especially the latter from their solubility, are highly poisonous, but were used in very small doses as a stimulant to the nervous system.
stryçh'nin·iṣm, *n.* in medicine, a diseased condition resulting from an overdose or improper use of strychnine.
stryçh'nīze, *v.t.* to put under the influence of strychnine.
Stryçh'nos, *n.* [L., from Gr. *strychnos*, nightshade.] a genus of plants, family *Loganiaceæ*,

found principally in the tropical parts of Asia and America. Among the species are *Strychnos nux vomica*, poison nut or ratsbane, and *Strychnos potatorum*, or clearing nut, an abundant plant in the woods and mountains of the East Indies. *Strychnos colubrina*, snakewood or snake poison nut, is native to the Coromandel Coast.

Stū'ărt, *n.* the family that ruled in Scotland from 1371 to 1603 and in England and Scotland from 1603 to 1714 except during the Commonwealth (1649–1660).

Stū·är'ti·ȧ, *n.* [named after John *Stuart*, an English patron of botany.]
1. a genus of ornamental shrubs of the camellia family, growing in the southern part of the United States and in Japan, characterized by thin leaves and handsome white flowers, blooming in late spring and early summer.
2. [s–] a shrub of this genus.

stub, *n.* [ME. *stubbe*; AS. *stybb*, a stub; akin to O.N. *stubbr.*; Dan. *stub*; Sw. *stubbe*, stump.]
1. the stump of a tree; that part of the stem of a tree or other plant which remains fixed in the earth after the main part is cut down.
2. a short piece or length remaining after the main part has been removed or used up; as, the *stub* of a tail, cigar, tree root, pencil, etc.
3. any short projection; as, a mere *stub* of a horn.
4. a pen having a short, blunt point.
5. a stub nail.
6. a short piece of a ticket, blank check, etc. kept as a record after the rest has been torn off.
7. stub iron.

stub, *v.t.*; stubbed, *pt., pp.*; stubbing, *ppr.* 1. to grub up by the roots; to extirpate; as, to *stub* up edible roots.
2. to strike (one's foot, toe, etc.) against something by accident.
3. to clear of stumps or stubs, as a piece of land.
4. to render stublike; as, to *stub* a pen or a pencil. [Rare.]

stubbed (stubd), *a.* 1. like a stub; stubby; short and thick; truncated; blunt; obtuse.
2. stocky; hardy; not sensitive or delicate.
3. covered with stubs or stumps; having many stubs.

stub'bed·ness, *n.* bluntness; obtuseness.

stub'bi·ness, *n.* the quality or condition of being stubby.

stub'ble, *n.* [ME. *stobil*; OFr. *estouble*, ult. from L. *stipula*, a stalk, stem.]
1. the stalk ends of wheat, rye, barley, oats, corn, etc. left in the ground after harvesting; the part of the stalk left by the scythe, sickle, etc.
2. something resembling the stubble of grain, as a short growth of beard or hair.

stub'bled, *a.* covered with stubble; stubbly.

stub'ble fiēld, a field from which the grain has just been cut; a field covered with stubble.

stub'ble goose, the common wild goose; the graylag. [Brit. Dial.]

stub'ble land, land from which a crop of grain has been cut; a stubble field.

stub'ble quāil, an Australian quail, *Coturnix pectoralis.*

stub'ble rāke, 1. a rake with long teeth for raking together stubble.
2. a rake for gleaning from the stubble after the harvesters have done their part.

stub'ble tûrn'ẽr, a device attached to a plow to turn the stubble so that it may be covered in the furrow.

stub'bly, *a.*; *comp.* stubblier; *superl.* stubbliest, 1. covered with or composed of stubble; having stubble; stubbled; as, *stubbly* fields.
2. resembling stubble; short, bristly, and stiff; as, a *stubbly* beard.

stub book, a book containing stubs bearing memoranda of checks or other papers which have been detached.

stub'bŏrn, *a.* [ME. *stubborne, stuborne, stoburn, stiborne*, etc.; prob. from AS. *stybb*, a stub; lit., like a stub, stockish, blockish, hence obstinate.]
1. refusing to yield, obey, or comply; resisting doggedly; determined; obstinate.
2. done or carried on in a stubborn, obstinate, or persistent manner; as, a *stubborn* campaign.
3. hard to handle, treat, or deal with; intractable; as, a *stubborn* piece of oak.
4. harsh; rough; rugged. [Obs.]
Syn.—obstinate, tough, unyielding, hard, intractable, obdurate, stiff, harsh, inflexible, headstrong, refractory, heady, contumacious, pigheaded.

stub'bŏrn·ly, *adv.* in a stubborn manner.

stub'bŏrn·ness, *n.* the quality or the state of being stubborn.

stub'by, *a*; *comp.* stubbier; *superl.* stubbiest, 1. covered with stubs or stubble.
2. short and heavy or dense; as, *stubby* bristles.
3. short and thickset; stocky.

stub dam'ȧsk, a strip of metal composed of steel and stub iron wound into a spiral and welded, used in making fine gun barrels: also called *stub twist.*

stub end, the enlarged end of a pitman rod.

stub feath'ẽr (feth'), a pinfeather.

stub ī'ron (-ūrn), iron made chiefly from old stubs of horseshoe nails and used in making gun barrels.

stub mor'tise, a mortise extending only part way through the timber in which it is cut.

stub nāil, 1. an old horseshoe nail, especially one broken off or worn down.
2. any short, thick nail.

stub pen, a pen having a short blunt point, or nib.

stub short, same as *stub shot.*

stub shot, 1. the unsawed part of a log at the end by which it is held while being sawed into parallel pieces; also, the corresponding part of one of the boards or timbers after it is separated by splitting.
2. in turning, the end, as of a piece of timber, which is not worked and which is detached as useless when the piece is finished.

stub ten'ŏn, in carpentry, a short tenon which prevents side movement.

stub twist, see *stub damask.*

stub'wŏrt, *n.* the wood sorrel: so named from its growing around stubs or stumps.

stuc'cō, *n.*; *pl.* **stuc'cōes, stuc'cōs,** [It., from O.H.G. *stucchi*, a crust.]
1. plaster or cement of any kind used as a coating for walls; especially, a fine plaster composed of lime or gypsum with sand and pounded marble, used for surfacing inside or outside walls, molding relief ornaments, cornices, etc.
2. work made of stucco.
bastard stucco; a very coarse stucco.
trowelled stucco; stucco applied with a trowel.

stuc'cō, *v.t.*; stuccoed (-kōd), *pt., pp.*; stuccoing, *ppr.* to cover or decorate with stucco.

stuc'cō·ẽr, *n.* one versed in stuccowork; a maker of stucco.

stuc'cō·wōrk, *n.* work made of stucco.

stuck, *v.* past tense and past participle of *stick.*

stuck, *n.* a thrust. [Obs.]

stuc'kle, *n.* a number of sheaves set together in a field. [Brit. Dial.]

stuck'ling, *n.* an apple fritter. [Brit. Dial.]

stuck'-up', *a.* snobbish; haughty; self-important; conceited; arrogant. [Colloq.]

stud, *n.* [AS. *studu*, a prop, a pillar, a post; akin to O.N. *stoth.*]
1. any of a series of small knobs or rounded nailheads used to ornament a surface, as of leather.
2. a small, double-headed, buttonlike device used as a collar fastener, shirt-front ornament, etc.
3. in a building, an upright support in the framework, to which horizontal boards or laths are nailed.
4. in machinery, (a) a projecting pin or peg used as a support, pivot, stop, etc., sometimes forming a journal; (b) a stud bolt.
5. a stem; a trunk. [Obs.]
6. a strengthening crosspiece set transversely in the link of a chain, as in a chain cable.

stud, *v.t.*; studded, *pt., pp.*; studding, *ppr.* 1. to set or decorate with studs or studlike objects.
2. to be set thickly on; to be scattered over; as, rocks *stud* the hillside.
3. to scatter or cluster (something) thickly; as, jewels *studded* on bracelets.
4. to provide (a building) with studs or upright members.

stud, *n.* [AS. *stud*; akin to G. *stute*, mare.]
1. a collection of horses, especially a group kept for breeding.
2. the place where such horses are kept.
3. a collection of well-bred horses kept for special purposes, as racing, driving, riding, or hunting.
4. a kennel of breeding dogs.
5. a stallion; a studhorse.
at stud; available for breeding: said of male animals.

stud, *a.* 1. of or having to do with a stud; as, a *stud* farm.
2. kept for breeding.

stud bōlt, in machinery, a bolt with a thread at either end, to be screwed into a fixed part at one end and to have a nut screwed on it at the other.

stud'book, *n.* a book containing a genealogy or register of pedigreed horses or cattle of particular breeds, especially of thoroughbred race horses: also *stud book.*

stud'dẽr·y, *n.* a stud (place where studhorses are kept). [Obs.]

stud'die, *n.* a stithy. [Scot. and Brit. Dial.]

stud'ding, *n.* 1. the studs of a building.
2. the material from which joists and studs are made.

stud'ding·sāil (*in nautical usage*, stun'sl), *n.* [perh. from D. *stooten*, to push, urge on; akin to G. *stossen*, to push; and *sail.*] an auxiliary sail, usually of light canvas, set outside the edge of a working sail in light weather by means of an extensible boom: also *studding sail.*

STUDDINGSAILS
a, royal studdingsail; *b*, topgallant studdingsail; *c*, topmast studdingsail; *d*, *e*, studdingsail booms

stud'dle, *n.* [AS. *stodle*; akin to O.N. *studhill*, dim. of *stoth*, a post.] a prop or stud used in timbering a mining shaft.

stū'dent, *n.* [ME. *studiante*, from OFr. *estudiant*; L. *studens* (-*entis*), ppr. of *studere*, to be eager about, to study.]
1. a person who studies, or investigates; as, a *student* of human behavior.
2. a person who is enrolled for study at a school, college, etc.
student lamp; see under *lamp.*

stū'dent·ry, *n.* students as a body. [Rare.]

stū'dent·ship, *n.* 1. the state of being a student.
2. a scholarship.

stu̇'dẽr·īte, *n.* [after B. *Studer* (1794–1887), a Swiss geologist.] a variety of tetrahedrite containing over five per cent of zinc, found at Ausserberg, Valais, Switzerland.

stud fārm, a farm for breeding horses.

stud'fish, *n.*; *pl.* **stud'fish** or **stud'fish·es,** any fish of the genus *Fundulus*: so called from having its sides studded with bright spots.

stud'flow"ẽr, *n.* a liliaceous flower, *Helonias bullata*, growing in bogs in the eastern United States.

stud groom, a groom of a stud.

stud'horse, *n.* a stallion; a male horse kept for breeding purposes.

stud'i·ȧ·ble, *a.* that can be studied.

stud'ied (-id), *a.* 1. prepared or planned by careful study.
2. deliberate; premeditated; as, *studied* indifference.
3. learned. [Rare.]

stud'ied·ly, *adv.* in a studied manner.

stud'i·ẽr, *n.* one who studies; a student. [Rare.]

stū'di·ō, *n.*; *pl.* **stū'di·ōs,** [It., a study.]
1. the building, room, etc. of an artist, a sculptor, a photographer, etc.
2. the place where motion pictures are made professionally.
3. a room or rooms especially designed for producing and transmitting television or radio programs.

stū'di·ō, *a.* pertaining to or suitable for use in a studio; similar to a studio.
studio apartment; an apartment, part of which is an artist's studio; also, an apartment suitable for an artist's studio, being equipped with large windows, high ceilings, etc.
studio couch; a bed or lounge, usually upholstered, so constructed that it may be closed during the day to be used as a sofa, and opened at night to form a bed, usually a double bed. It is so named because it was originally designed for studio use.

stū'di·ous, *a.* [ME. *studiouse*; L. *studiosus*, eager, zealous.]
1. fond of, or often engaged in, study; devoted to the acquisition of knowledge from books by study; as, a *studious* scholar.
2. contemplative; given to thought, or to the examination of subjects by contemplation. [Rare.]
3. characterized by careful heed or attention; diligent; earnest; eager; as, be *studious* to please; *studious* to find new friends.
4. planned with study; deliberate; studied. [Rare.]
The frigid villainy of *studious* lewdness. —Rambler.
5. favorable to study; suitable for thought and contemplation; as, the *studious* shade. [Poet.]
Syn.—literary, diligent, desirous, attentive, careful, thoughtful, assiduous, reflective.

stū'di·ous·ly, *adv.* in a studious manner.

stū'di·ous·ness, *n.* the quality or practice of being studious.

stud pōk'ẽr, a variety of the game of poker in which each player is dealt five cards, the first face down and the others face up, the betting being done on each round of open cards dealt: sometimes seven cards are dealt, the first two, and often the last, face down.

stud'y, *n.*; *pl.* **stud'ies,** [ME. *studie*; OFr. *estudie*; L. *studium*, a busying oneself about a thing, zeal, study, application to learning, from *studere*, to busy oneself about, to apply oneself to, to study.]
1. the act or process of applying the mind in order to acquire knowledge, as by reading, investigating, etc.
2. careful attention to, and critical examination and investigation of, any subject, event, etc.; as, after *study* of the matter, the judge gave his decision; the *study* of human nature.
3. a branch of learning; a department of knowledge.
4. [*pl.*] education; schooling.
5. a product of study (senses 1 and 2); specifically, (a) an essay, monograph, or thesis embodying the results of a particular investigation; (b) a work of literature or art treating a subject in careful detail and made primarily as an instructive exercise for the maker; (c) a first sketch for a story, picture, etc.; (d) a short musical composition as an exercise in technique; étude.
6. an earnest effort; deliberate intention; as, his constant *study* is to do a job well.
7. abstracted state of mind; deep thought or mental absorption.
8. a room designed for study, writing, reading, etc., usually with books, a desk, and similar furnishings.
9. a person, especially an actor, with reference to his ability to memorize or learn; as, John is a quick *study*.

stud'y, *v.i.*; studied, *pt., pp.*; studying, *ppr.*
1. to fix the mind closely upon a subject; to muse; to dwell upon something in thought; to meditate; to ponder.
I found a moral first, and then *studied* for a fable. —Swift.
2. to apply the mind in order to acquire knowledge.
3. to be a student; to take a regular course in some branch of knowledge.
4. to endeavor diligently and zealously.

stud'y, *v.t.* 1. to apply the mind to attentively; to read and examine for the purpose of learning and understanding; as, to *study* law or theology; to *study* languages.
2. (a) to examine or investigate carefully; as, I shall *study* your problem; (b) to look at carefully; to scrutinize; as, he *studied* the map.
3. to read (a book, lesson, etc.) so as to know and understand it.
4. to memorize.
5. to take a course in, as at a school or college.
6. to pay attention to; to give care and thought to; as, he *studies* to do the right thing.

stud'y hall, in some schools, a room where groups of students can study during free periods between classes.

stū'fȧ, *n.* [It., a stove.] a jet of steam issuing from a fissure of the earth in volcanic regions.

stuff, *n.* [OFr. *estoffe* (Fr. *étoffe*, stuff, matter, substance, material), prob. from L. *stuppa*, *stupa*, tow, oakum, whence also G. *stopfen*, to stop or stuff up.]
1. the material or substance out of which anything is or can be made; raw material.
2. constituent elements; basic parts; essence; character; as, he is made of sterner *stuff* than his brother.
3. any kind of matter, indefinitely.
4. cloth, especially woolen cloth.
5. (a) household goods; (b) personal belongings; (c) objects; things.
6. something to be drunk or swallowed; especially, a medicine or potion.
7. worthless objects; refuse; junk.
8. foolish or worthless ideas, words, etc.; nonsense: often used as an interjection expressing disagreement, derision, irritation, etc.
9. money; cash. [Slang.]
10. a composition of fish oil and tallow for filling the pores of leather.
11. a melted mass of turpentine, tallow, etc., with which the masts, sides, and bottoms of ships are smeared for preservation.
12. paper stock, ground ready for use.
13. salt and alum, for whitening bakers' bread.
clear stuff; see under *clear*.
small stuff; see under *small*.
stuff gown; a gown made of stuff; hence, the wearer of a stuff gown, as a junior barrister not entitled to wear a silk gown. [Brit.]

stuff, *v.t.*; stuffed (stuft), *pt., pp.*; stuffing, *ppr.* [ME. *stoffen*; OFr. *estoffer*, from *estoffe*.]
1. to fill the inside of (something); to pack; specifically, (a) to fill (a cushion, chair, etc.) with padding or stuffing, as an upholsterer does; (b) to fill the skin of (a dead animal, bird, etc.) as part of the process of mounting and preserving, as a taxidermist does; (c) to fill (a chicken, turkey, etc.) with seasoning, bread crumbs, etc. before roasting.
2. (a) to fill too full; to cram; to overload; as, the drawer is *stuffed* with papers; (b) to fill to excess with food.
3. to fill with; to pack or cram with; to crowd in.
4. to fill with information, ideas, etc.; as, he *stuffed* his head with facts.
5. to put fraudulent votes into (a ballot box.)
6. (a) to plug; to block; (b) to choke; to stop up, as with phlegm.
7. to force; push; as, he *stuffed* a handkerchief into his pocket.
8. to treat (leather) with a preparation of oil and tallow for preserving it.
9. to cause to swell out. [Obs.]
10. to put together the various parts of (a newspaper) when it is made up of a number of sheets printed singly. [Slang.]

stuff, *v.i.* to eat too much or too quickly; to feed gluttonously.

stuffed shīrt, a pompous, pretentious, but actually insignificant person. [Slang.]

stuff'ẽr, *n.* 1. one who stuffs; specifically, one who stuffs the skins of animals for the purpose of preserving as specimens, etc.; as, a bird *stuffer*.
2. that which stuffs; specifically, a machine or instrument for filling in stuffing or seasoning; as, a sausage *stuffer*.

stuff'i·ly, *adv.* in a stuffy manner.

stuff'i·ness, *n.* the state or quality of being stuffy, close, or musty; as, the *stuffiness* of a room.

stuff'ing, *n.* 1. the action of filling, packing, or gorging.
2. something used to fill or stuff; specifically, (a) soft, springy material used as padding in cushions, upholstered furniture, etc.; (b) a mixture, as of bread crumbs, seasoning, etc., for stuffing a fowl, roast, or the like before cooking; (c) a dressing composed of oil and tallow for filling and softening leather; (d) any material used for the purpose of extending or padding, as in a book, sermon, etc.

stuff'ing box, a chamber that holds packing tightly around a moving part, as a piston rod, boat propeller shaft, etc., to prevent leakage of fluid along the part.

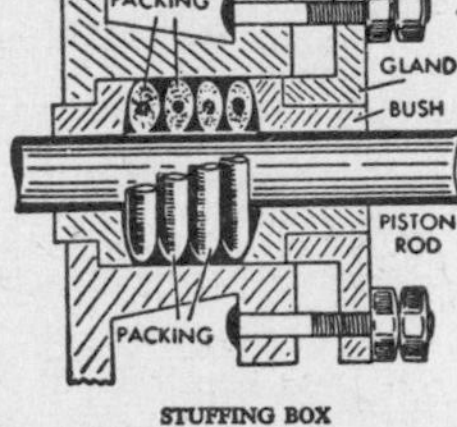

STUFFING BOX

stuff'y, *a.*; *comp.* stuffier; *superl.* stuffiest, [*stuff* and *-y*.]
1. poorly ventilated; having little fresh air; close.
2. having the nasal passages stopped up, as from a cold.
3. dull; stodgy; not interesting or stimulating. [Colloq.]
4. conservative; old-fashioned. [Colloq.]
5. prim; strait-laced. [Colloq.]
6. sulky; obstinate. [Colloq.]
7. stout; mettlesome; resolute. [Scot.]
8. fat; stuffed out. [Brit. Dial.]

Stụ'kȧ, *n.* [from G. *sturzkampfflugzeug*; *sturz*, a fall, *kampf*, a battle, and *flugzeug*, aircraft.] a German dive bomber of World War II so constructed that it could dive low over a small strategic objective, drop a heavy bomb, and ascend again swiftly into the air.

stull, *n.* [perh. from G. *stollen*, a support, prop.] any of several kinds of supports or frameworks used in mines to prevent cave-ins, support a platform, etc.

stul''ti·fi·cā'tion, *n.* a stultifying or being stultified.

stul'ti·fī·ẽr, *n.* one who or that which stultifies.

stul'ti·fȳ, *v.t.*; stultified, *pt., pp.*; stultifying, *ppr.* [L. *stultus*, foolish, and *facere*, to make.]
1. to cause to appear foolish, stupid, inconsistent, etc.; to make absurd or ridiculous.
2. to cause to be of no effect; to make worthless or useless; as, his present behavior *stultifies* his previous efforts.
3. in law, to allege (oneself or another) to be of unsound mind and, hence, not legally responsible.
4. to look upon as foolish. [Rare.]

stul·til'ō·quence, *n.* foolish or silly talk; babble. [Rare.]

stul·til'ō·quent, *a.* [L. *stultus*, foolish, and *loquens* (*-entis*), ppr. of *loqui*, to talk.] given to or characterized by stultiloquence, or silly talk. [Rare.]

stul·til'ō·quent·ly, *adv.* in a stultiloquent manner; with silly talk. [Rare.]

stul·til'ō·quy, *n.* [L. *stultiloquium*.] foolish talk; silly discourse; babble. [Rare.]

stul'ty, *a.* silly; senseless; given to foolish talk. [Obs.]

stum, *n.* [D. *stom*, unfermented wine, must, wine that has not worked, from *stom*, dumb, mute.]
1. unfermented or partly fermented grape juice; must or new wine, often mixed with dead or vapid wine to raise a new fermentation.
2. wine revived by increased fermentation, through the addition of stum.

stum, *v.t.*; stummed, *pt., pp.*; stumming, *ppr.* to renew, as wine, by adding stum and raising a new fermentation.

stum'ble, *v.i.*; stumbled, *pt., pp.*; stumbling, *ppr.* [ME. *stomblen*, *stomelen*, prob. from O.N.]
1. to trip or miss one's step in walking, running, etc.
2. to walk or go in an unsteady or awkward manner, as from age, weakness, etc.
3. to speak, act, or proceed in a confused, blundering manner; as, he *stumbled* through his recitation.
4. to fall into sin or error; to do wrong.
5. to come by chance; to happen; as I *stumbled* across a clue.

stum'ble, *v.t.* 1. to cause to stumble.
2. to confound; to puzzle; to perplex; to embarrass.

stum'ble, *n.* 1. the act of stumbling; a trip or blunder in walking or running.
2. a blunder; an error; a sin; a failure; a slip.

stum'blẽr, *n.* one who stumbles or makes a blunder.

stum'bling block, any cause of stumbling; that which forms a difficulty in one's way; an obstacle, hindrance, or difficulty.

stum'bling·ly, *adv.* in a stumbling manner.

stum'bling stōne, a stumbling block. [Rare.]

stump, *n.* [ME. *stumpe*, *stompe*, prob. from O.N. *stumpr*; akin to Sw. and Dan. *stump*, end, bit.]
1. the lower end of a tree or plant remaining in the ground after most of the stem or trunk has been cut off.
2. anything like a stump; specifically, (a) the part of a limb or tooth left after the rest has been cut off, broken off, etc.; (b) the part of anything left after the main or important part has been removed, worn off, etc.; butt; stub; as, the *stump* of a pencil.
3. a short, stocky person or animal.
4. the place where a political speech is made; political rostrum: so called because speeches were originally made from tree stumps.
5. (a) the sound of a heavy, clumsy, tramping step; (b) such a step.
6. a pointed rubber stick or a heavy, pointed roll of paper used for shading charcoal or pencil drawings.

7. a dare; challenge. [Former Colloq.]
8. [*pl.*] the legs. [Slang.]
9. in cricket, one of the three posts that compose the wicket, the one nearest the batsman being called the *leg stump*, the next one the *middle stump*, and the farthest one the *off stump*.
10. a stud, small pillar, or post.
11. in a lock, a projection on which the tumbler rests, to prevent the improper retraction of the bolt, or to guide a moving part; in a hinge, an obstruction that prevents it from folding but one way.
up a stump; unable to act, think, answer, etc.; in a dilemma; perplexed; nonplussed. [Colloq.]

stump, *v.t.*; stumped (stumpt), *pt., pp.*; stumping, *ppr.* 1. to reduce to a stump; to lop.
2. to remove stumps from (land).
3. to canvass, or travel over (a district), making political speeches.
4. to tone down or soften with a stump (sense 6).
5. to stub (one's toes, etc.). [Colloq.]
6. to puzzle; perplex; baffle; foil. [Colloq.]
7. to challenge; dare. [Colloq.]
8. in cricket, to put (a batsman) out by striking a bail from the wicket with the ball while the batsman is out of his ground: said of the wicketkeeper.
to stump it; (a) to make an escape; to take flight; to run off; (b) to travel about making political speeches. [Colloq.]

stump, *v.i.* 1. to walk stiffly, heavily, or noisily, as with a wooden leg.
2. to travel about making political speeches.
to stump up; to pay or hand over money; as I will make him *stump up* for my lost time. [Brit. Colloq.]

stump, *a.* pertaining to or delivered on the stump (sense 4); as, a *stump* speech.

stump'ăġe, *n.* 1. standing timber.
2. the value of standing timber as figured from the price per stump.
3. the right to cut such timber.
4. a tax levied on cut timber.

stump'ẽr, *n.* 1. one who or that which stumps.
2. a puzzling difficulty; a difficult question. [Colloq.]
3. a stump speaker.

stump'i·ness, *n.* the quality or condition of being stumpy.

stump'-tāiled, *a.* having a stubby tail; bobtailed; as, the *stump-tailed* lizard, a scincoid reptile of Australia.

stump'y, *a.*; *comp.* stumpier; *superl.* stumpiest. 1. covered with or full of stumps.
2. like a stump; short and thick; stubby.

stun, *v.t.*; stunned, *pt., pp.*; stunning, *ppr.* [ME. *stonien, stunien*; OFr. *estoner*, to stun, resound; hyp. L. *extonare*; *ex-* intens., and *tonare*, to thunder, crash.]
1. to make senseless or unconscious, as by a blow.
2. to daze or stupefy; to shock deeply; astound; overwhelm; as, we were *stunned* by the sight.
3. to overpower or bewilder as by a loud noise or explosion.

stun, *n.* 1. something that stuns; a blow; a shock.
2. the condition of being stunned.

Stun'diṣm, *n.* [G. *stunde*, hour, lesson.] the doctrines of a religious body of Russians, originated in 1860 by emigrants from Germany and emphasizing the idea of brotherly love and the necessity of manual labor.

Stun'dist, *n.* a believer in Stundism.

stung, *v.* past tense and past participle of *sting*.

stuñk, *v.* past participle and alternative past tense of *stink*.

stun'nẽr, *n.* 1. one who or that which stuns.
2. anything that stuns or astonishes by its appearance or other qualities; anything wonderfully or extraordinarily good; something first-rate; specifically, a person who is remarkably beautiful, excellent, etc. [Colloq.]

stun'ning, *a.* 1. that stuns.
2. remarkable, especially for beauty, smartness, etc. [Colloq.]

stun'ning·ly, *adv.* in a stunning manner.

stun'săil, stun's'le (stun'sl), *n.* a studding-sail.

stunt, *v.t.*; stunted, *pt., pp.*; stunting, *ppr.* [AS. *stintan*, to be weary, *stunt*, blunt, stupid; O.Sw. *stutt, stunt*, docked, short.]
1. to hinder from growth; to shorten or check the growth or development of; to dwarf.
2. to hinder (growth or development).

stunt, *n.* 1. the act or process of stunting or dwarfing; a check in growth.
2. that which has been checked in its growth; a stunted creature or thing.
3. a whale two years old.

stunt, *n.* [Late 19th-c. college slang: said to be from G. *stunde* in sense "a lesson," but *stump* was used earlier in the same sense and *stunt*, dial. var. of *stint*, may have influenced the word.] something done for a thrill, to attract attention, etc.; exhibition of skill or daring; feat. [Colloq.]

stunt, *v.i.* to perform a stunt or stunts. [Colloq.]

stunt, *v.t.* to perform stunts in or with (an airplane, etc.).

stunt'ed, *a.* undersized; dwarfed.

stunt'ed·ness, *n.* the quality or condition of being stunted.

stunt man, in motion pictures, a professional acrobat, etc. who takes the place of an actor in dangerous scenes involving falls, leaps, or the like.

stunt'ness, *n.* stuntedness. [Rare.]

stū'pȧ, *n.* [Sans. *stūpa*, an accumulation, a stupa, or tope.] a domelike mound containing a Buddhist shrine: also called *tope*.

stūpe, *n.* [L. *stupa*, tow.] in medicine, a soft cloth dipped in hot water, wrung dry, often medicated, and applied to the body to relieve pain.

stūpe, *v.t.*; stuped, *pt., pp.*; stuping, *ppr.* to foment with a stupe.

stūpe, *n.* a stupid person. [Slang.]

stū·pē·fā'cient (-shent), *a.* [L. *stupefaciens* (*-entis*), ppr. of *stupefacere*, to benumb, stupefy.] having a stupefying power.

stū·pē·fā'cient, *n.* a drug, etc. that produces stupor; a narcotic.

stū·pē·faç'tion, *n.* [L. *stupefacio* (*-onis*), from *stupefactus*, pp. of *stupefacere*, to stupefy.]
1. a stupefying or being stupefied.
2. great amazement or bewilderment; astonishment.

stū·pē·faç'tive, *a.* and *n.* same as *stupefacient*.

stū'pē·fīed·ness, *n.* stupefaction.

stū'pē·fī·ẽr, *n.* one who or that which stupefies.

stū'pē·fȳ, *v.t.*; stupefied, *pt., pp.*; stupefying, *ppr.* [Fr. *stupéfier*; L. *stupefacere*; *stupere*, to be amazed, and *facere*, to make.]
1. to bring into a state of stupor; to make dull or lethargic; to stun; to blunt the faculty of perception or understanding in.
2. to astound; to amaze; to astonish.
3. to deprive of the power of motion. [Obs.]

stū·pen'dous, *a.* [L. *stupendus*, amazing, gerundive of *stupere*, to be struck senseless.] overwhelming; astonishingly great in some quality; amazing; especially, amazingly large; immense; as, a *stupendous* lie.

stū·pen'dous·ly, *adv.* in a stupendous manner.

stū·pen'dous·ness, *n.* the quality or state of being stupendous, or astonishing.

stū'pē·ous, *a.* [L. *stupa*, tow.] towlike; stupose.

stū'pid, *a.* [Fr. *stupide*; L. *stupidus*, senseless, from *stupere*, to be amazed.]
1. in a state of stupor; dazed; stunned; stupefied.
2. lacking normal intelligence or understanding; slow-witted; dull.
3. showing or resulting from a lack of normal intelligence; foolish; irrational; as, what a *stupid* idea.
4. dull and boring; tiresome; as, a very *stupid* party.
Syn.—dull, senseless, stolid, doltish, besotted, insensate, obtuse, addlepated, dull-witted.

stū'pid, *n.* a stupid person.

stū·pid'i·ty, *n.* [Fr. *stupidité*; L. *stupiditas* (*-atis*), senselessness, from *stupidus*, senseless.]
1. the quality or condition of being stupid.
2. *pl.* **stū·pid'i·tieṣ,** something stupid; a foolish remark; irrational act, etc.
3. stupefaction; surprise. [Rare.]

stū'pid·ly, *adv.* in a stupid manner.

stū'pid·ness, *n.* stupidity.

stū'pi·fȳ, *v.t.* to stupefy. [Obs.]

stū'pŏr, *n.* [L.] 1. a state in which the mind and senses are dulled; great diminution or suspension of sensibility, as from the use of a narcotic; numbness.
2. intellectual insensibility; moral or mental dullness or apathy.

stū'pŏr·ous, *a.* of or in a stupor.

stū'pōse, *a.* [L. *stupa*, tow.] having a tuft of hairs; composed of matted filaments like tow.

stū'prāte, *v.t.* to ravish; to debauch. [Obs.]

stū·prā'tion, *n.* rape; violation by force. [Obs.]

stū'prum, *n.* [L., dishonor.] in Roman law, stupration; any sexual intercourse forbidden by law.

stū'pū·lōse, *a.* finely stupose; covered with fine short hairs.

stũrb, *v.t.* to disturb. [Obs.]

stũr'died, *a.* diseased with sturdy, as sheep.

stũr'di·ly, *adv.* in a sturdy manner.

stũr'di·ness, *n.* the quality or condition of being sturdy; stoutness; hardiness.

stũr'dy, *a.*; *comp.* sturdier; *superl.* sturdiest. [ME. *stourdi, sturdi*; OFr. *estourdi*, stunned, dazed, reckless.]
1. firm; resolute; that will not yield or compromise; as, *sturdy* defiance, a *sturdy* policy.
2. strong; vigorous; stout; hardy.
3. foolishly obstinate; stupidly hardened. [Obs.]

stũr'dy, *n.* [OFr. *estourdi*, giddiness.] gid, a disease in sheep, characterized by staggering.

stũr'ġeŏn, *n.*; *pl.* **stũr'ġeŏnṣ** or **stũr'ġeŏn,**

STURGEON (*Acipenser sturio*)

[ME. *sturgiun*; OFr. *esturgeon, estourgeon*; LL. *sturionem*, acc. of *sturio*, a sturgeon; Sw. *störa*; G. *stören*, to stir.] any of several large cartilaginous fishes of the genus *Acipenser*, found in northern Europe and North America. They have rows of spiny plates along the body and a projecting snout. Their flesh is valued for food. Caviar is prepared from the roe, and isinglass from the air bladder.

Stū·ri·ō'nēs, *n.pl.* the *Chondrostei*.

Stụrm'äb"tei·lụng (shtoorm'äp"), *n.* [G., lit., storm division, from *sturm*, a storm, and *abteilen*, to divide.] the Storm Troopers, a political militia of the Nazi party, organized about 1923 to keep order at party demonstrations and carry on propaganda by terrorist methods: after the liquidation of its leaders in 1934, it was reorganized to give premilitary and postmilitary indoctrination to German men: also called *Brown Shirts*.

Stụrm ụnd Dräng (shtoorm oont dräng), [G., lit., storm and stress.] a movement in eighteenth-century German literature away from the influence of French neoclassicism: it is the early phase of German romanticism; hence, any period characterized by a violent departure from old ideas and methods.

stũr'noid, *a.* [L. *sturnus*, a starling, and *-oid*.] relating to or like a starling.

stũrt, *v.t.* and *v.i.* to vex; to startle; to trouble. [Scot.]

stũrt, *n.* trouble; vexation; wrath. [Scot.]

stũrt, *n.* in mining, an extraordinary profit made by a tributer by taking the excavation or cutting of a course of ore at a high price. [Brit.]

stũr'tion, *n.* a corruption of *nasturtium*.

stut'tẽr, *v.t.* and *v.i.*; stuttered, *pt., pp.*; stuttering, *ppr.* [D. *stotteren*; L.G. *stötern*; G. *stottern*, to stutter; freq. forms corresponding to ME. and Prov. Eng. *stut*, to stutter, to stagger; Scot. *stot*, to rebound; L.G. *stöten*, to knock; Ice. *stauta*, to strike.] to speak or say with involuntary pauses, spasms, and repetition or prolongation of sounds and syllables, generally as a symptom of some psychic disturbance.

stut'tẽr, *n.* the act or an instance of stuttering.

stut'tẽr·ẽr, *n.* one who stutters.

stut'tẽr·ing, *n.* a hesitation in speaking in which there is a spasmodic and uncontrollable reiteration of the same syllable or sound.

stut'tẽr·ing·ly, *adv.* with stuttering.

stȳ, *n.*; *pl.* **stīeṣ,** [AS. *stīgu*; Ice. *stīa*, a sty.]
1. a pen for pigs.
2. any foul, filthy, or depraved place.

stȳ, *v.t.* and *v.i.*; stied, *pt., pp.*; stying, *ppr.* to lodge in or as in a sty.

stȳ, stȳe, *n.*; *pl.* **stīeṣ,** [from faulty interpretation of obs. *styany* (*styan-eye*) as *sty on eye*, from dial. *styan*, rising; AS. *stigend*, ppr. of *stigan*, to climb, rise.] a small, inflamed swelling of a sebaceous gland on the rim of the eyelid.

stȳ'çȧ, *n.* [AS. *stic, styc.*] an Anglo-Saxon copper coin of small value.

STYCA (front and back)

stȳ'cẽr·in, *n.* a trivalent alcohol obtained by heating a mixture of styryl tribromide and water.

stȳe, *n.* a sty (swelling).

Styġ′i·ăl, *a.* Stygian. [Rare.]

Styġ′i·ăn, *a.* [L. *Stygius*; Gr. *Styx, Stygos*, the Styx, said to mean literally, the Hateful, from *stygein*, to hate.]

1. of or characteristic of the river Styx and the infernal regions.
2. [*also* s–] infernal; dark; gloomy; hellish.
3. [*also* s–] inviolable; completely binding, as an oath sworn by the river Styx.

stȳ″lȧ·gal·mā′iç, *a.* [Gr. *stylos*, a pillar, and *agalma*, a statue.] in architecture, taking the place of a column, as a caryatid.

stȳ′lăr, *a.* of or relating to a style (in various senses): also spelled *stilar*.

Stȳ·las′tẽr, *n.* [Gr. *stylos*, a pillar, and *astēr*, a star.]

1. a genus of polyps of the order *Hydrocorallinæ*.
2. [s–] any polyp of this genus.

stȳ′lāte, *a.* 1. styliform. [Rare.]

2. in botany, having a persistent style.

stȳle, *n.* [ME. *stile*; OFr. *stile, style*, from L. *stilus*, an iron-pointed instrument for writing on wax tablets; also, a manner of writing.]

1. a sharp, slender, pointed instrument of iron or other material, used by the ancients for writing by scratching on wax tablets. One end was blunt and smooth, and was used to make erasures.
2. any of several devices, etc. similar in shape or use; specifically, (a) [Obs.] a pen; (b) an etching needle; (c) a phonograph needle; (d) an engraving tool; (e) the pointer on a dial, chart, etc.; (f) in botany, a small pointed process or part, especially the stalklike part of a pistil between the stigma and the ovary; (g) a hard point for tracing, in manifold writing; (h) a surgical probe; (i) in zoology, a stylus or stylet; a slender process, organ, or part.
3. (a) manner or mode of expression in language; way of putting thoughts into words; (b) specific or characteristic manner of expression, execution, construction, or design, in any art, period, work, employment, etc.; as, the Byzantine *style*, modern *style*.
4. distinction, excellence, originality, and character in any form of artistic or literary expression; as, this author lacks *style*.
5. the way in which anything is made or done; manner.
6. the way in which people of fashionable society dress, speak, conduct themselves, etc.; current and elegant mode.
7. distinction and elegance of manner and bearing.
8. form of address; title; as, he is entitled to the *style* of Mayor.
9. something stylish; especially, a dress, coat, etc. of current, smart design.
10. sort; kind; variety; type.
11. a way of reckoning time, dates, etc.
12. in printing, manner of dealing with spelling, punctuation, word division, etc. of any particular press, publisher, etc.

New Style; see under *new*.
Old Style; see *Old Style* following *old*.

stȳle, *v.t.*; styled, *pt., pp.*; styling, *ppr.* 1. to call; to name; to denominate; to give a title to in addressing.

2. to design the style of.
3. to bring into accord with accepted style, as of a printer; to normalize spelling, punctuation, etc.

stȳle′book, *n.* a book consisting of examples or rules of style (esp. sense 12).

stȳle brȧnch, a branch of the style, as in certain composite flowers.

stȳle sheet, a written or printed sheet of rules, etc., to govern typographical style, as of a book, magazine, or newspaper.

stȳ′let, *n.* [OFr., from It. *stiletto*, a dagger, from L. *stilus*, a pointed instrument.]

1. a slender, pointed weapon; especially, a stiletto.
2. in surgery, a thin probe for examining wounds; also, a wire used to stiffen a flexible catheter.
3. in zoology, a small style; a stiff, pointed process or part.

stȳle′wŏrt, *n.* any plant of the genus *Stylidium* or of the order *Stylidiaceæ*.

stȳ′lī, *n.* obsolete plural of *stylus*.

Stȳ·lid·i·ā′cē·ae, *n.pl.* a family of monopetalous dicotyledons, typified by the genus *Stylidium*; the styleworts.

Stȳ·lid′i·um, *n.* [Gr. *stylos*, a column.]

1. a genus of Australian plants, characterized by a sensitive column which bears the stamens and pistil: when touched at a certain point it throws itself with force from one side of the flower to the other, bursting the anther lobes and scattering the pollen on the stigma.

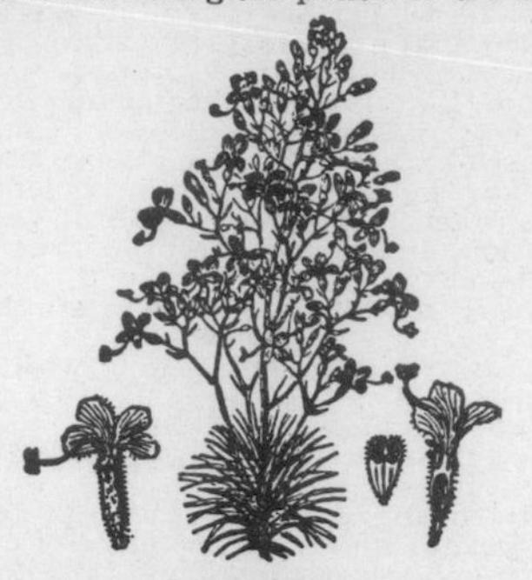

STYLIDIUM
(*Stylidium laricifolium*)

The species are herbaceous plants or small shrubs, with pink, white, violet, or yellow flowers.

2. [s–] any plant of this genus.

stȳ·lif′ẽr·ous, *a.* in botany, bearing styles.

stȳ′li·fọrm, *a.* shaped like a style (instrument).

stȳ′line, *a.* in botany, of or relating to a style.

stȳ′lish, *a.* conforming to current style in dress, decoration, behavior, etc.; being in style; fashionable.

stȳ′lish·ly, *adv.* in a stylish manner.

stȳ′lish·ness, *n.* the quality or condition of being stylish.

stȳ′list, *n.* 1. a writer, speaker, etc. whose work has style (sense 4) or is characterized by a particular style; a master of style.

2. a professional designer or adviser on current styles in clothing, home decorating, furniture, etc.; as, a fashion *stylist*.

stȳ·lis′tiç, stȳ·lis′tiç·ăl, of or relating to style, especially literary style.

stȳ·lis′tiç·ăl·ly, *adv.* with respect to style; in a stylistic fashion.

stȳ′līte, *n.* [Gr. *stylos*, a column.] any of a class of religious ascetics of the early Middle Ages who, by way of penance, lived on the tops of high columns or pillars: also called *pillar saint, pillarist*.

stȳl·i·zā′tion, *n.* a stylizing or being stylized.

stȳl′īze, *v.t.*; stylized, *pt., pp.*; stylizing, *ppr.* to make conform to a given style; specifically, to design or represent according to the rules of a style rather than according to nature; to conventionalize.

stȳ′lō-, [from L. *stylus*, incorrect for *stilus*, pointed instrument.] a combining form meaning *pointed, sharp*, as in *stylo*graph: also, before a vowel, *styl-*.

stȳ′lō·bāte, *n.* [Gr. *stylobatēs*, from *stylos*, a pillar, and *bainein*, to go.] in architecture, a continuous unbroken base or pedestal upon which an entire series of columns stands.

S, STYLOBATE

stȳ·lō·glos′săl, *a.* [*stylo-*, and Gr. *glōssa*, tongue.] of or pertaining to the styloid process and the tongue.

stȳ·lō·glos′săl, *n.* the styloglossus.

stȳ·lō·glos′sus, *n.*; *pl.* **stȳ·lō·glos′sī,** a small muscle arising from the styloid process and attached to the side of the tongue.

stȳ′lō·grȧph, *n.* [*stylo-* and *-graph*.] a fountain pen having a pierced conical point, rather than a nib, through which the ink flows.

stȳ·lō·graph′iç, stȳ·lō·graph′iç·ăl, *a.* 1. of or like a stylograph.

2. of or used in stylography.

stylographic pen; a stylograph.

stȳ·lō·graph′iç·ăl·ly, *adv.* in a stylographic manner; by means of a style.

stȳ·log′rȧ·phy, *n.* the art of tracing with a style; a method of drawing, writing, or engraving with a style or similar instrument.

stȳ·lō·hȳ′ăl, *n.* in zoology and anatomy, one of the bones of the hyoid arch near the proximal extremity of the arch, and above the epihyal.

stȳ·lō·hȳ′oid, *a.* of or pertaining to the styloid process and the hyoid bone.

stȳ·lō·hȳ′oid, *n.* the stylohyoid muscle.

stȳ″lō·hȳ·oi′dē·ăn, *a.* same as *stylohyoid*.

stȳ″lō·hȳ·oi′dē·us, *n.*; *pl.* **stȳ″lō·hȳ·oi′dē·ī,** the stylohyoid muscle.

stȳ′loid, *a.* resembling a style or pen; styliform; specifically, in anatomy, designating or of any of various long, slender processes, especially that at the base of the temporal bone.

styloid process; any of several long, slender processes, as (a) the conical projection behind the head of the fibula; (b) a projection on the outer part of the distal end of the radius; (c) a long spine extending downward from the lower surface of the temporal bone; (d) a projection on the inner side of the distal end of the ulna.

stȳ′lō·līte, *n.* a form of columnar structure with a slightly striated surface forming part of a rock deposit, usually of limestone and occurring transversely to the bedding, perhaps due to unequal pressure.

stȳ·lō·lit′iç, *a.* of, pertaining to, or containing a stylolite or stylolites.

stȳ·lō·mas′toid, *a.* of or pertaining to the styloid and mastoid processes.

stȳ·lō·max′il·lăr·y, *a.* of or pertaining to the styloid process and the lower maxilla.

stȳ·lom′ē·tẽr, *n.* [Gr. *stylos*, column, and *-meter*.] an instrument for the measurement of columns.

Stȳ·lom′mȧ·tȧ, *n.pl.* same as *Stylommatophora*.

Stȳ·lom·mȧ·toph′ō·rȧ, *n.pl.* [Gr. *stylos*, a pillar, *omma* (*-atos*), the eye, and *pherein*, to bear.] a suborder of pulmonate terrestrial mollusks, having two tentacles, usually retractile, with the eyes at the distal end.

stȳ·lom·mȧ·toph′ō·rous, stȳ·lom′mȧ·tous, *a.* 1. having eyes at the top of a horn or tentacle.

2. of or pertaining to the *Stylommatophora*.

stȳ·lō·phar·yn·ġē′ăl, *a.* of or pertaining to the styloid process and the pharynx.

stȳ·lō·phar·yn·ġē′ăl, *n.* the stylopharyngeus.

stȳ″lō·phȧ·ryn′ġē·us, *n.*; *pl.* **stȳ″lō·phȧ·ryn′ġē·ī,** a long, slender muscle having its origin in the styloid process of the temporal bone and connecting with the side of the pharynx.

Stȳ·lop′i·dae, *n.pl.* a family of insects parasitic on hymenopterous insects.

stȳ′lō·pod, *n.* a stylopodium. [Rare.]

stȳ·lō·pō′di·um, *n.*; *pl.* **stȳ·lō·pō′di·ȧ,** [Gr. *stylos*, pillar, and *pous, podos*, foot.] the fleshy support at the base of the style in flowers of the carrot family.

Stȳ′lops, *n.* [Gr. *stylos*, pillar, and *ōps*, eye.]

1. the type genus of the *Stylopidæ*.
2. [s–] an insect of this genus.

stȳ′lō·spōre, *n.* [Gr. *stylos*, a pillar, and *spora*, seed.] a naked spore in certain genera of fungi: so called from its being produced at the tips of short, threadlike cells, or, more rarely, on branched threads. In some genera, as in *Tympanis*, naked spores and asci are produced from the same hymenium.

stȳ·los′pō·rous, *a.* of the nature of or resembling a stylospore.

stȳ·lō·stē′ġi·um, *n.*; *pl.* **stȳ·lō·stē′ġi·ȧ,** [Gr. *stylos*, a pillar, and *stegein*, to cover closely.] in botany, the inner corona covering the style in *Stapelia* and related asclepiads.

stȳ′lō·tȳ·pīte, *n.* [Gr. *stylos*, a pillar, *typos*, type, impression, and *-ite*.] a sulfide of antimony, copper, iron, and silver, closely related to bournonite.

stȳ′lus, *n.* [L. *stylus*, a pointed instrument.]

1. a style or other needlelike marking device.
2. (a) a sharp, pointed device for cutting the grooves of a phonograph record; (b) the needle for reproducing the sound of such a record.
3. in entomology, a small, rigid, bristlelike anal organ; a stylet.
4. a sponge spicule having one sharp and one blunt end.

stȳme, *n.* same as *stime*.

stȳ′mie, *n.* [prob. a use of earlier Scot. *stymie*, a person partially blind, from *styme*; ME. *stime*, in the phr. *not able to see a stime*, not able to see at all: the reference is to the blind shot caused by a stymie.]

1. in golf, the condition that exists on a putting green when an opponent's ball lies in a direct line between the player's ball and the hole.
2. a golf ball lying in such a position.

Also spelled *stimy, stymy*.

stȳ′mie, *v.t.*; stymied, *pt., pp.*; stymieing, *ppr.* 1. to hinder or obstruct as with a stymie.

2. to check or block; to offer opposition to.

Also spelled *stimy, stymy*.

Stym·phā′li·ăn, *a.* of or pertaining to Stymphalus, the ancient name of a valley, lake, river, and town in Arcadia, Greece.

Stymphalian birds; in Greek mythology, birds of prey which infested Stymphalus, having wings, beaks, and claws of iron. The destruction or expulsion of these birds constituted one of the labors of Hercules. Also called *Stymphalides*.

stȳ′my, *n.*; *pl.* **stȳ′mieṣ,** a stymie.

stȳ′my, *v.t.*; stymied, *pt.*, *pp.*; stymying, *ppr.* to stymie.

Stȳ·phē′li·ȧ, *n.* [Gr. *styphelos*, solid, hard, rough.] a genus of shrubs of the family *Epacridaceæ*, having a one-sided ovary and fruit.

styph′nāte, *n.* a salt of styphnic acid.

styph′niç, *a.* [Gr. *styphein*, to draw together.] of, pertaining to, or forming a dibasic acid, $C_6H_3N_3O_8$, produced by the action of nitric acid on resorcinol and many gum resins, or by boiling extract of logwood, brazilwood, etc. with nitric acid.

styp′sis, *n.* [LL.; Gr. *stypsis*.] the action or use of a styptic.

styp′tiç, styp′tiç·ăl, *a.* [Fr. *styptique*; L. *stypticus*; Gr. *styptikos*, astringent, from *styphein*, to draw together, contract.] tending to halt bleeding by contracting the tissues or blood vessels; astringent.

styp′tiç, *n.* any styptic substance.

styp′tiç bũr, a perennial, verbenaceous herb, *Priva echinata*, native to Florida and the West Indies: the calyx is covered with hooked hairs.

styp′ti·cine, *n.* a yellow crystalline substance, $C_{12}H_{15}O_4N \cdot HCl$, used medicinally for its styptic properties.

styp·tic′i·ty, *n.* the quality of being styptic; astringency.

styp′tiç pen′cil, a small stick of a styptic substance used to stop bleeding, as from surface nicks or cuts.

styp′tiç weed, a tall herb, *Cassia occidentalis*, native to the tropics of America and the southern part of the United States: so called because the leaves are used in dressing slight wounds.

Stȳ·rȧ·çā′cē·ae, *n.pl.* a small family of trees and shrubs found in the temperate and tropical parts of North and South America, and also in Nepal and China. They have a fleshy or dry fruit and clusters of flowers, usually white, whose petals are united all around. They furnish the storax and benzoin of commerce, and some of the species are used for dyeing yellow. The family includes the snowdrop tree of North America, *Halesia tetraptera*.

stȳ·rȧ·çā′ceous, *a.* of, pertaining to, or belonging to the *Styracaceæ*.

styr′ȧ·cin, styr′ȧ·cine, *n.* a crystalline substance extracted by means of alcohol, ether, etc. from storax, of which it is the chief constituent. It is neutral and has the properties of a resin.

stȳ′rȧ·çol, *n.* an antiseptic substance used medicinally in intestinal catarrh and in tuberculosis.

Stȳ′rax, *n.* [Gr., a fragrant gum; also, the tree producing it.]

1. the type genus of the *Styracaceæ*, native to America and Asia; one species is also found in Europe, and one in Africa. *Styrax officinalis*, or officinal storax, is native to Syria, Italy, and most parts of the Levant. It yields the storax of commerce and is used in medicine. *Styrax benzoin*, the gum-benjamin tree, is native to Sumatra and Java and yields the benzoin of commerce.

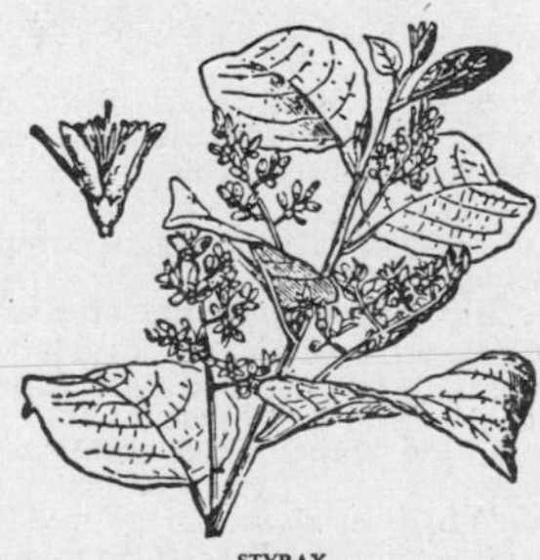

STYRAX
(*Styrax benzoin*)

2. [s–] any plant or flower of this genus; also, storax.

stȳ′rēne, *n.* a colorless or yellowish, aromatic liquid, $C_6H_5CH \cdot CH_2$, used in organic synthesis, especially in the manufacture of synthetic rubber.

stȳ′rol, *n.* same as *styrene*.

stȳ′rō·lēne, *n.* same as *styrene*.

stȳ′rōne, *n.* a crystalline compound, $C_9H_{10}O$, of fragrant odor and sweet taste, derived from styracin which has been acted upon by caustic potash: also called *styryl alcohol*.

stȳ′ryl, *n.* cinnamyl.

styryl alcohol; see *styrone*.

stȳthe, *n.* choke damp. [Brit. Dial.]

styth′y, *n.* and *v.t.* same as *stithy*.

Styx, *n.* [L., from Gr. *Styx*, lit., the Hateful, from *stygein*, to hate.] in Greek mythology, the river encircling the lower world, across which dead souls were ferried by Charon.

sū·ȧ·bil′i·ty, *n.* liability to be sued; the state of being subject by law to civil process.

sū′ȧ·ble, *a.* liable to be sued; subject by law to be called to answer in court.

suāde, *v.t.* to persuade. [Obs.]

suād′i·ble, *a.* suasible. [Obs.]

Sū·ae′dȧ, *n.* [name from the Ar.] the type genus of the *Suædeæ*. There are about forty-five species, widely distributed. They are saline herbs or shrubs with semicylindrical leaves, generally perfect flowers, and five-partite calyxes, usually fleshy.

Sū·ae′dē·ae, *n.pl.* a suborder of apetalous plants of the order *Chenopodiaceæ*.

suāġe, *v.t.* to assuage. [Obs.]

sū′ănt, *a.* [Fr. *suivant*, from *suivre*, to follow.]

1. even; uniform; spread equally over the surface. [U.S. and Brit. Dial.]

2. following; pursuant. [U.S. and Brit. Dial.]

sū′ănt, *n.* the plaice. [Brit. Dial.]

sū′ănt·ly, *adv.* evenly; smoothly. [U.S. and Brit. Dial.]

sụ·ar′rōw, *n.* same as *souari*.

sụ·ar′rōw nut, same as *souari nut*.

suā′si·ble, *a.* persuasible.

suā′sion, *n.* the act or effort of persuading: chiefly used in the phrase *moral suasion*.

suā′sive, *a.* persuasive.

suā′sive·ly, *adv.* in a persuasive manner; so as to persuade.

suā′sō·ry, *a.* tending to persuade; persuasive. [Rare.]

suȧs′ti·kȧ, *n.* variant of *swastika*.

suäve (*or* swāv), *a.* [Fr., sweet, pleasant, from L. *suavis*, sweet.] smoothly gracious or polite; polished; blandly ingratiating; urbane.

suäve′ly, *adv.* in a suave manner.

suäv′i·fy, *v.t.*; suavified, *pt.*, *pp.*; suavifying, *ppr.* to make suave. [Rare.]

suȧ·vil′ō·quent, *a.* speaking suavely, blandly, or affably; using soft and agreeable speech. [Rare.]

suäv′i·ty, *n.* [Fr. *suavité*; L. *suavitas* (*-atis*), sweetness, pleasantness, from *suavis*, sweet, pleasant.]

1. sweetness to the taste. [Obs.]

2. the quality of being suave; graciousness and pleasantness of manner; affability; blandness; as, *suavity* of conversation, *suavity* of manner.

3. *pl.* **suäv′i·tieṣ,** a suave action, speech, etc.

sub, *n. a contracted form of* sublieutenant, submarine, subordinate, subscription, substitute, and other words beginning with *sub-*. [Colloq.]

sub, *v.i.* subbed, *pt.*, *pp.*; subbing, *ppr.* to be a substitute (*for* someone). [Colloq.]

sub-, [L., from *sub*, under, below.]

a prefix meaning:

1. *under, beneath, below*, as in *sub*marine, *sub*soil.

2. *lower in rank* or *position than, inferior* or *subordinate to*, as in *sub*altern, *sub*agent.

3. *to a lesser degree than, somewhat, slightly*, as in *sub*human, *sub*tropical, *sub*conscious.

4. (a) *so as to form a division into smaller* or *less important parts*, as in *sub*let, *sub*divide; (b) *forming such a division*, as in *sub*section, *sub*division.

5. in chemistry, (a) *with less than the normal amount of* (the specified substance), as in *sub*chloride; (b) *basic*, as in *sub*carbonate.

6. in mathematics, *designating a ratio inverse to a given ratio*, as in *sub*duplicate. In words of Latin origin, *sub-* assimilates to *suc-* before *c*, as in *suc*ceed; *suf-* before *f*, as in *suf*fer; *sug-* before *g*, as in *sug*gest; *sum-* before *m*, as in *sum*mon; *sup-* before *p*, as in *sup*plant; *sur-* before *r*, as in *sur*render: *sub-* often changes to *sus-* before *c*, *p*, and *t*, as in *sus*tain, *sus*pend.

Below is a list of words whose meanings are self-evident, the prefix *sub-* signifying either *subordinate, secondary*, or *not quite, nearly*. Words formed with *sub-* which have special meanings will be found defined in their proper order in the vocabulary.

subacidulous
subacrid
subacuminate
subacutely
subaduncate
subadvocate
subagency
subalate
subalmoner
subangled
subangular
subangulate
subarborescent
subarcuate
subassociation
subastringent
subbeadle
subbrigadier
subcalcareous
subcarbureted
subcircular
subcolumnar
subcommission
subcommissioner
subcompressed
subconcave
subconchoidal
subconformable
subconical
subconnate
subconstellation
subcontiguous
subcontinuous
subconvex
subcordate
subcrescentic
subcrystalline
subcylindric
subcylindrical
subdentate
subdepressed
subdialect
subdichotomy
subdilated
subdistinction
subdistrict
subdivine
subelliptic
subelliptical
subelongate
subemarginate
subentry
subequal
subequilateral
suberect
subfactor
subfalcate
subfalciform
subfastigiate
subfebrile
subfibrous
subflavor
subflexuose
subflora
subform
subfusiform
subgelatinous
subgeniculate
subglabrous
subglobose
subglobular
subglobulose
subglumaceous
subgovernor
subgranular
subhexagonal
subicteric
subimbricate
subimpressed
subindividual
subinflammation
subinflammatory
subinspector
subinspectorship
subinvoluted
sublanate
sublanceolate
sublecturer
sublessee
sublessor
sublibrarian
sublimitation
sublinear
sublunate
submarshal
submaster
submedial
submembranous
submetallic
submiliary
subminimal
submucronate
subnarcotic
subnatural
subnude
subnumber
subobscure
subobtuse
subofficer
subopposite
suborbicular
suborbiculate
suboval
subovate
subovoid
subpalmate
subparallel
subpectinate
subpellucid
subpentangular
subpermanent
subpilose
subplantigrade
subpolygonal
subporphyritic
subprehensile
subprimary
subprovince
subpubescent
subpurchaser
subpyriform
subquadrangular
subquadrate
subquinquefid
subrectangular
subrector
subreniform
subrhomboidal
subrigid
subrotund
subsaline
subsaturated
subsaturation
subsensation
subserrate
subsessile
subsimious
subsphere
subspherical
subspherically
substriate
subtepid
subterminal
subtranslucent
subtransparent
subtransverse
subtriangular
subtrifid
subtrihedral
subtutor
subtypical
subumbellate
subuncinate
subvermiform
subvertical
subverticillate
subvesicular
subvitreous
subworker

sub·ac′ē·tāte, *n.* a basic acetate.

sub·ac′id, *a.* [*sub-*, and L. *acidus*, sour, acid.]

1. somewhat sour or acid; as, *subacid* wine.

2. slightly sharp or biting, as a remark.

sub·ȧ·cid′i·ty, *n.* the character of being subacid; also, that which is subacid.

sub·ȧ·çrō′mi·ăl, *a.* situated under the acromion.

sub·açt′, *v.t.* to subdue; to reduce. [Obs.]

sub·aç′tion, *n.* the act or process of reducing to any state, as of mixing two bodies completely, or beating anything to a powder. [Obs.]

sub·ȧ·cūte′, *a.* between acute and chronic with reference to duration: said of a disease.

sub·ā·ēr′i·ăl, *a.* being or lying under the air or sky; in geology, taking place or produced in the open air or at the earth's surface; as, *subaerial* erosion.

sub·ā′ġent, *n.* a person representing an agent; the agent of an agent.

sub·aġ·i·tā′tion, *n.* sexual intercourse. [Obs.]

sụ′bȧh, *n.* [Anglo-Ind.] a former state or province in India; also, a subahdar.

sụ·bȧh·där′, *n.* [Anglo-Ind.] formerly, the governor of a subah; also, a native who had a rank equivalent to captain in the British native army in India.

sụ·bȧh·där′y, sụ′bȧh·ship, *n.* the position, office, or jurisdiction of a subahdar.

sub·āid′, *v.t.* to aid secretly. [Rare.]

sub·al′pīne, *a.* 1. designating or of regions at the foot of the Alps.
 2. designating or of mountain regions at an altitude of between four and six thousand feet, below the timber line.

sub·ąl′tērn, *a.* [Fr. *subalterne*; LL. *subalternus*, subordinate; L. *sub-*, and *alternus*, alternate.]
 1. subordinate; of lower rank.
 2. holding an army commission below that of captain. [Chiefly Brit.]
 3. in logic, particular, with reference to a universal of which it is part.

sub·ąl′tērn, *n.* 1. a subordinate.
 2. a subaltern officer. [Chiefly Brit.]
 3. in logic, a subaltern proposition.

sub·ąl·tēr′nănt, *n.* in logic, a universal.

sub·ąl′tēr·nāte, *a.* 1. successive; succeeding by turns.
 2. in an alternate arrangement, but tending to become opposite: said of leaves.
 3. inferior; subaltern. [Obs.]

sub·ąl′tēr·nāte, *n.* in logic, a particular.

sub·ąl′tēr·nā·ting, *a.* succeeding by turns; successive.

sub·ąl·tēr·nā′tion, *n.* the condition of being subalternate.

sub·ant·ärc′tiç, *a.* designating or of the area surrounding the Antarctic Circle.

Sub-Ap′en·nīne, *a.* under or at the foot of the Apennine mountains: applied to a series of Tertiary strata of the older Pliocene period.

sub·ap′iç·ăl, *a.* situated under the apex.

sub″ap·os·tol′iç, *a.* relating to the period immediately after that of the Apostles.

sub·ȧ·quat′iç, *a.* partly aquatic.

sub·ā′quē·ous, *a.* [*sub-*, and L. *aqua*, water.]
 1. being or living under water or beneath the surface of water.
 2. adapted for use under water.
 3. in geology, formed under water; as, *subaqueous* strata.

sub·ȧ·rach′noid, *a.* in anatomy, situated or occurring beneath the arachnoid.

sub″ar·ach·noid′ăl, sub″ar·ach·noid′ē·ăn, *a.* subarachnoid.

sub·ärc′tiç, *a.* designating the region or climate immediately surrounding the Arctic Circle.

sub·ar′id, *a.* slightly arid; moderately dry.

sub·ar·rhā′tion (-rā′), *n.* [LL. *subarrare*, to betroth.] the ancient custom of betrothing by the bestowal, on the part of the man, of marriage gifts or tokens, as money, rings, or other articles, upon the woman.

sub·as′trăl, *a.* beneath the stars or heavens; terrestrial.

sub·at′ŏm, *n.* a constituent part of an atom.

sub·ȧ·tom′iç, *a.* of or pertaining to the inner part of an atom or to a particle smaller than an atom.

sub·ąud′, *v.t.* to understand or supply (the necessary words) mentally when an ellipsis occurs. [Rare.]

sub·ąu·di′tion (-dish′un), *n.* [L. *subauditio* (*-onis*), from *subaudire*, to understand or supply a word omitted; *sub-*, and L. *audire*, to hear.] the act of understanding or mentally supplying something not expressed; also, that which is understood or inferred from what is expressed.

sub·ąu·riç′ū·lăr, *a.* situated below the auricle of the ear.

sub·ax′il·lăr·y, *a.* 1. in botany, placed under the axil or angle formed by the branch of a plant with the stem, or by a leaf with the branch.
 2. in anatomy, situated below the armpit.

sub·bās′ăl, *a.* in zoology, situated close to the base.

sub′bāse, *n.* in architecture, the lowest horizontal section of a base consisting of more than one layer.

sub′bāse·ment, *n.* any floor or room below a basement.

sub′bȧss, *n.* in music, the deepest pedal stop of 16 or 32 feet, producing the lowest notes of an organ: also called *subbourdon*.

sub·bōur′dŏn, *n.* same as *subbass*.

sub·brach′i·ăl, *a.* and *n.* same as *subbrachiate*.

Sub·brach·i·ā′lēş, *n.pl.* the *Subbrachiati*.

sub·brach′i·āte, *a.* pertaining to or characteristic of the *Subbrachiati*.

sub·brach′i·āte, *n.* a member of the *Subbrachiati*.

Sub·brach·i·ā′tī, *n.pl.* [*sub-*, and L. *brachiatus*, with branches like arms, from *brachium*, an arm.] an order of fishes characterized by soft fins and having the ventrals under the pectorals.

sub′brȧnch, *n.* a division of a branch.

sub′breed, *n.* a distinctly marked subdivision of a breed; an incipient breed.

sub·bron′chi·ăl, *a.* situated under the bronchi, as the air sacs in birds.

sub·cal′i·bēr, *a.* 1. smaller than the caliber of the firearm from which it is fired: said of a projectile fired through a tube of proper caliber inserted in the barrel.
 2. of or having to do with a subcaliber projectile.

Sub″cär·bŏn·if′ēr·ous, *n.* the lower division of the Carboniferous series; the Mississippian.

Sub″cär·bŏn·if′ēr·ous, *a.* of or pertaining to the Subcarboniferous.

sub″cär·ti·laġ′i·nous, *a.* 1. partially cartilaginous.
 2. situated under or beneath cartilage.

sub·çąu′dăl, *a.* situated beneath the tail; as, the *subcaudal* plates of a snake.

sub·cē·les′tiăl, *a.* 1. beneath the heavens; terrestrial.
 2. mundane.
 3. in astronomy, situated exactly beneath the zenith.

sub·cē·les′tiăl, *n.* a subcelestial being.

sub′cel″lăr, *n.* a cellar beneath another cellar.

sub·cen′trăl, *a.* 1. being under the center.
 2. almost central.

sub·chȧnt′ēr, *n.* an underchanter; a succentor.

sub·chē′lȧ, *n.*; *pl.* **sub·chē′lae,** a terminal claw of a crustacean that bends like a hook on the joint to which it is articulated.

sub·chē′lāte, *a.* not completely chelate.

sub·chē′li·fọrm, *a.* subchelate.

sub·chlō′rīde, *n.* a chloride containing a relatively small proportion of chlorine.

sub·cinç·tō′ri·um, *n.* same as *succinctorium*.

sub′clȧss, *n.* a subdivision of a class.

sub·clā′vāte, *a.* shaped somewhat like a club; slightly clavate.

sub·clā′vi·ăn, *a.* situated under the clavicle, or collarbone; as, the *subclavian* arteries.
 subclavian groove; either of two grooves in the first rib, one for the main artery (*subclavian artery*) and the other for the main vein (*subclavian vein*) of the arm.

sub·clā′vi·ăn, *n.* a subclavian vein, artery, etc.

sub·clin′i·căl, *a.* without clinical symptoms, as a disease in its early stages.

sub′cŏm·mit·tee, *n.* a subordinate committee chosen from the members of a main committee.

sub·com′pact, *n.* a small, light, economical model of automobile.

sub″con·junç·tī′văl, *a.* beneath the conjunctiva.

sub·con′scious (-shus), *a.* 1. occurring without conscious perception, or with only slight perception, on the part of the individual: said of mental processes and reactions.
 2. not fully conscious; imperfectly aware.

sub·con′scious, *n.* that portion of mental activity of which the individual has little or no conscious perception.

sub·con′scious·ness, *n.* 1. the subconscious.
 2. a subconscious quality or condition.

sub·con′ti·nent, *n.* a large land mass, smaller than that usually called a continent.

sub·con′tract, *n.* a secondary contract undertaking some of the obligations of a primary or previous contract: construction companies often let *subcontracts* for the electrical work, plumbing, etc. in a new building.

sub·cŏn·tract′, *v.t.* and *v.i.* to make a subcontract (for).

sub·cŏn·tract′ed, *a.* 1. contracted under a subcontract.
 2. betrothed a second time. [Obs.]
 3. in entomology, slightly narrowed: said of wing cells.

sub·cŏn·tract′ŏr, *n.* one who contracts to fulful a part or the whole of a contract made by a principal contractor.

sub·con′trăr·y, *a.* 1. contrary in an inferior degree.
 2. in earlier geometry, designating two triangles having a common angle at the vertex but nonparallel bases, the angles at the bases being equal but on contrary sides.
 3. in logic, designating (a) either of two particular propositions when one is affirmative and the other negative; as, some *x* is *y* and some *x* is not *y* are subcontraries to all *x* is *y* and no *x* is *y*; (b) the relation between two attributes which coexist in the same substance, yet in such a way that the more there is of one the less there is of the other.

sub·con′trăr·y, *n.*; *pl.* **sub·con′trăr·ieş,** in logic, a subcontrary proposition.

sub·cor′ȧ·coid, *a.* beneath the coracoid.

sub·cor′nē·ous, *a.* 1. somewhat horny.
 2. beneath a horn or a horny part or layer.

sub·cor′ti·căl, *a.* beneath the cortex.

sub·cos′tȧ, *n.*; *pl.* **sub·cos′tae,** a subcostal vein or nervure of an insect's wing.

sub·cos′tăl, *a.* situated under or between the ribs.

sub·cos′tăl, *n.* 1. a subcostal muscle.
 2. in entomology, a subcostal vein or nervure.

sub·crā′ni·ăl, *a.* under the cranium or skull.

sub·crē′nāte, *a.* partially or slightly crenate.

sub·crust′ăl, *a.* in geology, being beneath the crust of the earth.

sub′cul″tūre, *n.* 1. (a) a group (within a society) of persons of the same age, social or economic status, ethnic background, etc. and having its own interests, goals, etc.; (b) the distinct cultural patterns of such a group.
 2. a culture, as of bacteria, grown on a fresh medium from a previous culture.

sub·cū·tā′nē·ous, *a.* being, used, or introduced beneath the skin.

sub·cū·tā′nē·ous·ly, *adv.* in a subcutaneous manner; hypodermically.

sub·cū·tiç′ū·lăr, *a.* being under the cuticle or scarfskin.

sub·cū′tis, *n.* the deeper portion of the true skin; the inner portion of the cutis.

sub·dēa′cŏn, *n.* a minister ranking next below a deacon; specifically, in the Roman Catholic Church, one who serves as a second deacon or attendant, as to the celebrant at Mass.

sub·dēa′cŏn·ry, *n.* subdeaconship.

sub·dēa′cŏn·ship, *n.* the order and office of subdeacon in the Roman Catholic Church.

sub′dēan, *n.* an underdean; a dean's substitute.

sub·dēan′ēr·y, *n.* the office or rank of subdean.

sub·deb′, *n.* 1. a girl in the years just preceding her debut into society.
 2. any girl of such age.

sub·deb′, *a.* of or suitable for a subdeb.

sub·deç′ȧ·năl, *a.* relating to a subdean or subdeanery.

sub·deç′ū·ple, *a.* containing one part of ten.

sub·dent′ed, *a.* indented beneath.

sub·dē·pärt′ment, *n.* a division of a department.

sub·dē·poş′it, *n.* that which is deposited beneath something else.

sub·dē·riv′ȧ·tive, *n.* a word derived from a derivative; as, "honorableness" is a *subderivative* from "honorable," the derivative of "honor."

sub·dī·aç′ō·nāte, *a.* relating to a subdeacon; as, *subdiaconate* duties.

sub·dī·aç′ō·nāte, *n.* the office of a subdeacon.

sub·di·vīde′, *v.t.* and *v.i.*; subdivided, *pt.*, *pp.*; subdividing, *ppr.* 1. to divide further after previous division has been made.
 2. to divide (land) into small parcels for ready sale.

sub·di·viş′i·ble, *a.* that can be subdivided.

sub·di·vi′şiŏn (-vizh′un), *n.* 1. a subdividing or being subdivided.
 2. the part of a thing made by subdividing; the part of a larger part.

sub′dō·lous, *a.* sly; crafty; cunning; artful; deceitful. [Rare.]

sub·dom′i·nănt, *n.* in music, the fourth tone of a diatonic scale; the tone next below the dominant.

sub·dū′ȧ·ble, *a.* that can be subdued.

sub·dū′ăl, *n.* the act of subduing; also, the state of being subdued.

sub·dūce′, *v.t.*; subduced (-dūst′), *pt., pp.*; subducing, *ppr.* [L. *subductus*, pp. of *subducere*, to draw or lead away; *sub-*, and *ducere*, to draw, lead.]

1. to withdraw; to take away. [Obs.]

2. to subtract by arithmetical operation. [Obs.]

sub·duçt′, *v.t.* and *v.i.* to withdraw; to subtract; to take away.

sub·duç′tion, *n.* 1. the act of taking away or withdrawing.

2. arithmetical subtraction.

sub·dūe′, *v.t.*; subdued, *pt., pp.*; subduing, *ppr.* [ME. *soduen, subduen*; OFr. *souduire*, to seduce, to subdue, from L. *subducere*, to draw away, remove; hence, to carry off, to overpower.]

1. to conquer; to bring into subjection; to vanquish; as, Caesar *subdued* the Gauls.

2. to tame; to make submissive, as by training; as, to *subdue* a stubborn child.

3. to reduce to mildness; to repress; as, to *subdue* the temper or passions.

4. to overcome by persuasion or other mild means; as, to *subdue* opposition by argument or entreaties.

5. to captivate, as by charms.

6. to make less intense or less harsh; to soften, as a tone or color.

7. to destroy the force of; to lower; as, medicines *subdue* a fever.

8. to till or cultivate (land).

sub·dūed′, *a.* 1. conquered; brought under subjection.

2. soft or softened, as color or tone.

sub·dūe′ment, *n.* a conquest. [Rare.]

sub·dū′ẽr, *n.* one who or that which subdues; one who conquers and brings into subjection; a conqueror; a tamer.

sub·dū′răl, *a.* in anatomy, situated beneath the dura.

sub·ed′it, *v.t.* to edit under the direction of a chief editor or general editor.

sub·ed′it·ŏr, *n.* an assistant editor.

sub″em·ployed′, *a.* designating or of those workers who are unemployed or employed at wages below a subsistence level.

sub″em·ploy′ment, *n.* the state of being subemployed.

sub″en·dō·çăr′di·ăl, *a.* beneath the endocardium.

sub·en′dy·măl, *a.* situated under the ependyma.

sub·en·tīre′, *a.* in botany, not quite entire; slightly toothed.

sub″ep·i·dẽr′măl, *a.* lying immediately under the epidermis; as, *subepidermal* layers of cellular tissue.

sub″ep·i·glot′tiç, *a.* lying under the epiglottis.

sub″ep·i·thē′li·ăl, *a.* lying under the epithelium.

sū′bẽr, *n.* same as *cork*, sense 2.

sū′bẽr·āte, *n.* a salt of suberic acid.

sū·bē′rē·ous, *a.* of the nature of cork; relating to cork.

sū·ber′iç, *a.* [L. *suber*, the cork tree.] pertaining to cork, or extracted from it; as, *suberic* acid.

suberic acid; an acid, $C_8H_{14}O_4$, produced by treating rasped cork with nitric acid: it is soluble in boiling water, alcohol, and ether, fuses at about 300° F., and sublimes in acicular crystals.

sū′bẽr·in, sū′bẽr·ine, *n.* a waxy or fatty substance contained in cork.

sū′bẽr·īte, *n.* [L. *suber*, the cork oak.] a sponge of the genus *Suberites*.

sū″bẽr·i·zā′tion, *n.* in botany, a suberizing or being suberized.

sū′bẽr·īze, *v.t.*; suberized, *pt., pp.*; suberizing, *ppr.* in botany, to change into cork by the formation of suberin in the cell walls.

sū′bẽr·ōne, *n.* a ketone, $C_{14}H_{24}O_2$, of suberic acid, obtained as an aromatic liquid.

sū′bẽr·ōse, *a.* 1. in botany, having the appearance of being gnawed, or slightly eaten.

2. corklike in appearance; suberized.

sū′bẽr·ous, *a.* of or like cork; suberose.

sub″ē·sō·phaġ′ē·ăl, *a.* in zoology, located under the esophagus.

subesophageal ganglion; a large ganglion found under the esophagus of certain invertebrates, as annelids and arthropods.

sub′fam″i·ly, *n.* any of the main subdivisions of a family of plants or animals.

sub·feū′, *v.t.* [*sub-* and *feu*, for *feud*.] in feudal law, to underlet or sublet; to make subinfeudation of; as, a vassal *subfeued* his lands.

sub·feū′dȧ·tō·ry, *n.* an inferior tenant who held a feud from a feudatory of the crown or other superior.

sub·flū′vi·ăl, *a.* 1. in geology, deposited in the bed of a river.

2. located beneath a stream, as a tunnel.

sub·fos′sil, *a.* of or pertaining to remains only partially fossilized.

sub′freez′ing, *a.* below freezing.

sub·fus′çous, *a.* subfusk.

sub·fusk′, *a.* duskish; moderately dark; brownish; tawny. [Rare.]

sub·ġē·ner′iç, *a.* pertaining to a subgenus.

sub·ġē′nus, *n.*; *pl.* **sub·ġen′ẽr·ȧ, sub·ġē′nus·eş,** a main subdivision of a genus of plants or animals.

sub·ġẽr′mi·năl, *a.* situated under the germ or embryo.

sub·glā′ciăl (-shăl), *a.* found or formerly deposited at the bottom of a glacier.

sub·glos′săl, *a.* sublingual.

sub·glot′tiç, *a.* located or occurring under the glottis.

sub′grāde, *n.* the surface or grade of a foundation layer, as for a street or sidewalk.

sub′group, *n.* a subdivision of a group, especially of a group in the periodic table of chemical elements.

sub′gum′, *a.* [Cantonese, lit., mixed vegetables.] designating any of various Chinese or Chinese-American dishes, as chow mein, prepared with water chestnuts, mushrooms, etc.

sub·has·tā′tion, *n.* [L. *subhastatio* (*-onis*), from *subhastare*, to sell by public auction; *sub-*, and *hasta*, a spear.] a public sale of property to the highest bidder; a sale by auction: so called from the Roman practice of planting a spear on the spot where a public sale was to take place. [Obs.]

sub′head (-hed), *n.* 1. the title of a subdivision of a chapter, article, etc.

2. a subordinate heading or title, as of a newspaper article.

3. the assistant to the head of a school, etc.

sub·head′ing, *n.* a subhead (senses 1 and 2).

sub·hē·pat′iç, *a.* situated beneath the liver or hepatic region.

sub·hū′măn, *a.* 1. below the human race in development; less than human.

2. nearly human.

sub·hū′mẽr·āte, *v.t.* to carry by placing on one's shoulders [Obs.]

sub·hy′ȧ·loid, *a.* in anatomy, occurring beneath the hyaloid membrane.

sub·hy·mē′ni·ăl, *a.* in botany, situated beneath the hymenium.

subhymenial layer; in some fungi, the layer of hyphal tissue below the hymenium; the subhymenium.

sub·hy·mē′ni·um, *n.* a subhymenial layer; a hypothecium.

sub·hy′oid, *a.* 1. lying under the hyoid bone; as, the *subhyoid* or cervical arch.

2. occurring after the hyoid arch, as the first branchial arch proper or the fourth visceral arch.

sub·i·mā′gō, *n.* in the development of insects, an incomplete winged state between the pupa and the imago in which the insect is able to fly but has to shed another skin.

sub·in′dex, *n.*; *pl.* **sub·in′di·çēş,** in mathematics, a figure or sign placed after and under a character to distinguish it from others; thus: A_1,bx.

sub·in′di·çāte, *v.t.*; subindicated, *pt., pp.*, subindicating, *ppr.* to indicate by signs; to indicate in a less degree or secondarily; to hint. [Rare.]

sub·in·di·çā′tion, *n.* the act of indicating by signs; a slight indication. [Rare.]

sub·in·dūce′, *v.t.* to insinuate; to suggest; to offer or bring into consideration indirectly. [Rare.]

sub·in·fẽr′, *v.t.* to infer or deduce from an inference already made. [Obs.]

sub·in·feū·dā′tion, *n.* 1. the transfer of feudal lands by a vassal lord to a subtenant with all the original privileges and responsibilities falling to the new holder.

2. tenure so established.

3. the lands or fief so held.

sub·in·feū′dȧ·tō·ry, *n.* a tenant by subinfeudation.

sub·in·gres′sion (-gresh′un), *n.* a subtle entrance. [Rare.]

sub·in·tes′ti·năl, *a.* occurring beneath an intestine.

sub·in·vō·lū′tion, *n.* an incomplete involution or return to normal dimensions.

sub·ir′ri·gāte, *v.t.* to irrigate (land) by a system of underground pipes.

sub·i·tā′nē·ous, *a.* sudden; hasty.

sub·i·tā′nē·ous·ness, *n.* suddenness.

sub′i·tā·ny, *a.* hasty; sudden. [Obs.]

sū′bi·tō, *adv.* in music, quickly; suddenly: a direction to the performer; as, volti *subito*, turn (the leaf) quickly.

sub·jā′cen·cy, *n.* a subjacent condition.

sub·jā′cent, *a.* [L. *subjacens* (*-entis*), ppr. of *subjacere*, to lie under; *sub-*, and *jacere*, to lie.]

1. lying directly under or below; underlying.

2. being in a lower situation, though not directly beneath.

sub′jeçt, *a.* [ME. *suget*, OFr. *sujet, suject, subject*, from L. *subjectus*, subject, pp. of *subjicere*, to place under, put under, subject.]

1. placed or situated under. [Obs.]

2. being under the power and dominion of, or owing allegiance to, another.

3 exposed; liable to receive (with *to*); as, a country *subject to* extreme heat or cold; a person *subject to* attacks of fever.

4. liable; having a disposition or tendency (with *to*); as, *subject to* criticism.

5. contingent or conditional upon (with *to*); as, it is *subject to* my approval.

6. submissive; obedient.

sub′jeçt, *n.* 1. one who or that which is under the power, control, influence, observation, or action of some other person or thing, especially a person who owes allegiance to a ruler, government, etc.; as, a *subject* of a king, or of a government.

2. that which is treated or handled in discussion, study, writing, painting, etc.; a theme, a topic; as, a *subject* of discussion, a *subject* of negotiation, the *subject* of a song or of a biography.

3. in music, the principal melody or theme of a movement or composition.

4. any of the various courses of study in a school or college; a branch of learning; as, mathematics is my favorite *subject*.

5. in grammar, the word or group of words in a sentence about which something is said and which serves as the starting point of the action except in passive constructions: subjects are nouns or pronouns or other words functioning as nouns or pronouns.

6. in logic, that term of a proposition concerning which anything is affirmed or denied.

7. in philosophy, that in which any characteristics inhere; a thing considered as apart from its attributes or qualities; hence, the ego; the thinking agent; the self, or personality of the thinker, as distinguished from everything outside of the mind.

8. that on which or the one on whom any operation or experiment is performed; hence, one susceptible to an action or influence, as (a) in anatomy, a dead body for the purposes of dissection; (b) a person used in experimental hypnotism; (c) a person affected by disease or susceptible to it.

9. one who or that which is the cause or occasion of something; reason; as, she was the *subject* of the outcry.

sub·jeçt′, *v.t.*; subjected, *pt., pp.*; subjecting, *ppr.* 1. to place under or below. [Obs.]

2. to place before; to submit; as, a plan *subjected* for approval. [Rare.]

3. to bring under the authority or control of; to cause to owe allegiance.

4. to cause to have a disposition or tendency; to expose (with *to*); as, his weakness *subjected* him to many diseases.

5. to cause to undergo or experience some action or treatment (with *to*); as, they *subjected* him to indignities.

sub·jeçt′, *v.i.* to be or become subject.

sub·jeç′tion, *n.* a subjecting or being subjected.

sub′jeçt·ist, *n.* a subjectivist.

sub·jeç′tive, *a.* [L. *subjectivus*.]

1. of, affected by, or produced by the mind or a particular state of mind; of or resulting from the feelings or temperament of the subject, or person thinking, rather than the attributes of the object thought of; as, a *subjective* judgment.

2. determined by and emphasizing the ideas, thoughts, feelings, etc. of the artist, writer, or speaker.

3. in grammar, nominative.

4. in philosophy, having to do with any of the elements in apprehension or apperception derived from the limitations of the mind rather than from reality independent of mind.

5. in medicine, designating or of a symptom or condition perceptible only to the patient.

6. in psychology, (a) existing or originating within the observer's mind and, hence, incapable of being checked externally or verified by other persons; (b) introspective.

7. submissive; relating to the subject of a sovereign. [Rare.]

subjective sensation; a sensation caused by an internal stimulus which gives an effect as of an external operating cause.

sub·jeç′tive·ly, *adv.* in a subjective manner.

sub·jeç′tive·ness, *n.* the state of being subjective.

sub·jeç′tiv·iṣm, *n.* 1. the philosophic theory that all knowledge is subjective and relative, never objective.

2. any philosophic theory of knowledge that gives great importance to the subjective or a priori elements of conscious experience.

3. an ethical doctrine that considers the supreme good to be some form of subjective feeling, usually of pleasure, or that measures supreme good by the criterion of such feeling.

sub·jeç′tiv·ist, *n.* one who maintains subjectivism.

sub·jeç·ti·vis′tiç, *a.* of or characterized by subjectivism.

sub·jeç·tiv′i·ty, *n.* a subjective quality or state; specifically, (a) the tendency to consider all things only in the light of one's own personality; (b) concern with only one's own thoughts and feelings; (c) the reflection of an artist's character and personality in his work.

sub′jeçt·less, *a.* without a subject.

sub′jeçt mat′tẽr, the matter or thought presented for consideration in a book, course of instruction, discussion, etc.

sub′jeçt·ness, *n.* subjection.

sub′jeçt-ob″jeçt, *n.* 1. an object possessing subjectivity.

2. the object perceived by cognition as opposed to the object as it really exists.

sub′jeçt-ob″jeç·tiv′i·ty, *n.* the state or condition of being a subject-object.

sub·jic′i·ble, *a.* in logic, capable of becoming a subject of a predicate.

sub·join′, *v.t.*; subjoined, *pt.*, *pp.*; subjoining, *ppr.* [OFr. *subjoindre*, from L. *subjungere*, to subjoin.] to add at the end; to add after something has been said or written; to append; to affix; to annex; as, to *subjoin* an argument or reason.

sub·join′dẽr, *n.* something subjoined.

sub jū′di·cē, [L.] before the judge; not decided; under judicial consideration.

sub′jụ·gāte, *v.t.*; subjugated, *pt.*, *pp.*; subjugating; *ppr.* [L. *subjugatus*, pp. of *subjugere*, to bring under the yoke; *sub-*, and L. *jugum*, yoke.]

1. to subdue and bring under the yoke by superior force; to conquer.

2. to cause to become subservient; to subdue.

sub·jụ·gā′tion, *n.* the act of subjugating or the state of being subjugated; subjection.

sub′jụ·gā·tŏr, *n.* one who subjugates.

sub·junç′tion, *n.* 1. the act of subjoining or the state of being subjoined.

2. that which is subjoined.

sub·junç′tive, *a.* [L. *subjunctivus*, subjunctive, lit., joining on at the end, from *subjunctus*, pp. of *subjungere*, to subjoin.]

1. subjoined or added to something said or written. [Obs.]

2. in grammar, designating or of that mood of a verb used to express condition, hypothesis, contingency, possibility, etc., rather than to state an actual fact: distinguished from *indicative*, *imperative*.

sub·junç′tive, *n.* a verb in the subjunctive mood; specifically, the subjunctive mood.

sub′king″dŏm, *n.* 1. a subordinate kingdom.

2. a primary division of the plant or animal kingdom: now called a *phylum*.

sub·lap·sār′i·ăn, *a.* and *n.* same as *infralapsarian*.

sub·lap·sār′i·ăn·iṣm, *n.* same as *infralapsarianism*.

sub·lap′sȧ·ry, *a.* same as *infralapsarian*.

sub·lāte′, *v.t.*; sublated, *pt.*, *pp.*; sublating, *ppr.* 1. to transport; to remove; to bear away. [Obs.]

2. in logic, (a) to contradict or deny; (b) to annul or wipe out.

sub·lā′tion, *n.* 1. the act of taking or carrying away. [Rare.]

2. in Hegelian philosophy, obliteration by a subsequent logical movement.

sub′lȧ·tive, *a.* tending to take away.

sub′lēase″ (-lēs″), *n.* a lease granted by a lessee to another person of all or part of the property.

sub·lēase′, *v.t.*; subleased (-lēst), *pt.*, *pp.*; subleasing, *ppr.* 1. to grant a sublease of.

2. to receive or hold a sublease of.

sub·let′, *v.t.*; sublet, *pt.*, *pp.*; subletting, *ppr.* 1. to lease or let, as a lessee, to another (property leased to oneself).

2. to let out (work) to a subcontractor.

sub·lē′thăl, *a.* not quite lethal; insufficient to cause death; as, a *sublethal* dose of poison.

sub·lē·vā′tion, *n.* 1. the act of raising on high; elevation.

2. an uprising or insurrection. [Rare.]

sub·lieū·ten′ănt (-lū-), *n.* in some armies and navies, an officer ranking next below a lieutenant.

sub·li·gā′tion, *n.* the act of binding underneath. [Rare.]

sub·lī′mȧ·ble, *a.* capable of being sublimated.

sub·lī′mȧ·ble·ness, *n.* the quality of being sublimable.

sub′li·māte, *v.t.*; sublimated, *pt.*, *pp.*; sublimating, *ppr.* [L. *sublimatis*, pp. of *sublimare*, to raise, elevate.]

1. to purify or refine (a substance) by subliming.

2. figuratively, to purify or refine.

3. to express (socially unacceptable impulses or biological drives) in constructive, socially acceptable forms, often unconsciously.

4. to extract by sublimation or a similar process. [Obs.]

5. to elevate; to idealize. [Obs.]

sub′li·māte, *v.i.* to undergo sublimation.

sub′li·măte (*or* -māt), *n.* a product of sublimation.

sub′li·măte (*or* -māt), *a.* 1. sublimated.

2. figuratively, elevated; purified.

sub·li·mā′tion, *n.* [L. *sublimatio*, from *sublimare*, to elevate, lift up.]

1. a sublimating or being sublimated.

2. the process of subliming.

3. a product of sublimating.

sub′li·mȧ·tō·ry, *a.* tending to sublimate; used in sublimation.

sub′li·mȧ·tō·ry, *n.*; *pl.* **sub′li·mȧ·tō·rieṣ,** a receptacle used in sublimation.

sub·līme′, *a.*; *comp.* sublimer; *superl.* sublimest, [Fr.; L. *sublimis*, uplifted, high, lofty, exalted.]

1. high in place; aloft; elevated. [Archaic.]

Sublime on these a tow'r of steel is rear'd.
—Dryden.

2. high in excellence; exalted; majestic; noble; as, a *sublime* leader.

3. inspiring awe, veneration, heroic or lofty feeling, and the like through grandeur, beauty etc.; as, *sublime* heights; a *sublime* deed.

Duty is the *sublimest* word in our language.
—R. E. Lee.

4. elevated by joy; elated. [Poet.]

5. lofty; proud; haughty. [Poet.]

6. in anatomy, near the surface.

sub·līme′, *n.* something sublime; sublime quality (with *the*).

sub·līme′, *v.t.*; sublimed, *pt.*, *pp.*, subliming, *ppr.* 1. to make sublime.

2. to purify (a solid) by heating directly to a gaseous state and condensing the vapor back into solid form.

sub·līme′, *v.i.* 1. to be brought or changed into a state of vapor by heat, and then condensed back into solid form, so as to be purified.

2. to become purified or exalted.

sub·līme′ly, *adv.* in a sublime manner.

sub·līme′ness, *n.* the state or quality of being sublime.

sub·līm′ẽr, *n.* one who or that which sublimes.

sub·lim″i·fi·çā′tion, *n.* [L. *sublimis*, exalted, elevated, and *facere*, to make.] the act of making sublime or the condition of being made sublime. [Obs.]

sub·lim′i·năl, *a.* [from *sub-*, and L. *limen*, threshold, and *-al*.] in psychology, too slight to be perceived; lying below the threshold of consciousness; subconscious.

sub·lim′i·năl, *n.* the subconscious.

sub·lim′i·ty, *n.* 1. the quality or condition of being sublime, majestic, noble, etc.

2. *pl.* **sub·lim′i·tieṣ,** that which is sublime.

3. climax; acme. [Rare.]

Syn.—grandeur.

sub·liñ′guȧ (-gwȧ), *n.*; *pl.* **sub·liñ′guae** (-gwē), a process of the mucous membrane of the floor of the mouth of certain animals.

sub·liñ′guăl, *a.* 1. situated under the tongue; as, the *sublingual* glands.

2. relating to the sublingua.

sub·lit′tō·răl, *a.* [*sub-*, and L. *litus*, *litoris*, the seashore.] in zoology, living near the seashore.

sub·lob′ū·lăr, *a.* situated under a lobe or lobule; as, the *sublobular* veins of the liver.

sub·lum′băr, *a.* in anatomy, located under or in front of the lumbar region.

sub′lū·nā·ry, sub·lū′năr, *a.* [*sub-*, and L. *luna*, the moon.]

1. beneath the moon.

2. earthly; mundane.

All things *sublunary* are subject to change.
—Dryden.

sub·lux·ā′tion, *n.* [*sub-*, and L. *luxatus*, pp. of *luxare*, to dislocate.] in medicine, an incomplete dislocation.

sub·mȧ·chïne′ gun, a portable, automatic or semiautomatic firearm with a short barrel and a stock, fired from the shoulder or hip.

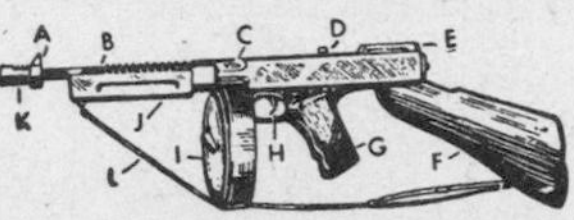

THOMPSON SUBMACHINE GUN

A, front sight; B, barrel; C, breech; D, rear sight; E, wind gauge; F, stock; G, pistol grip; H, trigger; I, magazine; J, hand grip; K, compensator; L, sling

sub·mam′mȧ·ry, *a.* situated under the mammae; as, *submammary* inflammation.

sub·mär′ġin·ăl, *a.* 1. considered to be below the standard that yields a satisfactory profit; as, a *submarginal* vein of coal.

2. below the margin.

3. in biology, near the margin.

sub·mär′ġin·āte, *a.* in biology, having characteristic submarginal markings; as, *submarginate* leaves.

sub·mȧ·rïne′, *a.* located, found, used, or living beneath the surface of the water, especially of the sea; as, *submarine* forms of life; a *submarine* cable.

submarine boat; a submarine (sense 1).

submarine gun, a gun designed for discharging projectiles under water.

submarine mine, a mine of explosives, commonly anchored so as to come in contact with a ship's bottom and be exploded by such contact. There are other kinds of submarine mines, as those that may be exploded from shore.

sub′mȧ·rïne, *n.* 1. a kind of warship that can operate under water.

2. a submarine plant or animal.

sub′mȧ·rïne, *v.t.*; submarined, *pt.*, *pp.*; submarining, *ppr.* to attack, especially to torpedo, with a submarine warship.

sub′mȧ·rïne chāṣ′ẽr, a small, fast naval patrol vessel carrying depth charges and light deck guns for use against submarines.

sub·max·il′lȧ, *n.*; *pl.* **sub·max·il′lae,** [L.] in anatomy, the lower jaw or jawbone.

sub·max′il·lā·ry, *a.* designating, of, or below the submaxilla; especially, designating or of either of two salivary glands, one on each side, below the inside edge of the submaxilla.

sub·max′il·lā·ry, *n.*; *pl.* **sub·max′il·lā·rieṣ,** a submaxillary part.

sub·mē′di·ăn, *a.* in zoology, adjacent to the median.

sub·mē′di·ănt, *n.* in music, the sixth tone of a diatonic scale, as A in the scale of C: also called *superdominant*.

sub·men′tăl, *a.* [*sub-*, and L. *mentum*, the chin.] in anatomy, under the chin; as, the *submental* tissues.

sub·men′tum, *n.*, *pl.* **sub·men′tȧ,** [L.] in entomology, one of two parts of the labium.

sub·mẽrġe′, *v.t.*; submerged, *pt.*, *pp.*; submerging, *ppr.* [Fr. *submerger*; L. *submergere*, to dip or plunge under.]

1. to put under or as under water; to plunge.

2. to cover or overflow with water, to drown.

So half my Egypt was *submerged*. —Shak.

3. to cover over; to suppress; to hide.

sub·mërge′, *v.i.* to plunge or sink under water, etc.

sub·mër′gence, *n.* the act of submerging or the state of being submerged.

sub·mër′gi·ble, *a.* that can be submerged.

sub·mërse′, *v.t.*; submersed (-mërst), *pt.*, *pp.*; submersing, *ppr.* [L. *submersus*, pp. of *submergere*, to submerge.] to submerge.

sub·mërse′, *a.* submersed.

sub·mërsed′ (-mërst′), *a.* submerged; specifically, in botany, growing under water, as the leaves of certain plants.

sub·mërs′i·ble, *n.* 1. a submarine. [Rare.]

2. formerly, a submarine capable of being but partly submerged, the conning tower, etc., remaining above water. It is submerged as desired by regulating the amount of water in the ballast tanks.

sub·mërs′i·ble, *a.* that can be submersed, especially so as to continue functioning.

sub·mër′sion, *n.* a submerging or being submersed.

sub″mī·crō·scop′ic, *a.* too small to be seen through a microscope.

sub·min′is·tẽr, *v.t.* to supply; to afford. [Obs.]

sub·min′is·tẽr, *v.i.* to subserve; to be useful. [Obs.]

Our passions *subminister* to the best and worst of purposes. —L'Estrange.

sub·min′is·trănt, *a.* subservient. [Obs.]

sub·min′is·trāte, *v.t.* to subminister. [Obs.]

sub·min·is·trā′tion, *n.* the act of furnishing or supplying. [Obs.]

sub·miss′, *a.* 1. submissive; humble. [Archaic.]

2. calm; soft; low; as, *submiss* voices. [Obs.]

sub·mis′sion (-mish′un), *n.* [ME.; OFr. *soubmission*; L. *submissio* (*-onis*), a letting down, submission, from *submissus*, pp. of *submittere*, to let down, submit.]

1. the act of submitting, yielding, or surrendering.

I determined to hammer continuously against the enemy until, by mere attrition, if in no other way, there should be nothing left to him but *submission*. —U. S. Grant.

2. the state or quality of being submissive; acknowledgment of inferiority or dependence; humble or suppliant behavior; meekness; resignation; obedience.

In all *submission* and humility.
York doth present himself unto your highness. —Shak.

3. the act of submitting something to another for decision, consideration, etc.

4. in law, an agreement by rival claimants to submit a matter in dispute to arbitration.

sub·mis′sive, *a.* inclined, disposed, or ready to submit without resistance; docile; yielding.

Syn.—obedient, docile, yielding, dutiful, humble, obsequious, subservient.

sub·mis′sive·ly, *adv.* in a submissive manner.

sub·mis′sive·ness, *n.* the state or quality of being submissive.

sub·miss′ly, *adv.* humbly; with submission. [Archaic.]

sub·miss′ness, *n.* humbleness; obedience. [Archaic.]

sub·mit′, *v.t.*; submitted, *pt.*, *pp.*; submitting, *ppr.* [L. *submittere*, to let down, submit, bow to; *sub*, under, down, and *mittere*, to send.]

1. to let down; to cause to sink; to lower. [Obs.]

Sometimes the hill *submits* itself a while. —Dryden.

2. to yield, resign, or surrender to the power, will, or authority of another or others: often used reflexively.

3. to refer; to leave or commit to the discretion or judgment of others; as, to *submit* a controversy to arbitrators; to *submit* a question to the court.

4. to put or place under. [Obs.]

The bristled throat
Of the *submitted* sacrifice with ruthless steel he cut. —Chapman.

5. to offer as one's own opinion; to suggest; to propose.

sub·mit′, *v.i.* 1. to surrender; to yield to the power, authority, or control of another or others; to give up resistance; as, the enemy *submitted*; on hearing the opinion of the court, the counsel *submitted* without further argument.

2. to be submissive, obedient, humble, etc.; to acquiesce in the authority of another.

3. to defer to another's judgment or decision.

sub·mit′tăl, *n.* the act of submitting.

sub·mit′tẽr, *n.* one who submits.

sub·mon′tāne, *a.* [from *sub* (below), and L. *montanus*, of a mountain, from *mons*, *montis*, mountain.]

1. located at the foot of a mountain or mountains.

2. of or characteristic of foothills.

3. beneath a mountain or mountains.

sub·mon′tāne·ly, *adv.* in a submontane position.

sub·mū·cō′sȧ, *n.* the submucous tissue; an areolar connective tissue underlying a mucous membrane.

sub·mū′cous, *a.* 1. in anatomy, underlying a mucous membrane.

2. of the character of or resembling mucus or mucous membrane.

sub·mul′ti·ple, *n.* [*sub-* (below) and *multiple*.] a number or quantity which is contained in another an exact number of times, or is an aliquot part of it; as, seven is the *submultiple* of fifty-six, being contained in it eight times.

sub·mul′ti·ple, *a.* referring to a submultiple; as, a *submultiple* ratio.

sub·mus′cū·lăr, *a.* underlying a muscle or muscles.

sub·nā′ṣăl, *a.* situated at the base of or beneath the nose.

sub·nas′cent, *a.* [L. *subnascens* (*-entis*), ppr. of *subnasci*, to grow up under; *sub*, under, and *nasci*, to be born.] growing underneath. [Rare.]

sub·nect′, **sub·nex′**, *v.t.* to tie, buckle, or fasten beneath. [Rare.]

sub·neū′răl, *a.* underlying the central nervous system.

sub·nī′trāte, *n.* a salt of nitric acid capable of forming a normal nitrate, by the addition of more nitric acid.

sub·nor′măl, *a.* below the normal; less than normal, especially in intelligence.

sub·nor′măl, *n.* 1. a subnormal person.

2. in geometry, that part of the axis of abscissas which is intercepted between the ordinate and the normal.

sub·nor·mal′i·ty, *n.* a subnormal quality or condition.

sub·nō·tō·chor′dăl, *a.* in anatomy, situated beneath the notochord.

sub·nū′vō·lăr, *a.* [*sub-*, and It. *nuvola*, cloud.] somewhat cloudy; partially covered or obscured by clouds.

sub·oc·cip′i·tăl, *a.* being under or behind the occiput or occipital bone; as, the *suboccipital* nerves.

sub·ō·cē·an′ic (-shē-), *a.* situated or taking place beneath the floor of the ocean.

sub·oc′tāve, *n.* 1. one eighth part. [Rare.]

2. in music, the octave below any given tone.

suboctave coupler; a mechanical device used on an organ to connect each note with the corresponding one in the octave below.

sub·oc′tū·ple, *a.* having the ratio of one to eight; being one eighth.

sub·oc′ū·lăr, *a.* being under the eye; suborbital.

sub·ō·pẽr′cū·lăr, *a.* placed under the operculum or gill flap of a fish; relating to the suboperculum.

sub·ō·pẽr′cū·lum, *n.* 1. the portion of the occipital gyrus that overlies the insula, or the island of Reil.

2. the lower section of the gill cover of a fish.

sub·or′bit·ăl, *a.* 1. located beneath the orbit of the eye; subocular.

2. designating or of a spaceflight in which the spacecraft follows a steep, short-range trajectory instead of going into orbit.

sub′or″dẽr, *n.* 1. in biological classifications, a subdivision of an order; a group of animals or of plants, greater than a family and smaller than an order.

2. in architecture, a secondary order.

sub·or′di·nȧ·cy, *n.* the state of being subordinate or subject to control; as, to bring the imagination to act in *subordinacy* to reason.

sub·or′di·năl, *a.* of or pertaining to a suborder.

sub·or′di·nănce, **sub·or′di·năn·cy**, *n.* subordinacy. [Obs.]

sub·or′di·năr·y, *n.* in heraldry, a figure of less importance than an ordinary.

sub·or′di·nāte, *a.* [ML. *subordinatus*, pp. of *subordinare*; L. *sub-*, under, and *ordinare*, to order.]

1. inferior to or placed below another in rank, power, importance, etc.; secondary.

2. under the power or authority of another.

3. subservient or submissive.

4. in grammar, (a) designating or of a clause that is dependent upon another clause and does not itself constitute a formal sentence; (b) introducing such a clause; as, *who, that, which, since, if*, etc. are *subordinate* conjunctions.

sub·or′di·nāte, *n.* a subordinate person or thing.

sub·or′di·nāte, *v.t.*; subordinated, *pt.*, *pp.*; subordinating, *ppr.* 1. to place in a subordinate position; to treat as inferior or less important.

2. to make obedient or subservient (*to*); to control; to subdue.

sub·or′di·nāte·ly, *adv.* in a subordinate manner.

sub·or′di·nāte·ness, *n.* the state or character of being subordinate.

sub·or·di·nā′tion, *n.* 1. the act of subordinating or the state of being subordinate.

2. a place of rank among inferiors. [Obs.]

3. subjection or submission to rank, power, authority, etc.; obedience.

sub·or·di·nā′tion·ism, *n.* in theology, the doctrine that in the Trinity, God the Father has priority over the second and third persons in order or in essence.

sub·or′di·nā·tive, *a.* 1. tending to or involving subordination.

2. in grammar, used to introduce a subordinate clause in a sentence; as, a *subordinative* conjunction.

sub·orn′, *v.t.*; suborned, *pt.*, *pp.*; suborning, *ppr.* [Fr. *suborner*, from L. *subornare*, to furnish or supply in an underhand way or secretly; *sub*, under, and *ornare*, to furnish.]

1. to get or bring about through bribery or other illegal methods.

2. to induce or instigate (another) to do something illegal, especially to commit perjury.

sub·or·nā′tion, *n.* [Fr.] 1. the act of procuring or inducing one by bribes, persuasion, or the like, to do something illegal.

2. in law, the crime of suborning; the act of secretly or in an underhand manner procuring, preparing, or instructing a witness to give false testimony; any act that allures or disposes to perjury. It is called *subornation of perjury*, and is punishable in the same manner as perjury.

sub·or′nȧ·tive, *a.* suborning or suborned.

sub·orn′ẽr, *n.* one who suborns.

sub·ox′ide, **sub·ox′id**, *n.* an oxide containing a relatively small proportion of oxygen.

sub·pē·dun′cū·lăr, *a.* in anatomy, situated beneath a peduncle.

sub·pē·dun′cū·lāte, *a.* having a very short peduncle.

sub·pē′nȧ, *n.* and *v.t.* same as *subpoena*.

sub·per·i·cär′di·ăl, *a.* situated beneath the pericardium.

sub·per·i·os′tē·ăl, *a.* situated beneath or under the periosteum.

sub·per″i·tō·nē′ăl, *a.* situated or occurring between the peritoneum and the body wall.

sub·pet′i·ō·lăr, *a.* situated within or beneath the base of the petiole: said of leaf buds, as in the plane tree.

sub·pet′i·ō·lāte, *a.* same as *subpetiolar*.

sub·phar·yn′gē·ăl, *a.* situated beneath the pharynx.

sub·phren′ic, *a.* situated below the diaphragm.

sub·phy̆′lum, *n.* any of the principal subdivisions of a phylum.

sub·pleū′răl, *a.* situated between the pleura and the body wall.

sub′plot, *n.* a secondary or subordinate plot in a play, novel, etc.

sub·pod·ō·phyl′lous, *a.* situated beneath the podophyllous layers in a horse's foot.

sub poe′nȧ, [L.] under penalty.

sub·poe′nȧ (*or* su-), *n.* [*sub-*, and L. *pœna*, pain, penalty.]

1. a writ directing the attendance in court of the person on whom it is served, under penalty, as a witness, etc.

2. a process requiring a defendant in equity to appear in court and answer to the bill of the plaintiff.

subpoena ad testificandum; a writ to bring a person into court to testify.

subpoena duces tecum; a writ ordering a person to appear in court and to bring with him books, writings, or papers in his possession.

sub·poe′nȧ, *v.t.*; subpoenaed, *pt.*, *pp.*; subpoenaing, *ppr.* to serve or summon with a subpoena; to direct the attendance of in court by a legal writ.

sub·poe′năl, *a.* required or performed under penalty.

sub·pō′lăr, *a.* 1. under or below the poles of the earth; adjacent to the poles.

2. in astronomy, under the celestial pole.

sub″pop·ū·lā′tion, *n.* a subdivision of a population, with distinguishing characteristics.

sub·prin′ci·păl, *n.* 1. a subordinate principal in a school, etc.

2. a secondary brace or rafter.

3. in music, an open diapason subbass in an organ.

sub·prī′ŏr, *n.* the vicegerent of a prior; a claustral officer who assists the prior.

sub·prō·fes′sion·ăl, *n.* paraprofessional.

sub·rā′mōse, *a.* in botany, so imperfectly ramose as to have only a few branches.

sub·rā′mous, *a.* subramose.

sub·rēad′ẽr, *n.* in English law, a reader in the Inns of Court who reads the law on which it is the intention of another reader, his superior to discourse.

sub′rē″ġiŏn, *n.* any of the divisions of a region, especially with reference to the distribution of plants and animals.

sub·rē·liġ′iŏn, *n.* a faith, doctrine, or belief approaching the sacredness of religion; an inferior religion.

sub·rep′tion, *n.* [L. *subreptio (-onis)*, a taking away secretly, stealing, from *subreptus*, pp. of *subripere*, to take away secretly, steal; *sub-*, and *rapere*, to take away, snatch.]

1. the fraudulent concealment or misrepresentation of facts.

2. a fase inference drawn from this.

3. the procurement of advantage, property, etc., especially of an ecclesiastical dispensation, by means of such fraudulent concealment of fact.

sub·rep·ti′tious (-tish′us), *a.* of, characterized by, or secured by subreption.

sub·rep·ti′tious·ly, *adv.* in a subreptitious manner.

sub·reṣ′in, *n.* the part of a resin soluble in hot alcohol and hardening into pseudocrystals on cooling.

sub′rō·gāte, *v.t.*; subrogated, *pt.*, *pp.*; subrogating, *ppr.* [L. *subrogatus*, pp. of *subrogare*, to cause to be chosen in place of another; *sub-*, under, and *rogare*, to ask, propose for election.] to substitute by transfer, as a person or thing, in the place of another; especially, to substitute (one creditor) for another.

sub·rō·gā′tion, *n.* the substitution of one person or thing for another; especially, the substitution of a new creditor for an old one.

sub rō′ṣȧ, [L.] under the rose, secretly, privately; in a manner that forbids disclosure: the rose in ancient times was the emblem of silence.

sub·röu·tïne′, *n.* 1. a short set of instructions, often used repeatedly, that directs a digital computer in the solution of part of a problem.

2. the set of instructions needed to direct a digital computer in completing a strictly defined mathematical or logical operation.

sub·sā′çrăl, *a.* in anatomy, situated under or on the ventral side of the sacrum.

sub′salt, *n.* a basic salt.

sub′sam·ple, *n.* a selected sample of a total sampling.

sub′sam·ple, *v.t.*; subsampled, *pt.*, *pp.*; subsampling, *ppr.* to take a subsample of.

sub·sçap′ū·lar, *a.* situated, passing, or located beneath the scapula; occupying the under surface of the scapula; as, a *subscapular* artery.

sub·sçap′ū·lăr·y, *a.* subscapular. [Rare.]

sub·sçlē·rot′iç, *a.* situated under the sclerotic coat.

sub·sçrīb′ȧ·ble, *a.* that can be subscribed.

sub·sçrībe′, *v.t.*; subscribed, *pt.*, *pp.*; subscribing, *ppr.* [L. *subscribere*; *sub*, under, and *scribere*, to write.]

1. to give consent to (something written); to bind oneself to by writing one's name beneath; as, parties *subscribe* a covenant or contract; a man *subscribes* a bond or articles of agreement.

2. to sign (one's name) at the end of a document, etc.

3. to support; to consent to; to favor; to sanction.

4. to promise to pay or contribute (money), especially by signing a pledge.

5. to submit. [Obs.]

6. to characterize by writing down, or as by writing down; as, to *subscribe* one a coward. [Obs.]

sub·sçrībe′, *v.i.* 1. to sign one's name at the end of a document, etc.

2. to give support, sanction, or approval; to consent; to agree; as, he would not *subscribe* to such a measure.

3. to promise to pay or contribute a sum of money.

4. to agree to receive and pay for a periodical, etc. for a specified period of time (with *to*).

5. to yield; to submit; to admit one's error or inferiority. [Obs.]

sub·sçrīb′ẽr, *n.* one who subscribes to something.

sub′sçript, *a.* written under or below.

sub′sçript, *n.* a figure, letter, symbol, etc. written underneath, as a mathematical subindex.

sub·sçrip′tion, *n.* 1. the act of subscribing.

2. something subscribed; specifically, (a) a written signature; (b) a signed document, etc.; (c) consent or sanction, especially in writing; (d) an amount of money subscribed; (e) a formal agreement to receive and pay for a periodical, books, theater tickets, etc. for a specified period of time; (f) the right to receive a periodical, etc., as by payment of a fixed sum.

3. in ecclesiastical usage, assent to certain doctrines for promoting uniformity; specifically, in the Anglican Church, acceptance of the Thirty-nine Articles of Faith and the Book of Common Prayer.

4. submission; obedience. [Obs.]

5. in pharmacy, the directions to a druggist, contained in a prescription.

sub·sçrip′tive, *a.* of, for, or indicating subscription.

sub·sçrip′tive·ly, *adv.* in a subscriptive manner.

sub·seç′tion, *n.* a part or division of a section; a subdivision.

sub′sē·çūte, *v.t.* to pursue; to follow closely so as to overtake. [Rare.]

sub·seç′ū·tive, *a.* following in a train or succession. [Rare.]

sub·sel′li·um, *n.*; *pl.* **sub·sel′li·ȧ,** [L. *subsellium*, bench, seat; *sub*, under, and *sella*, seat.] a misericord, sense 3.

sub·sem′i·tōne, *n.* in medieval music, the leading note of any key: also called *subtonic*.

sub·sen′si·ble, *a.* too deep or profound for the senses to reach or grasp.

sub·sep′tū·ple, *a.* containing one of seven parts; having a ratio of one to seven.

sub′sē·quence, *n.* 1. the fact or condition of being subsequent.

2. a subsequent happening, etc.

sub′sē·quen·cy, *n.* subsequence.

sub′sē·quent, *a.* [L. *subsequens (-entis)*, ppr. of *subsequi*, to follow close after.] following in time, place, or order; coming after; as, *subsequent* events.

subsequent to; after; following after; following.

sub′sē·quent·ly, *adv.* at a later time; at a time after something else; afterward.

sub·sē′rous, *a.* being beneath a serous membrane.

sub·sẽrve′, *v.t.*; subserved, *pt.*, *pp.*; subserving, *ppr.* [L. *subservire*, to serve under a person; *sub*, under, and *servire*, to serve.] to be useful or helpful to (a purpose, cause, etc.); to serve; promote; aid.

sub·sẽrve′, *v.i.* to serve in an inferior capacity; to be subservient or subordinate. [Rare.]

sub·sẽrv′i·ence, *n.* 1. the state or quality of being subservient.

2. subservient behavior or manner; submissiveness; servility.

sub·sẽrv′i·en·cy, *n.* same as *subservience*.

sub·sẽrv′i·ent, *a.* [L. *subserviens (-entis)*, ppr. of *subservire*, to serve under a person.]

1. that is useful, helpful, or of service, especially in an inferior or subordinate capacity.

2. submissive; obsequious.

> These ranks of creatures are *subservient* one to another. —Ray.

sub·sẽrv′i·ent·ly, *adv.* in a subservient manner.

sub·ses′qui-, a prefix used in chemistry to denote that the elements are combined in the proportion of two to three; as, *subsesquiacetate*, a salt containing two equivalents of acetic acid for every three of the base.

sub·sex′tū·ple, *a.* containing one part in six.

sub′shrub, *n.* an undershrub.

sub·sīde′, *v.i.*; subsided, *pt.*, *pp.*; subsiding, *ppr.* [L. *subsidere*, to settle down; *sub*, under, and *sidere*, to settle, from *sedere*, to sit.]

1. to sink or fall to the bottom; to settle, as lees.

2. to become quiet; to cease to rage; to be calmed; to become tranquil; as, the storm has *subsided*.

3. to tend downward; to sink to a lower level.

Syn.—abate, calm, decline, decrease, quiet, settle, sink, moderate, lull.

sub·sī′dence, sub·sī′den·cy, *n.* the act or process of subsiding.

sub·sid′i·ăr·i·ly, *adv.* in a subsidiary manner or capacity.

sub·sid′i·ăr·y, *a.* [L. *subsidiarius*, from *subsidium*, help, relief, aid.]

1. acting as a supplement; giving aid, support, service, etc.; auxiliary, especially in a secondary or subordinate capacity.

2. relating or pertaining to a subsidy; founded on or connected with a subsidy or subsidies; as, a *subsidiary* treaty.

subsidiary quantity or *symbol*; in mathematics, a quantity or symbol that is not essentially a part of the problem, but is introduced to help in the solution: used especially in trigonometry.

subsidiary troops; troops of one nation hired by another for military service. [Rare.]

sub·sid′i·ăr·y, *n.*; *pl.* **sub·sid′i·ăr·ieṣ,** 1. an assistant; an auxiliary; one who or that which contributes aid, support, or service.

2. a company controlled by another company which owns most of its shares: in full, *subsidiary company*.

3. in music, a subordinate theme.

sub″si·di·zā′tion, *n.* a subsidizing or being subsidized.

sub′si·dīze, *v.t.*; subsidized, *pt.*, *pp.*; subsidizing, *ppr.* 1. to furnish with a subsidy.

2. to purchase the assistance of by the payment of a subsidy; to assist, as an individual or an undertaking, with money: now often implying bribery.

sub′si·dy, *n.*; *pl.* **sub′si·dieṣ,** [L. *subsidium*, help, aid, lit., that which sits behind or in reserve; *sub*, under, and *sidere*, to settle.]

1. a grant of money; specifically, (a) in England, an aid or tax formerly granted by Parliament to the king for the urgent occasions of the realm, and levied on every subject of ability according to the value of his lands or goods; (b) a sum paid by one government to another, especially to meet the expenses of carrying on a war against a third.

> The continental allies of England were eager for her *subsidies*, and lukewarm as regarded operations against the common enemy. —Sir E. Creasy.

2. a grant of money from a government to a private enterprise considered as beneficial to the public.

Syn.—tribute, bounty, indemnity, grant, pension, bonus, allowance, premium.

sub·sīgn′ (-sīn′), *v.t.* to sign under; to subscribe; to write beneath. [Obs.]

sub·sig·nā′tion, *n.* the act of subsigning. [Obs.]

sub·sil′i·çāte, *n.* a basic silicate.

sub·sist′, *v.i.*; subsisted, *pt.*, *pp.*; subsisting, *ppr.* [Fr. *subsister*; L. *subsistere*, to stand still, stay, abide; *sub*, under, and *sistere*, to place, stand.]

1. to be; to have existence.

2. to continue to be or exist as a reality or in a given state; to abide.

3. to continue to live; to remain alive (*on* sustenance, *by* specific means, etc.).

4. to consist or inhere (*in*).

5. in philosophy, to be logically conceivable and, hence, to hold true.

sub·sist′, *v.t.* to maintain; to support with sustenance; as, to *subsist* a regiment.

sub·sist′ence, sub·sist′en·cy, *n.* 1. being; existence.

2. means of support or livelihood; that which supplies the means of living; as, a scanty *subsistence*.

3. the quality of being inherent.

4. the act of providing sustenance.

5. in philosophy, the status of something that subsists.

6. in theology, hypostasis (sense 3).

subsistence department; in the United States Army, formerly, the department in charge of the purchase and distribution of subsistence stores.

subsistence stores; army supplies, as food, clothing, etc.

sub·sist′ent, *a.* [L. *subsistens* (*-entis*), ppr. of *subsistere*, to abide, subsist.]
1. having existence; subsisting; being.
2. inherent.

sub·sī′zăr, *n.* formerly, in Cambridge University, an under sizar; a student ranking below a sizar.

sub′soil, *n.* the bed or stratum of earth lying below the surface soil.
subsoil plow; a plow for loosening the subsoil at the bottom of a furrow, without raising the subsoil to the surface.

sub′soil, *v.t.* to loosen or turn up the subsoil of.

sub′soil·ẽr, *n.* one who or that which subsoils land; also, a subsoil plow.

sub·sō′lăr, *a.* 1. located under the sun.
2. worldly; terrestrial; mundane.
3. characterized by having the sun in the zenith.
4. being between the tropics; equatorial.

sub′sō·lăr·y, *a.* subsolar. [Rare.]

sub·son′iç, *a.* [from *sub-*, and L. *sonus*, sound; and *-ic*.] designating or of speeds that are less than that of sound through air (about 738 miles per hour).

sub spē′ci·ē (-shi-), [L.] under the aspect (of).

sub·spē′cieṣ (-shiz), *n.* [Mod. L.] a division of a species.

sub·sphē·noid′ăl, *a.* located at the ventral, or lower, side of the sphenoid bone.

sub·spī′nous, *a.* situated under the spinal column; also, resembling a spine.

sub′stāġe, *n.* an apparatus placed underneath the stage of a microscope, capable of being made to approach or recede by rack-and-pinion movement, with centering screws and fittings for holding mirrors, etc.

sub′stănce, *n.* [L. *substantia*, essence, material, from *substare*, to be present, exist.]
1. the real or essential part or element of anything; essence; reality; matter.
2. the physical matter of which a thing consists; material.
3. (a) solid quality; substantial character; (b) consistency; body.
4. the real content of a statement, speech, etc.; true meaning; purport.
5. matter of a particular kind; stuff.
6. material possessions; property; resources; wealth.
7. in philosophy, the essence or substratum which underlies and is capable of having attributes or causing phenomena, but which in spite of changes in outward manifestation remains the same; that which really is or exists, as distinguished from its qualities, attributes, and the phenomena by which it is perceived.
8. in theology, the divine essence or personality, as considered common to each member of the Trinity.

The Son is said to be the same *substance* as the Father—that is, truly and essentially God as the Father is. —Eden.

in substance; (a) with regard to essential elements; substantially; (b) actually; really.

sub′stănce, *v.t.* to enrich or endow with substance. [Obs.]

sub′stănce·less, *a.* without substance; unsubstantial.

sub·stand′ărd, *a.* below standard; specifically, (a) below a standard established by law; (b) in linguistics, deviating from the standard language patterns of cultivated speakers of the language; as, obscenities, solecisms, slang, etc. are generally considered *substandard*.

sub′stănt, *a.* constituting substance. [Rare.]

sub·stan′ti·ȧ (-shi·ȧ), *n.* substance: used chiefly in a few anatomical phrases.

sub·stan′tiăl (-shăl), *a.* [L. *substantialis*.]
1. belonging to or having substance.
2. real; true; not seeming or imaginary.
3. with regard to essential elements; corporeal; material.

The rainbow appears like a *substantial* arch in the sky. —Watts.

4. having strong substance; strong; stout; solid; as, a *substantial* fence.
5. having property or possessions; wealthy; as, a *substantial* citizen.
6. of considerable worth or value; vital; important; as, they agree on all *substantial* issues.
7. of considerable size or amount; large; as, a *substantial* gift.
8. in philosophy, of, or having the nature of, substance.
substantial being; a material being; one that has substance.
substantial damages; a sum awarded by a jury intended to cover the real damage, instead of a nominal sum.
substantial right; a constitutional or legal right.
Syn.—hard, firm, compact, strong, stable, sound, real, valid, true, just, weighty, profound, grave, important.

sub·stan′tiăl, *n.* [*usually pl.*] a substantial thing.

sub·stan·ti·ā′li·ȧ (-shi-), *n.pl.* [LL.] in Scots law, those parts of a deed which are essential to its validity as a formal instrument.

sub·stan′tiăl·iṣm, *n.* in philosophy, (a) the doctrine that substantial realities underlie all phenomena; (b) the doctrine that matter is a real substance.

sub·stan′tiăl·ist, *n.* one who believes in the doctrine of substantialism.

sub·stan·ti·al′i·ty (-shi-), *n.* 1. the state or quality of being substantial; real existence.
2. genuineness; true worth.
3. physical firmness; solidity.

sub·stan′tiăl·īze (-shăl-), *v.t.*; substantialized, *pt.*, *pp.*; substantializing, *ppr.* to make substantial.

sub·stan′tiăl·ly, *adv.* 1. in a substantial manner; solidly; firmly; with strength.
2. to a substantial degree; specifically, (a) truly; really; actually; (b) largely; essentially; in the main.

sub·stan′tiăl·ness, *n.* the state or quality of being substantial.

sub·stan′ti·āte (-shi-), *v.t.*; substantiated, *pt.*, *pp.*; substantiating, *ppr.* [Mod. L. *substantiatus*, pp. of *substantiare*, from L. *substantia*, a substance.]
1. to give substance or true existence to.
2. to give concrete form or body to; convert into substance.
3. to establish by proof or evidence; to verify; to confirm; as, to *substantiate* a charge or allegation.

sub·stan·ti·ā′tion, *n.* the act of substantiating or the state of being substantiated; evidence; proof; verification.

sub·stan·tī′văl, *a.* pertaining to, or of the nature of, a substantive.

sub·stan·tī′văl·ly, *adv.* in a substantival manner.

sub′stăn·tive, *a.* [LL. *substantivus*, self-existent.]
1. existing independently; not dependent upon or subordinate to another.
2. of considerable amount; substantial.
3. having a real existence; actual.
4. of or containing the essential elements; essential.
5. of or consisting of legal rights and principles as distinguished from rules of form.
6. of a dye, becoming fixed without the use of a mordant.
7. in grammar, (a) showing or expressing existence; as, the *substantive* verb, "to be"; (b) of or used as a substantive.

sub′stăn·tive, *n.* 1. something substantive; one who or that which is independent.
2. in grammar, (a) a noun; (b) any word or group of words used as an equivalent for a noun.

sub′stăn·tive, *v.t.* to convert into or use in place of a substantive. [Rare.]

sub′stăn·tive·ly, *adv.* 1. in substance; essentially.
2. in grammar, as a substantive or noun.

sub′stăn·tive·ness, *n.* the state or quality of being substantive. [Rare.]

sub′stăn·tiv·īze, *v.t.*; substantivized, *pt.*, *pp.*; substantivizing, *ppr.* to convert into or use as a substantive.

sub′stā·tion, *n.* a branch station.

sub′stīle, *n.* same as *substyle*.

sub·stit′ū·ent, *n.* in chemistry, a radical, as an atom or group, which enters a molecule in the place of another eliminated by chemical reaction.

sub′sti·tūte, *n.* [Fr. *substitut*, a substitute; L. *substitutus*, one substituted, pp. of *substituere*, to put instead of.] a person or thing acting or used in place of another; specifically, (a) formerly, a person who, for a payment, entered military service in another's place; (b) in grammar, any word, as a pronoun, the verb *to do*, etc., used in place of another word or words (e.g., *did* for *shouted* in "she shouted and so did he.").

sub′sti·tūte, *a.* substitutional.

sub′sti·tūte, *v.t.*; substituted, *pt.*, *pp.*; substituting, *ppr.* 1. to put or use in the place of another.
2. to take the place of.
3. to appoint. [Obs.]

sub′sti·tūte, *v.i.* to act or serve in place of another: often with *for*.

sub·sti·tū′tion, *n.* 1. the act of substituting or the state of being substituted.
2. in grammar, syllepsis, or the use of one word for another.
3. the office of a substitute; delegated authority. [Rare.]
4. in civil law, a conditional appointment of an heir.
5. in Scots law, the enumeration or designation of a succession of heirs in a settlement of property.
6. in chemistry, the act or process of substituting an atom or radical for another atom or radical in a molecule: also called *metalepsy*.
7. in algebra, (a) the putting of one quantity in the place of another, to which it is equal but differently expressed; (b) an operation that changes the order of a finite series of symbols.

sub·sti·tū′tion·ăl, *a.* 1. of or characterized by substitution.
2. that is a substitute.

sub·sti·tū′tion·ăl·ly, *adv.* in a substitutional manner; by way of substitution.

sub·sti·tū′tion·ăr·y, *a.* substitutional.

sub′sti·tū·tive, *a.* 1. of or having to do with substitution.
2. being or capable of being a substitute.

sub·straçt′, *v.i.* and *v.t.* same as *subtract*.

sub·straç′tion, *n.* same as *subtraction*.

sub·straçt′ŏr, *n.* same as *subtractor*.

sub′strāte, *n.* 1. a substratum.
2. in biochemistry, the substance that is acted upon by an enzyme or ferment.

sub′strāte, *a.* forming or relating to a substratum.

sub·strā′tŏr, *n.* in the early Christian Church, a penitent or catechumen who was allowed to join only in parts of the ceremony of worship, but was obliged to kneel near the door until the services were completed.

sub·strat′ō·sphēre, *n.* the stratum of the atmosphere just below the stratosphere, from about 3½ miles to about 7 miles above the earth's surface.

sub·strā′tum, *n.*; *pl.* **sub·strā′tȧ,** [L. *substratus*, spread under.]
1. a part, substance, element, etc. which lies beneath and supports another; foundation.
2. figuratively, any basis or foundation.
3. in agriculture, subsoil.
4. in biology, the medium upon which an organism grows.
5. in metaphysics, substance, with reference to the events or causes which act upon it.

sub·struçt′, *v.t.* to lay or build as a foundation; to build beneath. [Rare.]

sub·struç′tion, *n.* [L. *substructio* (*-onis*), a foundation.] a substructure.

sub·struç′tūr·ăl (-chūr-) *a.* of a substructure.

sub·struç′tūre, *n.* a foundation; a part or structure acting as a support.

sub·stȳ′lăr, *a.* of, pertaining to, or consisting of the substyle.

sub′stȳle, *n.* a right line on which the style, or gnomon, of a dial is erected, being the common section of the face of the dial and a plane perpendicular to it passing through the style.

sub·sul′fāte, *n.* a basic sulfate.

sub·sul′fīde, *n.* a basic sulfide.

sub·sul′tive, *a.* subsultory.

sub·sul′tō·ri·ly, *adv.* in a bounding manner; by leaps, starts, or twitches.

sub·sul′tō·ry, *a.* bounding; leaping; moving by sudden leaps or starts, or by twitches.

sub·sul′tus, *n.* [LL., a leap.] in medicine, a starting, twitching, or convulsive motion.

sub·sūm′ȧ·ble, *a.* that can be subsumed.

sub·sūme′, *v.t.*; subsumed, *pt.*, *pp.*; subsuming, *ppr.* [*sub-*, and L. *sumere*, to lay hold of, take.]
1. to include in a class, group, order, etc.; to classify.
2. to show (an idea, instance, etc.) to be covered by a rule, principle, etc.

sub·sump′tion, *n.* 1. a subsuming or being subsumed.
2. something subsumed; especially, a minor concept or premise.

sub·sump′tive, *a.* characteristic of or pertaining to a subsumption.

sub′tack, *n.* in Scots law, a sublease; a lease of a farm, tenement, etc., granted by the principal leaseholder.

sub·tan′ġent, *n.* in geometry, the part of the axis of abscissas included between the ordinate of a point on a curve and the tangent at that point.

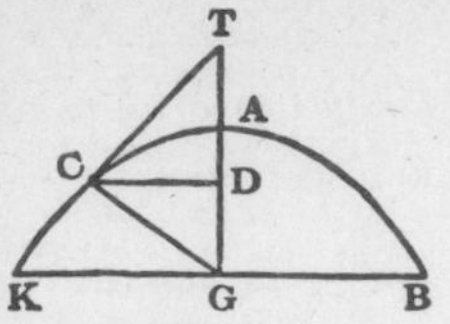

SUBTANGENT

CA, part of a parabola; GT, its axis; CT, tangent; CD, ordinate; DT, subtangent

sub·tär·tar′ē·ăn, *a.* being under Tartarus; infernal. [Obs.]

sub·teç′tà·çle, *n.* a covered place; a tent or tabernacle. [Obs.]

sub·teg·ū·lā′nē·ous, *a.* covered by a roof or eaves; indoors. [Rare.]

sub·tem′pẽr·āte, *a.* of or occurring in the colder areas of the Temperate Zones.

sub·ten′ăn·cy, *n.* 1. the status or occupancy of a subtenant.

2. the period of such occupancy.

sub·ten′ănt, *n.* a person who rents from a tenant; tenant of a tenant.

sub·tend′, *v.t.*; subtended, *pt., pp.*; subtending, *ppr.* [*sub-*, and L. *tendere*, to stretch.]

1. to extend under; to be opposite to; as, each side of a triangle *subtends* the opposite angle.

2. in botany, to enclose in an angle, as between a leaf and its stem.

sub·tense′, *n.* [*sub-*, and L. *tensus*, pp. of *tendere*, to stretch.] the chord of an arc. [Rare.]

sub′tẽr-, [from L. *subter*, under.] a prefix meaning *below, under, less than, secretly.*

sub·tẽr′flū·ent, *a.* running under or beneath.

sub·tẽr′flū·ous, *a.* subterfluent.

sub′tẽr·fūġe, *n.* [*subter-*, and L. *fugire*, to escape.] any plan or action used for escape or concealment; an evasion; an artifice used to escape censure or the force of an argument, to justify opinions, conduct, etc.

Syn.—excuse, artifice, blind, wile, dodge, chicanery, stratagem, sophistry, evasion.

sub·tẽr·nat′ū·răl (-nach′), *a.* below, or less than, what is natural.

sub′tẽr·rāne, *a.* subterranean.

sub′tẽr·rāne, *n.* 1. a cave or room underground.

2. in geology, an underlying formation; a basal terrane. [Rare.]

sub·tẽr·rā′nē·ăn, *a.* [L. *subterraneus*, underground; *sub*, and *terra*, the earth.]

1. lying beneath the earth's surface; underground.

2. secret; hidden.

sub·tẽr·rā′nē·ous, *a.* same as *subterranean.*

sub·tẽr·rā′nē·ous·ly, *adv.* in a subterraneous manner; under the ground; secretly.

sub·tẽr·rēne′, *a.* subterranean.

sub·tẽr·res′tri·ăl, *a.* subterranean. [Rare.]

sub′text, *n.* [*sub-* and *text.*]

1. the complex of feelings, motives, etc., conceived of by an actor as underlying the actual words and actions of the character being portrayed.

2. an underlying meaning, theme, etc.

sub·thȧ·lam′iç, *a.* beneath the optic thalamus.

sub′tile (sut′l *or* sub′tl), *a.* [ME. *sotil, sotel*; L. *subtilis*, fine, thin, precise, originally closely woven; *sub*, beneath, hence, closely, and *tela*, web.] subtle. [Rare.]

sub′tile·ly, *adv.* subtly.

sub′tile·ness, *n.* subtleness.

sub·til′i·āte, *v.t.* to make thin; rarefy. [Obs.]

sub·til·i·ā′tion, *n.* the act of making thin or rare. [Obs.]

sub′til·iṣm, *n.* the condition of being subtile; subtileness. [Rare.]

sub·til′i·ty, *n.*; *pl.* **sub·til′i·tieṣ,** subtlety.

sub″til·i·zā′tion (sut″il- *or* sub″til-), *n.* a subtilizing or being subtilized.

sub′til·ize (sut′l- *or* sub′til-), *v.t.* and *v.i.*; subtilized, *pt., pp.*; subtilizing, *ppr.* to make or become subtle; especially, to discuss or argue with subtle distinctions.

sub′til·ī·zẽr, *n.* one who or that which subtilizes; one given to making subtle distinctions.

sub′til·ty (sut′l- or sub′tl-), *n.*; *pl.* **sub′til·tieṣ,** subtlety.

sub′tī·tle, *n.* 1. a secondary or explanatory title, as of a book or play.

2. a book title repeated at the top of the first page of text.

3. lines of dialogue or of descriptive material shown on a motion-picture screen or television tube either by interrupting a scene with them or by superimposing them on the scene.

sub′tī·tle, *v.t.*; subtitled, *pt., pp.*; subtitling, *ppr.* to add a subtitle or subtitles to.

sub′tle (sut′l), *a.*; *comp.* subtler; *superl.* subtlest, [L. *subtilis*, fine, thin, precise, originally closely woven; *sub*, under, and *tela*, web.]

1. thin; rare; tenuous; not dense or heavy.

2. keen; acute; penetrating; discriminating.

3. delicately skillful or clever; deft; ingenious.

4. crafty; artful; wily; designing.

5. strangely suggestive; mysterious; sly; as, a *subtle* wink.

6. hard to solve, detect, or understand; intricate; abstruse; as, a *subtle* problem.

7. acting in an insidious way; as, a *subtle* poison.

sub′tle·ness, *n.* the quality or condition of being subtle.

sub′tle·ty, *n.*; *pl.* **sub′tle·tieṣ,** 1. the quality or condition of being subtle; craftiness.

2. acuteness of intellect; refinement of discrimination.

3. something subtle; especially, a fine distinction.

sub′tly, *adv.* in a subtle manner.

sub·ton′iç, *n.* in music, the semitone or note immediately below the upper tonic; the seventh tone of a diatonic scale.

sub·tor′rid, *a.* subtropical.

sub·traçt′, *v.t.* and *v.i.*; subtracted, *pt., pp.*; subtracting, *ppr.* [L. *subtractus*, pp. of *subtrahere*, to draw away underneath, subtract; *sub*, under, and *trahere*, to draw.]

1. to withdraw or take away, as a part from the whole or one quantity from another; as, *subtract* 5 from 9, and the remainder is 4.

2. to take away or deduct (one number or quantity from another).

sub·traçt′ẽr, *n.* one who or that which subtracts.

sub·traç′tion, *n.* [L. *subtractio* (*-onis*), from *subtractus*, pp. of *subtrahere*, to subtract.]

1. a subtracting or being subtracted.

2. in mathematics, the taking of a number or quantity from another of the same kind or denomination; a process of finding the difference between two quantities.

3. in law, a withdrawing or neglecting, as when a person who owes any suit, duty, custom, or service to another withdraws or fails to perform it.

sub·traç′tive, *a.* 1. tending to subtract.

2. capable of or involving subtraction.

3. that is to be subtracted; marked with the minus sign (−).

sub′trȧ·hend, *n.* [L. *subtrahendus*, gerundive of *subtrahere*, to subtract.] in mathematics, a number or quantity to be subtracted or taken from another (the *minuend*).

sub·treaṣ′ūr·ẽr (-trezh′), *n.* the assistant treasurer in charge of a subtreasury.

sub·treaṣ′ūr·y, *n.*; *pl.* **sub·treaṣ′ūr·ieṣ,** a subordinate treasury; specifically, in the United States, a branch of the national treasury; as, the *subtreasury* at Chicago.

sub·trīb′ăl, *a.* pertaining to a subtribe.

sub′trībe, *n.* 1. in ethnology, a tribal body that has separated from the parent tribe.

2. in zoology and botany, a group lower in rank than a tribe.

sub·tri′ple, *n.* in mathematics, one third. [Obs.]

sub·trip′li·çāte, *a.* in mathematics, having the inverse ratio of the cubes.

sub·trop′iç, *a.* subtropical.

sub·trop′i·çăl, *a.* 1. designating or of regions bordering on the tropical zone.

2. characteristic of such regions; nearly tropical.

sub·trūde′, *v.t.* to put under. [Rare.]

sū′bū·lāte, *a.* [L. *subula*, an awl, and *-ate.*] awl-shaped; slender and tapering gradually to a fine point.

sū′bū·lāt·ed, *a.* same as *subulate.*

Sū″bū·li·çor′ni·ȧ, *n.pl.* [L. *subula*, an awl, and *cornu*, a horn.] a division of neuropterous insects, having awl-shaped antennae. It includes the dragonflies and *Ephemeræ*, or May flies.

sū′bū·li·form, *a.* same as *subulate.*

sub·um′bō·năl, *a.* beneath the umbones in bivalves.

sub·um·brel′lȧ, *n.*; *pl.* **sub·um·brel′lae,** in zoology, the under part of the bell of a jellyfish.

sub·un·dā′tion, *n.* a deluge. [Obs.]

sub·uṅ′guăl (-gwăl), *a.* situated under the nail or hoof.

sub′ũrb, *n.* [L. *suburbium*, from *sub*, under, and *urbs, urbis*, a town.]

1. a district, especially a residential district, on the outskirts of a city: often a separately incorporated city or town.

2. [*pl.*] outlying parts, or confines.

the suburbs; the residential areas near, or on the outskirts of, a city.

sub·ũr′băn, *a.* 1. of, in, or residing in a suburb or the suburbs.

2. characteristic of the suburbs or suburbanites: variously connoting a combination of rural and urban features, middle-class conservatism, etc.

sub·ũr′băn, *n.* a resident of a suburb.

sub·ũr′băn·īte, *n.* a person living in a suburb.

sub·ũr·ban′i·ty, *n.* suburban character or life.

sub·ũr′băn·īze, *v.t.* and *v.i.*; suburbanized, *pt., pp.*; suburbanizing, *ppr.* to make or become suburban.

sub·ũr′bi·ȧ, *n.* the suburbs or suburbanites collectively: usually used to connote the values, attitudes, and activities regarded as characteristic of suburban life.

sub·ũr·bi·çār′i·ăn, *a.* [LL. *suburbicarius*, situated near the city.] being in the suburbs of Rome; specifically, designating or of the six dioceses surrounding Rome.

sub·ũr′bi·çăr·y, *a.* same as *suburbicarian.*

sub·ū·rē′thrăl, *a.* in anatomy, under the urethra.

sub·vaġ′i·năl, *a.* in anatomy, under a vaginal membrane.

sub·vȧ·rī′e·ty, *n.*; *pl.* **sub·vȧ·rī′e·tieṣ,** a subordinate variety, or a division of a variety.

sub·vēne′, *v.i.*; subvened, *pt., pp.*; subvening, *ppr.* [L. *subvenire*, to come to one's assistance; *sub*, under, and *venire*, to come.] to come or happen so as to aid or support. [Rare.]

sub·ven′tion, *n.* [L. *subvenire*, to aid.]

1. a subvening.

2. money granted, as by a government, in support of a study, institution, or undertaking; a subsidy; a grant.

sub·ven′tion, *v.t.* to support; to relieve; to subsidize. [Rare.]

sub·ven′tion·īze, *v.t.* to subvention. [Rare.]

sub·ven·ti′tious (-tish′us), *a.* subvening; supporting; helping. [Rare.]

sub vẽr′bō, [L.] under the word (specified): with reference to an entry in a dictionary, index, etc.

sub·vẽrse′, *v.t.* to subvert. [Rare.]

sub·vẽr′sion (*or* -zhun), *n.* [OFr., from L. *subversio* (*-onis*), an overturning, upsetting, from *subvertere*, to overturn, subvert.]

1. a subverting or being subverted; ruin; overthrow.

2. something that subverts.

sub·vẽr′sion·ăr·y, *a.* subversive.

sub·vẽr′sive, *a.* tending to subvert; having a tendency to overthrow and ruin (something established).

sub·vẽr′sive, *n.* a person regarded as subversive.

sub·vẽrt′, *v.t.*; subverted, *pt., pp.*; subverting, *ppr.* [OFr. *subvertir*; L. *subvertere*, to turn from beneath, overthrow; *sub*, under, and *vertere*, to turn.]

1. to overthrow or destroy (something established).

2. to corrupt; to undermine, as in morals.

Syn.—overthrow, pervert, destroy, corrupt, overturn.

sub·vẽrt′, *v.i.* to be subversive.

sub·vẽr′tē·brăl, *a.* on the under or ventral side of the vertebrae.

sub·vẽrt′ẽr, *n.* one who or that which subverts.

sub·vẽrt′i·ble, *a.* capable of being subverted.

sub·vir′ile, *a.* lacking virility; weak.

sub·vī′tăl·īzed, *a.* deficient in vitality; lacking vital power.

sub vō′ce, [L., under the voice.] sub verbo.

sub′wāy, *n.* 1. an underground way or passage.

2. an underground, metropolitan electric railway or the tunnel through which this runs.

sub·zō′năl, *a.* in anatomy, situated beneath a zone, as the zona pellucida.

sub′zōne, *n.* a subdivision of a zone.

sub·zy·gō·mat′iç, *a.* in anatomy, beneath the zygoma.

suç-, see *sub-.*

suç·çāde′, *n.* [L. *succus*, juice.] fruit candied or preserved in sirup. [Now Rare.]

succade gourd; same as *vegetable marrow* under *marrow.*

suç·cē·dā′nē·ous, *a.* [L. *succedaneus*, succeeding or filling the place or room of another, from *succedere*, to follow after, succeed.] supplying the place of something else; being, or employed as, a substitute or succedaneum.

suç·cē·dā′nē·um, *n.*; *pl.* **suç·cē·dā′nē·ȧ,** one who or that which supplies the place of another; that which is put or used for something else; a substitute; specifically, a medicine that is substituted for another of like properties.

suc̹·ceed′, *v.i.*; succeeded, *pt.*, *pp.*; succeeding, *ppr.* [ME. *succeden*; OFr. *succeder*, to succeed; L. *succedere*, to go beneath or under, follow after; *sub*, under, and *cedere*, to go.]
1. to come next after another; to follow; ensue; as, all *succeeding* laws were null and void.
2. to follow another into office, possession, etc.; as, the vice-president *succeeds* in case of the president's death.
3. to have success; to accomplish something planned or attempted; also, formerly, to have (a specified) success; as, he *succeeded* badly.
4. to devolve, as an estate. [Obs.]
5. to approach. [Obs.]

suc̹·ceed′, *v.t.* 1. to take the place left by; to be heir or successor to; to follow into office, possession, etc.; as, the king's eldest son *succeeds* his father on the throne.
2. to fall heir to; to inherit. [Obs.]
3. to follow; to come after; to be subsequent or consequent to.
The curse of heaven and men *succeed* their evils. —Shak.
4. to prosper; to make successful. [Obs.]

suc̹·ceed′ẽr, *n.* one who follows or comes in the place of another; a successor.

suc̹·ceed′ing, *n.* the act of one who or that which succeeds; a success.

suc̹·cen′tŏr, *n.* 1. the assistant to the leader in certain church choirs.
2. a precentor's deputy.

suc̹·cess′, *n.* [OFr. *succes*; L. *successus*, result, event, from *succedere*, to succeed.]
1. result; outcome. [Obs.]
2. a favorable or satisfactory outcome or result.
3. the gaining of wealth, fame, rank, etc.
4. a successful person or thing.
Syn.—achievement, luck, consummation, prosperity, victory.

suc̹·ces′sȧ·ry, *n.* succession. [Obs.]

suc̹·cess′fu̇l, *a.* 1. coming about, taking place, or turning out to be as was hoped for; having a favorable result; as, a *successful* mission.
2. achieving or having achieved success; specifically, having gained wealth, fame, rank, etc.
Syn.—fortunate, prosperous, lucky, effectual.

suc̹·cess′fu̇l·ly, *adv.* with success; prosperously; favorably; in a successful manner.

suc̹·cess′fu̇l·ness, *n.* prosperous conclusion; success; the quality or state of being successful.

suc̹·ces′sion (-sesh′un), *n.* [OFr., from L. *successio (-onis)*, a coming into the place of another, a succeeding, from *succedere*, to succeed.]
1. the act of succeeding or coming after another in order or sequence or to an office, estate, etc.
2. the right to succeed to an office, estate, etc.
3. a number of persons or things coming one after another in time or space; a series; sequence; as, a *succession* of piercing screams.
4. (a) a series of heirs or rightful successors of any kind; (b) the order or line of such a series.
5. in music, (a) the order in which the notes of a melody proceed; (b) same as *progression*.
apostolic succession; see under *apostolic*.
in succession; one after another in a regular series or sequence.
succession duty; in England, a tax imposed on every succession to property.
succession of crops; in agriculture, the cultivation of a different kind of crop each year, to prevent the exhaustion of the soil: generally called *rotation of crops*.

suc̹·ces′sion·ăl, *a.* of, involving, or occurring in a regular sequence or succession.

suc̹·ces′sion·ăl·ly, *adv.* in a successional manner.

suc̹·ces′sion·ist, *n.* one who adheres to the validity or necessity of succession, especially apostolic succession.

suc̹·ces′sive, *a.* 1. following in order or uninterrupted course, as a series of persons or things, either in time or place; coming in succession; consecutive; as, the *successive* revolutions of years; the *successive* kings of Egypt.
Send the *successive* ills through ages down. —Prior.
2. of or involving succession.
3. inherited by succession; having or giving the right of succeeding to an inheritance; hereditary. [Obs.]

suc̹·ces′sive·ly, *adv.* 1. in succession.
2. by order of succession and inheritance.

suc̹·ces′sive·ness, *n.* the state of being successive.

suc̹·cess′less, *a.* without success. [Rare.]

suc̹·cess′less·ly, *adv.* in a successless manner; without success. [Rare.]

suc̹·cess′less·ness, *n.* the state or quality of being successless. [Rare.]

suc̹·ces′sŏr, *n.* [L.] one who or that which succeeds, or follows; one who takes the place which another has left, and sustains the like part or character: correlative to *predecessor*; as, the *successor* of a deceased king, the *successor* to the world's heavyweight championship.

suc̹·ces′sŏr·ship, *n.* the office of a successor; also, the power or right of succession.

suc̹·ces′sō·ry, *a.* pertaining to succession.

suc̹·cif′ẽr·ous, *a.* [L. *succus*, juice, and *-ferous*.] producing or conveying sap. [Obs.]

suc̹·cin·am′āte, *n.* a salt or ester of succinamic acid.

suc̹·cin·am′ic̹, *a.* of, relating to, or designating an amide compound, $C_2H_4(CONH_2)CO_2H$, derived from succinic acid.

suc̹′ci·nāte, *n.* a salt or ester of succinic acid.

suc̹·cinc̹t′, *a.* [L. *succinctus*, prepared, short, contracted, pp. of *succingere*, to gird below, tuck up, prepare; *sub*, under, and *cingere*, to gird.]
1. tucked up; girded up. [Archaic.]
His habit fit for speed *succinct*.—Milton.
2. clearly and briefly stated; terse; as, a *succinct* account of the proceedings of the council.
3. characterized by brevity and conciseness of speech.
Syn.—brief, terse, concise, laconic, short.

suc̹·cinc̹t′ly, *adv.* in a succinct manner.

suc̹·cinc̹t′ness, *n.* the quality or state of being succinct.

suc̹·cinc̹·tō′ri·um, *n.*; *pl.* **suc̹·cinc̹·tō′ri·ȧ**, in the Roman Catholic Church, (a) a style of girdle formerly worn by priests or bishops; (b) a vestment embroidered with an Agnus Dei, worn by the Pope on solemn occasions.

suc̹·cinc̹′tō·ry, *n.*; *pl.* **suc̹·cinc̹′tō·ries**, same as *succinctorium*.

suc̹·cin′ic̹ ac′id, [Fr. *succinique*, from L. *succinum*, amber.] a colorless, crystalline dibasic acid, $(CH_2CO_2H)_2$, found in amber, lignite, and many plants, and produced synthetically or during alcoholic fermentation: it is used in medicine and organic synthesis.

suc̹·cin·im′īde, suc̹·cin·im′id, *n.* a white crystalline substance, $C_4H_5NO_2$, obtained from succinic anhydride by the action of ammonia gas.

suc̹′cin·īte, *n.* [L. *succinum*, amber, and *-ite*.]
1. an amber-colored variety of garnet.
2. amber.

suc̹′cin·yl, *n.* a radical of succinic acid, $C_4H_4O_2$.

suc̹·cīse′, *a.* [L. *succisus*, pp. of *succidere*, to cut off, *sub*, from under, off, and *cædere*, to cut.] in botany, appearing as if cut off at the end.

suc̹·ci′ṣion (-sizh′un), *n.* the act of cutting off or down. [Obs.]

suc̹′cŏr, *v.t.*; succored, *pt.*, *pp.*; succoring, *ppr.* [ME. *socouren*; OFr. *sucurre*; L. *subcurrere*, *succurrere*, to run up to, aid; *sub*, under, and *currere*, to run.] to help or relieve when in difficulty, want, or distress; to assist and deliver from suffering; as, to *succor* a besieged city.
Syn.—aid, assist, help, relieve, comfort, deliver.

suc̹′cŏr, *n.* 1. aid; help; assistance; especially, assistance that relieves and delivers from difficulty, want, or distress.
Flying for *succor* to his servant Banister. —Shak.
2. the person or thing that succors.

suc̹′cŏr·ȧ·ble, *a.* that can be succored or relieved.

suc̹′cŏr·ẽr, *n.* one who succors; a helper; a deliverer.

suc̹′cŏr·less, *a.* without succor; helpless.

suc̹′cō·ry, *n.* same as *chicory*.

suc̹′cō·tash, *n.* [Am. Ind.] a dish consisting of corn kernels and beans cooked together.

suc̹′cŏur, *n.* and *v.t.* succor: British spelling.

suc̹′cū·bȧ, *n.*; *pl.* **suc̹′cū·bae**, a succubus.

suc̹′cū·bīne, *a.* pertaining to or characteristic of a succubus.

suc̹′cū·bous, *a.* in botany, having the anterior margin of each leaf pass beneath the posterior margin of that succeeding it: opposed to *incubous*.

suc̹′cū·bus, *n.*; *pl.* **suc̹′cū·bī**, [LL., from L. *succuba*, strumpet, from *succubare*, to lie under, from *sub-*, under, and *cubare*, to lie.] in folklore, a female demon thought to have sexual intercourse with sleeping men: cf. *incubus*.

suc̹′cū·lȧ, *n.*; *pl.* **suc̹′cū·lae**, [L. *sucula*, winch, windlass.] a kind of winch or cylinder with levers for turning it, but having no drum.

suc̹′cū·lence, suc̹′cū·len·cy, *n.* the state or quality of being succulent; juiciness; as, the *succulence* of a peach.

suc̹′cū·lent, *a.* [Fr., from L. *succulentus*, full of juice, from *sucus*, juice.]
1. full of juice; juicy.
2. interesting; fascinating; vital; not dry or dull.
3. in botany, having juicy tissues, as a cactus.

suc̹′cū·lent·ly, *adv.* in a succulent manner; juicily.

suc̹′cū·lous, *a.* succulent. [Rare.]

suc̹·cumb′ (-kum′), *v.i.*; succumbed, *pt.*, *pp.*; succumbing, *ppr.* [L. *succumbere*, to lie or fall under, yield; *sub*, under, and *cumbere*, nasalized form of *cubare*, to lie.]
1. to give way; yield; submit (often with *to*); as, he *succumbed to* her persuasion.
2. to die (often with *to*); as, he *succumbed to* cancer.

suc̹·cum′bent, *a.* yielding; submissive. [Rare.]

suc̹·cũr′săl, *a.* [Fr. *succursale*, supplementing, from LL. *succursus*, succor.] subsidiary; especially, designating a church or monastery that is a branch of a principal one.

suc̹′cus, *n.*; *pl.* **suc̹′cī**, [L. *sucus*, juice.] in medicine, any juice secreted by or extracted from a plant; also, in anatomy, a fluid secretion.
succus entericus; the juice of the intestines, which is secreted by certain glands of the intestinal walls in small quantities; the intestinal juice.

suc̹·cuss′, *v.t.*; succussed (-kust), *pt.*, *pp.*; succussing, *ppr.* [L. *succussus*, pp. of *succutere*, to toss up, shake, jolt; *sub*, from below, up, and *quatere*, to shake.] to shake forcibly; specifically, in medicine, to shake (a patient) in order to detect the presence of a liquid in some body cavity, especially in the thorax.

suc̹·cus·sā′tion, *n.* 1. a trot or trotting (of horses). [Obs.]
2. a shaking; succussion.

suc̹·cus′sion, *n.* [L. *succussio (-onis)*, a shaking, from *succutere*, to shake, succuss.] the act or method of succussing.

suc̹·cus′sive, *a.* of the character of or pertaining to succussion.

such, *a.* [ME. *swulc*, *swilch*, *swich*; AS. *swylc*, *swilc*, *swelc*; akin to G. *solch*; orig. a compound from base of *so* and base of *like*.]
1. of this or that kind; of the same or similar kind; like or similar to something mentioned or implied; specifically, (a) being the same as what was stated before; as, *such* happiness was all he wished; (b) being the same in quality or kind; as, hats, coats, and *such* objects.
2. not named; indefinite; some; certain; as, on *such* a day as you may go.
3. so extreme, so much, so great, etc.: used, according to the context, for emphasis; as, he never expected *such* honor. *Such* is a term of comparison, although that with which comparison is made is not always expressed. When expressed, *as* or *that* is used as a correlative with *such* (e.g., *such* love *as* his is seldom experienced; we had *such* fun *that* nobody left.) It is not preceded by an article, although the article may occur between it and the noun it modifies (e.g., *such* a fellow!).
such as; (a) for example; (b) like or similar to (something specified).

such, *adv.* to such a degree; so; as, he was *such* a good man. [Colloq.]

such, *pron.* 1. such a person (or persons) or thing (or things); as, *such* as live by the sword.
2. the person or thing mentioned or implied; as, *such* was his nature.
as such; (a) as being what is indicated or suggested; (b) in itself; as, a name, *as such*, means nothing.

such and such, being a particular one but not named or specified; as, he went to *such and such* a place.

such′līke, *a.* of such a kind; of like or similar kind.

such′līke, *pron.* persons or things of such a kind.

such′wīṣe, *adv.* in such a manner; so.

suck, *v.t.*; sucked (sukt), *pt.*, *pp.*; sucking, *ppr.* [AS. *sûcan*, *sûgan*; akin to G. *saugen*.]
1. to draw (liquid) into the mouth by forming a partial vacuum with the lips and tongue.
2. to take up or in by or as by sucking; to absorb, inhale, etc.; as, he *sucked* air into his lungs; the pumps soon *sucked* the water from the hold.

3. to draw liquid from (a breast, fruit, etc.) by action of the lips and tongue.
4. to dissolve or consume by holding in the mouth or licking, as candy, ice, etc.
5. to hold (the thumb, etc.) in the mouth.
6. to bring into a specified state by sucking; as, he *sucked* the orange dry.
to suck in; to take advantage of; to swindle, etc. [Slang.]

suck, *v.i.* 1. to draw in water, air, etc. by creating a partial vacuum; to suck something.
2. to suck milk from the breast or udder.
3. to make the sound of sucking.
4. to draw in air instead of liquid: said of a faulty pump.

suck, *n.* 1. the act of sucking with the mouth; sucking action or force; suction.
2. that which is sucked, as milk drawn from the breast
3. the amount sucked at one time; a sip. [Colloq.]
4. the sound of sucking.

suck″à·ụ′hock, *n.* [Am. Ind.] same as *sewan.*

suck′à·tash, *n.* same as *succotash.*

suck′en, *n.* [AS. *socn*, privilege, jurisdiction, from *soc*, a soke, liberty, privilege.] in Scots law, the district attached to a mill, or the whole lands astricted to a mill, the tenants of which are bound to bring their grain to the mill to be ground: also called *soken.*

suck′ẽr, *n.* 1. one who or that which sucks; a suckling; particularly, a baby pig or whale.
2. a part or device used for sucking; specifically, (a) a pipe or conduit through which something is sucked; (b) the piston or piston valve of a suction pump; (c) an organ used by the snail, leech, etc. for sucking or holding fast to a surface by suction.
3. any of several varieties of fishes, as the sucking fish, lumpfish or lumpsucker, hagfish, northern sucker, white sucker, buffalo, chub, and others of the family *Catostomidæ.*
4. in botany, any of the rootlike sucking organs of certain parasitic plants; a haustorium.
5. in horticulture, a shoot springing from the roots or stem of a plant.
6. one who lives on others; a parasite; a sponger. [Rare.]
7. a lollipop. [Colloq.]
8. a toy consisting of a small piece of leather having a string attached to the center of it: when wet, it picks up by suction stones, etc. with which it is brought into contact.
9. a person easily cheated or taken in; a dupe; a simpleton. [Slang.]
cherry sucker; the spotted flycatcher of Europe. [Brit. Dial.]

suck′ẽr, *v.t.*; suckered, *pt., pp.*; suckering, *ppr.* to strip off shoots from; to deprive of suckers; as, to *sucker* maize.

suck′ẽr, *v.i.* to bear suckers, or shoots; as, corn *suckers* abundantly.

suck′ẽr·el, *n.* a fish, the black horse.

suck′ẽr foot, in zoology, (a) a proleg; (b) a tube foot.

suck′ẽr list, a list of persons regarded as easy victims for a swindle. [Slang.]

suck′fish, *n.*; *pl.* **suck′fish** or **suck′fish″eṣ,**
1. the remora.
2. a small sea fish of the blenny family, having a sucking disk on the underside.

suck′ing, *a.* 1. making use of suction; absorbing.
2. unweaned.
3. figuratively, very young; still in the infantile stage.

suck′ing fish, a remora.

suck′ing pump, same as *suction pump.*

suck′ing stŏm′ăçh, the first stomach of certain crustaceans and insects.

suck′le, *n.* a teat. [Obs.]

suck′le, *v.t.*; suckled (-ld), *pt., pp.*; suckling, *ppr.* [a freq. of *suck.*]
1. to cause to suck at the breast or udder; to nurse.
2. to bring up; to rear; to foster.

suck′le, *v.i.* to suck at the breast.

suck′lẽr, *n.* 1. a suckling.
2. a mammal.

suck′ling, *n.* [ME. *sokeling*, dim. of *sokel*, one who sucks.]
1. an unweaned child or young animal.
2. any of various plants sucked for honey; (a) the white clover; (b) the red clover; (c) the honeysuckle. [Brit. Dial.]

suck′stōne, *n.* a fish, the remora.

sū′crāte, *n.* [Fr. *sucre*, sugar, and *-ate.*] in chemistry, a salt of sucrose or some related carbohydrate.

sụ′çre (-çrā), *n.* [Am. Sp., after Antonio José de *Sucre* (1795–1830), S. Am. liberator.] the monetary unit of Ecuador.

sū′çrōse, *n.* [Fr. *sucre*, sugar.] a crystalline sugar, $C_{12}H_{22}O_{11}$, found in sugar cane, sugar beets, etc.

suç′tion, *n.* [OFr., from L. *suctus*, pp. of *sugere*, to suck.]
1. the act of process of sucking.
2. the production of a vacuum or partial vacuum in a container or over a surface, so that the external atmospheric pressure forces the surrounding fluid into the space or causes something to adhere to the surface.
3. the sucking force created in this way.

suç′tion an·e·mom′e·tẽr, an anemometer indicating a diminution of pressure corresponding to the diminution in the velocity of the wind.

suç′tion chām′bẽr, the chamber, barrel, or cylinder of a pump into which the water or other fluid is delivered from the suction pipe.

suç′tion pīpe, the pipe leading from the bottom of a pump barrel or cylinder to the well, cistern, or reservoir from which the water or other liquid is to be drawn up.

suç′tion pump, a pump in which water is drawn by means of suction induced by a piston and retained in the tube or barrel by means of a set of valves.

suç′tion stop, in phonetics, a stop sound made by drawing the breath into the mouth and clicking the lips or tongue.

suç′tion valve, the valve of a suction pump at the bottom of the cylinder; also, a similar valve in a feed pump.

Suç·tō′ri·à, *n.pl.* in zoology, any of several groups of animals; specifically, (a) an order of *Infusoria* in which the body is generally provided with a number of radiating filamentous tubes which have at their extremities suctorial disks; (b) that order of parasitic insects which contains the fleas, and which live by sucking the blood of man and some species of quadrupeds and birds; (c) an order of *Annelida*, containing the leeches, which are provided with a sucking disk at both extremities of the body; (d) a group of lower fishes comprising those which have a circular mouth adapted for suction, as the lamprey.

suç·tō′ri·ăl, *a.* [L. *suctus*, pp. of *sugere*, to suck.]
1. of or adapted for sucking or suction.
2. having organs used for sucking.
3. feeding by sucking fluids.

suç·tō′ri·ăn, *n.* any suctorial animal.

suç·tō′ri·ous, *a.* suctorial. [Rare.]

sū·dam′i·nà, *n.pl.*; *sing.* **sū·dā′men,** [L. *sudus*, without moisture, dry, from *sudare*, to sweat.] in pathology, minute transparent vesicles caused by the retention of sweat in the upper layers of the skin after heavy perspiration, as in certain fevers.

sū·dam′i·năl, *a.* of or pertaining to sudamina.

Sụ·dà·nēṣe′, *a.* of or pertaining to the Sudan, a region in Africa, or its people.

Sụ·dà·nēṣe′, *n.*; *pl.* **Sụ·dà·nēṣe′,** an inhabitant or native of the Sudan.

Sụ·dan′ grȧss, [after the *Sudan*, Africa, where it is cultivated.] a kind of grass grown for hay.

Sụ·dan′iç, *a.* designating or of a family of languages, variously spoken across nothern Africa, including Yoruba, Mandingo, and Tshi.

Sụ·dan′iç, *n.* the Sudanic family of languages.

sū·dâr′i·um, *n.*; *pl.* **sū·dâr′i·à,** [L.] 1. a sudatorium.
2. a handkerchief or cloth for wiping sweat from the face; specifically, the Veronica or a veronica.

sū′dà·ry, *n.*; *pl.* **sū′dà·rieṣ,** a sudarium.

sū·dā′tion, *n.* [L. *sudatio* (-*onis*), a sweating, from *sudare*, to sweat.] a sweating. [Rare.]

sū·dà·tō′ri·um, *n.*; *pl.* **sū·dà·tō′ri·à,** [L.] a heated room used for sweat baths.

sū′dà·tō·ry, *n.*; *pl.* **sū′dà·tō·rieṣ,** [L. *sudatorius*, belonging to or serving for sweating from *sudare*, to sweat.]
1. a sudatorium.
2. a sudorific.

sū′dà·tō·ry, *a.* 1. of a sudatorium.
2. sudorific.

sudd, *n.* [from Ar. *sudd*, to obstruct.] a mass of vegetable matter that forms floating islands in the White Nile, and obstructs navigation.

sud′den (sud′n), *a.* [ME. *sodain*; OFr. *sodain, sudain*; L. *subitaneus*, sudden, extended from *subitus*, pp. of *subire*, to go stealthily; *sub-*, and *ire*, to go or come.]
1. happening without previous notice; coming or appearing unexpectedly; not foreseen or prepared for; as, a *sudden* emergency.
2. done, coming, or taking place quickly or abruptly; hasty.
3. violent; rash; precipitate; impetuous. [Archaic.]
4. rapidly effective; prompt in effect. [Archaic.]
Syn.—unanticipated, unexpected, unlooked-for.

sud′den, *n.* an unexpected occurrence: obsolete except in the phrase *all of a sudden*, suddenly or unexpectedly.

sud′den in′fănt death syn′drōme, the sudden death of an apparently healthy infant, of unknown cause but believed to be related to some faulty mechanism in respiration control.

sud′den·ly, *adv.* in a sudden manner.

sud′den·ness, *n.* the state or quality of being sudden; a coming or happening without previous notice.

sud′den ty, *n.* suddenness. [Scot.]

Sụ·dẹ′ten, *n.* a native or inhabitant of the Sudetenland, Czchoslovakia.

Sụ·dẹ′ten, *a.* of the Sudetenland or its people.

sū′dŏr, *n.* [L.] sweat; perspiration.

sū′dŏr·ăl, *a.* of, characterized by, or relating to sweat or perspiration.

sū·dŏr·if′ẽr·ous, *a.* [L. *sudor, sudoris*, sweat, and *-ferous.*] causing or secreting perspiration.
sudoriferous gland; a sweat gland.

sū·dŏr·if′iç, *a.* [Fr. *sudorifique*; L. *sudorificus*, causing sweat, from *sudor, sudoris*, sweat, and *ficus*, making, from *facere*, to make.] causing or increasing sweating.

sū·dŏr·if′iç, *n.* a medicine, etc. that causes or increases sweating.

sū·dŏr·ip′à·rous, *a.* same as *sudoriferous.*

Sū′dra, *n.* [Sans. *sūdra.*] formerly, the lowest of the four great castes among the Hindus.

sudṣ, *n.pl.* [prob. (via East Anglican dial.) from M.D. *sudse*, marsh, marsh water.]
1. soapy water.
2. a froth on the surface of soapy water; foam.
3. beer. [Slang.]

sudṣ′y, *a.*; *comp.* sudsier; *superl.* sudsiest; full of or like suds or froth; foamy.

sūe (*or* sụ), *v.t.*; sued, *pt., pp.*; suing, *ppr.* [ME. *suen, sewen, suwen*; OFr. *sevre, suir, sivir*; LL. (hyp.) *sequere*, for L. *sequi*, to follow.]
1. to follow. [Obs.]
2. to act as a suitor to; to woo. [Archaic.]
3. to appeal to; to petition; to beseech.
4. in law, (a) to petition (a court) for justice or redress through legal action; (b) to bring civil action against or prosecute in a court of law in seeking redress of wrongs or justice; (c) to carry (an action) through to its final decision.
5. to beg; to ask for. [Archaic.]
When you *sued* staying. —Shak.
to sue out; in law, to apply for and obtain, as a pardon, a writ, or the like.

sūe, *v.i.* 1. to make an appeal; to petition; to plead.
2. to pay suit; to woo. [Archaic.]
3. to institute legal proceedings in court; to bring suit.

suede, suède (swād), *n.* [Fr. *Suède*, Sweden, in *gants de Suède*, Swedish gloves.]
1. tanned leather, formerly kid, and now usually calf, having the flesh side buffed into a nap.
2. a kind of cloth made to resemble this: also *suede cloth.*

sū′ẽr, *n.* one who sues.

sū′et, *n.* [ME., dim. of Anglo-Fr. *sue*; OFr. *sieu, seu*, from L. *sebum*, fat, tallow.] the fatty tissue of cattle and sheep, particularly the hard, crumbly fat deposited around the kidneys and loins: used in cooking and making tallow.

sū′et·y, *a.* consisting of, containing, or resembling suet; as, a *suety* substance.

suf-, see *sub-.*

suf′fẽr, *v.t.*; suffered, *pt., pp.*; suffering, *ppr.* [ME. *soffren, suffren*; OFr. *soffrir, suffrir*; L. *sufferre*, to undergo, endure; *sub*, under, and *ferre*, to bear.]
1. to undergo (something painful or unpleasant, as injury, grief, etc.); to endure; to bear; to be afflicted with.
2. to undergo or experience (any operation or process, especially change).
3. to allow; permit; tolerate.
4. to bear up under; to endure: now only in negative constructions; as, he could not *suffer* criticism.
Syn.—feel, bear, experience, sustain, permit, allow.

suf′fẽr, *v.i.* 1. to experience pain, harm, injury, loss, etc.
2. to be punished; to receive a penalty, especially death.
The father was first condemned to *suffer* on a day appointed, and the son afterward, the day following. —Clarendon.
3. to sustain loss or damage; as, foreign trade *suffers* from the high tariff rate.
4. to tolerate or endure evil, injury, etc. [Archaic.]

suf′fẽr·ȧ·ble, *a.* 1. that can be suffered, endured, or allowed; tolerable.
2. able to suffer. [Obs.]

suf′fẽr·ȧ·ble·ness, *n.* the state or quality of being sufferable.

suf′fẽr·ȧ·bly, *adv.* in a sufferable manner; tolerably.

suf′fẽr·ănce, *n.* [ME. *suffrance*; OFr. *soffrance, souffrance*; L. *sufferentia*, endurance.]
1. a suffering; the bearing of pain, affliction, or misery. [Archaic.]
2. patient endurance; moderation; submission. [Archaic.]
3. the power or capacity to endure or tolerate pain, distress, etc.
4. consent, permission, or sanction implied by failure to interfere; toleration.
5. in England, a permit to remove imported goods previous to the payment of duties.
estate at sufferance; an estate which is not surrendered at the expiration of a lease but is held by the tenant without positive leave of the owner.
on sufference; allowed or tolerated but not actually supported or encouraged; as, to hold an office or position *on sufferance.*
Syn.—pain, misery, inconvenience, endurance, patience, moderation, toleration, permission.

suf′fẽr·ẽr, *n.* one who or that which suffers.

suf′fẽr·ing, *n.* 1. the bearing or undergoing of pain, distress, or injury.
2. something suffered; pain; distress; injury.
Syn.—agony, pain, distress, torment, anguish, injury.

suf′fẽr·ing, *a.* being under stress of pain or grief; sustaining injury or loss.

suf′fẽr·ing·ly, *adv.* in a suffering manner; with suffering.

suf·fīce′, *v.i.*; sufficed (-fīst), *pt., pp.*; sufficing, *ppr.* [ME. *suffisen*; OFr. *suffire*, to suffice; L. *sufficere*, to provide, suffice, from *sub-*, under, and *facere*, to make.]
1. to be enough; to be sufficient or adequate.
2. to be competent or able. [Obs.]

suf·fīce′, *v.t.* 1. to answer the purpose or requirements of; to meet the needs of; to be enough for; to satisfy; as, this sum *suffices* all his needs.
2. to supply; to furnish. [Obs.]

suf·fi′cience (-fish′ens), *n.* sufficiency. [Obs.]

suf·fi′cien·cy, *n.* 1. sufficient means, ability, or resources; specifically, (a) an ample amount or quantity (*of* what is needed); (b) enough wealth or income.
2. the state or quality of being sufficient or adequate; adequacy.
3. self-sufficiency; self-confidence; conceit.
Syn.—abundance, ampleness, competency, adequacy, efficiency.

suf·fi′cient, *a.* [L. *sufficiens* (*-entis*), ppr. of *sufficere*, to suffice.]
1. enough; equal to the end proposed; adequate to wants; as much as is needed; enough; as, food *sufficient* for an army.
2. qualified; competent; possessing adequate talents or accomplishments; fit; capable; as, a scholar *sufficient* for such work. [Archaic.]
3. responsible; solvent; financially able. [Obs.]
4. self-sufficient. [Obs.]
principle of sufficient reason; the principle of Leibnitz that everything in the universe has adequate ground for its existence.
Syn.—ample, satisfactory, enough, full, adequate, qualified.

suf·fi′cient·ly, *adv.* so as to be sufficient; to a sufficient degree; enough.

suf·fī′cing, *a.* that suffices; satisfying; affording enough.

suf·fī′cing·ly, *adv.* in a sufficing manner.

suf·fī′cing·ness, *n.* the state, quality, or condition of being sufficient.

suf·fī′ṣănce, *n.* sufficiency; abundance; plenty. [Obs.]

suf·fī′ṣănt, *a.* sufficient; enough. [Obs.]

suf′fix, *n.* [L. *suffixus*, pp. of *suffigere*, to fasten on beneath; *sub*, under, and *figere*, to fix.]
1. a sound, syllable, or syllables added at the end of a word or word base to change its meaning, give it grammatical function, or form a new word, as *-ish* in small*ish*, *-ed* in walk*ed*, and *-ness* in dark*ness*.
2. in mathematics, a subindex.

suf·fix′, *v.t.*; suffixed (-fixt′), *pt., pp.*; suffixing, *ppr.* to add as a suffix.

suf′fix·ăl, *a.* of the nature of or relating to a suffix.

suf·fix′iŏn (-fik′shun), **suf·fix′ment,** *n.* a suffixing or being suffixed.

suf·flam′i·nāte, *v.t.* [L. *sufflamen*, a clog.] to retard the motion of, as a wheeled vehicle, by means of a clog or otherwise. [Rare.]

suf·flāte′, *v.t.* [from L. *sufflare*, from *sub-*, under, and *flare*, to blow.] to blow up; to inflate. [Obs.]

suf·flā′tion, *n.* [L. *sufflatio* (*-onis*), a blowing up, inflation, from *sufflatus*, pp. of *sufflare*, to inflate.] the act of blowing up or inflating. [Obs.]

suf′fō·cāte, *v.t.*; suffocated, *pt., pp.*; suffocating, *ppr.* [L. *suffocatus*, pp. of *suffocare*, to choke; lit., to put something under the gullet; *sub*, under, and *fauces*, the gullet, throat.]
1. to kill by cutting off the supply of air to the lungs, gills, etc. so as to cause asphyxiation.
2. to hinder the free breathing of; to deprive of fresh air.
3. to smother, suppress, extinguish, etc. by, or as by, cutting off the supply of air.
Syn.—stifle, smother, choke.

suf′fō·cāte, *v.i.* 1. to die by being suffocated.
2. to be unable to breathe freely; to choke; to stifle; to smother.

suf′fō·cāte, *a.* suffocated. [Obs.]

suf′fō·cā·ting, *a.* choking; stifling.

suf′fō·cā·ting·ly, *adv.* in a suffocating manner; so as to suffocate; as, *suffocatingly* hot.

suf·fō·cā′tion, *n.* a suffocating or being suffocated.

suf′fō·cā·tive, *a.* tending to suffocate; as, *suffocative* catarrh.

suf·fos′siŏn (-fosh′un), *n.* a digging under; an undermining. [Obs.]

suf′frȧ·găn, *a.* [L. *suffragans*, ppr. of *suffragari*, to assist.] assisting; as, a *suffragan* bishop; of or relating to a suffragan.

suf′frȧ·găn, *n.* 1. an assistant bishop; a bishop who has been consecrated to assist the bishop of a see in a particular portion of his diocese.
2. any bishop in his capacity as subordinate to his archbishop.

suf′frȧ·găn·ship, *n.* the office or position of suffragan.

suf′frȧ·gănt, *n.* an assistant. [Obs.]

suf′frȧ·gănt, *a.* assisting. [Obs.]

suf′frȧ·gāte, *v.t.* and *v.i.*; suffragated, *pt., pp.*; suffragating, *ppr.* to vote for or to vote with; also, to act as an assistant or suffragant. [Obs.]

suf′frȧ·gā·tŏr, *n.* one who assists. [Obs.]

suf′fraġe, *n.* [OFr. *suffrage*; L. *suffragium*.]
1. a short prayer of intercession or supplication.
2. a vote or voting; especially, a vote in favor of someone or something.
3. the right to vote, especially in political matters; the franchise.
4. approval; consent. [Archaic.]
5. testimony; attestation; witness. [Obs.]
6. aid; assistance. [Obs.]
female suffrage; the right of women to vote in public elections.
household suffrage; see under *household.*
manhood suffrage; the political right of voting, as extended to all male citizens who have attained majority.
universal suffrage; the right of voting as extended to all adult citizens of either sex, and not restricted by property qualifications.

suf′fraġe, *v.t.* to vote for; to elect to office. [Obs.]

suf·frȧ·ġette′ (-jet′), *n.* a woman who militantly advocates female suffrage.

suf·frȧ·ġet′tiṣm, *n.* the principles or practices of suffragettes.

suf·fraġ′i·nous, *a.* [L. *suffrago*, the hock.] pertaining to the kneejoint of an animal. [Obs.]

suf′frȧ·ġist, *n.* a person who believes in extending political suffrage, especially to women.

suf·frā′gō, *n.*; *pl.* **suf·fraġ′i·nēṣ,** [*sub-*, and L. *frago*, from *frangere*, to break.]
1. in a quadruped, a joint between the tibia and tarsus; the hock.
2. the heel of a bird.

suf′frănce, *n.* sufferance. [Obs.]

suf·frụ·tes′cent, *a.* moderately frutescent.

suf′frụ·tex, *n.*; *pl.* **suf·frụ′ti·cēṣ,** [*sub-*, and L. *frutex*, a shrub.]
1. an undershrub or shrub of a small size, herbaceous at the ends of the shoots, but woody at the base, as thyme.
2. any small shrub; a short plant with woody stems, as the trailing arbutus.

suf·frụ′ti·çōse, *a.* [*sub-*, and L. *frutex* (*-icis*), a shrub.] in botany, woody at the base, but herbaceous above, as sage, thyme, hyssop, etc.

suf·frụ′ti·çous, *a.* suffruticose.

suf·frụ·tiç′ū·lōse, *a.* in botany, slightly or imperfectly fruticulose, as some lichens.

suf·fū′mi·gāte, *v.t.*; suffumigated, *pt., pp.*; suffumigating, *ppr.* [L. *suffumigare*, to smoke from below: *sub-*, and *fumigare*, to smoke, from *fumus*, smoke.] to fumigate from below; to apply fumes or smoke upward to the parts of, as to the body in medical treatment.

suf·fū·mi·gā′tion, *n.* 1. the operation of applying fumes from below; fumigation upward.
2. the act of burning incense, as in magic rites.
3. a substance to be burned in suffumigation.

suf·fū′miġe, *n.* a medicinal fume. [Obs.]

suf·fūṣe′, *v.t.*; suffused, *pt., pp.*; suffusing, *ppr.* [L. *suffusus*, pp. of *suffundere*, to pour beneath, diffuse beneath or upon; *sub*, under, and *fundere*, to pour.] to overspread, as with a liquid, light, color, etc.; to fill or cover, as with something fluid; as, eyes *suffused* with tears.

suf·fū′ṣion, *n.* [ME.; L. *suffusio*.]
1. the act of suffusing or overspreading, as with a liquid, light, or color.
2. the state of being suffused or spread over.
3. that which is suffused or spread over.
4. a coloring or tint spread over a surface; specifically, a flush or blush.

Sụ′fī, *n.* formerly, a title or surname of the shah of Persia.

Sụ′fī, *n.* [Ar. *ṣūfī*, ascetic, lit., a man of wool, from *ṣūf*, wool.] a person who believes in or practices Sufism.

Sụ′fiç, *a.* belonging or relating to Sufism; Sufistic.

Sụ′fiṣm, *n.* a system of Moslem mysticism practiced chiefly in Persia, from which has developed a literature of symbolical poetry.

Sụ·fis′tiç, *a.* of, characteristic of, or practicing Sufism.

sug-, see *sub-*.

sug, *n.* an unidentified parasite on trout. [Obs.]

sụg′ăr (shụg′), *n.* [ME. *sugre*; Fr. *sucre*; Sp. *azucar*; Ar. *sakkar, sokkar*; Per. *shakar*, sugar; Sans. *çarkarā*, gravel, clayed or candied sugar.]
1. a sweet, usually crystalline, substance, $C_{12}H_{22}O_{11}$, extracted chiefly from sugar cane and sugar beets and used as a food and sweetening agent: also called *cane* (or *beet*) *sugar, saccharose, sucrose.*
2. any of a class of sweet, soluble, crystalline carbohydrates, as the disaccharides (sucrose, lactose, and maltose) and the monosaccharides (glucose and fructose).
3. flattery; honeyed words.
4. that which resembles sugar in any of its properties; as, *sugar* of lead.
5. money. [Slang.]
bastard sugar; sugar made from old syrup.
black sugar; licorice.
confectioners' sugar; fine powdered sugar that will dissolve readily.
malado sugar; a conglomerate sugar in which the crystalline form is obscured by the presence of invert sugar.

sụg′ăr (shụg′), *v.t.*; sugared, *pt., pp.*; sugaring, *ppr.* 1. to impregnate, season, cover, sprinkle, or mix (food) with sugar.
2. to sweeten with sugar.
3. to cause to seem less disagreeable; to disguise, so as to render acceptable what is otherwise distasteful; to make pleasant with flattery, etc.

sụg′ăr, *v.i.* 1. to make maple sugar.
2. to form sugar crystals or granules by long, slow boiling (usually with *off*).

sụg′ăr älm′ŏnd (äm′), almond praline.

sụg′ăr bāk′ẽr, one who refines sugar.

sụg′ăr bēan, a kidney bean, *Phaseolus lunatus.*

sụg′ăr beet, a variety of the beet *Beta vulgaris*

having a root with white flesh and a high sugar content, extensively cultivated for use in sugar making.

sug'ăr·ber·ry, *n.*; *pl.* **sug'ăr·ber·ries,** the hackberry.

sug'ăr·bīrd, *n.* 1. any bird of the genus *Coereba*, which sucks the nectar of flowers.
2. a honey eater or honeybird.
3. the evening grosbeak, *Hesperiphona vespertina*. [Dial.]

sug'ăr bōwl, a small container of glass, china, etc., usually with a cover, for sugar at the table.

sug'ăr·bush, *n.* 1. any South African shrub of the genus *Protea*; particularly, *Protea mellifera*, which gives out a sweet liquid.
2. a grove or orchard of sugar maples.

sug'ăr camp, a place in or near a sugar maple orchard where the sap from the trees is collected and manufactured into sugar.

sug'ăr can'dy, sugar clarified and concreted or crystallized.

sug'ăr cāne, a plant, *Saccharum officinarum*, cultivated as the main source of sugar. It is a very tall grass, with jointed stems, large, firm, thin leaves, and numerous flowers arranged in a regular ample panicle, and each enveloped in a dense tuft of silky hairs.

SUGAR CANE

African sugar cane; imphee.
Chinese sugar cane; sorghum.
sugar-cane beetle; *Euetheola rugiceps*, a beetle that is destructive to sugar cane.
sugar-cane borer; the larva of the moth *Diatræa saccharalis*, which bores into sugar cane.

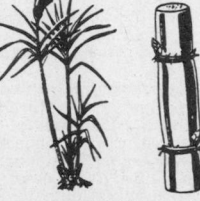

sug'ăr-cōat, *v.t.* 1. to cover or coat with sugar.
2. to make seem more pleasant or attractive, as with flattery, euphemism, etc.

sug'ăr-cōat·ing, *n.* 1. the act or process of coating with sugar.
2. that which makes something seem more pleasant or attractive, as flattery, etc.

sug'ăr corn, sweet corn.

sug'ăr-cūred', *a.* treated with a pickling preparation of sugar, salt, and nitrate or nitrite: said of ham, bacon, etc.

sug'ăr dad'dy, a wealthy, especially older, man who lavishes gifts on young women in return for their attentions. [Slang.]

sug'ăred, *a.* sweetened with or as with sugar; sugar-coated.

sug'ăr gum, the Australian tree, *Eucalyptus corynocalyx*.

sug'ăr·house, *n.* a place where sugar is processed; especially, a building where maple sap is boiled for producing maple sirup and sugar.

sug'ăr·i·ness, *n.* the quality or condition of being sugary.

sug'ăr·ing, *n.* 1. the act of sweetening with sugar; also, the sugar used in sweetening.
2. the process of making sugar, especially that part in which the cooling product granulates or turns to sugar.

sug'ăr·less, *a.* free from sugar.

sug'ăr-lōaf, *a.* shaped like a sugar loaf.

sug'ăr lōaf, 1. a conical mass of crystallized sugar.
2. something shaped like this, as a hill or mound.

sug'ăr mā'ple, a North American maple, *Acer saccharinum*, valued for its hard wood and for its sap from which maple sirup and maple sugar are made by boiling.

sug'ăr mill, a machine for pressing out the juice of the sugar cane: also called *cane mill*.

sug'ăr mil'let, sorghum.

sug'ăr mīte, a wingless insect, *Lepisma saccharina*, covered with silvery scales, found frequently in unrefined sugar.

sug'ăr of lead, lead acetate.

sug'ăr of milk, lactose.

sug'ăr or'chărd, a grove of sugar maple trees which annually furnish sap for making maple sugar and maple sirup.

sug'ăr pīne, any of a number of tall related pines of the Pacific coast, with soft, reddish-brown wood, large cones, and sugarlike resin.

sug'ăr·plum, *n.* a sweetmeat made up in small round or oval pieces; a bonbon; hence, something pleasing, as a compliment.

sug'ăr press, a device for pressing the juice from sugar cane.

sug'ăr squir'rel (skwĩr'), a small Australian marsupial, *Petaurus breviceps*, having a long bushy tail, but otherwise resembling a flying squirrel.

sug'ăr-tit, *n.* an artificial nipple sweetened with sugar and used to quiet a restless infant.

sug'ăr tongs, small tongs for serving lump sugar at the table.

sug'ăr tree, the sugar maple.

sug'ăr·y, *a.* 1. of or containing sugar.
2. like sugar; specifically, (a) sweet; (b) granular.
3. sweetly flattering or pleasant; honeyed.
4. fond of sugar or of sweet things.

sū'gent, *a.* [L. *sugens* (*-entis*), ppr. of *sugere*, to suck.] in zoology, pertaining to or adapted for sucking.

sū·ges'cent, *a.* sugent. [Rare.]

sug·gest' (*also* su-jest'), *v.t.*; suggested, *pt., pp.*; suggesting, *ppr.* [L. *suggestus*, pp. of *suggerere*, to carry or lay under, to furnish; *sub*, under, and *gerere*, to carry.]
1. to bring (a thought, problem, desire, etc.) to the mind for consideration.
2. to arouse (a thought) in the mind through association of ideas; as, what does this shape *suggest* to you?
3. to propose (someone or something) as a possibility; as, can you *suggest* a course of study?
4. to show indirectly; to imply; to intimate; as, her dark skin *suggests* a Latin background.
5. to serve as a motive for; to prompt; as, my success *suggested* further attempts.
6. to tempt; to seduce; to prompt to evil acts. [Obs.]
Syn.—insinuate, hint, instill, intimate.

sug·gest', *v.i.* to make suggestions; to prompt; to tempt.

sug·gest'ẽr, *n.* one who or that which suggests.

sug·gest·i·bil'i·ty, *n.* the quality or condition of being suggestible.

sug·gest'i·ble, *a.* 1. capable of being influenced by suggestion; especially, susceptible to hypnotic suggestion.
2. that can be suggested.

sug·ges'tion (-chun), *n.* [ME. and OFr. *suggestioun*; L. *suggestio* (*-onis*), from *suggestus*, pp. of *suggerere*, to suggest.]
1. a suggesting or being suggested.
2. something suggested.
3. the process through which an idea is brought to the mind because of its connection or association with an idea already in the mind.
4. a faint hint or indication; a small amount; a trace; as, there was a *suggestion* of boredom in her tone.
5. in psychology, (a) the inducing of an idea, decision, etc., by means of a verbal or other stimulus, in another individual, who accepts it uncritically, as in hypnosis; (b) an idea so induced, or the stimulus by which such uncritical acceptance is effected.
6. in law, information without oath.
7. a false accusation. [Obs.]
negative suggestion; the phase of suggestion which results in inaction or the repression of normal action, as in the hypnotic state.
suggestion on the record; in law, an entry upon the record of some important fact concerning a given case which necessarily makes an end of proceedings, as the death of one of the parties in the case.
Syn.—hint, allusion, intimation, insinuation, proposal.

sug·gest'ive, *a.* 1. that suggests or tends to suggest thoughts or ideas; containing a hint or intimation; full of suggestions.
2. tending to suggest something considered improper or indecent.
3. relating to or characterized by hypnotic suggestion; as, *suggestive* medicine, in which the treatment consists of suggestions made to a hypnotized subject.

sug·gest'ive·ly, *adv.* in a suggestive manner.

sug·gest'ive·ness, *n.* the state or character of being suggestive.

sug·gest'ment, *n.* suggestion [Rare.]

sug·gest'ress, *n.* a woman who suggests. [Rare.]

sug'gill, *v.t.* [L. *suggillare*, to beat, to revile.]
1. to make livid by bruises. [Obs.]
2. to defame; to sully; to blacken. [Obs.]

sug'gil·lāte, *v.t.* to beat black and blue. [Obs.]

sug·gil·lā'tion, *n.* a livid or black-and-blue mark; a bruise.

sú'gi, *n.* a coniferous tree, *Cryptomeria japonica*, of Japan; the Japanese cedar, growing very tall with a straight stem, the valuable wood of which is white and soft.

sū·i·cīd'ăl, *a.* 1. of, involving, or leading to suicide.
2. having an urge to commit suicide.

sū·i·cīd'ăl·ly, *adv.* in a suicidal manner.

sū'i·cīde, *n.* [Fr., from L. *sui*, of oneself, and *-cidium*, a slaying, from *cædere*, to slay.]
1. the act of killing oneself intentionally; in law, the act of self-destruction by a person sound in mind and capable of measuring his moral responsibility; legal suicide.
2. by extension, destruction of one's moral, social, political, or business life by one's own act; ruin of one's plans or interests because of one's own neglect or action.

> Throughout these years they had died to each other by that soul *suicide* of mutual indifference.
> —Katherine Holland Brown.

3. a person who commits suicide.

sū'i·cīde, *v.t.*; suicided, *pt., pp.*; suiciding, *ppr.* to commit suicide. [Colloq.]

sū·i·cī·dol'ō·gy, *n.* the study of suicide, its causes, and its prevention, and of the behavior of those who threaten or attempt suicide.

sū'i·cism, *n.* egoism. [Obs.]

Sū'i·dae, *n.pl.* [L. *sus*, *suis*, a sow, and Gr. *eidos*, resemblance.] a family of ungulate artiodactylous mammals consisting of the swine and typified by the genus *Sus*. The family includes the wild boar, *Sus scrofa*, and the domestic hog.

sū'ī gen'ẽr·is, [L.] of his, her, or its own kind; singular; unique; in a class by itself.

sū'ī jū'ris, [L., lit., in his (or her) own right.] in law, legally competent to manage one's own affairs, because of legal age and of sound mind.

sū'il·lāge, *n.* a drain of filth. [Obs.]

sū'il·line, *a.* relating to or resembling a hog.

sū'il·line, *n.* one of the *Suidæ*; a hog.

sū'ine, *n.* a preparation consisting of suet, lard, etc., used as a substitute for butter.

sū'ing, *n.* [verbal noun of *sue*.]
1. a making or paying suit; a wooing.
2. the bringing of a suit at law.

sū'ing·ly, *adv.* subsequently. [Obs.]

sū'int (*or* swint), *n.* [Fr.] the grease obtained in washing sheep's wool, consisting of insoluble saponaceous matter and a soluble salt containing potash.

sū'ist, *n.* an egoist. [Obs.]

sūit, *n.* [ME. *siute*, *seute*; OFr. *suite*; L. *secta*, a following, in LL. extended to mean a suit at law, a series, order, set, a suit of clothes, etc.; from the base of *sequi*, to follow.]
1. a set of clothes to be worn together; now, especially, a coat, trousers (or skirt), and, often, a vest, usually all of the same material.
2. a group of similar things forming a set or series.
3. any of the four sets of thirteen playing cards each (*spades*, *clubs*, *hearts*, and *diamonds*) forming a pack.
4. historically, the act of following or attending a feudal court in an effort to secure justice.
5. action to secure justice in a court of law; attempt to recover a right or claim through legal action.
6. (a) an act of suing, pleading, or requesting; (b) a petition.
7. a wooing.
8. pursuit; chase. [Obs.]
9. succession; series; regular order. [Obs.]
10. a following; a company; a retinue. [Obs.]
fresh suit; in law, immediate pursuit of an offender. [Obs.]
out of suits; at discord or out of favor. [Obs.]
suit and service; in feudal law, the attendance of a vassal upon his lord at court in return for the tenure and protection afforded him by the lord.
suit at law; same as *suit* (sense 5).
suit covenant; in feudal law, a covenant to attend the court of the superior lord.
to bring suit; to institute legal action; to sue.
to follow suit; see under *follow*.

sūit, *v.t.*; suited, *pt., pp.*; suiting, *ppr.* 1. to adapt; to accommodate; to fit or make suitable; as, to *suit* oneself to one's circumstances.
2. to become; to be adapted or fitted to; to be suitable for or appropriate to; to agree with.

3. to be agreeable to; to fall in with the wishes or convenience of; to please; to satisfy; as, that arrangement did not *suit* him at all.

4. to dress; to clothe. [Rare.]

to suit oneself; to act according to one's own wishes.

sūit, *v.i.* 1. to correspond or harmonize (usually with *to* or *with*). [Archaic.]

2. to be fit, suitable, or convenient.

to suit up; to put on a spacesuit, athletic uniform, etc. in preparation for a particular activity.

sūit·ȧ·bil′i·ty, *n.* the condition or quality of being suitable; appropriateness; applicability.

sūit′ȧ·ble, *a.* fitting; appropriate; applicable; agreeable; becoming; as, language *suitable* to the subject.

Syn.—apt, becoming, appropriate, expedient, fit.

sūit′ȧ·ble·ness, *n.* fitness; propriety; the state of being suitable.

sūit′ȧ·bly, *adv.* in a suitable manner; so as to be suitable.

sūit′çase, *n.* a valise or traveling bag that is flat and rectangular in shape: originally it was called a *dress-suit case* and was designed to contain a suit of clothes and accessories.

suite (swēt), *n.* [Fr. *suite*, a following, *suit*, from L. *secutus*, pp. of *sequi*, to follow.]

1. a company or number of attendants or followers; train; retinue; as, the *suite* of a visiting prince.

2. a set or series of related things; specifically, (a) a group of connected rooms used as a unit; (b) a number of pieces of matched furniture for a given room; as, a dining room *suite*.

3. a sequel. [Rare.]

4. in music, (a) an early form of instrumental composition consisting of a series of dances in the same or related keys; (b) a modern instrumental composition in a number of movements.

sūit′hōld, *n.* in feudal law, a tenure granted for attendance and services rendered a superior lord.

sūit′ing, *n.* material from which a suit of clothes can be made.

sūit′ŏr, *n.* 1. who sues or prosecutes at law, as a plaintiff, petitioner, or appellant.

2. a petitioner; an applicant.

3. a man who courts or woos a woman; a wooer; a lover.

sūit′ress, *n.* a woman suitor. [Rare.]

sụ′ki·yä′ki, *n.* [Japan.] a Japanese dish of sliced meat, onions, and other vegetables fried together and seasoned with soya sauce, sake, and sugar.

sụk′kȧh, *n.*; *pl.* **sụk′kōt, sụk′kōth** (-ōt, -ōs), [see next entry.] a temporary structure with a roof of leafy boughs, straw, etc., built by Jews for Sukkoth to commemorate the tabernacles of the Exodus.

Sụk·kōth′ (*or* sụk′ōs), *n.pl.* [*construed as sing.*] [Heb. *sūkōth*, lit., tabernacles.] a Jewish holiday, the Feast of Tabernacles, celebrating the fall harvest: also *Succos*.

sụ′jee, *n.* [Anglo-Ind.] a kind of fine flour made from the heart of Indian wheat: also written *soojee, soujee, suji*.

Sū′lȧ, *n.* [Ice. *sūla*, the solan goose or gannet.] a genus of conical-billed sea birds including the gannets.

sul′çāte, sul′çā·ted, *a.* [L. *sulcatus*, pp. of *sulcare*, to furrow, from *sulcus*, a furrow.] furrowed; grooved; scored with deep, parallel furrows or grooves.

sul·çā′tion, *n.* 1. any of a series of deep, parallel grooves or furrows.

2. the state of being sulcate; the act, process, or mode of grooving or making sulcate.

sul′çū·lus, *n.*; *pl.* **sul′çū·lī,** [L.] a small or minute sulcus.

sul′çus, *n.*; *pl.* **sul′cī,** [L.] a groove or furrow; a channel or fissure; specifically, in anatomy, one of the shallow grooves separating the convolutions of the brain.

sulf-, a combining form meaning *of* or *containing sulfur*: also *sulph-*.

sul′fȧ, *a.* designating or of a family of drugs of the sulfanilamide type, used in combating certain bacterial infections: words beginning with *sulfa-* may also be spelled *sulpha-*.

sul·fȧ·dī′ȧ·zīne, *n.* a sulfa drug, $C_{10}H_{10}N_4O_2S$, used in treating certain pneumococcus, streptococcus, and staphylococcus infections.

sul·fȧ·guȧ′ni·dīne (-gwan′ȧ-), *n.* a sulfa drug, $C_7H_{10}N_4O_2S{\cdot}H_2O$, used in the treatment of various intestinal infections.

sulf·am′āte, *n.* a salt of sulfamic acid.

sul·fȧ·mer′ȧ·zīne, *n.* a sulfa drug, $C_{11}H_{12}N_4$-O_2S, a methyl derivative of sulfadiazine that is more rapidly absorbed.

sul″fȧ·meth″yl·thī′ȧ·zōle, *n.* a sulfa drug, $C_{10}H_{11}N_3O_2S_2$, used especially in treating staphylococcus infections.

sulf·am′iç, *a.* having sulfur and ammonium as the characteristic constituents.

sulfamic acid; an acid the ammonium salt of which is produced by the action of dry ammonia on dry sulfur trioxide. It is a monobasic acid, known only in its salts, called sulfamates.

sulf·am′īde, *n.* an amido compound produced when dry ammonia gas is passed over sulfuryl chloride.

sulf·ȧ·nil′a·mīde, *n.* a white crystalline compound, $NH_2C_6H_4SO_2NH_2$, used in treating gonorrhea, septicemia, streptococcus infections, etc.: a synthetic coal-tar product.

sulf·ȧ·nil′iç, *a.* derived from or containing sulfuric acid and aniline.

sulf·an·ti·mō′nāte, *n.* a salt of sulfantimonic acid.

sulf·an·ti·mon′iç, *a.* pertaining to or designating a compound derived from an antimonic sulfide.

sulf·an·ti·mō′ni·ous, *a.* pertaining to or designating a compound derived from a sulfacid of antimony.

sulf·an′ti·mō·nīte, *n.* a salt of sulfantimonious acid.

sul·fȧ·pyr′ȧ·zīne, *n.* a sulfa drug, $C_{10}H_{10}N_4O_2S$, used in treating certain pneumococcus, streptococcus, and staphylococcus infections.

sul·fȧ·pyr′i·dīne, *n.* a sulfa drug, $C_{11}H_{11}N_3O_2S$, used especially in the treatment of pneumonia.

sulf·är·sē′ni·āte, *n.* a salt of sulfarsenic acid.

sulf·är·sen′iç, *a.* designating a compound derived from a sulfide of arsenic.

sulf·är′se·nīde, *n.* a double salt of sulfide and arsenide.

sulf·är·sē′ni·ous, *a.* designating a compound derived from an arsenious sulfide.

sulf·är′se·nīte, *n.* a salt of sulfarsenious acid.

sul·fȧ·sux′i·dīne, *n.* a sulfa drug, $C_{14}H_{13}N_3O_5$-S_2, used especially in treating infections in the intestinal and urinary tracts: a trade-mark (*Sulfasuxidine*).

sul′fāte, *n.* [Fr.; Mod. L. *sulphas, sulphatis*, from L. *sulphur*, sulfur.] a salt of sulfuric acid.

sul′fāte, *v.t.*; sulfated, *pt., pp.*; sulfating, *ppr.* 1. to treat with sulfuric acid or a sulfate.

2. to convert into a sulfate.

3. to cause a deposit of sulfates to form on (the plates of a storage battery).

sul′fāte, *v.i.* to become sulfated.

sul·fȧ·thī′ȧ·zōle, *n.* a sulfa drug, $C_9H_9N_3O_2S_2$, used especially in treating pneumonia and staphylococcus infections.

sul·fat′iç, *a.* characteristic of or containing a sulfate or sulfates.

sul′fȧ·tīze, *v.t.*; sulfatized, *pt., pp.*; sulfatizing, *ppr.* to turn (sulfide ores, etc.) into sulfate, as by roasting.

sul·fat′ō-, a combining form meaning *containing a sulfate*.

sul′fīde, sul′fid, *n.* a compound of sulfur with another element or a radical.

sul′fi·nāte, *n.* a salt of sulfinic acid.

sulf·in·di·got′iç, *a.* pertaining to, derived from, or containing sulfuric acid and indigo.

sul′fine, *n.* any compound formed principally by the union of sulfur with a hydrocarbon radical.

sul·fin′iç, *a.* designating any of a series of acids derived from sulfine.

sul′fi·nīde, *n.* same as *saccharin* (sense 1).

sul′fi·ŏn, *n.* a supposed radical, SO_4, resulting from the electrolysis of sulfuric acid.

sulf′i·ō·nīde, *n.* a sulfate. [Obs.]

sul′fīte, *n.* a salt of sulfurous acid.

sul·fit′iç, *a.* of, like, or using sulfite.

sul′fō-, a combining form used in chemistry meaning: (a) *having divalent sulfur*; (b) *replacing oxygen with sulfur*; (c) *having the sulfonic or sulfonyl group*. Also *sulpho-*.

sul″fō·är·sen′iç, *a.* belonging to, relating to, or containing sulfur and arsenic.

sul·fō·çär′bŏn·āte, *n.* a sulfocarbonic acid salt.

sul″fō·çär·bon′iç, *a.* designing a sulfacid resembling carbonic acid.

sul·fō·cy̆′ȧ·nāte, *n.* same as *thiocyanate*.

sul″fō·cy̆·an′iç ac′id, same as *thiocyanic acid*.

sul·fō·cy̆′ȧ·nīde, *n.* same as *thiocyanate*.

sul·fō·hā′līte, *n.* a greenish-yellow mineral containing sodium sulfate and sodium chloride.

sul·fō·hy′drāte, *n.* any compound of a base with the radical SH, or hydrogen sulfide: also written *sulphydrate*.

sul′fō·nǎl, *n.* a white, crystalline compound, $C_7H_{16}S_2O_4$, used in medicine as a soporific.

sul·fon′ȧ·mīde, *n.* any of the sulfa drugs, as sulfathiazole or sulfapyridine, containing the monovalent radical $-SO_2NH_2$ and used in the treatment of various bacterial diseases.

sul′fō·nāte, *n.* the ester of a sulfonic acid.

sul′fō·nāte, *v.t.* sulfonated, *pt., pp.*; sulfonating, *ppr.* to introduce the sulfonic group into (an aromatic hydrocarbon) by treating with sulfuric acid.

sul′fōne, *n.* [G. *sulfon*, from *sulfur*, sulfur.] any of a group of compounds containing the radical SO_2, the sulfur atom of which is linked chemically with a carbon atom of each of two alkyl groups.

sul·fon′iç, *a.* designating or of the univalent acid group SO_3H.

sul·fon′iç ac′id, any acid containing the sulfonic group and derived from sulfuric acid by the replacement of an OH group.

sul·fō′ni·um, *n.* [Mod. L.; *sulf*ur, and am*monium*.] a univalent electropositive radical made up of three alkyl radicals and one atom of sulfur, as the triethyl sulfonium radical $(C_2H_5)_3S-$.

sul·fōn·meth′āne, *n.* same as *sulfonal*.

sul′fō·nyl (*or* -nēl), *n.* the divalent radical SO_2: also *sulfuryl*.

sul·fō·phos′phāte, *n.* a salt of sulfophosphoric acid.

sul·fō·phos′phīte, *n.* a salt of sulfophosphorous acid.

sul″fō·phos·phor′iç, *a.* designating a compound derived from phosphoric sulfide.

sul·fō·phos′phō·rous, *a.* designating a derivative of phosphorous sulfide.

sul′fō salt, a salt in which oxygen is replaced by sulfur; sulfur salt.

sul·fō·stan′nāte, *n.* a sulfostannic acid salt.

sul·fō·stan′niç, *a.* designating a derivative of stannic sulfide.

sul·fō·vin′iç, *a.* designating a derivative of sulfuric acid and alcohol.

sul′fūr, *n.* [ME. *sulphre*; L. *sulphur*, sulfur.] a pale-yellow, nonmetallic chemical element found in crystalline or amorphous form: it burns with a blue flame and a stifling odor and is used in vulcanizing rubber, making matches, paper, gunpowder, insecticides, sulfuric acid, etc.: symbol S; atomic weight, 32.06; atomic number, 16: see also *sulphur*: see *sulf-*.

flowers of sulfur; the condensed vapor of heated sulfur.

roll sulfur; purified sulfur in stick form.

sublimed sulfur; flowers of sulfur.

sulfur acid; same as *sulfacid*.

sulfur alcohol; same as *mercaptan*.

sulfur dioxide; a heavy, colorless, suffocating gas, SO_2, easily liquefied and used as a bleach, disinfectant, and refrigerant.

sulfur ether; a sulfide of a hydrocarbon radical, having sulfur in the place of the oxygen of ordinary ethers.

sulfur trioxide; a white crystalline compound, SO_3, formed by oxidizing sulfur dioxide. It forms sulfuric acid on uniting with water.

vegetable sulfur; same as *lycopode*.

sul′fū·rāte, *a.* of, like, or containing sulfur.

sul′fū·rāte, *v.t.*; sulfurated, *pt., pp.*; sulfurating, *ppr.* to treat or combine with sulfur; to sulfurize.

sul·fū·rā′tion, *n.* a sulfurating or being sulfurated.

sul′fū·rā·tŏr, *n.* a device for fumigating or bleaching with sulfur fumes.

sul·fū′rē·ous, *a.* [L. *sulfureus*, of or like sulfur.]

1. of, like, or containing sulfur.

2. greenish-yellow.

sul·fū′rē·ous·ly, *adv.* in a sulfureous manner.

sul·fū′rē·ous·ness, *n.* the state or quality of being sulfureous.

sul′fū·ret, *n.* a sulfide.

sul′fū·ret, *v.t.*; sulfuretted, *pt., pp.*; sulfuretting, *ppr.* to combine or impregnate with sulfur.

sul′fū·ret·ted, *a.* having sulfur in combination.

sulfuretted hydrogen; same as *hydrogen sulfide* under *hydrogen*.

sul·fū′riç, *a.* of, pertaining to, derived from, or containing sulfur, especially sulfur with a valence of six.

sulfuric acid; a heavy, oily, colorless, very corrosive liquid, H_2SO_4, used in making dyes, paints, explosives, fertilizers, etc.: also called *oil of vitriol.*

sulfuric anhydride; same as *sulfur trioxide* under *sulfur.*

sulfuric ether; same as *ether* (sense 4).

sul′fūr·ine, *a.* sulfureous. [Rare.]

sul′fūr·ing, *n.* a process of bleaching by exposure to the fumes of sulfur, or by means of sulfuric acid.

sul″fū·ri·zā′tion, *n.* a sulfurizing or being sulfurized.

sul′fū·rīze, *v.t.*; sulfurized, *pt., pp.*; sulfurizing, *ppr.* to combine, treat, or impregnate with sulfur or a compound of sulfur, especially with sulfur dioxide fumes in bleaching or disinfecting.

sul′fūr ōre, pyrite, from which sulfur and sulfuric acid are obtained.

sul·fū′rous, *a.* 1. consisting of, containing, or impregnated with sulfur, especially sulfur having a valence of four.

2. like burning sulfur in color, odor, etc. See also *sulphurous.*

sulfurous acid; a colorless acid, H_2SO_3, known only in the form of its salts or in aqueous solution and used as a chemical reagent, a bleach, in medicine, etc.

sulfurous anhydride; same as *sulfur dioxide* under *sulfur.*

sulfurous oxide; same as *sulfur dioxide* under *sulfur.*

sul′fūr sa̤lt, a sulfo salt. [Obs.]

sul′fūr wa̤′tērs, waters impregnated with hydrogen sulfide.

sul′fūr·y, *a.* of or like sulfur.

sul′fūr·yl, *n.* sulfonyl.

sulfuryl chloride; a colorless liquid, SO_2Cl_2, obtained by uniting sulfur dioxide and chlorine.

sul·fȳ′drāte, *n.* same as *sulfohydrate.*

sul·fȳ′driç, *a.* sulfureted.

Sū′li·dae, *n.pl.* a family of web-footed sea birds, of which *Sula* is the type genus.

sulk, *v.i.*; sulked (sulkt), *pt., pp.*; sulking, *ppr.* [back-formation from *sulky.*] to be silently sullen; to be morose or obstinate; to be sulky.

sulk, *n.* 1. a state of sulkiness; a sullen mood or humor: often in the plural.

2. a sulky person.

sulk′ēr, *n.* one who sulks.

sulk′i·ly, *adv.* sullenly; morosely; in a sulky manner.

sulk′i·ness, *n.* sulky manner or behavior.

sulk′y, *a.*; *comp.* sulkier; *superl.* sulkiest, [AS. *solcen,* slothful, remiss.]

1. showing resentment and ill-humor by sullen, withdrawn behavior.

2. gloomy; dismal; sullen; as, a *sulky* day.

3. sluggish in growth, development, or movement: said of things.

sulk′y, *n.*; *pl.* **sulk′ieṣ,** [so called from accommodating only one person, who may be regarded as sulkily desiring to be left alone.] a light, two-wheeled carriage for a single person.

sulky cultivator, harrow, plow, rake, etc.; a cultivator, etc., having a seat for the driver.

sull, *n.* a plow. [Brit. Dial.]

sul′lāġe, *n.* [OFr. *souiller,* to soil.]

1. filth, as that collected by drains from a house, street, etc.; sewage.

2. that which renders filthy or defiles. [Obs.]

3. silt and mud deposited by water.

4. in founding, the scoria on molten metal.

sul′lāġe piēce, in founding, a deadhead.

sul′len, *a.* [ME. *solein, solain,* originally solitary, later hating company; OFr. *solain,* solitary, lonely; ult. from L. *solus,* alone.]

1. showing resentment and ill-humor by morose, unsociable withdrawal; sulky; glum.

2 gloomy; dismal; sad; depressing.

3. somber; dull.

4. slow-moving; sluggish.

5. baleful; threatening; as, *sullen* clouds.

6. alone; solitary; desolate. [Obs.]

Syn.—gloomy, obstinate, intractable, morose, petulant, sulky, sour, grim, cross.

sul′len, *v.t.* to make sullen. [Rare.]

sul′len, *n.* 1. a recluse or hermit. [Obs.]

2. [*pl.*] a morose temper; gloominess; sulks. [Archaic.]

sul′len·ly, *adv.* in a sullen manner.

sul′len·ness, *n.* the quality or condition of being sullen.

sul′lē·vāte, *v.t.* to incite or stir up. [Obs.]

sul′li·āġe, *n.* same as *sullage.*

sul′lōw, *n.* a plow. [Brit. Dial.]

sul′ly, *v.t.* and *v.i.*; sullied, *pt., pp.*; sullying, *ppr.* [prob. from Fr. *souiller*; perh. ult. from L. *suculus,* dim. of *sus,* a boar, swine.] to make or become soiled, stained, tarnished, or defiled.

sul′ly, *n.*; *pl.* **sul′lieṣ,** soil; tarnish; a stain; defilement; a blemish.

sulph- (sulf), sulf-: for words beginning *sulph-,* see forms under *sulf-.*

sul′phȧ, *a.* same as *sulfa.*

sul′phūr, *n.* 1. sulfur.

2. any of a number of small, yellow butterflies: *Colias philodice* is the clouded sulphur.

sul′phūr-bot″tŏm, *n.* the largest of all whales, *Sibbaldius sulfureus,* bluish gray in color, found in the Antarctic and in the colder parts of the Atlantic and Pacific Oceans: also called *sulfur whale.*

sul′phūr·ous (*for 1, usually* sul-fū′rus), *a.* 1. sulfurous.

2. infernal; hellish.

3. violently passionate; heated; fiery.

sul′phūr rāin, pollen from the *Coniferæ* which has been floating in the air, and is brought to the ground by rain.

sul′phūr·weed, *n.* same as *sulphurwort.*

sul′phūr whāle (hwāl), same as *sulphur-bottom.*

sul′phūr·wŏrt, *n.* a plant, *Peucedanum officinale,* the root of which has a smell resembling sulfur.

sul′phūr yel′lōw, a light yellow.

Sul·pi′ciăn, Sul·pi′tiăn (-pish′ăn), *n.* [named after the parish of St. *Sulpice,* Paris, where the order was founded.] one of an order of secular priests, founded in 1642. The members are specially devoted to training candidates for the priesthood. Besides their seminaries in France, the Sulpicians have establishments in Canada and the United States.

sul′tăn, *n.* [Fr., from Ar. *sulṭān,* victorious, also a ruler, prince.]

1. a Moslem ruler; especially [S–], formerly, the ruler of Turkey.

2. [S–] any of a breed of chicken with heavily feathered feet and legs.

3. a sultana (sense 5).

sul·tan′ȧ, *n.* [It., f. of *sultano*; Ar. *sulṭān,* a sultan.]

1. the wife of a sultan.

2. the mother, sister, or daughter of a sultan.

3. a mistress, especially of a king, prince, etc.

4. a small, white, seedless grape used for raisins and in wine-making; also, the raisin from this grape.

5. a game bird of either of the genera *Porphyrio* and *Ionornis,* belonging to the rail family. *Ionornis martinica,* the purple gallinule, is a species of marshbird found in the West Indies and the southern part of the United States: it has bright blue and green feathers.

sul·tan′ȧ bīrd, same as *sultana,* sense 5.

sul′tăn·āte, *n.* 1. the authority, position, or reign of a sultan.

2. the territory or jurisdiction of a sultan.

sul′tăn·ess, *n.* a sultana (senses 1 and 2).

sul′tăn flow′ēr, either of two species of composite plants, *Centaurea suaveolens* and *Centaurea moschata,* known respectively as the yellow and white sweet sultan.

sul·tan′iç, *a.* or or pertaining to a sultan.

sul′tăn red, a deep red.

sul′tăn·ry, *n.* same as *sultanate.*

sul′tăn·ship, *n.* the office or state of a sultan.

sul′tăn·y, *n.* sultanate. [Obs.]

sul′tri·ly, *adv.* in a sultry manner; so as to be sultry.

sul′tri·ness, *n.* the state of being sultry.

sul′try, *a.*; *comp.* sultrier; *superl.* sultriest, [a form of *sweltry*; ME. *sueltrie,* sultry, from *swelter,* which again is from *swell,* to faint, be oppressed with heat.]

1. very hot and moist, or hot, close, stagnant, and heavy; sweltering; as, a *sultry* day.

2. very hot; burning; as, Libya's *sultry* deserts.

3. hot or inflamed, as with passion or lust.

Sụ′lụ, *n.* 1. a member of a Moro tribe of the Sulu Archipelago.

2. the dialect of the Sulus.

Sụ·lụ′ăn, *a.* of the Sulus or their language.

Sụ·lụ′ăn, *n.* a Sulu.

sum, *n.* [OFr. *sume, some*; L. *summa,* a sum, f. of *summus,* highest, superl. of *superus,* that is above, from *super,* above.]

1. an amount of money; as, they paid a great *sum* for the painting.

2. the whole amount; total result; aggregate; as, that is the sum of our experience.

3. gist; summary; substance.

4. the result obtained by adding together two or more numbers or quantities; the total.

5. numbers to be added together.

6. a problem in arithmetic. [Colloq.]

7. the highest degree; height; summit. [Archaic.]

in sum; in short; in brief.

sum, *v.t.*; summed, *pt., pp.*; summing, *ppr.* 1. to determine the sum of by adding; to add up or collect into a whole or total: usually followed by *up.*

The hour doth rather *sum up* the moments,
than divide the day. —Bacon.

2. to sum up; recapitulate; summarize.

to sum to; to total; to add up to.

to sum up; (a) to state in a few words; to summarize; to review briefly; (b) to give a brief review or summary; to recapitulate.

sum-, see *sub-.*

sụ′maç, sụ′mach (*or* shụ′), *n.* [Fr. *sumac,* from Ar. *summāk,* sumac, from *sumaka,* to be tall.]

1. a plant or shrub of the genus *Rhus,* of many species, some of which are used in tanning, some in dyeing, and some in medicine.

2. the powdered leaves, peduncles, and young branches of certain species of the sumac plant, used in tanning and dyeing.

3. the wood of the sumac plant.

Canadian sumac; a low bush of North America, *Rhus canadensis* or *Rhus aromatica.*

dwarf sumac; a North American plant, *Rhus copallina,* which thrives in dry ground.

myrtle-leaved sumac; a shrub of Europe, *Coriaria myrtifolia,* the leaves of which are used in tanning.

Sicilian sumac; a plant, *Rhus coriaria* cultivated in Sicily.

stag-horn sumac; a North American shrub, *Rhus typhina,* the aromatic wood of which is used in dyeing.

tanners' or *tanning sumac*; the Sicilian sumac.

Virginian sumac; the stag-horn sumac.

Sụ·mä′trȧ, *n.* 1. a severe windstorm common between the Malay peninsula and Sumatra.

2. a breed of game birds.

Sumatra camphor; in chemistry, $C_{10}H_{17}OH$, a variety of camphor obtained from the tree *Dryobalanops aromatica* and much used in the Orient as an embalming substance and as incense.

Sụ·mä′trăn, *a.* of or relating to Sumatra, its people, or culture.

Sụ·mä′trăn, *n.* a native or inhabitant of Sumatra.

sum′bō, *n.* [native name.] a species of kingfisher, *Corythornis cyanostigma,* native to South Africa.

sum′bul, *n.* [E.Ind.] the muskroot, *Euryangium* (or *Ferula*) *sumbul,* or the spikenard, *Nardostachys jatamansi.* The commercial name is *muskroot.*

Sū·mē′ri·ăn, Sū·mir′i·ăn, *a.* 1. of Sumer, an ancient region in the lower Euphrates River Valley.

2. designating or of an ancient people of Babylonia, probably of non-Semitic origin.

Sū·mē′ri·ăn, Sū·mir′i·ăn, *n.* 1. one of the Sumerian people.

2. the language of the Sumerians, of undetermined relationship, extinct since the 3d century B.C.: its tablets and inscriptions date back to 4000 B.C.

sum′less, *a.* not capable of being summed up or counted; innumerable; incalculable; inestimable; countless.

Welcom'd with gifts of price, a *sumless* store! —Pope.

sum′mȧ çum la̤u′dē, [L.] with the greatest praise: phrase used to signify graduation with the highest honors from a university or college.

sum′mȧ·ri·ly, *adv.* in a summary manner.

sum′mȧ·ri·ness, *n.* the quality of being summary.

sum′mȧ·rist, *n.* one who summarizes.

sum″mȧ·ri·zā′tion, *n.* a summarizing or being summarized.

sum′mȧ·rīze, *v.t.*; summarized, *pt., pp.*; summarizing, *ppr.* 1. to make a summary or condensed statement of; to state briefly.

2. to be a summary of.

sum′mȧ·ry, *a.* [L. *summarium,* a summary, from *summa,* sum.]

1. that presents the substance or general idea in brief form; summarizing; concise; condensed.

2. prompt and informal; done without delay or ceremony; as, *summary* punishment, *summary* procedure.

summary conviction; a conviction obtained in a case tried without formal indictment or the intervention of a jury.

summary court-martial; the least formal military court, consisting of one officer, for judging minor offenses.

summary proceeding; a court proceeding carried out without the formalities required by the common law, as for certain minor offenses.

sum'mȧ·ry, *n.*; *pl.* **sum'mȧ·rieș,** a short, abridged, or condensed statement or account; an abstract; an abridgment or compendium containing the sum or substance of a fuller statement.

Syn.—abridgment, brief, abstract, digest.

sum·mā'tion, *n.* 1. the act of finding a sum or total amount.

2. a total or aggregate.

3. a final summing up of arguments, as in a court trial or debate, before the decision is to be rendered.

summation of series; in mathematics, the act or process of finding the sum of a series.

summation tone; a combinational tone (a tone made by the blending of two tones): so called when the frequency is the sum of the two components: the opposite of *differential tone*, where the frequency is the difference.

sum'mẽr, *n.* one who sums up an account.

sum'mẽr, *n.* [Fr. *sommier*, a packhorse, a rafter, from LL. *sagmarius*, a packhorse, from L. and Gr. *sagma*, a pack saddle.]

1. a large, horizontal supporting beam or girder.

2. a lintel.

3. the capstone of a column supporting an arch or lintel.

sum'mẽr, *n.* [AS. *sumor, sumer*; akin to G. *sommer*.]

1. that season of the year when the heat of the sun is most directly felt; the warmest season of the year. In the North Temperate Zone, it is regarded as including June, July, and August. In the astronomical year, it is that period between the summer solstice and the autumnal equinox.

2. a year, as reckoned by the summer season; as, a girl of sixteen *summers*.

3. any period regarded, like summer, as a time of growth, development, fulfillment, perfection, etc.

Indian summer; see under *Indian*.

St. Luke's summer or *little summer of St. Luke*; in Great Britain, a short period of warm weather occurring about St. Luke's day, October 18.

sum'mẽr, *v.i.*; summered, *pt., pp.*; summering, *ppr.* to pass the summer; as, we *summer* on Cape Cod.

sum'mẽr, *v.t.* to keep, feed, or maintain during the summer.

sum'mẽr, *a.* of or pertaining to summer; occurring in the summer; suitable for summer; characteristic of summer; as, *summer* flowers, *summer* sports.

summer complaint; diarrhea occurring in the summer time. [Colloq.]

summer coot; a wading bird, the gallinule. [Dial.]

summer cypress; a plant of the genus *Kochia, Kochia scoparia*.

summer duck; in zoology, (a) the migratory North American duck, *Dendronena sponsa* or *Aix sponsa*; (b) the garganey.

summer house; a house or cottage, as in the country, used during the summer.

summer rash; an eruption popularly known as *prickly heat*.

summer sausage; dried or smoked, uncooked sausage, that keeps well in warm weather.

summer sheldrake; the hooded merganser. [Dial.]

summer snipe; (a) the dunlin; (b) the green sandpiper; (c) the European sandpiper.

summer solstice; the time during the summer when the sun is farthest from the equator; June 21 or 22 in the Northern Hemisphere.

summer spore; in botany, a spore of brief vitality which propagates a plant only during the summer.

summer squash; any of a number of small squashes grown in summer and eaten before fully ripe.

summer tanager; the American rose tanager, *Piranga rubra*, the male of which is of a rosy or vermilion tint.

summer teal; the garganey.

summer warbler; the yellow warbler.

sum'mẽr·bīrd, *n.* the wryneck. [Brit. Dial.]

sum'mẽr fal'lōw, land that has been worked, plowed, and harrowed throughout the summer in preparation for sowing in the fall.

sum'mẽr-fal''lōw, *v.t.*; summer-fallowed, *pt., pp.*; summer-fallowing, *ppr.* to plow (land) repeatedly in the summer and let it lie fallow.

sum'mẽr·house, *n.* a small, open structure in a garden, park, etc., for providing a shady rest.

sum'mẽr·līke, *a.* summery.

sum'mẽr·li·ness, *n.* the state or quality of being summerly or resembling summer. [Rare.]

sum'mẽr·ly, *a.* summery.

sum'mẽr·sault, sum'mẽr·set, *n.* and *v.i.* same as *somersault*.

sum'mẽr·stīr, *v.t.*; summerstirred, *pt., pp.*; summerstirring, *ppr.* to summer-fallow. [Dial.]

sum'mẽr·tīde, *n.* summertime.

sum'mẽr·tīme, *n.* the season of summer.

sum'mẽr·tree, *n.* a beam full of mortises for the reception of the ends of joists; a lintel.

sum'mẽr·y, *a.* of, like, or characteristic of summer; summerlike.

sum'ming up, a concise summation; as, the state's attorney began his *summing up*.

sum'mist, *n.* one who makes an abridgment. [Rare.]

sum'mit, *n.* [Fr. *sommet*, dim. of OFr. *som*, a summit, from L. *summum*, the highest part.]

1. the top or apex; the highest point, part, or elevation; as, the *summit* of a mountain.

2. the highest state or degree; the acme; as, the general arrived at the *summit* of fame.

3. (a) the highest level of officialdom; specifically, in connection with diplomatic negotiations, the level restricted to heads of government; as, a meeting at the *summit*; (b) a conference at the summit.

4. in mathematics, the point at which three or more surfaces of a polyhedron meet.

Syn.—apex, peak, top, pinnacle, crown.

sum'mit, *a.* of the heads of government; as, a *summit* parley.

sum'mit·less, *a.* having no summit.

sum'mit lev'el, the highest level of a canal or railroad, etc., in surmounting an ascent.

sum'mit·ry, *n.*; *pl.* **sum'mit·rieș,** the use of, or reliance upon, summit conferences to resolve problems of international diplomacy.

sum'mit·y, *n.* 1. the height or top of anything. [Obs.]

2. the utmost degree; perfection. [Obs.]

sum'mŏn, *v.t.*; summoned, *pt., pp.*; summoning, *ppr.* [OFr. *somondre*; L. *summonere*, to remind privily; *sub*, under, secretly, and *monere*, to advise, warn.]

1. to call together; to order to meet or convene.

2. to call or send for with authority; to order to come or appear.

3. to issue a legal summons against.

4. to call upon to act, especially to surrender.

5. to call forth; to rouse; gather; collect (often with *up*); as, *summon* (*up*) your strength.

sum'mŏn·ẽr, *n.* one who summons or cites by authority; specifically, formerly, one employed to serve court summonses.

sum'mŏnș, *n.*; *pl.* **sum'mŏnș·eș,** a call or order to come, attend, appear, or perform some action; specifically, (a) in law, an official order to appear in court; also, the writ containing such an order; (b) a call, command, knock, or other signal that summons.

sum'mŏnș, *v.t.*; summonsed, *pt., pp.*; summonsing, *ppr.* to serve with a court summons. [Colloq.]

sum'mū·lȧ, *n.*; *pl.* **sum'mū·lae,** [L., dim. of *summa*, sum.] a summing up or synopsis.

sum'mum bō'num, [L.] the highest, or greatest, good.

sum'nẽr, *n.* a summoner. [Obs.]

su·mōōm', *n.* same as *simoom*.

sump, *n.* [L.G., Sw., and Dan. *sump*; D. *somp*; G. *sumpf*, a swamp, marsh, pool.]

1. a pit or well in which liquids collect; specifically, (a) a cesspool; (b) an oil trap or reservoir at the bottom of the lubricating system of an internal-combustion engine.

2. in mining, a pit or pool at the bottom of a shaft or mine, in which water collects and from which it is pumped.

3. in metallurgy, a round pit of stone lined with clay for receiving the metal on its first fusion.

4. a pond of salt water reserved for saltworks.

5. a puddle or pool of dirty water. [Brit. Dial.]

sump fūșe, a waterproof fuse used in blasting in a sump or under water.

sumph (sumf), *n.* a blockhead. [Scot. and Brit. Dial.]

sum'pit, *n.* [Malay.] a small poisoned dart or arrow thrown by means of a sumpitan.

sum'pi·tan, *n.* [Malay.] a blowgun with which natives of Borneo and neighboring islands shoot darts or arrows, usually with poisoned heads.

sump pump, a pump set in the sump of a mine to raise water to the hogger pump or to the hogger pipe.

sump shaft, the shaft leading directly up from the sump of a mine.

sump'si·mus, *n.* a correct form taking the place or which should take the place of an incorrect one; usually, a pedantic correction: see *mumpsimus*.

sump'tẽr, *n.* [OFr. *sometier*; LL. *saumarius, salmarius*, from L. *sagmarius*, a packhorse, from L. and Gr. *sagma*, a packsaddle, a load.]

1. a pack horse, mule, or other animal used for carrying baggage.

2. the driver of a pack horse. [Obs.]

3. a porter. [Rare.]

4. a pack. [Obs.]

sump'tẽr, *a.* carrying or designed to carry burdens or baggage, as of an army; as, a *sumpter* mule.

sump'tion, *n.* 1. a taking; an assumption. [Obs.]

2. in logic, the major premise of a syllogism.

sump'tū·ā·ry, *a.* [L. *sumptuarius*, from *sumptus*, expense.] relating to expense or to expenditures; fixing, regulating, or limiting expenses; as, *sumptuary* laws.

sumptuary laws; see under *law*.

sump·tū·os'i·ty, *n.* expensiveness; costliness; lavishness; magnificence; also, a sumptuous thing.

sump'tū·ous, *a.* [L. *sumptuosus*, from *sumptus*, cost, expense.]

1. involving great expense; costly; lavish.

2. magnificent; splendid.

sump'tū·ous·ly, *adv.* in a sumptuous manner.

sump'tū·ous·ness, *n.* the state, condition, or quality of being sumptuous.

sump winze, a winze to facilitate exploration on a level below that of the sump in a mine.

sun, *n.* [AS. *sunne*; akin to Ice., O.H.G., and Goth. *sunna*, G. *sonne*, L.G. *sunne*, D. *zon*.]

1. the incandescent body of gases about which the earth and other planets revolve and which furnishes light, heat, and energy for the solar system: it is the star nearest the earth, whose mean distance from it is nearly 93,000,000 miles: its diameter is about 865,000 miles; its mass is about 322,000 times, and its volume more than 1,300,000 times, that of the earth, and its density, about one fourth that of the earth.

2. the light, heat, and vitalizing energy of the sun; as, a plant flourishes in the *sun*.

3. a place illuminated and warmed by the sun; as, to stand in the *sun*: distinguished from *shade*.

4. any incandescent heavenly body that is the center of a solar system.

5. something like the sun, as in warmth, brilliance, splendor, etc.

6. a day. [Poet.]

7. a year. [Poet.]

8. sunrise or sunset. [Archaic.]

9. in heraldry, a bearing representing the sun's disk, sometimes with a human face and radiant lines.

a place in the sun; a prominent or favorable position or situation.

from sun to sun; from sunrise to sunset; all the day. [Archaic.]

sun-and-planet wheels; an invention by James Watt in the early history of the steam engine for converting the reciprocating motion of the beam into a rotatory motion. In the accompanying figure, the sun wheel *a* is a notched wheel fixed fast to the axis of the fly wheel, and the planet wheel *b* is a similar wheel bolted to the lower end of the connecting rod *c*; it is retained in its orbit by a link at the back of both wheels. By the reciprocating motion of the connecting rod, the wheel *b* is compelled to circulate round the wheel *a*, and in so doing carries the latter along with it, communicating to the fly wheel a velocity double that of its own.

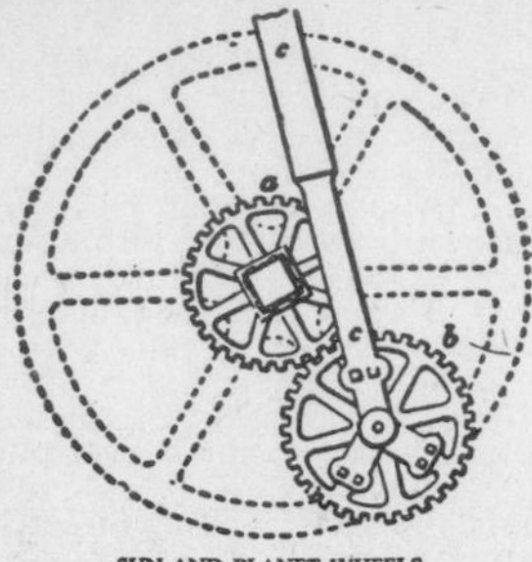
SUN-AND-PLANET WHEELS

under the sun; in the whole world; on earth; as, where *under the sun* are you going?

sun, *v.t.*; sunned, *pt., pp.*; sunning, *ppr.* to expose to the sun's rays; to warm, dry, bleach, tan, etc. in or as in the sunlight.

sun, *v.i.* to sun oneself.

sun, *n.* same as *sunn.*

sun ān′ġel, a hummingbird of the genus *Heliangelus*, distinguished for its brilliant plumage.

sun an·i·mal′çūle, *n.* a spherical heliozoan having numerous radial pseudopodia.

sun bȧth, exposure of the body to the sun's rays, especially for the improvement of one's health.

sun′-bāthe″, *v.i.*; sun-bathed, *pt., pp.*; sun-bathing, *ppr.* to expose the body to the rays of the sun.

sun′bēam, *n.* a ray or beam of sunlight.

sun beãr, a bear, *Helarctos malayanus*, indigenous to southern Asia and Borneo, having a small head, a long tongue, and short glossy fur: also called *bruang* and *Malay bear*.

sun bee′tle, any beetle of the genus *Amara* or related genera, having wing covers with a bright metallic luster.

Sun′belt″, *n.* that part of the United States comprising most of the States of the South and the Southwest, characterized by a warm, sunny climate and regarded as an area of rapid population and economic growth: also *Sun Belt.*

sun′bīrd, *n.* 1. any member of the family *Nectariniidæ*, the honeysuckers, indigenous to the tropics of the Old World and Australia. They closely resemble hummingbirds in external appearance and habits, and have a muscular vocal apparatus.
2. the sun bittern.

sun bit′tẽrn, an aquatic bird, *Eurypyga helias*, native to South America and remarkable for its finely variegated plumage: also called *peacock bittern*, from the brilliancy of its plumage.

sun′bliñk, *n.* a gleam, glimpse, or flash of the sun. [Scot.]

sun′bon″net, *n.* a bonnet for women and girls, having a large brim and a flap at the back for shading the face and neck from the sun.

sun′bōw, *n.* a rainbow. [Poet.]

sun′-brīght (-brīt), *a.* bright as the sun; like the sun in brightness; as, a *sun-bright* shield, a *sun-bright* chariot.

sun′bũrn, *v.t.* and *v.i.*; sunburned *or* sunburnt, *pt., pp.*; sunburning, *ppr.* to get or cause to get sunburn.

sun′bũrn, *n.* 1. an inflammation of the skin resulting from prolonged exposure to the sun's rays.
2. the reddish or tan color of sunburned skin.
3. in botany, same as *heliosis.*

sun′bũrned, sun′bũrnt, *a.* 1. reddened or tanned by the rays of the sun, as the skin.
2. dried or baked by the sun, as bricks.

sun bũrn′ẽr, a large reflecting cluster of gas burners placed near the ceiling for lighting a large room.

sun′bũrst, *n.* 1. the sudden appearance of sunlight, as through a break in clouds.
2. a firework in imitation of the sun spreading rays.
3. a jeweled brooch, etc. representing the sun with spreading rays.

sun çrack, in geology, a crack left upon a rock at the time when it was being consolidated.

sun′-çūred, *a.* cured, as meat, by drying in the sun.

sun′dae, *n.* [prob. an invented term; perh. from *Sunday*; from being orig. sold only on this day.] a serving of ice cream covered with a sirup, fruit, nuts, whipped cream, etc.

sun dȧnce, a religious dance of certain plains tribes of North American Indians, performed in worship of the sun at the summer solstice.

Sun·dȧ·nēṣe′, Sun·dȧ·nē′siăn (-shăn), *a.* of or pertaining to the Sunda Islands or their natives or inhabitants.

Sun·dȧ·nēṣe′, Sun·dȧ·nē′siăn, *n.* one of a section of the Malay race inhabiting the Sunda Islands.

sun′dȧ·ree, *n.* see *sundoree.*

sun′dȧ·ri, *n.* [Bengal.] an East Indian tree, *Heritiera minor*, of moderate size with a dark durable wood used in building and for fuel. The name is also applied to *Heritiera littoralis*, which is very abundant but less useful: also called *sundra tree, sunder tree.*

sun′därt, *n.* a sunbeam. [Rare.]

Sun′dāy, *n.* [AS. *sunnon dæg*, day of the sun; used as transl. of LL. *dies solis*, day of the sun.] the first day of the week: it is observed as the Sabbath by most Christian denominations.
Advent Sunday; the first Sunday in the season of Advent.
Alb Sunday; see *alb.*
cycle of Sundays; same as *cycle of the sun* under *cycle.*
fisherman's Sunday; Friday: so called in Pennsylvania when it was against the law to fish on that day.
God's Sunday; Easter.
Great or *Holy Sunday*; in the Orthodox Eastern Church, Easter.
Green Sunday; in the Armenian church, the second Sunday after Easter.
Hosanna Sunday; same as *Palm Sunday.*
hospital Sunday; a Sunday on which collections are taken in churches for the support of hospitals.
Low Sunday; the first Sunday after Easter.
Mid-Lent Sunday; the fourth Sunday in Lent.
month of Sundays; an indefinitely long time. [Colloq.]
New Sunday; same as *Low Sunday.*
Palm Sunday; see following *palm.*
Passion Sunday; see under *passion.*
Quadragesima Sunday; see under *Quadragesima.*
Quinquagesima Sunday; see under *Quinquagesima.*
Refreshment Sunday: Mid-Lent Sunday: the Gospel for the day tells of the miracle of feeding the five thousand: also called *Bragget, Jerusalem, Mothering, Refection, Rose, Golden Rose,* or *Simnel Sunday.*
Renewal Sunday; the second Sunday after Easter.
Rogation Sunday; the fifth Sunday after Easter.
Show Sunday; at Oxford University, the Sunday preceding commemoration day.
Shrove Sunday; Quinquagesima Sunday: so called because it precedes Shrove Tuesday.
Sunday best; best clothes, as if worn only on Sundays. [Colloq.]
Sunday of St. Thomas; same as *Low Sunday.*

Sun′dāy, *a.* of, pertaining to, or occurring on the first day of the week, or Sunday.
Sunday letter; same as *dominical letter* under *dominical.*
Sunday saint; one whose religion consists principally in observing forms of worship on Sunday: used chiefly in the phrase *Sunday saint and weekday sinner.*
Sunday salt; large crystals of salt: so called in saltworks because they form in the pans on Sunday when work is stopped.

Sun′dāy-gō-tö-meet′ing, *a.* appropriate to Sunday church services; i.e., best or most presentable, as clothes, manners, etc. [Colloq.]

Sun′dāy sçhool, 1. a school, usually affiliated with some church, giving religious instruction on Sunday.
2. its teachers and pupils.

sun deck, an open porch or deck for rest or recreation in the sun.

sun′dẽr, *v.t.* and *v.i.*; sundered, *pt., pp.*; sundering, *ppr.* [AS. *sundrian, syndrian*, from *sundor, sunder*, asunder, separate, apart; similarly Ice. *sundra*, Dan. *söndre*, D. *zonderen*, G. *sondern*, to separate.] to part; to separate; to break apart; to divide; to split; as, to *sunder* a rope; to *sunder* friends or the ties of friendship.

sun′dẽr, *n.* a separation or severance: used chiefly in the phrase *in sunder*, in parts or pieces; asunder.

sun′dẽr, *v.t.* to expose to the sun; to dry in the sun, as hay. [Brit. Dial.]

sun′dẽr·ănce, *n.* a sundering or being sundered; separation.

sun′dẽr·ment, *n.* the state of being sundered; separation. [Rare.]

sun′dẽr tree, see *sundari.*

SUNDEW (*Drosera rotundifolia*)

sun′dew, *n.* any plant of the genus *Drosera*, characterized by slender stems, leaves covered with sticky hairs, and clusters of pink, red, or white flowers.

GNOMON

SUNDIAL

sun′dī″ăl, *n.* an instrument that indicates time by the position of the shadow of a pointer or gnomon cast by the sun on the face of a dial marked in hours.

sun disk, a disk flanked by two serpents and set in a pair of outspread wings, a symbol of the Egyptian sun god, Ra.

sun′dog, *n.* 1. a bright, often colored spot near the sun; a parhelion.
2. a small halo or rainbow on the parhelic circle.

sun′dō·ree, *n.* [Assamese.] a cyprinoid fish, *Semiplotus macclellandi*, native to Assam: also spelled *sundaree, sentoree.*

sun′down, *n.* 1. sunset.
2. a hat with a broad brim which protects the eyes, worn by women.

sun′down″ẽr, *n.* a tramp who makes a practice of arriving at a station at sundown, receiving food and shelter, and leaving in the morning to avoid working in payment. [Australian Slang.]

sun′drȧ tree, see *sundari.*

sun′-drīed, *a.* dried by the sun.

sun′drieṣ, *n.pl.* various small things, or miscellaneous matters; sundry items.

sun′dri·ly, *adv.* in sundry ways. [Obs.]

sun′drops, *n.* a hardy perennial or biennial herb, *Œnothera fruticosa*, native to the eastern coast of North America. It has large, usually yellow flowers which remain open during the sunlight hours.

sun′dry, *a.* [AS. *syndrig*, separate, from *sunder*, apart.]
1. various; miscellaneous; divers; as, *sundry* items of clothing.
2. separate; distinct; individual. [Obs.]
all and sundry; all, both collectively and individually; as, be it known to *all and sundry* whom it may concern.

sun′dry·măn, *n.*; *pl.* **sun′dry·men,** a dealer in sundries or a variety of small articles.

sun′fȧst, *a.* that will not fade if exposed to sunlight.

sun fẽrn, a fern, *Phegopteris polypodioides.*

sun′fish, *n.*; *pl.* **sun′fish** or **sun′fish″eṣ,** 1. an ocean fish of the genus *Orthagoriscus*, belonging to the family *Diodontidæ*, having a short, thick, almost tailless body, a small mouth, and very long dorsal and anal fins.
2. the basking shark.
3. any of various small, fresh-water fishes of North America including the crappie, bluegill, and, especially, the pumpkinseed.
4. any one of the large jellyfishes.

SUNFISH (*Orthagoriscus mola*)

sun′flow″ẽr, *n.* 1. a plant of the genus *Helianthus*, so named from the form and color of the flower. The common American sunflower is the *Helianthus annuus.* It has yellow, daisylike flowers with yellow, brown, purple, or almost black disks that contain edible seeds from which an oil is extracted.

2. the rockrose or sun rose.

3. in civil engineering, a circular protractor, used in the measurement of the sectional areas of tunnels.

4. in electrical apparatus, (a) a commutator resembling a sunflower in appearance; (b) a form of flat or disk commutator.

Sung, *n.* [Chin.] a dynasty (960–1279 A.D.) of the Chinese Empire, famous for achievement in art, literature, and philosophy.

sung, *v.* past participle and rare past tense of *sing.*

sun ġem, a Brazilian hummingbird, *Heliactin cornutus.*

sun′glȧss, *n.* 1. a convex lens used to produce heat by converging the sun's rays at a single point; a burning glass.

2. [*pl.*] eyeglasses having special lenses to protect the eyes from the sun's glare.

sun′glōw, *n.* a colored glow seen in the sky at sunrise or sunset as a result of the diffraction of the sun's rays by particles in the air.

sun god, the sun personified and worshiped as a god, as the Egyptian Ra, the Roman Apollo, the Greek Helios.

sun grēbe, a bird of the rail family, the finfoot.

suñk, *v.* past tense and alternative past participle of *sink.*

suñk, *n.* [AS. *sang;* Sw. *säng,* a bed.]

1. a low seat of grass or straw. [Scot. and Brit. Dial.]

2. a kind of saddle filled with straw. [Scot. and Brit. Dial.]

suñk′en, *a.* [Obs. pp. of *sink.*] 1. sunk in liquid; especially, at the bottom of a body of water; as, a *sunken* ship.

2. situated beneath the surface of the surrounding medium; as, a *sunken* rock.

3. that is below the usual or general level; as, a *sunken* garden.

4. depressed; hollow; as, *sunken* cheeks.

sunken battery; in military usage, a battery placed beneath the surface of the ground.

suñ′ket, *n.* a dainty. [Scot. and Brit. Dial.]

sunk fence, a fence, wall, etc. set in a ditch; a ha-ha.

sun lamp, 1. an electric lamp that radiates ultraviolet rays, used therapeutically as a substitute for sunlight.

2. a lamp with parabolic mirrors for intensifying and reflecting light, as in a motion-picture studio.

sun′less, *a.* without sun or sunlight; dark.

sun′less·ness, *n.* the condition of being sunless.

sun′līght (-līt), *n.* the light of the sun.

sun′līke, *a.* resembling the sun, as in brilliance.

sun′lit, *a.* lighted by the sun.

sunn, *n.* [E. Ind.] 1. an East Indian plant, *Crotalaria juncea,* with silvery, lance-shaped leaves, yellow flowers, and stems yielding fiber used in canvas, rope, etc.

2. the fiber of this plant.

SUNN (*Crotalaria Juncea*)

Sun′nȧ, Sun′nȧh, *n.* [Ar. *sunnah,* tradition.] Moslem law based, according to tradition, on the teachings and practices of Mohammed and observed by orthodox Moslems: it is supplementary to the Koran.

sunn hemp, same as *sunn.*

Sun′nī, Sun′nee, *n.* same as *Sunnite.*

Sun′ni·ȧh, *n.* same as *Sunnite.*

sun′ni·ly, *adv.* in a sunny manner.

sun′ni·ness, *n.* the condition of being sunny.

sun′nish, *a.* sunny. [Obs.]

Sun′nīte, *n.* [Ar. *sunna*h and *-ite.*] a member of one of the two great sects of Moslems: Sunnites approve the historical order of the first four caliphs as the rightful line of succession to Mohammed and accept the Sunna as an authoritative supplement to the Koran: opposed to *Shiite.*

sun′ny, *a.;* *comp.* sunnier; *superl.* sunniest. 1. having or full of sunshine; bright with sunlight.

2. of, like, or coming from the sun.

3. warm; cheerful; bright; as, a *sunny* smile or disposition.

sun′ny, *n.;* *pl.* **sun′nieṣ,** the common sunfish.

sun′ny sīde, 1. the side exposed to sunlight.

2. the more pleasing or favorable part, feature, or aspect.

on the sunny side of; somewhat younger than (a specified age).

sun pär′lŏr, a sitting room having many large windows to admit much sunlight.

sun′prōof, *a.* impervious to or unaffected by the rays of the sun.

sun′rāy, *n.* 1. a ray of sunlight.

2. a representation of this in art.

sun′rīṣe, *n.* 1. the daily appearance of the sun above the eastern horizon.

2. the varying time of this.

3. the atmospheric phenomena at this time.

sun′ro͞of, *n.* an automobile roof with a panel that slides back or lifts out to let in light or air: also written *sun roof.*

sun′ro͞om, *n.* a sun parlor.

sun rōṣe, the rockrose.

sun sçald, a plant disease resulting from excessive transpiration.

sun′set, *n.* 1. the daily disappearance of the sun below the western horizon.

2. the varying time of this.

3. the atmospheric phenomena at this time; especially, the color of the western sky at sunset.

4. the final phase or decline (*of* a period).

sun′set, *a.* designating or of a law, bill, etc. requiring that certain government agencies, programs, etc. come to an end after a specified period unless they get legislative approval.

sun′set shell, a bivalve of the genus *Psammobia,* found in the West Indies: the shell is marked with bands of various colors.

sun′shāde, *n.* something used as a protection from the rays of the sun, as (a) an umbrella or parasol; (b) a broad hat; (c) an awning.

sun′shīne, *n.* 1. the shining of the sun.

2. the light and heat given off by the sun.

3. a surface or area on which the sun shines.

4. (a) cheerfulness, happiness, etc.; (b) a source or cause of cheerfulness, etc.

sun′shīne, *a.* 1. sunny; sunshiny; hence, prosperous, cheerful, etc.

2. designating or of a law, bill, etc. requiring that certain meetings, records, etc. of public bodies be open to the public.

sun′shīn″y, *a.* 1. bright with the rays of the sun; sunny; as, a *sunshiny* day.

sun′spot, *n.* any of the dark spots sometimes seen on the surface of the sun: they are believed to have some connection with magnetic disturbances on earth. In a typical spot there is an exterior shade called the penumbra, an inner darker one called the umbra, and very often one deeper still in the center called the nucleus. In some there are many umbrae for one penumbra. Large spots commence as little dots, often in groups, and grow very rapidly, often extending as much as 140,000 miles across. Sometimes spots last for days, weeks, or months; sometimes they disappear on one part of the sun's disk and appear on another. They are rare at the sun's equator.

sun spūrġe, a plant, *Euphorbia helioscopia,* the wartwort.

sun′squa̤ll (-skwa̤l), *n.* a jellyfish, as *Aurelia flavidula.*

sun stär, a starfish having many rays, as *Solaster papposa.*

sun′stead (-sted), *n.* a solstice. [Obs.]

sun′stōne, *n.* 1. a variety of oligoclase having a reddish or yellowish reflection caused by the hematite particles in it.

2. a variety of orthoclase having a similar appearance.

sun′strōke, *n.* a form of heatstroke produced by excessive exposure to the sun and marked by convulsions, a high body temperature, and, often, coma.

sun′struck, *a.* affected with sunstroke.

sunt, *n.* the wood of the bablah tree.

sun tan, 1. a darkened condition of the skin resulting from exposure to the sun.

2. a yellowish red-brown color.

sun trout, same as *weakfish.*

sun′up, *n.* sunrise.

sun′wărd, sun′wărdṣ, *adv.* toward the sun.

sun′wărd, *a.* facing the sun.

sun wheel (hwēl), same as *sun-and-planet wheels* under *sun.*

sun′wīṣe, *adv.* in the direction of the sun's apparent motion across the sky: in the Northern Hemisphere, in the direction of the hands of a watch, or clockwise.

sun wŏr′ship, the worship or adoration of the sun as the symbol of the deity, as the most glorious object in nature, or as the source of light and heat.

sun wŏr′ship·ēr, a worshiper of the sun; one who practices sun worship.

sū′ō jụ′rē, [L.] in one's own right.

sū′ō lō′çō, [L.] in its own (i.e., proper) place.

sup-, see *sub-.*

sup, *v.t.* and *v.i;* supped (supt), *pt., pp.;* supping, *ppr.* [AS. *sūpan,* to sup, drink; Ice. *súpa.*] to take into the mouth in small amounts, as a liquid; to sip. [Archaic or Dial.]

There I'll *sup*
Balm and nectar in my cup.
—Crashaw.

sup, *n.* a small mouthful, as of liquor or broth; a little taken at one time; a sip. [Archaic or Dial.]

sup, *v.i.;* supped (supt), *pt., pp.;* supping, *ppr.* [ME. *soupen, sopen;* OFr. *soper.*] to eat the evening meal; to have supper.

sup, *v.t.* to provide with supper.

sū·pa̤wn′, *n.* [Am. Ind.] boiled corn meal; mush. [Dial.]

sū′pēr-, [L., from *super,* above.] a prefix meaning: (a) *over, above, on top of,* as in *super*structure, *super*scribe; (b) *higher in rank or position than, superior to,* as in *super*intendent, *super*visor; (c) *greater in quality, amount, or degree than, surpassing,* as in *super*fine, *super*abundance; (d) *greater or better than others of its kind,* as in *super*market; (e) *to a degree greater than normal,* as in *super*heat, *super*saturate; (f) *extra, additional,* as in *super*tax; (g) *to a secondary degree,* as in *super*parasite; (h) in chemistry, *with a large or unusually large amount of* (the specified substance), as in *super*phosphate: an earlier prefix now largely replaced by *bi-, di-, per-,* etc.

sū′pēr, *n.* [from *super-* as used in numerous Eng. compounds.]

1. an extra person, especially an actor having a small nonspeaking part; a supernumerary. [Colloq.]

2. a product of superior grade, extra-large size, etc.: a trade term. [Colloq.]

3. a superintendent. [Colloq.]

4. in bookbinding, a kind of starched cotton mesh used for reinforcing books.

5. the removable top part of a beehive.

sū′pēr, *a.* superfine; of great excellence: often ironical; as, a *super* patriot.

sū′pēr, *v.t.* in bookbinding, to reinforce with super.

sū′pēr·ȧ·ble, *a.* [L. *superabilis,* that may be overcome, from *superare,* to overcome.] that can be overcome, conquered, or surmounted; as, these are *superable* difficulties.

sū′pēr·ȧ·ble·ness, *n.* the quality of being conquerable or surmountable.

sū′pēr·ȧ·bly, *adv.* so as to be overcome.

sū″pēr·ȧ·bound′, *v.i.;* superabounded, *pt., pp.;* superabounding, *ppr.*

1. to be very abundant; to be in great abundance.

2. to be too abundant; to be in excess.

sū″pēr·ȧ·bun′dănce, *n.* 1. the state of being superabundant.

2. more than is usual or needed; surplus; excess.

sū″pēr·ȧ·bun′dănt, *a.* being more than is usual or needed; surplus; excess; overly abundant.

sū″pēr·ȧ·bun′dănt·ly, *adv.* in a superabundant manner; more than sufficiently.

sū″pēr·ȧ·cid′ū·lā·ted, *a.* acidulated to excess.

sū·pēr·add′, *v.t.;* superadded, *pt., pp.;* superadding, *ppr.* to put in as extra; to add over and above; to add (something) to what has been added already.

sū″pēr·ad·di′tion (-dish′un), *n.* 1. a superadding or being superadded.

2. that which is superadded.

sū″pēr·ad·vēn′ient (-yent), *a.* 1. coming upon; coming to the increase or assistance of anything. [Rare.]

2. coming unexpectedly. [Rare.]

sū″pēr·al·i·men·tā′tion, *n.* excess in eating.

sū′pēr·al·tăr, *n.* 1. a ledge or shelf over or at the back of an altar for supporting the cross, etc.; a retable.

2. a consecrated altar of stone or marble laid on the top of an unconsecrated altar.

sū·pēr·an′nū·āte, *v.t.*; superannuated, *pt.*, *pp.*; superannuating, *ppr.* [back-formation from *superannuated.*]

1. to retire from service, especially with a pension, because of old age or infirmity.

2. to set aside as old-fashioned or obsolete.

sū·pēr·an′nū·āt·ed, *a.* [from ML. *superannatus* (with *-u-* after L. *annus*), from L. *super annum*, beyond a year.]

1. discharged from service, especially on a pension, because of old age or infirmity.

2. obsolete; old-fashioned; outdated.

3. too old or worn for further work, service, etc.

sū·pēr·an·nū·ā′tion, *n.* 1. a superannuating or being superannuated.

2. a pension received by a superannuated person.

sū·pēr·ax′il·lăr·y, *a.* same as *supra-axillary.*

sū·pērb′, *a.* [L. *superbus*, proud, lit., one who thinks himself lifted above others.]

1. grand; magnificent; stately; august; noble; majestic; as, a *superb* edifice.

2. rich; elegant; luxurious; as, *superb* furniture or decorations.

3. of the highest quality; extremely fine; excellent; as, a *superb* entertainment.

superb bird of paradise; a velvety-black Papuan bird, *Lophorina superba*, burnished and spangled with various iridescence, bearing a shieldlike mantle and a rich metallic-green breastplate.

superb warbler; an Australian wren of the genus *Malurus*, the male of which has a plumage of an intense blue color.

Syn.—grand, magnificent, elegant, princely, splendid, showy, august, gorgeous.

sū·pēr′bi·āte, *v.t.* to render haughty or overbearingly proud. [Rare.]

sū′pēr·block, *n.* an urban area of several acres, usually closed to through traffic, having interrelated residences and industries along with commercial, social, and recreational facilities.

sū·pērb′ly, *adv.* in a superb manner; magnificently; richly; elegantly.

sū·pērb′ness, *n.* the state of being superb; magnificence.

sū·pēr·çal′en·dēr, *n.* [*super-* and *calender.*] a series of polished rollers used to give an extra-high gloss to paper, rubber, etc.

sū·pēr·çal′en·dēr, *v.t.* to process with a supercalender.

sū·pēr·cär′bū·ret·ed, *a.* bicarbureted. [Obs.]

sū′pēr·cär·gō, *n.*; *pl.* **sū′pēr·cär·gōeṣ, sū′pēr·cär′gōṣ,** [from Sp. *sobrecargo*, supercargo, substituting L. *super* for Sp. *sobre*, both meaning over.] an officer or person in a merchant ship who has charge of the cargo, representing the shipowner in all transactions.

sū·pēr·cär′păl, *a.* in anatomy, above or on the upper side of the carpus.

sū″pēr·cē·les′tiăl, *a.* situated above the firmament or great vault of heaven; higher than celestial.

sū′pēr·chärġe, *v.t.*; supercharged, *pt.*, *pp.*; supercharging, *ppr.* 1. in heraldry, to place (one bearing) on another.

2. to fill to excess; to overload.

3. to increase the power of (an engine), as by the use of a supercharger.

sū′pēr·chärġe, *n.* in heraldry, one figure borne upon another.

sū′pēr·chär″ġēr, *n.* an apparatus consisting of a pump, compressor, or blower used to increase the volume of air over and above that which would normally be drawn into an internal combustion engine by the action of its pistons: designed to increase the power output of the engine.

sū·pērch′ēr·y, *n.* fraudulent representation; imposition. [Obs.]

sū·pēr·cil′i·ăr·y, *a.* [*super-*, and L. *cilium*, the eyebrow.]

1. situated above the eyelid; over the eye.

2. of, or in the region of, the eyebrows; supraorbital.

3. distinguished by marked supercilia; as, a *superciliary* bird.

superciliary arch; the bony superior arch of the orbit.

sū·pēr·cil′i·ous, *a.* [L. *supercilium*, an eyebrow, or pride, haughtiness, as expressed by raising the eyebrows.]

1. disdainful or contemptuous; full of or characterized by pride or scorn; arrogant; haughty.

2. dictatorial; overbearing; as, a *supercilious* officer. [Rare.]

sū·pēr·cil′i·ous·ly, *adv.* in a supercilious manner; haughtily; with an air of contempt.

sū·pēr·cil′i·ous·ness, *n.* the quality or character of being supercilious.

sū·pēr·cil′i·um, *n.*; *pl.* **sū·pēr·cil′i·ȧ,** 1. the eyebrow; the projecting arch above the eyelid.

2. in zoology, a patch or line of color situated over an eye or ocellus.

sū′pēr·cit·y, *n.*; *pl.* **sū′pēr·cit·ieṣ,** same as *megalopolis.*

sū′pēr·çlȧss, *n.* in biology, (a) a subdivision of a subphylum; (b) sometimes, a subphylum.

sū″pēr·çō·lum′năr, *a.* in architecture, having one order of columns above another.

sū″pēr·çō·lum·ni·ā′tion, *n.* in architecture, the placing of one order of columns above another; also, the effect or work produced by such placing.

sū″pēr·çŏn·duç′tion, *n.* superconductivity.

sū″pēr·çon·duç·tiv′i·ty, *n.* in physics, the phenomenon, exhibited by certain metals and alloys, as cadmium, aluminum, mercury, etc., of continuously conducting electrical current without resistance when cooled to temperatures near absolute zero.

sū·pēr·çọọl′, *v.t.* and *v.i.* to cool, as a liquid, below its freezing point without solidification.

sū·pēr·çres′cence, *n.* that which grows upon another growing thing. [Rare.]

sū·pēr·çres′cent, *a.* growing on some other growing thing. [Rare.]

sū·pēr·dom′i·nănt, *n.* in music, the sixth tone of a diatonic scale; the submediant.

sū·pēr·dread′nọught, sū·pēr·dread′nạught (-dred′nạt), *n.* a battleship of the dreadnought class, but larger and with greater firepower.

sū·pēr·ē′gō, *n.* in psychoanalysis, that part of the psyche which controls at an unconscious level the impulses of the id; the conscience of the unconscious: distinguished from *ego*, *id.*

sū·pēr·em′i·nence, *n.* eminence superior to others; distinguished eminence; as, the *supereminence* of Cicero as an orator.

sū·pēr·em′i·nen·cy, *n.* supereminence.

sū·pēr·em′i·nent, *a.* eminent in a superior degree; surpassing others in excellence, rank, dignity, character, etc.

sū·pēr·em′i·nent·ly, *adv.* in a superior degree of excellence; with unusual distinction.

sū·pēr·er′ō·gănt, *a.* supererogatory. [Rare.]

sū·pēr·er′ō·gāte, *v.i.*; supererogated, *pt.*, *pp.*; supererogating, *ppr.* [L. *supererogatus*, pp. of *supererogare*, to pay out beyond what is expected; *super*, above, and *rogare*, to ask.]

1. to do more than duty requires or than is expected.

2. to make up for some deficiency in another by extraordinary effort. [Obs.]

sū·pēr·er·ō·gā′tion, *n.* the performance of more than duty requires; the act or an instance of supererogating.

works of supererogation; in the Roman Catholic Church, good deeds performed, as by saints, over and above what is required for their own salvation.

sū″pēr·ē·rog′ȧ·tive, *a.* supererogatory.

sū″pēr·ē·rog′ȧ·tō·ry, *a.* 1. done or observed beyond the degree required or expected.

2. superfluous; unnecessary.

sū″pēr·es·sen′tiăl (-shal), *a.* essential above others; also, of the highest essence.

sū·pēr·eth′iç·ăl, *a.* transcending the ordinary rules of ethics; more than ethical.

sū′pēr·ette, *n.* [*super*market, and *-ette.*] a small self-service grocery store.

sū″pēr·ex·ạlt′ (-egz-), *v.t.*; superexalted, *pt.*, *pp.*; superexalting, *ppr.* to exalt to a superior degree.

sū″pēr·ex·ạl·tā′tion, *n.* exaltation to a superior degree.

sū·pēr·ex′cel·lence, *n.* superior excellence.

sū·pēr·ex′cel·lent, *a.* excellent in an uncommon or high degree; very excellent.

sū·pēr·fam′i·ly, *n.* in biology, a category ranking above a family and below an order.

sū·pēr·feç′tȧ, *n.* [*super-*, and per*fecta.*] a bet or betting procedure in which one wins if one correctly picks the first four finishers in a horse race in the order in which they finish.

sū·pēr·feç·un·dā′tion, *n.* in physiology, the fertilization of two ova at separate times during the same menstrual period.

sū″pēr·fē·çun′di·ty, *n.* superabundant fecundity or multiplication of the species.

sū·pēr·fē′tāte, *v.i.*; superfetated, *pt.*, *pp.*; superfetating, *ppr.* [from LL. *superfetatus*, pp. of *superfetare.*] in physiology, to conceive a second time while still pregnant from an earlier conception.

sū″pēr·fē·tā′tion, *n.* [L. *superfetatus*, pp. of *superfetare*, to bring forth anew when already pregnant; *super*, above, and *fetare*, to bring forth, breed.] a second conception during a pregnancy from an earlier conception.

sū·pēr·fēte′, *v.i.* to superfetate. [Obs.]

sū·pēr·fēte′, *v.t.* to conceive by superfetation. [Obs.]

sū″pēr·feū·dā′tion, *n.* same as *superinfeudation.*

sū′pēr·fice, *n.* superficies; surface. [Obs.]

sū·pēr·fi′ciăl (-fish′ăl), *a.* [L. *superficialis*, of the surface.]

1. lying on or pertaining to the superficies or surface; not penetrating the substance of a thing; not sinking deep; as, a *superficial* covering.

2. in geology, designating the formation overlying all others; designating or of the surface of the land.

3. in anatomy, near the surface; not deep-seated.

4. square: said of measurements.

5. concerned with and understanding only the easily apparent and obvious; not profound; shallow.

6. quick and cursory; as, a *superficial* reading.

7. apparent, but not real; external; as, a *superficial* resemblance.

Syn.—shallow, flimsy, cursory, hasty, desultory, summary.

sū·pēr·fi′ciăl·ist, *n.* a superficial person; one who does things superficially; one of superficial attainments; a sciolist; a smatterer.

sū·pēr·fi·ci·al′i·ty (-fish-i-), *n.* 1. the state or quality of being superficial.

2. *pl.* **sū·pēr·fi·ci·al′i·tieṣ,** that which is superficial.

sū·pēr·fi′ciăl·īze (-fish′ăl-), *v.t.*; superficialized, *pt.*, *pp.*; superficializing, *ppr.* to treat or regard in a superficial, slight, or shallow manner. [Rare.]

sū·pēr·fi′ciăl·ly, *adv.* 1. in a superficial manner.

2. to a superficial degree.

sū·pēr·fi′ciăl·ness, *n.* the state or character of being superficial.

sū·pēr·fi′ci·ăr·y (-fish′i-), *a.* 1. of or pertaining to the surface; superficial.

2. in law, located or built on another's land.

sū·pēr·fi′ci·ăr·y, *n.* in law, one who holds the surface right on the land of another; especially, one who pays quit rent for a structure built on another's land.

sū·pēr·fi′cīēṣ (-fish′ēz), *n.*; *pl.* **sū·pēr·fi′cīēṣ,** [L. *superficies*, upper face, surface; *super*, above, and *facies*, face.]

1. the surface; the area of a surface; the boundaries of a body.

2. the outward form or aspect.

3. in law, the right to build on another's land, granted by a lease, subject to annual payment; also, everything that constitutes part of the land, connected with it by art or nature, as houses, trees, etc.

sū′pēr·fīne, *a.* 1. of exceptionally fine quality; extra fine; as, *superfine* cloth.

2. excessively subtle, delicate, or refined; over-nice; as, *superfine* distinctions.

sū′pēr·fīne·ness, *n.* the state or quality of being superfine.

sū·pēr′flū·ence, *n.* superfluity; more than is necessary. [Obs.]

sū·pēr′flū·ent, *a.* [*super-*, and L. *fluens* (*-entis*), ppr. of *fluere*, to flow.]

1. floating or flowing above. [Obs.]

2. superfluous. [Rare.]

sū·pēr·flū′i·tănce, *n.* [L. *super*, above, and *fluitare*, to float.] matter floating above or on the surface. [Archaic.]

sū·pēr·flū′i·ty, *n.*; *pl.* **sū·pēr·flū′i·tieṣ,** [ME. *superfluite*; OFr. *superfluité*; L. *superfluitas* (*-tatis*), that which is overflowing, unnecessary, from *superfluus*, overflowing, superfluous, unnecessary.]

1. the state or quality of being superfluous.

2. a quantity or number beyond what is needed; excess; superabundance.

3. [*usually in pl.*] something superfluous; a thing not needed.

sū·pēr′flū·ous, *a.* [L. *superfluus*, overflowing,

unnecessary, from *superfluere*, to overflow; *super*, above, and *fluere*, to flow.]

1. more than is wanted, needed, or useful; surplus; excessive; as, a composition abounding with *superfluous* words.

2. not needed; unnecessary; as, a *superfluous* remark.

3. in music, augmented: said of an interval.

sū·pẽr′flū·ous·ly, *adv.* in a superfluous manner.

sū·pẽr′flū·ous·ness, *n.* the state or condition of being superfluous.

sū′pẽr·flux, *n.* that which is more than is needed; a superfluity.

sū″pẽr·foe·tā′tion, *n.* same as *superfetation*.

sū·pẽr·fō·li·ā′tion, *n.* excessive foliation.

sū·pẽr·fron′tăl, *a.* pertaining to or specifying the upper part of the frontal lobe of the brain.

sū·pẽr·fron′tăl, *n.* the cloth covering the top of an altar, sometimes overhanging the upper part of the frontal.

sū·pẽr·fūse′, *v.t.* and *v.i.*; superfused, *pt.*, *pp.*; superfusing, *ppr.* [L. *superfusus*, pp. of *superfundere*, to pour out, overflow; *super*, over, and *fundere*, to pour out.]

1. to pour or be poured over or on something.

2. in chemistry, to supercool.

sū·pẽr·fū′sion, *n.* a superfusing or being superfused.

sū·pẽr·hēat′, *v.t.*; superheated, *pt.*, *pp.*; superheating, *ppr.* 1. to overheat.

2. to heat (a liquid) above its boiling point without vaporization.

3. to heat (steam not in contact with water) beyond its saturation point, so that a drop in temperature will not cause reconversion to water.

sū′pẽr·hēat, *n.* the number of degrees by which the temperature of superheated steam exceeds the temperature of the steam at its saturation point.

sū·pẽr·hēat′ẽr, *n.* an apparatus for superheating steam.

sū·pẽr·het′ẽr·ō·dȳne″, *a.* [*super*sonic and *heterodyne*.] designating or of a form of radio reception in which part of the amplification is carried out at an intermediate supersonic frequency produced by beating the frequency of the received carrier waves with that of locally generated oscillations.

sū·pẽr·het′ẽr·ō·dȳne″, *n.* a radio set for this method of reception.

sū·pẽr·high′wāy (hī′), *n.* a highway for high-speed traffic, consisting generally of four or more lanes and connecting with crossroads by means of cloverleaves.

sū·pẽr·hū′măn, *a.* 1. regarded as having powers or a nature above that of man; divine; supernatural.

2. greater than that of a normal human being.

sū″pẽr·im·pōṣe′, *v.t.*; superimposed, *pt.*, *pp.*; superimposing, *ppr.* 1. to lay or impose on top of something else; as, a stratum of earth *superimposed* on a different stratum.

2. to add.

sū·pẽr·im·pō·ṣi′tion (-zish′un), *n.* the act of superimposing, or the state of being superimposed; also, something superimposed.

sū·pẽr·im·preg·nā′tion, *n.* 1. superfecundation.

2. superfetation.

sū″pẽr·in·çum′bence, sū″pẽr·in·çum′ben·cy, *n.* the state or quality of being superincumbent.

sū″pẽr·in·çum′bent, *a.* [L. *superincumbens*, ppr. of *superincumbere*, from *super-*, above, and *incumbere*, to lie.]

1. lying or resting on something else.

2. suspended above; overhanging.

sū″pẽr·in·dūce′, *v.t.*; superinduced (-dust), *pt.*, *pp.*; superinducing, *ppr.* to bring in or introduce in addition to some already existing condition.

sū″pẽr·in·dūce′ment, *n.* the act of superinducing; also, that which is superinduced.

sū″pẽr·in·duç′tion, *n.* a superinducing or being superinduced.

sū·pẽr·in·feū·dā′tion, *n.* the creation of a feudal estate out of or upon the feudal estate of another.

sū″pẽr·in·fūṣe′, *v.t.*; superinfused, *pt.*, *pp.*; superinfusing, *ppr.* to infuse or pour over or upon. [Rare.]

sū·pẽr·in·sti·tū′tion, *n.* one institution upon another, as when one person is instituted and admitted to a benefice to which another has already been instituted and admitted.

sū·pẽr·in·tel·leç′tū·ăl, *a.* extremely intellectual; of superior intellect.

sū″pẽr·in·tend′, *v.t.*; superintended, *pt.*, *pp.*; superintending, *ppr.* [LL. *superintendere*, to superintend; L. *super*, above, and *intendere*, to attend to, apply the mind to.] to have or exercise the charge and oversight of; to oversee with the power of direction; to take care of or direct with authority; to control; to regulate; to supervise; as, the officer *superintended* the construction of a fort.

sū″pẽr·in·tend′ence, *n.* the act of superintending; the function of a superintendent; care and oversight for the purpose of direction, and with authority to direct.

Syn.—supervision, direction.

sū″pẽr·in·tend′en·cy, *n.* 1. superintendence.

2. the office or rank of a superintendent.

sū″pẽr·in·tend′ent, *a.* superintending; as, a *superintendent* architect.

sū″pẽr·in·tend′ent, *n.* [OFr. *superintendant*, from LL. *superintendens* (*-entis*), ppr. of *superintendere*, to superintend; L. *super*, over, and *intendere*, to attend to, apply the mind to.] one who has the oversight and charge of a department, institution, project, etc.; as, the *superintendent* of a hospital, the *superintendent* of public works.

Syn.—overseer, inspector, curator, manager, director, supervisor.

sū″pẽr·in·tend′ẽr, *n.* a superintendent.

sū·pē′ri·ŏr, *a.* [ME.; OFr.; L. *superior* (*-oris*), higher, comp. of *superus*, that is above.]

1. having greater elevation; higher; upper.

2. printed or written above another figure or letter or above the rest of the line: in $n^2 = y^x$, *2* and *x* are *superior*.

3. higher in rank, position, authority, etc.

4. greater in value, quality, amount, power, etc.

5. far above the average; of high quality, worth, ability, etc.; excellent.

6. having or showing a feeling that one is better than others; arrogant; haughty; supercilious.

7. more comprehensive or inclusive; generic: said of words, terms, concepts, etc.

8. in astronomy, (a) farther from the sun than the earth is: said of certain planets; (b) designating a conjunction that is farther from the earth than the sun is.

9. in botany, (a) growing above some other organ: thus, a calyx is said to be *superior* when it appears to grow from the top of an ovary, and the ovary is *superior* when growing above the origin of the calyx; (b) next to the axis; belonging to the part of an axillary flower which is toward the main stem; (c) pointing toward the apex of the fruit; ascending: said of the radicle.

10. in anatomy and zoology, relatively higher in position or direction.

superior planets; those planets which are more distant from the sun than the earth, as Mars, Jupiter, Saturn, Uranus, and Neptune.

superior to; (a) higher than; (b) greater than; (c) unaffected by; not yielding to or influenced by; indifferent to (something painful, unpleasant, etc.).

Syn.—higher, better, surpassing, loftier, eminent, conspicuous.

sū·pē′ri·ŏr, *n.* 1. one who is superior to or above another; one who is higher or greater than another in social station, rank, office, dignity, power, excellence, ability, or qualities of any kind.

Behold him humbly cringing wait
Upon the minister of state:
View him soon after to inferiors
Aping the conduct of *superiors*.
—Goldsmith.

2. the head of a monastery, convent, or abbey.

3. in feudal law, one who or whose predecessor has made an original grant of heritable property on condition that the grantee, termed the *vassal*, shall annually pay to him a certain sum (commonly called feu duty) or perform certain services.

4. in printing, a superior letter or figure.

sū·pē′ri·ŏr·ess, *n.* a woman who acts as head of a convent, abbey, nunnery, and the like.

sū·pē·ri·or′i·ty, *n.* 1. the state or quality of being superior; the condition of one who or that which is superior, more advanced, or higher, greater or more excellent than another in any respect; as, *superiority* in age, rank, or dignity.

2. the position, authority, rights, etc. of a superior.

Syn.—pre-eminence, excellence, predominancy, ascendancy, odds, advantage.

sū·pē·ri·or′i·ty com′plex, popularly, a feeling of superiority or exaggerated self importance, often accompanied by excessive aggressiveness, a domineering attitude, etc. which are actually compensation for feelings of inferiority.

sū·pē′ri·ŏr·ly, *adv.* in a superior manner or position.

sū·pẽr·jā′cent, *a.* [*super-*, and L. *jacens* (*-entis*), ppr. of *jacere*, to lie.] lying above or upon.

sū·pẽr·lā′tion, *n.* exaltation of anything beyond truth or propriety; undue exaltation. [Obs.]

sū·pẽr′lȧ·tive, *a.* [OFr. *superlatif*; LL. *superlativus*, superlative, from L. *superlatus*, carried beyond.]

1. superior to or excelling all other or others; of the highest kind, quality, degree, etc.; supreme.

2. excessive; exaggerated.

3. in grammar, expressing the extreme degree of the quality or attribute indicated by the simple, or positive, form of an adjective or adverb: usually indicated by the suffix *-est* (*hardest*) or by the use of *most* with the positive form (*most beautiful*).

sū·pẽr′lȧ·tive, *n.* 1. the highest or utmost degree; the acme; height; peak.

2. something superlative.

3. in grammar, (a) the superlative degree; the extreme degree of comparison of an adjective or adverb; (b) a word or form in this degree.

sū·pẽr′lȧ·tive·ly, *adv.* in a superlative manner.

sū·pẽr′lȧ·tive·ness, *n.* the quality or state of being superlative.

sū″pẽr·lū·crā′tion, *n.* excessive profit. [Obs.]

sū·pẽr·lū′năr, *a.* superlunary.

sū·pẽr·lū′nȧ·ry, *a.* [from *super-*, and L. *luna*, moon; and *-ary*.]

1. located above or beyond the moon.

2. celestial; not earthly.

sū′pẽr·man, *n.*; *pl.* **sū′pẽr·men,** [*super-* and *man*, transl. of G. *übermensch*.]

1. in the philosophy of Nietzsche, an idealized superior, dominating man, regarded as the goal of the evolutionary struggle for survival.

2. a man having apparently superhuman powers.

sū′pẽr·mär″ket, *n.* a large food store or market in which shoppers serve themselves from open shelves and pay for their purchases at the exit: also *super market*.

sū″pẽr·mȧ·tē′ri·ăl, *a.* superior to matter.

sū″pẽr·max·il′lȧ, *n.* the upper jaw; the maxilla.

sū·pẽr·max′il·lăr·y, *a.* pertaining to the upper jaw.

sū·pẽr·mun′dāne, *a.* being above the world.

sū·pẽr·naç′ū·lăr, *a.* having the quality of supernaculum; very good, first rate.

sū·pẽr·naç′ū·lum, *adv.* [*super-*, and G. *nagel*, nail.] to the last drop: with reference to the practice of turning up the emptied glass on one's thumbnail to show that there is not a drop of liquor left. [Archaic.]

sū·pẽr·naç′ū·lum, *n.* good liquor, such as one will drink till not enough is left to wet one's nail; hence, anything excellent.

sū·pẽr′năl, *a.* [Fr. *supernel*, from L. *supernus*, upper, from *super*, above.]

1. of, from, or being in the sky or heaven.

2. high in rank, merit, power, etc.; lofty.

3. celestial; ethereal; heavenly; divine.

sū·pẽr·nā′tănt, *a.* [L. *supernatans* (*-antis*), *ppr.* of *supernatare*, to float; *super*, above, and *natare*, to swim.] floating on the surface, as, oil *supernatant* on water.

sū″pẽr·nȧ·tā′tion, *n.* the act or condition of floating on the surface of a fluid.

sū·pẽr·nat′ū·răl, *a.* [LL. *supernaturalis*, from L. *super*, above, and *natura*, nature.]

1. existing or occurring outside the normal experience or knowledge of man; caused by other than the known forces of nature.

2. attributed to hypothetical forces beyond nature; miraculous; divine.

the supernatural; (a) something supernatural; (b) the intervention of supernatural forces in nature.

sū·pẽr·nat′ū·răl·ism, *n.* 1. the state or quality of being supernatural.

2. belief in the supernatural, especially a belief that some supernatural, or divine, force controls nature and the universe.

sū·pẽr·nat′ū·răl·ist, *n.* a person who believes in the supernatural or in supernaturalism.

sū·pẽr·nat′ū·răl·ist, *a.* supernaturalistic.

sū·pẽr·nat″ū·răl·is′tiç, *a.* of or characteristic of supernaturalism.

sū·pẽr·nat·ū·ral′i·ty, *n.* the state or quality of being supernatural.]Rare.]

sū·pẽr·nat′ū·răl·īze, *v.t.*, supernaturalized, *pt.*, *pp.*; supernaturalizing, *ppr.* 1. to make supernatural.

2. to think of or treat as supernatural.

sū·pẽr·nat′ū·răl·ly, *adv.* in a supernatural manner; in a manner exceeding the established course or laws of nature.

sū·pẽr·nat′ū·răl·ness, *n.* the state or quality of being supernatural.

sū·pẽr·nọr′măl, *a.* above or beyond the normal.

It may seem odd, in beginning an account of occurrences apparently involving intrusion by *supernormal* agency, to start with so commonplace a happening. —René Bache.

sū·pẽr·nū′mẽr·ăr·y, *a.* [LL. *supernumerarius*, excessive in number, from L. *super*, above, and *numerus*, number.]

1. exceeding the number stated or prescribed; extra; as, a *supernumerary* officer.

2. exceeding a necessary or usual number; superfluous; as, *supernumerary* expense.

supernumerary buds; in botany, buds exceeding the usual number.

sū·pẽr·nū′mẽr·ăr·y, *n.*; *pl.* **sū·pẽr·nū′mẽr·ăr·ieṣ,** 1. a supernumerary person or thing.

2. in the theater, an actor having a small, nonspeaking part, as in a mob scene: colloquially contracted to *super*.

sū″pẽr·oc·cip′i·tăl, *a.* at the upper part of the occipital; belonging or relating to the superoccipital; especially, referring to one of the lateral occipital gyri of the brain.

sū″pẽr·oc·cip′i·tăl, *n.* the superior element of the occipital bone.

sū·pẽr·ọr′dẽr, *n.* in biology, a category between an order and a class or subclass.

sū·pẽr·ọr′di·năl, *a.* relating to a superorder.

sū·pẽr·ọr′di·nāte, *a.* related as a superorder to an order or as a universal proposition to a particular included in it.

sū·pẽr·ọr·di·nā′tion, *n.* 1. the ordination of a person to fill an office still occupied, as the ordination by an ecclesiastic of one to fill his office when it becomes vacant by his own death or otherwise.

2. in logic, the relation of a universal proposition to a specific proposition of the same nature.

sū″pẽr·ọr·gan′ic, *a.* above or beyond the organic.

sū·pẽr·ox′ide, *n.* peroxide. [Obs.]

sū·pẽr·par′ȧ·sīte, *n.* an organism that lives as a parasite upon another parasite.

sū″pẽr·pär·tic′ū·lăr, *a.* noting a ratio when the excess of the greater term over the less is a unit, as the ratio of 1 to 2, or of 3 to 4. [Obs.]

sū·pẽr·pär′tient (-shent), *a.* noting a ratio when the excess of the greater term over the less is more than a unit, as that of 3 to 5, or of 7 to 10. [Obs.]

sū·pẽr·pā′tri·ŏt, *n.* a person who is or professes to be a devout patriot, often to the point of fanaticism.

sū·pẽr·phos′phāte, *n.* an acid phosphate, especially a mixture of monocalcium phosphate, CaH_4PO_4, and calcium sulfate made by treating bone, phosphate rock, etc. with sulfuric acid and used as fertilizer.

sū·pẽr·phyṣ′i·căl, *a.* above or beyond the physical; not explainable by the known laws of physics.

sū′pẽr·plant, *n.* a plant growing on another plant; a parasitic growth. [Obs.]

sū·pẽr·plēaṣe′, *v.t.* to please exceedingly. [Obs.]

sū′pẽr·plus, *n.* surplus. [Obs. or Scot.]

sū′pẽr·plus″ăge, *n.* surplusage. [Obs.]

sū·pẽr·pol′i·tic, *a.* excessively politic. [Obs.]

sū·pẽr·pon′dẽr·āte, *v.t.* to weigh over and above. [Obs.]

sū·pẽr·pōṣ′ȧ·ble, *a.* capable of being superposed.

sū·pẽr·pōṣe′, *v.t.*; superposed, *pt.*, *pp.*; superposing, *ppr.* [Fr *superposer*; L. *superponere*, from *super*, above, and *ponere*, to place.] to lay or place on, over, or above something else; specifically, in geometry, to suppose (one figure) to be placed upon another in such a way that the parts of one coincide with the parts of the other; to superimpose.

sū″pẽr·pō·ṣi′tion (-zish′un), *n.* 1. a superposing or being superposed; a lying or being situated above or upon something; specifically, (a) in geology, the order in which mineral masses are placed upon or above each other, as more recent strata upon those that are older, secondary rocks upon primary, tertiary upon secondary, etc.; (b) in geometry, the process by which one magnitude may be conceived to be placed upon another, so as exactly to cover it, or so that every part of each shall exactly coincide with every part of the other; (c) in botany, the position of leaves on an axis when lying directly above one another and not alternating.

sū·pẽr·pow′ẽr, *n.* 1. a state having political power over other powerful states.

2. electrical power secured by linking together a number of electrical power systems in a single area into one main power system, so as to increase the efficiency of distribution.

sū·pẽr·prāiṣe′, *v.t.* to praise to excess.

sū″pẽr·prō·pōr′tion, *n.* overplus of proportion; excess of proportion.

sū″pẽr·pūr·gā′tion, *n.* excessive purgation. [Obs.]

sū″pẽr·rē·flec′tion, *n.* the reflection of an image reflected; the echo of an echo. [Obs.]

sū·pẽr·rē′găl, *a.* of more than regal quality.

sū″pẽr·rē·wạrd′, *v.t.* to reward to excess. [Obs.]

sū·pẽr·roy′ăl, *a.* larger than royal: denoting a certain size of paper for writing and printing.

sū·pẽr·sā′crăl, *a.* in anatomy, situated dorsally from the sacrum.

sū·pẽr·sā′li·en·cy, *n.* the act of leaping upon anything. [Rare.]

sū·pẽr·sā′li·ent, *a.* leaping upon. [Rare.]

sū′pẽr·sạlt, *n.* in chemistry, a salt with a greater number of equivalents of acid than base.

sū·pẽr·sat′ū·rāte, *v.t.*; supersaturated, *pt.*, *pp.*; supersaturating, *ppr.* [*super-* and *saturate*, after Fr. *sursaturer*.] to cause to contain more of a solution than is normally possible; to saturate beyond the normal point for the given temperature.

sū·pẽr·sat·ū·rā′tion, *n.* a supersaturating or being supersaturated.

sū·pẽr·scrībe′, *v.t.*; superscribed, *pt.*, *pp.*; superscribing, *ppr.* [L. *superscribere*, to write above; *super*, above, and *scribere*, to write.]

1. to write, mark, or engrave (an inscription, name, etc.) on the top or outer surface of something.

2. to write a name, address, etc. on the outside of (a letter, parcel, etc.).

sū′pẽr·script, *a.* written above the line.

sū′pẽr·script, *n.* a number, symbol, letter, etc. written above and to the side of another, as an algebraic exponent.

sū·pẽr·scrip′tion, *n.* [L. *superscriptio* (*-onis*), a writing above, from *superscriptus*, pp. of *superscribere*, to write above.]

1. the act of superscribing.

2. that which is written or engraved on the outside, or above something else; specifically, the address on a letter.

3. in pharmacy, that part of a prescription containing the Latin word *recipe*, take, usually represented by the symbol ℞.

sū·pẽr·sec′ū·lăr, *a.* being above the world or secular things. [Obs.]

sū·pẽr·sēde′, *v.t.*; superseded, *pt.*, *pp.*; superseding, *ppr.* [OFr. *superseder*, *superceder*, to surcease, leave off, give over; L. *supersedere*, lit., to sit upon, also to preside over, forbear, refrain, desist from, *super*, above, and *sedere*, to sit.]

1. to cause to be set aside or dropped from use as inferior or obsolete and replaced by something else.

2. to take the place or office of; to succeed.

3. to remove or cause to be removed so as to make way for another; to supplant.

sū·pẽr·sē′dē·as, *n.* [L., lit., you shall forbear.]

1. in law, a writ having in general the effect of a command to stay, on good cause shown, some ordinary proceedings which ought otherwise to have proceeded.

2. a stoppage; a stay.

sū″pẽr·sē·dē′rē, *n.* in Scots law, a private agreement among creditors, or a court order, granting protection to a debtor.

sū·pẽr·sē′dūre, *n.* a superseding or being superseded.

sū·pẽr·sem′i·nāte, *v.t.* [*super-*, and L. *seminare*, to sow.] to sow (seed) where seed has already been sown.

sū·pẽr·sem·i·nā′tion, *n.* the sowing of seed where seed has already been sown.

sū·pẽr·sen′si·ble, *a.* beyond the reach of the senses; above the natural powers of perception.

sū·pẽr·sen′si·bly, *adv.* in a supersensible manner.

sū·pẽr·sen′si·tive, *a.* sensitive to an excessive or abnormal degree.

sū·pẽr·sen′si·tive·ness, *n.* the quality or state of being supersensitive.

sū·pẽr·sen′sō·ry, *a.* beyond or apart from normal sense perception; extrasensory; supersensible.

sū·pẽr·sen′sụ·ăl (-shụ-), *a.* 1. supersensory.

2. spiritual.

sū·pẽr·sen′sụ·ous, *a.* supersensual.

sū·pẽr·sẽrv′ice·ȧ·ble, *a.* overofficious; doing more than is required or desired.

sū·pẽr·ses′sion (-sesh′un), *n.* supersedure; the act of superseding or the condition of being superseded.

sū·pẽr·sō′lăr, *a.* situated above the sun. [Rare.]

sū·pẽr·son′ic, *a.* 1. designating or of vibrations or waves with frequencies higher than those audible to the human ear (above about 20,000 per second).

2. designating or of a speed greater than the speed of sound (above about 1,087 feet per second, or 738 miles per hour).

3. traveling at such a speed.

sū·pẽr·son′ics, *n.pl.* [construed as sing.] the science dealing with supersonic phenomena.

sū·pẽr·spī′nous, *a.* in anatomy, situated above a spinous process; supraspinous.

sū′pẽr·stär, *n.* a very prominent performer, as in sports or the entertainment industry, considered to have exceptional skill and talent.

sū′pẽr·stāte, *n.* a state or government having power over other subordinated states.

sū·pẽr·sti′tion (-stish′un), *n.* [OFr.; L. *superstitio* (*-onis*), a standing still over or near a thing; amazement, wonder, dread, from *superstes* (*-itis*), one who stands by or is present; *super*, above, and *sistere*, causal of *stare*, to stand.]

1. any belief or attitude that is inconsistent with the known laws of science or with what is generally considered in the particular society as true and rational; especially, such a belief in charms, omens, the supernatural, etc.

2. any action or practice based on such a belief or attitude.

3. such beliefs or attitudes collectively.

sū·pẽr·sti′tion·ist, *n.* one addicted to superstition.

sū·pẽr·sti′tious (-stish′us), *a.* [OFr. *superstitieux*; L. *superstitiosus*, full of superstition.]

1. of, characterized by, or resulting from superstition.

2. having or manifesting superstitions.

3. overexact; scrupulous beyond need. [Rare.]

superstitious use; in English law, the use of land for a religious purpose or by a religious corporation, not tolerated by law.

sū·pẽr·sti′tious·ly, *adv.* in a superstitious manner.

sū·pẽr·sti′tious·ness, *n.* the state or character of being superstitious; superstition.

sū·pẽr·strā′tum, *n.*; *pl.* **sū·pẽr·strā′tȧ,** a stratum or layer above another.

sū·pẽr·struct′, *v.t.*; superstructed, *pt.*, *pp.*; superstructing, *ppr.* [L. *superstructus*, pp. of *superstruere*, to build upon or over; *super*, over, and *struere*, to pile up, arrange.] to build upon; to erect on a foundation.

sū·pẽr·struc′tion, *n.* 1. the act of erecting or building upon something else. [Rare.]

2. that which is erected on something else; a superstructure. [Rare.]

sū·pẽr·struct′ive, *a.* built or erected on something else. [Obs.]

sū·pẽr·struct′ŏr, *n.* one who builds on something else. [Obs.]

sū′pẽr·struc·tūre, *n.* 1. a structure built on top of another.

2. that part of a building above the foundation.

3. that part of a ship, especially of a warship, above the main deck.

4. the rails and ties of a railroad as distinguished from the ballast or roadbed.

sū″pẽr·sub·stan′tiăl (-shăl), *a.* 1. more than substantial; transcending the domain of matter: used especially with reference to the phrase in the Lord's Prayer, Matt. vi. 11, where the word *daily* in the King James version reads *supersubstantialis* in the Vulgate.

2. transcending all natures and the distinction of existence and nonexistence.

sū·pẽr·sub′tle (-sut′), *a.* too subtle.

sū·pẽr·sub′tle·ty, *n.* the quality of being supersubtle.

sū·pẽr·sul′fāte, *n.* sulfate with a greater number of equivalents of acid than base. [Obs.]
sū·pẽr·sul′fū·ret·ed, *a.* consisting of a greater number of equivalents of sulfur than of the base with which the sulfur is combined. [Obs.]
sū·pẽr·sul′fūr·īze, *v.t.*; supersulfurized, *pt.*, *pp.*; supersulfurizing, *ppr.* in chemistry, to use an excess of sulfur in (any combination). [Obs.]
sū′pẽr·tañk·ẽr, *n.* an extremely large tanker, of about 300,000 tons or more.
sū′pẽr·tax″, *n.* an additional tax; especially, a surtax.
sū·pẽr·tem′pō·răl, *a.* transcending time, or independent of time.
sū·pẽr·tem′pō·răl, *n.* that which is independent of time.

Plotinus and Numenius, explaining Plato's sense, declare him to have asserted three *supertemporals* or eternals, good, mind or intellect, and the soul of the universe. —Cudworth.

sū·pẽr·tem′pō·răl, *a.* in anatomy, situated above the temporal bone or high up in the temporal lobe.
sū″pẽr·tẽr·rā′nē·ăn, *a.* being on or above the ground: opposed to *subterranean.*
sū″pẽr·tẽr·rēne′, *a.* being above ground or above the earth; superterrestrial.
sū″pẽr·tẽr·res′tri·ăl, *a.* being above the earth or above what belongs to the earth.
sū·pẽr·ton′iç, *n.* in music, the second tone of a scale, next above the tonic.
sū·pẽr·traġ′iç·ăl, *a.* tragical to excess. [Rare.]
sū′pẽr·tū·niç, *n.* an upper tunic or gown.
sū″pẽr·vȧ·çā′nē·ous, *a.* [L. *supervacaneus,* over and above what is necessary, needless; *super,* above, and *vacuus,* empty.] superfluous; unnecessary; needless; serving no purpose. [Obs.]
sū·pẽr·vēne′, *v.i.*; supervened, *pt.*, *pp.*; supervening, *ppr.* [L. *supervenire,* to come over or upon, to follow; *super,* over, and *venire,* to come.]
1. to come or happen as something additional, unexpected, or foreign to the normal course of events.
2. to take place; to ensue.
sū·pẽr·vēn′ient (-yent), *a.* coming upon as something additional or extraneous; supervening; additional.

That branch of belief was in him *supervenient* to Christian practice. —Hammond.

sū·pẽr·ven′tion, *n.* 1. the act of supervening.
2. a supervening event.
sū·pẽr·viṣ′ăl, *n.* the act of supervising or overseeing. [Rare.]
sū·pẽr·vīṣe′, *n.* inspection. [Obs.]
sū′pẽr·vīṣe, *v.t.*; supervised, *pt.*, *pp.*; supervising, *ppr.* [*super-*, and L. *visus,* pp. of *videre,* to see.]
1. to oversee or direct (work, workers, a project, etc.); to superintend.
2. to look over so as to peruse; to read; to look through. [Obs.]
sū′pẽr·vīṣe, *v.i.* to oversee or direct work, workers, etc.
sū·pẽr·vi′ṣiŏn, *n.* a supervising or being supervised; direction; superintendence.
sū′pẽr·vī·ṣŏr, *n.* 1. a spectator. [Obs.]
2. in some of the United States, an officer, elected annually or biennially, having general charge of the administrative business of a town or township.
3. a person who supervises; a superintendent; a manager; a director.
4. in certain school systems, an official in charge of the courses of study for a particular subject and of all teachers of that subject.
sū·pẽr·vī′ṣŏr·ship, *n.* the position, duties, or administration of a supervisor.
sū·pẽr·vī′ṣō·ry, *a.* 1. pertaining to supervision or a supervisor.
2. supervising.
sū·pẽr·viṣ′ū·ăl (-vizh′), *a.* being beyond the ordinary visual power.
sū″pẽr·vō·lūte′, *a.* [*super-*, and L. *volutus,* pp. of *volvere,* to roll, turn about.] having one edge rolled inward and enveloped by the opposite edge; also, rolled inward, as the leaves of an apricot tree or of the morning-glory.
sū′pi·nāte, *v.t.* and *v.i.*; supinated, *pt.*, *pp.*; supinating, *ppr.* [from L. *supinare,* to lay backward, from *supinus,* backward.] in anatomy, to turn, as the arm or forelimb, so that the palm is upward or away from the body.
sū·pi·nā′tion, *n.* [L. *supinatus,* pp. of *supinare,* to bend or lie back, put back.]
1. a supinating or being supinated.
2. the position resulting from this.
Opposed to *pronation.*
sū′pi·nā·tŏr, *n.* in anatomy, the muscle in the forearm that turns the palm of the hand upward.
sū·pīne′, *a.* [L. *supinus,* backward, lying on one's back.]
1. lying on the back, face upward: opposed to *prone.*
2. with the palm upward or away from the body: said of the hand.
3. leaning or sloping backward. [Poet.]
4. mentally or morally inactive; sluggish; listless; passive.
sū′pīne, *n.* in Latin grammar, a part of the verb, really a verbal noun formed from the stem of the past participle. It has two forms or cases; the first ending in *-um* is an accusative case; it always follows verbs of motion. The second supine ends in *-u,* and is an ablative case, and follows substantives or adjectives.
sū·pīne′ly, *adv.* in a supine manner.
sū·pīne′ness, *n.* the condition or quality of being supine.
sū·pin′i·ty, *n.* supineness. [Obs.]
sup·pal·pā′tion, *n.* the act of enticing by soft words. [Obs.]
sup·par″ȧ·si·tā′tion, *n.* the act of flattering merely to gain favor. [Obs.]
sup·par′ȧ·sīte, *v.t.* to flatter; to cajole. [Obs.]
sup·pạwn′, *n.* same as *supawn.*
sup·pē·dā′nē·ous, *a.* being under the feet. [Obs.]
sup·ped′i·tāte, *v.t.* to supply. [Obs.]
sup·ped·i·tā′tion, *n.* supply; aid afforded. [Obs.]
sup′pẽr, *n.* [OFr. *soper, super, souper,* a supper.] the evening meal; the last meal of the day, regardless of the time, but usually following dinner.
The Last Supper; (a) the last supper eaten by Jesus with his disciples before the Crucifixion, on the night of his betrayal by Judas; (b) a famous painting by Leonardo da Vinci depicting this supper.
sup′pẽr, *v.i.* to partake of supper.
sup′pẽr, *v.t.* to furnish with supper.
sup′pẽr club, an expensive nightclub, especially one featuring fine food and liquors.
sup′pẽr·less, *a.* without supper; as, to go *supperless* to bed.
sup′pẽr·tīme, *n.* the time when supper is eaten.
sup·plāce′, *v.t.*; supplaced (-plāst′), *pt.*, *pp.*; supplacing, *ppr.* to displace; to replace. [Rare.]
sup·plant′, *v.t.*; supplanted, *pt.*, *pp.*; supplanting, *ppr.* [Fr. *supplanter*; L. *supplantare,* to put something under the sole of the foot, trip up; *sub,* under, and *planta,* the sole of the foot.]
1. to trip up. [Rare.]
2. to take the place of; to supersede, especially through force, scheming, or treachery.
3. to remove or uproot in order to replace with something else.
sup·plan·tā′tion, *n.* a supplanting or being supplanted.
sup·plant′ẽr, *n.* one who or that which supplants.
sup′ple, *a.* [ME. and OFr. *souple*; L. *supplicare,* to kneel down, humble oneself, beseech; *sub,* under, and *plicare,* to fold, double up.]
1. easily bent or twisted; flexible; pliant.
2. lithe; limber; as, a *supple* body.
3. easily changed or influenced; yielding; compliant.
4. yielding too easily; obsequious; servile.
5. adaptable; resilient; elastic: said of the mind, etc.
6. that makes pliant. [Obs.]
sup′ple, *v.t.*; suppled, *pt.*, *pp.*; suppling, *ppr.* to make supple.
sup′ple, *v.i.* to become supple.
sup′ple·jack, *n.* 1. a tough-stemmed climbing shrub with greenish-white flowers and dark-purple fruit, as (a) any one of various climbers of the genus *Paullinia,* especially *Paullinia curassavica*; (b) *Clematis aristata,* of Australia; (c) *Berchemia scandens* of the southern part of the United States, a woody climber of the buckthorn family.
2. a cane or walking stick made from the stem of one of the above plants.
sup′ple·ly, *adv.* in a supple manner; flexibly.
sup′plē·ment, *n.* [Fr., from L. *supplementum,* that with which anything is made full or whole, a filling up; *sub,* under, and *plere,* to fill.]
1. something added, especially to make up for a lack or deficiency.
2. a section added to a book or the like to give additional information, correct errors in the body of the work, etc.
3. a separate section containing feature stories, comic strips, etc., issued with a newspaper.
4. the amount to be added to a given angle or arc, to make 180° or a semicircle.
5. store; supply. [Obs.]
Syn.—appendix, addition, appendage, adjunct.
sup′plē·ment, *v.t.*; supplemented, *pt.*, *pp.*; supplementing, *ppr.* to fill up, supply, or complete by additions; to add something to, especially so as to make up for a lack or deficiency.
sup·plē·men′tăl, *a.* of the nature of a supplement; serving to supplement, fill up, or complete by additions; supplementary.
supplemental air; air which may be expelled from the lungs in excess of that normally breathed out: also called *reserve air.*
supplemental arcs; in trigonometry, arcs of a circle or other curve which have a common extremity, and together subtend an angle of 180 degrees or two right angles at the center.
supplemental chord; the chord of a supplemental arc.
sup·plē·men′tȧ·ri·ly, *adv.* in a supplementary manner; so as to be supplementary.
sup·plē·men′tȧ·ry, *a.* 1. supplying what is lacking; serving as a supplement; additional.
2. equaling 180° when added together: said of arcs or angles.
sup″plē·men·tā′tion, *n.* the act or instance of supplementing, filling up, or adding to.
sup′ple·ness, *n.* the quality or state of being supple.
sup′plē·tive, *a.* same as *suppletory.*
sup·plē′tion, *n.* [ME. *supplecioun*; OFr.; hyp. L. *suppletio.*]
1. a supplementing.
2. in linguistics, the supplying of deficient forms of a word by forms drawn from another word. Example: *went,* originally the past tense of *wend,* is used, as a result of *suppletion,* to express the past tense of *go.*
sup′plē·tō·ry, *a.* [L. *suppletus,* pp. of *supplere,* to fill up, supply.] supplying deficiencies; supplementary; as, a *suppletory* oath.
sup′plē·tō·ry, *n.*; *pl.* **sup′plē·tō·rieṣ,** a supplement. [Obs.]
sup·plī′ăl, *n.* the act of supplying; also, supply. [Rare.]
sup·plī′ănce, *n.* the act of supplying. [Rare.]
sup′pli·ănce, *n.* supplication; the state of being suppliant. [Rare.]
sup′pli·ănt, *a.* [Fr.; L. *supplicare,* to supplicate.]
1. entreating; beseeching; supplicating; asking earnestly and submissively.
2. manifesting entreaty; expressive of humble supplication.
Syn.—supplicating, suing, begging, beseeching, entreating.
sup′pli·ănt, *n.* a humble petitioner; one who supplicates.
sup′pli·ănt·ly, *adv.* in a suppliant or submissive manner.
sup′pli·ănt·ness, *n.* the state or quality of being suppliant.
sup′pli·căn·cy, *n.* suppliance; the act of supplicating [Rare.]
sup′pli·çănt, *a.* [L. *supplicans* (*-antis*), ppr. of *supplicare,* to supplicate.] entreating; supplicating submissively.
sup′pli·çănt, *n.* one who supplicates; a suppliant.
sup′pli·çănt·ly, *adv.* in a supplicating manner; entreatingly.
sup′pli·çat, *n.* in English universities, a petition; a written application with a certificate that the requisite conditions have been complied with.
sup′pli·çāte, *v.t.*; supplicated, *pt.*, *pp.*; supplicating, *ppr.* [L. *supplicatus,* pp. of *supplicare,* to kneel down, pray; *sub,* under, and *plicare,* to fold, double up.]
1. to entreat for; to seek by earnest prayer; as, to *supplicate* blessings.

2. to address in prayer; to petition earnestly; as, to *supplicate* the throne of grace.

Syn.—beseech, entreat, implore, petition, crave, importune, beg, pray.

sup′pli·çāte, *v.i.* to entreat; to beseech; to implore; to petition with earnestness and submission.

That part of her life had been as something in the past which *supplicated* for tolerance.
—Susan Keating Glaspell.

sup′pli·çā·ting·ly, *adv.* in a supplicating manner.

sup·pli·çā′tion, *n.* [Fr., from L. *supplicatio* (*-onis*), a public prayer or supplication, from *supplicatus*, pp. of *supplicare*, to supplicate.]
1. entreaty; the act of supplicating.
2. a humble request, prayer, petition, etc.
3. in ancient Rome, a religious solemnity observed in consequence of some military success, and also in times of distress and danger to avert the anger of the gods.

Syn.—prayer, entreaty, petition, craving, solicitation, appeal.

sup′pli·çā·tŏr, *n.* one who supplicates.

sup′pli·çȧ·tō·ry, *a.* supplicating; humble; submissive.

sup·plī′ẽr, *n.* one who supplies; anything, as an agency, that supplies.

sup·plȳ′, *v.t.*; supplied, *pt., pp.*; supplying, *ppr.* [ME. *supplyen*; OFr. *supplier*; L. *supplere*, to fill up; *sub*, under, and *plere*, to fill.]
1. to fill up; to furnish with what is wanted; to afford or furnish a sufficiency to or for; as, to *supply* the poor with bread and clothing; to *supply* the daily wants of nature.
2. to serve instead of; to take the place of; to fill, as places that have become vacant; to fill up; as, in the absence of the president the secretary *supplied* his place.
3. to give; to grant; to afford; to bring or furnish in general; as, to *supply* a table with food.
4. to compensate for; to make good; as, friends have *supplied* their loss.

Syn.—furnish, afford, provide, accouter, give, minister, yield, contribute.

sup·plȳ′, *n.*; *pl.* **sup·plieṣ′,** 1. the act of supplying.
2. an amount or quantity available for use; stock; store.
3. the amount of a commodity available for purchase at a given price: opposed to *demand*.
4. [*pl.*] materials, provisions, etc. for supplying an army, an expedition, a business, etc.
5. [*pl.*] an amount of money granted for government expenses; appropriation.
6. a temporary substitute, as for a minister or teacher.
7. (a) aid; assistance; (b) reinforcements. [Obs.]

stated supply; a minister not called to the pastorate of a church but occupying its pulpit for a given term.

sup·plȳ′, *a.* 1. having to do with a supply or supplies.
2. serving as a substitute.

sup′ply, *adv.* supplely.

sup·plȳ′-sīde, *a.* designating or of an economic theory that an increase in money for investment, as supplied by lowering taxes, will increase productivity.

sup·pōrt′, *v.t.*; supported, *pt., pp.*; supporting, *ppr.* [Fr. *supporter*, to support; L. *supportare*, to carry, bring to a place; hence, to endure, sustain; *sub*, near, and *portare*, to carry.]
1. to bear; to sustain; to uphold; to prop up; to keep from falling or sinking; as, a prop or pillar *supports* a structure; an abutment *supports* an arch; the stem of a tree *supports* the branches.
2. to endure without being overcome; to suffer; to undergo; as, to *support* pain, distress, or misfortunes.
3. to uphold by aid, encouragement, or countenance; to keep from fainting, sinking, failing, or declining; as, to *support* the courage or spirits.
4. in the theatre, (a) to represent, as a character, on the stage; to act; as, to *support* the character of King Lear; to *support* the part assigned; (b) to assist as a subordinate character; as, the star was admirably *supported* throughout.
5. to be able to supply funds for or the means of continuing; as, to *support* the annual expenses of government.
6. to be able to carry on; to be able to continue; as, to *support* a war or a contest; to *support* an argument or debate.
7. to maintain with the necessary means of living; to provide for; to supply a livelihood to; as, to *support* a family; to *support* a son at college; to *support* the ministers of the gospel.
8. to keep up by nutriment; to sustain; to keep from failing; as, to *support* life; to *support* the strength by nourishment.
9. to keep up in reputation; to maintain; as, to *support* a good character.
10. to verify; to make good; to substantiate; as, the testimony is not sufficient to *support* the charges; the evidence will not *support* the statements or allegations.
11. to assist; to further; to forward; to second; to aid; to help; as, to *support* a friend or a party.
12. to vindicate; to maintain; to defend successfully; as, to be able to *support* one's own cause.
13. to accompany as an honorary assistant; to act as the aid or attendant of; as, the chairman of the meeting was *supported* by every officer of the association.
14. to second, as a proposal or motion at a public meeting; as, the amendment was strongly *supported* by other speakers.
15. in politics, (a) to favor and to work for the election of, as a candidate for office; (b) to approve and labor for the adoption of, as a platform or a measure of public policy; as, to *support* a candidate and the platform upon which he was nominated.

Syn.—prop, uphold, sustain, assist, carry, maintain.

sup·pōrt′, *n.* 1. a supporting or being supported.
2. one who or that which supports.
3. a means of support; subsistence.
4. specifically, (a) in music, a subordinate part; (b) in military operations, a body of soldiers immediately in the rear of the line actively engaged in fighting; (c) in photography, a plate holding a film.

right of support; in law, (a) the right of a wife to maintenance by her husband; (b) the right of an owner to rely upon the support naturally afforded his property by the premises adjoining.

Syn.—prop, stay, buttress, maintenance, subsistence, encouragement, comfort, help.

sup·pōrt′ȧ·ble, *a.* capable of being supported; endurable; tolerable; maintainable.

sup·pōrt′ȧ·ble·ness, *n.* the quality or the state of being supportable.

sup·pōrt′ȧ·bly, *adv.* in a supportable manner.

sup·pōrt′ănce, *n.* maintenance; support. [Obs.]

sup·pōr·tā′tion, *n.* maintenance; aid; support. [Obs.]

sup·pōrt′ed, *a.* in heraldry, designating an ordinary having another under it by way of support; as, a chief *supported*.

A
B

CHIEF SUPPORTED
A, a chief; B, a bar supporting it

sup·pōrt′ẽr, *n.* 1. one acting as a means of support or maintenance, as (a) a defender or furtherer; as, a *supporter* of the law; (b) a disciple; a partisan; as, a *supporter* of a church or party; (c) one who supports the presiding officer of a social organization.
2. that which supports or acts as a prop; specifically, (a) in shipbuilding, a knee placed under the cathead; also, same as *bibb*; (b) in heraldry, a figure on each side of a shield of arms appearing to support the shield; (c) an elastic appliance used to support or bind some part of the body, as a jockstrap; (d) in mechanics, a bracket or part serving as a bracket or cleat.

sup·pōrt′less, *a.* without support.

sup·pōrt′ment, *n.* support. [Obs.]

sup·pōrt′ress, *n.* a woman supporter.

sup·pōṣ′ȧ·ble, *a.* that can be assumed or supposed.

sup·pōṣ′ȧ·bly, *adv.* in a supposable manner.

sup·pōṣ′ăl, *n.* the imagining of something to exist; supposition.

sup·pōṣe′, *v.t.*; supposed, *pt., pp.*; supposing, *ppr.* [ME. *supposen*; OFr. *supposer*, to put, lay, or set upon; also, to suppose, imagine.]
1. to assume to be true, as for the sake of argument or to illustrate a proof; as, *suppose* A equals B.
2. to believe to be; to imagine; to think; to presume.
3. to involve the assumption of; to presuppose.
4. to consider as a proposed or suggested possibility: used in the imperative; as, *suppose* I write him first.
5. to expect; to obligate: always in the passive; as, I'm *supposed* to be there at eight o'clock.

Syn.—assume, presume, believe, divine, fancy, deem, think, regard, conceive, imagine, imply, presuppose, conjecture, guess, conclude, judge, consider.

sup·pōṣe′, *v.i.* to formulate a supposition or opinion.

sup·pōṣe′, *n.* a supposition; position without proof.

sup·pōṣed′, *a.* 1. regarded as true, genuine, etc., without actual knowledge.
2. merely imagined.

sup·pōṣ′ed·ly, *adv.* according to what is, was, or may be supposed.

sup·pōṣ′ẽr, *n.* one who supposes.

sup·pō·ṣi′tion, *n.* [Fr., from L. *suppositio* (*-onis*), a putting or placing under, a substitution, from *suppositus*, pp. of *supponere*, to put, place, or set under; *sub*, under, and *ponere*, to place, put.]
1. the act of supposing; the act of laying down a hypothesis; reasoning by hypothesis; as, to argue by *supposition*.
2. that which is supposed or assumed hypothetically; an assumption; hypothesis.
3. a surmise; a conjecture; a guess; an opinion; as, I thought it was he, but that was a mere *supposition*.

sup·pō·ṣi′tion·ăl, *a.* founded or based on supposition; conjectural.

sup·poṣ·i·ti′tious (-tish′us), *a.* [L. *suppositicius*, put in the place of, substituted.]
1. substituted with intent to deceive or defraud; spurious; counterfeit.
2. suppositional.

sup·poṣ·i·ti′tious·ly, *adv.* in a supposititious manner.

sup·poṣ·i·ti′tious·ness, *n.* the state or quality of being supposititious.

sup·poṣ′i·tive, *a.* supposed; having the nature of, based on, or involving supposition.

sup·pos′i·tive, *n.* in grammar, a conjunction introducing a supposition, as *if*, *granted*, *provided*, etc.

sup·poṣ′i·tō·ry, *n.*; *pl.* **sup·poṣ′i·tō·rieṣ,** [L. *suppositorium*, that which is placed underneath, from *suppositus*, pp. of *supponere*, to place beneath.] a medicated substance in the form of a cylinder or cone, becoming liquid at the temperature of the body, to be introduced into the vagina, urethra, rectum, etc., where it is melted and diffused by the body temperature.

sup·poṣ′i·tum, *n.* [L.] 1. something assumed.
2. in philosophy, the individual.

sup·press′, *v.t.*; suppressed (-prest′), *pt., pp.*; suppressing, *ppr.* [L. *suppressus*, pp. of *supprimere*, to press under, suppress; *sub*, under, and *premere*, to press.]
1. (a) to put down by force; to subdue; to quell; to crush; (b) to abolish by authority.
2. to keep from appearing or being known; to keep back; to restrain; to conceal; as, I *suppressed* a laugh, newspapers have *suppressed* the story.
3. to prevent or prohibit the publication of (a book, passage in a book, etc.).
4. to check the flow or discharge of; to stop.
5. in psychiatry, to conceal or withhold from consciousness.

Syn.—repress, crush, subdue, quell, put down, overthrow, overpower, overwhelm, restrain, retain, conceal, stifle, stop, smother.

sup·press′ănt, *n.* something, especially a drug, that tends to suppress an action, condition, etc.; as, appetite, pain, and cough *suppressants*.

sup·pressed′ (-prest′), *a.* 1. restrained; stopped; obstructed.
2. in forestry, etc., undeveloped.

sup·press′i·ble, *a.* capable of being suppressed.

sup·pres′sion, *n.* [Fr., from L. *suppressio* (*-onis*), a keeping back, a suppression, from *supprimere*, to suppress.]
1. a suppressing or being suppressed.
2. the state of being suppressed; concealment; as, the *suppression* of truth, of reports, of evidence, and the like.
3. the stoppage, obstruction, or morbid retention of discharges; as, the *suppression* of urine.

4. in grammar, omission; as, the *suppression* of a word.
5. in biology, the nondevelopment of any part or organ; abortion.
6. in psychoanalysis, the deliberate exclusion of an idea, desire, or feeling from consciousness or overt action.
Syn.—concealment, obstruction, overthrow, destruction.

sup·pres′sive, *a.* tending to suppress; that suppresses.

sup·pres′sŏr, *n.* one who or that which suppresses, subdues, or prevents utterance, disclosure, or communication.

sup·prīṣe′, *v.t.* to surprise. [Obs.]

sup′pū·rănt, *n.* a suppurative medicine.

sup′pū·rāte, *v.i.*; suppurated, *pt., pp.*; suppurating, *ppr.* [L. *suppuratus*, pp. of *suppurare*, to gather pus underneath; *sub*, under, and *pus, puris*, pus, matter.] to form or discharge pus; to fester; as, a boil or abscess *suppurates.*

sup′pū·rāte, *v.t.* to cause to suppurate. [Rare.]

sup·pū·rā′tion, *n.* [Fr., from L. *suppuratio* (*-onis*), a purulent gathering, suppuration, from *suppuratus*, pp. of *suppurare*, to suppurate.]
1. the process of suppurating.
2. the matter produced by suppuration; pus.

sup′pū·rā·tive, *a.* of, causing, or characterized by suppuration.

sup′pū·rā·tive, *n.* a medicine, etc. inducing suppuration.

sup′pū·tāte, *v.t.* to compute. [Obs.]

sup·pū·tā′tion, *n.* a reckoning; account; computation. [Obs.]

sup·pūte′, *v.t.* to reckon; to compute. [Obs.]

sū′prȧ (*or* sū′prȧ), *adv.* [L.] above.

sū′prȧ- (*or* sū′), [from L. *supra*, above.] a prefix meaning *above, over, beyond*, as in *supra*maxillary.

sū″prȧ·ȧ·crō′mi·ăl, *a.* above the acromion.

sū·prȧ·ā′năl, *a.* in entomology, situated above the anus.

sū·prȧ·aṅ′gū·lăr, *a.* same as *surangular.*

sū″prȧ·au·riç′ū·lăr, *a.* situated above the external ear.

sū·prȧ·ax′il·lăr·y, *a.* in botany, growing above the axil; inserted above the axil, as a peduncle.

sū·prȧ·braṅ′chi·ăl, *a.* situated above the branchiae or gills.

sū·prȧ·chō′roid, sū″prȧ·chō·roid′ăl, *a.* situated above or upon the choroid.

sū″prȧ·chō·roid′ē·ȧ, *n.* the outermost layer of the choroid coat; the loose tissue between the sclerotic and the choroid coat of the eye.

sū·prȧ·cil′i·ăr·y, *a.* in anatomy, superciliary. [Rare.]

sū·prȧ·clav′i·cle, *n.* in ichthyology, a bone which usually joins the clavicle and posttemporal.

sū″prȧ·clȧ·viç′ū·lăr, *a.* 1. in anatomy, situated above the clavicle.
2. in ichthyology, pertaining to the supraclavicle.

sū·prȧ·çon′dy·lăr, sū·prȧ·çon′dy·loid, a. in anatomy, situated above a condyle or condyles.

sū·prȧ·ços′tăl, *a.* situated above a costa or rib, or outside of the ribs.

sū·prȧ·çrā′ni·ăl, *a.* situated above, or on the upper part of, the cranium.

sū″prȧ·çrē·tā′ceous, *a.* in geology, designating certain deposits lying above the Cretaceous formation, or of more recent origin than the chalk.

sū″prȧ·dē·cŏm·pound′, *a.* more than decompound; very much divided; as, a *supradecompound* leaf.

sū″prȧ·ē·sō·phaġ′ē·ăl, *a.* situated above the esophagus, or on its dorsal side, as a ganglion of a crustacean.

sū·prȧ·eth′moid, *a.* situated above the ethmoid bone, or on its dorsal side.

sū·prȧ·fō·li·ā′ceous, *a.* [*supra-*, and L. *folium*, leaf.] in botany, inserted into the stem above the leaf, petiole, or axil, as a peduncle or flower. [Rare.]

sū·prȧ·glot′tiç, *a.* situated above the glottis.

sū″prȧ·hē·pat′iç, *a.* situated above the liver, or on its dorsal side.
suprahepatic abscess; an abscess situated in the suspensory ligament between the liver and diaphragm.

sū·prȧ·hy′oid, *a.* situated above the hyoid bone.

sū·prȧ·il′i·um, *n.* an epiphysis which some animals have at the sacral end of the ilium.

sū″prȧ·lap·sār′i·ăn, *a.* [*supra-*, and L. *lapsus*, fall.] pertaining to the supralapsarians or to their opinions.

sū″prȧ·lap·sār′i·ăn, *n.* any of the Calvinists who hold that God's plan of salvation for some preceded the fall of man from grace, which had been predestined: opposed to *infralapsarian.*

sū″prȧ·lap·sār′i·ăn·iṣm, *n.* the doctrine or tenets of the supralapsarians.

sū·prȧ·lap′sȧ·ry, *a.* supralapsarian. [Obs.]

sū·prȧ·lim′i·năl, *a.* [*supra-* and *liminal.*] above the threshold of consciousness; conscious; opposed to *subliminal.*

sū·prȧ·lō′răl, *a.* situated above the lores of a bird.

sū·prȧ·lō′răl, *n.* a supraloral feather.

sū·prȧ·lū′năr, sū·prȧ·lū′nȧ·ry, *a.* beyond the moon; hence, of very great height; very lofty.

sū·prȧ·mam′mȧ·ry, *a.* situated above the mammary gland.

sū″prȧ·max·il′lȧ, *n.*; *pl.* **sū″prȧ·max·il′lae,** the supramaxillary.

sū·prȧ·max′il·lăr·y, *n.*; *pl.* **sū·prȧ·max′il·lăr·ieṣ,** the upper jawbone.

sū·prȧ·max′il·lăr·y, *a.* in anatomy, (a) pertaining to the upper jaw; (b) situated above the maxilla.

sū·prȧ·men′tăl, *a.* situated above the chin.

sū″prȧ·mō·leç′ū·lăr, *a.* composed of more than one molecule.

sū·prȧ·mun′dāne, *a.* being or situated above the world; in philosophy, supernatural.

sū·prȧ·nat′ū·răl, *a.* supernatural.

sū·prȧ·nat′ū·răl·iṣm, *n.* same as *supernaturalism.*

sū·prȧ·nat′ū·răl·ist, *n.* and *a.* same as *supernaturalist.*

sū·prȧ·nat″ū·răl·is′tiç, *a.* same as *supernaturalistic.*

sū·prȧ·neū′răl, *a.* above a nerve or above a neural axis.

sū·prȧ·nū′çlē·ăr, *a.* situated or occurring above or on the cortical side or surface of a nucleus.

sū″prȧ·oç·cip′i·tăl, *a.* and *n.* same as *supeoccipital.*

sū·prȧ·oç′u·lăr, *a.* in zoology, located over the eyes, as certain scales.

sū·prȧ·oe·soph′ȧ·găl, *a.* same as *supra-esophageal.*

sū·prȧ·or′bit·ăl, *a.* in anatomy, situated above the orbit of the eye.

sū·prȧ·or′bit·ăr, sū·prȧ·or′bit·ā·ry, *a.* supraorbital. [Rare.]

sū·prȧ·ped′ăl, *a.* located above the foot, as of a mollusk.

sū·prȧ·prō′test, *n.* in law, an acceptance or payment of a bill of exchange by someone other than the drawer, after protest for nonacceptance or nonpayment by the drawee.

sū·prȧ·pū′bi·ăn, *a.* suprapubic.

sū·prȧ·pū′biç, *a.* situated or performed above the pubic arch.

sū·prȧ·pȳ′găl, *a.* [*supra-*, and L. *puga*, the rump.] located above the rump.

sū·prȧ·rē′năl, *a.* [*supra-*, and L. *renes*, the kidneys.] situated above the kidneys; specifically, designating or of an adrenal gland.
suprarenal body (or *capsule*); a flat triangular organ on the upper side of the kidney. It consists of an internal medullary matter and an external cortex covered by a sheath of connective tissue, from which septa are given off into the interior of the organ.
suprarenal extract; in pharmacy, a principle extracted from the suprarenal bodies, having the property of producing constriction of vessels when applied locally.

sū·prȧ·rē′năl, *n.* an adrenal gland.

sū·prȧ·sçap′ū·lȧ, *n.*; *pl.* **sū·prȧ·sçap′ū·lae,** the posttemporal bone of a fish, connecting the shoulder girdle with the cranium.

sū·prȧ·sçap′ū·lăr, *a.* situated upon or on the upper part of the scapula.

sū·prȧ·sep′tăl, *a.* situated above a septum.

sū·prȧ·spī′năl, *a.* situated upon or above a spine.

sū·prȧ·spī′nāte, *a.* supraspinous. [Rare.]

sū·prȧ·spī′nous, *a.* situated above a spine or spinous process.

sū″prȧ·stȧ·pē′di·ăl, *a.* located above the stapes.

sū″prȧ·stȧ·pē′di·ăl, *n.* a suprastapedial part.

sū·prȧ·ster′năl, *a.* situated above the sternum.

sū″prȧ·tem′pō·răl, *a.* situated above the temporal bone, fossa, or region.

sū·prȧ·tem′pō·răl, *n.* a supratemporal bone.

sū·prȧ·troch′lē·ăr, *a.* situated above the trochlea.

sū·prȧ·vaġ′i·năl, *a.* situated above or outside of a sheath, or above the vagina.

sū·prȧ·vi′ṣion, *n.* supervision. [Obs.]

sū·prȧ·vīṣ′ŏr, *n.* a supervisor. [Obs.]

sū·prȧ·vul′găr, *a.* being above the vulgar or common people. [Obs.]

sū·prem′ȧ·cy, *n.*; *pl.* **sū·prem′ȧ·cieṣ,** 1. the state or quality of being supreme or in the highest station of power.
2. supreme authority or power; as, the *supremacy* of a king; the *supremacy* of a parliament.

> The usurped power of the pope being destroyed, the crown was restored to its *supremacy* over spiritual men and causes.
> —Blackstone.

Act of Supremacy; in English history, (a) an act passed by Parliament in 1534, proclaiming the sovereign the supreme head on earth of the Church of England; (b) a similar act passed in 1558, giving supreme spiritual authority to the sovereign.
oath of supremacy: in Great Britain, an oath which acknowledges the supremacy of the king or ruler in spiritual affairs, and renounces or abjures the supremacy of the Pope in ecclesiastical or temporal affairs.

sū·prēme′, *a.* [Fr. *suprême*; L. *supremus*, highest.]
1. highest in authority, rank, power, etc.; dominant.
2. highest in quality, achievement, etc.; most excellent; as, *supreme* love; *supreme* glory; *supreme* degree.
3. highest in degree; utmost; as, a *supreme* fool.
4. final; ultimate.
Supreme Being; God.
Supreme Court; (a) the highest Federal court, consisting of nine judges: its decisions are final and take precedence over those of all other judicial bodies in the country; (b) the highest court in any of the States.
Supreme Court of Judicature; in England, the court constituted in 1875 by the union and consolidation of the Courts of Chancery, of Queen's Bench, of Common Pleas, of Exchequer, of Admiralty, Probate, and of Divorce and Matrimonial Cases; it consists of two permanent divisions, called the *High Court of Justice* and the *Court of Appeal.*
supreme good; that which is perfectly good; the ultimate good.
Supreme Pontiff; the Pope.
supreme sacrifice; the sacrifice of one's life, especially in war.
Supreme Soviet; the parliament of the Soviet Union: it consists of two equal chambers, the Council of the Union (whose members are elected on the basis of population) and the Council of the Nationalities (whose members are elected by the various nationality groups).

sū·prēme′ly, *adv.* with the highest authority; in the highest degree; to the utmost extent; as, *supremely* blest.

sū·prēme′ness, *n.* the state or quality of being supreme.

sū·prem′i·ty, *n.* same as *supremacy.*

sŭr-, [from OFr. *sur*, from L. *super, supra*, over, above.] a prefix meaning *over, upon, above, beyond*, as in *sur*coat, *sur*face.

sŭr-, same as *sub-.*

su′rȧ, *n.* [Ar. *sūra*, a step.] a division or chapter of the Koran.

sū′rȧh, *n.* [from *Surat*, India.] a light, soft, twilled fabric of silk or of silk and rayon: also called *surah silk.*

sū′răl, *a.* [L. *sura*, calf of the leg.] being in or petaining to the calf of the leg; as, the *sural* arteries.

sŭr·ā′năl, *a.* same as *supra-anal.*

sŭr·ā′năl, *n.* in entomology, a supra-anal plate or tergite of a caterpillar.

sŭr·aṅ′gū·lăr, *a.* referring to one of several bones of the lower jaw of birds, reptiles, etc., situated above the angular bone.

sŭr·aṅ′gū·lăr, *n.* the surrangular bone.

sŭr′bāse, *n.* 1. a cornice or series of moldings on the top of the base of a pedestal.
2. a molding or upper base running around the walls of a room above the baseboard or wainscoting.

sŭr′bāsed (-bāst), *a.* [from *surbase* and *-ed.*] in architecture, having a surbase, or molding above the base.

sŭr′bāsed, *a.* [from Fr. *surbaissé*; *sur-* (from L. *super*), over, and *baissé*, pp. of *baisser*, to lower.] designating an arch whose rise is less than half its span.

sŭr·bāse′ment, *n.* the condition of being surbased (having a rise less than half the span).

sŭr·bāte′, *v.t.* to bruise or batter (the feet) by travel. [Obs.]

sŭr·bed′, *v.t.*; surbedded, *pt.*, *pp.*; surbedding, *ppr.* to place or set (a stone) edgewise.

sŭr·cēas′ănce, *n.* cessation. [Obs.]

sŭr·cēase′, *v.i.*; surceased (-cēst), *pt.*, *pp.*; surceasing, *ppr.* [OFr. *sursis*, masc., *sursise*, f., surceased, intermitted; L. *supersedere*, to refrain from, desist.] to cease; to stop; to be at an end; to leave off; to practice no longer; to refrain finally. [Archaic.]

sŭr·cēase′, *v.t.* to stop; to cause to cease. [Archaic.]

sŭr·cēase′, *n.* cessation; stop. [Archaic.]

sŭr·chärġe′, *v.t.*; surcharged, *pt.*, *pp.*; surcharging, *ppr.* [Fr. *surcharger*; *sur*, over, and *charger*, to load.]
1. to overload; to overburden; as, to *surcharge* a beast or a ship; to *surcharge* a cannon.
2. to overcharge; to make an extra charge upon.
3. to fill to excess or beyond normal capacity.
4. to mark (a postage stamp) with a surcharge.
5. in law, to show an omission, as of a credit, in (an account).

sŭr′chärġe, *n.* 1. an excessive load or burden; a load greater than can well be borne.
2. (a) an additional amount added to the usual charge; (b) an excessive charge; overcharge.
3. a new valuation overprinted on a postage stamp, etc., to change its denomination.
4. in law, (a) [Obs.] the excessive use by one party of land held in common, especially of pasturage on a common; (b) an omission of items from an account, for which credit should be given; (c) an extra or additional lien or liability on real property, as a second or third mortgage.
5. in ceramics, a decoration in an enamel of lighter shade than that which is used as a ground color.

sŭr·chär′ġẽr, *n.* one who surcharges.

sŭr′cin·gle, *n.* [*sur-*, and L. *cingulum*, a belt.]
1. a belt, band, or girth, which passes around a horse's body to bind on a saddle, blanket, pack, etc.
2. a girdle, especially that of a cassock, by which it is fastened around the waist.

sŭr′cin·gle, *v.t.*; surcingled, *pt.*, *pp.*; surcingling, *ppr.* to furnish with a surcingle; to bind or attach with a surcingle.

sŭr′cle, *n.* a little shoot; a twig; a sucker. [Obs.]

sŭr′cōat, *n.* [ME. and OFr. *surcote.*] an outer coat or gown; especially, in the Middle Ages, a loose, short cloak worn over armor.

sŭr′cū·lāte, *v.t.* to prune. [Obs.]

sŭr·cū·lā′tion, *n.* the act of pruning. [Obs.]

sŭr′cū·lī, *n.* plural of *surculus*.

sŭr·cū·liġ′ẽr·ous, *a.* [L. *surculus*, a shoot, graft, sucker, and *gerere*, to carry.] in botany, producing or resembling suckers.

sŭr′cū·lōse, sŭr′cū·lous, *a.* [L. *surculosus*, from *surculus*, a twig, a sucker.] in botany, producing suckers or suckerlike outgrowths.

sŭr′cū·lus, *n.*; *pl.* **sŭr′cū·lī**, [L.] in botany, a sucker; a leafy shoot projecting from an underground base.

sŭr·çur′rent, *a.* in botany, running up the stem, as a leafy expansion: opposed to *decurrent*.

sŭrd, *a.* [L. *surdus*, deaf.]
1. deaf; not having the sense of hearing. [Obs.]
2. unheard. [Obs.]
3. devoid of meaning; senseless. [Obs.]
4. in mathematics, not capable of being expressed in rational numbers; irrational; as, a *surd* expression, quantity, or number.
5. in phonetics, uttered with breath and not with voice; voiceless.

sŭrd, *n.* 1. in mathematics, a surd, or irrational, number or quantity; as, the square root of 2 is a *surd*.
2. in phonetics, a consonantal sound uttered with breath and not with voice; a voiceless sound, as *p, f, s, t, k*.

sŭrd, *v.t.* to make soft; to soften the sound of. [Rare.]

sŭrd′ăl, *a.* surd. [Obs.]

sŭr′din·y, *n.* a sardine. [Obs.]

sŭrd′i·ty, *n.* deafness. [Rare.]

sụre (shụr), *a.*; *comp.* surer; *superl.* surest, [ME. *sur*, *seur*; OFr. *sur*, *seür*, *segur*; L. *securus*, secure, sure.]
1. secure; safe; stable. [Rare.]
2. that will not fail; always effective; as, a *sure* method.
3. that can be relied or depended upon; trustworthy; as, he is my *sure* lieutenant and adviser.
4. that cannot be doubted, questioned, or disputed; absolutely true.
5. having or showing no doubt or hesitancy; positive; confident; certain; as, he approached with a *sure* step, are you *sure* of your facts?
6. (a) that can be counted on to be or happen; as, he's heading for *sure* defeat; (b) having confidence in some future contingency; as, I'm *sure* he'll come.
7. bound or destined to do, experience, or be something specified; as, he is *sure* to lose, it's *sure* to snow.
8. never missing; unerring; steady; as, a *sure aim*.
9. betrothed. [Obs.]
as sure as a gun; most certainly; most assuredly; unfailingly; absolutely. [Slang.]
for sure; certainly; without doubt.
sure enough; certainly; without doubt. [Colloq.]
to be sure; certainly; surely.
to have a sure thing; to have a certainty; to be certain of sucess.
to make sure; (a) to be or cause to be certain or secure; to secure so that there can be no possibility of failure or disappointment; (b) formerly, to make fast by betrothal.

sụre, *adv.* 1. surely; inevitably. [Colloq.]
2. certainly; indeed: an intensive, often used as an affirmative answer to questions. [Colloq.]
3. securely. [Obs.]

sụre′-ē·nough′ (-nuf′), *a.* genuine; real; actual. [Colloq.]

sụre′-fīre″, *a.* sure to be successful or as expected; that will not fail. [Colloq.]

sụre′-foot″ed, *a.* not liable to stumble, slip, fall, or err; as, a *sure-footed* horse.

sụre′ly, *adv.* 1. with assurance or confidence; in a sure, unhesitating manner.
2. without a doubt; assuredly; unquestionably; certainly: often used as an intensive emphasizing belief or supposition; as, *surely* you don't believe that!
3. firmly; securely. [Archaic.]

sụre′ment, *n.* security for payment. [Obs.]

sụre′ness, *n.* certainty.

sụre′ti·ship, *n.* suretyship. [Obs.]

sū·rette′, *n.* [Fr. *suret*, dim. of *sur*, sour.] a tropical tree, *Byrsonima spicata*, the bark of which is used in tanning and dyeing.

sụre′ty, *n.*; *pl.* **sụre′ties**, [ME. *seurte*; OFr. *seurte*, from L. *securitas* (-*atis*), freedom from care, unconcern.]
1. the state of being sure; sureness; assurance.
2. something sure; certainty.
3. something that makes sure, protects, or gives assurance, as against loss, damage, or default; guarantee; security.
4. a person who makes himself responsible for another; specifically, in law, one who makes himself liable for another's debts, defaults of obligations, etc.
5. evidence; ratification; confirmation. [Obs.]

sụre′ty, *v.t.* to become a surety for. [Obs.]

sụre′ty·ship, *n.* the state of being surety; the position, responsibility, or obligation of a person answerable as a surety.

sŭrf, *n.* [prob. a variant of *sough*, as it was formerly spelled *suffe*, and, like *sough*, has the sense of a rushing noise.]
1. the waves or swell of the sea which breaks upon the shore or upon shoals or rocks.
2. the foam or spray caused by this.

sŭrf, *v.i.*; surfed, *pt.*, *pp.*; surfing, *ppr.* to engage in the sport of surfing.

sŭr′fāce, *n.* [Fr., from L. *superficies*; *super*, above, and *facies*, face.]
1. (a) the outer face, or exterior, of an object; (b) any of the faces of a solid.
2. superficial features, as of a personality; outward appearance.
3. in geometry, an extent or magnitude having length and breadth, but no thickness.
4. in aeronautics, an airfoil.
5. in fortifications, that part of the side which is terminated by the flank prolonged, and the angle of the nearest bastion.
algebraic surface; a surface, the relations of the co-ordinates of whose points can be expressed by an equation which may be reduced to a finite number of terms involving positive integral powers of the variables.
doubly ruled surface; one wherein each element of one generation, while intersecting no other elements of its own set, meets all of the other set; and any three of either set might be taken as directrices for the other. There are but two doubly ruled surfaces, the hyperboloid and hyperbolic paraboloid.
surface condensation; a method of condensing steam by contact with cold metallic surfaces instead of by the injection of cold water.
surface condenser; see under *condenser*.
tangent surfaces; two surfaces so related to each other at a given point that at that point they have a common tangent plane.

sŭr′fāce, *v.t.*; surfaced (-fāst), *pt.*, *pp.*; surfacing, *ppr.* 1. to treat the surface of; to give a specified kind of surface to; especially, to make smooth or level.
2. to bring (a submarine) to the surface of the water.

sŭr′fāce, *v.i.* 1. to work at or near the surface, as in mining.
2. to rise to the surface of the water; as, the fish *surfaced* and jumped.
3. to become known, especially after being concealed.

sŭr′fāce, *a.* 1. of, on, or at the surface.
2. exterior; superficial.

sŭr′fāce çär, a car running on a track laid on the surface of the ground.

sŭr′fāce gāuġe, an instrument for testing the accuracy of plane surfaces.

sŭr′fāce grub, a cutworm.

sŭr′fāce·măn, *n.*; *pl.* **sŭr′fāce·men**, a person whose duty it is to keep the tracks and bed of a railroad in order.

sŭr′fāce mīn′ing, strip mining.

sŭr′fāce noiṣe, noise produced by the friction of a phonograph needle in passing along the grooves of a record.

sŭr′fāce ŏf rev·ō·lū′tion, the surface generated by a plane curve revolving around an axis in its plane.

sŭr′fāce plāte, a steel plate having a tooled flat surface used as a standard of flatness, as in manufacturing.

sŭr′fāce print′ing, a printing from a raised surface, as type, as distinguished from an engraved surface.

sŭr′fā·cẽr, *n.* a machine for giving a smooth surface to stone, wood, etc; a planer.

sŭr′fāce rib, a rib of a vault used for decoration, not support.

sŭr′fāce rōad, a railroad having its tracks on the surface of the ground, as distinguished from an *elevated* or an *underground road*.

sŭr′fāce struç′tūre, in transformational grammar, the formal structure of a sentence as expressed phonetically and as distinguished from the underlying deep structure.

sŭr′fāce ten′sion, a property of liquids in which the exposed surface tends to contract to the smallest possible area, as in the spheroidal formation of drops: it is a phenomenon attributed to the attractive forces, or cohesion, between the molecules of the liquid.

sŭr′fāce wa̤′tẽr, water falling on the surface of the earth, which runs off into lakes and streams, as distinguished from *spring water* or *well water*.

sŭr′fāce wŏrm, a surface grub.

sŭr′fā·cing ma̤·çhīne′, a machine for finishing the surface of a metal, as by means of emery wheels.

sŭrf′bīrd, *n.* a shore bird of the plover family, *Aphriza virgata*, of the Pacific coast of North and South America, related to the sandpipers, having a rather plump body, a short bill, and a broad, notched tail, white at the base and black at the tip.

sŭrf′bōard, *n.* a long, narrow board used in the water sport of riding in toward shore on the crests of waves.

SURFBOARD

sŭrf′bōat, *n.* a sturdy, light boat of great buoyancy designed for passing through heavy surf, as in lifesaving.

sŭrf çlam, same as *sea clam*.

sũrf duck, any one of various scoters or sea ducks, especially of the genus *Œdemia.*

sũr′feit (-fit), *n.* [ME. *surfet, surfait;* OFr. *sorfait,* excess, and *sor,* L. *super,* above, and *fait,* pp. of *faire,* L. *facere,* to make.]

1. too great an amount or supply; excess (usually with *of*); as, a *surfeit of* complaints.

2. overindulgence, especially in food or drink.

3. discomfort or disorder resulting from overindulgence in food or drink.

4. disgust, nausea, etc. resulting from any kind of excess; satiety.

sũr′feit, *v.t.*; surfeited, *pt., pp.*; surfeiting, *ppr.* 1. to feed or supply to satiety or excess; as, I am *surfeited* with sweets.

2. to cloy; as, he *surfeits* us with his eulogies.

sũr′feit, *v.i.* to indulge or be supplied to satiety or excess; to overindulge.

sũr′feit·ẽr, *n.* one who surfeits; a glutton; a reveler.

sũr′feit wa̤′tẽr, a water for the cure of surfeit. [Obs.]

sũr′fel, sũr′fle, *v.t.* to surphul. [Obs.]

sũrf′ẽr, *n.* same as *surf duck.*

sũrf fish, any of a group of small, perchlike, embiotocoid fishes living in shallow water along the Pacific coast: they bear living young.

sũrf′ing, *n.* the sport of riding in toward shore on the crest of waves, especially on a surfboard.

sũrf′măn, *n.*; *pl.* **sũrf′men,** one experienced in handling a surfboat; specifically, one of a lifesaving crew.

sũrf′măn·ship, *n.* the skill of a surfman; the art of handling a surfboat and of saving life.

sũr′foot, *a.* weary; footsore. [Obs.]

sũrf sçō′tẽr, any of a group of sea ducks living in northern waters, especially *Œdemia perspicillata,* a large sea duck of North America: the male is distinguished by black plumage with white on the forehead and nape, the females and young are grayish-brown.

sũrf smelt, a Californian sea fish, *Hypomesus pretiosus.*

sũrf whit′ing, a sciaenoid marine food fish, *Menticirrus littoralis,* native to the coast of South Carolina.

sũrf′-wo̤rn, *a.* worn by the beating and washing of the surf: said of rocks.

sũrf′y, *a.*; comp. *surfier*; superl. *surfiest,* 1. of, like, or forming surf.

2. having surf, especially heavy surf.

sũrġe, *n.* [prob. via Fr. from L. *surgere,* to rise.]

1. (a) a large mass of or as of moving water; a wave; a swell; a billow; (b) such waves or billows collectively.

2. a movement of or like that of a mass of water; violent rolling, sweeping, or swelling motion; as, the *surge* of the sea.

3. a short, sudden rush or excess of electric current in a circuit.

4. in nautical usage, the concave part of a capstan or windlass, upon which the rope slips, or surges.

5. a source of water; a spring. [Obs.]

sũrġe, *v.t.*; surged, *pt., pp.*; surging, *ppr.* to slacken or release (a rope or cable) suddenly; to slack up (a rope) suddenly when it renders round a pin, a winch, a windlass, or a capstan.

sũrġe, *v.i.* 1. to have a heavy, violent swelling motion; to move in or as in a surge or surges.

2. to be tossed about on waves, as a vessel.

3. to increase suddenly or oscillate abnormally: said of an electric current.

4. to slip, as a rope or cable on a capstan or windlass.

sũrġe′fu̇l, *a.* full of surges.

sũrġe′less, *a.* free from surges; smooth; calm.

sũr′ġent, *a.* mounting up; swelling and rising like a surge.

sũr′ġeŏn, *n.* [ME. *surgien;* OFr. *cirurgien, serurgien,* from *cirurgie, sirurgie;* LL. *chirurgia,* surgery.]

1. a doctor who practices surgery, as distinguished from a physician.

2. a medical officer attached to a military unit; as, a regimental *surgeon.*

3. a surgeonfish.

assistant surgeon; formally, a surgeon of junior grade in the Medical Corps.

barber surgeon; formerly, a barber who was authorized to practise surgery.

flight surgeon; a medical officer who ministers to injured airmen.

passed assistant surgeon; formerly, a surgeon who had passed the grade of assistant surgeon and was eligible to a place in the corps of surgeons.

post surgeon; a medical officer having charge of the medical department of a post, camp, or garrison.

sũr′ġeŏn ȧ·poth′ē·çā·ry, in Great Britain, a practitioner holding license as a surgeon and as an apothecary.

sũr′ġeŏn a̤u′rist, a practitioner who treats diseases of the ear; an otologist.

sũr′ġeŏn·cy, *n.* the office, profession, or position of a surgeon.

sũr′ġeŏn den′tist, a practitioner who performs dental surgery; a dental surgeon.

sũr′ġeŏn·fish, *n.*; *pl.* **sũr′ġeŏn·fish** or **sũr′ġeŏn·fish·eṣ,** any of several bright-colored tropical fishes with sharp, lancelike spines on either side of the base of the tail, as *Teuthis achilles* of Hawaii: also called *doctorfish* and *lancet fish.*

Sũr′ġeŏn Ġen′ẽr·ăl, *pl.* **Sũr′ġeŏnṣ Ġen′ẽr·ăl, Sũr′ġeŏn Ġen′ẽr·ălṣ,** 1. in the United States Army or Navy, the chief general officer or admiral in charge of the medical department.

2. in the United States Bureau of Public Health, the chief medical officer.

3. [s– g–] in the British Army, a member of the medical staff.

sũr′ġeŏn·ry, *n.* surgery. [Obs.]

sũr′ġeŏn·ship, *n.* the office, rank, or position of a surgeon.

sũr′ġeŏn′ṣ knot (not), a knot used as by surgeons in tying ligatures, etc.; see *knot,* illus.

sũr′ġẽr·y, *n.*; *pl.* **sũr′ġẽr·ieṣ,** [ME. *surgerie;* OFr. *cirurgie, sirurgie;* LL. *chirurgia,* surgery, from Gr. *cheirourgia,* a working with the hands, handicraft, skill; *cheir, cheiros,* hand, and *ergein,* to work.]

1. the treatment of disease, injury, or deformity by manual or instrumental operations, as the removal of diseased parts or tissue by cutting.

2. the branch of medicine dealing with this.

3. the laboratory or operating room of a surgeon or hospital.

4. in Great Britain, a doctor's office.

dental surgery; dentistry.

orthopedic surgery; that branch of surgery which concerns the bones, joints, and related structures, together with the correction and prevention of skeletal diseases and deformities.

veterinary surgery; the surgical treatment of horses and other domestic animals.

sũr′ġi·căl, *a.* 1. of surgeons or surgery.

2. used in or connected with surgery.

3. resulting from or after surgery.

surgical fever; the fever caused by the inflammation which sometimes results from a surgical operation.

sũr′ġi·căl·ly, *adv.* 1. by surgery.

2. with reference to surgery.

sũr′ġing, *n.* a swelling and rolling, as of billows.

electric surgings; (a) electric oscillations set up in a conductor that is undergoing rapid discharging, or in neighboring conductors that are being rapidly charged and discharged; (b) electric oscillations, direct or induced.

sũr′ġy, *a.*; *comp.* surgier; *superl.* surgiest, 1. surging; having a surge or surges.

2. characteristic of a surge or surges.

sũ′ri·çāte, *n.* [native name.] a small, four-toed, burrowing, carnivorous mammal, *Suricata tetradactyla,* found in South Africa, related to the civet and mongoose. It is somewhat smaller than the domestic cat, and when tamed is useful in killing rats, mice and other vermin. Also called *zenick.*

Sụ·ri·năm′ bärk, [from *Surinam,* South America.] the bark of the tree *Andira inermis,* or cabbage tree, a leguminous plant of the West Indies, with alternate pinnate leaves and terminal panicles of reddish-lilac flowers: used in medicine, especially as an anthelmintic: also called *worm bark.*

Sụ·ri·năm′ tōad, same as *Pipa.*

sũr·in·ten′dănt, *n.* a superintendent. [Obs.]

sũr′li·ly, *adv.* in a surly manner.

sũr′li·ness, *n.* a surly state or quality; gloomy moroseness; crabbed ill nature; as, the *surliness* of a dog.

sũr′ling, *n.* a sour, morose fellow. [Obs.]

sũr′loin, *n.* same as *sirloin.*

sũr′ly, *a.*; *comp.* surlier; *superl.* surliest, [earlier *serly, sirly,* masterful, imperious, from *sir.*]

1. bad-tempered; uncivil; sullenly rude.

2. rough; dark; tempestuous: said of weather. [Obs.]

3. haughty; arrogant. [Rare or Obs.]

sũr′mȧ, *n.* a chemical, black sulfide of antimony, used by oriental women for darkening the eyes: also spelled *soorma.*

sũr′märk, *n.* in shipbuilding, (a) one of the stations of the ribbands and harpings which are marked on the timbers; (b) a cleat temporarily placed on the outside of a rib to give a hold to the ribband by which, through the shores, it is supported on the ways.

sũr·mīṣ′ȧ·ble, *a.* capable of being surmised; conjecturable.

sũr·mīṣ′ăl, *n.* surmise. [Obs.]

sũr·mīṣe′ (*or* sũr′mīz), *n.* [ME. *surmyse;* OFr. *surmise,* accusation, f. of *surmis,* pp. of *surmettre,* lit., to put upon, hence, to accuse; *sur-* (from L. *super*), above, and *mettre,* to put, from L. *mittire,* to send.]

1. an idea or opinion formed from evidence that is neither positive nor conclusive; a conjecture; a guess.

2. the act or process of surmising; conjecture in general.

sũr·mīṣe′, *v.t.* and *v.i.* surmised, *pt., pp.*; surmising, *ppr.* to imagine or infer (something) without certain knowledge or upon slight evidence; to conjecture; to guess.

sũr·mīṣ′ẽr, *n.* one who is given to surmising.

sũr·mount′, *v.t.*; surmounted, *pt., pp.*; surmounting, *ppr.* [Fr. *surmonter.*]

1. to surpass; to exceed; to go beyond. [Rare.]

2. to get the better of; to conquer; to overcome.

3. to be or lie at the top of; to be or rise above.

4. to climb up and across; to get over (a height, obstacle, etc.).

5. to place something on top of or above.

Syn.—vanquish, subdue, conquer, overcome.

sũr·mount′ȧ·ble, *a.* that can be surmounted.

sũr·mount′ȧ·ble·ness, *n.* the state or character of being surmountable.

sũr·mount′ed, *a.* 1. overcome; conquered; surpassed.

2. in architecture, denoting an arch or dome which rises higher than a semicircle.

3. in heraldry, designating a charge having another charge of a different metal or color laid over it.

sũr·mount′ẽr, *n.* one who surmounts.

sũr·mul′let, *n.*; *pl.* **sũr·mul′lets** or **sur·mul′let,** [Fr. *surmulet,* the red mullet, for *sormulet,* from OFr. *sor,* Fr. *saur,* reddish-brown, sorrel, and *mulet,* a mullet.] any of the fishes of the family *Mullidæ*; especially, the red or plain surmullet, *Mullus barbatus,* a perchlike salt-water food fish with two barbels attached to the lower lip, which inhabits the Mediterranean and attains a length of about 12 inches. Its flesh is highly esteemed, and was formerly greatly prized by the Romans. It is remarkable for the brilliancy of its colors. The striped or common surmullet, *Mullus surmuletus,* is somewhat larger, but equal to the red surmullet in delicacy.

SURMULLET (*Mullus barbatus*)

sũrn, *n.* the hawk owl, *Surnia ulula.*

sũr′nāme, *n.* [altered, after *name,* from ME. *surnoun,* from OFr. *surnom; sur-,* over, and *nom,* a name.]

1. a family name as distinguished from a given or Christian name; last name.

2. a name or epithet added to a person's given name; agnomen; as, King Richard had the *surname* "the Lionhearted."

sũr′nāme (*also* sũr-nām′), *v.t.*; surnamed, *pt., pp.*; surnaming, *ppr.* [Fr. *surnommer.*] to give a surname (especially sense 2) to.

And Simon he *surnamed* Peter.
—Mark iii. 16.

sũr·nom′i·năl, *a.* of or relating to surnames.

sũr·ox′īde, *n.* peroxide. [Obs.]

sũr·ox′i·dāte, *v.t.*; suroxidated, *pt., pp.*; suroxidating, *ppr.* to peroxidize. [Obs.]

sũr·pȧss′, *v.t.*; surpassed (-pȧst), *pt., pp.*; surpassing, *ppr.* [OFr. *surpasser; sur-,* beyond, and *passer,* to pass.]

1. to excel or be superior to.

A nymph of late there was,
Whose heav'nly form her fellows did *surpass.*
—Dryden.

2. to exceed in quantity, degree, amount, etc.

3. to go beyond the limit, capacity, range, etc. of; as, his luck *surpassed* his wildest dreams.

Syn.—exceed, eclipse, excel, outdo, transcend, outstrip.

sũr·pȧss'ȧ·ble, *a.* capable of being surpassed.

sũr·pȧss'ing, *a.* excellent in an eminent degree; exceeding or excelling.

sũr·pȧss'ing, *adv.* excellently. [Obs. or Poet.]

sũr·pȧss'ing·ly, *adv.* in a surpassing manner.

sũr·pȧss'ing·ness, *n.* the state or quality of surpassing or excelling all others.

sũr'phul, *v.t.* to bathe with medicated water, as the face with a liquid cosmetic. [Obs.]

sũr'plice, *n.* [ME. *surplis*; Anglo-Fr. *surpliz*; OFr. *surplis*; LL. *superpelliceum*, a surplice; *super*, above, and *pelliceum*, neut. of L. *pelliceus, pellicius*, made of skins.] a white garment worn by the clergy of the Roman Catholic and Anglican churches, over the cassock or gown during the performance of religious services: also worn by choristers. It is a loose, flowing vestment of linen, reaching almost to the feet, having sleeves broad and full.

SURPLICE

sũr'pliced (-plist), *a.* wearing a surplice; as, a *surpliced* choir.

sũr'plice feeṣ, fees paid to the clergy for such services as baptisms, marriages, funerals, etc.

sũr'plus, *n.* [ME.; OFr., from L. *super*, above, and *plus*, more.]

1. a quantity or amount over and above what is needed; something left over; excess.

2. the excess of assets of a business over its liabilities for a given period.

3. the excess of the total accumulated assets of a business over its liabilities and capital stock outstanding.

sũr'plus, *a.* being over and above what is used or required; excess; extra.

sũr'plus·ăġe, *n.* 1. that which is in excess; surplus; redundancy.

2. irrelevant or unnecessary words; specifically, in law, any part of a pleading or proceeding not necessary or relevant to the case.

sũr'plus val'ūe, in Marxist economics, the amount by which the value of the worker's product exceeds that of his pay: regarded as the source of the capitalist's profit.

sũr'print, *v.t.* to print (something new) over matter already printed.

sũr'print, *n.* something surprinted.

sũr·prīṣ'ăl, *n.* the act or state of surprising or being surprised; a surprise.

sũr·prīṣe', *v.t.*; surprised, *pt., pp.*; surprising, *ppr.* [OFr. *surpris*, pp. of *sorprendre, surprendre*, to surprise; *sur-*, above, and *prendre*, to take.]

1. to come or fall upon (someone or something) suddenly and unexpectedly; to come upon unawares; to take unawares.

The castle of Macduff I will *surprise*.
—Shak.

2. to seize suddenly; to take prisoner. [Rare.]

3. to capture by an unexpected or sudden attack; to take by surprise.

And seizing at the last upon the Britons here,
Surpris'd the spacious isle.
—Drayton.

4. to hold possession of; to hold; to retain. [Obs.]

5. to overpower; to affect strongly. [Obs.]

I am *surprised* with an uncouth fear.
—Shak.

6. to strike with wonder and astonishment, as at something sudden, unexpected, or remarkable in conduct, words, story, etc., or by the appearance of something unusual; to astound.

People were not so much frightened as *surprised* at the bigness of the camel.
—L'Estrange.

7. (a) to cause (someone) by some sudden or unexpected action to do or say something unintended: often with *into*; (b) to bring out or elicit (something) by such means; as, we *surprised* an admission from him.

sũr·prīṣe', *n.* 1. the act of surprising; unexpected seizure or attack.

2. the state of being surprised; feeling aroused by something unusual or unexpected; astonishment.

3. something that surprises; especially, a sudden or unexpected event or unusual thing that causes wonderment or astonishment.

Syn.—astonishment, awe, wonder, bewilderment, amazement.

to take by surprise; (a) to come upon suddenly or without warning; to surprise; (b) to amaze; astonish; astound.

sũr·prīṣ'ed·ly, *adv.* with surprise; in a manner showing surprise.

sũr·prīṣe'ment, *n.* surprisal. [Rare.]

sũr·prīṣe' pär'ty, a social gathering of people, at a time and in a manner previously agreed upon, uninvited, at the house of a common friend. A gift of some sort, for which the money has previously been taken up by subscription, is often presented to the surprised host or hostess.

sũr·prīṣ'ẽr, *n.* one who or that which surprises.

sũr·prīṣ'ing, *a.* arousing surprise; amazing; extraordinary; of a nature to excite wonder and astonishment; as, *surprising* bravery; *surprising* patience; a *surprising* escape from danger.

sũr·prīṣ'ing·ly, *adv.* in a surprising manner.

sũr·prīṣ'ing·ness, *n.* the state or quality of being surprising.

sụr'rȧ, *n.* [E. Ind.] a kind of infectious anemia in horses, mules, camels, etc.

sũr·rē'ăl·iṣm, *n.* [Fr. *surréalisme*; *sur-*, over, beyond, and *réalisme*, realism.] a modern movement in art and literature, in which an attempt is made to portray or interpret the workings of the subconscious mind as manifested in dreams: it is characterized by an irrational, noncontextual arrangement of material.

sũr·rē'ăl·ist, *n.* a surrealist painter, writer, etc.

sũr·rē'ăl·ist, *a.* of, practicing, or characterized by surrealism.

sũr·rē·ăl·is'tiç, *a.* of surrealism.

sũr·rē·but', *v.i.*; surrebutted, *pt., pp.*; surrebutting *ppr.* in law, to reply, as a plaintiff, to a defendant's rebutter.

sũr·rē·but'tăl, *n.* in law, the act of giving evidence to support or maintain a surrebutter.

sũr·rē·but'tẽr, *n.* in law, a plaintiff's reply to a defendant's rebutter.

sur·rein', *v.t.* to exhaust or injure by overriding; to override. [Obs.]

sũr·rē·join', *v.i.* in law, to reply, as a plaintiff, to a defendant's rejoinder.

sũr·rē·join'dẽr, *n.* in law, a plaintiff's reply to a defendant's rejoinder.

sur·ren'dẽr, *v.t.*; surrendered, *pt., pp.*; surrendering, *ppr.* [OFr. *surrendre*, to deliver up into the hands of justice; *sur-*, upon, up, and *rendre*, to render.]

1. to yield to the power of another; to give or deliver up possession of upon compulsion or demand; as, to *surrender* one's person to an enemy; to *surrender* a fort or a ship.

2. to yield, especially voluntarily, in favor of another; to resign in favor of another; to cease to claim or use; as, to *surrender* a right or privilege; to *surrender* a place or an office.

3. to give up or abandon; to make surrender of.

4. to yield or resign (oneself) to any influence, passion, or power; as, to *surrender oneself* to grief, to despair, to indolence, etc.

5. to return; to restore. [Obs.]

Syn.—cede, deliver, resign.

sur·ren'dẽr, *v.i.* to yield; to give up oneself into the power or control of another, especially as a prisoner; as, seeing no way of escape, he *surrendered* at the first summons.

sur·ren'dẽr, *n.* 1. the act of surrendering; the act of yielding, resigning, or giving up; as, the *surrender* of a castle to an enemy; the *surrender* of a right or of claims.

2. in insurance, the abandonment of an insurance policy by the party insured on receiving a cash payment (*surrender value*), thus freeing the company of liability.

3. in law, (a) the yielding up of an estate for life, or for years, to one who has the immediate estate in reversion or remainder; (b) the giving of a principal into custody by his bondsmen; (c) the delivery up of fugitives from justice, as by a foreign state; extradition; (d) in old English bankruptcy acts, the appearing of the one bankrupt before the commissioners in order to satisfy the legal requirements.

sur·ren·dẽr·ee', *n.* in law, one to whom a surrender is made.

sur·ren'dẽr·ẽr, *n.* one who surrenders.

sur·ren'dẽr·ŏr, *n.* in law, a person who makes a surrender.

sur·ren'dry, *n.* a surrender. [Obs.]

sũr·rep'tion, *n.* the act or process of getting in a surrepitious manner, or by stealth or craft. [Obs.]

2. a coming unperceived. [Obs.]

sũr·rep·ti'tious (-tish'us), *a.* [L. *surrepticius*, stolen, done stealthily, from L. *surreptus*, pp. of *surripere*, to take away secretly; *sub*, under, and *rapere*, to seize.]

1. done by stealth, or without proper authority; made or introduced fraudulently; clandestine; underhand.

2. acting in a secret, stealthy way.

sũr·rep·ti'tious·ly, *adv.* in a surreptitious manner; by stealth; without authority; fraudulently.

sũr·rey, *n.*; *pl.* **sũr'reyṣ,** [said to be after *Surrey*, England.] a light, four-wheeled, pleasure carriage, with or without a top, having end springs and two seats, both facing forward.

SURREY

sũr'rō·gāte, *n.* [L. *surrogatus*, pp. of *surrogare*, to elect in place of another, substitute; *sub*, under, in place of, and *rogare*, to ask, elect.]

1. in a general sense, a deputy; a delegate; a substitute; a person appointed to act for another; particularly, the deputy of an ecclesiastical judge, most commonly of a bishop or his chancellor.

2. in some States, a probate court judge in charge of probating wills, administering estates, etc.

sũr'rō·gāte, *v.t.*; surrogated, *pt., pp.*; surrogating, *ppr.* 1. to put in another's place as a substitute or deputy.

2. in law, to subrogate.

sũr'rō·gāte·ship, *n.* the office of a surrogate.

sũr·rō·gā'tion, *n.* subrogation.

sur·round', *v.t.*; surrounded, *pt., pp.*; surrounding, *ppr.* [ME. *sourrounden*; Anglo-Fr. *surounder*; OFr. *suronder*, to overflow, from L. *super*, over, and *undare*, to move in waves, to rise, from *unda*, wave.]

1. to encompass; to environ; to enclose; to cause to encircle on all or nearly all sides, as a town; as, to *surround* a city; they *surrounded* a body of the enemy.

2. to lie or be on all or nearly all sides of; to form an enclosure round; to environ; to encircle; as, a wall or ditch *surrounds* the city.

3. to pass around; to travel about; to circumnavigate; as, to *surround* the globe. [Obs.]

4. to cut off (a fort, military unit, etc.) from communication or retreat by enclosing or shutting in with enemy troops; to beset; to invest.

Syn.—encompass, encircle, environ, enclose, invest, hem in, fence about.

sur·round', *v.i.* to overflow. [Obs.]

sur·round', *n.* a method of hunting animals in herds by surrounding them. [Now Rare.]

sur·round'ing, *a.* that surrounds, or encompasses.

sur·round'ing, *n.* that which surrounds; especially, [*pl.*] the things, conditions, circumstances, influences, etc. that surround a given place or person; environment.

sũr·roy'ăl, *n.* the crown antler of a stag.

sũr'sȧ·nūre, *n.* a sore healed outwardly but not inwardly. [Obs.]

sũr'sē·ănce, *n.* cessation (of hostilities); peace. [Obs.]

sũr·sīze', *n.* [OFr. *sursise*.] a feudal penalty for not paying castle guard-rent. [Obs.]

sũr·sol'id, *n.* in mathematics, the fifth power of a number; the product of the fourth multiplication of a number considered as the root. Thus 3 × 3 = 9, the square of 3, and 9 × 3 = 27, the third power or cube, and 27 × 3 = 81, the fourth power, and 81 × 3 = 243, which is the *sursolid* of 3. [Obs.]

sũr·style', *v.t.* to surname. [Obs.]

sũr'sum çọr'dȧ, [L.] literally, lift up (your) hearts: an incitement to courage, fervor, etc.: opening words of the Preface of the Mass.

sũr'tax, *n.* 1. an extra tax or a special charge assessed on certain goods or accommodations, or on a certain class of people, over and above the normal rates.

2. a graduated income tax levied in addition to the normal tax, on the amount of net income which exceeds a certain sum.

sûr′tax (*also* sûr-tax′), *v.t.* [Fr. *surtaxer.*] to levy a surtax on.

sûr·tout′ (*or* -tö′), *n.* [Fr., lit., over-all; *sur-*, over, and *tout*, from L. *totus*, all.] a man's coat to be worn over his other garments; a man's long overcoat, especially one that resembles a frock coat.

sûr′tūr·brand, *n.* [Ice. *surtarbrandr*; *svartr*, black, and *brandr*, a firebrand.] fibrous brown coal found in the north of Iceland.

sûr·veil′lănce (-vāl′ăns), *n.* 1. inspection or superintendence.

2. watch or observation kept over a person, especially one under suspicion or a prisoner.

sûr·veil′lănt, *n.* [Fr., ppr. of *surveiller*, to watch over; *sur-*, from L. *super*, over, and *veiller*, from L. *vigilare*, to watch.] one who watches or observes; a supervisor or overseer.

sûr·veil′lănt, *a.* keeping surveillance; watching over another or others; overseeing; observant; watchful.

sûr·vēne′, *v.t.* to supervene. [Obs.]

sûr′vē·nūe, *n.* a sudden or unexpected intervention. [Obs.]

sûr·vey′, *v.t.*; surveyed, *pt., pp.*; surveying, *ppr.* [Fr. *sur-*, over, and OFr. *veoir*, to see, from L. *super*, over, and *videre*, to see.]

1. to overlook; to inspect or take a view of, especially in a general or comprehensive way.

2. to see; to perceive. [Obs.]

3. to examine carefully with reference to condition, situation, or the like, with a view to ascertaining the precise state or value of; to inspect or consider carefully.

4. to determine the boundaries, form, extent, area, position, contour, etc. of (a tract of land) by means of linear and angular measurements, and the application of the principles of geometry and trigonometry.

sûr′vey (*or* sûr-vā′), *n.*; *pl.* **sûr′veys,** 1. the act of surveying; a general study or inspection.

To take a *survey* of our own understandings.
—Locke.

2. a general view; comprehensive study or examination; as, the course presents a *survey* of Italian art.

3. (a) the operation of surveying the boundaries, form, extent, area, position, contour, etc. of a tract or area of land; (b) the measured plan, account, or description of such an observation; (c) an area that has been surveyed.

coast and geodetic survey; a survey, under the authority of the Commerce Department, of the coasts and rivers of the United States, for purposes of air and naval navigation.

United States Geological Survey; a government commission acting under the supervision of the Department of the Interior, which is concerned with the geologic conditions within the borders and dependencies of the United States and consists of the description of the mineral and water deposits.

sûr·vey′ȧ·ble, *a.* capable of being surveyed; suitable to be surveyed.

sûr·vey′ăl, *n.* survey. [Rare.]

sûr·vey′ănce, *n.* survey; inspection. [Rare.]

sûr·vey′ing, *n.* 1. the act of surveying.

2. the science or occupation of surveying land.

marine or *nautical surveying*; the surveying of the forms of coasts and harbors, the positions and distances of objects on the shore, of islands, rocks, and shoals, the entrances of rivers, the depth of water, etc.

sûr·vey′ŏr, *n.* 1. an overseer; one placed to superintend others.

2. one who surveys or measures land; one skilled in surveying.

3. an inspector or superintendent, especially a customs official who ascertains the amount and value of imported merchandise.

surveyor of the customs or *of the port*; in the United States, a revenue officer who has general supervision of the loading and unloading of ships, and who has charge of the staff of measurers, inspectors, gaugers, etc.

surveyor's chain; see *chain* (sense 5).

surveyor's cross; see under *cross*.

surveyor's level; a revolving telescope mounted on a tripod and fitted with cross hairs and a spirit level: used by surveyors in finding points of identical elevation.

surveyor's measure; a system of measurement used in surveying:

7.92 inches	=	1 link
100 links	=	1 chain, or 66 feet
80 chains	=	1 mile
625 square links	=	1 square pole
16 square poles	=	1 square chain
10 square chains	=	1 acre
640 acres	=	1 section, or 1 square mile
36 sections	=	1 township

sûr·vey′ŏr ġen′ẽr·ăl, *pl.* **sûr·vey′ŏrs ġen′ẽr·ăl,** 1. a principal surveyor. [Brit.]

2. in the United States government, the chief surveyor of public lands: an officer of the Department of the Interior.

sûr·vey′ŏr·ship, *n.* the office or position of a surveyor.

sûr·view′, (-vū′), *v.t.* to survey. [Archaic.]

sûr·view′, *n.* a survey. [Archaic.]

sûr·vīse′, *v.t.*; survised, *pt., pp.*; survising, *ppr.* [Fr. *sur-*, over, and *viser*, to see.] to look upon. [Obs.]

sûr·vīv′ăl, *n.* 1. a living beyond the life of or continuing longer than another person, thing, or event; an outliving; the act, state, or fact of surviving.

2. something that survives, as a habit, usage, or belief remaining from ancient times.

survival of the fittest; see **natural selection** under *natural*.

sûr·vīv′ănce, sûr·vīv′ăn·cy, *n.* survivorship. [Rare.]

sûr·vīve′, *v.t.*; survived, *pt., pp.*; surviving, *ppr.* [Fr. *survivre*, to survive, from L. *supervivere*, to outlive; *super*, above, and *vivere*, to live.]

1. to outlive; to live beyond the life or existence of; to last longer than; as, the wife *survived* her husband.

2. to continue to live after or in spite of; as, we *survived* the wreck.

sûr·vīve′, *v.i.* to remain alive or in existence, as after an event or after the death of another.

sûr·vīv′ẽr, *n.* same as *survivor*.

sûr·vīv′ing, *a.* remaining alive or in existence; as, *surviving* relatives, *surviving* customs.

sûr·vīv′ŏr, *n.* 1. one who or that which exists after the death of another or others, or after some event or time.

2. in law, the longer liver of two joint tenants, or of any two persons who have a joint interest in anything.

sûr·vīv′ŏr·ship, *n.* 1. the state of being a survivor.

2. in law, the right of a surviving joint owner or owners to take the share of another upon his death.

sus·cep·ti·bil′i·ty, *n.*; *pl.* **sus·cep·ti·bil′i·ties,** 1. the quality or state of being susceptible.

2. [*pl.*] capacities for feeling or emotional excitement; sensitivities.

3. a susceptible temperament or disposition; capacity for receiving impressions.

4. the capacity of a substance for being magnetized, expressed in the ratio of the extent of magnetization to the strength of the magnetizing force.

Syn. —sensibility, capability, feeling.

sus·cep′ti·ble, *a.* [Fr., from L. *susceptibilis*, ready to undertake; *sub*, under, and *capere*, to take.] easily affected emotionally; having a sensitive nature or feelings; responsive.

susceptible of; that can be affected with; admitting; allowing; as, testimony *susceptible of* error.

susceptible to; easily influenced by or affected with; especially liable to; as, *susceptible to* tuberculosis.

Syn.—capable, impressible, tender, sensitive.

sus·cep′ti·ble·ness, *n.* susceptibility.

sus·cep′ti·bly, *adv.* so as to be susceptible.

sus·cep′tion, *n.* the act of taking upon oneself. [Rare.]

sus·cep′tive, *a.* 1. susceptible.

2. receptive.

sus·cep′tive·ness, *n.* susceptibility.

sus·cep·tiv′i·ty, *n.* the quality of being susceptive.

sus·cep′tŏr, *n.* [L.] one who undertakes; specifically, a godfather. [Rare.]

sus·cip′i·en·cy, *n.* reception; admission. [Obs.]

sus·cip′i·ent, *a.* receiving; admitting. [Obs.]

sus·cip′i·ent, *n.* one who takes or admits; one who receives. [Obs.]

sus″ci·tȧ·bil′i·ty, *n.* the state or quality of being readily roused, raised, or excited; excitability. [Obs.]

sus′ci·tāte, *v.t.* to rouse; to excite; to call into life and action.

sus·ci·tā′tion, *n.* the act of raising or exciting.

sū′si, *n.* [Hind.] a fine cotton fabric striped with silk or cotton.

sus′lik, *n.* [Russ.] 1. a small gopher or ground squirrel, *Spermophilus citillus*, of north central Eurasia; a spermophile.

SUSLIK (*Spermophilus citillus*)

2. its mottled, grayish-brown fur.

sus·ō·tox′in, *n.* [L. *sus*, *suis*, hog, pig, and Eng. *toxin.*] a ptomaine, $C_{10}H_{26}N_2$, isolated from cultures of the hog-cholera bacillus.

sus·pect′, *v.t.*; suspected, *pt., pp.*; suspecting, *ppr.* [Fr. *suspecter*, from L. *suspectus*, pp. of *suspicere*, to look under, to look up to, admire, also, to mistrust; *sub*, under, and *spicere*, to look.]

1. to look up to; to respect. [Obs.]

2. to believe (someone) to be guilty of something specified on little or no evidence.

3. to believe to be bad, wrong, harmful, questionable, etc.; to distrust.

4. to imagine to be; to think probable or likely; suppose; presume; surmise.

sus·pect′, *v.i.* to imagine guilt; to be suspicious.

sus′pect, *a.* doubtful; suspected; under suspicion.

sus′pect, *n.* 1. suspicion. [Archaic.]

2. a suspected person, especially one suspected of a crime, etc.

sus·pect′ȧ·ble, *a.* that can be suspected. [Rare.]

sus·pect′ed·ly, *adv.* so as to excite suspicion; so as to be suspected.

sus·pect′ed·ness, *n.* the state of being suspected.

sus·pect′ẽr, *n.* one who suspects.

sus·pect′ful, *a.* apt to suspect or mistrust; suspicious. [Rare.]

sus·pec′tion, *n.* suspicion. [Obs.]

sus·pec′tious·ness (-shus-), *n.* suspiciousness. [Obs.]

sus·pect′less, *a.* 1. not suspecting; having no suspicion. [Obs.]

2. not suspected; not mistrusted. [Obs.]

sus·pend′, *v.t.*; suspended, *pt., pp.*; suspending, *ppr.* [ME. *suspenden*; Fr. *suspendre*, to suspend, from L. *suspendere*, to hang up; *sub*, under, and *pendere*, to hang.]

1. to bar or exclude from an office, privilege, position, etc., usually for a specified time, as a penalty; to debar.

2. to cause to cease or become inoperative for a time; to stop or withhold temporarily; as, train service has been *suspended*.

3. to keep undecided or in abeyance; to hold back (judgment, sentence, etc.).

4. to hang; to attach to something above so as to allow free movement; as, to *suspend* a chandelier.

5. to hold without attachment, as dust in the air; to keep in suspension.

6. to keep in suspense, wonder, etc.

7. to make to depend on. [Rare.]

God hath *suspended* the promise of eternal life on the condition of faith and obedience.
—Tillotson.

8. in music, to hold back (a tone) into the next chord, creating a temporary dissonance.

Syn.—defer, withhold, hang, interrupt, intermit, stay, delay, hinder, debar.

sus·pend′, *v.i.* 1. to stop temporarily.

2. to stop payment, or be unable to meet one's debts or obligations.

sus·pend′ed, *a.* 1. hung from something; pendent.

2. interrupted; delayed temporarily.

3. in botany, hanging downward from the apex of a cell, as many seeds or ovules.

4. in entomology, attached in a pendent position by the cremaster, as the chrysalises of many butterflies.

sus·pend′ed an·i·mā′tion, a temporary cessation of the vital functions resembling death, as in asphyxiation.

sus·pend′ẽr, *n.* 1. one who or that which suspends.

2. something suspended, as a hanging basket or vase for plants or flowers.
3. [*pl.*] a pair of straps or bands passed over the shoulders to support the trousers.
4. [*pl.*] garters. [Brit.]
5. one of a series of vats or pits used by tanners.

sus·pen·sā′tion, *n.* a temporary cessation. [Obs.]

sus·pense′, *n.* [L. *suspensus,* suspended, uncertain, lit., hung up, pp. of *suspendere,* to suspend.]
1. the state of being undecided or undetermined.
2. the state of being uncertain, as in awaiting a decision, usually characterized by some anxiety or apprehension.
3. uncertainty; indecisiveness.
4. suspension or interruption, as of a legal right. [Rare.]
5. stop; cessation for a time. [Obs.]
Syn.—doubt, cessation, hesitancy, perplexity, uncertainty.

sus·pense′, *a.* 1. held from proceeding. [Obs.]
2. held in doubt or expectation; expressing doubt. [Obs.]

sus·pense′ ac·çount′, in bookkeeping, an account in which sums received or disbursed are temporarily entered, until their disposition can be determined.

sus·pense′ly, *adv.* in suspense. [Obs.]

sus·pen·si·bil′i·ty, *n.* the quality or capacity of being suspensible; as, the *suspensibility* of indurated clay in water.

sus·pen′si·ble, *a.* capable of being suspended.

sus·pen′sion, *n.* [Fr., from L. *suspensio (-onis),* a hanging up, suspension.]
1. a suspending or being suspended; specifically, (a) a barring from office, etc. (b) a stoppage of payment, etc.; (c) a holding back of a judgment, etc.
2. a supporting device upon or from which something is suspended.
3. the system of springs, etc. supporting a vehicle upon its undercarriage or axles.
4. the act or means of suspending the balance or pendulum in a timepiece.
5. the condition of a solid whose particles are dispersed through a fluid but not dissolved in it.
6. a substance in this condition.
7. in music, (a) the holding back of one or more tones in a chord while the others progress, so that a temporary dissonance is created; (b) the tone or tones so held.
8. in rhetoric, a keeping of the hearer in suspense of what is to follow, or what is to be the inference or conclusion from the arguments or observations.
plea in suspension; in law, a plea which shows some matter of temporary incapacity to proceed with the action or suit.
suspension and interdict; in Scots law, a judicial remedy of the Court of Session when the object is to stop or interdict any unlawful proceeding: the remedy is applied for by a note of suspension and interdict.

SUSPENSION BRIDGE

suspension bridge; a bridge suspended from chains or cables which are anchored at either end and supported by towers at regular intervals.
suspension of arms; a short truce or cessation of operations in a war agreed upon by the commanders of the contending armies, as for burying the dead, making proposals for surrender or for peace, etc.
suspension point; any of a series of dots, properly three, indicating the omission of words or sentences, as in something quoted.
suspension railway; a railway in which the body of the carriage is suspended from an elevated track or tracks on which the wheels run.
Syn.—cessation, interruption, delay, intermission.

sus·pen′sive, *a.* 1. that suspends, defers, or temporarily stops something.
2. tending to suspend judgment; undecided in mind.
3. of, characterized by, or in suspense; apprehensive.
4. expressing or creating suspense; as, a *suspensive* sentence.
5. of or characterized by physical suspension. [Rare.]
suspensive conditions; conditions that make the beginning of a legal transaction or title dependent upon the happening of some event.

sus·pen′sive·ly, *adv.* in a suspensive manner.

sus·pen′sŏr, *n.* [LL., from L. *suspensus,* pp. of *suspendere,* to suspend.]
1. a suspensory.
2. in botany, a cellular cord by which the embryo of some plants is suspended from the foramen or opening of the seed.
3. in anatomy, the longitudinal ligament of the liver.

sus·pen·sō′ri·ăl, *a.* pertaining to or of the nature of a suspensory; specifically, in anatomy, of or pertaining to the suspensorium of the lower jaw.

sus·pen·sō′ri·um, *n.*; *pl.* **sus·pen·sō′ri·ȧ,** [LL.] that which suspends; a suspensory; specifically, (a) in the vertebrates below mammals, the bone or series of bones, either cartilaginous or ligamental, by means of which the lower jaw is suspended from the skull; (b) in the *Acanthocephala,* the ligament which traverses the anenterous body and supports the generative organs.

sus·pen·sō′ri·us, *n.*; *pl.* **sus·pen·sō′ri·ī,** a suspensory muscle.

sus·pen′sō·ry, *a.* 1. suspending, supporting, or sustaining; as, a *suspensory* muscle or bandage.
2. suspending or delaying, especially so as to leave something undecided.
suspensory ligament; a ligament supporting the lens of the eye.

sus·pen′sō·ry, *n.*; *pl.* **sus·pen′sō·rieș,** a suspensory muscle, bone, truss, bandage, etc.; a suspensorium.

sus″pi·cȧ·bil′i·ty, *n.* the state or quality of being suspicable. [Obs.]

sus′pi·çȧ·ble, *a.* that can be suspected; liable to suspicion. [Obs.]

sus·pi′cien·cy (-pish′en-), *n.* suspiciousness. [Obs.]

sus·pi′ciŏn (-pish′un), *n.* [Fr., from L. *suspicio (-onis),* mistrust, from *suspectus,* pp. of *suspicere,* to look up at, admire; also, to look secretly at, mistrust, suspect.]
1. the act or an instance of suspecting; a believing of something bad, wrong, harmful, etc. with little or no supporting evidence.

Suspicions among thoughts are like bats among birds; they ever fly by twilight.
—Bacon.

2. the feeling or state of mind of a person who suspects.
3. a very small amount or degree; suggestion; inkling; trace.
above suspicion; not to be suspected; honorable.
on suspicion; on the basis of suspicion; because suspected.
under suspicion; suspected.
Syn.—distrust, mistrust, doubt, fear.

sus·pi′ciŏn, *v.t.* to regard with suspicion; to suspect; to mistrust; to doubt. [Dial. or Colloq.]

sus·pi′cious, *a.* [L. *suspiciosus,* mistrustful.]
1. arousing or likely to arouse suspicion in others.
2. showing or expressing suspicion.
3. (a) suspecting; feeling suspicion; (b) tending habitually to suspect, especially to suspect fault, evil, etc.
Syn.—distrustful, mistrustful, doubtful, dubious, questionable.

sus·pi′cious·ly, *adv.* in a suspicious manner.

sus·pi′cious·ness, *n.* the state or quality of being suspicious.

sus′pir·ăl, *n.* 1. a breathing hole; a vent or ventiduct. [Obs.]
2. a spring of water passing under ground toward a cistern or conduit. [Obs.]

sus·pi·rā′tion, *n.* [L. *suspiratio (-onis),* a deep breath, sigh, from *suspirare,* to draw a deep breath, sigh.] the act of sighing or taking a long, deep breath; a prolonged sigh.

sus·pīre′, *v.i.*; suspired, *pt., pp.*; suspiring, *ppr.*
1. to sigh; to take a long, deep breath. [Poet.]
2. to breathe. [Obs.]

sus·pīre′, *v.t.* to utter with a sigh. [Obs.]

sus·pīre′, *n.* a sigh; a deep breath. [Obs.]

sus·tāin′, *v.t.*; sustained, *pt., pp.*; sustaining, *ppr.* [ME. *susteinen*; OFr. *sustenir*; L. *sustinere,* to uphold; *sub,* under, and *tenere,* to hold.]
1. to maintain; keep in existence; keep going; prolong; as, this pedal *sustains* the tones.
2. to keep supplied with necessities; to provide for.
3. to support from or as from below; to carry the weight or burden of.
4. to strengthen the spirits, courage, etc. of; to comfort; buoy up; encourage.
5. to endure; to bear up against; withstand.
6. to undergo; to experience; to suffer, as an injury or loss.
7. to uphold or support the validity or justice of.
8. to confirm; prove; corroborate.
9. to support in any condition by aid; to assist or relieve. [Obs.]
Syn.—bear, support, uphold, prop, subsist, nourish, assist, relieve, suffer, undergo, endure.

sus·tāin′, *v.i.* 1. to suffer; to endure. [Obs.]
2. to rest for support. [Obs.]

sus·tāin′, *n.* one who or that which upholds; a sustainer. [Obs.]

sus·tāin′ȧ·ble, *a.* capable of being sustained or maintained; maintainable.

sus·tāined′, *a.* kept at one pitch or level, especially a high pitch or degree.

sus·tāin′ẽr, *n.* 1. one who or that which sustains.
2. in entomology, a sustentor.

sus·tāin′ing, *a.* having the ability to sustain; enduring; supporting; giving strength; corroborating.
sustaining fund; an amount of money or other resources used as a foundation or a means of permanent support, as of an organization or business.
sustaining program; any radio program presented and paid for by a radio station or network rather than by a commercial sponsor.

sus·tāin′ment, *n.* a sustaining or being sustained; support; also, a supporter.

sus′tē·nănce, *n.* [LL. *sustinentia,* patience, endurance, from L. *sustinere,* to uphold, sustain.]
1. sustainment.
2. support; maintenance; subsistence; means of livelihood; as, the *sustenance* of the body; the *sustenance* of life.
3. that which supports life; food; nourishment.

sus·ten·taç′ū·lăr, *a.* [from L. *sustentaculum,* a support, and *-ar.*] in anatomy, supporting: said of connective-tissue cells, etc.

sus·ten·taç′ū·lum, *n.*; *pl.* **sus·ten·taç′ū·lȧ,** a part or organ acting as a support.

sus′ten·tāte, *v.t.* to support. [Archaic.]

sus·ten·tā′tion, *n.* [L. *sustentatio (-onis),* maintenance, from *sustinere,* to uphold, sustain.]
1. a sustaining or being sustained; maintenance; support; preservation.
2. something that sustains or supoprts; sustenance.
sustentation fund; a fund established by any religious body for the support of its churches or ministers.

sus′ten·tā·tive, *a.* of or providing sustentation; sustaining.

sus′ten·tā·tŏr, *n.* in anatomy and zoology, a part or structure acting as a support.

sus·ten′tion, *n.* [coined from *sustain* by analogy with *detention, retention,* etc.] a sustaining or being sustained; as, the *sustention* of a musical tone.

sus·ten′tŏr, *n.* in entomology, one of a pair of posterior projections of the chrysalis of a butterfly.

sus′tẽr, sus′tre, *n.* a sister. [Obs.]

sụ′sụ, *n.* [Bengalese.] a cetacean, *Platanista gangetica,* found in the rivers of India.

sū·sur′rănt, *a.* [L. *susurrans (-antis),* ppr. of *susurrare,* to whisper.] whispering; murmuring; rustling.

sū·sur′rāte, *v.i.*; susurrated, *pt., pp.*; susurrating, *ppr.* [L. *susurratus,* pp.] to whisper; murmur; rustle.

sū·sur·rā′tion, *n.* [L. *susurratio (-onis),* a whispering, from *susurrare,* to whisper.] the act of whispering; a soft murmur; a rustle.

sū·sur′ring·ly, *adv.* whisperingly. [Obs.]

sū·sur′rous, *a.* whispering; susurrant.

sū·sur′rus, *n.* [L., a whisper, murmur.] a whispering, murmuring, or rustling sound.

Suth·ẽr·lan′di·ȧ, *n.* [named after James *Sutherland,* Scot. botanist.] a genus of leguminous plants having one species, *Sutherlandia frutescens,* the Cape bladder senna, a shrub having unequally pinnate leaves, large scarlet flowers, and bladdery legumes with many seeds.

sū'tile, *a.* done by stitching. [Rare.]

sut'lẽr, *n.* [O.D. *soeteler*, D. *zoetelaar*, a sutler, from *soetelen*, to perform menial offices or dirty work.] one who follows an army for the purpose of selling the troops provisions, liquor, etc.

sut'lẽr·ship, *n.* the occupation or business of a sutler.

sū'trȧ, *n.* [Sans., a thread, a string.]
 1. in Brahmanism, (a) a precept or maxim; (b) a collection of these.
 2. in Buddhism, scriptural narratives, especially the dialogues of the Buddha.

sụt'tȧ, *n.* same as *sutra*.

sut·tee', *n.* [Hind. *satī*; Sans. *satī*, from *sat*, good, pure; properly, a chaste and virtuous wife.]
 1. a Hindu widow who throws herself alive, and is cremated, on the funeral pile of her husband.
 2. the voluntary self-cremation of Hindu widows on the funeral pile of their husbands: a former practice now virtually obsolete.

sut·tee'iṣm, *n.* the custom or practice of suttee.

sut'tle, *a.* designating the weight of goods when the tare has been deducted and, formerly, when the tret was yet to be allowed.

sut'tle, *v.i.*; suttled (-tld), *pt., pp.*; suttling, *ppr.* to carry on the business of a sutler. [Archaic.]

sū'tūr·ăl, *a.* [L. *sutura*, a seam.] of, belonging to, situated at, or taking place at or near a suture.

sū'tūr·ăl·ly, *adv.* in the manner of a suture.

sū·tūr·ā'tion, *n.* the act of suturing; also, the thing sutured.

sū'tūre, *n.* [L. *sutura*, a seam, from *sutus*, pp. of *suere*, to sew.]
 1. the act of joining together by or as by sewing; also, the line along which two things are joined, united, or sewn together, so as to form a seam, or something resembling a seam.
 2. in anatomy, the joining together, or the line of junction, of two bones, especially of the skull.
 3. in botany, (a) a seam formed when two parts unite; (b) a line along which a fruit, as a pod or capsule, splits.
 4. in entomology, the line formed by the meeting of the elytra when they are confluent.
 5. in surgery, (a) the uniting of the lips or edges of a wound or incision by stitching or other means; (b) any of the stitches of gut, thread, wire, etc. so used.
 6. in zoology, the outline of a septum in the *Tetrabranchiata*, resembling a suture in the skull.

sū'tūre, *v.t.*; sutured, *pt., pp.*; suturing, *ppr.* to make a suture in; to join together by or as by stitching or sewing.

sū'um çui'quē (kwī'kwē), [L.] to each his own.

sụ·wär'rōw, *n.* same as *saguaro*.

sụ·wär'rōw nut, the souari nut.

sū'ze·rāin, *n.* [Fr., formed from prefix *sus*, above, over, L. *sursum*; on type of *sovereign*, from L. *super*, above.]
 1. a ruler, especially a feudal lord or baron.
 2. a state in its relation to another over which it has political control.

sū'ze·rāin·ty, *n.*; *pl.* **sū'ze·rāin·tieṣ,** [Fr. *suzeraineté*, from *suzerain*, a lord paramount.] the position or power of a suzerain.

svas'ti·kȧ, *n.* same as *swastika*.

svelte, svelt, *a.* [Fr. *svelte*.] slender and graceful; lithe.

swä, *adv.* so. [Obs.]

swäb, *n.* [back-formation from *swabber*.]
 1. a mop for cleaning floors, ships' decks, or the like.
 2. (a) a small piece of cotton, cloth, sponge, etc. used to apply medicine to, or clean discharged matter from, the throat, mouth, etc.; (b) the matter collected in this way.
 3. a long-handled brush for cleaning the barrel of a gun, etc.
 4. an epaulet: humorously compared to a swab or mop. [Slang.]
 5. a cod or pod, as of beans, peas, or the like. [Brit. Dial.]
 6. in founding, a soft brush made of some strands of gasket tied together at one end and beaten and combed out at the other, used to wet the parting edge before drawing the pattern, to moisten parts of the mold requiring repairs, etc.
 7. a clumsy, loutish fellow. [Slang.]
 Also *swob*.

swäb, *v.t.*; swabbed, *pt., pp.*; swabbing, *ppr.* to use a swab on; to clean, medicate, etc. with a swab: also *swob*.

swäb'bẽr, *n.* 1. one who uses a swab, as to clean the deck of a ship.
 2. a clumsy, loutish person.
 3. a swab.
 4. [*pl.*] certain cards in an old-fashioned game of whist, the holders of which were entitled to part of the stakes.

Swā'bi·ăn, *n.* 1. a native or inhabitant of Swabia, a former duchy of Germany, now a district of Bavaria.
 2. the language of the Swabians, a dialect of High German.

Swā'bi·ăn, *a.* of or relating to Swabia, its people, their language, etc.

swäd, *n.* 1. a pod, as of beans or peas. [Brit. Dial.]
 2. a lump, mass, or bunch; also, a crowd. [Slang.]
 3. a silly, coarse fellow; a bumpkin. [Brit. Dial.]
 4. in mining, a thin layer of stone or refuse coal at the bottom of a coal seam. [Brit.]

swäd'dle, *v.t.*; swaddled, *pt., pp.*; swaddling, *ppr.* [ME. *swadil*, *swadel*, *swathele*, to bind, from AS. *swæthil*, *swethel*, a swaddling band.]
 1. to wrap (a newborn baby) in long, narrow bands of cloth.
 2. to bind in or as in bandages; to swathe.
 3. to beat; to cudgel. [Obs.]

swäd'dle, *n.* a cloth or bandage used for swaddling.

swäd'dle·bill, *n.* a duck, the shoveler. [Dial.]

swäd'dlẽr, *n.* a Protestant, especially an early Methodist: a term of contempt applied by Roman Catholics in Ireland.

swäd'dling bandṣ, swaddling clothes.

swäd'dling çlōtheṣ, 1. formerly, the long, narrow bands of cloth wrapped around a new-born baby.
 2. baby clothes.
 3. the period of infancy or of close parental control.
 4. any rigid control or restrictions, as of the immature.

swäd'dling çlouts, swaddling clothes.

Swȧ·de̤'shi, *n.* [Sans. *svadesin*, native, from *svadeśa*, native land.] in India, a policy of boycotting foreign goods to encourage home production.

swag, *v.i.*; swagged, *pt., pp.*; swagging, *ppr.* [Ice. *svegja*, to make to sway; *sveigja*, to sway; G. *schwanken*, to sway; hence, swagger.]
 1. to sink down by its weight; to sag.
 2. to sway or lurch.
 3. in Australia, to travel carrying a swag.

swag, *v.t.* to cause to sway.

swag, *n.* 1. the proceeds of theft or robbery; plunder. [Slang.]
 2. in Australia, the pack carried by a foot traveler, miner, etc., as a long roll of blankets, etc. borne on the back.
 3. a lurching or swaying motion.
 4. a swale; a tract of low land. [Dial.]

swag'bel"lied, *a.* having a prominent, overhanging belly.

swag'bel"ly, *n.* a prominent or projecting belly; also, a swagbellied person. [Dial.]

swāġe, *v.t.* and *v.i.* to ease; to mitigate; to assuage. [Archaic.]

swāġe, *n.* [ME.; OFr. *souage*, from LL. *soca*, a rope.]
 1. a kind of tool for bending or shaping metal.
 2. a die or stamp for shaping or marking metal by hammering.

swāġe, *v.t.*; swaged, *pt., pp.*; swaging, *ppr.* to use a swage on; to shape, bend, etc. with a swage.

swāġe block, a large perforated block of metal, having grooved sides, and adapted for heading bolts and swaging objects of larger size than can be worked in the ordinary heading tools and swages fitted to the anvil.

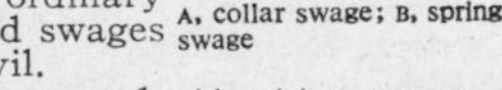

SWAGES
A, collar swage; B, spring swage

swag'gẽr, *v.i.*; swaggered, *pt., pp.*; swaggering, *ppr.* [prob. freq. of *swag*.]
 1. to strut with an insolent or arrogant air; to strut about with an affected superiority.
 2. to boast, brag, or show off in a loud, superior manner.

swag'gẽr, *v.t.* to influence by blustering; to bluff.

swag'gẽr, *n.* swaggering walk, manner, or behavior.

swag'gẽr, *n.* in Australia, a tramping bushman who carries a swag.

swag'gẽr, *a.* regarded as ultrafashionable; stylish; swell. [Colloq.]

swag'gẽr·ẽr, *n.* a person who swaggers.

swag'gẽr stick, a short stick or cane as carried by some army officers, etc.

swag'gy, *a.* sinking, hanging, or leaning by its weight. [Dial.]

swag'măn, swagṣ'măn, *n.* in Australia, a swagger. [Slang.]

Swä·hi'li, *n.* [from Ar. *sawāḥil*, pl. of *sāḥil*, coast, and *-i*, belonging to.]
 1. *pl.* **Swä·hi'li,** one of a Bantu people inhabiting Zanzibar and the near-by mainland, characterized by a large admixture of Arab stock.
 2. their Northern Bantu language, used as a lingua franca in east central Africa.

Swä·hi'li, *a.* same as *Swahilian*.

Swä·hi'li·ăn, *a.* of the Swahili or their language.

swāin, *n.* [ME. *swein*; O.N. *sveinn*, a boy, servant; Sw. *sven*, a page, young man; Dan. *svend*, a servant, journeyman.]
 1. a young man in attendance on a knight; a squire. [Obs.]
 2. a servant. [Obs.]
 3. a young man living in the country. [Poet. or Archaic.]
 4. a young rustic lover or gallant; also, any lover. [Poet. or Archaic.]

swāin'ish, *a.* rustic; boorish. [Rare.]

swāin'ish·ness, *n.* the condition of being swainish. [Rare.]

swāin'ling, *n.* a little or young swain. [Obs.]

swāin'mōte, *n.* an old English forest court, formerly held three times a year by the officers of the forest.

swāin'ship, *n.* the state or condition of being a swain.

swāl, *v.* obsolete past tense of *swell*.

swāle, *n.* [Ice. *svalr*; Sw. *sval*, cool.]
 1. a hollow or depression, especially one in wet, marshy ground.
 2. a shade or shady place. [Dial.]

swāle, *v.i.* same as *sweal*.

swäl'let, *n.* water breaking in upon miners at their work. [Brit. Dial.]

swäl'lōw, *n.* [ME. *swalu*, *swalwe*; AS. *swalewe*, *swealwe*.]
 1. any small, swift-flying bird of the family *Hirundinidæ*, with long, pointed wings and forked tail, known for its regular migrations.
 2. any of certain swifts resembling swallows, as the chimney swift.
 3. a variety of domestic pigeon.

EUROPEAN SWALLOW
(*Hirundo rustica*)

swäl'lōw, *v.t.*; swallowed, *pt., pp.*; swallowing, *ppr.* [ME. *swalwen*, *swolwen*; AS. *swelgan*, *swilgan*, to swallow.]
 1. to pass (food, etc.) from the mouth through the gullet or esophagus into the stomach, usually by a series of muscular actions in the throat.
 2. to take in; to absorb; to engulf; to overwhelm: usually followed by *up*; as, *swallowed up* by the night.
 3. to take back (words said); to retract; to withdraw.
 4. to put up with; to tolerate; to bear humbly; as, he had to *swallow* their insults.
 5. to refrain from expressing; to hold back; to suppress; as, *swallow* your pride.
 6. to receive or accept, as opinions or belief, without examination or scruple; to receive gullibly; to drink in; as, he *swallowed* everything she told him. [Colloq.]

swäl'lōw, *v.i.* to perform the muscular actions characteristic of swallowing something, especially as in emotion.

swäl'lōw, *n.* 1. the gullet or esophagus; the throat.
 2. as much as is swallowed at one time.
 3. the act of swallowing.
 4. relish; appetite. [Rare.]
 5. the opening or space in a hoisting block or pulley through which the rope passes.
 6. a swellfish or puffer.

swäl′lōw·ẽr, *n.* one who or that which swallows; also, a glutton.
swäl′lōw fish, the tubfish, *Trigla hirundo*: also called *sapphirine gurnard*.
swäl′lōw flȳ′catch·ẽr, the swallow shrike.
swäl′lōw hawk, a swallow-tailed kite.
swäl′lōw hōle, a sink hole.
swäl′lōw·ing, *n.* the reception of food into the stomach through the throat; deglutition.
swäl′lōw plŏv′ẽr, a pratincole.
swäl′lōw shrīke, an East Indian and Australian bird resembling the swallows and the shrikes, as the ashy *swallow shrike* of India, *Artamus fuscus*.
swäl′lōw·tāil, *n.* 1. something having a forked shape like that of a swallow's tail.
2. in carpentry, a dovetail.
3. a plant, a species of willow.
4. in fortification, an outwork composed of two redans.
5. a swallow-tailed coat.
6. an arrowhead, or the arrow itself.
7. any of various butterflies, especially *Papilio machaon*: so called because the lower wings are prolonged to form pointed tails or projections.
8. a common British moth, *Urapteryx sambucaria*, having long, pointed lower wings.
swäl′lōw-tāiled, *a.* 1. having or resembling the form of a swallow's tail.
2. in carpentry, dovetailed.
swallow-tailed duck; the old squaw, a northern sea duck.
swallow-tailed flycatcher; the scissortail.
swallow-tailed gull; *Xema furcata*, a gull of the Arctic Ocean.
swallow-tailed hawk or *kite*; a kite, *Elanoides forficatus*, with a deeply forked tail.
swallow-tailed moth; same as *swallowtail* (sense 8).
swäl′lōw-tāiled çōat, a man's coat that tapers down in two long tails, or skirts, at the back; full-dress coat.
swäl′lōw wąr′blẽr, a species of singing bird, common to India, Africa, and Australia.
swäl′lōw·wing, *n.* a fissirostral barbet or puffbird of the genus *Chelidoptera*.
swäl′lōw·wŏrt, *n.* 1. the common celandine, *Chelidonium majus*.
2. a kind of vine whose root is used in medicine.
3. a plant related to the milkweed.
white swallowwort; *Vincetoxicum officinale*, an herb allied to the milkweed.
swam, *v.* past tense of *swim* (to move through water).
swam, *v.* past tense of *swim* (to be dizzy).
swä′mi, *n.*; *pl.* **swä′miș,** [Hind. *svami*; Sans. *svamin*, a lord.] lord; master: a Hindu title of respect, especially for a Hindu religious teacher.
swămp, *n.* [Dan. and Sw. *svamp*; Ice. *svöppr*, sponge, fungus; hence applied to spongy ground; Sw. *svampig*, swampy.]
1. spongy land; low ground filled with water; soft, wet ground; a marsh; a bog.
2. in coal mining, a hollow space in a coal bed where water may collect.
swămp, *v.t.*; swamped (swompt), *pt.*, *pp.*; swamping, *ppr.* 1. to plunge or sink in a swamp, or as in a swamp.
2. to flood or submerge with or as with water.
3. to overcome or overwhelm; to ruin; as, heavy debts soon *swamped* them.
4. to sink (a boat) by filling with water.
5. to make (a road or path) in a swamp or wood.
6. to draw, as logs, etc., to a skidway.
swămp, *v.i.* to become swamped; to be plunged or caught in a swamp, or as in a swamp.
swămp ap′ple, the honeysuckle apple.
swămp black′bīrd, the red-winged blackbird.
swămp çab′bāġe, the skunk cabbage.
swămp deer, an East Indian deer, *Servus duvaucelli*, living in swamps.
swămp fē′vẽr, malaria.
swămp hen, 1. the purple gallinule.
2. an Australian waterfowl of the genus *Porphyrio*.
3. a species of crake or rail of Australia.
swămp hŏn′ey·suç·kle, a flowering shrub, *Azalea viscosa*, of American swamps.
swămp hook, a kind of hook used with a long chain to roll logs.
swămp′land, *n.* swampy land.
swămp lau′rel, an evergreen shrub, *Kalmia glauca*, with leaves bluish white on the under surface.
swămp lil′y, 1. a plant of the genus *Zephyranthes*, bearing white lilylike flowers.
2. the Turk's-cap lily, bearing red flowers.
swămp mā′ple, the red maple, *Acer rubrum*.
swămp ōak, the swamp post oak, *Quercus lyrata*; also, the swamp white oak, *Quercus bicolor*; also, the swamp Spanish oak or pin oak, *Quercus palustris*.
swămp ōre, an ore of iron found in swamps and morasses; bog ore; limonite.
swămp pär′tridġe (-trij), the spruce partridge.
swămp pīne, the southern pine, *Pinus australis*, growing from Virginia to Florida.
swămp piñk, the swamp honeysuckle, *Azalea viscosa*, and other azaleas.
swămp quāil, an Australian quail, *Synæcus australis*.
swămp rob′in, the chewink.
swămp sas′sȧ·fras, the sweet bay, *Magnolia glauca*.
swămp spar′rōw, a species of sparrow, *Melospiza palustris*, which lives in swamps and thickets: abundant in the eastern United States.
swămp wil′lōw, pussy willow.
swămp′wood, *n.* the leatherwood, *Dirca palustris*.
swămp′y, *a.*; *comp.* swampier; *superl.* swampiest, 1. of or consisting of a swamp or swamps.
2. like a swamp; low, wet, and spongy; as, *swampy* land.
swä′my, *n.*; *pl.* **swä′mieș,** a swami.
swän, *n.*; *pl.* **swänș** or **swän,** [ME.; AS. *swan*; akin to D. *zwaan*; Ice. *svanr*; Sw. *svan*; Dan. *svane*; G. *schwan*.]

WILD SWAN (*Cygnus musicus*)

1. any large-bodied, web-footed water bird of the genus *Cygnus*, having a long neck and short legs placed far back. On the under surface, the plumage is thick and furlike; on the upper side the feathers are broad, but both above and below, the body is thickly covered with down. With two exceptions, all adults have pure white plumage. They are graceful swimmers and strong flyers.
2. [S–] Cygnus, a constellation.
3. a poet or singer of great ability: from the myth that swans sing a melodious song just before dying.
swän, *v.i.* [variant of *swear*.] to swear: principally in the phrase *I swan!*, an exclamation of surprise, impatience, etc.
swän an·i·mal′çūle, an infusorian having a long process resembling a neck.
swän dīve, a forward dive in which the legs are held straight and together, the back is curved, and the arms are stretched out to the sides.
swän′flow″ẽr, *n.* any of several species of orchids, of the South American tropics. In the flower there is an arched column like a swan's neck.
swang, *v.* archaic or dialectal past tense of *swing*.
swang, *n.* a piece of low, wet land or greensward. [Brit. Dial.]
swän gōose, the Chinese goose, *Cygnopsis cygnoides*.
swän′hẽrd, *n.* a person who tends swans.
swän′-hop″ping, *n.* same as *swan-upping*.
swän′i·mōte, *n.* same as *swainmote*.
swañk, *n.* [orig. in slang from dial. *v.i.*]
1. stylish display or ostentation in dress, etc. [Slang.]
2. swaggering, ostentatious behavior, speech, etc. [Slang.]
swañk, *a.* 1. ostentatiously stylish. [Slang.]
2. active; lively. [Dial.]
swañk, *v.i.* to act in a showy, pretentious manner; to swagger. [Slang.]
swañk, *v.* alternative past tense of *swink*.
swañk′i·ly, *adv.* in a swanky manner. [Slang.]
swañk′i·ness, *n.* the quality of being swanky. [Slang.]
swañk′y, *a.*; *comp.* swankier; *superl.* swankiest, ostentatiously stylish; swaggering; showy. [Slang.]
swañk′y, swañk′ie, *n.*; *pl.* **swañk′ieș,** a slender, agile, or clever youth or maid. [Scot.]
swañk′y, *n.* inferior ale or beer. [Dial.]
swän′līke, *a.* like a swan.
swän māid′en, in various ancient mythologies, a creature with the supernatural power of taking on at will the form of a swan or of a beautiful maiden.
swän′märk, *n.* a mark on a swan's bill to designate the owner, as one made at swan-upping.
swän′neck, *n.* 1. the swanflower.
2. a long slender neck like that of a swan.
swän′nẽr·y, *n.*; *pl.* **swän′nẽr·ieș,** a place in which swans are kept or bred.
swän′ny, *a.* like a swan.
swän′ș′-down, *n.* 1. a fine, soft, thick cloth of wool mixed with silk, cotton, or rayon, used for making baby clothes, etc.
2. Canton flannel.
3. the soft, fine underfeathers, or down, of the swan, used for trimming clothes, making powder puffs, etc.
Also *swansdown*.
swän′skin, *n.* 1. any of various soft, thick, warm flannels of wool or cotton.
2. the skin of a swan, with its feathers and down.
swän sǫng, 1. the song supposed in ancient fable to be sung by a dying swan.
2. the last act, final creative work, etc. of a person, as before his death.
swän′-up″ping, *n.* 1. the practice of marking annually the upper mandible of young swans, as a sign of ownership.
2. a yearly expedition on the Thames for this purpose.
swän′wŏrt, *n.* the swanflower.
swäp, *v.t.* swapped (swopt), *pt.*, *pp.*; swapping, *ppr.* [ME. *swappen*, to strike, move quickly; prob. echoic.]
1. to exchange; to barter. [Colloq.]
2. to strike; to cut. [Rare.]
Also spelled *swop*.
swäp, *v.i.* 1. to make an exchange or trade. [Colloq.]
2. to sweep down; to rush; to fall. [Obs.]
Also spelled *swop*.
swäp, *n.* 1. a blow; a stroke. [Obs.]
2. an exchange; a trade. [Colloq.]
Also spelled *swop*.
swäp, *adv.* hastily; at a stroke. [Brit. Dial.]
swāpe, *n.* [collateral form of *sweep*, *swipe*.]
1. a device for raising water, consisting of a bucket hung on the end of a counterpoised lever; a sweep or swipe.
2. a sconce or lightholder.
3. a pump handle.
4. a long oar; a sweep.
[Brit. Dial. in all senses.]
swȧ·räj′, *n.* [Hind.; Sans. *svarāj*, self-ruling; *sva-*, own, and *rāj*, rule.] in India, home rule; political independence; self-government: during the period of British rule it was [S–] the name of the political party seeking Indian autonomy.
swąrd, *n.* [AS. *sweard*; akin to D. *zwoord*; Dan. *svær*; Ice. *svördhr*; G. *schwarte*, all signifying the skin of bacon, and then sward or surface of the earth.]
1. the skin of bacon; rind. [Brit. Dial.]
2. a grassy surface of land; turf; that part of the soil which is filled with the roots of grass, forming a kind of mat, as green*sward*.
swąrd, *v.t.* and *v.i.*; swarded, *pt.*, *pp.*; swarding, *ppr.* to cover or become covered with sward.
swąrd′-çut″tẽr, *n.* an instrument for cutting sward, as a plow.
swąrd′ed, *a.* covered with sward.
swąrd′y, *a.* covered with sward or grass; as, *swardy* land.
swāre, *v.* archaic past tense of *swear*.
swärf, *v.i.*; swarfed (swärft), *pt.*, *pp.*; swarfing, *ppr.* [Sw. *svarfva*, to turn in a lathe, from *svarf*, a lathe.] to faint; to swoon. [Scot.]
swärf, *n.* stupor; a fainting fit; a swoon. [Scot.]
swärf, *n.* 1. iron filings.
2. the grit worn away from grindstones used in grinding cutlery wet.
swąrm, *n.* [AS. *swearm*, a swarm; akin to Ice. *svarmr*, a tumult; O.H.G. *swaram*, G. *schwarm*, noisy revelry, a swarm, from *schwärmen*, to buzz, riot, swarm.]
1. a large number or body of insects in motion.
2. a great number of bees, led by a queen, which emigrate from a hive together and

seek another; also, a colony of bees united and settled permanently in a hive.
3. a moving crowd or throng; a multitude of people in motion.
4. in biology, a mass of motile one-celled organisms.
swarm, *v.i.*; swarmed, *pt., pp.*; swarming, *ppr.* 1. to collect and depart, as from a hive, by flight in a body; as, bees *swarm* on warm, clear days in summer.
2. to appear or collect in a crowd; to throng together; to congregate in a multitude.
3. to be crowded; to be thronged with a multitude of objects in motion; to teem (usually with *with*).
Every place *swarms* with soldiers. —Spenser.
4. in biology, to burst forth in a swarm.
swarm, *v.t.* to crowd or throng.
swarm, *v.i* and *v.t.* [perhaps akin to *swerve*, but more probably to the preceding *swarm.*] to climb, as a tree, mast, etc., by embracing it with the arms and legs; to shin.
swarm cell, a swarm spore.
swarm'ẽr, *n.* 1. a person or thing that swarms; a member of a swarm.
2. in biology, a swarm spore.
swarm'ing, *n.* the act of coming off in swarms, as bees.
swarm spōre, 1. one of a mass of motile spores; a zoospore.
2. a gemmule; a flagelliform spore; a ciliate sponge embryo.
swart, *a.* [ME. *swerte, swarte*; AS. *swart, sweart*; akin to Goth. *swarts*; L.G. *swart*; Ice. *svartr*; G. *schwarz*; D. *zwart*, black, dark.]
1. being of a dark hue; moderately black; tawny: used of the skin. [Dial. or Poet.]
2. gloomy; malignant. [Poet.]
swart, *v.t.* to make tawny; to tan. [Obs.]
swart'back, *n.* the great black-backed gull, *Larus marinus*. [Brit. Dial.]
swarth, *a.* swarthy.
swarth, *n.* an apparition of a person about to die; a wraith. [Brit. Dial.]
swarth, *n.* [variant of *sward.*] sward. [Dial.]
swarth, *n.* [prob. a variant of *swath.*] a swath.
swarth'i·ly, *adv.* duskily; with a tawny hue.
swarth'i·ness, *n.* tawniness; a dusky or dark complexion; the quality of being swarthy.
swarth'ness, *n.* same as *swarthiness.*
swarth'y, *a.*; *comp.* swarthier; *superl.* swarthiest, being of a dark hue or dusky complexion; dusky; dark.
swarth'y, *v.t.* to make swarthy. [Obs.]
swart'i·ness, *n.* a tawny color; swarthiness.
swart'ish, *a.* somewhat dark or tawny.
swart'ness, *n.* same as *swarthiness.*
swart stär, Sirius, the dog star: so called because it appears during the summer when complexions are swarthy from exposure to the sun.
swart'y, *a.* swarthy; tawny. [Obs.]
swarve, *v.i.* to swerve. [Scot. and Brit. Dial.]
swarve, *v.t.* to climb. [Scot. and Brit. Dial.]
swäsh, *n.* in architecture, an oval figure whose moldings are oblique to the axis of the work. [Obs.]
swäsh, *n.* 1. a body of swift, dashing water; specifically, a channel cutting through or behind a sandbank.
2. a bar washed over by the sea.
3. the splashing of water or the sound of this.
4. a swaggering; blustering.
5. a braggart; a swaggerer.
6. liquid filth; hogwash. [Brit.]
swäsh, *v.i.* swashed (swosht), *pt., pp.*; swashing, *ppr.* [compare Sw. dial. *svasska*, to make a washing noise.]
1. to swagger; to bluster.
2. to splash; to dash, strike, wash, etc. with a splashing sound.
swäsh, *v.t.* to dash about or spill violently, as water; to splash (a liquid), as in a container.
swäsh, *a.* soft, like overripe fruit. [Brit. Dial.]
swäsh'buck''lẽr, *n.* [*swash* and *buckler*, a shield.] a blustering fighting man; a swaggerer; a braggadocio.
swäsh'buck''lẽr·ing, *n.* and *a.* swashbuckling.
swäsh'buck''lẽr·y, *n.* brazen effrontery; swashbuckling.
swäsh'buck''ling, *n.* the characteristic behavior of a swashbuckler; loud boasting or bullying.
swäsh'buck''ling, *a.* of or typical of a swashbuckler.
swäsh'ẽr, *n.* a swashbuckler.
swäsh'ing, *a.* 1. swashbuckling.
2. splashing.
3. violent; slashing. [Archaic.]
swäsh let'tẽrs, italic capital letters formed with long tails and flourishes.
swäsh plāte, in mechanics, a disk fixed on a revolving axis in an inclined position, for the purpose of communicating a reciprocating motion to a bar in the direction of its length.

SWASH PLATE

swäsh'y, *a.* 1. insipid. [Brit.]
2. swash; squashy. [Brit.]
swäs'ti·kȧ, *n.* [Sanskrit, from *svasti*, well-being, benediction, from *su*, well, and *asti*, being, is.]
1. a design or ornament of ancient origin in the form of a Greek cross with each arm bent in a right-angle extension: it exists as a mystic symbol among various American Indian tribes and in India, Japan, Persia, etc.
2. this design with the extensions bent in a clockwise direction, used in Nazi Germany as the party emblem and symbol of anti-Semitism.

SWASTIKA

Swät, *n.*; *pl.* **Swä'ti,** one of an East Indian people of Moslem faith who live in Swat, a district of Pakistan: also called *Swati.*
swät, *v.* obsolete past tense of *sweat.*
swät, *v.t.*; swatted, *pt., pp.*; swatting, *ppr.* [echoic.] to hit with a quick, sharp blow: also *swot.* [Colloq.]
swät, *n.* a quick, sharp blow: also *swot.* [Colloq.]
swätch, *n.* 1. a swath. [Obs.]
2. a small piece of cloth or other material cut off as for a sample.
swäth, *n.* [AS. *swathu*, a track; D. *zwad*; G. *schwad*, a row of mown grass.]
1. a line or row of grass or grain cut in one course by a scythe or a mowing machine.
2. the whole breadth or sweep covered with one cut of a scythe or mowing machine; as, a wide *swath.*
3. a stroke with a scythe. [Rare.]
4. a strip, track, row, band, or fillet.
to cut a wide swath; to make an ostentatious display; to make a great stir; to appear important.
swäth bañk, a row or ridge of newly cut grass. [Brit. Dial.]
swāthe, *v.t.*; swathed, *pt., pp.*; swathing, *ppr.* [Ice. *svatha*, to swathe; AS. *swethian*, to bind.]
1. to wrap or bind up in a long strip or bandage.
2. to wrap (a bandage, etc.) around something.
3. to surround; to envelop; to enclose.
swāthe, *n.* a bandage or wrapping; a swaddling band.
swāthe, *n.* a swath.
swāth'ẽr, *n.* a contrivance used on a reaper or mower to straighten up fallen uncut grain and to mark the boundary of the swath.
Swä'ti, *n.*; *pl.* **Swä'ti,** a Swat.
swät'te, *v.* obsolete past tense of *sweat.*
swät'tẽr, *n.* 1. a person who swats.
2. a device, as of fine wire mesh at the end of a handle, for swatting flies, etc.: in full, *fly swatter.*
swāy, *v.t.*; swayed, *pt., pp.*; swaying, *ppr.* [Ice. *sveigja*, to bow, to bend as a switch; Sw. dial. *svega*, from *sviga*, to bend.]
1. to cause to swing or move from side to side.
2. to cause to lean or incline to one side.
3. to cause (a person, one's opinion, etc.) to incline in a particular direction.
4. to cause to turn from a given course; to divert; as, his threats will not *sway* us.
5. (a) to wield (a scepter, etc.); (b) to rule over or control; to dominate. [Archaic.]
This was the race
To *sway* the world, and land and sea subdue. —Dryden.
6. in nautical usage, to hoist into place, as yards: usually with *up.*
Syn.—influence, govern, rule, bias, wave, swing, wield.
swāy, *v.i.* 1. to be drawn to one side by weight; to lean or incline to one side; to veer; as, a wall *sways* to the west.
2. to move or incline to one side and then the other; to swing backward and forward; to fluctuate; to oscillate; as, the branches *sway* in the wind.
3. to have the judgment or feelings inclining to one side.
4. to have weight or influence; to rule; to govern.
5. to advance steadily onward. [Obs.]
swāy, *n.* 1. a swaying or being swayed; movement to the side; a swinging, leaning, fluctuation, etc.
2. impetus; influence; force; control; as, moved by the *sway* of passion.
3. rule; dominion; sovereign power or authority.
4. the motion of a thing moving heavily. [Obs.]
5. preponderance; turn or cast of the balance. [Obs.]
Syn.—influence, rule, authority, government, superiority, bias, dominion, control, preponderance, domination, supremacy, mastery, ascendancy, weight, force, power.
sway'-back, sway'back, *n.* the condition of being sway-backed.
sway'-back, sway'back, *a.* sway-backed.
swāy'-backed, *a.* having an abnormal inward curve in the spine, usually as a result of strain or overwork: said of horses, cattle, etc.
swāy bär, in a vehicle, a bar fastened to the rear end of the fore hounds, which slides on the coupling poles in the turning of the wagon.
swāy brā'cing, the horizontal bracing of a bridge, to prevent lateral swaying.
swāyed, *a.* sway-backed.
swāy'fụl, *a.* able to exercise sway; powerful. [Rare.]
swāy'ing, *n.* the condition of being sway-backed.
Swä'zi, *n.* a member of a Bantu tribe of Swaziland, in southeastern Africa.
swēal, *v.i.*; swealed, *pt., pp.*; swealing, *ppr.* [AS. *swelan*, to burn slowly without flame, from *swol*, heat; akin to L. G. *swelen*, G. *schwelen*, to burn slowly, to sweal; Ice. *svæla*, thick, choking smoke.]
1. to melt and run down, as the tallow of a candle. [Brit. Dial.]
2. to burn unsteadily and slowly. [Brit. Dial.]
swēal, *v.t.* to dress, as a hog, by burning or singeing. [Brit. Dial.]
swēar, *v.i.*; swore *or archaic* sware, *pt.*; sworn, *pp.*; swearing, *ppr.* [AS. *swerian*, to swear; akin to D. *zweren*; G. *schwören*; Ice. *sverja*; Sw. *svarja*, Dan. *sværge*, to swear.]
1. to make a solemn declaration or affirmation with an appeal to God or to someone or something held sacred, for confirmation; as, he *swore* by the Bible.
2. to make a solemn pledge or promise; to vow.
3. to use profane or blasphemous language; to curse.
4. in law, to give evidence or state under oath.
5. to be inharmonious, as one color with another: followed by *at.* [Colloq.]
to swear by; (a) to name (a person or thing held sacred) in taking an oath; (b) to have great faith in; to place absolute confidence in; to depend upon, as an infallible authority.
swēar, *v.t.* 1. to declare solemnly in the name of God or of someone or something held sacred.
2. to pledge or vow on oath.
3. to assert or promise with great conviction or emphasis; as, I *swear* the man's a fool!
4. to take (an oath) by swearing.
5. to administer a legal oath to.
6. to appeal to by an oath; to call to witness. [Obs.]
to swear in; to administer an oath to (a person taking office, a witness, etc.).
to swear off; to promise to give up, leave off, or renounce.
to swear out; to obtain (a warrant for someone's arrest) by making a charge under oath.
to swear the peace against one; to make oath that one is under the actual fear of death or bodily harm from some person, in order to cause the accused to find sureties of the peace. [Brit.]
swēar'ẽr, *n.* 1. one who swears, or takes an oath.
2. a profane person; one who habitually utters profane oaths.
swēar'ing, *n.* the act of taking or administering an oath; also, the use of oaths in speech.
swēar'wŏrd, *n.* a word or phrase used in swearing or cursing; a blasphemous or profane oath.
sweat (swet), *v.i.*; sweat *or* sweated, *pt., pp.*; sweating, *ppr.* [ME. *sweten*; AS. *swætan*, to sweat.]
1. to give forth a characteristic salty mois-

ture through the pores of the skin; to perspire.
2. (a) to give forth moisture in droplets on its surface; as, a ripening cheese *sweats*; (b) to collect and condense water in droplets on its surface; as, he stirred his iced drink until the glass *sweated*.
3. to ferment: said of tobacco leaves, etc.
4. to come forth in drops through pores or a porous surface; to ooze.
5. to work so hard as to cause sweating: often used metaphorically. [Colloq.]
6. to suffer; to pay a penalty. [Slang.]

sweat (swet), *v.t.* 1. (a) to give forth (moisture) through its pores or a porous surface; (b) to collect and condense (moisture) on its surface.
2. to cause to sweat, or perspire, as by drugs, exercise, heat, etc.
3. to cause to give forth moisture; especially, to ferment; as, the tobacco leaves are being *sweated*.
4. to make wet with sweat, or perspiration; as, he *sweated* his shirt.
5. to try to get rid of by sweating: often with *out*, as, he is *sweating out* his cold.
6. to heat (a metal) in order to extract an easily fusible constituent.
7. (a) to heat (solder) until it melts; (b) to unite (metal parts) by heating at the point of contact.
8. to remove particles of metal from (a coin) illegally, as by shaking in a bag with other coins.
9. to cause to work so hard as to sweat; to overwork.
10. to cause (employees) to work long hours at low wages under poor working conditions; to exploit.
11. to get information from by torture or by long, grueling questioning; to subject to the third degree. [Colloq.]
12. to extort money from; to fleece; to bleed. [Slang.]
13. to pawn. [Slang.]
14. in charcoal burning, to dry (wood) by covering the pile.
15. in the manufacture of leather, to subject to fermentation, as hides, in order to loosen the hair.
to sweat blood; (a) to work very hard; to overwork; (b) to be impatient, apprehensive, anxious, etc. [Slang.]
to sweat (something) out; (a) to wait through (a line, etc.); (b) to anticipate or wait anxiously or impatiently for (something). [Slang.]

sweat (swet), *n.* [altered, after the *v.*, from ME. *swet, swat, swote*; AS. *swat*, sweat.]
1. the clear, alkaline, salty liquid given forth in drops through the pores of the skin; perspiration.
2. the moisture given forth or collected in droplets on the surface of something.
3. a sweating or being sweated; especially, an artificially induced sweating.
4. a condition of eagerness, anxiety, impatience, etc. regarded as strong enough to cause sweating.
5. hard work; drudgery.
6. exercise, as a run, given a horse before a race.
7. that which causes sweat; a sudorific medicine.
8. sweating sickness. [Obs.]
cold sweat; a sweat marked by chilliness.

sweat'band, *n.* a band of leather, etc. placed inside a hat to protect it against sweat from the brow.

sweat'box, *n.* 1. a small cell in which prisoners are given the third degree. [Colloq.]
2. a box in which the process of sweating hides, etc. is carried on.

sweat'ed, *a.* 1. soiled, dampened, etc. by sweat.
2. that has been made to sweat; specifically, employed for long hours at low wages under poor working conditions; exploited.

sweat'ẽr (swet'), *n.* 1. one who or that which sweats.
2. a knitted or crocheted outer garment for the upper part of the body, with or without sleeves and either a pull-over or a jacket.
3. a sudorific.
4. an employer who sweats his employees.

sweat gland, one of the glands that secrete the sweat, consisting of a tube so coiled as to form a round mass located in the subcutaneous tissue and opening by a duct upon the surface of the skin.

sweat'i·ly, *adv.* in a sweaty manner.

sweat'i·ness, *n.* the state of being sweaty.

sweat'ing bȧth, a sudatory.

sweat'ing house, a house for sweating persons in sickness. [Obs.]

sweat'ing ī'ron (-ũrn), an instrument for scraping sweat from horses.

sweat'ing rọom, 1. a room for sweating persons; the hot room in a Turkish bath.
2. in dairy farming, a room for sweating cheese and carrying off the superfluous juices.

sweat'ing sick'ness, an acute infectious, rapidly fatal disease that was epidemic in England in the 15th and the 16th centuries and was characterized by a high fever and profuse sweating.

sweat shīrt, a long-sleeved heavy shirt, usually fleece-lined, used by athletes to absorb sweat during or after their exercises.

sweat'shop, *n.* a shop or plant where employees are forced to work long hours at low wages under poor working conditions.

sweat'y, *a.*; *comp.* sweatier; *superl.* sweatiest, 1. sweating; covered with sweat.
2. like or like that of sweat; as, a *sweaty* odor.
3. causing sweat.
4. calling for great effort; laborious.

Swēde, *n.* 1. a native or inhabitant of Sweden.
2. a Swedish turnip.

Swē·den·bọr'ġi·ăn, *a.* of or pertaining to Emanuel Swedenborg (1688–1772), Swedish theologian, to the church named after him, or to his teachings.

Swē·den·bọr'ġi·ăn, *n.* a believer in the doctrines of the Church of the New Jerusalem as taught by Emanuel Swedenborg. He professed to be the founder of the Church of the New Jerusalem, alluding to the New Jerusalem spoken of in the book of Revelation, and claimed to receive special scriptural revelations from God.

Swē·den·bọr'ġi·ăn·ism, *n.* the religious doctrines of the Swedenborgians.

Swē·den·bọrg'ism, *n.* Swedenborgianism.

swedġe, *v.t.* and *n.* same as *swage*.

Swēd'ish, *a.* pertaining to Sweden, its inhabitants, or their language.

Swēd'ish mȧs·säġe' (-säzh'), massage combined with Swedish movements, as in treating certain diseases.

Swēd'ish möve'ments, a set or system of exercises involving various muscle groups of the body, used in the treatment of certain diseases.

Swēd'ish, *n.* the language of Sweden.

swee'ny, *n.* atrophy of the shoulder muscles of horses: also called *swinney*.

sweep, *v.t.*; swept, *pt.*, *pp.*; sweeping, *ppr.* [ME. *swepen*, altered from AS. *swapan*, after *swepe, n.*]
1. to clear or clean (a surface, room, etc.) as by brushing with a broom.
2. to remove, clear away, or clean up (dirt, debris, etc.) with or as with a brush or broom or with a brushing movement.
3. to clear (a space, path, etc.) with or as with a broom.
4. to strip, clear, carry away, or destroy with force of movement.
5. to move or carry along with a sweeping movement; as, he *swept* the cards into a pile; she *swept* her hand through her hair.
6. to touch or brush in moving across; as, his hands *swept* the keyboard; her dress *sweeps* the ground.
7. to pass swiftly over or across; to traverse, as in search; as, armed bands *sweep* the countryside; his eyes *swept* the terrain.
8. to drag (*v.t.*, 2).
9. to rake (*v.t.*, 5).
10. (a) to win all the games or events of (a series, set, or match); (b) to win overwhelmingly; as, the Democrats *swept* the election. [Colloq.]
11. to propel by means of a sweep or long oar.
to sweep or *sweep up a mold*; in founding, to form a mold by means of a sweep.

sweep, *v.i.* 1. to clean a surface, room, etc. with or as with a broom or the like.
2. to move, pass, or progress steadily or smoothly, especially with speed, force, or gracefulness; as, the planes *sweep* across the sky; the music *sweeps* to a thrilling close.
3. (a) to trail one's skirts, etc. in moving; (b) to trail, as skirts.
4. to reach or extend in a long, graceful curve or line; as, the road *sweeps* up the hill.
5. to swing or slat the flukes: said of a whale, as when wounded.

sweep, *n.* 1. the act of sweeping; a cleaning, clearing, or removing with or as with a broom.
2. (a) a steady sweeping or driving movement; as, the *sweep* of a scythe; (b) a stroke or blow resulting from this.
3. a trailing, as of skirts.
4. range or scope; as, they came within the *sweep* of our guns.
5. a stretch; extent; reach; as, a long *sweep* of meadow.
6. a line, contour, curve, etc. that gives an impression of flow or movement.
7. a person whose work is sweeping; as, a chimney *sweep*.
8. [*usually pl.*] sweepings.
9. the taking or winning of all; complete victory or success, as in a series of contests.
10. a long oar.
11. a long pole mounted on a pivot, with a bucket at one end: used for raising water, as from a well.
12. a sweepstakes.
13. in physics, the irreversible process by which a substance tends to settle into thermal equilibrium.
14. violent and general destruction; as, the *sweep* of an epidemic disease.
15. a rapid survey with the eye.
16. in shipbuilding, the mold of a ship when she begins to compass in at the rungheads; also, any part of a ship shaped by the segment of a circle. [Obs.]
17. in card playing, (a) in the game of cassino, a pairing or combining of all the cards on the board and so removing them all; (b) in whist, the winning of all the tricks in a hand.
18. in heraldry, a ballista.
sweep of the tiller; a circular frame on which the tiller travels in large ships.

sweep'ăġe, *n.* the hay crop from a meadow.

sweep'back, *n.* the angle formed by the line of declination of an airplane wing and the lateral axis of the airplane.

sweep'ẽr, *n.* one who or that which sweeps.

sweep'ing, *a.* 1. that sweeps; cleansing or carrying away with or as with a broom.
2. extending over the whole range or a great space.
3. extensive; complete; comprehensive; thoroughgoing.

sweep'ing, *n.* the act, work, etc. of a person or thing that sweeps.

sweep'ing·ly, *adv.* in a sweeping or comprehensive manner.

sweep'ing·ness, *n.* the state or quality of being sweeping or comprehensive.

sweep'ings, *n.pl.* things swept up; dirt, etc. swept from a floor.

sweep rāke, a rake in a harvester that clears the table.

sweep sạw, a bow saw.

sweep'stāke, *n.* a sweepstakes.

sweep'stākes, *n. sing.* and *pl.* [so named because the winner "sweeps" in all of the stakes.]
1. a lottery in which each person taking part puts up a stake of money in a common fund which is given as the prize to the winner or in shares to several winners.
2. a contest, especially a horse race, the result of which determines the winner or winners of such a lottery.
3. the prize or prizes won in such a lottery.

sweep tick'et, a chance or ticket in a sweepstakes.

sweep'wäsh·ẽr, *n.* the person who extracts the small particles of precious metal from the sweepings, etc. of refineries of gold and silver.

sweep'y, *a.* 1. passing or moving with a sweeping motion. [Poet.]
2. having long sweeps or turns, as a river. [Poet.]

sweet, *a.* [AS. *swete, swet*; akin to Ice. *sætr, sötr*; Goth. *sutis*, for *svotis*; seen also in L. *suavis*, for *suadvis*, sweet; Gr. *hēdys*, agreeable.]
1. (a) having an agreeable taste or flavor, like that of honey or sugar; as, *sweet* grapes: opposed to *sour* or *bitter*; (b) containing sugar in some form; as, *sweet* wines.
2. pleasant to the smell; fragrant; as, *sweet* violets.
3. pleasing to the ear; melodious; harmonious; as, a *sweet* song.
4. pleasing to the eye; beautiful; lovely; charming; as, a *sweet* face.
5. kind; gentle; mild; meek.

Canst thou bind the *sweet* influences of Pleiades? —Job xxxviii. 31.

6. gracious; kind; soft; bland; as, a *sweet* smile.

7. pleasing to the mind; gratifying; as, a *sweet* word of approval.

8. good, delightful, etc.: a generalized epithet of approval. [Slang.]

9. not salty or salted; as, *sweet* water.

10. not rancid or spoiled; fresh.

11. good for growing crops: said of soil.

12. in chemistry, free from excessive acid, sulfur, etc.

13. in jazz music, (a) designating or of playing characterized by more or less strict adherence to melody, blandness, and a relatively moderate tempo: distinguished from *hot*; (b) designating or of music played in this way.

sweet alyssum; same as *alyssum*, sense 3.

sweet basil; a plant with bluish-white flowers and fragrant leaves used in cooking.

sweet calabash; a passionflower, *Passiflora maliformis*, with large red, white, and blue flowers, and an applelike fruit, yellow when ripe, with black seeds, a thick rind, and a sweetish edible pulp.

sweet calamus; same as *sweet flag*.

sweet cicely; see *cicely*.

sweet clover; a sweet-scented plant of the genus *Melilotus*, with butterfly-shaped, white or yellow flowers, and leaves in groups of three, grown for fodder: also called *melilot*.

sweet coltsfoot; same as *butterbur*.

sweet corn; a variety of Indian corn, rich in sugar and eaten as a table vegetable in its unripe, or milky, stage.

sweet fennel; see under *fennel*.

sweet herbs; aromatic and fragrant herbs cultivated for culinary purposes, as sage, thyme, etc.

sweet marjoram; a fragrant herb whose leaves are used in cooking.

sweet violet; a species of violet, *Viola odorata*, with deep-purple, sometimes reddish-purple, lilac, or white fragrant flowers: common in grassy places throughout Europe and northern Asia. *Viola blanda*, of the United States, is also sweet-scented.

to be sweet on; to be in love with. [Colloq.]

sweet, *n.* 1. the quality of being sweet; sweetness.

2. something sweet; specifically, (a) [*usually in pl.*] a candy; sweetmeat; (b) [Brit.] a sweet dish served as dessert; (c) [*often in pl.*] pleasure or a pleasurable experience; (d) [Colloq.] a sweet potato.

3. a perfume.

4. a beloved one; a darling: a term of endearment.

sweet, *adv.* sweetly.

sweet ap′ple, the sweetsop.

sweet bāy, 1. a plant, *Laurus nobilis*, of Europe, with sweet-smelling leaves.

2. the swamp sassafras of the genus *Magnolia*.

sweet′bread (-bred), *n.* 1. the pancreas of a calf or other animal, used for food: also called *stomach sweetbread*.

2. the thymus of an animal: also called *throat sweetbread* or *neck sweetbread*.

sweet′-breast″ed (-brest″), *a.* sweet-voiced; having a musical voice, as the thrush or the lark. [Obs.]

sweet′brī″ẽr, sweet′brī″ăr, *n.* a shrubby plant, *Rosa rubiginosa*, with fragrant leaves, pink flowers, and tall, prickly stems; eglantine.

sweet cī′dẽr, cider that has not fermented.

sweet′en (sweet′n), *v.t.*; sweetened, *pt., pp.*; sweetening, *ppr.* 1. to make sweet with or as with sugar; as, to *sweeten* tea or coffee.

2. to make pleasant or agreeable.

3. to mollify; to alleviate; to appease.

4. in finance, to increase the value of (collateral for a loan) by adding valuable securities. [Colloq.]

5. in poker, to add further stakes to (the pot) before opening. [Slang.]

6. to make pure by destroying noxious matter; to restore to purity; as, to *sweeten* rooms or apartments that have been infected; to *sweeten* the air.

7. to make (soil) fertile and free of sourness.

sweet′en, *v.i.* to become sweet.

sweet′ened, *a.* made sweet or mild.

sweet′en·ẽr, *n.* one who or that which sweetens.

sweet′en·ing, *n.* the act of sweetening; also, that which sweetens.

sweet fẽrn, a small North American shrub, *Comptonia asplenifolia*, having sweet-scented leaves resembling fern leaves.

sweet flag, an araceous plant, *Acorus calamus*, growing in wet ground and sending up two-edged, sword-shaped leaves two feet or more in height, from a horizontal, aromatic, edible rootstock.

SWEET FLAG (*Acorus calamus*)

sweet gāle, see third *gale*.

sweet gråss, any grass of the genus *Glyceria*. [Brit. Dial.]

sweet gum, a tree, *Liquidambar styraciflua*, with shining maplelike leaves, spiny balls of fruit, and fragrant juice.

sweet′heärt, *n.* a lover; especially, a woman with reference to her lover: sometimes used as a term of endearment.

sweet′heärt, *v.t.* to act the part of a lover to; to pay court to; to gallant; as, to *sweetheart* a lady. [Colloq.]

sweet′heärt, *v.i.* to act the part of a sweetheart. [Colloq.]

sweet′ie, *n.* a sweetheart. [Colloq.]

sweet′ing, *n.* 1. a variety of sweet apple.

2. a sweetheart. [Archaic.]

sweet′ish, *a.* somewhat sweet.

sweet′ish·ness, *n.* the quality of being sweetish.

sweet John, a plant, the narrow-leaved variety of sweet William, *Dianthus barbatus*.

sweet′lēaf, *n.* see *horse sugar*.

sweet′ly, *adv.* in a sweet manner.

sweet′mēat, *n.* 1. any sweet food or delicacy prepared with sugar or honey, as a cake, confection, preserve, etc.; specifically, a candy, candied fruit, etc.

2. a mollusk, the slipper shell. [Dial.]

3. a varnish used on patent leather.

sweet′ness, *n.* the quality of being sweet.

sweet oil, olive oil.

sweet pēa, a climbing plant with large, variously colored fragrant flowers.

sweet pep′pẽr, 1. a kind of pepper plant producing a mild fruit.

2. its fruit.

sweet pō·tā′tō, 1. a tropical trailing plant with purplish flowers and a large, fleshy, orange or yellow root used as a vegetable.

2. its root.

sweet reed, sorghum. [South Africa.]

sweet′ro̤ot, *n.* the licorice, *Glycyrrhiza glabra*.

sweet rush, same as *sweet flag*.

sweet′-scent″ed, *a.* having a sweet smell; fragrant.

sweet-scented grass; same as *vernal grass* under *vernal*.

sweet-scented shrub; a shrub, *Calycanthus floridus*, bearing purple flowers having the odor of allspice.

sweet′sop, *n.* 1. an evergreen shrub or tree of tropical America, *Anona squamosa*, having green, scaly, egg-shaped fruit with a sweet pulp and black seeds.

2. the fruit of this plant.

sweet tañ′gle, a seaweed, *Laminaria saccharina*, much used for food in Japan: also called *kambou*.

sweet′tem″pẽred, *a.* having a sweet or pleasant disposition.

sweet to̤oth, a fondness or craving for sweets. [Colloq.]

sweet′wa̤″tẽr, *n.* a variety of European grape with very sweet juice.

sweet′weed, *n.* 1. same as *West Indian tea* under *tea*.

2. a West Indian figwort, *Scoparia dulcis*: also called *sweet broomweed*.

sweet Wil′liăm, sweet wil′liam (-yăm), 1. a perennial pink, *Dianthus barbatus*, of many varieties, cultivated in gardens for its bright flowers.

2. in zoology, (a) the willow warbler; (b) the European goldfinch. [Brit. Dial.]

Barbados sweet William; the cypress vine.

wild sweet William; the *Phlox maculata*, with white or pinkish flowers.

sweet wil′lōw, the sweet gale.

sweet′wood, *n.* any one of various trees or shrubs of the laurel family, native to the West Indies and South America.

sweetwood bark; same as *cascarilla*.

sweet′wŏrt, *n.* any plant with a sweet taste.

swe̤igh (swe̤), *n.* sway. [Obs.]

swe̤in, *n.* swain. [Obs.]

swe̤in′mōte, *n.* swainmote. [Obs.]

swell, *v.i.*; swelled, *pt.*; swelled *or* swollen, *pp.*; swelling, *ppr.* [AS. *swellan*; akin to Ice. *svella*, to swell, to grow wrathful; D. *zwellen*, G. *schwellen*, to swell, dilate.]

1. to increase in volume or become larger as a result of pressure from within; to expand; to dilate.

2. to become larger at a given point; to curve out; to bulge; to protrude.

3. to extend beyond or above the normal or surrounding level; as, clouds that *swell* above the horizon.

4. to be or become filled (*with* pride, indignation, a sense of importance, etc.); to puff up.

5. to increase within one: said of an emotion, etc.; as, anger *swelled* in him.

6. to increase in size, force, intensity, degree, etc.; as, our ranks *swelled* to over a hundred.

7. to increase in volume or loudness: said of sound, musical instruments, etc.

swell, *v.t.* to cause to swell; specifically, (a) to cause to increase in size, volume, extent, degree, etc.; (b) to cause to bulge or protrude; (c) to fill with pride, indignation, etc.; to inflate; to puff; (d) to cause (a tone, chord, etc.) to increase in loudness.

swelled head; egotism; undue self-esteem; as, prosperity gave him a *swelled head*. [Colloq.]

swell, *n.* 1. a part that swells; a bulge; curve; protuberance; specifically, (a) a swollen part or area of the body; (b) a large wave that moves steadily without breaking; (c) a piece of rising ground; a rounded hill or slope.

2. a swelling or being swollen.

3. an increase in size, amount, extent, degree, etc.

4. a person who is strikingly stylish or fashionable, especially in dress. [Colloq.]

5. in music, (a) a gradual increase in volume (*crescendo*), usually followed by a gradual decrease (*diminuendo*); (b) a sign (**<>**) indicating this; (c) a device for controlling the loudness of tones in an organ, harpsichord, etc.

6. in geology, an extensive area in which the strata dip outward and downward in all directions, at a low angle.

swell, *a.* [ME. *swelle*, tumid, proud.]

1. stylish; very fashionable. [Colloq.]

2. first-rate; excellent: a generalized epithet of approval. [Slang.]

swell blīnd, in an organ, one of the movable slats, usually vertical, forming the front of the swell box.

swell box, in an organ, the compartment in which the pipes of the swell organ are arranged: the front is made of movable blinds or slats, operated by a pedal.

swell′dŏm, *n.* swells collectively; the world of fashion and wealth. [Slang.]

swell′fish, *n.* any fish of the *Tetrodon, Diodon*, and allied genera: so called because they are capable of inflating or swelling up by swallowing air.

swell′ing, *n.* 1. an increasing or being increased in size, volume, etc.

2. something swollen; especially, an abnormally swollen part of the body.

3. an inundation; a flood; an overflow. [Obs.]

4. arrogance; pride; conceit. [Obs.]

swell′ing, *a.* that swells, or curves outward.

swell′ish, *a.* pertaining to or characteristic of a swell or dandy; foppish; dandified; as, he puts on *swellish* airs. [Slang.]

swell kēy′bōard, in a swell organ, the keyboard or manual.

swell o̤r′găn, an organ or partial organ next in importance to the great organ. The pipes are enclosed in a swell box and are governed by a pedal.

swell ped′ăl, in an organ, a pedal by means of which the swell blinds are moved, to increase or decrease sound.

swell shärk, a small shark of the waters of northwest North America, *Scyllium ventricosum*: so called because it swells up when caught.

swell′tōad, *n.* same as *swellfish*.

swelt, *v.* obsolete past tense and past participle of *swell*.

swelt, *v.i.* 1. to faint, to swoon. [Obs.]

2. to die. [Obs.]

swelt, *v.t.* 1. to overpower, as with heat; to cause to faint. [Obs.]

2. to kill; to destroy. [Obs.]

swel′tẽr, *v.i.*; sweltered, *pt., pp.*; sweltering, *ppr.* [ME. *swelten*, to die, swoon away, or faint; AS. *sweltan*, to die; Ice. *svelta*; Sw.

svälta, to die, starve.] to perspire, languish, or faint with heat.

swel′tẽr, *v.t.* 1. to cause to swelter.
2. to exude (venom or poison). [Archaic.]
3. to soak; to steep; to welter. [Obs.]

swel′tẽr, *n.* 1. the condition of sweltering.
2. oppressive heat.

swel′tẽr·ing, *a.* 1. that swelters or suffers with the heat.
2. very hot; sultry.

swel′try, *a.*; *comp.* sweltrier; *superl.* sweltriest; sweltering.

swel′we, *v.t.* and *v.i.* to swallow. [Obs.]

swept, past tense and past participle of *sweep.*

swẽrd, *n.* and *v.* sward. [Obs.]

swẽrve, *v.i.*; swerved, *pt., pp.*; swerving, *ppr.* [ME. *swerven*; AS. *sweorfan*; akin to Ice. *svarfa*, to swerve, sweep aside; D. *zwerven*, to swerve, rove, wander.]
1. to wander; to rove; to stray. [Obs.]
2. to turn aside from a straight line or course.
3. to depart from what is established by law, duty, or custom; to deviate.
4. to climb or move upward by winding or turning. [Obs.]

The tree was high;
Yet nimbly up from bough to bough I
swerved. —Dryden.

swẽrve, *v.t.* to cause to turn aside from a straight line, course, etc.

swẽrve, *n.* 1. the act or degree of swerving; a turning aside.
2. something that swerves.

swē′ven, swē′ven·ing, *n.* a dream; a vision. [Archaic.]

Swiē·tē′ni·ȧ, *n.* [named after Gerard Van *Swieten*, Dutch botanist.] a genus of South American and Mexican trees, which includes the mahogany, *Swietenia mahogani.*

swift, *a.* [AS. *swift*, from the stem of *swifan*, to move quickly.]
1. moving or capable of moving with great speed; fleet; rapid; quick; speedy.
2. ready; prompt.

Let every man be *swift* to hear, slow to speak, slow to wrath. —James i. 19.

3. of short continuance; short; happening quickly; rapidly passing; undelayed.

Syn.—fast, fleet, ready, hasty, rapid, quick, speedy, expeditious.

swift, *adv.* swiftly.

swift, *n.* 1. the rapid current of a stream.
2. an expanding reel used to hold skeins of silk, etc. that are being wound off.
3. a sooty-brown, swift-flying bird of the family *Cypselidæ*, resembling the swallow. The common swift is *Cypselus* or *Micropus apus.* The swifts pass most of their time in the air, where they pursue their insect prey. They build their nests in holes in the walls of houses, in rocks, hollow trees, etc. The American swift, *Chætura pelagica*, has the hind toe directed backward, and the tail feathers stiff, as in woodpeckers. It is commonly called the *chimney swift. Chætura caudacuta* is the Australian swift, and *Cypselus melba*, the European Alpine swift.
4. any one of various species of newts or lizards that move swiftly, as the fence lizard.
5. the ghost moth.
6. the main cylinder of a carding machine.

swift′ẽr, *n.* in nautical usage, (a) a rope used to confine the bars of the capstan in their sockets while men are turning it; (b) [Obs.] a rope used to encircle a boat longitudinally, to strengthen or protect its sides; (c) a shroud from the head of a lower mast to the ship's side before the other shrouds.

swift′ẽr, *v.t.* to tighten, as shrouds.

swift′foot, *a.* swift-footed.

swift′foot, *n.* in zoology, a courser.

swift′-foot′ed, *a.* that can run swiftly.

swift′let, *n.* any small swift of the genus *Collocalia*, found in the East Indies and in Asia; a salangane.

swift′ly, *adv.* in a swift manner; fleetly; rapidly; with celerity.

swift′ness, *n.* the quality or state of being swift; celerity; rapidity.

swift shrīke, any of the wood swallows.

swig, *v.t.* and *v.i.*; swigged, *pt., pp.*; swigging, *ppr.* [from Early Mod. Eng. slang.] to drink, especially in great gulps or large quantities. [Colloq.]

swig, *n.* 1. an instance of swigging; a deep draft, especially of liquor. [Colloq.]
2. in nautical usage, a tackle with ropes which are not parallel.

swig, *v.t.* [evidently a variant of *swag.*]
1. to castrate, as a ram, by binding the testicles so that they mortify and slough off. [Rare.]
2. in nautical usage, to make taut, as a tackle, by successively jerking the fall with the weight of the body and taking in the slack around a belaying pin or cleat.
3. to suck greedily. [Obs.]

swig′gẽr, *n.* a person or animal that swigs.

swill, *v.t.*; swilled, *pt., pp.*; swilling, *ppr.* [ME. *swilen*; AS. *swilian*; Scot. *sweel*, to wash.]
1. to drink greedily or in large quantity.
2. to flood with water so as to wash or rinse.
3. to fill with drink: used reflexively.

swill, *v.i.* to drink, especially liquor, excessively or greedily; also, to wash; to drench oneself.

swill, *n.* 1. garbage, table scraps, etc. mixed with liquid and used for feeding animals, especially pigs; wash.
2. garbage.
3. the act of swilling.
4. a swig; a deep drink of liquor.

swill′ẽr, *n.* one who swills.

swill′ings, *n.pl.* same as *swill* (sense 1).

swim, *v.i.*; swam *or archaic or dial.* swum, *pt*; swum, *pp.*; swimming, *ppr.* [ME. *swimmen*; AS. *swimman*; akin to Ice. *svimma*; G. *schwimmen*, to swim.]
1. to float; to be supported on water or other liquid; as, any substance will *swim* whose specific gravity is less than that of the liquid in which it is immersed.
2. to move through water by means of the motion of the hands, feet, fins, etc.
3. to be flooded; to be overflowed or drenched.
4. to glide along with a smooth motion, as though swimming.
5. to be covered or saturated with or as with a liquid.

swim, *v.t.* 1. to pass over or across by swimming; to move on, in, or over (a body of water) by swimming; as, to *swim* a stream.
2. to cause to swim or float; as, to *swim* a cow across a lake.
3. to immerse in water so that the lighter parts may float; as, to *swim* wheat for seed.

swim, *n.* 1. the act or motion of swimming.
2. a period of swimming for sport; as, I had a *swim.*
3. a distance swum or to be swum.
4. a swimming bladder.
5. the part of a stream where fish are abundant.

in the swim; identified with the successful or fashionable in business, current social affairs, etc.; as, he is *in the swim.*

swim, *n.* [ME. *swime*; AS. *swima.*] the condition of being dizzy; as, her head was in a *swim.*

swim, *v.i.*; swam, *pt.*; swum, *pp.*; swimming, *ppr.* 1. to be dizzy.
2. to have a hazy, reeling, or whirling appearance; as, the room *swam* before his eyes.

swim′ble, *n.* a dizzy motion. [Obs.]

swim′mẽr, *n.* 1. one who or that which swims.
2. a protuberance on the leg of a horse. [Obs.]
3. any bird that can swim; one of the *Natatores.*

swim′mẽr·et, *n.* any of a series of abdominal legs or appendages in certain of the *Crustacea*, so modified as to serve for a swimming organ. In the lobster, there are five pairs of swimmerets, the last pair being greatly expanded and forming, with the telson, a powerful caudal fin. In the female, the fine hairs fringing the swimmerets serve as supports for the eggs during the spawning season.

swim′ming, *n.* the act of a person or animal that swims, especially for sport.

swim′ming, *a.* 1. that swims.
2. used in swimming.
3. flooded or overflowing with or as with water; as, *swimming* eyes.

swim′ming, *n.* dizziness.

swim′ming, *a.* affected with a dizzy, whirling sensation.

swim′ming bell, a nectocalyx.

swim′ming belt, an air-inflated belt worn around the body as a support in the water.

swim′ming blad′dẽr, the air bladder of a fish.

swim′ming çrab, a crab with some of its legs modified for swimming.

swim′ming foot, a swimmeret or pleopod.

swim′ming hōle, a pool or a deep place in a river, creek, etc. used for swimming.

swim′ming·ly, *adv.* smoothly; without obstruction; with great success.

swim′ming·ness, *n.* a moist appearance, as of the eyes; tearfulness. [Rare.]

swim′ming pool, a pool of water used for swimming; especially, an artificially created pool, or tank, either indoors or outdoors.

swim′ming stōne, floatstone (sense 1).

swim sūit, a garment designed for swimming; bathing suit.

swin′dle, *v.t.*; swindled (-dld), *pt., pp.*; swindling, *ppr.* [back-formation from *swindler.*]
1. to get money or property from (another) under false pretenses; to cheat; to defraud.
2. to get by false pretenses or fraud.

swin′dle, *v.i.* to engage in swindling others.

swin′dle, *n.* 1. the act or process of swindling; a fraudulent scheme; a cheat; a fraud.
2. that which is not what it seems or is supposed to be. [Colloq.]

swin′dlẽr, *n.* [G. *schwindler*, from *schwindeln*, to be dizzy, defraud, cheat.] a person who swindles; a cheat.

swin′dlẽr·y, *n.* an act of swindling.

swīne, *n.*; *pl.* **swīne**, [ME. and AS. *swīn*, swine; akin to D. *zwijn*; Ice. *svīn*; Goth. *swein*; Pol. *swinia*; same root as *sow*; L. *sus.*]
1. a pig or hog: generally used collectively.
2. a vicious, contemptible person.

swīne′-backed (-bakt), *a.* convex.

swīne′bread (-bred), *n.* 1. the truffle.
2. sowbread.

swīne′çōte, *n.* a pigpen. [Brit. Dial.]

swīne çress, the herb ivy, *Senebiera coronopus.*

swīne′çrūe, *n.* a pigpen. [Brit. Dial.]

swīne fē′vẽr, hog cholera.

swīne′fish, *n.* the wolf fish.

swīne grȧss, knotgrass.

swīne′hẽrd, *n.* a keeper of swine.

swīne′pīpe, *n.* a bird, the redwing. [Brit. Dial.]

swīne plāgue (plāg), an infectious disease of swine caused by a specific bacterium. The disease closely resembles hog cholera.

swīne pox, a variety of chicken pox. [Archaic.]

swīn′ẽr·y, *n.* a piggery.

swīne′s′-çress, *n.* swine cress.

swīne′s′-feath″ẽr (-feth″), *n.* a small spear fitted into a musket rest and used as a defense against cavalry. [Obs.]

SWINE'S-FEATHER

swīne′sty̆, *n.* a pigpen.

swīne this′tle (this′l), the sow thistle.

swing, *v.i.*; swung *or archaic or dial.* swang, *pt.*; swung, *pp.*; swinging, *ppr.* [ME. *swingen*; AS. *swingan*, to beat, dash, scourge; Dan. *svinge*; Sw. *svinga*; G. *schwingen.*]
1. to sway to and fro with regular movement, as a body suspended in the air; to oscillate.
2. to move backward and forward in a swing (n. 10).
3. to move, float, or turn round a fixed point, hinge, or swivel; as, a ship *swings* with the tide.
4. to be hanged or suspended; specifically, to be hanged in execution.
5. to move with a freely swaying, relaxed motion, as in walking.

to swing round the circle; to take a circular course, covering a wide territory, in a political campaign.

swing, *v.t.* 1. (a) to move or wave (a weapon, tool, bat, etc.) with a sweeping motion; to flourish; to brandish; (b) to lift or hoist with a sweeping motion; as, he *swung* the bag onto his back.
2. to cause (a hanging object) to sway backward and forward; specifically, to cause (a person on a swing) to move backward and forward by pushing or pulling.
3. to cause to turn or pivot, as on a hinge or swivel; as, he *swung* the door open.
4. to cause to hang freely, so as to be capable of easy movement; as, the sailors *swung* their hammocks below decks.
5. to cause to come about successfully; to manage or handle with the desired results; as, I think we can *swing* the election.
6. to play or arrange (a piece of music) in the style of swing.
7. in machinery, to receive so as to shape: said of a lathe.

swing, *n.* 1. the act or process of swinging.
2. the arc, or the length of the arc, through which something swings; as, what is the *swing* of that pendulum?
3. the manner of swinging; specifically, the manner of striking with a golf club, baseball bat, etc.
4. freedom to do as one wishes or is naturally inclined; as, he gave us full *swing* in the matter.
5. a free, relaxed motion, as in walking.
6. a sweeping blow or stroke.
7. the course, development, or movement of some activity, business, etc.

8. the power, or force, behind something swung or thrown; impetus.
9. rhythm, as of poetry or music.
10. a device consisting of a seat hanging from two or more ropes or chains, on which one can sit and swing backward and forward as a form of recreation.
11. (a) jazz music, especially in its development after about 1935, characterized by the use of larger bands, contrapuntal improvisation, and written arrangements for ensemble playing; (b) the characteristic rhythmic element of such music.
12. in commerce, regular upward and downward change in the price of stocks or in some other business activity. [Colloq.]
13. in vehicles, the dish of a wheel.
14. the distance from the head center of a lathe to the bed or ways, or to the rest. The swing determines the diametric size of the object which is capable of being turned in the lathe.
15. an animal or team hitched to the wagon tongue in front of the wheel horses; also, the chain or rope used in fastening the singletree to the wagon tongue.
16. in photography, a swing back.
in full swing; in complete working order; going on without reserve or restraint.
swing, *a.* of, in, or playing swing (music).
swing back, a device in a camera by means of which the plate holder may be brought into real or approximate parallelism with the object to be photographed.
swing bēam, a swing bolster.
swing bōat, a form of swing having a boatlike arrangement containing seats. [Brit.]
swing bōl'stẽr, in railroad-car construction, a bolster bearing on springs so as to swing laterally to the truck.
swing bridġe, a bridge that can be swung back in a horizontal plane to allow tall vessels, etc. to pass.
swing'dev"il, *n.* a bird, the swift. [Brit. Dial.]
swinġe, *v.t.*; swinged, *pt., pp.*; swingeing, *ppr.* [ME. *swengen*; AS. *swengan*, caus. of *swingan*, to swing.]
1. to punish with blows; to beat soundly; to whip. [Archaic.]
And *swinges* his own vices in his son.
—Dryden.
2. to lash (a tail). [Obs.]
swinġe, *n.* 1. the sweep of anything in motion; a swing; a lash. [Brit. Dial.]
2. sway; authority; control; rule. [Obs.]
swinġe'buck"lẽr, *n.* swashbuckler. [Obs.]
swinġe'ing, *a.* 1. very large; great. [Colloq.]
2. extremely good; first-rate. [Colloq.]
swinġe'ing·ly, *adv.* 1. largely; vastly. [Colloq.]
2. extremely well. [Colloq.]
swiñ'gel, *n.* same as *swingle.*
swin'ġẽr, *n.* 1. one who or that which swinges.
2. a stunner; anything very great or astonishing. [Colloq.]
swing'ẽr, *n.* one who or that which swings.
swing'ing dōor, a door hung so that it can be opened in either direction and swings shut of itself.
swiñ'gle, *v.t.*; swingled (-gld), *pt., pp.*; swingling, *ppr.* [ME. *swinglen*; MD. *swinghelen*, from *swinghel*, a swingle.] to clean (flax or hemp) by beating or scraping with a swingle.
swiñ'gle, *n.* 1. a wooden instrument like a large knife, about two feet long, with one thin edge, used for cleaning flax or hemp by beating or scraping.
2. the swiple, or striking part, of a flail.
3. a spoke or lever for turning the barrel in wire drawing.
4. a hand lever for turning a plate press roller.
swiñ'gle, *v.i.* 1. to dangle; to hang. [Obs.]
2. to swing for pleasure. [Obs.]
swiñ'gle·bär, *n.* same as *swingletree.*
swiñ'gle·tāil, *n.* same as *fox shark.*
swiñ'gle·tree, *n.* a whipple tree or singletree.
swiñ'gling tōw, the coarse part of flax, separated from the finer by swingling and hatcheling.
swing plow, any plow without wheels.
swing shift, in those factories operating on a 24-hour basis, the evening work shift, from about midafternoon to about midnight. [Colloq.]
swing'tree, *n.* same as *swingletree.*
swing wheel, the wheel which drives the pendulum in a clock; also, the balance wheel in a watch.
swīn'ish, *a.* of, fit for, characteristic of, or like swine; gross; hoggish; brutal; as, a *swinish* drunkard or sot; *swinish* gluttony.
swīn'ish·ly, *adv.* in a swinish manner.
swīn'ish·ness, *n.* the state or character of being swinish.
swiñk, *v.i.*; swank *or* swonk, *pt.*; swonken, *pp.*; swinking, *ppr.* [ME. *swinken*; AS. *swincan*, from the base seen in *swing.*] to labor; to toil; to drudge. [Archaic.]
swiñk, *v.t.* to cause to drudge. [Obs.]
swiñk, *n.* labor; toil; drudgery. [Archaic.]
swiñk'ẽr, *n.* a laborer; a plowman. [Obs.]
swin'ney, *n.* same as *sweeny.*
swīpe, *n.* [ME. *swipe*; O.N. *svipr*, a stroke.]
1. a lever or handle, as on a pump; a swape or sweep.
2. a strong, sweeping blow. [Colloq.]
3. in golf, cricket, etc., a full driving stroke. [Colloq.]
swīpe, *v.t.*; swiped (swīpt), *pt., pp.*; swiping, *ppr.* 1. to strike with a long or wide sweeping blow; to give a swipe to. [Colloq.]
2. to steal; to pilfer. [Slang.]
swīpe, *v.i.* to make a sweeping blow or stroke. [Colloq.]
swī'pẽr, *n.* one who swipes. [Colloq.]
swīpes, *n.pl.* beer, especially thin, watery beer. [Brit. Slang.]
swip'le, swip'ple (-l), *n.* [prob. from or akin to *swipe.*] the part of a flail that strikes the grain in threshing.
swip'pẽr, *a.* nimble; quick. [Obs.]
swĩrl, *v.i.*; swirled, *pt., pp.*; swirling, *ppr.* [prob. from O.N. *svirla*, to whirl.]
1. to move with a twisting, whirling motion; to eddy.
2. to swim, or be dizzy, as the head.
swĩrl, *v.t.* to cause to swirl; to whirl.
swĩrl, *n.* 1. a swirling motion; a whirl; an eddy.
2. something swirled or swirling; a twist; a curl; a whirl; a whorl.
swĩr'ly, *a.* 1. full of swirls.
2. knotted; tangled. [Scot.]
swish, *v.i.* [echoic.] 1. to move with a sharp, hissing sound, as a cane swung through the air.
2. to rustle, as skirts in walking.
swish, *v.t.* 1. to cause to swish.
2. to whip or flog.
swish, *n.* 1. a hissing or rustling sound, as of rapid motion through the air, or of waves lapping the shore; also, that which produces or tends to produce such a sound.
2. (a) a rod or cane for flogging; (b) a stroke with this.
Swiss, *n.*; *pl.* **Swiss,** [Fr. *suisse.*] a native or inhabitant of Switzerland.
the Swiss; the Swiss people.
Swiss, *a.* of or pertaining to Switzerland, its people, or culture.
Swiss chard; a chard (sense 2).
Swiss cheese; [orig. made in Switzerland.] a white or pale-yellow hard cheese with many large holes.
Swiss Guards; (a) a corps of mercenary soldiers from Switzerland, employed at various periods as bodyguards, etc., by European sovereigns; (b) a company of bodyguards to the Pope at the Vatican, Rome.
Swiss steak; a thick cut of round or shoulder steak pounded with flour and cooked, usually with a sauce of tomato and onion.
Swiss'ẽr, *n.* same as *Switzer.*
switch, *n.* [O.D. *swick*, a scourge, whip.]
1. a small, flexible twig or rod, especially one used for whipping.
2. the bushy part of the tail in some animals, as the cow.
3. a movable section of railroad track by which a train is changed from one set of rails to another.
4. in electricity, any device for readily opening, closing, or diverting an electric circuit.
5. a tress of human hair, or of some substance made to resemble hair, fastened together at one end, used by women in hairdressing.
6. an abrupt, sharp, lashing movement, as with a switch.
7. the act or process of changing the position of a switch.
8. a shift or transference; a change; a turn.
double-break switch; in electricity, a switch which breaks a circuit in two places, as distinguished from a switch which breaks a circuit at a single point only.
double-pole switch; in electricity, a switch which simultaneously breaks the circuit of both positive and negative leads.
flying switch; a switch which transfers a car or cars from one track to another or others while the train is in motion.
plug switch; in electricity, a switch operated by the insertion of a metallic plug between two insulated metallic segments connected to a circuit, and separated by air spaces for the reception of the plug key.
time switch; in electricity, a switch arranged to open or close a circuit at a certain time.
switch, *v.t.*; switched (switcht), *pt., pp.*; switching, *ppr.* 1. to strike with or as with a switch or small twig or rod; to beat.
2. to jerk or swing sharply; to lash; as, the cat *switched* its tail in anger.
3. to shift; transfer; change; turn aside; divert.
4. (a) to operate the switch of (an electric circuit) so as to connect, disconnect, or divert; (b) to turn (an electric light or appliance) *on* or *off* in this way.
5. to change or exchange; as, we *switched* places. [Colloq.]
6. in railroading, to transfer (a train or car) from one set of rails to another by use of a switch; as, to *switch* an engine to another track.
7. to trim, as a hedge. [Rare.]
switch, *v.i.* 1. to move from or as from one set of tracks to another.
2. to shift; transfer; change.
switch'back, *n.* 1. a road or railroad following a winding or zigzag course up a steep grade.
2. a roller coaster. [Brit.]
switch'bōard, *n.* a board or panel equipped with apparatus for controlling the operation of a system of electric circuits, as in a telephone exchange.
switch box, a box containing a switch or switches, usually mounted on a wall or panel.
switch'el, *n.* [etym. uncertain.] a beverage made of molasses and water, ginger, vinegar, or rum sometimes being added; hence, any strong beverage sweetened and flavored.
switch'ẽr, *n.* 1. a switchman.
2. a switching engine.
switch grȧss, a variety of panic grass, *Panicum virgatum*, of the United States.
switch'ing en'ġine, an engine used about a railroad station or yard for switching.
switch'măn, *n.*; *pl.* **switch'men,** a man who has charge of one or more railroad switches.
switch'y, *a.* of or pertaining to a switch.
switch'yärd, *n.* a railroad yard where cars are shifted from one track to another by means of a system of switches, as in making up trains.
swith, swīthe, *adv.* quickly; rapidly; promptly. [Archaic and Dial.]
swith'ẽr, *v.i.* [AS. *swetherian, swethrian*, to fail, abate.] to fear; to hesitate; to doubt. [Scot.]
swith'ẽr, *n.* hesitation; doubt; fear; a fright. [Scot.]
Switz'ẽr, *n.* [M.H.G., from *Switz, Swiz*, Switzerland.] a Swiss; one who lives in or is a native of Switzerland; also, a Swiss mercenary soldier: also *Swisser.*
swīve, *v.t.* to have sexual intercourse with. [Obs.]
swiv'el, *n.* [ME. *swiuel*, from base of AS. *swīfan*, to move quickly, to be turned round, revolve.]
1. a fastening so contrived as to allow the thing fastened to turn freely in any direction; specifically, (a) a twisting link in a chain consisting of a ring or hook ending in a headed pin which turns in a link of the chain so as to prevent kinking; (b) the platform support for a swivel chair or swivel gun.
2. a swivel gun.

SWIVEL

swiv'el, *v.t.*; swiveled *or* swivelled, *pt., pp.*; swiveling *or* swivelling, *ppr.* 1. to cause to turn or rotate on or as on a swivel.
2. to fit, fasten, or support with a swivel.
swiv'el, *v.i.* to turn on or as on a swivel.
swiv'el bridġe, a swing bridge.
swiv'el chāir, a chair mounted on a swivel in the base so that the seat can be turned completely around.
swiv'el-eȳed (-īd), *a.* squint-eyed. [Slang.]
swiv'el gun, an artillery piece mounted on a platform in such a way that it can be turned horizontally or vertically for aiming.
swiv'el hook, a hook that turns in the end of the strap of a pulley block, as for taking the turns out of a tackle.
swiv'el mus'ket, same as *jingal.*
swiz'zle, *n.* [var. of *switchel*; prob. from *switch*, *v.* with reference to the mixing.]

1. any of several alcoholic drinks containing rum or other liquor, crushed ice, sugar, bitters, etc.
2. intoxicating drink generally. [Colloq.]
swiz′zle, *v.t.* to drink to excess.
swiz′zle stick, a stick or rod for stirring mixed drinks.
swob, *n.* and *v.*; swobbed, *pt.*, *pp.*; swobbing, *ppr.* same as *swab.*
swob′bẽr, *n.* same as *swabber.*
swōll′en, swōln, *v.* alternative past participle of *swell.*
swōll′en, *a.* inflated or enlarged, as from swelling; blown up; distended; bulging; as, *swollen* streams; *swollen* eyes.
swŏm, *v.* obsolete past tense of *swim.*
swoñk, *v.* alternative past tense of *swink.*
swoñk′en, *v.* past participle of *swink.*
swoon, *v.i.*; swooned, *pt.*, *pp.*; swooning, *ppr.* [ME. *swounen*, from *swoweninge*, swooning, from AS. *geswogen*, unconscious, pp. of a lost v.] to faint.
He seemed ready to *swoon* away in the surprise of joy. —Tatler.
swoon, *n.* a fainting fit; syncope.
swoon′ing, *n.* the act of fainting; syncope.
swoop, *v.t.*; swooped (swoopt), *pt.*, *pp.*; swooping, *ppr.* [ME. *swopen*, *swapen*; AS. *swapan*, to sweep along, rush; also to sweep; Ice. *sveipa*, to sweep, swoop, from *sópa*; Sw. *sopa*, to sweep.] to snatch or seize suddenly, with a sweeping movement: often with *up*, etc.
swoop, *v.i.* 1. to pass with pomp. [Obs.]
2. to descend upon prey suddenly and swiftly; to pounce or sweep (*down* or *upon*).
swoop, *n.* the act of swooping; a sudden violent descent, as of a rapacious fowl on its prey.
swoop′stāke, *n.* and *adv.* sweepstake. [Obs.]
swop, *n.*, *v.t.* and *v.i.*; swopped (swopt), *pt.*, *pp.*; swopping, *ppr.* same as *swap.*
swōrd (sōrd), *n.* [ME.; AS. *sweord*, *swurd*, *sword*, sword. Origin uncertain.]
1. a hand weapon having a long strong blade usually of fine polished steel, either straight and with a sharp point for thrusting, as the modern rapier; with a sharp point and one or two cutting edges for thrusting and striking, as the broadsword; or curved, and with a sharp convex edge for striking, as the scimitar, etc. The blade is secured by means of a tang to the handle which commonly consists of a hilt, a grip, and a pommel.
2. the sword regarded as an instrument of death, destruction, etc.
3. power or authority, especially military power.
4. the military profession.
5. war; conflict.
6. in weaving, one of the arms by which the lay of a hand loom is supported.
at swords' points; ready to quarrel or fight.
sword of state; the sword carried before a sovereign on state occasions, emblematic of military power.
to cross swords; (a) to fight; (b) to argue violently.
to put to the sword; (a) to slay with a sword or swords; (b) to slaughter, especially in war.
swōrd ärm, the arm that wields the sword or other weapon; the right arm.
swōrd bāy′ō·net, a short sword that can be mounted on a rifle for use as a bayonet: see illustration under *bayonet.*
swōrd bēan, same as *horse bean.*
swōrd belt, a belt from which a sword is suspended.
swōrd′bill, *n.* a South American hummingbird, *Docimastes ensiferus*, with an extremely long, slender bill that is longer than its body.
swōrd′-billed hum′ming·bird, a swordbill.
swōrd break′ẽr, an archaic sword-shaped weapon, much broader than an ordinary sword, and having long teeth on one edge intended to catch and break an enemy's sword; also, a notch in the guard of a sword, or a small piece of steel parallel with the blade, intended for the same purpose.
swōrd cāne, a cane or walking stick containing a long pointed blade, that may be used as a sword or dagger.
swōrd′craft, *n.* 1. swordsmanship.
2. the use of military force; tactics of warfare.
swōrd cut, a cut or wound made with a sword.
swōrd cut′lẽr, one who makes or mounts swords.
swōrd dȧnce, 1. a dance in which swords are clashed together by the dancers.
2. a dance of the Scottish Highlanders, in which bare swords are laid crosswise on the ground, the skill of the dancer being shown in never touching the swords with his feet while dancing over them.
swōrd′ed, *a.* armed with a sword.
swōrd′ẽr, *n.* a soldier; a cutthroat. [Obs.]
swōrd′fish, *n.*; *pl.* **swōrd′fish** or **swōrd′fish·es,** a large marine food fish of the genus *Xiphias*, family *Xiphiidæ*, named for its elongated upper jaw, which extends in a swordlike point.

SWORDFISH (7 ft. long)

swordfish sucker; a remora, *Echeneis brachyptera*, often found attached to the swordfish.
swōrd flag, the yellow flag, *Iris pseudacorus.*
swōrd grȧss, any of several plants, as (a) the gladden; (b) the sweet rush, and many other sedges or grasses with toothed or sword-shaped leaves.
swōrd′ick, *n.* a small marine fish, the rock eel, *Murænoides gunnellus.*
swōrd knot (not), a loop of leather, ribbon, etc. attached to a sword hilt as an ornament or, originally, for support around the wrist during swordplay.
swōrd law, government by force; martial law.
swōrd′less, *a.* without a sword.
swōrd lil′y, same as *gladiolus.*
swōrd′măn, *n.*; *pl.* **swōrd′men,** a swordsman; a fighting man. [Rare.]
swōrd mat, in nautical usage, a mat woven with a sword-shaped piece of wood, and used to prevent chafing.
swōrd′plāy, *n.* a contest with swords; fencing; swordsmanship.
swōrd′plāy″ẽr, *n.* a fencer; a gladiator; one who exhibits his skill in the use of the sword. [Rare or Obs.]
swōrd′proof, *a.* impenetrable to a cut or thrust of the sword.
swōrd sedge, an Australian seacoast sedge, from which a paper is manufactured.
swōrd′-shāped (-shāpt), *a.* shaped like a sword; as, a *sword-shaped* leaf.
swōrds′măn, *n.*; *pl.* **swōrds′men,** 1. one who uses a sword in fencing or fighting.
2. one who uses the sword with skill; a fencer.
swōrds′măn·ship, *n.* the art, skill, or practice of a swordsman.
swōrd′stick, *n.* a sword cane.
swōrd′tāil, *n.* 1. any insect of the genus *Uroxiphus.*
2. a small, vividly colored fresh-water fish of Mexico and Central America, often kept in aquariums.
swōre, *v.* alternative past tense of *swear.*
swōrn, *v.* past participle of *swear.*
swōrn, *a.* bound, pledged, promised, etc. by or as by an oath.
sworn brothers; brothers or companions in arms, who according to the laws of chivalry vowed to share danger or success; hence, close companions or associates.
sworn enemies; determined or irreconcilable enemies.
sworn friends; loyal, close, or firm friends.
swot, *n.* and *v.t.*; swotted, *pt.*, *pp.*; swotting, *ppr.* same as *swat.*
swough (swou), *n.* a sigh or moan; a murmur. [Obs.]
swound, *v.i.* to swoon. [Archaic.]
swound, *n.* a swoon; a fainting fit. [Archaic.]
'swounds, 'swouns, *interj.* God's wounds: a euphemistic contraction used as an oath: also *zounds.* [Archaic.]
swum, *v.* past participle and archaic or dialectal past tense of *swim*, (to move through water).
swum, *v.* past participle of *swim* (to be dizzy).
swung, *v.* past participle and alternative past tense of *swing.*
swȳthe, *adv.* swith; quickly. [Obs.]
sȳ, *v.* obsolete past tense of *see.*
syb, *n.* and *a.* sib. [Obs.]
Syb′ȧ·rīte, *n.* [L. *Sybarita*; Gr. *Sybaritēs*, an inhabitant of Sybaris, Italy, a town proverbial for its luxury.]
1. any of the people of ancient Sybaris, in southern Italy.
2. [s–] anyone very fond of luxury and pleasure; a voluptuary.
Syb·ȧ·rit′iç, *a.* 1. of or characteristic of Sybaris or the Sybarites.
2. [s–] luxurious; voluptuous.
syb·ȧ·rit′i·çăl, *a.* sybaritic.
syb′ȧ·rī·tism, *n.* the practices or habits of a sybarite; voluptuousness.
syç′ȧ·mine, *n.* [L. *sycaminus*; Gr. *sykaminos*, the mulberry tree.] a tree mentioned in Luke xvii. 6, believed to be the black mulberry.
syç′ȧ·mōre, *n.* [L. *sycomorus*; Gr. *sykomoros*, the fig mulberry tree; *sykon*, a fig, and *moron*, a black mulberry.] in botany, (a) a tree, *Ficus sycomorus*, very common in Palestine, Arabia, and Egypt, growing large and to a great height, much used in building, and very durable; (b) the sycamore maple, *Acer pseudoplatanus*, with yellow flowers and coarse-toothed leaves, found in Europe and Asia; (c) any of a number of related American plane trees; especially, the buttonwood.
sȳce, *n.* [Ar. *sa'is.*] in India, a groom (for horses).
sȳ·cee′, sȳ·cee′ sil′vẽr, [Chinese *si szĕ*, fine silk, so called because if pure it may, when heated, be spun into threads as fine as silk.] silver cast into ingots, usually stamped, used in China as money.
sych·nō·cär′pous, *a.* [Gr. *sychnos*, many, and *karpos*, fruit.] capable of bearing fruit many times. [Rare.]
syç·ō·cer′iç, *a.* relating to or designating a resinous acid derived from sycoceryl.
syç·ō·cē′ryl, *n.* [Gr. *sykon*, fig, *kēros*, wax, and *-yl.*] an aromatic radical obtained from the waxy resin of an Australian fig.
syç″ō·cē·ryl′iç, *a.* sycoceric.
sȳ′cock, *n.* the mistle thrush of England. [Brit. Dial.]
sy·çō′mȧ, *n.* [Gr. *sykōma*, from *sykon*, a fig.] a wart shaped like a fig.
Sȳ·çō′nēs, *n.pl.* [Gr. *sykon*, a fig.] a family of the chalk sponges.
sȳ·çō′ni·um, *n.*; *pl.* **sȳ·çō′ni·ȧ,** [Mod. L., from Gr. *sykon*, a fig.] in botany, a fleshy, hollow receptacle containing numerous flowers which are combined in the fruit, as in a fig.
syç′ō·noid, *a.* of, pertaining to, or like the *Sycones.*
sȳ·çō′nus, *n.*; *pl.* **sȳ·çō′nī,** a syconium.
syç′ō·phăn·cy, *n.*; *pl.* **syç′ō·phăn·cies,** the behavior or character of a sycophant; obsequious flattery.
syç′ō·phănt, *n.* [L. *sycophanta*, an informer; Gr. *sykophantēs*, lit., a fig shower; *sykon*, fig, and *phainein*, to show.]
1. originally, an informer; a talebearer.
2. a parasite; a person who seeks favor by flattering people of wealth or influence; a toady.
syç′ō·phănt, *v.t.* to play the sycophant toward.
syç′ō·phănt, *v.i.* to act as a sycophant.
syç·ō·phan′tiç, syç·ō·phan′ti·çăl, *a.* characteristic of or relating to a sycophant.
syç′ō·phănt·ish, *a.* characteristic of a sycophant.
syç′ō·phănt·ish·ly, *adv.* in a sycophantish manner.
syç′ō·phănt·ism, *n.* sycophancy.
syç′ō·phănt·īze, *v.i.*; sycophantized, *pt.*, *pp.*; sycophantizing, *ppr.* to act as a sycophant.
syç′ō·phănt·ry, *n.* sycophancy.
sȳ·çō′sis, *n.* [Mod. L.; Gr. *sykōsis*, from *sykon*, fig.] a chronic disease of the hair follicles, especially of the beard, caused by certain staphylococci and characterized by the formation of papules and pustules.
sȳ′en·īte, *n.* [Fr. *syénite*; L. *syenites*, from *Syene*, Gr. *Syēnē*, Syene, a town in upper Egypt.] a kind of gray, igneous rock containing feldspar, hornblende, and some silicates.
sȳ·e·nit′iç, *a.* 1. characteristic of or pertaining to syenite.
2. [S–] pertaining to Syene, a town in upper Egypt.
syenitic gneiss; see *gneiss.*
sȳke, *n.* [a variant of *sike.*] a small brook or rill in low ground. [Dial.]
syk′ẽr, *a.* and *adv.* sicker. [Obs.]
syl-, same as *syn-.*
syl·lȧ·bär′i·um, *n.* [LL.] a syllabary.
syl′lȧ·bãr·y, *n.*; *pl.* **syl′lȧ·bãr·ies,** [L. *syllaba*; Gr. *syllabē*, a syllable.]
1. a set or table of syllables.
2. a system of written characters representing spoken syllables rather than individual sounds.

syl'labe, *n.* a syllable. [Rare.]
syl'là·bī, *n.* alternative plural of *syllabus.*
syl·lab'iç, *a.* 1. of a syllable or syllables.
2. designating a consonant that in itself forms a syllable with no appreciable vowel sound, as the *l* in *tattle* (tat'l).
3. pronounced distinctly, syllable by syllable.
4. designating a form of verse arranged according to the number of syllables per line rather than by rhythm or accent.
syl·lab'iç, *n.* a syllabic sound; a sonant.
syl·lab'i·çăl, *a.* same as *syllabic.*
syl·lab'i·çăl·ly, *adv.* syllable by syllable; by syllables.
syl·lab'i·çāte, *v.t.*; syllabicated, *pt., pp.*; syllabicating, *ppr.* to syllabify.
syl·lab·i·çā'tion, *n.* syllabification.
syl·lab"i·fi·çā'tion, *n.* formation of or division into syllables.
syl·lab'i·fȳ, *v.t.*; syllabified, *pt., pp.*; syllabifying, *ppr.* to form or divide into syllables.
syl'là·bişm, *n.* 1. the use of syllabic characters, rather than letters, in writing.
2. division into syllables.
syl'là·bīze, *v.t.*; syllabized, *pt., pp.*; syllabizing, *ppr.* to syllabify.
syl'là·ble, *n.* [ME. *sillable*; OFr. *sillabe*; L. *syllaba*, from Gr. *syllabē*, a syllable, lit., that which holds together; *syl*, for *syn*, together, and *lambanein*, to hold.]
1. a word or part of a word pronounced with a single, uninterrupted sounding of the voice; unit of pronunciation, consisting of a single sound of great sonority (usually a vowel) and generally one or more sounds of lesser sonority (usually consonants).
2. one or more letters or symbols written to represent, more or less, a spoken syllable.
3. the least bit of expression; slightest detail; as, don't mention a *syllable* of this.
syl'là·ble, *v.t.* and *v.i.*; syllabled, *pt., pp.*; syllabling, *ppr.* to pronounce in or as in syllables.
syl'là·bub, *n.* same as *sillabub.*
syl'là·bus, *n.*; *pl.* **syl'là·bus·eş** or **syl'là·bī,** [Mod. L., from *syllabas* in a 15-c. edition of Cicero, a misprint for *sittybas*, pl. of *sittyba*, a list, from Gr. *syttyba*, piece of parchment used as a label.]
1. a summary or outline containing the main points, especially of a course of study.
2. in law, notes preceding and explaining the decision in the written report of a trial.
3. in the Roman Catholic Church, a summary enumeration of propositions considered erroneous by an act or decree of ecclesiastical authority; especially, a document issued by Pope Pius IX in 1864 in which eighty current doctrines, institutions, etc. of the age are condemned as heresies, including pantheism, rationalism, socialism, secret societies, Bible societies, etc.; also, a document issued by Pope Pius X in 1907 in which sixty-five doctrines of Modernism are condemned as heresies.
syl·lep'sis, *n.*; *pl.* **syl·lep'sēs,** [L.; Gr. *syllēpsis*, a putting together, from *syllambanein*, to take together, lay hold of.]
1. in grammar, a construction in which a single word is used to modify or govern syntactically two or more words in the same sentence, though it can grammatically agree with only one of them. Example: He or his friends *were* responsible.
2. in rhetoric, a figure by which the sense of words is conceived otherwise than the words import and construed according to the intention of the author; the taking of words in two senses at once, the literal and metaphorical, as the word *sweeter* in the following quotation.
The judgments of the Lord are true and righteous altogether ... *sweeter* also than honey and the honeycomb.—Ps. xix. 9, 10.
syl·lep'tiç, *a.* of, having the nature of, or involving syllepsis.
syl·lep'ti·çăl, *a.* sylleptic.
syl·lep'ti·çăl·ly, *adv.* in a sylleptical manner; by the use of syllepsis.
syl·lid'i·ăn, *n.* [LL. *Syllis*, the typical genus.] any marine worm of the family *Syllidæ*, many species of which are phosphorescent.
syl'lō·ġişm, *n.* [ME. *silogime*; OFr. *silogime, sillogisme*; L. *syllogismus*; Gr. *syllogismos*, a reckoning all together, from *syllogizesthai*, to reckon together, sum up.]
1. an argument or form of reasoning in which two statements or premises are made and a logical conclusion drawn from them.
Major Premise. All ruminants are quadrupeds.
Minor Premise. All deer are ruminants.
Conclusion ∴ All deer are quadrupeds.
The figure of a syllogism consists in the situation of the middle term with respect to the major and minor. In the first figure, the middle is the subject of the major and the predicate of the minor, M—P, S—M, S—P; in the second, it is the predicate of both premises, P—M, S—M, S—P; and in the third, it is the subject of both premises, M—P, M—S, S—P; the fourth figure is the reverse of the first, the middle term being the predicate of the major and the subject of the minor, P—M, M—S, S—P. Every proposition in logic must have one of four possible forms: (a) universal affirmative, all S is P; (e) universal negative, no S is P; (i) particular affirmative, some S is P; (o) particular negative, some S is not P. Each syllogism has three propositions, and by permutation of the four possible forms, there may be constructed sixty-four modes (or moods), of which only nineteen are valid forms of reasoning.
2. reasoning from the general to the particular; deductive logic.
3. subtle, tricky, or specious reasoning.
syl·lō·ġis'tiç, *a.* of, pertaining to, resembling, consisting of, or using a syllogism.
syl·lō·ġis'tiç, *n.* reasoning by syllogisms.
syl·lō·ġis'ti·çăl, *a.* same as *syllogistic.*
syl·lō·ġis'ti·çăl·ly, *adv.* in the form or manner of a syllogism.
syl"lō·ġi·zā'tion, *n.* a reasoning by syllogisms.
syl'lō·ġīze, *v.i.* and *v.t.*; syllogized, *pt., pp.*; syllogizing, *ppr.* to reason or infer by use of syllogisms.
syl'lō·ġi·zēr, *n.* one who reasons by syllogisms.
sylph, *n.* [from Mod. L. *sylphes*, pl.; perhaps coined by Paracelsus from L. *sylvestris*, of a forest, and *nympha*, nymph.]
1. in Paracelsus' system, any of a class of mortal, but soulless, beings supposed to inhabit the air.
2. a slender, graceful woman or girl.
3. in zoology, a hummingbird of South America, with a long, forked tail.
sylph'id, *n.* [Fr. *sylphide.*] a little or youthful sylph.
sylph'id·ine, *a.* of or like a sylphid.
sylph'ish, *a.* sylphlike.
sylph'līke, *a.* resembling a sylph; slender; graceful.
syl'và, *n.*; *pl.* **sil'vàş, syl'vae,** [L. *silva*, a wood, forest.] same as *silva.*
syl'văn, *a.* [L. *silvanus*, belonging to a wood or forest, from *silva*, wood; chiefly used of the god *Silvanus.*]
1. of or characteristic of the woods or forest.
2. living, found, or carried on in the woods or forest.
3. wooded.
syl'văn, *n.* 1. one who lives in the woods.
2. a deity or spirit of the woods.
Also spelled *silvan.*
syl'văn·īte, *n.* [from Tran*sylvan*ia (where it was first found), and *-ite.*] a gray or silvery crystalline telluride of gold and silver, $AgAuTe_2$.
syl'vāte, *n.* a salt of sylvic acid.
syl·vat'iç, *a.* sylvan. [Rare.]
Syl·ves'tri·ăn, *n.* a member of a religious body founded in Italy in 1231, by Sylvester Gozzolini: also written *Sylvestrine.*
syl·ves'tri·ăn, *a.* sylvan. [Rare.]
syl'vi·ăn, *a.* of, relating to, or resembling the *Sylviidæ.*
Syl'vi·ăn, *a.* described by or named for Jacques Dubois (*Sylvius*), a French anatomist of the fifteenth century.
Sylvian aqueduct; a passage which connects the third and fourth ventricles of the brain.
Sylvian artery; the middle cerebral artery.
Sylvian fissure; see *fissure of Sylvius* under *fissure.*
Sylvian fossa; a depression on the cerebral hemispheres between the arms of the Sylvian fissure: its bottom is occupied by the island of Reil, or central lobe.
Sylvian ventricle; the fifth ventricle of the brain.
syl'viç ac'id, an acid, $C_{20}H_{30}O_2$, obtained from resin.
syl'vi·çul·tūre, *n.* [L. *sylva*, a forest, and *cultura*, culture.] same as *silviculture.*
Syl·vī'i·dae, Syl'vi·dae, *n.pl.* a family of dentirostral birds widely distributed, but most common in the Eastern Hemisphere; the Old World warblers.
Syl·vi·ī'nae, *n.pl.* 1. the *Sylviidæ* as a subfamily of some other family, as the *Turdidæ.*
2. the typical subfamily of *Sylviidæ*, with six genera and thirty-three species; most abundant in the Palearctic region.
syl'vi·ine, *a.* of or pertaining to the *Sylviinæ*, or typical Old World warblers.
syl'vin, syl'vine, *n.* sylvite.
syl'vīte, *n.* [from Mod. L. *sal digestivus sylvii*, old name of the salt (prob. after Franz de la Boë *Sylvius*, 1614–1672, physician and professor of medicine at Leyden); and *-ite.*] native potassium chloride, KCl, occurring in crystalline masses and used as a fertilizer: also *sylvine, sylvin.*
sym-, same as *syn-.*
sy·mär', *n.* same as *simar.*
sym'bi·ont, sym'bi·on, *n.* an organism which lives in a state of symbiosis.
sym·bī·ō'sis, *n.* [Gr., a living together.] in biology, the living together of two dissimilar organisms in close association or union, especially where this is advantageous to both, as in the case of the fungus and alga which together form the lichen: distinguished from *parasitism*: also called *mutualism* and *commensalism.*
sym·bī·ot'iç, *a.* of, pertaining to, or characterized by *symbiosis.*
sym·bī·ot'i·çăl, *a.* symbiotic.
sym·bī·ot'i·çăl·ly, *adv.* in a symbiotic manner.
sym·bleph'à·ron, *n.* [*sym-*, and Gr. *blepharon*, the eyelid.] adhesion of the lids to the eyeball.
sym'bŏl, *n.* [Fr. *symbole*; L. *symbolum*; Gr. *symbolon*, a token, pledge, a sign by which one infers a thing, from *symballein*, to throw together, compare; *syn*, together, and *ballein*, to throw.]
1. something that stands for or represents another thing; especially, an object used to represent something abstract; an emblem; as, the dove is a *symbol* of peace, the cross is the *symbol* of Christianity.
2. a written or printed mark, letter, abbreviation, etc. standing for an object, quality, process, quantity, etc., as in music, mathematics, or chemistry.
3. in psychoanalysis, an act or object representing an unconscious desire that has been repressed.
4. in theology, an abstract or compendium, creed, or a summary of the articles of religion.
Syn.—type, sign, image, emblem, representation.
sym'bŏl, *v.t.*; symboled, *pt., pp.*; symboling, *ppr.* to symbolize.
sym'bŏl, *n.* [L. *symbola*; Gr. *symbolē*, a contribution to a common feast; also the feast itself.] a contribution to a common fund, especially for a feast; a share; a portion. [Rare.]
sym"bol·ae·og'rà·phy, *n.* [Gr. *symbolon*, a sign, and *-graphy.*] the art or science of properly framing or drawing up legal instruments.
sym·bol'iç, sym·bol'i·çăl, *a.* [Gr. *symbolikos*, from *symbolon*, symbol.]
1. of or expressed in a symbol or symbols.
2. that serves as a symbol (*of* something).
3. using symbols; characterized by symbolism.
4. in grammar, connective; relational: said of pronouns, prepositions, conjunctions, etc.
5. in mathematics, dealing with symbols of operation.
symbolical books; such books as contain the fundamental doctrines, or creeds and confessions, of the different churches, as the Confession of Augsburg received by the Lutherans, the Thirty-nine Articles of the Church of England, etc.
symbolical delivery; in law, the delivery of property sold or resigned, by delivering something else as a symbol, token, or representative of it.
sym·bol'iç, *n.* same as *symbolics*, sense 2.
sym·bol'i·çăl·ly, *adv.* in a symbolic manner; by means of symbols.
sym·bol'i·çăl·ness, *n.* the state, condition, or quality of being symbolic.
sym·bol'içs, *n.* 1. the study of ancient symbols.
2. the study of the history and contents of Christian creeds and confessions of faith; symbolism.
sym'bŏl·işm, *n.* 1. the representation of things by use of symbols, especially in fine art or literature.
2. a system of symbols.
3. symbolic meaning.
4. a group of symbolists, as in art or literature.
5. the theories or practices of such a group.

6. in chemistry, a combining of parts or ingredients. [Obs.]

sym'bŏl·ist, *n.* 1. a person who uses symbols.

2. a person who practices symbolism in representing ideas, etc., especially in fine art or literature; specifically, any of a group of French and Belgian writers and artists of the late nineteenth century who rejected realism and tried to express ideas, emotions, and attitudes by the use of symbolic words, figures, objects, etc.

3. a person who studies or is expert in interpreting symbols or symbolism.

4. in theology, a person who regards the Eucharist as merely symbolical and denies the doctrine of transubstantiation.

sym·bŏl·is'tiç, sym·bŏl·is'ti·căl, *a.* of or characteristic of symbolism or symbolists.

sym''bŏl·i·zā'tion, *n.* a symbolizing or being symbolized.

sym'bŏl·īze, *v.t.*; symbolized, *pt.*, *pp.*; symbolizing, *ppr.* [Fr. *symboliser*; Mod. L. *symbolizare.*]

1. to be a symbol of; to typify; to stand for.

2. to represent by a symbol or symbols.

3. to make into a symbol; to treat as a symbol.

sym'bŏl·īze, *v.i.* 1. to use symbols or symbolism.

2. to agree; to conform; to harmonize; especially, to hold the same faith or religious belief. [Rare.]

sym'bŏl·ī·zẽr, *n.* one who or that which symbolizes.

sym·bō·loġ'i·căl, *a.* of or pertaining to symbology.

sym·bol'ō·ġist, *n.* an expert in symbology.

sym·bol'ō·ġy, *n.* [from *symbol* and *-logy.*]

1. the study or interpretation of symbols.

2. representation or expression by means of symbols; symbolism.

3. a system of symbols; symbolism.

Sym·brăn'çhi·à, *n.pl.* [Gr. *syn*, together, and *branchia*, gills.] an order of physostomous fishes, having long, eellike bodies and confluent inferior branchial apertures: also written *Symbranchii.*

sym·brañ'çhi·āte, *a.* of, pertaining to, or having the characteristics of the *Symbranchia.*

sym·brañ'çhi·āte, *n.* one of the *Symbranchia.*

Sym·brañ'çhi·ī, *n.pl.* same as *Symbranchia.*

sym·brañ'çhous, *a.* of or pertaining to the *Symbranchia.*

sym·met'ăl·lişm, *n.* [from *sym-* and *metal* and *-ism.*] a system of coinage based on a unit of two or more metals in combination, each of a specified minimum weight.

sym'mē·trăl, *a.* commensurable; symmetrical; pertaining to symmetry. [Rare.]

sym·met'ri·ăn, *n.* a student of proportion or symmetry of parts. [Obs.]

sym·met'riç, *a.* same as *symmetrical.*

sym·met'ri·căl, *a.* having or showing symmetry, or correspondence in form, size, or arrangement of parts; specifically, (a) in botany, that can be divided into similar parts by a plane passing through the center; also, having the same number of parts in each whorl of leaves: said of a flower; (b) in chemistry, exhibiting a regular repeated pattern of atoms in the structural formula; specifically, designating a compound (benzene derivative) in which substitution takes place at the alternate carbon atoms; (c) in mathematics and logic, designating an equation, relation, etc. whose terms can be interchanged without affecting its validity; (d) in medicine, affecting corresponding parts of the body simultaneously in the same way: said of a disease, etc.

sym·met'ri·căl·ly, *adv.* in a symmetrical manner.

sym·met'ri·căl·ness, *n.* the state or quality of being symmetrical.

sym'mē·trist, *n.* one studious or observant of symmetry or due proportion.

sym''mē·tri·zā'tion, *n.* a symmetrizing or being symmetrized.

sym'mē·trīze, *v.t.*; symmetrized, *pt.*, *pp.*; symmetrizing, *ppr.* to make symmetrical.

sym'mē·try, *n.*; *pl.* **sym'mē·trieş,** [Fr. *symétrie*; L. and Gr. *symmetria*, due proportion, from Gr. *symmetros*, measured together; *syn*, together, and *metron*, a measure.]

1. similarity of form or arrangement on either side of a dividing line or plane; correspondence of opposite parts in size, shape, and position; condition of being symmetrical: an attribute of the whole or of the parts of which it is composed.

2. excellence or beauty of form or proportion as a result of such correspondence.

3. in mathematics, the correspondence of parts or relations; similarity of arrangement. Thus, a figure has symmetry with respect to a point called the *center of symmetry*, or with respect to a line called the *axis of symmetry*, if, on being turned round on that point or line as a pivot for less than a complete revolution, it coincides with its original position. It has symmetry with respect to a *plane of symmetry*, if that plane bisects all the lines joining corresponding points.

4. in crystallography, the symmetrical arrangement of nonparallel equivalent elements in a crystal with respect to axes or planes of symmetry. Every symmetrical crystal may be classed in one of thirty-two groups or classes of symmetry.

axis of symmetry of a body; see under *axis.*

bilateral symmetry; that form of symmetry in which the plane of symmetry is vertical and through the longitudinal axis.

center of symmetry; see *symmetry*, sense 2.

kinetic symmetry; the condition in which the moments of inertia about the axes through the center of mass of any body are equal.

plane of symmetry; a plane with respect to which any figure is symmetrical.

radial symmetry; symmetry in which similar parts radiate from an axis.

zonal symmetry; the symmetry of annulose or ringed organisms, as earthworms, in which bilateral symmetry is not well marked.

sym·pal'mō·gràph, *n.* [Gr. *syn*, together, *palmos*, vibration, from *pallein*, to vibrate, and *-graph.*] a device by which the composition of two simple harmonic motions at right angles may be illustrated graphically.

sym·pà·thet'iç, *a.* 1. of, expressing, resulting from, feeling, or showing sympathy; sympathizing.

2. in agreement with one's tastes, mood, feelings, disposition, etc.; congenial.

3. showing favor, approval, or agreement; as, he was *sympathetic* to our plan. [Colloq.]

4. in anatomy and physiology, designating or of that part of the autonomic nervous system whose nerves originate in the lumbar and thoracic regions of the spinal cord and whose functions include the innervation of smooth muscles, heart muscle, and glands: cf. *parasympathetic.*

5. in physics and acoustics, caused by vibrations transmitted from a neighboring vibrating body: said of vibrations, sound, etc.

6. operating as if by sympathy or occult influence; as, *sympathetic* ink.

sympathetic ink; see *invisible ink* under *ink.*

sympathetic nerve; a nerve of the sympathetic nervous system; particularly, one of two cords connecting a series of ganglia along the spinal column.

sympathetic nervous system; one of the two parts of the autonomic nervous system: see sense 4, above.

sympathetic powder; in alchemy, a preparation reputed to have the property of curing a wound if applied to the weapon that inflicted it or to a cloth dipped in the blood which flowed from it.

sym·pà·thet'i·căl, *a.* sympathetic. [Rare.]

sym·pà·thet'i·căl·ly, *adv.* in a sympathetic manner; with sympathy.

sym'pà·thist, *n.* a sympathizer. [Rare.]

sym'pà·thīze, *v.i.*; sympathized, *pt.*, *pp.*; sympathizing, *ppr.* [Fr. *sympathiser.*]

1. to share or understand the feelings or ideas of another; to be in sympathy.

2. to feel or express sympathy, especially in pity or compassion; to commiserate (*with* someone or something).

3. to be in harmony or accord.

sym'pà·thīze, *v.t.* to have sympathy for; to share or participate in; to correspond to. [Obs.]

sym'pà·thī·zẽr, *n.* one who sympathizes.

sym'pà·thy, *n.*; *pl.* **sym'pà·thieş,** [Fr. *sympathie*; L. *sympathia*; Gr. *sympatheia*, like feeling, fellow-feeling, from *sympathēs*, of like feelings; *syn*, together, and *pathos*, feeling, from *paschein*, to suffer, feel.]

1. sameness of feeling; affinity between persons or of one person for another.

2. an action or response arising from this.

3. agreement in qualities; harmony; accord.

4. a mutual liking or understanding arising from sameness of feeling.

5. the entering into or ability to enter into another person's mental state, feelings, emotions, etc.; especially, pity or compassion for another's trouble, suffering, etc.

6. in physics, a relation or harmony between bodies of such a nature that vibrations in one cause sympathetic vibrations in the other or others.

7. in physiology, a relation between parts of the body of such a nature that a disorder, pain, etc. in one induces a similar effect in other.

8. a supposed tendency of certain things to unite with or act on each other; as, the *sympathy* between the lodestone and iron. [Obs.]

Syn.—fellow feeling, congeniality, commiseration, compassion, pity, tenderness, agreement, condolence.

sym'pà·thy (or **sym·pà·thet'iç**) **strīke,** a strike by a group of workers in support of another group of workers who are on strike.

sym·pel'mous, *a.* [Gr. *syn*, together, and *pelma*, the sole of the foot.] having the deep flexor tendons of the toes united: said of some birds.

sym·pet'ăl·ous, *a.* gamopetalous.

sym·phon'iç, *a.* 1. pertaining to, resembling, or characteristic of a symphony; as, a composition in *symphonic* form.

2. of or having to do with harmony of sound.

3. having a similar sound or sounds.

symphonic poem; an extended musical composition for full symphony orchestra, usually in one movement, programmatic in nature, and freer in form than the symphony: also called *tone poem.*

sym·phō'ni·ous, *a.* agreeing in sound; harmonious.

sym'phō·nist, *n.* a composer of symphonies.

sym'phō·nīze, *v.t.* and *v.i.*; symphonized, *pt.*, *pp.*; symphonizing, *ppr.* to harmonize.

sym'phō·ny, *n.*; *pl.* **sym'phō·nieş,** [L. *symphonia*; Gr. *symphōnia*, music, from *symphōnos*, agreeing in sound, harmonious; *syn*, together, and *phōnein*, to sound, from *phōnē*, sound.]

1. harmony of sounds, especially of instruments.

2. harmony of any kind, especially of color.

3. anything, as a picture, characterized by harmonious composition.

4. in music, (a) an extended composition in sonata form for full orchestra, having several (usually four) movements related in subject, but varying in form and execution; (b) an instrumental passage in a composition that is largely vocal or choral; (c) a symphony orchestra; (d) [Colloq.] a symphony concert.

sym'phō·ny ọr'çhes·trà, a large orchestra for playing symphonic works, composed of string, wind, and percussion sections: distinguished from *band.*

Sym''phō·ri·cär'pos, *n.* [LL., from Gr. *symphorein*, to yield together, and *karpos*, fruit: so named from the cluster of berries.] a genus of North American shrubs of the honeysuckle family. *Symphoricarpos racemosus* is the snowberry of the United States. *Symphoricarpos vulgaris* is the Indian currant, or coralberry.

sym''phō·ri·cär'pous, *a.* in botany, bearing fruits clustered together. [Rare.]

Sym'phy·là, *n.pl.* [Gr. *symphylos*, of the same stock or race; *phylon*, a clan, tribe.] an order or suborder of arthropods resembling in some respects true insects and myriapods.

sym·phyl'lous, *a.* gamophyllous.

sym'phy·lous, *a.* pertaining to the *Symphyla.*

sym'phy·nōte, *a.* [Gr. *symphyēs*, growing together, and *nōton*, back.] having the valves firmly fixed at the back or hinge, as some river mussels.

sym'phy·ō-, [from Gr. *syn*, together, and *phyein*, to grow.] a combining form meaning *growing together.*

sym''phy·ō·ġen'e·sis, *n.* in botany, production by union of formerly separate elements.

sym''phy·ō·ġē·net'iç, *a.* pertaining to symphyogenesis.

sym''phy·ō·stem'ō·nous, *a.* [*symphyo-*, and Gr. *stēmōn*, stamen.] in botany, monadelphous. [Obs.]

sym·phyş'ē·ăl, *a.* of or pertaining to symphysis.

sym''phy·şē·ot'ō·my, *n.* [Gr. *symphysis*, symphysis, and *temnein*, to cut.] in surgery, the division of the fibrocartilage of the symphysis pubis, in order to facilitate childbirth by increasing the anteroposterior diameter of the pelvis.

sym·phyş'iç, *a.* characterized by fusion of adjacent parts.

sym·phys'i·ŏn, *n.* the middle point of the outer border of the alveolar process of the lower jaw.

sym"phy·si·or'rha·phy (-rȧ-), *n.* [Gr. *symphysis*, symphysis, and *rhaphē*, suture.] suture of a divided symphysis.

sym'phy·sis, *n.*; *pl.* **sym'phy·sēs,** [LL., from Gr. *symphysis*, a growing together; *syn*, together, and *phyein*, to grow.]

1. in anatomy and zoology, (a) the growing together of bones originally separate, as of the two halves of the lower jaw or the two pubic bones; (b) the line of junction of such bones.

2. in botany, the growing together of similar parts of a plant; coalescence.

symphysis pubis; the junction of the pubic bones.

sym"phy·sō·daç·tyl'i·ȧ, *n.* [Gr. *symphysis*, symphysis, and *daktylos*, finger.] fusion of the fingers or toes.

sym·phy·sot'ō·my, *n.* symphyseotomy.

sym'phy·tiṣm, *n.* [Gr. *symphytos*, growing together; *syn*, together, and *phytos*, shaped by nature, grown, from *phyein*, to grow.] coalescence; fusion. [Rare.]

Sym'phy·tum, *n.* [LL.] a genus of plants of the borage family. *Symphytum officinale* is the comfrey of Europe and North America.

sym"pi·ē·ṣom'ē·tẽr, *n.* [Gr. *sympiesis*, compression; *syn*, together, and *piezein*, to press, and *-meter*.]

1. an instrument for measuring the weight of the atmosphere by the compression of a column of gas. It consists of a column of oil, supported by atmospheric pressure, and rising against a body of hydrogen gas, which acts like a spring against the column of oil, and as the elasticity of the hydrogen varies with every change of temperature, a movable thermometer scale is attached for making the necessary corrections.

2. an instrument for determining the pressure exerted by currents of water.

sym"pi·ē·zom'ē·tẽr, *n.* same as *sympiesometer*.

sym·pleç'tiç, *a.* [Gr. *symplektikos*, twining together; *syn*, together, and *plekein*, to twine.] related or pertaining to the symplectic.

sym·pleç'tiç, *n.* a bone found in many fishes, situated in the midst of the bones which form the tympanic pedicle.

sym'plē·sīte, *n.* [Gr. *syn*, together, and *plēsiazein*, to approach.] a green monoclinic hydrous iron arsenate, occurring in tufts of small prismatic crystals in cavities in siderite.

Sym·plō·çãr'pus, *n.* [Gr. *symplokē*, an interweaving, and *karpos*, fruit.] a genus of araceous plants containing but one species, the skunk cabbage.

sym'plō·cē, *n.* [Gr. *symplokē*, an intertwining; *syn*, together, and *plekein*, to twine.] in rhetoric, the repetition of a word at the beginning and another at the end of successive clauses. Example: *Mercy* descended from heaven to dwell on the *earth*; *Mercy* fled back to heaven and left the *earth*.

Sym'plō·ços, *n.* [Gr., intertwined.] a genus of trees and shrubs of which the horse sugar is a species. The genus includes between 160 and 170 species, native to America, Asia, and Australia.

sym'pōde, *n.* same as *sympodium*.

sym·pō'di·ăl, *a.* pertaining to or characteristic of a sympodium.

sym·pō'di·ăl·ly, *adv.* in the manner of a sympodium.

sym·pō'di·um, *n.*; *pl.* **sym·pō'di·ȧ,** [LL., from Gr. *syn*, with, and *pous*, *podos*, foot.] in botany, a stem made up of a series of branches growing on each other, giving the effect of a simple stem.

sym·pō'ṣi·aç, *a.* having the nature of, appropriate to, or pertaining to a symposium; as, *symposiac* meetings.

sym·pō'ṣi·aç, *n.* a symposium.

sym·pō'ṣi·ăl, *a.* symposiac.

sym·pō'ṣi·ärch, *n.* [Gr. *symposion*, a drinking party, and *archein*, to rule.]

1. in ancient Greece, the master of a feast or symposium.

2. one who presides at a banquet; a toastmaster.

sym·pō'ṣi·ast, *n.* one of the participants in a symposium. [Rare.]

sym·pō'ṣi·ŏn, *n.* a symposium.

sym·pō'ṣi·um, *n.*; *pl.* **sym·pō'ṣi·umṣ, sym·pō'ṣi·ȧ,** [L., from Gr. *symposion*, a drinking party, from *sympinein*, to drink together; *syn*, together, and *pinein*, to drink.]

1. in ancient Greece, an entertainment characterized by drinking, music, and intellectual discussion.

2. any meeting or social gathering at which ideas are freely exchanged.

3. a conference organized for the discussion of some particular subject.

4. a collection of opinions or essays on a given subject.

symp'tŏm, *n.* ME. *symthoma*, from Gr. *symptōma*, anything that has befallen one, a casualty: usually in a bad sense; *syn*, together, and *piptein*, to fall.]

1. in medicine, any condition accompanying or resulting from a disease and serving as an aid in diagnosis; a perceptible change in the body or its functions which indicates disease.

2. a sign or token; that which indicates the existence or occurrence of something else; as, open murmurs of the people are a *symptom* of disaffection to law or government.

Syn.—indication, mark, sign, token.

symp·tō·mat'iç, symp·tō·mat'i·çăl, *a.* 1. of or having to do with symptoms.

2. that constitutes a symptom (*of* something, especially disease).

3. in accordance with symptoms; as, a *symptomatic* treatment.

symp·tō·mat'i·çăl·ly, *adv.* by means of symptoms; with regard to symptoms.

symp'tō·mȧ·tīze, *v.t.*; symptomatized, *pt.*, *pp.*; symptomatizing, *ppr.* to exhibit symptoms of; to show by symptoms; to indicate.

symp·tō·mat·ō·loġ'i·çăl, *a.* pertaining to symptomatology.

symp·tō·mat·ō·loġ'i·çăl·ly, *adv.* in a symptomatological manner.

symp"tō·mȧ·tol'ō·ġy, *n.* the branch of medicine which treats of the symptoms of diseases; semiology.

symp·tō'sis, *n.* [Gr. *symptōsis*, meeting, from *syn*, together, and *ptōsis*, fall.] the gradual wasting of the whole body or of any organ or part.

syn-, [from Gr. *syn*, with.] a prefix meaning *with, together with, at the same time, by means of*, as in *syn*agogue, *syn*apse: *syn-* assimilates to *syl-* before *l*, as in *syl*logism; *sym-* before *m*, *p*, *b*, as in *sym*biosis; *sys-* before *s* and before an aspirate *h*, as in *sys*tole, *sys*tem.

syn·aer'e·sis, *n.* same as *syneresis*.

syn·aes·thē'si·ȧ (-zhȧ), *n.* same as *synesthesia*.

syn·ȧ·goġ'i·çăl, *a.* pertaining to a synagogue.

syn'ȧ·gogue (-gog), *n.* [Fr. from LL. *synagoga*, from Gr. *synagōgē*, a bringing together, assembly; *syn*, together, and *agein*, to bring, drive.]

1. a congregation or assembly of Jews for worship and religious study.

2. a building or place used by Jews for worship and religious study.

3. the Jewish religion as organized in such local congregations.

4. any assembly of men. [Obs.]

The Great Synagogue; in Jewish history, an assembly or council of 120 members said to have been founded and presided over by Ezra after the return from the captivity.

syn·ȧ·lē'phȧ, *n.* see *synaloepha*.

syn·ȧ·lē'phē, syn·ȧ·loe'phē, *n.* same as *synaloepha*.

syn·al'ġi·ȧ, *n.* referred pain; pain at one place caused by a hurt at another.

syn"ăl·lag·mat'iç, *a.* [Gr. *synallagma*, a mutual agreement, from *synallassein*, to have dealings with, to enter into contracts; *syn*, with, and *allassein*, to repay, interchange.] in civil law, imposing reciprocal obligations upon the parties.

syn·ăl·lax'ine, *a.* of or belonging to the genus *Synallaxis*.

Syn·ăl·lax'is, *n.* [Gr. *synallaxis*, commerce, exchange.] a genus of birds resembling the true creepers, ranging from Patagonia to Mexico.

syn·ȧ·loe'phȧ, syn·ȧ·lē'phȧ, *n.* [L. *synalœpha*; Gr. *synaloiphē*, lit., a melting together, from *syn-*, together, and *aleiphein*, to smear, anoint.] the contraction into one syllable of two adjacent vowels, usually by elision. Example: *th'eagle* for *the eagle*.

syn'ange, *n.* same as *synangium*, sense 2.

syn·an'ġi·ăl, *a.* of, relating to, or designating a synangium.

syn·an'ġi·um, *n.*; *pl.* **syn·an'ġi·ȧ,** [*syn-*, and Gr. *angeion*, a vessel, jar.]

1. in anatomy and zoology, a common trunk from which several arteries branch; also, in the lower vertebrates, the terminal part of an arterial trunk.

2. in botany, a boat-shaped spore case produced from a group of epidermal cells, characteristic of ferns of the genus *Marattia*, or allied genera.

Syn'ȧ·non, *n.* [after a treatment center founded (1958) in Santa Monica, California: supposedly from a patient's slurred pronunciation of "symposium," and "seminar."] [*also* s-]

1. a method of group psychotherapy for treating narcotic addiction.

2. a group of inpatients undergoing such therapy.

syn·an'thous, *a.* [*syn-*, and Gr. *anthos*, a flower.] in botany, (a) characterized by synanthy; (b) having the flowers and leaves appearing at the same time.

syn·an'thy, *n.* in botany, the more or less complete union of several flowers that are usually distinct.

syn·apse', *n.* [Mod. L. *synapsis*; Gr. *synapsis*, union, joining.] the point of contact between adjacent neurons, where nerve impulses are transmitted from one to the other.

syn·ap'sis, *n.*; *pl.* **syn·ap'sēṣ,** 1. in genetics, the conjugation of maternal and paternal pairs of homologous chromosomes. It is the first step in meiosis.

2. in physiology, a synapse.

syn·ap'tiç, sȳn·ap'ti·çăl, *a.* of synapsis or a synapse.

syn·ap·tiç'ū·lȧ, *n.*; *pl.* **syn·ap·tiç'ū·lae,** [LL., from Gr. *synaptos*, bound together.] one of the various transverse calcareous bars which stretch across the interseptal loculi in the *Fungiidæ*, and form a kind of trelliswork, uniting the opposite faces of adjacent septa.

syn·ap'tō·sōme, *n.* [from *synapse*, and *-some*.] a nerve ending pinched off at the synapse.

syn·är·tē'sis, *n.* [from Gr. *synartan*, to fasten together.] a fastening or knitting together; the state of being closely united; close or intimate union.

syn·är·thrō'di·ȧ, *n.* same as *synarthrosis*.

syn·är·thrō'sis, *n.* [Gr. *synarthrōsis*, a being joined together; *syn*, together, and *arthroun*, to fasten by a joint.] in anatomy, any of various immovable articulations, or joints.

syn'as·try, *n.* [*syn-*, and Gr. *astēr*.] coincidence as regards stellar influence; the state of having similar starry influences presiding over one's fortunes as determined by astrological calculation.

syn·ax'is, *n.*; *pl.* **syn·ax'ēṣ,** [Gr., from *synagein*, to bring together; *syn*, together, and *agein*, to bring.] in the early church, a congregation; also, a celebration of the Eucharist.

syn'çärp, *n.* [LL. *syncarpium*, from Gr. *syn*, together, and *karpos*, fruit.] in botany, an aggregate fruit having the pericarps adherent into a solid mass; a collective fruit, as a blackberry.

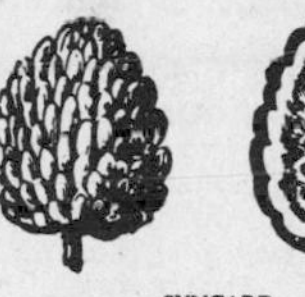

SYNCARP (fruit of *Anona squamosa*)

syn·çär'pi·um, *n.*; *pl.* **syn·çär'pi·ȧ,** same as *syncarp*.

syn·çär'pous, *a.* [*syn-*, and Gr. *karpos*, fruit.]

1. composed of two or more pistils growing together.

2. of a syncarp.

syn·çat·ē·gor·ē·mat'iç, *a.* [Gr. *synkatēgorēmatikos*; *syn*, together, and *katēgorēma*, a predicate.] in logic, designating a word which cannot be used as a term by itself, as an adverb or preposition.

syn·çat·ē·gor·ē·mat'iç, *n.* a syncategorematic word.

syn·çat·ē·gor·ē·mat'i·çăl·ly, *adv.* after the manner of a syncategorematic.

syn·cer'ē·brăl, *a.* pertaining to a syncerebrum.

syn·cer'ē·brum, *n.* [*syn-*, and L. *cerebrum*, the brain.] in entomology, a compound brain.

syn̄·çhon·drō'si·ăl, *a.* pertaining to or resembling synchondrosis.

syn̄·çhon·drō'sis, *n.* [*syn-*, and Gr. *chondros*, cartilage.] a synarthrosis in which the union is of cartilage.

syn̄·çhon·drot'ō·my, *n.* in surgery, symphyseotomy.

syn̄·çhō·rē'sis, *n.* [Gr. *synchōrēsis*, concession, from *synchōrein*, to come together, meet.] in rhetoric, a concession allowed, in order to make a more pointed retort.

syn̄′çhrō·mesh, *a.* [*synchro*nized and *mesh*.] in motor vehicles, designating or employing a device by which synchronized shifting can be effected.

syn̄′çhrō·mesh, *n.* 1. a synchromesh gear system.
 2. any gear in such a system.

syn̄′çhrō·năl, *a.* [*syn-*, and Gr. *chronos*, time.] same as *synchronous*.

syn̄′çhrō·năl, *n.* that which happens at the same time with something else, or pertains to the same time.

syn·çhron′iç, *a.* same as *synchronous*.

syn·çhron′i·căl, *a.* same as *synchronic*.

syn·çhron′i·căl·ly, *adv.* in a synchronic manner; simultaneously.

syn̄′çhrō·nişm, *n.* [Gr. *synchronismos*, agreement of time, from *synchronos*, contemporaneous; *syn*, together, and *chronos*, time.]
 1. the fact or state of being synchronous; concurrence of two or more events in time; simultaneousness.
 2. a chronological listing of persons or events in history.
 3. in painting, the representation, in the same picture, of events happening at different times.

syn̄·çhrō·nis′tiç, *a.* pertaining to synchronism; synchronous.

syn̄·çhrō·nis′ti·căl, *a.* synchronistic.

syn̄″çhrō·ni·zā′tion, *n.* a synchronizing or being synchronized; as, the *synchronization* of sound and action in motion pictures.

syn̄′chrō·nīze, *v.i.*; synchronized, *pt.*, *pp.*; synchronizing, *ppr.* to move or occur at the same time or rate; to have the same timing; to be synchronous; as, the clocks are *synchronized*.

syn̄′chrō·nīze, *v.t.* 1. to cause to agree in rate or speed; to regulate (clocks, a flashgun and camera shutter, etc.) so as to make synchronous.
 2. to assign (events, etc.) to the same date or period; to represent as or show to be coincident or simultaneous.
 3. in motion pictures, (a) to add or adjust (sound effects or dialogue) so as to coincide with the action of a picture; (b) to add or adjust such sound effects or dialogue to (a picture).

syn̄′çhrō·nīzed shift′ing, a type of gear shifting in motor vehicles, in which the gears to be meshed are automatically brought to the same speed of rotation before the shift is completed.

syn̄′çhrō·nī·zer, *n.* one who or that which synchronizes; specifically, an instrument for synchronizing clocks.

syn̄·çhrō·nol′ō·ġy, *n.* [Gr. *synchronos*, contemporaneous, and *-logy*.] chronological arrangement of synchronous events side by side.

syn̄·çhron′ō·sçōpe, *n.* a synchroscope.

syn̄′çhrō·nous, *a.* [LL. *synchronus*; Gr. *synchronos*.]
 1. happening at the same time; occurring together; simultaneous.
 2. having the same period between movements, occurrences, etc.; having the same rate and phase, as vibrations.
 synchronous curve; a synchrone.
 synchronous machine; an alternating-current motor, generator, or converter whose normal operating speed is exactly proportional to the frequency of the current by which it is supplied.
 synchronous speed; a fixed speed for an alternating-current machine, determined by the frequency of the current by which it is supplied.

syn̄′çhrō·nous·ly, *adv.* at the same time.

syn̄′çhrō·ny, *n.* same as *synchronism*, senses 1 and 2.

syn̄′çhrō·sçōpe, *n.* [*synchro*nism and *-scope*.] a device for indicating the degree of synchronism, as between two or more airplane engines: also *synchronoscope*.

syn̄′çhrō·tron, *n.* [*synchro*nize and elec*tron*.] a type of cyclotron for accelerating the velocities of charged particles, especially of electrons, through the use of a low-frequency magnetic field in combination with a high-frequency electrostatic field.

syn̄′çhrō·tron rā·di·ā′tion, the electromagnetic radiation given off by high-energy particles, as electrons, as they spiral at a speed close to the speed of light in a strong magnetic field, as in combination with a high-frequency electrostatic field.

syn̄′çhy·sis, *n.* [Gr. *synchysis*, a commixture; *syn*, together, and *chysis*, a pouring, from *chein*, to pour.] confusion; specifically, (a) confusion of words in a sentence; (b) a softening of humors in the eye.

syn·çlas′tiç, *a.* [*syn-*, and Gr. *klastos*, broken.] having curvatures all in the same direction, that is, all convex or all concave, at any given point: said of a surface, as of a sphere: opposed to *anticlastic*.

syn·çlī′năl (*or* sing′kli-), *a.* [Gr. *synklinein*, to incline together; *syn*, together, and *klinein*, to incline.]
 1. inclined downward from opposite directions, so as to meet in a common point or line.
 2. of, formed by, or forming a syncline.
 synclinal valley; a valley formed by synclinal strata.

syn·çlī′năl, *n.* in geology, a synclinal line, axis, or fold; a syncline.

syn̄′çlīne, *n.* in geology, a fold of stratified rock inclining upward in opposite directions from both sides of its axis: opposed to *anticline*.

syn·çlin′i·căl, *a.* synclinal.

syn̄·çli·nō′ri·um, *n.*; *pl.* **syn̄·çli·nō′ri·á**, [LL.] in geology, a mountain or a group of mountains supposed to have been formed by the upheaval of a pre-existent geosynclinal.

syn·çlit′iç, *a.* pertaining to or marked by synclitism.

syn̄′çlit·işm, *n.* in obstetrics, parallelism between the planes of the fetal head and those of the maternal pelvis.

syn̄′çō·păl, *a.* pertaining to or characterized by syncope.

syn̄′çō·pāte, *v.t.*; syncopated, *pt.*, *pp.*; syncopating, *ppr.* [LL. *syncopatus*, pp. of *syncopare*, to swoon; L. *syncope*, *syncopa*, a swooning, in grammar, a syncope, from Gr. *synkopē*, a cutting short; *syn*, together, and *koptein*, to cut.]
 1. to shorten (a word) by syncope.
 2. in music, (a) to begin (a tone) on an unaccented beat and continue it through the next unaccented beat, or to begin (a tone) on the last half of a beat and continue it through the first half of the following beat; (b) to use such shifted accents in (a musical composition, passage, etc.).

syn̄·çō·pā′tion, *n.* 1. a syncopating or being syncopated.
 2. syncopated music.
 3. in grammar, syncope.

SYNCOPATION

syn̄′çō·pā·tŏr, *n.* one who syncopates.

syn̄′çō·pē, *n.* [L., from Gr. *synkopē*, a cutting short; *syn*, together, and *koptein*, to cut.]
 1. in music, syncopation.
 2. in grammar, an elision of one or more letters or sounds from the middle of a word, as in *Wooster* for *Worcester*.
 3. in medicine, a fainting, swooning, or loss of consciousness, caused by a temporary deficiency of blood supply to the brain.

syn̄′çō·pist, *n.* one who shortens words by the use of syncope. [Rare.]

syn̄′çō·pīze, *v.t.*; syncopized, *pt.*, *pp.*; syncopizing, *ppr.* to syncopate.

syn·çot·y·lē′dŏn·ous, *a.* [*syn-*, and Gr. *kotylēdōn*, a cup-shaped hollow.] having cotyledons united as if grown together.

syn·çran·tē′ri·ăn, *a.* [*syn-*, and Gr. *krantēres*, the wisdom teeth.] having a continuous row of teeth, as certain reptiles: opposed to *diacranterian*.

syn·çret′iç, *n.* a syncretist.

syn·çret′iç, *a.* same as *syncretistic*.

syn̄′çrē·tişm, *n.* [Fr. *syncrétisme*, from Gr. *synkrētismos*, the union of two parties against a third, from *synkrētizein*, to make two parties join against a third.]
 1. the combination or reconciliation of differing beliefs in religion, philosophy, etc., or an attempt to effect such compromise.
 2. in philology, the merging into one of two or more differently inflected grammatical categories.

syn̄′çrē·tist, *n.* one who advocates or practices syncretism; especially, a follower of Calixtus, a Lutheran divine of the seventeenth century.

syn̄·çrē·tis′tiç, *a.* of or pertaining to the syncretists or to syncretism; characterized by syncretism.

syn̄′çrē·tīze, *v.t.* and *v.i.*; syncretized, *pt.*, *pp.*; syncretizing, *ppr.* to attempt to harmonize or blend; to combine or reconcile, as varying principles or parties.

syn̄′çri·sis, *n.* [Gr., a comparison; *syn*, together, and *krisis*, a choosing, from *krinein*, to decide, judge.] in rhetoric, a figure of speech in which opposite things or persons are compared; contrast.

syn·çyt′i·ăl, *a.* pertaining to a syncytium.

syn·çyt′i·um, *n.*; *pl.* **syn·çyt′i·á**, [LL., from Gr. *syn*, together, and *kytos*, the hollow of a shield, breastplate, vessel, or jar.] tissue consisting of a mass of protoplasm, wholly lacking cell walls but containing nuclei, as in striped muscle, or a sponge ectoderm.

syn·daç′tyl, syn·daç′tyle, *a.* [from *syn-* and Gr. *-daktylos*, fingered, from *daktylos*, finger, toe.] having two or more digits united, as by webbing.

syn·daç′tyl, syn·daç′tyle, *n.* a syndactyl animal or bird or, abnormally, person.

syn·daç·tyl′i·á, *n.* syndactylism.

syn·daç·tyl′iç, *a.* syndactyl.

syn·daç′tyl·işm, *n.* the condition of being syndactyl.

syn·daç′tyl·ous, *a.* syndactyl.

syn·des·mog′rȧ·phy, *n.* [Gr. *syndesmos*, a ligament, and *-graphy*.] in anatomy, a description of the ligaments and joints of the body.

syn·des·mol′ō·ġy, *n.* [Gr. *syndesmos*, a ligament, and *-logy*.] the anatomy of the ligaments.

syn·des·mō′sis, *n.* [Gr. *syndesmos*, a ligament.] in anatomy, the union of one bone with another by ligaments or membranes.

syn·des·mot′iç, *a.* of, having the nature of, or characterized by syndesmosis; united by ligaments.

syn·det′iç, syn·det′i·căl, *a.* [Gr. *syndetikos*, from *syndetos*, bound hand and foot; *syn*, together, and *dein*, to bind.] connecting or connected by means of conjunctions; connective; conjoining: opposed to *asyndetic*.

syn·det′i·căl·ly, *adv.* conjunctively; in a syndetic manner.

syn′diç, *n.* [Fr.; LL. *syndicus*, from Gr. *syndikos*, adj., helping in a court of justice, as n., a syndic; *syn*, with, and *dikē*, justice.]
 1. the business agent or manager of a corporation, especially of a university.
 2. variously, any of certain government officials; especially, a civil magistrate or the like.
 3. in law, one chosen to transact business for others; an assignee or an advocate; as, in France, *syndics* are appointed by the creditors of a bankrupt to manage the property.

syn′di·căl, *a.* of a syndic.

syn′di·căl·işm, *n.* [Fr. *syndicalisme*, from *syndical*, of a syndic or labor union (*chambre syndicale*), from *syndic*.] a theory and movement of trade unionism, originating in France, in which all means of production and distribution would be brought under the control of federations of labor unions by the use of direct action, such as general strikes.

syn′dic·ăl·ist, *n.* one who believes in or advocates syndicalism.

syn″di·căl·is′tiç, *a.* of, like, or characteristic of syndicalism.

syn′di·çāte, *n.* [Fr. *syndicat*; ML. *syndicatus*, from *syndicus*, a syndic.]
 1. a body, group, or council of syndics; the office of a syndic.
 2. an association of bankers, corporations, etc. formed to carry out some financial project requiring much capital, especially to gain control of the market in a particular commodity.
 3. any group organized to further some undertaking.
 4. an association of criminals set up to control vice, gambling, etc.
 5. a group of similar organizations, as of newspapers, owned by one company.
 6. an organization that sells special articles or features to a number of different newspapers for simultaneous publication.

syn′di·çāte, *v.t.*; syndicated, *pt.*, *pp.*; syndicating, *ppr.* [from ML. *syndicatus*, pp. of *syndicare*, to censure.] 1. to judge or to censure. [Obs.]
 2. to manage as or form into a syndicate.
 3. to sell (an article, feature, etc.) through a syndicate for simulataneous publication in a number of newspapers.

syn′di·çāte, *v.i.* to form a syndicate.

syn·di·cā'tion, *n.* a syndicating or being syndicated.

syn'drōme, *n.* [Gr. *syndromē*, a running together; *syn*, together, and *dromos*, a running, a course.]
 1. concurrence. [Rare.]
 2. in medicine, a number of symptoms occurring together and characterizing a specific disease.

syn·dy·aṣ'mi·ăn, *a.* [Gr. *syndyasmos*, a pairing; *syn*, together, and *dyo*, two.] of or relating to sexual pairing, as of animals while procreating and rearing their young.

sȳne, *adv.* 1. since; ago. [Scot.]
 2. afterward; then; next; as, he did that and *syne* something else. [Scot.]
 auld lang syne; see under *auld*.
 soon or syne; sooner or later.

sȳne, *conj.* and *prep.* since; ago. [Scot.]

syn·eç'dō·çhē, *n.* [L., from Gr. *synekdochē*, lit., a receiving together; *syn*, together, and *ekdechesthai*, to receive.] in rhetoric, a figure of speech, by which the whole of a thing is put for a part, or a part for the whole. Example: *bread* for *food*, or *the army* for *a soldier*.

syn·eç·doçh'i·çăl, *a.* of the nature of or expressed by synecdoche; implying a synecdoche.

syn·eç·doçh'i·çăl·ly, *adv.* in a synecdochical manner; by means of synecdoche.

syn·ē·çhī'ȧ, *n.* [Gr. *synecheia*, continuity, adherence, from *synechein*, to hold together; *syn*, together, and *echein*, to hold.] a diseased adhesion of parts, especially of the iris to the cornea.
 annular or *circular synechia*; adhesion of the rim of the iris to the lens.
 anterior synechia; adhesion of the iris to the cornea.
 posterior synechia; adhesion of the iris to the capsule of the lens.
 total synechia; adhesion of the whole surface of the iris to the lens.

syn·ē'cious, *a.* synoecious.

syn·eç·phō·nē'sis, *n.*, [Gr., from *synekphōnein*, to utter together; *syn*, with, and *ekphōnein*, to cry out; *ek*, out, and *phōnein*, to sound, to call, from *phōnē*, sound, voice.] in grammar, a contraction of two syllables into one; syneresis.

syn·ē'drăl, *a.* in botany, growing on the angles of a stem: said of leaves, etc.

Syn·ed'ri·ŏn, Syn·ed'ri·um, *n.* same as *Sanhedrin*.

syn·ē'drous, *a.* [Gr. *synedros*, sitting together; *syn*, together, and *hedra*, seat.] in botany, same as *synedral*.

syn·en'tog·nath, *n.* in zoology, any fish of the *Synentognathi*.

Syn·en·tog'nȧ·thī, *n.pl.* [*syn-*, Gr. *entos*, within, and *gnathos*, jaw.] a group of teleocephalous fishes with spineless fins and closed sounds.

syn·en·tog'nȧ·thous, *a.* pertaining to or possessing the characteristics of the *Synentognathi*.

syn·er'e·sis, syn·aer'e·sis, *n.* [Mod. L. *synæresis*; Gr. *synairesis*, a taking together; *syn*, together, and *hairein*, to take.]
 1. the contraction of two consecutive vowels or syllables into one syllable, especially so as to form a diphthong: opposed to *dieresis*.
 2. synizesis.

syn·ẽr·ġet'iç, *a.* [Gr. *synergētikos*, a working together; *syn*, together, and *ergon*, work.] working in co-operation.

syn·ẽr'ġiç, *a.* of or characterized by synergy.

syn·ẽr'ġid, *n.* in botany, a synergida.

syn·ẽr'ġi·dȧ, *n.*; *pl.* **syn·ẽr'ġi·dae,** [Gr. *synergos*, working together, and *-ida*.] in botany, either of the two naked co-operating cells at the apex of the embryo sac.

syn·ẽr'ġi·dăl, *a.* of or pertaining to synergidae.

syn'ẽr·ġiṣm, *n.* [Mod. L. *synergismus*, from Gr. *synergos*, working together.]
 1. in theology, a doctrine of a faction in the Lutheran church who, about the end of the sixteenth century, denied that God was the sole agent in effecting regeneration and affirmed that man co-operated with divine grace in the accomplishment of this.
 2. the simultaneous action of separate agencies which, together, have greater total effect than the sum of their individual effects: said especially of drugs.

syn'ẽr·ġist, *n.* 1. in theology, a supporter of the doctrine of synergism.
 2. a synergetic organ, muscle, drug, etc.

syn·ẽr·ġis'tiç, *a.* same as *synergetic*.

syn'ẽr·ġy, *n.* [Gr. *synergia*, joint work, from *synergein*, to work together.] combined or co-operative action or force; specifically, in medicine, (a) the combined or correlated action of different organs or parts of the body, as in performing complex movements; (b) the combined or correlated action of two or more drugs.

syn'ē·sis, *n.* [Gr. *synesis*, sagacity, quick perception.] grammatical construction which conforms to the meaning rather than to strict syntactical agreement or reference. Example: *Most* of the team *are* invalided.

syn·es·thē'ṣi·ȧ (-zhȧ), *n.* [Mod. L. *synæsthesia*, from Gr. *syn-*, together, and *aisthēsis*, sensation.]
 1. in physiology, sensation felt in one part of the body when another part is stimulated.
 2. in psychology, a process in which one type of stimulus produces a secondary, subjective sensation, as when a specific color evokes a specific smell sensation.
 Also spelled *synaesthesia*.

syn'fū·el, *n.* [*syn*thetic and *fuel*.] a fuel produced as by extracting oil from coal or methane from plant cellulose, and used as a substitute, as for petroleum or natural gas.

syn·gam'iç, *a.* of or characteristic of syngamy.

syn̄'gȧ·mous, *a.* same as *syngamic*.

syn̄'gȧ·my, *n.* [*syn-* and *-gamy*.]
 1. sexual reproduction; union of male and female gametes to form a fertilized ovum.
 2. conjugation.

Syn·ġē·nē'si·ȧ, *n.pl.* [LL., from Gr. *syn*, with, and *genesis*, origin, generation.] in botany, a Linnaean class of plants whose stamens are united in a cylindrical form by the anthers.

syn·ġē·nē'siăn (-shăn), **syn·ġē·nē'sious** (-shus) *a.* of, pertaining to, or having the characteristics of the *Syngenesia*.

syn·ġen'e·sis, *n.* [LL., from Gr. *syn*, with, and *genesis*, generation, origin.] sexual reproduction; also, a theory that the embryo is the joint product of the male and female elements, and that the original germ sometimes contains the germs of all subsequent generations: opposed to *epigenesis*.

syn·ġen'iç, *a.* same as *syngenetic*.

syn·ġē·net'iç, *a.* of or characteristic of syngenesis; reproduced sexually.

Syng'nȧ·thī, *n.pl.* [*syn-*, and Gr. *gnathos*, jaw.] a suborder of lophobranchiate fishes, including the pipefish, sea horse, etc., named from their jaws being united and elongated to form a tubular snout.

syng'nȧ·thid, *n.* one of the *Syngnathi*.

syng'nȧ·thous, *a.* having the jaws united and drawn out into a tube-shaped snout.

syn̄'grȧph, *n.* a writing signed by all the parties to a contract or bond.

syn·i·zē'sis, *n.* [L.; Gr., a settlement, collapse, from *synizanein*, to sink in, collapse.]
 1. the contraction of two adjacent vowels into a single syllable, as in Latin, without forming a diphthong.
 2. in biology, the massing of the chromatin in meiosis just before the maturation division.
 3. an obliteration of the pupil of the eye; a closure of the pupil.

syn·neū·rō'sis, *n.* same as *syndesmosis*.

syn'ō·çhȧ, syn'ō·çhus, *n.* [Gr. *synochos*, continued.] in medicine, a continued fever. [Rare.]

syn·oç'rē·āte, *a.* in botany, noting stipules uniting on the opposite side of a stem from the leaf and enclosing the stem in a sheath.

syn'ŏd, *n.* [ME. *sinod*, from *sinoth*; AS. *synoth*; L. *synodus*, from Gr. *synodos*, lit., a coming together; *syn*, together, and *hodos*, way.]
 1. a meeting or assembly of churches or church delegates for mutual deliberation on matters affecting the churches to which they belong, and designed for their guidance; ecclesiastical council.
 2. among the Presbyterians, a court intermediate between the general assembly and a presbytery, or, if no assembly exist, it is then itself the highest court. It is divided into presbyteries, of which there are never less than three. Each congregation is represented by a minister and an elder.
 3. any assembly or council.
 4. in astronomy, a conjunction of two or more planets or stars. [Obs.]
 General Synod; a council of supreme authority in the Evangelican Lutheran, the Reformed (Dutch), and the Reformed (German) churches in the United States.
 Holy Synod; see under *holy*.
 Particular Synod; an ecclesiastical court, of the Reformed (German) Church in the United States and of the Reformed (Dutch) Church, more limited than the General Synod.

syn'ŏd·ăl, *a.* pertaining to, occasioned by, or proceeding from a synod.

syn'ŏd·ăl, *n.* 1. formerly, in England, a pecuniary tribute paid to the bishop or archdeacon at the time of his Easter visitation by every parish priest; a procuration. [Obs.]
 2. a constitution made in a provincial or diocesan synod.

syn·od'iç, *a.* synodical.

syn·od'i·çăl, *a.* 1. synodal; pertaining to a synod; transacted in a synod; as, *synodical* proceedings or forms; a *synodical* epistle.
 2. in astronomy, of or having to do with conjunction, especially with the period in which two heavenly bodies pass from one conjunction to another; as, a *synodical* month.
 Synodical Conference; a conference of strict Evangelical Lutherans of the central western States of the United States, organized in 1872.
 synodical month; the period from one conjunction of the moon with the sun to another; a lunation.

syn·od'i·çăl·ly, *adv.* in the manner of or by means of a synod.

syn'ŏd·ist, *n.* one who adheres to a synod.

syn·oe'cious, *a.* [Gr. *synoikos*, dwelling in the same house, from *syn*, together, and *oikos*, house.] in botany, having male and female organs in the same flowers, as some composite plants, or in the same receptacle, as certain mosses: also spelled *synecious*.

syn·om'ō·sy, *n.* [Gr. *synōmosia*; *syn*, together, and *omnunai*, to swear.] sworn brotherhood; a society in ancient Greece closely resembling a modern political society: its members were leagued by oath.

syn'ō·nym, *n.* [Fr. *synonyme*; L. *synonyma*, from Gr. *synōnymon*, of like meaning or like name; *syn*, with, and *onyma*, name.]
 1. a word having the same or nearly the same meaning in one or more senses as another of the same language: opposed to *antonym*.
 2. a metonym.
 3. in biology, an incorrect or outmoded systemic name.

syn·on'y·măl, *a.* synonymous. [Obs.]

syn·on'y·măl·ly, *adv.* synonymously. [Obs.]

syn·on·y·mat'iç, *a.* synonymic.

syn'ō·nyme, *n.* same as *synonym*.

syn·ō·nym'iç, *a.* of, using, constituting, or relating to a synonym or synonyms.

syn·ō·nym'i·çăl, *a.* synonymic.

syn·ō·nym'i·çŏn, *n.* a book containing a list of synonyms. [Rare.]

syn·on'y·mist, *n.* one who lists and explains synonymous words.

syn·ō·nym'i·ty, *n.* the state or fact of being synonymous; identity of nature or meaning.

syn·on'y·mīze, *v.t.*; synonymized, *pt.*, *pp*; synonymizing, *ppr.* to express in different words of the same meaning; to furnish a synonym or synonyms for (a word).

syn·on'y·mous, *a.* [ML. *synonymus*; Gr. *synōnymos*, of like meaning or like name.] expressing the same or nearly the same meaning.

syn·on'y·mous·ly, *adv.* in a synonymous manner.

syn·on'y·my, *n.*; *pl.* **syn·on'y·mieṣ,** 1. the quality of expressing the same or nearly the same meaning by different words.
 2. the study of synonyms.
 3. a list or listing of synonyms.
 4. (a) the scientific names used in different nomenclature systems to designate the same species, etc.; (b) a list of such names.
 5. in rhetoric, a figure by which synonymous words are used to amplify a discourse.

syn·op'sis, *n.*; *pl.* **syn·op'sēṣ,** [LL., from Gr. *synopsis*, a general view; *syn*, together, and *opsis*, sight.] a statement giving a brief, general review or condensation; summary, as of a story.
 Syn.—abridgment, epitome, condensation, compendium.

syn·op'tiç, *a.* [Mod. L. *synopticus*; Gr. *synoptikos*, seeing the whole together, from *synopsis*, a general view, synopsis.]
 1. of or constituting a synopsis; presenting a general view or summary.
 2. giving an account from the same point of view: said especially [*often* S-] of the *Synoptic Gospels*.
 Synoptic Gospels; the Gospels of Saints Matthew, Mark, and Luke, because they present a synopsis or general view of the same series of events, whereas in the fourth, or St. John's, Gospel the narrative and discourses are different.

syn·op′tiç, *n.* one of the Synoptic Gospels; also, a synoptist.
syn·op′ti·çăl, *a.* synoptic.
syn·op′ti·çăl·ly, *adv.* in a synoptic manner.
syn·op′tiç chärt, a chart showing meteorological conditions over a region at a given time; weather map.
syn·op′tist, *n.* one of the writers of the Synoptic Gospels.
syn·os·tē·ō′sis, *n.* [*syn-*, and Gr. *osteon*, bone.] in anatomy, union by means of bone; union of bones by growth; ankylosis.
syn·os·tō′sis, *n.* same as *synosteosis.*
syn·os·tot′iç, syn·os·tot′i·çăl, *a.* in medicine, of, indicating, or relating to synosteosis.
syn·ō·veç′tō·my, *n.* excision of a synovial membrane.
syn·ō′vi·ȧ, *n.* [*syn-*, and L. *ovum*, egg.] a thick, viscid, yellowish-white fluid, somewhat resembling white of egg in appearance, secreted, for the purpose of lubricating the joints of the body, by a membrane which lines the joint cavities, tendon sheaths, etc.
syn·ō′vi·ăl, *a.* pertaining to synovia; secreting synovia; as, the *synovial* membrane; *synovial* gland.
synovial capsule; a closed membranous sac between movable articular surfaces.
synovial fluid; same as *synovia.*
synovial membrane; a dense smooth membrane of connective tissue in synovial cavities, which secretes synovia.
syn·ō′vin, *n.* the mucin found in synovia.
syn·ō·vī′tis, *n.* inflammation of a synovial membrane.
syn·pel′mous, *a.* same as *sympelmous.*
syn·sep′ăl·ous, *a.* in botany, having the sepals united.
syn·taç′ti·çăl, syn·taç′tiç, *a.* pertaining to or according to the rules of syntax.
syn·taç′ti·çăl·ly, *adv.* in a syntactical manner; according to the rules of syntax.
syn′tax, *n.* [Fr. *syntaxe*; LL. *syntaxis*; Gr. *syntaxis*, an arrangement, arranging; *syn*, together, and *taxis*, order.]
1. orderly or systematic arrangement. [Obs.]
2. (a) in grammar, the arrangement of words as elements in a sentence to show their relationship; sentence structure; (b) the branch of grammar dealing with this.
syn·tax′is, *n.* syntax. [Rare.]
syn·teç′tiç, syn·teç′ti·çăl, *a.* pertaining to syntexis; consumptive; wasting.
syn·tē·rē′sis, *n.* [Gr., a watching closely, from *syntērein*, to watch closely together; *syn*, together, and *tērein*, to watch, guard.]
1. in medicine, preservative or preventive treatment; prophylaxis.
2. in metaphysics, conscience regarded as the internal repository of the laws of right and wrong.
syn·tex′is, *n.* [Gr., from *syntēkein*, to waste away.] in medicine, a wasting of the body; consumption.
syn·thĕr′măl, *a.* alike in degree of heat.
syn′thē·sis, *n.*; *pl.* **syn′thē·sēş,** [L. *synthesis*, from Gr. *synthesis*, a putting together; *syn*, together, and *tithenai*, to place.]
1. composition; the putting of two or more things together so as to form a whole: opposed to *analysis.*
2. a whole made up of parts or elements put together.
3. in philosophy, deductive reasoning, from the simple elements of thought into the complex whole, from cause to effect, from a principle to its application, etc.
4. in chemistry, the act or process of making a compound by joining together elements, simpler compounds, or radicals.
5. in surgery, the union of the edges of a wound or the broken ends of a fractured bone.
syn′thē·sist, *n.* one who uses synthesis or follows a synthetic method.
syn′thē·sīze, *v.t.*; synthesized, *pt., pp.*; synthesizing, *ppr.* 1. to unite in one; to combine or produce by synthesis.
2. to form by bringing together separate parts; specifically, in chemistry, to produce by synthesis rather than by extraction, refinement, etc.
3. to treat synthetically.
syn′thē·sīz″ẽr, *n.* a person or thing that synthesizes; specifically, an electronic device containing filters, oscillators, and voltage-control amplifiers, used to produce sounds unobtainable from ordinary musical instruments.
syn·thet′iç, syn·thet′i·çăl, *a.* [Fr. *synthétique*; Gr. *synthetikos.*]
1. of, involving, or using synthesis: opposed to *analytic.*
2. produced by synthesis; specifically, produced by chemical synthesis, rather than of natural origin.
3. artificial; not real or genuine; as, *synthetic* enthusiasm.
4. characterized by the use of inflectional adjuncts, or affixes, to express syntactical relationships: opposed to *analytical.*
5. in biology, of a comprehensive type; comprising in a single organism characters which in the process of evolution will be specialized in different organisms.
synthetic geometry; elementary geometry, not involving the use of algebraic symbols or analysis: opposed to *analytic geometry.*
synthetic philosophy; the philosophy of Herbert Spencer: so called by him as being an attempt at fusing all the sciences into a coherent whole.
synthetic rubber; any of several substances resembling natural rubber, prepared by polymerization of butadiene, chloroprene, and other hydrocarbons.
syn·thet′iç, *n.* something synthetic; specifically, any substance produced by chemical synthesis.
syn·thet′i·çăl·ly, *adv.* in a synthetic manner; by synthesis.
syn·thet′i·cişm, *n.* the principles of synthesis; a tendency toward synthetic methods.
syn′thē·tist, *n.* one who synthesizes or is versed in synthesis.
syn′thē·tīze, *v.t.*; synthetized, *pt., pp.*; synthetizing, *ppr.* to synthesize.
syn′tō·my, *n.* [Gr. *syntomos*, strained, tight, from *syntemnein*, to cut short, to cut down.] brevity; conciseness: also written *syntomia.* [Rare.]
syn·ton′iç, *a.* [from *syn-*, and Gr. *tonos*, a tone; and *-ic.*] in radio, of, or having to do with, resonance.
syn′tō·nin, *n.* [Gr. *syntonos*, strained, tight.] muscle fibrin; the basis and principal constituent of the contractile tissues.
syn″tō·ni·zā′tion, *n.* the act or process of syntonizing.
syn′tō·nīze, *v.t.*; syntonized, *pt., pp.*; syntonizing, *ppr.* to tune or harmonize (radio transmitters and receivers) with each other.
syn′tō·nous, *a.* same as *syntonic.*
syn′tō·ny, *n.* in radio, resonance.
syn·traç′trix, *n.* the locus of a point on the tangent to a tractrix, which divides the constant line into parts of a determined length.
syn·trop′iç, syn·trop′i·çăl, *a.* [*syn-*, and Gr. *trepein*, to turn.] turning or pointing in the same direction; specifically, in anatomy, designating parts, or the position of such parts, which form a series of similar segments, as the ribs on one side.
syn·typ′iç, *a.* of or relating to the same type.
syn·typ′i·cişm, *n.* the state or quality of being syntypic.
sȳ′phẽr, *v.t.* [var. of *cipher.*] to overlap the chamfered edges of (planks, etc.) so as to form a smooth joint.
sȳ′phẽr joint, a lap joint for chamfered boards, leaving a flush surface.
syph′i·lide, *n.* a syphilitic skin lesion.
syph′i·lis, *n.* [from *Syphilus*, the name of a shepherd in Hieronymus Fracastorius' poem entitled *Syphilis, sive Morbus Gallicus*, published in 1530.] an infectious venereal disease, caused by a spirochete and usually transmitted by sexual intercourse or acquired congenitally: if untreated, it usually passes through three stages, the first (*primary syphilis*) characterized by a hard chancre on the genitals or other point of inoculation, the second (*secondary syphilis*) by variable lesions of the skin and mucous membranes, and the third (*tertiary syphilis*) by the infection and disablement of bones, muscles, nerve tissue, etc.
syph·i·lit′iç, *a.* pertaining to, caused by, or diseased with syphilis.
syph·i·lit′iç, *n.* a syphilitic person.
syph·i·lit′i·çăl·ly, *adv.* in a syphilitic manner.
syph″i·li·zā′tion, *n.* inoculation with the spirochete of syphilis in an attempt to cure or prevent the disease.
syph′i·līze, *v.t.*; syphilized, *pt., pp.*; syphilizing, *ppr.* to inoculate with the spirochete of syphilis.
syph′i·lō·dẽrm, *n.* [*syphilis*, and Gr. *derma*, skin.] a dermal lesion or eruption due to syphilis: also written *syphiloderma.*
syph″i·lō·dẽr′mȧ·tous, *a.* relating to syphilitic eruptions.
syph′i·loid, *a.* of a syphilitic character.
syph·i·lol′ō·ġist, *n.* a specialist in syphilology.
syph·i·lol′ō·ġy, *n.* the study and treatment of syphilis.
syph′i·lous, *a.* syphilitic.
sȳ′phŏn, *n.* and *v.* same as *siphon.*
Syr′ȧ·çūse, *n.* an Italian red wine.
syr·ette′, *n.* [*syringe* and *-ette.*] an injection unit consisting of a small, collapsible tube fitted with a hypodermic needle and filled with a single dose of medication: a trademark (*Syrette*).
Syr′i·aç, *n.* the ancient Aramaic language of Syria, spoken from the 3d century A.D. to the 13th.
Syr′i·aç, *a.* pertaining to Syria or its language; as, the *Syriac* version of the Pentateuch.
Syr′i·ȧ·cişm, *n.* a Syriac idiom.
Syr′i·ăn, *a.* pertaining to Syria, its people, their language, etc.
Syr′i·ăn, *n.* 1. a member of the Semitic people of Syria.
2. the modern Arabic dialect of the Syrians.
Syr′i·ăn·işm, *n.* same as *Syriacism.*
Syr′i·ärch, *n.* [LL. *Syriarcha*, from Gr. *Syriarchēs*, the chief priest of Syria; *Syria*, Syria, and *archein*, to rule.] the governor or chief priest of the province of Syria under the Roman Empire.
Syr′i·aşm, *n.* same as *Syriacism.*
Sy·rin̄′gȧ, *n.* [Mod. L., from Gr. *syrinx, syringos*, a pipe, a tube: said to be so called from the use of the plants for making pipes or pipestems.]
1. a genus of plants of the family *Oleaceæ*, with large, fragrant clusters of white, pink, red, purplish, or bluish flowers; also [s–], any plant of this genus; a lilac.
2. [s–] any of a group of ornamental shrubs of the saxifrage family, with white or creamy flowers; the mock orange, *Philadelphus coronarius.*
syr′inġe, *n.* [ME. *siringe*; ML. *sirynga*, from Gr. *syrinx, syringos*, a reed, pipe, tube.]
1. a device consisting of a narrow tube fitted at one end with a rubber bulb or piston by means of which a liquid can be drawn in and then ejected in a stream: used to inject fluids into the body, cleanse wounds, etc.
2. a syringium.
fountain syringe; an apparatus that injects a liquid by the force of gravity.
syr′inġe, *v.t.*; syringed, *pt., pp.*; syringing, *ppr.* to inject by means of a syringe; also, to wash and cleanse by injections from a syringe.
sy·rin′ġē·ăl, *a.* of or pertaining to the syrinx.
sy·rin′ġin, *n.* a bitter, crystalline glucoside obtained from lilac bark.
syr·in·ġī′tis, *n.* [Gr. *syrinx, syringos*, a pipe, tube, and *-itis.*] inflammation of the Eustachian tube.
sy·rin′ġi·um, *n.*; *pl.* **sy·rin′ġi·ȧ,** [Mod. L.] a syringelike organ in certain insects and larvae, from which a defensive liquid can be discharged.
sy·rin̄′gō·coēle, *n.* [LL., from Gr. *syrinx, syringos*, a pipe, tube, and *-coele.*] the canal in the center of the spinal cord.
sy·rin̄″gō·mȳ·ē′li·ȧ, *n.* [Mod. L., from Gr. *syrinx, syringos*, a reed, pipe, tube, and *myelos*, marrow.] a chronic, progressive disease of the spinal cord, characterized by the formation of cavities filled with liquid in the spinal substance and occurring most frequently in young adults.
sy·rin̄′gō·tōme, *n.* [Gr. *syringotomion.*] a kind of bistoury used in syringotomy.
syr·in·got′ō·my, *n.* [Gr. *syrinx, syringos*, a fistula, and *tomē*, a cutting, from *temnein*, to cut.] the operation of cutting a fistula.
syr′in̄x, *n.*; *pl.* **sy·rin′ġēş, syr′in̄x·eş,** [Mod. L.; Gr. *syrinx, syringos*, a pipe, tube.]
1. a Panpipe.
2. [S–] the nymph who was metamorphosed into the reed from which Pan made pipes.
3. in songbirds, the vocal organ near the point of union of the bronchi and the trachea.
4. the Eustachian tube.
5. in archaeology, a tunnellike passage in the stone tombs of Egypt.
syr′mȧ (sũr′), *n.* [Gr.] a long robe reaching to the floor, worn by actors in ancient Greek tragedy.
Syr′ni·um (sũr′), *n.* [Gr. *syrnion*, bird of ill omen.] a genus of owls represented by the family *Bubonidæ*, including the North American barred owl, *Syrnium barium.*
Sȳ′rō-, [from Gr. *Syros*, Syrian.] a combining form meaning *Syrian and*; as, *Syro*-Arabian.
syr′phi·ăn, syr′phid (sũr′), *a.* relating to the syrphus fly or the *Syrphidæ.*

syr′phi·ăn, syr′phid, *n.* any one of the *Syrphidæ.*

Syr′phi·dae, *n.pl.* [Gr. *syrphos, serphos,* a small, winged insect.] a family of dipterous flies, some of which have larvae that feed on plant lice.

Syr′phus, *n.* a large and extensive genus of flies, typical of the family *Syrphidæ.*

syr′phus fly, any fly of the family *Syrphidæ,* resembling the hive bee.

syr′tis (sŭr′), *n.*; *pl.* **syr′tēş,** [L.] a quicksand. [Rare.]

syr′up (sir′), *n.* same as *sirup.*

syr′up·y, *a.* same as *sirupy.*

sys·săr·çō′sis, *n.* [Mod. L.; Gr. *syssarkōsis,* to be grown, over with flesh, from *syn,* together, and *sarkōsis,* fleshy growth.] in anatomy, the union of two or more bones by muscle.

sys′si·dĕr·īte, *n.* [Gr. *syn* and *sideros,* iron, and *-ite.*] a meteorite containing silicates held together by metallic iron.

sys·sit′i·ȧ, *n.pl.* [Gr. *syn,* together, and *sitos,* food.] the practice among ancient Spartans and Cretans of eating the main meal together in public in order to strengthen political and social bonds.

sys·tal′tiç, *a.* [LL. *systalticus;* Gr. *systaltikos,* drawing together, from *systellein,* to draw together; *syn,* together, and *stellein,* to send.] characterized by or having alternate dilatation and contraction; as, the *systaltic* action of the heart.

sys′tȧ·sis, *n.* a union; a political federation or alliance. [Obs.]

sys′tem, *n.* [Fr. *système;* L. *systema;* Gr. *systēma,* from *synistanai,* to place together; *syn,* with, together, and *histanai,* to set.]

1. a set or arrangement of things so related or connected as to form a unity or organic whole; as, a solar *system,* irrigation *system,* supply *system.*

2. the world or universe.

3. the body considered as a functioning organism; as, my *system* needs toning up.

4. a set of facts, principles, rules, etc. classified or arranged in a regular, orderly form so as to show a logical plan linking the various parts.

5. a method or plan of classification.

6. a regular, orderly way of doing something; order; method; regularity.

7. a number of bodily organs acting together to perform one of the main bodily functions; as, the circulatory *system,* digestive *system.*

8. an arrangement of rocks showing evidence, as through fossils, of having been formed during a given geological period; as, the Devonian *system.*

9. a group of transportation lines under a common owner.

10. in chemistry, a group of substances in or approaching equilibrium: a system with two components is called binary, one with three, ternary, etc.

11. in zoology, a cluster of zooids, parasitic upon certain ascidians and furnished with a common cloaca.

12. in ancient music, an interval regarded as compounded of several lesser intervals.

13. in musical notation, a number of staffs connected by brackets, as in concerted scores.

conservative system; see under *conservative.*

cumulative system of voting; same as *cumulative voting* under *cumulative.*

decimal system; see under *decimal.*

Syn.—method, manner, mode, order, rule.

sys·tem·at′iç, *a.* 1. forming or constituting a system.

2. based on or involving a system.

3. made or arranged according to a system, method, or plan; regular; orderly.

4. characterized by the use of method or orderly planning; methodical.

5. of or having to do with classification, especially in biology.

sys·tem·at′i·çăl, *a.* same as *systematic.*

sys·tem·at′i·çăl·ly, *adv.* in a systematic manner; in the form of a system; methodically.

sys·tem·at′içs, *n.pl.* [*construed as sing.*] the science or a method of classification.

sys′tem·ȧ·tişm, *n.* the practice or process of systematizing.

sys′tem·ȧ·tist, *n.* one who works according to a system; also, a taxonomist.

sys·tem·ȧ·ti·zā′tion, *n.* a systematizing or being systematized.

sys′tem·ȧ·tīze, *v.t.*; systematized, *pt., pp.*; systematizing, *ppr.* to make into a system; arrange according to a system; make systematic.

sys′tem·ȧ·tīz·ĕr, *n.* one who systematizes.

sys″tem·ȧ·tol′ō·ġy, *n.* the science of systematizing.

sys·tem′iç, *a.* pertaining to a system; specifically, in physiology, of or affecting the entire bodily system.

sys″tem·i·zā′tion, *n.* systematization.

sys′tem·īze, *v.t.*; systemized, *pt., pp.*; systemizing, *ppr.* to systematize.

sys′tem·i·zĕr, *n.* a systematizer.

sys′tem·less, *a.* 1. without system.

2. undifferentiated into organic systems or specialized structures: said of *Algæ* and *Protozoa.*

sys′tō·lē, *n.* [Mod. L.; Gr. *systolē,* from *systellein,* to shorten; *syn,* together, and *stellein,* to draw, put.]

1. in Latin and Greek prosody, the shortening of a naturally long syllable: opposed to *diastole.*

2. the usual rhythmic contraction of the heart, especially of the ventricles, following each dilatation (*diastole*), during which the blood is driven onward from the chambers.

sys·tol′iç, *a.* pertaining to or characterized by systole.

sys′tȳle, *n.* [Gr. *systylos; syn,* together, and *stylos,* a column.] in architecture, the placing of columns so that the space between the two shafts is equal to twice the diameter of the shaft.

sys′ty·lous, *a.* 1. having coherent or united styles: said of a flower.

2. in mosses, having the lid and columella united.

syz′y·gănt, *n.* [Gr. *syzygos,* coupled; *syn,* together, and *zygon,* a yoke.] any rational integral function of a covariant or invariant of a quantic of such a nature that it vanishes when stated as a function of the coefficients.

syz·i·ġet′iç, *a.* in mathematics, syzygial.

syz·yġ′i·ăl, *a.* of or relating to a syzygy.

sy·zyġ′i·um, *n.*; *pl.* **sy·zyġ′i·ȧ,** in zoology, the union of two organisms, as gregarines, without blending.

syz′y·ġy, *n.*; *pl.* **syz′y·ġieş,** [LL. *syzgia;* Gr. *syzygia; syn,* together, and *zygon,* a yoke.]

1. in astronomy, either of two opposite points in the orbit of a planet or satellite, especially the moon, where it is in opposition to or conjunction with the sun; also, the points in the orbit of the moon when it is new and when it is full: the line joining these two points is called the *line of the syzygies.*

2. in ancient prosody, a group of two feet, as a dipody: sometimes restricted to a combination of dissimilar feet.

3. in mathematics, a linear function.

4. in biology, (a) a syzygium; (b) a firm union of two segments or joints of a crinoid arm; (c) a segment formed by such a union.

T

T, t (tē), *n.*; *pl.* **T's, t's, Ts, ts** (tēz), 1. the twentieth letter of the English alphabet: from the Greek *tau,* derived from the Hebrew *taw.*

2. the sound of T or t, usually a voiceless tongue apex stop.

3. a type or impression for T or t.

4. a symbol for the twentieth in a sequence or group (or the nineteenth if J is omitted).

T, t, *a.* 1. of T or t.

2. twentieth (or nineteenth if J is omitted) in a sequence or group.

T, t, *n.* 1. an object shaped like T.

2. a medieval Roman numeral for 160; with a superior bar ($\bar{T}$), 160,000.

to a T; to perfection; exactly.

T, t, *a.* shaped like T.

T bandage; a surgical bandage made in the shape of the letter T, used on the perineum.

T bar; a metal bar shaped like a T in cross section.

T bolt; a bolt whose head is formed of a transverse piece, so that with its body it makes the outline of a letter T.

T bone; a bone shaped like T.

T bulb; a metal bar having a cross section resembling a T with a bulb-shaped stem.

T cart; a form of phaeton having a body that resembles a T.

T cloth; a cotton cloth marked with a large T, made in Great Britain and sold especially in Asia.

T cross; a tau cross.

T iron; (a) a rolled wrought-iron bar whose cross section is like a letter T; (b) any T-shaped iron piece.

T joint; a welded joint for uniting pieces of bar iron at right angles with each other.

T plate; a metal plate shaped like a T.

T rail; see under *rail.*

T square; a T-shaped ruler for drawing parallel lines.

-t, a suffix used to form past participles and adjectives derived from participles, as in slep*t,* gil*t*: variant of *-ed.*

't, it: a contraction used with a verb initially, as in *'t*was, or, finally, as in do*'t.*

Ta, in chemistry, tantalum.

tā, *v.t.* to take. [Obs.]

Täal, *n.* [D., language, speech.] the Dutch dialect spoken in South Africa; Afrikaans.

täas, *n.* a pile; a heap. [Obs.]

tab, *n.* [earlier also *tabb,* from Eng. dial.; in some senses contr. of *tablet;* in others, associated or merged with *tag.*]

T SQUARE

1. a small, flat loop or strap fastened to something for pulling it, hanging it up, etc

2. a small, usually ornamental, flap or piece fastened to the edge or surface of something, as a dress, coat, etc.

3. an attached or projecting piece of a card or paper, useful in filing.

4. a record; a reckoning. [Colloq.]

5. in aeronautics, a small auxiliary airfoil set into the trailing edge of an aileron, etc.

6. a strap on a shoe. [Brit. Dial.]

7. the metallic binding on the end of a shoe lace, etc.; a tag.

8. the hanging sleeve of a child's garment.

9. a flap of a cap falling over the ear: also called *eartab.*

to keep tab (or *tabs*) *on;* to keep a check on. [Colloq.]

tab′ȧ·nid, *a.* pertaining to the *Tabanidæ.*

tab′ȧ·nid, *n.* any fly of the *Tabanidæ,* as a gadfly, or horsefly.

Tȧ·ban′i·dae, *n.pl.* a large family of blood-sucking flies, typified by the genus *Tabanus.*

Tȧ·bā′nus, *n.* [L., a horsefly.] a genus of dipterous insects, family *Tabanidæ,* including the gadflies, or horseflies.

tab′ărd, *n.* [ME. *tabard*; OFr. *tobart*; LL. *tabardus*, a cloak, from L. *tapete* (-*etis*), a painted hanging.]

TABARD

1. originally, a loose, sleeved or sleeveless jacket worn out of doors.
2. a short-sleeved, blazoned cloak worn by knights over their armor.
3. a herald's official coat, blazoned with his king's or lord's arms.

tab′ărd·ẽr, *n.* one who wears a tabard; specifically, a scholar belonging to the foundation of Queen's College, Oxford, who formerly wore a tabard.

tab′ȧ·ret, *n.* [trade name, prob. from *tabby*.] a satin-striped silk cloth, used in upholstering.

Tȧ·bas′çō, *n.* [from *Tabasco*, a Mexican state.] a very hot sauce made from a kind of pepper: a trade-mark.

tab·ȧ·sheer′, tab·ȧ·shïr′, *n.* [Ar. *tabāshīr*.] a form of silica found in the joints of the bamboo and other large grasses.

tab′bi·net, *n.* a watered fabric of silk and wool: also written *tabinet*.

tab′by, *n.*; *pl.* **tab′bieṣ,** [Fr. *tabis*; LL. *attabi*, from Ar. *'attābī*, a rich kind of watered silk, from *'Attābī*, a quarter of Bagdad where it was manufactured: so named after a prince called *'Attāb*.]
1. a silk taffeta with stripes or wavy markings; watered silk.
2. a mixture of lime with shells, gravel, or stones in equal proportions, with an equal amount of water, forming a mass, which, when dry, becomes as hard as rock: used in Morocco and in some parts of the United States instead of bricks for building.
3. a gray or brown cat with dark stripes.
4. any domestic cat, especially a female.
5. an old maid.
6. a female gossip.

tab′by, *a.* 1. having wavy markings; made of, or like, tabby.
2. having dark stripes over gray or brown; brindles.

tab′by, *v.t.*; tabbied, *pt.*, *pp.*; tabbying, *ppr.* to make wavy markings in (silk, etc.).

tab′by çat, same as *tabby*, sense 3.

tab′by mọth, any moth of the genus *Aglossa*; a grease moth.

tab·ē·fac′tion, *n.* [L. *tabere*, to waste, and *facere*, to make.] a wasting away; a gradual losing of flesh by disease. [Rare.]

tab′ē·fȳ, *v.i.* to waste away gradually; to lose flesh. [Rare.]

tȧ·bel′liŏn, *n.* a secretary or notary under the Roman Empire, or in France during the old monarchy.

tā′bẽr, *v.i.* to tabor. [Dial.]

tab′ẽrd, *n.* a tabard. [Obs.]

tab′ẽr·naç·le, *n.* [L. *tabernaculum*, a tent, dim. of *taberna*, a hut, a shed, a tavern, from root of *tabula*, a board.]
1. (a) a temporary shelter, as a tent; (b) a dwelling place.
2. the human body considered as the dwelling place of the soul.
3. [T–] (a) the portable sanctuary carried by the Jews in their wanderings from Egypt to Palestine: Ex. xxv, xxvi, xxvii; (b) later, the Jewish temple.
4. a shrine, niche, etc. with a canopy.
5. a place of worship; especially, a church with a large seating capacity.
6. in ecclesiastical usage, an ornamental container for the consecrated Host: now usually placed on the middle of the altar.
7. an elevated socket for a ship's mast, or a projecting post to which a mast may be hinged when it is fitted for lowering to pass beneath bridges.

Feast of Tabernacles; a Jewish holiday, Sukkoth.

tab′ẽr·naç·le, *v.i.*; tabernacled, *pt.*, *pp.*; tabernacling, *ppr.* 1. to live in a tabernacle, or temporary shelter.
2. to dwell temporarily; as, the soul is said to *tabernacle* in the body.

tab′ẽr·naç·le, *v.t.* to place in or as in a tabernacle.

tab′ẽr·naç·le wŏrk, carved canopy work over a pulpit, choir stall, niche, etc.

tab·ẽr·naç′ū·lăr, *a.* 1. sculptured with delicate tracery or openwork; latticed.
2. of, like, characteristic of, or pertaining to a tabernacle.
3. common; low.

Tȧ·bẽr″nae·mon·tā′nȧ, *n.* [named after J. T. *Tabernæmontanus*, a German botanist.] a genus of tropical apocynaceous plants comprising about 150 species some of which are cultivated for their ornamental foliage and flowers.

tā′bēṣ, *n.* [L., a wasting away, from *tabere*, to waste away.]
1. formerly, any wasting disease of the body; progressive atrophy of the body or a part of it; consumption.
2. locomotor ataxia.

diabetic tabes; a peripheral neuritis occurring in diabetic patients with symptoms of locomotor ataxia.

tabes dorsalis; locomotor ataxia.

tabes mesenterica; tuberculosis of the mesenteric glands in children, resulting in digestive derangement and wasting of the body.

tȧ·bes′cence, *n.* the quality or condition of being tabescent; an emaciated condition; gradual decay.

tȧ·bes′cent, *a.* wasting or withering away; shriveling.

tȧ·bet′iç, *a.* pertaining to or affected with tabes.

tȧ·bet′iç, *n.* a person affected with tabes.

tȧ·bet′i·fọrm, *a.* resembling tabes.

tab′iç, *a.* tabetic.

tab′id, *a.* [Fr. *tabide*; L. *tabidus*, from *tabere*, to waste away.] wasting away; tabetic.

tab′id·ly, *adv.* in a tabid manner.

tab′id·ness, *n.* the condition of being tabid.

tȧ·bif′iç, tȧ·bif′iç·ăl, *a.* causing consumption or wasting away; wasting.

tab′i·net, *n.* same as *tabbinet*.

tab′i·tūde, *n.* the condition of one affected with tabes.

tab′lȧ·tūre, *n.* [Fr., from L. *tabula*, a table or board.]
1. an obsolete form of musical notation; specifically, a form used for the lute and other stringed instruments, in which the lines of the staff represented the strings and the letters or figures on them indicated the finger stops.
2. a flat surface or tablet with an inscription, painting, or design on it. [Archaic.]
3. in anatomy, the separation of the chief cranial bones into inner and outer tables, with intervening space.

tā′ble, *n.* [Fr. *table*, a table, a tablet, a list, from L. *tabula*, a board, a painting, a tablet, from root *ta*, to extend, and dim. suffix *-bula*.]
1. originally, a thin, flat tablet or slab of metal, stone, or wood, used for inscriptions.
2. a painting; a drawing. [Obs.]
3. [*pl.*] a memorandum tablet; a tablet on which something is written. [Obs.]
4. a piece of furniture consisting of a flat top set horizontally on legs.
5. such a table set with food for a meal.
6. food served at table; feasting as entertainment; as, the host's *table* was sumptuous.
7. the people seated at a table to eat, talk, etc.
8. a compact, systematic list of details, contents, etc.
9. a compact arrangement of related facts, figures, values, etc. in orderly sequence, and usually in rows and columns, for convenience of reference; as, the multiplication *table*.
10. a tableland.
11. in anatomy, the hard inner or outer layer of the bony tissue of the skull.
12. in architecture, (a) any horizontal, projecting piece, as a molding or cornice; stringcourse; (b) a plain or decorated rectangular piece set into or raised on a wall; a panel.
13. in backgammon, (a) either of the two folding leaves of a backgammon board; (b) [*pl.*] [Obs.] backgammon.
14. in geology, a horizontal stratum.
15. in jewelry, (a) the upper, flat surface cut in a precious stone; (b) a diamond or other stone cut with such a surface.
16. in palmistry, part of the palm of the hand.
17. in glassmaking, (a) a circular sheet of crown glass, usually about four feet in diameter; (b) a flat plate with a raised rim, on which plate glass is formed.
18. in machinery, the part of a machine tool on which work is placed to be operated upon.

commutation tables or *columns*; in life insurance, two columns of numbers, headed respectively D and N, indicating denominator and numerator, used in conjunction with a third column of numbers headed *x*, representing age: by dividing a number in the N column by one in the D column corresponding to the proper age, *x*, the immediate annuity on any life may be determined: the numbers indicate the ratios of equal benefits at different ages.

extension table; a table that can be extended by the insertion of leaves.

gate-leg table; a table with drop leaves supported by gatelike legs that are swung back against the frame to permit the leaves to drop: also *gate-legged table*.

on the table; postponed or shelved: said of a bill, etc. referred to the table of the presiding officer.

Round Table; see *Knights of the Round Table* under *knight*.

the Lord's table; see under *lord*.

the tables; laws, as the Ten Commandments or ancient Roman codes, inscribed on flat stone slabs.

to turn the tables; to reverse completely a situation existing between oneself and another person or between two opposing groups.

twelve tables; in ancient Rome, the tables containing the body of Roman law drawn up by the decemvirs, 451 B.C.: originally there were only ten of these tables, but two more were later added.

tā′ble, *v.i.*; tabled, *pt.*, *pp.*; tabling, *ppr.* to board; to live at the table of another. [Obs.]

tā′ble, *v.t.* 1. to represent, as in a picture or painting; to delineate, as on a tablet. [Obs.]
2. to board; to supply with food. [Obs.]
3. to make a list or compact arrangement of; to tabulate. [Rare.]
4. to put on a table.
5. to postpone indefinitely the discussion or consideration of, as a legislative bill, motion, etc., by referring it to the table of the presiding officer.
6. to enter in a record or list. [Obs.]
7. in carpentry, to insert, as one piece of timber into another, by alternate grooves and projections to prevent loosening.
8. in nautical usage, to stiffen the edge of (a sail) with wide hems for attaching the boltrope.

tā′ble, *a.* 1. of, belonging to, or used at a table.
2. having the form of a table.

tab′leau (-lō), *n.*; *pl.* **tab′leaux, tab′leauṣ** (-lōz), [Fr., dim. of *table*.]
1. a graphic scene; picture.
2. a tableau vivant.

tȧb·leau′ vi·vänt′ (-väṅ′), *n.*; *pl.* **tȧb·leaux′ vi·vänts′** (-blō′, -väṅ′), [Fr., lit., living tableau.] a representation of a scene, picture, etc. by a person or group of persons appropriately costumed and posing silently without moving.

tā′ble bōard, meals without rental of a room: distinguished from *room and board*.

tā′ble bōard′ẽr, one who takes meals at a house, but lodges elsewhere.

tā′ble book, 1. a memorandum book; a notebook; a tablet. [Obs.]
2. a book, usually ornamented and illustrated, displayed on a table.

tā′ble·çloth, *n.* a cloth for covering a table, especially at meals.

tā′ble çov′ẽr, a covering for a table, usually ornamented, for use between meals.

ta′ble d'hôte (tä′bl dōt′), *pl.* **ta′bles d'hôte** (tä′blṣ), [Fr., lit., table of the host.]
1. a common table for guests at a hotel or restaurant.
2. a complete meal with courses as specified on the menu, served at a restaurant or hotel for a set price: distinguished from *à la carte*.

tā′ble dī′ȧ·mŏnd, a diamond with a flat top surface, the sides being cut in angles.

tā′ble flap, a hinged table leaf at the end or side of a table, which can be folded down when not in use.

tā′ble grāpe, a grape cultivated for table use: distinguished from *raisin grape, wine grape*.

tā′ble·land, *n.* a high, broad, generally level region; a plateau.
tā′ble lēaf, 1. a removable board for use in an extension table.
2. same as *table flap.*
tā′ble lin′en, linen, as tablecloths, napkins, etc., for table service; napery.
tā′ble·măn, *n.*; *pl.* **tā′ble·men,** a man or piece used in backgammon. [Obs.]
tā′ble mŏn′ey, in the British army and navy, an allowance to officers for the purpose of extending official hospitality.
tā′ble mōv′ing, same as *table tipping.*
tā′blẽr, *n.* 1. one who boards; a boarder. [Obs.]
2. one who keeps boarders. [Obs.]
tā′ble rap′ping, the sounds of raps on tables, believed by spiritualists to be a method of communication employed by the spirits of the dead.
tā′ble shōre, a low, level shore.
tā′ble·spoon, *n.* 1. a large spoon used for eating soup, for serving at the table, and as a measuring unit in cookery.
2. a tablespoonful.
tā′ble·spoon″ful, *n.*; *pl.* **tā′ble·spoon″fuls,** as much as a tablespoon will hold; 3 teaspoonfuls or 1/2 fluid ounce.
tā′ble stākes, in poker, the restriction that a player can bet only what money or chips he has in front of him at the time the cards are dealt.
tab′let, *n.* [ME. *tablett*; OFr. *tablete*; LL. *tabuleta*, dim. of L. *tabula*, table.]
1. a flat, thin piece of stone, wood, metal, etc. shaped for a specific purpose.
2. such a piece with an inscription, used as a memorial wall panel.
3. a smooth, flat leaf made of wood, ivory, metal, etc. and used to write on.
4. a set of such leaves fastened together.
5. a writing pad containing sheets of paper fastened together at one edge.
6. a small, flat piece of solid or compressed material, as medicine, soap, etc.
tā′ble talk (tak), informal conversation at a table or at meals; familiar conversation.
tā′ble talk′ẽr, a person who talks at the table, especially a distinguished conversationalist.
tā′ble ten′nis, a game somewhat like tennis in miniature, played on a large, rectangular table, usually indoors, with a small, hollow celluloid ball and small, racket-shaped paddles.
tā′ble tip′ping, the moving of a table without any apparent physical or mechanical cause: called also *table moving, table turning.*
tā′ble tūrn′ing, same as *table tipping.*
tā′ble·wāre, *n.* articles for service at the table for meals, as dishes, knives, forks, spoons, etc.
tā′ble·wīse, *adv.* in the form of a table.
tȧ·bli·ẽr′ (-ā′), *n.* [Fr.] an apron, or a part of a woman's dress resembling an apron.
tā′bling, *n.* 1. the act of tabulating or forming into tables. [Rare.]
2. in carpentry, the inserting of one timber into another by alternate scores or projections, as in shipbuilding.
3. a broad hem made on a sail by turning over the edge of the canvas, and sewing it down.
4. material for table linen.
5. the act of playing backgammon. [Obs.]
6. board; maintenance. [Obs.]
7. in architecture, the cap or top course of a wall; a coping.
tā′bling house, a gambling house. [Obs.]
tab′loid, *a.* of or pertaining to a condensed or abbreviated form of anything; characterized by compactness or brevity; concentrated; short.
tab′loid, *n.* [from *tablet* and *-oid.*]
1. a small tablet of medicine, a drug, etc. in compressed or concentrated form: a trademark (*Tabloid*).
2. a newspaper, usually half the ordinary size, with many pictures and short news stories.
tȧ·boo′, *n.* [Tongan *tabu.*]
1. among primitive tribes, a sacred prohibition put upon certain people, things, or acts which makes them untouchable, unmentionable, etc.
2. the highly developed system or practice of such prohibitions.
3. any social prohibition or restriction that results from convention or tradition.
4. in linguistics, the substitution of one term for another because of taboo.
Also spelled *tabu.*
tȧ·boo′, *a.* 1. sacred and prohibited by taboo.
2. restricted by taboo: said of people.
3. prohibited or forbidden by tradition, convention, etc.
Also spelled *tabu.*
tȧ·boo′, *v.t.*; tabooed, *pt.*, *pp.*; tabooing, *ppr.*
1. to put under taboo.
2. to prohibit or forbid because of tradition, convention, etc.
Also spelled *tabu.*
tā′bŏr, tā′bŏur, *n.* [OFr. *tabour*; Sp. and Port. *tambor*, prob. from Ar. *tambūr*, and from Per. *tabīr*, a tabor.] a small drum, formerly often used as an accompaniment to a pipe or fife.
tā′bŏr, tā′bŏur, *v.i.* to beat or drum on or as on a tabor.
tā′bŏr, tā′bŏur, *v.t.* to drum. [Obs.]
tā′bŏr, *n.* [Bohem.] a stronghold; a fortified camp.
tā′bŏr·ẽr, *n.* one who plays the tabor.
tab′ō·ret, tab′ŏu·ret, *n.* [OFr., a stool, lit., a little drum, dim. of *tabour*, a drum.]
1. a small tabor.
2. a stool; a seat without a back or arms.
3. a low ornamental stand.
4. an embroidery frame.
tab′ō·rin, tab′ō·rine, *n.* [OFr. *tabourin*, dim. of *tabour.*] a small tabor played with only one stick: also spelled *tabourine.*
Tā′bŏr·īte, *n.* a radical Hussite.
tā′bŏur, *n.*, *v.i.* and *v.t.* same as *tabor.*
tā′bŏur·ẽr, *n.* same as *taborer.*
tab′ŏu·ret, *n.* same as *taboret.*
tab′ŏu·rine, *n.* same as *taborin.*
tā′brēre, *n.* a taborer. [Obs.]
tab′ret, *n.* 1. a small tabor; a taboret.
2. a person who plays a tabret. [Obs.]
tȧ·bu′, *n.*, *a.*, and *v.* same as *taboo.*
tab′ū·lȧ, *n.*; *pl.* **tab′ū·lae,** [L., a board, plank, table.]
1. a table or tablet.
2. in zoology, any of the horizontal plates extending across the cavity of the theca of certain corals.
tabula rasa; an erased tablet: applied figuratively to the mind on which no impression has been made by experience, as the mind of an infant.
tab′ū·lăr, *a.* [L. *tabularis*, from *tabula*, table.]
1. in the form of a table; having a flat surface.
2. having the form of laminae, or plates.
3. (a) of or arranged in a table or tabulated scheme; (b) computed from or calculated by such a table or tables.
tabular difference; the difference between two consecutive numbers as ascertained from a table, as of logarithms.
tab″ū·lăr·i·zā′tion, *n.* the act of tabularizing; tabulation.
tab′ū·lăr·īze, *v.t.*; tabularized, *pt.*, *pp.*; tabularizing, *ppr.* to tabulate.
tab′ū·lăr·ly, *adv.* in or by means of a table.
Tab·ū·lā′tȧ, *n. pl.* a group of stony corals, having rudimentary partitions, or none at all, and well-developed tabulae, which divide the visceral chamber into a series of stories.
tab′ū·lāte, *v.t.*; tabulated, *pt.*, *pp.*; tabulating, *ppr.* [from L. *tabula*, a table; and *-ate.*]
1. to put (facts, statistics, etc.) in a table or tables (senses 8 and 9); to list or arrange systematically.
2. to give a flat, tablelike surface to.
tab′ū·lāte, *a.* 1. having a flat surface.
2. having or made of thin, horizontal plates, as some corals.
tab·ū·lā′tion, *n.* the act of tabulating or the state of being tabulated; orderly arrangement, as in a table.
tab′ū·lā·tŏr, *n.* 1. a person or machine that tabulates.
2. a typewriter device used to put figures into columns.
taç′ȧ·mȧ·haç, taç′mȧ·hack, *n.* [Sp. *tacamahaca*, earlier *tecomahaca*, from Nahuatl *tecomahca*, lit., stinking copal.]
1. any of several trees yielding a strong-smelling gum resin; specifically, *Icica tacamahaca*, a tree of South America; the *Calophyllum inophyllum*, of Madagascar and the Isle of Bourbon, and the balsam poplar, *Populus balsamifera*, of North America.
2. a resin, the product of *Calophyllum inophyllum*: it has a strong smell and a bitterish aromatic taste.
3. the gum resin yielded by the *Populus balsamifera*, used in ointments and incenses.
taç·ȧ·mȧ·haç′ȧ, *n.* same as *tacamahac.*
Taç′ça, *n.* [Malay.] a genus of tropical herbs, the type of the family *Taccaceæ*, having tuberous roots, simple or pinnate radical leaves, and greenish or brown flowers arranged in an umbel at the top of a leafless scape.
tāce, *n.* same as *tasse.*
tā′cē, *v.imp.* [L., imper. of *tacere.*] be silent.
tā′cet, *v.imp.* [L., from *tacere*, to be silent.] be silent (for an indicated time): a direction used in music.
tache, tach, *n.* [ME.; OFr., a nail, hook.] a device, as a buckle, hook and eye, etc., for fastening two parts together. [Archaic.]
taçhe, *n.* same as *tack* (spot).
taçh′ȳ″drīte, *n.* [Gr. *tachys*, swift, and *hydōr*, *hydros*, water.] a yellowish chloride of calcium and magnesium, hydrous in character.
Taçh′i·nȧ, *n.* a genus of gray and black, parasitic dipterous flies.
taçh′i·nȧ flȳ, [Mod. L. *tachina*, from Gr. *tachinos*, swift, for *tachys*, swift.] any fly of the genus *Tachina*, whose larvae are parasitic on and destructive to caterpillars, grubs, etc.
Tä Ch′ing (dä ching), the Manchu dynasty of China, overthrown in 1911.
taçh′i·ōl, *n.* silver fluoride, $AgF \cdot H_2O$, used as an antiseptic.
taçh′isme (tash′iz′m), *n.* [Fr., from *tache*, a spot, and *-isme*, -ism.] a method of painting in which nonrepresentational compositions are created by splashing, dribbling, etc. paint upon the canvas in apparently random patterns.
ta·çhis′tō·sçōpe, *n.* [from Gr. *tachistos*, superl. of *tachys*, swift; and *-scope.*] an apparatus for testing attention, memory, etc. by throwing images of objects on a screen for a brief measured period, a fraction of a second.
taçh′ō·grȧph, *n.* a tachometer that records or registers its measurements; also, its record.
tȧ·çhom′e·tẽr, *n.* 1. an instrument employed for measuring the velocity of machines or the revolutions per minute of a revolving shaft.
2. an instrument for measuring the velocity of a current in a river, the blood stream, etc.
tȧ·çhom′e·try, *n.* the use of a tachometer.
taçh′y-, [from Gr. *tachys*, swift.] a combining form meaning *rapid, swift, fast*, as in *tachymeter.*
taçh·y·cär′di·ȧ, *n.* [*tachy-*, and Gr. *kardia*, a heart.] an abnormally fast heartbeat.
taçh·y·drō′mi·ăn, *n.* [*tachy-*, and Gr. *dromos*, a running.] any of a family of wading birds, related to the plovers.
Taçh·y·glos′sus, *n.* [*tachy-*, and Gr. *glōssa*, a tongue.] a genus of monotrematous mammals, including the spiny anteaters.
taçh′y·grȧph, *n.* [Fr. *tachygraphe*, from Gr. *tachygraphos*, swift writer, from *tachys*, swift, and *graphein*, to write.]
1. something written in tachygraphy.
2. a tachygrapher.
tȧ·çhyg′rȧ·phẽr, *n.* a person skilled in tachygraphy.
taçh·y·graph′iç, *a.* of or in tachygraphy.
taçh·y·graph′i·çăl, *a.* tachygraphic.
tȧ·çhyg′rȧ·phy, *n.* [*tachy-* and *-graphy.*] the art or use of rapid writing; especially, ancient Greek and Roman shorthand or the medieval cursive writing, with abbreviations, etc., in these languages.
taçh′y·lȳte, taçh′y·līte, *n.* [*tachy-*, and Gr. *lytos*, dissolving: so called because of its rapid decomposition in acids.] a black basaltic glass, occurring in amorphous fragments in the softer trap rocks.
taçh·y·lyt′iç, *a.* of, like, or consisting of tachlyte.
tȧ·çhym′e·tẽr, *n.* a surveying instrument by which distance, elevation, etc. can be quickly ascertained.
tȧ·çhym′e·try, *n.* the use of a tachymeter.
taçh·y·phrā′si·ȧ, *n.* [Gr. *tachys*, swift, and *phrasis*, speech.] a speech disorder characterized by extreme volubility.
taçh·y·phrē′ni·ȧ, *n.* [Gr. *tachys*, swift, and *phrēn*, mind.] abnormally fast mental activity.
taçh·yp·nē′ȧ, taçh·yp·noe′ȧ, *n.* [Gr. *tachys*, swift, and *pnoiē*, breathing.] abnormally fast respiration.
taçh′y·sçōpe, *n.* [*tachy-*, and Gr. *skopein*, to view.] a form of kinescope in which the pictures were attached to the perimeter of a rotating glass plate and revolved rapidly to give the impression of actual motion.
tac′it, *a.* [Fr. *tacite*; L. *tacitus*, silent.]
1. making no sound; saying nothing; still.
2. unspoken; silent.

3. not expressed or declared openly, but implied.

4. in law, happening without contract but by operation of law.

Syn.—implied, silent, understood, unspoken.

tac′it·ly, *adv.* in a tacit manner; silently; by implication; without words; as, he *tacitly* assented.

tac′i·tūrn, *a.* [L. *taciturnus.*] habitually silent; not apt to talk.

Syn.—silent, uncommunicative, reserved, reticent, mute, dumb.

tac·i·tūrn′i·ty, *n.* [Fr. *taciturnité*, from L. *taciturnitas*, from *tacere*, to be silent.] the quality or state of being taciturn; habitual silence.

tac′i·tūrn·ly, *adv.* silently; without speech.

tack, *n.* 1. a spot, stain, etc.: also *tache.* [Obs.]

2. a flavor; a taste. [Obs.]

tack, *n.* [ME. *takke*; O.Norm. Fr. *taque*; OFr. *tache*, a nail, fibula.]

1. a short nail or pin with a sharp point and a relatively large, flat head.

2. (a) a stitch; especially, a long stitch used for temporary sewing; (b) a fastening, especially in a slight or temporary way.

3. a zigzag course, or movement in such a course.

4. a course of action or policy, especially one differing from another or preceding course.

5. food; foodstuff; as, hard*tack.*

6. that which is tacked on or attached.

7. in nautical usage, (a) a rope used to confine the foremost lower corners of the courses and staysails, when the wind crosses the ship's course obliquely; also, a rope used to pull the lower corner of a studdingsail to the boom; (b) the part of a sail to which the tack is usually fastened; the foremost lower corner of the courses; (c) the course of a ship in regard to the position of the sails; as, the starboard *tack*, the port *tack*; (d) a change of direction made by changing the position of the sails; (e) a course against the wind; (f) one of a series of zigzag movements in such a course.

on the right tack; in the right course.

on the wrong tack; in the wrong course.

tack of a flag; a line spliced into the eye at the bottom of the tabling for securing the flag to the halyards.

to hold tack; to last or hold out.

tack, *v.t.*; tacked (takt), *pt., pp.*; tacking, *ppr.*

1. to fasten or attach with tacks.

2. to unite temporarily, as by stitching together.

3. to add as a supplement to, as to a bill in its progress through Congress; to append.

4. in nautical usage, (a) to change the course of (a ship) by turning it with its head to the wind; (b) to maneuver (a ship) against the wind by a series of tacks.

tack, *v.i.* 1. to go in a zigzag course.

2. to change suddenly one's policy or course of action.

3. in nautical usage, (a) to tack a ship; (b) to change its course by being tacked, or sail against the wind by a series of tacks: said of a ship.

tack claw, a forked tool for drawing tacks from a carpet, etc.

tack drīv′ẽr, 1. a tack hammer.

2. a tool for automatically placing tacks in succession, and driving them into place.

tack dū′ty, in Scots law, rent reserved on a lease.

tack′ẽr, *n.* one who or that which tacks.

tack′et, *n.* a small nail with a broad flat head. [Obs.]

tack ham′mẽr, a small hammer used for driving and extracting tacks.

tack′i·ness, *n.* the quality or state of being tacky.

taç′kle, *n.* [ME. *takel*; Sw. *takel*; Dan. *takkel*, tackle, from Ice. *taka*, to take or grasp.]

1. apparatus; equipment; as, fishing *tackle.*

2. a rope and pulley block, or a system of ropes and pulleys, used to lower, raise, or move weights.

3. the act of tackling, as in football.

4. in football, either of the two players (*right tackle* and *left tackle*) between the guard and the end on either side of the line of scrimmage.

5. in nautical usage, (a) originally, a ship's rigging; (b) later, the running rigging and pulleys to operate the sails.

6. an arrow. [Obs.]

taç′kle, *v.t.*; tackled, *pt., pp.*; tackling, *ppr.*

1. to fasten by means of tackle.

2. to harness (a horse).

3. to seize; to lay hold of.

4. to supply with tackle. [Obs.]

5. in football, to stop or throw (an opponent running with the ball).

6. to attack or fasten upon, as something difficult; to undertake; to set to work upon; as, to *tackle* a problem.

taç′kle block, a block or pulley over which a rope runs.

taç′kle bōard, in ropemaking, a frame at the head of a ropewalk, containing the whirls to which yarns are attached to be twisted into strands.

taç′kled, *a.* made of or equipped with tackle.

taç′kle fall, the rope or the end of the rope of a pulley by which it is operated.

taç′kle pōst, same as *tackle board.*

taç′klẽr, *n.* one who or that which tackles; specifically, [Brit.] in mining, any of several small chains having a hook at one end and a ring at the other, to be put around the corves to keep the coal from falling out.

taç′kling, *n.* gear; tackle. [Rare.]

tacks′măn, *n.*; *pl.* **tacks′men,** [from *tack*, to fasten.] one who holds a tack, or lease, of land from another; a lessee. [Scot.]

tack′y, *a.*; *comp.* tackier; *superl.* tackiest, [*tack*, in sense of "slight fastening," and *-y.*] adhesive; sticky, as undried paint, varnish, etc.

tack′y, *a.* [prob. specialized use of *tacky* (sticky).] dowdy; shabby. [Colloq.]

tack′y, *n.*; *pl.* **tack′ieṣ,** an ill-fed, neglected, bony horse: sometimes used also of persons in such condition. [Dial.]

taç′lō·bō, *n.* [Tag.] a large mollusk, the giant clam, *Tridacna gigas.*

taç′lō″çus, *n.* [L. *tactus*, touching, and *locus*, place.] in geometry, the locus of the points of tangency of two curves, whether of different families or nonconsecutive ones of the same family.

taç′mȧ·hack, *n.* same as *tacamahac.*

taç′nōde, *n.* in geometry, the point of tangency of two or more branches of the same curve.

tä′çō, *n.* [Mex. Sp.] a tortilla folded over a filling, as of chopped meat, tomato, lettuce, etc., and served hot.

Tȧ·çō′ni·ăn, *a.* relating to the Taconic system.

Tȧ·çŏn′iç, *a.* relating to the system, or series, of upper Cambrian or lower Silurian rocks found in the Taconic range on the western slope of the Green Mountains in Vermont.

taç′ŏn·īte, *n.* [perh. from *Taconic*, old name for a rock series in the Lake Superior region which resembles the rocks of the Taconic range, Vt., and *-ite.*] a dull-colored quartz containing from 25 to 35 per cent hematite and magnetite: it is a low-grade iron ore.

Taç·sō′ni·ȧ, *n.* [Peruv. *tacso.*] a genus of polypetalous plants of the family *Passifloraceæ.* The twenty-five species are native to tropical America, and are distinguished from the genus *Passiflora*, or true passionflowers, by the elongated tubular part of the calyx.

taçt, *n.* [Fr.; L. *tactus*, pp. of *tangere*, to touch.]

1. touch; a touching. [Obs.]

2. the sense of touch. [Now Rare.]

3. intuitive perception, especially a quick and fine perception of the proper thing to say or do to avoid giving offense; sensitive skill in dealing with people.

4. in music, the beat with which a measure begins; hence, a measure. [Obs.]

taç′tȧ·ble, *a.* capable of being touched or of being felt by the sense of touch. [Obs.]

taçt′ful, *a.* showing or having tact.

taç′tiç, *a.* [Mod. L. *tacticus*; Gr. *taktikos*, fit for arranging.] in biology, of, showing, or characteristic of taxis.

taç′tiç, *n.* 1. tactics.

2. a detail or branch of tactics.

taç′tiç, *a.* of arrangement or system.

taç′tiç·ăl, *a.* of the nature of or pertaining to tactics; pertaining to the art of military and naval maneuvers; also, characterized by or showing cleverness and skill in tactics.

tactical diameter; in naval tactics, the diameter of a half circle made by a ship in turning from its course.

tactical unit; in military usage, any unit organized primarily for tactical purposes, as the battalion in infantry or the squadron in cavalry.

taç′tiç·ăl·ly, *adv.* according to tactics; in a tactical manner.

taç·ti′ciăn (-tish′ăn), *n.* an expert in tactics; hence, an adroit manager or skillful director in any line of action.

taç′tiçs, *n.* [Gr. (*ta*) *taktika*, lit., (the) matters of arrangement, from *taktikos*, fit for arranging, from *tassein*, to arrange.]

1. the science and art of disposing military and naval forces in action or before the enemy.

2. actions in accord with this science; hence, any skillful management for effecting a desired result; adroit devices for gaining an end.

Syn.—strategy, policy, diplomacy.

taç′tile, *a.* [Fr. *tactile*, from L. *tactilis*, tangible, from *tangere*, to touch.]

1. tangible; that can be perceived by touch; that may be felt.

2. of or having the sense of touch; adapted for feeling or touching; tactual.

tactile cells; cells found in the deeper layer of the epidermis, in which the axis cylinders of the medullated nerve fibers terminate.

tactile corpuscle; a rounded or elliptical body contained in a tactile papilla of the corium.

taç·til′i·ty, *n.* 1. the quality or condition of being tactile; tangibleness.

2. touchiness. [Rare.]

taç·tin·vār′i·ănt, *n.* in mathematics, the invariant which, equated to zero, expresses the condition that two quantic curves or surfaces touch each other.

taç′tion, *n.* [Fr., from L. *tangere*, to touch.] a touching or being touched; contact.

taçt′less, *a.* not having or showing tact.

taçt′less·ness, *n.* lack of tact.

taç·tom′e·tẽr, *n.* in medicine, a device for measuring the sensitiveness of the sense of touch.

taç′tŏr, *n.* [LL.] an organ of touch.

taç′tū·ăl, *a.* [from L. *tactus* (pp. of *tangere*, to touch); and *-al.*]

1. of the sense or organs of touch.

2. causing a sensation of touch; caused by touch.

taç′tū·ăl·ly, *adv.* by means of touch.

taç′tus, *n.* the sense of touch.

tad, *n.* [prob. short for *tadpole.*] a little child.

tad′pōle, *n.* [ME. *taddepol*, from *tade*, *tadde*, toad, and *pole*, head; hence, the toad that seems all head.]

1. the larva of certain amphibians, as frogs and toads, having gills and a tail and living in water: as it matures, the gills and tail are lost and legs develop.

2. the hooded merganser. [Dial.]

tad′pōle fish, the tadpole hake.

tad′pōle hāke, a hake, *Raniceps raninus*, of the Scottish, Cornish, and Devon coasts. It is about one foot long and dark in color.

Tä′dzhik (-jik), *n.*; *pl.* **Tä′dzhik,** one of a people of Iranian descent living in the region of the Tadzhik S.S.R., a republic of the U.S.S.R. in Central Asia.

tāe, *n.* a toe. [Scot.]

tāe, *prep.* to. [Scot.]

tāe, *a.* the one, not the other. [Scot.]

tae′di·um, *n.* [L.] tedium; weariness.

taedium vitae; weariness of life.

tael (tāl), *n.* [Port., from Malay *tahil*, a measure of weight, from Hindu *tolā*, from Sans. *tulā*, a balance.]

1. any of various units of weight of eastern Asia; especially, a Chinese unit equal to $^{1}/_{16}$ catty.

2. a Chinese unit of money equal in value to a tael of silver.

tā′en, *v.* taken. [Poet.]

tae′ni-, [from L. *tænia*, Gr. *tainia*, a ribbon.] a combining form meaning ***like a ribbon*** or ***band***: also *taenia-*, *taenii-.*

tae′ni·ȧ, *n.*; *pl.* **tae′ni·ae,** [L., from Gr. *tainia*, a ribbon, or tape.]

1. an ancient Greek headband or fillet.

2. in architecture, the fillet or band that separates the Doric frieze from the architrave.

3. in surgery, a long and narrow bandage.

4. in anatomy, a ribbonlike part or structure, as of muscle or nerve tissue.

5. [T-] the leading genus of tapeworms, typical of the family *Tæniidæ.*

6. any one of the genus *Tænia.*

Also spelled *tenia.*

tae′ni·ȧ·cīde, *n.* [*taenia* and *-cide.*] a drug, etc. that destroys tapeworms: also spelled *teniacide.*

Tae·nī′ȧ·dȧ, *n.pl.* a division of internal parasites, the tapeworms.

tae′ni·ȧ·fūġe, *n.* [from *taenia*, and L. *fugare*, to drive away.] a drug, etc. that expels tapeworms from the body: also spelled *teniafuge.*

tae·nī′ȧ·sis, *n.* infestation with tapeworms: also spelled *teniasis.*

Tae·ni·ā′tȧ, Tae·ni·ā′tae, *n.pl.* a family of taeniform ctenophores.

tae′ni·āte, *a.* resembling a ribbon in form.

tae′ni·cīde, *n.* [*tæni-*, and L. *cædere*, to kill.] any substance that kills tapeworms.

tae·nid′i·um, *n.*; *pl.* **tae·nid′i·ȧ,** one of the bands of the spiral chitinous covering of the trachea of an insect.

tae'ni·i·fọrm, *a.* taeniform.

Tae"ni·ō·brañ'çhi·ȧ, *n.pl.* [*tænio-*, and Gr. *branchia*, gills.] a division of ascidians containing the salps.

tae"ni·ō·brañ'çhi·āte, *a.* having taeniate gills; specifically, pertaining to the *Tænio-branchia*.

Tae"ni·ō·glos'sȧ, *n.pl.* [*tænio-*, and Gr. *glōssa*, a tongue.] a division of gastropods characterized by a ligulate odontophore bearing several transverse rows of teeth.

tae"ni·ō·glos'sāte, *a.* pertaining to the *Tænioglossa*.

tae"ni·ō·glos'sāte, *n.* a taenioglossate mollusk.

tae'ni·oid, *a.* 1. resembling a ribbon in shape.
2. of or pertaining to *Tænia*, or tapeworms.

Tae"ni·ō·sō'mī, *n.pl.* [*tænio-*, and Gr. *sōma*, body.] a suborder of long, ribbon-shaped fishes, with a long dorsal fin and no anal fin.

TAF, T.A.F. [*t*umor *a*ngiogenesis, development of blood vessels, *f*actor.] a substance of protein and nucleic acid developed in a malignant tumor, stimulating the formation of capillaries that nourish the tumor and carry off its waste.

taf'fȧ·rel, taf'fẽr·el, *n.* [D. *tafereel*, a panel, picture; dim. of *tafel*, table, from L. *tabula*, a table.]
1. formerly, the upper, flat part of a ship's stern: so called because ornamented with carved panels.
2. a taffrail.

taf'fē·tȧ, *n.* [ME. *taffata*; OFr. *tafetas*, *taffetas*; Sp. *tafetan*, from Per. *tāftan*, to weave.]
1. a fine, rather stiff, fabric of silk with a sheen.
2. loosely, a similar cloth of cotton, linen, etc.

taf'fe·ty, *n.* taffeta.

taf'fi·ȧ, *n.* same as *tafia*.

taff'rāil, *n.* [D. *tafereel*, dim. of *tafel*, table, from L. *tabula*, a table.]
1. a taffarel. [Rare.]
2. the rail around a ship's stern.

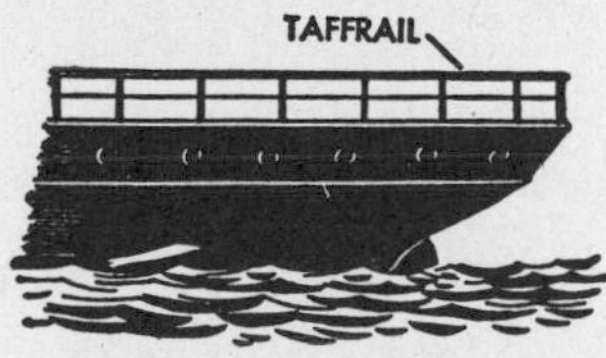

TAFFRAIL

taf'fy, *n.* [an early form of *toffee*.]
1. a chewy candy made by boiling down and pulling sugar or molasses.
2. flattery. [Colloq.]

taf'i·ȧ, *n.* [Fr., from Malay *tāfīa*, a spirit distilled from molasses.] a low-grade rum made in the West Indies from cheap molasses or refuse sugar.

tag, *n.* [ME. *tagge*; prob. from ON.]
1. originally, a hanging end, or rag, as on a torn skirt.
2. any small part or piece hanging from or loosely attached to the main piece.
3. a hard-tipped end, as of metal, on a string or lace, to give stiffness for drawing through holes.
4. a bright piece of material next to the fly on a fishhook.
5. a card, paper, etc. tied or attached to something as a label.
6. an ornamental or instructive ending for a speech, story, etc.
7. a short, familiar quotation used as such an ending.
8. the last words of an actor's speech, a song, etc.
9. the last part of any proceeding.
10. a loop on a garment for hanging it up, or on a boot for pulling it on.
11. a flourish or decorative stroke in writing.
12. (a) a lock of hair; (b) a matted lock of wool.
13. the rabble: now only in combination with *rag*, as "*rag, tag*, and *bobtail*." [Obs.]
14. a children's game in which one player, called "it," chases the others with the object of touching, or tagging, one of them and making him "it" in turn.

tag, *v.t.*; tagged, *pt., pp.*; tagging, *ppr.* 1. to provide with a tag; to fasten a tag to.
2. to end (a speech, story, etc.) with a tag.
3. to overtake and touch in or as in the game of tag.
4. to follow closely after. [Colloq.]

tag, *v.i.* to follow close behind a person or thing (usually with *along, after*, etc.).

Tȧ·gä'lȧ, *n.* same as *Tagalog* (sense 1).

tag ạl'dẽr, a plant, either the smooth alder, *Alnus serrulata*, or the red alder, *Alnus rubra*, of the Pacific coast.

Tȧ·gä'log (*or Eng.* tag'ȧ-log), *n.* 1. a member of a Malayan people of the Philippine Islands.
2. their Indonesian language, the chief native language of the Philippine Islands.

tag dāy, a day on which funds are publicly solicited for a stated fund, each contributor receiving a tag.

tag end, 1. any loosely attached or hanging end.
2. the last part of something; remnant.

Tȧ·ġē'tēṣ, *n.* [L. *Tages*, an Etruscan deity.] a genus of showy tropical herbs of the composite family, some species of which are cultivated for their ornamental flowers; the marigolds.

tag'gẽr, *n.* 1. one who or that which tags or attaches one thing to another.
2. something pointed like a tag. [Obs.]
3. a device for removing taglocks from sheep.
4. [*pl.*] very thin sheet metal, usually coated with tin.
5. in the game of tag, the pursuer. [Dial.]

tag'let, *n.* a small tag. [Rare.]

Tȧgl·iȧ·çō'tiăn (tȧl-yȧ-), *a.* same as *Taliacotian*.

tȧgl·iō'ni (tȧl-yō'), *n.* [after a celebrated Italian family of ballet dancers.] a kind of overcoat fashionable in the early 19th century.

tag'lock, *n.* a lock of tangled wool or hair.

tag'rag, *n.* 1. a loose rag; a tatter.
2. same as *ragtag*.

tag'uȧ (-wȧ), *n.* [Panama native name.] the palm that yields vegetable ivory, *Phytelephas macrocarpa*.

tag'uȧn, *n.* a large Asiatic flying squirrel of the genus *Pteromys*; particularly, *Pteromys petaurista*.

Tä'hȧ, *n.* [Afr.] a genus of weaverbirds resembling *Pyromelana*.

tä·hï'nï, *n.* [Ar.] a sauce made from sesame seed oil mixed with spicy seasonings, used in various Middle Eastern dishes.

Tä·hï'ti·ăn, *n.* 1. a native or inhabitant of Tahiti; especially, a member of the native Polynesian people of Tahiti.
2. the Polynesian language of the Tahitians.

Tä·hï'ti·ăn, *a.* belonging or relating to Tahiti, its people, their language, etc.

tȧ·hō'nȧ, *n.* [Sp., from Ar. *tohōna*, a mill.] same as *arrastre*.

tähr, *n.* in zoology, same as *thar*.

täh·sïl·där', *n.* in India, a local revenue officer or collector of taxes.

Tä'ï (*or* tī), *n.* and *a.* Thai.

taī, *n.* [Japan.] a brilliantly colored edible fish, *Chrysophrys cardinalis* or *Pagrus cardinalis*, of Japan and China.

taī' chï' (jē'), [Chin.] a series of postures and exercises developed in China as a system of self-defense and as an aid to meditation, characterized by slow, relaxed, circular movements.

taī' chï' ch'uan' (jē' chwän'), same as *tai chi*.

taī'gȧ, *n.* [Russ.] the coniferous forests in the far northern regions of Eurasia and North America.

tāi'gle (-gl), *v.t.*; taigled (-gld), *pt., pp.*; taigling, *ppr.* [from *tag*, to follow after.]
1. to impede; to delay; to hinder. [Scot.]
2. to fatigue; to weary. [Scot.]

tāil, *n.* [OFr. *taille*, a cutting.] a limitation on the inheritance of an estate.
estate in tail; an estate restricted in succession to particular heirs.

tāil, *a.* limited in a specified manner as to inheritance; as, fee *tail*.

tāil, *n.* [ME. *tayl*; AS. *tægel*, a tail.]
1. the rear end of an animal's body, especially when extending from the trunk as a distinct flexible appendage; specifically, (a) in mammals, the cauda; (b) in birds, the tail feathers; (c) in reptiles, the end of the body; (d) in fishes, that part of the body which is behind the anus and ends in the caudal fin; (e) in crustaceans, the stomach or region including and about the abdomen; (f) in insects, the pygidium; (g) in worms, that part of the body opposite to the head; (h) in some arachnidans, a postabdominal part of the body back of the thorax; (i) [Dial. or Slang.] the buttocks.
2. formerly, in Turkey, the tail of a horse mounted on a lance and borne as a standard of rank before a pasha.
3. anything like an animal's tail in form or position, as (a) in botany, a downy or feathery appendage to certain seeds; (b) that tendon of a muscle which is fixed to the movable part; (c) the stem of a musical note; (d) in nautical usage, a strap connected with a block, by which it may be secured to a rope, spar, or the like; (e) the outer corner of the eye.
4. a luminous train behind a comet or meteor.
5. the hind, bottom, last, or inferior part of anything, as, (a) in architecture, the bottom or lower part, as of a slate or tile; (b) the inner end of a stone or brick built into a wall so as to project; (c) the beginning and ending of a surgical incision which does not go through the whole skin; also, a strip at the end of a bandage made by ripping the bandage; (d) [*pl.*] chaff; (e) [*pl.*] in mining, tailings; (f) the final portion of what takes place or has duration; as, the *tail* of an entertainment; the *tail* of a storm.
6. [*usually pl.*] the reverse side of a coin from the side with the head, date, etc.
7. a long braid or tress of hair; a switch.
8. (a) a line of people waiting their turn; a queue; (b) a retinue.
9. [*pl.*] (a) a swallow-tailed coat; (b) full-dress attire for men. [Colloq.]
10. the lower end of a stream or pool.
11. in aeronautics, the rear part of an airship; especially, a set of stabilizing planes at the rear of an airplane.
12. in printing, the bottom of a page.
13. in prosody, the short line or lines ending certain stanzas or verse forms.
14. in bookbinding, the lower edge of a book.
15. in heraldry, the tail of a hart.
16. the handle of a rake.
tail of a comet; same as sense 4, above.
tail of a lock; on a canal, the lower end or entrance into the lower pond.
to turn tail; to run from danger, difficulty, hardship, etc.
to twist the lion's tail; see under *twist*.
with the tail between the legs; in defeat or in escape from expected defeat; with fear or dejection.

tāil, *v.t.*; tailed, *pt., pp.*; tailing, *ppr.* 1. to attach a tail to; as, to *tail* a kite.
2. to cut or detach the tail or taillike part from.
3. to form the tail or end of, as a group or procession; to be at the rear or end of.
4. to fasten or connect at or by the tail.
5. to follow stealthily; to shadow. [Slang.]
6. in architecture, to fasten one end of (a brick, board, etc.) into a wall, etc. (with *in* or *on*).
7. to pull by the tail. [Rare.]
8. in Australia, to herd, as cattle.

tāil, *v.i.* 1. to become scattered in a line; to straggle.
2. to become gradually smaller or fainter; to almost disappear; as, the noise *tailed* away.
3. to form, or become part of, a line or tail.
4. to follow close behind. [Colloq.]
5. in architecture, to be fastened into a wall, etc. by one end: said of a brick or board.
6. in nautical usage, to go aground or be anchored stern foremost.

tāil, *a.* 1. at the rear or rear end.
2. from the rear; as, a *tail* wind.

tāil, *v.t.* 1. to cut; to carve. [Obs.]
2. to set down on a tally. [Obs.]
3. to limit as by an entail.

tāil'band, *n.* 1. in bookbinding, the bottom headband of a book: formerly so called.
2. a crupper. [Dial.]

tāil bāy, in architecture, one of the main divisions of a framed roof or floor.

tāil bēam, a timber tailed in, as to a wall.

tāil block, on shipboard, a single block having a short piece of rope, strap, etc. attached to it by which it may be fastened to any object at will.

tāil'bōard, *n.* the board that forms the back of a wagon, cart, etc.: it is completely removed or swung down on hinges for loading or unloading.

tāil çōat, a man's coat with long tails in back, usually worn on formal occasions.

tāil çorn, wheat unfit for market but available for home use. [Brit. Dial.]

tāil cŏv'ẽrts, the feathers that cover the bases of the tail feathers.

tāil dīve, a tail-forward, downward plunge of an airplane.

tāiled, *a.* having a (specified kind of) tail; caudate: principally in combination, as in short-*tailed*, bob*tailed*, ring-*tailed*, etc.
2. in botany, having a taillike appendage.
3. shaped like a tail.

tāil end, 1. the rear or bottom end of anything.
2. the concluding or last part of anything.
3. [*pl.*] inferior samples of corn.

tāil feath′ẽr (feth′), a rectrix; one of the feathers of a bird's tail.

tāil fin, the caudal fin of a fish.

tāil′flow″ẽr, *n.* any plant of the genus *Anthurium.*

tāil gāte, the gate at the lower end of a canal lock.

tāil′gāte, *n.* a tailboard, as of a wagon.

tāil grāpe, any climbing shrub of the genus *Artabotrys,* native to tropical Africa and Asia, the fruit of which is supported by a recurving peduncle.

tāil′ing, *n.* 1. [*pl.*] waste or refuse in various processes of milling, mining, distilling, etc.
2. in building, the part of a projecting brick, stone, etc. embedded in a wall.
3. a defect in printing calico caused by an imperfect process.
4. in electricity, (a) a residual discharge affecting the receiver of a telegraph system, tending to make the signals run together; (b) a residual or return charge or current in the transmission of electromagnetic waves through a dielectric.

tāil lamp, a taillight.

tāille (tāl), *n.* [Fr., from *tailler,* to cut.]
1. a tally. [Obs.]
2. a French feudal tax imposed by the king or a lord.
3. form or shape, especially of the bust.
4. the waist of a dress or its fit, cut, etc.

tāil′less, *a.* having no tail.

tail·lèur′ (tä-yẽr′), *n.* [Fr. *tailler,* to cut.] the dealer or banker in various French card games.

tāil′lie, *n.* [Fr. *tailler,* to cut.] in Scots law, tail.

tāil′light, *n.* a light at the back of a vehicle to warn approaching vehicles of its presence at night: also *tail lamp.*

tail·loir′ (tä-ywär′), *n.* [Fr. *tailler,* to cut.] in architecture, an abacus.

tāi′lŏr, *n.* [Fr. *tailleur,* from *tailler,* to cut.]
1. a person who makes, repairs, or alters clothes, especially suits, coats, etc.
2. in zoology, (a) a tailorbird; (b) the silversides.
merchant tailor; see under *merchant.*
tailor's chair; a legless seat with a back rest, allowing the occupant to sit crosslegged.
tailor's muscle; the sartorius.

tāi′lŏr, *v.i.*; tailored, *pt., pp.*; tailoring, *ppr.*
1. to work as a tailor.
2. to deal with tailors, as for clothing.

tāi′lŏr, *v.t.* 1. to make (clothes) by tailor's work.
2. to fit or provide (a person) with clothes made by a tailor.
3. to cut, form, produce, alter, etc. so as to meet requirements or particular conditions; as, her novel is *tailored* to popular tastes.
4. to fashion (women's garments, etc.) with trim, simple lines like those of men's clothes.

tāi′lŏr·bīrd, *n.* one of various birds, as those of the genus *Orthotomus* or allied genera, constructing a nest by sewing leaves together and lining the case with some soft substance.

tāi′lŏr·ess, *n.* a woman tailor.

tāi′lŏr·ing, *n.* 1. the business of a tailor.
2. the workmanship or skill of a tailor.

tāi′lŏr-māde, *a.* made by or as by a tailor or according to his methods; specifically, (a) made with trim, simple lines: said of a woman's garment; (b) made to order or to meet particular conditions; as, furniture *tailor-made* for the small apartment.

tāil′pïece, *n.* 1. a piece or part added to or forming the end of something, as (a) in a lathe, the tailpin; (b) in mining, a snore piece.
2. the small triangular piece of wood at the lower end of a violin, cello, etc., to which the strings are attached.
3. a short beam or rafter with one end tailed in a wall and the other supported by a header.
4. in printing, an ornamental design, engraving, etc. put at the end of a chapter or at the bottom of a page.
5. in entomology, one of the parts making up a pygidium.

tāil′pin, *n.* the adjustable screw on a rear spindle.

tāil′pīpe, *n.* 1. an exhaust pipe at the rear of an automotive vehicle.
2. the exhaust duct of a jet engine.

tāil plāne, a horizontal supporting surface at the rear of an aircraft; a stabilizer.

tāil′rāce, *n.* 1. the lower part of a millrace.
2. the channel through which water flows after going over a water wheel.
3. a water channel to carry away tailings from a mine.

tāil′spin, *n.* the descent of an airplane with nose down and tail spinning in circles overhead: often used figuratively: also *tail spin.*

tāil′stock, *n.* the adjustable part of a lathe, containing the dead center which holds the work.

tāil switch′ing (swich′), a method of switching trains at stations by means of which they may be drawn out tail end first.

tāil wạ′tẽr, the water flowing from the buckets of a water wheel in motion.

tāil wind, a wind blowing from behind an airplane, ship, etc. in motion.

tāil′zie, *n.* [Fr. *tailler,* to cut.] in Scots law, tail.

tāin, *n.* [ME. *teine,* a thin plate, L. *tænia,* a band.] thin tin plate; also, tin foil for mirrors.

Taī′nō, *n.*; *pl.* **Taī′nōs,** 1. [*pl.*] a member of an extinct, aboriginal Indian tribe of the West Indies.
2. its Arawakan language.

tāint, *v.t.*; tainted, *pt., pp.*; tainting, *ppr.* [contr. from *attaint*; meaning influenced by Fr. *teint,* pp. of *teindre,* from L. *tingere,* to wet, moisten.]
1. to affect with something physically injurious, unpleasant, etc.; to infect; to spoil.
2. to make morally corrupt or depraved; as, greed *tainted* his mind.
3. to dye; to color. [Obs.]
4. to sully or stain (a person's honor). [Obs.]
5. to mollify. [Obs.]

tāint, *v.i.* 1. to become tainted.
2. to be affected with incipient putrefaction, as meat.

tāint, *n.* 1. tincture; stain; color. [Obs.]
2. an infectious or contaminating trace; infection; contamination.
3. a trace of corruption, evil, disgrace, etc.

tāint, *n.* [shortened form of *attaint.*] a hit in tilting. [Obs.]

tāint, *v.i.* to make a thrust in tilting. [Obs.]

tāint, *v.t.* to touch as in tilting; also, to thrust, as a lance. [Obs.]

tāint′less, *a.* without taint or infection; pure.

tāint′less·ly, *adv.* without taint; in a taintless manner or way.

tāint′ŏr, *n.* a dyer. [Rare.]

tāint′ūre, *n.* taint; tinge; defilement; stain; spot. [Obs.]

tāint′wŏrm, *n.* any parasitic worm injurious to plant or animal life.

Taī′ping (tī′), *a.* [Chin. *t'ai-p'ing,* great peace: designation of the dynasty that was to be established.] designating or of a rebellion (1850–1864) against the Manchu dynasty, led by Hung Siu-tsuan.

taī′rà, taȳ′rà, *n.* [S.Am.] a South American carnivore, *Galera barbara,* resembling the weasel.

tāirġe, *v.t.* [ME. *taryen,* to tarry, delay; OFr. *targer,* to delay.] to censure. [Scot.]

tāirn, *n.* a tarn. [Scot.]

tāisch, *n.* [Gael.] the phantom or voice of a person about to die. [Scot.]

tāit, *n.* [Australian.] an Australian marsupial, *Tarsipes rostratus,* about the size of the mouse, feeding principally upon honey and insects.

täj, *n.* [Per., from Ar.] a distinguishing headdress; a high cap such as is worn by Mohammedan dervishes.

Tä′jik, *n.*; *pl.* **Tä′jik,** same as *Tadzhik.*

Täj Mȧ·häl′, [Per., best of buildings.] the famous mausoleum at Agra, India, built (1630?–1648?) by Shah Jahan for his favorite wife.

tä′kä, *n.*; *pl.* **tä′kä,** [from Sans. *tŏnkō,* silver coins.] the monetary unit of Bangladesh.

tāke, *v.t.*; took, *pt.*; taken, *pp.*; taking, *ppr.* [ME. *taken*; (late) AS. *tacan,* from ON. *taka.*]
1. to get by conquering; to capture; to seize.
2. to trap or snare (a bird, animal, or fish).
3. (a) to win, as a game, a part of a game, or a trick at cards; (b) to remove (an opponent's piece) from play by capturing.
4. to get hold of; to grasp.
5. to hit (a person) *in* or *on* some part.
6. to affect; to attack; as, he was *taken* by violent shaking.
7. to catch (a person) in some act, especially a fault.
8. to capture the fancy of; to charm.
9. to get into one's hand or hold; to transfer to oneself.
10. to eat, drink, swallow, etc. for bodily nourishment.
11. to get benefit from by exposure to; as, she *took* the air. [Rare.]
12. to enter into a special relationship with; as, she *took* students to add to her income; he *took* a wife.
13. to buy; as, he *took* the first suit that the clerk offered.
14. to rent or lease; as, we *took* a cottage for the summer.
15. to get regularly by paying for; as, we *take* two daily newspapers.
16. to assume as a responsibility, task, etc.; as, he *took* the job.
17. to assume or adopt (a badge or symbol of duty, office, etc.); as, the president *took* the chair.
18. to obligate oneself by; as, he *took* a vow.
19. to become a member of; to join, as a party or side in a contest, disagreement, etc.
20. to assume (something) as if granted or due one; as, he *took* the blame; she *took* her leave.
21. to cheat; to trick. [Slang.]
22. in grammar, to have or admit of according to usage, nature, etc.; to be used with in construction; as, a transitive verb *takes* an object.
23. to choose; to select.
24. to use or employ; to resort to; as, he *took* a whip to his son.
25. to travel by; to get in or on as a means of traveling; as, she *took* a train.
26. to go to (a place) for shelter, safety, etc.; as, the birds *took* cover.
27. to deal with; to consider; as, he *took* the matter gravely.
28. to occupy; as, *take* a chair.
29. to require; to demand; to need: used impersonally, as, it *takes* money to make money. [Colloq.]
30. to derive or draw, as a name, quality, etc., from.
31. to extract, as for quotation; to excerpt; as, he *took* a verse from the Bible.
32. to obtain by observation, experiment, study, etc.; as, he *took* a poll.
33. to write down; to copy; as, *take* notes.
34. to draw, photograph, etc. a likeness of; as, let me *take* your picture.
35. to win, as a prize, reward, etc.
36. to be the object of; to undergo; as, *take* punishment.
37. to occupy oneself in; to enjoy; as, *take* a nap.
38. to accept (something offered); as, *take* a bet; *take* advice.
39. to have a specified reaction to; as, he *took* the joke in earnest.
40. to confront and get over, through, etc.; as, the horse *took* the jump.
41. to be affected by (a disease, etc.); as, he *took* cold.
42. to absorb; to become impregnated with, as a dye, polish, etc.
43. (a) to understand the remarks of (a person); (b) to comprehend the meaning of (words, remarks, etc.); (c) to understand or interpret in a specified way.
44. to suppose; to presume; as, I *take* him to be an intelligent person.
45. to have or feel, as an emotion, mental state, etc.; as, *take* pity, *take* notice.
46. to hold and act upon, as an idea, resolution, etc.
47. to do; to perform (an act); as, *take* a walk.
48. to make or put forth as the result of thought, as a resolution or objection.
49. to aim and execute (a specified action) at an object; as, he *took* a short jab at his opponent. [Colloq.]
50. to conduct; to lead; as, this path *takes* you to the river.
51. to carry; as, *take* your skates with you.
52. to remove from a person or thing; to extract; as, the thief *took* the silver.
53. to remove by death.
54. to subtract; as, the storekeeper *took* a dollar from the price.
55. to direct (oneself); to go.
to take amiss; (a) originally, to be wrong concerning; to mistake; (b) to misunderstand the reason behind (an act); to become offended at.
to take at one's word; to accept as true, correct, etc.

to take back; (a) to regain use or possession of; (b) to retract (something said, promised, etc.).

to take care of; to superintend or oversee; to have the charge of.

to take down; (a) to remove from a higher place and put in a lower one; to pull down; (b) to unfasten; to take apart; (c) to make less conceited; to humble (a person); (d) to put in writing; to record.

to take for; (a) to consider to be; to regard as; (b) to regard wrongly as; to mistake for; (c) [Slang.] to cheat (a person) of.

to take ground; in military usage, to extend the line in order to cover specified territory.

to take heed; to be careful or cautious.

to take hold; (a) to seize; to grasp; (b) to gain control or power: used with *of*.

to take in; (a) to admit; to receive; (b) to shorten (a sail) by reefing or furling; (c) to make smaller or more compact; (d) to include; to comprise; (e) to understand; to comprehend; (f) to cheat; to trick; to deceive; (g) to visit; as, we *took in* all the sights; (h) to receive into one's home for pay, as roomers, work, etc.

to take it; (a) to suppose; believe; (b) [Slang.] to withstand difficulty, criticism, hardship, ridicule, etc.

to take it lying down; to submit without protest to oppression, etc.; to offer no resistance; to be meek. [Colloq.]

to take it on the chin; to be defeated; to undergo punishment, pain, difficulties, etc. [Slang.]

to take it out of; (a) to exhaust; tire; (b) to obtain payment or satisfaction from. [Colloq.]

to take it out on; to make (another) suffer for one's own anger, irritation, bad temper, etc. [Colloq.]

to take off; (a) to remove, as a garment; (b) to draw or conduct away; (c) to go away; depart (used reflexively); (d) to deduct; subtract; (e) to kill, as an assassin, disease, etc.; (f) to make a copy or likeness of; (g) [Colloq.] to imitate in a burlesque manner; to mimic.

to take on; (a) to acquire; to assume, as form, quality, etc.; (b) to employ; to hire; (c) to begin to do, as a task, etc.; to undertake; (d) to oppose in a game or contest; to play against.

to take one's life in one's hands; to subject oneself to danger; to risk one's life.

to take (one's) time; to be slow or unhurried: to delay.

to take out; (a) to remove or extract from a place, or from a number of other things; (b) to remove by cleansing or the like; as, *to take out* a stain, a blot, etc.; (c) to cause to be no longer operative; to put an end to; as, *to take* the strength *out* of one; (d) to obtain or accept as an equivalent; as, he *took* the amount of the debt *out* in goods; (e) to obtain by application to the proper authority; as *to take out* a patent; (f) in bridge, to bid higher than (one's partner) but in a different suit; (g) [Colloq.] to escort.

to take over; to assume the control or management of; to undertake; as, *to take over* a business.

to take to pieces; to separate into individual parts; hence, to analyze; as, *to take* an argument *to pieces*.

to take up; (a) to raise; to lift; (b) to make tighter or shorter; (c) to pay off; to recover by buying, as a mortgage, note, etc.; (d) to absorb (a liquid); (e) to accept, as a challenge, bet, etc.; (f) to assume protection, custody, etc. of (a person); (g) to interrupt (a person) in disapproval, rebuke, etc.; (h) to resume (something interrupted); (i) to become interested in or devoted to, as an occupation, study, belief, etc.; to adopt (an idea); (j) to occupy or fill (place or time).

to take upon (or *on*) *oneself*; (a) to take the responsibility for; to accept as a charge or duty; (b) to begin (to do anything); to undertake.

tāke, *v.i.* 1. to get possession.

2. to hook or engage with another part: said of a mechanical device.

3. to take root; to begin growing: said of a plant.

4. to lay hold; to catch; as, the fire *took* rapidly.

5. to gain public favor; to be popular; as, the play *took* from its first performance.

6. to be effective in action, operation, etc.; as, the smallpox vaccination *took*; the dye *takes* well.

7. to remove a part; to detract (with *from*); as, nothing *took from* the scene's beauty.

8. to be made or adapted to be taken in a specified way.

9. to go; to proceed; as, the horse *took* to the roadside.

10. to become (ill or sick). [Colloq. or Dial.]

11. to be photographed in a specified way; as, she *takes* well. [Colloq.]

12. in law, to take possession of property.

to take after; to be, act, or look like.

to take off; (a) to leave the ground or water in flight, as an airplane; (b) [Colloq.] to start.

to take on; to show violent emotion, especially anger or sorrow. [Colloq.]

to take to; (a) to develop a habit or practice of doing, using, etc.; (b) to go to, as for hiding, rest, etc.; (c) to become fond of; to care for; to be attracted to.

to take up with; to become an associate or companion of; to be friendly with. [Colloq.]

tāke, *n.* 1. the act or process of taking.

2. something that has been taken.

3. the amount or quantity of something taken; as, the day's *take* of fish.

4. the money received; receipts or profit. [Slang.]

5. in motion pictures, (a) a scene photographed or to be photographed with an uninterrupted run of the camera; (b) the process of photographing such a scene.

6. in England, a holding of property, as land leased for coal mining.

tāke′down, *n.* 1. the act or process of taking down, especially of disassembling mechanically.

2. humiliation; mortification.

tāke′down, *a.* made to be easily taken apart; as, a *takedown* firearm.

tāke′-hōme pāy, wages or salary after deductions for income tax, social security, etc. have been made.

tāke′-in, *n.* 1. imposition; fraud; deception. [Colloq.]

2. one who cheats or deceives; as, he is a *take-in*. [Colloq.]

tāk′en, *v.* past participle of *take*.

taken aback; suddenly confused or startled; dumbfounded.

tāke′-ōff, *n.* 1. the act of leaving the ground, as in jumping or flight.

2. the spot from which one leaves the ground.

3. a forward and upward motion made in leaving the ground in an airplane; as, his *take-off* was perfect.

4. an amusing or mocking imitation; a caricature; a burlesque. [Colloq.]

5. in mechanics, a device for transferring power from an engine or other source for the operation of another mechanism.

tāke′-out, *n.* in bridge, a bid made by a player, indicating to his partner his ability to assist the latter, or, in general, a bid that gives one's partner a clue as to the strength or the weakness of one's hand.

tāke′-out, *a.* pertaining to a take-out; as, a *take-out* bid.

tāk′ẽr, *n.* one who takes something, as a bet, tickets, etc.

tāke′-up, *n.* 1. the act or process of taking up, making tight, etc.

2. a mechanical device for tightening something.

3. a device for winding up material as it leaves a loom.

4. a device for tightening the stitch on a sewing machine, by taking in the slack of the upper thread while the needle is rising.

5. the part between the smoke box of a steam boiler and the bottom of the funnel.

tā′kin, *n.* same as *yakin*.

tāk′ing, *a.* 1. alluring; attracting; engaging; pleasing.

2. infectious; contagious; catching: said of a disease. [Colloq.]

tāk′ing, *n.* 1. the act of one who or that which takes.

2. a state of agitation or excitement. [Colloq.]

3. something taken; a catch.

4. [*pl.*] earnings; profits; receipts.

5. that which takes, as a sickness; an evil influence. [Obs.]

tāk′ing·ly, *adv.* in a taking or attractive manner.

tāk′ing·ness, *n.* the quality of pleasing.

tāk′ing ōff, 1. the act of bearing off or away.

2. assassination; murder; death.

tak·ō′sis, *n.* [Gr. *tēkein*, to waste away.] a contagious disease of goats, characterized by failing appetite, and a gradual weakening and wasting away.

tal′ȧ·poin, tel′ȧ·poin, *n.* [E. Ind.] 1. a Buddhist monk.

2. a species of small, longtailed monkey, *Cercopithecus talapoin*, of West Africa.

tȧ·lā′ri·ȧ, *n.pl.* [L., from *talus*, the ankle.] winged sandals or wings on the ankles, represented as an attribute of Hermes, or Mercury, and other gods.

tal′bŏt, *n.* [probably from the *Talbot* family, who bear the figure of a dog in their coat of arms.] an extinct breed of hound, having a broad mouth, deep chops, large, pendulous ears, and a smooth coat, usually white: probably the origin of the bloodhound.

tal′bō·tȳpe, *n.* [after Fox *Talbot*, the English inventor.] same as *calotype*.

talç, *n.* [Fr., from Ar. *talq*.] a very soft mineral, magnesium silicate, $H_2Mg_3(SiO_3)_4$, used to make talcum powder, lubricants, etc.

talç, *v.t.*; talcked *or* talced, *pt.*, *pp.*; talcking *or* talcing, *ppr.* to use talc on.

tal′çȧ gum, a kind of gum arabic secreted by the tree *Acacia stenocarpa*.

talç′ōse, talç′ous, *a.* of, pertaining to, or containing talc.

tal′çum, *n.* [LL., from Ar. *talq*, talc.]

1. talc.

2. talcum powder.

tal′çum pow′dẽr, a powder for the body and face made of powdered talc that has been purified and, usually, perfumed.

tāle, *n.* [AS. *talu*, tale, speech, number.]

1. something told or related; relation or recital of happenings.

2. (a) a story or account of true, legendary, or fictitious events; a narrative; (b) a literary composition in narrative form.

3. idle or malicious gossip.

4. a fiction; falsehood; lie.

5. a tally; count; enumeration. [Archaic or Poetic.]

6. a complete tally; total; as, the flood's *tale* of dead.

7. the act of telling; talk. [Obs.]

8. in law, a count or declaration. [Obs.]

Syn.—story, legend, incident, fable, narrative, anecdote, relation, memoir, account.

tāle, *v.i.* to tell stories. [Obs.]

tāle, *n.* same as *tael*.

tāle′beăr″ẽr, *n.* a person who gossips or tells secrets, scandal, etc.

tāle′beăr″ing, *a.* of or relating to the telling of secrets or scandal.

tāle′beăr″ing, *n.* the act of circulating gossip or scandal.

tāle′çar″ri·ẽr, *n.* a talebearer.

tāle′fụl, *a.* having many stories.

Tal·ē·gal′lus, *n.* [native name.] a genus of rasorial birds, typical of the family *Talegallinæ*, native to Australia and New Guinea: the best-known species is the brush turkey.

tāle′mŏn·gẽr, *n.* a talebearer.

tal′ent, *n.* [Fr., from L. *talentum*; Gr. *talanton*, a talent or weighed amount of money, a weight.]

1. a gift committed to one's trust to use and improve: from the parable of the talents, in St. Matthew xxv. 14–30; hence, any natural faculty, ability, or power.

2. a special, superior ability in an art, mechanics, learning, etc.

3. talented persons collectively; as, he encouraged young *talent*.

4. disposition; inclination; affection; will. [Obs.]

The nation generally was without any ill *talent* to the church in doctrine or discipline. —Clarendon.

5. a unit of weight or of money (the value of a talent weight in gold, silver, etc.) used in ancient Greece, Rome, the Middle East, etc.: it varied widely in value at different times and in different places but was usually large, the lowest estimated weight being about 58 pounds avoirdupois.

6. habitual bettors or gamblers. [Slang.]

Syn.—gift, ability, capacity, genius, endowment.

tal′ent·ed, *a.* having talent; possessing skill or talent; highly gifted.

tä′lẽr, *n.*; *pl.* **tä′lẽr,** [G.] a former German silver coin: also spelled *thaler*.

tā′lēş, *n.pl.* [L. *talis*, pl. *tales*, such, of such a kind: from use in *tales de circumstantibus*, such of those standing about, phrase in writ summoning them.]

1. in law, people summoned to fill jury vacancies when the regular panel has become deficient in number by challenge, etc.

2. [*construed as sing.*] the writ that summons them.

tāleṣ′măn (*or* tal′is-măn), *n.*; *pl.* **tāleṣ′men,** a person summoned as one of the tales.

tāle′tell″ẽr, *n.* 1. one who tells stories.
 2. a talebearer.

tāle′wīṣe, *adv.* in the manner of a tale.

Tal″i·ȧ·çō′tiăn, *a.* relating to or named after G. Taliacotius or Tagliacozzi, a Bolognese surgeon of the sixteenth century.
 Taliacotian operation; the surgical operation of making a nose out of the flesh of the arm: also called *Taliacotian rhinoplasty.*

tal·i·ā′tion, *n.* retaliation. [Obs.]

tal·i·ẹ′rȧ, *n.* [E. Ind.] in botany, the *Corypha taliera,* a species of palm growing in Bengal, related to the talipot.

tal′i·grāde, *a.* [L. *talus,* an ankle, and *gradi,* to step or walk.] in zoology, walking on the heel or side of the foot, as the sloth.

Tȧ·lī′num, *n.* [Senegal.] a genus of herbs of the order *Portulaceæ,* chiefly American, having bright-colored flowers.

ta′li·ŏn, *n.* [Fr., from L. *talio (-onis),* from *talis,* such.] punishment that exacts a penalty just like the crime; retaliation, as the principle of an eye for an eye, a tooth for a tooth.

tal·i·on′iç, *a.* of, relating to, or having the character of retaliation.

tal′i·ped, *n.* [L. *talus,* an ankle, and *pes, pedis,* a foot.] a person or animal having a clubfoot.

tal′i·ped, *a.* clubfooted; having talipes.

tal′i·pēṣ, *n.* [L. *talus,* an ankle, and *pes,* a foot.] a deformity of the foot in which it is twisted out of shape or position; clubfoot.

tal′i·pŏt, tal′i·put, *n.* [Bengali *tālipāt,* palm leaf, from Sans. *tālī,* fan palm, and *pattra,* leaf.] the fan palm, *Corypha umbraculifera,* native to India, Ceylon, and the Malabar coast, with fanlike leaves, which are used for thatch, umbrellas, fans, and writing paper: also *talipot palm.*

tal′is·măn, *n.*; *pl.* **tal′is·mănṣ,** [Fr. and Sp. *talisman*; Ar. *tilsam,* a magic figure, a horoscope, from Gr. *telesma,* incantation.]
 1. something, as a ring or stone, bearing engraved figures or symbols supposed to bring good luck, keep away evil, etc.
 2. anything supposed to have magic power; a charm.

tal·is·man′iç, *a.* of, like, or used as a talisman.

tal·is·man′iç·ăl, *a.* same as *talismanic.*

tal′ith, *n.* same as *tallith.*

tạlk (tạk), *v.i.*; talked, *pt., pp.*; talking, *ppr.* [ME. *talken*; prob. based on AS. *talian,* to reckon.] 1. to put ideas into, or exchange ideas by, spoken words; to speak; to converse.
 2. to express ideas by speech substitutes; as, *talk* by signs.
 3. to speak emptily or trivially; to chatter.
 4. to gossip.
 5. to confer; to consult.
 6. to make noises suggestive of speech.
 to talk at; to make comments intended for (a person) without directly speaking to him.
 to talk away; to talk continuously; to chatter.
 to talk back; to answer impertinently, brazenly, or rudely.
 to talk big; to boast; to brag. [Slang.]
 to talk down to; to talk to (people of less or supposedly less intelligence than oneself) so that they will understand; to patronize by pointedly simple speech.
 to talk into; to persuade (someone) to do something.
 to talk of; (a) to speak about; to discuss; (b) to express the possibility or intention of (doing something).
 to talk out; to speak loudly and clearly. [Colloq.]
 to talk out of; to dissuade (someone) from doing something.
 to talk up; (a) to speak loudly and clearly; (b) to speak boldly or impertinently. [Colloq.]
 to talk with; (a) to speak or discuss with; (b) to try to persuade, convince, etc.
 Syn.—chat, confer, converse, discourse.

tạlk, *v.t.* 1. to put into spoken words; utter.
 2. to make use of in speaking; as, to *talk* Spanish, to *talk* slang.
 3. to speak at length about; discuss.
 4. to put (oneself or another) into a specified condition, state of mind, etc. by talking; as, *talk* oneself hoarse, *talk* him into agreement.
 to talk around; to talk (a person) over; persuade.
 to talk away; to pass (a specified length of time) by talking.
 to talk down; to talk louder, longer, or more effectively than (a person); to silence (an argument or person).
 to talk one's arm (or *head*) *off*; to talk without pause or for a long time: also *to talk to death.* [Slang.]
 to talk out; (a) to exhaust (a subject) by discussing it; (b) [Brit.] to discuss (a proposed parliamentary bill) so long that adjournment prevents a vote on it.
 to talk over; (a) to talk about; to discuss; to debate; (b) to win (a person) over by talking or argument; to persuade.
 to talk up; to discuss in order to create interest; to praise.

tạlk, *n.* 1. (a) the act of talking; speech; (b) conversation, especially of an informal nature.
 2. a speech or lecture.
 3. a formal discussion; conference.
 4. rumor; gossip.
 5. the subject of conversation, gossip, etc.
 6. empty, frivolous discussion or conversation; as, it's just *talk.*
 7. a particular kind of speech; dialect; lingo. [Colloq.]
 big talk; a bragging, or boasting. [Slang.]
 to make talk; (a) to talk in an idle, forced manner in an effort to pass time; (b) to cause gossip.
 Syn.—conversation, colloquy, discourse, chat, dialogue, conference, communication.

tạlk′ȧ·tive (tạk′), *a.* given to much talking; chatty; loquacious; garrulous.
 Syn.—talkative, loquacious, garrulous.

tạlk′ȧ·tive·ly, *adv.* in a talkative manner.

tạlk′ȧ·tive·ness, *n.* loquacity; garrulity; the practice or habit of speaking a great deal.

tạlk′ee-tạlk′ee, *n.* 1. a corrupt or broken dialect.
 2. incessant chatter or talk. [Colloq.]

tạlk′ẽr, *n.* one who talks; especially, a loquacious or talkative person; a chatterer; a boaster.

tạlk′ie, *n.* a talking picture. [Colloq.]

tạlk′ing, *a.* 1. given to talking; talkative; garrulous; loquacious.
 2. having the ability to speak; as, a *talking* parrot.

tạlk′ing, *n.* the act of a person who talks; discussion; conversation.

tạlk′ing mȧ·chïne′, a phonograph.

tạlk′ing piç′tūre, a motion picture with a synchronized sound track for reproducing dialogue, music, etc. to accompany the action.

tạlk′ing-tö, *n.* a reprimand; a scolding; as, to give one a good *talking-to.* [Colloq.]

tạlk shōw, in radio and television, a program in which a host interviews or converses informally with guest celebrities, experts, etc., often with questions and comments by telephone from listeners or viewers.

tạlk′y, *a.*; *comp.* talkier; *superl.* talkiest, 1. talkative.
 2. containing too much talk, or dialogue; as, a *talky* novel.

tạll, *a.*; *comp.* taller; *superl.* tallest, [ME. *tal,* dexterous, seemly; AS. *(ge)tæl,* swift, prompt.]
 1. high in stature; higher than the average.
 2. having a stated height; as, five feet *tall.*
 3. (a) fine; handsome; (b) bold; brave. [Obs.]
 4. exaggerated; hard to believe; as, a *tall* tale. [Colloq.]
 5. large; huge; as, a *tall* drink. [Colloq.]
 6. high-flown; pompously eloquent; as, *tall* talk. [Colloq.]

tal′lāġe, *n.* [ME. *talliage*; OFr. *taillage*; from *tail,* a tax, and *-age.*] a portion cut out of a whole; a share; a share of a man's substance paid away as tribute; hence, a tax or toll; especially, a tax levied by the Anglo-Norman kings upon demesne lands of the crown and royal towns.

tal′lāġe, *v.t.*; tallaged, *pt., pp.*; tallaging, *ppr.* to levy a tallage upon; to tax.

tạll′boy, *n.* 1. a long-stemmed glass for drinking.
 2. a kind of tall chimney pot.
 3. a tall chest of drawers mounted on legs; a highboy. [Brit.]

tal′lēs, *n.* same as *tallith.*

tal′lis, *n.* same as *tallith.*

tạll′ish, *a.* rather tall.

tal′lith, *n.* [Heb.] 1. in Judaism, a shawl or scarf with fringes (*zizith*) on each corner, worn over the shoulders or head during morning prayer: Deut. xxii. 12.
 2. a similarly fringed undergarment covering the chest and back, worn by orthodox Jews.

tạll′ness, *n.* the state or quality of being tall; height.

täll oil, [Sw. *tallöl,* pine beer.] a resinous liquid obtained as a by-product in the manufacture of chemical wood pulp: it is used in the manufacture of soap, varnishes, etc.

tal′lōw, *n.* [ME. *talgh*; akin to AS. *tælg,* a color: supposedly so called from its use as a hair coloring among ancient Germanic tribes.] the harder and less fusible fat in cows, sheep, etc.: it is melted and used to make candles, soap, etc.
 vegetable tallow; any of various tallowlike substances obtained from various plants, used for making soap or candles.

tal′lōw, *v.t.*; tallowed, *pt., pp.*; tallowing; *ppr.*
 1. to grease or smear with tallow.
 2. to fatten (animals) so as to cause to have a large quantity of tallow; as, to *tallow* sheep.

tal′lōw çan′dle, a candle made of tallow.

tal′lōw chan′dlẽr, one whose occupation is to make or to make and sell tallow candles.

tal′lōw chan′dlẽr·y, the business or place of business of a tallow chandler.

tal′lōw çup, a lubricator supplying melted tallow.

tal′lōw·ẽr, *n.* 1. an animal that produces tallow.
 2. a tallow chandler.

tal′lōw-fāce, *n.* a person having a pale, sickly complexion.

tal′lōw-fāced (-fāst), *a.* having a sickly complexion; pale.

tal′lōw gōurd, the wax gourd.

tal′lōw·ing, *n.* the act or practice of causing animals to produce tallow; also, the property in animals of forming tallow.

tal′lōw·ish, *a.* having the properties of tallow; rather tallowy.

tal′lōw shrub, the wax myrtle, or bayberry.

tal′lōw tree, any of various trees which produce a vegetable tallow that can be used for making candles. The tallow tree of Malabar is *Vateria indica,* that of China, *Stillingia sebifera,* and that of Sierra Leone, *Pentadesma butyracea.*

tal′lōw·wood, *n.* a large Australian tree having hard, durable wood, used for railroad ties, etc.

tal′lōw·y, *a.* 1. like tallow in consistency; oily; greasy.
 2. like tallow in color; pale yellow.
 3. full of tallow; fat: said of an animal.

tạll′wood, *n.* billets of firewood. [Archaic.]

tal′ly, *n.*; *pl.* **tal′lieṣ,** [ME. *talie, talye*; Anglo-Fr. *tallie*; Anglo-Lat. *talia*; L. *talea,* a stick, cutting.]
 1. originally, a stick with cross notches representing the amount of a debt owing or paid: usually the stick was split lengthwise, half for the debtor and half for the creditor.
 2. anything used as a record for an account.
 3. an account; a reckoning; a score.
 4. either of two corresponding parts of something; counterpart.
 5. agreement; correspondence.
 6. a notch or mark made on a tally.
 7. a mark representing a certain number of objects in a tally.
 8. any number of objects used as a unit in counting.
 9. an identifying tag or label.
 10. a tally shop. [Brit.]
 tally system; a credit system of trade by which customers agree to pay the price of purchases in installments. Both parties keep books, in which are entered the terms of the transaction and the payments of the installments. [Brit.]
 tally trade; credit business using the tally system. [Brit.]

tal′ly, *v.t.*; tallied, *pt., pp.*; tallying, *ppr.* 1. to put on or as on a tally; to record.
 2. to count (usually with *up*).
 3. to put a label or tag on.
 4. to make (two things) agree or correspond.
 to tally on; in nautical usage, to pull aft, as the sheets or lower corners of the mainsail and foresail.

tal′ly, *v.i.* 1. to correspond; to agree; as, the accounts *tally.*
 2. to make or keep a tally, as in a game.

tal′ly·hō′, *interj.* [altered from Fr. *taiaut, tayaut.*] the cry of a hunter on sighting the fox.

tal′ly·hō′, *n.* 1. a cry of "tallyho."
 2. a coach drawn by four horses.

tal′ly·măn, *n.*; *pl.* **tal′ly·men,** 1. one who keeps tally.
 2. one who sells goods to be paid for in installments.

tal'ly sheet, a sheet upon which a score or tally is recorded; a record sheet of votes.

tal'mȧ, *n.* [after F. J. *Talma* (1763–1826), a French actor.] a kind of large cape, or short, full cloak worn in the first half of the nineteenth century.

Tal'mud, *n.* [Heb. *talmūdh*, instruction, from *lāmadh*, to learn.] the collection of writings constituting the Jewish civil and religious law: it consists of two parts, the Mishnah (text) and the Gemara (commentary), but the term is sometimes restricted to the Gemara.

Tal·mud'iç, Tal·mud'i·căl, *a.* of, pertaining to, or contained in the Talmud; as, *Talmudic* teachings.

Tal'mud·ist, *n.* 1. one versed in the Talmud.
2. one who accepts its teachings.
3. any of the authors or compilers of the Talmud.

Tal·mud·is'tiç, *a.* Talmudic.

tā'lō-, [from L. *talus*, heel, ankle.] a combining form meaning *in connection with* or *relation to the astragalus*.

tā''lō·cal·çā'nē·ăl, *a.* pertaining to the astragalus and the calcaneum.

tā·lō·çrū'răl, *a.* [*talo-*, and L. *crus*, leg.] pertaining to the astragalus and the bones of the leg.

tā·lō·fib'ū·lăr, *a.* pertaining to the astragalus and the fibula.

tal'ŏn, *n.* [ME. *talon*, a talon, claw; OFr. *talon*, a heel.]
1. [*usually in pl.*] the claw of an animal or bird of prey, as the hawk, vulture, etc.
2. [*pl.*] human fingers or hands like claws in appearance or grasp.
3. in a lock, the part of the bolt upon which the key presses as it is turned.
4. in architecture, an ogee molding.
5. in card games, the cards remaining after the hands are dealt; the stock.
6. the heel of a sword blade.

tal'ŏned, *a.* having talons.

tȧ·lo͝ok'där, *n.* same as *talukdar*.

Tā'los, *n.* in Greek mythology, (a) an inventor killed because of jealousy by Daedalus, his uncle; (b) a man of brass given by Zeus to Minos, King of Crete, as a watchman.

tā·lō·sçaph'oid, *a.* pertaining to the astragalus and the scaphoid bone.

tā·lō·tib'i·ăl, *a.* pertaining to the astragalus and the tibia.

Tal'pȧ, *n.* [L., a mole.]
1. the type genus of the *Talpidæ*, comprising about six old-world species.
2. [t–] in pathology, a tumor under the skin; also, an encysted tumor or wen on the head: so called because it was supposed to burrow like a mole.

täl·pä·tä'te, täl·pe·tä'te, *n.* [Sp. *tepetate*, from Nahuatl *tepetatl*, from *tetl*, a stone, and *petlatl*, a mat.]
1. in geology, a Central and South American rock containing volcanic ash.
2. a Central American volcanic soil of low grade.

Tal'pi·dae, *n.pl.* a family of *Insectivora*, limited to the temperate regions of Europe, Asia, and North America; the moles.

tal'poid, *a.* belonging to or resembling the *Talpidæ*.

tal'poid, *n.* one of the *Talpidæ*.

tȧ·luk', tȧ·lo͝ok', *n.* [Ar. *ta'alluq*, from *alaqa*, to adhere.] in India, (a) an estate inherited by the native owner; (b) a part of a district subdivided for tax collection.

tä·luk'där, tä·lo͝ok'där, *n.* [from prec., and Per. *-dār*, holding.] in India, the holder of a taluk, who pays the revenue due the government from his estate.

tā'lus, *n.*; *pl.* **tā'lī,** [L., the ankle, heel.]
1. in anatomy, (a) the anklebone; the astragalus; (b) the entire ankle.
2. an analogous part in birds and insects.
3. a variety of clubfoot, in which the heel rests on the ground, and the toes are drawn toward the leg.

tā'lus, *n.* [Fr.; OFr. *talu*; said to be from L. *talus*, an ankle, in special sense.]
1. a slope.
2. the sloping face of a wall, narrow at the top and wide at the base, in a fortification.
3. in geology, a sloping pile of rock fragments at the foot of a cliff.

Tal'win, *n.* [arbitrary name chosen in a contest for naming the product.] a pain-killing, synthetic drug derived from coal tar: used in place of morphine because it is nonaddictive: a trade-mark.

tam, *n.* a tam-o'-shanter.

tām·ȧ·bil'i·ty, *n.* the state or character of being tamable; tamableness.

tām'ȧ·ble, *a.* that can be tamed or reclaimed from wildness.

tām'ȧ·ble·ness, *n.* the quality of being tamable.

tȧ·mä'lē, tȧ·mäl', *n.* [Sp.] a native Mexican dish of crushed Indian corn mixed with finely chopped meat and oil. It is highly seasoned with red pepper, rolled in a corn shuck, and steamed or baked, to be eaten hot. Also called *hot tamale*.

tä·män·duä' (-dwä'), **tȧm'ȧn·dū,** *n.* [S. Am.]
1. a small, tree-dwelling, four-toed anteater, *Tamandua tetradactyla*, of tropical America.
2. [T–] the genus to which this species belongs.

tä·mȧ·noir' (-nwor'), *n.* [Fr., from *tamandua*, S. Am. name of an anteater.] the ant bear or three-toed anteater, *Myrmecophaga jubata*, of South America.

tam'ȧ·nū, *n.* [E. Ind.] a large tree, *Calophyllum inophyllum*, native to Polynesia and the East Indies, yielding a heavy, green resin.

tam'ȧ·rȧ, *n.* [E. Ind.] a spice or condiment much used in Italy, composed of cinnamon, cloves, coriander seeds, aniseed, and fennel seed, ground together.

tam'ȧ·rack, *n.* [Am. Ind.] 1. the American or black larch, *Larix laricina*, found in cool swamps or uplands of Canada and the northern part of the United States; also, the wood of this tree.
2. the black pine, *Pinus murrayana*, found along the Pacific coast from Alaska to California: also called *tamarack pine*.

tä·mȧ·rau' (-row'), *n.* a small, wild buffalo native to the island of Mindoro in the Philippines.

tam'ȧ·riç, tam'ȧ·rick, *n.* tamarisk. [Obs.]

Tam''ȧ·ri·çā'cē·ae, *n.pl.* [L. *tamariscus*, tamarisk.] the tamarisk family, including five genera, native to the warmer parts of the Northern Hemisphere and South Africa. They are usually shrubs, rarely herbs or trees, with fleshy leaves and small, showy, pink or white flowers.

tam''ȧ·ri·çā'ceous, *a.* of, resembling, or belonging to the *Tamaricaceæ*.

tam'ȧ·rin, *n.* [S.Am.] any marmoset of the genus *Midas*, of South America, resembling a squirrel and having long, silky fur.

tam'ȧ·rind, *n.* [Ar. *tamr hindī*, the Indian date tree.]
1. a leguminous tree, *Tamarindus indica*, cultivated in tropical regions, and having a large trunk, terminal racemes of yellow flowers streaked with red, and brown pods with an acid pulp.
2. a seed pod of the tamarind, used for culinary purposes and in medicine.
velvet tamarind; a small tree, *Dialium guineense* or *Codarium acutifolium*, of western Africa: so called because it bears edible pods covered with a black down resembling velvet. Also called *black* or *brown tamarind*.
wild tamarind; any one of several trees resembling the tamarind, as the *Pithecolobium filicifolium* of Jamaica, the *Pentaclethra filamentosa* of Central and South America, etc.

tam'ȧ·rind fish, a preparation of a kind of East Indian fish with the acid pulp of the tamarind fruit.

tam'ȧ·rind plum, a tree, *Dialium indicum*, of the East Indies, the fruit of which resembles the tamarind.

Tam·ȧ·rin'dus, *n.* a genus of leguminous trees, having but one species, *Tamarindus indicus*, widely diffused through the tropics of Africa and Australia, and cultivated in Asia and America.

tam'ȧ·risk, *n.* [L. *tamariscus*, *tamarix*, from Ar. *tamr*, a date.] a plant of the genus *Tamarix*, with slender branches and feathery clusters of pinkish flowers: sometimes called *flowering cypress*. The common tamarisk is *Tamarix gallica*, native to France and to the Mediterranean region, and naturalized on parts of the southern English coast.

TAMARISK
(*Tamarix gallica*)

German tamarisk; a European shrub, *Myricaria germanica*, closely related to and resembling the common tamarisk.
Indian tamarisk; a species of tamarisk, *Tamarix indica*, producing galls which are used in dyeing and in photography.
Oriental tamarisk; a species of tamarisk, *Tamarix orientalis*, native to Arabia, Persia, and the East Indies, encrusted with salt, which is used by the natives: also called *Indian* or *tamarisk salt tree*.

Tam'ȧ·rix, *n.* the type genus of the tamarisk family.

tȧ·mä'shȧ, *n.* [Ar. *tamāsha*, a walking around.] in India, a show; a spectacle; an entertainment.

tam'baç, *n.* same as *tombac*.

tam'bŏr, *n.* [from *tambour*, a drum.]
1. a swellfish.
2. the red rockfish of California.

tam'bōur (*or* -bŏr), *n.* [Fr., a drum.]
1. a drum or drumlike contrivance; a bass drum.
2. an embroidery frame of two closely fitting hoops that hold the cloth stretched between them; also, the piece of embroidery worked on such a frame.
3. in fortification, a stockade to defend an entrance.
4. in architecture, (a) the core of Corinthian and Composite capitals, which bears some resemblance to a drum; (b) the wall of a circular temple surrounded with columns; (c) the circular vertical part of a cupola; also, the base of the cupola when it is circular; (d) a kind of lobby or vestibule of timberwork with folding doors, and covered with a ceiling, as within the porches of churches, etc., to break the current of wind from without; (e) a cylindrical stone, such as one of the courses of the shaft of a column.
5. in physiology, a device for recording the movements of the pulse.

tam'bōur, *v.t.* and *v.t.*; tamboured, *pt.*, *pp.*; tambouring, *ppr.* to embroider with or on a tambour.

tam·bōur'ġi, *n.* [Turk.] a drummer.

tam'bōu·rin (*or Fr.* tän-bö-raṅ'), *n.* [Fr., dim. of *tambour*.]
1. a kind of long drum used in Provence.
2. (a) a quick, sprightly dance of Provence, originally accompanied by such a drum; (b) the music for this dance.

tam·bŏur·ïne', *n.* [Fr. *tambourin*, dim. of *tambour*, drum.]
1. a musical instrument resembling the drum, formed of a hoop over one end of which parchment is stretched and in which jingling metal disks are inserted. It is played by shaking, hitting with the knuckles, etc.
2. a species of dove, *Tympanistria bicolor*, indigenous to South Africa: it has a very resonant call.

TAMBOURINE

tam·breet', *n.* in Australia, the duckbill.

tāme, *v.t.* to open; to broach; to divide; to carve. [Now Dial.]

tāme, *a.*; *comp.* tamer; *superl.* tamest, [AS. *tam*, tame.]
1. changed from a wild to a domesticated state, as animals trained for man's use.
2. like a domesticated animal in nature; gentle; docile.
3. submissive; subdued; servile; crushed by or as by domestication.

He's no swaggerer, hostess; a *tame* cheater, i' faith. —Shak.

4. unanimated; without spirit; insipid; dull; lacking in interest; flat; as, a *tame* performance; a *tame* anecdote.
5. without earnest feeling or fervor; listless; cold.

He that is cold and *tame* in his prayers hath not tasted of the goodness of God. —Jer. Taylor.

6. accommodated to one's habits; grown into a custom; wonted; accustomed. [Obs.]
7. harmless; ineffectual; impotent. [Obs.]

His remedies are *tame* i' the present peace. —Shak.

8. in agriculture, cultivated: said of plants or land.

tāme, *v.t.*; tamed, *pt.*, *pp.*; taming, *ppr.* 1. to make tame; to change from a wild to a domestic state.
2. to overcome the wildness or fierceness of; to subdue; to curb.

3. to deprive of spirit or animation; as, to *tame* the passions of youth.
4. to make less intense; to soften, as colors.

tāme·ȧ·bil′i·ty, *n.* same as *tamability.*

tāme′ȧ·ble, *a.* same as *tamable.*

tāme′less, *a.* 1. not tamed.
2. not tamable.

tāme′ly, *adv.* in a tame manner.

tāme′ness, *n.* the quality or condition of being tame.

tāme poi′ṣŏn, a European herb, *Cynanchum vincetoxicum,* of the milkweed family, whose root was formerly thought to be an antidote for poisons.

tām′ẽr, *n.* one who or that which tames; as, a lion *tamer.*

Tā′mi·as, *n.* [Gr., a steward, a storekeeper, from its habit of laying up large stores.] a genus of rodent mammals, allied to the true squirrels, but distinguished from them by their cheek pouches and their habit of retreating into underground holes. They are of small size and marked with stripes on the back and sides. The ground squirrel or chipmunk is the most common species in North America.

tam′i·dine, *n.* a modified form of trinitrocellulose, formerly used for the filaments of incandescent lamps.

Tam′il, *n.* [Tamil. *Tamiṛ, Tamiḷ,* native name of the people and their language.]
1. any of a Dravidian people of southern India and northern Ceylon.
2. the Dravidian language of the Tamils, ancient or modern, spoken over a wide area of southern India and in northern Ceylon.

Tȧ·mil′i·ăn, Tȧ·mil′iç, *a.* of or pertaining to the Tamils or their language.

tam′ine, tam′in, *n.* [Fr. *étamine.*] a strainer or bolter of hair or cloth. [Obs.]

Tām′ing of the Shrew, a comedy (c. 1594) by Shakespeare.

tam′is, *n.* [Fr., a sieve.]
1. a worsted cloth used for the purpose of straining sauces.
2. a sieve made of tamis.

tam′kin, *n.* same as *tampion.*

Tam′mȧ·ny, *n.* [altered from *Tamanend,* lit., the affable, name of a 17th-c. chief of the Delaware Indians celebrated for his wisdom and friendliness toward white men, and hence, as *Saint Tammany,* humorously regarded as patron saint of the U.S.] a powerful Democratic political organization of New York City, founded in 1789: also *Tammany Society.*

Tam′mȧ·ny, *a.* of Tammany's theories, practices, members, etc.

Tam′mȧ·ny Hạll, 1. Tammany.
2. the headquarters of Tammany.

Tam′muz (*or* tä′mooz), *n.* [Heb. *tammūz;* Assyr.-Bab. *Du'uzu;* Sumerian *dummuzi;* lit., prob. son of life, son who rises.]
1. a Babylonian and Assyrian god whose supposed annual death and resurrection symbolized the winter and spring cycle.
2. the tenth month of the Jewish year.
Also spelled *Thammuz.*

tam′my, *n.* same as *tamin.*

tam′-ō′-shan′tẽr, *n.* [from the name of the main character of Burns's poem "Tam o' Shanter."] a Scottish cap with a round, flat top and, often, a center tassel: also *tam.*

TAM-O'-SHANTER

tamp, *v.t.;* tamped (tampt), *pt., pp.;* tamping, *ppr.* [prob. from *tampion.*]
1. in blasting, to pack clay, sand, etc. around the charge in (the drill hole).
2. to pack or pound down by frequent blows or taps; as, to *tamp* earth so as to make a smooth place.

tam′pan, *n.* [S. Afr.] a poisonous South African tick.

tamp′ẽr, *n.* 1. one who or that which tamps.
2. an instrument used in tamping; a heavy bar or timber with a flat, metal tip.

tam′pẽr, *v.i.* [a form of *temper.*] to contrive something secretly; to plot; to scheme.
to tamper with; (a) to make secret, illegal arrangements with; to bribe; (b) to interfere with; to meddle; (c) to change by meddling; to make corrupt, illegal, etc.

> The Tudors, far from considering the law of succession as a divine and unchangeable institution, were constantly *tampering with* it. —Macaulay.

tam′pẽr·ẽr, *n.* one who tampers.

Tam·pi′çō fī′bẽr, [from *Tampico,* Mexico.] a tough palm fiber used in the manufacture of brooms and brushes.

tamp′ing, *n.* the act of filling up a hole in a rock for the purpose of blasting; also, the material used in thus filling up.

tamp′ing bär, an iron bar with a broad head used in tamping a blast hole.

tam′pi·ŏn, *n.* [OFr. *tampon,* a nasalized form from *tapon, tape,* a bung.]
1. the stopper of a cannon or other piece of ordnance, consisting of a cylinder of wood.
2. a plug for stopping closely the upper end of an organ pipe.

tam′pŏn, *n.* [Fr.] in surgery, a plug of cotton or other absorbent material put into a wound, cavity, etc. for the control of hemorrhage or the absorption of secretions.

tam′pŏn, *v.t.* to put a tampon into.

tam′pŏn·ȧġe, *n.* the act or the operation of applying tampons; also, the use of tampons.

tam·pọọn′, *n.* a plug or bung, as of a barrel, etc.

tam′-tam (tum′tum), *n.* [Hind.; of echoic origin.]
1. a large, slightly convex, disk-shaped gong, struck with a felt-covered drumstick.
2. a tom-tom.

Tam′ul, *n.* same as *Tamil.*

Tȧ·mū′liç, *a.* same as *Tamilian.*

tȧ·mūre′, *n.* [Maori.] a kind of fish, *Pagrosomus auratus,* inhabiting Australian waters.

Tā′mus, *n.* [LL.] an old-world genus of wild climbing plants of the yam family.

Tam′wŏrth, *n.* [from *Tamworth* in Staffordshire, England, where first raised.] one of a breed of large English pigs: they are reddish-brown with black patches, and yield a fine grade of bacon.

tan, *n.* [Fr.; ML. *tannum.*]
1. the bark of oak and certain other trees, crushed to make tannin.
2. bark from which tannin has been extracted, used to cover racecourses, etc.
3. tannin or a solution made from it, used to tan leather.
4. a yellowish-brown color.
5. such a color given to the skin by exposure to the sun.

tan, *a.; comp.* tanner; *superl.* tannest, 1. of or for tanning.
2. yellowish-brown.

tan, *v.t.;* tanned, *pt., pp.;* tanning, *ppr.* 1. to change (hide) into leather by soaking in tannin.
2. to produce a tan color in, as by exposure to the sun.
3. to whip severely; to flog. [Colloq.]
to tan one's hide; to whip one severely; to flog. [Colloq.]

tan, *v.i.* to get or become tanned; as, the leather *tans* easily; my face *tans* quickly.

tan, *n.* same as *picul.*

tä′nȧ, tan′nȧ, *n.* [Hind. *thānā.*] in India, a police station or a military post.

tä′nȧ, *n.* same as *banxring.*

Tan·ȧ·cē′tum, *n.* [LL., from OFr. *tanasie,* tansy, and L. *-etum.*] a genus of perennial herbs of the composite family, including over thirty species, among which is the common tansy.

tä′nȧ·där, tan′nȧ·där, *n.* [Hind. *thānā,* a fort, and *-dar,* holding.] the officer in charge of a tana.

tan′ȧ·ġẽr, *n.* [Braz.] any of several small American songbirds of the genus *Tanagra* and allied genera: the males are usually brilliantly colored.

TANAGER (*Tanagra cyanocephala*)

Tan′ȧ·grȧ, *n.* [Braz. *tangara,* a tanager.] a genus of passerine birds of the finch family, having a conical beak, triangular at the base, the upper mandible notched toward the tip, and its ridge arched.

Tan′ȧ·grȧ, *n.* any of the figurines found at Tanagra, an ancient Greek town in Boeotia.

tan′ȧ·grine, *a.* relating to the genus *Tanagra.*

tan′ȧ·groid, *a.* resembling a tanager.

tan′bärk, *n.* any bark containing tannin, used to tan hides and, after the tannin has been extracted, to cover race tracks, circus rings, etc.

tan bed, in gardening, a bed made of tan; a bark bed.

tan′-çōl″ōred (-ũrd), *a.* having the color of tan.

tan′dem, *adv.* [orig. punning use of L. *tandem,* at length (of time).] in a single line, one behind another; as, horses driven *tandem;* also, in electricity, in series; not abreast.

tan′dem, *a.* having two parts or things placed tandem.
tandem engine; a steam engine having two cylinders placed axially in line.

tan′dem, *n.* 1. a two-wheeled carriage drawn by horses harnessed tandem.
2. a team, as of horses, harnessed tandem.
3. a bicycle with two seats and two sets of pedals placed tandem.

tan·ē·kä′hȧ, *n.* [Maori.] a pine tree, *Phyllocladus trichomanoides,* of New Zealand, the bark of which contains a high percentage of tannin.

tang, *n.* [echoic.] a loud, ringing sound; a twang.

tang, *v.t.* and *v.i.* to sound with a loud ringing.

tang, *n.* [ME. *tange;* ON. *tangi,* a sting, point, dagger.]
1. a projection, tongue, or shank used to fasten an article to a handle, as (a) the smaller end of a knife or a sword blade, chisel, file, rake, etc., set into the handle; (b) an extension of a gun barrel, used to fasten it to the stock.
2. a tongue or tine, as of a buckle or a fork. [Brit. Dial.]
3. a knife, dagger, or bodkin. [Brit. Dial.]
4. a sting, as of a snake or bee.
5. a strong and penetrating taste or odor.
6. a special or characteristic flavor, quality, etc.

tang, *v.t.* to provide with a tang.

tang, *n.* [Dan. *tang;* Ice. *thang,* seaweed.] any of several large seaweeds.
black tang; a coarse black seaweed, *Fucus vesiculosus.*

Täng, *n.* a Chinese dynasty that flourished from the beginning of the 7th century to the beginning of the 10th century, marked by great progress, especially the invention of printing and the advancement of literature.

tañ′gȧ·lung, *n.* [native name.] a civet of Sumatra, *Viverra tangalunga.*

tan′ġē·lō, *n.; pl.* **tan′ġē·lōṣ,** [*tangerine* and *pomelo.*] a fruit produced by crossing a tangerine with a grapefruit, or pomelo.

tan′ġence, *n.* tangency. [Rare.]

tan′ġen·cy, *n.* the state or condition of being tangent.

tan′ġent, *a.* [L. *tangens* (*-entis*), touching, *ppr.* of *tangere,* to touch.]
1. touching.
2. in geometry, meeting a curved line or surface at one point but ordinarily not intersecting it: said of a line or surface.

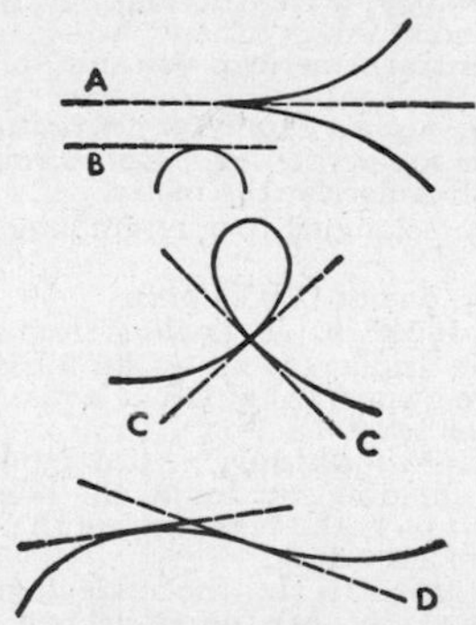

TANGENTS
A, tangent at a cusp; B, ordinary tangent; C, C, tangents at a node; D, tangent at a point of inflection, cutting curve at point of tangency

tangent line; a line tangent to a curve or plane at a definite point.
tangent plane; a plane tangent to a curve or surface.
tangent scale; (a) a rear sight for a cannon: its base has a curvature corresponding to the circumference of the breech of the gun, and its face is cut into steps corresponding to angles of elevation; (b) an addition to the surveyors' compass for the purpose of measuring the slopes of ground so that the proper allowance in chaining may be made.
tangent screw; a screw which acts in the direction of a tangent to an arc or circle.
tangent wheel; a wheel whose spokes are tangent to the hub.

tan′ġent, *n.* 1. a tangent curve, line, or surface.
2. in trigonometry, the ratio of the side opposite the given acute angle in a right-angled triangle to the side opposite the other acute angle: the tangent of an obtuse angle is numerically equal to that of its supplement, but is of opposite sign.
3. the sounding pin upon the end of a clavichord key, which strikes the strings.
4. in engineering, the part of the line of a railroad which lies between any two curves; specifically, the straight portion of railroad line as distinct from the curved portion: so called because they are tangent to the curves. [Colloq.]
artificial tangent; a natural tangent expressed by logarithms.
cuspidal tangent; a line tangent to a curve at a cusp.
logarithmic tangent; same as *artificial tangent*.
method of tangents; a method of determining certain values, as areas, etc., by the relations of the tangents of curves.
multiple tangent; a tangent having more than one contact point with the same curve or surface.
natural tangent; a tangent expressed by natural numbers, as opposed to an *artificial tangent*.
to go (or *fly*) *off at* (or *on*) *a tangent*; to break off suddenly from one line of action, train of thought, etc. and pursue another course.

tan·ġen′tăl, *a.* tangential.

tan·ġen′tiăl (-shăl), *a.* 1. of, like, or in the direction of, a tangent.
2. drawn as a tangent.
3. turned aside from a straight course; digressing.
4. merely touching a subject, not dealing with it at length.
tangential force; (a) the same as centrifugal force; (b) in machinery, a force which acts upon a wheel in the direction of a tangent to the wheel is said to be tangential, and this is the direction in which motion is communicated between wheels and pinions, or from one wheel to another.

tan·ġen′tiăl·ly, *adv.* in a tangential manner; so as to be tangential.

tan·ġĕr·ine′, *n.* [from Fr. *Tanger*, Tangier, Morocco.]
1. a small, loose-skinned orange with a deep, reddish-yellow color and segments that are easily separated
2. a deep reddish-yellow color.
3. [T–] a native or inhabitant of Tangier.

taṅg′fish, *n.*; *pl.* **taṅg′fish** or **taṅg′fish″eṣ,** the seal: so called in the Shetland Islands.

taṅ′ghăm, taṅ′ghăn, *n.* the tangum.

taṅ′ghin (-gin), *n.* [Malagasy.] a poison found in the seeds of the ordeal tree, *Tanghinia venenifera*; also, the ordeal tree.
trial by tanghin; an ordeal formerly practiced in Madagascar to determine the guilt or innocence of an accused person, by use of the tanghin poison. The seed was pounded and a small piece swallowed by each person to be tried. If the accused retained the poison in the system, death quickly resulted—a proof of guilt; if the stomach rejected the dose, innocence was established

Taṅ·ghin′i·ȧ, *n.* a genus of plants belonging to the family *Apocynaceæ*. *Tanghinia venenifera* is the ordeal tree of Madagascar, which produces the tanghin poison.

TANGHIN (branch, drupe, and kernel) (*Tanghinia venenifera*)

tan·ġi·bil′i·ty, *n.* the quality or state of being tangible.

tan′ġi·ble, *a.* [from L. *tangere*, to touch.]
1. that can be touched; that can be felt by touch; having actual form and substance.
2. that can be appraised for value; as, *tangible* assets.
3. that can be understood; definite; objective.

tan′ġi·ble·ness, *n.* the state or quality of being tangible; tangibility.

tan′ġi·bleṣ, *n.pl.* property that can be appraised for value; assets having real substance; material things.

tan′ġi·bly, *adv.* in a tangible manner; perceptibly to the touch.

tan′ġi·lin, *n.* a pangolin, or scaly anteater.

taṅ′gle, *v.t.*; tangled, *pt.*, *pp.*; tangling, *ppr.* [Ice. *thöngull*, *thang*; Dan. *tang*, tangle, seaweed; nasalized forms corresponding to AS. *tægl*, hair, a tail.]
1. to hinder, obstruct, or confuse by covering, circling, entwining, etc.
2. to catch in or as in a net or snare; to trap.
3. to make a knot or snarl of; to intertwine.

taṅ′gle, *v.i.* to become tangled; to be entangled or united confusedly.

taṅ′gle, *n.* 1. an intertwined, confused mass of things, as string, branches, etc.; a snarl.
2. a jumbled, confused condition; a muddle.
3. a perplexed state.
4. a deep-sea dredge used to obtain delicate and fragile organisms. It is a bar or frame of iron with mops of hemp to drag upon the bottom and entangle the minute forms.

taṅ′gle, *n.* 1. either of two kinds of large, edible seaweed, *Laminaria digitata* or *Laminaria saccharina*.
2. a tall, lank person. [Scot.]

taṅ′gle·ber″ry, *n.*; *pl.* **taṅ′gle·ber″ries,** [*tangle* (intertwine) and *berry*.] a kind of huckleberry found especially in the eastern United States.

taṅ′gle·fish, *n.*; *pl.* **taṅ′gle·fish** or **taṅ′gle·fish·eṣ,** the pipefish, *Syngnathus acus*.

taṅ′gle pick′ẽr, the turnstone, a bird. [Brit. Dial.]

taṅ′gle swäb, the mop or swab of a deep-sea tangle.

taṅ′gle tent, a tent or cylinder of compressed tangle (*Laminaria*) used to dilate the cervix of the uterus by absorbing moisture.

taṅ′gling·ly, *adv.* in a tangling manner.

taṅ′gly, *a.* in a tangle; full of tangles; snarled; confusing; involved.

taṅ′gly, *a.* strewn with tangle; as, a *tangly* shore.

taṅ′gō, *n.*; *pl.* **taṅ′gōṣ,** [Am. Sp., a dance; Sp., a Negro dance from Cuba.]
1. a South American dance with long gliding steps and intricate movements and poses.
2. music for this dance in $^2/_4$ or $^4/_4$ time.

taṅ′gō, *v.i.* to dance the tango.

taṅ′grăm, *n.* [prob. arbitrary coinage on analogy of *anagram*, *cryptogram*, etc.] a Chinese puzzle made by cutting a square into five triangles, a square, and a rhomboid, and using these pieces to form different figures and designs.

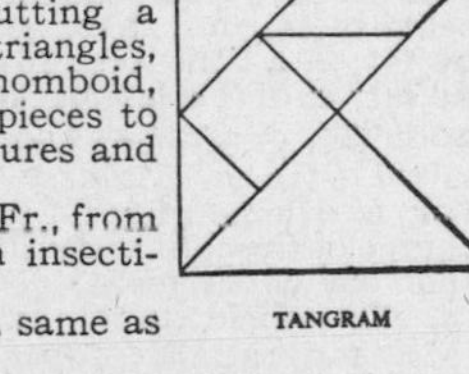
TANGRAM

taṅgue (tang), *n.* [Fr., from native name.] an insectivore, the tenrec.

taṅ′guin (-gin), *n.* same as *tanghin*.

taṅ′gum, taṅ′gun, *n.* [Tibetan.] a variety of piebald pony found in Tibet

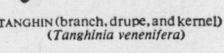

TANGUM

taṅg′whaup (-hwạp), *n.* [*tang*, seaweed, and *whaup*.] the whimbrel, a curlew. [Scot. and Brit. Dial.]

taṅg′y, *a.*; *comp.* tangier; *superl.* tangiest; having a tang, or flavor.

tan house, a building in which tanners' bark is stored; also, a tannery.

tan′i·ẽr, *n.* same as *tannier*.

tan′ist (*or* thọn′), *n.* [Gael. *tānaiste*, a lord, the governor of a country; in Ireland, the heir apparent of a prince; probably from *tan*, a region or territory.] the elected heir of a Celtic chief.

tan′ist·ry, *n.* [Gael. *tanaisteachd*.] in ancient Ireland, the system of electing a tanist from among the chief's relatives during his lifetime.

tā′nīte, *n.* a material composed of scrap leather, emery, cement, etc., used to make grinding and polishing disks, etc.

tä′ni·whä (-hwä), *n.* a dragonlike beast in Maori legend.

taṅk, *n.* [in sense 1, from Gujarati *tānkh*; in other senses, from or influenced by Port. *tanque*, a tank, pond, pool, from L. *stagnum*, a pond, standing water.]
1. originally, in India, a natural or artificial pool or pond used for water storage.
2. any large container for liquid or gas; as, a gasoline *tank*, a swimming *tank*.
3. [name orig. used for purpose of secrecy during manufacture.] an armored, self-propelled vehicle moving on caterpillar treads: valuable in modern warfare for its fire power, rapid movement, and ability to operate over most kinds of terrain.

TANK

taṅk, *v.t.* to put, store, or process in a tank.

taṅk, *n.* a weight of 68 grains, used in Bombay.

taṅ′kȧ, *n.* [Chinese.] 1. a portion of the population of Canton and neighborhood living in boats.
2. the kind of boat in which the tanka live: also called *tanka boat*.

taṅk′āġe, *n.* 1. storage of fluids, gases, etc. in tanks.
2. the charge for such storage.
3. the capacity of a tank or tank system.
4. refuse from tanks, as the residue left in rendering out soap fats, etc.: it is dried, ground, and used as a stock food or for fertilization.

taṅk′ărd, *n.* [OFr. *tanquart*.] a large drinking vessel with a handle and, often, a hinged lid.

taṅk′ărd tũr′nip, a sort of turnip that stands high above the ground.

taṅk çär, 1. on railroads, a car so constructed that gases or liquids may be transported safely within it, requiring no other receptacle.
2. a tank truck.

taṅk de·stroy′ẽr, a highly mobile, armored half-track on which antitank guns are mounted.

taṅk drä′mȧ, melodrama requiring a tank of water or other sensational stage effect for the climax of the plot; also, plays touring tank towns.

taṅked (taṅkt), *a.* drunk; inebriated. [Slang.]

taṅk en′ġine, any engine designed to carry its own water and fuel supply.

taṅk′ẽr, *n.* 1. a ship fitted with tanks in which oil or other liquids can be carried in bulk: also called a *tank ship*.
2. a tank car.
3. a tank truck.
oil tanker; a tanker carrying oil in its hold.

taṅk·ette′, *n.* a small tank for military use.

taṅk färm′ing, the growing of plants in nutrient solutions instead of in soil; hydroponics.

taṅk′fụl, *n.* as much as a tank will hold.

taṅk fũr′nace (-nis), in glass manufacturing, a hearth, from one end of which molten glass may be drawn after the raw materials have been introduced into it from another opening.

taṅ′ki·ȧ, *n.* same as *tanka*.

taṅk ī′ron (-ũrn), plate iron thick enough for tanks.

taṅk stā′tion, same as *tank town*.

taṅk town, 1. a railroad stop for locomotives to fill their boilers with water: it usually became the site of a small town.
2. any small or unimportant town.

taṅk truck, a motor truck built to transport gasoline, oil, or other liquids.

taṅk wŏrm, a nematoid worm of East Indian water tanks.

tan′ling, *n.* a suntanned person. [Rare.]

tan′nȧ, *n.* same as *tana* (police station).

tan′nȧ·ble, *a.* capable of being tanned.

tan′nāġe, *n.* 1. the act or process of tanning.
2. something that has been tanned.

tan′nāte, *n.* a salt of tannic acid.

tan′nẽr, *n.* 1. one whose occupation is to tan hides for leather.
2. a sixpence. [Brit. Slang.]

tan′nẽr·y, *n.*; *pl.* **tan′nẽr·ieṣ,** 1. a place where the operations of tanning hides to make leather are carried on.
2. the art or practice of tanning.

Tann'häu·ser (tän'hoi-zẽr), *n.* [G.] 1. a German knight and minnesinger of the 13th century, identified with a legendary knight who seeks absolution after giving himself up to revelry in the Venusberg.
2. an opera by Wagner (1845) based on this legend.

tan'niç, *a.* of, like, or derived from tan (sense 1) or tannin.

tan'niç ac'id, [from *tan, n.* and *-ic.*]
1. a yellowish, astringent substance, $C_{14}H_{10}O_9$, derived from oak bark, gallnuts, etc. and used in tanning, dyeing, medicine, etc.
2. any of a number of similar substances.

tan'ni·ẽr, *n.* a plant, *Caladium sagittæfolium*, allied to the taro and cultivated for its edible leaves and tubers: also called *blue eddoes.*

tan·nif'ẽr·ous, *a.* yielding tannic acid.

tan'nin, *n.* tannic acid.

tan'ning, *n.* [*tan* and *-ing.*]
1. the art or process of making leather from hides.
2. the act of making the skin brown by exposure to the sun or weather.
3. a severe whipping; a flogging. [Colloq.]

tan piç'kle, the brine of a tan pit.

tan pit, a sunken vat in which hides are laid in tan.

tan'reç, *n.* same as *tenrec.*

tan'ṣy, *n.*; *pl.* **tan'ṣieṣ,** [Fr. *tanaisie*; Sp. *atanasia*, tansy, from Gr. *athanasia*, immortality, from the medicinal properties of some of the plants, or because the dried flowers retain their natural appearance.]
1. any plant of the genus *Tanacetum*, especially *Tanacetum vulgare*, a plant one to three feet high, with bipinnatifid serrate leaves, and small, yellow flowers in a terminal corymb. The whole plant is bitter and aromatic. It is used in cooking, and medicinally as an anthelmintic and a febrifuge.
2. any of various similar plants, especially *Potentilla anserina*, so named because the leaves are much divided like those of the tansy: also called *goose tansy* and *silverweed.*
3. a dish of the seventeenth century, made of eggs, cream, rose water, sugar, and the juice of herbs, as endive, spinach, sorrel, or tansy, baked with butter in a shallow pewter dish.

tan'ṣy mus'tãrd, a mustard plant, *Sisymbrium canescens*, which bears leaves resembling those of the tansy.

tan'tȧ·lāte, *n.* a salt of tantalic acid.

tan·tal'iç, *a.* 1. of, derived from, or containing tantalum, especially with a valence of five.
2. designating a colorless crystalline acid, $HTaO_3$, that forms complex salts.

tan'tȧ·liṣm, *n.* the punishment of Tantalus; a teasing or tormenting by the hope or near approach of good which is unattainable. [Obs.]

tan'tȧ·līte, *n.* a heavy, black, crystalline mineral, $Fe(TaO_3)_2$, a tantalate of iron.

tan·tā'li·um, *n.* tantalum. [Obs.]

tan″tȧ·li·zā'tion, *n.* the state of being tantalized or the act of tantalizing.

tan'tȧ·līze, *v.t.*; tantalized, *pt., pp.*; tantalizing, *ppr.* [from *Tantalus.*] to tease or torment by presenting some good to the view and exciting desire, but continually frustrating the expectations by keeping that good out of reach; to arouse hope and then disappointment in; to tease.

Syn.—taunt, tease, twit, torment, annoy, vex, irritate, provoke.

tan'tȧ·lī·zẽr, *n.* one who tantalizes.

tan'tȧ·lī·zing, *a.* [ppr. of *tantalize.*] that tantalizes; teasing.

tan'tȧ·lī·zing·ly, *adv.* in a tantalizing manner.

tan'tȧ·lous, *a.* of, derived from, or containing tantalum, especially with a valence of three.

tan'tȧ·lum, *n.* [Mod. L., from *Tantalus*: so named because its insolubility in most acids made extraction from the mineral difficult.] a rare, steel-blue, corrosion-resisting, metallic chemical element found in various minerals and used for electric light filaments, grids and plates in radio tubes, surgical instruments, etc.: symbol, Ta; atomic weight, 180.88; atomic number, 73.

Tan'tȧ·lus, *n.* [ME. *Tantale*; L.; Gr. *Tantalos.*]
1. in Greek mythology, a king, son of Zeus, whose punishment in the lower world was eternal hunger and thirst: he was doomed to stand in water that always receded when he tried to drink it and under branches of fruit he could never reach.
2. [t—] a stand with decanters that, although plainly visible, cannot be removed until the bar that locks them in place is raised.
3. a genus of waders including various ibises.

tan'tȧ·mount, *v.i.* to be equal or equivalent. [Obs.]

tan'tȧ·mount, *a.* [from L. *tantus*, so much, and OFr. *amonter*, to increase, ascend.] equal; equivalent in force, value, effect, or signification.

tan'tȧ·rȧ, *n.* [echoic.]
1. a trumpet blast or fanfare.
2. a sound like this.

tan·tiv'y, *adv.* [prob. echoic of sound of a horse galloping.] at full gallop; headlong.

tan·tiv'y, *a.* swift; fast.

tan·tiv'y, *v.i.* to hurry away; to go off in a hurry. [Obs.]

tan·tiv'y, *n.*; *pl.* **tan·tiv'ieṣ,** 1. a rapid, violent gallop.
2. a devoted adherent of the English court in the time of Charles II; a royalist.
3. rapid movement; a rush.
4. a hunting cry to signal a faster chase.

tȧṅt mieux' (täṅ myu'), [Fr.] so much the better.

tän'tō, *adv.* [It.; L. *tantum*, so much.] in music, too much; so much: a direction to the performer, as, allegro non *tanto.*

tȧṅt pïs' (täṅ pī'), [Fr.] so much the worse.

tan'trȧ, *n.* [Sans., from *tan*, to stretch.] a division or chapter of certain Hindu sacred works in Sanskrit.

tan'triṣm, *n.* the doctrines of the tantras.

tan'trist, *n.* one who advocates tantrism.

tan'trum, *n.* [earlier form *tantarum* suggests pseudo-L. coinage on *tantara.*] a violent, willful outburst of annoyance, rage, etc.; a fit of bad temper.

tan vat, a vat containing the liquid and tan in which hides are steeped.

tan'yȧ, *n.* [etym. unknown.] a tropical plant, *Colocasia antiquorum*, cultivated for its farinaceous thick rootstocks; the taro.

Tan·y·stō'mȧ·tȧ, *n.pl.* [Gr. *tanyein*, to stretch, and *stoma*, a mouth.] a group of dipterous insects characterized by a long proboscis furnished with a lance, including horseflies and other stinging flies.

Tan'zi·mat, *n.* [Ar., pl. of *tansim*, a regulation.] an organic law or statute constituting the first contribution toward constitutional government in Turkey, issued in 1839 by Sultan Abdul Medjid.

Tao'iṣm (tou' *or* dou'), *n.* [Chinese *tao*, the way, and *-ism.*] a Chinese religion and philosophy based on the teachings of Lao-tse (6th century B.C.) and advocating simplicity, selflessness, etc.

Tao'ist, *n.* a believer in Taoism.

Tao'ist, *a.* of Taoism or Taoists.

Tao·is'tiç, *a.* same as *Taoist.*

tao'taī (-tī), *n.* [Chinese *tao*, the way, and *t'aī*, a title.] formerly, a Chinese officer in charge of the civil and military affairs of more than one department.

tap, *v.t.*; tapped (tapt), *pt., pp.*; tapping, *ppr.* [ME. *tappen*; OFr. *taper*, to tap, to strike; *tape*, a tap, a slap, probably ultimately from the sound, though directly from the Teutonic.]
1. to strike lightly and rapidly.
2. to strike something lightly with; as, he *tapped* a stick against the window.
3. to make or do by tapping; as, he *tapped* a message with his fingers.
4. to repair (a shoe) by adding a thickness of leather to the heel or sole.

tap, *v.i.* to strike a light, rapid blow; to make a tapping sound.

tap, *n.* 1. a light, rapid blow, or the sound made by it.
2. a piece of leather used in repairing the sole or heel of a shoe.

tap, *n.* [ME. *tappe*; AS. *tæppe.*]
1. a device for starting or stopping the flow of liquid in a pipe, barrel, etc.; a faucet.
2. a plug, cork, etc. for stopping or opening a hole in a container holding a liquid.
3. liquor of a certain kind or quality, as drawn from a certain tap.
4. a tool used to cut threads in internal screws.
5. a place that serves liquor; a bar; a taproom. [Colloq.]
6. in electricity, a place in a circuit where a connection can be made.
on tap; (a) in a tapped cask ready to be drawn: said of liquors, especially malt liquors; (b) [Colloq.] ready for consideration or action.

tap, *v.t.*; tapped (tapt), *pt., pp.*; tapping, *ppr.*
1. to put a tap or spigot on.
2. to put a hole in for drawing off liquid; as the farmer *tapped* a sugar maple tree.
3. to pull out the tap or plug from.
4. to draw (liquid) from a container, etc.
5. to drain liquid from (a cavity, abscess, etc.) by surgical operation.
6. to make an opening in or connection with; as, they *tapped* the water main to supply the new building.
7. to cut threads on the inner surface of (a nut, etc.).
8. to make a connection with secretly; as the detective *tapped* the telephone wires to overhear what was said.
to tap the admiral; to tap surreptitiously a cask of liquor: from the story that when a certain admiral's body was being conveyed to England in spirits, the sailors tapped the cask containing it and drank the liquor. [Slang.]

tap, *n.* a variety of East Indian jungle fever.

tä'pä, *n.* [from native Polynesian name.] an unwoven cloth made by people in the Pacific islands from the treated inner bark of a kind of mulberry tree: also written *tapa cloth.*

tap·ȧ·dẹ'rȧ, tap·ȧ·dẹ'rō, *n.* [Sp., a cover. the hood used on the stirrup of a Mexican saddle.

tä·pȧ·yax'in, *n.* [Mex.] same as *horned toad* under *horned.*

tap bōlt, a bolt with a square head, to be screwed into a part instead of passing through it and taking a nut.

tap cin'dẽr, the slag produced in the process of puddling.

tap'-dȧnce, *v.i.* to perform or dance a tap dance.

tap dȧnce, a dance performed with sharp, loud taps of the foot, toe, or heel at each step.

tāpe, *n.* [ME. *tappe, tape*; AS. *tæppe*, a fillet.]
1. a strong, narrow, woven strip of cotton, linen, etc. used to bind seams in garments, tie bundles, etc.
2. a narrow strip or band of steel, paper, etc.
3. a strip of cloth stretched between posts as the finishing line of a race track.
4. a thin plastic ribbon coated with a suspension of ferromagnetic iron oxide particles, used as a storage medium for recording electrical signals, as from sound, video material, digital computer data, etc.: in full, *magnetic tape.*
5. shortened form of *adhesive tape, friction tape, ticker tape, tape measure*, etc.

tāpe, *v.t.*; taped, *pt., pp.*; taping, *ppr.* 1. to put tape on or around, as for binding, tying, etc.
2. to measure by or as by using a tapeline.

tāpe deck, a simplified tape (sense 4) assembly, without an amplifier or speaker but having tape reels, drive, and recording and playback heads.

tāpe grȧss, an aquatic grass, *Vallisneria spiralis*, with a yellowish tubular perianth.

tȧ·peī·nō·ceph'ȧ·ly, *n.* [Gr. *tapeinos*, lowlying, and *kephalē*, head.] the condition of having a low form of skull, which is also flattened at the front.

tāpe'līne, *n.* a tape or metal ribbon, graduated, as in inches or centimeters, and usually enclosed in a case, used in measuring.

tāpe meaṣ'ūre (mezh'), same as *tapeline.*

tāpe nee'dle, a needle with a slot in the head for receiving a tape; a kind of bodkin.

tā'pẽr, *n.* [ME.; AS. *taper*, from Ir. *tapar*, a taper; W. *tampr*, a torch, taper.]
1. (a) originally, a wax candle used in religious services; (b) a very slender candle.
2. a long wick coated with wax, used for lighting candles, lamps, etc.
3. any feeble light.
4. (a) a gradual decrease in width or thickness; as, the *taper* of a pyramid; (b) a gradual decrease in action, power, etc.
5. something that tapers.

tā'pẽr, *a.* regularly narrowed toward the point; becoming smaller toward one end; conical; pyramidal; as, *taper* fingers.

tā'pẽr, *v.t.* and *v.i.*; tapered, *pt., pp.*; tapering, *ppr.* 1. to decrease gradually in width or thickness.
2. to lessen; to diminish; as, the conversation *tapered* into silence.
to taper off; (a) to taper; to become gradually smaller toward one end; (b) to discontinue or stop gradually; as, *to taper off* the use of tobacco.

tāpe rē·çord'ẽr, a device for recording on tape (sense 4).

tā'pẽred, *a.* lighted up with candles; as, a *tapered* room.

tā'pẽr·ing, *a.* gradually diminishing in size toward one end.

tā'pēr·ing·ly, *adv.* in a tapering manner.
tā'pēr·ness, *n.* the quality or condition of being taper; as, the *taperness* of her fingers.
tap'es·try, *n.*; *pl.* **tap'es·tries,** [Late ME. *tapsterie,* earlier *tapicerie;* OFr. *tapis,* a carpet; *tapisserie,* hangings, tapestry, from L. *tapete,* hangings, cloth.]
1. a heavy cloth woven by hand or machinery with decorative designs and pictures and used as a wall hanging, furniture covering, etc.
2. tapestry carpet.
tapestry carpet; a kind of two-ply carpet, the warp or weft being printed before weaving so as to produce a figured effect.
tap'es·try, *v.t.*; tapestried, *pt., pp.*; tapestrying, *ppr.* 1. to adorn with, or as if with, tapestry.
2. to depict by weaving in a tapestry.
tap'es·try moth, same as *carpet moth.*
tap'es·try pāint'ing, a painting on material giving the effect of tapestry.
tap'et, *n.* tapestry. [Obs.]
tap'e·tăl, *a.* relating to the tapetum.
tap'e·ti, *n.* [Braz.] a small rabbit of South America, *Lepus brasiliensis.*
tȧ·pē'tum, *n.*; *pl.* **tȧ·pē'tȧ,** [LL., from L. *tapete,* a carpet.]
1. in botany, the group of cells borne contiguous to the outer part of the archespore, later being absorbed on the maturation of the spores.
2. in anatomy and zoology, (a) a layer of cross fibers of the corpus callosum spreading outward on the roof of the lateral ventricles of the cerebrum; (b) any of various membranous layers; especially, the iridescent portion of the choroid coat of the eye, giving the luminous effect seen in the eye of the cat and certain other animals.
tāpe'wŏrm, *n.* a parasitic worm, resembling a tape in form, found in the mature state in the intestines of man and various other warm-blooded vertebrates. Tapeworms are composed of a number of flattened joints or segments, the anterior of which, or head, is furnished with a circlet of hooks and suckers which enable it to maintain its hold on the mucous membrane of the intestines of its host. The other segments, called *proglottides,* are simply generative organs budded off by the head, the oldest being farthest removed from it and each containing when mature male and female organs. The ova of tapeworms are taken into the alimentary canal of the host, whence they make their way into the tissues, where they form small cystlike masses, called *scoleces* or *cysticerci.* When the flesh of the original host is eaten, the scoleces develop within the intestines of the new host into a *strobilus,* or adult tapeworm. *Tænia solium* is the pork tapeworm. The common tapeworm of man is *Tænia saginata,* the beef tapeworm. The largest is *Bothriocephalus latus,* the broad tapeworm, three-fourths of an inch broad and often twenty feet in length. Its larvae are found in fish.
tap'hōle, *n.* the hole in a puddling furnace through which the tap cinder is let out, and which during puddling is stopped up.
tap'house, *n.* a tavern, inn, or bar: also *tap house.*
taph·reñ'ehy·mȧ, *n.* [Gr. *taphros,* a trench, and *enchyma,* something poured in.] in botany, pitted, dotted, or porous tissue; bothrenchyma.
Taph·rī'nȧ, *n.* [LL., from Gr. *taphros,* a trench.] a genus of parasitic fungi, including about twenty species that cause damage to fruit trees, as the peach and plum.
tap'i·nāġe, *n.* the act of hiding or lying in wait. [Obs.]
tap·i·ō'çȧ, *n.* [Port. and Sp., from Braz. (Tupi) *tipyoca,* from *ty,* juice, and *pya,* heart, and *oc, og,* to squeeze out.] a starchy granular substance prepared from the root of the cassava plant, used to make puddings, thicken soups, etc.
tap'i·ō·līte, *n.* in mineralogy, a tantalate of iron found in Finland.
tā'pīr, *n.*; *pl.* **tā'pīrs,** *or* **tā'pīr,** [Sp.; Braz. (Tupi) *tapyra,* large mammal, tapir.] any of several large hoglike mammals of the genus *Tapirus,* of tropical America and the Malayan peninsula: they have flexible snouts, and four toes to the fore feet and three to the hind ones. Tapirs feed on plants and move about at night. The South American tapir, *Tapirus americanus,* is the size of a small ass, with a brown skin, nearly naked. Another American species found in the Cordilleras has the back covered with hair and the nose more elongated. The tapirs are related to the rhinoceros, but they are much smaller.

MALAYAN TAPIR
(*Tapirus indicus*)

Tȧ·pir'i·dae, *n.pl.* the tapir family of animals.
tap'i·roid, *a.* belonging to or resembling the *Tapiridæ.*
tap'is (tap'ē *or* tap'is), *n.* [Fr., carpet.] tapestry used as a curtain, tablecloth, carpet, or the like. [Archaic.]
to be on or *upon the tapis;* to be under consideration.
tap'is, *v.t.*; tapised (-ist), *pt., pp.*; tapising, *ppr.* to cover with figures like tapestry. [Archaic.]
tap'is·ēr, *n.* an upholsterer; also, a maker of tapestry. [Obs.]
tap'ish, *v.t.* and *v.i.* tapis. [Obs.]
tap'lash, *n.* [etym. doubtful.] the last running of small beer; the dregs or refuse of liquor. [Now Dial.]
tap'ling, *n.* [etym. doubtful.] the strong double leather made fast to the end of each piece of a flail.
tap'net, *n.* [etym. doubtful.] a frail or basket made of rushes, etc., in which figs are imported.
tȧ·pō'ȧ, *n.* [Australian.] the sooty phalanger, *Trichosurus fuliginosus,* of Australia.
tapoa tafa; a bushy-tailed flesh-eating marsupial, *Phascogale penicillata,* of Australia.
tap'pen, *n.* [from *tap,* a plug.] an obstructive mass found occasionally in the intestines of hibernating animals.
tap'pēr, *n.* 1. one who or that which taps; specifically, a telegraph key.
2. a woodpecker. [Brit. Dial.]
tap'pet, *n.* [L. *tapete,* hangings, cloth.] tapestry.
tap'pet, *n.* in machinery, a projection on a moving part, designed to touch and move or be moved by some other part at certain intervals.
tappet motion; the motion working the steam valve of a steam engine.
tap'ping, *n.* 1. the act of a person or thing that taps.
2. [*pl.*] that which runs from a tap or is drawn by tapping.
3. in surgery, the operation of removing fluid from any of the serous cavities of the body in which it has collected in large quantity; paracentesis.
tap'ping bär, in founding, a round bar with a sharp point, used for letting out the metal from a furnace.
tap'ping drill, a drill for boring holes in water mains and pipes.
tap'ping gouġe, a gouge used in tapping the sugar maple.
tap'pish, *v.t.* and *v.i.* to hide; to conceal. [Obs.]
tap'pit, *a.* crested. [Scot.]
tap'pit-hen, *n.* 1. a hen with a crest or topknot. [Scot.]
2. a kind of drinking vessel containing from one to three quarts: so named from the knob on the lid. [Scot.]
tap'rọọm, *n.* a place where liquor is sold and consumed; a barroom.
tap'rọọt, *n.* the main root of a plant, which grows directly downward with small branch roots spreading out from it.
taps, *n.pl.* [from *tap* (to strike), because originally a drum signal.] a bugle call or drum signal to put out lights in retiring for the night, as in an army camp: also sounded at the burial of a soldier, sailor, etc.
tap'stēr, *n.* [ME. *tappestere;* AS. *tæppestre,* barmaid, from *tæppe,* tap (faucet).]
1. originally, a barmaid.
2. a bartender.
tȧ·pù', *n., a.,* and *v.* same as *taboo.*
Tä·pù'yä, *n.*; *pl.* **Tä·pù'yä,** a Tapuyan Indian.
Tä·pù'yăn, *a.* [Port. *Tapuya,* Tapuyan Indian; Tupi *tapuya,* a savage, enemy; and *-an.*] designating or of a linguistic group of South American Indians that occupied a large part of Brazil, particularly the Amazon Valley.
tä'quȧ nut, [S. Am.] the ivory nut.
tär, *n.* [ME. *tere, terre;* AS. *teru, tero.*] a thick, sticky, brown to black liquid with a pungent odor, obtained by the destructive distillation of wood, coal, peat, shale, etc.: tars are composed of hydrocarbons and their derivatives, and are used for protecting and preserving surfaces, in making various organic compounds, etc.
tär, *a.* 1. of or like tar.
2. tarred.
tär, *v.t.*; tarred, *pt., pp.*; tarring, *ppr.* to smear or cover with or as with tar; as, to *tar* ropes.
to be tarred with the same brush (or *stick*); to possess similar faults or obnoxious traits.
to tar and feather a person; see under *feather, v.t.*
tär, *n.* [abbrev. of *tarpaulin.*] a sailor. [Colloq.]
tä'rȧ, *n.* 1. same as *taro.*
2. same as *taliera.*
tä'rȧ fērn, a species of fern, *Pteris aquilina* or *esculenta,* the root of which was used by the natives of New Zealand and Tasmania as an article of food. It is a variety of the common brake.
tar'ȧ·gon, *n.* same as *tarragon.*
tȧ·raī'rẹ, *n.* [Maori.] a tree of New Zealand, *Beilschmiedia tarairi,* producing a hard wood.
tä·rȧ·kī'hī, *n.* [Maori.] the morwong.
Tar'ȧ·nis, *n.* a Celtic divinity, regarded as the evil principle, but identified by the Romans with Jupiter.
tä·rän·täss', tä·rän·täs', *n.* [Russ.] a large, low, four-wheeled traveling carriage without springs, but balanced on long poles: used in Russia.
tar·ăn·tel'lȧ, *n.* [It.] 1. a rapid, whirling southern Italian dance for couples, in 6/8 time: so called because it was popularly thought to be a remedy for tarantism.
2. the music for such a dance.
tar'ănt·iṣm, *n.* [It. *tarantismo,* from *Taranto,* a town in southern Italy.] a nervous disease characterized by hysteria and a mania for dancing, especially as prevalent in southern Italy in the 16th and 17th centuries: popularly supposed to be caused by the bite of the tarantula: also spelled *tarentism.*
tar'ănt·ist, *n.* a person who has tarantism.
tȧ·ran'tū·lȧ, *n.* [from L. *Tarentum,* now *Taranto,* a town in the south of Italy, in whose vicinity the spider was found.] any of a number of large, hairy, somewhat poisonous spiders found in southern Europe, the southern United States, and tropical America. The bite of *Lycosa tarantula,* the European species, was popularly but wrongly supposed to cause tarantism.

TARANTULA
(1-3 in. long)

tȧ·ran'tū·lȧ kill'ēr, a large wasp, *Pompilus formosus,* that paralyzes the Texan tarantula with its sting.
tȧ·ran'tū·lăr, *a.* pertaining to or caused by the tarantula.
tȧ·ran'tū·lā·ted, *a.* suffering from tarantism; bitten by a tarantula.
tȧ·ran'tū·liṣm, *n.* same as *tarantism.*
tȧ·rä'tȧ, *n.* [Maori.] a small evergreen tree, *Pittosporum eugenioides,* with fragrant yellow flowers.
tar·ax·aç'ēr·in, *n.* a crystalline and soluble substance, $C_8H_{16}O$, obtained from dandelion root.
tȧ·rax'ȧ·cin, *n.* a bitter substance from the root of the common dandelion.
Tȧ·rax'ȧ·çum, *n.* [prob. of Arabic or Persian origin; compare Per. *tarashqūn,* wild succory, dandelion.]
1. a genus of herbs of the aster family, embracing some thirty species found in temperate regions. *Taraxacum officinale* is the common dandelion.
2. [t–] a plant of this genus; also, a drug obtained from the dried rhizome and roots of the dandelion, used as a tonic.
tär'bōard, *n.* a stout kind of millboard made from junk, tarred rope, etc.
tär·bog'gin, *n.* and *v.* same as *toboggan.*

tär·boosh′, *n.* [Ar. *tarbūsh.*] a red cap of cloth or felt, usually ornamented with a blue silk tassel, and worn by the Egyptians, Turks, and Arabs, sometimes as the inner part of a turban; a kind of fez.

tär·dā′tion, *n.* the act of retarding or delaying; retardation. [Obs.]

Tär·dig′rȧ·dȧ, *n.pl.* [LL., slow-paced.]
1. in former classifications, a division of edentate mammals or quadrupeds, comprising, of living genera, the sloth only.
2. a class of minute water animals with segmented bodies and four pairs of legs, usually considered as belonging to the arthropods.

tär′di·grāde, *a.* [Fr.; L. *tardigradus*; *tardus*, slow, and *gradus*, step.]
1. slow-paced; moving or stepping slowly.
2. of or pertaining to the *Tardigrada.*

tär′di·grāde, *n.* one of the *Tardigrada.*

tär·dig′rȧ·dous, *a.* same as *tardigrade.*

tär′di·ly, *adv.* in a tardy manner; late.

tär′di·ness, *n.* the state or quality of being tardy.

tär′di·ty, *n.* [L. *tarditas.*] slowness; tardiness. [Obs.]

tär′dō, *a.* and *adv.* [It.] in music, slow: a direction to the performer.

tär′dy, *a.*; *comp.* tardier; *superl.* tardiest, [Fr. *tardif*; L. *tardus*, slow.]
1. slow; moving with a slow pace or motion; sluggish.
2. late; dilatory; behind time; delayed.
3. characterized by or proceeding from reluctance; unwilling to move or act; hanging back.

tär′dy, *v.t.* to delay; to make tardy. [Obs.]

tär′dy-gāit″ed, *a.* sluggish; having a slow step or pace.

tãre, *n.* [ME., orig., small seed: present sense from Biblical transl.; prob. from M.D. *tarwe*, *terwe*, wheat.]
1. any of a number of related species of *Vicia*, a genus of trailing or climbing plants with many small leaflets, grown for fodder; especially, the common tare, *Vicia sativa*; vetch.
2. the seed of any of these plants.
3. in the Bible, a noxious weed supposed to be the *Lolium temulentem*, or darnel: Matt. xiii. 36.

tãre, *n.* [Fr. *tare*; It. and Sp. *tara*; O. Sp. *atara*, tare, from Ar. *ṭarḥa*, from *ṭaraḥa*, to reject.]
1. a deduction made from the gross weight in allowance of the weight of the container, wrapper, box, truck, etc. in order to determine the weight of the contents or load. Tare is said to be *real* when the true weight of the container is known and allowed for, *average* when it is estimated from similar known cases, and *customary* when a uniform rate is deducted. When the tare is deducted, the remainder is called the *net* weight.
2. the weight deducted.
3. in chemistry, an empty vessel similar to one being used in an experiment and placed beside it to show or counterbalance any change in its weight.
tare and tret; in arithmetic, a rule or process for calculating allowances, as for tare, tret, cloff, etc. [Obs.]

tãre, *v.t.*; tared, *pt.*, *pp.*; taring, *ppr.* to ascertain, allow for, or mark the amount of tare of (any merchandise).

tãre, *v.* archaic or dialectal past tense and past participle of *tear* (to pull apart).

tȧ·rente′ (-ront′), *n.* [Fr. prob. from *Tarentum*, Italy.] the common gecko, *Platydactylus mauritanicus*, of southern Europe.

tar′ent·ism, *n.* same as *tarantism.*

tȧ·ren′tō·lȧ, *n.* 1. the common gecko.
2. [T—] a genus of such geckos.

tȧ·ren′tū·lȧ, *n.* same as *tarantula.*

tãre vetch, a kind of vetch, *Vicia hirsuta*, native to Europe and cultivated along the Atlantic coast of the United States. It closely resembles the common vetch.

tärġe, *n.* [ME.; Late AS.; ON.] a buckler; a shield. [Obs.]

tärġe, *v.t.*; targed, *pt.*, *pp.*; targing, *ppr.* [AS. *tyrgan*, D. *tergen*, to vex, provoke, irritate.]
1. to cross-examine; to question.
2. to keep in order or under discipline.
3. to rate or reprimand severely.
Also written *tairge.*
[Scot. in all senses.]

tärġe′măn, *n.*; *pl.* **tärġe′men**, one who carries a targe or shield.

tär′get, *n.* [ME. *targuet*, from OFr. *targue*, AS. *targe*, a shield.]

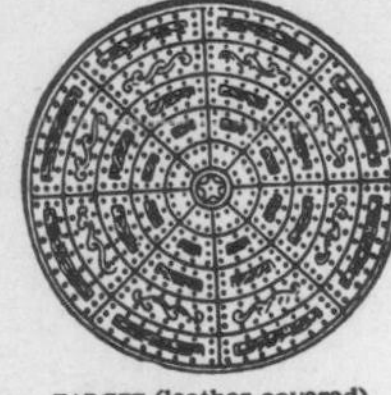
TARGET (leather-covered)

1. a circular shield or buckler of a small kind, mounted on wood, and strengthened by bosses, formerly used in warfare defensively; also, a shield as a bearing in heraldry.
2. a round, flat board, straw coil, etc., usually marked with concentric circles, set up to be aimed at, as in archery or rifle practice.
3. any object that is shot at.
4. a ship, building, site, etc. that is the object of a military attack.
5. one who or that which is a marked object of verbal attack, ridicule, criticism, etc.
I do not fix upon him as the *target* for retribution. —Susan Keating Glaspell.
6. in an X-ray tube, the metallic surface upon which the stream of cathode rays impinge and from which X rays emanate.
7. in surveying, the sliding sight on a leveling rod.
8. on a railway, the disk-shaped signal at a switch.
9. a shred; a slice; a strip. [Brit. Dial.]
10. a pendant or tassel, often jeweled. [Scot.]

tär′get·ed, *a.* furnished or equipped with a target.

tär·get·eer′, *n.* formerly, one equipped with a target (shield).

Tär′gum, *n.*; *pl.* **Tär′gums** or Heb. **Tär·gu·mim′**, [Heb.; Aram. *targūm*, interpretation.] a translation or paraphrase of parts of the Old Testament in the Aramaic language or dialect of Judea. All the Targums taken together form a paraphrase of the whole of the Old Testament except Nehemiah, Ezra, and Daniel.

Tär·gum′iç, *a.* of or pertaining to the Targums.

Tär′gum·ist, *n.* the writer of a Targum; also, one versed in the language and literature of the Targums.

Tär·gum·is′tiç, *a.* of or pertaining to a Targumist or the Targumists.

Tär′heel, *n.* one who lives in the pine barrens of North Carolina; hence, any native or inhabitant of North Carolina. [Colloq.]

tär′hood, *n.* sailors collectively. [Slang.]

tar′iff, *n.* [It. *tariffa*; Ar. *ta'rīf*, explanation, information, a list of things, particularly of fees to be paid, from *'arafa*, to inform.]
1. a list or system of taxes placed by a government upon exports or, especially, imports.
2. a tax of this kind, or its rate.
3. any list or scale of prices, charges, etc.
tariff reform; the reform of a tariff or a tariff system; specifically, in United States politics, a movement favoring a reduction of import duties, especially on raw materials, and opposed to the principle of protection.

tar′iff, *v.t.*; tariffed (-ift), *pt.*, *pp.*; tariffing, *ppr.*
1. to make a schedule of tariffs on; to set a tariff on.
2. to fix the price of according to a tariff.

tar′iff-rid″den, *a.* burdened with a heavy tariff.

tar′in, *n.* [Fr.] a bird, the siskin.

tar′ing, *n.* the common tern. [Brit. Dial.]

tär′lȧ·tăn, **tär′le·tăn**, *n.* [Fr. *tarlatane*, earlier *tarnatane*; prob. of East Indian origin.] a thin, stiff, open-weave muslin.

tärn, *n.* [Ice. *tjörn*, a tarn.]
1. a small mountain lake or pool.
Fled like a glittering rivulet to the *tarn.* —Tennyson.
2. a bog; a marsh; a fen. [Brit. Dial.]

'tär′năl, *a.* 1. eternal. [Dial.]
2. confounded; damned; as, he's a *'tarnal* liar. [Dial.]

'tär′năl, *adv.* confoundedly; damned; very. [Dial.]

tär·nā′tion, *n.* and *interj.* [blend of *'tarnal* and *damnation.*] damnation. [Dial.]

tär·nā′tion, *adv.* damned; very. [Dial.]

tär′nish, *v.t.*; tarnished (-nisht), *pt.*, *pp.*; tarnishing, *ppr.* [Fr. *ternir*, to make dim, ppr. *ternissant*, from O.H.G. *tarnjan*, to cover, conceal; AS. *dernan*; Scot. *dern*, to conceal, hide; AS. *derne*, secretly.]
1. to dull the luster of, as a metallic surface by oxidation.
2. to besmirch or sully (a reputation, etc.).

tär′nish, *v.i.* 1. to lose luster; to become dull; to discolor, as from oxidation.
2. to become sullied or soiled.

tär′nish, *n.* 1. the condition of being tarnished; dullness.
2. a stain; blemish.
3. a tarnished surface.
4. in mineralogy, a change in luster or color of a mineral, due to the alteration of the original color or to the deposition of some foreign substance.

tär′nish·ȧ·ble, *a.* capable of being tarnished.

tär′nished (-nisht), *a.* having lost its luster.

tär′nish·ẽr, *n.* one who or that which tarnishes.

tä′rō, *n.*; *pl.* **tä′rōs**, [Tahitian.] 1. in botany, a tropical plant of the arum family, *Colocasia esculenta*, cultivated in the Pacific islands for its starchy, tuberous root that is edible.
2. the root of this plant.

tä′rō, *n.* [It.] a maltese money of account.

tar′ōt, **tar′ōç**, *n.* [It.] 1. a card game played with seventy-eight cards.
2. any one of the cards used in tarot.

tär′pan, *n.* [Tatar.] the wild horse of Central Asia, not larger than an ordinary mule, and tan or dun in color, with black mane and tail.

TARPAN

tär pā′pẽr, a heavy tarred paper, used in building.

tär·pau′lin, *n.* [*tar* and *-paulin* (said to be from *palling*, from *pall*, a covering, but at least influenced by ME. *palyoun*, a canopy, esp. in early form *tarpaulian*, etc.; orig. sense, "canopy, awning").]
1. canvas waterproofed with tar, paint, etc., or a sheet of this used to spread over anything to protect it from getting wet.
2. a hat or coat of tarpaulin.
3. a sailor; a tar. [Archaic or Rare.]

Tär·pē′iȧ (-yȧ), *n.* [L., fem. of *Tarpeius*, Roman proper name.] in Roman legend, a girl who treacherously opened the Capitoline citadel to the invading Sabines on their promise of giving her what they wore on their arms: instead of the gold bracelets she meant, they threw their shields on her and crushed her to death.

Tär·pē′iăn, *a.* designating or of a cliff on the Capitoline hill at Rome over which persons convicted of treason to the state were hurled: so named from Tarpeia.

tär′pon, *n.*; *pl.* **tär′pons** or **tär′pon**, [same word as D. *tarpoen*; prob. from W.Ind. native name.] a large, silvery game fish of the herring group, found in the warmer parts of the western Atlantic: tarpons measure up to seven feet in length and weigh up to two hundred pounds: also called *silverfish.*

tär′pum, *n.* same as *tarpon.*

Tär′quin·ish, *a.* like Tarquin, the last king of early Rome; proud; haughty.

tar′răce, *n.* a terrace. [Obs.]

tar′rȧ·gon, *n.* [OFr. *targon*; Sp. *taragona*, tarragon, from L. *dracunculus*, a dim. of *draco*, a dragon.]
1. a plant of the aster family, *Artemisia dracunculus*, whose fragrant leaves are used in seasoning.
2. the leaves of this plant.

tar′răs, *n.* and *v.* terrace. [Obs.]

tärre, *v.t.* to tar. [Obs.]

tar′ri·ănce, *n.* a tarrying; delay; lateness. [Archaic.]

tar′ri·ẽr, *n.* 1. one who tarries or delays.
2. one who causes delay. [Obs.]

tar′ri·ẽr, *n.* a terrier. [Dial.]

tar′rŏck, *n.* [Eskimo.] 1. the kittiwake gull.
2. the common tern; a sea swallow.
3. a guillemot.

tar′rōw, *v.i.* to hesitate; to feel reluctance. [Scot.]

tär′ry, *a.*; *comp.* tarrier; *superl.* tarriest, 1. consisting of tar or like tar.
2. smeared or covered with tar.

tar′ry, *n.* 1. a stay; stop; sojourn.
2. a delay. [Obs.]

tar′ry, *v.t.* 1. to cause to delay; to postpone; to impede. [Obs.]
2. to wait for. [Archaic.]

tar′ry, *v.i.*; tarried, *pt., pp.*; tarrying, *ppr.* [ME. *tarien*, to delay, vex, hinder, from AS. *tergan*, to vex, provoke, merged with OFr. *targer*, to delay, from LL. *tardicare*, from L. *tardare*, to delay, from *tardus*, slow.]
1. to delay; linger; loiter; be tardy.
2. to stay, as in a town, etc., especially longer than originally intended; to remain temporarily.
3. to wait.

tar′ry·ing, *n.* the act of lingering or delaying.

tär′săl, *a.* [LL. *tarsus*, instep.]
1. of or pertaining to the tarsus of the foot or the tarsi of the eyelids.
2. in ornithology, belonging or relating to the tarsometatarsus of a bird.
3. belonging or relating to the terminal segment of the leg of an insect.
tarsal tetter; an inflammation of the lids of the eyes; a form of bleareye.

tär′săl, *n.* a tarsal bone or plate; a tarsal cartilage; a tarsale.

tär′săl, *n.* a tercel. [Obs.]

tär·sā′lē, *n.*; *pl.* **tär·sā′li·ȧ,** any bone of the tarsus; especially, one belonging to the distal row.

tär·seç′tō·my, *n.* [LL. *tarsus*, and Gr. *ektomē*, a cutting out.] in surgery, (a) excision of the tarsus, or a part of it; (b) excision of a tarsal cartilage.

tär′sel, *n.* a tercel. [Obs.]

Tär′shish, *n.* an ancient region mentioned in the Bible and believed to have been on the southern coast of Spain: 1 Kings, x. 22.

tär′sī, *n.* plural of *tarsus.*

tär′si·ȧ, *n.* [It.] a kind of mosaic woodwork or marquetry executed by inlaying pieces of wood of different colors and shapes into panels so as to represent landscapes, architectural scenes, figures, fruit, flowers, etc.

tär″si·ȧ·tū′rȧ, *n.* tarsia.

tär′si·ẽr, *n.* [Fr., from Gr. *tarsos*, a broad flat surface: so called from the peculiar form of the foot.] any of several small animals of the genus *Tarsius* of the East Indies and the Philippines, with large, gogglelike eyes, large ears, a long, tufted tail, and unusually long tarsal bones: tarsiers are related to the lemurs, live in trees, are active at night, and feed on insects.

Tär·sī′i·dae, *n.pl.* a family of lemuroids, typified by the genus *Tarsius.*

Tär′si·us, *n.* 1. in zoology, the genus of lemuroids comprising the tarsiers.
2. [t—] a lemuroid mammal of this genus, as the malmag, *Tarsius spectrum.*

tär′sō-, [from Mod. L. *tarsus.*] a combining form meaning *tarsus* or *tarsal*: also, before a vowel, *tars-.*

tär·sō·met·ȧ·tär′săl, *a.* 1. of or relating to the tarsus and the metatarsus.
2. pertaining to the tarsometatarsus.

tär·sō·met·ȧ·tär′sus, *n.*; *pl.* **tär·sō·met·ȧ·tär′sī,** in birds, a large bone in the lower part of the leg, connecting with the tibia and the toes, produced by the union and ankylosis of the lower or distal portion of the tarsus with the whole of the metatarsus.

tär·sor′rhȧ·phy (-rȧ-), *n.* [*tarso-*, and Gr. *raphē*, a seam.] in surgery, the operation of suturing an eyelid or suturing the eyelids together.

tär·sot′ō·my, *n.* [*tarso-*, and Gr. *temnein*, to cut.] the operation of incising the tarsus, or an eyelid.

tär′sus, *n.*; *pl.* **tär′sī,** [Mod. L.; Gr. *tarsos*, any broad flat surface.]
1. in anatomy, (a) the ankle; (b) the seven bones forming the ankle; (c) the small plate of connective tissue stiffening the eyelid.
2. in zoology, (a) the tarsometatarsus; (b) the terminal segment of the leg in insects and certain other arthropods.

tärt, *a.* [AS. *teart*, acid, sharp, from *teran*, to tear (to pull apart).]
1. acid; sharp to the taste; sour; acidulous; as, a *tart* apple.
2. sharp in meaning or implication; cutting; keen; as, a *tart* reply.

tärt, *n.* [Fr. *tarte*, *tourte*; It. *torta*, tart, from L. *tortus*, pp. of *torquere*, to twist: so called from the original twisted form.]
1. a small shell of pastry containing fruit, jam, or jelly, without a top crust.
2. in England, a fruit pie, with a top crust.

tärt, *n.* [orig., slang term of endearment, for *sweetheart.*] a prostitute or any woman of loose morals.

tär′tăn, *n.* [prob. merging of ME. *tirtaine* (from OFr. *tiretaine*), mixed, fabric and ME. *tartarin*, *tartayne* (from OFr. *tartarin*, lit., cloth of Tartary), a rich material from China.]
1. woolen cloth with a woven pattern of straight lines of different colors and widths crossing at right angles, worn especially in the Scottish Highlands, where each clan had its own pattern.
2. any plaid cloth like this.
3. any tartan pattern.
4. any article made of such a fabric.
silk tartan; a silk textile having a tartan pattern.

tär′tăn, *a.* consisting of, made from, or resembling tartan; having the pattern of a tartan.
tartan velvet; a velvet with a short nap and woven in tartan patterns.

tär′tăn, *n.* [Sp. and It. *tartana.*] a small Mediterranean coasting vessel with one mast, a large lateen sail, and a jib.

TARTAN

tär′tăr, *n.* [OFr. *tartre*; ML. *tartarum*, from Ar. *durd*, dregs, sediment, the tartar of wine; also, Ar. *darad*, a shedding of the teeth, tartar.]
1. potassium bitartrate, $KHC_4H_4O_6$, present in grape juice, and forming a reddish, crustlike deposit in wine casks: its purified form is cream of tartar: see also *cream of tartar.*
2. a hard deposit on the teeth, consisting of saliva proteins and calcium phosphate.

Tär′tăr, *n.* [ML. *Tartarus*, a Tartar; altered (after *Tartarus*, hell) from Per. *Tatar.*]
1. a Tatar.
2. [*usually* t—] a person of an irritable, violent, or intractable temper; as applied to a woman, a shrew; a vixen; as, she's a regular *tartar.*
to catch a tartar; to make an attack upon or oppose a person who proves able to overmatch his assailant; to get more than one bargained for.

Tär′tăr, *a.* of Tatary or the Tatars.

Tär′tăr, *n.* Tartarus; hell. [Obs.]

tär′tăr·ā·ted, *a.* containing tartaric acid.

Tär·tār′ē·ăn, *a.* of, or pertaining to Tartarus; infernal. [Obs.]

tär′tăr ē·met′iç, potassium antimonyl tartrate, $KSbOC_4H_4O_6{\cdot}{}^1\!/_2H_2O$, a poisonous white salt used in medicine to cause expectoration, vomiting, and perspiring, and in dyeing as a mordant.

Tär·tār′ē·ous, *a.* Tartarean. [Obs.]

tär·tār′ē·ous, *a.* 1. like or consisting of tartar.
2. having a rough crumbling surface, like the thallus of some lichens.
tartareous moss; a lichen, *Lecanora tartarea*, the source of litmus and cudbear.

tär′tāre (-tẽr) **sauce,** [Fr. *sauce tartare.*] a sauce, as for fried fish, consisting of mayonnaise with chopped pickles, olives, chives, capers, etc.

Tär·tār′i·ăn, Tär·tar′iç, *a.* of Tatary or the Tatars.
Tartarian lamb; the barometz.

tär·tar′iç, *a.* of, containing, pertaining to, or derived from tartaric acid or tartar.

tär·tar′iç ac′id, a clear, colorless crystalline acid, $(CHOH{\cdot}COOH)_2$, found in vegetable tissues and fruit juices and obtained commercially from tartar: it is used in dyeing, photography, medicine, etc.

tär′tăr·ine, *n.* potash. [Obs.]

tär″tăr·i·zā′tion, *n.* 1. a tartarizing or being tartarized.
2. the forming of tartar.

tär′tăr·īze, *v.t.*; tartarized, *pt., pp.*; tartarizing, *ppr.* 1. to treat, impregnate, or combine with tartar.
2. to rectify with cream of tartar.
tartarized antimony; tartar emetic.

Tär′tăr·īze, *v.t.* same as *Tatarize.*

tär′tăr·ous, *a.* of, like, or containing tartar.

tär′tȧ·rum, *n.* argol.

Tär′tȧ·rus, *n.* [L., from Gr. *Tartaros.*] in Greek mythology, (a) the infernal abyss below Hades, where Zeus hurled the rebel Titans; (b) Hades; hell.

Tär′tȧ·ry, *n.* 1. Tartarus. [Obs.]
2. Tatary.

Tär·tī′ni's tōne, [after Guiseppe *Tartini* (1692–1770), Italian musician.] in music, a tone whose frequency of vibration is the difference between the frequency of its components: also called *difference tone* and *differential tone.*

tärt′ish, *a.* rather tart.

tärt′let, *n.* a small tart (pastry).

tärt′ly, *adv.* in a tart manner; with acidity.

tärt′ness, *n.* the condition or quality of being tart.
Syn.—sourness, severity, asperity, harshness, keenness, acrimony, acerbity.

tär′tr-, tar′trō-, a combining form meaning *having or related to tartar or tartaric acid.*

tär·tral′iç, *a.* derived from tartar.
tartralic acid; an acid, $C_8H_{10}O_{11}$, produced by heating tartaric acid and keeping it at a high temperature.

tär·tram′iç, *a.* derived from tartaric acid.
tartramic acid; an acid, $C_4H_7NO_5$, obtained by the action of ammonia on the tartaric anhydride.

tär·tram′ide, *n.* an amide of tartaric acid, $C_4H_8N_2O_4$.

tär′trāte, *n.* a salt or ester of tartaric acid.

tär′trā·ted, *a.* 1. derived from or containing tartar.
2. combined with tartaric acid.

tär′trȧ·zine, tär′trȧ·zin, *n.* a phenyl hydrazine used to dye textiles yellow.

tär′trō-, see *tartr-.*

tär′trō·nāte, *n.* a salt or ester of tartronic acid.

tär·tron′iç, *a.* designating or of an acid derived from mesoxalic acid by reduction.

tär′trō·nyl, *n.* a bivalent radical, $C_3H_2O_3$, existing in tartronic acid.

Tär·tụfe′ (*or Fr.* tȧr-tüf′), *n.* [Fr.; It. *tartufo*, lit., a truffle.]
1. the hero of Molière's satirical comedy of the same name, who was a religious hypocrite.
2. [t—] a hypocrite.

Tär·tụffe′, *n.* Tartufe.

Tär·tụff′ish, Tär·tụf′ish, *a.* hypocritical; resembling Tartufe.

tärve, *n.* a bend or turn.

tär wạ′tẽr, 1. a cold infusion of tar, formerly regarded as having curative powers.
2. ammoniacal water; a by-product of gasworks.

tär′weed, *n.* any one of several coarse, viscid, highly scented herbs of the genus *Madia.*

tas′çō, *n.* [L. *tasconium*, clay.] a sort of clay for making melting pots.

tȧsh·lik′, *n.* [Heb.] a propitiatory rite of orthodox Jews, performed on the afternoon of Rosh Hashana, in which they assemble on the bank of a river or stream and pray, while shaking part of their garments over the water in a symbolic washing away of their sins.

tȧ·sim′ē·tẽr, *n.* [from Gr. *tasis*, a stretching, from *teinein*, to stretch; and *-meter.*] an electric instrument for measuring minute expansions or motions of solids and the variations in temperature that cause these.

tas·i·met′riç, *a.* having to do with a tasimeter or tasimetry.

tȧ·sim′ē·try, *n.* the use of or measurement by a tasimeter.

tȧsk, *n.* [OFr. *tasque*; LL. *taxa*, a tax, from L. *taxare*, to rate, value.]
1. originally, a tax.
2. a piece of work assigned to or demanded of a person.

It is rather for us to be here dedicated to the great *task* remaining before us.
—Abraham Lincoln.

3. any undertaking or piece of work.
4. an undertaking involving labor or difficulty.
to take to task; to reprove; to reprimand; to call to account; as, *to take* one *to task* for idleness.
Syn.—work, function, labor, job, operation, undertaking, drudgery, toil, lesson.

tȧsk, *v.t.*; tasked (tȧskt), *pt., pp.*; tasking, *ppr.* 1. originally, to tax.
2. to assign a task to; to require or demand a piece of work of.
3. to burden; strain; overtax.

tȧsk'ẽr, *n.* 1. one who imposes a task or stint.
2. one who performs a piece of labor. [Dial.]

tȧsk fōrce, a specially trained, self-contained military unit assigned a specific mission or task, as the raiding of enemy shore installations.

tȧsk'mȧs"tẽr, *n.* one who imposes a task or burdens with labor; one who assigns tasks to others, especially when exacting or severe; an overseer.

tȧsk'wŏrk, *n.* 1. work assigned as a task.
2. distasteful or oppressive work.
3. piecework.

tas'let, *n.* same as *tasset.*

Tas·mā'ni·ăn, *n.* a native or inhabitant of Tasmania.

Tas·mā'ni·ăn, *a.* of Tasmania or its people.
Tasmanian cider tree; a species of eucalyptus.
Tasmanian devil; see *devil,* sense 7.
Tasmanian wolf (or *tiger*); a striped marsupial of wolflike character; the thylacine.

Täss, *n.* [Russ. *T*elegraphnoye *A*genstvo *S*ovyetskovo *S*oyuza, Telegraph Agency of the Soviet Union.] a Soviet agency for gathering and distributing news.

tȧss, *n.* [OFr. *tasse*; Ar. *ṭass, ṭassah,* from Per. *tast,* a cup.]
1. a drinking cup; a small goblet. [Obs. or Scot.]
2. its contents; a small draft. [Obs. or Scot.]

tȧsse, *n.* one of a series of plates forming the tasses of a suit of armor: see *tasses.*

tas'sel (tas'l), *n.* [OFr. *tassel,* a knob or knot, a button; prob. from LL. *tessella,* a small piece of mosaic.]
1. a sort of pendent ornament, usually consisting of a roundish mold covered with twisted threads of silk, wool, and the like, which hang down in a thick fringe. Tassels are attached to the corners of cushions and to curtains, umbrella handles, sword hilts, etc.
2. anything resembling a tassel, as the pendent head or flower of some plants, especially the inflorescence at the top of a stalk of corn, or the silk protruding from an ear of corn.
3. a small ribbon of silk sewed to a book, to be put between the leaves as a bookmark.
4. a clasp or fibula. [Obs.]

tas'sel, *v.i.*; tasseled *or* tasselled, *pt., pp.*; tasseling *or* tasselling, *ppr.* to put forth or bear a tassel, as a plant.

tas'sel, *v.t.* 1. to make into tassels.
2. to ornament with tassels.
3. to remove tassels from (corn, etc.) to strengthen the plants.

tas'sel, *n.* same as *tercel.*

tas'sel·fish, *n.* a threadfin of Australia.

tas'sel flow'ẽr, a composite summer annual, *Senecio sonchifolia,* from India, cultivated as a house plant.

tas'sel grȧss, sea grass, *Ruppia maritima.*

tȧss'eş, tas'sets, *n.pl.* [OFr. *tassette,* dim. of *tasse,* a pouch.] armor for the thighs; the series of connected plates hanging from the corselet and forming a skirt that covered the thighs.

CORSELET WITH TASSES

tas'sie, *n.* a small tass or cup. [Scot.]

tāst'ȧ·ble, *a.* that can be tasted.

tāste, *v.t.*; tasted, *pt., pp.*; tasting, *ppr.* [OFr. *taster,* to handle, taste; from *taxitare,* a hypothetical freq. of L. *taxare,* to touch sharply; to judge of.]
1. originally, to test by touching.
2. to test the flavor of by putting a little in one's mouth.
3. to detect or distinguish the flavor of by the sense of taste; as, I *taste* sage in the dressing.
4. to eat or drink a small amount of.
5. to eat or drink; as, he hasn't *tasted* a thing.
6. to receive the sensation of, as for the first time; to experience; to have; as, at last they *tasted* freedom.
7. to have limited experience of; as, I have merely *tasted* manhood.
8. to like the taste of; to like. [Archaic or Rare.]

tāste, *v.i.* 1. to tell flavors by the sense of taste; to have the sense of taste.
2. to eat or drink a small amount (often with *of*).
3. to have a specific flavor; as, the salad *tastes* of garlic.
4. to have a sensation, experience, or anticipating sense (*of* something).

The valiant never *taste of* death but once. —Shak.

5. to enjoy or partake (*of*) sparingly.

For age but *tastes of* pleasures, youth devours. —Dryden.

tāste, *n.* 1. originally, (a) a test; a trial; (b) a tasting.
2. that one of the five senses that is stimulated by contact of a substance with the taste buds on the surface of the tongue and is capable of distinguishing between sweet, sour, salt, and bitter: the flavor of any specific substance is usually recognized by its combined taste, smell, and texture.
3. the quality of a thing that is perceived through the sense of taste; flavor; savor.
4. a small amount put into the mouth to test the flavor.
5. the distinguishing flavor of a substance; as, a chocolate *taste.*
6. a slight experience of something; a sample; as, he got a *taste* of her anger.
7. a bit; trace; suggestion; touch.
8. the ability to notice, appreciate, and judge what is beautiful, appropriate, or harmonious, or what is excellent in art, music, decoration, clothing, etc.
9. a specific preference; partiality; predilection; as, a *taste* for red ties.
10. a liking; inclination; fondness; bent; as, he has no *taste* for business.
11. scent; odor. [Obs.]
in bad (*poor,* etc.) *taste*; in a form, style, or manner showing lack or impairment of a sense of beauty, excellence, fitness, propriety, etc.
in good (*excellent,* etc.) *taste*; in a form or manner showing a sense of beauty, excellence, fitness, etc.
in taste; in good taste.
to one's taste; (a) pleasing or satisfying to one; (b) so as to please or satisfy one.
Syn.—flavor, relish, savor, sensibility, judgment, gustation, sapidity, perception, discernment, nicety, critique, choice, zest, predilection, delicacy, elegance, refinement.

tāste, *n.* a kind of narrow silk ribbon.

tāste bud, any of the clusters of cells at the base of the papillae of the tongue, functioning as the sense organs of taste.

tāste'fụl, *a.* 1. having a high relish; savory; tasty. [Rare.]
2. characterized by or showing good taste (sense 8); produced, arranged, constructed, or regulated by good taste, or in accordance with it; as, a *tasteful* design or pattern.

tāste'fụl·ly, *adv.* in a tasteful manner; with good taste.

tāste'fụl·ness, *n.* the state or quality of being tasteful.

tāste'less, *a.* having no taste; specifically, (a) exciting no sensation in the organs of taste; insipid; as, a *tasteless* medicine; (b) [Rare.] incapable of experiencing the sense of taste; as, the tongue when furred is nearly *tasteless*; (c) having no power of giving pleasure; stale; flat; insipid; as, *tasteless* amusements; (d) not originating from or in accordance with the principles of good taste; as, a *tasteless* arrangement of drapery; (e) not possessing appreciation or enjoyment of what is good, excellent, beautiful, sublime, or the like; having bad taste; as, the only true poet or painter of a *tasteless* age.

tāste'less·ly, *adv.* in a tasteless manner.

tāste'less·ness, *n.* the state or quality of being tasteless.

tāst'ẽr, *n.* 1. a person who tastes; specifically, (a) a person employed to test the quality of (wines, teas, etc.) by tasting; (b) a servant, as of a royal house, who tastes his master's food and drink to detect poisoning.
2. any of several devices used for tasting, sampling, or testing.

tāst'i·ly, *adv.* in a tasty manner.

tāst'i·ness, *n.* the quality or state of being tasty.

tas'tō, *n.* in music, something touched to produce a tone; a key.
tasto solo; in music, one key at a time: a direction indicating that a passage should be played with no other chords than unisons and octaves.

tāst'y, *a.*; *comp.* tastier; *superl.* tastiest, 1. that tastes good; flavorful; savory.
2. showing good taste; tasteful: now seldom used. [Colloq.]

tat, *v.t.*; tatted, *pt., pp.*; tatting, *ppr.* [back-formation from *tatting.*] to make by tatting: see *tatting.*

tat, *v.t.* to entangle; to confuse. [Brit. Dial.]

tat, *v.i.* to do tatting.

tat, *n.* [Hind.] a coarse kind of cloth made from jute and used for gunny bags.

tat, *n.* [Anglo-Ind.] a native East Indian pony.

tat, *n.* [perh. from *tap,* a blow.] a tap or blow: now only in *tit for tat.*
tit for tat; (a) blow for blow; (b) like for like, given in retaliation.

tä'-tä', *interj.* good-by: a familiar expression at parting.

Tä'tär, *n.* [Per.] 1. a member of any of the Mongolian and Turkic tribes who took part in the invasion of central and western Asia and eastern Europe in the Middle Ages.
2. any of a Turkic people who live in the Tatar A.S.S.R., the Crimea, and parts of Asia.
3. any of their Turkic languages.

Tä'tär, *a.* of or pertaining to the Tatars, their country, languages, etc.

Tä·tär'i·ăn, *a.* of or relating to the Tatars.
Tatarian bread; the fleshy root of a European herb, *Crambe Tartarica,* which is used as food; also, the plant itself.
Tatarian buckwheat; see *fagopyrum.*
Tatarian lamb; same as *barometz.*

Tä·tär'iç, *a.* of or pertaining to the Tatars.

Tä'tär·ize, *v.t.*; Tatarized, *pt., pp.*; Tatarizing, *ppr.* to cause to resemble the Tatars.

Tä'tär·y, *n.* in European history, a vast region of central and western Siberia and southern Russia, invaded and inhabited by Tatar tribes: also *Tartary.*

tatch, *n.* (a) a blemish; (b) a strain; (c) a trick or plot. [Obs.]

tāte, *n.* a wisp, as of hay or hair. [Scot.]

'tā'tẽr, *n.* a potato. [Dial.]

tath, *n.* [ON. *tath,* dung, manure, whence *tatha,* a manured field.] the dung or manure left on land where livestock is fed; also, strong grass growing round the dung of cattle. [Obs. or Dial.]

tath, *v.t.*; tathed (tatht), *pt., pp.*; tathing, *ppr.* to manure, as a field, by allowing livestock to feed on it. [Obs. or Dial.]

Tat'lẽr, the, a tri-weekly English periodical composed of short essays, published and chiefly written by Richard Steele with contributions by Joseph Addison: 271 issues appeared from 1709 to 1711.

tȧ·tọọ', tȧ·tủ', *v.t.* and *v.i.* same as *tattoo.*

tat'öu, *n.* the giant armadillo of South America, *Tatusia* (or *Prionodonta*) *gigas.*

tat'öu·āy, *n.* [from Braz. *tatu,* armadillo, and *aí,* worthless: so named because its flesh is not edible.] a large, South American armadillo, *Dasypus tatouay* or *Xenurus unicinctus.*

tat'öu pē'bȧ, same as *peba.*

tatt, *v.t.* and *v.i.* same as *tat.*

tat'tȧ, *n.* same as *tatty.*

tat'tẽr, *n.* one who makes tatting.

tat'tẽr, *n.* [ON. *tötturr,* tatters, rags.]
1. a torn and hanging shred or piece, as of a garment.
2. a separate shred or scrap; a rag.
3. [*pl.*] torn, ragged clothes.

tat'tẽr, *v.t.*; tattered, *pt., pp.*; tattering, *ppr.* to rend or tear into rags; to reduce to tatters; to make ragged.

tat'tẽr, *v.i.* to become ragged.

tat"tẽr·dē·māl'iŏn, *n.* [*tatter* and extension of *demon.*] a person in torn, ragged clothes; a ragamuffin.

tat'tẽred, *a.* 1. ragged; torn; as, a *tattered* garment.
2. dilapidated; showing gaps or breaks.
3. dressed in tatters; wearing ragged clothes.

tat'ting, *n.* [formed from *tat,* to entangle.]
1. a kind of lace made by looping and knotting heavy thread that is wound on a hand shuttle.
2. the act or process of making such lace.

tat'tle, *v.i.*; tattled, *pt., pp.*; tattling, *ppr.* [from M.D. *tatelen*; of echoic origin.]
1. to chatter; to talk idly; to use many words with little meaning.
2. to tell tales; to reveal other people's secrets.

tat'tle, *v.t.* to reveal (a secret) through gossiping; to say in tattling.

tat'tle, *n.* gossip; idle talk or chat; trifling talk.

tat′tlẽr, *n.* 1. one who tattles; an idle talker; one who tells tales.
2. a North American bird of the genus *Totanus*, as the long-legged plover, yellow-legged plover, etc.: so called from their cry.

tat′tle·tāle, *n.* a telltale; a talebearer; a tattler.

tat·to͞o′, *n.*; *pl.* **tat·to͞os′,** [ME. *taptoo*, from D. *doe het tap toe*, do the tap to; that is, shut it up; a signal for closing public houses.]
1. a signal for soldiers or sailors to return to quarters for the night, given by a prolonged continuous drum beating or by a bugle call.
2. any continuous drumming, rapping, etc.

tat·to͞o′, *v.i.* to beat or sound the tattoo. [Rare.]

tat·to͞o′, *v.t.*; tattooed, *pt., pp.*; tattooing, *ppr.* [Tahitian *tatu*, from *ta*, a mark.]
1. to make permanent marks or designs on (the skin) by puncturing it and inserting indelible colors.
2. to make (marks or designs) on the skin in this way.

tat·to͞o′, *n.*; *pl.* **tat·to͞os′,** a tattooed mark or design.

tat·to͞o′, *n.* same as *tat* (a pony).

tat·to͞o′ẽr, *n.* one who tattoos; one skilled in tattooing.

tat·to͞o′ing, *n.* the act of one who tattoos; the design produced by a tattooer; the art of a tattooer.

tat′ty, *a.* same as *tauted*.

tat′ty, *n.*; *pl.* **tat′ties,** in India, a fragrant grass mat which is kept wet and hung at the doors and windows of a house for the purpose of reducing the temperature of the air indoors during the hot season.

tat′ū, *n.* same as *tatou*.

tȧ·tū′si·id, *a.* [S.Am.] pertaining to the family *Tatusiidæ*.

tȧ·tū′si·id, *n.* any armadillo, as the peba, belonging to the family *Tatusiidæ*.

Tat·ū·si′i·dæ, *n.pl.* a family of armadillos found from Texas to Paraguay; the pebas.

tau, *n.* [ME. *tau*; L. *tau*; Gr. *tau*.]
1. the nineteenth letter of the Greek alphabet, corresponding to English letter *T, t*.
2. in heraldry, a tau cross.
3. any of several insects shaped like or marked with a tau cross.
4. the toadfish, *Batrachus tau*.

Tau′be, *n.* [G. *taube*, a dove.] a type of German monoplane having pigeon-shaped wings.

tau cross, the cross of St. Anthony. It derives its name from the Greek letter *tau*, which it resembles in shape.

TAU CROSS

taught (tạt), *a.* taut. [Obs.]

taught, *v.* past tense and past participle of *teach*.

taunt, *a.* [OFr. *tant*, from L. *tantus*, so great.] in nautical usage, very high or tall: specifically applied to unusually high masts.

taunt, *v.t.*; taunted, *pt., pp.*; taunting, *ppr.* [prob. from Fr. *tant pour tant*, tit for tat.]
1. to reproach with scornful or insulting words; to jeer at; to revile; to upbraid; to deride.

When I had at my pleasure *taunted* her.
—Shak.

2. to drive or provoke (a person) by taunting.
3. to tease. [Dial.]

Syn.—jeer, deride, flout, revile, upbraid, mock, ridicule.

taunt, *n.* 1. a scornful or jeering remark; a gibe.
2. a taunted person. [Obs. except in the Bible.]

taunt′ẽr, *n.* one who taunts.

taunt′ing·ly, *adv.* in a taunting manner; with bitter and sarcastic words; insultingly; scoffingly.

taunt′ress, *n.* a woman who taunts.

taupe (tōp), *n.* [Fr., from L. *talpa*, a mole.] a dark, brownish gray, the color of moleskin.

tau′pie, taw′pie, *n.* [a Scand. word; Ice. *tópi*, a fool; Sw. *tapig*, simple, foolish; Dan. *taabe*, a fool.] a foolish, thoughtless young woman. [Scot.]

Taur, *n.* [ME.; Fr. *taure*, from L. *taurus*, a bull.] the sign of the zodiac Taurus. [Obs.]

tau′ri·form, *a.* [L. *taurus*, a bull, and *-form*.] having the form of a bull or of the horns of a bull.

tau′rine, *n.* [L. *taurus*, a bull: so called because first found in the bile of the ox.] a colorless, neutral, crystalline compound, $C_2H_7SNO_3$, found in bile and formed by the hydrolysis of taurocholic acid.

tau′rine, *a.* [L. *taurinus*, of or relating to a bull.]
1. relating to Taurus, the sign of the zodiac.
2. pertaining or relating to a bull; resembling a bull.

tau′rō-, [from Gr. *tauros*, a bull.] a combining form meaning (a) *of* or *like a bull*; (b) in chemistry, *relationship with taurine*.

tau·rō·chō′lāte, *n.* [*tauro-*, and Gr. *cholos*, gall.] a salt of taurocholic acid.

tau·rō·chol′ic ac′id, [*tauro-* and *cholic*.] a colorless crystalline acid, $C_{26}H_{45}O_7NS$, found as the sodium salt in bile.

tau′rō·col, tau·rō·col′lȧ, *n.* [*tauro-*, and Gr. *kolla*, glue.] glue made from a bull's hide.

tau·rō·mā′chi·ăn, *a.* [*tauro-*, and Gr. *machē*, a fight.] pertaining to bullfights or bullfighting.

tau·rō·mā′chi·ăn, *n.* one who engages in bullfights; a toreador. [Rare.]

tau·rō·mach′ic, *a.* pertaining to tauromachy. [Rare.]

tau·rom′ȧ·chy, *n.* bullfighting; a bullfight.

Tau′rus, *n.* [L.] 1. a northern constellation containing the Pleiades, supposedly resembling the forequarters of a bull in shape.
2. the second sign of the zodiac (♉), entered by the sun on or about April 20.
3. in zoology, a former name for the genus of ruminant quadrupeds including the domestic cattle; the genus *Bos*.

taut, *a.* [ME. *toght*, tight, firm; prob. from pp. of *togen*, (AS. *togian*), to pull.]
1. tightly stretched, as a rope.
2. tense; as, a *taut* smile.
3. neat; trim; tidy; snug.

tau·taug′, *n.* same as *tautog*.

tau′ted, *a.* matted together, as wool or hair. [Scot.]

tau·tē·gor′ic·ăl, *a.* [Gr. *tauto*, the same, and *agoreuein*, to speak.] expressing the same thing in different words. [Rare.]

tau′ten, *v.t.* and *v.i.* to make or become taut.

taut′ly, *adv.* in a taut manner; so as to be taut.

taut′ness, *n.* the state or quality of being taut.

tau′tō-, [Gr. *tauto-*, from *to auto*, the same.] a combining form meaning *the same*, as in *tautology*.

tau′tō·chrōne, *n.* [Gr. *tauto*, the same, and *chronos*, time.] in mathematics, a curve such that a heavy body rolling down it, under the influence of gravity, will always reach the same point at the same time, from whatever point it may start. The inverted cycloid, in a vertical plane, having its base horizontal, is a tautochronous curve. Also, when any number of curves are drawn from a given point, and another curve is so drawn as to cut off from every one of them an arc which is described by a falling particle in one given time, that arc is called a tautochrone.

tau·toch′rō·nous, *a.* pertaining to, or having the character of, a tautochrone; isochronous.

tau·tog′, *n.* [Am. Ind.] a labroid fish, *Tautoga onitis*, found on the eastern coast of the United States, and valued as a food fish: also called *blackfish* and *oysterfish*.

tau·tō·log′ic·ăl, tau·tō·log′ic, *a.* of, involving, or using tautology.

tau·tō·log′ic·ăl·ly, *adv.* in a tautological manner.

tau·tol′ō·gism, *n.* 1. the use of tautology.
2. an example of tautology.

tau·tol′ō·gist, *n.* one who habitually uses tautology.

tau·tol′ō·gīze, *v.i.*; tautologized, *pt., pp.*; tautologizing, *ppr.* to repeat the same thing in different words; to use tautology.

tau·tol′ō·gous, *a.* tautological. [Rare.]

tau·tol′ō·gy, *n.*; *pl.* **tau·tol′ō·gies,** [Gr. *tauto*, the same, and *-logia*.]
1. needless repetition of an idea in a different word, phrase, or sentence; redundancy; pleonasm. Example: necessary essentials.
2. an example of this.

Syn.—repetition.—There may be frequent *repetitions* (as in legal instruments) which are warranted either by necessity or convenience; but *tautology* is always a fault, being a sameness of expression which adds nothing either to the sense or the rhetorical effect.

tau·tō·mer′ic, *a.* of or having tautomerism.

tau·tom′ẽr·ism, *n.* [Gr. *tauto*, same, and *meros*, part; and *-ism*.] in chemistry, the property of some substances of being in a condition of equilibrium between two isomeric forms and of reacting to form either.

tau′tō·nym, *n.* [*tauto-*, and Gr. *onyma*, a name.] in botany and zoology, a name consisting of two terms, in which the generic and specific names are the same: this kind of name is no longer approved by the International Code of Botanical Nomenclature.

tau·tō·ou′si·ăn, *a.* tautoousious. [Rare.]

tau·tō·ou′si·ous, *a.* [Gr. *tauto*, same, and *ousia*, essence.] in theology, having the same essence; of identically the same nature. [Rare.]

tau·tō·phon′ic·ăl, *a.* repeating the same sound.

tau·toph′ō·ny, *n.* [Gr. *tauto*, same, and *phōnē*, sound.] repetition of the same sound.

tau·tō·zōn′ăl, *a.* of the same zone, as the planes of a crystal.

täv (*or Heb.* tof), *n.* [Heb.] the twenty-third letter of the Hebrew alphabet, corresponding to English *T, t*: also *tau, taw*.

tav′ẽrn, *n.* [ME. and OFr. *taverne*; L. *taberna*, a tavern, booth, stall made of boards.]
1. a place where liquors, beer, etc. are sold to be drunk on the premises; a saloon; a bar.
2. an inn.

tä·ver′nȧ, *n.* [Mod. Gr. *taberna*, from L.: see preceding.] an inexpensive tavern or restaurant in Greece, often with music and dancing.

tav′ẽrn·ẽr, *n.* 1. one who keeps a tavern.
2. one who frequents a tavern.

taw, *v.t.*; tawed, *pt., pp.*; tawing, *ppr.* [AS. *tawian*, to prepare, scourge.]
1. to prepare (a natural product) for further treatment or use.
2. to make (skins) into leather by treating with alum, salt, etc.
3. to whip; to flog. [Obs. or Dial.]

taw, *n.* [also *tor, alley-tor*; perh. an abbrev. or from *tau*, the Gr. letter with reference to method of indicating a mark as the juncture of two straight lines (T).]
1. a marble used to shoot with: it is usually large and fancy.
2. a game of marbles.
3. the line or mark from which players at marbles shoot.
to come to taw; to come to the mark, figure, or proposition designated.

tä′wȧ, *n.* [Maori.] a variety of evergreen tree found in New Zealand, closely allied to the taraire.

taw′dri·ly, *adv.* in a tawdry manner.

taw′dri·ness, *n.* the state or quality of being tawdry.

taw′dry, *a.*; *comp.* tawdrier; *superl.* tawdriest, [by syllabic merging of *St. Audrey*, esp. in *St. Audrey lace* or *St. Audrey's laces*, women's neckpieces sold at St. Audrey's fair, Norwich, England.] gaudy and cheap; sleazy; showy.

taw′dry, *n.*; *pl.* **taw′dries,** a gaudy ornament; a piece of cheap finery.

taw′ẽr, *n.* one who taws skins; a maker of white leather.

taw′ẽr·y, *n.*; *pl.* **taw′ẽr·ies,** a place where skins are tawed.

taw′ie, *a.* tame; tractable. [Scot.]

taw′ni·ness, *n.* the quality of being tawny.

taw′ny, *a.*; *comp.* tawnier; *superl.* tawniest, [OFr. *tanné*, from *tanner*, to tan.] brownish-yellow; tan: also spelled *tawney*.

taw′ny, *n.* tawny color: also spelled *tawney*.

taws, tawse, *n.* [AS. *tawian*, to scourge.] a leather strap, usually with a slit or fringelike end, used as an instrument of punishment by schoolmasters and others. [Scot.]

tax, *n.* [OFr. *taxe*, from *taxer*, to tax, from L. *taxare*, to appraise, tax, censure.]
1. (a) a compulsory payment of a percentage of income, property value, sales price, etc. for the support of a government; (b) a special assessment, as in a society, labor union, etc.
2. a heavy demand; a burden; a strain.
3. a charge, as in a restaurant, etc. [Colloq.]
capitation tax; a poll tax.
direct tax; see following *direct*.
indirect tax; see under *indirect*.

Syn.—assessment, contribution, custom, impost, duty, rate, tribute, toll.

tax, *v.t.*; taxed (takst), *pt., pp.*; taxing, *ppr.*
1. originally, to determine the value of; to assess.
2. (a) to require (a person) to pay a percentage of his income, property value, etc. for the support of the government; (b) to require (a person) to pay a special assessment, as in a society, labor union, etc.
3. to assess a tax on (income, property, purchases, etc.).
4. to impose a burden on; to put a strain on; as, the work *taxed* his strength.
5. to accuse; to charge; as, he was *taxed* with negligence.
6. in law, to go through and allow or disallow the items of charge in.

tax·ȧ·bil′i·ty, *n.* the state or quality of being taxable.

tax′ȧ·ble, *a.* 1. that can be taxed; liable by law to the assessment of taxes; as, a *taxable* estate.

2. that can be legally charged by a court against the plaintiff or defendant in a suit; as, *taxable* costs.

tax′ȧ·ble, *n.* one who or that which can be taxed.

tax′ȧ·ble·ness, *n.* the state or quality of being taxable.

tax′ȧ·bly, *adv.* in a taxable manner.

Tax·ā′cē·ae, *n.pl.* [L. *taxus*, from Gr. *taxos*, a yew tree.] the yew family of evergreen trees and shrubs, characterized by needle- or scale-like leaves, berrylike fruit, and stamens and pistils in separate flowers on the same plants.

tax·ā′ceous (-shus), *a.* of or belonging to the *taxaceæ*, or yew family.

tax·as·pid′ē·ăn, *a.* [Gr. *taxis*, an arrangement, and *aspis* (-*idos*), a shield.] having regularly arranged rectangular scutella, as the tarsi of certain birds.

tax·ā′tion, *n.* [OFr., from L. *taxatio* (-*onis*), taxing.]

1. a taxing or being taxed.
2. a tax or tax levy.
3. the principle of levying taxes.
4. revenue from taxes.
5. in law, the act of taxing or assessing a bill of costs.

tax′-dē·duçt′i·ble, *a.* that is allowed as a deduction in computing income tax.

tax dū′pli·çāte, 1. the certification of real-estate assessments to the taxing authorities.

2. the basis upon which the tax collector prepares tax bills and for which he is held accountable to the auditor.

tax′ēme, *n.* [Gr. *taxis*; and phon*eme*.] in linguistics, a feature in grammatical construction; specifically, selection of words, order of words or morphemes, modulation in stress and pitch, or phonetic modification.

tax′ē·ō·pod, *a.* of or pertaining to the *Taxeopoda*.

tax′ē·ō·pod, *n.* one of the *Taxeopoda*.

Tax·ē·op′ō·dȧ, *n.pl.* [Gr. *taxis*, order, and -*poda*.] an order of the *Ungulata*, characterized by apposition of the bones of one tarsal row with those of the other row, and including the fossil *Condylarthra*, and fossil and existing *Proboscidea*, as the elephants.

tax·ē·op′ō·dous, *a.* taxeopod.

tax·ē·op′ō·dy, *n.* arrangement of the tarsal bones as exhibited by taxeopods.

tax′ēr, *n.* one who taxes.

tax′-ex·empt′, *a.* 1. exempt from or not subject to taxation; as, *tax-exempt* property.

2. producing income that is exempt from taxation; as, *tax-exempt* bonds.

tax′gath″ēr·ēr, *n.* a collector of taxes. [Archaic.]

tax′gath″ēr·ing, *n.* the collection of taxes. [Archaic.]

tax′i, *n.*; *pl.* **tax′iș,** [short for *taxicab*.] a taxicab.

tax′i, *v.i.*; taxied, *pt., pp.*; taxiing *or* taxying, *ppr.* 1. to ride in or be transported by a taxi.

2. to move under its own power across land or water without rising into the air: said of an airplane.

tax′i, *v.t.* to cause (an airplane) to taxi.

tax′i·arçh, *n.* [Gr. *taxis*, order, and *archein*, to rule.] a Greek military officer commanding a taxis.

tax′i·çab, *n.* [short for *taximeter cab*.] an automobile in which passengers are carried for a fare at a rate usually recorded by a taximeter.

Tax·i·çor′nēș, *n.pl.* in a former classification, a family of winged insects having the antennae perfoliated.

tax′i danc′ēr, [so called (after *taxicab*) because hired to dance.] a girl or woman who may be hired at a dance hall or cabaret as a dance partner at a fixed charge for each dance.

tax·i·dēr′măl, tax·i·dēr′miç, *a.* pertaining to taxidermy.

tax′i·dēr·mist, *n.* one practicing or skilled in taxidermy.

tax′i·dēr·my, *n.* [Gr. *taxis*, order, and *derma*, skin.] the art of preparing and preserving skins of animals, birds, etc., and of stuffing and mounting them in a lifelike manner.

tax′i·mē·ter, *n.* [Fr. *taximètre*, from *taxe*, a tax, and *mètre*, a meter.] an automatic device installed in taxicabs, that computes and registers the fare due.

tax′ine, *n.* [L. *taxus*, a yew tree.] a poisonous, resinous alkaloid obtained from the leaves of the yew.

tax′is, *n.* [Gr., order, arrangement, from *tassein*, to arrange.]

1. in surgery, the replacement by hand of a displaced part, as of a hernial protrusion, without cutting any tissue.

2. in ancient Greece, a division of troops, varying in size from the modern company to the regiment.

3. in biology, the movement of an organism in response to some external stimulus.

-tax′is, [Mod. L.; Gr. -*taxis*, from *taxis*.] a combining form meaning *arrangement*, *order*, *taxis*, as in para*taxis*, thermo*taxis*: also -*taxy*.

tax′i squăd, [after such a group kept on the payroll of a taxi company also owned by the owner of the Cleveland Browns in the 1940's.] a group of reserve players in professional football who practice with the team but are not eligible to play in the games.

tax′ite, *n.* [from Gr. *taxis*; and -*ite*.] volcanic rock that appears to be a combination of two or more minerals or kinds of rock fragments.

tax′i·wāy, *n.* any of the paved strips at an airport for use by airplanes in taxiing between the terminals or hangars and the runways.

tax′less, *a.* free from taxes; tax-free.

Tax·ō′di·um, *n.* [Gr. *taxos*, yew, and *eidos*, form.] a genus of coniferous trees with the male catkins arranged in racemose panicles. *Taxodium distichum*, or red cypress, is native to North America, and its wood is valued for its durability.

tax·ō·nom′iç, tax·ō·nom′iç·ăl, *a.* pertaining to or involving taxonomy.

tax·ō·nom′iç·ăl·ly, *adv.* according to the principles of taxonomy.

tax·on′ō·mist, *n.* one skilled in the classification of animals and plants according to some system; one versed in taxonomy.

tax·on′ō·my, *n.* [Gr. *taxis*, order, and *nomos*, a law.]

1. the science of classification; the laws and principles covering the classifying of objects.

2. classification, especially of animals and plants into phyla, species, etc.

tax′pāy″ēr, *n.* any person who pays a tax; a person subject to taxation.

tax rāte, the percentage of income, property value, etc. assessed as tax.

tax shel′tēr, any financial investment made for the purpose of acquiring expenses, depreciation allowances, etc., which can be used to reduce one's income tax.

tax stamp, a stamp that shows that a tax has been paid.

tax tī′tle, the title conveyed to the purchaser of property sold for nonpayment of taxes.

Tax′us, *n.* [L.] a genus of evergreen coniferous trees and plants, the yews.

-tax′y, same as -*taxis*.

Tāy′-Sachs′ diș·ēașe′, [after W. *Tay*, an English physician, and B. *Sachs*, a U.S. neurologist, who described it.] a hereditary condition, found chiefly among descendants of some Eastern European Jews, caused by an enzyme deficiency and characterized by mental retardation, paralysis, and death in early childhood.

täz′zȧ (tät′sȧ), *n.* [It.] a large ornamental cup or vase with a foot and handles.

Tb, in chemistry, terbium.

T′-bär, *n.* a T-shaped bar suspended from a power-driven endless cable, used to pull two skiers at a time uphill as they stand on their skis.

T′-bill, *n.* shortened form of *treasury bill*.

T′-bōne steăk, any steak with a T-shaped bone, as club steak or porterhouse.

Tc, in chemistry, technetium.

T cell, [from *t*hymus.] any of the lymphocytes that are affected by the thymus and are involved in rejecting foreign tissue, regulating cellular immunity, and controlling the production of antibodies in the presence of an antigen.

Tcheb·y·shef′fi·ăn (cheb-), *a.* relating or belonging to Tchebysheff (1821–1894), Russian mathematician.

Tchebysheffian function; the sum of the logarithms of all prime numbers not greater than the variable.

tẹ, *n.* in music, ti.

Te, in chemistry, tellurium.

tēa, *n.* [D. *thee*; Malay *teh*; Chin. dial. *t'e*, for Mandarin *ch'a*, tea.]

1. a white-flowered evergreen plant, *Thea sinensis*, grown in China, India, Japan, etc.

2. its dried and prepared leaves, used to make a beverage.

3. the beverage made by soaking tea leaves in boiling water.

4. any of several plants resembling or used as tea.

5. a tealike beverage made from such a plant or from a meat extract; as, camomile *tea*; beef *tea*.

6. a light meal in the late afternoon or the evening, at which tea is the usual beverage. [Chiefly Brit.]

7. a reception or other social gathering in the afternoon, at which tea, coffee, etc. are served.

8. same as *marijuana*. [Slang.]

Abyssinian tea; the leaves of *Catha edulis*, which are stimulant, antisoporific, and antinarcotic.

Appalachian tea; the leaves of either the inkberry or the withe rod, used for tea in certain localities.

TEA SHOOT

TEA LEAVES AND FLOWERS

Arabian tea; Abyssinian tea.

Assam tea; a cultivated variety of tea plant, *Thea assamica*, grown extensively in Assam.

Blue Mountain tea; the sweet goldenrod, *Solidago odora*, whose leaves are used in a medicinal beverage.

Bourbon tea; faham tea.

Brazilian tea; gervao.

cambric tea; see following *cambric*.

Carolina tea; same as *Appalachian tea*.

New Jersey tea; redroot.

Oswego tea; *Monarda didyma*, an aromatic American herb.

St. Helena tea; a plant, *Frankenia portulacæfolia*, native to St. Helena.

Swiss tea; an aromatic infusion of various herbs, generally used for medicinal purposes and common in the Swiss Alps.

West Indian tea; an herb, *Capraria biflora*, native to tropical America and Africa: the leaves are used as tea in the West Indies.

tēa, *v.i.* to take or drink tea. [Colloq.]

tēa bąll, 1. a hollow, perforated metal ball used to hold tea leaves in making tea.

2. a small, porous bag of cloth or paper, containing tea leaves and used in making an individual cup of tea: also *tea bag*.

tēa′ber″ry, *n.*; *pl.* **tēa′ber″rieș,** 1. a creeping plant with shiny leaves, bell-shaped white flowers, and red fruit; checkerberry; wintergreen.

tēa bis′çuit (-kit), any of a variety of cookies often served with tea.

tēa′bōard, *n.* a board or tray for holding and carrying a tea service.

tēa bug, an insect which injures tea plants by puncturing the tender, more juicy, and most valued leaves with its long, slender proboscis.

tēach, *v.t.*; taught (tąt), *pt., pp.*; teaching, *ppr.* [ME. *techen*; AS. *tæcan*, to show, to teach.]

1. to show how to do something; to give instructions to; to train; as, he *taught* his child how to write.

2. to give lessons to (a student or pupil); to guide the study of; to instruct.

3. to give lessons in (a subject); to hold classes in.

4. to provide with knowledge, insight, etc.; as, experience will *teach* him common sense.

Syn.—impart, direct, instruct, inform,

counsel, admonish, educate, inculcate, enlighten, advise, indoctrinate, train.

tēach, *v.i.* to give lessons or instruction; to be a teacher; to instruct.

Nothing *teaches* like experience.—Bunyan.

tēach·ȧ·bil′i·ty, *n.* the condition or quality of being teachable.

tēach′ȧ·ble, *a.* that can be taught; apt to learn; also, readily receiving instruction; docile.

tēach′ȧ·ble·ness, *n.* the quality of being teachable; readiness or aptness to receive instruction.

tēache, *n.* [Sp. *tacho.*] in sugar making, an evaporating pan or boiler, especially the last one of a series.

tēach′ẽr, *n.* 1. one who teaches or instructs; an instructor; a preceptor; a tutor; one whose occupation is to instruct others.

2. one who instructs others in religion; a preacher; a minister of the gospel.

The *teachers* in all the churches assemble themselves. —Raleigh.

3. one who preaches without regular ordination.

Syn.—instructor, schoolmaster, preceptor, tutor, professor, pedagogue, educationist, educator, schoolmistress.

tēach′ẽr bĩrd, 1. an ovenbird (American warbler).

2. a red-eyed vireo.

tēa chest, a cubical box, made of light wooden material and lined with thin sheet lead or tin, in which tea is exported from China and other tea-producing countries.

tēach′ing, *n.* 1. the action of a person who teaches; the profession of a teacher.

2. [*often pl.*] something taught; precept, doctrine, or instruction.

tēach′less, *a.* unteachable; indocile.

tēa çlam, a small hard-shelled clam or quahog found along the Atlantic coast of North America.

tēa′çup, *n.* 1. a cup in which tea is served.

2. a teacupful.

tēa′çup·fụl, *n.*; *pl.* **tēa′çup·fụlṣ,** as much as a teacup will contain, about four fluid ounces.

tēa dȧnce, 1. a dance at which afternoon tea is served.

2. a dance held in the afternoon.

tēa gär′den, 1. a garden, generally attached to a house of entertainment, where tea and other refreshments are served.

2. a plantation in which tea plants are cultivated.

tēa′gle, *n.* [variant of *tackle.*] an elevator; a hoist; a crane. [Brit. Dial.]

tēa gown, a gown to be worn at tea.

Tēague (tēg), *n.* [Ir. *Tadhg.*] an Irishman: used in contempt.

tēa′house, *n.* in the Orient, a place where tea and other refreshments are served.

tēak, *n.* [Port. *teca*; Malayalam *tēkka.*] a large tree of the East Indies, *Tectona grandis*, the hard, yellowish-brown wood of which is highly valued for shipbuilding, furniture, and many other purposes; also, the wood itself.

African teak; a large tree, *Oldfieldia africana*, of Sierra Leone, which yields a heavy valuable wood: also called *African oak.*

New Zealand teak; a tall tree, *Vitex littoralis*, yielding hard timber that is very durable under water.

tēa′ket″tle, *n.* a covered kettle, having a spout and handle, in which water is boiled for making tea, coffee, etc.

tēak′wood, *n.* teak.

tēal, *n.* [ME. *tele*; akin to D. *teling, taling,* a teal.]

1. *pl.* **tēalṣ** or **tēal,** any of various small, fresh-water ducks of the genus *Querquedula*, having short necks and a grayish-blue color. The common teal of Europe is *Querquedula crecca.*

COMMON TEAL (*Querquedula crecca*)

2. a dark grayish blue: also *teal blue.*

tēal duck, a teal.

tēam, *n.* [AS. *team,* offspring, a succession, a long row.]

1. (a) [Obs.] progeny, race, or lineage; (b) [Dial.] a brood of young animals, especially of ducks or pigs.

2. two or more horses, oxen, etc. harnessed to the same vehicle or plow.

3. (a) two or more draft animals and their vehicle; (b) one draft animal and its vehicle.

4. a group of people working or playing together, especially as one side in a contest.

5. any number of animals or birds passing in a line; a flock, as of wild ducks, flying in a line.

Like a long *team* of snowy swans on high. —Dryden.

tēam, *v.t.*; teamed, *pt., pp.*; teaming, *ppr.* 1. to harness or yoke together in a team.

2. to work, convey, or haul with a team.

tēam, *v.i.* 1. to drive a team.

2. to join in co-operative activity (often with *up*); as, the boys *teamed up* on the paper route.

tēam′ing, *n.* 1. the act or business of hauling or carrying merchandise, lumber, or other materials with a team.

2. a certain mode of contract work, which is given out to a foreman, who hires a gang or team to do it, and is responsible to the owner of the stock.

tēam′māte, *n.* a person on the same team.

tēam′stẽr, *n.* one who drives a team (now, often, a truck) for hauling loads.

tēam′wŏrk, *n.* 1. joint action by a group of people, in which each person subordinates his individual interests and opinions to the unity and efficiency of the group; co-ordinated effort, as of an athletic team.

2. work done by or with a team.

tēa oil, an oil obtained from the seeds of *Camellia oleifera*, a Chinese plant, and used in cooking.

tēa pär′ty, *n.*; *pl.* **tēa pär′tieṣ,** a party or entertainment at which tea, among other things, is served.

tēa plant, any plant which yields tea; specifically, the Chinese tea shrub, from which the tea of commerce is obtained.

tēa′pot, *n.* a vessel with a lid, spout, and handle for making and pouring tea.

tēa′poy, *n.* [Hind. *tipāī*, from *tīn*, three, and Per. *pāe*, foot; sp. affected by association with *tea.*]

1. a small, three-legged stand.

2. a small table used in serving tea.

tēar, *n.* [AS. *tear, teagor*; akin to G. *zähre.*]

1. a drop of the salty fluid secreted by the lachrymal gland, which serves normally to lubricate the eyeball and in weeping flows from the eye.

2. anything resembling this, as a drop of transparent gum; a tearlike mass.

3. [*pl.*] sorrow; grief.

in tears; crying; weeping.

tēar, *v.i.* to shed, or fill with, tears.

teãr, *v.t.*; tore, *pt.*; torn, *pp.*; tearing, *ppr.* [AS. *teran*, to rend; akin to G. *zehren*, to destroy.]

1. to pull apart or separate into pieces by force; to rip; to rend, as cloth or paper.

2. to make or cause by tearing or puncturing; as, the nail *tore* a hole in her dress.

3. to wound by tearing; to lacerate; as, the saw *tore* his skin.

4. to force apart or divide into factions; to disrupt; to split; as, their ranks were *torn* by dissension.

5. to divide with doubt, uncertainty, etc.; to agitate; to torment; as, his mind was *torn* between duty and desire.

6. to remove by or as by tearing, pulling, etc. (with *up, out, away, off,* etc.); as, he *tore* the plant *up* by its roots; he *tore* himself *away.*

to tear down; (a) to dismantle; wreck; demolish, as a building; (b) to controvert or disprove (an argument, etc.) point by point.

to tear from; to separate and take away by force.

to tear off; to pull off by violence; to strip.

to tear up; to rip up; to remove from a fixed state by violence or force; as, to *tear up* a floor.

teãr, *v.i.* 1. to be torn.

2. to move violently or with speed.

to tear at; to make violent, pulling motions at in an attempt to tear or remove.

to tear into; to attack impetuously and, often, devastatingly. [Colloq.]

teãr, *n.* 1. the act of tearing.

2. the result of a tearing; a torn place; a rent.

3. a violent outburst; a rage.

4. a carousal; a spree. [Slang.]

tēar bag, the tearpit; the lachrymal sinus.

tēar bomb (bom), a bomb that releases tear gas upon explosion.

tēar′drop, *n.* a tear.

tēar′drop, *a.* shaped like a tear.

teãr′ẽr, *n.* 1. one who or that which tears or rends anything.

2. one who tears along; a roisterer, ranter, etc.

tēar′-fạll″ing, *a.* shedding tears; tender; as, *tear-falling* pity. [Poet.]

tēar′fụl, *a.* weeping; shedding tears; as, *tearful* eyes; also, giving cause for tears; sad.

tēar′fụl·ly, *adv.* in a tearful manner.

tēar′fụl·ness, *n.* the state or quality of being tearful.

tēar gȧs, see under *gas.*

teãr′ing, *a.* violent; impetuous; hasty.

tēar-jẽrk′ẽr, *n.* a play, motion picture, etc. with a very sad or sentimental theme. [Slang.]

tēar′less, *a.* 1. shedding no tears; without tears.

2. unable to weep.

tēar′less·ly, *adv.* in a tearless manner.

tēar′less·ness, *n.* the state or quality of being tearless.

tēa′rọọm, *n.* a restaurant that serves tea, coffee, light lunches, etc.

tēa rōṣe, 1. a kind of rose having an odor supposedly resembling that of tea.

2. its yellowish-pink color.

tēar′pit, *n.* a tear sac (sense 2).

tēar saç, 1. in anatomy, a lachrymal gland.

2. in zoology, a sebaceous gland found in some antelope and deer: it is a lachrymal sinus which opens under the lower eyelid and is controlled by voluntary muscles: it yields a waxlike substance having a characteristic smell.

teãr sheet, a page or sheet taken in unbound form from a periodical or other publication for special distribution by the publisher, and on which is printed an advertisement or other matter of interest to the person or persons to whom it is sent.

tēar shell, a shell containing tear gas.

tēar′stāin, *n.* in plant pathology, a streaky discoloration of citrus fruits occurring in certain diseases.

tēar′-stāined, *a.* stained with tears.

teãr′thumb (-thum), *n.* any of several species of *Polygonum*, or knotweed: so called from the hooked prickles on the angles of their stems.

tēar′y, *a.*; *comp.* tearier; *superl.* teariest, 1. resembling tears; falling in drops like tears.

2. tearful; wet with or full of tears; crying.

tēa sçrub, the tea tree of New Zealand.

tēaṣe, *v.t.*; teased, *pt., pp.*; teasing, *ppr.* [ME. *tesen*; AS. *tæsan*, to gather, tease; Dan. *tæse*, to tease wool.]

1. to separate the fibers of; to comb or card, as wool or flax.

2. to scratch, as cloth in dressing, for the purpose of raising a nap; to teasel.

3. to harass, annoy, or disturb by persistent, irritating actions or remarks, or by poking fun at.

4. to urge persistently; to beg; to importune.

Syn.—vex, taunt, tantalize, torment, harass, annoy, disturb, irritate, plague, mortify, chagrin.

tēaṣe, *v.i.* to indulge in teasing.

tēaṣe, *n.* 1. one who or that which teases.

2. the act of teasing or the state of being teased.

tēa′ṣel, *n.* [ME. *tesel*; AS. *tæsel*, from base of *tæsan*, to tease.]

1. any of a number of thistlelike plants of the genus *Dipsacus*, with bristly yellowish or purplish flowers.

2. the flower of the species *fuller's teasel*, used when dried for raising a nap on cloth.

3. any device for raising a nap on cloth.

Also spelled *teasle, teazel, teazle.*

tēa′ṣel, *v.t.*; teaseled *or* teaselled, *pt., pp.*; teaseling *or* teaselling, *ppr.* to raise a nap on (cloth) by means of teasels: also spelled *teasle, teazel, teazle.*

tēa′ṣel·ẽr, tēa′ṣel·lẽr, *n.* 1. a person who teasels.

2. a machine for teaseling.

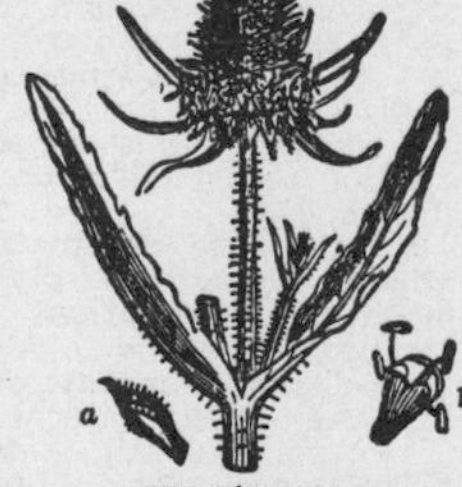

FULLER'S TEASEL (*Dipsacus fullonum*)
a, scale of the receptacle; *b*, corolla

tēaṣ′ẽr, *n.* 1. one who or that which teases.
2. the stoker who tends the furnace in glassworks.
3. a hunting dog. [Obs.]
4. something that is the cause of vexation or annoyance; an annoying or puzzling problem.
5. a bird, the gull teaser.
6. in electricity, (a) an additional coil of fine wire placed on the field magnets of a dynamo; (b) a series coil used for preliminary excitation, being placed on a field magnet in addition to a regular shunt field.

tēa sẽrv′ice, the articles employed in serving tea, taken as a whole; as, a silver *tea service.*

tēaṣ′ing·ly, *adv.* in a teasing manner.

tēa′sle, *n.* and *v.* same as *teasel.*

tēa′spọọn, *n.* 1. a small spoon used in stirring tea, coffee, etc. or in eating soft substances.
2. a teaspoonful.

tēa′spọọn·fụl, *n.*; *pl.* **tēa′spọọn·fụlṣ,** as much as a teaspoon holds, or about one and one-third fluid drams: the equivalent of one-third tablespoonful.

tēat, *n.* [ME. *tete, titte*; AS. *tit*; OFr. *tette*; Ice. *tata*; W. *didi,* a teat.]
1. the projecting organ through which milk is drawn from the breast or udder of female mammals in suckling the young; the pap; the nipple.
2. any small protuberance resembling a teat, as a nozzle, the point of certain drills, etc.

tēa tā′ble, a small table on which tea, etc. is set or at which tea is drunk.

tēa′-tā″ble, *a.* supposedly characteristic of people at a tea; as, *tea-table* talk.

tēa′tāst·ẽr, *n.* a person whose business is testing tea for grading.

tēat′ed, *a.* having teats; having teatlike formations.

tēathe, *n.* and *v.* same as *tath.*

tēa′-things, *n.pl.* the teapot and accessories used at tea; a tea service.

Tē′ȧ·tin, *n.* same as *Theatin.*

tēat′ish, *a.* fretful; peevish. [Obs.]

tēa trāy, a tray for carrying cups, plates, spoons, etc. in serving tea or other light refreshment.

tēa tree, any plant or shrub that produces leaves which are used for tea; particularly, the tea plant of China. Other varieties are *Lycium afrum,* of Africa, and various species of the genera *Leptospermum* and *Melaleuca,* of Africa and Australia.

tēa wag′ŏn, a small table on wheels, used in serving tea and light refreshments.

tēaze′hōle, *n.* the opening in a glass furnace through which the fuel is supplied.

tēa′zel, *n.* and *v.* same as *teasel.*

tēa′zel·ẽr, *n.* same as *teaseler.*

tēaz′ẽr, *n.* same as *teaser.*

tēa′zle, *n.* and *v.* same as *teasel.*

Te̤·bet′, Te̤·beth′ (tā-vāth′ *or* tā′vis), *n.* [Heb.] the fourth month of the Jewish year.

tech′i·ly, *adv.* peevishly; fretfully; frowardly.

tech′i·ness, *n.* peevishness; fretfulness.

tech·nē′ti·um (-shi-um), *n.* [Mod. L., from Gr. *technētos,* artificial; and *-ium.*] a metallic chemical element obtained by the irradiation of molybdenum with deuterons and in the fission of uranium: symbol Tc; atomic weight, 99?; atomic number, 43 (formerly designated as *masurium*).

tech′niç, *a.* [Gr. *technikos,* from *technē,* an art, artifice.] technical. [Now Rare.]

tech′niç, *n.* 1. technique. [Now Rare.]
2. same as *technics,* sense 1.

tech′niç·ăl, *a.* [*technic* and *-al.*]
1. having to do with the practical, industrial, or mechanical arts or the applied sciences; as, *technical* schools offer courses in welding, engineering, etc.
2. of, used in, or peculiar to a specific science, art, profession, craft, etc.; specialized; as, *technical* vocabulary.
3. of, in, or showing technique; as, *technical* skill.
4. in terms of some science, art, etc.; according to principles or rules; as, a *technical* difference.
5. in finance, designating or of a market in which prices are sharply affected by manipulation and speculation.

tech·ni·çal′i·ty, *n.*; *pl.* **tech·ni·çal′i·tieṣ,**
1. the quality or state of being technical.
2. the use of technical terms, methods, etc.
3. a point, detail, term, method, etc. of or peculiar to an art, science, code, or skill; a rule, etc. that only a technical expert would be aware of.

tech′niç·ăl knock′out (nok′), in boxing, a victory won when the opponent, though not knocked out, is so badly beaten that the referee stops the match.

tech′niç·ăl·ly, *adv.* 1. in a technical manner; according to technical principles.
2. in a technical sense; in technical terms.

tech′niç·ăl·ness, *n.* the quality or state of being technical; technicality.

tech′niç·ăl ser′ġeănt (sär′), 1. in the United States Army, formerly, the second grade of enlisted man (now *sergeant first class*).
2. in the United States Marine Corps and Air Force, the second grade of enlisted man, ranking just below master sergeant.

tech·ni′ciăn (-nish′ăn), *n.* 1. one versed in the technicalities of some subject; specifically, an artist, writer, musician, etc. who has great technical skill or knowledge.
2. in the United States Army, formerly, any of several alternative ranks of enlisted man, of the third, fourth, and fifth grades.

tech′ni·cist, *n.* a technician; one versed or skilled in technics or in the practical arts.

tech″ni·çō·loġ′iç·ăl, *a.* same as *technological.*

tech·ni·çol′ō·ġy, *n.* same as *technology.*

tech′ni·çŏl·ŏr, *n.* the process of reproducing colors on a motion-picture film by combining several separate, synchronized films each of which is sensitive to a single color: a trademark (*Technicolor*).

tech′niçs, *n.pl.* [*construed as sing.*] 1. the study or principles of an art or of the arts in general, especially practical arts.
2. technique.

tech·nïque′ (-nēk′), *n.* [Fr., from Gr. *technikos,* from *technē,* an art, artifice.]
1. the method of procedure (with reference to practical or formal details) in rendering an artistic work or carrying out a scientific or mechanical operation.
2. the degree of expertness in following this; as, the pianist had pleasing interpretation but poor *technique.*

tech′niṣm, *n.* technicality.

tech′nō-, [from Gr. *technē,* an art, artifice.] a combining form meaning: (a) *art, science, skill,* as in *techno*cracy; (b) *technical, technological,* as in *techno*chemistry.

tech″nō·chem′is·try, *n.* industrial chemistry.

Tech·noc′rȧ·cy, *n.* government by technicians; specifically, the theory or doctrine of a proposed system of government, regarded by its proponents as suitable for a technological age, in which all economic resources, and hence the entire social system, would be controlled by scientists and engineers.

tech′nō·crat, *n.* an advocate of the teachings and principles or technocracy.

tech·nō·crat′iç, *a.* of technocracy or technocrats.

tech·nog′rȧ·phy, *n.* the description of arts and techniques.

tech·nō·loġ′iç·ăl, tech·nō·loġ′iç, *a.* 1. of or having to do with technology.
2. due to developments in technology; resulting from technical progress in the use of machinery in industry, agriculture, etc.; as, *technological* productivity, *technological* unemployment.

tech·nō·loġ′iç·ăl·ly, *adv.* 1. by means of technology.
2. according to, or from the viewpoint of, technology.

tech·nol′ō·ġist, *n.* one versed in technology.

tech·nol′ō·ġy, *n.* [Gr. *technē,* art, and *logos,* word or discourse.]
1. the science or study of the practical or industrial arts.
2. the terms used in a science, art, etc.; technical terminology.
3. applied science.

tech′y, *a.*; *comp.* techier; *superl.* techiest, [from ME. *teche, tecche, tache,* manners, quality; OFr. *tache,* a stain, blemish.] peevish; irritable; touchy: also spelled *tetchy.*

Tē·çō′mȧ, *n.* [shortened from *tecomaxochitl,* the Mexican name of the species.] a genus of plants, of the family *Bignoniaceæ.* The species are erect trees or shrubs or climbing plants, with unequally pinnate or digitate simple leaves and terminal panicles of dusky red or orange flowers. They are native to tropical and subtropical climates. A climbing species, *Tecoma radicans,* or trumpet flower, is native to North and South Carolina, Florida, and Virginia.

teç′ti·branch, *a.* and *n.* same as *tectibranchiate.*

Teç·ti·brañ′chi·ȧ, *n.pl.* same as *Tectibranchiata.*

teç·ti·brañ′chi·ăn, *a.* and *n.* same as *tectibranchiate.*

Teç·ti·brañ·chi·ā′tȧ, *n.pl.* [L. *tectus,* concealed or covered, and *branchiæ,* gills.] a division of gastropodous *Mollusca,* comprising those species in which the gills are attached along the right side or on the back in the form of leaves more or less divided. The mantle covers them more or less, and contains nearly always in its thickness a small shell, which may be entirely concealed or partly exposed.

teç·ti·brañ′chi·āte, *a.* of or belonging to the *Tectibranchiata.*

teç·ti·brañ′chi·āte, *n.* any one of the *Tectibranchiata.*

teç′ti·fọrm, *a.* like a roof in form or use; serving as a covering or lid.

teçt′ly, *a.* [L. *tectum,* a roof.] in a private, secret, or covert manner. [Obs.]

Teç·tō′nȧ, *n.* [from its name in Malabar.] a genus of trees of the family *Verbenaceæ*; the teak or Indian oak. There are three species: *Tectona grandis,* native to India and Malaysia, *Tectona hamiltoniana,* native to Burma, and *Tectona philippinensis,* native to the Philippines.

teç·ton′iç, *a.* [L. *tectonicus*; Gr. *tektonikos,* from *tektōn* (*-onos*), a carpenter, builder.]
1. pertaining to building or construction; constructional; hence, architectural.
2. in geology, of or resulting from changes in the structure of the earth's crust; as, a *tectonic* valley.

teç·ton′içs, *n.pl.* [*construed as sing.*] 1. the science or art of combining the useful and artistic in building or constructing edifices, implements, vessels, etc.
2. geology that deals with land structure.

teç·tō′ri·ăl, *a.* [L. *tectorium,* a covering, roof, and *-al.*] in anatomy, serving as a cover; roofing over; as, the *tectorial* membrane of the ear.

teç·tō′ri·um, *n.*; *pl.* **teç·tō′ri·ȧ,** [L., a covering.] the membranous covering of the organ of Corti, in the internal ear; the membrane of Corti.

teç′tri·çēṣ, *n.pl.*; *sing.* **teç′trix,** [LL. f. pl. of *tector,* from L. *tegere,* to cover.] in ornithology, the feathers of a bird which cover the tail and the wings; the coverts.

teç·tri′ciăl (-trish′ăl), *a.* of the nature of or pertaining to the tectrices.

teç′trix, *n.* any feather of the tectrices.

tē′çum, *n.* same as *tucum.*

ted, *v.t.*; tedded, *pt., pp.*; tedding, *ppr.* [ME. *tedden*; prob. from ON. *tethja,* to manure.] to turn over and spread or scatter out to dry, as newly cut grass.

ted′dẽr, *n.* one who or that which teds; specifically, an implement that spreads and turns newly mown grass or hay from the swath, for the purpose of drying.

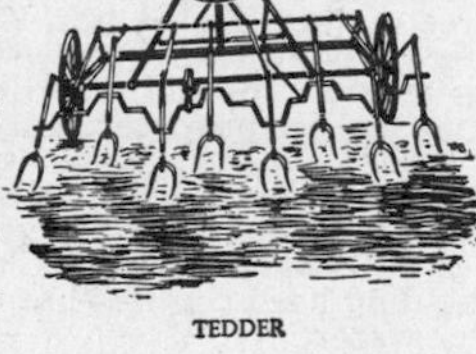
TEDDER

ted′dẽr, *n.* and *v.* tether. [Obs.]

ted′dy, *n.*; *pl.* **ted′dieṣ,** [prob. from the nickname *Teddy.* [*usually pl.*] a woman's one-piece undergarment consisting of a top combined with loose-fitting drawers.

ted′dy beār, [c. 1907, after *Teddy,* nickname for *Theodore,* with reference to Theodore Roosevelt.] a stuffed toy for children resembling a bear in miniature.

te·des′çō, *a.* [It.] German: used chiefly in regard to art, music, etc.

Tē Dē′um, 1. an old Christian hymn of praise commencing *Te Deum laudamus* (We praise thee, O God).
2. a religious service in which this hymn forms a principal part.
3. a musical setting for this hymn.

tedġe, *n.* [etym. obscure.] in founding, same as *ingate.*

tē·di·os′i·ty, *n.* tediousness. [Rare.]

tē′di·ous, *a.* [ME.; LL. *tædiosus,* from L. *tædium,* wearisomeness.]
1. wearisome; tiresome from continuance; boring.

Life is as *tedious* as a twice-told tale,
Vexing the dull ear of a drowsy man.
—Shak.

2. slow; as, a *tedious* course. [Obs. or Dial.]
Syn.—wearisome, tiresome, fatiguing, sluggish, irksome.

tē′di·ous·ly, *adv.* in a tedious manner; so as to weary.

tē′di·ous·ness, *n.* the state or quality of being tedious.

tē′di·um, *n.* [L. *tædium*, from *tædet*, it disgusts, offends.] the condition or quality of being tiresome, wearisome, or monotonous; wearisomeness.

Evidently she, too, was beguiling the *tedium* of the journey. —Elizabeth Phipps Train.

tee, *n.*; *pl.* **tees,** 1. the letter T, t.
2. something shaped like the letter T.
to a tee; exactly; precisely.

tee, *a.* shaped like a T.

tee, *n.* [Burmese *h'ti*, an umbrella.] an umbrella-shaped structure as a termination or finial crowning the Buddhist topes and Hindu pagodas.

tee, *n.* [from *tee* (T): the mark was orig. T-shaped.] a mark aimed at in quoits, curling, etc.

tee, *n.* [prob. contr. from earlier *teaz*, Scot. dial. word, but now associated with prec. in form and sense.] in golf, (a) a small, cone-shaped mound of sand, earth, etc. on which the ball is placed when a player drives; (b) a small, pointed, wooden or plastic holder now generally substituted for this; (c) the place from which a player makes the first stroke on each hole.

tee, *v.t.* and *v.i.*; teed, *pt.*, *pp.*; teeing, *ppr.* to place (a golf ball) on a tee.
to tee off; to play (a golf ball) from a tee.

teek, *n.* teak. [Obs.]

teel, *n.* [E. Ind.] same as *til*.

teem, *v.i.*; teemed, *pt.*, *pp.*; teeming, *ppr.* [ME. *temen*; AS. *tieman*, to produce, to bear.]
1. originally, to bring forth young, as an animal; to produce fruit, as a plant; to bear.
2. to be full as if ready to bring forth young; to be stocked to overflowing; to be prolific or abundantly fertile; to abound; to swarm.

On we went past open plazas *teeming* with the life of the city. —Howard M. Raymond.

teem, *v.t.* 1. to produce; to bring forth. [Rare.]
2. to bring about. [Obs.]

teem, *v.t.* [ME. *temen*; ON. *tæma*, to empty.] to empty; to pour out; specifically, in steel manufacturing, to pour (molten metal) from a crucible into a mold.

teem, *v.i.* to pour; to come down in torrents: said of rain, water, etc.

teem′ẽr, *n.* one who or that which teems, or is prolific, etc.

teem′ẽr, *n.* one who pours; specifically, in steel manufacturing, one who pours the molten metal into the mold.

teem′ful, *a.* pregnant; prolific. [Obs.]

teem′ing, *a.* prolific; abounding; swarming.

teem′less, *a.* not fruitful or prolific; barren; as, the *teemless* earth. [Poet.]

-teen, [ME. *-tene*; AS. *-tene*, *-tyne*, inflected form of *tien*, ten.] a suffix meaning *ten and*, used to form the cardinal numbers from *thirteen* to *nineteen*.

teen, *n.* [ME. *tene*; AS. *teona*, basic sense "accusation."]
1. injury.
2. anger.
3. grief.
[Archaic or Dial. in all senses.]

teen, *v.t.* [AS. *teona*, accusation, injury.] to excite; to provoke. [Obs. or Dial.]

teen, *v.t.* [AS. *tȳnan*, to enclose, to shut in, to hedge.] to enclose; to shut. [Scot. and Brit. Dial.]

teen′āge, *n.* wood for fences or enclosures. [Brit. Dial.]

teen′-āge, *a.* 1. in one's teens.
2. of, characteristic of, or for persons in their teens.

teen′-āg·ẽr, *n.* a person in his teens.

teend, *v.i.* to tind. [Obs.]

teen′ful, *a.* full of grief; sorrowful. [Obs.]

teens, *n.pl.* the numbers, or years of one's age, between thirteen and nineteen inclusive; as, she is in her *teens*.

tee′ny, *a.*; *comp.* teenier; *superl.* teeniest; tiny; very small. [Colloq.]

teen′y, *a.* fretful; irritable; peevish. [Obs. or Dial.]

tee′pee, *n.* same as *tepee*.

tee shirt, same as *T-shirt*.

teest, *n.* [variant spelling of *test*.] in mechanics, a small anvil; a tinsmith's stake.

tee′tee, *n.* [S. Am.] a squirrel monkey of the genus *Callithrix*, found in South America; the titi.

tee′tee, *n.* the Australian diving petrel, *Pelecanoides urinatrix*.

tee′tẽr, *n.*, *v.i.* and *v.t.*; teetered, *pt.*, *pp.*; teetering, *ppr.* [dial. *titter*, to move unsteadily, *teeter*; ME. *titeren*; ON. *titra*, to tremble, quiver.] seesaw, waver.

tee′tẽr·tāil, *n.* the common spotted sandpiper.

tee′tẽr-tot″tẽr, *n.* and *v.* same as *seesaw*.

teeth, *n.* plural of *tooth*.

teethe, *v.i.*; teethed, *pt.*, *pp.*; teething, *ppr.* [ME. *tethen*, from *tethe*, teeth.] to grow teeth; to cut teeth, as a child.

teeth′ing, *n.* the operation or process of the first growth of teeth; dentition.

teeth′ing ring, a ring of ivory, plastic, etc. for teething babies to bite on.

teeth′ridge, *n.* 1. the ridge of the jaw where the teeth sockets are located.
2. in phonetics, the upper front teethridge.

tee·tō′tăl, *a.* [formed by reduplication of initial letter of *total*, for the sake of emphasis.]
1. total; entire; complete. [Colloq.]
2. pertaining to or advocating total abstinence from alcoholic drinks.

tee·tō′tăl·ẽr, tee·tō′tăl·lẽr, *n.* one pledged to total abstinence from all intoxicating drinks.

tee·tō′tăl·ism, *n.* the principles or practice of teetotalers; total abstinence.

tee·tō′tăl·ly, *adv.* fully; wholly. [Colloq.]

tee·tō′tum, *n.* [from *T*, the initial of L. *totum*, total, and the word *totum* itself.] a kind of top twirled by the fingers, especially one with four lettered sides used in a game of chance.

tee′wit, *n.* the pewit. [Brit. Dial.]

teff, *n.* [Abyss.] a grain plant, *Eragrostis abyssinica*, of Abyssinia, from which flour is made.

teg, *n.* 1. a doe, or female deer, in its second year. [Obs.]
2. a sheep in its second year.

teg′men, *n.*; *pl.* **teg′mi·nȧ,** [L., a covering.]
1. a tegument; a covering.
2. in botany, the inner skin which covers a seed.
3. an elytrum of certain orthopterous insects.
4. in anatomy, a plate of the temporal bone covering the middle ear.

teg·men′tăl, *a.* in biology, pertaining to or of the nature of a tegmentum or tegmen.

teg·men′tum, *n.*; *pl.* **teg·men′tȧ,** [L., from *tegere*, to cover.]
1. in anatomy, the upper and larger of the two principal parts of either crus cerebri.
2. in botany, one of the scales which cover the leaf buds.

tē·guex′in (-gwex′), *n.* [Braz.] a large lizard, *Teius teguexin*, of South America, which attains a length of nearly five feet and has a very long tail. The name is sometimes applied to other species of the family *Teiidæ*, as *Teius rufescens*, which is known as the red teguexin.

teg′ū·lȧ, *n.*; *pl.* **teg′ū·lae,** [L., a tile.] a kind of callosity at the origin of the forewings of the *Hymenoptera*.

teg′ū·lăr, *a.* [L. *tegula*, a tile, from *tegere*, to cover or make close.]
1. pertaining to or resembling a tile or tiles; also, arranged like tiles.
2. pertaining to a tegula.

teg′ū·lăr·ly, *adv.* in the manner of tiles, as on a roof.

teg′ū·lā·ted, *a.* composed of plates or scales overlapping like tiles: said specifically of ancient armor.

teg′ū·ment, *n.* [L. *tegumentum*, a covering.] the natural covering of the body, or of some organ, of an animal or plant; an integument.

teg·ū·men′tăl, *a.* of, pertaining to, or serving as a tegument; covering; tegumentary.

teg·ū·men′tȧ·ry, *a.* tegumental.

tē·hee′, *interj.* and *n.* [ME.; echoic.] the sound of a titter or light, derisive laugh.

tē-hee′, *v.i.*; te-heed, *pt.*, *pp.*; te-heeing, *ppr.* to titter; to giggle; to snicker.

Tē·hil′lim, *n.* [Heb.] the Book of Psalms: the Hebrew name.

Te·huel′che (-wel′), *n.* [native word in Patagonia, lit., southeast, but said of northern Patagonian natives.] the dominant aboriginal tribe of Patagonia, known for their tallness.

Tē′iăn, *a.* of or relating to ancient Teos, in Asia Minor, the birthplace of the poet Anacreon.

tē ig′i·tũr, [L.] in the Roman Catholic Church, the prayer or paragraph beginning the Canon of the Mass: so called from the first two words, literally, "Thee therefore."

tēil, *n.* [OFr., from L. *tilia*, a lime tree.] the linden or lime tree: also *teil tree*.

tēind, *n.* [Ice. *tīund*; Sw. *tiende*, tenth.] a tithe or tenth part paid from the produce of land or cattle. [Scot.]

tēin′land, *n.* thaneland.

tek·non′y·mous, *a.* of teknonymy.

tek·non′y·my, *n.* [Gr. *teknon*, child, and *onyma*, name.] in ethnology, a custom of some primitive peoples of naming parents from their offspring.

tek′tīte, *n.* [from Gr. *tēktos*, molten, and *-ite*.] any of certain small, dark green to black glassy bodies of various shapes, found especially in areas of the East Indies, Australia, North America, central Europe, and eastern Africa, and assumed to have originated in outer space.

tel-, same as *tele-*.

tel-, same as *telo-* (end).

tē′lȧ, *n.* [L., a web.] any weblike tissue, especially the membranous roof of the third and fourth ventricles of the brain, known as *tela choroidea*.

tel·aes·thē′si·ȧ, *n.* same as *telesthesia*.

tel′ȧ·mon, *n.*; *pl.* **tel·ȧ·mō′nēs,** [L.; Gr. *telamōn*, bearer.] a supporting column in the form of a man's figure: see also *atlantes*.

tel·an·gi·eç·tā′sis, tel·an″gi·eç·tā′si·ȧ, *n.* [Gr. *telos*, end, and *angeion*, vessel, and *ektasis*, extension.] in medicine, chronic dilatation of the capillary vessels and minute arteries, forming small, reddish tumors in the skin, as of the face.

tel·an·gi·eç′tȧ·sy, *n.* telangiectasis.

tel·an″gi·eç·tat′iç, *a.* pertaining to or of the nature of telangiectasis.

tel·an·gi·ō′sis, *n.* [Gr. *telos*, end, and *angeion*, vessel.] any disease of the capillary vessels.

tē·lăr′i·ăn, *a.* [L. *tela*, a web.] web-spinning, as a spider.

tē·lăr′i·ăn, *n.* a web-spinning spider.

tel′ȧ·ry, *a.* [L. *tela*, a web.]
1. pertaining to a web; spun.
2. spinning webs; as, a *telary* spider.

tel·au′tō·gram, *n.* a reproduction by a telautograph.

tel·au′tō·grȧph, *n.* [*tel-*, and Gr. *autos*, self, and *graphein*, to write.] a telegraphic apparatus by means of which handwriting, drawings, etc. are reproduced at a distance by an electrically controlled pen that makes the same motions as the transmitting pen: a trade-mark (*TelAutograph*).

tel′ē-, [Gr. *tēle-*, from *tēle*, far off.] a combining form meaning: (a) *operating at a distance*, as in *tele*graph; (b) *of, in,* or *by television*, as in *tele*cast. Also, before a vowel, *tel-*.

tel·ē·bar′ō·grȧph, *n.* a barograph electrically recording indications made at a distance.

tel″ē·bȧ·rom′e·tẽr, *n.* a barometer electrically registering indications made at a distance.

tel′ē·çȧst, *n.* a television broadcast.

tel′ē·çȧst, *v.t.* and *v.i.*; telecast *or* telecasted, *pt.*, *pp.*; telecasting, *ppr.* to broadcast by television.

tel″ē·çom·mū″ni·çā′tion, *n.* communication by radio, telephone, telegraph, television, etc.

tel′e·çon·fẽr·ence, *n.* a conference of individuals in different locations, as by telephone, television, etc.

tel′e·çon·fẽr·ence, *v.i.*; teleconferenced, *pt.*, *pp.*; teleconferencing, *ppr.* to hold a teleconference.

tel′ē·çourse, *n.* a course of televised lectures offered for credit by a college or other school.

tē·leç′trō·sçōpe, *n.* an instrument electrically transmitting optical images of objects at a distance.

tel′ē·dū, *n.* [Malay *teledu*.] a small, flesh-eating, burrowing animal, *Mydaus meliceps*, resembling a skunk, native to Java, Borneo, and Sumatra.

tel′ē·fō·tō, *n.*, *v.i.* and *v.t.* telephotograph: a trade-mark (*Telefoto*).

tē·le′gȧ, *n.* [Russ.] a Russian vehicle having a rude box mounted on four wheels without springs.

tel·e·gen′iç, *a.* [*tele-* and *-genic*.] that looks or is likely to look attractive on television: said especially of persons.

tel·ē·gon′iç, *a.* of or affected by telegony.

te·leg′ō·ny, *n.* [*tele-* and *-gony*.] the supposed transmission of hereditary characteristics of one sire to offspring subsequently borne to other sires by the same female.

tel′ē·gram, *n.* [*tele-*, and Gr. *gramma*, writing.] a telegraphic message, or dispatch.

tel·ē·gram′mic̦, *a.* of the nature of a telegram; hence, concise. [Rare.]

tel′ē·gråph, *n.* [Fr. *télégraphe*, see *tele-* and *-graph*.]

1. originally, any signaling apparatus.

2. an apparatus or system for transmitting messages by electric impulses sent through a wire or converted into radio waves: basically it involves the use of a code of short and long signals, called *dots* and *dashes*, produced by the closing and opening of an electric circuit by means of a lever, or key.

3. a telegram.

acoustic telegraph; (a) a telephone; (b) a system of telegraphy in which a sounder is used as a receiving instrument.

automatic telegraph; apparatus for transmitting a telegraph message automatically, a perforated fillet of paper being prepared and inserted in the transmitting apparatus, some form of registering apparatus receiving and recording the message sent. Other forms of automatic telegraph are in use, as those in which the operation of keys resembling those of a typewriter records a message at a distant point.

chemical telegraph; telegraphic apparatus in which the receiver records the signals on a sheet of chemically prepared paper.

copying telegraph; telegraphic apparatus, as the telautograph, reproducing drawings or writing.

dial telegraph; a system of telegraphy in which the movements of a needle over a dial are duplicated by the receiving apparatus.

duplex telegraphy; see *duplex*, a., 2.

electrochemical telegraph; a chemical telegraph.

electromagnetic telegraph; the common system of telegraphy or the apparatus used in such system.

facsimile telegraph; see under *facsimile*.

fire-alarm telegraph; the apparatus necessary to send in alarms to a central station or to the fire-engine houses in a district from call boxes or from fire-alarm contacts working automatically.

harmonic multiple telegraph; a system of telegraphy transmitting a number of separate and distinct musical notes over a single wire, the separate tones of which are utilized in affecting apparatus tuned in unison with such tones, the receiving operator being in communication with but one operator whose sender is tuned to his receiver.

magnetic telegraph; see under *magnetic*.

mechanical telegraph; any form of telegraphy in which communication is made by mechanical means.

morse telegraph; any system of telegraphy employing the Morse alphabet.

multiplex telegraph; a system of telegraphy for the simultaneous transmission of more than four separate messages over a single wire.

optical telegraph; a semaphore; also, an electric telegraph making use of a needle or pointer.

pneumatic telegraph; (a) a system of communication formerly used employing a column of water under pneumatic pressure; (b) a system by which signals may be transmitted by the compression of air confined in a tube.

quadruple telegraph; a telegraph by means of which four separate messages may be transmitted simultaneously over one wire.

space telegraph; same as *wireless telegraph*.

submarine telegraph; a system of telegraphy in which a submarine cable is used instead of a line wire.

wireless telegraph; see *wireless telegraphy* under *wireless*.

tel′ē·gråph, *v.t.*; telegraphed (-gråft), *pt., pp.*; telegraphing, *ppr.* 1. to convey or communicate (a message) by telegraph.

2. to send a telegram to.

tel′ē·gråph, *v.i.* 1. to send a message or messages by telegraph.

2. to signal by any means.

tel′ē·gråph c̦ā′ble, an insulated cable containing wires for use in telegraphy.

tel′ē·gråph c̦lock, 1. a clock regulating other clocks by electricity.

2. one of a system of clocks regulated by telegraphic impressions from a standard clock.

tel′ē·gråph dī′ăl, a lettered dial with a pointer moved by means of electromagnetism.

tē·leg′rȧ·phẽr (*or* tel′ē-graph-er), *n.* one skilled in telegraphy; a telegraph operator.

tel″ē·gråph·ēṣe′, *n.* the shortened, sometimes cryptic, language typical of telegrams.

tel·ē·graph′ic̦, *a.* 1. of or pertaining to the telegraph; made by a telegraph.

2. transmitted or communicated by a telegraph.

3. in the concise style of a telegram.

tel·ē·graph′i·c̦ăl, *a.* telegraphic.

tel·ē·graph′i·c̦ăl·ly, *adv.* 1. by means or use of the telegraph.

2. in a telegraphic manner; in the manner or style of a telegram; concisely; briefly.

tē·leg′rȧ·phist, *n.* a telegrapher.

tel′ē·gråph kēy, the instrument used to make and break an electric circuit, as in Morse telegraphy.

TELEGRAPH KEY

tel·ē·graph′ō·phōne, *n.* a device for making phonographic or graphophonic records at a distance; the system used in making such a record.

tel·ē·graph′ō·scōpe, *n.* [*tele-* and *-graph* and *-scope*.] an instrument which transmits a picture telegraphically and reproduces its image as a positive or negative.

tel′ē·gråph plant, a plant of East India, *Desmodium gyrans*, the leaves of which attract attention by their curious movements.

tel′ē·gråph pōle, one of a number of poles bearing brackets or insulators for the support of a telegraph line.

tel′ē·gråph pōst, a telegraph pole.

tel′ē·gråph reġ′is·tẽr, a device in telegraphy which registers the signals it receives.

tē·leg′rȧ·phy (*or* tel′ē-graph-y), *n.* 1. the operation of telegraph apparatus or the study of this.

2. transmission of messages by telegraph.

3. the making of telegraph instruments.

Tel′e·gụ, *n.* Telugu.

tel·ē·hȳ″drō·bȧ·rom′ē·tẽr, *n.* an electrical device registering the height of water at a distance, as in a reservoir or standpipe.

tel″ē·ī·c̦on′ō·gråph, *n.* [*tele-*, and Gr. *eikōn*, image, and *-graph*.] a device combining the principles of the telescope and the camera lucida, by means of which the images of distant objects are thrown upon a screen.

tel″ē·ki·nē′sis, *n.* [*tele-*, and Gr. *kinēsis*, movement.] the movement of an object caused while not in contact with the body generating the force, and supposedly caused by spiritualistic methods.

tel″ē·ki·net′ic̦, *a.* of or pertaining to telekinesis.

tel·ē·lec̦′tric, *a.* [*tel-* (tele-) and *electric*.] designating or of the transmission of music, etc. to a distance by electricity.

tē·lel′ō·gråph, *n.* a modification of the semaphore introduced about the close of the eighteenth century.

Tē·lem′ȧ·c̦hus, *n.* [L.; Gr. *Tēlemachos*.] in Greek legend, the son of Odysseus and Penelope, who helped his father slay his mother's suitors.

tel″ē·mȧ·nom′ē·tẽr, *n.* a device for recording, at a distance, the movements of a manometer.

tel″ē·mē·c̦han′ic̦s, *n.pl.* [*construed as sing.*] [*tele-* and *mechanics*.] the science of operating mechanisms by remote control through radio transmission.

tē·lem′ē·tẽr, *n.* 1. an instrument for determining the distance of an object remote from the observer, as the distance of a target in gunnery; a range finder.

2. an electric instrument adapted for recording at a distance the readings of other instruments.

tel·ē·met′ric̦, *a.* of, determined by, or pertaining to a telemeter or telemetry.

tē·lem′ē·try, *n.* the science of the use of the telemeter.

tel′ē·mō·tŏr, *n.* a hydraulic or electrical device controlling the action of mechanical apparatus at a distance; specifically, such a device controlling the steering gear of a ship.

tel″en·c̦ē·phal′ic̦, *a.* of the telencephalon.

tel·en·ceph′ȧ·lon, *n.* [Mod. L.; *tel-* and *encephalon*.] the anterior end of the embryonic brain structure of a vertebrate, from which the cerebral hemispheres are developed.

tē·len′ġi·sc̦ōpe, *n.* [*tele-*, and Gr. *engus*, near, and *skopein*, to view.] a combined telescope and microscope.

tel′ē·ō-, tel′e-, [from Gr. *teleos*, complete.] combining forms used in various scientific terms to signify *perfect, whole*.

Tē″lē·ō·ceph′ȧ·lī, *n.pl.* an order of fishes, widely distributed, including those in which the cranium has the full complement of bones.

tē″lē·ō·ceph′ȧ·lous, *a.* pertaining to or resembling the *Teleocephali*.

Tel″ē·ō·des·mā′c̦ē·ȧ, *n.pl.* in zoology, an order of bivalves with strongly developed hinges.

tē″lē·ō·loġ′i·c̦ăl, *a.* having to do with teleology; relating to final causes; concerned with design or purpose in nature.

tē″lē·ō·loġ′i·c̦ăl·ly, *adv.* in a teleological manner.

tē·lē·ol′ō·ġist, *n.* a student of or believer in teleology.

tē·lē·ol′ō·ġy, *n.* [Gr. *telos, teleos*, an end, and *-logy*.]

1. the study of final causes.

2. the fact or quality of being directed toward a definite end or of having an ultimate purpose, especially as attributed to natural processes.

3. a belief, as that of vitalism, that natural phenomena are determined not only by mechanical causes but by an over-all design or purpose in nature: opposed to *mechanism*.

4. the study of evidence for this belief.

tē′lē·ō·phōre, *n.* same as *gonangium*.

tē′lē·ō·phȳte, *n.* [*teleo-*, and Gr. *phyton*, plant.] a plant composed of a number of cells arranged in tissues.

tē″lē·ọr·gan′ic̦, *a.* essential to organic life.

tē′lē·ō·sạur, *n.* a fossil saurian of the genus *Teleosaurus*.

Tē″lē·ō·sạu′rus, *n.* [*teleo-*, and Gr. *sauros*, a lizard.] in paleontology, a genus of fossil saurians with long and narrow snouts. They are confined to the oölitic division of the secondary rocks.

tē′lē·ost, tē·lē·os′tē·ăn, *a.* of, belonging to, or pertaining to the *Teleostei*.

tē′lē·ost, tē·lē·os′tē·ăn, *n.* a teleost fish.

Tē·lē·os′tē·ī, *n.pl.* [*teleo-*, and Gr. *osteon*, bone.] a subclass of fishes including the great majority of those having a well-ossified skeleton: it comprises almost all the common fishes, and includes the groups *Malacopteri, Acanthini, Acanthopteri, Plectognathi*, and *Lophobranchii*.

Tē·lē·os′tō·mī′, *n.pl.* a division of fishes including the ganoids and the ordinary fishes.

tē″lē·ō·trō′c̦hȧ, *n.* same as *telotrocha*.

tē″lē·ō·zō′ic̦, *a.* of or pertaining to a teleozoon.

tē″lē·ō·zō′ŏn, *n.* [*teleo-*, and Gr. *zōon*, an animal.] any animal composed of a number of cells and arranged in tissues.

tel·ē·path′ic̦, *a.* of, pertaining to, or acting through telepathy.

tel·ē·path′i·c̦ăl·ly, *adv.* by telepathy.

tē·lep′ȧ·thist, *n.* 1. a believer in or student of telepathy.

2. a person supposedly possessing telepathic power.

tē·lep′ȧ·thy, *n.* [*tele-* and *-pathy*; coined (1882) by F. W. Myers (1843–1901).] supposed communication between minds by some means other than the normal sensory channels; transference of thought.

tel′ē·phēme, *n.* a telephonic communication. [Rare.]

tel′ē·phōne, *n.* [*tele-* and *-phone*; adopted by Bell (1876) after use for other sound instruments.] an instrument or system for conveying speech over distances by converting sound into electric impulses sent through a wire: it consists of a transmitter and receiver, often with a dialing mechanism for connecting lines: often shortened to *phone*.

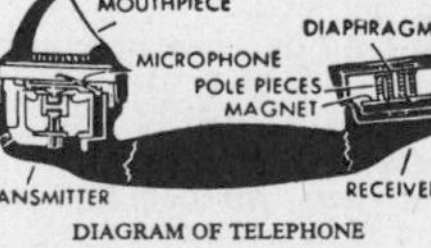

DIAGRAM OF TELEPHONE

automatic telephone; a system of telephony, or the apparatus used in such a system, by which an automatic switchboard places the person making a call in direct communication with the number called, thus eliminating the need for a central operator.

dial telephone; a telephone having a dial attached to it by means of which a telephone number may be called.

DIAL TELEPHONE

local telephone; a telephone or telephone system for use in a certain district, as in a city or town.

long-distance telephone; a telephone or telephone system for communication with a place at a considerable distance.

string telephone; the simplest form of telephone, often sold as a toy, consisting of two cups having the bottoms of tightly stretched membranes connected by a cord: a true mechanical telephone.

tel′ē·phōne, *v.i.*; telephoned, *pt., pp.*; telephoning, *ppr.* to communicate by telephone; to convey a message by telephone: often shortened to *phone.*

tel′ē·phōne, *v.t.* 1. to convey (a message) by telephone.
2. to speak to or reach (a person) by telephone; to call.
Often shortened to *phone.*

tel′ē·phōne bo̤oth, a booth in which one using a telephone may talk without being overheard or disturbed by outside noises.

tel′ē·phōne ex·chānġe′, a central office where telephonic connections are made so that telephone conversations may be carried on between any two stations.

tel′ē·phōne ġirl, a girl operator at a switchboard: also called *telephone operator.*

tel′ē·phōne num′bẽr, in telephony, a number, or more commonly an exchange call name and a number, by which a subscriber may be called on the telephone.

tel′ē·phōne rē·ceiv′ẽr, that part of a telephone which is held to the ear and converts the varying electrical impulses into sound: it is either a separate unit or a part of a handset.

tel′ē·phōne set, in telephony, a group of devices consisting of a telephone transmitter and receiver, together with the necessary circuit and signaling connections.

tel·ē·phon′iç, *a.* 1. of or having to do with a telephone or telephones.
2. transmitted by a telephone.

tel·ē·phon′i·căl·ly, *adv.* in a telephonic manner; by telephone.

tē·leph′ō·nist, *n.* a person versed in telephony, or who operates a telephone.

tel·ē·phō′nō·gråph, *n.* an instrument for recording telephonic communications.

tē·leph′ō·ny, *n.* 1. the art, science, or practice of transmitting communications by the telephone.
2. the making or operation of telephones.

tel′ē·phōte, *n.* [*tele-*, and Gr. *phōs, phōtos,* light.] any of various devices for reproducing pictures or photographic images of visible objects at a distance by electricity.

tel″ē·phō′tō, *a.* 1. telephotographic.
2. designating or of a compound lens that produces a large image of a distant object in a camera of ordinary focal length.

tel″ē·phō′tō, *n.* a telephotograph.

tel·ē·phō′tō·gråph, *n.* 1. a photograph taken with a telephoto lens.
2. a photograph transmitted by telephotography.

tel·ē·phō′tō·gråph, *v.t.* and *v.i.* 1. to take (photographs) with a telephoto lens.
2. to transmit (photographs) by telephotography.

tel″ē·phō″tō·graph′iç, *a.* of, pertaining to, having to do with, or used in telephotography.
telephotographic lens; a telephoto lens.

tel″ē·phō·tog′rȧ·phy, *n.* 1. the art or process of photographing distant objects by using a telephoto lens or a telescope with the camera.
2. the science or process of transmitting photographs over distances by converting light rays into electric signals which are sent over wire or radio channels: the receiver converts the electric signals back into light rays to which a photographic film is exposed.

tel″ē·pō·lar′i·sçōpe, *n.* a polariscope and telescope combined.

tel′ē·pōst, *n.* [Gr. *tele,* and *post,* a dispatch.] an automatic, high-speed telegraph system, the transmitter being operated by a perforated tape.

tel′ē·print·ẽr, *n.* a teletypewriter. [Chiefly Brit.]

tel′ē·ran, *n.* [from *tele*vision *r*adar *a*ir *n*avigation.] an electronic aid to aerial navigation by which data received by radar, maps of the terrain, etc. are transmitted to aircraft by television.

tel′ẽr·ġy, *n.* the influence one brain is supposed to have over that of another at a distance through hypothetical mental force.

tel·ē·ryth′rin, *n.* in chemistry, a crystalline compound of a red color, derived from erythrin.

tel′ē·sçope, *n.* [It. *telescopio* (Galileo, 1611); Mod. L. *telescopium,* from Gr. *tēleskopos,* seeing from a distance, from *tēle,* far, off and *skopein,* to view.] an instrument for making distant objects, as the stars, appear nearer and consequently larger: it consists of a tube or series of tubes containing lenses and is of two types, *refracting,* in which the image is focused on a lens, and *reflecting,* in which the image is focused on a mirror.

HAND TELESCOPE

astronomical telescope; a telescope provided with a simple eyepiece by which the image of the object is inverted.

broken telescope; a telescope the tube of which is bent at right angles about midway between the focus and the object glass, a prism or mirror doing the reflecting.

Cassegrainian telescope; a form of the reflecting telescope in which the great speculum is perforated like the Gregorian telescope, but the rays converging from the surface of the mirror are reflected back by a small convex mirror in the axis of the telescope, and come to a focus at a point near the aperture in the speculum, where they form an inverted image, which is viewed by the eyepiece screwed into the tube behind the speculum.

equatorial telescope; see *equatorial, n.*

Galilean telescope; see under *Galilean.*

Gregorian telescope; see under *Gregorian.*

Herschelian telescope; a reflecting telescope in which only one speculum is employed, by means of which an image of the object is formed near one side of the open end of the tube, and to this the eyeglass is applied directly.

Keplerian telescope; a refracting telescope employing a convex lens of a short focus for an eyepiece, available only for astronomical observations.

Newtonian telescope; see under *Newtonian.*

photographic telescope; a telescope constructed so as to photograph celestial bodies.

prism telescope; a teinoscope.

reflecting telescope; a telescope with a concave mirror at the lower end of the tube, which receives the light from the object and reflects it to a focus near the top of the tube.

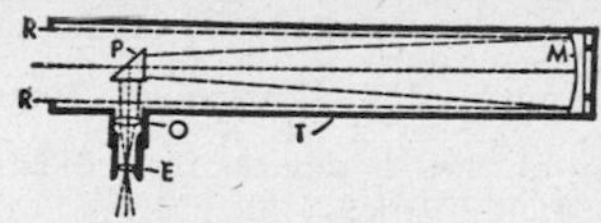

DIAGRAM OF REFLECTING TELESCOPE
T, tube; R, rays reflected from M, mirror to P, prism to O, objective lens to E, eyepiece

refracting telescope; 1. a telescope in which a large double-convex lens (*object glass*) causes light rays to converge to a focus, forming an image magnified by a double-convex eyepiece.
2. a similar telescope, in which the converging rays are intercepted by a double-concave eyepiece.

REFRACTING TELESCOPE

sciatheric telescope; see under *sciatheric.*

terrestrial telescope; a telescope having an eyepiece with two more lenses than an astronomical one. It inverts the image and shows objects in an erect position.

tel′ē·sçōpe, *a.* having parts that slide one inside the other.

tel′ē·sçōpe, *v.i.*; telescoped (-sçōpt), *pt., pp.*; telescoping, *ppr.* to slide or be forced one into another like the concentric tubes of a small collapsible telescope.

tel′ē·sçōpe, *v.t.* 1. to cause to telescope.
2. to condense; to shorten.

tel′ē·sçōpe bag, a handbag having two stiff cases, the one capable of containing the other.

tel′ē·sçōpe çärp, a variety of the goldfish, *Carassius auratus,* having the tail much enlarged, and the eyes, which are large and protruding, set on pedicels.

tel′ē·sçōpe drīv′ẽr, the mechanism for moving a telescope to keep it within the same field of exploration.

tel′ē·sçōpe eȳe (ī), an eye carried at the end of a retractile stalk, as in certain gastropods.

tel′ē·sçōpe fish, same as *telescope carp.*

tel′ē·sçōpe flȳ, a dipterous insect of the genus *Diopsis.*

tel′ē·sçōpe shell, a gastropod, *Telescopium fuscum,* the pyramidal shell of which has numerous whorls.

tel′ē·sçōpe sīght (sīt), in firearms, a telescopic glass mounted on the barrel, used as a sight.

tel·ē·sçop′iç, tel·ē·sçop′i·căl, *a.* 1. of a telescope or telescopes.
2. seen or obtained by a telescope.
3. visible only with the aid of a telescope.
4. having distant vision; farseeing.
5. having sections that slide one inside another; as, a *telescopic* drinking tumbler.
6. in machinery, constructed or composed of concentric tubes; as, a *telescopic* boiler; a *telescopic* smokestack, as of a river boat.
telescopic sight; see under *sight.*

tel·ē·sçop′i·căl·ly, *adv.* 1. in a telescopic manner.
2. by means of a telescope.

tel′ē·sçop·i·fo̤rm, *a.* having the form or construction of a telescope; jointed like a telescope.

tel′ē·sçō·pist (*or* tē-les′), *n.* one skilled in the use of the telescope and in making telescopic observations.

Tel·ē·sçō′pi·um, *n.* [Mod. L.] a southern constellation.

tel′ē·sçō·py (*or* tē-les′), *n.* 1. the art or practice of using the telescope.
2. the science of making telescopes.

tel′ē·sçrībe, *n.* [*tele-*, and L. *scribere,* to write.] a phonograph used to record messages received by telephone. [Obs.]

tel·ē·sçrip′tŏr, *n.* a particular form of printing telegraph.

tel′ē·sēme, *n.* [*tele-*, and Gr. *sēma,* sign.] in electricity, a self-registering device by means of which a dial operated in a room indicates the character of the service required: used in connection with hotel annunciators, police signals, etc.

tel·ē′si·ȧ, *n.* [Fr. *télésie,* from Gr. *telesios,* making perfect.] same as *telesis.*

tel′ē·sis, *n.* [Mod. L., from Gr. *telein,* to fulfill, complete, from *telos,* an end.] the purposeful use of natural and social forces; planned progress.

tel′eṣm, *n.* [Ar.] an amulet, a talisman. [Obs.]

tel·eṣ·mat′iç, *a.* telesmatical. [Obs.]

tel·eṣ·mat′i·căl, *a.* talismanic. [Obs.]

tel·ē·speç′trō·sçōpe, *n.* an instrument composed of a telescope and spectroscope, used for forming and examining spectra of the sun and other planets or their atmospheres.

tel·ē·ster′ē·ō·sçōpe, *n.* a binocular telescope which provides a stereoscopic view of distant objects.

tel·es·thē′ṣi·ȧ, *n.* [Mod. L., from *tele-* and *esthesia.*] extrasensory perception of distant objects, events, etc.

tē·les′tiç, *a.* pertaining to the final end or purpose; tending or serving to the end or finish. [Rare.]

tē·les′tich (*or* tel′ē-), *n.* [Gr. *telos,* end, and *stichos,* a verse.] a poem in which the final letters of the lines spell a word or words when taken in order: also *telestic.*

tel·ē·thẽr′mō·gråph, *n.* 1. a registering telethermometer.
2. the record made by a telethermometer.

tel″ē·thẽr·mom′ē·tẽr, *n.* an electrical recording thermometer, for indicating and recording temperature at a distance.

tel″ē·thẽr·mom′ē·try, *n.* the art of registering temperature at a distance.

Tel′ē·tȳpe, *n.* 1. [*often* t–] a form of teletypewriter: a trade-mark.
2. [*often* t–] communication by means of Teletype.

Tel'ē·ty̆pe, *v.t.* and *v.i.*; Teletyped (-tȳpt), *pt.*, *pp.*; Teletyping, *ppr.* [*often* t–] to send (messages) by Teletype.

tel'e·ty̆p"ẽr, *n.* one who operates a teletypewriter.

tel"e·ty̆pe'set"tẽr, *n.* a machine which simultaneously sets type in each of several receiving stations: the messages are transmitted electrically from a central master machine which is connected to each of the receiving stations.

tel"e·ty̆pe'writ"ẽr, *n.* a form of telegraph in which the receiver prints messages typed on the keyboard of the transmitter: the striking of the keys produces electrical impulses that cause the corresponding keys on the instrument at the distant point to register.

tel'e·ty̆p"ing, *n.* act of transmitting by means of the teletype.

tē·leū'tō·fọrm, *n.* [Gr. *teleutē*, completion, and L. *forma*, form.] same as *teliostage*.

tē·leū'tō·spōre, *n.* [Gr. *teleutē*, completion, and E. *spore*.] same as *teliospore*.

tel'ē·view (-vū), *v.t.* and *v.i.* to view or watch (a performance, event, etc.) by television.

tel'ē·vīṣe, *v.t.* to transmit or receive by television.

tel'ē·vi·ṣiŏn, *n.* [*tele-* and *vision*.]

1. the process of transmitting scenes or views by radio or, rarely, by direct wire: the transmitting televisor, by means of an electronic tube (either an *iconoscope* or *Orthicon*), converts light rays into electronic impulses for further conversion into radio waves; the receiving televisor reconverts the corresponding impulses into electron beams that are projected against the luminescent screen of the *kinescope*, reproducing the original image.

2. the science of making or operating television apparatus.

3. the field of radio broadcasting that employs television.

tel'ē·vi·ṣŏr, *n.* a television transmitter or receiver.

tel'fẽr, *n.* and *v.t.* telpher.

tel'fẽr·ăġe, *a.* telpherage.

tel'fŏrd, *a.* [after T. *Telford* (1757–1834), Scot. civil engineer.] designating or of a road pavement made of stones and gravel rolled smooth.

tel'fŏrd, *n.* a telford pavement.

tel'fŏrd·īze, *v.t.* and *v.i.*; telfordized, *pt.*, *pp.*; telfordizing, *ppr.* to build (roads) after the method invented by Thomas Telford.

tel"hăr·mō'ni·um, *n.* an instrument consisting of a keyboard that controls alternating currents of electricity for producing music at a distant point.

tē'li·ăl, *a.* 1. of a telium.

2. designating or of the final and teliospore-bearing stage in the life cycle of the rust fungi.

tel'iç, *a.* [Gr. *telos*, end.] directed toward an end; purposeful.

tē'li·ō·spōre, *n.* a resting spore that develops in the telial stage of the rust fungi and germinates at the end of the winter.

tē'li·ō·stāġe, *n.* the last stage in the life cycle of rust fungi, in which they develop two-celled, resting spores.

tē'li·um, *n.*; *pl.* **tē'li·ȧ,** the teliospore-bearing sorus of the rust fungi.

tell, *v.t.*; told, *pt.*, *pp.*; telling, *ppr.* [AS. *tellan*, to tell, announce, reckon, count.]

1. to enumerate; to count; to reckon; as, *tell* one's beads.

2. to relate in order; to narrate; to recount; as, he *told* a story.

3. to express in spoken or written words; to utter; to say; as, *tell* the facts, *tell* the truth.

4. to report; announce; publish.

5. to reveal; disclose; make known; as, her face *told* her joy.

> She never *told* her love,
> But let concealment, like a worm i' the bud,
> Feed on her damask cheek. —Shak.

6. to solve; to explain; to interpret.

> Whoso asked her for his wife,
> His riddle *told* not, lost his life. —Shak.

7. to recognize; distinguish; discriminate; as, I can *tell* the difference.

8. to decide; know; as, I can't *tell* what to do.

9. to give instruction to; to make acquainted with; to inform.

> I *told* him of myself; which was as much
> As to have asked him pardon. —Shak.

10. to give an order, command, or request to; as, I *told* him to stay at home.

11. to declare or inform with emphasis; to assert positively; to assure; as, I *tell* you it is late.

12. to set store by; to make account of; to regard. [Obs.]

to tell off; (a) to count (persons, etc.) and separate from the total number; (b) [Colloq.] to rebuke severely.

to tell on; (a) to tire; wear out; (b) [Colloq.] to carry tales about; to inform against.

tell, *v.i.* 1. to give an account or description; to make report: with *of*; as, the speaker *told of* his experiences.

2. to give evidence or be an indication (*of* something).

3. to carry tales; to reveal secrets; as, kiss and *tell*.

4. to produce a result; to be effective; to have a marked effect; as, every hammer blow *told*.

tell, *n.* a story; an account. [Rare.]

tell, *n.* [Ar.] a mound or hill.

Tell, Wil'liăm (-yăm), in Swiss legend, a hero in the fight for independence from Austria: at the command of the Austrian governor on pain of death, he is supposed to have shot an apple off his son's head with bow and arrow: German name, *Wilhelm* (vil') *Tell*.

tell'ȧ·ble, *a.* 1. capable of being told.

2. worth being told.

tel'len, *n.* any species of the *Tellina* or related genera.

tell'ẽr, *n.* 1. one who tells, relates, or communicates (a story, etc.); a narrator.

2. a bank clerk who receives or pays out money; as, a paying *teller*; a receiving *teller*.

3. one of several persons appointed, as in a legislative or deliberative body, or in a public meeting, to count the ballots or votes, in balloting, and, in a division, to count the ayes and noes.

4. one of four officers formerly employed in the Exchequer of England to receive and pay out all moneys for the king: the offices were abolished in 1834.

tell'ẽr·ship, *n.* the position of a teller.

Tel·lī'nȧ, *n.* [LL., from Gr. *telinē*, a kind of shellfish.] a genus of marine and fresh-water mollusks, characterized by the hinge of the shell having one tooth on the left, and two teeth on the right valve, with a strong external ligament, and two slender siphons twice as long as the shell.

tell'ing, *a.* highly effective; impressive; forceful; striking; as, a *telling* discourse; a *telling* look.

tell'ing·ly, *adv.* so as to make an impression; in a telling manner.

tel'li·nid, *n.* any species of the *Tellina* or of the family *Tellinidæ*.

Tel·lin'i·dae, *n.* a family of bivalves, of which *Tellina* is the typical genus.

tel'li·nīte, *n.* a petrified or fossil bivalve shell of the genus *Tellina*.

tel'li·noid, *a.* of or pertaining to the *Tellinidæ*.

tel'li·noid, *n.* one of the *Tellinidæ*.

tell'tāle, *a.* being or serving as a telltale.

tell'tāle, *n.* 1. a person who carries tales; a talebearer; a tattler.

2. an outward indication of something secret.

3. any of various devices for indicating or recording information; an indicator; specifically, (a) a row of strips hung over a railroad track to warn of an approaching low bridge; (b) a device indicating the position of a ship's rudder; (c) a time clock; (d) in music, a gauge on an organ showing the air pressure.

4. in ornithology, same as *tattler*.

tel'lū·răl, *a.* [L. *tellus* (*-uris*), the earth.] of or pertaining to the earth. [Rare.]

tel'lū·rāte, *n.* a salt of telluric acid.

tel'lū·ret, *n.* a telluride. [Obs.]

tel'lū·ret·ed, tel'lū·ret·ted, *a.* combined with tellurium.

telluretéd hydrogen; a gaseous compound obtained by the action of hydrochloric acid on an alloy of tellurium. It is a feeble acid, analogous in composition, smell, and other characters to hydrogen sulfide.

tel·lūr·hy̆'driç, *a.* of or pertaining to tellureted hydrogen.

tellurhydric acid; same as *tellureted hydrogen* under *tellureted*.

tel·lū'ri·ăn, *a.* of or pertaining to the earth.

tel·lū'ri·ăn, *n.* 1. an inhabitant of the earth.

2. an apparatus for demonstrating how the earth's position and movement (diurnal rotation, annual revolution, etc.) causes day and night and the cycle of the seasons.

tel·lū'riç, *a.* of, derived from, or containing tellurium, especially in a higher valence than in the corresponding tellurous compounds.

tel·lū'riç, *a.* 1. tellurian.

2. of or arising from the earth, or soil.

telluric acid; an oxyacid of tellurium which is formed when tellurium is oxidized.

telluric bismuth; same as *tetradymite*.

telluric lines; lines of the solar spectrum which owe their presence to the absorption of the earth's atmosphere.

telluric silver; hessite. [Obs.]

tel'lū·rīde, tel'lū·rid, *n.* a compound of tellurium with an electropositive element or with a radical.

tel·lū'ri·ŏn, *n.* a tellurian (sense 2).

tel'lū·riṣm, *n.* 1. a modification of the hypothesis of animal magnetism, introduced by a German, Dr. Kieser, who attributed the phenomena to a telluric influence. [Rare.]

2. the effect of certain soils in causing disease.

tel'lū·rist, *n.* one who believes in tellurism.

tel'lū·rīte, *n.* 1. a salt of tellurous acid, containing tetravalent tellurium.

2. native tellurium dioxide, TeO_2.

tel·lū'ri·um, *n.* [L. *tellus* (*-uris*), the earth.] a rare nonmetallic chemical element discovered in 1782, usually combined with gold and silver, but sometimes found in a native state. It is tin-white and brittle and belongs to the same family of elements as sulfur and selenium: symbol, Te; atomic weight, 127.61; atomic number, 52.

tel'lū·rīze, *v.t.*; tellurized, *pt.*, *pp.*; tellurizing, *ppr.* to combine or treat with tellurium: used chiefly in the past participle.

tel'lū·rous, *a.* of, pertaining to, or obtained from tellurium, especially in a lower valence than in the corresponding telluric compounds.

tellurous acid; an oxyacid of tellurium formed by the action of nitric acid on the metal. It is a white insoluble powder, forming with alkalis crystallizable salts.

Tel'lus, *n.* [L.] in Roman mythology, the goddess of the earth.

tel'ō-, same as *tele-*.

tel'ō-, [from Gr. *telos*, an end, completion.] a combining form meaning *end*, as in *telophase*: also, before a vowel, *tel-*.

tel'ō·blȧst, *n.* [*telo-*, and Gr. *blastos*, germ.] a segmentation sphere at the end of a germinal band.

tel·ō·blas'tiç, *a.* of, pertaining to, or having the characteristics of a teloblast.

tel"ō·dy̆·nam'iç, *a.* [*telo-* (tele-) and *dynamic*.] of or for the transmission of mechanical power to a distance by cables and pulleys.

tel·ō·lec'i·thăl, *a.* [*telo-* (end), and Gr. *lekithos*, yolk of an egg.] in embryology, having a large amount of eccentric food yolk, usually collected near one pole, as the ova of certain birds.

tel·ō·lem'mȧ, *n.* [*telo-* (end), and Gr. *lemma*, husk.] the covering of the end of a nerve where it connects with muscle tissue.

Tel'ọọ·gọọ, *n.* same as *Telugu*.

tel'ō·phāṣe, *n.* [*telo-* (end) and *phase*.] in biology, the final stage of mitosis, in which the parent cell becomes completely divided into two cells, each having a nucleus.

tē·lot'rō·chȧ, *n.* [*telo-* (end), and Gr. *trochos*, wheel.] a larval annelid having a ring of cilia around the body in front of the mouth and another around the caudal end.

tē·lot'rō·chăl, tē·lot'rō·chous, *a.* having both oral and anal bands of cilia; of the character of a telotrocha.

tel'ō·ty̆pe, *n.* [*telo-* (tele-), and Gr. *typos*, impression.]

1. a printing electric telegraph.

2. a telegram printed by means of the telotype.

telotype printing; printing done by means of the telotype.

tel'phẽr, *a.* of, pertaining to, or carried by a telpher; relating to telpherage: also written *telfer*.

tel'phẽr, *n.* an electrically driven carriage running on an overhead track, to which the carriers, buckets, etc. are attached: also written *telfer*.

tel'phẽr, *v.t.* to transport by telpher: also written *telfer*.

tel'phẽr·ăġe, *n.* a transportation system using telphers: also spelled *telferage*.

tel'phẽr·măn, *n.* one who travels with and operates a train of telphers: also spelled *telferman*.

tel′phẽr·wāy, *n.* the road, line, or way over which transportation is carried on by telpherage: also spelled *telferway.*

tel′sŏn, *n.* [Gr., a limit.] the last joint in the abdomen of the *Crustacea.* The telson may be broad and spreading, as in the lobster, or sword-shaped, as in the king crab, while in the extinct *Eurypterida* its form was extremely variable. The name is also applied to the last joint of scorpions, which has been modified into a weapon of offense.

Tel′ụ̈·gụ̈, *n.* 1. a Dravidian language spoken in eastern India.

2. *pl.* **Tel′ụ̈·gụ̈, Tel′ụ̈·gụ̈ṣ,** a member of a Dravidian people living in Hyderabad, India, who speak this language.

Tel′ụ̈·gụ̈, *a.* of or pertaining to the Telugus or to their language.

tem·blōr′, *n.*; *pl.* **tem·blōrṣ′, tem·blō′reṣ,** [Sp.] an earthquake.

tem·ẽr·ăr′i·ous, *a.* [Fr. *téméraire,* from L. *temerarius;* imprudent.]

1. rash; headstrong; as, *temerarious* folly.

2. careless; reckless.

tē·mer′i·ty, *n.* [L. *temeritas* (*-tatis*), rashness, from *temere,* rashly.] heedlessness; foolish boldness; recklessness; daring; audacity; as, the *temerity* to offer an affront.

tem′ẽr·ous, *a.* reckless; careless; venturesome. [Rare.]

tem′i·ak, *n.* [Eskimo.] a coat or jacket of bird skins worn by Eskimos of both sexes.

Tem′pē·ăn, *a.* resembling or pertaining to Tempe, a valley in Thessaly between Mounts Olympus and Ossa, which has been made famous by Greek poets for its beautiful scenery and mild climate: it was anciently regarded as sacred to Apollo.

tem′pẽr, *v.t.*; tempered, *pt., pp.*; tempering, *ppr.* [Fr. *temperer,* from L. *temperare,* to regulate, temper.]

1. to make suitable, desirable, or free from excess by mingling with something else; to reduce in intensity, especially by the admixture of some other quality; to moderate; to assuage; to mollify; as, *temper* your criticism with reason.

2. to bring to the proper texture, consistency, hardness, etc. by mixing with something or treating in some way; as, some paints are *tempered* with oil; steel and glass are *tempered* by heating and sudden cooling; clay is *tempered* by moistening and kneading.

3. to fit; adapt. [Rare.]

4. to mix in proper proportions. [Archaic.]

God hath *tempered* the body together.
—1 Cor. xii. 24.

5. in music, to adjust the pitch of (a note, instrument, etc.) by temperament; to tune.

6. to accommodate; to modify.

7. to govern. [Obs.]

tem′pẽr, *v.i.* 1. to correspond; to agree. [Obs.]

2. to be or become tempered.

tem′pẽr, *n.* 1. the state of being tempered; specifically, (a) [Archaic.] properly proportioned mixture; (b) the state of a metal with regard to the degree of hardness and resiliency.

2. frame of mind; disposition; mood; as, in a bad *temper.*

3. calmness of mind; composure: now used only in the phrases *lose one's temper, keep one's temper.*

4. a tendency to become angry readily; as, she has a *temper.*

5. anger; rage; as, he went into a *temper.*

6. something used to temper a mixture, etc.

7. middle course; mean; medium. [Archaic.]

8. (a) character; quality; (b) bodily constitution. [Obs.]

9. in sugarworks, white lime or other substance stirred into a clarifier filled with cane juice, to neutralize the superabundant acid.

good temper; good disposition as shown in good will, amiability, and freedom from irritation.

to keep one's temper; to avoid becoming angry.

to lose one's temper; to become angry.

to show one's temper; to be exasperated, as by a trifling circumstance: said especially of a child.

tem′pẽr·à, *n.* [It.] 1. a process of painting in which pigments are mixed with size, casein, or egg, especially egg yolk, to produce a dull finish.

2. the paint used in this process.

tem′pẽr·à·ble, *a.* that can be tempered.

tem′pẽr·à·ment, *n.* [Fr., from L. *temperamentum.*]

1. originally, a tempering; proportionate mixture or balance of ingredients.

2. in medieval physiology, any one of the four conditions of body and mind, the *sanguine, phlegmatic, choleric* (or *bilious*), and *melancholic temperaments,* attributed to an excess of one of the four corresponding humors.

3. a middle course or an arrangement reached by mutual concession, or tempering of the extreme claims on either side; adjustment of opposing influences, as passions, interests, doctrines, and the like; also, the means used to make such an adjustment; a compromise, as between conflicting opinions, etc. [Rare.]

4. frame of mind; disposition; nature; as, he has an excitable *temperament.*

5. a disposition that rebels at restraints and is often moody or capricious; as, many artists have *temperament.*

6. (a) climate; (b) temperature. [Obs.]

7. in music, a system of adjustment of the intervals between the tones of an instrument of fixed intonation: it may be *pure temperament,* in which the intervals are set exactly according to theory, or *equal temperament* (as in a piano), in which the pitch of the tones is slightly adjusted to make them suitable for all keys.

equal temperament, pure temperament; see *temperament,* sense 7.

tem″pẽr·à·men′tăl, *a.* 1. of or caused by temperament.

2. having an excitable temperament; easily upset; moody.

tem″pẽr·à·men′tăl·ly, *adv.* by temperament; as, *temperamentally* unsuited for office work.

tem′pẽr·ănce, *n.* [Fr., from L. *temperantia,* moderation.]

1. the state or quality of being temperate; self-restraint in conduct, expression, indulgence of the appetites, etc.; moderation, originally as one of the four cardinal virtues.

2. moderation in eating and drinking, especially in drinking alcoholic liquors.

3. total abstinence from alcoholic liquors.

4. temper. [Obs.]

5. temperature. [Obs.]

tem′pẽr·ăn·cy, *n.* temperance. [Obs.]

tem′pẽr·ăte, *a.* [L. *temperatus.*]

1. moderate in the indulgence of the appetites; abstemious, especially in the use of alcoholic liquors.

2. moderate in one's actions, speech, etc.; self-restrained.

3. characterized by moderation or restraint, as things, actions, etc.

4. neither very hot nor very cold: said of climate, etc.

5. in music, tempered: said of a scale or interval.

6. proceeding from temperance. [Rare.]

tem′pẽr·āte, *v.t.* to moderate; to temper. [Obs.]

tem′pẽr·ăte·ly, *adv.* in a temperate way.

tem′pẽr·ăte·ness, *n.* moderation; temperance.

Tem′pẽr·ăte Zōne, either of two zones of the earth (*North Temperate Zone* and *South Temperate Zone*) between the tropics and the polar circles: also called *Variable Zone.*

tem′pẽr·à·tive, *a.* having the power or quality of tempering.

tem′pẽr·à·tūre, *n.* [Fr., from L. *temperatura.*]

1. the degree of hotness or coldness of anything, usually as measured on a thermometer.

2. (a) the degree of heat of a living body; (b) the excess of this over the normal (about 98.6°F or 37°C in man).

3. (a) temperateness, as of climate; (b) temperament. [Obs.]

4. moderation; freedom from passions. [Obs.]

5. alloy; mixture; compound. [Obs.]

6. temper, as of metals. [Obs.]

critical temperature; see under *critical.*

tem′pẽr·à·tūre grā′di·ent, the rate of temperature change with increase in altitude.

tem′pẽred, *a.* 1. having been given the desired temper, consistency, hardness, etc.; as, *tempered* steel.

2. modified by addition of or mixture with other qualities, ingredients, etc.; as, *tempered* boldness.

3. having a (specified kind of) temper; as, bad-*tempered.*

4. in music, adjusted to a temperament, especially equal temperament.

tem′pẽr·ẽr, *n.* one who or that which tempers; specifically, a machine in which articles are ground together with water to mix thoroughly.

tem′pẽr sçrew (skrụ̈), an adjusting screw used to connect the beam and tools in well-boring.

tem′pest, *n.* [OFr. *tempeste,* from L. *tempestas,* portion of time, weather, a calamity, storm, tempest, from *tempus,* time.]

1. a violent storm; a gale; a hurricane; a violent and extensive wind, especially one accompanied by heavy rain, hail, or snow.

2. any violent tumult or commotion, as of words.

3. a noisy, fashionable gathering; a drum. [Rare.]

a tempest in a teapot; a great commotion over a small matter.

tem′pest, *v.t.* to agitate as by a storm.

tem′pest, *v.i.* to rage or storm. [Obs.]

tem·pes′tive, *a.* seasonable. [Archaic.]

tem·pes′tive·ly, *adv.* seasonably. [Archaic.

tem·pes·tiv′i·ty, *n.* seasonableness. [Obs.]

tem·pes′tū·ous, *a.* 1. pertaining to or resembling a tempest.

2. stormy; violent; turbulent.

tem·pes′tū·ous·ly, *adv.* in a tempestuous manner.

tem·pes′tū·ous·ness, *n.* the state or quality of being tempestuous.

tem′pi, *n.* alternative plural of *tempo.*

tem′plăr, *n.* [ME. *templer;* OFr. *templier,* from L. *templum,* a temple; so named from occupying quarters near the site of Solomon's Temple in Jerusalem.]

1. [T–] a member of a military and monastic order called Knights Templars, Knights of the Temple, or Brethren of the Temple of Solomon at Jerusalem, founded in 1118 or 1119 by Crusaders to protect pilgrims and the Holy Sepulcher. The order was suppressed in 1312 by the Council of Vienne.

2. a law student or barrister residing at the Temple in London, a group of buildings owned by legal societies.

3. [T–] a member of the Masonic order of Knights Templar; also *Knight Templar.*

TEMPLAR

4. one of a temperance society called Good Templars.

tem′plăr, *a.* 1. pertaining to a temple. [Rare.]

2. [T–] pertaining to a Templar or to the Templars.

tem′plāte, *n.* [Fr. *templet, templette,* dim. of *temple,* from L. *templum,* small timber, purlin.]

1. in architecture, (a) a short stone or timber placed under a beam to help distribute the pressure; (b) a beam for supporting joists over an open space, as a doorway.

2. a pattern, usually in the form of a thin plate, for testing accuracy of form in woodworking, etc.

tem′ple, *n.* [Fr.; see *template.*] a device for keeping the cloth in a loom stretched to its correct width during weaving.

tem′ple, *n.* [OFr. *temple,* one of the temples of the head, from L. *tempora,* the temple, the right place, the fatal spot.]

1. either of the flat surfaces behind the forehead and in front of the ear.

2. either of the sidepieces of a pair of glasses that fit against the temples and over the ears.

3. an ornament for the side of the head, worn in the fifteenth century.

tem′ple, *n.* [AS. *templ, tempel,* from L. *templum,* a temple, originally a part cut off and set apart for religious purposes.]

1. a place regarded by the ancients as a dwelling place for a god or gods; hence, a building for the worship of a god or gods.

2. [T–] any of three buildings for worshiping Jehovah, successively built in Jerusalem.

3. the place of worship of a reformed Jewish congregation: distinguished from *synagogue.*

4. a Christian church; especially, in France, a Protestant church.

5. [T–] either of two (*Inner* and *Middle Temple*) of four sets of London buildings housing England's principal law societies: their site was formerly occupied by the London branch of Knights Templars.

6. a building, usually of imposing size, etc., serving the public or an organization in some

special way; as, a *temple* of art, a Masonic *temple*.

tem′ple, *v.t.*; templed, *pt., pp.*; templing, *ppr.* to build a temple for; to appropriate a temple to; to supply with temples. [Rare.]

Tem′ple Bär, a former London gateway before the Temple buildings: the heads of traitors and criminals were exhibited on it.

tem′pled, *a.* 1. having many temples (places of worship).
2. enshrined in or as in a temple.

tem′plet, *n.* a template.

tem′pō, *n.*; *pl.* **tem′pōs, tem′pi,** [It.; L. *tempus*, time.]
1. the rate of speed at which a musical composition is, or is supposed to be, played: it is indicated by such notations as *allegro, andante*, etc. or by reference to metronome timing.
2. rate of activity; as, the *tempo* of modern living.
tempo commodo; in easy or moderate time.
tempo di ballo; in dance time.
tempo di marcia; in march time.
tempo di valse; in waltz time.
tempo giusto; in strict time.
tempo primo; in the time of the original movement, another having intervened.
tempo rubato; in irregular or borrowed time, some notes being held longer than their legitimate time and others proportionally shortened for the sake of expression.

tem′pō, *n.* [Japan.] in Japanese currency, an obsolete oval brass coin with a square hole in the middle: so called because first coined during the period called *tempo* (1830–43).

tem′pō·răl, *a.* [Fr. *temporel*, from L. *temporalis*, from *tempus*, time.]
1. lasting only for a time; transitory; temporary: opposed to *eternal*.
2. pertaining to this life, or this world, or the body only: opposed to *spiritual*.
3. secular; civil or political: opposed to *ecclesiastical*.
4. of or limited by time: distinguished from *spatial*.
5. in grammar, of, pertaining to, or expressing relations of time; relating to a tense; as, *temporal* conjunctions or clauses.
lords temporal; see under *lord*.
temporal augment; in Greek, a lengthening of the initial vowel.
temporal power; the rule of an ecclesiastic in civil or secular matters as distinguished from spiritual matters; specifically, the dominion of the Pope over the states of the Roman Catholic Church, which was abolished in 1870.
Syn.—secular, worldly, sublunary, transient, transitory.

tem′pō·răl, *n.* 1. [*usually pl.*] anything temporal.
2. [*pl.*] temporalities.

tem′pō·răl, *a.* [Fr. *temporal*, of or in the temples, from L. *temporalis*, temporal, belonging to the temples.] of or near the temple or temples of the head; as, the *temporal* bone; a *temporal* artery or vein.
temporal bone; either of a pair of compound bones forming the sides of the skull.

tem′pō·răl, *n.* in anatomy, the temporal bone.

tem·pō·rā′lē, *n.* that part of the missal or breviary in which are given, in regular order, the daily offices for the entire ecclesiastical year, beginning with Advent.

tem·pō·ral′i·ty, *n.*; *pl.* **tem·pō·ral′i·ties,** 1. the quality or state of being temporal or temporary: distinguished from *perpetuity*.
2. [*usually pl.*] secular properties of a church, especially church revenues.
3. the laity.

tem′pō·răl·ly, *adv.* with respect to time or this life only.

tem′pō·răl·ness, *n.* the quality or state of being temporal.

tem′pō·răl·ty, *n.*; *pl.* **tem′pō·răl·ties,** 1. the laity. [Obs.]
2. a secular possession; a temporality.

tem·pō·rā′nē·ous, *a.* temporary. [Obs.]

tem′pō·rār·i·ly, *adv.* for a time only; for the time being.

tem′pō·rār·i·ness, *n.* the quality or state of being temporary.

tem′pō·rār·y, *a.* [L. *temporarius*, from *tempus* (*-oris*), time.]
1. lasting for a time only; existing or continuing for a limited time; as, the patient has obtained *temporary* relief.
2. intended to last for a time only; not permanent; as, a *temporary* support.
3. contemporary. [Obs.]
temporary star; a star which, for a time, bursts into great brillance and then fades away.
temporary way; in railroad construction, (a) a track laid for trains while alterations or repairs are being made on the main line; (b) a railroad roughly built for immediate use, to be improved and straightened later: opposed to *permanent way*.
Syn.—transient, transitory, fleeting.

tem′pō·rist, *n.* a temporizer. [Obs.]

tem″pō·ri·zā′tion, *n.* the act of temporizing; procrastination; gaining of time.

tem′pō·rīze, *v.i.*; temporized, *pt., pp.*; temporizing, *ppr.* [Fr. *temporiser*, from L. *tempus*, *temporis*, time.]
1. to suit one's actions to the time or occasion; to conform to the circumstances.
2. (a) to give temporary compliance or agreement, evade immediate decision, etc., so as to gain time or avoid argument; (b) to parley or deal (*with* a person, etc.) so as to gain time.
3. to effect a compromise (*with* a person, etc., or *between* persons or parties).

tem′pō·rī·zēr, *n.* one who temporizes.

tem′pō·rī·zing·ly, *adv.* in a temporizing manner.

tem′pō·rō-, [from L. *tempora*.] a combining form, used in anatomical terms, meaning *temporal and*, as in *temporo*maxillary.

tem″pō·rō·ā′lăr, *a.* in ornithology, pertaining to the temporal region and to the wing.

tem″pō·rō·ā·lā′ris, *n.*; *pl.* **tem″pō·rō·ā·lā′rēs,** in ornithology, the temporoalar muscle.

tem″pō·rō·au·riç′ū·lăr, *a.* pertaining to the temporal and auricular regions of the head.

tem″pō·rō·fā′ciăl (-shăl), *a.* of or pertaining to the temporal and facial regions of the head.

tem″pō·rō·mā′lăr, *a.* of or pertaining to the temporal and malar bones.

tem″pō·rō·max′il·lār·y, *a.* of or pertaining to the temporal bone and a maxilla, usually the upper.

temps (*or Fr.* tăṅ), *n.* 1. time. [Obs.]
2. in legerdemain, the exact moment for executing a required movement, as when the attention of the audience is distracted by some other act.

temps, tempse, *n.* tense. [Obs.]

tempt, *v.t.*; tempted, *pt., pp.*; tempting, *ppr.* [OFr. *tempter*, from LL. *temptare*, from L. *tentare*, to try the strength of, to urge, intens. of *tendere*, to stretch.]
1. originally, to test; to try.
2. to try to persuade (a person); to induce; to entice; to allure, especially to something sensually pleasurable or immoral.
3. to rouse desire in; to be inviting to; to attract; as, that pie *tempts* me.
4. to provoke or run the risk of provoking (fate, etc.).
5. to dispose or incline strongly; as, I am *tempted* to accept.
Syn.—decoy, allure, attract, seduce, entice.

tempt·ȧ·bil′i·ty, *n.* the state or character of being temptable.

tempt′ȧ·ble, *a.* capable of being tempted.

temp·tā′tion, *n.* 1. the act of testing; trial. [Archaic.]
2. a tempting or being tempted.
3. something that tempts; an enticement.

temp·tā′tion·less, *a.* having no temptation.

temp·tā′tious, *a.* tempting. [Brit. Dial.]

tempt′ēr, *n.* one who tempts.

> Those who are bent to do wickedly will
> never want *tempters* to urge them on.
> —Tillotson.

the Tempter; the Devil; Satan.

tempt′ing, *a.* that tempts; alluring; attractive; seductive; as, *tempting* pleasures.

tempt′ing·ly, *adv.* in a tempting manner; in a manner to entice to evil; so as to allure.

tempt′ing·ness, *n.* the state of being tempting.

tempt′ress, *n.* a woman who tempts or entices, especially sexually.

tem′pus fū′ġit, [L.] time flies.

temse, *n.* [AS. *temes*, a sieve, from *temsian*, to sift.] a sieve; a strainer; a bolter. [Brit. Dial.]

temse′bread (-bred), *n.* bread made of flour better sifted than common flour. [Brit. Dial.]

tem′ū·lence, *n.* intoxication. [Rare.]

tem′ū·len·cy, *n.* temulence. [Rare.]

tem′ū·lent, *a.* intoxicated. [Rare.]

tem′ū·lent·ive, *a.* somewhat intoxicated. [Rare.]

ten, *a.* [AS. *ten, tyn, tene*; Goth. *taihun*; L. *decem*; Sans. *dáça*, ten.] twice five; denoting the sum of nine and one: often used indefinitely for *many*.

> There's a proud modesty in merit,
> Averse from begging, and resolv'd to pay
> *Ten* times the gift it asks.
> —Dryden.

ten bones; the ten fingers. [Obs.]
ten-cent store; see *five-and-ten-cent store*.
Ten Commandments; in the Bible, the ten rules of living and religious observance given to Moses by God on Mount Sinai; the Decalogue: Ex. xx. 2–17.
Ten Words; the Ten Commandments. [Archaic.]

ten, *n.* 1. a cardinal number; the sum of nine and one or of five and five; the number between 9 and 11; 10; X.
2. any group of ten persons or things.
3. the tenth in a series.
4. a playing card marked with the number 10 and ten spots of its suit.
5. a ten-dollar bill. [Colloq.]
6. the hour of ten; ten o'clock; as, carriages at *ten* sharp.
7. an English coal weight varying between 48 and 50 tons. [Brit. Dial.]
upper ten or *upper ten thousand*; the so-called aristocratic social circles; those regarded as eminent in society. [Colloq.]

ten-, same as *teno-*.

ten·ȧ·bil′i·ty, *n.* the state or quality of being tenable; tenableness.

ten′ȧ·ble, *a.* [Fr. *tenable*, from L. *tenere*, to hold.]
1. capable of being held, maintained, or defended, as against an assailant, or against attempts to take it; as, a *tenable* fortress.
2. capable of being retained; not let out; not uttered; kept secret. [Obs.]

ten′ȧ·ble·ness, *n.* tenability.

ten′āce, *n.* in bridge, etc., a combination in one hand of the ace and queen or the king and jack of the same suit.

Te·nȧch′, *n.* the sacred writings of the Hebrews.

tē·nā′cious, *a.* [L. *tenax, tenacis*, from *tenere*, to hold.]
1. holding fast or firmly; as a *tenacious* grip.
2. retentive; apt to retain long what is committed to it; as, a *tenacious* memory.
3. that holds together strongly; cohesive; tough; as, a *tenacious* wood.
4. that clings; adhesive; sticky.
5. persistent; stubborn; as, *tenacious* courage.
6. niggardly; closefisted. [Obs.]

tē·nā′cious·ly, *adv.* in a tenacious manner, as (a) with a disposition to hold fast what is possessed; firmly; determinedly; (b) adhesively; with cohesive force.

tē·nā′cious·ness, *n.* tenacity.

tē·nac′i·ty, *n.* the state or quality of being tenacious; firmness of hold, retentiveness, cohesiveness, adhesiveness, or persistence.

tē·naç′ū·lum, *n.*; *pl.* **tē·naç′ū·lȧ,** [LL., instrument for holding, from L. *tenere*, to hold.]
1. in surgery, a pointed, hooklike instrument for lifting and holding parts, as blood vessels, during operations, dissections, etc.
2. in entomology, a pair of chitinous processes on podurans, which secure the elater.

ten′ȧ·cy, *n.* [L. *tenax*, a holder, from *tenere*, to hold.] tenacity. [Obs.]

te·naille′, te·nāil′, *n.* [Fr. *tenaille*, from *tenir*, L. *tenere*, to hold.] in fortification, an outwork or rampart raised in the main ditch immediately in front of the curtain, between two bastions.

tē·nāil′lŏn (-nā′lyŏn), *n.* in fortification, a work constructed on each side of ravelin.

ten′ăn·cy, *n.*; *pl.* **ten′ăn·cies,** 1. the condition of being a tenant; the renting of land, a building, etc.
2. property occupied by a tenant.
3. the duration of such an occupancy.
4. possession of lands, etc. by any kind of title.

ten′ănt, *n.* [ME. *tenaunt*; OFr. *tenant*, from *tenir*, to hold; L. *tenere*, to hold.]
1. a person who pays rent to occupy or use land, a building, etc.: distinguished from *landlord*.

2. a person who holds or possesses lands, etc. by any kind of title.

3. one who has possession of any place; a dweller; an occupant.

tenant in capite or *tenant in chief*; formerly, in England, one who held land immediately of the king. According to the feudal system, all lands in England were considered as held immediately or mediately of the king, but the tenants, however, were considered as having the fee of the lands and permanent possession.

tenant in common; one who holds or occupies lands or possesses chattels along with another or other persons, each having an equal interest.

ten'ănt, *v.t.*; tenanted, *pt., pp.*; tenanting, *ppr.* to hold or possess as a tenant; to occupy.

ten'ănt·ȧ·ble, *a.* suitable for a tenant; fit to be occupied.

ten'ănt·ȧ·ble·ness, *n.* the state of being tenantable.

ten'ănt färm'ẽr, a person who farms land owned by another and pays rent in cash or in a share of the crops.

ten'ănt·less, *a.* having no tenant; unoccupied.

ten'ănt·ry, *n.*; *pl.* **ten'ănt·ries,** 1. tenants collectively; as, the *tenantry* of a manor or a kingdom.

2. the condition of being a tenant; tenancy.

tench, *n.*; *pl.* **tench'es** or **tench,** [OFr. *tenche*, from LL. *tinca*, a tench.] a cyprinoid freshwater fish, *Tinca vulgaris*, native to Europe and noted for its tenacity of life.

tench'weed, *n.* an aquatic plant, *Potamogeton natans*, the pondweed, supposed to be eaten by tench.

tend, *v.t.*; tended, *pt., pp.*; tending, *ppr.* [ME. *tenden*; contr. of *attenden*, to attend.]

1. to accompany as a protector or assistant; to look after; to guard; to watch over; to be attentive to; as, to *tend* a flock, to *tend* a child.

2. to be in charge of; manage; operate; as, they *tend* the store.

3. in nautical usage, to be on the alert to keep (a rope, etc.) from fouling.

tend, *v.i.* 1. to pay attention; to be attentive; as, to *tend* to your own business.

2. to wait; to expect. [Obs.]

to tend on; to wait upon; to serve.

tend, *v.i.* [L. *tendere*, to stretch out.]

1. to move in a certain direction; to be directed; as, the road *tends* to the east.

2. to be apt; to incline; to have or give a leaning; to have an inclination, disposition, bias, etc. to do something; as, he *tends* to exaggerate, she *tends* toward selfishness.

3. to lead or be directed (*to* or *toward* a specified result.

tend'ănce, *n.* 1. attendance; attention; care.

2. persons attending; attendants collectively. [Obs.]

tend'ence, *n.* tendency.

ten·den'cious, *a.* same as *tendentious*.

tend'en·cy, *n.*; *pl.* **tend'en·cies,** [ML. *tendentia*, from L. *tendens*, extending.]

1. the character of tending toward some end; inclining or contributing influence; inclination; proclivity; bent; as, a *tendency* toward luxury.

> Its inconsiderate *tendency* to set aside national good faith. —Grover Cleveland.

2. a course toward some purpose, object, or result; a drift.

3. a definite purpose or point of view in a literary work: usually used attributively, as *tendency* drama.

Syn.—drift, scope, aim, proneness, bias, gravitation, disposition, predisposition, proclivity, leaning, inclination.

ten·den'tious (-shus), *a.* [G. *tendenziös*, from *tendenz*, tendency.] characterized by a deliberate tendency or aim; especially, advancing a definite point of view or doctrine; as, *tendentious* writings.

ten'dẽr, *v.t.*; tendered, *pt., pp.*; tendering, *ppr.* [Fr. *tendre*, to reach or stretch out; L. *tendere*, to stretch.]

1. to present for acceptance; to offer; as, to *tender* one's resignation.

2. to offer in payment or satisfaction of an obligation; as, to *tender* the amount of rent or debt.

ten'dẽr, *n.* 1. an offer of money, services, etc. made to satisfy an obligation in order to avoid prosecution.

2. a formal offer, as of marriage, contractual terms, etc.

3. something offered in payment, especially money; as, the currency of any country is legal *tender* in that country.

tend'ẽr, *n.* 1. one who attends or takes care of something; as, a bar*tender*.

2. a small ship employed to attend a larger one; also, a boat to supply a larger one close to shore with provisions and other stores, or to carry passengers, etc.

3. a railroad car attached to the rear of a steam locomotive and fitted with a tank for water, a fuel bin, etc.

ten'dẽr, *a.*; *comp.* tenderer; *superl.* tenderest, [Fr. *tendre*, from L. *tener*, tender, from same root as *tenuis*, thin, fine, *tendere*, to stretch.]

1. easily impressed, broken, bruised, or injured; not tough, firm, or hard; delicate in texture; soft, fragile, succulent, etc.; as *tender* plants, *tender* flesh.

2. very sensitive, especially to pain; easily pained.

3. weak of constitution or physique; not hardy; not able to endure hardship, severe weather, etc.

4. weak; immature; young; as, *tender* age.

5. that requires careful handling; ticklish; delicate; as, a *tender* question.

6. that has or expresses affection, love, consideration, etc.; gentle; affectionate; as, a *tender* smile.

7. sparing; chary; as, *tender* of one's praise.

8. sensitive to impressions, emotions, moral influences, etc.; impressionable; as, *tender* conscience.

9. sensitive to others' feelings; sympathetic; compassionate; as, a *tender* heart.

> It is impossible to speak of William McKinley without remembering that no truer, *tenderer* knight to his chosen lady ever lived among mortal men. —John Hay.

10. careful; considerate; as, be *tender* of your neighbor's reputation.

11. gentle; mild; unwilling to pain; not rough or heavy; as, a *tender* touch.

12. of soft or delicate quality; subdued; as, *tender* colors.

13. frail; slender; thin; fine; tenuous. [Obs.]

14. keen of scent; sharp. [Obs.]

15. in nautical usage, careening too readily under sail; crank.

Syn.—delicate, frail, impressible, susceptible, yielding, soft, effeminate, weak, feeble, compassionate, affectionate, careful, gentle, mild, meek, merciful.

ten'dẽr, *v.t.* 1. to make tender.

2. to treat with tenderness. [Archaic.]

ten'dẽr, *n.* regard; kind concern. [Obs.]

ten'dẽr·foot, *n.*; *pl.* **ten'dẽr·foots** or, rarely, **ten'dẽr·feet,** 1. one who is not accustomed to the hardships and privations of the ranching and mining country of the West; a greenhorn.

2. any newcomer, novice, or inexperienced person.

3. a beginner in the Boy Scouts.

ten'dẽr·heärt'ed, *a.* having a tender heart; easily moved to pity; sympathetic.

ten·dẽr·heärt'ed·ly, *adv.* with tender affection; sympathetically.

ten·dẽr·heärt'ed·ness, *n.* the state or quality of being tenderhearted.

ten'dẽr-heft'ed, *a.* having great tenderness. [Obs.]

ten'dẽr·īze, *v.t.*; tenderized, *pt., pp.*; tenderizing, *ppr.* to make tender, as meat.

ten'dẽr·ling, *n.* 1. a weakling; one made tender by too much kindness.

2. one of the first horns of a deer.

ten'dẽr·loin, *n.* 1. the tenderest part of a loin of beef, pork, etc., located under the short ribs and consisting of the psoas muscle.

2. [*usually* T–] (a) formerly, a district in New York City, below 42d Street west of Broadway, in which there was much vice and corruption: so called because regarded as a choice assignment for police grafters; (b) any similar district in another city.

ten'dẽr·ly, *adv.* 1. with tenderness; mildly; gently; softly; in a manner not to injure or give pain.

2. kindly; with pity or affection.

3. with too much tenderness or care; effeminately.

ten'dẽr·ness, *n.* the state or quality of being tender or easily broken, bruised, or injured; softness; brittleness.

Syn.—kindness, pity, humanity, benignity, mildness.

ten·di·nī'tis, *n.* same as *tenonitis*.

ten'di·nous, *a.* [Fr. *tendineux*, from LL. *tendines*, tendons, from *tendere*, to stretch.]

1. pertaining to or like a tendon or tendons.

2. consisting of tendons; sinewy; as, nervous and *tendinous* parts.

tend'ment, *n.* attendance; care. [Obs.]

ten'dŏn, *n.* [Fr.; ML. *tendo*, from Gr. *tenōn*, a sinew, from *teinein*, to stretch.] in anatomy, a hard, inelastic cord or bundle of connective tissue by which a muscle is attached to a bone or other part or in which muscle fibers end; a sinew.

ten'dŏn cell, a cell of connective tissue lying between the fibrous bundles of a tendon.

ten'dŏn·ous, *a.* tendinous. [Rare.]

ten'dŏn rē'flex, reflex action produced in a muscle by a blow upon its tendon.

ten'draç, *n.* same as *tenrec*.

ten'dresse, *n.* tenderness. [Obs.]

ten'dril, *n.* [OFr. *tendrille*, a tendrill, a little gristle, from *tendre*, tender.] a filiform spiral shoot of a climbing plant that clings or coils around an object for the purpose of support.

ten'dril, *a.* clasping; climbing. [Rare.]

ten'driled, ten'drilled, *a.* having tendrils, as a vine.

ten'drŏn, *n.* tendril. [Rare.]

ten'dry, *n.* a proposal for acceptance; a tender. [Obs.]

Ten'ē·brae, *n.pl.* [L., darkness.] in the Roman Catholic Church, the service of matins and lauds sung for the following day in the afternoon or evening of the last three days of Holy Week, at which the Crucifixion is commemorated by the extinguishing of candles.

tē·neb'ri·çōse, *a.* same as *tenebrous*.

ten·ē·brif'iç, *a.* making dark or gloomy; obscuring.

ten·ē·brif'iç·ous, *a.* tenebrific. [Obs.]

tē·nē'bri·ous, *a.* tenebrous.

ten'ē·brōse, *a.* tenebrous.

ten·ē·bros'i·ty, *n.* the state or quality of being tenebrous.

ten'ē·brous, *a.* [L. *tenebrosus*, from *tenebræ*, darkness.] dark; gloomy.

ten'ē·brous·ness, *n.* darkness; gloom; tenebrosity.

ten'ē·ment, *n.* [Fr.; LL. *tenementum*, from L. *tenere*, to hold.]

1. a dwelling house; a building for a habitation.

2. a room or set of rooms tenanted as a separate dwelling.

3. a tenement house.

4. in law, any species of permanent property that may be held of another by tenure, as lands, houses, rents, commons, offices, franchises, etc.

5. a place of occupancy; an abode; as, the body is the *tenement* of the soul. [Poet.]

ten·ē·men'tăl, *a.* 1. pertaining to tenements.

2. that is or can be held by a tenant or tenants.

ten·ē·men'tȧ·ry, *a.* 1. that is or can be leased to tenants.

2. tenemental.

ten'ē·ment house, a house divided into a number of tenements, or apartments: often used to denote such a dwelling that is in the poorer section of a city and is overcrowded, dirty, or deteriorated.

tē·nen'dum, *n.* in law, formerly, that clause in a deed defining a tenure.

ten'ent, *a.* holding; clasping; specifically, in zoology, adapted for holding or clasping, as hairs or tentacles. [Rare.]

ten'ẽr·ăl, *a.* [L. *tener*, soft, delicate, and *-al*.] relating to the condition of a neuropterous insect just after it has passed the pupal state and before it has reached the imaginal state.

Ten·ẽr·iffe', *n.* a wine made in Tenerife (or Teneriffe), one of the Canary Islands, similar to madeira wine in appearance, but slightly more acid in taste.

tē·nes'miç, *a.* pertaining to, or of the nature of, tenesmus.

tē·nes'mus, *n.* [ML.; L. *tenesmos*; Gr. *teinesmos*, from *teinein*, to stretch.] in medicine, a feeling of urgent need to defecate or urinate, with a straining but unsuccessful effort to do so.

ten'et, *n.* [L. *tenet*, he holds.] any opinion, principle, dogma, or doctrine which a person, sect, school, etc., believes or maintains; as the *tenets* of Plato or of Cicero.

Syn.—opinion, principle, doctrine, dogma, belief, precept.

ten'fōld, *a.* 1. having ten times as much or as many; multiplied by ten.

2. having ten parts.

ten'fōld, *adv.* ten times as much or as many; by tens; in tens.

ten'-gal'lŏn hat, a very tall, wide-brimmed felt hat, originally worn by American cowboys.

tē′ni·ȧ, *n.*; *pl.* **tē′ni·ae,** same as *taenia.*
tē′ni·ȧ·cīde, *n.* same as *taeniacide.*
tē′ni·ȧ·fūge, *n.* same as *taeniafuge.*
te·nī′ȧ·sis, *n.* same as *taeniasis.*
tē′ni·oid, *a.* same as *taenioid.*
ten′nănt·īte, *n.* [from Smithson *Tennant*, an English chemist.] a blackish lead-gray ore consisting of copper, iron, arsenic, and sulfur.
ten·né′ (-nā′), *n.* [OFr. *tenné*, tawny.] in heraldry, a chestnut or orange-brown color seldom used.
Ten·nes·sē′ăn, *a.* of Tennessee.
Ten·nes·sē′ăn, *n.* a native or inhabitant of Tennessee.
Ten·nes·see′ walk′ing hǫrse, any of a breed of saddle or light utility horse with an easy, ambling gait.
ten′nis, *n.* [ME. *teneiz*; prob. from Anglo-Fr. *tenetz*, receive, hold, from OFr. *tenir*, to hold: a cry before play by the server.] any of various games played by batting a ball back and forth with rackets or paddles; specifically, (a) a game, usually played outdoors, in which players bat a fabric-covered, hollow rubber ball back and forth over a net stretched across a specially prepared court of turf, clay, asphalt, etc.: officially called *lawn tennis*; (b) an old indoor game (*court tennis*), in which players batted a ball back and forth over an embankment or against a wall, originally with the palms of their hands, later with paddles: modern modifications of this game are racquets, squash, handball, etc.
ten′nis çourt, the ground, space, or building marked with lines and divided by a net, where the game of tennis is played.
ten′nis shōe, 1. a light, rubber-soled, heelless shoe of canvas or leather, worn in playing tennis, etc.
2. a similar leather shoe with short spikes, sometimes worn in playing tennis on a grass court.
Ten′nō, *n.* [Japan.] heavenly ruler: a title given to the emperor of Japan.
Ten·ny·sō′ni·ăn, *a.* of, like, or characteristic of Alfred, Lord Tennyson or his poetry.
ten′ō-, [from Gr. *tenōn*, tendon.] a combining form meaning *tendon*, as in *teno*tomy: also, before a vowel, *ten-*.
ten′ŏn, *n.* [ME. *tenon*, *tenoun*; (early) Fr. *tenon*, from *tenir*, to hold.] a projecting part cut on the end of a piece of wood for insertion into a corresponding hole (*mortise*) in another piece to make a joint.

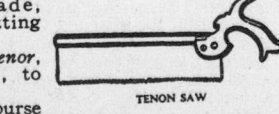

TENON
a a, mortises; *b b*, tenons

ten′ŏn, *v.t.* and *v.i.* 1. to make a tenon (on).
2. to joint by mortise and tenon.
Te·nō′ni·ăn, *a.* of, pertaining to, or named after J. R. Tenon, a French anatomist (1724–1816).
Tenonian or *Tenon's capsule*; a delicate sheet of connective tissue in the orbit of the eye, forming a lymphatic cavity, and separating the fatty tissue from the eyeball.
ten·ŏn·ī′tis, *n.* 1. inflammation of a tendon.
2. inflammation of the Tenonian capsule.
ten′ŏn sąw, a saw with a brass or steel back and a thin, fine-toothed blade, used for cutting tenons.

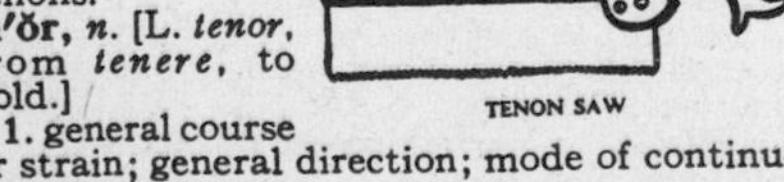
TENON SAW

ten′ŏr, *n.* [L. *tenor*, from *tenere*, to hold.]
1. general course or strain; general direction; mode of continuance.

Along the cool sequester'd vale of life
They kept the noiseless *tenor* of their way.
—Gray.

2. general character or nature.

This success would look like chance, if it were not perpetual and always of the same *tenor*. —Dryden.

3. that course of thought which holds on or runs through the whole of a discourse; general course, drift, or direction of thought; purport; substance.

Bid me tear the bond,
When it is paid according to the *tenor*.
—Shak.

4. the exact wording or an exact copy of a legal document.
5. the highest adult male voice, usually ranging from about an octave below middle C to an octave above: see also *falsetto*.
6. the part written for or sung by this voice.
7. a person or instrument having this range or performing this part.
8. that bell of a peal or set having the lowest tone.
ten′ŏr, *a.* of, in, for, or having the range of the tenor; as, a *tenor* saxophone.
ten′ŏr çlef, the C clef on the fourth line, used in notation for the tenor trombone, the upper range of the cello and bassoon, etc.
tē·nor′rhȧ·phy, *n.*; *pl.* **tē·nor′rhȧ·phieş,** [Gr. *tenōn*, a tendon, and *rhaphe*, a seam.] in surgery, the suture or uniting of the ends of a divided tendon.
ten·ō·sī′tis, *n.* inflammation of a tendon.
ten·os·tō′sis, *n.* ossification of a tendon.
ten·ō·sū′tūre, *n.* same as *tenorrhaphy.*
ten′ō·tōme, *n.* a cutting instrument used in performing a tenotomy.
tē·not′ō·mist, *n.* an expert in performing a tenotomy.
tē·not′ō·mīze, *v.t.* and *v.i.* to divide a tendon or tendons.
tē·not′ō·my, *n.* in surgery, the cutting or dividing of a tendon.
ten′pen″ny (*also, for* 1, ten′pă n-i), *a.* 1. in England, worth ten pence.
2. designating a nail of large size (three inches in length).
ten′pinṡ, *n.pl.* 1. [*construed as sing.*] a game of bowling, in which ten pins are arranged in the form of a triangle at one end of a bowling alley and bowled at.
2. the pins used in this game.
ten′-pound″ẽr, *n.* 1. an ocean fish, about three feet long, inhabiting tropical waters.
2. anything that weighs ten pounds.
3. a cannon that fires a ball weighing ten pounds.
ten′reç, *n.* [Fr. *tanrac*, *tenrec*, from Malagasy *tāndraka*.] any of a number of small insectivorous animals of the genus *Centetes*, related to the hedgehog, native to Madagascar and the Isle of France: also written *tanrec*, *tendrac*.

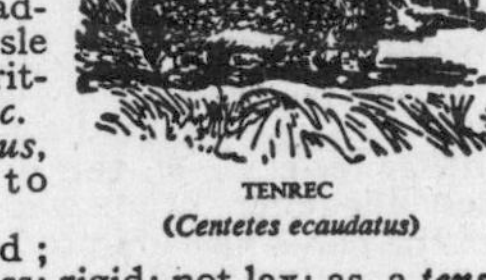
TENREC
(*Centetes ecaudatus*)

tense, *a.* [L. *tensus*, from *tendere*, to stretch.]
1. stretched; strained to stiffness; rigid; not lax; as, a *tense* fiber.
2. undergoing or showing mental or nervous strain.
3. in phonetics, spoken with tensed muscles, especially of the tongue: opposed to *lax*, *flaccid*.
tense, *v.t.* and *v.i.*; tensed (tenst), *pt.*, *pp.*; tensing, *ppr.* to make or become tense.
tense, *n.* [OFr. *tans*, *tenzs*, *temps*, from L. *tempus*, time.]
1. any of the forms of a verb that show the time of its action or state of being: the English tenses are usually listed as *present*, *past*, *future*, *perfect*, *past perfect* (*pluperfect*), and *future perfect*, in accordance with Latin models; but the use of English verbal forms is determined more by the manner of action (aspect, mode) than by the time of action.
2. a set of such inflectional forms for any given time; as, decline the present *tense* of *be*.
tense′ly, *adv.* with tension; in a tense manner.
tense′ness, *n.* the state or condition of being tense.
ten·si·bil′i·ty, *n.* the state or quality of being tensible.
ten′si·ble, *a.* capable of being extended or stretched out; tensile; ductile.
ten′si·bly, *adv.* by means of tension.
ten′sile, *a.* 1. of, undergoing, or exerting tension; as, *tensile* strength.
2. capable of being extended or stretched.
ten′siled, *a.* made tensile. [Rare.]
ten′sile strength, resistance to lengthwise stress, measured by the greatest load in weight per unit area pulling in the direction of length that a given substance can bear without tearing apart.
ten·sil′i·ty, *n.* the state or quality of being tensile.
ten·sim′e·tẽr, *n.* an instrument for measuring the tension, or pressure, of gases or vapors; manometer.
ten·si·om′e·tẽr, *n.* an instrument for measuring the tautness of a stretched wire, rope, etc.
ten′sion, *n.* [from Fr. or L.; Fr. *tension*; L. *tensio*, from *tensus*, pp. of *tendere*, to stretch.]
1. a tensing or being tensed.
2. mental or nervous strain, often accompanied by muscular tautness.
3. a state of strained relations; uneasiness due to mutual hostility.
4. a device for making something tense or taut, as thread in a sewing machine.
5. electromotive force; electric potential or potential difference.
6. the expansive force, or pressure, of a gas or vapor.
7. (a) stress on a material produced by the pull of forces tending to cause extension; (b) a force or combination of forces exerting such a pull against the resistance of the material.
ten′sion·ăl, *a.* of or pertaining to tension.
ten′sion mem′bẽr, a separate piece or unit serving to bear the tensile strain of a framed structure.
ten′sion rod, a rod in a truss or structure used as a tension member.
ten′si·ty, *n.* the state or quality of being tense; tenseness.
ten′sive, *a.* causing, or giving the sensation of, tension; as, a *tensive* pain.
ten′sŏn, *n.* [Fr., from LL. *tensio* (-*onis*), a contention, from L. *tendere*, to stretch.] a contest in verse between rival troubadours; hence, a verse or song composed for such a contest: written also *tenzon*.
ten′sŏr, *n.* 1. any muscle that extends or stretches a part of the body.
2. in mathematics, the ratio in which the modulus of a quaternion stretches the length of a vector.
ten′-strīke, *n.* 1. in tenpins, a strike.
2. any entirely successful stroke or move.
ten′sūre, *n.* tension. [Obs.]
tent, *n.* [Fr. *tente*; LL. *tenta*, a tent, lit., something stretched out or extended, from L. *tendere*, to stretch.]
1. a portable shelter consisting of canvas or other coarse cloth stretched over poles and attached to stakes.
2. anything more or less like this, as an airtight shelter (*oxygen tent*) placed over the bed of a patient receiving oxygen.
tent of meeting; in the Bible, a tabernacle.
tent, *v.i.* to live in a tent; to encamp.

We're *tenting* tonight on the old camp ground. —Kittredge.

tent, *v.t.* to lodge in tents. [Rare.]
tent, *n.* [ME. *tente*; OFr. *tente*, a probe, from *tenter*, to try, test; L. *tentare*.]
1. in surgery, a roll of lint or linen, used to dilate an opening in the flesh, or to prevent the healing of an opening from which matter or other fluid is discharged.
2. a probe for examining a wound. [Obs.]
tent, *v.t.* 1. to insert a tent in.
2. to probe; to search as with a tent; as, to *tent* a wound. [Obs.]

I'll *tent* him to the quick. —Shak.

tent, *n.* [Sp. *tinto*, deep colored, from L. *tinctus*.] a kind of wine of a deep-red color, chiefly from Galicia or Malaga in Spain.
tent, *n.* [contr. of *attend*, to note.] attention; notice; caution; care. [Scot. and Brit. Dial.]
tent, *v.t.* to give heed to; to attend to; also, to prevent; to observe. [Scot. and Brit. Dial.]

If there's a hole in a' your coats,
I rede you *tent* it.
A chield's amang you taking notes,
An', faith, he'll prent it. —Burns.

ten′tȧ′çle (-kl), *n.* [Mod. L. *tentaculum*, from L. *tentare*, to handle, touch.]
1. any of various kinds of long, slender, flexible growths about the head or mouth of some invertebrate animals, used variously to feel, grasp food, propel, or cling.
2. in botany, a sensitive hair, as on some leaves.
ten′tȧ·çled (-kld), *a.* having tentacles.
ten′tȧ·çle shēath, a sheath surrounding the base of the tentacles of many mollusks.
ten·taç′ū·lăr, *a.* pertaining to, of the nature of, or serving as a tentacle or tentacles.
ten·taç′ū·lāte, ten·taç′ū·lā·ted, *a.* having tentacles.
ten·taç′ū·li·cyst, *n.* same as *tentaculocyst.*
Ten·taç·ū·lif′ẽr·ȧ, *n.pl.* same as *Suctoria.*
ten·taç·ū·lif′ẽr·ous, *a.* producing or provided with tentacles.
ten·taç′ū·li·fọrm, *a.* having the form of a tentacle.
ten·taç′ū·līte, *n.* one of a group of small, annulated, pointed shells, fossil in the Silurian strata.
ten·taç′ū·lō·cyst, *n.* [LL. *tentaculum*, and Gr. *kystis*, bladder.] a modified tentacle, as of certain medusae.

ten·tac̦′ū·lum, *n.*; *pl.* **ten·tac̦′ū·lȧ,** [LL., from L. *tentare*, to touch.]
1. a tentacle of any kind; a feeler.
2. a tactile hair, as one of the whiskers of a cat or other animal.

tent′āġe, *n.* any supply or collection of tents; as, the regiment was without *tentage*.

ten·tā′tion, *n.* [Fr., from L. *tentatio* (*-onis*), trial.] experimental adjustment.

ten′tȧ·tive, *a.* [ME. *tentativus*, from pp. of L. *tentare*, to try, to touch.] based on or consisting in trial or experiment made or done provisionally; experimental; empirical.

ten′tȧ·tive, *n.* an essay; a trial; an experiment.

ten′tȧ·tive·ly, *adv.* in a tentative manner.

tent bed, 1. a bedstead having curtains that hang from a central point overhead, forming a tentlike canopy.
2. a small bed for use in a tent.

tent c̦at′ẽr·pil·lăr, a gregarious caterpillar, the larva of a moth, *Malacosoma americanum*: it lives in colonies in large tentlike webs which it spins on trees.

tent′ed, *a.* covered by or living in a tent or tents.

tent′ẽr, *n.* one who lives in a tent.

tent′ẽr, *n.* [from *tent*, to tend.] a person in a factory who tends or looks after a machine or set of machines; as, a loom *tenter*. [Chiefly Brit.]

ten′tẽr, *n.* [ME. *tentoure*, from L. *tentus*, stretched, from *tendere*, to stretch.]
1. a machine or frame for stretching cloth by means of tenterhooks, so that it will dry evenly without shrinking.
2. a tenterhook.
3. a bristle on a fly's foot; a tentacle.

ten′tẽr, *v.t.* and *v.i.*, tentered, *pt.*, *pp.*; tentering, *ppr.* to stretch on a tenter or tenters.
Woolen cloth will *tenter*. —Bacon.

ten′tẽr ground, ground on which tenters are erected and operated.

ten′tẽr·hook, *n.* a sharp hooked nail, used in stretching cloth on a tenter.
on tenterhooks; in suspense; filled with anxiety.

tent flȳ, an outer sheet of canvas, etc. stretched over a tent roof to provide double protection.

tent′fu̇l, *n.* as many or as much as a tent will contain.

tenth, *a.* 1. first after the ninth, or last in order in a series of ten.
2. being one of the ten equal parts of anything.

tenth, *n.* 1. any of ten equal parts into which anything is or may be divided; a **tithe**.
2. the one following the ninth.
3. in old English law, the tenth part of income, or property, which was paid as a tithe to the sovereign.
4. the tenth part of the annual profit of each benefice in the Church of England, payable to the crown, and made by statute part of the fund called Queen Anne's Bounty.
5. in music, the octave of the third; also, an interval comprising ten degrees diatonically divided.

tenth′ly, *adv.* in the tenth place.

tenth′mē·tẽr, tenth′mē·tre, *n.* in physics, the ten-millionth part of a millimeter.

ten·thred′i·nid, *a.* of or pertaining to the family *Tenthredinidæ*.

ten·thred′i·nid, *n.* one of the *Tenthredinidæ*.

Ten·thrē·din′i·dae, *n.pl.* a family of hymenopterous insects, of which the genus *Tenthredo* is the type.

Ten·thrē′dō, *n.* [Gr. *tenthrēdōn*, a kind of wasp.] a genus of hymenopterous insects, popularly known as the sawflies.

ten′tie, *a.* same as *tenty*.

tent′i·fọrm, *a.* tent-shaped, as the nests of certain insects.

ten·tiġ′i·nous, *a.* exciting lasciviousness; as, a *tentiginous* humor. [Obs.]

tent′māk″ẽr, *n.* one who makes tents.

ten·tō′ri·ăl, *a.* of or pertaining to the tentorium.

ten·tō′ri·um, *n.*; *pl.* **ten·tō′ri·ȧ,** [L., a tent.]
1. in anatomy, a process of the dura mater, which separates the cerebrum from the cerebellum.
2. in zoology and anatomy, the endocranium.

tent′ō·ry, *n.*; *pl.* **tent′ō·rieṣ,** [L. *tentorium*, a tent.] the awning of a tent. [Obs.]

tent peg, same as *tent pin*.

tent peg′ging, a sport, especially among British cavalrymen, in which the contestants, riding at full gallop, attempt to uproot with their lances tent pins which have been fixed in the ground.

tent pin, a stout peg of wood or iron driven into the ground to secure one of the ropes of a tent.

tent shōw, a show, as a traveling carnival, given in a tent.

tent stitch, an embroidery stitch that forms a series of parallel slanting lines.

tent tree, a tall screw pine, *Pandanus forsteri*, found on Lord Howe's Island, New South Wales.

ten′tūre, *n.* [Fr.] paper or tapestry for a wall.

tent′wŏrt, *n.* a fern, *Asplenium ruta-muraria*; the wall rue.

tent′y, *a.* careful; cautious. [Scot.]

ten′ū·āte, *v.t.*; tenuated, *pt.*, *pp.*; tenuating, *ppr.* to make thin. [Rare.]

ten′ū·ēṣ, *n.* pl. of *tenuis*.

ten″ū·i·fō′li·ous, *a.* [L. *tenuis*, stretched, and *folium*, a leaf.] having thin or narrow leaves.

tē·nū′i·ous, *a.* tenuous. [Rare.]

ten″ū·i·ros′tẽr, *n.* a slender-billed bird; specifically, one of the *Tenuirostres*.

ten″ū·i·ros′trăl, *a.* slender-beaked; pertaining to the *Tenuirostres*.

Ten″ū·i·ros′trēṣ, *n.pl.* [L. *tenuis*, slender, and *rostrum*, a beak.] a former group of passerine or insessorial birds, comprising those which have the beak long and slender, gradually tapering to a point. Most of the *Tenuirostres* live upon insects, but some live partially or wholly upon the juices of flowers. The chief families are the creepers, the honey birds, the hummingbirds, the sunbirds, and the hoopoes.

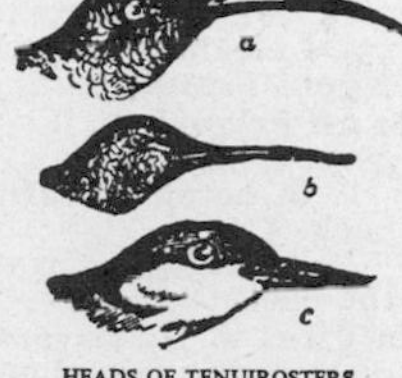

HEADS OF TENUIROSTERS
a, sunbird; *b*, hummingbird; *c*, European nuthatch

ten′ū·is, *n.*; *pl.* **ten′ū·ēṣ,** [L., thin, slender.] formerly, in phonetics, one of the three surd mutes (voiceless stops) of the Greek alphabet κ, π, τ; also, the corresponding letters and sounds in any language, as *k*, *p*, *t*.

tē·nū′i·ty, *n.*; *pl.* **tē·nū′i·tieṣ,** [Fr. *tenuité*; L. *tenuitas*, from *tenuis*, thin.] the state or quality of being tenuous; specifically, (a) smallness in diameter; thinness; slenderness; fineness; as, the *tenuity* of a hair or filament; (b) rarity; rareness; as, the *tenuity* of the air in the higher regions of the atmosphere; (c) faintness, as of light or voice; (d) meagerness; slightness.

ten′ū·ous, *a.* [L. *tenuis*, thin.]
1. physically thin, slender, or fine.
2. rare; not dense, as air at high altitudes.
3. unsubstantial; slight; flimsy; as, a *tenuous* plot.

ten′ūre, *n.* [ME. *tenur*; OFr., from *tenir*, L. *tenere*, to hold.]
1. the act, manner or right of holding property, office, etc. In United States law, the whole right and title of the land rests with the owner, subject only to the laws of the State. In British law, the person possessing the land holds it from a superior, ultimately from the crown.
2. the right to hold or possess something.
3. the length of time something is held; as, *tenure* of office.
4. conditions of possession.
5. permanent possession, as of an office or position.

tẹn·ū′ri·ăl, *a.* of or dependent on tenure.

tẹ·nū′tō, *a.* [It., held.] in music, held for its full value: said of a tone or chord.

tē·ō·c̦al′li (*or* -yi), *n.*; *pl.* **tē·ō·c̦al′liṣ,** [Nahuatl, God's house.] a temple of the ancient Mexicans and Central Americans, generally a solid truncated pyramid, built terracewise, with the temple proper on the platform at the summit.

tē·ō·sin′tē, *n.* [Sp.; Nahuatl *teocentli*, lit., divine maize, from *teotl*, god, and *centli*, maize.] a tall annual grass, *Euchlæna luxurians*, native to Mexico and Central America. It resembles Indian corn and is cultivated for fodder in various parts of the world. Also called *Guatemala grass*.

tē′pee, *n.* [Am. Ind. (Siouan) *tīpi*, from *ti*, to dwell, and *pi*, used for.] a cone-shaped tent used by the American Indians: also spelled *teepee*.

tep·ē·fac̦′tion, *n.* [L. *tepefacio* (*-onis*); *tepidus*, warm, and *facere*, to make.] the act of making tepid or the state of being made tepid.

tep′ē·fȳ, *v.t.* and *v.i.* tepefied, *pt.*, *pp.*; tepefying, *ppr.* [L. *tepefacere*.] to make or become tepid, or moderately warm.

tē·phil′lin, *n.pl.* phylacteries (sense 1).

teph′rīte, *n.* [L. *tephritis*, from Gr. *tephra*, ashes.] one of certain volcanic rocks consisting of a plagioclastic feldspar, associated with either nephelite or leucite, and sometimes with both.

teph·rit′ic̦, *a.* of the nature of or pertaining to tephrite.

teph′ri·toid, *n.* a variety of tephrite lacking nephelite.

teph′rō·īte, *n.* [Gr. *tephros*, ash-gray.] a silicate of manganese of an ash-gray color.

teph′ro·man·cy, *n.* [Gr. *tephra*, ashes, and *manteia*, divination.] divination by the inspection of the ashes of a sacrifice.

Tē·phrō′ṣi·ȧ, *n.* [Gr. *tephros*, ash-gray: from the color of some of the species.] a genus of plants of the pea family. It consists of shrubs, undershrubs, or herbs found throughout the world and most abundant in warm regions. *Tephrosia apollinea*, or Egyptian indigo, is native to Egypt and Nubia and yields a fine blue dye. *Tephrosia toxicaria* is native to the West Indies and Cayenne. The whole plant yields a narcotic poison. *Tephrosia virginiana* is a powerful vermifuge.

tep′id, *a.* [L. *tepidus*, lukewarm.] moderately warm; lukewarm; as, a *tepid* bath.

tep·i·dãr′i·um, *n.*; *pl.* **tep·i·dãr′i·ȧ,** [L.] in the ancient Roman baths, the warm room, situated between the steam room and the cooling room.

tē·pid′i·ty, *n.* the state or quality of being tepid; lukewarmness.

tep′id·ly, *adv.* in a tepid manner; lukewarmly.

tep′id·ness, *n.* tepidity.

tep′ŏr, *n.* [L.] gentle heat; moderate warmth.

tē′poy, *n.* same as *teapoy*.

tẹ·qui′lȧ (-kē′), *n.* [from *Tequila*, a district in Mexico.]
1. a century plant growing in Mexico.
2. an alcoholic liquor distilled from the juice of the stem of this plant.

ter·ȧ·c̦on′ic̦, *a.* in chemistry, designating or of a crystalline acid obtained by the distillation of terebic acid and resembling citraconic acid.

ter·ȧ·c̦ryl′ic̦, *a.* in chemistry, designating or of an acid of the acrylic series, resembling terpene.

ter′ȧ·phim, *n.pl.*; *sing.* **ter′ăph,** [Heb. *tĕrāphīm*.] small idols representing household gods, used in divination among the ancient Hebrews and other Semitic peoples.

ter′ȧ·pin, *n.* same as *terrapin*.

tē·rat′ic̦·ăl, *a.* [Gr. *teras*, *teratos*, a sign, a wonder.] incredible; prodigious. [Obs.]

ter′ȧ·tiṣm, *n.* [Gr. *teratikos*, monstrous.] a monstrosity; a malformed fetus.

ter′ȧ·tō-, [from Gr. *teras*, *teratos*, a wonder, monster.] a combining form meaning *monster*, *monstrosity*, as in *teratology*: also, before a vowel, *terat*-.

ter″ȧ·tō·ġen′ic̦, *a.* producing monsters; of or pertaining to teratogeny.

ter·ȧ·toġ′e·ny, *n.* [Gr. *teras*, *teratos*, a wonder, and *gennān*, to produce.] in pathology, the development of fetal monsters.

ter′ȧ·toid, *a.* [*terat-* and *-oid*.] in biology, having the appearance or qualities of a monster; monstrous.

ter″ȧ·tō·loġ′ic̦, ter″ȧ·tō·loġ′ic̦·ăl, *a.* of or pertaining to teratology.

ter·ȧ·tol′ō·ġy, *n.* [Gr. *teras*, a prodigy, and *logos*, discourse.]
1. that branch of biological science which deals with monsters or malformations.
2. bombast in language; affectation of sublimity; exaggeration; also, narration of the marvelous. [Obs.]

ter·ȧ·tō′mȧ, *n.*; *pl.* **ter·ȧ·tō′mȧ·tȧ,** a tumor containing material not ordinarily found at the place where the tumor is growing, such as teeth, hair, etc.

tẽr′bi·ȧ, *n.* [Mod. L.] terbium oxide, Tb_2O_3, a white powder soluble in dilute acids.

tẽr′bic̦, *a.* of, pertaining to, derived from, or containing terbium.

tẽr′bi·um, *n.* [LL., from *Ytterby*, Sweden.] a metallic chemical element of the rare-earth group, found in gadolinite and other minerals: symbol, Tb; atomic weight, 159.2; atomic number, 65.

tẽrce, *n.* [OFr. *tierce*, a third.]
1. a third; a third part. [Obs.]
2. in Scots law, the right of a widow who has not by will or otherwise accepted any

special provision, to a life rent of one-third of her deceased husband's estate, provided she had been his wife for a year and a day or had given birth to a living child.

3. same as *tierce* (in various senses).

tēr'cel, *n.* [Fr. *tiers*, third: said to be so named because a third smaller than the female.]

1. the male of the common falcon, *Falco peregrinus*.

2. the male of any other species of falcon or hawk.

tērce'let, *n.* a male falcon or hawk.

tēr'cel·lēne, *n.* a small tercelet. [Obs.]

tēr·cen'tē·nār·y, *n.*; *pl.* **tēr·cen'tē·nār·ies,** [L. *ter*, three times; and *centenary*.]

1. a period of 300 years.

2. a 300th anniversary or a celebration of this.

tēr·cen'tē·nār·y, *a.* of, comprising, or relating to a period of 300 years.

tēr'cēr, *n.* [OFr. *tercier*, belonging to a third.] in Scots law, a widow entitled to terce.

tēr'cet, *n.* [Fr.; It. *terzetto*, dim. of *terzo* (from L. *tertius*), a third.]

1. a group of three lines that rhyme with one another or are connected by rhyme with an adjacent triplet or triplets.

2. in music, a triplet.

tēr'cine, *n.* [Fr., from L. *tertius*, third.] in botany, the outer coat of the nucleus of the ovule of a plant, now considered a layer of the secundine.

ter'ē·bāte, *n.* a salt of terebic acid.

ter·ē·bel'lid, *n.* [LL. *terebella*, dim. of L. *terebra*, a borer.] a marine annelid of the order *Tubicola*, inhabiting a tube a foot in length composed of sand and fragments of shell cemented together by a glutinous secretion.

ter·ē·bel'loid, *a.* relating to or like a terebellid.

ter'ē·bēne, *n.* [*tereb*inth and *-ene*.] a mixture of terpenes obtained by the action of sulfuric acid on turpentine: used as a deodorizer and disinfectant.

ter·ē·ben'thēne, *n.* an isomer of terpene found in certain kinds of oil of turpentine.

tē·reb'iç, *a.* [from *tere*binth and *-ic*.] of, relating to, or derived from turpentine.

terebic acid; a white crystalline acid, $C_7H_{10}O_4$, a product of the action of nitric acid on turpentine.

ter'ē·binth, *n.* [L. *terebinthus*; Gr. *terebinthos*, the turpentine tree.] a small European tree of the sumac family, the turpentine tree, *Pistacia terebinthus*, which yields turpentine.

ter·ē·bin'thiç, *a.* terebinthine.

ter·ē·bin'thi·nāte, *a.* terebinthine; also, impregnated with turpentine.

ter·ē·bin'thine, *a.* [L. *terebinthinus*, from *terebinthus*, turpentine.]

1. of or pertaining to turpentine; consisting of or like turpentine.

2. of the terebinth tree.

ter'ē·brȧ, *n.* [L., a borer, auger, from *terere*, to pierce.]

1. the borer of female hymenopterous insects, into which the oviduct opens.

2. [T-] a genus of turreted marine univalves; the auger shells.

3. an individual of this genus.

ter'ē·brănt, *a.* [L. *terebrans* (*-antis*), boring.] fitted for boring.

Ter·ē·bran'ti·ȧ (-shi-), *n.pl.* [L. *terebrans* (*-antis*), ppr. of *terebrare*, to bore.] a group of hymenopterous insects, comprising those in which the females have a boring ovipositor.

ter'ē·brāte, *a.* 1. possessing a terebra.

2. arranged for boring.

ter'ē·brāte, *v.t.*; terebrated, *pt.*, *pp.*; terebrating, *ppr.* to bore; to perforate, as with a gimlet. [Rare.]

ter·ē·brā'tion, *n.* the act of boring. [Obs.]

Ter·ē·brat'ū·lȧ, *n.* [dim. form from L. *terebratus*, pp. of *terebrare*, to bore, in allusion to the perforation of the beak.] a genus of deep-sea bivalve mollusks. One of the valves is perforated for the passage of a fleshy peduncle, by which the animal attaches itself to rocks, shells, etc. There are few recent species but the fossil ones are numerous.

ter·ē·brat'ū·lid, *n.* any brachiopod of or resembling *Terebratula*.

ter″ē·brȧ·tū'li·fọrm, *a.* shaped like the shell of a terebratulid.

ter'ē·dine, *n.* a borer, as the teredo.

ter·ē·din'id, *n.* a teredo or a member of an allied genus.

Te·rē'dō, *n.* [L., from Gr. *terēdōn*, a borer.]

1. a genus of mollusks that bore and penetrate the hulls of ships and other submerged wood.

2. [t-] any mollusk of this genus: also called *shipworm*.

ter'ek, *n.* a Eurasian sandpiper whose bill has a slight upward curvature.

ter·eph'thȧ·lāte, *n.* a salt of terephthalic acid.

ter·eph·thal'iç, *a.* relating to or derived from an isomer of phthalic acid.

terephthalic acid; an acid occurring in white crystals, derived by oxidation from turpentine.

Tē·rē'siăn, *n.* one of the friars or nuns of the branch of barefooted Carmelites founded by St. Teresa.

ter'et, *a.* terete. [Obs.]

te·rēte', *a.* [L. *teres*, *teretis*, round, smooth.] cylindrical or slightly tapering in form and circular in cross section; columnar, as some stems of plants.

te·rē'tiăl (-shăl), *a.* terete. [Obs.]

ter'ē·tous, *a.* terete. [Obs.]

Tē'reūs, *n.* [L.; Gr. *Tēreus*.] in Greek mythology, a king of Thrace.

tēr'găl, *a.* [L. *tergum*, back.] relating to the tergite or tergum; dorsal.

tēr'gănt, *a.* [L. *tergum*, the back.] in heraldry, having the back displayed, as an eagle; recursant.

tēr·ġem'i·năl, *a.* same as *tergeminate*.

tēr·ġem'i·nāte, *a.* [L. *ter*, thrice, and *geminatus*, doubled.] thrice double; having three petioles growing from a common point, with a pair of leaflets on each; as, a *tergeminate* leaf.

tēr·ġem'i·nous, *a.* same as *trigeminous*.

tēr·ġif'ēr·ous, *a.* [L. *tergum*, the back, and *ferre*, to bear.]

1. in botany, bearing, as spores, upon the back.

2. in zoology, carrying, as the young, upon the back.

tēr'ġite, *n.* [L. *tergum*, the back.] the dorsal plate covering a somite of an articulate animal.

tēr'ġi·vēr·sāte″, *v.i.*; tergiversated, *pt.*, *pp.*; tergiversating, *ppr.* [from L. *tergiversatus*, pp. of *tergiversari*, to turn one's back, decline, shift, from *tergum*, the back, and *versari*, to turn.]

1. to desert a cause, party, etc.; to become a renegade; to apostatize.

2. to use evasions or subterfuge; to equivocate.

tēr″ġi·vēr·sā'tion, *n.* 1. subterfuge; evasion.

2. desertion of a cause, etc.; apostasy.

tēr'ġi·vēr·sā″tŏr, *n.* one who tergiversates.

tēr·gō·lat'ēr·ăl, *a.* pertaining to the back and a side.

tēr'gum, *n.*; *pl.* **tēr'gȧ,** [L., the back.]

1. the back of an animal, especially of an articulated animal.

2. a tergite.

3. a dorsal plate of the shell of a cirriped.

ter'in, *n.* a tarin. [Obs.]

tẽrm, *n.* [Fr. *terme*, end, limit, from L. *terminus*, a limit, bound, end.]

1. originally, a point of time designating the beginning or end of a period; a set date.

2. a date set for payment, termination of tenancy, etc.

3. a period of time having definite limits; time during which anything lasts; duration; specifically, (a) a regularly set period of time during which courses of study are taken and completed; (b) a stipulated length of time that a person may hold office.

4. [*pl.*] conditions of a contract, agreement, sale, etc. that limit or define its scope or the action involved; as, *terms* of payment, the *terms* of a treaty.

5. [*pl.*] (a) mutual relationship between or among persons; footing; as, on speaking *terms*; (b) good or equal footing.

6. a word or phrase having a limiting and definite meaning in some science, art, etc.; as, *tergum* is a zoological *term*.

7. any word or phrase used in a definite or precise sense; expression; as, patriot is the *term* he deserves.

8. [*pl.*] words that express ideas in a limited or special form; as, he spoke in derogatory *terms*.

9. a limit; boundary; extremity. [Archaic or Rare.]

10. [*pl.*] condition; circumstances. [Obs.]

11. in architecture, a boundary post, especially one consisting of a pedestal topped by a bust, as of the god Terminus.

12. in law, (a) the time a court is in session; (b) the length of time for which an estate is granted; (c) the estate itself; (d) time allowed a debtor to pay.

13. in logic, (a) either of two concepts that have a stated relation, as the subject and predicate of a proposition; (b) any one of the three parts of a syllogism.

14. in mathematics, (a) either of the two quantities of a fraction or a ratio; (b) each of the quantities in a series; (c) each of the quantities connected by plus or minus signs in an algebraic expression.

15. in geometry, a point, line, or surface that limits; as, a line is the *term* of a surface, and a surface the *term* of a solid. [Rare.]

16. (a) [Obs.] the menstrual discharge or period; (b) the completion of the normal period of gestation.

17. in shipbuilding, a term piece.

term of thought; a conclusion reached as the result of consideration.

to bring to terms; to reduce to submission or to conditions.

to come to terms; to agree; to come to an agreement.

to make terms; to come to an agreement.

Syn.—limit, boundary, condition, time, season, period, expression, designation, word, name, article, proviso, stipulation.

tẽrm, *v.t.*; termed, *pt.*, *pp.*; terming, *ppr.* to name; to call by a term; to denominate.

She doesn't wish to *term* you unreasonable.
—Dickens.

tẽr'mȧ, *n.* [Mod. L., from Gr. *terma*, a limit.] the thin lamina forming the terminal layer of the anterior portion of the third ventricle of the cerebrum.

tẽr'mȧ·găn·cy, *n.* the quality or state of being a termagant; shrewishness.

tẽr'mȧ·gănt, *a.* [OFr. *Tervagant*, idol, imaginary Moslem deity: prob. brought over by the Crusaders.] quarrelsome; scolding; of the nature of a termagant.

tẽr'mȧ·gănt, *n.* 1. a boisterous, brawling, scolding woman; a shrew; a virago.

2. [T-] an imaginary deity supposed by medieval Christians to be worshiped by Moslems and represented as a boisterous, overbearing figure.

tẽr'mȧ·gănt·ly, *adv.* in a termagant manner.

tẽrm dāy, the day set for payment of rent due, etc.

tẽrm'ẽr, *n.* 1. formerly, one who traveled to attend a court term; especially, one who visited London in term time for some disreputable or dishonest purpose. [Obs.]

2. a termor [Obs.]

3. a person serving a term, especially in prison: usually in hyphenated compounds; as, a third-*termer*.

Tẽr'mēṣ, *n.* [L. *termes*, *termitis*, a wood worm.] a genus of insects typical of the family *Termitidæ*, which includes the termites, or white ants.

tẽrm fee, a small fee allowed an attorney as costs at each term while his client's cause is in court.

tẽr″mi·nȧ·bil'i·ty, *n.* the quality or state of being terminable.

tẽr'mi·nȧ·ble, *a.* 1. that can be terminated.

2. that terminates after a specified time, as a contract.

tẽr'mi·nȧ·ble·ness, *n.* the state of being terminable.

tẽr'min·ȧ·bly, *adv.* so as to be terminable.

tẽr'mi·năl, *a.* [LL. *terminalis*, from L. *terminus*, a boundary.]

1. of, at, or forming the end, extremity, or terminus of something.

2. occurring at the end of a series; concluding; closing; final.

3. having to do with a term or established period of time; occurring regularly in terms.

4. connected with, charged at, etc. the end of a railroad line; as, *terminal* rates.

5. in botany, growing at the end of a stem or branch; as, a *terminal* leaflet.

terminal leave; the final leave granted to a member of the armed forces immediately before his discharge, extending over a period equal to his accumulated unused leave.

terminal value or *terminal form*; in mathematics, the last and most complete value or form given to an expression.

terminal velocity; the greatest velocity which a body can acquire by falling freely through the air, the limit being arrived at when the increase of the atmospheric resistance becomes equal to the weight of the body.

tẽr'mi·năl, *n.* 1. a terminating part; end; extremity; limit.

2. either end of an electric circuit or a connection at either end.

3. either end of a transportation line, as a railroad, including station, yards, etc.

4. (a) a station or city at such a terminus; (b) a station at an important point or junction of a transportation line.

5. in architecture, (a) a term (sense 11); (b) an ornamental carving at the end of a structural element.

Tẽr·mi·nā'li·ȧ, *n.pl.* [L.] the annual festival held by the ancient Romans in February in honor of Terminus, the god of boundaries.

Tẽr·mi·nā'li·ȧ, *n.* a genus of combretaceous trees or shrubs, including numerous species in the tropical regions of both the Old and the New World.

tẽr'mi·năl·ly, *adv.* 1. at the end.
2. as concerns termination.
3. every term.

tẽr'mi·nāte, *v.t.*; terminated, *pt.*, *pp.*; terminating, *ppr.* [L. *terminatus*, pp. of *terminare*, to end, to limit.]
1. to bound; to limit; to form the extreme point or side of; to set a boundary or limit to; as, to *terminate* a surface by a line.
2. to end; to put an end to; to close; as, to *terminate* a controversy.
3. to complete; to finish.

tẽr'mi·nāte, *v.i.* 1. to come to an end in space or time; to stop; to end.
2. to have its end (*in* something); as, the road *terminates* in woods.

tẽr'mi·nāte, *a.* that can terminate or come to an end; terminable; limited; bounded; as, a *terminate* decimal.
terminate number; in mathematics, a number, especially a decimal, that can be expressed in a finite number of terms.

tẽr·mi·nā'tion, *n.* 1. a terminating or being terminated.
2. the end of something in space or time; limit, bound, conclusion, or finish.
3. the end of a word; final sound, morpheme, or syllable.
4. a thing's outcome or result; as, a friendly *termination* of a dispute.

tẽr·mi·nā'tion·ăl, *a.* 1. of, pertaining to, or forming a termination or terminations.
2. in grammar, formed by inflectional endings.

tẽr'mi·nā·tive, *a.* terminating or tending to terminate; definitive; absolute; not relative.

tẽr'mi·nā·tive, *n.* in linguistics, a suffix.

tẽr'mi·nā·tive·ly, *adv.* in a terminative manner.

tẽr'mi·nā·tŏr, *n.* 1. one who or that which terminates.
2. in astronomy, the line dividing the illuminated and dark parts of the disk of the moon or a planet.

tẽr'mi·nȧ·tō·ry, *a.* 1. terminative.
2. terminal.

tẽr'mi·nẽr, *n.* [OFr., to end, limit.] in law, a determining.

tẽr'mi·niṣm, *n.* the doctrine of the terminists.

tẽr'mi·nist, *n.* in theology, one who maintains that God has fixed a certain term for the probation of individual persons, during which period, and no longer, they have the offer of grace.

tẽr″mi·nō·loġ'iç·ăl, *a.* relating to terminology.

tẽr″mi·nō·loġ'iç·ăl·ly, *adv.* in a terminological manner; according to terminology.

tẽr·mi·nol'ō·ġy, *n.* [Fr. *terminologie*; L. *terminus*, a limit, hence a term, appellation; and *-logy*.]
1. the doctrine or science of technical terms; the theory regarding the proper use of terms. [Rare.]
2. the terms collectively used in any art, science, or the like; nomenclature; as, the *terminology* of botany.

tẽr'mi·nus, *n.*; *pl.* **tẽr'mi·nī, tẽr'mi·nus·eṣ**, [L., bound or limit.]
1. a boundary or limit. [Rare.]
2. a boundary stone or marker.
3. [T-] in Roman mythology, the deity presiding over boundaries and landmarks.
4. an end; extremity or goal.
5. either end of a railroad, bus, or air line.
6. the station or city at the end of such a line. [Chiefly Brit.]

tẽr'mi·nus ad quem, [L., lit., end toward which.] a destination; conclusion.

tẽr'mi·nus ā quō, [L., lit., end from which.] a starting point.

tẽr·mi·tăr'i·um, *n.*; *pl.* **tẽr·mi·tăr'i·ȧ**, [LL.] a termites' nest.

tẽr'mi·tăr·y, *n.*; *pl.* **tẽr'mi·tăr·ieṣ**, a termitarium.

tẽr'mīte, *n.* one of the *Termitidæ*: also called *white ant*.

Tẽr·mit'i·dae, *n.pl.* [L. *termes* (*-itis*), a wood worm.] a family of pseudoneuropterous insects, the termites, or white ants, having little affinity with the true ants, which are hymenopterous, although they resemble them in their social mode of life. They are found in the Temperate Zones and in the tropics and are very destructive to wooden structures.

tẽr'mi·tine, *a.* of the *Termitidæ*.

tẽr'mi·tine, *n.* a termite.

tẽr'mi·tō·phīle, *n.* an insect that inhabits the nests of termites.

tẽr·mi·toph'i·lous, *a.* inhabiting the nests of termites, as certain insects.

tẽrm'less, *a.* 1. unlimited; without end; boundless.
2. beyond expression; indescribable. [Rare.]
3. unconditional.

tẽrm'ly, *a.* occurring every term: as, a *termly* fee.

tẽrm'ly, *adv.* term by term; every term.

tẽrm'ŏn, *n.* [Ir. *termonn* or *termann*, boundary or sanctuary, from L. *terminus*, a boundary.] in Irish ecclesiastical history, any land which belonged to a religious organization or church and was therefore exempt from state tax.

tẽrm'ŏr, *n.* [ME; Anglo-Fr. *termer*, from *terme*, a term.] in law, a person holding an estate for a certain period or for life.

tẽrm pā'pẽr, the chief written exercise required in a collegiate course of study during a term.

tẽrm'tīme, *n.* the period of time during a legal or school term.

tẽrm piēce, in shipbuilding, a piece of carved work placed under each end of the taffrail and extending to the footrail of the balcony.

tẽrn, *n.* [from ON. *therna*.] any of several natatorial birds of the gull family, *Laridæ*, but smaller, with a more slender body and beak, and a deeply forked tail: they are found on both sides of the Atlantic. There are several species, as the great or common tern or sea swallow, *Sterna hirundo*, the black tern, *Hydrochelidon fissipes*, the roseate tern, *Sterna dougalli*, the European least tern, *Sterna minuta*, etc.

LEAST TERN (*Sterna minuta*)

hooded tern; the least tern, *Sterna minuta*: also called *fairy bird*.

tẽrn, *a.* [L. *terni*, thrice each, from *tres*, three.] threefold; consisting of three; triple; ternate.
tern schooner; a three-masted schooner.

tẽrn, *n.* [Fr. *terne*, from L. *terni*, three each, from *tres*, three.]
1. that which consists of three things or numbers together; specifically, a prize in a lottery gained by drawing a combination of three numbers; also, the three numbers themselves.

She'd win a *tern* in Thursday's lottery.
—E. B. Browning.

2. a tern schooner. [Archaic or Dial.]

tẽr'năl, *a.* composed of three; threefold; triple; tern.

tẽr'nȧ·ry, *a.* [ME.; L. *ternarius*, from *terni*, three each.]
1. made up of three parts; threefold; triple.
2. third.
3. in chemistry, of or containing three different elements, radicals, etc.
4. in mathematics, (a) having three as a base; (b) involving three variables.
5. in metallurgy, of an alloy of three metals.
ternary form or *quantic*; in mathematics, a form or quantic having three variables.
ternary time; in music, triple time.

tẽr'nȧ·ry, *n.*; *pl.* **tẽr'nȧ·rieṣ**, a group or set of three; a triad. [Rare.]

tẽr'nāte, *a.* [LL. *ternatus*, from L. *terni*, three each.]
1. arranged in threes.
2. consisting of threes.
3. in botany, growing in groups of three, as some leaves.

tẽr'nāte·ly, *adv.* in a ternate manner.

tẽr″nāte-pin'nāte, *a.* same as *ternatopinnate*.

tẽr·nat'i·sect, *a.* in botany, divided into three parts or lobes, as some leaves.

tẽr·nā·tō·pin'nāte, *a.* in botany, ternately compound: applied to secondary petioles, on the sides of which the leaflets are attached, which appear in groups of threes from the summit of a common petiole.

tẽrne, *n.* same as *terneplate*.

tẽrne'plāte, *n.* [Fr. *terne*, dull, and Eng. *plate*.] a thin iron or steel plate coated with an alloy of tin and lead, used for roofing, lining packing cases, etc.: it has a dull finish and is considered inferior to standard tin plate.

tẽrn'ẽr·y, *n.*; *pl.* **tẽrn'ẽr·ieṣ**, a place where terns breed.

tẽr'ni·ŏn, *n.* [L. *ternio*, a triad, from *terni*, three each.] a set of three, especially of three folded sheets of paper.

Tẽrn·stroe'mi·ȧ, *n.* the typical genus of the order *Ternstrœmiaceæ*.

Tẽrn·stroe·mi·ā'cē·ae, *n.pl.* [after *Ternström*, a Swedish naturalist.] an order of polypetalous dicotyledonous plants, consisting of trees or shrubs, with alternate simple, usually coriaceous, leaves without stipules. The flowers are usually white and are arranged in axillary or terminal peduncles, articulated at the base.

tẽr·ox'ide, *n.* same as *trioxide*.

tẽr'pēne, *n.* [from *terpentine*, obs. form of *turpentine*, and *-ene*.] any of a series of isomeric hydrocarbons of the general formula $C_{10}H_{16}$, found in resins, essential oils, etc.

tẽr·pē·nyl'iç, *a.* designating an acid, $C_8H_{12}O_4$, derived from oil of turpentine and chromic acid.

tẽr'pi·lēne, *n.* a polymeric modification of terpene.

tẽr'pin, *n.* same as *terpinol*.

tẽr·pin'ē·ol, *n.* [*terpin* and *-ol*.] any of three isomeric alcohols, $C_{10}H_{17}OH$, with a lilac odor, found in certain volatile oils and used in perfumes.

tẽr'pin·ol, *n.* a white crytalline compound, $C_{10}H_{18}(OH)_2$, found in two isomeric forms.

Tẽrp·siçh'ō·rē, *n.* [Gr., f. of *terpsichoros*, delighting in the dance; *terpein*, to delight in, and *choros*, a dance.] in Greek mythology, the Muse of dancing, daughter of Jupiter and Mnemosyne.

TERPSICHORE

tẽrp″siçh·ō·rē'ăn, *a.* 1. [T-] of or pertaining to Terpsichore.
2. having to do with dancing.

tẽrp″siçh·ō·rē'ăn, *n.* a dancer: literary or humorus usage.

ter'rȧ, *n.* [L.] (the) earth.
terra alba; any of several white earths, as gypsum, magnesia, kaolin, etc.
terra cariosa; same as tripoli.
terra di Siena; same as *sienna*.
terrae filius; formerly, one appointed to write a satirical Latin poem at the public acts in the University of Oxford.
terra firma; firm earth; solid ground.
terra incognita; (a) an unknown or unexplored region; (b) an unknown or unexplored field of knowledge.
terra japonica; a substance obtained from the juice of a species of acacia, formerly supposed to be a kind of earth from Japan.
terra ponderosa; in old chemistry, baryta.

ter'rȧce, *n.* [Fr. *terrasse*, a terrace, earthwork, from LL. *terracia*, terrace, from L. *terra*, earth.]
1. a raised, flat mound of earth with sloping sides.
2. any of a series of flat platforms of earth with sloping sides, rising one above the other, as on a hillside.
3. a geological formation of this nature.
4. an unroofed, paved area immediately adjacent to a house and overlooking a lawn or garden.
5. a flat roof, especially of a house of Spanish or Oriental architecture.
6. a row of houses on ground raised from the street.
7. a street in front of such houses: often used in street names.
8. a parklike strip in the middle of a boulevard, etc.
cut terrace; see under *cut*.
shore terrace; a terrace formed by the action of the waves on a shore.
stream terrace; a terrace formed at the edges of a stream by the action of the current, and laid bare by the deepening of the stream channel or a withdrawal of a part or the whole of the volume of water.

ter'rȧce, *v.t.*; terraced (-răst), *pt.*, *pp.*; terracing, *ppr.* to make into a terrace; to lay out in, or surround with, a terrace or terraces.

ter'rȧ-çot'tȧ, *a.* of terra cotta.

ter'rȧ çot'tȧ, [It., lit., baked earth, from L.]

1. a hard, brown-red, usually unglazed earthenware used for pottery, statuettes, ornamental facing, etc.

2. its brown-red color.

ter·rȧ·çul′tūr·ăl, *a.* of or pertaining to terraculture. [Rare.]

ter·rȧ·çul′tūre, *n.* [L. *terra,* earth, and *cultura,* culture.] cultivation of the earth; agriculture. [Rare.]

ter·rāin′, *n.* [Fr. *terrain,* soil, ground, rock, from L. *terra,* earth.]

1. in geology, a terrane.

2. a portion of land, especially considered with regard to its natural features or fitness for some particular purpose.

Ter·rȧ·mȳ′cin, *n.* [from L. *terra,* earth, and Gr. *mykēs,* fungus; and *-in.*] an antibiotic drug derived from an earth and used in treating some virus diseases: a trade-mark.

ter·rāne′, *n.* [Fr. *terrain.*] a geological formation or series of continuously related formations.

ter′rȧ·pin, *n.* [of Am. Ind. origin.]

1. any of several species of North American fresh-water or tidewater turtles constituting the family *Emydidæ,* characterized by a horny beak, a shield covered with epidermic plates, and partly webbed feet. One species, the diamondback terrapin, *Malaclemys terrapin,* is abundant along the Atlantic and Gulf Coasts.

2. any of various tortoises or turtles of other families.

3. the flesh of the terrapin used as food.

painted terrapin; same as *painted turtle* under *painted.*

speckled terrapin; a small fresh-water tortoise, *Clemmys guttata,* having bright-yellow spots on its shell.

ter·rā′quē·ous, *a.* [L. *terra,* earth, and *aqua,* water.] consisting of both land and water.

ter′rãr, *n.* the treasurer of a monastery or other religious organization. [Obs.]

ter·rãr′i·um, *n.*; *pl.* **ter·rãr′i·umṣ, ter·rãr′i·ȧ,** [from L. *terra,* earth, and *-arium* as in *aquarium.*]

1. an enclosure for keeping small animals.

2. a bottle, bowl, or other container enclosing a garden of small plants.

ter′răs, *n.* same as *trass.*

ter·răz′zō (-rät′sō), *n.* [It.] a flooring of small chips of marble set in cement and polished.

ter·rē′i·ty, *n.* earthiness. [Obs.]

ter·rēne′, *a,* [L. *terrenus,* from *terra,* the earth.]

1. of or pertaining to the earth; earthy; terrestrial; as, *terrene* substance.

2. worldly; mundane.

ter·rēne′, *n.* 1. the earth.

2. a land or territory.

ter·ren′i·ty, *n.* the state or quality of being terrene; worldliness. [Obs.]

ter′rē·ous, *a.* [L. *terreus,* from *terra,* earth.] earthy; consisting of earth. [Obs.]

terre′plein, *n.* [Fr. *terre,* earth, and *plein,* level.] in fortification, a platform or horizontal surface behind a rampart, on which guns are placed and worked; also, the level surface about a fieldwork.

ter·res′tre (-tẽr), *a.* terrestrial. [Obs.]

ter·res′tri·ăl, *a.* [L. *terrestris,* from *terra,* the earth.]

1. pertaining to the earth; existing on earth; earthly; worldly; mundane: opposed to *celestial.*

2. representing or consisting of the earth; as, a *terrestrial* globe.

3. pertaining to or consisting of land as distinguished from water.

4. confined to, inhabiting, or living on land or the ground: opposed to *aquatic, arboreal, aerial.*

5. growing on land or in the ground: distinguished from *aquatic, marine, parasitic, epiphytic.*

ter·res′tri·ăl, *n.* an inhabitant of the earth.

ter·res′tri·ăl·ly, *adv.* in an earthly manner.

ter·res′tri·ăl·ness, *n.* the state or quality of being terrestrial.

ter·res′tri·fȳ, *v.t.*; terrestrified, *pt., pp.*; terrestrifying, *ppr.* to reduce to earth or to an earthly or mundane state. [Obs.]

ter′ret, *n.* [ME. *teret, toret;* OFr. *toret,* dim. of *tour,* a turn.]

1. a ring for attaching a leash, as on a dog collar.

2. any of the rings on a harness, through which the reins pass.

terre′-ten″ănt, *n.* in law, the actual possessor or occupant of land; also, the owner and holder of the legal estate in land.

terre′-verte, *n.* [Fr. *terre,* earth, and *vert, verte,* green.] any of several greenish earths used as a green pigment; especially, a kind of glauconite.

burnt terre-verte; same as *Vandyke brown.*

ter′ri·ble, *a.* [Fr., from L. *terribilis,* from *terrere,* to frighten.]

1. causing terror; fearful; frightful; dreadful.

2. extreme; intense; severe.

3. very bad, unpleasant, or disagreeable. [Colloq.]

Syn.—frightful, dreadful, fearful, grim, awful, shocking, horrible.

ter′ri·ble·ness, *n.* dreadfulness; the quality or state of being terrible.

ter′ri·bly, *adv.* 1. in a terrible manner.

2. extremely; exceedingly; very. [Colloq.]

ter·riç′ō·line, *a.* terricolous.

ter·riç′ō·lous, *a.* [from L. *terricola,* earth dweller, from *terra,* earth, and *colere,* to dwell.] in botany and zoology, inhabiting the earth; living in or on the ground.

ter′ri·ẽr, *n.* [ME. *terrere, terryare;* (early) Fr. (*chien*) *terrier,* hunting (dog), from *terrier,* hillock, burrow, from ML. *terrarius,* of earth, from L. *terra,* earth.] any of several breeds of active, intelligent, typically small dog, formerly used to burrow after small game: they include the Airedale, schnauzer, bull terrier, fox terrier, Bedlington terrier, Boston terrier, Clydesdale terrier, Dandie Dinmont terrier, Irish terrier, Scottish (or Scotch) terrier, Sealyham terrier, etc.

ter′ri·ẽr, *n.* [Fr. *terrier,* from LL. *terrarius liber,* a land book, from L. *terra,* the earth.]

1. formerly, a collection of acknowledgments of the vassals or tenants of a lordship, containing the rents and services owed to the Lord.

2. a book or roll in which the lands of private persons or corporations are described by their site, boundaries, number of acres, etc.

ter·rif′iç, *a.* [L. *terrificus,* from *terrere,* to frighten, and *facere,* to make.]

1. causing great fear; terrifying; dreadful; appalling.

2. unusually great, intense, excellent, etc.; extraordinary. [Colloq.]

ter·rif′iç·ăl, *a.* terrific. [Obs.]

ter·rif′iç·ăl·ly, *adv.* 1. in a terrific manner.

2. to a terrific degree.

ter·rif′iç·ly, *adv.* terrifically.

ter′ri·fȳ, *v.t.*; terrified, *pt., pp.*; terrifying, *ppr.* 1. to fill with terror; to frighten; to alarm; to shock.

They were *terrified* and affrighted.
—Luke xxiv. 37.

2. to make terrible. [Obs.]

ter·rig′ē·nous, *a.* [L. *terrigena,* one born of the earth.]

1. earthborn; produced by the earth.

2. designating or of sediments, etc. on the sea bottom derived from eroded land as distinguished from deposits made by oceanic organisms.

ter·rine′, *n.* 1. a tureen.

2. a small earthenware dish or jar in which table delicacies are sold.

3. a kind of stew.

ter′rit, *n.* same as *terret.*

ter″ri·tē·lăr′i·ăn, *a.* of or pertaining to a group of spiders, the *Territelaria,* which have vertically moving mandibles.

ter″ri·tē·lăr′i·ăn, *n.* any spider belonging to the *Territelaria,* as the trap-door spider.

ter·ri·tō′ri·ăl, *a.* 1. of territory or land.

2. of, belonging to, or limited to a specific territory or district; as, a *territorial* industry, waters, etc.

3. [T–] of the territory of a state; of a Territory or Territories.

4. [*often* T–] organized primarily for home defense; as, the *Territorial* Army of Great Britain.

ter·ri·tō′ri·ăl, *n.* a member of a territorial force; specifically, [T–] a member of the Territorial Army of Great Britain.

ter·ri·tō′ri·ăl·iṣm, *n.* 1. a system giving the landowning class predominance in a state; landlordism.

2. a system of church government under which the supreme authority is placed in the civil power: also *territorial system.*

Ter·ri·tō′ri·ăl·iṣm, *n.* formerly a theory or program for the establishment of a Jewish national settlement that would be autonomous or self-governing.

ter″ri·tō·ri·al′i·ty, *n.* the state or quality of being territorial.

ter″ri·tō·ri·ăl·i·zā′tion, *n.* a territorializing or being territorialized.

ter·ri·tō′ri·ăl·īze, *v.t.*; territorialized, *pt., pp.*; territorializing, *ppr.* 1. to add territory to.

2. to reduce to the status of a territory.

3. to distribute among territories; to establish on a territorial basis.

ter·ri·tō′ri·ăl·ly, *adv.* in regard to territory or territories.

ter·ri·tō′ri·ăl sys′tem, territorialism (sense 2).

ter′ri·tō·ried, *a.* having territory. [Rare.]

ter′ri·tō·ry, *n.*; *pl.* **ter′ri·tō·rieṣ,** [Fr. *territoire;* L. *territorium,* from *terra,* earth.]

1. the land and waters under the jurisdiction of a nation, state, ruler, etc.

2. a part of a country or empire that does not have the full status of a principal division; specifically, (a) [T–] formerly, a part of the United States having its own legislature but without the status of a State and under the administration of an appointed governor: Alaska and Hawaii were U.S. Territories; (b) [T–] a similar region in Canada or Australia without the status of a Province or State.

3. any large tract of land; region; district.

4. an assigned area, as of a traveling salesman.

5. a sphere or province of action, existence, thought, etc.

6. in football, hockey, etc., either half of the field with regard to its possession by a team; as, deep in Notre Dame's *territory.*

Syn.—country, domain, land, tract, district, region, province.

ter′rŏr, *n.* [L. *terror,* from *terrere,* to frighten.]

1. intense fear.

2. (a) a person or thing that causes intense fear; (b) the quality of causing dread; terribleness.

3. [T–] a period characterized by political executions, as during revolution, especially such a period (also called the *Reign of Terror*) during the French Revolution, from May, 1793, to July, 1794.

4. a program of terrorism or a party, group, etc. resorting to this.

5. a very annoying or unmanageable person; a pest. [Colloq.]

Syn.—alarm, apprehension, dread, consternation, fear, fright.

ter′rŏr·iṣm, *n.* 1. a terrorizing; use of terror and violence to intimidate, subjugate, etc., especially as a political weapon or policy.

2. intimidation and subjugation so produced.

ter′rŏr·ist, *n.* a person who practices or favors terrorism; specifically, (a) an agent or supporter of the revolutionary tribunal during the French Reign of Terror; (b) a member of any of certain extreme revolutionary societies in czarist Russia.

ter·rŏr·ist′iç, *a.* characterized by or practicing terrorism.

ter″rŏr·i·zā′tion, *n.* a terrorizing or being terrorized.

ter′rŏr·īze, *v.t.*; terrorized, *pt., pp.*; terrorizing, *ppr.* 1. to fill with terror; to terrify; to appall; to frighten.

2. to coerce, maintain power, etc. by inducing terror; to practice terrorism.

ter′rŏr·ī·zẽr, *n.* one who terrorizes.

ter′rŏr·less, *a.* without terror.

ter′rŏr-smit″ten, *a.* struck or affected with terror; terrified; terror-stricken.

ter′rŏr-strick″en, ter′rŏr-struck, *a.* stricken with terror; terrified.

ter′ry, *n.*; *pl.* **ter′rieṣ,** [Fr. *tirer,* to draw.]

1. any of the loops forming the pile of a fabric, when left uncut.

2. a cloth having a pile in which the loops are left uncut: also *terry cloth.*

Tẽr·sanç′tus, *n.* [L., thrice holy.] same as *Trisagion.*

tẽrse, *a.* [L. *tersus,* wiped off, clean, pp. of *tergere,* to wipe.]

1. free of superfluous words; concise; succinct; to the point; as, a *terse* style.

Again and again he read the *terse* message, unable to grasp at once the full import of those few, fatal words. —Timov.

2. wiped or rubbed; appearing wiped or rubbed; polished; smooth; clean; clear. [Obs.]

Syn.—concise, neat, smooth, compact, brief, succinct, pithy.

tẽrse′ly, *adv.* in a terse manner or style.

tẽrse′ness, *n.* the quality or state of being terse; conciseness.

tẽr′sion, *n.* dry cleaning; cleaning by rubbing. [Rare.]

tẽr·sul′fīde, tẽr·sul′fid, *n.* same as *trisulfide.*

tẽr·sul′fū·ret, *n.* a trisulfide. [Rare.]

tẽr'ten·ănt, *n.* same as *terre-tenant.*

tẽr'tiăl (-shăl), *a.* designating or of the third row of flight feathers on a bird's wing, along the humerus.

tẽr'tiăl, *n.* a tertial feather or quill.

tẽr'tiăn, *a.* [L. *tertianus,* from *tertius,* third.] occurring every other day (i.e., every third day, counting both days of occurrence).

tẽr'tiăn, *n.* 1. a form of fever occurring every other day.

2. a wine measure equal to one-third of a tun, or 84 wine gallons. [Obs.]

double tertian; an intermittent fever in which there are two sets of recurrences falling on alternate days.

tẽr'ti·ăr·y (-shi-), *a.* [L. *tertiarius,* from *tertius,* third.]

1. of the third rank, order, formation, etc.; third.

2. of the third order in a monastic system.

3. in chemistry, (a) third in order or type; involving the substitution of three atoms or radicals; (b) characterized by or designating a carbon atom attached to three other carbon atoms in a chain or ring.

4. [T-] in geology, designating or of the first period of the Cenozoic Era or its system of rocks.

5. in zoology, tertial.

tertiary alcohol; alcohol formed by the replacement of three hydrogen atoms in carbinol with alkyls.

tertiary amide; an amide formed by the replacement of three hydrogen atoms with alkyls.

tertiary syphilis; a stage in the development of syphilis characterized by skin eruptions, including rupia, gumma, syphilitic pemphigus, and ecthyma.

tẽr'ti·ăr·y, *n.*; *pl.* **tẽr'ti·ăr·ieș,** 1. a member of the third order of a monastic system.

2. a color, as russet, citrine, olive, and the like, produced by the mixture of two secondary colors.

3. a tertial feather.

the Tertiary; the Tertiary Period or its rocks.

tẽr'ti·āte, *v.t.*; tertiated, *pt., pp.*; tertiating, *ppr.* [L. *tertiatus,* pp. of *tertiare,* to do every third day.]

1. to do for the third time. [Obs.]

2. to measure (a firearm, etc.) at several points in order to ascertain its thickness.

tẽr'ti·um quid, [L., lit., third something.] something related to but distinct from two other things; an intermediate person or thing.

ter·tū'li·ȧ, *n.* [Sp.] a social gathering; an informal party.

Tẽr·tul'li·ăn·ișm, *n.* Montanism as it was modified about 203 A.D. by Tertullian, Latin church father who opposed second marriages and the absolution of penitents.

Tẽr·tul'li·ăn·ist, *n.* a believer in Tertullianism.

ter·ū·ter'ō, *n.* [echoic.] a South American lapwing, *Vanellus* or *Belonopterus cayennensis.*

tẽr·vā'lence, *n.* same as *trivalence.*

tẽr·vā'lent, *a.* [L. *ter,* thrice; and *-valent.*]

1. having three valences.

2. having a valence of three.

Also, especially for 2, *trivalent.*

ter'zä ri'mä (-tsä), [It., lit., third rhyme.] a verse form of Italian origin, consisting of a continuous series of tercets in which the second line of each tercet rhymes with the first and third lines of the following one (*aba, bcb, cdc,* etc.): it was used by Dante in the *Divine Comedy.*

ter·zet'tō (-tset'), *n.* [It.] a short musical composition, piece, or movement for three performers, vocal or instrumental; a short trio.

tes''sȧ·rȧ·deç'ad, *n.* [Gr. *tessares,* four, and *dekas,* the number ten.] a group of fourteen individuals; an aggregate of fourteen.

tes·sel'lȧ, *n.*; *pl.* **tes·sel'lae,** a small tessera.

tes'sel·lăr, *a.* composed of tesserae.

tes'sel·lāte, *v.t.*; tessellated, *pt., pp.*; tessellating, *ppr.* [L. *tessella,* a little square stone.] to inlay, lay out, or pave in a mosaic pattern of small, square blocks.

tes'sel·lāte, *a.* tessellated.

tes'sel·lā·ted, *a.* 1. formed by inlaying differently colored materials in small squares, as mosaic work.

2. in botany and zoology, checkered.

tes·sel·lā'tion, *n.* 1. tessellated work; mosaic.

2. a tessellating or being tessellated.

tes'sē·rȧ, *n.*; *pl.* **tes'sē·rae,** [L., a cube, a die, from Gr. *tessares,* four.]

1. a small cube or square of different materials, as marble, precious stones, ivory, glass, wood, etc., used in mosaic work.

2. in ancient Rome, a small square of bone, wood, etc., used as a ticket of admission, a token, etc.

tes·sē·rā'iç, *a.* tessellar. [Obs.]

tes'sē·răl, *a.* 1. tessellar.

2. in crystallography, isometric.

tes'sū·lăr, *a.* same as *tesseral.*

test, *n.* [OFr. *test,* from L. *testum,* an earthen vessel, from *testa,* a piece of burned clay, shell, or skull: the modern meaning derives from use of the cupel in examining metals.]

1. a cupel, a cuplike porous vessel used in the assaying or refining of precious metals.

2. an examination or assaying of metal by means of the cupel.

3. an examination or trial, as to prove the value or ascertain the nature of something.

4. (a) the method, process, or means used in making such an examination or trial; (b) a standard or criterion by which the qualities of a thing are tried.

5. an event, set of circumstances, etc. that proves or tries a person's qualities; as, the delay was a *test* of his patience.

6. a set of questions, problems, or exercises for determining a person's knowledge, abilities, aptitude, or qualifications; an examination.

7. in chemistry, (a) a trial or reaction for identifying a substance or ingredient; (b) the reagent used in the procedure; (c) a positive indication obtained by it.

8. a witness. [Obs.]

9. proof; evidence; testimony. [Obs.]

impact test; in engineering, a test in which the load is violently applied, the force of the blow being nearly all due to the speed or velocity of the moving body and only slightly due to its static weight.

Nessler's test; a test for ammonia consisting of mercuric iodide dissolved in an aqueous solution of caustic potash and potassium iodide; if free ammonia is present in a solution the reagent gives a yellow-brown precipitate.

test act; an act imposing a test, especially a religious one; specifically, in English history, an act passed in the reign of Charles II, providing that all persons holding any important office, civil or military, from the crown, or receiving money therefrom, should take the oaths of supremacy and allegiance, and subscribe a declaration against transubstantiation, and also receive the sacrament of the Lord's supper according to the usage of the Church of England.

test case; in law, a case in which the decision sets a precedent with respect to the points of law involved; also, a legal proceeding, frequently for an injunction, brought by the parties involved for the purpose of obtaining a decision regarding the constitutionality of a law.

test flight; in aviation, a trial or preliminary flight to determine the fitness of an aircraft for use.

test furnace; a refining furnace of the reverberatory kind, for treating silver-bearing alloys.

test glass; a glass vessel, often with a foot, used to hold liquids for testing.

test meal; a meal given to test the digestive tract, furnishing material for examination.

test object; a minute object for testing the power of a microscope.

test paper; (a) a paper on which a test has been written; (b) paper prepared with a reagent for making chemical tests: see also *litmus paper.*

test pilot; a pilot who tests new or newly designed airplanes in flight, subjecting them to various strains to prove their fitness for use.

test tube; a tube of thin, transparent glass closed at one end, used in chemical experiments, etc.

vocabulary test; a test conducted to determine an individual's knowledge of words, often used as part of an intelligence test.

test, *v.t.*; tested, *pt., pp.*; testing, *ppr.* 1. in metallurgy, to refine (metal), as in a cupel.

2. to put to the test; to bring to trial and examination; to prove the genuineness or truth of by experiment, or by some fixed principle or standard; to compare with a standard; to try; as, to *test* the soundness of a principle.

3. in chemistry, to examine by means of a reagent or reagents.

4. to make trial of the power, strength, endurance, or purity of.

test, *n.* [L. *testa,* a shell.]

1. in zoology, the outside hard covering of certain animals, as (a) the shell of *Mollusca,* which are for this reason sometimes called *Testacea*; (b) the calcareous shell of sea urchins; (c) the thick leathery outer tunic of the sea squirts.

2. in botany, same as *testa.*

tes'tȧ, *n.*; *pl.* **tes'tae,** [L.] 1. in botany, the hard outer covering or integument of a seed.

2. in zoology, same as *test.*

test'ȧ·ble, *a.* [L. *testabilis,* from *testari,* to testify.]

1. that can be tested.

2. in law, (a) that can be devised or given by will; (b) capable of witnessing or of being witnessed.

Tes·tā'cē·ȧ, *n.pl.* [L. *testaceus,* covered with a shell, testaceous, from *testa,* a shell.] an order of shell-covered rhizopods.

tes·tā'ceăn (-shun), *n.* any representative of the *Testacea.*

tes·tā'ceăn, *a.* relating to the *Testacea.*

tes·tā·cē·og'rȧ·phy, *n.* the description of testaceans. [Rare.]

tes·tā·cē·ol'ō·ġy, *n.* conchology; the description of shellfish. [Rare.]

tes·tā'ceous, *a.* [L. *testaceus,* from *testa,* a shell.]

1. of, or of the nature of, a shell or shells.

2. having a hard shell.

3. in botany and zoology, of the color of unglazed earthenware; reddish-brown or brownish-yellow.

testaceous animals; formerly, animals having a strong thick entire shell, as oysters and clams: distinguished from crustaceous animals, whose shells are thin and softer, and consist of several pieces jointed, as lobsters.

tes'tȧ·cy, *n.* in law, the circumstance of leaving a valid will at death; the state of being testate.

tes'tȧ·ment, *n.* [Fr., from L. *testamentum,* from *testari,* to testify, make a will.]

1. in the Bible, a covenant.

2. [T-] either of the two parts of the Bible, the *Old Testament* and the *New Testament*: so called because considered covenants between God and man.

3. [T-] the New Testament. [Colloq.]

4. in law, a will: now rare except in the phrase *last will and testament.*

holographic testament; a will made wholly in the handwriting of the testator.

New Testament; see under *new.*

Old Testament; see under *old.*

tes·tȧ·men'tăl, *a.* relating to a testament or will; testamentary.

tes·tȧ·men'tȧ·ry, *a.* 1. pertaining to a will or to wills; as, *testamentary* causes in law; also, relating to administration of the estates of deceased persons.

2. bequeathed by will; given by testament; as, *testamentary* charities.

3. set forth or contained in a will.

4. done in accordance with a testament, or will; as, the *testamentary* guardian of a minor; that is, one appointed by testament, or will.

tes''tȧ·men·tā'tion, *n.* the act or power of giving by will. [Rare.]

tes'tȧ·men·tize, *v.i.* to make or execute a will or testament. [Obs.]

test·tā'mũr, *n.* [L., we testify.] a certificate given to an English university student certifying that he has successfully passed a certain examination: so called from the opening words, *Ita testamur.*

tes'tāte, *a.* [L. *testatus.*] having made and left a legally valid will: said of a deceased person.

tes'tāte, *n.* one who has died testate.

tes·tā'tion, *n.* 1. a witnessing. [Obs.]

2. act of disposing of property by will.

tes·tā'tŏr, *n.* [L.] one who makes and leaves a legally valid will or testament at death.

tes·tā'trix, *n.*; *pl.* **tes·tā'tri·ceș,** a female testator.

tes'tē, *n.* [abl. sing. of L. *testis,* a witness.] the witnessing clause of a writ or other legal precept which expresses the date of its issue.

test'ĕd, *a.* having the teste, or witnessing clause, properly attached and filled in: said of a legal document.

tes'tẽr, *n.* [OFr. *testiere,* a headpiece, the crown of a hat; Fr. *tête,* the head, from L. *testa,* an earthen pot, the skull, the head.]

1. the square canopy over a bed.

2. in architecture, a flat canopy, as over a pulpit, tomb, or the like.

3. a headpiece; a helmet. [Obs.]

tes'tẽr, *n.* same as *teston.*

test'ẽr, *n.* 1. one who tests, tries, assays, proves, or the like; as, a good *tester.*

2. any instrument or apparatus used in testing; as, a steam-gauge *tester.*

tes′tērn, *v.t.* to present with a sixpence. [Obs.]

tes′tēṣ, *n.* plural of *testis.*

Tes·ti·cär′di·nēṣ, *n.pl.* [LL. *testa,* a shell, and *cardo* (*-inis*), a hinge.] a division of brachiopodous mollusks, including those which have a hinged calcareous shell; the *Arthropomata.*

tes′ti·çle, *n.* [L. *testiculus,* dim. of *testis,* a testicle.] the sex gland of the male; either of two oval structures that are suspended in the scrotum and secrete spermatozoa; testis.

tes′ti·çond, *a.* [L. *testis,* a testicle, and *condere,* to hide.] having the testicles naturally concealed within the body, as the *Cetacea.*

tes·tiç′ū·lăr, *a.* 1. of or relating to a testicle.

2. same as *testiculate.*

tes·tiç′ū·lāte, tes·tiç′ū·lā·ted, *a.* in botany, shaped like a testicle; also, having two tubers resembling testicles, as some species of orchids.

TESTICULATE ROOT

tes·ti·ere′ (-âr′), *n.* [OFr. *teste,* the head.] a headpiece. [Obs.]

tes′tif, *a.* testy. [Obs.]

tes·tif′i·çāte, *n.* in Scots law, a solemn written assertion, not on oath, formerly used in judicial procedure.

tes″ti·fi·çā′tion, *n.* [L. *testificatio* (*-onis*), a testifying.]

1. the act of testifying or giving testimony or evidence.

2. testimony.

tes′ti·fi·çā·tŏr, *n.* a testifier.

tes′ti·fī·ēr, *n.* one who testifies.

tes′ti·fȳ, *v.i.*; testified, *pt., pp.*; testifying, *ppr.* [OFr. *testifier,* from L. *testificari,* to testify; *testis,* a witness, and *facere,* to make.]

1. to make a solemn declaration, verbal or written, to establish some fact; to give testimony for the purpose of communicating to others a knowledge of something not known to them.

2. in law, to make a solemn declaration under oath, for the purpose of establishing or making proof of some fact to a court.

3. to serve as an indication; to be evidence; as, his letters *testify* against him.

tes′ti·fȳ, *v.t.*. 1. to affirm or declare solemnly; to bear witness to.

2. in law, to affirm or declare under oath before a tribunal, for the purpose of proving some fact.

3. to be evidence of; to indicate.

4. to profess and declare publicly, as one's belief.

tes′ti·ly, *adv.* in a testy manner; fretfully.

tes·ti·mō′ni·ăl, *n.* [Fr., from L. *testimonium.*]

1. a written statement in favor of one's character, worth, attainments, conduct, qualifications, etc., or in favor of some product, service, etc.; a letter or statement of recommendation.

2. a gift raised by subscription in acknowledgment of an individual's services, or as a token of respect for his worth, presented to him in the form of a sum of money, piece of plate, his portrait, or the like, or if done after death, taking the form of a monument, benevolent endowment, or the like.

tes·ti·mō′ni·ăl, *a.* 1. relating to or containing testimony. [Rare.]

2. pertaining to or regarded as a testimonial (sense 2); as, a *testimonial* banquet.

tes·ti·mō′ni·ăl·īze, *v.t.* to present with a testimonial. [Rare.]

tes′ti·mō·ny, *n.*; *pl.* **tes′ti·mō·nieṣ,** [L. *testimonium,* from *testis,* a witness.]

1. a declaration or statement, written or verbal, made for the purpose of establishing or proving some fact, especially one made under oath by a witness in court.

2. the act of bearing witness; open attestation; profession.

3. a statement or declaration of facts; representation; declaration; evidence; witness.

The difficulty is, when *testimonies* contradict common experience. —Locke.

4. proof; attestation; support of a statement made.

5. anything equivalent to a declaration or protest; manifestation.

Shake off the dust under your feet for a *testimony* against them. —Mark vi. 11.

6. in the Bible, the two tables of the law. Thou shalt put into this ark the *testimony* which I shall give thee. —Ex. xxv. 16.

7. in the Bible, (a) [*pl.*] the precepts of God; (b) the Scriptures; divine revelations.

The *testimony* of the Lord is sure, making wise the simple. —Ps. xix. 7.

tes′ti·mō·ny, *v.t.* to witness. [Obs.]

tes′ti·ness, *n.* the state or character of being testy; peevishness; petulance.

tes′tis, *n.*; *pl.* **tes′tēṣ,** [L.] 1. a testicle.

2. [*pl.*] the posterior pair of the corpora quadrigemina.

tes′tō, *n.* [It., from L. *textus,* text.] in music, (a) the theme or subject; (b) the text or libretto.

tes′tŏn, tes′toon, *n.* [Fr.; It. *testone,* from *testa,* the head.] formerly, any of several coins with the image of a head on one side; especially, (a) a silver French coin of the sixteenth century; (b) an English coin with the head of Henry VIII, originally worth a shilling, later, sixpence.

tes·tos′tēr·ōne, *n.* [from *testes* and *ster*ol and *-one.*] a male sex hormone, $C_{19}H_{28}O_2$, produced as a white, crystalline substance by isolation from animal testes, or synthesized.

tes·tū′di·năl, *a.* [L. *testudo,* a tortoise.] of or resembling a tortoise or its shell.

tes·tū·di·nā′ri·ous, *a.* [L. *testudo,* tortoise, and *-arious.*] testudinal.

Tes·tū·di·nā′tȧ, *n.pl.* [L., from *testudo,* a tortoise.] an order of reptiles having the body encased in a bony box or leathery shell, consisting of a carapace and a plastron; the turtles and tortoises; the *Chelonia.*

tes·tū′di·nāte, tes·tū′di·nā·ted, *a.* [L. *testudo,* a tortoise.]

1. shaped like the back of a tortoise; roofed; arched; vaulted.

2. of or pertaining to the *Testudinata;* chelonian.

tes·tū′di·nāte, *n.* one of the *Testudinata* or *Chelonia;* a tortoise.

tes·tū·din′ē·ăl, *a.* same as *testudinal.*

tes·tū·din′ē·ous, *a.* 1. resembling the shell of a tortoise.

2. slow in moving, like a tortoise.

Tes·tū·din′i·dae, *n.pl.* the land tortoises, a family of chelonian reptiles distinguished by their highly arched carapace and short clubby feet.

tes·tū′dō, *n.*; *pl.* **tes·tū′di·nēṣ,** [L., a tortoise shell.]

1. a movable shelter or screen with a strong arched roof, used as a protection by ancient Roman soldiers.

2. a protective covering formed by a body of ancient Roman soldiers by interweaving their shields above their heads.

ROMAN TESTUDO

3. in medicine, an encysted tumor, supposed to resemble the shell of a turtle.

4. formerly, in music, a lyre: so called because the lyre of Mercury was said to have been fashioned from the shell of a tortoise.

5. (a) [T-] the type genus of the *Testudinidæ;* (b) a member of this genus; any of a number of land tortoises.

tes′tūle, *n.* in botany, a frustule. [Obs.]

test′y, *a.*; *comp.* testier; *superl.* testiest, [ME. *testif,* from OFr. *teste,* the head, from L. *testa.*] fretful; peevish; petulant; easily irritated.

tē·tan′iç, *a.* [L. *tetanicus,* from Gr. *tetanikos,* from *tetanos,* spasm.] of the nature of, pertaining to, characterized by, or producing tetanus.

tē·tan′iç, *n.* any drug, as strychnine, which in overdoses can cause tetanic spasms of the muscles, often resulting in death.

tet·ȧ·nil′lȧ, *n.* [LL., dim. of *tetanus.*] a form of tetany without rigidity but attended by mental changes.

tet′ȧ·nīne, *n.* a poisonous ptomaine, $C_{13}H_{30}N_2O_4$, obtained from cultures of the tetanus bacillus or the tissues of patients affected with tetanus. It produces paralysis, tetanic convulsions, and death.

tet″ȧ·ni·zā′tion, *n.* a tetanic state or condition; the production of tetanus.

tet′ȧ·nīze, *v.t.*; tetanized, *pt., pp.*; tetanizing, *ppr.* to affect with or cause tetanus in.

tet′ȧ·noid, *a.* [Gr. *tetanos,* spasm, and *eidos,* form.] resembling tetanus.

tet″ȧ·nō·mō′tŏr, *n.* a device for the mechanical production of tetanic motor spasm in a muscle.

tet″ȧ·nō·tox′in, *n.* [Gr. *tetanos,* spasm; and *toxin,* poison.] a ptomaine obtained from the cultures of the tetanus bacillus.

tet′ȧ·nus, *n.* [Gr. *tetanos,* a spasm, lit., stretched.]

1. in medicine, an acute infectious disease, often fatal, caused by the toxins of a specific bacillus which usually enters the body through wounds: it is characterized by spasmodic contractions and rigidity of some or all of the voluntary muscles.

2. in physiology, the state of continuous contraction of a muscle undergoing a series of rapidly repeated stimuli.

tet′ȧ·ny, *n.* [from Mod. L. *tetania,* from Gr. *tetanos,* spasm.] an abnormal condition characterized by tetanic spasms of the arm and leg muscles, resulting usually from the faulty metabolism of calcium salts.

tē·tärd′, *n.* a gobioid fish, *Eleotris gyrinus,* found in the southern part of the United States.

tē·tär′tō-, [from Gr. *tetartos,* fourth.] a combining form meaning *one fourth,* as in *tetart*ohedral.

tē·tär·tō·hē′drăl, *a.* [*tetarto-* and *-hedral.*] having one fourth of the planes needed for crystallographic symmetery.

tē·tär·tō·hē′drăl·ly, *adv.* in a tetartohedral form or arrangement.

tē·tär·tō·hē′driṣm, *n.* the state or property of being modified tetartohedrally.

tē·tär·tō·hē′drŏn, *n.* a tetartohedral form.

tetched (techt), *a.* touched; demented. [Dial. or Humorous.]

tetch′i·ness, *n.* the state or quality of being tetchy.

tetch′y, *a.*; *comp.* tetchier; *superl.* tetchiest, [var. of *techy.*] touchy; irritable; peevish: also spelled *techy.*

tête (tāt), *n.* [Fr., head.] false hair; a kind of ornamented wig worn by women in the eighteenth century. [Obs.]

tête′-à-tête′ (tāt′ȧ-tāt′), *adv.* [Fr., lit., head to head.] together privately: said of two people; as, they spoke *tête-à-tête.*

tête′-à-tête′, *a.* for or of two people in private; as, a *tête-à-tête* conversation.

tête′-à-tête′, *n.* 1. a private or intimate conversation between two people.

2. an S-shaped seat on which two people can sit facing each other.

tête′-bêche′ (tet′besh′), *a.* [Fr., *tête,* head, and *bêche,* from *bechevet,* double bed head.] printed so that one is inverted in relation to the other: said of a pair of postage stamps.

tête′-de-pont′ (tet′dē-pọṅ′), *n.*; *pl.* **têtes′-de-pont′** (tet′dē-pọṅ′), [Fr., head of a bridge.] a bridgehead.

tet′el, *n.* [Ar.] the tora, an African antelope, *Alcelaphus tora.*

teth (*or* tes), *n.* the ninth letter of the Hebrew alphabet, corresponding to English *T, t.*

teth′ēr, *n.* [ME. *tedir;* ON. *tiōthr;* akin to M.D. *tudder.*]

1. a rope or chain fastened to an animal so as to keep it within certain bounds.

2. the range or limit of one's abilities, resources, etc.

at the end of one's tether; at the end of one's endurance, resources, etc.

teth′ēr, *v.t.*; tethered, *pt., pp.*; tethering, *ppr.* to fasten or confine, as a grazing animal, with a tether; figuratively, to tie or restrain (anything) within certain limits.

tē·thȳ′dăn, *n.* a tunicate.

Tē′thys, *n.* [Gr. *Tēthys.*]

1. in Greek mythology, a Titaness, daughter of Uranus, wife of Oceanus, and mother of the Oceanides.

2. a genus of large marine mollusks.

tet′rȧ-, [from Gr. *tettares,* four.] a combining form meaning *four,* as in *tetra*chord; also, before a vowel, *tetr-.*

tet·rȧ·bā′siç, *a.* [*tetra-* and *basic.*] designating or of an acid having four replaceable hydrogen atoms per molecule.

tet·rȧ·bō′riç, *a.* same as *pyroboric.*

tet′rȧ·braçh, *n.* [*tetra-*, and Gr. *brachys*, short.] in ancient prosody, a foot or word of four short syllables; a proceleusmatic.

tet′rȧ·brañçh, *a.* and *n.* same as *tetrabranchiate.*

Tet·rȧ·brañ·çhi·ā′tȧ, *n.pl.* an order of *Cephalopoda*, comprising the two families *Nautilidæ* and *Ammonitidæ*. Of this order, the pearly nautilus may be regarded as the type, being the only living member of the order, though its fossil representatives, *Orthoceras*, *Ammonites*, etc., are abundant. The characteristic features of the order are the external many-chambered shell, the septa between the chambers of which are perforated by the tube, called a siphuncle, and the four branchiae.

tet·rȧ·brañ′çhi·āte, *a.* of or belonging to the *Tetrabranchiata*; having four gills (branchiae).

tet·rȧ·brañ′çhi·āte, *n.* one of the *Tetrabranchiata.*

tet·rȧ·çär′pel·lãr·y, *a.* in botany, having four carpels.

tet·rac′ẽr·ous, *a.* [*tetra-*, and Gr. *keras*, horn.] having four horns or processes resembling horns, as a snail.

tet·rȧ·çhlō′rīde, *n.* any chemical compound with four chlorine atoms to the molecule.

tet′rȧ·çhord, *n.* [Gr. *tetrachordon*, musical instrument, from *tetrachordos*, four-stringed.]
 1. in music, a series of four consecutive full tones comprising a total interval of a fourth; half an octave.
 2. a four-stringed lyre.

tet·rȧ·çhord′ăl, *a.* of a tetrachord.

tet·rȧ·çhot′ō·mous, *a.* [Gr. *tetracha*, in four parts, and *tomos*, a cutting, from *temnein*, to cut.] having a division by four; separated into four parts or series, or into series of fours.

tet·rac′id, *a.* [*tetr-* and *acid.*] in chemistry, capable of replacing four atoms of hydrogen in an acid; also, having four atoms of hydrogen replaceable by acid radicals.

te·trac′id, *n.* 1. a base that can react with four molecules of a monobasic acid to form a salt.
 2. an alcohol having four OH groups per molecule.

tet·rȧ·coç′çous, *a.* [*tetra-*, and Gr. *kokkos*, a berry.] in botany, having four cells elastically dehiscing and separating.

Tet·rȧ·coç′çus, *n.* a genus or form of microscopic plants made up of a tetrad or of tetrads of cells.

tet·rȧ·cō′lŏn, *n.* [*tetra-*, and Gr. *kōlon*, a member.] in Greek and Latin prosody, a stanza or division of lyric poetry consisting of four verses.

tet″rȧ·çor′ăl, *n.* any of the *Tetracoralla.*

Tet″rȧ·çō·ral′lȧ, *n.pl.* same as *Rugosa.*

tet′rȧ·çō·sāne″, *n.* [Gr. *tetra*, four, and *eikosi*, twenty.] in chemistry, $C_{24}H_{50}$, a solid hydrocarbon of the paraffin series, particularly the normal type which melts at 54° C.

tet′raçt, *a.* [*tetra-*, and Gr. *aktis*, a ray.] having four rays, as a sponge spicule.

tet′raçt, *n.* a four-rayed sponge spicule.

tet·raç′ti·năl, tet·raç′tine, *a.* tetract.

tet·raç·ti·nel′lid, *a.* pertaining to or characteristic of the *Tetractinellida.*

tet·raç·ti·nel′lid, *n.* one of the *Tetractinellida.*

Tet·raç·ti·nel′li·dȧ, *n.pl.* [*tetra-*, and Gr. *aktis* (*-inis*), a ray.] a division of siliceous sponges with four-rayed spicules. It includes the families *Choristida* and *Lithistida.*

tet·raç·ti·nel′li·dăn, *a.* tetractinellid.

tet·raç·ti·nel′line, *a.* tetractinellid.

te·traç′ti·nōse, *a.* tetractinal.

te·traç′tys, *n.* [Gr. *tetraktys*, a group of four.] ten as the total obtained by adding one, two, three and four. [Obs.]

tet·rȧ·cyç′liç, *a.* having four circles or whorls of floral parts, as flowers.

tet″rȧ·cy′çlo-, a combining form meaning *having four circles* or *four atomic rings.*

tet′rad, *a.* in chemistry, quadrivalent.

tet′rad, *n.* [Gr. *tetras* (*-ados*), the number four.]
 1. the number four.
 2. a group or set of four things.
 3. in chemistry, an atom, radical, or element having a valence of four.
 4. a group of four chromosomes formed by the division of a pair during meiosis.

tet·rȧ·daç′tyl, tet·rȧ·daç′tyle, *a.* having four digits on each limb.

tet·rȧ·daç′tyl, *n.* a tetradactyl animal.

tet″rȧ·daç·tyl′i·ty, *n.* the state or quality of being tetradactyl.

tet·rȧ·daç′tyl·ous, *a.* tetradactyl.

tet′rȧ·därçh″y (-därk″y), *n.* a tetrachy.

tet·rȧ·deç′āne, *n.* [*tetra-*, and Gr. *deka*, ten.] one of the paraffins, $C_{14}H_{30}$, found in petroleum and in the light oils obtained by the distillation of coal.

tet·rȧ·deç′ȧ·pod, *a.* having fourteen feet; pertaining to the *Tetradecapoda.*

tet·rȧ·deç′ȧ·pod, *n.* one of the *Tetradecapoda.*

Tet″rȧ·dē·çap′ō·dȧ, *n.pl.* the *Arthrostraca*, an order of crustaceans the typical adult of which has seven pairs of feet.

tet″rȧ·dec′yl al′çō·hol, [*tetra-*, *decyl* and *alcohol.*] in chemistry, $C_{14}H_{29}OH$, one of the higher alcohols of the methane series, particularly that obtained by reducing myristic aldehyde, which yields a waxlike solid.

tet″rȧ·dī·ȧ·pā′sŏn, *n.* a quadruple diapason or octave: also called a *quadruple eighth* or *twenty-ninth.*

tet·rad′iç, *a.* of or pertaining to a tetrad.

Tet′rȧ·dīte, *n.* [from Gr. *tetras*, four.] one of certain sects, as the Manichees, who believed there were four persons in the Godhead.

tet′rȧ·drachm (-dram), *n.* a silver coin of ancient Greece worth four drachmas.

tet·rad′y·mīte, *n.* [Gr. *tetradymos*, fourfold: so named because it occurs in compound twin crystals.] a native bismuth telluride, Bi_2Te_3, a pale, steel-gray mineral in foliated form.

Tet″rȧ·dy·nā′mi·ȧ, *n.pl.* [*tetra-*, and Gr. *dynamis*, power.] in botany, a former classification of plants having six stamens, four of which are longer than the others.

tet″rȧ·dy·nā′mi·ăn, tet·rȧ·dyn′ȧ·mous, *a.* having six stamens, four of which are uniformly longer than the others; pertaining to the *Tetradynamia.*

tet·rȧ·eth′yl lead (led), same as *lead tetraethyl.*

tē·traġ′ē·nous, *a.* splitting into groups of four: said of bacteria.

tet′rȧ·gon, *n.* [*tetra-*, and Gr. *gōnia*, angle.]
 1. in geometry, a plane figure with four sides and four angles; a quadrangle.
 2. in astrology, an aspect of two planets with regard to the earth, when they are distant from each other ninety degrees, or the fourth of a circle.

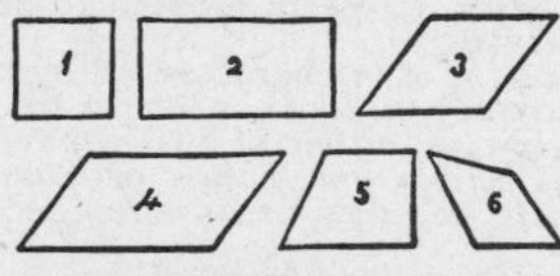

TETRAGONS

1. square, 2. parallelogram or oblong, 3. rhombus, 4. rhomboid, 5. trapezoid, 6. trapezium

tet·rag′ō·năl, *a.* 1. of, or having the form of, a tetragon; quadrangular.
 2. designating or of a system of crystallization in which the three axes are at right angles, the two lateral axes being of equal length, and the third shorter or longer.
 3. in botany, having four prominent longitudinal angles, as a stem.

te·trag′ō·nous, *a.* tetragonal.

tet′rȧ·gram, *n.* 1. a word of four letters.
 2. [*also* T–] the Tetragrammaton.

Tet·rȧ·gram′mȧ·ton, *n.* [*tetra-*, and Gr. *gramma*, a letter.] the four consonants of the ancient Hebrew name for God (variously written JHVH, IHVH, JHWH, YHVH, YHWH), considered too sacred to pronounce: the word *Adonai* (Lord) is substituted for this name in utterance, and the vowels of *Adonai* or *Elohim* (God) are inserted in Hebrew texts, so that the modern reconstructions are *Yahweh, Jehovah*, etc.

tet′rȧ·ġyn, *n.* one of the *Tetragynia.*

Tet·rȧ·ġyn′i·ȧ, *n.pl.* [*tetra-*, and Gr. *gynē*, a female.] in botany, a former classification of hermaphrodite plants having four styles.

tet·rȧ·ġyn′i·ăn, *a.* tetragynous.

te·traġ′y·nous, *a.* in botany, hermaphrodite with four styles; pertaining to the *Tetragynia.*

tet·rȧ·hē′drăl, *a.* 1. pertaining to or having the form of a tetrahedron.
 2. in crystallography, (a) having the form of the regular tetrahedron; (b) pertaining or relating to a tetrahedron, or the system of forms to which the tetrahedron belongs.
 tetrahedral angle; a solid angle which has four plane angles for its boundaries.

tet·rȧ·hē′drăl·ly, *a.* in a tetrahedral manner.

tet·rȧ·hē′drīte, *n.* [Gr. *tetraedril.*] a gray to blackish mineral occurring in tetrahedral crystals, essentially a sulfide of copper and antimony, $3Cu_2S \cdot Sb_2S$: in many forms the copper is partly replaced by iron, lead, silver etc.

tet·rȧ·hē′droid, *n.* in geometry, the envelope of a quadric surface contiguous to eight given lines.

tet·rȧ·hē′drŏn, *n.*; *pl.* **tet·rȧ·hē′drŏns, tet·rȧ·hē′drȧ,** [*tetra-*, and Gr. *hedra*, a base.] a solid figure with four triangular surfaces.

TETRAHEDRON

tet·rȧ·hex·ȧ·hē′drăl, *a.* pertaining to or of the form of a tetrahexahedron.

tet·rȧ·hex·ȧ·hē′drŏn, *n.* a solid bounded by twenty-four equal faces, four corresponding to each face of the cube.

tet″rȧ·kis·hex·ȧ·hē′drŏn, *n.* a tetrahexahedron.

tet′rȧ·kō·sāne, *n.* [*tetra-*, and Gr. *eikosi*, twenty.] same as *tetracosane.*

TETRAHEXAHEDRON

te·tral′ō·ġy, *n.*; *pl.* **te·tral′ō·ġies,** [Gr. *tetralogia*; see *tetra-* and *-logy.*]
 1. a series of four dramas, three tragic and one satiric, performed together at ancient Athens at the festival of Dionysus.
 2. any series of four related dramatic, operatic, or literary compositions.

Te·tram′ẽ·rȧ, *n.pl.* [*tetra-*, and Gr. *meros*, a part.] a division of coleopterous insects, distinguished by having all the tarsi four-jointed, as in the *Rhynchophora.*

te·tram′ẽr·ăl, *a.* tetramerous.

te·tram′ẽr·ous, *a.* consisting of or divided into four parts; characterized by having four parts; specifically, (a) in botany, applied to a flower or other complex organ having its parts in fours: often written 4-*merous*; (b) in zoology, having or seeming to have four joints in the tarsi.

te·tram′e·tẽr, *n.* [Gr. *tetrametros*; see *tetra-* and *meter* (rhythm).]
 1. a line of verse containing four metrical feet or measures. Example: "Tḗrĕnce, / thĭs ĭs / stū́pĭd / stŭ́ff."
 2. verse consisting of tetrameters.

te·tram′e·tẽr, *a.* having four metrical feet or measures.

tet·rȧ·meth′yl·ēne, *n.* [*tetra-* and *methylene.*] a bivalent radical, $-CH_2CH_2CH_2CH_2-$.

tet′rȧ·morph, *n.* [*tetra-*, and Gr. *morphē*, form.] in Christian art, the union of the four attributes of the evangelists in one figure, winged, and standing on winged fiery wheels, the wings being covered with eyes.

Te·tran′dri·ȧ, *n.pl.* [*tetra-*, and Gr. *anēr*, *andros*, a male.] formerly, the fourth class of plants in the Linnaean system, including those that have four stamens.

te·tran′dri·ăn, *a.* in botany, belonging to the class *Tetrandria.*

te·tran′drous, *a.* tetrandrian.

tet·rā′ō·nid, *n.* one of the *Tetraonidæ.*

Tet·rā·on′i·dae, *n.pl.* the grouse family, a family of birds belonging to the order *Gallinæ*, type genus *Tetrao.*

tet·rȧ·pet′ăl·ous, *a.* [*tetra-*, and Gr. *petalon*, leaf.] in botany, having four distinct petals.

tet·rȧ·phär′mȧ·çon, *n.* [*tetra-*, and Gr. *pharmakon*, a drug.] a combination of wax, resin, lard, and pitch, composing an ointment.

tet·rȧ·phē′nōl, *n.* furan. [Rare.]

tet·rȧ·phyl′lous, *a.* [*tetra-*, and Gr. *phyllon*, leaf.] in botany, having four leaves; consisting of four distinct leaves or leaflets.

Tet′rȧ·plȧ, *n.* [*tetra-*, and Gr. *-ploos*, fold.] an edition of the Old Testament in four versions, specifically, an edition of the Greek Testament compiled by Origen, containing four different versions.

Tet·rap·neū′mō·nȧ, *n.pl.* [*tetra-*, and Gr. *pneumōn*, lung.] a division of *Araneida*, four-lunged spiders having two pairs of lung sacs and two pairs of spinnerets. The division includes the trap-door spiders.

tet″rap·neū·mō′ni·ăn, *n.* a member of the *Tetrapneumona.*

tet′rȧ·pod, *a.* having only four perfect legs, as certain butterflies.

tet′rȧ·pod, *n.* a four-footed animal; specifically, an insect having only four perfect legs, as certain *Lepidoptera.*

te·trap′ō·dy, *n.* in prosody, a set or measure of four feet.

te·trap′ō·lis, *n.* [*tetra-*, four, and Gr. *polis*, city.] four cities grouped or confederated; a grouping or alliance of four municipalities.

tet·rȧ·pol′i·tăn, *a.* of or relating to a tetrapolis.

Tetrapolitan Confession; in church history, a confession of faith submitted by the municipalities of Constance, Strasbourg, Memmingen, and Lindau to the Diet of Augsburg, in 1530.

te·trap′tẽr·ăn, *n.* [*tetra-*, and Gr. *pteron*, wing.] any four-winged insect.

te·trap′tẽr·ous, *a.* 1. in biology, having four wings.
2. in botany, having four winglike parts; as, *tetrapterous* fruit.

tet′trap·tōte, *n.* [*tetra-*, and Gr. *ptōsis*, a case.] in grammar, a noun that has four cases only.

tet″rȧ·pȳ·rē′nous, *a.* [*tetra-*, and Gr. *pyrēn*, a fruit stone.] in botany, four-stoned, as certain fruit.

te·tra·quē′trous (-tra-kwē′), *a.* [*tetra-*, and L. *quadratus*, square.] having four very sharp and almost winged corners, as the stalks of some plants.

tē′trärch (*or* tet′), *n.* [ME. *tetrarche*; LL. *tetrarcha*; L. *tetrarches*; Gr. *tetrarchēs*, from *tetra-*, four, and *archos*, ruler.]
1. in the ancient Roman Empire, the ruler of part (originally a fourth part) of a province.
2. a subordinate prince, governor, etc.

tē′trärch, *a.* in botany, having four points of origin.

tē′trärch·āte, *n.* the fourth part of a province under a Roman tetrarch; also, the territory under the jurisdiction of a tetrarch.

tē·trärch′i·căl, *a.* pertaining to a tetrarch or a tetrarchy.

tē′trärch·y, *n.*; *pl.* **tē′trärch·ieṣ,** 1. the rule, jurisdiction, or territory of a tetrarch.
2. government by four persons.
3. a group of four rulers.
4. a country divided into four subordinate governments.

tet·rȧ·schis′tiç, *a.* in biology, divided into four parts by fission.

tet′rȧ·sēme, *a.* [*tetra-*, and Gr. *sēma*, a sign.] in prosody, constituted of or having the measure of four morae.

tet·rȧ·sep′ăl·ous, *a.* in botany, having four sepals.

tet·rȧ·spas′tŏn, *n.* [*tetra-*, and Gr. *span*, pull, stretch.] in mechanics, a machine in which four pulleys act together.

tet·rȧ·spẽr′mous, *a.* [*tetra-*, and Gr. *sperma*, seed.] in botany, having four seeds.

tet′rȧ·spō·ranġe, *n.* a tetrasporangium.

tet″rȧ·spō·ran′ġi·um, *n.* in botany, a tetraspore-producing sporangium.

tet′rȧ·spōre, *n.* in botany, any of the asexual spores, usually four in number, produced in certain algae.

tet·rȧ·spor′iç, *a.* of or pertaining to tetraspores.

tet′rȧ·stich, *n.* [L. *tetrastichon*; Gr. *tetrastichon*, from *tetra-*, four, and *stichos*, verse.] a stanza, epigram, or poem consisting of four lines.

tet·rȧ·stich′iç, *a.* 1. of a tetrastich.
2. in tetrastichs.
3. having four lines.

tē·tras′ti·chous, *a.* [*tetra-*, and Gr. *stichos*, row.] in botany, in four vertical rows, as the flowers on some spikes.

tet′rȧ·stȳle, *n.* in architecture, a building with four columns in front.

tet′rȧ·stȳle, *a.* in architecture, having four columns in front.

TETRASTYLE TEMPLE

tet″rȧ·syl·lab′ic, tet″rȧ·syl·lab′i·căl, *a.* consisting of four syllables.

tet·rȧ·syl′lȧ·ble, *n.* a word consisting of four syllables.

tet·rȧ·thē′căl, *a.* [*tetra-*, and Gr. *theka*, a case.] in botany, having four cells or cavities in the ovary.

tet′rȧ·thē·iṣm, *n.* in theology, the doctrine of a Godhead, in which there are four distinct offices or functions, the Father, the Son, the Holy Ghost, and a Divine Essence.

tet·rȧ·thī′on·āte, *n.* a salt of tetrathionic acid.

tet″rȧ·thī·on′iç, *a.* [*tetra-*, and Gr. *theion* sulfur.] designating an unstable acid of sulfur containing oxygen and hydrogen, $H_2S_4O_6$.

tet·rȧ·tom′iç, *a.* 1. designating or of a molecule consisting of four atoms.
2. having four replaceable atoms or groups.
3. tetravalent. [Rare.]

te·tra·vā′lence, *n.* quadrivalence.

te·tra·vā′lent, *a.* 1. having a valence of four.
2. having four valences.
Also, esp. for 2, *quadrivalent*.

te·trax′i·ăl, *a.* in biology, provided with four axes; as, *tetraxial* spicules.

te·trax′ile, *a.* tetraxial.

te·trax′ŏn, *n.* a tetraxial spicule.

te·trax′ŏn, *a.* having four axes; tetraxial.

te·traz′o-, a combining form used in chemistry to designate, (a) a compound containing four atoms of nitrogen; (b) the presence of four azo groups.

tet′rȧ·zōne, *n.* any member of a series of basic compounds characterized by four atoms of nitrogen.

tet′riç, tet′ri·căl, *a.* froward; perverse; harsh; sour; rugged. [Rare.]

tet′ri·căl·ness, *n.* frowardness; perverseness. [Obs.]

te·tric′ity, *n.* crabbedness; perverseness. [Rare.]

tet′riç·ous, *a.* tetric. [Obs.]

te·trin′iç, *a.* containing a radical with four carbon atoms; as, *tetrinic* acid, $C_4H_3O_3(CH_3)$.

tet′rōde, *n.* [*tetr-* and *-ode*.] an electron tube having four elements (usually a cathode, a plate, a control grid, and a screening grid).

Tet′rō·don, *n.* 1. a genus of teleostean fishes, apparently having four large teeth, the jaws being each divided by a central suture.
2. [t–] a fish of the genus *Tetrodon*.

tet′rō·dont, *n.* a tetrodon: also written *tetraodont*.

tet′rō·dont, *a.* of or relating to tetrodons.

tet′rŏl, *n.* [Gr. *tetra*, four.] a hypothetical hydrocarbon, C_4H_4.

tet·rol′iç, *a.* designating a monobasic acid, $C_4H_4O_2$.

te·trox′id, *n.* same as *tetroxide*.

te·trox′īde, *n.* any oxide with four atoms of oxygen in each molecule.

tet′ry·lēne, *n.* same as *butylene*.

tet′tẽr, *n.* [AS. *teter*, prob. from Celt.]
1. any of various skin diseases characterized by itching, as eczema, psoriasis, etc.
2. a cutaneous disease of animals which spreads on the body in different directions and causes a troublesome itching.

tet′tẽr, *v.t.*; tettered, *pt., pp.*; tettering, *ppr.* to affect with tetter in any of its types.

tet′tẽr ber′ry, a plant, *Bryonia dioica*; also, its red berry, formerly reputed to be a cure for tetter. [Brit.]

tet′tẽr·ous, *a.* of or characterized by tetter.

tet′tẽr-tot″tẽr, *n.* same as *titter-totter*.

tet′tẽr·wŏrt, *n.* either of two papaveraceous plants, *Chelidonium majus*, or *Sanguinaria canadensis*: so called because reputed to cure tetter.

tet′tix, *n.* [Gr. *tettix*, a cicada.]
1. a cicada. [Obs.]
2. [T–] a genus of acridian grasshoppers.

teūçh′it, *n.* a bird, the lapwing. [Scot.]

Teū′cri·ăn, *a.* and *n.* [from *Teucer*, first king of Troy.] Trojan.

teū′crin, *n.* a crystalline glucoside, $C_{21}H_{24}O_{11}$, extracted from the plant *Teucrium fruticans*.

Teū′cri·um, *n.* a genus of labiate plants, including many species, some of which are valued for their medicinal qualities.

teū′fit, *n.* [imitative.] teuchit. [Brit. Dial.]

teūk, *n.* a snipe, the redshank. [Brit. Dial.]

Teū′tŏn, *n.* [from L. *Teutones*.]
1. a member of the Teutones.
2. a member of any Teutonic people; especially, a German.

Teū′tō·neṣ, *n.pl.* [L.] an ancient tribe, variously considered as Teutonic or Celtic, that lived north of the Elbe in Jutland.

Teū·ton′iç, *a.* 1. of the ancient Teutons.
2. German.
3. designating or of a group of north European peoples including the German, Scandinavian, Dutch, English, etc.
4. in ethnology, Nordic: term now seldom used.
5. in linguistics, Germanic: term now seldom used.

Teutonic cross; in heraldry, a cross potent from its having been the original badge of the Teutonic Order.

Teutonic Order; a military and religious order of German knights (*Teutonic Knights*) originally organized in 1191 for service in the Holy Land and later active in the military conquests by medieval Germany of Baltic and Slavic lands.

Teū·ton′iç, *n.* the language or languages collectively of the Teutons.

Teū·ton′i·ciṣm, *n.* 1. a Teutonic or German idiom, expression, or manner of speech.
2. Teutonic or German spirit, custom, etc.

Teū′tŏn·iṣm, *n.* 1. belief in the supposed racial superiority of the Teutons, especially of the Germans.
2. Teutonic culture.

Teū′tŏn·īze, *v.t.* and *v.i.*; Teutonized, *pt., pp.*; Teutonizing, *ppr.* to make or become Teutonic or German.

tew, *v.t.*; tewed, *pt., pp.*; tewing, *ppr.* [AS. *tawian*, to taw, work, prepare, beat.]
1. to fatigue.
2. to tease.
3. to beat or press, as leather or hemp; to soften or render pliable.
[Brit. Dial. in all senses.]

tew, *v.i.* to hurry and work fussily. [Brit. Dial.]

tē′whit, *n.* [imitative.] the lapwing: also called *teuchit* and *teufit*. [Brit. Dial.]

Tex′ăn, *n.* a native or inhabitant of the State of Texas.

Tex′ăn, *a.* of or pertaining to the State of Texas.

Texan fever; same as *Texas fever*.

Tex′ȧs, *n.*; *pl.* **Tex′ȧs,** [Sp., from Am. Ind. (Caddo) *techas*, allies (against the Apaches).]
1. a member of a Caddoan tribe of American Indians.
2. [t–] [name given to the officers' quarters on Mississippi steamboats because they were the largest of the staterooms, which were named after States.] the low boxlike structure on the hurricane deck of a steamboat, containing the cabins of the officers, etc. and having the pilothouse standing on the top or front part of it.

Tex′ȧs blūe′bon″net, a plant with blue flowers, the state flower of Texas.

Tex′ȧs fē′vẽr, an infectious disease of cattle, carried by ticks.

Tex′ȧs lēa′guẽr (-gẽr), in baseball, a fly ball that falls between the infield and outfield and is a safe hit. [Slang.]

Tex′ȧs Rān′ġẽr, a member of the mounted State police of Texas.

Tex′ȧs spar′rōw, an olive-green finch of southeastern Texas and eastern Mexico.

Tex′ȧs tow′ẽr, [so named after such structures, originally for oil drilling, off the coast of *Texas*.] an offshore platform erected on firm foundations or steel legs planted deeply in the sea bottom: used for supporting radar installations, navigation beacons, etc.

text, *n.* [ME. and OFr. *texte*; L. *textus*, woven; also fabric, structure, text, from *texere*, to weave.]
1. the actual or original words of an author, as distinguished from notes, commentary paraphrase, translation, etc.
2. the main body or substance of a book or manuscript, as distinguished from headings, marginal notes, etc.
3. the actual structure of words in a piece of writing or printing; wording.
4. (a) the wording set forth by an editor as most nearly representing the author's original work, or an edition containing this; as, the Caxton *text* of Chaucer; (b) any form in which a writing exists; as, a corrupt *text*.
5. letterpress, as distinguished from illustrations, etc.
6. a Biblical passage quoted as authority for a belief or as the topic of a sermon.
7. a topic; subject.
8. large handwriting; text hand.
9. any of several bold-faced styles of type.
10. a textbook.
11. any of various versions or recensions of all or part of the Scriptures, taken to represent the authentic reading.

text, *v.t.* to write in large letters. [Rare.]

text′book, *n.* 1. a book of which the printed lines are so spaced as to give ample room for notes.
2. a book giving instructions in the principles of a subject of study; any book used as the basis or partial basis of a course of study.

Syn.—handbook, manual, guide, libretto, treatise.

text ē·di′tion, that edition of a book prepared for use in schools or colleges.

text hand, a large, carefully formed and executed handwriting: so called from its former use to distinguish the texts of manuscripts from notes.

tex′tile, *a.* [L. *textilis*, from *textus*, fabric.]
1. having to do with weaving or woven fabrics.
2. woven.
3. that can be woven; as, *textile* material.

textile cone; a large shell, *Conus textilis*, whose markings give it a resemblance to a textile fabric.

tex'tile, *n.* 1. a woven fabric; cloth.
2. raw material suitable for weaving, as cotton, flax, wool, etc.

text'măn, *n.*; *pl.* **text'men,** a man always ready to quote texts, or one overstrict in adhering to the letter of texts.

tex·tō'ri·ăl, *a.* [L. *textorius*, of or pertaining to weaving.] pertaining to weaving. [Rare.]

tex'tū·ăl, *a.* 1. of, pertaining to, or contained in a text; as, *textual* commentary, a *textual* error.
2. serving for or based on texts; hence, literal; word for word.
3. skilled in texts; acquainted with and capable of quoting texts. [Obs.]

tex'tū·ăl·ism, *n.* 1. strict adherence to the text, especially of the Scriptures.
2. the art of textual criticism.

tex'tū·ăl·ist, *n.* a person who is versed in, or adheres strictly to, the text, especially of the Scriptures.

tex'tū·ăl·ly, *adv.* in a textual manner; in the text, or according to the text; as regards the text.

tex'tū·ăr·y, *a.* same as *textual*.

tex'tū·ăr·y, *n.*; *pl.* **tex'tū·ăr'ies,** a textualist.

tex'tūr·ăl, *a.* of or pertaining to texture.

tex'tūre, *n.* [L. *textura*, from *texere*, to weave.]
1. the act, art, or process of weaving. [Obs.]
2. originally, a woven fabric; a textile.
3. the character of a woven fabric resulting from the arrangement, size, quality, etc. of the fabric's threads; as, a fine or coarse *texture*, a ribbed or twilled *texture*.
4. the arrangement of the particles or constituent parts of any material, as wood, metal, etc.; structure, composition.
5. the structural quality of a work of art, resulting from the artist's method of using his medium

tex'tūre, *v.t.*; textured, *pt.*, *pp.*; texturing, *ppr.* to form into a texture. [Rare.]

tex'tus, *n.* [L., text.] the text of any literary work; authoritative text; especially, the text of the Bible or of any part of it.
textus receptus; a received text; a text which, as being the best accessible, is used by translators.

T'-group' (tē'), *n.* [*t*raining *group*.] a group engaging in sensitivity training.

-th, [ME. *-th*, *-the*; AS. *-thu*, *-tho*, *-th*.] a suffix used in forming nouns from verbs and adjectives, meaning: (a) *the action of -ing*, as in steal*th*; (b) *the state or quality of being or having*, as in weal*th*.

-th, [ME. *-the*; AS. *-tha*, *-the*, *-otha*, *-othe*.] a suffix used in forming ordinal numerals, as four*th*, nin*th*: also, after a vowel, *-eth*.

-th, [ME. and AS. *-th*.] contracted form of *-eth*, archaic ending of the third person singular, present indicative, of verbs, as in ha*th*, do*th*.

Th, in chemistry, thorium.

Thä'i (tä'ē *or* tī), *n.* 1. a group of Asian languages considered to be a subbranch of the Sino-Tibetan language family.
2. the official language of Thailand.
3. a member of a group of Thai-speaking peoples of Indochina.
Also spelled *Tai*.

Thä'i, *a.* of the Thai or their language: also spelled *Tai*.

Thä·is' (tä-ēs'), *n.* the heroine of a French opera (1894) by Jules Massenet, after a novel (1890) by Anatole France: she is an Alexandrian courtesan converted by a monk who, however, in the end succumbs to her charms: also spelled *Thaïs*.

thal"ȧ·men·ceph'ȧ·lon, *n.* [Mod. L., from Gr. *thalamos*, an inner room, and *enkephalos*, brain.] the posterior part of the embryonic forebrain, from which the thalamus develops: also called *diencephalon*.

thȧ·lam'iç, *a.* pertaining to the thalamus, especially the optic thalamus.

Thal"ȧ·mi·flō'rae, *n.pl.* a class of exogenous or dicotyledonous plants in which the petals are distinct and inserted with the stamens on the receptacle, not on a disk or on the calyx.

thal"ȧ·mi·flō'răl, thal"ȧ·mi·flō'rous, *a.* in botany, having the stamens arising immediately from the thalamus; belonging to the *Thalamifloræ*.

thal'ȧ·mō·coele, *n.* [Gr. *thalamos*, inner room, and *koilia*, hollow.] the third ventricle of the brain.

Thal·ȧ·moph'ō·rȧ, *n.pl.* same as *Foraminifera*.

thal'ȧ·mus, *n.*; *pl.* **thal'ȧ·mī,** [L., from Gr. *thalamos*, an inner room.]
1. in anatomy, a large, ovoid mass of gray matter situated at the base of the brain and involved in the transmission and integration of certain sensations: also *optic thalamus*.
2. in botany, the receptacle of a flower; torus.

thȧ·las'si·ăn, *n.* [Gr. *thalassios*, of or belonging to the sea.] any sea turtle.

thȧ·las'siç, *a.* 1. of the sea or ocean; marine.
2. of or pertaining to bays, gulfs, etc. and inland or smaller seas: distinguished from *oceanic*.

thal·ăs·sin'i·ăn, *a.* of or pertaining to the *Thalassinidæ*.

Thal·ăs·sin'i·dae, *n.pl.* a family of burrowing macrurous decapods, noted for the elongation of their abdomen: the typical genus is *Thalassina*, and the most common species is the scorpion lobster, *Thalassina scorpionida*.

thal·ăs·soç'rȧ·cy, *n.* same as *thalassocraty*.

thal·ăs·soç'rȧ·ty, *n.* [Gr. *thalassa*, the sea, and *kratein*, to rule.] dominion of the seas; naval supremacy.

thal·ăs·sog'rȧ·phy, *n.* [Gr. *thalassa*, the sea, and *-graphy*.] oceanography.

thal"ăs·sō·ther'ȧ·py, *n.* [Gr. *thalassa*, the sea; and *therapy*.] the treatment of disease by sea bathing, sea voyages, sea air, etc.

thāle'-çress', *n.* [after Johann *Thal* (1542–1583), a German physician.] the mouse-ear cress, *Sisymbrium thaliana*, a low, slender herb of Europe, naturalized, to some extent in the United States.

thä'lẽr (tä'), *n.*; *pl.* **thä'lẽr,** a taler.

Thȧ·lī'ȧ, *n.* [Gr. *Thaleia*, from *thallein*, to flourish, bloom.] in Greek mythology, (a) the Muse of comedy and pastoral poetry; (b) one the three Graces.

Thȧ·li·ā'cē·ȧ (-shē-), *n.pl.* [from *Thalia*, the Muse, and *-acea*.] an order of tunicates including certain free-swimming pelagic forms.

Thȧ·lī'ăn, *a.* pertaining or relating to Thalia, the Muse of pastoral and comic poetry; hence, [t-] comic.

Thȧ·liç'trum, *n.* [Gr. *thaliktron*, meadow rue, from *thallein*, to bloom, in allusion to the bright color of the young shoots.] a genus of herbs of the family *Ranunculaceæ*, with apetalous flowers borne in panicles or corymbs; the meadow rues.

thal'liç, *a.* designating or of a chemical compound containing thallium with a valence of three; as, *thallic* acid.

thal'li·fọrm, *a.* having the form of a thallus.

thal'line, thal'lin, *n.* an antiseptic crystalline substance derived from coal tar.

thal'line, *a.* pertaining to a thallus; of the character of a thallus.

thal'li·ous, *a.* same as *thallous*.

thal'li·um, *n.* [Gr. *thallos*, a young, green shoot, from the green line it gives in the spectrum, which led to its discovery.] a rare, bluish-white, soft, metallic chemical element, the lightest of the elements having naturally radioactive isotopes: used in making antiknock compound, rat poisons, etc.: symbol, Tl; atomic weight, 204.39; atomic number, 81.

thal'li·um glȧss, a glass of great density and refracting power, in the preparation of which thallium is used instead of lead or potassium.

thăl·lod'iç, *a.* same as *thalloid*.

thal'lō·ġen, *n.* [Gr. *thallos*, a young shoot, a sprout, a frond, and *-gen*.] same as *thallophyte*.

thal·loġ'e·nous, *a.* of or belonging to the thallogens.

thal'loid, *a.* of or resembling a thallus.

thal'lōme, *n.* a thallus. [Rare.]

Thăl·loph'y·tȧ, *n.pl.* [Gr. *thallos*, a young shoot, and *phyton*, a plant.] a primary division of plants including all forms consisting of one cell and cell aggregates not clearly differentiated into root, stem, and leaf, including bacteria, algae, fungi, and lichens.

thal'lō·phȳte, *n.* any plant of the division *Thallophyta*.

thal·lō·phyt'iç, *a.* of or pertaining to the *Thallophyta*.

thal'lōse, *a.* same as *thalloid*.

thal'lous, *a.* of or pertaining to a chemical compound containing thallium with a valence of one.

thal'lus, *n.*; *pl.* **thal'lī, thal'lus·eṣ,** [Mod. L.; Gr. *thallos*, a young shoot, a sprout, a frond.] the plant body of a thallophyte, showing no clear distinction of roots, stem, or leaves.

THALLUS OF LICHEN (*Parmella pityrea*) *t*, thallus; *a*, apothecia

thăl'weġ (täl'väk), *n.* [G.] a line on a topographical surface having everywhere the direction of greatest slope, and distinguished by having the lines of straight horizontal projection which cut all contours at right angles.

Tham'muz (tä'mooz), *n.* same as *Tammuz*.

tham'nō·phile, *n.* a member of the subfamily *Thamnophilinæ*.

Tham"nō·phi·lī'nae, *n.pl.* the American ant shrikes; a subfamily of *Formicariidæ*, with ten genera, from the forest districts of equatorial America.

Tham·noph'i·lus, *n.* [Gr. *thamnos*, a thicket, and *philein*, to love.] the type genus of *Thamnophilinæ*, with more than fifty species, from tropical America.

than, *conj.* [ME. *than*, *thene*, *thonne*; AS. *thenne thanne*, *thonne*, than, then, the latter being the original meaning.]
1. a particle used to introduce the second element in a comparison, following an adjective or adverb in the comparative degree; as, I am taller *than* Bruce, we arrived earlier *than* they did.
2. a particle used to express exception, following an adjective or adverb; as, it was none other *than* Sam.

than, *prep.* compared to: used only in the phrases *than whom*, *than which*; as, a writer *than whom* there is none finer.

A tragedy *than which*, since the days of the ancients, there had been nothing more classic or elegant. —Thackeray.

than, *adv.* then. [Obs.]

thān'āġe, *n.* 1. the land held by a thane; also, the tenure of such holding.
2. the dignity, office, or jurisdiction of a thane.

than'ȧ·tō-, [from Gr. *thanatos*, death.] a combining form meaning *death*, as in *thanato*phobia: also, before a vowel, *thanat-*.

than'ȧ·toid, *a.* 1. similar to death.
2. deadly, as a poisonous serpent.

than·ȧ·tol'ō·ġy, *n.* the study of death, especially of the medical, psychological, and social problems associated with dying.

than"ȧ·tō·phid'i·ȧ, *n.pl.* [*thanato-*, and Gr. *ophis*, serpent.] poisonous snakes.

than"ȧ·tō·phō'bi·ȧ, *n.* an abnormally great fear of death.

than·ȧ·top'sis, *n.* [Mod L.; *thanat-* and *-opsis*.] a view of or meditation on death.

Than'ȧ·tos, *n.* [Gr.] in Greek mythology, death personified.

thāne, *n.* [ME. *thein*, *theign*; AS. *thegen*, *thegn*, a soldier, a servant of the king, a minister, a nobleman.]
1. among the Anglo-Saxons and Scandinavians in early England, a member of a class of freemen who held land of the king or a lord in return for military services, and who corresponded to the later knights and barons.
2. in early Scotland, a person of rank who held land of the king; any chief of a clan who became a baron under the king.
Also spelled *thegn*.

thāne'dŏm, *n.* the property or jurisdiction of a thane; also, the judicial power of a thane.

thāne'hood, *n.* the office, dignity, or character of a thane; also, the collective body of thanes.

thāne'land, *n.* land granted to a thane and over which a thane had jurisdiction.

thāne'ship, *n.* the state or dignity of a thane.

thaṅk, *v.t.*; thanked (thaṅkt), *pt.*, *pp.*; thanking, *ppr.* [ME. *thankien*; AS. *thancian*.]
1. to give one's thanks to; to express appreciation or gratitude to.
2. to hold responsible; to blame: an ironic use, as, he can be *thanked* for our failure.
to have oneself to thank; to be oneself the agent or cause of (something unpleasant).

thaṅk'ẽr, *n.* one who gives thanks.

thaṅk'fụl, *a.* 1. impressed with a sense of kindness received, and ready to acknowledge it; grateful.

Be *thankful* unto him, and bless his name. —Ps. c. 4.

As I am a gentleman, I will live to be *thankful* to thee for't. —Shak.
2. expressive of or by way of thanks; as, a *thankful* sacrifice.
3. claiming or deserving thanks; meritorious. [Obs.]

thañk'ful·ly, *adv.* in a thankful manner.

thañk'ful·ness, *n.* the state or quality of being thankful.

thañk'less, *a.* 1. not thankful; ungrateful; not feeling or expressing thanks; not acknowledging favors.
How sharper than a serpent's tooth it is
To have a *thankless* child. —Shak.
2. not obtaining, deserving, or likely to gain thanks; unappreciated; as, a *thankless* task.

thañk'less·ly, *adv.* in a thankless manner.

thañk'less·ness, *n.* the state or quality of being thankless.

thañk of'fẽr·ing, an offering made as an expression of thanks or gratitude; an offering for benefits received; a peace offering.

thañks, *n.pl.* [pl. of ME. *thank, thanc*; AS. *thanc, thonc*, thanks.] an expression of gratitude; grateful acknowledgment of something received by or done for one.
thanks to; (a) thanks be given to; (b) on account of.

thañks, *interj.* I thank you.

thañks·give', *v.t.* to celebrate in token of thankfulness. [Rare.]

thañks·giv'ẽr, *n.* one who gives thanks or acknowledges a kindness.

thañks·giv'ing, *n.* 1. a giving of thanks.
2. an expression of this.
3. a formal, often public, expression of thanks to God in the form of a prayer, etc.
4. [T-] an annual United States holiday, the fourth Thursday of November, instituted by the Pilgrims to give thanks to God for their survival: in full, *Thanksgiving Day*.
General Thanksgiving; in the Book of Common Prayer, a form of thanks prescribed for the ordinary blessings of life.

thañk'wŏr″thi·ness, *n.* the state of being thankworthy.

thañk'wŏr″thy, *a.* deserving thanks; meritorious; as, a very *thankworthy* labor.

thañk'-yöu (-ū), *n.* same as *thanks.*

thañk'-yöu-ma'am, *n.* a ridge or furrow made across a sloping road so as to deflect water or melting snow that would otherwise follow the track and spoil the road: so called in humorous allusion to its causing a person to bow in riding over it: also written *thank-you-mam.* [Colloq.]

Thap'si·ȧ, *n.* [Gr. *thapsia*, a plant from the island of Thapsos; used as a yellow dye.]
1. a genus of umbelliferous plants, of the countries of the Mediterranean. *Thapsia silphium*, native to the north of Africa, is supposed to be the plant which produced the deadly carrot of the ancients.
2. [t-] any plant of this genus.

thär, *n.* [E. Ind.] a species of antelope, *Hemitragus jemlahicus*, found in Nepal.

thär, *adv.* there. [Obs.]

thär, thärf, *v.i.* to need. [Obs.]

thärf, *a.* unleavened. [Brit. Dial.]

thärm, *n.* [AS. *thearm.*] an intestine; a gut. [Obs.]

thā'ros, *n.* a small American butterfly, *Phyciodes tharos*, having orange wings spotted with black and white.

Thas'pi·um, *n.* a genus of umbelliferous plants including the meadow parsnip.

that, *pron.*; *pl.* **thōse,** [AS. *thæt*, neut. of the demonstrative and def. art. *se*, also *the* (masc.), *seo* (f.), *thæt* (neut.); Goth. *sa, so, thata*; Ice. *that*; Sans. *sa, sā, tat.*]
In senses 1–4, *that* is used as a demonstrative pronoun; in senses 5–7, *that* is used as a relative pronoun.
1. the person or thing mentioned or understood; as, *that* is John, *that* tastes good.
2. the thing farther away: distinguished from *this*; as, I can see this more clearly than *that.*
3. one of two things which are compared or contrasted, as contradistinguished from *this*; as, of the two possibilities, this is more likely than *that.*
4. that which; as, have you *that* I ordered? [Archaic.]
5. who, whom, or which: used generally in restrictive clauses (e.g., the road *that* we took) and often omitted (e.g., the road we took).
6. where; at which; on which; as, the place *that* I saw him.
7. when; in which; on which; as, the year *that* he was born.
at that; (a) at that point; with no further discussion, etc.; (b) all things considered; even so. [Colloq.]
that's that!; that is done (or settled or decided, etc.)!

that, *a.* 1. designating the person or thing mentioned or understood; as, *that* man is John, *that* pie tastes good.
2. designating the thing farther away: distinguished from *this*; as, I can see this house more clearly than *that* one across the street.
3. designating one of two things that are compared or contrasted, as contradistinguished from *this*; as, of the two, this possibility is more likely than *that* one.
4. designating something or someone that is not described but that is well known or easily recognizable: sometimes with implications of disparagement; as, *that* certain feeling, there comes *that* smile!; *that* George!

that, *conj.* 1. used to introduce a noun clause; as, *that* he's gone is obvious, the truth was *that* we never saw him.
2. used to introduce a clause expressing purpose; as, they died *that* we might live.
3. used to introduce a clause expressing result; as, he ran so fast *that* I couldn't catch up.
4. used to introduce a clause expressing cause; as, I'm sorry *that* I caused you such annoyance.
5. used to introduce an elliptical sentence expressing surprise, indignation, or desire; as, *that* he should say such a thing!; oh, *that* this day were over!
6. used to supply the place of another conjunction in the second part of a clause. [Archaic.]
7. added to other conjunctions and adverbs without modifying their sense. [Archaic.]
After that the holy rites are ended. —Shak.
in that; for the reason that; seeing that; because.

that, *adv.* 1. to that extent; so; as, I can't see *that* far ahead: also used colloquially before an adjective modified by a clause of result; as, I'm *that* tired I could drop.
2. very; so very: used in negative constructions; as, I didn't like the book *that* much. [Colloq.]

thatch, *n.* [altered (after the v.), from older *thack*; ME. *thac*; AS. *thæc*, a thatch, roof.]
1. a roof or roofing of straw, rushes, palm leaves, etc.
2. material for such a roof.
3. any of a number of palms whose leaves are used for thatch: also *thatch palm.*
4. the hair growing on the head.

thatch, *v.t.*; thatched (thacht), *pt., pp.*; thatching, *ppr.* [ME. *thecchen*; AS. *thecc(e)an.*] to cover with or as with thatch.

thatch'ẽr, *n.* one whose occupation is to thatch.

thatch'ing, *n.* 1. the act or art of covering buildings with thatch.
2. the materials used for this purpose.

thatch pälm, any palm having leaves suitable for thatching, as *Sabal umbraculifera*, the royal palmetto.

thatch tree, any thatch palm.

thatch'y, *a.*; *comp.* thatchier; *superl.* thatchiest, of or like thatch.

thau'mȧ·site, *n.* [Gr. *thaumazein*, to be surprised, and *-ite.*] an amorphous mineral consisting of calcium sulfate, carbonate, and silicate with water.

thau·mȧ·tol'ȧ·try, *n.* idolatry of wonders or marvelous things. [Rare.]

thau·mȧ·tol'ō·gy, *n.* [from Gr. *thauma, thaumatos*, a miracle, wonder; and *-logy.*] the study or lore of miracles.

thau'mȧ·trōpe, *n.* [Gr. *thauma, thaumatos*, a wonder, and *tropos*, a turning.] a device consisting of a card with different designs on either side, which, when the card is twirled, appear to blend into one: it demonstrates the persistence of vision.

thau'mȧ·tūrge, *n.* [Fr.; ML. *thaumaturgus*; Gr. *thaumaturgos*, working wonders, from *thauma*, a wonder, and *-ergos*, working.] a conjurer or magician; one who supposedly performs miraculous feats.

thau·mȧ·tūr'gic, thau·mȧ·tūr'gi·căl, *a.* of or involving thaumaturgy; of a nature to excite wonder; miraculous.

thau·mȧ·tūr'gics, *n.pl.* feats performed by conjurers, magicians, prestidigitators, etc.

thau'mȧ·tūr·gist, *n.* a thaumaturge, especially a magician.

thau·mȧ·tūr'gus, *n.*; *pl.* **thau·mȧ·tūr'gī,** a miracle worker: a title given to some of the saints specially noted for working miracles.

thau'mȧ·tūr·gy, *n.* [Gr. *thaumatourgia*, from *thauma (-atos)*, a wonder, and *ergon*, work.] the supposed working of miracles; magic.

thaw, *v.i.*; thawed (thad), *pt., pp.*; thawing, *ppr.* [AS. *thawian.*]
1. (a) to melt; to become liquid or semiliquid, as ice, snow, etc.; (b) to pass to an unfrozen state: said of frozen foods.
2. to have its contents melt; as, our water pipe hasn't *thawed.*
3. to rise above freezing, so that snow, etc. melts: with the impersonal *it*, in reference to the weather; as, *it* will *thaw* tomorrow.
4. to lose one's coldness or reserve of manner.
Syn.—melt, dissolve, fuse, liquefy.

thaw, *v.t.* to cause to thaw.

thaw, *n.* 1. a thawing; the melting of ice or snow.
2. a spell of weather warm enough to allow thawing.
3. a becoming less reserved in manner.

thaw'y, *a.* having a tendency to thaw. [Colloq.]

the (thu; *before vowels*, thi), *a., def. art.* [ME. indeclinable article, from AS. *se* (nom. masc. article) with *th-*, from other AS. case and gender forms (*thone, thæs, thære, thæm, thy*); the meaning is controlled by the basic notion "a previously recognized, noticed, or encountered" in distinction to *a, an.*]
1. that (one) being spoken of or already mentioned; as, *the* story ended.
2. that (one) which is present, close, nearby, etc., as distinguished from all others, which are considered remote; as, *the* day just started, *the* heat is oppressive.
3. that (one) designated or identified, as by a title; as, *the* President (of the United States), *the* Mississippi (River).
4. that (one) considered outstanding, most fashionable, etc.; as, that's *the* restaurant in town: usually given special emphasis when spoken and italicized when printed.
5. that (one) belonging to a person previously mentioned; as, take me by *the* hand, rub into *the* face: equivalent to *your, his, her, my, our, one's*, etc.
6. that (one) considered as a unit of purchase, etc.; as, at five dollars *the* half ton: equivalent to *a, per, each*, etc.
7. that (one) who has a specific family relationship to one; as, *the* wife, *the* kid sister. [Colloq.]
In the preceding senses, *the* (as opposed to *a, an*) is used to refer to a particular person, thing, or group.
8. *the* is used to refer to that one of a number of persons or things which is identified by a modifier, as by (a) an attributive adjective; as, *the* front door; (b) a relative clause; as, "ask *the* man who owns one"; (c) a prepositional phrase; as, *the* hit of the week; (d) an infinitive phrase; as, *the* right to strike; (e) a participle; as, follow *the* directions given.
9. *the* is used to refer to a person or thing considered generically or universally, as (a) one taken as a representative of the entire genus or type; as, he learned to use *the* typewriter; *the* cow is a domestic animal; (b) an adjective used substantively; as, none but *the* brave deserves *the* fair.

the, *adv.* 1. that much; to that extent; as, *the* better to see you with.
2. by how much . . . by that much; to what extent . . . to that extent: used in a correlative construction expressing comparison; as, *the* sooner the better.

Thē'ȧ, *n.* [LL., from Chinese *tcha.*] a genus of trees and shrubs of the tea family, that includes the species yielding the tea of commerce.

thē·ā'ceous, *a.* [from Mod. L. *Theaceæ*, name of the family, from *Thea*, generic name, after Gr. *thea*, goddess (as being a divine herb), but from source of Eng. *tea.*] of the tea family of trees and shrubs, having five-petaled flowers and dry or fleshy fruit.

thē·an'dric, *a.* [Gr. *theos*, god, and *anēr, andros*, man.] relating to or existing by the union of divine and human operation in Christ, or the joint agency of the divine and human nature.

thē·an·throp'ic, thē·an·throp'i·căl, *a.* [Gr. *theos*, god, and *anthrōpos*, man.] having or of a nature both divine and human.

thē·an'thrō·pism, *n.* 1. a state of being God and man. [Rare.]
2. (a) the attributing of human characteristics to God or gods; anthropomorphism;

(b) belief in a theanthropic being or beings.
3. the theological doctrine of the union of divine and human natures in Jesus Christ.

thē·an′thrō·pist, *n.* a believer in theanthropism.

thē·an′thrō·py, *n.* theanthropism.

thē·är′çhiç, *a.* divinely sovereign or supreme. [Rare.]

thē′är·çhy, *n.*; *pl.* **thē′är·çhies,** [Gr. *theos*, god, and *archē*, rule.]
1. government by God or gods; theocracy.
2. a body of divine rulers; an order or system of ruling gods or deities.

thē′à·tēr, thē′à·tre, *n.* [Fr. *théâtre*, from L. *theatrum*, from Gr. *theatron*, theater, from *thea*, a view, sight.]
1. a place where plays, operas, motion pictures, etc. are presented; especially, a building expressly designed for such presentations. The Greek and Roman theaters very closely resembled each other. The building was of an oblong, semicircular form, resembling the half of an amphitheater, and was not covered by a roof. The seats were all concentric with the orchestra and arranged in ascending rows.

ROMAN THEATER

2. any place resembling a theater, especially one having ascending rows of seats, as a lecture hall, surgical clinic, etc.
3. any place where events take place; scene of operations; as, the Pacific *theater* of war.
4. (a) the dramatic art; drama; (b) the theatrical world; people engaged in theatrical activity.
5. theatrical technique, production, etc. with reference to its effectiveness; as, the play was good *theater*.

thē′à·tēr·gō″ēr, thē′à·tre·gō″ēr, *n.* a person who goes to the theater, especially one who goes habitually.

thē′à·tēr·gō″ing, thē′à·tre·gō″ing, *n.* the practice of going to the theater, especially habitually.

thē′à·tēr of the ab·sūrd′, unconventional, mid-20th-century drama made up of apparently absurd, incongruous, or pointless situations and dialogue, typically expressing man's self-isolation, anxiety, frustration, etc.

thē′à·tēr pär′ty, a form of entertainment in which the guests attend a theater in a party, sometimes preceded or followed by a dinner.

Thē′à·tine, Thē′à·tin, *n.* [LL. *Theatinus*, from a place in Italy.]
1. one of an order of Italian monks, established, in 1524, expressly to oppose the Reformation, and to raise the tone of piety among Roman Catholics. They hold no property, nor do they beg, but depend on voluntary contributions.
2. one of a corresponding order of nuns.

thē′à·trăl, *a.* belonging to a theater. [Obs.]

thē·at′riç, *a.* theatrical.

thē·at′ri·căl, *a.* [LL. *theatricus*; Gr. *theatrikos*.]
1. having to do with the theater, the drama, a play, actors, etc.
2. characteristic of the theater; dramatic; histrionic; especially (in disparagement), melodramatic; pompous; affected.
Syn.—dramatic, scenic, showy, melodramatic, pompous.

thē·at′ri·căl·ism, *n.* theatrical style, manner, etc.; especially, affectation, show, etc.

thē·at·ri·cal′i·ty, *n.* the quality or state of being theatrical; theatricalism.

thē·at·ri·căl·i·zā′tion, *n.* a theatricalizing or being theatricalized.

thē·at′ri·căl·ize, *v.t.*; theatricalized, *pt.*, *pp.*; theatricalizing, *ppr.* 1. to make theatrical; give a dramatic, sometimes overly dramatic, quality to.
2. to put in a theatrical setting.

thē·at′ri·căl·ly, *adv.* in a theatrical manner.

thē·at′ri·căl·ness, *n.* same as *theatricality*.

thē·at′riç·ăls, *n.pl.* performances of stage plays, especially by amateurs.

thē·at′riçs, *n.pl.* [*construed as sing.*] the art of the theater.

thēave, *n.* [W. *dafad*, a sheep, a ewe.] a ewe of the first year. [Brit. Dial.]

Thē·bā′iç, *a.* of Thebes in Egypt.

Thē′bā·id, *n.* [L. *Thebais*, *Thebaidis*, from *Thebae*, Thebes, name of two ancient cities, one in Egypt, the other in Boeotia.] a poem about the siege of Boeotian Thebes, especially an epic by the Latin poet Statius (1st century A.D.).

thē′bà·in, *n.* thebaine.

thē′bà·ine, *n.* [L. *Thebæ*, Thebes, Egypt; and *-ine*.] a crystalline, colorless, poisonous, and anodyne alkaloid, $C_{19}H_{21}NO_3$, obtained from opium, having properties similar to those of strychnine, and used in medicine.

thē′bà·ism, *n.* the habitual use of opium, or its consequences.

Thē′băn, *a.* of or relating to Thebes in Greece or Thebes in Egypt.
Theban year; in ancient chronology, the Egyptian year of 365 days and six hours.

Thē′băn, *n.* a native or inhabitant of Thebes in Greece or Thebes in Egypt.

Thē·bē′siăn, *a.* pertaining to or named after Thebesius, a German anatomist of the eighteenth century; as, the *Thebesian* valve; *Thebesian* veins.

thē′çà, *n.*; *pl.* **thē′cae,** [L., from Gr. *thēkē*, a case.]
1. in botany, a spore case, sac, or capsule, as of ferns, mosses, and other cryptogamic plants.
2. any sac enclosing an organ or a whole organism, as (a) in anatomy, the strong fibrous sheaths in which certain soft parts of the body are enclosed, as the canal of the vertebral column; (b) in zoology, a calicle, as of a coral; the covering of an insect pupa, etc.

thē·çà·glos′sāte, *a.* same as *thecoglossate*.

thē′çăl, *a.* of, pertaining to, or of the nature of a theca.

thē′çà·phōre, *n.* in botany, (a) the stalk of an ovary; specifically, the long stalk supporting the ovary in *Passiflora*, etc.; (b) a surface or receptacle bearing a theca or thecae.

thē·çà·spō′răl, *a.* thecasporous.

thē′çà·spōre, *n.* in botany, an ascospore.

thē·çà·spō′rous, *a.* of or pertaining to fungi which have their spores in thecae.

Thē·çā′tà, *n.pl.* same as *Thecophora*.

thē′çāte, *a.* enclosed by or furnished with a theca; sheathed.

thē·cif′ēr·ous, *a.* bearing thecae.

thē′ci·form, *a.* having the shape of a theca.

thē·cī′tis, *n.* [Gr. *thēkē*, a case, and *-itis*.] inflammation of the sheath of a tendon.

Theç′là, *n.* [*Thecla*, a woman's name.]
1. a genus of diurnal lepidopterous insects; the hairstreaks.
2. [t–] a butterfly of this genus.

thē·çō·daç′tyl, thē·çō·daç′tyle, *n.* [Gr. *thēkē*, case, and *daktylos*, a finger.] any one of the geckos which has the toes widened throughout, and is furnished beneath with transverse scales divided by a deep longitudinal furrow, in which the claw may be concealed.

thē·çō·daç′tyl, thē·çō·daç′tyle, *a.* having the characteristics of a thecodactyl.

thē·cō·daç′tyl·ous, *a.* thecodactyl.

thē′çō·dont, *a.* [Gr. *thēkē*, a case, and *odous* (*-ontos*), tooth.] of or pertaining to the *Thecodontia*; having the teeth implanted in a bony socket.

thē′çō·dont, *n.* any member of the *Thecodontia*.

Thē·çō·don′ti·à (-shi-), *n.pl.* a group of extinct saurians with thecodont dentition and biconcave vertebrae.

thē·çō·glos′sāte, *a.* [Gr. *thēkē*, case, and *glōssa*, tongue.] pertaining to the *Thecoglossæ*, a group of lizards including the agamas, having a smooth sheathed tongue.

Thē·çoph′ō·rà, *n.pl.* [Gr. *thēkē*, a case, and *-phoros*, bearing.] a group of hydroids having hydranths in thecae and the sexual zooids protected by gonangia.

Thē·çō·sō′mà·tà, *n.pl.* [Gr. *thēkē*, a case, and *sōma*, body.] a formerly recognized group of pteropodous mollusks having the body protected by an external shell, and the organ of respiration contained within a mantle cavity.

thē·çō·sō′mà·tous, thē·çō·sō′māte, *a.* pertaining to the *Thecosomata*.

thé dan·sant′ (tā däṅ-säṅ′), *n.*; *pl.* **thés dan·sant′** (tā däṅ-säṅ′), [Fr., from *thé*, tea, and *dansant*, ppr. of *danser*, to dance.] a tea dance.

thee, *pron.* [ME. and AS. *the*, dat. and acc. of *thu*, thou.] the objective case of *thou*: also used in place of thou by Friends (Quakers) with the verb in the third person singular; as, *thee* speaks harshly.

thee, *v.i.* [AS. *theón*.] to thrive; to prosper. [Obs.]

thee′lin, *n.* [from Gr. *thēlys*, female; and *-in*.] in biochemistry, estrone, a female sex hormone.

thee′lōl, *n.* estriol, a female sex hormone.

theet′see, *n.* [Burma.] the black-varnish tree, *Melanorrhœa usitata* or *usitatissima*.

thee′zăn tēa, a shrubby Eastern plant of the genus *Sageretia*: its leaves are sometimes used in place of tea.

theft, *n.* [ME. *thefte*, *thiefthe*; AS. *theófth*, *thȳfth*. Final *th* became *t*, as in *height*.]
1. the act or instance of stealing; larceny.
2. something stolen. [Obs.]

thegn (thān), same as *thane*.

thē′i·form, *a.* having the form of tea.

thē′ine, thē′in, *n.* [Fr. *théine*, from *thé*, tea.] caffeine, especially as found in tea.

their (thār), *pron.* [ME. *their*, *theyr*, from ON. *theirra*, genit. pl. of the demonstrative pron. replacing ME. *here*, AS. *hira*.] possessive form of they.

their, *possessive pronominal adj.* of, belonging to, or done by them.

theirs (thārz), *pron.* [*their*, and *-s* by analogy with *his*.] that or those belonging to them: the absolute form of *their*, used without a following noun, often after *of*, as, a friend *of theirs*, that book is *theirs*, *theirs* are better.

thē′ism, *n.* [from Gr. *theos*, god; and *-ism*.]
1. belief in the existence of a god or gods.
2. belief in one God; monotheism: opposed to *pantheism*, *polytheism*.
3. belief in one God who is creator and ruler of the universe and known by revelation: distinguished from *deism*.

thē′ism, *n.* the ill effect of habitual excess in tea drinking.

thē′ist, *n.* one who believes in theism.

thē′ist, *a.* same as *theistic*.

thē·is′tiç, thē·is′ti·căl, *a.* pertaining to theism, or to a theist.

thē·is′ti·cal·ly, *adv.* according to theistic doctrine.

thē·lī′tis, *n.* [Mod. L., from Gr. *thēlē*, nipple; and *-itis*.] inflammation of the nipple.

Thel·phū′sà, *n.* a genus of fresh-water crabs, typical of the family *Thelphusidæ*, as the river crab, *Thelphusa depressa*, from southeastern Europe.

thel·phū′si·ăn, *a.* of or pertaining to the genus *Thelphusa* or the family *Thelphusidæ*.

thel·phū′si·ăn, *n.* a river crab of the genus *Thelphusa* or family *Thelphusidæ*.

Thel·phū′si·dae, *n.pl.* [*Thelphusa*, a city in Arcadia.] a family of brachyural crustaceans of which the *Thelphusa* is the typical genus. Most of the species are tropical or subtropical and live in or on the banks of rivers.

thel′y·blast, *n.* [Gr. *thēlys*, female, and *blastos*, germ.] the active element of the female generative cell.

Thel·y·phon′i·dae, *n.pl.* [Gr. *thēlys*, a female, and *phonos*, murder.] a family of arachnids, closely resembling the true spiders.

thē·lyt′ō·kous, *a.* [Gr. *thēlys*, a female, and *tekein*, to produce.] of or relating to a form of parthenogenetic reproduction from which females only are produced.

them, *pron.* [ME. *theim*; ON. *theim*.] the objective case of *they*: also used colloquially as a predicate complement with a linking verb (e.g., that's *them*).

thē′mà, *n.*; *pl.* **thē′mà·tà,** [LL., from Gr. *thema*, a theme.] a thesis.

thē·mat′iç, *a.* of, relating to, or consisting of a theme or themes.
thematic catalogue; in music, a catalogue of musical works, giving not only their titles, but also, in musical notation, their opening themes, and sometimes also the opening themes of their several movements.

thē·mat′i·căl·ly, *adv.* 1. in or by means of a theme or themes.
2. by the nature of its theme or themes.

thē′mà·tist, *n.* a writer of themes.

thēme, *n.* [ME. and OFr. *teme*; L. *thema*; Gr. *thema*, what is laid down.]
1. a subject or topic on which a person writes or speaks; anything proposed as a subject of discussion or discourse; as, the speaker made education his *theme*.

2. a short essay, especially one composed by a student on a given subject, as a school or college exercise.

3. that which is said or thought on a given subject; discourse. [Obs.]

4. the base or stem of a word to which the inflectional endings are added.

5. the means or instrument by which a thing is done. [Obs.]

6. a short, melodic series of notes constituting the subject of a musical composition or a phrase upon which variations are developed.

7. in radio, etc., a theme song, or signature.

8. a division for the purpose of provincial administration under the Byzantine Empire. There were twenty-nine themes, twelve in Europe and seventeen in Asia.

theme pärk, an amusement park built around some central theme, as a land of fantasy, future world, or past age.

thēme sọng, 1. a song repeated several times during a musical play or motion picture and popularly associated with it: it is often intended to set the mood of the dramatic theme.

2. in radio, etc., a song or tune used to identify a program, performer, etc.; a signature.

Thē′mis, *n.* [Gr.] 1. in Greek mythology, a goddess of law and justice, daughter of Uranus and Gaea: represented as holding aloft a scale for weighing opposing claims.

2. in astronomy, one of the asteroids, discovered by De Gasparis, in 1853.

Thē·mis′ti·ănş, *n.pl.* same as *Agnoetae*, sense 2.

them·selveş′, *pron.* [Late (Northern) ME. *thaim selfe* for ME. *hemselve(n)*, and *-s* pl. suffix.] a form of the third person plural pronoun, used: (a) as an intensive; as, they went *themselves*; (b) as a reflexive; as, they hurt *themselves*.

then, *adv.* [AS. *thænne, thanne, thonne*, then, an acc. form belonging to the pronominal stem *the, thæt*, correlative to *hwanne*, when.]

1. at that time; as, we were young *then*, *then* I shall go.

2. soon afterward; next in time; as, he got up, took his hat, and *then* left.

3. next in order; as, first there is Fred's desk, *then* there is David's.

4. in that case; therefore; accordingly; as, if he read it, *then* he knows; do it your own way, *then*.

5. besides; moreover; as, but I like to walk, and *then* it's cheaper.

6. at another time: used as a correlative with *now, sometimes*, etc., as, now she's sullen, *then* gay.

but then; but on the other hand; but at the same time.

then and there; at that time and in that place; at once.

what then? what would happen in that case?

then, *a.* of that time; being such at that time; as, the *then* director.

then, *n.* that time; as, by *then*, they were gone.

then, *conj.* than. [Obs.]

then′ȧ·dāyş, *adv.* in those days; in time past; then.

thē′när, thē′năl, *a.* of or pertaining to a thenar; as, the *thenar* muscle; the *thenar* eminence or the ball of the thumb.

thē′när, *n.* [Mod. L.; Gr. *thenar*, the palm.]

1. the palm of the hand or, sometimes, the sole of the foot.

2. the fleshy bulge at the base of the thumb.

thē·närd′īte, *n.* [after L. J. Thénard (1777–1857), Fr. chemist.] in mineralogy, anhydrous sulfate of sodium, occurring in crystalline coatings at the bottom of some salt lakes.

thence, *adv.* [ME. *thens, thennes, thannes*, from AS. *thanan, thonon*, thence, with change of suffix, the suffix *es* being a genitive termination, as in *hence, whence*.]

1. from that place; therefrom; as, he went to breakfast and *thence* to work.

2. from that time; after that time; thenceforth.

3. for that reason; from that source; therefore.

4. formerly, elsewhere; absent.

thence″fōrth′, *adv.* from that time forward; thereafter; as, he was *thenceforth* an outcast.

from thenceforth; from thenceforth: a pleonasm.

thence″fọr′wărd, thence″fọr′wărdş, *adv.* from that time onward; thenceforth.

thence″from′, *adv.* from that place. [Archaic.]

thē′ō-, [from Gr. *theos*, god.] a combining form meaning *a god* or *God*, as in *theo*centric: also, before a vowel, *the-*.

Thē·ō·brō′ma, *n.* [LL., from Gr. *theos*, god, and *brōma*, food.]

1. a genus of plants of the family *Sterculiaceæ*. They are small trees with large simple leaves, with the flowers in clusters, and are all of them native to South America. The most important species is *Theobroma cacao*, the common cacao or chocolate-nut tree.

2. [t–] a plant of this genus.

thē·ō·brō′miç, *a.* relating to or derived from *Theobroma cacao*; as, *theobromic* acid, a waxy, crystalline acid found in peanuts and cacao butter.

thē·ō·brō′mine, thē·ō·brō′min, *n.* [from *theobroma* and *-ine*.] a bitter crystalline alkaloid, $C_7H_8O_2N_4$, extracted from the leaves and seeds of *Theobroma cacao*, used in medicine as a diuretic and nerve stimulant: it is related to theophylline and caffeine.

thē·ō·cen′triç, *a.* holding God as its center or center of interest.

thē·oç′rȧ·cy, *n.*; *pl.* **thē·oç′rȧ·cieş,** [Gr. *theokratia*; *theos*, god, and *kratein*, to rule, from *kratos*, strength.]

1. literally, the rule of a state by God or a god.

2. government by priests claiming to rule with divine authority.

3. a country governed in this way.

4. a group of clerics with political power.

thē·oç′rȧ·sy, *n.* [Gr. *theos*, god, and *krasis*, mixture.]

1. the mystic union of the soul with God.

2. polytheism; a mingled worship of two or more gods.

3. a mixture of several deities in one.

thē′ō·crat, *n.* [Gr. *theos*, god, and *kratein*, to rule.]

1. one who believes in or advocates a theocracy.

2. the ruler or one of the rulers in a theocracy.

thē·ō·çrat′iç, thē·ō·çrat′i·căl, *a.* of or under a theocracy; as, the *theocratic* state of the Israelites.

thē·oç′rȧ·tist, *n.* one who believes in the principle of theocracy.

Thē·oç·ri·tē′ăn, *a.* relating to or in the style of Theocritus, the Greek poet of the third century B.C.; pastoral; idyllic; bucolic.

thē″ō·di·cae′ȧ, thē″ō·di·cē′ȧ, *n.* same as *theodicy*.

thē″ō·di·cē′ăn, *a.* of or pertaining to theodicy.

thē·od′i·cy, *n.*; *pl.* **thē·od′i·cieş,** [Gr. *theos*, god, and *dikē*, justice.]

1. a vindication of divine justice in allowing the existence of evil.

2. in philosophy, that branch which treats of the being, perfections, and government of God, and the immortality of the soul.

thē·od′ō·līte, *n.* [perhaps from Gr. *thea*, a seeing, *hodos*, a way, and *litos*, plain, smooth, or from *thea*, and *doulos*, a slave.] a surveying instrument which is a combination of transit and level, used for measuring horizontal and vertical angles.

thē·od·ō·lit′iç, *a.* of, pertaining to, or made by means of a theodolite.

Thē·ō·dō′siăn, *a.* of or pertaining to any one of the name of Theodosius; specifically, to either of the Roman emperors of that name.

Theodosian code; a code of Roman laws, published during the reign of Theodosius II in the first half of the fifth century.

Thē·ō·dō′siăn, *n.* one of a body of Russian dissenters, so named from their leader, Theodosius, a monk of the sixteenth century. Their characteristic belief was that all articles purchased from unbelievers required purification by prayer.

Thē·ō·dō′tiăn, *n.* one of a religious sect in the third century, which denied the divinity of Christ: so called from their leader, Theodotus, of Byzantium.

thē·ō·gon′iç, *a.* of or pertaining to theogony.

thē·og′ō·nişm, *n.* theogony.

thē·og′ō·nist, *n.* one versed in theogony.

thē·og′ō·ny, *n.*; *pl.* **thē·og′ō·nieş,** [Fr. *théogonie*; Gr. *theogonia*; *theos*, god, and *gonos*, generation.] the origin or genealogy of the gods, as told in myths.

thē·ol′ō·gas·tēr, *n.* a quack in theology. [Rare.]

thē·ol′ō·gāte, *n.* the course in theology prescribed by the Roman Catholic Church for students or novices preparing for the priesthood.

thē·ol′ō·ġēr, *n.* a theologian. [Rare.]

thē·ō·lō′ġi·ăn, *n.* a person who is a student of or an authority on theology, especially Christian theology; a professor of or writer on theology.

thē·ō·loġ′i·căl, thē·ō·loġ′iç, *a.* 1. of the nature of or pertaining to theology.

2. of the word of God; of divine revelation; scriptural; specifically, designating the three virtues: faith, hope, and charity.

thē·ō·loġ′i·căl·ly, *adv.* in a theological manner; according to theology.

thē·ō·loġ′içs, *n.* theology. [Rare.]

thē·ol′ō·ġist, *n.* a theologian. [Rare.]

thē″ō·lō·ġī′um, *n.*; *pl.* **thē″ō·lō·ġī′ȧ,** [Gr. *theologeion*, from *theos*, god, and *logeion*, a place for speaking.] in the ancient theater, a small upper stage, where the impersonators of the gods in a play appeared.

thē·ol′ō·ġize, *v.t.*; theologized, *pt.*, *pp.*; theologizing, *ppr.* to put into theological terms; to render theological.

thē·ol′ō·ġize, *v.i.* to speculate theologically; to reason upon or discuss theology.

thē·ol′ō·ġī·zēr, *n.* one who theologizes.

thē′ō·logue (-log), *n.* 1. a theologian. [Rare.]

2. a student of theology. [Colloq.]

thē·ol′ō·ġy, *n.*; *pl.* **thē·ol′ō·ġieş,** [ME. *theologie, teologie*; OFr. *theologie*; L. *theologia*, from Gr. *theologia*; *theos*, god, and *logos*, discourse.]

1. the study of God and the relations between God and the universe; study of religious doctrines and matters of divinity.

2. a specific form or system of this study, as expounded by a particular religion or denomination.

ascetical theology; a system of theology, which teaches that perfection and the practice of the virtues are attained only through asceticism.

Biblical theology; that branch of theology which aims to set forth the knowledge of God and the divine life by means of the Bible as a whole, and not by isolated passages.

dogmatic theology; theology as authoritatively held and taught by the church.

moral theology; see under *moral*, a.

natural theology; see *natural religion* under *natural*.

New England theology; a phase of Calvinism developed in the orthodox Congregational churches of New England.

new theology; a reaction against dogmas and creeds of orthodox Protestant churches, first gaining prominence in the last quarter of the nineteenth century.

polemic theology; the learning and practice involved in defending one system of theology or disputing another, by scientific and philosophical arguments.

rational theology; theology based on opinions deduced from reason.

revealed theology; theology which depends on revelation or the teachings of the Bible for its authority.

speculative theology; theology in which theory predominates over Scripture and all other authority.

systematic theology; a constructive method of theology which aims at a complete, philosophic, and systematic statement of the entire sum of theological knowledge.

thē·om′ȧ·çhist, *n.* one who fights against God or the gods, or one who rebels at carrying out divine commands.

thē·om′ȧ·çhy, *n.*; *pl.* **thē·om′ȧ·çhieş,** [Gr. *theos*, a god, and *machē*, combat.]

1. a fighting against the gods, as the battle of the giants with the gods.

2. opposition to the divine will.

3. a strife or combat among gods.

thē′ō·man·cy, *n.* [Gr. *theos*, a god, and *manteia*, divination.] a kind of divination drawn from the responses of oracles.

thē·ō·mā′ni·ȧ, *n.* [Gr. *theos*, a god, and *mania*, madness.] religious insanity; especially, insanity in which the patient believes himself inspired by or possessed of divinity.

thē·ō·mā′ni·aç, *n.* one who is affected with theomania.

thē·ō·mọr′phiç, *a.* [Gr. *theos*, a god, and *morphē*, form.] having the form, image, or likeness of God or a god.

thē·ō·mọr′phişm, *n.* theomorphic character.

thē″ō·my·thol′ō·ġy, *n.* [Gr. *theos*, a god, and *mythologia*, mythology.] a mixture or combination of theology and mythology; as, the *theomythology* of the Iliad. [Rare.]

Thē·ō·pas′çhite, *n.* [L.Gr. *Theopaschitēs*, from *theos*, a god, and *paschein*, to suffer.] one who believes that God suffered in Christ's crucifixion; a Monophysite.

thē·ō·pas′çhi·tişm, *n.* the doctrine taught by the Theopaschites.

thē″ō·pȧ·thet′iç, thē·ō·path′iç, *a.* pertaining to theopathy.

thē·op′ȧ·thy, *n.*; *pl.* **thē·op′ȧ·thieş,** [Gr. *theos,* a god, and *pathos,* passion.] religious emotion; mystical ecstasy.

thē·ō·phan′iç, *a.* relating to a theophany; making an actual appearance to man, as a god.

thē·oph′ȧ·ny, *n.*; *pl.* **thē·oph′ȧ·nieş,** [Gr. *theos,* god, and *phainesthai,* to appear.]
 1. a supposed manifestation of God or of gods to man by actual appearance.
 2. [T–] the festival of the Epiphany.

thē·ō·phil·ăn·throp′iç, *a.* relating to theophilanthropism or to its adherents.

thē″ō·phi·lan′thrō·pişm, *n.* love of both God and man; the doctrines or tenets of the theophilanthropists: also written *theophilanthropy.*

thē″ō·phi·lan′thrō·pist, *n.* [Gr. *theos,* a god, and *philanthrōpos,* a lover of man.]
 1. one who practices or professes theophilanthropism.
 2. one of a society formed at Paris during the first French revolution. It had for its object to establish a new religion in place of Roman Catholicism, which had been abolished by the Convention. The system of belief thus attempted to be established was pure deism.

thē″ō·phi·lan′thrō·py, *n.* same as *theophilanthropism.*

thē′ō·phile, *n.* [Gr. *theos,* a god, and *philein,* to love.] one who loves or is loved by God.

thē·ō·phil·ō·soph′iç, *a.* combining or pertaining to the combination of theism and philosophy.

Thē·ō·phrō′ni·ănş, *n.pl.* same as *Agnoetae,* sense 1.

thē·ō·phyl′līne, thē·ō·phyl′lin, *n.* [from Mod. L. *thea,* tea, and Gr. *phyllon,* leaf; and *-ine.*] a colorless, crystalline alkaloid, $C_7H_8O_2N_4 \cdot H_2O$, extracted from tea leaves: an isomer of, and used like, theobromine.

thē·op·neū′stiç, thē·op·neūs′ted, *a.* given by inspiration of the Spirit of God. [Rare.]

thē′op·neūs·ty, *n.* [Gr. *theopneustos,* inspired of God, from *theos,* a god, and *pnein,* to breathe.] divine inspiration; the mysterious power which the Divine Spirit exercises in making men know and communicate the revealed truth.

thē·or′bist, *n.* a performer on the theorbo.

thē·or′bō, *n.* [It. *tiorba;* Fr. *théorbe.*] an obsolete musical instrument, very popular in the seventeenth century. It resembled a large lute, but had two heads, to each of which some of the strings were attached.

thē′ō·rem, *n.* [Fr. *théorème,* from Gr. *theōrēma,* from *theōrein,* to look at, to view.]
 1. a propostion that is not self-evident but that can be proved from accepted premises and so is established as a law or principle.
 2. an expression of relations in an equation or formula.
 3. in mathematics and physics, a proposition embodying something to be proved.
 binomial theorem; see under *binomial.*
 universal theorem; a theorem which is applicable to any quantity whatever.

thē′ō·rem, *v.t.* theoremed, *pt., pp.;* theoreming, *ppr.* to reduce to a theorem; to express as a theorem. [Rare.]

thē″ō·rem·at′iç, *a.* pertaining to a theorem; comprised in a theorem; consisting of theorems; as, *theorematic* truth.

thē″ō·rem·at′i·căl, *a.* theorematic.

thē·ō·rem′ȧ·tist, *n.* one who formulates theorems.

thē·ō·rem′iç, *a.* theorematic.

thē·ō·ret′iç, *a.* same as *theoretical.*

thē·ō·ret′iç, *n.* same as *theoretics.*

thē·ō·ret′i·căl, *a.* [LL. *theoreticus;* Gr. *theōrētikos.*]
 1. of or constituting theory.
 2. limited to or based on theory; hypothetical; ideal: opposed to *practical* or *applied.*
 3. tending to theorize; speculative.

thē·ō·ret′i·căl·ly, *adv.* in or by theory; in speculation; speculatively; according to a theory; as, some things appear to be *theoretically* true which are found to be practically false.

thē·ō·re·ti′ciăn, *n.* a person who is a student of or authority on the theory of some art, science, etc.

thē·ō·ret′içs, *n.pl.* [*construed as sing.*] that part of any field of knowledge which deals in theories or speculations.

thē·or′iç, *a.* of or pertaining to the theorica.

thē′ō·riç, *a.* of or pertaining to theory; theoretical. [Obs.]

thē′ō·riç, *n.* speculation; theory. [Obs.]

thē·or′i·çȧ, *n.pl.; sing.* **thē·or′i·çon,** in ancient Greece, public money devoted to the formation of a fund for furnishing to all citizens not absent from Attica the sum of two oboli, the price of seats at the great dramatic festivals.

thē·or′i·căl, *a.* theoric. [Obs.]

thē·or′i·căl·ly, *adv.* theoretically. [Obs.]

thē′ō·rist, *n.* one who forms theories; especially, one who specializes in the theory of some art, science, etc.

thē″ō·ri·zā′tion, *n.* the process or the result of theorizing; the formulation of theories.

thē′ō·rīze, *v.i.;* theorized, *pt., pp.;* theorizing, *ppr.* to form a theory or theories; to speculate.

thē′ō·rīz·ēr, *n.* a theorist.

thē′ō·ry, *n.*; *pl.* **thē′ō·rieş,** [Fr. *théorie,* from L. *theoria,* a theory, from Gr. *theōria,* a looking at, contemplation, speculation, theory.]
 1. originally, a mental viewing; contemplation.
 2. an idea or mental plan of the way to do something.
 3. a systematic statement of principles involved; as, the *theory* of equations in mathematics.
 4. a formulation of apparent relationships or underlying principles of certain observed phenomena which has been verified to some degree: distinguished from *hypothesis.*
 5. that branch of an art or science consisting in a knowledge of its principles and methods rather than in its practice; pure, as opposed to applied, science, etc.
 6. popularly, a mere hypothesis, conjecture, or guess; as, my *theory* is that he never got the letter.
 Syn.—hypothesis, speculation, scheme, ideal.

thē′ō·soph, thē·os′ō·phēr, *n.* a theosophist.

thē·ō·soph′iç, *a.* pertaining to theosophy or theosophists.

thē·ō·soph′i·căl, *a.* theosophic.

thē·os′ō·phişm, *n.* belief in theosophy, or one of its doctrines.

thē·os′ō·phist, *n.* one who believes in theosophy.

thē·os·ō·phis′tiç·ăl, *a.* theosophic.

thē·os′ō·phīze, *v.i.;* theosophized, *pt., pp.;* theosophizing, *ppr.* to practice theosophy.

thē·os′ō·phy, *n.* [ML. *theosophia;* L. Gr. *theosophia,* knowledge of divine things; *theos,* god, and *sophia,* wisdom, from *sophos,* wise.]
 1. any of various philosophies or religious systems that propose to establish direct contact with divine principle through contemplation, revelation, etc. and to gain thereby a spiritual insight superior to empirical knowledge.
 2. [*often* T–] the doctrines and beliefs of a modern sect of this nature that incorporates elements of Buddhism and Brahmanism.

thē·ō·teçh′niç, *a.* pertaining to the action or intervention of the gods; operated or carried on by the gods.

thē′ō·teçh·ny, *n.* [Gr. *theos,* god, and *technē,* art.] the introduction of supernatural beings into any piece of literary composition.

thē·ō·ther′ȧ·py, *n.* [Gr. *theos,* god, and *therapeia,* treatment.] the treatment of disease by prayer and religious exercises.

Thē·ot′ō·ços, *n.* [Gr. *theotokos,* bringing forth or giving birth to a god; *theos,* god, and *tokos,* bringing forth, from *tiktein,* to bring forth.] in theology, the Mother of God: an epithet applied to the Virgin Mary.

Ther·ȧ·peū′tae, *n.pl.* [LL., from Gr. *therapeutēs,* an attendant or servant, from *therapeuein,* to serve.] a mystic Jewish sect of devotees of the first century: so called from the extraordinary purity of their religious worship.

ther·ȧ·peū′tiç, ther·ȧ·peū′ti·căl, *a.* [Gr. *therapeutikos,* from *therapeuein,* to nurse, serve, or cure.]
 1. serving to cure or heal; curative; concerned in discovering and applying remedies for diseases.
 2. of therapeutics.

Ther·ȧ·peū′tiç, *n.* a member of the traditional sect of Therapeutae.

ther·ȧ·peū′ti·căl·ly, *adv.* in a therapeutic manner.

ther·ȧ·peū′tiçs, *n. pl.* [*construed as sing.*] that part of medical science which relates to the treatment and cure of diseases; therapy.

ther·ȧ·peū′tist, *n.* one skilled in therapeutics.

ther′ȧ·pist, *n.* a therapeutist. [Rare.]

ther′ȧ·py, *n.*; *pl.* **ther′ȧ·pieş,** [Mod. L. *therapia;* Gr. *therapeia,* from *therapeuein,* to nurse, cure.]
 1. therapeutics: often used in compounds, as, hydro*therapy.*
 2. therapeutic nature or power.
 maggot therapy; in pathology, treatment with live maggots, usually those of the bluebottle fly, to remove dead tissue in suppurative infections.
 physical therapy; see under *physical.*
 serum therapy; in immunology, the treatment of disease by injection with blood serum from an animal that has been inoculated with the causative agents of the disease.

there (thār), *adv.* [ME. *ther,* there, where; AS. *ther, thær,* there, where.]
 1. at or in that place: often used as an intensive, as, John *there* is a good ball player.

> Darkness *there* might well seem twilight here. —Milton.

 2. toward, to, or into that place; thither; as, go *there.*
 3. at that point in action, speech, etc.; then.
 4. in that matter, respect, etc.; as to that; as, *there* you are wrong.
 5. at the moment; right now; as, *there* goes the whistle.
 There is also used (a) in interjectional phrases of approval, encouragement, etc. (e.g., *there's* a fine fellow!); (b) with pronominal force in impersonal constructions in which the real subject follows the verb (e.g., *there* is very little time, *there* are three men here).
 all there; being prepared for any action. [Slang.]
 here and there; see under *here.*

there, *n.* that place; as, we left *there* at six.

there, *interj. there* is used as an exclamation expressing: (a) defiance, dismay, satisfaction, etc. (e.g., *there,* that's done!); (b) sympathy, concern, etc. (e.g., *there, there!* don't worry).

there′ȧ·bouts″, there′ȧ·bout″, *adv.* 1. near that place.
 2. near that time or point in action, speech, etc.
 3. nearly; near that number, degree, or quantity; as, ten men or *thereabouts.*
 4. concerning that. [Rare.]

there·ȧft′ēr, *adv.* [AS. *thæræfter,* after that.]
 1. after that; afterward.
 2. according to that; accordingly. [Archaic or Rare.]
 3. of or after that sort. [Obs.]

there′ȧ·gain″ (-gen″), *adv.* thereagainst. [Obs.]

there′ȧ·gainst″ (-genst″), *adv.* against or contrary to that; in opposition.

there′ȧ·nent″, *adv.* concerning, or with reference to anything. [Scot.]

there·at′, *adv.* 1. at that place.
 2. at that time; when that occurred.
 3. at that; on that account.

> Every error is a stain to the beauty of nature; for which cause it blusheth *thereat.* —Hooker.

there′ȧ·wāy″, *adv.* 1. away; from that place or direction.
 2. about there or that; thereabouts. [Colloq.]

there″bē·fōre′, *adv.* beforehand; before that time. [Obs.]

there·bȳ′, *adv.* 1. by that; by that means; in consequence of that.
 2. connected with that: used chiefly in expressions such as *thereby hangs a tale.*
 3. thereabouts.
 to come thereby; to come into possession of it.

there·for′, *adv.* for that; for this; for it.

there′fōre, *conj.* and *adv.* for that; for this or that reason; consequently; hence.

> I have married a wife, and *therefore* I cannot come. —Luke xiv. 20.
> He blushes; *therefore* he is guilty. —*Spectator.*

there·from′, *adv.* from this; from that; from it.

there·in′, *adv.* 1. in there; in or into that place or thing.
 2. in that writing, speech, etc.
 3. in that matter, detail, etc.

there·in·ȧft′ēr, *adv.* in the following part (of that document, speech, etc.).

there·in′tö, *adv.* 1. into that place or thing.
 2. into that matter, condition, etc.

ther′e·min, *n.* [after Leo *Theremin* (1896–), Russ. inventor.] an electronic musical instrument whose tone and pitch are controlled by moving the hands through the air varying distances from two projecting antennas: a trade-mark (*Theremin*).

there·of′ (-ov′), *adv.* 1. of that; of it; concerning that or it.
2. from that as a cause, reason, etc.; therefrom.

there·on′, *adv.* 1. on that; concerning that subject, etc.
2. immediately following that; thereupon.

there·out′, *adv.* 1. out of that or this. [Archaic.]
2. without; out of doors. [Obs.]

there′ṣ, there is.

there·thrŏugh′ (-thrö′), *adv.* through that; by that means.

there·tö′, *adv.* 1. to that place, thing, etc.; thereunto.
2. moreover; also; besides; in addition to that. [Archaic or Poet.]

there·tö·fōre′, *adv.* before that time; before that; until then.

there·un′dẽr, *adv.* 1. under that; under it.
2. under that in number; fewer than that.
3. under that title, etc.; by that authority.

there·un·tö′, *adv.* thereto (sense 1).

there·up·on′, *adv.* 1. upon that; concerning that subject, etc.
2. in consequence of that.
3. immediately; promptly; quickly.

there·whīle′ (-hwīl′), *adv.* at the same time; for that time; also, presently. [Obs.]

there·with′, *adv.* 1. with that, this, or it.
2. in addition to that; withal.
3. straightway; thereupon.

there·with·ạl′, *adv.* 1. over and above; besides; with all that or this.
2. at the same time. [Obs.]
3. with that or this; therewith. [Obs.]

thē′ri·aç, *n.* [L. *theriaca*; Gr. *thēriakē*, treacle.] a former antidote for poison, *Theriaca andromachi*, or Venice treacle, a compound of sixty-four drugs, prepared, pulverized, and reduced by means of honey to an electuary.

thē′ri·aç, *a.* theriacal.

thē·rī′ȧ·çȧ, *n.* same as *theriac.*

thē·rī′ȧ·çăl, *a.* pertaining to theriac; medicinal.

thē′ri·ăl, *a.* theriacal. [Rare.]

thē″ri·an·throp′iç, *a.* 1. that combines human and animal form, as the centaur.
2. of religions having therianthropic gods.

thē·ri·od′iç, *a.* malignant.

thē′ri·ō·dont, *a.* belonging or pertaining to the *Theriodontia.*

thē′ri·ō·dont, *n.* any reptile of the *Theriodontia.*

Thē″ri·ō·don′ta, *n.pl.* same as *Theriodontia.*

Thē″ri·ō·don′ti·ȧ (-shi-), *n.pl.* [Gr. *thērion*, a wild beast, and *-odont.*] a group of extinct South African reptiles having turtlelike heads and biconcave vertebrae.

thē″ri·ō·mor′phiç, *a.* [Gr. *thērion*, a wild beast, and *morphē*, form.] conceived of as having the form of an animal: said of gods.

thē″ri·ō·mor′phous, *a.* theriomorphic.

thẽrm, *n.* [Gr. *thermē*, heat; *thermai*, hot baths.]
1. a hot bath; also, a pool of water. [Obs.]
2. in physics, (a) a great calorie or, occasionally, a small calorie; (b) a unit of heat equal to 1,000 great calories; (c) a unit of heat equal to 100,000 B.T.U.'s.
Also spelled *therme.*

thẽrm-, see *thermo-.*

thẽr′mae, *n.pl.* hot springs or baths; specifically, the public baths of the ancient Romans.

thẽrm·aes·thē·si·om′e·tẽr, *n.* same as *thermesthesiometer.*

thẽr′măl, *a.* [Fr. *thermal*, from Gr. *thermē*, heat.]
1. having to do with heat, hot springs, etc.
2. warm or hot.
3. designating or of a loosely knitted material with air spaces for insulation to help retain body heat; as, *thermal* underwear.
thermal capacity; the amount of heat required to raise the temperature of a body one degree.
thermal conductivity; the amount of heat that passes in unit time through a plate whose surfaces differ by one degree in temperature, with unit area and thickness.
thermal diffusion; heat diffusion by radiation, convection, or conduction.
thermal equator; on the earth's surface, the line of greatest heat.
thermal paradox; in physics, an experiment in which a closed beaker of boiling water is removed from the heat to which it has been subjected, and is inverted and made to boil again by the application of cold.
thermal pollution; the discharge of heated liquid or air into lakes, rivers, etc., as by an industry or nuclear power plant, causing such a rise in the water temperature as to affect the life cycles within the water and disrupt the ecological balance.
thermal unit; a heat unit.

thẽr′măl·ly, *adv.* by means of heat.

thẽr″man·es·thē′si·a, thẽr″man·aes·thē′si·ȧ, *n.* same as *thermoanesthesia.*

thẽr·man′ti·dōte, *n.* an East Indian apparatus for producing a current of cool air.

thẽrm·es·thē′si·ȧ, thẽrm·aes·thē′si·ȧ, *n.* [Mod. L.] in physiology, the sense by which heat and cold are perceived; temperature sense.

thẽrm″es·thē·si·om′e·tẽr, *n.* an instrument for measuring sensibility to heat and cold.

thẽr′miç, *a.* [Gr. *thermē*, heat.] of or caused by heat; thermal.
thermic anomaly; the difference between the mean temperature of a place and the average temperature of its parallel of latitude.
thermic fever; sunstroke.

Thẽr·mi·dor′, *n.* [Fr., from Gr. *thermē*, heat, and *dōron*, gift.] the eleventh month (July 19–August 17) of the French Revolutionary Calendar, adopted by the First Republic in 1793.

Thẽr·mi·dō′ri·ăn, *n.* [from the 9th *Thermidor*, when the Reign of Terror ended.] one of those who in 1794 took part in the overthrow of Robespierre and the Jacobins in France.

thẽrm′ī·on, *n.* [*therm-* and *ion.*] an electrically charged particle emitted by an incandescent material: positively charged thermions are called *ions*, and negatively charged, *electrons.*

thẽrm·ī·on′iç, *a.* of or operating by means of thermions.
thermionic current; an electric current caused by directed thermionic emission.
thermionic emission; emission of thermions from a heated cathode, as in a vacuum tube: also called *Richardson effect.*
thermionic rectifier; a vacuum tube rectifier or valve which permits the passage of current in one direction only, using the principle of thermionic emission: usually composed of a heated cathode or electron emitter and a cold anode or electron receiver.
thermionic tube; a vacuum tube which depends on the emission of electrons from a heated cathode for its function.
thermionic valve; an electron tube. [Brit.]

thẽrm·ī·on′içs, *n.pl.* [*construed as sing.*] the study and science of thermionic activity.

thẽr′mit, *n.* a mixture of powdered aluminum and an oxide of iron or other metal, which produces great heat and is used in welding and in incendiary bombs: a trade mark (*Thermit*).

thẽr′mīte, *n.* thermit.

thẽr′mō-, [from Gr. *thermē*, heat.] a combining form meaning: (a) *heat*, as in *thermo*dynamics; (b) *thermoelectric*, as in *thermo*couple. Also, before a vowel, *therm-*.

thẽr″mō·an·es·thē′si·ȧ, thẽr″mō·an·aes·thē′si·ȧ, *n.* [Mod. L.] the lack or loss of the ability to perceive heat and cold: also *thermanesthesia, thermanaesthesia.*

thẽr·mō·bar′ō·grȧph, *n.* a combination of a thermograph and a barograph for determining both the pressure and the temperature of a gas.

thẽr″mō·bȧ·rom′e·tẽr, *n.* 1. a barometric instrument for measuring atmospheric pressure and, hence, altitudes, by the boiling point of water.
2. a siphon barometer that can be adapted for use as a thermometer.

thẽr·mō·çau′tẽr·y, *n.* cauterization by means of a heated wire or point.

thẽr·mō·çhem′iç, *a.* thermochemical.

thẽr·mō·çhem′iç·ăl, *a.* belonging or relating to thermochemistry.

thẽr·mō·çhem′is·try, *n.* the branch of chemistry that deals with the relationship of heat to chemical change.

thẽr′mō·chrō·sy, *n.* [*thermo-*, and Gr. *chrōsis*, a coloring.] the property of being composed, like light, of rays of different refrangibilities, varying in rate or degree of transmission through diathermal substances: said of heat.

thẽr′mō·çou·ple (-kup-l), *n.* a thermoelectric couple for measuring differences in temperature.
thermocouple instrument; an instrument consisting of a thermocouple and a highly sensitive direct-current meter, used in determining various electromotive forces.
thermocouple meter; a meter used to measure voltage or amperage, consisting of one or more thermocouples that are heated by the current to be measured, together with a suitable deflecting instrument which is actuated by the electromotive force of the thermocouple.

thẽr′mō·çũr·rent, *n.* a current, as of electricity, caused by heating a compound circuit consisting of two or more different metals.

thẽr′mō dē·vel′ŏp·ment, in photography, a method for developing negatives in which the time allowed for developing is related to the temperature of the developing solution.

thẽr″mō·dif·fū′ṣion, *n.* diffusion by heat.

thẽr′mō·din, *n.* a white crystalline powder derived from urethane; an antipyretic and analgesic.

thẽr″mō·dȳ·nam′iç, *a.* 1. having to do with thermodynamics.
2. operated by heat converted into motive power.

thẽr″mō·dȳ·nam′içs, *n.pl.* [*construed as sing.*] the science that deals with the relationship of heat and mechanical energy and the conversion of one into the other.

thẽr″mō·ē·leç′triç, *a.* pertaining to thermoelectricity.
thermoelectric couple; a junction of any two bars, wires, etc. of dissimilar metals which will produce thermoelectric current when heated: it is used in temperature measurements, etc.: also *thermoelectric pair.*
thermoelectric multiplier; a thermopile.
thermoelectric pair; a thermoelectric couple.

thẽr″mō·ē·leç′tri·căl, *a.* thermoelectric.

thẽr″mō·ē·leç·tric′i·ty, *n.* 1. electricity produced by heat, as by means of a thermoelectric couple.
2. the branch of electricity dealing with the properties and action of electricity developed by heat.

thẽr″mō·ē·leç·trom′e·tẽr, *n.* an instrument for measuring the power of an electric current by the amount of heat it produces, or for measuring the heating power of an electric current.

thẽr″mō·ē·leç″trō·mō′tive, *a.* designating or of the electromotive force produced as by a thermoelectric couple.

thẽr·mō·el′ē·ment, *n.* a thermoelectric couple.

thẽr″mō·ex·cī′tō·ry, *a.* exciting or stimulating the production of heat in the body.

thẽr′mō·ġen, *n.* [*thermo-*, and Gr. *-genēs*, producing.] caloric.

thẽr·mō·ġen′e·sis, *n.* the production of heat; especially, the physiological process of generating heat within the animal body.

thẽr″mō·ġē·net′ic, *a.* of thermogenesis.

thẽr·mō·ġen′iç, *a.* relating to the production of heat; thermogenous.

thẽr·moġ′e·nous, *a.* producing heat.

thẽr·moġ′e·ny, *n.* thermogenesis.

thẽr′mō·gram, *n.* a record made by a thermograph.

thẽr′mō·grȧph, *n.* a thermometer for automatically recording variations of temperature.

thẽr″mō·in·hib′i·tō·ry, *a.* preventing abnormal production of heat: applied to certain nerves.

thẽr″mō·kin·ē·mat′içs, *n.pl.* [*construed as sing.*] the science that deals with the relationship of heat and motive power.

thẽr·mō·lā′bile, *a.* designating or of substances, as some toxins, enzymes, etc., that are destroyed or lose their special properties when heated to 55°C. or above: opposed to *thermostable.*

thẽr·mol′ō·ġy, *n.* the science of heat.

thẽr·mol′y·sis, *n.* [*thermo-*, and Gr. *lysis*, a loosening.]
1. in chemistry, dissociation of a compound by heat.
2. in physiology, the dispersion or loss of heat from the body by any process.

thẽr·mō·lyt′iç, *a.* pertaining to thermolysis.

thẽr′mō·lȳze, *v.t.* to dissociate by heat.

thẽr·mō·mag′net·iṣm, *n.* magnetism as produced or affected by heat.

thẽr·mom′e·tẽr, *n.* [LL. *thermometrum*, from Gr. *thermē*, heat, and *-meter.*]

1. an instrument for measuring temperatures, consisting of a graduated glass tube with a sealed, capillary bore in which mercury, colored alcohol, etc. rises or falls as it expands or contracts from changes in temperature.

2. any similar instrument, as one operating by means of a thermocouple.

The three principal types of thermometers are: *Fahrenheit*, in which the freezing point of water is 32° and the boiling point 212°; *centigrade*, in which the freezing point is 0° and the boiling point 100°; and *Reaumur*, in which the freezing point is 0° and the boiling point 80°.

clinical thermometer; see under clinical.

maximum thermometer; a thermometer registering the maximum temperature since its last adjustment.

metallic thermometer; a thermometer indicating the temperature by the unequal expansion or contraction of two different metals.

minimum thermometer; see under *minimum*.

registering thermometer; a thermometer that registers the temperature it indicates, as in a continuous record, at given times, or at the maximum or minimum point.

upsetting thermometer; a thermometer that registers when inverted.

thẽr·mō·met′riç, *a.* of or measured by a thermometer.

thẽr·mō·met′riç·ăl, *a.* same as *thermometric*.

thẽr·mō·met′riç·ăl·ly, *adv.* by means of a thermometer.

thẽr·mō·met′rō·grȧph, *n.* [*thermo-*, Gr. *metron*, measure, and *graphein*, to write.] a self-registering thermometer, especially one that registers the maximum and minimum degrees of temperature during long periods.

thẽr·mom′e·try, *n.* 1. measurement of temperature.

2. the science of making or using thermometers.

thẽr·mō·mō′tŏr, *n.* an engine operated by heat, especially by the expansion of heated air.

thẽr·mō·mul′ti·plī·ẽr, *n.* same as *thermopile*.

thẽr·mō·nū′çlē·ar, *a.* designating, of, or employing the heat energy released in nuclear fission.

thẽr″mō·pen·ē·trā′tiŏn, *n.* in medicine, a method of heating the deeper, internal portions of the body by means of electric currents of low tension and high amperage.

thẽr′mō·phōne, *n.* a telephone in which the sounds are produced by variations of temperature of a fine wire attached to the diaphragm of the receiver, and in which a heated wire forms part of the primary circuit of the transmitter.

thẽr′mō·phōre, *n.* an electric heating pad.

thẽr′mō·pīle, *n.* an instrument consisting of a series of thermocouples, used for measuring minute changes in temperature or for generating thermoelectric current.

thẽr·mō·plas′tiç, *a.* becoming or remaining soft and moldable when subjected to heat: said of certain plastics.

thẽr·mō·plas′tiç, *n.* a thermoplastic substance.

thẽr″mō·rā″di·ō·ther′ȧ·py, *n.* in medicine, a system of applying heat and X rays to tissue for treatment.

thẽr″mō·rē·duç′tion, *n.* in metallurgy and chemistry, reduction by the application of heat.

thẽr·mō·reg′ū·lā·tŏr, *n.* a thermostat (sense 1).

thẽr′mŏs bot′tle (or **flȧsk, jug**), [Gr. *thermos*, hot.] a bottle, flask, or jug for keeping liquids at almost their original temperature for several hours: it has two walls enclosing a vacuum and is fitted in a metal outer case: a trademark (*Thermos*).

THERMOS BOTTLE

thẽr′mō·sçōpe, *n.* an instrument for indicating changes in temperature without accurately measuring them.

thẽr·mō·sçop′iç, *a.* of or indicated by a thermoscope.

thẽr·mō·sçop′i·căl, *a.* thermoscopic.

thẽr′mō·set·ting, *a.* becoming permanently hard and unmoldable when once subjected to heat: said of certain plastics.

thẽr′mō·sī·phŏn, *n.* an apparatus consisting of an arrangement of siphon tubes for inducing the circulation of a liquid, as in the water-cooling system of an internal-combustion engine.

thẽr·mō·stā′ble, *a.* designating or of substances, as some toxins, enzymes, etc., that can be heated to moderately high temperatures without losing their special properties: opposed to *thermolabile*.

thẽr′mō·stat, *n.* [*thermo-*, and Gr. *statos*, standing.]

1. an apparatus for regulating temperature, especially one that automatically controls a heating unit.

2. a device that sets off a sprinkler, etc. at a certain heat.

thẽr·mō·stat′iç, *a.* of or operated by a thermostat.

thẽr·mō·stat′i·căl·ly, *adv.* by means of a thermostat.

thẽr·mō·stat′içs, *n. pl.* [*construed as sing.*] the science that deals with the equilibrium of heat.

thẽr·mō·syn′thē·sis, *n.* in chemistry, synthesis produced by the application of heat.

thẽr″mō·sys·tal′tiç, *a.* pertaining to the influence of heat on muscular contraction or expansion.

thẽr·mō·taç′tiç, *a.* regulating or controlling the body temperature.

thẽr′mō·tañk, *n.* a tank for heating or cooling air passing through it, by means of pipes through which water, steam, etc. circulates.

thẽr·mō·tax′iç, *a.* 1. of thermotaxis.

2. regulating body temperature.

thẽr·mō·tax′is, *n.* [*thermo-*, and Gr. *taxis*, arrangement.]

1. in biology, movement of an organism toward or from a source of heat.

2. in physiology, the normal regulation of body temperature.

thẽr·mō·tel′ē·phōne, *n.* same as *thermophone*.

thẽr·mō·ten′sile, *a.* relating to tensile strength as affected by changes in temperature.

thẽr·mō·ten′sion, *n.* a process of increasing the strength of wrought iron by heating the metal to a determinate temperature, and giving it a mechanical strain in the direction in which the strength is to be exerted.

thẽr″mō·ther·ȧ·peū′tiçs, *n.* same as *thermotherapy*.

thẽr·mō·ther′ȧ·py, *n.* the treatment of disease by the application of heat.

thẽr·mot′iç, thẽr·mot′iç·ăl, *a.* of or relating to heat; resulting from or dependent on heat.

thẽr·mot′içs, *n.* the science of heat.

thẽr·mō·trop′iç, *a.* of or having thermotropism.

thẽr·mot′rō·piṣm, *n.* [*thermo-*, and Gr. *trepein*, to turn.] the tendency of a plant to grow toward or away from a source of heat. Growth toward a source of heat is called *positive thermotropism*; growth away from a source of heat, *negative thermotropism*.

thẽr′mō·tȳpe, *n.* [*thermo-*, and Gr. *typos*, impression.] a picture, as of a slice of wood, obtained by first wetting the object with dilute acid, as sulfuric or hydrochloric acid, then printing it, and afterward developing the impression by heat.

thẽr′mō·tȳ·py, *n.* the art or process of producing a thermotype.

thẽr″mō·vol·tā′iç, *a.* pertaining to heat and electricity, or to the thermal effects produced by voltaic electricity.

-thẽr′my, [from Gr. *thermē*, heat.] a combining form meaning *heat* or *the production of heat*, as in dia*thermy*.

thē′rō·dont, *n.* same as *theriodont*.

thē′roid, *a.* [Gr. *thēr*, a wild beast, and *-oid.*] beastlike; like or characteristic of an animal.

thē·rol′ō·ġy, *n.* mammalogy.

thē′rō·mọrph, *n.* one of the *Theromorpha*.

Thē·rō·mọr′phȧ, *n.pl.* an order of fossil reptiles of the Permian Period.

thē·rō·mọr′phi·ȧ, *n.* [Gr. *thēr*, *thēros*, a wild beast, and *morphē*, form.] an abnormality in human anatomy showing assimilation of form or structure to that of lower animals.

thē·rō·mọr′phiç, thē·rō·mọr′phous, *a.* pertaining to or resembling the *Theromorpha*.

thē·rō·mọr′phiç, *a.* of or showing theromorphia.

Thē·rop′ō·dȧ, *n.pl.* an order of extinct carnivorous dinosaurs in which the structure of the feet resembled quadrupeds rather than birds. They were large and predatory. The order includes *Megalosaurus* and *Creosaurus*.

Thẽr·sī′tēṣ, *n.* in Greek legend, an ugly, loud, abusive Greek soldier in the Trojan War, killed by Achilles.

thẽr·sit′iç·ăl, *a.* characteristic of Thersites; loud and abusive; scurrilous.

thē·sau′rus, *n.*; *pl.* **thē·sau′rī, thē·sau′rus·eṣ** [L. *thesaurus*, from Gr. *thēsauros*, a treasure.]

1. a treasury; a storehouse or repository.

2. a book containing a store of words, as a dictionary, encyclopedia, book of classified synonyms and antonyms, etc.

thēṣe, *pron* and *a.* plural of *this*.

Thē·sē′ăn, *a.* of or like Theseus.

Thē′seūs, *n.* in Greek legend, the principal hero of Attica, son of Aegeus and king of Athens: he is famed for many exploits, especially for his killing of the Minotaur.

thē′si·çle, *n.* a little or subordinate thesis; a proposition. [Rare.]

thē′sis, *n.*; *pl.* **thē′sēṣ**, [L. *thesis*; Gr. *thesis*, a position, from *tithenai*, to put, place.]

1. in classical poetry, the accented syllable of a foot.

2. the unaccented syllable of a foot in poetry: usage due to misinterpretation of the classical Greek word.

3. an accented note in music, indicated by a downward stroke in conducting.

4. a proposition to be maintained or defended in argument, formerly one publicly disputed by a candidate for a degree in a medieval university.

5. an essay or dissertation presented by a candidate for an academic degree as evidence of his knowledge of an individual research in a subject.

6. in logic, an unproved statement assumed as a premise; a postulate: distinguished from *hypothesis*.

Opposed to *arsis* (in senses 1, 2, 3).

Thē·sī′um, *n.* [L. *thesium*; Gr. *thēseion*, said to be from Gr. *thēs*, a serf or villain.] a genus of plants of the order *Santalaceæ*. The species are scentless and slightly astringent.

Thes·mō·phō′ri·ȧ, *n.pl.* [Gr., from *thesmophoros*, lawgiving, an epithet of Demeter; *thesmos*, a law, and *pherein*, to bear.] a famous ancient Greek festival celebrated by married women in honor of Demeter (Ceres) as the mother of beautiful offspring.

thes′mō·thēte, *n.* 1. a lawgiver; a legislator.

2. originally, any of the six inferior archons at Athens.

Thes·pē′si·ȧ, *n.* [from Gr. *thespesios*, divine, in allusion to *Thespesia populnea* being planted in sacred or religious localities.] a genus of tropical trees of the order *Malvaceæ*, having large, undivided leaves and large flowers. *Thespesia populnea*, the umbrella tree, is included in this genus.

Thes′pi·ăn, *a.* [from *Thespis*, ancient Greek poet, considered the originator of Greek tragedy.]

1. of Thespis.

2. having to do with the drama, especially with tragedy.

Thes′pi·ăn, *n.* an actor; especially, a tragedian: a somewhat humorous or pretentious usage.

Thes·sā′li·ăn, *a.* of or pertaining to Thessaly (an ancient region in northeastern Greece), its people, etc.

Thes·sā′li·ăn, *n.* 1. a native or inhabitant of ancient Thessaly.

2. the ancient Greek dialect spoken in Thessaly.

Thes·sȧ·lō′ni·ăn, *a.* of or pertaining to Thessalonica (now Salonika), an important city of ancient Macedonia.

Thes·sȧ·lō′ni·ăn, *n.* a native or inhabitant of Thessalonica.

Thes·sȧ·lō′ni·ănṣ, *n.pl.* [*construed as sing.*] either of the Epistles to the Thessalonians, two books of the New Testament which were messages from the Apostle Paul to the Christians of Thessalonica.

thē′tȧ (*or* thē′tȧ), *n.* [Gr. *thēta*; of Sem. origin.] the eighth letter of the Greek alphabet, corresponding to English *th*; called the unlucky letter from being used on the ballots by judges in ancient Greece in passing condemnation on the prisoner, it being the first letter of the Greek *thanatos*, death.

theta function; in mathematics, one of the functions employed in developing the properties of elliptic functions.

thet′iç, *a.* [Gr. *thetikos*, fit for placing, from *thetos*, placed, from base of *tithenai*.]

1. set forth dogmatically; prescribed.
2. in Greek and Latin poetry, pertaining to or constituting the thesis; also, beginning with a thesis.

thet'iç·ăl, *a.* [Gr. *thetikos*, positive.] prescriptive; arbitrary; thetic.

thē'tine, *n.* in chemistry, any one of a series of basic sulfur compounds, analogous to the sulfines.

Thē'tis, *n.* in Greek mythology, a Nereid who became the spouse of the mortal Peleus, despite her efforts to escape him by countless transformations, and was by him the mother of Achilles.

thē·ūr'ġiç, thē·ūr'ġiç·ăl, *a.* of or pertaining to theurgy or the power to perform supernatural things; magic.
theurgic hymns; songs of incantation.

thē'ūr·ġist, *n.* one who practices theurgy, or magic; a magician.

thē'ūr·ġy, *n.*; *pl.* **thē'ūr·ġieṣ,** [Gr. *theourgia*, from *theos*, god, and *ergon*, work.]
1. supposed divine or supernatural intervention in human affairs.
2. magic; sorcery, especially that practiced by certain Neoplatonists who professed to worked miracles by the intervention of beneficent, divine spirits.

Thē·vē'ti·ȧ (-shi-), *n.* [after André *Thevet*, a French traveler.] a genus of shrubs and trees of four known species: *Thevetia nereifolia*, the yellow oleander, is cultivated as an ornamental plant.

thev'e·tin, *n.* a poisonous glucoside extracted from the seeds of certain apocynaceous plants: there are many such plants and trees, all tropical, and all belong to the dogbane family: from the nuts of one of them, the yellow oleander, a crystalline form of thevetin is extracted which is effective in the treatment of cardiac affections.

thew (thū), *n.* [AS. *theāw*, custom, manner, behavior, from *theōn*, to flourish, prosper.] manner; custom; habit; form of behavior. [Obs.]

thewed (thūd), *a.* 1. accustomed; educated; mannered. [Obs.]
2. having thews, muscle, or strength; as, a well-*thewed* limb.

thew'less, *a.* lacking thews, or bodily strength; without vigor or spirit. [Chiefly Scot.]

thewṣ, *n.pl.*; *sing.* **thew,** [ME. *theawes*, good qualities, hence, later, good physical qualities, strength, from AS. *theaw*, custom, habit, hence characteristic quality; akin to OS. *thau*, custom.]
1. muscular power; bodily strength.
2. [*rarely in sing.*] muscles or sinews.

thew'y, *a.*; *comp.* thewier; *superl.* thewiest; having thews; brawny; muscular; sinewy; vigorous; strong.

thẹy (thā), *pron.* [ME. *thei*, from O.N. *thei-r*, nom. masc. pl. of the demonstrative pron.; like *their* and *them* (ME. *theim*), also from the O.N. demonstrative forms, *thei* replaced earlier ME. *he* (*hi*) because the native pronouns were phonetically confused with the forms of the pers. pron. (ME. *he, hire, hem, him*, etc.).]
1. the persons, animals, or things previously mentioned: *they* is the nominative case form, *them* the objective, *their* and *theirs* the possessive, and *themselves* the intensive and reflexive, of the third personal plural pronoun: for the singular see *he, she, it*.
2. people (or a person) generally or indefinitely; as, *they* say it's so.

thẹy'd (thād), 1. they had.
2. they would.

thẹy'll (thāl), 1. they will.
2. they shall.

they're (thâr), they are.

thẹy've, (thāv), they have.

thī-, see *thio-*.

thī·al'din, thī·al'dīne, *n.* [from Gr. *theion*, sulfur.] the nitrogenous sulfur base, $C_6H_{13}NS_2$.

thī'ȧ·min, *n.* thiamine.

thī'ȧ·mīne, *n.* [*thi-* and *amine.*] a complex white, crystalline compound, $C_{12}H_{17}ON_4SCl{\cdot}HCl$, found in the outer coating of cereal grains, green peas, beans, egg yolk, liver, etc., and also prepared synthetically; vitamin B_1: a deficiency of this vitamin results in beriberi and certain nervous disorders: also *thiamine chloride, thiamine hydrochloride*.

thī'ȧ·sus, thī'ȧ·sos, *n.*; *pl.* **thī'ȧ·sī,** in ancient Greece, an organization of men having a divinity as a patron and honoring him with festal and pompous observances; also, any such observance in honor of a god, as a feast or procession.

thī'ȧ·zin, *n.* thiazine.

thī'ȧ·zīne, *n.* [*thi-* and *azine.*] any of a group of heterocyclic compounds whose molecules contain one atom of nitrogen, one atom of sulfur, and four atoms of carbon, arranged in a ring.

thī'ȧ·zōl, *n.* thiazole.

thī'ȧ·zōle, *n.* [*thi-* and *azole.*]
1. a colorless liquid, C_3H_3NS, with a five-membered ring.
2. any of its various derivatives, used in dyes and drugs.

Thi·bet'ăn (ti-), *a.* and *n.* same as *Tibetan*.

thick, *a.*; *comp.* thicker; *superl.* thickest, [AS. *thicce*; akin to Ice. *thykkr*, Dan. *tyk*, G. *dick*, D. *dik*, thick.]
1. having relatively great depth; of considerable extent from one surface or side to the opposite; as, a *thick* layer of stones, a *thick* board.
2. having relatively large diameter in relation to length; as, a *thick* rod, *thick* pipe.
3. measured in the third dimension or between opposite surfaces; as, three inches *thick*: distinguished from *long, wide*.
4. having the constituent elements arranged close together; dense; compact; abundant; specifically, (a) filled or covered completely; dense; luxuriant; as, a *thick* head of hair, *thick* woods; (b) great in number; abundant; crowded; as, a *thick* crowd; (c) of great density or consistency; not very fluid; viscous; heavy; as, *thick* soup, *thick* smoke; (d) not clear; turbid; muddy; foggy; close; as, the air was *thick* with fumes.
5. not clear; husky; hoarse; as, a *thick* voice.
6. not clear in understanding; stupid; dull.
7. very friendly; intimate. [Colloq.]
8. too much to be tolerated; excessive. [Brit. Colloq.]
9. somewhat deaf; dim, indistinct, weak, or defective, as the sense of sight. [Dial.]
Opposed to *thin* (in senses 1, 2, 4a, 4b, 4c).
Syn.—dense, condensed, inspissated, close, compact, turbid, coagulated, muddy, dull, misty, foggy, vaporous, crowded, numerous, solid, bulky, deep, confused, inarticulate, intimate.

thick, *n.* 1. the thickest part; as, the *thick* of the arm.
2. the period of greatest activity; the time when or place where anything is thickest; as, the *thick* of the fight.
3. a thicket. [Obs.]
through thick and thin; in good times and hard times; without regard to hindrance or obstruction; perseveringly; without wavering in loyalty; as, to stand by a friend *through thick and thin*.

thick, *adv.* in a thick manner; thickly; as, bread covered *thick* with butter.
thick and threefold; in quick succession, or in great numbers. [Archaic or Dial.]
to lay it on thick; to exaggerate; especially, to give exaggerated blame or praise. [Colloq.]

thick, *v.t.* to thicken. [Rare.]

thick, *v.i.* to become thick or dense. [Rare.]

thick'-ănd-thin', *a.* constant; devoted; faithful; as, a *thick-and-thin* friend.

thick'bill, *n.* the bullfinch. [Brit. Dial.]

thick'-brāined, *a.* stupid; dull; obtuse; thickheaded.

thick'en, *v.t.*; thickened, *pt., pp.*; thickening, *ppr.* [AS. *thiccian.*]
1. to make thick or thicker.
2. to make close; to fill up interstices; as, to *thicken* cloth.
3. to inspissate; as, to *thicken* paint, mortar, or a liquid.
4. to strengthen; to confirm. [Obs.]
5. to make frequent, or more frequent; as, to *thicken* blows.
6. to make close, or more close; to make more numerous; as, to *thicken* the ranks.
7. to make more complex or involved.
Syn.—condense, inspissate, incrassate, compact, solidify, befoul, obscure, bemire, becloud, increase, coagulate, amalgamate, commingle, intermix, crowd, multiply, enlarge, expand, extend, broaden, deepen, obstruct, confuse.

thick'en, *v.i.* 1. to become thick or thicker; to become dense; as, the fog *thickens*.
2. to become dark or obscure.
3. to become more complex or involved; as, the plot *thickened*.
4. to be inspissated; as, vegetable juices *thicken* as the more volatile parts are evaporated.
5. to become close, more close, or more numerous.
6. to become quick and animated.
The combat *thickens*. —Addison.

thick'en·ẽr, *n.* one who or that which thickens; especially, something added to a liquid to make it thicker, as in cookery, dyeing, etc.

thick'en·ing, *n.* 1. the action of a person or thing that thickens.
2. a material used to thicken soup, etc.
3. something thickened or the thickened part.

thick'et, *n.* [AS. *thiccet*, from *thicce*, thick.] a thick growth of underbrush, small trees, or shrubs; a copse.

thick'head (-hed), *n.* 1. a thickheaded, or stupid, person.
2. in ornithology, (a) a pachycephalic Australian shrike; (b) a scansorial barbet.

thick'head'ed (-hed'), *a.* having a thick skull; dull; stupid.

thick'ish, *a.* somewhat thick.

thick'knee (-nē), *n.* a European ploverlike bird, *Œdicnemus crepitans*.

thick'lēaf, *n.* any plant belonging to the genus *Crassula*, characterized by thick, succulent leaves.

thick'ly, *adv.* in a thick manner; deeply; closely; compactly; in quick succession.

thick'ness, *n.* 1. the state or quality of being thick in any sense.
2. dimension from surface to opposite surface: distinguished from *length, width*.
3. a layer, stratum, etc.; as, three *thicknesses* of cloth.
4. the thickest place or part.

thick'set, *a.* 1. close-planted; as, a *thickest* wood.
2. having a thick body; stout; stocky.

thick'set, *n.* 1. a thicket; also, a dense or thick hedge.
2. a fabric from which men's working clothes are made; a fustian corduroy.

thick'skin, *n.* a thick-skinned person.

thick'-skinned', *a.* 1. having a thick skin or rind; as, a *thick-skinned* animal; *a thick-skinned* apple.
2. insensitive to criticism, insult, etc.; callous; stolid; gross.

thick'skull, *n.* a dull person; a blockhead.

thick'-skulled', *a.* dull; thickheaded; stupid; slow to learn.

thick stā'men, a plant of the genus *Pachysandra*.

thick'wind, *n.* rough breathing in horses, usually occurring after pneumonia.

thick'-wind''ed, *a.* troubled with thickwind, as a horse.

thick'-wit'ted, *a.* thickheaded.

thid'ẽr, *adv.* thither. [Obs.]

thiēf, *n.* [AS. *thefe*, the bramble.] a bramble, *Rubus fruticosus*. [Brit. Dial.]

thiēf, *n.*; *pl.* **thiēveṣ,** [AS. *theōf, thiōf, thēf*, thief.]
1. one who steals, especially secretly; a person who is guilty of theft, or larceny; one who takes the goods or personal property of another without his knowledge or consent, and without any intention of returning it.
2. an excrescence or waster in the snuff of a candle. [Dial.]
Syn.—robber.—a *thief* takes property by stealth; a *robber* uses force or the threat of force.

thiēf'tāk·ẽr, *n.* one whose business is to find and take thieves, and bring them to justice; a thief catcher; a detective. [Brit.]

thiēve, *v.i.*; thieved, *pt., pp.*; thieving, *ppr.* to steal; to practice theft.

thiēve, *v.t.* to take by theft; to purloin; to steal.

thiēv'ẽr·y, *n.* 1. the act or practice of stealing or an instance of this; theft.
2. that which is stolen. [Rare.]

thiēveṣ, *n.* plural of *thief*.

thiēv'ish, *a.* 1. addicted to thieving, or stealing.
2. of, like, or characteristic of a thief; stealthy; furtive.

thiēv'ish·ly, *adv.* in a thievish manner.

thiēv'ish·ness, *n.* the state or character of being thievish.

thīgh (thī), *n.* [ME. *thi, thih*; AS. *theoh.*]
1. the part of the human leg between the knee and the hip.
2. a corresponding part in other vertebrates; the region of the femur or, as in birds, the next lower segment of the leg.
3. the third segment (from the base) of an insect's leg; the femur.

thīgh'bōne (thī'), *n.* the bone of the thigh, articulating with the tibia and the pelvis; femur: also *thigh bone.*

thīgh joint, the hip joint; the coxa.

thig·mō·tac'tic, *a.* of thigmotaxis.

thig·mō·tax'is, *n.* [Mod. L., from Gr. *thigma,* touch; and *-taxis.*] in biology, involuntary reaction to simple contact with some outside object or body, as in motile cells.

thig·mot'rō·pism, *n.* [Mod. L., from Gr. *thigma,* touch; and *-tropism.*] stereotropism.

thilk, thilke, *pron.* that; that same. [Archaic or Dial.]

thill, *n.* [AS. *thil, thill,* a stake, pole, plank, also *thel,* a board or plank.] one of the two shafts between which a horse is hitched to a wagon or carriage.

thill coup'ling (kup'), a device for coupling thills or shafts to the front axle of a vehicle.

thill'ẽr, *n.* a thill horse.

thill horse, the horse which goes between the thills, or shafts, and supports them.

thim'ble, *n.* [ME. *thimbel, thymel;* AS. *thymel,* thumbstall, from *thuma,* a thumb, with *-el,* dim. suffix.]

1. a small, pitted cap of metal, plastic, etc. worn on the finger in sewing to protect it in pushing the needle through the fabric, etc.

2. in mechanics, any thimble-shaped device, used to join the ends of tubes, pipes, shafting, etc., as the coupling box in a thimble coupling; a fixed or movable ring, tube, or lining placed in a hole; a tubular cone for expanding a flue.

3. an iron ring with a hollow or groove round its whole circumference, to receive the rope which is spliced about it: used to keep the rope from being chafed.

thim'ble·ber"ry, *n.*; *pl.* **thim'ble·ber"ries,** any of various raspberries or blackberries with fruit shaped like a thimble; especially, the black raspberry, *Rubus occidentalis,* common in North America.

thim'ble coup'ling (kup'), in machinery, a kind of permanent coupling in which the two ends of the shafts are connected by a common thimble bored to fit the two connected ends of the shafts.

THIMBLE COUPLING

thim'ble-eȳe (-ī), *n.* the chub mackerel, *Scomber colias.*

thim'ble·ful, *n.*; *pl.* **thim'ble·fuls,** as much as a thimble will hold; hence, a very small quantity.

thim'ble·măn, *n.*; *pl.* **thim'ble·men,** a thimblerigger.

thim'ble·rig, *n.* 1. a swindling game in which spectators are challenged to bet on the location of a small object ostensibly concealed under one of three cups or nutshells manipulated by a sleight-of-hand operator: also called *shell game.*

2. a thimblerigger.

thim'ble·rig, *v.t.*; thimblerigged, *pt., pp.*; thimblerigging, *ppr.* to swindle by means of thimblerig or sleight of hand; hence, to trick or defraud by low cunning.

thim'ble·rig"gẽr, *n.* 1. an operator of a thimblerig.

2. a swindler.

thim'ble·weed, *n.* 1. any of various coneflowers of the genus *Rudbeckia,* with cone-shaped disks and daisylike flowers.

2. a plant, *Anemone virginiana,* the floral receptacles of which are thimble-shaped.

thin, *a.*; *comp.* thinner; *superl.* thinnest. [ME. *thinne;* AS. *thynne, thyn;* Ice. *thunnr;* D. *dun;* Sw. *tunn,* thin, from the root of AS. *thenian;* Ice. *thenja,* to stretch; L. *tenuis,* thin.]

1. having little thickness or extent from one surface to the opposite; as, *thin* paper, a *thin* board, a *thin* covering.

2. of little opacity; flimsy; transparent; as, a *thin* veil.

3. having small diameter in relation to length; as, *thin* thread.

4. deficient in such ingredient as gives body or substance; of little body, richness, strength, etc.; as, a *thin* soup.

5. not close; not crowded; not filling the space; not having the individuals that compose the thing in a close or compact state; sparse; not abundant; as, the audience was *thin.*

6. of little density or consistency; very fluid; rare; tenuous; as, *thin* milk, *thin* air.

7. of little intensity; dim; faint; pale; as, *thin* colors.

8. having little fat or flesh; slender; lean.

9. of little resonance or volume, as sound; high-pitched and weak; as, a *thin* voice.

10. easily seen through; slight; as, a *thin* excuse.

11. of little substance or content; unsubstantial; inadequate; scanty; as, a *thin* plot, a *thin* argument.

12. in photography, lacking contrast of light and shade: said of a negative or print.

Syn.—slim, slender, flimsy, attenuated, diluted, watery, meager, unsubstantial, lean, slight.

thin, *adv.* not thickly or closely; in a scattered state; thinly; as, seed sown *thin.*

thin, *v.t.* and *v.i.* thinned, *pt., pp.*; thinning, *ppr.* to make or become thin or thinner: with *out, down,* etc.

thīne, *pron.* [ME. *thin;* AS. *thīn,* thine, genit- of *thū,* thou; like Ice. *thīn;* Sw. and Dan. *dīn;* Goth. *theina; n* being the sign of the genitive.] the possessive case of *thou.*

thīne, *a.* thy: used before a vowel or unaspirated *h, thy* taking its place before a consonant.

thing, *n.* [ME.; AS. *thing,* a council, court, controversy.]

1. any matter, circumstance, affair, or concern.

2. that which constitutes an end to be achieved, a step in a process, etc.; as, the next *thing* is to mix thoroughly.

3. that which is conceived, spoken of, or referred to as existing as an individual, distinguishable entity

4. any single entity distinguished from all others; as, every *thing* in the universe.

5. a tangible object, as distinguished from a concept, quality, etc.; as, the book is a *thing;* its color is a quality.

6. an item, detail, etc.; as, not a *thing* has been overlooked.

7. that which is represented as distinguished from the word or symbol that represents it.

8. an inanimate object; any lifeless material or object.

Ye meads and groves, unconscious *things!*
—Cowper.

9. a person: often used in pity or contempt, sometimes with an idea of fondness, tenderness, etc.; as, poor *things!* [Colloq.]

10. an act; a deed; a transaction; a matter; an event; an action; that which is done, has been done, or is to be done; as, he'll accomplish great *things.*

11. something mentioned but unnamed, as in contempt, or because the name is not known or remembered; as, It's that other *thing* I want. [Colloq.]

12. [*pl.*] clothes; also, personal belongings; as, pack up my *things.*

13. in law, that which may be owned; a property, as distinguished from a *person.*

a thing or two; something of interest or importance connected with an affair, but not generally known; as, I can tell you *a thing or two* about that. [Colloq.]

the thing; (a) that which is proper, right, essential, etc.; (b) that which is the height of fashion or style.

to know a thing or two; to be particularly knowing; to be shrewder than reputed to be. [Colloq.]

to make a good thing of; to profit by (some enterprise or investment). [Colloq.]

to see things; to have hallucinations. [Colloq.]

thing (*or* ting), *n.* [O.N. *thing,* an assembly.] a judicial or legislative assembly among the Scandinavian peoples: also *ting.*

Likewise the Swedish king
Summoned in haste a *thing,*
Weapons and men to bring
In aid of Denmark. —Longfellow.

thing'-in-it·self', *n.* [transl. of G. *ding an sich.*] in Kantian philosophy, that aspect of a thing which has reality beyond human perception and knowledge and, hence, can never be known.

thing'um·à·jig", *n.* a thingumbob. [Colloq.]

thing'um·bob, *n.* [extension of older *thingum,* from *thing.*] any device; a contrivance; a gadget: humorous substitute for a name not known or temporarily forgotten. [Colloq.]

thiñk, *v.t.*; thought, *pt., pp.*; thinking, *ppr.* [from ME. *thenchen,* to think, confused with *thinchen,* to seem; AS. *thencan,* to think, caus. of *thyncan,* to seem.]

1. to form or have in the mind; to conceive; as, I am *thinking* black thoughts.

2. to hold in one's opinion; to judge; consider; as, I *think* her charming.

3. to believe; surmise; expect; as, they *think* they can come; I did not *think* to see you.

4. to determine, resolve, work out, etc. by reasoning; as, he *thought* his way out of the dilemma.

5. to have in intent; to purpose; intend; as, he *thinks* to deceive me.

6. to put, throw, etc. (into a specified condition) by mental concentration; as, she *thought* herself into this dilemma.

7. to bring to mind, or recollect; as, *think* how we were once friends.

8. to keep continually in the mind; to be obsessed with; as, he *thinks* model airplanes all day long.

to think out; (a) to think about completely or to the end; (b) to work out, solve, discover, or plan by thinking.

to think over; to give thought to; to ponder well, as for reconsideration.

to think through; to think about until one reaches a conclusion or resolution.

to think up; to invent, contrive, plan, etc. by thinking.

thiñk, *v.i.* 1. to bring the intellectual faculties into play; to use the mind for arriving at conclusions, making decisions, drawing inferences, etc.; to perform any mental operation; to reason.

For that I am
I know, because I *think.* —Dryden.

2. to judge; to conclude; to decide; to hold as a settled opinion; to believe; as, to *think* nobly of a person.

3. to purpose; to intend; as, I *thought* to help him.

4. to muse; to meditate; to reflect; to recollect; to weigh something mentally; as, he *thought* on the past; *think* much, speak little.

5. to presume; to venture.

Think not to say within yourselves, We have
Abraham to our father. —Matt. iii. 9.

to think aloud; to speak one's thoughts as they occur: also *think out loud.*

to think better of; see under *better, adv.*

to think much of; to hold in high esteem.

to think nothing of; (a) to attach no importance to; (b) to regard as easy to do.

to think of; (a) to call to mind; recall; remember; (b) to have an opinion, judgment, etc. of; (c) to discover; invent; conceive of; (d) to allow oneself to consider; (e) to have regard for; to consider the welfare of.

to think twice; to reconsider; to pause to think about again.

Syn.—cogitate, muse, imagine, suppose, expect, fancy, guess.

thiñk, *v.i.*; thought, *pt., pp.*; thinking, *ppr.* [from ME. *thinchen,* to seem, confused with *thenchen,* to think; AS. *thyncan, thincan,* to seem, to appear, pt. *thuhte,* often used impersonally with a dative; Goth. *thugkjan;* L.G. and D. *dunken;* G. *dünken;* allied to the other verb *think.*] to seem; to appear: used impersonally and now only in the compounds *methinks* and *methought.*

thiñk, *n.* thought; a thinking; as, take a long *think.* [Colloq.]

thiñk'à·ble, *a.* that can be thought; conceivable.

thiñk'ẽr, *n.* one who thinks; specifically, one who thinks in a specified manner; as, a deep *thinker,* a coherent *thinker.*

thiñk'ing, *a.* 1. having the faculty of thought; cogitative; capable of a regular train of ideas; as, man is a *thinking* being.

2. thoughtful or reflective by nature.

thiñk'ing, *n.* mental action; cogitation; judgment; a thought; also, the act of thinking.

I heard a bird so sing,
Whose music, to my *thinking,* pleased the king. —Shak.

thiñk'ing·ly, *adv.* by thought.

thin'ly, *adv.* in a thin manner; not thickly; as, ground *thinly* covered with trees; a country *thinly* inhabited.

thin'nẽr, *n.* one who or that which thins; especially, a substance or liquid added, as turpentine to paint, for thinning.

thin'ness, *n.* the state, property, or quality of being thin.

thin'nish, *a.* rather thin.

thin'ō·līte, *n.* [Gr. *this, thinos,* the beach, and *lithos,* a stone.] a light-colored crystalline tufa found as a shore deposit and in the dried basins of many lakes in the western part of the United States.

thin'-skinned', *a.* having a thin skin; also, sensitive to criticism, insult, etc.; touchy.

thī'ō-, [from Gr. *theion,* brimstone.] a combining form meaning *sulfur,* used in chemical terms to indicate the replacement of oxygen in an acid radical by negatively divalent sulfur: also, before a vowel, *thi-*.

thī·ō·al′dē·hȳde, *n.* any of a group of organic chemical compounds containing the monovalent radical -CHS; an aldehyde in which sulfur has replaced the oxygen.

thī″ō·an′ti·mō·nāte″, *n.* any of a group of chemical compounds considered salts of thioantimonic acid.

thī″ō·an·ti·mō′ni·āte, *n.* thioantimonate.

thī″ō·an·ti·mon′iç ac′id, a hypothetical acid, H_3SbS_4, known only in the form of its salts.

thī″ō·an·ti·mō′ni·ous ac′id, any of a group of hypothetical acids, H_3SbS_3, $HSbS_2$, $H_4Sb_2S_5$, and $H_2Sb_4S_7$, known only in the forms of their salts in solution.

thī″ō·an′ti·mō·nīte″, *n.* any of a group of chemical compounds known only in solution and considered salts of the thioantimonious acids.

thī·ō·är′sē·nāte, *n.* any of a group of chemical compounds considered salts of the thioarsenic acids.

thī″ō·är·sen′iç ac′id, any of three hypothetical acids, H_3AsS_4, $HAsS_3$, and $H_4As_2S_7$, known only in the forms of their salts.

thī″ō·är·sē′ni·ous ac′id, any of a group of hypothetical acids, H_3AsS_3, $HAsS_2$, $H_4As_2S_5$, known only in the forms of their salts.

thī·ō·är′sē·nīte, *n.* any of a group of chemical compounds considered salts of the thioarsenious acids.

thī·ō·çär′bŏn·āte, *n.* same as *sulfocarbonate*.

thī″ō·çär·bon′iç, *a.* same as *sulfocarbonic*.

thī·ō·çȳ′ȧ·nāte, *n.* a salt or ester of thiocyanic acid, containing the monovalent radical -SCN.

ferric thiocyanate; a red crystalline substance used as a test for ferric iron.

thī″ō·cy·an′iç ac′id, a colorless, unstable acid, HSCN, with a penetrating odor, known chiefly in the form of its salts.

thī′ōl, *n.* any of a class of chemical compounds analogous to the alcohols and characterized by the substitution of sulfur for oxygen in the OH radical; a mercaptan.

thī·ō·naph′thēne, *n.* a base, C_8H_6S, known by its derivatives.

thī·on′iç, *a.* [from Gr. *theion*, brimstone, sulfur; and *-ic*.] of, containing, or derived from sulfur.

thī·on′iç ac′id, 1. any organic chemical compound containing the monovalent CS·OH radical.

2. any of a group of acids with the general formula $H_2S_nO_6$, in which *n* varies from 2 to 5.

thī′ō·nīne, *n.* a dark-green dye or stain, $C_{12}H_9N_3S$, giving a purple color in solution and used as a stain in microscopy.

thī′ō·nyl, *n.* the divalent radical SO.

thī′ō·phēne, thī′ō·phen, *n.* a heterocyclic chemical compound, C_4H_4S, a colorless liquid resembling benzene and found in coal tar.

thī·oph′thēne, *n.* an oily compound, $C_6H_4S_2$, consisting of two thiophene nuclei.

thī″ō·sin·am′ine, thī″ō·sin·am′in, *n.* [*thio-*, and *sinamine* (from L. *sinapis*, mustard; and *amine*.] a colorless, crystalline chemical compound, $C_4H_8N_2S$, produced by the reaction of ammonia on mustard oil and used in medicine for resolving scar tissue.

thī·ō·sul′fāte, *n.* a salt of thiosulfuric acid; especially, sodium thiosulfate: see *hypo*.

thī″ō·sul·fū′riç ac′id, an unstable acid, $H_2S_2O_3$, whose salts are used in photography, as an antichlor in bleaching, etc.

thī·ō·tō′lēne, *n.* an oily compound, C_5H_6S, contained in coal tar.

thī·ox′ēne, *n.* [*thio*phene and *xylene*.] any one of three dimethyl derivatives of thiophene.

thī″ō·ū·rē′ȧ, *n.* a colorless, crystalline chemical compound, $CS(NH_2)_2$, used in organic synthesis and as a reagent for bismuth.

third, *a.* [ME. *thridde*; AS. *thridda*, *thyrdda*, the common metathesis of *r* and the vowel giving *third*; compare Goth. *thridja*, Ice. *thridi*, *thridja*, Sw. and Dan. *tredie*, D. *derde*, L. *tertius*, third.]

1. preceded by two others in a series: the ordinal of three.

2. designating any of the three equal parts of something.

third estate; see *estate*, *n.* sense 2.

Third International; the international organization of Communist parties, founded in Moscow in 1919 and dissolved in 1943: also called *Communist International*, *Comintern*.

third order; in the Roman Catholic Church, a minor order attached to one of the monastic orders, composed of associates not bound by vows, but conforming, to a certain extent, to the general designs of the order.

third person; in grammar, that form of a pronoun or verb which refers to the person or thing spoken of: in *he does*, *he* and *does* are in the third person.

third, *n.* 1. one of three equal parts of anything.

2. the sixtieth of a second of time or of an arc of an angle.

3. the one following the second.

4. the third forward gear ratio of an automotive vehicle: in most automobiles it is the highest.

5. [*pl.*] in law, (a) the third part of a deceased man's estate, which, under certain conditions, goes unrestrictedly to his widow; (b) loosely, a widow's dower.

6. in music, (a) an interval of three degrees in a diatonic scale; (b) a tone three degrees above or below a given tone; (c) the combination of two notes separated by this interval; (d) the third tone of a diatonic scale.

7. in baseball, third base.

third bāse, in baseball, the base between second base and home plate, located on the pitcher's right.

third bŏr′ōugh (-ō), in English history, an underconstable.

third′-çlȧss′, *a.* of the class, rank, excellence, etc. next below the second; specifically, (a) designating or of accommodations next below the second; as, a *third-class* railway carriage; (b) designating or of a class of mail consisting of books, circulars, etc.

third′-çlȧss′, *adv.* 1. with accommodations next below the second; as, they traveled to Berlin *third-class*.

2. as or by third-class mail.

third′-dē·gree′, *a.* of the third degree.

third dē·gree′, 1. in Freemasonry, the degree of master mason, conferred with elaborate ceremonies.

2. severe treatment or torture of a prisoner or suspect in order to extort a confession or information.

third di·men′sion, 1. (a) the dimension of depth in something as distinguished from the two dimensions of any of its flat surfaces; (b) the quality of having, or of seeming to have, such depth, or solidity.

2. the quality of being true to life or seeming real.

third eȳe′lid (ī′), the nictitating membrane.

third′ings, *n.pl.* the third part of the corn or grain growing on the ground at the tenant's death, due to the lord of the manor for a heriot. [Brit.]

third′ly, *adv.* in the third place; third: used chiefly in enumerating topics.

third pär′ty, 1. a political party organized to compete against the two major parties in a two-party system.

2. a person in a case or matter other than the two principals.

third rāil, an extra rail used in some electric railroads, instead of an overhead wire, for supplying power.

third′-rāte′, *a.* 1. third in quality or other rating; third-class.

2. definitely inferior; very poor.

Third Rē·pub′liç, the republic established in France in 1870, after the fall of Napoleon III, lasting until the German occupation of France in World War II.

third wŏrld, [*often* T- W-] the underdeveloped or emergent countries of the world, especially of Africa and Asia.

thirl, *n.* [AS. *thyrel*, hole.]

1. an opening or entrance. [Brit. Dial.]

2. in coal mining, a cross hole between two headings, made for ventilating purposes. [Brit. Dial.]

thirl, *v.t.* and *v.i.*; thirled, *pt.*, *pp.*; thirling, *ppr.* 1. to pierce. [Dial.]

2. to thrill. [Dial.]

thirl, *v.t.* to enthrall; to enslave; also, to bind by the terms of thirlage. [Scot.]

thirl′ȧ·ble, *a.* capable of being penetrated or pierced. [Obs.]

thirl′ăġe, *n.* in Scots law, the right which the owner of a mill possesses, by contract or law, to compel the tenants of a certain district to bring all their grain to his mill for grinding and pay a specified fee for this; also, the fee paid.

thirl′ing, *n.* 1. the act of boring, drilling, or perforating.

2. in mining, same as *thirl* (cross hole).

thirst, *n.* [ME. *thirst*, *thurst*; AS. *thurst*.]

1. the uncomfortable or distressful feeling caused by a desire or need for water or other drink and characterized generally by a sensation of dryness in the mouth and throat.

2. a craving for alcoholic liquor. [Colloq.]

3. a strong desire; a craving; a longing; as, a *thirst* for worldly honors; a *thirst* for praise.

I speak this in hunger for bread, not in *thirst* for revenge. —Shak.

thirst, *v.i.*; thirsted, *pt.*, *pp.*; thirsting, *ppr.* 1. to want to drink; to be thirsty.

2. to have a vehement desire or craving.

thirst, *v.t.* to have a thirst or craving for. [Rare.]

thirst′ẽr, *n.* one who or that which thirsts.

thirst′i·ly, *adv.* in a thirsty manner.

thirst′i·ness, *n.* the state of being thirsty; thirst.

thirs′tle, *n.* the throstle. [Brit. Dial.]

thirst′y, *a.*; *comp.* thirstier; *superl.* thirstiest.

1. wanting to drink; suffering from thirst.

2. very dry; having no moisture; parched; as, *thirsty* fields.

3. having a vehement desire or craving.

4. causing thirst; as, *thirsty* work. [Colloq.]

thir′teen′, *a.* [ME. *thrittene*; AS. *threotȳne*, thirteen, lit., three-ten, from *threo*, three, and *tyne*, ten.] consisting of ten and three; being one more than twelve; as, *thirteen* years.

thir′teen′, *n.* 1. the number which consists of ten and three; the cardinal number between twelve and fourteen.

2. a symbol representing thirteen units, as 13 or XIII.

3. an Irish coin worth thirteen pence, current in the early part of the nineteeth century. [Obs.]

thir·teen′ẽr, *n.* 1. same as *thirteen*, sense 3.

2. in the game of whist, the last or thirteenth card of a suit remaining after the others have been played. [Colloq.]

thir′teenth′, *a.* 1. the third after the tenth; preceded by twelve others in a series: the ordinal of thirteen; as, the *thirteenth* day of the month.

2. designating one of thirteen equal parts of anything.

thir′teenth′, *n.* 1. one of thirteen equal parts of anything.

2. the next after the twelfth.

3. in music, an interval between two notes thirteen diatonic degrees apart.

thir′ti·eth, *a.* [AS. *thrītigotha*.]

1. preceded by twenty-nine others in a series: the ordinal of thirty; as, the *thirtieth* day of May.

2. designating one of thirty equal parts of anything.

thir′ti·eth, *n.* 1. the one following the twenty-ninth.

2. any of the thirty equal parts of something.

thir′ty, *a.* [ME. *thirti*, *thritti*; AS. *thrītig*, *thrittig*, from *thrī*, *threo*, three, and suffix *-tig*, ten.] being thrice ten; ten three times repeated; twenty and ten; as, the month of June consists of *thirty* days.

Thirty Years' War; a series of wars carried on between the Protestant and Roman Catholic leagues in Germany, later involving other European countries. It began with the Bohemian war, 1618, and ended with the Peace of Westphalia, 1648.

thir′ty, *n.*; *pl.* **thir′ties**, 1. the cardinal number between twenty-nine and thirty-one; the number which consists of three times ten.

2. a symbol representing thirty units, as 30 or XXX.

the thirties; the years from thirty through thirty-nine (of a century or a person's age).

Thir′ty-Nīne Ar′ti·çles (-klz), the thirty-nine points of doctrine of the Church of England and the Episcopal Church.

thir′ty-seç′ŏnd nōte, in music, a note (♬) having 1/32 the duration of a whole note: also called *demisemiquaver*.

thir·ty-twō′mō (-tö′mō), *n.* 1. the page size of a book made up of printer's sheets folded into 32 leaves, each leaf approximately 3½ by 5½ inches.

2. a book consisting of pages of this size: written *32mo* (no period).

thir·ty-twō′mō, *a.* consisting of 32 leaves to a sheet.

this, *pron.*; *pl.* **thēse**, [ME. *this*, *thes*; AS. *thes*, masc., *this*, neut., from the base of the demonstrative pronoun.]

1. the person or thing mentioned or understood; as, *this* is John; *this* tastes good.

2. the thing that is nearer: distinguished from *that*; as, I can see *this* more clearly than that.

3. one of two things that are compared or contrasted: distinguished from *that*; as, of the two possibilities, *this* is more likely than that.

4. the fact, idea, etc. that is about to be stated; as, "*this* above all: to thine ownself be true."

5. the fact, idea, etc. that has just been mentioned; as, *this* leads us to the following conclusion.

this, *a.* 1. designating the person or thing mentioned or understood; as, *this* man was John; *this* pie tastes good.

2. designating the thing that is nearer: distinguished from *that*; as, I can see *this* house more clearly than that one across the street.

3. designating one of two things that are compared or contrasted, as contradistinguished from *that*; as, of the two, *this* possibility is more likely than that one.

4. designating something about to be stated; as, *this* claim I make: I was his friend.

5. designating something that has just been mentioned; as, *this* evidence leads us to the following conclusion.

6. these: used of things considered collectively or as a unit; as, by *this* means.

this, *adv.* to this extent; so; as, it was *this* big.

This'bē, see *Pyramus and Thisbe.*

this'tle (this'l), *n.* [ME. and AS. *thistel.*] any of various carduaceous plants of the genera *Carduus, Cirsium, Cnicus,* etc., with prickly leaves and heads of white, purple, pink, or yellow flowers.

THISTLE

blue thistle; the viper's bugloss: see *bugloss.*

bull thistle; the common thistle, *Cnicus lanceolatus.*

Canada thistle; a species of thistle, *Cnicus arvensis,* with purplish flowers, wavy leaves, and creeping roots.

common thistle; any plant of the genus *Cnicus,* especially *Cnicus lanceolatus.*

distaff thistle; a thistle, *Carthamus lanatus,* of Europe, central Asia, and northern Africa, which has large pale-yellow heads.

golden thistle; any species of *Scolymus,* a genus of yellow-flowered composite herbs indigenous to Europe.

Mexican thistle; a tall thistle, *Cnicus conspicuus,* of Mexico and Central America.

Order of the Thistle; a Scottish order of knighthood, sometimes called *the order of St. Andrew.* It was instituted by James VII (James II of England) in 1687, when eight knights were nominated. It fell into abeyance during the reign of William and Mary, but was revived by Queen Anne in 1703. The order consists of the sovereign and sixteen nobles, besides extra knights (princes), and a dean, a secretary, the Lyon king-of-arms, and the gentleman usher of the green rod.

ORDER OF THE THISTLE
star, jewel, badge, and collar

Our Lady's thistle; the milk thistle.

pine thistle; a European plant, *Atactylis gummifera,* the involucres of which discharge a gum.

Russian thistle; a prickly, many-branched, small-leaved weed, *Salsola tragus,* which matures into a tumbleweed: it grows abundantly in the western part of the United States.

Scotch thistle; see under *Scotch.*

Syrian thistle; a thistle, *Cnicus syriacus,* of the Mediterranean region.

tall thistle; a common thistle of the United States, *Cnicus altissimus.*

Virgin Mary's thistle; the milk thistle.

wool thistle or *wooly-headed thistle*; same as *friar's-crown.*

yellow thistle; a yellow-headed thistle, *Cnicus horridulus,* characterized by sharply spinose foliage.

this'tle-bīrd, *n.* the American goldfinch, *Spinus* or *Chrysomitris tristis,* popularly known as the *yellowbird.*

this'tle but'tẽr-flȳ, *n.* the painted lady.

this'tle-ḉrown, *n.* an English gold coin of the value of a dollar, struck in the reign of James I.

this'tle dol'lăr, a Scottish silver coin issued in the sixteenth century.

this'tle·down, *n.* the pappus of the thistle; the down attached to the ripe flower head.

this'tle finch, any of several finches that feed on thistle seeds; especially, the goldfinch.

this'tle fun'nel, a bulging, flaring-mouthed funnel, in form somewhat resembling a thistle.

this'tle·wa̤rp, *n.* the thistle finch. [Obs.]

this'tly (-ly), *a.*; *comp.* thistlier; *superl.* thistliest, 1. full of or overgrown with thistles; as, *thistly* ground.

2. resembling a thistle or thistles; prickly.

thith'ẽr (*or* thith') *adv.* [ME. *thider*; AS. *thider, thyder.*]

1. to or toward that place or direction: opposed to *hither.*

2. to that end, point, or result. [Rare.]

hither and thither; see under *hither.*

thith'ẽr, *a.* being or situated in that (more distant) place or direction.

thith'ẽr·tō, *adv.* to that point; so far; up to then.

thith'ẽr·wărd, *adv.* thither; toward that place or point; in that direction.

thith'ẽr·wărdṣ, *adv.* thitherward.

thit'see, *n.* same as *theetsee.*

Thlas'pi, *n.* [L., from Gr. *thlaspi,* a kind of cress.] a genus of herbaceous plants of the order *Cruciferæ.* Field pennycress, or Mithridate mustard, *Thlaspi arvense,* occurs as a weed in cornfields, in some places in great abundance.

thlips·en·ceph'ȧ·lus, *n.*; *pl.* **thlips·en·ceph'ȧ·lī,** [Gr. *thlipsis,* pressure, and *enkephalos,* brain.] a monster with a deficient skull or with the upper part of the skull lacking.

thlip'sis, *n.* [Gr., pressure.] in medicine, compression or constriction of vessels, especially by an external cause.

thō', thō, *conj.* and *adv.* though.

thō, *def. art.* the. [Obs.]

thō, *pron.* those; they. [Obs.]

thō, *adv.* then; thereupon. [Obs.]

thōle, *n.* [AS. *thol*; Ice. *thollr,* a thole, a wooden peg.]

1. a pin or either of a pair of pins, made of metal or wood and set vertically in the gunwale of a boat to serve as a fulcrum for an oar.

2. the pin, or handle, of a snath.

thōle, *n.* [Gr. *tholos,* a dome.] in architecture, (a) a tholus; (b) the scutcheon or knot at the center of a timber vault; (c) a place in temples where votive offerings were suspended.

thōle, *v.t.*; tholed, *pt., pp.*; tholing, *ppr.* [AS. *tholian,* to bear, endure, suffer; O.H.G. *doljan, dolên, dultan*; G. *dolen,* to bear, endure, tolerate.]

1. to bear; to endure; to undergo. [Archaic or Brit. Dial.]

2. to allow or permit. [Archaic or Brit. Dial.]

thōle, *v.i.* 1. to suffer pain or grief; to bear. [Archaic or Brit. Dial.]

2. to wait. [Archaic or Brit. Dial.]

thōle'pin, *n.* a thole.

thol'ō·bāte, *n.* [Gr. *tholos,* a covered roof, and *basis,* basis.] the substructure on which a dome or cupola rests. [Rare.]

thō'lus, *n.*; *pl.* **thō'lī,** [Gr., a dome or any circular building.] in classical architecture, any round building which terminated at the top in a point; a dome or cupola: also written *tholos.*

> The Thirty Tyrants on one occasion summoned him, together with four others, to the *Tholus,* the place in which the Prytanes took their meals. —G. H. Lewes.

Thō·mae'ăn, Thō·mē'ăn (tō-), *n.* one belonging to a church of early Christians said to have been founded on the Malabar Coast of India by St. Thomas: also called *Christians of St. Thomas.*

Thō'mȧ·iṣm, *n.* same as *Thomism.*

Thom'ăs (tom'), *n.* [LL.; Gr. *Thōmas*; Ar. *tĕ'ōma,* lit., a twin.] one of the twelve apostles, who doubted at first the resurrection of Jesus: John xx. 24–29.

Thom'ăs·īte (tom'), *n.* same as *Christadelphian.*

Thō'miṣm (tō'), *n.* the doctrines of Thomas Aquinas, theologian of the thirteenth century, who attempted to reconcile the philosophy of Aristotle with the Christian faith. He held faith and reason to be the sources of knowledge and taught unconditional predestination and a physical as well as moral efficacy in the sacraments. His doctrines formed the basis of thirteenth century scholasticism.

Thō'mist, *n.* a follower of Thomas Aquinas; an adherent of Thomism.

Thō'mist, *a.* having to do with Thomas Aquinas, his doctrines, or his followers.

Thō·mis'tiç, *a.* of, or in the manner of, the *Thomists*: also *Thomistical.*

Thō'mīte, *n.* same as *Thomaean.*

Thomp'sŏn sub·mȧ·ḉhīne' gun (tom'), a type of submachine gun: a trade-mark.

thom'sen·ō·līte (tom'), *n.* [after Dr. J. *Thomsen,* of Copenhagen.] a hydrous fluoride of sodium, calcium, and aluminum. It is found occurring with pachnolite and cryolite in Greenland and Colorado.

Thom'sen'ṣ diṣ·ēaṣe', [after A. J. *Thomsen,* 19th-c. Dan. physician.] a disease, believed to be congenital, characterized by tonic spasms and rigidity of certain muscles after a period of inactivity. The stiffness disappears as the muscles are used. Also called *myotonia congenita.*

Thom'sŏn ef·fect', see under *effect.*

Thom·sō'ni·ăn, *a.* of or pertaining to Thomsonianism.

Thom·sō'ni·ăn, *n.* one who practices or believes in Thomsonianism.

Thom·sō'ni·ăn·iṣm, *n.* [after its founder, Dr. Samuel *Thomson,* of Massachusetts.] a system of botanical medicine, which proposed that only vegetable drugs be used.

thom'sŏn·īte, *n.* [after Thomas *Thomson,* early 19th-c Scot. chemist.] a mineral of the zeolite family, occurring generally in masses of a radiated structure, with a glassy or vitreous luster. It is a hydrous silicate of aluminum, calcium, and sodium.

thoṇg, *n.* [ME. *thong, thwang*; AS. *thwang,* a twisted string, thong.]

1. a narrow strip of leather, etc. used as a lace, strap, etc.

2. a whiplash, as of plaited strips of hide.

thoṇg sēal, the bearded seal, *Erignathus barbatus.*

thō'oid, *a.* [Gr. *thōs,* a jackal.] wolflike; related to or resembling the wolf; lupine: applied to a series of canine carnivores, including wolves, dogs, and jackals.

thō'oid, *n.* one of the thooid, or lupine, series of canine carnivores.

Thor, *n.* [Ice. *Thórr,* contr. from an older form *Thonor,* equivalent to AS. *thunor,* MnE. *thunder.*] in Norse mythology, the god of thunder, war, and strength, and the son of Odin: he had a magic hammer with which he destroyed the foes of the gods.

thō″rȧ·cen·tē'sis, *n.* [Gr. *thōrax,* thorax, and *kentēsis,* a pricking.] a surgical puncture or tapping of the chest wall.

thō'rȧ·ḉēṣ, *n.* alternative plural of *thorax.*

thō·rȧ·cē'trŏn, *n.*; *pl.* **thō·rȧ·cē'trȧ,** [Gr. *thōrax,* the thorax, and *ētron,* the abdomen.] the thorax, or second division of the body, of some crustaceans.

thō·rac'iç, *a.* [Gr. *thōrax,* the breast.] of, in, near, or pertaining to the thorax; as, the *thoracic* arteries.

thoracic duct; the main canal of the lymphatic system, passing along the front of the spinal column to the junction of the left subclavian and left internal jugular veins. It acts as a channel for the collection of the lymph from the portions of the body below the diaphragm, and from the left side of the body above the diaphragm.

thō·rac'iç, *n.* in zoology, one of a group of fishes having the ventral fins placed underneath the thorax, or directly beneath the pectoral fins.

Thō·rac'i·çȧ, *n.pl.* in zoology, the principal group of the *Cirripedia,* having the body formed of six thoracic segments, generally furnished with six pairs of limbs, the abdomen rudimentary, but often bearing caudal appendages. The common barnacle is the typical species.

thō·rac'i·çō-, thoraco- (sense 2).

thō·rac″i·çō·lum'băr, *a.* thoracolumbar.

thō'rȧ·çō-, [Gr. *thōrako-.*] a combining form meaning: (a) *the thorax,* as in *thoraco*plasty; (b) *the thorax and,* as in *thoraco*lumbar: also, before a vowel, *thorac-.*

thō″rȧ·çō·cyr·tō′sis, *n.* abnormal curvature of the thorax, resulting in a chest of unusual prominence.

thō″rȧ·çō·lum′băr, *a.* of the thoracic and lumbar regions.

thō·rȧ·çom′e·tẽr, *n.* same as *stethometer.*

thō′rȧ·çō·plas″ty, *n.* [Gr. *thōrax* (-*akos*), thorax, and *plassein*, to put into a certain form.] plastic surgery of the thorax; operative repair of defects of the chest.

Thō·rȧ·ços′trȧ·çȧ, *n.pl.* [Gr. *thōrax* (-*akos*), thorax, and *ostrakon*, a shell.] a large group of malacostracous crustaceans, having the thoracic somites covered and united with the head by an overlying shield or carapace, as the lobsters, crabs, shrimps, etc.

thō·rȧ·çot′ō·my, *n.* [Gr. *thōrax* (-*akos*), thorax, and *tamein*, to cut.] surgical incision of the thorax.

thō′răl, *a.* [L. *torus*, a couch or bed.] of or pertaining to a bed, especially to the marriage bed. [Rare.]

thō′rax, *n.*; *pl.* **thō′rax·eṣ, thō′rȧ·çēṣ,** [Gr. *thōrax*, the chest, a breastplate.]

1. in man and the higher vertebrates, the chest, or that cavity of the body formed by the spine, ribs, and breastbone, and situated between the neck and the abdomen, which contains the pleura, lungs, heart, esophagus, thoracic duct, etc.: in mammals the thorax is completely separated from the abdomen by the diaphragm.

2. the less sharply defined cavity in the lower vertebrates, as birds, fishes, etc.: in serpents and fishes the thorax is not completed below by a breastbone.

3. the middle one of the three main segments of an insect's body: three sections form the thorax: (a) the *prothorax*, bearing the first pair of legs, (b) the *mesothorax*, bearing the second pair of legs and first pair of wings, and (c) the *metathorax*, bearing the third pair of legs and the second pair of wings.

4. in the crustaceans and arachnidans, the chest segment united with the head into a single mass called the *cephalothorax*.

5. a breastplate, cuirass, or corselet.

thō′ri·ȧ, *n.* a white, earthy powder, thorium oxide, ThO_2, obtained by Berzelius in 1829 from thorite: also called *thorina*.

thō′ri·ȧ·nīte, *n.* a black, crystalline, radioactive mineral found in Ceylon, consisting chiefly of the oxides of thorium and uranium: it has a specific gravity of 9.32.

thō′riç, *a.* of, pertaining to, or containing thorium.

thō′rīte, *n.* [from *Thor*, the Norse deity.] a dark-brown or black mineral, $ThSiO_4$, a native silicate of thorium.

thō′ri·um, *n.* [Mod. L., from *Thor*.] a rare, grayish, radioactive chemical element occurring in monazite and thorite: symbol, Th; atomic weight, 232.12; atomic number, 90.

thorn, *n.* [AS. *thorn*.]

1. a very short, hard, leafless branch or stem with a sharp point.

2. any small tree or shrub bearing thorns.

3. the wood of any of these plants.

4. a sharp, pointed protuberance on an animal; spine.

5. any tenacious cause of hurt, irritation, annoyance, or worry: from the manner in which thorns prick.

6. in Old English and Old Norse, the runic character (þ), corresponding to either sound of English *th*, as in *this* or *thick*: so called because it was the first letter of the word *thorn*.

thirsty thorn; a small variety of thorny acacia, *Acacia seyal*, found in the Libyan and Nubian deserts.

thorn, *v.t.* to prick or pierce as with a thorn.

thorn ap′ple, 1. a hawthorn or its applelike fruit; haw.

2. a Jimson weed or any other related plant.

thorn′back, *n.* 1. a European ray with many tubercles on its back and a double row of spines on its tail.

2. a large spider crab with a spiny back.

thorn′bill, *n.* a hummingbird of the genus *Rhamphomicron*.

thorn′bīrd, *n.* a South American bird of the genus *Anumbius*: so called on account of its huge nest built of thorns and twigs.

thorn brooṃ, the furze, *Ulex europæus*.

thorn′but, *n.* a fish, the turbot.

thorn dev′il, the moloch, a spiny lizard.

thorned, *a.* thorny.

thorn′-head″ed (-hed″), *a.* having the head set with spines, as certain worms of the order *Acanthocephala*.

thorn′i·ness, *n.* the state or quality of being thorny.

thorn′less, *a.* without thorns.

thorn let′tẽr, a thorn (sense 6).

thorn′tāil, *n.* any hummingbird of the genus *Gouldia*, having pointed tail feathers.

thorn tree, any of various thorny trees; especially, the hawthorn.

thorn′y, *a.*; *comp.* thornier; *superl.* thorniest.

1. full of thorns; brambly; prickly.

2. having thorns or spines: said of some animals.

3. like a thorn; sharp.

4. full of obstacles, vexations, pain, etc.; as, the *thorny* road to peace.

5. full of controversial points; difficult; contentious; as, a *thorny* problem.

thŏr′ō, *a.*, *prep.*, *adv.* thorough.

thō′ron, *n.* [Mod. L., from *thor*ium and *-on* as in *argon*.] a radioactive isotope of radon, resulting from the disintegration of thorium: symbol, Tn; atomic weight, 220; atomic number, 86.

thŏr′ōugh (-ō), *a.* [ME. *thuruh*: an emphatic var. of *through*.]

1. originally, passing through: now chiefly in combination, as in *thorough*fare.

2. done or proceeding through to the end; thoroughgoing; complete; finished.

3. that is completely (as described); out-and-out; absolute; as, a *thorough* rascal.

4. very exact, accurate, or painstaking, especially with regard to details; as, a *thorough* person.

thŏr′ōugh, *prep.* through. [Obs.]

thŏr′ōugh, *adv.* 1. through. [Obs.]

2. thoroughly. [Dial.]

thŏr′ōugh, *n.* 1. a trench between two ridges; a channel for water. [Archaic and Brit. Dial.]

2. [T–] in English history, the thorough, ruthless administrative policies under Charles I, as carried out by William Laud and the Earl of Strafford.

thŏr′ōugh băss, 1. formerly, a system of indicating accompanying chords by placing figures representing complete chords under the notes of the bass.

2. the figures so used.

3. loosely, the theory of harmony.

thŏr′ōugh brāce, a leather thong serving as a spring in a carriage or other horse-drawn vehicle.

thŏr′ōugh·bred, *a.* 1. of pure or unmixed breed or race; bred from a sire and dam of official pedigree; as, a *thoroughbred* horse.

2. thoroughly trained, educated, cultured, etc.; well-bred.

thŏr′ōugh·bred, *n.* 1. a thoroughbred animal; specifically, [T–] any of a breed of race horses developed originally by crossing English with Turkish and Arabic horses.

2. a cultured, well-bred person.

thŏr′ōugh·fāre, *n.* [ME. *thurgh fare*, from *thurgh*, through, and *fare*.]

1. a way or passage through.

2. a public, unobstructed street open at both ends, especially one through which there is much traffic; highway; main road.

3. the act of passing through; transit.

thŏr′ōugh·foot, *n.* in nautical usage, a condition in which one or both blocks of a tackle have become twisted through the fall.

thŏr′ōugh·gō″ing, *a.* very thorough (senses 2, 3, 4).

thŏr′ōugh-līght″ed (-līt″), *a.* lighted so that the light passes through, as a room which has windows on opposite sides. [Rare.]

thŏr′ōugh·ly, *adv.* in a thorough manner.

thŏr′ōugh·ness, *n.* the condition or quality of being thorough; completeness.

thŏr′ōugh·pāced (-pāst), *a.* 1. thoroughly trained in all paces or gaits: said of horses.

2. thoroughgoing; out-and-out.

thŏr′ōugh·pin, *n.* a disease in horses which consists of enlarged mucous capsules growing on each side of the hocks, giving somewhat the appearance of a pin thrust through and occasionally causing lameness.

thŏr′ōugh·wax, *n.* an umbelliferous plant of the genus *Bupleurum*.

thŏr′ōugh·wŏrt, *n.* a short plant, *Eupatorium perfoliatum*, with flat clusters of grayish-white flowers and a stem passing through the leaf blade, native to North America: also called *boneset*.

thorp, thorpe, *n.* [ME. *thrope*; AS. *throp*; akin to G. *dorf*, village.] a hamlet or village; a small group of dwellings in the country: now mainly in place names; as, Copmans*thorpe*.

Thos, *n.* [Gr. *thōs*, a jackal.]

1. a genus of dogs including several species of jackal.

2. [t–] any animal of this genus.

thōṣe, *a.* and *pron.* [ME. *thas, thos*; AS. *thas, thæs*, pl. of *thes*, this.] pl. of *that*.

Thōth (*or* tōt), *n.* [L.; Gr. *Thōth*; Egypt. *Teḥuti*.] the ancient Egyptian god of learning and magic, the measurer of time and inventor of numbers, represented as having a human body and the head of a dog or of an ibis.

THOTH

thou, *pron.*; *pl. nom. and obj.* **yōu, yē,** *poss.* **yŏur, yŏurṣ,** [ME. *thu, thou*; AS. *thu*; akin to G. *du*.] the nominative second person singular of the personal pronoun: formerly used in familiar address but now replaced by *you* except in poetic or religious use, the speech of Friends or Quakers, and some British dialects: *thee* is the objective case form, *thy* or *thine* the possessive, and *thyself* the intensive and reflexive.

thou, *v.t.*; thoued, *pt.*, *pp.*; thouing, *ppr.* to address with the pronoun *thou*.

thou, *v.i.* to use *thou* and its forms in discourse.

thōugh (thō), *conj.* [ME. *thoh, thowgh, theah*; AS. *theah*, influenced by O.N. *tho*; akin to G. *doch*, yet, still.]

1. in spite of the fact that; notwithstanding that; although; as, *though* the car was repaired, it still rattled.

2. all the same; yet; still; as, they finally made it, *though* I never thought they would.

3. even if; supposing that; as, *though* he may fail, he will have tried.

Also spelled *tho, tho'*.

as though; as it (or I, you, he, etc.) would if; as if.

thōugh, *adv.* notwithstanding this or that; however; nevertheless: used as a conjunctive adverb: also spelled *tho, tho'*.

thought (thạt), *n.* [AS. *thoht, gethoht*, from *thencan*, to think; akin to G. *gedachtnis*, memory.]

1. the act or process of thinking; reflection; meditation; cogitation.

2. the power of reasoning or of conceiving ideas; capacity for thinking; intellect; imagination.

3. a result of thinking; idea, concept, opinion, etc.

4. the ideas, principles, opinions, etc. prevalent at a given time, among a given people, or in a given place; as, modern *thought* in child education.

5. attention; consideration; heed; as, don't give it a moment's *thought*.

6. mental engrossment; preoccupation; concentration; as, deep in *thought*.

7. intention or expectation; as, I had no *thought* of seeing her.

8. a little; trifle; as, please be a *thought* more careful.

Syn.—cogitation, conception, conceit, contemplation, deliberation, fancy, idea, imagination, notion, reflection, supposition.

thought, *v.* past tense and past participle of *think*.

thought′fụl, *a.* 1. full of thought; meditative; thinking; as, John was quiet and *thoughtful*.

2. showing or characterized by thought; serious; as, a *thoughtful* essay.

3. heedful, careful, attentive, etc.; especially, considerate of others; kind.

4. full of anxiety or care; anxious; solicitous. [Obs.]

thought′fụl·ly, *adv.* in a thoughtful manner.

thought′fụl·ness, *n.* the state or quality of being thoughtful; solicitude; consideration.

thought′less, *a.* 1. not stopping to think; careless; heedless; reckless.

2. not given thought; ill-considered; rash.

3. not considerate of others; inconsiderate; remiss.

4. stupid; dull-witted.

thought′less·ly, *adv.* in a thoughtless manner.

thought′less·ness, *n.* the state or quality of being thoughtless.

thought rēad′ing, telepathic reading; mind reading.

thought trans′fẽr, thought trans·fẽr′ence, telepathy.

thought wāve, a vibration supposed to communicate telepathic sensations or impressions.
Thō'us, *n.* same as *Thos.*
thou'ṣănd, *n.* [AS. *thūsend*; akin to G. *tausend.*]
1. the number of ten hundred; hence, indefinitely, a great number.
A thousand shall fall at thy side, and ten *thousand* at thy right hand.—Ps. xci. 7.
2. a symbol representing the number ten hundred, as M or 1,000.
thou'ṣănd, *a.* 1. indicating ten hundred.
2. denoting an indefinitely great number; as, it is a *thousand* chances to one that you succeed.
thou'ṣănd·fōld, *a.* 1. having a thousand parts.
2. having a thousand times as much or as many.
thou'ṣănd·fōld, *adv.* a thousand times as much or as many: with *a.*
thou'ṣănd·fōld, *n.* a number or amount a thousand times as great.
Thou'ṣănd Ī's'lănd dress'ing (ī'lănd), mayonnaise with minced capers or pickles, parsley, chili sauce, catsup, etc., used as a salad dressing.
thou'ṣănd-legṣ, *n.* any myriapod, as the gallyworm: called also *thousand-legger.*
thou'ṣăndth, *a.* 1. next after the nine hundred and ninety-ninth; coming last in a series of a thousand.
2. constituting or being one of a thousand equal parts into which anything is divided.
3. occurring as or being one of a very great number; as, to do a thing for the *thousandth* time.
thou'ṣăndth, *n.* 1. the thousandth one of a series.
2. any of the thousand equal parts of something.
thōw'el, thōwl, *n.* a thole.
thow'less, *a.* thewless. [Scot.]
Thrā'ciăn, *a.* of or relating to Thrace, an ancient region in the eastern Balkan Peninsula, or to its people, or culture.
Thrā'ciăn, *n.* a native or inhabitant of Thrace.
thrack, *v.t.* to load or burden. [Obs.]
thrạll, *n.* [AS. *thræl*; O.N. *thræl.*]
1. a slave; a bondman; a serf; hence, one who is in moral or psychological bondage.
2. slavery; bondage; thralldom.
thrạll, *a.* enslaved. [Rare.]
thrạll, *v.t.* to enslave; to put in thralldom. [Archaic.]
thrạll, *n.* a shelf or stand, as for barrels. [Brit. Dial.]
thrạll'dŏm, thrạl'dŏm, *n.* the state of being a thrall; bondage; servitude; as, the Greeks lived in *thralldom* under the Turks nearly 400 years.
thrạll'-less, *a.* without thrall; free.
thrạll'-līke, *a.* like one in thrall; slavish.
thrȧ'nīte, *n.* [Gr. *thranitēs*, from *thranos*, a bench, a form, especially the topmost bench in a trireme.] in ancient Greece, one of the rowers on the topmost bench in a trireme, who had the longest oars and the hardest work.
thrȧ·nit'iç, *a.* pertaining to or like a thranite.
thrap, *v.t.*; thrapped (thrapt), *pt., pp.*; thrapping, *ppr.* in nautical usage, to strap about; to bind on; to fasten round. [Rare.]
thrap'ple, *n.* same as *thropple.*
thrash, *v.t.* [ME. *threschen*; AS. *threscan*; akin to G. *dreschen*, to thresh.]
1. to thresh.
2. to beat or flog, as with a flail.
3. to defeat completely or mercilessly.
to thrash out; to discuss thoroughly and conclusively.
thrash, *v.i.* 1. to thresh.
2. to move violently, especially swinging one's arms about like threshing flails; to toss about; to lash.
3. in nautical usage, to force one's way against opposing wind, tide, etc.
thrash, *n.* the act of thrashing; specifically, in swimming, a kick, or movement of the legs, used in the crawl and backstroke.
thrash, thresh, *n.* a rush (plant). [Scot.]
thrash'ẽr, *n.* 1. a person or thing that thrashes.
2. a thresher (shark).
thrash'ẽr, *n.* [Brit. Dial. *thresher*, ultimately from same source as *thrush.*] any of a group of American songbirds resembling the thrush but having a long, stiff tail and a long bill.
thrash'ing, *n.* a beating; flogging.

thrȧ·son'iç·ăl, *a.* [from *Thraso*, a boaster in a comedy by Terence.] boastful; bragging.
thrȧ·son'iç·ăl·ly, *adv.* boastfully; in a thrasonical manner.
thrăst, *v.* obsolete past tense of *thrust.*
thrāve, thrēave, *n.* [ME. *threve*, from O.N. *threfi.*] a measure generally containing twenty-four sheaves, as of wheat. [Dial.]
thrạw, *v.t.*; thrawed, *pt., pp.*; thrawing, *ppr.* [AS. *thrawan*, to throw, twist.] to twist; to wrench; to distort; to wrest; to frustrate; to thwart. [Scot.]
thrạw, *v.i.* 1. to cast; to warp. [Scot.]
2. to twist, as in agony; to writhe. [Scot.]
thrạw, *n.* 1. a twist; a distortion; a wrench. [Scot.]
2. a pang; a throe. [Scot.]
dead thraw; the death throes. [Scot.]
thrạwn, *a.* [from *thraw*, dial. form of *throw.*]
1. distorted; twisted. [Scot.]
2. perverse; obstinate. [Scot.]
thread (thred), *n.* [AS. *thræd*, lit., what is twisted; from base of *thrawan*, to twist, to throw; akin to G. *draht.*]
1. a very fine cord composed of a strand or strands of spun silk, flax, cotton, etc., used in sewing: used without the article to mean such cords collectively; as, use black *thread.*
2. any of the yarns of which a fabric is woven.
3. a fine, threadlike filament, as of organic tissue, metal, glass, plastic, etc.
4. a thin line, stratum, vein, stream, ray, etc. of something.
5. an element suggestive of a thread in its continuousness, length, sequence, etc.; as, the *thread* of a story; the *thread* of life.
6. the spiral or helical ridge of a screw, bolt, nut, etc.
7. quality; composition. [Obs.]
8. a clew.
thread and thrum; good and bad together.
thread lace; lace made of thread.
thread, *v.t.*; threaded, *pt., pp.*; threading, *ppr.*
1. to put a thread through the eye of (a needle, etc.).
2. to string (beads, etc.) on or as on a thread.
3. (a) to pass through like a thread; to weave in and out of; as, he *threaded* the streets; (b) to pervade; as, a note of hope threaded the story; (c) to follow or proceed on in a threadlike fashion; as, *thread* one's way.
4. to fashion a thread (sense 6) on or in (a screw, pipe, etc.).
thread, *v.i.* 1. to go along or proceed in a threadlike fashion; to wind one's way or its way.
2. to form a thread when dropped from a spoon: said of boiling sirup, etc. that has reached a certain consistency.
thread'bāre, *a.* 1. worn down so that the threads show; having the nap worn off; as, a *threadbare* coat.
2. wearing old, worn clothes; shabby; as, a *threadbare* person.
3. worn out; trite; hackneyed; having no novelty or interest; as, a *threadbare* subject.
thread'bāre·ness, *n.* the state or quality of being threadbare.
thread cell, a lasso cell or nematocyst.
thread'en, *a.* made of thread; as, *threaden* sails. [Archaic or Dial.]
thread'ẽr, *n.* 1. one who or that which threads.
2. a device for threading a needle.
thread'fin, *n.* any fish of the genus *Polynemus* and related genera, having pectoral fins ending in threadlike rays.
thread'fish, *n.* 1. the cobblerfish.
2. the cutlass fish.
thread'foot, *n.* a riverweed.
thread her'ring, 1. a fish, *Opisthonema thrissa*, of the herring family, found in West Indian waters and along the eastern coast of the United States.
2. the gizzard shad.
thread'i·ness, *n.* the state or quality of being thready.
thread märk, a marking of paper currency by incorporating colored silk fibers in the paper pulp to make counterfeiting difficult.
thread'-nee"dle, thread'-the-nee"dle, *n.* a game in which children stand in a row holding hands, and the leader of the chain runs between every other one.
thread'-shaped (-shāpt), *a.* filiform; shaped like a thread.
thread'wŏrm, *n.* any of a group of long, threadlike parasitic worms of the order *Nematoidea*; specifically, the pinworm.

thread'y, *a.*; *comp.* threadier; *superl.* threadiest, 1. of or like a thread; stringy; fibrous; filamentous.
2. forming threads; viscid: said of liquids.
3. of or covered with threads or threadlike parts; fibrous.
4. resembling a thread in thinness or feebleness; as, a *thready* voice.
thrēap, *v.t.*; threaped (thrēpt), *pt., pp.*; threaping, *ppr.* [AS. *threapian*, to rebuke.]
1. to chide, scold, or rebuke. [Scot. or Brit. Dial.]
2. to pommel or thrash. [Brit. Dial.]
3. to maintain or assert obstinately. [Scot. or Brit. Dial.]
thrēap, *v.i.* to insist on some assertion; to contend; to quarrel. [Scot. or Brit. Dial.]
thrēap, *n.* a stubborn insistence; an obstinate decision or determination. [Scot. or Brit. Dial.]
threat (thret), *n.* [ME. *threte*; AS. *threat*, a throng, painful pressure; akin to G. *(ver)driessen*, to grieve, annoy.]
1. a statement or expression of intention to hurt, destroy, punish, etc., as in retaliation or intimidation.
There is no terror, Cassius, in your *threats.* —Shak.
2. an indication of imminent danger, harm, evil, etc.; as, the *threat* of war.
threat, *v.t.* and *v.i.* to threaten. [Obs.]
threat'en (thret'n), *v.t.*; threatened, *pt., pp.*; threatening, *ppr.* [AS. *threatian*, to reprove, threaten.]
1. to declare an intention of hurting or punishing; to make threats against.
2. to be a menacing indication of (something dangerous, evil, etc.); as, the clouds *threaten* rain or a storm.
3. to express intention to inflict (injury, retaliation, etc.).
4. to be a source of danger, harm, etc. to.
threat'en, *v.i.* 1. to use or make threats or menaces.
2. to have a menacing aspect; to give indication of impending danger or mischief; as, a *threatening* sky.
threat'en·ẽr, *n.* one who or that which threatens.
threat'en·ing, *a.* 1. indicating a threat or menace; as, a *threatening* look.
2. indicating something impending; as, the weather is *threatening.*
Syn.—menacing, intimidating, minatory, comminatory, foreboding, unpromising, imminent, impending.
threat'en·ing·ly, *adv.* in a threatening manner.
threat'fụl, *a.* full of threats; having a menacing appearance. [Rare.]
threat'fụl·ly, *adv.* in a threatful manner; with threats. [Rare.]
thrēave, *n.* same as *thrave.*
three, *a.* [AS. *thri*, *threo*, three; akin to G. *drei.*] totaling one more than two.
three, *n.* 1. the cardinal number between two and four.
2. a symbol representing the number three, as 3 or III.
3. a playing card, domino, or die with three spots.
rule of three; see under *rule.*
three'-bag'gẽr, *n.* a three-base hit. [Slang.]
three'-bāse hit, in baseball, a hit by which the batter can reach third base without benefit of an error: also called *triple.*
three'-çōat, *a.* having or requiring three coats, as of paint or plaster.
three'-çŏl'ŏr proc'ess, a process of printing, lithographing, etc. in full color by making superimposed impressions from three separate plates, each reproducing one primary color.
three'-çọr"nẽred, *a.* having three corners or angles; as, a *three-cornered* shelf.
3-D (thrē'dē'), three dimensions or three-dimensional: used of a motion-picture system in which a stereoscopic picture is projected on a flat screen and viewed through polaroid glasses.
three'-deck"ẽr, *n.* 1. a ship with three decks; especially, a former type of warship with three decks of cannon.
2. a structure with three levels.
3. a sandwich made with three slices of bread.
three'-flow"ẽred, *a.* bearing three flowers only; bearing flowers in clusters or groups of three.
three'fōld, *a.* 1. having three parts.
2. having three times as much or as many.

three′fōld, *n.* the bog or buck bean, *Menyanthes trifoliata.*

three′fōld, *adv.* in a threefold manner or degree; three times as much or as many.

three′-hand″ed, *a.* 1. having three hands.
2. done, played, or engaged in by three persons; as, a *three-handed* game of pool.

three′-lēaved (-lēvd), **three′-lēafed** (-lēft), *a.* having three leaves or leaflets; trifoliate.
three-leaved nightshade; same as *trillium.*

three′ling, *n.* same as *trilling.*

three′-lōbed, *a.* having three lobes; trilobate.

three′-mȧst″ed, *a.* having three masts.

three′-mȧst″ẽr, *n.* a vessel, especially a schooner, having three masts.

three′-mīle lim′it, the outer limit of a zone of water extending three miles offshore, regarded under international law as the extent of the territorial jurisdiction of the adjacent country.

three′-nẽrved, *a.* in botany, having three nerves; triple-nerved, as a leaf.

threep, *v.* and *n.* same as *threap.*

three′-pärt″ed, *a.* containing, consisting of, or divided into three parts.

three′pence (*or* thrip′ens), *n.* 1. the sum of three pence; three British pennies.
2. a British silver coin of this value, equal to about six cents.
Also *thrippence.*

three′pen·ny (*or* thrip′en-), *a.* 1. worth three pence.
2. of little worth; poor; mean; cheap.

three′-phāṣe, *a.* in electricity, designating or of a system of alternating-current circuits, each of which differs in phase by 120 degrees.

three′-phāṣ″ẽr, *n.* that which has three phases.

three′-piēce, *a.* designating a garment or costume composed of three separate pieces, as of a skirt, jacket, and topcoat.

three′-pīle, *n.* three-piled velvet.

three′-pīled, *a.* having a triple pile or nap, as a kind of fine velvet; hence, having the qualities or characteristics of three-pile.

three′-plȳ, *a.* consisting of three parts, layers, strands, or thicknesses; threefold.

three′-point″ed, *a.* having three points; tricuspidate.

three′-point land′ing, 1. a perfect airplane landing in which both main wheels and the tail wheel or skid touch the ground at the same time.
2. a successful conclusion to any venture. [Colloq.]

three′-quar′tẽr, three′-quar′tẽrṣ, *a.* 1. of or involving three fourths of something.
2. showing the face intermediate between profile and full face; as, a *three-quarter* portrait.

three′-quar′tẽr bind′ing, a type of bookbinding in which the material of the back, usually leather, is extended onto the covers for one third of their width: usually the outer corners are tipped with triangles of the same material.

three′-ring cīr′çus, 1. a circus having three rings for simultaneous performances.
2. any event or occasion characterized by a variety of simultaneous occurrences.

three′sçore, *a.* three times twenty; sixty; as, *threescore* years.

three′-sīd″ed, *a.* having three sides, especially three plane faces.

three′sōme, *a.* [ME. *thresum.*] triple; of or engaged in by three; as, a *threesome* reel; a *threesome* game of golf.

three′sōme, *n.* 1. a group of three persons.
2. a game played by three persons; specifically, in golf, a match in which one participant plays against two others, who alternate strokes on a single ball.

three′-squāre, *a.* having three plane surfaces of equal width: applied especially to certain files of triangular cross section.

three′-step, *n.* a dance in triple time or with three steps in each movement.

three′-valved (-valvd), *a.* trivalvular; having, splitting, or opening by three valves; as, *three-valved* fruit.

three′-wāy, *a.* having, controlling, connected with, or opening into three pipes, channels, or passages: generally noting a form of pipe connection; as, a *three-way* valve or stopcock.

threm·mȧ·tol′ō·ġy, *n.* [Gr. *thremma* (*-atos*), nursling, and *-logy.*] in biology, artificial evolution; the science of breeding or propagating animals and plants under domestication, of their congenital variations, and of the perpetuation of such variations.

thrēne, *n.* [L. *threnus*, from Gr. *thrēnos*, a lamentation.] a threnody; a dirge; also, lamentation. [Obs.]

thrē·net′iç, thrē·net′iç·ăl, *a.* [L. *threneticus*, from Gr. *thrēnētikos*, sorrowful.] of or pertaining to a threne; mournful; sorrowful.

thrē′nōde, *n.* same as *threnody.*

thrē·nō′di·ăl, *a.* threnodic.

thrē·nod′iç, *a.* of or like a threnody.

thren′ō·dist, *n.* a writer of threnodies; one who composes or sings dirges.

thren′ō·dy, *n.*; *pl.* **thren′ō·dieṣ,** [Gr. *thrēnōdia*, from *thrēnos*, lamentation, and *ōdē*, song.] a song of lamentation; a dirge.

thrēpe, *v.t.* same as *threap.*

threp·sol′ō·ġy, *n.* [Gr. *threpsis*, nourishment, and *-logy.*] the science of the nutrition of living organisms.

thresh, *v.t.*: threshed (thresht), *pt.*, *pp.*; threshing, *ppr.* [ME. *threshen*; AS. *threscan.*]
1. to beat out (grain) from its husk, as with a flail.
2. to beat grain out of (husks).
3. to flog; to thrash. [Rare.]
to thresh out; to discuss thoroughly and conclusively.

thresh, *v.i.* 1. to beat out grain from straw, as with a flail.
2. to toss oneself about; to thrash.

thresh, *n.* same as *thrash.*

thresh′el, *n.* an instrument to thresh with; a flail. [Obs. or Brit. Dial.]

thresh′ẽr, *n.* 1. a person who threshes.
2. a threshing machine.
3. a large shark of temperate and tropical seas, having a long tail with which it is said to thresh the water and drive its prey together.

thresh′ing mȧ·chïne′, a large, power-driven farm machine for threshing.

thresh′ōld, *n.* [AS. *therscwold*, threshold, from *threscan*, to thresh, to tread.]
1. a doorsill; a plank, stone, or piece of timber placed under a door.
2. the place or point of entering or beginning; an entrance; as, on the *threshold* of a career.
3. in psychology and physiology, the point at which a stimulus is just strong enough to be perceived or produce a response; as, the *threshold* of pain.

threst, *v.t.* to thrust. [Obs.]

thret′ty, *a.* thirty. [Obs.]

threw (thrụ), *v.* past tense of *throw.*

thrib′ble, *a.* [var. of *treble.*] threefold; triple. [Scot. and Brit. Dial.]

thrīce, *adv.* [ME. *thries*, from *thrie*, three, with genit. form.]
1. three times.
2. three times as much or as many; threefold.
3. very; greatly; highly.

thrīce′çock, *n.* the missel thrush. [Brit. Dial.]

thrid, *a.* third. [Obs.]

thrid, *n.* and *v.* thread. [Archaic or Brit. Dial.]

thrift, *n.* [ME.; O.N., from *thrifa*, to thrive, and noun suffix *-t.*]
1. originally, the condition of thriving; prosperity.
2. economical management; economy; frugality.
3. physical thriving; vigorous growth. [Rare.]
4. any of a number of short plants with narrow leaves and small white, pink, red, or purplish flowers.
5. a means of thriving; work; labor. [Scot.]
prickly thrift; a species of the genus *Acantholimon*, having prickly foliage.

thrift′i·ly, *adv.* 1. in a thrifty manner; frugally; economically.
2. becomingly; punctiliously. [Obs.]

thrift′i·ness, *n.* the state or quality of being thrifty; frugality.

thrift′less, *a.* without thrift; wasteful.

thrift′less·ly, *adv.* in a thriftless manner; extravagantly.

thrift′less·ness, *n.* the state or quality of being thriftless.

thrift′y, *a.*; *comp.* thriftier; *superl.* thriftiest, 1. characterized by or practicing thrift; frugal; sparing; using economy and good management.

> I am glad he has so much youth and vigor left, of which he has not been *thrifty.*
> —Swift.

2. thriving; successful; prosperous; fortunate.
3. growing vigorously, as a plant.
4. appearing prosperous. [Obs.]
5. useful; profitable. [Obs.]
Syn.—careful, economical, sparing, frugal.

thrill, *v.t.* [ME. *thrillen, thyrlen*; AS. *thyr*(*e*)*lian*, to pierce, from *thyrel*, perforation.]
1. to cause emotional excitement in, as though by piercing; to make shiver or tingle with excitement.
2. to produce vibrations or quivering in; to cause to tremble.
3. to perforate; to drill or penetrate. [Obs.]
4. to hurl; to throw; to cast. [Obs.]

thrill, *v.i.* 1. to feel emotional excitement; to shiver or tingle with excitement.
2. to tremble; to vibrate; to quiver.

thrill, *n.* [new formation from the *v.*]
1. a thrilling or being thrilled; tremor of excitement.
2. the quality of thrilling; as, this movie lacks *thrill.*
3. a vibration; a tremor; a quiver; specifically, in medicine, an abnormal tremor, as of the circulatory system, that can be felt on palpation.
4. a thriller.

thrill, *n.* a warbling; a trill.

thrill, *v.i.* to warble; to trill.

thrill′ănt, *a.* penetrating; thrilling; piercing. [Obs.]

thrill′ẽr, *n.* a person or thing that thrills; specifically, a thrilling story, motion picture, etc.

thrill′ing, *a.* 1. piercing; penetrating. [Obs.]
2. that thrills or causes emotional excitement; as, a *thrilling* experience.

thrill′ing·ly, *adv.* with thrilling sensations; in a thrilling manner.

thrill′ing·ness, *n.* the quality of being thrilling.

Thrī′nax, *n.* [Gr., a trident.] a genus of palm trees of the tribe *Corypheæ*, including nine species, mostly native to the West Indies.

thring, *v.t.* to thrust; to crowd. [Obs.]

thring, *v.i.* to push; to force one's way. [Obs.]

thrip′pence, *n.* threepence.

Thrips, *n.* [L.; Gr. *thrips*, a woodworm.]
1. a genus of small, destructive insects typical of the family *Thripidæ* or *Thripsidæ*: they live by sucking the juices of plants, as of tobacco.
2. [t—] any insect of this genus.

thrist, *n.* thirst. [Obs.]

thrīve, *v.i.*; throve *or* thrived, *pt.*; thrived *or* thriven, *pp.*; thriving, *ppr.* [ME. *thrifen*; O. N. *thrifask*, to have oneself in hand, a reflexive verb, from *thrifa*, to grasp.]
1. to prosper; to flourish; to be successful, especially as the result of industry, economy, and good management.
2. to grow; to increase in bulk or stature; to flourish; as, trees *thrive* in a good soil.

thriv′en, *v.* alternative past participle of *thrive.*

thrīv′ẽr, *n.* one who thrives, or prospers.

thrīv′ing·ly, *adv.* in a thriving or prosperous way.

thrīv′ing·ness, *n.* the state or quality of one who thrives; prosperity.

thrō′, thrö, *prep.*, *adv.*, and *a.* through.

thrōat, *n.* [AS. *throte*; akin to G. *drossel*, the gullet.]
1. the front of the neck below the chin and above the collarbone; the jugular region.
2. the upper part of the passage leading from the mouth and nose to the stomach and lungs, including the pharynx and the upper larynx, trachea, and esophagus.
3. any narrow, throatlike passage.
4. the part of a chimney between the gathering, or portion of the funnel which contracts in ascending, and the flue.
5. the narrow, contracted neck of a vase or jar.
6. the orifice of a gamopetalous flower.
7. in nautical usage, (a) that end of a gaff which is next to the mast; (b) the rounded angular point at which the arm of an anchor is joined to the shank; (c) the inside of the knee timber at the middle or turns of the arms.
a lump in the throat; a feeling of constriction in the throat, as from restrained emotion.
to cut one another's throats; to ruin one another, as by underselling or underbidding in business. [Colloq.]
to cut one's own throat; to be the means of one's own destruction or ruin. [Colloq.]
to jump down one's throat; to attack or critize one suddenly and violently. [Colloq.]
to ram (*something*) *down one's throat*; to force one to accept, hear, etc. something.
to stick in one's throat; to be hard to say, as from reluctance.

thrōat, *v.t.* 1. to utter in the throat, i.e., with a harsh, guttural quality.

So Hector hereto *throated* threats to go to sea in blood. —Chapman.

2. to channel or groove; to make a throat in.

thrōat′band, *n.* a throatlatch.

thrōat′bōll, *n.* the Adam's apple in the neck. [Obs.]

thrōat brāil, in nautical usage, a brail attached to the gaff for trussing up the sail close to the gaff as well as the mast.

thrōat hal′yärd, one of the ropes or tackles applied to hoist the inner part of the gaff and its portion of the sail.

-thrōat′ed, a combining form used in hyphenated compounds, meaning *having a* (specified kind of) *throat,* as in ruby-*throated.*

thrōat′i·ly, *adv.* in a throaty manner.

thrōat′i·ness, *n.* a throaty quality.

thrōat′ing, *n.* in architecture, the undercutting of a projecting molding, so as to prevent rain water from dripping down the surface of the wall.

thrōat′latch, *n.* a strap that passes under a horse's throat, for holding a bridle or halter in place.

thrōat pipe, the windpipe, or trachea.

thrōat′rọọt, *n.* an American species of avens, *Geum virginianum.*

thrōat′wŏrt, *n.* [from being formerly used in remedies for throat ailments.] any plant of several species of the genus *Campanula.*

thrōat′y, *a.*; *comp.* throatier; *superl.* throatiest; produced in the throat, as some speech sounds or tones, or characterized by such sounds, as the voice; guttural; hoarse.

throb, *v.i.*; throbbed, *pt., pp.*; throbbing, *ppr.* [ME. *throbben,* to throb.]

1. to beat, pulsate, vibrate, etc.

2. to beat strongly or fast; to palpitate, as the heart under exertion.

3. to feel or show emotional excitement, as by quivering, shivering, etc.

throb, *n.* the act of throbbing; a beat or pulsation, especially a strong one, as of the heart.

throb′bẽr, *n.* a person or thing that throbs.

throd′den, *v.i.*; throddened, *pt., pp.*; throddening, *ppr.* to grow; to thrive. [Brit. Dial.]

thrōe, *n.* [prob. from AS. *thrawu,* pain, affliction, influenced by *thrawen,* to twist.]

1. a spasm or pang of pain.

2. [*pl.*] pangs of childbirth; labor pains.

3. [*pl.*] desperate or agonizing struggle; agony, as the pangs of death.

thrōe, *v.i.*; throed, *pt., pp.*; throeing, *ppr.* to suffer throes; to struggle in extreme pain.

thrōe, *v.t.* to put in agony. [Rare.]

throm′bī, *n.pl.* of *thrombus.*

throm′bin, *n.* [from *thrombus* and *-in.*] the enzyme of the blood that causes clotting by forming fibrin.

throm′bō·ġen, *n.* [from Gr. *thrombos,* a lump, clot, and *-gen.*] prothrombin.

throm·bō·ġen′iç, *a.* producing a clot.

throm′boid, *a.* like a thrombus.

throm′bōsed (-bōst), *a.* having a thrombus.

throm·bō′sis, *n.* [Mod. L.; Gr. *thrombōsis,* coagulation, from *thrombos,* a clot, lump.] coagulation of the blood in some part of the circulatory system, forming a clot that obstructs circulation in that part.

throm·bot′iç, *a.* of or having thrombosis.

throm′bus, *n.*; *pl.* **throm′bī,** [Mod. L.; Gr. *thrombos,* a clot, lump.] a fibrinous coagulum or clot formed in thrombosis.

thrōne, *n.* [OFr. *trone*; L. *thronus,* from Gr. *thronos,* a seat.]

1. a seat occupied by one having power or authority; especially, the chair of state of a sovereign: it is usually on a dais, covered with a canopy, and highly decorated.

2. the power or rank of a king, cardinal, etc.; sovereignty.

3. a sovereign, ruler, etc.; as, orders from the *throne.*

4. in theology, an order in the hierarchy of angels.

thrōne, *v.t.*; throned, *pt., pp.*; throning, *ppr.*

1. to place on a throne; to enthrone.

2. to place in an elevated position; to give an elevated place to; to exalt.

thrōne, *v.i.* to sit on a throne; to sit in state as a king.

thrōne′less, *a.* without a throne.

thrọng, *n.* [ME. *throng, thrang*; AS. (*ge*)*thrang,* from the base of *thringan,* to press, crowd.]

1. a great number of people gathered together; a crowd.

2. a crowding together of people; a crowded condition.

3. any great number of things considered together; a multitude.

4. a time of pressing work or active business; as, the *throng* of the harvest. [Scot.]

thrọng, *v.i.*; thronged, *pt., pp.*; thronging, *ppr.* [AS. *thringan,* to crowd.] to crowd; to gather together, move, or press in a throng.

thrọng, *v.t.* 1. to crowd or press upon in large numbers.

2. to crowd into; to fill with a throng; as, to *throng* a hall.

3. to gather together into a throng.

thrọng, *a.* 1. thickly crowded together; thronged; crowded. [Obs.]

2. very occupied or engaged; busy. [Obs.]

thrọng′ly, *adv.* in crowds. [Obs.]

thrōpe, *n.* a thorp or village. [Obs.]

throp′ple, *n.* the windpipe. [Brit. Dial.]

throp′ple, *v.t.* to strangle; to throttle. [Brit. Dial.]

thros′tle (thros′l), *n.* [AS. *throstle*; akin to G. *drossel.*]

1. a bird, *Turdus musicus,* the song thrush. [Scot.]

2. a form of spinning machine in which the thread is spun from roves by the continuous operation of a set of drawing rollers with bobbins and fliers: so named from the humming sound it makes.

thros′tle çock, the male missel thrush. [Brit. Dial.]

throt′tle, *n.* [dim. of *throat.*]

1. the throat or windpipe. [Rare.]

2. the valve in an internal-combustion engine that regulates the amount of fuel vapor entering the cylinders.

3. the hand lever or foot pedal that controls this valve.

throt′tle, *v.t.*; throttled (-tld), *pt., pp.*; throttling, *ppr.* 1. to choke; to strangle.

2. to stop the utterance of; to suppress; to silence.

3. to reduce the flow of (fuel vapor) by means of a throttle.

4. to slow (*down*) by this or similar means.

5. to utter with breaks and interruptions, as a person half suffocated. [Rare.]

throt′tle, *v.i.* 1. to choke; to strangle.

2. to breathe hard, as when nearly suffocated.

throt′tle lev′ẽr, the hand lever by which the throttle valve is operated.

throt′tlẽr (-lẽr), *n.* one who or that which throttles.

throt′tle valve, a throttle (sense 2).

through (thrö), *prep.* [ME. *thurgh, thuruh*; AS. *thurh*; akin to G. *durch.*]

1. in one side and out the other side of; from end to end of; between the parts of.

2. in the midst of; among.

3. by way of.

4. over the entire extent or surface of.

5. to various places in; around; as, he toured *through* France.

6. from beginning to end of; throughout; during the time of.

7. by means of; as, *through* her help.

8. as a result of; because of; as, done *through* error.

through, *adv.* 1. in one side and out the other; from end to end; between the parts.

2. from the beginning to the end.

3. completely to the end; to a conclusion; as, he saw it *through.*

4. thoroughly; completely; as, soaked *through* (often reduplicatively, *through and through*).

through, *a.* 1. extending from one place to another; allowing free passage; as, a *through* street.

2. traveling to the destination without stops; as, a *through* train.

3. not necessitating changes; good for traveling without intermediate transfer; as, a *through* ticket.

4. arrived at the end; finished; as, I'm *through* with this assignment.

5. at the end of one's usefulness, resources, etc.; as, he's *through* in politics.

6. having no further dealings, connections, etc.; as I'm *through* with that crowd.

Also spelled *thro', thro, thru.*

through bōlt, a bolt which passes through the thickness of what it fastens.

through bridġe, a bridge so constructed that the track or roadway is between the trusses, and not on top.

through çōld, a deep-seated cold. [Obs.]

through′ly, *adv.* thoroughly. [Archaic.]

through·out′, *prep.* all the way through; in or during every part of.

through·out′, *adv.* in or during every part; everywhere; the whole time; in every respect.

through stōne, in architecture, a bondstone; a stone that passes entirely through a wall.

thrōve, *v.* alternative past tense of *thrive.*

thrōw, *n.* agony of travail; throe. [Obs.]

thrōw, *n.* [AS. *thrah, thrāg,* a short time.] a brief space of time; as little while; a trice. [Obs.]

thrōw, *v.t.*; threw, *pt.*; thrown, *pp.*; throwing, *ppr.* [AS. *thrāwan,* to throw, twist; akin to G. *drehen,* to twist, turn.]

1. to twist strands of (silk, etc.) into thread.

2. to cause to fly through the air by releasing from the hand at the end of a rapid motion of the arm; to cast; to hurl.

3. to discharge through the air from a catapult, pump, etc.

4. to hurl violently, as in anger, etc.; to dash; as, she *threw* the vase on the ground.

5. to cause to fall; to upset; to overthrow; dislodge; as, he *threw* the other wrestler, she was *thrown* by her horse.

6. to move or send rapidly; to advance; as, they *threw* reinforcements into the battle.

7. to put suddenly and forcibly into or onto a specified object or place; as, she *threw* the clothes into the suitcase.

8. to put suddenly and forcibly into a specified condition or situation; as, he was *thrown* into prison, the meeting was *thrown* into confusion.

9. to cast or roll (dice).

10. to make (a specified cast) at dice; as, he *threw* a five.

11. to cast off; to shed; as, snakes *throw* their skins, the horse *threw* its shoe.

12. to bring forth (young); to give birth to: said of domesticated animals.

13. to move (the lever of a switch, clutch, etc.) or connect, disconnect, engage, etc. by so doing.

14. to direct, cast, turn, project, etc. (variously with *at, on, upon, over, toward,* etc.); as, she *threw* a glance *at* me, his shadow was *thrown on* the ground, the window *threw* an eerie light.

15. to put (blame *on,* influence *into,* obstacles *before,* etc.).

16. to lose (a game, race, etc.) deliberately, as by prearrangement. [Colloq.]

17. to give (a party, dance, etc.). [Slang.]

18. in card games, to play or discard (a card) from the hand.

19. in ceramics, to shape on a potter's wheel.

to throw across; to construct transversely; as, *to throw* a bridge *across* a stream.

to throw away; (a) to rid oneself of; to discard; (b) to be wasteful of; to waste; (c) to fail to make use of.

to throw a (*monkey*) *wrench into*; to stop or obstruct by direct interference; to sabotage.

to throw back; (a) to cause to be reflected; (b) to reject as unfit.

to throw by; to lay aside or reject as useless.

to throw cold water on; see under *cold.*

to throw down; to subvert; to overthrow; to destroy.

to throw dust in (*someone's*) *eyes*; see under *dust.*

to throw good money after bad; to continue to invest in a failing enterprise.

to throw in; (a) to inject; (b) to put in; to deposit with others; (c) to add extra or free, as to complete a sale or a bargain; (d) to engage (a clutch) or cause (gears) to mesh.

to throw in the sponge; see under *sponge.*

to throw light on or *upon*; to illumine; to make more clear; as, *to throw light on* a mystery or a subject.

to throw off; (a) to cast aside; to rid oneself of, as an incumbrance; (b) to evade (a pursuer); (c) to expel; to emit, etc.; (d) [Colloq.] to write or utter quickly, in an offhand manner.

to throw on; to put on (a garment) hastily or carelessly.

to throw oneself at; to try very hard to win the affection, friendship, or love of.

to throw oneself into; to engage in with great zeal and energy.

to throw oneself upon (or *on*); to beg the mercy or indulgence of; to rely on for support; as, *to throw oneself upon* the mercy of the court.

to throw open; (a) to open promptly and suddenly, as a door; (b) to remove all restrictions from; to give free access to; as, competition was *thrown open* to all.

to throw out; (a) to discard; (b) to reject; (c) to put forth or utter, as a hint or sugges-

tion; (d) to disengage (a clutch); (e) in baseball, to throw the ball to a baseman so as to put out (a runner).
to throw over; (a) to give up; to abandon; (b) to jilt.
to throw overboard; to throw from a vessel into the sea; to abandon; to betray.
to throw the bull; to talk glibly, especially untruthfully or insincerely. [Slang.]
to throw together; to make or assemble hurriedly and carelessly.
to throw up; (a) to give up or abandon; (b) to vomit; (c) to construct rapidly; (d) to mention (something) repeatedly (*to* someone), as in reproach or criticism.
Syn.—cast, fling, hurl, pitch, toss.

thrōw, *v.i.* to perform the act of throwing, flinging, or casting.
to throw about; to cast about; to try expedients.
to throw back; to revert in type or character to an ancester; to show atavism.

thrōw, *n.* 1. the action of a person who throws; a cast.
2. a cast of dice, or the numbers cast.
3. a venture; a risk.
4. the distance something is or can be thrown; as, a stone's *throw*.
5. (a) a spread or coverlet for draping over a bed, etc.; (b) a scarf or the like for throwing around the shoulders.
6. (a) the motion of a moving part, as a cam, eccentric, etc.; (b) the extent of such a motion.
7. in geology, the amount of displacement at a fault.
8. in wrestling, (a) the act of throwing an opponent; (b) a particular way of doing this.
9. a stroke; a blow. [Obs.]
10. in electricity, an agitation of a galvanometer needle or a suspended coil because of a sudden sufficient variation in a current acting upon it.
11. in ceramics, the wheel, jigger, or table of a potter.

thrōw'ȧ·wāy, *n.* a leaflet, handbill, etc. distributed as in the streets or from house to house.

thrōw'back, *n.* 1. a throwing back; a check.
2. reversion to an ancestral type or characteristic, or an instance of this.

thrōw'-crook, *n.* 1. a machine for twisting hay or straw into ropes. [Scot.]
2. a potter's wheel. [Scot.]

thrōw'down, *n.* a severe rebuff. [Slang.]

thrōw'ẽr, *n.* one who or that which throws; specifically, (a) a person who winds or twists silk; a throwster; (b) a potter who works a throwing engine or wheel.

thrōw'ing en'ġine, a revolving disk or table, carried by an upright spindle, on which the mass of clay is first roughly molded by the hand of the potter; a potter's wheel: also called *throwing mill, throwing table, throwing wheel*.

thrōw'ing stick, an instrument for hurling spears, used by certain native tribes.

thrōw lāthe, a hand lathe.

thrōwn, *v.* past participle of *throw*.

thrōwn, *a.* 1. pitched; hurled.
2. unseated from a horse.
3. cast to the ground, as in wrestling.
thrown silk; see under *silk*.
thrown singles; silk cord or thread made by first combining two or three singles to make cords, three or more of which are then twisted together.

thrōw'off, *n.* 1. a start in a race or hunt.
2. in a printing press, a device for preventing an impression at any time by displacing the platen while the machinery continues in motion.
3. something thrown off.

thrōw'out, *n.* 1. the act of throwing or casting out; rejecting.
2. an apparatus for throwing a machine out of gear; specifically, a device or group of devices for separating the driving and driven plates of a clutch.
3. an apparatus which removes the carcasses of scalded hogs from the scalding tub.
4. any person or thing cast aside or rejected.

thrōw'stẽr, *n.* one who throws; specifically, one who twists or winds silk into threads; a thrower.

thrōw stick, 1. a throwing stick.
2. a stick, usually with a nob at the end, used for hurling, as a boomerang.

thru̇, *prep., adv., and a.* through.

thrum, *n.* [ME. and AS. *thrum*, ligament.]
1. [*pl.*] the row of warp thread ends left on a loom when the web is cut off.
2. any of these ends.
3. any short end thread or fringe.
4. any coarse yarn.
5. anything resembling a thrum, as a filamentous or fringelike appendage.
6. [*pl.*] in nautical usage, short pieces of woolen or hempen yarn for thrumming canvas.

thrum, *v.t.*; thrummed, *pt., pp.*; thrumming, *ppr.* 1. to fringe; to furnish with thrums.
2. in nautical usage, to insert short pieces of woolen or hempen yarn in (canvas) to make a rough surface for chafing, stopping leaks, etc.

thrum, *v.t.*; thrummed, *pt., pp.*; thrumming, *ppr.* [echoic.]
1. to play on (a stringed instrument) monotonously, idly, or unskillfully; to strum.
2. to tell in a monotonous, tiresome way.
3. to drum on with the fingers.

thrum, *v.i.* 1. to thrum a stringed instrument.
2. to sound when so played: said of a guitar, etc.
3. to drum with the fingers.

thrum, *n.* a thrumming or the sound of this.

thrum'-eȳed (-īd), *a.* in botany, having anthers projecting from the throat of the corolla.

thrum'my, *a.*; *comp.* thrummier; *superl.* thrummiest; consisting of, covered with, or resembling thrums; shaggy; rough.

thrum'wŏrt, *n.* 1. a species of amaranth, *Amarantus caudatus*, or love-lies-bleeding.
2. same as *starfruit*.

thrush, *n.* [ME. *thrusch*; AS. *thrysce*.]
1. a songbird of the family *Turdidæ*, and especially of the genus *Turdus*, including the robin, wood thrush, bluebird, hermit thrush, etc. of North America and the common thrush, blackbird, ouzel, etc. of Europe; specifically, the mavis, throstle, or song thrush, *Turdus musicus*.

SONG THRUSH OR MAVIS (*Turdus musicus*)

2. any bird, not of the thrush family, but resembling a true thrush or mistaken for one: usually with a qualifying epithet.

thrush, *n.* [Dan. *troske*; Sw. *trosk*.]
1. a disease, especially of children, caused by a fungus and characterized by the formation of milky-white lesions on the membranes of the mouth, lips, and throat.
2. a disease of a horse's foot, characterized by the formation of pus.

thrush black'bīrd, the rusty grackle. [Dial.]

thrush'el, *n.* the throstle. [Brit. Dial.]

thrush'ẽr, *n.* a thrush; specifically, the song thrush or mavis. [Brit. Dial.]

thrush nīght'in·gāle (nīt'), a large nightingale having a spotted breast.

thrush tit, any of several birds of the genus *Cochoa*. They are mostly blue, green, or purple and are native to Southeastern Asia and Java.

thrust, *v.t.*; thrust, *pt., pp.*; thrusting, *ppr.* [ME. *thristen*, from O.N. *thrȳsta*, to thrust.]
1. to push with sudden force; to shove; to drive.
2. to pierce; to stab.
3. to put (a person) in some position or situation against his wishes or the wishes of others: often used reflexively; as, she *thrust* herself upon us two months ago.
4. to interject or interpose; as, he *thrust* a question in occasionally.
5. to extend, as in growth; as, the tree *thrusts* its branches high.
to thrust aside; to push out of the way; to displace.
to thrust forth; (a) to drive out; to expel; (b) to cause to project.
to thrust on; to impel; to urge.
to thrust oneself in or *into*; to obtrude; to intrude; to enter where one is not invited or not welcome.
to thrust out; to drive out or away; to expel.
to thrust upon; to force or impose upon.

thrust, *v.i.* 1. to push or shove against something.
2. to make a thrust, or stab.
3. to force one's way: with *into, through*, etc.
4. to extend, as in growth.

thrust, *n.* 1. the act of thrusting; specifically, (a) a sudden, forceful push or shove; (b) a lunge or stab, as with a weapon.
2. continuous pressure of one part against another, as of a rafter against a wall.
3. (a) the driving force of a propeller in the line of its shaft; (b) the forward force produced in reaction by the escaping gases in jet propulsion.
4. in geology, an almost horizontal fault.
5. in mining, the breaking down of the roof of a gallery, or any similar opening, by the pressure of the superincumbent rocks.

thrust beãr'ing, in shipbuilding, the bearing which receives and transmits to the hull the thrust of a screw propeller: also called *thrust block*.

thrust'ẽr, *n.* one who thrusts; specifically, a swordsman.

thrust hōe, a hoe worked by pushing.

thrust'ing, *n.* 1. the act of pushing with force.
2. [*pl.*] in cheese making, the white whey pressed out by squeezing curds: also called *thrutchings*.

thrust'ing sçrew (skru̇), a screw of a press, as one for pressing curd in cheese making.

thrus'tle (thrus'l), *n.* a throstle. [Obs.]

thrust plāne, in geology, the line of junction of the dissevered parts of a reversed fault, where the upper rocks have been so moved as to be superimposed upon underlying beds.

thrust shȧft, the part of a shaft of a screw propeller which carries the thrust bearings.

thrutch'ingṣ, *n.* same as *thrusting*, sense 2.

thud, *n.* [prob. from dial. var. of ME. *thidden* (AS. *thyddan*), to strike, thrust; influenced by echoism.]
1. a blow.
2. a dull sound, as that of a heavy, solid object dropping on a soft but solid surface.

thud, *v.t.*; thudded, *pt., pp.*; thudding, *ppr.* 1. to beat; to hit; to strike. [Scot.]
2. to drive rapidly or impetuously. [Scot.]

thud, *v.i.* to hit or fall with a thud.

thug, *n.* [Hind. *ṭhag*, swindler (euphemism); Prakrit *ṭhaga*; Sans. *sthaga*, a cheat, rogue.]
1. [*also* T-] a member of a former religious organization of India who murdered and robbed in the service of Kali, a god of destruction.
2. any assassin, cutthroat, or ruffian.

thug'gee, *n.* [Hind. *ṭhagī*, robbery.] murder and robbery as formerly practiced by the thugs of India.

thug'gee·iṣm, *n.* thuggee.

thug'gẽr·y, *n.* thuggee; the practices of thugs.

thug'giṣm, *n.* thuggee; lawless violence.

Thū'jȧ, *n.* [Mod. L., from Gr. *thyia*, African tree with aromatic wood.]
1. a genus of trees of the pine family, with fragrant, soft, waxy, scalelike leaves.
2. [t-] any tree of this genus; arbor vitae.

Thū'lē, *n.* [L.; Gr. *Thoulē, Thylē*.] in ancient geography, the northernmost region of the world, possibly Norway, Iceland, or Mainland (the largest of the Shetland Islands): often in *ultima Thule* (farthest Thule).

thū'li·ȧ, *n.* in chemistry, thulium oxide, Tm_2O_3.

thū'līte, *n.* in mineralogy, a reddish variety of epidote, found in the granite districts of Norway.

thū'li·um, *n.* [Mod. L.; see *Thule*.] a metallic chemical element of the rare-earth group: symbol, Tm; atomic weight, 169.4; atomic number, 69.

thumb (thum), *n.* [AS. *ṭhūma*, a thumb.]
1. the short, thick inner digit of the human hand, apposable to the other fingers; pollex.
2. a corresponding part in other animals.
3. that part of a glove or mitten which covers the thumb.
4. in architecture, an ovolo.
all thumbs; clumsy; fumbling.
thumbs down; a signal of rejection or disapproval.
thumbs up; a signal of acceptance or approval.
under one's thumb; under one's influence or sway.

thumb, *v.t.*; thumbed, *pt., pp.*; thumbing, *ppr.* 1. to handle awkwardly; to play with the fingers; as, to *thumb* over a tune.

2. to handle, turn, soil, or wear with or as with the thumb.

3. to turn over the thumb, as a glass: an old custom among drinkers who wished to demonstrate that they had drained their glasses to the last drop. [Obs.]

4. (a) to solicit (a ride) in a passing automobile by extending a thumb in the direction one wishes to travel; (b) to make (one's way) in this manner. [Colloq.]

to thumb one's nose; to raise one's thumb to the nose with the fingers extended, as a coarse gesture of defiance or insult.

thumb, *v.i.* to play with the fingers; to thrum.

to thumb through; to glance rapidly through (a book), as by releasing pages along their edge with the thumb.

thumb çlēat, in nautical usage, a small cleat, resembling a thumb, for preventing the topsail reef earings from slipping, and other purposes.

thumbed, *a.* 1. having thumbs.

2. marked by handling; as, *thumbed* books.

thumb'i·kin, *n.* a thumbkin. [Scot.]

thumb'-in'dex, *v.t.* to furnish (a book) with a thumb index.

thumb in'dex, a reference index for books, consisting of a series of rounded notches cut in the front edge of a book with a tab at the base of each notch bearing a letter or title: the desired section can be turned to quickly by placing the thumb or a finger on the proper notch.

thumb'kin, *n.* a thumbscrew (sense 2).

thumb latch, a kind of door latch, operated by the thumb being placed on the lever to raise the latch.

thumb'less, *a.* without a thumb; hence, clumsy; awkward.

thumb'märk, *n.* a mark left by the impression of the thumb, as on the leaves of a book; hence, any mark resembling this.

thumb'nāil, *n.* 1. the nail of the thumb.

2. something as small as a thumbnail.

thumb'nāil, *a.* of the size of a thumbnail; very small, brief, or concise; as, a *thumbnail* sketch.

thumb nut, a nut for a bolt or screw, having wings which give a purchase to the thumb in turning it.

thumb'print, *n.* an impression or print of the thumb made for purposes of identification.

thumb ring, a ring worn on the thumb.

thumb'sçrew (-skrū), *n.* 1. a screw having a broad, flat head which may be turned with the thumb and fingers.

2. a former instrument of torture for squeezing the thumbs.

thumb'stall, *n.* 1. a kind of thimble or ferule of iron, horn, or leather, with the edges turned up to receive the thread in making sails. It is worn on the thumb to tighten the stitches.

2. a case or sheath of leather or other substance to be worn on the thumb.

3. a buckskin cushion worn on the thumb, and used to close the vent of a gun while it is being sponged.

4. a fisherman's cot worn on the thumb to protect it from friction.

5. a gold or silver cap formerly worn on the thumb by English bishops; a pouncer.

thumb'tack, *n.* a kind of tack with a broad, flat head that can be pressed into a board, etc. with the thumb.

Thum'mim, *n.pl.* [Heb. *tummūn*, pl. of *tōm*, perfection.] see *Urim and Thummim.*

thump, *n.* [imitative.]

1. a blow with something heavy and blunt, as with a cudgel.

2. the dull sound made by such a blow.

thump, *v.t.*; thumped (thumpt), *pt., pp.*; thumping, *ppr.* 1. to strike with a thump or thumps.

2. to thrash; to beat severely.

thump, *v.i.* 1. to hit or fall with a thump.

2. to make a dull, heavy sound; to pound; to throb.

thump'ẽr, *n.* 1. a person or thing that thumps; specifically, a heavy blow.

2. a person or thing that is huge or great; a whopper. [Slang.]

thump'ing, *a.* 1. that thumps.

2. very large; whopping. [Colloq.]

thun'dẽr, *n.* [AS. *thunor*, thunder; akin to G. *donner*.]

1. the sound that follows a flash of lightning, caused by the sudden disturbance of air by electrical discharge.

2. any sound resembling this.

3. a threatening, menacing, or extremely vehement utterance.

4. a thunderbolt. [Obs. or Poetic.]

to steal one's thunder; to use one's ideas or methods without permission and without giving credit; especially, to lessen the effectiveness of another's statement or action by anticipating him in this.

thun'dẽr, *v.i.*; thundered, *pt., pp.*; thundering, *ppr.* 1. to produce the noise of thunder; to make thunder: usually in the impersonal construction; as, it *thundered* yesterday.

2. to make a sound resembling thunder.

3. to utter loud denunciations or threatenings.

thun'dẽr, *v.t.* 1. to emit as with the noise of thunder; to utter with a loud and threatening voice; to utter or issue by way of threat or denunciation.

2. to strike, drive, attack, etc. with the sound or violence of thunder.

thun·dẽr·ā'tion, *interj.* an exclamation of surprise, emphasis, etc. [Slang.]

thun'dẽr·bīrd, *n.* 1. an Australian bird, *Pachycephala pectoralis*, a kind of shrike.

2. in the mythology of certain North American Indians, an enormous bird supposed to produce thunder, lightning, and rain.

thun'der·bōlt, *n.* 1. a flash of lightning and the accompanying thunder.

2. in heraldry, a bearing represented as a twisted bar in pale, inflamed at each end, surmounting two jagged darts in saltire, between two wings expanded, with streams of fire issuing from the center.

3. something that stuns with the speed and force of a thunderbolt; as, the news was a *thunderbolt*.

4. a person acting with sudden violence or force.

5. a bolt or missile imagined as hurled to earth by a stroke of lightning.

6. a thunderstone. [Rare.]

thun'dẽr·bōlt bee'tle, a long-horned, wood-boring beetle, *Arhopalus fulminans*; so called from the zigzag markings on the elytra.

thun'dẽr·çlap, *n.* 1. a clap or burst of thunder.

2. anything resembling this in being sudden, startling, violent, etc.

thun'dẽr·çloud, *n.* a storm cloud charged with electricity and producing lightning and thunder.

thun'dẽr·egg, *n.* [perhaps from a Pueblo ceremony involving their use in invoking thunder.] a cryptocrystalline variety of quartz, often found in egg-shaped nodules.

thun'dẽr·ẽr, *n.* one who or that which thunders; specifically, [T-] Jupiter; Zeus; also, in England, the London *Times*.

thun'dẽr·fish, *n.* 1. same as *raad*.

2. a cyprinoid fish frequenting European waters; a loach.

thun'dẽr·flow"ẽr, *n.* the cornpoppy, the stitchwort, or the white campion.

thun'dẽr·head (-hed), *n.* a round mass of cumulus clouds appearing before a thunder storm.

thun'dẽr·ing, *a.* 1. producing or characterized by a loud noise, as that of thunder.

2. extraordinary; very great; tremendous: used as an intensive; as, he went at a *thundering* pace. [Colloq.]

thun'dẽr·ing, *n.* the report of an electrical explosion; thunder.

thun'dẽr·ing·ly, *adv.* in a thundering manner.

thun'dẽr·less, *a.* without thunder.

thun'dẽr·ous, *a.* 1. producing or full of thunder.

How he before the *thunderous* throne doth lie. —Milton.

2. making a noise like thunder.

thun'dẽr·ous·ly, *adv.* in a thunderous manner; attended by thunder or loud noise.

thun'dẽr·pēal, *n.* a peal, or loud crash, of thunder.

thun'dẽr·pump, *n.* same as *thunder pumper*.

thun'dẽr pump'ẽr, an American bird, the bittern.

thun'dẽr·show"ẽr, *n.* a shower accompanied by thunder and lightning.

thun'dẽr snāke, 1. a snake of the genus *Ophibolus*, as the milk snake and king snake.

2. the worm snake.

thun'dẽr·squall", *n.* a squall accompanied by thunder and lightning.

thun'dẽr·stōne, *n.* 1. a rounded stone, fossil, prehistoric implement, etc. formerly thought to have been hurled to earth by lightning and thunder.

2. a belemnite.

thun'dẽr·stọrm, *n.* a storm accompanied by lightning and thunder.

thun'dẽr·strick"en, *a.* thunderstruck.

thun'dẽr·strīke, *v.t.*; thunderstruck, *pt.*; thunderstruck *or* thunderstricken, *pp.*; thunderstriking, *ppr.* 1. to strike, blast, or injure by lightning. [Rare.]

2. to astonish or strike dumb, as with something terrible: rarely used except in the past participle.

thun'dẽr·struck", *a.* struck with amazement, terror, etc., as if by a thunderbolt.

thun'dẽr tūbe, a fulgurite. [Colloq.]

thun'dẽr·wŏrm, *n.* a snakelike lizard, *Rhineura floridana*: so called because it leaves its burrows after a thunderstorm.

thun'dẽr·y, *a.* 1. accompanied by or betokening thunder.

2. that sounds like thunder.

thun'drous, *a.* same as *thunderous*.

thuñk, *n.* [echoic.] an abrupt, muffled sound, as of an ax blade hitting a tree trunk.

thuñk, *v.i.* to make a thunk.

thū'ri·ble, *n.* [L. *thuribulum*, from *thus*, *thuris*, frankincense.] a censer.

thū'ri·fẽr, *n.* [L. *thus*, *thuris*, incense, and *ferre*, to bear.] an acolyte or altar boy who carries a thurible.

thū·rif'ẽr·ous, *a.* [L. *thurifer*; *thus*, *thuris*, incense, and *ferre*, to bear.] producing or bearing frankincense.

thū"ri·fi·çā'tion, *n.* [L. *thus*, *thuris*, incense, and *facere*, to make.] the act of fuming with incense; the act of burning incense.

thū'ri·fȳ, *v.t.*; thurified, *pt., pp.*; thurifying, *ppr.* to cense.

thū'ri·fȳ, *v.i.* to scatter incense.

Thū·rin'ġi·ăn, *a.* relating to Thuringia, a region of central Germany, or to its people, or culture.

Thū·rin'ġi·ăn, *n.* 1. a member of an ancient Germanic tribe of central Germany.

2. a native or inhabitant of Thuringia, a region of central Germany.

thū·rin'ġite, *n.* [from *Thuringia*, where it is found.] a silicate of iron and aluminum occurring as an aggregate of minute scales, which are distinctly cleavable in one direction, and have an olive-green color and nacreous luster.

thūrl, *n.* thirl. [Obs.]

thur'rock, thur'rok, *n.* the hold or bilge of a ship. [Obs.]

Thūrṣ'dāy, *n.* [ME. *Thoresdai*, *Thunres dai*, from AS. *Thunres dæg*, O.N. *Thorsdagr*, Thor's day, rendering LL. *Jovis deis*: cf. Fr. *jeudi*, G. *Donnerstag*.] the fifth day of the week.

Holy Thursday; see under *holy*.

thus, *n.* [L., frankincense.] the resin of the spruce fir, so called from its use as frankincense.

thus, *adv.* [AS. *thus*.]

1. in this or that manner; in the way just stated or in the following manner.

2. to this or that degree or extent; so.

3. according to this or that; consequently; therefore; hence.

Thū'yȧ, *n.* same as *Thuja*.

thū'yin, *n.* a substance extracted from the arbor vitae.

Thū·yop'sis, *n.* [*Thuya*, and Gr. *opsis*, resemblance.] a genus of coniferous trees. *Thuyopsis dolabrata*, the only species, is native to Japan.

thwack, *v.t.*; thwacked (thwakt), *pt., pp.*; thwacking, *ppr.* [AS. *thaccian*, to stroke, to clap; basically echoic.]

1. to strike with something flat or heavy; to bang; to beat or thrash.

2. to fill too full; to pack tightly. [Obs.]

thwack, *n.* a heavy blow as with something flat or heavy.

thwāite, *n.* a fish, the twaite.

thwāite, *n.* a piece of land cleared of wood and stumps and converted to tillage. [Brit. Dial.]

thwạrt, *a.* [O.N. *thvert*, lying across, transverse.]

1. transverse; oblique; being across something else.

Moved contrary with *thwart* obliquities. —Milton.

2. contrary; perverse. [Obs.]

thwạrt, *prep.* and *adv.* athwart. [Archaic.]

thwạrt, *n.* 1. a rower's seat extending across a boat.

2. a brace extending across a canoe.

thwạrt, *v.t.*; thwarted, *pt., pp.*; thwarting, *ppr.*

1. originally, to extend or place over or across; also, to move across.

Swift as a shooting star
In autumn *thwarts* the night. —Milton.

2. to hinder, obstruct, frustrate, or defeat (a person, plans, wishes, etc.).

thwa̤rt, *v.i.* 1. to be in opposition; to conflict. [Rare.]

2. to go or move obliquely. [Rare.]

thwa̤rt'ẽr, *n.* a disease in sheep, indicated by shaking, trembling, or convulsive motions.

thwa̤rt'ing·ly, *adv.* in a thwarting manner.

thwa̤rt'ly, *adv.* obliquely; crossly; perversely.

thwa̤rt'ness, *n.* the quality or state of being thwart.

thwīte, *v.t.* to cut with a knife; to whittle. [Obs.]

thwit'tle, *v.t.* to whittle. [Obs.]

thwit'tle, *n.* a whittle; a knife. [Obs.]

thȳ, *poss. pronominal a.* [ME. *thi*, contr. of *thin*, thy, used before consonants.] of, belonging to, or done by thee: archaic or dialectal variant of *your*.

These are *thy* glorious works, Parent of good. —Milton.

Thȳ·es'tē·ăn ban̄'quet (or **fēast**), [see *Thyestes*.] a banquet at which human flesh is served.

Thȳ·es'tēṣ, *n.* [L.; Gr. *Thyestēs*.] in Greek legend, a brother of Atreus and son of Pelops

thȳ'ine, *a.* [Gr. *thyinos*, pertaining to the tree *thyia*, *thya*, an African tree with sweet-smelling wood.] designating a precious wood, mentioned in Rev. xviii. 12. It is supposed to be that of *Callitris quadrivalvis*, the resin of which is used in varnish making under the name of *sandarac*.

thȳ'lȧ·cīne, *n.* [Gr. *thylax*, a pouch, and *kyon*, a dog.] a carnivorous marsupial, *Thylacinus cynocephalus*, inhabiting Tasmania: it is fierce and somewhat like a dog in appearance, but with dark stripes on the back: it is about extinct: also called *Tasmanian tiger*, *Tasmanian wolf*.

Thȳ·lac'i·nus, *n.* a genus of carnivorous marsupials including the thylacine.

thȳ·lȧ·cī'tis, *n.* [Gr. *thylax*, a pouch, and *-itis*.] inflammation of the oil glands of the skin.

thȳm·ac'e·tin, *n.* [Gr. *thymon*, thyme, and L. *acetum*, vinegar.] a white crystalline thymol derivative, $C_{14}H_{21}NO_3$.

thȳm'āte, *n.* a salt of thymic acid.

thyme (tīm), *n.* [Fr. *thym*; L. *thymum*; Gr. *thymos*, thyme.] any of several related plants of the mint family belonging to the genus *Thymus*: they have white, pink, or red flowers and fragrant leaves used for seasoning.

cat thyme; a plant, *Teucrium marum*, of the mint family, native to the Mediterranean region: so called because cats are said to be fond of rolling in it.

horse thyme; the wild basil. [Obs.]

wild thyme; a plant, *Thymus serpyllum*, which thrives in hilly parts of Europe.

Thym·ē·lae'ȧ (thim-), *n.* [Gr. *thymelaia*, the plant *Daphne gnidium*, from *thymos*, thyme, and *elaia*, an olive tree.] a genus of plants typical of the family *Thymelæaceæ*, consisting of herbs and shrubs whose flowers are sessile and apetalous. They are native to Europe and Asia.

Thym″ē·lae·ā'cē·ae, *n.pl.* a family of trees, shrubs, and herbs, comprising thirty-eight genera and 500 species, native to the temperate parts of the Eastern Hemisphere.

thym″ē·lae·ā'ceous, *a.* pertaining to plants of the family *Thymelæaceæ*, having very tough bark.

thym'e·lē, *n.* [Gr. *thymelē*, an altar, from *thyein*, to sacrifice.] an altar; specifically, the altar of Dionysus which was erected in the center of the orchestra of a Greek theater.

thȳm'ēne (tīm'), *n.* [LL. *thymus*, thyme, and *-ene*.] a clear, oily hydrocarbon, $C_{10}H_{16}$, from the oil of thyme.

thȳ'miç, *a.* in anatomy, relating to the thymus.

thymic acid; an acid derived from the nucleic acid obtained from the thymus gland.

thȳm'iç (tīm'), *a.* contained in or derived from thyme.

thȳm'in (thīm'), *n.* in physiological chemistry, a crystalline compound, $C_5H_6N_2O_2$, obtainable from the decomposition of the thymic acid derivable from the thymus.

thȳ·mī'tis, *n.* inflammation of the thymus.

thȳ'mōl, *n.* [*thyme* and *-ol*.] an aromatic, colorless, crystalline compound, $C_{10}H_{14}O$, obtained from oil of thyme or made synthetically, and used in medicine as an antiseptic and deodorant.

thȳ'mus (thī'), *n.* [L., from G. *thymos*, thyme: so called because shaped like the thyme flower.]

1. a ductless, glandlike body, of undetermined function, situated in the upper thorax near the throat: it is most prominent at puberty, after which it disappears or becomes vestigial: the thymus of an animal, when used as food, is called sweetbread: also *thymus gland*.

2. see *acrothymion*.

Thȳ'mus, *n.* a genus, of the mint family, of perennial, aromatic herbs with small entire leaves and bilabiate calyx and corolla.

thȳm'y (tīm'), *a.* 1. overgrown with thyme.

2. having the scent of thyme.

thȳ'rē·ō- (thī'), [from Gr. *thyreos*, *thyrios*, a large shield, shaped like a door, from Gr. *thura*, a door.] a combining form meaning *thyroid*, as in *thyreo*tomy: also *thyro-*, *thyre-*.

thȳ″rē·ō·an·ti·tox'in, *n.* an antitoxin developed in thyroid poisoning.

thȳ'rē·oid, *n.* and *a.* thyroid.

thȳ″rē·oid·eç'tō·my, *n.* thyroidectomy.

thȳ″rē·ō·prō'tē·ide, *n.* a toxic proteide of the thyroid gland, supposed to contain its characteristic properties.

thȳ″rō·ȧ·ryt'ē·noid, *a.* of or pertaining to the thyroid and arytenoid cartilage.

thȳ·rō·çal'ci·tō'nin, *n.* [*thyro-* (see *thyreo-*), and *calci-*, and *tone*, and *-in*.] a hormone secreted by the thyroid gland, regulating the balance of calcium in the blood and bone.

thȳ·ro·hȳ'ăl, *n.* a segment of the hyoid arch, frequently united with the hyoid bone and constituting one of its cornua, as in man.

thȳ·rō·hȳ'oid, *a.* of or belonging to the hyoid bone and the thyroid axis.

thȳ'roid, *n.* [from Gr. *thyreos*, a large shield, and *eidēs*, form.]

1. the thyroid gland.

2. the thyroid cartilage.

3. a preparation consisting of the thyroid gland of certain domesticated animals, used in treating goiter, myxedema, etc.: also *thyroid extract*.

thȳ'roid, *a.* 1. in anatomy, shield-shaped.

2. designating or of a large ductless gland lying in front and on either side of the trachea and secreting the hormone thyroxine, which regulates the growth of the body: the malfunctioning or congenital absence of this gland can cause goiter, cretinism, etc.

3. designating or of the principal cartilage of the larynx, forming the Adam s apple.

thyroid extract; thyroid, *n.* 3.

thȳ·roid'ē·ăl, *a.* thyroid.

thȳ·roid·eç'tō·my, *n.* in surgery, removal of all or part of the thyroid gland.

thȳ·roid·ī'tis, *n.* [Mod. L.] inflammation of the thyroid gland.

thȳ·rō·ther'ȧ·py, *n.* in medicine, the treatment of disease with prepared thyroid glands, usually those of sheep.

thȳ·rox'in, *n.* thyroxine.

thȳ·rox'ine, *n.* [from *thyr*oid and *oxy-* and *ine*.] a colorless, crystalline compound, $C_{15}H_{11}O_4NI_4$, the active hormone of the thyroid gland, often prepared synthetically and used in treating goiter, cretinism, and myxedema.

thyrse (thẽrs), *n.* [L. *thyrsus*, from Gr. *thyrsos*, a stalk.] a thyrsus.

thyrse'flow″ẽr, *n.* any species of the genus *Thyrsacanthus*, herbs and shrubs bearing bright scarlet flowers in dense racemes, indigenous to tropical America and much cultivated in hothouses.

thyr·sif'ẽr·ous, *a.* in botany, having thyrsoid inflorescence.

thyr'si·fo̤rm, *a.* resembling or having the form of a thyrsus.

thyr'soid, thyr·soid'ăl, *a.* resembling a thyrsus; thyrsiform.

thyr'sus, *n.*; *pl.* **thyr'sī,** [L., from Gr. *thyrsos*, a stalk or shaft.]

1. a staff tipped with a pine cone and sometimes entwined with ivy or vine leaves, which Dionysus, the satyrs, etc. were represented as carrying.

2. in botany, a flower cluster in which the main stem is racemose and the secondary stems are cymose, as in the lilac.

THYRSUS of horse chestnut)

thȳ·sȧ·nop'tẽr, *n.* a member of the *Thysanoptera*.

Thȳ·sȧ·nop'tē·rȧ, *n.pl.* [LL., from Gr. *thysanos*, a fringe, and *pteron*, a wing.] a group of small insects having wings with rudimentary nervures, feeding upon vegetable juices and very destructive to growing crops.

thȳ·sȧ·nop'tẽr·ăn, *a.* of or pertaining to the *Thysanoptera*.

thȳ·sȧ·nop'tẽr·ăn, *n.* a thysanopter.

thȳ·sȧ·nop'tẽr·ous, *a.* thysanopteran.

Thȳ·sȧ·nū'rȧ, *n.pl.* [LL., from Gr. *thysanos*, fringe, and *oura*, a tail.] an order of wingless insects, with rudimentary masticating mouth parts and bristlelike appendages at their rear ends, and including the *Cinura*, or bristletails.

thȳ·sȧ·nū'răn, *a.* of, designating, or pertaining to the *Thysanura*.

thȳ·sȧ·nū'răn, *n.* one of the *Thysanura*; a bristletail.

thȳ·sȧ·nū'rous, *a.* of or like a thysanuran or thysanurans; thysanuran.

thȳ·self', *pron.* [ME. *thi self*, superseding earlier *the self*, lit., thee self; AS. *the self*; in ME., *self*, orig. adj., was regarded as n.] the reflexive or emphatic form of *thou*: an archaic or dialectal variant of *yourself*.

Thyself and thy belongings
Are not thine own. —Shak.

tī, *n.* any species of the genus *Cordyline*, family *Liliaceæ*, trees native to southern Asia and Polynesia. One species, *Cordyline terminalis*, yields edible roots, and the leaves of *Cordyline australis* furnish a fiber used in the manufacture of paper and cordage: also *ti palm*.

tī, *n.* [altered from *si*.] in music, a syllable representing the seventh tone of the diatonic scale: also *te*.

Ti, in chemistry, titanium.

tī'ăr, *n.* a tiara. [Poet.]

tī·ăr'ȧ, *n.* [L., from Gr. *tiara*; prob. of Oriental origin.]

1. the head covering of the ancient Persians; the crown of the ancient Persian kings.

2. (a) the triple crown worn by the Pope; (b) the position or authority of the Pope.

3. a woman's crownlike headdress of jewels, flowers, etc.; any rich ornament for the head; a coronet; a frontal.

tī·ăr'ăed, *a.* covered by or adorned with a tiara.

tib'-çat″, *n.* a female cat. [Brit. Dial.]

ti·bet', *n.* 1. a dress fabric made of goat's hair.

2. a fine woolen cloth used for ladies' dresses: also written *thibet*, *tibet cloth*, *thibet cloth*.

Ti·bet'ăn, *a.* of Tibet, its people, their language, etc.: also spelled *Thibetan*.

Ti·bet'ăn, *n.* 1. a member of the Mongolic people of Tibet.

2. the Sino-Tibetan language of Tibet.

Also spelled *Thibetan*.

ti·bet' clo̤th, see *tibet*.

Ti·bē'tiăn, *a.* and *n.* same as *Tibetan*.

Ti·bet″ō-Būr'măn, *a.* designating or of a subdivision of the Sino-Tibetan family of languages, including Tibetan and Burmese.

tib'i·ȧ, *n.*; *pl.* **tib'i·ae** or **tib'i·ȧṣ,** [L., the shinbone, also, a pipe, flute, because first made of bone.]

1. the inner and thicker of the two bones of the human leg between the knee and the ankle; the shinbone.

2. a corresponding bone in the leg of other vertebrates.

3. the fourth segment or joint (from the base) of an insect's leg, situated between the femur and tarsus.

4. an ancient type of flute, originally made from an animal's tibia.

tib'i·ăl, *a.* of, pertaining to, or resembling a tibia.

tibial spur; a spine on the tibia of many insects.

tib'i·ăl, *n.* a tibia muscle, artery, etc.

ti·bī'cen, *n.* anciently, one who performed on the tibia.

ti·bic'i·nāte, *v.i.* to play on the tibia. [Rare.]

tib″i·ō·tăr'săl, *a.* of or relating to the tibia and the tarsus, or to the tibiotarsus.

tib″i·ō·tăr'sus, *n.*; *pl.* **tib″i·ō·tăr'sī,** the tibia of a bird's leg, formed by the fusion of the tibia with the proximal tarsals.

Tib·ö̤u·chī'nȧ, *n.* [native Guiana.] a genus of melastomaceous plants, chiefly shrubs with entire leaves, and panicles of large purple flowers, indigenous to tropical America.

tiç, *n.* [Fr.; It. *ticchis*; of Gmc. origin.] any involuntary, regularly repeated, spasmodic contraction of a muscle, generally of neurotic origin; especially, tic douloureux.

ti·cäl′, *n.* [Malay *tikal.*]
1. the former monetary unit of Siam, replaced by the baht.
2. a former Siamese unit of weight equivalent to about half an ounce.
3. a Burmese weight.

tic dou·lou·reux′ (-rö′) [Fr., lit., painful tic] a tic of the facial muscles, accompanied by severe neuralgic pains; trigeminal neuralgia.

tīce, *v.t.* to entice. [Obs.]

tīce, *n.* same as *yorker.*

tīce′ment, *n.* enticement. [Obs.]

tī′chō·rhine (-rin), *a.* [Gr. *teichos*, wall, and *rhis* (*rhinos*), nose.] having an osseous septum between the nostrils.

tī′chō·rhine, *n.* a fossil rhinoceros, *Rhinoceros tichorhinus*: so called from the bony septum supporting the nose.

tick, *n.* [contr. of *tick*et.] credit; trust; as, to buy on *tick*. [Chiefly Brit. Colloq.]

tick, *v.i.* to purchase on credit or to give or sell on credit. [Chiefly Brit. Colloq.]

tick, *n.* [ME. *tike, teke*; AS. *ticia.*]
1. any of a large group of wingless, blood-sucking insects or mites that infest man, cattle, sheep, and other animals.
2. any of various degenerate, two-winged, parasitic insects.
3. a variety of horse bean, *Faba vulgaris.*

tick, *n.* [ML. *teca*; L. *theca*; Gr. *thēkē*, case.]
1. the cloth case or covering that is filled with cotton, feathers, hair, etc. to form a mattress or pillow.
2. ticking. [Colloq.]

tick, *n.* [ME. *tek, tekk*; prob. from Gmc. echoic base.]
1. originally, a light touch; a pat.
2. a light clicking or tapping sound, as that made by the escapement of a watch or clock.
3. a mark made to check off items; a check mark (✓, /, etc.).
4. the time between two ticks of a clock; a moment; an instant. [Colloq.]

tick, *v.i.* to make a tick or series of ticks.

tick, *v.t.* 1. to indicate, record, or count by a tick or ticks.
2. to mark or check off (an item in a list, etc.) with a tick.

tick, *n.* a bird, the whinchat. [Brit. Dial.]

tick′bēan, *n.* [prob. from its likeness in shape to the insect.] a small bean used in feeding horses and other animals.

ticked (tikt), *a.* speckled or spotted: said of the coat of an animal, as of a dog.

tick′en, *n.* cloth for bedticks; ticking. [Brit.]

tick′ēr, *n.* 1. one who or that which ticks.
2. the sounder or receiving part of a telegraph instrument.
3. a telegraphic device that automatically prints stock market quotations and other reports, such as baseball scores, etc. on a paper tape.
4. a watch. [Slang.]
5. the heart. [Slang.]
stock ticker; same as *ticker*, sense 3.
ticker tape; a paper ribbon or tape attached to a ticker: stock market quotations and other news are automatically printed on this paper as they are received by the ticker.

tick′et, *n.* [Fr. *étiquette*; OFr. *estiquete*, from *estiquer*, to stick.]
1. a note or memorandum, or a slip of paper containing this. [Now Rare.]
2. a printed card or piece of paper that gives a person a specified right, as to attend a theater, ride on a train, claim a purchase, etc.
3. a license or certificate, as of a ship's captain or of an airplane pilot.
4. a card, piece of paper, or piece of cloth fastened to goods to tell the size, color, price, quantity, etc.; a label; a tag.
5. a slip recording a transaction or a sum paid or due, to be entered in a permanent account book.
6. the list of candidates nominated by a political party in an election; a ballot.
7. a notice of arrest for a traffic violation. [Colloq.]
8. a visiting card. [Obs.]
scratched ticket; a ticket from which the names of certain regular candidates of a party have been erased.
split ticket; a ballot cast for candidates of more than one party: opposed to *straight ticket.*
straight ticket; a ballot cast for all the candidates of one party.
that's the ticket! that's the correct or proper thing! that's right! [Slang.]

tick′et, *v.t.*; ticketed, *pt., pp.*; ticketing, *ppr.*
1. to distinguish by a ticket; to attach a ticket to; to label; to tag.
2. to supply with tickets; to give a ticket to, as a passenger.

tick′et ā′gent, a person or agency that sells theater tickets, railroad tickets, etc.

tick′et chop′pēr, an employee at a railway station or the like, whose duty it is to see that passengers entering deposit their tickets in a box, where they are canceled by chopping. [Slang.]

tick′et dāy, on the London stock exchange, the day on which the brokers make known to each other the names of the actual purchasers. It precedes settling day.

tick′et·ing, *n.* in England, a method of sale of ores that occurs periodically in the mining districts, when bids are presented on tickets and the sale is made to the highest bidder.

tick′et of′fice, an office, as in railroad stations, where tickets are sold.

tick′et-ŏf-lēave′, *a.* having a ticket of leave. [Brit.]

tick′et ŏf lēave, formerly, a permit allowing a convict to be at liberty, with certain restrictions, before his sentence had expired: equivalent to *parole.* [Brit.]

tick′et pōr′tēr, a licensed porter wearing a ticket by which he may be identified. [Brit.]

tick fē′vēr, any infectious disease transmitted by the bite of a tick, as Rocky Mountain spotted fever.

tick′ing, *n.* a closely-woven, strong, often striped linen or cotton fabric, used for the ticks of beds, mattresses, awnings, etc.

tic̦′kle, *v.t.*; tickled (-ld), *pt., pp.*; tickling, *ppr.* [ME. *tikelen*; akin to G. dial. *zickeln.*]
1. to please; gratify; as, this dessert will *tickle* the palate.
2. to amuse; delight; as, the story *tickled* him.
3. to excite the surface nerves of by touching or stroking lightly with the finger, a feather, etc. so as to cause involuntary twitching, laughter, etc.
4. to rouse, stir, move, get, etc. by or as by touching lightly.
to tickle one pink; to please one greatly. [Slang.]

tic̦′kle, *v.i.* 1. to have an itching or tingling sensation; as, my palm *tickles.*
2. to be affected by excitation of the surface nerves; to be ticklish.
3. to have an impatient desire to get something; to itch; to be thrilled with pleasure. [Rare.]

tic̦′kle, *n.* 1. a tickling or being tickled.
2. a tickling sensation.

tic̦′kle, *a.* 1. tottering; unstable; easily overthrown; ticklish. [Obs.]
2. subject to change; inconstant.

tic̦′kle-foot″ed, *a.* slippery; fickle. [Obs.]

tick′len·bŭrg, *n.* [etym. doubtful.] a linen fabric of coarse texture.

tic̦′kle·ness, *n.* unsteadiness. [Obs.]

tic̦′klēr, *n.* 1. one who or that which tickles.
2. a memorandum pad, file, or other device for aiding the memory.
3. something puzzling or perplexing.
4. in accounting, an account book showing notes due and the dates of these.
5. a bung-extracting prong. [Brit.]

tic̦′klish, *a.* 1. sensitive to tickling.
2. easily upset; unstable; unsteady; touchy; fickle.
3. needing careful handling; precarious; delicate.

tic̦′klish·ly, *adv.* in a ticklish manner.

tic̦′klish·ness, *n.* the state or quality of being ticklish.

tick′seed, *n.* 1. any plant of the genus *Coreopsis* or *Corispermum*, having yellow, red, orange, or purplish flowers with toothed petals and wiry stems; coreopsis.
2. a tick trefoil.
3. any seed or fruit that resembles an insect or bug in shape.

tick′seed sun′flow″ēr, a variety of bur marigold with large petals.

tick′tack, *n.* [echoic redupl. of *tick.*]
1. an old form of backgammon.
2. a noise resembling the ticking of a clock.
3. a device for tapping on windows and house walls from a distance, by means of a cord and weight: used in practical jokes.

tick-tack-tōe′, *n.* a game in which two players take turns marking either crosses or circles in a block of nine squares, the object being to complete a straight or diagonal line of one's mark before the other player does: also *tit-tat-toe.*

tick′tock, *n.* the sound made by a clock or watch.

tick′tock, *v.i.* to make the sound of a clock or watch.

tick trē′foil, a plant of the genus *Desmodium* of the pea family, with clusters of small purple flowers: so named from the trifoliate leaves and the prickly pod joints which adhere closely to clothing, to the wool of sheep, etc.

tic̦·pō·loṅ′gȧ, *n.* an extremely venomous Indian snake, *Vipora* or *Daboia russelli.*

tid, *a.* [AS. *tidder*, tender.] tender; soft; nice. [Brit. Dial.]

tīd′ăl, *a.* 1. of or pertaining to tides; periodically rising and falling, or flowing and ebbing; as, *tidal* waters.
2. depending on or regulating its time by the tides; as, a *tidal* steamer; *tidal* trains.
tidal air; the air which passes in and out in breathing, generally estimated at about thirty cubic inches at each respiration.
tidal basin; a basin in which the tide ebbs and flows.
tidal day; same as *tide day.*
tidal wave; (a) an unusually great, destructive wave sent inshore by an earthquake or a very strong wind; (b) any great or widespread movement, expression of prevalent feeling, etc.

tid′bit, *n.* [dial. *tid*, small object, and *bit.*] a pleasing or choice bit of food, gossip, etc.: also *titbit.*

tid′dle, *v.t.* to use with tenderness; to fondle. [Obs.]

tid′dle·dy·wiṅks, *n.* tiddlywinks.

tid′dly·wiṅk, *n.* an unlicensed pawnbroker's shop or beer shop. [Brit. Slang.]

tid′dly·wiṅks, *n.* [prob. from *tiddly*, child's form of *little*; the word first occurs in sense "illicit grogshop."] a game in which the players try to snap little colored disks from a table, etc. into a cup by pressing their edges with larger disks.

tīde, *n.* [AS. *tīd*, time, season, opportunity, hour.]
1. originally, a period of time; season: now used only in combination, as in *Eastertide*, *eventide*, or in the proverb "Time and *tide* wait for no man."
2. [prob. influenced by M.L.G. or M.D.] the alternate rise and fall of the surface of oceans, seas, and the bays, rivers, etc. connected with them, caused by the attraction of the moon and sun. The tide occurs twice in each period of 24 hours and 51 minutes (*lunar day*). During its rise, tide is called *flood tide*, and during its fall, *ebb tide.* When the moon is new or full, the tide is unusually high and is called *spring tide*; when the moon is at first or third quarter, the tide is unusually low and is called *neap tide.*
3. something that rises and falls like the tide.
4. a stream, current, tendency, etc.; as, the *tide* of public opinion.
5. the period during which something is at its highest or fullest point.
6. an opportune time or occasion. [Archaic.]
7. in mining, the period of twelve hours. Hence, to work *double tides*, to work night and day.
acid tide; a temporary increase of the acidity of the urine which sometimes follows fasting.
alkaline tide; a temporary increase of the alkalinity of the urine during digestion.
atmospheric tide; motions of the atmosphere resembling ocean tides, but not caused by the attraction of the sun or the moon.
lagging or *retardation of the tides*; see under *retardation.*
priming or *acceleration of the tides*; the acceleration of the tide wave, or amount of shortening of the tide day in the first and third quarters of the moon.
weather tide; a tide running against the wind.

tīde, *a.* tidal.

tīde, *v.t.*; tided, *pt., pp.*; tiding, *ppr.* to carry with or as with the tide.
to tide over; (a) to help along temporarily, as through a period of difficulty; (b) to overcome; survive; endure.

tīde, *v.i.* 1. to happen; to betide. [Obs.]
2. to flow or surge like a tide.
3. in nautical usage, to drift with the tide, especially so as to work in or out of a river or harbor.

tīd′ed, *a.* affected by or having a tide; tidal.

tīde dāy, at any one point, the time between two successive high tides.

tīde gāte, 1. a gate through which water passes into a basin when the tide flows, and which is shut to retain the water from flowing back at the ebb.
2. in nautical usage, a place where the tide runs with great velocity.
tīde gāuġe, an instrument, sometimes self-registering, used on coasts and in harbors to measure the rise and fall of the tide.
tīde′land, *n.* land covered by flood tide.
tīde′less, *a.* having no tide.
tīde lock, a lock between the tidewater of a harbor or river and an enclosed basin when their levels vary. It has double gates by which vessels can pass either way at all times of the tide.
tīde′märk, *n.* a mark indicating the highest point of flood tide or, sometimes, the lowest point of ebb tide.
tīde mill, a mill that is moved by tidewater; also, a mill for clearing lands from tidewater.
tīde′rip′, *n.* water made rough by currents or tides flowing in opposing directions: also *rip*.
tīde′-rōde, *a.* in nautical usage, swung by the tide, as a boat at anchor.
tīdeṣ′măn, *n.*; *pl.* **tīdeṣ′men,** 1. one who is employed only during certain states of the tide.
2. a tidewaiter.
tīde tā′ble, a table showing the time of high water at any place, or at different places, for each day throughout the year.
tīde′wāit″ēr, *n.* formerly, a customhouse officer who watched the landing of goods to see that the customs regulations were observed and the revenue laws obeyed.
tīde′wa̤″tēr, *n.* 1. water brought into an area by the action of the rising tide.
2. water, as of a certain area or in certain streams, that is affected by the tide.
3. an area in which water is affected by the tide; specifically, [T–] the eastern part of Virginia.
4. [T–] the English dialect of eastern Virginia.
tīde′wa̤″tēr, *a.* 1. of or along a tidewater.
2. [T–] of (the) Tidewater.
tīde wāve, an undulation of water as the tides move around the Earth.
tīde′wāy, *n.* 1. a channel in which the tide runs.
2. the tidal part of a river.
3. a tidal current.
tīde wheel (hwēl), a water wheel so constructed as to be moved by the flow of the tide.
tī′di·ly, *adv.* neatly; with neat simplicity; as, a woman *tidily* dressed.
tī′di·ness, *n.* the quality of being tidy.
tī′ding, *n.* tidings. [Obs.]
tī′ding·less, *a.* having no tidings.
tī′dingṣ, *n.pl.* [*sometimes construed as sing.*] [ME. *tithinge*, from Ice. *tīthindi*, news.] news; information; intelligence.
tid′ley, *n.* [etym. uncertain.]
1. the European wren. [Brit. Dial.]
2. the goldcrest. [Brit. Dial.]
tīd·ol′ō·ġy, *n.* the doctrine, theory, or science of tides.
tī′dy, *a.*; *comp.* tidier; *superl.* tidiest, [from *tide*, time, season; Dan. and Sw. *tidig*, seasonable, fit]
1. being in proper time; seasonable; favorable. [Obs.]
2. neat in personal appearance, ways, etc.; orderly.
3. neat in arrangement; in order; trim.
4. fairly good; satisfactory. [Colloq.]
5. considerable; moderately large or great; as, he has left a *tidy* sum of money. [Colloq.]
6. smart; brave; expert. [Obs.]
tī′dy, *n.*; *pl.* **tī′dieṣ,** 1. a covering, usually of knitted or crochet work, for the back of a chair, the arms of a sofa, or the like.
2. a pinafore or apron. [Brit. Dial.]
tī′dy, *v.t.* and *v.i.*; tidied, *pt., pp.*; tidying, *ppr.* to make (things) tidy: often with *up*.
tī′dy·tips, *n.*; *pl.* **tī′dy·tips,** a California plant, *Layia platyglossa*, with yellow, daisylike flowers, often tipped with white.
tīe, *v.t.*; tied, *pt., pp.*; tying, *ppr.* [ME. *tien*; AS. *tigan, tegan*, from base of *teag, teah*, a rope.]
1. to fasten, attach, or bind (one thing to another or two or more things together) by entwining with a piece of string, cord, rope, etc., which is then knotted.
2. to draw together or join the parts, ends, or sides of by tightening and knotting laces, strings, etc.; as, he *tied* his shoes, she *tied* her apron.
3. to make (a knot).
4. to make a knot in; as, he *tied* his bow tie.
5. to fasten, connect, or join in any way.
6. to confine; restrain; restrict.
7. (a) to equal the score of (an opponent) in a contest; (b) to equal (the score of an opponent).
8. to join in marriage. [Colloq.]
9. in music, to connect with a tie.
10. in building, to bind together, as two bodies, by means of a piece of timber or metal.
11. in surgery, to ligate, as a vein or artery, so as to prevent a loss of blood.
12. to furnish with ties, as a railway roadbed.
to tie down; to confine; restrain; restrict.
to tie up; (a) to tie firmly or securely; (b) to wrap up and tie with string, etc.; (c) to moor to a dock; (d) to obstruct; hinder; stop; (e) to cause to be already in use, retained, committed, or other wise rendered unavailable.
tīe, *v.i.* 1. to be capable of being tied; to make a tie.
2. to make the same score in a contest.
tīe, *n.* [ME. *tege, teige*; AS. *teag, teah*, a rope.]
1. the act of tying. [Rare.]
2. a string, lace, cord, etc. used to tie things.
3. something that connects, binds, or joins; a bond; a link; as, a business *tie, ties* of affection.
4. something that confines, limits, or restricts; as, legal *ties*.
5. a necktie, or cravat.
6. a beam, rod, etc. that holds together parts of a building and strengthens against stress.
7. any of the parallel crossbeams to which the rails of a railroad are fastened; sleeper.
8. any of various similar things that tie or unite, as, (a) a knot of hair, as on a wig; (b) a ribbon used to tie a wig; (c) a bale tie, a device used to join the ends of the straps used on bales of cotton, etc.; (d) a halyard of a topsail or topgallant yard; (e) a line connecting letters in proofreading to show that they are to be set as a logotype; (f) a pattern used by a weaver.
9. an equality of scores in a contest.
10. a contest or match in which there is such an equality; a draw; a stalemate.
11. in music, a curved line above or below two notes of the same pitch, indicating that the tone is to be held unbroken for the duration of their combined values.
12. [*pl.*] low shoes, laced in front; oxfords.
tīe′back, *n.* a sash, ribbon, tape, etc. used to tie curtains or draperies to one side.
tīe bär, a bar which forms a tie.
tīe bēam, a beam serving as a tie in a roof, etc.
tīe′-in, *a.* designating or of a sale in which two or more articles are offered together, often at a reduced price, or something scarce, desirable, etc. can be bought only in combination with some other, generally undesired item.
tīe′-in, *n.* 1. such a sale.
2. an article sold in this way.
tīe līne, a line used in surveying as a substitute for the diagonals in a field survey when a modification of the diagonal method of survey is necessary: so called because it ties the sides of the field together. This modification is called surveying by tie lines.
tīe′măn·nīte, *n.* [from W. *Tiemann*, its discoverer.] a grayish selenide of mercury, HgSe, with a metallic luster.
tī·en′dȧ, *n.* [Sp.] a booth or shop.
tīe′pin, *n.* a decorative pin for fastening a necktie.
tiēr, *n.* [OFr. *tier*, a row, rank.]
1. a row; a rank; a range, particularly when two or more rows are placed one above another; as, a *tier* of seats in a church or theater.
2. any of a series of rows, or ranks, arranged one above or behind another.
3. in organ building, a rank.
4. [*pl.*] the ranges of fakes or windings of a cable, laid one within another when coiled.
tiēr, *v.t.* to lay or arrange in tiers.
tiēr, *v.i.* to be set, or to stand, in tiers.
tī′ēr, *n.* 1. one who or that which ties.
2. a pinafore worn by children.
3. the larva of a moth which fastens leaves together with silk: sometimes called a *leaf tier*.
tiērce, *n.* [Fr., a third part, also *tiers*, a third, from L. *tertius*, third, from *tres*, three.]
1. originally, a third.
2. the third canonical hour (9 A.M.) or its office.
3. an old liquid measure, equal to $^1/_3$ pipe (42 gallons).
4. a cask of this capacity, between a barrel and a hogshead in size.
5. in card games, a sequence of three cards in the same suit.
6. in fencing, the third position, from which a lunge or parry can be made.
7. in music, a major third.
8. in heraldry, the division of a field into three equal parts of different tinctures.
arch of the tierce or *third point*; an arch consisting of two arcs of a circle intersecting at the top; a pointed arch.
tierce major; a sequence of ace, king, queen in whist.
tier·cé′ (tēr-sā′), *a.* [Fr.] in heraldry, having three equal divisions, each of a different tincture.
tiēr′cel, *n.* a tercel.
tiēr′cē·rŏn, *n.* [Fr.] in the vaulting of Gothic architecture, a minor rib, usually simply ornamental, rising from the point of junction of two others.
tiēr′cet, *n.* same as *tercet*.
tīe rod, a rod acting as a tie; specifically, (a) a crosstie; (b) in architecture, building, etc., a bar or rod for bracing together the frames of roofs, etc.
tier′ràṣ (tyer′), *n.pl.* [Sp.] a mixture of powdery ore with dirt or rock.
tiers é·tat′ (tyärz ā-tȧ′), [Fr.] in French history, the third estate, that is, the people exclusive of the nobility and clergy; the commonalty; the commons. The nobles and clergy constituted the first and second estates, previous to the French Revolution.
tīeṣ, *n.pl.* same as *tie, n.* 12.
tīe strut, a cross brace used in center-frames for arches, acting both as a tie and a strut: sometimes called a *strut tie*.
tīe′tick, *n.* the meadow pipit. [Brit. Dial.]
tīe′-up, *n.* 1. a temporary stoppage or interruption of production, traffic, etc.
2. connection; relation. [Colloq.]
tīe′wig, *n.* 1. a wig having its curls or tail tied with a ribbon.
2. a wig tied to the head; a queue; a pigtail.
tiff, *n.* [also early and dial. *tift*; perh. echoic or same word as *tiff* (drink).]
1. a slight fit of anger or bad humor; a huff; a pet.
2. a slight quarrel; a spat.
tiff, *v.i.* to be in or have a tiff.
tiff, *n.* [also early and dial. *tift*; perh. O.N. *thefr*, a smell.]
1. liquor; especially, weak liquor. [Rare or Obs.]
2. a sip or little drink of diluted liquor or punch. [Rare or Obs.]
tiff, *v.i.* [Anglo-Ind.] in India, to take lunch or tiffin.
tiff, *v.t.* to dress. [Obs.]
tif′fȧ·ny, *a.* gauzy; composed of tiffany.
tif′fȧ·ny, *n.*; *pl.* **tif′fȧ·nieṣ,** [OFr. *tiphanie*, Epiphany; LL. *theophania*; Gr. *theophania*, lit., manifestation of God: perh. so called because worn on Epiphany.]
1. a thin gauze of silk or muslin.
2. a flour sieve made of tiffany.
tif′fin, *n.* [Anglo-Ind.] lunch. [Brit.]
tiff′ish, *a.* peevish; pettish; capricious.
tift, *n.* a tiff in any sense; also, a whiff; a sniff. [Scot. and Brit. Dial.]
tig, *n.* [variant of *tick*, to touch.]
1. a child's game; tag. [Scot. and Brit. Dial.]
2. a touch, or tag, as in the game. [Scot. and Brit. Dial.]
tig, *n.* a large, flat-bottomed cup.
tiġe (tēzh), *n.* [Fr., a stalk, from L. *tibia*, a pipe.]
1. the shaft of a column.
2. in botany, a stalk; a stem.
3. a pin at the base of the breech in a system of firearms, for expanding the base of the ball; also, an anvil or support for the cap or primer in a center-fire cartridge.
ti·ġel′lȧ, *n.* [LL., from, Fr. *tige*, a stalk.] see *tigelle*.
tiġ′el·lāte, *a.* having or resembling a tigelle.
ti·ġelle′, *n.* in botany, the caulicle or radicle of an embryo: also called *tigellus, tigellum*, and *tigella*.
tī′ġēr, *n.*; *pl.* **tī′ġērṣ** or **tī′ġēr,** [ME. and OFr. *tigre*, from L. *tigris*, from Gr. *tigris*, from Per. *tīghri*, a tiger, from *tighra*, sharp, pointed.]
1. a large, fierce, carnivorous animal of the cat family, *Felis tigris*. Its coat is bright reddish-yellow or tawny with irregular stripes of black. It has short hair and no

mane and is as large or larger than a lion and much more agile.

BENGAL TIGER

2. any of several similar animals, as (a) the South American jaguar; (b) the South African leopard; (c) the Tasmanian tiger or wolf.

3. a cruel, bloodthirsty person.

4. a loud yell (often the word "tiger") at the end of a round of cheers.

5. a servant in livery who rides with his master or mistress. [Old Slang.]

Mexican tiger; the jaguar.

royal tiger or *royal Bengal tiger*; the common tiger, *Felis tigris*.

tī′gẽr bee′tle, a beetle of the family *Cicindelidæ* with larvae that burrow in soil and feed on other insects.

tī′gẽr bĭrd, *n.* 1. a nonpasserine, tropical bird, subfamily *Capitoninae*.

2. *Sporaeginthus amandava*, the amadavat, a small Indian songbird.

3. the tiger bittern.

tī′gẽr bit′tẽrn, a sun bittern

tī′gẽr ça̤t, 1. any of various wildcats smaller than, but somewhat resembling, the tiger, as the serval, ocelot, margay, etc.

2. the Tasmanian spotted dasyure, *Dasyurus maculatus*.

3. a domestic cat with tigerlike markings.

tī′gẽr chop, *Mesembryanthemum tigrinum*, a fig marigold of South Africa.

tī′gẽr çow′ry, the tiger shell.

tī′gẽr·eȳe (-ī), *n.* a semiprecious yellow-brown stone, usually oxidized crocidolite, used for ornament.

tī′gẽr·flow″ẽr, *n.* a bulbous plant, *Tigridia pavonia*, order *Iridaceæ*, native to Mexico, and bearing bright orange flowers.

tī′gẽr gråss, an Indian species of dwarf fan-palm.

tī′gẽr heärt, in medicine, a condition of the heart in which the inner surface of the ventricular wall presents a striped and spotted appearance similar to that of a tiger's skin.

tī′gẽr·ine, *a.* tigrine; like a tiger.

tī′gẽr·ish, *a.* 1. like or characteristic of a tiger.

2. cruel; ferocious.

tī′gẽr lil′y, 1. a plant, *Lilium tigrinum*, native to China, common in English gardens, having orange flowers with purplish-black spots.

2. any of several kinds of lilies resembling this flower.

TIGER LILY

tī′gẽr mọth, any of various species of moths of the genera *Arctia, Hypercampa*, and *Nemeophila*. They are generally large, with hairy wings, richly streaked so as somewhat to resemble the skin of a tiger.

tī′gẽr pȳ′thŏn, an Indian rock snake, *Python molurus*.

tī′ger'ş-eȳe (-ī), *n.* a tigereye.

tī′gẽr's-foot, *n.* a plant of the genus *Ipomæa*, or *Convolvulus*.

tī′gẽr shärk, 1. a shark with tigrine markings, found in the Indian Ocean.

2. a spotted shark of the genus *Galeocerdo*.

tī′gẽr shell, a red gastropodous shell, *Cypræa tigris*, with large white spots: also called *tiger cowry*.

tī′gẽr'ş-milk, *n.* the milklike juice of a tree, *Excœcaria agallocha*, growing from Polynesia to India.

tī′gẽr wolf (wulf), 1. the thylacine.

2. the spotted hyena.

tī′gẽr·wood, *n.* 1. a valuable wood for cabinetmakers, imported from British Guiana. It is the heartwood of *Machærium schomburgkii*.

2. a kind of citron wood.

tīght (tīt), *a.*; *comp.* tighter; *superl.* tightest, [ME. *tight, thight*; AS. *thiht* (in comp.), strong.]

1. originally, dense.

2. so close or compact in structure that water, air, etc. cannot pass through; as, the boat is *tight*.

3. drawn, packed, etc. closely together; as, a *tight* weave.

4. snug; trim; neat. [Dial.]

5. fixed securely; held firmly; firm; as, a *tight* joint.

6. fully stretched; taut: opposed to *slack, loose*.

7. fitting closely, especially so as to be uncomfortable.

8. strict; restraining; severe; as, she kept *tight* control over her children.

9. difficult to manage: especially in a *tight corner, squeeze*, etc., a difficult situation.

10. showing tension or strain; as, a *tight* smile.

11. almost even or tied; close; as, a *tight* race.

12. (a) difficult to get; scarce in relation to demand: said of commodities on a market; (b) characterized by such scarcity; as, a *tight* market.

13. concise; condensed: said of language.

14. well-proportioned; shapely. [Archaic or Dial.]

15. competent; capable. [Dial.]

16. stingy; parsimonious. [Colloq.]

17. drunk. [Slang.]

18. intimate; familiar; friendly (usually with *with*). [Slang.]

tight end; in football, an end whose position is close to the tackle on the offensive line.

tight ship; an institution, business, etc. that is highly organized and efficiently run, like a naval vessel on which discipline is strictly enforced. [Colloq.]

to sit tight; (a) to maintain one's opinion; to remain firm; (b) to maintain one's position; to refrain from action.

Syn.—firm, compact, fast, close, tidy, neat, smart, tense, stretched.

tīght, *adv.* tightly.

tīght, *v.t.* to tighten. [Obs.]

-tīght, [from *tight*.] a combining form meaning *impervious to*, as in water*tight*, air*tight*.

tīght′en, *v.t.* and *v.i.*; tightened; *pt., pp.*; tightening, *ppr.* to make or become tight or tighter.

tīght′en·ẽr, *n.* one who or that which tightens; specifically, (a) in anatomy, a tensor; (b) in mechanics, a tightening pulley.

tīght′en·ing pụl′ley, a pulley that tightens a belt or band against which it rests.

tīght′ẽr, *n.* tightener. [Obs.]

tīght′fist′ed, *a.* stingy; closefisted.

tīght′-lipped′ (-lipt); *a.* 1. having the lips closed tightly.

2. not saying much; secretive.

tīght′ly, *adv.* in a tight manner; compactly; neatly; adroitly.

tīght′ness, *n.* the state, quality, or character of being tight.

tīght′rōpe, *n.* a tightly stretched rope or cable on which acrobats walk or do balancing acts.

tīghts, *n.pl.* a tightly fitting garment for the lower half of the body and legs, worn by acrobats, dancers, etc.

tīght′wäd, *n.* a stingy person; a miser. [Slang.]

tig′liç, *a.* of, pertaining to, or derived from *Croton tiglium*.

tiglic acid; an unsaturated, monobasic acid, C_4H_7COOH, occurring as a glyceride in croton oil and camomile oil.

tī′gress, *n.* 1. a female tiger.

2. a cruel, ferocious woman.

Ti·grid′i·ȧ, *n.* a genus of bulbous plants, the tigerflowers, of the family *Iridaceæ*, native to Central America and the northern part of South America. There are seven species, noted for their evanescent flowers.

tī′grine, *a.* like a tiger, as in color; of, relating to, or resembling a tiger or tigers: also written *tigerine*.

tī′grish, *a.* same as *tigerish*.

tig′tag, *n.* the game of tag.

tīke, *n.* a tick or mite. [Obs.]

tīke, *n.* same as *tyke*.

tik′lin, *n.* [Tag. *tikling*.] a rail of the Philippine Islands, *Hypotænidia philippinensis*.

tī′kọr, *n.* [Hind.] the long yellow tubers of an East Indian plant, *Curcuma augustifolia*; also, a starchy preparation from them.

til, *prep.* and *conj.* till. [Obs.]

til, *n.* [Hind.] sesame, a plant with small, edible seeds.

til′bur·y, *n.*; *pl.* **til′bur·ieş,** [after the inventor, a London coach builder.] a kind of light gig, or two-wheeled carriage for two persons, with or without a top or cover.

til′dẹ, *n.* [Sp., from L. *titulus*, inscription, title.] a diacritical mark (~) used: (a) in Spanish, over an *n* to indicate a palatal nasal sound (ny), as in *señor*; (b) in Portuguese, over a vowel or the first vowel of a diphthong to indicate nasalization, as in *lã, pão*: the same mark is also used in some phonetic systems to indicate any of various other sounds.

tīle, *n.* [ME. *tile, tegele*; AS. *tigele*; L. *tegula*, a tile, from *tegere*, to cover.]

1. a thin, usually rectangular piece of unglazed, fired clay, stone, or concrete, used for roofing, flooring, etc.

2. a thin, usually rectangular piece of glazed, fired clay, often decorated, used for fireplace borders, bathroom walls, etc.

3. a similar piece of other material, as of metal or plastic, used in the same way.

4. any of the pieces, or counters, in mahjongg.

5. in metallurgy, a small flat piece of dried earth or earthenware, used to cover vessels in which metals are fused.

6. a section of earthenware pipe, forming a drain or sewer.

7. tiles collectively; tiling.

8. a high, stiff hat. [Colloq.]

encaustic tile; see under *encaustic*.

tile tea; same as **brick tea** under **brick**.

tīle, *v.t.*; tiled, *pt., pp.*; tiling, *ppr.* 1. to cover or furnish with tiles; as, to *tile* a house or a floor.

2. to drain by means of tiles; as, to *tile* a farm.

3. in Freemasonry, to guard against the entrance of the uninitiated by placing the tiler at the closed door; as, to *tile* a lodge; to *tile* a meeting.

4. to bind to keep what is said or done in strict secrecy.

tīle çrēas′ing, in architecture, two rows of plain tiles placed horizontally under the coping of a wall, and projecting about $1^1/_2$ inches over each side to throw off the rain water.

tīle drāin, a drain constructed of tiles.

tīle′-drāin, *v.t.* to furnish with a tile drain; to drain with tiles.

tīle ẽarth, a strong, clayey earth used for making tiles.

tīle′fish, *n.*; *pl.* **tīle′fish** or **tīle′fish·eş,** a large, deep-sea food fish, *Lopholatilus chamæleonticeps*, with a golden-spotted blue or purple body, yellow-spotted fins, and a fleshy crest on its head: it was found in abundance off the Atlantic coast of the United States in 1879, three years later it was nearly exterminated, but since then its numbers have increased.

tīle kiln (kil), a kiln for baking tiles.

tīle ōre, a variety of earthy cuprite, varying in color from brick-red to black.

tīl′ẽr, *n.* 1. one who lays tiles.

2. one who makes tiles.

3. a tile kiln.

4. in Freemasonry, the doorkeeper of a lodge.

tīle red, a light, brownish red, the color of brick or burnt tile.

tīle′rọọt, *n.* any plant of the iridaceous genus *Geissorhiza*, characterized by a scaly rootstock, the scales of which consist of the bases of dead foliage.

tīl′ẽr·y, *n.*; *pl.* **tīl′ẽr·ieş,** a place where tiles are made.

tīle′seed, *n.* any tree of the genus *Geissois*, found in the South Sea islands: so called from the imbricate seed.

tīle′stōne, *n.* 1. in geology, any laminated sandstone fit for roofing; a flagstone; specifically, the reddish, thin-bedded, slightly micaceous sandstone lying at the base of the Devonian and forming the transition between it and the Silurian.

2. a tile. [Obs.]

Til′i·ȧ, *n.* [L., the linden.] a genus of trees, comprising sixteen or seventeen species, native to the north temperate zone and including the American basswoods and the European lindens or limes.

Til·i·ā′cē·ae, *n.pl.* a family of polypetalous dicotyledonous herbs, trees, or shrubs (the linden family), with simple, toothed, alternate leaves, furnished with stipules. The flowers are axillary, and usually white or pink; they have a valvate calyx, indefinite hypogynous stamens, and a free, many-celled ovary. The species are generally diffused throughout the tropical and temperate parts of the globe. They have a mucilaginous sap and are noted for the toughness of the fibers of their inner bark.

til·i·ā'ceous, *a.* of or relating to the *Tiliaceæ.*

tīl'ing, *n.* 1. a covering or structure of tiles.
2. tiles in general.
3. the operation of covering with tiles.

till, *n.* [contr. of *lentil.*] a vetch; a tare. [Obs. except Brit. Dial.]

till, *n.* [ME. *tiller* or *till,* a drawer, from *tillen,* to draw.]
1. originally, a drawer or tray in a trunk.
2. a drawer or tray in a store, warehouse, etc. for keeping money; a cash drawer, as in a store, counter, or the like; a money drawer in a counter or desk.
3. ready cash.

till, *n.* [var. of ME. *thill,* in same sense.] in geology, stiff, stony, unstratified, glacial drift, forming poor subsoil impervious to water. It is found largely in all regions of extended glacial action, and has been traced over vast regions of the northern part of the United States and Canada. Stones of all sizes and shapes are disseminated through it.

till, *prep.* [ME. and AS. *til;* O.N.]
1. up to the time of; until.
2. up to the place of; as far as. [Obs. or Scot.]
3. to, concerning, for, by, etc. [Scot.]

till, *conj.* until.

till, *v.t.*; tilled, *pt., pp.*; tilling, *ppr.* [AS. *tilian,* to labor, cultivate; lit., to make fit, from *til,* fit, good.]
1. to cultivate; to plow and prepare for raising crops, as by plowing, fertilizing, etc.; as, to *till* the land.
2. to prepare; to set, as a snare. [Brit. Dial.]

till, *v.i.* to cultivate land.

till'ȧ·ble, *a.* capable of being tilled; arable.

till'ăġe, *n.* 1. the tilling of land.
2. the state of being tilled; cultivation.
3. land that is tilled.
4. the crops on such land.

till ȧ·lärm', an apparatus by which an alarm is given when a drawer, as a cash till, is tampered with.

Til·land'si·ȧ, *n.* [after E. *Tillands,* a Swedish botanist.]
1. a genus of mosslike plants of the pineapple family, having slender, gray stems covered with tiny leaves, found hanging in strands from many trees in the South. *Tillandsia utriculata* is the wild pine of Jamaica. The leaves of most of the species are dilated at the base so as to form a bottlelike cavity into which the rain and dew flow.
2. [t-] any plant of this genus; Spanish moss.

till'ẽr, *n.* one who tills; a husbandman; a cultivator; a farmer.

till'ẽr, *n.* [AS. *telgor,* a branch.]
1. in botany, the shoot of a plant, springing from the root or bottom of the original stalk.
2. a young timber tree.

till'ẽr, *v.i.*; tillered, *pt., pp.*; tillering, *ppr.* to put forth tillers, or new shoots from the root: said of plants.

till'ẽr, *n.* [OFr. *telier;* ML. *telarium,* weaver's beam, from *tela,* a web.]
1. any handle. [Brit. Dial.]
2. in nautical usage, the bar or lever fitted to the head of a rudder, and used for turning it.
3. a small drawer; a till.
4. the handle of a crossbow; also, the crossbow itself. [Obs.]

till'ẽr-chāin, *n.* in nautical usage, one of the chains leading from the tiller-head round the barrel of the wheel, by which a vessel is steered.

till'ẽr-head (-hed), *n.* the extremity of the tiller, to which the tiller-rope or tiller-chain is attached.

till'ẽr-rōpe, *n.* a rope used in the same way as a tiller-chain; also, a rope extending to each side of the deck from the tiller-head, used to aid the helmsman in controlling the rudder in a strong breeze.

Til·lē'ti·ȧ (-shi-), *n.* [after M. *Tillet,* a French scientist.] a genus of fungi causing the stinking smut of various cereal grasses. *Tilletia tritici* is the stinking smut of wheat.

til'ley, *a.* same as *tilly.*

til'ley seed, same as *tilly seed.*

till'măn, *n.* a man who tills the earth. [Obs.]

til'lō·dont, *a.* pertaining to the *Tillodontia.*

til'lō·dont, *n.* one of the *Tillodontia.*

Til·lō·don'ti·ȧ (-shi-), *n.pl.* [LL., from Gr. *tillein,* to pluck, tear, and *odous, odontos,* tooth.] a family of fossil mammals found in remains from the Middle and Lower Eocene of North America. They seem to combine the characters of the *Ungulata, Rodentia,* and *Carnivora.*

til'lot, *n.* [etym. doubtful.] a kind of muslin bag used as a wrapping for dress goods.

til'lōw, *v.i.* to tiller (put forth new shoots).

til'ly, *a.* characteristic of till, or glacial drift.

til'ly seed, the seed of a Malayan tree, *Croton pavana,* nearly identical with *Croton tiglium,* from which croton oil is obtained.

til'ly-val''ly, *interj.* [etym. obscure.] nonsense! bosh!: also written *tilly-fally.* [Archaic.]

til'mus, *n.* [Gr. *tillein,* to pluck or tear.] in medicine, picking at bedclothes, or floccillation.

til seed, the seed of til, or sesame.

tilt, *n.* [ME. *tilde, teld;* AS. *teld,* a tent.]
1. a tent; a covering overhead. [Obs.]
2. the cloth covering of a cart, wagon, etc.
3. the cloth cover of a boat; a small canopy or awning of canvas or other cloth, extended over the stern sheets of a boat.
4. in Newfoundland, a hut or house used as a place of shelter for woodmen, fishermen, etc.

tilt, *v.t.* to cover with a cloth or awning.

tilt, *v.t.*; tilted, *pt., pp.*; tilting, *ppr.* [ME. *tilten,* to be overthrown, totter, from AS. *tealt,* shaky, unstable.]
1. to cause to slope; to slant; to tip; as, to *tilt* a barrel.
2. to point or thrust, as a lance.
3. to hammer or forge with a tilt hammer; as, to *tilt* steel to render it more ductile.
4. to attack (one's opponent) with a spear in the contest called tilt.

tilt, *v.i.* 1. to slope; incline; slant; tip.
2. to poise or thrust one's lance, or to charge (*at* one's opponent), in a tilt.
3. to take part in a tilt or joust.
4. to dispute; argue.
5. to move unsteadily; to ride, float, and toss.

The fleet swift *tilting* o'er the surges flew.
—Pope.

tilt, *n.* 1. a medieval contest in which two armed horsemen thrust with lances in an attempt to unseat each other; a joust.
2. any spirited contest between two persons, as a debate.
3. a thrust or parry, as with a lance.
4. a tilting or being tilted (sense 1).
5. a slope.
6. a seesaw.
7. a tilt hammer.
(*at*) *full tilt;* at full speed; with the greatest force.

tilt bōat, a boat covered with canvas or other cloth.

tilt'ẽr, *n.* 1. one who tilts; one who practices the contest called tilt.
2. one who uses a tilt hammer.
3. one who or that which tilts, tips, or inclines something.

tilth, *n.* [AS. *tilth,* culture, from *tilian,* to till.]
1. a tilling or being tilled; tillage.
2. that which is tilled; tilled land.
3. crop; harvest. [Obs.]

tilt ham'mẽr, a large drop hammer used in forging.

tilt'ing, *n.* the process by which blister steel is rendered ductile, by beating with the tilt hammer.

tilt'ing hel'met, a large helmet sometimes worn over the ordinary helmet at tilts or tournaments.

tilt mill, a mill where tilt hammers are used; also, the machinery by which tilt hammers are operated.

til tree, [L. *tilia,* a linden.] the European linden.

tilt ro̤of, a round-topped roof, shaped like a tilt or wagon cover.

tilt'up, *n.* a small spotted sandpiper; the teetertail.

tilt'yärd, *n.* a place where tilts were held.

til'yẽr, *n.* the rose-colored starling of India.

tim'ȧ·līne, *a.* [etym. unknown.] relating to the *Timeliidæ,* a family of passerine birds including the babbling thrushes, bulbuls, babblers, etc.

tī·mȧ·rau', *n.* [from the native name in Mindoro.] a small, stocky Philippine buffalo with brownish-black hide and short, thick horns.

ti·mä'ri·ot, *n.* [Turk. *tīmār,* from Per. *tīmār,* care, attendance.] a member of the Turkish feudal militia. [Obs.]

tim'băl, *n.* [Fr. *timbale;* Sp. *atabal,* from Ar. *at-tabl,* drum, timbal.]
1. a kettledrum.
2. a cicada's vibrating membrane.

tim'bāle (*or Fr.* tañ-bȧl'), *n.* [Fr., so called because shaped like a drum.]
1. a custardlike, highly flavored dish made of chicken, lobster, fish, etc. baked in a small, drum-shaped mold.
2. a type of fried pastry shell, filled with a cooked food: also *timbal case.*

tim'bẽr, *n.* [ME. and AS. *timber.*]
1. originally, (a) a building; (b) building material.
2. wood suitable for building houses, ships, etc., whether cut or in the form of trees.
3. trees collectively.

Natives began to appear from the bamboo thickets and the intricate pathways through the *timber.*—Gen. Charles King.

4. a large piece of dressed wood for building; a beam.
5. personal quality or character; as, a man of his *timber.*
6. lumber. [Brit.]
7. timberland.
8. in shipbuilding, one of the curved frames which form the ribs of a ship.
9. the wooden part of something, as the handle of a weapon. [Obs.]

tim'bẽr, *v.t.* to provide, build, shore, or prop up with timbers.

tim'bẽr, *v.i.* to make a nest. [Obs.]

tim'bẽr, *a.* of or for timber.

tim'bẽr, *interj.* a warning shout by a lumberman that a cut tree is about to fall.

tim'bẽr, *n.* [Fr. *timbre;* Sw. *timmer;* L.G. *timmer;* G. *zimmer,* a certain number of skins. Origin doubtful.] a certain number of skins: in the case of the skins of martens, ermines, sables, and the like, forty; of some other skins, one hundred and twenty.

tim'bẽr, *n.* [Fr. *timbre,* a crest, a helmet.] in heraldry, a crest on a coat of arms.

tim'bẽr, *v.t.* to surmount and decorate, as a crest does a coat of arms. [Obs.]

tim'bẽr bee'tle, any one of many species of beetles, the larvae of which bore into timber, as *Lymexylon sericeum.*

tim'bẽr brick, a piece of timber of the size and shape of a brick, inserted in brickwork to attach the finishings to.

tim'bẽr çru̇iṣ'ẽr, a man who is employed in seeking for valuable tracts of timber, as for a lumbering concern.

tim'bẽred, *a.* 1. made or furnished with timber or timbers: frequently in composition; as, a well-*timbered* house.
2. built; formed; contrived.
3. covered or abounding with growing timber; wooded; as, the country is well-*timbered.*

tim'bẽr grouse, any one of several species of grouse that frequent wooded land, as the ruffed grouse.

tim'bẽr·head (-hed), *n.* in ships, the top end of a timber, rising above the gunwale, and serving for belaying ropes, etc.

tim'bẽr hitch, in nautical usage, a knot used for tying a rope to a spar: see *knot,* illus.

tim'bẽr·ing, *n.* work made of timber; timberwork; also, timbers collectively.

tim'bẽr·land, *n.* land with trees suitable for timber; wooded land.

tim'bẽr-līne, *a.* of a timber line.

tim'bẽr līne, the imaginary line on mountains and in polar regions beyond which trees do not grow.

tim'bẽr·ling, *n.* a small tree whose wood is suitable for use in building.

tim'bẽr·măn, *n.*; *pl.* **tim'bẽr·men,** a man who erects wooden supports in a mine.

tim'bẽr māre, a kind of wooden horse on which soldiers were formerly made to ride as a punishment.

tim'bẽr sçrībe, an instrument used in marking timber.

tim'ber sow, a wood louse.

tim'bẽr tree, a tree suitable for timber.

tim'bẽr wolf (wu̇lf), a large, gray or brindled wolf of North America.

tim'bẽr·wŏrk, *n.* work made of wood; timbering.

tim'bẽr wŏrm, the larva of any timber-boring insect; the timber sow.

tim'bẽr yärd, a yard or place where timber is stored or sold.

tim'bre (-bẽr), *n.* [Fr.; OFr., small bell.]
1. in heraldry, a crest on a coat of arms; a timber.
2. in music, the characteristic quality of sound that distinguishes one voice or musical instrument from another: it is determined by the harmonics of the sound and is distinguished from the *intensity* and *pitch.*

3. in phonetics, the degree of resonance of a voiced sound, especially of a vowel.

tim′brel, *n.* [dim. of ME. *timbre*; OFr. *tymbre*, from L. *tympanum*, a drum.] An ancient type of tambourine.

And Miriam took a *timbrel* in her hand.
—Ex. xv. 20.

tim′breled, tim′brelled, *a.* sung to the sound of the timbrel. [Rare.]

tim·brol′ō·gy, *n.* [Fr. *timbre*, stamp, and *-logy*.] the science or study of postage stamps.

tim·bu·rine′, *n.* a tambourine. [Obs.]

tīme, *n.* [ME.; AS. *tīma*, time, hour, season.]

1. the period between two events or during which something exists, happens, or acts; measured or measurable interval.

2. [*usually pl.*] a period of history, characterized by a given social structure, set of customs, etc.; as, medieval *times*.

3. [*often pl.*] a period of history or of the history of a region, with reference to a famous person living then; as, in Lincoln's *time*.

4. [*usually pl.*] prevailing conditions, past, present, or future; as, *times* are bad.

5. a period characterized by a prevailing condition; as, a *time* of sorrow.

6. a period or occasion with reference to one's personal reaction to it; as, I had a good *time*.

7. a period of duration set or thought of as set; specifically, (a) a period of existence; a lifetime; as, my *time* is almost over; (b) the period of pregnancy; (c) a term of apprenticeship; (d) a term of imprisonment.

8. a period or periods necessary, sufficient, or available for something; as, I have not *time* to speak with you now.

I have resolved to take *time*, and in spite of all misfortunes, to write you, at intervals, a long letter. —Swift.

9. the usual, shortest, or allotted period during which something is done; as, the runner's *time* was 1.47 minutes; baking *time*, 20 minutes.

10. (a) the period worked or to be worked by an employee; (b) the pay due for this.

11. rate of speed in marching, driving, working, etc.; as, go at double *time*.

12. a point in duration; a moment; an instant.

13. a precise instant, second, minute, hour, day, week, month, or year, determined by clock or calendar; as, the *time* of the accident was 5:46 P.M., March 12, 1954.

14. the point at which something has happened, is happening, or will happen; occasion; as, at the *time* they arrived, I was away.

15. the usual, natural, traditional, or appointed moment for something to happen, begin, or end; as, *time* to get up; specifically, (a) the moment of death; as, my *time* is close at hand; (b) the moment of childbirth: said of a pregnant woman; as, she is near her *time*.

16. the suitable, proper, favorable, or convenient moment; as, now is the *time* to act.

17. any one of a series of moments at which the same or nearly the same thing recurs; a repeated occasion; as, this is the fifth *time* I've told you; *time* and *time* again.

18. duration; continuance.

19. indefinite, unlimited duration in which things are considered as happening in the past, present, or future; every moment there has ever been or ever will be.

20. (a) the entire period of existence of the known universe; finite duration, as distinguished from infinity; (b) the entire period of existence of the world or of humanity; earthly duration, as distinguished from eternity.

21. a system of measuring duration; as, solar *time*, standard *time*, etc.

22. [T—] Father Time.

23. in music, (a) the grouping of rhythmic beats into measures of equal length; (b) the characteristic rhythm of a composition or passage in terms of this grouping, indicated by the time signature: also called *meter*, *rhythm*; (c) the rate of speed at which a composition or passage is played; tempo; (d) loosely, the rhythm and tempo characteristic of a kind of composition; as, waltz *time*, march *time*; (e) the duration of a note or rest.

24. in prosody, (a) a unit of quantitative meter; especially, (b) a mora, or short syllable.

25. in grammar, tense. [Obs.]

26. in drama, one of the three unities.

27. in phrenology, the perceptive faculty for judging or measuring time intervals.

28. in fencing, a division of a movement.

29. one of the larger divisions of geologic chronology.

abreast of the times; (a) up-to-date; modern in ideas, dress, etc.; (b) informed about current matters.

absolute time; a system intended to indicate the same instant by the same standard in all parts of the world, irrespective of local standards and without reference to the meridian under which an event takes place.

against time; trying to finish in a given time; as fast as possible.

ahead of time; sooner than due; early.

apparent time; time regulated by the diurnal motion of the sun; time as shown by a sun dial; solar time.

astronomical time; mean solar time reckoned from noon through the twenty-four hours.

at one time; (a) simultaneously; (b) formerly.

at the same time; (a) simultaneously; in the same period; (b) nonetheless; however.

at times; occasionally; sometimes.

behind the times; out-of-date; old-fashioned.

behind time; late.

between times; now and then; occasionally.

equation of time; see under *equation*.

for the time being; for the present; temporarily.

from time to time; at intervals; now and then.

high time; see under *high*.

in good time; see under *good*.

in no time; almost instantly; very quickly.

in time; (a) at the right moment; sufficiently early; before it is too late; (b) in the course of things; by degrees; eventually; as, you will *in time* recover your health; (c) keeping the set rhythm, tempo, pace, etc.

many a time; often; frequently.

mean time or *mean solar time*; see under *mean* (middle), *a*.

on one's own time; during time for which one is not paid; during other than working hours.

on time; (a) at the appointed time; punctual or punctually; (b) to be paid for in installments over a period of time.

out of time; (a) not at the usual time; unseasonable; (b) not keeping the set rhythm, tempo, pace, etc.

sidereal time; see under *sidereal*.

solar time; same as *apparent time*.

standard time; the official civil time for any given region; mean solar time, determined by

UNITED STATES TIME ZONES

distance east or west of Greenwich, England: the earth is divided into twenty-four time zones extending from pole to pole, four of them (*Eastern*, *Central*, *Mountain*, and *Pacific*) falling within the borders of the United States and using the civil times of the 75th, 90th, 105th, and 120th meridians respectively; adjacent time zones are one hour apart, but some slight variations occur in legal time, as when a country extending across more than one time zone keeps a uniform legal time nationally.

time after time; again and again; continually: also *time and again*.

time enough; early enough.

time of day; greeting; salutation: chiefly in *to give one*, or *pass, the time of day*.

time of life; age (of a person).

time of one's life; an experience of unusual pleasure for one. [Colloq.]

time out of mind; same as *time immemorial*.

times; multiplied by: symbol, ×.

to gain time; (a) to go too fast: said of a timepiece; (b) to prolong a situation until a desired occurrence can take place.

to keep time; (a) to register time, as a watch; (b) in music, to observe the rhythmic beats; (c) to move rhythmically with another.

to kill time; see *kill*, *v.t.*, sense 4.

to lose time; (a) to let time go by without advancing one's objective; (b) to go too slow; as, a watch or clock *loses time*.

to make time; (a) to compensate for lost time by going faster, as a train; (b) to travel, work, etc. at a specified, especially fast, rate of speed; as, we *made* (good) *time* between Boston and Albany.

true time; (a) mean time; (b) apparent time.

Syn.—age, duration, period, season.

tīme, *v.t.*; timed, *pt.*, *pp.*; timing, *ppr.* 1. to adapt to the time or occasion; to bring, begin, or perform at the proper time; as, he *timed* his visit to find her in.

2. to regulate for a given speed or length of operation; as, he *timed* the stroke.

3. to calculate or record the time, duration, or rate of; as, to *time* a race or other performance; to *time* the speed of a horse.

4. to adjust, set, play, etc. so as to coincide in time with something else; as, *time* your watch with mine.

5. to set the duration of (a syllable or musical note) as a unit of rhythm.

tīme, *v.i.* 1. to keep time; to move in time. [Rare.]

2. to waste time; to defer; to procrastinate. [Obs.]

tīme, *interj.* in sports, etc., a signal that a period of play or activity is ended or that play is temporarily suspended.

tīme, *a.* 1. having to do with time.

2. set or regulated so as to explode, open, etc. at a given time; as, a *time* bomb.

3. payable later or on a specified future date; as, a *time* loan.

4. having to do with purchases in which payment is made over a period of time; as, a *time* payment.

tīme and ȧ hȧlf (hȧf), a rate of payment one and a half times the usual rate, as for working overtime.

tīme ball, a ball on a pole dropped to mark certain predetermined hours, noon being that in general use.

tīme bär′gain (-gen), a contract for the sale or purchase of merchandise or of stock at a certain future date.

tīme bill, a timetable. [Brit.]

tīme book, a book in which is kept a record of the time persons have worked.

tīme′çärd, *n.* an employee's card on which a daily record of working time as well as the time of arrival and departure is kept.

tīme çlock, a clock having a mechanical arrangement which records on a timecard the time of arrival and departure of employees.

tīme dē·poṣ′it, a bank deposit payable at a specified future date or upon advance notice.

tīme dē·teçt′ŏr, an instrument for recording the time at which a watchman was at different stations on his beat; a telltale.

tīme drȧft, a draft payable at a future date specified on the draft.

tīme ex·pō′ṣūre (-zhūr), 1. an exposure of photographic film for a relatively long period, generally longer than half a second.

2. a photograph taken in this way.

tīme frāme, a specified period of time.

tīme′fụl, *a.* seasonable; timely; sufficiently early.

tīme fūṣe, a fuse which can be so arranged as to explode a charge at a certain determinate interval after the time of its ignition.

tīme′-hon″ŏred (-on″), *a.* honored or observed because in existence or usage for a long time; as, a *time-honored* institution.

tīme im·mē·mō′ri·ăl, 1. time so long past as to be forgotten or vague.

2. in English law, time beyond legal memory, fixed by statute as prior to 1189, the beginning of the reign of Richard I.

tīme′keep″ẽr, *n.* 1. a clock, watch, or other timepiece.

2. a person who keeps time; specifically, (a) a person employed to keep account of the hours worked by employees; (b) a person who beats time for a band, etc.; (c) a person who keeps account of the elapsed time in the periods of play in certain sports.

tīme′less, *a.* 1. that cannot be measured by time; unending; eternal.

2. referred or restricted to no specific time; always valid or true; dateless.

3. untimely. [Obs.]

tīme lim′it, a fixed period of time during which something must be done or ended.

tīme′li·ness, *n.* the quality or condition of being timely; seasonableness.

The common school is supereminent in the *timeliness* of the aid it proffers.
—Horace Mann.

tīme′ling, *n.* a timeserver. [Obs.]

tīme lōan, a loan to be paid by a specified time.

tīme lock, a lock having clockwork attached which prevents opening before the time set.

tīme′ly, *a.*; *comp.* timelier; *superl.* timeliest. 1. happening, done, said, etc. at a suitable time; well-timed; opportune.
 2. being in good time; early; as, the defendant had *timely* notice. [Obs. or Rare.]
tīme′ly, *adv.* early; soon. [Archaic or Poet.]
tim·ē·nog′uy (-nog′i), *n.* [etym. unknown.] a rope made fast to the stock of an anchor of a ship, to keep the tacks and sheets from fouling on the stock.
tīme′ous, *a.* timely; as, a *timeous* measure. [Scot.]
tīme′ous·ly, *adv.* in a timeous manner. [Scot.]
tīme out, 1. any time not counted toward a work record, score, etc.
 2. in football, basketball, etc., any time requested during play to make substitutions, discuss strategy, etc. and not counted in the playing time.
tīme′piēce, *n.* a clock, watch, or other instrument to measure or record time; a chronometer.
tīme′plēaṣ·ēr, *n.* one who complies with the prevailing opinions of the time, whatever they may be; a timeserver.
tīm′ẽr, *n.* 1. a person who keeps time or time records; a timekeeper.
 2. a timepiece; especially, a stop watch.
 3. in internal-combustion engines, a mechanism for causing the spark to be produced in the cylinder at the required instant.
tīme′sāv″ing, *a.* saving time because of greater efficiency, etc.; intended to save time; as, a *timesaving* device.
tīme′sẽrv″ẽr, *n.* a person who for his own advantage deliberately surrenders his principles and acts in conformity with the patterns of behavior prevailing at the time or sanctioned by those in authority.
tīme′sẽrv″ing, *n.* the action or behavior of a timeserver.
tīme′sẽrv″ing, *a.* of, or having the nature of, a timeserver.
tīme sig′nȧ·tūre, in music, a sign, after the key signature, indicating the time, or tempo.
tīme stud′y, study of operational or production procedures and the time consumed by them, for the purpose of devising methods of increasing efficiency or productivity of workers.
tīme′tā·ble, *n.* 1. a table or schedule of the times certain things are to happen, especially of the departure and arrival of trains, busses, ships, etc.
 2. in music, a table containing the relative value of every note.
tīme′-test′ed, *a.* having value proved by long use or experience.
tīme wạrp, the condition or process of being displaced from one point in time to another, as in science fiction.
tīme′wŏrk, *n.* work which is paid for by the hour or day: distinguished from *piecework.*
tīme′wōrn, *a.* worn or deteriorated by long use or existence.
tīme zōne, see *standard time* under *time.*
tim′id, *a.* [L. *timidus*, from *timere*, to fear.]
 1. easily frightened; lacking self-confidence; shy; timorous.
 2. showing fear or lack of self-confidence; hesitant; as, a *timid* reply.
 Syn.—fearful, shy, diffident, afraid, fainthearted.
ti·mid′i·ty, *n.* [Fr. *timidité*; L. *timiditas.*] the quality or condition of being timid; fearfulness; shyness.
tim′id·ly, *adv.* in a timid manner.
tim′id·ness, *n.* timidity.
tīm′ing, *n.* the regulation of the speed with which something is performed so as to produce the most effective results; as, the *timing* of a play, of an engine, of a golfer's swing, etc.
tīm′ist, *n.* 1. in music, a performer who keeps correct time.
 2. one who conforms to the times; a timeserver. [Obs.]
tim′mẽr, *n.* timber. [Scot. and Brit. Dial.]
tī·moç′rȧ·cy, *n.*; *pl.* **tī·moç′rȧ·cieṣ,** [OFr. *tymocracie*; ML. *timocratia*; Gr. *timokratia*; *timē*, honor, worth, and *kratein*, to rule.]
 1. in Plato's politics, a state in which love of honor and glory is the guiding principle of the rulers.
 2. in Aristotle's politics, a state in which political power is in direct proportion to property ownership.
tī·mō·crat′iç, *a.* of or characteristic of a timocracy.
tim·ō·neer′, *n.* [Fr. *timonier*, from *timon*, a helm or tiller, from L. *temo* (-*onis*), a pole.] a helmsman. [Rare.]

Tī′mŏn·ist, *n.* a misanthrope.
tim′ŏr·ous, *a.* [from L. *timor*, fear.]
 1. fearful; full of or subject to fear; timid; as, a *timorous* deer.
 2. showing or caused by timidity; as, *timorous* doubts; *timorous* beliefs.
tim′ŏr·ous·ly, *adv.* fearfully; timidly; in a timorous manner.
tim′ŏr·ous·ness, *n.* fearfulness; timidity; the state of being timorous.
tim′ŏr·sōme, *a.* easily frightened; timorous. [Obs. or Dial.]
Tī·mō′thē·ăn, *n.* [L. *Timotheus*, from Gr. *Timotheos*, one who honors God.] any of a group of Monophysites who, in the fifth century, followed Timotheus Aelurus of Alexandria.
Tim′ō·thy, *n.* in the Bible, (a) a disciple of the Apostle Paul; (b) either of the Epistles to Timothy, two books of the New Testament which were messages from the Apostle Paul.
tim′ō·thy, *n.* [after *Timothy* Hanson, who did much to promote its cultivation in the United States and Canada.] a grass, *Phleum pratense*, with long, narrow leaves and bearded spikes of flowers, used for fodder: also called *timothy grass.*
tīm′ous, *a.* early; timely. [Obs.]
tim′pȧ·ni, *n.pl.*; *sing.* **tim′pȧ·nō,** [It.] kettledrums; especially, a set of kettledrums of different pitches played by one performer in an orchestra: also spelled *tympani.*
tim′pȧ·nist, *n.* a person who plays kettledrums.
tim′-whis″ky (-hwis″), *n.* [etym. unknown.] a light one-horse chaise without a top.
tin, *n.* [ME. and AS.]
 1. a soft, silver-white, metallic chemical element, malleable at ordinary temperatures, capable of a high polish, and used as an alloy in tin foils, solders, utensils, type metals, etc. and in making tin plate: symbol, Sn; atomic weight, 118.70; atomic number, 50.
 2. tin plate.
 3. a can in which foodstuffs are preserved. [Brit.]
 4. money. [Obs. Slang.]
 5. anything made of tin or of tin plate, as a can, pot, pan, box, etc.
 butter of tin; chloride of tin.
 salt of tin; tin dissolved in hydrochloric acid: used as a mordant.
tin, *a.* made of tin or of tin plate; as, a *tin* pan, a *tin* soldier.
tin, *v.t.*; tinned, *pt.*, *pp.*; tinning, *ppr.* 1. to cover or plate with tin.
 2. to pack, put up, or preserve in tins; as, to *tin* vegetables. [Brit.]
tin′ăge, *n.* an earthenware wine jar. [Obs.]
ti·nä′jä (-hä), *n.* [Sp.] 1. a water jar, made of porous material, in which water is cooled by evaporation.
 2. a hole holding water, in a crevice of rock or deep ravine. [Mex.]
Ti·nam′i·dae, *n.pl.* a South American family of birds, including the tinamou.
tin′ȧ·mine, *a.* pertaining to the tinamou.
tin′ȧ·mōu, *n.* [native name.] any of a number of South and Central American birds belonging to the genus *Tinamus*: they resemble the partridge and quail but belong to the ratite group. The great tinamou, *Tinamus brasiliensis*, is about 18 inches long, and inhabits the great forests of Guiana.

GREAT TINAMOU (*Tinamus brasiliensis*)

tiñ′çăl, *n.* [Malay *tingkal.*] crude borax.
tin′chel, *n.* [Ir. and Gael. *timchioll*, a going round or about.] a circle of sportsmen, who, by surrounding an extensive space, and gradually closing in, bring a number of deer and game within a small space. [Scot.]
tiñçt, *v.t.* to tincture; to stain or color; to imbue. [Obs.]

tiñçt, *n.* stain; color; tint. [Poet.]
tiñçt, *a.* tinged; tinted; slightly colored. [Poet.]
tiñç′tion, *n.* the process of coloring or dyeing; also, the coloring material used in such an operation.
tiñç·tō′ri·ăl, *a.* having to do with color, dyeing, or staining; as, the *tinctorial* principle of madder.
tiñç′tūre, *n.* [Fr. *teinture*, from L. *tinctura*, from *tinctus*, *pp.* of *tingere*, to dye.]
 1. originally, a dye.
 2. a light color; a tint; a tinge.
 3. a slight trace, smattering, shade, vestige, taste, etc.
 4. a medicinal substance in solution, especially in an alcoholic solvent; as, *tincture* of iodine: distinguished from *spirit.*
 5. in heraldry, any color, metal, or fur.
 alcoholic tinctures; tinctures such as are prepared with alcohol. When ether spirit is used as the solvent, they are termed *ethereal tinctures*; when ammonia is used, they are termed *ammoniated tinctures*; and when wine is used, they are called *medicated wines.*
 simple tinctures; tinctures which hold only one substance in solution: *compound tinctures* are those in which two or more ingredients are in solution.
tiñç′tūre, *v.t.*; tinctured, *pt.*, *pp.*; tincturing *ppr.* 1. to color lightly; to tint; to tinge.
 2. to imbue or permeate slightly with a trace, taste, odor, etc.
 3. to affect slightly with a quality; as, a message *tinctured* with hope.
tind, *v.t.* and *v.i.* to kindle. [Dial.]
tin′dăl, *n.* [Malay *tandal.*] in the East Indies, a native petty officer of lascar sailors or soldiers; also, a gang foreman.
tin′dẽr, *n.* [AS. *tynder.*] an inflammable substance composed of partially burned linen, used for kindling fire from a spark struck from a flint with a piece of steel; any dry, easily inflammable material used in this way.
tin′dẽr·box, *n.* 1. formerly, a metal box for holding tinder, flint, and steel for starting a fire.
 2. any highly inflammable object or structure, excitable person, etc.
tin′dẽr fuñ′gus, a tree fungus, *Polyporus fomentarius*, from which tinder is made.
tin′dẽr·līke, *a.* like tinder; very inflammable.
tin′dẽr·y, *a.* like tinder; inflammable.
tīne, *v.t.* to kindle; to set on fire. [Obs.]
tīne, *v.t.* 1. to lose. [Dial.]
 2. to wipe out; to destroy. [Dial.]
tīne, *v.i.* to perish; to be lost. [Dial.]
tīne, *v.t.* to shut or enclose. [Brit. Dial.]
tīne, *v.i.* to enclose; to hedge in. [Brit. Dial.]
tīne, *n.* [ME. *tind*; AS. *tind*; Ice. *tindr*, a spike.] a sharp, projecting point; a spike; a prong, as one of the spikes or projections of a fork, one of the projections of a deer's antler, a tooth of a harrow or drag, etc.
tīne, *n.* trouble; distress. [Obs.]
tīne, *n.* a wild vetch or tare; a plant that tines or encloses other plants. [Obs.]
tin′ē·ȧ, *n.* [L., gnawing worm, a moth.] any of various skin diseases caused by a fungus; especially, ringworm.
Tin′ē·ȧ, *n.* 1. a genus of moths including the clothes moth, distinguished by having the head covered with coarse hairs, with five-jointed maxillary palpi and cylindrical labial palpi. The front wings are oblong-ovate, and the hind wings ovate and scaly. The genus includes a large number of species, the larvae of several of which are very destructive to cloth, especially *Tinea pellionella* and *Tinea tapetzella.*

TINEA (*Tinea pellionella*)

 2. [t—] any moth of this genus.
tin′ē·ăn, *n.* and *a.* same as *tineid.*
tīned, *a.* furnished with tines; as, a three-*tined* fork.
tin′ē·id, *n.* a member of the *Tineidæ.*
tin′ē·id, *a.* designating, of, or pertaining to the *Tineidæ.*
Ti·nē′i·dae, *n.pl.* a family of lepidopterous insects, consisting of small moths, some of which infest woolen cloths and furs, upon which their larvae feed. The principal genera are *Tinea, Scardia, Incurvaria,* and *Lampronia.*
tī′net, *n.* brushwood and thorns for making and repairing hedges. [Obs.]
tin flōor, in tin mining, the small vein or thin flat mass of tinstone interposed between

certain rocks and parallel to their beds; also, a large irregular mass of tin ore.
tin'-foil, *a.* made of tin foil.
tin foil, pure tin, or the metal alloyed with a little lead, beaten and rolled into thin sheets: used in wrapping small articles, as protection from moisture or the air.
ting, *n.* [echoic.] a single, light, ringing sound, as of a small bell being struck.
ting, *v.t.* and *v.i.* to make or cause to make a ting.
ting, *n.* a thing (assembly).
ting'-à-ling, *n.* the tinkle of a bell; the sound of a small bell ringing.
tinge, *v.t.*; tinged, *pt., pp.*; tingeing *or* tinging, *ppr.* [L. *tingere*, to dye, stain.]
1. to color slightly; to give a tint to.
2. to give a trace, slight flavor or odor, shade, etc. to; as, his memory was *tinged* with sorrow.
Syn.—dye.
tinge, *n.* 1. a slight coloring; a tint.
2. a slight trace, flavor, odor, etc.; a smack; a touch; as, there was a *tinge* of sarcasm in his voice.
tin'gent, *a.* having the power to tinge. [Rare.]
tin'gĕr, *n.* one who or that which tinges.
tiñ'gi, *n.* a Brazilian forest tree *Magonia glabrata*, family *Sapindaceæ*. Soap is made from its broad flat seeds, and an infusion of the roots is used to poison fish: also spelled *tinguy*.
tin'gi·ble, *a.* susceptible to stain.
tin'gid, *a.* pertaining to the genus *Tingis*.
Tin'gis, *n.* 1. a genus of hemipterous insects, typical of the family *Tingitidæ*, which prey on other insects, vegetables, and trees.
2. [t—] one of the *Tingitidæ*.
Tin·git'i·dae, *n.pl.* a family of hemipterous insects which collect in large numbers on the leaves of trees and shrubs.
tin'-glȧss, *n.* bismuth. [Obs.]
tiñ'gle, *v.i.*; tingled (-gld), *pt., pp.*; tingling, *ppr.* [var. of *tinkle*.]
1. to tinkle; to jingle. [Now Rare.]
2. to have a thrilling sensation, or a slightly stinging, prickly sensation, as from cold, a sharp slap, emotional excitement, etc.
3. to cause this sensation.
tiñ'gle, *v.t.* 1. to cause to jingle or tinkle. [Now Rare.]
2. to cause to have a prickling, slightly stinging feeling.
tiñ'gle, *n.* a prickling, slightly stinging feeling.
tiñ'gly, *a.*; *comp.* tinglier; *superl.* tingliest, having or characterized by a tingling.
tin hat, a soldier's steel helmet (especially in World War I).
tin'horn, *a.* [from the flashy appearance and cheap quality of tin horns.] pretending to have money, influence, ability, etc., though actually lacking in these; cheap and showy; as, a *tinhorn* sport. [Slang.]
tiñk, *v.t.*; tinked (tiñkt), *pt., pp.*; tinking, *ppr.* [imitative.] to make a sharp, shrill noise; to tinkle. [Obs.]
tiñk, *n.* a tinkle; a tinkling. [Obs.]
tiñk'ẽr, *n.* [W. *tincerz*, the ringer, from *tinciaw*, to ring.]
1. a mender of metal kettles, pans, and the like, usually going from house to house.
2. the act of mending, as metalwork; the doing the work of a tinker.
3. one who is able to do minor repairing of any kind; a jack-of-all-trades.
4. a clumsy or unskillful worker; a bungler; a botcher.
5. the action of such a person; a bungling attempt.
6. a small piece of ordnance consisting of a small mortar fixed on a stake. [Obs.]
7. any of various fishes, as the skate, the silversides, the chub mackerel, a young mackerel about two years old, and a variety of stickleback.
8. any of various birds, as the razorbill and the guillemot. [Dial.]
9. a kind of seal. [Newfoundland.]
tiñk'ẽr, *v.t.*; tinkered, *pt., pp.*; tinkering, *ppr.*
1. to work on or at as a tinker; to mend, repair, or make small improvements in.
2. to mend bunglingly; to patch up in an unskillful manner.
tiñk'ẽr, *v.i.* 1. to work at tinkering; to patch up defects; to work upon a thing by making small repairs.
2. to work in a bungling way; to make clumsy, unsuccessful attempts to mend or repair something.
3. to fuss or putter aimlessly or uselessly.
tiñk'ẽr·ing, *n.* the act or employment of a tinker.
tiñk'ẽr·ly, *a.* of or characteristic of a tinker.
tiñ'kẽr's damn (or **dam**), [from *tinker* and *damn*: with reference to the lowly status and profane speech of tinkers.] something of no value: especially in *not worth a tinker's damn*.
tiñk'ẽr·shïre, tiñk'ẽr·shüe, *n.* the guillemot. [Brit. Dial.]
tiñk'ẽr's weed, [after Dr. *Tinker* of New England.] feverroot: also called *tinker's root*.
tiñ'kle, *v.i.*; tinkled (-kld), *pt., pp.*; tinkling, *ppr.* [imitative.]
1. to make a series of small, quick, light, clinking sounds like those of a very small bell.
2. to tingle. [Now Rare.]
tiñ'kle, *v.t.* 1. to cause to tinkle.
2. to indicate, signal, etc. by tinkling.
tiñ'kle, *n.* 1. the act of tinkling.
2. a tinkling sound.
tiñ'klẽr, *n.* a tinker. [Brit. Dial.]
tiñ'kling, *n.* 1. a tinkle or tinkles.
2. a Jamaican grackle with a tinkling call.
tiñ'kly, *a.*; *comp.* tinklier; *superl.* tinkliest, characterized by tinkling.
tin liq'uŏr (lik'ẽr), a solution of tin filings and hydrochloric acid used as a mordant in dyeing.
tin'măn, *n.*; *pl.* **tin'men,** a manufacturer of tinware; a tinsmith; also, a dealer in tinware.
tin mor'dănt, same as *tin liquor*.
tin'mouth, *n.* a fish, the crappie. [Colloq.]
tinned, *a.* 1. plated, covered, or coated with tin; as, *tinned* spoons.
2. packed in tin cans or cases; canned; as, *tinned* peaches. [Brit.]
Tin'neh, *n.pl.* a family of American Indians including several of the tribes in the Northwest; the Athapascans.
tin'nen, *a.* consisting or made of tin. [Obs.]
tin'nẽr, *n.* 1. one who works in the tin mines.
2. a worker in tin; one who makes tinware; a tinsmith.
3. a canner. [Brit.]
tin'ni·ent, *a.* emitting a ringing sound. [Obs.]
tin'ni·ly, *adv.* in a tinny manner.
tin'ni·ness, *n.* a tinny quality or state.
tin'ning, *n.* 1. the act or practice of covering or lining anything with tin, or of preserving in tin.
2. the covering or lining thus put on.
3. the work of a tinsmith.
tin·nī'tus, *n.* [L., a ringing.] a sound as of ringing or whistling in the ear, not resulting from an external stimulus.
telephone tinnitus; tinnitus thought to be due to the continual use of the telephone.
tin'nŏck, *n.* the blue titmouse. [Brit. Dial.]
tin'ny, *a.*; *comp.* tinnier; *superl.* tinniest, 1. of, containing, or yielding tin.
2. like tin in appearance or strength; bright but cheap; not durable.
3. of or like the sound made in striking a tin object.
4. tasting of tin.
Tī·noc'e·ras, *n.* [Gr. *teinein*, to stretch, and *keras*, horn.]
1. an Eocene genus of gigantic fossil herbivorous mammals, having a long narrow head and two or three pairs of horns.
2. [t—] an animal of this genus.
tin'-pan al'ley, 1. a street or part of a city, especially of New York, where there are many musicians, publishers of popular music, etc.
2. the publishers, writers, and promoters of popular music.
tin'-plāte', *v.t.* to plate with tin.
tin plāte, thin sheets of iron or steel plated with tin.
tin'sel, *n.* [OFr. *estincelle*, from L. *scintilla*, a spark or flash.]
1. formerly, a cloth of wool, etc. interwoven with glittering threads of gold, silver, or other metal.
2. thin sheets, strips, or threads of tin, metal foil, etc., used for inexpensive decoration.
3. cloth overlaid with metal foil.
4. something that glitters like precious metal but has little worth; empty show; sham splendor.
tin'sel, *a.* 1. made of or decorated with tinsel.
2. having sham splendor; showy; gaudy.
tin'sel, *v.t.*; tinseled *or* tinselled, *pt., pp.*; tinseling *or* tinselling, *ppr.* 1. to adorn with tinsel or with something glittering and showy like tinsel.

She, *tinseled* o'er in robes of varying hues.
—Pope.

2. to give a false appearance of splendor to.
tin'sel·ly, *a.* resembling tinsel; gaudy; showy and superficial.
tin'sel·ly, *adv.* in a gaudy and superficial manner.
tins'măn, *n.*; *pl.* **tins'men,** a tinsmith.
tin'smith, *n.* one who makes articles of tin or tin plate; a worker in tin.
tin'stōne, *n.* cassiterite, a native dioxide of tin: the principal ore of tin found in the mines of Cornwall.
tint, *n.* [for earlier *tinct*, from L. *tinctus*, a hue, dye.]
1. a delicate color or hue; a tinge.
2. a color; especially, a gradation of a color with reference to its mixture with white.
3. in engraving, an even shading produced by fine parallel lines.
4. in printing, a light colored background, as for an illustration.
Syn.—color, hue, tinge, dye, complexion.
tint, *v.t.*; tinted, *pt., pp.*; tinting, *ppr.* to tinge; to give a slight coloring or tint to.
tin·tȧ·märre', tin·tȧ·mär', *n.* a hideous or confused noise. [Archaic.]
tint block, in printing, an electrotype, or surface of wood or metal, often bearing a design, for printing the background of an illustration in color.
tint'ẽr, *n.* 1. one who or that which tints.
2. a plain colored glass slide used for giving a tinted effect to stereopticon projections.
tin'tẽr·nell, *n.* an old-time dance. [Obs.]
tin'tie, *n.* the wren. [Brit. Dial.]
tint'ing, *n.* in engraving, the method of shading by cutting a series of fine parallel lines.
tin·tin·nab'ū·lăr, tin·tin·nab'ū·lăr·y, *a.* of or relating to bells or their sound.
tin·tin·nab·ū·lā'tion, *n.* a tinkling or ringing sound, as of bells.

The *tintinnabulation* that so musically wells
From the bells. —Poe.

tin·tin·nab'ū·lous, *a.* same as *tintinnabular*.
tin·tin·nab'ū·lum, *n.* [L., a little bell, from *tintinnare*, a freq. and aug. from *tinnire*, to ring, to jingle.]
1. a bell. [Rare.]

Beating alternately in measured time
The clockwork *tintinnabulum* of rime.
—Cowper.

2. a jingling toy of small bells or metal plates.
tint'less, *a.* without tint; colorless.
tin'tō, *n.* [Sp., colored.] a Madeira wine, red in color and not highly aromatic.
tint·om'e·tẽr, *n.* an instrument for determining color by comparison with an arbitrary standard.
tint tool, a tool for engraving parallel lines or stipples.
tin'tȳpe, *n.* a positive photograph taken directly on a sensitized plate of enameled tin or iron; a stannotype or ferrotype.
tin'wāre, *n.* pots, pans, etc. made of tin plate.
tin'wŏrk, *n.* 1. work done in tin.
2. *pl.* [*construed as sing.*] a place where tin is smelted, rolled, etc.
tī'ny, *a.*; *comp.* tinier; *superl.* tiniest, [from ME. *tine*, *n.*, a little (something), always preceded by *litel*, little.] very small; diminutive; minute.

And the *tiny* mark, like the mark of Cain.
—J. B. Wilbur, Jr.

-tion, [from Fr., OFr., or L.; Fr. *-tion*; OFr. *-cion*; L. *-tio, -tionis*, from *-t-* of pp. stem and *-io, -ionis*, suffix.] a suffix, used to form nouns from verbs, meaning: (a) *a* ——*ing* or *being* ——*ed*, as in rela*tion*; (b) *something* ——*ed*, as in crea*tion*.
-tious (-shus), [from Fr. or L.; Fr. *-tieux*; L. *-tiosus*, from *-t-* of pp. stem and *-iosus*, *-ous*.] a suffix used in forming adjectives corresponding to nouns in *-tion*, as cau*tious*.
tip, *n.* [ME. *tip*, *tippe*, tip; compare D. *tip*, tip.]
1. the pointed, tapering, or rounded end or top of something long and slim.
2. something attached to the end, as a cap, ferrule, etc.
3. a top or apex, as of a mountain.
4. in gilding, a tool made of camel's hair, used by the gilder in transferring gold leaf from the cushion to the sized surface of the work.
5. in hatmaking, (a) a circular piece of pasteboard pasted on the inside of a hat crown to stiffen it; (b) the upper part of the crown of a hat.
6. the last piece of a jointed fishing rod.
7. a sandal (sense 3).
tip, *v.t.*; tipped (tipt), *pt., pp.*; tipping, *ppr.*
1. to make a tip on.

2. to cover the tip or tips of (*with* something).

3. to serve as the tip of.

tip, *v.t.* [prob. from ME. *tippe*, a tip, or its base.]

1. to strike lightly and sharply; to tap.

2. to give a small present of money to (a waiter, porter, etc.) for some service.

3. to give secret information to in an attempt to be helpful: often with *off*. [Colloq.]

4. in baseball, etc., to hit (the ball) a glancing blow.

5. to give, communicate, or direct toward another generally; as, *tip* me your fist. [Slang.]

to tip the wink to; to wink at as a sign of warning or suggestion. [Slang.]

tip, *v.i.* to give a tip or tips.

tip, *n.* 1. a light, sharp blow; tap.

2. a piece of information given secretly or confidentially in an attempt to be helpful; as, he gave me a *tip* on the race.

3. a suggestion, hint, warning, etc.

4. a small present of money given to a waiter, porter, etc. for services: gratuity.

tip, *v.t.*; tipped (tipt), *pt., pp.*; tipping, *ppr.* [ME. *tipen* (short vowel prob., from pt. *tipte*); Northern word, prob., from O.N.]

1. to overturn or upset: often with *over*.

2. to cause to tilt or slant.

3. to raise slightly or touch the brim of (one's hat) in salutation.

tip, *v.i.* 1. to tilt or slant.

2. to overturn or topple: often with *over*.

tip, *n.* 1. a tipping or being tipped; tilt; slant.

2. rubbish from a quarry; also, the place where the rubbish is dumped.

tip, *n.* a drink of alcoholic liquor. [Obs. Brit. Slang.]

tï pälm (päm), a ti (tree).

tip'bŭrn, *n.* a disease affecting the leaf of the potato plant, usually caused by dry hot weather.

tip çär, in railroading, a gravel, sand, or coal car, pivoted on its truck, so that it can be tilted to discharge its contents.

tip çärt, a cart that can be tilted to empty its contents.

tip'çat, *n.* [*tip* (to overturn) and *cat*.]

1. a game in which a small piece of wood, usually tapered at both ends, is struck on one end with a bat or stick so that it is sprung into the air where it can be batted for distance.

2. the small piece of wood used in this game. Also called *cat, catty*.

tï'pï, *n.* a tepee.

tip'-off, *n.* 1. the act of tipping off.

2. a tip; confidential disclosure, hint, or warning.

Tip'pē-çà-nōe', *n.* nickname of William Henry Harrison: from his leadership of American troops in a battle (1811) with Tecumseh's Indians, fought near the Tippecanoe.

tip'pẽr, *n.* a kind of ale brewed in England: named after its originator, Thomas Tipper.

tip'pẽr, *n.* one who or that which tips (in various senses).

tip'pet, *n.* [AS. *tæppet*, a tippet, from L. *tapete*, from Gr. *tapēs*, hanging, rug, tapestry, covering.]

1. formerly, a long, hanging part of a hood, cape, or sleeve.

2. a scarflike garment of fur, wool, etc. for the neck and shoulders, hanging down in front.

3. in the Anglican Church, a long, black scarf worn by the clergy.

4. a length of twisted hair or gut in a fishing line. [Scot.]

5. a bundle of straw bound together at one end and used in thatching. [Scot.]

6. in entomology, a patagium.

7. in ornithology, a ruff or ruffle.

8. a hood of chain mail. [Obs.]

tip'ping, *n.* 1. in music, same as ***tonguing***.

2. in bookbinding, the act or method of inserting an extra page, illustration, etc. in a bound book by pasting it to the binding edge of a section.

3. the act or habit of giving tips.

tip'ple, *v.t.*; tippled (-pld), *pt., pp.*; tippling, *ppr.* 1. to sip; to drink (alcoholic liquor) often and habitually.

2. to affect by tippling; to make drunk.

tip'ple, *v.i.* to drink alcoholic liquors often and habitually.

tip'ple, *n.* drink; alcoholic liquor.

tip'ple, *n.* a device for unloading tip cars; also, the place where such cars are tipped.

tip'plẽr, *n.* one who habitually drinks alcoholic liquors.

tip'pling, *n.* the habitual drinking of alcoholic liquors.

tip'pling house, a house where alcoholic liquor is sold and drunk; a tavern. [Obs.]

tip'py, *a.* apt to tip over; shaky. [Colloq.]

tip'si·fȳ, *v.t.* to make tipsy; to inebriate.

tip'si·ly, *adv.* in a tipsy manner.

tip'si·ness, *n.* a tipsy condition or quality.

tip'stȧff, *n.*; *pl.* **tip'stȧffs, tip'stāveṣ,** 1. a staff with a metal tip, formerly carried as an emblem by certain officials.

2. an official who carried such a staff, especially, in England, a bailiff or constable.

tip'stẽr, *n.* one who sells tips, or confidential information, about horse races, stocks and bonds, etc. [Colloq.]

tip'sy, *a.*; *comp.* tipsier; *superl.* tipsiest, 1. that tips easily; not steady; shaky.

2. crooked; awry.

3. somewhat drunk; intoxicated enough to be somewhat unsteady, fuddled, etc.

tip'sy çāke, a cake over which wine has been poured, served as a dessert.

tip'tōe, *n.*; *pl.* **tip'tōeṣ,** the tip of a toe or the tips of the toes.

on tiptoe; (a) on one's tiptoes; (b) eager or eagerly; (c) silently; stealthily.

tip'tōe, *a.* 1. standing on one's tiptoes.

2. (a) lifted up; exalted; (b) eager; excited; alert; (c) stealthy; cautious.

tip'tōe, *adv.* on tiptoe.

Night's candles are burnt out, and jocund day
Stands *tiptoe* on the misty mountain tops.
—Shak.

tip'tōe, *v.i.*; tiptoed, *pt., pp.*; tiptoeing, *ppr.* to walk stealthily or cautiously on tiptoe.

tip'top, *n.* [*tip* (end) and *top*.]

1. the highest point; the very top.

2. the highest in quality or excellence; the best. [Colloq.]

tip'top, *a.* and *adv.* 1. at the highest point, or top.

2. at the highest point of excellence, health, etc. [Colloq.]

Tip'ū·lȧ, *n.* [L., a crane fly.]

1. a genus of dipterous insects, characterized by long legs, including the various species of crane fly.

2. [t–] any fly of this genus.

Tip·ū·lā'ri·ȧ, *n.* a genus of terrestrial orchids comprising only two species, one of which grows in the Himalayan region and the other, *Tipularia unifolia*, in the eastern part of the United States. The latter bears a long raceme of greenish-purple flowers and has a solitary leaf which in shape resembles the crane fly.

tip'ū·lār·y, *a.* pertaining to the genus *Tipula*.

tip'ū·lid, *a.* tipuloid.

tip'ū·loid, *a.* belonging or relating to the crane flies.

tip'up, *n.* 1. a bird, the sandpiper or teeter-tail.

2. a fishing hut; a tilt.

tip wŏrm, the larva of a gallfly, *Cecidomyia vaccinii*, found on the tips of cranberry vines. [Dial.]

ti·rāde', *n.* [Fr., from It. *tirata*, a volley, from *tirare*, to draw, to fire.]

1. a long, vehement speech; especially, a declamatory speech of censure or reproof; a harangue.

2. in music, the filling of an interval between two consecutive notes several degrees apart by a rapid run.

tï·räil·lēur' (tē-rä-yēr'), *n.* [Fr., from *tirailler*, to tease, skirmish, from *tirer*, to draw, to fire.] a sharpshooter or skirmisher in the French army.

tīre, *n.* a tier. [Obs.]

tīre, *n.* [ME. *tiren*.]

1. attire; dress. [Archaic.]

2. a woman's headdress; an ornament for the head, generally of gold and precious stones; a tiara. [Archaic.]

3. a child's sleeveless apron; a pinafore.

4. equipment; furniture; apparatus. [Obs.]

tīre, *v.t.*; tired, *pt., pp.*; tiring, *ppr.* to attire; to dress. [Archaic.]

tīre, *n.* [ME. *tyre*, short for *attire*, in sense "equipment".]

1. a hoop of iron or rubber around the wheel of a vehicle, forming the tread.

2. (a) a rubber tube filled with air, fixed about the wheel of a vehicle to reduce shock: an automobile tire consists of a rubber inner tube filled with air at a specified pressure and enclosed in a heavy, treaded, rubber casing; (b) the casing alone, as distinguished from the inner tube.

tīre, *v.t.*; tired, *pt., pp.*; tiring, *ppr.* to furnish with a tire or tires.

tīre, *v.t.* and *v.i.*; tired, *pt., pp.*; tiring, *ppr.* [ME. *tyren*; OFr. *tirer*, to draw, pull.]

1. to seize or tear at (something). [Obs.]

2. to be mentally absorbed (in). [Obs.]

tīre, *v.t.*; tired, *pt., pp.*; tiring, *ppr.* [AS. *teorian*, to be tired.]

1. to weary; to fatigue; to exhaust the physical strength of by toil or labor; as, to *tire* a horse or an ox.

2. to exhaust the patience or interest of, as with dullness or tediousness.

to tire out; to tire completely; to weary or fatigue to excess; to exhaust.

Syn.—weary, exhaust, jade.

tīre, *v.i.* 1. to become weary; to be fatigued; to have the strength fail; as, a feeble body soon *tires* with hard labor.

2. to lose interest or patience; to become bored or impatient.

to tire of; to lose patience with or interest in; to become bored by.

tīred, *a.* wearied; fatigued.

tīred'ness, *n.* the state of being tired; weariness.

tīre·fōnd' (-fōṅ'), *n.* [Fr.] a former surgical instrument like a corkscrew for raising depressed portions of a bone. [Obs.]

tīre'less, *a.* untiring; not easily fatigued.

tīre'ling, *a.* wearied; fatigued. [Obs.]

Tī·rē'si·ȧs, *n.* in Greek legend, a blind soothsayer of Thebes.

tīre'sŏme, *a.* wearisome; fatiguing; exhausting; tedious; as, a *tiresome* day's work; a *tiresome* journey.

tīre'sŏme·ly, *adv.* with fatigue; in a tiresome manner.

tīre'sŏme·ness, *n.* the state or quality of being tiresome; wearisomeness.

tīre'wom"ăn (-woom"), *n.*; *pl.* **tīre'wom"en** (-wim"), a lady's maid, especially one employed in the dressing room of a theater. [Archaic.]

ti·rï'bȧ, *n.* a Brazilian parakeet, *Conurus leucotis*.

tīr'ing ī'ronṣ (-ŭrnz), a puzzle or game, the object of which is to remove one or more rings from an interlinked group in which there is but one opening.

tīr'ing rọọm, a dressing room, especially one in a theater. [Archaic.]

tirl, *v.t.* and *v.i.* [variant of *trill*.] to cause (a string) to make a vibrating sound by plucking or striking. [Scot.]

to tirl at the pin; to twirl or rattle the doorlatch, as a signal to those within that a person desires or intends to enter. [Scot.]

Sae licht's he jumped up the stair
And *tirled at the pin*;
And wha sae ready as hersel
to let the laddie in.—Jacobite Song.

tirl, *n.* the vibrating sound caused by plucking or striking a string. [Scot.]

tirl, *v.t.* to uncover; to remove a roof or clothing from; also, to twist; to twirl. [Scot.]

tir'mȧ, *n.* same as *oyster catcher*.

tī'rō, *n.*; *pl.* **tī'rōṣ,** a tyro.

tir·ō·cin'ī·um, *n.*; *pl.* **tir·ō·cin'ī·ȧ,** [L.] the first campaign of a young soldier; hence, a first experience.

Tir·ō·lēṣe', *a.* and *n.* Tyrolese.

T ī'ron (-ŭrn), an iron bar shaped like the letter T, used in structural work; also, any rod or bar having a crossbar at one end.

Tī·rō'ni·ăn, *a.* [from *Tiro*, the freedman, pupil, and amanuensis of Cicero.] designating a system of shorthand practised by Tiro.

Tironian notes; the shorthand signs and symbols used in the stenographic system of ancient Greece and Rome.

tir'rȧ·lir'rȧ, *n.* a conventionalized echoic representation of the note of a lark or of a similar sound.

tir'rit, *n.* terror; fright: a fanciful word said by Mrs. Quickly, in Shakespeare's *Henry IV*.

tir'whit (-hwit), *n.* same as *tirwit*.

tir'wit, *n.* [imitative of its cry.] the lapwing.

'tiṣ, it is.

tiṣ'ăn, *n.* same as *tisane*.

tï·ṣāne', *n.* [Fr.] in pharmacy, a decoction, as of herbs.

tï'ṣär, *n.* [Fr. *tisard*, from L. *titio* (-*onis*), cinder.] in making plate glass, the heating furnace attached to the annealing chamber.

Tish'äh b'Ab (bọv), [Heb. *tishāh b'ab*, ninth (day) of Ab.] a Jewish fast day commemorating the destruction of the Temple.

Tish'ri, *n.* [Heb., to open.] the first month of the Jewish year.

Tī·siph'ō·nē (-sif'), *n.* in Greek and Roman mythology, one of the three Furies.

tis'sūe (tish'ū), *n.* [ME. *tissu, tissewe*; OFr. *tissu*, woven, from L. *texere*, to weave.]

1. a woven or textile fabric; specifically, (a) [Archaic.] cloth interwoven with gold or silver, or with figured colors; (b) light, thin cloth, as gauze.

2. tissue paper.

3. in biology, (a) the substance of an organic body or organ, consisting of cells and intercellular material; (b) any of the distinct structural materials of an organism, having a particular function; as, epithelial *tissue*.

4. any chain or series of facts, circumstances, etc. intricately interwoven as if to form a tissue; a mesh; a network; a web; as, a *tissue* of falsehoods.

TISSUE

1. prosenchyma or woody tissue; 2. horizontal section of prosenchymatous tissue; 3. section of a single cell, showing the successive layers of deposit in the interior which give hardness and firmness to the wood of plants; 4. cylindrical parenchyma; 5. round or elliptical parenchymatous tissue; 6. spongiform or stellate tissue

adenoid tissue; a kind of tissue like that forming the lymphatic glands: it consists of a network of fibers in the meshes of which lodge lymphoid cells.

adipose tissue; see under *adipose*.

areolar tissue; connective tissue made up largely of interlacing fibers.

cancellous tissue; the loose, spongy tissue of the interior and articular ends of bone.

cellular tissue; see under *cellular*.

elastic tissue; see under *elastic*.

erectile tissue; see under *erectile*.

fatty tissue; same as *adipose tissue*, under *adipose*.

interstitial tissue; the connective tissue between the cellular elements of an organ or part; the stroma.

lymphoid tissue; same as *adenoid tissue*.

mucoid tissue; same as *mucous tissue*.

mucous tissue; see under *mucous*.

tis'sūe (tish'ū), *v.t.* tissued, *pt., pp.*; tissuing, *ppr.* to form into tissue; to interweave; to variegate. [Rare.]

tis'sūe çul'tūre, in biology, the process or science of growing tissue artificially in a special medium.

tis'sūed, *a.* woven; formed with variegated work; ornamented with or characterized by tissue.

tis'sūe pā'pēr, a very thin, unsized, nearly transparent paper, such as is used for wrapping fine and delicate articles, for toilet use, etc.

tit, *n.* [from *titmouse*.] a titmouse, titlark, or other small bird.

tit, *n.* [ME. *titte*; AS. *titt*; var. of *teat*.] a teat, a nipple; hence, a breast: in this latter sense now vulgar.

tit, *n.* [ME. *tit-* in *titmouse, titling*, etc.; prob. children's term for "little".]

1. a small, worn-out, inferior horse; a nag; a jade.

2. a girl or woman: usually in depreciation. [Slang.]

tit, *n.* [var. of *tip* (to strike) in earlier *tip for tap*, tit for tat.] a blow; a tap: now only in *tit for tat*, blow for blow; retaliation in kind.

Tī'tăn, *n.* 1. in Greek mythology, any one of the twelve children (six sons and six daughters) of Uranus (Heaven) and Gaea (Earth). They rebelled against their father and deposed him, raising Kronos, one of their number, to the throne. After a long contest they were defeated by Zeus and succeeded by the Olympian gods; also, any of their descendants.

2. the sun personified; Helios, the sun god: so called by certain Latin poets.

3. the sixth of the eight satellites of Saturn.

4. [t–] any person or thing of great size or power.

Tī'tăn, *a.* [*also* t–] Titanic.

tī'tăn, *n.* 1. titanite.

2. titanium.

tī'tăn·āte, *n.* a salt of titanic acid.

Tī·tā'ni·ăn, *a.* Titanic. [Rare.]

tī·tā'ni·ăn, *a.* pertaining to titanium; titanic.

Tī·tăn·esque' (-esk'), *a.* same as *Titanic*.

Tī'tăn·ess, *n.* a female Titan.

Tī·tā'ni·ȧ, *n.* the queen of fairyland and wife of Oberon in Shakespeare's *Midsummer Night's Dream*.

Tī·tan'iç, *a.* of, pertaining to, or characteristic of the Titans; hence [t–], enormous in size or strength; gigantic; superhuman; huge; vast.

tī·tan'iç, *a.* designating or of a chemical compound containing titanium with a valence of four.

titanic acid; either of two weak acids, H_2TiO_3 or H_4TiO_4, derived from titanic oxide.

titanic iron ore; ilmenite.

titanic oxide; a crystalline compound, TiO_2, used as a pigment, ceramic glaze, etc.: also *titanic dioxide*.

tī·tăn·if'ēr·ous, *a.* containing titanium; as, *titaniferous* pyrites.

Tī'tăn·iṣm, *n.* [*also* t-] the characteristic quality or spirit of the Titans, who overthrew Uranus; spirit of revolt or defiance, as against the established order or social conventions.

tī'tăn·īte, *n.* same as *sphene*, a mineral.

tī·tăn·it'ic, *a.* same as *titanic*.

tī·tā'ni·um, *n.* [Mod. L., from L. *Titani* or *Titanes*; Gr. *Titanes*, pl. of *Titan*, a Titan.] a dark-gray, lustrous, metallic chemical element found in rutile and other minerals and used as a cleaning and deoxidizing agent in molten steel, etc.: symbol, Ti; atomic weight, 47.90; atomic number, 22.

Tī·tăn·om'ȧ·çhy, *n.* in Greek mythology, the war between the Titans and the Olympian gods.

Tī″tăn·ō·sau'rus, *n.* [Gr. *Titan*, a Titan, and *sauros*, lizard.] same as *Atlantosaurus*.

tī'tăn·ō·thēre, *n.* an animal of the genus *Titanotherium*.

Tī″tăn·ō·thē'ri·um, *n.* [Gr. *Titan*, a Titan, and *thērion*, a wild beast.]

1. a genus of animals of gigantic size, resembling the rhinoceros, from the Miocene of America.

2. [t–] any animal of this genus.

tī'tăn·ous, *a.* of or designating a chemical compound containing titanium with a valence of three.

tī'tär, *n.* [Hind.] the gray partridge.

tit bab'blēr, a bird, *Trichostoma rostratum*, found in the Malay peninsula and adjacent islands.

tit'bit, *n.* a tidbit.

tīte, *adv.* [ME. *tite, tit*, from Ice. *titt*, fast.] fast; quickly; as, he ran as *tite* as he could. [Obs. except Brit. Dial.]

tīte, *a.* tight. [Obs.]

tīte'ly, *adv.* quickly; soon. [Obs.]

tī'tēr, *n.* [Fr. *titre*, standard, title.] in chemistry, physiology, and immunology, (a) a standard strength or degree of concentration of a solution as established through titration; (b) the minimum weight or volume of a substance necessary to cause a given result in titration.

tīth'ȧ·ble, *a.* 1. subject to the payment of tithes; that may be tithed, as property.

2. that may pay or be made to pay a tithe or tithes, as a person. [Rare.]

tīth'ȧ·ble, *n.* one subject to tithes.

tīthe, *n.* [AS. *teótha*, for *teóntha*, tenth.]

1. the tenth part or any small part; a tenth.

2. a tenth of the annual produce of one's land, etc., or its equivalent in money, paid as a tax for the support of the church or the clergy.

3. a small part or proportion.

4. any tax or levy.

tīthe, *a.* tenth.

tīthe, *v.t.*; tithed, *pt., pp.*; tithing, *ppr.* 1. to exact tithes from; to levy a tenth part on.

2. to pay tithes on; to pay the tenth part of.

tīthe, *v.i.* to pay tithes. [Obs.]

tīth'ēr, *n.* one who collects or pays tithes.

tīth'ing, *n.* 1. in old English law, a unit of civil administration originally consisting of a number or company of ten householders.

2. a tithe.

3. a levying or paying of tithes.

tīth'ing·măn, *n.*; *pl.* **tīth'ing·men,** 1. in old English law, the chief man of a tithing.

2. a peace officer; an underconstable. [Brit.]

3. in early New England history, a parish officer annually elected to preserve good order in the church during divine service, and to make complaint of any disorderly conduct.

tīth'ly, *adv.* titely. [Obs.]

tī·thon'iç, *a.* [Gr. *Tithōnos*, the consort of Aurora.] pertaining to or denoting rays of light which produce chemical effects; actinic. [Rare.]

tith·ō·nic'i·ty, *n.* actinism. [Rare.]

tī·thō·nom'e·ter, *n.* an actinometer.

Ti·thō'nus, *n.* [L.; Gr. *Tithōnos*.] in Greek mythology, the son of Laomedon, loved by Eos, who got for him immortality but not eternal youth, so that he shriveled up and was turned into a grasshopper.

tī'ti, *n.* [Sp., from Aymara Indian name.]

1. a small evergreen tree or shrub with fragrant, white or pinkish flowers, found in swamps in the southern United States.

2. any of a number of related trees, as the white titi.

ti·tī', *n.* [Sp. *tití*; Guarani *titi*.] any of several small South American monkeys.

Ti'tiăn (-shun), *n.* 1. a painting by Titian, the artist.

2. [t–] a brilliant, yellowish-red color; auburn: so called because Titian often painted hair this shade in his portraits.

3. [t–] one who has titian hair.

tit'il·lāte, *v.t.*; titillated, *pt., pp.*; titillating, *ppr.* [L. *titillare*, to tickle.] to tickle; also, to excite or stimulate pleasurably.

tit·il·lā'tion, *n.* the act of titillating or the state of being titillated.

tit'il·lā·tive, *a.* titillating or tending to titillate.

tit'i·vāte, *v.t.* and *v.i.*; titivated, *pt., pp.*; titivating, *ppr.* [perhaps from *tidy*.] to make to look smart or spruce; to dress up; to adorn: also spelled *tittivate*. [Colloq.]

tit·i·vā'tion, *n.* a titivating or being titivated: also spelled *tittivation*.

tit'lärk, *n.* a pipit, a larklike bird.

tī'tle, *n.* [ME.; OFr., from L. *titulus*, a title.]

1. an inscription or superscription set over or on anything. [Archaic.]

2. the name of a poem, essay, chapter, book, picture, statue, piece of music, etc.

3. an appellation; a descriptive name; an epithet.

4. an appellation of dignity, distinction, or pre-eminence given to persons or families; as, *titles* of office, nobility, distinction, degree, etc.

5. a claim; a right.

Make claim and *title* to the crown of France.
—Shak.

6. a title page.

7. a division of a law book, statute, etc., usually larger than a section or article.

8. (a) in the Church of England, etc., a source of income or field of work required of a candidate for ordination; (b) in the Roman Catholic Church, any of the parish churches in Rome having a cardinal for its head.

9. in law, (a) the name of a statute or act; (b) the heading designating a proceeding; (c) a right to ownership, especially of real estate; (d) evidence of such right of ownership; (e) a document stating such a right; a deed.

10. in sports, etc., a championship.

tī'tle, *v.t.*; titled, *pt., pp.*; titling, *ppr.* to give a title to; to name; to entitle.

tī'tled (-tld), *a.* having a title, especially one of nobility.

tī'tle deed, a document that establishes title to property.

tī'tle·less, *a.* not having a title or name.

tī'tle pāġe, the page in the front of a book that contains its full title, the names of its author and publisher, etc.

tit'lēr, *n.* [etym. doubtful.] a large truncated loaf or cone of refined sugar.

tī'tle rōle (or **pärt**), the character in a play, motion picture, etc. whose name is used as the title.

tit'ling, *n.* [dim. of *tit*, something small.]

1. (a) the titlark; (b) the hedge sparrow.

2. stockfish: former name in customhouses.

tit'măl, *n.* a blue titmouse.

tit'mouse, *n.*; *pl.* **tit'mīce,** [altered, after *mouse*, from ME. *titemose*; prob. from *tit-*, little, and AS. *māse*, a kind of bird.] any of a number of small birds of the genus *Parus* or allied genera, with dull-colored feathers. There are numerous species, including the chickadee, which feed on insects, seeds, etc. Among the common species are the blue titmouse, *Parus cæruleus*, the greater titmouse, *Parus major*, the coal titmouse, *Parus ater*, the marsh titmouse, *Parus palustris*, the crested titmouse, *Parus cristatus*, the bearded

BLUE TITMOUSE
male and female (*Parus cæruleus*)

titmouse, *Panurus biarmicus*, and the long-tailed titmouse, *Acredula caudata*.
tī′trāte, *v.t.*; titrated, *pt., pp.*; titrating, *ppr.* to test by or be subjected to the process of titration.
tī′trā·ted, *a.* analyzed by titration.
tī·trā′tion, *n.* in chemistry, physiology, and immunology, the process of finding out how much of a certain substance is contained in a solution by measuring how much of another substance it is necessary to add to the solution in order to produce a given reaction.
tī′tre (-tẽr), *n.* same as *liter*.
tī′tree, *n.* same as *ti*.
tit″-tat-tōe′, *n.* same as *tick-tack-toe*.
tit′tẽr, *v.i.*; tittered, *pt., pp.*; tittering, *ppr.* [imitative.] to laugh in a half-suppressed way, suggestive of foolishness, nervousness, etc.; to giggle.
tit′tẽr, *n.* the act or an instance of tittering.
tit′tẽr, *v.i.* to teeter or seesaw.
tit′tẽr·el, *n.* a bird, the whimbrel. [Brit. Dial.]
tit′tẽr-tot″tẽr, *v.i.* [reduplication from Ice. *titra*, to tremble.] to teeter. [Brit. Dial.]
tit′tẽr-tot″tẽr, *n.* the game of seesaw. [Brit. Dial.]
tit′tẽr-tot″tẽr, *adv.* unsteadily. [Brit. Dial.]
tit′tie (-i), *n.* a sister: also spelled *titty*. [Scot.]
tit′ti·vāte, *v.t.* and *v.i.*; tittivated, *pt., pp.*; tittivating, *ppr.* to titivate.
tit′tle, *n.* [L. *titulus*, a mark over a word.]
1. a small particle; a minute part; a jot; an iota.
2. a dot or other small mark used as a diacritic.
tit′tle·bat, *n.* a stickleback. [Brit. Dial.]
tit′tle-tat″tle, *n.* [reduplication of *tattle*.]
1. idle, trifling talk; empty prattle; gossip.
2. an idle, trifling talker; a gossip. [Obs.]
tit′tle-tat″tle, *v.i.* tittle-tattled (-tld), *pt., pp.*; tittle-tattling, *ppr.* to gossip; to talk idly; to prate.
tit′tle-tat″tling, *n.* the act of gossiping or prating idly.
tit′tup, *n.* [prob. echoic of hoof beats.] an action portraying gaiety or liveliness; the act of prancing or capering; a frisk; a caper.
tit′tup, *v.i.*; tittuped *or* tittupped (-tupt), *pt., pp.*; tittuping *or* tittupping, *ppr.* to behave in a frolicsome manner; to caper.
tit′ty, *n.*; *pl.* **tit′tieṣ,** a teat or nipple: a childish diminutive, now regarded as vulgar.
tit′ū·bāte, *v.i.*; titubated, *pt., pp.*; titubating, *ppr.* [L. *titubare*, to stumble.] to stumble; to stagger. [Rare.]
tit·ū·bā′tion, *n.* [L. *titubatio*, a staggering or stammering.] a stumbling or staggering gait characteristic of certain nervous disorders.
tit′ū·lăr, *a.* [Fr. *titulaire*, from L. *titulus*, a title.]
1. existing in title or name only; nominal; having the title only; as, a *titular* king or prince.
2. of, having the nature of, or possessing a title.
3. from whose name the title is taken; as, the *titular* character of a novel.
4. designating a bishop holding the title of a defunct see.
tit′ū·lăr, *n.* a person invested with a title, in virtue of which he holds an office or benefice, whether he performs the duties of it or not.
titular of a church; the origin of the name of a church which may be a person, incident, or thing.
tit·ū·lar′i·ty, *n.* the state of being titular.
tit′ū·lăr·ly, *adv.* nominally; by title only.
tit′ū·lăr·y, *a.* titular.
tit′ū·lăr·y, *n.*; *pl.* **tit′ū·lăr·ieṣ,** one who holds a title; a titular.
tit′ūled, *a.* having or bearing a title; entitled. [Rare.]
tit′up; *n.* and *v.i.* same as *tittup*.
Tī′tus, *n.* in the Bible, (a) a disciple of the Apostle Paul; (b) an Epistle to Titus, a book of the New Testament, which was a message from Paul.
Tī′ù, *n.* in Germanic mythology, a god of war and of the sky: identified with the Norse god Tyr.
tiv′ẽr, *n.* [AS. *teafor*, a red color.] a kind of ocher which is used in marking sheep in some parts of England. [Brit. Dial.]
tiv′ẽr, *v.t.*; tivered, *pt., pp.*; tivering, *ppr.* to mark (sheep) with tiver. [Brit. Dial.]
tiv′y, *adv.* [contr. of *tantivy*.] with great speed: a huntsman's word or call.
tiz′zy, tiz′zieṣ, *n.*; *pl.* **tiz′zieṣ,** [corruption of *tester*, a sixpence.] a sixpence. [Brit. Slang.]
tiz′zy, *n.* a state of frenzied excitement or distraction, especially over some trivial matter. [Slang.]
Tl, in chemistry, thallium.
Tliñ′git, *n.pl.* [from Am. Ind. (Tlingit).]
1. the members of several tribes of seafaring American Indians of the coastal areas of southern Alaska and northern British Columbia.
2. [*construed as sing.*] their language, consisting of several dialects.
Tliñ′kit, *n.pl.* same as *Tlingit*.
Tm, in chemistry, thulium.
tmē′mȧ, *n.*; *pl.* **tmē′mȧ·tȧ,** [Gr., a part cut off.] a division; a section; a separated part. [Rare.]
tmē′sis, *n.* [Gr. *tmēsis*, a cutting.] in rhetoric and prosody, separation of the parts of a compound word by an intervening word or words. Example: *what person soever* for *whatsoever person*.
Tn, in chemistry, thoron.
tö-, [ME. and AS.] an obsolete prefix, formerly used as an intensive in composition with verbs, participles, or adjectives, signifying *asunder, in pieces*, as in *to*-broken, broken to pieces.
tö, *prep.* [ME.; AS. *to*, to, toward.]
1. (a) in the direction of; toward; as, turn *to* the left; he was traveling *to* Pittsburgh; (b) in the direction of and reaching; as far as; as, he went *to* Boston; it dropped *to* the ground.
2. as far as; as, wet *to* the skin; honest *to* a fault.
3. toward or into a condition of; as, he grew *to* manhood; her rise *to* fame.
4. on, onto, against, at, next, etc.: used to indicate nearness or contact; as, apply the lotion *to* the skin; a house *to* the right.
5. at or in (a specified place); as, he's *to* home. [Dial.]
6. until; as, no parking from four *to* six.
7. for the purpose of; for; as, they came *to* our aid.
8. as concerns; in respect of; involving; as, that's all there is *to* it; open *to* attack.
9. producing, causing, or resulting in; as, *to* my amazement nothing happened; torn *to* pieces.
10. with; along with; accompanied by; as an accompaniment for; as, add this *to* the others; dance *to* the music.
11. being the proper appurtenance, possession, or attribute of; of; as, the key *to* the house.
12. compared with; as against; as, the score was 7 *to* 0.
13. in agreement, correspondence, or conformity with; as, not *to* my taste.
14. comprising; constituting; in; as, twenty *to* the bushel.
15. with (a specified person or thing) as the recipient, or indirect object, of the action; as, they listened *to* me; give the book *to* her.
16. in honor of; as, a toast *to* your success.
17. with; as, a field planted *to* corn. [Colloq.]
To is also used before a verb as a sign of the infinitive (e.g., I came *to* listen; it was easy *to* read; *to* live is sweet) or, elliptically, to denote the infinitive (e.g., tell him if you want *to*).
tö, *adv.* 1. forward; as, his hat is on wrong side *to*.
2. to the matter at hand; as, they took off their coats and fell *to*.

I will stand *to* and feed. —Shak.

3. in the normal or desired direction, position, or condition; especially, shut or closed.

The wind has been and blown the door *to*,
and I can't get in. —Dickens.

4. at hand; as, we were close *to* when it happened.
5. in nautical usage, close to the wind: said of a sailing vessel.
6. into a normal or conscious state; as, he came *to* after a while.
7. on, forward: used as a command. [Obs.]

To, Achilles! *to*, Ajax! *to*! —Shak.

to and fro; first in one direction and then in the opposite; back and forth.
tö, *conj.* till. [Obs.]
tōad, *n.* [ME. *tode*; AS. *tadige, tadie*, toad.]
1. any of a group of small, froglike animals of the genus *Bufo*, family *Bufonidæ*, which is almost universally distributed. Toads eat insects and are usually terrestrial except in the breeding season, when they are aquatic. The common toad of North America is *Bufo lentiginosus*. *Bufo vulgaris* is the common European species. Also applied to other tailless amphibians, including frogs.
2. a person considered as an object of contempt, aversion, etc.
obstetrical toad; same as *nurse frog*.
tōad′back, *a.* in architecture, shaped like a toad's back, as a handrail.
tōad′ēat″ẽr, *n.* 1. a flatterer; an obsequious parasite; a sycophant.
2. a quack doctor's assistant who ate or pretended to eat supposedly poisonous toads in order that the employer might demonstrate his ability to expel poison.
tōad′fish, *n.*; *pl.* **tōad′fish** or **tōad′fish·eṣ,**
1. any of a group of scaleless fishes of the genus *Batrachus*; especially, *Batrachus tau*, the sapo or oysterfish, noted for its broad, froglike head, found in shallow water on the Atlantic coast of America.
2. a teleostean fish, *Lophius piscatorius*, the angler.
3. the mousefish, *Pterophryne histrio*.
4. a swellfish.
tōad′flax, *n.* 1. a common weed of the genus *Linaria*, especially *Linaria vulgaris*, having a dense raceme of yellow flowers spotted with orange, native to Europe: also called *flaxweed, ranstead, butter and eggs*.
2. any other related plant.
bastard toadflax; (a) in the United States, any species of the genus *Comandra*, perennial herbs with alternate leaves and terminal or axillary umbels of greenish-white flowers; (b) in England, a similar plant, *Thesium linophyllon*.
tōad′flow″ẽr, *n.* a plant of the genus *Stapelia*.
tōad′head (-hed), *n.* the golden plover, *Charadrius dominicus*. [Dial.]
tōad′ish, *a.* toadlike; resembling a toad. [Obs.]
tōad′let, *n.* a little or young toad.
tōad lil′y, 1. a liliaceous plant, *Tricyrtis hirta*, native to Japan and China, having spotted, white flowers.
2. *Castalia odorata*, the white water lily; also, *Fritillaria pyrenaiea*, a species of water lily.
tōad liz′ărd, a horned toad.
tōad or′chis, an orchid, *Megaclinium bufo*, indigenous to tropical West Africa, having purple-spotted flowers.
tōad′pīpe, *n.* any species of *Equisetum* or horsetail.
tōad rush, a low rush, *Juncus bufonius*.
tōad snatch′ẽr, the reed bunting. [Brit. Dial.]
tōad spit (or **spit′tle**), cuckoo spit.
tōad′stōne, *n.* any stone or similar object formerly thought to have been formed inside a toad's head or body and often worn as a charm.
tōad′stōne, *n.* [from G. *todtstein*, dead stone.] in Derbyshire, England, bands of rock, generally basaltic, alternated with bands of limestone of the Carboniferous series, which are unproductive of ore: miner's term.
toad′stool, *n.* any fungus having an umbrellalike disk, or pileus, borne on a stalk, especially fungi of the genus *Agaricus* and related genera; a mushroom; especially, in popular usage, any poisonous mushroom: also called *frogstool, toad's meat*.
tōad′y, *n.*; *pl.* **tōad′ieṣ,** [short for *toadeater* (sense 2).] a hanger-on or servile flatterer; a sycophant; a toadeater.
tōad′y, *v.t.* and *v.i.*; toadied, *pt., pp.*; toadying, *ppr.* to fawn upon; to act in a servile or obsequious manner; to flatter.
tōad′y·iṣm, *n.* the behavior of a toady; sycophancy; servile adulation.
tö′-and-frō′, *a.* moving forward and backward; back-and-forth.
tōast, *v.t.*; toasted, *pt., pp.*; toasting, *ppr.* [OFr. *toster*, to toast, from L. *tostus*, pp. of *torrere*, to parch.]
1. to brown the surface of (bread, cheese, etc.) by heating in a toaster, over or near a fire, or in an oven.
2. to warm thoroughly; as, to *toast* the feet.
tōast, *v.i.* to become toasted.
tōast, *n.* 1. sliced bread browned by heat; also, bread thus prepared and buttered or put in some liquid, such as gravy, milk, etc.
2. one who drinks intemperately. [Obs.]
tōast, *n.* [from the use of toasted spiced bread to give flavor to the wine, and the notion that the person, etc. honored also added flavor.]
1. a person, institution, sentiment, etc. in honor of which a person or persons raise their glasses and drink.
2. a proposal to drink to some person, etc.
3. a drink in honor of a person, etc.

tōast, *v.t.* to propose or drink a toast to.
tōast, *v.i.* to drink a toast or toasts.
tōast'ẽr, *n.* one who drinks or proposes a toast.
tōast'ẽr, *n.* 1. any of various utensils or appliances used to toast cheese, bread, etc.
2. one who toasts bread, cheese, etc.
3. something suitable for toasting. [Colloq.]
tōast'ing, *a.* pertaining to toast or the act of browning bread, etc.
tōast'ing, *n.* the act of toasting or giving a toast.
tōast'ing fork, 1. a long-handled fork used in toasting bread, marshmallows, etc. over a fire.
2. a sword. [Humorous.]
tōast'mȧs"tẽr, *n.* one who presides at a banquet, and proposes or announces the toasts, introduces after-dinner speakers, etc.
tōast rack, a small rack used to hold slices of toast. [Chiefly Brit.]
tōat, *n.* [etym. doubtful.] the curved handle attached to a planing tool.
tō'ȧ·tō·ȧ, *n.* [Maori.] same as *tanekaha.*
tō·baç'çō, *n.*; *pl.* **tō·baç'çōṣ,** [Sp. *tabaco,* from W. Ind. (Carib) *tabaco,* the pipe or tube in which the Indians smoked the plant, transferred by the Spaniards to the plant itself.]
1. any of a number of solanaceous plants of the genus *Nicotiana,* with white or pink flowers and large, lance-shaped leaves: cultivated throughout the Temperate and Tropical Zones for its leaves. *Nicotiana macrophylla,* Maryland tobacco, and *Nicotiana angustifolia,* Virginia tobacco, are popular cultivated varieties. The Cuban and Manila tobacco is a variety of Maryland tobacco.
2. the leaves of any of these plants, prepared for smoking, chewing, or snuffing.
3. products prepared from these leaves; cigars, cigarettes, snuff, etc.
4. the use of tobacco for smoking, etc.

VIRGINIA TOBACCO (*Nicotiana angustifolia*)

tō·baç'çō bee'tle, a ptinoid beetle, *Lasioderma serricorne,* that infests stored tobacco.
tō·baç'çō box, 1. a box for holding tobacco.
2. the sunfish, *Pomotis gibbosus,* or any fish of the same genus. [Dial.]
3. the ray, *Raia erinacea.* [Dial.]
tō·baç'çō bug, an insect, *Dicyphus minimus,* that injures growing tobacco by sucking its juice.
tō·baç'çō çam'phŏr, nicotianin.
tō·baç'çō çut'tẽr, 1. a machine for shredding tobacco.
2. a tobacco knife.
tō·baç'çō grāt'ẽr, a grinding machine used in the manufacture of smoking tobacco.
tō·baç'çō heart, a cardiac disturbance characterized by irregular action and due to excessive use of tobacco.
tō·baç'çō·iṣm, *n.* nicotinism.
tō·baç'çō knife (nīf), a knife, usually having a pivoted handle, used in cutting plug tobacco.
tō·baç'çō·măn, *n.*; *pl.* **tō·baç'çō·men,** a tobacconist. [Rare.]
tō·baç'çō·nẽr, *n.* a tobacconist. [Obs.]
tō·baç'çō·ning, *n.* the act or practice of using tobacco. [Obs.]
tō·baç'çō·nist, *n.* [from *tobacco*; originally applied to a user of tobacco.]
1. a dealer in tobacco and other smoking supplies; also, a manufacturer of tobacco. [Chiefly Brit.]
2. a smoker of tobacco. [Obs.]
tō·baç'çō·nīze, *v.t.*; tobacconized, *pt., pp.*; tobacconizing, *ppr.* to impregnate with tobacco or its smoke; to fumigate with tobacco.
tō·baç'çō pīpe, 1. a pipe used for smoking tobacco.
2. the Indian pipe, a plant.
tō·baç'çō-pīpe çlāy, same as *pipe clay.*
tō·baç'çō plant, same as *tobacco* (sense 1).
tō·baç'çō·root, *n.* the bitterroot.
tō·baç'çō stop'pẽr, a device for pressing down the tobacco as it is smoked in a pipe.
tō·baç'çō wŏrm, either of two large green caterpillars, the larvae of the sphinx moth, with slanting white markings, which feed upon tobacco plants, often doing great damage.
tō·bēat', *v.t.* to beat severely. [Archaic.]
Tō·bī'ȧs fish, same as *sand eel* (sense 1).
tō'bine, *n.* a stout twilled silk formerly used for dresses.
Tō'bit, *n.* one of the books of the Old Testament Apocrypha.
tō·bog'găn, *n.* [Canad. Fr. *tabagan,* from Am. Ind. (Algonquian).]
1. a long, narrow, flat sled without runners, made of thin boards curved back at the front end and often having side rails: now used for the sport of coasting down a prepared slope or chute.
2. a similar sled with very low runners.

TOBOGGAN

tō·bog'găn, *v.i.*; tobogganed, *pt., pp.*; tobogganing, *ppr.* 1. to coast, travel, etc. on a toboggan.
2. to decline rapidly; as, prices *tobogganed.*
tō·bog'găn·ist, tō·bog'găn·ẽr, *n.* one who toboggans.
tō·bog'găn slīde, a steep decline prepared for coasting on toboggans: also called *toboggan chute.*
tō·brēak', *v.t.* to break in pieces; to destroy. [Obs.]
tō·bŭrst', *v.t.* and *v.i.* to burst or break into pieces. [Obs.]
Tō'by, *n.*; *pl.* **Tō'bieṣ,** [from the personal name *Toby,* dim. or familiar form of *Tobias.*]
1. a small jug, pitcher, or mug, usually in the form of a stout man wearing a three-cornered hat, the angles of which form the pouring spouts: also *Toby jug.*
2. a type of long, slender, inferior cigar. [Slang.]
toç·çä'tȧ, *n.* [It., pp. of *toccare,* to touch.] a composition in free style for the organ, piano, etc., generally characterized by the use of full chords and running passages and often used as the prelude of a fugue: it was originally designed to display the technique of the performer.
toç·çȧ·tī'nȧ, *n.* [It., dim. of *toccato.*] in music, a short toccata.
Tō·chär'i·ăn, *n.* [from *Tochrī,* word used to designate the language in certain accompanying (Uigur) writings.]
1. a member of a people living in central Asia until about 1000 A.D.
2. their Indo-European language, comprising two dialects: the earliest record known is from the seventh century A.D.
Also *Tokharian, Tokharic.*
Tō·chär'i·ăn, *a.* of the Tocharians or their language: also *Tokharian, Tokharic.*
toch'ẽr, *n.* [Gael. *tochar,* a dowry.] the dowry of a bride. [Scot.]
toch'ẽr, *v.t.*; tochered, *pt., pp.*; tochering, *ppr.* to give a tocher, or dowry, to. [Scot.]
toch'ẽr·less, *a.* without a tocher, or dowry. [Scot.]
tock, *n.* [African.] a hornbill; specifically, the red-billed hornbill of Africa, *Toccus erythrorhynchus.*
tō'çō, *n.* the common toucan, *Rhamphastos toco.*
tō'çō, *n.* [Gr. *tokos,* interest.] punishment: a term used by schoolboys. [Brit. Slang.]
tō·çog'ō·ny, *n.* [Gr. *tokos,* a birth, and *-gony.*] parental generation; biogenesis.
tō·çol'ō·ġy, *n.* [Gr. *tokos,* childbirth, and *logos,* discourse.] obstetrics or midwifery: also written *tokology.*
tō·çoph'ẽr·ōl, *n.* [from Gr. *tokos,* childbirth, and *pherein,* to carry, bear; and *-ol.*] any of those alcohols having the properties of vitamin E, the antisterility vitamin, and occurring in wheat-germ oil, cottonseed oil, lettuce, etc.
tō·çō·rō'rō, *n.* [Cuban.] the Cuban trogon.
toç'sin, *n.* [OFr. *toquesin*; *toque,* a stroke, and *sin, sein,* a bell.]
1. an alarm bell; also, its sound.
2. any warning signal.
tō·çus'sō, *n.* [native name.] an Abyssinian millet, *Eleusine tocusso.*
tod, *n.* [ME. *todde*; prob. from L.G. source.]
1. a bushy clump, especially of ivy; a thick mass of growing foliage.
2. a former English weight used chiefly in buying wool, equal to about 28 pounds.
tod, *n.* [perh. from *tod* (bushy clump), with reference to the fox's tail.] a fox. [Scot.]
tod, *n.* a drink; a toddy. [Colloq.]
tö·dāy', tö·dāy', *adv.* [ME. *to-daye,* from AS. *to dæg*; *to,* prep., on, for, and *dæg,* day.]
1. on or during the present day; as, I shall go *today.*
2. at the present time; in the present age; nowadays.
tö·dāy', tö·dāy', *n.* 1. the present day; this day; as, *today* is a holiday.
2. the present time, period, or age; as, the spirit of *today.*
tod'dle, *v.i.*; toddled, *pt., pp.*; toddling, *ppr.* [perh. freq. of *totter.*] to walk with short, unsteady steps, as a child.
tod'dle, *n.* 1. the act of walking with short, unsteady steps.
2. a careless, idle stroll. [Colloq.]
3. a toddler. [Rare.]
tod'dlẽr, *n.* one who toddles; especially, a young child.
tod'dy, *n.*; *pl.* **tod'dieṣ,** [Anglo-Ind., from Hind. *tārī,* from *tār,* a palm tree.]
1. the sweet sap of various East Indian palms, used as a beverage.
2. an intoxicating liquor made by fermenting this sap.
3. a drink of brandy, whisky, etc. mixed with hot water, sugar, and, usually, spices.
tod'dy bĩrd, any of several birds of India that feed on the juices of palms.
tod'dy çat, a paradoxure; a palm cat.
tod'dy pälm (päm), any palm secreting a sap or juice from which toddy can be prepared.
tōde, *n.* [of uncertain origin.] a rough sled used in hauling logs.
Tō'di·dae, *n.pl.* a family of insectivorous, tropical American birds, the todies.
tō'dine, *a.* of or pertaining to the todies or *Todidæ.*
tö·dö', *n.* ado; bustle; hurry; commotion. [Colloq.]
tod stōve, a box-shaped stove for burning wood.
Tō'dus, *n.* [LL.] a genus of small birds native to the West Indies.
tō'dy, *n.*; *pl.* **tō'dieṣ,** [L. *todus,* small bird.] any of several small, insect-eating birds of the West Indies, of the genus *Todus,* family *Todidæ,* related to the kingfishers, especially the Jamaican species that is green with a red throat.
tōe (tō), *n.* [AS. *tā*; Ice. *tā*; Dan. *taa*; D. *teen,* toe.]
1. any of the five digits of the human foot.
2. any of the digits of an animal's foot.
3. the fore part of the human foot: distinguished from *heel.*
4. that part of a shoe, sock, etc. which covers the toes.
5. anything suggesting a toe in location, shape, or function; specifically, (a) a pivot or journal extending vertically in a bearing; (b) a projecting arm raised or moved by a cam.
on one's toes; mentally or physically alert. [Colloq.]
tōe, *v.t.*; toed, *pt., pp.*; toeing, *ppr.* 1. to provide with a toe or toes; as, she *toed* the stockings.
2. to touch, follow, or kick with the toes; as, they *toed* the starting line.
3. (a) to drive (a nail) slantingly; (b) to fasten with nails driven slantingly; to toenail.
to toe the line (or *mark*); (a) to stand or crouch with the toes touching the starting line of a race, etc.; (b) to follow orders, rules, doctrines, etc. strictly.
tōe, *v.i.* to stand, walk, or be formed so that the toes are in a specified position; as, he *toes* in, she *toes* out.
tōe bit'ẽr, a tadpole.
tōe'çap, *n.* that part of a shoe or boot which covers the toes.
tōe çrack, a lesion (*sand crack*) in the front part of a horse's hoof.
tōed, *a.* 1. having (a specified kind or number of) toes: usually in hyphenated compounds, as pigeon-*toed.*
2. (a) driven obliquely: said of a nail; (b) fastened by obliquely driven nails.
tōe'-dȧnce, *v.i.* to do a toe dance.
tōe dȧnce, a dance performed on the tips of the toes, as in ballet.
tōe drop, paralysis of the extensor muscles of the toes causing inability to raise the foot and toes.
tōe hōld, 1. a small space or ledge for supporting the toe of the foot in climbing, etc.

2. any means of surmounting obstacles, gaining entry, etc.
3. a slight footing or advantage.
4. in wrestling, a hold in which one wrestler twists the other's foot.

tōe′-in, *n.* an adjustment of the front wheels of an automobile or other motor vehicle so that they are not perfectly parallel but tend to converge slightly toward the front.

tōe′less, *a.* 1. having no toe or toes.
2. having the toe open or uncovered; as, a *toeless* shoe.

tōe′nāil, *n.* 1. the nail of a toe.
2. in carpentry, a nail driven obliquely, as through the side of a vertical plank to fasten it to the horizontal plank on which it is based.

tōe′nāil, *v.t.* in carpentry, to fasten with a toenail.

tö′fall, *n.* 1. decline; setting; end; as, *tofall* of the day. [Scot. and Brit. Dial.]
2. a lean-to. [Scot. and Brit. Dial.]

toff, *n.* a dandy; a fop; a swell. [Brit. Slang.]

tof′fee, tof′fy, *n.* [variant of *taffy*.] a hard, chewy candy made with brown sugar or molasses, often coated with nuts.

Tō·fiēl′di·à, *n.* [after *Tofield*, English botanist.] a small genus of liliaceous plants of the order *Melanthaceæ*.

tö·fōre′, tö·forn′, *prep.* and *adv.* before; formerly. [Obs.]

toft, *n.* [Ice. *toft, tupt,* a knoll, a homestead.]
1. originally, a house site or homestead.
2. a homestead with its arable land.
3. a knoll; a hillock.
[Brit. Dial. in all senses.]

toft′măn, *n.* one who owns or occupies a toft. [Brit. Dial.]

tō′fū′, *n.* [Japan.] a bland, custardlike food, rich in protein, coagulated from an extract of soybeans and eaten in soups, in various cooked dishes, etc.

tog, *n.* [prob. from cant *togeman(s), togman,* a cloak, coat; ult. from L. *toga,* toga.]
1. a coat. [Old Slang.]
2. [*pl.*] clothes; as, tennis *togs.* [Colloq.]

tog, *v.t.* and *v.i.*; togged, *pt., pp.*; togging, *ppr.* to put clothes on; to dress (often with *up* or *out*). [Colloq.]

tō′gȧ, *n.*; *pl.* **tō′gȧs, tō′gae,** [L., from *tegere,* to cover.]
1. in ancient Rome, the principal outer garment worn in public by citizens. It was a loose, flowing, one-piece garment made of wool or silk, usually undyed.
2. a robe of office; a characteristic gown of a profession.
toga candida; a white toga worn by a candidate for office.
toga picta; an ornamented toga worn by high officers on special occasions.
toga praetexta; see *praetexta*.
toga pulla; a black or gray toga worn by mourners.
toga virilis; the toga of manhood, put on by boys of ancient Rome about the time of completing their fourteenth year.

ROMAN TOGA

tō′gȧed (-gȧd), *a.* wearing a toga.

tō′gā·ted, *a.* [L. *toga,* a gown; *togatus,* gowned.]
1. dressed in a toga or robe.
2. dignified.

tō′ged, *a.* togated. [Obs.]

tö·geth′ēr, *adv.* [ME. *togeder*; AS. *togædre, togadere*; *to,* to, and *gædre,* together, from base of *gaderian,* to gather.]
1. in or into one gathering, group, mass, or place; as, the employees were called *together.*
2. in or into contact, collision, companionship, union, etc. with each other; as, the cars skidded *together,* they live *together.*
3. considered collectively; added up; as, he's lost more than all of us *together.*
4. with one another; in association; as, the books were compared *together.*
5. at the same time; simultaneously; as, the shots were fired *together.*
6. in succession; continuously; as, he worked for eight hours *together.*
7. in or into agreement, co-operation, etc.; as, let's get *together* on this.
Together is also often used colloquially as an intensive after *add, join,* etc.
together with; in union with; in company or mixture with.

tö·geth′ēr, *a.* having fully developed one's abilities, ambitions, etc.; having an integrated personality. [Slang.]

tog′gēr·y, *n.* [from *tog.*]
1. clothes; garments; dress; togs. [Colloq.]
2. *pl.* **tog′gēr·ieș,** a clothing store; especially, a haberdashery. [Colloq.]

tog′gle, *n.* [prob. from *tug.*]
1. a rod, pin, or bolt for inserting between the strands or through a loop of a rope, through a link of a chain, etc. to make an attachment, prevent slipping, or tighten by twisting.
2. a toggle joint or a device having one.

tog′gle, *v.t.*; toggled (-gld), *pt., pp.*; toggling, *ppr.* to provide or fasten with a toggle or toggles.

tog′gle ī′ron (-ŭrn), the form of harpoon used for killing whales and walruses, having a pivoted cross blade instead of fixed barbs.

tog′gle joint, a knee-shaped joint consisting of two bars pivoted together at one end: when pressure is put on the joint to straighten it, opposite, outward pressures are transmitted to the open ends.

tog′gle press, a press, as for printing, compressing cotton, etc., in which the action of parts forming a toggle joint operate the press.

tog′gle riv′et·ēr, a riveter that forms the rivethead and upsets the stem through the action of a toggle mechanism.

tog′gle switch, a switch consisting of a projecting lever moved back or forth through a small arc to open or close an electric circuit.

togș, *n. pl.* articles of clothing. [Colloq.]

tōgue (tōg), *n.* [Am. Ind.] the namaycush.

tö·hew′, *v.t.* to hew asunder; to hack to pieces. [Obs.]

tō′hū·bō′hū, *n.* [imitative of the Heb. words meaning without form and void.] chaos.

toil, *v.i.*; toiled, *pt., pp.*; toiling, *ppr.* [Anglo-Fr. *toiler,* to strive, dispute; OFr. *toeillier,* to trouble, begrime.]
1. to labor untiringly; to work hard and continuously.
2. to proceed laboriously; to move or progress slowly and with difficulty.

> But they, while their companions slept,
> Were *toiling* upward in the night.
> —Longfellow.

toil, *v.t.* 1. to drag about; to tug. [Obs.]
2. to weary; to overlabor; to exhaust by toil. [Archaic.]
3. to make or accomplish with great effort; to gain or obtain by toil; as, they *toiled* their way.
4. to labor; to work; to till. [Obs.]

toil, *n.* [Anglo-Fr., turmoil, struggle, from the *v.*]
1. originally, contention; struggle; strife.
2. hard, exhausting work or effort; tiring labor.
3. a task performed by such effort.
Syn.—labor, drudgery, task, work, travail, exertion.—*Labor* implies strenuous exertion, but not necessarily such as overtasks the faculties; *toil* denotes an intensity of *labor* that is painful and exhausting; *drudgery* implies work that wearies or disgusts from its minuteness or dull uniformity.

toil, *n.* [OFr. *toile,* cloth, web, from L. *tela,* web.]
1. a net for trapping. [Archaic.]
2. [*pl.*] any snares or traps suggestive of a net.

toile (twäl), *n.* [Fr.] 1. a variety of sheer linen cloth.
2. a variety of fine cretonne.

toil′ēr, *n.* one who toils; one who labors hard and unceasingly.

toi′let, *n.* [Fr. *toilette,* from *toile,* cloth, from L. *tela,* a web.]
1. a covering or cloth used in shaving or hairdressing. [Obs.]
2. a dressing table; a toilet table.
3. the articles used in dressing or grooming.
4. the act or process of dressing or grooming oneself, especially, formerly, of dressing one's hair.
5. the mode of dressing; the style and makeup of a person's dress; toilette; also, any specific costume; as, her *toilet* was in good taste.
6. the cleansing and dressing of a wound after surgery.
7. (a) a room or booth equipped with a washbowl, water closet, etc.; (b) a water closet.
to make one's toilet; to bathe and dress, arrange one's hair, etc.

toi′let, *a.* of or for the toilet; as, *toilet* articles, *toilet* paper.

toi′let glȧss, a mirror for a toilet table or dressing room.

toi′let·ry, *n.*; *pl.* **toi′let·rieș,** soap, powder, cologne, a comb, etc. used in making one's toilet.

toi′let sẽrv′ice, a toilet set.

toi′let set, a set of articles for use in the toilet, as brushes, combs, etc.

toi′let sōap, a hard, milled soap for personal use.

toi′let tā′ble, a table with a mirror, for use while putting on cosmetics, etc.

toi·lette′, *n.* [Fr.] 1. the process of grooming oneself including hairdressing, putting on cosmetics, and dressing: said of women.
2. dress or manner of dress; attire; costume.

toi′let trāin′ing, the training of a young child to control defecation and urination.

toi′let wa′tēr, a perfumed, slightly alcoholic liquid, as cologne, applied to the skin in making one's toilet.

toil′ful, *a.* laborious; full of toil; toilsome.

toil′ful·ly, *adv.* in a toilful manner.

toi·li·nette′, *n.* [dim. of Fr. *toile,* a cloth.] a cloth, the weft of which is of woolen yarn, and the warp of cotton and silk.

toil′less, *a.* without toil.

toil′sōme, *a.* attended with or involving toil; laborious; wearisome; as, a *toilsome* climb.

toil′sōme·ly, *adv.* in a toilsome manner.

toil′sōme·ness, *n.* laboriousness; wearisomeness.

toil′worn, *a.* wearied by or showing the effects of toil.

toișe, *n.* [Fr.] a fathom or long measure in France, containing six French feet, or about 2.13 English yards, or 1.95 meters.

toi′șōn, *n.* [Fr., from LL. *tonsio* (-*onis*), a shearing, from *tondere,* to clip or shear.] the fleece of a sheep.
toison d'or; (a) in heraldry, the figure for a golden fleece or the Holy Lamb; (b) same as *Golden Fleece* (sense b) under *golden.*

TOISON D'OR

tō′kȧ·mak, *n.* [from Russ. acronym for a "toroidal magnetic chamber."] a reactor designed to control nuclear fusion in a plasma of ions and electrons inside a doughnut-shaped, or toroidal, magnetic bottle.

tō·kāy′, *n.* 1. a sweet, rich wine made in Tokay, Hungary.
2. any wine like this.
3. a large, sweet, whitish or purplish grape used for the wine.

tōke, *n.* a piece of dry bread. [Brit. Slang.]

tōke, *n.* [perhaps from **token.**] a puff on a cigarette, especially one of marijuana or hashish. [Slang.]

tōke, *v.t.*; toked, *pt., pp.*; toking, *ppr.* to puff (a marijuana or hashish cigarette). [Slang.]

tō′ken, *n.* [AS. *tācn, tācen,* a token; akin to G. *zeichen.*]
1. a sign, indication, or symbol; as, this gift is a *token* of my affection.
2. something serving as a sign of authority, identity, genuineness, etc.
3. a distinguishing mark or feature.
4. a keepsake.
5. a piece of stamped metal with a face value higher than its real value, issued as a substitute for currency.
6. any of various similar devices of metal, paper, etc. used as for transportation fares or the payment of a sales tax.
7. in printing, ten quires of paper. [Obs.]
8. a small disk of metal formerly issued in the Scottish church to every one connected with the congregation who was entitled to receive communion. Tokens have given place to communion cards.
9. a signal. [Archaic.]
10. in mining, a small vein of mineral, indicating the proximity of a larger vein; also, a leathern tag attached to cars or tubs sent to the surface, to show to whom credit for the work should be given. [Brit.]
by this (or *the same*) *token*; following from this.
in token of; as evidence of.
token money; money issued by a government and made legally current for more than its real value.
token payment; a partial payment made as a token of intention to pay the remainder of the debt later.

tō′ken, *v.t.*; tokened, *pt., pp.*; tokening, *ppr.* to make known; to betoken; to be a sign of.

tō′ken, *a.* 1. by way of a token, symbol, indication, etc.; as, a *token* gesture.

2. merely simulated; slight or of no real account; as, *token* resistance.

tō'ken·ism, *n.* a show of accommodation to a demand, principle, etc. by small, often merely formal concessions to it; specifically, token integration of Negroes, as in schools, jobs, etc.

tō'ken·less, *a.* without a token.

Tō·khär'i·ăn (-kär'), *n.* and *a.* Tocharian.

Tō·khär'iç, *n.* and *a.* Tocharian.

tō·kol'ō·ġy, *n.* same as *tocology.*

tō·kō·pat', *n.* a palm, *Livistona jenkinsiana,* native to Assam, the broad leaves of which are used by the natives in making hats, thatching the roofs of huts, etc.

tōl, *v.t.* [L. *tollere.*] to take away. [Obs.]

tō'lā, *n.* [Hind., from Sans. *tulā,* a balance.] in India, a weight for gold and silver, the standard being 180 grains troy (the weight of one silver rupee).

tō'lan, *n.* tolane.

tō'lāne, *n.* [*tol*uene and *-ane.*] a colorless, crystalline hydrocarbon, $C_{14}H_{10}$.

tōl'bo̤oth, *n.* a jail or prison: also spelled *tollbooth.* [Scot.]

tōld, *v.* past tense and past participle of *tell.*
all told; all (being) counted; in all; as, there were forty *all told.*

tōle, *v.t.* and *v.i.* to toll, as a bell. [Obs.]

tōle, *v.t.*; toled, *pt., pp.*; toling, *ppr.* [var. of *toll,* to allure.] to allure; to entice. [Dial or Archaic.]

tole, tôle (tōl), *n.* [Fr. *tôle,* sheet iron, plate.] a type of lacquered or enameled metalware popular in the eighteenth century and reproduced today in the form of trays, lamps, etc.: it is commonly dark-green or black with gilt decoration.

Tō·lē'dō, *n.*; *pl.* **Tō·lē'dōṣ,** a fine-tempered sword or sword blade made in Toledo, Spain.

tol''ēr·ȧ·bil'i·ty, *n.* the quality or state of being tolerable.

tol'ēr·ȧ·ble, *a.* [Fr., from L. *tolerabilis.*]
1. that can be tolerated; endurable; bearable.
2. fairly good; passable.
3. in reasonably good health. [Colloq.]
Syn.—endurable, bearable, supportable, allowable, permissible, passable.

tol'ēr·ȧ·ble·ness, *n.* tolerability.

tol'ēr·ȧ·bly, *adv.* 1. in a tolerable manner.
2. moderately; to a tolerable degree.

tol'ēr·ănce, *n.* [L. *tolerantia,* from *tolerare,* to bear.]
1. a tolerating or being tolerant, especially of others' views, beliefs, practices, etc.; freedom from bigotry or prejudice.
2. the amount of variation allowed from a standard, accuracy, etc.; specifically, (a) the amount that coins are legally allowed to vary from a standard of weight, fineness, etc.; (b) the difference between the allowable maximum and minimum sizes of some mechanical part, as a basis for determining the accuracy of a fitting.
3. an enduring or the ability to endure. [Rare.]
4. in medicine, the natural or developed ability to endure, or resist the harmful effects of, the continued or increasing use of a drug, etc.

tol'ēr·ănt, *a.* 1. inclined to tolerate others' beliefs, practices, etc.
2. in medicine, of or having tolerance.

tol'ēr·āte, *v.t.*; tolerated, *pt., pp.*; tolerating, *ppr.* 1. to allow; permit; not interfere with.
2. to recognize and respect (others' beliefs, practices, etc.) without necessarily agreeing or sympathizing.
3. to put up with; to bear; as, he *tolerates* his brother-in-law.
4. in medicine, to have tolerance for (a specified drug, etc.).
Syn.—permit, allow, suffer, endure.

tol·ēr·ā'tion, *n.* [L. *toleratio (-onis),* from *tolerare,* to endure.] tolerance; specifically, freedom to hold religious views that differ from the established ones.
Act of Toleration; in England, the Act of 1689, by which Protestant dissenters from the Church of England, on condition of taking the oaths of supremacy and allegiance and repudiating the doctrine of transubstantiation, were relieved from the restrictions under which they had formerly lain with regard to the exercise of their religion according to their own forms.

tol·ēr·ā'tion·ist, *n.* one who advocates toleration, especially in religious matters.

tol'ēr·ā·tive, *a.* tolerating or tending to tolerate.

tol'ēr·ā·tŏr, *n.* one who tolerates.

tol'i·dīne, tol'i·din, *n.* [*tol*uol and benz*idine.*] any of a group of isomeric dimethyl derivatives of benzidine, $C_{14}H_{16}N_2$.

tōll, *v.t.* [L. *tollere,* to take away.] to take away; to vacate; to annul.

tōll, *v.t.*; tolled, *pt., pp.*; tolling, *ppr.* [ME. *tollen,* to pull; prob. var. from AS. *-tillan,* to touch, influenced by echoism.]
1. to allure or entice; especially, to decoy (game, etc.). [Dial. or Rare.]
2. to ring (a church bell, etc.) slowly with regularly repeated strokes, as for summoning public bodies or religious congregations to their meetings, for announcing the death of a person, or to give solemnity to a funeral.

Toll ye the church bell sad and slow.
—Tennyson.

3. to indicate by tolling or striking, as the hour.

The clocks do *toll* the third hour.—Shak.

4. to draw attention to or give notice of by slowly repeated sounds of a bell; to ring for or on account of; as, to *toll* the passing of a friend.
5. to announce the death of (someone) in this way.

tōll, *v.i.* to sound or ring slowly in strokes uniformly repeated at intervals, as at funerals, or in calling assemblies, or to announce the death of a person: said of a bell.

tōll, *n.* 1. the act or sound of tolling a bell.
2. a single stroke of the bell.

tōll, *n.* [AS. *toll;* akin to G. *zoll.*]
1. a tax paid or a duty imposed for some liberty or privilege or other consideration, such as a fixed charge made for the passage of persons, goods, and cattle over roads, streets, bridges, etc.; also, the right to demand toll.
2. the payment claimed by the owners of a port for goods landed at or shipped from that port.
3. the sum charged by the owners of a market or fair for goods brought to be sold there or for liberty to break the soil for the purpose of erecting temporary structures. [Brit.]
4. formerly, a portion of grain taken by a miller as a compensation for grinding.
5. in old English law, a liberty to buy and sell within the bounds of a manor.
6. a charge for transporting goods by rail, canal, or steamship.
7. a charge made for a long-distance telephone call.
8. the number lost, taken, exacted, etc.; exaction; as, the accident took a heavy *toll* of lives.
Syn.—duty, custom, tax, impost.

tōll, *v.t.* to collect in toll. [Rare.]

tōll, *v.i.* 1. to pay toll or tollage. [Rare.]
2. to take or levy toll. [Rare.]

tōll'ȧ·ble, *a.* that may be taxed or tolled; as, *tollable* merchandise.

tōll'ăġe, *n.* 1. toll (tax).
2. payment or demand of toll.

tōll bāit, bait chopped up and cast into the water to attract fish. [Dial.]

tōll bär, a bar, gate, etc. for stopping travel at a point where toll is taken.

tōll bōard, 1. in telegraphy, a switchboard, such as is used in telephony, for making connections over toll lines.
2. a schedule of railroad rates posted for public information. [Brit.]

tōll'bo̤oth, *n.* same as *tolbooth.*

tōll bridġe, a bridge at which toll is paid for passage.

tōll çall, a long-distance telephone call, for which there is a charge beyond the local rate.

tōll çol·leç'tŏr, 1. a device employed in gristmills which automatically separates from the grist the portion of grain taken by the miller as his fee.
2. a gatherer or exactor of tolls.

tōll dish, a dish for measuring toll in mills.

tōll'ēr, *n.* one who collects taxes; a toll gatherer.

tōll'ēr, *n.* a person or thing that tolls; specifically, (a) a dog trained to toll, or decoy, ducks; (b) a person who tolls a bell; (c) a bell for tolling.

Tol'lē·tăn, *a.* relating to Toledo, Spain; of Toledo workmanship. [Obs.]

tōll'gāte, *n.* a gate for stopping travel at a point where toll is taken.

tōll'gath''ēr·ēr, *n.* the man who takes toll.

tōll'house, *n.* 1. a house or shed placed by a road, bridge, etc., where the tollgatherer stays.
2. a booth, etc. where toll is taken.

tōll'house cook'y, [made according to a recipe used at the *Toll House* in Whitman, Massachusetts.] a kind of cooky containing bits of solid chocolate.

tōll'ing, *n.* 1. the act of sounding a bell at uniform intervals of unusual length.
2. the sounding of such a bell.

tōll'keep''ēr, *n.* one who takes toll at a tollgate.

tōll līne, a long-distance telephone line.

tōll'măn, *n.*; *pl.* **tōll'men,** a man who collects toll.

tol'lŏn, *n.* same as *toyon.*

tōll rōad, a road for travel on which payment of toll is required.

tō·lō'sȧ wood, a tree, *Pittosporum bicolor,* of Tasmania.

tōlt, *n.* [L. *tollere,* to take away.] in old English law, a writ whereby a cause depending in a court-baron was removed into a county court.

Tol'teç, *n.* [Nahuatl *Tolteca.*] a member of an ancient group of Nahuatl Indians who lived in Mexico before the Aztecs: their culture shows Mayan influence.

Tol'teç, *a.* of the Toltecs or their culture.

Tol'tē·çăn, *a.* Toltec.

tō·lū', *n.* [Sp. *tolú,* from Santiago de *Tolú,* Colombia, S. Am.] the balsam produced by the tolu tree of South America: also called *tolu balsam.*

tol'ū·āte, *n.* a salt or ester of toluic acid.

tol'ū·ēne, *n.* [*tolu* and benz*ene.*] a colorless liquid hydrocarbon, $C_6H_5CH_3$, obtained originally from tolu balsam but now generally from coal tar and used in making dyes, explosives, etc. and as a solvent.

tō·lū'iç ac'id, any of four isomeric acids, $C_8H_8O_2$, carboxyl derivatives of toluene.

tol'ū·id, *n.* a toluide.

tol'ū·īde (*or* -id), *n.* any of a class of chemical compounds having the general formula $RCONHC_6H_4CH_3$, derived from the toluidines by the substitution of an acid radical for one of the amino H atoms.

tō·lū'i·din, *n.* a toluidine.

tō·lū'i·dīne, *n.* any of three isomeric amino derivatives, C_7H_9N, of toluene, used in the synthesis of dyes and medicines.

tol'ū·ōl, *n.* [*tolu* and *-ol.*] toluene; especially, crude commercial toluene.

tol'ū·ōle, *n.* toluol.

tō·lū'riç, *a.* derived from or containing toluic and uric acids.
toluric acid; any of several isomeric crystalline acids, $C_7H_7CO{\cdot}NH{\cdot}CH_2CO_2H$.

tol·ū·tā'tion, *n.* a pacing or ambling. [Obs.]

tō·lū' tree, [from *tolu.*] a large South American tree with rough, thick bark, yielding a fragrant balsam used in perfume, medicine, etc. The fruit is a one-celled oblique-winged legume.

tol'ū·yl, *n.* [*toluic* and *-yl.*] the monovalent acid radical C_7H_7CO.

tol'ū·yl·ēne, *n.* 1. stilbene.
2. tolylene.

tol'yl, *n.* the monovalent radical $CH_3C_6H_4$, derived from toluene.

tol'yl·ēne, *n.* the bivalent radical, $CH_3C_6H_3$, derived from toluene.

Tol·y·peū'tēṣ, *n.* [Gr. *tolypeuein,* to wind off, from *tolypē,* a ball.] a genus of armadillos, typical of the subfamily *Tolypeutinæ;* the matacos.

tol·y·peū'tīne, *a.* pertaining to the *Tolypeutes.*

tol·y·peū'tīne, *n.* one of the *Tolypeutes.*

tom, *n.* [from *Tom,* dim. of *Thomas;* esp. after *tomcat,* earlier *Tom the Cat* (c. 1760).]
1. the male of some animals, especially of the cat.
2. [T-] a man or boy; a fellow.
3. the knave of trumps in the game of gleek. [Obs.]
long tom; a long gun.
Old Tom; gin without sugar.
Tom and Jerry; a sweet spiced drink of rum, water, etc., served hot, with beaten eggs: so called from names of two chief characters in Egan's *Life in London* (1821).
Tom Collins; see under *Collins.*
Tom, Dick, and Harry; everyone; anyone; people taken at random: usually preceeded by *every* and used in a disparaging sense.
Tom o' Bedlam; an insane man; a crazy-appearing migratory beggar.

tom, *a.* male; as, a *tom* turkey. Sometimes used in compounds, occasionally with derived senses, as *tomcod.*

tom'ȧ·hawk, *n.* [of Am. Ind. (Algonquian) origin.] a light ax, originally having a stone or bone head, used by North American Indians as a tool and a weapon.
to bury the tomahawk; same as *to bury the hatchet* under *bury.*

to take up the tomahawk; same as *to take up the hatchet* under *hatchet*.
tom′ȧ·hạwk, *v.t.*; tomahawked, *pt.*, *pp.*; tomahawking, *ppr.* to cut, hit, or kill with a tomahawk.
tom′al″ley, *n.* [prob. from Carib name.] the liver of a lobster, which turns green when boiled and is considered a delicacy.
tō·män′, tō·mạun′, *n.* [Mongol. *tōmān*, ten thousand.]
1. a Persian gold coin.
2. a division of ten thousand Tatar or Mongol soldiers.
tō̆·mā′tō (*or* -mä′), *n.*; *pl.* **tō·mā′tōeṣ,** [Sp. *tomate*; Nahuatl *tomatl*.]
1. the edible fruit of *Lycopersicum esculentum*, a plant of the nightshade family; also, the plant itself. It is an annual from two to six feet in height, and is native to South America. The fruit is fleshy, usually red or yellow and glossy, more or less round, and used as a vegetable: botanically it is a berry.
2. a woman or girl. [Slang.]

TOMATO (*Lycopersicum esculentum*)

cherry or *currant tomato*, a species of tomato bearing small fruit in racemes like cherries or currants.
tō·mā′tō frụit′wŏrm, the bollworm.
tō·mā′tō gạll, a mass of irregular swellings, made by the gall midge, *Lasioptera vitis*, on the stems and leaves of American grapevines.
tō·mā′tō sphinx, a hawk moth, the larva of which is the tomato worm.
tō·mā′tō wŏrm, *n.* the larva of *Protoparce celeus*, a hawk moth known as the tomato sphinx, which infests the leaves of the tomato in America.
tömb (tōm), *n.* [Fr. *tombe*; LL. *tumba*, from Gr. *tymbos*, a tomb.]
1. a grave for the dead.
2. a house or vault, formed wholly or partly in the earth, with walls and a roof, for the dead.
3. a tombstone or burial monument erected to preserve the memory of the dead.
the tomb; death.
the Tombs; New York City prison.
tömb, *v.t.*; tombed, *pt.*, *pp.*; tombing, *ppr.* to bury; to inter. [Rare.]
tom′baç, tom′back, tom′bak, *n.* [Fr. *tombac*; Sp. *tumbaga*; Port. *tambaque*, from Malay *tĕmbaga*, copper.] an alloy consisting of copper and zinc, used in making cheap jewelry. When arsenic is added, it is called white tombac.
tömb bat (tōm), any one of several species of bats of the Eastern Hemisphere which inhabit tombs and similar places.
tom′bes·tēre, tom′bes·tẽr, *n.* same as *tumbester*.
tömb′iç (tōm′) *a.* relating to tombs.
tömb′less, *a.* without a tomb or sepulchral monument.
tom′bō·lȧ, *n.* [It.] a game of chance, to win at which one must draw each number of a set on a certain card.
tom′boy, *n.* 1. a rude, boisterous boy. [Obs.]
2. a girl who behaves like a boisterous boy; a hoyden.
tom′boy·ish, *a.* of or like a tomboy.
tömb′stōne (tōm′), *n.* a stone, usually with an engraved inscription, erected over a grave to preserve the memory of the deceased; a monument.
tom′çat, *n.* a male cat; especially, a full-grown male cat.
tom′çod, *n.* a small North American food fish, *Microgadus tomcodus*, about ten or twelve inches long, resembling the cod; a frostfish. The name is applied to other small fishes of the cod family.
tōme, *n.* [Fr., from L. *tomus*, from Gr. *tomos*, a section.]
1. originally, any volume of a work of several volumes.
2. a book, especially a large, heavy one.
-tōme, [from Gr. *tomē*, a cutting.] a combining form meaning *cutter*, used in forming names of surgical instruments, as micro*tome*, osteo*tome*.
tōme′let, *n.* [dim. of *tome*.] a small tome.
tō′ment, *n.* same as *tomentum*.
tō·men′tōse, tō·men′tous, *a.* [L. *tomentum*, down.] in botany, entomology, etc., covered with short, matted, woolly hairs.
tō·men′tū·lōse, *a.* somewhat or slightly tomentose.
tō·men′tum, *n.*; *pl.* **tō·men′tȧ,** [L. *tomentum*, down.]
1. in botany, a kind of pubescence, consisting of longish, soft, entangled hairs, pressed close to the surface.
2. in anatomy, a network of minute blood vessels of the pia mater and the cortex of the cerebrum.
tom′fool′, *n.* 1. a foolish, stupid, or silly person.
2. the Jamaican rainbird, *Saurothera vetula*.
tom′fool′, *a.* foolish, stupid, or silly.
tom′fool′, *v.i.*, tomfooled, *pt.*, *pp.*; tomfooling, *ppr.* to act foolishly. [Colloq.]
tom″fool′ẽr·y, *n.*; *pl.* **tom″fool′ẽr·ieṣ,** 1. foolish trifling; nonsense; absurd behavior.
2. silly trifles; absurd ornaments or knickknacks: also written *tomfoolishness*.
tom′fool′ish, *a.* foolish; silly.
tō′mi·ȧ, *n.* plural of *tomium*.
tō′mi·ăl, *a.* in ornithology, cutting; of or pertaining to the tomia or to a tomium.
-tom′iç, a combining form used to form adjectives corresponding to nouns ending in *-tome*.
tō′mi·um, *n.*; *pl.* **tō′mi·ȧ,** [LL., from Gr. *tomē*, a cutting.] in ornithology, one of the cutting edges of a bird's bill.
tom′john (-jon), *n.* a tonjon. [Colloq.]
tom′kin pōst, in a grain mill, the post which serves as a support for the pivot end of the bridgetree.
tom′my, *n.*; *pl.* **tom′mieṣ,** 1. a penny roll; hence, bread; provisions; goods given to a workman in lieu of wages. [Brit. Slang.]
2. a tommy shop. [Brit. Slang.]
3. the system of paying workmen in goods in place of money; the truck system. [Brit. Slang.]
4. a tomcat. [Colloq.]
5. a simpleton. [Brit. Slang.]
6. a small lever used to tighten screw bolts by inserting it in a hole in the screw head.
tom′my, *v.t.*; tommied, *pt.*, *pp.*; tommying, *ppr.* to enforce the tommy or truck system on; to oppress or defraud by the tommy system. [Brit. Slang.]
Tom′my, tom′my, *n.*; *pl.* **Tom′mieṣ, tom′mieṣ,** a Tommy Atkins; British soldier: a nickname.
Tom′my At′kinṣ, [from the use of the fictitious name *Thomas Atkins* in sample forms used in the British Army.] a British (noncolonial) soldier: a nickname.
tom′my gun, 1. a Thompson submachine gun. [Colloq.]
2. loosely, any submachine gun. [Colloq.]
tom′my nod′dy, a tomnoddy.
tom′my·rot, *n.* [from *Tommy*, in dial. sense of "fool", and *rot*.] foolishness; nonsense; rubbish. [Slang.]
tom′my shop, a shop or store conducted on the tommy system. [Brit. Slang.]
tom′nod′dy, tom′nor′ry, *n.* 1. the puffin. [Scot. and Brit. Dial.]
2. a blockhead; a dolt; a dunce.
tō·mog′rȧ·phy, *n.* [from Gr. *tomos*, a piece cut off, section; and *-graphy*.] in medicine, a technique of X-ray photography by which a single selected plane is photographed, with the outline of structures in other planes eliminated.
Tō·mop′tē·ris, *n.* [Gr. *tomē*, a cutting, and *pteron*, wing.]
1. a genus of marine annelids having long, transparent, unringed bodies and deeply forked finlike organs.
2. [t–] any annelid of this genus.
tō̈·mọrn′, *adv.* tomorrow [Obs.]
tō̈·mor′rōw, tō̈-mor′rōw, *adv.* [AS. *to*, on, and *morgen*, morrow.] on or for the day after today; on the morrow.
tō̈·mor′rōw, tō̈-mor′rōw, *n.* 1. the day after the present day; the morrow.
2. an indefinite time in the near future.
tom′pi·ŏn, *n.* 1. same as *tampion*.
2. the inking pad of a lithographic printer: also written *tompon*.
tom′pi·ŏn, *n.* a watch; specifically, one made by Thomas Tompion (1639–1713). [Obs.]
tom′rig, *n.* a rude, wild girl; a tomboy. [Obs.]
Tom Thumb (thum), 1. a tiny hero of many English folk tales.
2. any dwarf or small person: so called from an American midget (*General Tom Thumb*), Charles S. Stratton (1838–1883), exhibited by P. T. Barnum.
tom′tit′, *n.* 1. a titmouse; a tit. [Brit.]
2. the tree creeper, *Certhia familiaris*. [Irish.]
3. a wren, chickadee, or any of various other small birds.
tom′-tom, *n.* [Hind. *tam-tam*, of echoic origin.]
1. any of various drums of primitive origin, played with the hands or with sticks.
2. a tam-tam.
tom′-tom, *v.i.* to beat or play on the tom-tom.
-tō·my, [from Gr. *tomē*, a cutting.] a combining form meaning (a) *a cutting, dividing*, as in dicho*tomy;* (b) a surgical operation, as in appendec*tomy*.
tōn, *n.* obsolete plural of *toe*.
tŏn, *n.* [AS. *tunne*, a butt, a large vessel.]
1. a unit of weight equal to 2,240 pounds avoirdupois (or 1,016.06 kilograms), commonly used in Great Britain: in full, *long ton, shipping ton*.
2. a unit of weight equal to 2,000 pounds avoirdupois (or 907.20 kilograms), commonly used in the United States, Canada, South Africa, etc.: in full, *short ton*.
3. a metric ton.
4. a unit of internal capacity of ships, equal to 100 cubic feet (or 2.8317 cubic meters).
5. a unit of carrying capacity of ships, usually equal to 40 cubic feet: in full, *measurement ton, freight ton*.
6. a unit for measuring displacement of ships, equal to 35 cubic feet: it is approximately equal to the volume of a long ton of sea water: in full, *displacement ton*.
7. a very large amount or number. [Colloq.]
8. a certain quantity of timber, as forty feet of rough or round timber, and fifty feet of hewn.
toṇ, *n.* [Fr.] the prevailing fashion; style; vogue; as, ladies of *ton*.
-tŏn, [from AS. *tūn*, town.] a combining form meaning *town*; as, Washing*ton*, Ash*ton*, etc.
tō′năl, *a.* of or pertaining to a tone or tones.
tō′năl·ite, *n.* [from *Tonale* in the Tyrol, Austria, and *-ite*.] a variety of quartz diorite, rich in mica containing magnesia.
tō·nal′i·ty, *n.*; *pl.* **tō·nal′i·tieṣ,** [Fr. *tonalité*, from *ton*, a sound.]
1. quality of tone.
2. in art, the arrangement of tones, or color scheme, in a painting.
3. in music, (a) a key; (b) the tonal character of composition or of a composition, as determined by the relationship of the tones to the tonic, or keynote.
tō′năl·ly, *adv.* as regards tone.
tō̈′-nāme, *n.* a name added to another name; a name in addition to the Christian and surname of a person to distinguish him from others of the same name; a nickname: also called *tee-name* in Scotland, where they are especially common. [Obs. except Scot.]
toñ′çȧ bēan, same as *tonka bean*.
ton·dĭ′nō, *n.* [It.] 1. in architecture, an astragal.
2. a small tondo.
ton′dō, *n.* [It.] a painting or a piece of sculpture done in circular form.
tōne, *indef. pron.* the one, or that one: used as correlative to *tother*. [Obs.]
tōne, *n.* [ME. *ton, tone*; OFr. *ton*, from L. *tonus*, a sound, from Gr. *tonos*, a stretching, a tone.]
1. (a) a vocal or musical sound; (b) its quality.
2. an intonation, pitch, modulation, etc. of the voice that expresses a particular meaning or feeling of the speaker; as, a *tone* of contempt.
3. a manner of speaking or writing that shows a certain attitude on the part of the speaker or writer, consisting in choice of words, phrasing, etc.; as, the letter had a friendly *tone*.
4. normal resiliency or elasticity; as, this wood has lost its *tone*.
5. (a) the prevailing or predominant style, character, spirit, trend, morale, or state of morals of a place or period; as, her house has a conservative *tone*; (b) distinctive style; elegance.
6. (a) a quality o value of color; a tint; a shade; (b) any of the slight modifications of a

particular color; hue; as, it has three *tones* of green.

7. in linguistics, (a) the musical pitch of a sound, word, etc.; (b) a rising, falling, or other inflection by which words otherwise pronounced the same are distinguished, as in ancient Greek or Pekingese Chinese.

8. in music and acoustics, (a) a sound that is distinct and identifiable by its regularity of vibration, or constant pitch, and that may be put into harmonic relation with other such sounds: distinguished from *noise*; (b) the simple or fundamental tone of a musical sound as distinguished from its overtones; (c) any one of the full intervals of a diatonic scale; a step: also called *whole* tone; (d) any of the nine psalm tunes in plainsong: also called *Gregorian tone*.

9. in painting, the effect produced by the combination of light, shade, and color.

10. in phonetics, (a) sound produced by vibration of the vocal cords; voice; (b) a pitch of voice; (c) syllabic stress.

11. in physiology, (a) the condition of an organism, organ, or part with reference to its normal, healthy functioning; (b) the normal tension, or resistance to stretch, of a healthy muscle, independent of that caused by voluntary innervation.

characteristic tone; (a) the seventh tone of the diatonic scale; (b) the distinguishing tone of a key.

combination tone; the third tone, produced by the simultaneous sounding of two primary tones.

difference or *differential tone*; a combination tone having a frequency of vibration which is the difference of the frequencies of its components.

partial tone; see under *partial*.

resultant tone; same as *combination tone*.

tōne, *v.t.*; toned, *pt., pp.*; toning, *ppr.* 1. to intone. [Rare.]

2. to give a tone to; specifically, to give the proper or desired tone to (a musical instrument, a painting, etc.).

3. to change the tone of.

to tone down; to give a lower or less intense tone to; to subdue the boisterous manners of; as, *to tone down* a child; to modify; as, *to tone down* expressions of opinion.

to tone in with; to harmonize with.

to tone up; to give a higher or more intense tone or quality to; to elevate; to strengthen; to brace up.

tōne, *v.i.* to harmonize, or blend in shade; to assume a tone.

to tone down; to become softened.

to tone up; to become strengthened or heightened.

tōne cŏl′ŏr, timbre.

tōne cŏn·trōl′, a device in a radio or electric phonograph by which the intensity of tones of varying frequencies is regulated.

tōned, *a.* having a tone; used in composition; as, high-*toned*; sweet-*toned*.

tōne′-deaf (-def), *a.* not able to distinguish accurately differences in musical pitch.

tō·ne·lä′dȧ (-thȧ), *n.* [Sp. and Port., from *tonel*; ult. from Pr. *tona*, a tub.]

1. in Spain, a unit of weight equal to 2,028.7 pounds.

2. in Brazil, a unit of weight equal to 1,748.79 pounds.

tōne′less, *a.* without tone; unmusical.

tōne pō′em, an elaborate, orchestral composition, usually in one movement, having no fixed form and based upon some nonmusical poetic or descriptive theme: also called *symphonic poem*.

tōne syl′lȧ·ble, an accented syllable.

tō·net′iç, *a.* [from *tone*, after *phonetic*.] in linguistics, designating tones (sense 7) or languages which distinguish word meanings by tone variations.

tō·net′içs, *n.pl.* [*construed as sing.*] the science of speech tones.

tọng, *v.t.* to seize, collect, handle, or hold with tongs.

tọng, *v.i.* to use tongs.

tọng, *n.* [Chin. *t'ang*, a hall, meeting place, hence society.]

1. a Chinese association or political party.

2. in the United States, a private or secret society of Chinese.

toṅ′gȧ, *n.* [Hind.] a light, two-wheeled carriage used in India.

toṅ′gȧ bēan, same as *tonka bean*.

Toṅ′găn, *n.* 1. a native of Tonga.

2. the Polynesian language of the Tongans.

tong′kang, *n.* [E. Ind.] a boat, a form of junk common in the Malay Archipelago.

tọngṣ, *n.pl.* [*sometimes construed as sing.*] [AS. *tange*, tongs; akin to G. *zange*.] a device for siezing or lifting objects, generally having two long arms pivoted or hinged together; as, blacksmiths' *tongs*; ice *tongs*, etc.: also called a *pair of tongs*.

tŏngue (tung), *n.* [AS. *tunge*, a tongue; akin to G. *zunge*.]

1. the movable muscular structure attached to the floor of the mouth: it is an important organ in the ingestion of food, the perception of taste, and, in man, the articulation of speech sounds.

2. an animal's tongue used as food.

3. the human tongue as the organ of speech.

4. ideas expressed by speaking; talk; speech.

5. the act or power of speaking.

6. a manner or style of speaking in regard to tone, meaning, intention, etc.

7. a language or dialect.

8. the cry of a hunting dog, etc. in sight of game.

9. something resembling a tongue in shape, position, movement, or use; specifically, (a) the flap under the laces or strap of a shoe; (b) the clapper of a bell; (c) the pin of a buckle; (d) the pole of a wagon, etc.; (e) the projecting tenon of a tongue-and-groove joint; (f) in machines, a projecting flange, rib, etc.; (g) the vibrating end of the reed in a wind instrument; (h) a narrow strip of land extending into a sea, river, etc.; (i) a narrow inlet of water; (j) the movable rail in a railroad switch; (k) a long, narrow flame; (l) the pointer of a scale, etc.

10. words or declaration only; mere speech or talk, as opposed to thoughts or actions.

Let us not love in word, neither in *tongue*, but in deed and in truth. —1 John iii. 18.

11. a nation, as distinguished by its language. [Archaic.]

I will gather all nations and *tongues*.
—Isa. lxvi. 18.

12. in a ship, (a) the upper main piece of a built mast; (b) a rope spliced into the upper part of a standing backstay.

13. in zoology, an organ or part resembling a tongue, as a ligula or a proboscis; as, the long, spirally-rolled *tongue* of a butterfly.

gift of tongues; a gift bestowed in connection with the pentecostal descent of the Holy Spirit, as related in The Acts of the Apostles ii. 1–21, whereby men of various tongues were miraculously endowed with the power of speaking and understanding one common language.

on everyone's tongue; prevailing as common gossip.

on the tip of one's (or *the*) *tongue*; (a) almost said by one; (b) about to be said: especially of something forgotten that is almost but not quite recalled.

to find one's tongue; to recover the power of speech, as on recovery from shock or from embarrassment.

to give tongue; see under *give*.

to hold one's tongue; to refrain from speaking; also, to cease speaking.

Syn.—speech, language, dialect, idiom, discourse.

tŏngue, *v.t.*; tongued (tungd), *pt., pp.*; tonguing, *ppr.* 1. to reproach or scold.

2. to speak or say. [Archaic.]

3. to touch, etc. with the tongue.

4. (a) to cut a tongue (sense 9e) on or in; (b) to join by means of a tongue-and-groove joint.

5. in music, to play by tonguing: see *tonguing*.

tŏngue, *v.i.* 1. to talk or talk much. [Rare.]

2. to project like a tongue.

3. in music, to use tonguing: see *tonguing*.

tŏngue′-and-grọove′ joint, a kind of joint in which a tongue or rib on one board fits exactly into a groove in another.

tŏngue′bĭrd, *n.* the wryneck. [Brit. Dial.]

tŏngued (tungd), *a.* having a tongue: usually in hyphenated compounds, meaning *having a* (specified kind of) *tongue*; as, sharp-*tongued*.

tŏngue′fish, *n.* a flatfish, *Aphoristia plagiusa*, found off the southern coast of the United States.

tŏngue′flow″ẽr, *n.* any orchid of the Australian genus *Glossodia*.

tŏngue′-flow″ẽred, *a.* provided with tonguelike flowers.

tongue-flowered orchis; an orchid, *Serapias lingua*, common to southern Europe.

tŏngue grȧft′ing, a method of grafting by inserting the split end of a scion into a stock which has also been split.

tŏngue grȧss, peppergrass.

tŏngue′-lash″ing, *n.* a vigorous scolding; wordy vituperation. [Colloq.]

tŏngue′less, *a.* 1. having no tongue.

2. speechless; dumb; as, a *tongueless* block.

3. unnamed; not spoken of. [Obs.]

tŏngue′let, *n.* 1. a little tongue, or small process shaped like a tongue.

2. the ligula.

3. an arachnid of the group *Linguatulina* or *Pentastomidea*.

tŏngue′-pad, *n.* a great talker. [Dial.]

tŏngue′-shāped (-shāpt), *a.* shaped like a tongue; specifically, in botany, linear and fleshy, blunt at the end, convex underneath, and having usually a cartilaginous border; as, a *tongue-shaped* leaf.

tŏngue shell, a brachiopod of the family *Lingulidæ*.

tŏngue′stẽr, *n.* a talkative, loquacious person; a chatterer; a babbler.

tŏngue′-tīe, *n.* impeded motion of the tongue in consequence of the shortness of the frenum, resulting in indistinct articulation.

tŏngue′-tīe, *v.t.*; tongue-tied, *pt., pp.*; tongue-tying, *ppr.* to deprive of speech or the power of speech, or of distinct articulation; to make tongue-tied.

tŏngue′-tīed, *a.* 1. having a condition of tongue-tie.

2. speechless from amazement, embarrassment, etc.

tŏngue twist′ẽr, a phrase or sentence hard to speak fast, usually because of alliteration or a sequence of nearly similar sounds. Example: She sells sea shells by the seashore.

tŏngue′wŏrm, *n.* 1. a parasitic wormlike arachnid belonging to the *Linguatulina*, which infests the nostrils and lungs of some animals.

2. a tonguelike worm; a tonguelet.

tŏngue′y, tŏngu′y, *a.* voluble or fluent in speech; loquacious.

tŏngu′ing, *n.* the use of the tongue to produce a rapidly staccato effect on a musical wind instrument or to modify the intonation.

ton′iç, *a.* [Gr. *tonikos*, from *tonos*, a stretching, a tone.]

1. of, producing, or tending to produce good muscular tone, or tension.

2. mentally or morally invigorating; stimulating.

3. having to do with tones; specifically, (a) in music, designating or based on the first tone (*keynote*) of a diatonic scale; as, a *tonic* chord; (b) in painting, having to do with the tone or tones of a picture; (c) in phonetics, designating or of sounds characterized by resonance in the head cavities: in this sense, no longer used; also, accented.

4. in linguistics, tonetic; as, Chinese is a *tonic* language.

5. in medicine and physiology, of or characterized by tone, or tonus.

tonic spasm; see *spasm*.

ton′iç, *n.* 1. anything which invigorates or stimulates; specifically, a tonic medicine.

2. in music, the first, or basic, tone of a diatonic scale; a keynote.

3. in phonetics, (a) a sound characterized by resonance in the head cavities: in this sense, no longer used; (b) an accented syllable.

ton′iç aç′cent, 1. a vocal accent, or stress, as distinguished from a written, or graphic, accent: term no longer used.

2. in phonetics, emphasis given to a syllable by changing, especially by raising, the pitch.

tō·nic′i·ty, *n.* the quality or condition of being tonic; especially, in physiology, the normal tension of a muscle at rest; tonus.

ton′i·çăl, *a.* tonic. [Obs.]

ton′iç sōl″-fä′, a system of musical notation based on the relationship between the tones of a key, using the syllables of solmization (*do, re, mi*, etc.), instead of the usual staff symbols: used especially in elementary singing instruction.

tö·nīght′ (-nīt′), *adv.* [ME. and AS. *to niht*.]

1. on or during the present or coming night.

2. on or during the preceding night. [Obs. or Dial.]

tö·nīght′, tö-nīght′, *n.* 1. the present night, or the night after the present day.

2. the night just past. [Dial.]

ton′ish, *a.* stylish; fashionable.

ton'ish·ness, *n.* the quality of being in the ton or prevailing fashion; modishness.

tŏn'ite, *n.* [from L. *tonare*, to thunder, and *-ite*.] a powerful explosive made of guncotton and barium nitrate.

ton'jon, *n.* [Hind.] in India, a chair or sedan suspended on a pole and carried by four bearers.

toñ'kȧ, *n.* the tonka bean.

toñ'kȧ bēan, [from native Guiana name.] the seed of a tall tree, *Dipteryx odorata*, of the northern regions of South America, or the tree itself. The seed is almond-like in shape, and contains coumarin, which gives it a fragrant odor and makes it valuable for perfuming and flavoring.

TONKA-BEAN TREE (*Dipteryx odorata*)

toñ'kȧ-bēan tree, the tree that bears the tonka bean.

toñ'kȧ-bēan wood, scentwood.

ton'kin', *n.* [after *Tonkin*, in Viet-Nam.] a kind of bamboo, used for fishing poles, etc.

tŏn'nāġe, *n.* [ME. *tonage*; OFr. *tonnage*.]
1. a duty or tax on ships, based on tons carried.
2. a charge per ton on cargo or freight on a canal, at a port, etc.
3. the total amount of shipping of a country or port, calculated in tons.
4. the carrying capacity of a ship, calculated in tons.
5. weight in tons.
Also spelled *tunnage*.
gross tonnage; the total internal capacity of a ship expressed in tons.
net tonnage; the cubic capacity of a ship available for the carrying of freight.

tonne, *n.* [Fr.] a ton.

tŏn·neau' (nō'), *n.*; *pl.* **tŏn·neauṣ', tŏn·neaux'** (nōz'), [Fr., lit., a cask, tun.]
1. an enclosed rear compartment for passengers in an early type of automobile.
2. the whole body of such an automobile.
3. a metric ton, or 1,000 kilograms.

ton'nish, *a.* same as *tonish*.

ton'nish·ness, *n.* same as *tonishness*.

tō·nom'e·tẽr, *n.* [Gr. *tonos*, tone, and *metron*, a measure.]
1. any instrument for measuring the pitch of tones, as a tuning fork or a graduated set of tuning forks.
2. an instrument for measuring vapor pressure.
3. in physiology and medicine, any instrument for measuring tension, as of the eyeball, or pressure, as of the blood.

ton·ō·met'riç, *a.* 1. of or determined by a tonometer.
2. having to do with tonometry.

tō·nom'e·try, *n.* the science of measuring with a tonometer; specifically, (a) in music, the measuring of tone vibrations; (b) in medicine, the measuring of tension, especially intraocular tension; (c) in chemistry, the measuring of molecular strain in liquids.

ton'ō·phănt, *n.* [Gr. *tonos*, sound, and *phainein*, to show.] a contrivance composed of two thin strips of steel welded together, of adjustable length, by which the composition of acoustic vibrations is made visible to the eye.

ton'ō·plast, *n.* [Gr. *tonos*, tone, and *plastos*, formed.]
1. in botany, the membranous wall surrounding a vacuole.
2. in physiology, a small intracellular body.

tōn'ous, *a.* full of tone or sound; sonorous. [Rare.]

toñ'quin bēan, same as tonka bean.

ton'sil, *n.* [Fr. *tonsille*, from L. *tonsilla*, the tonsil.]
1. either of a pair of oval masses composed mainly of lymphoid tissue and covered with mucous membrane, containing various crypts and many lymphoid follicles. The tonsils are located one on each side of the back of the mouth leading to the pharynx, and are supposed to act as sources for the supply of phagocytes to the mouth and pharynx.
2. a lobe on either side of the lower surface of the cerebellum.

ton'sil·lăr, ton'sil·ăr, *a.* of or pertaining to the tonsils.

ton·sil·leç'tō·my, *n.*; *pl.* **ton·sil·leç'tō·mieṣ,** [L. *tonsilla*, a tonsil, and Gr. *ektomē*, a cutting out.] in surgery, the cutting out or removal of the tonsils.

ton·sil·lit'iç, *a.* 1. tonsillar.
2. pertaining to or affected with tonsillitis.

ton·sil·lī'tis, *n.* inflammation of the tonsils.

ton·sil'lō·tōme, *n.* an instrument used in tonsillotomy.

ton·sil·lot'ō·my, *n.* the surgical incision of a tonsil; especially, a tonsillectomy.

ton'sŏr, *n.* [L.] a barber; one who shaves.

ton·sō'ri·ăl, *a.* [L. *tonsorius*, pertaining to clipping.] pertaining to a barber or his work: often used humorously; as, a *tonsorial* artist.

ton'sụre (-shụr), *n.* [Fr., from L. *tonsura*, a shaving, from *tonsus*, pp. of *tondere*, to shave.]
1. the act of clipping the hair or of shaving the crown of the head; also, the state of being shorn.
2. in the Roman Catholic and Orthodox Eastern churches, the first ceremony used for devoting a person to the service of God and the church; the first step preparatory to entering the priesthood, given by a bishop, a mitred abbot, or a cardinal priest, who shaves off a part of the hair of the candidate with prayers and benedictions; hence, entrance or admission into holy orders.
3. the portion of a priest's or monk's head made bare by shaving.

ton'sụre, *v.t.*; tonsured, *pt.*, *pp.*; tonsuring, *ppr.* to clip the hair of or shave the crown of the head of; to give the tonsure to, as a priest in the Roman Catholic and Orthodox Eastern churches, thus devoting him to the service of the church.

ton'sụred, *a.* 1. having received the tonsure; shaven; hence, clerical.
2. having a bald spot on the head like a tonsure.

ton'tīne, *n.* [Fr.; It. *tontina*, from Lorenzo *Tonti*, Neapolitan banker who introduced the system into France in the 17th c.]
1. an annuity shared among a group of persons, or a loan based on a group of annuities, with the provision that as each beneficiary dies, his share is divided among the survivors until the entire amount accrues to the last or last two or three survivors.
2. the subscribers to such an annuity, collectively.
3. the total annuity or the share of each subscriber.
4. any similar insurance system.

ton·tīne', *a.* of, pertaining to, or embracing the principle of tontine; as, a *tontine* policy.

tō'nus, *n.* [Gr. *tonos*, sound.] tone or tonicity; especially, muscular tone.

tō'ny, *n.*; *pl.* **tō'nieṣ,** [abbreviation of *Antony*.] a simpleton. [Old Slang.]

tō'ny, *a.*; *comp.* tonier; *superl.* toniest; high-toned; in the height of fashion; stylish: often ironic.

tọọ, *adv.* [stressed form of *to*, *prep.*, with differentiated spelling.]
1. more than enough; superfluously; overly; as, the hat is *too* big.
2. likewise; also; in addition; besides; as well; as, beautiful, and clever *too*.
3. in an excessive degree; to a regrettable extent; as, that's *too* bad!
4. extremely; very; as, it was just *too* delicious!
Too is often used as a mere emphatic; as, I will *too* go!
too too; altogether too: a repetition emphasizing excess. [Colloq.]

tọọ'ärt, *n.* [native name.] the Australian white gum tree.

took, *v.* past tense of *take*.

tọọl, *n.* [AS. *tōl*; akin to O.N. *tōl*.]
1. any implement, instrument, or utensil held in the hand and used for cutting, hitting, digging, rubbing, etc.: knives, saws, hammers, shovels, rakes, etc are tools.
2. (a) any similar instrument that is the working part of a power-driven machine, as a drill, band-saw blade, etc.; (b) the whole machine; a machine tool.
3. anything that serves in the manner of a tool; a means; as, books are a scholar's *tools*.
4. a person used by another to accomplish his purposes, especially when these are illegal or unethical; a dupe; a stooge.
5. in law, any instrument or device necessary to one's profession or occupation.
6. a shiftless, lazy fellow. [Dial. or Slang.]
Syn.—utensil, implement, machine, instrument, dupe, cat's paw, hireling.

tọọl, *v.t.*; tooled, *pt.*, *pp.*; tooling, *ppr.* 1. to form, shape, or work with a tool.
2. to provide tools or machinery for (a factory, industry, etc.).
3. to drive (a vehicle) or convey (a person in a vehicle). [Brit. Colloq.]
4. in bookbinding, to impress letters or designs on (a book cover) with special tools.

tọọl, *v.i.* 1. to use a tool or tools.
2. to ride or drive in a vehicle. [Brit. Colloq.]

tọọl'ing, *n.* 1. work or decoration done with tools.
2. the process of fitting out a factory with machine tools in readiness for going into production.

tọọl'māk·ẽr, *n.* a maker of tools; especially, a machinist who makes, maintains, and repairs machine tools.

tọọl'märk, *n.* a specific or characteristic mark left by a tool upon any article.

tọọl pōst, a circular post attached to the top of a slide or tool rest on a lathe for the clamping down of the cutting tools.

tọọl rest, in a lathe, a device for supporting a tool post or tool, often in various positions.

tọọl'si, tọọl'sy, *n.* [Sans. *tulasī*.] the holy basil: a plant held sacred by the Hindus.

tọọl'stock, *n.* same as *tool post*.

tọọm, *a.* empty. [Scot. and Brit. Dial.]

tọọm, *v.t.* to evacuate; to empty. [Scot. and Brit. Dial.]

tọọn, *n.* obsolete plural of *toe*.

tọọn, tọọn'wood, *n.* [Hind. *tūn*; Sans. *tunna*.]
1. a wood of a reddish-brown color, used in India for cabinetwork.
2. the tree from which the wood is obtained, *Cedrela toona*.

tọọ'nȧ, *n.* same as *toon* (the tree).

tọọn'drȧ, *n.* same as *tundra*.

tọọ'rọọ, *n.* [S. Am. *turu*.] a South American palm, *Œnocarpus bataua*, whose wood is much used for inlaid work, canes, etc.

tọọt, *v.i.*; tooted, *pt.*, *pp.*; tooting, *ppr.* [from D. or L.G. *tuten*, from a Gmc. echoic base.]
1. to blow a horn, whistle, etc., especially in short blasts.
2. to sound in short blasts: said of a horn, whistle, etc.
3. to make a sound like a horn or whistle.

tọọt, *v.t.* 1. to cause to sound in short blasts.
2. to sound (tones, blasts, etc.), as on a horn.

tọọt, *n.* 1. a short blast of a horn or whistle, or a similar sound.
2. a spree; as, to go on a *toot*. [Slang.]

tọọt, *n.* an idle, shiftless person. [Slang.]

tọọt, *v.i.* 1. to stand out or be prominent. [Dial.]
2. to peep; to look narrowly. [Dial.]

tọọt'ẽr, *n.* one who or that which toots.

tọọth, *n.*; *pl.* **teeth,** [AS. *tōth*, pl. *teth*; akin to G. *zahn*.]
1. any of a set of hard, bonelike structures (normally 32 in the human adult) set in the jaws of most vertebrates and used for biting, tearing, and chewing: a tooth consists typically of a sensitive, vascular pulp surrounded by dentine and coated on the crown with enamel and on the root with cement.

ENAMEL
CROWN
PULP
DENTINE
CEMENT
ROOT
CEMENT

DIAGRAM OF TOOTH

2. something resembling a tooth; a toothlike part, as on a saw, fork, rake, gear, etc.; a tine; prong; cog.
3. appetite or taste for something; as, a sweet *tooth*.

These are not dishes for thy dainty *tooth*. —Dryden.

4. in invertebrates, any of various hard calcareous or chitinous bodies, presenting great variety of position and structure, which may occur in the alimentary canal from the mouth to the stomach; as, a *tooth* or mouthplate of a starfish.
5. in botany and zoology, any of various

A B C D E F G H

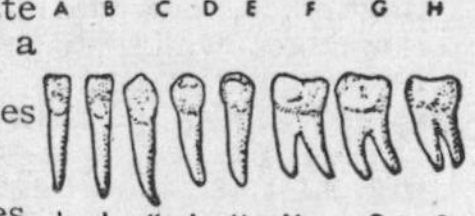

PERMANENT TEETH OF RIGHT SIDE

Upper Jaw: A, central incisor; B, lateral incisor; C, canine; D, first premolar; E, second premolar; F, first molar; G, second molar; H, third molar. Lower Jaw: I, central incisor; J, lateral incisor; K, canine; L, first premolar; M, second premolar; N, first molar; O, second molar; P, third molar

small projections resembling or likened to a tooth, as the pointed marginal lobes of a leaf, an appendage at the mouth of the capsule of a moss, a process at or near the hinge of the shell in many bivalves, or a horny process of the cutting edge of the beak of many birds, as the falcon and shrike.

6. [*pl.*] the lower zone of facets in a rose-cut diamond.

7. the corrugated surface made by scoring the under face of a veneer or the outer face of the piece to which it is to be glued, to afford a good hold for the glue.

8. in masonry, any of a series of bricks or stones left projecting at the end of a wall to provide for an extension.

9. figuratively, something that bites, pierces, or gnaws like a tooth; as, the *teeth* of the storm.

armed to the teeth; fully armed.

in the teeth of; (a) in opposition to; (b) straight against; as, to walk *in the teeth of* the wind; (c) in the face or presence of.

sweet tooth; see following *sweet*.

to cast in the teeth of; see under *cast*.

tooth and nail; as if by biting and scratching; with one's utmost power; by all possible means.

to put teeth in (*a law*, etc.); to enforce or facilitate the enforcement of (a law, etc.).

to set one's teeth; to prepare to meet firmly something difficult or unpleasant.

to show one's teeth; to show hostility; to threaten angrily.

to throw (*something*) *in one's teeth*; (a) to reproach one for (something); (b) to hurl (a challenge, taunt, etc.) at one.

tooth, *v.t.*; toothed, *pt.*, *pp.*; toothing, *ppr.* 1. to furnish with teeth; as, to *tooth* a rake.

2. to indent; to cut into teeth; to jag; as, to *tooth* a saw.

3. to lock one in another, as the teeth of gear wheels.

4. to bite; to chew.

tooth, *v.i.* 1. to teethe. [Dial.]

2. to interlock, as cogwheels.

tooth'āche (-āk), *n.* pain in a tooth or the teeth; odontalgia.

tooth'āche grȧss, a tall grass, *Ctenium americanum*, of the southern United States, having a very pungent taste.

tooth'āche tree, 1. the prickly ash.

2. the angelica tree, *Aralia spinosa*: also called *wild orange*.

tooth'back, *n.* a tooth-backed moth of the family *Notodontidæ*, whose caterpillars have large humps on the back.

tooth'bill, *n.* a fruit-eating pigeon, *Didunculus strigirostris*, of the Samoan Islands, having toothlike projections at the end of its mandible.

tooth'brush, *n.* a small brush used for cleaning the teeth.

tooth'brush tree, a small Asiatic evergreen, *Salvadora persica*, the twigs of which are sometimes made into brushes for cleaning the teeth.

tooth çor'ăl·ine, any hydroid of the family *Sertularidæ*.

tooth çress, an herb of the genus *Dentaria*; English pepperroot.

tooth'draw″ẽr, *n.* one who extracts teeth with instruments; a dentist.

toothed (tootht), *a.* 1. having teeth, jags, or notches.

2. in botany, dentate; having projecting points about the margin; notched; serrate.

toothed whale; a whale having developed teeth; one of the *Denticete*.

toothed wheel; a wheel the periphery of which has teeth or cogs which transmit motion by engaging the teeth or cogs of another wheel.

-toothed, a combining form used in hyphenated compounds, meaning *having* (a specified number or kind of) *teeth*, as in big-toothed.

tooth'flow″ẽr, *n.* a rubiaceous herb, *Dentella repens*, of Asia, Australia, and Polynesia, the sole species of its genus, a creeping annual growing in dense patches. Its corolla lobes have a small tooth on each side.

tooth'fu̇l, *n.* a small draught of drink or bite of food.

tooth'ing, *n.* in masonry, bricks or stones left projecting at the end of a wall, so that they may be bonded into an extension or angle of such wall when required.

tooth'ing plāne, a plane the iron of which is formed into a series of small teeth. It is used to roughen a surface intended to be covered with veneer or cloth, in order to give a better hold to the glue.

tooth kēy, an instrument formerly used for extracting teeth: so called because it was turned like a key.

tooth'less, *a.* having no teeth; without teeth.

tooth'let, *n.* a little tooth, or small toothlike projection.

tooth'let·ed, *a.* in botany, denticulate; having very small teeth or projecting points, as a leaf.

tooth ọr'nȧ·ment, in architecture, a Gothic ornament generally having the form of a square, four-leaved flower, the center projecting in a point.

TOOTH ORNAMENT

tooth pāste, a paste for brushing the teeth.

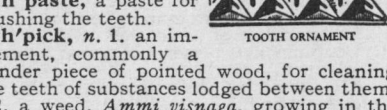

tooth'pick, *n.* 1. an implement, commonly a slender piece of pointed wood, for cleaning the teeth of substances lodged between them.

2. a weed, *Ammi visnaga*, growing in the Mediterranean region and having rays which dry and may be used for toothpicks.

3. a bowie knife. [Slang.]

tooth'pick, *a.* pointed; specifically, designating shoes having the toes shaped to a sharp point. [Slang.]

tooth'pick″ẽr, *n.* a toothpick. [Obs.]

tooth plug'gẽr, in dentistry, an instrument used in filling teeth.

tooth pow'dẽr, a powder for brushing the teeth.

tooth pulp, the soft vascular tissue filling the pulp cavity of a tooth.

tooth rash, red gum; an eruption on the face and neck occurring in teething.

tooth saç, the connective tissue that encloses the developing tooth.

tooth shell, a gastropod of the genus *Dentalium*.

tooth'sŏme, *a.* [*tooth* and *-some*.] palatable; pleasing to the taste.

tooth'sŏme·ly, *adv.* in a toothsome manner.

tooth'sŏme·ness, *n.* the quality or state of being toothsome.

tooth vī'ō·let, a plant, coralwort.

tooth'wŏrt, *n.* (a) a leafless, parasitic plant, *Lathræa squamaria*, having toothlike scales, covering its rootstock; (b) any of a number of related plants with white, toothlike roots and clusters of white, purplish, or rose flowers.

tooth'y, *a.* 1. having large or prominent teeth.

2. toothsome. [Colloq.]

too'tle, *v.i.*; tootled (-tld), *pt.*, *pp.*; tootling, *ppr.* [freq. of *toot*.] to toot in a gentle continuous manner, as on a flute.

tootle, *n.* the act or sound of tootling.

toot plant, the tutu.

toots, *n.* [from *tootsy*.] darling; dear: affectionate or playful term of address. [Slang.]

toot'sy, *n.*; *pl.* **toot'sieṣ,** [child's term of endearment.]

1. a child's or woman's small foot. [Slang.]

2. toots. [Slang.]

too'zoo, *n.* [imitative.] the ringdove. [Brit. Dial.]

top, *n.* [ME.; late AS.; akin to D. dial. *top*.]

1. a child's toy shaped somewhat like an inverted cone, with a point at its apex upon which it is spun, usually by unwinding a string.

2. in ropemaking, a conical piece of wood placed between the strands of a rope to keep the twist tight during the twisting process.

to sleep like a top; to sleep soundly.

top, *n.* [AS. *top*, a tuft or ball at the point or top of anything.]

1. originally, (a) a tuft of hair; (b) the hair of the head.

2. the head, or crown of the head.

3. the highest part, point, or surface of anything; as, the *top* of the hill.

4. the part of a plant that grows above ground; as, beet *tops*.

5. something that constitutes the uppermost part or covering of something else; specifically, (a) a lid, cover, cap, etc.; as, a box *top*, bottle *top*; (b) the upper part of an automobile body, especially a folding roof or cover; (c) a platform around the head of each lower mast of a sailing ship, to which the rigging of the topmast is attached.

SHIP'S TOP

6. a person or thing that is first in order, excellence, importance, etc.; specifically, (a) the highest degree or pitch; zenith; acme; as, at the *top* of his voice; the *top* of her career; (b) the highest rank, position, etc.; as, he's at the *top* in his profession; (c) a person in this rank, etc.; (d) the choicest part; the pick; the cream; as, the *top* of the crop.

7. the beginning, or earliest part; as, the *top* of the year.

8. in card games, the card or (in *pl.*) cards that will win the first or second round of a suit.

9. in chemistry, the most volatile part of a mixture.

10. in sports and games, (a) a stroke that hits the ball above center or near its top; (b) the forward spin given the ball by such a stroke.

11. in woolen manufacture, the combed wool ready for the spinner, from which the noils, or shorts and dust, have been removed.

12. that portion of a cut gem which is between the girdle or extreme margin and the table or flat face.

13. a method of cheating at dice by keeping one at the top of the box between the fingers.

14. [*pl.*] top boots.

on top; at the top; successful.

on top of; (a) on or at the top of; (b) resting upon; (c) in addition to; besides; (d) following immediately after.

on top of the world; in a position of great success, prosperity, happiness, etc. [Colloq.]

over the top; (a) over the front of the trench, as in attacking; (b) exceeding the assigned quota or goal.

to blow one's top; (a) to lose one's temper; (b) to become insane. [Slang.]

(*the*) *tops*; pre-eminent in quality, ability, popularity, etc.; the very best: used predicatively. [Slang.]

top, *a.* of, situated at, or being the top; uppermost; highest; as, the *top* drawer, *top* honors.

top, *v.t.*; topped (topt), *pt.*, *pp.*; topping, *ppr.* 1. to take off the top of (a plant, etc.).

2. to provide or cover with a top.

3. to be a top for.

4. to reach the top of; to be on a level with.

5. to equal or exceed in amount, height, etc.; as, the fish *topped* 75 pounds.

6. to surpass; to outdo; as, he *tops* them all at tennis.

7. to go over the top of (a rise of ground, etc.).

8. to be at the top of; to head; to lead.

9. in chemistry, to remove the volatile parts from, by distillation.

10. in dyeing, to finish with a certain dye.

11. in sports and games, (a) to hit (the ball) above center or near its top, giving it a forward spin; (b) to make (a stroke) by hitting the ball in this way.

to top off; to complete by adding a finishing touch.

top, *v.i.* to top someone or something (in any sense).

tō'pärçh, *n.* [L. *toparcha*, from Gr. *toparchēs*; *topos*, place, and *archein*, to rule.] the head of a toparchy.

tō'pärçh·y, *n.* a little state, consisting of a few cities or towns; a petty country governed by a toparch; as, Judea was formerly divided into ten *toparches*.

top'-är″mŏr, *n.* formerly, in a ship, a railing on the top supported by stanchions and equipped with netting.

tō'paz, *n.* [ME. and Fr. *topace*; L. *topazus*, from Gr. *topazos*, the yellow or oriental topaz.]

1. a native aluminum silicate, $Al_2SiO_4F_2$, occurring in white, yellow, pale-blue, or pale-green crystals: the yellow variety is used as a gem.

2. any of various similarly colored gems or semiprecious stones, as a yellow variety of sapphire and a yellow variety of quartz.

3. either of two large, brightly colored hummingbirds (genus *Topaza*) of South America.

4. in heraldry, or (tincture) in blazoning by precious stones.

false topaz; a kind of pale-yellow quartz.

smoky topaz; same as *smoky quartz* under *smoky*.

Tō·pā'zȧ, *n.* a genus of South American hummingbirds, having brilliant plumage, a long tail, and a long bill.

tō'paz·ine, *a.* resembling a topaz in yellowness and luster: used in describing the ocelli or the eyes of an insect.

tō·paz'ō·līte, *n.* [Gr. *topazos*, topaz, and *-lite*.]

a variety of garnet of a topaz-yellow or an olive-green color.

top block, in a ship, a block hung to an eyebolt in the cap, used in swaying and lowering the topmast.

top boots, boots having tops, often of a different material from the rest: used chiefly for riding.

top chain, in a ship, a chain to sling the lower yards in time of action to prevent their falling when the ropes by which they are hung are shot away. [Obs.]

top cloth, in a ship, a piece of canvas used to cover the hammocks which are lashed to the top in action. [Obs.]

top'coat, *n.* an overcoat; especially, a lightweight overcoat.

top'-drain, *v.t.*; top-drained, *pt., pp.*; top-draining, *ppr.* to drain the surface of (land).

top'-drain"ing, *n.* the act or practice of draining the surface of land.

top'-draw'er, *a.* of first importance, rank, privilege, etc.

top'-dress, *v.t.*; top-dressed (-drest), *pt., pp.*; top-dressing, *ppr.* to put top-dressing on (land).

top'-dress"ing, *n.* 1. material applied to a surface, as fertilizer on land or crops, or stones on a road.

2. the applying of such material.

tōpe, *n.* [Cornish.] a fish of the shark family, *Galeus canis*, resembling the dogfish.

tōpe, *n.* a wren, *Troglodytes parvulus*. [Brit. Dial.]

tōpe, *n.* [Tamil *tōpu*.] in India, a grove or clump of trees; as, a mango *tope*.

tōpe, *n.* [Sans. *stûpa*, a mound.] a Buddhist shrine in the form of a dome with a cupola.

tōpe, *v.t* and *v.i.*; toped (tōpt), *pt., pp.*; toping, *ppr.* [Fr. *toper*, to accept the stakes in gambling; present Eng. meaning prob. from the custom of drinking to the conclusion of the wager.] to drink hard; to drink (alcoholic liquor) to excess. [Archaic.]

tō·pee', *n.* [Hind. *topī*.] in India, a hat or cap, especially a pith sun helmet: also *topi*.

tō'pēr, *n.* a person who topes; one who drinks intoxicants to excess; a drunkard.

top'-flight' (-flīt'), *a.* best; first-rate. [Colloq.]

top'full', *a.* full to the brim.

top"gal'lănt (*nautically*, tŏ-gal'ănt), *a.* 1. situated above the topmast and below the royal mast on a sailing ship.

2. higher than the adjoining parts of the ship: said of a rail, deck, etc.

3. highest; splendid; lofty.

top"gal'lănt, *n.* 1. a topgallant mast, sail, spar, etc.

2. anything high; an elevated part.

3. summit; zenith. [Rare.]

toph, *n.* [L. *tophus*, sandstone.] tufa.

tō·phā'ceous, *a.* gritty; sandy; rough; stony.

top'-ham"pēr, *n.* 1. the upper masts, spars, and rigging of a sailing ship, usually kept aloft.

2. rigging, spars, etc. not needed immediately and an encumbrance aloft or on deck. Also *top hamper*.

top hat, a tall, black, cylindrical hat, usually of silk, worn by men in formal dress.

tōphe (tōf), *n.* tufa.

top'-heav"i·ness (-hev"), *n.* the quality or state of being top-heavy.

top'-heav"y, *a.* heavier at the top than below, so as to be likely to fall over or collapse; overweighted at the top with stacked objects: also used figuratively, as of an overcapitalized financial structure.

Tō'phet, Tō'pheth (tō'fet), *n.* [ME.; Heb. *tōpheth*, perh. altar; perh. from Aram.]

1. in the Old Testament, apparently a place where human sacrifices by fire were made to Moloch, possibly in the Valley of Hinnom.

2. hell.

toph'in, *n.* same as *toph*.

top'-hōle', *a.* first-rate. [Brit. Slang.]

tō'phus, *n.*; *pl.* **tō'phī,** [L., *tufa*.]

1. in medicine, an abnormal mineral deposit, as of calcium carbonate, about the joints, on the roots of the teeth, etc., in a person who has the gout.

2. tufa.

toph"y·per·i·drō'sis, *n.* [Gr. *topos*, place, *hyper*, over, and *hidros*, sweat.] excessive local sweating.

tō·pī', *n.* [Anglo-Ind.] in India, a topee.

top·i·ār'i·ăn, *a.* pertaining to or practicing topiary work.

top'i·ār·y, *a.* [L. *topiarius*, an ornamental gardener.] designating or of the art of trimming and training shrubs or trees into unnatural, ornamental shapes.

tō'pi·ăr·y, *n.*; *pl.* **tō'pi·ăr·ies,** 1. topiary art or work.

2. a topiary garden.

top'iç, *n.* [Fr. *topique*, from L. *topica*, from Gr. *topikos*, local.]

1. formerly, a kind of consideration suitable for rhetorical discourse.

2. the subject of a paragraph, essay, speech, etc.

3. a subject for discussion.

The principles of freedom and the *topics* of government shall always be interesting to mankind. —George Washington.

4. a heading or item in an outline.

5. a principle of persuasion. [Obs.]

Contumacious persons whom no *topics* can work upon. —Wilkins.

6. in medicine, an external remedy, as a plaster, a poultice, etc. [Obs.]

Syn.—question, theme, subject.

top'iç, *a.* local; topical. [Obs.]

top'iç·ăl, *a.* 1. pertaining to a particular place; limited; local; localized.

2. of or using a topic or topics.

3. having to do with topics of the day; of current or local interest; as, *topical* allusions in literature.

4. in medicine, of or for a particular part of the body; as, a *topical* remedy.

5. characteristic of a topic; hence, merely probable. [Obs.]

top'iç·ăl·ly, *adv.* in a topical manner.

top kick, a first sergeant. [Military Slang.]

top'knot (-not), *n.* 1. a knot or bow, as of ribbon, worn by women on the top of the head.

2. (a) a tuft of hair on the crown of the head of a person or animal; (b) a tuft of feathers on a bird's head.

3. a flatfish of European seas.

4. any domestic fowl having a tufted crest.

top'less, *a.* 1. having no top; specifically, designating or wearing a costume that exposes the breasts.

2. seeming to have no top; very high; as, a *topless* tower.

3. supreme; having no superior; that cannot be topped. [Obs.]

top'-lev'el, *a.* 1. of or by persons of the highest office or rank.

2. in the highest office or rank.

top light (līt), a large lantern hung in the upper rigging of a vessel.

top"loft'i·ness, *n.* the quality of being toplofty. [Colloq.]

top'loft'y, *a.* lofty in manner; haughty; pompous; supercilious. [Colloq.]

top'măn, *n.*; *pl.* **top'men,** 1. the man who stands above in sawing.

2. a sailor whose station is in a top.

top'măst, *n.* the second mast above the deck of a sailing ship, supported by the lower mast and often supporting a topgallant mast in turn.

top min'nōw, any of a group of small surface-feeding fish that produce their young fully formed, as a small fresh-water fish, *Gambusia patruelis*, of the southern parts of the United States; also, any fish of the genus *Zygonectes*.

top'mōst, *a.* at the very top; highest; uppermost; as, the *topmost* cliff, the *topmost* branch of a tree.

top'-notch', *a.* first-rate; best. [Colloq.]

tō·pog'ră·phēr, *n.* 1. an expert or specialist in topography.

2. a person who describes or maps the topography of a place or region.

top·ō·graph'iç, *a.* topographical.

top·ō·graph'iç·ăl, *a.* of, pertaining to, or done by topography.

topographical adolescence or *youth*; in physical geography, the second stage in the development of the topographical features of a land area, characterized by the presence of well-defined valleys cut by main streams but the absence of a highly developed system of drainage.

topographical infancy; in physical geography, the character of a region newly exposed to the action of water, when lakes abound in slight hollows, and the smooth nearly level tracts have narrow stream channels not well established.

topographical maturity; in physical geography, the third stage in the development of the topographical features of a region, wherein is found the greatest degree and variety of relief caused by the processes of denudation, such as the sea cutting back the coast line in one place, and building it out in another, rivers establishing themselves by conformation to the underlying rocks cutting deep trenchlike valleys, while the atmospheric agencies widen the valleys, slowly wearing down and washing away the sides and tops of the hills.

topographical old age; in physical geography, the fourth stage in the development of the topographical features of a district. The featureless condition of old age is the result of the continued effect of the denuding or degrading processes. The region becomes worn down to a nearly plane surface, through which sluggish streams meander. When this process is complete the country is said to be base-leveled.

top·ō·graph'iç·ăl·ly, *adv.* as regards topography; in the manner of topography.

top·ō·graph'içs, *n.* topography. [Rare.]

tō·pog'ră·phist, *n.* a topographer.

tō·pog'ră·phy, *n.*; *pl.* **tō·pog'ră·phies,** [Gr. *topos*, a place, and *-graphy*.]

1. originally, the accurate and detailed description of a particular place, city, town, district, estate, parish, or tract of land.

2. the science of drawing on maps and charts or otherwise representing the surface features of a region, including hills, valleys, rivers, lakes, canals, bridges, roads, etc.

3. these surface features.

4. topographic surveying.

5. a study or description of a region, system, or part of the body showing specific relations of component parts as to shape, size, position, etc.; as, cerebral *topography*.

military topography; the minute description of places with special reference to their adaptability to military purposes.

tō·pol'ā·try, *n.* [Gr. *topos*, a place, and *latreia*, service, worship.] worship of or excessive reverence for a place or places. [Rare.]

tō·pol'ō·ġy, *n.* [Gr. *topos*, a place, and *-logy*.]

1. a topographical study of a specific object, entity, place, etc.; as, the *topology* of the mind.

2. in mathematics, the study of those properties of geometric figures that remain unchanged even when under distortion, so long as no surfaces are torn.

3. in medicine, the topographical anatomy of a body region.

tō"pō·neū·rō'sis, *n.* [Gr. *topos*, place, and *neurosis*.] a neurosis affecting a limited region.

tō·pon'ō·my, *n.* [Gr. *topos*, a place, and *onoma*, a name.] the place names of a country or district, or a register of such names.

top'ō·nym, *n.* [from *toponymy*.]

1. a name of a place.

2. a name that indicates origin, natural locale, etc., as in zoological nomenclature.

tō·pon'y·măl, *a.* toponymic. [Rare.]

top·ō·nym'iç, *a.* 1. of a toponym or toponyms.

2. having to do with toponymy.

top·ō·nym'iç·ăl, *a.* toponymic.

tō·pon'y·my, *n.* [Gr. *topos*, place, and *onoma*, *onyma*, name.]

1. the place names of a country, district, etc. or the study of these.

2. in anatomy, the nomenclature of the regions of the body. [Rare.]

tō·pō·phō'bi·ȧ, *n.* [Gr. *topos*, place, and *phobos*, fear.] a marked dread of particular places.

top'ō·phōne, *n.* [Gr. *topos*, place, and *phōnē*, voice.] an instrument for localizing the direction of sounds, as in a fog at sea.

top pen'dănt, in nautical usage, a stout rope by which topmasts are hoisted or lowered.

top'pēr, *n.* 1. a device for removing tops, as of vegetables.

2. a top-notch person or thing. [Slang.]

3. (a) a top hat; (b) a topcoat; especially, a woman's short, loose-fitting topcoat. [Slang.]

top'ping, *a.* 1. that tops in degree, rank, etc.

2. superior; excellent; first-rate. [Brit. Colloq.]

3. proud; haughty. [Colloq.]

4. fine; noble; gallant. [Colloq.]

top'ping, *n.* 1. the act of one who or that which tops.

2. [*pl.*] that which is cut off, as a top of a tree.

3. in nautical usage, the act of pulling one extremity of a yard or boom higher than the other.

4. [*pl.*] that which comes from hemp in the process of hatcheling.

5. that which tops, sets off, of forms the upper part of anything, as a crest of hair upon the head.

6. the tail of an artificial fly.

top′ping lift, in nautical usage, a large, strong tackle employed to lift or top the outer end of a gaff or boom, especially of a mainsail.

top′ping·ly, *adv.* in a topping manner.

top′ple, *v.i.*; toppled (-pld), *pt., pp.*; toppling, *ppr.* 1. to fall top forward; to pitch or tumble down; to fall over from top-heaviness, etc. (often with *over*).

Though castles *topple* on their warders heads. —Shak.

2. to overhang, as if ready to fall; to overbalance; to totter.

top′ple, *v.t.* to cause to topple; to overturn; to upset.

top′-proud, *a.* proud to the highest degree. [Obs.]

top′rōpe, *n.* in nautical usage, a rope to sway up a topmast, etc.

top′sāil (*or* -sl), *n.* in nautical usage, (a) in a square-rigged vessel, a sail directly above the lowest sail of a mast; (b) in a fore-and-aft-rigged vessel, the sail next above the gaff of a fore-and-aft sail.

double topsails; two sails on a square-rigged vessel corresponding in width to the topsail formerly carried on a square-rigger, but only half as high. The upper sail has a yard which may be hoisted or lowered, but the yard of the lower sail is stationary.

rolling topsail; a topsail which may be taken in around a roller under the yard.

topsail schooner; a fore-and-aft-rigged schooner carrying a square topsail and a topgallant sail on the foretopmast.

top′sāil yärd, a yard to which a topsail is bent.

tops and bot′tŏms, small rolls of dough baked, halved, and browned in an oven: used as food for infants.

top saw, the upper saw of a pair in a circular sawmill.

top saw′yẽr, 1. the sawyer who takes the upper stand in a saw pit.

2. figuratively, one who holds a higher position than another; a chief over others. [Colloq.]

3. a prominent person [Colloq.]

top′-sē′çret, *a.* designating or of military information or diplomatic material of the greatest secrecy.

top ser′ġeănt (sär′), in the United States Army, a first sergeant. [Colloq.]

top′-shāped (-shāpt), *a.* in botany, having the shape of a top; inversely conical.

top shell, any of the shells of the various species of the family *Trochidæ*. Many of them are large and handsome.

top′sīde′, *n.* [*usually in pl.*] the part of a ship's side above the water line.

top′sīde′, *adv.* on or to the upper side of a ship; on deck.

tops′măn, *n.*; *pl.* **tops′men,** 1. a chief or head cattle drover. [Scot. and Brit. Dial.]

2. in nautical usage, a topman.

top′soil, *n.* the uppermost layer of soil, usually darker and richer than the subsoil; surface soil.

top′soil, *v.t.* to remove the topsoil from (land).

top′stōne, *n.* a stone that is placed on the top or that forms the top.

top″sy-tûr′vi·ly, *adv.* in a topsy-turvy manner.

top″sy-tûr′vi·ness, *n.* the quality or state of being topsy-turvy.

top′sy-tûr′vy, *a.* and *adv.* [earlier *topsytervy*; prob. from *top*, highest part, and ME. *terven*, to roll.]

1. upside down; in a reversed condition.

2. in confusion or disorder.

top′sy-tûr′vy, *n.* 1. a topsy-turvy condition; inverted state.

2. a state of confusion.

top′sy-tûr′vy, *v.t.*; topsy-turvied, *pt., pp.*; topsy-turvying, *ppr.* to turn upside down; to turn topsy-turvy.

top taç′kle, a large tackle hooked to the lower end of the topmast toprope, and to the deck.

top-tim″bẽr, *n.* any of the highest timbers in the side of a vessel.

tōque (tōk), *n.* [Fr., a cap, from Celt. *toc*, a hat or bonnet.]

1. a woman's small, round, close-fitting hat, with or without a brim: a modification of a 16th-century, small, plumed hat, worn by men and women.

2. a long woolen cap; as, the *toque* of a toboggan club.

3. the bonnet macaque, *Macacus sinicus*; also, any monkey resembling it.

4. a small nominal money of account used in trading on some parts of the west coast of Africa.

tọr, *n.* [ME.; AS. *torr*, a tower, rock; L. *turris*.] a high, rocky hill.

tō′rȧ, *n.* an African antelope, *Alcelaphus tora*.

tō′rȧh, tō′rȧ, *n.*; *pl.* **tō′rōth,** [Heb. *tōrāh*, a law.] in Judaism, (a) learning, law, instruction, etc.; (b) the whole body of Jewish religious literature, including the Scripture, the Talmud, etc.; (c) [*usually* T–] the Pentateuch; also, a parchment scroll containing the Pentateuch.

tọr′bẽrn·īte, *n.* [after *Torbern* O. Bergmann, a Swedish chemist.] a mineral, occurring native in tabular crystals, being a phosphate of uranium and copper: called also *copper uranite*.

tọrç, *n.* same as *torque*.

tọr′cel, *n.* the larva of a South African fly parasitic beneath the human skin.

tọrch, *n.* [OFr. *torche*; LL. *tortia*, a torch, from L. *tortus*, twisted.]

1. a portable light consisting of a long piece of resinous wood, or twisted tow dipped in tallow, etc., flaming at one end; a link; a flambeau.

2. anything considered as a source of enlightenment, illumination, inspiration, etc.; as, the *torch* of science.

3. any of various portable devices for producing a very hot flame, used in welding, burning off paint, etc.

4. a flashlight. [Brit.]

torch dance; a dance in which lighted torches are carried.

torch singer; a person who sings torch songs.

torch song; a popular and sentimental song, especially portraying unrequited love.

tọrch, *v.t.*; torched (tọrcht), *pt., pp.*; torching, *ppr.* in plastering, to point, as the inside joints of slating laid on lath, with lime and hair.

tọrch′beăr″ẽr, *n.* 1. one who carries a torch.

2. the highest rank awarded a Campfire Girl.

3. one who brings enlightenment, inspiration, truth, etc.

tọrch′ẽr, *n.* one who or that which gives light. [Rare.]

tọrch·iēr′, tọrch·iēre′, *n.* [from Fr. *torchère*, small, high candlestand, from OFr. *torche*, a torch.] a floor lamp with a reflector bowl and no shade, for casting light upward so as to give indirect illumination.

tọrch′light (-līt,) *a.* done or carried on by torchlights.

tọrch′light, *n.* the light of a torch or torches.

tọrch lil′y, the flameflower.

tọr·chon′, *n.* [Fr.] a dishcloth; a duster.

torchon board; a pasteboard of torchon paper, used by artists.

torchon lace; (a) a strong, bobbin lace made of coarse linen thread in simple, open, geometric patterns; (b) an imitation of this made by machine.

torchon paper; a paper with a rough surface used by painters in water colors.

tọrch rāce, a race held at certain festivals among the ancient Greeks, in which the runners carried lighted torches: the torches were passed from one runner to another, and the contestant who first reached the goal with his torch still burning won the race.

tọrch this′tle (this′l), a cactus of the genus *Cereus*, sometimes used by North American Indians as torches.

tọrch′wood, *n.* any resinous wood suitable for torches; also, any of a number of related trees furnishing such wood, as *Amyris sylvatica*, Florida torchwood.

tọrch′wŏrt, *n.* the mullein.

tōre, *v.* alternative past tense of *tear* (to pull apart).

tōre, *n.* [W. *tori*, to cut.] the dead grass that remains on mowing land in winter and spring. [Brit. Dial.]

tōre, *n.* [L. *torus*, a raised ornament.] in architecture and geometry, a torus.

tọr′ē·ȧ·dọr″, *n.* [Sp., from *toro*, a bull.] a bullfighter, especially one who fights on horseback: term no longer used in bullfighting.

tō·re′rō, *n.*; *pl.* **tō·re′rōs,** [Sp., from *torear*, to fight bulls.] a bullfighter on foot.

tor′et, *n.* a turret. [Obs.]

tō·reu̇·mȧ·tog′rȧ·phy, *n.* [Gr. *toreuma*, work in relief, and *-graphy*.] the description of works in toreutics.

tō·reu̇·mȧ·tol′ō·ġy, *n.* the science or art of toreutics, or a treatise on it.

tō·reu̇′tiç, *a.* [Gr. *toreutikos*, pertaining to work in relief.] designating or of embossed or chased work, especially in metal.

tō·reu̇′tiçs, *n.pl.* [*construed as sing.*] the art of making toreutic work.

tọr′goch, *n.* [W., lit., red belly.] the red-bellied lake trout, *Salmo salvelinus*.

tō′rī, *n.* plural of *torus*.

tọr′iç, *a.* of or shaped like a torus.

tọr′iç lens, a lens of which one surface is a segment of the surface of a torus: used especially in eyeglasses.

tō′ri·ī, *n.*; *pl.* **tō′ri·ī,** [Japan.] a gateway at the entrance to a Japanese Shinto temple, consisting of two uprights supporting a curved lintel, with a straight crosspiece below.

TORII

Tō·rin·ēse′, *a.* of or belonging to Turin, a city in northwestern Italy.

Tō·rin·ēse′, *n.* a native or inhabitant of Turin.

tọr′ment, *n.* [OFr., from L. *tormentum*, a rack, an instrument of torture.]

1. an engine for casting stones. [Obs.]

2. originally, an instrument of torture; also, torture.

3. that which gives pain, anxiety, or annoyance.

4. extreme pain or anguish, physical or mental; suffering; agony.

5. a victim. [Rare.]

tọr·ment′, *v.t.*; tormented, *pt., pp.*; tormenting, *ppr.* 1. to torture. [Rare.]

2. to put to extreme physical pain or mental anguish; to inflict excruciating pain and misery upon.

3. to twist.

4. to tease; to subject to annoyance; to plague.

5. to put into great agitation; to stir up. [Obs.]

tọr·ment′ed, *a.* agonized; suffering.

tọr·ment′ẽr, *n.* same as *tormentor*.

tọr′men·til, *n.* [Fr. *tormentille*, from L. *tormentum*, pain.] a yellow-flowered, trailing plant, *Potentilla tormentilla*, whose root is used in medicine, dyeing, and tanning: also called *septfoil*.

TORMENTIL (*Potentilla tormentilla*)

Tọr·men·til′lȧ, *n.* 1. a former genus of the rose family: now included in the genus *Potentilla*.

2. [t–] same as *tormentil*.

tọr·ment′ing, *a.* that torments; that causes pain, distress, or anguish; teasing; vexing; as, a *tormenting* toothache, a *tormenting* child.

tọr·ment′ing·ly, *adv.* in a tormenting manner.

tọr·ment′ŏr, *n.* 1. one who or that which torments.

2. one who inflicts penal anguish or tortures. [Obs.]

3. an instrument for breaking up stiff soil, resembling a harrow, but running on wheels.

4. a meat fork used by a ship's cook.

5. in the theater, either of the wings or curtains projecting out onto each side of the stage, directly behind the proscenium: so called because it obstructs a full view of the stage by those sitting at the sides.

6. in motion pictures, a covered screen for absorbing echoes on a set.

tọr·ment′ress, *n.* a woman who torments.

tọr′ment·ry, *n.* pain; anguish. [Archaic.]

tọr·men′tum, *n.*; *pl.* **tọr·men′tȧ,** [L.] any ancient war machine used in hurling projectiles.

tọr′mi·nȧ, *n.pl.* [L.] severe griping pains in the bowels; gripes; colic.

tọr′mi·nous, *a.* of the character of tormina; griping.

tọr′mō·dont, *a.* [Gr. *tormos*, a hole, socket, and *-odont*.] socketed, as teeth. [Rare.]

tọrn, *v.* alternative past participle of *tear* (to pull apart)

tọr·nad′iç, *a.* of or like a tornado.

tọr·nā′dō, *n.*; *pl.* **tọr·nā′dōeṣ, tōr·nā′dōṣ,** [Sp. *tronado,* thunder, thunderstorm, from *tronar,* to thunder; L. *tonare,* to thunder; prob. merged with Sp. *tornar,* to turn.]
 1. a violent whirling wind, especially in the central United States, accompanied by a rapidly rotating, funnel-shaped cloud that usually destroys everything along its narrow path.
 2. any whirlwind or hurricane.

tọr·nā′dō cel′lăr, a cyclone cellar.

tọr·nā′dō lamp, a lamp so constructed that violent currents of air cannot reach the flame.

tọr·nā′dō lan′tērn, a tornado lamp.

tọr·nā′ri·ȧ, *n.* [L. *tornus,* a lathe, and *-aria.*] the free-swimming larva of any species of *Balanoglossus.*

tọr·nil′lȧ, tọr·nil′lō, *n.* [Sp., a screw.] a kind of bean, the screw-pod mesquite.

tō′roid, *n.* [from *tore* (torus), and *-oid.*] in geometry, a surface, or its enclosed solid, generated by any closed plane curve rotating about a straight line in its own plane: a *torus* is a specialized form of *toroid.*

tō·roid′ăl, *a.* in geometry, of or pertaining to a tore or toroid.

tō·rōse′, *a.* [L. *torosus,* full of muscle, brawny, from *torus,* muscle.]
 1. bulging, knobbed, protuberant, swollen, etc.
 2. in botany, cylindrical, with swellings at intervals.

tō·ros′i·ty, *n.* the state of being torose.

tō′rō·tō′rō, *n.* [native name.] a kingfisher, *Syma torotoro,* native to New Guinea.

tō′rouṣ, *a.* same as *torose.*

tọr·ped′i·nous, *a.* pertaining to or resembling a torpedo. [Rare.]

tọr·pē′dō, *n.*; *pl.* **tọr·pē′dōeṣ,** [L., from *torpere,* to be stiff, numb, or torpid.]
 1. a fish of the genus *Torpedo*; an electric ray; a crampfish; a numbfish.
 2. [T–] a genus of elasmobranchiate fishes, the electric ray.
 3. a large, cigar-shaped, self-propelled, underwater projectile for launching against enemy ships from a submarine, airplane, etc.: it explodes on contact by means of a timing mechanism or by radio control.
 4. a metal case containing explosives, especially one used as an underwater mine.
 5. a small firework consisting of a percussion cap and gravel wrapped in tissue paper, which explodes with a loud report when thrown against a hard surface.
 6. an explosive cartridge placed on a railroad track and detonated by a train wheel as a signal to the crew.
 7. an explosive cartridge lowered into oil wells, where it is detonated to clear the bore or break through into the oil pocket.
 8. a gangster or gunman serving as a bodyguard, ready to shoot or attack with no warning. [Slang.]

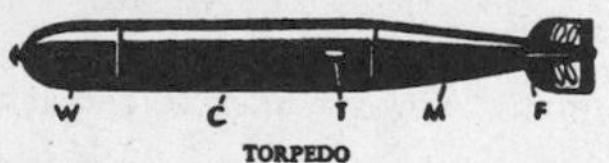

TORPEDO
W, war head; C, compressed air chamber; T, trigger; M, motor; F, fins, propellers, and rudder

tọr·pē′dō, *v.t.*; torpedoed, *pt., pp.*; torpedoing, *ppr.* to destroy, attack, damage, or ruin with or as with a torpedo.

tọr·pē′dō, *v.i.* to use torpedoes.

tọr·pē′dō bōat, a small, fast, maneuverable warship for attacking with torpedoes, armed with only light guns.

tọr·pē′dō-bōat de·stroy′ēr, a warship like a torpedo boat but larger and more heavily armed, originally designed to destroy enemy torpedo boats but later used offensively as a torpedo boat.

tōr·pē′dō bod′y, a design of automobile body somewhat like that of a submarine torpedo, with flush sides for reducing wind resistance.

tọr·pē′dō net, a network of chains or metal bars, suspended beneath the surface of the water around a ship as a protection against torpedoes.

tọr·pē′dō tūbe, a tube for launching torpedoes, located in surface vessels below or close to the water line.

tọr′pent, *a.* [L. *torpens,* benumbed.] benumbed; torpid; having no motion or activity; incapable of motion. [Rare.]

tọr′pent, *n.* in medicine, that which lessens the exertion of the irritative motions.

tọr·pes′cence, *n.* a state of insensibility; torpidness; numbness; stupidity.

tọr·pes′cent, *a.* [L. *torpescens,* growing numb.] becoming torpid or numb.

tọr′pid, *a.* [L. *torpidus,* torpid.]
 1. having lost temporarily all or part of the power of motion or sensation, as a hibernating animal; dormant; inactive; numb.
 2. dull; stupid; sluggish; apathetic.

tọr′pid, *n.* at Oxford University, a second-class racing boat; also, a member of its crew.

tọr·pid′i·ty, *n.* the condition or quality of being torpid.

tọr′pid·ly, *adv.* in a dull, inactive manner.

tọr′pid·ness, *n.* torpidity.

tọr′pi·fȳ, *v.t.*; torpified, *pt., pp.*; torpifying, *ppr.* to make torpid.

tọr′pi·tūde, *n.* torpor. [Rare.]

tọr′pŏr, *n.* [L.] 1. the state of being dormant or inactive; temporary loss of all or part of the power of motion or sensation; stupor.
 2. dullness; laziness; sluggishness; apathy.

tọr·pŏr·if′iç, *a.* producing or tending to produce torpor.

tọr′quāte, *a.* having a torques; collared.

tọr′quā·ted, *a.* 1. decorated or supplied with a torque; wearing a torque.
 2. torquate.

tọrque (tọrk), *n.* [L. *torquis,* from *torquere,* to twist.]
 1. a necklace or collar of twisted metal, worn in ancient times by the Teutons, Gauls, Britons, etc. as a symbol of rank and command.
 2. in physics, (a) a force or combination of forces that produces or tends to produce a twisting or rotating motion (called *torsion*); (b) the tendency to produce torsion.
 3. in optics, a rotary effect produced by some crystals and liquids on the plane of polarization of light passing through them.

tọrqued (tọrkt), *a.* twisted; formed like a torque.

tọr′quēṣ, *n.* 1. a torque (sense 1). [Rare.]
 2. a natural collar; a ring or collar of feathers, hair, or modified skin around the neck of an animal or bird, of a color distinct from the color of the rest of the body.

tor·rē·faç′tion, *n.* the act of torrefying or the state of being torrefied.

tor′rē·fȳ, *v.t.*; torrefied, *pt., pp.*; torrefying, *ppr.* [Fr. *torréfier*; L. *torrefacere*; *torrere,* to dry or roast by heat, and *facere,* to make.] to dry, parch, scorch, or roast by exposure to heat; specifically, (a) [Rare.] in metallurgy, to roast or scorch, as metallic ores; (b) in pharmacy, to dry or parch, as some drugs. Also spelled *torrify.*

Tor′renṣ sys′tem, a system of registering land titles, long existing in parts of Europe, perfected and drafted as a law for South Australia in 1858, by Sir Robert Richard Torrens, and since then adopted by several States of the United States.

tor′rent, *n.* [Fr. *torrent,* from L. *torrens (-entis),* a torrent.]
 1. a violent, rushing stream, especially of water.
 2. a violent, rapid, or profuse flow of mail, words, etc.; a flood; a rush.
 3. a heavy fall of rain.

tor′rent, *a.* of or like a torrent; as, waves of *torrent* fire. [Rare.]

tor′rent bōw, a bow or arch of rainbowlike or prismatic colors formed by the refraction and reflection of rays of light from the spray of a torrent.

tor′rent duck, a merganser inhabiting the swift streams and rivers of the Andes.

tor·ren′tiăl (-shăl), *a.* 1. of, or having the nature of, a torrent.
 2. like a torrent, as in violence, swiftness, copiousness, etc.; overwhelming; outpouring.
 3. resulting from the action of a torrent.

tor·ren′tiăl·ly, *adv.* in the manner of a torrent; overwhelmingly.

tor′ren·tine, *a.* torrential. [Rare.]

Tor′rey·ȧ, *n.* [after Dr. J. *Torrey,* an American botanist.] a genus of conifers, including the California nutmeg, *Torreya californica,* and the Florida stinking cedar, *Torreya taxifolia.*

Tor·ri·cel′li·ăn, *a.* of or relating to Torricelli (1608–1647), an Italian physicist and mathematician, who discovered the principle of the barometer.
 Torricellian tube; a glass tube, open at one end and hermetically sealed at the other, such as is used in the barometer.
 Torricellian vacuum; a vacuum produced by filling a Torricellian tube with mercury and, after immersing the open end in a vessel of mercury, allowing the enclosed mercury to descend till it is counterbalanced by the weight of an equal column of the atmosphere, as in the barometer.

tor′rid, *a.* [L. *torridus,* from *torrere,* to roast.]
 1. dried by or subjected to intense heat, especially of the sun; scorched; parched; arid.
 2. so hot as to be parching or oppressive; scorching.
 3. highly passionate, ardent, zealous, etc.
 Torrid Zone; the area of the earth between the Tropic of Cancer and the Tropic of Capricorn and divided by the equator.

tor·rid′i·ty, *n.* the state or quality of being torrid; severe heat.

tor′rid·ness, *n.* torridity.

tor′ri·fy, *v.t.*; torrified, *pt., pp.*; torrifying, *ppr.* to torrefy.

tọr·sāde′, *n.* [Fr.] 1. molded decoration in the shape of a twisted rope or cord.
 2. a twisted cord used in draperies, etc.

tọrse, *n.* a torso.

tọrse, *n.* [OFr. *torse,* from L. *torquere,* to twist.]
 1. in heraldry, a wreath.
 2. in mathematics, a single curved surface, the consecutive positions of whose rectilinear generatrix lie in the same plane.

tọr′sel, *n.* [dim. from *torse.*] a piece of timber, etc. laid in brickwork or masonry as a support for the end of a crossbeam.

tọr′sï, *n.* alternative plural of *torso.*

tọr·si·bil′i·ty, *n.* ability to undergo, or resistance to, torsion.

tọr′sion, *n.* [LL. *torsio,* from L. *torquere,* to twist.]
 1. the act of twisting or the state of being twisted; specifically, (a) in physics, the alteration in the relative position of the parts of any solid due to rotation about a common axis, as by twisting one end of a wire or rod while the other remains fixed; (b) the tendency of a twisted wire, bar, etc. to return to its untwisted condition; (c) in botany, a spiral twist, as of a vine.
 2. griping, as in colic. [Obs.]
 3. distortion. [Rare.]
 angle of torsion; (a) the angle passed through by any point at one end of a body that is twisted, while the other end remains fixed; (b) in a tortuous curve, or curve of double curvature, the angle between any two consecutive osculating planes.
 torsion balance; see under *balance.*
 torsion electrometer; a torsion balance used to measure the intensity of electricity.
 torsion scale; a form of scale having wires or metal strips as fulcrums which are subjected to torsion by the addition of a weight.

tọr′sion·ăl, *a.* relating to, producing, or caused by torsion.

tọr′sive, *a.* in botany, twisted spirally.

tọrsk, *n.*; *pl.* **tọrsk** or **tọrsks,** [Sw. and Dan. *torsk,* a codfish.]
 1. a large, edible sea fish of the genus *Brosmius,* related to the cod, found among the Orkney and Shetland Islands: also called *cusk.*

TORSK (*Brosmius brosme*)

 2. a codfish.

tọr′sō, *n.*; *pl.* **tọr′sōṣ, tọr′sï,** [It., a stump, trunk of a statue; L. *thyrsus,* a stalk, stem; Gr. *thyrsos,* a stem, wand.]
 1. the trunk of a statue of the nude human figure, especially of such a statue lacking the head and limbs.
 2. the trunk of the human body.
 3. any unfinished or fragmentary piece of work.

tọr′sō mūr′dēr, a murder in which the victim's body is dismembered.

tọrt, *n.* [Fr., from L. *tortus,* twisted.]
 1. in law, a wrongful act (not involving a breach of contract) resulting in an injury, loss, or damage, for which the injured party can bring civil action, as trespass, assault and battery, defamation, and the like.
 2. injury. [Obs.]
 tort feasor; one guilty of tort.

tọrt, *a.* taut. [Rare.]

tọr'tȧ, *n.* [Sp., a cake.] the silver ore mixture of the patio process of amalgamation as spread out in a layer.

tọr'teau (-tō), *n.* [OFr., a round cake.] in heraldry, a red roundel.

tọr·ti·çol'lis, *n.* [LL., from L. *tortus*, twisted, and *collum*, neck.] in medicine, a condition of persistent involuntary contraction of the cervical muscles, producing a twisting of the neck and an unnatural position of the head; wryneck.

tọr'tile, *a.* [L. *tortilis*.] twisted or coiled.

tọr·til'i·ty, *n.* the state of being twisted.

tọr·til'lȧ (-tē'yȧ), *n.* [Sp.] a large, round, thin, unleavened cake prepared from a paste made of corn, baked on a heated iron plate or stone slab: used as a substitute for bread in Mexico.

tọr'tion, *n.* torsion. [Obs.]

tọr'tious (-shus), *a.* 1. injurious; wicked; wrong. [Obs.]

2. in law, involving or implying tort.

tọr'tious·ly, *adv.* by tort or injury; wrongfully.

tọr'tive, *a.* [L. *tortus*, twisted.] twisted; wreathed. [Rare.]

tọr'toise (-tis), *n.*; *pl.* **tọr'tois·eṣ** or **tọr'toise,** [ME. *tortuce*; ML. *tortuca*; prob. from It. *tortuca*, altered from *tartaruca*, from Gr. *tartaruchos*, evil demon: so called because in Greek belief the tortoise was a demon.]

1. a turtle; any reptile of the order *Chelonia* or *Testudinata*, especially one that lives on land.

2. a testudo (movable shelter).

tọr'toise bee'tle, any of a group of small beetles of the family *Cassididæ*, having elytra shielding the body and projecting somewhat like the carapace of a tortoise.

tọr'toise flow'ēr, the turtlehead, a plant of the genus *Chelone*.

tọr'toise plant, a South African plant, *Testudinaria elephantipes*, related to the yams: so called from the resemblance of its rootstock to a tortoise shell: also called *elephant's-foot*.

tọr'toise shell, 1. the hard, mottled, yellow-and-brown shell or horny plates of the tortoise, especially the shell of the hawkbill turtle, *Eretmochelys imbricata*, used extensively in the manufacture of combs, spectacle frames, etc., and in inlay and other ornamental work: it becomes very plastic when heated.

2. a tortoise-shell butterfly.

tọr'toise-shell, *a.* 1. made of tortoise shell or of a synthetic substance like it.

2. resembling tortoise shell, either in coloration or appearance.

tortoise-shell butterfly; any of several species of black and yellow-brown butterflies of the genus *Aglais* with markings resembling those of tortoise shell.

tortoise-shell cat; a variety of the domestic cat, of a color resembling tortoise shell.

tortoise-shell turtle; a species of turtle inhabiting tropical seas: also called *hawksbill* and *caret*.

tọr'tri·cid, *a.* 1. of or belonging to the lepidopterous family *Tortricidæ*.

2. belonging to the ophidian family *Tortricidæ*.

tọr'tri·cid, *n.* 1. a moth of the family *Tortricidæ*.

2. a snake of the family *Tortricidæ*.

Tọr·tric'i·dae, *n.pl.* 1. a family of small, broad-bodied moths, the leaf rollers.

2. a family of narrow-bodied snakes, native to the tropics, typified by the genus *Tortrix*.

Tọr'trix, *n.* [from L. *tortor*, a torturer.]

1. a genus of lepidopterous insects, the type of the family *Tortricidæ*; the leaf roller moths. The *Tortrix pomonana*, or apple moth, in the larval state, feeds on the pulpy substance of the apple and plum. *Tortrix viridana* feeds on the leaves of the oak, and *Tortrix vitana*, in the larval state, eats the leaves of vines in France.

2. the typical genus of a family of cylindrical snakes, having rudimentary hind limbs and a short conic tail, and inhabiting tropical America.

tọr'tū·lous, *a.* torulose. [Rare.]

tọr'tū·ōse (-chū), *a.* wreathed; twisted; winding.

tọr·tū·os'i·ty, *n.* 1. the quality or condition of being tortuous.

2. *pl.* **tọr·tū·os'i·tieṣ,** a twist, turn, winding, etc.

tọr'tū·ous, *a.* [L. *tortuosus*, tortuous, from *torquere*, to twist.]

1. twisted; full of turns, curves, or windings; crooked; winding; as, a *tortuous* train.

2. not straightforward; devious; specifically, deceitful; immoral.

3. oblique: applied in astrology to the six zodiacal signs which ascend most rapidly and obliquely.

Syn.—sinuous, circuitous, devious, serpentine, roundabout, indirect.

tọr'tū·ous·ly, *adv.* in a tortuous or winding manner.

tọr'tū·ous·ness, *n.* the state of being tortuous.

tọr'tūr·ȧ·ble, *a.* capable of being tortured.

tọr'tūre, *n.* [Fr., from LL. *tortura*, a twisting, torture, from L. *torquere*, to twist.]

1. the inflicting of severe pain to force information or confession, get revenge, etc.

2. any method by which such pain is inflicted.

3. any severe physical or mental pain; agony; anguish.

Ghastly spasm or racking *torture*.—Milton.

4. a cause of such pain or agony.

5. a violent twisting, distortion, perversion, etc. [Rare.]

Syn.—agony, anguish, pain, distress, torment.

tọr'tūre, *v.t.*; tortured, *pt., pp.*; torturing, *ppr.*

1. to subject to torture.

2. to cause (a person) extreme physical or mental pain; to agonize.

3. to twist or distort (meaning, etc.).

4. to keep on the stretch, as a bow. [Obs.]

tọr'tūre, *v.i.* to give excruciating pain; to cause torture.

tọr'tūr·ēr, *n.* one who or that which tortures.

tọr'tūr·ing·ly, *adv.* in a torturous manner.

tọr'tūr·ous, *a.* pertaining to or involving torture; causing torture.

Tor'ū·lȧ, *n.* [L. *torulus*, a little swelling or protuberance.]

1. same as *Saccharomyces*.

2. [t–] in botany, a small torus.

tor'ū·li·form, *a.* having the form of a torula; like a string of beads; moniliform. [Rare.]

tor'ū·loid, *a.* pertaining to or resembling the genus *Torula*.

tor'ū·lōse, tor'ū·lous, *a.* in botany and zoology, somewhat torose.

tor'ū·lus, *n.*; *pl.* **tor'ū·lī,** the socket that holds the antenna of an insect.

tor'up, *n.* the great snapping turtle of America.

tō'rus, *n.*; *pl.* **tō'rī,** [L., a bulge, a protuberance.]

1. in architecture, a semicircular projecting molding used at the base of columns, etc., just above the plinth: also called *tore*.

a, TORUS

2. in zoology, one of the ridges of an annelid, usually furnished with hooked setae.

3. in anatomy, any rounded projection or swelling.

4. in botany, that part of a plant on which the floral leaves grow; a receptacle.

5. in geometry, a surface, or its enclosed solid, generated by the revolution of a conic section, especially a circle, about any axis in its plane other than its diameter: also *tore*.

tọrve, tọr'vous, *a.* [L. *torvus*, stern.] sour or severe of countenance; stern; grim. [Obs.]

tọr'vi·ty, *n.* [L. *torvitas*, sternness.] sternness or severity of countenance; grimness. [Obs.]

Tō'ry, *n.*; *pl.* **Tō'rieṣ,** [Ir. *tōruidhe*, robber, pursuer, from *tōir*, to pursue.]

1. [*sometimes* t–] (a) in the 17th century, any of the dispossessed Irish who became outlaws, killed English settlers and soldiers, and lived by plundering; (b) later, any armed Irish Papist or Royalist.

2. in 1679–1680, a person who opposed the exclusion of James, Duke of York, from succession to the English throne.

3. after 1689, a member of one of the two major political parties of England: opposed to *Whig*, and later, to *Liberal, Radical, Laborite*: changed officially c. 1830 to *Conservative*.

4. one who sided with Great Britain and against the colonists during the American Revolution.

5. [*often* t–] any extreme conservative; a reactionary.

Tō'ry, *a.* [*also* t–] of, being, or characteristic of Tories; specifically, of or pertaining to the party of Tories; as, a *Tory* government.

Tō'ry·iṣm, *n.* the principles and practices of the Tories, specifically of the British Tories.

tos'çȧ, *n.* 1. a marshy limestone embedded in layers in the earth or mud of the pampas of South America. It underlies the Pampean formation.

2. any one of a variety of pumiceous tuffs of Sicily and southern Italy.

tö-sçat'tēr, *v.t.* to scatter in pieces. [Obs.]

tōṣe, *v.t.* 1. to pull about; to tousle. [Obs.]

2. to comb or tease (wool). [Obs.]

tō'ṣēr, *n.* one who toses; specifically, one who toses wool. [Obs.]

tosh, *a.* [OFr. *tousé*, shorn, clipped, from L. *tonsus*, clipped.] trim or neat; proper. [Scot.]

tö-shred', *v.t.* to tear into shreds. [Obs.]

tọss, *v.t.*; tossed (tọst) *or obs. or poet.* tost, *pt., pp.*; tossing, *ppr.* [prob. from O.N. via dial.; cf. Norw. dial. *tossa*, to spread, strew.]

1. to throw about; to fling about; to pitch about; to buffet; as, the waves *tossed* the boat.

2. to disturb; agitate; disquiet.

3. to throw, especially upward, lightly, and easily, from the hand.

4. to lift quickly; to jerk upward; as, the horse *tossed* its head.

5. to toss up with (someone *for* something): see phrase below.

6. to busy oneself with; to tumble over; as, to spend four years in *tossing* the rules of grammar.

7. to pass from one to another, as in discussion; to bandy; as, the word was *tossed* from mouth to mouth.

8. in mining, to separate (ore) from the gangue by agitating the slimes in a vessel, thus forcing the heavier valuable parts to settle.

to toss in a blanket or *sheet*; to toss (a person) into the air from a blanket or sheet held slackly at the corners and edges and jerked quickly up and down.

to toss off; (a) to make, do, write, etc. quickly, casually, and without effort; (b) to drink up in one draft.

to toss up; (a) to toss a coin for deciding something according to which side lands uppermost; (b) to make hurriedly, as something to eat or drink.

tọss, *v.i.* 1. to be flung to and fro; to be thrown about or pitched about.

2. to fling oneself about in sleep, etc.; to be restless in bed; as, I *tossed* all night long.

3. to move or go impatiently, angrily, or disdainfully, as with a toss of the head.

4. to toss up: see phrase below.

to toss for; to toss up for; to gamble for.

to toss up; to throw up a coin for deciding something.

tọss, *n.* 1. a tossing or being tossed; a fling; as, a *toss* of the head.

2. a tossup.

3. the distance that something is or can be tossed.

4. a state of anxiety or agitation; commotion.

to win the toss; to have something decided in one's favor by tossing up a coin; hence, to gain advantage; to have luck on one's side.

tos'sel, *n.* tassel. [Obs.]

tos'sel, *n.* in architecture, same as *torsel*.

tọss'ēr, *n.* one who or that which tosses.

tọss'i·ly, *adv.* in a tossy manner; with affected indifference, carelessness, or contempt.

tọss'ing, *n.* the act of one who or that which tosses; specifically, a process in mining which separates ore from the gangue by forcing the heavier valuable parts to settle.

tọss'ment, *n.* the act of tossing or being tossed. [Rare.]

tọss'pot, *n.* a toper; a heavy drinker; a drunkard.

tọss'up, *n.* 1. the act of tossing or flipping a coin, etc. to decide something according to which side lands uppermost.

2. an even chance.

tọss'y, *a.* tossing; especially, tossing the head as in scorn or contempt; hence, affectedly indifferent; offhand; contemptuous.

tọst, *v.* obsolete or poetic past tense and past participle of *toss*.

tos'tō, *a.* [It.] in music, quick; rapid.

più tosto; in music, faster.

tö-swink', *v.i.* to labor or work hard; to toil incessantly. [Obs.]

tot, *n.* [prob. (via dial.) from O.N. *tuttr*, dwarf.]

1. a very small amount or thing.

2. a young child.

3. a small drinking cup; also, a small quantity or drink of alcoholic liquor. [Brit. Dial.]

tot, *n.* in a literal sense, so much: formerly, in the English exchequer, often written opposite an item to indicate that it was collectable, or good for so much cash.

tot, *n.* [contr. of *total.*] 1. total.
2. an example in addition. [Colloq.]

tot, *v.t.*; totted, *pt., pp.*; totting, *ppr.* 1. to designate (an item) as collectable by entering opposite it the word *tot.*
2. in accounts, to add; to sum up; to count: usually with *up*; as, to *tot up* a long column of figures. [Brit. Colloq.]

tō'tȧ, *n.* in zoology, same as *grivet.*

tō'tăl, *a.* [ME.; Late OFr.; LL. *totalis,* from L. *totus,* the whole.]
1. constituting the (or a) whole; complete in all its parts; entire; as, a *total* sum or amount.
2. complete in degree; absolute; thorough; as, a *total* wreck or rout; a *total* loss.
3. putting everything into a small compass; summary; curt; abrupt. [Obs.]
total abstinence; see under *abstinence.*
total depravity; see under *depravity.*
total eclipse; an eclipse in which the entire surface of the eclipsed luminary is hidden.

tō'tăl, *n.* the whole; the whole sum or amount.

tō'tăl, *v.t.*; totaled *or* totalled, *pt., pp.*; totaling *or* totalling, *ppr.* 1. to bring to a total; to add: often with *up.*
2. to amount to; to reach the sum of; to add up to.

tō'tăl, *v.i.* to amount (*to*) as a whole.

tō″tăl·i·ṣā'tion, *n.* same as *totalization.*

tō'tăl·i·ṣā″tŏr, *n.* same as *totalizer.*

tō·tal″i·tăr'i·ăn, *a.* designating, of, or characteristic of a government or state in which one political party or group maintains complete control and refuses to recognize, and as a consequence suppresses, all other political parties.

tō·tal·i·tăr'i·ăn·iṣm, *n.* totalitarian government, doctrines, etc.

tō·tal'i·ty, *n.* [Fr. *totalité.*]
1. the state or character of being total; entirety.
2. the whole sum; a whole quantity or amount; an aggregate.
3. in astronomy, the period of an eclipse, while it is total.
in totality; as a whole; altogether.

tō″tăl·i·zā'tion, *n.* the act or process of totalizing; also, the state of being totalized.

tō'tăl·i·zā″tŏr, *n.* any machine for computing and showing totals of measurements, etc.; especially, a machine for computing and showing the total number and amount of bets, as at a horse race; pari-mutuel: also *totalisator, totalizer.*

tō'tăl·ize, *v.t.*; totalized, *pt., pp.*; totalizing, *ppr.* to make a total of; to combine into a total.

tō'tăl·ize, *v.i.* to use a totalizer.

tō'tăl·i·zẽr, *n.* 1. a totalizator.
2. an adding machine.

tō'tăl·ly, *adv.* wholly; entirely; fully; completely; as, to be *totally* exhausted, all hope *totally* failed.

tō'tăl·ness, *n.* entireness.

tō'tăl wạr, warfare that uses all possible means of attack, military, scientific, and psychological, against both enemy troops and civilians.

tō·tä'rȧ, *n.* [Maori.] a large New Zealand tree, *Podocarpus totara,* of the pine family, whose red, fine-grained wood is used for veneering as well as for furniture and cabinetwork.

tōte, *v.t.*; toted, *pt., pp.*; toting, *ppr.* [earlier *toat*; perh. from early Fr *tauter,* to remove on rollers.]
1. to carry or haul, especially in the arms or on the back. [Colloq.]
2. to be armed with (a gun, etc.). [Colloq.]

tōte, *n.* 1. a toting. [Colloq.]
2. something toted; load; haul. [Colloq.]

tōte, *n.* [L. *totus,* the whole.] the entire body, or all; as, the whole *tote.* [Colloq.]

tōte, *n.* [Ice. *tuta,* a peak, projection.] the handle of a plane: so called by a joiner.

tōte, *v.t.* to sound; to toot. [Obs.]

tōte, *v.i.* to look; to observe; to peep. [Obs.]

tö-teär', *v.t.* to tear, rend, or agitate. [Obs.]

tōte bōard, a totalizator. [Colloq.]

tō'tem, *n.* [Am. Ind.] 1. among primitive peoples, an animal or natural object considered as being related by blood to a given family or clan and taken as its symbol.
2. an image of this.

And they painted on the grave posts
Each his own ancestral *totem,*
Each the symbol of his household.
—Longfellow.

tō·tem'iç, *a.* relating or belonging to a totem or totems.

tō'tem·iṣm, *n.* 1. belief in totems and totemic relationships.
2. the use of totems to distinguish families.
3. social customs based on this.

tō'tem·ist, *n.* one having a totem, or one of a family or clan having a totem.

tō·tem·is'tiç, *a.* of or pertaining to totemism or totemists.

tō'tem pōle, a pole or post carved and painted with totems, often erected in front of their dwellings by Indian tribes of the northwest coast of North America.

TOTEM POLE

tō'tem pōst, a totem pole.

tōt'ẽr, *n.* 1. one who totes, in any sense of the word.
2. a stone roller.

tŏth'ẽr, t'ŏth'ẽr, 'tŏth'ẽr, *a.* and *pron.* [ME. *the tother,* earlier *thet other, that other.*] that (or the) other. [Chiefly Dial.]

How happy could I be with either
Were *tother* dear charmer away. —Gay.

tō'ti-, [from L. *totus,* whole.] a combining form meaning *whole, entire, wholly, entirely,* as in *toti*palmate.

tot'i·dem vẽr'bis, [L.] in so many words.

tō'tient (-shent), *n.* [L. *toties,* so many, and *-ent.*] in mathematics, the number of totitives in any specific number.

Tō″ti·pal·mā'tae, *n.pl.* [L. *totus,* entire, and *palma,* a palm.] a tribe of swimming birds having the hind toes united with the others in a continuous membrane, as ducks, geese, pelicans, cormorants, frigate birds, etc

tō·ti·pal'māte, *a.* being full web-footed; having the hind toe connected with the other three in a continuous membrane.

tō·ti·pal'māte, *n.* one of the *Totipalmatæ.*

tō″ti·pal·mā'tion, *n.* 1. the complete union of the hind toe with the others in a continuous membrane.
2. the state of being totipalmate.

Tō·ti·pal'mī, *n.pl.* a group of swimming birds including those which are characterized by totipalmation.

tō·tip'ō·tent, *a.* in zoology, pertaining to those organisms, as flatworms, which are capable of complete regeneration of any or all of its severed parts or of the parts themselves.

tot'i·tive, *n.* any integer smaller than a specific number and having with it unity as the only common divisor.

tot'tẽr, *v.i.*; tottered, *pt., pp.*; tottering, *ppr.* [ME. *toteren,* from AS. *tealtrian,* to totter.]
1. to rock or shake as if about to fall; to be unsteady.
2. to be unsteady on one's feet; to stagger; to toddle.

tot'tẽr, *v.t.* to shake out of a steady position. [Obs.]

tot'tẽr, *n.* a tottering.

tot'tẽr·ẽr, *n.* one who or that which totters.

tot'tẽr·ing·ly, *adv.* in a tottering manner.

tot'tẽr·y, *a.* unsteady; trembling; shaky.

tot'tle, *v.i.* [variant of *toddle.*] to toddle. [Brit. Dial.]

tot'tlish, *a.* tottering; trembling; unsteady; insecure. [Colloq.]

tot'ty, *a.* [contr. from *totter.*] tottery; wavering; unsteady; dizzy. [Brit. Dial.]

tot'y, *a.* totty. [Obs.]

tō'ty, *n.* [native.] a sailor or a fisherman: used among the islanders of the Pacific.

töu'ărt, *n.* same as *tooart.*

töu'çan, *n.* [Fr. *toucan*; Braz. *tucano,* from the cry of the bird.]
1. any brightly colored, fruit-eating bird of the genus *Rhamphastos* of tropical America, distinguished by a large, down-curved beak. The species are easily tamed and are remarkable among birds for regurgitation of food, sending it back into the bill to undergo a kind of mastication. Their feet, like those of parrots, are formed for grasping.

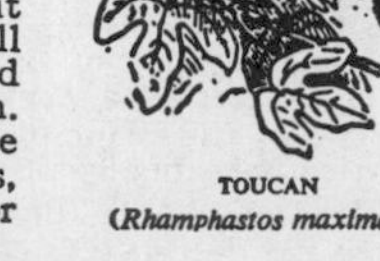

TOUCAN
(*Rhamphastos maximas*)

2. [T—] in astronomy, a modern constellation of the Southern Hemisphere.

töu'çan·et, *n.* a diminutive toucan.

töu·çang', *n.* [E. Ind.] a kind of boat much used at Malacca and Singapore, propelled by either oar or sail, speedy, rather flat in the center, but sharp at the extremities.

tŏuch, *v.t.*; touched, *pt., pp.*; touching, *ppr.* [ME. *touchen*; OFr. *tochier, tuchier.*]
1. to put the hand, finger, or other part of the body on, so as to feel; to perceive by the sense of feeling.
2. to bring (something) into contact with (something else); as, he *touched* the paper with his pencil, he *touched* a lighted match to the kindling.
3. formerly, to lay the hand on (a person with scrofula), as some kings, in order to effect a miraculous cure.
4. to be or come into contact with.
5. to adjoin; to border on.
6. to strike lightly.
7. to affect through contact; to have a physical effect on; as, water won't *touch* these grease spots.
8. to injure slightly; as, frost *touched* the plants.
9. to test by a touchstone or something similar.
10. to stamp (tested metal).
11. to strike the keys of, pluck the strings of, etc. (a musical instrument).
12. to play (a few notes, an air, etc.) on a musical instrument.
13. to draw, change the color of, etc. (the details of a painting, etc.) by using a brush or pencil.
14. to give a light tint, aspect, etc. to: used chiefly in the past participle; as, clouds *touched* with pink.
15. to stop at in passing, as a ship.
16. to lay hands on; to handle; to use.
17. to mishandle; to molest; to affect so as to injure.
18. to taste or partake of: usually used in the negative, as he didn't *touch* his supper.
19. to come up to; to reach; to attain.
20. to compare with; to equal; to rival: usually in the negative; as, my cooking can't *touch* yours.
21. to take or make use of without permission or wrongly; to misappropriate.
22. to deal with; to refer to; to mention, especially in a light or passing way.
23. to have to do with; to affect; to concern; as, a subject that *touches* our welfare.
24 to taint slightly, as in morals.
25. to cause to be slightly ill mentally: usually in *touched in the head,* somewhat demented.
26. to arouse an emotion in, especially one of sympathy, gratitude, etc.
27. to provoke; irritate; sting; as, it *touched* me to the quick.
28. to ask for, or get by asking, a loan or gift of money from. [Slang.]
29. in geometry, to be tangent to.
30. to infect; as, men *touched* with pestilent diseases. [Rare.]
31. to influence by impulse; to impel forcibly.
32. among sailors, to luff, as a vessel, until the edges of the sails touch.
to touch elbows; among veterans, to march together in rank, as in a campaign or a reunion; to rub elbows.
to touch off; (a) to represent accurately or aptly; (b) to make explode or detonate; to fire; (c) to motivate or initiate.
to touch the wind; in seamen's language, to keep the ship as near the wind as possible.
to touch up; (a) to stimulate or rouse, as by touching; (b) to improve or finish (a painting, literary work, etc.) by minor changes or additions.

tŏuch, *v.i.* 1. to touch a person or thing (especially in sense 3).
2. to be or come in contact.
3. in geometry, to be tangent.
4. to fasten; to act; to take effect. [Obs.]
5. to treat (a subject) slightly in discourse: with *on* or *upon.*
6. in nautical usage, to have the edge of a sail so struck by the wind that a tremulous motion is caused in it.
7. to salute by touching the hat. [Brit. Dial.]
to touch and go; in sailing, to rub slightly against the ground with the keel and pass on with little or no hindrance.
to touch at; to stop briefly at (a port, etc.): said of ships and travelers.

tŏuch, *n.* 1. a touching or being touched; contact; specifically, (a) a light tap, stroke, etc.;

(b) a delicate stroke made with a brush in painting, etc.

But O, for the *touch* of a vanished hand,
And the sound of a voice that is still.
—Tennyson.

2. the sense of feeling, one of the five senses; tactile sense; as, a thing is cold or warm to the *touch*; silk is soft to the *touch*.

3. a sensation caused by this, especially one characteristic of a particular substance; tactile quality; feel.

4. an impression received as if by touching; a mental response; slight emotion

5. a mental capacity analogous to the sense of touch; mental or moral sensitivity.

No beast so fierce but knows some *touch* of pity. —Shak.

6. an effect of being touched; specifically, (a) a mark, impression, etc. left by touching; (b) a subtle change or addition in a painting, story, or other work.

7. a very small amount, degree, etc.; specifically, (a) a trace, tinge, etc., especially a characteristic one; as, a *touch* of humor; (b) a slight attack; as, a *touch* of the flu.

8. (a) touchstone; (b) the quality of gold, silver, etc. as determined by touchstone; (c) an official stamp indicating this.

9. any test or criterion.

10. (a) the act of asking for, or getting in this way, a gift or loan of money; (b) money so acquired.

11. in music, (a) the manner in which a performer strikes the keys of a keyboard instrument; as, a delicate *touch*; (b) the manner in which the action of a piano, etc. responds to the fingers; as, a piano with a heavy *touch*; (c) in bell ringing, a set of changes less than a peal.

12. in rugby, the part of the field outside the sidelines.

13. a trait; a characteristic; a lineament; a feature or peculiar feature.

One *touch* of nature makes the whole world kin. —Shak.

14. a hint; a suggestion; a slight notice.

15. animadversion; censure; reproof; as, a *touch* of conscience. [Obs.]

16. a particular application of anything to a person. [Obs.]

17. the characteristic handling usual to an artist by which his works may be known.

18. in obstetrics, the examination of the mouth of the womb by actual contact of the hand or fingers.

19. a brief or slight essay. [Obs.]

20. in shipbuilding, the broadest part of a plank worked top and butt; also, the angles of the stern timbers at the counters.

a near touch; an exceedingly narrow miss or escape; a close shave. [Colloq.]

in touch; in football, outside the touch lines and between the goal lines.

in touch with; (a) in communication or contact with; (b) responsive or sensitive to; as, a statesman must be *in touch with* every interest of his country.

out of touch with; no longer well-informed on or in close communication with.

to keep touch; (a) [Obs.] to fulfill duly a part or function; (b) to be in sympathy with anything or any one.

to make a touch; to borrow money. [Slang.]

true as touch; completely true. [Obs.]

tŏuch'ȧ·ble, *a.* that can be touched; tangible.

tŏuch'ȧ·ble·ness, *n.* the quality of being touchable.

tŏuch'-ănd-gō', *a.* 1. hurried; temporary; superficial; as, a *touch-and-go* manner.

2. uncertain; risky; precarious; ticklish; as, a *touch-and-go* situation of affairs.

tŏuch ănd gō, 1. a hasty or casual act.

2. an uncertain or dangerous situation.

tŏuch'back, *n.* in football, the act of a player in grounding the ball behind his own goal line when the ball has been caused to pass the goal line by an opponent: distinguished from *safety*.

tŏuch bod'y, a touch corpuscle.

tŏuch'box, *n.* a box for lighted tinder, formerly carried by soldiers who used matchlocks, the match being lighted at it.

tŏuch çor'pus·cle (-sl), a corpuscle connected with the sense of touch.

tŏuch'down, *n.* 1. (a) the act of landing, or touching down: said of an aircraft or spacecraft; (b) the moment at which a landing aircraft or spacecraft touches the landing surface.

2. in football, (a) a play in which a player grounds the ball on or past the opponent's goal line; (b) a score (6 points) so made.

tou·ché' (tọọ-shā'), *a.* [Fr., pp.] in fencing, touched: said of a point scored by a touch.

tou·ché' (tọọ-shā'), *interj.* that hit the mark! good point!: an exclamation used to acknowledge a successful point in debate or a witty retort.

tŏuched (tŏcht), *a.* [pp. of *touch.*] that has undergone touching; specifically, (a) emotionally affected; moved; (b) slightly demented; somewhat unbalanced mentally.

tŏuch'ẽr, *n.* one who or that which touches; a good marksman; one who hits or touches the mark often.

tŏuch foot'ball, an informal variety of football: a defensive player downs the ball carrier by touching him in any of various specified ways, usually with both hands and below the waist, rather than tackling him.

tŏuch'hōle, *n.* the vent of a cannon or early firearm through which the charge was touched off.

tŏuch'i·ly, *adv.* in a touchy manner.

tŏuch'i·ness, *n.* the quality or state of being touchy.

tŏuch'ing, *a.* arousing feeling; affecting; full of pathos.

tŏuch'ing, *n.* 1. the act of one that touches.

2. the sense of touch.

tŏuch'ing, *prep.* relating to; concerning; as, he was asked to give an opinion *touching* the case in hand.

tŏuch'ing·ly, *adv.* in a touching manner.

tŏuch'līne, *n.* in rugby and football, either of the sidelines bounding the field.

tŏuch'-mē-not, *n.* 1. a plant of the genus *Impatiens*, whose seed pods when ripe burst upon the slightest touch or disturbance, as *Impatiens nolitangere*, *Impatiens fulva*, or *Impatiens pallida*, common in the United States: also called *jewelweed* and *balsam*.

2. in medicine, a tubercular affection, occurring especially about the face. [Obs.]

tŏuch nee'dle, a small bar of gold and silver, either pure or alloyed with copper, etc., used for testing articles of gold, silver, and other metals by rubbing them upon a touchstone.

tŏuch'pan, *n.* the pan of an old-pattern gun that holds the priming.

tŏuch pā'pẽr, paper steeped in niter so that it catches fire from a spark and burns slowly: used for firing gunpowder and the like.

tŏuch'piēce, *n.* a coin given by the sovereigns of England to those whom they touched for the cure of scrofula or king's evil.

tŏuch'stōne, *n.* 1. a variety of compact siliceous schist formerly used to test the purity of gold or silver by the streak left on it when it was rubbed with the metal.

2. any test or criterion for determining genuineness or value; as, money, the *touchstone* of common honesty.

Irish touchstone; basalt, the stone which composes the Giant's Causeway.

tŏuch sys'tem, a method of typing without looking at the keyboard, by regularly touching a given key with a specific finger.

tŏuch'-tȳpe, *v.i.*; touch-typed, *pt.*, *pp.*; touch-typing, *ppr.* to type by means of the touch system.

tŏuch'wood, *n.* 1. dried, decayed wood or dried fungus used as tinder; punk.

2. a fungus, *Polyporus igniarius*.

tŏuch'y, *a.*; *comp.* touchier; *superl.* touchiest, 1. easily offended; oversensitive; irritable.

2. sensitive to touch; easily irritated, as a part of the body.

3. very risky or precarious; as, a *touchy* situation.

4. highly inflammable, as touchwood.

5. in decorative art, made up of points or broken lines or touches, instead of firm, long lines.

tŏugh (tuf), *a.*; *comp.* tougher; *superl.* toughest, [AS. *tōh*, tough.]

1. strong but pliant; that will bend, twist, etc. without tearing or breaking.

2. that will not cut or chew easily; as, *tough* steak.

3. strongly cohesive; glutinous; viscous; sticky; as, *tough* putty.

4. strong of physique; robust; hardy.

5. hard to convince or influence; stubborn.

6. overly aggressive; brutal; rough.

7. very difficult; toilsome.

8. vigorous; violent; as, a *tough* fight.

Syn.—resistant, hardened, fibrous, hard, unmanageable, tenacious, firm, strong.

tŏugh, *n.* a rowdy; a tough person; a ruffian.

tŏugh çāke, refined copper which has been cast into cakes: also called *tough pitch*.

tŏugh'en, *v.i.*; toughened, *pt.*, *pp.*; toughening, *ppr.* to grow tough or tougher.

tŏugh'en, *v.t.* to make tough or tougher.

tŏugh'head (-hed), *n.* the hardhead, or ruddy duck. [Dial.]

tŏugh'ish, *a.* somewhat tough.

tŏugh'ly, *adv.* in a tough manner.

tŏugh'-mīnd'ed, *a.* shrewd and unsentimental; practical; realistic.

tŏugh'ness, *n.* the state or quality of being tough.

tou·pee', *n.* [Fr. *toupet*, dim. from OFr. *toupe*, a tuft of hair.]

1. formerly, a curl or lock of artificial hair worn on top of the head, sometimes as part of a wig.

2. a small wig for covering a bald spot.

tou·pet' (-pā'), *n.* [Fr.] 1. same as *toupee*.

2. the crested or tufted titmouse: also called *toupettit*.

tour, *n.* [Fr., a turn, from *tourner*, to turn.]

1. a turn, spell, or shift, as of work; especially, in military usage, a period of duty at a single place.

2. a long trip, as for sightseeing.

3. any trip, as for inspection; a round; a circuit; specifically, a trip by a theatrical company to give performances at a number of cities.

4. a turn; a revolution; as, the *tours* of the heavenly bodies. [Obs.]

5. turn; cast; manner. [Rare.]

6. a course or drive for horses or carriages, or a ride or drive in such a course. [Obs.]

on tour; touring.

Syn.—journey, circuit, ramble, excursion.

tour, *v.t.*; toured, *pt.*, *pp.*; touring, *ppr.* 1. to take a tour through or around; as, to *tour* the Continent.

2. to take (a play, theatrical company, etc.) on a tour.

tour, *v.i.* to go on a tour.

tou'rä·çō, *n.* any of a group of brightly colored tropical birds related to the cuckoo.

tour·bil'liŏn (-yun), *n.* [Fr. *tourbillon*, whirlwind.]

1. originally, a whirlwind.

2. a firework that rises with a spiral motion.

tour de fōrce', [Fr.] a feat of strength, skill, or ingenuity, often one that is merely clever or spectacular.

tour'ing, *a.* of or pertaining to that which is used or can be used on a tour; as, a *touring* car.

tour'ing çär, an early type of open automobile, often with a folding top, seating five or more passengers.

tour'iṣm, *n.* tourist travel, especially when regarded as a source of income for a country, business, etc.

tour'ist, *n.* 1. one who makes a tour; one who makes a journey for pleasure.

2. tourist class.

tour'ist, *a.* of or for tourists.

tourist agency; an agency for serving or providing information for tourists.

tourist cabin; a cabin for tourists; specifically, one of a row of small, one room buildings for overnight accommodation.

tourist camp; an area of land for tourists as a camp or stopping place: usually a site on which tourist cabins have been erected.

tourist class; the lowest-priced accommodations, as on a ship.

tourist court; same as *motel*.

tourist home; a private home in which bedrooms are rented to tourists or travelers.

tour'ist, *adv.* in or by means of tourist class.

tour'mȧ·line, tūr'mȧ·line, *n.* [Fr., from *tournamal*, the Ceylon name.] a semiprecious mineral occurring crystallized and used as a gem and in optical instruments. It consists principally of a compound silicate and borate of alumina and magnesia, but frequently contains iron, lithia, and other substances.

tour'mȧ·line gran'ite, a variety of granite in which tourmaline is a principal constituent.

tour'mȧ·line tongṣ, a simple variety of polariscope in which two flat, transparent pieces of tourmaline are fixed to the ends of a device resembling tongs, enabling the examiner to hold an object between them: they are used by jewelers in distinguishing stones.

tourn, *n.* [old spelling of *turn.*] in old English law, the turn or circuit made by the sheriff twice every year for the purpose of holding in each hundred the great court leet of the county.

tour'nȧ·ment (*or* tẽr'), *n.* [OFr. *tornoiement*, from *torner*, to turn.]

1. in the Middle Ages, (a) a sport consisting of an encounter between knights on horse-

back, in which the opponents tried to unseat one another with lances, the winner receiving a prize; jousting contest; (b) a series of such encounters presented as an entertainment.

2. a series of contests in some sport, usually a competition for championship.

3. any similar series of contests, as in chess or bridge.

4. a sport in which horsemen riding at full speed endeavor to carry off on their lances rings hung above their heads. [Now Rare.]

Tour·ne·for'ti·a, *n.* [after J. P. de *Tournefort*, a French botanist.] a large genus of tropical plants of the order *Boraginaceæ*. It is related to the genus *Heliotropium*, but is distinguished from it by its fruit, which is a small, fleshy, four-celled drupe containing either two or four nutlets.

tourn'er·y, *n.* turnery. [Obs.]

tourne'sol, *n.* same as *turnsole*.

tour'ney (*or* tēr'), *n.*; *pl.* **tour'neys**, a tournament.

tour'ney, *v.i.* to tilt; to perform in a tournament.

tour'ni·quet (-ket), *n.* [Fr.] 1. any device for compressing a blood vessel to stop bleeding or control the circulation of blood to some part, as a bandage twisted about a limb or a pad pressed down by a screw.

2. a turnstile. [Obs.]

BLOOD VESSELS

TOURNIQUET

tour·nois' (-nwä'), *a.* of Tours: used only in certain phrases, as *livre tournois*, an old French money of account worth twenty sous.

tour·nure', *n.* [Fr.] 1. turn; contour; shape.

2. a pad tied around the waist by women, to give the hips a graceful curve; hence, the drapery at the back of a skirt.

touse, *n.* [ME. *tosen*, to tease wool.] a pulling; a disturbance. [Dial.]

touse, *v.t.*; toused, *pt., pp.*; tousing, *ppr.* 1. to rend; to tear apart. [Dial.]

2. to tease; to worry; to plague. [Dial.]

3. to pull about roughly; to dishevel; to tousle. [Dial.]

touse, *v.i.* to hustle; to stir about. [Dial.]

tous'ēr, *n.* one who or that which touses. [Brit. Dial.]

tou'sle, *v.t.*; tousled (-zld), *pt., pp.*; tousling, *ppr.* [freq. of ME. *tusen*, to pull, tear.] 1. to disarrange; to rumple; to dishevel; as, to *tousle* one's hair.

2. to pull or jerk about playfully; to tease. Also spelled *touzle*.

tou'sle, *n.* a tousled condition, mass of hair, etc.: also spelled *touzle*.

tous-les-mois' (tö-lā-mwä'), *n.* [Fr.] a starchy matter resembling arrowroot, procured from the rhizomes of several South American species of *Canna*.

tou'sy, *a.* disordered; unkempt; tousled; rough; shaggy. [Colloq.]

tout, *v.i.*; touted, *pt., pp.*; touting, *ppr.* [AS. *tōtian*, to peep, look out after.]

1. to solicit customers, patrons, votes, etc. [Colloq.]

2. (a) especially in England, to spy on race horses in training, etc. in order to secure tips for betting; (b) to provide betting tips on horse races. [Slang.]

tout, *v.t.* 1. to solicit or importune. [Colloq.]

2. to praise or recommend highly; to puff. [Colloq.]

3. (a) to spy out or otherwise get information on (race horses); (b) to give a tip on (a race horse) for a price. [Slang.]

tout, *n.* a person who touts; especially, a person who makes a business of selling tips on race horses.

tout, *n.* in the game of solo, a play when a single player takes or proposes to take all the tricks.

tout, *n.* the sulks; a fit of ill humor; also, a slight illness. [Scot.]

tout à fait (tọọ-tȧ-fā'), [Fr., lit., all done.] entirely; completely; quite.

tout de suite' (töt swēt'), [Fr., lit., all in succession.] immediately; right away.

tout en·sem'ble (tö-toṅ-soṅ'bl), see under *ensemble*.

tout'ēr, *n.* a person who touts; a tout.

tout le monde' (tö le mōṅd'), [Fr., lit., all the world.] everyone.

touze, *v.t.* and *v.i.* to touse. [Obs.]

tou'zle, *n.* and *v.t.*; touzled, *pt., pp.*; touzling, *ppr.* tousle.

tō·vä'risch (-rish), *n.* [Russ. *tovarishch*.] comrade: a title used among Communists in the Soviet Union.

tōw, *v.t.*; towed, *pt., pp.*; towing, *ppr.* [AS. *togian*, to drag, tug.]

1. to pull by a rope or chain; as, one ship or automobile is sometimes *towed* by another.

2. to pull or drag behind.

tōw, *n.* 1. the act of towing or the state of being towed.

2. a vessel, automobile, etc. that is being towed; anything towed.

3. a towing rope; a towline.

in tow; (a) being towed; (b) in one's company or retinue; (c) under one's influence or charge.

tōw, *n.* [AS. *tow-*, for spinning or weaving; prob. from base seen in *taw*, v., and *tool*.]

1. the coarse and broken part of flax or hemp, separated from the finer part by the hatchel or swingle.

2. in heckling, flax or hemp fibers in sufficient quantity for spinning a yarn 160 fathoms long.

tōw, *a.* of or resembling tow.

tōw'age, *n.* 1. the act of towing or the state of being towed.

2. a charge for towing.

towage service; in law, aid rendered in the propulsion of a vessel through the water merely to expedite her voyage: opposed to *salvage service*, or the rendering of aid to relieve her from distress.

tō'wärd (*or* tọrd), *prep.* [AS. *tōweard* from *tō*, to, and *weorlhan*, to become.]

1. in the direction of.

He set his face *toward* the wilderness.
—Num. xxiv. 1.

2. facing.

3. in a manner designed to achieve or along a course likely to result in; as, efforts *toward* a peaceful settlement; steps *toward* war.

4. concerning; regarding; about; as, his attitude *toward* me.

5. close to or just before (in time); as, they left *toward* four o'clock.

6. in anticipation of; for; as, they're saving *toward* a new car.

Also *towards*.

tō'wärd, *a.* 1. favorable; propitious.

2. ready to learn; promising; apt.

3. docile; compliant; tractable.

4. at hand; imminent.

5. being done; in progress: used predicatively.

[Archaic or Rare in all senses.]

tō'wärd·li·ness, *n.* the character of being towardly; readiness to do or learn; aptness; docility. [Archaic or Rare.]

tō'wärd·ly, *a.* [*toward* and *-ly*.]

1. favorable; propitious.

2. tractable; docile.

3. forward; precocious; making good progress.

[Archaic or Rare in all senses.]

tō'wärd·ness, *n.* docility; towardliness. [Obs.]

tō'wärds, *prep.* same as *toward*.

tō'wärds, *adv.* forward; near; toward the place in question; at hand. [Rare.]

tō'wärds, *a.* toward (senses 2, 3, 4). [Obs.]

tōw'bōat, *n.* any boat employed in towing a ship or vessel; a tugboat.

tōw'cock, *n.* [Chinese.] an Asiatic species of bean, *Vigna sinensis*: also called *cowpea* and *chowlee*.

tow'el, *n.* [OFr. *touaille*; LL. *toacula*, a towel.]

1. a piece of cloth or absorbent paper used for wiping the hands, face, or body after washing or bathing, or for wiping or drying things in domestic use.

2. in ecclesiastical usage, (a) the rich covering of silk and gold which used to be laid over the top of the altar, except during Mass; (b) a linen altar cloth. [Obs.]

an oaken towel; a cudgel. [Brit. Slang.]

tow'el, *v.t.*; toweled *or* towelled, *pt., pp.*; toweling *or* towelling, *ppr.* 1. to wipe or dry with a towel.

2. to beat with a cudgel. [Brit. Slang.]

tow'el, *v.i.* to use a towel; to rub or wipe with a towel.

tow'el gōurd, same as *sponge gourd*.

tow'el·ing, tow'el·ling, *n.* material for making towels.

tow'ēr, *n.* [OFr. *tur*, from L. *turris*, a tower.]

1. a structure that is relatively high for its length and width, either a separate building or part of another.

2. such a structure used as a fortress or prison.

3. a person or thing that resembles a tower in height, strength, dominance, etc.

4. in early and medieval warfare, a tall, movable wooden structure used in storming a fortified place.

5. a high headdress, worn by women in England in the reigns of William III and Queen Anne.

6. in astrology, a mansion. [Obs.]

7. in heraldry, a bearing representing a fortified tower with battlements and usually a gate with a portcullis.

TOWER HEADDRESS

Gay-Lussac tower; in the manufacture of sulfuric acid, a tower in which is intercepted the nitrous anhydride contained in the gas coming from the lead chambers.

Glover's tower; in the manufacture of sulfuric acid, a large tower or chamber in which the crude acid is condensed, and the nitrous anhydride that trickles from the Gay-Lussac tower is received and utilized.

Martello tower; a small circular fort with thick walls, built chiefly on seacoasts to prevent the landing of enemies.

mural tower; a tower flush with the line of the wall or structure of which it forms a part.

round tower; see under *round*.

Tower of London; a large assemblage of buildings which occupies an elevated area of twelve or thirteen acres, just beyond the old walls of the city of London, on the northern bank of the Thames. This collection of buildings is used as an arsenal, garrison, and repository of various objects of interest. The oldest portion, the White Tower, was built by William the Conqueror. It was anciently a palace, and in English history was frequently used as a state prison. To the northwest is Tower Hill, where traitors were publicly executed.

tower of silence; the tower upon which the Parsees expose their dead, that they may be dissipated without contaminating earth.

tow'ēr, *v.i.*; towered, *pt., pp.*; towering, *ppr.* 1. to rise above surrounding objects; to be lofty.

2. in falconry, to rise like a hawk in order to descend on its prey; also, to soar as a lark in the act of singing; to rise straight up in the air, as a wounded bird.

tow'ēr, *v.t.* to rise aloft into. [Obs.]

tōw'ēr, *n.* a person or thing that tows.

tow'ēr bas'tion, in fortification, a small tower in the form of a bastion, with rooms or cells underneath for men and guns.

tow'ēred, *a.* 1. adorned or defended by towers; having or bearing a tower or towers.

2. rising into the air like a tower.

tow'ēr·ing, *a.* 1. that towers; very high; elevated; as, a *towering* height.

2. very violent; intense; extreme; surpassing; as, a *towering* rage.

tow'ēr·let, *n.* a little tower. [Rare.]

tow'ēr mus'tärd, an annual plant of the genus *Arabis*, found in Europe, Asia, North America, and Australia, the leaves and seeds of which give the stem a pyramidal form.

tow'ēr wag'ŏn, a wagon or truck having a movable platform which can be raised to enable workmen to repair overhead trolley wires.

tow'ēr·wŏrt, *n.* the tower mustard or some allied species of *Arabis*.

tow'ēr·y, *a.* 1. having towers; adorned or defended by towers; as, *towery* cities.

2. lofty; towering.

tōw'head (-hed), *n.* 1. a head of pale-yellow hair or, rarely, tousled hair.

2. a person having such hair.

3. an alluvial obstruction in a river. [Dial.]

4. the hooded merganser. [Dial.]

tōw'head"ed, *a.* having pale-yellow hair or, rarely, tousled hair.

tow'hee, *n.* [so called from its note.] any of various small North American finches related to the sparrows and buntings; especially, the chewink, or marsh robin: also called *towhee bunting*.

tō·wil'ly, *n.* the sanderling. [Brit. Dial.]

tōw'ing brī'dle, in nautical usage, a chain

with a hook at each end, or in the middle, used for attaching a towline.

tōw'ing net, a net to be towed behind a moving ship for collecting specimens of marine animals and plants.

tōw'ing path, same as *towpath.*

tōw'ing pōst, a towing timber.

tōw'ing tim'bẽr, in nautical usage, a stout post on the deck of a tugboat to fasten the towline to.

tōw'līne, *n.* a hawser, rope, chain, etc. used in towing vessels; a towrope.

town, *n.* [AS. *tūn,* an enclosure, enclosed space, field, homestead, village, town; Ice. and L.G. *tūn,* with similar meanings; D. *tuin,* a fence; O.H.G. *zūn,* a hedge, a rampart; G. *zaun,* a hedge.]

1. a place enclosed or fenced in; a collection of houses enclosed within walls, hedges, or the like; a walled place. [Obs.]

2. a group of houses; a hamlet; a village. [Dial.]

3. a more or less concentrated group of houses and private and public buildings, larger than a village but smaller than a city; especially, (a) in most of the United States, a township; (b) in New England, a rural or urban unit of local government smaller than a city, a political subdivision of a State, having its sovereignty vested in a town meeting.

4. in England, (a) a village that holds a market periodically; (b) a large, thickly populated place, as a borough, city, etc.

5. the business center of a city; as, I'm going into *town.*

6. the town or city being spoken of or understood; as, they just got into *town.*

7. the inhabitants, voters, etc. of a town.

8. any populated place spoken of familiarly; as, New York's an exciting *town.* [Colloq.]

9. a farm or farmstead; a farmhouse with its outbuildings. [Scot.]

county town; see under *county.*

man about town; a well-to-do man who spends much of his time in clubs and public places in a city.

on the town; (a) dependent on the public charity of the town or city; (b) [Slang.] out for a good time at the theater, night clubs, etc.

to go to town; (a) to go on a spree; (b) to work or act fast and efficiently; (c) to be eminently successful. [Slang.]

to paint the town red; to go on a boisterous spree; to carouse. [Slang.]

town, *a.* of, for, or characteristic of a town.

town ad'jū·tănt, in England, formerly, a military officer on the staff of a garrison, and ranking as a lieutenant. His duties were to maintain discipline, etc.

town çär, an automobile with an enclosed rear seat separated by a glass partition from the open or partially enclosed driver's seat.

town çlērk, an official in charge of the records, legal business, etc. of a town.

town çress, the garden peppergrass, *Lepidium sativum.*

town çrī'ẽr, see under *crier.*

tōw'net, *n.* a towing net.

town'fōlk (-fōk), *n.pl.* same as *townspeople.*

town hall, a large hall or building belonging to a town, in which the meetings of the town council are held, and which contains the public offices of the town.

town'house, *n.* a town hall.

town house, a city residence, especially as distinguished from a country residence of the same owner.

town'ish, *a.* pertaining to the inhabitants of a town; like the town.

town'less, *a.* having no town.

town'let, *n.* a little town.

town mā'jŏr, in England, formerly, a military officer performing duties similar to those of a town adjutant.

town meet'ing, 1. a meeting of the people of a town.

2. especially in New England, a meeting of the qualified voters of a town to act upon town business.

Town'şend·īte, *n.* an adherent of the *Townsend Plan,* a social insurance measure proposed by Dr. Francis E. Townsend, according to which all wage earners would retire at the age of sixty and receive a monthly pension from the U. S. government.

townş'fōlk (-fōk), *n.pl.* same as *townspeople.*

town'ship, *n.* [ME. *tunscipe*; AS. *tūnscipe,* people living in a *tūn.*]

1. originally, in England, a parish or division of a parish, as a unit of territory and administration.

2. in most of the United States, a division of a county, constituting a unit of local government with administrative control of local schools, roads, etc.

3. in New England, a town.

4. a unit of territory in the United States land survey, generally six miles square, containing thirty-six mile-square sections, and sometimes, but not necessarily, coextensive with a governmental township.

5. in Canada, a subdivision of a province.

townş'măn, *n.*; *pl.* **townş'men,** 1. a person who lives in, or has been reared in, a town.

2. a person who lives in one's own or the same town.

3. in New England, a selectman.

townş'pēo"ple, *n.pl.* 1. people of a town.

2. people brought up in a town or city, as distinguished from those brought up in the country.

town tạlk (tạk), the common talk of a town, or the subject of such talk.

town'wărd, town'wărdş, *adv.* in the direction of a town; toward a town.

town'y, *n.*; *pl.* **town'ieş,** a townsman; one born in the same town with the speaker; as, he is a *towny* of mine. [Slang.]

tōw'path, *n.* a path along the bank of a river or canal, used by men or animals in towing boats.

tōw'rōpe, *n.* a rope used in towing.

tow'şẽr, *n.* same as *touser.*

tow'zie, *a.* same as *tousy.*

tōw'y, *a.* containing or resembling tow.

tox·ae'mi·ȧ, *n.* see *toxemia.*

tox·ae'miç, *a.* see *toxemic.*

tox·al·bū'min, *n.* any poisonous albumin whether of bacterial or other origin. Some like abrin and ricin are found in plant juices; others in serpent venoms, bacterial cultures, etc.

tox·al'bū·mōse, *n.* a poisonous albumose.

tox·ȧ·nē'mi·ȧ, tox·ȧ·nae'mi·ȧ, *n.* [Gr. *toxikon,* poison, and *anemia.*] anemia due to a poison.

tox·ē'mi·ȧ, tox·ae'mi·ȧ, *n.* [LL., from Gr. *toxikon,* poison, and *haima,* blood.] any condition of blood poisoning, especially poisoning caused by bacterial toxins transported through the blood stream from a focus of infection.

tox·ē'miç, tox·ae'miç, *a.* 1. of, having the nature of, or caused by toxemia.

2. having toxemia.

tox·en'zȳme, *n.* any poisonous enzyme.

tox'iç, tox'iç·ăl, *a.* [Gr. *toxikon,* poison, originally poison in which arrows were dipped, from *toxikos,* of or for a bow, from *toxon,* a bow.]

1. poisonous.

2. of, pertaining to, affected by, or caused by a toxin, or poison.

tox'iç·ăl·ly, *adv.* by toxicants.

tox'i·çănt, *a.* poisonous; toxic.

tox'i·çănt, *n.* a poison.

tox·i·çā'tion, *n.* the condition of being poisoned; poisoning.

tox'i·cīde, *a.* [Gr. *toxikon,* poison, and L. *cædere,* to kill.] overcoming toxic agents.

tox'i·cīde, *n.* a toxicide drug.

tox·ic'i·ty, *n.*; *pl.* **tox·ic'i·tieş,** a poisonous quality or state, especially the degree of virulence of a toxic microbe or of a poison.

tox'i·çō-, [from Gr. *toxikon.*] a combining form meaning *poison,* as in *toxico*genic: also, before a vowel, *toxic-.*

Tox"i·çō·den'drŏn, *n.* a genus of poisonous plants of the spurge family, native to South Africa. *Toxicodendron capense* is known as the hyena poison.

tox"i·çō·dẽr'mȧ, *n.* toxicodermatitis.

tox"i·çō·dẽr·mȧ·tī'tis, *n.* [from Gr. *toxikon,* poison, and *derma,* skin; and *-itis.*] any skin inflammation due to a poison.

tox"i·çō·dẽr·mī'tis, *n.* toxicodermatitis.

tox"i·çō·ġen'iç, *a.* [Gr. *toxikon,* poison, and *gennan,* to produce.]

1. produced by a toxic substance.

2. producing a poison.

tox'i·çoid, *a.* [Gr. *toxikon,* poison, and *-oid.*] resembling a poison.

tox"i·çō·loġ'iç·ăl, tox"i·çō·loġ'iç, *a.* pertaining to toxicology.

tox"i·çō·loġ'iç·ăl·ly, *adv.* in a toxicological manner.

tox·i·çol'ō·ġist, *n.* one who specializes in the study of poisons; one versed in toxicology.

tox·i·çol'ō·ġy, *n.* [Gr. *toxikon,* poison, and *-logy.*] the scientific study of poisons, their effects, their detection, and the treatment of the conditions produced by them.

tox"i·çō·mā'ni·ȧ, *n.* [Gr. *toxikon,* poison, and *mania.*]

1. an intense desire for poisons or narcotic drugs.

2. same as *toxiphobia.*

tox"i·çō·mū'cin, *n.* [L. *toxicus,* poisonous, and *mucus,* slime.] a poisonous albuminoid substance derived from cultures of the tubercle bacillus.

tox"i·çō·path'iç, *a.* pertaining to toxicopathy.

tox·i·çop'ȧ·thy, *n.* [Gr. *toxikon,* poison, and *-pathy.*] any disease induced by a poison.

tox"i·çō·phid'i·ȧ, *n.pl.* [Gr. *toxikon,* poison, and *ophidion,* serpent.] venomous snakes collectively. [Rare.]

tox·i·çō'sis, *n.* any diseased condition due to poisoning.

exogenic toxicosis; poisoning by the ingestion of toxic material, as in the food.

retention toxicosis; poisoning due to nonexcretion of noxious waste products.

Tox·if'e·rȧ, *n.pl.* same as *Toxoglossa.*

tox·if'ẽr·ous, *a.* [Gr. *toxikon,* poison, and *-ferous.*] conveying or producing a poison.

tox'in, *n.* [Gr. *toxikon,* poison.]

1. any of various unstable poisonous compounds produced by some microorganisms and causing certain diseases.

2. any of various similar poisons, related to proteins, secreted by plants and animals, as snake venom.

tox'in-an·ti·tox'in, *n.* a mixture of toxin and antitoxin for producing active immunity against a specific disease, especially diphtheria: now largely superseded by toxoids.

tox'ine, *n.* a toxin.

tox·in·ē'mi·ȧ, tox·in·ae'mi·ȧ, *n.* [*toxin,* and Gr. *haima,* blood.] the poisoning of the blood with toxins.

tox·in·feç'tion, *n.* infection by a toxin the causative microbe of which is not identified.

tox·in'i·cīde, *n.* [*toxin,* and L. *cædere,* to kill.] any agent destructive to toxins.

tox·i·nō'sis, *n.* any diseased condition due to the presence of a toxin.

tox·i·phō'bi·ȧ, *n.* [Gr. *toxikon,* poison, and *phobos,* fear.] an abnormal dread of poisons or of being poisoned.

tox'in, *n.* poisoning; especially, poisoning by toxins.

tox·i·ther'ȧ·py, *n.* [Gr. *toxikon,* poisoning, and *therapeuein,* to treat medically.] the therapeutic use of antitoxins.

tox'i·us, *n.*; *pl.* **tox'i·ī,** [Gr. *toxon,* bow.] in spongology, a spicule curved like a bow.

tox"ō·ȧ·lex'in, *n.* [Gr. *toxikon,* poison, and *alexein,* to ward off.] an alexin which tends to produce immunity to bacterial toxins.

Tox'ō·don, *n.* [Gr. *toxon,* a bow, and *odous, odontos,* a tooth.]

1. a genus, typical of the *Toxodonta,* of gigantic fossil quadrupeds.

2. [t—] a fossil quadruped of the genus *Toxodon.*

tox'ō·dont, *a.* pertaining to the *Toxodonta.*

tox'ō·dont, *n.* one of the *Toxodonta.*

Tox·ō·don'tȧ, Tox·ō·don'ti·ȧ (-shi-), *n.pl.* an extinct order of large quadrupeds discovered in the upper Tertiary formation in South America.

Tox·ō·glos'sȧ, *n.* [Gr. *toxikon,* poison, and *glōssa,* tongue.] a division of gastropods having poison sacs and fangs.

tox'oid, *n.* [Gr. *toxikon,* poison, and *-oid.*] a toxin that has been treated, as with chemical agents, so as to eliminate the toxic qualities while retaining the antigenic properties.

tox·oph'i·līte, *a.* toxophilitic.

tox·oph'i·līte, *n.* [Gr. *toxon,* a bow, and *philos,* a lover.] a lover of archery; one skilled in archery.

tox·oph·i·lit'iç, *a.* pertaining to archery or archers.

tox"ō·plaş·mō'sis, *n.* [Mod.L.] a disease of man, dogs, cats, and certain other mammals, caused by a parasitic microorganism and affecting especially the nervous system.

tox·ō·sō'zin, *n.* any sozin which destroys the poisons produced by microorganisms.

Tox·os'tō·mȧ, *n.* [Gr. *toxo-, toxon,* bow and *stoma,* mouth.] in zoology, a genus of American songbirds closely related to the mocking-birds and including most of the thrashers.

Tox'ō·tēş, *n.* [Gr., a bowman.]

1. a genus of fishes, the archerfishes of East Indian waters.

TOXOTES
(*Toxotes jaculator*)

2. [t–] any fish of this genus.

toy, *n.* [D. *tuig*, tools, implements, trifles; Dan. *töi*, G. *zeug*, stuff, gear, etc., whence respectively D. *speeltuig*, toys; Dan. *legetöi*, a toy, a plaything, *lege*, to play.]
1. originally, (a) amorous behavior; flirtation; (b) pastime; sport.
2. a thing of little value or importance; a trifle.
3. a little ornament; bauble; trinket.
4. a plaything, especially one for children.
5. any small thing, person, or animal; specifically, a small breed of dog, etc.; as, a *toy* terrier.
6. in Scotland, a woman's headdress of linen or wool, with flaps that hang over the shoulders. [Obs. or Rare.]
7. a trifling practice; a silly opinion; a wild fancy; an odd conceit. [Obs.]

toy, *a.* 1. like a toy, or plaything, in size, use, etc.
2. made as a toy; especially, being a miniature imitation; as, a *toy* stove.

toy, *v.i.*; toyed, *pt.*, *pp.*; toying, *ppr.* to trifle or play (*with* a piece of food, another's affection, an idea, etc.).

toy, *v.t.* to treat foolishly. [Obs.]

tö-yēar′, *adv.* in this year. [Obs. or Brit. Dial.]

toy′ẽr, *n.* one who toys; one who is full of trifling tricks.

toy′ful, *a.* full of trifling play. [Rare.]

toy′ing·ly, *adv.* triflingly; in a toying manner.

toy′ish, *a.* 1. trifling; wanton. [Rare.]
2. like a toy; small. [Rare.]

toy′ish·ly, *adv.* in a toyish or trifling manner. [Rare.]

toy′ish·ness, *n.* disposition or inclination to toying or trifling. [Rare.]

toy′măn, *n.*; *pl.* **toy′men,** one who deals in or makes toys.

tō′yŏn, *n.* an American evergreen shrub, *Heteromeles arbutifolia*, of the Pacific Coast, having shiny, toothed leaves, clusters of white flowers, and bright-red berries: also called *tollon*, *California holly*, etc.

toy′shop, *n.* 1. a shop where toys are sold.
2. a shop where trinkets, knickknacks, etc. were sold. [Obs.]

toy′sŏme, *a.* inclined to trifle; wanton. [Rare.]

toy′wŏrt, *n.* same as *shepherd's-purse*.

tōze, *v.t.* to tose. [Obs.]

tō′zi·ness, *n.* the state or quality of being tozy. [Obs. or Brit. Dial.]

tō′zy, *a.* resembling teased wool; soft. [Brit. Dial.]

Tr, in chemistry, terbium.

trab′ăl, *a.* [L. *trabalis*, from *trabs*, a beam.] of or pertaining to the trabs, or the trabs cerebri.

trā′bē·ȧ, *n.* [L.] in ancient Rome, the purple-striped robe of state worn by kings, consuls, augurs, etc.

trā′bē·ā·ted, *a.* [L. *trabs*, a beam.]
1. built with horizontal beams or lintels, instead of arches.
2. of such construction.

trā·bē·ā′tion, *n.* 1. trabeated construction or structure.
2. an entablature. [Obs.]

trȧ·bec̦′ū·lȧ, *n.*; *pl.* **trȧ·bec̦′ū·lae,** 1. in anatomy and zoology, a small septum of fibers forming, with others of its kind, an essential part of the framework of an organ or part.
2. in botany, a row or bridge of cells extending across the cavity of the sporangium of a moss.

trȧ·bec̦′ū·lăr, *a.* of or pertaining to a trabecula or trabeculae.

trȧ·bec̦′ū·lāte, *a.* marked with crossbars.

trabs, *n.* [L., a beam.] the corpus callosum: called also *trabs cerebri*.

trāce, *n.* [OFr., from *tracier*; see the **v.**]
1. originally, a way followed or path taken.
2. a mark, footprint, etc. left by the passage of a person, animal, or thing.
3. a beaten path or trail left by the passage of persons, vehicles, etc.; as, the Natchez *Trace*.
4 a visible mark left by a past person, thing, or event; a sign; evidence; vestige; as, the war left its *traces*.
5. a barely observable amount; a very small quantity; as, a *trace* of anger, a *trace* of salt.
6. a drawn or traced mark.
7. the traced record of a recording instrument.
8. in psychology, an engram.
9. in chemistry, a very small amount, usually one quantitatively immeasurable.
10. in geometry, the intersection of a plane with one of the planes of projection.
11. in fortification, a ground plan of a work.
Syn.—mark, vestige, track, imprint, token, remnant.

trāce, *v.t.*; traced (trāst), *pt.*, *pp.*; tracing, *ppr.* [Fr. *tracier*, to trace, delineate, mark; LL. *tractiare*, from L. *tractus*, pp. of *trahere*, to draw.]
1. to move along, follow, or traverse (a path, route, etc.).
2. to follow the trail or footprints of; to track.
3. to follow the development, process, or history of, especially by proceeding from the latest to the earliest evidence, etc.
4. to find or determine (an origin, source, date, etc.) by this procedure.
5. to discover or ascertain by investigating traces or vestiges of (something prehistoric, etc.).
6. to draw with lines; to delineate.
7. (a) to make a drawing, diagram, etc. of; (b) to mark the course of on a map, plan, etc.
8. to ornament with tracery: used chiefly in the past participle.
9. to copy (a drawing, etc.) by following its lines on a superimposed, transparent sheet; to make a tracing of.
10. to form (letters, etc.) carefully or laboriously.
11. to make or copy with a tracer.
12. to record by means of a curved, broken, or wavy line, as in a seismograph.
13. to define or present in general terms; as, he *traced* the policy afterward carried out by his henchmen.

trāce, *v.i.* to follow a path, route, development, etc.; to make one's way.

trāce, *n.* [ME. *traice*, *trais*; OFr. *traiz*, *trais*, pl. of *trait*; L. *tractus*, pp. of *trahere*, to draw.]
1. either of two straps, chains, etc. connecting a draft animal's harness to the vehicle drawn.
2. a rod, pivoted at each end, that transmits motion from one moving part of a machine to another.
to kick over the traces; to shake off control; to show insubordination or independence.

trāce, *v.t.* to hitch up (a horse, etc.).

trāce′ȧ·ble, *a.* that can be traced.

trāce′ȧ·bly, *adv.* in a traceable manner.

trāce′less, *a.* leaving or exhibiting no mark or trace; that cannot be traced.

trāce′less·ly, *adv.* in a traceless manner.

trā′cẽr, *n.* 1. a person or thing that traces; specifically, (a) a person whose work is tracing lost or missing articles; (b) an instrument for tracing designs on cloth, etc.
2. an inquiry sent out for a letter, package, etc. that is missing in transport.
3. (a) the chemical added to a tracer bullet or shell to leave a trail of smoke or fire; (b) a tracer bullet or shell.

trā′cẽr bul′let (or **shell**), a bullet or shell that traces its own course in the air with a trail of smoke or fire, so as to facilitate adjustment of the aim.

trā′cẽr·ied, *a.* consisting of or decorated with tracery.

trā′cẽr·y, *n.*; *pl.* **trā′cẽr·ieṣ,** [from *trace*, v., and *-ery*.]
1. in architecture, the ornamental openwork formed in the head of a Gothic window by the mullions there diverging into arches, curves, and flowing lines, intersecting in various ways and enriched with foliations; also, the subdivisions of groined vaults, or any ornamental design of the same character, for doors, paneling, ceilings, etc.
2. in decorative art, any ornamental work of interlacing or branching lines; scrollwork.
3. any natural or artificial linear pattern suggesting tracery; as, the *tracery* of a leaf; the *tracery* of a glaciated pebble.

trā′c̦hē-, tracheo-.

trā′c̦hē·ȧ (*or* trȧ-kē′ȧ), *n.*; *pl.* **trā′c̦hē·ae,** [LL. *trachia*, the windpipe, from Gr. *tracheia*, lit., the rough, from the rings of gristle of which it is composed.]
1. in the respiratory tract of vertebrates, that part which conveys air from the larynx to the bronchi; the windpipe.
2. in the respiratory system of insects and other invertebrates, any of the small tubules for conveying air.
3. in botany, a tubelike duct in plants, formed by a row of cells whose partitioning cell walls have disappeared.
book-leaf trachea; a sac with leaflike divisions, forming the respiratory organ of certain species of *Arachnida*.
trachea retractor; an instrument for holding back the edges of the slit trachea during surgical operations.

trā′c̦hē·ăl (*or* trȧ-kē′ăl), *a.* 1. of, like, or having a trachea or tracheae.
2. of or composed of tracheal tissue.
tracheal commissure; one of the transverse tubes serving to connect the lateral stems of a tracheal system in insects.
tracheal sac; a respiratory sac in insects.
tracheal tissue; the essential tissue of the xylem of plants, composed of tracheae or tracheids, or both. It has both a supporting and a vascular function and serves to transport watery solutions from the root.

trā·c̦hē·al′gi·ȧ, *n.* pain in the trachea.

trā·c̦hē·ā′lis, *n.*; *pl.* **trā·c̦hē·ā′lēṣ,** [L.] in anatomy, a muscle which lessens the caliber of the trachea.

trā′c̦hē·ăn, *a.* 1. having tracheae or similar organs.
2. breathing by or having the functions of tracheae.

Trā·c̦hē·ā′ri·ȧ, *n.pl.* an order of the class *Arachnida*, including those arachnids breathing by tracheal tubes alone.

trā′c̦hē·ăr·y, *a.* 1. having a trachea or tracheae.
2. making use of tracheae in breathing.
tracheary tissue; same as *tracheal tissue* under *tracheal*.

trā′c̦hē·ăr·y, *n.* a member of the *Trachearia*.

Trā·c̦hē·ā′tȧ, *n.pl.* same as *Trachearia*.

trā′c̦hē·āte, *a.* 1. respiring by means of tracheae.
2. of or pertaining to the *Trachearia* or *Tracheata*.

trā′c̦hē·āte, *n.* any arthropod furnished with tracheae.

trā′c̦hē·id, *n.* [*trache-* and *-id.*] in botany, any of the large, thick-walled, water-conducting, tubelike cells found in woody tissue, as of the conifers.

trā·c̦hē′i·dăl, *a.* of or like a tracheid.

trā·c̦hē·ī′tis, *n.* [Mod. L.] inflammation of the trachea.

trac̦h′ē·lāte, trȧ·c̦hē′li·āte, *a.* [Gr. *trachēlos*, the neck, throat.] resembling or similar to a neck, as the tapering prosternum of certain insects.

trȧ·c̦hel′i·dăn, *n.* any beetle having the head borne on a pedicle.

trȧ·c̦hel′i·pod, *n.* one of the *Trachelipoda*.

Trā·c̦hē·lip′ō·dȧ, *n.pl.* [*trachelo-*, and Gr. *pous*, *podos*, foot.] a former classification of gastropods comprising species having a spiral shell and the foot attached to the base of the neck.

trā·c̦hē·lip′ō·dous, *a.* having the foot united with the neck; having the characters of a trachelipod.

trā′c̦hē·lō-, trā′c̦hel-, [from Gr. *trachēlos*, neck.] a combining form meaning *neck*.

trā·c̦hē·lō·brañ′c̦hi·āte, *a.* [*trachelo-*, and Gr. *branchia*, gills.] furnished with branchia growing from the neck.

trā·c̦hē·lō·dyn′i·ȧ, *n.* [*trachel-*, and Gr. *odynē*, pain.] pain in the neck.

trā·c̦heñ′c̦hy·mȧ, *n.* same as *tracheal tissue* under *tracheal*.

trā′c̦hē·ō-, [from *trachea*.] a combining form meaning (a) *of the trachea*, as in *tracheo*tomy; (b) *the trachea and*, as in *tracheo*bronchial: also, before a vowel, *trache-*.

trā·c̦hē·ō·brañ′c̦hi·ȧ, *n.*; *pl.* **trā·c̦hē·ō·brañ′c̦hi·ae,** [*tracheo-*, and Gr. *branchia*, gills.] a breathing organ of the nature of a gill as well as a trachea: seen in the aquatic larvae of certain insects.

trā·c̦hē·ō·broñ′c̦hi·ăl, *a.* pertaining to the bronchial and tracheal tubes: used of the syrinx of some birds.

trā·c̦hē′ō·cēle, *n.* [*tracheo-*, and Gr. *kēlē*, a tumor.]
1. goiter.
2. hernial protrusion of the mucous membrane of the trachea.

Trā·ċhē·oph′ō·nae, *n.pl.* [*tracheo-*, and Gr. *phōnē*, voice.] a group of passerine birds in which the syrinx is situated at the proximal end of the trachea: also written *Tracheophones.*

trā·ċhē·ot′ō·my, *n.* [*tracheo-*, and Gr. *temnein*, to cut.] in surgery, the operation of making an opening into the trachea, or windpipe, as in cases of suffocation.

trā′ċhi·noid, *a.* of or pertaining to the genus *Trachinus.*

Trā·ċhī′nus, *n.* a genus of fishes typical of the *Trachinidæ*, a family of acanthopterygious fishes; the weevers.

trȧ·ċhō′mȧ, *n.* [Gr. *trachōma*, roughness, from *trachys*, rough.] a contagious form of conjunctivitis, characterized by the formation of inflammatory granulations on the inner eyelid.

trȧ·ċhom′ȧ·tous, *a.* of, having, or pertaining to trachoma.

trā′ċhy-, [from Gr. *trachys*, rough.] a combining form meaning *rough*, as in *trachy*carpous.

trā·ċhy·cär′pous, *a.* [Gr. *trachys*, rough, and *karpos*, fruit.] bearing rough fruit.

Trā″ċhy·mē·dū′sae, *n.pl.* [Gr. *trachys*, rough, and *Medusæ.*] a group of *Cœlenterata* with a firm gelatinous umbrella supported by cartilaginous ridges.

trā·ċhy·spẽr′mous, *a.* [Gr. *trachys*, rough, and *sperma*, seed.] having rough seeds.

Trā·ċhy·stō′mȧ·tȧ, *n.pl.* [Gr. *trachys*, rough, and *stoma*, *stomatos*, mouth.] a group of perennibranchiate amphibians with eellike bodies and rudimentary anterior limbs, represented in North America by *Siren lacertina*, native to South Carolina.

trā′ċhȳte, *n.* [Gr. *trachytēs*, roughness, sharpness, from *trachys*, rough.] a nearly compact, light-colored, feldspathic, pyrogenous rock, breaking with a rough surface, and often containing crystals of glassy feldspar, sometimes with hornblende and mica. This rock is extremely abundant among the products of modern volcanoes, and forms whole mountains in countries where igneous action is very slightly or not at all perceived.

trȧ·ċhyt′iç, *a.* of, characteristic of, or occurring in trachyte: trachytic rock contains long feldspar crystals in nearly parallel lines.

traċh′y·toid, *a.* belonging to or resembling trachyte.

trā′cing, *n.* 1. the act of one who traces.
2. something made by tracing; specifically, (a) a copy of a drawing, etc. made by tracing the lines on a superimposed, transparent sheet; (b) the record of a recording instrument, in the form of a traced line.

trā′cing ċloth, smooth linen, coated with size, used for making tracings of architectural drawings, etc.

trā′cing pā′pẽr, thin, strong, transparent paper on which tracings can be made.

trā′cing wheel (hwēl), a toothed wheel, manipulated by a handle, which is used to mark out a pattern in dotted lines; also, any wheel used to make tracings.

track, *n.* [OFr. *trac*, a track, tract, or trace, a beaten way or course; O.D. *treck*, D. *trek*, a draft, from *trekken*, to draw, pull, tow, travel, march.]
1. a mark or series of marks left by a person, animal, or thing that has passed, as a footprint, wheel rut, wake of a boat, etc.
2. a trace or vestige.
3. a beaten path or trail left by the passage of persons, animals, or vehicles.
4. a course or line of motion or action; route; way.
5. a sequence of ideas, events, etc.; a succession.
6. a path or circuit laid out for running, horse racing, etc.
7. a pair of parallel metal rails with their crossties and roadbed, on which trains, streetcars, etc. run.
8. the distance in inches between parallel wheels, as of an automobile.
9. (a) athletic sports performed on a track, as running, hurdling, etc.: distinguished from *field sports*; (b) track and field sports together.
10. in anatomy, the path of a vessel, nerve, or duct.
11. in zoology, the sole of the foot, especially of birds.
12. a tract of land. [Obs.]
in one's tracks; where one is at the moment.
off the track; straying from the subject, objective, or goal; in error.
on the track; keeping to the subject, objective, or goal; correct.
to keep track of; to keep an account of; to stay informed about.
to lose track of; to fail to keep informed about; to lose sight or knowledge of.
to make tracks; to proceed or depart hurriedly. [Colloq.]

track, *v.t.*; tracked (trakt), *pt.*, *pp.*; tracking, *ppr.* 1. (a) to follow the track of; as, they *track* game; (b) to follow (a track, etc.).
2. to trace by means of vestiges, evidence, etc.
3. to tread or travel.
4. to leave tracks or footprints on (often with *up*).
5. to leave in the form of tracks; as, he *tracked* dirt over the floor.
6. to provide with tracks or rails.
7. to mark out (a path).
to track down; (a) to pursue until caught, as by following tracks; (b) to investigate or search for until found, by examining evidence, etc.

track, *v.i.* 1. to run in the same (width) track.
2. to be in alignment, as wheels or gears.
3. to have a (specified) width between the wheels; as, a narrow-gauge car *tracks* less than 56 inches.

track, *a.* 1. having to do with a railroad track.
2. of or performed on an athletic track.

track, *v.t.* to tow or draw, as a vessel or boat, by a line reaching from it to the shore or bank.

track′āġe, *n.* a drawing or towing, as of a boat; towage.

track′āġe, *n.* 1. all the tracks of a railroad.
2. permission for a railroad to use the tracks of another.
3. a charge for this.

track and fiēld, a series of contests in running, jumping, shot-putting, etc. performed on a track and on a field (*n.* 11b).

track edġe, the sloping edge of the furrow of a millstone.

track′ẽr, *n.* one who or that which tracks, or traces; one who pursues or hunts by following a track or trail.

track′ẽr, *n.* 1. one who or that which tows a boat, as by a line from the shore.
2. a wooden strip in pipe organs, serving to connect levers.

track in′di·cā·tŏr, on a railroad car, a device for indicating the alignment, level, etc. of the track on which the car is running.

track′less, *a.* without a track, trail, or path; specifically, not running on tracks; as, a *trackless* trolley.

track′less·ness, *n.* the state of being without a track.

track′less trol′ley, a passenger bus which, instead of being motivated by a gasoline engine, is operated electrically by an overhead trolley. The bus is steered like an automobile and requires no tracks.

track′măn, *n.*; *pl.* **track′men,** a man hired to inspect and take care of a railroad track; a trackwalker.

track man, an athlete who competes in track events.

track′mȧs″tẽr, *n.* an official who has charge of a railroad track.

track reç′ord, [probably with reference to the running records of race horses.] the record of the performance of a person, organization, etc. as in some field of activity or on some issue. [Colloq.]

track rōad, a towing path.

track sçāle, a scale with tracks, for weighing railroad cars with or without loads.

track sys′tem, a system of education in which students are put in different groups according to test performance and are kept in them through the grades.

track′walk″ẽr (-wąk″), *n.* a man employed to walk along, and inspect, sections of railroad track; a trackman.

traçt, *n.* [L. *tractus*, a drawing out, a region, from *tractus*, pp. of *trahere*, to draw.]
1. (a) duration or lapse of time; (b) a period of time. [Poet.]
2. a continuous expanse of land, etc.; a stretch; extent; area.
3. in anatomy and zoology, (a) a system of parts or organs having some special function; as, the genito-urinary *tract*; (b) a bundle of nerve fibers having the same origin, termination, and function.
4. [ML. *tractus.*] in the Roman Catholic Church, a penitential chant of Lent, etc., consisting either of a complete psalm or of a few verses of Scripture, often from the Psalms: it is sung straight through without interruption.
5. in ornithology, a pteryla.

traçt, *v.t.* 1. to trace; to follow. [Obs.]
2. to draw out; to protract. [Obs.]

traçt, *n.* [L. *tractatus*, a handling, treatise.]
1. formerly, a short treatise.
2. a pamphlet or leaflet, especially one on a religious subject.
Tracts for the Times; see *Tractarianism.*

traçt·ȧ·bil′i·ty, *n.* the quality or state of being tractable.

traçt′ȧ·ble, *a.* 1. easily led, taught, or managed; docile; manageable; governable; as, *tractable* children.
2. palpable; that can be handled. [Obs.]
3. easily worked or wrought; malleable.

traçt′ȧ·ble·ness, *n.* tractability.

traçt′ȧ·bly, *adv.* in a tractable manner; with ready compliance.

Traç·tār′i·ăn, *n.* a founder of or believer in Tractarianism.

Traç·tār′i·ăn, *a.* pertaining to the Tractarians or their doctrines.

Traç·tār′i·ăn·iṣm, *n.* the principles of the Oxford Movement, opposed to the tendency toward evangelical Protestantism in the Church of England and favoring a return to early Catholic doctrines and practices: so called from the ninety "Tracts for the Times," a series of pamphlets issued at Oxford from 1833 to 1841; also called *Puseyism.*

traçt′āte, *n.* [L. *tractatus*, a handling, a treatise.] a treatise; a tract.

traç·tā′tion, *n.* treatment or handling of a subject; discussion. [Obs.]

traç·tā′tŏr, *n.* a writer of tracts; specifically, [T-] one who favors Tractarianism; a Tractarian.

traç·tā′trix, *n.* [L.] same as *tractrix.*

traç′tile, *a.* [L. *tractus*, pp. of *trahere*, to draw.] capable of being drawn out in length; ductile.

traç·til′i·ty, *n.* the property of being tractile; ductility.

traç′tion, *n.* [ML. *tractio*, from L. *tractus*, pp. of *trahere*, to draw.]
1. (a) a pulling or drawing, especially of a load over a road, track, or other surface; (b) the state of being pulled or drawn.
2. a pulling, as of the muscles of the leg, arm, etc., in order to bring a fractured or dislocated bone into place.
3. the pulling power of a locomotive, etc.; as, steam *traction.*
4. adhesive friction, as of a wheel on a rail; as, the train got little *traction* on the hill.
angle of traction; the angle which the force of traction makes with the plane along which a body is drawn.
force of traction; the power exerted in order to draw a body along a plane.

traç′tion·ăl, *a.* of or pertaining to traction.

traç′tion en′ġine, a steam locomotive for pulling heavy wagons, plows, etc. on roads or in fields.

traç′tion wheel (hwēl), a wheel that draws or impels a vehicle, as the driving wheel of a locomotive.

Traç′tīte, *n.* same as *Tractarian.*

traçt′ive, *a.* serving or used to pull or draw.

traçt′ŏr, *n.* [Mod. L., from L. *tractus*, pp. of *trahere*, to draw.] that which draws or is used for drawing; specifically, (a) a small, powerful vehicle with a gasoline or Diesel engine and, sometimes, caterpillar treads, for pulling farm machinery, hauling loads, etc.; (b) a kind of truck with a driver's cab and no body, designed for hauling one or more large vans, or trailers; (c) an airplane with a tractor propeller or propellers.

TRACTOR

metallic tractors; two small pointed bars, one of brass and one of steel, which, on being drawn over diseased parts of the body, were formerly used to relieve pain through electricity or magnetism.
tractor propeller; an airplane propeller mounted in front of the wings.

traç·tō·rā′tion, *n.* the use of metallic tractors for the cure of diseases. [Obs.]

traçt′ō·ry, *n.*; *pl.* **traçt′ō·rieṣ,** a tractrix. [Rare.]

traçt′rix, *n.* in geometry, a curve whose tangent is always equal to a given line. It may be described by a small weight attached to a string, the other end of which is moved along a given straight line or curve.

trāde, *n.* [M.L.G., a track; OS. *trada*, a trace, trail.]

1. a footstep; track; trail. [Obs.]

2. a particular course of action or effort; a regular procedure. [Obs.]

3. custom; habit; standing practice. [Obs.]

4. a means of earning one's living; occupation; work; especially, skilled work, as distinguished from unskilled work or from a profession or business; a craft.

5. the act or business of exchanging commodities for other commodities or for money; the business of buying and selling; commerce; barter.

6. all the persons engaged in the same line of business.

7. customers; clientele.

8. an exchange; a swap.

9. [*pl.*] trade winds.

10. the instruments, collectively, of any occupation. [Dial.]

11. rubbish; debris. [Dial.]

12. a purchase or sale; a bargain; a deal.

Syn.—business, traffic, sale, exchange.

trāde, *a.* pertaining to or characteristic of trade.

trade dollar; see under *dollar*.

trade price; the reduced price at which manufacturers or wholesalers sell to dealers in the same trade.

trade sale; a special auction sale by manufacturers, publishers, or others to persons in the trade.

trāde, *v.t.*; traded, *pt.*, *pp.*; trading, *ppr.* to exchange; to buy and sell; to barter.

They *traded* the persons of men.
—Ezek. xxvii. 13.

trāde, *v.i.* 1. to barter; to traffic; to carry on a trade or business.

2. to make an exchange (*with* someone).

3. to have business dealings or transactions (*with* someone).

How did you dare
To *trade* and traffic *with* Macbeth?
—Shak.

4. to go to for the purpose of buying or selling, as a merchantman. [Rare.]

5. to be a customer (*at* a specified store or shop). [Colloq.]

to trade in; to give (one's used automobile, etc.) as part payment in the purchase of a new one.

to trade on (or *upon*); to take advantage of; to presume or impose upon.

trāde aç·cept'ănce, a bill of exchange or draft drawn upon the purchaser by the seller and accepted by the purchaser for payment at a specified time.

trāde as·sō·ci·ā'tion, an association of merchants or business firms for the unified promotion of their common interests.

trāde dis'çount, a deduction from the list price allowed a retailer by a manufacturer, wholesaler, or distributor, or allowed one firm by another in the same trade.

trāde ē·di'tion, that edition of a book sold through regular channels to the general public, as distinguished from a school edition, etc. of the same book.

trāde'fụl, *a.* commercial; busy in trade.

trāde'-in, *n.* 1. something given or taken as payment or, especially, part payment for something else.

2. an exchange involving a trade-in.

3. the valuation allowed by the seller on a trade-in.

trāde joūr'năl, a magazine in which matters pertaining to a particular business, trade or industry are printed.

trāde'-lȧst, *n.* a compliment reported by someone on the condition that the one about whom the compliment was made will report a similar compliment about the reporter in exchange. [Colloq.]

trāde'less, *a.* without trade.

trāde mag·ȧ·zīne', same as *trade journal*.

trāde'-märk, trāde'märk, *n.* a distinguishing symbol, design, word, etc. used by a manufacturer or dealer on his goods, labels, etc., to distinguish them from those of competitors, and usually registered and protected by law.

trāde'-märk, trāde'märk, *v.t.* 1. to put a trade-mark on (a product).

2. to register (a symbol, etc.) as a trade-mark.

trāde nāme, 1. the name by which a commodity is commonly known in trade.

2. a name used as a trade-mark, especially one registered and protected by law.

3. the name under which a company carries on business.

trāde'-ọff, *n.* an exchange; especially, a giving up of one benefit, advantage, etc. in order to gain another regarded as more desirable: also *tradeoff*.

trāde pā'pēr, same as *trade journal*.

trād'ēr, *n.* 1. one who is engaged in trade or commerce; a merchant.

2. a ship used in trade.

3. a member of a stock exchange who trades for himself and not as an agent for customers.

trāde rou̇te, any route customarily taken by trading ships, caravans, etc.

Trad·es·çan'ti·ȧ (-shi-), *n.* [named after John *Tradescant*, 17th-c. Eng. naturalist and traveler.]

1. a genus of lilylike plants of the spiderwort family, *Commelinaceæ*, native to America and characterized by having three sepals, three petals, a three-celled capsule, and filaments covered with jointed hairs. *Tradescantia virginica*, a North American species, has succulent stems, shiny, glasslike leaves, and blue, red, or white flowers.

2. [t-] any plant of this genus.

TRADESCANTIA
(*Tradescantia virginica*)

trāde sçhool, a school where a trade or trades are taught.

trāde sē'çret, any device, method, formula, etc. known to the manufacturer who uses it but not to his competitors.

trādeṣ'fōlk (-fōk), *n.pl.* tradespeople.

trādeṣ'măn, *n.*; *pl.* **trādeṣ'men,** 1. one who is engaged in trade, especially a shopkeeper.

2. a man having a trade; a craftsman or artisan. [Dial.]

trādeṣ'pēo''ple, *n.pl.* people employed in trade, especially storekeepers and their families.

trādeṣ ūn'iŏn (-yun), a trade union. [Chiefly Brit.]

trādeṣ'wom''ăn (-woom''), *n.*; *pl.* **trādeṣ'wom''en** (-wim''), a girl or woman storekeeper.

trāde'-ūn''iŏn (-yun), *a.* of a trade union or trade unions.

trāde'-ūn''iŏn, *n.* a trade union.

trāde ūn'iŏn, an association of workers to promote and protect the welfare, interests, and rights of its members, primarily by collective bargaining; a labor union.

trāde ūn'iŏn·iṣm, 1. the principles or practices of organizing into trade unions.

2. the policies and activities of trade unions.

Also *trade-unionism*.

trāde ūn'iŏn·ist, 1. a member of a trade union.

2. a person who believes in or supports trade unionism.

Also *trade-unionist*.

trāde wind, a wind that blows toward the equator from the same quarter throughout the year. The general direction is from northeast to southwest on the north side of the equator, and from southeast to northwest on the south side of the equator.

trād'ing, *a.* 1. that trades; carrying on commerce; engaged in trade; as, a *trading* company.

2. corrupt; unprincipled; as, a *trading* politician.

trād'ing, *n.* the action of a person who trades; buying and selling; commerce.

trād'ing pōst, a store or station in an outpost, settlement, etc., where trading is done, as with natives.

trād'ing stamp, a stamp given by some merchants as a premium to customers, redeemable in a specified quantity for merchandise from those dealers.

trȧ·di'tion, *n.* [L. *traditio* (*-onis*), a surrender, delivery, tradition, from *traditus*, pp. of *tradere*, to deliver.]

1. delivery; the act of delivering into the hands of another: usually a legal term.

A deed takes effect only from the *tradition* or delivery.
—Blackstone.

2. originally, a surrender; a betrayal.

3. the delivery of opinions, doctrines, practices, rites, and customs from generation to generation by oral communication.

4. a statement, opinion, or belief handed down orally from one generation to another.

5. in theology, (a) among the Jews, an unwritten code of laws said to have been given to Moses on Mt. Sinai when he received the decalogue, and handed down by the teachings of the prophets and rabbis; (b) among Christians, the unwritten teachings regarded as handed down from Jesus and the Apostles; also, in the Roman Catholic Church, the decrees of the councils and the popes, which are considered to have been prompted by the Holy Ghost and therefore are authoritative; (c) among Moslems, the sayings and acts attributed to Mohammed, not contained in the Koran, but handed down orally.

6. a long-established custom or practice that has the effect of an unwritten law; specifically, any of the usages of a school of art or literature handed down through the generations, and generally observed.

Tradition Sunday; Palm Sunday: formerly so called because candidates for baptism or for confirmation on Easter were taught the creed on that day.

trȧ·di'tion, *v.t.* to hand down as a tradition.

trȧ·di'tion·ăl, *a.* of, pertaining to, or handed down by tradition; conventional; customary.

trȧ·di'tion·ăl·iṣm, *n.* 1. adherence to or excessive respect for tradition.

2. the doctrine that the only valid religious belief is that handed down from an original divine revelation.

trȧ·di'tion·ăl·ist, *n.* one who observes tradition or believes in its authority; also, one who believes in traditionalism.

trȧ·di''tion·ăl·is'tiç, *a.* of, pertaining to, or characterized by traditionalism.

trȧ·di'tion·ăl·ly, *adv.* according to tradition.

trȧ·di'tion·ăr·i·ly, *adv.* by tradition.

trȧ·di'tion·ăr·y, *a.* same as *traditional*.

trȧ·di'tion·ăr·y, *n.*; *pl.* **trȧ·di'tion·ăr·ieṣ,** one who acknowledges the authority of traditions; a traditionalist.

trȧ·di'tion·ist, trȧ·di'tion·ēr, *n.* 1. a traditionalist.

2. a specialist in or recorder of traditions.

trad'i·tive, *a.* traditionary; traditional.

trad'i·tŏr, *n.*; *pl.* **trad·i·tō'rēṣ,** [L., from *traditus*, pp. of *tradere*, to draw.] among the early Christians, a traitor during the Roman persecution.

trȧ·dūce', *v.t.*; traduced (-dūst), *pt.*, *pp.* traducing, *ppr.* [L. *traducere*, to lead along, exhibit as a spectacle, disgrace, transfer; *trans*, across, over, and *ducere*, to lead.]

1. to exhibit; to display; to make an example of. [Obs.]

2. to defame; to slander; to malign; to calumniate; to vilify.

3. to translate from one language into another. [Obs.]

4. to draw aside from duty; to seduce. [Obs.]

trȧ·dūce'ment, *n.* the act of traducing; misrepresentation; defamation; calumny.

trȧ·dū'cent, *a.* slandering; slanderous. [Rare.]

trȧ·dū'cēr, *n.* one who traduces; a slanderer; a calumniator.

trȧ·dū'ciăn, *n.* one who believes in the doctrine of traducianism.

trȧ·dū'ciăn·iṣm, *n.* [LL. *traducianus*, from L. *tradux*, a branch of a vine.] in theology, (a) the doctrine that the soul as well as the body is begotten by reproduction from the substance of the parents: opposed to *creationism*; (b) [Rare.] the doctrine of the transmission of original sin from parent to child.

trȧ·dū'ciăn·ist, *n.* a traducian.

trȧ·dū'cing·ly, *adv.* in a traducing manner; slanderously; by way of defamation.

trȧ·duçt', *v.t.* to transmit; to pass on; to propagate. [Obs.]

trȧ·duç'tion, *n.* 1. derivation from one of the same kind; propagation. [Obs.]

2. tradition; transmission from one to another. [Obs.]

3. conveyance; transportation; act of transferring. [Obs.]

4. a translation. [Obs.]

trȧ·duç'tive, *a.* derivative; that can be deduced. [Obs.]

traf'fiç, *n.* [Fr. *trafic*, *trafique*, traffic; It. *traffico*, from *trafficare*, to trade.]

1. originally, (a) transportation of goods for trading; (b) trading over great distances; commerce; (c) [Rare.] merchandise; commodities for market.

2. buying and selling; barter; trade.

3. corrupt or illegal trade.

4. dealings, business, or intercourse (*with* someone).

5. (a) the movement or number of automobiles along a street, pedestrians along a sidewalk, ships in a port, etc.; (b) the automobiles, pedestrians, ships, etc.

6. the business done by a transportation company, measured by the number of passengers, quantity of freight, etc. carried during a given period.

7. the business done by a communications company, measured by the telegrams, calls, etc. transmitted during a given period.

8. the passengers, freight, communications, etc. thus measured.

traf'fiç, *a.* of, for, or regulating traffic; as, a traffic policeman.

traffic cop; a traffic policemen. [Slang.]

traffic court; a local court having jurisdiction over those charged with violating statutes or ordinances governing the flow of traffic on streets and highways.

traffic light; a set of signal lights placed at intersections of streets to regulate traffic.

traffic policeman; a policeman stationed at intersections of streets, whose duty it is to direct traffic and guide pedestrians.

traffic tower; a raised booth from which traffic, especially city traffic, is directed by a traffic policeman.

traf'fiç, *v.i.*; trafficked (-fikt), *pt., pp.*; trafficking, *ppr.* [Fr. *trafiquer*, to traffic, trade.]

1. to pass goods and commodities from one person to another for an equivalent in goods or money; to carry on commerce, especially illegal trade (*in* a commodity).

2. to have trade, traffic, or dealings (*with* someone).

traf'fiç, *v.t.* 1. to exchange in traffic; to barter.

2. to negotiate; to bargain for. [Rare.]

traf'fiç·ȧ·ble, *a.* marketable.

traf'fick·ẽr, *n.* one who carries on commerce; a trader; a merchant.

traf'fiç·less, *a.* without trade.

traf'fiç man'ȧ·ġẽr, the manager or superintendent of traffic of any commercial or industrial establishment.

traf'fiç pat'tẽrn, a pattern of flight in the air above or around an airport normally followed by aircraft before landing or after taking off.

trag'ȧ·çanth, *n.* [L. *tragacantha*; Gr. *tragakantha*; *tragos*, a goat, and *akantha*, a thorn.]

1. a tasteless, odorless, white or reddish gum obtained from several shrubs of the genus *Astragalus*, used in pharmacy, calico printing, cloth finishing, etc.: also called *gum dragon*, *dracanth*, *gum tragacanth*.

2. goat's-thorn, a leguminous plant, *Astragalus tragacantha*, that yields a gummy juice used in confections.

3. any of several other species of the genus *Astragalus*.

TRAGACANTH (*Astragalus gummifer*)

trā'gȧl, *a.* of or pertaining to the tragus of the ear.

trȧ·ġē'di·ăn, *n.* [ME. and OFr. *tragedien*.]

1. a writer of tragedies.

2. an actor of tragedy.

trȧ·ġē·di·enne' (-en'), *n.* an actress of tragedy.

traġ'e·dy, *n.*; *pl.* **traġ'e·dieş**, [Fr. *tragédie*; L. *tragædia*; Gr. *tragōdia*, a tragedy, lit., the song of the goat; from *tragōdos*, lit., a goat singer, a tragic poet and singer, from *tragos*, a he-goat, and *ōidē*, song; variously explained as referring to a goat offered as a prize or to the goatskin dress of the performers in early plays of this sort.]

1. a serious play having an unhappy or disastrous ending brought about by the characters or central character impelled, in ancient drama, by fate or, more recently, by moral weakness, psychological maladjustment, or social pressures.

2. the branch of drama consisting of plays of this type.

3. the writing, acting, or theoretical principles of this kind of drama.

4. a novel or other literary work with similar characteristics.

5. the tragic element of such a literary work, or of a real event.

6. a very sad or tragic event or events; a disaster.

Syn.—disaster, calamity, affliction, adversity, catastrophe, grief.

traġ'iç, traġ'iç·ăl, *a.* [Fr. *tragique*; L. *tragicus*; Gr. *tragikos*, goatish, tragic, from *tragos*, a goat.]

1. pertaining to tragedy; of the nature of tragedy; as, a *tragic* poem.

2. like or characteristic of tragedy; fatal, mournful, sorrowful, calamitous, etc.

3. appropriate to the acting of tragedy; expressive of tragedy; as, a *tragic* voice.

4. writing or acting in tragedy.

traġ'iç, *n.* 1. a writer of tragedy; a tragedian. [Rare.]

2. a tragedy. [Rare.]

the tragic; the tragic elements of art and literature, or of life.

traġ'iç·ăl·ly, *adv.* in a tragic manner.

traġ·i·çom'e·dy, *n.*; *pl.* **traġ·i·çom'e·dieş**, [Fr. *tragicomédie*, from L. *tragicocomœdia*; Gr. *tragikokomōdia*.]

1. a play or other literary work combining tragic and comic elements.

2. a real situation or incident like this.

traġ·i·çom'iç, *a.* pertaining to or having the nature of tragicomedy; having both tragic and comic elements.

traġ·i·çom'iç·ăl, *a.* same as *tragicomic*.

traġ·i·çom'iç·ăl·ly, *adv.* in a tragicomical manner.

traġ·i·çom·i·pȧs'tŏr·ăl, *a.* blending tragic, comic, and pastoral elements. [Rare.]

Trag'ō·pan, *n.* [Gr. *tragos*, a goat, and *Pan*, the deity; so called from the protuberances on its head.]

1. a genus of pheasants of the Himalayas. The plumage is spotted with eyelike markings and on the head of the male are two fleshy protuberances which can be erected until they look like a pair of horns.

2. [t—] any bird of this genus: also called *horned pheasant*.

Trag·ō·pō'gŏn, *n.* [Gr. *tragos*, goat, and *pōgōn*, the beard.] a genus of the *Compositæ*, including the salsify, or vegetable oyster, and the goat's beard.

trā'gus, *n.*; *pl.* **trā'ġī**, [Gr. *tragos*, a goat.] the cartilaginous projection before the external meatus or entrance of the ear, partly extending over the opening of the ear and, in men, often bearing a tuft of hair.

trāik, *v.i.* 1. to rove idly; also, to go astray. [Scot.]

2. to decline in strength.

trāil, *v.t.* [ME. *trailen*; OFr. *trailler*, from L. *trahere*, to draw or drag along.]

1. (a) to drag or let drag behind one, especially on the ground, etc.; (b) to bring along behind; as, he *trailed* dirt into the house.

2. (a) to make or mark (a path, track, etc.), as by treading down; (b) to make a path in (grass, etc.).

3. to follow the tracks of; to track.

4. to hunt by tracking.

5. to follow behind, especially in a lagging manner.

6. in military usage, to carry (a rifle, etc.) in the right hand with the arm extended downward so that the muzzle is slightly forward and the butt near the ground.

7. to draw out, or protract, the discussion of.

to trail a pen; to be a writer.

to trail a pike; to be a soldier.

to trail arms; in military usage, to carry a rifle so that the butt is raised a few inches from the ground with the muzzle pushed forward to bring the rifle barrel to an angle of approximately thirty degrees.

trāil, *v.i.* 1. to hang down, especially behind, so as to drag on the ground, etc.

2. to grow so long as to extend along the ground, over rocks, etc.: said of some plants.

3. to extend in an irregular line; to straggle.

4. to flow behind in a long, thin stream, wisp, etc.; as, smoke *trailed* from the chimney.

5. to move, walk, go along, etc. wearily, heavily, or slowly; to crawl; to drag.

6. to follow or lag behind.

7. to track game: said of hounds.

to trail off; to wander aimlessly away; also, to diminish or dwindle, as, the conversation began *to trail off*.

trāil, *n.* 1. the track followed by a hunter; the scent, mark, footprint, etc. left on the ground, as by an animal being pursued; hence, a clue.

2. anything drawn or trailed behind; also, the path or mark made by something drawn or passing through; a train; a wake; as, the *trail* of a meteor; a *trail* of smoke; the *trail* of a skirt.

3. a path or track made by continual passing or deliberately blazed.

4. a vehicle dragged along; a sled or sledge.

5. the act of playing upon or taking advantage of another's ignorance. [Brit. Dial.]

6. in military usage, (a) the position of trailing a rifle; (b) a beamlike part of a gun carriage, which may be lowered to the ground to form a rear brace.

7. in architecture, a running enrichment of leaves, flowers, tendrils, etc., in the hollow moldings of Gothic architecture.

trāil, *n.* a trellis or frame for climbing plants. [Obs.]

trāil blāz'ẽr, 1. a person who blazes a trail.

2. a pioneer in any field.

trāil bōard, a carved or ornamented board on each side of the stem of a vessel, stretching forward to the figurehead.

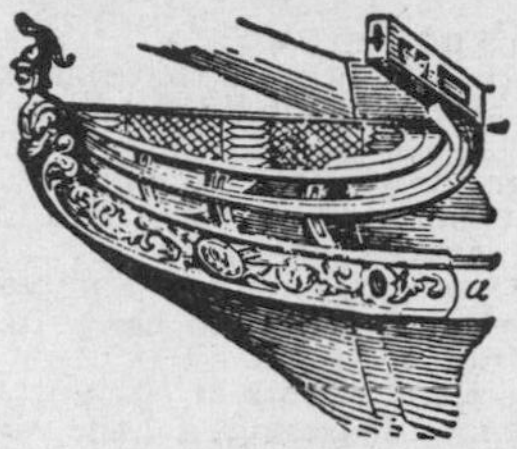

a, TRAIL BOARD

trāil'ẽr, *n.* 1. a person, animal, or thing that trails; specifically, (a) a trailing plant or vine; (b) a car, as on an electric or cable system, drawn by another connected with the source of power; (c) a wheel, as in a telpherage system, trailing the telpher along the overhead rail or wire, when the carrier is large, and helping to sustain the weight; (d) the fringe on the heel of a moccasin, believed by some Indians to be a protection against snakes; (e) a person who follows a trail, as a hunter, a tracker, or a detective; also, a dog that scents a trail.

2. a cart, wagon, or large van for hauling furniture, produce, etc., designed to be pulled by an automobile, truck, or tractor.

3. a closed vehicle designed to be pulled by an automobile and equipped as a place to live in, usually with a bed or beds, cooking facilities, etc.

4. in motion pictures, a short film containing scenes from a feature picture to be shown later, used for advertising: so called because originally attached to the end of a reel of film.

trailer camp; a number of parked trailers serving as a temporary housing project for workers, tourists, etc.

trāil'ing, *a.* 1. of or pertaining to a trailer.

2. that trails.

trailing arbutus; see under *arbutus*.

trailing edge; in aeronautics, the rear edge of a plane, propellor, etc.

trailing wheels; the wheels placed behind the driving wheels of a locomotive engine; also, the hind wheels of a carriage.

trāil rōpe, a rope used in trailing.

trāin, *v.t.*; trained, *pt., pp.*; training, *ppr.* [OFr. *trainer*, *trahiner*, to draw; LL. *trahinare*, a derivative from L. *trahere*, to draw.]

1. to draw along; to trail. [Rare.]

In hollow cube
Training his devilish enginery. —Milton.

2. to guide the growth of (a plant), as by tying, pruning, etc.

3. to guide the mental, moral, etc. development of; to bring up; to rear.

4. to instruct so as to make proficient or qualified; as, nurses are *trained* at this hospital.

5. to discipline or condition (animals) to perform tricks.

6. to prepare or make fit for an athletic contest, etc.

7. to aim (a gun, binoculars, etc.) at something; to bring to bear (usually with *on*).

8. to train (a child, puppy, etc.) to defecate and urinate in the proper place. [Colloq.]

9. in mining, to trace, as a lode or any mineral appearance, to its head.

Syn.—lead, rear, accustom, habituate, inure, drill, exercise, practice, discipline, instruct, bend, educate, aim, direct.

trāin, *v.i.* 1. to drill; to undergo a course of exercise and instruction, physical, mental, or moral; as, to *train* for an athletic contest; to *train* with the militia.

2. to carry out the process of training persons, animals, or plants.

3. to trail; to drag; to follow. [Rare.]

4. to travel by railroad train. [Colloq.]
5. to fraternize or take part; as, he has *trained* with that faction for years. [Colloq.]
6. to romp; to be sportive. [Colloq.]

trāin, *n.* 1. that which is drawn along or after; that which is the hinder part or rear; a trail, as (a) that part of a gown, robe, or the like, which trails behind the wearer; (b) the tail of a comet, meteor, etc.; (c) the tail of a bird; (d) the after part of a gun carriage; the trail.
2. that which draws along; specifically, (a) something used to allure and entice; an artifice; a stratagem; a device; (b) something tied to a lure to entice a hawk; (c) a trap for an animal.

Devilish Macbeth
By many of these *trains* hath sought to win me
Into his power. —Shak.

3. a group of persons that follow after another as attendants in a procession; a retinue; suite.
4. a group of persons, animals, vehicles, etc. that follow one another in a line; a procession; caravan; cortege.
5. the persons, animals, and vehicles accompanying an army to carry its supplies, ammunition, food, etc.
6. a series of events or circumstances that follow some happening; as, the war brought famine and disease in its *train*.
7. any connected order or arrangement; a series; sequence; as, a *train* of thought.
8. a series of connected mechanical parts for transmitting motion; as, a *train* of gears.
9. a line of connected railroad cars pulled or pushed by a locomotive or locomotives.
10. a line of gunpowder that serves as a fuse for an explosive charge.
bridge train; a part of an army, with its necessary equipment, which builds temporary bridges; a pontoon train.
Syn.—series, following, trail, procession, course.

trāin'ȧ·ble, *a.* capable of being trained.

trāin'band, *n.* [contraction of *trained band.*] a band or company of militia; specifically, a volunteer body trained as a kind of militia, raised in England by James I and dissolved by Charles II.

trāin'beăr''ẽr, *n.* one who holds up the train of a robe.

trāin·ee', *n.* a person or animal being trained; especially, a military recruit.

trāin'ẽr, *n.* 1. one who trains; an instructor.
2. one who trains or prepares men, horses, etc. for athletic exercises or contests.
3. an apparatus used in training; specifically, a frame of wood or wire for supporting or displaying flowers and plants; a trellis.
4. a militiaman in training. [Obs.]

trāin'ing, *n.* 1. the action of one who trains, educates, or develops.
2. a being trained or undergoing training.
3. drill; manual exercises.
4. education; instruction and practice, especially in a branch of the useful arts; as, manual *training*.
horizontal training; in horticulture, the training of fruit trees so that their main branches extend horizontally, as against a wall.
manual training; training or practice in work done with the hands, as basket weaving, sewing, metalworking, carpentry, and the like.
physical training; the training of the muscles and organs of the body by means of systematic exercise.

trāin'ing dāy, formerly, a day on which the militia met for drill or exercise.

trāin'ing school, a school that gives training in a specific field or profession, as nursing, acting, etc.

trāin'ing ship, a ship on which persons are trained in seamanship, especially in a navy.

trāin'less, *a.* without a train, as a dress.

trāin'măn, *n.*; *pl.* **trāin'men,** a person who works on a railway train, usually as a conductor's assistant; especially, a brakeman.

trāin'mȧs·tẽr, *n.* a railroad official in charge of some division or subdivision of a line.

trāin'-mīle, *n.* in railroading, a unit in railroad accounts, used in the calculation of average earnings and expenses per running mile of one train.

trāin oil, [D. and L.G. *traan*; Dan. and Sw. *tran*, train oil.] oil obtained from blubber, or from seals, codfish, etc.

trāin taç'kle, formerly, a tackle hooked to the train of a gun, to hold it in place.

trāin'wāy, *n.* a platform used at ferry slips to enable railroad trains to run on and off the ferry boat.

trāin'y, *a.* resembling train oil. [Rare.]

trāipse, *v.i.*; traipsed, *pt.*, *pp.*; traipsing, *ppr.* [earlier *trapass*; prob. from OFr. *trapasser*, to pass beyond; hence a var. of *trespass*.]
1. to walk or wander idly; to gad; to trudge. [Dial. or Colloq.]
2. to trail untidily. [Dial. or Colloq.]

trāipse, *v.t.* to tramp; to trample. [Dial.]

trāipse, *n.* an idle, sluttish woman. [Dial.]

trāit, *n.* [Fr. *trait*, a draft, line, stroke, from *trait*, pp. of *traire*; L. *trahere*, to draw.]
1. a stroke; a touch; trace; flash. [Rare.]
2. a distinguishing quality or characteristic, especially of personality.

trāi·tēur', *n.* [Fr.] one who keeps a restaurant.

trāi'tŏr, *n.* [OFr. *traitor*, *traiteur*, a traitor; L. *traditor*, one who betrays, from *traditus*, pp. of *tradere*, to hand over, deliver, betray.] one who betrays his country, cause, friends, etc.; one guilty of treason.

trāi'tŏr, *a.* traitorous; characteristic of a traitor; as, his *traitor* eye.

trāi'tŏr, *v.t.*; traitored, *pt.*, *pp.*; traitoring, *ppr.* to fail or be false to; to betray; as, my old limbs *traitored* me. [Obs.]

trāi'tŏr·ess, *n.* a traitress.

trāi'tŏr·ly, *a.* treacherous. [Obs.]

trāi'tŏr·ous, *a.* 1. of, or having the nature of, a traitor; treacherous; faithless.
2. of or involving treason; treasonable.

trāi'tŏr·ous·ly, *adv.* in a traitorous manner; treasonably.

trāi'tŏr·ous·ness, *n.* the quality of being traitorous; treachery.

trāi'tŏr·y, *n.* treachery. [Obs.]

trāi'tress, *n.* a woman who is a traitor.

trȧ·jeçt', *v.t.*; trajected, *pt.*, *pp.*; trajecting, *ppr.* [L. *trajectus*, pp. of *trajicere*, to throw, cast, or fling over or across; *trans*, across, and *jacere*, to throw.] to throw or cast (through space or some other medium); as, to *traject* the sun's light through three or more cross prisms. [Rare.]

traj'eçt, *n.* 1. a ferry; a passage or place for crossing water with boats.
2. the act of throwing or carrying across. [Rare.]
3. a trajectory. [Rare.]

trȧ·jeç'tion, *n.* 1. the act of casting through or across.
2. in grammar, transposition.

trȧ·jeçt'ō·ry, *n.*; *pl.* **trȧ·jeçt'ō·ries,** 1. the curved path of something hurtling through space, especially that of a projectile from the time it leaves the muzzle of the gun.
2. in mathematics, a curve or surface that passes through all the curves of a given system at the same angle.

trȧ·lā'tion, *n.* the use of a word in a figurative sense. [Obs.]

tral·ȧ·ti'tion (-tish'un), *n.* a figurative expression; a metaphor. [Rare.]

tral·ȧ·ti'tious, *a.* metaphorical; not literal.

tral·ȧ·ti'tious·ly, *adv.* metaphorically; not in a literal sense.

trȧ·lin'ē·āte, *v.i.* to deviate from any direction or course. [Obs.]

trȧ·lū'cen·cy, *n.* translucency. [Obs.]

trȧ·lū'cent, *a.* transparent; clear; translucent. [Obs.]

tram, *n.* [Eng. dial. *tram*, shaft, wooden frame for carrying; prob. from L.G. *traam*, a beam; current senses from *tramroad*.]
1. an open railway car for carrying loads in mines.
2. a tramcar; streetcar. [Brit.]
3. the basket or car of an overhead conveyor.
4. a tramline.
5. a tramway.

tram, *v.t.*; trammed, *pt.*, *pp.*; tramming, *ppr.* to move or transport by means of a tramcar or tramway.

tram, *v.i.* to operate or travel on a tramcar.

tram, *n.* 1. a trammel (sense 6).
2. correct adjustment.

tram, *v.t.* and *v.i.*; trammed, *pt.*, *pp.*; tramming, *ppr.* to adjust, align, or measure with a trammel.

tram, *n.* [It. *trama*, from L. *trama*, weft.] a kind of doubled silk thread in which two or more strands are twisted together, used for the weft or cross threads of certain velvets and the best varieties of silk goods.

trā'mȧ, *n.* [L., weft.] in botany, the substance intermediate between the layers of hymenium in the gills of agarics or pores of *Polyporus*.

tram'çär, *n.* 1. a tram (mine car).
2. a streetcar. [Brit.]

tram'līne, *n.* a streetcar line. [Brit.]

tram'mel, *n.* [Fr. *tramail*, *trêmail*, a net of three layers; It. *tramaglio*, from LL. *tramacula*, *tremaculum*, a kind of fishing net, from L. *tres*, three, and *macula*, a mesh.]
1. a fishing net consisting of two outer layers of coarse mesh and a loosely hung middle layer of fine mesh: also *trammel net*.
2. a kind of shackle for a horse, especially one to teach ambling.
3. [*often pl.*] something that confines, restrains, or shackles.
4. a pothook.
5. an instrument for drawing ellipses.
6. any of several devices for adjusting or aligning parts of a machine.
7. a braid of hair. [Obs.]
8. a beam compass.

TRAMMEL

tram'mel, *v.t.*; trammeled *or* trammelled, *pt.*, *pp.*; trammeling *or* trammelling, *ppr.* 1. to entangle, as in a trammel: often with *up*.
2. to confine; to hamper; to shackle.

tram'meled, *a.* 1. caught; confined; shackled.
2. marked as if by shackles: said of a horse whose forefoot and hind foot on one side are marked alike.

tram'mel·ẽr, tram'mel·lẽr, *n.* a person or thing that trammels.

tram'mel net, a kind of net for sea fishery, anchored and buoyed, the back rope being supported by cork floats and the footrope kept close to the bottom by weights; also, a loose net of small meshes between two tighter nets of large meshes.

tram'mel wheel (hwēl), a wheel having two slots crossing each other at right angles and forming guides for two sliding blocks to which a pitman is connected. As the wheel rotates the sliders keep in their own grooves, crossing each other's tracks, and the pitman makes two up and two down strokes for each revolution of the wheel. It is used for operating the needle of a sewing machine or for driving a saw or a gang of saws.

tram'ming, *n.* in silk manufacture, the making of trams.

trȧ·mōn·tä'nȧ, *n.* [It.] the north wind in the Mediterranean; also, a cold and blighting wind of the Adriatic.

trȧ·mon'tāne, *a.* [OFr. *tramontain*; It. *tramontano*, from L. *transmontanus*, beyond the mountains; *trans*, beyond, and *mons*, *montis*, mountain.]
1. lying or being beyond the mountain; hence, foreign; barbarous.
2. beyond the Alps as seen from Italy; ultramontane.

trȧ·mon'tāne, *n.* 1. one living beyond the mountain; a stranger; a foreigner.
2. the tramontana.

tramp, *v.t.*; tramped (trampt), *pt.*, *pp.*; tramping, *ppr.* [L.G. *trampen*, to trample.]
1. to tread under foot; to trample.
2. to cleanse or scour, as clothes, by treading on them in water. [Scot.]
3. to walk or ramble through; as, to *tramp* a country.

tramp, *v.i.* 1. to step or walk firmly and heavily.
2. to travel about on foot, especially doing odd jobs or begging for a living.

tramp, *n.* 1. a person who travels about on foot, especially one doing odd jobs or begging for a living; a hobo; a vagrant.
2. the sound of heavy steps, as of people marching.
3. the act of tramping; especially, a journey on foot; a hike; a trudge.
4. a freight ship that has no regular schedule, but picks up cargo and passengers wherever it may be.
5. an iron plate on the sole of a shoe to protect it in spading, etc.
6. a prostitute or any woman or girl of loose morals; a tart. [Slang.]

tramp'ẽr, *n.* a stroller; a vagrant or vagabond; a tramp.

tram plāte, a flat iron plate laid as a rail.

tram'ple, *v.t.*; trampled (-pld), *pt.*, *pp.*; trampling, *ppr.* [ME. *trampelen*, a freq. of *tramp*.]

1. to tread under foot; to tread down; to hurt by treading; as, to *trample* grass.

2. to crush, destroy, or violate, as by tramping.

to trample under foot; (a) to crush or hurt by trampling; (b) to treat harshly or ruthlessly; to domineer over: also *trample on, trample upon.*

tram'ple, *v.i.* 1. to tread in contempt; as, to *trample* on one's pride.

2. to tread heavily; to tramp.

tram'ple, *n.* the act of treading under foot; also, the noise made by trampling.

tram'plẽr, *n.* one who tramples; one who treads down.

tram·poose', *v.i.* same as *trampous.*

tram'pō·line, tram'pō·lin, *n.* [from It. *trampoli*, stilts.]

1. originally, a performance by an acrobat on stilts.

2. a net of strong canvas stretched tightly on a frame, used by acrobats, as in a circus, for performing various feats of tumbling.

tram'pot, *n.* in milling, the support or step for the foot of the spindle.

tram'pous, tram·poose', *v.i.* to walk heavily; to wander about; to tramp. [Slang.]

tram'rōad, *n.* a road for trams, especially in a mine, in which the track for the wheels is made of timbers, flat stones, or iron plates arranged in a line; a tramway.

tram'wāy, *n.* 1. a tramroad.

2. a streetcar line; a tramline. [Brit.]

trȧ·nā'tion, *n.* the act of passing over by swimming. [Obs.]

trȧnce, *n.* [OFr. *transe*, great apprehension, from *transir*, to perish; L. *transire*, to die, from *trans*, across, beyond, and *ire*, to go.]

1. a state resembling sleep, in which consciousness may remain although voluntary movement is lost, as in catalepsy or hypnosis.

2. a stunned condition; a daze; stupor.

3. a condition of great mental concentration or abstraction, especially one induced by religious fervor or mysticism.

4. a condition in which a spiritualist medium allegedly loses consciousness and passes under the control of some external force, as for the supposed transmission of communications from the dead during a seance.

5. a passage; especially, a passage inside a house. [Scot.]

trȧnce, *v.t.*; tranced (trȧnst), *pt., pp.*; trancing, *ppr.* 1. to entrance; to place in or as in a trance.

2. to traverse. [Dial.]

trȧnce, *v.i.* to tramp; to travel. [Dial.]

trañ'gȧm, *n.* an odd thing intricately contrived. [Obs.]

trañ'quil, *a.*; *comp.* tranquiler *or* tranquiller; *superl.* tranquilest *or* tranquillest, [Fr. *tranquille*; L. *tranquillus*, calm, quiet, still; from *trans*, beyond, hence, surpassingly, and base akin to *quies*, rest, calm.]

1. free from emotional disturbance or agitation; calm; serene; placid.

2. quiet or motionless; even; steady; as, *tranquil* waters.

trañ·quil'i·ty, *n.* see tranquillity.

trañ"quil·i·zā'tion, trañ"quil·li·zā'tion, *n.* the act of tranquilizing or state of being tranquilized.

trañ'quil·īze, trañ'quil·līze, *v.t.*; tranquilized *or* tranquillized, *pt., pp.*; tranquilizing *or* tranquillizing, *ppr.* to cause to be tranquil; to make calm and peaceful; as, to *tranquilize* the mind.

trañ'quil·īze, trañ'quil·līze, *v.i.* to become calm; to exert a quieting effect.

Syn.—quiet, allay, compose, appease, pacify, soothe, calm, lull.

trañ'quil·ī·zẽr, trañ'quil·lī·zẽr, *n.* one who or that which tranquilizes.

trañ'quil·ī·zing·ly, trañ'quil·lī·zing·ly, *adv.* so as to tranquilize.

trañ·quil'li·ty, trañ·quil'i·ty, *n.* [L. *tranquillitas (-atis)*, quietness, stillness, from *tranquillus*, tranquil.] quietness; a calm state; freedom from disturbance or agitation; the state or quality of being tranquil.

Syn.—quiet, quietness, peace, calm, repose, stillness, rest.

trañ'quil·ly, *adv.* in a tranquil manner.

trañ'quil·ness, *n.* tranquility.

trans-, [from L. *trans*, across, over.] a prefix meaning: (a) *on the other side of, to the other side of, over, across*, as in *trans*atlantic: opposed to *cis-*; (b) *so as to change thoroughly*, as in *trans*literate; (c) *above and beyond, transcending*, as in *trans*-sonic.

trans·aċt', *v.t.*; transacted, *pt., pp.*; transacting, *ppr.* [L. *transactus*, pp. of *transigere*, to drive through, to settle; *trans-*, through, and *agere*, to drive.] to do; to perform; to complete; as, to *transact* commercial business.

Syn.—conduct, negotiate, manage.

trans·aċt', *v.i.* to do business or a piece of business; to negotiate. [Rare.]

trans·aċ'tion, *n.* [L. *transactio (-onis)*, from *transactus*, pp. of *transigere*, to transact.]

1. a transacting or being transacted.

2. that which is transacted or completed; specifically, a business deal.

3. [*pl.*] the published accounts or reports of the proceedings, discussions, etc. of the meetings of a society, convention, etc.

Syn.—proceeding, process.

trans·aċ'tion·ăl, *a.* having to do with transacting or a transaction.

trans·aċ'tion·ăl ȧ·nal'y·sis, a form of popular psychotherapy conducted on the premise that there are three states of the ego (*parent, adult, child*) in each individual which must be brought into balance.

trans·aċt'ŏr, *n.* one who transacts.

trans·al'pīne, *a.* [L. *transalpinus*.] on the other (northern) side of the Alps: from the viewpoint of Rome.

trans·al'pīne, *n.* a native or inhabitant of a transalpine country.

trans·am·i·nā'tion, *n.* [*trans*, and *amine*, and *-ation*.] the transfer of an amino group from one molecule to another usually by the action of an enzyme (*transaminase*).

trans·an·i·mā'tion, *n.* metempsychosis; transmigration. [Rare.]

trans·at·lan'tiç, *a.* 1. on the other side of the Atlantic.

2. crossing the Atlantic; as, *transatlantic* steamers.

trans·çā'lent, *a.* [L. *trans-*, through, and *calens (-entis)*, ppr. of *calere*, to be warm.] pervious to heat; permitting the passage of heat.

Trans·çau·çā'siăn, *a.* of Transcaucasia, the region of the U.S.S.R. south of the Caucasus Mountains, or its people.

Trans·çau·çā'siăn, *n.* a native or inhabitant of Transcaucasia.

trans·cēiv'ẽr, *n.* [*trans*mitter, and re*ceiver*.]

1. an apparatus contained in a single housing, functioning alternately as a radio transmitter and receiver.

2. an electronic device that transmits and receives facsimile copies of printed material, pictures, etc. over a telephone line.

tran·scend', *v.t.*; transcended, *pt., pp.*; transcending, *ppr.* [L. *transcendere*, to climb over; *trans-*, over, and *scandere*, to climb.]

1. to go beyond the limits of; to overstep; to exceed; as, the story *transcends* belief.

2. to be superior to; to surpass; to excel.

3. in philosophy and theology, to be separate from or beyond (experience, the material universe, etc.): said of God or a god.

tran·scend', *v.i.* 1. to climb. [Obs.]

2. to be transcendent; to excel. [Archaic.]

tran·scend'ence, tran·scend'en·cy, *n.* superior excellence; supereminence; the state or character of being transcendent.

tran·scend'ent, *a.* [L. *transcendens (-entis)*, ppr. of *transcendere*, to transcend.]

1. transcending; surpassing; excelling; extraordinary.

2. in philosophy, beyond the limits of possible experience and, hence (in Kantianism), beyond human knowledge.

3. in theology, that exists apart from the material universe: said of God, divine spirit, etc.: distinguished from *immanent*.

trans·scend'ent, *n.* 1. that which surpasses or excels; anything greatly superior.

2. in philosophy, (a) a reality above the categories or predicaments; (b) that which is altogether beyond the bounds of human cognition and thought.

tran·scen·den'tăl, *a.* 1. transcendent; surpassing others; as, *transcendental* qualities.

2. in Kantian philosophy, not derived from experience but based on the a priori elements of experience, which are the necessary conditions of human knowledge; transcending human experience but not knowledge.

3. abstract; metaphysical; hence, vague; obscure; as, *transcendental* poetry.

4. supernatural.

5. in mathematics, of any equation, curve, or quantity which cannot be represented or defined by an algebraic expression of a finite number of terms, with numeral and determinate indexes. Transcendental quantities include all exponential, logarithmic, and trigonometrical lines, because there are no finite algebraic formulas by which these quantities can be expressed.

transcendental curve; a curve that is the graph of a transcendental function.

transcendental equation; an equation containing transcendental functions: the term sometimes indicates such differential equations as can only be integrated by means of some curve, logarithm, or infinite series.

transcendental function; see under *function*.

transcendental idealism; the Kantian doctrine that those things to which the conceptions of reality, actuality, etc. are applicable are merely phenomena or appearances.

transcendental meditation; intense meditation as practiced in Hinduism, often while chanting a mantra, with the objective of relieving tension and of increasing awareness.

transcendental quantity; in algebra, a quantity which cannot be represented by an algebraic expression of a finite number of terms, as the quantity π.

transcendental reality; in metaphysics, reality as it exists independently of all thought about it.

transcendental unity; the unity resulting from the action of the mind in cognition.

tran·scen·den'tăl, *n.* a transcendent conception.

tran·scen·den'tăl·iṣm, *n.* 1. any of various philosophies that propose to discover the nature of reality by investigating the process of thought rather than the objects of sense experience: the philosophies of Kant, Hegel, and Fichte are types of transcendentalism.

2. by extension, the philosophical ideas of Ralph Waldo Emerson and some other 19th-century New Englanders, based on a search for reality through spiritual intuition.

3. popularly, any obscure, visionary, or idealistic thought.

4. the state or quality of being transcendental.

tran·scen·den'tăl·ist, *n.* one who believes in transcendentalism.

tran"scen·den·tal'i·ty, *n.* the quality or condition of being transcendental.

tran·scen·den'tăl·ly, *adv.* in a transcendental manner.

tran·scend'ent·ly, *adv.* to a transcendent degree; supereminently; supremely.

tran·scend'ent·ness, *n.* the quality or condition of being transcendent; superior or unusual excellence.

tran·scen'sion, *n.* a passage over or beyond; a transcending. [Rare.]

trans'cō·lāte, *v.t.* to strain; to filter. [Obs.]

trans"con·ti·nen'tăl, *a.* 1. that crosses a (or the) continent.

2. on the other side of a (or the) continent.

trans·çor'pō·rāte, *v.i.*; transcorporated, *pt., pp.*; transcorporating, *ppr.* to pass from one body to another.

tran·sçrib'blẽr, *n.* one who transcribes hurriedly and inaccurately.

tran·sçrībe', *v.t.*; transcribed, *pt., pp.*; transcribing, *ppr.* [L. *transcribere*, to transfer in writing; *trans*, across, and *scribere*, to write.]

1. to make a written or typewritten copy of (shorthand notes, a speech, etc.).

2. to arrange or adapt (a piece of music) for an instrument, voice, or ensemble other than that for which it was originally written.

3. in radio, to record (a program, commercial, etc.) for broadcast at some later time.

tran·sçrīb'ẽr, *n.* one who transcribes.

tran'sçript, *n.* [L. *transcriptus*, pp. of *transcribere*, to transcribe.]

1. a written or typewritten copy of an original.

2. a copy or reproduction of any kind.

tran·sçrip'tion, *n.* [Fr.] 1. the act or process of transcribing.

2. something transcribed; specifically, (a) a transcript; copy; (b) an arrangement of a piece of music for an instrument, voice, or combination of instruments or voices other than that for which it was originally written; (c) a recording made for radio broadcasting; also, the act or practice of using such recordings; as, a program brought you by *transcription*.

tran·sçrip'tive, *a.* resembling a copy in style or appearance; imitative.

tran·sçrip'tive·ly, *adv.* in the manner of a copy; by way of transcription.

trans·çur'rent, *a.* [L. *transcurrens (-entis)*, ppr. of *transcurrere*, to run over or across; *trans*, across, and *currere*, to run.] extending crosswise; lying in a transverse direction.

trans·çūr'sion, *n.* a passage beyond certain limits; extraordinary deviation. [Obs.]

trans·dī′ȧ·lect, *v.t.* to translate from one dialect into another. [Rare.]

trans·dūc′ẽr, *n.* [from L. *transducere*, to lead across (*trans-*, over, and *ducere*, to lead); and -er.] in physics, a device that transmits power from one system to another system.

trans·duc′tion, *n.* the act of conveying over. [Rare.]

tran·sect′, *v.t.*; transected, *pt.*, *pp.*; transecting, *ppr.* [L. *trans*, across, and *sectus*, pp. of *secare*, to cut.] to cut across or divide transversely by cutting.

tran·sec′tion, *n.* 1. a transecting or being transected.

2. a transverse section.

trans·el′ē·ment, trans·el·ē·men′tāte, *v.t.* to change the elements of; to transubstantiate.

trans·el″ē·men·tā′tion, *n.* the change of the elements of one body into those of another.

tran·sen′nȧ, *n.* [L., a grating of any kind, latticework.] a carved latticework or grating of marble, silver, etc., used for exposing but protecting a shrine.

TRANSENNA

tran′sept, *n.* [lit., a cross-enclosure, from L. *trans*, across, and *septum*, an enclosure.]

1. the part of a cross-shaped church at right angles to the long, main section, or nave.

2. either arm of this part, outside the nave.

tran·sep′tăl, *a.* of or pertaining to a transept.

trans′ē·unt, *a.* [L., from *transire*, to go across.] operating outside itself; having an outside effect: opposed to *immanent*.

tran·sex′ion, *n.* change of sex. [Obs.]

trans·fem′i·nāte, *v.t.* to change in sex from female to male. [Obs.]

trans·fẽr′, *v.t.*; transferred, *pt.*, *pp.*; transferring, *ppr.* [L. *transferre*; *trans*, across, and *ferre*, to bear.]

1. to convey, carry, remove, or send from one person, place, or position to another.

2. to make over the legal title, right, or ownership of to another.

3. to convey (a picture, design, etc.) from one surface to another by any of several processes.

trans·fẽr′, *v.i.* 1. to transfer oneself; as, he *transferred* to the New York office.

2. to be transferred.

3. to change from one bus, streetcar, etc. to another, usually by presenting a transfer (sense 3).

trans′fẽr, *n.* 1. (a) a transferring or being transferred; (b) a means of transferring.

2. a thing or person that is transferred; specifically, a picture or design transferred or to be transferred from one surface to another.

3. a ticket, provided free or at a small extra charge, entitling the bearer to change from one bus, streetcar, etc. to another at a specified place and within a specified period.

4. a place for transferring.

5. a form or document effecting a transfer, as of a student.

6. in law, (a) the transferring of a title, right, or property from one person to another; (b) the document effecting this.

7. in railway transportation, (a) a point on a railway where a train is ferried over a body of water; also, the ferry used for this purpose; (b) the system by which passengers and their baggage are conveyed from one depot to another: also used adjectively; as, a *transfer* line.

trans·fẽr·ȧ·bil′i·ty, *n.* the condition or quality of being transferable.

trans·fẽr′ȧ·ble, *a.* 1. capable of being transferred or conveyed from one place or person to another.

2. capable of being legitimately passed or changed into the possession of another, and conveying to the new holder all its claims, rights, or privileges; as, a note, bill of exchange, or other evidence of property is *transferable* by endorsement.

trans′fẽr dāy, one of certain regular days at the Bank of England for registering transfers of bank stock and government funds in the books of the corporation.

trans·fẽr·ee′, *n.* 1. a person to whom something is transferred, especially legally.

2. a person who is transferred.

trans·fẽr′ence, *n.* 1. a transferring or being transferred.

2. in psychoanalysis, a reproduction of emotions relating to repressed experiences, especially of childhood, and a replacement of another person, as the psychoanalyst, for the original object of the repressed impulses.

trans·fẽr·en′tiăl (-shăl), *a.* of or involving a transfer or transference.

trans·fẽr′ŏr, *n.* one who legally transfers a right, property, etc.

trans′fẽr pā′pẽr, a prepared paper used in lithography or copying presses for transferring impressions.

trans·fẽr′rence, *n.* same as *transference*.

trans·fẽr′rẽr, *n.* one who or that which transfers.

trans·fẽr′ri·ble, *a.* same as *transferable*.

trans′fẽr tā′ble, a traverse table on a railroad.

trans·fig·ū·rā′tion, *n.* [Fr., from L. *transfiguratio* (*-onis*), from *transfigurare*, to transfigure.]

1. a transfiguring or being transfigured.

2. [T–] the change in the appearance of Jesus on the mountain: Matt. xvii; Mark ix.

3. [T–] a church festival commemorating this, held on August 6.

trans·fig′ūre, *v.t.*; transfigured, *pt.*, *pp.*; transfiguring, *ppr.* [ME. *transfiguren*; OFr. *transfigurer*; L. *transfigurare*, to change the figure of; *trans*, across, and *figura*, figure, outward appearance.]

1. to transform; to change the outward form, figure, or appearance of.

2. to transform so as to exalt; to elevate and glorify; to idealize.

Yet it lies in my little one's cradle,
  And sits in my little one's chair,
And the light of the heaven she's gone to
  Transfigures its golden hair. —Lowell.

trans·fix′, *v.t.*; transfixed (-fikst), *pt.*, *pp.*; transfixing, *ppr.* [L. *transfixus*, pp. of *transfigere*, to thrust through.]

1. to pierce through with or as with something pointed.

2. to fasten in this manner; to impale.

3. to make motionless, as if pierced through; as, *transfixed* with horror.

trans·fix′iŏn (-fik′shun), *n.* 1. the act of transfixing or piercing through.

2. the state of being transfixed or pierced.

3. in surgery, a cutting through, as in amputation.

trans′flū·ent, *a.* [L. *trans-*, through, and *fluens* (*-entis*), ppr. of *fluere*, to flow.]

1. flowing or running across or through; as, a *transfluent* stream.

2. in heraldry, represented as running through the arches of a bridge: said of water.

trans·fō·rā′tion, *n.* [L. *transforatio* (*-onis*), a boring through, from *transforatus*, pp. of *transforare*, to bore through.] the act of perforating; especially, in surgery, the piercing of the fetal skull.

trans·fọrm′, *v.t.*; transformed, *pt.*, *pp.*; transforming, *ppr.* [ME. *transformen*; OFr. *transformer*; L. *transformare*, to change the form of; *trans*, across, implying change, and *forma* form.]

1. to change the form or outward appearance of.

2. to change the condition, nature, or function of; to convert; as, the mansion was *transformed* into a hospital.

3. to change the personality or character of.

4. in electricity, to change in potential or type: said of currents.

5. in mathematics, to change (an expression, figure, etc.) in form but not in value.

6. in physics, to change (one form of energy) into another.

trans·fọrm′, *v.i.* to be or become changed in form; to be metamorphosed. [Rare.]

trans′fọrm, *n.* [from the verb.]

1. in mathematics, a figure or expression which is the result of the geometrical or analytical transformation of another figure or expression.

2. in linguistics, (a) any of a set of rules for producing grammatical transformations of a kernel sentence; (b) a sentence so produced.

trans·fọrm′ȧ·ble, *a.* capable of being transformed.

trans·fọr·mā′tion, *n.* 1. the act or operation of changing the form or external appearance; the state of being transformed; a change in form, appearance, nature, disposition, condition, character, etc.

2. in biology, change of form in insects; metamorphosis, as from a caterpillar to a butterfly.

3. in alchemy, the change of one metal into another; transmutation of metals.

4. in mathematics, the operation or process of changing in form or expression, as (a) the change of a given geometrical figure into another of equal area, but of a different number of sides, or of a given solid into another of equal solidity, but having a different number of faces; (b) the change of the form of an equation without destroying the equality of its members; (c) the change of the form of a fraction without altering its value.

5. in pathology, a morbid change in a part, which consists in the conversion of its texture into one which is natural to some other part, as when soft parts are converted into cartilage or bone.

6. in physiology, the change of one form into another form; metamorphosis; metabolism.

7. in chemistry, change from solid to liquid or from liquid to gaseous state, or the converse.

8. in physics, a change from one form of energy into another.

9. in electricity, a change in potential or type: said of currents.

10. that appearance or character taken by a person or thing that has been transformed.

11. a kind of wig worn by a woman.

12. in linguistics, (a) the process of obtaining, by the application of certain rules, all the sentences of a given language from a basic group of kernel sentences; (b) the result obtained by applying any of these rules.

biquadratic transformation; a transformation in which the variables of one system are substituted for the variables of another system of which they are biquadratic functions.

orthogonal transformation; a linear transformation or substitution in which the sum of the squares of the variables remains the same.

trans·fọr·mā′tion·ăl, *a.* of or having to do with transformation.

trans·fọr·mā′tion·ăl (gen′ẽr·ā·tive) gram′mär, a grammatical system characterized by the view that all sentences in a given language are either kernel sentences or transformations of kernel sentences resulting from the application of transformational rules.

trans·fọrm′ȧ·tive, *a.* transforming or tending to transform.

trans·fọrm′ẽr, *n.* 1. a person or thing that transforms.

2. an apparatus for transforming the voltage of an electric current: there are two types, a *step-down transformer*, which changes high voltage into low voltage, and a *step-up transformer*, which changes low voltage into high voltage.

multiple transformer; (a) any form of transformer the coils or circuits of which are connected in multiple; (b) the ordinary alternating current transformer connected across a supply circuit as distinguished from a *series transformer*.

parallel transformer; (a) a transformer connected with a parallel system of distribution; (b) a transformer that is connected to mains in parallel; (c) a transformer whose secondary coils are connected in parallel.

series transformer; a converter whose primary coil is connected in series with the primary coils of other similar transformers in the primary circuit.

trans·fọrm′işm, *n.* evolutionism.

trans·fọrm′ist, *n.* a believer in the doctrine of transformism.

trans′fūge, *n.* a soldier who goes over to the enemy in a time of war; a deserter; one who changes sides; a turncoat; an apostate. [Rare.]

trans·fūşe′, *v.t.*; transfused, *pt.*, *pp.*; transfusing, *ppr.* [L. *transfusus*, pp. of *transfundere*, to pour out of one vessel into another; *trans*, across, and *fundere*, to pour.]

1. to transfer (liquid) by pouring from one container into another.

2. to make permeate; to instill; to imbue; to infuse.

3. in medicine, (a) to transfer (blood) from one individual into a blood vessel, usually a vein, of another; (b) to inject (a saline solution, etc.) directly into a blood vessel; (c) to give a transfusion to.

trans·fū′şi·ble, *a.* capable of being transfused.

trans·fū′şiŏn (-zhun), *n.* the act of transfusing; especially, the transfusing of the blood of one individual into the blood vessels of another.

trans·fū′sive, *a.* tending or serving to transfuse.

trans·gress′, *v.t.*; transgressed (-grest), *pt.*, *pp.*; transgressing, *ppr.* [Fr. *transgresser*, from L. *transgressus*, pp. of *transgredi*, to step over, pass over; *trans*, across, and *gradi*, to step, walk.]

1. to pass over or beyond; to surpass, as a limit or boundary.

2. to overpass, as some law or rule prescribed; to break or violate; to infringe.

3. to offend against. [Obs.]

trans·gress′, *v.i.* to break a law, commandment, etc.; to sin.

trans·gres′sion (-gresh′un), *n.* [Fr., from L. *transgressio* (*-onis*), a stepping over, from *transgressus*, pp. of *transgredi*, to transgress.] the act of transgressing; the breaking or violation of any law, civil or moral, expressed or implied; a trespass; an offense.

Syn.—fault, crime, sin, violation.

trans·gres′sion·ăl, *a.* due to transgression; pertaining to transgression.

trans·gres′sive, *a.* transgressing or tending to transgress.

trans·gres′sive·ly, *adv.* by transgressing.

trans·gress′ŏr, *n.* one who transgresses.

tran·shāpe′, *v.t.* to transshape.

tran·ship′, *v.t.*; transhipped (-shipt), *pt.*, *pp.*; transhipping, *ppr.* to transship.

tran·ship′ment, *n.* same as *transshipment*.

trans·hū′măn, *a.* superhuman.

trans·hū′măn·ize, *v.t.*; transhumanized, *pt.*, *pp.*; transhumanizing, *ppr.* to elevate or transform to something beyond what is human; to change from a human into a higher, purer, nobler, or celestial nature.

tran′sience (-shens), *n.* a transient quality or state.

tran′sien·cy (-shen-), *n.* transience.

tran′sient (-shent), *a.* [L. *transiens* (*-entis*), ppr. of *transire*, to go across; *trans*, across, and *ire*, to go.]

1. (a) passing away with time; not permanent; temporary; transitory; (b) passing quickly or soon; fleeting; ephemeral.

2. transeunt.

3. staying only for a short time; not permanently settled, etc.; as, a *transient* lodger.

4. in music, designating or of a temporary modulation.

Syn.—fleeting, fugitive, transitory, temporary, passing, evanescent, ephemeral.

tran′sient (-shent), *n.* a transient person or thing; especially, a temporary lodger, hotel guest, etc.

tran′sient·ly, *adv.* in a transient manner.

tran′sient·ness, *n.* the state or quality of being transient.

tran·sil′i·ence, *n.* the state or quality of being transilient.

tran·sil′i·en·cy, *n.* transilience. [Rare.]

tran·sil′i·ent, *a.* [L. *transiliens*, ppr. of *transilire*, to leap across, from *trans-*, over, across, and *salire*, to leap.] passing abruptly or leaping from one thing, condition, form, etc. to another.

trans·il·lū′mi·nāte, *v.t.*; transilluminated, *pt.*, *pp.*; transilluminating, *ppr.* in medicine, to pass a strong light through (an organ or part) in examination.

trans·il·lū·mi·nā′tion, *n.* the act of illuminating a thing by throwing a light through it; particularly, in medicine, the inspection of the interior of a cavity by means of a strong light made to pass through its walls.

trans·ī′rē, *n.* a customhouse permit to allow the removal of goods from one place to another.

tran·ṣis′tŏr, *n.* [*trans*fer, and res*istor*.]

1. a solid-state, electronic device, composed of semiconductor material, as germanium, silicon, etc., that controls current flow without use of a vacuum: transistors are similar in function to electron tubes, but have the advantages of being compact, long-lived, and low in power requirements.

2. popularly, a transistorized radio.

tran·ṣis′tŏr·ize, *v.t.*; transistorized, *pt.*, *pp.*; transistorizing, *ppr.* to equip (a device) with transistors.

trans′it, *n.* [L. *transitus*, pp. of *transire*, to go across.]

1. (a) passage through or across; (b) a transition; a change.

2. a carrying or being carried through or across; conveyance; as, goods in *transit*.

3. a surveying instrument for measuring horizontal angles, a kind of theodolite: called in full *transit theodolite*.

4. in astronomy, (a) the apparent passage of a heavenly body across a given meridian or through the field of a telescope; (b) the apparent passage of a smaller heavenly body across the disk of a larger one, as of Mercury across the sun.

5. same as *transit instrument*.

lower transit; a transit across the meridian below the pole.

upper transit; a transit across the meridian above the pole, or toward the zenith from the polar axis.

trans′it, *v.t.* 1. to make a transit through or across, especially in astronomical senses.

2. to revolve (the telescope of a transit) around its horizontal transverse axis.

trans′it, *v.i.* to make a transit (senses 1 and 4).

trans′it cīr′çle, a meridian circle.

trans′it çŏm′păss, same as *transit*, n. 3.

trans′it dē·pärt′ment, in banking, the office or offices which clears and collects checks.

trans′it dū′ty, a tax levied against goods traveling through a country.

tran′sit·ẽr, *n.* an attachment to a transit, consisting usually of a wire, which may be made to cross a transit's field in such a manner and at such a rate as to continuously bisect an object in its field of view: usually connected with another instrument which registers its passage across certain points in the field.

trans′it flōat′ẽr, in marine insurance, a blanket policy covering the entire cargo.

trans′it in′strụ·ment, 1. a telescope mounted at right angles to a horizontal east-west axis so that it can be rotated only in the vertical plane of the meridian at its site, thereby affording accurate observation of the transit of heavenly bodies across the meridian.

2. a transit (sense 3).

tran·ṣi′tion (-zizh′un), *n.* [L. *transitio* (*-onis*), a passing over, from *transitus*, pp. of *transire*, to pass over.]

1. a passing from one condition, form, stage, activity, place, etc. to another.

2. the period when this occurs.

3. a word, phrase, sentence, or group of sentences that relates a preceding topic with a succeeding one.

4. in music, (a) a modulation; especially, a brief or passing modulation; (b) an abrupt change into a remote key.

tran·ṣi′tion·ăl, *a.* of, showing, or characterized by transition.

tran·ṣi′tion·ăr·y, *a.* transitional.

tran·ṣi′tion tint, the almost neutral tint seen in the polariscope of a saccharimeter.

tran′si·tive, *a.* [LL. *transitivus*, from L. *transitus*: see *transit*.]

1. transitional. [Rare.]

2. transeunt.

3. expressing an action that is thought of as passing over to and taking effect on some person or thing; taking a direct object to complete the meaning: said of certain verbs.

transitive group; a mathematical group in which an element may be placed in any desired position by its substitutions: said to be doubly transitive when two elements may be simultaneously changed as desired.

tran′si·tive·ly, *adv.* in a transitive manner.

tran′si·tive·ness, *n.* the state or quality of being transitive.

tran′si·tō·ri·ly, *adv.* in a transitory manner.

tran′si·tō·ri·ness, *n.* the state or quality of being transitory.

tran′si·tō·ry, *a.* [Fr. *transitoire*; L. *transitorius*, liable to pass away, passing away.] of a passing nature; ephemeral; transient; speedily vanishing.

> O Lord, comfort and succor all those who,
> in this *transitory* life, are in trouble.
> —Book of Common Prayer.

transitory action; in law, an action which may be brought in any county, as actions for debt, detinue, slander, and the like: opposed to *local action*.

Syn.—brief, transient, short, fleeting, temporary, evanescent, ephemeral, short-lived.

Trans-Jọr·dā′ni·ăn, *n.* a native or inhabitant of Trans-Jordan.

Trans-Jọr·dā′ni·ăn, *a.* of Trans-Jordan or its people.

trans·lāt′ȧ·ble, *a.* capable of being translated.

trans·lāte′, *v.t.*; translated, *pt.*, *pp.*; translating, *ppr.* [ME. *translaten*, from L. *translatus*, transferred, used as pp. of *transferre*; *trans*, across, and *ferre*, to bear.]

1. to change from one place, position, or condition to another; to transfer; specifically, (a) to convey to heaven, originally without death; (b) to transfer (a bishop) from one see to another; (c) to move (a saint's body, relics, etc.) from one place of interment to another.

2. to change from one language into another.

3. to change into another medium or form; as, *translate* ideas into action.

4. to put into different words; to interpret.

5. to repeat or retransmit (a telegraphic message) by means of an automatic relay.

6. to enrapture; entrance. [Archaic or Rare.]

7. in mechanics, to impart translation to.

8. to cause to remove from one part of the body to another; as, to *translate* a disease. [Obs.]

Syn.—interpret, define, explain, elucidate, transfer, change, transform.

trans·lāte′, *v.i.* 1. to make translations (into other languages).

2. to be capable of being translated; as, this poetry does not *translate* easily.

trans·lā′tion, *n.* 1. a translating or being translated.

2. the result of a translating, especially a translated version of a literary work.

3. in mechanics, motion in which every point of the moving object has simultaneously the same velocity and direction of motion: distinguished from *rotation*.

4. in rhetoric, transference of the meaning of a word or phrase; metaphor. [Obs.]

Syn.—interpretation, description, explanation, transference.

trans·lā′tion·ăl, *a.* having to do with translation.

trans·lȧ·ti′tious (-tish′us), *a.* transposed; metaphorical; figurative; transported. [Obs.]

trans·lāt′ive, *a.* figurative; metaphorical. [Rare.]

trans·lāt′ŏr, *n.* 1. a person who translates; specifically, (a) a person who translates books, articles, etc.; (b) a person who translates speech; an interpreter.

2. an automatic repeater in a long-distance telegraph relay.

trans·lāt′ŏr·ship, *n.* the office of a translator.

trans·lāt′ō·ry, *a.* transferring; serving to translate.

trans·lāt′ress, *n.* a woman translator.

trans·lit′ẽr·āte, *v.t.*; transliterated, *pt.*, *pp.*; transliterating, *ppr.* [*trans-*, and L. *litera*, letter.] to write or spell (words, etc.) in the alphabetical characters of another language that represent the same sound or sounds.

trans·lit·ẽr·ā′tion, *n.* 1. a transliterating or being transliterated.

2. a transliterated word, text, etc.

trans·lō′çāte, *v.t.*; translocated, *pt.*, *pp.*; translocating, *ppr.* to cause to change location or position; to dislocate; to displace.

trans·lō·çā′tion, *n.* [*trans-*, and L. *locatio* (*-onis*), a placing, from *locatus*, pp. of *locare*, to place.]

1. a translocating; dislocation.

2. in botany, the transference of food materials from one part of a plant to another.

trans·lū′cence, *n.* the quality or state of being translucent.

trans·lū′cen·cy, *n.* translucence.

trans·lū′cent, *a.* [L. *translucens* (*-entis*), ppr. of *translucere*, to shine through; *trans*, through, and *lucere*, to shine.]

1. originally, shining through.

2. transparent. [Rare.]

3. letting light pass but diffusing it so that objects on the other side cannot be distinguished; partially transparent, as frosted glass.

trans·lū′cent·ly, *adv.* in a translucent manner.

trans·lū′cid, *a.* translucent.

trans′lū·năr·y, *a.* lying or situated beyond the moon.

trans·mȧ·rīne′, *a.* [L. *transmarinus*, beyond the sea; *trans*, beyond, and *mare*, the sea.]

1. crossing the sea.

2. on the other side of the sea.

trans·mē′di·ăn, *a.* passing across the median line or plane: said of muscles in certain animals.

trans·mē′di·ăn, *n.* a transmedian muscle.

trans·mew′, *v.t.* to transmute; to transform; to metamorphose. [Obs.]

trans·mī′grănt, *a.* [L. *transmigrans* (*-antis*), ppr. of *transmigrare*, to transmigrate.] transmigrating from one place to another; as, a *transmigrant* people.

trans·mī′grănt, *n.* a person or thing that transmigrates; specifically, an emigrant passing through a country or place on his way to the country in which he will be an immigrant.

trans·mī′grāte, *v.i.*; transmigrated, *pt.*, *pp.*; transmigrating, *ppr.* [L. *transmigratus*, pp. of *transmigrare*, to migrate across from one place to another.]

1. to migrate; to pass from one country, habitation, etc. to another for the purpose of residing in it.
2. in some religions, to pass from one body into another at death: said of the soul.

trans·mī′grāte, *v.t.* to cause to pass from one region or condition to another.

trans·mī·grā′tion, *n.* [Fr., from L. *transmigratio* (*-onis*), a moving from one place to another.]
1. the act or process of transmigrating; passage from one place or state to another.
2. the supposed passing of the soul into another body after death; metempsychosis.

trans·mī′grā·tŏr, *n.* one who or that which transmigrates.

trans·mī′grà·tō·ry, *a.* 1. of transmigration.
2. accustomed or likely to transmigrate.

trans·mis·si·bil′i·ty, *n.* the quality or state of being transmissible.

trans·mis′si·ble, *a.* capable of being transmitted.

trans·mis′sion (-mish′un), *n.* [L. *transmissio*, from *transmissus*, pp. of *transmittere*.]
1. a transmitting or being transmitted.
2. something transmitted.
3. the part of an automobile, truck, etc. that transmits motive force from the engine to the wheels, usually by means of gears or hydraulic cylinders.
4. the passage of radio waves through space between the transmitting station and the receiving station.
transmission case; in automobiles, a case or jacket used to cover the transmission.

trans·mis′sive, *a.* [from L. *transmissus*, pp. of *transmittere*.]
1. having the quality of transmitting or of being transmitted.
2. transmitting or capable of transmitting.

trans·mit′, *v.t.*; transmitted, *pt.*, *pp.*; transmitting, *ppr.* [L. *transmittere*, to cause to go across, send over, dispatch; *trans*, across, and *mittere*, to send.]
1. to send or cause to go from one person or place to another, especially across intervening space or distance; to transfer; to convey.
2. to hand down to others by heredity, inheritance, etc.
3. to communicate.
4. to cause (light, heat, sound, etc.) to pass through air or some other medium.
5. to allow the passage of; to conduct; as, water will *transmit* sound.
6. to convey (force, movement, etc.) from one mechanical part to another.
7. to send out (radio or television signals) by electromagnetic waves.

trans·mit′tà·ble, *a.* transmissible.

trans·mit′tăl, *n.* a transmitting; transmission.

trans·mit′tănce, *n.* the act of transmitting or the state of being transmitted; transmission.

trans·mit′tẽr, *n.* 1. a person who transmits.
2. a thing that transmits; specifically, (a) the part of a telegraphic instrument by which messages are sent; (b) the part of a telephone, behind or including the mouthpiece, that converts speech sound into electric impulses for transmission; (c) the apparatus that generates radio waves, modulates their amplitude or frequency, and sends them through space by means of an antenna: also called *transmitting set*.

trans·mit′ti·ble, *a.* that can be transmitted; transmissible.

trans·mit′ting set, a transmitter (sense 2 c).

trans·mit′ting stā′tion, a station at which equipment for sending out radio messages or signals is located.

trans·mog″ri·fi·çā′tion, *n.* the act of transmogrifying or the condition of being transmogrified.

trans·mog′ri·fȳ, *v.t.*; transmogrified, *pt.*, *pp.*; transmogrifying, *ppr.* [humorous pseudo-L. formation.] to transform or change completely, especially in a grotesque or strange manner.

trans·mon′tāne, *a.* [L. *transmontanus*.] tramontane.

trans·mun′dāne, *a.* beyond the world; beyond worldly matters.

trans·mū·tà·bil′i·ty, *n.* the quality or state of being transmutable.

trans·mūt′à·ble, *a.* capable of being changed into a different form, nature, or substance.

trans·mūt′à·ble·ness, *n.* transmutability.

trans·mūt′à·bly, *adv.* so as to be transmutable; by or through transmutation.

trans·mū·tā′tion, *n.* [Fr., from L. *transmutatio* (*-onis*), a changing, from pp. of *transmutare*, to transmute, change.]
1. a transmuting or being transmuted; a change of one thing into another.
2. a fluctuation. [Rare.]
3. in the Middle Ages, the supposedly possible conversion of base metals into gold and silver by alchemy.
4. the conversion of one element into another, as in radioactive disintegration or by nuclear bombardment.
transmutation hypothesis; in biology, the theory that the operations of nature as observed at the present time sufficiently account for all existing species.

trans·mū·tā′tion·ist, *n.* one who believes in transmutation.

trans·mū′tà·tive, *a.* 1. tending to transmute.
2. having to do with transmutation.

trans·mūte′, *v.t.*; transmuted, *pt.*, *pp.*; transmuting, *ppr.* [L. *transmutare*, to change into another form; *trans*, across, and *mutare*, to change.] to change from one nature, form, species, condition, or substance into another; to transform.

trans·mūt′ed, *a.* changed into another substance, condition, or nature; transformed.

trans·mūt′ẽr, *n.* one who or that which transmutes.

trans″ō·cē·an′iç (-shē-), *a.* 1. crossing or spanning the ocean.
2. on the other side of the ocean.

tran′sŏm, *n.* [prob. from L. *transtrum*, a transom, lit., that which is across.]
1. a crosspiece in a structure; specifically, (a) a lintel; (b) a horizontal crossbar across the top or middle of a window or the top of a door.
2. a small window or shutterlike panel directly over a door or window, usually hinged to the transom (sense 1b): also called *transom window*.
3. any crosspiece; specifically, (a) the horizontal beam of a cross or gallows; (b) the seat of a throne, boat's cabin, etc.; (c) any of the transverse beams attached to the sternpost of a wooden ship.

tran′sŏmed, *a.* having a transom or transoms, as doors or windows.

tran′sŏm knee (nē), a ship's knee connecting a transom with an after timber.

tran·son′iç, *a.* same as *transsonic*.

trans·pà·cif′iç, *a.* 1. crossing or spanning the Pacific.
2. on the other side of the Pacific.

trans′pà·dāne, *a.* [L. *transpadanus*; *trans*, across, and *Padus*, the river Po.] lying or situated on the other (or northern) side of the river Po: from the viewpoint of Rome.

trans·păr′ence, *n.* the quality or state of being transparent; transparency.

trans·păr′en·cy, *n.* 1. the quality or state of being transparent.
2. *pl.* **trans·păr′en·cieṣ,** something transparent; specifically, a piece of transparent or translucent material having a picture or design that is visible when light shines through it.

trans·păr′ent, *a.* [Fr., from L. *trans*, through, and *parens* (*-entis*), ppr. of *parere*, to appear.]
1. transmitting light rays so that objects on the other side may be distinctly seen; capable of being seen through; as, window glass is *transparent*: opposed to *opaque* and distinguished from *translucent*.
2. so fine in texture or open in mesh that objects on the other side may be seen relatively clearly; sheer; gauzy; diaphanous.
3. easily understood; very clear.
4. easily recognized or detected; obvious.
5. open; frank; candid.
6. luminous; penetrating. [Obs. or Poetic.]

trans·păr′ent·ly, *adv.* in a transparent manner; clearly; so as to be easily seen through.

trans·păr′ent·ness, *n.* the state or quality of being transparent.

trans·pȧss′, *v.t.* and *v.i.* to pass over; to pass by or away. [Obs.]

trans·pȧss′à·ble, *a.* capable of being transpassed. [Obs.]

trans·pat′rŏn·ize, *v.t.* to transfer the patronage of. [Obs.]

tran·spē′ci·āte (-shi-), *v.t.* to change the species of; to transform. [Rare.]

tran·spiç′ū·ous, *a.* [L. *transpicere*, to look through; *trans*, through, and *specere*, to look.] transparent; easily seen through.

trans·piērce′, *v.t.*; transpierced (-pērst), *pt.*, *pp.*; transpiercing, *ppr.* [Fr. *transpercer*.]
1. to pierce through completely.
2. to penetrate; to pierce.

tran·spīr′à·ble, *a.* capable of transpiring or being transpired.

tran·spi·rā′tion, *n.* [Fr.] 1. the act or process of transpiring; specifically, the giving off of moisture, etc. through the pores of the skin or through the surface of the leaves and other parts of plants.
2. in physics, the passage of gases through a capillary tube or a porous substance by pressure.

tran·spīr′à·tō·ry, *a.* 1. of or pertaining to transpiration.
2. that can be transpired.

tran·spīre′, *v.t.*; transpired, *pt.*, *pp.*; transpiring, *ppr.* [L. *trans*, through, and *spirare*, to breathe.] to cause (vapor, moisture, etc.) to pass through tissue or other permeable substances, especially through the pores of the skin or the surface of leaves and other parts of plants.

tran·spīre′, *v.i.* 1. to give off vapor, moisture, etc., as through the pores of the skin.
2. to be given off, passed through pores, exhaled, etc.
3. to leak out; to become known.
4. to come to pass; to happen: in this sense, regarded by some grammarians as a loose usage.

trans·plāce′, *v.t.*; transplaced (-plāst), *pt.*, *pp.*; transplacing, *ppr.* to remove and put in a new place. [Rare.]

trans·plant′, *v.t.*; transplanted, *pt.*, *pp.*; transplanting, *ppr.* [Fr. *transplanter*; LL. *transplantare*; L. *trans*, across, and *plantare*, to plant.]
1. to remove and plant in another place; as, to *transplant* trees.
2. to remove (people) from one place and resettle in another place.
3. in surgery, to transfer (tissue or an organ) from one part of the body or from one individual to another; to graft.

trans·plant′, *v.i.* 1. to do transplanting.
2. to be capable of enduring transplantation.

trans′plant, *n.* 1. a transplanting.
2. something transplanted, as a seedling or body tissue.

trans·plant′à·ble, *a.* capable of being transplanted.

trans·plan·tā′tion, *n.* 1. a transplanting or being transplanted.
2. something transplanted.

trans·plant′ẽr, *n.* 1. one who transplants.
2. a machine for transplanting plants.

tran·splen′den·cy, *n.* supereminent splendor. [Rare.]

tran·splen′dent, *a.* resplendent in the highest degree. [Rare.]

tran·splen′dent·ly, *adv.* in a transplendent manner. [Rare.]

trans·pleū′răl, *a.* extending across the pleural sac.

trans·pō′ni·ble, *a.* [from L. *transponere*, to transpose, and *-ible*.] capable of being transposed.

trans·pon′tine, *a.* [L. *trans*, across, and *pons*, *pontis*, bridge.]
1. on the other side of a bridge; specifically, south of the Thames (and its bridges) in London.
2. of or characteristic of a type of melodrama in which the characters are overdrawn and the situations improbably romantic: such plays were formerly popular at certain London theaters on the south side of the Thames. [Brit.]

trans·pōrt′, *v.t.*; transported, *pt.*, *pp.*; transporting, *ppr.* [Fr. *transporter*; L. *transportare*, to carry across; *trans*, across, and *portare*, to carry.]
1. to carry from one place to another, especially over long distances.
2. to carry away with emotion; to enrapture; to entrance.
3. to carry off to a penal colony, etc.; banish; deport.
4. to carry off by death; kill. [Obs.]

He cannot be heard of. Out of doubt he is *transported*. —Shak.

trans′pōrt, *n.* 1. the act or process of transporting; transportation; conveyance.
2. the condition of being carried away with emotion; rapture.
3. a ship used for transporting soldiers, military supplies, etc.
4. a large commercial airplane for carrying passengers, freight, etc.
5. a convict sentenced to transportation.

trans·pōrt·à·bil′i·ty, *n.* the state or quality of being transportable.

trans·pōrt′à·ble, *a.* 1. that can be transported.

2. implying or involving transportation; subject to transportation; as, a *transportable* offense.

trans·pōrt′ăl, *n.* transportation. [Rare.]

trans·pōrt′ănce, *n.* transportation. [Rare.]

trans·pōr·tā′tion, *n.* 1. a transporting or being transported.
2. a means of conveyance; as, our *transportation* was camel.
3. cost of being transported; fare.
4. a ticket for transport.
5. banishment for crime, as to a penal colony; deportation.
6. transport; ecstasy. [Obs.]

trans·pōrt′ed·ly, *adv.* in a state of rapture; in a transported manner.

trans·pōrt′ed·ness, *n.* the state of being transported, or enraptured.

trans·pōrt′ẽr, *n.* one who or that which transports or removes.

trans·pōrt′ing, *a.* that carries away with delight; ecstatic; as, *transporting* joy.

trans·pōrt′ing·ly, *adv.* in a transporting manner.

trans·pōrt′ment, *n.* transportation. [Obs.]

trans′pōrt ship, a transport (sense 3).

trans·pōṣ′ȧ·ble, *a.* capable of being transposed.

trans·pōṣ′ăl, *n.* the act of transposing or the state of being transposed; transposition. [Rare.]

trans·pōṣe′, *v.t.*; transposed, *pt., pp.*; transposing, *ppr.* [Fr. *transposer*; L. *transpositus*, pp. of *transponere*, to set over; *trans*, across, and *ponere*, to place.]
1. to change the usual, normal, relative, or respective place or order of; to cause to change places; as, to *transpose* letters or words.
2. to alter in form; to transform. [Obs.]
3. to transfer. [Rare.]
4. to transfer (an algebraic term) from one side of an equation to the other, reversing the plus or minus value.
5. to write or play (a musical composition) in a different key.

trans·pōṣe′, *v.i.* 1. to write or play music in a different key.
2. to be capable of being transposed.

trans·pōṣ′ẽr, *n.* one who or that which transposes.

trans·pōṣ′ing, *a.* having the quality of changing or transposing: applied specifically to musical instruments which do not play the actual notes written down, but others, according to the modifications in the instrument itself.

trans·pō·ṣi′tion, *n.* [Fr.] 1. (a) the act of transposing or the state of being transposed; (b) the result of this; something transposed.
2. the transfer of an algebraic term from one side of an equation to the other, without changing the value of the equation.
3. in grammar, a change of the natural order of words in a sentence; as, Latin and Greek admit *transposition* without inconvenience to a much greater extent than English.
4. in music, a change in a composition, either in the transcript or the performance, into another key.
5. in medicine, (a) a displacement of a visceral organ to the opposite side; (b) the surgical operation of carrying a tissue flap from one location to another without severing its connection entirely, until it is united at its new location.

trans·pō·ṣi′tion·ăl, *a.* of the nature of or pertaining to transposition.

trans·poṣ′i·tive, *a.* made by transposing; involving transposition.

trans·poṣ′i·tive·ly, *adv.* by transposition; in a transpositional manner.

trans·poṣ′i·tŏr, *n.* a transposer. [Rare.]

trans·print′, *v.t.* to print in the wrong place; to transpose by error in printing. [Rare.]

trans·proc′ess, *n.* a diapophysis.

trans·prōṣe′, *v.t.* to change from verse into prose.

trans·rē′ġiŏn·āte, *a.* foreign. [Obs.]

trans′seç·tion, *n.* same as *transection.*

trans·seg·men′tăl, *a.* in anatomy, extending across a segment of a limb.

trans·shāpe′, *v.t.* to change into another form. [Rare.]

trans·ship′, *v.t.*; transshipped, *pt., pp.*; transshipping, *ppr.* to transfer from one ship, train, etc. to another for reshipment: also *tranship.*

trans·ship′ment, *n.* 1. the act or process of transshipping.
2. something transshipped.

trans·son′iç, *a.* [from *trans-* and L. *sonus*, sound, and *-ic.*] of, designating, or traveling at speeds approximating the speed of sound in air (which is about 738 miles per hour): the limits are variously set from as low as 550 miles per hour to as high as 900 miles per hour.

trans·tem′pō·răl, *a.* in anatomy, crossing the temporal lobe of the brain.

trans·thȧ·lam′iç, *a.* in anatomy, crossing the optic thalamus.

tran·sub·stan′ti·āte (-shi-), *v.t.*; transubstantiated, *pt., pp.*; transubstantiating, *ppr.* [from ML. *transubstantiatus*, pp. of *transubstantiare*, to transubstantiate, from L. *trans*, across, and *substantia*, substance.] to change one substance into another; to transmute; to transform; specifically, in the Roman Catholic and Orthodox Eastern Churches, to bring about transubstantiation in (bread and wine).

tran·sub·stan·ti·ā′tion, *n.* a change of one substance into another; specifically, in the Roman Catholic and Orthodox Eastern Churches, the doctrine of the conversion of the bread and wine in the Eucharist into the body and blood of Christ, only the accidents of bread and wine remaining.

tran·sub·stan′ti·ā·tŏr, *n.* one who maintains the doctrine of transubstantiation. [Obs.]

tran′sū·dāte, *n.* something transuded.

tran·sū·dā′tion, *n.* 1. the act or process of transuding.
2. a transudate.

tran·sū′dȧ·tō·ry, *a.* passing by, or pertaining to, transudation.

tran·sūde′, *v.i.*; transuded, *pt., pp.*; transuding, *ppr.* [Fr. *transsuder*, from L. *trans*, through, and *sudare*, to sweat.] to ooze, exude, or pass through pores or interstices as or like sweat.

tran·sūme′, *v.t.* to take from one to another; to convert. [Obs.]

tran·sumpt′, *n.* a copy or exemplification of a record. [Archaic.]

tran·sump′tion, *n.* the act of taking from one place to another. [Obs.]

tran·sump′tive, *a.* taken from one to another; also, metaphorical. [Obs.]

trans·ū·ran′iç, *a.* designating or of the elements having atomic numbers higher than that of uranium, as plutonium, etc.

trans·val′ūe, *v.t.*; transvalued, *pt., pp.*; transvaluing, *ppr.* to evaluate by a new principle, especially one rejecting conventional or accepted standards.

trans·vā′sāte, *v.t.* to transvase. [Obs.]

trans·vȧ·sā′tion, *n.* the process or act of transvasing. [Obs.]

trans·vāse′, *v.t.*; transvased (-vāst), *pt., pp.*; transvasing, *ppr.* to pour from one vessel into another.

trans·veç′tion, *n.* the act of conveying or carrying over. [Rare.]

trans·vẽr′bẽr·āte, *v.t.* to strike through. [Rare.]

trans·vẽr′săl, *a.* lying across; transverse; as, a *transversal* line.

trans·vẽr′săl, *n.* in geometry, a straight or curved line that transverses or intersects two or more other lines, as a line intersecting the three sides of a triangle.

trans·vẽr·sā′lis, *n.* [LL., transverse.] in anatomy, a muscle, part, etc. that lies across another.

trans·vẽr·sal′i·ty, *n.* the state or quality of being transversal.

trans·vẽr′săl·ly, *adv.* in a transverse direction.

trans·vẽrse′, *a.* [L. *transversus*, turned across; hence, athwart; pp. of *transvertere*, to turn across; *trans*, across, and *vertere*, to turn.]
1. lying, situated, placed, etc. across; crossing from side to side; crosswise.
2. in geometry, designating the axis that passes through the foci of a conic section (in an ellipse, the longer axis).
transverse bone; in some reptiles, a bone of the skull connecting the palatine and pterygoid bones with the maxilla.
transverse flute; the modern orchestral flute, which is sounded by blowing into the side of the tube: formerly called *German flute.*
transverse magnet; a bar magnet in which the magnetization is at right angles to its length.
transverse process; in anatomy, a process projecting laterally from a vertebra.

trans·vẽrse′, *n.* 1. a transverse beam, part, etc.; especially, in anatomy, a transversalis.
2. in geometry, a transverse axis.

trans·vẽrse′, *adv.* transversely; crosswise.

trans·vẽrse′, *v.t.* 1. to overturn. [Rare.]
2. to transpose. [Rare.]

trans·vẽrse′ly, *adv.* in a transverse direction; as, to cut a thing *transversely.*

trans·vẽr′sion, *n.* the act or process of transversing.

trans·vẽr·sō·çū′bit·ăl, *a.* in entomology, running transversely and dividing the cubital cells of the wings, as certain nervures.

trans·vẽr·sō·mē′di·ăl, *a.* in entomology, crossing the medial cells of the wings, as certain nervures.

trans·vẽr″sō·spī·nā′lis, *n.* one of a series of muscular structures connecting the transverse and spinous processes of the vertebrae.

trans·vẽr′sum, *n.*; *pl.* **trans·vẽr′sȧ,** in reptiles, the transverse bone of the skull.

trans·vẽr′sus, *n.*; *pl.* **trans·vẽr′sī,** in anatomy, a transverse muscle; a transversalis.

trans·vẽrt′, *v.t.* to transform. [Obs.]

trans·ves′tite, *n.* [from *trans-*, across, and L *vestire*, to clothe.] a person who derives sexual pleasure from dressing in the clothes of the opposite sex.

trans·vō·lā′tion, *n.* the act of flying beyond ordinary limits. [Obs.]

Tran·syl·vā′ni·ăn, *a.* of or pertaining to Transylvania, a province in Romania, its people, their language, etc.

Tran·syl·vā′ni·ăn, *n.* a native or an inhabitant of Transylvania.

trant, *v.i.* to peddle. [Brit. Dial.]

trant′ẽr, *n.* a peddler, usually with a horse and cart. [Brit. Dial.]

trap, *n.* [AS. *træppe*, a trap; O.D. *trappe*; O.H.G. *trapo*, snare, trap.]
1. an instrument or device for ensnaring animals, as one that shuts suddenly, often by means of a spring; a gin, snare, or pitfall.
2. an ambush; a stratagem; a device or contrivance to catch one unawares.
3. a device worked by a trigger and spring for throwing clay pigeons, glass balls, etc. into the air to be struck or shot at, as in trapball or trapshooting.
4. (a) trapball; (b) [Slang.] [*pl.*] trapshooting.
5. any of various devices for preventing the escape of gas, offensive odors, etc.; especially, a U-shaped or S-shaped part of a drainpipe, in which water seals off sewer gas.
6. a trap door.
7. a light, two-wheeled carriage on springs.
8. a rattletrap.
9. a policeman. [Brit. Slang.]
10. a kind of fish net.
11. sagacity; cunning; craft. [Slang.]
12. [*pl.*] the drums, cymbals, bells, etc. in an orchestra or band.
13. the mouth. [Slang.]
14. in golf, any of various hazards; as, a sand *trap.*

trap, *v.t.*; trapped (trapt), *pt., pp.*; trapping, *ppr.* 1. to catch in a trap; to ensnare; to take by stratagem.
2. to hold back or seal off by a trap (also with *out*).
3. to furnish with a trap or traps.
4. to attach a trap to, as a drain.
5. in trapshooting, to place in or send up from a trap, as clay pigeons, glass balls, etc.

trap, *v.i.* 1. to set traps for game; as, to *trap* for beaver.
2. to trap animals, especially for their furs.
3. to work the trap in trapshooting.
4. to be hindered or stopped, as liquid, etc.

trap, *n.* [D. *trap*, a step; Sw. *trappa*, a stair.] a kind of portable stepladder.

trap, *n.* [Sw. *trapp*, from *trappa*, a stair, stairs, a kind of ladder: so named from the terraced or steplike arrangement which may be traced in many of these igneous rocks.] any of several kinds of heavy igneous rock, of a greenish-black or grayish color, found in other rock in steplike formations: also called *traprock.*

trap, *v.t.* [ME. *trappen*, from *trappe*, the trappings or ornaments of a horse; prob. from OFr. *drap*, a cloth. The *t* occurs in Sp. and Port. *trapo*, and LL. *trapus*, a cloth.] to array with trappings; to caparison.

trap, *n.* 1. trappings, as for a horse. [Obs.]
2. [*pl.*] belongings; baggage. [Colloq.]

Trā′pȧ, *n.* [abbrev. of LL. *calcitrapa*, a caltrop.] a genus of aquatic polypetalous plants of the *Onagraceæ* or evening-primrose family. The large seeds are sweet and edible. *Trapa bispinosa* of China yields Singhara nuts or water nuts. Also called *water caltrops.*

trȧ·pan′, *n.* same as *trepan* (trick).

trȧ·pan′, *v.t.*; trapanned, *pt., pp.*; trapanning, *ppr.* to trepan (trick).

trȧ·pan′nẽr, *n.* same as *trepanner.*

trap′ball, *n.* an old game played with a trap, a ball, and a bat: the ball is placed in the hollow end of the trap and sent into the air by a blow on its opposite end or handle, and the striker endeavors to hit it as far as possible with the bat before it falls to the ground; also, the ball used in this game. Also *trap ball.*

trap cel′lăr, in a theater, the room or space immediately under the stage, from which the traps are operated.

trap dōor, 1. a sliding or hinged door in a floor, ceiling, or roof.
 2. same as *weather door.*

TRAP-DOOR SPIDER
1. the spider; 2, 3. the nest, in front and profile; 4. section of the nest

trap-door spider; any of a number of large spiders that dig a burrow and cover the entrance with a hinged lid like a trap door. The best known of these spiders are the mason spider, *Cteniza* (or *Mygale*) *cæmentaria,* and *Cteniza californica,* a species native to the southwestern part of the United States.

trāpe, *v.i.;* traped, *pt., pp.;* traping, *ppr.* to traipse. [Obs.]

trāpes, *v.i.;* trapesed (trāpst), *pt., pp.;* trapesing, *ppr.* to traipse.

trāpes, *n.* same as *traipse.*

trap′ē·zāte, *a.* trapeziform.

trȧ·pēze′, *n.* [Fr. *trapèze;* L. *trapezium;* Gr. *trapezion,* a trapezium.]
 1. a trapezium (senses 1 and 2).
 2. a short horizontal bar, hung at a height by two ropes, on which gymnasts, circus performers, etc. swing.

trȧ·pē′zi·ăl, *a.* of or pertaining to the trapezius.

trȧ·pē′zi·fọrm, *a.* having the form of a trapezium.

trȧ·pē′zi·um, *n.; pl.* **trȧ·pē′zi·umṣ, trȧ·pē′zi·ȧ,** [Mod. L., from Gr. *trapezion,* a trapezium, lit., a small table or counter, dim. of *trapeza,* table, lit., a four-footed bench; *tra-* for *tetra,* four, and *peza,* a foot, akin to *pous,* foot.]

TRAPEZIUM

 1. in geometry, a quadrilateral no two sides of which are parallel.
 2. a trapezoid. [Brit.]
 3. in anatomy, (a) a small bone of the wrist near the base of the thumb; (b) the trapezoid body.

trȧ·pē′zi·us, *n.; pl.* **trȧ·pē′zi·ī,** either of a pair of large muscles of the back and neck, which draw the head backward or sidewise, rotate the scapula, etc.

trȧ·pē·zō·hē′drăl, *a.* of, pertaining to, or having the form of a trapezohedron.

trȧ·pē·zō·hē′drŏn, *n.* [Mod. L., from *trapezium,* and Gr. *hedra,* seat.]
 1. a solid bounded by twenty-four equal and similar trapezoidal planes; a tetragonal trisoctahedron.
 2. a solid figure all of whose faces are trapeziums.

trap′ē·zoid, *n.* [Mod. L. *trapezoides,* from Gr. *trapezoeides,* shaped like a trapezoid.]

TRAPEZOID

 1. a quadrilateral, of which two sides only are parallel.
 2. a trapezium (sense 1). [Brit.]
 3. in anatomy, a small bone of the wrist near the base of the index finger.

trap′ē·zoid, *a.* 1. shaped like a trapezoid.
 2. in anatomy, designating or of a bundle of transverse fibers (*trapezoid body*) in the pons of the brain.

trap·ē·zoid′ăl, *a.* 1. trapezoid.
 2. trapezohedral.
 trapezoidal masonry; a style of masonry in which the facing stones are in trapezoid form.

trap′hōle, *n.* 1. a hole with a trap-door covering.
 2. same as *trous-de-loup.*

trä·pï′chę, *n.* [Sp.] 1. a sugar mill; also, a sugar plantation.
 2. in Spanish America, a kind of grinding mill made of two stones, the upper of which is manipulated horizontally by means of a pole: used in crushing and grinding ores.

trap′pē·ăn, *a.* relating or pertaining to trap (rock).

trap′pẽr, *n.* 1. one who traps; especially, one who sets traps to catch fur-bearing animals, usually for their skins.
 2. in mining, a boy in a coal mine who opens the air doors of the galleries for the passage of the coal wagons.
 3. a horse for driving with a trap. [Colloq.]

trap′pingṣ, *n.pl.* the ornamental covering of a horse; also, any external and superficial decorations; ornaments generally; finery; dress.

Trap′pist, *n.* [Fr. *Trappiste,* named from the abbey of La *Trappe,* in Normandy, the headquarters of the body.] a member of a religious body belonging to the Roman Catholic Church, a branch of the Cistercian order, known for perpetual silence and the austere life led by the monks.

Trap′pist, *a.* of or pertaining to the Trappists.

trap′pist·ine, *n.* [named after the *Trappists,* who manufacture it.]
 1. a liqueur manufactured by the Trappists.
 2. [T-] one of an order of nuns.

trap′poid, *a.* like trap (rock).

trap′pous, trap′pōse, *a.* trappy; trappean.

trap′rock, *n.* trap (rock).

traps, *n.pl.* personal belongings; trap.

trap′shọọt″ẽr, *n.* a person who does trapshooting.

trap′shọọt″ing, *n.* the sport of shooting at clay pigeons, glass balls, etc. thrown into the air from traps.

trap′stick, *n.* a stick used in the game of trapball.

trapt, *v.* occasional past tense of *trap.*

trash, *n.* [prob. from Anglo-N. etymon of Norw. dial. *trask,* lumber, trash.]
 1. parts that have been broken off, stripped off, etc., especially leaves, twigs, husks, and other plant trimmings.
 2. any waste or worthless matter; good-for-nothing stuff; rubbish; refuse; dross; dregs.
 Who steals my purse, steals *trash.*—Shak.
 3. worthless ideas, talk, or writing; nonsense.
 4. a worthless or disreputable person or people.
 5. the refuse of sugar cane after the juice has been pressed out.

trash, *v.t.* 1. to trim (trees or plants) of trash.
 2. to regard or treat as trash; to discard as worthless.

trash, *v.t.* to wear out with exertion. [Brit. Dial.]

trash, *v.i.* to walk or run until fatigued. [Brit. Dial.]

trash, *v.t.* [OFr. *trachier,* var. of *tracier;* LL. *tractiare,* from L. *tractus,* a drawing along, track.] to hold back by a leash or halter, as a dog in pursuing game; hence, to retard; to clog; to encumber; to hinder.

trash, *n.* 1. a collar, halter, or leash for trashing a dog.
 2. any restraint or hindrance.

trash′ẽr·y, *n.; pl.* **trash′ẽr·ieṣ,** trash in the aggregate; refuse.

trash house, a house for storing the refuse in sugar making.

trash īce, ice in small pieces, floating in and mixed with water.

trash′i·ly, *adv.* in a trashy manner.

trash′i·ness, *n.* the state or quality of being trashy.

trash′y, *a.; comp.* trashier; *superl.* trashiest, composed of or resembling trash, rubbish, or dross; waste; rejected; worthless; useless; as, a *trashy* novel.

trass, *n.* [G.; D. *tras,* from earlier *terras;* OFr. *terrace,* terrace.] an earth of volcanic origin, resembling a tufa, but containing abundant fragments of pumice, and also fragments of many other volcanic rocks: it is used in hydraulic cement.

trau′liṣm, *n.* a stammering.

trau′mȧ, *n.; pl.* **trau′mȧ·tȧ, trau′mȧṣ,** [Mod. L.; Gr. *trauma.*]
 1. in medicine, (a) an injury or wound violently produced; (b) the condition or neurosis resulting from this.
 2. in psychiatry, an emotional experience, or shock, which has a lasting psychic effect.

trau·mat′iç, *a.* [LL. *traumaticus;* Gr. *traumatikos.*]
 1. of, having the nature of, or resulting from a trauma.
 2. used in the treatment of wounds.

trau·mat′iç, *n.* a medicine useful in the treatment of wounds. [Obs.]

trau′mȧ·tiṣm, *n.* [from Gr. *trauma, traumatos;* and *-ism.*]
 1. the abnormal condition caused by a trauma.
 2. a trauma.

trau′mȧ·tīze, *v.t.;* traumatized, *pt., pp.;* traumatizing, *ppr.* 1. to injure or wound (tissues).
 2. in psychiatry, to subject to a trauma.

trau″mȧ·tō·nē′sis, *n.* [Gr. *trauma, traumatos,* a wound, and *nēsis,* a spinning.] in surgery, suture.

trau″mȧ·top·nē′ȧ, trau″mȧ·top·noe′ȧ, *n.* [Gr. *trauma,* wound, and *pnoiē,* breath.] the passage of air in and out of a wound in the chest wall.

trau·mȧ·top′y·rȧ, *n.* [Gr. *trauma, traumatos,* a wound, and *pyr, pyros,* fire.] traumatic fever.

träunce, *n.* a trance. [Obs.]

träunt, *v.i.* to carry about wares for sale; to hawk goods. [Obs.]

träunt′ẽr, *n.* one who traunts. [Obs.]

Trau̇t·vet·tē′ri·ȧ, *n.* a genus of ranunculaceous plants, of a single species, *Trautvetteria palmata,* a slender plant with palmately-lobed leaves and bearing corymbose, apetalous, white flowers.

trav′āil, *v.i.;* travailed, *pt., pp.;* travailing, *ppr.* [ME. *travaillen;* OFr. *travaillier,* to labor, to toil; LL. hyp. *tripaliare,* to torment.]
 1. to work very hard; to toil.
 2. to suffer the pangs of childbirth; to have labor pains.

trav′āil, *v.t.* to harass; to torment; as, troubles sufficient to *travail* the realm. [Archaic.]

trav′āil, *n.* [ME.; OFr.; LL. hyp. *tripalium,* instrument of torture composed of three stakes, from *tria,* three, and *palus,* a stake.]
 1. very hard work; toil.
 2. labor pains; pains of childbirth.
 3. intense pain; agony.

trȧ·vāil′ (-vȧ′y), *n.* same as *travois.*

trāve, *n.* [ME.; OFr., a crossbeam, from L. *trabs, trabis,* a beam.]
 1. a crossbeam; also, a division made by crossbeams, as in a ceiling.
 2. a wooden frame to confine a restive horse while the smith is setting his shoes.
 3. a shackle used in training a horse to pace. [Obs.]

trav′el, *v.i.;* traveled *or* travelled, *pt., pp.;* traveling *or* travelling, *ppr.* [var. of *travail.*]
 1. to pass or make a journey from one place to another; to make a journey or journeys; to journey; as, to *travel* for health, for pleasure, for improvement, or the like.
 2. to go from place to place as a traveling salesman; as, he has *traveled* over ten years for the same firm.
 3. to proceed or advance in any way; to move; to pass from one point or place to another.
 4. in mechanics, to traverse, as a movable part of a machine which moves in a fixed path or over a fixed distance.
 5. to labor; travail. [Obs.]
 6. to walk or run.
 7. to move or advance with speed. [Colloq.]

trav′el, *v.t.* 1. to harass; trouble; torment. [Obs.]
 2. to journey through; to pass over; to traverse; as, to *travel* every country in Europe.
 I *travel* this profound. —Milton.
 3. to force to journey; to cause to move from place to place.

trav′el, *n.* 1. the act or process of traveling.
 2. [*pl.*] (a) the trips, journeys, tours, etc. taken by a person or persons; (b) a written account of these.
 3. passage or movement of any kind.
 4. the number of persons, vehicles, or ships traveling on a route, through a given place, etc.; traffic.
 5. (a) mechanical motion, especially reciprocating motion; (b) the distance of a mechanical stroke, etc.
 6. travail; toil. [Obs.]
 Syn.—journey, wandering, migration, pilgrimage, excursion, tramp, expedition, trip, ramble, voyage, tour, peregrination.

trav′eled, *a.* 1. that has traveled much; having made journeys; especially, having gained knowledge or experience by traveling.

I am not much *traveled* in the history of modern times. —Fielding.

2. much used by travelers; as, a *traveled* road.

trav'el·ẽr, *n.* 1. one who travels.

2. one who visits foreign countries; one who explores regions more or less unknown; as, he had been a great *traveler* in his time.

3. a traveling salesman; a commercial traveler. [Chiefly Brit.]

4. a thing that travels; specifically, (a) any mechanical part or apparatus, as a traveling crane, that moves or slides along a support; (b) in nautical usage, a metal ring that slides on a rope, rod, or spar; also, the rope, rod, or spar it slides on.

5. a slip on which a customer's various purchases are noted so that they may all be paid for at once.

6. in Australia, a tramp or wanderer.

7. in ring-spinning, the loop round the bobbin in a spinning machine, known as the ring spinner.

trav'el·ẽr's check, a check or draft, usually one of a set, issued by a bank, etc. in any of several denominations and sold to a traveler who signs it at issuance and can cash it by having the payer witness and verify his signature of endorsement.

trav'el·ẽr's-joy', *n.* a climbing plant with white flowers, the *Clematis vitalba*.

trav'el·ẽr's tree, see *Ravenala*.

trav'el·ing, *n.* 1. a passing from place to place; the act of performing a journey.

2. motion of any kind; change of place.

3. labor; toil. [Obs.]

trav'el·ing, *a.* 1. pertaining to or connected with travel; as, a *traveling* companion; *traveling* expenses, fees, etc.

2. movable; as, a *traveling* crane.

trav'el·ing crāne, a crane fixed on a carriage which may be moved on rails.

trav'el·ing sāleṣ'măn, a salesman who travels from place to place soliciting orders for the business firm he represents.

trav'elled, *a.* same as *traveled*.

trav'el·ling, *a.* and *n.* same as *traveling*.

trav'el·lẽr, *n.* same as *traveler*.

trav'e·logue, trav'e·log, *n.* [*travel* and *-logue*.]

1. a travel lecture, usually accompanied by the showing of stereopticon pictures or the like.

2. a motion picture of travels.

trav'el-stāined (-stānd), *a.* having the clothes, etc. soiled with the marks of travel.

trav'ẽrs·ȧ·ble, *a.* 1. capable of being traversed; as, *traversable* deserts.

2. in law, capable of being traversed or denied; as, a *traversable* allegation.

trav'ẽrs·ăl, *n.* a traversing or being traversed.

trav'ẽrse, *v.t.*; traversed, *pt.*, *pp.*; traversing, *ppr.* [ME *traversen*; OFr. *traverser*; L. *transversus*, pp. of *transvertere*, to turn across.]

1. (a) to pass over, across, or through; to cross; (b) to go back and forth over or along; to cross and recross.

2. to go counter to; to oppose; to thwart.

3. to survey or examine carefully.

4. to turn (a gun, lathe, etc.) laterally; to swivel.

5. in law, (a) to deny or contradict formally (something alleged by the opposing party in a lawsuit); (b) to take issue upon (an indictment) or upon the validity of (an inquest of office).

6. in nautical usage, to brace (a yard) fore and aft.

7. in carpentry, to plane in a direction across the grain of the wood; as, to *traverse* a board.

trav'ẽrse, *v.i.* 1. to turn, as on a pivot; to move round; to swivel; as, the needle of a compass *traverses*.

2. in horsemanship, to move crosswise, as a horse that throws his croup to one side and his head to the other.

3. to cross; to cross over.

4. to march to and fro; to cross and recross.

5. in fencing, to move one's blade toward the opponent's hilt while pressing one's foil hard against his.

To see thee fight, to see thee *traverse*. —Shak.

trav'ẽrse, *n.* 1. something that traverses or crosses; specifically, (a) a line that intersects others; (b) a crossbar, crossbeam, transom, etc.; (c) a screen, curtain, etc. placed crosswise; (d) a parapet or wall of earth, etc. across a rampart or trench; (e) a gallery, loft, etc. crossing a building; also, a transverse piece in a timber roof; (f) a straight line surveyed across a plot, region, etc.

2. something that opposes or thwarts; an obstacle.

3. a traversing; specifically, (a) a passing across or through; a crossing; (b) a lateral, pivoting, oblique, or zigzagging movement.

4. a part, device, etc. that causes a traversing movement.

5. a passage by which one may cross; a way across.

6. (a) a zigzagging course or route taken by a vessel, as in sailing against the wind; (b) a single leg of such a course.

7. a formal denial in a lawsuit.

trav'ẽrse, *a.* [OFr. *travers*; L. *transversus*, pp. of *transvertere*, to turn across.]

1. passing or extending across; transverse.

2. designating or of drapes (and the rods and hooks for them) hung in pairs that can be drawn together or apart by pulling cords at the side.

trav'ẽrse, *adv.* across; crosswise. [Obs.]

trav'ẽrse bōard, in nautical usage, formerly, a small board hung in the steerage, and bored with holes upon lines, showing the points of the compass. By means of pegs, the steersman kept an account of the course steered during a watch.

trav'ẽrse cĩr'çle, a flat, circular iron track on which the wheels of a gun carriage move when the gun is traversed.

trav'ẽrsed (-ẽrst), *a.* in heraldry, turned to the sinister side of the shield.

trav'ẽrs·ẽr, *n.* 1. one who or that which traverses; specifically, in law, one who traverses or denies a plea.

2. in railroading, a traverse table.

trav'ẽrse tā'ble, 1. in navigation, a table of difference of latitude and departure.

2. in railroading, a platform arranged to move laterally on wheels, for shifting carriages, etc., from one line of rails to another; a traverser.

trav'ẽrs·ing, *a.* having a lateral adjustment; adapted for giving lateral motion.

trav'ẽr·tine, trav'ẽr·tin, *n.* [It. *travertino*, *tibertino*, *tiburtino*; L. *lapis Tiburtinus*, from being formed by the waters of Anio at *Tibur*, now Tivoli.] a light-colored limestone, usually hard and semicrystalline, deposited from the water of springs holding lime in solution: it is quarried in Italy.

trav'es·ty, *a.* [from Fr. *travesti*, pp. of *travestir*, to disguise; It. *travestire*, from L. *trans*, over, and *vestire*, to dress.] disguised by dress so as to be ridiculous; burlesqued. [Obs.]

trav'es·ty, *n.*; *pl.* **trav'es·tieṣ,** 1. a burlesque treatment, imitation, or translation for purposes of ridicule.

2. a crude and ridiculous representation; a ludicrous distortion.

trav'es·ty, *v.t.*; travestied, *pt.*, *pp.*; travestying, *ppr.* to translate, treat, or imitate so as to render ridiculous or ludicrous; to burlesque.

trȧ·vois' (-voi'), *n.*; *pl.* **trȧ·vois'** (-voiz'), **trȧ·vois'eṣ,** [Canad. Fr. from *travail*, a brake.] a crude sledge of the North American Plains Indians, consisting of a net or platform dragged along the ground on the two poles that support it and serve as shafts for the draft animal.

trȧ·voiṣe', *n.* same as *travois*.

trawl, *n.* [doubtful Late ME. *trawelle*; prob. var. of *trail*.]

1. a long line, sometimes more than a mile in length and supported by buoys, from which short lines with baited hooks are suspended: used especially in deep-sea fishing, as for cod or haddock; a bultow.

TRAWL
a, trawlwarp; *b*, bridle; *c*, trawl beam; *d d*, trawlheads; *e*, ground-rope; *l*, tail of net, which is tied for the convenience of opening and examining the net

2. a large, bag-like net dragged along the bottom of a fishing bank by a boat: also called *trawlnet*.

trawl, *v.i.*; trawled, *pt.*, *pp.*; trawling, *ppr.* to fish with a trawl.

trawl, *v.t.* 1. to drag, as a trawl.

2. to catch or take with a trawl.

trawl an̄'chŏr, an anchor with which a trawl (line) is moored.

trawl bēam, the beam of a trawl net for holding it open.

trawl'bōat, *n.* a boat which is used for fishing when trawls or trawl nets are employed.

trawl'ẽr, *n.* 1. one who trawls; a fisherman who uses a trawl or trawlnet.

2. a fishing boat which trails or drags a trawl.

trawl'head (-hed), *n.* a frame of iron at each end of a trawl beam.

trawl keg, a keg used as a buoy for a trawl (line) or to indicate its position.

trawl'net, *n.* same as *trawl*, sense 2.

trawl rōll'ẽr, a roller which is placed on the gunwale of a trawlboat or dory to aid in hauling a trawl (net).

trawl'warp, *n.* a rope forming the connection between the boat and the trawl (net) when the latter is overboard.

trāy, *n.* [ME. *treie*; AS. *treg*, *trig*, wooden board.]

1. a flat receptacle made of wood, metal, glass, plastic, etc. with slightly raised edges or low sides, used for holding or carrying articles.

2. a tray with its contents; as, a *tray* of food.

3. a shallow, boxlike, removable compartment of a trunk, cabinet, etc.

trāy ag'ri·çul·tūre, hydroponics.

trāy'fụl, *n.* as much as a tray will hold.

trāyṣ, *n.* in harness, a trace. [Obs.]

trāy trip, an ancient game of dice in which success probably depended upon the throwing of a three. [Obs.]

treach'ẽr (trech'), *n.* a traitor. [Obs.]

treach'ẽr·ous, *a.* [ME. *trecherous*; OFr. *trecheros*.]

1. violating allegiance or faith pledged; faithless; traitorous; perfidious; betraying a trust; characteristic of a traitor.

2. having a false appearance of safety, honesty, etc.; deceptive; not to be depended upon; insecure; as, *treacherous* rocks.

Syn.—traitorous, treasonable, perfidious, false, faithless.

treach'ẽr·ous·ly, *adv.* in a treacherous manner.

treach'ẽr·ous·ness, *n.* the quality or state of being treacherous; faithlessness; perfidiousness.

treach'ẽr·y, *n.*; *pl.* **treach'ẽr·ieṣ,** [ME. *trecherie*; OFr. *tricherie*, trickery, from *tricher*, to cheat.]

1. violation of allegiance or faith and confidence; perfidy.

2. treason.

3. an act of perfidy or treason.

treach'ē·tōur, *n.* a traitor. [Obs.]

trēa'çle, *n.* [OFr. *triacle*, corrupted from L. *theriaca*, from Gr. *thēriakē* (*pharmaka*, drugs, understood), antidotes against the bites of venomous animals, from *thērion*, a wild beast, dim. of *thēr*, an animal.]

1. molasses; a viscid syrup, which drains from the sugar-refining molds: sometimes called *sugarhouse molasses*. [Brit.]

2. a saccharine fluid, consisting of the inspissated juices or decoctions of certain vegetables, as the sap of birch, sycamore, etc. [Rare.]

3. formerly, a remedy for poison; hence, any effective remedy.

countryman's treacle; (a) the common rue; (b) the valerian; (c) the garlic. [Brit. Dial.]

English treacle; the water germander.

trēa'çle mus'tȧrd, a cruciferous plant, *Erysimum cheiranthoides*: the seeds are said to have been used for destroying worms in children.

trēa'çle wạ'tẽr, a compound cordial, distilled with a spirituous menstruum from several other cordial and sudorific drugs and herbs.

trēa'çle wŏrm'seed, treacle mustard.

trēa'çly, *a.*; *comp.* treaclier; *superl.* treacliest.

1. similar to or made of treacle; thick and sticky.

2. covered with treacle.

tread (tred), *v.t.*; trod *or archaic* trode, *pt.*; trodden *or* trod, *pp.*; treading, *ppr.* [ME. *treden*; AS. *tredan*.]

1. to walk on, in, along, across, over, etc.

2. to beat or press with the feet so as to crush or injure; to trample; as, to *tread* a path.

3. to accomplish, perform, or execute by walking, dancing, stepping, etc.

4. to oppress or subdue, as if by stepping on.

5. to copulate with: said of the male bird.

6. to put a tread on (a pneumatic tire).

to tread the boards or *the stage*; to act as a stageplayer; to perform parts on the stage.

to tread water; in swimming, to move the feet and hands regularly up and down, while keeping the body in an erect position, in order to keep the head above the water.

tread (tred), *v.i.* 1. to set the foot down; to make a step; to step.

Fools rush in where angels fear to *tread*.
—Pope.

2. to walk or step; to move on foot.

3. to copulate, as birds: used especially of male birds.

4. to trample (with *on* or *upon*).

to tread on air; (a) to walk gaily; (b) to be gay or happy.

to tread on one's toes; to offend one.

to tread on or *upon*; to follow closely.

tread (tred), *n.* 1. a mark made by treading; a footprint. [Rare.]

2. way; track; path. [Obs.]

3. the act of the male bird in copulation.

4. a treading; also, manner or sound of stepping; as, a horse has a good *tread*.

5. something on which a person treads or moves, as the part of a shoe, etc. that makes contact or the horizontal upper surface of a stair.

6. the distance between the points of contact (with the ground) of paired wheels, as of an automobile.

7. the outer, grooved rim of a pneumatic tire, on which the tire moves.

8. the cicatricle or chalaza of a bird's egg.

9. the length of a ship's keel.

10. the part of a rail on which the wheels run.

11. an injury to a horse's foot made by interfering.

tread'ẽr, *n.* one who or that which treads.

tread'le, *n.* [ME. *tredyl*; AS. *tredel*.]

1. a lever or pedal moved by the foot and connected to the crank of a small machine, as a lathe, sewing machine, etc., to operate it.

2. the chalaza of a bird's egg: so called because formerly supposed to have been produced by copulation.

tread'le, *v.i.*; treadled (-ld), *pt., pp.*; treadling, *ppr.* to work a treadle.

tread'mill, *n.* 1. a kind of mill wheel turned by the weight of persons treading steps arranged around its circumference: it was formerly used as an instrument of prison discipline.

2. a mill driven by an animal treading a sloping, endless belt.

3. any monotonous round of duties, work, etc. in which one seems to get nowhere.

tread'-sọft″ly, *n.* the spurge nettle.

tread'wheel (-hwēl), *n.* a wheel resembling a treadmill (sense 1) in manner of propulsion.

trēague (trēg), *n.* a truce. [Obs.]

trēa'ṣŏn, *n.* [ME. *trezoun, tresun, traison*; OFr. *traison, traisson*; L. *traditio* (-*onis*), from *tradere*, to give or deliver over or up; *trans*, over, and *dare*, to give.]

1. violation of the allegiance owed to one's sovereign or state; betrayal of one's country: the Constitution of the United States (Article III, Section 3) declares, "Treason against the United States shall consist only in levying war against them or in adhering to their enemies, giving them aid and comfort."

2. any betraying, treachery, breach of faith, or betrayal of trust. [Rare.]

trēa'ṣŏn·ȧ·ble, *a.* pertaining to treason; consisting of treason; involving the crime of treason.

Syn.—traitorous.

trēa'ṣŏn·ȧ·bly, *adv.* 1. in a treasonable manner.

2. by an act of treason.

trēa'ṣŏn·ous, *a.* treasonable.

treaṣ'ūre (trezh'ũr), *n.* [ME. *tresoure*; OFr. *tresor*; L. *thesaurus*, from Gr. *thēsauros*, a store, treasure, from *the*, the root of *tithenai*, to put or place.]

1. wealth accumulated or stored in the form of money, precious jewels, etc.

2. a great quantity of anything collected for future use.

3. something or someone considered very valuable.

4. a treasury. [Obs.]

treaṣ'ūre, *v.t.*; treasured, *pt., pp.*; treasuring, *ppr.* 1. to hoard; to collect or save up (money, valuables, etc.) as for future use; as, to *treasure* gold and silver: usually with *up*.

2. to attach great value to; to cherish.

treaṣ'ūre house, a house or building where treasures and stores are kept.

treaṣ'ūr·ẽr, *n.* one who has the care of a treasure or treasury; specifically, an officer who has charge of the funds or finances of a government, an incorporated company, a private society, etc.

Lord High Treasurer; formerly, in England, the principal officer of the crown, having charge of all the national revenue.

treaṣ'ūr·ẽr·ship, *n.* the office of treasurer.

treaṣ'ūr·ess, *n.* a woman treasurer.

treaṣ'ūre-trōve', *n.* [*treasure*, and Fr. *trové*, pp. of *trover, trouver*, to find.]

1. any money, bullion, and the like, found hidden, the owner of which is not known.

2. any valuable discovery.

treaṣ'ūr·y, *n.*; *pl.* **treaṣ'ūr·ieṣ,** [ME. and OFr. *tresorie*.]

1. a place where treasure is kept; a room or building where valuable objects are preserved.

2. a place where public or private funds are kept, received, disbursed, and recorded.

3. the funds or revenues of a state, corporation, society, etc.

4. [T-] the department of a state or nation that is in charge of revenue, taxation, and public finances.

5. a collection of treasures in art, literature, etc.; as, a *treasury* of verse.

6. treasure. [Obs.]

treasury bench; a bench or row of seats in the House of Commons, to the right of the Speaker, occupied by those members of the House who are also members of the government. [Brit.]

treasury bill; a short-term obligation of the United States Treasury, usually maturing in 91 days, bearing no interest and sold periodically on the open market on a discount basis.

treasury bond; any of various series of bonds issued by the United States Treasury, usually maturing over long periods.

treasury certificate; an intermediate-term obligation of the United States Treasury, usually maturing in one year, paying interest periodically on a coupon basis.

treasury note; any of the interest-bearing obligations of the United States Treasury with maturities between one and five years.

trēat, *v.t.*; treated, *pt., pp.*; treating, *ppr.* [ME. *treten*; OFr. *traitier*, to handle, meddle, treat, from L. *tractare*, a freq. of *trahere*, to draw.]

1. to behave to or toward (a person, animal, etc.) in a specified manner; to conduct oneself in a certain manner with respect to.

2. to handle or develop in a particular manner, in writing, speaking, painting, etc.; as, to *treat* a subject diffusely; the composer *treated* the theme skillfully.

3. to pay for the food, drink, entertainment, etc. of (another); as, to *treat* the whole company.

To *treat* a poor wretch with a bottle of Burgundy, and fill his snuff box, is like giving a pair of laced ruffles to a man that had never a shirt on his back.—Tom Brown.

4. to have a specified opinion or view of and behave accordingly in regard to; as, he *treated* the mistake as a joke.

5. to subject to some process, usually for a definite purpose; specifically, (a) to give medical or surgical care to; (b) to subject to chemical action; (c) to cover or coat with some preparation for protection, appearance, etc.

6. to entreat; to beseech; to solicit. [Obs.]

7. to negotiate; to discuss. [Rare.]

Syn.—entertain, discourse, manipulate, handle, arrange.

trēat, *v.i.* 1. to discourse; to handle in writing or speaking; to make discussions: followed usually by *of*.

Then, sir, awful odes she wrote,
Too awful, sure, for what they *treated of*.
—Tennyson.

2. to carry on business or discuss terms (*with* a person); to negotiate.

Inform us, will the emp'ror *treat*?—Swift.

3. to stand the cost of another's entertainment.

If we do not please, at least we *treat*.
—Prior.

trēat, *n.* 1. a meal, drink, entertainment, etc. given or paid for by someone else.

This is the ceremony of my fate;
A parting *treat*, and I'm to die in state.
—Dryden.

2. anything which gives great or unusual pleasure; a delight.

Carrion is a *treat* to dogs, ravens, vultures, fish.
—Paley.

3. (a) the act of treating or entertaining; (b) one's turn to treat.

4. parley; conference; treaty. [Obs.]

Bid him battle without further *treat*.
—Spenser.

trēat'ȧ·ble, *a.* 1. moderate; not violent. [Obs.]

2. tractable; affable; as, a *treatable* disposition.

trēat'ȧ·bly, *adv.* in a treatable manner.

trēat'ẽr, *n.* one who or that which treats.

trēa'tise, *n.* [ME. *tretis*; OFr. *tretis, treitis, traictis*, from L. *tractare*, to handle.]

1. a formal, systematic essay or book on some subject, especially a discussion of facts, evidence, or principles and the conclusions based on these.

He had written an exhaustive *treatise* on the discovery of America by the Norseman.
—W. A. Fraser.

2. a narrative; a tale. [Obs.]

Syn.—tract, essay, paper, disquisition, dissertation, tractate, monograph, article.

trēa'tis·ẽr, *n.* one who writes a treatise. [Obs.]

trēat'ment, *n.* [Fr. *traitement*, from L. *tractare*, to handle.]

1. act, manner, method, etc. of treating, as a person, a substance in processing, or a subject in art or literature.

2. medical or surgical care, especially a systematic course of this.

3. the act of treating or entertaining; entertainment. [Rare.]

Carrel-Dakin treatment; in medicine and surgery, a method of treating wounds by periodic bathing, by means of a specially devised system of rubber tubes, with a solution of chlorinated soda and sodium bicarbonate, to promote healing: named for Alexis Carrel, French surgeon, and H. D. Dakin, English chemist.

trēa'tūre, *n.* treatment. [Obs.]

trēa'ty, *n.*; *pl.* **trēa'tieṣ,** [ME. *tretee*; OFr. *traité*, a treaty, properly pp. of *traiter*, to treat, from L. *tractare*, to handle, manage, treat.]

1. formerly, (a) treatment; (b) negotiation; (c) entreaty; (d) any agreement or contract; (e) discourse.

2. (a) a formal agreement, league, or contract, between two or more nations or sovereigns, formally signed and solemnly ratified by the supreme power of each state. Treaties are of various kinds, as for regulating trade, for forming alliances, offensive and defensive, for making peace, etc.; (b) the document embodying such an agreement.

Syn.—contract, agreement, league, covenant, alliance, negotiation, convention.

trēa'ty-māk″ing, *a.* authorized to make or form treaties.

trēa'ty pọrt, a port that must be kept open for foreign trade according to the terms of a treaty, as, formerly, any of certain ports in China.

treb'le, *a.* [ME.; OFr.; L. *triplex, triplus*; *tres*, three, and *plexus*, fold.]

1. threefold; triple; as, a lofty tower with *treble* walls.

2. (a) of or for the highest part in musical harmony; (b) playing or singing this part.

3. high-pitched; shrill.

treb'le, *n.* 1. the highest part in musical harmony; soprano.

2. a singer or instrument that takes this part.

3. a high-pitched or shrill voice or sound.

4. in short whist, a game which counts three points to the winners, their opponents not having scored.

treb'le, *v.t.*; trebled (-ld), *pt., pp.*; trebling, *ppr.* 1. to make thrice as much; to make threefold.

2. to utter in a treble tone; hence, to whine. [Obs.]

treb'le, *v.i.* to become threefold; as, a debt at compound interest soon *trebles* in amount.

treb'le clef, 1. a sign on a staff (𝄞), indicating that the notes on the staff are above middle C.

2. the range so indicated.

Also called *G clef*, and distinguished from *F*, or *bass, clef*.

treb'le·ness, *n.* the state or quality of being treble.

treb'let, *n.* same as *triblet*.

treb'ly, *adv.*; *comp.* treblier; *superl.* trebliest; three times; triply; in a threefold number or quantity; as, a good deed *trebly* recompensed.

treb'ū·chet, *n.* [ME. and OFr., from *trebucher*, to stumble, from *tre-, tra-* (from L. *trans*, over) and *buc*, trunk, body, from OS. *buk*, trunk.]

1. a medieval war engine for hurling large stones. A heavy weight on the short end of a lever was suddenly released, raising the light

end of the longer arm containing the missile, and discharging it with great force.

2. a kind of balance or scales used in weighing coins.

3. a cucking stool.

4. a kind of trap for small game.

trē′buck·et, *n.* a trebuchet.

tre·cen′tist (-chen′), *n.* a follower of the style of the trecento.

tre·cen′tō (-chen′), *n.* [It.] the period of the fourteenth century in Italian art, literature, etc.

trē·chom′e·tēr, *n.* [Gr. *trechein*, to run, and *-meter.*] a kind of odometer or contrivance for registering the distance run, especially by vehicles.

treck, *v.i.* and *n.* same as *trek*.

treck′schuyt (-skoit), *n.* same as *trekschuit*.

tred′dle, *n.* the dung of sheep or of hares. [Brit. Dial.]

tred′dle, *n.* same as *treadle*.

trē·dille′, trē·drille′, *n.* a game at cards for three people.

tree, *n.* [AS. *treow, treo, tre*; akin to Goth. *triu*, tree, wood; compare W. *derw*, Gr. *drus*, an oak, Sans. *dru*, a tree.]

1. a woody, perennial plant with one main stem or trunk which develops many branches: most trees are over ten feet tall.

2. a treelike bush or shrub; as, a rose *tree*.

3. a wooden beam, bar, pole, post, stake, etc.

4. a gallows.

5. anything resembling a tree as in having a stem and branches; specifically, (a) a diagram of family descent (*family* or *genealogical tree*); (b) in chemistry, a treelike formation of crystals.

6. shortened form of *boot tree, saddletree, crosstree, Christmas tree*, etc.

7. the cross on which Jesus was crucified. [Archaic.]

8. wood. [Obs.]

9. in mathematics, a diagram of branching lines.

big tree; a California tree, *Sequoia gigantea*.

genealogical tree; see under *genealogical*.

mammoth tree; same as *big tree*.

tree of Buddha; the Bo Tree.

tree of heaven; a fast-growing tree with smooth, brown bark, pinnate leaves, and greenish flowers; ailanthus: the stamen-bearing flowers smell bad.

tree of knowledge; in the Bible, the tree whose fruit Adam and Eve tasted in disobedience to God: Gen. ii, iii: also *tree of knowledge of good and evil*.

tree of life; (a) the arborvitae; (b) in the Bible, a tree in the Garden of Eden bearing fruit which, if eaten, gave everlasting life: Gen. ii. 9; iii. 22; (c) in the Bible, a tree in the heavenly Jerusalem whose leaves are for healing the nations: Rev. xxii. 2.

tree of long life; a small hardy tree of the genus *Glaphyria* or *Leptospermum*, belonging to the myrtle family, growing in the Malayan islands.

tree of Porphyry; in logic, a diagram representing the relation of genera.

tree of the gods; same as *tree of heaven*.

tree of the sun; a Japanese forest tree, *Retinospora obtusa*, so called because dedicated by the natives to the god of the sun. It rises to the height of eighty or ninety feet, with a straight trunk, having a diameter at the base of five feet, and yields a fine-grained timber: also called *Japanese cypress*.

trembling tree; the American aspen.

Tyburn tree; the gallows.

up a tree; in a situation without escape; in a difficult position; cornered. [Colloq.]

tree, *v.t.*; treed *pt., pp.*; treeing, *ppr.* 1. to drive to a tree; to cause to ascend a tree; as, a dog *trees* a squirrel.

2. to gain complete advantage over; to corner, as if chased up a tree; to place in a difficult position; as, to *tree* an opponent in an argument. [Colloq.]

3. to stretch or place on a boot tree.

tree ag′āte, a species of agate with dendritic markings, found in India and Brazil.

tree al′ōe, same as *quiver tree*.

tree ȧsp, a venomous South African tree-climbing snake of the genus *Dendraspis*.

tree ȧ·zā′lē·ȧ, a North American shrub with large rose-colored flowers.

tree beãr, the raccoon. [Dial.]

tree′bēard, *n.* 1. the long moss.

2. a lichen, *Usnea barbata*, which grows on trees.

tree bee′tle, any one of many beetles which subsist on the leaves of trees and shrubs.

tree belt, same as *tree lawn*.

tree′bīne″, *n.* any cultivated vine of the genus *Cissus*.

tree bō′ȧ, an arboreal serpent of the family *Boidæ*, especially *Corallus hortulanus*.

tree brack′et, any fungus shaped like a bracket.

tree bug, one of numerous species of insects which feed on the sap of trees and shrubs.

tree bur′i·ăl (ber′), a custom, formerly prevalent among North American Indians, of placing their dead on a platform in a tree or in the hollow trunk of a tree.

tree çaç′tus, the saguaro.

tree çȧlf (kȧf), *n.* in bookbinding, a brown calf binding with markings resembling the limbs and foliage of a tree.

tree çat, a paradoxure.

tree cel′an·dīne, any herb of the genus *Macleaya*: it is native to Asia and is often cultivated for its plumelike flowers.

tree clȧss, in forestry, one of the common age groups or size classifications into which forest trees are divided for identification, as sapling, veteran, and the like.

tree çlīmb′ēr (klīm′), any animal given to climbing trees; specifically, a climbing fish.

tree çlō′vēr, the sweet clover, *Melilotus alba*.

tree çō′brȧ, any one of the tropical and South African venomous snakes of the genus *Dendraspis*: they are related to the true cobras but do not have a dilatable hood. Of the many species, *Dendraspis angusticeps* is the quickest and most pugnacious.

tree çŏm′pȧss, in forestry, a device with which the diameters of trees may be measured. A scale bar and a pair of dividers comprise the instrument.

tree çō′ny, any one of several species of *Dendrohyrax*, a type of wild African rabbit.

tree çot′tŏn, a tall East Indian cotton plant of the genus *Gossypium*.

tree çrab, a purse crab.

tree çreep′ēr, any one of numerous species of birds which creep about trees, especially of the genus *Certhia* and related genera.

tree çrick′et, an arboreal American cricket of the genus *Œcanthus*, which infests grapevines.

tree çrōw, an Asiastic crow of the genus *Crypsirhina* and related genera, intermediate between the true crows and the jays.

tree çuck′ōō, any arboreal cuckoo, as opposed to a *ground cuckoo*.

tree çult, tree worship, formerly a general practice among civilized as well as primitive people: it invested trees with supernatural powers and included sacrifices to them as well as ornamentation of them with various offerings.

tree dig′gēr, an appliance used in transplanting trees.

tree dŏve, an arboreal pigeon of the genus *Macropygia*, native to the Moluccas.

tree duck, an arboreal duck of the *Dendrocygna* or an allied genus, native to the tropics.

tree fērn, any one of several species of tropical ferns which attain the size of trees, have a woody trunk, and bear at their summits clusters of large, drooping fronds. A handsome species, *Cyathea medullaris*, contains in its trunk a mucilaginous pulp comparable to sago, which is used extensively for food in Polynesia and New Zealand.

tree′fish″, *n.*; *pl.* **tree′fish″** or **tree′fish″eș,** a California rockfish, *Sebastichthys serriceps*, valued for food.

tree frog, a batrachian living in trees, as (a) a tree toad; (b) any of various frogs that live in trees.

tree′fụl, *n.* that quantity which fills a tree; as, a *treeful* of plums.

tree gōōse, a goose mussel or goose barnacle.

tree hēath, a short European shrub with globe-shaped flowers.

tree hop′pēr, any of certain homopterous insects which injure the trees in which they deposit their eggs. Many species, as *Ceresa bubalus*, the buffalo tree hopper, are of curious shapes.

tree ī′ron (-ũrn), in a vehicle, (a) an iron connecting the singletree to the doubletree, or the latter to the tongue; (b) a hook or clip used in attaching the traces.

tree job′bēr, a woodpecker. [Obs.]

tree kañ·gȧ·rōō′, any of a number of tree-dwelling kangaroos of New Guinea and northern Australia, of the genus *Dendrolagus*.

tree lärk, a bird, the tree pipit. [Brit. Dial.]

tree lạwn, the unpaved strip of ground between a city street and its parallel sidewalk: lawns and trees are often planted here.

tree′less, *a.* without trees.

tree liz′ärd, a lizard of the group *Dendrosauria*, including the chameleons.

tree louse, a plant louse, an insect of the genus *Aphis*.

tree mi·gnŏn·ette′ (min-yun-et′), ordinary mignonette made a perennial by nipping off the flower buds.

tree mō·lȧs′seș, maple syrup. [Colloq.]

tree mọss, in botany, (a) a moss, *Usnes plicata*, growing on trees; (b) a moss in the form of a miniature tree.

tree mouse, an arboreal mouse of the family *Muridæ*.

tree′nāil″ (*or* tren′l), *n.* [ME. *trenayle*, from *tre* in early sense "wood".] a wooden peg used to join timbers: it swells from moisture and is therefore used in shipbuilding, etc.: also *trenail, trunnel*.

tree nymph, same as *hamadryad*.

tree ŏn′iŏn (-yun), a species of onion, *Allium proliferum*, the stalks of which, when allowed to run up, produce small bulbs instead of flowers at the top.

tree oys′tēr, a small American oyster which attaches itself to the roots of the mangrove tree: also called *mangrove oyster* and *raccoon oyster*.

tree pīe, an Asiatic bird of the genus *Dendrocitta*, allied to the crow and magpie.

tree pig′eŏn, a species of pigeon, allied to the true pigeons, but presenting more points of resemblance to insessorial birds. The tree pigeons are native to Asia, Africa, and Australia. They have long wings, and live among trees, feeding on fruits and berries.

tree pop′py, a shrubby plant, *Romneya coulteri*, of California, having large showy white flowers; also, a papaveraceous plant, *Dendromecon rigidum*, of California, having showy yellow flowers and thick inflexible leaves.

tree pọr′çū·pīne, any one of several species of South American arboreal porcupines, of the genus *Sphingurus*.

tree rat, an arboreal rodent found in the West Indies and belonging to the genus *Capromys* or the genus *Plagiodon*.

tree′sçāpe, *n.* a wooded landscape.

tree sẽr′pent, a tree snake.

tree shrew (shrö), an animal of the genus *Tupaia*; a banxring; a squirrel shrew.

tree shrīke, a bush shrike.

tree snāke, an arboreal harmless snake found in the warmer parts of the world.

tree sor′rel, a species of sorrel, *Rumex lunaria*. It grows to the height of a small tree and is sometimes cultivated for its greenish flowers.

tree spar′row, 1. a sparrow, *Passer montanus*, closely related to the house sparrow, but somewhat smaller, common in Great Britain, and naturalized in the United States.

2. in the United States, a common sparrow, *Spizella monticola*.

tree squĩr′rel (skwĩr′), a true or typical squirrel of the genus *Sciurus*, as distinguished from the *flying squirrel, ground squirrel, marmot squirrel, prairie squirrel*, etc.

tree sụg′ăr (shụg′), maple sugar. [Dial.]

tree sũr′ġeŏn, a person skilled in tree surgery.

tree sũr′ġēr·y, treatment of damaged trees as by filling cavities, removing parts, treating fresh wounds, etc.

tree swäl′lōw, 1. a swallow of Australia which lays its eggs in holes in trees.

2. the white-bellied swallow, *Tachycineta bicolor*, which nests in trees in North America.

tree swift, a long-tailed swift of the genus *Dendrochelidon*, found in the Orient.

tree tī′gēr, the leopard.

tree tōad, any of many tree-dwelling, toadlike amphibians with small, adhesive pads on the toes; especially, any toad of the genus *Hyla* or related genera of the family *Hylidæ*. There are many species, found for the most part in the American tropics, although there is one European species, *Hyla arborea*. *Hyla versicolor* is common in the United States. The latter and many other species are noted for the facility with which they change colors so as to blend with the surroundings.

tree′top, *n.* the topmost branches of a tree.

tree vī′ō·let, a shrubby species of violet, *Viola arborescens*, having erect, branching stems and pale blue flowers, growing in the western Mediterranean district.

tree wạr'blẽr, any one of several species of arboreal typical warblers of the genus *Hypolais* or a related genus.

tree wool, same as *pine-needle wool* under *pine needle.*

tree wŏrm, the shipworm. [Obs.]

tref'le, *n.* [OFr. *treffle,* trefoil.]

1. a trefoil or object representing a trefoil.
2. in fortification, a mine shaped like a trefoil.

tré·flé', tre·flée' (trā-flā'), *a.* in heraldry, (a) having arms which end in a trefoil or triple leaves, as a cross; (b) semé with triple leaves or flowers, as a bend.

CROSS TRÉFLÉ

trē'foil, *n.* [OFr. *trifoil;* L. *trifolium,* a three-leaved plant; *tri-,* prefix allied to *tres,* three, and *folium,* leaf.]

1. any of a number of plants with leaves divided into three leaflets; especially, any plant of the genus *Trifolium,* including white clover, red clover, etc.; also, the medic, *Medicago lupulina,* or nonesuch, cultivated for fodder.
2. in architecture, an ornament of three cusps in a circle, resembling a threefold leaf: used in Gothic architecture in the heads of window lights, tracery, etc.

TREFOILS

3. in heraldry, a charge representing the clover leaf, always depicted as slipped, that is, furnished with a stalk.
4. a European bombycid moth or egger, *Lasiocampa trifolii,* the larva of which feeds on clover.

hare's-foot trefoil; same as *hare's-foot,* sense 1.

shrubby trefoil; same as *hop tree.*

thorny trefoil; a thorny annual shrub of the genus *Fagonia;* especially, *Fagonia cretica,* found chiefly in the Mediterranean region, but also in warm parts of Asia and America.

trē'foiled, trē·fō'li·ā·ted, *a.* 1. having the form or outline of a trefoil, as an arch or tracery.

2. in heraldry, same as *bottony.*

trē'foil knot (not), a kind of knot: see *knot,* illus.

treġ'et, *n.* jugglery; trickery; legerdemain. [Obs.]

treġ'et·öur, *n.* a juggler; one who practices legerdemain; a magician who employs mechanical contrivances to produce illusions; also, an impostor. [Archaic.]

treġ'et·ry, *n.* sleight of hand; legerdemain; also, a trick; deception. [Obs.]

trē·hä'lȧ, *n.* the substance of cocoons excreted by a lepidopterous insect, *Larinus maculatus,* of Persia and Turkey. The larvae eat the branches of *Echinops persica* for the sugar, starch, and gum contained in them, and of these substances the cocoons chiefly consist. Also called *Turkish manna.*

trē'hȧ·lōse, *n.* a crystalline sugar, $C_{12}H_{22}O_{11}$, obtained from certain lichens and fungi: so called because first obtained from trehala; mycose.

treil'läġe (trāl'), *n.* [Fr., from *treille,* a trellis.] in gardening, a sort of latticework, consisting of light posts and rails for supporting vines, espaliers, and wall trees; a trellis.

treille (trāl), *n.* 1. in heraldry, a lattice. [Rare.]

2. in lacemaking, a net ground.

trek, *v.i.;* trekked (trekt), *pt., pp.;* trekking, *ppr.* [S. Afr.D., from D. *trekken,* to draw.]

1. in South Africa, to travel by ox wagon.
2. to travel slowly or laboriously.

trek, *v.t.* in South Africa, to draw (a wagon): said of an ox.

trek, *n.* 1. in South Africa, a journey made by ox wagon, or one leg of it.

2. a journey or leg of a journey.
3. a migration.

trek'kẽr, *n.* one who treks.

trek'schuit (-skoit), *n.* [D.] a boat built to be towed; a Dutch canalboat.

trek tōw, [S. Afr.] a chain or cable, which attaches the yokes of an ox team to the wagon pole.

trel'lis, *n.* [OFr. *treliz,* latticework, from *treille;* L. *trichila,* a bower or arbor.]

1. a structure of thin wooden or metal strips crossing each other in an open pattern of squares, diamonds, etc., on which vines or other creeping plants are trained; a lattice.

TRELLIS
1. wooden; 2. wire

2. a bower, archway, etc. of this.
3. in heraldry, a lattice.

trel'lis, *v.t.;* trellised (-list), *pt., pp.;* trellising, *ppr.* 1. to furnish with or as with a trellis or trellises.

2. to train or support on a trellis.
3. to cross or interweave like a trellis; to interlace; to form into a trellis or latticework.

trellised armor; an armor of the middle ages. It was composed of bands interlaced over a background of cloth or leather. Some varieties had rivets or studs at each intersection of the bands.

trel'lis·wŏrk, *n.* 1. open network of wooden or metal strips; latticework.

2. a kind of modern appliqué lace or embroidery.

Trē'mȧ, *n.* [LL., from Gr. *trēma,* a hole.] a genus of apetalous plants bearing polygamous flowers, which are succeeded by small drupes. There are between twenty and thirty species, widely distributed through the tropics and subtropics of both hemispheres.

trẹ·män'dō, *adv.* [It.] in music, same as *tremolando.*

Trem·ȧ·tō'dȧ, *n.pl.* [Gr. *trēma, trēmatos,* a hole, a pore.] a class of parasitic flatworms commonly known as suctorial worms, flukes, or flukeworms. They are usually of a flattened or rounded form, and are found in the internal organs of various animals, being furnished with one or more suctorial pores for adhesion. Also written *Trematodea.*

trem'ȧ·tōde, *a.* of or pertaining to the *Trematoda.*

trem'ȧ·tōde, *n.* a member of the *Trematoda.*

trem'ȧ·toid, *a.* and *n.* trematode.

trem'ble, *v.i.;* trembled, *pt., pp.;* trembling, *ppr.* [ME. *tremblen;* OFr. *trembler;* LL. *tremulare,* from L. *tremulus,* trembling, from *tremere,* to tremble.]

1. to shake involuntarily, as with fear, cold, excitement, or weakness; to shiver; to shudder.
2. to feel great fear or anxiety; as, I *tremble* for your safety.
3. to quiver, quake, totter, vibrate, etc.

trem'ble, *n.* 1. (a) a trembling; (b) [*sometimes pl.*] a fit or state of trembling.

2. [*pl.*] a disease of cattle and sheep caused by eating any of various poisonous weeds and characterized by muscular tremors and a stumbling gait: it is communicated to man as milk sickness: cf. *milk sickness.*

all of a tremble; highly excited or agitated, so as to tremble all over. [Colloq.]

trem'ble·ment, *n.* [Fr.] 1. in music, a trill or shake.

2. a tremor; a quivering. [Rare.]

trem'blẽr, *n.* one who or that which trembles.

trem'bling, *a.* shaking, as with fear, cold, or weakness; quaking; as, *trembling* palsy.

trem'bling·ly, *adv.* so as to tremble; with shivering or quaking.

trem'bly, *a.;* *comp.* tremblier; *superl.* trembliest; trembling; tremulous.

Trē·mel'lȧ, *n.* [LL., from L. *tremere,* to tremble.] a genus of gelatinous fungi found on old and dead trees.

Trem·el·lā'cē·ae, *n.pl.* a family of fungi including the genus *Tremella,* characterized by small gelatinous gyroidal fruit bodies.

trem·el·lā'ceous, *a.* pertaining to or resembling the *Tremellaceæ.*

trem'el·line, *a.* of or pertaining to the genus *Tremella.*

trem'el·loid, *a.* similar to a member of the genus *Tremella.*

trem'el·lōse, *a.* [from L. *tremere,* to tremble.] gelatinous; jellylike in consistency.

trē·men'dous, *a.* [L. *tremendus,* lit., to be trembled at, dreadful, from *tremere,* to tremble.]

1. such as to make one tremble; terrifying; dreadful.
2. (a) very large; great; enormous; (b) wonderful, amazing, extraordinary, etc. [Colloq.]

Syn.—terrible, dreadful, awful, fearful, appalling.

trē·men'dous·ly, *adv.* in a tremendous manner.

trē·men'dous·ness, *n.* the state or quality of being tremendous.

Trē'mex, *n.* [LL., from Gr. *trēma,* a hole.]

1. a genus of *Hymenoptera* including the pigeon tremex, *Tremex columba,* a North American horntail. By means of her long ovipositor, the female bores a hole in the trunk of a tree and deposits eggs. The larvae injure the tree by boring into the wood.
2. [t–] any horntail of this genus.

trem·ō·län'dō, *adv.* [It.] in music, tremulously; quaveringly; with a tremolo.

trem'ō·līte, *n.* a mineral, $CaMg_3Si_4O_{12}$, a white or green variety of amphibole: it is a silicate of calcium and magnesium.

trem'ō·lō, *n.;* *pl.* **trem'ō·lōṣ,** [It., from L. *tremulus;* see *tremulous.*] in music, (a) a tremulous effect produced by the rapid reiteration of the same tone, as by the rapid up-and-down movement of the bow or plectrum: in singing, sometimes interchangeable with *vibrato;* (b) a device, as in an organ, for producing such a tone.

trem'ŏr (*or* trē'mŏr), *n.* [ME. and OFr. *tremour;* L. *tremor,* from *tremere,* to tremble.]

1. a trembling, shaking, or shivering.
2. a vibratory or quivering motion.
3. a nervous thrill; a trembling sensation.
4. a trembling sound.
5. a state of tremulous excitement; as, she was in a *tremor* of delight all afternoon.

trem'ū·lănt, trem'ū·lent, *a.* same as *tremulous.*

trem·ū·lā'tion, *n.* agitation which results in perceptible trembling. [Rare.]

trem'ū·lous, *a.* [L. *tremulus,* from *tremere,* to tremble.]

1. trembling; quivering; palpitating.
2. fearful; timid; timorous.
3. marked by or showing trembling or quivering; as, *tremulous* excitement.

trem'ū·lous·ly, *adv.* in a tremulous manner; with quivering or trepidation.

trem'ū·lous·ness, *n.* the state or quality of being tremulous.

tren, *n.* a fish spear. [Obs.]

trē'nāil, *n.* same as *treenail.*

trench, *v.t.;* trenched (trencht), *pt., pp.;* trenching, *ppr.* [OFr. *trencher,* to cut, carve, slice, hack, hew, from L. *truncare,* to cut, lop off.]

1. to cut or make by cutting.
2. to cut into, cut off, cut to pieces, etc.; to slice; slash; gash.
3. (a) to cut a deep furrow or furrows in; (b) to dig a ditch or ditches in.
4. to surround or fortify with trenches.

trench, *v.i.* 1. to cut or make a cutting; to cut its way.

2. to dig a ditch or ditches, as for fortification.
3. to stretch out or extend. [Obs.]

to trench on (or *upon*); (a) to infringe upon (another's land, rights, time, etc.); (b) to come close to in meaning, relationship, etc.

trench, *n.* 1. a long narrow cut in the earth; a deep furrow; a ditch; as, a *trench* for draining land.

2. something resembling a trench; as, a deep facial wrinkle.
3. in military usage, a long, narrow ditch from which the earth is thrown up in front as a parapet, used in battle for cover or concealment.

to mount the trenches; to mount guard in the trenches or upon the parapets.

to open the trenches; to begin to dig, to form the lines of approach to a besieged place.

trench'ăn·cy, *n.* the quality of being trenchant.

trench'ănt, *a.* [OFr., cutting, ppr. of *trencher,* to cut.]

1. originally, cutting; sharp.
2. keen; penetrating; incisive; as, *trenchant* words.
3. forceful; vigorous; energetic; as, a *trenchant* argument.
4. clear-cut; distinct; as, a *trenchant* pattern.

trench'ănt·ly, *adv.* in a trenchant manner.

trench çav·ȧ·lïer', in fortification, a high parapet made by the besiegers upon the glacis to command and enfilade the covered way of the fortress.

trench çōat, a heavy, belted raincoat in a military style.
trenched (trencht), *a.* cut into long hollows or ditches; deep-furrowed.
trench'ēr, *n.* one who trenches; specifically, (a) one who digs trenches or ditches; (b) formerly, one who carved at table.
trench'ēr, *n.* [ME. *trenchere*; OFr. *trencheoir.*]
1. (a) a wooden board or platter on which meat was formerly carved or served; (b) any platter.
2. (a) food served on a trencher; (b) a supply of food. [Archaic.]
3. a slice of bread used as a plate or platter. [Obs.]
4. a knife [Obs.]
5. pleasures of the table. [Archaic.]
trench'ēr friend (frend), one who frequents the tables of others; a sponger.
trench'ēr·măn, *n.*; *pl.* **trench'ēr·men,** 1. an eater; especially, a heavy eater; a person with a hearty appetite.
2. a person who frequents a patron's table; a sponger; parasite; hanger-on.
3. a cook. [Obs.]
trench'ēr māte, a table companion; a guest at any meal.
trench fē'vēr, an infectious, probably rickettsial, disease transmitted by body lice and characterized by a remittent fever, muscular pains, etc.: it affected troops in the trenches in World War I.
trench foot, a diseased condition of the feet resulting from prolonged exposure to wet and cold and the circulatory disorders caused by inaction, as of soldiers in trenches.
trench'ing, *n.* in agriculture, the act or operation of preparing or improving land by cutting trenches or by bringing up the subsoil to the surface by means of a trench plow.
trench knīfe (nīf), a double-edged military knife or dagger, for hand-to-hand combat.
trench'mōre, *n.* 1. a kind of lively dance, performed in a rough, boisterous manner. [Obs.]
2. the music for this dance, in triple time. [Obs.]
trench'mōre, *v.i.* to perform the dance called a trenchmore. [Obs.]
trench mọr'tăr (or **gun**), any of various portable mortars or guns for shooting projectiles at a high trajectory, used especially in trench warfare.
trench mouth, an infectious disease of the mucous membranes of the mouth and throat, caused by a spirochete and commonly affecting troops in trenches: also called *Vincent's angina.*
trench plow, a kind of plow for opening land to a greater depth than that of common furrows; a ditching plow.
trench'-plow, *v.t.* to plow with deep furrows.
trench plow'ing, the practice or operation of plowing with deep furrows, for the purpose of loosening the land to a greater depth than usual.
trend, *v.i.*; trended, *pt., pp.*; trending, *ppr.* [AS. *trendan*, to turn, roll; akin to AS. *trinde*, round lump.]
1. to extend, turn, incline, bend, etc. in a specific direction; to tend; to run; as, the river *trends* northward.
2. to have a general tendency: said of events, discussions, opinions, etc.
3. to roll or turn about. [Obs.]
4. to go round a region; to skirt. [Obs.]
trend, *v.t.* 1. to cause to turn; to bend. [Rare.]
2. to coast along. [Obs.]
3. to cleanse, as wool. [Brit. Dial.]
trend, *n.* 1. the general direction of a coast, river, road, etc.
2. the general tendency or course, as of events, a discussion, etc.; drift.
3. in nautical usage, the thickening of an anchor shank as it approaches the arms; also, in a ship riding at anchor, the angle made by the line of the keel and the direction of the anchor cable.
4. a stream. [Brit. Dial.]
5. clean or cleansed wool. [Brit. Dial.]
6. a vogue, or current style, as in fashions.
trend'i·ly, *adv.* in a trendy manner. [Colloq.]
trend'i·ness, *n.* the state or quality of being trendy. [Colloq.]
trend'ing, *n.* 1. an inclination.
2. the operation of freeing wool from filth of various kinds. [Brit. Dial.]
tren'dle, *n.* [AS. *trendel*, a circle, ring.]
1. anything round used in turning or rolling; a little wheel; a trundle; also, the turning beam of a spindle. [Obs.]
2. in a brewery, a cooler. [Brit. Dial.]
trend'y, *a.*; *comp.* trendier; *superl.* trendiest, of or in the latest style, or trend; ultrafashionable; faddish. [Colloq.]
tren'nel, *n.* same as *treenail.*
Trent, Coun'cil of, the council of the Roman Catholic Church held intermittently at Trent, Italy, 1545–1563: it condemned the Reformation, undertook Catholic reform, and defined Catholic doctrines.
tren'tăl, *n.* [OFr. *trentel, trental*, from *trente*, from L. *triginta*, thirty.]
1. a group, series, or collection of thirty. [Obs.]
2. formerly, an office for the dead in the Roman Catholic service, consisting of thirty Masses celebrated for thirty days successively after the person's death.
3. a dirge; an elegy. [Obs.]
trente et quà·rànte' (trän̈-tā-kȧ-ränt'), [Fr., lit., thirty and forty.] a gambling game in which cards are dealt and added up for each of the two colors, red and black, on which bets have been laid: the winners are those who have bet on that color for which the total of points is closest to thirty but not more than forty: also called *rouge et noir.*
Tren'tŏn, *a.* [named from *Trenton* Falls, New York.] in American geology, pertaining to or designating a subdivision in the Lower Silurian system.
Trenton period; a subdivision in the Lower Silurian system of North America: the formation is highly developed in the interior, particularly in the Appalachian region.
trē·pan', *n.* [Fr. *trépan*; LL. *trepanum*, from Gr. *trypanon*, a carpenters' tool, an auger, also a surgical instrument, trepan, from *trypan*, to bore.]
1. any instrument for boring.
2. a war engine or instrument used in sieges for piercing or making holes in the walls. [Obs.]
3. in surgery, an obsolete form of the trephine, resembling a carpenters' bit and brace.
4. a heavy boring tool for sinking deep wells and mining shafts.
trē·pan', *v.t.*; trepanned, *pt., pp.*; trepanning, *ppr.* 1. to trephine.
2. to cut a disk out of (a metal plate, ingot, etc.).
trē·pan', *n.* [older *trapan*; prob. from *trap*, but influenced by fig. use of preceding.]
1. a person or thing that tricks, traps, or ensnares.
2. a trick; stratagem; trap.
Also *trapan.*
trē·pan', *v.t.*; trepanned, *pt., pp.*; trepanning, *ppr.* to trick; to trap; to ensnare; to lure: also *trapan.*
trep·ȧ·nā'tion, *n.* [Fr. *trépanation.*] a trepanning or being trepanned.
trē·pang', *n.* [Malay *trīpang.*] the sea slug, a marine animal of the genus *Holothuria*, belonging to phylum *Echinodermata*, class *Holothurioidea*, popularly known as *sea cucumbers*, or *bêches-de-mer.* They are found chiefly on coral reefs in the eastern seas, and are highly esteemed as an article of food in China, where they are boiled, dried, and smoked, and used in making soup. The trepang is an animal somewhat resembling the land slug in shape, but having rows of longish suckers on its body, and a radiated mouth. It varies in length, from six to twenty-four inches.

TREPANG (*Holothuria edulis*)

trep'ăn·īze, *v.t.*; trepanized, *pt., pp.*; trepanizing, *ppr.* to trepan. [Rare.]
trē·pan'nēr, *n.* one who trepans.
trē·pan'ning, *n.* the operation of making an opening in the skull.
treph, *a.* [Heb.] in Judaism, not kosher; not in accordance with the dietary laws: said of food.
tre'phȧ, *n.*; *pl.* **tre'phọth,** [Heb.] in Judaism, food that is not kosher, or not fit to eat according to the dietary laws.
trē·phīne' (*or* -fēn'), *n.* [Fr. *tréphine*, mod. form for *trépan.*] a type of small crown saw used in surgery for removing a circular disk of bone from the skull.
trē·phīne', *v.t.*; trephined, *pt., pp.*; trephining, *ppr.* to operate on with a trephine.
trep'id, *a.* trembling; quaking. [Obs.]
trep·i·dā'tion, *n.* [L. *trepidatio*, a trembling, from *trepidatus*, pp. of *trepidare*, to tremble, from *trepidus*, disturbed, alarmed.]
1. tremulous or trembling movement; quaking; tremor.
2. fear; alarm; dread.
3. a trembling of the limbs, as in paralytic affections.
4. in the Ptolemaic system of astronomy, a libration of the eighth sphere, or a motion ascribed to the firmament, to account for the changes and motion of the axis of the world.
Syn.—tremor, agitation, disturbance, fear.
trē·pid'i·ty, *n.* trepidation.
trep·ō·nē'mȧ, *n.* [Mod. L., from Gr. *trepein*, to turn, and *nēma*, a thread.] any of a group of spirochetes, genus *Treponema*, including the causative agents of syphilis and yaws.
tres'păss, *v.i.*; trespassed (-păst), *pt., pp.*; trespassing, *ppr.* [OFr. *trespasser*; ML. *transpassare*, to pass across; L. *trans*, across, and *passare*, to pass.]
1. to go beyond the limits of what is considered right or moral; to commit a transgression; to transgress; offend; sin.
2. to go on another's land or property unlawfully.
3. to intrude; encroach; as, he is always *trespassing* on my time.
4. in law, to commit a trespass.
5. to depart from life; to go; to die. [Obs.]
tres'păss, *n.* [OFr. *trespas.*] a trespassing; specifically, (a) an offense; sin; transgression; (b) an encroachment; intrusion; (c) in law, an illegal act done with violence against another's person, rights, or property; also, legal action for damages resulting from this: any injuries committed against land or buildings are in the most ordinary sense of the word trespasses, as entering another's house without permission, walking over the ground of another, or allowing any cattle to stray upon it, or any detrimental act or any practice which damages in the slightest degree the property, or interferes with the owner's or occupier's right of possession. Trespass against the person may be by menace, assault, battery, or maiming.
Syn.—offense, breach, infringement, transgression, misdemeanor, misdeed.
tres'păss·ēr, *n.* 1. one who commits a trespass; an offender; a sinner.
2. one who enters upon another's land or violates his rights.
tres'păss of'fēr·ing, an offering, among the Israelites, in expiation of a trespass.
tress, *n.* [ME. *tresse*; OFr. *tresce.*]
1. originally, a braid or plait of hair, etc.
2. a lock or curl of human hair.
3. [*pl.*] a woman's or girl's hair, especially when long and hanging loosely.
4. anything resembling a tress.
There stood a marble altar, with a *tress*
Of flowers budded newly. —Keats.
-tress, see *-ess.*
tressed (trest), *a.* 1. having tresses.
2 curled; formed into ringlets or tresses.
tres'sel, *n.* same as *trestle.*
tress'fụl, *a.* having a luxuriant growth of hair.
tres'sūre (tresh'ēr), *n.* [Fr., a heraldic term meaning border, from *tresser*, to twist, to plait.] in heraldry, the diminutive of the orle, and generally reckoned one-half of that ordinary. It passes round the field, following the shape and form of the escutcheon, and is usually borne double. It is often ornamented with fleur-de-lis.

DOUBLE TRESSURE

tres'sūred, *a.* provided with a tressure; arranged in the form or occupying the place of a tressure.
tress'y, *a.*; *comp.* tressier; *superl.* tressiest, of, adorned with, or having the form of tresses.
tres'-tīne, *n.* the third tine from the head in the antler of a deer.
tres'tle (tres'l), *n.* [OFr. *trestel*; hyp. LL. *transtellum*, dim. of L. *transtrum*, a beam.]

TRESTLE (frame)

1. a frame consisting of a horizontal beam fastened to two pairs of spreading legs, used to support planks to form a table, etc.

2. a framework of vertical or slanting uprights and crosspieces, supporting a bridge, etc.

TRESTLE (bridge)

3. same as *trestletree*.
4. [*pl.*] the framework on the ways, which supports a vessel under construction.
5. in heraldry, a low, usually three-legged, stool, used as a bearing.

tres′tle bōard, a movable board or tabletop, supported on trestles, used by draftsmen.

tres′tle·tree, *n.* either of two horizontal fore-and-aft beams, one on each side of a mast, that support the crosstrees, top, and fid of the mast above.

tres′tle·wŏrk, *n.* 1. a trestle or system of trestles for supporting a bridge, etc.
2. a bridge or other structure supported by trestles.

tres′-tȳne, *n.* same as *tres-tine*.

tret, *n.* [Norm. Fr. *trett*, a draft; Fr. *trait*, from OFr. *traire*, to draw, from L. *trahere*, to draw.] in commerce, formerly, an allowance to purchasers, for waste or refuse matter, of four pounds on every 104 pounds of suttle weight, or weight after the tare was deducted.

trēt′ȧ·ble, *a.* obsolete spelling of *treatable*.

trē′tis, trē′tys, *n.* treatise. [Obs.]

trē′tis, trē′tys, *a.* well-formed. [Obs.]

trē·val′ly, *n.* [corruption of *cavally*.] a carangoid fish found in Australian waters; also, any species resembling it; a cavally.

trev′et, *n.* same as *trivet*.

trew, *a.* true. [Obs.]

trewṣ, *n.pl.* trousers, especially close-fitting plaid trousers as worn in the Scottish Highlands. [Scot.]

trewth, *n.* truth. [Obs.]

trey, *n.* [OFr. *trei, treis*, L. *tres*, three.]
1. a die, card, or domino having three spots.
2. a throw or play of three at dice, dominoes, or cards.

tri-, [from Fr., L., or Gr.; Fr. *tri-*, from L. *tri-* (from *tres*, three) or Gr. *tri* (from *treis*, three, *tris*, thrice).] a combining form meaning: (a) *of three, having three parts*, etc., as in *tri*plane; (b) *three times, into three*, as in *tri*sect; (c) *every three, every third*, as in *tri*annual; (d) in chemistry, *having three atoms, groups*, or *equivalents of* (the thing specified), as in *tri*basic.

trī′ȧ·ble, *a.* 1. capable of being tried or subjected to trial or test.
2. subject to trial in a law court; as, a cause may be *triable* before one court, which is not *triable* before another.

trī′ȧ·ble·ness, *n.* the state or quality of being triable.

trī·ac′id, *a.* 1. capable of reacting with three molecules of a monobasic acid: said of a base.
2. containing three replaceable hydrogen atoms: said of an acid or acid salt.

trī′ȧ·çle, *n.* treacle. [Obs.]

trī·ȧ·çon·tȧ·hē′drăl, *a.* [Gr. *triakonta*, thirty, and *hedra*, side.]
1. having thirty sides.
2. in crystallography, bounded by thirty rhombs.

trī′ȧ·çon·tēr, *n.* [Gr. *triakontērēs*, from *triakonta*, thirty.] in ancient Greece, a vessel having thirty oars.

trī′açt, trī·aç′tin·ăl, *a.* having three rays, as a sponge spicule.

trī′ad, *n.* [Fr. *triade*; L. *trias*, from Gr. *trias, triados*, a triad.]
1. a union or set of three; a group of three persons, things, ideas, etc.; a trinity.
2. in music, a chord of three tones, especially one consisting of a root tone and its third and fifth: a triad with a major third and perfect fifth is called a *major triad*; a triad with a minor third and perfect fifth is called a *minor triad*.
3. in chemistry, a trivalent atom, element, or radical.
4. in Welsh literature, a form of composition dating from the twelfth century, in which subjects or statements are arranged in groups of three.
5. a conception of three associated or correlated deities, as the Hindu Indra, Agni, and Surya or Savitri; or Brahma, Vishnu, and Siva.

trī·ȧ·del′phous, *a.* [*tri-*, and Gr. *adelphos*, a brother.] in botany, having stamens combined in sets of three.

Trī·ȧ·dē′num, *n.* a genus of plants of the family *Hypericaceæ*, growing in water or on marshy land, with pale, often purple-veined, leaves and close clusters of flowers. The genus was for---ly known as *Elodea* or *Elodes*. The common name of the plants is *marsh St.-John's-wort*.

trī·ad′iç, *a.* of, pertaining to, or characteristic of a triad.

trī′ad·ist, *n.* one who composes poetic triads.

trī′aene, *n.* [Gr. *triaina*, a trident.] a form of three-rayed sponge spicule. The rays are secondary, and branch from one end.

trī·ae′nōse, *a.* pertaining to or having a triaene.

trī″ȧ·kis·oç″tȧ·hē′drŏn, *n.* [Gr. *triakis*, thrice, *okto*, eight, and *hedra*, side.] a solid having twenty-four equal triangular faces.

trī″ȧ·kis·tet″rȧ·hē′drŏn, *n.* [Gr. *triakis*, thrice, *tetra*, for *tessara*, four, and *hedra*, side.] a solid having twelve equal triangular faces.

trī′ăl, *n.* [Anglo-Fr., from *trier*, to try.]
1. (a) the act or process of trying, testing, or putting to the proof; a test; (b) a testing of qualifications, attainments, or progress; probation; (c) experimental treatment or operation; an experiment.
2. a being tried by suffering, temptation, etc.
3. a hardship, pain, etc. that tries one's endurance.
4. a source of annoyance or irritation; as, his son is a great *trial*.
5. a formal examination of the facts of a case by a court of law to decide the validity of a charge or claim.
6. an attempt; endeavor; effort.
7. verification; proof. [Obs.]

trī′ăl, *a.* 1. of a trial or trials.
2. made, done, or used for the purpose of trying, testing, or putting to the proof.

trī′ăl and er′rŏr, the process of making repeated trials, experiments, tests, etc. to find a desired result or solution.

trī′ăl bal′ănce, a statement of the debit and credit balances of all open accounts in a double-entry bookkeeping ledger to test their equality.

trī′ăl băl·lo͞on′, 1. a balloon equipped with instruments for testing air currents, wind velocities, etc.
2. any action, statement, etc. intended to test public opinion on an issue or pending project.

trī′ăl frāme, a frame for holding trial lenses in testing vision.

trī′ăl hēat, in racing, (a) a preliminary test of speed before a race; (b) one of the preliminary heats in a race with many competitors, run off for the purpose of weeding out the contestants for the final.

trī·al′i·ty, *n.* the state of being three or three united.

trī′ăl jū′ry, a jury of twelve persons impaneled to decide a court case; petit jury: distinguished from *grand jury*.

trī′ăl lenṣ′eṣ, a set of lenses used in testing vision.

trī′ȧ·logue (-log), *n.* [Gr. *treis, tria*, three, and *logos*, discourse.] a discourse by three speakers; a colloquy of three persons. [Rare.]

trī·am′ide, trī·am′id, *n.* an amide having three amido radicals in combination.

trī·am·īne′, *n.* any amine having three amino radicals in combination.

trī·an′dēr, *n.* a plant of the class *Triandria*.

Trī·an′dri·ȧ, *n.pl.* [Gr. *treis*, three, and *anēr, andros*, a male.] formerly, a class of hermaphrodite plants, having three distinct and equal stamens: third in the Linnean system.

TRIANDRIA

trī·an′dri·ăn, trī·an′drous, *a.* having three distinct and equal stamens, in the same flower with a pistil or pistils.

trī′añ·gle, *n.* [OFr.; L. *triangulum*, from *tri-*, and *angulus*, angle.]
1. in geometry, a figure bounded by three lines, and containing three angles. If the three lines or sides of a triangle are all straight, it is a plane or rectilinear triangle, as figs. 1, 2, 3, 4. If all the three sides are equal, it is an equilateral triangle, fig. 2. If only two of the sides are equal, it is an

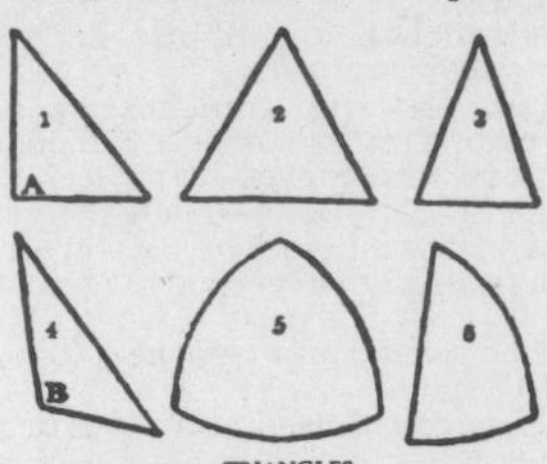

TRIANGLES

isosceles triangle, fig. 3. If all the three sides are unequal, it is a scalene triangle, fig. 4. If one of the angles is a right angle, the triangle is right-angled, as fig. 1, having the right angle A. If one of the angles is obtuse, the triangle is called obtuse-angled, as fig. 4, having the obtuse angle B. If all the angles are acute, the triangle is acute-angled, figs, 2, 3. If the three lines of a triangle are all curves, the triangle is said to be curvilinear, fig. 5. If some of the sides are straight and others curved, the triangle is said to be mixtilinear, fig. 6. If the sides are all arcs of great circles of the sphere, or arcs of the same circle, the triangle is said to be spherical, fig. 5.
2. anything having a triangular form; specifically, (a) a musical percussion instrument, made of a rod of polished steel, bent into the form of a triangle, and open at one of its angles: it produces a high-pitched, tinkling sound; (b) in astronomy, [T–] one of the forty-eight ancient constellations, in the Northern Hemisphere, surrounded by Perseus, Andromeda, Aries, and Musca; also, a small constellation near the South Pole, having three bright stars; the Triangulum Australe; (c) the equilateral triangle, symbolizing the Trinity, found in many figures in Christian ornament; (d) a right-angled, flat, triangular instrument used in drafting; (e) a kind of gin for raising heavy weights, formed of three spars joined at the top; (f) in the British army, formerly, a frame of three halberds stuck in the ground, and united at the top, to which soldiers were bound when flogged; (g) a group of three fishhooks joined so that the points spread to form a triangle, as used with a trolling spoon; (h) any of various tripods or stilts used in firing pottery; (i) certain leaf roller moths of the genus *Tortrix*; (j) a three-sided fish of the genus *Ostracion*; the trunkfish; (k) a triangular wing cell of certain dragon flies.
3. (a) a group of three involved in some situation as one in which two men are in love with the same woman; (b) such a situation.
surgical triangle; any triangular area or region in which certain nerves, vessels, or organs are located. Such areas are established for reference in surgical operations.
triangle of forces; a triangle representing graphically the magnitude and direction of three forces at equilibrium at a point.

trī′añ·gled (-gld), *a.* having three angles; also, enclosed in a triangle.

trī′añ·gle spī′dēr, any of several species of spider that spins a web in the form of a triangle, so constructed that one corner can be released to snare any insect touching the web.

trī·añ′gū·lăr, *a.* 1. having three angles; of or shaped like a triangle.
2. in botany, (a) flat or lamellar, and having three sides; as, a *triangular* leaf; (b) oblong, and having three lateral faces; as, a *triangular* stem, seed, column, and the like.
3. relating to or involving three elements, issues, factions, persons, or things; as, a *triangular* discussion.
4. having bases that are triangles, as a prism.
triangular compass; a compass having three legs, two opening in the usual manner, and the third turning round an extension of the central pin of the other two, besides having a motion on its own central joint. By means of this instrument any three points may be taken off at once.
triangular crab; a crab of the genus *Maia*.
triangular numbers; the series of figurate numbers which consists of the successive sums of the terms of an arithmetical series, whose first term is 1, and the common difference 1; thus, 1, 3, 6, 10, 15, 21, 28, etc., are *triangular numbers*: so called because the number of points expressed by any one of

them may be arranged in the form of an equilateral triangle.

triangular pyramid; a pyramid whose base is a triangle.

triangular scale; in mechanics, a drawing scale having three faces each differently divided. The dimensions on each side can therefore be set off directly on the paper without resorting to the use of compasses or separate scales.

trī·añ·gū·lar′i·ty, *n.* the state or quality of being triangular.

trī·añ′gū·lăr·ly, *adv.* in the shape of a triangle.

trī·añ′gū·lāte, *v.t.*; triangulated, *pt., pp.*; triangulating, *ppr.* 1. to divide into triangles.

2. to survey or map (a region) by dividing into triangles and measuring their angles.

3. to make triangular.

4. to measure by trigonometry.

trī·añ′gū·lāte, *a.* 1. of triangles; triangular.

2. marked with triangles.

trī·añ·gū·lā′tion, *n.* 1. the act or process of triangulating, especially in surveying.

2. the triangles marked out in this process.

primary triangulation; the first triangulation, characterized by the greatest length of the sides of the triangle practicable in the country traversed, and by the greatest accuracy in measurement. The length of the sides of the triangle averages 20 to 25 miles in a flat or rolling country, and increases to 90 and sometimes to 180 or 190 miles as the country becomes more mountainous.

radiating triangulation; the method of triangulating where a center point is used from which lines are measured and the angles about the point are formed. The boundary required to complete the polygon thus started is then easily calculated.

secondary triangulation; triangulation intermediate between primary and tertiary triangulation, serving to connect the long sides of the triangle used in the former to the short sides of the triangle of the latter. The length of its sides may therefore vary considerably.

tertiary triangulation; the lowest in order of triangulations, designed to furnish positions of points for use in topographic or hydrographic surveys or for engineering purposes in general. The sides of the triangle in this case are usually about 12 miles.

Trī·añ′gū·lum, *n.* [L., triangle.] a small northern constellation.

Trī·añ′gū·lum Aus·trā′lē, [L., southern triangle.] a southern constellation.

trī·an′tē·lōpe, *n.* in Australia, a tarantula. [Colloq.]

trī·an′thous, *a.* [*tri-*, and Gr. *anthos*, flower.] three-flowered.

trī·ap′si·dăl, trī·ap′săl, *a.* having three apses.

trī′är·çhy, *n.*; *pl.* **trī′är·çhieṣ**, [*tri-*, and Gr. *archein*, to rule.]

1. government by three persons; a triumvirate.

2. a country governed by three rulers.

trī·ā′ri·ăn, *a.* [L. *triarii*, soldiers of the third rank.] occupying the third post or place in a military line. [Obs.]

trī·är·tiç′ū·lāte, *a.* with or having three joints.

Trī′ăs, *n.* [LL.; see *Triad*: so called because divisible into three groups.] the series of geological strata lying immediately below the Jurassic.

Trī·as′siç, *a.* designating or of the first period of the Mesozoic Era, characterized by the dominance of reptiles and the appearance of cycadaceous trees.

the Triassic; the Triassic Period or its rocks.

trī·at′iç stāy, [*tri-*, *-atic*, and *stay*.] a rope secured to the heads of the foremast and mainmast, to which hoisting tackles can be attached.

trī·ȧ·tom′iç, *a.* 1. containing three atoms; as, a *triatomic* molecule.

2. trivalent; as, a *triatomic* element.

3. having three replaceable atoms or groups.

trī·ax′i·ăl, *a.* having three axes.

trī·ax′ŏn, *n.* [*tri-*, and Gr. *axōn*, axis.] a triaxial figure, as a sponge spicule.

trī·ax′ŏn, *a.* having three axes diverging at equal angles from a common center.

trī·ax·ō′ni·ăn, *a.* same as *triaxon*.

trī′ȧ·zin, *n.* triazine.

trī′ȧ·zīne (*or* -zin), *n.* [*tri-* and *azine*.]

1. any of three isomeric heterocyclic compounds having the formula $C_3H_3N_3$.

2. any derivative of these.

trī·ȧ·zō′iç, *a.* hydrazoic.

trī′ȧ·zōle, *n.* [*tri-* and *azole*.] any of four isomeric heterocyclic compounds having the formula $C_2H_3N_3$.

trib′ȧ·diṣm, *n.* [from Gr. *tribein*, to rub.] Lesbianism.

trīb′ăl, *a.* belonging to or characteristic of a tribe or tribes; as, *tribal* customs.

trīb′ăl·iṣm, *n.* tribal organization, culture, loyalty, etc.

trīb′ăl·ly, *adv.* by or in a tribe or tribes.

trī·bā′siç, *a.* [*tri-* and *basic*.]

1. containing in its molecule three atoms of hydrogen that are replaceable by basic atoms or radicals: said of an acid.

2. producing three hydrogen ions per molecule in solution: said of an acid.

trib′ble, *n.* a kind of frame used in drying newly made paper.

trībe, *n.* [L. *tribus*, one of the three bodies into which the Romans were originally divided, from *tres*, *tria*, three.]

1. a group of persons, families, or clans descended from a common ancestor and forming, together with their slaves, adopted strangers, etc., a community.

2. a group of this kind having recognized ancestry; specifically, (a) any of the three divisions of the ancient Romans, traditionally of Latin, Sabine, and Etruscan origin; (b) any of the later political and territorial divisions of the ancient Romans, originally thirty and subsequently thirty-five in number; (c) any of the phylae of ancient Greece; (d) any of the twelve divisions of the ancient Israelites.

3. any primitive or nomadic group of people of generally common ancestry, possessing common leadership.

4. any group of people having the same occupation, habits, ideas, etc.: chiefly in a derogatory sense; as, the *tribe* of daubers.

5. a subdivision of an order or suborder of animals or plants.

6. any group, class, or kind of animals, plants, etc.

7. in stock breeding, the animals descended from the same female through the female line.

8. a number or company of persons or animals.

9. a family: a humorous or derogatory usage.

Syn.—horde, race, stock, breed, people.

trībe, *v.t.* to arrange in tribes; to classify. [Rare.]

trībeṣ′măn, *n.*; *pl.* **trībeṣ′men**, a member of a tribe.

trib′let, trib′ō·let, *n.* [Fr. *tribolet*.]

1. a mandrel used in forging tubes, nuts, and rings, and for other purposes.

2. a mandrel in a machine for making pipe.

trib″ō·lū·mi·nes′cence, *n.* [Gr. *tribein*, to rub or wear, and Eng. *luminescence*.] luminosity induced by friction.

trī·bom′e·tēr, *n.* [Gr. *tribein*, to rub or wear, and *-meter*.] an instrument for measuring the force of friction in rubbing surfaces.

trī′braçh, *n.* [L. and Gr. *tribrachys*, from Gr. *tri-*, for *treis*, three, and *brachys*, short.] a metrical foot consisting of three short syllables, two belonging to the thesis and one to the arsis.

trī·braç′tē·āte, *a.* having three bracts, as the leaves of some plants.

trī·brō·mō·eth′ȧ·nōl, *n.* [from *tri-* and *bromine* and *ethanol*.] a colorless, crystalline bromine derivative of ethyl alcohol, $CBr_3 \cdot CH_2OH$, used as a general anesthetic.

trib′ū·ăl, trib′ū·lăr, *a.* pertaining to a tribe; tribal.

trib·ū·lā′tion, *n.* [LL. *tribulatio* (*-onis*), distress, tribulation, from pp. of L. *tribulare*, to thrash, to beat, from *tribulum*, a threshing sledge.]

1. a state of affliction or trial; great misery or distress, as from oppression; deep sorrow.

The way to fame is like the way to heaven—
through much *tribulation*. —Sterne.

2. something that causes suffering or distress; an affliction; a trial.

Trib′ū·lus, *n.* [Gr. *tribolos*, three-pointed, three-pronged; *tri-*, for *treis*, three, and *belos*, a dart.] a genus of subtropical plants of the bean-caper family.

trī·bū′năl, *n.* [L. *tribunal*, from *tribunus*, a tribune, who administered justice.]

1. the seat of a judge; the bench on which a judge or judges sit for administering justice.

2. a court of justice.

3. any real or imagined seat of judgment; as, the *tribunal* of popular sentiment.

trib′ū·nār·y, *a.* pertaining to tribunes.

trib′ū·nāte, *n.* [Fr. *tribunat*; L. *tribunatus*.]

1. the rank, office, or authority of a tribune.

2. a group of tribunes.

trib′ūne, *n.* [L. *tribunus*, a tribune, lit., the chief of a tribe, from *tribus*, tribe.]

1. any of several ancient Roman magistrates, especially one appointed to protect the interests and rights of plebeians against violation by patricians.

2. a champion of the people.

3. any of the six officers of an ancient Roman legion who rotated command over a period of a year.

trib′ūne, *n.* [Fr., from L. *tribunal*, a platform.]

1. in a Roman basilica, the platform or elevated place from which speeches were delivered.

2. a pulpit or elevated place where a speaker stands to address an assembly.

trib′ūne·ship, *n.* the rank, office, or term of office of a tribune.

trib·ū·ni′tiăl, trib·ū·ni′ciăl (-nish′ăl), *a.* suitable to, pertaining to, or having the dignity of a tribune.

trib·ū·ni′tiăn, trib·ū·ni′ciăn, *a.* same as *tribunitial*

trib·ū·ni′tious, trib·ū·ni′cious, *a.* pertaining to tribunes; tribunitial. [Obs.]

trib′ū·tăr·i·ly, *adv.* as a tributary or tributaries.

trib′ū·tăr·i·ness, *n.* the state of being tributary.

trib′ū·tăr·y, *a.* [L. *tributarius*, of or belonging to tribute.]

1. paying tribute.

2. subject; subordinate; inferior; as, a *tributary* province.

3. paid in tribute; of the nature of tribute.

4. yielding supplies or making additions; subsidiary; contributing; as, a *tributary* river.

trib′ū·tăr·y, *n.*; *pl.* **trib′ū·tăr·ieṣ**, 1. a tributary individual, government, or state.

2. an affluent; a stream that flows into a larger stream or body of water; as, the *tributaries* of the Mississippi.

trib′ūte, *n.* [Fr. *tribut*; L. *tributum*, tribute, lit., a thing contributed or paid, neut. of *tributus*, pp. of *tribuere*, to assign, allot, pay, originally to allot or pay to a tribe, from *tribus*, tribe.]

1. money paid regularly by one ruler or nation to another as acknowledgment of subjugation, for protection from invasion, etc.

2. a tax levied for this.

3. under feudalism, a tax paid by a vassal to his overlord.

4. the obligation to make such a payment.

5. any forced payment, as through bribery.

6. a gift, statement, testimonial, etc. that shows gratitude, respect, or honor.

7. praise; laudation.

8. in mining, (a) work performed in the excavation of ore; (b) the proportion of ore or its value that a person engaged in such work receives for his labor.

trib′ūte, *v.t.*; tributed, *pt., pp.*; tributing, *ppr.* to pay as tribute.

trib′ūte mŏn′ey, money paid as tribute.

trib′ūte pitch, in mining, a limited part of a lode beyond which a tributer is not permitted to work. [Brit.]

trib′ū·tēr, *n.* in mining, one who excavates ore and works on tribute, or shares.

trī′çȧ, *n.*; *pl.* **trī′cae**, [L. *tricæ*, trifles.] in botany, the reproductive organ of a lichen.

trī·çap′sū·lăr, *a.* in botany, three-capsuled; having three capsules to each flower.

trī·çär·băl·lyl′iç, *a.* in chemistry, pertaining to or designating a compound having three atoms of carboxyl and derived from a compound of allyl.

trī·çär′bi·mide, *n.* same as *cyanuric acid*.

trīce, *v.t.*; triced (trīst), *pt., pp.*; tricing, *ppr.* [ME. *trycen*, from M.D. *trise*, a windlass.]

1. to haul up (a sail, etc.) and secure with a small rope; to hoist (usually with *up*).

2. to pull; to drag; to haul. [Obs.]

trīce, *n.* 1. originally, one pull or effort: in *at a trice*.

2. a very short time; an instant; a moment: now only in *in a trice*.

trī·cen·nār′i·ous, *a.* tricennial. [Rare.]

trī·cen′ni·ăl, *a.* [LL. *tricennium*, thirty years, from L. *triginta*, thirty, and *annus*, year.] pertaining to thirty years; occurring once in every thirty years. [Rare.]

trī·cen′tē·nãr·y, *a.* and *n.* same as *tercentenary.*

trī·cen·ten′ni·ăl, *a.* and *n.* tercentenary.

trī′ceps, *n.*; *pl.* **trī·cep′seş,** [Mod. L., from L. *triceps,* triple-headed, from *tri-,* three, and *caput,* a head.] a muscle having three heads, or points of origin; especially, the large muscle at the back of the upper arm that extends the forearm when contracted.

trī′ceps, *a.* three-headed.

triçh-, see *tricho-.*

tri·çhī′ȧ·sis, *n.* [LL., from Gr. *trichiasis*; *thrix, trichos,* hair.] in medicine, (a) a disease of the kidneys or bladder, in which filamentous substances resembling hairs are passed in the urine; (b) an abnormal condition in which hairs, especially the eyelashes, grow inward.

Trī·chil′i·ȧ, *n.* [Gr. *tricheilos,* three-lipped; *treis,* three, and *cheilos,* a lip.] a genus of meliaceous plants, with pinnate leaves and axillary panicles of white flowers, including *Trichilia emetica,* the mafurra tree.

Tri·çhī′nȧ, *n.* [Gr. *thrix, trichos,* a hair.]
1. a genus of nematoid endoparasitic worms, typical of the *Trichinidæ.* The larvae of *Trichina spiralis* infest the intestines and voluntary muscles of man, causing trichinosis.
2. [t–] *pl.* **tri·çhī′nae,** any endoparasite of the genus *Trichina.*

triçh·i·nī′ȧ·sis, *n.* same as *trichinosis.*

triçh′i·nīze, *v.t.*; trichinized, *pt., pp.*; trichinizing, *ppr.* to infect with trichinae: generally used only in the past participle; as, *trichinized* pork.

tri·çhī′nō·sçōpe, *n.* [Gr. *thrix, trichos,* a hair, and *skopein,* to view.] an instrument for the inspection of meat in order to detect trichinae.

triçh′i·nōşed, *a.* trichinous.

triçh·i·nō′sis, *n.* a disease caused by the presence of trichinae in the intestines and muscle tissues and usually acquired by eating insufficiently cooked pork from an infected hog: it is characterized by fever, nausea, diarrhea, and muscular pains.

triçh′i·nous, *a.* 1. infected with trichinae; trichinized.
2. of or having trichinosis.

triçh′īte, *n.* 1. a hairlike spicule found in certain sponges.
2. a crystallite resembling a tuft of hairs, seen in vitreous rocks, especially obsidian.

triçh·i·ū′ri·fọrm, *a.* [*trichiurus,* and L. *forma,* form.] having that form which is characteristic of the hairtails, a genus of fishes belonging to the family *Trichiuridæ.*

Triçh·i·ū′ri·dae, *n.pl.* a family of fishes of which *Trichiurus* is the type genus.

triçh·i·ū′roid, *a.* same as *trichiuriform.*

Triçh·i·ū′rus, *n.* [*trichi-,* and Gr. *oura,* tail.] a genus of acanthopterygious teleostean fishes, belonging to the family *Trichiuridæ,* or hairtails: so called from the elongated hairlike filament that terminates the tail. The silvery hairtail, *Trichiurus lepturus,* an inhabitant of the Atlantic, attains a length of 12 feet: also called *cutlass fish.*

trī·chlō′rid, *n.* trichloride.

trī·chlō′rīde, *n.* a chloride containing three atoms of chlorine in the molecule.

trī·chlō″rō·phē·nox″y·ȧ·cē′tiç aç′id, [*tri-, chloro-, phenoxy, acetic.*] a trichloride derivative of phenoxy acetic acid, $Cl_3C_6H_2OCH_2·COOH$, used as a weed killer.

triçh′ō-, [from Gr. *thrix, trichos,* a hair.] a combining form meaning *hair,* as in *tricho*sis.

triçh·ō·braṅ′çhi·ȧ, *n.* [*tricho-,* and Gr. *branchia,* gills.] a filamentous gill characteristic of most long-tailed, ten-footed crustaceans, as crawfishes, lobsters, etc.; a gill in which the branchial filaments are slender and cylindrical.

triçh·ō·çär′pous, *a.* [*tricho-,* and Gr. *karpos,* fruit.] in botany, having hairy carpels or fruit.

Triçh·ō·ceph′ȧ·lus, *n.* [*tricho-,* and Gr. *kephalē,* the head.] a genus of nematode worms, one species of which, *Trichocephalus dispar,* is parasitic in the intestines of man.

triçh·ō·çlā′si·ȧ, *n.* [*tricho-,* and Gr. *klasis,* fracture.] a condition of the hair, especially after sickness, in which it is very brittle.

triçh′ō·cyst, *n.* [*tricho-,* and Gr. *kystis,* a bag.] any of many tiny stinging organs on the body of some infusorians.

trī·çhoġ′en·ous, *a.* producing hair: said of cells.

Triçh·ō·glos′si·dae, *n.pl.* [*tricho-,* and Gr. *glōssa,* tongue.] a genus of Australian birds of the parrot family, having hairy tongues with which they collect honey; the lorikeets.

triçh′ō·ġyne, *n.* [*tricho-,* and Gr. *gynē,* a female.] a long, thin, hairlike part of a procarp in red algae, acting as a receptor for the male fertilizing bodies.

triçh·ō·ġyn′iç, of or pertaining to the trichogyne.

tri′çhoid, *a.* hairlike.

tri·çhol′ō·ġy, *n.* in medicine, the science relating to the hair, its functions, diseases, etc.

trī·çhō′mȧ, *n.* [Gr. *trichōma,* growth of hair, from *thrix, trichos,* hair.]
1. introversion of the edge of the eyelid or of any similar structure.
2. a matted and crusted condition of the hair.
3. any of the threadlike structures, or filaments, of certain algae.

Trī·chom′ȧ·nēş, *n.* [Gr., a kind of fern.] a genus of ferns with free veins and urn-shaped or tubular involucres.

trī·çhom′ȧ·tōse, *a.* [Gr. *trichōma, trichōmatos,* a growth of hair, and *-ose.*] matted together; having trichoma: said of hair.

trī′çhōme, *n.* [Gr. *trichōma,* a growth of hair.]
1. any hairlike outgrowth on a plant, as a bristle, prickle, root hair, etc.
2. a trichoma (sense 3).

tri·çhom′iç, *a.* having the nature of a trichome or trichoma.

triçh″ō·mon′ad, *n.* [*tricho-* and *monad.*] any flagellated protozoan of a group parasitic in man and lower animals.

triçh″ō·mȳ·çō′sis, *n.* [*tricho-,* and Gr. *mykēs, mykētos,* fungus.] any disease of the hair caused by fungi.

triçh′ō·phōre, *n.* [*tricho-,* and Gr. *pherein,* to bear.] the part in red algae, usually consisting of several cells, that bears the trichogyne.

trī·çhop′tẽr, *n.* any of the *Trichoptera.*

Trī·çhop′tē·rȧ, *n.pl.* [*tricho-,* and Gr. *pteron,* a wing.] an order of insects consisting of the caddis flies, having four hairy membranous wings.

trī·çhop′tẽr·ăn, *n.* any of the *Trichoptera*; a caddis fly.

trī·çhop′tẽr·ous, *a.* of or pertaining to the *Trichoptera.*

trī′çhọrd, *n.* [*tri-,* and Gr. *chordē,* a string.] a musical instrument with three strings, as some lyres.

trī′çhọrd, *a.* having three strings.

Triçh·ō·san′thēş, *n.* [Gr. *thrix, trichos,* hair, and *anthos,* a flower.] a genus of trailing or climbing plants native to Asia.

tri·çhō′sis, *n.* [Mod. L., *trich-* and *-osis.*] any disease of the hair.

triçh·ō·tom′iç, *a.* pertaining to or involving trichotomy; divided into three parts.

trī·çhot′ō·mous, *a.* [Gr. *tricha,* thrice, and *tomos,* a cutting, from *temnein,* to cut.] divided into three parts; trichotomic.

trī·çhot′ō·my, *n.* [Gr. *tricha,* thrice, and *tomia,* the parts cut up, from *temnein,* to cut.] division into three parts; specifically, the theological division of human nature into body, soul, and spirit.

trī·çhrō′iç, *a.* 1. having or showing three colors.
2. exhibiting trichroism.

trī′çhrō·işm, *n.* [*tri-,* Gr. *chroia,* color, and *-ism.*] the property that some crystals have of transmitting light of three different colors in three different directions.

trī·çhrō·mat′iç, *a.* of, having, or using three colors, as in the three-color process in printing and photography.

trī·çhrō′mȧ·tişm, *n.* 1. the condition of being trichromatic.
2. the use or combination of three colors.
3. trichroism.

trī·çhrō′miç, *a.* [*tri-,* and Gr. *chrōma,* color.] of or relating to three colors; trichromatic.

trī·cin′i·um, *n.*; *pl.* **trī·cin′i·ȧ,** [*tri-,* and L. *canere,* to sing.] a trio for unaccompanied voices.

trī·cip′i·tăl, *a.* [L. *triceps, tricipitis,* three-headed, and *-al.*] in anatomy, (a) three-headed; (b) pertaining to the triceps.

trick, *n.* [from OFr. *trichier,* to trick, to cheat; Pr. *tric,* deceit; It. *treccare,* to cheat.]
1. an action or device designed to deceive, swindle, etc.; artifice; a dodge; ruse; stratagem; deception.
2. a practical joke; a mischievous or playful act; prank.
3. a freakish, foolish, mean, or stupid act.
4. (a) a clever or difficult act intended to amuse; especially, an act of jugglery or sleight of hand; also, an illusion of the kind created by legerdemain; (b) any feat requiring skill.
5. the art, method, or process of doing something successfully or of getting a result quickly; a knack; as, the *trick* of making good pastry.
6. an expedient or convention of an art, craft, or trade; as, he learned the *tricks* of the trade: often used in an unfavorable sense.
7. a personal mannerism; as, a *trick* of stroking his nose.
8. a turn or round of duty.
9. any child, girl, etc. regarded playfully. [Colloq.]
10. in card games, the cards played and won in a single round.
to do (or *turn*) *the trick*; to bring about the desired result.
Syn.—stratagem, artifice, device, wile, fraud, cheat, juggle, finesse, sleight, deception, imposture, delusion, imposition.

trick, *v.t.*; tricked (trikt), *pt., pp.*; tricking, *ppr.* 1. to deceive; to impose on; to cheat; as, to *trick* another in the sale of a horse.
2. in heraldry, to draw an outline, as with a pen; to delineate without color, as heraldic arms; to emblazon.
to trick out (or *up*); to dress up; to deck; to adorn; to array.

trick, *v.i.* 1. to use trickery; to practice deception.
2. to perform with juggling or sleight-of-hand feats.
3. to trifle; to toy. [Rare.]

trick, *a.* 1. having to do with a trick or tricks.
2. that tricks.

trick′ẽr, *n.* one who tricks; a trickster.

trick′ẽr, *n.* a trigger. [Dial.]

trick′ẽr·y, *n.*; *pl.* **trick′ẽr·ieş,** the act or practice of tricking; imposture; artifice; stratagem.

trick′i·ly, *adv.* in a tricky way.

trick′i·ness, *n.* the quality or condition of being tricky.

trick′ing, *n.* 1. articles of dress; finery.
2. the act of ornamenting with trifles.
3. in heraldry, a delineation or representation of a heraldic subject. [Rare.]

trick′ing, *a.* practicing trickery; artful; tricky.

trick′ish, *a.* 1. given to deception and cheating; knavish.
2. characterized by or full of tricks.

trick′ish·ly, *adv.* in a trickish manner; artfully; knavishly.

trick′ish·ness, *n.* the state of being trickish or deceitful.

trick′le, (-kl), *v.i.*; trickled, *pt., pp.*; trickling, *ppr.* [ME. *triklen*; prob. from *striklen,* freq. of *striken,* to strike.]
1. to flow slowly in a thin stream or fall in drops.
2. to move, enter, etc. slowly or little by little; as, the crowd began to *trickle* away.

trick′le, *v.t.* to cause to trickle.

trick′le, *n.* 1. a trickling.
2. a slow flow or thin stream; drip.

trick′let, *n.* a tiny stream; a rill.

trick′ly, *adv.* deftly; artfully; cleverly. [Rare.]

trick′ment, *n.* a decoration; especially, a heraldic decoration. [Rare.]

trick′si·ness, *n.* the condition or quality of being tricksy or playful; playfulness.

trick′stẽr, *n.* one who tricks; a deceiver; a cheat; a tricker.

trick′sy, *a.*; *comp.* tricksier; *superl.* tricksiest.
1. full of tricks and devices; tricky; artful.
2. tricked out; neat; smart.
3. sportive; playful; mischievous.

trick′track, *n.* [Fr. *trictrac,* backgammon.] backgammon, especially a variety played with both pegs and pieces.

trick′y, *a.*; *comp.* trickier; *superl.* trickiest. 1. given to or characterized by trickery; deceitful.
2. like a trick in deceptiveness; intricate; catchy.

triç′li·nāte, *a.* same as *triclinic.*

trī·çlin′i·ãr·y, *a.* [L. *tricliniaris,* from *triclinium,* a dining room.] pertaining to a triclinium, or the ancient custom of reclining at table.

trī·çlin′iç, *a.* [*tri-,* and Gr. *klinein,* to incline, and *-ic.*] in crystallography, pertaining to the inclination of three intersecting axes to each other; specifically, pertaining to a system of crystallization in which the three axes are unequal, and their intersections oblique, as in the oblique rhomboidal prism.

trī·çlin′i·um, *n.*; *pl.* **trī·çlin′i·ȧ,** [L., from Gr. *triklinion*; *tri-, treis,* three, and *klinē,* a couch.]
1. a couch extending around three sides of

an ancient Roman dining table, for reclining at meals.

2. an ancient Roman dining room, especially one containing such a couch.

trī·coc′cous, *a.* [*tri-*, and Gr. *kokkos*, a berry.] in botany, having three cocci, or carpels, as in *Euphorbia*.

tric·ō·lette′, *n.* a kind of knitted fabric, usually made of cotton or, sometimes, of fiber silk.

trī′cŏl·ŏr, trī′cŏl·ŏur, *n.* [Fr. *tricolore*, of three colors; L. *tres*, three, and *color*, color.] a flag or banner having three colors in large areas; especially, the flag of France, which has three broad, vertical stripes of blue, white, and red, respectively, from the hoist out.

trī′cŏl·ŏr, trī′cŏl·ŏred, *a.* having three colors.

trī′corn, *a.* [Fr. *tricorne*; L. *tricornis*, from *tri-* and *cornu*, horn.] having three horns or corners, as a hat with the brim folded up against the crown so as to form three sides.

trī′corn, *n.* a tricorn hat.

trī·cor′pō·răl, *a.* [*tri-*, and L. *corpus*, *corporis*, body.] in heraldry, tricorporate.

trī·cor′pō·rāte, *a.* having three bodies; specifically, in heraldry, having the bodies of three beasts represented as issuing from the dexter, sinister, and base points of the escutcheon, and meeting, conjoined to one head, in the center point.

trī·cos′tāte, *a.* [*tri-*, and L. *costa*, a rib.]

1. in zoology, having three costae.

2. in botany, having three ribs from the base; three-ribbed.

trī′cot (-kō), *n.* [Fr., from *tricoter*, to knit.]

1. a woolen silk, cotton, rayon, or nylon cloth, knitted, or woven so as to resemble knitting.

2. a type of ribbed cloth for dresses.

tric′ō·tīne, *n.* [Fr.] a woolen cloth resembling twill.

trī″cot·y·lēd′ŏn·ous, *a.* [*tri-*, and Gr. *kotylēdōn*, anything hollow.] in botany, having three cotyledons.

trī·crot′iç, *a.* having three separate rhythmic waves to one beat of the pulse.

trī′crō·tism, *n.* the quality or condition of being tricrotic.

trī′crō·tous, *a.* tricrotic.

tric′traç, tric′-traç, *n.* tricktrack.

trī·cūr′vāte, *a.* in zoology, triple-curved; curved in three separate directions or places.

trī·cus′pid, *a.* 1. having three cusps, or points; as, a *tricuspid* tooth.

2. designating or of a valve with three flaps, between the right auricle and right ventricle of the heart.

trī·cus′pid, *n.* the tricuspid valve.

trī·cus′pi·dāte, *a.* three-pointed; having three cusps.

trī′cy·cle (-si-kl), *n.* [*tri-*, and Gr. *kyklos*, a circle, a wheel.]

1. a light, three-wheeled vehicle operated by pedals or, rarely, hand levers; especially, such a vehicle for children.

2. a three-wheeled motorcycle.

trī′cy·cle, *v.i.*; tricycled, *pt.*, *pp.*; tricycling, *ppr.* to ride a tricycle.

trī′cy·clẽr, trī′cy·clist, *n.* one who rides a tricycle.

trī·cȳ′cliç, *a.* of or having three cycles.

Trī·dac′nȧ, *n.* [Gr. *tridaknos*, eaten at three bites; *tri-*, for *treis*, three, and *daknein*, to bite.] a genus of equivalve, lamellibranchiate mollusks, including some forms known as clams, and forming the type of the family *Tridacnacea* or *Tridacnidæ*. *Tridacna gigas* is the giant clam of the East Indies, attaining a weight of five hundred pounds or more.

trī·dac′tyl, trī·dac′tyle, *a.* having three digits, or three digital parts or processes.

trid′dlẽr, *n.* a species of sandpiper, *Tringa maculata*. [Dial.]

trī′dent, *n.* [Fr., from L. *tridens* (*-entis*); *tri-* for *tres*, three, and *dens*, *dentis*, tooth.]

1. any instrument having the form of a fork with three prongs; specifically, a three-pronged fish spear.

2. in classical mythology, a kind of spear with three barb-pointed prongs, borne as a scepter by Poseidon (Neptune), the sea god; hence, marine supremacy or power.

3. in ancient Rome, a three-pronged spear used in gladiatorial combats by the retiarius.

4. a cubic curve of the third order having branches extending in such directions as to give it the shape of a trident.

trī′dent, *a.* having three teeth, points, or prongs.

trī·den′tăl, *a.* of, pertaining to, or provided with a trident.

trī·den′tāte, trī·den′tā·ted, *a.* [*tri-*, and L. *dentatus*, toothed.] having three teeth, points, or prongs.

trī·den·tif′ẽr·ous, *a.* bearing a trident.

Trī·den′tine, *a.* [ML. *Tridentum*, Trent.]

1. of or pertaining to Trent, Italy.

2. of the Ecumenical Council of Trent (see under Trent), or in accord with its decrees.

Trī·den′tine, *n.* one who accepts the decrees of the Council of Trent; a Roman Catholic.

trī·dī·ȧ·pā′şŏn, *n.* [*tri-*, and Gr. *diapason*.] in music, a triple octave.

trī·di·men′sion·ăl, *a.* [*tri-*, and L. *dimensio* (*-onis*), dimension, and *-al*.] having three dimensions.

trid′ū·ăn, *a.* lasting three days, or happening every third day. [Rare.]

trid′y·mīte, *n.* [Gr. *tridymos*, threefold.] a triclinic form of silica occurring in hexagonal tables and presenting a pseudohexagonal aspect through the twinning of three individuals.

trī·ē′cious, *a.* trioecious.

tried, *v.* past tense and past participle of *try*.

tried, *a.* 1. tested; proved.

2. trustworthy; faithful.

trī·ē′drăl, *a.* same as *trihedral*.

trī·en′ni·ăl, *a.* [L. *triennium*, the space of three years; *tri-*, for *tres*, three, and *annus*, a year.]

1. continuing or lasting three years; as, a *triennial* parliament.

2. happening every three years; as, *triennial* elections.

trī·en′ni·ăl, *n.* anything taking place once in three years; also, a third anniversary.

trī·en′ni·ăl·ly, *adv.* once in three years.

trī′ens, *n.*; *pl.* **trī·en′tēs,** [L., the third part of anything.] an ancient Roman bronze coin, equal to one third of the as.

Trī·en·tā′lis, *n.* [L., containing a third, from *triens* (*-entis*), a third part.] a small genus of plants, family *Primulaceæ*, including two species, *Trientalis europæa* and *Trientalis americana*: commonly called star flower.

trī′ẽr, *n.* 1. one who tries, as (a) one who makes experiments; one who examines anything by a test or standard; (b) one who tries judicially; a judge who tries a person or cause; (c) in law, same as *trior*; (d) an ecclesiastical commissioner appointed by the Parliament under the Commonwealth to examine the character and qualifications of clergymen.

2. that which tries; a test.

trī′ẽr·ärch, *n.* [Gr. *triērarchos*, from *triērēs*, a trireme, and *archos*, chief.] in ancient Greece, the commander of a trireme; particularly, at Athens, one who, at his own expense, built, equipped, and maintained a trireme for public service.

trī·ẽr·ärch′ăl, *a.* of or pertaining to a trierarchy or trierarch.

trī′ẽr·ärch·y, *n.*; *pl.* **trī′ẽr·ärch·ies,** 1. the rank, authority, or duties of a trierarch.

2. trierarchs collectively.

3. in ancient Athens, the system by which citizens built, outfitted, and maintained triremes for the service of the state.

trī·ē·ter′iç, *a.* [Gr. *tri-* and *etos*, year.] in ancient Greece, occurring or taking place every third (i.e., every alternate) year.

trī·ē·ter′iç, *n.* a celebration or festival occurring every alternate year.

trī·ē·ter′i·căl, *a.* trieteric. [Obs.]

trī·eth′yl-, in chemistry, a combining form indicating the presence of *three ethyl groups*, particularly when they replace hydrogen.

trī·eth″yl·ȧ·mīne′, *n.* in chemistry, a tertiary amine, $N(C_2H_5)_3$: it is an oily liquid having strong alkaline properties.

trī·eth″yl·stib′ine, *n.* in chemistry, $Sb(C_2H_5)_3$, a liquid with an odor like that of garlic: it is easily combustible in air and exhibits some of the characteristics of metal in various reactions.

trī·fā′ciăl (-shăl), *a.* and *n.* [*tri-*, and L. *facies*, face.] same as *trigeminal*.

trī·fā′r′i·ous, *a.* [L. *trifarius*, threefold.] arranged in three rows.

trī·fec′tȧ, *n.* [*tri-* and per*fecta*.] a bet or betting procedure in which one wins if one correctly picks the first, second, and third place finishers in a race.

trī′fid, *a.* [L. *trifidus*; *tri-*, for *tres*, three, and *fidus*, from *findere*, to divide.] in botany, divided into three lobes or parts by linear sinuses with straight margins; three-cleft.

trī·fis′tū·lăr·y, *a.* [*tri-*, and L. *fistula*, a pipe.] having three pipes. [Rare.]

trī·flaġ′el·lāte, *a.* in zoology, having or characterized by three whiplike appendages or flagella, as some Protozoa.

trī′fle, *n.* [ME. *truffle*; OFr. *trufle*, *truffle*, mockery, dim. of *truffe*, gibe, mock.]

1. something of little value or importance; a trivial thing, idea, etc.; a paltry matter.

2. a small amount of money.

3. a small amount; a little.

4. a dessert consisting of spongecake soaked in wine and covered with macaroons, almonds, whipped cream, etc.

5. (a) a kind of pewter; (b) [*pl.*] utensils made of this.

Syn.—bauble, bagatelle, triviality.

trī′fle, *v.i.*; trifled, *pt.*, *pp.*; trifling, *ppr.* 1. to act or talk without seriousness, weight, or dignity; to act or talk with levity.

2. to dally; to play fast and loose (*with* a person's affections, etc.).

3. to play; to toy: used with *with*.

trī′fle, *v.t.* 1. to make of no importance. [Rare.]

2. to waste (usually with *away*); to spend idly.

3. to make sport of. [Rare.]

trī′flẽr, *n.* one who trifles or acts with levity.

trī′fling, *a.* 1. being of small value or importance; trivial; as, a *trifling* debt; a *trifling* affair.

2. that trifles; frivolous.

Syn.—futile, frivilous, inconsiderable, light, petty, unimportant, insignificant, little, shallow, inconsequential.

trī′fling, *n.* concern with things of little or no importance; trifling talk or action.

trī′fling·ly, *adv.* in a trifling manner; with levity; without seriousness or dignity.

trī′fling·ness, *n.* the quality of being trifling.

trī·flō′răl, *a.* same as *triflorous*.

trī·flō′rous, *a.* [*tri-*, and L. *flos*, *floris*, flower.] three-flowered; bearing three flowers; as, a *triflorous* peduncle.

trī·flu′ō·rīde, *n.* in chemistry, a compound consisting of an element or a radical joined with three atoms of fluorine.

trī·fō′căl, *a.* adjusted or ground to three different focal lengths.

trī·fō′căl, *n.* a lens like a bifocal but with an additional narrow area ground to adjust the eye for intermediate focus (about 30 inches).

trī·fō′li·āte, *a.* [*tri-*, and L. *folium*, leaf.]

1. having three leaves.

2. loosely, trifoliolate.

trī·fō′li·ā·ted, *a.* trifoliate.

trī·fō′li·ō·lāte, *a.* having three folioles, as the leaf of a clover.

Trī·fō′li·um, *n.* a genus of leguminous plants, usually characterized by leaves with three leaflets and including over one hundred fifty species. *Trifolium pratense*, red clover, has conspicuous stipules, oval leaflets marked with a pale spot, and a head of red florets closely surrounded by the uppermost leaves. *Trifolium fucatum* is the fodder plant of California. *Trifolium alexandrinum*, called *berseem*, is the forage crop of the Nile valley.

trī·fō′ri·um, *n.* [*tri-*, and L. *foris*, a door.] a gallery or arcade between the vaulting and the roof of the nave, choir, or transept of a church: also called *blindstory*.

trī′form, *a.* [L. *triformis*; *tri-*, for *tres*, three, and *forma*, form.] having a triple form, nature, or shape; as, the *triform* countenance of the moon.

trī′formed (-formd), *a.* triform.

trī·form′i·ty, *n.* the state of being triform.

trī·fūr′cāte, trī·fūr′cā·ted, *a.* [*tri-*, and L. *furca*, fork.] having three branches or forks.

trig, *a.* [ME. *trigg*; ON. *tryggr*, trusty, firm, true; base as in *true*.]

1. trim; neat; spruce.

2. in good condition; strong; sound.

3. prim; precise. [Rare.]

trig, *v.t.*; trigged, *pt.*, *pp.*; trigging, *ppr.* to make trig (often with *out* or *up*). [Dial.]

trig, *v.t.*; trigged, *pt.*, *pp.*; trigging, *ppr.* [prob. back-formation from dial. *trigger*, brake.]

1. to prevent (a wheel, etc.) from rolling by placing a wedge, stone, etc. under it.

2. to prop or support.

trig, *n.* a stone, wedge of wood, or the like laid under a wheel, etc. to prevent its rolling.

trig′ȧ·mist, *n.* a person who commits trigamy.

trig′ȧ·mous, *a.* [Gr. *trigamos*, thrice married.]

1. of or relating to trigamy.

2. guilty of trigamy.

3. in botany, having three sorts of flowers in the same head, male, female, and hermaphrodite.

trig'ȧ·my, *n.* [*tri-*, and Gr. *gamos*, marriage.] the state of being married three times; specifically, the criminal offense of having three husbands or three wives at the same time.

trī·ġem'i·năl, *a.* [L. *trigeminus*, three at a birth.] in anatomy, of, relating to, or indicating the fifth pair of nerves which arise from the crura of the cerebellum and are divided within the cranium into three branches, viz., the orbital, the superior maxillary, and the inferior maxillary: also called *trifacial*.

trī·ġem'i·năl, *n.* a trigeminal nerve.

trī·ġem'i·nous, *a.* [L. *trigeminus*, three at a birth; *tri-*, for *tres*, three, and *geminus*, a twin.]

1. being one of three born together; born three at a time.

2. threefold. [Rare.]

trī·ġes''i·mō-sē·çun'dō, *a.* [L.] in the manufacture of books, having thirty-two leaves, or sixty-four pages, to a sheet; 32mo.

trī·ġes''i·mō-sē·çun'dō, *n.* [L.] a 32mo book, made of sheets each of which contains thirty-two leaves, or sixty-four pages.

trig'gẽr, *n.* [ME. *tricker*; D. *trekker*, a trigger, from *trekken*, to draw, pull.]

1. the finger piece of a gun lock; a small lever in firearms which when pressed back by the finger releases the firing hammer.

2. a small lever or part which when pulled or pressed releases a catch, spring, etc.

quick on the trigger; (a) quick to fire a gun; (b) quick to act, understand, etc.; alert. [Colloq.]

trig'gẽr fiñ'gẽr, 1. the finger used in pressing a trigger; especially, the forefinger.

2. a condition in which there is a momentary spasmodic arrest of movement inflexing or extending the finger, followed by a snapping of the finger into place.

trig'gẽr·fish, *n.*; *pl.* **trig'gẽr·fish, trig'gẽr·fish·eș,** [so called because depression of the second spine of the fin causes the first to snap down.] any of a group of brightly colored tropical fishes having an anterior dorsal fin with two or three spines.

trig'gẽr plant, any one of several plants of the genus *Candollea*.

trī·ġin'tăl, *n.* same as *trental*.

trī'glot, *a.* [*tri-*, and Gr. *glōssa*, tongue.] containing or compiled in three different languages; as, a *triglot* textbook.

trī·glyc'ẽr·īde, *n.* a glyceride produced by the chemical substitution of acid radicals for three hydrogen atoms in glycerin.

trī'glyph, *n.* [*tri-*, and Gr. *glyphē*, sculpture.] an ornament in the frieze of the Doric order, repeated at equal intervals. Each triglyph has two vertical channels cut to a right angle, called *glyphs*, separated by three fillets, with a half-channel on either side.

trī·glyph'iç, trī·glyph'i·çăl, *a.* of or ornamented with triglyphs.

trig'ness, *n.* the state or quality of being trig or trim; neatness.

trī'gō, *n.* [Sp.] wheat.

trī'gon, *n.* [Fr. *trigone*; L. *trigonum*; Gr. *trigōnon*, triangle, lyre; *tri-*, for *treis*, three, and *gōnia*, angle.]

1. a triangle.

2. in astrology, a division consisting of three signs; also, the aspect of two planets distant 120 degrees from each other; trine.

3. an ancient triangular lyre or harp.

4. a ball game played by three persons standing so as to be at the angles of a triangle.

trig'ō·năl, *a.* 1. triangular; having three angles or corners.

2. in botany, trigonous.

3. of a trigon.

trig'ō·năl·ly, *adv.* triangularly.

trī'gōne, *n.* in anatomy, a triangular area of the interior of the bladder between the openings of the ureters and the orifice of the urethra: also called *trigonum*.

Trig·ō·nel'lȧ, *n.* [a dim. formed from *trigon*: from the triangular appearance of the flower.] a genus of plants of the natural order *Leguminosæ*, strong-scented herbs with trifoliate leaves and small blue, yellow, or white flowers, growing singly or grouped in the axils of the leaves. They are chiefly native to Europe, Asia, and North Africa.

trī·gō·neū'tiç, *a.* [*tri-*, and Gr. *goneuein*, to beget.] having three broods in one year, as certain insects.

trī·gō·neū'tișm, *n.* the quality or state of being trigoneutic.

Trī·gō'ni·ȧ, *n.* [Gr. *trigōnos*, triangular, three-cornered.] in zoology, a genus of lamellibranchiate mollusks, belonging to the family *Trigoniidæ*. They are triangular or suborbicular, equivalve, transverse bivalves, living species of which have been discovered near Australia only, in sandy mud. The fossil species are abundant in the strata between the Lias and the Chalk.

trig·ō·nī'tis, *n.* inflammation or localized hyperemia of the trigone of the bladder.

trig''ō·nō·ceph'ȧ·lous, *a.* [Gr. *trigōnos*, triangular, and *kephalē*, head.] having a flat, triangular head, as some snakes.

trig·ō·noc'ẽr·ous, *a.* [Gr. *trigōnos*, triangular, and *keras*, horn.] having horns with three angles or ridges, as some goats and sheep.

trig·ō·nom'e·tẽr, *n.* [Gr. *trigōnon*, triangle, and *-meter*.] an instrument for plotting angles and laying down distances upon paper, and for solving problems in plane trigonometry by inspection. It consists of a semicircular protractor, with a long arm carrying a T square and graduated sliding scale.

trig''ō·nō·met'riç, trig''ō·nō·met'ri·çăl, *a.* pertaining to trigonometry; performed by or according to the rules of trigonometry.

trigonometric canon; a table that gives the values of trigonometric functions.

trigonometric curve; a curve that is the graph of the trigonometric functions of right-angled co-ordinates.

trigonometrical survey; any survey of a country which is carried on from a single base, by the computation of observed angular distances: the term is usually confined to measurements on a large scale, embracing a considerable extent of country, and requiring a combination of astronomical and geodetical operations.

trig''ō·nō·met'ri·çăl·ly, *adv.* according to the rules or principles of trigonometry.

trig·ō·nom'e·try, *n.*; *pl.* **trig·ō·nom'e·trieș,** [Gr. *trigōnon*, a triangle, and *-metry*.]

1. the branch of mathematics that deals with the ratios between the sides of a right triangle with reference to either acute angle (*trigonometric functions*), the relations between these ratios, and the application of these facts in finding the unknown sides or angles of any triangle, as in surveying, range-finding, navigation, engineering, etc.

2. a treatise or textbook on this subject.

analytic trigonometry; trigonometry which deals with the general relations and properties of angles and trigonometrical functions of angles.

trig'ō·nous, *a.* [Gr. *trigōnos*, triangular.]

1. trigonal.

2. in botany, having three prominent longitudinal angles, as a style or ovary.

trī'gram, *n.* an inscription of three letters; also, a figure formed of three lines.

trī·gram·mat'iç, *a.* [*tri-*, Gr. *gramma*, a letter, and *-ic*.] of or forming a trigram.

trī·gram'miç, *a.* same as *trigrammatic*.

trī'gràph, *n.* a group of three letters forming a single phoneme, as *eau* (ō) in b*eau*.

trī'ġyn, *n.* [*tri-*, and Gr. *gynē*, a female.] in botany, a plant having three styles; one of the *Trigynia*.

Trī·ġyn'i·ȧ, *n.pl.* formerly, an order of plants in the Linnaean system, having three styles or pistils, as in the bladdernut.

trī·ġyn'i·ăn, trig'y·nous, *a.* in botany, having three styles; of or relating to the *Trigynia*.

trī·hal'īde, *n.* in chemistry, a compound of either an element or a radical with three atoms of halogen.

trī·hē'drăl, *a.* [*tri-*, and Gr. *hedra*, side.] of, or having the form of, a trihedron.

trihedral angle; a solid angle formed by three plane surfaces meeting in a point.

trī·hē'drŏn, *n.*; *pl.* **trī·hē'drŏnș, trī·hē'drȧ,** [ML.] a solid figure with three plane surfaces meeting in a point.

trī''hē·mim'ẽr, *n.* in classical prosody, a group of three half feet.

trī''hē·mim'ẽr·al, *a.* pertaining to or after a trihemimer: said of a caesura.

trī·hē''mi·ō·bō'li·on, *n.* an ancient Greek silver coin, equivalent to one and one half obols.

trī·hō'răl, *a.* happening once every three hours.

trī·hour'ly, (-our'), *a.* happening once every three hours, as an occurrence, or lasting for three hours, as a period of time.

trī·hȳ'brid, *n.* in biology, a crossbred organism, the parents of which differ by three pairs of contrasting Mendelian characters.

trī·hȳ'drāte, *n.* a compound in which there is one radical of hydroxyl to three atoms of a base.

trī·hȳ'driç, *a.* containing three hydrogen atoms that are replaceable by bases.

trī·hȳ·drox'y, *a.* containing three hydroxyl groups.

trī'jū·gāte, trī'jū·gous, *a.* [*tri-*, and L. *jugum*, yoke.] in botany, having three pairs of leaflets on a common stem: said of a leaf.

trī'kō·sāne, *n.* [*tri-*, and Gr. *eikosi*, twenty.] in chemistry, a hydrocarbon, $C_{23}H_{48}$, of the paraffin series.

trī'lābe, *n.* [*tri-*, and Gr. *labē*, a handle.] a three-pronged instrument for taking calculi from the bladder.

trī·lat'ẽr·ăl, *a.* [*tri-*, and L. *latus*, *lateris*, side.] having three sides; as, a *trilateral* figure.

trī·lat·ẽr·al'i·ty, *n.* the quality of being trilateral.

trī·lat'ẽr·ăl·ly, *adv.* with three sides.

trī·lat'ẽr·ăl·ness, *n.* trilaterality.

trī·lau'rin, *n.* a crystalline glyceride, the chief constituent of coconut oil: it is a fat similar to palmitin.

trī·lem'mȧ, *n.* [*tri-*, and Gr. *lēmma*, anything received, an assumption, from *lambanein*, to receive.]

1. in logic, a syllogism with three conditional propositions, the major premises of which are disjunctively affirmed in the minor.

2. in general, any choice between three alternatives.

trī·lin'ē·ăr, *a.* [*tri-*, and L. *linea*, a line.] of, enclosed by, or involving three lines.

trī·liñ'guăl (-gwăl), *a.* [*tri-*, and L. *lingua*, language.] of, using, written in, or spoken in three languages.

trī·liñ'guăr, *a.* trilingual. [Rare.]

trī·lin·ō'lē·in, *n.* a glyceride found in linseed oil, hempseed oil, sunflower oil, etc.

Tril'i·sȧ, *n.* [LL., an anagram of *Liatris*.] a genus of plants of the aster family, the two species of which are native to the southern part of the United States. One of these, *Trilisa odoratissima*, is known as the wild vanilla or deer's-tongue.

trī·lit'ẽr·ăl, *a.* [*tri-*, and L. *litera*, letter.] consisting of three letters; as, a *triliteral* root or word.

trī·lit'ẽr·ăl, *n.* a three-letter word or base.

trī·lit'ẽr·ăl·ișm, *n.* the quality of being triliteral; specifically, the characteristic quality of Semitic languages of containing many bases having three consonants, on which words are formed by the addition of various vowel sounds.

trī·lit·ẽr·al'i·ty, trī·lit'ẽr·ăl·ness, *n.* the quality or state of being triliteral.

trī'lith, *n.* [*tri-*, and Gr. *lithos*, a stone.] in archaeology, a monument, probably sepulchral, either standing alone or forming part of a larger work, and consisting of three stones, two uprights connected by a continuous impost or architrave.

trī·lith'iç, *a.* of or relating to a trilith; consisting of three stones.

tril'i·thon, *n.* a trilith.

trill, *n.* [Fr. *trille*; It. *trilla*, *trillo*, from *trillare*, to trill; echoic.]

1. (a) a rapid alternation of two musical tones a degree or half degree apart; (b) musical vibrato.

2. a similar sound, as of birds; a warble.

3. a rapid vibration of the tongue or uvula, as in pronouncing *r* in some languages.

4. a consonant pronounced with such a vibration.

trill, *v.t* and *v.i.*; trilled, *pt.*, *pp.*; trilling, *ppr.* to sound, speak, sing, or play with a trill or trills.

trill, *v.i.* to flow in a small stream or in drops rapidly succeeding each other; to trickle. [Archaic.]

trill, *v.t.* to turn; to twist; to twirl. [Archaic.]

tril'lȧ·çhăn, *n.* the oyster catcher. [Brit. Dial.]

tril'ling, *n.* 1. any one child of three born at the same time; a triplet.

2. in crystallography, a composite crystal made up of three individuals: also called *threeling*.

tril'liŏn (-yun), *n.* [Fr.; *tri-* and *million*.]

1. in the United States and France, a thousand billions (1,000,000,000,000).

2. in Great Britain and Germany, a million billions (1,000,000,000,000,000,000).

tril'lĭŏn, *a.* amounting to one trillion in number.

tril'liŏnth, *a.* 1. being the last in a series of a trillion.
 2. being one of a trillion; as, a *trillionth* part.

tril'liŏnth, *n.* 1. the last in a series of a trillion.
 2. any of the trillion equal parts of something.

Tril'li·um, *n.* [LL., from L. *tri-*, for *tres*, three.]
 1. a genus of low, perennial, liliaceous herbs, having a short, fleshy rootstock, bearing at its summit a whorl of three large leaves, and a solitary flower, with its three outer segments green and its three inner segments either red, purple, white, or green. Of the fifteen species, fourteen are native to North America and two to Asia.
 2. [t–] any plant of this genus, including the wake-robin, three-leaved nightshade, wood lily, birthroot, nosebleed, etc.

tril'lō, *n.* [It.] in music, same as *trill*.

trī·lō'băl, *a.* trilobate.

trī·lō'bāte, trī·lō'bāt·ed, *a.* having three lobes, as some leaves.

trī·lō·bā'tion, *n.* the state or quality of being trilobate.

trī'lōbed, *a.* trilobate.

Trī·lō·bī'tȧ, *n.pl.* a Paleozoic group of *Crustacea*, extinct since the Carboniferous age and regarded as the early and more generalized type from which the more specialized *Isopoda* have descended.

trī'lō·bīte, *n.* [*tri-*, and Gr. *lobos*, a lobe.] any one of the *Trilobita*: so called because their bodies are composed of three lobes or segments, the cephalic, thoracic, and abdominal. There were more than 500 species.

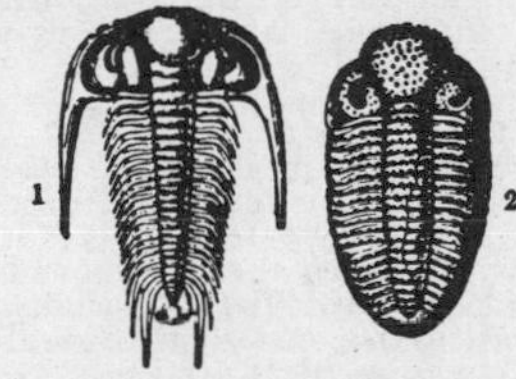

TRILOBITES
1. *Paradoxides bohemicus*; 2. *Phacops latifrons*

trī·lō·bit'iç, *a.* pertaining to, containing, or resembling the trilobites.

trī·loç'ū·lăr, *a.* [*tri-*, and L. *loculus*, a cell.] having three cells, chambers, or cavities; as, a *trilocular* pericarp.

tril'ō·ġy, *n.*; *pl.* **tril'ō·ġieṣ,** [*tri-*, and Gr. *logos*, a discourse, from *legein*, to speak.]
 1. in ancient Greek drama, a group of three tragedies which were related in subject and intended for consecutive performance.
 2. any set of three related plays, novels, etc. which, though each has its own unity, form together a larger whole.

trī·lū'mi·năr, trī·lū'mi·nous, *a.* [*tri-*, and L. *lumen*, light.] having three lights.

trim, *v.t.*; trimmed, *pt.*, *pp.*; trimming, *ppr.* [AS. *trymian*, *trymman*, to make firm, set in order, array.]
 1. to make tidy or neat; to put in proper order, especially by clipping, lopping, etc.
 2. to furnish or embellish with ornaments; to decorate; as, to *trim* a gown with lace.
 3. to clip, pare, cut, or prune (often with *off*); as, he *trimmed* dead branches *off* the tree.
 4. to dress, as timber; to make smooth.
 5. (a) to balance (a ship) by adjusting or shifting the cargo, persons, or ballast; (b) to adjust or arrange in the best order for sailing, as the yards or sails.
 6. to balance (an airplane) in flight by regulating the surface controls and tabs.
 7. to modify according to expediency; to adjust; to adapt.
 8. (a) to scold; to chide; to rebuke; (b) to beat, punish, thrash, etc.; (c) to defeat; (d) to cheat. [Colloq.]
 9. to prepare; to fit out; to dress. [Obs.]
 to trim in; in carpentry, to fit, as a piece of timber, into other work.
 to trim up; to put in order.

trim, *v.i.* 1. to change one's opinions or viewpoint so as to satisfy opposing factions, etc.; to keep a middle-of-the-road policy; to compromise.
 2. (a) to keep in balance: said of a ship; (b) to keep a ship in balance; to adjust the sails or yards in managing a vessel.

trim, *n.* 1. order; arrangement; condition; as, in proper *trim*.
 2. good condition or order; as, he got into *trim*.
 3. equipment; gear; dress.
 4. a trimming by clipping, cutting, etc.
 5. window dressing.
 6. the lighter interior or exterior woodwork of a building, especially around windows and doors.
 7. the interior furnishings of an automobile body.
 8. any ornamental trimming.
 9. (a) the condition of being trimmed or ready to sail: said of ships; (b) the position of a boat or ship in the water; (c) the balance of a ship; (d) the difference between the draft forward and draft aft; (e) the adjustment of the sails or yards in managing a vessel.
 10. the degree of buoyancy of a submarine.
 11. the position of an airplane in relation to a fore-and-aft horizontal axis.
 12. something that is trimmed, as sections of motion-picture film cut out in editing.
 13. character (of a person). [Obs.]
 trim of the masts; the position of the masts in regard to the ship and to each other, as near or distant, far forward or much aft, erect or raking.

trim, *a.*; *comp.* trimmer; *superl.* trimmest, 1. orderly; neat; tidy.
 2. well-proportioned; smartly designed.
 3. in good condition.
 4. fine; nice. [Obs.]

trim, *adv.* in a trim manner.

trī·maç'ū·lā·ted, trī·maç'ū·lăr, *a.* [*tri-*, and L. *macula*, spot.] marked with three spots.

trī·mel·lit'iç, *a.* of or pertaining to a colorless crystalline triacid, obtained from mellitic acid.

trī·mem'brăl, *a.* having three members.

Trim'ẽr·ȧ, *n.pl.* [*tri-*, and Gr. *meros*, a part.] a division of *Coleoptera*, including those which have each tarsus composed of three articulations, as the ladybugs.

trim'ẽr·ăn, *n.* any member of the *Trimera*; a trimerous insect.

trim'ẽr·ăn, *a.* same as *trimerous*.

trim'ẽr·ous, *a.* 1. in botany, having three members in each set: said of a flower.
 2. in entomology, (a) having three segments or joints, as the tarsus of a beetle; (b) of or pertaining to the *Trimera*.

trī·mē·sit'iç, *a.* [*tri-*, *mesit*ylene, and *-ic*.] of or pertaining to a tribasic compound obtained from mesitylene by oxidation.

trī·mes'tẽr, *n.* [Fr. *trimestre*, from L. *trimestris*, of three months; *tri-*, for *tres*, three, and *mensis*, month.] a term or period of three months.

trī·mes'tri·ăl, *a.* of or pertaining to a trimester; occurring every three months.

trim'ē·tẽr, *n.* [*tri-*, and Gr. *metron*, measure.]
 1. a line of verse containing three metrical feet or measures.
 2. a poetical division of verse, consisting of trimeters.

trim'ē·tẽr, *a.* having three metrical feet.

trī·meth'yl, *a.* containing three methyl groups.

trī·meth'yl-, a combining form indicating the *presence of three methyl groups*, as in *trimethyl*amine.

trī·meth″yl·am·ïne', *n.* a substituted ammonia containing three methyl groups, or one in which the three hydrogen atoms are replaced by methyl, $N(CH_3)_3$.

trī·meth'yl·ēne, *n.* a gaseous hydrocarbon, C_3H_6, derived indirectly from propylene, furnishing the base of a series of compounds similar to the aromatic hydrocarbons.

trī·met'riç, *a.* 1. same as *orthorhombic*.
 2. having three metrical feet.

trī·met'ri·căl, *a.* same as *trimetric*.

trī·met'riç prō·jeç'tion, a type of geometric projection in which the three dimensions are measured by different scales according to arbitrarily chosen angles.

trī·met'rō·gon, *n.* [from *tri-*, and Gr. *metron*, a measure, and *gōnia*, an angle.] a system of aerial photography in which three high-speed, wide-angled cameras are so placed in an airplane as to take photographs of the earth from horizon to horizon.

trim'ly, *adv.* in a trim manner; neatly; in good order.

trim'mẽr, *n.* 1. one who or that which trims (in any sense).
 2. a person who trims a ship during loading or unloading, by distributing the cargo.
 3. a machine for trimming lumber, etc.
 4. a person who changes his opinions, policies, etc. to suit the occasion; a timeserver.
 5. in architecture, a piece of timber inserted in a floor frame, to support the ends of headers, as around a stairwell.
 6. one who chastises or reprimands; a sharp, shrewish person; also, that by which a reprimand or chastisement is administered. [Colloq. or Dial.]

trim'ming, *n.* 1. the action of a person who trims; specifically, (a) a scolding; (b) a beating; thrashing; (c) a defeat; (d) a cheating. [Colloq.]
 2. something used to trim; specifically, (a) decoration; ornament; (b) [*pl.*] the side dishes or garnishings of a meal; as, turkey with all the *trimmings*.
 3. [*pl.*] parts trimmed off.

trim'ming joist, in architecture, a small beam into which are framed the ends of other joists.

trim'ming·ly, *adv.* in a trimming manner.

trim'ness, *n.* neatness; snugness; the state of being trim.

trī·mō·leç'ū·lăr, *a.* of or formed from three molecules.

trī·mŏnth'ly, *a.* happening or appearing every three months.

trī'mọrph, *n.* [*tri-*, and Gr. *morphē*, form.]
 1. a substance that crystallizes in three distinct forms.
 2. any one of the forms in which such a substance exists.

trī·mọr'phiç, *a.* same as *trimorphous*.

trī·mọr'phiṣm, *n.* [*tri-*, Gr. *morphē*, form, and *-ism*.]
 1. in zoology, the existence of three distinct forms in the same species.
 2. in crystallography, the property of crystallizing in three distinct forms.
 3. in botany, the existence of three distinct forms of flowers, leaves, stamens, or other organs on the same plant or on different plants of the same species.

trī·mọr'phous, *a.* of, pertaining to, or characterized by trimorphism; having three distinct forms.

Trī·mụr'ti, *n.* [Sans., from *tri*, three, and *mūrti*, body, shape.] the Hindu trinity of gods, Brahma, Vishnu, and Siva, conceived as an inseparable unity: considered separately, Brahma is the creating, Vishnu the preserving, and Siva the destroying principle. The trimurti is represented symbolically as one body with three heads, Vishnu at the right, Siva at the left, and Brahma in the middle.

TRIMURTI

Trī·nā'çri·ăn, *a.* [from L. *Trinacria*, Sicily.] Sicilian.

trī'năl, *a.* [LL. *trinalis*, from L. *trinus*, three.] having three parts; triple; threefold.

trī'nȧ·ry, *a.* [LL. *trinarius*, of three kinds, for L. *ternarius*, ternary.] threefold; ternary.

trin'dle, *n.* 1. a trundle. [Scot. and Brit. Dial.]
 2. in bookbinding, formerly, one of several forked pieces of wood or metal placed over the back of a book to flatten the round back before trimming the front.

trin'dle, *v.t.* and *v.i.* to trundle. [Obs.]

trīne, *a.* [ME.; OFr.; L. *trinus*, triple.]
 1. threefold; triple; as, *trine* dimension, that is, length, breadth, and thickness.
 2. in astrology, in trine; hence, favorable.

trīne, *n.* 1. in astrology, the aspect of two planets distant from each other 120 degrees: it was supposed to be a favorable aspect.
 2. a group of three; a triad; as, a single *trine* of brazen tortoises.
 3. [T–] the trinity.

trīne, *v.t.*; trined, *pt.*, *pp.*; trining, *ppr.* to put in the aspect of a trine. [Rare.]

trī·nẽrv'āte, *a.* [*tri-*, L. *nervus*, nerve, and *-ate*.] in botany, having three nerves, as a leaf.

trī·nẽrve', trī·nẽrved', *a.* same as *trinervate*.

Triñ'gȧ, *n.* [Gr. *tryngas*, a bird.] a genus of grallatorial birds, of the family *Tringidæ*, including many species of sandpipers.

triñ'gle, *n.* [Fr.] 1. in architecture, a small, straight molding; especially, a little, square ornament fixed exactly over every triglyph.
 2. a rod upon which rings may be run, as for a curtain.

triñ'goid, *a.* resembling the genus *Tringa*; like a member of the sandpiper family.

Trin·i·tār′i·ăn, *a.* 1. [*also* t–] (a) pertaining to the Trinity or to the doctrine of the Trinity; (b) believing in this doctrine.
2. [t–] forming a trinity; threefold.

Trin·i·tār′i·ăn, *n.* 1. one who believes in the doctrine of the Trinity.
2. one of a monastic order, founded at the close of the twelfth century to redeem captive Christians from the Moslems: also called *Mathurin, Redemptionist.*

Trin·i·tār′i·ăn·ism, *n.* the doctrine of the Trinity; also, belief in this.

trī·nī′trāte, *n.* a nitrate containing three nitric acid radicals in combination.

trī·nī′trō-, a combining form used in chemistry to indicate the presence of *three atoms of nitrogen*, as in *trinitro*glycerin.

trī·nī·trō·cre′sŏl, *n.* [*trinitro-* and *cresol.*] a yellow, crystalline chemical compound, $C_7H_5O(NO_2)_3$, used as an antiseptic and in explosives.

trī·nī·trō·glyc′ẽr·in, *n.* nitroglycerin.

trī·nī·trō·meth′āne, *n.* a chemical compound, $CH(NO_2)_3$, in which three of the hydrogen atoms of methane are replaced by the nitro group.

trī·nī·trō·phē′nŏl, *n.* in chemistry, picric acid.

trī·nī·trō·tol′ū·ēne, *n.* in chemistry, a powerful explosive, $CH_3C_6H_2(NO_2)_3$; any of the isomeric derivatives of toluene, used for blasting, in artillery shells, etc.: abbreviated T. N. T. or TNT.

trī·nī·trō·tol′ū·ŏl, *n.* same as *trinitrotoluene.*

trin′i·ty, *n.*; *pl.* **trin′i·ties**, [ME. *trinite*; OFr. *trinité*; L. *trinitas*, from *trinus*, threefold, from *tres, tria*, three.]
1. the condition of being three or threefold.
2. [T–] in Christian theology, the union of the three divine persons in one Godhead, the Father, the Son, and the Holy Spirit, or Holy Ghost.
3. any symbolical representation of the Trinity.
4. any combination of three parts, persons, characters, etc. that form a unit.
5. [T–] Trinity Sunday.
Trinity House; an association in London to promote commerce and navigation by licensing pilots, erecting and maintaining lighthouses, etc.
Trinity Sunday; the Sunday next after Whitsunday: so called from the feast held on that day in honor of the Trinity.
Trinity term; formerly, in England, a term of court beginning on the Friday next after Trinity Sunday.

SYMBOLS OF THE TRINITY

trin·i·ū′ni·ty, *n.* trinity. [Obs.]

triñk, *n.* a kind of net for catching fish. [Obs.]

triñ′ket, *n.* a small topsail. [Obs.]

triñ′ket, *n.* [ME. *trenket*, a shoemakers' knife, later a toy knife carried by ladies, finally, any ornament, from Fr. *trancher, trencher*; Sp. *trinchar*, to cut.]
1. a small ornament, as a jewel, a ring, and the like; a fancy article of small size.
2. a trifle or toy.

triñ′ket, *v.i.* to traffic secretly; to intrigue. [Rare.]

triñ′ket·ẽr, *n.* one who trinkets. [Rare.]

triñ′ket·ry, *n.* ornaments of dress; trinkets collectively.

triñ′kle, *v.i.* to meddle; to act in a sneaking manner. [Obs.]

trī·noc′tiăl (-shăl), *a.* [*tri-*, and L. *nox, noctis*, night.] continuing for three nights.

trī·nōd′ăl, *a.* [*tri-*, and L. *nodus*, knot.] having three nodes or nodal points.

trī·nō′mi·ăl, *a.* [*tri-* and bi*nomial.*] having three names or three terms.

trī·nō′mi·ăl, *n.* a quantity consisting of three terms, as (a) a mathematical expression consisting of three terms connected by plus or minus signs, as $a + b - c$; (b) a technical name of a plant or animal having three terms to denote genus, species, and subspecies or variety; a trionym.

trī·nom′ĭ·năl, *n.* and *a.* trinomial. [Obs.]

trī′ō (*or* trē′), *n.*; *pl.* **trī′ōs**, [Fr.; It., from L. *tres, tria*, three.]
1. three persons or things united in a group.
2. in music, a composition for three voices or three instruments; also, the three persons or instruments performing such a composition.
3. the middle section of a minuet, scherzo, etc., originally written in three voices, or parts.
4. in card playing, three cards of the same kind.

trī·ob′ō·lăr, trī·ob′ō·lā·ry, *a.* of the value of three oboli; mean; worthless. [Obs.]

trī·oc′tīle, *n.* [*tri-* and *octile.*] in astrology, an aspect of two planets with regard to the earth when they are three octants, 135 degrees, distant from each other.

trī′ōde, *n.* [*tri-* and *-ode.*] a three electrode vacuum tube composed of a cathode, an anode, and a control grid, and used to produce, detect, or amplify radio waves.

trī·ō′di·on, *n.*; *pl.* **trī·ō′di·ȧ**, in the Orthodox Eastern Church, a liturgical book in which the offices beginning with the fourth Sunday before Lent and continuing to Easter eve are contained: the name derives from the fact that no more than three odes are ever used in the canons.

Trī′ō·don, *n.* 1. the only type of a genus of puff-fishes, native to the eastern coast of Asia and the East Indies: the fused teeth of the upper jaw form two plates, one to a side, while those of the lower jaw form a single plate.
2. [t–] any fish of this genus.

Trī″ō·don·toph′ō·rus, *n.* a genus of Nematoda, or roundworms, found as parasites in animals.

Trī·oe′ci·ȧ (-shi-), *n.pl.* [*tri-*, and Gr. *oikos*, a house.] the third order of plants in the class *Polygamia*, in the Linnaean system. It comprises plants with unisexual and bisexual flowers on three separate plants, or having flowers with stamens only on one, pistils only on another, and bisexual flowers on a third. [Obs.]

trī·oe′cious, *a.* 1. belonging to or having the characteristics of the order *Triœcia*. [Obs.]
2. having male, female, and two-sexed flowers on separate plants: also spelled *triecious.*

trī·oe′cism, *n.* the condition or quality of being trioecious.

trī·oi′cous, *a.* same as *trioecious.*

trī′ōle, *n.* in music, a triplet.

trī·ō′lē·āte, *n.* a salt of oleic acid.

trī·ō′le·fin, *n.* in chemistry, any of the aliphatic series of hydrocarbons containing three double bonds: they have the general formula C_nH_{2n-4}.

trī·ō′lē·in, *n.* an olein containing three oleic acid radicals.

trī′ō·let, *n.* [Fr., dim. of *trio*, three.] a poem or stanza having eight lines and two rhymes, the first line being repeated as the fourth and seventh, and the second as the eighth: the rhyme scheme is *abaaabab.*

-trī′ōne, in organic chemistry, a combining form used to indicate the presence of three ketone groups or, in one that is not a true ketone but a cyclic compound, three carbonyl groups.

trī·ōn′fō, *n.*; *pl.* **trī·ōn′fī**, in Italy, during the Middle Ages, an extravagant procession.

trī·on′y·chid, *n.* a soft-shelled turtle.

Trī·ō·nych′i·dae, *n.pl.* [*trionyx* and *-idæ.*] a family of fresh-water carnivorous turtles having a depressed carapace covered with a soft shell, native to the rivers of the Northern Hemisphere.

trī′ō·nym, *n.* [*tri-*, and Gr. *onyma*, name.] a name composed of three terms; a trinomial.

Trī′ō·nyx, *n.* [*tri-*, and Gr. *onyx, onychos*, a nail.] a genus of turtles, the type of the *Trionychidæ.*

trī′ŏr, *n.* in law, a person appointed by the court to examine whether a challenge to a panel of jurors or to any juror is just.

trī·or′chis, *n.* [Gr. *treis*, three, and *orchis*, testicle.] a person or animal having three testicles.

trī·or·thog′ō·năl, *a.* of, pertaining to, or consisting of three lines or systems of lines intersecting each other at right angles.

trī′ōse, *n.* a sugar containing three atoms of oxygen.

Trī·os′tē·um, *n.* [*tri-*, and Gr. *osteon*, bone.] a genus of coarse leafy plants of the *Caprifoliaceæ*, or honeysuckle family, with leaves narrowed at the base, but united around the simple stem, sessile flowers single or in clusters, and fleshy fruit. The most common species, *Triosteum perfoliatum*, is also called *feverwort.*

trī·ō′vū·lāte, *a.* having three ovules.

trī·ox′īde, trī·ox′id, *n.* a compound containing three atoms of oxygen to the molecule.

trip, *v.i.*; tripped (tript), *or occas.* tript, *pt., pp.*; tripping, *ppr.* [ME. *trippen*; OFr. *triper, treper*; prob. from M.D. *trippen*, to tread, trip.]
1. to run or step lightly; to move or walk with quick, light steps; to move the feet nimbly, as in running, walking, dancing, or the like.
2. to take a voyage or journey; to make a jaunt or excursion. [Rare.]
3. to stumble.
4. to make a wrong step, inaccuracy, or mistake; to err; to go wrong.
5. to falter in speaking.
6. to run past the pallet of the escapement: said of a tooth of the escapement wheel of a watch, etc.
7. to tilt; to tip.
8. to experience a trip (*n.* 10). [Slang.]

trip, *v.t.* 1. to cause to fall by striking the feet suddenly from under the person; to cause to stumble, make a false step, or lose the footing: often followed by *up*; as, to *trip* or *trip up* a man in wrestling.
2. to perform, as a dance, in a nimble, light manner.
3. to catch in a lie, offense, mistake, etc. (also with *up*).
4. (a) to cause to make a false step or mistake; (b) to cause to fail or stop; to obstruct.
5. (a) to release (a spring, wheel, or other mechanical part), as by the action of a detent; (b) to start or operate by this.
6. to tilt; to tip up.
7. in nautical usage, (a) to raise (an anchor) clear of the bottom; (b) to tilt (a yard) into position for lowering; (c) to raise (an upper mast) so that the fid may be removed before lowering.

trip, *n.* 1. a light, quick tread.
2. a going from one place to another, or a going to a place and returning; a journey, especially a short one; an excursion, voyage, jaunt, etc.
3. a stumble.
4. a mistake; blunder.
5. a faltering; a slip; a lapse.
6. a maneuver for causing someone to stumble or fall, as by catching his foot.
7. (a) any mechanical contrivance for tripping a part, as a pawl; (b) its action.
8. in nautical usage, a single board or tack in plying to windward. [Rare.]
9. in the fisheries, the catch of fish during a voyage; as, a good *trip* of seals; a bumper *trip.*
10. (a) the hallucinations, sensations, etc. experienced under the influence of a psychedelic drug, especially LSD; (b) the period or experience of being under such an influence; (c) an experience that is pleasing, exciting, unusual, etc.; (d) any activity, mode of conduct, state of mind, etc.; as, a spiritual *trip.* [Slang.]
round trip; see under *round.*
Syn.—stumble, failure, mistake, excursion, jaunt, ramble, tour.

trī·pal′mi·tin, *n.* same as *palmitin.*

tri·pang′, *n.* same as *trepang.*

trip′ȧ·rȧ, *n.* a woman who has borne three children.

trī′pärt·ed, *a.* [*tri-*, and L. *pars, partis*, part.] divided into three parts.

trī·pär′tīte, *a.* [L. *tripartitus*; *tri-*, for *tres*, three, and *partitus*, pp. of *partiri*, to divide.]
1. divided into three parts; threefold.
2. existing in three corresponding parts or copies.
3. made or existing between three parties; as, a *tripartite* treaty.
4. in botany, divided into three parts nearly to the base; as, a *tripartite* leaf.

trī·pär·ti′tion, *n.* 1. a division into three parts or among three parties.
2. a division by three, or the taking of a third part of any number or quantity.

trī·pas′chăl, *a.* continued through or embracing three Passovers.

trīpe, *n.* [ME.; OFr. *tripe, trippe*, from Ar. *tharb*, entrails, a net.]
1. the entrails generally; hence, the belly: generally used in the plural. [Obs.]
2. part of the stomach of ruminating animals when dressed and prepared for food.
How say you to a fat *tripe* finely broiled?
—Shak.
3. anything worthless, offensive, etc.; rubbish; trash. [Slang.]

trīpe′-dē-rōche′, *n.* [Fr., lit., tripe of the rock.] any of various lichens of the genera *Gyrophora* and *Umbilicaria.* It is used as an article of food in the arctic regions when no better food may be found. Although nutritious, it is bitter and purgative.

trip′el, *n.* same as *tripoli.*

trī·pen′nāte, *a.* same as *tripinnate.*

trī·pẽr′sŏn·ăl, *a.* in theology, of, relating to, or consisting of three persons: said of the Godhead.

trī·pẽr′sŏn·ăl·ist, *n.* a believer in a tripersonal Godhead or the Trinity; a Trinitarian.

trī·pẽr·sŏn·al′i·ty, *n.* the state or quality of existing as three persons in one Godhead; trinity.

trīp′ẽr·y, *n.* a place where tripe is prepared, or a store in which it is put on sale.

trīpe′stōne, *n.* a variety of anhydrite contorted in form and somewhat resembling tripe.

trī·pet′ăl·oid, *a.* in botany, appearing to have three petals.

trī·pet′ăl·ous, *a.* in botany, having three petals.

trip ġēar, a valve gear in which the valves are opened and closed by means of cams, levers, or catches.

trip′ham″mẽr, *n.* a heavy, power-driven hammer, alternately raised and allowed to fall by a tripping device: also *trip hammer.*

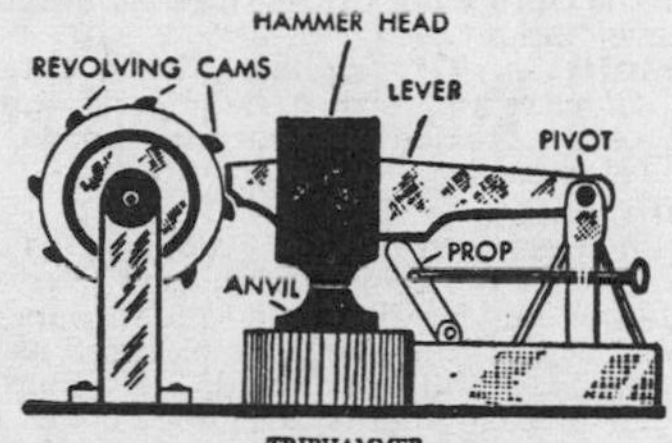

TRIPHAMMER

trī′phāne, *n.* same as *spodumene.*

trī′phāṣe, *a.* same as *three-phase.*

trī′phāṣ·ẽr, *n.* same as *three-phaser.*

Trī·phā′si·ȧ, *n.* [Gr. *triphasios,* triple.] a genus of Malayan plants of the family *Rutaceæ*: the species are thorny shrubs, with trifoliate leaves. The fruit of *Triphasia aurantiola,* which is preserved or eaten raw, has an acid taste.

trī·phā′ṣiç, *a.* triply varied or in triple phases.

trī·phen″yl·meth′āne (*or* trī-fē″nil-), *n.* a colorless, crystalline hydrocarbon, $CH(C_6H_5)_3$, used in organic synthesis and in making dyes.

triph′thoṅg, *n.* [*tri-* and di*phthong.*] a combination of three vowel sounds in a single syllable forming a simple or compound sound; also, loosely, a trigraph.

triph·thoṅ′găl, *a.* pertaining to a triphthong; consisting of a triphthong.

triph′y·līne, *n.* triphylite.

triph′y·līte, *n.* [from *tri-*, and Gr. *phylē,* a class; and *-ite.*] a greenish-blue, crystalline mineral, $LiFePO_4$, a native phosphate of lithium and iron.

trī·phyl′lous, *a.* [*tri-*, and Gr. *phyllon,* leaf.] in botany, having three leaves.

trī·pin′nāte, *a.* [*tri-*, and L. *pinnatus,* winged.] in botany, threefold pinnate; bipinnate with each division pinnate, as the leaves of some ferns.

trī·pin′nā·ted, *a.* tripinnate.

trī·pin·nat′i·fid, *a.* in botany, pinnatifid, with the segments twice divided in a pinnatifid manner.

trī·pin·nat′i·seçt, *a.* in botany, parted to the base in a tripinnate manner, as a leaf.

trī′plāne, *n.* an early type of airplane with three wings arranged one above another.

trī·plā′siăn (-zhăn), *a.* threefold. [Rare.]

trip′le, *a.* [Fr., from L. *triplus*; *tri-*, for *tres,* three, and *-plus,* related to *plenus,* full.]

1. threefold; consisting of or including three.
2. treble; three times repeated.
3. three times as much or as many.
4. being last of three. [Obs.]

Triple Alliance; (a) an alliance of England, Sweden, and the Netherlands against France in 1668; (b) an alliance of Great Britain, France, and the Netherlands against Spain in 1717; (c) an alliance of Great Britain, Austria, and Russia against France in 1795; (d) the Dreibund, an alliance of Germany, Austria, and Italy in 1882.

triple crown; the papal crown or tiara; also, in heraldry, a bearing.

Triple Entente; see under *entente.*

triple measure; triple time.

triple play; in baseball, a play by which three players are put out.

triple ratio; any ratio of three to one.

triple salt; in chemistry, a salt considered to be a molecular combination of three different salts.

triple star; three stars closely grouped.

triple time; musical time or rhythm having three beats to the measure, with the first beat accented.

trip′le, *n.* 1. an amount three times as much or as many.
2. a group of three; a triad.
3. in baseball, a three-base hit.

trip′le, *v.t.*; tripled, *pt., pp.*; tripling, *ppr.* to make threefold, or thrice as much or as many.

trip′le, *v.i.* 1. to become three times as much or as many.
2. in baseball, to hit a triple.

trip′le-crowned′, *a.* 1. having three crowns.
2. wearing a triple crown, as the Pope.

trip′le-ex·pan′sion, *a.* designating a system of utilizing steam by means of three cylinders or sets of cylinders, in which the steam is expanded.

trī′ple-ex·pan′sion en′ġine, a steam engine with three cylinders or sets of cylinders, in which the steam is successively expanded.

trip′le-head″ed (-hed″), *a.* having three heads.

trip′le·nẽrved′, *a.* in botany, having three nerves, or veins; specifically, having three nerves arising from or near the base, as some leaves.

trip′le-ribbed, *a.* in botany, having a pair of large ribs branching off from the main one above the base, as in the leaves of many species of sunflower.

trip′let, *n.* 1. a collection or group of three, usually of one kind.
2. in poetry, a group of three successive lines, usually rhyming.
3. in music, three notes sung or played in the time of two of the same value.
4. (a) one of three children brought forth at the same birth; (b) [*pl.*] three offspring born at a single birth.
5. in optics, a system of three lenses so disposed as to counteract the effects of spherical and chromatic aberration; loosely; any three lenses in combination.
6. [*pl.*] three links of a chain, as those joining the cable and ring of the anchor of a ship.

trip′le·tāil, *n.* any of a group of large food fishes of warm seas, of the genus *Lobotes,* having long hind fins that extend back along the caudal fin so as to give the effect of a three-lobed tail.

trī′plex, *a.* [L.; *tri-*, and *-plex-*, -fold, from base of *plaga,* surface.] triple; threefold.

trī′plex, *n.* 1. a thing that is triplex.
2. triple time.

trip′li·çāte, *v.t.*; triplicated, *pt., pp.*; triplicating, *ppr.* to treble or make threefold.

trip′li·çāte, *a.* [L. *triplicatus,* pp. of *triplicare,* to treble; *tri-*, for *tres,* three, and *plicare,* to fold.]
1. made in or forming three identical copies.
2. threefold; triple.

triplicate ratio; the ratio of the cubes of two quantities.

trip′li·çāte, *n.* one of three identical copies or things.

in triplicate; in three identical copies.

trip′li·çāte-tẽr′nāte, *a.* in botany, thrice ternate; triternate.

trip·li·çā′tion, *n.* 1. the act of triplicating or being triplicated.
2. anything triplicate or threefold.
3. in civil law, surrejoinder.

trī·plic′i·ty, *n.*; *pl.* **trī·plic′i·tieṣ,** [Fr. *triplicité,* from L. *triplex,* threefold.]
1. trebleness; the state or quality of being triple.
2. a union or group of three; a triad.
3. in astrology, a trigon.

trip·li·cos′tāte, *a.* triple-ribbed.

trip′līte, *n.* [G. *triplit,* from Gr. *triplous,* threefold.] an imperfectly crystallized, dark-brown mineral, a fluophosphate of manganese and iron, $(Fe, Mn)_2 FPO_4$.

trip·lō·blas′tiç, *a.* [Gr. *triploos,* triple, and *blastos,* germ.] having three blastodermic layers or membranes, as most animals.

trip′loid, *a.* in biology, having three times the haploid number of chromosomes.

trip′loi·dīte, *n.* a brownish, translucent, hydrous phosphate, similar to triplite.

trip′lō·py, trip·lō′pi·ȧ, *n.* [Gr. *triploos,* triple, and *ōps, opos,* eye.] an ailment of the eye which causes objects to appear threefold.

trip′ly, *adv.* in a triple amount or degree.

trip′mad″ăm, *n.* a plant, *Sedum reflexum,* a variety of stonecrop.

trī′pod, *n.* [L. *tripus*; Gr. *tripous*; *tri-*, for *treis,* three, and *pous, podos,* foot.]
1. a caldron, stool, table, etc. having three legs; specifically, the bench, stool, or seat upon which the priests and sibyls in ancient times were placed to render oracles.
2. a frame or support, having three legs, used for cameras, telescopes, etc., usually adjustable for height.
3. in anatomy and zoology, a formation resembling a tripod.

trī′pod, *a.* having three legs; adapted for use with a tripod; as, a *tripod* camera.

trip′ō·dăl, *a.* [*tripod* and *-al.*] having three legs or feet, as a stool.

trī·pō′di·ăn, *n.* a stringed instrument of ancient times, formed like a tripod.

trī·pod′iç, *a.* [*tripod* and *-ic.*] of the form of a tripod; having or using three feet.

trip′ō·dy, *n.*; *pl.* **trip′ō·dieṣ,** a verse or phrase of three metrical feet.

trip′ō·li, *n.* [from *Tripoli,* Africa.] a light, porous rock, white, gray, pink, red, buff, or yellow in color, consisting of weathered chert and siliceous limestones: it is used as a polishing powder and abrasive: also called *rottenstone, tripoli powder* (or *stone*).

trip′ō·line, *a.* pertaining to tripoli.

Trip′ō·line, *a.* and *n.* Tripolitan.

Tri·pol′i·tăn, *a.* of Tripoli, its people, or culture.

Tri·pol′i·tăn, *n.* a native or inhabitant of Tripoli.

trip′ō·līte, *n.* tripoli.

trī′pos, *n.*; *pl.* **trī′pos·eṣ,** [L. *tripus,* tripod.]
1. originally, a tripod.
2. at Cambridge University, (a) formerly, a scholar who sat on a three-legged stool at commencement and disputed humorously with candidates for a degree; (b) any of the examinations for the B. A. degree with honors, originally for honors in mathematics.
3. a tripos paper.
4. one who prepares a tripospaper.

trī′pos pā′pẽr, at Cambridge University, any one of the sets of questions in a tripos (sense 2a).

trip′pănt, *a.* in heraldry, tripping: a term applied to beasts of chase, as *passant* is to beasts of prey, etc. The animal is represented with the right foot lifted up, and the other three feet upon the ground.

STAG TRIPPANT

trip′pẽr, *n.* 1. one who or that which trips; one who walks nimbly.
2. a tourist; a traveler. [Brit. Colloq.]
3. in machinery, a piece of mechanism that releases, or trips, a catch, as a cam, pawl, etc.; also, a tripping device that operates a signal on a railroad.
4. a conductor or motorman having no regular run but working as an extra man. [Colloq.]

trip′pet, *n.* in machinery, a part designed to strike another part at regular intervals.

trip′ping, *a.* 1. stepping nimbly and lightly.
2. quick; nimble.

trip′ping, *n.* 1. the act of one who or that which trips.
2. a light, graceful dance.
3. in nautical usage, the loosing of an anchor from the ground by its cable or buoy-rope.

trip′ping çoil, in electricity, a coil that forms part of an automatic circuit breaker.

trip′ping līne, in nautical usage, (a) a line attached to a yard to assist in lowering it to the deck of a vessel; (b) a line for tripping the anchor.

trip′ping link, in nautical usage, a link comprising a hook closed by a ring which may be opened by pulling on the tripping line.

trip′ping·ly, *adv.* in a tripping manner.

Trip′sȧ·çum, *n.* [etym. uncertain.] a genus of American grasses, including the gama grass: they are perennial, tall, and coarse, and have flowering spikelets.

trip′sis, *n.* [Gr., a rubbing, from *tribein,* to rub.] trituration; also, the process of shampooing.

trip′tāne, *n.* [contr. from *tripentane.*] a high antiknock fuel for use in internal-combustion engines, especially in airplanes.

trip′tẽr·ous, *a.* [from *tri-*, and Gr. *pteron*, wing; and *-ous.*] having three winglike parts, as some fruits or seeds.

Trip·tol′e·mus, Trip·tol′e·mos, *n.* in Greek mythology, a legendary hero who was supposed to have given man the secret of cultivating grain.

trip′tych, *n.* [from Gr. *triptychos*, threefold, from *tri-*, for *treis*, three, and *ptyx*, *ptychos*, a fold.]

1. an ancient writing tablet of three leaves hinged or tied together.

2. a set of three panels with pictures, designs, or carvings, often hinged so that the two side panels may be folded over the central one: it is used as an altarpiece, etc.

TRIPTYCH

trī·pū′di·ăr·y, *a.* [L. *tripudium*, a religious dance.] pertaining to dancing; performed by dancing. [Rare.]

trī·pū′di·āte, *v.i.* [L. *tripudiatus*, pp. of *tripudiare*, to dance as a religious act.] to dance. [Rare.]

trī·pū·di·ā′tion, *n.* the act of dancing. [Rare.]

trī·quäd·ran′tăl, *a.* having three quadrants: said of a spherical triangle.

trī·quē′trăl, *a.* same as *triquetrous.*

trī·quē′trous, *a.* [L. *triquetrus*, three-cornered.]

1. triangular.
2. having a triangular cross section.
3. trihedral.

trī·quē′trum, *n.*; *pl.* **trī·quē′trȧ**, 1. the cuneiform bone of the wrist.

2. any Wormian bone.

trī·rā′di·ăl, *a.* triradiate.

trī·rā′di·āte, *a.* [*tri-*, and L. *radiatus*, beaming.] having three rays or raylike projections; radiating in three directions; three-forked.

trī·rā′di·ā·ted, *a.* same as *triradiate.*

trī·rec·tan′gū·lăr, *a.* having three right angles, as a spherical triangle.

trī′rēme, *n.* [Fr. *trirème*, from L. *triremis*, having three banks of oars; *tri-*, for *tres*, three, and *remus*, oar.] an ancient Greek or Roman galley, usually a warship, with three benches or ranks of oars on each side.

trī·rhom·boid′ăl, *a.* having three rhomboidal faces or sides.

trī·sac′chȧ·rīde, *n.* a carbohydrate yielding three monosaccharides upon hydrolysis.

trī·sac″rȧ·men·tãr′i·ăn, *n.* one of a religious sect who maintain that three sacraments and no more are essential to salvation, namely, baptism, the Eucharist, and penance.

Tris·ag′i·on, *n.* [Gr. *tris-*, for *treis*, three, and *agion*, neut. of *agios*, holy.] an ancient hymn in whose beginning the word *holy* is repeated three times in addressing God.

trī·sect′, *v.t.*; trisected, *pt.*, *pp.*; trisecting, *ppr.* 1. to cut or divide into three parts.

2. in geometry, to divide into three equal parts.

trī·sec′tion, *n.* [*tri-*, and L. *sectus*, pp. of *secare*, to cut.] the division of a thing into three parts; in geometry, the division of an angle or of an arc into three equal parts.

trī·sec′tŏr, *n.* a line, plane, etc. that trisects.

trī·sep′ȧ·lous, *a.* having three sepals.

trī·sep′tāte, *a.* [*tri-* and *septate.*] in botany and zoology, having three septa, or dividing walls.

trī·sē′ri·ăl, *a.* 1. arranged in three series or rows.

2. in botany, having only three verticils.

trī·sē′ri·āte, *a.* same as *triserial.*

tris′kēle, *n.* a triskelion.

tris·kel′i·ŏn, *n.* a design, usually symbolic, consisting of three curved branches or three bent legs or arms radiating from a center.

Tris·mē·gis′tus, see *Hermes Trismegistus.*

tris′mic, *a.* of, or having the nature of, trismus.

tris′mus, *n.* [Gr. *trismos*, a grinding, from *trizein*, to grind the teeth.] lockjaw.

tris·nī′trāte, *n.* [Gr. *tris*, thrice, and *nitrate.*] trinitrate. [Obs.]

tris·oc·tȧ·hē′drăl, *a.* of, or having the form of, a trisoctahedron.

tris·oc·tȧ·hē′drŏn, *n.* [Gr. *tris*, thrice; and *octahedron.*] a solid figure or crystal with twenty-four plane surfaces, every three of which correspond to a single surface of an octahedron imagined as underlying them: trisoctahedrons are of two kinds, the *trigonal trisoctahedron*, having triangular surfaces, and the *tetragonal trisoctahedron*, or *trapezohedron*, having quadrilateral surfaces.

trī′spast, trī·spas′ton, *n.* [*tri-*, and Gr. *span*, to draw.] a machine with three pulleys for raising great weights.

trī·spẽr′mous, *a.* [*tri-*, and Gr. *sperma*, seed.] three-seeded; containing three seeds.

trī·splan̄ch′nic, *a.* in anatomy, supplying the three great body cavities and their viscera; as, the *trisplanchic* nerves.

trī·spŏr′ic, *a.* having three spores.

trī·spŏr′ous, *a.* trisporic.

trist, *n.* and *v.* trust. [Obs.]

trist, triste, *n.* and *v.* tryst. [Obs.]

trïste, *a.* [Fr.] sad; sorrowful.

trī·stē′ȧ·rin, *n.* same as *stearin.*

trïs·tesse′, *n.* [Fr.] sadness; melancholy.

trist′ful, *a.* sad; sorrowful; gloomy.

trist′fụl·ly, *adv.* sadly.

tris′tich, *n.* a group or stanza of three lines of verse; a triplet.

tris′tich·ous, *a.* [Gr. *tris-*, for *treis*, three, and *stichos*, a row.] in botany, arranged or standing in three vertical rows, as parts, leaves, etc.

trī·stig·mat′ic, *a.* having three stigmas, as a flower.

trī·stig′mȧ·tōse, *a.* tristigmatic.

Tris′tăn, *n.* see *Tristram.*

tris·ti′ti·āte (-tish′i-), *v.t.* to make sad. [Obs.]

Tris′tō·mȧ, *n.* [Gr. *tri-*, for *treis*, three, and *stoma*, mouth.]

1. a genus of trematode worms, mostly of a broad oval shape, infesting the skin and gills of fishes.

2. [t–] any worm of the genus *Tristoma.*

Tris′trăm, *n.* in medieval legend, a knight sent to Ireland by King Mark of Cornwall to bring back the princess Isolde to be the king's bride: Isolde (called *the Fair*) and Tristram unwittingly drink a magic potion, fall in love, and ultimately die together; in some versions, Tristram is married to another Isolde (called *Isolde of the White Hand*): the story is the subject of a number of poems and of an opera by Wagner (*Tristan und Isolde*).

trist′y, *a.* trist. [Obs.]

trī·stȳ′lous, *a.* in botany, having three styles.

trī′sulc, *n.* something having three furrows or three prongs. [Obs.]

trī·sul′cāte, *a.* having three furrows: used in botany and zoology; as, a *trisulcate* foot; a *trisulcate* stem.

trī·sul′fīde, trī·sul′fid, *n.* a sulfide containing three atoms of sulfur to the molecule.

trī·syl·lab′ic, *a.* having three syllables.

trī·syl·lab′ic, *n.* a metrical foot of three syllables.

trī·syl·lab′i·căl, *a.* same as *trisyllabic.*

trī·syl·lab′i·căl·ly, *adv.* in or as three syllables.

trī·syl′lȧ·ble (*or* tri-), *n.* a word of three syllables.

trīte, *a.*; *comp.* triter; *superl.* tritest, [L. *tritus*, pp. of *terere*, to rub, wear.] worn out; common; used till so common as to have lost its novelty and interest; hackneyed; stale; as, a *trite* remark; a *trite* subject.

trīte′ly, *adv.* in a trite manner.

trīte′ness, *n.* the quality or state of being trite.

trī·tẽr′nāte, *a.* in botany, three times ternate: applied to a petiole which separates into three and is again divided at each point into three and on each of these nine points bears three leaflets.

trī′thē·ism, *n.* [*tri-*, Gr. *theos*, god, and *-ism.*] the doctrine of the existence of three distinct gods; specifically, in Christian theology, the doctrine that the Father, Son, and Holy Spirit are separate and distinct Gods.

trī′thē·ist, *n.* one who believes in the doctrine of tritheism.

trī·thē·is′tic, *a.* pertaining to tritheism.

trī·thē·is′ti·căl, *a.* tritheistic.

trī′thē·īte, *n.* a tritheist.

trī′thing, *n.* one of the three administrative divisions of Yorkshire, England; a riding. [Brit.]

trī·thī′ŏn·āte, *n.* a salt of trithionic acid.

trī·thi·on′ic, *a.* pertaining to or designating an acid, $H_2S_3O_6$.

trit′i·căl, *a.* trite; common. [Obs.]

trit′i·căl·ness, *n.* triteness. [Obs.]

trī·ti′ceous, *a.* [L. *triticeus.*] in anatomy, resembling a grain of wheat; nodular.

Trit′i·cum, *n.* [L. *triticeus*, of wheat, wheaten.] an important genus of grasses, containing two distinct groups; one, which includes wheat, *Triticum vulgare*, consists of annual plants, with ovate-oblong, boat-shaped glumes; the other includes perennials, with nearly lanceolate glumes and two ranked spikes. To the former belong all the varieties of wheat; the latter includes the troublesome weed, couch grass or quitch, *Triticum repens.*

trit′i·um (*or* trish′), *n.* [Mod. L., from Gr. *tritos*, third, and L. *-ium*, n. suffix.] an isotope of hydrogen having an atomic weight of 3: symbol, T or H^3.

trī′tō·cēre, *n.* [Gr. *tritos*, third, and *keras*, horn.] that development in a stag's antlers after the third year, or the third tine in order of development.

trī′tō·mīte, *n.* [Gr. *tritomos*, thrice cut, and *-ite.*] a vitreous, brown, isometric mineral composed of calcium, thorium, boron, and other elements.

Trī′tŏn, *n.* [L.; Gr. *Tritōn*, a Triton.]

1. in Greek and Latin mythology, (a) a son of Poseidon and Amphitrite, who lived with his father and mother in a golden palace on the bottom of the sea. He is pictured as having the head and upper body of a man and the tail of a fish and as carrying a conch-shell trumpet; (b) later, one of many attendants of the sea gods.

2. a genus of gastropodous mollusks, including the sea trumpet, triton shell, or conch shell; also, [t–] a shell of this genus.

3. a genus of batrachian reptiles or aquatic salamanders. Among the best known species are the crested newt, *Triton* or *Hemisalamandra cristatus*, the straight-lipped newt, *Triton bibronii*, and the marbled newt, *Molge marmorata*; also, [t–] a member of this genus.

trī′tōne, *n.* [ML. *tritonus*; Gr. *tritonos*, of three tones; *tri-*, for *treis*, three, and *tonos*, a tone.] in music, an interval of three whole tones.

Trī′tŏn's horn, a trumpet shell.

tri·tō′pin, *n.* an alkaloid of opium, $C_{42}H_{54}N_2O_7$, crystallizing in scales and prisms.

trī·tō′ri·um, *n.* same as *triturium.*

trī·tō′vum, *n.*; *pl.* **trī·tō′vȧ**, [LL., from Gr. *tritos*, third, and L. *ovum*, egg.] an ovum in its third stage.

trī·tō·zō′oid, *n.* [Gr. *tritos*, third, *zōon*, a living being, and *-oid.*] in zoology, a zooid produced by a deuterozooid; a zooid of the third generation.

trit′ū·rȧ·ble, *a.* capable of being triturated.

trit′ū·răl, *a.* adapted for grinding, as the teeth of certain animals.

trit′ū·rāte, *v.t.*; triturated, *pt.*, *pp.*; triturating, *ppr.* [from LL. *trituratus*, pp. of *triturare*, to grind, from L. *tritura*, a rubbing, from *terere*, to rub.] to grind; to rub; to crush; specifically, to grind to powder; to pulverize.

trit′ū·rāte, *n.* 1. a triturated substance.

2. a trituration (sense 2).

trit·ū·rā′tion, *n.* 1. the act of triturating or being triturated.

2. in pharmacy, a triturated drug, especially one containing a pulverized mixture of a medicinal substance with lactose.

trit′ū·rā·tŏr, *n.* a person or thing that triturates.

trit′ūre, *n.* a rubbing or grinding. [Obs.]

trī·tū′ri·um, *n.*; *pl.* **trī·tū′ri·ȧ**, [L. *tritus*, pp. of *terere*, to rub.] a vessel for separating liquids of different densities.

trit′yl, *n.* [Gr. *tritos*, third, and *-yl.*] propyl. [Obs.]

trit′yl·ēne, *n.* propylene. [Obs.]

Trī·tyl′ō·don, *n.* [L. *tri-*, three, and Gr. *tylos*, knob, and *odon*, *odontos*, tooth.] in paleontology, a genus of lower Mesozoic mammals, closely allied to the reptiles: they were multituberculate and had premolars resembling true molars.

Trī·um·fet′tȧ, *n.* [LL., named after G. B. *Trionfetti*, Italian botanist.] a genus of tropical shrubs and herbs of the linden family, which bear flowers with numerous stamens.

Triumfetta rhomboidea and *Triumfetta semitriloba* yield valuable fiber.

trī'umph, *n.* [OFr. *triumphe, triomphe*; L. *triumphus*, from Gr. *thriambos*, a hymn to Bacchus sung in festal processions to his honor.]
1. in ancient Rome, a procession celebrating the return of a victorious general and his army.
2. the state of being victorious.
3. achievement; successful undertaking; success; victory.
4. joy or exultation for success; great gladness; rejoicing.
5. any public spectacle or celebration. [Obs.]
6. an old game of cards; also, a trump card. [Obs.]
to ride triumph; to be in full career; to take the lead.

trī'umph, *v.i.*; triumphed (-umft), *pt., pp.*; triumphing, *ppr.* [OFr. *triumpher*; L. *triumphare*, from the n.]
1. to gain victory or success; to be victorious or successful; to win mastery.
2. to rejoice or exult over victory, achievement, etc.
3. to celebrate a Roman triumph.
4. to be prosperous; to flourish.
5. to play a winning card; to trump. [Obs.]

trī'umph, *v.t.* 1. to succeed in overcoming; to surmount; to subdue; to conquer. [Obs.]
2. to cause to triumph. [Obs.]

trī·um'phăl, *a.* [L. *triumphalis*.]
1. of, or having the nature of, a triumph.
2. celebrating or commemorating a triumph.
triumphal arch; originally, a temporary arch erected for the triumph of a Roman general, and through which he and his army passed; afterward, a permanent structure, often having a central and two side archways. Besides the Arch of Titus there are several other triumphal arches at Rome. Arches of a similar kind have also been erected in modern times.

TRIUMPHAL ARCH—Arch of Titus, Rome

triumphal column; among the Romans, a column erected in commemoration of a victor or a victory.

trī·um'phăl, *n.* a token of victory. [Obs.]

trī·um'phănt, *a.* [L. *triumphans (-antis)*, ppr. of *triumphare*, to triumph.]
1. successful; victorious.
2. rejoicing for victory; exulting in success; elated.
3. triumphal. [Now Rare.]
4. magnificent. [Obs.]
A most *triumphant* lady. —Shak.

trī·um'phănt·ly, *adv.* in a triumphant manner.

trī'umph·ẽr, *n.* 1. one who triumphs or rejoices for victory.
2. in ancient Rome, one who was honored with a triumph.

trī'umph·ing·ly, *adv.* in a triumphing manner.

trī·um'vir, *n.*; *pl.* **trī·um'virs, trī·um'vi·rī,** [L. *trium*, genit. of *tres*, three, and *vir*, man.]
1. in ancient Rome, any of a group of three administrators sharing authority equally.
2. any of three persons associated in office or authority.

trī·um'vi·răl, *a.* relating to a triumvir or triumvirate.

trī·um'vi·rāte, *n.* [L. *triumviratus*.]
1. the office, functions, or term of a triumvir.
2. government by three men or by a coalition of three parties.
3. any association of three in authority.
4. any group or set of three persons or, rarely, things.

trī·um'vi·ry, *n.* a triumvirate. [Obs.]

trī'ūne, *a.* [from *tri-*, and L. *unus*, one.] three in one: an epithet applied to God, to express the unity of the Godhead in a trinity of persons.

trī'ūne, *n.* 1. a triad.
2. [T–] the trinity.

trī·uñ'gū·lin, *n.* the earliest larval stage of certain species of beetle, as the oil beetle.

trī·uñ'gū·lus, *n.* [*tri-*, and L. *ungula*, a claw, talon, hoof.] the parasitic triungulin form of the larva of the oil beetle.

trī·ū″ni·tăr'i·ăn, *n.* a Trinitarian.

trī·ū'ni·ty, *n.* the state or quality of being triune; trinity.

trī'vā·lence (*or* triv'ȧ-), *n.* the condition or quality of being trivalent.

trī·vā'len·cy (*or* triv'ȧ-), *n.* trivalence.

trī'vā·lent (*or* triv'ȧ-), *a.* [*tri-* and *-valent*.]
1. having a valence of three.
2. having three valences.
Also, esp. for sense 2, *tervalent*.

trī'valve, *a.* having three valves, as a shell.

trī'valve, *n.* a trivalvular shell.

trī·val'vū·lăr, *a.* three-valved; having three valves.

triv'ănt, *n.* a truant. [Obs.]

trī·vẽr'bi·ăl, *a.* in ancient Rome, of or pertaining to certain days in the Roman calendar which were juridical, or allowed to the praetor for deciding causes: so named from the three special words of his office, *do, dico, addico*.

triv'et, *n.* [L. *tripes*; *tri-*, for *tres*, three, and *pes, pedis*, foot.]
1. a three-legged stand for holding pots, kettles, etc. over or near a fire.
2. a short-legged metal plate for holding hot dishes on a table.
right as a trivet; firm; stable; solid; in good order.

triv'et, *n.* [etym. uncertain.] a knife used by velvet weavers to cut the loops formed over wires and thus form the pile.

triv'et tā'ble, a table with three legs.

triv'i·ȧ, *n.pl.* [Mod. L., pl.: see *trivial*.] unimportant matters; trivialities; trifles.

triv'i·ăl, *a.* [L. *trivialis*, of the crossroads, hence commonplace, from *trivium*, a place where three roads meet; *tri-*, three, and *via*, road.]
1. trifling; of little worth or importance; as, a *trivial* subject; a *trivial* affair.
2. commonplace. [Archaic.]
3. occupying oneself with trifles; trifling. [Rare.]
4. relating to or of the trivium.
5. in botany and zoology, (a) popular, as distinguished from technical; as, the *trivial* name of a tree; (b) specific, as distinguished from generic; as, in the name *Pinus sylvestris*, the Scotch pine, *sylvestris* is the *trivial*, or specific, name.

triv'i·ăl, *n.* 1. any one of the studies of the trivium.
2. [*often pl.*] a trivial matter.

triv'i·ăl·ism, *n.* 1. trivial character.
2. a triviality.

triv·i·al'i·ty, *n.* 1. a trivial state or quality.
2. *pl.* **triv·i·al'i·ties,** a trivial thing or matter.

triv'i·ăl·ly, *adv.* in a trivial way.

triv'i·ăl·ness, *n.* triviality.

triv'i·um, *n.*; *pl.* **triv'i·ȧ,** [L., a place where three roads meet.]
1. in the Middle Ages, the lower division of the seven liberal arts, consisting of the three arts, grammar, logic, and rhetoric: the other four were called the *quadrivium*.
2. the three anterior radii of a holothurian or other echinoid considered collectively, as distinguished from the *bivium*, or posterior pair.

trī·vol'tin, *n.* [*tri-*, It. *volto*, turn, and *-in*.] a kind of silkworm having three generations each year, or three crops of cocoons.

trī·week'ly, *a.* and *adv.* 1. (occurring, performed, or appearing) every three weeks.
2. (happening, performed, or appearing) thrice a week; as, a *triweekly* newspaper.

trī·week'ly, *n.*; *pl.* **trī·week'lies,** a publication that appears triweekly.

-trix, *pl.* **-trix'es, -tri·cēs'** (*or* -trī'sēs), [L.] an ending of some feminine nouns of agent, corresponding to the masculine form *-(t)or*, as in avia*trix*.

Trō'ad, *n.* Troas: also *the Troad*.

Trō'as, *n.* the ancient region in Asia Minor in which Troy was located: also called *the Troad*.

trōat, *v.i.* [prob. imitative.] to cry, as a buck in rutting time.

trōat, *n.* the cry of a buck at rutting time.

trō'căr, *n.* [Fr., from *trois*, three, and *carre*, a side, face.] a surgical instrument consisting of a sharp stylet enclosed in a tube (cannula) and inserted through the containing wall of a body cavity: the stylet is withdrawn permitting fluid to drain off through the tube.

trō'chȧ, *n.* [Sp.] in Spanish America, a barrier; usually, a sort of fence with intrenchments, forts, etc., to obstruct the movements of an armed force.

trō·chā'iç, *a.* [from Fr. *trochaïque* or L. *trochaicus*; Gr. *trochaikos*.] of or made up of trochees.

trō·chā'iç, *n.* 1. a trochaic verse.
2. a trochee.

trō·chā'i·căl, *a.* trochaic.

trō'chăl, *a.* [Gr. *trochos*, a wheel.] in zoology, resembling a wheel.

trō·chan'tẽr, *n.* [Gr. *trochantēr*, a runner, the ball on which the hip bone turns in its socket, from *trechein*, to run.]
1. any of several jutting processes at the upper end of the femur of many vertebrates. In man there are two, the major and minor.
2. a short ring next to the coxa, forming the second joint of the leg of an insect.

trō·chan·tē'ri·ăn, *a.* trochanteric.

trō·chan·ter'iç, *a.* relating to trochanters or to a trochanter.

trō·chan'tin, trō·chan'tine, *n.* 1. the trochanter minor. [Rare.]
2. a sclerite forming a part either of the trochanter or of the coxa of the leg of an insect.

trō'chăr, *n.* same as *trocar*.

trō'chāte, *a.* [Gr. *trochos*, a wheel.]
1. wheel-shaped.
2. having a wheel-shaped disk.

trō'chē, *n.* [shortened from *trochisk*; Fr. *trochisque*; L. *trochiscus*, a pill; Gr. *trochiskos*, a lozenge, from *trochos*, a round cake.] a small, usually round, medicinal lozenge. It is intended to be gradually dissolved in the mouth and slowly swallowed, as a demulcent, etc.

trō'chee, *n.* [L. *trochæus*; Gr. *trochaios*, running, from *trechein*, to run.] a metrical foot consisting of two syllables, the first long and the second short; or, in accented verse, a foot with the accent on the first syllable only; thus: What' a | pret'ty | tale' you | told' me, | etc.

Troch'i·dae, *n.pl.* a family of marine gastropods typified by the genus *Trochus*.

trō·chif'ẽr·ous, *a.* in zoology, having a wheel-like part.

trō'chil, *n.* [Gr. *trochilos*.] a bird, the trochilus. [Obs.]

Troch'i·lī, *n.pl.* same as *Trochilidæ*.

trō·chil'iç, *a.* [Gr. *trochilia*, a revolving cylinder, from *trochos*, a wheel.] having power to turn round. [Rare.]

trō·chil'içs, *n.* the science of rotary motion. [Rare.]

Trō·chil'i·dae, *n.pl.* the humming birds, a family of extremely minute, passerine birds, chiefly tropical American.

trō·chil'i·dist, *n.* a specialist in the study of the *Trochilidæ*. [Rare.]

troch'i·line, *a.* relating to the *Trochilidæ*.

troch'i·lus, *n.*; *pl.* **troch'i·lī,** [L., from Gr. *trochilos*, a small bird.]
1. a small Egyptian bird thought by the ancients to accompany the crocodile and pick its teeth; crocodile bird.
2. a kind of hummingbird.
3. any of several European warblers.
4. [T–] the type genus of the *Trochilidæ*.

troch'i·lus, *n.*; *pl.* **troch'i·lī,** [L.] in architecture, same as *scotia*.

trō'chin, *n.* [L. *trochinus*.] in anatomy, the lesser tuberosity of the humerus.

trō'ching, *n.* one of the small branches surmounting the antler of a stag.

trō·chin'i·ăn, *a.* of or pertaining to the trochin.

trō·chis'çus, *n.*; *pl.* **trō·chis'cī,** in pharmacy, a troche (lozenge).

trō'chisk, *n.* a troche (lozenge). [Obs.]

trō'chīte, *n.* [Gr. *trochos*, a wheel, and *-ite*.] a wheelstone; an entrochite.

troch'i·tẽr, *n.* in anatomy, the greater tuberosity of the humerus.

troch·i·tē'ri·ăn, *a.* of or pertaining to the trochiter.

trō·chit'iç, *a.* of or pertaining to a trochite.

troch'lē·ȧ, *n.*; *pl.* **troch'lē·ae,** [L., from Gr.

trochilia, a pulley.] in anatomy, a pulley-shaped part or structure; specifically, the lower part of the humerus, which articulates with a corresponding part of the ulna.

troch'lē·ăr, *a.* of the nature of, resembling, or serving as a pulley; specifically, (a) in anatomy of or like a pulley; also, situated near or connected with a trochlea; (b) in botany, short, circular, compressed, and contracted in the middle.

trochlear muscle; same as *pathetic muscle* under *pathetic*.

trochlear nerve; same as *pathetic nerve* under *pathetic*.

troch·lē·ăr'i·form, *a.* trochlear.

troch·lē·ā'ris, *n.* in anatomy, (a) the trochlear muscle; (b) the trochlear nerve.

troch'lē·ā·ry, *a.* in anatomy, same as *trochlear*.

troch'lē·āte, *a.* in botany, same as *trochlear*.

trō'choid, *a.* [Gr. *trochos*, a wheel, and *-oid*.]
1. having a wheellike rotary motion, as, in anatomy, a pivotal organ or part.
2. in geometry, same as *trochoidal*.
3. in conchology, (a) conical with a flat base; (b) of or pertaining to the genus *Trochus*.

trō'choid, *n.* 1. a curve produced by a point on or connected with a circle rolling along a straight line.
2. in geometry, same as *cycloid*.
3. in conchology, a shell shaped like a top; any shell of the genus *Trochus* or family *Trochidæ*.

trō·choid'ăl, *a.* 1. in geometry, of the nature of or pertaining to a trochoid.
2. in anatomy and conchology, same as *trochoid*.

trō·choi'dēs, *n.* in anatomy, a pivotlike joint; an articulation by a pivot turning within a ring or by a ring turning around a pivot.

trō·chom'e·tēr, *n.* [Gr. *trochos*, a wheel, and *-meter*.] an instrument for computing the revolutions of a wheel.

troch'ō·phōre, *n.* [Gr. *trochos*, a wheel; and *-phore*.] a free-swimming ciliated larva of marine annelid worms and certain other aquatic invertebrates.

troch'ō·sphēre, *n.* a trochophore.

troch·ō·spher'i·căl, *a.* of the nature of or pertaining to a trochosphere.

Troch·ō·zō'ȧ, *n.pl.* [LL., pl. of *trochozoön*.] a group of invertebrates, as annelids, mollusks, polyzoans, etc., whose larval forms in one stage are trochophores.

troch·ō·zō'on, *n.* [LL., from Gr. *trochos*, a wheel, and *zōon*, a living being, animal.] any one of the *Trochozoa*, or any one of the hypothetical ancestors of such invertebrates.

trō'chus, *n.*; *pl.* **trō'chi**, [L. *trochus*, a hoop or top; Gr. *trochos*, a wheel.]
1. a shell of the genus *Trochus*.
2. [T–] the top shells, a genus of gastropods of the family *Trochidæ*. The shell has a flattened base, and is of pyramidal shape.

trō'cō, *n.* [Sp. *truco*, a kind of table.] an old English game played on a lawn with wooden balls and a cue ending in a spoon-shaped iron projection: also called *lawn billiards*.

trod, *v.* past tense and alternative past participle of *tread*.

trŏd'den, trod, *a.* trampled; crushed; degraded.

trod'den, *v.* alternative past participle of *tread*.

trōde, *v.* archaic past tense of *tread*.

trog'lō·dȳte, *n.* [Fr., from Gr. *trōglodytēs*, one who creeps into holes, a cave dweller; *trōglē*, a cave, and *dyein*, to creep in, enter.]
1. a cave dweller; a member of an ancient or prehistoric people that lived in caves.
2. (a) a hermit; recluse; (b) anyone who lives in a primitive, low, or degenerate fashion.
3. a wren.
4. an anthropoid ape, as the chimpanzee or gorilla.

Trog·lō·dȳ'tēs, *n.* 1. a genus of insessorial birds; the wrens.
2. a genus of anthropoid apes.

trog·lō·dyt'iç, trog·lō·dyt'i·căl, *a.* of a troglodyte or troglodytes.

trō'gon, *n.* [Gr. *trōgōn*, gnawing, ppr. of *trōgein*, to gnaw.]
1. a genus of bright-colored tropical birds. There are many species, including the peacock trogon, *Trogon pavoninus* or *Calurus resplendens*, which is native to Central America.

TROGON

2. [t–] any bird of the genus *Trogon*.

Trō·gon'i·dae, *n.pl.* a family of birds, of which the *Trogon* is the type genus.

trō'gon·oid, *a.* of or resembling the trogons; belonging to the *Trogonidæ*.

trōgue, *n.* [variant of *trough*.] in mines, a troughlike drain, made of wood. [Brit. Dial.]

Trō'iç, *a.* [L. *Troicus*; Gr. *Trōicos*, of Troy.] of or pertaining to ancient Troy or the Trojans; Trojan; relating to the Trojan War.

troi'kȧ, *n.* [Russ.] a carriage drawn by three horses abreast; also, a team consisting of three horses.

trō'i·līte, *n.* [named after D. *Troili*, an 18th-c. Italian scientist.] ferrous sulfide (FeS), found in meteorites.

Trō'i·lus (*or* troi'), *n.* [L.; Gr. *Trōilos*.] in Greek legend, a son of King Priam, killed by Achilles: in medieval romance and in works by Boccaccio, Chaucer, and Shakespeare, Troilus was the lover of Cressida.

trō'i·lus but'tēr·flȳ, *n.* an American butterfly, *Euphæades troilus* (*Papilio troilus*), having large black forewings marked with yellow spots, its hind wings marked with blue spots.

Trō'jan, *a.* of or referring to ancient Troy, its people, or culture.

Trojan horse; (a) in classical legend, a huge, hollow wooden horse filled with Greek soldiers and left at the gates of Troy: when it was brought into the city, the soldiers came out at night and opened the gates to the Greek army, which destroyed the city: also called *wooden horse*; (b) the infiltration of troops or agents (or those so infiltrated) into enemy territory for disrupting or weakening the defense; fifth column.

Trojan War; in Greek legend, the war waged against Troy by the Greeks in order to get back Helen, the wife of King Menelaus, who had been abducted by Paris, son of King Priam of Troy.

Trō'jăn, *n.* 1. a native or inhabitant of ancient Troy.
2. a person of energy and determination; as, he worked like a *Trojan*.

trōke, *n.*, *v.t.* and *v.i.* trade; barter. [Scot.]

trōll, *v.t.*; trolled, *pt.*, *pp.*; trolling, *ppr.* [ME. *trollen*; OFr. *troller*, from M.H.G. *trollen*, to roll.]
1. to move in a circular direction; to roll; to revolve.
2. to circulate; to pass round, as a vessel of liquor at table. [Now Rare.]
3. to sing the parts of in succession, as of a catch or round; also, to sing in a full, jovial voice; to chant merrily.
4. to fish for with a moving line, especially one with a revolving lure; hence, to allure; to entice; to draw on; as, to *troll* for pickerel.
5. to fish in (a lake, etc.) by this method.

trōll, *v.i.* 1. (a) to speak fast; (b) to wag: said of the tongue. [Now Rare.]
2. to sing in a round, catch, etc.
3. (a) to sing lustily or in a full, rolling voice; (b) to be uttered in such a voice.
4. to fish with a moving line, especially one with a revolving lure, as from a boat.
5. to roll, spin, or whirl.
6. to stroll; to ramble. [Archaic.]

trōll, *n.* 1. the act of going or moving round; a trolling.
2. a song the parts of which are sung in succession; a round.
3. a reel on a fishing rod. [Now Rare.]
4. (a) the method of trolling in fishing; (b) a lure or lure and line used in trolling.
5. same as *trolley* (sense 1).

trōll, *n.* [ON. and Sw. *troll*, a troll.] in Scandinavian folklore, one of certain supernatural beings represented as a kind of giant, but in modern Scandinavia often regarded as dwarfs or imps inhabiting caves or living underground.

trōll'ēr, *n.* one who trolls for fish.

trol'ley, *n.*; *pl.* **trol'leys**, [from East Anglican dial., from *troll*, *v.*]
1. any of various low carts or trucks. [Brit.]
2. a wheeled carriage, basket, etc. that runs suspended from an overhead track.
3. an apparatus for collecting electric current from an overhead wire and transmitting it to a motor of a streetcar, etc.: it is of two types, the *bow trolley*, having a bow-shaped contact on a flexible frame, and the *wheel trolley*, having a wheel contact at the end of a pole.
4. a trolley car; streetcar.
Also spelled *trolly*.

trol'ley, *v.t.* and *v.i.* to carry or ride on a trolley car: also spelled *trolly*.

trol'ley bus, an electric bus that gets its motive power from an overhead wire by means of a trolley, but does not run on tracks; trackless trolley.

trol'ley çär, an electric streetcar propelled by a motor receiving its current from an overhead wire by means of a trolley.

trol'ley līne, an electric streetcar system or route.

trol'ley pōle, the pole serving to connect a trolley with a car.

trol'ley wīre, a wire carrying a current to be transmitted by means of a trolley.

trōll'flow''ēr, *n.* same as *globeflower*.

Trol'li·us, *n.* [prob. from G. *troll*, a troll.] a genus of ranunculaceous plants of which the globeflower, *Trollius europæus*, is a type.

trōll mad'ăm, an old English game, nineholes. [Obs.]

trol'lŏp, *n.* [Scot., from ME. *trollen*, to roll, troll, wander.] an untidy or dirty woman; a slattern: also, a prostitute.

trol·lŏp·ee', *n.* formerly, a loose dress worn by women.

trōll plāte, in machinery, a rotating plate or disk adapted for opening and closing the jaws of a tool, as of a chuck or the dies in a stock.

trol'ly, *n.*; *pl.* **trol'lies**, a trolley.

trol'ly, *v.t.* and *v.i.*; trollied, *pt.*, *pp.*; trollying, *ppr.* to trolley.

trom'bȧ, *n.* [It.] a trumpet.

trom''bi·dī'ȧ·sis, *n.* [Mod. L., from *Trombidium*, a genus of mites; and *-iasis*.] the state of being infested with chiggers.

trom'bōne, *n.* [Fr., from It. *trombone*, from *tromba*, a trumpet.] a large, brass-wind instrument consisting of a long tube bent parallel to itself twice and ending in a bell mouth: it is of two types, the *slide trombone*, in which different tones are produced by moving the slide, or movable section of the tube, in or out, and the *valve trombone*, played, like the trumpet, with valves.

TROMBONES
1. valve trombone; 2. slide trombone

trom'bōn·ist, *n.* a person who plays the trombone.

trom'mel, *n.* [G., a drum.] a sieve, usually a revolving cylindrical one, for cleaning or for sizing ore, coal, etc.

trō·mom'e·tēr, *n.* [from Gr. *tromos*, trembling; and *-meter*.] an instrument for detecting or measuring very slight earth tremors.

tromp, trompe, *n.* a trump. [Obs.]

trompe, *n.* [Fr. *trompe*, a tube, a trumpet.] an apparatus for producing a blast in a forge, blast furnace, etc. by means of air which is drawn into the upper part of a vertical tube through side holes by a stream of water within, and is carried down with the water into a box or chamber below from which it can escape only by a pipe leading to the furnace.

tromp'il, *n.* [Fr.] an aperture in a trompe.

tron, *n.* a trone. [Obs.]

trō'nȧ, *n.* [Sw., from Ar. *tron*, contr. from *natrūn*, natron.] a monoclinic hydrous sodium carbonate, $Na_2CO_3 \cdot NaHCO_3 \cdot 2H_2O$, gray or yellowish-white, found on the banks of soda lakes: also called *urao*.

trōn'āġe, *n.* a toll or duty formerly paid for weighing wool. [Obs.]

trōne, *n.* throne. [Obs.]

trōne, *n.* [Scot. *tron*; OFr. *trone*; L. *trutina*; Gr. *trytanē*, a balance.]
1. a machine for weighing heavy articles. [Scot.]
2. a post supporting such a machine, used as a pillory. [Scot.]
trone weight; a former Scottish standard of weight: in this weight the pound differed in various counties from twenty-one ounces to twenty-eight ounces avoirdupois.

trọọ'lie päłm (päm), same as *bussu*.

trọọp, *n.* [Fr. *troupe*; back-formation from *troupeau*, from LL. *troppus*, a flock.]
1. a collection of people, animals, or, formerly, things; a herd, flock, band, etc.
2. loosely, a great number; a lot.
3. [*usually pl.*] soldiers.
4. in cavalry, a subdivision of a regiment, under the command of a captain, and corresponding to a company of infantry.
5. a particular roll or call of the drum; a signal for marching.
6. a group of sixteen or thirty-two boy scouts.
7. a band or company of performers or actors; a troupe. [Archaic.]

trọọp, *v.i.*; trooped (trọọpt), *pt., pp.*; trooping, *ppr.* 1. to gather or go in or as in troops; as, the crowd *trooped* out of the stadium.
2. to walk, go, etc.; as, the children *trooped* along the sidewalk.
3. to associate or consort. [Archaic.]

trọọp, *v.t.* to form into a troop or troops.

trọọp'ẽr, *n.* 1. a cavalryman.
2. a cavalry horse.
3. a troopship. [Chiefly Brit.]
4. a mounted policeman.
5. a State policeman. [Colloq.]

trọọp'fowl, *n.* the scaup of North America. [Dial.]

trọọp'i·ăl, *n.* same as *troupial*.

trọọp'mēal, *adv.* by troops; in crowds. [Obs.]

trọọp'ship, *n.* a ship for the conveyance of troops; a transport.

trọọst'īte, *n.* [after G. *Troost* (1776–1850), Am. metallurgist.] a variety of willemite occurring in large, reddish crystals which are mostly impure from the presence of manganese, which partially replaces zinc.

trō·pae'ō·lin, trō·pae'ō·line, *n.* [from *tropaeolum* and *-ine.*] any of a group of orange or orange-yellow azo dyes: also spelled *tropeolin, tropeoline*.

Trō·pae'ō·lum, *n.* [Gr. *tropaios*, of a turning, from *trepein*, to turn.] a genus of plants, including the nasturtium, having shield-shaped, finely cut or lobed leaves, and trumpet-shaped, red, yellow, or orange flowers with spurs: also, [t–] any plant of this genus; a nasturium.

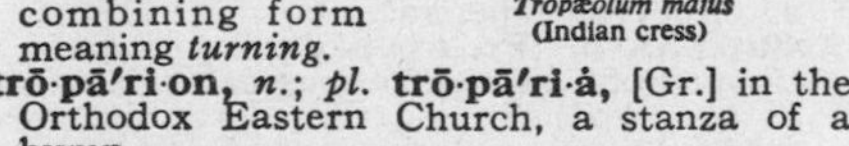

TROPAEOLUM
Tropæolum malus
(Indian cress)

-trō'păl, [Gr. *tropos*, turning; and *-al*.] a combining form meaning *turning*.

trō·pā'ri·on, *n.*; *pl.* **trō·pā'ri·ȧ,** [Gr.] in the Orthodox Eastern Church, a stanza of a hymn.

trōpe, *n.* [L. *tropus*; Gr. *tropos*, a turn, a figure of speech, from *trepein*, to turn.]
1. (a) the use of a word in a figurative sense; (b) a figure of speech; (c) figurative language in general.
2. any of various short, formulistic phrases used in Gregorian chants.
3. in the medieval church, (a) the interpolation of a phrase or passage into the authorized service: such passages were later developed into semi-dramatic dialogues; (b) any such passage.
4. a heading of subject matter.

-trōpe, [Gr. *-tropos*, a turning, a turn.] a combining form meaning *turning*.

trō·pē'iç, *a.* [Gr. *tropis*, keel.] like a keel; as, the *tropeic* fold of certain sharks.

trō·pē'in, trō·pē'ine, *n.* any ester of tropin.

troph'ē·sy, *n.* [Gr. *trophē*, nourishment.] in medicine, defective nutrition due to disorder of the trophic nerves.

trō'phī, *n.pl.* [Gr. *trophos*, one who feeds, from *trephein*, to feed.] in entomology, the organs about the mouth in arthropods: the trophi of masticatory insects, such as beetles, consists of (a) an upper lip, or labrum; (b) a pair of mandibles, for biting; (c) a pair of maxillae, for chewing; (d) a lower lip, or labium.

troph'iç, troph'i·çăl, *a.* [Gr. *trophē*, food, from *trephein*, to feed.] of or pertaining to nutrition; having to do with the processes of nutrition.

trō·phic'i·ty, *n.* a trophic function or relation.

trō'phied, *a.* adorned with trophies.

trōph'işm, *n.* direct trophic influence.

troph'ō-, [from Gr. *trophē*, nourishment.] a combining form meaning *of nutrition*, as in *tropho*plasm: also, before a vowel, *troph-*.

troph'ō·blast, *n.* [*tropho-* and *-blast.*] a layer of ectoderm outside the blastoderm, by which the fertilized ovum is attached to the uterine wall and the developing embryo receives its nourishment.

troph·ō·blas'tiç, *a.* pertaining to the trophoblast.

troph″ō·neū·rō'sis, *n.* any functional nervous disease due to failure of nutrition from defective nerve influence.

troph″ō·neū·rot'iç, *a.* pertaining to or of the nature of trophoneurosis.

Trō·phō'ni·ăn, *a.* pertaining to the mythical Grecian architect Trophonius, his cave, or his architecture.

troph·op'ȧ·thy, *n.* [Gr. *trophē*, nourishment, and *pathos*, suffering.] any derangement of the function of nutrition.

troph'ō·phōre, *n.* [*tropho-*, and Gr. *pherein*, to bear.] a nutritive amoebiform cell of a sponge.

trō·phoph'ō·rous, *a.* pertaining to or of the nature of trophophores.

troph'ō·plaşm, *n.* [*tropho-* and *-plasm.*]
1. the nutritive or vegetative substance of an organic cell: distinguished from *idioplasm*.
2. formerly, a cytoplasmic substance distinguished from archoplasm.

troph'ō·plast, *n.* [Gr. *trophē*, nourishment, and *plastos*, formed.] a granular protoplasmic body; a plastid.

troph'ō·sōme, *n.* [*tropho-*, and Gr. *sōma*, body.] the nutritive zooids of a hydrozoan, collectively.

troph'ō·spẽrm, *n.* [*tropho-*, and Gr. *sperma*, seed.] a trophospermium. [Obs.]

troph·ō·spẽr'mi·um, *n.* in botany, a placenta. [Obs.]

troph·ō·trop'iç, *a.* pertaining to trophotropism.

troph'ō·trō·pişm, *n.* [*tropho-*, and Gr. *tropē*, from *trepein*, to turn.] the phenomenon of the movement of cells in regard to nutritive matter.

-trō'phy, [Gr. *-trophia*, from *trophein*, to nourish.] a combining form meaning *nutrition*, *nourishment*, as in hyper*trophy*.

trō'phy, *n.*; *pl.* **trō'phieş,** [Fr. *trophée*; L. *tropæum*, a sign of victory, from Gr. *tropaion*, a monument of an enemy's defeat.]
1. in ancient Greece and Rome, a monument or memorial in commemoration of a victory, consisting originally of some of the arms and other spoils of the vanquished enemy erected either on the field of battle or in a public place.
2. a representation of this on a medal.
3. anything taken from the enemy and preserved as a memorial of victory, as arms, flags, standards, and the like.
4. a lion's skin, deer's head, etc. displayed as evidence of hunting prowess.
5. a prize, usually a silver cup, awarded in an athletic or sports contest.
6. in architecture, an ornament representing a group of weapons.
7. any memento or memorial.

trō'phy çress, Indian cress.

trō'phy mŏn'ey, a duty formerly paid in England annually, by housekeepers, toward providing harness, drums, colors, etc., for the militia. [Brit.]

trō'phy·wŏrt, *n.* the Indian cress.

-trop'iç, [from Gr. *tropos*, turning.] a combining form meaning *turning, changing, tending to turn, tending to change, responding to a* (specified kind of)*stimulus*, as in photo*tropic*.

trop'iç, *n.* [ME. *tropik*; LL. *tropicus*; Gr. *tropikos*, belonging to a turn (of the sun at the solstices), from *tropē*, a turn.]
1. either of the two circles of the celestial sphere, on each side of the equator, at a distance of 23°27′ and parallel to it, which the sun apparently reaches at its greatest declination north or south, and from which it turns again toward the equator, the northern circle being called the *Tropic of Cancer*, and the southern the *Tropic of Capricorn*, from the names of the two signs at which they touch the ecliptic.

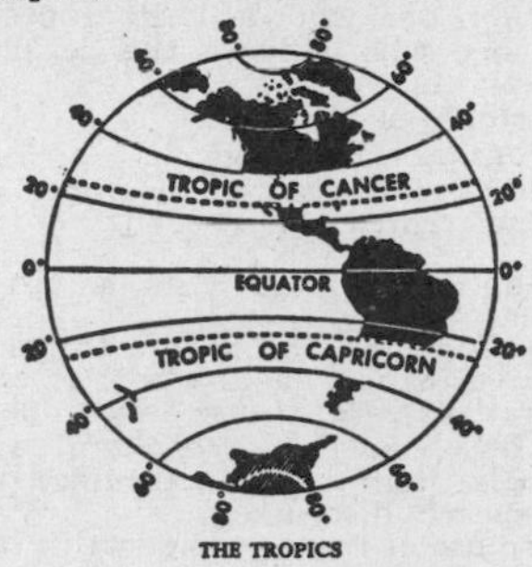

THE TROPICS

2. either of the two parallels of terrestrial latitude corresponding to the celestial tropics, being at the same distance from the terrestrial equator as the celestial tropics are from the celestial equator. Over these circles the sun is vertical when its declination is greatest, and they include that portion of the globe called the Torrid Zone, a zone 46° 54′ wide, having the equator for a central line.
3. [*also* T–] [*pl.*] the region of the earth lying between the tropics or near them on either side.

trop'iç *a.* tropical; pertaining to the tropics.

trop'i·çăl, *a.* pertaining to, characteristic of, or in the tropics; hence, very hot; sultry; torrid; as, *tropical* climates.
tropical month; see under *month*.
tropical year; see under *year*.

trop'i·çăl, *a.* [from *trope.*] figurative; of, or having the nature of, a trope.

Trop·i·çā'li·ȧ, *n.* the marine realm included within the tropics.

trop'i·căl·ly, *adv.* in a tropical or figurative manner.

trop'iç bīrd, any of a number of tropical sea birds of the genus *Phaëthon*, characterized by white plumage with black markings, a pair of long tail feathers, and webbed toes: in general appearance they resemble gulls and terns. In two species from the Atlantic Ocean, *Phaëthon æthereus* (or *candidus*) and *Phaëthon flavirostris*, the tail feathers are white; in a third species, *Phaëthon phœnicurus*, from the Pacific Ocean, they are red.

TROPIC BIRD (*Phaëthon phœnicurus*)

Trop'iç of Çan'cẽr, the parallel of latitude that is the northern boundary of the Torrid Zone: it is 23°27′ north of the equator.

Trop'iç of Çap'ri·çorn, the parallel of latitude that is the southern boundary of the Torrid Zone: it is 23°27′ south of the equator.

trop″i·çō·pol'i·tăn, *a.* [*tropic*, and Gr. *politēs*, a citizen.] belonging to or inhabiting the tropics; found only in the tropics.

trop″i·çō·pol'i·tăn, *n.* a tropicopolitan animal.

trop'i·din, *n.* an oily liquid base, $C_8H_{13}N$, formed by the dehydration of tropine.

trō'pin, *n.* same as *tropine*.

trō'pīne, *n.* [from *atropine.*] a poisonous, colorless heterocyclic alkaloid, $C_8H_{15}ON$, produced by the hydrolysis of atropine or hyoscyamine.

-trō'pişm, a combining form meaning *tropism, tendency to turn toward* or *away from* (something specified), as in thermo*tropism*, helio*tropism*.

trō′pism, *n.* [from Gr. *tropē*, a turn; and *-ism.*] the tendency of a plant, animal, or part to move or turn in response to an external stimulus, either by attraction or repulsion, as a sunflower turns toward light.

trō′pist, *n.* one who deals in tropes; specifically, one who explains the Scriptures by tropes and figures of speech.

trō·pis′tic, *a.* of a tropism.

trop·ō·log′ic, *a.* tropological.

trop·ō·log′i·căl, *a.* varied by tropes; changed from the original import of the words; figurative.

trop·ō·log′i·căl·ly, *adv.* in a tropological manner.

trō·pol′ō·gize, *v.t.* to use in a tropological or figurative manner, as a word; to change to a figurative sense; to use as a trope. [Rare.]

trō·pol′ō·gy, *n.* [LL. *tropologia*; Late Gr. *tropologia*, from *tropos*, a turning, turn, and *logos*, speech, discourse.]

1. the use of tropes or figurative language.

2. a method of considering or interpreting Scripture in a figurative as well as a literal sense.

3. *pl.* **trō·pol′ō·gies**, a treatise on figurative language.

trō·pom′ē·tēr, *n.* 1. an instrument for measuring the rotation of the eyeball.

2. an instrument for measuring the torsion of a long bone.

trop′ō·pause, *n.* [from *tropo*, as in *troposphere*, and Gr. *pausis*, a stopping.] a transition zone between the troposphere and the stratosphere, at which the drop in temperature with increasing height ceases.

trō·poph′i·lous, *a.* [from Gr. *tropos*, a turning; and *-philous.*] in botany, able to adjust to conditions of heat or cold, dryness or moisture, etc., as in seasonal changes: said of plants.

trop′ō·phȳte, *n.* [from Gr. *tropos*, a turning; and *-phyte.*] any tropophilous plant, as the deciduous trees of temperate zones.

trop·ō·phyt′ic, *a.* of, or having the nature of, a tropophyte.

trop′ō·sphēre, *n.* [Gr. *tropos*, a turning, and Fr. *sphère*, a ball.] the portion of the atmosphere included between the earth's surface and the stratosphere and in which the temperature falls as the altitude increases, cloud formation takes place, and air currents are active.

-trō′pous, [from Gr. *tropos*, a turning; and *-ous.*] a combining form meaning *turning* or *turned* (in some specified way or in response to some specified stimulus): used in forming botanical terms, as photo*tropous*.

trōp′pō (*or Eng.* trop′ō), *adv.* [It.; LL. (hyp.) *troppus*; prob. from Frank. (hyp.) *throp*, a crowd.] too; too much so: used in musical directions (e.g., *adagio ma non troppo*, slowly but not too much so).

-trō′py, [from Gr. *tropē*, a turning.] a combining form meaning *turning*, equivalent to: (a) -tropism; (b) -tropous.

tros′sērs, *n.pl.* trousers. [Obs.]

trot, *v.i.*; trotted, *pt.*, *pp.*; trotting, *ppr.* [ME. *trotten*; OFr. *troter*; O.H.G. *trottōn*, to tread.]

1. to move, ride, drive, run, or go at a trot.

2. to move quickly; hurry; run.

trot, *v.t.* 1. to cause to trot; to ride at a trot.

2. to go about or over at a trot.

3. to use a crib or pony in studying (a lesson); as, to *trot* Greek. [Slang.]

to trot out; (a) to bring out for others to see or admire; (b) to submit for consideration or approval. [Colloq.]

trot, *n.* 1. a gait of a horse, etc. in which the legs are lifted in alternating diagonal pairs.

2. a jogging gait of a person, at a pace between a walk and a run.

3. the sound of a trotting horse.

4. a trotting race. [Rare.]

5. a small child; a tot. [Rare.]

6. an old woman: contemptuous term. [Archaic.]

7. a trotline.

8. a literal translation of a literary work in a foreign language, used in doing school work, often dishonestly: also called *pony*, *crib*. [Slang.]

troth (*or* trōth), *n.* [formed from the verb *trow.*]

1. belief; faith; fidelity; loyalty; faithfulness; as, to plight one's *troth*; also, betrothal. [Archaic.]

2. truth; verity; veracity; as, in *troth*; by my *troth*. [Archaic.]

troth, *v.t.* to pledge; to betroth. [Archaic.]

troth′less, *a.* faithless; treacherous. [Archaic.]

troth′plight (-plīt), *v.t.* to betroth or affiance. [Archaic.]

troth′plight, *a.* betrothed; affianced. [Archaic.]

troth′plight, *n.* betrothal. [Archaic.]

trot′līne, *n.* a strong fishing line suspended over the water, with short, baited lines hung from it at intervals; a trawl line.

Trot′sky·ism, *n.* the doctrines, methods, and practices of Leon Trotsky (1877–1940), Russian revolutionist and writer, and of his followers.

Trot′sky·ist, *n.* same as *Trotskyite*.

Trot′sky·īte, *n.* an adherent of Trotskyism.

trot′tēr, *n.* 1. one that trots; specifically, a horse trained for trotting races: distinguished from *pacer* or *runner*.

2. the foot of an animal, especially of a sheep or pig, used as food; also, jocularly, the human foot.

3. a person who moves about energetically and constantly.

trot·toir′ (-twär′), *n.* [Fr.] the sidewalk on each side of a street; a pavement. [Rare.]

trō′tyl, *n.* same as *trinitrotoluene*.

tröu′bȧ·dour, *n.* [Fr.; Pr. *trobador*, from *trobar*, to find, compose in verse.]

1. any of a class of lyric poets and poet-musicians who lived in Provence, Catalonia, southern France, and northern Italy in the 11th, 12th, and 13th centuries and wrote poems of love and chivalry, usually with intricate stanza form and rhyme scheme.

2. loosely, any minstrel or ballad singer.

troub′lȧ·ble (trub′), *a.* causing trouble; troublesome. [Obs.]

troub′le (trub′l), *v.t.*; troubled, *pt.*, *pp.*; troubling, *ppr.* [ME. *trublen*; OFr. *trubler*, *troubler*; from L. *turbula*, dim. of *turba*, crowd.]

1. to put into confused motion; to agitate; to disturb; to confuse; to disorder: now used chiefly in the passive; as, the waters were *troubled*.

2. to annoy; to pester; to bother; to tease; to fret.

3. to cause pain or discomfort to; to afflict.

4. to put to some labor, exertion, or inconvenience; to incommode; as, may I *trouble* you to pass the salt?

5. to cause (a person) mental agitation; to worry; harass; perturb; vex.

Syn.—disturb, perplex, afflict, distress, grieve, harass, annoy, tease, vex, molest.

troub′le, *v.i.* 1. to make an effort; to bother; to take pains; to give oneself trouble; as, do not *trouble* about a reply.

2. to be distressed; to worry.

troub′le, *a.* troubled. [Obs.]

troub′le, *n.* 1. a state of mental distress; worry.

2. (a) a misfortune; calamity; mishap; (b) a distressing or difficult situation.

3. one who or that which gives trouble, annoyance, disturbance, etc. or causes grief, affliction, pain, or the like.

4. pains; labor; exertion; effort; as, she took the *trouble* to visit them.

5. in mining, a fault or interruption in a stratum, especially a stratum of coal.

6. sickness; disease; ailment.

7. public disturbance; civil disorder.

Syn.—distress, perplexity, annoyance, molestation, vexation, inconvenience, affliction, calamity, misfortune, adversity, embarrassment, anxiety, sorrow, misery.

troub′led (-ld), *a.* disturbed; agitated; afflicted; annoyed.

troub′lēr, *n.* one who or that which troubles.

troub′le·māk″ēr, *n.* a person who habitually makes trouble for others.

troub′le-shoot″ēr, *n.* a person who locates and repairs mechanical breakdowns; a person charged with locating and eliminating the source of trouble in any flow of work: also *trouble shooter*.

troub′le·sōme, *a.* 1. giving or causing trouble; characterized by trouble.

2. agitated; turbulent; as, *troublesome* rapids. [Archaic.]

Syn.—uneasy, harassing, irksome, afflictive, burdensome, wearisome.

troub′le·sōme·ly, *adv.* in a troublesome manner.

troub′le·sōme·ness, *n.* the state or quality of being troublesome; as, the *troublesomeness* of a creditor.

troub′le·stāte, *n.* a disturber of the community. [Obs.]

troub′lous, *a.* 1. troubled; agitated; disturbed; unsettled.

2. that causes trouble; troublesome. Now chiefly a literary usage.

troub′ly, *a.* violent; stormy; turbulent; riotous; also, confused; troubled. [Obs.]

tröu-dē-löup′ (-lö′), *n.*; *pl.* **tröus-dē-löup′** (trö-), [Fr., wolf hole.] in military usage, any of the conical pits with a vertical pointed stake in the center of each, formerly built in rows as an obstacle to the enemy, especially to enemy cavalry.

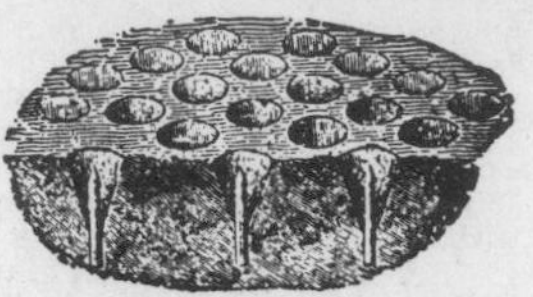

TROUS-DE-LOUP

trough (trôf), *n.* [ME. *trogh*, *trough*; AS. *trog*, *troh*, trough.]

1. a container of wood, stone, or metal, generally rather long and not very deep, open along the top, for holding water or food for animals.

2. any similarly shaped vessel, as one for kneading or washing something.

3. a gutter under the eaves of a building, for carrying off rain water.

4. a channel or spout for conveying water, as to a mill. [Dial.]

5. the array of connected cells of a galvanic battery, in which the copper and zinc plates of each pair are on opposite sides of a partition.

6. a frame, vat, buddle, or rocker in which ores or slimes are washed and sorted in water.

7. anything resembling a trough in shape, as a depression between two ridges or between two waves; a basin-shaped or oblong hollow; as, the *trough* of the sea.

8. in printing, a metal box in which forms and inking rollers are cleaned.

9. a canoe or dugout; any small boat. [Obs.]

10. the line in a cyclonic area which marks the greatest barometric depression.

11. in electroplating, a vat or tray containing the metallic solution in which the articles to be plated are immersed.

12. in chemistry, a water-containing receptacle used in the distillation of gas.

trough, *v.i.* to feed grossly, as a hog from a trough. [Rare.]

trough, *v.t.* to shape like a trough.

trough bat′tēr·y, a galvanic battery with cells arranged in a trough (sense 5).

trough gut′tēr, a gutter in the form of a trough placed below the eaves of buildings.

trough shell, any shell of a mollusk belonging to the genus *Mactra*.

troul, *v.* to troll. [Obs.]

trounce, *v.t.*; trounced (trounst), *pt.*, *pp.*; trouncing, *ppr.* [OFr. *troncer*, to cut or break in two, from *tronche*, a big piece of timber.]

1. to beat; to thrash; to flog.

2. to defeat. [Colloq.]

tröupe, *n.* [Fr.] a troop; a company; particularly, a company of players, singers, dancers, acrobats, or the like.

tröupe, *v.i.* to travel as a member of a company of actors or entertainers.

tröup′ēr, *n.* a member of a troupe; hence, any actor of long experience.

tröup′i·ăl, *n.* [Fr. *troupiale*, from *troupe*, a troop: from their gregarious habit.] any bird of a group including the North American orioles, meadow larks, cowbirds, grackles, and blackbirds, and the Central American caciques.

tröus-dē-löup′ (trö-dē-lö′), *n.* plural of *trou-de-loup*.

trouse, *n.* trousers. [Obs.]

troused, *a.* trousered. [Obs.]

trou′sered, *a.* wearing trousers; masculine.

> The inferior or *trousered* half of the creation. —T. Hughes.

trou′sēr·ing, *n.* cloth for making trousers.

trou′sēr leg, one of the legs of a pair of trousers.

trou′sērs, *n.pl.* [lengthened (prob. after *drawers*), from obs. *trouse*; Ir. *triubhas.*] an outer garment, especially for men and boys, covering the lower half of the body from the waist to the ankles (or, sometimes, as in boy's trousers, to the knees) and divided into separate coverings for the legs: also called *pants*.

trōus·seau′ (trō-sō′ *or* trō′sō), *n.*; *pl.* **trōus·seaux′, trōs·seaus′** (-sōz′ *or* -sōz), [from Fr., small bundle, dim. of *trousse*, a bundle, truss.]
1. originally, a bundle.
2. a bride's outfit of clothes, linen, jewelry, etc.

trout, *n.*; *pl.* **trout** or **trouts,** [AS. *truht*; L. *tructa*, from Gr. *trōktēs*, a kind of fish, from *trōgein*, to gnaw.]
1. any of various game and food fishes of the family *Salmonidæ* and genus *Salmo* or related genera of the salmon family, usually spotted and found chiefly in fresh water; as, the speckled *trout*, rainbow *trout*, Great Lakes *trout*, brook *trout*, etc.
2. any of various fishes resembling the trout, but of different family, as the California rock trout and the common squeteague.
Mackinaw trout; see following *Mackinaw*.
speckled trout; see under *speckled*.

trout′bĭrd, *n.* the golden plover, *Pluvialis dominica*. [Dial.]

trout′-çŏl″ŏred, *a.* white with spots of black, bay, or sorrel; as, a *trout-colored* horse.

trout′let, *n.* a little or young trout.

trout′ling, *n.* a troutlet.

trout pērch, 1. an American fresh-water fish, *Percopsis omiscomaycus*, resembling the trout, but with scales and mouth like a perch.
2. the black bass. [Dial.]

trout spoon, a small spoon bait used in trolling for trout.

trou·vère′ (trō-vār′), [Fr., OFr. *trovere*, from *trover*, to find, compose (Pr. *trobar*; see *troubadour*).] any of a class of narrative poets in northern France from the 11th to the 14th century.

trōu·vēur′, *n.* a trouvère.

trōve, *n.* treasure-trove. [Colloq.]

trō′vēr, *n.* [OFr. *trover* (Fr. *trouver*), to find.] in law, (a) originally, an action against a person who found another's goods and refused to return them; (b) an action to recover damages for goods withheld or used by another illegally.

trōw, *v.i.* and *v.t.* [AS. *treowian*, *trywian*, to have trust in, from *treowe*, true.]
1. to believe; to trust. [Obs.]
2. to think; to suppose; to imagine; to be inclined to believe. [Archaic.]

trōw, *n.* any of various small fishing boats. [Brit.]

trow′el, *n.* [OFr. *truelle*; LL. *truella*, a variant of L. *trulla*, a small ladle, scoop, trowel.] any of several small hand tools for spreading, smoothing, scooping, etc.; specifically, (a) a thin, flat, rectangular tool of wood or metal, used for smoothing plaster; (b) a

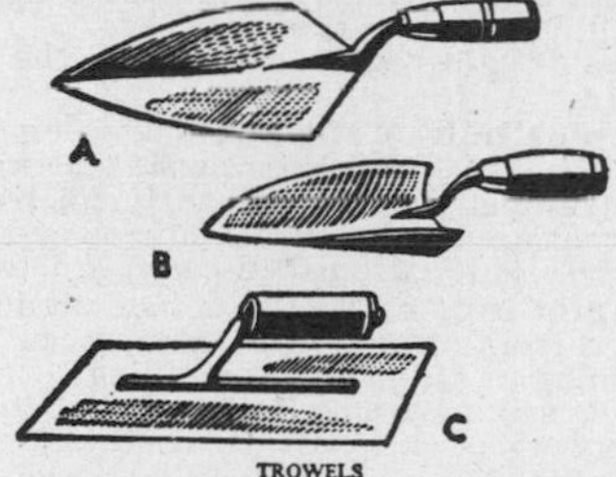

TROWELS
A, brick trowel; B, garden trowel; C, cement trowel

thin, flat, pointed metal tool for applying and shaping mortar, as in bricklaying; (c) a pointed, scooplike metal tool for loosening soil, digging holes, etc., as in transplanting.

trow′el, *v.t.*; troweled *or* trowelled, *pt., pp.*; troweling *or* trowelling, *ppr.* to spread, smooth, shape, dig, etc. with a trowel.

trow′eled, *a.* formed with a trowel; as, *troweled* stucco, that is, stucco laid on and ready for the reception of paint.

trow′el·fụl, *n.*; *pl.* **trow′el·fụls,** the quantity a trowel will hold.

trōwl, *n.* troll. [Obs.]

trow′sērs, *n.pl.* trousers. [Obs.]

troy, *n.* troy weight.

troy, *a.* by or in troy weight.

troy weight (wāt), [named from *Troyes*, France, where it was first used.] a system of weights for gold, silver, precious stones, etc., based on a pound containing 5,760 grains (0.82286 lb. avoirdupois), in which 24 grains = 1 pennyweight, 20 pennyweights = 1 ounce and 12 ounces = 1 pound.

trụ′āge, *n.* 1. a pledge of peace given on payment of a tax. [Obs.]
2. an impost; tribute. [Obs.]

trụ′ăn·cy, *n.* 1. *pl.* **trụ′ăn·cies,** the act or an instance of playing truant.
2. the state of being truant; truant behavior.

trụ′ănd, *n.*, *a.*, and *v.* truant. [Obs.]

trụ′ănt, *n.* [OFr. *truant*; Fr. *truand*, a vagabond, from W. *tru*, *truan*, wretched.]
1. formerly, a lazy, idle person.
2. a pupil who stays away from school without permission.
3. a person who shirks or neglects his work or duties.

trụ′ănt, *a.* 1. that is a truant; that plays truant.
2. idle; shiftless.
3. characteristic of a truant; errant; straying.

trụ′ănt, *v.i.* to idle away time; to shirk one's duty, attendance at school, etc.; to play truant.

trụ′ănt, *v.t.* to idle away; to waste, as time. [Obs.]

trụ′ănt·ly, *adv.* like a truant; as a truant; in idleness.

trụ′ănt of′fi·cēr, a school official who deals with cases of truancy.

trụ′ănt·ship, *n.* idleness; the conduct of a truant. [Obs.]

trub, *n.* a truffle. [Obs.]

trụce, *n.* [ME. *triwes*, *treowes*, *trewes*, pl. of *trewe*, a pledge; AS. *treowa*, *truwa*, compact, faith, from *treowe*, true.]
1. a temporary suspension of warfare by agreement of the belligerents; a temporary cessation of hostilities, either for negotiation or other purpose.
2. any pause or respite, especially from trouble, pain, etc.
flag of truce; see under *flag*.
Truce of God; a suspension of arms which occasionally took place in the Middle Ages, and was introduced by the church to mitigate the evils of private feuds or private war.

trụce′break″ēr, *n.* one who violates a truce.

trụce′less, *a.* 1. without truce; as, a *truceless* war.
2. granting or holding no truce; unforbearing.

truch′măn, *n.* an interpreter; a dragoman. [Obs.]

trụ·ci·dā′tion, *n.* the act of killing. [Obs.]

truck, *n.* [L. *trochus*, a hoop, from Gr. *trochos*, a wheel, a disk, etc., from *trechein*, to run.]
1. a small, solid wheel or roller, especially one for a gun carriage.
2. a small wooden block or disk with holes for halyards, especially one at the top of a flagpole or mast.
3. a kind of barrow, consisting of an open frame with a pair of wheels at one end, used to carry trunks, crates, etc.
4. any of various low frames or platforms on wheels, sometimes motor-driven, for carrying heavy articles, as in a warehouse.
5. an automotive vehicle for hauling loads along highways, streets, etc.: also *motor truck*.
6. an open railroad freight car. [Brit.]
7. a swiveling frame with two, three, or four pairs of wheels, usually provided with brakes and springs, forming the wheel unit under each end of a railroad car, streetcar, etc.

truck, *v.t.* to carry on a truck or trucks.

truck, *v.i.* 1. to do trucking.
2. to drive a truck.
truck (on) down; to walk in a carefree, leisurely manner; stroll. [Slang.]

truck, *n.* [Fr. *troc*, from *troquer*, to exchange, barter.]
1. barter.
2. payment of wages in goods produced instead of money.
3. small commercial articles.
4. small articles of little value.
5. vegetables raised for sale in markets.
6. dealings. [Colloq.]
7. trash; rubbish. [Colloq.]
truck farm; a farm devoted to the growing of vegetables for the market.
truck farmer; one who operates a truck farm.
truck garden; a garden devoted to the cultivation of vegetables for the market.
truck system; the practice of paying the wages of workmen in goods instead of money.

truck, *v.t.* and *v.i.*; trucked (trukt), *pt., pp.*; trucking, *ppr.* 1. to exchange; to barter.
2. to peddle; to huckster; to hawk. [Rare.]

truck, *n.* an old game of bowls. [Obs.]

truck′āge, *n.* barter; exchange. [Rare.]

truck′āge, *n.* 1. conveyance of goods by trucks.
2. money paid for the conveyance of goods in trucks.

truck′ēr, *n.* 1. one who engages in barter; one who traffics by exchange of goods.
2. a truck farmer; a market gardener.

truck′ēr, *n.* 1. a person who drives a truck; a truck driver.
2. a person or company engaged in trucking.

truck′ing, *n.* the business or process of moving or transporting goods in trucks.

truç′kle, *n.* [OFr. *trocle*; L. *trochlea*, a pulley, roller; Gr. *trochilea*, from *trochos*, wheel.]
1. originally, a small wheel or caster.
2. a truckle bed.

truç′kle, *v.i.*; truckled, *pt., pp.*; truckling, *ppr.* [from *truckle* in *truckle bed*.]
1. to move on small wheels or casters.
2. to be servile; to cringe; submit, toady, etc. (with *to*).

truç′kle, *v.t.* to move (something) on small wheels or casters.

truç′kle bed, a low bed on wheels or casters, that can be pushed under another bed when not in use; a trundle bed.

truç′klēr, *n.* one who truckles or submits meekly or obsequiously to another's will.

truç′kling, *a.* apt to truckle; cringing; fawning; slavish; servile.

truck′măn, *n.*; *pl.* **truck′men,** a trucker.

truç′ū·lence, truç′ū·len·cy (*or* trö′kū-), *n.* the state or quality of being truculent; savageness of manner; fierceness.

truç′ū·lent, *a.* [L. *truculentus*, from *trux*, *trucis*, fierce, savage.]
1. fierce; cruel; savage; ferocious.
2. rude, harsh, mean, scathing, etc.: said especially of speech or writing.

truç′ū·lent·ly, *adv.* in a truculent manner.

trudġe (truj), *v.i.*; trudged, *pt., pp.*; trudging, *ppr.* [earlier *tredge*, *tridge* beside *trudge* suggest hyp. AS. *trycgan* (via dial., akin to AS. *trucian*, to fail, run short).] to walk, especially wearily or laboriously.

trudġe, *n.* a walk or tramp, especially a wearying, tedious one.

trudġe′măn, *n.* a truchman. [Obs.]

trudġ′en strōke, [after John *Trudgen*, Eng. amateur who introduced it (1873) from Argentina.] a swimming stroke in which a double overarm motion and a scissors kick are used: also *trudgen*.

trụe, *a.*; *comp.* truer; *superl.* truest, [AS. *treōwe*, *trywe*, true.]
1. faithful; loyal; constant.
2. reliable; certain; as, a *true* indication.
3. in accordance with fact; that agrees with reality; not false.
4. truthful.
5. conforming to an original, pattern, rule, standard, etc.; exact; accurate; right; correct.
6. rightful; lawful; legitimate; as, the *true* heirs.
7. accurately fitted, placed, or shaped; as, the board is not *true*.
8. (a) real; genuine; authentic; as, a *true* diamond; (b) conforming to the ideal character of such; rightly so called; as, a *true* scholar.
9. honest; virtuous. [Archaic.]
10. in biology, conforming to the essential characteristics of a genus, class, etc.
11. in navigation, surveying, etc., determined by the poles of the earth's axis, not by the earth's Magnetic Poles; as, *true* north.
to come true; to happen according to prediction or expectation; to become a realized fact.

trụe, *adv.* 1. truly.
2. in biology, in accordance with the parental type; without variation: in phrase *to breed true*.

trụe, *n.* that which is true (with *the*).
in true; properly set, adjusted, etc.; exact.
out of true; not properly set, adjusted, etc.; inexact.

trụe, *v.t.*; trued, *pt., pp.*; truing *or* trueing, *ppr.* to make true; especially, to fit, place, or shape accurately.
to true up; to fit, place, or shape accurately.

trụe bill, in law, a bill of indictment returned and endorsed by a grand jury as supported by evidence sufficient to warrant a hearing of the case.

trụe′-blūe′, *a.* unswervingly honest, faithful, and loyal.

trụe blūe, 1. originally, a fast blue dye or color.

2. a 17th-century Scottish Presbyterian, or Covenanter: so called from the blue worn by the Covenanters in contradistinction to the red of the Royalists.
3. great loyalty.
4. a very loyal person.

trüe′bǫrn′, *a.* being a (specified) type of person from the nature of birth or early environment; as, a *trueborn* New Yorker.

trüe′bred′, *a.* 1. well-bred.
2. purebred.

trüe bug, in zoology, any one of the *Hemiptera* or *Homoptera*.

trüe çōurse, in navigation, the angle formed with the true meridian by the ship's track.

trüe dag′gȧ, Indian hemp, used by the natives of South Africa as a narcotic.

trüe′-fąlse′, *a.* containing both truth and untruth.

trüe′-fąlse′ test, a test in which a person is required to discriminate between true and false statements.

trüe′heärt″ed, *a.* being of a faithful heart; honest; sincere; loyal; not faithless or deceitful; as, a *true-hearted* friend.

trüe′heärt″ed·ness, *n.* fidelity; loyalty.

trüe lev′el, an imaginary surface that is perpendicular at every point to the plumb line; specifically, the mean sea level thought of as extending throughout the globe; the geoid.

trüe′lŏve, *n.* 1. a sweetheart; a loved one.
2. the herb Paris, a plant having a whorl of four leaves which, with the flower or berry in the center, suggests a truelove knot.
3. a truelove knot. [Obs.]

trüe′lŏve knot (not), a kind of a bowknot that is hard to untie, a symbol of lasting love.

trüe′-lŏv′ẽr′ṣ knot, a truelove knot.

TRUELOVE KNOTS

trüe′ness, *n.* the state or quality of being true; faithfulness; sincerity; reality; genuineness; exactness.

trüe′pen″ny, *n.* an honest or trusty person. [Archaic.]

trüe ribṣ, see *rib*.

trüe stitch, in embroidery, a stitch alike on both sides of the cloth.

truf′fle (*or* trŭf′), *n.* [Fr. *truffe*, prob. from L. *tuber*, an esculent root.] a subterranean fungus of the genus *Tuber*, of a fleshy, roundish figure and of a dark color: an esculent substance, much esteemed as a delicacy. There being no appearance aboveground to indicate the existence of the truffle, dogs are trained to find it by the scent and scratch it up. Hogs, which are extremely fond of it, are also employed to discover and root it up.

truf′fled (-fld), *a.* furnished, cooked, or stuffed with truffles; as, a *truffled* turkey.

truf′fle dog, a dog trained to scent and find truffles.

truf′fle wŏrm, a worm found in truffles, the larva of a fly, a species of *Leiodes*.

trug, *n.* a measure of wheat; two-thirds of a bushel. [Obs.]

trug, *n.* a concubine; a prostitute. [Obs. or Dial.]

trug′ging house, a house of prostitution. [Obs.]

trü′iṣm, *n.* a statement the truth of which is obvious and well-known; a platitude; a commonplace.

> It is, of course, the merest *truism* to say a party is of use only so far as it serves the nation. —Theodore Roosevelt.

trü·iṣ·mat′iç, *a.* relating to or composed of truisms. [Rare.]

trü·is′tiç, *a.* of, or having the character of, a truism.

trull, *n.* [G. *trolle*, *trulle*.]
1. a prostitute; a harlot.
2. a girl; a lass; a wench. [Obs.]

Trul′lăn, *a.* [LL. *trullus*, a dome, from L. *trulla*, a trowel.] relating to the two eccelsiatical councils held in the trullus, or domed chamber, of the imperial palace at Constantinople in 680 and 692 A.D.

trul·li·zā′tion, *n.* the act of laying on plaster with a trowel.

trü′ly, *adv.* 1. in fact; indeed; in reality; really: often used as an expletive; as, *truly*, you are kind.
2. according to truth; in agreement with fact; as, to see things *truly*; the facts are *truly* represented.
3. sincerely; honestly; faithfully; as, to be *truly* attached to a lover; the citizens are *truly* loyal to the constitution.
4. exactly; justly; accurately; as, to estimate *truly* the weight of evidence.

trü·meau′ (-mō′), *n.*; *pl.* **trü·meaux′** (-mōz′), [Fr., a pier.] a pillar which supports the arch of a double door or opening.

trump, *n.* [OFr. *trompe*, prob. from L. *tuba*, a tube, trumpet.]
1. a trumpet; as, the last *trump*, the day of final judgment. [Archaic or Poet.]
2. a jew's-harp. [Scot.]

trump, *v.i.* and *v.t.* to trumpet. [Archaic or Poet.]

trump, *n.* [corruption of *triumph*.]
1. any playing card of a suit that for the duration of a particular hand is ranked higher than any other suit, as through a winning bid: a trump can take any card of a suit other than its own, regardless of its denomination.
2. [*sometimes pl.*] a suit of trumps.
3. an old game with cards. [Obs.]
4. a good fellow; a person upon whom one can depend. [Colloq.]
call for trumps; a sign by which, in whist, a player indicates that his partner shall lead trumps.
to put to one's trumps, to put on one's trumps; to force a card player to play out his trumps; hence, to reduce to the last expedient, or to the utmost exertion of power.

trump, *a.* of a superior quality; outrivaling all others.

trump, *v.t.*; trumped (trumpt), *pt., pp.*; trumping, *ppr.* 1. to take (a trick, another card, etc.) with a trump; to put a trump card upon in order to win, or in accordance with the rules of the game.
2. to surpass; to beat; to outdo; to cap.
to trump up; to devise or concoct deceitfully or fraudulently, as a charge against a person.

trump, *v.i.* in card playing, to play a trump.

trump, *v.t.* [Fr. *tromper*, to trick, deceive.] to trick; to impose upon; to gull; to deceive. [Obs.]

trump çärd, a trump; any card of a suit which has precedence over the cards of other suits; also, the card which determines the suit of trumps.

trump′ẽr·y, *n.*; *pl.* **trump′ẽr·ies,** [Fr. *tromperie*, from *tromper*, to deceive, cheat.]
1. deceit; fraud. [Obs.]
2. anything calculated to deceive by false show; anything externally splendid but intrinsically of little value; worthless finery.
3. things worn out and of no value; useless matter; trifles; rubbish; nonsense.

> This idolatrous *trumpery* and superstition. —South.

trump′ẽr·y, *a.* trifling; showy but worthless; trashy; paltry.

trump′et, *n.* [OFr. *trompette*; dim. of *trompe*, a trump.]
1. a brass-wind instrument with a powerful tone, consisting of a tube in an oblong loop, with a flared bell at one end, a cupped mouthpiece at the other, three valves for producing changes in tone, and small, secondary, looped tubes.
2. a person who plays this instrument in an orchestra, etc.

TRUMPET

3. [*pl.*] any of several plants with trumpet-shaped leaves.
4. a sound like that of a trumpet, especially one made by an elephant.
5. a trumpet-toned organ stop.
6. anything in the form of a trumpet; specifically, (a) a bell-shaped tube serving to conduct anything, as yarn in a knitting machine; (b) the bell-shaped mouth of the drawhead of a railway car to receive the coupling pin; (c) a trumpet shell; a triton; (d) an ear trumpet.
electric trumpet; an electromagnetic buzzer whose sound is strengthened by a trumpet-shaped resonator.
Feast of Trumpets; Rosh Hashana: so called from the blowing of trumpets in the temple.

trump′et, *v.t.*; trumpeted, *pt., pp.*; trumpeting, *ppr.* 1. to sound on a trumpet.
2. to sound or utter with a trumpetlike tone.
3. to proclaim loudly; to noise abroad.
4. to give the shape of a funnel or mouth of a trumpet to.

trump′et, *v.i.* 1. to sound or blow a trumpet.
2. to emit a trumpetlike sound, as an elephant.

trump′et an·i·mal′çūle, a stentor (protozoan).

trump′et ash, see *trumpet creeper*.

trump′et çall, a call sounded on the trumpet; hence, figuratively, an urgent or imperative summons to action.

trump′et çonçh, a trumpet shell.

trump′et çreep′ẽr, a hardy, woody, climbing vine, *Tecoma radicans*, bearing large, red, trumpet-shaped flowers. It is native to the southern part of the United States, but is cultivated elsewhere for ornament: also called *trumpet flower*, *trumpet ash*, and *trumpet vine*.

trump′et·ẽr, *n.* 1. a person who plays a trumpet.
2. a soldier, herald, etc. who signals on a trumpet.
3. a person who proclaims or heralds something.
4. any of a group of long-legged, long-necked South American birds of the genus *Psophia*, having a loud cry; the agami.
5. a trumpeter swan.
6. a pigeon with a crested crown and feathered feet.
7. a large, edible fish, *Latris hecateia*, found in New Zealand and Australia.

trump′et·ẽr pẽrch, a percoid sea fish of Australia.

trump′et·ẽr swän, a North American wild swan, *Cygnus buccinator*, with a loud, resonant cry.

trump′et fish, a sea fish, *Centriscus scolopax*; the bellows fish, sea snipe, or snipefish: so called on account of its tubular snout.

trump′et flow′ẽr, 1. any of a number of plants with trumpet-shaped flowers, as the trumpet creeper and the trumpet honeysuckle.
2. the flower of any of these plants.

trump′et flȳ, a botfly.

trump′et gąll, a trumpet-shaped gall produced on grapevines of the United States by a gallfly, *Cecidomyia vitis-viticola*.

trump′et gōurd, a variety of the bottle gourd.

trump′et hŏn′ey·suç·kle, a twining American honeysuckle, *Lonicera sempervirens*, bearing trumpet-shaped, brilliantly colored flowers that are scarlet on the outside and yellow on the inside: also called *trumpet flower*.

trump′et·ing, *n.* 1. the act of producing a sound from or as from a trumpet, or of proclaiming or publishing something.
2. in mining, a small channel cut behind the brickwork of the shaft. [Brit. Dial.]

trump′et·lēaf, *n.* in botany, any one of several species of the genus *Sarracenia*, of the southern part of the United States: so called because the long leaves resemble trumpets.

trump′et mā′jŏr, a head trumpeter in a band or regiment.

trump′et mȧ·rïne′, a sea trumpet (musical instrument).

trump′et milk′weed, the wild lettuce, *Lactuca canadensis*.

trump′et-shāped (-shāpt), *a.* shaped like a trumpet; specifically, in zoology and botany, hollow and dilated at one extremity like the end of a trumpet.

trump′et shell, a shell of the genus *Triton*; a sea trumpet: so called because it can be blown upon as a trumpet.

trump′et tōne, the sound produced by a trumpet; hence, a loud voice; as, to expose the traitor in *trumpet tones*.

trump′et-tŏngued (-tungd), *a.* having a tongue vociferous as a trumpet.

trump′et tree, a tree, *Cecropia peltata*, of the West Indies and South America: so called because the hollow stems are used for musical instruments: also called *trumpetwood* and *snakewood*.

trump'et vīne, see *trumpet creeper.*

trump'et·weed, *n.* 1. boneset, a shrubby plant with flat clusters of grayish-white or purple flowers.

2. joe-pye weed, a tall plant with large clusters of rose or purplish flowers.

3. same as *trumpet milkweed.*

4. the sea trumpet (seaweed).

trump'et·wood, *n.* see *trumpet tree.*

trum'pie, *n.* a gull, the skua.

trump'līke, *a.* resembling a trumpet; as, a *trumplike* tone.

truñ'căl, *a.* [L. *truncus,* trunk, and *-al.*] of or pertaining to the trunk, as of a body or tree.

truñ'çāte, *v.t.;* truncated, *pt., pp.;* truncating, *ppr.* 1. to cut off a part of; to shorten by cutting; to lop.

2. in crystallography, to cut off or replace (an angle) by a plane.

truñ'çāte, *a.* [L. *truncatus,* pp. of *truncare,* to cut off.]

1. truncated.

2. in botany and zoology, having a square or broad end; appearing as if cut off at the tip; ending in a transverse line; as, a *truncate* leaf; a *truncate* tail.

truñ'çā·ted, *a.* 1. cut short or appearing as if cut short.

2. (a) cut off or replaced by a plane face: said of the angles or edges of a crystal or solid figure; (b) having its angles or edges cut off or replaced in this way: said of a crystal or solid figure.

3. having the vertex cut off by a plane: said of a cone or pyramid: cf. *frustum, ungula.*

truñ'çāte·ly, *adv.* in a truncate manner.

truñ·çā'tion, *n.* 1. the act of truncating or the state of being truncated.

2. in crystallography, the replacement of an edge by a plane, especially by one equally inclined to the adjoining faces.

truñ'çȧ·tūre, *n.* in zoology, truncation.

trunch, *n.* a small stake or post. [Obs.]

trun'cheŏn, *n.* [OFr. *tronson, tronchon,* dim. of *tronc;* L. *truncus,* a trunk, stock.]

1. a short, thick staff; a cudgel; a club: now used chiefly of a policeman's baton.

2. any staff or baton of authority.

3. the shaft of a spear. [Archaic.]

4. a trunk or stem, especially one with the branches lopped off. [Obs.]

trun'cheŏn, *v.t.* to beat with a truncheon; to cudgel.

trun'cheŏned, *a.* furnished with a truncheon.

trun'cheŏn·ēr, trun·cheŏn·eer', *n.* a person armed with a truncheon. [Rare.]

truñ'çus, *n.; pl.* **trun'cī,** [L., trunk, stock.]

1. in botany and zoology, the trunk.

2. in anatomy, the trunk or body; also, the main stem of a vessel or nerve.

3. in entomology, the thorax.

trun'dle (-dl), *n.* [altered (after the *v.*) from earlier *trendle, trindle;* AS. *trendel,* a circle.]

1. a little wheel; a roller; a caster.

2. a kind of small cart or truck with low roller wheels.

3. (a) that motion characteristic of moving on small roller wheels; a rolling motion; (b) its sound.

4. a lantern wheel; also, any of its bars.

5. a trundle bed.

6. in heraldry, a spool of gold thread.

trun'dle, *v.t.* and *v.i.;* trundled, *pt., pp.;* trundling, *ppr.* 1. to roll along.

2. to rotate.

trun'dle bed, a low bed that is moved on trundles, or casters; a truckle bed.

trun'dle·head, (-hed), *n.* 1. in nautical usage, the head of a capstan having peripheral sockets into which the capstan bars are inserted.

2. one of the end disks of a lantern wheel or trundle wheel.

trun'dle·tāil, *n.* a curled tail; also, a dog with such a tail. [Archaic.]

truñk, *n.* [OFr. *tronc;* L. *truncus,* a trunk, stock, stem, from *truncus,* maimed, mutilated.]

1. the main stem or body of a tree, considered apart from its roots and branches.

2. the body of a human being or animal considered apart from the head and limbs.

3. the main body of a nerve, blood vessel, etc., as distinguished from the branches.

4. a long, flexible snout or proboscis, as of an elephant.

5. in architecture, the shaft of a column.

6. a box or chest, often reinforced with metal, cloth, or leather, used to carry clothing and personal effects, as for a vacation.

7. a long tube through which pellets of clay, beans, peas, etc. are blown. [Obs.]

8. a large, long, boxlike shaft, pipe, etc., used to convey water, air, etc. from one point to another.

9. in trunk engines, a large pipe passing longitudinally through the cylinder attached to the piston and moving with it, its diameter being sufficient to allow one of the connecting rods to be attached to the crank and the other end pivoted to the piston; also, a trunk engine.

10. a lobster pot.

11. [*pl.*] trunk hose.

12. [*pl.*] tight-fitting, very short breeches worn by men for athletics, etc.

13. a trunk line.

14. the thorax of an insect.

15. in nautical usage, (a) the part of a cabin above the upper deck; (b) a boxlike or funnellike casing, as for a centerboard, for connecting upper and lower hatches, etc.

truñk, *a.* pertaining to or designating a main line, as of a railroad or telephone system.

truñk, *v.t.;* trunked (truñkt), *pt., pp.;* trunking, *ppr.* to truncate. [Obs.]

truñk'back, *n.* the leatherback, a soft-shelled turtle, *Dermochelys coriacea:* also called *trunk turtle.*

truñked (truñkt), *a.* 1. having a trunk.

2. beheaded. [Obs.]

truñk en'ġine, a steam or internal-combustion engine in which the connecting rod is pivoted directly to the piston.

truñk'fish, *n.; pl.* **truñk'fish** or **truñk'fish·eṣ,** any of a group of tropical fishes whose bodies are encased in fused, bony plates, with only the mouth, eyes, fins, and tail projecting through.

truñk'fųl, *n.* as much as a trunk will hold.

truñk hōṣe, a kind of full, baglike breeches reaching about halfway to the knee, worn by men in the sixteenth and seventeenth centuries.

TRUNK HOSE

truñk līne, a main line of a railroad, canal, telephone system, etc.

truñk nāil, a short nail having a convex head, used in decorating trunks, etc.

truñk'nōṣe, *n.* the sea elephant.

truñk'wŏrk, *n.* underhand or secret work. [Obs.]

trun'nel, *n.* a treenail.

trun'niŏn (-yun), *n.* [Fr. *trognon,* a stump, trunk, dim. of *tron, tronc,* a trunk, stem.]

1. either of two cylindrical projections from the sides of a cannon, mortar, etc. which rest in the cheeks of the carriage, forming supports for the piece and an axis on which it pivots.

2. one of the hollow axes on which the cylinder of an oscillating steam engine reciprocates, and through which steam is received and exhausted.

trun'niŏned, *a.* having trunnions.

trun'niŏn plāte, 1. a plate acting as a shoulder for a gun trunnion.

2. a metal plate on a gun carriage under the trunnion and covering the upper part of the sidepiece.

trun'niŏn ring, a ring on a cannon directly in front of the trunnions.

trụ'ṣion, *n.* the act of pushing or thrusting. [Rare.]

truss, *n.* [ME. *trusse,* from *trussen,* to truss; OFr. *trousse,* from *trousser.*]

1. a bundle or pack.

2. a bundle of hay, especially one of a certain weight (usually 56-60 lbs.), or of straw (usually 36 lbs.).

3. in botany, a tuft of flowers formed at the top of the main stalk or stem.

4. in nautical usage, an iron band having a gooseneck used to keep the center of a yard to the mast.

5. in building, a framework of wood, metal, or both for supporting a roof, bridge, etc. The simplest example of a truss is the principal or main couple of a roof, in which *a a,* the tiebeam, is suspended in the middle by the king post *b* to the apex of the angle formed by the meeting of the rafters *c c.* The feet of the rafters being tied together by the beam *a,* and being thus incapable of yielding

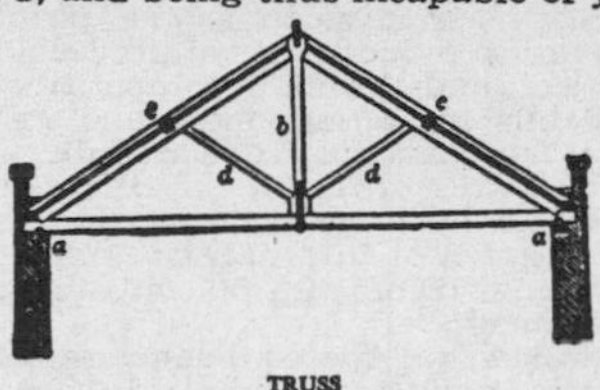

TRUSS

in the direction of their length, their apex becomes a fixed point, to which the beam *a* is trussed or tied up to prevent its sagging; to prevent the rafters from sagging there are inserted the struts *d d.*

6. in architecture, a bracket or modillion supporting a projection from the face of a wall.

7. an appliance for giving support in cases of rupture or hernia, usually consisting of a pad on a special belt.

8. a padded jacket or dress worn under armor to protect the body from the effects of friction. [Obs.]

truss, *v.t.;* trussed (trust), *pt., pp.;* trussing, *ppr.* [ME. *trussen;* OFr. *trusser, trosser, trousser,* to pack, bind, or gird up, truss.]

1. originally, to put or make up into a truss or bundle; to bundle.

2. to seize and hold firmly; to seize and carry off or aloft: said especially of birds of prey. [Archaic.]

3. to tie up: sometimes with *up.*

4. to hang: frequently with *up.* [Archaic.]

5. (a) to enclose or gird (the body) with a garment; (b) to tie, fasten, or tighten (a garment, etc.). [Now Rare.]

6. to skewer or bind the wings, etc. of (a fowl) before cooking; by extension, to prepare for cooking; to disembowel, etc.

7. in building, to furnish with a truss or trusses; to strengthen or support by a truss.

truss, *a.* stocky; round and thick. [Obs.]

truss bēam, a metal frame serving as a beam, girder, or summer; also, a wooden beam or frame with a tie rod to strengthen it.

truss bridġe, a bridge supported largely by trusses.

TRUSS BRIDGE

truss hoọp, in nautical usage, a hoop round a yard or mast to which an iron truss is fixed.

truss'ing, *n.* 1. the beams, rods, etc. that form a truss.

2. the act of one who trusses.

3. constructional trusses collectively.

4. bracing by or as by trusses.

trust, *n.* [ME. *trust, tryst;* ON. *traust,* trust, protection, firmness.]

1. confidence; a reliance or resting of the mind on the integrity, veracity, justice, friendship, or other sound principle of another person or thing.

> Whoso putteth his *trust* in the Lord shall be safe. —Prov. xxix. 25.

2. one who or that which is trusted.

> O Lord God, thou art my *trust* from my youth. —Ps. lxxi. 5.

3. something received in confidence; that which is confided to one's faith; as, to violate a sacred *trust.*

> Reward them well, if they observe their *trust.* —Denham.

4. responsibility or obligation resulting from this.

5. confident expectation of any event; anticipation; hope.

> His *trust* was with th' *Eternal* to be deemed Equal in strength. —Milton.

6. trustworthiness; loyalty. [Rare.]

7. keeping; care; custody.

8. confidence in a purchaser's intention or future ability to pay for goods, etc. delivered; credit; as, he sells on *trust.*

9. something entrusted to a person; a charge, duty, etc.

10. (a) a combination of corporations in the same industry or allied industries, usually

the largest producers, in which the stockholders turn over their stock to a board of trustees, who issue trust certificates to them and pay them dividends: the purposes of trusts are to reduce costs of production, control prices, and eliminate competition, thereby establishing a monopoly and increasing profits; they have been declared illegal in the United States; (b) any association of industrialists, business firms, etc. for establishing a national or international monopoly by price fixing, ownership of controlling stock, etc.; a cartel.

11. in law, (a) the confidence reposed in a person by giving him nominal ownership of property, which he is to keep, use, or administer for another's benefit; (b) an estate or property under the charge of a trustee or trustees; (c) a trustee or group of trustees; (d) a person's right to property held in trust for him.

in trust; in the condition of being entrusted to another's care.

Syn.—belief, confidence, credit, faith, hope, dependence.

trust, *a.* 1. held in trust; as, *trust* property.

2. relating to a trust or trusts.

3. managing for an owner; acting as a trustee.

trust buster; a government officer who seeks to dissolve trusts (sense 10) through the vigorous enforcement of antitrust laws.

trust certificate; see *trust*. n. (sense 10a).

trust company; (a) a bank organized under the laws of the State in which it transacts business, for the purpose of dealing in trusts and engaging in the general business of banking: such banks do not issue bank notes; (b) any corporation whose function is to act as trustee.

trust deed; see *deed of trust* under *deed*.

trust fund; money, stock, etc. held in trust.

trust territory; a region, colony, etc. placed under the administrative authority of a country by the United Nations: such territories include former mandates held under the League of Nations and colonies, etc. taken from Axis countries following World War II.

trust, *v.t.*; trusted, *pt., pp.*; trusting, *ppr.* 1. to place confidence in; to rely on; to believe in the honesty, integrity, justice, etc. of; as, we cannot *trust* those who have deceived us.

2. to show confidence by entrusting to (a person); to entrust: followed by *with*; as, I *trusted* him *with* my car.

3. to commit (*to* one's care); to entrust (*to* a person).

4. to allow to do something without fear of consequences; to allow to be exposed.

I wonder men dare *trust* themselves with men. —Shak.

5. to give business credit to.

6. to be confident; to feel sure; to expect; to hope.

I *trust* it will grow to a most prosperous perfection. —Shak.

7. to believe; to suppose.

Syn.—confide, rely, credit, believe, charge, deposit, entrust, repose, hope.

trust, *v.i.* 1. to have trust or faith; to place reliance; to be confident.

2. to hope (with *for*).

3. to give business credit.

to trust to; to depend on; to have confidence in; to rely on.

trus·tee′, *n.* 1. a person to whom another's property or the management of another's property is entrusted.

2. any of a group or board of persons appointed to manage the affairs of a college, hospital, etc.

3. a person in whose hands the property of a debtor is attached by the trustee process; a garnishee.

trustee process; garnishment.

trus·tee′, *v.t.* trusteed, *pt., pp.*; trusteeing, *ppr.* 1. to attach by the trustee process.

2. to commit (property or management) to a trustee or trustees.

trus·tee′ship, *n.* 1. the office, duties, or functions of a trustee.

2. (a) a commission from the United Nations to a country to administer some region, colony, etc. (called the *trust territory*); (b) the condition or fact of being a trust territory.

trust′ẽr, *n.* 1. one who trusts or gives credit.

2. in Scots law, one who grants a trust deed.

trust′fụl, *a.* 1. full of trust; confiding; trusting.

2. trusty; faithful; trustworthy. [Obs.]

trust′fụl·ly, *adv.* in a trustful manner.

trust′fụl·ness, *n.* the quality of being trustful.

trust′i·ly, *adv.* in a trusty manner.

trust′i·ness, *n.* the quality of being trusty.

trust′ing, *a.* trustful; confiding; having trust.

trust′ing·ly, *adv.* with trust or implicit confidence.

trust′less, *a.* 1. not worthy of trust; unfaithful; treacherous.

2. distrustful.

trust′less·ness, *n.* unworthiness of trust.

trust′wŏr″thi·ly, *adv.* in a trustworthy manner.

trust′wŏr″thi·ness, *n.* the quality of being trustworthy.

trust′wŏr″thy, *a.* worthy of trust or confidence; dependable; reliable.

trust′y, *a.*; *comp.* trustier; *superl.* trustiest. 1. that can be safely trusted or relied upon; justly deserving of trust or confidence; trustworthy; reliable; as, a *trusty* sentinel.

2. trustful. [Now Rare.]

trust′y, *n.*; *pl.* **trust′ieṣ,** 1. a trusted person.

2. a convict or prisoner to whom special privileges are granted because of good behavior.

trụth, *n.*; *pl.* **trụthṣ** (*or* trụths), [ME. *trewthe, trouthe*; from AS. *treowthu*, faith, truth.]

1. the quality or state of being true; specifically, (a) formerly, loyalty; trustworthiness; (b) sincerity; genuineness; honesty; (c) the quality of being in accordance with experience, facts, or reality; conformity with fact; (d) reality; actual existence; (e) agreement with a standard, rule, etc.; correctness; accuracy.

2. that which is true; a fact; a reality; that which conforms to fact or reality; the real or true state of things.

3. a verified fact; a true statement or proposition; an established principle, a fixed law, or the like.

in truth; for a certainty; in fact.

of a truth; certainly.

trụth, *v.t.* to declare true. [Rare.]

trụth′fụl, *a.* 1. telling the truth; presenting the facts; veracious; honest.

2. corresponding with fact or reality, as an artistic representation.

trụth′fụl·ly, *adv.* in a truthful manner.

trụth′fụl·ness, *n.* the state of being truthful.

trụth′less, *a.* lacking truth; without foundation; faithless.

trụth′less·ness, *n.* the state of being truthless.

trụth lŏv′ẽr, one who loves the truth.

trụth′ness, *n.* truth. [Obs.]

trụth′tell″ẽr, *n.* one who tells the truth.

trụth′y, *a.* truthful. [Dial.]

trụ′ti·nāte, *v.t.* to weigh; to consider. [Obs.]

trụ·ti·nā′tion, *n.* the act of weighing or considering. [Obs.]

trut·tā′ceous, *a.* [LL. *trutta*, a trout, and *-aceous.*] pertaining to trout.

trȳ, *v.t.*; tried, *pt., pp.*; trying, *ppr.* [ME. *trien, tryen*; OFr. *trier*, perh. from LL. *tritare*, to *triturate*, also to grind or thresh corn, to separate the corn from the stalk, select, from L. *tritus*, pp. of *terere*, to rub, thresh corn.]

1. to separate; to sift or pick out: usually with *out*. [Obs.]

2. (a) to melt out or render, as fat; (b) to extract or refine by heating, as metal. Usually with *out*.

3. to examine; to test; to put to the proof.

4. to subject to a severe test or strain; as, rigors that *try* one's stamina.

5. to subject to trials, annoyance, etc.; to afflict; as, he was sorely *tried*.

6. to settle (a matter, quarrel, etc.) by a test or contest; to fight out; as, the knights *tried* the dispute in a joust. [Now Rare.]

7. (a) to examine and decide (a case) in a law court; (b) to determine legally the guilt or innocence of (a person); (c) to preside as judge at the trial of (a case or person).

8. to test the operation or effect of; to experiment with; to make a trial of; as, *try* his new recipe.

9. to attempt to find out by experiment or effort; as, he left the farm to *try* his fortune in the city.

10. to make an effort to do; to attempt; to undertake.

11. to experience; to have knowledge of by experience; to prove. [Obs.]

12. to make smooth or even with a trying plane.

to try conclusions; see under *conclusion*.

to try on; to put on, as a garment, to see if it fits properly.

to try out; (a) to test or find out the quality result, value, etc. of; to experiment with; (b) to test one's ability to qualify in a competition, for a job, etc.

Syn.—endeavor, attempt, test, assay, essay, strive, aim, examine.

trȳ, *v.i.* 1. to find, show, or prove by experience what a person or thing is; to make an experiment.

2. to make an effort, attempt, or endeavor: colloquially, *try* in this sense is often followed by *and* and a co-ordinate verb, as, please *try and* behave.

3. to do; to fare. [Brit. Dial.]

trȳ, *n.*; *pl.* **trīeṣ,** 1. the act of trying; an attempt; an endeavor; a trial; an experiment; as, let us give it a *try*.

2. a sieve; a screen. [Obs.]

3. in Rugby football, a grounding of the ball on or behind the opponent's goal line: this play counts 3 points and entitles the scoring team to try to kick a goal for 2 additional points.

trȳ′ȧ·ble, *a.* same as *triable*.

trȳ çock, a gauge cock.

trȳ′gon, *n.* [Gr. *trygōn*.] a sting ray.

trȳ′ing, *a.* adapted to try; exasperating, irksome; painful; perplexing; as, a *trying* situation; a *trying* voyage.

trȳ′ing plāne, a long finishing plane for use on edges, etc. that must be accurate.

trȳ′mȧ, *n.* [Mod. L., from Gr. *tryma, trymē*, a hole, from *tryein*, to rub down, to wear away.] a nut having a fleshy or fibrous epicarp that bursts upon ripening, as the walnut and hickory.

trȳ′out, *n.* an opportunity to prove, or a test to determine, fitness or qualifications, as for competition in sports, a role in a play, etc. [Colloq.]

trȳ′pȧ, *n.* [Gr. *trype*, a hole.] in zoology, an aperture in the front wall of the zooecium of a polyzoan.

Tryp″ȧ·nō·sō′mȧ, *n.* [Gr. *trypanon*, borer, and *sōma*, body.]

1. a genus of flagellate protozoans that live as parasites in the blood of man and other vertebrates and often cause serious diseases, as sleeping sickness.

2. [t–] any protozoan of this genus.

tryp′ȧ·nō·sōme, *n.* a trypanosoma.

tryp′sin, *n.* [G., from Gr. *tripsis*, a rubbing, from *tribein*, to rub; and *-in*.]

1. a digestive enzyme in the pancreatic juice: it changes proteins into peptones.

2. any of several similar enzymes.

tryp·sin′ō·ġen, *n.* [from *trypsin* and *-gen*.] the zymogen occurring in the pancreas, from which trypsin is formed during the secretion of the pancreatic juice.

tryp′tiç, *a.* relating to or produced by trypsin.

tryp′tōne, *n.* any peptone produced by the digestion of trypsin.

tryp′tō·phan, tryp′tō·phāne, *n.* an amino acid, $C_{11}H_{12}O_2N_2$, produced in digestion by the action of trypsin on proteins.

trȳ′sāil (*or* -sl), *n.* a small, stout, fore-and-aft sail hoisted when other canvas has been lowered, to keep a vessel's head to the wind in a storm.

trȳ squāre (skwãr), an instrument used by carpenters and joiners for testing the accuracy of square work or for marking off right angles. It consists of a thin blade of steel about six inches long, set into a wooden piece of similar length and securely fastened at right angles to it.

tryst, *n.* [ME. *trist*; OFr. *tristre*, hunting station.]

1. an appointment to meet at a specified time and place, as one made by lovers.

2. a meeting held by appointment.

3. a trysting place.

4. a market; a fair. [Scot.]

tryst, *v.t.* 1. to engage to meet at a certain time and place. [Scot.]

2. to bespeak; to order in advance; as, to *tryst* a pair of boots. [Scot.]

tryst, *v.i.* to agree to meet at any particular time or place. [Scot.]

tryst′ẽr, *n.* one who trysts; one who fixes a time and place of meeting.

tryst′ing, *n.* a tryst.

tryst′ing dāy, an appointed day of meeting or assembling, as of troops.

tryst′ing plāce, an arranged meeting place, as of lovers; a rendezvous.

tsä′di, *n.* the eighteenth letter of the Hebrew alphabet, corresponding phonetically to English *ts*.

tsär, *n.* a czar.
tsär′dŏm, *n.* a czardom.
tsär′e·vitch, *n.* a czarevitch.
tsär·ev′nȧ, *n.* a czarevna.
tsä·ri′nȧ, *n.* a czarina.
tsär′iṣm, *n.* czarism.
tsär′ist, *a.* and *n.* czarist.
tsär·it′zȧ, *n.* a czarina.
tscheff′kin·īte (chef′), *n.* [named after the Russ. Gen. *Tscheffkin.*] a rare titanian silicate occurring in velvety black, massive formations.
tset′sē, *n.* [S. Afr.] an African dipterous insect of the family *Tipulidæ* and genus *glossina*, akin to the gadfly: one species is a carrier of nagana and another a carrier of sleeping sickness: also called *tsetse fly*.

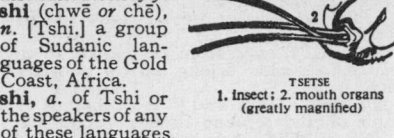

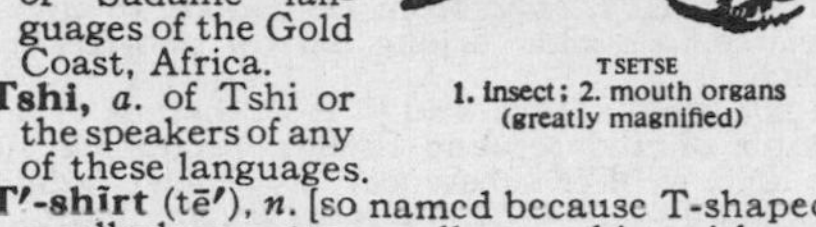
TSETSE
1. insect; 2. mouth organs (greatly magnified)

Tshi (chwē *or* chē), *n.* [Tshi.] a group of Sudanic languages of the Gold Coast, Africa.
Tshi, *a.* of Tshi or the speakers of any of these languages.
T′-shirt (tē′), *n.* [so named because T-shaped.] a collarless, cotton, pull-over shirt with very short sleeves.
T squāre, see under *T*.
tsü′bȧ, *n.* [Japan.] the highly decorated guard of a Japanese sword.
Tsū′gȧ, *n.* [Japan.] a genus of coniferous trees, the hemlocks, intermediate between *Picea*, the spruces, and *Abies*, the firs. The six species have pendulous branches, narrowly linear leaves, white underneath, and small brown cones.
Tu, in chemistry, thulium.
Tuȧ′reg (twä′), *n.* [from Arab. *tereq*, to give up.]
1. a member of a group of Berber tribes of the western and central Sahara.
2. their Hamitic language.
tū′ärt, *n.* same as *tooart*.
tū·ȧ·tę′rȧ, *n.* a lizard of the genus *Hatteria*.
tub, *n.* [ME. *tubbe*; M.D. *tubbe*.]
1. a round, broad, open, wooden container, usually formed of staves and hoops fastened around a flat bottom.
2. any similarly large, open container of metal, stone, etc., as for washing.
3. the contents of a tub, or a tub and its contents.
4. a small cask holding about four gallons.
5. (a) a bucket or tram for carrying coal, ore, etc. in a mine; (b) the lining of a mining shaft.
6. a bathtub.
7. a bath in a tub. [Brit. Colloq.]
8. a slow-moving, clumsy ship or boat. [Colloq.]
tub, *v.t.* and *v.i.* tubbed, *pt.*, *pp.*; tubbing, *ppr.*
1. to wash in a tub. [Colloq.]
2. to bathe (oneself). [Brit. Colloq.]
tū′bȧ, *n.*; *pl.* **tū′bȧṣ, tū′bae,** [L., a trumpet.]
1. in ancient Rome, a straight war trumpet.
2. a large brass-wind instrument of the saxhorn group.
3. a powerful reed organ stop of 8-foot pitch.

TUBA

tūb′ăge, *n.* 1. formerly, the act of lining a gun with a cylindrical tube of wrought iron or steel to increase the power by decreasing the caliber.
2. the insertion of a tube into one of the passages of the body; intubation.
tūb′ăl, *a.* relating to a tube, especially to a Fallopian or a Eustachian tube.
tūb′ăl, *n.* a Fallopian tube.
Tū′bȧl-çāin′, *n.* in the Bible, a worker in brass and iron: Gen. iv. 22.
tūb′āte, *a.* furnished with or having the shape of a tube; tubular.
tub′bing, *n.* [verbal noun of *tub*.]
1. the materials from which tubs are made.
2. the act of one employed in making tubs.
3. the metal or wooden lining of the shaft of a mine, usually cylindrical in form.
4. the act or process of bathing or of being bathed in a tub.
tub′by, *a.*; *comp.* tubbier; *superl.* tubbiest, 1. shaped like a tub.
2. short and fat.
3. having a dull, wooden sound.
tūbe, *n.* [Fr., from L. *tubus*, a pipe.]
1. a hollow cylinder or pipe of metal, glass, rubber, etc., usually long in proportion to its diameter, used for conveying fluids, etc.
2. an enclosed, hollow cylinder of thin, soft metal, fitted at one end with a screw cap and used for holding toothpaste, artist's paints, etc.
3. an instrument, part, organ, etc. resembling a tube; as, a bronchial *tube*.
4. an electron tube.
5. (a) an underground tunnel for an electric railroad; (b) [Colloq.] the electric railroad itself.
6. a telescope. [Archaic.]
7. in botany, the lower, united part of a gamopetalous corolla or a gamosepalous calyx.
8. in electricity, a tubular space bounded by lines of force or induction: also *tube of force, tube of induction*.
bronchial tubes; see under *bronchial*.
capillary tubes; see under *capillary*.
down the tube (or *tubes*); in or into a condition of failure, defeat, etc. [Colloq.]
electron tube; see under *electron*.
Eustachian tube; see under *Eustachian*.
Malpighian tube; see under *Malpighian*.
pneumatic tube; a tube that uses compressed air for carrying packets, letters, etc. in a box fitted to the tube and containing a compartment for receiving whatever is to be carried.
safety tube; in anatomy, a small part of the upper termination of the Eustachian tube: it is partly open, thus allowing a recoil of air from the tympanum when the membrane of the drum is driven inward suddenly: pressure in the tympanic cavity is thus equalized from the pharynx.
screen-grid tube; a vacuum tube using a fine wire mesh grid or screen to reduce to a minimum the effective capacity between the electrodes.
the tube; television. [Colloq.]
vacuum tube; see following *vacuum*.
tūbe, *v.t.*; tubed, *pt.*, *pp.*; tubing, *ppr.* 1. to furnish with, place in, or pass through a tube or tubes.
2. to make tubular.
tūbe çor′ăl, same as *tubipore*.
tūbe foot, a locomotive process or ambulacral sucker of an echinoderm.
tūbe′-nōṣed (nōzd), *a.* having tubiform nostrils, as certain birds.
tūbe plāte, same as *tube sheet*.
tū′bēr, *n.* [L., lit., a swelling or knob on plants.]
1. in botany, a fleshy, rounded part of a subterranean stem, as the potato or arrowroot: new plants develop from the buds, or eyes, that grow in the axils of the minute scale leaves of a tuber.
2. [T-] a genus of fungi including the truffles.
3. in anatomy, a tubercle.
Tū·bē·rā′cē·ae, *n.pl.* [LL., from L. *tuber*, a tuber, and *-aceæ*.] a family of fungi analogous among the sporidiferous kind with the hypogeal fungi among the sporiferous. All the genera, with a single exception, are strictly subterranean. The order includes the genus *Tuber*, the common truffles, and *Rhizopogon*, the white truffles.
tū·bē·rā′ceous, *a.* pertaining or belonging to the order *Tuberaceæ*.
tū′bēr·çle (-kl), *n.* [Fr., from L. *tuberculum*, double dim. of *tuber*, a swelling.]
1. a nodule or small prominence, especially a solid elevation of the skin larger in size than a papula.
2. in anatomy, a rough, rounded prominence on a bone.
3. any abnormal hard nodule; especially, the typical nodular lesion produced by the bacillus of tuberculosis, and consisting of a translucent mass, gray in color, made up of small spheric cells, which contain giant cells, and are surrounded by a layer of spindle-shaped connective tissue cells known as epithelioid cells.
4. in botany, a little knob or rough point on the fronds of some lichens; also, a small tuber or tuberlike root growth.
5. in the *Echinidæ*, a small eminence of the body wall which is immediately connected with the spines.
Darwinian tubercle; see under *Darwinian*.
tū′bēr·çle bȧ·cil′lus, the bacillus causing tuberculosis.
tū′bēr·çled (-kld), *a.* having tubercles; affected with tubercles; as, a *tubercled* lung.
tū·bēr′çū·lăr, *a.* [L. *tuberculum*, tubercle.]
1. shaped like a tubercle; having the form and appearance of a tubercle.
2. full of tubercles; tuberculate.
3. in medicine, affected with or having tuberculosis; tuberculous.
tū·bēr′çū·lăr, *n.* a tuberculous person.
Tū·bēr″çū·lā·ri·ā′cē·ae, *n.pl.* [L. *tuberculum*, a tubercle, and *-aceæ*.] a large family of fungi, having the conidia borne laterally or terminally on hyphae. Growths of this class cause many plant diseases.
tū·bēr″çū·lăr·ĭ·zā′tion, *n.* infection with tuberculosis.
tū·bēr′çū·lăr·īze, *v.t.*; tubercularized, *pt.*, *pp.*; tubercularizing, *ppr.* to infect with tuberculosis.
tū·bēr′çū·lāte, *a.* [LL. *tuberculatus*, from L. *tuberculum*, a tubercle.]
1. tubercular.
2. tuberculated.
tū·bēr′çū·lā·ted, *a.* characterized by, shaped like, or having a tubercle or tubercles.
tū·bēr·çū·lā′tion, *n.* the development of tubercles.
tū·bēr′çū·lin, *n.* [*tubercul*um and *-in*.] a sterile liquid preparation made from the growth products or extracts of a tubercle bacillus culture and injected into the skin as a test for the presence of tuberculosis.
tū·bēr′çū·line, *n.* tuberculin.
tū·bēr″çū·li·zā′tion, *n.* the formation of tubercles; the condition of becoming tubercled.
tū·bēr′çū·lō-, [from L. *tuberculum*.] a combining form meaning (a) *tuberculous*; (b) *tubercle bacillus*; (c) *tuberculosis*: also, before a vowel, *tubercul-*.
tū·bēr″çū·lō·cī′din, *n.* an albumose derived from tuberculin by treating it with platinum chloride. It is used like tuberculin but is said to be free from the impurities of the latter.
tū·bēr′çū·loid, *a.* [*tubercul*um and *-oid*.] like a tubercle.
tū·bēr′çū·lōse, *a.* tubercular.
tū·bēr′çū·lōsed (-lōst), *a.* having tuberculosis.
tū·bēr·çū·lō′sis, *n.* [L. *tuberculum*, tubercle.] an infectious disease caused by the tubercle bacillus and characterized by the formation of tubercles in various tissues of the body; especially, tuberculosis of the lungs; pulmonary phthisis; consumption. To a lesser extent the spleen, kidneys, lymph glands, liver, intestines, and brain may become involved. The disease is attended by symptoms due to the destruction it produces and varying with the location of the infection. When not strictly localized, the general symptoms of septic infection are present, such as hectic fever, increasing emaciation, and night-sweats.
tū·bēr′çū·lous, *a.* 1. tubercular.
2. having tuberculosis.
tū·bēr′çū·lum, *n.* [L., tubercle.] a tubercle.
tū·bēr·if′ēr·ous, *a.* [L. *tuber*, *tuberis*, a tuber, and *-ferous*.] producing or bearing tubers.
tū′bēr·in, *n.* in physiological chemistry, a proteide typical of the potato tuber.
tū′bēr·ŏn, *n.* a shark. [Obs.]
tūbe·rōṣe, *n.* [an alteration of LL. *tuberosa*, from L. *tuberosus*, knobby.] a plant with a tuberous root, short, grasslike leaves, and a liliaceous flower, the *Polianthes tuberosa*.
tū′bēr·ōse, *a.* tuberous.
tū·bēr·os′ĭ·ty, *n.*; *pl.* **tū·bēr·os′ĭ·tieṣ,** 1. the state or quality of being tuberous.
2. a swelling or prominence; specifically, in anatomy, a projection or elevation on a bone, having a rough uneven surface, to which muscles and ligaments are attached.

TUBEROSE (*Polianthes tuberosa*)

tū′bēr·ous, *a.* [L. *tuberosus*.]
1. covered with knobby or wartlike lumps or prominences; knobbed.
2. in botany, consisting of or containing tubers; also, resembling a tuber.
tū′bēr·ous·ness, *n.* the quality of being tuberous; tuberosity.

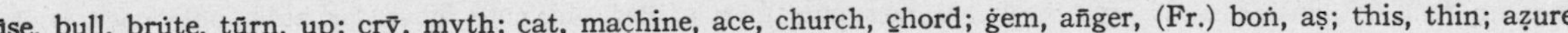

tū′bẽr·ous ro̤ot, a tuberlike root without buds or scale leaves, as of the dahlia.
tūbe sheet, an iron plate or sheet in which are fastened the ends of boiler tubes.
tūbe spin′nẽr, a tube weaver.
tūbe wēav′ẽr, any spider of the *Tubicolæ* or *Tubitelæ*.
tūbe well, an apparatus consisting of a cylindrical iron tube, which is driven into the earth to a stratum containing water, and which serves as a temporary well.
tūbe′wŏrm, *n.* a tube-constructing annelid.
tub′fish, *n.*; *pl.* **tub′fish, tub′fish·eṣ,** the sapphirine gurnard, *Trigla hirundo*.
tub′fụl, *n.* a quantity sufficient to fill a tub; as much as a tub will hold.
tū′bi-, [from L. *tubus*, tube.] a combining form meaning *of* or *pertaining to a tube*.
Tū·biç′ō·lae, *n.pl.* [*tubi-*, and L. *colere*, to inhabit.]
1. a family of spiders that enclose themselves in tubular webs: it includes two genera, *Dysdera* and *Segestria*.
2. an order of annelids comprising those which live in calcareous tubes composed of secretions from the animal itself, as the *Serpulidæ*; in tubes composed of sand and fragments of shell connected by a glutinous secretion, as the *Terebellidæ*; in tubes composed of granules of sand and mud, as the *Sabellidæ*; or in membranous tubes, as the families which include the less known genera *Pectinaria*, *Phoronis*, etc.
tū·biç′ō·lăr, *a.* same as *tubicolous*.
tū·biç′ō·lous, *a.* in zoology, inhabiting, secreting, or having a tube.
tū′bi·çorn, *n.* [*tubi-*, and L. *cornu*, horn.] one of a family of hollow-horned ruminants; an animal having horns composed of a horny axis enclosed in a horny sheath.
tū·bi·çor′nous, *a.* hollow-horned.
tū·bi·fā′cient (-shent), *a.* [*tubi-*, and L. *faciens* (*-entis*), ppr. of *facere*, to make.] tube-building, as an annelid.
tū·bi·flō′rous, *a.* [*tubi-*, and L. *flos*, *floris*, a flower.] bearing tubular flowers.
tū′bi·fọrm, *a.* having the form of a tube; tubular.
tū·bi·liṅ′guăl, *a.* having a cylindrical or tubular tongue.
Tū·bi·nā′rēṣ, *n.pl.* [*tubi-*, and L. *nares*, nostrils.] a large family of sea birds, characterized by tubular nostrils, including the petrels, albatrosses, etc.
tū·bi·nãr′i·ăl, *a.* 1. of or belonging to the *Tubinares*.
2. having tubular nostrils.
tū·bi·nā′rine, *a.* tubinarial.
tūb′ing, *n.* 1. the process of making tubes.
2. a series or system of tubes.
3. tubes collectively.
4. material in the form of a tube.
5. a piece of a tube.
Tü′bing·en sçho̤ol, a school of theology, founded at Tübingen, Germany, in 1826, which attempted to apply a Hegelian philosophy of history to an explanation of the evolution of Christianity.
tū·bip′ȧ·rous, *a.* [*tubi-*, and L. *parere*, to produce.] forming tubular structures; as, a *tubiparous* gland.
Tū·bip′ō·rȧ, *n.* [*tubi-*, and L. *porus*, a pore.] the organ-pipe corals, a genus of actinozoans, or corals, order *Alcyonaria*, including those which are provided with internal ovaries and eight pinnated tentacula, contained in elongated cylindrical cells, which are calcareous or coriaceous and attached by the base.
tū′bi·pōre, *n.* [*tubi-*, and L. *porus*, pore.] one of a genus of coral zoophytes; an organ-pipe coral.
tub′măn, *n.*; *pl.* **tub′men,** in English law, formerly, a barrister who had a preaudience in the Exchequer division of the High Court: he stood beside the tub used as a measure in excise cases.
tū″bō-ō·vãr′i·ăn, *a.* of or pertaining to an oviduct and an ovary.
tub prēach′ẽr, a dissenting minister; hence, a ranting, ignorant preacher: a term of contempt.
tū′bū·lăr, *a.* [L. *tubulus*, a small tube.]
1. having the form of a tube or pipe; consisting of a pipe; fistular; as, a *tubular* snout.
2. made or furnished with tubes; as, a *tubular* calyx.
3. designating a sound similar to that produced by a current of air through a tube: applied to certain respiratory sounds.
tubular bridge; see under *bridge*.
tubular girder; any hollow girder of metal.
Tū·bū·lā′ri·ȧ, *n.* [LL., from L. *tubulus*, a small tube.] in zoology, a genus of *Hydrozoa*, of the subclass *Hydroida*, order *Corynidæ* or *Tubularida*. In this genus, the hydrosoma consists of clustered, horny, strawlike tubes, each of which is filled with a soft, semifluid, reddish coenosarc, and gives exit at its distal extremity to a single bright red, unretractile polypite.
Tū·bū·lā′ri·ae, *n.pl.* an order of tubularian hydroids, the gymnoblastic *Hydromedusæ*.
tū·bū·lăr′i·ăn, *n.* a member of the order *Tubulariæ*.
tū·bū·lăr′i·ăn, *a.* of or pertaining to the *Tubulariæ*.
Tū″bū·lȧ·rī′i·dae, *n.pl.* in zoology, a family of tubularian *Hydromedusæ*, represented by the genus *Tubularia*: also called *Athecata*, *Gymnoblastea*, and *Tubularidæ*.
tū′bū·lāte, *a.* 1. tubular (senses 1 and 2).
2. of, shaped like, or provided with a tubulure.
tū′bū·lāte, *v.t.*; tubulated, *pt.*, *pp.*; tubulating, *ppr.* 1. to form into a tube.
2. to furnish with a tube or tubulure.
tū′bū·lā·ted, *a.* [L. *tubulatus*.] made in the form of, or furnished with, a small tube, or tubulure.
tū·bū·lā′tion, *n.* the act of making hollow, as a tube; the act of forming a tube or the process of being formed into a tube; also, the arrangement of a number of tubes.
tū′bū·lȧ·tūre, *n.* a tubulure.
tū′būle, *n.* [L. *tubulus*, a small tube.]
1. a small pipe or fistular body.
2. a small tubular structure in an animal or plant.
tū′bū·li-, [from L. *tubulus*.] a combining form meaning *tubule*.
tū″bū·li·braṅ′chi·ăn, *n.* a mollusk of the order *Tubulibranchiata*.
Tū″bū·li·braṅ·chi·ā′tȧ, *n.pl.* [L. *tubulus*, a small tube, and *branchiæ*, gills.] in Cuvier's classification, those gastropods whose branchiae are lodged in a more or less regularly shaped tube, including the genera *Vermetus*, *Magilus*, and *Siliquaria*.
tū″bū·li·den′tāte, *a.* [L. *tubulus*, a small tube, and *dentatus*, toothed.] having teeth composed of tubular bundles of denticles, as the aardvark, or Cape anteater of South Africa.
tū·bū·lif′ẽr·ous, *a.* [L. *tubulus*, a small tube, and *-ferous*.] in entomology, provided with tubules, as some insects with tubular ovipositors.
tū″bū·li·flō′rous, *a.* [L. *tubulus*, a small tube, and *flos*, *floris*, a flower.] having flowers in heads with tubular corollas, as certain composite flowering plants.
tū′bū·li·fọrm, *a.* [L. *tubulus*, small tube, and *-form*.] having the form of a small tube.
tū′bū·li·pōre, *n.* [L. *tubulus*, small tube, and *porus*, pore.] a polyzoan of the family *Tubuliporidæ*.
Tū″bū·li·por′i·dae, *n.pl.* a family of polyzoans of which *Tubulipora* is the typical genus, characterized by tubular calcareous calycles.
tū′bū·lōse, *a.* [L. *tubulus*, a small tube, and *-ose*.] tubulous.
tū′bū·lous, *a.* longitudinally hollow; resembling a tube or pipe; tubular; specifically, in botany, containing small tubes, or composed wholly of tubulous florets; as, a *tubulous* compound flower.
tū′bū·lūre, *n.* [Fr.] in chemistry, a short open tube or tubular opening at the top of a retort, etc.
tū′bū·lus, *n.*; *pl.* **tū′bū·lī,** [L.] a little tube or pipe; specifically, in anatomy, a minute duct, as the *tubuli lactiferi*, or milk ducts.
tụ′çăn, *n.* [Mex.] the pocket gopher, *Geomys mexicanus*, of Mexico: also written *tuca*, and *tuza*.
Tū·cā′nȧ, *n.* a southern constellation.
tuch, *n.* touch. [Obs.]
tuçk, *v.t.* [OFr. *toucher*, to touch.] to beat; to tap. [Scot.]
tuck, *n.* the sound produced by beating a drum; a beat. [Scot.]

Leslie's foot and Leven's troopers
Marching to the *tuck* of drum.
—Aytoun.

tuck, *v.t.*; tucked (tukt), *pt.*, *pp.*; tucking, *ppr.* [ME. *tuken*, from M.D. *tucken*, to tuck, and cognate AS. *tucian*, to ill-treat, lit., to tug.]
1. to pull up or gather up in a fold or folds; to draw together, as to make shorter (usually with *up*).
2. (a) to thrust the edges of (a sheet, napkin, etc.) under or in, in order to make secure (usually with *up*, *in*, etc.); (b) to cover or wrap snugly in or as in this way; as, she *tucked* the baby in bed.
3. to put or press snugly into a small space; to cram; to fit; as, she managed to *tuck* her shoes in the suitcase.
4. to make a sewed fold or folds in (a garment).
5. to full, as cloth. [Brit. Dial.]
to tuck away (or *in*); to eat or drink heartily. [Brit. Slang.]
tuck, *v.i.* 1. to contract; to draw together; to pucker.
2. to make tucks in a fabric, etc.
tuck, *n.* 1. a kind of small net used in removing fish caught in a larger net.
2. in a ship, the part where the ends of the bottom planks meet under the stern.
3. a fold sewed in a garment for ornamentation or to make it shorter or smaller; a plait.
4. in bookbinding, a flap attached to one book cover which folds over and tucks into a pocket on the other.
5. food, especially sweets, pastry, etc. [Brit. Slang.]
tuck, *n.* [OFr. *estoc*, from D. *stocken*, to stick, pierce.] a rapier; a long narrow sword. [Archaic.]
tuck′ȧ·hōe, *n.* [Am. Ind.] 1. a tuberous vegetable or underground fungus, producing an edible, weblike substance: also called *Indian bread*, *Indian head*, *Virginia truffle*, and *Indian loaf*.
2. formerly, either the Virginia wakerobin, or the goldenclub. [Obs.]
tuck′ẽr, *n.* 1. a person who makes tucks.
2. a sewing machine attachment for making tucks.
3. a neck and shoulder covering worn with a low-cut bodice by women in the seventeenth and eighteenth centuries.
4. a detachable collar or chemisette of thin muslin, etc.
5. a fuller of cloth. [Dial.]
6. food. [Australian Slang.]
tuck′ẽr, *v.t.*; tuckered, *pt.*, *pp.*; tuckering, *ppr.* to tire; to exhaust physically: used with *out*; as, when he finished the race he was completely *tuckered out*. [Colloq.]
tuck′et, *n.* [from *tuck* (to beat a drum).] a flourish on a trumpet; a fanfare. [Archaic.]
tuck′et, *n.* an ear of green Indian corn. [Dial.]
tuck net, a small net used to take out fish from a larger one.
tū′çum, *n.* [Braz.] any of several species of palm, *Astrocaryum vulgare*, of great importance to the Brazilian Indians, who make cordage, bowstrings, fishing nets, hats, fans, hammocks, etc., from the fine durable fiber of the epidermis of its unexpanded leaves; also, the fiber or thread.
tụ·çū′mȧ, *n.* same as *tucum*.
tụ′çū-tụ′çū, tụ′çō-tụ′çō, *n.* [Braz.] a small, burrowing South American rodent, *Ctenomys brasiliensis*, about as large as a rat but resembling a squirrel.
-tūde, [Fr.; L. *-tudo*, *-tudinis*.] a noun-forming suffix corresponding to *-ness*, as in certi*tude*.
Tū′dŏr, *a.* 1. of or belonging to a ruling family of England (1485–1603), descended from Owen Tudor, a Welsh nobleman who married the widow of Henry V: it included Henry VII, Henry VIII, Edward VI, Mary I, and Elizabeth I.
2. of the period of their reigns.
3. designating or of a style of architecture that prevailed during the reign of the Tudors: it is characterized by flat arches, shallow moldings, profuse paneling, etc.
Tū′dŏr, *n.* 1. a sovereign of the Tudor line.
2. a poet, artist, etc. of the time of the Tudors.
Tū′dŏr flow′ẽr, a trefoil ornament much used in Tudor architecture. It is placed upright on a stalk, and is employed in long rows as a crest or ornamental finishing on cornices, ridges, etc.

TUDOR FLOWER

Tū′dŏr rōṣe, a conventionalized representation of a rose adopted by Henry VII as a royal emblem of England and used in Tudor decoration.
tū′ē, *n.* same as *poebird*.
tūe′ī·ron (-ũrn), *n.* [corruption of *tuyère*.]
1. a tuyère.
2. [*pl.*] a smith's tongs.
Tūeṣ′dāy, *n.* [AS. *Tiwes dæg*, Tiw's day, the day of *Tiw*, the northern Mars, or god of

war.] the third day of the week; the day after Monday and preceding Wednesday.

tū'fȧ, *n.* [It. *tufa*; Fr. *tuf*, a kind of porous stone, from L. *tofus*, tuff, tufa.]

1. a porous limestone formed by deposits from springs and streams.

2. tuff.

Also *toph, tophe.*

tū·fā'ceous, *a.* [*tufa* and *-aceous.*] pertaining to tufa; consisting of tufa or resembling it.

tuff, *n.* a porous rock, usually stratified, consisting of accumulations of scoria and ashes about the crater of a volcano, which are agglutinated together so as to make a coherent or solid mass. Sometimes tuff is composed of volcanic ashes and sand, transported and deposited by rainwater.

tuff·ā'ceous, *a.* having the nature of tuff; relating to tuff.

tuf'fet, *n.* 1. tuft. [Dial.]

2. a mound or hillock: in the nursery rhyme, *tuffet* is of doubtful meaning.

Little Miss Muffet sat on a *tuffet*.
—Nursery Rhyme.

tuf·fọọn', *n.* a typhoon. [Obs.]

tuft, *n.* [ME.; OFr. *tuffe.*]

1. a bunch of hairs, feathers, grass, etc. growing closely together or attached at the base.

2. any similar cluster; specifically, (a) a clump of plants or trees; (b) any of the clusters of threads drawn tightly through a mattress, quilt, etc. to hold the padding in place: also, a button to which such a tuft is fastened.

3. in English universities, a young nobleman student at a university: so called from the *tuft* formerly worn on the cap. [Slang.]

tuft, *v.t.*; tufted, *pt., pp.*; tufting, *ppr.* 1. to provide or decorate with a tuft or tufts.

2. to secure the padding of (a quilt, mattress, etc.) by means of regularly spaced tufts.

tuft, *v.i.* to grow in tufts; to form a tuft or tufts.

tuf·taf'fē·tȧ, *n.* a kind of taffeta with the nap formed into tufts. [Obs.]

tuft'ed, *a.* 1. having, provided with, or decorated with a tuft or tufts.

2. formed into or growing in a tuft or tufts.

tufted duck; (a) a scauplike duck, *Fuligula cristata*, common in the northern parts of the Old World, the male having a tuft of long feathers on the head; (b) [Dial.] the ringnecked duck.

tufted titmouse; a North American titmouse, *Parus bicolor*, common in the eastern part of the United States and characterized by a conspicuous crest.

tuft'hunt"ẽr, *n.* [*tuft* (in Eng. university slang sense of "titled undergraduate": from the tuft or tassel formerly worn by titled undergraduates at Oxford and Cambridge) and *hunter.*] a person who tries to get acquainted with distinguished or wealthy people; a social climber; a sycophant; a toady; a snob.

tuft'hunt"ing, *n.* the practices of a tufthunter.

tuft'y, *a.* 1. full of or covered with tufts.

2. growing in or forming a tuft or tufts.

tug, *v.t.*; tugged, *pt., pp.*; tugging, *ppr.* [ME. *tuggen*, prob. from ON. *toga*, to draw, pull.]

1. to pull at with great force; to strain at.

2. to drag; haul.

3. to tow with a tugboat.

tug, *v.i.* 1. to pull with great effort; as, to *tug* at the oar; to *tug* against the stream.

2. to labor; to strive; to struggle.

tug, *n.* 1. a pull exerting the utmost effort.

2. a violent effort; the severest strain or struggle.

When Greeks joined Greeks, then was the *tug* of war. —Lee.

3. a tugboat.

4. a trace of a harness; also, any rope or chain used for pulling.

5. in mining, an iron hoop to which a tackle is fastened.

6. an English type of timber wagon.

tug'bōat, *n.* a small, strongly built steamboat used for towing or pushing other vessels: also called *steam tug.*

tug'gẽr, *n.* one who or that which tugs.

tug'ging, *n.* the act of pulling or dragging.

tug'ging·ly, *adv.* with laborious pulling; by tugging.

tug ī'ron (-ūrn), an iron used to hold a tug, as on a wagon shaft.

tug'măn, *n.*; *pl.* **tug'men,** a person employed on a tugboat.

tug of wạr, 1. a contest in which two teams pull at opposite ends of a rope, each trying to drag the other across a central line.

2. any hard struggle between two parties.

tū'ī, *n.* same as *poebird.*

Tuï'lẽr·ieṣ (twē'; Fr. twēl"rē'), *n.* a former royal palace in Paris, burned in 1871.

tuïlle (twēl), *n.* [OFr., from L. *tegula*, tile.] in medieval plate armor, a guard plate attached to the tassets and covering the upper part of the thigh.

tū·i'tion, *n.* [Fr., from L. *tuitio* (*-onis*), protection, from *tuitus*, pp. of *tueri*, to watch, protect.]

1. guardianship; the watch and care of a tutor or guardian over his pupil or ward. [Obs.]

2. instruction; the act or business of teaching the various branches of learning.

3. the money paid for instruction; tuition fee; as, the *tuition* is very high.

tū·i'tion·ăl, *a.* having to do with tuition.

tū·i'tion·ăr·y, *a.* same as *tuitional.*

tū'lȧ met'ăl, [from *Tula*, in Russia.] an alloy of silver, copper, and lead, which forms the base of a variety of Russian metalwork: also called *black silver.*

tū·lä'rẹ, *n.* [Sp.] in western United States, marshy ground that abounds with tule.

tū·lȧ·rē'mi·ȧ, tū·lȧ·rae'mi·ȧ, *n.* [from *Tulare* county, Calif., and *-emia*, from Gr. suffix *-aimia*, designating a blood condition.] an infectious disease of rodents, especially rabbits, caused by a bacterium and transmitted to man in handling the flesh of infected animals or by the bite of certain insects: it is characterized by an irregular fever, aching, inflammation of the lymph glands, etc.: also called *rabbit fever.*

tū'lȧ·si, *n.* same as *toolsi.*

tū'lȧ wŏrk, decorative work, somewhat similar to enameling, done in tula metal: also called *niello* or *niello work.*

Tul·bagh'i·ȧ (-bag'), *n.* [after Ryk *Tulbagh*, a Dutch governor (1751–1771) at the Cape of Good Hope.] a genus of plants of the lily family, native to Africa.

tul'çhan, tul'çhin, *n.* a calfskin stuffed with straw, and set beside a cow, to make her give her milk. [Scot.]

tulchan bishops; titular bishops to the Scottish sees immediately after the Reformation, in whose names the revenues of the sees were drawn by the lay barons who had given them the office: used derisively. [Obs.]

tū'le, *n.* [Sp. Am.] a large kind of bulrush, *Scirpus lacustris*, found in marshy places in the western and southwestern United States.

tū'lip, *n.* [Fr. *tulipe*; It. *tulipano*; Turk. *tülbend*, for *dülbend*, turban, from Per. *dulband*, turban: so called because of its likeness to a turban.]

1. a liliaceous plant of the genus *Tulipa*, of a great variety of colors, mostly spring-blooming, with long, broad, pointed leaves and, usually, a single, large cup-shaped flower; also, this flower or the bulb. About forty species have been described, of which the most noted are the common garden tulip, *Tulipa gesneriana*, native to the Levant, introduced into England about 1577, and the sweet-scented tulip or Van Thol tulip, *Tulipa suaveolens*, cultivated for its fragrance.

2. a tuliplike expansion of a gun muzzle. [Rare.]

African tulip; a plant of the amaryllis family, genus *Hæmanthus.*

butterfly tulip; the mariposa lily.

Tū'li·pȧ, *n.* a genus of liliaceous plants, the tulips. They are bulbous, bearing a solitary erect bell-shaped flower on a simple stem.

tū'lip-ēared, *a.* having a pointed ear, as some dogs.

tū'lip·ist, *n.* a cultivator of tulips.

tū"lip·ō·mā'ni·ȧ, *n.* a violent passion for the acquisition or cultivation of tulips, which arose in Europe and especially in Holland about 1634, leading to great financial catastrophes. The mania raged for several years till the government found it necessary to interfere.

tū"lip·ō·mā'ni·aç, *n.* a speculator in tulips; one affected with tulipomania.

tū'lip pop'lăr, same as *tulip tree.*

tū'lip rọọt, *n.* a disease of oats, caused by a worm, in which the stalk swells like a tulip bulb.

tū'lip shell, a gastropod of the genus *Fasciolaria*, or its shell.

tū'lip tree, 1. an American tree of the magnolia family, *Liriodendron tulipifera*, growing to a large size, and bearing greenish-yellow flowers resembling the tulip, bluish-green leaves, and long, conelike fruit.

2. any of a number of trees with tuliplike flowers.

Chinese tulip tree; a small shrub from China, *Magnolia fuscata*, whose flowers are shaped like a tulip.

FLOWER OF TULIP TREE (*Liriodendron tulipifera*)

Queensland tulip tree; the Queensland fire tree, a large tree of the genus *Ctenocarpus*, having fiery-red blossoms.

West Indian tulip tree; a large tree, *Hibiscus elatus*, yielding a lacy inner bark called Cuba bast.

tū'lip·wood, *n.* 1. the light, soft wood of the tulip tree, used in cabinetwork, etc.

2. any one of various showy cabinet woods with stripes or streaks of color, as (a) the wood of *Physocalymma floribunda*, finely striped and of a rose color; (b) the wood of *Harpullia pendula*, variegated with dark markings on a light ground: also called *Queensland tulipwood.*

3. one of the trees producing such wood.

tūlle, *n.* [after city of *Tulle*, France.] a kind of thin, fine netting of silk, rayon, or nylon, used for thin dresses, veils, etc.

Tul'li·ăn, *a.* of or like Tully, or Marcus Tullius Cicero.

tul'li·bee, *n.* [Canad. Fr. *toulibi.*] a kind of whitefish, *Coregonus tullibee*, found in the Great Lakes, etc.

tūl'si, *n.* same as *toolsi.*

tūm'bek·i, *n.* [Turk.] a kind of Persian tobacco.

tum'bes·tẽr, *n.* a female tumbler or dancer. [Obs.]

tum'ble, *v.i.*; tumbled, *pt., pp.*; tumbling, *ppr.* [ME. *tumblen*, freq. of *tumben, tomben*; AS. *tumbian*, to dance.]

1. to do somersaults, handsprings, or other acrobatic feats.

2. to fall suddenly, clumsily, or helplessly.

3. to stumble; trip.

4. to toss about or roll around.

5. to move, go, etc. in a hasty, awkward, or disorderly manner; as, she *tumbled* out of bed half awake.

6. to understand something suddenly (with *to*). [Slang.]

7. to dance. [Rare.]

to tumble home; in shipbuilding, to slope inward above the greatest width, as a vessel's sides.

tum'ble, *v.t.* 1. to turn over; to throw by chance or with violence; used with words limiting the sense; as, to *tumble over* books or papers; to *tumble* casks *out* of a door; to *tumble down* a pile of bricks.

2. to disturb; to rumple; as, to *tumble* a bed.

3. to cause to tumble; to make fall, throw down, toss about, roll over, etc.

4. to whirl in a tumbling box or barrel.

tum'ble, *n.* 1. a tumbling; specifically, (a) a somersault, handspring, etc.; (b) a fall; (c) a stumble.

2. disorder; confusion.

3. a confused heap.

tum'ble·bug, *n.* any of several dung beetles, common in the United States, which roll balls of dung containing its eggs.

tum'ble-down, *a.* dilapidated; rickety.

tum'ble·dung, *n.* same as *tumblebug.*

tum'ble hōme, the part of a ship which inclines inward above the extreme breadth.

tum'blẽr, *n.* 1. a person who does somersaults, handsprings, etc.; an acrobat.

2. a kind of dog formerly used to catch rabbits: so called from the manner in which it caught its prey.

3. a kind of pigeon that does somersaults during flight.

4. an ordinary drinking glass, having no foot or stem: so called because originally it had a rounded or pointed bottom and could not be set down until emptied.

5. its contents.

6. a tumbrel. [Brit. Dial. or Scot.]

7. the part of a gunlock through which the mainspring acts upon the hammer.

8. a part of a lock whose position must be changed by a key in order to release the bolt.

9. on a revolving or rocking part, a projecting piece that strikes and moves another part.

10. a part moving a gear into place in an automobile transmission.

11. an easily tipped, self-righting toy.

12. a tumbling box or barrel.

13. in nautical usage, one of the movable pins with which the cathead stopper and shank painter are respectively engaged. By the coincident movement of the pins, the ends of the anchor are simultaneously freed.

14. the aquatic larva of any member of the *Culicidæ*.

tumbler pigeon; same as *tumbler*, sense 3.

tum′blẽr·fụl, *n.*; *pl.* **tum′blẽr·fụlṣ**, a quantity sufficient to fill a tumbler; as much as a tumbler can contain.

tum′ble·weed, *n.* any of a number of plants, as the pigweed, Russian thistle, etc., which break off near the ground in autumn and are blown about by the wind.

tum′bling, *n.* the act of falling or rolling; the performances of a tumbler.

tum′bling bar′rel (or **box**), a device consisting of a box or cylindrical container pivoted at the ends or at two corners so that it can be revolved: used for mixing materials, polishing metal objects by letting them tumble about together with an abrasive, etc.: also called *rumble, rumbler*.

tum′bling bāy, in a canal, an overfall or weir.

tum′bly, *a.* uneven, lumpy, or rough, as if with tumbled debris.

tum′brel, tum′bril, *n.* [OFr. *tumbrel, tumberel*, tip cart, from *tomber*, to fall.]

1. formerly, an instrument of punishment, as the cucking stool.

2. a farmer's cart or wagon, especially one that may be tilted for emptying.

3. any of the carts used to carry the condemned to the guillotine during the French Revolution.

4. a two-wheeled military cart for carrying ammunition, etc.

5. a basket or cage of osiers, willows, etc., for keeping hay and other food for sheep. [Brit. Dial.]

tū·mē·fā′cient (-shent), *a.* [L. *tumefaciens (-entis)*, ppr. of *tumefacere*, to swell, tumefy.] tending to cause or causing a swelling; puffy.

tū·mē·fac′tion, *n.* 1. a tumefying or being tumefied.

2. a swollen part.

tū′mē·fȳ, *v.t.*; tumefied, *pt., pp.*; tumefying, *ppr.* [Fr. *tuméfier*; L. *tumefacere*, to cause to swell; *tumere*, to swell, and *facere*, to make.] to swell; to cause to swell.

tū′mē·fȳ, *v.i.* to swell; to rise in a tumor.

tū·mes′cence, *n.* 1. a swelling.

2. a swollen part.

tū·mes′cent, *a.* [L. *tumescens (-entis)*, ppr. of *tumescere*, to swell up, inceptive of *tumere*, to swell.] swelling; becoming tumid or swollen; also, in botany, partially tumid.

tū′mid, *a.* [L. *tumidus*, swelling, from *tumere*, to swell.]

1. swollen, enlarged, or distended; as, a *tumid* leg; *tumid* flesh.

2. protuberant; rising above the level.

So high as heaved the *tumid* hills.
—Milton.

3. swelling in sound or sense; pompous; puffy; bombastic; falsely sublime; as, a *tumid* expression; a *tumid* style.

4. teeming; bursting. [Rare.]

tū·mid′i·ty, *n.* the condition or quality of being tumid.

tū′mid·ly, *adv.* in a tumid manner.

tū′mid·ness, *n.* the condition of being tumid.

tum′mālṣ, *n.* in mining, a heap; a pile. [Brit. Dial.]

tum′my, *n.* stomach: a child's word.

tū′mŏr, *n.* [L., a swelling, from *tumere*, to swell.]

1. in pathology, (a) swelling; morbid enlargement; (b) a neoplasm; a mass of new tissue which persists and grows independently of its surrounding structures, and which has no physiologic use. Tumors are classified as benign or malignant.

2. affected pomp; bombast; high-flown language. [Obs.]

adipose tumor; same as *lipoma*.

cystic tumor; a tumor not solid, but more or less hollow.

dermoid tumor; a tumor which contains fatty, cutaneous elements and sometimes hair, nails, etc.

encysted tumor; a tumor enclosed in a membranous sac.

follicular tumor; a sebaceous cyst; a dilated sebaceous follicle.

fungating tumor; a tumor which fungates, or produces granulations rapidly.

heterologous tumor; a tumor made up of tissue which differs from that in which it grows.

muscular tumor; a myoma.

sebaceous tumor; a cyst formed by the retention of the secretions of a sebaceous gland.

tū′mŏred, *a.* distended; swollen with or as with a tumor.

tū′mŏr·ous, *a.* 1. of, or having the nature of, a tumor.

2. having a tumor or tumors.

3. vainly pompous; bombastic, as language or style. [Obs.]

tū′mour, *n.* tumor; British spelling.

tūmp, *n.* [W. *twmp*, a round mass, a hillock.] a little hillock; a clump. [Brit. Dial.]

tump, *v.t.*; tumped (tumpt), *pt., pp.*; tumping *ppr.* to form a mass of earth or a hillock round (a plant); as, to *tump* teazel. [Brit. Dial.]

tump, *v.t.* to drag or draw along, as an animal, after killing it; as, to *tump* a deer. [Dial.]

tump′līne, *n.* a strap placed across the forehead to assist a man carrying a pack on his back. [Dial.]

tum′-tum, *n.* [Anglo-Ind.] a dish made in the West Indies by beating boiled plantain in a wooden mortar until it is soft.

tū′mū·lăr, *a.* of or like a tumulus.

tū′mū·lăr·y, *a.* tumular.

tū′mū·lāte, *v.t.* to cover with a mound; to bury. [Rare.]

tū′mū·lōse, tū′mū·lous, *a.* full of tumuli, or mounds.

tū·mū·los′i·ty, *n.* hilliness; the quality or state of being tumulose.

tū′mult, *n.* [OFr. *tumulte*; L. *tumultus*, a restless swelling or surging up, tumult, from *tumere*, to swell.]

1. the commotion, disturbance, or agitation of a multitude, usually accompanied with great noise, uproar, and confusion of voices; an uproar.

Till in loud *tumult* all the Greeks arose.
—Pope.

2. violent commotion or agitation, with confusion of sounds; as, the *tumult* of the elements.

3. great emotional disturbance; agitation of mind or feeling.

Syn.—agitation, commotion, confusion, bustle, stir, riot, uproar, hubbub, clamor, disturbance, ferment.

tū′mult, *v.i.* to make a tumult; to be in great commotion.

tū′mult·ẽr, *n.* one who creates a tumult. [Obs.]

tū·mul′tū·ăr·i·ly, *adv.* in a tumultuary or disorderly manner. [Rare.]

tū·mul′tū·ăr·i·ness, *n.* disorderly or tumultuous conduct; turbulence; disposition to tumult. [Rare.]

tū·mul′tū·ăr·y, *a.* [L. *tumultuarius*, hurried, from *tumultus*, tumult.]

1. disorderly; irregular; unsystematic; confused.

Men, who live without religion, live always in a *tumultuary* and restless state.
—Atterbury.

2. tumultuous.

tū·mul′tū·āte, *v.i.* [L. *tumultuare*.] to make a tumult. [Rare.]

tū·mul·tū·ā′tion, *n.* commotion; irregular or disorderly movement. [Rare.]

tū·mul′tū·ous, *a.* [OFr.; L. *tumultuosus*, full of tumult, from *tumultus*, tumult.]

1. full of or characterized by tumult; noisy; as, a *tumultuous* assembly or meeting.

2. making a tumult; turbulent.

3. greatly disturbed or agitated.

Syn.—violent, disorderly, noisy, confused, agitated, turbulent, boisterous, riotous.

tū·mul′tū·ous·ly, *adv.* in a tumultuous manner.

tū·mul′tū·ous·ness, *n.* the state of being tumultuous; disorder; commotion.

tū′mū·lus, *n.*; *pl.* **tū′mū·lī**, an artificial hillock, such as was raised over graves in ancient times; a barrow, or artificial burial mound of earth.

tun, *n.* [AS. *tunne*, a large vessel, a butt; akin to G. *tonne*, cask, tun.]

1. a large cask, especially for wine, beer, or ale.

2. a fermenting vat used in brewing, usually in the form of a truncated cone.

3. a varying measure for liquids, as for wine, formerly equal to two pipes, four hogsheads, or 252 wine gallons.

4. a chimney or its projecting top. [Brit. Dial.]

5. a drinking bowl or cup. [Archaic.]

tun, *v.t.*; tunned, *pt., pp.*; tunning, *ppr.* to put into or store in a tun or tuns, as wine or malt liquor.

tū′nȧ, *n.* 1. any of a number of related plants of the cactus family, the prickly pears, especially, *Opuntia tuna*; opuntia.

2. the edible fruit of any of these plants.

tụ′nȧ, *n.*; *pl.* **tụ′nȧ** or **tụ′nȧṣ**, [Am. Sp.; ult. from same source as *tunny*.] a tunny, a large food fish of the mackerel group; specifically, (a) the variety caught off the Pacific coast; (b) the variety caught off the coast of Florida, Central America, and the West Indies: also *tuna fish*.

tụ′nȧ, *n.* the common eel, *Anguilla aucklandii*, of New Zealand.

tūn′ȧ·ble, *a.* 1. in tune.

2. tuneful.

3. capable of being put in tune.

Also written *tuneable*.

tūn′ȧ·ble·ness, *n.* the state or quality of being tunable; harmony; melodiousness.

tūn′ȧ·bly, *adv.* in a tunable manner; tunefully.

tun′bel″lied, *a.* having a large, protuberant belly.

tun′bel″ly, *n.* a large, protuberant belly.

tun′dish, *n.* a funnel. [Brit. Dial.]

tụn′drȧ, *n.* [Russ.] one of the vast stretches of flat, boggy, treeless plains of the arctic regions.

tūne, *n.* [ME. and Anglo-Fr., from OFr. *ton*; L. *tonus*, a sound, from Gr. *tonos*, a tone.]

1. originally, a tone.

2. a rhythmical succession of musical tones; a melody; an air.

3. a musical setting of a hymn or psalm, for use in public worship.

4. (a) the condition of being in proper musical pitch or of agreeing in pitch; hence, (b) harmony; agreement; concord; adjustment: now used chiefly in phrases *in tune, out of tune*; as, the violin is *in tune*, he's *out of tune* with the times.

to change one's tune; to change one's attitude or manner, as from scorn to respect.

to sing a different tune; to talk or act differently; to change one's tune.

to the tune of; to the sum of; at the price of. [Colloq.]

tūne, *v.t.*; tuned, *pt., pp.*; tuning, *ppr.* 1. to adjust (a musical instrument) to some standard of pitch; to put in tune.

2. to adapt (music, the voice, etc.) to some pitch, tone, or mood.

3. to adapt to some condition, mood, etc.; to bring into harmony or agreement.

4. to utter or express musically.

to tune in (on); to adjust a radio receiver to a given frequency so as to receive (a station, program, etc.).

to tune out; to adjust a radio receiver so as to eliminate (interference, etc.).

to tune up; (a) to adjust (musical instruments) to the same pitch, as in an orchestra; (b) to adjust to the proper or required condition, as a motor.

tūne, *v.i.* 1. to be in tune; to harmonize.

2. to utter inarticulate musical sounds with the voice; to hum a tune. [Dial.]

tūne′fụl, *a.* 1. harmonious; melodious; musical.

2. producing musical sounds.

tūne′fụl·ly, *adv.* in a tuneful manner; harmoniously; musically.

tūne′fụl·ness, *n.* the state or quality of being tuneful.

tūne′less, *a.* 1. unmusical; inharmonious.

2. not making music; as, a *tuneless* harp.

3. not expressed musically; silent.

tūn′ẽr, *n.* a person or thing that tunes; specifically, (a) a person who tunes musical instruments; as, a piano *tuner*; (b) the part of a radio receiver that detects signals; especially, such a part in the form of a separate unit.

tūne′-up″, *n.* an adjusting, as of a motor, to the proper or required condition.

tung oil, [from Chin. *yu-t'ung* from *yu*, oil, and *t'ung*, name of the tree.] a yellow, poisonous oil from the nuts of a tree grown in China, Japan, and Florida, used instead of linseed oil in paints, varnishes, etc. for a higher gloss and more water-resistant finish.

tun′-greāt, *a.* having a circumference of the size of a tun. [Obs.]

tung′stāte, *n.* a salt of tungstic acid.

tung′sten, *n.* [Sw. *tungsten*, lit., heavystone; *tung*, heavy, and *sten*, stone.]

1. wolfram: the former name.
2. the native tungstate of lime. [Obs.]

tungsten lamp; an electric lamp with filaments of metallic tungsten and a very low wattage.

tungsten ocher or *tungstic ocher*; same as *tungstite*.

tungsten steel; see under *steel*.

tung·sten'iç, *a.* pertaining to or containing tungsten; tungstic.

tung'stiç, *a.* of, pertaining to, or obtained from tungsten, especially with a valence of five or six.

tung'stiç ac'id, any of a group of acids produced by the combination of tungstic trioxide, WO_3, with water; specifically, the monohydrate acid, H_2WO_4.

tung'stīte, *n.* a yellow or yellow-green mineral, WO_3, native tungstic trioxide.

tung tree, [from native name.] a Chinese tree, *Aleurites fordii*, valuable for the oil produced from its seeds; also, the *Dipterocarpus turbinatus*, an East Indian tree which yields wood oil or tung oil, as well as gurjun and a fine timber for boatbuilding.

Tụn·gụş', *n.* 1. *pl.* **Tụn·gụş'eş, Tụn·gụş',** a member of a group of Tungusic-speaking tribes (*Tunguses*) of Mongolian descent, including the Manchu, living in Siberia east of the Yenisei in the Amur basin, and, formerly, in Manchuria.
2. their Tungusic language.
Also spelled *Tunguz*.

Tụn·gụş', *a.* of the Tunguses or their language; Tungusic: also spelled *Tunguz*.

Tụn·gụş'iç, *n.* a family of languages spoken in central and eastern Siberia and Manchuria: it includes Tungus and Manchu, and may be related to the Mongolian and Turkic language families.

Tụn·gụş'iç, *a.* 1. of the Tunguses.
2. of Tungusic.

tun'hoof, *n.* the ground ivy, *Glechoma hederacea*. [Brit. Dial.]

tū'niç, *n.* [L. *tunica*.]
1. a loose, gownlike garment worn by men and women in ancient Greece and Rome.
2. a blouselike garment extending to the hips or lower, usually gathered at the waist, often with a belt.
3. a short coat forming part of the uniform of soldiers, policemen, etc. [Chiefly Brit.]
4. a tunicle.
5. in anatomy, a membrane that covers some part or organ.
6. a natural covering; an integument; a mantle, as (a) in zoology, one of the layers which form the covering of a tunicate; (b) in botany, any loose membranous skin not formed from epidermis; the skin of a seed; also, the peridium of certain fungi.

tū'ni·çȧ, *n.*; *pl.* **tū'ni·cae,** [Mod. L.; see *tunic*.] in anatomy and zoology, an enclosing or covering layer of tissue or membrane, as of the ovaries.

tū'ni·çār·y, *n.*; *pl.* **tū'ni·çār·ieş,** one of the *Tunicata*; a tunicate. [Obs.]

Tū·ni·çā'tȧ, *n.pl.* [L. *tunicatus*, pp. of *tunicare*, to put on a tunic, from *tunica*, a tunic.] a subphylum and class of chordates, which are enveloped in a coriaceous tunic, or mantle, having two orifices, the one branchial, and the other anal, and covering beneath it a second tunic, which adheres to the outer one at the orifices; the ascidians. These animals are popularly named sea squirts. Also called *Ascidia* and *Urochorda*.

tū'ni·çāte, *a.* [L. *tunicatus*, pp. of *tunicare*, to put on a tunic.]
1. in botany, of or covered with concentric layers or tunics, as an onion.
2. in zoology, having a tunic or mantle.
3. in entomology, covered by one another like a set of funnels, as the joints of some antennae.

tū'ni·çāte, *n.* an ascidian or sea squirt; any member of the *Tunicata*.

tū'ni·çā·ted, *a.* same as *tunicate*.

tunicated bulb; a bulb composed of numerous concentric coats, as an onion.

tū'ni·cin, *n.* a substance resembling vegetable cellulose, found in the tunic of the tunicates.

tū'ni·çle, *n.* [ME.; L. *tunicula*, dim. of *tunica*, a tunic.]
1. a small and delicate natural covering; a fine integument; as, the *tunicles* that make the ball of the eye. [Rare.]
2. in the Roman Catholic Church, the vestment worn by a subdeacon over the alb or by a bishop under the dalmatic.

tūn'ing, *n.* the art or operation of one who or that which tunes; specifically, in radio, the act of bringing the circuit into resonance with an external source of similar character.

tūn'ing çrook, a hook inserted in a wind instrument to vary the pitch.

tūn'ing fọrk, a small steel instrument with two prongs, which when struck sounds a certain fixed tone in perfect pitch: it is used as a guide in tuning instruments.

TUNING FORK

tūn'ing ham'mẽr, a wrench resembling a hammer, used by a piano tuner.

Tu·ni'si·ăn (tū-nish'i-ăn, tū-nish'ăn, tū-nē'zhăn), *a.* of Tunis or Tunisia, their people, or culture.

Tū·ni'si·ăn, *n.* a native or inhabitant of Tunis or Tunisia.

tuñk, *n.* [echoic.] a thump; a quick blow. [Dial.]

Tuñk'ẽrş, *n.pl.* same as *Dunkers*.

tun'nāġe, *n.* same as *tonnage*.

tun'nel, *n.* [OFr. *tonnel*, dim. of *tonne*, a tun.]
1. originally, (a) a flue; (b) a funnel.
2. an underground or underwater passageway, as for motor traffic, a railroad, etc.
3. an animal's burrow.
4. any tunnellike passage, as one in a mine.
5. in mining, a transverse opening that may serve as an adit.
6. a tunnel net. [Rare.]

tun'nel, *v.t.*; tunneled *or* tunnelled, *pt.*, *pp.*; tunneling *or* tunnelling, *ppr.* 1. to dig (a passage) in the form of a tunnel.
2. to make a tunnel through or under.
3. to make (one's way or a way) by digging a tunnel.
4. to catch in a tunnel net.

tun'nel, *v.i.* to make a tunnel.

tun'nel diş·ēaşe', decompression sickness.

tun'nel·ẽr, tun'nel·lẽr, *n.* a person or thing that tunnels.

tun'nel head (hed), the cylindrical chimney or mouth of a blast furnace.

tun'nel kiln (kil), a limekiln constructed to permit the use of coal as fuel.

tun'nel net, a wide-mouthed fishing net tapering toward its end.

tun'nel pit, tun'nel shȧft, a shaft beginning at the surface of the ground to meet a tunnel at a point between its ends.

tun'nel vi'şiŏn, a narrow outlook; specifically, the focus of attention on a particular problem without proper regard for possible consequences or alternative approaches.

tun'ny, *n.*; *pl.* **tun'nieş** or **tun'ny,** [Fr. *thon*; L. *thynnus*, from Gr. *thynnos*, a tunny, lit., a darter, from *thynein*, to dart along.]
1. any of several large, edible sea fishes of the mackerel group, with coarse, somewhat oily flesh, weighing up to 1,000 pounds; a tuna.

TUNNY
(*Thunnus thynnus*)

2. any of certain related fishes, as the albacore.

tup, *n.* [ME. *tupe, tope, toup*; prob. from ON.]
1. a male sheep; a ram.
2. the striking part of a pile driver or power hammer.

tup, *v.t.* and *v.i.* 1. to butt like a ram. [Brit. Dial.]
2. to copulate with (a ewe): said of a ram.

Tū·pā'iȧ, *n.* [Malay.] a genus of squirrel shrews: they feed on fruit and insects, living on trees like squirrels, which they resemble in general appearance, having long bushy tails: some are called *banxrings*.

tū·pāi'id, *n.* any one of the *Tupaiidæ*; a banxring or squirrel shrew.

Tū·pā·ī'i·dae, *n.pl.* the banxrings or squirrel shrews, a family of insectivorous vertebrate animals consisting of the single genus *Tupaia*.

tū'pe·lō, *n.*; *pl.* **tū'pe·lōş,** [Am. Ind.]
1. any one of various cornaceous American trees of the genus *Nyssa*, with small, greenish flowers and blue or purple fruit; among them are the black or sour gum, or pepperidge, tree, *Nyssa sylvatica*, the swamp tupelo, *Nyssa biflora*, and the water tupelo, *Nyssa aquatica*.
2. the tough wood of any of these trees. Also *tupelo gum*.

Tụ·pī', *n.* [Tupi, comrade.]
1. *pl.* **Tụ·pīş', Tụ·pī',** a member of a group of South American Indian tribes living in parts of Brazil, chiefly along the coast and along the lower Amazon, and in part of Paraguay.
2. their language, especially the northern dialect, used as a lingua franca in the Amazon region.

Tụ·pī'ăn, *a.* 1. of the Tupis or their language.
2. designating or of a large linguistic stock of South American Indians, comprising the Tupis and the Guaranis.

tup'pence, *n.* twopence.

tūque (tūk), *n.* [Fr. *toque*, cap.] a winter cap consisting of a knitted bag tapered and closed at both ends, worn with one end tucked into the other.

tụ quō'que, [L.] thou also; you too: a retort accusing an accuser of the same charge.

tụr, *n.* [Russ.] same as *urus*.

tū'rȧ·cin, *n.* [*turacou* and *-in*.] an animal pigment found in the primary and secondary pinion feathers of four species of the touraco, containing nearly six per cent of copper.

tụ'rȧ·çō, tụ'rȧ·çōu, *n.* same as *touraco*.

tū''rȧ·çō·vẽr'din, *n.* [*turaco*, and Fr. *vert*, green color.] a green organic compound existing in the plumage of certain touracos.

Tū'rȧ·çus, *n.* a genus of touracos.

tụ'rȧ·kọọ, *n.* any of a group of brightly colored tropical birds: also spelled *touraco*.

Tū·rā'ni·ăn, *n.* [Per. *Tūrān*, the area north of the Oxus River; and *-ian*.] 1. the Ural-Altaic family of languages.
2. a member of any of the peoples who speak them.

Tū·rā'ni·ăn, *a.* designating or of Turanian or of the Turanians.

tũr'băn, *n.* [Fr.; Port. *turbante*; Turk. *tülbend, dülbend*, Ar. and Per. *dulband*, turban; *dul*, a turn, a round, and *band*, a band.]
1. a headdress of Moslem origin, consisting of a cap with a scarf wound round it.
2. a similar headdress consisting of a scarf or cloth wound round the head.
3. a kind of hat worn by women, with no brim or a very short brim turned up closely.
4. the spiral of a univalve shell. [Rare.]

tũr'bănd, *n.* a turban. [Obs.]

tũr'bāned, *a.* wearing a turban.

tũr'băn shell, the naked shell of a sea urchin.

tũr'bȧ·ry, *n.*; *pl.* **tũr'bȧ·ries,** [OFr. *turberie*, from *tourbe*, turf.] in English law, a right of digging turf or peat on another man's land; also, the place where turf or peat is dug.

Tũr·bel·lā'ri·ȧ, *n.pl.* [L. *turba*, a crowd, a stir: from the currents caused by their moving cilia.] a class of flatworms, mostly aquatic and nonparasitic, characterized by leaf-shaped bodies covered with many cilia.

tũr·bel·lār'i·ăn, *a.* having the characteristics of the *Turbellaria*.

tũr·bel·lār'i·ăn, *n.* a flatworm belonging to the *Turbellaria*.

tũr·bel·lar'i·fọrm, *a.* shaped like or resembling a turbellarian.

tũr'bid, *a.* [L. *turbidus*, troubled, disturbed, from *turbare*, to trouble, from *turba*, a crowd.]
1. having the sediment stirred up; muddy; cloudy.
2. thick, dense, or dark, as clouds or smoke.
3. confused; perplexed; muddled.

tũr·bi·dim'e·tẽr, *n.* [from *turbidity* and *-meter*.] a device for measuring the turbidity of a liquid, as in a water-purification plant.

tũr·bid'i·ty, *n.* the state or quality of being turbid.

tũr'bid·ly, *adv.* in a turbid manner.

tũr'bid·ness, *n.* turbidity.

tũr·bil'liŏn (-yun), *n.* same as *tourbillion*.

tũr·bi·nā'ceous, *a.* turfy; peaty. [Rare.]

tũr·bi·nä'dō, *n.* [Am. Sp., from Sp., spiral.] a partially refined, granulated, pale brown sugar obtained by washing raw sugar in a centrifuge until most of the molasses is removed: also called *turbinado sugar*.

tũr'bi·năl, *a.* [from L. *turbo*, *turbinus*, a whirl, and *-al*.] same as *turbinate*.

tũr'bi·năl, *n.* a turbinate bone.

tũr'bi·nāte, *v.i.* to turn or whirl; to revolve or spin.

tũr'bi·nāte, tũr'bi·nā·ted, *a.* [L. *turbinatus*, from *turbo*, a whirl, rotation.]

1. shaped like a cone resting on its apex; top-shaped; specifically, in botany, narrow at the base and broad at the apex; as, a *turbinate* germ or nectary.

2. shaped like a scroll or spiral; specifically, in anatomy and zoology, designating or of any of certain spiral spongy bones in the nasal passages.

tûr′bi·nāte, *n.* 1. a turbinate shell.
2. a turbinate bone.

tûr′bine (*or* -bīn), *n.* [L. *turbo, turbinis,* that which spins or whirls round, a top.] an engine or motor driven by the pressure of steam, water, or air against the curved vanes of a wheel or set of wheels.

Tûr·bi·nel′lȧ, *n.* [LL., from L. *turbo, turbinis,* a top, and dim. suffix *-ella.*] a genus of marine gastropods with a stout columelliform shell.

tûr′bi·ni·fọrm, *a.* turbinoid; top-shaped.

tûr′bi·nīte, *n.* a fossil shell of the genus *Turbo* or a related genus.

tûr′bi·noid, *a.* [L. *turbo* (*-inis*), a top, and *-oid.*] of or relating to the genus *Turbo.*

tûr′bit, *n.* [perh. from L. *turbo,* a top: from the shape.] any of a variety of domestic pigeons having a short head and beak and a ruffled breast.

Tûr′bō, *n.* [L. *turbo* (*-inis*), a whirl, top.] a genus of the family *Turbinidæ,* marine gastropods with conical shells having a spiral operculum.

tûr′bō-, [from L. *turbo,* thing that spins.] a combining form meaning; (a) *consisting of a turbine;* (b) *driven by and directly coupled to a turbine,* as in *turbo*generator.

tûr′bō·chärġe, *v.t.*; turbocharged, *pt., pp.*; turbocharging, *ppr.* to increase the power of (an engine) by the use of a turbocharger.

tûr′bō·chärġ·ẽr, *n.* a device using a turbine driven by exhaust gases to drive a supercharger on an engine, especially of a racing car.

tûr′bō·fan, *n.* 1. a turbojet engine in which additional thrust is obtained from the part of the air that bypasses the engine and is accelerated by a fan in an enclosed duct: in full, *turbofan engine.*
2. a fan driven by a turbine.

tûr′bō·ġen′ẽr·ā·tŏr, *n.* [*turbo-,* and *generator.*] a generator driven by and directly coupled to a turbine.

tûr′bō·jet, *n.* 1. a jet engine using a turbine to drive an air compressor that takes in and compresses air for fuel combustion and employing the resulting hot gases to rotate the turbine before forming the propulsive stream: in full, *turbojet engine.*
2. an aircraft propelled by such an engine.

tûr′bō·prop, *n.* [*turbo-,* and *prop*eller.]
1. a turbojet engine whose turbine shaft, through reduction gears, drives a propeller that develops most of the thrust, with some thrust usually being added by a jet of the turbine exhaust gases: in full *turboprop engine.*
2. an aircraft propelled by such an engine.

tûr′bō·sū′pẽr·chärġ″ẽr, *n.* a device using a turbine driven by exhaust gases to compress air before delivering it to the intake of a reciprocating engine: used to maintain air-intake pressure at high altitudes.

tûr′bŏt, *n.*; *pl.* **tûr′bŏt** or **tûr′bŏts,** [ME. *turbut;* OFr. *tourbout.*]
1. a large European flatfish, *Psetta maxima,* having a compressed, disk-shaped, asymmetrical body, attaining large size, often weighing from thirty to forty pounds.

TURBOT
(*Psetta maxima*)

2. any of a number of other flatfishes resembling the turbot.

tûr′bū·lence, tûr′bū·len·cy, *n.* the condition or quality of being turbulent.
Syn.—tumultuousness, agitation, disorder, commotion, refractoriness, insurbordination.

tûr′bū·lent, *a.* [Fr.; L. *turbulentus,* full of commotion or disturbance, from *turbare,* to disturb, from *turba,* crowd.]
1. causing disturbance; disorderly; unruly; boisterous.
2. characterized by disturbance; disturbed; agitated; tumultuous.
3. marked by wildly irregular motion; as, *turbulent* air currents.

tûr′bū·lent·ly, *adv.* in a turbulent manner.

Tûr′ciṣm, *n.* same as Turkism.

tûr′çō, *n.* a Chilean wren, *Hylactes megapodius.*

Tûr′çō-, Turko-.

Tûr′çō·măn, *n.*; *pl.* **Tûr′çō·măns,** same as Turkoman.

Tûr′di·dae, *n.pl.* a family of passerine birds, the thrushes and thrushlike birds.

tûr′di·fọrm, *a.* having the form or appearance of a thrush.

tûr′dīne (*or* -din), *a.* [from L. *turdus,* a thrush; and *-ine.*] of or belonging to a large and widely distributed group of songbirds comprising the true thrushes and allied groups.

Tûr′dus, *n.* [L., thrush.] a genus of birds including the thrushes only.

tū·reen′, *n.* [from L. *terrenus,* earthy, from *terra,* earth.] a large, deep dish with a lid, for serving soup, etc.

tū·reen′ful, *n.* as much as a tureen will hold.

tûrf, *n.*; *pl.* **tûrfs,** archaic **tûrveṣ,** [ME. *turf, torf;* AS. *turf,* turf.]
1. a surface layer of earth containing grass plants with their matted roots; sod; sward.
2. a piece of this layer.
3. peat, or a piece of it for use as fuel.
4. (a) a track for horse racing; (b) horse racing. Usually with *the.*
5. one's own territory or domain. [Slang.]

tûrf, *v.t.*; turfed (tûrft), *pt., pp.*; turfing, *ppr.* to cover with turf; as, to *turf* a bank.

tûrf ȧnt, a small European ant, *Lasius flavus.*

tûrf drāin, a drain covered with turf or peat.

tûrf′en, *a.* made of turf; covered with turf.

tûrf′i·ness, *n.* the state or quality of being turfy.

tûrf′ing, *n.* the operation of laying down turf, or covering with turf.

tûrf′ing ī′ron (-ûrn), an implement for paring off turf.

tûrf′ing spāde, a turfing iron.

tûrf′less, *a.* without turf.

tûrf′măn, *n.*; *pl.* **tûrfmen,** one who is interested in horse racing.

tûrf′wŏrm, *n.* same as *sodworm.*

tûrf′y, *a.*; *comp.* turfier; *superl.* turfiest, 1. of or covered with turf; grassy.
2. of the nature of or resembling turf.
3. having to do with horse racing.

tûr′ġent, *a.* [L. *turgens* (*-entis*), from *turgere,* to swell.]
1. swelling; swollen; tumid. [Now Rare.]
2. turgid; bombastic; pompous. [Obs.]

tûr·ġesce′, *v.i.*; turgesced (-ġest′), *pt., pp.*; turgescing, *ppr.* [L. *turgescere,* inceptive of *turgere,* to *swell.*] to become turgid; to swell; to inflate. [Obs.]

tûr·ġes′cence, *n.* [from *turgescent.*]
1. a swelling.
2. swollen condition.
3. empty pompousness; inflation; bombast.

tûr·ġes′cen·cy, *n.* the quality or state of being turgescent.

tûr·ġes′cent, *a.* [L. *turgescens* (*-entis*), ppr. of *turgescere,* to begin to swell.] swelling; growing turgid or inflated.

tûr′ġid, *a.* [L. *turgidus,* swollen, distended, from *turgere,* to swell.]
1. swollen; bloated; inflated; distended.
2. grandiloquent; tumid; pompous; inflated; bombastic; as, a *turgid* style; a *turgid* manner of talking.

tûr·ġid′i·ty, *n.* the state or quality of being turgid.

tûr′ġid·ly, *adv.* in a turgid manner.

tûr′ġid·ness, *n.* same as *turgidity.*

tûr′ġid·ous, *a.* turgid. [Obs.]

tûr′ġīte, *n.* [*Turg*insk, a copper mine in the Ural Mountains, and *-ite.*] a crimson iron ore, occurring in fibrous masses, probably a solid solution of goethite with hematite: also called *hydrohematite.*

tûr′gŏr, *n.* [LL., a swelling, from L. *turgere,* to swell.]
1. turgescence or turgidity.
2. the normal distention and resiliency of living animal and plant cells.
turgor vitalis; the normal fullness of the blood vessels and capillaries. When the surrounding tissues lose their normal resistance this turgor becomes preternaturally increased and swelling results.

tū·ri·cä′tȧ, *n.* a Mexican tick, *Argas turicata,* very troublesome to men and animals.

Tū′rin grȧss, same as *couch grass.*

Tū′rin nut, a fossil walnut-shaped fruit, found in the Upper Tertiary deposits near Turin, Italy.

tū′ri·ō, *n.* same as *turion.*

tū′ri·ŏn, *n.* [L. *turio* (*-onis*), shoot.] in botany, a scaly solitary shoot springing out of the ground, as asparagus or hop; also, a young scaly sucker.

tū″ri·ō·nif′ẽr·ous, *a.* [L. *turio* (*-onis*), shoot, and *-ferous.*] having or producing shoots.

Tûrk, *n.* [Fr. *Turc,* from Tat. *Turk,* Turk.]
1. a native or inhabitant of Turkey; especially, a member of the Moslem people of Turkey or, formerly, of the Ottoman Empire.
2. a follower of Mohammed; a Mohammedan. [Obs.]
3. a member of any of the Turki peoples.
4. a fierce, cruel person: in allusion to the conquering Turks of the Ottoman Empire. [Now Rare.]
5. [t-] a sword or scimitar. [Obs.]
6. [t-] in entomology, the plum weevil.
7. a Turkish horse.

tûr′key, *n.*; *pl.* **tûr′keyṣ** or **tûr′key,** [earlier *Turkey-cock,* term orig. applied to the Guinea fowl, sometimes imported through Turkey and for a time identified with the Am. fowl.]

AMERICAN WILD TURKEY
(*Meleagris gallopavo*)

1. either of two varieties of large, wild or domesticated, North American birds with a small, naked head and spreading tail, bred as poultry in many parts of the world. The plumage of the wild male turkey is a golden bronze, shot with violet and green, and banded with black. It has a tuft of hairlike feathers projecting from the breast.
2. its flesh, prized as food.
3. a failure: said of a play, musical comedy, etc. [Slang.]
to talk turkey; to talk candidly and bluntly.

tûr′key·bēard, *n.* in botany, a perennial herb of the genus *Xerophyllum:* also called *turkey's-beard.*

tûr′key·ber″ry, *n.* one of the berries of some species of *Rhamnus,* which form an article of commerce from the Mediterranean on account of the coloring matter which they yield, which varies from yellow to green.

tûr′key bîrd, the wryneck, *Jynx torquilla.* [Brit. Dial.]

tûr′key blos′sŏm, a yellow-blossomed herb from the West Indies, *Tribulus cistoides,* of the family *Zygophyllaceæ.*

tûr′key buz′zärd, a dark-colored vulture, *Cathartes aura,* of South and Central America and the southern United States, having a resemblance to a turkey in its naked, reddish head.

Tûr′key çär′pet, same as *Turkish carpet.*

tûr′key çock, 1. the male turkey.
2. a vain, strutting, pompous person.

tûr′key çọrn, squirrel corn.

tûr′key gnat (nat), a small black fly of the southern United States, that infests poultry.

tûr′key gob′blẽr, the turkey cock. [Colloq.]

tûr′key grȧss, goose grass. [Brit. Dial.]

Tûr′key gum, gum exuded by some species of *Acacia.*

tûr′key hen, the hen or female turkey.

Tûr′key hōne, a Turkey stone.

Tûr′key leath′ẽr (leth′), leather prepared by tawing with oil. [Brit.]

tûr′key louse, a bird louse infesting the turkey.

tûr′key pōult, a young turkey.

Tûr′key red, 1. a bright red produced on cotton cloth by alizarin.
2. cotton cloth of this color.

Tûr′key slāte, a Turkey stone.

Tûr′key spŏnġe, a fine quality of sponge found in the Mediterranean.

Tûr′key stōne, 1. a slate or oilstone from Turkey, from which hones are made.
2. turquoise. [Obs.]

tûr'key-trot, *v.i.* to dance the turkey trot.

tûr'key trot, a ballroom dance to ragtime music, popular in the early twentieth century.

tûr'key vul'tûre, the turkey buzzard.

Tur'kï, *a.* [Per.] 1. designating or of the Southern branch of the Turkic languages, including Turkish, Osmanli, Turkoman, etc.

2. designating or of the peoples who speak them.

Tur'kï, *n.* 1. the Turki languages.

2. a member of any Turki people.

Tûr'kiç, *a.* 1. designating or of a subfamily of Altaic languages divided into Southern, or Turki, and Eastern, Western, and Central branches.

2. designating or of the peoples who speak any of these languages.

3. loosely, Turkish.

Tûr'kiç, *n.* the Turkic subfamily of languages.

tûr'kis, *n.* a turquoise. [Obs.]

Tûrk'ish, *n.* Osmanli, the Turkic language of Turkey.

Tûrk'ish, *a.* of or pertaining to Turkey, the Turks, their language, etc.

Tûrk'ish bȧth, 1. a kind of bath in which the bather, after a period of heavy perspiration in a room of hot air or steam, is washed, massaged, and cooled.

2. a place where such a bath is given.

Tûrk'ish çär'pet, a wool carpet with large loops that are cut so as to give the appearance of velvet.

Tûrk'ish dē·light' (-līt') (or **pāste**), a kind of candy consisting of cubes of a sweetened and flavored jellylike substance covered with powdered sugar.

Tûrk'ish·ly, *adv.* in the manner of the Turks.

Tûrk'ish·ness, *n.* the character or condition of the Turks; Turkism.

Tûrk'ish pound, the Turkish lira: symbol £T.

Tûrk'ish tow'el, tûrk'ish tow'el, a thick cotton towel with a rough nap of uncut loops.

Tûrk'ism, *n.* Turkish culture, beliefs, customs, principles, etc.

tûr'kle, *n.* a turtle. [Dial.]

Tûrk'măn, *n.*; *pl.* **Tûrk'men,** a native or inhabitant of the Turkmen S.S.R.

Tûrk'men, *n.* the East Turkic language of the Turkomans: also *Turkoman.*

Tûrk·mē'ni·ăn, *a.* of the Turkmen S.S.R., its people (*Turkmen*), etc.

Tûr'kō-, a combining form meaning (a) *of Turkey, of the Turks*; (b) *Turkey and, the Turks and.* Also *Turco-.*

Tûr'kō, *n.* same as *Turco.*

tûr'kois, *a.* and *n.* same as *turquoise.*

Tûr'kō·măn, *n.* [Per. *Turkumān,* one like a Turk.]

1. *pl.* **Tûr'kō·măns,** a member of a group of seminomadic tribes living in the Turkmen, Uzbek, and Kazakh Soviet Socialist Republics and in parts of Iran and Afghanistan.

2. the language of the Turkomans; Turkmen.

Also spelled *Turcoman.*

Tûrk's'-çap, *n.* 1. a Turk's-cap lily.

2. a plant, *Cactus intortus*: also called *Turk's-cap cactus* or *Turk's-head.*

3. a variety of winter squash.

Tûrk's'-çap lil'y, 1. a lily having purplish-red to violet-rose flowers with rolled-back petals; martagon.

2. a lily resembling the martagon, having orange-red flowers spotted with purple.

Tûrk's'-head (-hed), *n.* 1. see *Turk's-cap,* sense 2.

2. in nautical usage, an ornamental knot shaped somewhat like a turban by weaving a small rope around a larger one.

3. a round brush having a long handle, used especially for cleaning ceilings.

4. a pan used for baking cakes, puddings, etc., having a pipe in the center to allow the heat to permeate more completely the middle of the cake or pudding.

Tûrk's'-tûr"băn, *n.* a plant of the genus *Ranunculus*; the crowfoot.

Tûr'lū·pin, *n.* [OFr.] in French ecclesiastical history, one of a sect of freethinkers in the thirteenth and fourteenth centuries: a nickname.

tûrm, *n.* [L. *turma.*] a troop. [Obs.]

tûr'mȧ, *n.*; *pl.* **tûr'mae,** in ancient Rome, a body of cavalry composed of thirty or thirty-two men.

tûr'mȧ·lin, tûr'mȧ·line, *n.* same as *tourmaline.*

tûr'mēr·iç, *n.* [Fr. *terre-mérite*; LL. *terra-merita,* as if excellent earth; *terra,* earth, and *meritus,* excellent; but prob. altered from Ar. *karkam, kurkum,* saffron.]

1. the root, usually in powdered form, of the *Curcuma longa* of the East Indies. It is used as a condiment, a dye, a medicine, and also as a chemical test for the presence of alkalis. It forms one of the chief ingredients of curry powder.

2. the plant, *Curcuma longa,* which yields turmeric.

3. bloodroot.

turmeric oil; see *turmerol.*

turmeric paper; paper impregnated with turmeric, used as a test for the alkalis, which turn it brown, and for boric acid, which turns it reddish brown.

turmeric root; (a) bloodroot; (b) yellowroot or orangeroot, *Hydrastis canadensis.*

tûr'mēr·iç tree, either of two rutaceous trees of Australia, *Acronychia baueri,* or a species of the genus *Zieria,* the inner bark of which yields a yellow dye.

tûr'mēr·ōl, *n.* [*turmer*ic and *-ol.*] a brownish-yellow oil obtained by the action of a petroleum on turmeric: also called *turmeric oil.*

tûr'moil, *n.* [prob. a merged word, based on OFr. *trumel,* tumult, noisy quarreling, but influenced by *moil.*] disturbance; tumult; confusion; uproar; commotion.

tûr·moil', *v.t.* to harass with commotion; to disquiet; to agitate. [Obs.]

tûr·moil', *v.i.* to be disquieted; to be in commotion. [Obs.]

tûrn, *v.t.*; turned, *pt., pp.*; turning, *ppr.* [from AS. *turnian* and OFr. *turner, tourner,* both from L. *tornare,* to turn in a lathe, turn, from *tornus,* lathe; Gr *tornos,* a lathe.]

1. to rotate (a wheel, etc.).

2. to give circular motion to; to move around or partly around; as, *turn* the key.

3. to do by a revolving motion; as, he *turned* a somersault.

4. to give circular shape to by rotating against a tool, as in a lathe.

5. to give rounded shape or form to in any way.

6. to give a well-rounded or graceful form to; as, he can *turn* fine phrases.

7. to change the position of, as by a rotating motion; as, *turn* your chair around.

8. to revolve in the mind; to ponder (often with *over*); as, she *turned* the plan *over* in her mind.

9. to bend, fold, twist, etc.; as, *turn* the sheet back.

10. to bend back (the cutting edge of a knife, etc.); to blunt.

11. to reverse the position or sides of; to invert; specifically, (a) to change so that the undersurface is on top and vice versa; as, he *turned* the pages; (b) to spade, plow, etc. so that the undersoil comes to the surface; (c) to alter (a collar, coat, etc.) so that the inner surface becomes the outer and vice versa.

12. to cause to become upside down, topsy-turvy, etc.

13. to upset (the stomach).

14. to bend the course of; to deflect; to divert; to avert; as, he *turned* the blow.

15. to cause to change one's intentions, actions, etc.; as, I *turned* him from his purpose; specifically, (a) to convert or persuade; as, I *turned* her to progressive views; (b) to prejudice; as, they *turned* his family against him.

16. to go around (a corner, an army's flank, etc.).

17. to reach or pass (a certain age, amount, etc.).

18. to reverse the course of; specifically, (a) to cause to move back or retreat; to repel; as, we *turned* the attack; (b) to cause to recoil, rebound, etc.; as, his own criticism was *turned* against him.

19. to drive, set, let go, etc. in some way; as, they *turned* him adrift.

20. to keep (money, goods, etc.) circulating or moving.

21. to change the direction of (one's eyes, face, etc.).

22. to direct, point, aim, etc.; as, he *turned* his gun on me.

23. to change the trend, focus, etc. of; as, *turn* your thoughts to practical matters.

24. to put to (a specified) use or result; to employ; to apply; as, he *turned* his knowledge to good account, he *turned* his hand to writing.

25. to change; convert; transmute; as, it *turns* cream into butter.

26. to exchange for; as, she *turns* her eggs into hard cash.

27. to subject; as, she *turned* his remarks to ridicule.

28. to translate or paraphrase.

29. to derange, dement, distract, or infatuate.

30. to make sour.

31. to affect (a person) in some way; as, it *turns* her nauseous.

32. to change the color of.

to turn a deaf ear to; to ignore; to refuse to listen to or believe, as an entreaty.

to turn around one's (little) finger; to have complete control of; to influence at will.

to turn aside; to avert; to ward off.

to turn away; (a) to dismiss; to send away; (b) to avert; as, *to turn away* wrath or evil; (c) to turn in a different direction.

to turn back; (a) to cause to return or retrace one's footsteps; hence, to drive off or away; (b) to send back; to return.

to turn down; (a) to fold or double down; (b) to lower by turning a valve, etc.; as, *to turn down* the gas; (c) to reject (a request, advice, etc.); (d) to reject the request, advice, etc. of (someone).

to turn in; (a) to point (toes) inward; (b) to deliver; hand in; (c) to give back; return; (d) to fold over; double.

to turn off; (a) to shut off; (b) to put out (a light); (c) to deflect; divert; (d) [Brit.] to discharge (employees); (e) formerly, to give over; to consign; (f) to accomplish; to perform; to complete; as, the printer *turned off* 10,000 copies.

to turn on; (a) to start the flow of; (b) to open; release; (c) to put on (a light); (d) to stimulate sexually. [Slang.]; (e) to make interested, enthusiastic, etc. [Slang.]

to turn one's coat; to change sides; to transfer one's services to the opposite party.

to turn one's hand to; to try; to undertake; to apply oneself to.

to turn one's head; see under *head,* n.

to turn out; (a) to put out (a light, etc.); (b) to shut off; (c) to put outside; (d) to drive out; to dismiss or discharge; (e) to produce as the result of labor; (f) to equip, dress, etc.; (g) to put to pasture, as cattle or horses; (h) to reverse; to show the inside of, as a pocket or glove.

to turn over; (a) to change the position of, as by rolling; (b) to reverse the position of; to turn upside down; to invert; (c) to think about carefully; to ponder; (d) to hand over; to transfer; (e) to relinquish; to delegate; (f) to put to a different use; to convert; (g) to sell and replenish (a stock of goods); (h) to buy and sell, or do business, to the amount of; (i) to open and turn the leaves of for the purpose of examining.

to turn the corner; see under *corner,* n.

to turn the die or *the dice*; to change fortune.

to turn the edge of; to blunt or render dull; to deprive of sharpness or keenness.

to turn the scale; to make one side of the balance go down; hence, figuratively, to decide in one way or another.

to turn turtle; to turn upside down; to capsize.

to turn under; to plow so as partly to cover with earth.

to turn up; (a) to fold or bend back or over upon itself; (b) to shorten (a dress, etc.) by folding back the bottom edge and making a new hem; (c) to lift up or turn face upwards, as to see the other side; (d) to bring to light by digging, etc.; (e) to increase the flow, speed, intensity, loudness, etc. of, as by turning a handle or knob; (f) to tilt up; to make point upward; to bring the end, tip, or point uppermost; as, *to turn up* one's nose in scorn; (g) to refer to in a book; as, *to turn up* a passage or text.

to turn upon or *on*; to cause to operate on or against; hence, to cast back; as, he *turned* his sword *upon* himself; *to turn* the arguments of an opponent *upon* the opponent himself.

to turn up one's toes; to die. [Slang.]

to turn upside down; to throw into confusion or disorder.

tûrn, *v.i.* 1. to move in a circle or around an axis; to rotate; revolve; pivot.

2. to move in a circular manner; to move around or partly around; as, the key won't *turn.*

3. to reel; to be in a whirl; as, my head is *turning.*

4. to run a lathe.

5. to be shaped on a lathe.
6. (a) to move in a rotary manner so as to change position; (b) to shift or twist the body as if on an axis.
7. to become curved or bent.
8. to reverse position so that bottom becomes top and top becomes bottom, etc.; to become inverted.
9. to become upset: said of the stomach.
10. to change one's or its course so as to be moving, going, etc. in a different direction; to deviate.
11. to reverse one's or its course; to start to move, go, etc. in the opposite direction; as, the tide has *turned*.
12. to change one's or its direction; to face about; to shift.
13. to direct or shift one's attention, abilities, thoughts, etc. to; as, he *turned* back to his work; she *turned* to music.
14. to reverse one's feelings, attitude, allegiance, etc., especially in relation to a specific person or thing; as, he *turned* against his former friends.

The smallest worm will *turn*, being trodden on. —Shak.

15. to vacillate. [Obs.]
16. to enter into a specified condition; to become; as, the milk *turned* sour.
17. to change into another form; as, the rain *turned* to sleet.
18. to become rancid, putrid, sour, etc.
19. to change color; as, the leaves are *turning*.
20. to become infatuated, mad, insane, or the like.

to turn again; to return; to turn back.

to turn away; (a) [Archaic.] to leave a straight or former course; to deviate; to forsake; (b) to move the face to another direction; to avert one's looks.

to turn back; to go or come back; to return.

to turn in; (a) to bend or double or point inward; as, his legs *turn in*; (b) to make a turn into; to enter; (c) [Colloq.] to retire; to go to bed.

to turn off; (a) to leave (a road) and enter another road branching off; (b) to branch off: said of a road.

to turn on; (a) to attack or oppose suddenly; (b) to be contingent on; to hinge on; to depend on.

to turn out; (a) to come or go out, as to assemble somewhere; (b) to result; to eventuate; (c) to prove to be; to be found; (d) to come to be; to become; (e) [Colloq.] to get out of bed. (f) to bend or point outward; as, his legs *turn out*; (g) to give up work to go on a strike; as, all the printers *turned out*.

to turn over; to shift one's position, as from one side to the other; to roll over.

to turn round; to move so as to face in another direction.

to turn to; (a) to refer to; to consult; (b) to go to for assistance; to apply to; to rely on; (c) to get to work; to get busy; (d) to be directed toward; as, the needle *turns to* the pole.

to turn under; to bend, double, or be folded downward or under.

to turn up; (a) to fold or bend back or over upon itself; (b) to have an upward direction; (c) to come about; to happen; (d) to make an appearance; to arrive; (e) to be found; (f) to make a turn onto and ascend (a street on a hill, etc.); also, to make a turn into any street or road.

tũrn, *n.* 1. a turning around; complete or partial rotation, as of a wheel, handle, etc.; a revolution.
2. (a) a winding of one thing around another; (b) a single twist, coil, winding, etc.; a convolution.
3. the condition of being twisted, bent, etc. in a circular form.
4. the direction of this.
5. a musical figure consisting of four tones the second and fourth of which are the same, or principal, tone, the first, normally, being a degree above, and the third a degree below: if the first is a degree below and the third a degree above, it is called an *inverted turn*.
6. a changing of position or posture, as by a rotating motion.
7. a change or reversal of course or direction; as, the *turn* of the tide, a *turn* to the right.
8. (a) a walk taken about a building, area, etc., as for inspection; a tour; (b) a short walk or ride, returning to the starting place, as for exercise.

Come, you and I must walk a *turn* together. —Shak.

9. the place where a change in direction occurs; a bend; a curve.
10. a change in trend, circumstances, events, policy, health, etc., often for better or for worse, sometimes occurring at a crisis.
11. the time of a chronological change; as, at the *turn* of the century.
12. a turning point.
13. a momentary shock, as from fright. [Colloq.]
14. an action that harms or, more usually, benefits another; as, he did me a good *turn*.
15. a bout; spell; try; as, a *turn* at gardening.
16. an attack of illness, dizziness, rage, etc.; a fit.
17. the right, duty, or opportunity to do something, usually in regular order, coming to each of a number of people; as, it's my *turn* to go.
18. a shift of work. [Brit.]
19. (a) a short performance given as part of a variety show; an act; (b) its performer or performers.
20. a transaction on the stock exchange involving both purchase and sale of particular securities.
21. a distinctive form, manner, cast, detail, etc.; as, a quaint *turn* to her speech, dress, etc.
22. natural inclination or aptitude; flair; as, an inquisitive *turn* of mind.
23. a tendency; drift; trend; as, the discussion took a new *turn*.
24. a variation or interpretation of the original; as, she gave the sonata a lively *turn*.
25. convenience; purpose; requirement; use; exigency; advantage. [Archaic.]
26. a hanging; an execution: so called from the practice of making the criminal stand on a ladder, which was turned over at a signal, leaving him suspended. [Obs.]
27. in law, a tourn. [Obs.]
28. [*pl.*] monthly courses; menses. [Colloq.]
29. in mining, a pit sunk in a drift. [Brit. Dial.]
30. as much as can be carried at one time by a person or an animal; as, a *turn* of wood. [Dial.]
31. a type turned upside down, showing black in proof, where a particular letter is missing.

at every turn; in every instance; constantly.

by turns; (a) one after another; alternately; in succession; (b) at intervals.

in turn; in proper sequence or succession.

on the turn; about to turn or change. [Colloq.]

out of turn; (a) not in proper sequence or order; (b) at the wrong time; (c) [Colloq.] rashly; imprudently.

to a turn; to just the right degree; exactly; perfectly; as, the meat is done *to a turn*: from the practice of roasting meat on a revolving spit.

to take turns; to speak, do, etc. one after another in regular order.

turn about; same as *turn and turn about*.

turn and turn about; alternately; by turns; successively.

turn of life; the menopause; change of life.

Syn.—revolution, rotation, change, alteration, vicissitude, winding, bend, deflection, curve, alternation, opportunity, occasion, time, deed, act, treatment, talent, gift, tendency, character, crisis, form, cast, shape, manner, mold, fashion, cut.

tũrn′ȧ-bout, *n.* 1. the act of turning about, as to face the other way.
2. a shift or reversal of allegiance, opinion, etc.; an about-face.
3. a merry-go-round.
4. one who favors change. [Obs. or Rare.]

tũrn′-ȧ-bout-fāce′, *n.* a turnabout (sense 2).

tũrn′-and-bank′ in·di·cā′tŏr, an airplane instrument that indicates the rate of turn and degree of bank at the same time, so that the pilot can judge whether the airplane is properly banked for a particular turn.

tũrn bench, a simple portable lathe, used by watchmakers.

tũrn bridġe, a swing bridge.

tũrn′brōach, *n.* [Fr. *tournebroche*.] a turnspit. [Obs.]

tũrn′buc″kle, *n.* 1. originally, a catch for shutters or casement windows, consisting of a flat bar that drops into into a slot.

TURNBUCKLE

2. a kind of coupling for use between lengths of rod or wire, consisting of a metal loop or sleeve with opposite internal threads at each end or with an internal thread at one end and a swivel at the other: the effective length of the rod or wire can be increased or decreased by turning the metal loop.
3. in ordnance, a device used for securing the free ends of the implement chains in a gun carriage.

Tũrn′bull's blūe, a deep-blue precipitate produced when potassium ferricyanide is added to a ferrous salt.

tũrn′çap, *n.* a chimney top which turns round with the wind so that the opening is on the side away from the wind.

tũrn′çōat, *n.* one who forsakes his party or principles; a renegade.

tũrn′çock, *n.* 1. a cock or faucet with a handle.
2. an employee of a water company who turns the water on or off in the mains, attends to the fireplugs, etc.

tũrn′down, *a.* 1. that can be turned down.
2. having the upper part folded down; as, a *turndown* collar.

tũrn′down, *n.* the act of ignoring, rejecting, or dismissing; as, he made application for the position but met with a *turndown*. [Slang.]

tũrned çom′mȧ, an inverted comma (‘).

tũr′nep, *n.* a turnip. [Obs. or Dial.]

tũrn′ẽr, *n.* 1. one who or that which turns; specifically, one whose occupation is to form things with a lathe.
2. a tumbler pigeon. [Obs.]
3. a seal advancing to maturity; a three-year-old seal: so called in Newfoundland.

tũr′nẽr, *n.* [G., from *turnen*, to exercise.] 1. a member of a Turnverein.
2. a gymnast; a tumbler.

Tũr′nẽr·ȧ, *n.* [after William *Turner*, an English physician and author.] a genus of plants of South America and the West Indies, type of the family *Turneraceæ*. They are mostly herbs and shrubs, with inconspicuous flowers, chiefly yellow. An infusion of the leaves of *Turnera apifera* is used as an astringent by the Brazilians.

Tũr·nẽr·ā′cē·ae, *n.pl.* a family of polypetalous exogenous plants. It contains six genera, of which *Turnera* is the best known.

tũrn′ẽr härp, a three-year-old harp seal. [Newfoundland.]

tũr′nẽr hood, a three-year-old hoodcap. [Newfoundland.]

tũr′nẽr·īte, *n.* [after Edward *Turner*, an English mineralogist.] a variety of monazite of a yellowish-brown color.

tũrn′ẽr·y, *n.*, *pl.* **tũrn′ẽr·ieṣ**, 1. the work, art, or technique of forming solid substances into cylindrical or other forms by means of a lathe.
2. things made by a turner or in the lathe.
3. the workshop of a turner.

tũr′ney, *n.* and *v.* tourney. [Obs.]

tũrn′hall, Tu̇rn′häl·le, *n.* [G., from *turnen*, to exercise, and *halle*, hall.] a building for the use of gymnasts; a gymnasium.

Tũr·nī·ci·mor′phae, *n.pl.* [*turnix*, and Gr. *morphē*, form.] a division of gallinaceous birds including the genus *Turnix*.

tũrn′ing, *n.* 1. the act of one who or that which turns; a revolving, winding, twisting, inverting, etc.
2. a bend or bending course; a flexure; the place where a road or street diverges from another road or street.
3. the art or operation of shaping things on a lathe; turnery.
4. [*pl.*] the chips detached in shaping material on a lathe.
5. a shaping or fashioning (of literary work).
6. a military maneuver by which an enemy or position is turned.
7. in obstetrics, the operation by which the feet of a child are brought down in order to facilitate delivery.
8. a deviation from the straight or established course.
9. gymnastics.

tũrn′ing bridġe, a swing bridge.

tũrn′ing en′ġine, a lathe operated by an engine.

tũrn′ing lāthe, a lathe suitable for general turnery.

tũrn′ing·ness, *n.* the quality of turning; tergiversation; subterfuge. [Obs.]

tŭrn′ing point, 1. the point at which a thing turns or changes direction.

2. a point in time at which a decisive change occurs; crisis; critical point; as, the *turning point* of a disease, one's fortune, an argument, etc.

3. in engineering, a temporary bench mark used in leveling when the instrument must be moved from one position to another.

tŭr′nip, *n.* [earlier *turnep*, prob. from Fr. *tour*, or E. *turn*, in the sense of "turned, round," and AS. *næp*, a turnip, from L. *napus*, a kind of turnip.]

1. either of two plants of the genus *Brassica* (the *white turnip* and the *Swedish turnip*, or *rutabaga*), with hairy leaves and a roundish, light-colored, fleshy root, used as a vegetable.

2. the root of either of these plants.

Indian turnip; see under *Indian*.

tŭr′nip ā′phid, any plant louse destructive to turnips; especially, *Brevicoryne brassicae*.

tŭr′nip çab′bāġe, the kohlrabi.

tŭr′nip flȳ, 1. a small coleopterous insect, *Phyllotreta striolata*, destructive to the seed leaves and young crops of turnips. It has two yellow stripes on its wing cases.

2. a hymenopter, *Athalia spinarum*. The larvae of this fly are very destructive to the leaves of the turnip, and pass their chrysalis stage on the ground.

3. *Anthomyia radicum*, a dipterous insect, family *Anthomyidae*, the larva of which lives in the turnip root.

tŭr′nip mag′gŏt, the larva of the turnip fly, *Anthomyia radicum*.

tŭr′nip shell, a gastropod of the genus *Rapa*, with a bulky shell shaped somewhat like a turnip.

tŭr′nip·wood, *n.* an Australian tree, the bark of which smells like a Swedish turnip.

Tŭr′nix, *n.* [an abbrev. of L. *coturnix*, a quail.]

1. a genus of small, three-toed game birds resembling the plovers, found in southern Europe, northern Africa, and Asia.

2. [t—] any bird of this genus.

tŭrn′kēy, *n.*; *pl.* **tŭrn′kēys̤,** a person who has charge of the keys of a prison; a jailer; a warder.

tŭrn′kēy, *a.* [because the new owner of a housing-project unit so constructed need only turn the door key to take occupancy.] designating, of, or by a method of construction whereby the contractor assumes total responsibility from design through completion of the project.

tŭrn′out, tŭrn′-out, *n.* 1. a turning out.

2. (a) a gathering of people, as at a meeting; (b) the number of people assembled.

3. a labor strike or striker. [Brit.]

4. things produced; output.

5. a wider part of a narrow road, or a short side road, enabling vehicles to pass one another.

6. a railroad siding.

7. a carriage with its horse or horses; equipage.

8. (a) equipment; outfit; array; (b) a set of clothes; costume.

tŭrn′ō″vẽr, *n.* 1. a turning over; specifically, (a) an upset; (b) a change from one use, side, opinion, etc. to another.

2. a tart or a small pie made by folding one half of a circular crust back over the filling and other half.

3. (a) the number of times a stock of goods is sold and replenished in a given period of time; (b) the amount of business done during a given period of time in terms of the money used in buying and selling; (c) the number of shares sold in a stock market during a given period of time; (d) the amount of money loaned on call during a given period of time.

4. (a) the number of workers hired to replace those who have left during a given period of time; (b) the ratio of this to the average number of workers employed.

5. an apprentice transferred from one master to another to complete his apprenticeship. [Brit.]

6. in basketball and football, loss of possession of the ball because of an error by the offensive team.

tŭrn′ō″vẽr, *a.* that turns over or is turned over; made to be turned or folded over; as, a *turnover* collar.

tŭrn′pīke, *n.* [ME. *turnpyke*, a spiked barrier across a road, used in war.]

1. formerly, a turnstile.

2. a tollgate.

3. a road having tollgates; a toll road.

4. loosely, any highway.

tŭrn′pīke, *v.t.*; turnpiked (-pikt), *pt.*, *pp.*; turnpiking, *ppr.* to form, as a road, in the manner of a turnpike road; to throw, as the center of a road, into a rounded form.

tŭrn′pīke man, a man who collects the toll at a turnpike.

tŭrn′plāte, *n.* same as *turntable*.

tŭrn′sçrew (-skrŭ), *n.* a screwdriver.

tŭrn′sick, *n.* a disease of sheep; the gid; the sturdy. [Dial.]

tŭrn′sōle, tŭrn′sōl, *n.* [Fr. *tournesol*, from *tourner*, to turn, and L. *sol*, the sun.]

1. any of a number of plants whose flowers turn toward the sun, as the sunflower, heliotrope, and sun spurge.

2. a Mediterranean plant, *Chrozophora tinctoria*, yielding a purple dye.

3. this dye.

tŭrn′spit, *n.* 1. a person who turns a spit.

2. a variety of dog allied to the terriers: so called from having formerly been employed to turn a spit by means of a treadmill.

tŭrn′stīle, *n.* 1. a post supporting two revolving horizontal crossed bars, placed in an entrance to allow the passage of persons but not of horses, cattle, etc.

2. a similar mechanical apparatus, used at entrances to subways, theaters, etc. to admit persons one at a time: it is is often coin-operated.

TURNSTILE

tŭrn′stōne, *n.* a migratory, grallatorial shore bird of the genus *Arenaria*, of the plover family: also called the *sea dotterel*. It takes its name from its practice of turning up small stones, in search of the marine worms, minute crustaceans, etc. upon which it feeds.

TURNSTONE
(*Arenaria interpres*)

tŭrn′tā″ble, *n.* 1. a circular revolving platform with a track, used for turning locomotives, as in a roundhouse.

2. any of various horizontal revolving platforms; as, a phonograph *turntable*.

tŭrn′up, *n.* something turned up; a turned-up part.

tŭrn′up, *a.* that turns up or is turned up.

tŭr′nus, *n.* [LL., from L. *Turnus*, a man's name.] the tiger swallowtail, *Papilio glaucus turnus*, a yellow butterfly with black stripes, common in the United States.

Tụrn′ve·reīn′ (-fe-), *n.* [G. *turnen*, to exercise, and *verein*, union.] an association of turners, or gymnasts; an athletic club; also, the building occupied by such a club.

tŭrn′wrest (-rest), *a.* having a reversible moldboard, by which a furrow may be turned either to the right or to the left: said of a plow.

Tū·rō′ni·ăn, *n.* [named from *Touraine*, in France.] in geology, a division of the Upper Cretaceous system in France.

tŭr′pen·tīne, *n.* [ME. *turpentyne*, *terbentyne*; OFr. *turbentine*; L. *terebinthinus*; Gr. *terebinthos*, made from the terebinth tree.]

1. the brownish-yellow, sticky, semifluid oleoresin (*Chian turpentine*) exuding from the terebinth.

2. any of various oleoresins flowing naturally or by incision from several species of coniferous trees, as from the pine, larch, fir, pistacia, etc. Common turpentine is obtained from the *Pinus sylvestris*, and some other species of *Pinus*. Venice turpentine is yielded by the larch, *Larix europæa*; Strasburg turpentine by *Abies picea*; Bordeaux turpentine by *Pinus pinaster*; and Canadian turpentine, or Canada balsam, by *Abies balsamea*.

3. a light-colored, volatile oil distilled from such oleoresins, used in paints, varnishes, etc., and in medicine: in full, *oil* (or *spirits*) *of turpentine*.

tŭr′pen·tīne, *v.t.*; turpentined, *pt.*, *pp.*; turpentining, *ppr.* 1. to apply turpentine to; to rub with turpentine.

2. to extract turpentine from (trees).

tŭr′pen·tīne mọth, a moth of the genus *Retinia*, the larvae of which attack pines and firs, causing a resinous exudation.

tŭr′pen·tīne tree, 1. the terebinth tree.

2. any tree yielding turpentine.

3. the Australian *Syncarpia laurifolia* or *Tristania conferta*, both of which yield an aromatic oil.

tŭr′peth, *n.* [ML. *turpethum*, ult. from Ar. (colloq.) and Per. *turbed*, *tirbid*, the name of the plant.]

1. the root of *Operculina turpethum*, from Ceylon, Malabar, and Australia, which has an emetic property: sometimes called *vegetable turpeth*.

2. an emetic made from this root; also, the plant itself.

3. basic sulfate of mercury, $HgSO_4 \cdot 2HgO$, a lemon-yellow powder which acts as a purgative: also called *turpeth mineral*.

tŭr′pi·tūde, *n.* [Fr., from L. *turpitudo*, baseness, from *turpis*, base.] baseness; vileness; depravity; shameful wickedness; also, an instance of this.

tŭrps, *n.* oil or spirits of turpentine. [Colloq.]

tŭr′quoiṣe (-koiz *or* -kwoiz), *n.* [ME. *turkeis*; OFr. *turqueise*, fem. of OFr. *turqueis*, Turkish: so named because brought through Turkey.]

1. a greenish-blue, sky-blue, or greenish-gray semiprecious stone, consisting essentially of a hydrous phosphate of aluminum colored by a little copper. Among gems, the turquoise is 6 in the scale of hardness, and from 2.6 to 2.8 in specific gravity. It is found in New Mexico, Arizona, and Nevada, Tibet, China, Silesia, and Saxony, the finest specimens coming from the northeastern part of Persia. Also written *turquois*, and, formerly, *turcois* and *turkois*.

2. the color of turquoise; greenish-blue: also *turquoise blue*.

tŭr′quoiṣe, *a.* greenish-blue.

tŭr′quoiṣe blūe, a greenish blue.

tŭr′quoiṣe green, a pale color intermediate between green and blue, characteristic of certain varieties of turquoise.

tŭrr, *n.* [Burmese.] a three-stringed viol used by the Burmese.

tŭr′rel, *n.* an auger used by coopers. [Obs.]

tŭr′ret, *n.* [ME. *touret*, *toret*; OFr. *tourete*, turret, small tower, dim. of *tour*; L. *turris*, tower.]

1. a little tower projecting from a building; a small tower, often crowning the angle of a wall: it is often only ornamental.

2. in ancient warfare, a movable building of a square form, consisting of as many as ten to twenty stories, usually moved on wheels, and carrying soldiers, engines, ladders, etc.: used in attacking fortresses or walled cities.

3. (a) a low, armored, usually revolving, towerlike structure for a gun and gunner or guns and their crew, as on a warship, tank, or fortress; (b) a transparent hemisphere of plexiglass, etc., for a gun and gunner, as on a bomber.

4. an attachment for a lathe, drill, etc., consisting of a block holding several cutting tools, which may be rotated to present any of the tools to the work: also *turrethead*.

5. an elevated part in the roof of a modern railroad car, either for ventilation or for a lookout.

6. in heraldry, a small slender tower, usually set upon a castle or a larger tower.

tŭr′ret·ed, *a.* 1. furnished with one or more turrets.

2. in zoology, designating a shell whose whorls form a high, conical spiral.

3. shaped like a turret; as, a *turreted* lamp.

tŭr′ret·head (-hed), *n.* same as *turret* (sense 4).

tŭr′ret lāthe, same as *turret* (sense 4).

tŭr′ret ship, an armor-plated warship with low sides, and having on the deck heavy guns mounted within one or more turrets.

tŭr′ret spī′dẽr, a spider that builds a turret or tower of twigs and mud above its burrow, as *Lycosa arenicola*, of North America.

tŭr′ri·bănt, *n.* turban. [Obs.]

tŭr′riç·ăl, *a.* [L. *turricula*, a little tower.] of or pertaining to a turret, or tower.

tŭr·riç′ū·lāte, *a.* [L. *turricula*, a little tower.]

1. resembling a turret; having the form of a turret; as, a *turriculate* shell.

2. turreted (sense 2).

tŭr·riç′ū·lā·ted, *a.* same as *turriculate*.

tŭr′ri·līte, *n.* [L. *turris*, tower, and *-lite*.] a fossil cephalopod belonging to an extinct Cretaceous genus of turreted chambered shells, allied to the ammonites.

tŭr′rit·ed, *a.* turreted. [Obs.]

Tũr·ri·tel′lȧ, *n.* [L. *turritus,* turreted, towered, and dim. suffix *-ella.*]
1. a genus of marine gastropods of the family *Turritellidæ,* characterized by a long screw-shaped shell furnished with a spiral operculum.
2. [t–] any marine gastropod of this genus.

tũr·ri·tel′loid, *a.* having the form of or relating to the turritellas; resembling a screw shell.

tũr′si·ō, *n.* [L.] a large dolphin of the North Atlantic Ocean, having few teeth.

tũr′tle, *n.*; *pl.* **tũr′tleṣ** or **tũr′tle,** [altered after *turtledove,* from Fr. *tortue* or Sp. *tortuga,* tortoise.]
1. any of a large and widely distributed group of land, fresh-water, and salt-water reptiles of the *Chelonia,* having a toothless beak and a soft body encased in a hard shell into which, in most species, the head, tail, and four legs may be withdrawn: although fresh-water and, particularly, sea species are usually called *turtle,* and land species are usually called *tortoise,* the terms are properly interchangeable for all species.
2. the flesh of some turtles, used as food.
3. a turtledove. [Archaic.]
4. in a printing press with a rotary cylinder, the curved detachable part of the cylinder which holds the plate or types.

GREEN TURTLE
(*Chelonia midas*)

green turtle; a large marine turtle of a greenish color, living in warm sea waters, much valued for food. One of the several species is *Chelonia midas,* of the West Indies.
to turn turtle; see under *turn, v.t.*

tũr′tle, *v.i.*; turtled, *pt., pp.*; turtling, *ppr.* to hunt for or catch turtles.

tũr′tle·back, *n.* 1. in archaeology, a rude stone implement whose chipped surface imperfectly resembles the back of a turtle.
2. a convex arched covering over the bow and, sometimes, the stern of a ship as a protection against heavy seas breaking on board: also *turtle deck.*
3. a similar structure protecting the decks of early gunboats from enemy fire.
4. a helmet shell.

tũr′tle çow′rie, a large marine shell or cowrie, *Cypræa testudinaria,* having somewhat the same color and form as a turtle.

tũr′tle çrąwl, 1. an enclosure for confining turtles.
2. the trail which a turtle makes between its nest and the water.

tũr′tle·dōve, *n.* [ME. *turtle, tortle*; AS. *turtle, turtla*; L. *turtur*; of echoic origin.] any dove of the genus *Turtur* of the family *Columbidæ*; specifically, *Turtur turtur,* a bird characterized by its devotion to its mate and its young, and recognized by its plaintive cooing note.

tũr′tle-foot″ed, *a.* slow-footed.

tũr′tle gräss, 1. a West Indian sea plant, *Thalassia testudinum.*
2. the true eelgrass, *Zostera marina.*

tũr′tle·head (-hed), *n.* a hardy American herb of the figwort family, *Chelone glabra,* having a white or purple blossom whose corolla has the shape of a turtle's head.

tũr′tle-neck, *a.* designating a sweater, etc. with a turtle neck.

tũr′tle neck, a high, turned-down collar that fits snugly about the neck, as on some pullover sweaters.

tũr′tle peg, a sharp steel spear used in harpooning sea turtles.

tũr′tlẽr, *n.* one who hunts turtles or their eggs; a turtle catcher.

tũr′tle shell, 1. the shell of a turtle.
2. this shell used as a material; tortoise shell.
3. a turtle cowrie.

tũr′tling, *n.* the occupation of a turtler; the catching of turtles.

tũrveṣ, *n.* archaic plural of *turf.*

tũr′wăr, *n.* [E. Ind.] a tanbark obtained in India from *Cassia auriculata.*

Tus′căn, *a.* [L. *Tuscanus,* from *Tuscus,* a Tuscan, Etruscan.]
1. of Tuscany, a region in western Italy, its people, etc.
2. designating or of a classical (Roman) order of architecture characterized by unfluted columns with a ringlike capital and a frieze like the Doric.

TUSCAN ORDER

Tus′căn, *n.* 1. a native or inhabitant of Tuscany.
2. any of the Italian dialects of Tuscany, especially that one accepted as standard literary Italian.

Tus·cȧ·rō′rȧ, *n.*; *pl.* **Tus·cȧ·rō′rȧ, Tus·cȧ·rō′rȧṣ,** a member of a tribe of Iroquoian Indians at one time living in North Carolina but later, after joining the Iroquois Confederacy in 1722, living in New York and Ontario.

tush, *interj.* an exclamation indicating impatience, rebuke, or contempt; as, *tush, tush!* never tell me such a story as that!

tush, *v.i.*; tushed, *pt., pp.*; tushing, *ppr.* to use such exclamations as tush, pshaw, etc., to express one's annoyance, impatience, or contempt.

tush, *n.* [ME. *tusch*; AS. *tucs, tux*; var. of *tusk.*] a tusk or long pointed tooth; especially, one of the four canine teeth of a horse.

tushed (tusht), *a.* tusked.

tusk, *n.* [ME. *tusk*; by metathesis from AS. *tucs, tux.*]
1. a very long, pointed tooth, usually one of a pair, projecting outside the mouth and used for defense, digging up food, etc., as in elephants, wild boars, or walruses.
> The wild boar of the forest does not glut his sharpened *tusks* upon a kindred boar.
> —Charles Sumner.

2. any long, protruding tooth.
3. a projecting, tusklike part.
4. in carpentry, a bevel shoulder made above a tenon to give additional strength to it.

tusk, *v.t.*; tusked (tuskt), *pt., pp.*; tusking, *ppr.* to dig, wound, or gore with a tusk or tusks.

tusk, *v.i.* to gnash the teeth, as a boar; to bare or to show the teeth. [Obs.]

tusked (tuskt), *a.* 1. having tusks.
2. in heraldry, having tusks of a tincture different from the rest of the bearing.

tusk′ẽr, *n.* an elephant, boar, etc. with large, well-devloped tusks.

tusk shell, a tooth-shaped marine mollusk of the genus *Dentalium.*

tusk′y, *a.* tusked.

tus′săç gräss, tussock grass.

tus′sȧh (-sȧ), *n.* [Hind. *tasar*; Sans. *tasara, trasara,* lit., a shuttle, kind of silkworm.]
1. an undomesticated Asiatic silkworm, *Antheræa mylitta,* that produces a coarse, tough silk.
2. this silk: also *tussah silk.*
Also *tusseh, tussa, tussar, tusser, tussor, tussore, tussur.*

tus′sȧh silk, same as *tussah* (sense 2).

tus′săl, *a.* [from L. *tussis,* a cough; and *-al.*] of or pertaining to a cough.

tus′sẽr, *n.* same as *tussah.*

tus·siç′ū·lăr, *a.* [L. *tussicularis,* from *tussis,* a cough.] pertaining to or having to do with a cough.

Tus·si·lā′gō, *n.* [L., the herb coltsfoot.] a genus of composite woolly plants whose only known species is the *Tussilago farfara,* the coltsfoot herb.

tus′sis, *n.* [L.] in medicine, a cough,.

tus′sive, *a.* relating to or caused by coughing.

tus′sle (tus′l), *v.i.*; tussled, *pt., pp.*; tussling, *ppr.* [freq. of obs. *touse,* to tease, pull; ME. *tusen,* to pull.] to engage in a scuffle; to fight, struggle, contend, etc. vigorously or vehemently; to wrestle.

tus′sle, *v.t.* to scuffle with; to engage in wrestling with.

tus′sle, *n.* a vigorous or vehement struggle, contest, or contention; a scuffle.

tus′sŏck, *n.* [modified from OE. *tuske,* a tuft, a bush.]
1. a thick tuft of twigs, grass, sedge, etc.
2. tussock grass.
3. a tussock moth.
4. a tuft or bunch of hair. [Now Rare.]

tus′sŏck gräss, 1. a strong grass, *Dactylis cæspitosa,* originally found in the Falkland Islands, used as fodder.
2. any sedge or strong, tufted grass that grows in tussocks on wet or swampy ground.

tus′sŏck mọth, any of a large group of moths, *Orgvia leucostigma,* whose caterpillars are covered with long tufts of hair.

tus′sŏck sedġe, a tufty sedge, *Carex stricta,* growing in swampy places.

tus′sŏck·y, *a.* 1. forming or resembling a tussock or tussocks.
2. covered with tussocks; tufty.

tus′suck, *n.* same as *tussock.*

tut, *interj.* an exclamation used to check or rebuke or to express impatience or contempt.

tut, *v.i.*; tutted, *pt., pp.*; tutting, *ppr.* to use the interjection *tut* to express one's contempt or impatience.

tut, *n.* an imperial ensign consisting of a golden globe with a cross on it. [Obs.]

tū·tā′ni·ȧ, *n.* [LL. *tutia*; Ar. *tūtiya,* oxide of zinc.] a white alloy used in making tableware, usually consisting of antimony, tin, bismuth, and brass mixed in approximately equal proportions.

tū′tē·lāġe, *n.* [from L. *tutela,* protection, and *-age.*]
1. the function of a guardian; guardianship; protection.
2. the condition of being under a guardian or of being tutored.
3. teaching; instruction.

tū′tē·lăr, *a.* and *n.* same as *tutelary.*

tū′tē·lăr·y, *a.* [L. *tutelarius,* from *tutela,* protection.]
1. protecting; watching over; guardian.
2. of or serving as a guardian.

tū′tē·lăr·y, *n.*; *pl.* **tū′tē·lăr·ieṣ,** a tutelary god, spirit, saint, etc.

tū′tēle, *n.* tutelage. [Obs.]

tū′tē·nag, *n.* [Fr. *tutenague,* from Ar. *tūtiya,* oxide of zinc.]
1. a white alloy of copper, nickel, and zinc, used for tableware, etc.
2. zinc.

tū′ti·ŏr·iṣm, *n.* [L. *tutior,* comp. of *tutus,* safe.] in church history and theology, the doctrine which, while holding that obedience to the law is always the safer and better way, allows that an opinion of the highest intrinsic probability in favor of liberty may sometimes be followed.

tū′ti·ŏr·ist, *n.* one who adopts and is guided by the principles of tutiorism.

tut′-mouthed (-moutht), *a.* having a projecting lower jaw. [Obs.]

tū′tŏr, *n.* [ME. *tutour*; OFr. *tutor, tutour,* from L. *tutor,* a guardian, from *tutus,* for *tuitus,* pp. of *tueri,* to look after, guard.]
1. a private teacher.
2. in some American universities and colleges, a teacher ranking below an instructor; a teaching assistant.
3. in English universities, a college official in charge of the studies of an undergraduate.
4. in law, the guardian of a minor and his property.
Syn.—guardian, governor, instructor, preceptor, teacher, professor, master.

tū′tŏr, *v.t.*; tutored, *pt., pp.*; tutoring, *ppr.* 1. to act as a tutor to; also, to instruct; to teach.
2. to train under discipline; to discipline; to admonish.
3. to have the guardianship, care, or charge of.

tū′tŏr, *v.i.* 1. to act as a tutor, or instructor.
2. to be tutored, or instructed, especially by a private teacher. [Colloq.]

tū′tŏr·āġe, *n.* 1. the office, occupation, or authority of a tutor; tutorship.
2. a charge for tutoring.

tū′tŏr·ess, *n.* a woman tutor; an instructress.

tū·tō′ri·ăl, *a.* belonging to or exercised by a tutor or tutors.

tū·tō′ri·ăl sys′tem, a system of instruction, as in some universities, in which a tutor directs the studies of and has general supervision over each of the small group of students assigned to him.

tū·tō′ri·ăl·ly, *adv.* in a tutorial manner.

tū′tŏr·iṣm, *n.* tutorship. [Rare.]

tū′tŏr·ize, *v.t.*; tutorized, *pt., pp.*; tutorizing, *ppr.* to act as a tutor for; to teach; to instruct. [Rare.]

tū′tōr·ly, *a.* like, suiting, or belonging to a tutor.

tū′tōr·ship, *n.* 1. the office, duties, or authority of a tutor.
2. guardianship; tutelage.

tū′tōr·y, *n.* tutorage; instruction. [Obs.]

tū′tress, *n.* a tutoress. [Rare.]

tū′trix, *n.* [LL.] a tutoress. [Rare.]

tut′tà, *a.* [It.] all; the whole.
tutta forza; in music, with full force; very loud: a direction to the performer.

tut′ti, *a.* [It., pl. of *tutto*, L. *totus*, pl. *toti*, all.] in music, for all voices or instruments together; concerted: a direction to the performers.

tut′ti, *n.*; *pl.* **tut′tis,** 1. a passage or movement in which all voices or instruments take part.
2. a tonal effect produced by the concerted playing or singing of all performers.

tut′ti-frut′ti, *n.* [It.] a confection containing or flavored with different kinds of fruits or fruit flavorings.

tut′ti-frut′ti, *a.* made or flavored with different fruits or fruit flavors.

tut′to, *n.* [It.] all; entire: a musical direction.

tut′ty, *n.* [ME. and Late OFr. *tutie*; Ar. *tūtiyā*, oxide of zinc.] a crude oxide of zinc, collected from the flues of smelting furnaces in the form of a waste product.

tu′tu, *n.* [Maori.] a shrub of New Zealand, *Coriaria ruscifolia*, of which the juice is harmless, but the fiber, bark, and foliage are poisonous.

tu′tu, *n.* [Fr.] a very short, full, projecting skirt worn by ballet dancers.

tut′wōrk, *n.* in mining, work done by the piece, paid for by measure. [Brit. Dial.]

tut′wōrk″măn, tut′wōrk″ēr, *n.* in mining, one who does tutwork. [Brit. Dial.]

tū′um, *pron.* [L.] thine.
meum and tuum; see *meum*.

tu-whit′ tu-whoo′ (-hwit′, -hwoo′), an imitation of the cry of the owl: sometimes also used as a verb.

tux, *n.* a tuxedo. [Colloq.]

tux·ē′dō, *n.*; *pl.* **tux·ē′dōs,** [from the name of a country club at *Tuxedo* Park, near *Tuxedo* Lake, New York.]
1. a man's tailless jacket for evening wear, usually black with satin lapels, considered less formal than a swallowtail coat; a dinner jacket.
2. a suit with such a jacket.

tu·yère′ (twē-yär′), *n.* [Fr. *tuyère*, nozzle, from *tuyau*, a pipe.] the pipe through which a current of air is forced into a blast furnace, forge, etc.: also called *twyer*.

tuz, *n.* a lock or tuft of hair. [Obs.]

twä, *a.* and *n.* two. [Scot.]

Twäd′dell, *n.* [after the inventor.] a hydrometer used for liquids heavier than water. The scale is graduated so that the specific gravity is found by multiplying the degree obtained on the scale by .005 and adding 1 to the sum.

twäd′dle (-dl), *v.t.* and *v.i.*; twaddled, *pt.*, *pp.*; twaddling, *ppr.* [a collateral form of *tattle*.] to talk or write in a senseless or silly manner; to prattle.

twäd′dle, *n.* 1. empty, silly talk or writing; nonsense.
2. a twaddler.

twäd′dlēr, *n.* one who twaddles.

twäd′dling, *n.* the act of one who twaddles; silly, empty talk.

twäd′dy, *n.* idle trifling; nonsense. [Rare.]

twag′gēr, *n.* a lamb. [Obs. exc. Brit. Dial.]

twāin, *a.* and *n.* [ME. *tweien*, *twein*, from AS. *twegen*, two.] two. [Archaic or Poet.]

Go with me
To bless this *twain*, that they may prosperous be. —Shak.

in twain; in two; asunder.

twāin çloud, same as *cumulo-stratus*.

twāite, *n.* 1. a species of European shad, *Alosa finta*: also called *thwaite*. [Brit. Dial.]
2. same as *thwaite* (land).

twang, *n.* tang; taste. [Obs.]

twang, *v.i.*; twanged, *pt.*, *pp.*; twanging, *ppr.* [echoic.] 1. to give out a quick, sharp, vibrating sound; to make the sound of a taut string suddenly plucked or released.
2. to speak with a sharp, nasal sound.
3. to be released with a quick, sharp, vibrating sound: said of an arrow.
4. to guess; to surmise. [Obs.]

twang, *v.t.* 1. to cause to sound with a sharp, vibrating noise.
2. to utter with a sharp, shrill, nasal tone.
3. to shoot (an arrow), release (a bowstring) etc., with a quick, sharp, vibrating sound.

twang, *n.* 1. a sharp, quick, vibrating sound; as, the *twang* of a bowstring.
2. a sharp, vibrant, nasal speech sound; a nasal intonation; as, to speak with a *twang*.
3. a way of speaking, especially a dialect, characterized by such sounds.
4. a twinge. [Dial.]

twañ′gle, *n.*, *v.i.* and *v.t.* [freq. of *twang*.] twang. [Rare.]

twang′y, *a.*; *comp.* twangier; *superl.* twangiest, having a twang.

twañk, *v.t.*; twanked, *pt.*, *pp.*; twanking, *ppr.* [echoic.] to cause to make a sharp, twanging sound; to twang. [Brit. Dial.]

twañ′kāy, *n.* [Chinese *t'un-k'i*, a brook in the province of Chĕ-kiang, China.] a kind of green tea.

'twāṣ, it was.

twät′tle (-tl), *v.i.*; twattled, *pt.*, *pp.*; twattling, *ppr.* [variant of *twaddle*.] to twaddle.

twät′tle, *v.t.* 1. to pet; to make much of. [Brit. Dial.]
2. to twaddle.

twät′tle, *n.* twaddle.

twät′tlēr, *n.* one who twattles.

twāy, *a.* and *n.* two. [Archaic.]

twāy′blāde, *n.* [archaic *tway*, two; and *blade*.]
1. a variety of orchid, *Listera ovata*, with two broad leaves and small, red-veined, yellow flowers.
2. any of several orchids of the genera *Listera* and *Liparis*, having two leaves springing from the roots.

twēag, *n.* and *v.t.* tweak.

twēak, *v.t.*; tweaked, *pt.*, *pp.*; tweaking, *ppr.* [var. of dial. *twick*, from ME. *twikken*; AS. *twiccan*, to twitch.] to twitch; to pinch and pull (the nose, ear, etc.) with a sudden jerk and, usually, twist.

twēak, *n.* 1. a sharp pinch or jerk; a twitch; as, a *tweak* of the nose.
2. distress; trouble; perplexity. [Obs.]
3. a lewd woman. [Obs.]

tweed, *n.* [from misreading of *tweel*, Scot. form of *twill*; later associated with the *tweed*, river flowing through the region where the cloth is woven.]
1. a wool fabric with a rough surface, in a plain, twill, or herringbone twill weave of two or more colors or shades of the same color.
2. a jacket, suit, etc. of this.
3. [*pl.*] clothes of tweed.

twee′dle, *v.i.*; tweedled, *pt.*, *pp.*; tweedling, *ppr.* [echoic of a reed pipe.] to play a series of shrill tones: said of a musical instrument or its player.

twee′dle, *v.t.* 1. to play carelessly or casually on (a musical instrument).
2. [influenced by *wheedle*.] to cajole or wheedle, as by music.

twee′dle, *n.* a sound produced by tweedling.

twee·dle·dum′ and twee·dle·dee′, [from *tweedle*: first used of rival musicians.]
1. two persons or things so much alike as to be almost indistinguishable.
2. [T– T–] two almost identical characters in *Alice's Adventures in Wonderland*, by Lewis Carroll.

Tweed Ring, a group of Tammany politicians, headed by William M. Tweed (1823–1878), who misappropriated millions of dollars while in control of New York City (1868–1871).

tweeg, *n.* [Am. Ind.] the hellbender.

tweel, *n.* and *v.* twill. [Scot.]

'tween, *prep.* between. [Poet.]

'tween′-brāin, *n.* the interbrain, or diencephalon.

'tween decks, between decks.

tweer, *n.* a tuyère. [Obs.]

tweet, *n.* and *interj.* [echoic.] a thin, chirping sound characteristic of small birds.

tweet, *v.i.* to utter a tweet.

tweeze, tweeṣe, *n.* [ME. *tweese*; Fr. *étui*, a case.]
1. a case of surgical instruments. [Obs.]
2. [*pl.*] tweezers.

tweeze, *v.t.* [back-formation from *tweezers*.] to pluck, remove, handle, etc. with or as with tweezers. [Colloq.]

twee′zēr, *n.* the American merganser. [Dial.]

twee′zēr, *n.* tweezers.

twee′zērṣ, *n.pl.* [altered from *tweeze*.]
1. small pincers for plucking out hairs, handling little objects, etc.: often *pair of tweezers*.
2. a tweeze. [Obs.]

TWEEZERS

twelfth, *a.* [ME. *twelfte*; AS. *twelfta*.] next in order after the eleventh in a series; 12th; also, designating any of the twelve equal parts of something.

twelfth, *n.* 1. the one following the eleventh.
2. any of the twelve equal parts of something; 1/12.
3. in music, (a) an interval of twelve degrees in a diatonic scale; (b) a tone twelve degrees above or below a given tone; (c) the combination of two tones separated by this interval.

twelfth′-çāke, *n.* a large cake containing a bean or coin, prepared for Twelfth-night festivities. On cutting the cake, the one receiving the bean or coin in his piece was declared monarch for the evening.

Twelfth′-dāy, *n.* the twelfth day after Christmas, January 6, on which the Epiphany is celebrated: formerly observed as the official end of the Christmas season.

Twelfth′-nīght (-nīt), *n.* evening preceding Twelfth-day, formerly celebrated with games and feasting.

twelfth′-seç″ŏnd, *n.* in physics, a unit of time, $.1^{12}$ of a second, for measuring small intervals.

Twelfth′-tīde, *n.* the season of Twelfth-night and Twelfth-day.

twelve, *a.* [ME. *twelfe*; AS. *twelf*.] two more than ten.
Twelve Tables; the early code of Roman law, written 451–450 B.C.

twelve, *n.* 1. the cardinal number between eleven and thirteen; 12; XII.
2. a group of twelve persons or things; a dozen.
3. [*pl.*] same as *duodecimo*.
the Twelve; the Twelve Apostles.

Twelve A·pos′tleṣ (-lz), the twelve disciples chosen by Jesus to go forth to teach the gospel.

twelve′fōld, *a.* 1. having twelve parts.
2. having twelve times as much or as many.

twelve′fōld, *adv.* twelve times as much or as many.

twelve′mō, *n.*; *pl.* **twelve′mōṣ,** same as *duodecimo*.

twelve′mŏnth, *n.* a year.

twelve′pence, *n.* an English shilling; the sum of twelve pennies.

twelve′pen″ny, *a.* sold for or costing a shilling; worth a shilling; as, a *twelvepenny* gallery.

twelve′sçōre, *a.* twelve times twenty; two hundred and forty.

twelve′-tōne, *a.* in music, designating or of a system or technique of composition, developed by Arnold Schönberg, in which the twelve tones of the chromatic scale are used without reference to a specific tonal center, or key, but in an arbitrary, fixed order.

twen′ti·eth, *a.* [AS. *twentigotha*, *twentogotha*.]
1. next in order after the nineteenth in a series; 20th.
2. designating any of the twenty equal parts of something.

twen′ti·eth, *n.* 1. the one following the nineteenth.
2. any of the twenty equal parts of something; 1/20.

twen′ty, *a.* [AS. *twentig*, *twegentig*, from *twegen*, twain, and the suffix *-tig*, ten.]
1. two times ten; as, *twenty* men, *twenty* years.
2. many.

twen′ty, *n.*; *pl.* **twen′tieṣ,** the cardinal number between nineteen and twenty-one; 20; XX.
the twenties; the years from twenty through twenty-nine (of a century or person's age).

twen′ty·fōld, *a.* 1. having twenty parts.
2. having twenty times as much or as many.

twen′ty·fōld, *adv.* twenty times as much or as many.

twen′ty·fōur′mō, *a.* in printing, having twenty-four leaves to one sheet of paper: usually written 24 mo.

twen′ty·fōur′mō, *n.* a book made of sheets folded into twenty-four leaves each.

twen'ty-one' (-wun'), *n.* a gambling game at cards, in which each player's aim is to obtain from the dealer cards whose pips total twenty-one or as near as possible to it without exceeding it: also called *blackjack, vingt et un.*

'twēre, it were.

twey, *a.* two. [Obs.]

twey'fōld, *a.* twofold. [Obs.]

twi-, [ME. *twi, twy-*; AS. *twi-.*] a prefix meaning *two, double, twice.*

twī'bil, twī'bill, *n.* [AS. *twibill,* from *twi,* double, and *bill, bil,* an ax, a bill.]
1. an ax with two cutting edges. [Obs.]
2. (a) a mattock; (b) a reaping hook. [Dial.]
3. a double-bladed battle-ax. [Archaic or Poetic.]

twī'billed, *a.* armed with a twibil.

twīce, *adv.* [ME. *twies*; AS. *twiges,* from *twi-,* double.]
1. on two occasions or in two instances.
2. two times.
3. doubly; in twofold amount or degree; as, *twice* the sum.
Twice is often used in hyphenated compounds, as *twice*-born, *twice*-planted, *twice*-conquered.

twīce'-lāid', *a.* 1. made from the yarns of old rope.
2. made from remnants or used material.

twīce'-tōld, *a.* 1. told twice.
2. told many times; hackneyed; trite.

twid'dle (-dl), *v.t.*; twiddled, *pt., pp.*; twiddling, *ppr.* [prob. via dial. from ON. *tvidla,* to stir.] to twirl or play with lightly.
to twiddle one's thumbs; (a) to twirl one's thumbs idly around one another; (b) to do nothing; to be idle.

twid'dle, *v.i.* 1. to play with something; to toy.
2. to be busy about trifles.
3. to move in a twirling manner.

twid'dle, *n.* a gentle twirling motion, as with the fingers.

twid'dlēr, *n.* one who twiddles.

twid'dling līne, in nautical usage, a string attached to one of the gimbals of a compass, by which the compass card can be jerked free if caught.

twī'fal·lōw, *v.t.* [AS. *twi-,* double, and Eng. *fallow.*] to plow a second time, as fallow land. [Obs.]

twī'fōld, *a.* twofold. [Archaic.]

twig, *v.t.* and *v.i.*; twigged, *pt., pp.*; twigging, *ppr.* [via thieves' slang, from Ir. *tuigim,* I understand.]
1. to notice; to observe keenly; to detect; to perceive. [Brit. Slang.]
2. to comprehend; to understand; as, I *twigged* what he said. [Brit. Slang.]

twig, *n.* [AS. *twigge.*]
1. a small shoot or branch of a tree or other plant.
2. a divining rod.

twig, *v.t.* to strike with twigs; to switch.

twig blīght (blīt), a blight injurious to apple twigs, produced by the bacillus *Bacillus amylovorus.*

twig bōr'ēr, any small beetle that bores the twigs of trees, as *Amphicerus bicaudatus,* the grape and apple twig borer.

twig bug, a twig insect.

twig'gen, *a.* 1. made of twigs; wicker. [Archaic.]
2. covered with twigs or wicker, as a wine bottle. [Archaic.]

twig'gēr, *n.* 1. one who or that which is active or energetic.
2. a fornicator. [Obs.]

twig gīr'dlēr, a beetle of the genus *Oncideres,* that girdles twigs of the apple, hickory, and other trees.

twig'gy, *a.* 1. like a twig; slender, delicate, etc.
2. full of or covered with twigs.

twīght (twīt), *v.t.* to twit. [Obs.]

twīght, *v.* obsolete past participle of *twitch.*

twig in'sect, a stick insect.

twig'less, *a.* having no twigs.

twig prun'ēr, a beetle of the genus *Elaphidion,* whose larvae bore into the plum, apple, and other trees of the United States and cut the twigs in two.

twig rush, a plant of the genus *Cladium,* of the sedge family; especially, *Cladium mariscus,* a British perennial plant, having spiny leaves and growing in marshy places.

twig'sōme, *a.* full of twigs. [Rare.]

twī'līght (-līt), *n.* [ME., from *twi-* and *light*; basic sense prob. "the light between."]
1. the subdued light just after sunset or, sometimes, just before sunrise.
2. the period from sunset to dark.
3. any faint light.
4. any condition or period preceding or, more commonly, following full development, victory, etc.

twī'līght, *a.* of or characteristic of twilight.

Twī'līght of the Gods, [from ON. *ragnar rökkr* via G. *Götterdämmerung.*] in Norse mythology, Ragnarok, the destruction of the gods and of the world in a final conflict with the powers of evil.

twī'līght sleep, a state of partial anesthesia and semiconsciousness induced by the injection of scopolamine and morphine derivative, as to lessen the pains of childbirth.

twill, *v.t.*; twilled, *pt., pp.*; twilling, *ppr.* [L.G. *twillen,* to make double.] to weave (cloth) so as to produce a diagonal ribbed appearance upon the surface.

twill, *n.* 1. a fabric woven so as to have parallel diagonal lines or ribs.
2. the pattern of this weave or its appearance.

twill, *n.* a reed; a quill; a spool on which to wind yarn. [Brit. Dial.]

'twill, it will.

twilled, *a.* woven in parallel diagonal lines or ribs.

twil'ly, *n.* a willowing machine.

twilt, *n.* a quilt. [Brit. Dial.]

twin, *a.* [ME.; AS. *twinn* and ON. *tvinnr,* double; both from base of *twi-.*]
1. (a) consisting of or being two separate but similar or closely related things; forming a pair; double; paired; (b) being one of a pair of such things; being a counterpart.
2. (a) being two that have been born at the same birth; as, *twin* girls; (b) being either one of two born at the same birth; as, a *twin* sister.
3. in botany, growing in pairs or divided into two equal parts.
4. in crystallography, designating or of a twin.
twin boat or *ship*; a vessel supported on two parallel hulls.
twin crystal; same as *twin,* n. 4.

twin, *n.* 1. either one of two born at the same birth: twins are either *identical* (produced from the same ovum) or *fraternal* (produced from separate ova).
2. either one of two persons or things very much alike in appearance, shape, structure, etc.
3. [T—] [*pl.*] Gemini, a constellation and sign of the zodiac.
4. a compound crystal of two crystals or parts in reversed positions with respect to each other.

twin, *v.i.*; twinned, *pt., pp.*; twinning, *ppr.*
1. to give birth to twins.
2. to be born at the same birth. [Rare.]
3. to be paired or coupled (with another).

twin, *v.t.* 1. to give birth to as twins.
2. to be or provide a counterpart to.
3. to pair or couple.
4. in crystallography, to unite or crystallize with in the form of a twin by a reversal of the molecular structure.

twin, *v.i.* 1. to be parted; to be divided; to come apart. [Obs.]
2. to part; to go away or asunder. [Obs.]
3. to be separated (from) or deprived (of); as, to *twin* with one's gear. [Scot.]

twin, *v.t.* 1. to part; to sever. [Obs.]
2. to part, as from another person or thing; to sunder; to deprive. [Scot.]

twin'bēr·ry, *n.*; *pl.* **twin'ber·ries,** 1. a variety of honeysuckle with purple flowers.
2. a trailing vine with red berries; partridgeberry.

twin'bọrn, *a.* born as a twin or twins.

twīne, *n.* [ME. and AS. *twin,* twisted thread, from base of *twi-.*]
1. strong thread, string, or cord of two or more strands twisted together.
2. a twining or being twined.
3. a twined thing or part; a twist; a convolution.
4. a tangle; a snarl.
5. a twining branch or spray of a plant.

twīne, *v.t.*; twined, *pt., pp.*; twining, *ppr.* [ME. *twinen*; prob. from D. *twijnen,* to twine, twist, lit. to double, and from the *n.*]
1. (a) to twist together; to intertwine; to interlace; (b) to form by twisting, intertwining, or interlacing.
2. to encircle or wreathe (one thing) with another.
3. to wind (something *around*) something else.
4. to encircle, enfold, embrace, etc.; as, a wreath *twined* his brow.
5. to unite; to mingle; to mix. [Obs.]

twīne, *v.i.* 1. to twist, interlace, wreathe, etc.
2. to twist and turn; to wind about.
3. to turn round; to whirl. [Obs.]

twīne, *v.t.* and *v.i.* to separate; to part. [Scot.]

twīn'ēr, *n.* 1. one who or that which twines; specifically, a machine for twining or twisting threads.
2. a plant that twines about a tree or other support.

twin'flow"ēr, *n.* *Linnæa borealis,* a creeping evergreen plant.

twinge, *v.t.*; twinged, *pt., pp.*; twinging, *ppr.* [ME. *twengen*; AS. *twengan,* to squeeze, press, pinch.]
1. to cause to have a sudden, sharp pain, pang, or qualm.
2. to pinch; to tweak; to pull with a jerk; as, to *twinge* one by the ears and nose. [Rare.]

twinge, *v.i.* to have a sudden, sharp pain, like a twitch.

twinge, *n.* 1. a sudden, sharp pain; a pang; as, a *twinge* in the arm or side.
2. a qualm, as of conscience.
3. a pinch; a tweak; as, a *twinge* of the ear.

twīn'ing, *a.* 1. twisting; winding round; embracing.
2. in botany, ascending spirally around a branch, stem, or prop.

twink, *v.i.* to wink. [Obs.]

twink, *n.* a wink; a twinkling. [Obs.]

twink, *v.t.* to twitter; to chirp, as in bird notes. [Rare.]

twink, *n.* the chaffinch. [Scot. and Brit. Dial.]

twin'kle, *v.i.*; twinkled, *pt., pp.*; twinkling, *ppr.* [ME. *twinklen*; AS. *twinclian,* to twinkle, shine faintly.]
1. to sparkle; to flash at intervals; to shine with a tremulous, intermitted light, or with a broken, quivering light; to scintillate; as, the fixed stars *twinkle,* the planets do not.

> These stars do not *twinkle,* when viewed through telescopes that have large apertures. —Newton.

2. to light up, as with amusement: said of the eyes.
3. to move rapidly to and fro in a sparkling manner, as dancers' feet; to flutter; to flicker.
4. to wink or blink. [Archaic.]

twin'kle, *v.t.* 1. to cause to twinkle.
2. to emit (light) in rapid, intermittent gleams.

twin'kle, *n.* 1. a wink or quick motion of the eyelid.
2. a gleam or sparkle of the eye; as, a humorous *twinkle.*
3. an intermittent gleam; a sparkle.
4. a twinkling; an instant; the time occupied by a wink.

twin'klēr, *n.* one who or that which twinkles; a sparkler.

twin'kling, *n.* 1. the act of one who or that which twinkles; especially, a quick movement of the eye; a wink.
2. a rapid gleam or little flash; a twinkle.
3. an instant; the time occupied by a wink.

twin'lēaf, *n.* *Jeffersonia diphylla,* an American perennial herb.

twin'līke, *a.* very much alike; resembling closely.

twin'ling, *n.* a twin.

twin-mō'tŏr, *a.* of or pertaining to a craft, as an airplane, having two motors.

twinned, *a.* 1. born as a twin or twins.
2. paired or coupled.
3. consisting of two crystals united so as to form a twin.

twin'nēr, *n.* a breeder of twins; a producer of twins.

twin'ning, *n.* 1. the bearing of twins.
2. a pairing or coupling.
3. the formation of a twin crystal or crystals.

twin'ning ax'is, in crystallography, an axis which is normal to the twinning plane.

twin'ning lạw, in a twin crystal, the law of twinning.

twin'ning plāne, the plane with which two parts of a twin crystal are symmetrical.

twin'-screw (-skrö), *a.* having two screw propellers, rotating in opposite directions, as some ships.

twin stock, a beehive in which two colonies of bees are kept.

twin'tēr, *n.* a farm animal two years old: said of sheep, cattle, and horses. [Scot. and Brit. Dial.]

twīre, *v.i.* to chirp, as a bird; to twitter. [Obs.]
twīre, *v.i.* 1. to twinkle; to gleam. [Obs.]
2. to look slyly askance; to peep. [Obs.]
twīre, *v.t.* to twirl or twist. [Obs.]
twīre, *n.* a twisted thread or filament. [Obs.]
twirl, *v.t.* and *v.i.*; twirled, *pt.*, *pp.*; twirling, *ppr.* [altered (with emphatic *tw-*) from ME. *tirlen*; by metathesis from *trillen*, to turn.]
1. to rotate rapidly; to spin.
2. to turn in a circle; to whirl around.
3. in baseball, to pitch.
twirl, *n.* 1. a twirling or being twirled.
2. something twirled; specifically, (a) a twist, coil, etc.; (b) a twisting line; a flourish.
twirl'ēr, *n.* one who or that which twirls; specifically, a baseball pitcher.
twist, *v.t.*; twisted, *pt.*, *pp.*; twisting, *ppr.* [ME. *twisten*, from AS. *twist*, a rope, occurring in the comp. *mæst-twist*, a stay, a rope used to stay a mast.]
1. to wind, entwine, etc.
2. (a) to wind (two or more threads or strands) around one another, as by spinning; (b) to wind two or more threads or strands of (cotton, silk, etc.) around one another so as to produce thread or cord; (c) to produce (thread, cord, etc.) by winding two or more threads or strands around one another.
3. to wreathe; twine.
4. to wind or coil (thread, rope, etc.) around something.
5. to encircle with a coil of.
6. to entwine or interweave in something else.
7. to make spiral, wrench, contort, etc.
8. to give spiral shape to by turning the ends in opposite directions.
9. to subject to torsion.
10. to put out of shape in this manner; to wrench; to sprain; as, he *twisted* his arm painfully.
11. to contort or distort (the face, etc.).
12. to wring; torment; harass.
13. to confuse; as, I'm all *twisted*.
14. to break off, snap off, etc. by turning the end (with *off*).
15. to wrest, distort, or pervert the meaning of.
16. to revolve, etc.
17. to cause to turn around or rotate.
18. to make (a ball) go in a curve by throwing or striking it so as to give it a spinning motion.
19. to trim, lop, or prune, as shrubbery. [Obs.]
to twist around one's (little) finger; to have completely under one's influence, power, or control.
to twist the lion's tail; to do something that will arouse British resentment: in allusion to the lion as emblematic of England.
Syn.—contort, convolve, complicate, pervert, distort, wrest, wreathe, wind, encircle, form, weave, insinuate, unite, intertwine.
twist, *v.i.* 1. to undergo twisting; as, the wire *twists* easily.
2. to spiral, coil, twine, etc. (*around* or *about* something).
3. to revolve or rotate.
4. to turn to one side; to change direction.
5. to turn one way and then another, as a path; to wind; to meander.
6. to twist something.
7. to squirm; writhe.
8. to move in a curved path, as a ball that has been thrown or struck so as to have a spinning motion.
twist, *n.* 1. something twisted or made by twisting or by uniting various elements, as (a) a heavy firm sewing silk used for making buttonholes, etc.; (b) a thread or cord of two or more twisted strands of hemp, cotton, silk, wool, etc.; (c) closely twisted cotton yarn used as warp thread; (d) tobacco in the form of a twisted roll; (e) a loaf of bread made of twisted dough; (f) a spiral in the bore of a rifled gun; (g) a mode of construction of gun barrels in which the iron, in the form of a ribbon, is heated and coiled spirally around a mandrel; (h) [Brit. Slang.] any kind of mixed liquor, as one of beer and whisky.
2. the act or manner of twisting; hence, a knot, etc. made by twisting.
3. rotation; spin, turn, twirl, etc.
4. a spin given to a ball in throwing or striking it.
5. spiral movement along and around on axis.
6. the condition of being twisted in a spiral; torsional stress.
7. the degree of this; angle of torsion.
8. a contortion, as of the face.
9. a wrench or sprain.
10. a turning aside; a turn; a bend.
11. a personal tendency, especially an eccentric one; bias.
12. a distorting or perverting of meaning.
13. capacity for swallowing; appetite. [Brit. Slang.]
14. a twig. [Obs.]
15. a kind of hinge. [Obs.]
twist'à·ble, *a.* capable of being twisted.
twist drill, a drill having spiral grooves around its body for throwing out chips.
twist'ed, *a.* (a) interwoven; (b) distorted; (c) winding.
twisted column; in architecture, a column having the appearance of being twisted or of having parts laid spirally together, as the strands of a rope.
twisted curve; a doubly-curved curve; a curve no two successive portions of which lie in the same plane.
twisted flower; any flower of the genus *Strophanthus*, of the dogbane family.
twisted pine; (a) same as *candlewood pine* under *pine*; (b) a scrub pine, *Pinus contorta*, of the Pacific coast.
twisted surface; a surface no two successive tangents to which lie in the same plane.
twisted suture; in surgery, a suture that closes a wound by the use of a large pin stuck through the edges and a thread twisted in a figure-of-eight position about the ends of the pin.
twist'ēr, *n.* 1. one who or that which twists.
2. a machine for twisting threads, etc.
3. a thrown or batted ball that has been given a twist.
4. a tornado or cyclone.
5. in carpentry, a girder. [Obs.]
6. the inner side of a rider's thigh.
twist'i·çăl, *a.* disposed to be crooked; odd; dishonest. [Slang.]
twist'ing mȧ·çhïne', a machine for twisting ropes, etc.
twist joint, a joint in which two ends of wires are overlapped and closely wrapped around each other; the joint used in splicing telegraph wires.
twit, *v.t.*; twitted, *pt.*, *pp.*; twitting, *ppr.* [by loss of initial *a*, from ME. *atwiten*, to twit, reproach; AS. *ætwitan*.] to reproach, to taunt, to upbraid, etc., especially by reminding of a fault or mistake.
twit, *n.* 1. act of twitting.
2. a reproach or taunt; a gibe.
twitch, *v.t.* and *v.i.*; twitched (twicht), *pt.*, *pp.*; twitching, *ppr.* [ME. *twicchen*; AS. *twiccian*, to pluck.]
1. to pull (at) with a sudden jerk; to pluck; to snatch.
2. to move with a quick, sudden motion or convulsively.
twitch, *n.* 1. a short, sudden, quick pull or jerk; as, a *twitch* by the sleeve.
2. a sudden, quick motion, especially a convulsive or spasmodic one; as, he has a *twitch* on one side of his face.
3. a noose attached to a stock or handle and twisted around the upper lip of a horse so as to keep it quiet when shoeing, etc.
4. in mining, a place where a vein becomes very narrow. [Obs.]
twitch'ēr, *n.* one who or that which twitches.
twitch grȧss, couch grass, a weedy kind of grass.
twīte, *n.* [imitative.] the mountain linnet, *Carduelis flavirostris*, native to northern Britain and Scandinavia.
twit'lärk, *n.* the titlark, or pipit. [Brit. Dial.]
twit'tēr, *v.i.*; twittered, *pt.*, *pp.*; twittering, *ppr.* [ME. *twiteren*.]
1. to make a succession of small, tremulous, intermittent vocal sounds; to chirp continuously or tremulously: said of birds.
2. to talk in a rapid, tremulous manner expressive of agitation, timidity, etc; to chatter.
3. to tremble; to quiver.
4. to titter.
twit'tēr, *v.t.* to express or say in a twittering manner.
twit'tēr, *n.* 1. a small, intermittent, tremulous noise or series of chirpings, as the sound made by a swallow.
2. any similar sound.
3. a slight trembling of the nerves; slight nervous excitement or agitation; tremulousness.
4. a titter; a sound as of half-suppressed laughter.
twit'tēr, *n.* one who twits, taunts, upbraids, or reproaches.
twit'tēr·ing, *n.* 1. the act of one who or of that which twitters; a sharp, intermittent chirping noise; a chirp.
2. slight nervous excitement; an agitation arising from suspense, desire, etc.
twit'ting·ly, *adv.* in a taunting or reproachful manner.
twit'tle-twät''tle, *n.* same as *tittle-tattle*.
'twixt, *prep.* between; betwixt. [Poet. or Dial.]
'twixt'brāin, *n.* the diencephalon.
twö (tö), *a.* [ME. *two*, *tu*; AS. *twa*, fem. and neut., *tu*, neut.] totaling one more than one.
twö (tö), *n.* 1. the cardinal number between one and three; 2; II.
2. something that has two of anything as its outstanding characteristic, as a playing card or domino marked with two spots.
in two; in two parts; asunder.
to put two and two together; to reach an obvious conclusion through a comparison of facts or statements.
twö'-bag'gēr, *n.* a two-base hit. [Slang.]
twö'-bāse hit, in baseball, a hit by which the batter can reach second base without benefit of an error: also called *double*.
twö'-bit', *a.* 1. worth or costing twenty-five cents. [Slang.]
2. cheap; worthless. [Slang.]
twö bits, twenty-five cents. [Slang.]
twö'-blocks, *adv.* in nautical usage, in the position of block to block; chockablock, as a tackle.
twö'-bȳ-fōur', *a.* 1. that measures two inches by four inches, two feet by four feet, etc.
2. small, narrow, cramped, etc. [Colloq.]
twö'-by-four', *n.* a piece of lumber two inches thick, four inches wide, and of varying length.
twö'-cap''sūled, *a.* in botany, bicapsular; having two distinct capsules.
twö'-celled, *a.* in biology, bilocular; having two cells.
twö'-çleft, *a.* in botany, bifid; divided half way from the border to the base into two segments.
twö'-çŏl''ŏr, *a.* of, in, or using two colors.
twö'-çȳ''çle, *n.* a two-stroke cycle in an internal-combustion engine.
twö'-çȳ''çle, *a.* having a two-stroke cycle.
twö'deck'ēr, *n.* 1. a vessel of war carrying guns on two decks.
2. anything having two layers, floors, stories, or decks, as an omnibus, a house, etc.
twö'-edġed', *a.* 1. that has two edges, usually on opposite sides.
2. that can have two different meanings; especially, that can be taken either as a compliment or insult.
twö'-fāced' (-fāst'), *a.* 1. having two faces, surfaces, etc.
2. deceitful; hypocritical; treacherous.
twö''-fāc'ed·ly (*or* -fāst'li), *adv.* in a two-faced manner; deceitfully.
twö'-fist'ed, *a.* 1. having, and able to use, both fists. [Colloq.]
2. vigorous; virile. [Colloq.]
twö'fōld, *a.* 1. having two parts.
2. having twice as much or as many.
3. in botany, having two and two together or growing from the same place; as, *twofold* leaves.
twö'fōld, *adv.* twice as much or as many; doubly.
Ye make him *twofold* more the child of hell than yourselves. —Matt. xxiii. 15.
twö'-foot, *a.* measuring two feet; as, a *two-foot* rule.
twö'-fọrked' (-fọrkt'), *a.* dichotomous; divided into two parts somewhat after the manner of a fork.
twö'-fōur', *a.* designating or of a musical rhythm with two quarter notes to a measure.
twö'-hand, *a.* same as *two-handed*.
twö'-hand'ed, *a.* 1. that needs to be used or wielded with both hands.
2. needing two people to operate; as, a *two-handed* saw.
3. that is engaged in by two people; for two people; as, a *two-handed* game.
4. having two hands.
5. able to use both hands equally well; ambidextrous.
6. formerly, large, stout, strong, powerful. [Colloq.]
twö'-head'ed (-hed'), *a.* 1. having two heads.
2. ruled by two chiefs or heads of state.
twö'-lēaved', *a.* in botany, diphyllous; having two distinct leaves.
twö'-leg'ged (*or* -legd'), *a.* having two legs.

twö′-lipped′ (-lipt′), *a.* 1. having two lips. 2. in botany, resembling the two lips when the mouth is more or less open; bilabiate.

twö′-lōbed′, *a.* bilobate; having two distinct lobes.

twö′-mast′ed, *a.* having two masts.

twö′-mast′ẽr, *n.* a sailing ship with two masts.

twö′-nāme, *a.* designating or of commercial paper bearing the names of two parties, the maker and the endorser, as liable.

twö′-pärt′ed, *a.* in botany, bipartite; divided from the border almost to the base into two distinct parts.

twö′-pärt′ tīme, musical time that has two beats or multiples of two beats to a measure.

two′pence (tup′ens), *n.* 1. the sum of two pence; two British pennies.

2. a former British silver coin of this value, since 1662 coined only as alms money for Maundy Thursday.

3. a British copper coin of this value, current in the reign of George III.

two′pen·ny (tup′en-i; *also, esp. of nails,* tö′ pen″i), *a.* 1. worth or costing twopence.

2. cheap; worthless.

twö′pen·ny gråss, same as *moneywort.*

twö′-pet′ăled, *a.* having two perfectly distinct petals; dipetalous.

twö′-phāṣe, *a.* in electricity, diphase.

twö′-phāṣ″ẽr, *n.* a diphase generator.

twö′-piēce′, *a.* consisting of two separate parts; as, a *two-piece* bathing suit.

twö′-plȳ′, *a.* 1. consisting of two thicknesses, as cloth; having two strands, as cord, thread, etc.

2. woven double.

twö′-rañked (-rañkt), *a.* in botany, ranked on opposite sides of the stem so as to form two rows.

twö′-seed′ed, *a.* in botany, dispermous; containing two seeds, as a fruit; having two seeds.

twö′-sīd′ed, *a.* 1. having two sides.

2. having two aspects; as, a *two-sided* question.

twö′sŏme, *n.* 1. two people together; a couple.

2. a game, etc. for or played by two people.

3. these people.

twö′sŏme, *a.* consisting of or engaged in by two.

twö′-spot, *n.* 1. a playing card, domino, etc. with two spots, or pips; a deuce.

2. (a) a two-dollar bill; (b) two dollars. [Colloq.]

twö′-step, *n.* 1. a ballroom dance in ²/₄ time.

2. a piece of music for this dance.

twö′-thīrdṣ rūle, formerly, a rule in Democratic presidential conventions requiring a vote of at least two-thirds of the delegates to nominate a candidate.

twö′-thrōw, *a.* in machinery, having two cranks forged upon it, as an axle or a shaft, usually situated near and at right angles to each other.

twö′-tīme, *v.t.* to deceive in love; to be unfaithful to (one's lover, wife, or husband). [Slang.]

twö′-tŏngued′ (-tungd′), *a.* double-tongued; deceitful.

twö′-tọọthed′ (-tötht′), *a.* having two teeth; bident.

’twould (twood), it would.

twö′-wāy′, *a.* 1. having two ways, lanes, etc.; allowing passage in either direction; as, a *two-way* street.

2. that connects a pipe, wire, etc. to two others.

3. in mathematics, (a) that extends in two directions or dimensions; (b) that has two modes of variation.

4. that is used for both transmission and reception; as, a *two-way* radio outfit.

twȳ′blāde, *n.* same as *twayblade.*

twȳ′ẽr, *n.* same as *tuyère.*

-ty, [AS. *-tig,* ten.] a suffix meaning *tens, times ten,* as in twen*ty,* thir*ty,* etc.

-ty, [ME. *-tie, -te;* OFr. *-tē;* L. *-tas.*] a suffix meaning *quality of, condition of,* found in some abstract nouns of Latin origin, as pauci*ty.*

tȳ′ạll, *n.* something that ties or secures. [Obs.]

Tȳ′bŭrn, *n.* a former place of public execution in London.

Tyburn ticket; in English law, a certificate formerly given to the prosecutor of a felon to conviction, exempting him from all parish and ward offices within the parish or ward where the felony had been committed.

Tȳ′ċhē, *n.* in Greek mythology, the goddess of chance, identified with the Roman Fortuna.

Tȳ·ċhon′iç, *a.* pertaining to Tycho Brahe, a Danish astronomer of the sixteenth century, or to his system of astronomy.

tȳ·çọọn′, *n.* [Japan. *taikun,* from Chinese *ta,* great, and *kiun,* prince.]

1. a title applied by foreigners to the former shogun of Japan.

2. a wealthy and powerful industrialist, financier, etc. [Colloq.]

tȳ·çọọn′āte, *n.* the shogunate of Japan.

Tȳ′deūs, *n.* [L.; Gr. *Tydeus.*] in Greek legend, the father of Diomedes, and one of the Seven against Thebes.

tȳe, *n.* 1. a tie; a bond; a fastening. [Archaic.]

2. in mining, an inclined trough for separating ore by means of a flowing stream of water. [Brit.]

3. in nautical usage, a rope by which a yard is hoisted. It passes through the mast; one end is attached to the middle of the yard, and the other end is hooked to a purchase composed of the tye block and fly block, by which the hoisting is effected.

tȳ′ẽr, *n.* a tier (one who or that which ties).

tȳ·fọọn′, *n.* same as *typhoon.*

tyg, *n.* a tig (a cup).

tȳ′ing, *n.* the act of fastening, with or as with a string, rope, or chain; also, a fastening, as a ribbon or cord.

tȳ′ing, *v.* present participle of *tie.*

tȳke, *n.* [ME. *tike;* ON. *tik,* a bitch.]

1. a dog; especially, a mongrel or cur.

2. a boor. [Scot.]

3. a small child: term of endearment, especially for a lively or mischievous child. [Colloq.]

Also spelled *tike.*

tyl′ȧ·rus, *n.; pl.* **tyl′ȧ·rī,** [Gr. *tylos,* knot, knob.] one of the callous pads on the underside of the toes of birds.

tȳle′ber″ry, *n.* the coral plant, *Jatropha multifida.*

tȳ′lō·pod, *n.* any member of the *Tylopoda,* as a camel or llama.

Tȳ·lop′ō·dȧ, *n.pl.* [Gr. *tylos,* knot, knob, and *pous, podos,* foot.] a family of selenodont artiodactyls: also called *Camelidæ.*

tȳ·lop′ō·dous, *a.* having the digits or ends of the digits like pads instead of hoofs; of or pertaining to the *Tylopoda.*

tȳ·lō′sis, *n.; pl.* **tȳ·lō′sēṣ,** [Gr. *tylos,* knot, and *-osis.*]

1. in botany, the filling up of punctated vessels with cellular tissue.

2. in medicine, an inflammation of the eyelids characterized by thickening and hardening of their margins.

3. a diseased condition characterized by the formation of white patches on the skin or on a mucous membrane.

4. callosity.

tȳ·lō·stȳ′lăr, *a.* of, pertaining to, or resembling a tylostyle.

tȳ′lō·stȳle, *n.* [Gr. *tylos,* knot, and *stylos,* pillar.] in sponges, a cylindrical spicule, knobbed at one end and pointed at the other.

tȳ·lō·stȳ′lus, *n.; pl.* **tȳ·lō·stȳ′lī,** a tylostyle.

tȳ′lō·tāte, *a.* in zoology, having knobs at both ends, as a sponge spicule or tylote.

tȳ′lōte, *n.* [Gr. *tylōtos,* knobbed, from *tylos,* a knob, knot.] in zoology, a cylindrical sponge spicule knobbed at each end.

tȳ·lot′iç, *a.* of or pertaining to tylosis.

tȳ·lō·tox′ē·ȧ, *n.* same as *tylostyle.*

tȳ·lō·tox′ē·āte, *a.* same as *tylostylar.*

tȳ·lō′tus, *n.; pl.* **tȳ·lō′tī,** a tylote.

tȳ′lus, *n.; pl.* **tȳ′lī,** [LL., from Gr. *tylos,* a knot, knob.] in entomology, a central projection on the upper surface of the head of some hemipterous insects.

tym′băl, *n.* same as *timbal.*

tymp, *n.* [abbrev. of *tympan.*] a rectangular iron casting placed at the top of the hearth of a blast furnace, through which water circulates.

tym′păn, *n.* [L. *tympanum;* Gr. *tympanon,* a drum, area of a pediment, panel of a door, from *typtein,* to strike, beat.]

1. a timbrel; a drum. [Obs.]

2. a piece of paper, parchment, etc. stretched over the platen or impression cylinder of a printing press to serve as a cushion behind the paper being printed and equalize type pressure: in some kinds of printing, packing is also used beneath the tympan.

3. any membranelike part of an apparatus.

4. in architecture, a tympanum.

5. in anatomy, a tympanum. [Obs.]

6. a stringed, Celtic instrument, played with a bow.

tym′pȧ·năl, *a.* same as *tympanic.*

tym′pȧ·ni, *n.pl.; sing.* **tym′pȧ·nō,** same as *timpani.*

tym·pan′iç, *a.* 1. of, pertaining to, or resembling a tympan or tympanum; of or like a drum or drumhead.

2. in anatomy and zoology, of or pertaining to the tympanum or eardrum; as, the *tympanic* canal; the *tympanic* membrane.

tym·pan′iç, *n.* a tympanic bone, membrane, etc.

tym·pan′iç bōne, a bone in the skull of mammals, supporting the eardrum and partly enclosing the tympanum.

tym·pan′iç mem′brāne, the eardrum.

tym′pan·i·fọrm, *a.* having the form of a tympanum.

tym′pȧ·niṣm, *n.* [Gr. *tympanon,* a drum, and *-ism.*] tympanites.

tym′pȧ·nist, *n.* [Fr. *tympaniste;* L. *tympanista;* Gr. *tympanistēs,* from *tympanon,* a drum.] a member of an orchestra who plays drums and other percussion instruments.

tym·pȧ·nī′tēṣ, *n.* [L., from Gr. *tympanitēs,* of a drum, from *tympanon,* a drum.] in medicine, a distention of the abdomen, from a collection of air or gas in the intestines or peritoneal cavity.

tym·pȧ·nit′iç, *a.* pertaining to, of the nature of, or having tympanites.

tym·pȧ·nī′tis, *n.* [*tympan*um and *-itis.*] inflammation of the lining membrane of the tympanum.

tym′pȧ·nīze, *v.t.* to stretch, as a skin over the head of a drum; to make into a drum. [Obs.]

tym′pȧ·nō, *n.* singular of *tympani.*

tym″pȧ·nō·hȳ′ăl, *n.* a small bone or cartilage at the base of the styloid process.

tym″pȧ·nō·hȳ′ăl, *a.* of or pertaining to the tympanum and the hyoid arch.

tym′pȧ·num, *n.; pl.* **tym′pȧ·numṣ, tym′pȧ·nȧ,** [L. *tympanum,* a drum, the triangular area of a pediment, from Gr. *tympanon, typanon,* a drum, from *typtein,* to beat.]

TYMPANUM, T
Façade of Doric Temple

1. the middle ear or, sometimes, the eardrum.

2. (a) a drum or drumlike instrument; (b) a drumhead.

3. one of the uncovered air sacs on the necks of certain birds.

4. in architecture, (a) the recessed, usually triangular, space in a pediment included between the cornices of the inclined sides and the horizontal cornice, often ornamented with sculpture; also, any similar space, as above a window, or the space included between the lintel of a door and the arch above it, often ornamented with carving or sculpture; (b) the die of a pedestal.

5. in machinery, a drum-shaped wheel with spirally curved partitions, by which water is raised to the axis, when the wheel revolves with the lower part of the circumference submerged.

6. in electricity, the diaphragm of a telephone.

7. in botany, a membranous substance closing the theca of a moss.

tym′pȧ·ny, *n.; pl.* **tym′pȧ·nieṣ,** [ML. *tympanias;* Gr. *tympanias,* from *tympan,* drum.]

1. inflated or distended condition; tympanites.

2. bombast; pomposity; conceit.

Tyn·dā′rē·us, *n.* [L.; Gr. *Tyndareos.*] a legendary Spartan king: see *Leda.*

tȳne, *n.* a tine.

tȳp′ăl, *a.* 1. pertaining to a type; typical; constituting or serving as a type.

2. typographical. [Rare.]

-tȳpe, [Gr. *-typon,* from *typos,* a blow, mark of the blow.] a combining form meaning: (a) *type, representative form, example,* as in proto*type;* (b) *stamp, print, printing type,* etc., as in daguerreo*type,* mono*type.*

tȳpe, *n.* [Fr. *type;* L. *typus,* from Gr. *typos,* a blow, the mark of a blow, figure, outline, character of a disease, from *typtein,* to beat, strike.]

1. a person, thing, or event that represents or symbolizes another, especially another that is to come; a symbol; an emblem; a token; a sign.

2. a distinguishing mark, sign, or impress. [Rare.]

3. the general form, structure, plan, style, etc. characterizing or distinguishing the members of a class or group.

4. a kind, class, or group having distinguishing characteristics in common; as, a new *type* of airplane, an animal of the dog *type*: in colloquial usage, often used elliptically immediately preceding the noun; as, a new *type* airplane.

5. a person, animal, or thing that is representative of, or has the distinctive characteristics of, a class or group; typical individual or instance.

6. (a) a perfect example; a model; a pattern; an archetype; as, John is the very *type* of an honest leader; (b) in biology, a genus or species that best exemplifies the characters of a larger group and often gives its name to it.

7. in chemistry, any compound representative of the composition of other compounds more complex in composition.

8. the design on the face of a medal or coin.

9. in medicine, the order in which the symptoms of a disease succeed each other: it may be continued, intermittent, or remittent. [Obs.]

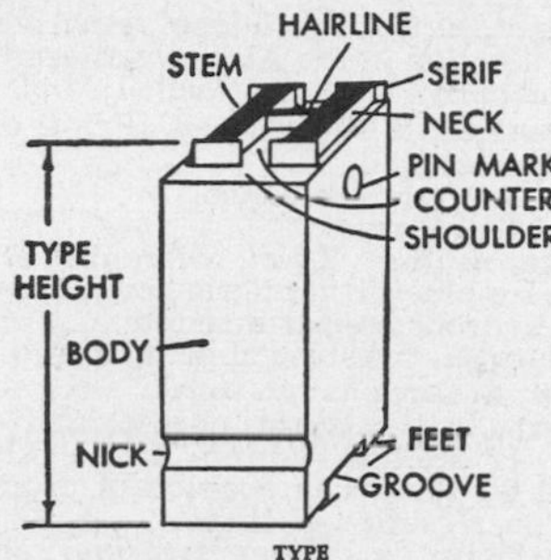

TYPE

10. in typography, (a) a rectangular solid or prism of metal, wood, or other hard material having a raised letter, figure, punctuation mark, or other character on the upper end in reverse, which, when inked, is used to make impressions on paper and other smooth surfaces; (b) types collectively; the quantity of types used in printing. The different parts of a type are technically named as follows: the *body* or *shank*, the rectangular solid itself; the *face*, the raised letter or character; the *shoulder*, the part of the end of the body unoccupied by the face; the *nicks*, notches made on one side of the prism, and designed to assist the compositor in distinguishing the bottom of the face from the top, etc.; the *groove*, a channel made in the bottom or foot of the type to make it stand steadily. The fine lines at the top and bottom of a letter are called *serifs*; the parts of the face of some letters, such as *j* and *f*, which project over the body, are called *kerns*. From the class, style, size, width, or weight of the letters, types are classified as CAPITALS, small or lower-case letters, roman, *italics*, script, etc.

The following table gives the names of the old bodies and their designation by points, 3½ point to 14 point being the sizes most used:

Brilliant	William	3½	point.
Diamond	William	4½	"
Pearl	William	5	"
Agate	William	5½	"
Nonpareil	William	6	"
Minion	William	7	"
Brevier	William	8	"
Bourgeois	William	9	"
Long Primer	William	10	"
Small Pica	William	11	"
Pica	William	12	"
English	William	14	"
Black Letter or Old English		8	"

11. a printed character or characters; as, small *type* is hard on the eyes.

12. in agriculture, the combination of characters of an animal or breed that make it most suitable for a particular use; as, beef *type*, dairy *type*.

13. in mathematics, the simplest of a set of equivalent forms.

point system of type; a standard system of sizes for type bodies, adopted by the Typefounders' Association of the United States. In this system, 996 points are equivalent to 35 centimeters, and one point is equal to .0138 of an inch.

tȳpe, *v.t.*; typed (tīpt), *pt., pp.*; typing, *ppr.* 1. to prefigure; to represent by a model or symbol beforehand.

2. typify; represent.

3. to classify according to type; as, he is *typed* as a villain in the theater.

4. to typewrite.

5. in medicine, to determine the type of (a blood sample).

tȳpe, *v.i.* to typewrite.

tȳpe bär, 1. in some typewriters, a bar which bears a type for making the impression.

2. a line of type cast in one piece, as by a linotype machine.

tȳpe found′ēr, one employed in the casting of metal type.

tȳpe found′ing, the art or operation of casting metal type.

tȳpe found′ry, a place where metal type is cast.

tȳpe ġē′nus, in biology, the genus that is theoretically most typical of a family or group and gives it its name.

tȳpe′-hīgh′ (-hī′), *a.* of the standard height of type (0.9186 inch); as, a *type-high* block.

tȳpe met′ăl, an alloy of tin, lead, and antimony used in making type, etc.

tȳpe′sçript, *n.* copy in typewritten form; typewritten matter.

tȳpe′set″tēr, *n.* 1. one who sets type; a compositor.

2. a typesetting machine.

tȳpe′set″ting, *n.* the act, art, or process by which type is set.

tȳpe′set″ting, *a.* of or used for setting type.

tȳpe′set″ting ma̤·chïne′, a machine for composing or setting up type.

tȳpe spē′ciēs (-shēz), in biology, the species that is theoretically most typical of a genus and gives it its name.

tȳpe spec′i·men, the individual animal or plant used as the basis of the scientific description of a species, etc.

tȳpe wheel, a wheel having raised letters on its circumference, used in some typewriters and in printing telegrams, etc.

tȳpe′wrīte (-rīt), *v.t.* and *v.i.*; typewrote, *pt.*; typewritten, *pp.*; typewriting, *ppr.*; to write with a typewriter: now usually shortened to *type*.

tȳpe′wrīt″ēr, *n.* 1. a writing machine with a keyboard for reproducing letters, figures, etc. that resemble printed ones: when the keys are struck, raised letters on bars are pressed against an inked ribbon, making the impression on an inserted piece of paper.

2. a typist.

3. a kind of printer's type made to appear like typewriter print.

tȳpe′wrīt″ing, *n.* the act or process of writing by means of a typewriter; also, the writing done by this process.

tȳpe′writ″ten (-rit″), *v.* past participle of *typewrite*.

tȳpe′writ″ten, *a.* written with a typewriter.

tȳpe′wrōte (-rōt), *v.* past tense of *typewrite*.

typh-, same as *typho-*.

Tȳ′phȧ, *n.* [Gr. *typhē*, cattail.] the type genus of the *Typhaceæ*; the cattails, bulrushes, or flags.

Tȳ·phā′cē·ae, *n.pl.* a family of plants, which includes two genera, *Typha* and *Sparganium*. They are herbaceous reedlike plants, growing in marshes and ditches.

tȳ·phā′ceous, *a.* of the nature of or pertaining to the *Typhaceæ*

tȳph′fē″vēr, *n.* typhus or typhoid. [Rare.]

tȳ·phin′i·ȧ, *n.* in medicine, a relapsing fever.

tȳph·i·zā′tion, *n.* the induction of a diseased condition by exposure to typhus.

typh·lit′iç, *a.* of the nature of, pertaining to, or affected with typhlitis.

typh·lī′tis, *n.* [Mod. L., from Gr. *typhlos*, blind; and *-itis*.] inflammation of the caecum.

typh′lō-, [from Gr. *typhlos*, blind.] a combining form meaning *caecum*: also *typhl-*.

typh·lō·em·py·ē′mȧ, *n.* an abdominal abscess accompanying appendicitis.

typh·lō·en·te·rī′tis, *n.* [*typhlo-*, Gr. *enteron*, intestine, and *-itis*.] same as *typhlitis*.

typh·lol′ō·ġy, *n.* [from Gr. *typhlos*, blind; and *-logy*.] the branch of medicine that deals with blindness.

typh′lon, *n.* the caecum.

Typh·lop′i·dae, *n.pl.* [*typhlo-*, and Gr. *ōps*, the eye.] a family of reptiles, distinguished from the typical snakes by the comparative narrowness of their gape, and by their habit of burrowing in the ground: they differ from all other reptiles in possessing teeth in only one of the jaws.

Typh′lops, *n.* the type genus of the *Typhlopidæ*.

typh·lō′sis, *n.* [Gr. *typhlōsis*.] in medicine, blindness.

typh·lō·sō′lăr, *a.* of the nature of or pertaining to a typhlosole.

typh′lō·sōle, *n.* [*typhlo-*, and Gr. *sōlēn*, a pipe, channel.] a fold in the dorsal wall of the intestinal cavity of certain annelids, mollusks, and tunicates.

typh·los′tō·my, *n.* [*typhlo-*, and Gr. *stoma*, mouth.] an operation in which the opening is made into the caecum.

tȳ′phō-, [from Gr. *typhos*, a vapor, fever, stupor.] a combining form meaning *typhus*, *typhoid*, as in *typho*genic: also *typh-*.

Ty·phō′ē·an (tī-fō′ē-an), *a.* pertaining to or resembling Typhoeus.

Tȳ·phō′eūs, *n.* in Greek mythology, a monster with a hundred heads, killed by Zeus.

tȳ·phō·ġen′iç, *a.* [*typho-* and *-genic*.] causing typhus or typhoid fever.

tȳ′phoid, *a.* [from Gr. *typhos*, a vapor, fever, stupor; and *-oid*.]

1. originally, of or like typhus.

2. designating or of an acute infectious disease (*typhoid fever*) caused by a bacillus and acquired through drinking infected milk, water, etc.: it was formerly considered a form of typhus and is characterized by fever, intestinal disorders, etc.

tȳ′phoid, *n.* typhoid fever.

tȳ′phoid·ăl, *a.* of, pertaining to, or characteristic of typhoid fever.

tȳ′phoid ba̤·cil′lus, the bacillus that causes typhoid fever.

tȳ·phoi′din, *n.* [*typhoid* and *-in*.] a preparation from a culture of the typhoid bacillus, injected in the skin for determining the presence of a typhoid infection.

tȳ″phō·mȧ·lăr′i·ăl, *a.* designating a fever believed to be of malarial origin, but having typhoid symptoms.

tȳ·phō·mā′ni·ȧ, *n.* [*typho-*, and Gr. *mania*, madness.] the state of muttering delirium accompanying typhus or typhoid fever.

Tȳ′phon, *n.* 1. in Greek mythology, the Egyptian divinity Set, the personification of the principle of evil.

2. in Greek and Roman mythology, the father of the winds and the son of Typhoeus, with whom he was sometimes confused.

tȳ·phō′ni·ȧ, *n.* same as *typhomania*.

tȳ·phon′iç, *a.* of or like a typhoon.

tȳ·phōōn′, *n.* [from Chin. dial. *tai-fung*, lit., great wind.] a violent cyclonic storm, especially one in the China Sea and adjacent regions; a hurricane.

tȳ·phō·sep′sis, *n.* [*typho-*, and Gr. *sepsis*, putrefaction.] the septic poisoning occurring in typhoid fever.

tȳ·phō′sis, *n.* typhoid state.

tȳ·phō·tox′in, *n.* a compound, $C_7H_{17}NO_2$, isomeric with gadinin, derived from cultures of the typhoid bacillus: in small animals it causes diarrhea, muscular paralysis, salivation, and dilatation of the pupil.

tȳ′phous, *a.* of the nature of or pertaining to typhus.

tȳ′phus, *n.* [Mod. L., from Gr. *typhos*, a vapor, fever, stupor.] an acute infectious disease caused by a rickettsia transmitted to man by the bite of fleas, lice, etc., and characterized by fever, nervous disorders, weakness, and an eruption of red spots on the skin: also *typhus fever*.

typ′iç, *a.* typical.

typ′i·căl, *a.* [Mod. L. *typicalis*, from L. *typicus*, from Gr. *typikos*, of a type, from *typos*, a type.]

1. serving as a type; symbolic.

2. having or showing the characteristics, qualities, etc. of a kind, class, or group so fully as to be a representative example.

3. of or belonging to a type or representative example; characteristic.

typ·i·çal′i·ty, *n.* the state of being typical.

typ′i·căl·ly, *adv.* in a typical manner; symbolically.

typ′i·căl·ness, *n.* the state of being typical.

typ′i·çum, *n.* [L.Gr. *typikon*, from Gr. *typikos*, of a type.] in the Orthodox Eastern Church, the directory, containing directions for service.

typ″i·fi·çā′tion, *n.* the act of typifying or the state of being typified.

typ′i·fi·ēr, *n.* one who or that which typifies.

typ′i·fȳ, *v.t.*; typified, *pt., pp.*; typifying, *ppr.* [L. *typus*, type, and *facere*, to make.]

1. to be a type or emblem of; to symbolize; to prefigure.

2. to embody the typical features or characteristics of; to be a type of; to exemplify; as, the genus *Typhlops typifies* the family *Typhlopidæ*.

tȳp'ist, *n.* a person who operates a typewriter, especially one hired to do so.

tȳ'pō-, [from Gr. *typos*, a blow, mark of the blow, figure.] a combining form meaning *type*, as in *typ*ography.

tȳ'pō, *n.* [short for *typographer*.] a compositor. [Colloq.]

tȳ'pō·çoș·my, *n.* [Gr. *typos*, an impression, and *kosmos*, the world.] a universal nomenclature. [Rare.]

tȳ'pō·gràph, *n.* [Gr. *typos*, type, and *-graph*.] a typographer.

tȳ·pog'rà·phẽr, *n.* a person skilled in typography; a printer.

tȳ·pō·graph'i·çăl, tȳ·pō·graph'iç, *a.* 1. of typography; pertaining to printing; as, *typographical* errors.

2. in print; printed.

3. emblematic; figurative; typical. [Obs.]

tȳ·pō·graph'i·çăl·ly, *adv.* in a typographical manner; as regards printing.

tȳ·pog'rà·phy, *n.* [Fr. *typographie*; ML. *typographia*; see *typo-* and *-graphy*.]

1. the process or act of setting and arranging types and printing from them; typesetting; composition.

2. the arrangement, style, or general appearance of matter printed from type; as, the *typography* of the book was good.

3. the art of printing with type.

4. emblematical or hieroglyphic representation. [Obs.]

tȳ·pō·loġ'i·çăl, *a.* of the nature of, pertaining to, founded on, or treating of typology.

tȳ·pō·loġ'i·çăl·ly, *adv.* by means of typology, in a typological manner.

tȳ·pol'ō·ġy, *n.* [*typo-* and *-logy*.]

1. the study of types, symbols, or symbolism.

2. symbolic meaning or representation; symbolism.

tȳ·poth'ē·tae (*or* -pō-thē'tē), *n.pl.* [Mod.L., from Gr. *typos*, type, and *tithenai*, to place, to set.]

1. an association of master printers.

2. printers: used in the names of organizations of printers.

Tyr (tēr), *n.* [ON.] in Norse mythology, the god of war and victory, and son of Odin.

tȳ'răn, *n.* and *v.* tyrant. [Obs.]

tȳ'răn·ness, *n.* a woman tyrant.

tȳ·ran'niç, *a.* same as *tyrannical*.

tȳ·ran'ni·çăl, *a.* [L. *tyrannicus*; Gr. *tyrannikos*.] pertaining to a tyrant; suiting a tyrant; arbitrary; despotic; hence, harsh; cruel; unjustly severe; as, a *tyrannical* ruler; *tyrannical* government or power.

Syn.—imperious, despotic, cruel, oppressive.

tȳ·ran'ni·çăl·ly, *adv.* in a tyrannical manner; with unjust exercise of power; arbitarily; oppressively.

tȳ·ran'ni·çăl·ness, *n.* tyrannical disposition or practice; the state of being tyrannical.

tȳ·ran'ni·cī·dăl, *a.* of or relating to tyrannicide.

tȳ·ran'ni·cīde, *n.* [L. *tyrannus*, tyrant, and *cædere*, to slay.]

1. the act of killing a tyrant.

2. one who kills a tyrant.

Tȳ·ran'ni·dae, *n.pl.* an American family of passerine birds named from the typical genus *Tyrannus*, including the flycatchers.

tyr'ăn·nīze, *v.i.*, tyrannized, *pt.*, *pp.*; tyrannizing, *ppr.* [Fr. *tyranniser*.]

1. to govern as a tyrant; to rule with absolute power.

2. to govern tyrannically; to rule with cruelty, injustice, etc.

3. to use power or authority harshly; to be oppressive.

tyr'ăn·nīze, *v.t.* to oppress; to tyrannize over; to rule despotically.

tȳ·ran'nō·saur, *n.* [from Gr. *tyrannos*, tyrant, and *sauros*, lizard.] a huge, two-footed, flesh-eating dinosaur of the Upper Cretaceous Period in North America.

tȳ·ran″nō·saur'rus, *n.* a tyrannosaur.

tyr'ăn·nous, *a.* 1. tyrannical; arbitrary; despotic.

2. involving tyranny; cruel, oppressive, unjust, etc.

tyr'ăn·nous·ly, *adv.* in a tyrannous manner; tyrannically; oppressively; violently; cruelly.

tyr'ăn·ny, *n.*; *pl.* **tyr'ăn·nieș,** [ME. *tyrannie*, *tirannye*; OFr. *tirannie*, from L. and Gr. *tyrannia*, sovereign sway.]

1. the office, authority, government, or jurisdiction of a tyrant or absolute ruler.

2. oppressive and unjust government; despotism.

3. very cruel and unjust use of power or authority.

4. harshness; rigor; severity.

5. a tyrannical act.

tȳ'rănt, *n.* [ME. *tirant*, *tiraunt*; OFr. *tiran*, *tyran*, tyrant; L. *tyrannus*; Gr. *tyrannos*, lord, absolute sovereign, usurper.]

1. an absolute ruler; specifically, in ancient Greece, etc., one who seized sovereignty illegally; a usurper.

2. a cruel, oppressive ruler; a despot.

3. one who exercises his authority in an oppressive manner; a cruel master.

4. any tyrannical power or influence; as, the *tyrant* habit.

5. one of the *Tyrannidæ*; a flycatcher: also called *tyrant flycatcher*.

the Thirty Tyrants; in ancient Greece, thirty oligarchs who ruled Athens with great severity and absolute power in 404–403 B.C.

Syn.—despot, oppressor, persecutor.

tȳ'rănt, *v.i.* to play the part of a tyrant; to tyrannize.

tȳre, *n.* [E. Ind.] a preparation of milk and rice used as food in the East Indies.

tȳre, *n.* a tire: British spelling.

Tyr'i·ăn, *n.* a native of Tyre, a seaport in ancient Phoenicia.

Tyr'i·ăn, *a.* 1. pertaining to the ancient city of Tyre, its people, culture, etc.

2. of Tyrian purple.

Tyrian Cynosure; the constellation *Ursa Minor*, which contains the polestar, the guide of Tyrian mariners.

Tyr'i·ăn-pūr'ple, *a.* of the color of Tyrian purple; bluish-red.

Tyr'i·ăn pūr'ple (or **dȳe**), 1. a purple or crimson dye used by the ancient Romans and Greeks: it was made from certain mollusks, originally at Tyre.

2. bluish red.

tȳ'rō, *n.*; *pl.* **tȳ'rōș,** [L. *tiro*, a young soldier, recruit.] a beginner in learning; a novice: also spelled *tiro*.

Syn.—beginner. learner, novice.

tȳ·rō·cī'din, *n.* same as *tyrocidine*.

tȳ·rō·cī'dīne, *n.* [*tyro*sine and *-cide* and *-ine*.] an antibiotic drug, similar to penicillin, obtained from a soil bacillus.

Ty·rō'lē·ăn, *a.* and *n.* same as *Tyrolese*.

Tyr·ō·lēșe', *a.* of the Tyrol, or its people: also spelled *Tirolese*.

Tyr·ō·lēșe', *n.*; *pl.* **Tyr·ō·lēșe',** a native of the Tyrol, a region in the Alps of western Austria and northern Italy: also spelled *Tirolese*.

Ty·rō·lienne' (tē-rō-lyen'), *n.* [Fr., f. of *Tyrolien*, Tyrolese.]

1. a Tyrolese folk dance.

2. music for this.

tyr'ō·līte, *n.* [from *Tyrol*, where it is found.] a fine azure-blue or verdigris-green ore of copper, a hydrous copper arsenate.

tȳ'rō·nișm, *n.* the state of being a tyro.

tȳ'rō·sin, *n.* same as *tyrosine*.

tȳ'rō·sīne, *n.* [Gr. *tyros*, cheese; and *-ine*.] a white, crystalline amino acid, $C_9H_{11}O_3N$, formed by the decomposition of proteins, as in the putrefaction of cheese.

tȳ·rō·thrī'cin, *n.* [from *tyrosine*; and Gr. *thrix*, a hair; and *-in*.] an antibiotic drug, similar to penicillin, obtained from a soil bacillus and used in localized infections.

tyr·ō·tox'i·çon, *n.* [Gr. *tyros*, cheese, and *toxikon*, poison.] a ptomaine in certain dairy products resulting in symptoms similar to those of cholera infantum.

tȳ'sŏn·īte, *n.* [named after S. T. *Tyson*, its discoverer.] a fluoride of the cerium metals: it is somewhat resinous, with a pale wax-yellow color.

tzär (tsär), *n.* same as *czar*.

tzär'dŏm, *n.* same as *czardom*.

tzär'e·vitch, *n.* same as *czarevitch*.

tzä·rev'nà (tsä-), *n.* same as *czarevna*.

tzä·rī'nà, *n.* same as *czarina*.

tzär'ișm (tsär'), *n.* same as *czarism*.

tzär'ist, *a.* and *n.* same as *czarist*.

tzä·rit'zà (tsä-rēt'sä), *n.* same as *czaritza*.

tzet'zē (set'sē), *n.* same as *tsetse*.

tzi·gàne' (tsē-), *n.* [Fr.; Hung. *czigány*.] a gypsy; especially, a Hungarian gypsy.

tzi·gàne' (tsē-), *a.* pertaining to or resembling a Hungarian gypsy.

Tzi'gä·ny, *n.* same as *tzigane*.

U

U, u (ū), *n.*; *pl.* **U's, u's, Us, us** (ūz), 1. the twenty-first letter of the English alphabet; formerly a variant of *V, v*; not until the 18th century was it established as a vowel symbol only.

2. a sound of U or u.

3. a type or impression for U or u.

4. *a symbol for* the twenty-first in a sequence or group (or the twentieth if J is omitted).

U, u (ū), *a.* 1. of U or u.

2. twenty-first (or twentieth if J is omitted) in a sequence or group.

U (ū), *n.* 1. an object shaped like U.

2. in chemistry, the symbol for uranium.

U (ū), *a.* shaped like U.

uà·kä'rī (wä-), *n.* same as *ouakari*.

Ub'ben·īte, *n.* a member of an Anabaptist sect founded in Germany in 1534 by Ubbe Phillips.

Ü'bẽr·mensch (-mensh), *n.* [G.] superman; overman: term used by Nietzsche.

ū'bẽr·ty, *n.* [L. *ubertas* (*-tatis*), from *uber*, fruitful or copious.] abundance; fruitfulness. [Rare.]

ū·bi·çā'tion, *n.* 1. situation; location. [Obs.]

2. ubiety; whereness.

ū·bī'e·ty, *n.* [L. *ubi*, where.] the state or quality of being in a place; local relationship; whereness.

ū·bi·quär'i·ăn (-kwär'), *a.* having existence everywhere; ubiquitous. [Rare.]

Ū·bi·quär'i·ăn, *n.* same as *Ubiquitarian*, sense 1.

ū·bī'quē, *adv.* [L.] everywhere.

Ū'bi·quist, *n.* a Ubiquitarian.

Ū·biq·ui·tär'i·ăn (-bik-wi-), *n.* 1. a believer in the bodily presence of Christ everywhere, especially in the Eucharist.

2. [u–] one who exists or is present everywhere. [Obs.]

ū·biq'ui·tär·i·ness, *n.* the state or quality of being ubiquitous. [Rare.]

ū·biq'ui·tär·y, *a.* [L. *ubique*, from *ubi*, where.] existing everywhere.

ū·biq′ui·tăr·y, *n.* 1. one who exists everywhere.
2. [Ū–] a Ubiquitarian.
Ū·biq′ui·tist, *n.* same as *Ubiquitarian*, sense 1.
ū·biq′ui·tous, *a.* present, or seeming to be present, everywhere at the same time; existing everywhere; omnipresent.
ū·biq′ui·tous·ly, *adv.* in a ubiquitous manner.
ū·biq′ui·tous·ness, *n.* the state or quality of being ubiquitous.
ū·biq′ui·ty, *n.* [Fr. *ubiquité*; LL. *ubiquitatem*, from L. *ubique*, everywhere.]
1. the state, fact, or capacity of existing everywhere at the same time; omnipresence; as, the *ubiquity* of God.
2. the doctrine of the Ubiquitarians.
ū′bī sū′prȧ, [L.] where (mentioned) above.
Ū′-bōat, *n.* [from G. *U-boot*, abbrev. of *Unterseeboot*, undersea boat.] a German submarine.
Ū bōlt, a U-shaped bolt with threads and a nut at each end.
ū′dăl, *a.* [Ice. *othal*; Norw. *odel*, hereditary property.] pertaining to that right in land which prevailed in northern Europe before the introduction of the feudal system; hereditary; alodial.
ū′dăl, *n.* a freehold in the Shetland and Orkney Islands; property held by udal tenure.
ū′dăl·ẽr, ū′dăl·lẽr, *n.* a freeholder in the Shetland and Orkney Islands without feudal dependencies.
ū′dăl·măn, *n.* same as *udaler*.
ud′dẽr, *n.* [AS. *uder*.]
1. a mammary gland, especially one that is relatively large and pendulous, with two or more teats, as in cows.
2. a teat or dug. [Rare.]
ud′dẽred, *a.* furnished with udders.
ud′dẽr·less, *a.* without an udder.
u′dō, *n.* [Japan.] a Japanese plant with crisp, blanched, edible shoots resembling celery.
ū·dom′ē·tẽr, *n.* [Fr. *udomètre*, from L. *udus*, moist, and *-meter*.] a rain gauge.
ū·dō·met′riç, *a.* of a udometer or udometry.
ū·dom′ē·try, *n.* the measurement of rainfall by means of a udometer.
ū·dom′ō·grȧph, *n.* [L. *udus*, moist, and *-graph*.] a rain gauge which is self-registering.
Ū′FŌ, *n.*; *pl.* **Ū′FŌs, Ū′FŌ′s**, [*u*nidentified *f*lying *o*bject.] any of the unidentified objects frequently reported, especially since 1947, to have been seen flying at varying heights and speeds and variously regarded as light phenomena, hallucinations, secret military missiles, spacecraft from another planet, etc.
ug′gũr oil, a distilled product of the agallochum, used in the Orient as a perfume.
ugh (ü), *interj.* [echoic.] an exclamation of horror, repugnance, annoyance, disgust, etc.
ug′gle·sōme, *a.* horrible; gruesome. [Archaic.]
ug′lī, *n.* [altered from *ugly*: from its misshapen appearance.] a Jamaican citrus fruit that is a three-way cross between a grapefruit, orange, and tangerine: also *ugli fruit*.
ug″li·fi·cā′tion, *n.* an uglifying or being uglified.
ug′li·fȳ, *v.t.*; uglified, *pt.*, *pp.*; uglifying, *ppr.* to make ugly; to disfigure.
ug′li·ly, *adv.* in an ugly manner; disagreeably.
ug′li·ness, *n.* 1. the state or quality of being ugly.
2. an ugly thing.
3. disgusting wickedness; moral offensiveness.
ug′ly, *a.*; *comp.* uglier; *superl.* ugliest, [Ice. *uggligr*, fearful, dreadful.]
1. very unpleasant to the sight; aesthetically offensive; unsightly.
2. bad; vile; disagreeable; repulsive; offensive; objectionable.
3. threatening; ominous; dangerous.
4. ill-tempered; cross. [Colloq.]
ugly duckling; [from a story by H. C. Andersen about a supposed ugly duckling that turns out to be a swan.] one whose lack of personal beauty, charm, etc. in childhood or youth turns out to be only temporary.
ug′ly, *v.t.* to render ugly; to disfigure.
ug′ly, *n.*; *pl.* **ug′lies**, an ugly person, animal, etc. [Colloq.]
Ū′gri·ăn, *a.* [from Russ. *Ugri*, an Asiatic people living east of the Urals; and *-an*.]
1. designating or of a group of Finno-Ugric peoples of western Siberia and Hungary, including the Magyars.
2. Ugric.
Ū′gri·ăn, *n.* 1. a member of any of the Ugrian peoples.
2. Ugric.
Ū′griç, *a.* 1. designating or of a branch of the Finno-Ugric family of languages comprising Hungarian (Magyar), Vogul, and Ostyak.
2. Ugrian.
Ū′griç, *n.* the Ugric languages.
Ū′grō-Fin′niç, *a.* Finno-Ugric.
ug′sōme, *a.* loathsome; ugly. [Scot. and Brit. Dial.]
ug′sōme·ness, *n.* the state or quality of being ugsome. [Scot. and Brit. Dial.]
uh′lăn, u′lăn (*or* ū′), *n.* [Polish *ulan*, a lancer, from Turk. *oglan*, a youth.]
1. a mounted soldier of a type formerly prominent in Poland, armed usually with a lance.
2. a cavalryman in the former German Army, similarly equipped.
Uī′gũr (wē′), *n.* [E. Turki *uighur*, from *ui*, to follow, and *-gur*, adj. suffix.]
1. a member of a Turkic people ruling in Mongolia and Turkestan from the 8th to the 12th century A.D.
2. their East Turki language.
ū·in′tȧ·īte, ū·in′tăh·īte, *n.* [after the *Uinta* Mountains, Utah.] a black kind of asphalt found in an almost pure state in parts of Utah and western Colorado: also called *gilsonite*.
Ū·in·tȧ·thē′ri·um, *n.* [*Uinta* Mountains in Utah, and Gr. *therion*, a wild beast.]
1. a genus typical of the *Uintatheriidæ*, a family of extinct mammals of the Eocene period, allied to the *Dinoceras*.
2. [u–] a fossil mammal of this genus.
uit, *prep.* [S. Afr. D.] out; out of.
uit′länd·ẽr, *n.* [S. Afr. D.] [*sometimes* U–] in South Africa, an outsider; a foreigner; an outlander.
uit′spȧn, *v.t.* and *v.i.* [S. Afr. D.] to unharness.
u′ji, *n.* [Japan., maggot.] a disease which affects silkworms in Japan.
u′ji flȳ, a fly, *Ujimyia sericaria*, the larvae of which attack, as parasites, the Japanese silkworm.
Ū·ji·mȳ′i·ȧ, *n.* [Japan. *uji*, maggot, and Gr. *myia*, fly.] a genus of flies of which the uji fly is the only species.
ū·kāse′, *n.* [Fr., from Russ. *ukaz*, an edict.]
1. in Czarist Russia, an imperial order or decree, having the force of law.
2. any official decree or proclamation.
Ū·krāin′i·ăn, *a.* of the Ukraine, its people, their language, etc.
Ū·krāin′i·ăn, *n.* 1. a native or inhabitant of the Ukraine.
2. the East Slavic language of the Ukrainians, very closely related to (Great) Russian: Little Russian.
ū·ku·le′lē (*Haw.* ü-koo-lā′lā), *n.* [Haw., lit., flea, from *uku*, insect, and *lele*, to jump: from the finger movements.] a small, four-stringed musical instrument resembling and played like a guitar: colloquially shortened to *uke*.
u′lăn, *n.* see *uhlan*.
u·lär′bū·rong, *n.* [Malay.] a large, but harmless, arboreal snake, *Dipsas dendrophila*, of Malaysia.
ū·lȧ·trō′phi·ȧ, ū·lat′rō·phy, *n.* [Gr. *oula*, gums, and *atrophia*, a wasting away.] in medicine, shrinkage or wasting of the gums.
ul′cẽr, *n.* [L. *ulcus*, *ulceris*, an ulcer; cognate with Gr. *helkos*, a wound, a sore, an abscess.]
1. an open sore (other than a wound) on the skin or some mucous membrane, as the lining of the stomach (*peptic ulcer*), characterized by the disintegration of the tissue and, often, the discharge of pus.
2. any corrupting or festering condition or influence.
Aden or *Aleppo ulcer*; a form of ulcer endemic chiefly in Asia and Africa, marked by the development on the face of a papula which passes successively through the stages of tubercle, scab, and circumscribed ulcer: also called *Aleppo evil*, *Oriental sore*, *Persian ulcer*, etc.
amputating ulcer; ulceration which encircles a part and destroys the tissues to the bone.
arterial ulcer; an ulcer of the skin caused by disease of an artery supplying blood to the affected part.
atonic ulcer; a chronic ulcer with unhealthy granulations.
carious ulcer; a gangrenous sore.
cold ulcer; a small noninflammatory ulcer of the extremities, sometimes gangrenous, due to imperfect nutrition. It is attended with coldness of the surface.
endemic ulcer; any form of ulcer prevailing in certain districts or regions.
hemorrhagic ulcer; an ulcer from which blood occasionally flows.
indolent ulcer; an ulcer with an indurated and elevated edge and a nongranulating base, usually occurring on the leg, and nearly painless.
Jacob's ulcer; rodent ulcer, especially that of an eyelid.
rodent ulcer; a carcinomatous ulcer of the face, neck, or scalp, which gradually involves and eats away the soft tissues and the bones.
varicose ulcer; an ulcer due to varicose veins.
ul′cẽr·ȧ·ble, *a.* capable of becoming ulcerated.
ul′cẽr·āte, *v.t.* and *v.i.*; ulcerated, *pt.*, *pp.*; ulcerating, *ppr.* to make or become ulcerous.
ul′cẽr·ā·ted, *a.* affected with an ulcer or ulcers; as, an *ulcerated* throat, an *ulcerated* gum.
ul·cẽr·ā′tion, *n.* [L. *ulceratio* (*-onis*), a breaking out in sores.]
1. an ulcerating; the formation of an ulcer.
2. an ulcer or group of ulcers.
ul′cẽr·ā·tive, *a.* 1. of, having the nature of, or causing an ulcer or ulcers.
2. ulcerative.
ul′cẽred, *a.* having become an ulcer; ulcerated.
ul″cẽr·ō·mem′brȧ·nous, *a.* characterized by ulceration and by a membranous exudation.
ul′cẽr·ous, *a.* 1. having an ulcer or ulcers.
2. ulcerative.
ul′cẽr·ous·ly, *adv.* in an ulcerous manner; so as to be ulcerous.
ul′cẽr·ous·ness, *n.* the state of being ulcerous.
ul′çus·cle, *n.* same as *ulcuscule*.
ul·çus′çūle, *n.* [L. *ulcusculum*, dim. of *ulcus*, an ulcer.] a little ulcer. [Rare.]
u′le, *n.* the ule tree.
-ūle, [Fr. or L.; Fr. *-ule*, from L. *-ulus*, *-ula*, *-ulum*.] a suffix added to nouns to form diminutives, as in spor*ule*, umbell*ule*.
ū·lē·mä′, *n.pl.* [Ar. *'ulemā*, pl. of *'ālim*, wise, from *'alama*, to know.]
1. Moslem scholars or men of authority in religion and law, especially in Turkey.
2. [*construed as sing.*] a council or college of such men.
ū″lem·or·rhā′gi·ȧ, ū″laem·or·rhā′gi·ȧ (-rā′), *n.* [Gr. *oulon*, gum, and *haimorrhagia*, bleeding.] bleeding or hemorrhage from the gums.
-ū·lent, [from Fr. *-ulent* or L. *-ulentus*.] a suffix meaning *full of*, *abounding in*, as in fraud*ulent*.
ū″ler·y·thē′mȧ, *n.* [Gr. *oulē*, scar, and Eng. *erythema*.] an erythematous disease of the skin characterized by the formation of cicatrices and by atrophy.
ū·let′iç, *a.* [Gr. *oulon*, gum.] pertaining to the gums.
u′le tree, a Mexican tree, *Castilloa elastica*, from the milky juice of which caoutchouc is obtained.
Ū′lex, *n.* [L., a shrub resembling rosemary.] a genus of plants of the bean family. The furze, *Ulex europæus*, is the best known of about twelve species.
ū′lex·ine, *n.* a diuretic and tonic alkaloid, $C_{11}H_{14}NC_2$, obtained from the seeds of the furze, *Ulex europæus*.
ū′lex·īte, *n.* [after G. L. *Ulex*, who first correctly analyzed it.] a white mineral occurring in roundish masses of capillary crystals. It is a hydrous borate of calcium and sodium.
ū·lig′i·nōse, ū·lig′i·nous, *a.* [L. *uligo*, *uliginis*, moisture.]
1. muddy; oozy; slimy.
2. in botany, growing in swampy places.
ū·lī′tis, *n.* [Gr. *oula*, gums, and *-itis*.] in pathology, inflammation of the gums.
ul′lāge, *n.* [OFr. *ouillage*, *eullage*, a filling up to the brim or the bunghole, from *ouiller*, to fill (a cask) to the bunghole, from *ueil*, an eye, fig. bunghole; from L. *oculus*, an eye.]
1. the amount by which a container of liquor falls short of being full.
2. the amount of grain, etc. lost through spilling or sifting through a bag.
3. the loss of liquor from a container through evaporation or leakage, or of grain, etc. through spilling or sifting.
ull′mănn·īte, *n.* [after J. C. *Ullmann* (1771–1821), German chemist by whom it was analyzed.] a sulfide of nickel and antimony, part of the latter being frequently replaced by arsenic. It generally occurs massive with a granular structure, and is of a gray color with a metallic luster.
ul·lū′çō, *n.* [S. Am.] the melluco.
Ul·mā′cē·ae, *n.pl.* [L. *ulmus*, elm.] the elm family of trees and shrubs, characterized by alternate leaves, one- or two-sexed flowers without petals, and upright anthers.
ul·mā′ceous, *a.* of or pertaining to the *Ulmaceæ*.

ul'māte, *n.* a salt of ulmic acid.

ul'miç, *a.* [L. *ulmus*, an elm.] of, pertaining to, or derived from ulmin; as, *ulmic* acid.

ulmic acid; a substance, $C_{20}H_{14}O_{6}$, isomeric with ulmin, obtained by neutralizing the ammoniacal solution of ulmin with an acid. It is precipitated in brown gelatinous flocks, soluble in water, but insoluble in water containing free acid.

ul'min, *n.* [L. *ulmus*, elm.]

1. a dark-colored substance obtained by boiling sugar for some time with dilute hydrochloric, nitric, or sulfuric acid, and washing the deposit with water. It forms black or brown scales, insoluble in water and alcohol, partially soluble in ammonia.

2. any of various substances which are present in vegetable mold, peat, etc. The name has also been applied to the dark-brown substance which exudes from the oak, elm, and various other trees. It has also been called *humus, humin, gein.*

ul'mō, *n.* in botany, same as *muermo.*

Ul'mus, *n.* [L., an elm.] a genus of urticaceous trees; the elms.

ul'nȧ, *n.*; *pl.* **ul'nae, ul'nȧs,** [L., from Gr. *ōlenē*, the elbow.]

1. in anatomy, the inner and larger bone of the forearm, on the side opposite to that of the thumb. It articulates with the humerus and the head of the radius above and with the radius below.

2. a corresponding bone in the forelimb of other vertebrates.

3. an ell.

ul'nad, *adv.* toward the ulna.

ul'năr, *a.* of or near the ulna; as, the *ulnar* nerve.

ulnar artery; the larger of the two branches into which the brachial artery divides. It commences just below the bend of the elbow, and runs along the inner side of the forearm, in an arched direction and at varying depth, to the hand, where it forms the superficial palmar arch. It gives off several branches.

ulnar nerve; a branch of the brachial plexus, distributed to the muscles and integument of the forearm and hand.

ulnar veins; two veins distributed to the forearm; (a) the posterior, arising from the basilic vein; (b) the anterior, arising from the median basilic.

ul·nā'rē, *n.*; *pl.* **ul·nā'ri·ȧ,** in anatomy, the cuneiform bone of the carpus.

ul'nō-, a combining form meaning *the ulna and.*

ul·nō·çär'păl, *a.* pertaining to the ulna and carpus.

ul·nō·rā'di·ăl, *a.* pertaining to the ulna and the radius.

ū'loid, *a.* [Gr. *oulē*, scar, and *-oid.*] scarlike.

ū·lon'çus, *n.* [Gr. *oulon*, gum, and *onkos*, tumor.] a swelling or tumor of the gums.

-ū·lōse', [from L. *-ulosus.*] a suffix meaning *characterized by, marked by*, as in gran*ulose.*

ū·lot'ri·chăn, *a.* [Gr. *oulos*, crisp, woolly, and *thrix*, hair.] ulotrichous.

ū·lot'ri·chăn, *n.* one of the Ulotrichi.

Ū·lot'ri·chī, *n.pl.* [Gr. *oulos*, crisp, woolly, and *thrix, trichos*, hair.] the woolly-haired peoples: one of the two great divisions into which T. H. Huxley classified man, in accordance with the character of the hair, the other division being the Leiotrichi, or smooth-haired people.

ū·lot'ri·chous, *a.* of or pertaining to the Ulotrichi; having crisp, woolly hair.

-ū·lous, [from L. *-ulosus.*] a suffix meaning *tending to, full of*, or *characterized by*, as in trem*ulous*, pop*ulous.*

ụl'pän, *n.*; *pl.* **ụl·pä'nim,** [Mod. Heb.] a course or school for teaching Hebrew by an intensive method; especially, such a school in Israel for immigrants.

ul'stēr, *n.* a long, loose, heavy overcoat, especially one with a belt, originally made of frieze cloth from Ulster, Ireland.

ul·tē'ri·ŏr, *a.* [L., comp. from *ulter*, beyond, further.]

1. lying beyond or on the farther side.

2. later, subsequent, or future.

3. further; more remote; especially, beyond what is expressed, implied, or evident; undisclosed; as, her true purpose was *ulterior* but praiseworthy.

ul·tē'ri·ŏr·ly, *adv.* in an ulterior manner; more distantly; remotely.

ul'ti·mȧ, *a.* [L.] most remote; farthest; final; last.

ultima ratio; the last argument or resort.

ultima ratio regum; the last resort of kings; resort to arms or war.

ul'ti·mȧ, *n.* [L.] in grammar, the last syllable of a word.

ul'ti·māte, *a.* [L. *ultimatus*, pp. of *ultimare*, to come to an end.]

1. beyond which it is impossible to go; farthest; most remote or distant.

2. in which a process or series comes to an end; final.

3. beyond which further analysis, division, etc. cannot be made; elemental; fundamental; primary.

4. greatest possible; maximum.

ultimate analysis; in chemistry, the resolution of a substance into its absolute elements: opposed to *proximate analysis*, or the resolution of a substance into its constituent compounds.

Syn.—final, terminal, conclusive, eventual.

ul'ti·māte, *v.t.* and *v.i.*; ultimated, *pt., pp.*; ultimating, *ppr.* to bring or come to an end; to terminate. [Rare.]

ul'ti·mȧte, *n.* something ultimate; final point or result, fundamental principle, etc.

ul'ti·mȧte·ly, *adv.* as an ultimate or final result; at last; in the end; finally; as, afflictions may *ultimately* prove blessings.

ul'ti·mȧ Thū'lē, [L.] 1. farthest Thule: to the ancients, the northernmost region.

2. any far-off, unknown region.

3. (a) the farthest possible point or limit; (b) the uttermost degree or goal attainable.

ul·ti·mā'tion, *n.* an ultimating or ultimatum. [Rare.]

ul·ti·mā'tum, *n.*; *pl.* **ul·ti·mā'tumṣ** or **ul·ti·mā'tȧ,** [LL.] any final proposal or statement of conditions; especially, in diplomatic negotiations, the final terms of the one party, the rejection of which by the other often involves an immediate rupture of diplomatic relations and a declaration of war.

> He delivered to the mediators an *ultimatum*, importing that he adhered to the treaties of Westphalia and Nimeguen.
> —Smollett.

ul'time, *a.* ultimate. [Obs.]

ul·tim'i·ty, *n.* the last stage or consequence. [Rare.]

ul'ti·mō, *adv.* [L. *ultimo* (*mense*), in the last (month).] in the month which preceded the present; in the last month, as distinguished from the current month.

ul″ti·mō·ġen'i·tūre, *n.* [from L. *ultimus*, last, and *-geniture* as in *primogeniture.*] inheritance or succession by which the youngest son succeeds to an estate: opposed to *primogeniture.*

ul'tion, *n.* [L. *ultio* (*-onis*), from *ulcisci*, to take vengeance on.] revenge. [Obs.]

ul'tra-, [from L. *ultra.*] a prefix meaning: (a) *beyond, on the further side of*, as in *ultra*violet; (b) (something) *excessive, to an extreme degree*, as in *ultra*modern, *ultra*ism; (c) *beyond the range of*, as in *ultra*microscopic.

ul'trȧ, *a.* [L., beyond, on the other side of.] beyond due limit; extreme; extravagant; fanatical; as, *ultra* principles.

ul'trȧ, *n.* one who proposes or advocates extreme measures or holds extreme opinions; an extremist; an ultraist.

ul″trȧ·çŏn·sērv'ȧ·tive, *a.* excessively or extremely conservative.

ul″trȧ·el·lip'tiç, *a.* same as *hyperelliptic.*

ul·trȧ·fash'ĭŏn·ȧ·ble, *a.* fashionable in the extreme; carrying the observance of fashion to excess.

ul·trȧ·gas'ē·ous, *a.* designating or having the properties exhibited by gases under infinitesimal pressures.

ul'trāġe, *n.* [L. *ultra.*] outrage. [Obs.]

ul'trȧ·iṣm, *n.* 1. the principles of men who advocate extreme measures, as a radical reform, etc.

2. an extremist statement or action.

ul'trȧ·ist, *n.* one who in opinions or action pushes a principle or measure to extremes; an extremist, especially in political, religious, and social matters.

ul'trȧ·ist, *a.* extremist.

ul″trȧ·mȧ·rīne', *a.* [L. *ultra*, beyond, and *marinus*, marine.]

1. beyond the sea.

2. deep-blue.

ul″trȧ·mȧ·rīne', *n.* 1. a blue pigment made from powdered lapis lazuli.

2. a blue pigment prepared artificially from other substances.

3. any of certain other pigments; as, yellow *ultramarine.*

4. deep blue.

artificial ultramarine; ultramarine produced by grinding together a mixture of clay, carbonate of soda, sulfur, and resin, which is then heated and slowly cooled into a greenish, porous cake: subsequent grinding, calcination, and cooling produces a blue color.

green ultramarine; see *artificial ultramarine.*

ultramarine ash or *ashes*; a pigment which is the residuum of lapis lazuli, after the ultramarine has been extracted.

yellow ultramarine; a yellow pigment produced from barium chromate.

ul″trȧ·mī·çrom'ē·tēr, *n.* a very sensitive micrometer, calibrated to a fine scale.

ul·trȧ·mī'çrō·sçōpe, *n.* an instrument equipped to pick up the reflections of light rays dispersed by ultramicroscopic objects lighted from the side and against a dark background, thus making them visible.

ul″trȧ·mī·çrō·sçop'iç, *a.* 1. too small to be seen with an ordinary microscope.

2. of an ultramicroscope.

ul″trȧ·mī·çrō·sçop'i·çăl, *a.* ultramicroscopic.

ul″trȧ·mī·çros'çō·py, *n.* the act or practice of using an ultramicroscope.

ul·trȧ·mod'ērn, *a.* extreme or excessive in modern style, taste, ideas, tendencies, etc.; as, *ultramodern* furniture.

ul·trȧ·mon'tāne, *a.* [ML. *ultramontanus.*]

1. beyond the mountains; especially, beyond the Alps: applied to the Italians by peoples to the north.

2. of the Italian party in the Roman Catholic Church.

3. of or favoring the doctrine of papal supremacy.

ul·trȧ·mon'tāne, *n.* 1. one who lives beyond the mountains, especially south of the Alps.

2. a member or adherent of the ultramontane party in the Roman Catholic Church.

ul·trȧ·mon'tȧ·niṣm, *n.* the doctrines and practices of the ultramontane party in the Roman Catholic Church.

ul·trȧ·mon'tȧ·nist, *n.* one of the ultramontane party; a promoter of ultramontanism.

ul·trȧ·mun'dāne, *a.* [L. *ultra*, beyond, and *mundus*, world.]

1. being beyond the world, or beyond the limits of the solar system.

2. beyond life.

ul·trȧ·na'tion·ăl·iṣm, *n.* nationalism that is excessive or extreme.

ul'trȧ·red, *a.* same as *infrared.*

ul'trȧ·sōme″, *n.* [*ultra-*, and *-some* (body).] an intracellular particle too small to be seen by usual microscopic methods.

ul·trȧ·son'iç, *a.* [*ultra-*, and *sonic.*] designating or of a frequency of mechanical vibrations above the range audible to the human ear, i.e., above 20,000 vibrations per second.

ul'trȧ·sound, *n.* ultrasonic waves, used in medical diagnosis and therapy, surgery, etc.

ul·trȧ·trop'iç·ăl, *a.* beyond the tropics; also, hotter than the tropics.

ul'trȧ vȧ·lō'rem, [L.] beyond the value.

ul·trȧ·vī'ō·let, *a.* lying beyond the violet end of the visible spectrum: said of certain light rays of extremely short wave length: cf. *infrared.*

ul'trȧ vī'rēṣ, [L.] beyond one's power; specifically, beyond the power of a person, court, or corporation legally or constitutionally.

ul·trȧ·vī'rus, *n.* [Mod. L.; *ultra-* and *virus.*] an ultramicroscopic virus, so small as to pass through the pores of the finest filter.

ul·trō'nē·ous, *a.* spontaneous; voluntary.

ul·trō'nē·ous·ly, *adv.* in an ultroneous manner; voluntarily.

ul·trō'nē·ous·ness, *n.* the character of being ultroneous; spontaneity.

ụ'lụ, *n.* [Esk.] a type of knife used by Eskimo women.

ụ·lụ'ȧ, *n.* [native name.] a large Hawaiian food fish, *Caranx sausun*, or a fish belonging to any other species of the same genus.

Ul'ū·lȧ, *n.* [L., a screech owl.] a former genus of the family *Strigidæ*, of which *Ulula cinerea*, the great gray owl, of arctic America is the type.

ul'ū·lănt, *a.* [L. *ululans*, ppr. of *ululare*, to howl.] ululating; howling; hooting; wailing or screeching, as an owl.

ul'ū·lāte, *v.i.*; ululated, *pt., pp.*; ululating, *ppr.* 1. to howl or hoot.

2. to wail or lament loudly.

ul·ū·lā'tion, *n.* the act or sound of ululating; a wailing, howling, or hooting.

Ul′vȧ, *n.* [L. *ulva*, sedge, allied to *ulmus*, an elm.] a genus of seaweeds, typical of the family *Ulvaceæ*, having flat membranaceous fronds of green color. *Ulva latissima* and *Ulva lactuca* are edible species, sometimes called *sea lettuce.*

Ū·lys′sēṣ, *n.* [L., var. of *Ulixes* (for Gr. *Odysseus*, but prob. from Etruscan *Uluxe*).]

1. Odysseus, king of Ithaca and one of the Greek chiefs in the Trojan War.

2. a celebrated psychological novel (1922) by James Joyce, divided into episodes paralleling those of Homer's *Odyssey*.

um-, a prefix signifying *around, about*, etc. [Obs.]

um′be, *prep.* around; about; after. [Obs.]

um′bel, *n.* [L. *umbella*, a parasol.]

1. in botany, an inflorescence which consists of a number of flower stalks or pedicels, nearly equal in length, spreading from a common center, their summits forming a level, convex, or even globose surface, more rarely a concave one. It is simple or compound; in the latter, each peduncle bears another little umbel called *umbellet*, or *umbellule.*

UMBEL OF HEMLOCK

2. in zoology, any umbelliform tuft or cluster of parts.

um′bel·lăr, *a.* same as *umbellate.*

um′bel·lāte, *a.* 1. in botany, bearing umbels; consisting of umbels; forming an umbel or umbels; as, *umbellate* plants or flowers.

2. in zoology, having an umbel, as a polyp; umbelliform.

um′bel·lā·ted, *a.* same as *umbellate.*

um′bel·let, *n.* an umbellule.

um·bel′liç, *a.* derived from or pertaining to umbelliferous plants; as, *umbellic* acid.

umbellic acid; (a) a compound identical with anisic acid; (b) a yellow substance derived from umbelliferone.

um·bel′li·fẽr, *n.* any plant of the order *Umbelliferæ.*

Um·bel·lif′e·rae, *n.pl.* [L. *umbella*, and *ferre*, to bear.] a family of plants, the parsley family, having their inflorescence in the form of an umbel. The *Umbelliferæ* abound in temperate climates in the Northern Hemisphere, but are rare in the tropics.

um·bel·lif′ẽr·ōne, *n.* a neutral white crystalline substance, $C_9H_6O_3$, obtained by the dry distillation of various resins, chiefly those derived from umbelliferous plants.

um·bel·lif′ẽr·ous, *a.* furnished with an umbel or umbels; umbellate; umbellated; of or pertaining to the *Umbelliferæ.*

um·bel′li·fọrm, *a.* having the form of an umbel; also, forming an umbel.

Um·bel·lū·lā′ri·ȧ, *n.* [LL. *umbellula*, a little umbel.] a genus of apetalous trees, of the order *Laurineæ.*

um·bel′lū·lāte, *a.* provided with or arranged in umbellules, or umbellets.

um·bel′lūle, *n.* [LL. *umbellula*, dim. of L. *umbella*, a sunshade.] one of the secondary umbels in a primary, or compound, umbel.

um·bel·lū·lif′ẽr·ous, *a.* having or bearing umbellules.

um′bẽr, *n.* [Fr. (*terre d'*)*ombre*; It. (*terra d'*)*ombra*, lit., (earth of) shade; prob. from L. *umbra*, a shade, shadow; but perhaps from *Umbria*, Italian province.]

1. a kind of earth containing oxides of manganese and iron, used as a pigment: *raw umber* is yellowish-brown; *burnt*, or calcined, *umber* is reddish-brown.

2. a yellowish-brown or reddish-brown color.

Cologne or *German umber*; a pigment procured from lignite.

um′bẽr, *a.* of the color of raw umber or burnt umber.

um′bẽr, *v.t.* to make umber-colored; to color with or as with umber.

um′bẽr, *n.* 1. a fresh-water fish of the salmon family, *Thymallus vulgaris*: also called *grayling.*

2. the umbrette: also *umber bird.*

3. the visor of a helmet; an umbrel. [Obs.]

4. a shade; a shadow. [Dial.]

um·bil′iç, *n.* 1. the navel; the center. [Obs.]

2. in geometry, an umbilicus.

um·bil′iç, *a.* umbilical. [Rare.]

um·bil′i·çăl, *a.* [L. *umbilicus*, the navel.]

1. of or like an umbilicus, or navel.

2. designating or of a cordlike structure (*umbilical cord*) connecting a fetus with the placenta of the mother and serving to convey food to, and remove waste from, the fetus.

3. descended through the female line. [Rare.]

umbilical arteries; in anatomy, certain arteries which exist in the fetus, conveying a part of the blood sent to the fetus by the umbilical vein to the placenta. Their functioning ceases when respiration is established.

umbilical cord; (a) in anatomy, the navel cord; the flexible structure which extends from the placenta to the fetal umbilicus; (b) in botany, an elongation of the placenta in the form of a little cord; a funicle.

umbilical points; in mathematics, same as *foci.*

umbilical region; the central portion of the abdomen.

umbilical vein; in anatomy, a vein which arises from the placenta and terminates at the fissure on the inferior surface of the liver of the fetus, to which it conveys the blood necessary for its nutrition.

Um·bil·i·çā′ri·ȧ, *n.* [L. *umbilicus*, the navel.] in botany, a genus of gymnocarpous lichens of the order *Parmeliacei*, so called because of a navel-shaped center by which the thallus is attached to the rocks. It is found in both temperate and arctic regions, and includes the tripe-de-roche or famine bread, *Umbilicaria arctica.*

um·bil′i·çāte, um·bil′i·çā·ted, *a.* 1. shaped like or resembling a navel; also, having an umbilicus or navel.

2. in botany, depressed in the center, as the ends of an apple.

um·bil·i·çā′tion, *n.* 1. the condition of being umbilicate.

2. a navellike pit or depression, as in a pustule.

um·bil′i·çus, *n.*; *pl.* **um·bil′i·cī,** [L.] 1. in anatomy, the navel; the cicatrix which marks the site of the entry of the umbilical cord.

2. in botany, (a) the part of a seed by which it is attached to the placenta; the hilum; (b) a depression or elevation about the center of a given surface.

3. in conchology, a circular depression in the base of the lower whorl or body of many spiral univalves.

4. in ancient Greece and Rome, an ornamented or painted ball or boss fastened at each end of the stick on which manuscripts were rolled.

5. in geometry, a focus; also, a point at which the radii of curvature are equal. [Obs.]

6. in ornithology, one of the depressions or apertures of the calamus of a feather.

um′bil·i·fọrm, *a.* having the shape of an umbilicus or navel.

um′ble pīe, a meat pie made from umbles; humble pie.

um′bleṣ, *n.pl.* [var. of *numbles*.] the entrails of a deer; hence, sometimes entrails in general. [Obs.]

um′bō, *n.*; *pl.* **um·bō′nēs, um′bōṣ,** [L. *umbo* (*-onis*), a knob or boss.]

1. the boss or protuberant part of a shield.

2. in botany, the knob in the center of the pileus or cap of certain fungus plants.

3. in conchology, that point of a bivalve shell immediately above the hinge; the beak.

4. any boss or rounded protuberance upon a surface; also, the corresponding depression.

um′bō·năl, *a.* 1. pertaining to, resembling, or near an umbo.

2. umbonate.

um′bō·nāte, um′bō·nā·ted, *a.* 1. having an umbo.

2. having the rounded or conical shape of an umbo.

um·bon′iç, *a.* 1. umbonate.

2. umbonal.

um·bon′ū·lāte, *a.* in botany, terminated by a very small boss or umbo.

um′bō·nūle, *n.* [LL. *umbonulus*, dim. of L. *umbo*, a boss or knob.] a small umbo.

um′brȧ, *n.*; *pl.* **um′brae,** [L.] 1. shade; shadow.

2. in astronomy, (a) the dark cone of shadow projected from a planet or satellite, on the side opposite to the sun; the total shadow of the earth or moon in an eclipse; (b) the dark central portion of a sun spot, which is surrounded by a brighter annular portion called the *penumbra.*

3. in physics, a perfect or complete shadow in which no direct light is received from the source of illumination.

4. in ancient Rome, one who went to a feast merely at the invitation of one directly invited, so called because he followed the guest as a shadow. [Rare.]

5. [U–] the sole genus of the *Umbridæ*, with two species: *Umbra krameri*, a small fish three or four inches long, from stagnant waters in central Europe, and *Umbra limi*, rather smaller, locally distributed in the United States, where it is known as the dogfish or mud minnow.

6. the umbrine.

um·braç′ū·lāte, *a.* having an umbrella-shaped projection on the head, as some *Orthoptera.*

um·braç·ū·lif′ẽr·ous, *a.* [L. *umbraculum*, an umbrella, and *ferre*, to bear.] in botany, bearing an umbrella-shaped organ or part.

um·braç′ū·li·fọrm, *a.* umbrella-shaped, as a mushroom.

um·braç′ū·lum, *n.*; *pl.* **um·braç′ū·lȧ,** [L., dim. of *umbra*, a shade.] in botany, an umbrella-shaped appendage.

um′brăġe, *n.* [ME.; OFr. *ombrage*, from L. *umbra*, a shade.]

1. shade; shadow. [Obs. or Poet.]

2. that which affords shade; especially, foliage.

3. offense; resentment and displeasure.

4. a semblance or shadowy appearance. [Archaic.]

Syn.—dissatisfaction, displeasure, offense, resentment.

um·brā′ġeous, *a.* [Fr. *ombrageux.*]

1. giving shade; shady; shaded; as, an *umbrageous* grotto or garden.

2. obscure; not easily perceived, as if from being darkened or shaded; hence, suspicious. [Obs.]

The present constitution of the court is very *umbrageous.* —Wotton.

3. easily offended or aroused to suspicion; feeling, taking, or inclined to take, umbrage.

um·brā′ġeous·ly, *adv.* in an umbrageous manner.

um·brā′ġeous·ness, *n.* the state or quality of being umbrageous.

um′brāte, *v.t.*; umbrated, *pt., pp.*; umbrating, *ppr.* to shadow. [Obs.]

um·brat′iç, um·brat′i·căl, *a.* [L. *umbraticus*, shady.]

1. foreshadowing. [Obs.]

2. confined, as to the shade; secluded; retired. [Obs.]

um′brȧ·tile, *a.* [L. *umbratilis.*]

1. being in the shade or retirement; secluded; as, an *umbratile* life.

2. unreal; unsubstantial. [Obs.]

um′brȧ tree, a South American tree with large dark leaves, which give it a gloomy appearance: the juice of the berries is used for coloring wine.

um′bre (-bẽr), *n.* umber. [Obs.]

um′brel, *n.* 1. an umbrella. [Obs.]

2. the visor of a helmet, protecting the face.

um·brel′lȧ, *n.* [It. *ombrella*, an umbrella, a dim. from L. *umbra*, a shade.]

1. a portable shade, screen, or canopy which opens and folds, carried in the hand as a shelter from the sun or rain. It is usually made of cloth extended on a folding radial frame of bars or strips of steel, cane, etc., inserted in or fastened to a rod or stick.

2. something shaped like or suggestive of this, as the disk or body of a jellyfish, or a force of military aircraft sent up to screen and protect ground or naval forces.

3. [U–] a genus of tectibranchiate mollusks: so called from a fanciful resemblance of the shell to an umbrella.

4. in zoology, the swimming bell of certain of the *Hydrozoa*, which is alternately contracted and expanded to propel the animal through the water.

um·brel′lȧ ȧnt, a sauba ant: so called because it carries bits of leaves across its back as if for protection: also called *parasol ant.*

um·brel′lȧ bĩrd, any one of several South and Central American birds of the genus *Cephalopterus*, especially *Cephalopterus ornatus*. They are related to the crows, and are noted for the erectile crest of blue-black feathers rising from the head and curving toward the end of the beak. Another long tuft of feathers hangs down from the neck. Also called *dragoon bird.*

um·brel′lȧ grȧss, 1. a semiaquatic plant of Australia, *Panicum decompositum*: also called *Australian millet.*

2. an Australian grass, *Aristida ramosa.*

3. a cyperaceous plant, of the genus *Fuirena*, of the United States.

um·brel′lȧ lēaf, a perennial plant, *Diphylleia cymosa*, of the *Berberidaceæ* or barberry family. It grows in damp or springy mountainous places in the United States from Virginia southward. From the thick horizontal root stalk arises a large, shield-shaped leaf, centrally peltate and cut-lobed, on a stem bearing two smaller leaves peltate near the side, a terminal cyme of white flowers, and blue berries.

um·brel′lȧ päl̇m, a tall palm, *Kentia canterburyana*, native to Lord Howe's Island in the Solomon Islands: the long pinnate leaves form a dense crown.

um·brel′lȧ shell, any shell of the genus *Umbrella*.

um·brel′lȧ tree, 1. a magnolia, *Magnolia tripetala* or *Magnolia umbrella*, so called from the way in which the oval, pointed leaves radiate from the ends of the branches: it has bad-smelling white flowers and reddish fruit.

2. any one of several other trees or shrubs whose leaves are umbrella-shaped or grow with an umbrellalike effect, as the screw pine, *Pandanus odoratissimus*, and the bendy tree, *Thespesia populnea*.

um·brēre′, *n.* an umbrel (sense 2). [Obs.]

um·brette′, *n.* [from Fr. or Mod. L.; Fr. *ombrette*, dim. of *ombre*, shade; or Mod. L. *umbretta*, dim.; both from L. *umbra*, a shade, shadow.] a dark-brown African wading bird, *Scopus umbretta*, related to the storks and herons: also *umber*, *umber bird*.

Um′bri·ăn, *a.* of or pertaining to Umbria in central Italy, its inhabitants, their language, etc.

Umbrian school of painting; the Italian school of painting developed in Umbria in the 15th century, known especially for the development of landscape painting.

Um′bri·ăn, *n.* 1. one of an Italian people inhabiting (ancient or modern) Umbria in central Italy.

2. the Italic language of ancient Umbria, regarded as one of the oldest of the Latin dialects, and preserved chiefly in the Eugubine tablets: extinct since ancient times.

um·brif′ẽr·ous, *a.* casting or affording shade.

um·brif′ẽr·ous·ly, *adv.* in an umbriferous manner; so as to cast or afford shade.

um′bril, *n.* an umbrel. [Obs.]

Um·brī′nȧ, *n.* [Sp.; from L. *umbra*, a shade.]

1. a genus of fishes of the family *Sciænidæ*; especially, the bearded umbrina, *Umbrina cirrosa*: species of the genus are common in tropical waters.

BEARDED UMBRINA (*Umbrina cirrosa*)

2. [u-] a fish of this genus; an umbrine.

um′brine, *n.* a fish of the genus *Umbrina*; specifically, *Umbrina cirrosa*.

um′brōse, *a.* shady. [Rare.]

um·bros′i·ty, *n.* shadiness. [Rare.]

ū′mi·ak, ū′mi·ack, *n.* [Esk. (eastern dial.).] a large open boat made of skins stretched on a wooden frame, used by Eskimos, especially Eskimo women: also spelled *oomiac*, *oomiak*.

ụm′laut (-lout), *n.* [G., change of sound, from *um*, indicating alteration, and *laut*, sound.]

1. a change in sound of a vowel, caused by its assimilation to another vowel or semivowel originally occurring in the next syllable but now generally lost; mutation: in English, the differences of vowel in certain singulars and plurals (e.g., *foot—feet*, *mouse—mice*) or causative verbs and the words from which they are derived (e.g., *gold—gild*) are due to the effects of umlaut on the second word of each pair.

2. a vowel resulting from such assimilation.

3. the diacritical mark (¨) placed over a vowel, especially in German, to indicate umlaut.

ụm′laut, *v.t.* to modify, sound, or write with an umlaut.

um′pi·rāġe, *n.* 1. the power, right, decision, or authority of an umpire.

2. an action, ruling, etc. of an umpire.

um′pīre, *n.* [OFr. *nonper*, peerless; *non*, not, and *per*, peer: altered to *numpire*: the initial *n* was lost through faulty separation of *a numpire*.]

1. a person to whose decision a controversy or question between parties is referred; a judge; an arbiter; specifically, in certain games, as baseball, a person selected to see that the rules of the game are observed and to decide all disputed points.

2. something that decides a matter.

3. in law, a third person called in to decide a controversy or question submitted to arbitrators, when the arbitrators do not agree.

um′pīre, *v.t.*; umpired, *pt.*, *pp.*; umpiring, *ppr.* to arbitrate; to decide as umpire; to settle, as a dispute; specifically, to act as umpire in or of (a game).

um′pīre, *v.i.* to act as umpire; as, he has *umpired* for years.

um′pīre·ship, *n.* umpirage.

ump′steen, *a.* [*umps-*, indefinite sound for an uncertain number, and *-teen* as in thir*teen*.] a great number of; very many. [Slang.]

ump′teen, *n.* umpsteen. [Slang.]

um′whīle (-hwīl), *a.* late; former: also written *umquhile*. [Archaic.]

um′whīle, *adv.* formerly: also written *umquhile*. [Archaic.]

un, *n.* one; as, a little *un*; we *uns*. [Colloq. or Dial.]

un-, 1. [ME. *un-*; AS. *un-*, *on-*; L. *in-*; Gr. *an-*, *a-*, not.] a prefix meaning *not*, *lack of*, *the opposite of*, as in *un*lucky, *un*truth, *un*happy.

2. [ME. *un-*, *on-*; AS. *un-*, *on-*, *an-*, *ond-*, *and-*, back.] a prefix meaning *back* and generally added to verbs to express a reversal of the action denoted by the verb, as in *un*arm, *un*do, *un*lock, or to nouns to form verbs indicating a release from the state expressed by the noun, as in *un*bosom. Sometimes it has a mere intensive force, as in *un*loosen.

Many self-explanatory words in present use, formed with the prefix *un-* in one or the other of its senses, *not* or *back*, will be found in the following list.

unabased
unabashed
unabated
unabating
unabbreviated
unable
unabsolvable
unabsolved
unabsorbable
unabsorbed
unacademic
unaccentuated
unacceptable
unaccepted
unaccessible
unacclimated
unaccommodating
unaccomplishment
unaccordant
unaccorded
unaccounted
unaccredited
unaccurate
unacquaintance
unacquirable
unacquired
unacted
unadaptable
unadapted
unadjustable
unadjusted
unadmired
unadmitted
unadmonished
unadorned
unadulterate
unadulterated
unadvantaged
unadventurous
unadvisable
unaesthetic
unaffable
unaffiliated
unafflicted
unafraid
unaggressive
unagreeable
unaided
unaimed
unalienable
unalienated
unalleviated
unalliable
unallied
unallotted
unallowable
unalloyed
unalterable
unalterably
unaltered
unambiguous
unambitious
unamendable
unamiability
unamiable
unamused
unamusing
unamusive
unanalytic
unanalytical
unanalyzable
unanalyzed
unancestried
unangular
unanimalized
unanimated
unannealed
unannexed
unannounced
unanswerable
unanswerably
unanswered
unanticipated
unanxious
unapocryphal
unapostolic
unappalled
unapparel
unapparent
unappeasable
unappeased
unappetizing
unapplicable
unapplied
unappreciated
unappreciative
unapprehended
unapprehensible
unapprised
unapproachably
unapproached
unapproved
unargumentative
unarrayed
unarrested
unartful
unartificial
unartistic
unascendable
unascended
unascertainable
unascertained
unashamed
unaspirated
unaspiring
unassailably
unassailed
unassayed
unassignable
unassigned
unassisted
unassociated
unassorted
unassumed
unattacked
unattainable
unattained
unattainted
unattempted
unattentive
unattested
unattired
unattracted
unattractive
unauspicious
unauthentic
unauthenticated
unauthoritative
unavailability
unavenged
unavoided
unavowed
unawaked
unawakened
unawed
unbailable
unballast
unballasted
unbandaged
unbanded
unbankable
unbarbed
unbare
unbargained
unbarricade
unbase
unbashful
unbathed
unbattered
unbearable
unbearded
unbearing
unbeauteous
unbeautiful
unbefitting
unbefriended
unbegot
unbegotten
unbeguile
unbegun
unbeholden
unbelievable
unbelieved
unbeloved
unbendable
unbendingly
unbeneficed
unbeneficial
unbenefited
unbenign
unbereft
unbeseeming
unbesought
unbestowed
unbetide
unbetrayed
unbetrothed
unbettered
unbewailed
unbias
unbiased
un-Biblical
unbid
unbigoted
unbitten
unblamable
unblamably
unblamed
unbleeding
unblemishable
unblemished
unblenching
unblessed
unblissful
unblithe
unblooded
unbloodily
unblotted
unblunted
unboastful
unboding
unboiled
unbookish
unbooted
unborrowed
unbottomed
unbowdlerized
unbraced
unbrained
unbranched
unbranded
unbreakable
unbreathable
unbreeched
unbrewed
unbribable
unbribed
unbridgeable
unbridged
unbridle
unbroached
unbrotherly
unbruised
unbrushed
unbudded
unbuilt
unbuoyed
unburdened
unburiable
unburied
unburnished
unbusinesslike
unbutton
unbuttressed
uncadenced
uncage
uncalcified
uncalcined
uncalculated
uncalculating
uncalendered
uncalked
uncanceled
uncancelled
uncandid
uncanonical
uncanonize
uncapsizable
uncaptious
uncareful
uncaring
uncarnate
uncarpeted
uncarved
uncatalogued
uncatechized
uncaught
unceasing
unceded
uncelebrated
uncemented
uncensored
uncensurable
uncensured
uncertified
unchain
unchalked
unchallengeable
unchallenged
unchangeable
unchangeably
unchanged
unchanging
unchanted
unchaperoned
uncharacterized
uncharged
uncharted
unchartered
unchary
unchaste
unchastened
unchastised
unchastity
uncheckable
unchecked
uncheerful
uncherished
unchewed
unchilled
unchiseled
unchivalrous
uncholeric
unchopped
unchosen
unchristened
unchristianize
unchristianly
unchurched
unchurchly
uncircumscribed
uncircumspect
uncircumstantial
uncited
uncivilly
unclaimed
unclarified
unclasped

fāte, fär, fȧst, fạll, finăl, cãre, at; mēte, prẹy, hẽr, met; pīne, marīne, bīrd, pin; nōte, mōve, fọr, atŏm, not; mọọn, book;

unclassed
unclassical
unclassifiable
unclassified
uncleaned
uncleansed
uncleared
uncleavable
uncleft
unclerical
unclipped
unclog
unclogged
uncloister
unclosed
unclothed
uncloud
unclouded
uncloyed
unclubable
unclutch
uncoacted
uncoagulated
uncoated
uncocked
uncoerced
uncoffined
uncogitable
uncoifed
uncoined
uncollapsible
uncollectable
uncollected
uncollectible
uncolonized
uncolored
uncombed
uncombinable
uncombined
uncomely
uncomforted
uncomforting
uncommanded
uncommemorated
uncommended
uncommensurable
uncommercially
uncommissioned
uncommonness
uncommunicable
uncommunicated
uncommuted
uncompact
uncompanionable
uncompanioned
uncompassionate
uncompellable
uncompensated
uncompetitive
uncomplaining
uncomplaisant
uncomplete
uncompleted
uncompliable
uncompliant
uncomplicated
uncomplimentary
uncomplimented
uncomplying
uncomposable
uncompounded
uncomprehending
uncomprehensible
uncompressed
uncompromised
uncomputed
unconcealable
unconcealed
unconceded
unconcernment
unconcerted
unconciliated
unconciliatory
unconcluded
unconcocted
unconcurrent
uncondemned
uncondensed
unconferred
unconfiding
unconfinable
unconfined
uncomformably
unconfused
unconfuted
uncongeal
uncongealable
uncongenial
uncongested
unconjugal
unconquerable
unconquered
unconscientious
unconsecrated
unconsenting
unconservative
unconsidered
unconsidering
unconsolidated
unconsoled
unconsoling
unconsonant
unconstant
unconstituted
unconstrained
unconstraint
unconstricted
unconsulted
unconsumed
uncontaminated
uncontemned
uncontemplated
uncontended
uncontracted
uncontradictable
uncontradicted
uncontrite
uncontrollability
uncontrollable
uncontrolled
uncontroversial
uncontroverted
uncontrovertible
unconventionally
unconversable
unconversant
unconvertible
unconvicted
unconvinced
unconvincing
uncookable
uncooked
un-co-operative
un-co-ordinated
uncopied
uncorrected
uncorrelated
uncorroborated
uncorroded
uncorrupt
uncorrupted
uncorruptible
uncorruption
uncostly
uncounseled
uncountable
uncourted
uncourteous
uncourtliness
uncourtly
uncoveted
uncowl
uncracked
uncrafty
uncredited
uncrippled
uncritical
uncriticizable
uncriticized
uncropped
uncross
uncrowded
uncrown
uncrushable
uncrystalline
uncrystallizable
uncrystallized
unculled
uncultivable
uncultivated
uncultured
uncumbered
uncurbable
uncurbed
uncurdled
uncured
uncurious
uncurled
uncurried
uncursed
uncurtailed
uncurtained
uncushioned
uncustomable
uncustomary
undamaged
undangered
undashed
undaughterly
undazzled
undealt
undebarred
undebased
undebatable
undebated
undebauched
undecayed
undecaying
undeceivable
undeceived
undecidable
undecipherable
undeciphered
undeck
undecked
undeclared
undeclinable
undeclined
undecomposable
undecomposed
undecorated
undeeded
undefaceable
undefaced
undefeatable
undefeated
undefecated
undefended
undefensible
undefiled
undefinable
undeformed
undefrauded
undefrayed
undegenerate
undegraded
undelayable
undelayed
undelectable
undelegated
undeliberate
undelighted
undelightful
undelineated
undeliverable
undelivered
undelved
undemanded
undemocratic
undemocratically
undemonstrable
undemonstrably
undenied
undenominational
undenounced
undependable
undeplored
undeposed
undepraved
undepreciated
undepressed
undeprived
underived
undescendible
undescribable
undescribed
undescried
undeserved
undeserving
undesignated
undesigned
undesirability
undesired
undesiring
undesirous
undesisting
undespairing
undespatched
undestined
undestroyed
undetachable
undetached
undetected
undeterminable
undeterred
undetesting
undeveloped
undeviating
undevised
undevoted
undevoured
undevout
undiaphanous
undifferentiated
undiffused
undigested
undigestible
undignified
undilated
undiluted
undiminishable
undiminished
undimmed
undinted
undiplomatic
undipped
undiscerned
undiscernible
undiscernibly
undiscerning
undischarged
undisciplined
undisclosed
undiscomfited
undisconcerted
undiscordant
undiscouraged
undiscoverable
undiscovered
undiscredited
undiscriminating
undiscussed
undisguised
undishonored
undisillusioned
undismantled
undismayed
undismembered
undismissed
undispatched
undispelled
undispensed
undispersed
undisputable
undisputed
undissected
undissembling
undissipated
undissolved
undissolving
undistempered
undistilled
undistinctive
undistinguishable
undistinguished
undistinguishing
undistracted
undistracting
undistraught
undistressed
undistributed
undisturbed
undiversified
undiverted
undivested
undividable
undivorced
undivulged
undock
undomestic
undomesticate
undomesticated
undoubtful
undoubting
undrainable
undrained
undramatic
undramatically
undramatized
undrape
undraped
undressed
undried
undrilled
undrinkable
undurable
unduteous
undutiful
undyed
uneatable
uneaten
unecclesiastic
uneclipsed
uneconomic
uneconomical
unedge
unedible
unedified
unedifying
unedited
uneducable
uneducated
uneffaced
uneffectuated
unelaborated
unelected
unelectrified
uneliminated
unemancipated
unembarrassed
unembellished
unembodied
unemotional
unemphatic
unemphatically
unemptiable
unemptied
unenchanted
unenclosed
unencumber
unencumbered
unendangered
unendeared
unended
unending
unendorsed
unendowed
unendurable
unenduring
unenforceable
unenforced
unenfranchised
unengaged
unengaging
unengrossed
unenjoyable
unenjoyed
unenlarged
unenlightened
unenlivened
unenriched
unenrolled
unenslaved
unentangled
unentered
unenterprising
unentertaining
unenthralled
unenthusiastic
unentitled
unentombed
unentranced
unenumerated
unenviable
unenvied
unenvious
unenvying
unepiscopal
unequipped
unequivocal
unerased
unescapable
unespied
unessayed
unessential
unestablished
unesthetic
unestimated
unetched
unethical
unevangelical
uneventful
unevident
unexacting
unexaggerated
unexalted
unexamined
unexcavated
unexcelled
unexchangeable
unexcised
unexcited
unexcluded
unexclusive
unexcogitable
unexcommunicated
unexcused
unexecuted
unexemplified
unexempt
unexercised
unexerted
unexhausted
unexhibited
unexpanded
unexpectant
unexpended
unexpendible
unexperienced
unexpert
unexpiated
unexpired
unexplainable
unexplained
unexplicit
unexploded
unexploited
unexplored
unexported
unexposed
unexpounded
unexpressed
unexpunged
unexpurgated
unextended
unexterminated
unextinct
unextinguishable
unextinguished
unextirpated
unextricated
unfabled
unfadable
unfaded
unfading
unfainting
unfallen
unfallowed
unfaltering
unfamed
unfamiliarly
unfashionable
unfashioned
unfatherly
unfathomable
unfathomed
unfatigueable
unfatigued
unfavored
unfeared
unfearful
unfearing
unfeasible
unfeathered
unfecundated
unfed
unfederated
unfeigning
unfelled
unfelt
unfeminine
unfenced
unfermentable
unfertile
unfertilized
unfettered
unfeudalize
unfiled
unfilial
unfilled
unfilleted
unfilling
unfilmed
unfiltered
unfinishable
unfired
unfirm
unfitted
unfixed
unflagging
unflattering
unflavored
unflickering
unflooded
unfluent
unflush
unfocused
unfoiled
unfoldment
unfoliated
unforbearing
unforbidden
unforced
unfordable
unforeboding
unforeknown
unforesee
unforeseeable
unforeseeing
unforeseen
unforested
unforetold
unforewarned
unforfeited
unforged
unforgetful
unforgettable
unforgetting
unforgivable
unforgiven
unforgiving
unforgotten
unformal
unformalized
unformulated
unforsaken
unfortified
unfossilized
unfostered
unfought
unframed
unfranchised
unfrankable
unfraternal
unfraught
unfree
unfreezable
unfreeze
unfreighted
un-French
unfrequent
unfrequented

unfrighted
unfrozen
unfulfilled
unfunded
unfurnish
unfurnished
unfurrowed
unfused
ungained
ungainful
ungallant
ungalvanized
ungarbled
ungarnished
ungarrisoned
ungartered
ungathered
ungear
ungenerated
ungenial
ungenteel
ungentle
ungentlemanly
ungently
ungenuine
ungifted
ungild
ungill
ungladdened
unglaze
ungleaned
unglorified
unglossed
unglove
unglue
unglutted
ungored
ungorged
ungot
ungotten
ungoverned
ungowned
ungraced
ungraceful
ungraded
ungrafted
ungrained
ungranted
ungratified
ungrave
ungreeted
ungrounded
ungrown
ungrudged
ungrudging
unguaranteed
unguessable
unguessed
unguidable
unguilty
unhabited
unhacked
unhackneyed
unhailed
unhammered
unhampered
unhandicapped
unhandily
unhandled
unhandy
unhang
unhanged
unharassed
unhardened
unhardy
unharmed
unharmful
unharmonious
unharnessed
unharrowed
unharvested
unhasp
unhasty
unhat
unhaunted
unhazarded
unhazardous
unhead
unhealable
unhealed
unheated
unhedged
unheeded
unheedful
unheeding
unheired
unhelmet
unhelped
unhelpful
unhemmed
unheralded
unheroic
unheroically
unhesitating
unhewed
unhewn
unhidden
unhindered
unhired
unhomelike
unhomogeneous
unhonored
unhooded
unhoop
unhopeful
unhosed
unhostile
unhouse
unhulled
unhumanize
unhung
unhurried
unhurt
unhurtful
unhusbanded
unhushed
unhusk
unhusked
unhygienically
unhyphenated
unhyphened
unideal
unidealism
unidentified
unidiomatic
unidiomatically
unignited
unilluminated
unillumined
unillusory
unillustrated
unimaginable
unimaginably
unimaginative
unimagined
unimitated
unimpaired
unimparted
unimpassioned
unimpeached
unimpeded
unimplored
unimportance
unimportant
unimposed
unimposing
unimpregnated
unimpressed
unimpressible
unimpressionable
unimpressive
unimproving
unimpugnable
unimpugned
uninaugurated
unincensed
unincorporated
unincubated
unincumbered
unindebted
unindemnified
unindexed
unindictable
unindicated
unindifferent
unindividualized
unindorsed
unindulged
uninfected
uninfectious
uninfested
uninflamed
uninflammable
uninflated
uninflected
uninfluenced
uninfluential
uninfringed
uninfringible
uningenious
uningenuous
uninhabitable
uninhabited
uninitiated
uninjured
uninoculated
uninquisitive
uninscribed
uninspired
uninspiring
uninstigated
uninstituted
uninstructed
uninstructive
uninsulated
uninsurable
uninsured
unintegrated
unintellectual
unintelligibility
unintelligible
unintelligibly
unintended
unintentional
uninterdicted
uninteresting
unintermitted
unintermittent
unintermitting
unintermittingly
unintermixed
uninterpolated
uninterpreted
uninterred
uninterrupted
unintimidated
unintoxicated
uninured
uninvaded
uninvented
uninventive
uninverted
uninvested
uninvestigated
uninvited
uninviting
uninvoked
uninvolved
unirrigated
unisolated
unissued
unjaded
unjaundiced
unjealous
unjoin
unjoined
unjoyful
unjoyous
unjudged
unjudicial
unjustifiable
unjustifiably
unjustified
unkept
unkilled
unkindled
unkindly
unkingly
unkissed
unkneaded
unknelled
unknightly
unknot
unknotted
unknowable
unknowing
unlabeled
unlabelled
unlabored
unlaboured
unlaborious
unlaced
unladen
unladylike
unlaid
unlamented
unland
unlap
unlarded
unlashed
unlaundered
unlearnable
unleased
unleavened
unlectured
unled
unlessened
unlessoned
unlet
unlevel
unlevied
unlibidinous
unlicensed
unlicked
unlifelike
unlighted
unlikable
unlikeable
unlime
unlineal
unlined
unlinked
unliquefiable
unliquefied
unliquidated
unlistening
unlit
unliterary
unlived
unliveliness
unlively
unlocalized
unlodge
unlogical
unlooped
unlovable
unloved
unloveliness
unloving
unlowered
unlubricated
unlustrous
unlying
unmacadamized
unmade
unmagisterial
unmagnetic
unmagnified
unmaidenly
unmailed
unmaimed
unmaintainable
unmakable
unmalleable
unmalted
unmanageable
unmanaged
unmanful
unmangled
unmanifested
unmanlike
unmanly
unmannered
unmannerly
unmannish
unmantle
unmanufacturable
unmanufactured
unmapped
unmarked
unmarketable
unmarketed
unmarred
unmarriageable
unmarried
unmasculine
unmasked
unmastered
unmasticated
unmatchable
unmatched
unmated
unmaternal
unmatriculated
unmatted
unmatured
unmeaning
unmeant
unmeasurable
unmeasured
unmechanical
unmeddling
unmedicated
unmeditated
unmellowed
unmelodious
unmelted
unmenaced
unmendable
unmended
unmensurable
unmentioned
unmercenary
unmerchantable
unmerciless
unmerited
unmeriting
unmeritorious
unmerry
unmesmerized
unmet
unmetaled
unmetamorphosed
unmetaphorical
unmethodical
unmethodized
unmetrically
unmilitary
unmilked
unmilled
unmingled
unministerial
unminted
unmiraculous
unmirthful
unmissed
unmistaken
unmitigable
unmixed
unmodernize
unmodifiable
unmodified
unmodish
unmodulated
unmoistened
unmold
unmolested
unmollified
unmolten
unmonastic
unmoneyed
unmoralizing
unmortgaged
unmortise
un-Mosaic
unmotherly
unmotivated
unmotived
unmourned
unmovable
unmoved
unmoving
unmown
unmunitioned
unmurmuring
unmuscular
unmutilated
unmuzzled
unmystified
unnail
unnamable
unnameable
unnamed
unnapped
unnative
unnaturalized
unnavigable
unnavigated
unneeded
unneedful
unnegotiable
unneighbored
unneighborly
unnest
unniggardly
unnoble
unnotched
unnoted
unnoticeable
unnoticed
unnotified
unnourished
unnumerable
unnurtured
unnutritious
unobjectionable
unobliged
unobliging
unobliterated
unobnoxious
unobscured
unobsequiousness
unobservable
unobservant
unobserved
unobserving
unobstructed
unobtainable
unobtained
unobtruding
unobtrusive
unobvious
unoccasioned
unoffended
unoffending
unoffensive
unoffered
unofficial
unofficinal
unofficious
unoiled
unopen
unoperated
unoperculate
unopposed
unoppressed
unordained
unordered
unorderly
unordinary
unorganizable
unoriginal
unoriginate
unornamental
unornamented
unornate
unorthodox
unossified
unostentatious
unowed
unoxidizable
unoxidized
unpacified
unpaid
unpaid-for
unpainful
unpainted
unpaired
unpalatable
unpampered
unpanel
unparagoned
unparaphrased
unpardonable
unpardonably
unpardoned
unpared
unparental
unparted
unparticipative
unpartisan
unpassable
unpassionate
unpassioned
unpasteurized
unpatented
unpatriotic
unpatriotically
unpatronized
unpatterned
unpaved
unpayable
unpeaceable
unpeaceful
unpedigreed
unpeeled
unpenciled
unpenetrated
unpenned
unpensioned
unperceivable
unperceived
unperceiving
unperfect
unperfected
unperforated
unperformed
unperishing
unperjured
unperplexed
unpersecuted
unpersonable
unpersonal
unpersuadable
unpersuaded
unpersuasive
unperturbed
unperused
unperverted
unpetrified
unphilanthropic
unphilological
unphilosophic
unphilosophical
unphonetic
unphysiological
unpickable
unpicked
unpicturesque
unpierced
unpile
unpillaged
unpillared
unpillowed
unpiloted
unpinned
unpiteous
unpitiable
unpitied
unpitiful
unpitying
unplaced
unplagued
unplanned
unplant
unplanted
unplastered
unplastic
unplated
unplausible
unplayed
unpleadable
unpleaded
unpleased
unpleasing
unpleasurable
unpledged
unpliable
unpliant
unplighted
unploughed
unplowed

unplucked
unplug
unplume
unpoetic
unpoetical
unpointed
unpoised
unpolarized
unpolicied
unpolish
unpolished
unpolite
unpolitic
unpolitical
unpolluted
unpondered
unpooled
unpopularity
unpopulated
unportioned
unpositive
unpossessed
unposted
unpotable
unpowdered
unpowerful
unpracticable
unpractical
unpraised
unprayerful
unpreceded
unprecise
unpredestinated
unpredictable
unprefaced
unpregnant
unprejudice
unprelatical
unpremeditation
unpreoccupied
unpreparation
unprepared
unprepossessing
unprescribed
unpresentable
unpresented
unpreserved
unpressed
unpresuming
unpresumptuous
unpretending
unpretentious
unprettiness
unpretty
unprevailing
unprevalent
unpreventable
unprevented
unpriest
unprimed
unprincely
unprinted
unprivileged
unprizable
unprized
unprobed
unprocessed
unproclaimed
unprocurable
unproduced
unprofessed
unprofessing
unproficiency
unprofitable
unprofited
unprogressive
unprohibited
unprojected
unprolific
unpromise
unpromising
unprompted
unpromulgated
unpronounceable
unpronounced
unprop
unprophetic
unpropitiable
unpropitiated
unpropitious
unproportionable
unproportioned
unproposed
unpropped
unprosecuted
unprostrated
unprotected
unprotruded
unprovable
unproved
unproven
unprovide
unprovincial
unprovoked
unprovoking
unpruned
unpucker
unpulled
unpulped
unpulverized
unpunctual
unpunishable
unpunished
unpurchasable
unpure
unpurged
unpurified
unpurposing
unpursuing
unpuzzle
unquailing
unquaking
unqualifying
unquantified
unquartered
unquellable
unquelled
unquenchable
unquenched
unquestionability
unquestioning
unquickened
unquiescence
unquizzable
unquotable
unquoted
unracked
unraised
unraked
unransacked
unransomed
unrated
unratified
unravaged
unrazed
unrazored
unreachable
unreached
unrealism
unrealizable
unrealized
unreaped
unreasoned
unreasoningly
unrebukable
unrebuked
unrebutted
unrecallable
unrecalled
unrecanted
unreceipted
unreceivable
unreceived
unreceptive
unreciprocated
unrecited
unreckonable
unreckoned
unreclaimable
unreclaimed
unrecognizable
unrecognized
unrecommended
unrecompensed
unreconciled
unrecorded
unrecounted
unrecoverable
unrecovered
unrecruited
unrectified
unrecumbent
unredeemable
unredeemed
unredressed
unreduced
unreducible
unrefined
unreflected
unreflecting
unreformable
unreformed
unrefreshed
unrefreshing
unrefunded
unrefuted
unregainable
unregal
unregarded
unregeneracy
unregistered
unregretful
unregretted
unregulated
unrehearsed
unrein
unrejoicing
unrelated
unrelative
unrelaxed
unrelaxing
unreliability
unreliable
unreliably
unrelievable
unrelieved
unrelinquished
unrelishable
unrelished
unreluctant
unremarked
unremedied
unremembered
unremembering
unreminded
unremittable
unremitted
unremittent
unremorseful
unremovable
unremoved
unremunerated
unremunerative
unrendered
unrenewed
unrenounced
unrenowned
unrented
unrepaid
unrepaired
unrepealed
unrepeated
unrepelled
unrepentance
unrepented
unrepenting
unrepined
unrepining
unreplaced
unreplenished
unreported
unrepresentative
unrepresented
unrepressed
unreprievable
unreprieved
unreprimanded
unreprinted
unreproachable
unreprovable
unreproving
unrepublican
unrepulsable
unreputable
unrequested
unrequitable
unrequited
unrequiting
unrescinded
unrescued
unresented
unresentful
unresigned
unresistant
unresisted
unresisting
unresolvable
unresolved
unresolving
unrespectable
unrespectful
unrespirable
unrespited
unresponsible
unresponsive
unrested
unrestful
unresting
unrestored
unrestrainable
unrestrained
unrestraint
unrestricted
unretarded
unretentive
unretracted
unretrieved
unreturned
unreturnable
unreturning
unrevealed
unrevenged
unrevengeful
unrevered
unreverence
unreverend
unreverent
unreversed
unreverted
unrevised
unrevoked
unrewarded
unrewarding
unrhetorical
unrhymed
unrhythmic
unrhythmical
unridden
unriddled
unridiculous
unrifled
unrigged
unright
unrighted
unrightful
unrimed
unring
unrinsed
unripened
unrisen
unrivet
unroasted
unrobbed
unrobe
unromantic
unromantically
unroost
unrope
unrough
unrounded
unroused
unroyal
unrubbed
unrude
unruffle
unruled
unrumple
unruptured
unrusted
unsaddled
unsafe
unsafety
unsaid
unsailable
unsaintly
unsalability
unsalable
unsalaried
unsaleability
unsaleable
unsalted
unsaluted
unsanctified
unsanctioned
unsanguine
unsanitary
unsapped
unsated
unsatiable
unsatiated
unsatiating
unsatisfactorily
unsatisfactory
unsatisfied
unsatisfying
unsaturation
unsaved
unsawed
unsawn
unsayable
unscale
unscaled
unscaly
unscanned
unscarified
unscarred
unscattered
unscented
unsceptered
unsceptical
unscheduled
unscholarly
unschooled
unscientific
unscientifically
unscissored
unscorched
unscorned
unscoured
unscourged
unscraped
unscratched
unscreened
unscriptural
unscutcheoned
unsealed
unsearched
unseated
unseaworthy
unseconded
unsecret
unsectarian
unsecularize
unsecured
unseduced
unseductive
unseeded
unseeing
unseemliness
unsegmented
unseizable
unseldom
unselected
unselective
unselfconscious
unselfish
unsensational
unsensitized
unsensualize
unsent
unsentenced
unsentimental
unseparated
unsepulchered
unsequestered
unserved
unserviceable
unsevered
unsewered
unsexual
unshackled
unshaded
unshadowed
unshady
unshakable
unshakeable
unshaken
unshamed
unshapely
unshared
unsharpened
unshattered
unshaved
unshaven
unsheared
unsheathed
unshell
unsheltered
unshelve
unshepherded
unshielded
unshocked
unshod
unshoe
unshorn
unshot
unshown
unshrined
unshrinkable
unshrinking
unshriven
unshroud
unshrouded
unshrubbed
unshrunk
unshunned
unshutter
unshy
unsifted
unsighted
unsightliness
unsignalized
unsigned
unsignified
unsilenced
unsimilar
unsimplicity
unsimulated
unsinful
unsingable
unsinkable
unsinning
unsisterly
unsized
unskinned
unslacked
unslain
unslaked
unslandered
unslaughtered
unsleeping
unsliced
unslipping
unsluice
unslumbering
unslurred
unsmelted
unsmiling
unsmirched
unsmitten
unsmoked
unsmooth
unsmotherable
unsmuggled
unsnare
unsoaked
unsoftened
unsoiled
unsold
unsoldered
unsoldierlike
unsoldierly
unsolemn
unsolemnize
unsolicited
unsolicitous
unsolid
unsolidified
unsoluble
unsolvable
unsolved
unsoothed
unsophisticate
unsophistication
unsorrowed
unsorted
unsought
unsounded
unsoured
unsowed
unsown
unspar
unspared
unspatial
unspatiality
unspecialized
unspecified
unspeculative
unspectacled
unspeedy
unspell
unspelled
unspent
unspied
unspike
unspilled
unsplit
unspin
unspiritual
unspiritualize
unspirituality
unspleened
unspliced
unsplit
unspoiled
unspoilt
unspoken
unspontaneous
unsportsmanlike
unsprinkled
unsprung
unsquandered
unsquared
unsqueamish
unsqueezed
unstack
unstaid
unstainable
unstained
unstalked
unstamped
unstanch
unstanchable
unstandardized
unstarch
unstarred
unstartled
unstated
unstatesmanlike
unstationed
unstatutable
unsteadfast
unsteadily
unsteadiness
unstemmed
unsterilized
unstiffened
unstifled
unstigmatized
unstilted
unstimulating
unstinted
unstitch
unstooping
unstopped
unstopper
unstopple
unstored
unstowed
unstrain
unstrained
unstrengthened

unstressed
unstretch
unstriated
unstringed
unstriped
unstripped
unstuffed
unstung
unsubdued
unsubjected
unsubmissive
unsubmitting
unsubordinate
unsubscribed
unsubsidized
unsubstantiality
unsubstantiated
unsucceeded
unsuccess
unsuccessful
unsuccessive
unsucked
unsuckled
unsued
unsuffocated
unsuggestive
unsuit
unsuited
unsullied
unsummoned
unsunk
unsunned
unsupped
unsupportable
unsupported
unsuppressed
unsure
unsurfeited
unsurgical
unsurmised
unsurmountable
unsurpassable
unsurpassed
unsurrendered
unsusceptible
unsuspecting
unsuspended
unsuspicion
unsuspicious
unsustainable
unsustained
unswaddle
unswallowed
unswayable
unswayed
unsweating
unsweet
unsweetened
unswept
unswerving
unsworn
unsyllabled
unsymmetry
unsympathetic
unsympathetically
unsympathizing
unsystematic
unsystematically
unsystematized
untack
untackle
untactful
untainted
untaken
untalented
untalked-of
untamable
untame
untamed
untameable
untanned
untapped
untarnishable
untarnished
untarred
untasked
untasted
untasteful
untax
untaxable
untaxed
unteachable
unteam
untearable
untechnical
untell
untellable
untemper
untempered
untenable
untenant
untenanted
untended
untender
untendered
unterminated
unterrified
untested
untether
unthatched
untheatrical
unthickened
unthorny
unthought
unthoughtful
unthought-of
unthrashed
unthreadable
unthreshed
unthriving
unthrone
unthwarted
untighten
untile
untillable
untilled
untimbered
untin
untinctured
untinged
untired
untiring
untithed
untooth
untoothsome
untormented
untorn
untowered
untraceable
untraced
untracked
untractable
untrading
untragic
untrained
untrammeled
untrammelled
untrampled
untransferable
untransferred
untransformed
untranslatable
untranslated
untransmissible
untransmitted
untransmutable
untransparent
untransplanted
untransportable
untransported
untransposed
untrapped
untraversable
untraversed
untreasured
untreated
untrembling
untrespassing
untrifling
untrim
untrimmed
untrodden
untroubled
untrumpeted
untrussed
untrusted
untrustful
untrustworthy
untrusty
untufted
untunable
untune
untuned
untuneful
unturf
unturned
untwilled
untwined
untwisted
untypical
unurged
unusable
unusefulness
unutilizable
unutilized
unuttered
unvaccinated
unvacillating
unvalidated
unvalued
unvamped
unvanquishable
unvanquished
unvariable
unvaried
unvariegated
unvarying
unvaryingly
unvascular
unvenerable
unvenomed
unventilated
unventured
unveracious
unveracity
unverdant
unverifiable
unverified
unvexed
unvictorious
unviolated
unvirtuous
unvisited
unvitiated
unvitrified
unvizard
unvocal
unvoidable
unvolatilized
unvoluptuous
unvouched
unvowed
unvulcanized
unvulgarize
unwaited
unwaked
unwakeful
unwakened
unwalkable
unwalled
unwallet
unwandering
unwanted
unwarlike
unwarmed
unwarned
unwarp
unwarped
unwarrantable
unwarranted
unwashed
unwasted
unwasting
unwatched
unwatchful
unwater
unwatered
unwavering
unwaxed
unweakened
unweaned
unwearable
unweary
unwearying
unweathered
unweave
unwebbed
unwed
unwedded
unwedgeable
unweeded
unweighed
unweighted
unwelcome
unweldable
unwelded
unwet
unwetted
unwhetted
unwhipped
unwhipt
unwhisperable
unwifelike
unwifely
unwill
unwilled
unwillful
unwincing
unwinking
unwily
unwiped
unwisely
unwished
unwished-for
unwithdrawing
unwithered
unwithering
unwithstood
unwitnessed
unwitty
unwomanlike
unwomanly
unwon
unwondering
unwooded
unwooed
unworded
unwork
unworkable
unworked
unworkmanlike
unwormed
unworn
unworshiped
unworshipped
unwounded
unwoven
unwrathfully
unwreaked
unwreathe
unwrecked
unwrinkle
unwrinkled
unwronged
unwrought
unwrung
unyielded
unyielding
unyoked
unyouthful
unzealous
unzoned

Ū'nȧ bōat, a catboat.

un·ȧ·bridġed', *a.* not shortened; complete; specifically, designating a dictionary that has not been abridged from a larger work.

un·aç·cent'ed, *a.* not accented; specifically, in music, receiving a relatively slight stress or rhythmical emphasis.

un·aç·çom'mō·dāt·ed, *a.* 1. not accommodated or adapted.
 2. having no accommodations.

un·ăç·cŏm'pȧ·nied, *a.* not accompanied; specifically, in music, having no accompaniment; as, an *unaccompanied* song.

un·aç·çom'plished, *a.* 1. not accomplished, completed, or achieved.
 2. having no accomplishments or skills.

un·ăç·çount·ȧ·bil'i·ty, *n.* 1. the state or quality of being unaccountable.
 2. that which is unaccountable or incapable of being explained.

un·ăç·çount'ȧ·ble, *a.* 1. not to be accounted for; inexplicable; strange; mysterious.
 2. not subject to account or control; not subject to answer; not responsible.
 3. not to be counted; countless; innumerable. [Obs.]

un·ăç·çount'ȧ·ble·ness, *n.* the state or quality of being unaccountable; unaccountability.

un·ăç·çount'ȧ·bly, *adv.* in an unaccountable manner; strangely.

un·ăç·çount'ed-fọr, *a.* not explained or accounted for.

un·ăç·cus'tŏmed (-tumd), *a.* 1. not accustomed; not used (*to*); not habituated; as, *unaccustomed to* work.
 2. new, not usual; not familiar; strange; as, *unaccustomed* work.

un·ăç·cus'tŏmed·ness, *n.* the state or character of being unaccustomed.

un·aç·knowl'edġed (-nol'ejd), *a.* not acknowledged; not recognized; as, an *unacknowledged* agent or consul.

un·ăç·quāint'ed (-kwānt'), *a.* 1. not well known; unusual. [Obs.]
 2. not acquainted: often with *with*.

un·ăç·quāint'ed·ness, *n.* the state or quality of being unacquainted.

un·ad·dressed' (-drest'), *a.* lacking an address: said of a letter, etc.

un·ad·vīṣed' (-vīzd'), *a.* 1. not prudent; not discreet; thoughtlessly hasty; rash; as, an *unadvised* measure or proceeding.
 2. without counsel or advice.

un·ad·vīṣ'ed·ly, *adv.* in an unadvised manner; imprudently; indiscreetly; rashly; without due consideration.

un·ad·vīṣ'ed·ness, *n.* the quality or state of being unadvised; imprudence; rashness.

un·ăf·feçt'ed, *a.* 1. not affected; plain; natural; sincere; simple; as, *unaffected* ease and grace.
 2. not changed, affected, or influenced.
 3. not moved; not having the emotions touched.

un·ăf·feçt'ed·ly, *adv.* in an unaffected manner.

un·ăf·feçt'ed·ness, *n.* the state of being unaffected.

un·ăf·fīed', *a.* not betrothed. [Rare.]

ū'năl·ist, *n.* the holder of but one benefice.

un·ăl·lāyed', *a.* not allayed; not appeased or quieted.

un-Ȧ·mer'i·çăn, *a.* not American; not agreeing with or conforming to the characteristics of the United States; especially, regarded as opposed or dangerous to the United States, its institutions, etc.

un·añ'çhŏr, *v.t.* and *v.i.* to release from anchorage; to become detached. [Rare.]

un·ȧ·nēled', *a.* not aneled; not having received extreme unction. [Archaic.]

ū·nȧ·nim'i·ty, *n.* [ME. and OFr. *unanimité*; L. *unus*, one, and *animus*, mind.] the state or quality of being unanimous; as, there was perfect *unanimity* among the members of the council.

ū·nan'i·mous, *a.* [L. *unanimus, unanimis*, from *unus*, one, and *animus*, the mind.]
 1. agreeing completely; united in opinion.
 2. showing, or based on, complete agreement.

ū·nan'i·mous·ly, *adv.* with one mind; with unanimity.

ū·nan'i·mous·ness, *n.* the state or quality of being unanimous.

un·an'swẽred (-sẽrd), *a.* 1. not answered; not replied to.
 2. not refuted.
 3. not suitably returned; unrequited.

un·ăp·păr'ent, *a.* not apparent; obscure; not visible.

un·ăp·pēal'ȧ·ble, *a.* 1. not appealable; admitting no appeal; that cannot be carried to a higher court by appeal; as, an *unappealable* action.
 2. not to be appealed from; as, an *unappealable* judge.

un″ap·prē·hen'sive, *a.* 1. not apprehensive; not fearful or suspecting.
 2. not intelligent; not quick to understand.

un″ap·prē·hen'sive·ly, *adv.* in an unapprehensive manner.

un″ap·prē·hen'sive·ness, *n.* the state of being unapprehensive.

un·ap·prōach'ȧ·ble, *a.* 1. not to be approached; inaccessible; distant; aloof.
 2. having no rival or equal; unmatched.

un·ăp·prō'pri·āte, *a.* inappropriate; also, unappropriated.

un·ăp·prō'pri·ā·ted, *a.* not appropriated; specifically, (a) not applied or directed to be applied to any specific use or purpose, as money or funds; (b) not owned by or granted to any person, company, or corporation; as, *unappropriated* lands.

un·apt', *a.* 1. not apt; unfit. [Obs.]
 2. dull; not ready to learn; not skillful.
 3. not likely or inclined; not disposed.
 4. unsuitable; inappropriate.

un·apt'ly, *adv.* unfitly; improperly.

un·apt'ness, *n.* the state or quality of being unapt.

un·är′gūed, *a.* 1. not argued or debated.
2. accepted without dispute.

un·ärm′, *v.t.* 1. to disarm.
2. to strip of armor. [Archaic.]

un·ärmed′, *a.* 1. having no weapons, especially firearms, or armor; defenseless.
2. not furnished with scales, prickles, or other defense, as animals and plants.

un·är′mŏred, un·är′mŏured, *a.* not furnished with armor, as a ship.

un·ärt′ed, *a.* not artificial; plain; also, ignorant of the arts. [Obs.]

un·ȧs·çrīed′, *a.* not seen. [Obs.]

un·ȧsked′ (-ȧskt′), *a.* 1. not asked; uninvited; as, he came *unasked.*
2. not sought; unsolicited; as, an *unasked* favor.

un·ȧs·sāil′ȧ·ble, *a.* not assailable; specifically, (a) that cannot be successfully assaulted; impregnable; (b) that cannot be successfully denied or contested.

un·as′suē·tūde (-swē-), *n.* the state or the quality of being unaccustomed.

un·ȧs·sūm′ing, *a.* not assuming; not bold or forward; not making lofty pretensions; not arrogant; modest; as, an *unassuming* youth; *unassuming* manners.

un·ȧs·sụred′ (-shụrd′), *a.* 1. not assured; not confident.
2. not to be trusted; as, an *unassured* foe. [Obs.]
3. not insured against loss; as, goods *unassured.*

un·ȧt·tached′ (-tacht′), *a.* 1. not attached or fastened.
2. not connected with any particular group, institution, etc.; independent.
3. not engaged or married.

un·ȧt·tend′ed, *a.* 1. not attended; not accompanied.
2. not medically attended to; not dressed; as, *unattended* wounds.

ū′nau, *n.* [Fr., from native Braz. (Tupi) name.] the two-toed sloth, *Cholopus didactylus,* of South America.

un·au′thŏr·īzed, *a.* not authorized; not warranted by proper authority; not duly commissioned.

un·ȧ·vāil′ȧ·ble, *a.* 1. not available; useless.
2. not effectual; vain.

un·ȧ·vāil′ing, *a.* not having the desired effect; futile; ineffectual; useless; as, *unavailing* efforts.

un·ȧ·vāil′ing·ly, *adv.* without effect.

un·ȧ·void′ȧ·ble, *a.* 1. that cannot be made null or void.
2. not avoidable; inevitable; as, *unavoidable* evils.
unavoidable hemorrhage; hemorrhage that results from the detachment of a placenta interfering with childbirth.

un·ȧ·void′ȧ·ble·ness, *n.* the state of being unavoidable; inevitableness.

un·ȧ·void′ȧ·bly, *adv.* inevitably; in a manner that cannot or could not be avoided.

un·ȧ·wāre′, *a.* 1. without thought; inattentive; heedless.
2. not aware or conscious; as, *unaware* of danger.

un·ȧ·wāre′, *adv.* same as *unawares.*

un·ȧ·wāreș′, *adv.* 1. suddenly; unexpectedly; by surprise; as, the storm came upon us *unawares.*
2. without knowing or being aware; unintentionally; as, he jostled the man *unawares.*
at unawares; unexpectedly.
He breaks *at unawares* upon our walks.
—Dryden.

un·ạwned′, *a.* in botany, without an awn or awns.

un·az′ō·tīzed, *a.* not azotized; not impregnated with nitrogen.

un·backed′ (-bakt′), *a.* 1. having no money bet in favor of it; as, an *unbacked* horse in a race.
2. not tamed; not taught to bear a rider: said of a horse.
3. unsupported; left without aid; not endorsed.

un·bāked′ (-bākt′), *a.* not baked; also, undeveloped; immature.

un·bal′ănce, *v.t.*; unbalanced, *pt., pp.*; unbalancing, *ppr.* 1. to disturb the balance or equilibrium of.
2. to disturb the functioning of; to derange (the mind).

un·bal′ănce, *n.* the condition of being unbalanced; lack of balance.

un·bal′ănced (-ănst), *a.* 1. not balanced; not in equilibrium.
2. not adjusted; not settled; not brought to an equality of debt and credit; as, an *unbalanced* account.
3. not functioning properly; deranged: said of the mind.
4. (a) mentally deranged; (b) not stable, steady, or sound in character or judgment.

un·bañk′, *v.t.* 1. to remove a bank from, as a road or a field.
2. to uncover, as a banked fire.

un·bap·tīzed′, *a.* not baptized; hence, not hallowed; profane.

un·bär′, *v.t.* to remove a bar or bars from; to unfasten; to open; as, to *unbar* a gate.

un·bärk′, *v.t.* to strip the bark from, as a tree.

un·bärk′, *v.i.* to disembark, to effect a landing. [Obs.]

un·bashed′ (-basht′), *a.* unabashed. [Obs.]

un·bāt′ed, *a.* 1. not dulled; not blunted, as a sword. [Archaic.]
2. not abated or diminished. [Poet.]

un·bāy′, *v.t.* to open; to free from restraint. [Obs.]

un·beār′, *v.t.* to free (a horse) from the pressure of a bearing rein.

un·bēat′en, *a.* 1. not beaten; not struck with blows.
2. untrod; not beaten by the feet; unfrequented; as, *unbeaten* paths.
3. not defeated, as in a contest.

un·bē·çōme′, *v.t.* to be unsuitable to; to misbecome.

un·bē·çōm′ing, *a.* 1. not becoming; unsuitable or inappropriate.
2. not proper or decent.

un·bē·çōm′ing·ly, *adv.* in an unbecoming manner.

un·bē·çōm′ing·ness, *n.* the state or the quality of being unbecoming.

un·bed′, *v.t.* to raise or rouse from bed.

un·bed′ded, *a.* 1. not yet married, as a bride.
2. in geology, not in beds, or layers.

un·bē·get′, *v.t.* to cancel the begetting of.

un·bē·jug′gled (-gld), *a.* not deceived by artifice.

un·bē·knōwn′, *a.* not known; unknown; unperceived: often used in an adverbial sense.
unbeknown to; without the knowledge of, or unperceived by (a specified person): also *unbeknownst to.*

un·bē·knōwnst′, *a.* unbeknown. [Dial.]

un·bē·liēf′, *n.* incredulity; a withholding or lack of belief, especially in religion or in the doctrines of a given religion.
Syn.—incredulity, disbelief, skepticism.

un·bē·liēv′ẽr, *n.* 1. one who does not believe; a doubter.
2. a person who does not accept the doctrines of a given religion, or who has no religious belief.

un·bē·liēv′ing, *a.* not believing; incredulous; doubting; skeptical.

un·bē·liēv′ing·ly, *adv.* in an unbelieving manner; with unbelief

un·belt′, *v.t.* 1. to loosen or remove a belt or belts from.
2. to remove (a sword, etc.) by detaching a belt.

un·bend′, *v.t.*; unbent *or* unbended, *pt., pp.*; unbending, *ppr.* 1. to release, as a bow, from strain or tension.
2. to relax, as from mental strain or effort.
3. to make straight (something bent or crooked).
4. in nautical usage, (a) to loosen or unfasten (a rope, sail, etc.); (b) to untie (a rope).

un·bend′, *v.i.* 1. to become straight or less bent.
2. to become free from constraint, stiffness, or severity; to relax and be less formal, more genial, etc.

un·bend′ing, *a.* 1. not bending; rigid; stiff; as, an *unbending* bar.
2. unyielding; resolute; firm; as, *unbending* beliefs.
3. that unbends; relaxing.

un·bend′ing, *n.* relaxation of restraint, severity, etc.

un·bī′ȧsed (-ȧst), *a.* free from bias, partiality, or prejudice; impartial.

un·bī′ȧsed·ly, *adv.* without bias; impartially.

un·bī′ȧsed·ness, *n.* the state of being unbiased.

un·bid′den, *a.* 1. not commanded.
2. uninvited.

un·bīnd′, *v.t.*; unbound, *pt., pp.*; unbinding, *ppr.* 1. to untie; to remove a band from; to unfasten.
2. to release from bonds or restraints; to release.

un·bish′ŏp, *v.t.* to divest of the rank of bishop.

un·bitt′, *v.t.* in nautical usage, to remove the turns of (a cable, etc.) from the bitts.

un·bit′ted, *a.* 1. having no bit or bridle on.
2. unrestrained; uncontrolled; ungoverned.

un·blēached′ (-blēcht′), *a.* not bleached: applied to textile fabrics; as, *unbleached* muslin.

un·blēach′ing, *a.* not bleaching; not becoming white or pale. [Rare.]

un·blenched′ (-blencht′), *a.* not daunted or disconcerted; unconfounded.

un·blessed′, un·blest′, *a.* 1. not hallowed or consecrated.
2. not blessed or given benediction.
3. accursed; wicked.
4. wretched; unhappy.

un·blīnd′, *v.t.* to free from blindness; to give sight to; to open the eyes of. [Rare.]

un·block′, *v.i.* in whist, to avoid interfering with a partner's long suit, by playing an unnecessarily high card.

un·blood′y (-blud′), *a.* 1. not marked with blood.
2. without bloodshed.
3. not bloodthirsty.

un·blōwn′, *a.* 1. not inflated.
2. not causing to sound, as a wind instrument.
3. not yet fully developed; still in the bud.

un·blush′ing, *a.* not blushing; also, shameless; as, an *unblushing* assertion.

un·blush′ing·ly, *adv.* in an unblushing manner.

un·bod′ied, *a.* 1. incorporeal; having no body or form.
2. disembodied; separated from the body.

un·bod′kined, *a.* not fastened with a bodkin.

un·bod′y, *v.i.* to become disembodied.

un·bōlt′, *v.t.* and *v.i.* to withdraw the bolt or bolts of (a door, etc.); to unbar; to open.

un·bōlt′ed, *a.* freed from fastening by bolts, as a door.

un·bōlt′ed, *a.* not bolted or sifted.

un·bōne′, *v.t.* 1. to bone.
2. to fling or twist about as if boneless. [Rare.]

un·bōned′, *a.* 1. having no bones; boneless.
2. not having the bones removed.

un·bon′net, *v.t.* and *v.i.* to take the bonnet or other head covering off, especially as a token of respect; to uncover.

un·bon′net·ed, *a.* having no bonnet or other headdress; bareheaded.

un·booked′ (-bookt′), *a.* not bookish.

un·book′lēarn″ed, *a.* illiterate.

un·bọrn′, *a.* 1. not born; not brought into life; not existing.
2. not yet born; yet to come or be; future.

un·boș′ŏm (-booz′), *v.t.* to reveal; to let out; to disclose, as one's feelings, secrets, etc.
to unbosom oneself; to tell or reveal one's feelings, secrets, etc.

un·boș′ŏm, *v.i.* to disclose what one feels, knows, etc.

un·boș′ŏm·ẽr, *n.* one who unbosoms, discloses, or reveals.

un·bọught′ (-bọt′), *a.* not bought; obtained without money or purchase.

un·bound′, *v.* past tense and past participle of *unbind.*

un·bound′, *a.* 1. released from bonds, ties, or shackles.
2. without a binding, as a book.

un·bound′ed, *a.* 1. having no bounds or limit; unlimited in extent; infinite; interminable.
2. having no check or control; unrestrained.
Syn.—boundless, infinite, unlimited, illimitable, interminable, unrestrained, uncontrolled.

un·bound′ed·ness, *n.* the state or quality of being unbounded.

un·bowed′, *a.* 1. not bowed or bent.
2. not yielding or giving in; unsubdued.

un·box′, *v.t.* to take out of a box.

un·brāce′, *v.t.*; unbraced, *pt., pp.*; unbracing, *ppr.* 1. to free from braces or bands.
2. to loosen; to relax.
3. to make slack or feeble.
4. to disjoint; to carve. [Obs.]

un·brāce′, *v.i.* to relax; to hang loose.

un·brāid′, *v.t.* to separate the braids or strands of.

un·bred′, *a.* 1. unbegot; unborn. [Obs.]
2. not well-bred; unmannerly.
3. not taught or trained; uninstructed.

un·breech′, *v.t.* 1. to remove the breeches of; to divest or strip of breeches.
2. to free the breech of, as a cannon, from its fastenings or coverings.

un·brī′dled, *a.* 1. having no bridle on: said of a horse, etc.
2. unrestrained; uncontrolled; ungoverned.

un·brō′ken, *a.* 1. not broken; whole; intact.
2. not disordered, impaired, or disorganized.
3. not tamed or subdued.
4. undisturbed; uninterrupted; even; as, *unbroken* sleep.

un·buc̦′kle, *v.t.*; unbuckled, *pt., pp.*; unbuckling, *ppr.* to unfasten the buckle or buckles of.

un·build′ (-bild′), *v.t.* to demolish (something built); to raze; to destroy.

un·bun′dle, *v.t.* to open; to disclose.

un·bũr′den, *v.t.* 1. to rid of a load; to free from a burden; to ease.
2. to throw off, as a burden; to discharge.
3. to relieve, as oneself or one's soul, mind, etc., by revealing or disclosing something hard to bear, as guilt.
4. to get rid of the burden of (anything heavy or hard to bear, as guilt, etc.), often by disclosure.

un·bũrned′, *a.* 1. not burned; not consumed by fire.
2. not baked, as brick.

un·bũrnt′, *a.* unburned.

un·bur′y (-ber′), *v.t.* 1. to disinter; to exhume.
2. figuratively, to disclose; to reveal.

un·c̦ā′bled, *a.* not fastened or secured by a cable.

un·c̦alled′, *a.* not called; not summoned; not invited.

un·c̦alled′-fọr, *a.* 1. not called for or required.
2. unnecessary and out of place; improperly brought forward; as, *uncalled-for* remarks.

un·c̦al′lōw, *n.* deposits of gravel found on chalk beds. [Brit. Dial.]

un·c̦älm′ (-käm′), *v.t.* to disturb. [Rare.]

un·c̦amp′, *v.t.* to cause to decamp; to dislodge from camp.

un·c̦an′dŏr, *n.* absence of candor.

un·c̦an′ni·ly, *adv.* in an uncanny manner.

un·c̦an′ni·ness, *n.* the quality of being uncanny.

un·c̦an′ny, *a.* 1. mysterious or unfamiliar, especially in such a way as to frighten or make uneasy; preternaturally strange; eerie; weird.
2. so good, acute, etc. as to seem preternatural; as, *uncanny* shrewdness.
3. (a) dangerous; (b) hard. [Scot. and North Eng. Dial.]

un·c̦ap′, *v.t.*; uncapped, *pt., pp.*; uncapping, *ppr.* 1. to remove a covering or cap from (a bottle, etc.).
2. to remove a cap from the head of (a person).

un·c̦ap′, *v.i.* to salute by removing the hat.

un·c̦ā′pȧ·ble, *a.* incapable. [Obs.]

un·c̦āred′-fọr, *a.* not regarded; not heeded.

Un̄·c̦ā′ri·ȧ, *n.* [L. *uncus*, a hook.] a genus of plants of the family *Rubiaceæ*. The species are chiefly native to India. They are permanent cirriferous ramblers, hanging to different trees by hooked peduncles. The most important species is *Uncaria gambier*, which yields the substance gambier, used in tanning.

un·c̦ärt′, *v.t.* to unload or discharge from a cart.

un·c̦āse′, *v.t.* 1. to disengage from a case or covering.
2. to unfurl and display, as the colors of a regiment; hence, to reveal.
3. to strip; to undress; also, [Obs.] to flay.

un·c̦auṣed′, *a.* not caused or created; self-existent; as, *uncaused* matter.

unce, *n.* a claw. [Obs.]

un·cer·ē·mō′ni·ous, *a.* 1. less formal and ceremonious than is usual or expected; informal; familiar.
2. curt; abrupt; lacking courtesy.

un·cẽr′tain (-tin), *a.* 1. not certainly known; questionable; problematical.
2. vague; not definite or determined.
3. doubtful; not having certain knowledge; not sure.
4. ambiguous.
5. not steady or constant; varying.
6. liable to change or vary; not dependable or reliable.

un·cẽr′tain·ly, *adv.* in an uncertain manner.

un·cẽr′tain·ness, *n.* the condition of being uncertain.

un·cẽr′tain·ty, *n.* 1. the quality or state of being uncertain; lack of certainty; doubt.
2. *pl.* **un·cẽr′tain·tieṣ,** something not certainly and exactly known; something not determined, settled, or established; a contingency.

un′chȧnce, *n.* calamity. [Scot.]

un·chȧn′cy, *a.* 1. unlucky; unfortunate.
2. dangerous.
3. inconvenient; poorly-timed; inopportune.
[Scot. in all senses.]

un·chärġe′, *v.t.* 1. to free from a charge, load, or cargo; to unload. [Rare.]
2. to acquit of blame, guilt, etc. [Obs.]

un·char′i·ŏt, *v.t.* to throw out of a chariot.

un·char′i·tȧ·ble, *a.* harsh or severe, as in opinion; unforgiving, ungenerous, or censorious.

un·char′i·tȧ·bly, *adv.* in an uncharitable manner.

un·chärm′, *v.t.* to release from some charm, fascination, or secret power.

un·chärm′ing, *a.* not charming; no longer able to charm.

un·chär′nel, *v.t.* to remove from a tomb; to disinter.

un·chīld′, *v.t.* 1. to bereave of children; to make childless.
2. to divest of the character of a child.

un·chīld′ish, *a.* not childish.

un·c̦hris′ten (-kris′n), *v.t.* 1. to annul the baptism of; to deprive of the rite or sacrament of baptism.
2. to make unchristian. [Obs.]

un·c̦hris′tiăn (-chăn), *a.* 1. contrary to the principles of Christianity.
2. not having or practicing a Christian religion; infidel.
3. not in keeping with people practicing a Christian religion; hence, cruel, improper, etc.
4. unbefitting or unworthy of a Christian or any decent, civilized person.

un·chŭrch′, *v.t.* 1. to expel from a church; to deprive (a person) of membership in a given church; to excommunicate.
2. to deprive (an entire congregation) of the name, rights, and character of a church.

un′ci·ȧ (-shi-), *n.* [L.] 1. in ancient Rome, the twelfth part of anything; an ounce, as being the twelfth part of the Roman as.
2. the numerical coefficient of any term of the binomial theorem. [Obs.]

un′ciăl (-shăl), *a.* [L. *uncia*, an inch.] designating or of a kind of large, rounded letters used in ancient Latin and Greek manuscripts. Uncial writing was used in Latin manuscripts as early as the third or fourth century, but was seldom used after the tenth.

CENTESIMO:

UNCIAL LETTERS (*centesimo*)

un′ciăl, *n.* an uncial letter; also, uncial writing or writings.

un·ci·ā′tim, *adv.* [L.] ounce by ounce.

un·cif′ẽr·ous, *a.* [L. *uncus*, hook, and *ferre*, to bear.] having a curved process or hook, as an ovipositor.

un′ci·fọrm, *a.* [L. *uncus*, hook, and *-form*.]
1. hooked; shaped like a hook.
2. in anatomy, (a) designating or of a bone in the distal row of the wrist, on the same side as the ulna; (b) designating a hooked process on the unciform bone, or a similar process on the ethmoid bone.

un′ci·fọrm, *n.* an unciform bone.

un′ci·năl, *a.* uncinate.

Un·ci·nā′ri·ȧ, *n.* a threadlike parasitic worm of the family *Strongylidæ*.

un″ci·nȧ·rī′ȧ·sis, *n.* [Mod. L., from *Uncinaria* (from L. *uncinus*, a hook); and *-iasis*.] infestation by hookworms; ancylostomiasis.

Un·ci·nā′tȧ, *n.pl.* a division of tubicolous annelids of the order *Chætopoda*.

un′ci·nāte, *a.* [L. *uncinatus*, from *uncus*, a hook.] hooked or barbed at the end; unciform.

un′ci·nāte, *n.* a process bearing a hook or barb at the end.

un′ci·nā·ted, *a.* same as *uncinate*.

un·ci·nā′tum, *n.*; *pl.* **un·ci·nā′tȧ,** the unciform bone.

un·cī′nī, *n.* plural of *uncinus*.

Un·cin′ū·lȧ, *n.* [LL. *uncinus*, a hook.] a genus of parasitic fungi, having curved appendages, as the common powdery mildew of the grape.

un·cī′nus, *n.*; *pl.* **un·cī′nī,** [LL.] 1. a hook or barb; a hamulus.
2. one of the hook-shaped teeth on the pleura or lateral tracts of the radula or lingual ribbon of the *Mollusca*.
3. one of the hooked or barbed cilia of the *Infusoria*.

un·cĩr′c̦um·cīṣed, *a.* 1. not circumcised.
2. Gentile.
3. heathen.

un·cĩr·c̦um·ci′ṣiŏn, *n.* 1. the absence of circumcision.
2. in the Bible, the Gentiles.

un·ci·ros′trāte, *a.* [L. *uncus*, hook, and *rostratus*, beaked, curved.] hook-beaked; hamirostrate. [Rare.]

un·civ′il, *a.* 1. not civilized; barbarous.
2. not civil or courteous; ill-mannered.

un·civ′il·īzed, *a.* not civilized; barbarous; savage; unenlightened.

un·c̦lad′, *v.* alternative past tense and past participle of *unclothe*.

un·c̦lad′, *a.* not clad; wearing no clothes; naked.

un·c̦lȧsp′, *v.t.* 1. to open or loosen the clasp of.
2. to release from a clasp or grasp.

un·c̦lȧsp′, *v.i.* 1. to become unfastened; to open.
2. to relax the clasp or grasp.

un̄′c̦le, *n.* [OFr. *oncle*, from L. *avunculum*, accus. of *avunculus*, one's mother's brother, lit., little grandfather, double diminutive of *avus*, a grandfather.]
1. the brother of one's father or mother.
2. the husband of one's aunt.
3. a pawnbroker. [Slang.]
4. an elderly man: a term of address. [Colloq.]
Uncle Sam; [extended from abbrev. U.S.] the United States (government or people), personified as a tall, spare man with chin whiskers, dressed in a red, white, and blue costume of swallowtail coat, striped trousers, and tall hat. [Colloq.]
Uncle Tom; the main character in Harriet Beecher Stowe's antislavery novel, *Uncle Tom's Cabin* (1852), an elderly Negro slave devoted to his kind master but mistreated by the cruel Simon Legree after the master's death: sometimes applied contemptuously to Negroes whose behavior toward whites is regarded as fawning or abjectly servile.

un·c̦lēan′, *a.* 1. not clean; foul; dirty; filthy.
2. ceremonially impure.
3. morally impure; obscene or vile; unchaste.

un·c̦lean′li·ness (-klen′), *n.* the quality or condition of being uncleanly.

un·c̦lean′ly, *a.* not cleanly; unclean; dirty.

un·c̦lēan′ly, *adv.* in an unclean manner.

un·c̦lench′, *v.t.* and *v.i.* to open or force open: said of something clenched, or clinched.

The fist *unclenches*, and the weapon falls.
—Garth.

un̄′c̦le·ship, *n.* the state, condition, or relationship of an uncle.

un·c̦linch′, *v.t.* and *v.i.* same as *unclench*.

un·c̦lōak′, *v.t.* and *v.i.* 1. to remove a cloak or other covering (from).
2. to reveal; to expose.

un·c̦lōṣe′, *v.t.* and *v.i.*; unclosed, *pt., pp.*; unclosing, *ppr.* 1. to open; as, to *unclose* the eyes.
2. to disclose or reveal.

un·c̦lōthe′, *v.t.*; unclothed *or* unclad, *pt., pp.*; unclothing, *ppr.* to strip of or as of clothes; to undress, uncover, or divest.

un̄′c̦ō, *a.* [contr. from *uncouth*; ME. *unkow*.]
1. unknown; strange.
2. weird; uncanny.
3. notable; great; remarkable.
[Scot. and N. Eng. Dial. in all senses.]

un̄′c̦ō, *adv.* very; remarkably; extremely; exceedingly. [Scot. and N. Eng. Dial.]

un̄′c̦ō, *n.*; *pl.* **un̄′c̦ōṣ,** 1. anything strange or prodigious.
2. a strange person; a stranger.
3. [*pl.*] rumors; news.
[Scot. and N. Eng. Dial. in all senses.]

un·c̦ock′, *v.t.* 1. to let down the cock of, as a gun.
2. to release the brim of or restore to its usual position, as a hat.

un·c̦ock′, *v.t.* to open or spread out from a cock, or heap, as hay.

un·c̦oil′, *v.t.* and *v.i.* [*un-* (back), and *coil*.] to unwind.

un-c̦ōme-at′-ȧ·ble, *a.* not attainable; not obtainable; not accessible.

un·c̦ŏm′fŏrt·ȧ·ble, *a.* 1. affording no comfort; feeling discomfort.

Christmas is in the most dead and the most *uncomfortable* time of the year.
—Addison.

2. causing discomfort; not pleasant or agreeable.
3. receiving no comfort; disagreeably situated; uneasy; ill at ease.

un·çŏm′fŏrt·ȧ·bly, *adv.* so as to be uncomfortable.

un·çŏm·mẽr′ciăl (-shăl), *a.* 1. of or concerned with things other than trade or commerce.

2. not in accordance with the principles or methods of commerce.

un·çŏm·mit′ted, *a.* 1. not committed or carried out, as a crime.

2. not bound or pledged, as to doing a certain thing.

3. not jailed or imprisoned.

un·çom′mŏn, *a.* not common; not usual; infrequent; rare; hence, remarkable; extraordinary; strange.

Syn.—rare, scarce, unwonted, unusual, remarkable, extraordinary, unique, singular.

un·çom′mŏn, *adv.* exceedingly; very; unusually; as, *uncommon* cheap. [Dial.]

un·çom′mŏn·ly, *adv.* 1. in an uncommon manner; rarely; not usually.

2. strangely; remarkably; as, *uncommonly* qualified.

un·çŏm·mū′ni·çȧ·tive, *a.* not communicative; tending to withhold information, expression of opinions, feelings, etc.; reserved; silent.

un·çom′prō·mīş·ing, *a.* not compromising or yielding; firm; inflexible; determined.

un·çŏn·cẽrn′, *n.* 1. absence of concern, anxiety, or solicitude; freedom from concern or anxiety.

2. lack of interest; apathy; indifference.

un·çŏn·cẽrned′, *a.* not concerned; not anxious; free from concern or anxiety; not interested.

un·çŏn·cẽrn′ed·ly, *adv.* in an unconcerned manner; indifferently; disinterestedly.

un·çŏn·di′tion·ăl, *a.* without conditions or reservations; absolute.

un·çŏn·di′tion·ăl·ly, *adv.* without conditions or reservations; absolutely.

un·çŏn·di′tioned, *a.* 1. unconditional.

2. in philosophy, infinite; absolute.

3. in psychology, not conditioned; natural; not learned; as, an *unconditioned* reflex.

un·çŏn·fĩrmed′, *a.* 1. not firmly established; not having full stability.

2. not confirmed by additional testimony.

3. not confirmed by authority.

un·çŏn·fọrm′ȧ·ble, *a.* 1. not conformable or conforming; not consistent; not agreeable.

2. in geology, showing unconformity.

un·çŏn·fọrm′i·ty, *n.*; *pl.* **un·çŏn·fọrm′i·tieş,** 1. a lack of conformity; inconsistency; incongruity.

UNCONFORMITY

2. in geology, a break in the continuity of strata lying next to each other, resulting from an interruption in formation.

un·çŏn·neç′ted, *a.* 1. not connected; not united; separate; also, without connections or relations.

2. not coherent; disconnected; loose; vague; rambling; as, an *unconnected* discourse.

un·çon′sciŏn·ȧ·ble (-shun-) *a.* 1. unreasonable; exceeding the limits of any reasonable claim or expectation; immoderate; as, an *unconscionable* demand.

2. not guided or influenced by conscience; unscrupulous.

un·çon′sciŏn·ȧ·ble·ness, *n.* the condition of being unconscionable.

un·çon′sciŏn·ȧ·bly, *adv.* 1. in an unconscionable manner.

2. to an unconscionable degree.

un·çon′scious, *a.* 1. (a) not endowed with consciousness; mindless; (b) temporarily deprived of consciousness.

2. not aware (*of*); as, he was *unconscious of* his mistake.

3. not known, realized, or intended by the person himself; as, an *unconscious* act, an *unconscious* insult.

4. not aware of one's own existence; not conscious of self.

5. having to do with those of one's mental processes that one is unable to bring into his consciousness.

collective unconscious; in psychology, a theory that each individual inherits, in his unconscious mind, certain racial experiences which cause him, upon environmental contact, to react accordingly: credited to C. G. Jung.

the unconscious; in psychoanalysis, the sum of all thoughts, impulses, desires, feelings, etc. of which the individual is not conscious but which influence his behavior; that part of one's psyche which comprises repressed desires and other matter excluded from, but often tending to affect, the consciousness.

un·çon′scious·ly, *adv.* in an unconscious manner; without perception; without knowledge.

un·çon′scious·ness, *n.* the quality or condition of being unconscious; lack of consciousness.

un″çon·sti·tū′tion·ăl, *a.* not authorized by the constitution; contrary to the principles of the constitution; not constitutional.

un″çon·sti·tū″tion·al′i·ty, *n.* the condition, fact, instance, or quality of being unconstitutional; as, the Supreme Court has power to decide upon the *unconstitutionality* of a law.

un″çon·sti·tū′tion·ăl·ly, *adv.* in a manner not warranted by or contrary to the constitution.

un·çŏn·tent′ed, *a.* discontented.

un·çŏn·test′ȧ·ble, *a.* incontestable.

un·çŏn·test′ed, *a.* not contested; not disputed.

un·çŏn·ven′tion·ăl, *a.* that violates the rules or customs established by society, as in dress, speech, or behavior; free from conventionality.

un·çŏn·ven·tion·al′i·ty, *n.* 1. the quality or state of being unconventional; freedom from precedents and regulations.

2. *pl.* **un·çŏn·ven·tion·al′i·tieş,** an unconventional act, remark, etc.

un·çŏn·vẽr′şion, *n.* impenitence. [Rare.]

un·çŏn·vẽrt′ed, *a.* 1. not converted; not changed in opinion; not turned from one faith to another.

2. in theology, not accepting the Christian religion; not regenerated; sinful.

un·çork′, *v.t.* to pull the cork out of.

un·çŏr·reçt′, *a.* incorrect.

un·çor′ri·ġi·ble, *a.* incorrigible.

un·çŏr·rupt′ness, *n.* integrity; uprightness.

un·çount′ed, *a.* 1. not counted.

2. inconceivably numerous; innumerable.

un·çŏup′le, *v.t.*; uncoupled, *pt., pp.*; uncoupling, *ppr.* 1. to loose (dogs, etc.) from a leash or couple.

2. to disconnect; unfasten (something coupled).

un·çŏup′le, *v.i.*, to break loose; to roam at liberty. [Obs.]

un·çŏup′led (-ld), *a.* not coupled; hence, single; not married.

un·çöuth′, *a.* [ME.; AS. *uncūth*, unknown; *un*, not, and *cūth*, pp. of *cunnan*, to know.]

1. unknown. [Obs.]

2. strange; not familiar. [Rare.]

3. awkward; clumsy; ungainly.

4. uncultured; crude; boorish.

5. rare; wonderful. [Rare.]

un·çöuth′ly, *adv.* in an uncouth manner.

un·çöuth′ness, *n.* the quality or state of being uncouth.

un·çŏv′e·nȧ·ble, *a.* inconvenient; unbecoming. [Obs.]

un·çŏv′e·nănt·ed, *a.* 1. not covenanted; not promised, secured, or sanctioned by a covenant; not resting on a covenant or promise.

2. not bound by or committed to the terms of a covenant, contract, or agreement; not having joined in a covenant.

3. not subscribing to the Scottish Solemn League and Covenant.

4. in theology, not proceeding from or belonging to the covenant made between God and his people through Christ and resting on acceptance of the appointed means.

un·çŏv′ẽr, *v.t.*; uncovered, *pt., pp.*; uncovering, *ppr.* 1. to make known; to disclose; to reveal.

2. to lay bare or open by removing a covering.

3. to remove the cover or protection from.

4. to remove the hat, cap, etc. from (the head), as in respect or reverence.

5. in military usage, to expose, as successive lines of formation, by marching out leading companies, divisions, etc. to the right or left.

un·çŏv′ẽr, *v.i.* 1. to take a cover or covering off anything.

2. to bare the head, as in respect or reverence; as, the company was ordered to *uncover*.

un·çŏv′ẽred, *a.* 1. having no covering; exposed.

2. not covered or protected by insurance, collateral, etc.

3. wearing no cap, hat, etc.; bareheaded.

un·çrē·āte′, *v.t.* to annihilate; to deprive of existence.

un·çrē·āte′, *a.* uncreated.

un·çrē·āt′ed, *a.* 1. deprived of existence; not yet created.

2. not produced by creation.

un·çred′i·ble, *a.* incredible.

un·çred′it, *v.t.* to discredit. [Obs.]

un·çred′it·ȧ·ble, *a.* discreditable.

un·çrowned′, *a.* 1. not crowned; not officially installed as ruler by a coronation ceremony; as, Edward VIII was an *uncrowned* king.

2. ruling without the title or position of king; queen, etc.

unç′tion, *n.* [ME. *unccioun*; L. *unctio* (*-onis*), from *ungere*, to anoint.]

1. the act of anointing, as (a) a symbol of consecration, dedication, etc. in religious ceremonies; (b) for medical purposes.

2. that which is used for anointing; an unguent; a salve; an ointment.

3. anything soothing or comforting.

4. that quality in language, tone of expression, mode of address, manner, and the like, which excites strong devotion, fervor, tenderness, sympathy, and the like; that which is meant to arouse religious fervor and tenderness.

His sermons want all that is called *unction*,
and sometimes even earnestness.
—Hallam.

5. a quality or manner of utterance characterized by a mere pretense or affectation of fervor, etc., or by unctuosity.

unç′tious, *a.* unctuous.

unç·tū·os′i·ty, *n.* [ME. and OFr. *unctuosite*; ML. *unctuositas*.] an unctuous quality.

unç′tū·ous, *a.* 1. of the nature of or resembling an unguent or ointment; greasy; oily; fat; soapy.

Ingrateful man, with liquorish draughts
And morsels *unctuous*, greases his pure
mind. —Shak.

2. made up of or containing fat or oil.

3. having a greasy, oily, or soapy feel when touched: a characteristic of steatite, talc, serpentine, and other minerals.

4. soft and rich: said of soil.

5. plastic.

6. characterized by a smug, smooth pretense of spiritual feeling, fervor, or earnestness, especially in an attempt to influence or persuade; too suave, bland, or oily, as in speech or manner.

unç′tū·ous·ly, *adv.* in an unctuous manner.

unç′tū·ous·ness, *n.* unctuosity.

un·çul′pȧ·ble, *a.* inculpable. [Obs.]

un·çul′tūre, *n.* lack of culture.

un·çun′ning, *a.* ignorant; unknowing.

un·çun′ning·ness, *n.* ignorance.

un·çūr′ȧ·ble, *a.* incurable.

un·çūrl′, *v.t.* to straighten out, as something which has once been curled.

un·çūrl′, *v.i.* to become straight, as hair.

un·çūrse′, *v.t.* to free from any execration. [Rare.]

uñ′çus, *n.*; *pl.* **un′çī,** [L.] a hook or hooklike structure.

un·çus′tŏmed, *a.* not subjected to customs or duty; not having paid duty or been charged with customs.

un·çut′, *a.* 1. not cut; specifically, (a) untrimmed; (b) having the margins untrimmed: said of the pages of a book.

2. not ground to shape: said of a gem; as, an *uncut* stone.

un·çŭth′, *a.* uncouth. [Obs.]

un·dam′, *v.t.* to free from a dam, mound, or obstruction. [Rare.]

un·damped′ (-dampt′), *a.* [*un*-(not) and *damped*.]

1. not disheartened or discouraged.

2. in electricity, not decreasing in amplitude.

un′dāte, *a.* [L. *undatus*, pp. of *undare*, to rise in waves, from *unda*, a wave.] in botany, undulate. [Rare.]

un′dā·ted, *a.* 1. waved; rising and falling in waves toward the margin. [Obs.]

2. in botany, undulate.

3. in heraldry, undé. [Obs.]

un·dāt′ed, *a.* having no date; not dated, as a letter.

un·däunt′ȧ·ble, *a.* not to be daunted.

un·däunt′ed, *a.* not daunted; not subdued or depressed by fear or discouragement; undismayed; intrepid.

un·däunt′ed·ly, *adv.* in an undaunted manner.

un·däunt′ed·ness, *n.* boldness; fearless bravery; intrepidity.

un·dawn′ing, *a.* not yet dawning; not growing light; not opening with brightness.

un′dé (-dā), *a.* [OFr. *unde*, from L. *unda*, a wave.] in heraldry, wavy: applied to ordinaries or division lines: also spelled *undée*.

A FESSE UNDÉ

un·dead′li·ness (-ded′), *n.* immortality. [Obs.]

un·dead′ly, *a.* immortal. [Obs.]

un·deaf′ (-def′), *v.t.* to free from deafness. [Obs.]

un·deç′ȧ·gon, *n.* [L. *undecim*, eleven, and Gr. *gōnia*, angle.] a plane figure of eleven angles and eleven sides.

un′de·çāne, *n.* [L. *undecim*, eleven.] same as *hendecane*.

un·dē·cēive′, *v.t.*; undeceived, *pt.*, *pp.*; undeceiving, *ppr.* to free from deception, mistake, error, or illusion.

un·dē′cen·cy, *n.* indecency.

un·dē·cen′nȧ·ry, *a.* same as *undecennial*.

un·dē·cen′ni·ăl, *a.* [L. *undecim*, eleven, and *annus*, a year.] belonging or relating to a period of eleven years; occurring or observed every eleven years, or on every eleventh year; as, an *undecennial* festival.

un·dē′cent, *a.* indecent. [Archaic, exc. Brit. Dial.]

un·dē′cent·ly, *adv.* indecently. [Archaic, exc. Brit. Dial.]

un·dē·cīde′, *v.t.* to reverse a decision concerning. [Rare.]

un·dē·cīd′ed, *a.* 1. that is not decided or settled.

2. not having come to a decision; irresolute.

un·dec′i·mōle, *n.* [It.] in music, a group of eleven notes to be played in the time of eight.

un·dē·cī′sive, *a.* indecisive.

un·dē·çol′iç, *a.* designating an acid of the propiolic series containing eleven carbon atoms.

un′de·cyl, *n.* the univalent radical of undecylenic acid.

un·dec·y·len′iç, *a.* designating an acid obtained by distillation from castor oil. It is a colorless, crystalline compound.

un·dē·cyl′iç, *a.* same as *hendecatoic*.

un·dē·fat′i·gȧ·ble, *a.* indefatigable.

un·dē·fēa′ṣi·ble, *a.* indefeasible.

un·dē·fīne′, *v.t.* to make indefinite; to confound or confuse.

un·dē·fīned′, *a.* not defined; indefinite; vague.

un·dē′i·fȳ, *v.t.* to reduce from the state or rank of deity.

un·dē·mon′strȧ·tive, *a.* not demonstrative; giving little outward expression of the feelings; restrained; reserved.

un·dē·nī′ȧ·ble, *a.* 1. not deniable; not capable of being denied; indisputable; as, *undeniable* evidence.

2. decidedly and unmistakably good; excellent; as, a man of *undeniable* character.

un·dē·nī′ȧ·bly, *adv.* so as to be undeniable; indisputably; incontestably.

un·dē·pärt′ȧ·ble, *a.* not capable of being parted or separated; inseparable. [Obs.]

un′dẽr, *prep.* [ME. and AS.]

1. in, at, or to a position down from; below; lower than; as, he hid *under* the bed; also, below and to the other side of; as, we drove *under* the bridge.

2. covered, surmounted, enveloped, or concealed by; as, he's wearing a jacket *under* his raincoat.

3. beneath the surface of; as, twenty thousand leagues *under* the sea.

4. loaded, oppressed, overwhelmed, or burdened by; as, to fall *under* a load.

Fainting *under* the pleasing punishment. —Shak.

5. in a position of inferiority or subordination to; subject to the rule, government, direction, guidance, instruction, or influence of; as, he is *under* my care; I served *under* his father.

6. in a state of liability, obligation, or limitation with respect to; as, *under* the penalty of fine or imprisonment; *under* the vow of chastity.

7. inferior to in point of rank, dignity, social position, or the like.

It was too great an honor for any man *under* a duke. Addison.

8. inferior to or less than in point of numbers, amount, quantity, value, or the like; falling short of; in or to a less degree than; as, the steak weighed *under* a pound.

9. lower than the required or standard degree of; as, *under* age.

10. comprehended by or in; included in, as in the same category, list, division, section, class, etc.; as, we will treat them both *under* one head.

11. during or in the time of; as, *under* the Roman emperors.

12. bearing or being in the form or style of; with the appearance or show of; with the character, designation, pretense, or cover of.

He does it *under* name of perfect love. —Shak.

13. with the sanction, authorization, permission, or protection of; attested by; as, *under* her signature.

14. being the subject of; subject to; as, the matter is now *under* discussion.

15. subjected to; undergoing; as, *under* an anesthetic, *under* repair.

16. having regard for; because of; as, *under* the circumstances.

17. planted with; sowed with; as, an acre *under* corn.

to be under a cloud; see under *cloud*.

under arms; see under *arms*.

under bare poles; see under *bare*.

under canvas; see under *canvas*.

under fire; see under *fire*.

under foot; see under *foot*.

under one's breath; see under *breath*.

under sentence; having been sentenced, as a criminal.

under the lee; see under *lee*.

un′dẽr, *adv.* 1. in or to a position below something; beneath; underneath.

2. in or to a condition that is inferior or subordinate.

3. so as to be covered, surmounted, enveloped, or concealed.

4. less than the required or assigned amount, etc.

un′dẽr, *a.* 1. located or moving below something else or on the lower surface.

2. lower in authority, position, power, etc.; subordinate.

3. held in control or restraint: used predicatively.

4. lower in amount, degree, etc.: used predicatively.

un′dẽr-, [ME. *under-*, *onder-*; AS. *under-*.] a prefix meaning: (a) *in, on, to,* or *from a lower place* or *side*; *beneath* or *below*, as in *under*shirt; (b) *in an inferior* or *subordinate position* or *rank*, as in *under*graduate; (c) *to a degree, extent,* or *amount that is below standard* or *inadequate*, as in *under*develop.

un·dẽr·ȧ·chiēve′, *v.i.*; underachieved, *pt.*, *pp.*; underachieving, *ppr.* to fail to do as well in school studies as might be expected from scores made on intelligence tests.

un·dẽr·ȧ·chiēv′ẽr, *n.* one who underachieves.

un·dẽr·açt′, *v.t.* and *v.i.* to act or perform (a theatrical role) with too great restraint and subtlety; to underplay.

un′dẽr·aç·tion, *n.* 1. subordinate action.

2. defective or insufficient action.

un′dẽr·aç·tŏr, *n.* a subordinate actor.

un·dẽr·āġe′, *a.* 1. not having reached adult age; immature.

2. below the usual or required age.

un′dẽr·ärm, *a.* 1. under the arm; in the armpit.

2. in cricket, etc., performed with the hand below the level of the shoulder, as a bowl, or characterized by such a method of delivery; underhand.

un·dẽr·ärm′, *adv.* with an underarm delivery or motion.

un′dẽr·back, *n.* in a brewery, a cistern or tank beneath the mash vat to receive the wort.

un·dẽr·beăr′, *v.t.* 1. to support; to endure. [Rare.]

2. to line; to face; as, cloth of gold *underborne* with blue tinsel. [Rare.]

un′dẽr·beăr·ẽr, *n.* a pallbearer. [Dial.]

un·dẽr·bid′, *v.t.*; underbid, *pt.*, *pp.*; underbidding, *ppr.* to bid or offer less than (another), as at auctions; to offer to do, sell, or contract at a lower price than (another), as when a contract or service is offered to the lowest bidder.

un·dẽr·bid′dẽr, *n.* one who underbids.

un·dẽr·bill′, *v.t.* to bill, as importations or freight, at less than actual weight or measurement.

un·dẽr·bīnd′, *v.t.* to bind underneath. [Obs.]

un·dẽr·bit′ten, *a.* in etching, insufficiently corroded or affected by the application of acid to print with the desired effect: said of copper plates or lines.

un·dẽr·bred′, *a.* 1. having or showing inferior breeding or manners; ill-bred.

2. not of pure breed; as, an *underbred* horse.

un′dẽr·brush, *n.* shrubs, small trees, etc. in a wood or forest, growing under large trees; undergrowth; brush.

un′dẽr·brush, *v.t.* and *v.i.* to clear away underbrush. [Colloq.]

un′dẽr·build·ẽr (-bild-), *n.* a subordinate builder.

un′dẽr·build·ing, *n.* same as *substructure*.

un·dẽr·bŭrn′, *v.t.* 1. to burn insufficiently.

2. to burn up. [Obs.]

un·dẽr·buȳ′ (-bī′), *v.t.*; underbought, *pt.*, *pp.*; underbuying, *ppr.* 1. to buy at less than the real value or asking price.

2. to buy at a lower price than (another).

un′dẽr·çar·riaġe (-rij), *n.* 1. a supporting frame or structure, as of an automobile.

2. the landing gear of an airplane.

un′dẽr·çȧst, *n.* in coal mining, an air passage carried under a mine road by means of a box or channel.

un·dẽr·chām′bẽr·lain (-lin), *n.* a deputy chamberlain of the exchequer.

un·dẽr·chȧnt′ẽr, *n.* same as *subchanter*.

un′dẽr·chäps (-chops), *n.pl.* the lower jaw.

un·dẽr·chärġe′, *v.t.* 1. to charge less than is usual or correct (for), as goods or services.

2. to load with an insufficient charge, as a gun.

undercharged mine; in military operations, a mine the crater of which is not as wide at the top as it is deep.

un′dẽr·chärġe, *n.* 1. a charge that is insufficient.

2. the act of undercharging.

un′dẽr·çlȧss, *n.* the social and economic class with incomes below subsistence level, including especially the underprivileged.

un·dẽr·çlȧss′măn, *n.*; *pl.* **un·dẽr·çlȧss′men,** a freshman or sophomore.

un′dẽr·çlāy, *n.* a stratum of clay lying beneath beds of coal, often containing stigmaria or roots of trees.

un′dẽr·çliff, *n.* a strip of broken ground, or subordinate cliff, on a shore, formed by material fallen from a cliff above.

un·dẽr·çlōthed′, *a.* not sufficiently clothed.

un′dẽr·çlōtheṣ (-klōz *or* -klōthz), *n.pl.* clothes worn under a suit, dress, etc. or next to the skin.

un′dẽr·çlōth·ing, *n.* same as *underclothes*.

un′dẽr·çōat, *n.* 1. a coat worn beneath another.

2. the under layer of short hair in an animal's coat.

3. a coating of tarlike material applied to the exposed undersurface of an automobile to prevent rust, etc.

un′dẽr·çōat, *v.t.* to apply an undercoat (sense 3) to.

un″dẽr·çŏn·sump′tion, *n.* consumption of less than is normal or than is produced.

un·dẽr·çŏv′ẽr, *a.* acting or carried out in secret.

un′dẽr·çrȧft, *n.* a sly or cunning trick. [Obs.]

un·dẽr·çrest′, *v.t.* to support as a crest. [Obs.]

un′dẽr·çroft, *n.* [*under*, and obs. *croft*, a vault.] an underground room or vault, especially in a church; also, a vault or secret walk underground.

un′dẽr·çur·rent, *n.* 1. a current flowing below the surface, or contrary to that on the surface.

2. a hidden or underlying tendency, influence, opinion, etc., usually one at variance with another that is more obvious.

un′dẽr·çur·rent, *a.* running below the surface; hidden.

un′dẽr·çut, *n.* 1. a cut made below or underneath another so as to leave an overhang or concave profile.

2. a part cut in this way.

3. a notch cut in a tree below the level of the major cut and on the side to which the tree is to fall.

4. a tenderloin or fillet of beef. [Chiefly Brit.]

5. in sports, (a) backspin, as in golf; (b) a cut, slice, or chop made with an underhand motion, as in tennis.

un′dẽr·çut, *a.* that is undercut.

un·dẽr·çut′, *v.t.*; undercut, *pt., pp.*; undercutting, *ppr.* 1. to make a cut below or under.
2. to make an undercut in.
3. to undersell or work for lower wages than.
4. in sports, (a) to impart backspin to (a ball), as in golf; (b) to cut, slice, or chop (a ball) with an underhand motion, as in tennis.

un·dẽr·çut′, *v.i.* to undercut something or someone (in various senses).

un′dẽr·dēal·ing, *n.* artifice; unfair practice; tricky dealing. [Obs.]

un″dẽr·dē·vel′ŏp, *v.t.* and *v.i.* to develop to a point below what is usual or needed.

un·dẽr·ditch′, *v.t.* to form a deep ditch or trench to drain the surface of; as, to *underditch* a farm.

un·dẽr·dö′, *v.i.*; underdid, *pt.*; underdone, *pp.*; underdoing, *ppr.* 1. to act below one's abilities.
2. to do less than is requisite.

un·dẽr·dö′, *v.t.* to do less than is usual, advisable, needed, or called for; especially, to cook insufficiently; as, the steak is *underdone.*

un·dẽr·dö′ẽr, *n.* one who does less than is required or expedient; a shirk.

un′dẽr·dog, *n.* 1. the losing or defeated dog in a dog fight.
2. a person or group that is losing, as in a contest or struggle; one that is handicapped or underprivileged, as in the struggle of life.

un′dẽr·dŏne′, *a.* [pp. of *underdo.*] not thoroughly cooked: said of food, especially beef.

un′dẽr·dōse, *n.* a dose smaller than is prescribed, necessary, or requisite.

un·dẽr·dōse′, *v.t.* and *v.i.* to give or take small or insufficient doses.

un′dẽr·drāin, *n.* a drain or trench below the surface, so formed as to admit water percolating through the soil above.

un·dẽr·drāin′, *v.t.* to drain by cutting an underdrain or underdrains in.

un·dẽr·dress′, *v.i.* to dress more plainly or informally than is indicated by the occasion.

un·dẽr·dressed′ (-drest′), *a.* not dressed elaborately enough for the occasion.

un·dẽr·driv′en, *a.* driven from beneath: said of certain machines driven by power transmitted from beneath.

un·dẽr·es′ti·māte, *v.t.* and *v.i.* to put too low an estimation or valuation on; to estimate below the actual value, amount, etc.

un·dẽr·es′ti·māte, *n.* an estimate or valuing that is too low.

un·dẽr·es·ti·mā′tion, *n.* an underestimating or underestimate.

un″dẽr·ex·pōṣe′, *v.t.* to expose (a photographic plate or film, etc.) for too short a time.

un″dẽr·ex·pō′ṣūre (-zhũr), *n.* 1. the act of underexposing.
2. an underexposed film or plate.

un′dẽr·faç·tion, *n.* a subordinate faction or party.

un′dẽr·faç·ul·ty, *n.* a subordinate faculty.

un·dẽr·fang′, *v.t.* 1. to undertake; also, to accept. [Obs.]
2. to circumvent; to ensnare. [Obs.]

un′dẽr·färm·ẽr, *n.* a subordinate farmer.

un·dẽr·feed′, *v.t.* underfed, *pt., pp.*; underfeeding, *ppr.* 1. to feed less than is needed; to supply with too little food.
2. to stoke (a fire) from below.

un′dẽr·fel·lōw, *n.* a mean, sorry wretch; an underling. [Obs.]

un′dẽr·fill·ing, *n.* the lower part of a building.

un·dẽr·fīred′, *a.* in ceramics, insufficiently baked; baked for too short a time or at too low a temperature.

un′dẽr·flōw, *n.* an undercurrent.

un·dẽr·fong′, *v.t.* to underfang. [Obs.]

un·dẽr·foot′, *adv.* 1. under the foot or feet; on the ground or floor at one's feet.
2. in the way.

un·dẽr·foot′, *a.* 1. under the foot or feet; on the ground or floor at one's feet.
2. in the way.
3. low; base; abject.

un·dẽr·foot′, *v.t.* to underpin.

un′dẽr·fũr, *n.* the softer, finer fur growing under the outer coat of some animals, as beavers and seals.

un·dẽr·fũr′nish, *v.t.* to supply with less than enough; to furnish scantily or insufficiently.

un·dẽr·fur′rōw, *v.t.* in agriculture, to cover, as seed, by plowing it in after it is sown

un′dẽr·gär·ment, *n.* a garment worn under another or others, especially next to the skin.

un·dẽr·gīrd′, *v.t.* to gird, strengthen, or brace from the bottom side, as a ship.

un′dẽr·glāze, *a.* in ceramics, designating a pigment, design, etc. placed on the surface of pottery before glazing; as, an *underglaze* color.
underglaze painting; in ceramics, painting on the surface before the glazing is applied.

un·dẽr·gō′, *v.t.*; underwent, *pt.*; undergone, *pp.*; undergoing, *ppr.* 1. to endure; to experience; to be subjected to; as, a nation may *undergo* many revolutions.
2. to be the bearer of; to possess. [Obs.]

un′dẽr·god, *n.* in polytheism, an inferior or subordinate deity.

un′dẽr·gown, *n.* a gown to be worn under another garment.

un′dẽr·grāde, *a.* having the truss below the track or roadway.

un·dẽr·grad′ū·āte, *n.* a student at a university or college who has not yet received the first, or bachelor's, degree.

un·dẽr·grad′ū·āte, *a.* 1. of, consisting of, or characteristic of undergraduates.
2. having the status of an undergraduate.

un·dẽr·grad′ū·āte·ship″, *n.* the state of being an undergraduate.

un·dẽr·grōan′, *v.t.* to groan under. [Obs.]

un′dẽr·ground (*or* un′dẽr-ground′), *a.* 1. occurring, working, placed, used, etc. beneath the surface of the earth.
2. secret; hidden; undercover.

un′dẽr·ground (*or* un′dẽr-ground′), *adv.* 1. beneath the surface of the earth.
2. in or into secrecy or hiding; so as to be undercover; surreptitiously.

un′dẽr·ground, *n.* 1. the entire region beneath the surface of the earth.
2. an underground space or passage.
3. a secret movement organized in a country to oppose or overthrow the government in power or enemy forces of occupation; as, the *underground* of France in World War II.
4. a subway: short for *underground railway.* [Brit.]

un′dẽr·ground, *v.t.* to arrange underground, as a system of telegraphy or telephony. [Colloq.]

un′dẽr·ground rāil′rōad, see under *railroad.*

un′dẽr·ground rāil′wāy, a railroad running through tunnels under the ground; especially, a subway: also, *underground railroad.*

un′dẽr·grōve, *n.* a collection of small trees or shrubs growing under taller ones.

un·dẽr·grōw′, *v.i.* to be stunted in growth; to fail to reach the usual size in growth. [Rare.]

un·dẽr·grōwn′, *a.* not grown to full or normal size or development; stunted in growth.

un′dẽr·grōwth, *n.* 1. small trees, shrubs, etc. that grow beneath large trees in woods or forests; underbrush.
2. an undercoat (sense 2).
3. the state of being undergrown.

un′dẽr·hand, *adv.* 1. with an underhand motion.
2. slyly; secretly; unfairly.

un′dẽr·hand, *a.* 1. secret; sly; deceitful; not open or straightforward; as, he obtained the place by *underhand* practices.
2. done with the hand below the level of the elbow or shoulder.

un′dẽr·hand′ed, *a.* 1. underhand; clandestine; sly.
2. short of hands, or workers, players, etc.; shorthanded.

un·dẽr·hand′ed·ly, *adv.* secretly; clandestinely; in an underhand way.

un′dẽr·head (-hed), *n.* a dunderhead; a dolt. [Obs.]

un·dẽr·hew′, *v.t.* 1. to hew (a piece of timber which should be square) in such a manner that it appears to contain a greater number of cubic feet than it really does.
2. to hew less than is required or usual.

un·dẽr·hon′est (-on′), *a.* not altogether honest. [Rare.]

un·dẽr·hung′, *a.* 1. projecting beyond the upper jaw: said of the lower jaw.
2. having such a lower jaw.
3. underslung.
4. in carpentry, rolling on a track below instead of above: said of some sliding doors.

un′dẽr·jaw, *n.* the lower jaw.

un·dẽr·keep′, *v.t.* to suppress. [Obs.]

un′dẽr·kīnd, *n.* a lower kind.

un′dẽr·king, *n.* a subordinate king.

un′dẽr·king″dŏm, *n.* a subordinate kingdom.

un·dẽr·lā′bŏr·ẽr, *n.* a subordinate workman.

un·dẽr·lāid′, *a.* 1. laid or placed underneath.
2. raised or supported by something lying underneath; having an underlay.

un·dẽr·lap′, *v.t.*; underlapped, *pt., pp.*; underlapping, *ppr.* to lie or extend partly under.

un′dẽr·lāy, *n.* 1. something laid underneath, especially a thickness of paper, etc. laid under type to raise the level of the face.
2. in mining, an inclination or dip of a vein from the vertical.

un·dẽr·lāy′, *v.t.*; underlaid, *pt., pp.*; underlaying, *ppr.* [ME. *underlein*; AS. *underlecgan*; *under*, and *lecgan*, to lay.]
1. to cover or extend over the bottom of.
2. to lay (something) under something else, especially as a support, wedge, etc.
3. to raise or support with something laid underneath; to provide with an underlay.
4. to furnish (a shoe) with a tap. [Obs.]

un·dẽr·lāy′, *v.i.* in mining, to incline from the vertical: said of a vein.

un·dẽr·lāy′, *v.* past tense of *underlie.*

un·dẽr·lāy′ẽr, *n.* one who or that which underlays.

un′dẽr·lēaf, *n.* a kind of apple used for cider.

un′dẽr·lēase, *n.* a sublease.

un·dẽr·let′, *v.t.* 1. to let at a price below the real value.
2. to let or lease to a subtenant; to sublet.

un·dẽr·let′tẽr, *n.* a tenant who sublets to another.

un·dẽr·līe′, *v.t.*; underlay, *pt.*, underlain, *pp.*; underlying, *ppr.* [ME. *underlien, underliggan*; AS. *underlicgan*; under, and *licgan*, to lie.]
1. to lie or be placed under; to be beneath.
2. to support; to form the basis or foundation of.
3. to be subordinate to. [Obs.]
4. in finance, to be prior to (another): said of a right, security, etc.; as, this claim *underlies* that.

un·dẽr·līe′, *v.i.* to lie beneath. [Obs.]

un′dẽr·līe, *n.* in mining, an underlay.

un′dẽr·līne′, *v.t.*; underlined, *pt., pp.*; underlining, *ppr.* 1. to mark with a line below, as words; to underscore.
2. to stress or emphasize.
3. to announce (a performance, a book, etc.) by a notice added to a bill of a play or other announcement.

un′dẽr·līne, *n.* 1. a line underneath, as an underscore.
2. the announcement of a following performance, etc. by a notice added to a bill or other announcement.

un′dẽr·lin·en, *n.* linen undergarments; sometimes, cotton or silk undergarments as distinguished from those knitted or made of flannel.

un′dẽr·ling, *n.* [ME.; AS.] a person who has little rank or authority in comparison with another whom he serves; a subordinate: usually contemptuous or disparaging.

un′dẽr·lip, *n.* the lower lip.

un′dẽr·lock, *n.* a lock of wool hanging from the belly of a sheep.

un′dẽr·look·ẽr, *n.* same as *underviewer.*

un′dẽr·ly, *a.* inferior; low. [Rare.]

un′dẽr·ly̆·ing, *a.* 1. lying under; placed beneath.
2. fundamental; basic.
3. obscure; not clearly evident.
4. in finance, prior, as a claim.

un·dẽr·man′, *v.t.* to man insufficiently; to understaff.

un·dẽr·mȧst′ed, *a.* denoting ships which have masts of less than the usual dimensions.

un·dẽr·mȧs′tẽr, *n.* a master subordinate to the principal master.

un′dẽr·match, *n.* one unequal or inferior to someone else. [Obs.]

un′dẽr·mēal, *n.* 1. the meal or nap taken at undern. [Obs.]
2. the division or portion of the day which included undern; originally, the morning, but later the afternoon. [Obs.]

un′dẽr·mīne′, *v.t.*; undermined, *pt., pp.*; undermining, *ppr.* 1. to dig beneath; to excavate ground from under, so as to form a tunnel or mine.
2. to wear away at the base or foundation.
3. to injure, weaken, or impair, especially by subtle or stealthy means.
He should be warned who are like to *undermine* him. —Locke.

un′dẽr·mīn′ẽr, *n.* one who undermines.
un·dẽr·min′is·tẽr, *v.t.* to minister to in an inferior capacity. [Obs.]
un′dẽr·min″is·try, *n.* a subordinate ministry.
un′dẽr·mōst, *a.* and *adv.* lowest in place, state, condition, rank, etc.
un′dẽrn, *n.* [AS. *undern,* from *under,* in the sense of meanwhile; allied to L. *inter,* between.] a time of day; originally 9:00 A.M.; later, some other hour of the forenoon; also, midday or afternoon. [Obs. or Brit. Dial.]
un·dẽr·nēath′, *adv.* 1. beneath; below; in a lower place.
2. on the underside; at a lower level.
un·dẽr·nēath′, *prep.* 1. under; beneath; below.
2. under the form, guise, or authority of.
un·dẽr·nēath′, *a.* under; lower.
un·dẽr·nēath′, *n.* the under part.
un·dẽr·nice′ness, *n.* insufficient niceness.
un′dẽr·nōte, *n.* an undertone.
un·dẽr·nour′ish (-nũr′), *v.t.* to give insufficient nourishment to; to provide with less than the least amount of food needed for health and growth.
un′dẽr·of″fi·cẽr, *n.* a subordinate officer.
un′dẽr·pärt, *n.* a subordinate part.
un′dẽr·pȧss, *n.* a passage, road, etc. passing under something; especially, a passageway for automobiles, pedestrians, etc. that runs under a railway or highway, from one side to the other.
un·dẽr·pāy′, *v.t.*; underpaid, *pt., pp.*; underpaying, *ppr.* to give inadequate pay to; as, to *underpay* workers.
un′dẽr·pēo·pled (-pld), *a.* not fully peopled.
un·dẽr·pin′, *v.t.*; underpinned, *pt., pp.*; underpinning, *ppr.* 1. to lay (stones or other foundation) under the sills of a building on which it is to rest.
2. to support by some solid foundation; to place something underneath for support, as props.
3. to support; to corroborate.
un′dẽr·pin·ning, *n.* 1. supports, temporary or permanent, introduced beneath a wall already constructed; undersetting.
2. a support.
3. a system of lining shafts with brickwork.
4. [*pl.*] the legs. [Colloq.]
un·dẽr·plāy′, *v.t.* and *v.i.* 1. to play, or act, with less than the usual emphasis, in an intentionally restrained manner; as, he likes to *underplay* Hamlet's scene with Gertrude.
2. to act (a role, etc.) with insufficient emphasis, in a bare or casual manner.
3. to play (one's hand at cards, etc.) without fully realizing, or taking advantage of, the potentialities.
un′dẽr·plāy, *n.* the act of underplaying.
un′dẽr·plot, *n.* 1. a secondary or subordinate plot in a play, novel, etc.
2. a clandestine scheme; a trick.
un·dẽr·poise′, *v.t.* to undervalue. [Obs.]
un″dẽr·pŏs·sess′ẽr, *n.* one having possession subservient to the superior right of another.
un·dẽr·prāise′, *v.t.* to praise inadequately.
un′dẽr·priv′i·leged, *a.* deprived of fundamental social rights, or privileges, and security through poverty, discrimination, etc.
the underprivileged; those who are underprivileged.
un·dẽr·prīze′, *v.t.* to value at less than the worth; to undervalue.
un″dẽr·prō·duc′tion, *n.* production not meeting economic demand, or production less than is usual or needed.
un′dẽr·proof′, *a.* containing less alcohol than proof spirit does.
un·dẽr·prop′, *v.t.*; underpropped, *pt., pp.*; underpropping, *ppr.* to prop underneath; to support; to uphold.
un″dẽr·prō·pōr′tioned, *a.* not in equal or adequate proportions.
un·dẽr·prop′pẽr, *n.* one who or that which underprops.
un·dẽr·pull′, *v.i.* to effect something without exposing the cause. [Obs.]
un·dẽr·pull′ẽr, *n.* one who underpulls. [Obs.]
un·dẽr·put′, *v.t.* to place under. [Obs.]
un·dẽr·quōte′, *v.t.* 1. to offer at a lower price than another price or than the market price, as goods or stocks.
2. to quote a lower price than (another or others).
un·dẽr·rāte′, *v.t.* to rate too low; to rate below the value; to undervalue; to underestimate.
un′dẽr·rāte, *n.* a price less than the worth; as, to sell a thing at an *underrate.*
un·dẽr·reck′ŏn, *v.t.* to underrate.
un·dẽr·run′, *v.t.*; underran, *pt.,* underrun, *pp.*; underrunning, *ppr.* to run, go, or pass under.
to underrun a tackle; in nautical usage, to separate the parts of a tackle and put them in order.
un′dẽr·run, *n.* something running or passing underneath, as a stream.
un·dẽr·sāil′, *v.i.* to sail near land. [Obs.]
un·dẽr·sāy′, *v.t.* to say by way of derogation or contradiction. [Obs.]
un′dẽr·sçōre′, *v.t.*; underscored, *pt., pp.*; underscoring, *ppr.* to underline.
un′dẽr·sçōre′, *n.* a line drawn beneath a printed or written word, passage, etc., as for emphasis.
un′dẽr·sēa′, *a.* and *adv.* beneath the surface of the sea.
un·dẽr·sēaṣ′, *adv.* same as *undersea.*
un·dẽr·seç′rē·tar·y, *n.*; *pl.* **un·dẽr·seç′rē·tãr·ieṣ,** an assistant secretary.
un·dẽr·sell′, *v.t.*; undersold, *pt., pp.*; underselling, *ppr.* 1. to sell at a lower price than.
2. to sell at a price lower than the actual value.
un′dẽr·sẽrv·ănt, *n.* a servant under the authority of another servant; a subordinate servant.
un·dẽr·set′, *v.t.* to prop; to support.
un′dẽr·set, *n.* an ocean undercurrent.
un′dẽr·set·tẽr, *n.* a prop; a pedestal; a support.
un′dẽr·set·ting, *n.* the lower part; a pedestal; an underpinning.
un·dẽr·shāp′en, *a.* dwarfish.
un′dẽr·sher·iff, *n.* a sheriff's deputy.
un′dẽr·sher·iff·ry, *n.* the office of an undersheriff.
un′dẽr·shīrt, *n.* a piece of underclothing worn under an outer shirt, next to the skin.
un·dẽr·shoot′, *v.t.* to shoot short of.
un′dẽr·shot, *a.* 1. moved or turned by water passing beneath: said of a water wheel.

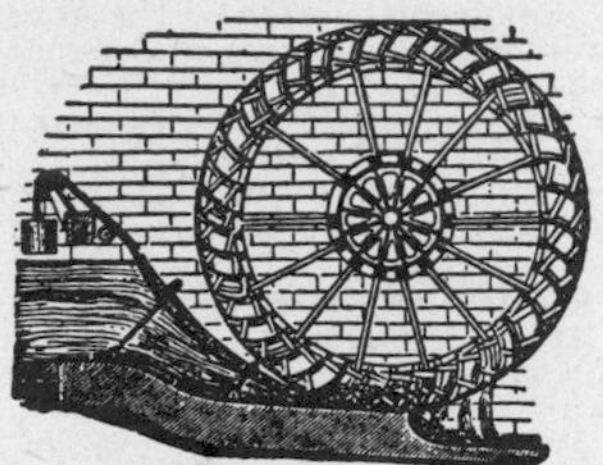

UNDERSHOT WATER WHEEL

2. having the lower jaw protruding, as a dog.
3. having the lower front teeth protruding beyond the upper front teeth when the mouth is closed.
undershot wheel; a water wheel moved by water passing beneath.
un′dẽr·shrīēve, *n.* an undersheriff. [Obs.]
un′dẽr·shrub, *n.* any low-growing, woody, bushy plant.
un′dẽr·shut, *a.* closed from beneath; having a lid, cover, or slide operated from below, as a valve.
un′dẽr·sīde, *n.* the side or surface that is underneath.
un′dẽr·sīgn′ (-sīn′), *v.t.* to sign one's name at the foot or end of, as a letter, document, etc.
un′dẽr·sīgned′, *a.* 1. signed at the end.
2. whose name is signed at the end.
the undersigned; the person or persons signing at the end.
un′dẽr·sīze′, *a.* same as *undersized.*
un′dẽr·sīzed′, *a.* smaller in size than is usual, average, or proper.
un′dẽr·skiṅk·ẽr, *n.* a helping tapster. [Obs.]
un′dẽr·skīrt, *n.* a skirt worn under another.
un′dẽr·sleeve, *n.* a sleeve worn under another.
un′dẽr·slung′, *a.* 1. designating an automobile frame attached to the underside of the axles.
2. having an underslung frame.
un′dẽr·soil, *n.* soil beneath the surface; subsoil.
un′dẽr·sọng, *n.* 1. a song or refrain sung as accompaniment to another song.
2. an underlying meaning.
un′dẽr·spärred′, *a.* not sufficiently sparred, as a ship.
un·dẽr·spend′, *v.t.* to spend less than.
un′dẽr·sphēre, *n.* a sphere of less extent than another.
un·dẽr·stȧffed′ (-stȧft′), *a.* having too small a staff; having insufficient personnel.
un·dẽr·stand′, *v.t.*; understood, *pt., pp.*; understanding, *ppr.* [ME. *understanden*; AS. *understandan*; lit., to stand under or among, hence, to comprehend.]
1. to apprehend or comprehend; to know or grasp the meaning, import, intention, or motive of; to perceive or discern the meaning of; as, to *understand* a problem, an argument, an oracle, a secret sign, indistinct speech, etc.
2. to be informed or receive notice of; to learn; as, I *understand* the bill has passed the House.
3. to accept or hold as signifying; to attach or give as a meaning or explanation to; to suppose to mean; to interpret.
4. to take as meant or implied; to infer; to assume.

War,
Open or *understood,* must be resolved.
—Milton.

5. to supply or leave to be supplied mentally (an idea, word, answer, etc.); as, in the phrase, "The good are happy," the word *persons* is *understood.*
6. to take as a fact; to accept as a condition.
7. to know thoroughly; to grasp or perceive clearly and fully the nature, character, functioning, etc. of.
8. to stand under. [Obs.]
My legs do better *understand* me, sir, than I understand what you mean. —Shak.
to give one to understand; to let one know in such a way as to remove all doubt.
Syn.—apprehend, comprehend, know, perceive, discern, conceive, learn, recognize, interpret, imply.
un·dẽr·stand′, *v.i.* 1. to have understanding, comprehension, or discernment, either in general or with reference to some specific statement, situation, etc.
2. to be informed; to believe; to assume (usually parenthetical); as, he is, I *understand,* no longer here.
un·dẽr·stand′ȧ·ble, *a.* that can be understood.
un·dẽr·stand′ȧ·bly, *adv.* so as to be understandable; in an understandable manner.
un·dẽr·stand′ẽr, *n.* one who understands. [Rare.]
un·dẽr·stand′ing, *a.* that understands; having or characterized by comprehension, discernment, sympathy, etc.
un·dẽr·stand′ing, *n.* 1. the mental act, quality, or state of one who understands; comprehension; knowledge; discernment.
There is a spirit in man, and the inspiration of the Almighty giveth him *understanding.*
—Job xxxii. 8.
2. the power or ability to think and learn; intelligence; judgment; sense.
3. a specific interpretation; as, this is my *understanding* of the matter.
4. mutual agreement, especially one that settles differences or is informal and not made public.
5. mutual comprehension, as of ideas, intentions, etc.
Syn.—knowledge, comprehension, apprehension, conception, sense, intellect, faculty, intelligence, ken, reason.
un·dẽr·stand′ing·ly, *adv.* in an understanding manner; intelligently; with full knowledge or comprehension; as, to vote upon a question *understandingly*; to act or judge *understandingly.*
un·dẽr·stāte′, *v.t.* and *v.i.*; understated, *pt., pp.*; understating, *ppr.* to make a weaker statement (of) than is warranted by truth, accuracy, or importance; to state (something) too weakly or moderately.
un′dẽr·stāte·ment, *n.* 1. the act of understating.
2. that which is understated; a statement that is too weak or moderate.
un′dẽr·stock, *n.* a plant or part of a plant upon which a graft is made.
un·dẽr·stock′, *v.t.* to supply insufficiently with stock, or goods.
un·dẽr·stood′, *v.* past tense and past participle of *understand.*
un·dẽr·stood′, *a.* 1. agreed upon.
2. implied but not expressed; assumed.

un′dẽr·strap″pẽr, *n.* [from *under-*, and *strap*, and *-er.*] a person having low rank or position; a subordinate; an underling.
un′dẽr·strap·ping, *a.* subservient; subordinate.
un′dẽr·strā·tum, *n.*; *pl.* **un′dẽr·strā·tȧ, un′dẽr·strā·tums,** a substratum.
un·dẽr·strōke′, *v.t.* to underline.
un′dẽr·stud·y, *n.*; *pl.* **un′dẽr·stud·ies,** *n.* 1. an actor who studies the part of another actor so that he can serve as a substitute when necessary.
2. any person who learns the duties of another so that he can serve as a substitute.
un′dẽr·stud·y, *v.t.* and *v.i.*; understudied, *pt., pp.*; understudying, *ppr.* 1. to act as an understudy (to).
2. to learn (a part) as an understudy.
un′dẽr·sũr·fȧce, *n.* the underside.
un·dẽr·tāk′ȧ·ble, *a.* that may be undertaken; feasible.
un·dẽr·tāke′, *v.t.*; undertook, *pt.*, undertaken, *pp.*; undertaking, *ppr.* 1. to engage in; to enter upon; to take in hand; to begin to perform; as, when I *undertook* this work, I had a very inadequate knowledge of the extent of my labors.
2. to give a promise or pledge that; to contract; as, he *undertook* to be our guide.
3. to promise; to guarantee.
4. to make oneself responsible for; to take over as a charge.
5. to respond to the challenge of; to take on in or as in combat. [Obs.]
6. to assume, as a character. [Obs.]
un·dẽr·tāke′, *v.i.* 1. to take on responsibility, pledge oneself, guarantee, or be surety (*for*). [Archaic.]
2. to perform the duties of an undertaker (sense 3). [Colloq.]
un·dẽr·tāk′ẽr (*for 3,* un′dẽr-tāk-ẽr), *n.* 1. one who undertakes something.
2. one who stipulates or covenants to perform any work for another. [Archaic.]
3. one whose business is preparing the dead for burial and managing funerals.
un·dẽr·tāk′ing, *n.* (*for 2,* un′dẽr-tāk-ing), 1. any business, work, project, etc. undertaken; an enterprise; a charge; a task.
2. the business of an undertaker (sense 3).
3. the act of one who undertakes some task, responsibility, etc.
4. a promise; a guarantee.
un′dẽr·ten″ănt, *n.* a subtenant.
un′dẽr·thing, *n.* 1. anything of little value; anything inferior. [Obs.]
2. [*pl.*] underclothes.
un′dẽr·tīme, *n.* undern. [Obs.]
un′dẽr·tint, *n.* a faint or subdued tint.
un′dẽr·tōne, *n.* 1. a low tone of sound or voice.
2. something said in an undertone.
3. a faint or subdued color, especially one seen through other colors, as in some glazes.
4. anything that exists in or as in the background; underlying quality, factor, element, etc.; as, an *undertone* of horror.
un·dẽr·took′, *v.* past tense of *undertake*.
un′dẽr·tōw, *n.* a current of water below, flowing in a different direction from that on the surface; specifically, the undercurrent flowing seaward beneath breaking surf.
un·dẽr·treaṣ′ũr·ẽr (-trezh′), *n.* a subordinate treasurer.
un·dẽr·trump′, *v.t.* 1. to trump with a trump of lower denomination than has previously been played.
2. to play a lower trump than (one's partner).
un′dẽr·val·ū·ā″tion, *n.* 1. the act of valuing below the real worth.
2. an estimate or valuation that is too low.
un·dẽr·val′ūe, *v.t.*; undervalued, *pt., pp.*; undervaluing, *ppr.* 1. to value, rate, or estimate below the real worth.
2. to esteem lightly; to treat as of little worth.
3. to lower the value of.
4. to depise; to hold in mean estimation. [Obs.]
un′dẽr·val″ūe, *n.* low rate or price; a price less than the real worth.
un·dẽr·val′ū·ẽr, *n.* one who undervalues.
un′dẽr·vest, *n.* an undershirt. [Brit.]
un′dẽr·view″ẽr (-vū″), *n.* in mining, a subordinate manager.
un′dẽr·wāist, *n.* a waist worn under another.
un′dẽr·wą·tẽr, *a.* 1. being, placed, done, etc. beneath the surface of the water.
2. used or for use under water.
3. below the water line of a ship.
un′dẽr·weär, *n.* clothing worn next to the skin under the outer garments; underclothes.
un·dẽr·ween′, *v.t.* to undervalue. [Obs.]
un′dẽr·weight (-wāt), *a.* weighing too little; deficient in weight.
un′dẽr·weight, *n.* weight below what is normal, required, etc.
un·dẽr·went′, *v.* past tense of *undergo*.
un′dẽr·wing, *n.* 1. a wing growing under and to the rear of another, as in some moths.
2. any noctuid moth of the genus *Catocala*, as *Catocala brephos*, the hind wings of which are of a conspicuous orange color.
un·dẽr·wit′ted, *a.* mentally deficient; weak-minded; silly.
un′dẽr·wood, *n.* small trees, shrubs, etc. that grow beneath large trees in woods or forests; undergrowth; underbrush.
un′dẽr·wŏrk, *n.* subordinate work.
un·dẽr·wŏrk′, *v.t.* 1. to destroy by clandestine measures; to undermine. [Obs.]
2. to work or labor upon (anything) less than is sufficient or proper.
3. to work at a lower price than (others in the like employment); as, one mason may *underwork* another.
un·dẽr·wŏrk′, *v.i.* 1. to work clandestinely. [Obs.]
2. to do less than the proper amount of work.
3. to work for a lower price than the established rate.
un′dẽr·wŏrk″ẽr, *n.* 1. one who underworks.
2. a subordinate workman.
un′dẽr·wŏrk″măn, *n.*; *pl.* **un′dẽr·wŏrk″men,** a subordinate workman.
un′dẽr·wŏrld, *n.* 1. the earth.
2. the opposite side of the globe; the antipodes.

Fresh as the first beam glittering on a sail,
That brings our friends up from the *underworld.* —Tennyson.

3. the world of the dead; hades.
4. the criminal members of society; people living by vice or crime; as, a woman of the *underworld*.
un·dẽr·wrīte′ (-rīt′), *v.t.*; underwrote, *pt.*; underwritten, *pp.*; underwriting, *ppr.* [ME. *underwriten*; used as transl. of L. *subscribere*, to subscribe.]
1. to write under something, especially under something written; to subscribe.
2. to sign one's name to.
3. to agree to pay or give (a specified sum of money) by signing one's name to a document, etc.
4. to agree to buy (an issue of stocks, bonds, etc.) on a given date and at a fixed price, or to guarantee the purchase of (stocks or bonds to be made available to the public for subscription).
5. to subscribe or agree to, especially by signature.
6. to agree to pay for or finance (an undertaking, etc.).
7. in insurance, (a) to write one's signature at the end of (an insurance policy), thus assuming liability in the event of specified loss or damage; (b) to insure; (c) to assume liability to the amount of (a specified sum).
8. to submit to. [Obs.]
un′dẽr·wrīte′, *v.i.* 1. to underwrite something.
2. to be in business as an underwriter.
un′dẽr·wrīt·ẽr, *n.* 1. a person or agent who underwrites insurance.
2. a person who underwrites issues of stocks, bonds, etc.
un′dẽr·wrīt·ing, *n.* the business of an underwriter.
un·dē·ṣign′ing (-zīn′), *a.* not designing; straightforward; honest; not crafty or underhanded.
un·dē·ṣīr′ȧ·ble, *a.* not desirable; objectionable.
un·dē·ṣīr′ȧ·ble, *n.* an undesirable person.
un·dē·tẽr′mined, *a.* 1. not determined; not settled; not decided.
2. not limited; not defined; indeterminate.
un·dev′il, *v.t.* to free from possession by the devil; to exorcise. [Archaic.]
un·did′, *v.* past tense of *undo*.
un′dieṣ, *n.pl.* [dim. euphemistic abbrev.] (women's or children's) underwear. [Colloq.]
un·dīne′, *n.* [G.; Mod. L. *Undina*, from L. *unda*, a wave.] in folklore, a female water spirit, resembling in character the sylphs or spirits of the air, and without a soul until married to a mortal and the mother of a child.
un·di·rect′ed, *a.* 1. not directed; not guided.
2. not addressed, as a piece of mail.
un·dis·pen′sȧ·ble, *a.* indispensable. [Obs.]
un·dis·pōṣed′, *a.* 1. indisposed as to health. [Rare.]
2. disinclined.
3. not disposed (of); not sold, settled, distributed, or arranged for; as, the stock is *undisposed* of.
un·di·vīd′ed, *a.* 1. not divided; not separated or disunited; unbroken; whole; as, *undivided* attention or affections.
2. in botany, not lobed, cleft, or branched.
3. not made separate; limited to a particular share; as, to own an *undivided* share of a business.
un·dö′, *v.t.*; undid, *pt.*; undone, *pp.*; undoing, *ppr.* [ME. *undon*; AS. *undon*; *un-* (back), and *don*, to do.]
1. to open, release, or untie (a fastening).
2. to open (a parcel, door, etc.) by this means.
3. to reverse, as something which has been done; to annul; to bring to nought; to cancel.
4. to find an answer or explanation to; to solve; to explain. [Obs.]
5. to put an end to; to bring ruin or distress upon.
un·dö′ẽr, *n.* one who undoes; one who reverses what has been done; one who ruins.
un·dö′ing, *n.* 1. the reversal of what has been done; a canceling or annulling.
2. the act of bringing to ruin or destruction.
3. the cause or source of ruin or destruction.
un·dŏne′, *v.* past participle of *undo*.
un·dŏne′, *a.* ruined; destroyed.
un·dŏne′, *a.* not done; not performed, accomplished, completed, etc.
un′dōse, *a.* having undulating lines; wavy; undate.
un·dou′ble (-dub′l), *v.t.*; undoubled, *pt., pp.*; undoubling, *ppr.* to cause to be no longer doubled or double; to unfold; to unclench; as, to *undouble* the fist.
un·doubt′ed (-dout′), *a.* 1. not doubted; not called in question; indubitable; indisputable.
2. not filled with doubt, apprehension, fear, or the like; hence, confident; bold; fearless. [Rare.]
un·doubt′ed·ly, *adv.* without or beyond doubt; without question; indubitably; certainly.
un·dra̤w′, *v.t.* and *v.i.*; undrew, *pt.*; undrawn, *pp.*; undrawing, *ppr.* to draw aside, back, or away.
un·dra̤wn′, *a.* 1. not drawn, pulled, dragged, or hauled.
2. not portrayed, delineated, or described.
3. not drawn, as from a cask.
un·drēamed′, un·drēamt′ (-dremt′), *a.* not dreamed; not thought of; not imagined.
un·drēam′ing, *a.* not dreaming.
un·dress′ (*or* un′dres), *n.* loose, informal dress; also, ordinary dress, as opposed to full dress or uniform.
un·dress′, *a.* pertaining to ordinary or informal dress; as, an *undress* uniform.
un·dress′, *v.t.*; undressed (-drest′), *pt., pp.*; undressing, *ppr.* 1. to take off the clothing of; to strip.
2. to divest of ornaments.
3. to take the dressing, bandages, or covering from (a wound).
un·dress′, *v.i.* to take off one's clothes.
u̇nd sō wēi′tẽr (oont zō vī′tẽr), [G.] and so forth; et cetera.
un·dūe′, *a.* 1. not due; not yet owing or payable; as, a debt, note, or bond.
2. not just; not lawful; not legal; as, an *undue* proceeding.
3. improper; not appropriate or suitable.
4. erring by excess; excessive; unreasonable; immoderate; as, an *undue* regard for the externals of religion; an *undue* rigor in the execution of law.
undue influence; in law, influence exerted when one acquires such an ascendancy over another as to prevent the latter from being a free agent.
un·dūke′, *v.t.* to deprive of dukedom. [Rare.]
un′dū·lănt, *a.* undulating.
un′dū·lănt fē′vẽr, a persistent infectious disease caused by a bacterium transmitted to man in the milk of infected cows and goats, and characterized by an undulating, or recurrent, fever, an enlarged spleen, sweating, and pains in the joints: also called *Malta* (or *Mediterranean*) *fever*.
un′dū·lăr·y, *a.* undulating. [Obs.]

un′dū·lāte, *v.t.*; undulated, *pt.*, *pp.*; undulating, *ppr.* [from L. *undulatus*, undulated, from *unda*, a wave.]

1. to cause to move in waves; to move up and down or to and fro in undulations.

2. to give a wavy form, margin, or surface to.

un′dū·lāte, *v.i.* 1. to move in or as in waves.

2. to have a wavy form, margin, or surface.

un′dū·lāte, *a.* having a wavy form, margin, or surface; undulating.

un′dū·lāte·ly, *adv.* in an undulate shape or manner.

un′dū·lāt·ing, *a.* waving; vibrating; rising and falling like waves; having a form or outline resembling that of a series of waves; wavy.

un′dū·lāt·ing·ly, *adv.* in an undulating manner; in the form of waves.

un·dū·lā′tion, *n.* 1. an undulating or undulating motion, as of a snake.

Worms and leeches move by *undulation*. —Sir T. Browne.

2. a wavy form or outline, especially one of a series; a form resembling that of a wave or waves.

3. pulsation.

4. in physics, wave motion, as of light or sound, or a wave or vibration.

5. in music, the effect of the simultaneous vibration of two slightly inharmonious tones; a beat; also, a tremolo or tone produced by the pressure of a finger on a string, as of a violin.

6. in geometry, the coming of a plane curve into a higher contact than usual with its tangent without opposing flexure.

7. vermiculation; a surface marked with waved lines; waved lines collectively.

un·dū·lā′tion·ist, *n.* one who advocates the undulatory theory of light.

un′dū·lā·tive, *a.* of or characterized by undulations; undulatory.

un′dū·lā·tō″ry, *a.* 1. of, caused by, or characterized by undulations.

2. wavelike.

3. undulating.

undulatory theory of light; the theory that light is transmitted by an undulatory or vibrating movement of the ether.

un·dull′, *a.* not dull. [Obs.]

un′dū·lōse, *a.* undulous. [Rare.]

un′dū·lous, *a.* undulating; with alternating swells and troughs, as the sea; rising and falling in waves.

un·dū′ly, *adv.* 1. improperly; unjustly.

2. beyond a due degree; excessively.

un·dust′, *v.t.* to free from dust.

un′dy, *a.* in heraldry, undé.

un·dȳ′ing, *a.* not dying or ending; eternal or immortal; as, the *undying* souls of men.

un·dȳ′ing·ly, *adv.* imperishably; immortally.

un·ēared′, *a.* not plowed; untilled. [Obs.]

un·ēarned′ (-ērnd′), *a.* 1. not earned by labor or services.

2. not deserved.

unearned increment; the increase in the value of land or other property in consequence of general causes, such as the growth of population, the institution of railroads, the building of factories, etc. in contradistinction to that increase which is the direct result of expenditure, labor, or improvements made on the land or property by its owner.

un·ēarth′, *v.t.* 1. to dig up or bring forth from out of the earth.

2. to bring to light; to discover or find out; to disclose.

un·ēarth′li·ness, *n.* the state or quality of being unearthly.

un·ēarth′ly, *a.* 1. not earthly; supernatural; not of this world.

2. weird; mysterious.

3. fantastic; outlandish. [Colloq.]

un·ēaṣe′, *n.* uneasiness; trouble.

un·ēaṣe′, *v.t.* to cause uneasiness to; to make uneasy. [Obs.]

un·ēaṣ′i·ly, *adv.* in an uneasy manner.

un·ēaṣ′i·ness, *n.* the quality or state of being uneasy.

un·ēaṣ′y, *a.*; *comp.* uneasier; *superl.* uneasiest, 1. having, showing, or allowing no ease of body or mind; uncomfortable.

2. disturbed by anxiety or apprehension; restless; unsettled; perturbed.

3. not easy or elegant in manner or style; not graceful; constrained; cramped; stiff; awkward.

4. not easy to be done or accomplished; difficult. [Rare.]

un·ēath′, *a.* not easy; difficult. [Archaic.]

un·ēath′, *adv.* not easily; scarcely. [Archaic.]

un·em·ploy′ȧ·ble, *a.* not employable; specifically, that cannot be employed, as in industry, because of age, physical or mental deficiency, or the like.

un·em·ploy′ȧ·ble, *n.* an unemployable person.

un·em·ployed′, *a.* 1. not employed; without work.

2. not in use; idle; as, *unemployed* capital.

un·em·ployed′, *n.* an unemployed person.

the unemployed; people who are out of work.

un·em·ploy′ment, *n.* the state of being unemployed; lack of employment.

unemployment compensation; payment, as by a State government, of a certain amount of money to the unemployed, usually at regular intervals during a fixed period of time.

un-Eñg′lish (iṅ′glish), *a.* not English; opposed in character, feeling, or the like to what is English.

un·eñg′lished, *a.* not translated into English. [Archaic.]

un·ē′quăl, *a.* [L. *inæqualis.*]

1. not equal; not even; not of the same size, length, breadth, quantity, strength, talents, acquirements, age, station, form, etc.

2. insufficient; inadequate; as, his strength is *unequal* to the task.

3. not equitable; unfair; partial; unjust; as, an *unequal* peace.

4. not regular; not uniform; variable; fluctuating; as, *unequal* pulsations.

5. not balanced or symmetrical.

un·ē′quăl, *n.* an unequal person or thing.

un·ē′quăl·ȧ·ble, *a.* not able to be equaled, matched, or paralleled. [Obs.]

un·ē′quăled, un·ē′quălled, *a.* not equaled; unparalleled; unrivaled; supreme.

un·ē·quiv′ō·căl, *a.* not equivocal; plain; clear; straightforward; not ambiguous.

un·ē·quiv′o·căl·ly, *adv.* in an unequivocal manner; plainly; clearly.

un·ē·quiv′o·căl·ness, *n.* the quality of being unequivocal; certainty; sincerity.

un·ẽrr′ing, *a.* 1. free from error.

2. not missing or failing; certain; sure; exact.

un·ēth′, un·ēthe′, *adv.* uneath. [Obs.]

un·ē′ven, *a.* 1. not even; specifically, (a) not level, smooth, or plain; rough; rugged; as, an *uneven* road; (b) not straight or parallel; crooked; (c) not uniform, regular, or continuous; changeable; varying; as, *uneven* time; (d) not equal in height, thickness, etc.; (e) [Rare.] not fair, just, or true; (f) in mathematics, odd; not divisible by 2 without a remainder; as, 3, 5, 7, etc. are *uneven* numbers.

2. ill-matched; unsuitable; ill-assorted. [Obs.]

un·ē′ven·ly, *adv.* in an uneven manner; not smoothly or regularly; as, the pulse beats *unevenly*.

un·ē′ven·ness, *n.* the state or quality of being uneven.

un·ex·am′pled (-eg-zam′pld), *a.* having no precedent, parallel, or similar case; without example; unprecedented.

un·ex·cep′tion·ȧ·ble, *a.* not liable to any exception or objection; unobjectionable; faultless; irreproachable; as, *unexceptionable* conduct, *unexceptionable* testimony.

un·ex·cep′tion·ȧ·ble·ness, *n.* the state or quality of being unexceptionable.

un·ex·cep′tion·ȧ·bly, *adv.* in an unexceptional manner; so as to be unexceptionable.

un·ex·cep′tion·ăl, *a.* 1. not being an exception; according to rule or usage; ordinary; usual.

2. not admitting of any exception.

3. unexceptionable.

un·ex·cep′tion·ăl·ly, *adv.* in an unexceptional manner; without any exception; altogether; entirely.

un·ex·peç·tā′tion, *n.* lack of expectation. [Obs.]

un·ex·peçt′ed, *a.* not expected; not looked for; sudden; unforeseen.

un·ex·peçt′ed·ly, *adv.* in an unexpected manner.

un·ex·peçt′ed·ness, *n.* the quality of being unexpected.

un·ex·press′ive, *a.* 1. inexpressive.

2. that cannot be expressed; inexpressible. [Obs.]

un·fāil′ing, *a.* 1. not failing.

2. never ceasing or falling short; incapable of being exhausted; as, an *unfailing* spring.

3. always reliable; sure; certain; as, an *unfailing* loyalty.

un·fāil′ing·ly, *adv.* in an unfailing manner.

un·fāil′ing·ness, *n.* the quality of being unfailing.

un·fâir′, *a.* [ME.; AS. *unfæger*, unfair, frightful; *un-*, not, and *fæger*, fair.]

1. not just or impartial; biased; inequitable.

2. dishonest, dishonorable, or unethical in business dealings involving relations with employees, customers, or competitors.

3. not comely or beautiful. [Archaic.]

un·fâir′ly, *adv.* in an unfair or unjust manner.

un·fâir′ness, *n.* the state or quality of being unfair.

un·fāith′fụl, *a.* 1. not faithful; not observant of promises, vows, allegiance, or duty; violating trust or confidence; faithless; disloyal.

2. not having faith; unbelieving; impious; infidel. [Obs.]

3. not exact or accurate; not trustworthy; not in accordance with the truth or to the standard set up; as, an *unfaithful* description; an *unfaithful* translation.

4. lacking good faith; dishonest.

5. adulterous; guilty of adultery.

Syn.—dishonest, disloyal, faithless, perfidious, treacherous.

un·fāith′fụl·ly, *adv.* in an unfaithful manner.

un·fāith′fụl·ness, *n.* the state or quality of being unfaithful.

un·fȧ·mil′iăr (-yăr), *a.* 1. not familiar or well known; strange.

2. having no experience (*with*); not conversant; as, he was *unfamiliar with* tools.

un″fȧ·mil·i·ar′i·ty, *n.* lack of familiarity; state or quality of being unfamiliar.

un·fȧs′ten (-fȧs′n), *v.t.* to loose; to unfix; to unbind; to untie.

un·fȧs′ten·ẽr, *n.* one who or that which unfastens.

un·fä′thered, *a.* 1. having no father; fatherless.

2. of unknown paternity; illegitimate; bastard.

3. of unknown authorship or unestablished authenticity.

un·fā′vŏr·ȧ·ble, un·fā′vŏur·ȧ·ble, *a.* not favorable; not propitious; adverse, contrary, or disadvantageous.

un·fā′vŏr·ȧ·ble·ness, un·fā′vŏur·ȧ·ble·ness, *n.* the quality of being unfavorable.

un·fā′vŏr·ȧ·bly, un·fā′vŏur·ȧ·bly, *adv.* in an unfavorable manner.

un·fēa′tūred, *a.* lacking regular features; deformed.

un·feel′ing, *a.* 1. incapable of feeling or sensation; insensible; void of sensibility.

2. cruel; hardhearted; lacking sympathy or mercy.

un·feel′ing·ly, *adv.* in an unfeeling or cruel manner.

un·feel′ing·ness, *n.* the state or quality of being unfeeling.

un·feịgned′ (-fānd′), *a.* not feigned; genuine; real; sincere.

un·fẽr·ment′ed, *a.* not fermented; not having undergone the process of fermentation.

un·fet′tẽr, *v.t.* to free from fetters; to free from restraint of any kind; to liberate.

un·fig′ūred, *a.* 1. representing no figures or forms; devoid of figures.

2. literal; devoid of figures of speech.

3. in logic, not according to mood and figure.

un·fin′ished, *a.* 1. not finished; not completed or perfected; incomplete.

2. having no finish, or final coat, as of paint.

3. not sheared or processed after looming, as woolen cloth.

un·fit′, *a.* 1. incapable of meeting requirements or qualifications; not suitable.

2. not physically fit or sound.

3. not adapted or fitted for a given purpose.

Syn.—improper, unsuitable, inconsistent, unqualified, unmeet, untimely, incompetent, unworthy.

un·fit′, *v.t.*; unfitted, *pt.*, *pp.*; unfitting, *ppr.* to render unfit; to disable; to make unsuitable; to deprive of the strength, skill, or proper qualities for anything; as, sickness *unfits* a man for labor.

Syn.—disable, incapacitate, disqualify.

un·fit′ly, *adv.* in an unfit manner; not properly; unsuitably.

un·fit′ness, *n.* the state or quality of being unfit.

un·fit′ting, *a.* not fitting; improper; unbecoming.

un·fit′ting·ly, *adv.* in an unfitting manner; unbecomingly; improperly.

un·fix′, *v.t.* 1. to loosen from any fastening; to unfasten; to detach.

2. to unsettle; as, to *unfix* the mind or affections.
3. to dissolve; to make fluid.

un·fledged′ (-flejd′), *a.* 1. not fully fledged; unfeathered, as a young bird.
2. immature; undeveloped.

un·flesh′ly, *a.* not fleshly or carnal; spiritual.

un·flinch′ing, *a.* not flinching, yielding, or shrinking; steadfast; resolute; firm.

un·fōld′, *v.t.* [ME. *unfolden*; AS. *unfealdan*; *un-*, back, and *fealdan*, to fold.]
1. to open the folds of; to spread out; as, to *unfold* a letter.
2. to lay open to view or contemplation; to make known in all the details; to disclose; to reveal; to display; to explain; as, to *unfold* one's designs; to *unfold* the principles of a science.
Nay, answer me; stand and *unfold* yourself. —Shak.
3. to develop.
4. to unwrap.

un·fōld′, *v.i.* to become unfolded; to be spread apart; to become disclosed or developed; to develop itself.

un·fōld′, *v.t.* to release from a fold or pen; as, to *unfold* sheep.

un·fōld′ẽr, *n.* one who or that which unfolds.

un·formed′, *a.* 1. having no regular form or shape; shapeless.
2. not organized or developed.
3. not made; uncreated.

un·for′tū·nāte, *a.* not fortunate; characterized by bad fortune; unhappy, inauspicious, or unlucky.
Syn.—calamitous, ill-fated, unlucky, miserable, wretched, unhappy.

un·for′tū·nāte, *n.* one who is unfortunate; specifically, a prostitute.

un·for′tū·nāte·ly, *adv.* in an unfortunate manner.

un·found′ed, *a.* 1. not founded on fact or truth; baseless.
2. not established.

un·friend′ed (-frend′), *a.* having no friends; friendless.

un·friend′li·ness, *n.* an unfriendly state or quality; an unfriendly manner or behavior.

un·friend′ly, *a.* 1. not friendly or kind; hostile.
2. not favorable or propitious.

un·friend′ly, *adv.* in an unfriendly manner.

un·frock′, *v.t.* to deprive of a frock; to divest of a frock; hence, to deprive of the rank of a priest or clergyman.

un·fruit′ful, *a.* 1. not reproducing; barren; unproductive.
2. yielding no worthwhile result; fruitless; unprofitable.

un·fūmed′, *a.* 1. not fumigated.
2. not extracted or drawn forth by fumigation; undistilled.

un·fūrl′, *v.t.* and *v.i.* to loose and unfold; to expand; to open or spread out from a furled state, as a flag or sail.

uñ′gȧ, ung′kȧ, *n.* the siamang.

un·gāin′, *a.* ungainly; clumsy. [Archaic.]

un·gāin′li·ness, *n.* the state or quality of being ungainly; awkwardness.

un·gāin′ly, *a.* [ME. *ungeinliche*, from *ungein*, perilous, from *un-*, and ON. *gegn*, ready, serviceable, and *-ly*.]
1. not gainly; clumsy; awkward; as, an *ungainly* strut.
2. unprofitable; unremunerative; vain; unfit. [Obs.]

un·gāin′ly, *adv.* in an ungainly manner.

un·ġen′ẽr·ous, *a.* 1. not generous; stingy; mean.
2. not liberal or charitable; harsh.

un·ġen′i·tūred, *a.* lacking genitals or the power of propagation; impotent. [Rare.]

un·ġen′tle, *a.* 1. not gentle; rude; harsh.
2. plebeian; not noble. [Archaic.]

un·gift′ed, *a.* not endowed with talents; not gifted.

un·gird′, *v.t.* [ME. *ungirden*; AS. *ongyrdan*, from *un-*, back, and *gyrdan*, to gird.]
1. to remove the belt or girdle of.
2. to move by unfastening a belt or girdle.

un·girt′, *a.* [ME. *ungyrt*, from *ungirden*.]
1. having the girdle off or slackened; not girded.
2. loose; not braced or drawn tight; slack.

ung′kȧ, *n.* same as *unga*.

ung′kȧ pū′ti, [native name.] the agile gibbon of Sumatra, *Hylobates agilis*.

un·glūed′, *a.* broken open; separated: said of things glued together.

un·god′, *v.t.* to divest of divinity; also, to deprive of a god. [Obs.]

un·god′li·ly, *adv.* impiously; wickedly.

un·god′li·ness, *n.* the state or quality of being ungodly.

un·god′ly, *a.* 1. not godly or religious; impious.
2. sinful; wicked.
3. outrageous; dreadful. [Colloq.]

un·god′ly, *adv.* 1. in an impious, sinful, or wicked manner. [Archaic.]
2. outrageously; dreadfully; as, it's *ungodly* early.

un·gov′ẽrn·ȧ·ble, *a.* that cannot be governed; that cannot be ruled or restrained; unruly; wild; rebellious.

un·gov′ẽrn·ȧ·ble·ness, *n.* the quality or the state of being ungovernable.

un·gov′ẽrn·ȧ·bly, *adv.* so as not to be governed or restrained.

un·gown′, *v.t.* to unfrock; to degrade from the position of priest or clergyman.

un·grā′cious, *a.* 1. wicked; odious; hateful. [Obs.]
2. unacceptable; unpleasant; unattractive.
3. rude; discourteous; impolite; not gracious or affable.

un·grā′cious·ly, *adv.* with disfavor; in an ungracious manner; as, the proposal was received *ungraciously*.

un·grā′cious·ness, *n.* the quality of being ungracious.

un″gram·mat′i·cȧl, *a.* 1. not in accordance with the principles or rules of grammar.
2. using ungrammatical language.

un·grāte′, *a.* and *n.* ingrate. [Obs.]

un·grāte′ful, *a.* 1. not grateful; not showing thanks or gratitude for favors.
2. making no returns for kindness.
3. making no response to cultivation; as, an *ungrateful* soil.
4. unpleasing; unacceptable; disagreeable; as, harsh sounds are *ungrateful* to his ear.

un·grāte′ful·ly, *adv.* in an ungrateful manner.

un·grāte′ful·ness, *n.* the state or quality of being ungrateful.

un·grāve′ly, *adv.* without gravity or seriousness. [Rare.]

uñ′guȧl (-gwăl), *a.* [L. *unguis*; Gr. *onyx*, nail, claw.] of, like, or having a nail, claw, or hoof.

un·guärd′ed (-gärd′), *a.* 1. not guarded; not watched; not defended; having no guard.
2. careless; negligent; thoughtless; imprudent; not cautious; as, to be *unguarded* in conversation.

un·guärd′ed·ly, *adv.* in an unguarded manner; without caution; carelessly.

uñ′guent (-gwent), *n.* [L. *unguentum*, from *unguere*, to anoint.] a salve or ointment.

uñ′guen·tȧr·y, *a.* of, having the nature of, like, or used in an ungent.

uñ·guen′tous, *a.* unguentary.

uñ′guic·ȧl (-gwik-), *a.* [L. *unguis*, a claw.] ungual.

uñ′gui·corn, *n.* the horny tip of a bird's upper mandible.

uñ·guic′ū·lăr, *a.* [L. *unguis*, the nail.] ungual.

Uñ·guic·ū·lā′tȧ, *n.pl.* a division of mammals with claws or nails, as distinguished from those with hoofs, *Ungulata*.

uñ·guic′ū·lāte, *a.* [from L. *unguiculus*, fingernail, dim. of *unguis*, fingernail, claw, talon; and *-ate*.]
1. having nails, claws, or talons instead of hoofs.
2. in botany, having an unguis.

uñ·guic′ū·lāte, *n.* any of the *Unguiculata*.

uñ·guic′ū·lā·ted, *a.* unguiculate (sense 1).

un·guīd′ed (-gīd′), *a.* 1. not guided; not led or conducted.
2. not regulated.

uñ·guif′ẽr·ous (-gwif′), *a.* having or producing nails or claws.

uñ′gui·form, *a.* shaped like a claw.

uñ′gui·năl, *a.* ungual. [Rare.]

uñ′gui·nous (-gwi-), *a.* [L. *unguinosus*.] oily; unctuous; like or consisting of fat or oil.

uñ·gui·ros′trăl, *a.* having a nail on the end of the bill, as some birds.

uñ′guis (-gwis), *n.*; *pl.* **uñ′guēs̱,** 1. a claw, nail, talon, or hoof.
2. in botany, the claw-shaped base of a petal.
3. in entomology, a hook at the end of a tarsus.
4. in anatomy, a structure resembling a claw, as the lachrymal bone, os unguis, or the calcar of the brain.

uñ′gū·lȧ, *n.*; *pl.* **uñ′gū·lae,** [L., a hoof.]
1. a hoof.
2. a nail or claw.
3. an unguis.
4. in geometry, a section or part of a cylinder, cone, or other solid remaining after the top has been cut off in a plane oblique to the base.

uñ′gū·lăr, *a.* of, having the nature of, or like an ungula; ungual.

Uñ·gū·lā′tȧ, *n.pl.* an extensive group of mammals having hoofs.

uñ′gū·lāte, *a.* [LL. *ungulatus*, from L. *ungula*, a hoof.]
1. having hoofs; of or belonging to the group of animals having hoofs.
2. shaped like a hoof.

uñ′gū·lāte, *n.* a mammal having hoofs.

uñ′gūled, *a.* in heraldry, having hoofs; especially, having hoofs of a tincture different from the rest of the body.

uñ′gū·li·grāde, *a.* walking upon hoofs; cloven-footed, as ruminants.

uñ′gū·lous, *a.* ungulate. [Rare.]

un·hab′it·ȧ·ble, *a.* uninhabitable. [Rare.]

un·hāir′, *v.t.* and *v.i.* to make or become free from hair, as hides before tanning.

un·hāle′, *a.* unsound; not healthy. [Obs.]

un·hal′lōw, *v.t.* to desecrate; to profane.

un·hal′lōwed, *a.* 1. not hallowed or consecrated; unholy.
2. wicked; profane; impious.

un·hand′, *v.t.* to loose from the hand or hands; to let go.

un·hand′sōme, *a.* 1. not handsome; plain; homely; not attractive.
2. rude; unbecoming; not gracious or courteous.
3. stingy; mean.
4. unhandy; unmanageable. [Obs.]

un·hand′sōme·ly, *adv.* in an unhandsome manner.

un·hand′sōme·ness, *n.* the quality or state of being unhandsome.

un·hap′, *n.* ill luck; misfortune. [Archaic.]

un·hap′pi·ly, *adv.* unfortunately; miserably; in an unhappy manner.

un·hap′pi·ness, *n.* 1. misfortune; bad luck. [Obs.]
2. the state or condition of being unhappy.

un·hap′py, *a.*; *comp.* unhappier; *superl.* unhappiest, 1. unfortunate; unlucky; as, an *unhappy* turn of events.
2. not happy; miserable or wretched; sad; sorrowful.
3. not suitable or appropriate; ill-chosen.
4. evil; reprehensible. [Obs.]
Syn.—miserable, wretched, sad, downcast, cheerless, dissatisfied, discontented.

un·här′bŏr, un·här′bŏur, *v.t.* to drive from harbor or shelter.

un·här′bŏred, un·här′bŏured, *a.* not sheltered; also, [Obs.] affording no shelter.

un·här′ness, *v.t.* 1. to free from harness or gear.
2. to disarm; to strip of armor.

un·hatched′, *a.* not hatched; not having left the egg.

un·health′ (-helth′), *n.* unhealthiness.

un·health′ful, *a.* not healthful; injurious to health; unwholesome; noxious; as, an *unhealthful* climate.

un·health′ful·ly, *adv.* in an unhealthful manner.

un·health′ful·ness, *n.* the state or condition of being unhealthful.

un·health′i·ly, *adv.* in an unhealthy manner.

un·health′i·ness, *n.* the state of being unhealthy.

un·health′y, *a.* 1. having or showing poor health; sickly; not well.
2. morally unhealthful.
3. insalubrious; unwholesome; harmful to health.

un·hēard′, *a.* 1. not heard; not perceived by the ear; as, the cry went *unheard*.
2. not given a hearing.
3. not known; not heard of before.

un·hēard′-ŏf (-uv), *a.* not heard of before; unprecedented.

un·heärt′, *v.t.* to discourage; to depress; to dishearten.

un·heav′en·ly (-hev′), *a.* not heavenly. [Rare.]

un·heed′ed·ly, *adv.* without being heeded or noticed. [Rare.]

un·heed′y, *a.* incautious; heedless. [Obs.]

un·helm′, *v.t.* and *v.i.* to remove the helm or helmet (of). [Archaic.]

un·hinġe′, *v.t.*; unhinged, *pt., pp.*; unhinging, *ppr.* 1. to remove from the hinges.
2. to remove the hinges from.
3. to dislodge or detach.
4. to throw (the mind, etc.) into confusion; to unbalance or upset.

un·hinġe′ment, *n.* the act of unhinging or state of being unhinged. [Rare.]

un·his·tor′iç, *a.* 1. not historic; having no place in history.
2. not in accordance with history. [Rare.]
un·his·tor′iç·ăl, *a.* unhistoric.
un·hitch′, *v.t.* 1. to free from a hitch.
2. to unfasten; to release; to detach.
un·hīve′, *v.t.* to drive from or as from a hive.
un·hōard′, *v.t.* to scatter; to dissipate.
un·hō′li·ly, *adv.* in an unholy manner.
un·hō′li·ness, *n.* lack of holiness.
un·hō′ly, *a.*; *comp.* unholier; *superl.* unholiest, [ME.; AS. *unhalig*; *un-*, not, and *halig*, holy.]
1. not sacred, hallowed, or consecrated.
2. wicked; profane; impious.
3. frightful; dreadful. [Colloq.]
un·hook′, *v.t.* 1. to remove or loosen from a hook.
2. to undo or unfasten the hook or hooks of.
un·hook′, *v.i.* to become unhooked.
un·hōped′, *a.* unexpected; not hoped for: usually with *for*; as, an *unhoped-for* advantage.
un·hoŗse′, *v.t.*; unhorsed, *pt.*, *pp.*; unhorsing, *ppr.* 1. to throw (a rider) from a horse.
2. to overthrow; to upset.
3. to take a horse or horses from.
un·hū′măn, *a.* 1. inhuman. [Rare.]
2. superhuman.
3. not human in kind, quality, etc.; as, an *unhuman* voice.
ū′ni-, [from L. *unis*, one.] a combining form meaning *having* or *consisting of one only*, as in *uni*cellular.
ū″ni·är·tiç′ū·lāte, *a.* articulating at one place; single-jointed.
Ū′ni·at, Ū′ni·āte, *n.*[Russ. *uniyat*, from *uniya*, a union, from L. *unus*, one: so named from the "union" with the Roman Church.] a member of any Eastern Christian Church that recognizes the Pope as primate but keeps to its own liturgy, rites, etc.
Ū′ni·at, Ū′ni·āte, *a.* pertaining to a Uniat or Uniats.
ū″ni·au·riç′ū·lāte, *a.* having a single small earlike process, as a bivalve.
ū·ni·ax′ăl, *a.* uniaxial.
ū·ni·ax′ăl·ly, *adv.* uniaxially.
ū·ni·ax′i·ăl, *a.* 1. in biology, having a single axis.
2. in crystallography, having one optic axis or direction within the crystal, along which a ray of light can proceed without being bifurcated: Iceland spar is a *uniaxial* crystal.
ū·ni·ax′i·ăl·ly, *adv.* in a uniaxial manner.
ū·ni·brañ′chi·āte, *a.* having only one gill, as some mollusks.
ū·ni·cam′ẽr·ăl, *a.* [L. *unus*, one, and *camera*, a chamber.] of or consisting of a single legislative chamber.
ū·ni·cap′sū·lăr, *a.* in botany, having a single capsule.
ū·ni·car′i·nāte, *a.* unicarinated.
ū·ni·car′i·nā·ted, *a.* having a single ridge or keel.
ū·ni·cel′lāte, *a.* [*uni-*, and L. *cella*, a cell.] having a single prong, as a sponge spicule.
ū·ni·cel′lū·lăr, *a.* having or consisting of a single cell.
ū·ni·cel′lū·lăr an′i·măl, a protozoan.
ū·ni·cen′trăl, *a.* in biology, having a single center of growth, as an animal.
ū·ni·cil′i·āte, *a.* having a single cilium or ciliate process.
ū·ni·cil′i·ā·ted, *a.* uniciliate.
ū′ni·cist, *n.* one who believes in unicity.
ū·nic′i·ty, *n.* [L. *unicus*, single.]
1. the state of being unique.
2. the state of being in unity, or of being united into one.
ū·ni·çlī′năl, *a.* same as *monoclinal.*
ū·ni·çŏl′ŏr, ū·ni·çŏl′ŏur, *a.* having only one color.
ū·ni·çŏl′ŏr·āte, *a.* same as *unicolor.*
ū·ni·çŏl′ŏred, ū·ni·çŏl′ŏured, *a.* same as *unicolor.*
ū·ni·çŏl′ŏr·ous, *a.* unicolor.
ū·ni·çon′stănt, *a.* designating, or characterized by, a single constant.
ū′ni·çorn, *n.* [ME. and OFr. *unicorne*, from L. *unicornis*, one-horned, from *unus*, one, and *cornu*, horn.]
1. a mythical horselike animal having a single horn growing from the center of its forehead.
2. in heraldry, a representation of this animal used as one of the supporters of the royal arms of Great Britain.

UNICORN

3. in the Bible, a two-horned, oxlike animal called *rĕ′ēm* in Hebrew: Deut. xxxiii. 17.
4. a kind of beetle having a horn upon its head.
5. a pair of horses with a third horse in front; also, the whole equipage.
6. the larva of a unicorn moth.
7. the kamichi.
8. a unicorn shell.
9. a unicorn fish; a narwhal.
10. a howitzer. [Obs.]
11. a Scottish gold coin of the fifteenth and sixteenth centuries, which had the figure of a unicorn on the obverse.
12. [U-] in astronomy, the constellation Monoceros.
ū′ni·çorn bīrd, same as *unicorn* (sense 7).
ū·ni·çor′nē·ăl, *a.* having a single cornea.
ū′ni·çorn fish, the narwhal.
ū′ni·çorn moth, a bombycid moth of the genus *Cælodasys*, whose larva has a hornlike dorsal prominence.
ū·ni·çor′nous, *a.* having a single horn, as certain beetles.
ū′ni·çorn root, either of two plants, *Chamælirium carolinianum* or *Aletris farinosa*. The latter is a North American iridaceous plant, with fibrous roots, thin lanceolate leaves, and small, white, spiked flowers.
ū′ni·çorn shell, a marine gastropod, as of the genus *Monoceros*, having a spiny process on the lips of the shell.
ū′ni·çorn′ș horn, same as *unicorn root.*
ū′ni·çorn whāle (hwāl), the narwhal.
ū·ni·çŏs′tāte, *a.* 1. in botany, having a single midrib, from which the secondary veins or nerves diverge: said of a leaf.
2. having one rib, costa, or riblike part.
ū·ni·çot·y·lē′dŏn·ous, *a.* monocotyledonous.
ū·ni·çũr′săl, *a.* [L. *unus*, one, and *currere*, to run.] in geometry, designating a curve expressible as the locus of a point defined by rational functions of a single parameter.
ū·ni·çus′pid, *a.* having one cusp or canine tooth.
ū·ni·çus′pi·dāte, *a.* unicuspid.
ū′ni·çȳ·çle, *n.* any vehicle with a single wheel.
ū·ni·daç′tyl, ū·ni·daç′tyle, *a.* unidigitate.
ū·ni·daç′tyl·ous, *a.* unidactyl.
un·ī·dē′ȧed (-ȧd), *a.* having no ideas; stupid.
ū·ni·diġ′i·tāte, *a.* having one functional digit; monodactylous.
ū″ni·di·men′sion·ăl, *a.* having a single dimension, as a line.
ū″ni·di·reç′tion·ăl, *a.* having, or moving in, only one direction, as rectified electric current.
ū·ni·em′bry·ō·nāte *a.* in botany, having only one embryo.
ū·ni·fā′ciăl (-shăl), *a.* having but one front surface; as, some foliaceous corals are *unifacial*, the polyp mouths being confined to one surface.
ū·ni·fãr′i·ous, *a.* in biology, arranged in a single rank, row, or series, as flowers.
ū′ni·fī·ȧ·ble, *a.* capable of being unified.
ū·nif′iç, *a.* making one; forming unity.
ū″ni·fi·çā′tion, *n.* the act of unifying or the state of being unified.
ū′ni·fī·ẽr, *n.* one who or that which unifies.
ū·ni·fī′lăr, *a.* consisting of or having only one thread, wire, etc., as a magnetometer consisting of a magnetic bar suspended by a single thread.
ū·ni·flaġ′el·lāte, *a.* having a single flagellum.
ū·ni·flō′rous, *a.* [*uni-*, and L. *flos*, flower.] bearing one flower only; as, a *uniflorous* peduncle.
ū·ni·fō′li·ăr, *a.* unifoliate.
ū·ni·fō′li·āte, *a.* 1. loosely, unifoliolate.
2. having a single leaf.
ū·ni·fō′li·ō·lāte, *a.* in botany, designating a compound leaf consisting of a single leaflet, as a leaf of the orange; also, having leaves of this sort.

UNIFOLIOLATE LEAF (of orange)

ū′ni·form, *a.* [Fr. *uniforme*, from L. *uniformis*, having one form.]
1. always the same; not varying or changing in form, rate, degree, manner, etc.
2. having the same form, appearance, manner, etc.; not varying among themselves; conforming to a given standard; always alike.
3. having a consistent action, effect, etc.; being identical throughout a state, country, etc.; as, a *uniform* minimum wage.
uniform motion; the motion of a body passing over equal spaces in equal times.
uniform with; having the same form, appearance, etc. as.
ū′ni·form, *n.* 1. the official or distinctive clothes worn by the members of a particular group, as policemen or soldiers, especially when on duty.
2. a suit or outfit of such clothes.
ū′ni·form, *v.t.* 1. to make uniform or conformable; to cause to conform; to adapt.
2. to attire in or supply with a uniform; as, to *uniform* militia.
ū·ni·form′ăl, *a.* same as *uniform.*
ū′ni·formed, *a.* wearing a uniform.
ū·ni·form″i·tãr′i·ăn, *a.* 1. of or holding the doctrine that all geological phenomena may be explained as resulting from observable processes that have operated in a uniform way.
2. of or adhering to uniformity in something.
ū·ni·form″i·tãr′i·ăn, *n.* a person who adheres to some doctrine of uniformity.
ū·ni·form·i·tãr′i·ăn·iṣm, *n.* the hypothesis or theory of the uniformitarians.
ū·ni·form′i·ty, *n.*; *pl.* **ū·ni·form′i·tieș,** [Late ME. and Late OFr. *uniformite*; L. *uniformitas.*] state, quality, or instance of being uniform; as, (a) conformity to one pattern or rule; resemblance, consonance, or agreement; as, the *uniformity* of different churches in ceremonies or rites; (b) continued or unvaried sameness or likeness; monotony.
Act of Uniformity; in English history, an act of Parliament by which the form of public prayers, administration of sacraments, and other rites is prescribed to be observed in the Established Church.
ū′ni·form·īze, *v.t.* to make uniform.
ū′ni·form·ly, *adv.* in a uniform manner.
ū′ni·form·ness, *n.* the state or quality of being uniform.
ū′ni·fȳ, *v.t.*; unified, *pt.*, *pp.*; unifying, *ppr.* [from Fr. or ML.; Fr. *unifier*; ML. *unificare*, from L. *unus*, one, and *facere*, to make.] to make or form into one; to make a unit of; to consolidate; to unite.
ū·ni·ġen′e·sis, *n.* asexual reproduction.
ū·ni·ġen′i·tăl, *a.* [*uni-*, and L. *genitus*, begotten.] only-begotten.
ū·ni·ġen′i·tūre, *n.* the state of being the only-begotten.
ū·niġ′e·nous, *a.* [L. *unigena.*] of one kind; of the same genus.
ū·ni·grav′i·dȧ, *n.* [*uni-*, and L. *gravida*, pregnant.] a woman pregnant for the first time.
ū·nij′ū·gāte, *a.* [*uni-*, and L. *jugum*, a yoke.] in botany, consisting of only one pair of leaflets: said of a pinnate leaf.
ū·ni·lā′bi·āte, *a.* in botany, having one lip only, as a corolla.
ū·ni·lat′ẽr·ăl, *a.* [Mod.L. *unilateralis*; *uni-*, and L. *latus*, *lateris*, side.]
1. of, occurring on, or affecting one side only.
2. involving or obligating one only of several persons or parties; done or undertaken by one only; not reciprocal; as, a *unilateral* contract.
3. taking into account one side only of an issue, matter, etc.; one-sided.
4. showing descent through only one line of the family.
5. inclined or turned to one side.
6. in biology, arranged, disposed, or produced on one side of an axis, or having the parts so arranged; specifically, in botany, of a raceme, having flowers growing on one side only of the common peduncle.
7. in medicine, affecting only one side of the body.
8. in phonetics, formed on one side of the tongue.
9. in psychology, preferring to use only one side of the body.
ū″ni·lat·ẽr·al′i·ty, *n.* the state or quality of being unilateral.
ū·ni·lat′ẽr·ăl·ly, *adv.* in a unilateral manner; one-sidedly.
ū·ni·lit′ẽr·ăl, *a.* [*uni-*, and L. *litera*, letter.] consisting of only one letter.
ū·ni·lō′băr, *a.* same as *unilobed.*
ū′ni·lōbed, *a.* having only one lobe; consisting of a single lobe.
ū·ni·loç′ū·lăr, *a.* [*uni-*, and L. *loculus*, cell, dim. of *locus*, a place.] having only one loculus, compartment, chamber, or cell; not divided by septa into chambers or cells.

ū·ni·loc′ū·lāte, *a.* same as *unilocular.*

ū·ni·mod′ū·lăr, *a.* having a single modulus.

unimodular transformation; in mathematics, a linear transformation the multiplier or modulus of which is equivalent to one.

un·im·pēach′ȧ·ble, *a.* not impeachable; that cannot be doubted, questioned, or discredited; blameless; irreproachable.

un·im·pröved′, *a.* 1. not bettered or improved, as by planting, building, etc.; as, *unimproved* land.

2. not made use of; not turned to advantage.

3. not improved in health.

ū·ni·mū′crō·nāte, *a.* [L. *unus,* one, and *mucro (-onis),* point.] having a single tip or point.

ū·ni·nẽr′vāte, *a.* [L. *unus,* one, and *nervus,* nerve.] one-ribbed; having only one nerve or rib, as some leaves.

ū′ni·nẽrved, *a.* same as *uninervate.*

un·in·fọrmed′, *a.* 1. not informed; not instructed; untaught.

2. not animated; not enlivened.

ū·ni·nō′mi·ȧl, *a.* same as *uninominal.*

ū·ni·nom′i·năl, *a.* [L. *unus,* one, and *nomen,* name.] having a single name or term.

un·in·tel′li·ġent, *a.* having or showing a lack or deficiency of intelligence.

un·in′tẽr·est·ed, *a.* 1. not interested; not personally concerned (with *in*).

2. paying no attention.

un″in·trō·dūced′ (-dūst′), *a.* not introduced; not properly conducted; obtrusive.

ū·ni·nū′clē·ăr, *a.* [L. *unus,* one, and *nucleus,* nucleus.] having a single nucleus.

ū·ni·nū′clē·āte, *a.* same as *uninuclear.*

Ū′ni·ō, *n.* [LL., lit., oneness, unity, from L. *unus,* one; hence, a fine, large pearl.]

1. a genus of lamellibranch bivalve mollusks of the family of *Unionidæ,* including *Unio margaritiferus,* the pearl mussel.

2. [u–] any species of this genus.

ū·ni·oc′ū·lăr, *a.* pertaining to or affecting only one eye.

Ū·nī′ō·lȧ, *n.* [L., a kind of plant.] a genus of North American grasses comprising five species known as spike grass and union grass. *Uniola latifolia* is a pasture grass.

ūn′iŏn (-yun), *n.* [ME.; Late OFr.; L. *unio,* oneness, from *unus,* one.]

1. a uniting or being united; combination; junction; fusion.

2. an agreeing or leaguing together for mutual benefit.

3. the unity or solidarity produced by this.

4. marriage.

5. that which is united or made into one; something formed by a combination of united parts; a coalition; specifically, a confederacy of two or more nations, states, political groups, etc. for some specific purpose.

6. (a) in England, two or more parishes consolidated into one for joint administration of relief for the poor; (b) a workhouse kept up by such a union; (c) two or more parishes or contiguous benefices consolidated for ecclesiastical purposes.

7. a labor union; a trade union.

8. a device symbolizing political union, used in a flag or ensign: it may cover the entire field, as the three crosses in the British national flag, or it may be placed in the upper inner corner, as the white stars on a blue field in the flag of the United States.

9. a joint, screw, or other connection uniting parts of machinery, or the like; especially, a coupling for connecting the ends of pipes.

10. a mixed fabric of two or more different kinds of material, as cotton and linen.

11. in breweries, one of a series of casks placed side by side and supported on pivots or trunions, in which fermentation is completed.

12. in medicine, the process of healing; the growing together of a broken bone, the lips of a wound, etc.

Act of Union; in English history, one of several statutes bringing about political union, as the act by which Scotland was united to England, or by which the two kingdoms were incorporated into one, in 1707, or the act by which Ireland was legislatively united to Great Britain in 1800.

industrial union; see under *industrial.*

Latin Union; a coalition formed in 1865 of France, Belgium, Italy, Switzerland, and, later, Greece, to secure uniform monetary relations between countries.

the Union; the United States of America.

union down; a signal of distress at sea made by reversing the flag or turning the union downward.

Syn.—junction, conjunction, connection, combination, coalition, confederacy, concord, harmony, alliance.

ūn′iŏn çȧrd, a card serving to identify one as a member in good standing of a specified labor union.

ūn′iŏn grȧss, any grass of the genus *Uniola.*

ū′ni·ō·nid, *n.* any member of the *Unionidæ*; a unio.

Ū·ni·on′i·dae, *n.pl.* a family of bivalve mollusks of which the genus *Unio* is the type.

ūn′iŏn·iṣm *n.* 1. the principle of union.

2. support of this principle or of a specified union.

3. the system or principles of labor unions.

4. [U–] loyalty to the federal union of the United States, especially during the Civil War.

5. in British politics, the tenets of the Unionists.

ūn′iŏn·ist, *n.* 1. one who promotes or advocates unionism.

2. a member of a labor union.

3. [U–] a supporter of the federal union of the United States, especially during the Civil War.

4. [U–] in British politics, one opposed to home rule, or the granting of a separate parliament to Ireland and the disruption of the legislative union existing between England and Ireland.

5. [U–] a member of the British Conservative party.

ūn′iŏn·ist, *a.* 1. pertaining to union, unionism, or unionists.

2. [U–] of or pertaining to the Unionists.

ūn·iŏn·is′tiç, *a.* 1. pertaining to unionism or unionists; relating to or promoting union.

2. [U–] of or pertaining to Unionism or Unionists.

ūn″iŏn·i·zā′tion, *n.* a unionizing or being unionized.

ūn′iŏn·īze, *v.t.*; unionized, *pt., pp.*; unionizing, *ppr.* 1. to form into a union.

2. to organize (a group of workers in a shop, industry, etc.) into a labor union.

3. to bring into conformity with the rules, standards, etc. of a labor union.

ūn′iŏn·īze, *v.i.* to join or organize a union, especially a labor union.

ūn′iŏn jack, 1. a jack or flag consisting only of a union, especially of the union of a national flag.

2. [U–J–] the national flag of the United Kingdom.

ūn′iŏn joint, a union or pipe coupling.

ūn′iŏn shop, 1. a shop, business establishment, etc. in which a contract between the employer and a labor union permits the hiring of nonunion workers but requires that all new employees join the union within a specified period, often thirty days, and remain members of the union throughout their employment.

2. a shop, business establishment, or part thereof in which wages, hours, and working conditions of all employees are fixed by contract between the employer and a labor union.

ūn′iŏn sụ̈it, a suit of men's underwear uniting shirt and drawers in a single garment.

ū·ni·ō′vū·lāte, *a.* provided with but one ovule.

ū·nip′ȧ·rȧ, *n.* a woman who has borne but one child.

ū·nip′ȧ·rous, *a.* [L. *unus,* one, and *parere,* to bear.]

1. producing only one egg or offspring at a time.

2. in botany, producing only one axis at each branching, as certain flower clusters.

ū′ni·ped, *a.* having only one foot.

ū′ni·ped, *n.* one who or that which has only one foot.

ū·ni·pẽr′sŏn·ăl, *a.* 1. having but one person; existing as or in, consisting of, or manifested in the form of only one person.

2. in grammar, used only in one person: said chiefly of verbs used only in the third person singular, as *methinks.*

ū·ni·pẽr′sŏn·ăl·ist, *n.* one who believes there is but a single person in the Deity.

ū″ni·pet′ăl·ous, *a.* in botany, having only one petal.

ū′ni·phāṣe, *n.* same as *single-phase.*

ū′ni·phō·nous, *a.* monophonic; giving but one sound, as a drum.

ū·ni·plān′ăr, *a.* located or occuring in one plane.

ū·nip′li·cāte, *a.* consisting of or having one fold only.

ū′ni·pod, *n.* [*uni-* and *-pod,* after *tripod.*] a one-legged prop or support.

ū′ni·pod, *a.* having one leg.

ūn·i·pō′lăr, *a.* 1. of or having only one pole or one kind of polarity.

2. designating a nerve cell, as in spinal ganglia, having only one process.

unipolar induction; (a) induction by only one pole of a magnet, as when a conductor is so moved through a magnetic field as to continuously cut its lines of force.

unipolar stimulation; the stimulation of a nerve produced by the application of a single electrode to that nerve.

ū·nïque′ (-nēk′), *a.* [Fr., single, from L. *unicus,* single.]

1. one and only; single; sole.

2. different from all others; having no like or equal.

3. singular; unusual; extraordinary; rare: still regarded by some as an objectionable usage.

ū·nïque′, *n.* a thing unique; a thing unparalleled or sole of its kind.

ū·nïque′ly, *adv.* in a unique manner.

ū·nïque′ness, *n.* the state or quality of being unique.

ū·nïq′ui·ty, *n.* uniqueness. [Rare.]

ū·ni·rā′di·āte, *a.* monactinal; possessing but one process or ray.

ū·ni·rā′di·ā·ted, *a.* uniradiate.

ū·ni·rā′mous, *a.* provided with but one ramus.

ū·ni·sep′ăl·ous, *a.* having only one sepal.

ū·ni·sep′tāte, *a.* in zoology and botany, having but one septum or partition.

ū·ni·sē′ri·ăl, *a.* having only one row or series; also, set in one series.

ū·ni·sē′ri·ăl·ly, *adv.* in one series.

ū·ni·sē′ri·āte, *a.* uniserial.

ū·ni·sē′ri·āte·ly, *adv.* uniserially.

ū·ni·sex′ū·ăl, *a.* having one sex only; specifically, (a) in botany, diclinous; (b) in zoology, either male or female; not hermaphroditic.

ū′ni·sŏn (*or* -zŏn), *n.* [OFr. *unisson,* from ML. *unisonus,* having the same sound; L. *unus,* one, and *sonus,* a sound.]

1. identity of musical pitch, as of two or more voices or tones.

2. the interval of a perfect prime.

3. a single unvaried tone. [Rare.]

4. accordance; agreement; harmony.

5. a unison string.

in unison; (a) sounding the same note at the same time; (b) sounding together in octaves; (c) with all the voices or instruments performing the same part: said of a musical composition or passage.

ū′ni·sŏn, *a.* 1. sounding together. [Obs.]

2. in music, coinciding or identical in pitch or sound; as, *unison* passages: said of two or more parts.

unison string; in stringed instruments, a string tuned in unison with a companion string.

ū·nis′ō·năl, *a.* same as *unisonous.*

ū·nis′ō·năl·ly, *adv.* in a unisonal manner.

ū·nis′ō·nănce, *n.* accordance of sounds; unison.

ū·nis′ō·nănt, *a.* same as *unisonous.*

ū·nis′ō·nous, *a.* [ML. *unisonus.*] characterized by or being in unison.

ū′nit, *n.* [abbrev. from *unity.*]

1. the smallest whole number; one.

2. any fixed quantity, amount, distance, measure, etc. used as a standard; specifically, (a) in education, a fixed amount of work used as a basis in awarding scholastic credits, usually determined by the number of hours spent in class; (b) in medicine, etc., the amount of a drug, vaccine, serum, or antigen needed to produce a given result, as on a certain animal or on animal tissues.

3. a single person or group of individuals, especially as distinguished from others or as part of a whole.

4. a single, distinct part or object, especially one used for a specific purpose; as, the power *unit* of a jet plane, the lens *unit* of a camera, etc.

5. in mathematics, a magnitude or number regarded as an undivided whole.

6. in military usage, any organized body of troops that is a subdivision of a larger body.

In physics, units are divided into two classes, *fundamental units* and *derived units.* Volume, velocity, force, and all other physical quantities are derivatives of and can be expressed in the terms of the three fundamental quantities, length, mass, and time.

complex unit; in mathematics, a complex number such that when $a^2+b^2=1$, it is expressed by the formula $a+b\sqrt{-1}$.

fractional unit; in mathematics, the unit of a fraction: thus in the fraction $\frac{3}{4}$, the *fractional unit* is $\frac{1}{4}$.

integral unit; the unit 1.

physical unit; an arbitrary value, measure, or magnitude adopted as a standard in physical measurements, as the meter, dyne, erg, etc.

thermal unit; a unit used in the measurement of quantities of heat.

unit angle; in circular measure, a radian.

unit magnetic pole; a magnetic pole of such strength that it is capable, in a vacuum, of acting on a similar pole one centimeter distant with a force of one dyne.

unit of force; a dyne.

unit of heat; a thermal unit.

unit of illumination; the lux.

unit of power; any unit which measures the rate at which energy is expended.

unit of resistance; same as *resistance* (sense 4a).

unit of work; the amount of work done by unit force operating through unit distance, commonly taken as (a) the foot-pound; (b) a dyne-centimeter or the amount of work done when a force of one dyne acts through a distance of one centimeter; (c) the erg.

unit rule; a rule, in some political conventions, by which the delegates in a delegation cast as a unit the entire ballot according to the vote of the majority of its members.

unit stress; stress per unit of area.

ū·nīt′ȧ·ble, *a.* capable of uniting or being united: also spelled *uniteable.*

ū′nit·ăģe, *n.* a designation of the amount or quantity of a unit of measure.

ū′nit·ăl, *a.* unitary.

Ū·ni·tăr′i·ăn, *n.* [from Mod. L. *unitarius*, unitary, and *-an.*]

1. a person who denies the doctrine of the Trinity, believing in the teachings, but rejecting the divinity, of Jesus, and holding that God is a single being.

2. a member of a Protestant denomination based on this doctrine and characterized by congregational autonomy, emphasis on the importance of character, and tolerance of differing religious views.

3. a monotheist.

4. [u-] a monist.

5. [u-] an advocate of unity or of any unitary system.

6. [u-] in politics, an advocate of centralization.

Ū·ni·tăr′i·ăn, *a.* 1. of Unitarians or their doctrines, or adhering to Unitarianism.

2. [u-] unitary.

Ū·ni·tăr′i·ăn·iṣm, *n.* 1. the doctrines or beliefs of the Unitarians or the Unitarian Church.

2. [u-] any unitary system.

Ū·ni·tăr′i·ăn·īze, *v.t.* and *v.i.*; Unitarianized, *pt., pp.*; Unitarianizing, *ppr.* to cause to conform, or to conform, to Unitarianism.

ū′ni·tăr·y, *a.* 1. of a unit or units.

2. of, pertaining to, or characterized by unity; specifically, in politics, centralized.

3. having the nature of or used as a unit.

unitary theory; a system of chemistry in which the molecules of all bodies are compared, as to their magnitude, with one unit molecule and all chemical reactions are, as far as possible, reduced to one typical form of reaction.

ū′nit çhar′aç·tẽr, a character, or trait, transmitted as a unit in heredity according to Mendelian principles.

ū·nīte′, *v.t.*; united, *pt., pp.*; uniting, *ppr.* [ME. *unyten*, from L. *unitus*, pp. of *unire*, to unite.]

1. to put or bring together so as to form into one; to make to be one, and no longer separate; to incorporate into one.

2. to connect, conjoin, or bring together by some tie or bond, legal or other; to join in interest, affection, fellowship, or the like; to associate; to couple; to conjoin.

3. to cause to adhere; to connect or join together; to attach; as, to *unite* with flesh.

4. to have or show (qualities, characteristics, etc.) in combination.

5. to join in marriage.

ū·nīte′, *v.i.* 1. to become incorporated; to grow together; to become one or as one by adhering, associating, consolidating, etc.

2. to join together in an act; to act in union.

Syn.—join, combine, link, attach, amalgamate, associate, coalesce, embody, merge, be mixed, conjoin, connect, couple, add, incorporate with, cohere, concatenate, integrate.

ū′nīte, *n.* [from *unite*, v., with reference to the union of England and Scotland.] a former English gold coin equal to 20 shillings, current during the reign of James I.

ū·nīt′ed, *a.* [pp. of *unite.*]

1. combined; joined; made one.

2. of or resulting from joint action or association.

3. in agreement or harmony.

United Irishmen; a secret society formed in 1791 by Theobald Wolfe Tone: its object was the establishment of a republic in Ireland.

ū·nīt′ed·ly, *adv.* in a united manner.

Ū·nīt′ed Nā′tionṣ, an international organization of nations pledged to promote world peace and security, maintain treaty obligations and the observance of international law, and cooperate in furthering social progress: the organization was formed at San Francisco in 1945 under a permanent charter (ratified by 51 countries) that had its inception in conferences (1941–45) held by nations opposed to the fascist coalition of Germany, Japan, and Italy, and their satellites: the headquarters has been in New York City since 1946, and the membership now consists of approximately 150 nations.

Ū·nīt′ed Press In·tẽr·na′tion·ăl, a large, privately owned agency for gathering and distributing news to subscribers to its services: formed (1958) by the merger of *United Press* and *International News Service.*

Ū·nīt′ed Stātes Āir Fōrce, the aviation branch of the United States military force.

Ū·nīt′ed Stātes Ār′my, the permanent, or standing, army of the United States; the Regular Army: compare *Army of the United States.*

Ū·nīt′ed Stātes Mȧ·rīne′ Cōrps, a branch of the United States Navy, responsible especially for amphibious operations.

Ū·nīt′ed Stātes Nā′vy, the naval branch of the United States military force.

ū·nīt′ẽr, *n.* one who or that which unites.

ū′nit faç′tŏr, a gene involved in the inheritance of a given unit character.

ū·ni′tion (-nish′un), *n.* junction; the act of uniting.

ū′ni·tive, *a.* [ML. *unitivus.*] 1. having unity.

2. tending to unite.

ū′ni·tive·ly, *adv.* in a unitive manner.

ū′nit·īze, *v.t.*; unitized, *pt., pp.*; unitizing, *ppr.* to unify; to form, construct, or organize into a single unit.

ū′nit prīc′ing, a supplementary system of pricing commodities, especially food items, by showing the prices in terms of standard units, as of an ounce or pint: it facilitates a comparison of prices of competing items.

ū′ni·ty, *n.*; *pl.* **ū′ni·tieṣ,** [ME. *unite*; OFr. *unité*, from L. *unitas* (*-atis*), oneness.]

1. the state or condition of being one; oneness; singleness; being united.

2. concord; agreement; harmony; the quality of being one in purpose, sentiment, affection, or the like.

3. something considered complete in itself; a single, separate thing.

4. unification.

5. a group or body formed by this.

6. the quality or fact of being a totality or whole, especially a complex that is a union of related parts.

7. an arrangement of parts or material that will produce a single, harmonious design or effect in an artistic or literary production.

8. a design or effect so produced.

9. constancy, continuity, or fixity of purpose, action, etc.

10. in mathematics, (a) any quantity, magnitude, etc., considered or identified as a unit or 1; (b) the numeral or unit 1.

11. in law, (a) a joint possession of two rights by several titles; (b) the holding of the same estate in undivided shares by two or more; joint tenancy.

the unities; the three principles of dramatic construction (the *unities of action, time, and place*) derived by French neoclassicists from Aristotle's *Poetics*, holding respectively that a play should have a single unified plot, that all the action should occur in the space of one day, and that the setting should be confined to one locale.

Syn.—indivisibility, singleness, individuality, concord, conjunction, agreement, uniformity, oneness.

ū·ni·vā′lence, ū·ni·vā′len·cy (*or* ū-niv′ȧ-), *n.* in chemistry, the quality or condition of being univalent.

ū·ni·vā′lent (*or* ū-niv′ȧ-), *a.* [from *uni-*, and L. *valens*, *ppr.* of *valere*, to be worth.]

1. in chemistry, (a) having a valence of one; (b) having one valence.

2. in biology, single; unpaired: said of a chromosome.

ū′ni·valve, *n.* [*uni-* and *valve.*]

1. a mollusk shell consisting of a single piece.

2. a mollusk with a shell composed of a single piece. The univalves include most of the *Gastropoda*, as land-snails, sea-snails, whelks, limpets, etc.

ū′ni·valve, *a.* 1. designating or having a one-piece shell.

2. having one valve only.

ū′ni·valved, *a.* univalve.

ū·ni·val′vū·lăr, *a.* univalve.

ū·ni·vẽr′săl, *a.* [ME. and OFr. *universel*; L. *universalis*, universal, from *universus*, universal, lit., turned into one; *unus*, one, and *versum*, pp. of *vertere*, to turn.]

1. of or relating to the universe; extending to or comprehending the whole number, quantity, or space; pertaining to or pervading all or the whole; all-embracing; all-reaching; as, *universal* ruin; *universal* good; *universal* benevolence.

> The *universal* cause,
> Acts not by partial, but by general laws.
> —Pope.

2. considered as or constituting a whole; entire; total; whole; as, the *universal* earth.

3. of, for, or including all or the whole of something specified; not limited or restricted.

4. broad in knowledge, interests, ability, etc.

5. that can be used for all kinds, forms, sizes, etc.; adaptable to any use; as, a *universal* voltage regulator, calculator, etc.

6. used, intended to be used, or understood by all.

7. in logic, not restricted or particular in application; predicating something of every member of a class; generic.

universal chuck; a chuck having two or more radial slots, fitted to its jaws and moved by screws so that it can hold objects of different sizes.

universal church; in theology, the Christian church.

universal dial; a sundial by which the hour may be found by the sun in any part of the world or under any elevation of the pole.

universal instrument; in astronomy, a kind of altitude and azimuth instrument: the telescope, instead of being a straight tube, is broken into two arms at right angles to each other in the middle of the length of the tube, and at the break a totally reflecting prism is placed, which turns the rays entering the object glass in a rectangular direction along the eye-end of the telescope which forms part of the horizontal axis of the circle, so that the telescope becomes free to move through all altitudes.

universal joint or *coupling*; a joint or coupling, as the ball-and-socket, that permits a swing at any angle within certain limits, especially one used to transmit rotary motion from one shaft to another not in line with it, as in the drive shaft of an automobile.

A

B

UNIVERSAL JOINTS
A, single; B, double

universal legatee; in civil law, a legatee to whom the whole estate of a deceased party is given, subject only to the burden of other legacies and debts.

universal lever; see under *lever.*

universal proposition; in logic, a proposition which refers to every member of a class. A universal proposition may be *affirmative* or *negative.* Thus, "all men are mortal" is a universal *affirmative* proposition; "no man is perfect" is a universal *negative* one.

universal successor; in civil law, an heir who succeeds to the whole of the heritage of a person who dies intestate.

universal suffrage; suffrage for all adult citizens of either sex.

Syn.—all-embracing, total, unlimited, boundless, comprehensive, entire, general, whole, exhaustive, complete.

ū·ni·vẽr′săl, *n.* 1. the universe. [Obs.]

2. in logic, (a) a universal proposition; (b) any of the five predicables (genus, species, difference, property, accident); (c) a general term or concept; (d) that which such a term or concept covers.

3. in philosophy, a metaphysical entity characterized by repeatability and unchanging nature through a series of changes or changing relations, as the ego.

Ū″ni·vẽr·sā′li·ăn, *a.* of or pertaining to Universalism. [Rare.]

Ū·ni·vẽr′săl·işm, *n.* 1. the theological doctrine that all souls will eventually find salvation in the grace of God.

2. [u-] universality.

Ū·ni·vẽr′săl·ist, *n.* 1. a believer in Universalism.

2. [u-] a person characterized by universality, as of interests or activities.

Ū·ni·vẽr′săl·ist, *a.* of or pertaining to Universalism.

ū·ni·vẽr·săl·is′tiç, *a.* 1. of, relating to, or affecting the whole; universal.

2. [U-] of or relating to Universalism; Universalist.

ū″ni·vẽr·sal′i·ty, *n.*; *pl.* **ū″ni·vẽr·sal′i·tieș,** 1. the state or character of being universal.

The common school is supereminent in its *universality.* —Horace Mann.

2. complete versatility; universal range, as of knowledge, interests, abilities, etc.

ū·ni·vẽr″săl·i·zā′tion, *n.* the act or process of making universal.

ū·ni·vẽr′săl·īze, *v.t.* and *v.i.*; universalized, *pt., pp.*; universalizing, *ppr.* to make universal.

ū·ni·vẽr′săl·ly, *adv.* in a universal manner; specifically, (a) in every instance; without exception; (b) in every part or place; as, air is a fluid *universally* diffused.

ū·ni·vẽr′săl·ness, *n.* universality.

Ū·ni·vẽr′săl Prod′uçt Çōde, a patterned series of vertical bars of varying widths printed on packages of many consumer products: it can be read by a computerized device for inventory control, pricing, etc.

ū′ni·vẽrse, *n.* [Fr. *univers*, from L. *universum*, the universe, neut. of the adj. *universus*, all together, all taken collectively, the whole.]

1. the totality of all things that exist; the cosmos; creation.

For nothing this wide *universe* I call,
Save thou, my rose; in it thou art my all.
—Shak.

2. the world; also, all mankind.

3. an area, province, or sphere, as of thought or activity, regarded as a distinct, comprehensive system or world.

ū′ni·vẽrse of dis′çourse, in logic, the totality of facts, things, or ideas implied or assumed in a given discussion, argument, or discourse.

ū·ni·vẽr′si·ty, *n.*; *pl.* **ū·ni·vẽr′si·tieș,** [ME. *universite*; OFr. *universitē*; L. *universitas*, the whole, universe, society, guild.]

1. the universe. [Obs.]

2. a corporation; a guild; an association. [Obs.]

3. an educational institution of the highest level, typically with one or more undergraduate schools, or colleges, together with a program of graduate studies and a number of professional schools, and authorized to confer various degrees, as the bachelor's, master's and doctor's: European universities generally comprise only graduate or professional schools, or both.

The *university* will be the training camp of the future. —Henry W. Grady.

4. the grounds, buildings, etc. of a university.

5. the faculty and student body of a university.

university extension; same as *extension*, sense 4.

ū·ni·vẽr·sō·log′iç·ăl, *a.* of or pertaining to the science of universology.

ū″ni·vẽr·sol′ō·ġist, *n.* one versed in the science of universology.

ū″ni·vẽr·sol′ō·ġy, *n.* [L. *universum*, the universe, and Gr. *logos*, discourse.] the science of the universe, or of the whole system of created things.

ū·niv′ō·çăl, *a.* [*uni-*, and L. *vox, vocis*, a voice, a word.] having a single meaning; having the meaning certain and unmistakable. A *univocal* word is opposed to an *equivocal*, which has two or more significations.

ū·niv′ō·çăl, *n.* a word having only one signification or meaning.

ū·niv′ō·çăl·ly, *adv.* in a univocal manner; in one sense; not equivocally; unmistakably.

ū·niv·ō·çā′tion, *n.* agreement of name and meaning. [Obs.]

un·joint′, *v.t.* 1. to separate (a joint).

2. to separate the joints of.

un·joint′ed, *a.* 1. having no joints; as, an *unjointed* stem of a plant.

2. deprived of a joint; disjointed; disconnected; hence, incoherent. [Archaic.]

un·just′, *a.* 1. not just; not acting or disposed to act according to law and justice; contrary to justice; unfair; wrongful; as, an *unjust* cause.

2. not giving a just account; not rendering what is just; dishonest or unfaithful. [Obs.]

un·jus′tice, *n.* injustice.

un̄′ked, *a.* [corruption of *uncouth.*]

1. unusual; odd; strange. [Brit. Dial.]

2. lonely; solitary. [Brit. Dial.]

Also written *unkid.*

un·kembed′ (-kemd′), *a.* unkempt. [Archaic.]

un·kempt′, *a.* [*un-*, and *kempt*, pp. of dial. *kemben*, to comb; ME. *kemben*; AS. *cemban*, from *camb*, a comb.]

1. uncombed; not cared for; as, an *unkempt* beard.

2. untidy; messy.

3. unpolished; not refined; crude; rough; as, *unkempt* rhymes.

un·kenned′, *a.* unknown; strange. [Obs. or Dial.]

un·ken′nel, *v.t.*; unkenneled *or* unkennelled, *pt., pp.*; unkenneling *or* unkennelling, *ppr.* 1. to drive or release from a kennel or hole.

2. to uncover; to bring to light.

un·ken′nel, *v.i.* to come out of a kennel or hole.

un·kind′, *a.* not kind, sympathetic, or considerate of the feelings of others; harsh; cruel.

un·king′, *v.t.* to deprive of royalty.

un·king′ship, *n.* the state or condition of being unkinged. [Obs.]

un·kiss, *v.t.* to cancel or retract by kissing again, as an oath taken by kissing the book.

un·knit′ (-nit′), *v.t.* and *v.i.*; unknitted *or* unknit, *pt., pp.*; unknitting, *ppr.* [ME. *unknytten*; AS. *uncnyttan.*] to untie, undo, or unravel, as something knitted or knotted, or smooth out, as something wrinkled.

un·knot′ty (-not′), *a.* having no knots. [Rare.]

un·knōw′ (-nō′), *v.t.*; unknew, *pt.*; unknown, *pp.*; unknowing, *ppr.* to become ignorant of, as something already known.

un·knōw′ȧ·ble, *a.* not knowable; that cannot be known; specifically, beyond the range of human comprehension or experience.

un·knōw′ȧ·ble, *n.* something unknowable, or that which is unknowable.

the Unknowable; in philosophy, absolute reality, postulated as lying beyond the range of human comprehension or experience.

un·knōw′ing·ness, *n.* the state of being unknowing; ignorance.

un·knowl′edġed (-nol′ejd), *a.* not acknowledged or recognized. [Obs.]

un·knōwn′, *a.* 1. not known; not in one's knowledge, understanding, or acquaintance; unfamiliar; strange.

2. not discovered, identified, or brought to knowledge; as, an *unknown* island.

un·knōwn′, *n.* one who or that which is unknown; specifically, (a) a person without prestige; (b) an unknown quantity in mathematics; also, a symbol for such a quantity.

un·knōwn′ness, *n.* the state or condition of being unknown.

Un′knōwn Sōl′diẽr, [*also* u- s-] an unidentified soldier whose body has been selected and enshrined to represent all those of a nation who were killed in World War I.

un·lāce′, *v.t.*; unlaced, *pt., pp.*; unlacing, *ppr.* 1. to loose from lacing or fastening; to unfasten (something laced); as, to *unlace* a helmet, a garment, or a shoe.

2. to loosen or remove the dress of by or as by unfastening laces.

3. to divest of proper coverings; to expose to disgrace or injury. [Obs.]

4. in nautical usage, to loose and take off (a bonnet) from a sail, or to cast off (any lacing in any part of the rigging of a vessel).

5. to disentangle. [Obs.]

un·lāde′, *v.t.* and *v.i.* 1. to unload (a ship, etc.).

2. to discharge (a cargo, etc.).

un·lash′, *v.t.* to loose, unfasten, untie, or separate, as something lashed down.

un·latch′, *v.t.* to open or unfasten by releasing a latch.

un·latch′, *v.i.* to come open or unfastened at the latch; to become unlatched.

un·lạw′, *n.* in law, (a) a transgression of the law, or an act of injustice; lawlessness; (b) a fine legally fixed and exacted from one who has transgressed the law.

un·lạw′, *v.t.* 1. to deprive of the authority of law. [Obs.]

2. in Scots law, to fine.

un·lạwed′, *a.* in old English forest law, not having the claws of the forefeet cut off: said of dogs.

un·lạw′fụl, *a.* 1. against the law; illegal.

2. illegitimate; bastard.

un·lāy′, *v.t.* and *v.i.*; unlaid, *pt., pp.*; unlaying, *ppr.* [*un-*, and *lay*, v.t., sense 14.] in nautical usage, to untwist: said of a rope.

un·lead′ (-led′), *v.t.* in printing, to remove the leads from (set-up matter).

un·lead′ed, *a.* 1. not covered or weighted with lead.

2. not mixed with lead tetraethyl: said of gasoline.

3. in printing, not spaced with leads.

un·lẽarn′, *v.t.* 1. to forget, as what has been learned; to discard; to put away; to get rid of.

2. to teach the contrary of (something learned, especially erroneously).

3. to fail to learn. [Obs.]

un·lẽarn′ed, *a.* 1. not learned or educated; ignorant.

2. showing a lack of learning or education.

3. (un-lẽrnd′), (a) not learned or mastered; as, *unlearned* lessons; (b) known or possessed, as knowledge, without being learned.

Syn.—ignorant.

un·lẽarn′ed·ly, *adv.* in an unlearned manner; ignorantly.

un·lẽarn′ed·ness, *n.* lack of learning; illiterateness.

un·lēash′, *v.t.* to release or let go from or as from a leash.

un·less′, *conj.* [for *on less*, earlier *on lesse that*, in less that, at less than, or for less.]

1. if it be not that; were it not the fact that; if not; except when; except that.

2. for fear that; in case; lest. [Obs.]

un·less′, *prep.* except; save (with a verb implied); as, *unless* disaster, nothing will result.

un·let′tẽred, *a.* 1. not lettered; ignorant; uneducated.

2. illiterate.

un·līght′sŏme (-līt′), *a.* dark; gloomy; lacking light. [Obs.]

un·līke′, *a.* 1. not alike; different; dissimilar; having little or no resemblance; as, never were two men more *unlike.*

2. improbable; unlikely. [Archaic or Dial.]

un·līke′, *adv.* not in a like or similar manner. [Rare.]

un·līke′, *prep.* different from; not like; as, this action is *unlike* him, she is *unlike* anyone I've known.

un·līke′li·hood, *n.* the state or quality of being unlikely or improbable; improbability.

un·līke′li·ness, *n.* same as *unlikelihood.*

un·līke′ly, *a.* [ME. *unlikly*; prob. after ON. *ūlīkligr.*] 1. such as cannot reasonably be expected; improbable; as, an *unlikely* event; the thing you mention is very *unlikely.*

2. not holding out a prospect of success or of a desired result; likely to fail; unpromising.

3. not calculated to inspire liking or affection; not likable or lovable. [Dial.]

un·līke′ly, *adv.* with no or little likelihood; improbably.

un·līk′en, *v.t.* to feign; to dissimulate. [Obs.]

un·līke′ness, *n.* lack of resemblance; dissimilarity.

un·lim′bẽr, *v.t.* and *v.i.* [*un-*, back, and *limber.*]

1. to prepare (a field gun) for use by detaching the limber, or front part of the gun carriage.

2. to get ready for use or action.

un·lim′it·ȧ·ble, *a.* illimitable.

un·lim′it·ed, *a.* 1. not limited; having no bounds; boundless; not restricted.

2. undefined; indefinite; not bounded by proper exceptions; as, *unlimited* terms.

3. vast; illimitable.

unlimited problem; in mathematics, a problem capable of an infinite number of solutions.

Syn.—boundless.

un·lim′it·ed·ly, *adv.* in an unlimited manner; to an unlimited extent.

un·lim′it·ed·ness, *n.* the state or the quality of being unlimited.

un·līne′, *v.t.* to deprive of lining; to empty. [Rare.]

un·liñk′, *v.t.* to separate or unfasten the links of (a chain, etc.).

un·liq′uŏred (-lik′ẽrd), *a.* 1. not moistened; not smeared with liquor.

2. not intoxicated; sober; not filled with liquor.

un·list′ed, *a.* 1. not listed; not constituting an entry in a list.

2. not listed among those admitted for the purpose of trading on the stock exchange: said of securities.

un·live′, *v.t.* 1. to live so as to wipe out the consequences or results of; to live down.

2. to annul or wipe out (past experience, etc.).

3. to deprive of life. [Obs.]

un·lōad′, *v.t.* 1. to take a load or cargo from; to discharge of a load or cargo; as, to *unload* a ship; to *unload* an animal.

2. to remove or take off, as a burden or load; as, to *unload* freight.

3. to relieve from anything burdening or troublesome.

4. to get rid of; to sell, as stocks, bonds, merchandise, etc.; as, to *unload* stock in a failing concern; to *unload* wheat.

The rumor started shortly after the exchange opened that morning. Confusion reigned. Orders began to pour in to *unload* steel but the powerful combine could not be shaken. —Rand.

5. to extract the charge from; as, to *unload* a gun.

un·lōad′, *v.i.* to discharge or get rid of something, especially a cargo or load; as, it is time to *unload.*

un·lōad′ẽr, *n.* one who or that which unloads; specifically, a device for unloading a wagon, a car, etc., as of hay, coal, and the like.

un·lō′çā·ted, *a.* 1. not placed; not fixed in a place.

2. not located definitely by survey and markings, as public lands.

un·lock′, *v.t.* 1. to unfasten or open, as what is locked; as, to *unlock* a door or a chest.

2. to open, release, or unfasten by or as by undoing a lock.

3. to expose; to reveal; to solve; to bring to light; as, to *unlock* a secret or a mystery.

un·lock′, *v.i.* to become unlocked.

un·looked′-fọr″ (-lookt′), *a.* not expected; not looked for; as, an *unlooked-for* piece of good fortune.

un·lọọse′, *v.t.* to loose; to loosen; to release.

un·lọọse′, *v.i.* to become loose or unfastened.

un·lọọs′en, *v.t.* to unloose; to loosen.

un·lọrd′, *v.t.* to deprive of a lordship.

un·lọrd′ed, *a.* not raised to a lordship; also, deprived of a lordship.

un·lŏve′, *v.t.* to love no longer; to despise. [Rare.]

un·lŏve′ly, *a.* not lovely, pleasing, or attractive; unpleasant; disagreeable; ugly.

un·luck′i·ly, *adv.* unfortunately; not luckily.

un·luck′i·ness, *n.* the state or the quality of being unlucky.

un·luck′y, *a.*; *comp.* unluckier; *superl.* unluckiest. 1. not lucky; bringing or presaging bad luck; unfortunate, ill-fated, or ill-omened.

2. mischievous. [Archaic and Dial.]

un·lust′, *n.* displeasure; lack of inclination. [Obs.]

un·maġ′is·trāte, *v.t.* to divest of magistracy. [Obs.]

un·māid′en, *v.t.* to deflower. [Obs.]

un·māil′ȧ·ble, *a.* that cannot be mailed; prohibited from the mails by law.

un·māke′, *v.t.*; unmade (-mād′), *pt., pp.*; unmaking, *ppr.* 1. to cause to be as before being made; to cause to revert to the original form, elements, or condition.

2. to ruin; destroy.

3. to depose from a position, rank, or authority.

un·man′, *v.t.*; unmanned, *pt., pp.*; unmanning, *ppr.* 1. to deprive of the distinctive qualities of a human being, as reason, affection, resolution, and the like. [Rare.]

2. to deprive of men; as, to *unman* a ship.

3. to emasculate; to deprive of virility; to castrate.

4. to deprive of the qualities considered characteristic of a man; to break or reduce into irresolution; to make weak, nervous, timid, etc.

un·man′ȧ·çle, *v.t.* to relieve of manacles; to liberate.

un·man′hood, *n.* the lack of manhood; also, the act of an inhuman person. [Obs.]

un·manned′, *a.* 1. deprived of manly qualities.

2. emasculated.

3. deprived of or lacking men.

4. uninhabited.

5. not tamed or broken: said of an animal, especially a hawk. [Obs.]

un·man′nẽr·li·ness, *n.* the state or quality of being unmannerly.

un·man′nẽr·ly, *a.* not having good manners; not in accordance with good manners; rude; discourteous.

un·man′nẽr·ly, *adv.* uncivilly; in violation of good manners; rudely.

un·mar′ry, *v.t.* to divorce.

un·mär′tyr (-tĩr), *v.t.* to degrade from the standing or dignity of a martyr. [Obs.]

un·mȧsk′, *v.t.* 1. to remove a mask or disguise from.

2. to disclose the true nature of; to expose; to reveal.

un·mȧsk′, *v.i.* 1. to take off a mask or disguise.

2. to appear in true character.

un·mȧs′tẽr·ȧ·ble, *a.* that cannot be mastered or subdued. [Rare.]

un·mēan′ing, *a.* 1. lacking in meaning, sense, or significance.

2. showing no sense or intelligence; empty; expressionless.

un·meçh′ăn·ize, *v.t.* to undo or destroy the mechanism of. [Rare.]

un·med′dle, *v.i.* to undo the effects of meddling.

un·mē·dic′in·ȧ·ble, *a.* 1. powerless to cure. [Obs.]

2. that cannot be cured.

un·med′i·tā·ted, *a.* not meditated; not prepared by previous thought; unpremeditated. [Rare.]

un·meet′, *a.* [ME. *unmete*; AS. *unmæte.*] not meet or fit; not proper; not worthy or suitable; unseemly.

un·meet′ly, *adv.* unsuitably; not fitly.

un·meet′ness, *n.* unfitness; unsuitableness.

un·mem′bẽr, *v.t.* to deprive of membership, as in a church or a lodge.

un·men′tion·ȧ·ble, *a.* considered improper for polite conversation; not fit to be mentioned.

un·men′tion·ȧ·bleṣ, *n.pl.* things regarded as improper to be mentioned or talked about; specifically, and humorously, undergarments or (formerly) trousers.

un·mẽr′cied, *a.* unmerciful. [Obs.]

un·mẽr′ci·fụl, *a.* having or showing no mercy; cruel; relentless; pitiless.

un·mer′it·ȧ·ble, *a.* having no merit; worthless. [Obs.]

un·mēt′ed, *a.* not meted or measured. [Rare.]

un·mew′, *v.t.* to set free as from a mew; to emancipate.

un·mīnd′fụl, *a.* forgetful; heedless; careless; not mindful or attentive.

un·miñ′gle, *v.t.* to separate, as things mixed.

un·miñ′gle·ȧ·ble, *a.* that cannot be mixed.

un·mīr′y, *a.* not miry; not muddy; not foul with dirt. [Rare.]

un·mis·tāk′ȧ·ble, *a.* that cannot be mistaken or misinterpreted; leaving room for no misunderstanding; clear; obvious.

un·mis·tāk′ȧ·bly, *adv.* so as to be unmistakable.

un·mī′tẽr, un·mī′tre (-tẽr), *v.t.* to deprive of a miter; to degrade or depose from the rank of a bishop.

un·mit′i·gā·ted, *a.* 1. not mitigated; not lessened; not softened in severity or harshness.

2. unmodified; clear-cut; absolute; as, an *unmitigated* liar; an *unmitigated* scoundrel.

un·mix′ed·ly, *adv.* purely; entirely; without mixture of other qualities.

un·mod′ẽrn·īze, *v.t.* to cause to appear old or antique.

un·mō′men·tär·y, *a.* at the same time, or without a moment's intervention. [Rare.]

un·mō·nop′ō·līze, *v.t.* to free from monopoly; to deprive of the character of a monopoly. [Rare.]

un·mō·nop′ō·lī·zing, *a.* not monopolizing; not obtaining the whole of anything. [Rare.]

un·mọọr′, *v.t.* 1. in nautical usage, to bring to the state of riding with a single anchor, after having been moored by two or more.

2. to free (a ship) from moorings.

un·mọọr′, *v.i.* to become unmoored.

un·mor′ăl, *a.* 1. having no morality; neither moral nor immoral; nonmoral.

2. unable to distinguish right from wrong.

un·mō·ral′i·ty, *n.* the state or quality of being unmoral.

un·mor′ăl·īzed, *a.* untutored by morality; not conformed to good morals.

un·mor′rised (-rist), *a.* not wearing the dress of a morris dancer. [Obs.]

un·mŏth′ẽred, *a.* deprived of a mother; motherless.

un·mō′tived, *a.* without motive; as, an *unmotived* part of a work of art.

un·mount′ed, *a.* 1. not mounted; not being affixed to a stiff back, as of cardboard; not provided with a backing or setting; as, an *unmounted* photograph; an *unmounted* diamond.

2. not mounted; not on horseback; as, *unmounted* police.

un·möv·ȧ·bil′i·ty, *n.* immovability.

un·möv′ȧ·bly, *adv.* immovably.

un·möv′ed·ly, *adv.* without being moved.

un·mud′dle, *v.t* and *v.i.* to free from muddle.

un·muf′fle, *v.t.*; unmuffled, *pt., pp.*; unmuffling, *ppr.* 1. to remove the covering from, as the face, head, etc.

2. to remove the muffling from (oars, a drum, etc.).

un·muf′fle, *v.i.* to take off something that muffles.

un·mul′ti·plȳ, *v.t.* to separate into factors; to reverse the process of multiplication in. [Rare.]

un·mũr′mũred, *a.* not murmured at. [Rare.]

un·mū′ṣiç·ăl, *a.* 1. not musical; not harmonious or melodious; not pleasing to the ear.

2. not fond of or skilled in music.

un·mū′tȧ·ble, *a.* immutable. [Obs.]

un·muz′zle, *v.t.* 1. to free (a dog, etc.) from a muzzle.

2. to free from restraint or censorship of what is written or spoken.

un·mys′tẽr·y, *v.t.* to divest of mystery; to make clear or plain. [Rare.]

un·nap′kined, *a.* having no napkin.

un·nat′ū·răl, *a.* 1. contrary to, or at variance with, nature or what is considered normal; abnormal; strange.

2. artificial, affected, or strained.

3. characterized by a lack of emotions, attitudes, or behavior regarded as natural, normal, or right.

4. abnormally evil or cruel.

un·nat′ū·răl·iṣm, *n.* the state or character of being unnatural.

un·nat·ū·ral′i·ty, *n.* the state or quality of being unnatural. [Rare.]

un·nā′tūre, *v.t.* to change or take away the nature of; to endow with a different nature.

un·nā′tūre, *n.* the absence of nature or of the order of nature; the contrary of nature; that which is unnatural. [Rare.]

un·nēar′, *prep.* not near; at a distance from. [Obs.]

un·nec′es·sär·i·ly, *adv.* in an unnecessary manner; without necessity; needlessly.

un·nec′es·sär·i·ness, *n.* the state of being unnecessary; needlessness.

un·nec′es·sär·y, *a.* not necessary; needless; not required by the circumstances of the case; useless; as, *unnecessary* labor or care; *unnecessary* vigor.

un·nec′es·sär·y, *n.*; *pl.* **un·nec′es·sär·ieṣ,** that which is unnecessary.

un·nē·ces′si·ty, *n.* the contrary of necessity; something unnecessary. [Obs.]

un·nẽrv′āte, *a.* not strong; feeble; enervated. [Obs.]

un·nẽrve′, *v.t.*; unnerved, *pt., pp.*; unnerving, *ppr.* to cause to feel weak, nervous, or incapable; to deprive of nerve, courage, self-confidence, etc.; to unman.

un·nes′tle (-nes′l), *v.t.* to deprive of or eject from a nest; to dislodge; to eject. [Obs.]

un·net′ted, *a.* not enclosed in a net or network; unprotected by nets, as cherries.

un·nimbed′ (-nimd′), *a.* not having a nimbus; depicted as without a nimbus. [Rare.]

un·nō′ti·fȳ, *v.t.* to contradict, as something previously made known, declared, or notified.

un·num′bẽred, *a.* 1. countless; innumerable.

2. having no identifying number or numbers.

3. not counted.

un·nun′, *v.t.* to release or depose from the condition of a nun; to cause to cease to be a nun. [Rare.]

un·ō·bē′di·ence, *n.* disobedience.
un·ō·bē′di·ent, *a.* disobedient.
un·oc′cū·pied, *a.* 1. vacant; empty; having no occupant.
2. at leisure; idle.
ū′nōde, *n.* in geometry, a conical point of a surface in which the tangent cone has become a pair of coincident planes: also called *uniplanar point.*
un·of′ten (of′n), *adv.* not often; rarely. [Rare.]
un·ōld′, *v.t.* to make young; to rejuvenate. [Obs.]
Ū·nō′nȧ, *n.* a genus of plants of the order *Anonaceæ.* The species consist of trees, large shrubs, or climbing plants, found in India and tropical Africa. The bark and fruit of many of the species are aromatic, with some degree of acridity, and are employed as stimulants and febrifuges.
un·or′dẽr, *v.t.* to counterorder. [Rare.]
un·or′di·nȧte, *a.* inordinate.
un·or′di·nȧte·ly, *adv.* inordinately.
un·or′gȧn·īzed, *a.* 1. having no organic structure.
2. having no regular order, system, or organization.
3. not being a member of a labor union.
4. not being a member of a fraternity or sorority, as at a college.
un·or′gȧn·īzed fẽr′ment, an enzyme.
un·or′thō·dox, *a.* not orthodox; not conforming to the usual beliefs or established customs.
un·ōwned′, *a.* 1. having no owner.
2. not admitted or acknowledged.
un·pack′, *v.t.* 1. to open and remove the contents of.
2. to take out of a package, trunk, etc.
3. to remove a pack from (a horse, etc.) or a load from (a truck, etc.).
un·pack′, *v.i.* 1. to unpack a packed trunk, bag, etc.
2. to admit of being unpacked.
un·pāġed′, *a.* having the pages not numbered: said of a book, etc.
un·palped′ (-palpt′), *a.* without palps, as an insect.
un·par′ȧ·dīse, *v.t.* to deprive of happiness like that of paradise; to render unhappy. [Rare.]
un·par′ȧl·leled, *a.* that has no parallel, equal, or counterpart; unmatched.
un·pärched′ (-pärcht′), *a.* not parched.
un″pär·liȧ·men′tȧ·ry, *a.* contrary to parliamentary law or usage.
un·pär′tiăl (-shăl), *a.* impartial. [Obs.]
un·pär′tiăl·ly, *adv.* impartially. [Obs.]
un·pȧs′tŏr, *v.t.* to deprive of or reduce from the office of pastor. [Obs.]
un·pȧthed′, *a.* pathless.
un·pȧth′wāyed, *a.* pathless. [Rare.]
un·pā′tience (-shens), *n.* impatience. [Chiefly Dial.]
un·pā′tient, *a.* impatient. [Chiefly Dial.]
un·pāy′, *v.t.* to undo. [Obs.]
un·pēace′, *n.* absence of peace.
un·peer′ȧ·ble, *a.* incapable of having a peer, or equal; unequaled.
un·peered′, *a.* having no peer; unpeerable.
un·peg′, *v.t.*; unpegged, *pt., pp.*; unpegging, *ppr.* 1. to remove a peg or pegs from.
2. to unfasten or detach in this way.
un·pen′, *v.t.* to release from being penned or dammed up; to free from confinement.
un·pen′, *v.t.* to remove the feathers of. [Obs.]
un·pen′ē·trȧ·ble, *a.* impenetrable. [Rare.]
un·pen′i·tent, *a.* impenitent. [Rare.]
un·pēo′ple, *v.t.*; unpeopled, *pt., pp.*; unpeopling, *ppr.* to remove people from; to remove the occupants or inhabitants from; to depopulate.
un·pẽr·cēived′, *a.* not perceived; not heeded; not observed; not noticed.
un·pẽr·fec′tion, *n.* imperfection. [Obs.]
un·pẽr′fect·ly, *adv.* imperfectly. [Obs.]
un·per′ish·ȧ·ble, *a.* imperishable.
un·per′ish·ȧ·bly, *adv.* imperishably.
un·pẽr·plex′, *v.t.* to free from perplexity. [Rare.]
un·pẽr·suā′ṣiŏn (-swā′), *n.* the state of not being persuaded. [Rare.]
un·pẽr·vẽrt′, *v.t.* to free from perversion.
un·pick′, *v.t.* 1. to unfasten; to open with a pointed instrument.
2. to pick out; to undo by picking; hence, to take to pieces.
un·pick′, *v.i.* to pick out stitches.
un·pin′, *v.t.*; unpinned, *pt., pp.*; unpinning, *ppr.* 1. to remove a pin or pins from; as, to *unpin* a frock; to *unpin* the frame of a building.
2. to unfasten or detach in this way.
un·piñked′ (-piñkt′), *a.* not pinked; not pierced with eyelet holes. [Obs.]
un·pit′y, *n.* impiety. [Obs.]
un·plāced′ (-plāst′), *a.* 1. not placed; jumbled; confused.
2. having no office under government.
3. in horse racing, not among the first three horses.
un·plāin′, *a.* not simple or plain.
un·plāined′, *a.* not deplored or lamented. [Obs.]
un·plāit′, *v.t.* [*un-*, back, and *plait.*] to unbraid.
un·plau′sive, *a.* not approving; not applauding. [Obs.]
un·pleaṣ′ănt (-plez′), *a.* not pleasant; disagreeable; offensive.
un·pleaṣ′ănt·ness, *n.* 1. an unpleasant quality or condition.
2. an unpleasant situation, relationship, etc.
3. a quarrel or disagreement.
the late unpleasantness; the most recent war: an ironic usage.
un·pleaṣ′ănt·ry, *n.*; *pl.* **un·pleaṣ′ănt·rieṣ,** 1. lack of pleasantry.
2. a quarrel or falling out.
un·plēaṣ′ive, *a.* unpleasant. [Obs.]
un·plight′ (-plīt′), *v.t.* to unfold; to lay open. [Obs.]
un·plumb′ (-plum′), *v.t.* to remove the lead from. [Rare.]

> They *unplumb* the dead for bullets to assassinate the living. —Burke.

un·plumbed′, *a.* 1. not plumbed, fathomed, or measured; unknown.
2. having no plumbing.
3. not sealed with lead.
un·point′ed, *a.* 1. having no point; not sharp.
2. without a point or definite aim; aimless; purposeless.
3. not having marks by which to distinguish sentences, members, and clauses in writing; not punctuated.
4. not having the vowel points or marks; as, an *unpointed* manuscript in Hebrew or Arabic.
un·poi′ṣŏn, *v.t.* to remove or expel poison from. [Rare.]
un·pōlled′, *a.* [*un-*, not, and *polled*, pp. of poll, v.]
1. not having voted.
2. not cast or entered: said of a vote.
un·pōpe′, *v.t.* 1. to deprive of the character, dignity, or authority of a pope. [Rare.]
2. to deprive of a pope. [Rare.]
un·pop′ū·lăr, *a.* not popular; not liked or approved of by the public or by the majority.
un·pōr′tū·ous, *a.* having no ports. [Obs.]
un·pos·si·bil′i·ty, *n.* impossibility. [Dial.]
un·pos′si·ble, *a.* impossible. [Dial.]
un·pow′ẽr, *n.* weakness; lack of power. [Obs.]
un·prac′ticed, un·prac′tised (-tist), *a.* 1. not practiced; not habitually or repeatedly done, performed, etc.
2. not skilled or experienced; inexpert.
un·prāiṣe′, *v.t.* to deprive of praise. [Obs.]
un·prāy′, *v.t.* to revoke, recall, or negative by a subsequent prayer. [Rare.]
un·prēach′, *v.t.* to preach the contrary of; to recant in preaching. [Rare.]
un·prec′ē·dent·ed, *a.* having no precedent or parallel; unheard-of; novel; unexampled.
un·prē·dict′, *v.i.* to retract prediction. [Obs.]
un·prē·jū′di·cāte, *a.* not prepossessed by settled opinions. [Obs.]
un·prej′ū·diced (-dist), *a.* 1. without prejudice or bias; impartial.
2. not impaired.
un·prē·med′i·tāte, *a.* unpremeditated. [Archaic.]
un·prē·med′i·tāt·ed, *a.* done without plan or forethought; not premeditated.
un·prīced′ (-prīst′), *a.* 1. having no fixed price.
2. priceless.
un·prince′, *v.t.* to deprive of principality or sovereignty. [Rare.]
un·prin′ci·ple, *v.t.* to destroy the moral principles of. [Rare.]
un·prin′ci·pled (-pld), *a.* 1. not having settled principles.
2. having no good moral principles; destitute of virtue; not restrained by conscience; unscrupulous.
unprincipled in; uninstructed in the principles of.
un·prin′ci·pled·ness, *n.* the quality or state of being unprincipled.
un·print′ȧ·ble, *a.* not printable; not fit to be printed, as because of obscenity.
un·priṣ′ŏn, *v.t.* to set free from prison. [Rare.]
un·prīz′ȧ·ble, *a.* not prized; also, invaluable.
un·prob′ȧ·bly, *adv.* improperly. [Obs.]
un·prob′ȧ·bly, *adv.* improbably. [Obs.]
un·prō·duc′tive, *a.* 1. not productive; not producing large crops; barren; sterile; not making any return for labor expended; as, *unproductive* soil.
2. not producing profit; not bringing in any return; as, *unproductive* capital.
3. not producing goods or articles for consumption; as, *unproductive* labor.
4. not producing a specified or expected effect or result: followed by *of.*
un·prō·duc′tive·ly, *adv.* in an unproductive manner.
un·prō·duc′tive·ness, *n.* the state of being unproductive.
un·prō·fāned′, *a.* not profaned; not violated.
un·prō·fes′sion·ăl, *a.* 1. violating the rules or ethical code of a given profession.
2. not of, characteristic of, belonging to, or connected with a profession; nonprofessional.
un·prof′it, *n.* lack of profit.
un·prop′ẽr, *a.* improper. [Obs.]
un·prop′ẽr·ly, *adv.* improperly. [Obs.]
un·pros′ē·lȳte, *v.t.* to prevent being made a proselyte; to win back from proselytism. [Rare.]
un·pros′pẽr·ous, *a.* not prosperous; not attended with success; unfortunate.
un·pros′pẽr·ous·ly, *adv.* unsuccessfully; unfortunately.
un·prot′es·tănt·īze, *v.t.* to lead or drive away from Protestantism; to divest of a Protestant character; to change from Protestantism to some other religion. [Rare.]
un·prov′i·dent, *a.* improvident.
un·prụ′dence, *n.* imprudence.
un·prụ′dent, *a.* imprudent.
un·pub′lished, *a.* 1. not published.
2. in copyright law, designating a literary work that has neither been given public distribution nor been made available for sale in reproduced form, as of the time of registration.
un·pūre′, *a.* not pure; impure.
un·pūre′ly, *adv.* impurely.
un·pūre′ness, *n.* impurity.
un·pũrsed′ (-pũrst′), *a.* 1. robbed of a purse. [Rare.]
2. taken out of the purse; expended. [Obs.]
un·quäl′i·fīed, *a.* 1. not qualified; not fit; not having the usual or requisite talents, abilities, or accomplishments.
2. not modified, limited, or restricted by conditions or exceptions; as, *unqualified* praise.
3. absolute; downright; as, an *unqualified* success.
un·quäl′i·fīed·ly, *adv.* in an unqualified manner.
un·quäl′i·fīed·ness, *n.* the condition of being unqualified.
un·quäl′i·fȳ, *v.t.* to disqualify.
un·quäl′i·tied, *a.* deprived of the usual faculties. [Obs.]
un·queen′ (-kwēn′), *v.t.* to divest of the dignity of queen. [Rare.]
un·ques′tion·ȧ·ble, *a.* 1. not to be questioned, doubted, or disputed; certain.
2. unexceptionable.
un·ques′tion·ȧ·bly, *adv.* beyond any question or doubt; indisputably; certainly.
un·ques′tioned (-chund), *a.* 1. not called in question; not subjected to inquiry.
2. not interrogated; having no questions asked.
3. indisputable; not to be opposed.
un·quī′et, *a.* 1. not quiet; restless; disturbed; agitated.
2. anxious; uneasy.
3. disturbing.
un·quī′et, *v.t.* to disquiet.
un·quī′e·tūde, *n.* inquietude.

un·quōte′, *v.t.* and *v.i.*; unquoted, *pt.*, *pp.*; unquoting, *ppr.* to end (a quotation): generally used absolutely.

un·rav′el, *v.t.* unraveled *or* unravelled, *pt.*, *pp.*; unraveling *or* unravelling, *ppr.* 1. to disentangle (something woven, tangled, or raveled up); to disengage or separate the threads of.
2. to explain; to clear from complication or difficulty; as, to *unravel* a mystery.
3. to bring to a climax, as the plot of a novel or play.
4. to separate the connected or united parts of; to throw into disorder. [Obs.]

un·rav′el, *v.i.* to become unraveled; to be unfolded; to be disentangled.

un·rav′el·ment, *n.* the act of unraveling; disentanglement.

un·rā′zŏred, *a.* unshaven. [Rare.]

un·read′ (-red′), *a.* 1. not read; as, the book remained *unread.*
2. having read little or nothing.

un·rēad′à·ble, *a.* not readable; specifically, (a) illegible; (b) uninteresting to read; (c) unsuitable for reading.

un·read′i·ly, *adv.* in an unready manner.

un·read′i·ness, *n.* the quality or state of being unready.

un·read′y, *a.* 1. not ready; not prepared, as for action.
2. not prompt or alert; slow; hesitant.
3. undressed; not fully clothed. [Obs. or Dial.]

un·read′y (-red′), *v.t.* to undress. [Obs.]

un·rē′ăl, *a.* not real or actual; fantastic; imaginary; fanciful; visionary; insubstantial.

un·rē·al′i·ty, *n.*; *pl.* **un·rē·al′i·ties**, 1. the state or quality of being unreal.
2. something unreal.
3. a tendency to be visionary or fanciful.

un·rē′ăl·īze, *v.t.* to divest of reality.

un·rēa′ṣŏn, *v.t.* to undo or refute by argument. [Rare.]

un·rēa′ṣŏn, *n.* lack of reason; irrationality; stupidity; absurdity.

un·rēa′ṣŏn·à·ble, *a.* 1. not reasonable or rational; having or showing little sense or judgment.
2. excessive; immoderate; exorbitant.

un·rēa′ṣŏn·à·ble·ness, *n.* the quality or state of being unreasonable.

un·rēa′ṣŏn·à·bly, *adv.* so as to be unreasonable; in an unreasonable manner.

un·rēa′ṣŏn·ing, *a.* not reasoning; without reason; blind; thoughtless; irrational.

un·rēave′, *v.t.* to unwind; to disentangle; to loose. [Now Chiefly Dial.]

un·reç·ŏn·cīl′à·ble, *a.* irreconcilable.

un·reç·ŏn·cīl′à·bly, *adv.* irreconcilably.

un·rē·çŏn·struçt′ed, *a.* not having been reconstructed; specifically, in United States history, that had not yet undergone, or was not reconciled to, the Reconstruction after the Civil War.

un·rē·çūr′ing, *a.* incurable. [Rare.]

un·reel′, *v.t.* and *v.i.* to unwind from or as from a reel.

un·reeve′, *v.t.*; unrove *or* unreeved, *pt.*, *pp.*; unreeving, *ppr.* to withdraw (a rope, etc.) from a block, deadeye, or the like.

un·reeve′, *v.i.* 1. to become unreeved, as a rope.
2. to unreeve a rope.

un·ref·ŏr·mā′tion, *n.* lack of reformation. [Obs.]

un·rē·ġen′ẽr·āte, *a.* 1. not regenerate; not spiritually reborn or converted.
2. loosely, wicked; sinful.

un·rē·ġen′ẽr·āt·ed, *a.* unregenerate.

un·rē·ġen·ẽr·ā′tion, *n.* the state of being unregenerate. [Obs.]

un·rē·lent′ing, *a.* 1. refusing to yield or relent; inflexible; relentless.
2. without mercy or compassion; cruel; merciless.
3. not relaxing or slackening, as in effort, speed, etc.

un·rē·li′ġious, *a.* 1. irreligious.
2. not connected with or involving religion; neither religious nor irreligious; nonreligious.

un·rē·mem′brănce, *n.* forgetfulness; lack of remembrance.

un·rē·mit′ting, *a.* [*un-*, not, and *remitting.*] not stopping, relaxing, or slackening; incessant; persistent.

un·rē·morse′less, *a.* having no remorse. [Rare.]

un·rē·pâir′, *n.* disrepair.

un·rē·pâir′à·ble, *a.* irreparable.

un·rē·prōved′, *a.* 1. not reproved; not censured.
2. not liable to reproof or blame.

un·rē·ṣẽrve′, *n.* lack of reserve or restraint; frankness; candor.

un·rē·ṣẽrved′, *a.* 1. not reserved in speech or behavior; frank; candid.
2. not restricted or qualified; unlimited.

un·rē·ṣẽrv′ed·ly, *adv.* in an unreserved manner; without reservation.

un·rest′, *n.* a troubled or disturbed state; restlessness; disquiet; uneasiness: sometimes applied euphemistically to a condition of angry discontent verging on revolt.

un·rid′dle, *v.t.*; unriddled, *pt.*, *pp.*; unriddling, *ppr.* to solve or explain, as a riddle.

un·rid′dlẽr, *n.* one who unriddles.

un·rig′, *v.t.*; unrigged, *pt.*, *pp.*; unrigging, *ppr.* to strip of rigging or of equipment, gear, etc.

un·rīght′eous (-rī′chus), *a.* 1. not righteous; wicked; sinful.
2. not right; unjust; unfair.

un·rip′, *v.t.*; unripped, *pt.*, *pp.*; unripping, *ppr.* to rip open; to take apart or detach by ripping.

un·ripe′, *a.* 1. not ripe or mature; green: said of fruit, etc.
2. premature: said especially of death. [Obs.]

un·rī′văled, un·rī′vălled, *a.* having no rival, equal, or competitor; matchless; peerless.

un·rōll′, *v.t.* 1. to open or extend (something rolled up); as, to *unroll* wallpaper.
2. to display; to expose to view.
3. to remove from a roll or register, as a name or a record. [Rare.]

un·rōll′, *v.i.* to become unrolled.

un·rōll′ment, *n.* the act of unrolling or of being unrolled.

un·ro͝of′, *v.t.* to take off the roof or covering of.

un·ro͝ot′, *v.t.* to uproot.

un·round′, *v.t.* in phonetics, (a) to pronounce without rounding the lips, as a vowel usually rounded; (b) to make (the lips) not rounded, as in pronouncing the vowel in *she.*

un·rōve′, *v.* alternative past tense and past participle of *unreeve.*

un·rōve′, *a.* withdrawn from a block, deadeye, or the like, as a rope.

un·ruf′fled, *a.* not ruffled, disturbed, or agitated; calm; smooth; serene.

un·rụ′ined, *a.* having escaped ruin; as, one building alone remained *unruined.*

un·rụ′li·ness, *n.* state, quality, or instance of being unruly; stubbornness; refractoriness.

un·rụ′ly, *a.*; *comp.* unrulier; *superl.* unruliest, hard to control, restrain, or keep in order; disobedient; unmanageable; disorderly; refractory; not submitting or conforming to rule or discipline.

un·sad′dle, *v.t.*; unsaddled, *pt.*, *pp.*; unsaddling, *ppr.* 1. to remove a saddle from (a horse, etc.).
2. to push or throw from a saddle, as a rider; to unhorse.

un·sad′dle, *v.i.* to remove a saddle from a horse, etc.

un·sad′ness, *n.* infirmity; weakness. [Obs.]

un·sāint′, *v.t.* to deprive of saintship; to divest of saintly character; to deny sanctity to. [Obs.]

un·sal′và·ble, *a.* beyond the possibility of being saved; not savable.

un·sat′ū·rāt·ed, *a.* 1. not saturated.
2. in chemistry, (a) designating or of a compound in which some element possesses the capacity of combining further with other elements; (b) designating or of a solution that is not in equilibrium with the undissolved solute; (c) designating an organic radical with a double or triple bond that links two atoms of carbon.

un·sā′vŏr·y, un·sā′vŏur·y, *a.* 1. without flavor; tasteless.
2. unpleasant to taste or smell.
3. offensive, disagreeable, or unpleasant, especially morally.

un·sāy′, *v.t.*; unsaid, *pt.*, *pp.*; unsaying, *ppr.* to take back or retract (what has been said).

un·sçāp′à·ble, *a.* that cannot be escaped; inevitable. [Obs.]

un·sçathed, *a.* not scathed; uninjured.

un·sçī′ence, *n.* lack of science or knowledge; ignorance. [Obs.]

un·sçram′ble, *v.t.*; unscrambled, *pt.*, *pp.*; unscrambling, *ppr.* to cause to be no longer scrambled, disordered, or mixed up; as, he *unscrambled* the coded message. [Colloq.]

un·sçrew′, *v.t.* 1. to remove a screw or screws from.
2. to remove, detach, or loosen by removing a screw or screws, or by turning.

un·sçrew′, *v.i.* to become unscrewed or admit of being unscrewed.

un·sçrụ′pū·lous, *a.* not restrained by ideas of right and wrong; having no moral principles; not scrupulous; unprincipled.

un·sçulp′tūred, *a.* having no sculptured marks, as prominences and depressions: said of an organ or part of an insect.

un·sēal′, *v.t.* 1. to break or remove the seal of.
2. to open (something sealed or closed as if sealed).

un·sēam′, *v.t.* to open or undo the seam or seams of; to rip; to cut open.

un·sẽarch′à·ble, *a.* that cannot be searched into or explored; mysterious; inscrutable.

un·sẽarch′à·bly, *adv.* so as to be unsearchable.

un·sēa′ṣŏn·à·ble, *a.* 1. not seasonable; not usual for or appropriate to the season; as, *unseasonable* heat.
2. not suited to the time or the occasion; unfit; untimely; ill-timed.

un·sēa′ṣŏn·à·ble·ness, *n.* the quality or the state of being unseasonable.

un·sēa′ṣŏn·à·bly, *adv.* in an unseasonable manner; so as to be unseasonable.

un·sēa′ṣŏned, *a.* 1. not kept and made fit for use; not ripened, dried, etc. by enough seasoning; as, *unseasoned* wood.
2. not inured; not accustomed (*to*); not fitted by use or habit to endure something; as, men *unseasoned* to tropical climates.
3. not qualified by use or experience; unripe; inexperienced; as, an *unseasoned* soldier.
4. not flavored with seasoning; as, *unseasoned* meat.
5. unseasonable; untimely; ill-timed. [Obs.]

un·sēat′, *v.t.* 1. to throw or dislodge from a seat.
2. to remove from office, deprive of rank, etc.
3. to unhorse.

un·seem′li·ness, *n.* the condition or the character of being unseemly; uncomeliness; indecency; indecorum; impropriety.

un·seem′ly, *a.* not seemly; not fit, decent, or becoming; uncomely; unbecoming; improper; indecorous; as, *unseemly* behavior.

un·seem′ly, *adv.* in an unseemly manner; indecently; unbecomingly.

un·seen′, *a.* 1. not seen; unperceived, unobserved, unnoticed, or undiscovered.
2. invisible.

un·sensed′ (-senst′), *a.* lacking a distinct meaning; without a certain signification. [Rare.]

un·sen′si·ble, *a.* not sensible; nonsensical; insensible; imperceptible. [Dial.]

un·sen′si·ble·ness, *n.* a being insensible; lack of sensibleness. [Dial.]

un·sep′à·rà·ble, *a.* inseparable. [Obs.]

un·sep′à·rà·bly, *adv.* inseparably. [Obs.]

un·sẽrv′ice, *n.* lack of service; neglect of duty; idleness. [Rare.]

un·set′, *a.* 1. not set; not placed; unmounted.
2. not sunk below the horizon.
3. not set, as a broken limb.

un·set′tle, *v.t.*; unsettled, *pt.*, *pp.*; unsettling, *ppr.* to make unsettled, insecure, or unstable; to disturb, displace, disarrange, or disorder.

un·set′tle, *v.i.* to become unsettled; to give way.

un·set′tled (-tld), *a.* 1. not settled or orderly; disordered.
2. not stable or fixed; changeable; uncertain.
3. not decided or determined.
4. not paid, allotted, or otherwise disposed of; as, an *unsettled* debt, estate, etc.
5. having no settlers; unpopulated.
6. not established in a place or abode.

un·set′tled·ness, *n.* the state of being unfixed, unsettled, or undetermined.

un·set′tle·ment, *n.* an unsettled state; irresolution.

un·sew′ (-sō′), *v.t.* to rip.

un·sex′, *v.t.* to deprive of the qualities considered characteristic of one's sex; especially, to make unwomanly.

un·shack′le, *v.t.*; unshackled, *pt.*, *pp.*; unshackling, *ppr.* 1. to loosen or remove the shackles from.
2. to free.

un·shāked′ (-shākt′), *a.* firm. [Obs.]
un·shāpe′, *v.t.* to confound; to derange.
un·shāped′ (-shāpt′), *a.* not shaped; shapeless; unformed; unshapen.
un·shāp′en, *a.* 1. unshaped; shapeless.
2. badly shaped; misshapen, malformed, or deformed.
un·shēathe′, *v.t.*; unsheathed, *pt., pp.*; unsheathing, *ppr.* to remove (a sword, knife, etc.) from or as from a sheath or scabbard.
un·shed′, *a.* 1. not spilled; as, blood *unshed.*
2. not parted, as the hair. [Obs.]
un·sher′iff, *v.t.* to depose from the position of sheriff. [Rare.]
un·ship′, *v.t.*; unshipped, *pt., pp.*; unshipping, *ppr.* 1. to take (cargo, etc.) out of or off from a ship.
2. to remove (an oar, mast, etc.) from the proper position for use.
3. to disembark (passengers).
4. to unload; to get rid of. [Colloq.]
un·ship′ment, *n.* an unshipping or being unshipped.
un·shout′, *v.t.* to retract a shout. [Rare.]
un·shut′, *v.t.* to open. [Obs.]
un·sīght′ (-sīt′), *a.* not examined or inspected: only in the phrase, *unsight unseen*; as, to buy a thing *unsight unseen*, that is, without having seen or examined it.
un·sīght′li·ness, *n.* disagreeableness to the sight; ugliness.
un·sīght′ly, *a.*; *comp.* unsightlier; *superl.* unsightliest, disagreeable to the eye; ugly.
un·sig·nif′i·cȧnt, *a.* insignificant. [Obs.]
un·sin·cēre′, *a.* insincere. [Obs.]
un·sin′ew, *v.t.* to deprive of strength. [Rare.]
un·sis′tēr, *v.t.* to part, as sisters. [Rare.]
un·sit′ting, *a.* unbecoming. [Obs.]
un·skill′, *n.* unskillfulness. [Archaic.]
un·skilled′, *a.* 1. having no special skill or training.
2. requiring or using no special skill or training; as, *unskilled* labor.
un·skill′fu̧l, un·skil′fu̧l, *a.* having little or no skill or dexterity; awkward; clumsy.
un·sling′, *v.t.*; unslung, *pt., pp.*; unslinging, *ppr.* 1. to take (a rifle, etc.) from a slung position.
2. in nautical usage, to release from slings.
un·snap′, *v.t.*; unsnapped, *pt., pp.*; unsnapping, *ppr.* 1. to undo the snap or snaps of.
2. to loosen or detach by so doing.
un·snärl′, *v.t.* to untangle; to free of snarls or entanglement.
un″sō·ciȧ·bil′i·ty (-shȧ-), *n.* 1. the quality or state of being unsociable.
2. unsociable behavior or character.
un·sō′ciȧ·ble, *a.* 1. avoiding association with others; not sociable or friendly.
2. not conducive to sociability.
un·sō′ciȧ·bly, *adv.* in an unsociable manner.
un·sō′ciăl (-shăl), *a.* having or showing a dislike for the society of others.
un·soft′, *a.* not soft; hard. [Obs.]
un·soft′, *adv.* not softly. [Obs.]
un·sold′ẽr, (-sod′), *v.t.* 1. to take apart (things soldered together).
2. to disunite; to separate; to sunder.
un·sō′nȧ·ble, *a.* that cannot be sounded. [Obs.]
un·son′sy, un·son′cy, *a.* [*un-* and *sonsy.*] bringing or indicating bad luck; ominous. [Scot. and Brit. Dial.]
un·sō·phis′ti·cā·ted, *a.* 1. not sophisticated; artless; simple; ingenuous; lacking worldly experience.
2. not adulterated; genuine or pure.
un·soul′, *v.t.* to take the soul away from (someone).
un·sound′, *a.* 1. not sound, whole, or perfect; not in perfect health or condition.
2. at variance with fact, truth, or reason; false; ill-founded.
3. not safe, firm, or solid; insecure.
4. not deep; light: said of sleep.
un·spăr′ing, *a.* 1. not parsimonious or stinting; lavish; liberal; profuse.
2. not merciful or forgiving; severe.
un·spăr′ing·ly, *adv.* in abundance; lavishly.
un·spăr′ing·ness, *n.* the quality of being liberal or profuse.
un·spēak′, *v.t.*; unspoke, *pt.*; unspoken, *pp.*; unspeaking, *ppr.* to take back (something spoken); to retract; unsay.
un·spēak′ȧ·ble, *a.* 1. that cannot be spoken.
2. unutterable; ineffable; inexpressible.
3. inexpressibly bad, evil, or objectionable.
un·spēak′ȧ·bly, *adv.* so as to be unspeakable; in an unspeakable manner; inexpressibly; unutterably.
un·sped′, *a.* not performed or dispatched. [Obs.]
un·sphēre′, *v.t.*; unsphered, *pt., pp.*; unsphering, *ppr.* to remove from its sphere or from one's sphere.
un·spir′it, *v.t.* to dispirit. [Obs.]
un·spot′ted, *a.* not stained; figuratively, free from moral stain; untainted with guilt; unblemished; immaculate; as, *unspotted* reputation.
un·spot′ted·ness, *n.* the state of being unspotted.
un·squīre′, *v.t.* to divest of the title or privileges of an esquire. [Rare.]
un·stā′ble, *a.* 1. not stable; not fixed, firm, or steady; easily upset, shifted, or unbalanced.
2. changeable; inconstant; variable; fluctuating.
3. unreliable; fickle.
4. emotionally unsettled or variable.
5. in chemistry, tending to decompose or change into other compounds.
unstable equilibrium; the equilibrium of a body by which it tends to move, when disturbed, away from its position at the time of disturbance.
un·stāte′, *v.t.* 1. to deprive of dignity.
2. to take away the character or privileges of a state or statehood. [Rare.]
un·stead′y (-sted′), *a.* 1. not steady, firm, or stable; shaky.
2. changeable; inconstant; wavering.
3. erratic in habits, purpose, or behavior.
un·steel′, *v.t.* 1. to make no longer steeled; to soften.
2. to disarm. [Rare.]
un·step′, *v.t.*; unstepped, *pt., pp.*; unstepping, *ppr.* in nautical usage, to remove (a mast) from its step or socket.
un·stick′, *v.t.*; unstuck, *pt., pp.*; unsticking, *ppr.* to cause to stick, or adhere, no longer; to loosen or free, as something stuck.
un·stock′, *v.t.* 1. to lessen the stock of; to remove the stock from; as, to *unstock* a store.
2. to remove the stock from (a gun).
3. to launch (a ship).
un·stop′, *v.t.*; unstopped, *pt., pp.*; unstopping, *ppr.* 1. to remove the stopper from.
2. to clear (a pipe, etc.) of a stoppage or obstruction; to open.
3. to open the stops of (an organ).
un·strap′, *v.t.*; unstrapped, *pt., pp.*; unstrapping, *ppr.* to loosen or remove the strap or straps of.
un·strat′i·fīed, *a.* not stratified; specifically, in botany, having no clearly marked layers, as the thalli of certain lichens.
un·strength′, *n.* weakness. [Obs.]
un·string′, *v.t.*; unstrung, *pt., pp.*; unstringing, *ppr.* 1. to loosen or remove the string or strings of.
2. to remove from a string.
3. to loosen; to relax.
4. to weaken or disorder; to make unstrung (usually in the passive).
un·strung′, *v.* past tense and past participle of *unstring.*
un·strung′, *a.* 1. weak; nervous; upset.
2. having the string or strings loosened or detached, as a bow.
un·stud′ied, *a.* 1. not got by study or conscious effort.
2. spontaneous; natural; unforced; unaffected.
3. not having studied; unlearned or unversed.
un·sub·stan′tiăl (-shăl), *a.* 1. not substantial; having no material substance.
2. not solid or heavy; flimsy; light.
3. unreal; visionary.
4. not giving strength or vigor; as, *unsubstantial* food.
un·sub·stan′tiăl·īze, *v.t.* to make unsubstantial. [Rare.]
un·sub·stan·ti·ā′tion (-shi-ā′), *n.* deprivation of substantiality.
un·sūit·ȧ·bil′i·ty, *n.* the state or quality of being unsuitable.
un·sūit′ȧ·ble, *a.* not suitable or fitting; unbecoming; inappropriate.
un·sūit′ȧ·bly, *adv.* in an unsuitable manner.
un·sung′, *a.* 1. not sung.
2. not honored or celebrated in song or poetry.
un·sus·pect′ed, *a.* 1. not suspected; not under suspicion.
2. not imagined to be existent, probable, etc.
un·swāthe′, *v.t.*; unswathed, *pt., pp.*; unswathing, *ppr.* to remove a swathe or wrappings from.
un·sweăr′, *v.t.* and *v.i.*; unswore, *pt.*; unsworn, *pp.*; unswearing, *ppr.* to recant or take back (something sworn to), as by another oath; to abjure.
un·sym·met′riç, *a.* same as *unsymmetrical.*
un·sym·met′riç·ăl, *a.* lacking symmetry; asymmetrical.
un·sym·met′riç·ăl·ly, *adv.* in an unsymmetrical manner; asymmetrically.
un·sym′mē·try, *n.* lack of symmetry; disproportion.
un·tañ′gle, *v.t.*; untangled, *pt., pp.*; untangling, *ppr.* 1. to free from a snarl or tangle; to disentangle.
2. to clear up; to put in order; to straighten out.
un·tau̧ght′ (-tạt′), *v.* past tense and past participle of *unteach.*
un·tau̧ght′, *a.* 1. not taught or instructed; uneducated; ignorant.
2. got without teaching; natural.
un·tēach′, *v.t.*; untaught, *pt., pp.*; unteaching, *ppr.* 1. to cause to forget something learned.
2. to teach, or cause to believe, the opposite of something previously taught.
3. to teach the opposite of.
U̧n·tẽr·şee′bōot, *n.* [G.] undersea boat; submarine: often shortened to *U-boat.*
un·thañked′ (-thañkt′), *a.* 1. not thanked; not repaid with thanks or acknowledgment.
2. not received with thanks or thankfulness. [Rare.]
un·thañk′fu̧l, *a.* 1. not thankful; ungrateful.
2. not acknowledged or repaid with thanks; not thankfully received or welcomed; thankless.
One of the most *unthankful* offices in the world. —Goldsmith.
un·thañk′fu̧l·ly, *adv.* in an unthankful manner; without thanks.
un·thañk′fu̧l·ness, *n.* the quality or state of being unthankful; ingratitude.
un·thiñk′, *v.t.*; unthought, *pt., pp.*; unthinking, *ppr.* to retract mentally, rid one's mind of, or change one's mind about.
un·thiñk′ȧ·ble, *a.* not thinkable; that cannot be thought, conceived, or considered.
un·thiñk′ing, *a.* 1. thoughtless; heedless; inconsiderate.
2. lacking the ability to think.
3. showing lack of thought.
un·thread′ (-thred′), *v.t.* 1. to draw or take out the thread or threads from; as, to *unthread* a needle.
2. to disentangle; to unravel.
3. to relax the ligaments of; to loosen. [Rare.]
4. to find one's way through.
They soon *unthreaded* the labyrinth of rocks. —De Quincey.
un·thrift′, *a.* profuse; prodigal; unthrifty. [Obs.]
un·thrift′, *n.* 1. thriftlessness.
2. a prodigal.
un·thrift′fu̧l·ly, *adv.* unthriftily.
un·thrift′i·head (-hed), *n.* thriftlessness. [Obs.]
un·thrift′i·ly, *adv.* 1. in an unthrifty manner; wastefully.
2. shabbily; poorly. [Obs.]
un·thrift′i·ness, *n.* the state or quality of being unthrifty; prodigality; profusion.
un·thrift′y, *a.* 1. not thrifty; prodigal; profuse; lavish; wasteful.
2. not thriving; not in good condition; not vigorous in growth.
3. preventing thrift or thriving.
un·tī′di·ly, *adv.* in an untidy manner.
un·tī′di·ness, *n.* the state or quality of being untidy.
un·tī′dy, *a.*; *comp.* untidier; *superl.* untidiest. 1. untimely; unseasonable. [Obs.]
2. not neat; not tidy; not in good order; disarranged; slovenly; careless.
3. improper. [Obs.]
un·tīe′, *v.t.*; untied, *pt., pp.*; untying *or* untieing, *ppr.* 1. to loosen, undo, or unfasten (something tied or knotted).
2. to free or make clear, as from difficulty, restraint, etc.
3. to resolve (perplexities, etc.).
un·tīe′, *v.i.* to become untied or unfastened.
un·tīed′, *a.* 1. not tied; not held by any tie or band.
2. unrestrained; dissolute. [Obs.]

un·til′, *prep.* [ME. *until, untill, ontil*; formed from *unto*, by substituting Scand. *till, til*, for AS. *to.*]
1. up to the time of; till (a time or occurrence specified); as, *until* your departure.
2. before (a time specified): used with a negative; as, the show doesn't begin *until* nine o'clock.
3. unto; to. [Scot. and Brit. Dial.]

un·til′, *conj.* 1. up to the time when or that.
2. to the point, degree, or place that; as, he walked slowly *until* he was out of sight.

In open prospect nothing bounds our eye,
Until the earth seems joined unto the sky
—Dryden.

3. before: used with a negative; as, he didn't arrive *until* the concert was over.

un·tīme′, *n.* an unseasonable time. [Obs.]

un·tīme′li·ness, *n.* the state or quality of being untimely.

un·tīme′ly, *a.* 1. coming, said, done, etc. before the usual or proper time; premature; as, his was an *untimely* end.
2. coming, said, done, etc. at the wrong time; poorly timed; inopportune; unseasonable.

un·tīme′ly, *adv.* 1. inopportunely.
2. prematurely.

un·tīme′ous, un·tīm′ous, *a.* untimely; unseasonable. [Scot.]

un·tīme′ous·ly, *adv.* in an untimeous manner; untimely. [Scot.]

un·tī′tled (-tld), *a.* 1. not having a title; as, an *untitled* book, *untitled* noblemen.
2. having no right or claim.

un′tö, *prep.* [ME., formed by prefix *und-*, against (not found in AS. though prob. related to the verbal preffix *un-*), and *to*, to.]
1. to (except as the sign of an infinitive).
2. until; till.
[Archaic or Poet.]

un′tö, *conj.* until; up to the degree or time that. [Obs.]

un·tōld′, *a.* 1. not told, related, or revealed.
2. too great or numerous to be counted or measured; incalculable.
3. not numbered or counted; as, money *untold.*

un″tŏuch·ȧ·bil′i·ty, *n.* 1. the state or quality of being untouchable.
2. the defiling character attributed by Hindus of high caste, especially Brahmans, to those of low caste or to non-Hindus: the doctrine of untouchability was abolished, and its practice forbidden, by constitutional law in 1949.

un·tŏuch′ȧ·ble, *a.* 1. being beyond reach of touch; out of reach.
2. not to be touched or handled, as because of a taboo or fear of defilement.
3. intangible or impalpable.

un·tŏuch′ȧ·ble, *n.* in India, a member of the lowest caste, whose touch is regarded as defiling to Hindus of high caste, especially to Brahmans.

un·tŏuched′ (-tucht′), *a.* 1. not touched; not reached.
2. not moved; not affected; not aroused by emotion.
3. not handled; as, books *untouched* for years.

un·tō′wãrd (-ãrd), *a.* [*un-* (not) and *toward.*]
1. hard to manage or deal with; perverse; stubborn; unruly.
2. inconvenient; unfortunate; unfavorable.
3. unseemly.
4. awkward. [Obs.]

un·tō′wãrd·li·ness, *n.* the quality or condition of being untowardly.

un·tō′wãrd·ly, *a.* untoward; awkward; refractory; perverse.

un·tō′wãrd·ly, *adv.* in an untoward manner; perversely.

un·tō′wãrd·ness, *n.* the state or quality of being untoward.

un·trād′ed, *a.* 1. having no trade or traffic. [Obs.]
2. without practice or skill. [Obs.]
3. not much in use; unusual; rare. [Obs.]

un·trav′eled, un·trav′elled, *a.* 1. not used or frequented by travelers: said of a road, etc.
2. not having done much traveling, as to relatively far places.

un·tread′ (-tred′), *v.t.*; untrod, *pt.*; untrodden *or* untrod, *pp.*; untreading, *ppr.* to retrace.

un·treaṣ′ūre (-trezh′), *v.t.* to rob of treasure; also, to show forth as a treasure. [Rare.]

un·trēat′ȧ·ble, *a.* 1. not treatable.
2. not to be placated. [Obs.]
3. not practicable. [Obs.]

un·trenched′ (-trencht′), *a.* without a trench or trenches.

un·trīed′, *a.* 1. not tried; not attempted.
2. not having passed trial; not tried in court.
3. not tested or proved; as, *untried* methods.

un·trī′umph·ȧ·ble, *a.* not subject to triumph; not admitting triumph. [Obs.]

un·trọth′, *n.* untruth. [Obs.]

un·troub′le (-trub′), *v.t.* to release from trouble. [Obs.]

un·trōw′ȧ·ble, *a.* incredible. [Obs.]

un·trụe′, *a.* 1. not true; false; contrary to the fact or truth; incorrect; as, the story is *untrue.*
2. not faithful or loyal.
3. not agreeing with or conforming to a standard, measure, pattern, or rule.

un·trụe′, *adv.* untruly.

un·trụe′ness, *n.* the quality of being untrue.

un·trụ′iṣm, *n.* something obviously untrue: opposed to *truism*. [Rare.]

un·trụ′ly, *adv.* in an untrue manner; falsely.

un·truss′, *v.t.* 1. to undo.
2. to undress.

un·truss′ẽr, *n.* one who untrussed culprits; one who prepared others for flogging by untrussing: also *untruss*. [Obs.]

un·trust′, *n.* distrust. [Obs.]

un·trụth′, *n.* 1. the quality or state of being untrue; falsity; lack of veracity.
2. treachery; lack of fidelity; faithlessness; disloyalty. [Obs.]
3. a false assertion; a falsehood; a lie.
Syn.—falsehood, falsity, lie.—*Untruth* may be unintentional or not; a *falsehood* and a *lie* are intentional false statements.

un·trụth′fụl, *a.* 1. not in accordance with the truth; untrue.
2. given to telling untruths; likely to tell lies.

un·trụth′fụl·ly, *adv.* in an untruthful manner.

un·trụth′fụl·ness, *n.* the state or quality of being untruthful.

un·tuck′, *v.t.* to undo a tuck or tucks in; to free from a tuck or fold.

un·tũrn′, *v.t.* to turn in the reverse way. [Rare.]

un·tũrned′, *a.* [*un-*, not and *turned*, pp. of *turn.*] not turned (in various senses).
to leave no stone unturned; see under *stone.*

un·tū′tŏred, *a.* 1. not tutored; untaught.
2. simple; naive; unsophisticated.

un·twīne′, *v.t.*; untwined, *pt., pp.*; untwining, *ppr.* to undo (something twined or twisted); to disentangle.

un·twīne′, *v.i.* to become untwined.

un·twist′, *v.t.* and *v.i.* [*un-* (back) and *twist.*] to turn in the opposite direction so as to loosen or separate; to untwine; unravel; disentangle.

un·tȳ′, *v.t.* to untie. [Obs.]

un·ū′ni·fọrm, *a.* not uniform; lacking uniformity.

un·ū′ni·fọrm·ness, *n.* the state or quality of being ununiform.

un·ūs′äġe, *n.* lack of usage. [Obs.]

un·ūṣed′, *a.* 1. not put to use; not employed.
2. that has never been used.
3. not accustomed; as, hands *unused* to labor.
4. unusual. [Rare.]

un·ūse′fụl, *a.* useless; serving no good purpose.

un·ūse′fụl·ly, *adv.* uselessly.

un·ū′ṣụ·ăl (-zhü-), *a.* not usual or common; strange; rare; exceptional.

un·ut″tẽr·ȧ·bil′i·ty, *n.* 1. the quality or state of being unutterable.
2. that which cannot be uttered.

un·ut′tẽr·ȧ·ble, *a.* [*un-* (not) and *utterable.*]
1. that cannot be pronounced.
2. that cannot be expressed or described.

un·ut′tẽr·ȧ·bly, *adv.* so as to be unutterable.

un·val′ū·ȧ·ble, *a.* 1. not valuable; of no value; valueless.
2. invaluable. [Obs.]

un·vär′nished (-nisht), *a.* 1. not varnished.
2. plain; simple; unadorned; not embellished.

un·vẹil′, *v.t.* to remove a veil or covering from; to make visible; disclose; reveal.

un·vẹil′, *v.i.* to take off a veil or covering; to reveal oneself.

un·vẹil′ed·ly, *adv.* without disguise. [Rare.]

un·vẽrsed′ (-vẽrst′), *a.* not versed; not skilled; not acquainted.

un·ves′sel, *v.t.* to empty. [Obs.]

un·viç′ăr, *v.t.* to deprive of the position or office of vicar. [Rare.]

un·vī′ō·lȧ·ble, *a.* not to be violated; inviolable. [Rare.]

un·viṣ′i·ble, *a.* invisible. [Obs.]

un·viṣ′i·bly, *adv.* invisibly. [Obs.]

un·vī′tăl, *a.* not vital; not essential to life. [Rare.]

un·voice′, *v.t.*; unvoiced, *pt., pp.*; unvoicing, *ppr.* in phonetics, to utter or pronounce without voice; to render surd in pronouncing; as, one normally *unvoices* the *s* in *has* when saying "has to."

un·voiced′ (-voist′), *a.* 1. not spoken; not uttered; not articulated.
2. in phonetics, voiceless; surd.

un·vol′un·tā·ry, *a.* involuntary. [Obs.]

un·vōte′, *v.t.* to annul by vote. [Rare.]

un·voy′äġe·ȧ·ble, *a.* 1. not voyageable; innavigable.
2. impassable; untraversable.

un·wãre′, *a.* 1. not aware; off one's guard; unaware. [Archaic.]
2. unforeseen; unexpected. [Archaic.]

un·wãre′, *adv.* unawares. [Archaic.]

un·wãre′ly, *adv.* unawares. [Archaic.]

un·wãre′ness, *n.* the state of not being expected. [Archaic.]

un·wãreṣ′, *adv.* unawares. [Archaic.]

un·wãr′i·ly, *adv.* in an unwary manner.

un·wãr′i·ness, *n.* the quality or state of being unwary.

un·wạrm′, *v.i.* to lose warmth; to become cold. [Rare.]

un·wãr′y, *a.* not wary; not watchful or cautious; careless of danger; rash; unguarded.

un·wäsh′en, *a.* unwashed. [Archaic.]

un·wāyed′, *a.* 1. not used to travel; unaccustomed to the road. [Obs.]
2. without roads; pathless. [Obs.]

un·wēa′ri·ȧ·ble, *a.* not weariable; not capable of being wearied; indefatigable.

un·wēa′ri·ȧ·bly, *adv.* in an unweariable manner; indefatigably.

un·wēa′ried, *a.* 1. not wearied; not tired or fatigued.
2. never wearying; tireless; indefatigable.

un·wēa′ried·ly, *adv.* in an unwearied manner; indefatigably.

un·wēa′ried·ness, *n.* the quality or state of being unwearied.

un·wēa′ry, *v.t.* to refresh after weariness or fatigue. [Rare.]

un·weep′ing, *a.* not weeping; not shedding tears. [Rare.]

un·weet′ing, *a.* not knowing; ignorant; unwitting. [Archaic.]

un·weet′ing·ly, *adv.* unwittingly; ignorantly. [Archaic.]

un·wẹigh′ing (-wā′), *a.* thoughtless; inconsiderate. [Obs.]

un·well′, *a.* 1. not well; sick; indisposed.
2. indisposed from menstruation; menstruant: a euphemistic use.

un·well′ness, *n.* the quality or state of being unwell. [Rare.]

un·wemmed′, *a.* unspotted; unstained; spotless; pure. [Archaic.]

un·wept′, *a.* 1. not shed: said of tears.
2. not wept for; unmourned.

un·whōle′ (-hōl′), *a.* not whole; not sound; infirm. [Obs.]

un·whōle′sŏme (-hōl′), *a.* not wholesome; specifically, (a) harmful to body or mind; unhealthful; (b) of unsound health, or of unhealthy appearance; (c) morally harmful or corrupt.

un·whōle′sŏme·ly, *adv.* in an unwholesome manner.

un·whōle′sŏme·ness, *n.* the quality or state of being unwholesome.

un·wiēld′i·ly, *adv.* in an unwieldy manner; so as to be unwieldy.

un·wiēld′i·ness, *n.* the state or quality of being unwieldy.

un·wiēld′y, *a.* 1. hard to wield, manage, handle, or deal with, as because of large size or weight.
2. awkward; clumsy.

un·wīld′, *v.t.* to tame. [Obs.]

un·willed′, *a.* not willed; not produced by the will; involuntary; undesigned; unintentional.

un·will′ing, *a.* 1. not willing or inclined; reluctant; loath; averse.
2. done, said, given, etc. reluctantly.

un·wīnd′, *v.t.*; unwound, *pt., pp.*; unwinding, *ppr.* 1. to wind off or undo (something wound).
2. to uncoil.

3. to straighten out or untangle (something confused or involved).

un·wind′, *v.i.* to admit of being unwound; to become unwound.

un·wis′dom, *n.* lack of wisdom; ignorance; foolishness; unwise conduct or speech.

un·wise′, *a.* having or showing a lack of wisdom or sound judgment; foolish; imprudent.

un·wish′, *v.t.* 1. to cease wishing (something).
2. to do away with by wishing. [Obs.]

un·wist′, *a.* not known; not thought of. [Obs.]

un·wit′, *v.t.* to deprive of understanding. [Obs.]

un·wit′, *n.* lack of wit or understanding; ignorance; folly. [Obs.]

un·witch′, *v.t.* to free from the effects or influence of witchcraft; to disenchant. [Rare.]

un·wit′ting, *a.* 1. not knowing or aware; unconscious; ignorant.
2. unintentional.

un·wit′ting·ly, *adv.* 1. not wittingly; not knowingly; without knowledge or consciousness.
2. inadvertently.

un·wom′ăn (-woom′), *v.t.* to deprive of the qualities of a woman. [Rare.]

un·wŏnt′, *a.* unwonted. [Obs.]

un·wŏnt′ed, *a.* [*un-* (not) and *wonted.*]
1. not accustomed, familiar, or used (usually with *to*).
2. uncommon; unusual; infrequent; rare.

un·wŏrld′li·ness, *n.* 1. the quality or state of being unworldly.
2. unworldly behavior.

un·wŏrld′ly, *a.* 1. not concerned with worldly things.
2. not of this world; spiritual or unearthly.

un·wŏrth′, *a.* unworthy. [Obs.]

un·wŏrth′, *n.* unworthiness. [Rare.]

un·wŏr′thi·ly, *adv.* so as to be unworthy; in an unworthy manner.

un·wŏr′thi·ness, *n.* the quality or state of being unworthy.

un·wŏr′thy, *a.*; *comp.* unworthier; *superl.* unworthiest. 1. without merit or value; worthless.
2. not deserving (usually with *of*).
3. not fit, becoming, or suitable (usually with *of*).
4. shameful; despicable.

un·wŏr′thy, *n.* a person who is unworthy. [Rare.]

un·wound′, *v.* past tense and past participle of *unwind.*

un·wrap′ (-rap′), *v.t.*; unwrapped, *pt., pp.*; unwrapping, *ppr.* to take off the wrapping of; to open or undo (something wrapped).

un·wrap′, *v.i.* to become unwrapped.

un·wrīte′ (-rīt), *v.t.* to cancel, as that which is written; to erase. [Rare.]

un·writ′ten, *a.* 1. not written; not in writing.
2. not written on; blank.
3. operating only through custom or tradition; not distinctly expressed, laid down, or formulated, but generally understood and acknowledged as binding; as, an *unwritten* constitution.

unwritten law; (a) law originating in custom, usage, court decisions, etc., rather than in the action of any law-making body: also called *common law*; (b) any rule or principle rigidly observed notwithstanding the fact that it is not law and may be contrary to law; (c) the assumed right of a person to avenge his honor or that of his family, especially in cases of seduction, adultery, or rape, as by criminally harming the person regarded as guilty.

un·yōke′, *v.t.*; unyoked, *pt., pp.*; unyoking, *ppr.* 1. to release from a yoke.
2. to separate or disconnect.

un·yōke′, *v.i.* 1. to become unyoked.
2. to remove a yoke.

up-, [ME. and AS. *up-*, identical with *up*, adv.] a combining form meaning *up*, as in *up*grade, *up*hill.

up, *adv.* [AS. *up, uppe,* up.]
1. from a lower to a higher place; away from the ground.
2. in or on a higher position or level; off the ground.
3. in a direction or place thought of as higher or above.
4. above the horizon.
5. from an earlier to a later period or person; as, from his childhood *up.*
6. from a lower to a higher or better condition or station.
7. to a higher amount, degree, etc.; as, prices are going *up.*
8. (a) in or into a standing position; (b) out of bed.
9. in or into existence, action, view, evidence, consideration, etc.; as, bring *up* the matter at the next meeting.
10. into an excited or troubled state; as, she was wrought *up* by the news.
11. aside; away; by; as, we must lay *up* grain for the winter.
12. so as to be even with in space, time, degree, etc.; as, keep *up* with the times.
13. in or into a close space; as, tie *up* the package.
14. completely; entirely; thoroughly.
15. in baseball, to one's turn at batting.
16. in nautical usage, to the windward point; as, put *up* the helm.
17. in sports, ahead of an opponent with reference to the number of points, goals, strokes, etc.
18. open. [Obs.]

The adverb *up* is used idiomatically (a) to form a verb-adverb combination which changes the meaning of the verb (e.g., look *up* this word, he didn't turn *up*); (b) as an intensive with verbs (e.g., dress *up*, eat *up*, clean *up*); (c) as a virtually meaningless element colloquially added to almost any verb (e.g., light *up* a cigarette, write *up* a story). Many phrases with the adverb *up* (e.g., *to blow up, to cut up*, etc.) can be found in this dictionary under their key words.

up, *prep.* 1. to, toward, or at a higher place on or in; along the ascent of.
2. to, toward, or at a higher condition or station on or in; as, *up* the social ladder.
3. to, toward, or at a point farther along; as, *up* the road.
4. toward the source of (a river, etc.); in a direction contrary to that of the movement of.
5. in or toward the interior, often the more elevated part, of (a country, territory, etc.).
6. on or upon. [Obs.]

up a tree; see under *tree.*

up, *a.* 1. tending or directed toward a position that is higher or is regarded as being higher.
2. in a higher position, condition, or station.
3. (a) above the ground; (b) above the horizon.
4. advanced in amount, degree, etc.; as, rents are *up.*
5. (a) in a standing position; (b) out of bed.
6. in an active, excited, or agitated state; as, the wind is *up*; her anger was *up.*
7. even with in space, time, degree, etc.
8. living or located in the inner or elevated part of a country, territory, etc.
9. at an end; over; as, the jig is *up.*
10. at stake in gambling; as, he has two dollars *up* on the horse.
11. going on; happening; as, what's *up?* [Colloq.]
12. in baseball, at bat.
13. in golf, on the green: said of the ball.
14. in sports, (a) ahead of an opponent with reference to the number of points, goals, strokes, etc.; (b) needed for winning or ending the game: said of the specified number of points, etc.

As an adjective, *up* is usually predicative.

it's all up with; there is no further hope for; the end is near for.

up against; face to face with; confronted with; as, he's *up against* trouble now. [Colloq.]

up against it; in difficulty; especially, in financial difficulty. [Colloq.]

up and around; out of bed and resuming one's normal activities, as after an illness: also *up and about.*

up and doing; busy; active.

up for; (a) presented or considered for (an elective office, an election, etc.); (b) before a court for (trial).

up front; (a) very honest or forthright; open; candid; (b) in or into the open; in or into public knowledge; (c) ahead of time; in advance; as, to pay for something *up front*; (d) at the beginning. [Colloq.]

up on (or *in*); well informed concerning or well versed in. [Colloq.]

up to; (a) occupied with; doing; scheming; devising; (b) equal to; capable of (doing, undertaking, etc.); (c) dependent upon the decision or action of; (d) incumbent upon. [Colloq.]

up, *n.* 1. a person or thing that is up; specifically, (a) an upward slope; (b) an upward movement or course; (c) an upbound train, bus, etc.
2. an amphetamine or other stimulant drug; upper. [Slang.]

on the up and up; open and aboveboard; honest. [Slang.]

ups and downs; changes in fortune.

up, *v.i.*; upped (upt), *pt., pp.*; upping, *ppr.* to get up; to rise. [Colloq.]

up, *v.t.* 1. to put up, lift up, or take up. [Colloq.]
2. to increase, or cause to rise; as, to *up* prices. [Colloq.]
3. to raise, or bet more than (a preceding bet or bettor). [Colloq.]

up, *adv.* [phonetic respelling of *a*piece, influenced by prec. *up.*] apiece; each; as, the score is seven *up.*

up′-and-cŏm′ing, *a.* enterprising, alert, and promising. [Colloq.]

up′-and-down′, *a.* 1. going alternately up and down, to and fro, etc.
2. variable; fluctuating.

Ū·pan′i·shad, *n.* [Sans. *upanisad.*] one of a group of late Vedic metaphysical treatises dealing with man in his relation to the universe and emphasizing the pantheism of the ancient Hindu religion.

ū′păs, *n.* [Malay *ūpas*, poison.]
1. a tall tree, *Antiaris toxicaria*, common in the forests of Java and some of the neighboring islands, whose whitish bark yields a poisonous, milky juice.
2. the poisonous, milky juice of this tree, used for arrow poison.
3. something harmful or deadly in its influence; as, the *upas* of drunkenness.

up·bēar′, *v.t.*; upbore, *pt.*; upborne, *pp.*; upbearing, *ppr.* to hold, raise, or carry aloft; to bear up; to support.

up′bēat, *n.* in music, an unaccented beat, especially when on the last note of a bar.

up·bōrne′, *v.* past participle of *upbear.*

up·bōrne′, *a.* borne up; lifted or carried aloft; elevated.

up′bōw, *n.* a stroke on a violin, etc. in which the bow is drawn across the strings from the tip to the handle; symbol (V).

up·brāid′, *v.t.*; upbraided, *pt., pp.*; upbraiding, *ppr.* [ME. *upbreiden*; AS. *upbregdan*; *up-*, up, and *bregdan*, to pull, shake, weave.]
1. to scold or chide for some wrongdoing, offense, or error; to take to task; reprove; reproach.

> Then began he to *upbraid* the cities wherein most of his mighty works were done.
> —Matt. xi. 20.

2. to bring reproach on; to be a reproach to.

Syn.—blame, reproach, chide, reprove, condemn, revile, censure.

up·brāid′, *v.i.* to utter words of reproach or censure.

up·brāid′, *n.* the act of upbraiding; reproach. [Obs.]

up·brāid′ẽr, *n.* one who upbraids or reproves.

up·brāid′ing, *n.* the act or utterance of a person who upbraids; the act of reproaching or reproving.

up·brāid′ing, *a.* reproachful.

up·brāid′ing·ly, *adv.* in an upbraiding manner.

up·brāy′, *v.t.* and *v.i.* to upbraid. [Obs.]

up·brāy′, *n.* an upbraiding; reproach. [Obs.]

up·breāk′, *v.i.* to break or force a way upward; to come to the surface; to appear. [Rare.]

up′breāk, *n.* a breaking or bursting up; an upburst. [Rare.]

up·brēathe′, *v.t.* to breathe up or out; to exhale. [Obs.]

up·breed′, *v.t.* to breed up; to nurse; to train up. [Obs.]

up′bring·ing, *n.* the training and education received during childhood; rearing; bringing up; nurture.

up·brought′ (-brọt′), *a.* brought up; educated. [Obs.]

up·build′ (-bild′), *v.t.*; upbuilt, *pt., pp.*; upbuilding, *ppr.* to build up (in various senses).

up·buoy′ănce (-boy′), *n.* the act of buoying up; uplifting. [Rare.]

up′bũrst, *n.* a bursting up; a breaking a way up and through; an uprush; as, an *upburst* of lava.

up′ċast, *a.* 1. thrown upward.
2. turned or directed upward; as, with *upcast* eyes.

up·ċast′, *v.t.* 1. to cast or throw upward.
2. to reproach; to upbraid; to taunt. [Scot.]

up′ċast, *n.* 1. a casting upward or being cast upward.

2. something cast or thrown up.
3. in mining, a ventilating shaft for carrying off foul air.
4. in bowling, a cast; a throw. [Archaic.]
5. the state of being overturned. [Scot.]
6. a taunt; a reproach. [Scot.]

up·caught' (-kat'), *a.* caught or seized up.
She bears *upcaught* a mariner away.
—Cowper.

up·cheer', *v.t.* to cheer up; to enliven. [Obs.]

up·climb' (-klīm'), *v.t.* and *v.i.* to climb up; to ascend.

up·coil', *v.t.* and *v.i.* to make or wind up into a coil.

up·coiled', *a.* made into a coil.

up'com·ing, *a.* coming soon; forthcoming.

up'coun"try (-kun"), *a.* 1. of or located in the interior of a country; interior; inland.
2. rustic; unsophisticated: used derogatorily.

up'coun"try, *n.* the interior of a country.

up'coun"try, *adv.* to, toward, or in the interior of a country; as, to spend the summer *upcountry.*

up·curl', *v.i.* to curl or wreathe upward, as smoke.

up·draw', *v.t.* to draw up. [Rare.]

up·end', *v.t.* and *v.i.* to set, turn, or stand on end.

up·fill', *v.t.* to fill up. [Obs.]

up·flōw', *v.i.* to stream upward; to ascend.

up'flōw, *n.* a flow in an upward direction.

up·flung', *a.* thrown up.

up·gath'ēr, *v.t.* to contract. [Obs.]

up·gāze', *v.i.* to look or gaze upward. [Rare.]

up·give', *v.t.* to give up; to surrender. [Archaic.]

up'grāde', *n.* an upward slope or incline.
on the upgrade; (a) rising; (b) progressing; improving.

up'grāde', *a.* and *adv.* uphill.

up'grāde', *v.t.* to raise to a higher grade, rate of pay, etc.; to grade upward, as an employee to a position requiring more skill and carrying more responsibility and pay.

up·grōw', *v.i.* to grow up. [Obs.]

up'grōwth, *n.* 1. the process of growing up; rise and progress; development.
2. that which grows up.

up'gush, *n.* a gushing forth or upward, as of water from a spring.

up·gush', *v.i.* to gush forth or upward. [Rare.]

up'hand, *a.* lifted by the hand or by both hands, as a hammer. [Rare.]

up·hang', *v.t.* to hang up; to suspend.

up·hasp', *v.t.* to close; to fasten up. [Rare.]

up·hēaped' (-hēpt'), *a.* piled in a heap.

up·hēav'ăl, *n.* 1. a heaving up or being heaved up, as by volcanic eruption.
2. a sudden, violent change or disturbance in affairs.

up·hēave', *v.t.*; upheaved, *pt., pp.*; upheaving, *ppr.* to heave or lift up; to raise from beneath.

up·hēave', *v.i.* to rise as if forced up; to be raised from beneath.

up·hēaved', *a.* heaved or lifted up from beneath.

up·held', *v.* past tense and past participle of *uphold.*

ū'phēr, *n.* in architecture, a fir pole used for scaffolding, etc. [Brit.]

up'hill', *a.* 1. passing to a higher level; going or sloping up; rising.
2. calling for prolonged effort; tiring; difficult.
3. located on high ground.

up'hill', *n.* a sloping rise or ascent.

up'hill', *adv.* to or toward a higher level on or as if on an incline; upward at an angle.

up·hilt', *v.t.* to thrust in (a sword) to the hilt. [Rare.]

up·hōard', *v.t.* to hoard up. [Obs.]

up·hōld', *v.t.*; upheld, *pt., pp.*; upholding, *ppr.*
1. to hold up; to raise; to lift on high; to elevate.
2. to support; to sustain; to keep from falling or slipping.
3. to give moral or spiritual support or encouragement to.
Honor shall *uphold* the humble in spirit.
—Prov. xxix. 23.
4. to decide in favor of; to agree with and support against opposition; to confirm; to sustain.

up·hōld'ēr, *n.* 1. one who or that which upholds; a supporter; a defender; a sustainer.
2. an undertaker; one who provides for funerals. [Obs.]
3. a dealer in furniture, etc. [Obs.]

up·hōl'stēr, *v.t.* and *v.i.*; upholstered, *pt., pp.*; upholstering, *ppr.* [back-formation from *upholsterer.*]
1. to fit out (furniture) with coverings, springs, cushions, padding, etc.
2. to furnish (a room) with curtains, carpets, etc.

up·hōl'stēr, *n.* 1. an upholder (sense 3). [Obs.]
2. an upholsterer. [Obs.]

up·hōl'stēr·ēr, *n.* [corruption of ME. *upholder*, a tradesman.] one who upholsters.

up·hōl'stēr·y, *n.*; *pl.* **up·hōl'stēr·ies**, [from *upholster.*]
1. the fittings and material used in upholstering.
2. the business or work of an upholsterer.

ū'phrōe, *n.* [from D. *juffrouw*, a young lady.] same as *euphroe.*

up'keep, *n.* 1. the act of keeping up buildings, equipment, etc.; maintenance.
2. the condition of being kept up; repair.
3. the cost of maintenance.

up'lănd, *n.* high land; ground elevated above the lowlands, as of a region or country.

up'lănd, *a.* 1. situated in or being on upland; as, *upland* inhabitants.
2. of or pertaining to upland; growing on upland; as, *upland* pasturage, *upland* cotton.
upland moccasin; a snake, *Ancistrodon atrofuscus*, which inhabits the uplands of the southern part of the United States. It resembles the rattlesnake, but is without rattles.
upland plover; a large, short-billed sandpiper, *Bartramia longicauda*, found in the fields and uplands of eastern North America.
upland sumac; a shrublike plant, *Rhus glabra*, of North America, the leaves of which are used in tanning.

up'lănd·ēr, *n.* one who dwells in or is a native of an upland district.

up·land'ish, *a.* 1. pertaining to uplands; dwelling on high lands or mountains. [Rare.]
2. rustic; rude; countrified; boorish; uncultured. [Obs.]

up·lāy', *v.t.* to lay up; to hoard.

up·lēad', *v.t.* to lead upward.

up·lēan', *v.i.* to incline; to lean against something. [Obs.]

up·lift', *v.t.* 1. to raise aloft; to lift up; to elevate; as, to *uplift* the arm.
2. to raise to a higher moral, social, or spiritual level or condition.

up'lift, *n.* 1. the act or process of lifting up; elevation; raising.
2. the act or process of raising to a higher moral, social, or spiritual level.
3. any influence, movement, etc. that tends or attempts to raise morally, spiritually, etc.
4. a type of brassiere designed to lift and support the breasts: in full, *uplift brassiere.*
5. in geology, an upheaval.

up·lock', *v.t.* to lock up.

up·look', *v.i.* to look up.

up'mōst, *a.* uppermost; topmost; highest.

up·on', *prep.* [ME., from ON. *upp* (akin to Eng. *up*) and *on*, on.] on (in various senses), or up and on: used generally as an equivalent of *on*, without much distinction except for reasons of rhythm, etc.

up·on', *adv.* 1. on: used only to complete the idea of a verb; as, the canvas has not been painted *upon.*
2. on it; on one's person. [Obs.]
3. thereupon; thereafter. [Obs.]

up'pēr, *a.* [ME.; orig., compar. of *up.*]
1. higher in place or physical position.
2. farther inland.
3. higher in rank, authority, dignity, etc.; superior.
4. worn outside others; outer: said of clothes.
5. [U–] in geology, more recent; later: used of a division of a period; as, *Upper* Cambrian.
Upper Bench; in English history, the Court of King's Bench during the Commonwealth.
upper case; in printing, the top one of a pair of cases, used to hold capital letters; also, the capital letters.
upper crust; (a) the top crust, as of a loaf of bread; (b) [Colloq.] people having wealth and high social position.
upper hand; the position of advantage or control.
Upper House; [*often* u- h-] in a legislature having two branches, that branch which is usually smaller and less representative, as the British House of Lords.
upper leather; the leather for the vamps and quarters of shoes.
upper story; (a) a story above the ground floor; (b) [Slang] the head; brains.
upper works; in nautical usage, those parts of a loaded ship that project above the surface of the water.

up'pēr, *n.* 1. the vamp and quarter of a shoe or boot; that part above the welt and sole.
2. [*pl.*] cloth gaiters to be worn above the shoes.
3. an upper berth. [Colloq.]
4. any drug containing a stimulant; especially, an amphetamine. [Slang.]
on one's uppers; (a) wearing worn-out shoes; (b) in need or want; poor; shabby. [Colloq.]

up'pēr bound, in mathematics, a number that is greater than or equal to any number in a set.

up'pēr-cāse', *a.* 1. capital: said of a letter, as distinguished from *small*, or *lower-case.*
2. in printing, of the upper case.

up'pēr-class', *a.* 1. of or characteristic of the upper class, or social class above the middle class.
2. of or characteristic of the junior and senior classes in a high school, college, etc.

up·pēr·class'măn, *n.*; *pl.* **up·pēr·class'men**, a student who is a member of the junior or senior class in a high school, college, etc.

up'pēr·cut, *n.* in boxing, a short, swinging blow directed upward, as to the chin.

up'pēr·cut, *v.t.* and *v.i.*; uppercut, *pt., pp.*; uppercutting, *ppr.* to hit with an uppercut.

up'pēr·mōst, *a.* 1. highest in place, power, authority, etc.; predominant; topmost; as, the *uppermost* class of society.
2. foremost in the mind; first to occur to the mind.

up'pēr·mōst, *adv.* in the highest place, position, rank, etc.; at the top; first.

up·pile', *v.t.* to pile or heap up.

up'pish, *a.* inclined to be arrogant, snobbish, haughty, etc. [Colloq.]

up'pish·ly, *adv.* in an uppish manner. [Colloq.]

up'pish·ness, *n.* the quality of being uppish. [Colloq.]

up'pi·ty, *a.* uppish. [Colloq.]

up·prop', *v.t.* to prop up.

up·rāise', *v.t.* to raise; to lift up.

up·rēar', *v.t.* 1. to rear up; to raise.
2. to exalt.
3. to bring up.

up·rēar', *v.i.* to rise up.

up·ridge' (-rij'), *v.t.* to raise into a ridge or ridges.

up'right (-rīt) *a.* 1. standing, pointing, or directed straight up; in a vertical or perpendicular position; erect.
2. honest; just; honorable; as, an *upright* man, *upright* conduct.
upright piano; a piano, the mechanism of which is enclosed in an upright or vertical rectangular case.
Syn.—vertical, erect, perpendicular, honest, honorable, pure, principled, conscientious, just, fair, equitable.

up'right (*or* up-rīt'), *adv.* in an upright position or direction.

up'right, *n.* 1. the state of being upright or vertical.
2. something having an upright position; a vertical part or member.
3. an upright piano.
4. [*pl.*] in football, the goal posts.
5. in architecture, an elevation. [Obs.]

up·right'eous·ly (-rī'chus-), *adv.* uprightly; honorably; justly.

up'right·ly (-rīt-), *adv.* in an upright manner.

up'right·ness, *n.* the state or quality of being upright.

up·rīse', *v.i.*; uprose, *pt.*; uprisen, *pp.*; uprising, *ppr.* 1. to get up; to rise.
2. to move or slope upward; to ascend.
3. to rise into view, being, or activity.
4. to be or become erect or upright.
5. to increase in size, volume, etc.; to swell, as sound.
6. to rise in revolt.

up'rīse, *n.* the act or process of rising up.
2. an upward slope or ascent.

up'rīs·ing, *n.* 1. the act or process of rising up.
2. an upward slope or ascent.
3. a revolt; a rebellion; an outbreak against proper authority.

up'rōar, *n.* [from D. *oproer*, a stirring up.]
1. violent disturbance or commotion, especially one accompanied by loud, confused noise, as of shouting; tumult.
2. loud, confused noise; din.

up·rōar'i·ous, *a.* 1. making, or characterized by, an uproar.

2. loud and boisterous, as laughter; noisy and confused, as sounds.

up·rōar′i·ous·ly, *adv.* in an uproarious manner.

up·rōar′i·ous·ness, *n.* the state or quality of being uproarious.

up·rōll′, *v.t.* to roll up.

up·ro͞ot′, *v.t.* 1. to root up; to tear up by the roots.
2. to destroy or remove utterly; to eradicate; to extirpate.

up·rōse′, *v.* past tense of *uprise.*

up·rouse′, *v.t.* to rouse from sleep; to awake; to arouse.

up·rush′, *v.i.* to rush upward.

up′rush, *n.* an upward rush.

up·seek′ *v.i.*; upsought (-sot′), *pt., pp.*; upseeking, *ppr.* to seek or strain upward.

up·set′, *v.t.*; upset, *pt., pp.*; upsetting, *ppr.* 1. to tip over; overturn; capsize.
2. to disturb or disorder the functioning or course of; as, the accident *upset* the railroad's schedule.
3. to defeat or overthrow, especially unexpectedly.
4. to perturb; discompose; distress; as, his death *upset* us all.
5. in mechanics, (a) to shorten and thicken (a red-hot iron) by beating on the end; to swage; (b) to shorten (a tire) in the process of resetting it.

up·set′, *v.i.* to become overturned or upset.

up′set, *n.* 1. an upsetting or being upset; overturn.
2. a disturbance; disorder; derangement.
3. an overthrow or defeat, specifically one that is unexpected.
4. in mechanics, (a) a swage used for upsetting; (b) an upset piece or part.

up·set′ (*or* up′set), *a.* 1. set up; erected. [Rare.]
2. established; fixed; as, an *upset* price.
3. tipped over; overturned.
4. disturbed; disordered.
5. perturbed; distressed.
upset price; the minimum selling price of any article to be auctioned off.

up·set′tēr, *n.* one who or that which upsets or sets up.

up·set′ting, *a.* uppish; conceited. [Scot.]

up·sho͞ot′, *v.i.* to shoot upward.

up′shot, *n.* [orig., the final shot in an archery match.] final issue; conclusion; end; result; as, the *upshot* of the matter.

up′sīde, *n.* that part which is upper; the upper side.

up′sīde-down′, *a.* that is upside down: used attributively; as, *upside-down* logic.

up′sīde down, [ME. *up so doun,* lit., up as if down: altered through popular etym.]
1. with the upper part underneath or turned over.
2. in disorder or confusion; topsy-turvy.

ūp′si·lon (*or Brit.* ūp-sī′lŏn), *n.* [Gr. *ypsilon,* lit., simple *u*: so called in contrast with the spelling *oi,* which represented the sound in Late Gr.] the twentieth letter of the Greek alphabet, corresponding to English *U, u,* or *Y, y.*

up·spring′, *v.i.*; upsprang, *pt.*; upsprung, *pp.*; upspringing, *ppr.* to spring up.

up′spring, *n.* a spring upward.

up′stāge′, *adv.* at the rear of the stage or toward the rear of the stage.

up′stāge′, *a.* 1. of or having to do with the rear of the stage.
2. haughtily or disdainfully aloof, conceited, or supercilious. [Colloq.]

up′stage′, *v.t.* to treat in a haughty or disdainful manner. [Colloq.]

up′stairs′, *adv.* 1. up the stairs; so as to climb a flight of stairs.
2. in, on, or toward an upper floor.
to kick upstairs; to promote so as to get rid of. [Colloq.]

up′stairs, *n.* an upper story or stories, especially the one next above the first floor.

up′stairs′, *a.* pertaining to an upper story or floor; situated above stairs; as, an *upstairs* apartment.

up·stand′, *v.i.* to stand up.

up·stand′ing, *a.* 1. erect.
2. having a well-formed figure and good posture.
3. honorable; straightforward; upright.

up·stâre′, *v.i.* to stand on end; to be erect or conspicuous: said of the hair, etc. [Obs.]

up·stärt′, *v.t.* and *v.i.* to start up or cause to start up.

up′stärt, *n.* 1. a person who has recently come into wealth, power, importance, etc.; especially, such a person who is pushing, presumptuous, etc.; a parvenu.
2. same as *meadow saffron.*

up′stärt, *a.* 1. suddenly raised to prominence or consequence; as, an *upstart* family.
2. of or characteristic of an upstart.

up′stāte′, *a.* designating, of, or from the more northerly part of a State: used especially of New York.

up′stāte′, *n.* an upstate region; especially, the northern part of New York.

up′stāte′, *adv.* in or toward an upstate region.

up′stāt′ēr, *n.* an inhabitant of an upstate region.

up·stāy′, *v.t.* to sustain; to support.

up′stīr, *n.* disturbance; insurrection. [Dial.]

up′strēam′, *adv.* against the stream or current; as, he swam *upstream.*

up′strēam′, *a.* 1. of or situated at the upper part of a stream.
2. moving against the stream or current.

up·strēam′, *v.i.* to stream or flame up; to burst out and upward; as, *upstreaming* fire.

up′street′, *adv.* toward the upper end or higher part of a street.

up′strōke, *n.* 1. an upward stroke or movement.
2. a mark, line, or part of a letter made by a stroke upward or away from the body, with pen, pencil, brush, etc.

up′sun, *n.* the period between the rising and setting of the sun. [Scot.]

up·sūrge′, *v.i.* to surge up.

up′sūrge, *n.* a surge upward.

up·swarm′, *v.t.* to raise in a swarm.

up·swarm′, *v.i.* to rise in a swarm.

up·swāy′, *v.t.* to sway upwards.

up′sweep, *n.* 1. a sweep or curve upward, as of the underjaw of the bulldog.
2. an upswept hair-do.

up·sweep′, *v.t.* and *v.i.*; upswept, *pt., pp.*; upsweeping, *ppr.* to sweep or curve upward.

up·swell′, *v.i.* to swell up; to rise up.

up′swept, *a.* 1. curved or sloped upward; having an upsweep.
2. designating or of a style of hair-do in which the hair is combed up smoothly in the back and piled on the top of the head.

up′swing, *n.* 1. a swing, trend, or movement upward.
2. an advance or improvement.

up·swing′, *v.i.* 1. to swing or move upward.
2. to advance or improve.

up·sy·tūr′vy, *adv.* topsyturvy. [Rare.]

up′tāils all, 1. confusion; high jinks. [Obs.]
2. a reveler. [Obs.]

up·tāke′, *v.t.* to take up or into the hands; to succor. [Obs.]

up′tāke, *n.* 1. the act of lifting or taking up.
2. the act of or capacity for understanding or comprehending.
3. a pipe carrying smoke and gases from a furnace to its chimney.
4. a ventilating shaft or pipe.

up·teār′, *v.t.* to tear up.

up·thrōw′, *v.t.* to throw up; to raise.

up′thrōw, *n.* a throwing up; upheaval.

up′thrust, *n.* a thrust or move upward; specifically, in geology, an upheaval of a part of the earth's crust.

up·thun′dēr, *v.i.* to send up a thunderous noise.

up·tīe′, *v.t.* to tie or twist up; to wind up.

up′-tīght′, up′tīght′, *a.* 1. very tense, nervous, anxious, etc. [Slang.]
2. overly conventional or strict in attitudes. [Slang.]
3. in a bad way or state. [Slang.]
Also **up tīght.**

up·till′, *prep.* up to; against. [Rare.]

up·tilt′, *v.t.* to tilt up.

up′-tö-dāte′, *a.* 1. extending to the present time; using or including the latest facts, methods, ideas, data, etc.
2. keeping up with or conforming to what is most recent or modern in style, taste, manners, methods, information, etc.

up′town′, *a.* of, going toward, or in the upper part of a city or town, or the part away from the main business district.

up′town′, *adv.* in or toward the upper part of a city or town.

up′town′, *n.* the upper part of a city or town.

up·trāce′, *v.t.* to trace up; to examine.

up·trāin′, *v.t.* to train up; to educate.

up·tūrn′, *v.t.* and *v.i.*; to turn up or over; as, to *upturn* the ground in plowing.

up′tūrn, *n.* an upward turn, curve, or trend.

up·tūrned′, *a.* 1. turned upward.
2. turned over, or upside down.
3. having the end or tip turned upward; as, an *upturned* nose.

Ū′pū·pȧ, *n.* [L. *upupa,* like Gr. *epops,* hoopoe, from the bird's cry.] a genus of insessorial or perching birds, the hoopoes, distinguished by a long, curved bill and an erectile crest.

up′wărd, *adv.* [AS. *upweard.*]
1. to or toward a higher place or position.
2. to or toward the source, center, interior, etc.
3. toward the body, head, or upper parts; as, the swelling spread from his legs *upward.*
4. toward a higher degree, amount, price, rank, etc.
5. on into future years or later life.
6. in a higher or the highest place or position.
7. more; above; over.
upward of; more than.

up′wărd, *n.* the top. [Obs.]

up′wărd, *a.* directed or moving toward, or situated in, a higher position.

up′wărd·ly, *adv.* in an upward manner or direction.

up′wărds, *adv.* upward.

up·whirl′ (-hwūrl′), *v.i.* to rise upward in a whirl; to whirl upward.

up·whirl′, *v.t.* to raise upward in a whirling direction.

up·wind′, *v.t.* to wind or roll up.

up·wrēathe′ (-rēth′), *v.i.* to curl upward, as smoke.

Ur, in chemistry, uranium.

ur-, see *uro-.*

ū′rȧ·chăl, *a.* of or pertaining to the urachus.

ū′rȧ·chus, *n.*; *pl.* **ū′rȧ·chī,** [Gr. *ourachos.*] a cord which extends from the apex of the bladder to the navel. It represents the remains of the canal in the fetus which joins the bladder with the allantois.

ū·rae′mi·ȧ, *n.* same as *uremia.*

ū·rae′miç, *a.* same as *uremic.*

ū·rae′us, *n.* [Gr. *ouraios,* of a tail, from *oura,* tail.] the figure of the sacred asp or cobra on the headdress of ancient Egyptian rulers.

HEADDRESS WITH URAEUS

ū′răl, *n.* a bitter crystalline substance, $C_5H_8NO_3Cl_3$, used in medicine as a hypnotic.

Ū″răl-Al·tā′iç, *a.* 1. of the region of the Ural and Altai Mountains.
2. designating or of a postulated group of languages which includes, among others, the Uralic and Altaic families.
3. of the peoples using these languages.

Ū″răl-Al·tā′iç, *n.* the Ural-Altaic group of languages.

Ū·ral′iç, Ū·rā′li·ăn, *a.* designating or of a family of languages including the Finno-Ugric and Samoyed subfamilies.

Ū·ral′iç, Ū·rā′li·ăn, *n.* the Uralic family of languages.

ū′răl·īte, *n.* amphibole, altered from pyroxene, found originally in the Ural Mountains.

ū·răl·it′iç, *a.* consisting of or similar to uralite.

ū·ram′il, *n.* same as *murexan.*

ū′răn, *n.* same as *varan.*

ū·rȧ·nal′y·sis, *n.* urinalysis.

ū′rȧ·nāte, *n.* a salt of uranic acid.

Ū·rā′ni·ȧ, *n.* [L., from Gr. *Ourania,* lit., the heavenly one.]
1. In Greek mythology, the Muse of astronomy. She was a daughter of Zeus by Mnemosyne, and is generally represented holding in her left hand a celestial globe to which she points with a little staff.
2. an epithet applied to Aphrodite.
3. a genus of lepidopterous insects, found chiefly in the West Indies.

Ū·rā′ni·ăn, *a.* of or pertaining to Uranus.

ū·ran′iç, *a.* [Gr. *ouranos,* heaven, the sky.] of or pertaining to the heavens; celestial.

ū·ran′iç, *a.* [from *uramium* and *-ic.*] pertaining to, obtained from, or containing uranium, especially in its higher valence.

ū′rȧ·nin, *n.* an alkaline salt of fluorescein, staining the mucous membranes yellow when injected into the veins.

ū·ran′i·nīte, *n.* [from *uranium.*] a black, opaque mineral containing uranium, radium, thorium, lead, and, sometimes, the gases helium and argon.

ū·rȧ·nis′çō·plas·ty, *n.* [Gr. *ouraniskos*, the palate, and *plastikos*, forming.] in surgery, the operation of ingrafting in case of deficiency of the soft palate.

ū″rȧ·nis·çor′rȧ·phy, *n.* suture of the palate.

ū′rȧ·nīte, *n.* [G. *uranit.*] any of a group of native phosphates of uranium with calcium and copper.

ū·rȧ·nit′iç, *a.* pertaining to or containing uranite or uranium.

ū·rā′ni·um, *n.* [Mod. L., from *Uranus*, the planet.] a very hard, heavy, moderately malleable, radioactive metallic chemical element: it is found only in combination, chiefly in pitchblende, and is important in work on atomic energy, especially in the isotope of mass number 235 (U-235), which can undergo continuous fission, and in the more plentiful U-238, from which plutonium is produced: symbol, U; atomic weight, 238.07; atomic number, 92.

ū″răn·ō·graph′iç, ū″răn·ō·graph′iç·ăl, *a.* pertaining to uranography.

ū·rȧ·nog′rȧ·phist, *n.* an expert in uranography.

ū·rȧ·nog′rȧ·phy, *n.* [Gr. *ouranographia*, from *ouranos*, heaven, and *graphein*, to write.] the branch of astronomy dealing with the description of the heavens and celestial bodies, as by the construction of maps, charts, etc.

ū·ran′ō·līte, *n.* a meteorite. [Rare.]

ū·rȧ·nol′ō·ġy, *n.* [Gr. *ouranos*; and *-ology.*]
1. a written description of or treatise on the heavens and celestial bodies.
2. uranography.

ū″rȧ·nom·e·trī′ȧ, *n.* same as *uranometry.*

ū·rȧ·nom′e·try, *n.* 1. the measurement of the heavens.
2. a map, chart, or listing of celestial bodies, especially of visible fixed stars.

ū·ran′ō·phāne, *n.* hydrous silicate of uranium and calcium.

ū′rȧ·nō·plas″ty, *n.* same as *uraniscoplasty.*

ū·rȧ·nŏs′çō·py, *n.* [Gr. *ouranos*, heaven, and *skopein*, to view.] observation of the heavenly bodies.

ū·rȧ·nō′sō-, in chemistry, a combining form meaning *uranous.*

ū′rȧ·nous, *a.* pertaining to or containing uranium, especially in its lower valence.

Ū′rȧ·nus, *n.* [LL., from Gr. *Ouranos*, from *ouranos*, heaven or sky.]
1. in Greek mythology, a god who was the personification of Heaven, regarded as the husband or son of Gaea (Earth) and father of the Titans, Furies, and Cyclopes: he was overthrown by his son Cronus (Saturn).
2. a planet of the solar system, seventh in distance from the sun: diameter, c. 31,000 mi.; diurnal rotation, apparently 10 hrs., 45 min.; period of revolution, c. 84 yrs.; symbol, ♅.

ū′rȧ·nyl, *n.* [from *uranium* and *-yl.*] the divalent radical UO_2, present in many compounds of uranium.

ū·rȧ·nyl′iç, *a.* of, like, or containing uranyl.

u̇·rä′ō, *n.* a native sodium carbonate and bicarbonate of South America.

u̇·rä′ri, *n.* same as *curari.*

ū′rāse (*or* -rāz), *n.* urease.

ū′rāte, *n.* a salt of uric acid.

ū·rat′iç, *a.* of, containing, or characterized by urates.

ũrb, *n.* an urban area, especially as contrasted with its suburbs.

ũr′băn, *a.* [L. *urbanus*, from *urbs*, a city.]
1. of, in, constituting, or comprising a city or town.
2. characteristic of the city as distinguished from the country; citified.
Opposed to *rural.*

ũr′băn, *n.* one living in a city. [Rare.]

ũr′băn dis′triçt, in the British Isles, a densely populated community, like a borough but lacking a borough charter.

ũr·bāne′, *a.* 1. courteous in manners; polite; suave; elegant or refined; as, a man of *urbane* manners.
2. urban. [Obs.]

ũr′băn·ișm, *n.* 1. (a) the character of life in the cities; urban life, organization, problems, etc.; (b) the study of this.
2. movement of the population to, or concentration of the population in, the cities.

Ũr′băn·ist, *n.* 1. in ecclesiastical history, an adherent of Pope Urban VI, in opposition to whom a faction set up Clement VII in 1378.
2. one of a branch of Franciscan nuns founded by Pope Urban IV.

ũr′băn·īte, *n.* a person living in a city.

ũr·ban′i·ty, *n.*; *pl.* **ũr·ban′i·ties,** [Fr. *urbanité*, from L. *urbanitas*, urbanity.]
1. the quality of being urbane.
2. [*pl.*] civilities, courtesies, or amenities.
Syn.—civility, courtesy, suavity.

ũr″băn·i·zā′tion, *n.* an urbanizing or being urbanized.

ũr′băn·īze, *v.t.*; urbanized, *pt.*, *pp.*; urbanizing, *ppr.* 1. to change from rural to urban in character; to make like or characteristic of a city.
2. to make urbane; polish; refine. [Rare.]

ũr·băn·ol′ō·ġist, *n.* [*urban*, and *-o-*, and *-logy*, and *-ist.*] a student of, or specialist in, urban problems.

ũr·băn·ol′ō·ġy, *n.* the study of urban problems.

ũr′băn rē·new′ăl, rehabilitation of deteriorated or distressed urban areas, as by slum clearance and redevelopment construction in housing and public facilities.

ũr′băn sprawl, the spread of urban congestion into adjoining suburbs and rural sections.

Ũr·biç′ō·lae, *n.pl.* a group of butterflies, popularly called skippers.

ũr·biç′ō·lous, *a.* [L. *urbs, urbis*, a city, and *colere*, to inhabit.] inhabiting a city; urban.

ũr′cē·ō·lăr, *a.* urceolate.

ũr′cē·ō·lāte, *a.* [from L. *urceolus*, dim. of *urceus*, a pitcher.] shaped like a pitcher or urn.

ũr′cē·ōle, *n.* same as *cruet*, sense 2.

Ur″cē·ō·lī′nȧ, *n.* a genus of plants of the family *Amaryllidaceæ*, having urn-shaped flowers. The three species are native to the western part of South America.

ũr·cē′ō·lus, *n.*; *pl.* **ũr·cē′ō·lī,** [dim. of L. *urceus*, a water pitcher.]
1. in botany, a pitcherlike part.
2. in zoology, the tubelike casing of a rotifer.

ũr′cē·us, *n.*; *pl.* **ũr′cē·ī,** [L., a pitcher.] in ancient Rome, a pitcher with one handle.

ũr′chin, *n.* [ME. *urchone*, from OFr. *ireçon*, from L. *ericius*, a hedgehog.]
1. a hedgehog. [Archaic or Dial.]
2. a sea urchin.
3. an elf or fairy. [Obs.]
4. a roguish, mischievous child, particularly a mischievous boy.
5. a small cylinder in a carding machine.

ũr′chin, *a.* 1. mischievous. [Rare.]
2. of or like an urchin.

ũr′chin fish, a prickly globular fish, as the *Diodon hystrix.*

ũr′chŏn, *n.* an urchin. [Obs.]

Ur′dü, *n.* [Hind., from Per. *urdu*, a camp.]
1. a language used by Moslems in India: it developed from Hindustani but with Arabic characters.
2. Hindustani.

ūre, *n.* use; practice. [Obs.]

ūre, *v.t.* and *v.i.* to inure; to practice; to accustom by use or practice. [Obs.]

ūre, *n.* [L. *urus*, a wild bull.] the urus. [Obs.]

-ūre (*or* ũr), [from L. *-ura*, Fr. *-ure.*] a suffix meaning *act* or *result of an action, agent* or *instrument of action, state of being*, etc., as in expos*ure*, compos*ure.*

ū·rē′ȧ, (*or* ū′rē-ȧ), *n.* [Mod. L.; Fr. *urée*; Gr. *ouron*, urine.] a very soluble, crystalline solid, $CO(NH_2)_2$, found in the urine of mammals and produced synthetically: used in making plastics, adhesives, etc.

ū·rē′ăl, *a.* of, containing, or relating to urea.

ū·rē·am′e·tẽr, *n.* an instrument for measuring and indicating the proportion of urea in urine.

ū·rē′ȧ reș′inș, a group of resins produced by the interaction of urea and formaldehyde.

ū′rē·āse (*or* -āz), *n.* [from *urea* and *-ase.*] an enzyme that promotes the hydrolysis of urea into ammonium carbonate: also *urase.*

ū·rē·çhī′tin, *n.* a poisonous glucoside, $C_{28}H_{42}O_8$, from *Urechites suberecta*, a tropical plant of the dogbane family.

ū′rē·çhi·tox′in, *n.* a poisonous glucoside, $C_{13}H_{20}O_5$, from the plant *Urechites suberecta.*

Ū·rē·din′ē·ae, *n.pl.* an order of minute fungi, parasitic on and injurious to flowering plants and ferns and producing the diseases called smut, brand, burnt-ear, rust, etc.

ū·rē·din′ē·ous, *a.* of or relating to the *Uredineæ.*

ū·red′i·nous, *a.* same as *Uredineous.*

Ū·rē′dō, *n.* [L., a blast, blight, from *urere*, to burn.]
1. the form genus or stage in the development of certain microscopic fungi of the group or section *Uredineæ* in which are produced the uredospores.
2. [u-] urticaria; hives.

ū·rē′dō·spōre, *n.* [L. *uredo*, a blight, a blast, and *spore.*] a nonsexual spore produced in some rusts in their uredo stage.

ū·rē·dō·spor′iç, *a.* of, relating to, or characterizing a uredospore.

ū·rē′dō·stāġe, *n.* [*uredo* and *stage.*] in botany, the stage in which rust fungi develop one-celled summer spores with reddish or yellowish spots.

ū′rē·id, *n.* a ureide.

ū′rē·īde, *n.* any of several compounds derived by the elimination of water in the reaction of urea with an acid or aldehyde.

ū·rē′mi·ȧ, ū·rae′mi·ȧ, *n.* [LL., from Gr. *ouron*, urine, and *haima*, blood.] a toxic condition caused by the presence of urinary constituents in the blood: it results from suppression or deficient secretion of urine.

ū·rē′miç, ū·rae′miç, *a.* of, having, or characterized by uremia.

Ū·rē′nȧ, *n.* [from *uren*, the Malabar name of one of the species.] a genus of malvaceous plants consisting of tall, rigid herbs or shrubs with small pink flowers, native to India, China, Mauritius, South America, and the West Indies. The fiber of *Urena lobata* and *Urena sinuata* is used like jute.

ū·rē·ō·tel′iç, *a.* [from *urea*, and *telic.*] designating those animals, as mammals, fish, etc., that eliminate unwanted nitrogen in the form of urea excreted in the urine.

-ū·ret, [Mod. L. *-uretum.*] a suffix equivalent to *-id, -ide*: formerly used to form chemical terms.

ū·rē′tẽr, *n.* [Gr. *ourētēr*, from *ourein*, to urinate.] the excretory duct of the kidney; one of two tubes conveying the urine from the kidney to the bladder.

ū·rē′tẽr·ăl, *a.* same as *ureteric.*

ū·rē·tẽr·al′ġi·ȧ, *n.* [*ureter*, and Gr. *algos*, pain.] pain in the ureter; neuralgia of the ureter.

ū·rē·ter′iç, *a.* of or relating to the ureter.

ū·rē·tẽr·ī′tis, *n.* inflammation of the ureter.

ū·rē′tẽr·ō-, [from *ureter.*] a combining form meaning *the ureter* or *the ureter and*, as in *ureterostomy*: also, before a vowel, *ureter-.*

ū·rē″tẽr·or·rhā′ġi·ȧ (-rā′), *n.* a discharge of blood from the ureter.

ū·rē″tẽr·os′tō·my, *n.* [*uretero-* and *-stomy.*] the surgical creation of an artificial opening for the direct discharge of urine from the ureter.

ū·rē·than′, ū·rē·thāne′, *n.* [Fr. *uréthane.*]
1. a white crystalline compound, $C_3H_7O_2N$, produced by the action of ammonia on ethyl carbonate or by heating urea nitrate and ethyl alcohol: it is used as a hypnotic and sedative.
2. any ester of carbamic acid.

ū·rē′thrȧ, *n.*; *pl.* **ū·rē′thrae, ū·rē′thrȧș,** [Gr. *ourēthra*, the ureter, from *ouron*, urine.] the membranous canal by which the urine is discharged from the bladder in most mammals: in the male, sperm is also discharged through the urethra.

ū·rē′thrăl, *a.* pertaining to the urethra.
urethral fever; fever following the use of the urethral catheter, or sound.

ū·rē·thrit′iç, *a.* of or relating to urethritis.

ū·rē·thrī′tis, *n.* inflammation of the urethra.

ū·rē′thrō-, [from *urethra.*] a combining form meaning *the urethra* or *the urethra and*, as in *urethroscope*: also, before a vowel, *urethr-.*

ū·rē′thrō·sçōpe, *n.* [*urethra*, and Gr. *skopein*, to view.] an instrument for examining the interior of the urethra.

ū·rē·thros′çō·py, *n.* examination of the urethra with a urethroscope.

ū·rē′thrō·tōme, *n.* an instrument for performing a urethrotomy.

ū·rē·throt′ō·my, *n.* a surgical operation for relieving a urethral stricture.

ū·ret′iç, *a.* of, relating to, or promoting the flow of urine.

ũrġe, *v.t.*; urged, *pt.*, *pp.*; urging, *ppr.* [L. *urgere*, to press hard.]
1. to press upon the attention; to present or speak of earnestly and repeatedly; to plead, allege, or advocate strongly.
2. to drive or force onward; to press forward vigorously.
3. to entreat or plead with; to ask, persuade, or solicit earnestly; to press; exhort.
4. to force; to incite; impel; drive.
5. to ply vigorously, as oars.
6. to provoke; to exasperate. [Dial.]
Syn.—press, constrain, force, incite, impel, importune, instigate, stimulate, encourage.

ûrġe, *v.i.* 1. to make an earnest presentation of arguments, claims, charges, entreaties, solicitations, etc.
2. to exert a force that drives or impels, as to action.

ûr'ġence, *n.* urgency.

ûr'ġen·cy, *n.*; *pl.* **ûr'ġen·cieṣ**, [from *urgent.*]
1. the quality or state of being urgent; need for action, haste, etc.; stress; pressure, as of necessity.
2. insistence; importunity.
3. something urgent.

ûr'ġent, *a.* [Fr.; L. *urgens*, ppr. of *urgere*, to press hard, urge.]
1. calling for haste, immediate action, etc.; grave; pressing.
2. insistent; importunate.

ûr'ġent·ly, *adv.* in an urgent manner; vehemently; forcibly.

ûr'ġẽr, *n.* one who urges; one who importunes.

Ūr·ġin'e·ȧ, *n.* [Mod.L.; after Ar. tribe, Ben *Urgin*, in whose territory the first specimen was found.] a genus of liliaceous plants of the Old World, closely related to *Scilla*, but differing in the more widely spreading segments of the perianth and in the greater number of seeds. The bulbs of *Urginea scilla* (*Scilla maritima*) are known in medicine as squills.

-ûr'ġy, [Gr. *-ourgia*, from *-ourgos*, worker.] a combining form meaning *a fabricating* or *working of* (a specified material), as in crystallurgy, zymurgy.

-ū'ri·ȧ, [Mod. L.; Gr. *-ouris*, from *ouron*, urine.] a combining form meaning *a (diseased) condition of the urine resulting from the presence of* (a specified substance), as in glycos*uria*, albumin*uria*.

Ū·rī'ȧh, *n.* [Heb. *ūriyāh*, lit., God is light.] in the Bible, a Hittite captain whose beautiful wife, Bathsheba, aroused David's lust: David arranged for Uriah to die in battle and then married Bathsheba: 2 Sam. xi. 15.

ū'riç, *a.* relating to or obtained from urine.
uric acid; a white, odorless crystalline substance, $C_5H_4N_4O_3$, found in urine, being one of the products of nuclein metabolism. It is nearly insoluble in water, alcohol, and ether, but soluble in solutions of alkaline salts.

ū'ri·çō- [from *uric.*] a combining form meaning *uric acid*, as in *urico*meter: also, before a vowel, *uric-*.

ū·ri·drō'sis, *n.* a condition in which constituents of urine, such as uric acid, urea, etc., appear in the sweat.

Ū'ri·el, *n.* [Heb. *ūrī'ēl*, lit., light of God.] one of the archangels: in Milton's *Paradise Lost* he is called "regent of the sun."

Ū'rim and Thum'mim, [Heb. *ūrīm*; *tummīm.*] certain unidentified objects mentioned in the Old Testament as being worn in the breastplate of the high priest and apparently serving as a device for determining the will of God: Ex. xxviii. 30.

ū'ri·năl, *n.* [Fr. *urinal*; L. *urinalis*, from *urina*, urine.]
1. formerly, a bottle in which urine was kept for inspection. [Obs.]
2. a vessel for containing urine; specifically, a vessel worn for receiving urine in cases of incontinence.
3. a place for urinating.
4. in plumbing, the fixture for use by men in urinating.

ū·ri·nal'y·sis, *n.*; *pl.* **ū·ri·nal'y·sēṣ**, the chemical analysis of urine: also spelled *uranalysis*.

ū'ri·nănt, *a.* [L. *urinari*, to duck or dive under water.] in heraldry, designating a dolphin or fish when borne with the head downward and the tail erect: opposed to *haurient*.

ū'ri·nār·y, *a.* of or pertaining to the urine or the organs which secrete it.
urinary calculus; a concretion of urinary constituents occurring in the urinary tract.

ū'ri·nār·y, *n.*; *pl.* **ū'ri·nār·ieṣ**, a reservoir or place for the reception of urine and dung for use as manure.
2. a urinal.

ū'ri·nāte, *v.i.*; urinated, *pt.*, *pp.*; urinating, *ppr.* to discharge urine from the body; to micturate.

ū·ri·nā'tion, *n.* the act or process of urinating.

ū'ri·nā·tive, *a.* stimulating the flow of urine; diuretic.

ū'ri·nā·tŏr, *n.* [L., from *urinari*, to dive.] a diver; one who dives under water in search of something, as pearls. [Rare.]

ū'rine, *n.* [OFr., from L. *urina.*] in mammals, the yellowish fluid, containing urea and other waste products, secreted from the blood by the kidneys, passed down the ureters to the bladder, where it is stored, and periodically discharged from the body through the urethra.

ū'rine ȧ·nal'y·sis, the analysis of urine; urinalysis.

ū·ri·nē'mi·ȧ, **ū·ri·nae'mi·ȧ**, *n.* [Gr. *ouron*, urine, and *haima*, blood.] same as *uremia*.

ū'ri·ni-, see *urino-*.

ū·ri·nif'ẽr·ous, *a.* conveying urine; as, a *uriniferous* duct.

ū·ri·nip'ȧ·rous, *a.* [*urini-*, and L. *parere*, to produce.] producing or secreting urine: said of certain tubes in the cortical portion of the kidney.

ū'ri·nō-, **ū'ri·ni-**, [from L. *urina*, urine.] a combining form meaning *urine*, *urinary tract*, as in *urino*genital, *urini*ferous: also, before a vowel, *urin-*.

ū″ri·nō·ġen'i·tăl, **ū″ri·nō·ġen'i·tăr·y**, *a.* designating or of the urinary and genital organs; genitourinary.

ū·ri·nol'ō·ġy, *n.* the scientific study of the urine.

ū·ri·nom'e·tẽr, *n.* an instrument used in ascertaining the specific gravity of urine.

ū″ri·nō·met'riç, *a.* of or pertaining to urinometry or the use of the urinometer.

ū·ri·nom'e·try, *n.* the ascertainment of the specific gravity of urine.

ū″ri·nō·sçop'iç, *a.* of the nature of or pertaining to urinoscopy: also *uroscopic*.

ū·ri·nos'çō·py, *n.* [*urino-*, and Gr. *skopein*, to view.] the diagnostic examination of urine: also *uroscopy*.

ū'ri·nous, **ū'ri·nōse**, *a.* 1. of, like, or containing urine.
2. having the odor of urine.

ū'rīte, *n.* [Gr. *oura*, a tail, and *-ite.*] the sternite of any abdominal or postabdominal segment of an arthropod.

ûrn, *n.* [L. *urna*, an urn, from *urere*, to burn: so called because made of burnt clay.]
1. a vase in any of various forms and materials, usually with a foot or pedestal.
2. such a vase used to hold the ashes of the dead after cremation.
3. figuratively, the grave; any place of burial.
4. in ancient Rome, a measure for liquids, containing about three and a half gallons.
5. in botany, the hollow vessel in which the spores of mosses are lodged; the sporangium; the theca.
6. a metal container with a faucet, used for making or serving coffee, etc. at the table.

ûrn, *v.t.* to put in an urn; to inurn. [Rare.]

ûrn'ăl, *a.* of, resembling, or pertaining to an urn.

ûrn'flow″ẽr, *n.* any of several plants of the genus *Urceolina*.

ûrn'fụl, *n.* the quantity that an urn will contain.

ûrn mọss'eṣ, the true mosses: so called because many species have urn-shaped sporangia.

ûrn'-shāped (-shāpt), *a.* having the shape of an urn.

ū'rō-, [from Gr. *oura*, a tail.] a combining form meaning *tail*, as in *uro*pod, *uro*chord.

ū'rō-, [from Gr. *ouron*, urine.] a combining form meaning *urine*, *urination*, *urinary tract*, as in *uro*lith: also, before a vowel, *ur-*.

ū·rō·bī'lin, *n.* [*uro-*, and L. *bilis*, bile.] an amorphous, brownish-yellow pigment, $C_{32}H_{40}N_4O_7$, found in the urine.

ū·rō·bī·lin·ē'mi·ȧ, **ū·rō·bī·lin·ae'mi·ȧ**, *n.* [*urobilin*, and Gr. *haima*, blood.] the presence of urobilin in the blood.

ū″rō·bī·lin'ō·ġen, *n.* [*urobilin*, and Gr. *gennān*, to produce.] a chromogen whose decomposition produces urobilin.

ū·rō·bī·li·nū'ri·ȧ, *n.* a condition in which an excessive amount of urobilin is contained in the urine.

ū'rō·cēle, *n.* [*uro-*, and Gr. *kēlē*, a tumor.] a swelling of the scrotum due to the abnormal absorption of urine.

Ū·rō·cer'i·dae, *n.pl.* [*uro-*, and Gr. *keras*, a horn.] a family of hymenopterous insects widely distributed in Europe and North America; the horntails.

ū'rō·çhord, *n.* [*uro-*, and Gr. *chordē*, a string.]
1. in zoology, the notochord of ascidians and tunicates, mainly or more noticeably present in the larva, and restricted chiefly to the caudal region.
2. one of the *Urochorda*.

Ū·rō·çhọr'dȧ, *n.pl.* a subphylum of animals, the tunicates or ascidians, regarded as a branch of the *Chordata*.

ū·rō·çhọr'dăl, **ū·rō·çhọr'dāte**, *a.* having a urochord; pertaining or belonging to the *Urochorda*.

ū'rō·çhrōme, *n.* [*uro-*, and Gr. *chrōma*, color.] a yellow, amorphous pigment of the urine, $C_{43}H_{51}NO_{26}$, giving it its characteristic yellow color.

ū'roçhs, *n.* same as *aurochs*.

ū'rō·cyst, *n.* [*uro-*, and Gr. *kystis*, a bladder.] the urinary bladder.

ū·rō·cyst'iç, *a.* of or pertaining to the urinary bladder.

Ū·rō·cys'tis, *n.* a genus of ustilaginous fungi, destructive to various plants.

ū″rō·cys·tī'tis, *n.* inflammation of the urinary bladder.

Ū·rō·dē'lȧ, *n.pl.* [*uro-*, and Gr. *dēlos*, evident.] same as *Caudata*.

ū'rō·dēle, **ū·rō·dē'lăn**, *a.* of or belonging to the *Urodela*.

ū'rō·dēle, **ū·rō·dē'lăn**, *n.* any species of the *Urodela*.

ū·rō·dē'li·ăn, **ū·rō·dē'lous**, *a.* same as *urodele*.

ū″rō·ē·ryth'rin, *n.* [*uro-*, and Gr. *erythros*, red.] a reddish coloring matter found in the urine in certain diseases. It produces the red color seen in deposits of urates.

ū·rō·gas'tẽr, *n.* [*uro-*, and Gr. *gastēr*, stomach.] the urinary tract, including the allantoic cavity, of an embryo.

ū·rō·gas'triç, *a.* of or pertaining to the urogaster.

ū·rō·ġen'i·tăl, *a.* same as *urinogenital*.

ū·rog'ē·nous, *a.* [*uro-*, and Gr. *gennān*, to produce.]
1. producing urine.
2. contained in or obtained from urine.

ū·rō·glau'cin, *n.* [*uro-*, and Gr. *glaukos*, bright.] an indigo blue coloring matter occurring in the urine by the oxidation of a colorless chromogen.

ū·rō·hem'ȧ·tin, **ū·rō·haem'ȧ·tin**, *n.* the red pigment of urine.

ū·rō·hȳ'ăl, *a.* of or pertaining to the posterior element of the composite hyoid bone.

ū·rō·hȳ'ăl, *n.* a urohyal bone.

ū'rō·lith, **ū'rō·līte**, *n.* a urinary calculus.

ū″rō·li·thī'ȧ·sis, *n.* the formation of urinary calculi; also, the diseased condition associated with the presence of urinary calculi.

ū·rō·lith'iç, *a.* of a urolith or uroliths.

ū″rō·li·thol'ō·ġy, *n.* the scientific study of urinary calculi.

ū·rō·loġ'iç, *a.* urological.

ū·rō·loġ'iç·ăl, *a.* pertaining to urology.

ū·rol'ō·ġist, *n.* an expert in urology.

ū·rol'ō·ġy, *n.* [*uro-* and *-logy.*] the branch of medicine dealing with the urinogenital system and its diseases.

ū·rō·lū'tē·in, *n.* [*uro-*, and L. *luteus*, yellow.] a yellow pigment of the urine.

ū·rō·mel'ȧ·nin, *n.* [*uro-*, and Gr. *melas*, black.] a black pigment found in the urine in certain diseases.

ū·rom'ē·lus, *n.* [*uro-*, and Gr. *melos*, limb.] a monster fetus with the legs fused and one foot.

ū'rō·mēre, *n.* [*uro-*, and Gr. *meros*, part.] an abdominal or posterior segment of the body of an arthropod.

ū·rō·mer'iç, *a.* relating to a uromere.

Ū·rom'y·cēṣ, *n.* [*uro-*, and Gr. *mykēs*, a mushroom.] an extensive genus of rust fungi including nearly 200 species.

ū·rō·nol'ō·ġy, *n.* same as *urinology*.

ū·rō·phē'in, *n.* [*uro-*, and Gr. *phaios*, gray colored.] an odoriferous gray pigment of the urine.

ū'rō·pod, *n.* an appendage of the urosome of an arthropod.

ū·rop'ō·dăl, *a.* pertaining to or resembling a uropod.

ū″rō·poi·ē'sis, *n.* [*uro-*, and Gr. *poiein*, to make.] the secretion of urine.

ū″rō·poi·et'iç, *a.* of or pertaining to the secretion of urine.

ū·rō·pyġ'i·ăl, *a.* [*uro-*, and Gr. *pygē*, rump.] relating to the uropygium of birds.
uropygial gland; an oil-secreting gland located at the base of the tail feathers of birds. The oil is used in preening the feathers.

ū·rō·pyġ'i·um, *n.*; *pl.* **ū·rō·pyġ'i·ȧ**, [*uro-*, and Gr. *pygē*, rump.] the protuberance at the posterior end of a bird's body, from which the tail feathers grow.

ū″rō·pȳ·lor′iç, *a.* relating to the posterior part of the pylorus of some crustaceans.

ū·rō·rū′bin, *n.* [*uro-*, and L. *ruber*, red.] a red pigment found in the urine.

ū·rō·sā′çrăl, *a.* relating to the sacral and caudal portions of the spinal column, as in birds.

ū·ro·sçop′iç, *a.* of uroscopy.

ū·ros′çō·py, *n.* [*uro-* and *-scopy.*] examination of the urine, as for the diagnosis of disease.

ū·rō·sep′sis, *n.* septic poisoning from the absorption and decomposition of urinary substances in the tissues.

ū·rō·sep′tiç, *a.* pertaining to or marked by urosepsis.

ū·rō′sis, *n.* any disease of the urinary system.

ū′rō·sōme, *n.* [*uro-*, and Gr. *sōma*, body.] the abdomen of an arthropod.

ū·rō·sō′mīte, *n.* same as *uromere.*

ū·rō·stē′ȧ·lith, *n.* [*uro-*, Gr. *stear*, fat, and *lithos*, a stone.] a fatty constituent of certain urinary calculi.

ū·ros′tē·găl, *a.* relating to a urostege.

ū′rō·stēġe, *n.* [*uro-* and Gr. *stegē*, a roof.] a large plate on the ventral side of a snake's tail.

ū·ros′tē·ġīte, *n.* a urostege.

ū·ros′tē·on, *n.* [*uro-*, and Gr. *osteon*, bone.] a median posterior element of the sternum of certain birds.

ū·rō·stẽr′nīte, *n.* the ventral part of any uromere of an arthropod.

ū′rō·sthēne, *n.* [*uro-*, and Gr. *sthenos*, strength.] any animal having the caudal region unusually well developed, as snakes and whales.

ū·rō·sthen′iç, *a.* having the characteristics of a urosthene: opposed to *prosthenic.*

ū·rō·stȳ′lăr, *a.* pertaining to or resembling a urostyle.

ū′rō·stȳle, *n.* [*uro-*, and Gr. *stylos*, a column.] a posterior prolongation of the vertebral column of certain fishes and amphibians.

ū·rō·tox′iç, *a.* pertaining to the toxicity of urine.

urotoxic coefficient; the number of urotoxic units produced in twenty-four hours per kilogram of body weight.

ū′rō·tox·y, ū·rō·tox′i·ȧ, *n.* [*uro-*, and Gr. *toxikon*, poison.]

1. the toxicity of urine; also, the toxic substance of the urine.

2. the unit of the toxicity of the urine, or a quantity sufficient to kill an animal weighing one kilogram.

ū′rox, *n.* same as *aurochs.*

ū·rox′ȧ·nāte, *n.* a salt or ester of uroxanic acid.

ū·rox·an′iç, *a.* derived from or containing uric acid and alloxan.

uroxanic acid; a dibasic acid, $C_5N_4H_8O_6$, obtained by slowly boiling uric acid in an alkaline solution.

ū·rō·xan′thin (-zan′), *n.* [*uro-*, and Gr. *xanthos*, yellow.] a yellow pigment of normal urine convertible into indigo blue; indican.

ū·rox′in, *n.* alloxantin.

ūr·rhō′din (-rō′), *n.* [from *uro-*, and Gr. *rhodon*, a rose.] a red pigment sometimes found in diseased urine.

Ūr′sȧ, *n.* [L., a she-bear.] 1. Ursa Major.

2. Ursa Minor.

Ūr′sȧ Mā′jŏr, [L., lit., Great Bear.] the most conspicuous of the constellations in the northern sky. It is near the pole and contains fifty-three visible stars, seven of which form the Big Dipper: also called *Great Bear.*

Ūr′sȧ Mī′nŏr, [L., lit., Little Bear.] the northernmost constellation. It contains twenty-three visible stars, including those forming the Little Dipper; the most important of these is Polaris, the North Star: also called *Little Bear.*

ūr′săl, *n.* the fur seal.

ūr′si·fọrm, *a.* [L. *ursus*, a bear, and *-form.*] having the shape or appearance of a bear.

ūr′sīne, *a.* [L. *ursinus.*]

1. of, like, or characteristic of a bear or the bear family.

2. covered with bristles, as certain caterpillars.

ursine baboon; same as *chacma.*

ursine dasyure; the Tasmanian devil.

ursine howler; the red howling monkey native to the northern part of South America.

ursine seal; the sea bear, or fur seal.

ūr′sŏn, *n.* [Fr. *ourson*, a bear's cub.] the Canada porcupine.

Ūr′sprä·che (ůr′shprä-khe), *n.* [G.; *ur-*, original, and *sprache*, language.] a (hypothetical) parent language; as, the Indo-European *Ursprache* has been reconstructed by the methods of comparative linguistics.

Ūr′sū·line, *a.* designating or of an order of nuns founded by St. Angela Merici at Brescia, Italy, in the early part of the sixteenth century, to carry on the work of nursing and teaching.

Ūr′sū·line, *n.* one of the nuns of the Ursuline order.

Ūr′sus, *n.* [L., a bear.] a genus of carnivorous mammals; the bears.

Ūr′ti·cȧ, *n.* [L., nettle, from *urere*, to burn.] a genus of herbaceous plants covered with stinging hairs; the nettles.

Ūr·ti·cā′cē·ae, *n.pl.* a family of exogenous trees and shrubs including a large number of genera, among which are the nettles, the hops, the elms, and the hemp.

ūr·ti·cā′ceous, *a.* relating to the order *Urticaceæ.*

ūr′tiç·ăl, *a.* pertaining to or resembling the nettles or the genus *Urtica.*

ūr·ti·cā′ri·ȧ, *n.* [L. *urtica*, a nettle.] an allergic skin condition characterized by the eruption of smooth, itching patches, or wheals; hives.

ūr·ti·cā′ri·ăl, *a.* of, or having the nature of, urticaria.

ūr′ti·cāte, *v.t.*; urticated, *pt., pp.*; urticating, *ppr.* 1. to sting with or as with nettles; to produce urtication in.

2. figuratively, to irritate; to annoy.

ūr′ti·cāte, *v.i.* to sting.

ūr·ti·cā′tion, *n.* 1. formerly, the flogging of a paralyzed limb, etc. with nettles for the stimulating effect produced.

2. any sensation of stinging or itching.

3. the formation of urticaria.

ū′rū·bū, *n.* [Braz.] an American vulture, *Catharista iota*, the black vulture or zopilote, closely related to the turkey buzzard, which it resembles.

ū·rū·çū′ri, *n.* a Brazilian palm, *Attalea excelsa*, bearing large oily nuts, the smoke of which, when they are burned, is used in curing Para rubber.

Ū·rụ·guāy′ăn (-gwā′ *or* -gwī′), *a.* of Uruguay, its people, or culture.

Ū·rụ·guāy′ăn, *n.* a native or inhabitant of Uruguay.

ū′rus, *n.* [L., a wild bull.] a shaggy, long-horned wild ox, now extinct, common in Europe at the beginning of the Christian Era.

ū′rū·shi·ōl″, *n.* [Japan. *urushi*, lacquer; and *-ol.*] a poisonous, irritant liquid, $C_{21}H_{32}O_2$, present in poison ivy and the Japanese lac tree.

ūr′vȧ, *n.* [LL., from E. Ind.] the crab-eating ichneumon of India, *Herpestes urva.*

us, *pron.* [ME. *ous, us*; used both as acc. and dat. of *we*; AS. *us*, dat.; *us, usic, ussic*, acc. pl., us.] the objective case of we: also used colloquially as a predicate complement with a linking verb (e.g., that's *us*).

ūṣ·ȧ·bil′i·ty, *n.* the state or quality of being usable: also spelled *useability.*

ūṣ′ȧ·ble, *a.* capable of being used; suitable, fit, or safe for use; as, the water is *usable.*

ūs′ăġe, *n.* [OFr.; ML. *usagium, usaticum.*]

1. the act or way of using or treating; treatment; use.

2. long-continued or established custom or practice; habitual or customary use or way of action; custom; habit.

3. the way in which a word, phrase, etc. is used to express a particular idea; customary manner of using a given language in speaking or writing, or an instance of this.

4. manners; behavior; conduct. [Obs.]

5. experience. [Obs.]

Syn.—custom, prescription, habit, use.

ūṣ′ăġ·ẽr, *n.* one who has the use of anything in trust for another. [Obs.]

ūṣ′ănce, *n.* [ME. *usaunce*; OFr. *usance*; ML. *usancia.*]

1. income or other benefits derived from wealth or the use of wealth.

2. the time allowed for the payment of a foreign bill of exchange, as established by custom and excluding any period of grace.

3. (a) use; (b) usage; custom; (c) interest paid for the use of money. [Obs.]

ūṣ′ănt, *a.* accustomed; using. [Obs.]

Us′beg, Us′bek, *n.* and *a.* same as *Uzbek.*

ūse, *n.* [OFr. *us*, use, from L. *usus*, use.]

1. the act of using or the state of being used; usage.

2. the power or ability to use; as, he has regained the *use* of his hand.

3. the right or permission to use; as, he granted them the *use* of his name.

4. the need, opportunity, or occasion to use; as, we will have no further *use* for his services.

5. way of using.

6. the quality that makes a thing useful or suitable for a given purpose; advantage; usefulness; worth; utility.

7. the object, end, or purpose for which something is used.

8. function; service.

9. constant, continued, customary, or habitual employment, practice, or exercise, or an instance of this; custom; habit; practice; wont.

10. in law, (a) the enjoyment of property, as from occupying, employing, or exercising it; (b) [influenced by OFr. *ues*, gain, from L. *opus*, a work.] profit, benefit, or advantage, especially that of lands and tenements held in trust by another.

11. in liturgy, the particular form of ritual or liturgy practiced in a given church, diocese, etc.; as, the Lutheran *use.*

12. common occurrence. [Rare.]

executed use; a use to which the statute applies by annexing it to the legal ownership.

future or *contingent use*; a use limited to a person not ascertained, or upon an uncertain event, but without derogation of a use previously limited.

in use; (a) in the process of being used; (b) in heat, as a mare.

to have no use for; (a) to have no need of; (b) to have no wish to deal with; to be impatient with; (c) to have no affection or respect for; to dislike strongly.

to make use of; to use; to have occasion to use.

to put to use; to use; to find a use for.

Syn.—custom, habit, practice, usage, service.

ūṣe, *v.t.*; used, *pt., pp.*; using, *ppr.* [Fr. *user*, from LL. *usare*, from *usus*, pp. of L. *uti*, to use.]

1. to put or bring into action or service; to employ for or apply to a given purpose.

2. to practice; to exercise; as, you must *use* your judgment.

3. to act or behave toward; to treat; as, she *used* her friends badly.

4. to consume, expend, or exhaust by use (often with *up*); as, he has *used up* all his energy.

5. to smoke or chew (tobacco).

6. to make familiar; to accustom (used in the passive with *to*); as, they were *used to* the old ways.

7. to exploit, as a person; to treat as a means to some selfish end. [Colloq.]

Syn.—employ, exercise, treat, practice, accustom, habituate, inure.

ūṣe, *v.i.* 1. to be accustomed; to be wont (now only in the past tense, with an infinitive expressed or implied); as, he *used* to enter every contest.

> They *used* to place him that shall be their captain upon a stone always reserved for that purpose. —Spenser.

2. to frequent; to resort. [Archaic or Dial.]

ūṣe·ȧ·bil′i·ty, *n.* usability.

ūṣe′ȧ·ble, *a.* usable.

ūse′fụl, *a.* that can be used to advantage; serviceable; helpful; beneficial; advantageous; often, having practical utility.

ūse′fụl·ly, *adv.* in a useful manner.

ūse′fụl·ness, *n.* the quality or state of being useful.

ūse′less, *a.* having or of no use; unserviceable; answering no valuable purpose; ineffectual; as, a *useless* garment; *useless* pity.

> No man is *useless* while he has a friend. —Robert Louis Stevenson.

ūse′less·ly, *adv.* in a useless manner.

ūse′less·ness, *n.* the quality or state of being useless.

ūṣ′ẽr, *n.* [sense 1 from *use*, v.; in sense 2 a substantive use of OFr. *user*, to use.]

1. a person or thing that uses.

2. in law, (a) the exercise of a right of use; (b) a right of use, based on long use.

Ū′-shāped (-shāpt), *a.* having the shape of a U.

Ụ′shȧs, *n.* [Sans. *Uṣas*, dawn.] the Hindu, or Vedic, goddess of dawn.

ush′ẽr, *n.* [OFr. *ussier, huissier*, from *huis*, a door, from L. *ostium*, a door.]

1. an official doorkeeper.

2. a person whose duty it is to show people to their seats in a church, theater, etc.

3. a person whose official duty is to precede someone of rank, as in a procession, or to make introductions between those unacquainted with one another.

4. in Great Britain, an assistant teacher. [Obs.]

ush'ēr, *v.t.*; ushered, *pt., pp.*; ushering, *ppr.* 1. to act as an usher to; to escort or conduct (others) to seats, etc.

2. to precede and introduce, as forerunner or harbinger: generally followed by *in, forth,* etc.

ush'ēr·ănce, *n.* introduction. [Rare.]

ush'ēr·dŏm, *n.* ushership; ushers in general. [Rare.]

ush·ēr·ette' (-et'), *n.* a woman or girl usher, as in a theater.

ush'ēr·less, *a.* without an usher or ushers.

ush'ēr·ship, *n.* the office or status of an usher.

ūs'i·tā·tive, *a.* [L. *usitatus*, usual.] indicating customary action: said of a Greek tense.

Us'nē·ȧ, *n.* [Ar. *ushnah*, a lichen.] a genus of lichens of the family *Usneaceæ*. The species are branched and filiform in their structure, growing on rocks and trunks of trees, and are often called *tree moss* or *tree hair*.

us·nē·ā'ceous, *a.* of or pertaining to the genus *Usnea*.

us'niç, *a.* obtained from the *Usnea* or similar lichens.

usnic acid; a yellow, crystalline acid found in the *Usnea* or similar lichens.

us'quē·baugh (-bą), *n.* [Ir. and Gael. *uisge*, water, and *beatha*, life.]

1. whisky (in Scotland or Ireland).

2. a strong compound cordial, made in Ireland of brandy or other spirits, and flavored with cinnamon, cloves, etc.

us'sŭk, *n.* [Eskimo.] the bearded seal, *Erignathus barbatus*.

Us''ti·lā·ġin'ē·ae, *n.pl.* a section of fungi in which the protospores are not disposed in orbital or elliptic sori, but form irregular, dusty masses. The genus *Ustilago*, or smut, is the type. Also called *Ustilaginales*.

us·ti·laġ'i·nous, *a.* of or relating to the *Ustilagineæ*.

Us·ti·lā'gō, *n.* [LL., from L. *ustulare*, to burn up.] a genus of fungi comprising the grain smuts.

us'tion (-chun), *n.* [Fr., from L. *ustio (-onis)*, a burning.] the act of burning or the state of being burnt; also in surgery, the use of cautery. [Rare.]

us·tō'ri·ous, *a.* having the quality of burning. [Rare.]

us'tū·lāte, *a.* discolored or blackened, as if by burning.

us·tū·lā'tion, *n.* [L. *ustulatus*, burnt up, from *ustulare*, to burn up.]

1. the act of burning or searing. [Rare.]

2. in metallurgy, the operation of expelling one substance from another by heat, as sulfur and arsenic from ores, in a muffle. [Obs.]

3. in pharmacy, (a) the roasting or drying of moist substances so as to prepare them for pulverization; (b) the burning of wine.

4. lustful passion; concupiscence. [Obs.]

ū'ṣū·ăl (-zhū-), *a.* [Fr. *usuel*, from L. *usualis*, usual.] customary; common; frequent; such as occurs in ordinary practice or in the ordinary course of events; as, rainy weather is not *usual* in this climate.

Syn.—ordinary, normal, regular, habitual, wonted, accustomed, general.

ū'ṣū·ăl·ly, *adv.* according to what is usual or customary; generally; commonly; ordinarily.

ū'ṣū·ăl·ness, *n.* the quality or state of being usual.

ū·sū·çā'pi·ent, *n.* in Roman law, a person holding or claiming title to an estate by usucaption.

ū·sū·cap'tion, *n.* [L. *usus*, use, and *captus*, pp. of *capere*, to take.] in Roman law, the acquisition of the title or right to property by the uninterrupted and undisputed possession of it for a certain term prescribed by law.

ū'sū·fruçt, *n.* [L. *usus*, use, and *fructus*, fruit.] in law, the right of enjoying a thing which belongs to another and of deriving from it all the profit or benefit it may produce, provided it be without altering or damaging the substance of the thing.

ū·sū·fruç'tū·ār·y, *n.*; *pl.* **ū·sū·fruç'tū·ār·ieṣ,** the person or agent having the usufruct of property.

ū·sū·fruç'tū·ār·y, *a.* relating to or having the qualities of a usufruct.

ū·ṣū·rãr'i·ous, ū'ṣū·rãr·y, *a.* usurious. [Obs.]

ū'ṣūre (-zhūr), *n.* usury. [Obs.]

ū'ṣūre, *v.i.* to practise usury. [Obs.]

ū'ṣū·rēr (-zhū-), *n.* [LL. *usurarius*, a usurer, from L. *usura*, use, interest.]

1. a person who lends money at interest; a moneylender. [Obs.]

2. one who lends money at a rate of interest that is excessive or unlawfully high.

ū·ṣū'ri·ous, *a.* 1. practising usury; taking exorbitant interest for money lent.

2. of or constituting usury.

ū·ṣū'ri·ous·ly, *adv.* in a usurious manner.

ū·ṣū'ri·ous·ness, *n.* the state or quality of being usurious.

ū·ṣūrp', *v.t.*; usurped (-zūrpt), *pt., pp.*; usurping, *ppr.* [Fr. *usurper*, from L. *usurpare*, to usurp; *usus*, use, and *rapere*, to seize.] to take or assume and hold in possession by force or without right: said of seizures of power, positions, rights, functions, etc.

ū·ṣūrp', *v.i.* to practice or commit usurpation: often with *on* or *upon*.

The parish churches *on* which the Presbyterians and fanatics had *usurped*.—Evelyn.

ū·ṣūrp'ănt, *a.* usurping. [Obs.]

ū·ṣūr·pā'tion, *n.* 1. the act of usurping; the act of seizing or occupying and enjoying the place, power, functions, or property of another without right; especially, the unlawful occupation of a throne.

2. in law, (a) intrusion into an office which is vacant, or the ousting of an incumbent without any color of title; (b) such intrusion without legal right; (c) the absolute ouster and dispossession of the patron of a church by presenting a clerk to a vacant benefice, who is thereupon admitted and instituted; intrusion.

3. an encroaching; encroachment.

4. use; usage. [Obs.]

ū·ṣūrp'ȧ·tō·ry, *a.* characterized or marked by usurpation; usurping.

ū·ṣūrp'ȧ·tūre, *n.* usurpation. [Rare.]

ū·ṣūrp'ēr, *n.* one who usurps; one who seizes power or property without right; as, the *usurper* of a throne.

ū·ṣūrp'ing·ly, *adv.* in a usurping manner; by usurpation; without just right or claim.

ū'ṣū·ry (-zhū-), *n.*; *pl.* **ū'ṣū·rieṣ,** [OFr. *usure*; L. *usura*, interest on money lent.]

1. the act or practice of lending money at a rate of interest that is excessive or unlawfully high.

2. an excessive or unlawfully high rate or amount of interest.

3. interest paid on a loan. [Obs.]

ū'sus, *n.* [L., use.] in Roman law, the right to make use of or enjoy a thing, without the right to transfer it to another.

ū'sus lō·quen'dī, [L.] the usual way of speaking; usage in speaking, as among persons of a particular class or profession.

ŭt, *n.* in music, a syllable formerly used in solmization: now replaced by *do*.

ū'tas, ū'tis, *n.* [Norm. *utes, utas, ute*, the eighth, *ut*, eight; OFr. *oit*, Fr. *huit*, eight, from L. *octo*, eight.] the octave of a legal term or of any festival; the space of eight days after it; also, the festival itself. [Obs.]

Ūte, *n.*; *pl.* **Ūte, Ūtes,** [Am. Ind.] 1. a member of a tribe of nomadic Shoshonean Indians that lived in Colorado and Utah, ranging down into New Mexico and Arizona.

2. their Uto-Aztecan language.

ū·ten'sil, *n.* [OFr. *utensile*, from L. *utensilis*, fit for use, from *uti*, to use.]

1. any implement or container ordinarily used in a kitchen, dairy, or the like; as, cooking *utensils*.

2. any implement or tool, as for use in farming, etc.

ū·tēr·al'ġi·ȧ, *n.* [L. *uterus*, womb, and Gr. *algos*, pain.] pain in the womb or uterus.

ū'tēr·ine, *a.* [Fr. *utérin*; L. *uterinus*, from *uterus*, the womb.]

1. pertaining to the uterus.

2. having the same mother but a different father; as, a *uterine* brother.

ū'tēr·ō-, [from *uterus*.] a combining form meaning *the uterus* or *the uterus and*, as in *utero*abdominal: also *uter-*.

ū''tēr·ō·ġes·tā'tion, *n.* gestation in the womb from conception to birth.

ū''tēr·ō·vaġ'i·năl, *a.* relating to or connected with both the vagina and the uterus.

ū'tēr·us, *n.*; *pl.* **ū'tēr·ī,** [L.] a hollow, muscular organ of female mammals in which the ovum is deposited and the embryo and fetus are developed and protected; womb.

Ū'thēr, *n.* a legendary king of Britain, father of King Arthur.

ū'ti·ȧ, *n.* [W. Ind.] any rodent of the West Indies belonging to the genus *Capromys*.

ū'tile, *a.* useful. [Obs.]

ū'ti·līṣe, *v.t.*; utilised, *pt., pp.*; utilising, *ppr.* to utilize: British spelling.

ū·til·i·tãr'i·ăn, *a.* [from *utility* and *-arian*: coined by Bentham.]

1. of or having to do with utility.

2. stressing the importance of utility over beauty or other considerations.

3. made for or aiming at utility.

4. of, or having belief in, utilitarianism.

ū·til·i·tãr'i·ăn, *n.* one who believes in utilitarianism.

ū·til·i·tãr'i·ăn·iṣm, *n.* 1. the doctrine that the greatest happiness of the greatest number should be the aim of all action.

2. the doctrine that the worth or value of anything is determined solely by its utility.

ū·til'i·ty, *n.*; *pl.* **ū·til'i·tieṣ,** [Fr. *utilité*; L. *utilitas*, from *uti*, to use.]

1. the quality or property of being useful; usefulness.

2. the greatest happiness of the greatest number.

3. something useful.

4. something useful to the public, especially the service of electric power, gas, water, telephone, etc.

5. a company providing such a service.

6. [*pl.*] shares of stock in such a company.

7. in economics, the power to satisfy the needs or wants of humanity.

utility man; (a) in baseball, a player who can substitute at any of several positions in the absence of the regular player; (b) in the theater, a person who plays minor roles and performs odd jobs.

Syn.—usefulness, advantage, benefit, convenience, service, use.

ū'til·ī·zȧ·ble, *a.* that can be utilized.

ū''til·i·zā'tion, *n.* a utilizing or being utilized.

ū'til·īze, *v.t.*; utilized, *pt., pp.*; utilizing, *ppr.* [Fr. *utiliser*, from *utile*, useful.] to put to profitable account or use; to make useful; as, to *utilize* natural resources.

ut in'frȧ, [L.] as below.

ū'tī pos·si·dē'tis, [L., lit., as you possess.]

1. an interdict of the civil law as to heritage whereby the colorable possession of a bona fide possessor is continued until the final settlement of a contested right.

2. in international law, the basis or principle of a treaty which leaves belligerent parties in possession of what they have acquired by their arms during the war.

ū'tis, *n.* same as *utas*.

ut'mōst, *a.* [AS. *ytemest, ylmest*, double superl. of *ut*, out.]

1. extreme; being at the farthest point or extremity; most extreme or distant; farthest.

2. of or to the greatest or highest degree, amount, number, etc.; greatest.

Also *uttermost*.

ut'mōst, *n.* the most that can be; the greatest power, degree, or effort; as, he has done his *utmost*: also *uttermost*.

Ū'tō-Az'teç·ăn, *a.* designating or of a large American Indian linguistic family of the western United States, Mexico, and Central America.

Ū'tō-Az'teç·ăn, *n.* the Uto-Aztecan languages, comprising the Shoshonean, Nahuatl, Piman, Hopi, Ute, etc.

Ū·tō'pi·ȧ, *n.* [Gr. *ou*, not, and *topos*, place.]

1. an imaginary island described as having a perfect political and social system: subject and title of a book written by Sir Thomas More in 1516.

2. [*often* u-] any place, state, or situation of ideal perfection.

3. [*often* u-] any visionary scheme or system for an ideally perfect social order.

Ū·tō'pi·ăn, *a.* 1. of or like Utopia.

2. [*often* u-] having the nature of, or inclined to draw up schemes for, a utopia; idealistic; visionary.

Ū·tō'pi·ăn, *n.* 1. an inhabitant of Utopia.

2. [*often* u-] a person who believes in a utopia, especially of a social or political nature; a visionary; idealist.

ū·tō'pi·ăn·iṣm, *n.* the ideas, doctrines, aims, etc. of a utopian; visionary schemes for producing perfection in social or political conditions.

ū·tō'pi·ăn·ist, *n.* a utopian.

ū·tō'pist, *n.* a utopian. [Rare.]

Ū'trȧ·quist, *n.* same as *Calixtine*.

ū'tri·çle, *n.* [L. *utriculus*, a little bag or bottle.]

1. a small sac, vesicle, or baglike part;

specifically, in anatomy, the larger of the two saclike cavities (the other being the *saccule*) in the membranous labyrinth of the inner ear.
2. in botany, a small, one-celled seed vessel with a thin, membranous wall and one or several seeds.
primordial utricle; see under *primordial*.

ū·tric′ū·lăr, *a.* 1. of, or having the nature of, a utricle.
2. having one or more utricles.

Ū·tric·ū·lā′ri·ȧ, *n.* a genus of plants; the bladderworts.

ū·tric′ū·lāte, *a.* utricular.

ū·tric·ū·lif′ẽr·ous, *a.* producing or bearing utricles or bladders.

ū·tric′ū·li·form, *a.* in botany, having the shape of a utricle; utricular.

ū·tric·ū·lī′tis, *n.* inflammation of the utricle of the inner ear.

ū·tric′ū·loid, *a.* same as *utriculiform*.

ū·tric′ū·lōse, *a.* in botany, same as *utricular*.

ū·tric′ū·lus, *n.*; *pl.* **ū·tric′ū·lī,** [L.] a utricle, especially of the inner ear.

ū′tri·form, *a.* [L. *uter*, leather bag, and *-form*.] shaped like a leather bottle.

ut′suk, *n.* same as *ussuk*.

ut sū′prȧ, [L.] as above.

ut′tẽr, *a.* [AS. *utor*, *uttor*, comp. of *ut*, out.]
1. being on the outside; outer. [Obs.]
2. situated at or beyond the limits of something; remote from some center; outside of any place or space. [Obs.]
3. complete; total.
4. absolute; unconditional; unqualified; as, an *utter* refusal.
utter loss; in marine insurance, a total loss of everything of value.
Syn.—extreme, perfect, complete, unqualified, absolute, thorough, consummate, entire, sheer, pure.

ut′tẽr, *n.* the utmost limit. [Rare.]

ut′tẽr, *v.t.*; uttered, *pt.*, *pp.*; uttering, *ppr.* [ME. *uttren*, *outren*, from *utter*, outward, from *ut*, *out*, out.]
1. originally, to give out; to put forth: obsolete except when used of the passing of counterfeit money or forgeries, or the publication of libel.
2. to pronounce, speak, or express audibly, as words, thoughts, vocal sounds, etc.
3. to express in any way.
4. to emit (nonvocal sounds), as if speaking.
5. to make known; to divulge; to reveal.
6. to publish (a book, etc.). [Obs.]
7. to sell. [Obs.]
Syn.—speak, articulate, pronounce.

ut′tẽr·ȧ·ble, *a.* capable of being uttered, pronounced, or expressed.

ut′tẽr·ănce, *n.* 1. the act of uttering, or expressing by voice.
2. the power or style of speaking.
3. that which is uttered; especially, a word or words uttered, whether written or spoken.
4. the act of uttering, or circulating (counterfeit money, etc.). [Rare.]

ut′tẽr·ănce, *n.* [Fr. *outrance*; L. *ultra*, beyond.] the last extremity; i.e., death. [Obs.]

ut′tẽr·ẽr, *n.* one who utters.

ut′tẽr·est, *a.* utmost. [Obs.]

ut′tẽr·less, *a.* unutterable; inexpressible.

ut′tẽr·ly, *adv.* in an utter manner; to the fullest extent; fully; absolutely; totally; as, *utterly* powerless.
Syn.—fully, entirely, completely, totally.

ut′tẽr·mōst, *a.* and *n.* same as *utmost*.

ut′tẽr·ness, *n.* the state or quality of being utter or extreme; extremity.

ū′vȧ, *n.* [L., a grape.] in botany, a succulent indehiscent fruit with a central placenta, as the grape.

ů·vä′rō·vīte (-fīt), *n.* [named after S. S. *Uvarov* (1786–1855), Russ. statesman and author.] an emerald-green variety of garnet containing chromium: also *ouvarovite*, *uwarowite*.

ū′vāte, *n.* a grape preserve.

ū′vȧ-ūr″sī, *n.* the bearberry.

ū′vē·ȧ, *n.* [L.] 1. the posterior, pigmentary surface of the iris. [Obs.]
2. the iris, ciliary body, and choroid, together forming the entire pigmentary layer of the eye.

ū′vē·ăl, *a.* of or pertaining to the uvea.

ū·vē·it′iç, *a.* pertaining to, or of the nature of, uveitis.

ū·vē·ī′tis, *n.* inflammation of the uvea.

ū′vē·ous, *a.* same as *uveal*.

ū′viç, *a.* [L. *uva*, a grape.] of, pertaining to, or formed from grapes.
uvic acid; an acid derived from grapes; pyrotartaric acid.

ū′vi·form, *a.* having the form of a grape.

ū·vit′iç, *a.* of, pertaining to, or formed from grapes; especially, designating a white crystalline acid formed by oxidizing mesitylene.

ū·vi·ton′iç, *a.* of, pertaining to, or formed from grapes; especially, designating a compound which when decomposed forms uvitic acid.
uvitonic acid; an acid formed from ammonia and pyrotartaric acid.

ū′vrou, *n.* same as *euphroe*.

ū′vū·lȧ, *n.*; *pl.* **ū′vū·lȧs, ū′vū·lae,** [L., dim. of *uva*, a grape.] the pendulum of the palate; a small fleshy mass hanging from the soft palate above the back of the tongue.

ū″vū·lap·tō′sis, *n.* same as *uvuloptosis*.

ū′vū·lăr, *a.* 1. of or having to do with the uvula.
2. in phonetics, pronounced with a vibration of the uvula, or with the back of the tongue near or in contact with the uvula.

ū′vū·lăr, *n.* in phonetics, a uvular sound.

Ū·vū·lā′ri·ȧ, *n.* a genus of North American herbs belonging to the lily family, having erect stems and bell-shaped flowers; the bellworts.

ū′vū·lȧ·tōme, *n.* same as *uvulotome*.

ū·vū·lī′tis, *n.* inflammation of the uvula.

ū″vū·lop·tō′sis, *n.* [*uvula*, and Gr. *ptōsos*, a falling.] falling of the palate; a pendulous condition of the palate.

ū′vū·lō·tōme, *n.* [*uvula*, and Gr. *temnein*, to cut.] an instrument for cutting out the uvula.

ū·vū·lot′ō·my, *n.* the operation of cutting out the uvula.

ů·wä′rō·wīte, *n.* same as *uvarovite*.

ux·ō′ri·ăl, *a.* [L. *uxor*, a wife.]
1. uxorious. [Rare.]
2. of, pertaining to, or befitting a wife.

ux·ōr′i·cī·dăl, *a.* of or pertaining to uxoricide.

ux·ōr′i·cīde, *n.* [L. *uxor*, a wife, and *cædere*, to kill.]
1. the murder of a wife by her husband.
2. a man who kills his wife.

ux·ō′ri·ous, *a.* [L. *uxorius*, from *uxor*, *uxoris*, a wife.] excessively or irrationally fond of or submissive to one's wife; doting on one's wife.

ux·ō′ri·ous·ly, *adv.* in an uxorious manner; with irrational or doting fondness for a wife.

ux·ō′ri·ous·ness, *n.* the state or quality of being uxorious.

Uz′beg, *n.* and *a.* Uzbek.

Uz′bek, *n.* 1. a member of a Turkic people living in the region of the Uzbek S. S. R., in central Asia.
2. the Central Turkic language of the Uzbeks.
Also *Usbek*, *Uzbeg*, *Usbeg*.

Uz′bek, *a.* of the Uzbek S. S. R., its people, their language, etc.: also *Usbek*, *Uzbeg*, *Usbeg*.

uz′zărd, *n.* the letter *Z.*; izzard. [Archaic or Dial.]

V

V, v (vē), *n.*; *pl.* **V's, v's, Vs, vs** (vēz), 1. the twenty-second letter of the English alphabet: from the Latin *V*, derived from one form of the Greek *Y* (upsilon): formerly used interchangeably in English with U both as a vowel and as a consonant, now only as a consonant.
2. the sound of V or v.
3. a type or impression for V or v.
4. a symbol for the twenty-second in a sequence or group (or the twenty-first if J is omitted).

V, v (vē), *a.* 1. of V or v.
2. twenty-second (or twenty-first if J is omitted) in a sequence or group.

V (vē), *n.* 1. an object shaped like V.
2. a Roman numeral for 5; with a superior bar (V̄), 5,000.
3. a symbol for victory of the nations allied against the Axis powers in World War II.
4. a five-dollar bill. [Colloq.]
5. in chemistry, a symbol for vanadium.

V (vē), *a.* shaped like V.

V-1, [from G. *vergeltungswaffe*, *eins*, vengeance weapon 1.] a German jet-propelled bomb resembling a pilotless airplane, used against England in World War II; a robot bomb.

V-2, [from G. *vergeltungswaffe*, *zwei*, vengeance weapon 2.] a German rocket-propelled bomb, used against England in World War II: at the height of its trajectory it reached the stratosphere and attained a speed said to be greater than that of sound.

vä, [It.] in music, go on; continue; as, *va crescendo*, go on increasing the strength of tone: a direction to the performer.

väal′īte, *n.* [*Vaal*, a South African river, and *-ite*.] a form of biotite found along with diamonds in South Africa.

vä′çȧ, *n.* [Sp.] in the Southwest, a cow.

vā′căn·cy, *n.*; *pl.* **vā′căn·cieș,** [ML. *vacantia*, from L. *vacans*.]
1. the state of being vacant, or empty; emptiness.
2. (a) empty space; (b) a vacant space; a gap, blank, break, or opening, as in a row or series.
3. the state of being empty in mind; lack of intelligence, interest, or thought; vacuity.
4. the state of being free from work, activity, etc.; inactivity; idleness. [Now Rare.]
5. (a) a vacating or being vacant, or unoccupied: of a position or office; (b) the time such position or office is unoccupied; (c) an unoccupied position or office; an unfilled post, situation, or job.
6. untenanted quarters, as in an apartment house.

vā′cănt, *a.* [L. *vacans* (*-antis*), ppr. of *vacare*, to be empty, free, to have leisure.]
1. having nothing in it, as a space; devoid of contents; empty; void.
2. not held, filled, or occupied, as a position or office.
3. having no occupant; as, a *vacant* seat.
4. untenanted; not in use, as a room or house.
5. not filled with activity or work; free; leisure.
6. (a) having or showing emptiness of mind or lack of intelligence, interest, thought, etc.; (b) empty of thought: said of the mind.
7. in law, (a) unoccupied or unused, as land; (b) having no claimant, as an estate or succession; (c) not yet granted, as public lands.
Syn.—empty, unfilled, unoccupied, void, unemployed, free, unencumbered, uncrowded, idle, thoughtless.

vā′ċant·ly, *adv.* in a vacant manner.

vā′ċāte, *v.t.*; vacated, *pt., pp.*; vacating, *ppr.* [L. *vacatus*, pp. of *vacare*, to be free, empty.]
1. in law, to annul; to make void.
2. to make vacant; specifically, (a) to cause (an office, position, etc.) to be unfilled or unoccupied, as by resignation; (b) to leave (a house, room, etc.) uninhabited or untenanted; to give up the occupancy of.

vā′ċāte, *v.i.* 1. to make an office, position, place, etc. vacant.
2. to leave; to go away. [Colloq.]

vā·ċā′tion, *n.* [Fr., from L. *vacatio* (*-onis*), freedom, from *vacatus*, pp. of *vacare*, to be free.]
1. the act of making void, vacant, or of no validity; as, the *vacation* of a charter; also, the act of leaving without an occupant. [Rare.]
2. a formal recess of judicial proceedings; the space of time between the end of one term of court and the beginning of the next; nonterm.
3. freedom from any activity; a rest; a respite; an intermission.
4. a period of rest and freedom from work, study, etc.; a time of recreation, usually a specific interval in a year; as, two weeks' *vacation*.

vā·ċā′tion, *v.i.* 1. to take a vacation.
2. to pass one's vacation; as, he *vacationed* in Maine last summer.

vā·ċā′tion·ẽr, *n.* a vacationist.

vā·ċā′tion·ist, *n.* one taking a vacation, especially a person who is traveling or at a resort.

vā·ċā′tūr, *n.* [LL., it is vacated.] an order of a court vacating, or annulling, a proceeding.

vaç′ċȧ·ry, *n.* a cow house, dairy, or cow pasture. [Obs.]

vaç·ciġ′ē·nous, *a.* yielding vaccine.

vaç·cī′nȧ, *n.* vaccinia; cowpox.

vaç′ci·năl, *a.* pertaining to or caused by vaccine or vaccination.

vaç′ci·nāte, *v.t.*; vaccinated, *pt., pp.*; vaccinating, *ppr.* to inoculate with a specific vaccine in order to prevent or lessen the effect of some disease; specifically, to inoculate with cowpox vaccine in order to immunize against smallpox.

vaç′ci·nāte, *v.i.* to perform vaccination.

vaç·ci·nā′tion, *n.* 1. the act or process of vaccinating; protective inoculation.
2. the scar on the skin where the vaccine has been applied.

vaç·ci·nā′tion·ist, *n.* one in favor of vaccination.

vaç′ci·nā·tŏr, *n.* one who or that which vaccinates; especially, an instrument used for scarifying the skin where the vaccine is to be applied.

vaç′cine, *a.* [L. *vaccinus*, from *vacca*, a cow.]
1. of or pertaining to cows; derived from cows; as, the *vaccine* disease or cowpox. [Rare.]
2. pertaining to vaccination or vaccinia.

vaç′cine, *n.* 1. lymph, or a preparation of this, from a cowpox vesicle, containing the causative virus and used in vaccination against cowpox or smallpox.
2. any preparation of dead bacteria introduced into the body to produce immunity to a specific disease by causing the formation of antibodies.
vaccine therapy; treatment of disease by the use of vaccine.

vaç·ci·nel′lȧ, *n.* a spurious form of vaccinia not producing the required effect.

vaç·cin′i·ȧ, *n.* [L. *vaccinus*, of a cow.] cowpox.

Vaç·cin·i·ā′cē·ae, *n.pl.* a family of shrubby plants, including the blueberries, huckleberries, cranberries, etc.

vaç·cin·i·ā′ceous, *a.* of or belonging to the *Vacciniaceæ*.

vaç·cin′i·fẽr, *n.* [*vaccina*, and L. *ferre*, to bear.] the source of vaccine virus; also, an instrument used in the process of vaccination.

vaç·cin·i·ō′lȧ, *n.* a secondary eruption resembling that of smallpox, sometimes following vaccination.

vaç′ci·nist, *n.* one in favor of vaccination; also, one who performs vaccination.

Vaç·cin′i·um, *n.* [L., the whortleberry.] a genus of plants, family *Vacciniaceæ*, of which it is the type; the blueberries.

vaç″cin·i·zā′tion, *n.* repeated vaccination with the same vaccine until the virus has no further effect.

vaç″cin·ō·syph′i·lis, *n.* syphilis transmitted by syphilitic impurity in the vaccine.

vaçhe, *n.* a cow or other beast. [Obs.]

vaçh′ẽr·y, *n.* a vaccary. [Obs.]

vac′il·lăn·cy, *n.* fluctuation; vacillation. [Rare.]

vac′il·lănt, *a.* wavering; fluctuating. [Rare.]

vac′il·lāte, *v.i.*; vacillated, *pt., pp.*; vacillating, *ppr.* [L. *vacillatus*, pp. of *vacillare*, to sway to and fro, waver.]
1. to sway to and fro; to waver; to totter; to stagger.
2. to fluctuate.
3. to waver in mind; to show indecision; to be irresolute.

vac′il·lā·ting, *a.* tending to vacillate; wavering or tending to waver in motion, opinion, etc.

vac′il·lā·ting·ly, *adv.* in a vacillating manner.

vac·il·lā′tion, *n.* [L. *vacillatio* (*-onis*), a wavering, from *vacillatus*, pp. of *vacillare*, to waver.]
1. the act, fact, or condition of vacillating; a swaying to and fro; unsteady movement.
2. the act, fact, or condition of wavering in mind, opinion, or course of action; irresolution.

vac′il·lȧ·tō″ry, *a.* inclined to vacillate; wavering; irresolute; uncertain.

vaç′ū·ȧ, *n.* alternative plural of *vacuum*.

vaç′ū·āte, *v.t.* to make empty; to evacuate. [Obs.]

vaç·ū·ā′tion, *n.* the act of emptying; evacuation. [Obs.]

vaç′ū·ist, *n.* in philosophy, one who believes that a vacuum can exist in nature: opposed to *plenist*.

vȧ·çū′i·ty, *n.*; *pl.* **vȧ·çū′i·ties,** [L. *vacuitas*, from *vacuus*, empty.]
1. the quality or state of being empty; emptiness.
2. an empty space; a void; a vacuum.
3. the quality or state of being empty in mind; lack of intelligence, interest, or thought.
4. anything pointless or inane; something foolish.
5. inanity.

Vȧ·çū′nȧ, *n.* [L.] in Latin mythology, the Sabine goddess of rural leisure, to whom husbandmen sacrificed at the close of harvest.

vaç′ū·ō·lăr, *a.* of the nature of, pertaining to, or resembling a vacuole.

vaç′ū·ō·lā″ted, vaç′ū·ō·lāte″, *a.* having one or more vacuoles; containing vacuoles.

vaç″ū·ō·lā′tion, *n.* the formation or arrangement of vacuoles; the condition of being vacuolated.

vaç′ū·ōle, *n.* [Fr., from L. *vacuus*, empty.]
1. a relatively clear, bubblelike space or cavity in the protoplasm of a cell, containing air, water, or partially digested fluid, and believed to have the function of discharging wastes.
2. a small cavity or vesicle in the tissues of an organism.

vaç·ū·ō·li·zā′tion, *n.* same as *vacuolation*.

vaç·ū·om′e·tẽr, *n.* [*vacuum* and *-meter*.] an instrument for comparing barometers at different pressures with the standard barometer.

vaç′ū·ous, *a.* [L. *vacuus*.]
1. empty; unfilled; void; vacant.
2. having or showing lack of intelligence, interest, or thought; stupid; senseless; inane.
3. characterized by lack of purpose, of profitable employment, etc.; idle; purposeless.

vaç′ū·ous·ness, *n.* the state or quality of being vacuous.

vaç′ū·um, *n.*; *pl.* **vaç′ū·ums, vaç′ū·ȧ,** [L., an empty space, a void or vacuity, neut. sing. of *vacuus*, empty.]
1. a space with nothing at all in it; a completely empty space.
2. (a) a space, as that inside a vacuum tube, out of which most of the air or gas has been taken, as by pumping; a space containing air or gas at a pressure below that of the atmosphere; (b) the degree to which pressure has been brought below atmospheric pressure.
3. a space left empty by the removal or absence of something usually found in it; a void: often figurative.

vaç′ū·um, *a.* 1. of a vacuum.
2. used to make a vacuum.
3. having a vacuum; partially or completely exhausted of air or gas.
4. working by suction or the creation of a partial vacuum.

vaç′ū·um, *v.t.* to clean with a vacuum cleaner. [Colloq.]

vaç′ū·um bot′tle, a bottlelike container used to keep liquids hot or cold by means of a vacuum between its inner and outer wall.

vaç′ū·um brāke, see under *brake*.

vaç′ū·um ċlean′ẽr, a machine for cleaning carpets, floors, upholstery, etc. by suction.

vaç′ū·um gāuġe, an instrument for indicating difference between the external atmospheric pressure and the pressure inside a partially exhausted vessel, as a cooled steam boiler in which the steam has condensed, the receiver of an air pump, etc.

vaç′ū·um mȧ·chïne′, in mechanics and refrigeration, the equipment used in producing and maintaining a vacuum.

vaç′ū·um pan, in the processes of making sugar, condensed milk, etc., a large metal vessel having a steam jacket, used in the evaporation of the syrup, milk, etc.

vaç′ū·um pump, 1. a pump used to draw air or gas out of sealed space.
2. a pump for water, worked by the sucking effect of condensing steam.

vaç′ū·um sweep′ẽr, a vacuum cleaner.

vaç′ū·um taṅk, a tank in which the fuel from the fuel tank is drawn by vacuum pressure so that it is in a position to be fed, usually by gravity, to the carburetor: used in some types of internal-combustion engines.

vaç′ū·um tūbe, 1. a sealed glass or metal tube containing highly rarefied air or gas and a cathode (or filament), an anode (or plate), and a grid for controlling the flow of electrons from one to the other: it is used in radio, television, etc. as a rectifier, detector, amplifier, etc.; electron tube.

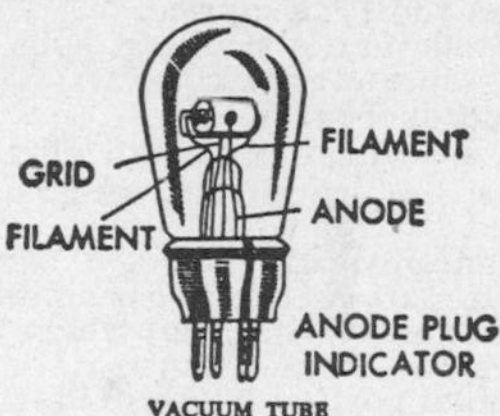

VACUUM TUBE

2. a sealed tube having the air or gas in it exhausted to a high degree and containing metallic electrodes between which electric discharges may be passed.

vaç′ū·um valve, 1. a reversed safety valve, opening inwardly to the pressure of the atmosphere when there is a negative pressure in the boiler.
2. a vacuum tube. [Brit.]

Vȧ·dan′tēs, *n.pl.* [L. *vadantes*, pl. of *vadans* (*-antis*), ppr. of *vadare*, to wade.] a former group of birds, including those which wade, swim, run, or walk.

vāde, *v.i.* to vanish; to pass away; to fade. [Obs.]

vā′dē mē′çum, [L., go with me.] a book or other thing that a person carries with him as a constant companion; specifically, a manual; a handbook.

vad′i·mō·ny, *n.* in old law, the giving of a vadium; bail. [Obs.]

vā′di·um, *n.* [L. *vas, vadis*, surety, bail.] in Scots law, a pledge or security.
vadium mortuum; a mortgage.
vadium vivum; a living pledge, differing from a *vadium mortuum* or mortgage in that the creditor retains possession of the debtor's property until the debt has been paid from the income of it.

vāe, *n.* same as *voe*.

vaē viç′tis, [L.] woe to the conquered.

vā′frous, *a.* crafty; cunning. [Obs.]

vag′ȧ·bond, *a.* [Fr., from L. *vagabundus*, adj., strolling about, from *vagari*, to wander.]
1. moving from place to place, with no fixed abode; wandering.
2. living an unsettled, drifting, or irresponsible life; vagrant.
3. shiftless; worthless; good-for-nothing.
4. of or characteristic of a wandering, shiftless, or irresponsible way of life.
5. aimlessly following an irregular course or path; drifting.
6. of or pertaining to the *Vagabundæ*.

vag′ȧ·bond, *n.* 1. a person who wanders from place to place, having no fixed abode.
2. a tramp; vagrant; wandering beggar.
3. an idle, disreputable, or shiftless person; a ne'er-do-well; a rascal
4. any one of the *Vagabundæ*.
5. a grass moth, *Crambus vulgivagellus*.

vag′ȧ·bond, *v.i.*; vagabonded, *pt., pp.*; vagabonding, *ppr.* to wander about in an idle manner; to play the vagabond.

vag′ȧ·bond·āġe, *n.* 1. the state, condition, ways, or habits of a vagabond.
2. vagabonds collectively; vagrants.

vag′ȧ·bond·ish, *a.* of, pertaining to, or like a vagabond; wandering.

vag′ȧ·bond·iṣm, *n.* vagabond way of life; vagabondage.

vag′ȧ·bond·īze, *v.i.*; vagabondized, *pt.*, *pp.*; vagabondizing, *ppr.* to wander or stroll about like a vagabond; to play the vagabond: sometimes followed by an indefinite *it*: also written *vagabondise.*

vag′ȧ·bond·ry, *n.* vagabondage. [Obs.]

Vag·ȧ·bun′dae, *n.pl.* [f. pl. of L. *vagabundus*, strolling about, vagabond.] a division of true spiders, which spin no web and prowl for their prey.

vā′găl, *a.* of or pertaining to the vagus, or pneumogastric nerve.

vā′găn·cy, *n.* vagrancy; also, extravagance. [Obs.]

Vȧ·gan′tēṣ, *n.pl.* same as *Vagabundæ.*

vȧ·gãr′i·ous, *a.* 1. full of vagaries; characterized by vagaries; erratic; unpredictable.
2. wandering; roaming.

vȧ·gãr′ish, *a.* wandering; given to vagaries.

vȧ·gãr′i·ty, *n.* the state or quality of being vagarious.

vȧ·gãr′y, *n.*; *pl.* **vȧ·gãr′ieṣ,** [L. *vagari*, to wander.]
1. an odd, eccentric, or unexpected action or bit of conduct.
2. an odd, whimsical, or freakish idea or notion; an oddity; a caprice.
3. a wandering; a strolling. [Obs.]

vȧ·gäs′, *n.* same as *vakass.*

vā′ġī, *n.* plural of *vagus.*

vā′ġi·ent, *a.* crying like a child. [Obs.]

vȧ·ġī′nȧ, *n.*; *pl.* **vȧ·ġī′nȧṣ, vȧ·ġī′nae,** [L., a sheath.]
1. in antomy and zoology, a sheath; a sheathlike part or organ; specifically, (a) in female mammals, the canal which leads from the vulva to the uterus; (b) in entomology, the terminal portion of the oviduct.
2. in botany, the sheath formed by the convolution of a flat petiole around a stem, as in grasses.
3. in architecture, the upper part of a terminus from which a bust or figure seems to issue.

vaġ′i·năl (*or* vȧ·jī′), *a.* 1. of, like, or pertaining to a sheath or vagina; resembling a sheath; as, a *vaginal* membrane.
2. of, for, or pertaining to the vagina of a female mammal; as, *vaginal* arteries.

vaġ′i·nănt, *a.* [L. *vagina*, a sheath.] in botany, sheathing; as, a *vaginant* leaf. [Obs.]

Vaġ·i·nā′tȧ, *n.pl.* [L. *vagina*, a sheath.] the sheathed polyps; a group of polyps comprising those enclosed in a calcareous or horny polypary.

vaġ′i·nāte, *n.* one of the *Vaginata.*

vaġ′i·nāte, vaġ′i·nā·ted, *a.* [L. *vagina*, a sheath.]
1. having a vagina or sheath; sheathed.
2. in the form of a sheath; like a sheath.

vaġ·i·nẽr′vōse, *a.* [L. *vagus*, wandering, and *nervus*, nerve.] in botany, having the veins in no definite order.

Vaġ·i·niç′ō·lȧ, *n.* a genus of infusorians secreting a lorica, erect or procumbent, in which they are sheathed.

vaġ·i·nif′ẽr·ous, *a.* [L. *vagina*, a sheath, and *-ferous.*] possessed of a sheath; as, *vaginiferous* insects.

vaġ″i·ni·pen′nāte, *a.* [L. *vagina*, a sheath, and *pennatus*, winged.] sheath-winged; having the wings covered with a hard case or sheath, as some insects.

vaġ·i·niṣ′mus, *n.* [L. *vagina*, a sheath, and *-ismus*, -ism.] spasmodic contraction of the sphincter muscle of the vagina.

vaġ·i·nī′tis, *n.* [L. *vagina*, a sheath, and *-itis.*] inflammation of the vagina.

vaġ′i·nō-, [from L. *vagina.*] a combining form meaning (a) *vagina*; (b) *vagina and.* Also, before a vowel, *vagin-.*

vaġ″i·nō·pen′nous, *a.* same as *vaginipennate.*

vaġ·i·not′ō·my, *n.* [L. *vagina*, a sheath, and Gr. *temnein*, to cut.] surgical incision of the vaginal wall.

vȧ·ġin′ū·lȧ, *n.*; *pl.* **vȧ·ġin′ū·lae,** [LL. *vaginula*, dim. of L. *vagina*, sheath.]
1. in botany, the sheath at the base of the seta of an urn moss.
2. in zoology, a little sheath.

vȧ·ġin′ū·lāte, *a.* furnished with a vaginula or with vaginulae; sheathed.

vaġ′i·nūle, *n.* in botany, a vaginula.

vaġ′is·sāte, *v.i.* to caper; to romp; to frisk. [Obs.]

vā′gous, *a.* wandering; unsettled. [Obs.]

vā′grăn·cy, *n.*; *pl.* **vā′grăn·cieṣ,** [from *vagrant.*]
1. a wandering in thought or talk; digression.
2. a wandering from place to place; vagabondage.
3. shiftless or idle wandering without money or work, as of tramps, beggars, etc.; conduct or way of life of a vagrant (sense 3).

vā′grănt, *n.* [ME. *vagarant*; prob. from OFr. *wa(u)crant*, ppr. of *wa(u)crer*, to wander about, walk; influenced in form by *vagabond* or L. *vagari*, to wander.]
1. a person who wanders from place to place or lives a wandering life; a rover.
2. a person who wanders from place to place without a regular job, supporting himself by begging, etc.; an idle wanderer; a vagabond; a tramp.
3. in law, a tramp, beggar, prostitute, or similar idle or disorderly person whose way of living makes him liable to be arrested and jailed.

vā′grănt, *a.* 1. wandering from place to place or living a wandering life; roaming; nomadic.
2. living the life of a vagabond or tramp.
3. of or characteristic of a vagrant.
4. characterized by straggling growth: said of plants.
5. following no fixed direction or course; moving at random; wayward: said of things.

vā′grănt·ly, *adv.* in a vagrant, wandering, or unsettled manner.

vā′grănt·ness, *n.* the state of vagrancy. [Rare.]

vā′grŏm, *a.* vagrant. [Archaic.]

vāgue (vāg), *a.*; *comp.* vaguer; *superl.* vaguest, [Fr., wandering, from *vaguer*, L. *vagari*, to wander, from *vagus*, wandering.]
1. not clearly, precisely, or definitely expressed or stated.
2. not clearly outlined; indefinite in shape or form; hazily, obscurely, or indistinctly seen or sensed.
3. not sharp, certain, or precise in thought or expression: said of persons, the mind, etc.
4. not precisely determined or known; uncertain.

Syn.—indefinite, loose, indistinct, indefinable, hazy, unsubstantial, dreamy.

vāgue, *n.* an undefined or indefinite expanse.

vāgue, *v.i.* to play the vagrant; to wander. [Obs.]

vāgue, *n.* a wandering. [Obs.]

vāgue′ly, *adv.* in a vague, uncertain, or unsettled manner.

vāgue′ness, *n.* the state of being vague, indefinite, unsettled, or uncertain; lack of clearness; ambiguousness; haziness.

> His speculations have none of that *vagueness* which is the common fault of political philosophy. —Macaulay

vā′gus, *n.*; *pl.* **vā′ġī,** [L., wandering.] either of the tenth pair of cranial nerves, arising in the medulla oblongata and innervating the larynx, lungs, heart, esophagus, and most of the abdominal organs; pneumogastric nerve: also *vagus nerve.*

vāil, *n.* and *v.t.* veil. [Obs.]

vāil, *n.* [ME. *vailen.*]
1. profit; proceeds. [Obs.]
2. an unlooked-for acquisition. [Obs.]
3. a perquisite; a tip; usually in the plural; as, the servants received *vails* above their wages. [Archaic.]

vāil, *v.i.* to be of use, service, or profit; to avail. [Archaic.]

vāil, *n.* submission; descent. [Obs.]

vāil, *v.t.* [ME. *valen.*] 1. to let sink down; to lower; to let fall. [Archaic.]
2. to take off (a hat, etc.) in token of respect or submission. [Archaic.]
3. to let sink, as through fear. [Obs.]

vāil, *v.i.* to yield or to recede; to give place; to show respect by yielding. [Obs.]

vāil′ẽr, *n.* a veiler. [Obs.]

vāil′ẽr, *n.* one who yields from respect; one who vails. [Obs.]

vāi′mūre, *n.* a vantmure. [Obs.]

vāin, *a.*; *comp.* vainer; *superl.* vainest, [OFr., from L. *vanus*, empty, vain.]
1. empty; worthless; hollow; having no genuine substance, value, or importance.

> Why do the people imagine a *vain* thing? —Ps. ii. 1.

2. without result or force; fruitless; ineffectual; producing no good result; as, all attempts, all efforts were *vain.*
3. having or showing an excessively high regard for one's self, looks, possessions, ability, etc.; indulging in or resulting from personal vanity; conceited.
4. lacking in sense; foolish. [Archaic.]
in vain; (a) fruitlessly; vainly; (b) lightly; profanely.

Syn.—empty, trivial, worthless, unsatisfying, fruitless, ineffectual, useless, idle, unreal, void, shadowy, delusive, unimportant, proud, conceited, inflated, showy, ostentatious, false, deceitful.

vāin·glō′ri·ous, *a.* [from *vainglory* and *-ous.*]
1. boastfully vain and proud of oneself.
2. showing or characterized by boastful vanity.

vāin·glō′ri·ous·ly, *adv.* with empty pride; in a vainglorious way.

vāin·glō′ri·ous·ness, *n.* the state of being vainglorious or of being filled with empty pride.

vāin·glō′ry, *n.* [ME. *vainglorie*; OFr. *vaine gloire*; ML. *vana gloria.*] extreme self-pride and boastfulness; excessive and ostentatious vanity.

vāin′ly, *adv.* 1. without effect; to no purpose; ineffectually; fruitlessly; in vain.
2. conceitedly; boastingly; with vaunting; proudly; arrogantly.
3. idly; foolishly; erroneously.

vāin′ness, *n.* 1. the quality or the state of being vain; inefficacy; ineffectualness; as, the *vainness* of efforts.
2. conceit; vanity.

vāir, *n.* [OFr. *vair*, from L. *varius*, spotted, variegated.]
1. a fur, usually from a gray and white squirrel, used for trimming and lining clothes in the 13th and 14th centuries.
2. in heraldry, a fur, represented by rows of small bells, usually azure and argent, one row upright, the next turned down.

VAIR

vai·ré′ (vā·rā′), *a.* [Fr.] in heraldry, checkered or charged with vair.

Vaīsh′nȧ·vȧ, *n.* [Sans.] a worshiper of Vishnu.

Vaīsh′nȧ·viṣm, *n.* the worship of Vishnu.

Vaīs′yȧ, *n.* [Sans. *vaiçya*, from *viç*, settler.] the third caste among the Hindus, including merchants, traders, and agriculturists.

vāi′vōde, *n.* same as *voivode.*

vȧ·käss′, *n.* an Armenian vestment bearing a breastplate on which are the names, heads, or figures of the twelve apostles.

vȧ·keel′, *n.* [Anglo-Ind.] in India, an ambassador or agent sent on a special commission, or residing at a court; a native attorney; a native law pleader.

Vȧ·lā′chi·ăn, *a.* and *n.* same as *Walachian.*

val′ănce, *n.* [perh. from *Valence*, in France.]
1. a short drapery or curtain hanging from the edge of a bed, shelf, table, etc., often to the floor.
2. a short drapery across the top of a window.
3. a facing of wood or metal imitating this.

val′ănce, *v.t.*; valanced, *pt.*, *pp.*; valancing, *ppr.* to furnish or decorate with a valance. [Rare.]

val′ănced, *a.* fitted with a valance.

vāle, *n.* [ME. *val*; Fr. *val*, from L. *vallis*, vale.]
1. a tract of low ground between hills; a valley. [Chiefly Poet.]
2. a little trough or canal; as, a pump *vale* to carry off the water from a ship's pump.
3. figuratively, a state of decline or wretchedness.

vāle, *n.* vail (descent). [Obs.]

vā′lē, *interj.* and *n.* [L.] farewell.

val·ē·diç′tion, *n.* [from L. *valedictus*, pp. of *valedicere*, to say farewell; *vale*, farewell, and *dicere*, to say.]
1. a farewell; a bidding or saying farewell.
2. something said in parting; a farewell utterance.

val″ē·diç·tō′ri·ăn, *n.* in schools and colleges, the student, usually the one ranking highest in scholarship, who delivers the valedictory at graduation.

val·ē·diç′tō·ry, *a.* said or done at parting, by way of farewell; uttered as a valediction.

val·ē·diç′tō·ry, *n.*; *pl.* **val·ē·diç′tō·rieṣ,** a farewell speech, especially one delivered at graduation from school or college.

val′ence, *n.* and *v.* same as *valance.*

vā′lence, *n.* [ML. *valentia*, strength, from L. *valens* (*-entis*), ppr. of *valere*, to be strong.]

1. in biology, the ability of chromosomes, serums, vaccines, etc. to combine with definite organisms, allergens, and allied matter, or produce a specific effect upon them.

2. in chemistry, the capacity of an element or radical to combine with another, as measured by the number of hydrogen atoms which one radical or one atom of the element will combine with or replace; as, oxygen has a *valence* of two (i.e., one atom of oxygen combines with two hydrogen atoms).

3. a unit of valence.

vȧ·len′ci·ȧ (-shi-), *n.* [prob. named from *Valence*, in France.] a stuff made of worsted, cotton, and silk, used for waistcoats.

Vȧ·len·ci·ennes′ (-enz), *n.* [from *Valenciennes*, in France.]

1. a flat bobbin lace made at Valenciennes, in France: it has a background of fine, diamond-shaped mesh.

2. a pyrotechnic composition used for setting off fireworks.

vā′len·cy, *n.* in chemistry, same as *valence*

-vā′lent, in chemistry, a suffix meaning: (a) *having a specified valence*; (b) *having a specified number of valences.* Although both the Greek set of prefixes (*mono-, di-, tri-, tetra-,* etc.) and the Latin (*uni-, bi-, ter-, quadri-,* etc.) are used with *-valent,* the latter set is preferred when designating the number of valences an element exhibits and the former when designating the specific valence of some atom or radical.

val′en·tīne, *n.* [Fr. *Valentin,* after Saint Valentine; L. *Valentinus,* from *valens* (*-entis*), ppr. of *valere,* to be strong.]

1. (a) a sweetheart chosen or complimented on Saint Valentine's day; (b) one's sweetheart.

2. (a) a greeting card or note sent to a real or pretended sweetheart on this day, and containing lines of sentimental love; (b) a burlesque of this, often sent anonymously.

3. a gift presented on Saint Valentine's day.

St. Valentine's day; see under *saint.*

Val·en·tin′i·ăn, *n.* one of the followers of Valentinus, the founder of a Gnostic sect in the second century A.D.

val′en·tin·īte, *n.* [named after Basil *Valentine,* an alchemist of the fifteenth century, who discovered the properties of antimony.] an orthorhombic mineral, occurring mostly in crystals, but occasionally massive, resulting from the decomposition of various antimonial ores.

val·ẽr·am′īde, *n.* [*valeric* and *amide.*] a crystalline amide derived from valeric acid.

val′ẽr·āte, *n.* a salt of valeric acid.

vȧ·lē′ri·ăn, *n.* [Fr. *valériane*; ML. *valeriana,* valerian; as if from the personal name *Valerius.*]

1. any plant belonging to the genus *Valeriana.*

2. a drug made from the roots of some of these plants and used as a sedative and antispasmodic.

Greek valerian; a plant, *Polemonium cæruleum,* the Jacob's-ladder.

red valerian; a plant, *Centranthis ruber,* native to the Mediterranean region.

Vȧ·lē·ri·ā′nȧ, *n.* a genus of perennial herbs with clusters or spikes of white, pink, red, or purplish flowers. The thick roots of most species have a strong odor, and that of *Valeriana officinalis* is used as a sedative and an antispasmodic.

Vȧ·lē″ri·ȧ·nā′cē·ae, *n.pl.* same as *Valerianeæ.*

vȧ·lē″ri·ȧ·nā′ceous, *a.* of or pertaining to the *Valerianeæ.*

vȧ·lē′ri·ăn·āte, *n.* a salt of valeric acid.

Vȧ·lē·ri·ā′nē·ae, *n.pl.* a family of herbs with opposite leaves and small flowers, as the spikenard, valerian, etc.

Vȧ·lē″ri·ȧ·nel′lȧ, *n.* a genus of the order *Valerianeæ,* comprising about fifty-five species of small annuals. The genus is common to the Mediterranean region, being found also in central Europe and North America. *Valerianella olitoria,* common corn salad, is an annual plant with pale-green leaves and heads of small slate-colored flowers, found abundantly in cultivated ground throughout Europe.

vȧ·lē·ri·an′iç, *a.* valeric.

vȧ·ler′iç, *a.* [Fr. *valérique.*] designating or of any of four isomeric acids, C_4H_9COOH, some originally found in valerian root, but all now made synthetically.

val′ẽr·in, *n.* [*valeric* and *glycerin.*] a salt formed by the combination of valeric acid and glycerin, found in butter and certain oils.

val′ẽr·ōne, *n.* a ketone derived from valeric acid in the form of an oily liquid.

val′ẽr·yl, *n.* the nucleus of some valeric acid derivatives, a hypothetical radical having the formula C_5H_9O.

val′ẽr·yl·ēne, *n.* a hydrocarbon of the acetylene series, C_5H_8.

val′et (*or* -ā), *n.* [Fr., a groom, yeoman. Same word as *varlet.*]

1. a personal manservant who takes care of one's clothes, helps one in dressing, etc.: also called *valet de chambre.*

2. a hotel employee who cleans or presses clothes or performs other personal services.

3. in horsemanship, a kind of goad or stick armed with a point of iron.

val′et, *v.t* and *v.i.* to serve (a person) as a valet.

vȧ·lęt′ dē chăm′bre (vȧ·lā′ dē shäṅ′br), a valet (sense 1).

val·ē·tū·di·nâr′i·ăn, *a.* [from L. *valetudinarius,* sickly, from *valetudo* (*-inis*), state of health, from *valere,* to be strong.]

1. in poor health; sickly; invalid.

2. anxiously concerned about one's health.

3. characterized by poor health.

val·ē·tū·di·nâr′i·ăn, *n.* 1. a person in poor health; an invalid.

2. a person who thinks constantly and anxiously about his health.

val·ē·tū·di·nâr′i·ăn·işm, *n.* a state of feeble health; infirmity.

val·ē·tū′di·nâr·i·ness, *n.* the state or quality of being valetudinarian.

val·ē·tū′di·nâr·y, *a.* same as *valetudinarian.*

val·ē·tū′di·nâr·y, *n.* valetudinarian.

val·ē·tū′di·nous, *a.* valetudinarian. [Obs.]

val′gus, *n.* [L., bowlegged.]

1. an abnormal turning outward of the foot so as to produce knock-knee.

2. varus. [Obs.]

val′gus, *a.* knock-kneed.

Val·hall′, *n.* Valhalla.

Val·hal′lȧ, *n.* [Ice. *valhöll,* genit. *valhallar,* the hall of the slain; *valr,* slaughter, and *höll,* a hall.]

1. in Norse mythology, the great hall where Odin receives and feasts the souls of heroes who have fallen bravely in battle: also *Walhalla, Valhall.*

2. any final resting place of many of the heroes or great men of a nation.

val′iănce, *n.* valiancy. [Archaic.]

val′iăn·cy, *n.* 1. bravery; courage.

2. *pl.* **val′iăn·cieş,** a brave deed.

val′iănt, *a.* [Fr. *vaillant,* from L. *valere,* to be strong.]

1. strong; vigorous in body; also, strong or powerful in a more general sense. [Obs.]

The scent thereof is somewhat *valiant.*
—Fuller.

2. brave; courageous: said of persons or their acts.

3. performed with valor; heroic; as, a *valiant* action or achievement.

val′iănt·ly, *adv.* in a valiant manner; stoutly; courageously; heroically.

val′iănt·ness, *n.* the state or quality of being valiant; valor; bravery.

val′id, *a.* [Fr. *valide*; L. *validus,* strong, powerful, from *valere,* to be strong, to have power.]

1. having legal force; properly executed and binding under the law.

2. sound; well grounded on principles or evidence; able to withstand criticism or objection, as an argument: opposed to *invalid.*

3. effective, effectual, cogent, etc.

4. robust; strong; healthy. [Rare.]

Syn.—powerful, cogent, weighty, sound, substantial, conclusive.

val′i·dāte, *v.t.*; validated, *pt., pp*; validating, *ppr.* 1. to make binding under the law; to give legal force to; to declare legally valid.

2. to prove to be valid; to confirm the validity of.

val·i·dā′tion, *n.* a making or declaring valid; proof; confirmation.

vȧ·lid′i·ty, *n.* [Fr. *validité*; L. *validitas* (*-tatis*), from *validus,* strong.]

1. the state or quality of being valid; specifically, (a) strength or force from being supported by fact; justness; soundness; as, the *validity* of an objection; (b) legal strength or force; as, the *validity* of a will.

2. strength or power in general. [Rare.]

Purpose is but the slave to memory,
Of violent birth, but poor *validity.* —Shak.

3. value. [Rare.]

val′id·ly, *adv.* in a valid manner; so as to be valid.

val′id·ness, *n.* the state or character of being valid.

val′īne, *n.* [from iso*val*eric acid, and *-ine.*] a white, crystalline, essential amino acid, $C_5H_{11}NO_2$, found in small quantities in many proteins.

val·in·ō·mȳ′cin, *n.* [from *valine,* and Gr. *mykēs,* fungus; and *-in.*] an antibiotic polypeptide, $C_{54}H_{90}N_6O_{18}$, isolated from a soil bacteria, *Streptomyces fulvissimus,* that promotes the movement of potassium ions in cells.

vȧ·līse′, *n.* [Fr.] a small suitcase.

Val′kyr, *n.* a Valkyrie.

Val·kyr′i·ȧ, *n.* same as Valkyrie.

Val·kyr′i·ăn, *a.* of, like, or characteristic of a Valkyrie.

Ourselves have often tried *Valkyrian* hymns. —Tennyson.

Val·kyr′ie, *n.* [ON. *valkyrja,* lit., chooser of the slain, from *valr,* those slain, and *kjosa,* to choose (akin to AS. *ceosan*).] in Norse mythology, any of the maidens of Odin who conduct the souls of heroes slain in battle to Valhalla and wait on them there: also *Walkyrie, Valkyr, Valkyria.*

val′lăn·cy, *n.* a large wig that shaded the face, worn in the seventeenth century.

val′lăr, *a.* [L. *vallaris,* of a rampart, from *vallum,* earth, a wall, rampart.] pertaining to a rampart or palisade.

vallar crown; among the ancient Romans, a crown made of gold, presented to the first soldier who surmounted the vallum and forced an entrance into the camp of the enemy: also called *vallary crown.*

val′lăr, *n.* a vallar crown.

val′lȧ·ry, *a.* same as *vallar.*

val′lāte, *a.* [L. *vallatus,* pp. of *vallare,* to surround with a rampart, intrench.]

1. in anatomy, surrounded with a rimmed depression.

2. in zoology, cup-shaped.

val′lā·ted, *a.* surrounded with or as with a rampart.

val·lā′tion, *n.* 1. a rampart or entrenchment for military defense.

2. the art or process of building such military defenses.

val′lȧ·tō·ry, *a.* pertaining to a rampart or vallum.

val·leç′ū·lȧ, *n.*; *pl.* **val·leç′ū·lae,** [LL., dim. of L. *vallis,* vale, valley.]

1. in anatomy, a depression, groove, or furrow.

2. in botany, a groove or hollow between the ribs of the fruit of umbelliferous plants.

val·leç′ū·lăr, *a.* of or pertaining to a vallecula.

val·leç′ū·lāte, *a.* having a vallecula or valleculae.

val′ley, *n.*; *pl.* **val′leyş,** [OFr. *valee,* formed with suffix *-ee,* from *val*; L. *vallis,* a vale.]

1. a stretch of low land lying between hills or mountains and usually having a river or stream flowing through it.

2. the land drained or watered by a great river system; as, Mississippi *valley.*

3. any dip or hollow like a valley, as the trough of a wave.

4. in architecture, the trough formed where two slopes of a roof meet, or where the roof meets a wall; gutter.

5. in anatomy, a depression on the inferior part of the cerebellum, which divides it into two symmetrical portions.

valley roof; a roof having two or more slopes that meet in an angle.

val′ley bōard, the board fixed on a valley rafter for the lead gutter to lie upon.

val′ley piēce, in a valley roof, the rafter which supports the valley; a valley rafter.

val′ley quāil, a crested quail, *Lophortyx californica,* of the Pacific coast of North America.

val′ley råft′ẽr, a valley piece.

val·liç′ū·lȧ, *n.* same as *vallecula.*

val·liç′ū·lăr, *a.* same as *vallecular.*

val·liç′ū·lāte, *a.* see *valleculate.*

Val·lis·nē′ri·ȧ, *n.* [named after Antonio *Vallisneri,* early 18th-c. Italian botanist.] a genus of aquatic plants that grow under water. *Vallisneria spiralis,* one of the two species, is commonly cultivated in aquariums. It is also widely found in running waters and is variously known as *tape grass, water celery, wild celery,* etc.

Val·lis·nē·ri·ā′cē·ae, *n.pl.* same as *Hydrocharideæ.*

val′lum, *n.*; *pl.* **val′lȧ,** [L.] a rampart; a line of entrenchment; specifically, the rampart with which the Romans enclosed their camps. It consisted of two parts, the *agger,* or mound of earth, and the *sudes,* or palisades, that were driven into the ground to secure and strengthen it.

và·lō′ni·à, *n.* [It. *vallonia,* from Gr. *balanos,* oak.] the acorn cups of an oak of Europe and Asia (*valonia oak*), used in dyeing, tanning, etc.

Và·lō·ni·ā′cē·ae, *n.pl.* a family of green-spored algae, characterized by the rooting, variously shaped fronds made up of a green watery endochrome.

val′ŏr, *n.* [OFr. *valour* from LL. *valor,* worth, hence, worthiness, courage, from L. *valere,* to be strong, to be worth.]

1. courage; fearlessness; bravery, especially in battle.

Fear to do base unworthy things is *valor;*
If they be done to us, to suffer them
Is *valor* too. —B. Jonson.

2. value; worth. [Obs.]

3. a courageous man. [Rare.]

val″ŏr·i·zā′tion, *n.* a fixing of prices, usually by government action, as by buying up a commodity at the fixed price or lending money to producers so that they can keep their goods off the market.

val′ŏr·ize, *v.t.* and *v.i.* to fix or control the price of (a commodity) by valorization.

val′ŏr·ous, *a.* brave; courageous; valiant; intrepid; as, a *valorous* knight.

val′ŏr·ous·ly, *adv.* in a valorous or brave manner; heroically.

val′ŏur, *n.* valor: British spelling.

Val·sal′văn, *a.* of or pertaining to the Italian anatomist Valsalva (1666–1723).

Valsalvan experiment; the act of forcing air into the middle ear by blowing while the nostrils and mouth are closed, to relieve partial deafness.

välse, *n.* [Fr.] a waltz.

val′ū·à·ble, *a.* 1. having material value; being worth money.

2. having great value in terms of money; as, a *valuable* diamond.

3. being highly thought of; being prized highly; being of great worth in some way, usually nonmaterial.

Syn.—precious, costly, rich, important, excellent, worthy, select, superior, estimable.

val′ū·à·ble, *n.* [*usually in pl.*] a thing, especially a small thing, of value, as a piece of jewelry.

Fra Diavolo learns that the travelers have saved the most of their *valuables.*
—George P. Upton.

val′ū·à·ble·ness, *n.* worth; the quality of being of value.

val′ū·à·bly, *adv.* so as to be of great value; usefully.

val·ū·ā′tion, *n.* 1. the act of estimating the value or worth; appraisement; evaluation; as, the just *valuation* of property.

2. determined or estimated value or price.

3. estimation of the worth, merit, etc. of anything; as, his *valuation* of our work was not high.

val′ū·ā·tŏr, *n.* one who sets a value; an appraiser.

val′ūe, *n.* [OFr. *value,* f. of *valu,* pp. of *valoir;* L. *valere,* to be strong, to be worth.]

1. a fair or proper equivalent in money, commodities, etc. for something sold or exchanged; fair price.

2. the worth of a thing in money or goods at a certain time; market price.

3. the equivalent (of something) in money; as, she lost jewels to the *value* of four thousand dollars.

4. estimated or appraised worth or price; valuation.

5. purchasing power; as, the *value* of a dollar fluctuates.

6. that quality of a thing according to which it is thought of as being more or less desirable, useful, estimable, important, etc.; worth or the degree of worth.

7. that which is desirable or worthy of esteem for its own sake; thing or quality having intrinsic worth.

8. precise meaning, as of a word.

9. in art, (a) relative lightness or darkness of a color; (b) proportioned effect, as of light and shade, in an artistic work.

10. in mathematics, the quantity or amount for which a symbol stands; as, 27 is the *value* of x in this equation.

11. in music, the relative duration of a note, tone, or rest.

12. in phonetics, the quality of sound of a letter or diphthong; as, each of the vowels has several *values* in English.

13. [*pl.*] in sociology, acts, customs, institutions, etc. regarded in a particular, especially favorable, way by a people, ethnic group, etc.

exchange value; same as *market price* under *market.*

nominal value; estimated market value, as value named in appraisement.

val′ūe, *v.t.;* valued, *pt., pp.;* valuing, *ppr.* 1. to estimate the worth of; to rate at a certain price; to appraise; as, to *value* lands or goods.

2. to place a certain estimate of worth on in a scale of values; as, I *value* health above wealth.

3. to think highly of; to esteem; to prize; as, I *value* your friendship.

4. to raise to estimation. [Obs.]

5. to be worth. [Obs.]

Syn.—appraise, rate, compute, reckon, estimate, esteem, respect, regard, appreciate, prize.

val′ūe-add′ed tax, a form of indirect sales tax paid on products and services at each stage of production or distribution, based on the value added at that stage and included in the cost to the ultimate consumer.

val′ūed, *a.* 1. estimated; appraised; as, a hat *valued* at ten dollars.

2. highly thought of; esteemed; as, a *valued* friend.

valued policy; see under *policy.*

val′ūe judg′ment, an estimate made of the worth, goodness, etc. of a person, action, event, or the like, especially when making such judgment is improper or undesirable.

val′ūe·less, *a.* having no value; worthless.

val′ū·ēr, *n.* 1. a person who values.

2. an appraiser. [Brit.]

vä·lü′tä, *n.* [It., value.] the value of a currency; specifically, the exchange value of a currency with reference to the currency of a specified country.

valv′ăl, *a.* relating to a valve or to valves.

valv′ăr, *a.* relating to or having to do with a valve; valvular.

val′và·sọr, *n.* same as *vavasor.*

Val·vā′tà, *n.* [L. *valvatus,* having folding doors, from *valva,* a leaf of a door.] a genus of small, fresh-water snails having a turbinate shell with a circular aperture.

valv′āte, *a.* [L. *valvatus,* having folding doors, from *valva,* a leaf of a door.]

1. meeting without overlapping, as the petals of some flower buds.

2. opening by valves, as a pea pod.

3. having a valve or valves.

valve, *n.* [L. *valva,* the leaf of a folding door.]

1. either of the halves of a double door or any of the leaves of a folding door. [Now Rare.]

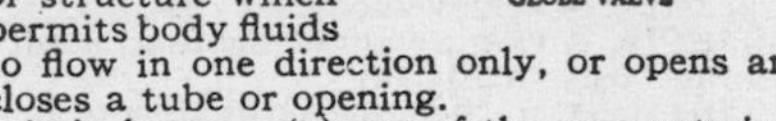

GLOBE VALVE

2. a gate regulating the flow of water in a sluice, channel, etc.

3. in anatomy, a membranous fold or structure which permits body fluids to flow in one direction only, or opens and closes a tube or opening.

4. in botany, (a) one of the segments into which a pod or capsule separates when it bursts open; (b) a lidlike part in some anthers, through which pollen is discharged.

5. in electricity, (a) an electrolytic cell or other device that permits a flow of current in one direction only; (b) [Brit.] an electron tube.

6. in mechanics, (a) any device in a pipe or tube that permits a flow in one direction only, or regulates the flow of whatever is in the pipe, by means of a flap, lid, plug, etc. acting to open or block passage; (b) the flap, lid, plug, etc. in such a device.

7. in music, a device in certain wind instruments, as the trumpet, that opens an auxiliary to the main tube, lengthening the air column and lowering the pitch.

8. in zoology, (a) one of the parts making up the shell of a mollusk, barnacle, clam, etc.; (b) a part forming the sheath of an ovipositor in certain insects.

ball valve; (a) a valve in which a ball closes the aperture, which is hemispherical; (b) a valve operated automatically by a floating ball.

valve, *v.t.* and *v.i.;* valved, *pt., pp.;* valving, *ppr.* 1. to fit with or make use of a valve or valves.

2. to regulate the flow of (a fluid) by means of a valve or valves.

valve buck′et, a bucket with a valve in the bottom, used in a pump or in drawing water from a well.

valve çāġe, in machinery, a perforated box placed over a valve to hold it in place and permit the passage of a fluid; also, a box containing one or more valves; the steam chest in a steam engine.

valve çock, a faucet in which the closure of the passage is by a valve on a seat.

valve çŏup′ling, a pipe coupling which includes a valve.

valved (valvd), *a.* having valves or hinges; composed of valves; valvate.

valve gēar, valve mō′tion, a device which gives the valves, as of a steam engine, the proper motion.

valve′-in-head′ (-hed′) **en′ġine,** an internal-combustion engine, as in some automobiles, having the intake and exhaust valves in the cylinder head instead of the block.

valve′less, *a.* without a valve.

valve′let, *n.* a little valve; valvule.

valve mō′tion, see *valve gear.*

valve sēat, the surface on which the valve rests.

valve shell, a shell of the genus *Valvata.*

valve stem, a rod like a piston rod, by which a valve is moved.

val·vif′ēr·ous, *a.* [L. *valva,* a leaf of a door, and *-ferous.*] having a valve or valves.

val′vū·là, *n.; pl.* **val′vū·lae,** [LL.] in anatomy, a small valve or valvelet; a valvule.

valv′ū·lăr, *a.* 1. having the form or function of a valve.

2. having a valve or valves.

3. of a valve or valves; especially, of the valves of the heart; as, a *valvular* disorder.

valv′ūle, *n.* [Fr., from L. *valvula,* dim. of *valva,* a leaf of a door.] a little valve; specifically, (a) in botany, one of the pieces which compose the outer covering of a pericarp; (b) in zoology, one of the valves of the venous and lymphatic system of animals.

val·vū·lī′tis, *n.* inflammation of a valve, especially a valve of the heart.

val′yl·ēne, *n.* an oily hydrocarbon, C_5H_6, volatile and having the odor of garlic.

vam′brāce, vant′brāce, *n.* [Fr. *avant-bras.*] formerly, in plate armor, the piece which protected the arm between the elbow and the wrist.

vam′brāced (-brāst), *a.* in heraldry, designating an arm protected by a vambrace.

va·mọose′, *v.t.* and *v.i.;* vamoosed (-mōst′), *pt., pp.;* vamoosing, *ppr.* [Sp. *vamos,* let us go.] to leave quickly; to go away or depart (from) hurriedly. [Slang.]

va·mōse′, *v.t.* and *v.i.* same as *vamoose.*

vamp, *n.* [ME. *vampe;* Fr. *avant-pied; avant,* before, and *pied,* foot.]

1. the part of a boot or shoe covering the instep and toe.

2. [from the *v.*] (a) something patched up; something fixed up to seem new; patchwork; (b) something patched on.

3. in music, a simple accompaniment improvised to fit a song.

vamp, *v.t.;* vamped (vampt), *pt., pp.;* vamping, *ppr.* 1. to put a vamp or upper leather on; as, to *vamp* a shoe.

2. to patch: often followed by *up.*

3. to make over (something old) by addition or alteration.

4. in music, to improvise an accompaniment to.

vamp, *v.i.* to improvise an accompaniment, variation of a tune, etc., as by striking different chords.

vamp, *n.* a vampire (sense 3) or unscrupulous flirt. [Slang.]

vamp, *v.t.* to seduce or beguile (a man) by the use of one's feminine charms and wiles. [Slang.]

vamp, *v.i.* to act the part of a vamp. [Slang.]

vamp, *v.i.* [etym. obscure.] to move forward; to travel; to proceed. [Rare.]

vamp′ēr, *n.* one who or that which vamps in any sense of the word.

vam′pīre, *n.* [Fr. *vampire;* G. *vampyr;* Serb. *vampir, vampira,* a vampire.]

1. in folklore, a corpse that becomes reanimated and leaves its grave at night to suck the blood of sleeping persons.

2. a person who preys ruthlessly on others; an extortioner or bloodsucker.

3. (a) a beautiful but unscrupulous woman who seduces men and leads them to their ruin; (b) an actress who plays the part of such a woman.

4. a vampire bat.

5. a spring trap in the stage floor of a theater.

vam'pīre, *a.* of, pertaining to, or of the character of a vampire; vampiric.

vam'pīre bat, 1. any of various tropical American bats, as those of the family *Phyllostomatidæ*, which live on the blood of animals.

VAMPIRE BAT
(*Phyllostoma spectrum*)

Others constitute the genus *Desmodus.*

2. any of various other bats mistakenly believed to be bloodsuckers.

vam·pir'iç, *a.* pertaining to or characteristic of a vampire.

vam'pir·iṣm, *n.* 1. superstitious belief in the existence of vampires.

2. the action of a vampire; the act of bloodsucking.

3. the practice of extortion or preying on others.

vam'plāte, *n.* [Fr. *avant-plat*, lit., a front or fore plate.] a circular shield of metal on the lower part of the staff of a tilting spear as a shield for the hand

Vam'py·rī, *n.pl.* a group of bats having well-developed nose leaves.

Vam'py·rus, *n.* a genus of phyllostomine bats, of the group *Vampyri*, native to America.

van, *n.* [Fr. *van*; L. *vannus*, a van or fan for winnowing grain.]

1. a winnowing fan or machine. [Archaic.]
2. a wing. [Poetic.]

van, *v.t.*; vanned, *pt., pp.*; vanning, *ppr.* [Fr. *vanner*, from *van*, a fan.] to winnow. [Obs.]

van, *n.* [abbrev. from *vanguard*.]

1. the front of an army on the march; also, the leading division of a fleet either sailing or when drawn up in battle.

2. the foremost position in a line, movement, field of endeavor, etc., or those in the foremost position.

van, *n.* [abbrev. of *caravan*.]

1. a large closed truck or wagon for carrying furniture, freight, etc.

2. a closed railway car for baggage, etc. [Brit.]

van, *v.t.* to carry or convey by means of a van.

van, *prep.* [D.] of; from: in Dutch family names it originally indicated place of origin: in American and British usage, it is often capitalized as part of a personal name.

van'ȧ·dāte, *n.* any salt or ester of vanadic acid.

vȧ·nā'di·āte, *n.* same as *vanadate*.

vȧ·nad'iç, *a.* designating or of chemical compounds containing trivalent or pentavalent vanadium.

vanadic acid; any of several acids containing vanadium.

van·ȧ·dif'ēr·ous, *a.* containing vanadium.

vȧ·nad'i·nīte, *n.* a mineral, lead vanadate and lead chloride, occurring in yellowish and brownish hexagonal crystals.

vȧ·nā'di·ous, *a.* vanadous.

van'ȧ·dīte, *n.* a salt of vanadous acid.

vȧ·nā'di·um, *n.* [ON. after *Vanadis*, one of the names of the goddess Freya.] a rare, malleable, ductile, silver-white metallic chemical element: it is alloyed with steel, to which it adds tensile strength. Symbol, V; atomic weight, 50.95; atomic number, 23.

vanadium bronze; a yellow pigment used in place of gold bronze; an acid derivative of vanadium.

vanadium steel; a steel alloy containing 0.15 to 0.25 per cent vanadium to harden and toughen it: used in the manufacture of machinery and tools.

van'ȧ·dous, *a.* of or pertaining to chemical compounds containing divalent or trivalent vanadium.

van'ȧ·dyl, *n.* the hypothetical radical V_2O_2.

Van Al'len (rā·di·ā'tion) belt, [named after James A. *Van Allen*, Am. physicist.] a broad, doughnut-shaped belt of radiation, composed of high-intensity protons and electrons temporarily trapped by the earth's magnetic field and encircling the earth at varying levels, starting at c.600 miles and extending to 40,000 miles or more.

van-çōu'ri·ēr, *n.* an avant-courier. [Obs.]

Van'dȧ, *n.* a genus of orchids having about twenty species, native to India and the Malay Archipelago.

Van'dăl, *n.* [L. *Vandalus*, one of the tribe of *Vandali*, lit., a wanderer, from G. *wandeln*, to wander.]

1. one of the most barbarous of the East Germanic tribes, that ravaged Gaul, Spain, and northern Africa, and invaded Rome in the fifth century; notorious for destroying the monuments of art and literature.

2. [v–] one who willfully or ignorantly destroys or disfigures, especially that which is beautiful or artistic.

Van·dal'iç, *a.* 1. of or characteristic of the Vandals.

2. [v–] ignorantly and willfully destructive.

3. of the East Germanic language of the Vandals, known only through proper names and scattered loan words in the Romance languages.

Van'dăl·iṣm, *n.* the spirit or conduct of Vandals; hence, [v–] malicious or ignorant destruction, especially of that which is beautiful or artistic.

van'dăl·īze, *v.t.*; vandalized, *pt., pp.*; vandalizing, *ppr.* to destroy or damage (public or private property) maliciously.

Van·dȳke', *n.* [named after Anthony *Van Dyck* (or *Vandyke*), the Flemish painter.]

1. a portrait or painting by Van Dyck.
2. a Vandyke collar.
3. a Vandyke beard.
4. one of a series of large points for edging, as of lace, ribbon, etc.

Van·dȳke', *a.* 1. of, or in the style of, Van Dyck.

2. of or imitating the dress, fashions, etc. depicted in portraits by Van Dyck.

Vandyke beard; a closely trimmed, pointed beard.

Vandyke brown; (a) a deep-brown pigment used by Van Dyck; hence, (b) any of several brown pigments or colors.

Vandyke collar (or *cape*); a broad linen or lace collar with a deeply indented edge.

Van·dȳke', *v.t.* to scallop the edge of, as some part of dress, after the manner of a Vandyke collar.

VANDYKE BEARD

vāne, *n.* [a variant of *fane*, a small flag or pennon, from AS. *fana*, a flag.]

1. a flat piece of metal, strip of cloth, etc. set up high to swing with the wind and show which way it is blowing; weather vane.

2. any of several flat or curved pieces set around an axle, forming a wheel to be rotated by moving air, water, etc., or, if mechanically rotated, to move the air or water; as, the *vane* of a windmill, propeller, etc.

3. a projecting fixed plate or strip of metal attached to a rocket, missile, etc. to provide stability or guidance.

4. a target set to slide on a leveling rod, for use in surveying.

5. one of the sights on a compass, quadrant, etc.

6. the web or flat part of a feather, containing the barbs.

Van·es'sȧ, *n.* [Gr. *Phanēs*, an Orphic divinity.]

1. a genus of lepidopterous insects belonging to the family *Nymphalidæ*. The larvae are covered with spines, and the chrysalids are suspended by the tail.

2. [v–] a butterfly of this genus.

Van·es·si'nae, *n.pl.* a subfamily of butterflies typified by the genus *Vanessa*.

vȧ·nes'soid, *a.* relating to the genus *Vanessa* or to the subfamily *Vanessinæ*.

vȧ·nes'soid, *n.* a vanesoid butterfly.

van'foss, *n.* [Fr. *avant-fosse*; *avant*, before, and *fosse*, ditch.] in fortification, a ditch on the outside of the counterscarp.

vang, *n.* [D. *vang*, catch, from *vangen*, to catch.] in nautical usage, one of two ropes running from the end of a gaff to the deck, used to steady the gaff.

Vañ'gȧ, *n.* [L. *vanga*, a spade, mattock.] a genus of Madagascar shrikes; also, [v–] a shrike of this genus, especially *Vanga curvirostris*, known as the hook-billed shrike.

van'ġee, *n.* [etym. obscure.] in nautical usage, a device for working the pumps of a ship by means of a barrel and crank brakes. [Rare.]

vañ'glō, vañ'glōe, *n.* the sesame: West Indian name.

van'guärd (-gärd), *n.* [ME. *vant-guard*; OFr. *avant-garde*.] 1. the troops who march in front of an army; the advance guard; the van.

2. the leading position in a movement.

3. those leading a movement.

Vȧ·nil'lȧ, *n.* [Sp. *vainilla*, a small pod, husk, from L. *vagina*, case, pod, sheath.]

1. a genus of orchidaceous plants, native to tropical America. The capsule of *Vanilla aromatica* is noted for its fragrant odor and for the volatile, odoriferous oil extracted from it.

VANILLA (branch with fruit 6-10 in. long)

2. [v–] a plant of the genus *Vanilla*, with fragrant, greenish-yellow flowers, especially one yielding the vanilla of commerce, as *Vanilla planifolia* and *Vanilla aromatica.*

3. [v–] the podlike capsule (*vanilla bean*) of this plant, or the flavoring extract prepared from it, used in cooking, baking, etc.

wild vanilla; a plant, *Trilisa* or *Liatris odoratissima*, of the aster family, growing in the southeastern part of the United States. Its dried leaves are sometimes mixed with tobacco.

VANILLA (vine)

vȧ·nil'lȧ bēan, the podlike capsule of the vanilla from which vanilla flavoring is obtained.

vȧ·nil'lȧ gräss, a grass, *Hierochloë borealis.*

vȧ·nil'lȧ plant, 1. any plant that yields the vanilla bean.

2. same as *wild vanilla.*

vȧ·nil'lāte, *n.* a salt of vanillic acid.

vȧ·nil'liç, *a.* pertaining to or obtained from vanilla or vanillin; as, *vanillic* acid.

vȧ·nil'lin, *n.* a fragrant, white, crystalline substance, $C_8H_8O_3$, produced from the vanilla bean or made synthetically, and used for flavoring.

vȧ·nil'liṣm, *n.* dermatitis from handling vanilla.

vȧ·nil'lōeṣ, *n.* an inferior quality of vanilla obtained from *Vanilla pompona.*

vȧ·nil'lyl, *n.* the monovalent radical, $C_8H_9O_2$, derived from vanillic alcohol.

vȧ·nil'ō·quence (-kwens), *n.* [L. *vaniloquentia*; *vanus*, vain, and *loquentia*, talk, from *loqui*, to speak.] vain talk; idle gossip. [Obs.]

vȧ·nil'ō·quent, *a.* talking vainly. [Obs.]

Vä'nir, *n.pl.* in Norse mythology, a race of gods who preceded the Aesir.

van'ish, *v.i.*; vanished, *pt., pp.*; vanishing, *ppr.* [ME. *vanissen*, from ppr. stem of OFr. *esvanir*; hyp. LL. *exvanire*, for L. *evanescere.*

1. to disappear; to pass suddenly from sight.

2. to decay or fade to nothing; to pass gradually out of existence.

3. to cease to exist; to come to an end.

4 in mathematics, to become zero.

van'ish, *n.* in phonetics, the faint last part of certain vowel sounds, as the faint *i* ending the vowel sound of *pay.*

van'ish·ēr, *n.* one who or that which vanishes.

van'ish·ing, *a.* fading away; disappearing.

vanishing fraction; in mathematics, a fraction which reduces to the form of $\frac{0}{0}$ for a particular value of the variable.

vanishing line; in perspective, a line ending at a vanishing point.

vanishing point; (a) in perspective, the point at which parallel lines receding from the observer seem to come together; (b) a time, place, or stage at which something disappears or ceases to exist.

vanishing stress; in phonetics, stress of voice upon the closing portion of a syllable.

van'ish·ing·ly, *adv.* in a vanishing manner.

van'ish·ment, *n.* a vanishing.

Vān'ist, *n.* a follower of Sir Henry Vane, governor of Massachusetts Bay colony in 1636, and leader of the New England Antinomians.

van'i·ty, *n.*; *pl.* **van'i·tieṣ,** [ME. *vanite*; OFr. *vanité*, from L. *vanitas* (-*atis*), emptiness, worthlessness, from *vanus*, vain.]

1. any thing or act that is vain, futile, idle, or worthless.

2. the quality or fact of being vain, or worthless; futility.

3. the quality or fact of being vain, or excessively proud of oneself or one's qualities or possessions; self-satisfaction.

4. a thing about which one is vain; a source of self-satisfaction.
5. a vanity case.
6. a dressing table.
7. [V-] in the old moralities and puppet shows, a personified vice.
vanity case (or *box*); a small case containing powder, rouge, a mirror, etc., carried by women.
Vanity Fair; (a) in Bunyan's *Pilgrim's Progress*, a fair always going on in the town of Vanity, symbolic of worldly folly, frivolity, and show; hence, (b) the world, especially the social world, or a city, society, etc. regarded as dominated by folly, frivolity, and show; (c) a novel (1847–1848) by Thackeray.
vanity table; a small dressing table in a lady's boudoir, usually fronted by a mirror: also called *vanity*.

van'jas, *n.* an Australian crow shrike, *Strepera graculina*.

van'nẽr, *n.* in mining, a machine for separating minerals from the gangue.

van'nẽr hawk, the kestrel. [Brit. Dial.]

van'ning mȧ·chïne', a vanner.

van'quish, *v.t.*; vanquished, *pt., pp.*; vanquishing, *ppr.* [ME. *venkisen*, from stem *veinquis-*, of OFr. *veincre*, L. *vincere*, to conquer.]
1. to conquer; to overcome or subdue in battle, as an enemy; to force into submission.
2. to overcome or defeat in any contest, as in an argument; to confute; to refute; to prove erroneous or unfounded; to upset.
This bold assertion has been fully *vanquished* in a late reply to the Bishop of Meaux's treatise. —Atterbury.
3. to overcome or subdue (a feeling, condition, etc.); to suppress; to overpower; to prostrate.
Sorrow and grief have *vanquished* all my powers. —Shak.
Syn.—conquer, overcome, subdue, defeat, confute, overthrow, surmount.

van'quish, *n.* a disease in sheep. [Scot.]

van'quish·ȧ·ble, *a.* capable of being vanquished.

van'quish·ẽr, *n.* one who or that which vanquishes; a conqueror; a victor.

van'quish·ment, *n.* the act of vanquishing or the state of being vanquished.

van'sīre, *n.* [Madagascar.] a small, weasel-like animal, *Herpestes galera*, from Madagascar. The color is deep brown speckled with yellow, the tail of equal thickness throughout. Also called *marsh ichneumon*.

vȧnt, *v.i.* to vaunt. [Obs.]

van'tăge, *n.* [OFr. *avantage*, advantage.]
1. advantage; superiority; favorable or advantageous position or chance against one's opponent; as, point of *vantage*.
2. in tennis, the first point scored after deuce; advantage.
3. advantage; gain; profit. [Archaic.]
coign of vantage; see under *coign*.
to have at vantage; to have the advantage of.

van'tăge, *v.t.* to profit; to assist. [Archaic.]

van'tăge ground, superiority of position or place; a place or condition which gives one an advantage over another.

van'tăge point, vantage ground.

vant'brāce, vant'bräs, *n.* a vambrace. [Obs.]

vant'-çou''ri·ẽr, *n.* a van-courier. [Obs.]

vant'mūre, *n.* [Fr. *avant-mur*; *avant*, before, and *mur*, wall.] in fortification, the walk or gangway on the top of a wall behind the parapet. [Obs.]

van'wărd, *a.* of, pertaining to, going toward, or situated in the van, or front, as of an army.

van'wạrd, *n.* a vanguard. [Obs.]

vap, *n.* wine which has become vapid or dead; vapid, flat, or insipid liquor. [Obs.]

vap'id, *a.* [L. *vapidus*, stale, insipid.]
1. tasteless; flavorless; flat.
2. uninteresting; lifeless; dull; unexciting; as, *vapid* talk.

va·pid'i·ty, *n.* the state or quality of being vapid; flatness; dullness; insipidity.

vap'id·ly, *adv.* in a vapid manner.

vap'id·ness, *n.* the state or quality of being vapid.

vā'pŏr, *n.* [OFr. *vapeur*; L. *vapor*.]
1. (a) a steamlike mist which rises into the air from water or damp objects subjected to heat; visible particles of moisture floating in the air; fog; mist; steam; (b) any cloudy or imperceptible exhalation, as smoke, noxious fumes, etc.
From the damp earth impervious *vapors* rise, Increase the darkness and involve the skies. —Pope.
2. the gaseous form of any substance which is usually a liquid or a solid.
3. (a) any substance vaporized for use in machinery, medical therapy, etc.; (b) a mixture of such a vaporized substance with air, as the explosive mixture in an automobile cylinder.
4. anything insubstantial.
5. [*pl.*] hypochondria or depressed spirits (often with *the*). [Archaic.]
6. [*pl.*] a hectoring or bullying; swaggering; braggadocio. [Obs.]
7. in medicine, any one of a class of remedies which are to be applied or administered by inhalation.
8. wind; flatulence. [Obs.]
saturated vapor; in physics, vapor which is at the point where it must condense if subjected to additional cooling or pressure.
superheated or *unsaturated vapor*; in physics, vapor which can be subjected to additional cooling or pressure without condensation.

vā'pŏr, *v.i.*; vapored, *pt., pp.*; vaporing, *ppr.*
1. to rise or pass off in the form of vapor; to dissolve or disappear, as into vapor, steam, or air; to evaporate.
2. to give off vapor, steam, or gas; to emit vapors or exhalations.
3. to boast or vaunt with ostentatious display; to bully; to hector; to brag; to bluster.

vā'pŏr, *v.t.* 1. to cause to pass into a vaporous state; to cause to dissolve, pass away, or disappear in a vaporous, gaseous, or aeriform condition; to vaporize.
2. to affect with the vapors; to make melancholy; to dispirit. [Archaic.]
3. to bully; to brag; to hector.

vā''pŏr·ȧ·bil'i·ty, *n.* the property or state of being vaporable.

vā'pŏr·ȧ·ble, *a.* capable of being vaporized or converted into vapor.

vā·pō·rā'ri·um, *n.* [L., a steam pipe in the sweating room of the Roman bath, from *vapor*, steam, vapor.] a vapor or steam bath.

vā'pŏr·āte, *v.i.* to emit vapor; also, to evaporate. [Obs.]

vā·pŏr·ā'tion, *n.* [L. *vaporatio* (*-onis*), from *vaporatus*, pp. of *vaporare*, to emit steam or vapor.] the act or process of converting into vapor, or of passing off in vapor; evaporation. [Obs.]

vā'pŏr bȧth, 1. the application of vapor or steam to the body in a close room or place; a bath in vapor.
2. the place where such a bath is taken.

vā'pŏr bũrn'ẽr, a device which vaporizes a liquid, as alcohol, gasoline, kerosene, etc., and from the vapor produces a flame for light or heat.

vā'pŏr den'si·ty, the relation between the weight of a given volume of any substance in the state of vapor and that of the same volume of hydrogen.

vā'pŏr dōuçhe, a topical vapor bath, which consists in the direction of a jet of aqueous vapor on some part of the body.

vā'pŏred, *a.* 1. affected with the vapors. [Rare.]
2. moist; hazy; misty. [Rare.]

vā'pŏr en'ġine, an engine driven by a vapor other than steam.

vā'pŏr·ẽr, *n.* 1. one who vapors, brags, or bullies; a braggart; a bully; a boaster.
2. a vaporer moth.

vā'pŏr·ẽr mọth, a common brown moth, *Orgyia antiqua*, the female of which cannot fly.

vā·pŏr·es'cence, *n.* formation of vapor.

vā·pŏr·es'cent, *a.* forming, or tending to form, vapor.

vā·pō·rif'ẽr·ous, *a.* [L. *vaporifer*, vaporous.] forming or conducting vapors.

vā·pō·rif'iç, *a.* [L. *vapor* (*-oris*), steam, vapor, and *facere*, to make.] 1. producing vapor.
2. vaporous.

vā'pŏr·i·fọrm, *a.* [L. *vapor* (*-oris*), vapor, and *-form*.] existing in the form or state of vapor.

vā·pō·rim'e·tẽr, *n.* [L. *vapor* (*-oris*), vapor, and *-meter*.] a device to measure vapor pressure and volume.

vā'pŏr·ing, *n.* the act of bragging or boasting; empty, ostentatious, or windy talk or behavior.

vā'pŏr·ing, *a.* 1. that vapors.
2. boasting; vaunting; given to boast or brag; as, *vaporing* talk.

vā'pŏr·ing·ly, *adv.* in a vaporing or boastful manner.

vā'pŏr·ish, *a.* 1. like vapor.
2. full of vapor or vapors.
3. having, or inclined to have, the vapors; in low spirits or easily depressed.

vā'pŏr·ī·zā·ble, *a.* capable of being converted into vapor.

vā''pŏr·i·zā'tion, *n.* 1. a vaporizing or being vaporized; specifically, the turning of water into steam, as in a boiler.
2. medical treatment with vapor.

vā'pŏr·īze, *v.t.*; vaporized, *pt., pp.*; vaporizing, *ppr.* 1. to convert into vapor, as by the application of heat or by spraying.
2. to affect with the vapors. [Archaic.]

vā'pŏr·īze, *v.i.* to be changed into vapor; to pass off in vapor.

vā'pŏr·ī·zẽr, *n.* a device for vaporizing liquids, as an atomizer, or a jet in a carburetor.

vā'pŏr·ōse, *a.* vaporous.

vā·pŏr·os'i·ty, *n.* the state or quality of being vaporous.

vā'pŏr·ous, *a.* [LL. *vaporosus*, from L. *vapor*, vapor.]
1. giving off or forming vapor.
2. full of vapor; foggy; misty.
3. like, having the nature of, or characteristic of vapor.
4. (a) fleeting, unsubstantial, fanciful, etc.: said of things, ideas, etc.; (b) given to such ideas or talk.
5. causing flatulence; as, *vaporous* food. [Obs.]

vā'pŏr·ous·ness, *n.* the state or character of being vaporous.

vā'pŏr plāne, the level of the atmosphere at which ascending moisture begins to form clouds by condensation.

vā'pŏr pres'sūre (presh'ũr), the pressure of a confined vapor that has accumulated above its liquid: it is determined by the nature of the liquid and the temperature.

vā'pŏr ten'sion, same as *vapor pressure*.

vā'pŏr·y, *a.* 1. full of vapors; of the nature of a vapor; vaporous.
2. affected with the vapors; melancholy. [Archaic.]

vā'pŏur, *n., v.i.* and *v.t.* vapor: British spelling.

vap·ū·lā'tion, *n.* the act of beating, whipping, or flogging. [Rare.]

vä·que̡'rō (-kā'), *n.*; *pl.* **vä·que̡'rōṣ,** [Sp.] in Spanish America and the southwestern United States, a cowboy; a herder of cattle.

vä'rä, *n.* [Sp. and Port., lit., a rod, stick; L., a forked pole, from *varus*, bent.] a Spanish, Portuguese, and Latin American unit of linear measure, varying in different countries from 32 to 43 inches: a square vara, as a unit of area, is sometimes called a *vara*.

vā'răn, *n.* [Ar. *waran*.] the monitor, a lizard.

Vā·ran'ġi·ăn, *n.* [LL. *Varangus*; Ice. *Væringi*, lit., confederates or sworn men, from *vārar*, troth.]
1. any of a Scandinavian people who settled in Russia in the ninth century and founded the first Russian dynasty, under Rurik.
2. any of those Scandinavians who entered the service of the Byzantine emperor about the eleventh century and became the imperial guard at Constantinople.

Var'ȧ·nus, *n.* [Ar. *waran*, a lizard.] the typical genus of *Varanidæ*, the monitor lizards, inhabiting Africa, Asia, and Australia.

vāre, *n.* [prob. a variant of *vair*.] a weasel. [Brit. Dial.]

vāre, *n.* a wand or staff of office or authority. [Obs.]

var'eç, *n.* [Fr. *varech*.] an impure carbonate of soda made from seaweed.

vāre'head''ed (-hed''), *a.* having a head shaped like that of a weasel. [Brit. Dial.]

vāre widġ'eŏn (wij'un), the weasel duck; the female or young male of the smew. [Brit. Dial.]

vär·gue̡'nō (-gā'), *n.* [Sp.] a decorative box-shaped cabinet of Spanish design, supported on a stand at a convenient height for use as a desk when the front cover is lowered. It was first made at Vargas, Spain, in the sixteenth century.

vä'rï, *n.* [from native name.] the ruffed lemur, or macaco, *Lemur varius* or *catta*.

vãr''i·ȧ·bil'i·ty, *n.* [from *variable* and *-ity*.]
1. the state or quality of being variable.
2. a tendency to vary.

vãr'i·ȧ·ble, *a.* [LL. *variabilis*, from L. *varius*, changing.]

1. able to vary or alter; capable of alteration in any manner; susceptible of change; changeable.

2. apt or likely to change; mutable; fickle; unsteady; inconstant; as, the affections of men are *variable.*

3. in mathematics, having no fixed value: opposed to *constant*, retaining the same value.

4. in astronomy, changing in brightness or apparent magnitude: said of certain stars.

5. in biology, tending to deviate in some way from the type; aberrant.

Variable Zone; Temperate Zone.

văr′i·ȧ·ble, *n.* 1. anything changeable; a thing that varies or may vary.

2. in astronomy, a variable star.

3. in mathematics, (a) a quantity that may have a number of different values; (b) a symbol for such a quantity.

4. in nautical usage, a shifting wind, or one which blows stronger or weaker at intervals: distinguished from *trade wind.*

complex variable; a variable consisting of an imaginary quantity of the type $x + y\sqrt{-1}$.

independent variable; any variable chosen arbitrarily as the one upon whose value that of another shall depend. There may be several thus chosen simultaneously in certain cases.

the variables; a region of shifting winds lying between the belts of the steady northeast and southeast trade winds.

văr′i·ȧ·ble·ness, *n.* variability: the state or quality of being variable.

văr′i·ȧ·bly, *adv.* in a variable way.

văr′i·ȧnce, *n.* [L. *varians (-antis)*, ppr. of *variare*, to change.]

1. the quality, state, or fact of varying or being variant; a changing or being changeable; tendency to change.

2. degree of change or difference; divergence; discrepancy.

3. an active disagreement; quarrel; dispute.

4. in law, a lack of agreement between two parts of a legal proceeding which should agree, as between a statement and the evidence offered in support of it.

at variance; (a) disagreeing; quarreling; not in accord: said of persons; (b) not in agreement with each other; differing; conflicting: said of things.

văr′i·ȧnt, *a.* 1. different; diverse; varying; especially, different in some way from others of the same kind or class, or from some standard or type.

2. variable; changeable; inconstant.

văr′i·ȧnt, *n.* anything that is variant; a variant form; as, (a) in biology, a form varying from the type; (b) a different spelling of the same word; (c) a different version of a myth or narrative.

văr′i·āte, *v.t.* and *v.i.*; variated, *pt., pp.*; variating, *ppr.* to alter; to vary.

văr′i·āte, *n.* in statistics, (a) loosely, a variable (sense 3); (b) a particular value of such a variable.

văr·i·ā′tion, *n.* [L. *variatio (-onis)*, a changing, from *variatus*, pp. of *variare*, to change.]

1. the act, fact, or process of varying; modification; change or deviation in form, condition, appearance, extent, etc. from a former or usual state, or from an assumed standard.

2. the degree or extent of such change; as, a *variation* of ten feet in height.

3. a thing which is somewhat different from another of the same kind.

4. in astronomy, a change in or deviation from the mean motion or orbit of a planet, satellite, etc.

5. in biology, (a) a deviation from the usual or parental type in structure or form; (b) an organism showing such deviation.

6. in magnetism, the deviation of a compass needle from true north and south; declination.

7. in mathematics, (a) [Obs.] any one of many arrangements of any number of quantities, a given number of them being considered together; the sequence of combinations that can be made of a number of terms or objects; (b) a relation between two quantities so that one changes with the other in the same ratio.

8. in music, the repetition of a melody or theme with changes or embellishments in harmony, rhythm, key, etc., especially one of a series of such repetitions.

annual variation, diurnal variation, etc.; the total change which takes place in a year, a day, etc., as in the orbit of a planet or in the declination and right ascension of a star.

irregular variation; any variation which takes place in an irregular degree or at irregular periods, as variations in winds, temperature, etc.

periodic variation; a variation which occurs periodically or in comparatively short periods: opposed to *irregular variation* or to *secular variation.*

secular variation; such a variation as continues to take place through a long period of time, yet tends to a well-defined change in a definite direction.

Syn.—change, modification, vicissitude, mutation, deviation, fluctuation, oscillation.

văr·i·ā′tion·ăl, *a.* 1. of variation.

2. showing or characteristic of variation.

3. involving variation.

var′i·çā·ted, *a.* [L. *varix (-icis)*, a dilated vein, varix.] having varices.

var·i·çā′tion, *n.* the state of having varices; also, the arrangement of varices; a combination of varices; a varix.

var·i·cel′lȧ, *n.* [dim. of *variola*, smallpox.] chicken pox.

var·i·cel′lāte, *a.* in zoology, marked with small ridges, as some shells.

var·i·cel′loid, *a.* resembling varicella, or chicken pox.

var′i·cēs̱, *n.* plural of *varix.*

var′i·ci·fọrm, *a.* having the form of a varix.

var′i·çō-, [from L. *varix.*] a combining form meaning *an enlarged vein*, as in *varico*cele: also, before a vowel, *varic-.*

var′i·çō·cēle, *n.* [L. *varix, varicis*, a dilated vein, and Gr. *kēlē*, tumor.] in medicine, a varicose condition of the veins of the spermatic cord in the scrotum.

var′i·çoid, *a.* same as *variciform.*

văr′i·çŏl·ŏred, *a.* [from *varius*, varied; and *colored.*]

1. of several or many colors.

2. varied; diversified.

var′i·çōse, *a.* [L. *varicosus*, having enlarged veins.]

1. abnormally and irregularly swollen or dilated; as, *varicose* veins.

2. of or having varicose veins.

3. designed for the treatment or relief of varicose veins; designating elastic fabrics made into stockings, bandages, and the like, used for this purpose.

var·i·çō′sis, *n.* [Mod. L.]

1. the formation of varices, or varicose veins.

2. varicosity.

var·i·ços′i·ty, *n.*; *pl.* **var·i·ços′i·tieṣ,** 1. the state of being varicose.

2. a varix.

var·i·çot′ō·my, *n.* [*varico-* and *-tomy.*] the surgical excision of a varix, especially of a varicose vein.

var·iç′ū·lȧ, *n.* a swelling or varicosity of the veins of the conjunctiva.

văr′ied, *a.* 1. altered; changed.

2. characterized by variety; consisting of various kinds or sorts; as, a *varied* assortment of goods.

3. variegated; marked in different colors.

văr′ied·ly, *adv.* diversely.

Vă″ri·ē·gā′tae, *n.pl.* [f. pl. of LL. *variegatus*, from *variegare*, to make of various kinds or colors.] a group of noctuid moths: so called because the hind and fore wings are of different colors.

văr′i·ē·gāte″, *v.t.*; variegated, *pt., pp.*; variegating, *ppr.* [LL. *variegatus*, pp. of *variegare*, to variegate, from L. *varius*, various, and *facere*, to make.]

1. to make varied in appearance by differences, as in colors.

2. to make varied; to give variety to; to diversify.

văr′i·ē·gāt″ed, *a.* [pp. of *variegate.*]

1. of different colors in spots, streaks, etc.; parti-colored.

2. varied; having variety in character, form, appearance, etc.; diversified.

văr″i·ē·gā′tion, *n.* 1. a variegating or being variegated.

2. diversity or variety in character or appearance; specifically, varied coloration.

3. in botany, (a) the presence of two or more colors in the petals, leaves, and other parts of plants; (b) a condition of plants in which the leaves become partially white or of a very light color from suppression or modification of the chlorophyll.

văr′i·ẽr, *n.* one who varies.

vȧ·rī′e·tăl, *a.* 1. of, connected with, or characterizing a variety.

2. constituting a variety.

vȧ·rī′e·tăl·ly, *adv.* in biology, as a variety.

vȧ·rī′e·tas, *n.* [L., difference, variety.] in biology, a variety: used only in technical terms.

vȧ·rī′e·ty, *n.*; *pl.* **vȧ·rī′e·ties,** [Fr. *variété*; L. *varietas*, from *varie*, variously, from *varius*, various.]

1. the state or quality of being varied or various; absence of monotony or sameness; intermixture of different things; diversity.

Age cannot wither her, nor custom stale
Her infinite *variety.* —Shak.

2. a different form of some thing, condition, or quality; sort; kind; as, *varieties* of cloth.

3. a number of different things thought of together; a collection of varied things; as, there is a *variety* of items in the basement.

The civilization of a people may be inferred
from the *variety* of its tools.
—Charles Norton Eliot.

4. difference; variation.

5. in biology, a group having characteristics of its own within a species; a subdivision of a species; a subspecies.

6. entertainment of the kind given in a variety show. [Chiefly Brit.]

7. in mineralogy, any of the forms of a mineral that may vary in color, structure, crystallization, etc.; as, *varieties* of quartz.

geographical variety; a variety of a species found only in a given geographical region and having its varietal peculiarities or differences caused by or dependent upon local influences, especially those of climate.

Syn.—diversity, change, difference, medley.

vȧ·rī′e·ty, *a.* of or in a variety show, or vaudeville.

vȧ·rī′e·ty hȳ′brid, an animal or plant resulting from a cross between two varieties of the same species; a mongrel.

vȧ·rī′e·ty shōw, a stage show made up of a number of different kinds of acts, as songs, dances, gymnastic or acrobatic feats, etc.; a vaudeville show.

vȧ·rī′e·ty thē′ȧ·tẽr, a theater where variety shows are the form of entertainment.

văr′i·fọrm, văr′i·fọrmed, *a.* [L. *varius*, various, and *-form.*] varied in form; having different shapes or forms.

vā′ri·fȳ, *v.t.* to make varied; to diversify. [Obs.]

văr″i·ō·çŏup′lẽr, *n.* [L. *varius*, diverse, and *coupler.*] in electricity, a coupler with a movable coil for changing the mutual inductance.

vȧ·rī′ō·lȧ, *n.* [LL., from L. *varius*, various.] in medicine, smallpox.

vȧ·rī′ō·lăr, *a.* same as *variolous.*

văr′i·ō·lāte″, *v.t.*; variolated, *pt., pp.*; variolating, *ppr.* [from *variola* and *-ate.*] to inoculate with the virus of smallpox.

văr′i·ō·lāte″, *a.* of the nature of or resembling smallpox: used in entomology and botany to designate foveae, pustules, etc. which resemble pockmarks.

văr′i·ō·lā″ted, *a.* inoculated with the virus of smallpox.

văr″i·ō·lā′tion, *n.* inoculation with the virus of smallpox.

văr′i·ōle, *n.* [Fr., from LL. *variola*, smallpox.]

1. a small pit or depression in the skin; a foveola.

2. in lithology, a spherule of variolite.

văr·i·ol′iç, *a.* variolous.

văr′i·ō·līte″, *n.* [L. *varius*, spotted, and *-lite.*] a rock, especially diorite, in which whitish spherules of other rock are embedded, making a pitted or specked surface.

văr″i·ō·lit′iç, *a.* 1. having a specked or pitted surface; pock-marked in appearance.

2. of or like variolite.

văr″i·ō·lit″i·zā′tion, *n.* conversion into variolite.

văr·i·ō·li·zā′tion, *n.* same as *variolation.*

văr′i·ō·loid″, *n.* [LL. *variola*, smallpox, and *-oid.*] a mild form of variola occurring in a person who has had a previous attack or who has been vaccinated.

văr′i·ō·loid″, *a.* 1. resembling variola, or smallpox.

2. of varioloid.

vȧ·rī′ō·lous, *a.* [LL. *variolosus*, from *variola*, smallpox.]

1. of or having variola, or smallpox.

2. having pitted scars, as pockmarks.

vȧ·rī″ō·lō·vaç′cine, *n.* a vaccine obtained from the lymph in lesions appearing in variolovaccinia.

vȧ·rī″ō·lō·vaç·cin′i·ȧ, *n.* cowpox in a heifer caused by inoculation with smallpox virus.

vãr·i·om′ē·tẽr, *n.* [from L. *varius*, various; and *-meter*.]
1. an instrument for comparing magnetic forces or determining variations of magnetic force, especially at different places on the earth.
2. an instrument for varying inductance in an electric circuit, consisting of a movable coil within a fixed coil, the two connected in series: used in radio tuning.

vãr·i·ō′rum, *n.* [L., of various (scholars).] an edition or text, as of a literary work, containing variant readings or notes by various editors, scholars, etc.

vãr·i·ō′rum, *a.* of such an edition or text.

vãr′i·ous, *a.* [L. *varius*, diverse.]
1. differing one from another; of several kinds.
2. several; many; as, *various* sections of the country.
3. many-sided; versatile.
4. characterized by variety; varied in nature or appearance.
5. changeable. [Rare.]

vãr′i·ous·ly, *adv.* in various ways; with change; with diversity; as, flowers *variously* colored.

vãr′i·ous·ness, *n.* variety.

var′i·scīte, *n.* [from *Variscia*, in Saxony.] a transparent, green, hydrous phosphate of aluminum.

vãr′ix, *n.*; *pl.* **vãr′i·cēṣ,** [L.] 1. in medicine, a permanently and irregularly swollen or dilated blood or lymph vessel, especially a vein; a varicose vein.
2. in conchology, any of the longitudinal thickened elevations which occur at irregular intervals on the outer surface of spiral shells.

vär′let, *n.* [OFr. *varlet*, *vaslet*.]
1. an attendant. [Archaic.]
2. a boy or youth serving as a knight's page. [Archaic.]
3. a rascal; scoundrel; knave. [Archaic.]
4. in playing cards, the knave or jack. [Obs.]

vär′let·ess, *n.* a girl or woman varlet. [Obs.]

vär′let·ry, *n.* 1. varlets collectively. [Archaic.]
2. the rabble; the crowd; the mob. [Archaic.]

vär′mint, vär′ment, *n.* [var. of dial. *vermin*, with unhistoric *-t*.] vermin; especially, a person or animal regarded as troublesome or objectionable: also used as a generalized epithet of disparagement. [Dial. or Colloq.]

vär′nish, *n.* [ME. *vernisch*; OFr. *vernis*, varnish.]
1. (a) a preparation made of resinous substances dissolved in oil (*oil varnish*) or in a liquid like alcohol which evaporates quickly (*spirit varnish*), and used to give a glossy surface to wood, metal, etc.; (b) any of various natural or prepared products used for the same purpose.
2. the smooth, hard, glossy surface of this after it has dried.
3. a surface gloss or smoothness, as of manner; outward attractiveness, often deceptive.

vär′nish, *v.t.*; varnished (-nisht), *pt.*, *pp.*; varnishing, *ppr.* [OFr. *vernisser*, to varnish.]
1. to cover with varnish; to brush varnish on.
2. to impart a smooth surface to, as with varnish; to give a varnished appearance to.
3. to make attractive on the surface; to embellish, often deceptively.

And bow the knee to pomp that loves to *varnish* guilt. —Byron.

4. to polish up; to brighten.

vär′nish·ẽr, *n.* one who varnishes or whose occupation is varnishing.

vär′nish·ing, *n.* the act of laying on varnish; also, varnish.

vär′nish·ing dāy, a day previous to the opening of an art exhibit, when the artists are given the opportunity of retouching or varnishing their pictures.

vär′nish tree, any one of various trees which exude resinous juices, either naturally or from incisions, which can be made into a lacquer or varnish.
black, *Burmese*, or *Martaban varnish tree*; the theetsee.
false varnish tree; same as *tree of heaven* under *tree*.
Japan varnish tree; the lacquer tree.
New Granada varnish tree; a rubiaceous tree of South America, *Elæagia utilis*.

vär′si·ty, *n.*; *pl.* **vär′si·tieṣ,** [contr., from *university* in 18th-c. pronun.] a team, usually athletic, that represents a university, college, or school in any competition.

vär′si·ty, *a.* designating or of a university, college, or school team or competition.

vär·sō·vi·enne′, *n.* [Fr., of Warsaw.] a 19th-century dance resembling the polka, redowa, and mazurka; also, the music for the dance.

vär′tȧ·bed, vär′tȧ·bet, *n.* [Armenian.] one of an order of ecclesiastics in the Armenian church intermediate between the bishops and priests, and devoted to teaching.

Var′ụ·nȧ, *n.* [Sans.] the Hindu god of the cosmos, represented in the Vedic hymns as of very great and manifold powers. He is depicted as four-armed and riding on a sea animal.

VARUNA

vãr′us, *a.* [Mod. L., from L., bent, grown inward.] an abnormal turning inward of the foot so as to produce bowleg.

vãr′us, *a.* bowlegged.

värve, *n.* [Sw. *varv*, layer.] in geology, a layer in a deposit of sedimentary material, showing seasonal variation caused by differences in summer and winter deposition: characteristic of certain recent deposits in glaciated regions, and used to estimate the length of glacial and interglacial periods.

vär′vel, *n.* in falconry, a ring attached to the end of a hawk's jess and used to fasten the jess to the leash.

vär′veled, vär′velled, *a.* having varvels or rings; in heraldry, designating a bearing in which the leather thongs or jesses which tie on the bells to the legs of hawks are borne flotant with rings at the ends.

VARVELED

vãr′y, *v.t.*; varied, *pt.*, *pp.*; varying, *ppr.* [ME. *varien*; OFr. *varier*, from L. *variare*, to vary, change, from *varius*, various.]
1. to change in form, appearance, nature, substance, etc.; to alter; to modify.
2. to make different from one another.
3. to give variety to; to diversify; as, *vary* your reading.
4. in music, to repeat (a melody or theme) with changes in harmony, rhythm, key, etc.

vãr′y, *v.i.* 1. to undergo change in any way; to become different.
2. to be different or diverse; to differ; as, the second edition *varied* little from the first.
3. to deviate, diverge, or depart (*from*).
4. to alter in succession; to alternate.
5. in biology, to show variation.
6. in mathematics, to change (directly or inversely) in the same ratio.
7. to disagree; to be at variance in opinion. [Obs.]

vãr′y, *n.* alteration; change.

vãr′y·ing, *a.* altering; changing; deviating.
varying hare; a hare, *Lepus variabilis*, whose coat of fur becomes white in winter.

vas, *n.*; *pl.* **vā′sȧ,** [L., a vessel, dish.] in anatomy and biology, a vessel; a duct.

vā′sạl, *a.* relating to a vessel or duct; pertaining to the blood vessels.

vas′çū·lăr, *a.* [L. *vasculum*, a small vessel, dim. of *vas*, a vessel, dish.] of or having vessels or ducts; specifically, (a) in anatomy and zoology, designating or of the vessels, or system of vessels, for conveying blood or lymph; (b) in botany, designating or of the ducts for conveying sap.
vascular bundle; in botany, a cluster of fibers and vessels.
vascular plants; plants whose structure is characterized by vascular tissue; the phanerogamous division of plants.
vascular system; in botany, the arrangement of all the vascular tissue in a plant.
vascular tissue; in botany, tissue composed of the ducts that carry sap through any of the higher plants.

Vas·çū·lā′rēṣ, *n.pl.* one of two great divisions of plants, consisting of those in which vascular tissue appears, and thus including all the phanerogamous plants, both exogenous and endogenous; vascular plants. [Obs.]

vas·çū·lar′i·ty, *n.*; *pl.* **vas·çū·lar′i·tieṣ,** vascular form or condition.

vas″çū·lăr·i·zā′tion, *n.* vascularity.

vas′çū·lōse, *n.* the substance constituting the principal part of the vascular tissue of plants.

vas′çū·lōse, *a.* of, full of, or supplied by or with ducts or vessels; vascular.

vas′çū·lous, *a.* vasculose.

vas′çū·lum, *n.*; *pl.* **vas′çū·lȧ,** [L., a small vessel.]
1. in botany, an ascidium.
2. a botanist's metal case for carrying specimens as he collects them.

vas de′fe·renṣ, *n.*; *pl.* **vā′sȧ def″ẽr·en′ti·ȧ** (-shi-ȧ), the convoluted excretory duct of a testicle, conveying sperm from the testicle to the ejaculatory duct of the penis.

vāse (*or* väz; *Brit.* väz), *n.* [Fr., from L. *vasum*, a collateral form of *vas*, a vessel, dish.]
1. an open container of metal, glass, pottery, etc., usually rounded and of greater height than width, used for decoration, displaying flowers, etc.

GRECIAN VASES

2. in architecture, a sculptured ornament resembling a vase.

vas·eç′tō·my, *n.* the surgical removal of all or part of the vas deferens.

vas′e·line, *n.* [irregular formation, from G. *wasser*, water, and Gr. *elaion*, oil; and *-ine* (suffix used to form commercial names).] a petroleum jelly, light yellow or white, used as a lubricant or ointment; petrolatum: a trade-mark (*Vaseline*).

Vash′tī, *n.* [Heb. *washtī*.] in the Bible, the queen of Ahasuerus of Persia: because she refused to present herself at his command at a feast, he repudiated her: Esth. i.

vas·i·faç′tive, *a.* [*vasi-*, and L. *factus*, pp. of *facere*, to make.] same as *vasoformative*.

vas′i·form, *a.* having the form, nature, or character of a vas or tube.

vas′ō-, vas′i-, vas-, [from L. *vas*, a vessel.] combining forms meaning: (a) *the blood vessels*, as in *vaso*motor; (b) *the vas deferens*, as in *vas*ectomy; (c) *vasomotor*.

vas″ō·çŏn·striçt′ŏr, *a.* causing constriction of the blood vessels.

vas″ō·çŏn·striçt′ŏr, *n.* a nerve or drug causing constriction of the blood vessels.

vas·ō·den′tīne, *n.* [*vaso-*, and L. *dens*, *dentis*, a tooth.] in anatomy, a modification of dentine in which capillary tubes of the primitive vascular pulp remain uncalcified and carry red blood into the substance of the tissue.

vas″ō·dī·lāt′ŏr, *a.* producing dilatation of the blood vessels.

vas″ō·dī·lāt′ŏr, *n.* a vasodilator nerve or drug.

vas·ō·fọrm′ȧ·tive, *a.* in physiology, building up new blood vessels or vascular tissue.

vas·ō·hȳ·pẽr·ton′iç, *a.* same as *vasoconstrictor*.

vas·ō·hȳ·pō·ton′iç, *a.* same as *vasodilator*.

vas″ō·in·hib′i·tŏr, *n.* any agent or drug that inhibits the action of the vasomotor nerves.

vas″ō·in·hib′i·tō·ry, *a.* hindering the action of the vasomotor nerves.

vas·ō·mō′tion, *n.* in anatomy, the contraction or dilatation of the caliber of a blood vessel.

vas·ō·mō′tŏr, *a.* [*vaso-* and *motor*.] in physiology, regulating the size (i.e., caliber) of blood vessels by causing contraction or dilatation: said of a nerve, nerve center, or drug.

vas″ō·mō·tō′ri·ăl, vas″ō·mō·tor′iç, vas·ō·mō′tō·ry, *a.* same as *vasomotor*.

vas·ō·pȧ·rē′sis, *n.* partial paralysis of vasomotor nerves.

vas·ot′ō·my, *n.*; *pl.* **vas·ot′ō·mieṣ,** [*vaso-*, and *-tomy*.] a surgical cutting of the vas deferens, as for the purpose of sterilizing sexually.

vas·ō·ton′iç, *a.* [*vaso-*, and Gr. *tonikos*, a tonic.] concerned in regulating the tone or tension of the blood vessels.

vas·ō·troph′iç, *a.* [*vaso-*, and Gr. *trophikos*, nursing.] affecting nutrition through the alteration of the caliber of the blood vessels.

vas′săl, *n.* [ME. *vassale;* OFr. *vassal;* ML. *vassalus,* manservant, extension of *vassus,* servant, from Celt.]
1. in the Middle Ages, a person who held land under the feudal system, doing homage and pledging fealty to an overlord, and performing military or other duties in return for his protection; a feudal tenant.
2. a subordinate, dependent, subject, etc.
3. (a) a servant; (b) a slave.

vas′săl, *a.* 1. of or like a vassal; dependent, subject, servile, subservient, etc.
2. being a vassal or vassals.

vas′săl, *v.t.*; vassaled *or* vassalled, *pt., pp.*; vassaling *or* vassalling, *ppr.* to subject to vassalage; to enslave.

vas′săl·ăġe, *n.* [Fr.] 1. the state of being a vassal.
2. the homage, loyalty, and service required of a vassal.
3. dependence; subordinate position; servitude.
4. lands held by a vassal; a fief.
5. a body of vassals.
6. valor; courage. [Obs.]

vas′săl·ess, *n.* a woman vassal. [Rare.]

vas′săl·ry, *n.* the whole body of vassals. [Rare.]

vȧst, *a.*; *comp.* vaster; *superl.* vastest, [Fr. *vaste,* from L. *vastus,* of large extent, vast.]
1. wide and vacant or unoccupied; waste; desert; desolate; lonely. [Obs.]
2. of great extent; very spacious or large; boundless; far-reaching.
3. huge in bulk and extent; enormous; massive; immense; as, the *vast* mountains of Asia.
4. very great in number, amount, or quantity.
5. very great in degree or intensity; as, *vast* knowledge.
Syn.—extensive, gigantic, enormous, immense, prodigious, far-reaching.

vȧst, *n.* 1. a boundless waste or space; immensity. [Poet.]

Far had he roam'd
With nothing save the *vast,* that foam'd
Above, around, and at his feet.—Keats.

2. a great deal; a large quantity. [Brit. Dial.]

vȧs·tā′tion, *n.* a laying waste; devastation. [Obs.]

vȧs·tid′i·ty, vȧst′i·ty, *n.* vastness; immensity.

vȧst′i·tūde, *n.* 1. the quality or condition of being vast; vastness.
2. a vast space or extent.
3. devastation. [Obs.]

vȧst′ly, *adv.* to a vast extent or degree; very; as, he was *vastly* enraged.

vȧst′ness, *n.* the state or quality of being vast; greatness; immensity.

vȧst′y, *a.*; *comp.* vastier; *superl.* vastiest, vast; boundless; of great extent; immense; huge.

vat, *n.* [ME. *fat,* from AS. *fæt,* a cask, vessel.]
1. a large tub, tank, or cask for holding liquids to be used in a manufacturing process or to be stored for fermenting or ripening.
2. a liquid measure used in Belgium and the Netherlands corresponding to the hectoliter, equal to 26.4 gallons.
3. in metallurgy, (a) a vessel used in the wet treatment of ores; (b) a square hollow place on the back of a calcining furnace in which tin ore is laid to dry.
4. a liquid containing a dye that does not color materials dipped in it until they are exposed to air.

vat, *v.t.*; vatted, *pt., pp.*; vatting, *ppr.* 1. to place or store in a vat.
2. to dip into a vat (dyeing solution).

vat dȳe, a dye used in a vat (sense 4).

Vȧ·tē′ri·ȧ, *n.* [named after Abraham *Vater* (1684–1751), a German botanist.] a genus of Asiatic trees, order *Dipterocarpeæ,* valuable for timber and also for copal and piny varnish which they yield.

vat′fụl, *n.* as much as a vat will hold; the contents of a vat.

vat′iç, *a.* [L. *vates,* a prophet.] of, relating to, or characteristic of a prophet or seer; prophetic; oracular; inspired.

vat′iç·ăl, *a.* vatic.

Vat′i·căn, *n.* [from L. *Vaticanus* (*mons*), the name of one of the hills of ancient Rome, on the west bank of the Tiber.]
1. the papal palace, consisting of a group of buildings in Vatican City.
2. the papal government, as distinguished from the Quirinal, or Italian civil government.
Vatican Codex; an uncial manuscript of the Greek Testament, dating from the fourth century, preserved at the Vatican.
Vatican Council; the Ecumenical Council of the Church of Rome which met in the Vatican in 1870, and declared the personal infallibility of the pope when speaking *ex cathedra* to be a dogma of the church.

Vat′i·căn·ișm, *n.* the doctrine of papal infallibility, and the system of theology and church government based upon it, beginning with the Vatican Council of 1869–1870: an opprobrious term.

Vat′i·căn·ist, *n.* one who believes in the doctrine of papal infallibility; an opprobrious term.

vat′i·cīde, *n.* [L. *vates,* a prophet, and *cædere,* to kill.]
1. the murder of a prophet.
2. the murderer of a prophet.

vȧ·tic′i·năl, *a.* having the nature of or characterized by prophecy; prophetic.

vȧ·tic′i·nāte, *v.t.* and *v.i.*; vaticinated, *pt., pp.*; vaticinating, *ppr.* [L. *vaticinatus,* pp. of *vaticinari,* to foretell, prophesy, from *vates,* a seer, prophet.] to prophesy; to foretell; to predict.

vȧ·tic·i·nā′tion, *n.* [L. *vaticinatio* (*-onis*), from *vaticinari,* to foretell, prophesy.]
1. prediction; prophecy.
2. a prophesying; a foretelling.

vȧ·tic′i·nā·tŏr, *n.* [L.] one who vaticinates or predicts; a prophet.

vat′i·cine, *n.* a prophecy or vaticination. [Obs.]

vaude′ville (vōd′vil *or* vọ′dȧ-), *n.* [Fr., earlier *vau-de-vire,* from *Vau-de-Vire,* the valley of the Vire (in Normandy), famous for light, convivial songs.]
1. (a) a stage show consisting of mixed specialty acts, including songs, dances, skits, acrobatic performances, etc.; a variety show; (b) such entertainment generally.
2. a comic theatrical piece interspersed with songs and dances. [Now Rare.]
3. a light popular song, usually satirical or topical, often accompanied by pantomime. [Obs.]

vaude′vil·list, *n.* a singer or composer of vaudevilles; also, an actor in vaudeville.

Vau·dois′ (vō-dwä′), *n.* 1. *pl.* **Vau·dois′,** a native or inhabitant of Vaud, a canton of Switzerland.
2. the dialect spoken in Vaud.

Vau·dois′ (vō-dwä′), *n.pl.* [ML. *Valdenses.*] the Waldenses.

vau·dọọ′, vau·döu′, vau·döux′ (vō-dö′), *n., a.* and *v.t.* same as *voodoo.*

vạult, *n.* [OFr. *vaulte, voulte;* from hyp. LL. *volta, voluta,* a vault, from L. *volutus,* pp. of *volvere,* to turn around, to roll; from the rounded or arched top of vaults.]

VAULTS
1. cylindrical, barrel, or wagon vault; 2. Roman vault, formed by the intersection of two equal cylinders; 3. Gothic groined vault; 4. spherical or domical vault

1. an arched roof, ceiling, or covering of masonry.
2. an arched chamber or space, especially when underground.
3. a cellar room used for storage, as of wine.
4. a burial chamber for the dead.
5. a room for the safekeeping of valuables or money, as in a bank.
6. an underground cave with a naturally arched roof.
7. the sky as a vaultlike canopy.
8. in anatomy, any arched cavity or structure; as, the cranial *vault.*
annular vault; a vaulted roof supported on circular walls.
barrel, cradle, cylindrical, tunnel, or *wagon vault;* in architecture, a semi-cylindrical vault with two parallel abutments.
coved vault; see under *coved.*

vạult, *v.t.* 1. to make a vault over; to cover with a vault.
2. to build in the form of a vault.

vạult, *v.i.* to curve like a vault.

vạult, *v.i.* [OFr. *volter, vouter,* from source of *vault* (arched roof); influenced in form by *vaulte, voulte,* etc., an arch.] to jump, leap, or spring, as over a barrier or from one position to another, especially with the help of the hands supported on the barrier, etc., or holding a long pole.

vạult, *v.t.* 1. to leap over; as, to *vault* a wall.
2. to mount (a horse, etc.) by leaping.

vạult, *n.* [Fr. *volte,* a bounding, from It. *volta,* a turn, a leap or vault, from L. *volutus,* pp. of *volvere,* to roll, to turn.]
1. a vaulting.
2. a leap or bound by a horse; a curvet.

vạult′ăġe, *n.* an arched cellar. [Obs.]

vạult′ed, *a.* 1. arched; concave; as, a *vaulted* roof.
2. covered or built with an arch or vault.
3. in botany, arched like the roof of the mouth, as the upper lip of many ringent flowers.
4. furnished with vaults or underground chambers.

vạult′ẽr, *n.* one who or that which vaults; a leaper; a tumbler.

vạult′ing, *n.* 1. the building of a vault or vaults.
2. the arched work forming a vault.
3. a vault, or vaults collectively.

vạult′ing, *n.* the art or practice of a vaulter or leaper.

vạult′ing, *a.* 1. leaping; leaping over.
2. overreaching; unduly confident; as, *vaulting* ambition.
3. used in vaulting.

vạult′ing çap′i·tăl, the capital of a vaulting shaft.

vạult′ing hợrse, in gymnastics, a padded block on legs, used for practice in vaulting.

vạult′ing house, a brothel. [Obs.]

vạult′ing pil′lăr, a vaulting shaft.

vạulting shȧft, in architecture, a pillar sometimes rising from the floor to the spring of the vault of the roof; more frequently, a short pillar attached to the wall rising from a corbel, and from the top of which the ribs of the vault spring.

vạult′ing tīle, a tile or brick used in vaulted ceilings.

vạult′y, *a.* arched; concave.

väunce, *v.i.* to advance. [Obs.]

väunt (*or* vạnt), *v.i.*; vaunted, *pt., pp.*; vaunting, *ppr.* [Fr. *vanter* (*se vanter,* lit., to speak vainly of oneself), from LL. *vanitare,* to speak vainly, boast, from L. *vanus,* vain.] to boast; to brag. [Now Rare.]

väunt, *v.t.* to boast about (something); to brag of.

väunt, *n.* a brag; ostentation from vanity; a boast.

väunt, *n.* the first part. [Obs.]

väunt′-çou″ri·ẽr, *n.* [Fr. *avant-courrier.*]
1. a soldier sent out in advance of an army. [Obs.]
2. a forerunner; precursor.

väunt′ẽr, *n.* a boaster; a braggart; a person given to vain ostentation.

väunt′fụl, *a.* boastful; vainly ostentatious. [Rare.]

väunt′ing·ly, *adv.* boastfully; with vain ostentation.

väunt′mūre, *n.* a vantmure. [Obs.]

vạunt′y, *a.* boastful; vain. [Scot.]

vauque′lin·īte (vōk′), *n.* [named after L. N. *Vauquelin,* French chemist.] a greenish monoclinic chromate of copper and lead.

vạut, *v.i.* and *n.* vault; leap. [Obs.]

väv (*or* vọv), *n.* [Heb. *vāv,* lit., a hook.] the sixth letter of the Hebrew alphabet, corresponding to English *V, v:* with diacritical marks, it often serves as a neutral vowel.

vav′ȧ·sŏr, vav′ȧ·söur, *n.* [OFr. *vavassor, vavasseur;* LL. *vavassor, vasvassor;* prob. from *vassus vassorum,* the vassal of vassals.] in the Middle Ages, a feudal vassal holding lands from a superior lord and having vassals under himself.

vav′ȧ·sō·ry, *n.* the quality or tenure of the fee held by a vavasor; also, lands held by a vavasor.

vā′wărd, *n.* the front part. [Obs.]

V′-dāy (vē′), *n.* Victory Day.

've, have: a contraction.

Vē′ȧ·där, *n.* [Heb.] the thirteenth or intercalary month added to the Jewish year about about every third year: it follows the month Adar.

vēal, *n.* [OFr. *veël, veau,* from L. *vitellus,* a little calf, dim. of *vitulus,* calf.]
1. the flesh of a calf used for food.
2. a calf, especially as intended for food. [Now Rare.]

vec'tion, *n.* [L. *vectio,* from pp. of *vehere,* to carry.] in medicine, passage of disease germs from an infected to a healthy person.

vec'tis, *n.* [L., a pole, a spike.] in obstetrics, a curved lever to assist delivery.

vec·ti·tā'tion, *n.* a carrying; the state of being carried. [Obs.]

vec'tŏr, *n.* [L., bearer, carrier, from *vectus,* pp. of *vehere,* to carry.]
1. in astronomy, an imaginary line joining the center of an attracting body, as the sun, with the center of a body revolving around it: also called *radius vector.*
2. in biology, any organism that is the carrier of a disease-producing virus, as one of the many insect hosts of microorganisms parasitic to man.
3. in mathematics, (a) a quantity, such as a force or velocity, having direction and magnitude; (b) a line representing such a quantity, drawn from its point of origin to its final position; (c) a radius vector.
vector potential; a vector quantity so distributed that some natural quantity may be deduced from it.
vector quantity; any quantity that can be entirely defined by its magnitude and direction.

vec·tō'ri·ăl, *a.* of or concerning a vector or vectors.

Ve'dȧ, *n.* [Sans., knowledge.] [*often in pl.*] the ancient sacred literature of Hinduism, consisting of four collections of psalms, chants, sacred formulas, etc., called the *Rig-Veda, Yajur-Veda, Sama-Veda,* and *Atharva-Veda.*

Ve'dȧ·iṣm, *n.* the religious doctrine and practices contained in the Vedas.

Vē·dā'li·ȧ, *n.* 1. a genus of ladybugs, native to subtropical regions and destructive to scale insects. An Australian variety, *Vedalia cardinalis,* was introduced into the United States to destroy the fluted scales, *Icerya purchasi.*
2. [v–] a member of this genus.

Ve·dän'tȧ, *n.* [Sans.] a system of Hindu monistic or pantheistic philosophy founded on the Vedas.

Ve·dän'tiç, *a.* of or pertaining to the Vedanta; founded on or derived from the Vedas.

Ve·dän'tiṣm, *n.* the philosophical doctrine of the Vedanta.

Ve·dän'tist, *n.* one versed in the Vedanta; an adherent of Vedantism.

V-E Dāy (vē'ē'), May 8, 1945, the day on which the surrender of the German forces in Europe was announced, officially ending the European phase of World War II.

Ved'dȧ, Ved'dȧh, *n.* any of the aboriginal people inhabiting the forests in the interior of Ceylon.

ve·dette', *n.* [Fr. *vedette*; It. *vedetta,* altered from *vedere,* to see, from *veletta,* sentry box, from L. *vigilia,* a watch, watching, vigil.]
1. in military usage, a mounted sentinel posted in advance of the outposts of an army.
2. in naval usage, a small scout boat, used to watch the enemy: also *vedette boat.*
Also spelled *vidette.*

Ve'diç, *a.* pertaining to or forming part of a Veda or the Vedas.

Ve'diç, *n.* the language in which the Vedas are written, an early form of Sanskrit.

ve'drō, *n.* [Russ.] a Russian liquid measure equal to 3.249 gallons.

vee, *n.* 1. the letter V, v, or anything shaped like it.
2. a five-dollar bill. [Colloq.]

vee, *a.* shaped like V.

veer, *v.i.*; veered, *pt., pp.*; veering, *ppr.* [altered, after *veer* (to let out) from Fr. *virer,* to turn around.]
1. to change direction; to shift; to turn or swing around.
2. to change sides; to shift, as from one opinion or attitude to another.
3. in meteorology, to shift; especially, to shift clockwise: said of the wind: opposed to *back.*
4. in nautical usage, (a) to change the direction of a ship by swinging its stern to the wind; to wear ship; (b) to be so turned: said of a ship.

veer, *v.t.* 1. to turn or swing; to change the course of.
2. in nautical usage, to change the direction or course of (a ship) by swinging its stern to the wind; to wear.

veer, *n.* a change of direction.

veer, *v.t.* and *v.i.* [ME. *veren*; M.D. *vieren,* to let out.] in nautical usage, to let out (a line, chain, anchor, etc.): often with *out.*
to veer and haul; in nautical usage, to pull tight and slacken alternately.

veer'ȧ·ble, *a.* shifting; changeable.

veer'ing, *n.* the act of turning or changing; a fickle or capricious change.

veer'ing, *a.* turning; changing; shifting.

veer'ing·ly, *adv.* in a veering manner; changeingly; shiftingly.

veer'y, *n.*; *pl.* **veer'ieṣ,** [prob. echoic.] a tawny thrush, *Turdus fuscescens,* native to the eastern United States: also called *Wilson's thrush.*

Vē'gȧ, *n.* [Ar. *waqi',* falling.] in astronomy, a blue-white star of the first magnitude in the northern constellation Lyra.

vē'gȧ, *n.* [Sp.] an open plain; a tract of level, fertile ground.

veġ''ē·tȧ·bil'i·ty, *n.* the state or quality of being vegetable. [Rare.]

veġ'ē·tȧ·ble, *n.* [Fr. *végétable,* from LL. *vegetabilis,* animating, hence, full of life, from L. *vegetare,* to enliven, quicken.]
1. broadly, any plant, as distinguished from animal or inorganic matter.
2. (a) specifically, any plant that is eaten whole or in part, raw or cooked, generally with an entree or in a salad but not as a dessert, as the tomato, potato, lettuce, cucumber, cabbage, etc.; (b) the edible part of such a plant, as the root of the carrot or seed of the pea.

veġ'ē·tȧ·ble, *a.* 1. of, having the nature of, made from, or produced by edible vegetables.
2. of, or having the nature of, plants in general; as, the *vegetable* kingdom.
vegetable acids; acids obtained from plants, as malic, citric, gallic, and tartaric acids.
vegetable alkali; in old chemistry, an alkaloid; also, potash.
vegetable anatomy; that branch of botany which deals with the form, disposition, and structure of the organs of plants.
vegetable brimstone; lycopode.
vegetable butter; an edible, fatty substance, solid at ordinary temperatures, yielded by some plants, as the cacao bean, coconut, nutmeg, etc.
vegetable earth; same as *vegetable mold.*
vegetable egg; (a) the eggplant; (b) the fruit of the marmalade tree.
vegetable ethiops; a charcoal made by burning common seaweed.
vegetable flannel; a fabric made from pineneedle wool.
vegetable fountain; same as *water vine.*
vegetable horsehair; the fiber of *Chamærops humilis,* the dwarf fan palm, used in upholstery.
vegetable ivory; (a) the ivorylike seed of a South American palm, used to make buttons, ornaments, etc.; ivory nut; (b) the shell of the coquilla nut.
vegetable jelly; pectin.
vegetable kingdom; the division of nature including all plant life.
vegetable leather; a shrubby West Indian plant, *Euphorbia punicea,* having leathery foliage.
vegetable marrow; (a) a large, smooth-skinned, meaty variety of squash; (b) its flesh.
vegetable mold; mold or soil consisting wholly or chiefly of humus.
vegetable naphtha; wood naphtha.
vegetable oyster; (a) a plant with a long, tapering, edible white root, grasslike leaves, and heads of purple flowers; salsify; (b) the root, used for food.
vegetable parchment; papyrin.
vegetable sheep; a woolly plant, *Raoulia eximia,* native to the mountains of New Zealand.
vegetable silk; the cottonlike fibrous material yielded by the seed coat of the fruit of *Chorisia speciosa,* a tree native to Brazil: used in pillows, etc.
vegetable sponge; the sponge gourd.
vegetable sulfur; lycopode.
vegetable tallow; see under *tallow.*
vegetable wax; a white, waxy substance found on the leaves or fruit of some plants and in the stems of others.

veġ'ē·tăl, *a.* [Fr. *végétal,* from L. *vegetus,* animated.]
1. of, or having the nature of, plants or vegetables.
2. of or having the characteristics common to both plants and animals, as absorption, nutrition, growth, etc. (as distinguished from rationality, sensibility, and volition).
3. vegetative (sense 3).

veġ'ē·tăl, *n.* a vegetable. [Rare.]

veġ·ē·tal'i·ty, *n.* the state or quality of being vegetal. [Rare.]

veġ'ē·tănt, *a.* [L. *vegetans, vegetantis,* ppr. of *vegetare.*]
1. stimulating growth and vigor; invigorating; animating.
2. of, or having the nature of, vegetation; vegetal.

veġ·ē·tār'i·ăn, *n.* a person who eats no meat, and sometimes no animal products (as milk, eggs, etc.); one who advocates a strict vegetable diet as the proper one for all people for reasons of health or because of principles opposing the killing of animals.

veġ·ē·tār'i·ăn, *a.* 1. of vegetarians or vegetarianism.
2. consisting wholly of vegetables.
3. advocating vegetarianism.

veġ·ē·tār'i·ăn·iṣm, *n.* the principles or practices of vegetarians.

veġ'ē·tāte, *v.i.*; vegetated, *pt., pp.*; vegetating, *ppr.* [from L. *vegetatus,* pp. of *vegetare,* to enliven, quicken, from *vegetus,* lively, from *vegere,* to excite, quicken, allied to *vigere,* to flourish; present meaning influenced by Eng. *vegetable.*]
1. to grow in the manner of plants.
2. to live an idle, unthinking life; to exist with little mental or physical activity.
3. in medicine, to become enlarged, as if by vegetable growth.

veġ·ē·tā'tion, *n.* [ML. *vegetatio* (*-onis*), a quickening, from L. *vegetare,* to quicken.]
1. the act or process of vegetating.
2. plant life in general.
3. dull, passive existence.
4. in medicine, any abnormal outgrowth on a part of the body.

veġ·ē·tā'tion·ăl, *a.* of or like vegetation.

veġ'ē·tā·tive, *a.* [ML. *vegetativus,* from L. *vegetatus,* pp. of *vegetare,* to quicken.]
1. (a) of vegetation, or plants; (b) of or concerned with vegetation, or plant growth.
2. growing, or capable of growing, as plants.
3. designating or of those functions or parts of plants concerned with growth and nutrition as distinguished from reproduction.
4. capable of causing growth in plants; as, *vegetative* soil.
5. involuntary or passive like the growth of plants; showing little mental activity; as, a *vegetative* existence.

veġ'ē·tā·tive·ly, *adv.* in a vegetative manner.

veġ'ē·tā·tive·ness, *n.* the state or quality of being vegetative.

vē·ġēte', *a.* vigorous; active. [Rare.]

veġ'ē·tive, *a.* vegetative.

veġ'ē·tive, *n.* a vegetable. [Obs.]

veġ''ē·tō·al'kȧ·lī, *n.* a vegetable alkali; an alkaloid.

veġ''ē·tō·an'i·măl, *a.* partaking of the nature of both vegetable and animal matter.

veġ'ē·tous, *a.* vegete. [Obs.]

vē'he·mence (vē'e-), *n.* [Fr. *véhémence*; L. *vehementia.*] the quality or state of being vehement; the quality exhibited by one who or that which is vehement, as (a) violent ardor; fervor; passion; intense feeling; as, the *vehemence* of anger, hate, etc.; (b) great force; violence; impetuosity; as, the *vehemence* of the wind.

vē'he·men·cy, *n.* same as *vehemence.*

vē'he·ment, *a.* [Fr. *véhément*; L. *vehemens* (*-entis*), eager, vehement, lit., carried out of one's mind; *vehere,* to carry, and *mens, mentis,* mind.]
1. acting or moving with great force; violent; impetuous.
2. fervent; passionate; intense, as feelings or thoughts.
3. characterized by intense feeling or passionate expression.
Syn.—impetuous, violent, furious, boisterous, passionate, fervid, ardent, fiery, glowing, burning, eager, urgent.

vē'he·ment·ly, *adv.* in a vehement manner; impetuously; ardently; passionately.

vē'hi·çle (*or* vē'i-), *n.* [L. *vehiculum,* carriage, from *vehere,* to carry.]
1. any device on wheels or runners for conveying persons or objects, as a cart, sled, automobile, etc.
2. any means of carrying, conveying, or communicating.

3. a means by which ideas are expressed or made known; as, music can be a *vehicle* for ideas.

4. in painting, a liquid, as water or oil, with which pigments are mixed for use.

5. in pharmacy, a substance, as sweet sirup, in which medicines are given.

6. in the theater, a play thought of as a means of communication or as a means of presenting a specified actor or company.

vē′hi·çled (-kld), *a.* conveyed in or imparted by means of a vehicle. [Rare.]

vē·hiç′ū·lăr, *a.* 1. of or for vehicles; as, a *vehicular* tunnel.

2. serving as a vehicle.

vē·hiç′ū·lăr·y, *a.* vehicular. [Rare.]

vē·hiç′ū·lāte, *v.t.* and *v.i.* to convey in or ride in a vehicle. [Rare.]

vē·hiç·ū·lā′tion, *n.* movement of or in vehicles; traffic. [Rare.]

vē·hiç′ū·là·tō·ry, *a.* vehicular. [Rare.]

Vęh′me (fā′), *n.* same as *Vehmgericht.*

Vęhm′gē·riçht (-rikht), *n.*; *pl.* **Vęhm′gē·riçh·te,** [G. *vehmgericht, fehmgericht*; *fehm*, criminal court, and *gericht*, law.] a system of secret tribunals which originated during the Middle Ages in Westphalia, and then spread over Germany when the regular administration of justice had fallen into complete disorder. This system provided great scope for the spirit of private revenge, malice, and interested motives, and many judicial murders were perpetrated. When the governments of the various states became more effective and society more settled, the regular executive struggled to destroy the power of the Vehmgericht, and ultimately succeeded, the last tribunal being held at Zell in 1568.

Vęh′miç, *a.* of or pertaining to the Vehme or Vehmgericht.

vęil (vāl), *n.* [OFr. *veile, voile*, veil, sail, curtain, etc., from L *velum*, a sail, covering, veil.]

1. a piece of light fabric, as of net or gauze, worn, especially by women, over the face or head or draped from a hat to conceal, protect, or enhance the face.

2. any piece of cloth used as a concealing or separating screen or curtain.

3. anything like a veil in that it covers or conceals; as, a *veil* of mist, a *veil* of silence.

4. a part of a nun's headdress, draped along the sides of the face and over the shoulders.

5. the state or life of a woman who has taken the vows of a nun or novice: used especially in *to take the veil*, to become a nun.

6. a caul. [Dial.]

7. in botany and zoology, a velum.

vęil, *v.t.*; veiled, *pt., pp.*; veiling, *ppr.* 1. to cover with or as with a veil.

2. to conceal; to hide, mask, or disguise.

vęiled, *a.* 1. wearing a veil.

2. covered with a veil.

3. concealed; hidden; disguised.

4. not openly expressing or expressed; as, a *veiled* threat.

vęil′ing, *n.* 1. the act of covering with or as with a veil.

2. a veil; a curtain.

3. thin, transparent fabric used for veils.

vęil′less, *a.* without a veil.

vęin (vān), *n.* [ME. *veine*; OFr. *veine*; L. *vena*, from base of *vehere*, to carry.]

1. any of a system of membranous canals or tubes distributed throughout the bodies of animals for the purpose of returning the impure blood from the organs and tissues to the heart. The veins like the arteries are composed of three coats.

2. any of the bundles of vascular tissue forming the framework of a leaf blade.

3. (a) a crack or fissure in a rock, filled up by substances different from the rock. When metallic, it is called by miners a *lode*; when filled with eruptive igneous material, a *dike*; (b) a deposit filling such a crack or fissure; (c) a stratum or bed of coal, etc. lying parallel with the fault of the rock.

4. a streak or marking of a different color, appearing in wood, in marble, and various stones; a long irregular streak of color.

5. a cavity, fissure, or cleft, as in the earth or other substance.

6. any distinctive quality or strain regarded as running through or being intermingled with others; a current; stream.

> Many a good poetic *vein* is buried under trade. —Locke.

7. a particular manner of speech or action; particular style, character, disposition, or cast of mind.

8. particular mood, temper, humor, or disposition for the time being.

> I am not in the giving *vein* to-day.—Shak.

9. one of the ribs, horny tubes, or nervures forming the framework of the wings of insects.

vęin, *v.t.*; veined, *pt., pp.*; veining, *ppr.* 1. to streak or mark with or as with veins.

2. to branch out through in the manner of veins.

3. to furnish with veins.

vęin′ăl, *a.* relating to veins. [Rare.]

vęined (vānd), *a.* having or showing veins or veinlike markings.

vęin′ing, *n.* 1. the act or process of forming veins.

2. a network of veins or veinlike markings.

3. in weaving, a stripe in the cloth formed by a vacancy in the warp.

vęin′less, *a.* not veined; without veins; as, a *veinless* leaf.

vęin′let, *n.* a small vein; a vein branching off from a larger vein.

vęin′ous, *a.* having veins; marked with veins.

vęin quartz, quartz of secondary origin, formed in mineral veins.

vęin′stōne, *n.* the rock or mineral material which accompanies or encloses ores in veins; gangue.

vęin′ūle, *n.* a veinlet; a venule.

vęin′y, *a.*; *comp.* veinier; *superl.* veiniest. 1. full of veins; as, *veiny* marble.

2. having or showing veins.

Vē′là, *n.* [L., a veil.] a subdivision of the constellation Argo.

vē′là, *n.* plural of *velum.*

ve·lā′men, *n.*; *pl.* **ve·lam′i·nà,** [L., a covering, from *velare*, to cover.]

1. in anatomy, a membrane or velum.

2. in botany, the corky outer layer of the aerial roots of certain orchids.

vē′lăr, *a.* [L. *velaris*, from *velum*, a veil.]

1. of a velum; especially, of the soft palate in the mouth.

2. in phonetics, pronounced with the back of the tongue touching or near the soft palate as the sound of *k* when followed by a back vowel such as *o͞o* or *o*.

vē·lăr′i·um, *n.*; *pl.* **vē·lăr′i·à,** [L.] 1. in ancient Rome, a kind of awning erected over the seats in a theater as a protection against sun or rain.

2. in zoology, the marginal membrane of a medusan.

vē′lăr·ize, *v.t.*; velarized, *pt., pp.*; velarizing, *ppr.* in phonetics, to change the pronunciation of (a sound) by bringing the back of the tongue up to or near the soft palate.

vē′lāte, *a.* [L. *velatus*, pp. of *velare*, to cover, veil.] in biology, having a velum or veil.

vē·lā′tion, *n.* 1. the act of veiling or the state of being veiled.

2. the development or formation of a velum.

veld, *n.* same as *veldt.*

veld′schōe, *n.*; *pl.* **veld′schōen,** [D.] a shoe made of rough or untanned leather, worn in South Africa.

veldt, *n.* [D. *veld.*] in South Africa, open grassy country, with few bushes and almost no trees; grassland.

vęle, *n.* a veil. [Obs.]

Vē·lel′là, *n.* [dim. of L. *velum*, veil.]

1. a genus of marine siphonophores, the best known species of which is *Velella vulgaris*, which floats on the surface of the sea, extending its vertical crest like a sail.

2. [v—] any member of this genus.

vē′liç, *a.* [L. *velum*, a sail, and *-ic.*] pertaining to a ship's sail.

vē·lif′ẽr·ous, *a.* [L. *velum, veli*, sail, and *-ferous.*]

1. bearing or carrying sails. [Obs.]

2. having a velum; velate.

vel′i·fọrm, *a.* [L. *velum*, veil, and *form.*] like a veil; resembling a velum.

vel′i·ġẽr, *n.* [LL. *veliger*, sail-bearing, from L. *velum, veli*, sail, and *gerere*, to bear.] a larval mollusk in the stage when it is provided with a velum or ciliated membrane for swimming.

vē·liġ′ẽr·ous, *a.* carrying a velum; resembling a veliger, as an embryonic mollusk.

vel·i·tā′tion, *n.* [L. *velitatio*, a skirmishing.] a dispute or contest; a skirmish. [Rare.]

vē′li·tēş, *n.pl.* [L., pl. of *veles, velitis*; akin to *velox*, swift.] in ancient Rome, lightly armed foot soldiers.

vell, *n.* [var. of *fell*, skin.] a rennet bag. [Brit. Dial.]

vell, *v.t.* to cut the turf or sward from (the land). [Brit. Dial.]

vel·lē′i·ty, *n.*; *pl.* **vel·lē′i·tieş,** [from Fr. or ML.; Fr. *velléité*; ML. *velleitas*, from *velle*, to wish.]

1. the weakest kind of desire or volition.

2. a mere wish that does not lead to the slightest action.

vel′let, *n.* velvet. [Obs.]

vel′li·çāte, *v.t.*; vellicated, *pt., pp.*; vellicating, *ppr.* [L. *vellicatus*, pp. of *vellicare*, to twitch, pinch, from *vellere*, to pluck.] to twitch; to pluck; to cause to twitch convulsively, as the muscles of an animal.

vel′li·çāte, *v.i.* to twitch; to move convulsively.

vel·li·çā′tion, *n.* 1. the act of twitching or of causing to twitch.

2. a twitching or convulsive motion of a muscle or muscles.

vel′li·çā·tive, *a.* having the power of vellicating, plucking, or twitching.

vel·lōn′ (vel-lyōn′), *n.* [Sp.] copper as used in Spanish coins.

vel′lum, *n.* [ME. *velim*; OFr. *velin*, vellum, prepared calfskin.]

1. a fine kind of parchment prepared from calfskin, lambskin, or kidskin, used as writing parchment or for binding books.

2. a manuscript written on vellum.

3. paper made to resemble vellum.

vel′lum, *a.* of or like vellum.

vel′lum·y, *a.* resembling vellum.

vē′lō, *n.* [from *velocity.*] a velocity of one foot per second: proposed as a unit for the measurement of velocity.

vē·lō′ce (-che), *adv.* [It.] in music, rapidly: a direction to the performer.

vel·ō·cim′e·tẽr, *n.* [L. *velox* (*-ocis*), swift, speedy, and *-meter.*] an apparatus for measuring velocities, especially the velocities of projectiles.

vē·loc′i·pēde, *n.* [Fr. *vélocipède*; from L. *velox* (*-ocis*), swift, speedy, and *pes, pedis*, foot.]

1. originally, any of various early bicycles or tricycles.

2. now, a child's tricycle.

3. a type of handcar for use on railroad tracks.

VELOCIPEDE

vē·loc′i·pē·dist, *n.* one who rides a velocipede.

vē·loc′i·ty, *n.*; *pl.* **vē·loc′i·tieş,** [Fr. *vélocité*, L. *velocitas* (*-atis*), from *velox* (*-ocis*), speedy, swift.]

1. quickness or rapidity of motion or action; swiftness; speed.

2. (a) rate of change of position, in relation to time; (b) rate of motion in a particular direction, as of the rotation of a sphere, in relation to time.

> The earth is rushing in its orbit round the sun at the rate of nineteen miles a second. Its surface at the equator is rotating at a *velocity* of 1,026 miles an hour.
> —Lewis Swift, F. R. A. S.

absolute velocity; see under *absolute.*

angular velocity; see under *angular.*

initial velocity; the rate of a moving body at the moment of starting, as that of a bullet leaving the barrel of a gun.

relative velocity; the rate at which a body approaches to or recedes from another body in motion, as distinguished from *absolute velocity.*

resolution of velocity; in physics, the finding of the components of a velocity represented by a straight line as the diagonal of a parallelogram, any two adjacent sides of which represent two component velocities.

uniform velocity; a rate of motion in which a body passes over equal linear units in equal units of time.

variable velocity; a rate of motion in which a body passes over unequal linear units in equal units of time.

virtual velocity; see under *virtual.*

vē·lō′ni·à, *n.* same as *valonia.*

ve·lọurs′ (-loor′), *n.*; *pl.* **ve·lọurs′** (-loor′), a fabric with a nap like velvet, made of wool, silk, linen, or cotton, and used for upholstery, draperies, hats, clothing, etc.: also spelled *velour.*

ve·lou·té′ (ve-lü-tā′), *n.* [Fr. *velouté*, velvety, soft and smooth to the palate.] a rich white sauce made from meat stock thickened with flour and butter: also *velouté sauce.*

vel·öu·tïne′, *n.* a kind of corded fabric made of fancy and merino wool.

velt′fāre, *n.* a small thrush, the fieldfare. [Obs.]

vē′lum, *n.*; *pl.* **vē′lȧ,** [L., a veil, sail.]
1. in botany, (a) the membranous covering of the sporangia of the *Isoëtes*; (b) the membranous covering of sporaphores of hymenomycetous fungi.
2. in anatomy, any of various veillike membranous partitions or coverings; specifically, the velum palati, or soft palate.
3. a membranous diaphragm serving as the chief organ of locomotion of the hydromedusans.
4. the membrane surrounding the flagellum of certain infusorians.
5. a ciliated swimming membrane of the larva of certain mollusks.

vē·lū′men, *n.*; *pl.* **vē·lū′mi·nȧ,** [L. *velumen*, a fleece.] in zoology and botany, a soft covering of short thick hairs.

ve·lūre′, *n.* [Fr. *velours*; OFr. *velous*; LL. *villosus*, shaggy, from *villus*, shaggy hair.]
1. velvet or a fabric like velvet, used for draperies, upholstery, etc.
2. a silk or plush pad used for brushing silk hats.

ve·lūre′, *v.t.*; velured, *pt., pp.*; veluring, *ppr.* to brush with a velure.

Vel·ū·tī′nȧ, *n.* [LL. *velutum*, velvet.]
1. a genus of taenioglossate gastropods inhabiting northern seas.
2. [v–] any member of this genus.

vē·lū′ti·nous, *a.* [from It. *velluto*, velvet.] in botany and zoology, having a velvety covering of short, dense, silky, upright hairs.

vel′vēr·et, *n.* a kind of velvet with a cotton back.

vel′vet (-vit), *n.* [ultimately from L. *villus*, shaggy hair.]
1. a rich fabric of silk, silk and cotton back, rayon, etc. with a soft, thick pile: *pile velvet* has the pile uncut, standing in loops; *cut velvet* has the loops cut apart.
2. anything with a surface like that of velvet.
3. a soft, furry skin on a deer's growing antlers.
4. clear profit; winnings; gain. [Slang.]
embossed velvet; velvet with a pattern in raised work.
to be or *play on velvet*; in gambling, to be playing with money won, hence, to be in easy circumstances, to be able to act without fear of consequences. [Slang.]

vel′vet, *v.i.* to imitate velvet in painting. [Rare.]

vel′vet, *v.t.* to adorn or cover with velvet; to make like velvet. [Rare.]

vel′vet, *a.* 1. made of or covered with velvet.
2. smooth and soft like velvet.
velvet ant; a spider ant.
velvet cork; cork best adapted for use by reason of its even substance.
velvet crab; a European crab, *Portunus puber*.
velvet duck or *coot*; the velvet scoter.
velvet flower; love-lies-bleeding.
velvet grass; a tall European grass, *Holcus lanatus*, so called from its pubescent stems and leaves.
velvet guards; velvet trimmings or persons wearing them. [Obs.]
velvet paper; flock paper.
velvet pile; (a) the pile of velvet, or a similar pile or nap; (b) a material, carpet, etc. having a nap like that of velvet.
velvet runner; the water rail. [Brit. Dial.]
velvet scoter; a marine duck, *Œdemia fusca*, the European black duck; also, the American white-winged scoter.
velvet sponge; see under *sponge*.

vel′vet·breast (-brest), *n.* the American merganser. [Dial.]

vel·vet·een′, *n.* 1. a cotton cloth with a short, thick pile, resembling velvet.
2. [*pl.*] clothes, especially trousers, made of velveteen.

vel′vet·ing, *n.* 1. the fine nap or shag of velvet.
2. [*pl.*] velvet goods.

vel′vet·lēaf, *n.* any one of a number of plants having silky down on their leaves, as (a) *Cissampelos pareira*, a tropical vine; (b) the Indian mallow.

vel′vet·y, *a.* 1. of the nature of velvet; like velvet in texture; having some of the characteristics of velvet.
2. smooth and soft to any of the senses; as, the *velvety* tread of a cat; *velvety* notes.
3. smooth-tasting; mellow; not harsh: said of liquors.

vē′nȧ, *n.*; *pl.* **vē′nae,** [L.] in anatomy, a vein.
vena cava inferior; a vein formed by the junction of the two common iliac veins and flowing into the right atrium of the heart.
vena cava superior; a vein formed by the union of the innominate veins, conveying the blood from the upper half of the body to the right atrium of the heart.
vena contracta; in hydraulics, the contracted part of a jet of liquid issuing from a vessel, at a short distance from the discharging orifice.

vē·nä′dȧ, *n.* [Sp. *venado*, a deer.] a very small Chilean deer, the pudu.

vē′năl, *a.* [L. *vena*, vein, and *-al*.] venous. [Rare.]

vē′năl, *a.* [L. *venalis*, salable, for sale, from *venus*, sale.]
1. that can readily be bribed or corrupted; mercenary; as, a *venal* judge.
2. capable of being obtained for a price; as, *venal* services.
3. characterized by corruption or bribery; as, a *venal* bargain.

vē·nal′i·ty, *n.*; *pl.* **vē·nal′i·ties,** the state, quality, or instance of being venal; mercenariness; willingness to be bribed or bought off, or to sell one's services to the highest bidder.

vē′năl·ly, *adv.* in a venal manner.

Vē·nan′tēs, *n.pl.* [LL., pl. of *venans* (*-antis*), ppr. of *venari*, to hunt.] a group of spiders which hunt their prey instead of catching it in a web.

vē·nat′iç, vē·nat′iç·ăl, *a.* [L. *venaticus*, of hunting, from *venatus*, hunting, the chase, from *venari*, to hunt.]
1. of or used in hunting.
2. fond of hunting.
3. living by hunting.

vē·nat′iç·ăl·ly, *adv.* in a venatic manner; by hunting.

vē·nā′tion, *n.* [L. *vena*, vein.]
1. the manner in which veins are arranged, as of leaves or insects' wings.
2. veins collectively.

vē·nā′tion, *n.* hunting. [Rare.]

ven·ȧ·tō′ri·ăl, *a.* venatic. [Rare.]

vend, *v.t.*; vended, *pt., pp.*; vending, *ppr.* [Fr. *vendre*; L. *vendere*, contr. from *venundare*, to sell, which itself stands for *venum dare*, to offer for sale; *venum*, sale, and *dare*, to give.]
1. to sell; to transfer to another person for a pecuniary equivalent; as, to *vend* meat and vegetables in market.
2. to give public expression to (opinions); to publish.

vend, *v.i* 1. to sell goods.
2. to be purchased; to find a market.

vend, *n.* 1. sale. [Brit.]
2. the total annual sales of coal from a colliery. [Brit.]

ven′dāce, *n.*; *pl.* **ven′dāce, ven′dā·ces,** [OFr. *vandoise*, dace.] a whitefish, *Coregonus vandesius*, native to England and Scotland.

Ven·dē′ăn, *a.* of the Vendée, a department of Western France, or its people.

Ven·dē′ăn, *n.* 1. a native of the Vendée.
2. a member of the royalist revolt against the French Republic that broke out in the Vendée in 1793.

vend·ee′, *n.* the person to whom a thing is sold.

Ven·dé·miaire′ (voṅ-dā-myăr′), *n.* [Fr., from *vindemia*, vintage.] the first month of the French revolutionary calendar, adopted by the First Republic in 1793. It began September 22 and ended October 21.

vend′ĕr, *n.* [Fr. *vendeur*.] a vendor.

ven·det′tȧ, *n.*; *pl.* **ven′det·tȧs,** [It.; L. *vindicta*, vengeance.] a blood feud in which the relatives of a murdered person try to kill the murderer or members of his family, as formerly in Corsica and parts of Italy.

vend·i·bil′i·ty, *n.* the state or quality of being vendible, or salable.

vend′i·ble, *a.* [L. *vendibilis*, from *vendere*, to sell.]
1. salable; that can be vended; as, *vendible* goods.
2. venal.

vend′i·ble, *n.* something to be sold or offered for sale.

vend′i·ble·ness, *n.* same as *vendibility*.

vend′i·bly, *adv.* in a vendible manner; so as to be vendible, or salable.

vend′ing mȧ·çhïne′, a coin slot machine for selling merchandise.

ven′dis, *n.* same as *vendace*.

ven′di·tāte, *v.t.* to spread out for sale, hence, to flaunt. [Obs.]

ven·di·tā′tion, *n.* a boastful display. [Obs.]

ven·di′tion (-dish′un), *n.* the act of selling; sale.

vend′ŏr, *n.* 1. one who vends, or sells.
2. a vending machine.

ven·dūe′, *n.* [OFr., a sale, from *vendu*, pp. of *vendre*, to sell.] a public auction.

ve·neer′, *v.t.*; veneered, *pt., pp.*; veneering, *ppr.* [G. *furniren*, to veneer, from Fr. *fournir*, to furnish.]
1. to cover with a thin layer of fine material; especially, to cover (wood) with wood of finer quality, as in furniture.
2. to cover (anything common or coarse) with a material having an attractive or superior surface.
3. to cement (thin layers of wood) into plywood.

ve·neer′, *n.* 1. a thin surface layer, usually of wood, laid over a base of common material.
2. any of the thin layers glued together in plywood.
3. any attractive but superficial appearance or display; as, a *veneer* of culture.

ve·neer′ing, *n.* 1. the act or art of one who veneers.
2. veneer (senses 1 and 2).

vē·nef′iç·ăl, *a.* same as *veneficial*.

ven′ē·fice, *n.* the practice of using poisons, as in sorcery. [Obs.]

ven·ē·fi′ciăl (-fish′ăl), *a.* [L. *veneficus*, poisonous, sorcerous.] acting by poisoning. [Rare.]

ven·ē·fi′cious (-fish′us), *a.* same as *veneficial*.

ven·ē·fi′cious·ly, *adv.* by means of poison. [Rare.]

ven′ē·nāte, *v.t.*; venenated, *pt., pp.*; venenating, *ppr.* to poison; to infect with poison. [Rare.]

ven′ē·nāte, *a.* poisoned. [Rare.]

ven·ē·nā′tion, *n.* [L. *venenatus*, pp. of *venenare*, to poison.] the act of poisoning; also, the condition of being poisoned.

vē·nēne′, *a.* poisonous; venomous. [Rare.]

ven·ē·nif′iç, *a.* [L. *venenum*, poison, and *facere*, to make.] yielding poison.

ven″en·ō·sal′i·vār·y, *a.* same as *Venomosalivary*.

ven′ē·nōse, *a.* poisonous. [Obs.]

ven·ē·nos′i·ty, *n.* the state or character of being poisonous. [Obs.]

ven′ē·nous, *a.* [LL. *venenosus*, poisonous.] poisonous or toxic. [Rare.]

ven·ē·punç′tūre, *n.* [from L. *vena*, vein; and *puncture*.] the surgical puncture of a vein, as with a hypodermic needle: also spelled *venipuncture*.

ven″ĕr·ȧ·bil′i·ty, *n.* the state or quality of being venerable.

ven′ĕr·ȧ·ble, *a.* [Fr., from L. *venerabilis*, to be reverenced, from *venerari*, to reverence, worship, adore.]
1. worthy of respect or reverence by reason of age and dignity, character, position, etc.
2. impressive on account of age or historic or religious associations; as, a *venerable* monument. In the Anglican Church, it is a title given to an archdeacon; in the Roman Catholic Church, it is a title given to persons who have attained the lowest of the three degrees of sanctity, the others being beatification and canonization.

ven′ĕr·ȧ·ble·ness, *n.* the state or quality of being venerable.

ven′ĕr·ȧ·bly, *adv.* in a venerable manner or so as to excite reverence.

Ven·ē·rā′cē·ȧ, *n.pl.* [L. *Venus*, *Veneris*, Venus.] a superfamily or suborder of bivalve mollusks, represented by the *Veneridæ* and other related families.

ven·ē·rā′cē·ăn, *a.* of or relating to the *Veneracea*.

ven·ē·rā′cē·ăn, *n.* any member of the *Veneracea*.

ven·ē·rā′ceous, *a.* same as *Veneracean*.

ven′ĕr·ănt, *a.* venerating; reverent. [Rare.]

ven′ĕr·āte, *v.t.*; venerated, *pt., pp.*; venerating, *ppr.* [L. *veneratus*, pp. of *venerari*, to worship, reverence.] to look upon with deep respect and reverence; to reverence; to revere; to regard as hallowed.
Syn.—honor, respect, adore, reverence, revere.

ven·ĕr·ā′tion, *n.* [L. *veneratio* (*-onis*), from *venerari*, to worship, reverence.]
1. a venerating or being venerated.
2. a feeling of deep respect and reverence.
3. an act of showing this.
4. in phrenology, the faculty of reverence or respect for what is great and good.
Syn.—reverence, awe, adoration.

ven′ĕr·ā·tive, *a.* reverent; pertaining to veneration.

ven′ẽr·ā·tŏr, *n.* [L.] one who venerates.
vē·nē′rē·ăl, *a.* [L. *venereus*, from *Venus*, *Veneris*, Venus, love.]
1. having to do with sexual love or intercourse.
2. transmitted by sexual intercourse with an infected person; as, syphilis and gonorrhea are *venereal* diseases.
3. infected with a venereal disease.
4. for the cure of such a disease; as, a *venereal* remedy.
vē·nē′rē·ăn, *a.* venereal. [Obs.]
vē·nē·rē·ol′ō·ġy, *n.* [*venereal*, and Gr. *logos*, discourse.] the study or science of venereal diseases.
vē·nē′rē·ous, *a.* [L. *venereus*.]
1. lustful; libidinous. [Obs.]
2. giving vigor for or inclination to venery; aphrodisiac; as, *venereous* drugs. [Obs.]
ven′ẽr·ẽr, *n.* a hunter.
Vē·ner′i·dae, *n.pl.* a family of lamellibranchiate mollusks, of which the Linnean genus *Venus* is the type.
ven′ẽr·ous, *a.* venereal. [Obs.]
ven′ẽr·y, *n.* [Fr. *venerie*, from OFr. *vener*, L. *venari*, to hunt.]
1. the act, art, or sport of hunting; the sports of the chase.
2. beasts of the chase; game. [Obs.]
ven′ẽr·y, *n.* [L. *Venus*, *Veneris*, Venus.] sexual intercourse; indulgence of sexual desire. [Archaic.]
vē·nē·seçt′, *v.t.* to open a vein of; to phlebotomize.
vē·nē·seçt′, *v.i.* to practice venesection or phlebotomy.
vē·nē·seç′tion, *n.* [L. *vena*, vein, and *sectio* (*-onis*), a cutting.] the opening of a vein for the purpose of letting blood; phlebotomy.
Vē·nē′tiăn (-shăn), *a.* [L. *Venetia*, Venice.] of or belonging to the city, province, or former state of Venice in northern Italy, or to its people, culture, etc.
Venetian architecture, Venetian Gothic; that style of Italian architecture developed by the Venetian architects from the twelfth to the early part of the sixteenth century. Typically, each story is provided with its own tier of columns or pilasters with their entablature, and is separated from the other stories by conspicuous friezes or belts, often in the form of balustrades broken by pedestals and ornamented by figures; the arched windows are ornamented with columns, the spandrels being often filled with figures; ornamental parapets are common; the coloring, derived from the use of marbles, mosaics, etc., is rich.
Venetian ball; an ornamental form of glass for paperweights, etc. It consists of waste pieces of filigree glass conglomerated together in a bulb of clear flint glass.
Venetian blind; a window blind made of a number of thin wooden or metal slats that can be set together at any angle to regulate the light and air passing through.
Venetian carpet; an inexpensive worsted carpet, formerly used for halls and stairs, generally arranged in stripes of different colors.
Venetian chalk; same as ***French chalk*** under *chalk*.
Venetian door; a door having long, narrow windows on the sides. [Rare.]
Venetian embroidery; embroidery on linen, or some thin fabric, in which all plain portions are cut away after the figures are done, and the parts connected by bars, or fancy stitches, so that it resembles lace.
Venetian glass; fine ornamental glass of various colors, the choicest varieties of which come from Murano, near Venice.
Venetian red; (a) a red pigment formerly made from native ferric oxides but now prepared synthetically; (b) a brownish-red color.
Venetian school; painting by artists in and near Venice in the 15th and 16th centuries, notably Giorgione, Tintoretto, Titian, and Veronese.
Venetian sumac; the European smoke tree.
Venetian white; a pigment made from carbonate of lead.
Venetian window; a window having three separate lights or apertures.
Vē·nē′tiăn (-shăn), *n.* 1. a native or inhabitant of Venice.
2. [*often* v–] (a) a Venetian blind; (b) [pl.] a tape or braid used on Venetian blinds. [Colloq.]
ven′ew, ven′ey, *n.* same as *venue*.
ve″ne·zō·lä′nō (-sō), *n.* a former coin of Venezuela.

Ven·ē·zue′lăn (-zwē′lăn *or* -zwā′lăn), *a.* of Venezuela, its people, or culture.
Ven·ē·zue′lăn, *n.* a native or inhabitant of Venezuela.
venġe, *v.t.* 1. to revenge; to punish. [Obs.]
2. to avenge; to take vengeance on behalf of (another). [Archaic.]
venġe′ȧ·ble, *a.* revengeful. [Obs.]
venġe′ȧ·bly, *adv.* revengefully. [Obs.]
venġe′ănce, *n.* [OFr. *vengeance*, from *venger*, to avenge, from L. *vindicare*, to avenge.]
1. the return of an injury for an injury, in punishment or retribution; the avenging of an injury or offense; revenge.

To me belongeth *vengeance* and recompense.
—Deut. xxxii. 35.

2. harm, mischief, or evil generally: in this sense used as an oath, curse, imprecation, etc.; as, a *vengeance* on you! [Obs.]
with a vengeance; (a) with great force or fury; (b) extremely; very; (c) excessively; to an unusual extent.
venġe′ănce·ly, *adv.* extremely; very. [Obs.]
venġe′fụl, *a.* 1. desiring revenge; seeking vengeance; vindictive.
2. arising from or showing a desire for vengeance: said of actions or feelings.
3. inflicting or serving to inflict vengeance.
venġe′fụl·ly, *adv.* in a vengeful manner.
venġe′ment, *n.* avengement. [Obs.]
ven′ġẽr, *n.* an avenger. [Chiefly Poet.]
vē′ni·ȧ·ble, *a.* venial; pardonable. [Obs.]
vē′ni·ȧ·bly, *adv.* pardonably; excusably. [Obs.]
vē′ni·ăl, *a.* [OFr., from LL. *venialis*, pardonable, from L. *venia*, grace, favor, kindness.]
1. that may be forgiven; pardonable; as, a *venial* sin: in theology, opposed to *mortal*.
2. excusable; that may be allowed to pass without censure; as, a *venial* error or fault.
3. allowed; unobjectionable. [Obs.]
venial sin; in the Roman Catholic Church, an offense against the law of God, as one committed without awareness of its seriousness or without full consent, that can be remitted by prayer or other good works and does not deprive the soul of sanctifying grace.
vē·ni·al′i·ty, *n.* the quality or fact of being venial.
vē′ni·ăl·ly, *adv.* in a venial manner; pardonably.
vē′ni·ăl·ness, *n.* veniality.
ven·i·puñç′tūre, *n.* same as *venepuncture*.
vē·nī′rē fā′ci·as (-shi-), [L., that you cause to come.] in law, a writ or precept directed to the sheriff or coroner, requiring him to summon persons to serve as jurors: also called *venire*.
vē·nī′rē·măn, *n.*; *pl.* **vē·nī′rē·men,** a person called to jury service on a writ of venire.
ven′i·ṣŏn (ven′i-zn *or Brit.* ven′zn), *n.* [ME. *veneison*; OFr. *veneisun*, *venaison*, from L. *venatio* (*-onis*), the chase, from *venatus*, pp. of *venari*, to hunt.]
1. the flesh of a game animal, used as food: now restricted to the flesh of the deer only.
2. beasts of the chase; game. [Obs.]
Vē·nī′tē, *n.* [L., come, 2d pers. pl., imperative, of *venire*, to come: from the opening word in the Latin version.]
1. the 95th Psalm in the King James Version (94th in the Vulgate), used as a canticle at matins or morning prayer.
2. music for this.
ven′ŏm, *n.* [ME. *venim*; OFr. *venim*; L. *venenum*, a poison.]
1. the poison secreted by some snakes, spiders, insects, etc., introduced into the body of the victim by bite or sting.
2. poison of any kind. [Rare.]
3. malignancy; spite; malice.
Syn.—bane, poison, virus, malice, spite, malignity, virulence.
ven′ŏm, *v.t.* and *v.i.*; venomed, *pt.*, *pp.*; venoming, *ppr.* to poison; to envenom or become envenomed. [Rare.]
ven′ŏm-mouthed (-moutht), *a.* having a mouth adapted for communicating venom, as a snake; figuratively, slanderous; malignant
ven″ō·mō·sal′i·văr·y, *a.* relating to venom and saliva; designating the salivary glands in certain animals, as snakes, that secrete venom instead of saliva.
ven′ŏm·ous, *a.* [ME. *venimous*; OFr. *venimeux*, from LL. *venenosus*, poisonous.]
1. containing or full of venom; poisonous.
2. malignant; spiteful; malicious.
3. in zoology, having a poison gland or glands; able to inflict a poisonous wound by biting or stinging.

ven′ŏm·ous·ly, *adv.* poisonously; malignantly; spitefully.
ven′ŏm·ous·ness, *n.* poisonousness; noxiousness to animal life; malignity; spitefulness.
ven′ŏm saç, one of the sacs in the head of a venomous snake, in which the venom is secreted and stored.
vē′nōse, *a.* in botany, venous.
vē·nos′i·ty, *n.* the state or quality of being venose or venous.
vē′nous, *a.* [L. *venosus*, full of veins, veiny, from *vena*, a vein.]
1. of a vein or veins.
2. in botany, having veins; veiny; full of veins: also *venose*.
3. in physiology, designating blood being carried in the veins back to the heart and lungs.
venous blood; blood that has given up oxygen and taken up carbon dioxide, and is characterized by a dark-red color.
venous congestion; same as ***hyperemia***.
venous hum; see under ***hum***.
venous pulse; a weak pulse that can be felt in some of the larger veins, as in the jugular.
venous sinus; an enlargement in a vein or venous duct, as at the junction of several smaller veins.
vē′nous·ly, *adv.* in a venous manner.
vent, *n.* sale; opportunity to sell; demand; market. [Rare.]
vent, *v.t.* to sell; to vend. [Obs.]
vent, *n.* a hostelry; an inn. [Obs.]
vent, *n.* [altered (after Fr. *vent*, a wind) from ME. *fent*, *fente*; OFr. *fente*, a cleft, rift, chink, slit, from *fendre*; L. *findere*, to cleave.]
1. the action of escaping or passing out, or the means or opportunity to do this; issue; outlet; passage; escape.
2. expression; release; as, giving *vent* to emotion.
3. a small hole or opening to permit passage or escape, as of a gas.
4. in old guns, the small hole at the breech through which a spark passes to set off the charge.
5. the crusted opening in a volcano from which gas and molten rock erupt.
6. in tailoring, a slit in a garment, especially the one at the back of a coat.
7. in zoology, the excretory opening of animals; especially, the external opening of the cloaca in birds, reptiles, amphibians, and fishes.
8. a discharge; an emission. [Obs.]
9. the coming to the surface of water for air, as a beaver. [Brit.]
vent, *v.t.* 1. to make a vent in.
2. to let out at an opening; to allow to escape through a hole.
3. to give release or expression to, as feelings.
4. to relieve or unburden by giving vent to feelings; as, he *vented* himself in an outburst of profanity.
5. to publish or utter as opinions.
vent, *v.i.* 1. to open or expand the nostrils to the air; to snuff; to snort; to scent. [Obs.]
2. to seek the surface of the water for air, as a beaver. [Brit.]
3. to have draft, as a chimney; to be ventilated.
vent, *n.* scent, as of the trail of an animal; also, the perception of such scent. [Obs.]
vent, *n.* a brand or mark on an animal showing that it has been sold. [Dial.]
ven′tȧ, *n.* [Sp.] an inn or tavern.
vent′ăġe, *n.* 1. a small hole; a vent.
2. a finger hole or vent in a flute or other musical wind instrument.
ven′tāil, *n.* [ME. *ventayle*; OFr. *ventaille*, from *vent* (L. *ventus*), a wind.] the movable piece of armor forming the lower front part of a metal helmet.
ven·ta′nȧ, *n.* [Sp.] a window.
vent′ẽr, *n.* one who vents or gives vent; especially, one who reports or publishes.
ven′tẽr, *n.* [L.] 1. in anatomy, (a) the abdomen or lower belly; (b) the protruding part of a muscle; (c) formerly, any large cavity containing viscera, as the head, thorax, and abdomen: called the *three venters*.
2. the womb; hence, in law, a mother in relation to her children.
3. in entomology, the lower part of the abdomen.
4. in botany, the enlarged basal part of an archegonium of a vascular cryptogam, in which the oösphere is developed.
vent feath′ẽr (feth′), any of the feathers of a bird that lie from the vent, or anus, to the tail underneath.

vent'hōle, *n.* a vent or opening.
ven'ti·duct, *n.* [L. *ventus*, wind, and *ductus*, leading, pp. of *ducere*, to lead.] a passage for wind or air; a ventilating pipe or duct.
ven'til, *n.* [L. *ventulus*, a slight wind, dim. of *ventus*, wind.] in certain musical wind instruments, a valve by means of which they may be made to sound the semitones and tones between the natural open harmonics.
ven'ti·lāte, *v.t.*; ventilated, *pt.*, *pp.*; ventilating, *ppr.* [L. *ventilatus*, pp. of *ventilare*, to fan, ventilate, from *ventus*, wind.]
1. to circulate fresh air in (a room, etc.), driving out foul air.
2. to circulate in (a room, etc.) so as to freshen: said of air.
3. to provide with an opening for the escape of air, gas, etc.; to furnish a means for airing.
4. to expose (a substance) to fresh air so as to keep in good condition.
5. to examine and discuss in public; to bring out into the open, as a grievance, problem, etc.
6. to aerate (blood); to oxygenate.
7. to winnow, as grain; to fan. [Obs.]
ven·ti·lā'tion, *n.* 1. the act or process of ventilating.
2. means of doing this; ventilating equipment.
3. the act of bringing out into view; public examination; open or free discussion.
4. vent; utterance.
ven'ti·lā·tive, *a.* 1 of or pertaining to ventilation.
2. serving to ventilate.
ven'ti·lā·tŏr, *n.* a thing that ventilates; especially, any opening or device used to bring in fresh air and drive out foul air.
ven'tōse, *a.* flatulent; windy. [Rare.]
ven'tōse, *n.* a cupping glass. [Obs.]
Ven·tōse' (väṅ-tōz'), *n.* [Fr., from L. *ventosus*, windy, from *ventus*, wind, so called from the usual windiness of the season.] the sixth month (February 19–March 20) of the French Revolutionary Calendar, adopted by the First Republic in 1793.
ven·tos'i·ty, *n.* 1. windiness; flatulence. [Obs.]
2. figuratively, empty pride or boasting; vainglory. [Obs.]
vent'piēce, *n.* in some breech-loading guns, a block which closes or assists in closing the rear of the bore. [Rare.]
ven'trad, *adv.* [L. *venter*, the belly, and *-ad*, to, toward.] in anatomy, to or toward the belly or ventral side of the body: opposed to *dorsad*.
ven'trăl, *a.* [L. *ventralis*, from *venter*, belly.]
1. in anatomy and zoology, of, near, on, or toward the belly or the side of the body where the belly is located; in man, anterior (or front), in most other animals, inferior (or lower): opposed to *dorsal*.
2. in botany, of or belonging to the inner or lower face.
ven'trăl, *n.* a ventral fin; one of the posterior pair of fins in fishes, corresponding to the hind limbs of higher vertebrates.
ven'trăl·ly, *adv.* in a ventral position or direction; toward the belly, or abdomen.
ven'tri·cle, *n.* [L. *ventriculus*, dim. of *venter*, belly.] in anatomy and zoology, any of various cavities or hollow organs; specifically, (a) either of the two lower chambers of the heart which receive blood from the auricles and pump it into the arteries; (b) any of the four small continuous cavities within the brain.
ventricles of the larynx; two deep depressions in the larynx between the superior and inferior ligaments.
ven'tri·cōse, *a.* [L. *venter*, belly.] 1. large-bellied; swelled out.
2. in botany and zoology, swelling out on one side.
ven·tri·cos'i·ty, *n.* a ventricose condition.
ven'tri·cous, *a.* same as *ventricose*.
ven·tric'ū·lăr, *a.* 1. of, or having the nature of, a ventricle.
2. having a bulge or belly; distended in the middle.
ven·tric'ū·līte, *n.* [L. *ventriculus*, ventricle.] any of a genus of fossil *Spongida* or sponges characteristic of the cretaceous or chalk rocks, and belonging to the *Ventriculitidæ*, a family of hexactinellid sponges.
ven·tric'ū·lōse, *a.* in botany, slightly ventricose.
ven·tric'ū·lous, *a.* [L. *ventriculus*, dim. of *venter*, belly.] same as *ventricular*.
ven·tric'ū·lus, *n.*; *pl.* **ven·tric'ū·lī,** [L.] 1. that part of the alimentary tract of an insect, analogous to the stomach, where digestion takes place.
2. the gizzard of a bird.
ven·tri·cum'bent, *a.* [L. *venter*, *ventris*, belly, and *-cumbens*, ppr. of *-cumbere*, in *incumbere*, to lie down.] lying on the belly or with the ventral side downward; prone: opposed to *dorsicumbent*.
ven"tri·lō·cū'tion, *n.* ventriloquism.
ven"tri·lō'quăl, *a.* ventriloquial.
ven·tri·lō'qui·ăl, *a.* pertaining to, belonging to, or using ventriloquism.
ven·tri·lō'qui·ăl·ly, *adv.* in a ventriloquial manner.
ven·tril'ō·quism, *n.* [from L. *ventriloquus*, lit., one who speaks from the belly, from *venter*, belly, and *loqui*, to speak; and *-ism*.] the art or practice of speaking in such a way that the voice seems to come from some source other than the speaker.
ven·tril'ō·quist, *n.* a person who practices ventriloquism; specifically, an entertainer who uses ventriloquism to carry on a pretended conversation with a large puppet, or dummy.
ven·tril·ō·quis'tic, *a.* of or pertaining to ventriloquism or ventriloquists.
ven·tril'ō·quīze, *v.t.* and *v.i.*; ventriloquized, *pt.*, *pp.*; ventriloquizing, *ppr.* to utter (words or sounds) as a ventriloquist.
ven·tril'ō·quous, *a.* same as *ventriloquial*.
ven·tril'ō·quy, *n.* same as *ventriloquism*.
ven·tri·mes'ăl, *a.* of or pertaining to the ventrimeson: also *ventromesal*.
ven·tri·mes'ŏn, *n.* the middle line on the ventral surface of the body.
ven·tri·pyr'ȧ·mid, *n.* the ventral pyramid of the medulla oblongata.
ven'trō-, [from L. *venter*, belly.] a combining form meaning: (a) *abdomen*; *belly*; (b) *ventral and*, as in *ventro*dorsal.
ven·trō·dor'săl, *a.* of or involving both the ventral and dorsal surfaces.
ven·trō·dor'săl·ly, *adv.* in a ventrodorsal manner.
ven"trō·fix·ā'tion, *n.* in surgery, the stitching of a visceral part to the abdominal wall.
ven·trō·hys'tĕr·ō·pex·y, *n.* ventrofixation of the uterus.
ven·trō·in'gui·năl (-gwi-), *a.* pertaining to the domen and the inguinal region.
ven·trō·lat'ĕr·ăl, *a.* of or pertaining to the abventral and lateral sides of the body.
ventrolateral mass or *muscle*; that portion of the primitive lateral mass of the embryo from which are developed the abdominal, thoracic, and anterior cervical muscles.
ven·trō·lat'ĕr·ăl·ly, *adv.* in a ventrolateral position or direction.
ven·trō·mes'ăl, *a.* same as *ventrimesal*.
ven·tros'i·ty, *n.* [LL. *ventrosus*, from L. *venter*, *ventris*, belly.] abdominal corpulence. [Rare.]
ven·trot'ō·my, *n.* in surgery, the opening of the abdomen by incision; laparotomy.
ven'tūre, *n.* [abbrev. of ME. *aventure* or *auenture*.]
1. a risky or dangerous undertaking; especially, a business enterprise in which there is danger of loss as well as chance for profit.
2. something on which a risk is taken, as the merchandise in a commercial enterprise or a stake in gambling.
3. chance; fortune: now only in *at a venture*, by mere chance, without consideration, at random.
ven'tūre, *v.t.*; ventured, *pt.*, *pp.*; venturing, *ppr.* 1. to expose to danger or risk; as, he *ventured* his life.
2. to expose to chance of loss, as money or merchandise.
3. to take the risk of; to brave.
4. to express at the risk of criticism, objection, denial, etc.; as, may I *venture* an opinion?
ven'tūre, *v.i.* to do or go at some risk; to dare.
ven'tūre cap'i·tăl, funds invested or available for investment at considerable risk of loss in potentially highly profitable enterprises.
ven'tūr·ĕr, *n.* 1. one who ventures or puts to hazard.
2. a prostitute. [Obs.]
ven'tūre·sŏme, *a.* 1. inclined to venture; daring.
2. venturous; risky; hazardous.
ven'tūre·sŏme·ly, *adv.* in a venturesome manner.
ven'tūre·sŏme·ness, *n.* the state or quality of being venturesome.
ven'tū·rine, *n.* same as *aventurine*.
ven·tu'rī tūbe, [after G. B. *Venturi* (1746–1822), It. physicist.] a short tube with a constricted, throatlike passage that increases the velocity and lowers the pressure of a fluid conveyed through it: used to measure the flow of a fluid or operate certain instruments, as in aircraft, to regulate the fuel mixture, etc.
ven'tūr·ous, *a.* 1. inclined to venture, or take chances; bold and enterprising; not timid.
2. involving danger or risk; risky; hazardous.
ven'tūr·ous·ly, *adv.* in a venturous manner; daringly; fearlessly.
ven'tūr·ous·ness, *n.* the state or quality of being venturous; boldness, intrepidity.
ven'ūe, *n.* [OFr. *venue*, coming, arrival, approach, from *venir*, to come.]
1. the county or locality in which a cause of action occurs or a crime is committed.
2. the county or locality in which a jury is drawn and a case tried.
3. that part of a declaration in an action that designates the county in which the trial is to occur.
4. the clause in an affidavit designating the place where it was sworn to. [Rare.]
change of venue; the change of the place of trial, as when the jury or court is likely to be prejudiced.
ven'ūe, *n.* in fencing, a match; a bout. [Obs.]
ven'ū·lȧ, *n.*; *pl.* **ven'ū·lae,** a small vein; a venule.
ven'ū·lăr, *a.* of a venule or venules.
ven'ūle, *n.* [L. *venula*, dim. of *vena*, vein.]
1. in anatomy, a small vein; a veinlet.
2. in zoology, any of the small branches of a vein in the wing of an insect.
ven'ū·lōse, ven'ū·lous, *a.* full of venules.
Vē'nus, *n.* [L.] 1. in Roman mythology, an ancient Italian goddess of spring, bloom, and beauty, later identified with the Greek Aphrodite as goddess of love.
2. a statue or image of Venus.
3. a very beautiful woman.
4. the most brilliant planet in the solar system, second in distance from the sun, anciently or poetically called Lucifer as the morning star and Hesperus as the evening star: diameter, 7,600 miles; year, 225 days; symbol, ♀.
5. in alchemy, copper.
6. in conchology, (a) the type genus of the family *Veneridæ*; (b) [v–] any shell of this genus.
7. in heraldry, the color green; vert.
Vē'nus·bĕrg (*or* G. vā'nus-berkh), *n.* [G., Venus mountain.] in medieval legend, a mountain in Germany between Eisenach and Gotha, where it was believed Venus held court in a cavern, enticing travelers who became loath to leave: in Wagner's opera *Tannhäuser*, the knight Tannhäuser struggles to free himself from her spell.
Vē'nus of Mī'lō (or **Mē'los**), a famous marble statue of Venus found on the island of Melos in 1820 and later placed in the Louvre in Paris.

VENUS OF MILO

Vē'nus'ṣ-bas"ket, *n.* same as *Venus's-flower-basket*.
Vē'nus'ṣ-bȧth, Vē'nus'ṣ-bā'sin (bās'n), *n.* the teazel plant: so called because its leaves collect and hold water.
Vē'nus'ṣ-cōmb (-kōm), *n.* 1. an annual plant, *Scandix pecten-veneris*, of the parsley family: so called because its clusters of fruit resemble a comb: also called *lady's-comb*, *shepherd's-needle*.
2. a snail, *Murex tenuispinatus*, found in the Indian Ocean and having many slender spines.
Vē'nus'ṣ-ēar, *n.* the abalone.
Vē'nus'ṣ-fan, *n.* a sea fan of Florida and the West Indies.
Vē'nus'ṣ-flow'ĕr-bas'ket, *n.* a glass sponge of the genus *Euplectella*.
Vē'nus'ṣ-flȳ'trap, *n.* a white-flowered plant of the North and South Carolina swamps, having leaves with two hinged blades which close upon insects.
Vē'nus'ṣ-gīr"dle, *n.* a ctenophorous, bandlike animal, *Cestum veneris*, found in warm seas.
Vē'nus'ṣ-gōld'en-ap'ple, *n.* a small East Indian rutaceous shrub, *Atalantia monophylla*, bearing a small, round, yellow fruit.
Vē'nus'ṣ-hāir, *n.* a maidenhair fern, *Adiantum capillus-veneris*.
Vē'nus'ṣ-hāir'stōneṣ, *n.* quartz crystals enclosing needlelike crystals of rutile.

Vē′nus'ṣ-look′ing-glȧss, *n.* any plant of the genus *Specularia.*
Vē′nus'ṣ-nā″vel·wŏrt, *n.* same as *navelwort* (sense 2).
Vē′nus'ṣ-nee′dle, *n.* same as *Venus's-comb* (sense 1).
Vē′nus'ṣ-prīde, *n.* the bluet.
Vē′nus'ṣ-pūrse, *n.* same as *Venus's-flower-basket.*
Vē′nus'ṣ-shell, *n.* 1. a veneroid bivalve mollusk; a venus.
2. a cowry.
3. Venus's-comb.
4. Venus's-slipper.
Vē′nus'ṣ-slip″pẽr, *n.* 1. any plant of the genus *Cypripedium.*
2. a heteropod of the genus *Carinaria.*
Vē′nus'ṣ-sū′maç (-shū′), *n.* same as *smoke tree.*
vē·nust′, *a.* beautiful. [Obs.]
ver′ȧ, *a.* and *adv.* very. [Scot.]
vē·rā′cious, *a.* [L. *verax* (*-acis*), speaking truly, from *verus,* true.]
1. habitually truthful; honest.
2. true; accurate.
vē·rā′cious·ly, *adv.* truthfully.
vē·rac′i·ty, *n.*; *pl.* **vē·rac′i·tieṣ,** [LL. *veracitas,* truthfulness, from L. *verus,* true.]
1. habitual truthfulness; honesty.
2. accuracy of statement; accordance with truth.
3. accuracy or precision, as of perception, measurement, etc.
4. that which is true; truth.
vē·ran′dȧ, vē·ran′dȧh, *n.* [Port. *varanda,* a balcony, of Hindu origin.] a kind of open portico or porch, usually roofed, extending along the outside of a building; a porch; a piazza.
ver·ȧ·tral′bine, *n.* an alkaloid derived from the plant *Veratrum album.*
ver′ȧ·trāte, *n.* a salt or ester of veratric acid.
vē·rā′tri·ȧ, *n.* veratrine.
vē·rat′riç, *a.* [from L. *veratrum,* hellebore; and *-ic.*] designating or of a white, crystalline acid, $(CH_3O)_2C_6H_3 \cdot COOH$, found in sabadilla seeds and also produced synthetically.
vē·rat′ri·dīne, vē·rat′ri·din, *n.* an amorphous alkaloid, $C_{36}H_{51}O_{11}N$, found in sabadilla seeds.
ver·ȧ·trī′nȧ, ver′ȧ·trin, *n.* veratrine.
ver′ȧ·trīne, *n.* [Fr. *vératrine,* from L. *veratrum,* hellebore.]
1. a mixture of alkaloids obtained from sabadilla seeds and used in treating neuralgia, arthritis, etc.
2. veratridine.
ver′ȧ·trīze, *v.t.*; veratrized, *pt., pp.*; veratrizing, *ppr.* to treat with veratrine.
ver′ȧ·trōl, *n.* an antipyretic oily compound, $C_8H_{10}O_2$, obtained from veratric acid.
Vē·rā′trum, *n.* [L., hellebore.] a genus of plants of the lily family, having poisonous rootstocks. *Veratrum album* and *Veratrum viride,* the hellebores, are used in medicine.
vẽrb, *n.* [Fr. *verbe,* from L. *verbum,* a word.]
1. in grammar, (a) any of a class of words expressing action, existence, or occurrence; as, *take, be,* and *appear* are *verbs*; (b) any phrase or construction used as a verb.
2. a word. [Obs.]
vẽr′băl, *a.* [Fr., from LL. *verbalis,* belonging to a word, from *verbum,* a word.]
1. of, by means of, or pertaining to words; as, a *verbal* dispute.
2. spoken; oral rather than written; as, *verbal* testimony.
3. literal; word for word; as, a *verbal* translation.
4. attending to words only as distinguished from facts or ideas.

Neglect the rules each *verbal* critic lays.
—Pope.

5. in grammar, (a) of, having the nature of, or derived from a verb; as, a *verbal* noun; (b) used to form verbs; as, *-ate* is a *verbal* suffix.
6. verbose. [Obs.]
verbal amnesia; a kind of aphasia in which the knowledge of the connection between words and objects is lost.
verbal inspiration; see under *inspiration.*
verbal note; in diplomacy, an unsigned memorandum or note when an affair has continued for a long time without any reply. It is designed to show that the matter is not urgent, but that at the same time it has not been overlooked.
verbal noun; in grammar, a noun derived from a verb and acting in some respects like a verb: in English it is either a noun ending in *-ing* (a gerund) or an infinitive; as, *walking* is healthful, *to err* is human.
Syn.—oral, vocal, literal.
vẽr′băl, *n.* a verbal noun or other word derived from a verb: in English, gerunds, infinitives, and participles are verbals.
vẽr′băl·iṣm, *n.* 1. a verbal expression; expression in words; a word or phrase.
2. words only, without any real meaning; mere verbiage.
3. any virtually meaningless phrase or form of words.
vẽr′băl·ist, *n.* 1. a person who is skilled in verbal expression; one who uses words well.
2. a person who fixes his attention or emphasis on mere words, rather than on facts or ideas.
vẽr·bal′i·ty, *n.* the state or quality of being verbal; bare literal expression. [Rare.]
vẽr″băl·i·zā′tion, *n.* the act of verbalizing; the state of being verbalized.
vẽr′băl·īze, *v.t.*; verbalized, *pt., pp.*; verbalizing, *ppr.* 1. to convert into a verb; to form a verb of.
2. to express in words.
vẽr′băl·īze, *v.i.* to be verbose or diffuse; to use many words.
vẽr′băl·ly, *adv.* 1. word for word.
2. in or with words only, often without real meaning or understanding.
3. in words; in writing or speech.
4. in spoken words; orally.
vẽr·bār′i·ăn, *a.* relating to words; verbal. [Rare.]
vẽr·bār′i·ăn, *n.* a word coiner; a verbalist. [Rare.]
vẽr·bār′i·um, *n.* [L. *verbum,* a word.] a game the object of which is the formation of words, either of the greatest possible number of words from the letters of a given one, or of one word from its own letters entangled in some way.
Vẽr·bas′çum, *n.* [L., mullen.] a large genus of tall, erect, tomentose, or woolly, usually biennial, plants of the family *Scrophulariaceæ,* characterized by its five perfect stamens. There are more than 100 species native to the Old World.
vẽr·bā′tim, *adv.* [LL., from L. *verbum,* a word.]
1. word for word; in the same words; as, to tell a story *verbatim* as another has related it.
2. by word of mouth; orally. [Obs.]
verbatim et literatim; word for word, and letter for letter; precisely as written or printed.
vẽr·bā′tim, *a.* following the original word for word; as, a *verbatim* account.
Vẽr·bē′nȧ, *n.* [L. *verbena,* foliage.]
1. a genus of plants of the family *Verbenaceæ.*
2. [v–] any of a number of plants of this genus with spikes or clusters of red, white, or purplish flowers.

VERBENAS

Vẽr·be·nā′cē·ae, *n.pl.* a family of gamopetalous herbs, shrubs, and trees, most of which are tropical.
vẽr·bē·nā′ceous, *a.* in botany, of the verbena family, a group of plants with opposite leaves and usually irregular flowers, including the verbena, vervain, lantana, and some trees, as the teak.
vẽr·bē′nȧ oil, an oil obtained from the lemon verbena. It is used in perfumery.
vẽr′bē·nāte, *v.t.*; verbenated, *pt., pp.*; verbenating, *ppr.* in ancient Rome, to strew or sanctify with sacred boughs, as in public rites.
vẽr′bēne, *n.* any verbenaceous plant.
vẽr′bẽr·āte, *v.t.* to beat; to strike. [Rare.]
vẽr·bẽr·ā′tion, *n.* 1. a beating or striking; a blow; a percussion. [Rare.]
2. the impulse of a body which causes sound. [Rare.]
Vẽr·bē·sī′nȧ, *n.* [LL., prob. from *verbena,* from a resemblance in the leaves of certain species.] a genus of plants of the aster family, mostly native to tropical America; the crown beards.
vẽr′bi·ăġe, *n.* [Fr.] verbosity; wordiness; use of many words without necessity; superabundance of words.
vẽr′bi·cīde, *n.* [L. *verbum,* a word, and *cædere,* to kill.] the perverting of the meaning of a word; punning; also, one who commits verbicide: used humorously.
vẽr′bid, *n.* in grammar, a gerund, infinitive, or participle that functions in part as a verb, as in taking an object (*watching* television can be tiring).
vẽrb′i·fy, *v.t.*; verbified, *pt., pp.*; verbifying, *ppr.* to verbalize; to change (a noun, etc.) into a verb.
vẽr″biġ·ẽr·ā′tion, *n.* the repetition of meaningless words and sentences.
vẽr·bōse′, *a.* [L. *verbosus,* full of words, from *verbum,* a word.] abounding in words; using or containing more words than are necessary; prolix; long-winded; wordy; as, a *verbose* speaker; a *verbose* argument.
vẽr·bōse′ly, *adv.* in a verbose manner.
vẽr·bōse′ness, *n.* verbosity.
vẽr·bos′i·ty, *n.* [Fr. *verbosité*; LL. *verbositas.*] the state or quality of being verbose; wordiness; prolixity.
ver·bō′ten (fer-), *a.* [G]. forbidden.
vẽr′bum sat sa·pi·en′ti (**est**), [L.] a word to the wise (is) enough.
vẽrd, *n.* [OFr.] 1. greenness; green color; freshness. [Obs.]
2. in English forest law, vert. [Obs.]
vẽr′dăn·cy, *n.* 1. the state or quality of being verdant; greenness.
2. rawness; inexperience; immaturity; as, the *verdancy* of youth.
vẽr′dănt, *a.* [prob. from *verdure* and *-ant.*]
1. green.
2. green with growing things; covered with green vegetation.
3. inexperienced; immature; innocent; as, *verdant* youth.
vẽrd an·tīque′ (-tēk′), [OFr., from *verd,* green, and *antique,* ancient.]
1. a green mottled or veined marble, used for interior decoration.
2. any of various green porphyritic rocks.
3. a green surface formed on bronze or brass by long exposure; patina; verdigris.
vẽr′dănt·ly, *adv.* in a verdant manner.
ver·dẹ′ȧ, *n.* [It.] 1. an Italian white grape used in making wine.
2. the wine made from this grape.
vẽr′dẽr·ẽr, *n.* [OFr. *verdier,* from *verd, vert*; L. *viridis,* green.] in medieval England, a judicial officer in the royal forests, appointed to take care of the vert, that is, the trees and underwood of the forest, and to keep the assizes, view, receive, and enroll attachments and presentments of all manner of trespasses.
vẽr′dẽr·ŏr, *n.* a verderer.
vẽr′diçt, *n.* [ME, *verdit*; OFr. *veirdit,* a verdict, from ML. *veredictum,* a true saying, verdict, from L. *vere dictum,* truly said.]
1. in law, the answer of a jury given to the court concerning any matter of fact in any cause, civil or criminal, committed to their trial and examination. In criminal causes, the usual verdict is "guilty" or "not guilty."
2. decision; judgment; opinion pronounced; as, to be condemned by the *verdict* of the public.
Syn.—finding, judgment, answer, opinion, decision, sentence.
vẽr′di·gris (*or* -gris), *n.* [ME. *verte grece*; OFr. *verd de Grece*; *verd,* green, *de,* of, and *Grece,* Greece.]
1. a green or greenish-blue poisonous compound prepared by treating copper with acetic acid, used as a medicine, pigment, and dye.
2. a green or greenish-blue coating that forms like rust on brass, bronze, or copper.
distilled verdigris; a copper acetate resulting from the dissolution of verdigris in hot acetic acid and the crystallization of the salt out of the cooled solution.
vẽr′di·gris, *v.t.*; verdigrised (-grēst), *pt., pp.*; verdigrising, *ppr.* to cause to be coated with verdigris; to cover or coat with verdigris. [Rare.]
vẽr′di·gris green, a bluish shade of green resembling verdigris.
vẽr′din, *n.* [Fr.] the yellow-headed titmouse, or goldtit, *Auriparus flaviceps,* found in the southwestern part of the United States.
vẽr′di·tẽr, *n.* [OFr. *verd de terre,* lit., green of the earth, earth green.] either of two basic copper carbonate pigments, the one (*blue verditer*) usually consisting of ground azurite, the other (*green verditer*) usually of ground malachite; bice.
vẽr′doy, *a.* [OFr. *verdoyer,* to be green or verdant.] in heraldry, charged with flowers, leaves, or other vegetable charges; as, a border *verdoy* of trefoils, cinquefoils, etc.
vẽr′dūre, *n.* [OFr., from *verd* (L. *viridis*), green.]
1. the fresh green color of growing things; greenness.

2. green growing plants and trees; green vegetation.
3. vigorous or flourishing condition.
4. decorative tapestry chiefly representing foliage and landscapes.

vẽr′dūred, *a.* covered or ornamented with verdure.

vẽr′dūre·less, *a.* without verdure; sterile.

vẽr′dūr·ous, *a.* 1. flourishing and richly green: said of vegetation.
2. covered with or consisting of verdure, or rich green vegetation.
3. of or characteristic of verdure.

ver′ē·çund, *a.* [L. *verecundus.*] bashful; modest. [Rare.]

ver·ē·çun′di·ty, *n.* the state or quality of being verecund; bashfulness; modesty. [Rare.]

Ver·eīn′ (fer-), *n.* [G.] a club, society, union, association, or social circle with a common interest; an organization, particularly one of Germans.

Ver·e·til′lum, *n.* [LL., dim. of L. *veretrum*, the penis.] the type genus of the *Veretillidæ*, a family of club-shaped pennatuloid polyps.

vẽrġe, *n.* [ME.; OFr., a rod, wand, stick, yard, hoop; L. *virga*, a twig, rod, wand; the semantic flow is from sense 5 through 6, 2, and 1.]
1. the edge, brink, or margin (*of* something); as, the *verge of* the forest: also used figuratively; as, on the *verge of* hysteria.
2. (a) an enclosing line or border; a boundary, especially of something more or less circular; (b) the area so enclosed.
3. the shaft of a column.
4. the edge of the tiling that projects over a gable.
5. a rod or staff symbolic of an office, as that carried before a church official in processions.
6. in English feudal law, (a) a rod held in the hand by a feudal tenant as he swore fealty to his lord; (b) the area over which an official had special jurisdiction, as the land surrounding the royal palace, under the jurisdiction of the king's marshal.
7. in watchmaking, the spindle of a balance wheel in a clock with a vertical escapement.
8. a yardland; a virgate. [Obs.]
9. an accent mark. [Obs.]
10. in a stocking frame, a metal piece which regulates the position of the needles.
11. in anatomy and zoology, the penis, as of an invertebrate.
12. in horticulture, the grass edging of a bed or border; a slip of grass dividing the walks from the borders in a garden.

vẽrġe, *v.i.*; verged, *pt., pp.*; verging, *ppr.* to be on the verge, edge, brink, or border (usually with *on* or *upon*); as, streets *verging on* the slum area: also used figuratively; as, such talk *verges on* the ridiculous.

vẽrġe, *v.i.* [L. *vergere*, to bend, turn.]
1. to tend; incline (with *to* or *toward*).
2. to be in the process of change or transition into something else; to come close to in gradation; to approach (with *into* or *on*); as, broad humor *verging on* slapstick.

vẽrġe′bōard, *n.* a bargeboard.

vẽr′ġen·cy, *n.* 1. the act of verging, tending, or inclining; approach. [Rare.]
2. in optics, the reciprocal of the focal distance of a lens, a measure of the divergence or convergence of a pencil of rays. [Rare.]

vẽr′ġẽr, *n.* 1. an inclosure; a garden or orchard. [Obs.]
2. one who carries a verge, especially (a) an officer who carries the verge, or staff of office, before a bishop, dean, canon, etc. in a procession; (b) the official who takes care of the interior of a church; (c) [Obs.] one in charge of procedure; a master of ceremonies.

Vẽr·ġil′i·ăn, *a.* Virgilian.

vē·rid′i·căl, *a.* [from L. *veridicus*, speaking the truth.] truth-telling; veracious.

vē·rid·i·căl′i·ty, *n.* [*veridical* and *-ity.*] the condition or quality of being veridical.

ver′i·est, *a.* [superl. of *very, a.*] utmost; greatest; as, the *veriest* nonsense.

ver′i·fī·ȧ·ble, *a.* capable of being verified; that can be proved or confirmed by examination or investigation.

ver″i·fi·çā′tion, *n.* [OFr. *verificacion.*]
1. a verifying or being verified.
2. the establishment or confirmation of the truth of a fact, theory, etc.
3. in law, a statement at the end of a pleading to the effect that the pleader is ready to prove his allegations.

ver′i·fi·çā·tive, *a.* [ML. *verificatus.*] serving or tending to verify; verifying.

ver′i·fī·ẽr, *n.* one who or that which verifies.

ver′i·fȳ, *v.t.*; verified, *pt., pp.*; verifying, *ppr.* [OFr. *verifier*, from ML. *verificare*, to make true, from L. *verus*, true, and *facere*, to make.]
1. to prove to be true by demonstration, evidence, or testimony; to confirm; to establish the proof of.
2. to fulfill, as a promise; to confirm the truth of, as a prediction: usually in passive.
3. to test or check the accuracy or correctness of, as by investigation, comparison with a standard, or reference to the facts.
4. to confirm or establish the authenticity of, as a title or power, by examination or competent evidence.
5. to maintain; to affirm. [Obs.]
6. to second or strengthen by aid; to back; to support the credit of. [Obs.]
7. to make to appear as true. [Obs.]
8. in law, (a) to affirm formally or upon oath; (b) to add a verification to (a pleading).

Syn.—establish, confirm, fulfill, authenticate, substantiate, identify, realize, test, warrant, demonstrate.

vē·ril′ō·quent, *a.* speaking truth; truthful. [Obs.]

ver′i·ly, *adv.* in truth; in very truth or deed; in fact; certainly; really; truly. [Archaic.]

ver′in, *n.* [contr. of *veratrine.*] a derivative of veratrine.

ver·i·sim′i·lăr, *a.* [L. *verisimilis*; *verus*, true, and *similis*, like.] seeming to be true or real; having the appearance of truth; probable; likely.

ver″i·si·mil′i·tūde, *n.* [L. *verisimilitudo*, from *verisimilis*; see *verisimilar.*]
1. the appearance of being true or real.
2. something that has the mere appearance of being true or real.

ver″i·si·mil′i·ty, *n.* verisimilitude. [Obs.]

ver·i·sim′i·lous, *a.* verisimilar. [Obs.]

vẽr′iṣm, *n.* [from L. *verus*, true; and *-ism.*] the theory that art and literature should adhere closely to reality, even in representing the ugly and distasteful aspects of life.

ver′i·tȧ·ble, *a.* [Fr.] 1. true; agreeable to fact; genuine; real; authentic; actual.
2. truthful. [Obs.]
3. having all the distinctive qualities of the person or thing specified; as, he is a *veritable* tyrant.

ver′i·tȧ·bly, *adv.* 1. truly; really; actually.
2. in a veritable manner.

Ver′i·tas, *n.* [Fr. *vêritas*, from L. *veritas*, truth, from *verus*, true.] same as *Bureau Veritas* under *bureau.*

ver′i·tiṣm, *n.* verism.

ver′i·tist, *n.* one who advocates or practices veritism, or verism.

ver′i·ty, *n.*; *pl.* **ver′i·tieṣ,** [Fr. *vérité*, from L. *veritas*, truth, from *verus*, true.]
1. truthfulness; conformity of a statement, proposition, or other thing to truth or fact; the quality of being real or actual.
2. a true assertion or tenet; a principle, belief, etc. taken to be fundamentally and permanently true; a truth or fact; a reality.
3. moral truth; honesty. [Obs.]

vẽr′jūice (-jūs), *n.* 1. an acid, sour juice of green or unripe fruit, as crab apples, grapes, etc., formerly used for culinary and other purposes.
2. sourness or acidity of temper, manner, or expression.

vẽr mȧ·çaque′ (-kak′), [Cayenne.] a larva, the torcel.

vẽr′meil (-mil), *n.* [ME. *vermayle*; OFr.; L. *vermiculus*, dim. of *vermis*, a worm.]
1. (a) vermilion; (b) the bright-red color of vermilion. [Obs. or Poetic.]
2. gilded copper, bronze, or silver.
3. in gilding, a liquid containing gamboge, dragon's blood, vermilion, etc., used to give a luster to a gilded surface.
4. a crimson-red to orange-red garnet.

vẽr′meil, *a.* vermilion.

vẽr·mē·ol′ō·ġist, *n.* a helminthologist. [Rare.]

vẽr·mē·ol′ō·ġy, *n.* helminthology. [Rare.]

Vẽr′mēṣ, *n.pl.* [L. *vermis*, a worm.] a former division of invertebrates, the worms: the classification is no longer used.

vẽr′mē·tid, *n.* a gastropod of the *Vermetidæ.*

Vẽr·met′i·dae, *n.pl.* a family of *Mollusca* of which *Vermetus* is the typical genus: the shell has the whorls at the apex close together and regular, but the lower ones disconnected, and more or less contorted.

Vẽr·mē′tus, *n.* [L. *vermis*, a worm.]
1. the typical genus of the *Vermetidæ*; the worm shells.
2. [v—] a member of this genus.

vẽr′mi-, [from L. *vermis*, a worm.] a combining form meaning *worm*, as in *vermicide.*

vẽr′mi·ăn, *a.* pertaining to the *Vermes*; like a worm.

vẽr·mi·cel′li (*or* -chel′), *n.* [It., lit., little worms, from L. *vermiculus*, dim. of *vermis*, a worm.] long, slender rolls or threads of dried paste made from a certain kind of wheat flour: so named from its wormlike appearance. It is thinner than spaghetti.

vẽr·mi′ceous (-mish′us), *a.* pertaining to worms; wormy. [Rare.]

vẽr′mi·cīde, *n.* [*vermi-* and *-cide.*] in medicine, a drug used to kill worms, especially intestinal worms; a worm killer.

vẽr·mi′cious, *a.* vermiceous. [Rare.]

vẽr′mi·çle, *n.* a vermicule. [Rare.]

vẽr·miç′ū·lăr, *a.* [L. *vermiculus*, dim. of *vermis*, a worm.]
1. shaped like a worm.
2. moving like a worm.
3. having wavy or winding marks or outlines, like worms or worm tracks.
4. made, done, or caused by worms; worm-eaten.

vẽr·miç′ū·lāte, *v.t.*; vermiculated, *pt., pp.*; vermiculating, *ppr.* [L. *vermiculatus*, pp. of *vermiculari*, to be full of worms, worm-eaten, wormy.]
1. to make worm-eaten.
2. to form, as by inlaying, with wavy or winding lines or marks like worm tracks.

vẽr·miç′ū·lāte, *v.i.* to be eaten by worms.

vẽr·miç′ū·lāte, *a.* 1. like a worm in shape or appearance.
2. having wavy or winding markings like worms or worm tracks.
3. moving like a worm; twisting or wriggling.
4. insinuating; sinuous.
5. worm-eaten; wormy.

vẽr·miç′ū·lāt·ed, *a.* vermiculate.

vermiculated work; (a) a sort of ornamental work consisting of frets or knots in mosaic pavements, winding and resembling the tracks of worms; (b) a species of rusticated masonry having the appearance of being worm-eaten, or formed by the tracks of worms.

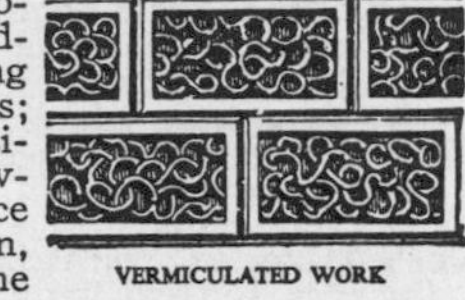

VERMICULATED WORK

vẽr·miç·ū·lā′tion, *n.* [L. *vermiculatio (-onis)*, a being worm-eaten, from *vermiculari*, to be worm-eaten.]
1. the act or operation of moving in the manner of a worm; continuation of motion from one part to another; especially, the peristaltic motion of the intestines.
2. decoration by vermicular work.
3. vermicular markings, as on certain birds.
4. the furrows or channels cut by worms; the state or condition of being vermiculate, or worm-eaten.

vẽr′mi·çūle, *n.* [L. *vermiculus*, dim. of *vermis*, a worm.] a little worm or grub.

vẽr·miç′ū·līte, *n.* [L. *vermiculus*, a little worm, and *-ite.*] any of a number of hydrous silicates resulting usually from alterations of mica and occurring in tiny leafy scales: when heated it breaks up with a vermicular motion, as if it were a mass of worms.

vẽr·miç′ū·lōse, *a.* [LL. *vermiculosus*, from *vermiculus*, dim. of *vermis*, a worm.] full of worms or grubs; resembling worms. [Rare.]

vẽr·miç′ū·lous, *a.* vermiculose. [Rare.]

vẽr·miç′ū·lus, *n.*; *pl.* **vẽr·miç′ū·lī,** [L.] a vermicule. [Obs.]

vẽr′mi·fọrm, *a.* [*vermi-* and *-form.*] having the form or shape of a worm; as, the *vermiform* process of the cerebellum.

vermiform appendix or *appendage*; see under *appendix.*

vermiform process; in anatomy, (a) the median lobe of the cerebellum, or either surface of this lobe; (b) the vermiform appendix.

Vẽr·mi·fọr′mi·ȧ, *n.pl.* a group of polyzoans of which *Phoronis* is the type.

vẽr·mif′ū·găl, *a.* tending to prevent, destroy, or expel worms.

vẽr′mi·fūġe, *a.* [L. *vermis*, a worm, and *fugare*, to expel.] serving to expel worms and other parasites from the intestinal tract.

vẽr′mi·fūġe, *n.* a vermifuge drug.

vẽr·mĭgl′iȧ (-mēl′yȧ), *n.* [It. *vermiglio*, red.] a Californian rock cod brightly colored with red, gold, green, and pink and their intermixtures.

vẽr′mi·grāde, *a.* wriggling; having a motion like a worm.

vẽr′mil, *n.* vermeil. [Obs.]

Vẽr·mi·liñ′gueṣ (-gwēz), *n.pl.* same as *Vermilinguia.*

Vẽr·mi·liñ′gui·ȧ (-gwi-ȧ), *n.pl.* [L. *vermis*, worm, and *lingua*, tongue.]

1. a division of toothless mammals having an extensile tongue flexible and wormlike, as the anteater.

2. a division of lizards having an extensile tongue: also called *Rhiptoglossa.*

vẽr·mil′iŏn (-yun), *n.* [OFr. *vermillon*, from *vermeil*, bright-red; from L. *vermiculus*, double dim. of *vermis*, worm.]

1. bright-red mercuric sulfide, used as a pigment.

2. any of several other red earths resembling this.

3. bright yellowish red.

4. cochineal. [Obs.]

vẽr·mil′iŏn, *a.* of the color of vermilion; scarlet; brilliantly red.

vermilion flycatcher; a bird of the genus *Pyrocephalus*, native to New Mexico and the surrounding regions, the male being characterized by a vermilion crest and under parts.

vẽr·mil′iŏn, *v.t.* to dye red or vermilion; to cover with a brilliant red.

vẽr′mi·ly, *n.* vermeil. [Obs.]

vẽr′min, *n.*; *pl.* **vẽr′min,** [ME. and OFr. *vermine*, from L. *vermis*, worm.]

1. any of a number of small animals with filthy, destructive, troublesome habits, as flies, lice, bedbugs, mice, rats, and weasels.

2. any bird or animal that kills game. [Brit.]

3. (a) a person who is vile, worthless, or objectionable; (b) such persons collectively.

vẽr′mi·nāte, *v.i.*; verminated, *pt., pp.*; verminating, *ppr.* to breed vermin; to become infested with vermin, as lice or other parasites.

vẽr·mi·nā′tion, *n.* [L. *verminatio.*]

1. the fact or condition of being infested with vermin or worms.

2. in zoology, rapid growth and breeding of vermin under favorable conditions.

vẽr·min·if′ẽr·ous, *a.* breeding, or bearing, vermin.

vẽr′min·ly, *a.* like vermin; of the nature of vermin. [Rare.]

vẽr′min·ous, *a.* [L. *verminosus.*]

1. of, having the nature of, or resembling vermin.

2. infested with vermin.

3. caused or produced by vermin.

vẽr·mip′ȧ·rous, *a.* [L. *vermis*, worm, and *parere*, to bear.] producing young in the form of worms; as, *vermiparous* animals.

vẽr·miv′ō·rous, *a.* [L. *vermis*, worm, and *vorare*, to devour.] devouring worms; feeding on worms; as, *vermivorous* birds.

Vẽr·mont′ẽr, *n.* a native or inhabitant of Vermont.

vẽr′mor·el sprāy′ẽr, a device used to spray trees and vines to destroy insects, larvae, etc.

vẽr·mouth′ (*or* vẽr′mụth), *n.* [G. *wermuth*, wormwood.] a fortified white wine flavored with wormwood and other aromatic herbs: it may be sweet or dry, and is used chiefly in cocktails: also written *vermuth.*

vẽr′nȧ·cle, *n.* same as *vernicle.*

vẽr′nȧ·çle, *n.* a vernacular term. [Rare.]

vẽr·naç′ū·lăr, *a.* [L. *vernaculus*, belonging to homeborn slaves, domestic, native, indigenous, from *verna*, a homeborn slave.]

1. using the native language of a country or place, as a writer.

2. commonly spoken by the people of a particular country or place: said of a language or dialect: often distinguished from *literary.*

3. of or in the native language.

4. native to a country; as, the *vernacular* arts of Brittany.

5. peculiar to a particular locality; as, a *vernacular* disease.

6. designating or of the common name of an animal or plant, as distinguished from the scientific term for it in Latin nomenclature.

vẽr·naç′ū·lăr, *n.* 1. the native speech, language, or dialect of a country or place.

2. the common everyday language of ordinary people in a particular locality.

3. the shop talk or idiom of a profession or trade.

4. (a) a vernacular word or term; (b) the vernacular name of an animal or plant.

vẽr·naç′ū·lăr·iṣm, *n.* 1. a vernacular word, phrase, or usage.

2. the use of vernacular language.

vẽr·naç″ū·lăr·i·zā′tion, *n.* the act or the process of making vernacular; the state of being vernacularized.

vẽr·naç′ū·lăr·īze, *v.t.*; vernacularized, *pt., pp.*; vernacularizing, *ppr.* to make vernacular.

vẽr·naç′ū·lăr·ly, *adv.* in a vernacular manner; also, in vernacular phrasing or usage.

vẽr·naç′ū·lāte, *v.t.* and *v.i.* to express in, or to use, the vernacular. [Rare.]

vẽr·naç′ū·lous, *a.* vernacular; also, scoffing; scurrilous; insolent. [Obs.]

vẽr′năġe, *n.* a sweet white Italian wine. [Obs.]

vẽr′năl, *a.* [L. *vernalis*, from *vernus*, belonging to spring, from L. *ver*, spring.]

1. belonging to the spring; appearing or occurring in spring; as, *vernal* bloom.

2. springlike; fresh, warm, and mild.

3. belonging to youth; youthful.

vernal equinox; the equinox that is reached about March 21: also called *vernal point.*

vernal grass; a sweet-scented grass, *Anthoxanthum odoratum*, which yields a sweet fragrance when dry.

vernal whitlow grass; same as *whitlow grass.*

vẽr·năl·i·zā′tiŏn, *n.* the act or process of vernalizing.

vẽr′năl·īze, *v.t.*; vernalized, *pt., pp.*; vernalizing, *ppr.* to stimulate the growth of (a plant) by artificially hastening the dormant period, as by subjecting the seed to low temperatures away from light.

vẽr′nănt, *a.* [L. *vernans* (-*antis*), ppr. of *vernare*, to bloom, flourish.] flourishing as in spring; as, *vernant* flowers. [Rare.]

vẽr·nā′tion, *n.* in botany, the disposition of leaves within a leaf bud.

Vẽr′nẽr′ṣ law (*or* **phē·nom′ē·non**), in linguistics, Karl Verner's explanation, published in 1876, of the apparent exceptions to Grimm's table of consonant correspondences between Indo-European and Germanic: the phenomenon is illustrated in *luxurious* (as compared with *luxury*), in which the cluster [ks] becomes voiced [gz] when the accent shifts to the following syllable.

vẽr′ni·çle, *n.* a veronica (sense 1b). [Obs.]

vẽr′ni·çōse, *a.* in botany, covered as if with a natural varnish: said of leaves.

vẽr′ni·ẽr, *n.* [named after the inventor, Pierre *Vernier*, of Franche Comté, 1580–1637.]

1. a short, graduated scale that slides along the fixed scale of a sextant, theodolite, barometer, or other graduated instrument, and is used for measuring a fractional part of one of the equal divisions on the fixed scale: also *vernier scale.*

2. any device that makes possible a finer setting of a tool or measuring instrument.

vẽr′ni·ẽr, *a.* of or fitted with a vernier; as, *vernier* calipers.

vẽr′nile, *a.* obsequious; servile; slavish. [Rare.]

vẽr·nil′i·ty, *n.* servility; fawning behavior, like that of a slave. [Rare.]

vẽr′nine, vẽr′nin, *n.* [*vernal* and -*ine*, -*in.*] an alkaloid, $C_{10}H_{13}N_5O_5$, found in young clover, vetches, and ergot. It yields guanin on treatment with hydrochloric and other acids.

vẽr′nish, *n.* varnish. [Obs.]

vẽr′nix çȧ·sē·ō′sȧ, an unctuous substance that covers the skin of the fetus.

Vẽr·nō′ni·ȧ, *n.* [named after W. *Vernon*, English botanist and traveler.] a very large genus of composite plants, including about 500 species chiefly found in the tropics; the ironweeds.

vẽr′nō·nin, *n.* a glucoside, $C_{10}H_{24}O_7$, from *Vernonia nigriliana*, an African plant, resembling digitalin in its action, but less toxic.

Ver·nụnft′ (fer-), *n.* [G.] in German philosophy, reason, theoretical and practical; the highest faculty of the mind; the source of ideas: distinguished from *Verstand.*

ver′ō·năl, *n.* [G., from L. *ver*, spring.] barbital: a trade-mark (*Veronal*).

Ver·ō·nēṣe′, *a.* of or relating to Verona, a city in northeastern Italy, its people, or culture.

Veronese green; a yellowish-green color.

Ver·ō·nēṣe′, *n.*; *pl.* **Ver·ō·nēṣe′,** a native or inhabitant of Verona.

vē·ron′i·çȧ, *n.* [ML., from LL. *veraiconica*, from L. *verus*, truth, and *iconicus*, of an image.]

1. (a) the image or representation of the face of Jesus as it was miraculously supposed to have appeared on the handkerchief used by Saint Veronica to wipe the bleeding face of Jesus on the road to Calvary; (b) [*often* V–] the handkerchief itself; (c) a similar representation of the face of Jesus on a cloth or garment.

2. [V–] a genus of plants and shrubs of the figwort family, with blue, pink, purple, or white flowers in spikes.

3. any plant of this genus; especially, the speedwell.

ver′rāy, *a.* very. [Obs.]

ver′rel, *n.* a ferrule. [Obs.]

ver·riç′ū·lāte, *a.* [L. *verriculum*, net, from *verrere*, to sweep, scour.] in zoology, covered with tufts of erect parallel hairs or bristles.

ver′ri·çūle, *n.* a thick tuft of close-set upright hairs.

ver·rụ′çȧ, *n.*; *pl.* **ver·rụ′cae,** [L., wart, orig. a steep place.]

1. a wart.

2. a wartlike elevation, as on the back of a toad.

ver·rụ′ci·fọrm, *a.* [L. *verruca*, wart, and -*form.*] in botany, wart-shaped.

ver′rụ·çōse, ver′rụ·çous, *a.* [L. *verrucosus*, full of warts, warty, from *verruca*, wart.] warty; having little warts or wartlike growths on the surface; as, a *verrucous* capsule.

ver·rụ·ços′i·ty, *n.* the condition of being verrucose.

ver·rụ′çū·lōse, *a.* [L. *verrucula*, dim. of *verruca*, wart.] having minute, wartlike prominences.

ver·rụ′gȧs, *n.* [Sp.] a disease prevalent in Peru; yaws.

vẽr·sȧ·bil′i·ty, vẽr′sȧ·ble·ness, *n.* aptness to be turned. [Rare.]

vẽr′sȧ·ble, *a.* capable of being turned. [Rare.]

vẽr′săl, *a.* universal. [Obs.]

vẽr′sănt, *a.* [Fr., from L. *versans* (-*antis*), ppr. of *versare*, to turn often, freq. of *vertere*, to turn.] familiar; acquainted.

vẽr′sănt, *n.* that part of a mountain or mountain chain which slopes in one direction; also, the general slope of a region.

vẽr′sȧ·tile, *a.* [Fr. *versatile*; L. *versatilis*, that turns round, movable, versatile, from *versatus*, pp. of *versare*, to turn often, freq. of *vertere*, to turn.]

1. that may be turned or moved around, as on a hinge or pivot.

2. liable to be turned in opinion; changeable; fickle; inconstant; as, a man of *versatile* disposition. [Rare.]

3. competent in many things; turning with ease from one thing to another; many-sided; as, a *versatile* actor.

4. in botany, freely movable on the filament to which it is attached; as, a *versatile* anther of a passionflower.

5. in ornithology, capable of either forward or backward movement, as the toe of a bird.

6. capable of motion in any direction, as the antenna of an insect or mollusk.

vẽr′sȧ·tile·ly, *adv.* in a versatile manner.

vẽr·sȧ·til′i·ty, vẽr′sȧ·tile·ness, *n.* [Fr. *versatilité.*] the quality or state of being versatile; specifically, (a) competence in many things; (b) ability to move freely, as on an axis, or in any direction.

vers″ de so·cié·té′ (vãr″ dē sō-syā-tā′), [Fr.] light, witty, polished poetry.

vẽrse, *n.* [ME. *vers*, from AS. *fers*, from L. *versus*, a turning, a line, row: so named from the turning to begin a new line, from *versus*, pp. of *vertere*, to turn.]

1. a line of poetry, consisting of a certain number of metrical feet, disposed according to some rule or design.

> Waller was smooth; but Dryden taught to join
> The varying *verse*, the full resounding line.
> —Pope.

2. metrical writing or speaking; poetry in general, especially when light or trivial or merely metered and rhymed, but without much serious content or artistic merit.

3. a particular form of metrical composition; as, blank *verse*, trochaic *verse.*

4. a single metrical composition; a poem.

5. a stanza or similar short subdivision of a metrical composition: sometimes distinguished from *chorus*, or *refrain.*

6. in the Bible, any of the single, usually numbered, short divisions of a chapter, generally a sentence or part of a sentence.

vẽrse, *v.t.*; versed (vẽrst), *pt., pp.*; versing, *ppr.* to tell in verse; to relate poetically; to versify. [Now Rare.]

> Playing on pipes of corn, and *versing* love.
> —Shak.

vẽrse, *v.i.* to produce verses; to compose poetry. [Now Rare.]

vẽrsed (vẽrst), *a.* [L. *versatus*, pp. of *versari*, to keep turning oneself about, passive form of *versare*, to turn often.] thoroughly acquainted; practiced; familiar; skilled; showing study.

Syn.—skilled, practiced, conversant, acquainted, initiated, indoctrinated, clever, familiar, proficient.

vẽrsed, *a.* [from L. *versus*, pp. of *vertere*, to turn; and *-ed.*] in mathematics, turned; as, a *versed* sine.

vẽrse′măn, *n.*; *pl.* **vẽrse′men,** a writer of verses; a versemonger.

vẽrse′mŏn·gẽr, *n.* a maker of verses; a rimer; a poetaster.

vẽrs′ẽr, *n.* a versifier. [Rare.]

vẽrs′et, *n.* a verse. [Obs.]

vẽr′si·cle, *n.* [ME.; L. *versiculus*, dim. of *versus*, verse.] a short or little verse; specifically, a short verse in a church service which is spoken or chanted by the priest or minister alternately with the response by the congregation.

vẽr′si·cŏl·ŏr, *a.* [L. *versicolor*; *versare*, to change, and *color*.] having various colors; also, changeable in color; iridescent.

vẽr′si·cŏl·ŏred, *a.* same as *versicolor*.

vẽr·sic′ū·lăr, *a.* [L. *versiculus*, dim. of *versus*, verse.] of, characterized by, or consisting of versicles or verses; as, a *versicular* division.

ver·sie′rȧ, *n.* [It.] in geometry, a plane cubic curve of the third order, discovered by Maria Agnesi (1718–1799), of the University of Bologna.

vẽr″si·fi·cā′tion, *n.* [L. *versificatio*.]

1. the act of versifying.
2. the art, practice, or theory of poetic composition.
3. the form or style of a poem; metrical structure.
4. a metrical version (*of* something).

vẽr′si·fī·ẽr, *n.* 1. one who versifies; one who makes verses; a poet.

2. one who converts into verse, or one who expresses in verse something written in prose; as, Dr. Watts was a *versifier* of the Psalms.

3. a person who writes light, cheap, or inferior verses; a poetaster.

vẽr′si·fọrm, *a.* [LL. *versiformis*, from L. *versus*, pp. of *vertere*, to turn, and *forma*, form.] varied in form; changing form.

vẽr′si·fȳ, *v.i.*; versified, *pt., pp.*; versifying, *ppr.* [Fr. *versifier*; L. *versificare*; *versus*, verse, and *facere*, to make.] to compose verses.

I'll *versify* in spite, and do my best
—Dryden.

vẽr′si·fȳ, *v.t.* 1. to relate or describe in verse; to treat as the subject of verse.

2. to turn or convert (prose) into verse; as, to *versify* the Psalms.

vẽr′ṣion, *n.* [Fr., from ML. *versio* (*-onis*), a turning, from *versus*, pp. of *vertere*, to turn, alter, translate.]

1. a turning; a change or transformation; conversion. [Obs.]
2. direction; change of direction. [Obs.]
3. the act of translating or rendering from one language into another.
4. (a) a translation; (b) [*often* V–] a translation of the Bible, in whole or part; as, the Douay and King James *versions*.
5. an account showing one point of view; a particular description or report given by one person or group; as, his *version* agreed with ours.
6. a particular form or variation of something.
7. in medicine, (a) displacement of the uterus in which it is deflected but not bent upon itself; (b) the operation of turning the fetus during childbirth to make delivery easier.

vẽr′ṣion·ăl, *a.* of a version or versions.

vẽr′ṣiŏn·ist, *n.* one who produces a version; a translator; also, one who prefers a certain translation or version, as of the Bible.

vers lī′bre (văr lē′br), [Fr.] same as *free verse*.

vers lī′brist (văr), [Fr.] a writer of free verse.

vẽr′sō, *n.*; *pl.* **vẽr′sōṣ,** [L. *verso*, abl. of *versus*, pp. of *vertere*, to turn.]

1. in printing, the left-hand page, as of a book or manuscript: opposed to *recto*.
2. the back of a coin or medal: opposed to *obverse*.

vẽr′sŏr, *n.* [L. *versus*, pp. of *vertere*, to turn.] in mathematics, a factor that turns a vector through an angle without changing its modulus, tensor, or length. Every quaternion is a product of a tensor and a versor, and that versor is represented by *U* before the quaternion.

quadrantal versor; a versor that expresses rotation through one right angle.

vẽrst, *n.* [Russ. *versta*.] a Russian measure of length, equal to about 3,500 feet or about ²/₃ mile.

Ver·ständ′ (fer-shtänt′), *n.* [G.] in German philosophy, understanding considered apart from reason.

vẽr′ṣụ·ăl (-shụ-), *a.* of or pertaining to a verse, verses, or short paragraphs; as, the *versual* divisions of the Bible.

vẽr′sus, *prep.* [L., toward, turned in the direction of.]

1. in law and sports, against; as, plaintiff *versus* defendant, Detroit *versus* Cleveland at baseball.
2. considered as an alternative to; contrasted with; as, they debated the open shop *versus* the closed shop.

vẽr·sūte′, *a.* [L. *versutus*, cunning, from *versus*, pp. of *vertere*, to turn.] crafty; wily. [Obs.]

vẽrt, *n.* [Fr., formerly also *verd*, from L. *viridis*, green.]

1. in English forest law, everything within a forest that grows and bears a green leaf, which may serve as a cover for deer; also, the right to cut green trees or wood.
2. in heraldry, the color green represented by diagonal lines from dexter (right) to sinister (left).

VERT

vẽrt, *n.* a convert.

vẽr′tē·bẽr, *n.* a vertebra. [Obs.]

vẽr′tē·brȧ, *n.*; *pl.* **vẽr′tē·brae, vẽr′tē·brȧṣ,** [L., a joint, vertebra, from *vertere*, to turn.]

1. any of the single bones or segments of the spinal column, articulating in the higher vertebrates with those adjacent to it by means of elastic fibrous discs: in man there are 7 cervical, 12 dorsal, and 5 lumbar vertebrae.

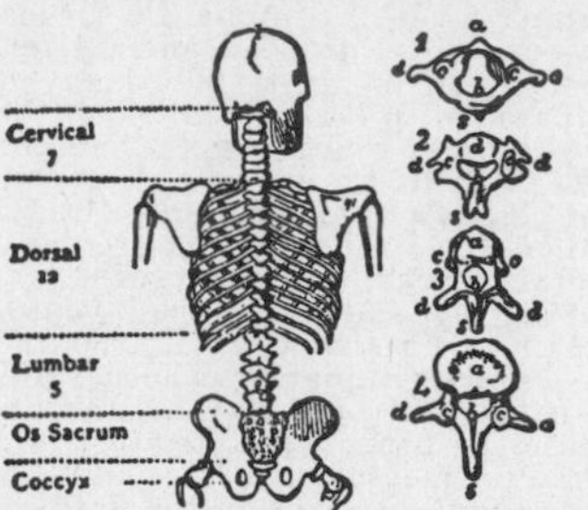

VERTEBRA

1. atlas, or vertebra supporting the head; 2. cervical vertebra; 3. dorsal vertebra; 4. lumbar vertebra; *a*, body; *b*, ring; *c*, oblique or articular process; *d*, transverse process; *s*, spinous process.

2. [*pl.*] loosely, the spine; as, to bend one's *vertebrae*.
3. in zoology, one of the axial ossicles or small bones in the arm of an ophiuran or starfish.

vẽr′tē·brăl, *a.* 1. of, or having the nature of, a vertebra or vertebrae; as, the *vertebral* column.

2. having or composed of vertebrae; as, *vertebral* animals.

vertebral ribs; the floating ribs.

vẽr′tē·brăl·ly, *adv.* at or within a vertebra.

vẽr″tē·brär·tē′ri·ăl, *a.* of or pertaining to a vertebra and an artery; specifically, pertaining to the vertebrarterial foramen in the transverse process of a cervical vertebra.

Vẽr·tē·brā′tȧ, *n.pl.* a large division of animals that have a backbone, or spinal column, of bone or cartilage, and in early life have a notochord. The *Vertebrata* include the classes *Pisces* (fishes), *Amphibia* (frogs, etc.), *Reptilia* (reptiles), *Aves* (birds), and *Mammalia* (quadrupeds and man).

vẽr′tē·brāte, *a.* [L. *vertebratus*, from *vertebra*, a joint, vertebra.]

1. having a backbone, or spinal column.
2. of or belonging to the vertebrates.

vẽr′tē·brāte, *n.* any animal of the *Vertebrata*.

vẽr′tē·brā·ted, *a.* 1. having a backbone; vertebrate.

2. consisting of vertebrae.

vẽr·tē·brā′tion, *n.* the quality or condition of developing vertebrae; segmentation into vertebrae.

vẽr′tē·bre (-bẽr), *n.* same as *vertebra*.

vẽr′tē·brō-, [from *vertebra*.] a combining form meaning: (a) *vertebrae*; (b) *vertebral and*. Also, before a vowel, *vertebr-*.

vẽr″tē·brō·il′i·ac, *a.* connecting the vertebral column and the ilium; as, *vertebroiliac* ligaments.

vẽr′tex, *n.*; *pl.* **vẽr′tex·eṣ, vẽr′ti·cēṣ,** [L., the top, properly the turning point, from *vertere*, to turn.]

1. the highest or principal point; apex; top; crown; summit.
2. in anatomy, the crown or top of the head.
3. in astronomy, the zenith; the point of the heavens directly overhead.
4. in geometry, (a) the point of intersection of two lines of a figure, opposite to the base and furthest from it; (b) the point in a curve at which the axis meets it; (c) the point of any angle of a triangle or polygon.
5. in optics, the point at which the axis cuts the curve of a lens.

vẽr′ti·căl, *a.* [Fr., from LL. *verticalis*, vertical, from L. *vertex* (*-icis*), a top or summit.]

1. relating to the vertex, or highest point; at or in the zenith; directly overhead.
2. being in a position perpendicular to the plane of the horizon; placed or acting perpendicularly or in an upright position or direction; upright; straight up and down.
3. in anatomy and zoology, pertaining to the vertex of the head.
4. in botany, (a) at a right angle to the horizon or to the supporting surface; (b) in the direction in which the axis lies; lengthwise.
5. in economics, of or controlling businesses concerned with all the processes in the manufacture and sale of a particular product; as, a *vertical* trust.

vertical angles; in geometry, the opposite angles formed by two insecting straight lines. In the accompanying example, the straight lines A B and C D intersect at point E. The opposite angles A E C and D E B are vertical angles, as are also A E D and C E B.

VERTICAL ANGLES

vertical anthers; anthers that terminate the filaments, and, being inserted by their base, stand no less upright than the filaments themselves.

vertical circle; in astronomy, a great circle in the celestial sphere passing through the zenith and the nadir, its plane cutting the plane of the horizon at a right angle at the point of observation.

vertical escapement; formerly, an escapement in watches, in which the scape wheel was in a vertical position.

vertical leaves; in botany, leaves that stand erect so that neither of the surfaces can be called the upper or under.

vertical line; in dialing, a line perpendicular to the horizon; in conics, a line drawn on the vertical plane and at right angles to any line or plane taken as a base.

vertical plane; (a) a plane perpendicular to the plane of the horizon; (b) in perspective, a plane perpendicular to the geometrical plane, passing through the eye, and cutting the perspective plane at right angles.

vertical steam engine; a steam engine in which the piston moves vertically up and down, as distinguished from a horizontal, inclined, or rotary steam engine.

vertical union; a labor union whose members all work in the same industry but not necessarily at the same trade; an industrial union: opposed to *horizontal union*.

vẽr′ti·căl, *n.* 1. the vertex; the point directly overhead; the zenith. [Obs.]

2. a vertical line, plane, circle, etc.
3. upright position.
4. a vertical or upright member in a truss.

vẽr·ti·cal′i·ty, *n.* 1. the condition of the sun at the zenith, when it is directly overhead.

2 vertical position; perpendicularity.

vẽr′ti·căl·ly, *adv.* 1. in a vertical manner, position, or direction.

2. straight overhead.

vẽr′ti·căl·ness, *n.* the state of being vertical.

vẽr′ti·cēṣ, *n.* alternative plural of *vertex*.

vẽr′ti·cil, *n.* [L. *verticillus*, dim. of *vertex*, a whirl.]

1. in botany, a whorl; an arrangement in which the leaves or flowers surround the stem in a circle upon the same plane.
2. in zoology, a whorl or circlet of hairs, scales, spines, etc., radiating from an axis. [Rare.]

vẽr″ti·cil·las′tẽr, *n.* [Mod.L., from L. *verticillus*, the whirl of a spindle, and dim. *-aster*.] in botany, an almost circular flower arrangement formed by a pair of clusters facing each other on the stem, as in some plants of the mint family.

vẽr″ti·cil·las′trāte, *a.* bearing or in the form of verticillasters.

vẽr·tic′il·lāte, vẽr·tic′il·lā·ted, *a.* in botany, (a) growing in a whorl or arranged on the same plane around an axis, as flowers, leaves, branches, etc.; (b) having leaves, flowers, etc. arranged in this way.

vẽr·tic·il·lā′tion, *n.* in botany, arrangement of flowers, leaves, etc. in verticils, or whorls.

vẽr·ti·cil′lus, *n.* same as *verticil.*

vẽr·tic′i·ty, *n.* [Fr. *verticité,* from L. *vertex,* a whirl.] the power or tendency to turn; revolution; rotation. [Rare.]

vẽr·tiġ′i·nāte, *a.* whirled about; dizzy. [Rare.]

vẽr·tiġ′i·nous, *a.* [L. *vertiginosus,* one having the vertigo.]

1. turning round; whirling; rotary; as, a *vertiginous* motion.

2. of or affected with vertigo; dizzy.

3. apt to turn or change; unstable; inconstant.

Inconstant they are in all their actions, *vertiginous,* restless. —Burton.

4. tending to cause vertigo; as, a *vertiginous* height.

vẽr·tiġ′i·nous·ly, *adv.* in a vertiginous manner; with a whirling or giddiness.

vẽr·tiġ′i·nous·ness, *n.* the state or quality of being vertiginous.

vẽr′ti·gō, *n.*; *pl.* **vẽr′ti·gōes, vẽr·tiġ′i·nieṣ,** [L. *vertigo,* from *vertere,* to turn.]

1. in medicine, a sensation of dizziness or giddiness.

2. [V–] a genus of marsh or land snails having a cylindrically fusiform shell, usually with a dentate aperture.

vẽr·ti·lin′ē·ăr, *a.* rectilinear. [Rare.]

vẽr′tū, *n.* virtue. [Obs.]

vẽr·tù′, *n.* same as *virtu.*

Vẽr·tum′nus, *n.* in Roman mythology, a deity who presided over gardens and orchards, and who was also worshipped as the god of spring or of the seasons in general.

vẽr″ū·mon·tā′num, *n.* [L., a mountain ridge.] a rounded projection in the urethra, on the floor of the prostatic portion.

vẽr′vāin, *n.* [OFr. *verveine,* from L. *vebena,* a shoot, a green branch.] any of a number of related plants of the verbena family, with spikes or clusters of red, white, or purplish flowers.

vẽr′vāin mal′lōw, a species of mallow, *Malva alcea.*

vẽr′vāin sāġe, the purple-flowered European sage, *Salvia verbenaca.*

vẽrve, *n.* [Fr., prob. from L. *verba,* pl. of *verbum,* a word.]

1. vigor and energy in ideas or expression of them.

2. vigor; enthusiasm.

3. aptitude. [Rare.]

vẽr′vel, *n.* same as *varvel.*

vẽr′vet, *n.* a small South African monkey, *Cercopithecus lalandi,* related to the grivet and green monkey, but with black hands, feet, and chin.

ver′y, *a.*; *comp.* verier; *superl.* veriest, [OFr. *verai,* true, from hyp. LL. *veraius,* from L. *verus,* true.]

1. in the fullest sense; complete; absolute; as, the *very* reverse of the truth.

2. the same; identical; as, that is the *very* hat I lost.

3. even; even the: used as an intensive; as, the *very* rafters shook.

4. actual; as, caught in the *very* act.

5. (a) real; true; genuine; (b) legitimate; lawful; rightful. [Archaic.]

ver′y, *adv.* 1. in a high degree; to a great extent; extremely; exceedingly.

2. truly; really: used as an intensive; as, the *very* same man.

Ver′y sig′năl (or **līght**), a colored flare fired from a special pistol (the *Very pistol*) at night and used for signalling: invented in 1877 by E. W. Very of the U. S. Navy.

vē·sā′ni·à, *n.* [L.] insanity.

vē·san′iç, *a.* of or pertaining to vesania.

vē·sī′cà, *n.*; *pl.* **vē·sī′cae,** [L., a bladder.] a bladder.

vesica piscis; [L., a fish bladder.] a pointed oval or egg-shaped aureole, made by the intersection of two equal circles cutting each other in their centers, often surrounding a sacred figure in a religious painting, etc.

ves′i·căl, *a.* relating to or having to do with a bladder, especially the urinary bladder.

ves′i·cănt, *a.* causing blisters; vesicatory.

ves′i·cănt, *n.* 1. a vesicant agent.

2. any agent, as mustard gas, used in chemical warfare to blister and burn body tissues by contact with the skin or inhalation.

ves′i·cāte, *v.t.*; vesicated, *pt., pp.*; vesicating, *ppr.* [L. *vesica,* a bladder.] to blister.

ves·i·cā′tion, *n.* the process of raising blisters on the skin.

ves′i·cà·tō″ry, *a.* [from *vesicate* and *-ory.*] causing or tending to cause blisters.

ves′i·cà·tō″ry, *n.*; *pl.* **ves′i·cà·tō″rieṣ,** a vesicatory agent.

ves′i·cle, *n.* [Fr. *vésicule*; L. *vesicula,* a little bladder, dim. of *vesica,* a bladder.] any small bladderlike structure, cavity, sac, or cyst; specifically, (a) in anatomy and zoology, a small blister; an orbicular elevation of the epidermis containing a serous liquid; (b) in botany, a small, bladderlike sac filled with air; (c) in geology, a small, spherical cavity in volcanic rock, produced by bubbles of air or gas when the mass was in a molten state. Also called *vesicule, vesiculus.*

seminal vesicle; see under *seminal.*

ves′i·cō-, [from L. *vesica,* a bladder.] a combining form meaning: (a) *bladder,* as in *vesicotomy*; (b) *bladder and.*

ves″i·cō·ab·dom′i·năl, *a.* pertaining to the abdomen and the urinary bladder.

ves′i·cō·cēle, *n.* [*vesico-,* and Gr. *kēlē,* a tumor.] hernial protrusion of the bladder.

ves″i·cō·fix·ā′tion, *n.* 1. the stitching of the uterus to the bladder.

2. the surgical fixation of the bladder.

ves″i·cō·pros·tat′iç, *a.* pertaining to the bladder and the prostate.

ves″i·cō·pū′biç, *a.* pertaining to the bladder and the pubes.

ves·i·çot′ō·my, *n.* [*vesico-,* and Gr. *temnein,* to cut.] a surgical incision of or cutting into the urinary bladder.

ves″i·cō·um·bil′iç·ăl, *a.* pertaining to the umbilicus and the bladder.

ves″i·cō·ū′tẽr·ine, *a.* of or pertaining to the bladder and the uterus.

ves″i·cō·vaġ′i·năl, *a.* pertaining to the bladder and the vagina.

vē·siç′ū·là, *n.*; *pl.* **vē·siç′ū·lae,** [L.] a vesicle.

vē·siç′ū·lăr, *a.* [L. *vesicula,* a little bladder.]

1. of, composed of, or having vesicles.

2. having the form or structure of a vesicle.

Vē·siç·ū·lā′ri·à, *n.* a typical genus of polyzoans of the family *Vesiculariidæ,* having tubular cells that grow in clusters on slender flexible stems.

vē·siç′ū·lăr·ly, *adv.* in a vesicular manner.

Vē·siç·ū·lā′tà, Vē·siç·ū·lā′tae, *n.pl.* the campanularian polyps or hydromedusians.

vē·sic′ū·lāte, *a.* vesicular.

vē·siç′ū·lāte, *v.t.*; vesiculated, *pt., pp.*; vesiculating, *ppr.* to make or cause vesicles to form in.

vē·siç′ū·lāte, *v.i.* to become vesicular.

vē·siç·ū·lā′tion, *n.* the condition of being filled or covered with vesicles; the formation of vesicles.

ves′i·çūle, *n.* same as *vesicle.*

vē·siç·ū·lif′ẽr·ous, *a.* having or full of sacs or vesicles; vesicular.

vē·siç′ū·lōse, vē·siç′ū·lous, *a.* vesicular.

vē·sic′ū·lus, *n.*; *pl.* **vē·siç′ū·lī,** a vesicle.

Ves′pà, *n.* [L., a wasp.] a genus of hymenopterous insects, of which the common wasp, *Vespa vulgaris,* is the type.

ves′pẽr, *n.* [L., evening; Gr. *hesperos,* the evening, the evening star.]

1. evening; eventide.

2. (a) an evening prayer, service, etc.; (b) a vesper bell.

3. [V–] the evening star, Hesperus; the planet Venus seen as the evening star.

ves′pẽr, *a.* 1. relating to the evening.

2. of vespers; as, *vesper* bells.

ves′pẽr·ăl, *a.* of evening or vespers. [Rare.]

ves′pẽr·ăl, *n.* in ecclesiastical usage, (a) a book containing the chants, psalms, etc. used at vespers; (b) a cloth cover for protecting the altar cloth.

ves′pẽr bīrd, the grass finch.

ves′pẽr mouse, *pl.* **ves′pẽr mīce,** a mouse, *Hesperomys leucopus,* of North America.

ves′pẽrṣ, *n.pl.* [OFr. *vespres*; ML. *vesperae,* from L. *vespera,* evening.]

1. (a) a church service held in the late afternoon or evening, as in the Anglican Church; (b) a prayer or song for this service.

2. in the Roman Catholic Church, (a) the sixth of the seven canonical hours; (b) the service for this hour; (c) a public ceremony in which part of this service is chanted on Sundays or holy days.

Also *Vespers.*

ves′pẽr spar′rōw, an American sparrow with white markings on its outer tail feathers: so called from its practice of singing in the evening.

Ves·pẽr·til′i·ō, *n.* [L., a bat.] a genus of bats.

ves·pẽr·til′i·ō·nid, *a.* vespertilionine.

ves·pẽr·til′i·ō·nid, *n.* a vespertilionine bat.

Ves·pẽr·til·i·on′i·dae, *n.pl.* a family of long-tailed insectivorous bats found throughout the Temperate Zones: the genus *Vespertilio* is the type.

ves·pẽr·til′i·ō·nine, *a.* of or belonging to the *Verspertilionidæ.*

ves′pẽr·tine, ves·pẽr·tī′năl, *a.* [L. *vespertinus,* belonging to evening.]

1. pertaining to the evening.

2. happening or appearing in the evening.

3. in botany, opening or blooming in the evening, as a flower.

4. in zoology, active or flying about in the early evening.

5. in astronomy, descending to the horizon from the meridian at the time of the setting of the sun: said of planets.

ves′pi·ăr·y, *n.*; *pl.* **ves′pi·ăr·ieṣ,** [from L. *vespa,* a wasp.] the nest or habitation of any of the social wasps, made of paperlike material and hung, as from a tree, or buried underground; also, a colony or community of such insects.

ves′pid, *a.* relating or belonging to the *Vespidæ.*

ves′pid, *n.* any of the *Vespidæ.*

Ves′pi·dae, *n.pl.* a family of social wasps, as the hornet and yellow jacket, of which the genus *Vespa* is the type: they live in colonies consisting of a queen, males, and workers.

ves′pi·fọrm, *a.* having the shape or form of a wasp.

ves·pil′lō, *n.* [L., from *vesper,* evening.] in ancient Rome, one who carried out the dead in the evening for burial. [Obs.]

ves′pine, *a.* of or like a wasp.

ves′sel, *n.* [OFr. *vessel,* from L. *vascellum,* dim. of *vas,* a vessel.]

1. a utensil for holding something, as a vase, bowl, pitcher, kettle, etc.

2. a person thought of as being the receiver or repository of some spirit, influence, etc.; as, a *vessel* of wrath. [Chiefly Biblical.]

3. a craft for traveling on water; a ship or boat, especially one larger than a rowboat.

4. an airship.

5. in anatomy and zoology, a tube or duct containing or circulating a body fluid; as, a blood *vessel.*

6. in botany, a tube or canal serving to conduct water.

acoustic vessels; see under *acoustic.*

the weaker vessel; a woman: humorous usage: from 1 Pet. iii. 7: "Giving honor unto the wife as unto *the weaker vessel.*"

ves′sel, *v.t.* to put into a vessel. [Obs.]

ves′sel·fụl, *n.* as much as a vessel will contain.

ves′seṣ, ves′setṣ, *n.pl.* a kind of worsted. [Obs.]

ves′sig·non, ves′siç·non, *n.* [Fr. *vessignon,* a windgall, from L. *vesica,* a bladder, a blister.] a soft swelling on a horse's leg; a windgall.

vest, *n.* [Fr. *veste,* from L. *vestis,* a garment, a vest.]

1. a short, tight-fitting, sleeveless garment worn under a suit coat by men; a waistcoat.

2. an undervest, or undershirt.

3. an insert or trimming worn under the bodice by women, simulating the front of a man's vest.

4. robe; garment; clothing. [Archaic.]

5. a long, cassocklike garment worn by men in the time of Charles II. [Obs.]

vest, *v.t.*; vested, *pt., pp.*; vesting, *ppr.* 1. to clothe; to dress, as in church garments.

2. to place (authority, power, property rights, etc.) in the control of a person or group (with *in*).

3. to put (a person) in possession or control of, as power or authority; to invest (*with* something).

vest, *v.i.* 1. to come or descend to a person; to become fixed upon or vested in a person, as property (with *in*).

2. to put on vestments or garments; to clothe oneself.

Ves′tà, *n.* [L.] 1. in Roman mythology, the goddess of the hearth and its fire, identified with the Greek Hestia: she was worshiped in a temple in which a sacred fire on the altar was tended by the vestal virgins.

2. in astronomy, one of the asteroids, discovered in 1807.

3. [v-] (a) orginally, a short wax friction match; (b) later, a short wooden match.

ves'tăl, *a.* [L. *Vestalis*, from *Vesta*, the goddess of fire.]

1. pertaining to, sacred to, or devoted to Vesta.

2. pure; chaste.

3. of the vestal virgins.

ves'tăl, *n.* 1. a virgin consecrated to Vesta, and to the service of watching the sacred fire, which was to be perpetually kept burning upon her altar; a vestal virgin. The vestals were six in number. They entered the service of the goddess at from six to ten years of age, their term of service lasting thirty years.

2. a virgin; a woman of spotless chastity.

3. a nun.

ves'tăl vĭr'ġin, same as *vestal*, n. 1.

vest'ed, *a.* 1. clothed in vestments; robed, especially in church vestments; as, a *vested* choir.

2. fixed; settled; absolute; not in a state of contingency or suspension; as, *vested* rights, a *vested* interest.

vested legacy; in law, a legacy the right to which commences *in præsenti*, and does not depend on a contingency.

vest·ee', *n.* [dim. of *vest.*] a vest (sense 3).

vest'ẽr, *n.* an investor; one who makes investments. [Rare.]

ves·ti·ăr'i·ăn, *a.* vestiary. [Rare.]

ves'ti·ăr·y, *a.* [OFr. *vestiairie*; ML. *vestiarium*; see *vestry*.] relating to clothes or vestments.

ves'ti·ăr·y, *n.* a vestry or cloakroom. [Obs.]

ves·tib'ū·lăr, *a.* pertaining to or like a vestibule.

ves'ti·būle, *n.* [Fr., from L. *vestibulum*, an entrance hall.]

1. a small entrance hall or room, either to a building or to a room within a building.

2. the enclosed passage between passenger cars of a train, having doors for entrance or exit.

3. in anatomy and zoology, any cavity or space serving as an entrance to another cavity or space; as, the *vestibule* of the inner ear leading into the cochlea.

ves'ti·būle, *v.t.*; vestibuled, *pt.*, *pp.*; vestibuling, *ppr.* to furnish with a vestibule.

ves'ti·būled, *a.* having vestibules; as, a *vestibuled* train.

ves·tib'ū·lum, *n.*; *pl.* **ves·tib'ū·lȧ,** [L.] in anatomy and zoology, a vestibule.

ves'ti·gāte, *v.t.* to investigate. [Obs.]

ves'tiġe, *n.* [Fr., from L. *vestigium*, a footprint.]

1. a trace, mark, or sign of something which has once existed but has passed away or disappeared; as, there was no *vestige* of the town.

2. a trace; bit; as, there was no *vestige* of woodland.

3. in biology, a degenerate, atrophied, or rudimentary organ or part, more fully developed or functional in an earlier stage of development of the individual or species.

Syn.—trace, mark, sign, evidence, token.

ves·tiġ'i·ăl, *a.* of, pertaining to, or of the nature of a vestige.

ves·tiġ'i·um, *n.*; *pl.* **ves·tiġ'i·ȧ,** in biology, a vestige; a vestigial organ or part.

vest'ing, *n.* cloth for vests; especially, a rich, heavy cloth used in vests for evening dress.

ves'ti·tūre, *n.* 1. investiture. [Obs.]

2. in zoology, the covering of a surface, as scales or hairs.

vest'let, *n.* a tube-inhabiting zoophyte of the genus *Cerianthus.*

vest'ment, *n.* [OFr. *vestement*, from L. *vestimentum*, from *vestire*, to clothe.]

1. a garment; robe; gown; especially, an official robe or gown.

2. in ecclesiastical usage, any of the garments worn by officiants and their assistants during certain services and rites.

vest'-pock''et, *a.* 1. made to fit into a vest pocket.

2. relatively small; as, a *vest-pocket* edition of a book.

ves'trăl, *a.* pertaining to a vestry.

ves'try, *n.*; *pl.* **ves'trieṣ,** [Fr. *vestiaire*, from L. *vestiarium*, a wardrobe, from *vestis*, a garment.]

1. a room in a church, where the clergy put on their vestments and the sacred vessels are kept; sacristy.

2. a room in a church or church building where prayer meetings, Sunday Schools, etc. are held.

3. in the Anglican and Episcopal churches, a group of church members who manage the temporal affairs of the church.

4. in the Anglican Church, (a) a meeting of such a group or of the parishioners in general; (b) the place where this is held.

ves'try bōard, same as *vestry*, sense 3.

ves'try çlẽrk, an officer chosen by the vestry, who keeps the parish accounts and books.

ves'try·măn, *n.*; *pl.* **ves'try·men,** one of the persons composing a vestry, other than a warden.

ves'tūre, *n.* [OFr. *vesture*, a garment.]

1. a garment; a robe; a vestment; apparel. [Rare or Archaic.]

2. that which invests or covers; covering generally; envelope; integument. [Rare or Archaic.]

3. in law, (a) all except trees that grows on or forms the covering of land; as, the *vesture* of an acre; (b) investiture; seizin; possession.

ves'tūre, *v.t.*; vestured, *pt.*, *pp.*; vesturing, *ppr.* to cover with vesture; to clothe; to envelop: usually in the past participle. [Rare or Archaic.]

ves'tūr·ẽr, *n.* one who has the care of ecclesiastical vestments; a sacristan; also, a subtreasurer of a collegiate church or cathedral. [Rare.]

Vē·sū'vi·ăn, *a.* of or like Mount Vesuvius; volcanic.

vē·sū'vi·ăn, *n.* 1. an early type of match, not easily extinguished, for lighting cigars or tobacco pipes.

2. vesuvianite.

vē·sū'vi·ăn·īte, *n.* a glassy mineral, brown to green in color, a basic silicate of calcium and aluminum, first found at Mt. Vesuvius; idocrase.

vet, *n.* a veterinarian. [Colloq.]

vet, *v.t.*; vetted, *pt.*, *pp.*; vetting, *ppr.* to examine or treat as a veterinarian does. [Colloq.]

vet, *v.i.* to be a veterinarian. [Colloq.]

vet, *n.* a veteran. [Colloq.]

ve̦'tȧ, *n.* [Sp.] mountain sickness; a feeling of being sick experienced by persons at very high altitudes.

vetch, *n.* [OFr. *veche*, from L. *vicia*, a vetch.] any of a number of short, leafy, climbing or trailing plants of the pea family, grown chiefly for fodder and as a soil restorer; especially, a leguminous plant of the genus *Vicia*. The name is also applied to many other leguminous plants of different genera, as the chickling *vetch*, of the genus *Lathyrus*; the horseshoe *vetch*, of the genus *Hippocrepis*; the milk *vetch*, of the genus *Astragalus*, etc. *Vicia sativa* is the common *vetch*. The licorice *vetch* is *Abrus precatorius*.

vetch'ling, *n.* a leguminous plant, of the genus *Lathyrus*. The meadow vetchling, *Lathyrus pratensis*, is a wild plant common in meadows, which makes good hay.

vetch'y, *a.* 1. consisting of vetches or of pea straw; as, a *vetchy* bed.

2. abounding with vetches.

vet'ẽr·ăn, *a.* [L. *veteranus*, from *vetus* (*-eris*), old.]

1. old and experienced; long practiced, especially in war or military service.

2. of a veteran or veterans.

vet'ẽr·ăn, *n.* 1. a person of long experience in some service or position, especially in military service.

2. a person who has served in the armed forces of a country, especially in time of war.

vet'ẽr·ăn·īze, *v.i.*; veteranized, *pt.*, *pp.*; veteranizing, *ppr.* to become a veteran. [Colloq.]

Vet'ẽr·ănṣ' Ad·min·is·trā'tion, a Federal agency, created in 1930, in which all agencies concerned with veterans' affairs were consolidated for administering all laws dealing with relief or benefits for veterans of the army, navy, etc.

vet''ẽr·i·nār'i·ăn, *n.* a person who practices veterinary medicine or surgery.

vet'ẽr·i·nār·y, *a.* [L. *veterinarius*, pertaining to beasts of burden, from *veterina*, beasts of burden.] designating or of the branch of medicine dealing with the investigation, treatment, and prevention of diseases in animals, especially domestic animals.

vet'ẽr·i·nār·y, *n.*; *pl.* **vet'ẽr·i·nār·ieṣ,** a veterinarian.

vet'i·tive, *a.* prohibiting; having the power to forbid or veto.

vet'i·vẽr, *n.* [Fr. *vétiver*, from Tamil *vettivēru*, lit., root that is dug up.]

1. an East Indian grass whose roots yield a fragrant oil used in perfumes.

2. its fibrous roots, also used for making screens, mats, etc.: also called *cuscus*.

vet'i·vẽr oil, a very fragrant oil obtained from the vetiver and used in perfumery: also called *cuscus oil.*

vē'tō, *n.*; *pl.* **vē'tōeṣ,** [L. *veto*, I forbid, from *vetare*, to forbid.]

1. an order prohibiting some proposed or intended act; prohibition, especially by a person in authority.

2. the power to prevent action by such prohibition.

3. the constitutional right or power of a ruler or legislature to reject bills passed by another branch of the government; specifically, in the United States, (a) the power of the President to refuse to sign a bill passed by Congress, preventing it from becoming law unless it is passed again (with a two-thirds majority) by both houses; (b) a similar power held by the governors of States; (c) the exercise of this power.

4. a document or message giving the reasons of the executive for rejecting a bill: also *veto message.*

5. in ancient Rome, the power possessed by the tribunes of the people of interfering so as at once to put a stop to any measure which they deemed injurious to their order, this power being exercised by pronouncing the solemn word *veto.*

vē'tō, *v.t.*; vetoed, *pt.*, *pp.*; vetoing, *ppr.* 1. to forbid; to refuse consent to.

2. to prevent (a bill) from becoming law by a veto.

vē'tō·ist, *n.* one who exercises the right of the veto; one who upholds the use of the veto.

vet·tū'rȧ, *n.*; *pl.* **vet·tū're̦,** [It., from L. *vectura*, a conveying, from *vehere*, to carry.] an Italian four-wheeled carriage.

vet·tū·rī'nō, *n.*; *pl.* **vet·tū·rī'nī,** in Italy, one who carries travelers from one place to another in a vettura at a price agreed on.

vē·tust', *a.* [L. *vetustus*, old, ancient.] old; ancient. [Rare.]

vēuve, *n.* [Fr., widow.] a whidah bird.

vex, *v.t.*; vexed (vekst), *pt.*, *pp.*; vexing, *ppr.* [ME. *vexen*; OFr. *vexer*, to vex, to torment, from L. *vexare*, a freq. or intens. of *vehere*, to carry.]

1. to make trouble for; to disturb; to to annoy; to irritate, especially in little things.

2. to afflict (a person): said of disease. [Rare.]

3. to trouble seriously; to torment.

4. to discuss at length; to bring up again and again for discussion; as a *vexed* point.

5. to shake up; to toss about; to agitate. [Obs.]

Syn.—tease, irritate, provoke, plague, torment, tantalize, bother, worry, pester trouble, disquiet, afflict, harass, annoy.

vex, *v.i.* to fret; to be teased or irritated. [Rare.]

vex·ā'tion, *n.* [ME. *vexacioun*; OFr.; L. *vexatio* (*-onis*), annoyance, from *vexare*, to agitate.]

1. the act of irritating, or of troubling, disquieting, and harassing.

2. the state of being irritated or disturbed in mind.

3. disquiet; agitation; great uneasiness; affliction.

4. the cause of trouble, disquiet, or annoyance.

5. a harassing by law; the act of troubling by a suit maliciously entered.

Syn.—mortification, chagrin, trouble, uneasiness.

vex·ā'tious, *a.* 1. causing vexation; troublesome; annoying.

2. characterized by vexation; disturbed.

3. in law, instituted without real grounds, chiefly to cause annoyance to the defendant: said of legal actions.

vex·ā'tious·ly, *adv.* in a vexatious manner; so as to be vexatious.

vex·ā'tious·ness, *n.* the quality of being vexatious.

vexed (vekst), *a.* 1. annoyed; troubled; agitated; disquieted; afflicted.

2. much disputed or agitated; much contested or discussed; brought up again and again; as, a *vexed* question.

vex'ed·ly, *adv.* with vexation; in a vexed manner.

vex'ẽr, *n.* one who vexes, irritates, or troubles.

vex'il, *n.* in botany, a vexillum.

vex'il·lăr, *a.* vexillary.

vex′il·lăr·y, *a.* [L. *vexillarius*, from *vexillum*; see *vexillum*.]
1. of an ensign or standard.
2. in botany, of or relating to a vexillum.
vexillary estivation; prefloration characterized by a vexillum which sheathes the remaining petals.

vex′il·lăr·y, *n.*; *pl.* **vex′il·lăr·ies,** in ancient Rome, (a) any of a class of veteran soldiers serving under a special standard; (b) one who carries a vexillum; a standard-bearer.

vex′il·lāte, *a.* having a vexillum or vexilla; as, a *vexillate* corolla.

vex·il·lā′tion, *n.* [L. *vexillatio*.] a company of troops under one vexillum, or ensign.

vex·il′lum, *n.*; *pl.* **vex·il′lȧ,** [L. *vexillum*, a standard, flag, dim., from base of *velum*, a sail, a curtain.]
1. in ancient Rome, (a) a military standard, consisting of a square piece of cloth hanging from a crossbar, sometimes surmounted by a figure; (b) the troops belonging to a vexillum; a company; a troop.
2. in ecclesiastical usage, (a) a banner used in processions; (b) a kind of flag or pennon attached to a bishop's pastoral staff. [Rare.]
3. in botany, the large, erect upper petal of a flower of the pea family.
4. in zoology, the web or vane of a feather.

vex′ing·ly, *adv.* in a manner causing vexation; with irritation.

V′-hook, *n.* the V-shaped opening of an eccentric rod of a steam engine.

Vi, in chemistry, virginium.

vī′ȧ (*or* vē′ȧ), *n.*; *pl.* **vī′ae,** [L., a way.] a way or road; as, the *via* Appia.
Via Lactea; same as *galaxy*, sense **1.**
via media; the middle way; the mean; specifically, the position of the Anglican church as a medium between Protestantism and Roman Catholicism.

vī′ȧ, *prep.* by the way of; passing through; as, a journey to Chicago *via* Cincinnati.

vī·ȧ·bil′i·ty, *n.* 1. the state or quality of being viable.
2. the state of being able to survive under conditions of wide geographical distribution, as species of animals and plants.

vī′ȧ·ble, *a.* [Fr., likely to live, from *vie*, L. *vita*, life.] able to live; specifically, (a) at that stage of development that will permit it to live and develop under normal conditions, outside of the uterus: said of a fetus or newborn, especially premature, infant; (b) able to take root and grow; as, *viable* seeds.

vī′ȧ·duct, *n.* [(after *aqueduct*) from L. *via*, a way.]
1. a long bridge consisting of a series of short concrete or masonry spans supported on piers or towers, usually to carry a road or railroad over a valley, gorge, etc.

VIADUCT

2. a similar structure of steel girders and towers.

vī′ăġe, *n.* a voyage. [Obs.]

vī′ăl, *n.* [OFr. *viole*, from L. *phiala*, a saucer, from Gr. *phialē*, a shallow cup.] a phial; a small bottle, usually of glass, for containing medicines or other liquids.
Leyden vial; same as *Leyden jar*.
to pour out vials of wrath; to inflict wrathful punishment.
Go your ways and *pour out the vials of the wrath* of God upon the earth.—Rev. xvi.1.

vī′ăl, *v.t.*; vialed *or* vialled, *pt., pp.*; vialing *or* vialling, *ppr.* to put or keep in or as in a vial.

vī·am′e·tẽr, *n.* [L. *via*, a way, and *-meter*.] an instrument for measuring the distance traveled by a carriage; an odometer.

vī′ănd, *n.* [OFr. *viande*, meat, food, from LL. *vivenda*, lit., things to be lived on, from L. *vivere*, to live.]
1. an article of food.
2. [pl.] food; victuals; especially, choice dishes.

vī′ănd·ẽr, *n.* one who eats or feeds; one who supplies or provides viands; a host. [Obs.]

vī′ap″ple, *n.* same as *Otaheite apple*.

vī·at′iç, *a.* [L. *viaticus*, pertaining to a way or road, from *via*, a way.] relating to a road or journey or to traveling.

vī·at′i·căl, *a.* viatic.

vī·at′i·çum, *n.*; *pl.* **vī·at′i·cȧ** or **vī·at′i·çums,** [L.] 1. provisions, money, or supplies for a journey.
2. in ancient Rome, an allowance of money or supplies to officers who were sent into the provinces to exercise any office or perform any service.
3. the Eucharist as given to a person in danger of death.

vī·ȧ·tom′e·tẽr, *n.* a viameter.

vī·ā′tŏr, *n.*; *pl.* **vī·ȧ·tō′rēş,** [L.] a traveler; a wayfarer.

vī′bex, *n.*; *pl.* **vi·bī′çēş,** [L., a wale.]
1. a discolored spot or blotch of the skin due to subcutaneous extravasation of blood, appearing in certain malignant fevers.
2. a narrow linear mark or streak; a linear subcutaneous effusion of blood.

vī·braç′ū·lăr, *a.* 1. relating to or having the character of vibracula.
2. having vibracula.

vī·braç·ū·lăr′i·um, *n.* same as *vibraculum*.

vī·braç′ū·loid, *a.* like a vibraculum or vibracula.

vī·braç′ū·lum, *n.*; *pl.* **vī·braç′ū·lȧ,** [LL., from L. *vibrare*, to brandish.] in zoology, any of the freely movable, spinelike or whiplike defensive organs of certain bryozoans.

vī′brăn·cy, *n.* the state or quality of being vibrant; resonance.

vī′brănt, *a.* [L. *vibrans* (*-antis*), shaking, from *vibrare*, to shake.]
1. quivering; vibrating; especially, vibrating in such a way as to produce sound.
2. produced by vibration; resonant: said of sound.
3. giving the impression of much energetic activity; pulsing; as, *vibrant* streets.
4. vigorous; energetic; as, a *vibrant* woman.
5. in phonetics, voiced.

vī′brănt, *n.* a voiced sound.

vī′brȧ·phōne, *n.* [from *vibrate* and *-phone*.] a musical instrument resembling the marimba, but with electrically operated valves in the resonators, that produce a gentle vibrato.

vī′brāte, *v.t.*; vibrated, *pt., pp.*; vibrating, *ppr.* [L. *vibrare*, to vibrate, brandish, shake.]
1. to move or wave to and fro; to cause to swing; to cause to oscillate.
2. to affect with vibratory motion; to cause to quiver.
3. to measure or indicate by vibrating or oscillating; as, a pendulum which *vibrates* seconds.
4. to give off (light or sound) by vibration.

vī′brāte, *v.i.* 1. to swing back and forth; to oscillate, as a pendulum.
2. to move rapidly back and forth; to quiver, as a plucked string.
3. to resound: said of sounds.
4. to be emotionally stirred; to thrill; as, she *vibrated* with joy.
5. to waver or vacillate, as between two choices.

vī′brȧ·tile, *a.* 1. of, characterized by, or having the nature of, vibration.
2. capable of vibrating or of being vibrated.
3. having a vibratory motion.

vī·brȧ·til′i·ty, *n.* the property or state of being vibratile.

vī·brā′tion, *n.* [L. *vibratio* (*-onis*), vibration.]
1. a vibrating; specifically, (a) motion back and forth, as of a pendulum; oscillation; (b) rapid rhythmic motion back and forth; quiver.
2. vacillation; wavering, as between two choices or opinions.
3. a stirring; a thrill, as of the emotions.
4. in physics, (a) rapid rhythmic motion back and forth across a position of equilibrium of the particles of a fluid or an elastic solid when its equilibrium has been disturbed, as in transmitting sound; (b) the vibrating motion of a string, etc. in producing sound; (c) a single, complete vibrating motion; a quiver.

vī·brā′tion·ăl, *a.* of, relating to, or resembling vibration.

vī·brā′ti·uñ·çle, *n.* [LL. *vibratiuncula*, dim. of L. *vibratio* (*-onis*), vibration.] a small vibration. [Rare.]

vī′brȧ·tive, *a.* vibratory; vibrating.

vi·brä′tō (*or It.* vē-), *n.* [It., pp. of *vibrare*, to vibrate.] in music, a tremulous effect obtained by rapidly alternating the original tone with a slightly perceptible variation in the pitch, as by the rapid pulsation of the finger on the string of a violin: in singing, sometimes interchangeable with *tremolo*.

vī′brā·tŏr, *n.* something that vibrates or causes vibration; specifically, (a) the hammer of an electric bell; (b) an electrical instrument with a vibrating rubber head or pad, used in massage, etc. (c) in electricity, an oscillator.

vī′brȧ·tō·ry, *a.* 1. of having the nature of, or consisting of vibration.
2. causing vibration.
3. vibrating or capable of vibration.
4. vibrant, as the voice.

Vib′ri·ō, *n.* [L. *vibrare*, to shake.]
1. a genus of short, flagellate, Gram-negative bacteria shaped like a comma or the letter S: one species is the causative agent of cholera.
2. [v–] any member of this genus.

vib′ri·oid, *a.* in botany, of or like a vibrio.

vib′ri·oid, *n.* a vibrioid body.

vib′ri·oid bod′y, in botany, any of the cylindrical, threadlike bodies in the cells of some algae and fungi.

vib′ri·on, *n.*; *pl.* **vib·ri·ō′nēş,** a vibrio.

vī·bris′sȧ, *n.*; *pl.* **vī·bris′sae,** [L. *vibrissæ*, from *vibrare*, to vibrate.] in anatomy and zoology, (a) any of the stiff hairs growing in or near the nostrils of certain animals and often serving as organs of touch, as a cat's whiskers; (b) any of the bristlelike feathers growing near the mouth of certain insect-eating birds, as the whippoorwill.

vī′brō·sçōpe, *n.* [from L. *vibrare*, to shake; and *-scope*.] an instrument for observing and recording vibrations.

Vī·bŭr′num, *n.* [L., the wayfaring tree.]
1. a large genus of shrubs and small trees of the honeysuckle family, with white flowers and black, green, or red berries.
2. [v–] a plant of this genus.
3. [v–] the bark of several species of this plant, used in medicine to relieve spasms.

viç′ăr, *n.* [OFr. *vicaire*; L. *vicarius*, from *vices*, changes, alterations.]
1. a person who acts in place of another; a deputy.
2. in the Anglican Church, the priest of a parish who is not a rector; priest of a parish in which the tithes go to a layman or a religious corporation, the priest himself receiving only a salary.
3. in the Episcopal Church, a minister in charge of one chapel in a parish, as deputy of another minister.
4. in the Roman Catholic Church, (a) a priest or other church officer acting as deputy of a bishop; (b) [V–] the Pope, regarded as earthly representative of Christ: in full, *Vicar of* (*Jesus*) *Christ*.
apostolic vicar, vicar apostolic; in the Roman Catholic Church, (a) formerly, a bishop or archbishop to whom the Pope delegated part of his jurisdiction; (b) a titular bishop administering a vacant diocese, etc., or a missionary bishop acting as a delegate of the Holy See in a region where no regular see has yet been organized.
clerk vicar, lay vicar, secular vicar; in the Anglican Church, a lay officer who assists in conducting services.
vicar capitular; in the Roman Catholic Church, a vicar who has charge of a diocese pending the election of a bishop.
vicar choral; in the Anglican Church, a clergyman or layman who assists in the musical part of the services.
vicar forane; in the Roman Catholic Church, a priest appointed by a bishop to a limited jurisdiction in a particular town or district in his diocese.
Vicar of (*Jesus*) *Christ*; in the Roman Catholic Church, the Pope, considered as head of the Church.

viç′ăr·ăġe, *n.* 1. the residence of a vicar.
2. the benefice or salary of a vicar.
3. the position or duties of a vicar. [Rare.]

viç′ăr·āte, *n.* a vicariate.

viç′ăr-ġen′ẽr·ăl, *n.*; *pl.* **viç′ărş-ġen′ẽr·ăl,**
1. in the Anglican Church, a layman serving as deputy to an archbishop or bishop in certain legal or administrative matters.
2. in the Roman Catholic Church, a priest or higher official acting as deputy to a bishop in administering his diocese.
3. in English history, the title given to Thomas Cromwell as vicegerent of Henry VIII.

vī·cār′i·ăl, *a.* 1. of a vicar or vicars.
2. acting as a vicar.
3. delegated; handed over to a deputy; vicarious; as, *vicarial* powers.

vī·cār′i·āte, *a.* having delegated power, as a vicar.

vī·cār′i·āte, *n.* 1. the office or authority of a vicar.
2. the district administered by a vicar.

vī·cãr′i·ous, *a.* [L. *vicarius*, substituted, from *vicis*, a change, alteration.]
1. taking the place of another thing or person; substitute; deputy.
2. endured, suffered, or performed by one person in place of another; as, *vicarious* punishment.
3. held or handled by one person as the deputy of another; delegated; as, *vicarious* authority or power.
4. enjoyed or experienced by someone through his imagined participation in another's experience; as, a *vicarious* thrill.
5. in physiology, designating or of a function abnormally performed by other than the usual organ or part; as, *vicarious* menstruation.

vī·cãr′i·ous·ly, *adv.* in a vicarious manner; by substitution.

vic′ăr·ship, *n.* the office or position of a vicar.

vic′ăr·y, *n.* a vicar. [Obs.]

vīce, *n.* [ME.; OFr.; L. *vitium*, vice, fault, from a root *vi*, meaning to twist.]
1. a serious fault of character; a grave moral failing.
2. evil or wicked conduct; corruption; depravity.
3. a particular immoral, depraved, or degrading habit.
4. [V–] in old English morality plays, a character, often a buffoon, representing a vice or vice in general.
5. a fault, defect, or blemish.
6. a physical defect or imperfection.
7. a bad or harmful trick or habit in a domestic animal, as in a horse or dog.
Syn.—corruption, fault, defect, evil, crime, immorality, sin, badness.

vīce, *n.* and *v.* same as *vise.*

vīce, *n.* one who acts in the place of another; a substitute or deputy. [Colloq.]

vī′cē, *prep.* [L.] in the place of; instead of; as, he becomes captain of Company K, *vice* Rawlins, resigned.

vīce-, [L. *vice*, in the place of another.] a prefix meaning *one who acts in the place of, subordinate, deputy,* as in *vice*-president.

vīce′-ad′mi·răl, *n.* a naval officer next in rank above a rear admiral and below an admiral.

vīce′-ad′mi·răl·ty, *n.* the office, rank, or command of a vice-admiral.
vice-admiralty court; a court in the British possessions beyond the seas, having admiralty jurisdiction.

vīce′-chãir′măn, *n.*; *pl.* **vīce′-chãir′men,** an assistant or deputy chairman.

vīce′-chām′bẽr·lain (-lin), *n.* the deputy of a chamberlain; in the English royal household, the deputy of the lord-chamberlain.

vīce′-chȧn′cel·lŏr, *n.* 1. an official next in rank below a chancellor, as of a university, and authorized to act as his deputy.
2. in law, a judge serving as assistant to a chancellor.
3. formerly, a judge in the chancery division of the High Court of Justice in England holding a separate court, whose decisions were subject to appeal to the lords justices of appeal and to the House of Lords.
4. formerly, in the Roman Catholic Church, the head cardinal of the papal chancery: now called *chancellor.*

vīce′-çon′sul, *n.* a subordinate or substitute consular officer, to whom special consular functions are delegated.

vīce′-çon′sul·āte, *n.* a consular office of subordinate rank.

vīced (vīst), *a.* vicious; corrupt. [Obs.]

vīce″ġē′răl, *a.* of a vicegerent.

vīce″ġē′ren·cy, *n.* 1. the office, function, or authority of a vicegerent.
2. a district ruled by a vicegerent.

vīce″ġē′rent, *n.* [L. *vicem gerens*, acting in the place of another.] a lieutenant; a vicar; a deputy; an officer deputed by proper authority to exercise the powers of another.

vīce″ġē′rent, *a.* 1. wielding the power of another.
2. characterized by delegated power.

vīce-kinġ′, *n.* one who acts in the place of a king; a viceroy.

vīce′-leg′āte, *n.* a subordinate, assistant, or deputy legate.

vīce′măn, *n.* same as *viseman.*

vic′e·nār·y, *a.* [L. *vicenarius.*]
1. of or consisting of twenty.
2. using twenty as the basic unit of notation.

vī·cen′ni·ăl, *a.* 1. lasting or existing for twenty years.
2. occurring every twenty years.

vīce′-preș′i·den·cy, *n.* the office or term of office of a vice-president.

vīce′-preș′i·dent, *n.* 1. an officer next in rank below a president, acting in his place during his absence or incapacity.
2. [V– P–] the elected officer of this rank in the government of the United States, acting as president of the Senate, but not as executive assistant to the President: he succeeds to the Presidency in the event that the President dies or otherwise leaves office.
3. in some corporations, any of several officers, each in charge of a separate department.
Also *vice president.*

vīce′-preș″i·den′tial (-shăl), *a.* of a vice-president.

vīce″rē′găl, *a.* pertaining to a viceroy or viceroyalty.

vīce″-rē′ġent, *a.* of, pertaining to, or occupying the office of, a vice-regent.

vīce″-rē′ġent, *n.* a substitute or deputy regent; one who acts in the place of a regent.

vīce′reine (rān), [Fr.] the wife of a viceroy.

vīce′roy, *n.* [Fr. *viceroi.*]
1. the governor of a country, province, or colony, ruling in the name of the king (or queen) with regal authority.
2. a strikingly colored American butterfly, *Limenitis archippus.* The orange-red wings are marked with black, and there are white spots at the margins.

vīce″roy′ăl·ty, *n.*; *pl.* **vīce″roy′ăl·ties,** 1. the office, dignity, or authority of a viceroy.
2. his term of office.
3. a district ruled by a viceroy.

vīce′roy·ship, *n.* viceroyalty.

vīce squäd, that division of a police force charged with the suppression or control of prostitution, gambling, and other vices.

vī′cē vẽr′sȧ (*now often* vīs′ vẽr′sȧ), [L.] the order or relation being reversed; on the contrary; conversely.

vi·chy·ssoise′ (vē-shē-swäz′), *n.* [Fr., orig. feminine of *Vichyssois*, of *Vichy*, a city in France.] a thick cream soup of potatoes, onions, etc., usually served cold.

Vich′y wa′tẽr, 1. a sparkling mineral water found at Vichy, France.
2. a natural or manufactured water resembling this.

Vic′i·ȧ, *n.* [L.] a genus of plants of the family *Leguminosæ.* They are usually climbing herbs with abruptly pinnate leaves and with many pairs of leaflets, the common petiole terminating in a tendril at the apex, which is mostly branched. Many of the species are used as green crops for feeding cattle and sheep, especially *Vicia sativa*, the common vetch or tare.

vic′i·năġe, *n.* [L. *vicinia*, neighborhood; *vicinus*, near.]
1. the region or area surrounding a particular place; neighborhood; vicinity.
2. the people living in a particular neighborhood.
3. the fact of being a neighbor; proximity.
jury of the vicinage; a jury whose members live in the county where a trial is held.

vic′i·năl, *a.* 1. neighboring; near-by.
2. designating a road that is local and not a highway.
3. in mineralogy, designating faces on a crystal which approximate or take the place of fundamental planes.

vi·cin′i·ty, *n.*; *pl.* **vi·cin′i·tieș,** [L. *vicinitas.*]
1. the quality or state of being near; nearness; proximity; propinquity.
2. neighborhood; a near-by or surrounding region; as, in the *vicinity* of Buffalo.
3. close relationship. [Obs.]
Syn.—nearness, neighborhood, vicinage.

vi′cious (vish′us), *a.* [Fr. *vicieux*; L. *vitiosus.*]
1. given to or characterized by vice or evil; wicked; depraved; immoral; as, a *vicious* person.
2. having a vice, flaw, fault, or defect; faulty; as, a *vicious* argument.
3. having bad habits; unruly; dangerous; as, a *vicious* horse.
4. malicious; spiteful; mean; as, a *vicious* rumor.
5. debasing; corrupting; as, the experience had a *vicious* effect on her.
6. impure, foul, or noxious, as air or water. [Obs.]
vicious circle; (a) a situation in which the solution of one problem gives rise to another, but the solution of this, or of other problems rising out of it, brings back the first, often with greater involvement; (b) in logic, an argument which is invalid because its conclusion rests on a premise which itself depends on the conclusion; also, the definition of a word by another which is in turn defined by the first; (c) in medicine, a situation in which one disease or disorder results in another which in turn aggravates the first.
vicious intromission; in Scots law, the unauthorized assumption of control or management of another's property; intermeddling in the affairs of another without authority.

vi′cious·ly, *adv.* in a vicious manner; so as to be vicious.

vi′cious·ness, *n.* the state or quality of being vicious.

vi·cis′si·tūde, *n.* [L. *vicissitudo*, from *vix, vicis*, a turn.]
1. [*usually pl.*] changes or variations occurring irregularly in the course of something; especially, change of circumstances in life; ups and downs of fortune.
2. regular succession or alternation, as of night and day.
3. change or alternation, as a natural process of life.

vi·cis·si·tū′di·nār·y, *a.* changing in succession; subject to vicissitudes; exhibiting or characterized by vicissitudes.

vi·cis·si·tū′di·nous, *a.* full of vicissitude; vicissitudinary.

vi·çomte′ (vē-kōṅt′), *n.*; *pl.* **vi·çomtes′** (-kōṅt′), [Fr.] same as *viscount* (sense 2).

vī·çon′ti·el, *a.* [OFr., from *viconte*, sheriff.] in old English law, pertaining to a viscount (sheriff).
vicontiel writs; writs triable in the county or sheriff court.

vī·çon′ti·elș, *n.pl.* in old English law, things belonging to the sheriff; particularly, farms for which the sheriff paid rent to the king.

vic′tim, *n.* [L. *victima*, a victim.]
1. a person or animal killed as a sacrifice to some god in a religious rite.
2. someone or something killed, destroyed, injured, or otherwise harmed by, or suffering from, some act, condition, agency, or circumstance; as, *victims* of war.
3. a person who suffers some loss, especially by being swindled; a dupe.

vic″tim·i·zā′tion, *n.* the act of victimizing or the state of being victimized.

vic′tim·īze, *v.t.*; victimized, *pt., pp.*; victimizing, *ppr.* to make a victim of; specifically, (a) to kill, destroy, etc. as or like a sacrificial victim; (b) to cheat; swindle; dupe.

vic′tim·ī·zẽr, *n.* one who victimizes.

vic′tim·less crime, a statutory crime, such as prostitution or gambling, regarded as having no clearly identifiable victim.

vic′tŏr, *n.* [L., a conqueror, from *vincere*, to conquer.]
1. one who wins in a contest; one who vanquishes another in any struggle; especially, one who wins a battle or war; a vanquisher; a conqueror.
2. a destroyer: used chiefly in poetry. [Rare.]

vic′tŏr, *a.* victorious.

Vic·tō′ri·ȧ, *n.* [L., victory.]
1. an asteroid discovered September 13, 1850, and named after the Roman goddess Victoria. It revolves round the sun in 1303.5 days, and is about two and one third times the distance of the earth from the sun: also called *Clio.*
2. (a) a genus of water lilies of the family *Nymphæaceæ*, named in honor of Queen Victoria of England. The species *Victoria regia*, native to Guiana and Brazil, has large, night-blooming, pineapple-scented flowers and floating leaves of a bright green above and a deep violet on the lower surface, measuring as much as from seven to eight feet in diameter, with a uniformly turned-up margin about three inches high; (b) [v–] a plant of this genus.
3. [v–] a low, four-wheeled carriage for two passengers, with a folding top and a high seat in front for the coachman.
4. [v–] an early touring automobile with a folding top over the rear seat.

VICTORIA

Victoria blue; a blue dyestuff obtained from rosaniline; spirit-blue.

Victoria Cross; the highest British military and naval decoration, consisting of a bronze Maltese cross having the royal crest in the center, with a scroll underneath bearing the words "For Valour," and worn, in the case of a sailor, with a blue ribbon, and in that of a soldier, a red one. It is awarded for deeds of exceptional valor, and the possessor is often honored with the abbreviation V.C. after his name.

VICTORIA CROSS

Victoria green; same as *brilliant green* under *green*.
Victoria pigeon or *crown pigeon*; same as *queen's pigeon*.
Victoria water lily; same as *Victoria*, sense 2.

vic·tō′ri·ăl, *a.* of or relating to victory; victorious. [Obs.]

Vic·tō′ri·ăn, *a.* 1. of or characteristic of the time when Victoria was queen of England (1837–1901).
2. showing the middle-class respectability, prudery, bigotry, etc. generally attributed to the Victorians.
3. designating or of a style of furniture of the 19th century, characterized by ornate, flowery carving and patterned upholstery.

Vic·tō′ri·ăn, *n.* a person, especially a writer, who lived in the reign of Queen Victoria.

Vic·tō′ri·ăn·ism, *n.* the quality or an instance of being Victorian in conduct, thought, style, etc.

vic·tŏr·ine′, *n.* [Fr., f. form of *victor*.] a small fur tippet worn by women.

vic·tō′ri·ous, *a.* [Fr. *victorieux*.]
1. having conquered in battle or contest; having overcome an enemy or antagonist; conquering; vanquishing; as, a *victorious* general, *victorious* troops.
2. associated or connected with victory; characterized by victory; producing conquest; as, a *victorious* day.

vic·tō′ri·ous·ly, *adv.* in a victorious manner; with conquest; triumphantly.

vic·tō′ri·ous·ness, *n.* the state or quality of being victorious.

vic′tō·ry, *n.*; *pl.* **vic′tō·ries,** [L. *victoria*, victory, from *victor*, a victor, from *vincere*, to conquer.]
1. final and complete supremacy or superiority in battle or war.
2. an instance of this; a military engagement ending in triumph.
3. success in any contest or struggle involving the defeat of an opponent or the overcoming of obstacles.
4. [V–] a female deity among the ancient Romans, the personification of victory.
Syn.—conquest, triumph, success.

vic′tress, *n.* a female victor.

vic′trice, *n.* [L., f. of *victor*, a victor.] a victress. [Obs.]

vic′trix, *n.* a victress. [Rare.]

vic·trō′lȧ, *n.* a phonograph: a trade-mark (*Victrola*).

vict′ŭal (vit′l), *n.* [OFr. *vitaille*, provisions; LL. *victualia*, provisions, from L. *victus*, food.]
1. food; provisions. [Archaic or Dial.]
2. [*pl.*] articles of food, especially when prepared for use. [Dial. or Colloq.]
3. grain of any kind. [Scot.]

vict′ŭal, *v.t.*; victualed *or* victualled, *pt.*, *pp.*; victualing *or* victualling, *ppr.* to supply with provisions; to store with food; as, to *victual* an army.

vict′ŭal, *v.i.* 1. to eat or feed. [Rare or Archaic.]
2. to lay in or take on a supply of food.

vict′ŭal·ăge, *n.* food; provisions.

vict′ŭal·ĕr, vict′ŭal·lĕr (vit′l-ĕr), *n.* 1. one who furnishes provisions, as to an army or a ship; a sutler.
2. an innkeeper. [Brit.]
3. a supply ship.
4. a grain dealer. [Scot.]

vict′ŭal·ing bill, a customhouse list warranting the shipment of the goods required for a voyage.

vict′ŭal·ing dē·pärt′ment, see *victualing office*.

vict′ŭal·ing house, an eating house.

vict′ŭal·ing yärd, a yard where supplies for a navy are kept, and where war vessels and transports are provisioned.

vi·cu′ña (vi-kū′nyȧ), *n.*; *pl.* **vi·cu′ñas** (-nyȧz), **vi·cu′ña,** [Sp.; of Quechuan origin.]
1. a cud-chewing animal found wild in the mountains of South America, related to the llama and alpaca of the camel family, and domesticated for its soft, shaggy wool.

VICUNA

2. a soft fabric made from this wool or from a substitute for it: also *vicuña cloth*.

vi′dȧ finch, same as *whidah bird*.

vi·dāme′, *n.* [Fr., from LL. *vice-dominus*; L. *vice*, in place of, and *dominus*, lord.] in France, an officer who, originally under the feudal system, represented the bishop, abbot, etc. in temporal affairs, as in the command of soldiers, the administration of justice, etc.

vī′dē, [L., imper. of *videre*, to see.] see; refer to: used to direct attention to a particular page, book, etc.

vī′dē an′tē, [L.] see before (in the book, etc.).

vī′dē in′frȧ, [L.] see below; see further on (in the book, etc.).

vi·del′i·cet, *adv.* [L., contr. for *videre licet*, it is permitted to see, one may see.] to wit; that is; namely: abbreviated *viz*.

vid′ē·ō, *adj.* [L., I see: used by analogy with *audio*.]
1. of or used in television.
2. designating or of the picture phase of a television broadcast, as distinguished from the *audio* (or sound) portion.

vid′ē·ō, *n.* same as *television*.

vid′ē·ō·cäs·sette′ (-set′), *n.* a cassette containing videotape, for playing back recorded material as on a television set: also *video cassette*.

vid′ē·ō·disc, *n.* a disc similar to a phonograph record, on which images and sounds, as of a motion picture, can be recorded for reproduction as on a home television receiver: also *video disc*.

vid′ē·ō·phōne, *n.* [*video*, and tele*phone*.] a telephone combined with a television receiver and transmitter so that users can see, as well as speak with, one another.

vid′ē·ō·tāpe, *n.* a magnetic tape on which the electronic impulses of the video and audio portions of a television program can be recorded as for later broadcasting.

vī′dē pōst, [L.] see after; see further on (in the book, etc.).

vī′dē sū′prȧ, [L.] see above (in the book, etc.).

vi·dette′, *n.* same as *vedette*.

vī′dē ut sū′prȧ, [L.] see what is stated above.

vid′i·con, *n.* [*vid*eo, and *icon*oscope.] a television camera pickup tube of high sensitivity in which the image is focused on a transparent, thin, metal film backed with a layer of photoconductive material that is scanned with a low-velocity electron beam.

vid′ū·ăl, *a.* of, pertaining, or relating to the state of a widow. [Rare.]

vi·dū′i·ty, *n.* widowhood. [Rare.]

vīe, *v.i.*; vied, *pt.*, *pp.*; vying, *ppr.* [contr. of ME. *envie*, from OFr. *envier*; to invite, vie in games, from L. *invitare*, to invite.]
1. in the old card games of gleek, primero, etc., to wager on the value of one's hand against an opponent. [Obs.]
2. to struggle for superiority (*with* someone) or enter into competition (*for* something); to compete.

vīe, *v.t.* 1. to bet; wager; hazard. [Obs.]
2. to do, offer, display, or match in competition or rivalry; as, they *vied* stories with each other. [Rare or Archaic.]

vīe, *n.* a contest for superiority; also, a challenge; a wager. [Obs.]

vi·elle′, *n.* [Fr., akin to *viol*.]
1. a stringed instrument played by means of a wheel; a hurdy gurdy.
2. a kind of medieval viol.

Vi·en′nȧ caus′tic, a caustic mixture of potash and lime: also called *Vienna paste*.

Vi·en′nȧ In·tĕr·na′tion·ăl, an international Socialist organization formed at Vienna in 1921: see *Labor and Socialist International*.

Vi·en·nēse′, *a.* of or pertaining to Vienna, Austria, or its people, culture, etc.

Vi·en·nēse′, *n.*; *pl.* **Vi·en·nēse′,** a native or inhabitant of Vienna.

vi·ē′rin, *n.* an aromatic, white, bitter substance from a tropical American tree, *Remijia vellozii*.

vī et är′mis, [L.] with force and arms; with actual violence: used in law with reference to a trespass which is the direct cause of damage to person or property.

Viēt Cong [from Vietnamese *Viet Nam Cong San*, Vietnamese Communist.]
1. collectively, native guerrilla and combat groups that compose the military force of the National Liberation Front of Vietnam.
2. any member of such a group.
3. of or having to do with these groups.
A loose, originally derogatory, term.

Viēt′cong′, *n.* same as *Viet Cong*.

Viēt′nam·ēse′, Viēt′-Nam·ēse′, *a.* of Vietnam, its people, etc.

Viēt′nam·ēse′, Viēt′-Nam·ēse′, *n.*; *pl.* **Viēt′-nam·ēse′, Viēt′-Nam·ēse′,** a native or inhabitant of Vietnam.

view (vū), *v.t.*; viewed, *pt.*, *pp.*; viewing, *ppr.*
1. to inspect; scrutinize.
2. to see; behold.
3. to survey mentally; to consider.

view, *n.* [OFr. *veue*, from *veoir*, to see, from L. *videre*, to see.]
1. a seeing or looking, as in inspection or examination.
2. sight or vision; especially, range of vision; as, not a person in *view*.
3. mental survey; intellectual inspection or examination; observation; consideration.
4. that which is viewed, seen, or beheld; something which is looked upon; scene.

'Tis distance lends enchantment to the *view*. —Campbell.

5. a picture, sketch, or photograph, particularly of a landscape; as, the artist has produced some charming *views* of this place.
6. visual appearance or aspect of something.
7. manner of regarding or considering something; judgment; opinion; as, may I have your *views* on the matter?
8. that which is worked toward or sought; object; aim; goal; as, he had a *view* to bettering his condition.
9. expectation; prospect; as, we had no *view* of failure.
10. a general survey or summary; as, the author gave a brief *view* of his book.
11. in law, a formal inspection by the jury of the scene of the alleged crime.
field of view; the whole region within the range of vision; especially, the whole area that can be seen through a microscope, telescope, or the like.
in view; (a) in sight; (b) under consideration; (c) in mind or memory; (d) as an end or object aimed at; (e) in expectation.
in view of; in consideration of; because of.
on view; displayed or exhibited publicly.
point of view; viewpoint.
to have in view; to have as one's object or aim; to have regard to.
view of frankpledge; in Anglo-Saxon law, inspection by the sheriff of the frankpledges of a hundred.
view of premises; in law, the inspection by the jury of the scene of a litigated transaction.
with a view to; (a) with the purpose of; intending; (b) with a hope or anticipation of; looking forward to.

view′ĕr, *n.* 1. one who views, surveys, or examines; specifically, (a) an official appointed to inspect or superintend something; an overseer; as, a *viewer* of the highway; (b) one who views a scene, exhibit, motion picture, television show, etc.; spectator.
2. an optical device for individual viewing of slides, filmstrips, etc.

view find′ĕr, a finder (sense 3).

view hal·loo′, the shout uttered by a huntsman on seeing the fox break cover: also *view hallo, view halloa*.

view′i·ness, *n.* the quality or condition of being viewy, or visionary. [Colloq.]

view′less, *a.* 1. offering no view, or prospect.
2. that cannot be seen; invisible.
3. having or expressing no views, or opinions.

view′less·ly, *adv.* in a viewless manner.

view′ly, view′sŏme, *a.* agreeable or pleasing to the sight. [Brit. Dial.]

view′point, *n.* 1. place of observation.
2. mental attitude or standpoint.
Also *point of view.*

view′y, *a.*; *comp.* viewier; *superl.* viewiest. 1. having odd or fantastic views or opinions; visionary. [Colloq.]
2. showy; ostentatious. [Colloq.]

vī·ġes′i·măl, *a.* [L. *vigesimus,* twentieth, from *viginti,* twenty.]
1. twentieth.
2. of or pertaining to twenty.
3. proceeding by twenties.

vī·ġes·i·mā′tion, *n.* [L. *vigesimus,* twentieth.] the act of putting to death every twentieth man. [Rare.]

vī·ġes′i·mō-quar′tō, *a.* with twenty-four leaves made from each sheet, as a book or pamphlet.

vī·ġes′i·mō-quar′tō, *n.* a book having pages of a certain size, 3⅝ x 5⅛ inches, made by folding a sheet into 24 leaves; 24mo.

vi·ġĭ′à, *n.* [Sp., a lookout.] a mark on hydrographic charts to denote obstructions to navigation, such as shoals or rocks.

viġ′il, *n.* [Fr. *vigile,* vigil, from L. *vigilia,* a watch, from *vigere,* to be vigorous or lively.]
1. a purposeful or watchful staying awake during the usual hours of sleep.
2. a watch kept, or the period of this.
3. in ecclesiastical usage, (a) the eve of a festival, especially when the eve is a fast; (b) a devotional watch kept on such an eve; (c) [*pl.*] devotional services held on such an eve.
vigils or *watchings of flowers*; the faculty belonging to the flowers of certain plants of opening and closing their petals at certain hours: a term used by Linneaeus.

viġ′i·lănce, *n.* [Fr., from L. *vigilans,* wakeful.]
1. the state or quality of being vigilant; watchfulness.
2. a guard or watch. [Obs.]
3. in medicine, insomnia; sleeplessness.
vigilance committee or *committee of vigilance*; (a) a group of persons organized without legal authorization professedly to keep order and punish crime when ordinary law enforcement agencies apparently fail to do so; (b) especially formerly in the South, such a group organized to terrorize and control Negroes and Abolitionists and, during the Civil War, to suppress support of the Union.

viġ′i·lănt, *a.* [Fr., from L. *vigilans.*] watchful; characterized by vigilance; especially, alert to danger.

viġ·i·lan′tē, *n.* [Sp.] one who serves on a vigilance committee.

viġ′i·lănt·ly, *adv.* in a vigilant manner; watchfully.

viġ′i·ly, *n.* vigil. [Obs.]

vī·ġin′ti-, [from L. *viginti,* twenty.] a combining form meaning *twenty,* as in *vigintiangular.*

vī·ġin″ti·an′ġū·lăr, *a.* having twenty angles.

Vig′nȧ, *n.* [after Domenico Vigna, an Italian botanist.] a genus of vines or erect herbs, of the family *Fabaceae*: it is characterized by trifoliate leaves and purple or yellow flowers.

vi·gnette′ (vin-yet′), *n.* [Fr. *vignette,* dim. from *vigne,* a vine.]
1. an ornamental design of vine leaves, tendrils, and grapes, used as a border, inset, headpiece, or tailpiece on a page.
2. any ornamental design or illustration used as an inset, headpiece, or tailpiece on a page.
3. a picture or illustration with no definite border, shading off gradually at the edges; especially, a photographic portrait showing only the head, or the head and shoulders, and shading off at the edges into the background.
4. a short literary composition characterized by compactness, subtlety, and delicacy.

vi·gnette′, *v.t.*; vignetted, *pt., pp.*; vignetting, *ppr.* to make a vignette of or on; to produce the vignette effect upon, as a photograph.

vi·gnet′tẽr, *n.* one who or that which vignettes; specifically, in photography, a device used in printing vignettes.

vi·gnet′tist, *n.* a maker of vignettes, as a painter, photographer, or writer.

vi·gō′ni·ȧ, *n.* the vicuña.

vig′ŏr, vig′ŏur, *v.t.* to invigorate. [Obs.]

vig′ŏr, *n.* [L., from *vigere,* to be strong.]
1. active physical or mental force or strength; vitality.
2. active or healthy growth; as, the vigor of a plant.
3. intensity, force, or energy; as, the *vigor* of her denial.
4. effective legal or binding force; validity; as, the *vigor* of a law.

vi·gō·rō′sō, *a.* [It.] in music, vigorous; energetic: a direction to the performer.

vig′ŏr·ous, *a.* 1. living or growing with full vital strength; strong; robust.
2. of, characterized by, or requiring vigor or strength.
3. forceful; powerful; strong; energetic.
4. acting, or ready to act, with energy and force.

vig′ŏr·ous·ly, *adv.* with vigor.

vig′ŏr·ous·ness, *n.* the quality of being vigorous.

vig′ŏur, *n.* vigor: British spelling.

vī′king, *n.* [O.N. *vikingr.*] any of the Scandinavian sea rovers and pirates who ravaged the coasts of Europe during the eighth, ninth, and tenth centuries.

vi·lä·yet′, *n.* [Turk.; Ar. *wilāyat.*] any of the main administrative districts into which Turkey is divided.

vīld, *a.* vile. [Obs.]

vīle, *a.*; *comp.* viler; *superl.* vilest, [Fr. *vil,* from L. *vilis,* cheap, base.]
1. morally base or evil; wicked; depraved; sinful.
2. offensive to the senses or sensibilities; repulsive; disgusting.
3. cheap; worthless.
4. degrading; lowly; mean: said of conditions, situations, etc.
5. of poor quality; very inferior: often a generalized counterword for anything objectionable; as,*vile* weather.

vīle′ly, *adv.* basely; shamefully; in a vile way.

vīle′ness, *n.* baseness; vile quality or state.

vil′ęynş, *a.* villainous. [Obs.]

vil·i·fi·cā′tion, *n.* a vilifying or being vilified.

vil′i·fī·ẽr, *n.* one who vilifies, defames, or traduces.

vil′i·fȳ, *v.t.*; vilified, *pt., pp.*; vilifying, *ppr.* 1. to use abusive or slanderous language about or of; calumniate; revile; defame.
2. to make vile; to debase; to degrade. [Rare.]
3. to behave toward as vile; to treat as of no importance. [Obs.]

vil′i·fȳ, *v.i.* to be guilty of slander.

vil′i·pend, *v.t.* to treat or regard contemptuously or slightingly; disparage; belittle.
2. to despise; to vilify.

vil·i·pend′en·cy, *n.* disesteem; slight. [Obs.]

vil′i·tȳ, *n.* vileness; baseness. [Obs.]

vill, *n.* [OFr. *ville,* a village, from L. *villa,* a country house, farm.] a village; a small collection of houses; also, a manor; a parish.

vil′lȧ, *n.* [L. *villa,* a country seat, farm.]
1. originally, a country house, with its outbuildings and grounds.
2. a rural or suburban residence, especially one that is large and pretentious.

vil′lȧ·dŏm, *n.* villas and their occupants, collectively; suburban society, regarded as smug, dull, and well-to-do. [Chiefly Brit.]

vil′lăġe, *n.* [OFr.; L. *villaticus,* belonging to a country house, from *villa,* a country house, a farm.]
1. a group of houses in the country, smaller than a town or city and larger than a hamlet.
2. such a community incorporated as a municipality.
3. the people of a village, collectively; villagers.
4. a collection of burrows or habitations of animals; as, a prairie-dog or beaver *village.*

vil′lăġe, *a.* of, pertaining to, or belonging to a village; rustic; provincial.
village community; a primitive type of organized farming community, regarded as the basic self-governing political unit from which the modern state developed, and characterized by communal ownership of land, part of which was apportioned among householders for cultivation, the nonarable part being left as common land.

vil′lȧ·ġẽr, *n.* an inhabitant of a village.

vil′lăġe·ry, *n.* villages collectively.

vil′lăin, *n.* [OFr. *vilain*; LL. *villanus,* a farm servant.]
1. one who is guilty or capable of gross wickedness or crimes; a vile wretch; a scoundrel; a rascal: sometimes used humorously.
2. a wicked or unprincipled character in a novel, play, etc. who opposes the protagonist or hero.
3. in the theater and motion pictures, an actor regularly cast in the role of such a character.
4. a villein.
5. a peasant; a clown; a boor. [Obs.]
Syn.—ruffian, wretch, knave, scamp.

vil′lăin, *a.* appropriate to a villain or slave; servile; base. [Rare.]

vil′lăin, *v.t.* to degrade; to enslave; to debase. [Obs.]

vil′lăin·ăġe, *n.* same as *villeinage.*

vil′lăin·ous, *a.* 1. suited to, like, or pertaining to a villain; very wicked or depraved; extremely vile.
There is nothing but roguery to be found in *villainous* man. —Shak.
2. denoting extreme wickedness or depravity; as, a *villainous* action.
3. arousing dislike or disgust; pitiful; sorry; mean; wretched: said of things.

vil′lăin·ous·ly, *adv.* basely; with extreme wickedness or depravity.

vil′lăin·ous·ness, *n.* the state or quality of being villainous.

vil′lăin·y, *n.*; *pl.* **vil′lăin·ieş,** 1. the state or fact of being villainous; as, the *villainy* of the seducer.
2. villainous conduct.
3. a villainous act; crime.
4. villeinage. [Obs.]
5. foul language or discourse; disgraceful or obscene speech. [Obs.]

vil′lȧ·kin, *n.* a little villa; also, a little village. [Rare.]

vil′lăn, *n.* a villain or villein.

vil′lăn·ăġe, *n.* same as *villeinage.*

vil·lȧ·nel′lȧ, *n.*; *pl.* **vil·lȧ·nel′le,** [It., from *villano,* rustic.]
1. an old rustic Italian song and accompanying dance.
2. a type of sixteenth-century part song for unaccompanied voices, like the madrigal, originating in Naples.

vil·lȧ·nelle′, *n.* [Fr., from It. *villanella.*] a short poem of fixed form, French in origin, consisting of several stanzas (usually five) of three lines each and a final stanza of four lines: it has only two rhymes throughout.

vil·lȧ·nette′, *n.* [dim. of *villa.*] a small villa or country residence. [Rare.]

vil′lăn·ous, *a.* same as *villainous.*

vil′lăn·ous·ly, *adv.* same as *villainously.*

vil′lăn·ous·ness, *n.* same as *villainousness.*

vil′lăn·y, *n.* same as *villainy.*

vil·lat′iç, *a.* [L. *villaticus.*] pertaining to a village or to a farm; rustic; rural.

vil·leġ·giȧ·tū′rȧ (-â-tu′), *n.* [It., from *villa,* a country house.] a temporary residence or stay in the country; rustication.

vil′lein (-en), *n.* [OFr., a farm servant.] in feudal England, any member of a class of serfs, or peasants, who by the thirteenth century had become freemen in their legal relations to all others except their lord, to whom they remained entirely subject as slaves.

vil′lein·ăġe, vil′len·ăġe, *n.* [OFr., servile tenure, from *villein,* a farm servant.]
1. the status or condition of a villein.
2. the conditions of tenure by which a villein held his land.

vil′lī, *n.* plural of *villus.*

vil′li·fọrm, *a.* resembling or fashioned like villi; like the pile or nap of velvet, as the small, closely set teeth of certain fishes.

vil·lī′tis, *n.* [LL., from L. *villus,* a tuft of hair, and *-itis.*] inflammation of the villous tissue of the coronet and of the plantar substance of a horse's foot.

vil′lōse, *a.* same as *villous.*

vil·los′i·ty, *n.*; *pl.* **vil·los′i·tieş,** 1. the quality or condition of being villous.
2. a villus.
3. a coating or surface of villi.

vil′lous, *a.* [L. *villosus,* hairy, from *villus,* a tuft of hair.] of, having the nature of, or covered with villi.

vil′lus, *n.*; *pl.* **vil′lī,** [L., shaggy hair.]
1. in anatomy, any of numerous hairlike or fingerlike vascular processes on certain mucous membranes of the body, as of the small intestine, serving to secrete mucus and absorb fats, etc.
2. in botany, any of the long, soft, fine hairs on certain plants.

vim, *n.* [L., acc. of *vis,* strength.] vigor; energy; activity; spirit.

vī′men, *n.*; *pl.* **vim′i·nȧ,** [L., a flexible twig.] in botany, a slender and elastic branch or shoot.

vim′i·năl, *a.* [L. *vimen, viminis,* a twig, from *viere,* to weave, to plait.] pertaining to twigs; consisting of twigs; producing twigs. [Rare.]

Vim′i·năl, *n.* one of the seven hills on which ancient Rome was built.

vi·min′ē·ous, *a.* [L. *vimineus,* from *vimen,* a twig.]
1. made or woven of twigs.
2. in botany, of or having long, flexible twigs.

viṅ (vaṅ), *n.* [Fr.] wine.

vī′nä, *n.* [Sans. *vīṇā.*] a Hindu musical instrument of the zither family: it has seven strings on a long, fretted fingerboard, which is attached to two gourds serving as resonators.

vī·nā′ceous, *a.* [L. *vinaceus,* from *vinum,* wine.]
1. similar or belonging to grapes or wine.
2. having the color of wine; claret-colored; red, as wine.

vin·āi·grette′, *n.* [Fr., from *vinaigre,* vinegar.]
1. a small box of gold, silver, etc., with perforations on the top, for holding aromatic vinegar, smelling salts, etc.
2. vinaigrette sauce.
3. a small two-wheeled vehicle to be drawn like a Bath chair. [Obs.]
vinaigrette sauce; a savory sauce made of vinegar, oil, herbs, etc., and used on cold meats.

vi·nāi′gri·ēr, *n.* same as *vinegarroon.*

vi·nāi′grous, *a.* sour like vinegar; hence, peevish or ill-tempered.

vi·nȧsse′, *n.* [Fr., from L. *vinacea,* a grape-skin.] the residue in the manufacture of beet-sugar or wine, from which potassium carbonate is prepared.

vi·nat′i·cō, *n.* [perhaps from Port. *vinhatico,* vinaceous, from its color.] a coarse mahogany obtained from *Persea indica,* which grows in Madeira.

viṅ blaṅç (vaṅ), [Fr.] white wine.

Viṅ′çȧ, *n.* [LL., from L., a periwinkle.] a genus of herbs, the periwinkles, with entire and chiefly opposite leaves and solitary flowers, comprising some five species, native to Europe. *Vinca minor* and *Vinca major* are well-known garden plants.

Vin·cen′tiăn, *a.* relating to Saint Vincent de Paul; as, the *Vincentian* Congregation.
Vincentian Congregation; an order of secular priests devoted to the hearing of confessions, education of the clergy, and to aiding the poor.

Vin·cen′tiăn, *n.* a member of an association founded by Saint Vincent de Paul to aid the poor.

Vin′cent's an·gi′nȧ (or **in·fec′tion**), [after J. H. *Vincent* (1862–1950), Fr. physician.] trench mouth.

Vin·cē·tox′i·cum, *n.* [L. *vincere,* to conquer, and *toxicum,* poison.] a genus of plants of the milkweed family: *Vincetoxicum officinale* of Europe was formerly used as an antidote to poisons.

vin·cē·tox′in, *n.* a bitter yellow extract of the root of *Vincetoxicum officinale.*

vin·ci·bil′i·ty, *n.* the quality or state of being vincible, or conquerable.

vin′ci·ble, *a.* [L. *vincibilis,* easily overcome.] capable of being conquered, overcome, or subdued.
vincible ignorance; in theology, ignorance which it is within the power of the subject to overcome; unpardonable ignorance: opposed to *invincible ignorance.*

vin′ci·ble·ness, *n.* capability of being conquered; vincibility.

vin′cit om′ni·ȧ ve′ri·tas, [L.] truth conquers all things.

viṅ′çū·lum, *n.*; *pl.* **viṅ′çū·lȧ,** [L., from *vincere,* to bind.]
1. that which binds; bond; tie.
2. in anatomy, a band, connecting fold, or ligament; frenum.
3. in mathematics, a line drawn over two or more terms of a compound quantity to show that they are to be treated together (e.g., $a-\overline{x+y}$).
4. the juncture of the two main pedal tendons in some birds.

viṅ′çū·lum ma·tri·mō′ni·ī, [L.] the bond of matrimony; marriage tie.

vin·dē′mi·ăl, *a.* [LL. *vindemialis,* from L. *vindemia,* vintage; *vinum,* wine, and *demere,* to remove.] belonging to a vintage or grape harvest. [Rare.]

vin·dē′mi·āte, *v.i.* to gather the vintage. [Rare.]

vin·dē·mi·ā′tion, *n.* the operation of gathering grapes. [Rare.]

vin″di·çȧ·bil′i·ty, *n.* the quality or state of being vindicable.

vin′di·çȧ·ble, *a.* [from L. *vindicare*; and *-able.*] that can be vindicated, justified, or supported; justifiable; defensible.

vin′di·çāte, *v.t.*; vindicated, *pt., pp.*; vindicating, *ppr.* [L. *vindicatus,* pp. of *vindicare,* to claim, avenge.]
1. to clear from criticism, censure, suspicion, etc.; to uphold by evidence or argument.
2. to defend or maintain (a cause, claim, etc.) against opposition.
3. to serve as justification for; to justify; as, his success *vindicated* their belief in him.
4. to claim or establish possession of (*for* oneself or another).
5. [Obs.] (a) to avenge; revenge; (b) to punish.
Syn.—maintain, support, aver, defend.

vin·di·çā′tion, *n.* [L. *vindicatio,* a claiming, from *vindicare,* to avenge.]
1. a vindicating or being vindicated; justification.
2. a fact or circumstance that vindicates, or justifies.
3. assertion or maintenance, as of a claim.

vin′diç·ā·tive (*or* vin·diç′ā-), *a.* 1. tending or serving to vindicate; defending; justifying.
2. revengeful; vindictive. [Obs.]

vin·diç′ā·tive·ness, *n.* vindictiveness.

vin′di·çā·tŏr, *n.* one who vindicates; one who justifies or maintains; one who defends.

vin′di·çȧ·tō·ry, *a.* 1. tending or serving to vindicate; vindicative; justificatory.
2. inflicting punishment; avenging; bringing retribution.

vin′di·çā·tress, *n.* a woman who vindicates.

vin·diç′tive, *a.* [abbrev. from *vindicative,* vindictive, the form being influenced by L. *vindicta,* revenge.]
1. revengeful in spirit; inclined to vengeance.
2. said or done in revenge; characterized by vengeance; as, *vindictive* punishment.
3. punitive. [Rare.]
vindictive damages; same as *exemplary damages.*

vin·diç′tive·ly, *adv.* by way of revenge; revengefully.

vin·dic′tive·ness, *n.* a revengeful temper; revengefulness.

vīne, *n.* [OFr., from L. *vinea,* a vine.]
1. any plant with a long, slender, more or less flexible stem which either trails on the ground or is supported by twining and climbing, sometimes supplied with tendrils which hold it in place.
2. the stem of such a plant.
3. a grapevine, a plant of the genus *Vitis,* having a woody stem and supporting itself by means of strong tendrils: often called *the vine.*
Allegheny vine; a fumariaceous plant, *Adlumia cirrhosa,* growing in low shady grounds and climbing over bushes or low trees by means of the stalks of its leaflets acting as tendrils, producing panicles of flesh-colored flowers all summer. It is cultivated for ornament, and is also called *climbing fumitory* and *mountain fringe.*
vine of Sodom; a plant named in Deut. xxxii. 32, but not certainly identified.

vin′ē·ȧ, *n.*; *pl.* **vin′ē·ae,** in ancient Rome, a kind of shed or shield on wheels for the protection of besiegers.

vin′ē·ăl, *a.* relating to or containing vines. [Obs.]

vīne bee′tle, any one of several species of beetles which are destructive to the branches or leaves of the grapevine, as the rose beetle, the rose chafer, etc.

vīne bŏr′ēr, any one of several species of insects whose larvae puncture the roots, stems, leaves, or twigs of the grapevine.

vīne bow′ēr, a handsome ornamental vine, *Clematis viticella,* of southern Europe.

vīne chăf′ēr, same as *rose chafer.*

vīne cī·dā′ri·ȧ, same as *vine inchworm.*

vīned, *a.* having leaves like those of the vine; ornamented or decorated with or as with vines.

vīne dis·ēașe′, a disease attacking vines, especially one caused by phylloxera.

vīne drag′ŏn, an old barren branch of a grapevine. [Obs.]

vīne′dress″ēr, *n.* one who dresses, trims, prunes, and cultivates vines, especially grapevines.

vīne for′est·ēr, same as *forester,* sense 5.

vīne fret′tēr, a small insect that injures vines; an aphis or plant louse. [Rare or Obs.]

vīne ġall, any gall formed on either the branches or the leaves of a grapevine.

vin′ē·găr, *n.* [Fr. *vinaigre,* from *vin,* wine, and *aigre,* sour.]
1. a sour liquid containing acetic acid, made by fermenting dilute alcoholic liquids, as cider, wine, malt, etc.: it is used as a condiment and preservative.
2. sour or ill-tempered speech, character, etc.
aromatic vinegar; vinegar that is flavored with aromatic spices.
mother of vinegar; see *mother* (substance formed by bacteria).
radical vinegar; same as *acetic acid* under *acetic.*
vinegar of opium; same as *black drop.*

vin′ē·găr, *v.t.*; vinegared, *pt., pp.*; vinegaring, *ppr.* 1. to make into vinegar to or make sour like vinegar. [Obs.]
2. to apply vinegar to; to pour vinegar over; also, to mix with vinegar. [Colloq.]

Vin′ē·găr Bī′ble, a Bible printed in 1717 by the Clarendon Press, Oxford, having the word *vinegar* misprinted for *vineyard* in the running headline for Luke xxii.

vin′ē·găr eel (or **wŏrm**), *Anguillula aceti-glutinis,* a minute species of nematode worm frequently found in vinegar and other fermenting liquids.

vin″ē·găr·ette′, *n.* same as *vinaigrette.*

vin′ē·găr flȳ, any fly of the genus *Drosophila,* whose larva lives in vinegar or similar liquids.

vin′ē·găr·ish, *a.* vinegary.

vin′ē·găr lamp, an apparatus used in oxidizing alcohol to acetic acid by the aid of platinum black.

vin′ē·găr māk′ēr, the vinegarroon.

vin′ē·găr plant, mother (substance formed by bacteria).

vin″ē·găr·rōōn′, *n.* [from Sp. *vinagre,* vinegar: so called from its odor when disturbed.] a large scorpion found in the Southwest and in Mexico.

vin′ē·găr tree, a tree, *Rhus typhina,* bearing acid berries which are sometimes used in making vinegar.

vin′ē·găr·y, *a.* 1. of, or having the nature of, vinegar.
2. sour in speech and disposition; ill-tempered.

vin″ē·gēr·ōne′, *n.* same as *vinegarroon.*

vīne grub, a little insect that infests vines; the vine fretter.

vīne hop′pēr, any one of several species of sap-sucking insects of the genus *Erythroneura*; a grape hopper.

vīne inch′wŏrm, the larva of any moth of the family *Geometridæ,* feeding on grapevines.

vīne leek, a European species of leek, *Allium ampeloprasum.*

vīne louse, a phylloxera.

vīne mā′ple, a maple, *Acer circinatum,* whose branches often bend over and take root in the ground.

vīne mil′dew (-dū), a fungus growth which is parasitic on grapevines.

vīne plūme, a plume moth whose larva feeds on grape leaves.

vīne prō′çris, any one of numerous species of moths of the family *Zygænidæ,* whose larvae are very destructive to grapevines.

vīn′ēr, *n.* a vinedresser. [Obs.]

vīn′ēr·y, *n.*; *pl.* **vīn′ēr·ieș,** [ME. *vinary*; OFr. *vignerie*; ML. *vinarium,* from L. *vinea,* a vine, vineyard.]
1. a greenhouse in which grapevines are grown.
2. vines collectively.
3. a vineyard. [Obs.]

vīne sạw′flȳ, a small, black sawfly, *Blennocampa pygmaea,* common in the United States, whose larvae eat the leaves of the grapevine.

vīne slug, the larval stage of the vine sawfly.

vīne sor′rel, an evergreen climbing plant, *Cissus acida,* closely allied to the grape: it is native to the West Indies.

vīne sphiṅx, a hawk moth which is destructive to the grape.

vīne tīe, a grass, *Ampelodesmos tenax,* growing in the region of the Mediterranean.

vi·nette′, *n.* barberry wine, used in finishing certain grades of leather.

vin′ewed (-ūd), *a.* finewed. [Obs.]

vīne wee′vil, a weevil destructive to grapevines.

vine'yärd, *n.* [AS. *wīngeard.*]
1. land devoted to cultivating grapevines.
2. a field of activity, especially of spiritual labor.

vine'yärd·ist, *n.* the owner of a vineyard; a person employed in the cultivation of grape vines.

vingt et un' (vant''ā-ẽn'), [Fr., lit., twenty and one, twenty-one.] blackjack, or twenty-one, a game at cards in which the object is to make the number or value of the spots on the cards add as nearly as possible to twenty-one, without exceeding it.

vingt''un' (vant''ẽn'), *n.* same as *vingt et un.*

vin'i-, [from L. *vinum*, wine.] a combining form meaning *wine grapes*, or *wine*, as in *vini*culture.

vī'nic (*or* vin'ik), *a.* [from L. *vinum*, wine; and *-ic.*] of, found in, or derived from wine.

vin·i·cul'tūr·ăl, *a.* of viniculture.

vin'i·cul·tūre, *n.* [*vini-* and *culture.*] the cultivation of wine grapes.

vin·i·cul'tūr·ist, *n.* one who is engaged in viniculture.

vin'i·fac·tẽur, *n.* any apparatus for making wine.

vī·nif'ẽr·ous, *a.* [L. *vinifer*, wine bearing, and *-ous.*] yielding wine; as, a *viniferous* country.

vin''i·fi·cā'tion, *n.* the forming of alcohol in a saccharine solution by fermentation.

vin'i·fi·cā''tŏr, *n.* [from *vini-* and L. *-ficatus*, pp. of *-ficare*, to make; and *-or.*] an apparatus for collecting and condensing the alcohol vapors that rise from fermenting wine.

vin'newed (-ūd), *a.* moldy; musty. [Obs.]

vin'newed·ness, *n.* mustiness; moldiness. [Obs.]

vin'ny, *a.* moldy; musty. [Obs.]

vin'ō·len·cy, *n.* [L. *vinolentia*, from *vinum*, wine.] drunkenness. [Obs.]

vin'ō·lent, *a.* addicted to the use of wine; intemperate. [Obs.]

vin·om'e·tẽr, *n.* [L. *vinum*, wine; and *-meter.*] a kind of hydrometer for determining the percentage of alcohol in a wine.

vin or·di·nāire' (van), [Fr., ordinary wine.] any cheap red wine customarily used in France as a table wine.

vī·nōse', *a.* same as *vinous.*

vī·nos'i·ty, *n.* [LL. *vinositas.*]
1. the state or quality of being vinous.
2. addiction to wine.

vī'nous, *a.* [L. *vinosus*, full of wine, from L. *vinum*, wine.]
1. of, having the nature of, or characteristic of wine.
2. (a) addicted to drinking wine; (b) resulting from such addiction; as, in a *vinous* state.
3. of the color of red wine; vinaceous.

vin'quish (-kwish), *n.* same as *vanquish.*

vin'tăge, *n.* [altered (after *vintner*) from ME. *vindage, vendage*; OFr. *vendange*, from L. *vindemia*, vintage, from *vinum*, wine, and *demere*, to remove.]
1. the crop or yield of a particular vineyard or grape-growing region in a single season, with reference either to the grapes or the resultant wine.
2. wine; especially, the wine of a particular region in a specified year.
3. the region or year of a particular wine.
4. the act or season of gathering grapes or of making wine.
5. the type or model of a particular, especially earlier, time; as, an automobile of ancient *vintage.*

vin'tăge, *a.* of a good vintage; choice; as, *vintage* wine.

vin'tăg·ẽr, *n.* [from *vintage* and *-er.*] a person who harvests wine grapes.

vint'nẽr, *n.* [altered from ME. *viniter*, a vintner; OFr. *vinetier, vinotier*, from *vinot*, dim. of *vin* (L. *vinum*), wine.] a person who sells wine, especially at wholesale; wine merchant. [Chiefly Brit.]

vint'ry, *n.*; *pl.* **vint'ries,** a place where wine is sold; a storehouse for wine. [Archaic.]

vī'num, *n.* [L.] wine.

vīn'y, *a.*; *comp.* vinier; *superl.* viniest, **1.** of, or having the nature of, vines.
2. abounding in vines; covered with vines.

vī'nyl (*or* vin'il), *n.* [from L. *vinum*, wine; and *-yl.*] the monovalent radical CH_2CH, characteristic of many derivatives of ethylene, its hydride: various vinyl compounds are polymerized to form resins and plastics, used as for high-fidelity, unbreakable phonograph records.

vī'ŏl, *n.* [Fr. *viole*, from LL. *vidula*, a fiddle, from L. *vitulus*, a calf.]
1. any of an early family of stringed instruments, forerunner of the violin family, characterized generally by six strings, frets, a flat back, and C-shaped sound holes.
2. any instrument of the violin family; as, the base *viol.*

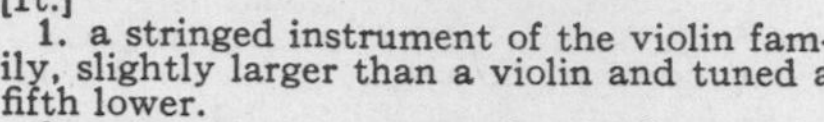

VIOL

vī'ŏl, *n.* in nautical usage, a large rope sometimes used in weighing anchor.

vi·ō'lȧ (*or* vī-), *n.* [It.]
1. a stringed instrument of the violin family, slightly larger than a violin and tuned a fifth lower.
2. an organ stop, generally of 8-foot pitch, producing a tone somewhat like that of a viola.

Vī'ō·lȧ, *n.* [L., a violet.]
1. an extensive genus of temperate plants including the violet, pansy, etc. They are low herbs, more rarely shrubs, with radical or alternate leaves or flowers. Several species are cultivated in gardens, as *Viola tricolor*, the pansy, and *Viola odorata*, the sweet-scented violet. There are a number of species native to the United States, of which *Viola cucullata*, the common blue violet, is much the best known. Other common species are *Viola palmata*, the hand-leaf violet, and *Viola pedata*, the bird's-foot violet, which bears large and handsome blue or purple flowers.
2. [v–] any plant of this genus.

vī''ō·lȧ·bil'i·ty, *n.* the state or condition of being violable.

vī'ō·lȧ·ble, *a.* [L. *violabilis.*] that can be violated, broken, or injured; easily violated.

vī'ō·lȧ·bly, *adv.* in a violable manner; so as to be violable.

Vī·ō·lā'cē·ae, *n.pl.* a family of polypetalous exogens, the violet family, including about fifteen genera of which *Viola* is the type.

vī·ō·lā'ceous, *a.* [L. *violaceus*, violet-colored.]
1. violet in color.
2. of or pertaining to the *Violaceæ*, the violet family.

vi·ō'lȧ clef, the C clef on the third line; alto clef.

vi·ō'lä dä brăc'ciō (brät'chō), [It., lit., viol for the arm.] an early stringed instrument of the viol family, forerunner of the viola.

vi·ō'lä dä găm'bä, [It., lit., viol for the leg.]
1. an early stringed instrument of the viol family, held between the knees like the violoncello of which it is the forerunner.
2. an organ stop of 8-foot pitch producing a stringlike tone.

vi·ō'lä d'ä·mō're, [It., lit., viol of love.] an early stringed instrument of the viol family having sympathetic strings of wire stretched behind the bowed strings, producing soft, clear, ringing tones.

vī·ō·lan'i·line, *n.* same as *nigrosine.*

vī·ō·lan'tin, *n.* a crystalline nitrogenous compound, $C_8N_6H_6O_8$, derived variously.

vī''ō·lȧ·quẽr'cit·rin (-kwẽr'), *n.* a crystalline glucoside obtainable from the pansy.

vī'ō·lāte, *v.t.*; violated, *pt., pp.*; violating, *ppr.* [L. *violatus*, pp. of *violare*, to use force or violence.]
1. to break (a law, rule, promise, etc.); to fail to keep or observe; to infringe on.

By him the *violated* law speaks out.
—Cowper.

2. to rape (a girl or woman); to ravish.
3. to treat without reverence; to desecrate or profane, as a sacred place.
4. to break in upon; interrupt; disturb; as, I shall not *violate* his privacy.

He who attempts to *violate* the happiness of another. —Wollaston.

5. to offend, insult, or outrage; as, his callousness *violates* my sense of decency.
6. to treat (someone) roughly or abusively; to mistreat. [Obs.]

Syn.—ravish, injure, abuse, disturb, hurt, rape, outrage, debauch, break, infringe, profane, transgress, disobey.

vī·ō·lā'tion, *n.* a violating or being violated; specifically, (a) infringement or breach, as of a law, right, etc.; (b) rape; ravishment; (c) desecration of something sacred, as a church; (d) interruption; disturbance; (e) [Obs.] rough, violent treatment.

vī'ō·lā·tive, *a.* violating; tending to or causing violation.

vī'ō·lā·tŏr, *n.* 1. one who violates, injures, interrupts, or disturbs; as, a *violator* of repose.
2. one who infringes or transgresses; as, a *violator* of law.
3. one who profanes or treats with irreverence; as, a *violator* of sacred things.
4. a ravisher.

vī'ō·lence, *n.* [L. *violentia*, from *violens* (*-entis*), violent.]
1. physical force used so as to injure or damage; roughness in action.
2. a use of force so as to injure or damage; a rough, injurious act.
3. natural or physical energy or force in action; intensity; severity; as, the *violence* of the storm.
4. unjust use of force or power, as in deprivation of rights.
5. great force or strength of feeling, conduct, or language; passion; fury.
6. distortion of meaning, phrasing, etc.; as, to do *violence* to a text.
7. desecration; profanation.

to do violence to; to outrage; to force; to injure; as, he *does violence to* his own opinions.

Syn.—vehemence, impetuosity, force, outrage, rage, profanation, injustice, fury, infringement, fierceness, oppression.

vī'ō·lence, *v.t.* to assault; to injure; also, to bring by violence; to force. [Obs.]

vī'ō·len·cy, *n.* violence. [Obs.]

vī'ō·lent, *a.* [L. *violens* (*-entis*), violent.]
1. acting with or characterized by great physical force, so as to injure or damage; rough.
2. acting or characterized by force unlawfully used.
3. caused by violence; as, a *violent* death.
4. showing, or resulting from, strong feeling or emotion; passionate; immoderate; furious; as, *violent* language.
5. extreme; intense; very strong; as, a *violent* storm.
6. tending to distort the meaning; as, a *violent* construction of a text.
7. forced; not voluntary; compulsory. [Obs.]

violent presumption; in law, presumption arising from circumstances which necessarily attend such facts. Such circumstances being proved, the mind infers with confidence that the fact has taken place, and this confidence is a *violent presumption*, which amounts to proof.

violent profits; in Scots law, the penalty due by a tenant who forcibly or unwarrantably retains possession after he ought to have removed.

Syn.—furious, boisterous, vehement, impetuous.

vī'ō·lent, *n.* an assailant. [Obs.]

vī'ō·lent, *v.t.* to urge or do with violence. [Obs.]

vī'ō·lent, *v.i.* to act or work with violence; to be violent. [Obs.]

vī'ō·lent·ly, *adv.* in a violent manner; with force; forcibly; vehemently.

vī·ō·les'cent, *a.* tending to a violet color.

vī'ō·let, *n.* [Fr. *violette*, dim. from L. *viola*, a violet.]
1. any of a number of related short plants of the genus *Viola*, with fragrant white, blue, purple, or yellow flowers.
2. the flower of any of these plants.
3. any of various similar but unrelated plants, or their flowers.
4. a bluish-purple color.
5. a pigment of this color.
6. in zoology, a small butterfly of a violet color, belonging to the *Polyommatus, Lycæna*, or related genera.

aniline violet; same as *mauveine.*

bird's-foot violet; a low stemless plant, *Viola pedata*, with large light-blue or white flowers, found in the eastern part of the United States.

Canada violet; a large erect plant, *Viola canadensis*, with white or light-blue flowers, found in the mountains of eastern North America.

dog violet; a stemmed violet, *Viola canina*, having light-blue or violet flowers, common in the northern parts of the Old World: one variety is found in North America.

English violet; the sweet violet.

green violet; a perennial herb with greenish-white flowers, *Solea concolor*, widely distributed in the eastern and central parts of the United States.

Hoffmann's violet; see *dahlia* (sense 3).

horned violet; a cultivated violet, *Viola cornuta*, of the Pyrenees and Switzerland, having pale-blue, sweet-scented spurred flowers.

Neapolitan violet; the sweet violet.

pansy violet; a variety of the bird's-foot violet with flowers that have dark-purple upper petals and light-purple lower petals: also called *velvet violet*.

paris violet; methyl violet.

spurless violet; an Australian violet, *Viola hederacea*, having small blue flowers and a spurless corolla.

spurred violet; a violet, *Viola calcarata*, of southern Europe, related to the horned violet and having large purple flowers and an awl-shaped spur.

sweet violet; see under *sweet*.

tricolored violet; the pansy.

velvet violet; see *pansy violet*.

vī'ō-let, *a.* having the color of violet; of a dark blue inclining to purple.

vī'ō-let-blūe, *n.* a shade of blue with a violet tinge.

vī'ō-let çär'mine, a bluish-purple color.

vī'ō-let çress, an annual cruciferous plant, *Ionopsidium acaule*, of Spain and Portugal, having violet, white, or pinkish flowers.

vī'ō-let-ēar, *n.* a hummingbird of the genus *Petasophora*, found in tropical America: so called from the violet-colored tufts on the ears.

vī'ō-let rāy, 1. the shortest ray of the visible spectrum, producing the color violet.

2. loosely, the ultraviolet ray.

vī'ō-let shell, any gastropod of the genus *Ianthina*.

vī'ō-let snāil, same as *ianthina*.

vī'ō-let tip, an American butterfly, *Polygonia interrogationis*, having violet tips on the wings.

vī'ō-let wood, any one of a number of woods of a violet color; as, (a) kingwood; (b) the wood of the myall; (c) the wood of a leguminous tree, *Andira violacea*, of Guiana.

vī-ō-lin', *n.* [It. *violino*, dim. of *viola*, a viol.]

1. any instrument of the modern family of string instruments played with a bow, developed from the viol and characterized by four strings, a lack of frets, a somewhat rounded back, and *f*-shaped sound holes; specifically, the smallest and highest pitched instrument of this family, held horizontally under the chin, resting against the collarbone; a fiddle.

2. a violinist, especially a member of an orchestra.

violin bow; the bow used in playing the violin.

violin clef; the G clef; treble clef.

violin diapason; a diapason stop in an organ of narrow scale and stringlike tone.

VIOLIN

A, scroll; B, pegbox; C, pegs; D, nut; E, neck; F, waist; G, sound holes; H, bridge; I, tailpiece; J, button; K, finger board

vī'ō-lin, *n.* an emetic substance found in the common violet.

vī-ō-lī'nȧ, *n.* an organ stop, usually of four-foot pitch and a stringlike quality.

vī'ō-līne, *n.* a blue-violet color.

vī-ō-lin'ist, *n.* one who plays on the violin.

vī-ō-lī'nō, *n.* [It.] a violin (musical instrument).

vī'ŏl-ist (*for 2*, vī-ō'list), *n.* 1. a player on the viol.

2. a player on the viola.

vī"ō-lon-cel'list (-chel'ist), *n.* one who plays on the violoncello; a cellist.

vī"ō-lon-cel'lō (-chel'), *n.*; *pl.* **vī"ō-lon-cel'lōṣ**, [It., dim. of *violone*, a bass viol.]

1. a cello.

2. an organ stop of eight-foot pitch, narrow scale, and a stringlike quality.

vī-ō-lō'ne, *n.* [It.] 1. the contrabass; the double bass.

2. an organ stop of sixteen-foot pitch of stringlike tone.

vī'ō-lous, *a.* violent. [Obs.]

vī-ō-lū'riç, *a.* of, pertaining to, or derived from violuric acid.

violuric acid; an acid whose salts are red, yellow, blue, and violet, obtained from various sources in yellowish crystals.

vī-os'tẽr-ōl, *n.* ultra*vio*let and ergo*sterol*.] a preparation of ergosterol, irradiated with ultraviolet rays and dissolved in oil, used in medicine to supply a vitamin D deficiency.

vī'pẽr, *n.* [Fr. *vipère*, from. L. *vipera*, short for *vivipara*, producing live young.]

1. a snake belonging to either of two worldwide groups of venomous snakes: the *true vipers*, found in Europe, Africa, and Asia, include the common, horned, or long-nosed vipers, puff adders, etc., and the *pit vipers*, found in Asia and America, include the water viper, copperhead, fer-de-lance, bushmaster, rattlesnake, etc.

2. any of various other venomous or supposedly venomous snakes.

3. a malicious or spiteful person.

4. a treacherous person.

vī'pẽr-fish, *n.* a long-toothed deep-sea fish of the genus *Chauliodus*, as *Chauliodus sloani*.

vī'pẽr gōurd, *a* vine, *Trichosanthes anguina* or *colubrina*, of the gourd family, native to India, having a snakelike, pendulous edible fruit.

vī'pẽr-id, *a.* viperine.

vī'pẽr-id, *n.* any snake of the *Viperidæ*.

Vī-pẽr-ī'dae, *n.pl.* a family of snakes, the vipers.

Vī-pẽr-ī'nȧ, *n.pl.* one of the groups of snakes: it includes the vipers.

vī'pẽr-ine, *a.* [L. *viperinus*.] pertaining to, having the nature of, or like that of a viper or vipers; venomous.

viperine snake; any snake of the family *Viperidæ*; also, any snake resembling a viper; especially, *Tropidonotus viperinus*, a small European snake.

vī'pẽr-ish, *a.* viperous; venomous; like a viper; especially, spiteful or malicious.

vī'pẽr-oid, *a.* relating to or like *Viperidæ*.

vī'pẽr-ous, *a.* of, having the nature of, or like a viper; especially, spiteful or venomous.

vī'pẽr'ṣ bū'gloss, blueweed, a plant of the genus *Echium*.

vī'pẽr'ṣ-grȧss, *n.* a plant of the genus *Scorzonera*.

vī-rȧ-ġin'i-ăn, *a.* having the qualities or characteristics of a virago.

vī-rȧ-ġin'i-ty, *n.* the quality or character of a virago. [Rare.]

vī-rā'gō, *n.*; *pl.* **vī-rā'gōeṣ**, **vī-rā'gōṣ**, [ME.; AS.; L., a manlike maiden, from *vir*, a man.]

1. a bold, quarrelsome, shrewish woman; a scold.

2. a strong, large, manlike woman; an amazon. [Archaic.]

vī'răl, *a.* of, involving, or caused by a virus.

vīre, *n.* [OFr., an arrow for the crossbow, from Sp. *vira*, a dart.] an arrow that whirls as it flies.

vīre-lāi', *n.* [Fr.] a virelay.

vir'e-lāy, *n.* [ME. *vyrelaye*; OFr. *virelai*; prob. altered after *lai*, lay (poem), from OFr. *virli*, *vireli*, a jingle used as the refrain of a song.]

1. an old French form of short poem, consisting of short lines with two rhymes and having two opening lines repeated at intervals.

2. any similar verse form, especially one with stanzas made up of alternating long lines and short lines, the rhyme of the short lines of one stanza being echoed by the rhyme of the long lines of the next stanza.

vī'rent, *a.* [L. *virens* (*-entis*), *ppr.* of *virere*, to be green.] green; verdant; fresh. [Rare.]

Vir'ē-ō, *n.* [L. *vireo*, a greenfinch.]

1. a genus of small, insect-eating, passerine singing birds, typical of the family *Vireonidæ*, with olive-green or gray plumage: they are mostly confined to North America.

2. [v–] *pl.* **vir'ē-ōṣ**, any member of the genus *Vireo* or family *Vireonidæ*.

vir'ē-ō-nīne, *a.* of or like a vireo; of the *Vireonidæ*.

vir'ē-ō-nīne, *n.* a bird of the family *Vireonidæ*.

vī-res'cence, *n.* [L. *virescens* (*-entis*), greenish, from *virescere*, to grow green.] in botany, a change to green of parts not normally so, due to an abnormal presence of chlorophyll.

vī-res'cent, *a.* turning or beginning to be green; also, greenish.

vir'gȧ, *n.* [Mod. L., from L., a twig, streak in the heavens.] in meteorology, long streamers or wispy streaks of water or ice particles falling from the base of a cloud but evaporating completely before reaching the ground.

vir'găl, *a.* [L. *virga*, a twig.] made of twigs.

vir'gāte, *a.* [L. *virga*, a twig.]

1. in botany, having the shape of a rod or wand.

2. having many small twigs.

vir'gāte, *n.* [ML. *virgata* (*terræ*), from L. *virga*, a rod, twig: used as transl. of AS. *gierland*, yardland.] an old English measure of land varying greatly in size, but most commonly equal to a quarter of a hide, or about thirty acres.

vir'gā-ted, *a.* virgate.

virġe, *n.* a wand; a verge. [Obs.]

vir'ġẽr, *n.* a verger. [Obs.]

Vir-ġil'i-ăn, *a.* of or like the poetry of Virgil: also spelled *Vergilian*.

vir'ġin, *n.* [L. *virgo* (*-inis*), a maiden.]

1. (a) a woman, especially a young woman, who has not had sexual intercourse; (b) a girl or unmarried woman.

2. less commonly, a man, especially a youth, who has not had sexual intercourse.

3. in ecclesiastical usage, a member of a religious order of women, as a nun, who has taken a vow of chastity.

4. [V–] the Virgin Mary, mother of Jesus: usually with *the*.

5. a Madonna; a representation of the Virgin Mary in art.

6. [V–] the constellation Virgo.

7. an insect producing fertile eggs without impregnation by the male.

8. a female animal that has not copulated.

9. a species of gossamer-winged butterfly.

10. the condition of virginity. [Rare.]

vir'ġin, *a.* 1. being a virgin.

2. composed of virgins.

3. characteristic of or proper to a virgin; chaste; modest.

4. like or suggesting a virgin because untouched, unmarked, pure, clean, etc.; as, *virgin* snow.

5. up to this time unused, untrod, uncultivated, undiscovered, etc. by man; as, *virgin* forest.

6. never having had contact with or experience (*of*); as, a forest *virgin of* hunters.

7. occurring uncombined in its native form; as, *virgin* silver.

8. being the first; initial; as, a *virgin* voyage.

9. (a) obtained from the first pressing, without the use of heat: said of an oil, as of olives; (b) obtained directly from an ore or from the first smelting: said of a metal.

10. parthenogenetic.

virgin birth; (a) in Christian theology, the doctrine that Jesus was born to Mary without prejudice to her virginity and that she was his only human parent; (b) in zoology, parthenogenesis.

virgin gold; pure, unalloyed gold.

Virgin Mary; Mary, the mother of Jesus.

Virgin Queen; Queen Elizabeth I of England.

virgin wool; wool that has never been processed.

vir'ġin, *v.i.* to play the virgin; to be chaste.

vir'ġin-ăl, *a.* 1. of, characteristic of, or proper to a virgin; maidenly.

2. remaining in a state of virginity.

3. pure; fresh; untouched; unsullied.

4. in zoology, not fertilized.

virginal generation; parthenogenesis.

virginal membrane; the hymen.

vir'ġin-ăl, *n.* [Fr. *virginale*; perh. from being commonly played by virgins, or young girls.] a harpsichord; especially, a small, rectangular harpsichord of the sixteenth century, placed on a table or held in the lap to be played: sometimes called *pair of virginals*.

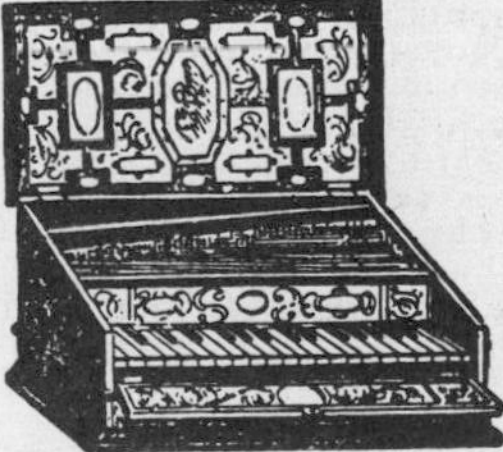

VIRGINAL

vir'ġin-ăl, *v.i.* to tap with the fingers; to strike as on a virginal.

Vir'ġin-ăl, **Vir-ġi-nā'lē**, *n.* in the Roman Catholic Church, the book of devotional services to the Virgin.

vir'ġin-hood, *n.* maidenhood; virginity.

Vir-ġin'i-ȧ, *n.* [L., f. of *Virginius*, *Verginius*, name of the Roman gens.]

1. one of the asteroids, discovered in 1857.
2. a kind of tobacco, grown in Virginia.
Virginia cowslip (or *bluebell*); a plant, *Mertensia virginica*, with clusters of blue or purple bell-shaped flowers that develop from pink buds.
Virginia creeper; a climbing vine, *Ampelopsis quinquefolia*, having leaflets in groups of five, greenish flowers, and bluish-black berries: also called *American ivy, woodbine.*
Virginia deer; any of a large group of American white-tailed deer having a white-spotted red coat in summer and a diffuse gray-brown coat in winter: found from Canada to Peru.
Virginia fence; a zigzag fence made of rails laid across each other at the ends; a worm fence: also *Virginia rail fence.*
Virginia nightingale; the cardinal bird.
Virginia quail; the bobwhite.
Virginia reel; (a) a country dance, the American variety of the reel, performed by a number of couples facing each other in two parallel lines; (b) music for this dance.
Virginia stock; a cruciferous herb, *Malcolmia maritima*, of the Mediterranean.
Virginia trumpet flower; any of a number of related climbing plants with clusters of orange-red, trumpet-shaped flowers; trumpet creeper.

Vĩr·ġin′i·ăn, *a.* of Virginia.

Vĩr·ġin′i·ăn, *n.* one born in or an inhabitant of Virginia.

vĩr·ġi′ni·bus pū·e·ris′que (-kwi), [L.] for girls and boys.

vĩr·ġin′i·ty, *n.* 1. the state or fact of being a virgin; maidenhood; celibacy.
2. condition of being new, fresh, unused, uninvestigated, or untried.

vĩr·ġin′i·um, *n.* [Mod. L., from *Virginia* (the State).] a name given to chemical element 87, supposedly discovered in 1930: symbol, Vi.

vĩr′ġin′ṣ-bow′ẽr, *n.* a white-flowered, rambling plant of the genus *Clematis*: called also *traveler's joy.*

Vĩr′gō, *n.* [L., a virgin.]
1. the sixth sign of the zodiac which the sun enters about August 22.
2. an equatorial constellation between Leo and Libra, supposedly outlining a woman, and containing 39 visible stars of which Spica is the brightest; the Virgin.

vĩr′gou·lēuṣe, *n.* [Fr., from *Virgoulée*, a village near Limoges, France.] a variety of pear.

Vĩr·gū·lā′ri·ȧ, *n.* [L. *virgula*, a little rod; dim. of *virga*, a rod.] a genus of coelenterates, closely allied to the genus *Pennatula*. One extremity, which is buried in the sand or mud, is always without polyps, and somewhat resembles the barrel of a feather.

vĩr·gū·lãr′i·ăn, *n.* a member of the genus *Virgularia.*

vĩr′gū·lāte, *a.* shaped like a rod.

vĩr′gūle, *n.* [Fr.; L. *virgula*, a small rod, twig.]
1. a comma. [Obs.]
2. a short diagonal line (/) placed between two words to indicate that either word can be used in interpreting the statement. Example: and/or; i.e., either "and" or "or."

vĩr′i·ăl, *n.* [L. *vis, viris*, force.] half of the product of the stress of attraction or repulsion by the distance between two particles.

vĩr′id, *a.* [L. *viridis*, green.] green; verdant. [Rare.]

vĩr·i·des′cence, *n.* [LL. *viridescens* (*-entis*), being green.] a viridescent state or quality; greenishness.

vĩr·i·des′cent, *a.* somewhat green; greenish.

vi·rid′i·ăn, *n.* [from L. *viridis*, green.] a bluish-green pigment, hydrated chromic oxide, Cr_2O_3, used in paints or dyes.

vĩr′i·dine, *n.* [L. *viridis*, green.] a greenish, oily coal-tar hydrocarbon.

vĩr′i·dīte, *n.* any of various greenish mineral silicates of iron and magnesium found in rocks.

vi·rid′i·ty, *n.* [L. *viriditas* (*-tatis*), from *virere*, to be green.]
1. greenness; verdure; the color of young vegetation.
2. freshness; liveliness.

vĩr′ile (*or, rarely*, vī′ril), *a.* [L. *virilis*, manly, from *vir*, a man.]
1. pertaining to, belonging to, or characteristic of an adult man; manly; masculine; male.
2. of or capable of procreation.
3. having manly strength or vigor; vigorous; forceful.

vĩr·i·les′cence, *n.* [L. *virilis*, manly, and *-escence.*] in zoology, that condition in an old female when certain of the characteristics of the male are assumed, as in some fowls.

vĩr·i·les′cent, *a.* in zoology, acquiring masculine qualities.

vī·ril′i·ȧ, *n.pl.* [L. *virilis*, manly.] the male generative organs.

vĩr′i·liṣm, *n.* [from *virile* and *-ism.*] the abnormal appearance of secondary male sexual characteristics in a woman, as the growth of facial hair.

vi·ril′i·ty, *n.* [Fr. *virilité*; L. *virilitas*, manhood.]
1. the state or quality of being virile; complete manhood.
2. the power of procreation.
3. strength; vigor; forcefulness.
4. the character or conduct of a man; masculinity.

vī·rip′ō·tent, *a.* [L. *vir, viri*, a man, and *potens* (*-entis*), able, fit.] sexually mature; marriageable.

vi·rōle′, *n.* [Fr.] in heraldry, a hoop or ring surrounding a bugle or hunting horn; also, a ferrule.

vi·rōled′, *a.* having a virole or viroles.

vī′rōse, *a.* [L. *virosus*, virulent, poisonous, from *virus*, poison.] virosis.

vī·rō′sis, *n.*; *pl.* **vī·rō′sēṣ,** [Mod. L.; *virus* and *-osis.*] any disease caused by a virus, especially a filtrable virus.

vir·tụ′, *n.* [It. *virtu*, excellence, virtue.]
1. a knowledge or love of, or taste for, artistic objects or curios.
2. the quality of being artistic, beautiful, rare, or otherwise such as to interest a collector.
3. such art objects and curios, collectively. Also spelled *vertu.*

vĩr′tū·ăl, *a.* [ME. *vertual*; ML. *virtualis*; L. *virtus*, strength, virtue.]
1. being in essence or effect, not in fact; not actual, but equivalent, so far as effect is concerned; as, he is a *virtual* stranger, although we've met.
2. effective because of some inherent virtues or powers. [Rare or Archaic.]
3. potential. [Archaic.]
virtual focus; the point from which rays which have been made divergent by reflection or refraction appear to issue.
virtual image; see under *image.*
virtual moment of a force; see under *moment.*
virtual velocity; in mechanics, the resolved part of the displacement in the direction of the force when the point of application of a force is displaced through an indefinitely small space.

vĩr·tū·al′i·ty, *n.* 1. the state or quality of being virtual.
2. potentiality; potential existence. [Obs.]

vĩr′tū·ăl·ly, *adv.* in a virtual manner; in effect if not in actuality; for all practical purposes; as, *virtually* identical.

vĩr′tū·āte, *v.t.* to make efficacious. [Obs.]

vĩr′tūe, *n.* [ME. and OFr. *vertu*, virtue, goodness, power, from L. *virtus*, manliness, worth.]
1. general moral goodness; right action and thinking; uprightness; rectitude; morality.
2. a particular moral quality regarded as good or meritorious; as, the *virtue* of generosity; specifically, in philosophy and theology, any of the cardinal virtues or theological virtues.
3. chastity, especially in a woman.
4. a specific excellence; any good quality, merit, or accomplishment; also, excellence in general; merit; value.

Pity is the *virtue* of the law.
And none but tyrants use it cruelly.—Shak.

5. effective power or force; efficacy; potency; especially, the ability to heal or strengthen; as, the *virtue* of a medicine.
6. [*pl.*] in theology, one of the orders of the angels.
7. bravery; valor; courage; daring. [Obs.]
8. a mighty work; a miracle. [Obs.]
by virtue of or *in virtue of*; because of; on the grounds of.
cardinal virtues; see under *cardinal.*
theological virtues; the three virtues, faith, hope, and charity.
to make a virtue of necessity; to do what one has to do as if from inclination or a sense of duty.

Syn.—chastity, efficacy, goodness, faithfulness, honesty, integrity, justice.

vĩr′tūe·less, *a.* 1. without virtue or moral goodness; vicious.
2. without efficacy or operating qualities.

vĩr·tụ·os′i·ty, *n.*; *pl.* **vĩr·tụ·os′i·tieṣ,** 1. interest in or taste for the fine arts; especially, a sensitive but amateur or trifling interest.
2. great technical skill in some fine art, especially in the performance of music; sometimes, mere technical skill.
3. virtuosos (sense 1) collectively.

vĩr·tụ·ō′sō, *n.*; *pl.* **vĩr·tụ·ō′sōṣ, vĩr·tụ·ō′si,** [It.] 1. a person with great interest and sensitive taste in the fine arts; a collector or connoisseur of art objects or curios.
2. a person having great technical skill in some fine art, especially in the performance of music.
3. a person learned in the arts and sciences; scholar; savant. [Obs.]
4. an empirical student; an experimental philosopher or investigator. [Obs.]

vĩr·tụ·ō′sō·ship, *n.* the pursuits, studies, and accomplishments of a virtuoso.

vĩr′tū·ous, *a.* 1. having, or characterized by, moral virtue; morally good; as, a *virtuous* man.
2. chaste; pure: applied to women.
3. efficacious; having effective virtue or potency. [Archaic.]
4. having or exhibiting strength and manly courage; brave; valorous. [Obs.]

vĩr′tū·ous·ly, *adv.* in a virtuous manner; in conformity with the moral law or with duty; as, a life *virtuously* spent.

vĩr′tū·ous·ness, *n.* the state or character of being virtuous.

vir′ū·lence, *n.* 1. the quality of being virulent; the quality or property of being poisonous, venomous, or injurious to life; as, the *virulence* of poison.
2. the relative infectiousness of a microorganism causing disease.
3. violent or bitter animosity.

vir′ū·len·cy, *n.* same as *virulence.*

vir′ū·lent, *a.* [ME. *verelent*; L. *virulentus*, full of poison.]
1. extremely injurious; deadly; very poisonous or venomous.
2. very bitter in enmity; violently antagonistic or spiteful; as, a *virulent* invective.
3. in medicine, pertaining to or characterized by malignancy and a rapid course: applied to diseases.
4. in bacteriology, having the property or ability to break down or overcome resistance of the host; highly infectious: said of a microorganism.

vir′ū·lent·ed, *a.* filled with poison; made poisonous. [Rare.]

vir′ū·lent·ly, *adv.* in a virulent manner.

vir·ū·lif′ẽr·ous, *a.* carrying or communicating virus or poison; containing a virus.

vī′rus, *n.* [L., poison.]
1. venom, as of a snake.
2. (a) any of a group of ultramicroscopic or submicroscopic infective agents that cause various diseases, as smallpox: viruses are capable of multiplying in connection with living cells and are variously regarded as living organisms and as complex proteins; (b) specifically, a filtrable virus; (c) the exudation from the vesicles of cowpox, used as a vaccine for smallpox.
3. that which corrupts or poisons the mind or character; evil or harmful influence.

vis, *n.*; *pl.* **vī′rēṣ,** [L.] force; power; strength; vigor; energy.
vis inertiae; (a) same as *inertia* (sense 1); (b) the resistance offered by the inertness of persons or their unwillingness to alter habits or what is established.
vis viva; kinetic energy.

vī′ṣȧ, *n.* [Fr ; L. f. of *visus*, pp. of *videre*, to see.] an endorsement stamped or written on a passport, showing that it has been examined by the proper officials of a country and granting entry into that country.

vī′ṣȧ, *v.t.*; visaed, *pt., pp.*; visaing, *ppr.* **1.** to put a visa on (a passport).
2. to give a visa to (someone).

viṣ′ăġe, *n.* [OFr. *visage*; from a hypothetical LL. form *visaticum*, from L. *visus*, a look, a seeing, from *videre*, to see.]
1. the face, with reference to the form and proportions of the features or to the expression; the countenance; as, a wolfish *visage.*
2. appearance; aspect.

viṣ′ăġe, *v.t.* to front; to face. [Obs.]

-viṣ′ăġed, a combining form meaning *having a* (specified) *kind of visage*, as in round-*visaged.*

viṣ′ăġed, *a.* having a visage or countenance.

viṣ′ărd, *n.* and *v.* same as *vizard.*

vis″-à-vis′ (vēz″à-vē′), *n.* [Fr., lit., face to face, from *vis*, a visage; L. *visus*, a look.]
1. one who or that which is opposite to or face to face with another, as in fencing.

2. a light carriage in which the seats face one another.

3. an S-shaped seat or sofa on which two people can sit facing each other.

vis″-à-vis′, *prep.* 1. face to face with; opposite to.

2. in comparison with; in relation to.

vis″-à-vis′, *a.* and *adv.* opposite; face to face.

Vī·sä′yăn, *n.* 1. a member of a large racial group of the Visayan Islands and northern Mindanao.

2. the Malay language of the Visayans.

Also *Bisayan.*

vis·çä′chȧ, viz·çä′chȧ, *n.* [Sp. *viscacha, bizcacha.*] *Lagostomus trichodactylus*, a large, burrowing South American rodent of the family *Chinchillidæ*, of the size of a badger.

vis′cē·rȧ, *n. pl.*; *sing.* (rare) **vis′çus**, [L., pl. of *viscus*, inner parts of the body.]

1. the internal organs of the body, especially of the thorax and abdomen, as the heart, lungs, liver, kidneys, intestines, etc.

2. popularly, the intestines.

vis′cẽr·ăl, *a.* 1. of, having the nature of, situated in, or affecting the viscera.

2. having deep sensibility or feeling. [Obs.]

visceral arch; in vertebrate animals, one of a series of parallel ridges in the wall of the oral and pharyngeal region: they are embryonic in the higher vertebrates.

visceral clefts; transverse clefts opening into the pharyngeal portion of the alimentary canal in embryonic vertebrates, and corresponding to the branchial clefts.

vis′cẽr·āte, *v.t.*; viscerated, *pt., pp.*; viscerating, *ppr.* to eviscerate.

vis′cẽr·ō·mō″tŏr, *a.* conveying motor impulses to the viscera, as certain nerves.

vis″cẽr·ō·skel′ē·tăl, *a.* relating or belonging to the skeleton on the visceral side.

vis′cid, *a.* [LL. *viscidus*, sticky, from L. *viscum, viscus*, birdlime.]

1. thick, sirupy, and sticky; viscous.

2. covered with a viscid substance: said of leaves.

vis·cid′i·ty, *n.* 1. the condition or quality of being viscid.

2. something viscid.

vis′cin, *n.* a glutinous substance obtainable from mistletoe.

vis′çoid, *a.* rather viscid; somewhat glutinous or sticky.

vis·çoi′dăl, *a.* viscoid.

vis·com′e·tẽr, *n.* a viscosimeter.

vis′cōse, *a.* [LL. *viscosus*, from L. *viscum, viscus*, birdlime.]

1. viscous.

2. of, containing, or made of viscose.

vis′cōse, *n.* an amber-colored, siruplike solution made by treating cellulose with potassium hydroxide and carbon disulfide: used in making rayon thread and fabrics, and cellophane.

vis·cō·sim′e·tẽr, *n.* an apparatus for measuring the viscosity of liquids, as by determining the rate of flow through a small opening.

vis·cos′i·ty, *n.*; *pl.* **vis·ços′i·tieş**, 1. the state or character of being viscous.

2. in physics, (a) that property or quality of gaseous or fluid bodies, resulting from molecular attraction, which makes them offer a resistance to flow; (b) the property of a solid of yielding steadily before a constant stress.

3. a viscous body.

vīs′çount (vī′), *n.* [ME. *viconte*; OFr. *visconte, viscomte*, from LL. *vice comes*, L. *vice*, in place of, and *comes*, a companion, a count.]

1. formerly, a deputy of a count or earl; specifically, a sheriff.

2. a nobleman next below an earl or count and above a baron.

vīs′çount·cy, *n.*; *pl.* **vīs′çount·cieş**, the rank, dignity, etc. of a viscount.

vīs′çount·ess, *n.* the wife of a viscount; also, a woman holding a viscountship in her own right.

vīs′çount·ship, *n.* a viscountcy.

vīs′çount·y, *n.*; *pl.* **vīs′çount·ieş**, 1. a viscountcy.

2. formerly, the territory under the jurisdiction of a viscount (sense 1).

vis′çous, *a.* [LL. *viscosus*, from L. *viscum, viscus*, birdlime.]

1. glutinous; thick, sirupy, and sticky; as, a *viscous* juice.

2. in botany, covered with a sticky substance, as leaves.

3. in physics, having the property of viscosity.

vis′çous·ness, *n.* same as *viscosity.*

Vis′çum, *n.* [L., mistletoe, birdlime.]

1. a genus of parasitic plants including the mistletoe. There are about thirty species, natives to the temperate and warm regions of the Old World. *Viscum album* is the well-known mistletoe.

2. [v–] birdlime.

vis′çus, *n.* singular of *viscera.* [Rare.]

vīse, *n.* [ME. and OFr. *vis*, a screw, from L. *vitis*, a vine, lit., that which winds.]

1. a device, usually attached to a workbench, for holding an object to be worked on in a firm position. It consists of a pair of steel-faced jaws moved by a screw or lever.

2. a spiral staircase. [Obs.]

Also spelled *vice.*

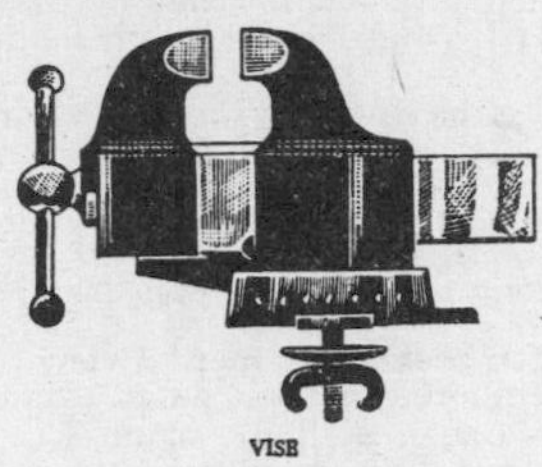

VISE

machine vise; a vise used for bolting to the table of a planing, shaping, or drilling machine.

standing vise; a vise at which the operator stands when working.

vīse, *v.t.*; vised, *pt., pp.*; vising, *ppr.* to hold or squeeze with or as with a vise: also spelled *vice.*

vi·sé (vē′zā *or* vē-zā′), *n.* and *v.t.*; viséed, *pt., pp.*; viséing, *ppr.* [Fr. *visé*, pp. of *viser*, to view, inspect, from L. *visus*, pp. of *videre*, to see.] visa.

vīse′măn, vīce′măn, *n.* one who works at a vise.

Vish′nụ, *n.* [Sans. *Visnu*, lit., prob. all-pervader.] in Hindu theology, the god who, with the other two great gods, Brahma and Siva, forms the trinity; the Preserver, considered by his worshipers to be the supreme god of the Hindu pantheon: he is popularly believed to have had several human incarnations, most important of which is Krishna.

VISHNU

viș·i·bil′i·ty, *n.*; *pl.* **viș·i·bil′i·tieş**, [LL. *visibilitas.*]

1. the fact or condition of being visible.

2. (a) the relative possibility of being seen under the conditions of distance, light, and atmosphere prevailing at a particular time; as, high *visibility*; (b) the relative distance at which an object can be seen under the prevailing conditions; range of vision; as, *visibility* is 300 yards.

3. a visible object.

viș′i·ble, *a.* [ME. *visible*; LL. *visibilis*, from L. *videre*, to see.]

1. that can be seen; perceptible by the eye.

2. that can be perceived or observed with the mind; evident; manifest.

3. on hand or available; as, *visible* supply.

4. so constructed as to bring to view parts or elements that are normally not perceptible.

visible church; in theology, the church of Christ on earth. It includes the whole body of professing Christians.

visible horizon; see *horizon* (sense 1).

visible speech; a system of characters designed to represent every possible articulate utterance of the organs of speech.

Syn.—perceivable, perceptible, discernible, apparent, obvious, manifest, clear, distinct, evident, plain.

viș′i·ble, *n.* that which is seen by the eye.

viș′i·ble·ness, *n.* the state or quality of being visible; visibility.

viș′i·bly, *adv.* in a visible manner; manifestly; clearly; observably; as, he was *visibly* tired.

viș′ie, viz′ie, *n.* [Fr. *visée*, an aim at, taking a sight at, from *viser*, to aim, mark.]

1. the aim taken at an object, as when one is about to shoot. [Scot.]

2. the knob or sight on the muzzle of a gun by which aim is taken. [Scot.]

Viș′i·goth, *n.* [LL. *Visigothi*; *visi-*, from Teut. stem, *west*, and *Gothi*, Goths.] any of the West Goths, a Teutonic people who invaded the Roman Empire late in the 4th century A.D., overran it, and set up a kingdom in France and Spain which lasted until about 700 A.D.

Viș·i·goth′iç, *a.* of or characteristic of the Visigoths.

vi′șiŏn (vizh′un), *n.* [ME. *visioun*; OFr. *vision*, from L. *visio (-onis)*, from *visus*, pp. of *videre*, to see.]

1. the act or power of seeing with the eye; the sense of sight.

2. that which is supposedly seen by other than normal sight; a supernatural, prophetic, or imaginary appearance; something seen in a dream, ecstasy, trance, or the like; an apparition; a phantom.

Beauteous as *vision* seen in dreamy sleep.
—Milman.

3. a mental image; especially, an imaginative contemplation; as, he has *visions* of power.

4. the ability to perceive something not actually visible, as through mental acuteness or keen foresight; as, his breadth of *vision* made this project possible.

5. force or power of the imagination; as, a dramatist of great *vision.*

6. something seen, especially something such as might be seen in a dream or trance.

7. something or someone, especially a woman, of extraordinary beauty.

arc of vision; in astronomy, the arc measuring the sun's distance below the horizon when a star or planet, previously concealed by its rays, becomes visible.

beatific vision; in theology, the sight of God in his divine glory: a term for the state of bliss in heaven.

binocular vision; the use of both eyes in perceiving three-dimensional space.

center of vision; see under *center.*

double vision; same as *diplopia.*

field of vision; same as *field of view* under *view.*

pseudoscopic vision; vision in which the object appears not as a solid body, but as a hollow one: the reverse of *stereoscopic vision.*

stereoscopic vision; perception of the relief of objects or of their depth; that in which objects seen appear solid.

Syn.—phantom, apparition, sight, view, picture, image.

vi′șiŏn, *v.t.*; visioned, *pt., pp.*; visioning, *ppr.* to see in or as in a vision; to dream.

vi′șiŏn·ăl, *a.* 1. of, or having the nature of, a vision.

2. perceived through or as through a vision; unreal.

vi′șiŏn·ăr·i·ness, *n.* the state or quality of being visionary.

vi′șiŏn·ăr·y, *a.* 1. seeing a vision; especially, habitually seeing visions.

2. characterized by impractical ideas or schemes.

3. of, having the nature of, or seen in a vision.

4. (a) not real; imaginary; (b) not capable of being carried out; merely speculative and impractical: said of an idea or scheme.

Syn.—imaginary, unreal, fantastic, fanciful, dreamy, whimsical.

vi′șiŏn·ăr·y, *n.*; *pl.* **vi′șiŏn·ăr·ieş**, 1. a person who sees visions.

2. a person who has impractical or fantastic ideas or schemes.

vi′șiŏned, *a.* 1. seen in a vision; formed by the fancy, or in a dream, trance, or the like; produced by a vision; spectral.

2. having the power of seeing visions; inspired.

vi′șiŏn·ist, *n.* a visionary.

vi′șiŏn·less, *a.* without vision; deprived of sight.

viș′it, *v.t.*; visited, *pt., pp.*; visiting, *ppr.* [OFr. *visiter*, from L. *visitare*, a freq. from *visere*, to go to see, itself a freq. from *videre*, to see.]

1. to go or come to see (someone) out of friendship or for social purposes.

2. to stay with as a guest for a more or less extended sojourn.

3. to go or come to see in a business or professional capacity; to attend, as a doctor.

4. to go or come to (a place) in order to inspect or investigate.

5. to go or come to (in a general sense); as, I *visited* the library last night.

6. to go or come to in order to comfort or help.

7. to come upon or afflict; to assail; as, a drought *visited* the valley.

Therefore hast thou *visited* and destroyed them.
—Isa. xxvi. 14.

8. (a) to inflict (punishment, suffering, etc.) upon someone; (b) to afflict (*with* punishment, suffering, etc.); (c) to inflict punishment for (wrongdoing); to avenge; as, *visiting* the sins of the fathers upon the children.

vis'it, *v.i.* to visit someone or something; specifically, (a) to inflict punishment or revenge; (b) to make a social call or calls: often followed by *with*; as, I'll *visit with* mother tomorrow; (c) [Colloq.] to converse or chat, as during a visit.

vis'it, *n.* a visiting; specifically, (a) a social call; (b) a stay as a guest; a sojourn; (c) an official or professional call, as of a doctor; (d) an official call as for inspection or investigation; especially, in marine law, the boarding of a ship of a neutral nation by an officer of a nation at war to search it for contraband, etc.; (e) [Colloq.] a friendly conversation or chat.

vis'it·à·ble, *a.* 1. that can be visited.
2. suitable for or worth visiting.
3. subject to visitation, or inspection.

vis'it·ănt, *n.* 1. a visitor; a guest.
When the *visitant* comes again, he is no more a stranger. —South.
2. a supernatural being, as revealed to a human being.
3. in zoology, a migratory bird in any of its temporary resting places.

vis'it·ănt, *a.* acting the part of a visitor; paying visits; visiting.

vis·it·ā'tion, *n.* [ME. and Anglo-Fr. *visitacioun*; LL. *visitatio* (*-onis*), appearance, sight, from L. *visitare*, to visit.]
1. the act or an instance of visiting; especially, an official visit to inpsect or examine, as that made by a bishop, etc. to a church in his diocese.
2. a visiting of reward or, especially, punishment, as by God.
3. any affliction or disaster thought of as an act of God.
4. [V-] in the Roman Catholic Church, (a) the visit of the Virgin Mary to Elisabeth; Luke i. 39–56; (b) a church feast (July 2) in commemoration of this.
5. in zoology, migration of animals or birds to a particular place at an unusual time or in unusual numbers.
6. the object of a visit. [Rare.]
7. same as *visit* (in marine law).

vis·it·ā'tion·ăl, *a.* of or characteristic of a visitation or visitations.

vis''it·à·tō'ri·ăl, *a.* 1. of or for visitation; as, *visitatorial* power.
2. having the power of visitation, or inspection.
To exercise *visitatorial* jurisdiction. —Macaulay.

vi·site', *n.* [Fr.] a thin cape formerly worn by women.

vis'it·ẽr, *n.* same as *visitor*.

vis'it·ing, *a.* authorized to visit and inspect; as, a *visiting* committee.

vis'it·ing, *n.* the act of going to see or of attending; visitation.

vis'it·ing book, a book containing a list of names of persons who are to be visited or from whom visits have been received.

vis'it·ing cärd, a calling card.

vis'it·ing fīre'măn, 1. an important person, especially any of a group, visiting a city, organization, etc. and given an official welcome, special entertainment, etc. [Colloq.]
2. a free-spending tourist, delegate to a convention, etc. [Colloq.]

vis'it·ing nûrse, a graduate nurse employed by a community agency, originally one who visited the sick in their homes to give nursing care.

vis'it·ing prō·fes'sŏr, a professor at a college or university invited to teach at another for a specified period.

vis'it·ing tēach'ẽr, a school teacher who gives instruction to bedridden students through regular visits to their homes.

vis'it·ŏr, *n.* [Fr. *visiteur*.]
1. a person making a visit.
2. a superior, or person authorized to visit an institution, etc., for the purpose of seeing that the laws and regulations are observed, or that the duties and conditions prescribed by the founder, or by law, are duly performed and executed.
3. in zoology, a visitant.

vis·it·ō'ri·ăl, *a.* visitatorial.

vis'it·ress, *n.* a female visitor.

vī'sive, *a.* [Fr. *visif*, from L. *videre*, to see.] pertaining to the power of seeing. [Rare.]

vis mā'jŏr, [L., greater force.] force majeure.

vïsne (vēn), *n.* [OFr. *visne*; L. *vicinia*, neighborhood.] in law, vicinage. [Rare.]

vis'nō·my, *n.* [var. of *physiognomy*.] face; countenance; visage. [Obs.]

vī'sŏn, *n.* the American mink.

vis'ŏr, *n.* [ME. *visere*; Anglo-Fr. *viser*; OFr. *visiere*, from *vis*, a face.]
1. in ancient armor, the movable part of a helmet, covering the face, especially a section that came down over and protected the eyes.
2. a mask, as for disguise; a vizard.
3. the projecting front brim of a cap, for shading the eyes.
4. a fixed or movable shade fastened to the windshield of a car, for shading the eyes.

vis'ŏr, *v.t.* to hide, protect, or shade with a visor.

vis'ŏred, *a.* having or wearing a visor.

vis'tà, *n.* [It., sight, from L. *videre*, to see.]
1. a view or outlook, especially one seen through a long passage, as between rows of houses or trees.
2. a long row of trees, etc., framing such a view.
3. a comprehensive mental view of a series of remembered or anticipated events.

vis'ū·ăl (vizh'), *a.* [OFr., from LL. *visualis*, visual, from L. *visus*, sight.]
1. of, connected with, or used in seeing.
2. that is or can be seen; visible.
3. of, having the nature of, or occurring as a mental image, or vision.
4. based on, designed for, or controlled by the use of sight; as, *visual* flight rules.
5. in optics, optical.
visual aids; motion pictures, lantern slides, charts, and other devices involving the sense of sight (other than books), used in teaching, illustrating lectures, etc.
visual angle; same as *optic angle* under *optic*.
visual point; in perspective, a point in the horizontal line in which all the visual rays unite.
visual purple; a purplish pigmentary substance in the rods of the retina, rapidly bleached to visual yellow by light and considered a factor in transforming light rays into the sensory impulses of vision.
visual rays; rays of light from an object to the eye.
visual yellow; the yellowish pigment into which visual purple is bleached by the action of light.

vis'ū·ăl, *n.* same as *visualizer*.

vis·ū·al'i·ty, *n.* the state or quality of being visual; also, a glimpse; a mental picture.

vis''ū·ăl·i·zā'tion, *n.* 1. a visualizing or being visualized.
2. anything visualized; a mental picture.

vis'ū·ăl·īze, *v.t.*; visualized, *pt.*, *pp.*; visualizing, *ppr.* to form a mental image, or vision, of (something not visible, as an abstraction).

vis'ū·ăl·īze, *v.i.* to form a mental image.

vis'ū·ăl·ī·zẽr, *n.* a person who visualizes; especially, one whose mental imagery is largely visual, rather than auditory, olfactory, etc.

vis'ū·ăl·ly, *adv.* in a visual manner; by sight.

vī'tà, *n.*; *pl.* **vī'tae,** [L., life.]
1. a biography or autobiography, often a brief one.
2. a summary of one's personal history and professional qualifications, as that submitted by a job applicant; résumé.

Vi·tā'cē·ae, *n.pl.* a family of plants, of which the genus *Vitis* (the grapes) is the type: they are climbing, woody vines with tendrils, clusters of small, greenish flowers, and berry-like fruits.

vi·tā'ceous, *a.* belonging to the family *Vitaceæ*.

Vī'tà·glȧss, *n.* a kind of glass which transmits ultraviolet rays: a trade-mark.

vī'tăl, *a.* [OFr. *vital*, from L. *vitalis*, vital, from *vita*, life.]
1. of, concerned with, or manifesting life; as, *vital* energy.
2. necessary or essential to life; being a source or support of life; as, *vital* organs.
3. destroying life; fatal; as, a *vital* wound.
4. (a) essential to the existence or continuance of something; indispensable; (b) of greatest importance; as, this matter is *vital*.
5. affecting the validity, truth, etc. of something; as, a *vital* error.
6. full of life and vigor; energetic; as, a *vital* personality.
7. capable of living. [Obs.]
vital air; oxygen. [Obs.]
vital capacity; the volume of air that can be forcibly expelled from the lungs after the maximum amount has been breathed in.
vital functions: see under *function*.
vital principle; the basic force or principle regarded as the source and cause of life in living organisms: also called *vital force*.
vital signs; indicators of the efficient functioning of the body; especially, pulse, temperature, and respiration.
vital statistics; data concerning births, deaths, marriages, etc.

vi·tal'iç, *a.* relating to life; vital.

vī'tăl·işm, *n.* [*vital* and *-ism*; Fr. *vitalisme*.] the doctrine that the life in living organisms is caused and sustained by a vital principle that is distinct from all physical and chemical forces and that life is, in part, self-determining and self-evolving: opposed to *mechanism*.

vī'tăl·ist, *n.* one who holds the doctrine of vitalism.

vī·tăl·is'tiç, *a.* of, or having the nature of, vitalism.

vī·tal'i·ty, *n.*; *pl.* **vī·tal'i·ties,** [L. *vitalitas*.]
1. vital principle or force.
2. power to live or go on living.
3. power to endure or survive, as of an institution.
4. mental or physical vigor; energy.

vī''tăl·i·zā'tion, *n.* a vitalizing or being vitalized.

vī'tăl·īze, *v.t.*; vitalized, *pt.*, *pp.*; vitalizing, *ppr.* 1. to make vital; to give life to.
2. to give vigor or animation to; as, to *vitalize* a dull report.

vī'tăl·ī·zẽr, *n.* any person or thing which vitalizes or gives life.

vī·tal'li·um, *n.* an alloy of cobalt, chromium, and molybdenum, used in bone surgery, etc.: a trade-mark (*Vitallium*).

vī'tăl·ly, *adv.* 1. so as to give life.
2. essentially; as, *vitally* important.

vī'tăls, *n.pl.* 1. the vital organs, as the heart, brain, lungs, etc. essential to life: used generally or specifically.
2. the parts of a complex whole essential to its life, existence, or sound state.

vī'tà·min, *n.* [L. *vita*, life, and *amine*.] any of a number of unrelated, complex organic substances found variously in most foods and essential, in small amounts, for the normal functioning of the body.
vitamin A, a fat-soluble aliphatic alcohol, $C_{20}H_{29}OH$, found in fish-liver oil, egg yolk, butter, etc., and (as carotene) in carrots and other vegetables: a deficiency of this vitamin results in night blindness and degeneration of epithelial tissue: it occurs in two forms, *vitamin* A_1 and *vitamin* A_2.
vitamin B (*complex*), a group of unrelated water-soluble substances including: (a) *vitamin* B_1 (see *thiamine*); (b) *vitamin* B_2 (see *riboflavin*); (c) *vitamin* B_6 (see *pyridoxine*); (d) nicotinic acid; (e) pantothenic acid; (f) biotin: also called *vitamin H*; (g) inositol; (h) para-aminobenzoic acid; (i) choline; (j) folic acid.
vitamin C, an organic compound, $C_6H_8O_6$, occurring in citrus fruits, tomatoes, and various vegetables: a deficiency of this vitamin tends to produce scurvy: also called *ascorbic acid*, *cevitamic acid*.
vitamin D, any of several related vitamins occurring in fish-liver oils, milk, egg yolks etc.: a deficiency of this vitamin tends to produce rickets; specifically, (a) *vitamin* D_1, a mixture of calciferol with another sterol prepared by the ultraviolet irradiation of ergosterol; (b) *vitamin* D_2 (see *calciferol*); (c) *vitamin* D_3, a substance similar to vitamin D_2, found chiefly in fish-liver oils.
vitamin E, a substance consisting of a mixture of tocopherols, believed to restore fertility to sterile mammals: formerly called *vitamin X*: see *tocopherol*.
vitamin G, vitamin B_2 (see *riboflavin*).
vitamin H, see *biotin*.
vitamin K, a vitamin occurring in certain green vegetables, fish meal, hempseed, etc. and used to promote blood clotting, and thus prevent hemorrhage, by aiding in the synthesis of prothrombin by the liver: the two varieties are *vitamin* K_1, found chiefly in alfalfa leaves, and *vitamin* K_2, found chiefly in fish meal.
vitamin P, a mixture of flavones occurring especially in citrus juice and paprika: a deficiency of this vitamin results in the increased permeability of capillary walls and, hence, greater susceptibility to hemorrhage: also called *citrin*.
vitamin X, a former name for *vitamin E*.

vī'tà·mine, *n.* a vitamin. [Rare.]

vī·tà·min'iç, *a.* of vitamins.

vī′tȧ·sçope, *n.* [L. *vita*, life, and Gr. *skopein*, to view.] an early type of motion-picture projector.

vī′tā·tive·ness, *n.* [L. *vita*, life.] in phrenology, the love of life and fear of extermination; also, the organ supposed to be the seat of the instinct of self-preservation.

vīte, *a.* [Fr.] in music, quick; swift: a direction to the performer.

vit·el·lãr′i·um, *n.*; *pl.* **vit·el·lãr′i·ȧ,** the gland of the female in some species of worms, which secretes the vitellus of the ova.

vī·tel′li·çle, *n.* [dim. of *vitellus*.] in biology, the yolk bag, or the sac containing that part of the yolk which has not been converted into the germ mass and embryo.

vit·el·liġ′e·nous, *a.* generating vitellus; designating the yolk or vitellus-producing cells in the ovaries of certain insects.

vī·tel′line, *n.* [from L. *vitellus*, the yolk of an egg.] in chemistry, a protein occurring in the yolk of eggs.

vī·tel′line, *a.* 1. of the yolk of an egg, as the *vitelline* membrane, which surrounds it.
2. of the yellow color of an egg yolk.

vī·tel′line, *n.* an egg yolk.

vī·tel′lō·ġēne, *n.* same as *vitellarium*.

vī·tel′lus, *n.* [LL., from L. *vitellus*, the yolk of an egg.]
1. the yolk of an egg.
2. in botany, a membrane enclosing the embryo in some plants.

Vī′tex, *n.* [L., from *viere*, to bind, in allusion to the flexible branches.] a genus of verbenaceous plants, including the chaste tree, *Vitex agnus-castus*, and several other species, all more or less aromatic.

vi′ti·ȧ·ble (vish′i-), *a.* that can be vitiated.

vi′ti·āte (vish′i-), *v.t.*; vitiated, *pt., pp.*; vitiating, *ppr.* [L. *vitiatus*, pp. of *vitiare*, to injure.]
1. to make imperfect, faulty, or impure; to spoil; to corrupt.
2. to weaken morally; to debase; to pervert.
3. to make legally ineffective; to invalidate, as a contract.
Syn.—defile, spoil, pollute, corrupt.

vi′ti·āt·ed, *a.* 1. made defective; spoiled.
2. debased; corrupted, as taste.
3. invalidated, as a contract.

vi·ti·ā′tion, *n.* a vitiating or being vitiated.

vi′ti·ā·tŏr, *n.* a person or thing that vitiates.

vī·tiç′ū·lōse, *a.* having vinelike twigs or stems; growing in a trailing manner.

vit·i·çul′tūr·ăl, *a.* relating to viticulture.

vit′i·çul·tūre, *n.* [L. *vitis*, a vine, and *cultura*, culture.] the cultivation of grapevines; the growing of grapes.

vit·i·çul′tūr·ist, *n.* one who makes a business of grape growing; an expert in viticulture.

vit·i·lī′gō, *n.* [L., tetter.] a skin disease characterized by the formation of smooth, white, pigmentless patches on various parts of the body: also called *piebald skin*.

vit·i·lit′i·gāte, *v.i.* to contend in law litigiously or captiously. [Obs.]

vit·i·lit·i·gā′tion, *n.* captious litigation. [Obs.]

vi·ti·os′i·ty (vish-i-), *n.* depravity; viciousness.

vi′tious, vi′tious·ly, vi′tious·ness (vish′us, etc.), obsolete forms of *vicious, viciously*, etc.

Vī′tis, *n.* [L., a vine.] a genus of plants, the grapevines, the type and principal genus of the order *Vitaceæ*.

vi·trel′lȧ, *n.* same as *retinophora*.

vit″rē·ō·ē·leç′triç, *a.* [L. *vitreus*, glassy, and E. *electric*.] containing or exhibiting positive electricity.

vit·rē·os′i·ty, *n.* the state or the quality of being vitreous; vitreousness.

vit′rē·ous, *a.* [L. *vitreus*, glassy, from *vitrum*, glass.]
1. of, having the nature of, or like glass; glassy.
2. derived from or made of glass.
3. of the vitreous humor.
vitreous body; same as *vitreous humor*.
vitreous china; chinaware of a hard, dense, glasslike or vitrified body.
vitreous copper; torbernite, a green crystalline mineral having a micalike structure.
vitreous electricity; positive electricity, as that produced by rubbing glass with silk.
vitreous fusion; gradual fusion like that of glass, not being confined to a melting point of any given temperature but occurring over a range of temperatures.
vitreous humor (or *body*); the transparent, colorless, jellylike substance occupying the greater part of the cavity of the eye, and all the space between the crystalline lens and the retina.
vitreous selenium; in chemistry, an allotropic form of selenium occurring as a brownish-black, glassy mass.
vitreous silver; in mineralogy, argentite.
vitreous sponge; same as *glass sponge*.
vitreous table; in anatomy, the inner layer of firmly united bony tissue of the chief bones of the skull.

vit′rē·ous·ness, *n.* the quality or state of being vitreous.

vi·tres′cence, *n.* [from L. *vitrum*, glass.] the state or quality of being vitrescent; a tendency to become vitreous, or glassy.

vi·tres′cent, *a.* 1. that can be formed into glass.
2. becoming or tending to become glass.

vi·tres′ci·ble, *a.* capable of being vitrified.

vit′riç, *a.* [L. *vitrum*, glass.] of, or having the nature of, glass: distinguished from *ceramic*.

vit′riçs, *n.pl.* 1. [*construed as sing.*] the art or study of making and decorating articles of glass.
2. glassware and glassy materials in general, as distinguished from *ceramics*.

vit·ri·faç′tion, *n.* [L. *vitrum*, glass, and *facere*, to make.] vitrification.

vit·ri·faç′tūre, *n.* [L. *vitrum*, glass.] the manufacture of glass or vitrified wares.

vit′ri·fī·ȧ·ble, *a.* capable of being vitrified, or converted into glass by heat and fusion; as, flint and alkalis are *vitrifiable*.

vit′ri·fi·çāte, *v.t.* to vitrify. [Obs.]

vit″ri·fi·çā′tion, *n.* a vitrifying or being vitrified; also, that which is vitrified.

vit′ri·fied, *a.* converted into glass; also, covered with a glaze or glassy exterior; as, *vitrified* tiles, *vitrified* brick, *vitrified* pottery.
vitrified fort or *wall*; in archaeology, any of a number of masonry remains, principally found on the crests of Scottish hills, but also in France, which are perfectly or partially vitrified or transformed into a kind of glass.

vit′ri·fọrm, *a.* [L. *vitrum*, glass, and *-form*.] having the form or appearance of glass; glasslike.

vit′ri·fȳ, *v.t.*; vitrified, *pt., pp.*; vitrifying, *ppr.* [L. *vitrum*, glass, and *-fy*.] to convert into glass or a glasslike substance by fusion due to heat; to make vitreous; as, to *vitrify* sand with alkaline salts.

vit′ri·fȳ, *v.i.* to become vitreous; to be converted into glass.

Vi·trī′nȧ, *n.* 1. a genus of land snails, the glass snails.
2. [v—] a glass snail of this or an allied genus, as *Vitrina limpida*, common in the United States.

vit′rine, *n.* [Fr., from *vitre*, window glass.] a glass showcase, made for the display of valuable or delicate articles, as in a shop, museum, or private house.

vit′ri·ŏl, *n.* [OFr. *vitriol*, from ML. *vitriolum*, vitriol, from L. *vitreus*, glassy: so called from the glassy appearance.]
1. any of several sulfates of metals, as copper sulfate (blue vitriol), iron sulfate (green vitriol), zinc sulfate (white vitriol), etc.
2. sulfuric acid: also *oil of vitriol*.
3. anything sharp or caustic; as, his language was pure *vitriol*.
copper vitriol; hydrous copper sulfate.
lead vitriol; sulfate of lead; anglesite.
nickel vitriol; hydrated sulfate of nickel.
red vitriol; (a) a sulfate of cobalt: also called *cobalt vitriol*; (b) red sulfate of iron: also called *vitriol of Mars*.

vit′ri·ŏl, *v.t.*; vitrioled *or* vitriolled, *pt., pp.*; vitrioling *or* vitriolling, *ppr.* to apply sulfuric acid to.

vit′ri·ō·lāte, *v.t.*; vitriolated, *pt., pp.*; vitriolating, *ppr.* in old chemistry, to convert into a vitriol, or sulfate.

vit′ri·ō·lāte, *n.* in old chemistry, a sulfate.

vit′ri·ō·lāte, *a.* converted into a sulfate. [Rare.]

vit′ri·ō·lā·ted, *a.* vitriolate. [Rare.]

vit″ri·ō·lā′tion, *n.* in old chemistry, the act or process of converting into a sulfate.

vit·ri·ol′iç, *a.* 1. pertaining to vitriol; having the qualities of vitriol, or obtained from vitriol.
2. extremely biting or caustic; sarcastic; sharp and bitter; as *vitriolic* talk.
vitriolic acid; in old chemistry, sulfuric acid.

vit′ri·ŏl·ī·zȧ·ble, *a.* capable of being converted into a vitriol.

vit″ri·ŏl·i·zā′tion, *n.* a vitriolizing or being vitriolized.

vit′ri·ŏl·īze, *v.t.*; vitriolized, *pt., pp.*; vitriolizing, *ppr.* 1. to convert into vitriol.
2. to subject to the action of vitriol.
3. to injure or try to injure (a person) as by throwing vitriol on the face.

vit′ri·ŏl·ous, *a.* vitriolic. [Obs.]

vit′rīte, *n.* [L. *vitrum*, glass.] a kind of very hard glass used for insulators and other electrical appliances.

vit′rō-di-trī′nȧ, *n.* [It., glass lace.] a kind of filigree or reticulated glasswork, invented by the Venetians in the fifteenth century, consisting of a lacework of white threads embedded in transparent glass.

vit′rō·phȳre, *n.* [L. *vitrum*, glass, and the *-phyr-* of porphyry.] a porphyritic rock composed partly of glassy matter.

Vi·trū′vi·ăn, *a.* of or pertaining to Marcus Vitruvius Pollio, Roman architect and engineer of the first century B. C.
Vitruvian scroll; an architectural ornament named after Vitruvius, and consisting of a series of convoluted scrolls. It occurs frequently in friezes of the Composite order.

VITRUVIAN SCROLL

vit′tȧ, *n.*; *pl.* **vit′tae,** [L.] 1. in ancient Rome, a headband, fillet, or garland.
2. in botany, one of the receptacles of oil which are found in the fruits of umbelliferous plants, as in those of anise, dill, fennel, caraway, etc.
3. in zoology and botany, a band; a stripe of color.

vit′tāte, *a.* 1. in botany, having a vitta or vittae.
2. in botany and zoology, striped lengthwise.

vit′tle, *n.* victual. [Dial.]

vit′ū·lăr, *a.* [L. *vitulus*, a calf.] of, pertaining to, or connected with a calf or calves.
vitular apoplexy; apoplexy which attacks cows during parturition.

vit′ū·lăr·y, *a.* same as *vitular*.

vit′ū·line, *a.* [L. *vitulinus*, pertaining to a calf.] pertaining to or resembling a calf, calves, or veal.

vī·tū′pēr·ȧ·ble, *a.* deserving of or liable to vituperation or abuse; blameworthy; censurable.

vī·tū′pēr·āte, *v.t.*; vituperated, *pt., pp.*; vituperating, *ppr.* [L. *vituperare*, to blame.] to speak abusively to or about; to berate; to revile.

vī·tū·pēr·ā′tion, *n.* [OFr., from L. *vituperatio* (*-onis*), blame.]
1. the act of vituperating.
2. bitter, abusive language.

vī·tū′pēr·ȧ·tive, *a.* having the nature of or characterized by vituperation; abusive.

vī·tū′pēr·ā·tive·ly, *adv.* in a vituperative manner; with vituperation.

vī·tū′pēr·ā·tŏr, *n.* one who vituperates; a reviler.

vī·tū·pē′ri·ous, *a.* worthy of vituperation; blameworthy; disgraceful. [Obs.]

vī′vä, *interj.* [It.] literally, (long) live (someone specified)!: an exclamation of acclaim.

vī′vä, *n.* a shout of "viva!"

vi·vä′çe (-chā), *a.* [It., lively.] in music, brisk; lively; spirited: a direction to the performer.

vī·vā′cious, *a.* [L. *vivax* (*-acis*), vigorous, from *vivere*, to live.]
1. long-lived; hard to kill or destroy. [Archaic.]
2. lively; active; spirited and full of life.
3. in botany, living throughout the winter, or from year to year; perennial. [Obs.]

vī·vā′cious·ly, *adv.* in a vivacious manner; with vivacity, life, or spirit.

vī·vā′cious·ness, *n.* 1. the state or quality of being vivacious; vivacity; liveliness.
2. the state of being long-lived; longevity. [Obs.]

vī·vac′i·ty, *n.* [Fr. *vivacité*, from L. *vivacitas*, natural vigor, from *vivax* (*-acis*), vigorous.]
1. liveliness; sprightliness of temper or behavior; animation.
2. power of living; longevity. [Obs.]
3. the quality or state of being vivacious.
4. *pl.* **vī·vac′i·tieṣ**, a vivacious act or expression.

vi·van·dière′ (vē-voṅ-dyãr′), *n.* [Fr., f. of *vivandier*, a food seller.] formerly, especially in France, a woman who accompanied troops and sold them wines, refreshments, and supplies.

vī·vãr′i·um, *n.*; *pl.* **vī·vãr′i·umṣ** or **vī·vãr′i·ȧ,** [L *vivarium*, from *vivere*, to live.] an enclosed place for raising plants or animals under conditions closely resembling those of their natural environment.

vī′vȧ·ry, *n.* same as *vivarium*.

vī′vȧ vō′cē, [L.] orally; by word of mouth; as, to vote *viva voce.*

vī′vȧ-vō′cē, *a.* expressed orally.

vïve, *interj.* [Fr., from L. *vivere,* to live.] long live (someone specified)!: an expression of acclaim.

vīve, *a.* [Fr., lively, from L. *vivus,* alive.] lively; forcible. [Chiefly Scot.]

vīve′ly, *adv.* in a lively manner. [Chiefly Scot.]

vī′ven·cy, *n.* [L. *vivens,* ppr. of *vivere,* to live.] vitality. [Obs.]

Vī·ver′rȧ, *n.* [L., a ferret.] the typical genus of the family *Viverridæ.*

Vī·ver′ri·dae, *n.pl.* a family of digitigrade carnivores, mostly long-bodied, short-legged animals, with bristly fur, a long tail, and a sharp muzzle. It includes the civet cat and the genet.

vī·ver′rīne, *a.* of or pertaining to the *Viverridæ.*

vī·ver′rīne, *n.* a member of the *Viverridæ.*

vï′vẽrș, *n.pl.* [Fr., provisions, from *vivre,* to live.] eatables; food; victuals. [Scot.]

vīveș, *n.pl.* [OFr. *avives,* prob. from Ar. *ad-dhība,* the she-wolf.] a disease of animals, particularly of horses, occurring in the glands under the ear, where a tumor is formed which sometimes ends in suppuration.

Viv′i·ăn, *n.* in Arthurian legend, an enchantress, mistress of Merlin: also called *Lady of the Lake.*

viv′i·ăn·īte, *n.* [named after J. H. *Vivian,* an English mineralogist.] a pearly and vitreous mineral crystallizing in the monoclinic system, but sometimes occurring in an earthy form. It is colorless when pure, but owing to the rapid oxidation of the iron, changes to blue or green when exposed to the air. It is a hydrous phosphate of protoxide of iron.

viv′id, *a.* [L. *vividus,* lively, from *vivere,* to live.]

1. full of life; vigorous; lively; striking; as, a vivid personality.

2. (a) bright; intense; brilliant: said of colors, light, etc.; (b) brightly colored; as, a *vivid* painting.

3. forming clear or striking mental images; strong; active; daring; as, a *vivid* imagination.

4. clearly perceived by the mind, as a recollection.

5. bringing strikingly real or lifelike images to the mind; as, *vivid* description.

Syn.—active, bright, clear, lively, lucid, quick, sprightly, striking.

vi·vid′i·ty, *n.* vividness.

viv′id·ly, *adv.* in a vivid manner.

viv′id·ness, *n.* the quality or state of being vivid.

vī·vif′iç, vī·vif′i·căl, *a.* [L. *vivificus.*] giving life; reviving; enlivening. [Obs.]

vī·vif′i·çāte, *v.t.* [LL. *vivificare,* to vivify; L. *vivus,* alive, and *facere,* to make.]

1. to give life to; to animate. [Rare.]

2. in chemistry, to restore or reduce to the metallic state, as from an oxide, solution, or the like. [Obs.]

viv″i·fi·çā′tion, *n.* 1. in physiology, the conversion of the lifeless matter of food into living proteide matter in the process of assimilation.

2. in chemistry, a vivificating. [Obs.]

3. a vivifying or being vivified.

vī·vif′i·çā·tive, *a.* able to animate or give life. [Rare.]

viv′i·fȳ, *v.t.*; vivified, *pt., pp.*; vivifying, *ppr.* [Fr. *vivifier*; LL. *vivificare*; L. *vivus,* alive, and *facere,* to make.]

1. to give life to; to make come to life; to animate.

2. to make more lively, active, striking, etc.

Vī·vip′ȧ·rȧ, *n.pl.* [LL., from L. *vivus,* alive, and *parere,* to bear.] the *Mammalia.* [Obs.]

viv·i·par′i·ty, *n.* a viviparous quality or condition.

vī·vip′ȧ·rous, *a.* [LL. *viviparus,* from L. *vivus,* alive, and *parere,* to produce.]

1. bearing or bringing forth living young (as most mammals and some other animals) instead of laying eggs: opposed to *oviparous.*

2. in botany, germinating while still on the parent plant, as certain seeds or bulbs.

3. producing such seeds or bulbs; proliferous.

vī·vip′ȧ·rous·ly, *adv.* in a viviparous manner.

vī·vip′ȧ·rous·ness, *n.* viviparity.

viv·i·seçt′, *v.t.* [back-formation from *vivisection,* after *dissect.*] to perform vivisection on.

viv·i·seçt′, *v.i.* to practice vivisection.

viv·i·seç′tion, *n.* [L. *vivus,* alive, and *sectio (-onis),* a cutting, from *secare,* to cut.]

1. a surgical operation performed on a living animal to study the structure and function of living organs and parts, and to investigate the effects of diseases and therapy.

2. experimental research involving such surgical operation.

viv·i·seç′tion·ăl, *a.* 1. relating to or having the nature of vivisection.

2. performing vivisection.

viv·i·seç′tion·ist, *n.* 1. a person who practices vivisection.

2. a person who advocates or defends vivisection as essential to scientific progress.

viv·i·seç′tŏr, *n.* a person who practices vivisection.

viv″i·seç·tō′ri·um, *n.* a place for vivisection.

vix′en, *n.* [AS. *fyxen, fixen,* a she-fox; compare G. *füchsinn,* a she-fox, from *fuchs,* a fox.]

1. a female fox.

2. a shrewish, ill-tempered, or malicious woman.

vix′en, *a.* vixenish.

vix′en·ish, *a.* of, like, or characteristic of a vixen; ill-tempered, quarrelsome, or malicious.

vix′en·ly, *a.* having the qualities of a vixen; ill-tempered.

viz′ărd, *n.* [altered from earlier *visar,* var. of *visor.*]

1. a visor.

2. a mask.

Also spelled *visard.*

viz·çä′chȧ, *n.* same as *viscacha.*

vi·ziēr′, vi·zïr′ (*or* viz′yẽr), *n.* [Fr. *vizir,* from Ar. *wazir,* a vizir, lit., a bearer of burdens, a porter, from *wazara,* to bear a burden.] in Moslem countries, a high officer in the government; especially, a minister of state.

vi·ziēr′āte, vi·zïr′āte, *n.* the rank, office, term, or authority of a vizier.

vi·ziēr′i·ăl, vi·zïr′i·ăl, *a.* relating to or decreed by a vizier.

vi·ziēr′ship, vi·zïr′ship, *n.* the authority, term of office, or position of a vizier.

vīz′ŏr, *n.* a visor.

vīz′ŏr, *v.t.* to visor.

vīz′ŏred, *a.* visored.

vīz′ŏr·less, *a.* without a vizor.

V-J Dāy, the day on which the fighting with Japan officially ended in World War II (August 14, 1945) or the day on which the surrender was formally signed (September 2, 1945).

Vlaçh, *a.* and *n.* same as *Wallachian.*

vleī (flī), *n.* [S. Afr. D.] a marsh; a swamp; a depressed place where water remains during the rainy season: also written *vley.*

V′-māil, *n.* a mail service of World War II, by which letters to or from the armed forces were reduced to microfilm to conserve shipping space, and enlarged and printed for delivery.

V′-neck, *n.* the neck of a dress or a blouse, cut in the shape of a V.

vō′cȧ·ble, *n.* [Fr., from L. *vocabulum,* from *vocare,* to call.] a word; a term; a name; specifically, a word considered as a unit of sounds or letters rather than as a unit of meaning.

vō·çab′ū·lăr·y, *n.*; *pl.* **vō·çab′ū·lăr·ieș,** [Fr. *vocabulaire,* from L. *vocabulum,* a word, from *vocare,* to call.]

1. a list of words and, sometimes, phrases, usually arranged in alphabetical order and defined; a dictionary, glossary, or lexicon.

2. all the words of a language.

3. all the words used by a particular person, class, profession, etc.: sometimes, all the words recognized and understood by a particular person, although not necessarily used by him (in full, *passive vocabulary*).

vō·çab′ū·list, *n.* the compiler or writer of a vocabulary; a lexicographer.

vō′căl, *a.* [L. *vocalis,* sounding, from *vox, vocis,* voice.]

1. uttered, produced, or performed by the voice; spoken or sung; oral; as, *vocal* music.

2. having a voice; capable of speaking or making oral sounds.

3. of, used in, connected with, or belonging to the voice; as, *vocal* organs.

4. full of voice or voices.

5. inclined to express oneself in speech; speaking freely or vociferously.

6. in phonetics, (a) vocalic; (b) voiced.

vocal cords; either of two pairs of membranous cords or folds in the larynx, consisting of a thicker upper pair (*false vocal cords*) and a lower pair (*true vocal cords*): voice is produced when air from the lungs causes the lower (true) cords to vibrate: pitch is controlled by varying the tension on the cords, and volume, by regulating the air passing through the larynx.

vocal fremitus; see under *fremitus.*

vō′căl, *n.* a vocal sound.

vō·cal′iç, *a.* 1. having many vowels; composed mainly or entirely of vowels.

2. of, consisting of, having the nature of, or affecting a vowel or vowels.

vō′căl·ișm, *n.* 1. the use of the voice, as in speaking or singing.

2. a vocalic sound; a vowel.

3. the act or art of singing.

4. a system of vowels, as of a particular language.

vō′căl·ist, *n.* a vocal musician; a singer.

vō·cal′i·ty, *n.* 1. the quality of having vocal powers, or voice.

2. the quality of being vocal or vocalic.

vō″căl·i·zā′tion, *n.* 1. the act of vocalizing or the state of being vocalized; the manner of vocalizing.

2. the formation and utterance of vowel sounds.

vō′căl·īze, *v.t.*; vocalized, *pt., pp.*; vocalizing, *ppr.* 1. to make vocal; to utter with the voice; to speak or sing.

2. to give a voice to; to make vocal, or articulate.

3. to add the diacritical marks of vowel sounds to (the characters of Hebrew, Arabic, or other languages lacking alphabetical letters for the vowels).

4. in phonetics, (a) to change into or use as a vowel; as, *w* is often *vocalized* at the end of a syllable; (b) to voice.

vō′căl·īze, *v.i.* 1. to utter sounds; to speak or sing; specifically, in singing, to practice tones sung on vowels.

2. to be changed into a vowel.

vō′căl·ly, *adv.* 1. in a vocal manner; with voice; with an audible sound.

2. in words; verbally.

3. as regards vowels or vocalic sounds.

4. in song.

vō′căl·ness, *n.* the quality of being vocal; vocality.

vō·cā′tion, *n.* [Fr., from L. *vocatio,* from *vocare,* to call.]

1. a call, summons, or impulsion to perform a certain function or enter a certain career, especially a religious one.

2. the function or career toward which one believes himself to be called.

3. any trade, profession, or occupation.

vō·cā′tion·ăl, *a.* of a vocation, trade, profession, occupation, etc.

vō·cā′tion·ăl guĭd′ănce (gīd′), the work of testing and interviewing persons in order to guide them toward the choice of a vocation suitable to their abilities or toward training for such vocation.

vō·cā′tion·ăl·ly, *adv.* in regard to a vocation.

voç′ȧ·tive, *a.* [L. *vocativus,* from *vocare,* to call, from *vox,* the voice.]

1. of, characteristic of, or used in calling.

2. in grammar, in certain inflected languages, designating or of the case of nouns, adjectives, etc., used in direct address to indicate the person or thing addressed.

voç′ȧ·tive, *n.* 1. in grammar, the vocative case.

2. a word in this case.

vō′çę (-chā), *n.*; *pl.* **vō′cï** (-chē), **[It., voice.]** voice.

voce di petto; chest voice.

voce di testa; head voice.

vō′cēș, *n.* plural of *vox.*

Vō·chys′i·ȧ, *n.* the type genus of the *Vochysiaceæ,* comprising about 55 species native to subtropical America and having flowers with not more than three petals, a single fertile stamen, and a three-celled ovary.

Vō·chys·i·ā′cē·ae, *n.pl.* a family of polypetalous dicotyledonous trees and shrubs, native to tropical America and comprising about 130 species distributed among seven genera.

vō·cif′ẽr·ănce, *n.* noise; clamor; vociferation.

vō·cif′ẽr·ănt, *a.* [L. *vociferans (-antis),* noisy.] clamorous; noisy; vociferous.

vō·cif′ẽr·ănt, *n.* a vociferous person; one who is clamorous.

vō·cif′ẽr·āte, *v.t.* and *v.i*; vociferated, *pt., pp.*; vociferating, *ppr.* [L. *vociferatus,* pp. of *vociferari,* to cry out.] to utter or cry out with a loud voice or clamorously; to shout.

Syn.—exclaim, bawl, shout, bellow, roar.

vō·cif·ẽr·ā′tion, *n.* the act of vociferating; a violent outcry; clamor; noisy exclamation.

vō·cif′ẽr·ā·tŏr, *n.* one who vociferates.

vō·cif′ẽr·ous, *a.* 1. making a loud outcry; shouting noisily; clamorous.

2. characterized by such outcry or clamor; as, a *vociferous* demand.

vō·cif′ẽr·ous·ly, *adv.* in a vociferous manner; with great noise in calling, shouting, etc.

vō·cif′ẽr·ous·ness, *n.* the quality or state of being vociferous; clamorousness.

voç′ū·lăr, *a.* [L. *vocula*, dim. of *vox, vocis*, voice.] vocal. [Rare.]

vod′kȧ, *n.* [Russ., brandy, dim. of *voda*, water.] a Russian alcoholic liquor distilled from wheat, rye, potatoes, etc.

vōe, *n.* [ON. *vāgr.*] in the Shetland Islands, an inlet, bay, or creek.

Vō·ē′tiăn (-shăn), *a.* in ecclesiastical history, of or pertaining to Gysbertus Voetius, literalist Theologian of Utrecht in the seventeenth century.

Vō·ē′tiăn, *n.* a believer in the theological teachings of Voetius.

vō′gie, *a.* vain; also, merry; cheerful; well-pleased. [Scot.]

vōgue (vōg), *n.* [Fr. *vogue*, fashion, reputation, lit., rowing of a ship, from *voguer*, to sail.]

1. the mode or fashion prevalent at any particular time; mode: often with *the*.

2. popularity; general favor or acceptance; as, ballad singers have acquired a great *vogue*.

3. sway; currency; authority. [Obs.]

Vō′gŭl, *n.* 1. a member of a Finno-Ugric people living in western Siberia.

2. the Ugric language of the Voguls.

voice, *n.* [OFr. *vois*, from L. *vox, vocis*, a voice.]

1. sound made through the mouth, especially by human beings, as in talking, singing, etc.

2. the ability to make sounds through the mouth; as, he lost his *voice*.

3. (a) any sound regarded as like vocal utterance; as, the *voice* of the sea; (b) anything regarded as like vocal utterance in communicating to the mind; as, the *voice* of his conscience.

4. a specified condition or quality of vocal sound; as, an angry *voice*.

5. the characteristic speech sounds normally made by a particular person; as, I recognized John's *voice*.

6. expressed wish, choice, opinion, etc.

7. the right to express one's wish, choice, opinion, etc., or to make it prevail; vote; as, we have a *voice* in our government.

8. expression; as, give *voice* to your opinion.

9. the person or other agency by which something is expressed or made known; as, this newspaper is the *voice* of the administration.

10. (a) rumor; report; (b) fame; reputation. [Obs.]

11. in grammar, (a) one of the forms of a verb showing the connection between the subject and the verb, either as performing (*active voice*) or receiving (*passive voice*) the action; (b) such forms or categories, collectively.

12. in music, (a) musical sound made with the mouth; singing; (b) the quality of a particular person's singing; as, a good *voice*; (c) a singer; (d) any of the parts of a musical phrase or composition in harmony; as, a song for three *voices*; (e) ability to sing; as, he really has no *voice*.

13. in phonetics, sound made by vibrating the vocal cords with air forced from the lungs, as in pronouncing all vowels and such consonants as *b, d, g, m*, etc.

in voice; with the voice in good condition, as for singing.

with one voice; unanimously.

voice, *v.t.*; voiced (voist), *pt., pp.*; voicing, *ppr.* 1. to give utterance to; to announce; to report.

2. in music, to regulate the tone of; as, to *voice* the pipes of an organ.

3. to nominate; to adjudge by vote; to vote. [Obs.]

4. to write voice parts for; as, to *voice* a quartette.

5. in phonetics, to utter with voice.

voice, *v.i.* to vote or give one's opinion. [Rare.]

voiced (voist), *a.* 1. having a voice.

2. having or using (a specified kind or tone of) voice: often in hyphenated compounds, as deep-*voiced*.

3. expressed by the voice.

4. in phonetics, made with voice; sonant; said of certain consonants.

voice′fụl, *a.* having, or as if having, voice or a voice; vocal; as, the *voiceful* sea.

voice′fụl·ness, *n.* the state or quality of being voiceful.

voice′less, *a.* 1. having no voice; dumb; mute.

2. not speaking; silent.

3. not spoken; not uttered; as, a *voiceless* wish.

4. lacking a musical voice or the ability to sing.

5. having no voice, or vote; lacking suffrage.

6. in phonetics, uttered without voice; surd; as, *k, p, t*, etc. are *voiceless* consonants.

voice′less·ly, *adv.* in a voiceless manner.

voice′less·ness, *n.* the state or quality of being voiceless; silence.

voice pärt, in music, the melody or part for a particular voice or instrument in a polyphonic composition.

voice′print, *n.* a pattern of wavy lines and whorls recorded by a device actuated by the sound of a person's voice: the pattern is supposed to be distinctive for each individual, like a fingerprint.

voi′cẽr, *n.* one who voices; specifically, one who regulates the pipes of an organ.

void, *a.* [OFr. *voide*, void, from L. *viduus*, deprived.]

1. empty; vacant; not occupied with any visible matter; as, a *void* space or place.

The earth was without form, and *void*, and darkness was upon the face of the deep.
—Gen. i. 2.

2. having no holder, possessor, or incumbent, as a benefice or office.

3. in law, (a) of no legal force; not binding; invalid; null; (b) loosely, voidable.

4. not taken up with business. [Rare.]

I chain him in my study, that, at *void* hours,
I may run over the story of his country.
—Massinger.

5. being without; devoid; destitute; wanting; *void* of reason or common sense.

6. not producing any effect; ineffectual.

void space; in physics, a vacuum.

Syn.—empty, vacant, unoccupied, unfilled, devoid, wanting, unfurnished, unsupplied.

void, *n.* 1. that which is void; an empty space; vacuum.

2. a feeling of emptiness or loss; as, his sudden death left a *void*.

3. a break or open space, as in a surface; a gap; opening.

void, *v.t.* 1. (a) to make empty or vacant; to clear; (b) to leave; to vacate. [Now Rare.]

2. to empty (the contents of something); to evacuate; discharge.

3. to make void, or of no effect; to nullify; annul.

void, *v.i.* 1. to be emitted or evacuated. [Rare.]

2. to go; to leave. [Obs.]

3. to have an evacuation.

void′ȧ·ble, *a.* in law, capable of being annulled, made void, or adjudged invalid.

void′ănce, *n.* [ME. *voydaunce*; Anglo-Fr. *voidaunce*; OFr. *vuidance*.]

1. a voiding; specifically, (a) annulment, as of a contract; (b) vacancy, as of a benefice.

2. evasion; subterfuge. [Obs.]

void′ed, *a.* 1. made void.

2. having an opening or hole cut.

3. in heraldry, pierced through so as to show the field and leave only an outline.

void′ẽr, *n.* 1. one who or that which voids, empties, vacates, annuls, or nullifies.

2. a tray or basket in which utensils or dishes, or remains of a meal, are carried away in clearing a table. [Obs. exc. Dial.]

3. in medieval armor, a contrivance, usually of chain mail, for protecting any part of the body left exposed by the plate armor.

void′ing, *n.* 1. the act of one who or that which voids.

2. that which is voided; a remnant.

void′ing knīfe (nīf), a knife used to collect fragments of food to put into a voider. [Obs.]

void′ly, *adv.* in a void manner.

void′ness, *n.* the state or character of being void, in any sense.

voi·là′ (vwȧ-lȧ′), [Fr., see there.] behold; there it is: often used as an interjection.

voile (vwȧl *or* voil), *n.* [Fr., veil.] a thin, sheer fabric of cotton, silk, rayon, or wool, used for dresses, curtains, etc.

voir dīre (vwor), [OFr., to speak true, from L. *verum dicere*.]

1. in law, an oath administered to a person intended as a witness, requiring him to make true answers to questions as to preliminary or collateral points, before he is allowed to testify as to the main point at issue.

2. the questions themselves.

voi·tūre′ (vwȧ-), *n.* [Fr.] a carriage or wagon.

voi·tūr·ette′ (vwȧ-), *n.* [Fr.] a small carriage.

voi′vōde, vāi′vōde, *n.* [Russ. *voyevoda*, army leader.] a title originally given to military commanders in various Slavonic countries, and afterward to governors of towns or provinces.

voi′vōde·ship, vāi′vōde·ship, *n.* the office or authority of a voivode.

voix cé·leste′ (vwȧ sā-lest′), [Fr., lit., heavenly voice.] an organ stop consisting of two soft-toned pipes for each tone, one of which is pitched slightly sharp so as to produce a wavering, tremulous effect.

vō′lȧ, *n.*; *pl.* **vō′lae,** [L.] the sole of the foot or palm of the hand.

vō·lā′cious, *a.* [L. *volare*, to fly.] apt or fit to fly. [Obs.]

vō·lä·dor′, *n.* [Sp., a flyer.]

1. a Californian flying fish, *Exocætus californicus*.

2. the flying gurnard.

vō′lae, *n.* plural. of *vola*.

vō·lāge′ (-lȧzh′), *a.* giddy; light; flighty. [Obs.]

Vō′lăns, *n.* [L. (*Piscis*) *Volans*, flying (fish).] a small southern constellation.

vō′lănt, *a.* [L. *volans* (-*antis*), ppr. of *volare*, to fly.]

1. flying or capable of flying.

2. nimble; active; as, *volant* touch.

3. in heraldry, represented as flying or having the wings spread.

4. moving about or passing from one place to another; hence, current. [Obs.]

CHARGE VOLANT

vō′lănt, *n.* 1. a shuttlecock; hence, one who fluctuates between two parties; a trimmer. [Obs.]

2. a flounce, as of a skirt, curtain, etc. [Obs.]

vō·län′te, *adv.* [It.] in music, lightly; with rapidity: a direction to the performer.

vō·län′te, *n.* [Sp.] a two-wheeled covered vehicle, drawn by two horses, one being ridden by a postilion: formerly used in Cuba.

vō′lănt piēce, in medieval armor, an additional covering for the front of a helmet. It stood somewhat forward, and the projecting salient angle was made sharp in order to cause the opposing lance to glance off.

VOLANT PIECE

Vo·la·pük′ (vō-lä-pük′), *n.* [from two words in the new language, *vol*, world, universe, and *pük*, speech, language.] an artificial language invented about 1879 by J. M. Schleyer of Baden, Germany, for proposed international use as an auxiliary language: also spelled *Volapuk*.

Vo·la·pük′ist, *n.* one versed in Volapük or favoring its adoption as a universal language.

vō′lăr, *a.* [L. *vola*, the palm of the hand, also the sole of the foot.] in anatomy, of or pertaining to the palm of the hand or the sole of the foot; as, the *volar* artery.

vol′ȧ·tile, *a.* [Fr. *volatil*, from L. *volatilis*, from *volare*, to fly.]

1. flying; having the power to fly. [Obs.]

2. evaporating rapidly; diffusing more or less freely in the atmosphere.

3. lively; brisk; gay; full of spirit.

4. changeable; fickle; transient.

volatile liniment; liniment of ammonia.

volatile oil; any of a number of highly volatile, non-saponifying oils distilled from the tissues of plants; essential oil: distinguished from *fixed oil*.

volatile salt; same as *sal volatile*.

vol′ȧ·tile, *n.* a winged animal; a bird; also, wild fowl, collectively. [Obs.]

vol′ȧ·tile·ness, *n.* same as *volatility*.

vol·ȧ·til′i·ty, *n.* [Fr. *volatilité*.] the state or quality of being volatile.

vol′ȧ·til·ī″zȧ·ble, *a.* capable of being volatilized.

vol·ȧ·til·i·zā′tion, *n.* the act of volatilizing or the condition of being volatilized.

vol′ȧ·til·īze, *v.t.*; volatilized, *pt., pp.*; volatilizing, *ppr.* [Fr. *volatiliser*.] to make volatile; to cause to pass off in vapor.

vol′ȧ·til·īze, *v.i.* to pass off in the form of vapor; to become volatile.

vōl·au·vent′ (-ō-voṅ′), *n.* [Fr., lit., flight in the wind.] a baked pastry shell of puff paste, filled with a stew of chicken, game, fish, etc.

vol′borth·īte, *n.* [after A. von *Volborth*, a Russ. scientist.] a mineral vanadate of calcium, barium, and copper, occurring in hexagonal green or yellow crystals.

vol·cā′ni·ăn, *a.* volcanic. [Rare.]

vol·căn′iç, *a.* [Fr. *volcanique*; It. *volcanico.*]

1. of, thrown from, caused by, or characteristic of a volcano.

2. having, or composed of, volcanoes.

3. like a volcano; violently and powerfully explosive or capable of explosion.

volcanic bomb; a more or less spherical lava mass formed by the rolling or projection of molten lava from a volcano.

volcanic focus; a center or focus of igneous action in a volcanic region.

volcanic glass; obsidian, a natural glass formed by the very rapid cooling of molten lava.

volcanic neck; a mass of lava solidified while filling the throat or vent of a volcano and remaining after the cone has been worn away.

volcanic rocks; igneous rocks of recent or modern origin, as lava from volcanoes.

vol·çan′i·căl·ly, *adv.* in a volcanic manner.

vol·căn·ic′i·ty, *n.* the state or quality of being volcanic; volcanic power.

vol′căn·işm, *n.* 1. volcanic processes and phenomena.

2. volcanicity.

vol′căn·ist, *n.* a student of or specialist in volcanoes.

vol·çan′i·ty, *n.* the state of being volcanic. [Rare.]

vol′căn·īze, *v.t.*; volcanized, *pt., pp.*; volcanizing, *ppr.* to subject to or change by volcanic heat.

vol·çā′nō, *n.*; *pl.* **vol·çā′nōeş** or **vol·çā′nōş,** [L. *Vulcanus*, Vulcan, the god of fire.]

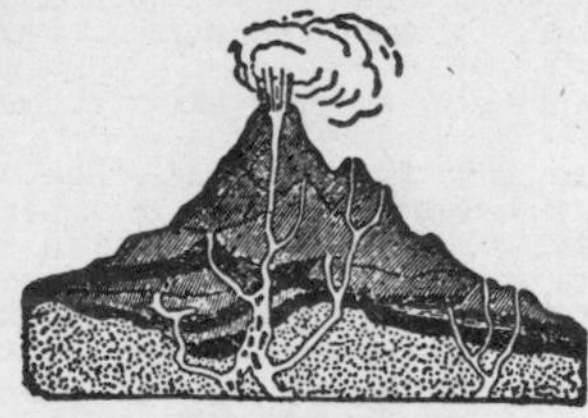

SECTION OF AN ACTIVE VOLCANO

1. a vent in the earth's crust through which rocks, dust, and ash, or molten rock in the form of liquid magma are ejected: a volcano is *active* while erupting, *dormant* during a long period of inactivity, or *extinct* when all activity has finally ceased.

2. a cone-shaped hill or mountain, wholly or chiefly of volcanic materials, built up around the vent.

vol″căn·ō·loġ′i·căl, *a.* of or having to do with volcanology.

vol·căn·ol′ō·ġy, *n.* the science dealing with volcanoes and volcanic phenomena.

vōle, *n.* [short for *vole mouse*, or *wold mouse*; *wold*, field.] any of various burrowing rodents of the genus *Arvicola*, including the European field mouse and the North American meadow mouse.

vōle, *n.* [Fr.; prob. from *voler* (L. *volare*), to fly.] in card games, the winning of all the tricks in a deal; a slam.

to go the vole; to risk everything in the hope of great gain.

vōle, *v.i.*; voled, *pt., pp.*; voling, *ppr.* in card games, to win all the tricks in a deal.

vol′ẽr·y, *n.pl.* **vol′ẽr·ieş,** [Fr. *volerie*, from L. *volare*, to fly.] 1. the birds in an aviary. [Rare.]

2. a place where birds are raised or kept; an aviary.

volġe, *n.* the mob; the crowd. [Obs.]

vol′i·tănt, *a.* [L. *volitans* (*-antis*), ppr. of *volitare*, to fly to and fro, freq. of *volare*, to fly.] volant; flying; also, capable of flying.

vol·i·tā′tion, *n.* 1. the act of flying; flight.

2. ability to fly.

vō·li′tient (-lish′ent), *a.* exercising volition. [Rare.]

vō·li′tion (-lish′un), *n.* [Fr., from L. *volo*, pres. ind. of *velle*, to be willing, to will.]

1. the act of willing; exercise of the will.

Volition is the actual exercise of the power which the mind has of considering or forbearing to consider an idea. —Locke.

2. settlement of vacillation or deliberation by a decision or choice; determination by the will.

3. the power of willing.

Syn.—preference, choice, will, purpose, determination.

vō·li′tion·ăl, *a.* 1. of, belonging to, or proceeding from volition.

2. having or exercising the power of volition.

vō·li′tion·ăl·ly, *adv.* by volition; by the will.

vol′i·tive, *a.* 1. having the power to will.

2. of or arising from the will.

3. in grammar, expressing a wish, as a verb, mood, etc.

Vōlk (fōlk), *n.* [G.] a folk; people; nation.

Vōlks′liēd (fōlks′lēt), *n.*; *pl.* **Vōlks′liēd·ẽr,** [G.] a folk song.

vōlks′raăd (-rät), *n.* [S. Afr. D.] a legislative body of any of the South African Dutch countries, as that of the former South African Republic or of the former Orange Free State.

Vōlks′sturm (fōlks′shtoorm), *n.* [G.] in Nazi Germany, a home guard army formed toward the end of World War II of men and boys unfit for regular military service.

vol′ley, *n.*; *pl.* **vol′leyş,** [Fr. *volée*; LL. *volatus*, a flying, flight, from L. *volatus*, pp. of *volare*, to fly.]

1. the simultaneous discharge of a number of firearms or other weapons.

2. the bullets, arrows, stones, etc. so discharged.

3. a burst or shooting forth of a number of things simultaneously or in quick succession; as, a *volley* of curses.

4. in cricket, a ball bowled so as to hit the wicket before touching the ground.

5. in soccer, a kick at a ball in play before it touches the ground.

6. in tennis, (a) the flight of a ball in play before it touches the ground; (b) a return of the ball before it touches the ground.

on the volley; at random. [Obs.]

vol′ley, *v.t.*; volleyed, *pt., pp.*; volleying, *ppr.* 1. to emit or discharge in or as in a volley: often with *out*.

2. in sports, to make a return of (a ball) before it touches the ground.

3. in cricket, to bowl or cast full to the head of the wicket.

vol′ley, *v.i.* 1. to be shot out in a volley; to be discharged simultaneously.

2. in cricket, to cast a ball directly to the head of the wicket.

3. in sports, to send the ball back over the net before it touches the ground.

vol′ley·bạll, *n.* 1. a game played on a court by two teams who hit a large, light, inflated ball back and forth over a high net with the hands, each team trying to return the ball before it touches the ground.

2. the ball used in this game.

vō′lost, *n.* [Russ.] 1. formerly, a small administrative district of peasants in czarist Russia.

2. a rural soviet in the Soviet Union.

vol′ōw, *v.t.* to baptize: a contemptuous variation of the L. *volo*, a response in the baptismal service. [Obs.]

vol′plāne, *v.i.*, volplaned; *pt., pp.*; volplaning, *ppr.* [Fr. *vol plané*; *vol*, flight, from *voler* (L. *volare*), to fly, and *plané*, pp. of *planer*, to glide, from *plan*, a level surface; L. *planus*.] to glide down with the engine cut off: said of an airplane or the pilot maneuvering it.

vol′plane, *n.* a glide with the engine cut off.

Vol′scī (-sī), *n.pl.* [L.] an ancient people of Latium who were conquered by the Romans in the 4th century B.C.

Vol′sciăn (-shăn), *a.* of or relating to the Volsci or to their language.

Vol′sciăn, *n.* any of the Volsci.

Vol′stead Açt (-sted), [after Rep. Andrew *Volstead* (1860–1947), who introduced the act.] an act of Congress to enforce the Eighteenth, or Prohibition, Amendment to the Constitution of the U. S., passed into law October 28, 1919, and effective the following January 19. The Eighteenth Amendment was repealed, 1933.

Vol′stead·işm, *n.* the policy of prohibiting the sale of intoxicating liquors or the enforcement of this policy by the Volstead Act.

Vol′suṇ·gȧ Sä′gȧ, [ON. *Völsunga saga*, lit., saga of the Volsungs, the descendants of *Volsi*, a legendary king.] an Icelandic saga relating the legend of Sigurd and the Nibelungs: it is also told, with variations, in a Germanic version, the Nibelungenlied.

vōlt, *n.* [Fr. *volte*; It. *volta*, a turn, from L. *volutus*, pp. of *volvere*, to roll, turn about or round.]

1. a circular tread; a gait in which a horse moves sideways round a center.

2. in fencing, a sudden movement to avoid a thrust.

vōlt, *n.* [named after Alessandro *Volta* (1745–1827), It. physicist.] the unit of electromotive force, or difference of potential, which will cause a current of one ampere to flow through a resistance of one ohm.

vōl′tȧ, *n.*;*pl.* **vōl′tẹ,** [It.] 1. in music, a time: used in directions, as, *una volta*, once.

2. an old dance.

vol′tȧ- [from *voltaic*.] in electricity, a combining form meaning *voltaic*, as in *volta*electric.

vol″tȧ·ē·leç′triç, *a.* relating to, due to, or causing voltaic electricity.

vol′tȧ·ē·leç·trom′e·tẽr, *n.* a device to measure the potential of a voltaic current.

vōl′tăġe, *n.* in electricity, electromotive force, or difference in electrical potential, expressed in volts.

vol·tag′rȧ·phy, *n.* the process of copying a pattern by electrolysis. [Rare.]

vol·tā′iç, *a.* [from Alessandro *Volta* and *-ic.*]

1. (a) designating or of electricity produced by chemical action; (b) used in producing electricity by chemical action.

2. designating or of electricity that moves in a current, as distinguished from static electricity.

3. [V–] of or relating to Alessandro Volta.

voltaic battery; in electricity, (a) a battery composed of voltaic cells; (b) a voltaic cell.

voltaic cell; in electricity, a device for producing an electric current by the action of two plates of different metals in an electrolyte.

voltaic couple; two dissimilar metallic plates acting in an electrolyte to produce an electric current.

voltaic pile; a column formed by successive pairs of dissimilar metallic disks, as silver and zinc, with moistened cloth between every two contiguous pairs; by extension, any battery.

Vol·tāir′ē·ăn, *a.* and *n.* Voltairian.

Vol·tāir′i·ăn, *a.* of, like, or characteristic of Voltaire.

Vol·tāir′i·ăn, *n.* an advocate of the principles of Voltaire.

Vol·tāir′işm, *n.* the principles or philosophy of Voltaire.

vol′tȧ·işm, *n.* voltaic electricity or the branch of electrical science dealing with this.

vol′tȧ·īte, *n.* [after A. *Volta*, It. physicist.] a resinous, dull-green to brown or black isometric mineral, occurring in octahedrons, cubes, and other forms. It is a hydrous sulfate of iron.

vol·tam′e·tẽr, *n.* an instrument for measuring the amount of electricity passing through a conductor by the amount of electrolysis produced.

vol·tȧ·met′riç, *a.* relating to or involving the use of the voltameter.

vōlt′am′mē·tẽr, *n.* an instrument for measuring voltage and amperage; a wattmeter.

vōlt′-am′pẽre, *n.* a unit of electrical measurement equal to the product of one volt and one ampere: in a direct current it is equal to one watt.

vol′tȧ·plast, *n.* [*volta*, and Gr. *plastos*, formed, molded.] a kind of voltaic battery used in electrotyping.

vol′tȧ·tȳpe, *n.* an electrotype. [Rare.]

vōlt box, in electricity, (a) a divided wire placed across the terminals of a voltmeter to be tested; (b) a resistance divided into such sections that any suitable fractional drop in potential in the entire resistance can be readily measured by a potentiometer.

vōlt′-çōu·lomb′ (-lom′) *n.* a joule.

vōlte′-fäçe′ (*or* vol′te-fäs), *n.* [Fr.] 1. a complete reversal of opinion, attitude, etc.

A *volte-face* worthy of a politician.
—W. Besant.

2. a turn so as to face the opposite way; about-face.

vōl′tï, *v. imper.* [It., from *voltare*, to turn.] in music, turn (the page): a direction to the performer.

vọl·ti·ġeur′ (-zhẽr′), *n.* [Fr., from *voltiger*, to vault.]

1. a leaper; a vaulter; a tumbler.

2. formerly, in the French army, a member of a select company of skirmishers attached to every regiment of French infantry.

vōlt′mē″tẽr, *n.* any instrument used to measure an electromotive force, or a difference in electrical potential, by volts.

voltz′ine, *n.* [named after P. L. *Voltz*, Fr. mining engineer.] a red, yellowish, or brownish, opaque or subtranslucent oxysulfide of zinc. It occurs in the form of small hemispheres, divisible into thin layers.

voltz'īte, *n.* same as *voltzine.*

vō·lū'bi·lāte, *a.* [L. *volubilis,* turning, spinning.] in botany, voluble. [Obs.]

vol'ū·bile, *a.* in botany, voluble. [Obs.]

vol·ū·bil'i·ty, *n.* voluble state or character.

vol'ū·ble, *a.* [Fr., from L. *volubilis,* easily turned about, from *volutus,* pp. of *volvere,* to roll, turn about or round.]

1. formed so as to roll with ease on an axis; rotating; as, *voluble* particles of matter. [Rare.]

2. speaking with ease or fluency; fluent; talkative; glib; garrulous.

3. in botany, twisting: applied to stems which twist or twine round other bodies, as that of the hop.

4. unstable; inconstant; changeable. [Rare.]

vol'ū·ble·ness, *n.* the quality of being voluble.

vol'ū·bly, *adv.* in a voluble manner; as, he talked *volubly* at times.

vol'ū·çrīne, *a.* [from L. *volucris,* a bird.] pertaining to or resembling birds.

vol'ūme, *n.* [Fr., from L. *volumen,* a roll, scroll, hence a book written on a parchment, roll, from *volutus,* pp. of *volvere,* to roll.]

1. originally, a roll of parchment, a scroll, etc.

2. (a) a collection of written, typewritten, or printed sheets bound together; a book; (b) one of the books in a set or a complete work.

3. the amount of space occupied in three dimensions; cubic contents or cubic magnitude.

4. a quantity, bulk, mass, or amount.

5. a large quantity; bulk, amount, etc.

6. the quantity, strength, or loudness of sound.

7. in music, fullness of tone.

specific volume; the result obtained by dividing the molecular weight of a compound body by the specific gravity.

to speak or *tell volumes*; to be very expressive or significant.

Syn.—size, body, bulk, dimensions, book, work, tome, capacity, magnitude, compass, quantity.

vol'ūmed, *a.* 1. having the form of a volume or roll; of a rounded form; as, *volumed* mist.

2. possessing volume; massive; large.

3. consisting of (a specified kind or number of) volumes: used in hyphenated compounds; as, a three-*volumed* book.

vol″ū·mē·nom'e·tẽr, *n.* [L. *volumen (-inis),* volume, and *meter.*] an instrument for measuring the volume of a solid body by the quantity of a liquid or of air which it displaces, and, hence, also for determining its specific gravity.

vol″ū·mē·nom'e·try, *n.* the act, skill, or practice of using a volumenometer.

vō·lū'mē·sçōpe, *n.* [L. *volumen (-inis),* volume, and Gr. *skopein,* to view.] a glass tube with a graduated scale for showing the changes of volume of various compounds resulting from chemical action.

vō·lū'mē·tẽr, *n.* [L. *volumen,* volume, and *-meter.*] an instrument used to determine the volumes of gases or liquids directly, and of solids by the amount of liquid they displace.

vol·ū·met'riç, vol·ū·met'ri·çăl, *a.* relating to the measurement of volumes.

volumetric analysis; the quantitative analysis of a chemical solution by determining the amount of reagent necessary to effect a reaction in a known volume of the solution.

vol·ū·met'ri·çăl·ly, *adv.* according to volumetric analysis.

vō·lū'me·try, *n.* 1. the measurement of volumes.

2. volumetric analysis.

vō·lū·mi·năl, *a.* pertaining to volume.

vō·lū·mi·nos'i·ty, *n.* the state or quality of being voluminous; prolixity; copiousness.

vō·lū'mi·nous, *a.* [LL. *voluminosus,* full of rolls or folds, from *volumen (-inis),* roll, volume.]

1. consisting of many coils, windings, or folds. [Rare or Archaic.]

2. writing, producing, consisting of, or forming such a mass of material as to fill volumes.

3. of great magnitude; bulky; spreading; wide.

vō·lū'mi·nous·ly, *adv.* in a voluminous manner; copiously.

vō·lū'mi·nous·ness, *n.* the state of being voluminous.

vol'ū·mist, *n.* one who writes a volume; an author. [Rare.]

vol'un·tăr·i·ly, *adv.* in a voluntary manner; of one's own free will.

vol'un·tăr·i·ness, *n.* the quality or state of being voluntary.

vol'un·tȧ·riṣm, *n.* in philosophy, any theory which holds that reality is ultimately of the nature of will or that the will is the primary factor in experience.

vol″un·tȧ·ris'tiç, *a.* of, having the nature of, or adhering to voluntarism.

vol'un·tăr·y, *a.* [Fr. *volontaire*; L. *voluntarius,* voluntary, from *voluntas,* free will, from *voluns,* var. of *volens (-entis),* ppr. of *velle,* to be willing, to will.]

1. brought about by one's own free choice; given or done of one's own free will; freely chosen or undertaken.

2. acting in a specified capacity willingly or of one's own accord.

3. intentional; not accidental; as, *voluntary* manslaughter.

4. controlled by the will; as, *voluntary* muscles.

5. able to will; having the power of free decision; as, man is a *voluntary* agent.

6. supported by contributions or freewill offerings; not supported or maintained by the state; as, *voluntary* churches.

7. arising in the mind without external constraint; spontaneous.

8. in law, (a) acting or done without compulsion or persuasion; (b) done without profit, payment, or any valuable consideration.

voluntary affidavit or *oath*; an affidavit or oath made in an extrajudicial matter or in a case for which the law has not provided.

voluntary conveyance; in law, a conveyance which may be made merely on a good but not a valuable consideration.

voluntary escape; in law, the escape of a prisoner with the express consent of the custodian.

voluntary jurisdiction; a jurisdiction exercised in matters admitting of no opposition or question, and therefore cognizable by any judge, in any place, and on any lawful day.

voluntary waste; waste which is the result of the voluntary act of the tenant of property, as where, without the consent of the proprietor, he cuts down timber, pulls down a wall, or the like.

Syn.—deliberate, spontaneous, free, intentional, optional, discretional, unconstrained, willing.

vol'un·tăr·y, *n.*; *pl.* **vol'un·tăr·ieṣ,** 1. one who engages in any affair of his own free will; a volunteer. [Rare.]

2. an advocate of voluntaryism.

3. a voluntary act or piece of work.

4. in music, a piece or solo, often an improvisation, played on the organ before, during, or after a church service.

vol'un·tăr·y, *adv.* voluntarily.

vol'un·tăr·y·iṣm, *n.* 1. the doctrine that churches, schools, etc. should be supported by voluntary contributions and not by the state.

2. a system based on this principle.

vol·un·teer', *n.* [Fr. *volontaire,* a voluntary.]

1. a person who enters or offers to enter into any service of his own free will.

2. a person who enters naval or military service of his own free will, without being compelled to do so by law: opposed to *conscript, draftee.*

3. in law, (a) a person who enters into any transaction of his own free will; (b) a person to whom property is transferred without valuable consideration.

4. in botany, a volunteer tree or shrub.

Volunteers of America; an undenominational society, similar to the Salvation Army, organized by Ballington Booth in 1896, in New York City, to bring religious and material help to those who need it.

vol·un·teer', *a.* 1. composed of volunteers, as an army.

2. serving as a volunteer.

3. of a volunteer or volunteers.

4. voluntary.

5. in botany, growing from self-sown or naturally fallen seed.

vol·un·teer', *v.t.*; volunteered, *pt., pp.*; volunteering, *ppr.* to offer or bestow voluntarily, or without solicitation or compulsion; as, to *volunteer* one's services.

vol·un·teer', *v.i.* to enter into or make an offer of or for any service of one's free will, without solicitation or compulsion.

Syn.—offer, proffer, tend, originate.

vol'ū·pẽr, *n.* a cap or hood worn by women in the fourteenth century. [Obs.]

vō·lup'tū·ăr·y, *n.*; *pl.* **vō·lup'tū·ăr·ieṣ,** [L. *voluptuarius,* from *voluptas,* pleasure.] one who is devoted to luxury or to the gratification of the appetite and to other sensual pleasures; a sensualist.

vō·lup'tū·ăr·y, *a.* of or characterized by luxury and sensual pleasure.

vō·lup'tū·ous, *a.* [Fr. *voluptueux*; L. *voluptuosus,* full of pleasure, from *voluptas,* pleasure.]

1. full of, producing, or characterized by sensual delights and pleasures; sensual.

2. fond of or directed toward luxury, elegance, and the pleasures of the senses.

3. suggesting or expressing sensual pleasure or gratification.

4. arising from sensual gratification.

vō·lup'tū·ous·ly, *adv.* in a voluptuous manner.

vō·lup'tū·ous·ness, *n.* the state or quality of being voluptuous.

vō·lup'ty, *n.* voluptuousness. [Obs.]

Vō·lū'tȧ, *n.* [L. *voluta,* volute; orig. f. of *volutus,* pp. of *volvere,* to roll.]

1. a genus of marine gastropods, including those which have a univalve spiral shell and a columella twisted or plaited, generally without lips or perforation.

2. [v–] a gastropod of this or an allied genus; a volute.

vol·ū·tā'tion, *n.* a wallowing; a rolling of a body on the earth; also, a similar motion of the sea.

vō·lūte', *n.* [Fr.; L. *voluta*; orig. f. of *volutus,* pp. of *volvere,* to roll.]

1. in architecture, a spiral scroll forming one of the chief features of Ionic and Corinthian capitals.

2. a spiral or twisting form; a turn; a whorl.

3. in zoology, any of the turns or whorls of a spiral shell.

4. a gastropod of the genus *Voluta* and allied genera.

vō·lūte', *a.* 1. rolled up; spiraled.

2. in machinery, (a) having a spirally shaped part; (b) having a combined circular and lateral motion.

vō·lūt'ed, *a.* 1. grooved or twisted in spirals.

2. in architecture, having a volute.

Vō·lū'ti·dae, *n.pl.* a family of marine gastropods of which the genus *Voluta* is the type.

vō·lū'tion, *n.* [from L. *volutus.*]

1. a revolving; rolling.

2. a spiral turn or twist; a coil; a convolution.

3. a whorl of a spiral shell.

vol'ū·toid, *a.* of or pertaining to the *Volutidæ*; resembling a volute.

vol'ū·toid, *n.* one of the *Volutidæ.*

vol'vȧ, *n.* [L., a wrapper.] the membranous covering enclosing some mushrooms in the early stage of growth.

vol'vāte, *a.* [*volva* and *-ate.*] in botany, having or pertaining to a volva.

Vol'vox, *n.* [L. *volvere,* to roll.] a genus of minute unicellular organisms formerly classed in the animal kingdom, but now regarded as vegetables and ranked among the *Protophyta.*

vol'vū·lus, *n.* [L. *volvere,* to turn, roll.] in pathology, a twisting of the intestine, producing obstruction to the passing of its contents and strangulation of the part involved.

vō'mẽr, *n.* [L., a plowshare.] in anatomy, a thin, flat bone forming part of the nasal septum separating the nasal passages.

vō'mẽr·ine, *a.* in anatomy, of or relating to the vomer.

vom'i·çȧ, *n.* [L., ulcer, abscess, from *vomere,* to vomit.]

1. a pus-filled cavity in some organ, especially the lungs.

2. the pus in such a cavity.

3. the coughing up of such pus in profuse quantities.

vom'i·cēne, *n.* same as *brucine.*

vom'iç nut, same as *nux vomica.*

vom'it, *n.* [L. *vomitus,* a discharging, vomiting, from *vomitus,* pp. of *vomere,* to discharge, vomit.]

1. the act or process of ejecting the contents of the stomach through the mouth.

2. matter ejected in this way.

3. a drug which causes vomiting; an emetic.

vom'it, *v.i.*; vomited, *pt., pp.*; vomiting, *ppr.* 1. to eject the contents of the stomach through the mouth; to throw up.

2. to be thrown up or out with force or violence; to rush out.

vom'it, *v.t.* 1. to throw up or eject from the stomach; to discharge from the stomach through the mouth: often followed by *up* or *out.*

> The fish *vomited out* Jonah upon the dry land. —Jonah ii. 10.

2. to discharge or throw out with force or in copious quantities; to belch forth; to disgorge; as, volcanoes *vomit* flames, ashes, stones, and liquid lava.

vom'it·ing, *n.* 1. the act of ejecting the contents of the stomach through the mouth; as, *vomiting* is essentially an inverted action of the stomach and esophagus.

2. the act of throwing out substances with violence from a deep hollow, as a volcano, etc.

vom'it·ing, *a.* causing to vomit.

vom'it·ing cen'tẽr, the nerve center in the medulla oblongata, the stimulation of which causes vomiting.

vom'it·ing gas, same as *chloropicrin*.

vō·mi'tion, *n.* the act or power of vomiting.

vom'i·tive, *a.* [Fr. *vomitif.*] of or causing vomiting; emetic.

vom'i·tive, *n.* an emetic.

vom'it nut, same as *nux vomica*.

vom'i·tō, *n.* [Sp.] 1. yellow fever.

2. the black vomit of yellow fever.

vom'i·tō·ry, *a.* [L. *vomitorius.*] vomitive; emetic.

vom'i·tō·ry, *n.*; *pl.* **vom'i·tō·ries,** [L. *vomitorius.*]

1. an emetic.

2. any opening, funnel, etc. through which matter is to be discharged.

3. in Roman amphitheaters, etc., any of the entrances leading to the tiers of seats.

vom''i·tū·ri'tion, *n.* [as if from a Latin verb *vomiturire*, to desire to vomit.] repeated but ineffectual attempts to vomit; retching; also, the vomiting of but little matter or vomiting with little effort.

von (fon *or Brit.* von), *prep.* [G.] of; from: a prefix occurring in many names of German and Austrian families, especially of the nobility.

vond·si'rȧ, *n.* same as *vansire*.

voo'doo, *n.*; *pl.* **voo'doos,** [Creole Fr., from a W. Afr. word.]

1. a body of primitive rites and practices, based on a belief in sorcery and in the power of charms, fetishes, etc., found among natives of the West Indies and in the southern United States, and ultimately of African origin.

2. a person who practices these rites.

3. a voodoo charm, fetish, etc.

voo'doo, *a.* of voodoos or voodooism.

voo'doo, *v.t.* to affect by charms, conjurations, and incantations of voodooism.

voo'doo·ism, *n.* the system of voodoo beliefs and practices.

voo·doo·ist'ic, *a.* of or characteristic of voodoo.

vōor'lōop''ẽr (fōr'lōp''), *n.* same as *forelooper*.

vōor'trek''kẽr (fōr'), *n.* [S. Afr. D.] in South Africa, a pioneer; the first to trek.

vō·rā'cious, *a.* [L. *vorax, voracis*, greedy to devour, from *vorare*, to devour.]

1. greedy in eating; devouring or eager to devour large quantities of food; ravenous; gluttonous.

2. very greedy or eager in some desire or pursuit; insatiable; as, a *voracious* reader.

vō·rā'cious·ly, *adv.* in a voracious manner; ravenously.

vō·rā'cious·ness, *n.* the quality or state of being voracious; eagerness to devour; rapaciousness; as, the *voraciousness* of a glutton.

vō·rac'i·ty, *n.* [Fr. *voracité*, from L. *voracitas* (*-tatis*), hungriness, from *vorax, voracis*, greedy to devour, voracious.] the quality or state of being voracious; ravenousness; voraciousness.

vō·rag'i·nous, *a.* [LL. *voraginosus*, from L. *vorago*, chasm, gulf.] full of gulfs; of or pertaining to a gulf or whirlpool; hence, devouring; swallowing. [Rare.]

vō·rā'gō, *n.* [L.] a gulf; an abyss; as, the *voragos* of subterranean cellars, wells, and dungeons.

-vō·rous, [from L. *vorare*, to devour.] a combining form meaning *feeding on, eating*, as in carni*vorous*.

Vōr'spiēl (fōr'shpēl), *n.* [G.] a prelude or overture.

Vōr'stel''lung (fōr'shtel-), *n.*; *pl.* **vōr'stel''lung·en,** [G.] in German philosophy, the ability to think in images or pictures; in the philosophy of Kant, any intellectual depiction of a proposition.

vor'tex, *n.*; *pl.* **vor'tex·es, vor'ti·cēs,** [L. *vortex, vertex*, from *vertere*, to turn, whirl.]

1. a whirling mass of water forming a vacuum at its center, into which anything caught in the motion is drawn; a whirlpool.

2. a whirl or powerful eddy of air; a whirlwind.

3. any activity, situation, or state of affairs that resembles a whirl or eddy in its rush, absorbing effect, irresistible and catastrophic power, etc.

4. in Cartesian philosophy, a collection of particles of matter forming an ether or fluid endowed with a rapid rotary motion around an axis. By means of these vortices, Descartes attempted to account for the formation of the universe.

5. [V-] in zoology, a genus typical of the *Vorticidæ*, a family of turbellarians.

vortex of the heart; a whorled arrangement of muscular fibers in the heart.

vor'tex at'ŏm, in chemistry, elementary matter in constant vortical motion arranged in hypothetical rings.

vor'tex fil'ȧ·ment, in physics, the fluid in a hypothetical tube represented by vortex lines drawn through an infinitely small closed curve in a rotating liquid.

vor'tex ring, in physics, a vortical molecular filament or column returning into itself so as to form a ring composed of a number of small rotating circles placed side by side, like beads on a string.

vor'tex sheet, in physics, an imaginary layer of fluid of infinite thinness on the surface of a series of vortex filaments rotating side by side.

vor'tex tūbe, in physics, an imaginary tubular surface formed by drawing vortex lines through all points of a closed curve.

vor'tex wheel (hwēl), a kind of water turbine.

vor'ti·căl, *a.* 1. of, characteristic of, or like a vortex.

2. moving in a vortex; whirling.

vor'ti·căl·ly, *adv.* in a vortical manner.

vor'ti·cel, *n.* a vorticella.

Vor·ti·cel'lȧ, *n.* [Mod. L., dim. of L. *vortex* (*-icis*), a whirl, eddy.]

1. a genus of one-celled animals living in water, with a bell-shaped body on a thin stem by which they attach themselves to other objects.

2. [v-] *pl.* **vor·ti·cel'lae,** any animal of this genus.

Vor·ti·cel'li·dae, *n.pl.* a family of infusorian animalcules having for its type the genus *Vorticella*.

vor'ti·cōse, *a.* [L. *vortex* (*-icis*), a vortex.] whirling; vortical.

vor·tic'ū·lăr, *a.* vorticose.

vor·tig'i·nous, *a.* [L. *vertiginosus*, from *vertigo* (*-inis*) a whirling round, giddiness.]

1. whirling: said of motion.

2. moving in or like a vortex.

vōt'ȧ·ble, *a.* that can be submitted to a vote; subject to a vote: also spelled *voteable*.

vō'tȧ·ress, *n.* a girl or woman votary: also spelled *votress*.

vō'tȧ·rist, *n.* a votary.

vō'tȧ·ry, *a.* [L. *votus*, pp. of *vovere*, to vow.]

1. consecrated by a vow or promise.

2. of, or having the nature of, a vow.

vō'tȧ·ry, *n.*; *pl.* **vō'tȧ·ries,** 1. a person bound by a vow or promise, especially one bound to religious vows, as a monk or nun.

2. a person devoted to a particular religion or a certain form of religious worship.

3. a devoted or ardent supporter, as of a cause, ideal, etc.

4. a person who is devoted to any game, study, pursuit, etc.

vōte, *n.* [L. *votum*, a wish; originally a vow, from *votum*, neut. of *votus*, pp. of *vovere*, to vow.]

1. a decision by one or more persons on a proposal, resolution, bill, etc., or a choice between candidates for office, expressed by written ballot, voice, show of hands, etc.

2. (a) the expression or indication of such a decision or choice; (b) the ticket, ballot, voice, or any other means by which it is expressed.

3. the right to exercise such a decision or choice, as in a meeting, election, etc.; suffrage.

4. (a) the total number of ballots cast; as, the *vote* was light; (b) votes collectively; as, get out the *vote*.

5. a voter. [Obs.]

6. a vow. [Obs.]

7. a prayer. [Obs.]

vōte, *v.t.*; voted, *pt., pp.*; voting, *ppr.* 1. (a) to decide, enact, or authorize by vote; (b) to grant or confer by vote; (c) to support (a specified party ticket) in voting.

2. to declare by general opinion; as, they *voted* the party a success.

3. to suggest. [Colloq.]

4. to cause to vote; as, to *vote* a gang. [Slang.]

to vote down; to decide against; to defeat by voting.

to vote in; to elect.

to vote out; to defeat an incumbent in an election.

vōte, *v.i.* to express or signify the mind, will, or preference in a matter by voice, ballot, etc.; to give or cast a vote; as, to *vote* for a resolution; to *vote* conscientiously.

vōte'less, *a.* having no vote; not eligible to vote.

vōt'ẽr, *n.* 1. one who votes.

2. one who has a legal right to vote; an elector.

vōt'ing mȧ·chine', a machine, working on the principle of an adding machine, for the automatic casting, recording, and counting of votes, consisting, in its most common form, of a vertical keyboard so arranged that the voter records his ballot by pressing a key or knob opposite the name of the candidate for whom he wishes to vote.

vōt'ing pā'pẽr, a ballot; specifically, one bearing the names of more candidates than there are vacancies to be filled, the voter signifying his choice by a cross in front of the candidate's name. [Brit.]

vōt'ist, *n.* a votary. [Obs.]

vō'tive, *a.* [L. *votivus*, from *votum*; see *vote*, n.]

1. given, dedicated, consecrated, done, etc., in fulfillment of a vow or pledge; as, *votive* offerings.

2. in the Roman Catholic Church, designating or of a special or extraordinary Mass said at the option of the priest.

votive medal; a medal struck in commemoration of some important deed or event.

votive offering; an offering, such as a tablet, picture, etc., dedicated in consequence of the vow of a worshiper.

vō'tive·ly, *adv.* by vow; in a votive manner.

vō'tive·ness, *n.* the state or quality of being votive.

vō'tress, *n.* a votaress.

vouch, *v.t.*; vouched (voucht), *pt., pp.*; vouching, *ppr.* [OFr. *voucher*, from L. *vocare*, to call, from *vox, vocis*, a voice.]

1. to attest; to give evidence for; to affirm or guarantee; as, *vouch* a statement.

2. to cite or appeal to (authority, example, books, authors, etc.) in support of one's views or actions.

3. to uphold by demonstration.

4. to call as witness. [Archaic.]

5. in law, to call (a person) into court to give warranty of title.

6. to back; to follow up; to support. [Rare.]

Syn.—declare, asseverate, assert, aver, protest, affirm, attest, warrant, guarantee, confirm, assure.

vouch, *v.i.* 1. to give assurance, affirmation, or a guarantee (with *for*); as, his friends *vouched for* his honesty.

2. to serve as evidence or assurance (with *for*); as, his references *vouch for* his ability.

vouch, *n.* a vouching; approving or attesting voice; warrant; attestation; testimony. [Rare or Archaic.]

vouch·ee', *n.* in law, a person called to attest or warrant.

vouch'ẽr, *n.* 1. one who vouches for, confirms, or attests, as the truth of a statement; one who gives surety for another.

2. a paper attesting or serving as evidence; specifically, a receipt or statement serving as evidence of payment of a debt or of the accuracy of an account.

3. in old English law, (a) the tenant in a writ of right; one who calls in another to establish his warranty of title: also called *vouchor*; (b) the act of calling a person into court to warrant another's title to a property.

vouch'ment, *n.* a declaration or solemn assertion. [Rare.]

vouch'ŏr, *n.* a voucher (sense 3a). [Rare.]

vouch·sāfe', *v.t.*; vouchsafed (-sāft), *pt., pp.*; vouchsafing, *ppr.* [ME. *vouchen safe*, to vouch as safe, the two words finally running into one.]

1. to be gracious enough to grant; to grant in condescension; to deign to give; to concede; to bestow.

2. to guarantee as safe; to secure. [Obs.]

3. to receive in a condescending manner. [Obs.]

vouch·sāfe', *v.i.* to permit; to yield; to condescend; to deign.

vouch·sāfe'ment, *n.* 1. the act or fact of vouchsafing

2. that which is vouchsafed, or granted in condescension.

vöu′dọọ, vöu′dŏu, *n.* same as *voodoo.*
vöu′dŏu·ịsm, *n.* same as *voodooism.*
vöuge (vözh), *n.* [OFr. *voulge, vouge*; origin unknown.] a medieval weapon consisting of a sharp-pointed knife on the end of a staff.
vöus·soir′ (vös-wor′), *n.* [Fr., from *voussure*, the curvature of a vault, from a verb *vousser*, hypothetical LL. *volutiare*, to round, make round, from L. *volutus*, pp. of *volvere*, to roll.] in architecture, a stone in the shape of a truncated wedge which forms part of an arch. The under sides of the voussoirs form the intrados, or soffit, of the arch, and the upper sides the extrados. The middle voussoir is termed the keystone.

a a, VOUSSOIRS

vöus·soir′, *v.t.*; voussoired, *pt., pp.*; voussoiring, *ppr.* to construct with or by means of voissoirs.
vow, *n.* [ME. *vow, vou*; OFr. *vou, vo, veu*, from L. *votum*, a vow, lit., a thing vowed, from *vovere*, to promise, vow.]
1. a solemn promise or pledge; especially, one made to God or a god, dedicating oneself to an act, service, or way of life, such as that of a nun.
2. a promise of love and fidelity; as, marriage *vows.*
3. a solemn affirmation or assertion.
to take vows; to enter a religious order; to become a monk, nun, etc.
vow, *v.t.*; vowed, *pt., pp.*; vowing, *ppr.* [ME. *vowen*; OFr. *vouer*, from L. *vovere*, to promise, vow.]
1. to promise solemnly.
2. to make a solemn resolution to do, get, etc.
3. to declare emphatically, earnestly, or solemnly.
vow, *v.i.* to make vows or solemn promises; to asseverate.
vow′el, *n.* [ME. *vowelle*; OFr. *vouele*; L. *vocalis*, vowel, from *vox, vocis*, voice, sound.]
1. a voiced speech sound characterized by generalized friction of the air passing in a continuous stream through the pharynx and opened mouth, with relatively no narrowing or other obstruction of the speech organs.
2. a letter, as *a, e, i, o,* and *u*, representing such a sound.
Distinguished from *consonant.*
vow′el, *a.* of or pertaining to a vowel or vowels; vocal.
vow′eled, *a.* furnished with vowels.
vow′el grā·dā′tion, in philology, ablaut.
vow′el·ish, *a.* having the quality or nature of a vowel. [Rare.]
vow′el·ịsm, *n.* the use of vowels. [Obs.]
vow′el·ist, *n.* one who uses many vowels.
vow″el·i·zā′tion, *n.* 1. the act of vowelizing.
2. the state of being vowelized.
vow′el·ize, *v.t.*; vowelized, *pt., pp.*; vowelizing, *ppr.* to add or insert vowel points or signs to, as a Hebrew or Arabic text.
vow′el·less, *a.* without vowels.
vow′el·ly, *a.* having many vowels.
vow′el point, in certain languages whose written form normally consists only of consonants, as Hebrew, a diacritical mark inserted above or below a consonant to indicate the following vowel sound.
vow′ẽr, *n.* one who makes a vow.
vow fel′lōw, one who is bound by the same vow as another. [Rare.]
vow′less, *a.* having no vow.
vox, *n.*; *pl.* **vō′cēṣ,** [L.] voice.
vox angelica; an organ stop having two rows of pipes, one row of which is tuned slightly sharper than the other, so that a tremulous, wavy tone is produced: also called *vox cœlestis, voix céleste.*
vox barbara; a barbarous word or phrase: used, in zoology and botany, of terms which are coined and which are ostensibly New Latin, but which belong to no language or are hybrids between Latin and Greek.
vox cœlestis; same as *vox angelica.*
vox cholerica; the peculiar suppressed voice due to Asiatic cholera.
vox humana; a reed stop in an organ which produces tones similar to those of the human voice.
vox populi; the voice of the people: also *vox pop.*
vox populi, vox Dei; the voice of the people (is) the voice of God.
voy′ăge, *n.* [ME. *viage, veage*; OFr. *veiage*, voyage, from L. *viaticum*, provision for a journey, from *viaticus*, of a journey, from *via*, way, journey.]
1. a relatively long journey or passage by sea or other large body of water, or, formerly, by land.
2. a journey by aircraft.
3. a written account of a voyage.
4. a project; an enterprise. [Obs.]
voy′ăge, *v.i.*; voyaged, *pt., pp.*; voyaging, *ppr.* to take a journey by sea, water, or air.
voy′ăge, *v.t.* to sail or travel over or on.
voy′ăge·ȧ·ble, *a.* capable of being sailed or traveled over; navigable.
voy′ȧ·gẽr, *n.* 1. a person who makes a voyage.
2. a person who makes a journey; a traveler.
vo·yȧ·gēur′ (vwȧ-yȧ-zhẽr′), *n.*; *pl.* **vo·yȧ·gēurs′** (-zhẽr′), [Fr.]
1. a traveler.
2. in Canada, (a) a person who transports goods and men by rivers and lakes to trading posts for the fur companies; (b) any woodsman or boatman of the Canadian wilds.
voy′ȧ·ġing, *n.* the act or process of taking a voyage; a journey by water.
vo·yēur′ (vwȧ-yẽr′), *n.* [Fr., from *voir*, to see.] a person given to voyeurism; a Peeping Tom.
vo·yēur′ịsm, *n.* a perversion in which sexual gratification is obtained by looking at sexual objects or scenes.
vrille, *n.* [Fr.] in aviation, a spinning nose dive.
vrouw, *n.* [D.] a woman; housewife: a title corresponding to Mrs.
V-shāped, *a.* shaped like the letter V.
V sīgn, [*V*ictory.] a gesture made by raising the hand with the middle and index fingers separated to form a V, showing a wish for victory or success, or expressing approval.
V/STOL, [*v*ertical or *s*hort *t*akeoff, and *l*anding.] an aircraft that can take off and land either vertically or on a short airstrip.
VTOL, [*v*ertical *t*akeoff, and *l*anding.] an aircraft, usually other than a helicopter, that can take off and land vertically.
V-type en′ġine, an engine, as a gasoline engine, in which the cylinders are set at an angle, or in two banks forming a V.
vug, vugg, vugh, *n.* [Corn. *vooga*, a cave.] in mining, a cavity or hollow in a rock or lode, often lined with crystals.
vug′gy, *a.*; *comp.* vuggier; *superl.* vuggiest, full of vugs, or cavities: said of rock.
Vul′căn, *n.* [L. *Vulcanus*, Vulcan, god of fire.]
1. in Roman mythology, the god who presided over fire and the working of metals: later identified with the Greek Hephaestus and considered to be lame.
2. a hypothetical planet between Mercury and the sun, the existence of which has never been established.
3. [v–] a volcano. [Obs.]
vulcan powder; an explosive compound consisting of nitroglycerin, sulfur, charcoal, and sodium nitrate.
Vul·cā′ni·ăn, *a.* [L. *Vulcanius*, of Vulcan.]
1. of, characteristic of, associated with, or made by, Vulcan.
2. [v–] having to do with metalworking.
3. [v–] in geology, (a) volcanic; (b) Plutonic.
Vul·can′iç, *a.* same as *Vulcanian.*
vul·căn·ic′i·ty, *n.* same as *volcanicity.*
vul′căn·ịsm, *n.* same as *volcanism.*
vul′căn·ist, *n.* one who supports the vulcanian, or Plutonic, theory, which ascribes the changes on the earth's surface to the agency of fire; also, a volcanist.
vul′căn·īte, *n.* [*Vulcan* and *-ite.*] a hard and nonelastic variety of vulcanized rubber, used for making combs, electrical insulation, etc.: it is made by treating crude rubber with a large amount of sulfur and subjecting it to a higher and more prolonged heat in curing than ordinary vulcanized rubber. It is of a brownish-black color, is hard and tough, cuts easily, and will take a good polish.
vul″căn·i·zā′tion, *n.* 1. the process of treating caoutchouc, or crude rubber, with sulfur or its compounds at a high temperature, by which its strength and elasticity are greatly increased, the changes in its properties resulting in the hard rubber called vulcanite, or ebonite: the degree of hardness varies directly with the degree of heat and amount of sulfur used.
2. a process somewhat like this, for hardening some substance.
vul′căn·īze, *v.t.*; vulcanized, *pt., pp.*; vulcanizing, *ppr.* to subject to the process of vulcanization, as crude rubber, or caoutchouc.
vul′çan·īze, *v.i.* to undergo vulcanization.
vul′căn·ī·zẽr, *n.* one who or that which vulcanizes; specifically, the steam apparatus used in vulcanizing crude rubber.
vul·çā′nō, *n.* a volcano. [Obs.]
vul·căn·ol′ō·ġy, *n.* same as *volcanology.*
vul′găr, *a.* [ME. *vulgare*; L. *vulgaris*, from *vulgus* or *volgus*, the common people.]
1. of, belonging to, or common to the great mass of people in general; common; popular; as, a *vulgar* superstition.
2. designating, of, or in the popular, or vernacular, speech.
3. commonly occurring or experienced; customary; usual; ordinary; commonplace.

> For what we know must be, and is as common
> As any the most *vulgar* thing to sense.
> —Shak.

4. characterized by a lack of culture, refinement, taste, sensitivity, etc.; coarse; crude.

> Be thou familiar but by no means *vulgar.*
> —Shak.

Vulgar Era; the common era used by Christians, dating from the birth of Christ.
vulgar fraction; a common fraction.
Vulgar Latin; the everyday speech of the Roman people, from which the Romance languages developed; popular Latin as distinguished from standard or literary Latin.
vul′găr, *n.* 1. the common people (with *the*). [Archaic.]
2. the vernacular. [Obs.]
vul·gār′i·ăn, *a.* vulgar. [Rare.]
vul·gār′i·ăn, *n.* a vulgar person; especially, a rich or well-to-do person with coarse, showy manners or tastes.

> The rich *vulgarians* of the Big Bonanza.
> —Robert Louis Stevenson.

vul′găr·ịsm, *n.* 1. a word, phrase, or expression occurring only in common colloquial usage or, especially, in coarse speech.
2. vulgar behavior, quality, etc.; vulgarity.
vul·gar′i·ty, *n.* 1. the state or quality of being vulgar; mean condition in life; as, *vulgarity* of birth.
2. the state or quality of being vulgar, crude, coarse, unrefined, etc.

> Modern generations have made both marriage and death more absurd, more banal, and more vulgar than any other period ever contrived to do. The essence and object of life is *vulgarity*—that is, publicity.
> —Ouida.

3. *pl.* **vul·gar′i·tieṣ,** a vulgar act, habit, usage in speech or writing, etc.
4. the commonalty; the mob. [Obs.]
vul″găr·i·zā′tion, *n.* a vulgarizing or being vulgarized.
vul′găr·īze, *v.t.*; vulgarized, *pt., pp.*; vulgarizing, *ppr.* to make vulgar.
vul′găr·īze, *v.i.* to conduct oneself in a vulgar manner. [Obs.]
vul′găr·ly, *adv.* in a vulgar manner.
vul′găr·ness, *n.* the state or character of being vulgar; vulgarity.
Vul′gāte, *n.* [ML. (*editio*) *vulgata*, the common (edition), from L. *vulgatus*, pp. of *vulgare*, to make public, to publish.]
1. a Latin version of the Bible prepared by St. Jerome in the fourth century, serving as the authorized version of the Roman Catholic Church.
2. [v–] any text or version in common acceptance.
Vul′gāte, *a.* 1. of, pertaining to, or in the Vulgate.
2. [v–] common; general; popular; usual.
vul″nẽr·ȧ·bil′i·ty, *n.* the state or property of being vulnerable; vulnerableness.
vul′nẽr·ȧ·ble, *a.* [LL. *vulnerabilis*, wounding, likely to injure; also, in pass. sense, vulnerable, from L. *vulnerare*, to wound, from *vulnus, vulneris*, a wound.]
1. capable of being wounded or physically injured; as, a *vulnerable* body.

> Achilles was *vulnerable* in his heel; and there will never be wanting a Paris to infix the dart.
> —Dwight.

2. open to criticism or attack; as, a *vulnerable* reputation.
3. open to attack or assault by armed forces; as, the Maginot line proved to be *vulnerable.*
4. in contract bridge, liable to increased penalties and entitled to increased bonuses: said of a team which has won one game.
vul′nẽr·ȧ·ble·ness, *n.* vulnerability.
vul′nẽr·ȧ·bly, *adv.* so as to be vulnerable.
vul′nẽr·ăr·y, *a.* [L. *vulnerarius*, suitable for wounds, from *vulnus*, a wound.] used for healing wounds.
vul′nẽr·ăr·y, *n.*; *pl.* **vul′nẽr·ăr·ieṣ,** any vulnerary plant, drug, etc.

vul′nẽr·āte, *v.t.* to wound; to hurt. [Obs.]

vul·nẽr·ā′tion, *n.* the act of wounding or the state of being wounded. [Obs.]

vul′nẽr·ōse, *a.* full of wounds; having wounds; wounded.

vul·nif′ic, vul·nif′i·căl, *a.* [L. *vulnificus*; *vulnus*, a wound, and *facere*, to make.] causing or inflicting wounds. [Rare.]

vul′nōse, *a.* vulnerose. [Rare.]

vul·pan′sẽr, *n.* a sheldrake.

Vul·peç′ū·lȧ, *n.* [L., dim. of *vulpes*, a fox.] in astronomy, the Little Fox, a small northern constellation between Cygnus and Aquila.

Vul·peç′ū·lȧ çum An′ser·ē, [L.; *vulpecula*, dim. of *vulpes*, a fox, and *cum*, with, and *ansere*, abl. of *anser*, a goose.] in astronomy, the Little Fox with the Goose: a name sometimes used for the constellation Vulpecula.

vul·peç′ū·lăr, *a.* of or pertaining to a fox, especially a young one; vulpine.

Vul′pēṣ, *n.* [L., fox.] a genus of foxes, including the common red fox.

vul′piç, *a.* of, pertaining to, or obtained from the lichen, *Cetraria vulpina*.

vulpic acid; a yellow crystalline compound, obtained from the lichen *Cetraria vulpina*.

vul′pi·cīde, *n.* [L. *vulpes*, a fox, and *cædere*, to kill.]

1. the act of killing a fox otherwise than by hunting with hounds. [Brit.]

2. a person who does this. [Brit.]

vul′pine, *a.* [Fr. *vulpin*; L. *vulpinus*, foxlike, from *vulpes*, a fox.]

1. of or pertaining to a fox or foxes; related to the foxes.

2. like a fox; clever; tricky; cunning; crafty; stealthy; foxy.

vulpine opossum, phalanger, or *phalangist*; an Australian arboreal marsupial, *Trichosurus vulpecula*, somewhat like a fox.

vul·pin′iç, *a.* same as *vulpic*.

vul′pin·iṣm, *n.* the quality of being foxlike or vulpine; craft; artfulness; cunning. [Rare.]

vul′pi·nīte, *n.* [named from *Vulpino*, in Italy.] a mineral of a grayish-white color, splendent and massive, with its fractures foliated. It is an anhydrous sulfate of lime, containing a little silica. It occurs along with granular foliated limestone at Vulpino, in Italy, and is sometimes used for ornamental work.

vul·sel′lȧ, *n.*; *pl.* **vul·sel′lae,** [L.] in surgery, a forceps with hooked blades.

vul·sel′lum, *n.*; *pl.* **vul·sel′lȧ,** same as *vulsella*.

vul′tūre, *n.* [ME. *vultur*, from L. *vultur*, vulture, lit., a plucker, from *vellere*, to pluck.]

1. any of a number of large birds of prey related to the eagles and hawks, with naked and usually brightly colored heads and dark plumage: vultures live on carrion and are found in tropical and temperate regions.

2. any greedy and ruthless person who preys on others.

VULTURE
(2 1/2 ft. long)

vul′tūre rā′ven, any of the ravens of the genus *Corvultur*, of Africa.

Vul·tū′ri·dae, *n.pl.* a family of birds, the vultures.

vul′tūr·īne, *a.* [L. *vulturinus*.]

1. of the vulture family.

2. of, characteristic of, or like a vulture or vultures.

vul′tūr·ish, *a.* vulturous.

vul′tūr·iṣm, *n.* the attributes or character of a vulture; rapacity.

vul′tūrn, *n.* the brush turkey of Australia.

vul′tūr·ous, *a.* like a vulture; rapacious; preying; ravenous.

vul′vȧ, *n.* [L. *vulva*, *volva*, a wrapper, a covering, the womb, from *volvere*, to roll or turn about.]

1. the external genital organs of the female, including the labia majora, labia minora, clitoris, and the entrance to the vagina.

2. in entomology, the orifice of the oviduct.

3. in conchology, a long and considerable depression often occurring behind the summit of bivalve shells at the dorsal part of the external surface.

vul′văl, *a.* of the vulva.

vul′văr, *a.* vulval.

vul′vāte, *a.* vulvar; vulviform.

vul′vi·fọrm, *a.* in zoology, like the vulva in form or appearance; oval.

vul·vis′mus, *n.* same as *vaginismus*.

vul·vī′tis, *n.* inflammation of the vulva.

vul′vō-, [from L. *vulva*, a covering, womb.] a combining form meaning: (a) *vulva*; (b) *vulva and*. Also *vulv-*.

vul·vō·vaġ′i·năl, *a.* of or pertaining to the vulva and vagina.

vul·vō·vaġ·i·nī′tis, *n.* inflammation of the vulva and vagina.

vum, *v.i.* to vow. [Dial.]

VX gas (vē′eks′), a highly lethal nerve gas of secret formula, absorbed through the skin and lungs.

vȳ′ing, *a.* [ppr. of *vie*.] that vies; that competes.

vȳ′ing·ly, *adv.* emulously.

W

W, w (dub′l-ū), *n.*; *pl.* **W's, w's, Ws, ws** (dub′l-ūz), 1. the twenty-third letter of the English alphabet: its sound was represented in Anglo-Saxon manuscripts by uu or u until about 900 A.D., then by ƿ (*wen*) borrowed from the runic alphabet, or sometimes by wu, v, wo, vo, uo, or o. In the 11th century a ligatured VV or vv was introduced by Norman scribes to replace the *wen*.

2. the sound of W or w: before r, as in *wrist*, and in some words, as *answer, sword, two*, it is silent.

3. a type or impression of W or w.

4. a symbol for the twenty-third in a sequence or group (or the twenty-second if J is omitted).

W, w, *a.* 1. of W or w.

2. twenty-third (or twenty-second if J is omitted) in a sequence or group.

W, in chemistry, wolfram (tungsten).

wạ, *n.* wall. [Scot.]

Waaf, *n.* in Great Britain, a member of the Women's Auxiliary Air Force: also written *WAAF, W.A.A.F.*

wäag, *n.* [native name.] the grivet, a monkey of Ethiopia and the Upper Nile.

wäa·hoọ′, *n.* same as *wahoo* (elm tree)

wăb′ble, *v.t.* and *v.i.*; wabbled, *pt., pp.*; wabbling, *ppr.* to wobble.

wăb′ble, *n.* a wobble.

wăb′ble, *n.* [var. of *warble* (tumor).] the larva of a botfly which is parasitic on squirrels.

wăb′blẽr, *n.* a wobbler.

wăb′bling, *a.* wobbling.

wăb′bly, *a.*; *comp.* wabblier; *superl.* wabbliest, wobbly.

Waç, *n.* a member of the Women's Army Corps.

wạçh′nȧ, *n.* [native name.] a fish, the little Alaskan cod, *Eleginus navaga*.

wack, *n.* a person whose behavior is eccentric, erratic, or so irrational as to seem crazy. [Slang.]

wack′e, wack′y, *n.* [G.; O.H.G. *wacko*, earlier *waggo*, gravel, stone.] a rock like sandstone in texture, resulting from the disintegration of volcanic rock.

wack′en, *a.* waken. [Obs.]

wack′y, *a.*; *comp.* wackier; *superl.* wackiest, [perh. from *whack* (a blow), and *-y*.] erratic, eccentric, or irrational: also *whacky*. [Slang.]

wäd, *n.* [formally akin to Sw. *vadd*.]

1. (a) a small, soft mass, as a handful of cotton, crumpled paper, etc.; (b) [Brit. Dial.] a bundle, especially a small one, as of straw or hay.

2. a lump or small, compact mass of something; as, a *wad* of chewing tobacco.

3. a mass of soft or fibrous material used for padding, packing, stuffing, etc.

4. a plug of hemp, tow, paper, etc., stuffed against a charge to keep it firmly in the breech of a muzzle-loading gun or in a cartridge.

5. a roll of paper money. [Colloq.]

6. a stock of wealth or money. [Slang.]

wäd, *v.t.*; wadded, *pt., pp.*; wadding, *ppr.* 1. to compress into a wad.

2. to roll up into a wad, as paper.

3. to plug or stuff with a wad.

4. to line or pad with or as with wadding.

5. to hold (a charge) in place by a wad, as in a gun or cartridge.

wäd, wädd, *n.* 1. an earthy ore of manganese combined with different oxides, as copper, cobalt, iron, etc.

2. graphite. [Obs. or Brit. Dial.]

wäd (*or unstressed* wăd), *v.* would. [Scot.]

wäd′dẽr, *n.* a person or thing that wads.

wäd′dic, *n.* same as *waddy*.

wäd′ding, *n.* 1. any soft material for wads; any pliable substance of which wads can be made, as for guns or cartridges.

2. any soft or fibrous material used for stuffing, padding, packing, etc.; especially, loose, fluffy sheets of cotton, or cotton batting.

wäd′dle, *v.i.*; waddled, *pt., pp.*; waddling, *ppr.* [freq. of *wade*.]

1. to sway from side to side in walking with short steps; to walk in a tottering or vacillating manner, as a duck.

2. to move clumsily with a motion like this; to toddle, as a baby.

wäd′dle, *v.t.* to tread down by wading or waddling through, as high grass. [Rare.]

wäd′dle, *n.* 1. the act of waddling.

2. a waddling gait or movement.

wäd′dlẽr, *n.* one who or that which waddles.

wäd′dling·ly, *adv.* with a waddling gait or motion.

wäd′dy, *a.* like a wad.

wäd′dy, *n.*; *pl.* **wäd′dieṣ,** [from the native name in Australia.] in Australia, (a) a short, thick club used by aborigines as a weapon; (b) a walking stick; a cane. Also spelled *waddie*.

wāde, *v.i.*; waded, *pt., pp.*; wading, *ppr.* [ME. *waden*; AS. *wadan*, to wade, trudge, go.]

1. to walk through any substance that impedes or hinders the free motion of the limbs; as, to *wade* through sand, snow, water, tall grass, etc.

2. to move forward with difficulty or labor; to make way against obstacles or circumstances that continually hinder, impede, or thwart.

3. to go; to proceed; to pass. [Obs.]

wāde, *v.t.* to cross over or pass through by wading; to ford; as, to *wade* a brook.

wāde, *n.* 1. the act or process of wading.

2. a place to be waded; a ford.

wād′ẽr, *n.* 1. one who or that which wades.
2. any of several long-legged shore birds of the group *Grallatores*, that wade the shallows and marshes for food, as the crane, heron, rail, coot, sandpiper, and snipe.
3. [*pl.*] high waterproof boots; hip boots.

wăd hook, a rod with a double screw at one end to draw wads out of a gun; also, the screw itself.

wä′di, wä′dy, *n.*; *pl.* **wä′diș, wä′dieș,** [Ar. *wādī*, the channel of a river, a river, a ravine, a valley.]
1. valley, ravine, or watercourse that is dry except in the rainy season.
2. the stream or rush of water that flows through it.
3. an oasis.

wād′ing bīrd, any of various unrelated long-legged shore birds that wade the shallows and marshes for food, as the crane, heron, rail, coot, sandpiper, and snipe.

wād′ing pool, a shallow pool of water, especially a small, portable unit in which small children can wade and play.

wäd′măl, *n.* a very coarse woolen cloth formerly made: also written *wadmol*.

wäd′nȧ, would not. [Scot.]

wäd′set, *n.* [Scot.; *wad*, a pledge, and *set*, to place.] in Scots law, the pledge of land, etc. as security for a debt; a mortgage.

wäd′set, *v.t.*; wadsetted, *pt.*, *pp.*; wadsetting, *ppr.* to put in pledge; to mortgage.

wäd′set·tẽr, *n.* in Scots law, one who holds a wadset, or mortgage.

wäd′y, *n.*; *pl.* **wäd′ieș,** a wadi.

wăe, *n.* woe; sorrow. [Scot. and Brit. Dial.]

wăe′sucks, wăe′suck, *interj.* [Scot. *wae*, and *sucks*, prob. for *sakes*, as in *sakes alive!*] alas! [Scot. and Brit. Dial.]

wā′fẽr, *n.* [ME. *wafre*; OFr. *waufre*; D. *wafel*, a wafer, waffle.]
1. a thin, flat, crisp cracker or cake; specifically, (a) a thin flat disk or piece of candy; (b) a thin cake of unleavened bread, generally stamped with the Christian monogram, the cross, or other sacred representation or symbol, used in the Eucharist, as in the Roman Catholic Church; (c) a thin disk of dried paste used for sealing letters, fastening documents together, and the like, usually made of flour, mixed with water, gum, and coloring matter.
2. anything resembling a wafer.

wā′fẽr, *v.t.*; wafered, *pt.*, *pp.*; wafering, *ppr.* to seal, close, attach, or fasten with a wafer or wafers.

wā′fẽr ash, a tall rutaceous shrub, *Ptelea trifoliata*, with winged fruit resembling a wafer: also called *hop tree*.

wā′fẽr cāke, same as *wafer* (senses 1a and 1b).

wā′fẽr ī′ron (-ũrn), a device in which wafers are held while being baked.

wā′fẽr tongs, same as *wafer iron*.

wā′fẽr·wom″ăn (-woom″), *n.* a woman who makes or sells wafers. [Obs.]

wā′fẽr·y, *a.* resembling a wafer.

waff, *n.* [var. of *wave*.]
1. a wave, or waving motion, as in signaling.
2. a puff, whiff, or gust, as of air.
3. a glimpse.
4. a ghost; a wraith.
[Scot. and Brit. Dial. in all senses.]

waff, *v.t.* and *v.i.* to wave. [Scot.]

waff, *a.* [var. of *waif*.]
1. worthless. [Scot.]
2. solitary. [Scot.]
Also spelled *waf*.

waff, *n.* a vagrant or vagabond: also spelled *waf*. [Scot.]

wäf′fle, *n.* [O.D. *waeffel*; D. *wafel*.] a batter cake baked in a waffle iron: it is somewhat crisper than a pancake.

wäf′fle, *a.* having a gridlike surface resembling a waffle.

wäf′fled, *a.* same as *waffle*.

wäf′fle ī′ron (-ũrn), a utensil for cooking waffles, having two flat, studded plates, now usually of aluminum, pressed together so that the waffle bakes between them.

wȧft, *v.t.*; wafted, *pt.*, *pp.*; wafting, *ppr.* [backformation from obs. *wafter*, a convoy.]
1. to convey or propel lightly through water or air, as objects, sounds, odors, etc.

> Speed the soft intercourse from soul to soul,
> And *waft* a sigh from Indus to the pole.
> —Pope.

2. to transport as if in this manner.
3. to buoy up; to cause to float; to keep from sinking. [Obs.]
4. [altered from dial. *waff*, to wave.] to signal to, as by waving the hand; to beckon to. [Obs.]
5. to turn (the eyes). [Obs.]

wȧft, *v.i.* 1. to float, as on the wind.

> And now the shouts *waft* near the citadel.
> —Dryden.

2. to blow gently: said of breezes.

wȧft, *n.* 1. the act or fact of floating or being carried lightly along.
2. an odor, sound, etc. carried through the air.
3. a breath or gust of wind.
4. a wave, waving, or wafting movement.
5. in nautical usage, a waif (sense 5).

wȧft, *n.* weft. [Scot.]

wȧft′āġe, *n.* the act of wafting or state of being wafted; conveyance by wafting. [Archaic.]

wȧft′ẽr, *n.* 1. one who or that which wafts; especially, a revolving fan in a blower.
2. a passenger ship. [Obs.]
3. a blunt sword, formerly used in military exercises.

wȧf′tūre, *n.* 1. the act of waving; a beckoning; a waving motion, as of the hand.
2. something wafted, as on or by a breeze.

wag, *v.t.*; wagged, *pt.*, *pp.*; wagging, *ppr.* [ME. *waggen*, prob. from OSw. *wagga*, to wag, fluctuate.]
1. to cause (something fastened at one end) to move up and down, backward and forward, or from side to side.
2. to move (the tongue) in talking, especially in idle or malicious gossip.

wag, *v.i.* 1. to move backward and forward, up and down, or from side to side, as a part of the body.
2. to make progress; to continue at a regular pace; to move along.

> Thus may we see, quoth he, how the world *wags*.
> —Shak.

3. to keep moving in talk, especially in idle or malicious gossip: said of the tongue.
4. to walk or move with a swaying motion; to waddle.
5. to play truant, as from school. [Brit. Slang.]
6. to move off or away; to be off; to depart; to be gone. [Brit. Colloq.]

wag, *n.* the act or an instance of wagging; as, the *wag* of a dog's tail.

wag, *n.* [prob. a shortening of the old term *waghalter*, a rogue, joker.] a person who is fond of a joke or of making jokes; one who is full of merry tricks or pranks; a humorist; a wit; a joker.

wāġe, *v.t.*; waged, *pt.*, *pp.*; waging, *ppr.* [OFr. *wager*, to gage, pledge, promise; Fr. *gager*, to stake, pledge, from LL. *vadium*, *wadium*; Goth. *vadi*, a pledge, the same word as AS. *wed*, a pledge.]
1. to pledge. [Obs.]
2. to wager; to bet.
3. to carry on; to engage in; to undertake; as, to *wage* war.
4. to hire out. [Obs.]
5. to hire; to employ for wages. [Obs. or Brit. Dial.]
6. in ceramics, to prepare (clay) by working and kneading.

wāġe, *v.i.* 1. to bind or engage oneself by a pledge; to pledge oneself. [Obs.]
2. to be opposed as equal stakes; to be equal. [Obs.]
3. to do battle; to fight. [Obs.]

wāġe, *n.* 1. [*usually pl.*] money paid to an employee for work done, and usually figured on an hourly, daily, or piecework basis: often distinguished from *salary*.

> I will be a swift witness against those that oppress the hireling in his *wages*.
> —Mal. iii. 5.

2. [*usually pl.*] what is given in return; a reward; a recompense: formerly the plural form was often construed as singular, as, "The *wages* of sin is death."

> That they may have their *wages* duly paid them.
> And something over to remember me.
> —Shak.

3. (a) a pledge; (b) the state of being pledged; a pawn. [Obs.]
4. [*pl.*] in economics, the share of the total product of industry that goes to labor, as distinguished from the share taken by capital.
living wage; see under *living*.
minimum wage; the lowest wage payable to an employee of a certain trade or class, as fixed by law or as agreed upon by the union representing the employees of the certain trade and the employer; also, a living wage.
minimum wage laws; laws specifying what the minimum wage for a certain class of employees shall be.

Syn.—remuneration, compensation, salary, stipend, hire, allowance.

wāġe ẽarn′ẽr, one who works for wages.

wag′el, *n.* the young of the great black-backed gull, *Larus marinus*. [Brit. Dial.]

wä′gen·boom, *n.* [D. *wagen*, wagon, and *boom*, tree.] same as *wagon tree*.

wā′ġẽr, *n.* [ME. *wageoure*; O.Norm.Fr. *wageure*, *gageure*, from LL. *vadiatura*, from *vadiare*, to pledge, wager.]
1. a bet (senses 1, 2, 3).
2. formerly, a pledge to do something or abide by an outcome: especially in *wager of battle*, a challenge by a defendant to prove his innocence by personal combat.
wager of law; see under *law*.
wager policy; see under *policy*.

wā′ġẽr, *v.t.* and *v.i.* to bet (all senses).

wā′ġẽr·ẽr, *n.* one who wages, or bets.

wāġe scāle, 1. a schedule of wages paid for the performance of related jobs or tasks in a given industry, plant, etc.
2. the schedule of wages paid by a given employer.

wā′ġeș fund, the amount of capital in a community available for or the amount used in the payment of wages, which, together with the total number of workers, determines the rate of wages.

wāġe′wŏrk·ẽr, *n.* one who works for wages.

wāġe′wŏrk·ing, *a.* doing work for wages.

wag′gel, *n.* same as *wagel*.

wag′gẽr·y, *n.*; *pl.* **wag′gẽr·ieș,** [from *wag* (joker), and *-ery*.]
1. mischievous merriment; sportive trick or gaiety; the words and actions of a wag; as, the *waggery* of a schoolboy.
2. a joke or jest; especially, a practical joke.

wag′gie, *n.* a bird, the wagtail. [Brit. Dial.]

wag′gish, *a.* 1. like a wag; full of sportive or jocular tricks, antics, sayings, etc.; roguish in merriment or good humor; frolicsome.
2. done, made, or said in waggery; playful; sportive; as, a *waggish* trick.

wag′gish·ly, *adv.* in a waggish manner; in sport.

wag′gish·ness, *n.* the state or quality of being waggish.

wag′gle, *v.t.*; waggled, *pt.*, *pp.*; waggling, *ppr.* [freq. of *wag*.] to wag, especially with short, abrupt motions; to move one way and the other; as, a bird *waggles* its tail.

wag′gle, *v.i.* to move with a wagging motion; to sway or move from side to side; to totter.

wag′gle, *n.* 1. the act or an instance of waggling.
2. in golf, the preliminary swinging of the club preparatory to making a stroke.

wag′gly, *a.* waggling or tending to waggle.

wag′gŏn, *n.* and *v.* wagon: British spelling.

wag′gŏn·āġe, *n.* wagonage: British spelling.

wag′gŏn·ẽr, *n.* wagoner: British spelling.

wag′hal·tẽr, *n.* one likely to be hanged. [Obs.]

Wäg·nē′ri·ăn (väg-), *a.* of or like Richard Wagner, German composer, or his music, theories, methods, etc.

Wäg·nē′ri·ăn, *n.* an admirer or follower of Wagner's music, theories, etc.

Wäg′nẽr·ișm, *n.* 1. Richard Wagner's theory, practice, and method of composing music dramas, characterized by emphasis on the co-ordination of all the components (vocal and instrumental music, text, action, setting, etc.), by constant use of the leitmotif, and by a general departure from the conventions of previous, especially Italian, opera.
2. the influence of Wagner's theories on other composers and musicians, or the tendency to imitate Wagner.

wag′nẽr·īte, *n.* [named after F. N. von *Wagner*, a German mineralogist.] a transparent mineral having a vitreo-resinous luster, yellow in color: it is a fluophosphate of magnesium, usually containing iron and manganese.

wag′ŏn, *n.* [D. *wagen*, a wagon.]
1. any of various four-wheeled vehicles, either open or covered, especially one for carrying heavy loads, as of freight.
2. an enclosed vehicle used by the police for carrying arrested people to the police station or jail: usually *the wagon*; in full *police* (or *patrol*) *wagon*. [Colloq.]

3. a railroad freight car. [Brit.]
4. a chariot. [Obs.]
5. in England, a car used in a mine for carrying ore, etc.
6. a tool having four edges of cane mounted in a frame, and used to trim goldleaf.
7. [W–] in astronomy, Charles's Wain.
on the (water) wagon; no longer drinking alcoholic liquors. [Slang.]
to fix someone's wagon; to hurt someone in some way so as to get even with him. [Slang.]
to hitch one's wagon to a star; to set oneself an ambitious goal.

wag'ŏn, *v.t.*; wagoned, *pt., pp.*; wagoning, *ppr.* to transport, convey, or carry in a wagon.

wag'ŏn, *v.i.* to transport goods on a wagon or wagons; to wagon goods as a business.

wag'ŏn·ăge, *n.* 1. transport by wagon; also, money paid for this.
2. a collection of wagons; wagons collectively.

wag'ŏn breast (brest), in mining, a breast in which mine cars may be run up to the working face.

wag'ŏn ceil'ing, a semicircular or wagon-headed ceiling.

wag'ŏn·ẽr, *n.* 1. one who drives a wagon; a wagon driver.
2. a charioteer. [Obs.]
3. [W–] in astronomy, (a) the northern constellation Auriga; (b) Charles's Wain.
4. an atlas. [Obs.]

wag·ŏn·ette', *n.* [dim. of *wagon.*] a kind of open, four-wheeled carriage of a very light construction having two seats set lengthwise facing each other behind the driver's seat.

wag'ŏn·ful, *n.* a wagonload.

wag'ŏn-head"ed (-hed"), *a.* in architecture, having an arched or semicircular top or head, like the top of a covered wagon; round-arched; as, a *wagon-headed* ceiling, roof, or vault.

wä·gōn·lit' (vä-gōn-lē'), *n.* [Fr.; *wagon*, a car, railway coach; and *lit*, a bed.] in Europe, a railroad sleeping car.

wag'ŏn·lōad, *n.* the load that a wagon carries or will carry.

wag'ŏn mas'tẽr, a person who has charge of one or more wagons; especially, an officer in charge of wagons in a military train.

wag'ŏn roof, a roof consisting of a semicylindrical or barrel vault.

wag'ŏn-roofed (-rooft), *a.* having a semicircular or wagon-headed roof.

wag'ŏn·ry, *n.* conveyance by means of wagons; wagonage. [Rare.]

wag'ŏn shōe, a brake or drag for checking the revolutions of a wagon wheel.

wag'ŏn top, 1. the part of a locomotive boiler which is raised above the rest of the shell, over the firebox.
2. the covering of a wagon.

wag'ŏn trāin, a line or convoy of wagons traveling together, especially one carrying military supplies.

wag'ŏn tree, a tree, *Protea grandiflora*, native to South Africa, having reddish-brown wood used in making wagon wheels.

wag'ŏn·wright (-rīt), *n.* a person who makes and repairs wagons.

wag'tāil, *n.* 1. any of numerous small birds of the family *Motacillidæ*, related to the pipits, mostly native to Europe, characterized by long wing feathers and a very long tail that wags up and down. The ordinary variety is the common or pied wagtail, *Motacilla alba.*

COMMON WAGTAIL (*Motacilla alba*)

2. any of various similar birds resembling the wagtail, as the American water thrush of the wood warbler family.
3. a pert person: a term of derision. [Obs.]

wag'tāil fly'catch"ẽr, a flycatcher, *Rhipidura* or *Sauloprocta tricolor*, common to Australia, New Guinea, and the Solomon Islands.

wäh (wä), *n.* the panda, *Ailurus fulgens.*

Wȧ·hä'bee, *n.* same as *Wahabi.*

Wȧ·hä'bi, *n.* [Ar. *Wahhabi.*] a follower of Abdel-Wahhab (1691–1787), the leader of a strict sect of Mohammedans who adhered religiously to the Koran and opposed all practices not countenanced by it. The sect now flourishes in Arabia. Also spelled *Wahhabi.*

Wȧ·hä'bi·ism, *n.* the doctrines and practices of the Wahabis.

Wȧ·hä'bism, *n.* same as *Wahabiism.*

Wȧ·hä'bit, Wȧ·hä'bīte, *n.* same as *Wahabi.*

Wȧ·hä'bīte, *a.* of or belonging to the Wahabis.

wȧ·hä'hẹ, *n.* [Maori.] a tree, *Disoxylum spectabile* or *Hartighsea spectabilis*, native to New Zealand, the leaves of which furnish a medicine used by the natives.

wä·hī'nẹ, *n.* [Maori, and Haw.] a Polynesian woman, especially of Hawaii.

wä·hoo', *n.* [Am. Ind. (Dakota) *wanhu*, lit., arrow wood.] a large shrub or tree, *Euonymus atropurpureus*, having small purple flowers and purple fruit with red seeds; burning bush.

wä·hoo', *n.* [Am. Ind. (Creek) *ûhawhu*, cork elm.]
1. a variety of elm with corky bark.
2. the basswood tree.
3. any of various other American trees or shrubs, as the cascara buckthorn, *Rhamus purshiana.*

wä·hoo', *n.*; *pl.* **wä·hoo', wä·hoos',** [origin unknown.] a large game and food fish, *Acanthocybium solanderi*, related to the mackerels and found in warm seas.

wāif, *n.* [ME; O.Norm.Fr. *waif, gaif*, prob. from ON. *veif*, anything flapping about, from *veifan*, to wave, swing.]
1. anything found by chance that is without an owner.
2. a person without home or friends; especially, a homeless child.
3. a strayed animal.
4. in law, goods stolen and thrown away by the thief in his flight.
5. in nautical usage, a signal flag or pennant, or a signal made with a flag or pennant; a waft.

wāil, *v.t.*; wailed, *pt., pp.*; wailing, *ppr.* [ME. *weilen, wailen*, from ON. *væla, vala*, to lament, from *væ*, woe.]
1. to lament; to mourn; to bewail.
2. to cry out in mourning or lamentation.

wāil, *v.i.* 1. to express grief or pain by long, loud cries.
2. to make a plaintive, sad, crying sound; as, the wind *wails.*

wāil, *n.* 1. a long, pitiful cry of grief and pain.
2. a sound like this.
3. a wailing.

wāil'ẽr, *n.* one who wails; specifically, in some countries, a professional mourner.

wāil'ful, *a.* 1. sorrowful; mournful.
2. lamentable; greatly to be mourned.
3. making a sorrowful sound.

wāil'ing·ly, *adv.* in a wailing manner.

Wāil'ing Plāce (or **Wall**) **of the Jews,** a courtyard in Jerusalem bordered by a high wall believed to contain stones from Herod's temple: Jews gather there weekly for prayer and lamentation: also *Wailing Wall.*

wāil'ment, *n.* lamentation. [Obs.]

wāil'sōme, *a.* 1. wailing; lamenting.
2. causing lamentation; lamentable.

wāi'ment, *v.i.* [OFr. *waimenter.*] to lament; to mourn; to complain; to fret: also written *wayment.* [Obs.]

wāin, *n.* [AS. *wægn, wæn*, a wagon.]
1. a wagon or cart. [Archaic.]
2. [W–] in astronomy, a constellation, Charles's Wain.

wāin, *v.t.* to carry; to convey; to transport. [Obs.]

wāin'ăge, *n.* same as *gainage.*

wāin'bōte, *n.* an allowance of timber for the repair of wagons or carts. [Obs.]

wāin house, a house or shed for wagons and carts. [Brit. Dial.]

wāin lōad, a wagonload.

wāin'rōpe, *n.* a cart rope. [Rare.]

wāin'sçŏt, *n.* [D. *wagenschot*, wainscot, prob. from *wagen*, a carriage, and *schot*, an enclosure or partition of boards; exact origin disputed.]
1. a wood lining or paneling on the walls of a room.
2. such a paneling on the lower part of a room only.
3. (a) the lower part of a room when it has a finish different from that of the upper; (b) any applied finish, as tile, linoleum, etc., laid on a wall.
4. a fine imported oak used for interior paneling. [Brit.]
5. in zoology, a European noctuid moth.

wāin'sçŏt, *v.t.*; wainscoted *or* wainscotted, *pt., pp.*; wainscoting *or* wainscotting, *ppr.* to line or panel (a wall or room) with boards or with other materials.

The other is *wainscoted* with looking glass.
—Addison.

wāin'sçŏt chāir, a chair with a boxlike seat filled in with panels.

wāin'sçŏt çlock, a tall encased clock with a long pendulum: so called because it usually stood against the wainscoting in old houses.

wāin'sçŏt·ing, wāin'sçŏt·ting, *n.* 1. paneling of wood, etc. on the walls of a room.
2. the material used for it.

wāin'sçŏt ōak, in botany, the European Turkey oak, *Quercus cerris.*

wāin'wright (-rīt), *n.* a person who builds or repairs wagons.

wāir, *v.t.* to ware (spend). [Scot. and Brit. Dial.]

wāir, *n.* [etym. obscure.] in carpentry, a piece of plank six feet long and a foot broad. [Obs.]

wä'ï·rẹ·pō, *n.* [native name.] in zoology, a sting ray of New Zealand, *Dasyatis brevicaudatus.*

wāist, *n.* [ME. *wast*, from AS. *weaxan*, to grow, wax.]
1. the part of the body between the ribs and the hips.
2. (a) the part of a garment that covers the waist; (b) the narrow part of a woman's dress, etc., worn at the waist or above or below it as the styles change; waistline; (c) the part of a garment covering the body from the shoulders to a line above the hips; (d) the upper part of a woman's dress; bodice; (e) a blouse; (f) a child's undershirt.
3. the narrow part of any object which is wider at the ends; as, the *waist* of a violin, shoe, etc.
4. in nautical usage, the middle part of the upper deck of a ship, or that part between the forecastle and the quarterdeck.
5. in zoology, the narrow part of the front of the abdomen of certain insects, as ants, wasps, etc.
6. the middle. [Obs.]

wāist an'chŏr, an anchor carried in the waist of a ship; a sheet anchor.

wāist'band, *n.* a band for a person's waist; specifically, the band at the top of a skirt, trousers, or other garment.

wāist bōat, a boat stowed and carried in the waist of a ship; specifically, in a whaler, the boat commanded by the second mate.

wāist bōat'ẽr, one who commands the waist boat of a whaler, usually the second mate.

wāist'çloth, *n.* 1. in nautical usage, the hammock coverings of the waist nettings.
2. a cloth worn around the waist, especially by natives of tropical countries, who wear it either hanging loosely or gathered in between the thighs; a loincloth.

wāist'çōat (*or* wes'kut), *n.* 1. a short coat or garment without sleeves, worn under the coat by men; a vest. [Brit.]
2. a similar garment worn by women.
3. a somewhat longer, heavily ornamented sleeveless jacket formerly worn under a doublet.

wāist·çōat·eer', *n.* one who wears a waistcoat; formerly, a woman who wore a waistcoat without gown, considered the mark of a loose woman; hence, a prostitute. [Obs.]

wāist'çōat·ing, *n.* a textile fabric specially designed for waistcoats.

wāist'-deep, *a.* and *adv.* of a depth sufficient to reach to the waist.

wāist'ed, *a.* having a waist: usually in hyphenated compounds, as, long-*waisted.*

wāist'ẽr, *n.* in nautical usage, one who is put to work in the waist of a ship, doing odd jobs not requiring much skill or knowledge of seamanship. [Rare.]

wāist'-hīgh' (-hī'), *a.* reaching up to the waist.

wāist'līne, *n.* 1. the line of the waist, between the ribs and the hips.
2. (a) the narrow part of a woman's dress, etc., worn at the waist or above or below it as styles change; (b) the line where the waist and skirt of a dress join.
3. the distance around the waist.

wāit, *v.i.*; waited, *pt., pp.*; waiting, *ppr.* [ME. *waiten*; OFr. *waiter*; O.H.G. *wahtēn*, from *wahta*, a guard, watch.]
1. to stay in a place or remain inactive or in anticipation until something expected takes

place (often with *for, until*, etc.); as, *wait* until we call; *wait* for us.
2. to be ready or at hand; as, dinner is *waiting* for us.
3. to remain temporarily undone or neglected; as, that work will have to *wait*.
4. to serve food at a meal (with *at* or *on*); as, she will *wait* at table.
5. to be on the watch; to be on one's guard. [Obs.]
to wait on or *upon*; (a) to attend upon or serve, as a waiter or servant; (b) to go to see; to visit; to call upon; (c) to attend or follow as a consequence; to be associated with; to accompany; as, may good digestion *wait on* you; (d) to look forward to; to await, as a result; (e) to attend to; to escort; to accompany, as a bride or bridegroom.
to wait on; in falconry, to hover aloft watching for the springing up of game: said of a hawk.
to wait up; to put off going to bed until someone expected arrives (often with *for*).

wāit, *v.t.* 1. to stay for; to rest or remain stationary in expectation or anticipation of; as, to *wait* orders to march.
2. to serve food at; as, he *waits* table.
3. to put off serving; to delay (a meal) until someone comes; as, *wait* dinner. [Colloq.]
4. to attend; to accompany or escort as a token of honor or respect. [Obs.]
5. to attend as a consequence. [Obs.]
to wait attendance; to be within call; to be near in readiness for service. [Obs.]

wāit, *n.* 1. the act or fact of waiting; as, we had a long *wait*.
2. a time of waiting; as, a four-hour *wait*.
3. an ambush; trap: usually in *lie in wait*.
4. in England, any of a group of singers and musicians who go through the streets at Christmas time playing and singing songs and carols for small gifts of money.
5. a member of a band of musicians formerly employed by a city or town in England to play at entertainments. [Obs.]
6. a watchman. [Obs.]
7. an old musical instrument of the hautboy, or oboe, kind. [Obs.]
to lay wait; to set an ambush.

wāit'-ȧ-bit, *n.* [transl. of S.Afr.D. *wacht-en-beetje*: so named for their clinging thorns.] any of a number of plants having sharp or hooked thorns.

wāit'ẽr, *n.* 1. one who waits or awaits.
2. a man who waits on table, as in a restaurant.

The *waiters* stand in ranks; the yeomen cry,
"Make room," as if a duke were passing by.
—Swift.

3. a tray on which dishes are carried; a salver.
4. a watchman or attendant. [Obs.]

wāit'ing, *a.* 1. that waits.
2. of or for a wait.
3. that serves or is in attendance.

wāit'ing, *n.* 1. the act of one that waits.
2. a period of waiting.
in waiting; (a) in attendance (on a king or other person of royalty); (b) in British military and naval usage, next in turn for some duty, privilege, etc.

wāit'ing·ly, *adv.* by waiting.

wāit'ing māid, a maid who attends a woman.

wāit'ing room, a room in which people wait, as in a railroad station, a dentist's office, etc.

wāit'ing wom'ăn (woom'), a woman who attends another as a servant; a waiting maid.

wāit'ress, *n.* a woman or girl who waits on table, as in a restaurant or hotel.

wāive, *n.* 1. a waif; a castaway. [Obs.]
2. in law, a woman outlaw. [Obs.]

wāive, *v.t.*; waived, *pt., pp.*; waiving, *ppr.* [ME. *waiven, weiven*, allied to *waif*, from Ice. *veifa*, to vibrate, swing about, move to and fro.]
1. to give up or forgo, as a right, claim, privilege, etc.
2. to refrain from insisting on or taking advantage of.
3. to put off until later; to postpone; to defer.
4. in law, to forgo or relinquish voluntarily, as a right which one is legally entitled to enforce.
5. to leave, reject, or abandon. [Obs.]

wāive, *v.i.* to deviate; to turn aside. [Obs.]

wāiv'ẽr, *n.* 1. in law, the act of waiving, or relinquishing, some right, claim, or privilege.
2. a formal written statement of such relinquishment; as, we signed a *waiver* of our claim.

wāi'wōde, *n.* same as *voivode*.

wāke, *n.* [Sw. *vak*; ON. *vök*, a hole, an opening in the ice.]
1. the track left by a moving boat or ship in the water.
2. any track or course; as, he followed in the *wake* of the procession.
in the wake of; (a) in nautical usage, following directly behind (a ship or boat); (b) following close behind; (c) following as a consequence.

wāke, *v.i.*; waked *or* woke, *pt.*; waked *or rarely* woken, *pp.*; waking, *ppr.* [AS. *wacan*, to arise, come to life, be born.]
1. to come out of sleep or a state like or suggestive of sleep, as a stupor, trance, etc.; to awake (often with *up*).
2. to be or stay awake.
3. to become active or animated after inactivity or dormance (often with *up*).
4. to become alert (*to* a realization, possibility, etc.).
5. to keep watch or vigil; especially, to hold a wake (sense 2). [Dial. or Archaic.]
6. to sit up late for festive purposes; to revel or carouse late at night. [Obs.]

The king doth *wake* tonight, and takes his rouse.
—Shak.

wāke, *v.t.* 1. to cause to wake (senses 1, 3, 4): often with *up*.
2. to arouse, excite, or stir up, as passions, or evoke, as a sound or echo.
3. to keep watch or vigil over; especially, to hold a wake over (a corpse). [Dial. or Archaic.]

wāke, *n.* 1. the act or state of waking or being awake. [Poet.]
2. a watch kept at night, or a vigil, as for some ritual purpose; especially, an all-night vigil over a corpse before burial, formerly often with festivities (common among the Irish).
3. in the Anglican Church, (a) an annual festival in honor of the dedication of a parish church; (b) a vigil held the night before this.

wāke'ful, *a.* 1. not sleeping or inclined to sleep; keeping awake.
2. watchful; vigilant; as, *wakeful* watches.
3. unable to sleep.
4. sleepless; as, a *wakeful* night.
5. rousing from or as from sleep; as, the *wakeful* trump of doom.

wāke'ful·ly, *adv.* in a wakeful manner; with watching or sleeplessness.

wāke'ful·ness, *n.* the state or quality of being wakeful.

wāke'less, *a.* unbroken; deep: said of sleep.

wāk'en, *v.i.*; wakened, *pt., pp.*; wakening, *ppr.* [AS. *wæcnan*, to become awake, from stem of *wacan*, to wake.]
1. to become awake; to come to one's senses after sleep or a state like sleep.
2. to become active, animated, or alive after inactivity or dormance.

wāk'en, *v.t.* 1. to rouse from sleep; to awaken.
2. to excite to action or motion; to rouse; to stir; as, to *waken* his conscience.
3. to produce; to call forth; as, to *waken* sympathy.
4. to guard. [Scot.]

wāk'en·ẽr, *n.* one who or that which wakens or rouses from sleep or as from sleep.

wāk'en·ing, *n.* the act of one waking from sleep.
wakening of a process; in Scots law, the reviving of a process in which, after calling a summons, no judicial proceeding has taken place for a year and a day.

wāk'ẽr, *n.* 1. one who wakes or rouses from sleep.
2. one who watches; a watcher. [Obs.]
3. one who attends a wake.

wāke'rīfe, *a.* wakeful. [Scot. and Brit. Dial.]

wāke'-rob''in, *n.* 1. any of a number of related plants with leaves in groups of three and white, pink, purple, or greenish three-part flowers; trillium.
2. any of a number of plants of the genus *Arum*, with variously colored, hoodlike leaves arching over flower spikes; especially the cuckoopint. [Brit.]
3. the jack-in-the-pulpit.

wāke'tīme, *n.* time during which one is awake. [Rare.]

wāke'-up, *n.* the flicker. [Colloq.]

wä'kï·kï, *n.* a shell money used in certain of the islands of the Pacific.

wāk'ing, *a.* 1. being awake; not sleeping.
2. rousing from sleep; exciting into motion or action.
waking hours; the hours when one is awake.

wāk'ing, *n.* 1. the condition or period of being awake.
2. the act of holding a wake or watching the dead.
3. watch. [Obs.]

wak'i·up, *n.* same as *wickiup*.

Wȧ·lā'chi·ăn, *a.* of Walachia, its people, or their language: also spelled *Wallachian*.

Wȧ·lā'chi·ăn, *n.* 1. a native or inhabitant of Walachia.
2. the language of the Walachians.
Also spelled *Wallachian*.

wä'lȧ·wāy, *interj.* wellaway. [Obs.]

Wal'chi·ȧ, *n.* [named after J. E. I. *Walch*, German naturalist.] an extinct genus of fossil conifers which existed in the Permian and Triassic periods. The modern genus *Araucaria* is closely related to it.

wal'chōw·īte, *n.* [from *Walchow*, in Moravia.] a yellow translucent mineral resin, occurring in the brown coal of Walchow; retinite.

Wäl·den'sēs, *n.pl.* [named after Peter *Waldo* or *Waldus*, a merchant of Lyons in the twelfth century, the founder of the sect.] a sect of puritan dissenters from the Roman Catholic Church which arose about 1170 in southern France through the preaching of Peter Waldo: they were excommunicated in 1184 and persecuted, but still survive in the Alps of France and Italy: also called *Vaudois*.

Wäl·den'si·ăn, *a.* pertaining or belonging to the Waldenses.

Wäl·den'si·ăn, *n.* one who accepts the doctrines of the Waldenses.

wäld'grāve, *n.* [G. *wald*, a forest, and *graf*, a ruler.]
1. in the old German empire, a head forest ranger.
2. in the Rhine districts, formerly, a nobleman of a certain rank.

Wäld·hei'mi·ȧ, *n.* [named after Fischer von *Waldheim*, German naturalist.] a genus of mostly extinct brachiopods.

Wal'dorf sal'ăd, [after the old *Waldorf-Astoria* Hotel in New York City.] a salad made of diced raw apples, celery, and walnuts, with mayonnaise.

wāle, *n.* [AS. *walu*, the mark of a stripe or blow, a wale; originally, a rod.]
1. a raised line or streak made on the skin by the slash of a stick or whip; a wheal; welt.
2. (a) a ridge on the surface of cloth, as corduroy; (b) texture of cloth.
3. a timber fastened to a row of piles in a dam, to strengthen and brace them.
4. in basketmaking, a band or ridge woven around the body of a basket to brace it.
5. in nautical usage, (a) the gunwale; (b) [*usually in pl.*] any of several strakes or heavy planks fastened to the outside of the hull of a wooden ship.
6. a rod. [Brit. Dial.]
7. a wale knot. [Obs.]
8. a tumor; a large swelling. [Brit. Dial.]

wāle, *v.t.*; waled, *pt., pp.*; waling, *ppr.* 1. to mark (the skin) with a wale or wales.
2. to fasten, protect, or brace with a wale or wales.
3. to make, as cloth, or weave, as wickerwork, with a wale or wales.

wāle, *n.* [ME. *wale*, from G. *wahl*, choice.]
1. a choosing; choice. [Scot. and Brit. Dial.]
2. that chosen as best. [Scot. and Brit. Dial.]

wāle, *v.t.* to seek; to select. [Scot. and Brit. Dial.]

He *wales* a portion with judicious care.
—Burns.

wāle, *a.* choice. [Scot. and Brit. Dial.]

wāle, *n.* weal. [Obs.]

wāle knot (not), same as *wall knot*.

wāle'pïece, *n.* a horizontal timber of a quay or jetty, bolted to the vertical timbers or secured by anchor rods to the masonry to receive the impact of vessels coming or lying alongside.

Wā'lẽr, *n.* [Anglo-Ind.] an Australian horse bred in New South Wales, especially one sent to India for cavalry service; hence, any Australian horse. [Colloq.]

Wäl·häl'lȧ, *n.* same as *Valhalla*.

wā'lie, *a.* and *n.* same as *waly*.

walk (wạk), *v.i.*; walked, *pt., pp.*; walking, *ppr.* [AS. *wealcan*, to roll, turn about, to rove, whence *wealcere*, a fuller of cloth.]
1. to go along or move about on foot at a moderate pace; specifically, (a) to move by placing one foot firmly on the ground before

lifting the other, as two-legged creatures do, or by placing two feet firmly on the ground before lifting either of the others, as four-legged creatures do: distinguished from *run, gallop, trot*, etc.; (b) to go about on foot for exercise or pleasure; to hike.

2. to return after death and appear on earth as a ghost.

3. to advance or move in a manner suggestive of walking: said of inanimate objects.

4. to follow a certain course of life; to conduct oneself in a certain way; as, let us *walk* in peace.

5. to be active or in motion, or to keep moving. [Obs.]

6. in baseball, to be advanced to first base as a result of being pitched four balls.

7. in basketball, to commit the foul of advancing more than two steps with the ball without either passing or dribbling it.

to walk off; to go away, especially without warning.

to walk off with; (a) to steal; (b) to win or gain.

to walk out; to go on strike. [Colloq.]

to walk out on; to leave; to desert; to abandon. [Colloq.]

walk (wạk), *v.t.* 1. to pass through or upon; as, to *walk* the streets.

2. to traverse on foot in order to survey, inspect, or repair, as a boundary, fence, tracks, etc.

3. (a) to cause (a horse, dog, etc.) to move at a walk; to lead, ride, or drive at a walk; (b) to train and exercise (a horse, dog, etc.) by walking.

4. to accompany (a person) on a walk or stroll; as, I'll *walk* you to the corner.

5. (a) to force (a person) to move at a walk, as by grasping the shoulders and pushing; (b) to help (a disabled person) to walk.

6. to bring (a person or animal) to a specified state by walking; as, they *walked* me to exhaustion.

7. to cause to move in a manner suggestive of walking.

8. in baseball, to advance (a batter) to first base by pitching four balls.

9. in basketball, to commit the foul of advancing more than two steps with (the ball) without passing or dribbling.

10. to subject to the process of fulling; to full. [Obs.]

to walk a chalk line; see under *chalk*.

to walk off; to get rid of by walking, as excess energy or fat.

to walk the plank; see under *plank*.

walk (wạk), *n.* 1. the act of walking.

2. a period or course of walking for pleasure or exercise; a stroll; a hike.

3. a route traversed by walking; as, his usual *walk* was along the bluff.

4. a distance walked, often in terms of the time required; as, the town was an hour's *walk* from us.

5. the pace of one who walks; as, the horse came home at a *walk*.

6. a manner of walking; as, I knew her by her *walk*.

7. a particular station in life, sphere of activity, occupation, etc.; as, people from all *walks* of life.

8. mode of living; general conduct or behavior.

9. a path or avenue specially prepared or set apart for walking.

10. a ropewalk.

11. (a) a plantation of trees in rows with a space between; (b) the space between any two such rows.

12. a place or enclosure for grazing or exercising animals; specifically, a sheepwalk.

13. the route covered by a vendor, hawker, etc. [Brit.]

14. in England, a part of a forest under the care of a keeper.

15. a resort or haunt. [Obs.]

16. in athletics, a walking race.

17. in baseball, an advancing to first base as the result of four balls pitched to the batter.

cock of the walk; see under *cock*.

walk'ȧ·ble, *a.* fit for walking; capable of being walked on; as, *walkable* roads. [Rare.]

walk'ȧ·wāy, *n.* an easily won victory.

walk'ẽr, *n.* 1. one who walks; a pedestrian.

2. a foot; a leg. [Obs.]

3. in English forest law, an officer appointed to walk over a certain space for inspection; a forester.

4. formerly, one who walked cloth; a fuller. The proper name *Walker* is from this sense. [Obs.]

5. one who trains young hounds by taking them out for exercise.

6. [*pl.*] the insects of the family *Phasmidæ*; the walking sticks.

walker! or *hookey walker!*; nonsense!: a slang expression of incredulity. [Brit. Slang.]

wạlk'ie-tạlk'ie (-tạk'), *n.* a compact radio transmitter and receiver that can be carried by one person: also spelled *walky-talky*.

wạlk'ing, *n.* 1. the act of one who or that which walks.

2. manner of walking; gait.

3. the condition of the ground, a path, etc. with reference to its suitability for walking on; as, easy *walking* along this road.

wạlk'ing, *a.* that walks; specifically, (a) that is drawn by an animal and guided by a person walking; as, a *walking* plow; (b) that moves back and forth; oscillating; as, a *walking* beam; (c) that moves forward in a manner suggestive of walking; as, a *walking* crane.

walking gentleman or *lady*; an actor or actress who plays minor parts requiring impressive appearance.

wạlk'ing bāss, a repeated figure, commonly in eighth notes, much used as the bass part in boogie-woogie music.

wạlk'ing del'ē·gāte, a labor-union official who goes from place to place inspecting working conditions, representing the union to its locals, negotiating with employers, etc.: term now seldom used.

wạlk'ing fẽrn, a walking leaf (sense 2).

wạlk'ing fish, 1. a fish of the genus *Antennarius*; a frogfish.

2. a fish of the family *Ophiocephalidæ*. The walking fishes use their pectoral fins as legs in crossing land.

wạlk'ing lēaf, 1. an insect of the genus *Phyllium*, family *Phasmidæ*, with wings and limbs resembling leaves.

2. a North American fern, *Camptosorus rhizophyllus*, having fronds that bend backward and often take root at the tip.

wạlk'ing pā'pẽrs, a dismissal, as from employment or public office. [Colloq.]

wạlk'ing stȧff, a staff or long strong stick used as a support in walking.

wạlk'ing stick, 1. a stick carried when walking; a cane.

2. an insect of the family *Phasmidæ*, resembling a twig; a stick bug.

wạlk'ing strạw, a large insect, *Diura* or *Cyphocrana titan*, of New South Wales.

wạlk'ing swōrd (sōrd), formerly, in England, a sword worn by gentlemen as part of their civil dress or costume.

wạlk'ing tick'et, an order of dismissal; walking papers. [Colloq.]

wạlk'ing wheel (hwēl), 1. a treadmill.

2. a pedometer.

wạlk'mill, *n.* a fulling mill. [Obs.]

wạlk'-on, *n.* a minor role in which the actor has no speaking lines.

wạlk'out, *n.* a strike of workers. [Colloq.]

wạlk'ō·vẽr, *n.* 1. a race in which the one horse entered has merely to walk over the course to win.

2. an easily won victory. [Colloq.]

wạlk'-up, *n.* an apartment house without an elevator. [Colloq.]

wạlk'-up, *a.* of or in a walk-up; as, a *walk-up* apartment.

Wal·kü're, Diē (väl-kü're), the second in a tetralogy of music dramas by Richard Wagner: see *Ring of the Nibelung*.

Wäl'kyr (väl') *n.* same as *Valkyr*.

Wäl·kyr'ie, *n.* 1. same as *Valkyrie*.

2. [w—] a fate reader; a wise woman. [Obs.]

wạlk'y-tạlk'y, *n.* a walkie-talkie.

wạll, *n.* [ME. *wal, walle*; AS. *weal, weall*, from L. *vallum*, a rampart, from *vallus*, a stake, pale, palisade; lit., a protection.]

1. an upright structure of wood, stone, brick, etc. serving to enclose, divide, support, or protect; specifically, (a) such a structure forming a side or inner partition of a building; (b) such a continuous structure serving to enclose an area, separate fields, etc.; (c) [*usually in pl.*] such a structure used as a military defense; fortification; (d) such a structure used to hold back water; a levee; dike.

2. something resembling a wall in appearance or function, as the side or inside surface of a container, body cavity, etc.

3. something suggestive of a wall in that it holds back, divides, hides, etc.; as, a *wall* of secrecy.

4. in mining, (a) the rock enclosing a vein: where the dip is considerable, the upper boundary is called the *hanging wall*, and the lower the *footwall*; (b) the side of a drift.

off the wall; (a) unsound of mind; crazy; (b) very eccentric or unconventional. [Slang.]

the wall; in narrow streets and lanes, the privilege or courtesy of allowing one, especially a lady, to pass or walk along the wall or inner side of a sidewalk: also used in the phrase *to give* or *take the wall*.

to drive (or *push*) *to the wall*; to place in a desperate or extreme position.

to go to the wall; (a) to be forced to retreat or yield in a conflict; to suffer defeat; (b) to fail in business; to become bankrupt.

wạll, *a.* 1. of a wall.

2. placed or growing on or against a wall.

wạll, *v.t.*; walled, *pt., pp.*; walling, *ppr.* 1. to furnish, line, enclose, divide, protect, etc. with or as with a wall or walls (often with *off*).

2. to close up (an opening) with a wall (usually with *up*).

3. to defend by walls; to fortify.

wạll, *n.* a spring of water. [Scot. and Brit. Dial.]

wäl'lȧ, *n.* a wallah.

wäl'lȧ·bȧ, *n.* [Guiana.] a leguminous tree of the suborder *Cæsalpineæ, Eperua falcata*, native to British Guiana. The wood, which is of a deep red color, and hard, heavy, and durable, is used for shingles, posts, house frames, etc.

wäl'lȧ·by, *n.*; *pl.* **wäl'lȧ·bieṣ** or **wäl'lȧ·by,** [from Australian native name.] any of several species of small and medium-sized Australian kangaroos belonging to the genus *Halmaturus*, some about the size of a rabbit. Also written *wallabee* and *whallabee*.

on the wallaby; out of work and in search of a job. [Australian Slang.]

Wäl'lăch, Wäl'lăck, *n.* and *a.* [G., from O.H.G. *walh*, a foreigner.] same as *Walachian*.

Wäl·lā'çhi·ăn, *n.* and *a.* same as *Walachian*.

wäl'läh, *n.* [Anglo-Ind., from Hind. *-vala*, a suffix of agency.] in Anglo-Indian usage, (a) a person, or sometimes a thing, connected with a particular thing or function; (b) [Colloq.] a person. Also spelled *walla*.

wạll är·çāde', an ornamental arcade or arched recess in a wall, constructed chiefly for decorative purposes.

wäl·lȧ·rọọ', *n.* any of a group of kangaroos of the genus *Macropus* characterized by their great size, long narrow hind feet, and thick gray fur.

wạll bär'ley, squirreltail grass, *Hordeum murinum*.

wạll bēar'ing, same as *wall box*.

wạll'bird, *n.* the spotted flycatcher, *Muscicapa grisola*; the beambird.

wạll'bōard, *n.* fibrous material made up into thin slabs for use in making or covering walls, partitions, and ceilings, in place of plaster, paneling, etc.

WALL BOX

wạll box, a device for supporting a plumber block on which a shaft rests in passing through a wall.

wạll çlamp, a clamp or tie for holding or bracing walls together.

wạll çreep'ẽr, any bird of the family *Certhiidæ* and subfamily *Tichodrominæ*, of which the best-known species is *Tichodroma muraria*, of Europe, Asia, and North Africa. It frequents ruins and the clefts and crevices of rocks, and feeds on insects.

WALL CREEPER

wạll çress, any plant of the genus *Arabis*. It grows on walls and in dry stony places.

wạlled, *a.* 1. having a wall or walls; enclosed by a wall.

2. fortified; as, a *walled* town.

3. enclosed or hedged in as if by a wall.

wa̤ll'ẽr, *n.* one who builds walls.

wa̤ll'ẽr, *n.* [G.] the sheatfish or wels.

Wäl·lē'ri·ăn, *a.* pertaining to, associated with, or named for A. Waller, an English physiologist of the nineteenth century.

Wallerian degeneration; fatty degeneration of a nerve fiber which has been severed from its nutritive centers.

Wallerian law; the law stating that when the sensory fibers of the root of a spinal nerve are divided on the central side of the ganglion, the fibers on the peripheral side of the cut do not degenerate, while those which remain connected with the cord do.

Wallerian method; the process of ascertaining the function of a nerve fiber by separating it from its nutrient vessels and noting the direction in which degeneration proceeds.

wäl'let, *n.* [ME. *walet*; prob. altered from *watel*, a hurdle, basket, hence bag.]

1. a bag for carrying provisions, clothing, food, etc. on a journey on foot; a knapsack. [Now Rare.]

2. a pocketbook, usually of leather, for carrying cards, unfolded paper money, etc.; a billfold.

3. anything protuberant and hanging. [Obs.]

4. a small kit carried by anglers and containing various small articles. [Brit.]

wäl·let·eer', *n.* one who carries a wallet; hence, a traveler on foot; a tramp; a begger. [Obs.]

wa̤ll'eȳe (-ī), *n.* [back-formation from *walleyed.*]

1. an eye, as of a horse, with a whitish iris or white, opaque cornea.

2. (a) an eye that turns outward, showing more white than is normal; (b) divergent strabismus. Opposed to *cross-eye.*

3. leucoma of the cornea.

4. a large, staring eye, as of some fishes.

5. any of several fishes with large, staring eyes; specifically, (a) the walleyed pike; (b) the walleyed pollack; (c) the walleyed surf fish; (d) the alewife.

wa̤ll'eȳed, *a.* [ME. *waldeyed, wawileyed*; ON. *valdeygthr*; altered from *vagl eygr*; *vagl*, a film on the eye, and *eygr*, having eyes.]

1. having one or both eyes with a whitish iris or white, opaque cornea.

2. having eyes that turn outward, showing more white than is normal, because of divergent strabismus.

3. having leucoma of the cornea.

4. having large, staring eyes, as some fishes.

5. glary-eyed; fierce-eyed.

6. drunk. [Slang.]

walleyed pike (or *perch*); any of several North American fresh-water food fishes of the perch family, with large, staring eyes.

walleyed pollack; any of a group of large, black ocean food fishes common off the west coast of North America.

walleyed surf fish; any of a group of common black salt-water fishes found off the coast of California, which bear live young.

wa̤ll fẽrn, a fern, *Polypodium vulgare*, with densely matted, creeping stems, found on walls and cliffs.

wa̤ll'flow″ẽr, *n.* 1. a plant of the genus *Cheiranthus* with lance-shaped leaves and clusters of fragrant yellow, red, orange, or purple flowers.

2. a person, especially a girl or woman, who sits by the wall, or only looks on, at a dance, sometimes from shyness but ordinarily from not having been sought as a partner. [Colloq.]

wa̤ll frāme, a frame of cast iron fitted in a wall to support a wall box.

wa̤ll geck'ō, a gecko, especially *Platydactylus muralis* of southern Europe; a wall lizard.

COMMON WALLFLOWER

wa̤ll ġil'ly·flow·ẽr, the wallflower, *Cheiranthus cheiri.*

wa̤ll grē·nāde', same as *rampart grenade* under *grenade.*

wa̤ll hawk'weed, a European hawkweed, *Hieracium murorum*: so called because it is often found growing on walls.

wa̤ll'hick, *n.* same as *hickwall.*

wa̤ll'ing, *n.* 1. walls in general; materials for walls.

2. the act of building a wall.

dry walling; walling constructed without mortar or cement.

wa̤ll'ing wax, wax used by etchers to make a wall about a plate to hold the acid used in etching the plate.

wa̤ll iñk, the brooklime, *Veronica beccabunga.*

wa̤ll knot (not), a knot made by sailors by weaving the strands of a rope in a particular manner.

wa̤ll let'tuce (-is), a wild lettuce of Europe, *Lactuca* or *Prenanthes muralis.*

wa̤ll liz'ărd, 1. a gecko; a wall gecko.

2. a European lizard, *Lacerta muralis.*

wa̤ll louse, a bedbug.

wa̤ll moss, 1. any moss which commonly grows on walls.

2. the stonecrop.

wa̤ll newt, same as *wall lizard.*

Wäl·lō'ni·ăn, *a.* and *n.* Walloon.

Wäl·loon', *n.* [Fr. *Wallon*; OFr. *Wallon*; LL. *Wallus*; L. *Gallus*, a Gaul, from O.H.G. *walh*, a foreigner.]

1. a member of a people living chiefly in southern and southeastern Belgium and near-by parts of France.

2. the French dialect of the Walloons.

Wäl·loon', *a.* of or pertaining to the Walloons or Walloon.

Walloon Church; a Dutch Protestant church composed of the descendants of the French and Flemish refugees of the seventeenth century.

Walloon guard; formerly, the bodyguard of a king or queen of Spain: so called because made up of Walloons only.

wäl'lŏp, *v.i.* [ME. *walopen*, to gallop; O. Norm.Fr. *waloper* (OFr. *galoper*).]

1. to boil with a continued, noisy bubbling or heaving of the liquor. [Brit. Dial.]

2. to move in a rolling, cumbersome manner; to flounder. [Dial or Colloq.]

3. to gallop. [Dial. or Colloq.]

4. to be slovenly or careless. [Brit. Dial.]

wäl'lŏp, *v.t.*; walloped (wol'lupt), *pt., pp.*; walloping, *ppr.* 1. to thrash or whip severely; to flog; to beat. [Colloq.]

2. to strike with a very hard blow. [Colloq.]

3. to defeat convincingly or crushingly. [Colloq.]

wäl'lŏp, *n.* 1. (a) a heavy, clumsy movement of the body; (b) a gallop. [Dial. or Colloq.]

2. (a) a hard blow; (b) the power to strike a hard blow. [Colloq.]

3. a chunk of fat. [Brit. Dial.]

wäl'lŏp·ẽr, *n.* 1. one who or that which wallops. [Colloq.]

2. something huge, enormous, or greatly exaggerated; a whopper. [Colloq.]

3. same as *pot-walloper.*

wäl'lŏp·ing, *a.* [ppr. of *wallop.*] enormous; very large; as, a *walloping* big boy. [Colloq.]

wäl'lŏp·ing, *n.* 1. a thrashing. [Colloq.]

2. a crushing defeat. [Colloq.]

wäl'lōw, *v.i.*; wallowed, *pt., pp.*; wallowing, *ppr.* [ME. *walwen*; AS. *wealwian*, to roll round.]

1. to roll about on the earth, in mire, or on other soft substance; to tumble and roll in water; as, swine *wallow* in the mud.

2. to move heavily and clumsily; to roll and pitch, as a ship.

3. to live or indulge oneself fully with animal pleasure or luxurious enjoyment (*in* a specified thing, condition, etc.); as, to *wallow in* riches, to *wallow in* vice.

wäl'lōw, *v.t.* to roll in some soft substance: often used reflexively. [Rare.]

wäl'lōw, *n.* 1. a rolling walk or gait. [Obs.]

2. the act of wallowing.

3. a muddy or dusty place in which an animal, as the buffalo, wallows; also, the traces of its wallowing left in the mud or earth.

wäl'lōw, *v.i.* to fade; to wither. [Obs. or Dial.]

wäl'lōw, *a.* insipid; tasteless. [Brit. Dial.]

wäl'lōw·ẽr, *n.* 1. one who or that which wallows.

2. same as *lantern wheel.*

wäl'lōw·ish, *a.* tasteless; stale; nauseous. [Obs. or Dial.]

wa̤ll'pā″pẽr, *n.* decorative paper for covering the walls and ceilings of a room.

wa̤ll'pā″pẽr, *v.t.* to hang or apply wallpaper on or in.

wa̤ll pel'li·tō·ry, a plant, *Parietaria officinalis*, growing on old walls, etc., in Europe: formerly used as a diuretic.

wa̤ll pen'ny·wŏrt, the navelwort.

wa̤ll pep'pẽr, the stonecrop.

wa̤ll pīe, same as *wall rue.*

wa̤ll'pièce, *n.* a piece of artillery mounted on a wall.

wa̤ll'-plat, *n.* 1. same as *wallbird.*

2. same as *wall plate*, sense 1.

wa̤ll plāte, 1. in building, a timber on a wall for supporting the ends of joists, girders, etc. and distributing their weight.

2. a metal plate fastened to a wall for attaching a bearing, bracket, etc.

3. in mining, one of the long timbers used in the timbering of a shaft.

wa̤ll rock, in geology and mining, the rock mass on either side of a fault.

wa̤ll rock'et, a perennial, *Diplotaxis tenuifolia*, having yellow flowers and found in quarries and on old walls.

wa̤ll rūe, a small delicate fern, *Asplenium ruta-muraria*, resembling the rue and often found on walls and cliffs.

wa̤ll'-sīd″ed, *a.* having sides nearly perpendicular, as a ship.

wa̤ll spāce, a plain expanse of wall; especially, such an expanse considered as a feature of design or a space for decoration.

wa̤ll spleen'wŏrt, same as *wall rue.*

Wa̤ll Street, 1. a street in lower Manhattan, New York City: the main financial center of the United States.

2. American financiers and their power, influence, policies, etc., or the American money market.

wa̤ll tent, a tent with upright walls and a peaked top.

wa̤ll'-tō-wa̤ll', *a.* 1. that completely covers a floor; as, *wall-to-wall* carpeting.

2. (a) in very large numbers or amounts; found throughout; pervasive; widespread; (b) comprehensive; all-inclusive; as, *wall-to-wall* health care. [Colloq.]

wa̤ll tree, a fruit tree trained along a wall for the better exposure of the fruit to the sun and protection from winds.

wa̤ll wăsp, a wasp that makes its nest in a wall; specifically, *Odynerus murarius*, a common European wasp.

wa̤ll'wŏrt, *n.* the Danewort.

wā'ly, *interj.* waly. [Scot.]

wā'ly, *a.* 1. fine; first-rate. [Scot.]

2. ample, large, strong, or robust. [Scot.]

3. pleasing; agreeable. [Scot.]

wā'ly, *n.*; *pl.* **wā'lieș,** 1. a toy, gimcrack, or bauble. [Scot.]

2. [*pl.*] finery. [Scot.]

wā'ly·drag, *n.* a weak, underdeveloped creature; sometimes, the last-born of a litter or brood. [Scot.]

wā'ly·drāi·gle, *n.* a wallydrag. [Scot.]

walm (wa̤m), *v.i.* to bubble; to boil. [Obs.]

wa̤lm, *n.* a bubble in boiling. [Obs.]

wa̤l'nut, *n.* [ME. *walnote, walnot*, from AS. *wealh*, foreign, and *hnutu*, a nut.]

1. a roundish, edible nut with a two-lobed seed.

WALNUT (*Juglans regia*)

2. any of a number of related trees bearing such a nut, as the *English walnut* (*Juglans regia*), the *black walnut* (*Juglans nigra*), etc.

3. the wood of any of these trees, used in furniture, woodwork, etc.

4. a shagbark tree (genus *Carya*), or its nut.

5. a shade of brown characteristic of the heartwood of the black walnut.

black walnut; see under *black.*

Caucasian walnut; a tree, *Pterocarya fraxinifolia*, native to the Caucasian region and distinguished from other varieties of the walnut by its two-winged fruit.

English walnut; see under *English.*

Indian walnut; a tree, *Aleurites triloba*, belonging to the spurge family.

walnut case-bearer; a small moth, *Acrobasis juglandis*, which, in its larval state, makes a case between the leaves of the walnut upon which it feeds.

white walnut; the butternut, *Juglans cinerea*.

wal'nut moth, any one of numerous species of moths whose larvae are destructive to the walnut, especially the *Citheronia regalis*.

wal'nut oil, an oil obtained from the kernels of walnuts.

wal'nut scāle, a flat gray scale, *Aspidiotus juglans-regiæ*, infesting the bark on the limbs of the walnut.

wal'nut sphinx, a large hawk moth, *Cressonia juglandis*, whose larva is injurious to the foliage of the black walnut.

Wäl·pur'gis·nächt (väl·poor'gis·näkht), *n.* [G.] Walpurgis Night.

Wäl·pur'gis Nīght (väl-), [G., from *Walburga*, *Walpurgis*, St. Walpurgis, English missionary in Germany in the 8th century; her feast day is April 30.]

1. April 30, the eve of May Day, when witches were supposed to gather and revel on Brocken peak in the Harz Mountains of Germany.

2. a witches' sabbath; diabolical revelry.

wäl·pūr'gīte, *n.* a yellow hydrated uranium-bismuth arsenate.

wäl'rus, *n.*; *pl.* **wäl'rus·es** or **wäl'rus,** [D. *walrus*; Sw. *valross*, walrus, lit., whale horse; OSw. *val*, a whale, and *ross*, a horse.] either of two massive sea animals of the seal family (genus *Odobenus*), one native to the North Pacific, the other to the North Atlantic, having two tusks projecting from the upper jaw, a thick mustache, a very thick hide, and a heavy layer of blubber.

WALRUS (10–11 ft. long)

wäl'rus, *a.* of, characteristic of, or suggestive of a walrus; specifically, designating a mustache with long, drooping ends.

wäl'rus bīrd, the pectoral sandpiper.

wäl'tẽr, *v.i.* to tumble; to roll; to wallow. [Dial.]

wäl'trŏn, *n.* the walrus. [Obs.]

wäl'ty, *a.* apt to roll over; crank: said of a ship. [Archaic.]

waltz (walts), *n.* [a shortened form of G. *walzer*, from *walzen*, to roll, dance about, waltz.]

1. a ballroom dance for couples, in moderate 3/4 time with marked accent on the first beat of the measure.

2. music for such a dance or in its characteristic rhythm.

waltz, *v.i.*; waltzed (waltst), *pt., pp.*; waltzing, *ppr.* 1. to dance a waltz.

2. to move lightly and nimbly; to whirl.

waltz, *v.t.* to cause to waltz.

waltz, *a.* of, for, or characteristic of a waltz.

waltz'ẽr, *n.* a person who waltzes.

waltz'ing, *n.* the act of dancing a waltz.

wā'ly, *a.* [a lengthening of *wale*.] beautiful; excellent; also, large; ample; robust. [Scot.]

wā'ly, *n.*; *pl.* **wā'lies,** an ornament; a toy. [Scot.]

wā'ly, *interj.* [corruption of *wellaway*.] an exclamation of sorrow or lamentation. [Scot.]

wä'mȧ·rȧ, *n.* [native name.] brown ebony, the wood of a tree native to British Guiana.

wäm'ble (wäm'l), *v.i.*; wambled, *pt., pp.*; wambling, *ppr.* [ME. *wamlen*; cf. Dan. *vamle*, to nauseate, to become squeamish, from *vammel*, nauseous.]

1. to turn, twist, writhe, roll, or wriggle about.

2. to move unsteadily; to stagger or reel.

3. (a) [Obs.] to be nauseated; (b) to give the sensation of nausea, as if turning about: said of the stomach or its contents.

[Chiefly Dial. in all senses.]

wäm'ble, *n.* 1. (a) a wambling; a turning, twisting, writhing, etc.; (b) an unsteady movement or staggering gait. [Chiefly Dial.]

2. a sensation of nausea. [Chiefly Dial.]

wäm'ble-cropped (-kropt), *a.* sick at the stomach. [Dial.]

wäm'bly (wäm'li), *a.* 1. unsteady, shaky, staggering, or reeling. [Chiefly Dial.]

2. feeling nausea; nauseated. [Chiefly Dial.]

wāme, *n.* the belly; also, the womb. [Scot. and Brit. Dial.]

wäm'mẽr·äh, *n.* same as *womera*.

wäm'mi·çăn, *n.* [Am. Ind.] a raft used by lumbermen, fitted with a shanty in which the raftsmen cook and sleep.

wam'mus, *n.* same as *wamus*.

wämp, *n.* the eider duck.

Wäm″pȧ·nō'ag, *n.*; *pl.* **Wäm″pȧ·nō'ag, Wäm″pȧ·nō'ags,** a member of a tribe of Algonquian Indians that lived in the region of Cape Cod: these were the first Indians met by the Pilgrims after the landing at Plymouth.

Wäm″pȧ·nō'ag, *a.* of this tribe.

wäm·pee', *n.* [Chinese.] a tree, *Cookia punctata*, cultivated in China and other countries in the Orient for its fruit, which is about the size of a pigeon's egg; also, the fruit.

WAMPEE (*Cookia punctata*)

wäm'pum, *n.* [short for *wampumpeag*.]

1. small beads made of shells and used by the North American Indians as money, for ornament, as in belts, etc.: they were of two varieties, white and black (or dark purple), the latter being worth twice the former.

2. money. [Slang.]

wäm'pum·pēag, *n.* [from Am. Ind. (Algonquian) *wampumpeage*, lit., white string of beads.]

1. white shell beads used by North American Indians as money.

2. shell money; wampum.

wäm'pum snāke, the hornsnake, *Farancia abacura*.

wäm'pus, *n.* same as *wamus*.

wä'mus, *n.* [D. *wammes*, earlier *wambuis*; OFr. *wambois*, *wambais*, leather doublet, from O.H.G. *wamba*, the belly.]

1. a kind of cardigan.

2. an outer jacket made of tough, long-wearing fabric.

Also *wammus*, *wampus*.

wän, *a.*; *comp.* wanner; *superl.* wannest, [ME.; AS. *wann*, *wonn*, dark.]

1. pale; having a sickly hue; pallid.

Sad to view, his visage pale and *wan*.
—Spenser.

2. indicative or suggestive of a sickly condition or great weariness, grief, etc.; faint or feeble; as, a *wan* smile.

3. (a) dark; gloomy; (b) sad. [Obs.]

wän, *n.* the condition of being wan. [Rare.]

wän, *v.t.* and *v.i.*; wanned, *pt., pp.*; wanning, *ppr.* to make or become sickly pale.

wän, *v.* obsolete past tense of win.

wänd, *n.* [ME., from Anglo-N.]

1. a slender, supple switch or shoot, as of a young tree, especially a willow.

2. a slender rod, as a musician's baton.

3. a rod or staff carried as a symbol of authority; a scepter.

4. (a) a magic rod, as used by a fairy; (b) the slender, batonlike rod of a magician or conjurer; (c) any rod of supposed magic power, as a divining rod.

5. in archery (as practiced in the United States), a slat used as a mark, 6 feet long and 2 inches wide: it is placed at a distance of 100 yards for men and 60 yards for women.

wand of peace; a small baton which forms part of the insignia of the messenger of a court in Scotland.

wän'dẽr, *v.i.*; wandered, *pt., pp.*; wandering, *ppr.* [ME. *wandrien*, *wandren*, from AS. *wandrian*, to wander, a freq. form of *wend*, to go.]

1. to ramble here and there, without any certain course or object in view; to travel or move from place to place without any fixed purpose or destination; to rove, range, or roam about; as, to *wander* in the woods.

2. to go to a place by any way or at any pace that suits the fancy; to idle; to stroll.

3. (a) to turn aside or astray (*from* a path, course, etc.); to lose one's way; (b) to stray from home, friends, familiar places, etc. (often with *off*).

4. to drift away from a subject, as in discussion.

5. to turn away from accepted thought or morals; to go astray morally or intellectually.

O let me not *wander* from thy commandments. —Ps. cxix. 10.

6. to be disordered, incoherent, delirious, etc.

7. to pass or extend in an irregular course; to meander, as a river.

8. to move idly from one object to another: said of the eyes, a glance, the hands, etc.

Syn.—rove, roam, stray, depart, range, stroll, straggle, ramble.

wän'dẽr, *v.t.* to roam through, in, or over without plan or destination. [Poet.]

Wandering many a famous realm.—Milton.

wän'dẽr·ẽr, *n.* one who or that which wanders; a rover; a rambler.

wän'dẽr·ing, *a.* 1. that wanders; moving from place to place; roaming, roving, straying, etc.

2. nomadic: said of tribes.

3. winding: said of rivers and roads.

wän'dẽr·ing, *n.* 1. an aimless going about.

2. [*pl.*] travels; especially, extended and apparently purposeless travels.

3. [*pl.*] incoherent or disordered thoughts or utterances, as in delirium.

wandering albatross; a large white sea bird with black wings, native to southern seas: see *albatross*.

wandering cell; in physiology, a leucocyte.

Wandering Jew; (a) a legendary Jew who, according to medieval folklore, was condemned to wander the earth until the second coming of Christ because of his scornful behavior just before the Crucifixion; (b) [w– J–] any of several trailing plants having smooth stems and leaves, and white, red, or blue flowers.

wandering kidney; a kidney which is loosened and displaced: also called *floating kidney*, *movable kidney*.

wandering liver; a displaced and movable liver.

wandering spider; any spider that wanders in quest of prey.

wän'dẽr·ing·ly, *adv.* in a wandering or unsteady manner.

Wän'dẽr·jähr (vän'der-yär), *n.* [G., lit. wander-year.] a year of travel before settling down to work: an old custom of European journeymen.

wän'dẽr·lust, *n.* [G.] an impulse, longing, or urge to wander or travel.

wän·dẽr·ọọ', *n.* [Singhalese *vanduru*, pl. of *vandurā*, from Sans. *vānara*, a monkey.]

1. any of a rare species of monkey of the macaque family, genus *Macacus*, native to southern India, with a black coat, a thick ruff of gray hair about the face, and a short, tufted tail.

WANDEROO (*Macacus silenus*)

2. any of a group of purple-faced langur monkeys of Ceylon.

wän'dle, *a.* [back-formation from AS. *wandlung*, changeableness.] supple; agile. [Scot.]

wän'dọọ, *n.* in botany, the western Australian white gum tree, *Eucalyptus redunca*, the heavy durable wood of which is much used by wheelwrights.

wänd'y, *a.* long and flexible, like a wand. [Brit. Dial.]

wāne, *v.i.*; waned, *pt., pp.*; waning, *ppr.* [ME. *wanien*; AS. *wanian*, *wonian*, to decrease, grow less, from *wan*, *won*, deficient.]

1. to grow gradually less in extent: said of

the illuminated part of the moon during the period after it has become full.

Waning moons their settled periods keep.
—Addison.

2. to decline in power, prosperity, importance, influence, etc.

Land and trade ever will wax and *wane* together. —Child.

3. to become less intense, bright, etc.; to grow dim or faint: said of light, etc.

4. to approach the end: said of a period of time; as, the day *wanes*.

Opposed to *wax*.

wāne, *v.t.* to cause to decrease. [Obs.]

wāne, *n.* 1. the gradual decrease of the illuminated part of the moon after it has become full; also, the time when this takes place.

2. a gradual decrease in power, importance, prosperity, intensity, etc., especially after a gradual climb to a peak.

3. a period of decline.

An age in which the church is in its *wane*.
—South.

4. the slanting or beveled defective edge of a board or plank cut from an unsquared log or block of wood.

on the wane; waning; declining, decreasing, etc.

wāne çloud, a cirro-stratus cloud.

wān′ey, *a.* same as *wany*.

wang, *n.* 1. the cheek. [Obs.]

2. a molar; a grinder. [Obs.]

waṅ′gȧ·lȧ, *n.* same as *vanglo*.

wang′ẽr, *n.* a pillow. [Obs.]

wang·hee′, *n.* [Chinese, yellow root.] a bamboo of the genus *Phyllostachys*, the slender stems of which are used for walking canes.

waṅ′gle, *v.t.*; wangled, *pt., pp.*; wangling, *ppr.* [prob. a slang formation on *angle*.]

1. to get, make, or bring about by persuasion, influence, adroit manipulation, contrivance, etc. [Colloq.]

2. to manipulate or change for a selfish or dishonest purpose, as statistics, etc.; to falsify; to juggle. [Colloq.]

3. to wiggle or wriggle. [Colloq.]

waṅ′gle, *v.i.* 1. to make use of contrivance, adroit manipulation, or tricky and indirect methods in order to achieve one's aims. [Colloq.]

2. to wriggle, as out of a difficult situation. [Colloq.]

waṅ′gle, *n.* an act of wangling. [Colloq.]

waṅ′gun, *n.* a place for keeping small supplies in a lumber camp.

wän′hōpe, *n.* 1. lack of hope; despair. [Archaic.]

2. vain hope; delusion. [Obs.]

wän′họrn, *n.* an East Indian plant, *Kæmpferia galanga*.

wän′i·änd, *n.* the moon's waning. [Obs.]

wän′iŏn (-yun), *n.* [altered from ME. *waneand*, Northern dial. ppr. of *wanien*, to wane; sense from notion of the waning of the moon as unlucky time.] bad luck; curse; plague; vengeance: in *with* (or *in*) *a wanion*. [Archaic.]

wäṅ′kȧ·pin, *n.* [Am. Ind.] the water chinkapin.

wäṅ′kle, *a.* [AS. *wancol*, unsteady, vacillating.] weak; unstable; not to be depended on. [Brit. Dial.]

wän′ly, *adv.* in a pale or wan manner.

wän′ness, *n.* the condition or quality of being wan.

wän′nish, *a.* somewhat wan.

wänt (*or* wọnt), *v.t.*; wanted, *pt., pp.*; wanting, *ppr.* [ME. *wanten*; O.N. *vanta*, to be lacking, want.]

1. to be without; to be destitute of; to lack; as, to *want* food.

2. to be short by (a specified amount) of a certain total or result; as, it *wants* twelve minutes of midnight.

3. to desire; to wish (followed by the infinitive); as, she *wants* to go with us.

4. to feel a desire for, as for something absent, needed, lost, or the like; to feel the need of; to wish or long for; to desire; to crave.

5. to desire to see or speak to or to do business with; to desire the presence or assistance of; as, he is the person we *want*.

6. to wish to apprehend, as for questioning or arrest: usually in the passive voice; as, *wanted* by the police.

7. to require; need; as, this *wants* attending to. [Chiefly Brit.]

Want is also used colloquially as an auxiliary meaning *ought* or *should*; as, you *want* to eat before you go.

wänt, *v.i.* 1. to suffer from the need of something; to have a need or lack (usually with *for*); as, we must not let him *want for* money.

2. to lack the necessaries of life; to be destitute or impoverished.

3. to be lacking or missing for completeness or a certain result; as, there *wants* but his approval. [Rare or Archaic.]

wänt, *n.* [ME.; O.N. *vant*, neut. of *vanr*, deficient.]

1. the state or fact of lacking, or having too little of, something needed or desired; the condition of being without anything; lack; deficiency; as, *want* of light, food, power, color, etc.

Evil is wrought by *want* of thought,
As well as *want* of heart. —Hood.

2. absence. [Obs.]

3. something needed or desired but lacking; need; necessity.

To supply the ripe *wants* of my friend.
—Shak.

4. lack of the necessities of life; destitution; poverty; as, he is in dire *want*.

5. a wish or desire for something; a craving.

Nature's *wants*, he knows how few they are.
—Wordsworth.

Syn.—deficiency, lack, scarcity, defect, destitution, poverty, indigence.

wänt, *n.* a mole. [Dial.]

wä′n't, a contraction of *was not*. [Dial.]

wänt ad, an advertisement, as in the classified advertising section of a newspaper, announcing that one wants a job, an apartment to rent, a specified type of employee, etc., or that one has something specified to sell or trade. [Colloq.]

wänt′äġe, *n.* deficiency; that which is wanting; shortage.

wänt′ing, *a.* 1. absent; lacking; missing; as, a coat with some buttons *wanting*.

2. not up to some standard; inadequate in some essential; as, weighed and found *wanting*.

wanting in; deficient in (some quality, part, etc.).

wänt′ing, *prep.* 1. lacking (something); without.

2. minus; less; as, a full payment, *wanting* ten dollars.

wänt′less, *a.* having no want.

wän′tŏn (*or* wọn′), *a.* [ME. *wantowen*, comp. of *wan-*, prefix (AS. *wan, won*), lacking, deficient, and *towen*, standing for AS. *togen*, pp. of *teōn*, to draw, educate, bring up; lit., illbred.]

1. originally, undisciplined; unmanageable; as, *wanton* boys.

2. unrestrained by the rules of chastity; lascivious; libidinous; lustful; lewd.

3. moving, wandering, or roving about in gaity or sport; playful; frolicsome; sportive; as, a *wanton* child. [Poet.]

4. moving or flying loosely, as if unconfined; playing freely or without constraint; as, *wanton* winds.

5. luxuriant in growth; overgrown; overfertile or abundant: said of vegetation, etc. [Poet.]

6. lavish, luxurious, or extravagant: said of speech, dress, etc.

7. senseless, unprovoked, unjustifiable, or deliberately malicious; as, *wanton* cruelty, a *wanton* insult.

8. reckless; heedless; with an utter disregard of right or consequences; as, *wanton* mischief.

Syn.—wandering, roving, sportive, playful, frolicsome, loose, unbridled, uncurbed, reckless, unrestrained, irregular, licentious, dissolute, inconsiderate, heedless, gratuitous.

wän′tŏn, *n.* 1. a wanton person or thing; especially, an immoral or unchaste man or woman.

2. a trifler; an insignificant flutterer.

3. a petted or pampered person. [Obs.]

wän′tŏn, *v.i.*; wantoned, *pt., pp.*; wantoning, *ppr.* 1. to be playful; to frolic heedlessly.

Nature here
Wantoned as in her prime. —Milton.

2. to indulge in playful, indiscriminate, or excessive lovemaking.

3. to indulge in excesses of conduct, language, etc.

4. to grow luxuriantly; to run riot.

wän′tŏn, *v.t.* 1. to make wanton. [Obs.]

2. to waste carelessly or in luxurious pleasures.

wän′tŏn·īze, *v.i.* to behave wantonly. [Archaic.]

wän′tŏn·ly, *adv.* in a wanton manner.

wän′tŏn·ness, *n.* the quality or state of being wanton.

wän′trust, *n.* distrust; diminishing trust. [Obs.]

want′wit (wọnt′), *n.* one who is lacking in wit or sense; a fool.

wän′ty, *n.* [etym. uncertain. Comp. D. *want*, cordage, tackling.] a leather tie or rope; a short wagon rope; also, a rope used for binding a load upon the back of a beast. [Brit. Dial.]

wān′y, *a.*; *comp.* wanier; *superl.* waniest. 1. waning.

2. having an edge or edges slanting or beveled: said of planks, etc. cut from an unsquared log or block.

Also spelled *waney*.

wäp, *n., v.t.* and *v.i.*; wapped, (wäpt) *pt., pp.*; wapping, ppr. whop. [Dial. or Archaic.]

wäp′ȧ·çut, *n.* [Am. Ind. *wapacuthu*, wapacut.] a spotted owl, *Strix wapacuthu*, native to the Hudson Bay region.

wäp′en·shaw, *n.* same as *wappenschaw*.

wäp′en·tāke, *n.* [AS. *wæpengetæc*, a district, wapentake; O.N. *vápnatak*, lit., a weapontaking or weapon-touching.] formerly, in England, (a) a subdivision of certain northern counties originally under Norse domination, corresponding to the hundred in other counties; (b) a law court in such a subdivision.

wäp′i·ti, *n.*; *pl.* **wäp′i·tis** or **wäp′i·ti,** [Am. Ind. *wapitik*, Rocky Mountain goat.] a species of deer or elk, *Cervus canadensis*, which resembles the European red deer, but larger, with long, branching antlers: it is native to North America.

wapp, *n.* [var. of *wap, wop*.] in nautical usage, a rope with which the shrouds of a vessel are set taut; also, a fair-lead.

Wäp′pȧ·tō, *n.* [Am. Ind.] among the Indians of Oregon, the edible tubers of *Sagittaria variabilis*, a common species of arrowhead.

wäp′pened, *a.* outworn: a word known only as occurring in the following passage from Shakespeare's *Timon of Athens*, and of doubtful meaning:

This yellow slave (gold)
Will knit and break religions. . . . This is it
That makes the *wappen'd* widow wed again.

wäp′pen·schaw, *n.* a wappenshawing: also spelled *wappenshaw, wapinschaw*.

wäp′pen·schaw·ing, *n.* [from *wapen*, weapon, and *schawing*, a showing.] in Scottish history, a review or mustering of men under arms, held at periodic intervals in each district: also spelled *wappenshawing*.

wäp′pẽr, *v.i.* to totter; to twitter; to blink. [Obs.]

wap′pẽr, *n.* a whopper. [Brit. Dial.]

wäp′pẽr·jaw, *n.* a misshapen or projecting underjaw. [Colloq.]

wäp′pẽr·jawed, *a.* having a wapperjaw. [Colloq.]

wap′ping, *n.* whopping. [Scot. and Brit. Dial.]

wạr, *n.* [ME. *werre*; O.H.G. *werra*, confusion, strife.]

1. open armed conflict between nations or states, or between parties in the same state, carried on by force of arms for various purposes; a conflict of arms between hostile parties or nations.

2. the profession, science, or art of military operations, or military operations as a department of activity.

Nation shall not lift up sword against nation, neither shall they learn *war* any more. —Isa. ii. 4.

3. any state of violent opposition or contest; act of opposition; inimical act or action; hostility; strife; as, the *war* between the sexes.

4. a battle. [Obs. or Poet.]

Articles of War; see under *article*.

at war; in a state of active armed conflict.

civil war; see under *civil*.

council of war; see under *council*.

declaration of war; a formal announcement, proclamation, or manifesto issued by authority of a state or nation declaring war against or upon another state or nation.

honors of war; see under *honor*.

international war; war between nations or sovereign states, as distinguished from *civil war*.

to declare war (*on*); (a) to make a formal declaration of being at war (with); (b) to announce one's hostility or open opposition (to).

to go to war; (a) to enter into a war; (b) to become a member of the armed forces during a war.

wạr, *a.* of, used in, or resulting from war.

wạr, *v.i.*; warred, *pt., pp.*; warring, *ppr.* 1. to make war; to carry on hostilities; to engage in military operations.

2. to contend; to strive; to be in a state of hostility or contention.

war, *v.t.* 1. to make war upon; as, to *war* the Japanese. [Obs.]
2. to carry on, as a contest. [Archaic.]

wär, *a.* and *adv.* [ME.; O.N. *verre,* a., *verr,* adv.] worse: also *waur.* [Scot. and N. Eng. Dial.]

war'ȧ·tȧh (-tȧ), *n.* [Australian.] 1. an Australian shrub, *Telopea speciosissima,* having a crimson flower borne in dense heads.
2. a camellia having a flower resembling the anemone.

War bē·tween' the Stātes, the American Civil War (1861–1865): so called generally in the South.

war'ble, *v.t.*; warbled, *pt., pp.*; warbling, *ppr.* [ME. *werblen;* O.Norm. Fr. *werbler,* from an unrecorded M.H.G. *werbelen,* G. *wirbeln,* to whirl, warble.]
1. to sing melodiously in a trilling, quavering, or vibrating manner; to modulate with turns or variations, as certain birds.
2. to tell in song or verse; to utter musically.

war'ble, *v.i.* 1. to sound with flowing, gliding flexible melody; to sing with a warble.
2. to make a musical sound; to babble, as a stream.
3. to yodel.

war'ble, *n.* 1. a trilling, flexible melody; a carol; a song.
2. an act of warbling.
3. a warbling sound; a trill.

war'ble, *v.t.* and *v.i.* in falconry, to cross (the wings) upon the back.

war'ble, *n.* [Early Mod. Eng.; perhaps from ME. *war,* pus.]
1. a small, hard tumor on the back of a horse produced by the friction and pressure of the saddle.
2. a lump or swelling under the hide of an animal, especially on the back, caused by the presence of a larva of the warble fly or botfly.
3. the larva of a warble fly; also, the warble fly.

war'ble flȳ, any of a number of two-winged flies, as the *Hypoderma bovis,* whose larvae burrow beneath the hides of cattle, horses, and other animals, producing warbles.

war'blẽr, *n.* 1. a bird or person that warbles; a singer; a songster.
2. any of a large family of small, insect-eating New World birds (*wood warblers*), many of which are brightly colored, as the yellow warbler, the golden warbler, the American redstart, etc.
3. any of a family of small songbirds, as the whitethroat, the reed warbler, etc., found chiefly in the Old World.

YELLOW WARBLER (*Dendroica æstiva*)

war'blet, *n.* a warble (sense 1).

war'bling·ly, *adv.* in a warbling manner.

war bon'net, a ceremonial headdress worn by some tribes of North American Indians, consisting of a headband and trailing part studded with feathers.

war brīde, (a) a girl or woman who marries a soldier while the latter is actively engaged in war service; (b) any speculative security based on war contracts. [Slang.]

war'crȧft, *n.* the science or art of war.

war crȳ, 1. a name, phrase, slogan, etc. shouted in a charge or battle.
2. a phrase or slogan adopted by a party in any conflict, contest, election, etc.

-wărd, [ME. *-werd, ward;* AS. *-weard, weardes,* from base of *weorthan,* to become.] a suffix meaning *in a* (specified) *direction* or *course,* as in back*ward,* east*ward:* also, in adverbial variants, *-wards.*

ward, *v.t.*; warded, *pt., pp.*; warding, *ppr.* [AS. *weardian,* to keep, watch.]
1. to turn aside; to fend off; to parry (usually with *off*).
2. to place (a person) in a ward, as in a hospital.
3. to keep in safety; to watch; to guard. [Archaic.]
4. to put in custody; to place under guard; to imprison. [Obs.]

ward, *v.i.* 1. to be vigilant; to keep guard. [Obs.]
2. to act on the defensive with a weapon; to guard oneself. [Obs.]

ward, *n.* [AS. *weard,* guard, watchman.]
1. a guarding: now only in *watch and ward.*
2. the state of being under guard.
3. (a) guardianship, as of a child or person not capable of handling his own affairs; (b) the condition of being under the control of a guardian; wardship; (c) a child or incompetent person placed by law under the care of a guardian or court; (d) a person under another's protection or care.
4. each of the parts or divisions of a jail or prison.
5. a room or division of a hospital, asylum, etc., set apart for a specific class or group of patients; as, a maternity *ward.*
6. a district or division of a city or town, for purposes of administration, representation, voting, etc.
7. one of the administrative districts into which some counties in northern England and Scotland are divided, corresponding to the hundred and wapentake.
8. a means of defense or protection.
9. a defensive posture, position, or motion, as in fencing.
10. an open space enclosed by the walls of a castle or fortification.
11. a garrison; the guard or watch. [Archaic.]
12. in lockmaking, (a) a projecting ridge in a keyhole or lock face that allows only the right key to enter; (b) the notch in a key that matches this ridge.
13. in feudal law, the heir of the king's tenant in capite, during his nonage.
14. a division of a forest. [Scot.]
15. any section of any army, as a regiment or brigade. [Obs.]
16. the extreme defenses or outworks of a castle. [Obs.]
condemned ward; a ward in a prison in which criminals condemned to death are placed to await execution.
isolation ward; a separate apartment in a hospital for patients suffering from contagious diseases.
ward in chancery; a minor or an incompetent person placed by law under the protection of a court of equity.

ward'ăġe, *n.* money paid and contributed for keeping guard: also called *ward penny.*

war dȧnce, 1. a ceremonial dance engaged in by primitive tribes before battle or after victory.
2. a dance simulating a battle.

ward'çorn, *n.* in old English law, wardage in the form of corn instead of money.

ward'çors, *n.* 1. a bodyguard. [Obs.]
2. a coat; a cloak. [Obs.]

ward'ed, *a.* having wards, or notches, etc., as a lock or key.

Ward'en, *n.* [ME. *wardon;* prob. from O.Norm. Fr. *warder,* to keep.] a medium-sized winter pear used chiefly for cooking: also *warden.*

ward'en, *n.* [ME. *wardein,* from an unrecorded OFr. *wardein,* later spelled *gardein,* a warden, guardian.]
1. a person who guards, or has charge of, something; a keeper, custodian, or special supervisory official; as, air-raid *warden,* game *warden.*
2. the head keeper or top administrative official of a prison.
3. in England, a high government officer: now obsolete except in titles; specifically, (a) a governor; (b) an officer in charge of a certain department of the government; (c) the superintendent of a port or market.
4. in England, a governing officer in certain colleges, guilds, hospitals, etc.; a trustee.
5. in Connecticut, the chief executive of a borough.
6. in the Episcopal Church, etc., a churchwarden.
7. a gatekeeper or watchman. [Rare.]
Warden of the Cinque Ports; in England, the governor of the Cinque Ports and their dependencies, who has the authority of an admiral.

ward'en pīe, a pie made of Warden pears.

ward'en·ry, *n.*; *pl.* **ward'en·rieṣ,** 1. the office or position of a warden.
2. the jurisdiction or district of a warden.

ward'en·ship, *n.* the office, jurisdiction, or term of office of a warden.

ward'ẽr, *n.* [ME. *wardere;* Anglo-Fr. *wardour;* OFr. *guarder.*]
1. one who guards; a watchman.
2. one who guards an entrance.
3. a warden, custodian, or jail official in charge of prisoners. [Chiefly Brit.]

ward'ẽr, *n.* [Late ME.] formerly, a staff or rod carried by a king, commander, etc. as a mark of authority, and used to signal his wishes.

ward heel'ẽr, a hanger-on of a ward committee or politician; a ward worker who solicits votes for his party and performs various small tasks for his political bosses: a contemptuous term.

Ward'i·ăn çase, [from the English inventor, Nathaniel B. *Ward* (1791–1868).] a case with glass sides and top for growing and carrying living plants.

ward'măn, *n.*; *pl.* **ward'men,** a minor officer of the law. [Brit.]

ward'mōte, *n.* a meeting of a ward; also, a court held in every ward in the City of London.

ward pen'ny, wardage. [Obs.]

ward pol·i·ti'ciăn, a politician who works in a ward.

ward'ress, *n.* a woman warder. [Chiefly Brit.]

ward'rōbe, *n.* [ME. *warderobe;* OFr. *warderobe,* later *garderobe,* from *warder,* to watch, keep, preserve, and *robe,* a robe.]
1. a closet or movable cabinet, usually relatively tall and provided with hooks, etc., for holding clothes.
2. a room where clothes are kept; especially, a room in a theater where costumes are kept.
3. a collection of clothes; especially, (a) the complete supply of clothes of a person; (b) a supply of clothes for a particular season or purpose; as, a spring *wardrobe;* (c) the clothes and costumes of a theater or theatrical company.
4. in a royal or similar household, the department in charge of clothes.
5. a privy. [Obs.]

ward'ro͝om, *n.* [*ward, n.* and *room.*]
1. in a warship, living or eating quarters for all officers above an ensign in rank, except the captain.
2. these officers collectively.
3. in military usage, a guardroom. [Brit.]

-wărdṣ, -ward.

ward'ship, *n.* 1. the office of a ward or guardian; guardianship; the care and protection of a ward; the right of guardianship.
2. the state of being a ward or in the care of a guardian.

wardṣ'măn, *n.*; *pl.* **wardṣ'men,** one who keeps guard; a guard.

ward wŏrk'ẽr, a ward politician.

wāre, *v.* obsolete past tense of *wear.*

wāre, *a.* [ME. *war,* from AS. *wær,* cautious.]
1. aware; conscious (of). [Archaic.]
2. on one's guard; ready; wary. [Archaic.]
3. prudent; cautious; wise. [Archaic.]

wāre, *v.t.*; wared, *pt., pp.*; waring, *ppr.* [ME *waren;* AS. *warian.*] to take heed to; to guard against; to beware of; to look out for: usually in the imperative, especially in hunting; as, *ware* hounds; *ware* hawk.

wāre, *n.* seaweed of various species, used as a manure and in the manufacture of kelp, etc. [Chiefly Dial.]

wāre, *n.* [ME. *ware;* AS. *waru,* merchandise; specialized use of *waru,* watchful care, in the sense "what is kept safe."]
1. anything made to be sold; anything that a store, merchant, peddler, etc. has to sell.
2. things, usually of the same general kind, which are for sale; a (specified) kind of merchandise, collectively; generally in compounds, as hard*ware,* earthen*ware,* glass*ware.*
3. dishes made of baked and glazed clay; pottery, or a specified kind or make of pottery.
4. [*pl.*] things for sale, collectively.

wāre, *v.t.*; wared, *pt., pp.*; waring, *ppr.* [ME., from Scand.]
1. to spend, as money, time, etc. [Scot. and Brit. Dial.]
2. to waste; to squander. [Scot. and Brit. Dial.]

war ēa'gle, the golden eagle.

wāre'fụl, *a.* wary; watchful; cautious. [Obs.]

wāre'fụl·ness, *n.* wariness; cautiousness. [Obs.]

wȧ·rẹ'gȧ flȳ, a kind of fly of Brazil whose larvae are said to be parasitic upon men and animals, forming swellings under the skin.

wāre go͝ose, the brant, whose chief food is ware, or seaweed. [Brit. Dial.]

wä'rẹ·hō·ụ, *n.* [New Zealand.] a carangoid fish of New Zealand waters, as *Seriolella brama.*

wāre'house, *n.* 1. a building where wares, or goods, are stored, as before being distributed to retailers; a storehouse.
2. a wholesale store or, sometimes, a large retail store. [Chiefly Brit.]

wāre'houṣe, *v.t.*; warehoused, *pt., pp.*; warehousing, *ppr.* to place or store in a warehouse;

 fāte, fär, fȧst, fạll, finăl, cãre, at; mēte, prẹy, hẽr, met; pīne, marīne, bīrd, pin; nōte, mōve, fọr, atŏm, not; mo͞on, bo͝ok;

especially, to store in a bonded or government warehouse until the duties are paid.

wāre′house·măn, *n.*; *pl.* **wāre′house·men,** 1. one who owns, manages, or works in a warehouse.
2. a wholesale dealer in goods. [Brit.]
warehousemen's itch; eczema of the hands affecting those who handle irritating goods in a warehouse.

wāre′house rē·cēipt′ (-sēt′), a receipt issued by a warehouse for goods stored there: it is usually negotiable.

wāre′hous″ing, *n.* the act of placing goods in a warehouse or in a customhouse store; also the business of running a warehouse.
warehousing system; a customs regulation by which imported articles may be lodged in public or bonded warehouses at a reasonable rent, without payment of the duties on importation, until they be withdrawn for home consumption. If they are re-exported, no duty is charged.

wāre′less, *a.* 1. unwary; incautious; careless. [Archaic.]
2. heedless; regardless; unaware. [Archaic.]

wāre′ly, *adv.* cautiously; warily. [Obs.]

wär′ence, *n.* madder. [Obs.]

wāre′room, *n.* a room used for the sale or storing of wares or merchandise.

war′fāre, *n.* 1. an armed contest or struggle carried on by enemies; hostilities; the action of waging war.
2. a contest; a struggle; conflict of any kind.

war′fāre, *v.i.*; warfared, *pt., pp.*; warfaring, *ppr.* to carry on warfare or engage in war; to contend; to struggle.

war′fār·ēr, *n.* one whose occupation is warfare.

war′fȧ·rin, *n.* [*W*isconsin *A*lumni *R*esearch *F*oundation, and couma*rin*.]
1. a colorless, odorless, tasteless rat poison, $C_{19}H_{16}O_4$, a crystalline powder that causes fatal internal bleeding in rodents.
2. this drug neutralized with sodium hydroxide, used in medicine as an anticoagulant.

war gāme, 1. same as *kriegspiel*.
2. [*pl.*] practice maneuvers involving actual troops and military equipment.

war′hā″ble, *a.* fit for war. [Obs.]

war ham′mēr, a pick and hammer united, carried by medieval horse soldiers to fracture armor.

war head (hed), the head, or forward section, of a self-propelled torpedo or of a rocket- or jet-propelled projectile, containing the explosive charge.

war horse, 1. a horse used in war; a trooper's horse; a charger.
2. a person who has been through many battles or struggles; a veteran. [Colloq.]

wār′i·an·gle, *n.* a shrike. [Obs.]

wār′i·ly, *adv.* in a cautious or wary manner.

wār′i·ment, *n.* caution; wariness. [Obs.]

war′ine, *n.* a species of monkey of South America; a sapajou.

wār′i·ness, *n.* the quality or state of being wary; caution; prudent care to foresee and guard against evil.

wār′ish, *v.t.* to ward off the ill effects of; to heal. [Obs.]

wār′ish, *v.i.* to be healed. [Obs.]

war′i·sŏn, *n.* [ME.; OFr.]
1. a reward or gift given by a superior. [Obs.]
2. a note sounded to signal an attack: erroneously so used by Scott. [Pseudoarchaic.]

wärk, *n.* and *v.i.* ache; pain. [Scot. and Brit. Dial.]

wärk, *n.* work. [Obs.]

wär·kȧ·moo′wee, *n.* [Singhalese.] a canoe with outriggers, used in Ceylon.

wärk′loom, *n.* a tool; an instrument. [Scot.]

war′līke, *a.* 1. fit for, fond of, or ready for war; bellicose; martial.
2. military; pertaining or belonging to war.
3. having a martial appearance; having the qualities of a soldier. [Rare.]
4. threatening war; indicative of war.

war′līke·ness, *n.* a warlike disposition or character.

war′lock, *n.* [ME. *warlawe, warloghe*; AS. *wærloga*, a traitor, deceiver, liar.]
1. a person presumed to have supernatural power and knowledge by a supposed pact with evil spirits; a wizard; a sorcerer.
2. a conjurer or the like.

war′lock, *a.* of or pertaining to a warlock.

war′lock·ry, *n.* the condition or practices of a warlock; sorcery. [Archaic.]

war lord, 1. a high military officer in a warlike nation.
2. an agressive tyrant.
3. in China, a local ruler or bandit leader with some sort of military following in a district where the established government is weak.

war′ly, *a.* warlike. [Obs.]

warm, *a.*; *comp.* warmer; *superl.* warmest, [AS. *wearm*, warm.]
1. (a) having or giving off a moderate degree of heat; as, *warm* iron, *warm* weather, *warm* coffee; (b) giving off heat; as, a *warm* fire.
2. having the natural heat of living beings: said of the body, blood, etc.
3. (a) heated or overheated, as with exercise or hard work; (b) such as to make one heated or overheated; as, *warm* exercise, work, etc.
4. made of a cloth or material which keeps body heat in; as, *warm* clothing.
5. characterized by lively disagreement: said of argument or controversy.
6. fervent; ardent; enthusiastic; as, *warm* encouragement.
7. lively, vigorous, brisk, or animated.
8. fiery; quick to anger; irascible; heated.
9. (a) genial; cordial; as, a *warm* welcome; (b) sincere; grateful; as, *warm* thanks; (c) sympathetic, affectionate, or loving; (d) passionate; amorous.
10. suggesting warmth; having yellow, orange, or red hue: said of colors: opposed to *cool*.
11. newly made; fresh; strong: said of a scent or trail.
12. close to discovering something; on the verge of guessing or finding, as in games. [Colloq.]
13. disagreeable; uncomfortable; hot; as, we made things *warm* for him. [Colloq.]
14. well-to-do; well off. [Colloq.]
Syn.—thermal, genial, irascible, hot, ardent, affectionate, fervid, fiery, glowing, enthusiastic, zealous, eager, excited, interested, animated.

warm, *adv.* so as to be warm; warmly.

warm, *v.t.* 1. to make warm; to raise the temperature of to a moderate extent.
2. to make excited, animated, ardent, enthusiastic, lively, etc.
3. to fill with pleasant or kindly emotions; as, the sight of the children *warms* my heart.
to warm up; (a) to heat or be heated; to make or become warm; (b) to heat again, after cooling: said of food: also *to warm over*; (c) to make or become more animated, excited, ardent, enthusiastic, lively, etc.

warm, *v.i.* 1. to become warm.
2. to become friendly, kindly, affectionate, or sympathetic (often with *to* or *toward*).
3. to become excited, ardent, enthusiastic, lively, etc.
to warm up; in sports, to practice or exercise a while before going into a game, test of skill, race, etc.

warm, *n.* a warming or being warmed. [Colloq.]

warm′-blood″ed (-blud″), *a.* 1. having warm blood and a constant natural body heat, specific for each species: said of mammals and birds.
2. having or characterized by an eager, lively, or passionate temperament; ardent; fervent; impetuous.

warm′ēr, *n.* one who or that which warms.

warm′ful, *a.* causing or retaining heat. [Rare.]

warm′heärt″ed, *a.* 1. kind; sympathetic; friendly.
2. loving; ardent.

warm′heärt″ed·ness, *n.* the quality or state of being warmhearted.

warm′ing, *n.* 1. the act of one who warms.
2. a thrashing. [Slang.]

warm′ing pad, a chemical or electrical heating device designed to supply external heat to any part of the body or to any place, as a bed.

warm′ing pan, a covered pan of brass, etc., having a long handle, formerly used to warm beds by means of live coals or hot water.

warm′ish, *a.* somewhat warm.

warm′ly, *adv.* in a warm manner.

warm′ness, *n.* warmth.

war′mŏn·gēr, *n.* an advocate of war; a person or agency trying to start a war.

war′mouth, *n.* a fish, *Chænobryttus gulosus*, the red-eyed bream.

warmth, *n.* [ME. *wermthe*.]
1. the state or quality of having or giving off a moderate degree of heat.
2. the natural heat of a living body.
3. the degree of heat in a substance, especially when it is moderate; mild heat.
4. excitement, strength, or vigor of feeling; enthusiasm; ardor; zeal.
5. slight anger.
6. a glowing or intense effect obtained by using red, yellow, or orange.

warmth′less, *a.* without warmth; cold.

warm′-up, *n.* the act of practicing or exercising before going into a game, contest, race, etc.

warn, *v.t.*; warned, *pt., pp.*; warning, *ppr.* [ME. *warnien, warnen*; AS. *wearnian, warnian*, to take heed, warn.]
1. to tell (a person) of a danger, coming evil, misfortune, etc.; to put on guard against a person or thing.
2. to advise to be wary or cautious.
3. to caution about certain acts; to admonish; as, you have been *warned* against smoking here.
4. to notify in advance; to inform.
5. to give notice to (a person), as that he must appear at a specified place and time, or that he must stay or keep (*off, out*, etc.).

warn, *v.i.* to give warning; as, a rattlesnake *warns* before it strikes.

warn′ēr, *n.* an admonisher; one who or that which warns.

warne′stōre, *v.t.* and *n.* supply; store. [Obs.]

warn′ing, *n.* 1. the act of one that warns, or the state of being warned.
2. something that serves to warn.

warn′ing, *a.* that warns; serving to warn.

warn′ing·ly, *adv.* in a warning way.

warn′ing piēce, 1. a warning gun.
2. in horology, an oscillating piece in a clock which causes a rustling noise before the striking.

war nōse, 1. the nose, or tip, of a shell, containing the primer and firing mechanism, and sometimes the explosive charge.
2. the explosive tip of a torpedo or other projectile.

War of 1812, a war (1812–1815) between the United States and Great Britain.

War of Ȧ·mer′i·căn In·dē·pen′dence, the American Revolution. [Brit.]

War of In·dē·pen′dence, the American Revolution; the Revolutionary War.

War of Sē·ces′sion.(1861–1865), the American Civil War: also called *War between the States*.

warp, *n.* [AS. *wearp*, a warp, from *wearp*, pt. of *weorpan*, to throw, cast.]
1. (a) a distortion, as a twist or bend, in wood or in an object made of wood, caused by contraction in drying; (b) any like distortion; (c) the state or fact of being so distorted.
2. a mental twist, quirk, aberration, or bias.
3. (a) silt, sediment, or mud dropped by water, as by a stream; (b) a deposit of this.
4. in nautical usage, a rope or line run from a ship to a pile, buoy, anchor, etc., and used to move or haul the ship into position.
5. in weaving, the threads running lengthwise in the loom and crossed by the weft or woof.

warp, *v.t.*; warped (warpt), *pt., pp.*; warping, *ppr.* [ME. *warpen*, to throw, bend; AS. *weorpan*, to throw.]
1. to bend, curve, or twist out of shape; to distort.
2. (a) to turn from the true, natural, or right course; (b) to turn from a healthy, sane, or normal condition; to pervert; to bias: said of the mind, character, judgment, etc.; (c) to twist; to distort in telling; misinterpret; as, a *warped* account.
3. to fasten by binding with rope, string, twine, etc.; as, *warp* two sticks together.
4. in aeronautics, to bend or twist (a wing) at one or both ends, as to keep or regain lateral balance.
5. in nautical usage, to move, as a ship, by hauling on a line fastened to a pile, dock, anchor, etc.
6. in weaving, to arrange (threads or yarns) so as to form a warp.
7. in agriculture, to let in the tide upon (land), so as to fertilize with a deposit of warp, or slimy substance.
8. in ropemaking, to run (yarn) off the winches into hauls to be tarred.

9. to cast (the young) prematurely: said of cattle, sheep, etc. [Brit. Dial.]
10. to utter; to throw out. [Obs.]
11. to contrive; to weave. [Dial.]

wa̤rp, *v.i.* 1. to become bent or twisted out of shape; as, a board *warps* in seasoning.
2. to turn or incline from a straight, true, or proper course; to deviate.
3. to fly with a bending or waving motion, as a flock of birds.
4. in weaving, to arrange yarn ready for weaving.
5. in nautical usage, to move by warping or being warped, as a ship.

wa̤rp′ăġe, *n.* 1. the act of warping.
2. the charge made for warping a vessel to its berth.

wa̤r pāint, 1. a pigment applied to the face and body by primitive tribes in preparation for war.
2. ceremonial dress; regalia. [Slang.]
3. cosmetics; powder, rouge, and lipstick, as used by women. [Slang.]

wa̤r′pȧth, *n.* the route or path taken by North American Indians on a warlike expedition.
on the warpath; (a) at war, ready for war, or looking for war; (b) actively angry; ready to fight.

wa̤rp bēam, in weaving, the roller on which the warp is wound in a loom.

wa̤rp′ẽr, *n.* one who or that which warps.

wa̤rp frāme, a frame used in making warp lace.

wa̤rp′ing, *n.* in geology, the gradual distortion of rock strata by general crustal disturbance.

wa̤rp′ing bank, in agriculture, a bank used to retain water on land for the purpose of warping or enriching it with the sediment deposited.

wa̤rp′ing hook, a hook used by ropemakers to hang the yarn on, when warping into hauls for tarring.

wa̤rp lāce, wa̤rp net, a lace made on a warp frame, having its threads arranged in such a way as to resemble the warp of a fabric.

wa̤r′plāne, *n.* any airplane for use in war.

wa̤r′proof, *n.* valor tried by war.

wär′rȧ·găl, *n.* 1. the dingo, or Australian wild dog.
2. an aboriginal Australian.

wär′rȧ·găl, *a.* wild; savage. [Australian.]

wär′răn·dice, *n.* [OFr. *warantie*, guarantee, warranty, or warrantise.] a form of warranty in Scots law, by which the grantor of a right guarantees the grantee its full enjoyment.

wär′rănt, *n.* [ME. *warant*; OFr. *warant, guarant*, later *garant*, warrant, from O.H.G. *weren*, a warranty.]
1. (a) authorization or sanction, as by a superior or the law; (b) justification or reasonable grounds for some act, course, statement, or belief.
2. something that serves as an assurance, or guarantee, of some event or result.
3. a writing serving as authorization or certification for something; specifically, (a) authorization in writing for the payment or receipt of money; a voucher; (b) [Brit.] a receipt for goods stored in a warehouse; (c) in law, a writ or order authorizing an officer to make an arrest, seizure, or search, or perform some other designated act; (d) in military usage, the certificate of appointment to the grade of warrant officer.
general warrant; see under *general*.
justice's warrant; a warrant issued by a justice of the peace for the arrest of a person on a civil or criminal charge.
Syn.—authority, license, power, writ, order, evidence, pledge, voucher.

wär′rănt, *v.t.*; warranted, *pt., pp.*; warranting, *ppr.* [OFr. *warantir, garantir, guarantir*, to warrant, from *warant, garant*, a warrant, from O.H.G. *warjan, werjan*, to protect, defend.]
1. (a) to give (someone) authorization or sanction to do something; (b) to authorize (the doing of something).
2. to serve as justification or reasonable grounds for (an act, belief, etc.); as, my remarks did not *warrant* her tears.
3. to give formal assurance, or guarantee, to (someone) or for (something); specifically, (a) to guarantee the quality, quantity, condition, etc. of (goods) to the purchaser; (b) to guarantee to (the purchaser) that goods sold are as represented; (c) to guarantee to (the purchaser) the title of goods purchased; to assure of indemnification against loss; (d) in law, to guarantee the title of granted property to (the grantee).
4. to state with confidence; to affirm emphatically; as, I *warrant* he'll be late. [Colloq.]
Syn.—justify, assure, guarantee, authorize, maintain, sanction, secure, support.

wär′rănt·ȧ·ble, *a.* 1. capable of being warranted.
2. of the proper age to be hunted; as, a *warrantable* deer.

wär′rănt·ȧ·ble·ness, *n.* the state or quality of being warrantable.

wär′rănt·ȧ·bly, *adv.* so as to be warrantable; justifiably.

wär·răn·tee′, *n.* in law, the person to whom a warranty is issued.

wär′rănt·ẽr, *n.* one who warrants.

wär′rănt·īse, *n.* warranty. [Obs.]

wär′rănt·ise, *v.t.* to warrant. [Obs.]

wär′rănt of′fi·cẽr, in the United States armed forces, an officer of either of two grades ranking above an enlisted man but below a second lieutenant or ensign, holding his office on a warrant instead of a commission.

wär′rănt·ŏr, *n.* in law, one who warrants, or gives a warranty.

wär′rănt·y, *n.*; *pl.* **wär′rănt·ieṣ,** [OFr. *warantie, garantie*, warranty; from *garant*, a warrant.]
1. in law, a guarantee; specifically, (a) a guarantee or an assurance, explicit or implied, of something having to do with a contract, as of sale; especially, the seller's assurance to the purchaser that the goods or property is or shall be as represented; (b) a guarantee by the insured that the facts are as stated in regard to an insurance risk, or that specified conditions shall be fulfilled: it constitutes a part of the contract and must be fulfilled to keep the contract in force; (c) a covenant by which the seller of real estate gives assurance of, and binds himself to defend, the security of the title: also called *covenant of warranty*; (d) a warrant or writ.
2. official authorization or sanction.
3. justification; reasonable grounds, as for an opinion or action.

From your love I have a *warranty*
To unburden all my plots and purposes.
—Shak.

wär′rănt·y deed, in law, a deed to real estate containing a covenant of warranty: distinguished from *quitclaim deed*.

wa̤r′rāy, *v.t.* to make war upon. [Obs.]

wa̤rre, *a.* worse. [Obs.]

wär·ree′, *n.* [E. Ind.] the white-lipped peccary of South America, *Dicotyles labiatus*.

wär′ren, *n.* [ME. *wareine*; OFr. *warenne*, from *warir*, to preserve.]
1. originally, a piece of ground enclosed and preserved for the breeding of game; hence, a space or limited area where rabbits breed or are numerous.
2. any building or group of buildings crowded like a rabbit warren.
3. in English law, a franchise or place privileged by prescription or grant from the king, for keeping certain animals.

wär′ren·ẽr, *n.* the owner or keeper of a warren.

wa̤r′rẽr, *n.* one who wars or creates wars.

wär′rin, *n.* a bright-colored lorikeet of Australia, the *Trichoglossus multicolor*.

wär′ri·ŏr (*or* wa̤r′yẽr), *n.* [ME. *werreour*, from OFr. *werreiur*, an unrecorded spelling of *guerreiur*, warrior, from *guerreier*, to make war.] a man experienced or engaged in warfare; a fighting man.

wär′ri·ŏr ănt, the predatory slavemaking ant, *Formica sanguinea*, of Europe and North America.

wär′ri·ŏr·ess, *n.* a woman warrior.

wa̤r risk in·sūr′ănce, United States government insurance carried in time of war by members of the armed forces.

wa̤r′saw, *n.* [altered from Sp. *guasa*.] a very large grouper, *Garruper nigrita*, found in the warm waters about the West Indies and Florida.

wa̤r′ship, *n.* any ship constructed or armed for combat use, as a battleship, destroyer, etc.

wär′sle, *n., v.i.* and *v.t.*; warsled, *pt., pp.*; warsling, *ppr.* to wrestle: also spelled *warstle*. [Scot., Irish, and N.Eng. Dial.]

Wa̤rṣ of the Rōṣ′eṣ, the English civil war (1455–1485) fought between the House of York, whose emblem was a white rose, and the House of Lancaster, whose emblem was a red rose: the war ended with the establishment of the House of Tudor on the English throne.

wa̤r sọng, a song having war or warlike deeds for its subject; a patriotic song inciting to war.

wa̤rt, *n.* [ME. *werte*; AS. *wearte*, wart.]
1. a small, usually hard, tumorous growth on the skin.
2. a small protuberance, as a glandular protuberance on a plant.
venereal wart; same as *condyloma*.

wa̤rt çress, the swine cress.

wa̤rt′ed, *a.* having little knobs on the surface; verrucose; as, a *warted* capsule.

wa̤rt grȧss, the sun spurge, *Euphorbia Helioscopia*: so called because its juice is supposed to remove warts.

wa̤rt hog, any of a group of wild African hogs having a broad flat face, very large incurved tusks, and a number of conical warts between the eyes and tusks.

WART HOG
(3 ft. high at shoulder)

wa̤r′tīme, *n.* any time or period of war.

wa̤rt′less, *a.* without warts.

wa̤rt snāke, a hornless viviparous snake of India, especially *Acrochordus javanicus*: so called from its warty scales.

wa̤rt spūrġe, the sun spurge.

wa̤rt′weed, *n.* same as *wart grass*.

wa̤rt′wŏrt, *n.* any one of various plants, as (a) the wartweed, or sun spurge; (b) the cudweed; (c) the wart cress, or swine cress.

wa̤rt′y, *a.*; *comp.* wartier; *superl.* wartiest, 1. having warts; full of warts.
2. of the nature of a wart or warts; resembling warts.
3. having lumps like warts.
warty egg; a small marine gastropod having warty tubercles at each end.

wa̤r whoop (hōp), a loud shout or yell uttered, as by North American Indians, on going into battle, etc.

wa̤r′wick·īte, *n.* [named from *Warwick*, N. Y., where it is found.] a dark-brown or black mineral consisting of borate and titanate of magnesium and iron, occurring in slender rhombic prisms in granular limestone.

wa̤r′wolf (-wulf), *n.* a werewolf. [Obs.]

wa̤r′wolf, *n.* 1. a medieval military engine used to hurl missiles.
2. a fierce warrior. [Obs.]

wa̤r′wọrn, *a.* worn from military service; as, a *warworn* soldier.

wa̤r′y, *a.*; *comp.* warier; *superl.* wariest, [from *ware*, a., and *-y*.]
1. cautious; on one's guard; circumspect; prudent.
2. characterized by caution; as, a *wary* look.
wary of; careful of; suspicious of.
Syn.—cautious, careful, circumspect, calculating, politic.

wäs (*or* wuz), *v.* [AS. *wæs*, 1st and 3d pers. sing. of *wesan*, to be.] the first and third person singular of the past tense indicative of the verb *to be*.

wä·sä′bi, *n.* a Japanese condiment resembling horseradish, eaten grated with fish, etc.

wāṣe, *n.* a wisp, bundle, or pad of hay or straw. [Obs. or Dial.]

wäsh (*or* wọsh), *v.t.*; washed (wäsht *or* wọsht), *pt., pp.*; washing, *ppr.* [ME. *waschen, weschen*; AS. *wæscan*, towash.]
1. to clean by means of water or other liquid, as by dipping, tumbling, or scrubbing, often with soap, etc.
2. to make clean in a religious or moral sense; to purify.
3. to make wet; to moisten; to drench or flush with water or other liquid.
4. to flow over, past, or against: said of a sea, river, lake, waves, etc.
5. (a) to soak out or flush off and carry away, as dirt, a dye, etc., by or as by the use or action of water, or like water (with *off, out*, or *away*); (b) to pick up and carry along or away; as, the waves *washed* the stick away.
6. (a) to make by flowing over and wearing away substance; as, the rain *washed* gullies

in the bank; (b) to cut into or erode; to wear away by flowing over (with *out* or *away*); as, the flood *washed out* the road.

7. to act as a suitable cleaning agent for; as, the soap will *wash* silks.

8. to cover with a thin or watery coating of paint, especially of water color.

9. to cover with a thin layer of metal.

10. in chemistry, (a) to pass distilled water through (a precipitate in a filter); (b) to pass (a gas) over or through a liquid in order to remove soluble matter.

11. in mining, (a) to pass water through or over (earth, gravel, etc.) in order to separate ore, metal, precious stones, etc.; (b) to separate (the ore, etc.) in this way.

to wash down; (a) to clean by washing, especially with a stream of water; (b) to follow (a bite of food, a meal, a drink of whisky, etc.) with a drink, as of water, beer, etc.

to wash one's hands of; to disclaim any further responsibility for or interest in.

wȧsh, *v.i.* 1. to wash oneself or one's hands, face, etc.: often with *up*.

2. (a) to wash clothes; (b) to clean anything in, or by means of, water, etc.

3. to undergo washing, especially without fading or other damage.

4. to be removed by washing (usually with *out*); as, the stain *washed out*.

5. to sweep, beat, or flow (*over, against, along,* etc.) with a characteristic sound, as, in, or as in waves.

6. to be cut, worn, or carried by the action of water (with *out* or *away*); as, the bridge had *washed out*.

7. to be eroded, as by the action of rain or a river.

8. to withstand a test or examination; as, his story won't *wash*. [Brit. Colloq.]

to wash out; to drop or be dropped from a course because of failure, especially from training in military aviation. [Slang.]

wȧsh, *n.* 1. the act or process of washing.

2. a quantity of clothes, etc. washed, or to be washed, in one batch.

3. waste liquid; refuse liquid food, as from cooking; swill; hogwash.

4. (a) the rush, sweep, or surge of water or waves; (b) the sound of this; (c) water rushing, sweeping, or surging in waves; (d) the surge or eddy of water caused by a propeller, oars, paddle wheel, etc.; (e) a disturbed eddy of air left behind a moving airplane, propeller, etc.

5. wear or erosion caused by a flow or falling of water, or by the action of waves.

6. silt, mud, debris, etc. carried and dropped by running water, as of a stream.

7. soil or earth from which metals, ores, precious stones, etc. may be washed.

8. (a) low ground which is flooded part of the time, and partly dry the rest, with water standing in pools; (b) a bog; a marsh; (c) a shallow pool or pond, or a small stream; (d) a shallow arm of the sea or part of a river.

9. a channel made by running water.

10. in the western United States, the dry bed of a stream which flows only occasionally, usually in a ravine or canyon.

11. a thin, watery layer of paint, especially of water color, applied with even, continuous movement of the brush.

12. a thin coating of metal applied to a surface in liquid form.

13. any of various liquids for cosmetic, medicinal, or toilet use; as, a mouth *wash*.

14. fermented liquor ready for distillation.

15. a liquid for washing, tinting, etc.

16. weak liquor or liquid food.

17. water, carbonated water, beer, etc. drunk after a drink of undiluted whisky or other strong liquor; a chaser. [Colloq.]

to come out in the wash; to be revealed or explained sooner or later. [Slang.]

wȧsh, *a.* 1. washy; watery; weak. [Obs.]

2. that can be washed without damage; washable; as, a *wash* dress.

wȧsh'ȧ·ble, *a.* capable of being washed without injury: said of fabric, dyes, etc.

wȧsh'-and-wear', *a.* designating or of fabrics or garments that need little or no ironing after washing.

wȧsh bạll, a ball of soap, sometimes combined with cosmetics.

wȧsh bar'rel, a barrel of brine in which split mackerel are immersed to extract the blood before further curing.

wȧsh'bā″sin (-bā″sn), *n.* a washbowl.

wȧsh beȧr, the raccoon.

wȧsh'bōard, *n.* 1. a board with a ribbed or corrugated surface of metal, glass, etc. on which to wash clothes by hand.

2. in nautical usage, a broad, thin plank fixed along the gunwale of a boat or on the sill of a lower deck port to keep out the sea and spray.

3. a board fixed along the base of a wall at the floor; a baseboard; a mopboard.

wȧsh bot'tle, 1. in chemistry, an apparatus for directing a fine jet or stream of liquid onto a precipitate for the purpose of washing it, or for removing any residue of a solution or solid particles from one vessel to another.

2. a bottle partly filled with some fluid through which gases are passed to purify them.

wȧsh'bōwl, *n.* a bowl or basin for use in washing one's face and hands, etc.

wȧsh'clọth, *n.* a small cloth used in washing the body.

wȧsh'dāy, *n.* a day, often the same day every week, when the clothes of a household are washed.

wȧsh dĩrt, in placer and hydraulic mining, earth rich enough in gold or other metal to pay for washing it: also called *washing stuff* and *wash gravel*.

wȧsh'dish, *n.* 1. same as *washbowl*.

2. the pied wagtail. [Brit. Dial.]

wȧsh drạw'ing, a drawing on which the coloring is done in washes, as distinguished from work done in stipple, in body color, etc.

wȧshed (wosht), *a.* 1. having been subjected to the process of washing.

2. in zoology, overlaid with a surface tint or color on a ground color; as, a fox's black fur *washed* with silver.

wȧshed'-out', *a.* 1. faded; having little color.

2. tired; spiritless. [Colloq.]

3. tired-looking; pale and wan. [Colloq.]

wȧshed'-up', *a.* 1. cleaned up.

2. tired; exhausted. [Colloq.]

3. finished; done for; discarded or dismissed as a failure. [Slang.]

wȧsh'en, *v.* archaic and dialectal past participle of *wash*.

wȧsh'ẽr, *n.* 1. a person who washes.

2. a small flat perforated disk, as of metal, leather, rubber, or wood, placed under a nut or pivot head, or at an axle bearing or pipe joint, to serve as a cushion or packing.

3. in papermaking, a machine used in washing rags or reducing them to pulp.

4. in plumbing, an outlet pipe, as for a cistern, tank, or basin, plugged when not in use; also, the plug.

5. in mining, (a) a machine for washing coal; (b) an apparatus for washing ore, as a jigger or slime table.

6. a bird, the pied wagtail: also called *washdish, dishwasher, washtail, washerwoman,* etc. [Brit. Dial.]

7. the raccoon.

8. a machine for washing something, as clothes, dishes, etc.

9. a device for washing gases.

wȧsh'ẽr, *v.t.*; washered, *pt., pp.*; washering, *ppr.* to fit or furnish with washers.

wȧsh'ẽr·măn, *n.*; *pl.* **wȧsh'ẽr·men,** a man whose occupation is washing clothes, etc., especially for hire; a laundryman.

wȧsh'ẽr·wom″ăn (-woom″), *n.*; *pl.* **wȧsh'ẽr·wom″en** (-wim″), 1. a woman whose work is washing clothes, etc., especially for hire.

2. the pied wagtail. [Brit. Dial.]

wȧsh gild'ing, a gilding made by means of an amalgam of gold from which the mercury is afterward driven off by heat, leaving a coating of gold. Also called *mercurial gilding* and *water gilding*.

wȧsh goods, fabrics or garments that can be washed without injury to fibers or finish.

wȧsh gōurd, same as *sponge gourd*.

wȧsh'house, *n.* a building or an apartment, furnished with boilers, tubs, etc., for washing clothes; a laundry.

wȧsh'-in, *n.* [*wash,* v. and *in.*] a warp of an airplane wing, giving an increase of the angle of attack toward the tip.

wȧsh'i·ness, *n.* the state or quality of being washy or watery; lack of strength.

wȧsh'ing, *n.* 1. the act or process of a person or thing that washes; especially, the act of cleaning with water, soap and water, or other liquid.

2. the act or process of drenching, flushing, or coating with a liquid, or of dipping into a liquid, etc.

3. (a) [*also pl.*] liquid which has been used to wash something; (b) matter, especially waste matter, removed by washing.

4. (a) the process of carrying away matter by the flow of running water; (b) matter carried away by this action; (c) metal, ore, gems, etc. obtained by washing; (d) a placer or similar deposit where metal, etc. may be obtained by washing.

5. a thin coating or covering, as of metal, put on in liquid form.

6. clothes or other things washed or to be washed, especially in one batch or at one time.

7. the act of making a wash sale.

wȧsh'ing, *a.* of, for, or used in washing.

wȧsh'ing beȧr, the raccoon, *Procyon lotor*: so called from its habit of dipping its food into water as if to wash it before eating it.

wȧsh'ing mȧ·chine', a machine for washing clothes, etc., by moving or tumbling them through suds, operated by electricity, hand, steam, etc.

wȧsh'ing pow'dẽr, a detersive powder, as of sodium carbonate, used in washing clothes.

wȧsh'ing sō'dȧ, a crystalline form of sodium carbonate, used in washing.

wȧsh'ing stuff, same as *wash dirt*.

Wȧsh·ing·tō'ni·ȧ, *n.* [after George *Washington.*] a genus of palms, found in southern California and Mexico: one of the species is the Washington palm.

Wȧsh·ing·tō'ni·ăn, *a.* 1. of or pertaining to George Washington, first president of the United States, to Washington, D.C., the capital of the United States, or to Washington (State).

2. of or relating to the temperance societies founded in the United States, about 1843.

Wȧsh·ing·tō'ni·ăn, *n.* 1. a native or resident of Washington (State) or Washington, D.C.

2. a member of a Washingtonian society.

Wȧsh'ing·tŏn pälm (päm), a tall, slender palm crowned with large, fan-shaped leaves, growing especially in southern California.

Wȧsh'ing·tŏn pīe, a layer cake with a filling of cream, custard, chocolate, fruit jelly, or the like.

wȧsh leath'ẽr (leth'), leather prepared, sometimes from chamois skin, but more usually from split sheepskins with oil, in imitation of chamois.

wȧsh'ọff, *a.* in calico printing, that can be washed off: applied to certain colors or dyes which will not stand washing.

wȧsh'out, *n.* 1. the washing away of soil, earth, rocks, etc. by a sudden, strong flow of water.

2. a hole or gap made by such washing away, as in a road or railroad bed.

3. a complete failure. [Slang.]

wȧsh'pot, *n.* 1. a vessel in which anything is washed.

2. in tin-plating, the vessel in which iron sheet receives its final coating of tin.

wȧsh'rag, *n.* a washcloth.

wȧsh'rọom, *n.* 1. a room for washing.

2. a room provided with washbowls, toilets, etc., as in a railroad station; a restroom.

wȧsh sāle, in the stock exchange, the illegal and pretended sale of a security, to make it seem that the market is active.

wȧsh'stand, *n.* 1. a table holding a bowl and pitcher, etc., for washing the face and hands.

2. a plumbing fixture consisting essentially of a bowl or basin fitted with water faucets and a drain, used for washing the face and hands, etc.

wȧsh'tāil, *n.* the pied wagtail. [Brit. Dial.]

wȧsh'tub, *n.* a tub for washing clothes, etc.: often, a stationary metal tub fitted with water faucets and a drain.

wȧsh'wom″an (-woom″), *n.*; *pl.* **wȧsh'wom″en** (-wim″), a washerwoman.

wȧsh'y, *a.*; *comp.* washier; *superl.* washiest, 1. watery; diluted; weak.

2. without force or substance; insipid.

3. bringing rain or moisture: said of wind or weather. [Rare.]

wạs'n't, was not.

WĂSP, Wăsp, *n.* a white Anglo-Saxon Protestant.

wäsp, *n.* [ME. *waspe*, from AS. *wæsp*.]

1. any of a large number of winged insects of various genera belonging chiefly to the family *Vespidæ*, order *Hymenoptera*, and characterized by a slender body with the abdomen attached by a narrow stalk, biting mouth parts, and, in the females and workers, a vicious sting: some wasps, as the hornet, are characterized by a colonial or social organization.

WASP (cicada killer, 1 1/5 in. long)

2. a waspish person.

Come, come, you *wasp*; you are too angry. —Shak.

social wasps; wasps living in colonies.
solitary wasps; wasps which do not live in colonies, as the mud dauber.

wäsp bee, same as *cuckoo bee*.

wäsp bee'tle, a beetle resembling the wasp, of the genus *Cyllene*.

wäsp flȳ, a species of fly resembling a wasp, but having no sting and only two wings.

wäsp'ish, *a.* 1. of or like a wasp.
2. having a slender waist, like a wasp.
3. bad-tempered; easily irritated and made spiteful; snappish.

wäsp'ish·ly, *adv.* petulantly; in a snappish manner.

wäsp'ish·ness, *n.* the quality or state of being waspish; snappishness.

wäsp wāist, a very slender or pinched-in waist.

wäsp'-wāist″ed, *a.* 1. having a slender waist.
2. having the waist pinched in; tightly corseted.

wäsp'y, *a.*; *comp.* waspier; *superl.* waspiest, of, like, or characteristic of a wasp.

wäs'sȧil, *n.* [ME. *wasseyl*, *wassayl*, from AS. *wes*, be thou, imper. sing. 2nd pers. of *wesan*, to be, and *hāl*, whole.]

1. a festive occasion or meeting with much drinking and pledging of healths; a drinking bout; a carouse.

The king doth wake tonight and takes his rouse,
Keeps *wassail*. —Shak.

2. the liquor used on such occasions, especially around Christmas or the new year. It consists of ale (sometimes wine) sweetened with sugar, and flavored with nutmeg, cinnamon, cloves, roasted apples, etc. Also called *lamb's wool*.

But let no footstep beat the floor,
Nor bowl of *wassail* mantle warm. —Tennyson.

3. a merry drinking song. [Obs. or Brit. Dial.]
4. the salutation formerly given in drinking the health of a person, as at a festivity.

wäs'sȧil, *v.t.*; wassailed, *pt.*, *pp.*; wassailing, *ppr.* to drink to the health or prospering of.

wäs'sȧil, *v.i.* to drink wassails; to carouse.

wäs'sȧil bōwl, the bowl in which wassail was mixed.

wäs'sȧil çan'dle, a candle used at a wassail.

wäs'sȧil çup, a cup from which wassail was drunk.

wäs'sȧil·ẽr, *n.* one who wassails; a merry-maker; a reveler.

Wäs'sẽr·männ test (väs' *or Eng.* wäs'ẽr-măn), a test for the diagnosis of syphilis by determining the presence of syphilitic antibodies in the blood serum: devised by August von Wassermann: also called *Wassermann reaction*.

wäst, *v.* archaic second person singular, past tense indicative of *be*: used with *thou*.

wāst'āge, *n.* 1. loss by use, decay, deterioration, etc.
2. the process of wasting.
3. what is wasted; waste.
4. in geology, the process by which snow and ice masses eventually become water or vapor.

wāste, *v.t.*; wasted, *pt.*, *pp.*; wasting, *ppr.* [ME. *wasten*; Anglo-Fr. and O.Norm. Fr. *waster*, from L. *vastare*, to lay waste.]

1. to destroy; devastate; ruin, as land.
2. to wear away; to consume gradually; to use up.
3. to make weak, feeble, or emaciated; to wear away the strength, vigor, or life of: said especially of disease, decay, age, etc.
4. to use up or spend without need, profit, or proper return; to squander.
5. to fail to take proper advantage of; as, you *wasted* a good opportunity.

wāste, *v.i.* 1. to lose strength, health, vigor, flesh, etc., as by disease; to become weak or enfeebled (often with *away*.)
2. to be used up or worn down gradually; to become smaller or fewer by gradual loss.
3. to pass or be spent: said of time. [Now Rare.]
4. to be wasted, or not put to full or proper use.

wāste, *a.* 1. resembling a desert or wilderness; desolate; wild; dreary; bare and dismal.

His heart became appalled as he gazed forward into the *waste* darkness of futurity. —Scott.

2. left over, superfluous, refuse, or no longer of use; as, a *waste* product, *waste* paper.
3. produced in excess of what is or can be used; as, *waste* energy.
4. excreted from the body as useless or superfluous material, as feces or urine.
5. (a) used to carry off waste; as, a *waste* pipe; (b) used to hold discarded waste; as, a *waste*basket.

wāste, *n.* 1. uncultivated or uninhabited land, as a desert or wilderness.
2. a desolate, uncultivated, or devastated stretch, tract, or area; as, Berlin was a *waste* of tumbled walls.
3. a wasting or being wasted; specifically, (a) a useless or profitless spending or consuming; squandering, as of money, time, etc.; (b) a failure to take advantage (*of* something); (c) a gradual loss, decrease, or destruction by use, wear, decay, deterioration, etc.
4. useless, unneeded, or superfluous matter; discarded or excess material, as ashes, garbage, by-products, etc.
5. superfluous matter excreted from the body, as feces or urine.
6. cotton fiber or yarn left over from the process of milling, used for wiping machinery, packing bearings, etc.
7. ruin or devastation, as by war, etc. [Archaic.]
8. in physical geography, material derived by erosion or disintegration of rock, such as is carried to the sea by rivers, etc.
9. in law, spoil, destruction, or injury done to houses, woods, fences, lands, etc., by a tenant for life or for years, to the prejudice of the heir, or of him in reversion or remainder.

to go to waste; to be or become wasted.
to lay waste; to destroy; to devastate; to make desolate.

Syn.—loss, desolation, destruction, extravagance.

wāste'bȧs″ket, *n.* a basket or open-topped box for holding discarded things, especially wastepaper: also *wastepaper basket*.

wāste'bōard, *n.* same as *washboard*, sense 2.

wāste book, a book or ledger in which rough entries of transactions are made, previous to their being carried into the journal. [Chiefly British.]

wāste dust'ẽr, a cleansing machine used to collect factory waste.

wāste'fụl, *a.* 1. using more than is needed; squandering; extravagant.
2. in the habit of wasting; characterized by waste.
3. desolate; unoccupied; untilled; uncultivated. [Obs.]

Syn.—prodigal, extravagant, lavish.

wāste'fụl·ly, *adv.* in a wasteful manner; with lavishness or prodigality.

wāste'fụl·ness, *n.* the state or quality of being wasteful; lavishness; prodigality.

wāste gāte, a discharge gate for the surplus water of a dam or pond.

wäs'tel, *n.* a kind of fine white bread. [Obs.]

wāste'land, *n.* land that is uncultivated, barren, or without vegetation: also *waste land*.

wäs'tel çāke, a cake of the finest wheat flour. [Obs.]

wāste'ness, *n.* the state of being desolate or waste; desolation; solitude. [Rare.]

wāste'pā″pẽr, *n.* paper thrown away after use or as useless: also *waste paper*.

wāste'pā″pẽr bas'ket, a wastebasket.

wāste pick'ẽr, same as *ragpicker*, sense 2.

wāste pīpe, a pipe used for conveying away waste steam or water: distinguished from *soil pipe*.

wāst'ẽr, *n.* [ME. *wastour*.]

1. one who or that which wastes; especially, a spendthrift or prodigal; a wastrel.

Sconces are great *wasters* of candles. —Swift.

2. an imperfection in a candle wick: so called because by increasing the combustion it wastes the material of the candle. [Dial.]
3. a kind of barbed spear or trident for striking fish. [Scot.]
4. a cudgel or blunt sword used in fencing or swordplay. [Obs.]
5. that which is wasted or spoiled; an article spoiled in the process of manufacturing, as a spoiled casting, a tin plate deficient in weight, etc.

wāste'thrift, *n.* a spendthrift. [Obs.]

wāste'wēir, *n.* a gate or sluice in the bank of a canal, wall of a cistern, or the like, for the escape of superfluous water.

wāst'ing, *a.* 1. desolating; destructive; ruinous; as, *wasting war*.
2. causing waste.
3. destructive to health or vigor, as a disease.

wasting palsy; progressive muscular atrophy.

wāst'rel, *n.* 1. anything cast away as bad; waste substances; refuse.
2. anything allowed to run to waste or neglected, as waste land. [Obs.]
3. a person who wastes; especially, one who squanders money; a spendthrift.
4. a good-for-nothing.

wāst'y, *a.* of or pertaining to waste; resembling waste; specifically, denoting cotton waste.

wät, *v.t.* wot. [Obs.]

wät, *n.* a hare. [Obs.]

wät, *a.* wet. [Scot.]

wät, *n.* a fellow. [Obs.]

watch (woch), *n.* [ME. *wacche*; AS. *wæcce*, a watch, from *wacian*, to watch, from *wacan*, to wake.]

1. the act or fact of keeping awake, especially of keeping awake and alert, in order to look after, protect, or guard.
2. (a) any of the several periods into which the night was divided in ancient times; (b) a part of the night; as, the still *watches* of the night.
3. (a) close observation for a time, in order to see or find out something; (b) vigilant, careful guarding; as, keep a close *watch* over the baby.
4. a person or group on duty, especially at night, to protect or guard; a lookout or guard.
5. (a) the period of duty of a guard; (b) the post of a guard.
6. a small spring-driven timepiece carried in the pocket, worn on the wrist, etc.
7. (a) a vigil; a wake; (b) vigilance. [Obs.]
8. a candle marked off into sections, used for keeping time: each section burned for a known period. [Obs.]
9. a watchman's cry. [Obs.]
10. in nautical usage, (a) any of the periods of duty (five of four hours, and two of two hours) into which the day is divided on shipboard, to split the labor of working the ship between alternating parts of the crew; (b) the part of the crew, usually half of all personnel, on duty during such periods; (c) a ship's chronometer.
11. in falconry, a flock or company, as of nightingales. [Obs.]

on the watch; watching; on the lookout, as for some thing or person expected.
watch and ward; the ancient custom of watching by night and by day in towns and cities; a continuous and uninterrupted watching and guarding; constant vigilance and protection by night and by day.

wätch, *v.i.*; watched (wächt), *pt.*, *pp.*; watching, *ppr.* [ME. *wacchen*, from AS. *wæcce*, watch.]

1. to stay awake at night in devotion; to keep religious vigil.
2. to stay awake and alert at night; to care for or guard something at night.
3. to be on the alert; to be on the lookout; to be on guard; to keep guard.
4. to be looking or waiting attentively (with *for*); as, *watch for* your chance.
5. to look; to observe; as, most people just *watched*.
6. in nautical usage, to float on the surface of the water: said of a buoy.

to watch out; to be alert and on one's guard; to be careful.
to watch over; to be cautiously observant of; to inspect, superintend, and guard from error and danger.

wätch, *v.t.* 1. to look with close attention at or on; to keep carefully and constantly in view or under supervision.
2. to guard; as, to *watch* sheep.
3. to view mentally; to keep informed about.

4. to be on the alert or lookout for; to wait for and look for; as, *watch* your chance.
5. to keep watch over; to tend, as a flock.
6. in falconry, to keep awake; to keep from sleep, as a hawk, for the purpose of exhausting and taming it.

wätch bell, a large bell in ships which is struck each half hour: now usually called *ship's bell*.

wätch bill, in nautical usage, a list of the officers and crew of a ship who are appointed to the watch, together with the several stations to which each man belongs.

wätch box, a sentry box.

wätch'çāse, *n.* 1. the outside cover or metal case of a watch.
2. a sentry box. [Obs.]

wätch chāin, a chain or guard by which a watch is secured to the wearer's clothing, worn as a safeguard against loss and breakage, or as an ornament draped across the vest.

wätch çlock, a time recorder used by a watchman while in the performance of his duties.

wätch'dog, *n.* 1. a dog kept to guard property, as by barking or by attacking intruders.
2. any watchful guardian.

wätch'ẽr, *n.* one who or that which watches; specifically, one who attends to the sick during the night.

wätch'et, *a.* pale blue. [Obs.]

wätch fīre, a fire kept up during the night as a signal or for the use of a watch, guard, sentinels, etc.

wätch'fụl, *a.* 1. vigilant; alert; attentive; closely observant.
2. characterized by vigilance.
3. wakeful; unsleeping. [Archaic.]
Syn.—attentive, observant, cautious, circumspect, wakeful, vigilant, heedful.

wätch'fụl·ly, *adv.* in a watchful manner.

wätch'fụl·ness, *n.* the quality or state of being watchful.

wätch glȧss, 1. a glass or crystal for covering the face of a watch.
2. an hour or half-hour glass such as is used on board ships to measure the time of a watch on deck.

wätch guärd (gärd), a cord, ribbon, chain, etc., by which a watch is attached to clothing.

wätch gun, a gun that is fired, as on board ships of war, at the setting of the watch.

wätch'house, *n.* 1. a house in which a watch or guard is placed.
2. a house where disturbers of the peace are kept in custody; a lockup.

wätch kēy, a key used for winding a watch.

wätch līght (līt), a light used while sitting up or watching during the night; especially, in former times, a candle with a rush wick.

wätch'māk″ẽr, *n.* one whose occupation is to make and repair watches.

wätch'māk″ing, *n.* the business of making or repairing watches.

wätch'măn, *n.*; *pl.* **wätch'men,** a person hired to watch or guard, especially at night; specifically, (a) one who guards a factory, warehouse, estate, etc., as against thieves or trespassers; (b) formerly, one whose duty was to guard or police the streets at night.
watchman's rattle; an instrument having at the end of a handle a revolving arm, which, by the action of a strong spring upon cogs, produces, when in motion, a harsh rattling sound.

wätch'măn bee'tle, a European beetle, the dorbeetle.

wätch märk, in nautical usage, a distinguishing badge formerly worn by sailors on a battleship to indicate the watch to which they were detailed: by those of the starboard watch it was worn on the right arm; by those of the port watch, on the left arm.

wätch meet'ing, a religious meeting, for thanksgiving and petition, held on New Year's Eve; a watch night service.

wätch nīght (nīt), 1. New Year's Eve.
2. a watch meeting.

wätch pā'pẽr, an old-fashioned fancy ornament made of cut paper for the inside of a watchcase.

wätch pock'et, a small pocket, usually in a vest or trousers, for carrying a watch.

wätch taç'kle, in nautical usage, a small tackle with a tail on a double block.

wätch'tow″ẽr, *n.* a tower on which a sentinel or watchman is stationed to watch for enemies, forest fires, etc.

wätch'wŏrd, *n.* 1. the word given to sentinels, and to such as have occasion to pass the guards: used as a signal by which a friend is known from an enemy, or a person who has a right to pass the watch from one who has not; a password.
2. a word or phrase used as a motto, as expressive of a principle or rule of action; a rallying cry.

wätch'wŏrk, *n.* the machinery of a watch or similar mechanism.

wạ'tẽr, *n.* [AS. *wæter*; akin to G. *wasser*, water.]
1. the colorless, transparent liquid occurring on earth as rivers, lakes, oceans, etc., and falling from the clouds as rain: it is chemically a compound of hydrogen and oxygen, H_2O, and under laboratory conditions it freezes hard, forming ice, at 32°F. (0°C.) and boils, forming steam, at 212°F. (100°C.).
2. water in any of its forms, or in any amount, or occurring or distributed in any specified way, or for any use, as drinking, washing, etc.
3. [*often pl.*] a large body of water, as a river, lake, sea, etc.
4. (a) water with reference to its depth; as, ten feet of *water* at the dam; (b) water with reference to the depth of displacement of anything in it; as, the boat draws six feet of *water*; (c) water with reference to its surface; as, above *water*, under *water*; (d) water with reference to its level in a sea, river, etc.; as, high *water*, low *water*.
5. a leaking, breaking, or slopping of water into a boat, etc.; as, the ship is making *water*.
6. each of the applications of water in any process; as, diapers must be rinsed in three *waters*.
7. [*pl.*] the water of a mineral spring or group of such springs, used in therapy, etc.; as, to take the *waters* at Saratoga.
8. any body fluid or secretion; specifically, (a) urine, saliva, tears, gastric and pancreatic juices, etc.; (b) the fluid surrounding the fetus in pregnancy; amniotic fluid.
9. a solution of any substance, often a gas, in water; as, mineral *water*, ammonia *water*.
10. (a) the degree of transparence and luster of a precious stone, as a measure of its quality; as, a diamond of the first *water*; hence, (b) degree of quality or conformity to type; as, an artist of the first or purest *water*.
11. a wavy, lustrous finish given to linen, silk, rayon, etc. or to a metal surface.
12. a water-colored painting: opposed to *oil* (painting).
13. in finance, (a) a valuation given to the assets of a business in excess of their real value; (b) an issue of capital stock which brings the face value of all the stock issued by a business to a figure higher than the actual value of its assets.
above water; out of difficulty or trouble; free from trouble, debt, worry, etc.; as, to keep one's head *above water*.
benediction of the waters; in the Greek Church, a ceremony at the feast of the Epiphany, in which the waters of the ocean, the sea, and the streams are blessed.
by water; by ship or boat.
first water; see following *first*.
hard water; water containing mineral matter to the amount of ten grains or more to the gallon.
heavy water; see following *heavy*.
high-water mark; see under *high*.
holy water; water consecrated and used for the purification of persons and things in ritualistic ceremonies.
inch of water; same as *water-inch*.
interdiction of fire and water; in medieval law, an order that no one supply a banished person with fire or water, two essentials to the support of life.
like water; with bountiful supply; abundantly; lavishly; plentifully; without stint; as, to let money flow *like water*.
low-water mark; the lowest mark reached by the tide; figuratively, the lowest position or degree that can be reached; extremity; distress.
mineral water; water naturally or artificially impregnated with mineral salts; especially, any such water considered to have medicinal values.
soft water; water containing little or no mineral matter, such as rain water or water flowing in beds free from soluble substances.
thermal waters; waters issuing from hot springs; waters heated by natural causes in the crust of the earth.
to cast oil on troubled waters; to allay excitement or turmoil.
to hold water; (a) to contain water without leaking; hence, (b) to remain sound, consistent, or logical, with no breaks or weaknesses; as, the argument should *hold water*; (c) to keep a boat at a standstill by holding the oars steady in the water.
to make (or *pass*) *water*; to urinate.
to tread water; see under *tread*.
troubled waters; excitement; turmoil, as in an assembly of discordant factions.
under water; below the surface of water; figuratively, in misfortune.
water of crystallization; water that occurs as a constituent of crystalline substances and can be removed from them by the application of heat: the loss of water usually results in the loss of crystalline structure.
water of hydration; water which is chemically combined with a substance to form a hydrate.

wạ'tẽr, *v.t.*; watered, *pt., pp.*; watering, *ppr.* [ME. *wateren*; AS. *wæterian*.]
1. to give (an animal) water to drink.
2. to supply with water; as, large tanks were there to *water* the troops.
3. to give water to (soil, crops, etc.) by sprinkling, pouring, or irrigating.
4. to bring water to (land): said of a river, canal, etc.
5. to put water on (a pavement, etc.), by sprinkling, hosing, etc.; to soak or moisten with water (often with *down*).
6. to add water to so as to weaken; to dilute; as, she *waters* the milk.
7. to give a wavy luster to the surface of (silk, etc.).
8. in finance, to add to the total face value of (stock) without increasing assets to justify this valuation (often with *down*).

wạ'tẽr, *v.i.* 1. to fill with tears: said of the eyes.
2. to secrete or fill with saliva; as, his mouth *watered* when he saw the food.
3. to get or take in water for any purpose; as, the ship put into port to *water*.
4. to drink water: said of animals.
to make one's mouth water; to create a desire or appetite in one; to be or seem tasty.

wạ'tẽr, *a.* 1. of or for water.
2. in or on water; as, *water* sports.
3. growing in or living on or near water; as, *water* plants, *water* birds.
4. (a) operated by water; as, a *water* wheel; (b) derived from running water; as, *water* power.
5. containing water or fluid; as, a *water* blister.
6. prepared with water, as for thinning or hardening.
7. ruling, or having dominion, over water; as, *water* gods.

wạ'tẽr ad'dẽr, (a) the water moccasin, a venomous snake; (b) the common American water snake, *Tropidonotus sipedon*.

wạ'tẽr·āġe, *n.* in England, transportation of goods by water or the fee charged for it.

wạ'tẽr ag'ri·mō·ny, a European plant, *Bidens tripartita*, found growing in wet places.

wạ'tẽr al'ōe, same as *water soldier*.

wạ'tẽr an'tē·lōpe, same as *water buck*.

wạ'tẽr ap'ple, same as *custard apple*.

wạ'tẽr ā'rum, a perennial aroid plant, *Calla palustris*, with a creeping rootstock, heart-shaped leaves, and flowers in a fleshy head or spike, growing in cold boggy places in North America.

wạ'tẽr ash, 1. a small tree, *Fraxinus platycarpa*, growing in the swamps of the southern United States.
2. the black ground ash, *Fraxinus sambucifolia*.

wạ'tẽr av'enṣ, the purple avens, *Geum rivale*.

wạ'tẽr back, 1. an iron chamber or reservoir at the back of a cooking range or stove, to utilize the heat of the fire in keeping a supply of hot water.
2. a tank or cistern used for the water supply in breweries.

wạ'tẽr bāil'iff, 1. an English customhouse officer in a port town, employed in searching ships. [Obs.]
2. a former officer of the London corporation who saw to the observance of the statutes and bylaws applicable to the River Thames.
3. one who polices a salmon river to prevent poaching. [Brit.]

wạ'tẽr bal'lȧst, water kept in tanks or compartments in a ship's hold to serve as ballast.

wạ'tẽr bär, a ridge or furrow made on a steep road to turn rain water to one side.

wạ'tẽr bȧ·rom'e·tẽr, a barometer in which a column of water is substituted for mercury.

wa̤′tẽr bȧth, 1. a large deep bath of water at a certain temperature, in which vessels containing chemical preparations, etc., may stand for the purpose of heat or evaporation.
2. a bath composed of water, as distinguished from a vapor bath.
3. a bath of clear water, used in the development of phototypes. Two baths are usually used, one before and the other after the acid bath, to remove all traces of the chemicals.

wa̤′tẽr bēan, a variety of water lily, *Nelumbo speciosa.*

wa̤′tẽr beãr, a minute aquatic arachnid, as one of the *Arctisca.*

Wa̤′tẽr Beãr′ẽr, 1. in astronomy, Aquarius.
2. [w– b–] one who conveys water from a spring, well, etc., to sell.

wa̤′tẽr beãr′ing, a journal box into which water under pressure is admitted to act as a lubricant for the bearings.

wa̤′tẽr·bed, *n.* same as *water bed.*

wa̤′tẽr bed, a heavy vinyl bag filled with water and used as a bed or as a mattress in a special bed frame.

wa̤′tẽr beech, same as *hornbeam.*

wa̤′tẽr bee′tle, any of many beetles that live in fresh-water ponds and streams, having the last pair of legs fringed and functioning as oars.

wa̤′tẽr bel′lōws̱, same as *trompe.*

wa̤′tẽr bet′ō·ny, a plant, *Scrophularia aquatica.*

wa̤′tẽr bīrd, any bird that swims in, or lives on or near, the water; an aquatic bird; a waterfowl.

wa̤′tẽr bis′çuit (-kit), a cracker made of water, flour, and shortening.

wa̤′tẽr·bliñk, *n.* same as *water sky.*

wa̤′tẽr bliñks, same as *water chickweed.*

wa̤′tẽr blis′tẽr, 1. a blister containing a thin, watery fluid without pus or blood.
2. an elevation on a leaf of a plant caused by the heat of the sun shining through a drop of water.

wa̤′tẽr bō′ȧ, same as *anaconda.*

wa̤′tẽr bōard, a board fastened to the weather side of a boat to keep the water or spray out.

wa̤′tẽr bōat′măn, the boat fly, a hemipterous insect.

wa̤′tẽr-bōrne, *a.* 1. floating on water.
2. floated on water; launched.
3. carried by water, as in a ship.

wa̤′tẽr bosh, 1. the tank which supplies the tuyère of a blacksmith's shop with water.
2. a tank in a foundry which supplies the water used for core making, and for watering green sand molds.

wa̤′tẽr bot′tle, a bottle made of glass, skin, rubber, etc., to contain water.

wa̤′tẽr box, a large compartment of iron filled with water, covering the bottom or sides of a furnace to keep the iron from being burned out.

wa̤′tẽr boy, 1. a boy who brings drinking water to workers, as in the fields.
2. an assistant who brings drinking water, towels, etc. to athletes during the time outs of a contest.

wa̤′tẽr brāin, *n.* gid, a kind of staggers in sheep.

wa̤′tẽr brash, a form of indigestion; pyrosis; heartburn.

wa̤′tẽr brēath′ẽr, any animal breathing by means of gills.

wa̤′tẽr bridġe, a hollow partition at the back of a furnace communicating with the other water spaces, and forming part of the heating surface.

wa̤′tẽr·buck, *n.*; *pl.* **wa̤′tẽr·buck** *or* **wa̤′tẽr·bucks,** [D. *waterbok.*] any of certain large African antelopes, as those of the genus *Kobus,* having reddish or grayish fur and lyre-shaped horns: also called *water antelope* or *waterbok.*

wa̤′tẽr buç′klẽr, same as *water shield.*

wa̤′tẽr budġ′et, a heraldic device representing two water vessels connected by a yoke.

WATER BUDGETS
1. modern form: 2 and 3. earlier forms

wa̤′tẽr buf′fȧ·lō, any of several slow, powerful, oxlike animals native to Asia, Malaya, Africa, and the Philippine Islands, having a pair of large, strong horns growing from the sides of the head: it likes to wallow in mud and water and is used as a draft animal: also called *water ox* and (in the Philippine Islands) *carabao.*

wa̤′tẽr bug, 1. any one of various species of aquatic hemipterous insects.
2. a small cockroach; the croton bug.

wa̤′tẽr butt, a large open-headed cask set up on end in an outhouse or close to a dwelling, to serve as a reservoir for rain or pipe water.

wa̤′tẽr çal′trop, same as *water chestnut.*

wa̤′tẽr çar′riaġe (-rij), 1. transportation or conveyance by water.
2. the means of transporting by water; vessels or boats collectively.
3. the carrying or conveying of water from one place to another.

wa̤′tẽr çar′ri·ẽr, one who or that which carries water.

wa̤′tẽr çärt, a cart constructed for the carrying of water, as for sprinkling streets, etc.

wa̤′tẽr çȧsk, a strong cask used for carrying water, especially on ships.

wa̤′tẽr çā′vy, the capibara.

wa̤′tẽr cel′ẽr·y, *Ranunculus sceleratus,* an annual acrid herb growing in wet places both in the Old and New World: also called *cursed crowfoot.*

wa̤′tẽr cell, any cell containing water; especially, a water storage cell of a camel's stomach.

wa̤′tẽr cē·ment′, same as *hydraulic cement* under *hydraulic.*

wa̤′tẽr cen′ti·pēde, same as *hellgrammite.*

wa̤′tẽr·chat, *n.* 1. a tyrant flycatcher.
2. an East Indian fork-tailed bird.

wa̤′tẽr chest′nut (ches′), 1. a water plant, *Trapa natans,* with floating leaves, small white flowers, and nutlike fruit; also, the fruit.
2. (a) a Chinese sedge, *Eleocharis dulcis,* with erect cylindrical leaves, growing in dense clumps in water; (b) the large, button-shaped, submerged tubers of this plant, used in Chinese cooking.

wa̤′tẽr chev′rō·tāin, an African species of chevrotain or water deer frequenting the streams in the western part of the continent. It is striped and spotted with white and has a larger body and shorter legs than the other species.

wa̤′tẽr chick′en, same as *gallinule.*

wa̤′tẽr chick′weed, a small smooth green-tufted plant of the genus *Montia,* found growing in wet places in warm climates.

wa̤′tẽr chiñ′quȧ·pin (-kȧ-), 1. a water plant with blue-green leaves, large yellow flowers, and nutlike seeds; the American lotus.
2. its seed.

wa̤′tẽr çlock, the clepsydra; an instrument or machine serving to measure time by the fall or flow of water.

wa̤′tẽr çlos̱′et, 1. a small room with a flush toilet in it.
2. a flush toilet.

wa̤′tẽr çock, a species of gallinule, *Gallicrex cinerea,* found in Australia and the East Indies.

wa̤′tẽr çol′ly, the water ouzel. [Scot. and Brit. Dial.]

wa̤′tẽr çŏl′ŏr, 1. a pigment mixed with water instead of oil.
2. a painting done with pigments mixed with water.
3. the art of painting with water colors.

wa̤′tẽr-çŏl′ŏr, *a.* painted with water colors.

wa̤′tẽr-çŏl′ŏr·ist, *n.* one who uses water colors in painting.

wa̤′tẽr çol′umn (-um), a column up which the supply water for a water crane passes.

wa̤′tẽr-çōōl, *v.t.* to keep (an engine, machine gun, etc.) from overheating by circulating water around or through it, as in pipes.

wa̤′ter-çōōled, *a.* kept from overheating by circulating water; as, a *water-cooled* engine: distinguished from *air-cooled.*

wa̤′tẽr çōōl′ẽr, a device for cooling water, as for drinking, by passing it in a coil through ice or other refrigerant.

wa̤′tẽr çōre, 1. a blemish in certain apples in which the tissue close to the core has a watery, transparent appearance.
2. in founding, a hollow core inside a mold, through which water is passed to hasten the cooling of the casting: used especially in the making of heavy ordnance.

wa̤′tẽr·çōurse, *n.* 1. a stream of water; a river or brook.
2. a channel for water, as a canal or stream bed.
3. in law, a right to the benefit or flow of a river or stream, including that of having the course of the stream kept free from any interruption or disturbance, whether owing to a diversion of the water or to its obstruction or pollution.

wa̤′tẽr çow, 1. a female water buffalo.
2. the manatee.

wa̤′tẽr·çrȧft, *n.* 1. skill in handling boats or ships.
2. skill in a water sport, as swimming.
3. a boat, ship, raft, etc.
4. ships or boats, collectively; as, the harbor was crowded with *watercraft.*
Also *water craft* (in senses 3 and 4).

wa̤′tẽr çrāke, 1. the water rail, *Rallus aquaticus.*
2. the water ouzel.
3. the spotted rail or crake of Europe.

wa̤′tẽr çrāne, 1. an apparatus for conveying water from an elevated tank to some receptacle below.
2. a crane worked by hydraulic power.

wa̤′tẽr çress, a small perennial creeping plant, *Nasturtium officinale,* growing in watery places. Its leaves have a pungent flavor and are eaten as a salad and used in flavoring and garnishing. The name is also applied to other species of the genus *Nasturtium.*

wa̤′tẽr-çress, *a.* of water cress.

wa̤′tẽr çrōw, 1. the water ouzel. [Scot. and Brit. Dial.]
2. the common coot of Europe, *Fulica atra.* [Brit. Dial.]

wa̤′tẽr çrōw′foot, any one of several species of *Ranunculus*; especially, *Ranunculus aquatilis,* an aquatic plant with showy white flowers found in the North Temperate Zone and in Australia. The great or yellow water crowfoot is *Ranunculus multifidus.*

wa̤′tẽr·çup, *n.* 1. the pennywort.
2. the trumpetleaf.

wa̤′tẽr çūre, 1. hydropathy or hydrotherapy.
2. a form of torture in which the victim is forced to swallow large quantities of water. [Colloq.]

wa̤′tẽr deck, a painted piece of canvas used for covering the saddle and bridle, girths, etc. of a dragoon's horse. [Brit.]

wa̤′tẽr deer, 1. a small antlerless Chinese deer, *Hydropotes inermis.*
2. the water chevrotain.

wa̤′tẽr deer′let, the water chevrotain.

wa̤′tẽr dev′il, 1. the larva of various aquatic insects, as of the genus *Hydrophilus.*
2. the dobson or hellgrammite, *Corydalus cornutus.*

wa̤′tẽr dock, any of several species of dock growing in wet places, as *Rumex verticillatus* or *Rumex hydrolapathum.*

wa̤′tẽr doç′tŏr, 1. one of a former school of physicians who claimed ability to diagnose all diseases by an examination of the urine. [Colloq.]
2. a hydropathist. [Colloq.]

wa̤′tẽr dog, 1. any dog having unusual swimming powers or accustomed to or fond of going into water, as the water spaniel; also, any of several hunting dogs trained to retrieve waterfowl.
2. any of various large salamanders; a mud puppy.
3. a small irregular floating cloud thought to portend rain. [Brit. Dial.]
4. an old sailor or any person who is at home in or on the water. [Colloq.]

wa̤′tẽr dress′ing, in surgery, the treatment of wounds and ulcers by the application of water or of dressings saturated with water only.

wa̤′tẽr drop′pẽr, an apparatus used in connection with an electrometer for measuring the atmospheric potential.

wa̤′tẽr drop′wŏrt, the umbelliferous plant, *Œnanthe fistulosa,* or any plant of this genus.

wa̤′tẽr dust, minute particles or drops of condensed atmospheric vapor, as in clouds, fogs, haze, etc., considered collectively.

wa̤′tẽr ēa′gle, same as *osprey.*

wa̤′tẽred (-tẽrd), *a.* 1. sprinkled with water.
2. supplied with water; having streams: said of land.
3. having a wavy, lustrous pattern: said of cloth, metal surfaces, etc.
4. treated, prepared, or diluted with water.
5. in finance, inflated above its real value: said of stock, etc.

wa̤′tẽr el′dẽr, the guelder rose.

wa̤′tẽr el′ē·phănt, the hippopotamus.

wa̤′tẽr elm, the common white elm.

wa̤′tẽr en′ġine, an engine to raise water; also, an engine moved by water.

wa′tēr ē-quiv′a-lent, the quantity of water whose thermal capacity is equal to that of a given body.

wa′tēr-ēr, *n.* 1. one who waters, in any sense.
2. that with which one waters; especially, a contrivance for sprinkling water on plants.

wa′tēr-fall, *n.* 1. a steep fall of water, as of a stream, from a height; a cascade; a cataract.
2. a neck scarf with long ends. [Colloq.]
3. a chignon, or roll of hair worn low on the neck. [Colloq.]

wa′tēr feath′ēr, wa′tēr feath′ēr-foil (feth′), the featherfoil or water violet.

wa′tēr fen′nel, one of the water dropworts, *Œnanthe aquatica.*

wa′tēr fērn, a fern of the genus *Osmunda*; especially, the flowering fern, *Osmunda regalis.*

wa′tēr-find′ēr, *n.* a person who seeks out underground water and determines where to sink wells, by means of a divining rod; a dowser.

wa′tēr flag, the yellow flag or iris, *Iris pseudacorus.*

wa′tēr flax′seed, the larger duckmeat, *Lemna polyrhiza.*

wa′tēr flēa, any one of several small crustaceans which move about on the surface of water with sudden leaps.

wa′tēr-flōōd (-flud), *n.* a flood of water; an inundation.

wa′tēr flōw, the water flowing in a stream or current.

wa′tēr flȳ, a stone fly; a perlid.

wa′tēr-fowl, *n.*; *pl.* **wa′tēr-fowl** *or* **wa′tēr-fowls,** a water bird, especially one that swims: the collective plural is used of swimming game birds especially.

wa′tēr frāme, the original frame for spinning cotton, invented by Arkwright and so called because at first driven by water.

wa′tēr fringe, any plant of the genus *Nymphoides.*

wa′tēr-frŏnt, *a.* of a water front.

wa′tēr frŏnt, 1. land at the edge of a stream, harbor, etc.
2. the part of a city or town on such land; wharf or dock area.

wa′tēr fur′rōw, in agriculture, a deep furrow made for conducting surface water away and keeping the ground dry.

wa′tēr-fur-rōw, *v.t.* to plow or open water furrows in; to drain with water furrows.

wa′tēr gall, 1. a cavity made in the earth by a torrent of water.
2. an appearance in the sky thought to presage the approach of rain; an imperfectly formed or a secondary rainbow. [Obs.]

wa′tēr gang, an opening for the passage of water; also, a sluiceway. [Obs.]

wa′tēr gap, a deep notch or ravine in a mountain, through which a river flows; as, the *water gap* of the Delaware.

wa′tēr gas, a poisonous mixture of hydrogen and carbon monoxide, made by forcing steam over incandescent carbon fuel, as coke, and used as a fuel gas, etc.

Wa′tēr-gāte, *n.* [after *Watergate*, building complex in Washington, D.C., housing Democratic Party headquarters, burglarized (June, 1972) under direction of government officials.] a scandal that involves officials violating public trust through subterfuge, bribery, burglary, and other abuses of power in order to maintain their positions of authority.

Wa′tēr-gāte, *v.t.*; Watergated, *pt.*, *pp.*; Watergating, *ppr.* to deal with in a covert or criminal manner.

wa′tēr gāte, 1. a floodgate.
2. a gate through which access is had to a river, well, or any supply of water.

wa′tēr gāuge, 1. a gauge for measuring the level or flow of water in a stream or channel.
2. a device, as a glass tube, that shows the water level in a tank, boiler, etc.

wa′tēr gēr-man′dēr, a creeping European marsh plant, *Teucrium scordium.*

wa′tēr gild′ing, see *wash gilding.*

wa′tēr glad′i-ōle, same as *flowering rush* under *flowering.*

wa′tēr glȧss, 1. (a) a drinking glass or goblet; (b) a glass container for water, etc.
2. a glass water gauge.
3. a glass-bottomed tube or box for looking at things under water.
4. sodium silicate or, sometimes, potassium silicate, occurring as a stony powder, usually dissolved in water to form a colorless, sirupy liquid used as a preservative for eggs, etc.
5. a water clock; a clepsydra.

wa′tēr-glȧss, *n.* same as *water glass.*

wa′tēr gram′pus, a hellgrammite; a grampus.

wa′tēr grȧss, a tall succulent grass of the genus *Paspalum*: so called in the southern United States.

wa′tēr grāte, a grate in a furnace or boiler having hollow bars through which water is passed.

wa′tēr grū′el, a liquid food composed of water and a small portion of meal; a thin gruel.

wa′tēr gum, a small myrtaceous tree of New South Wales, *Tristania neriifolia.* Its flowers are yellow and its close-grained, elastic timber is used in building; also, in the United States, the tupelo.

wa′tēr gun, a toy gun that shoots water in a stream.

wa′tēr gut, an alga, *Ulva enteromorpha*, found in fresh and salt water, and so called because when floating in the water it resembles the intestines of an animal.

wa′tēr ham′mēr, 1. a sealed glass tube containing water and no air: when it is shaken, the water strikes against the ends with a hammerlike sound, demonstrating that solids and liquids fall at the same rate in a vacuum.
2. (a) the sound caused in a pipe containing water when live steam is passed through it; (b) the thump of water in a pipe when a faucet is suddenly closed.

wa′tēr hāre, the water rabbit.

wa′tēr hēat′ēr, 1. a heater for water.
2. any apparatus in which the heating of water is an essential.

wa′tēr hem′lock, any one of several species of plants of the genus *Cicuta*, with strong-smelling leaves, clusters of small white flowers, and a poisonous root; also, dead tongue, or a related plant, *Œnanthe aquatica.*

wa′tēr hemp, see under *hemp.*

wa′tēr hen, 1. the American coot.
2. any of various birds of the rail family, as the gallinule, moor hen, etc.

wa′tēr hōar′hound, a British plant, *Lycopus europæus*, or any other of the same genus.

wa′tēr hog, (a) the African river hog; (b) the capibara.

wa′tēr hōle, a dip or hole in the surface of the ground, in which water collects; a pond; a pool, especially one left in the dry bed of a stream.

wa′tēr horse′tāil, any plant of the genus *Chara*; a stonewort.

wa′tēr hȳ′a-cinth, any of several tropical aquatic plants belonging to the genus *Eichhornia.*

wa′tēr hys′sŏp, a creeping herb, *Bacopa monniera*, of the figwort family.

wa′tēr īce, 1. ice formed directly by the freezing of fresh water or salt water, as in a lake, bay, etc., rather than by the packing down of snow.
2. sherbet. [Brit.]

wa′tēr-inch, *n.* a former unit of hydraulic measure, calculated as the discharge of water through a circular opening one inch in diameter from a reservoir in which the water level stays just high enough to cover the mouth of the opening, equal to about fourteen pints per minute, or about 500 cubic feet per 24 hours.

wa′tēr-i-ness, *n.* the state or quality of being watery.

wa′tēr-ing, *n.* 1. the act of a person or thing that waters.
2. a wavelike, lustrous appearance on silk fabric, etc.
3. a watering place. [Obs.]

wa′tēr-ing, *a.* 1. that waters.
2. having water, as for animals.
3. of or having mineral springs or resort facilities for bathing, boating, etc.; as, a *watering* place.

wa′tēr-ing call, a call or sound of a trumpet on which the cavalry assemble to water their horses.

wa′tēr-ing plāce, 1. a place where a supply of water may be obtained.
2. a town or place to which people resort in order to drink mineral waters, or for bathing, etc., as at the seaside.

wa′tēr-ing pot, 1. a container, especially a can with a spout having a perforated nozzle, for sprinkling water on plants and the like.
2. any true bivalve somewhat resembling the teredos, of the genus *Brechites.*

wa′tēr-ing trough (trof), a trough where animals are watered.

wa′tēr-ish, *a.* 1. having the appearance of water; thin; watery; figuratively, weak; insipid.
2. having water; aqueous.
3. juicy; succulent. [Obs.]

wa′tēr-ish-ness, *n.* the state of being watery.

wa′tēr jack′et, a casing holding water, placed around something to be cooled or kept at a constant temperature, as by the circulation of the water; especially, such a casing around the cylinder or cylinders of an internal-combustion engine.

wa′tēr-jack′et, *v.t.* to encase or equip with a water jacket.

wa′tēr joint, a water tight joint.

wa′tēr jump, a pond, ditch, or other small body of water that a horse has to jump over, as in a steeplechase.

wa′tēr juñ′ket, the sandpiper. [Brit. Dial.]

wa′tēr-lāid, *a.* cable-laid.

Wa′tēr-lănd-ēr, Wa-tēr-land′i-ăn, *n.* a member of the more moderate of the two sections into which the Dutch Anabaptists became divided in the sixteenth century.

wa′tēr-lēaf, *n.* 1. any plant of the genus *Hydrophyllum.*
2. in paper manufacture, the pulp after having passed the felts.

wa′tēr leg, in steam boilers, a vertical water space connecting other water spaces and crossing a flue space, by which its contents are heated.

wa′tēr lem′ŏn, a tropical American plant *Passiflora laurifolia*; also, its fruit.

wa′tēr lens, a lens formed by water enclosed in a transparent material so as to act as a refractive medium.

wa′tēr-less, *a.* dry; without water.

wa′tēr let′tuce (-is), the plant *Pistia stratiotes.*

wa′tēr lev′el, 1. (a) the surface of still water; (b) the height of this.
2. the upper limit of ground water; water table.
3. a leveling instrument containing water in a glass tube.
4. the line to which the surface of the water comes on the side of a ship or boat; the water line.

wa′tēr lil′y, any plant or flower of the family *Nymphæaceæ*; specifically, any member of the genus *Castalia* (*Nymphæa*), found throughout the world. These aquatic plants are readily distinguishable by their orbicular floating leaves and their large, showy flowers, borne on long scapes at the surface of the water.
fringed water lily; same as *water fringe.*
New Zealand water lily; a species of crowfoot, *Ranunculus lyallii.*
prickly water lily; an East Indian plant, *Euryale ferox*, having the calyx and under side of the leaves covered with stiff spines.
royal water lily; the Victoria water lily of South America.
Victoria water lily; see *Victoria*, sense 2.
yellow water lily; the pond lily, *Nymphæa advena* or *Nuphar lutea.*

wa′tēr līme, same as *hydraulic lime* under *hydraulic.*

wa′tēr līne, 1. the line to which the surface of the water comes on the side of a ship or boat; water level.
2. any of several lines parallel with this, marked at various heights on the hull of a ship, indicating the various degrees of submergence when the ship is fully or partly loaded, or unloaded, and on an even keel.
3. a watermark.

wa′tēr liz′ărd, any aquatic reptile of the genus *Varanus.*

wa′tēr lō′cust, a variety of honey locust tree, *Gleditsia aquatica*, having a heavy hard wood. The tree is common in southern parts of the United States.

wa′tēr-logged, *a.* 1. soaked or filled with water so as to be almost awash, and heavy and sluggish in movement: said of boats or floating objects.
2. soaked with water; swampy.

Wa′tēr-lōō, *n.* [after the site of Napoleon's final defeat in Belgium, 1815.] any disastrous or decisive defeat.

wa′tēr lot, a submerged lot of ground, particularly one which may be redeemed by filling.

wa′tēr lō′tus, a species of the *Nelumbo.*

wa′tēr lung, any of the respiratory trees having a cleansing or excretory function, found in the cloaca of holothurians.

wa′tēr māin, a main pipe in a system of pipes which carry water.

wa′tēr māize, the Victoria water lily.

wa′tēr-măn, *n.*; *pl.* **wa′tēr-men,** 1. a boatman; a ferryman; a man who manages watercraft.

2. a person skilled in rowing, etc.; an oarsman.

wa̤′tẽr·măn·ship, *n.* 1. the work, business, or skill of a waterman (sense 1).
2. skill in rowing, etc.; oarsmanship.

wa̤′tẽr mar′i·gōld, an aquatic plant, *Bidens beckii*, having dissected submerged leaves.

wa̤′tẽr·märk, *n.* 1. a mark indicating the rise and fall of the tide; a water line.
2. in papermaking, (a) a mark in paper, produced by pressure of a projecting design, as in the mold, during manufacture: it can be seen when the paper is held up to the light; (b) the projecting design that produces this.

wa̤′tẽr·märk, *v.t.*; watermarked (-märkt), *pt.*, *pp.*; watermarking, *ppr.* 1. to mark (paper) with a watermark.
2. to impress (a design) as a watermark.

wa̤′tẽr mead′ōw (med′), a meadow so situated that it can become overflowed with water from an adjoining stream.

wa̤′tẽr meas′ūre (mezh′), a former measure for articles brought by water, as coal, oysters, etc. This bushel was larger than the Winchester measure by about three gallons. [Brit.]

wa̤′tẽr meas′ūr·ẽr, an aquatic hemipterous insect; a skater.

wa̤′tẽr·mel″ŏn, *n.* 1. a large, round or oblong fruit with a hard, green rind and juicy, pink or red pulp containing many seeds.
2. the vine on which it grows, *Citrullus vulgaris*.

wa̤′tẽr mē′tẽr, an instrument that measures and records the quantity of water flowing through a pipe, etc.

wa̤′tẽr mil′foil, any one of several aquatic plants of the genus *Myriophyllum*.

wa̤′tẽr mill, a mill whose machinery is driven by water.

wa̤′tẽr mint, the bergamot mint, *Mentha aquatica*, a European herb which grows in wet places and furnishes a perfumers' oil.

wa̤′tẽr mīte, any aquatic insect of the family *Hydrachnidæ*.

wa̤′tẽr moc′ca̤·sin, 1. a large, poisonous, olive-brown viper with dark cross bars, related to the copperhead and found along river banks and swamps of the southern United States: also called *cottonmouth*.
2. any of several harmless water snakes resembling this.

wa̤′tẽr mōle, 1. a desman; any mole of the genus *Myogale*.
2. same as *duckbill*.

wa̤′tẽr mon′i·tŏr, a large aquatic lizard of the family *Varanidæ* or *Monitoridæ*.

wa̤′tẽr mŏn′key, an earthenware vessel, globular in shape and with a straight, vertical neck, used in tropical countries for holding water.

wa̤′tẽr mo̤th, a caddis fly.

wa̤′tẽr mō′tŏr, any water wheel or water engine; particularly, any small motor using water under pressure for driving light machinery, as folding presses.

wa̤′tẽr mouse, a beaver rat.

wa̤′tẽr myr′tle (mẽr′), same as *water gum*.

wa̤′tẽr net, a species of green-spored algae, of the genus *Hydrodictyon*, which has the appearance of a green net, composed of filaments enclosing pentagonal and hexagonal spaces.

wa̤′tẽr newt, any aquatic newt; a triton.

wa̤′tẽr nut, one of the large edible seeds of plants of the genus *Trapa*; a Singhara nut.

wa̤′tẽr nymph, 1. in Greek and Roman mythology, a goddess having the form of a lovely young girl, supposed to dwell in a stream, pool, lake, etc.; naiad, Nereid, Oceanid, etc.
2. a water lily of the genus *Nymphæa*.
3. any plant of the genus *Naias*.

wa̤′tẽr ōak, 1. any of several American oaks.
2. an oak, *Quercus nigra*, of the southeastern United States, found mainly along rivers, streams, etc.

wa̤′tẽr ōats, a species of water grass; Indian rice.

wa̤′tẽr ō·pos′sum, the yapok of South America.

wa̤′tẽr o̤r·dēal′, a form of ordeal in which water is the testing medium.

wa̤′tẽr ou̇′zel, a bird, *Cinclus aquaticus*; the dipper.

wa̤′tẽr ox, the water buffalo.

wa̤′tẽr pad′dȧ, a toad, *Breviceps gibbosus*, found in South Africa.

wa̤′tẽr pärs′nip, a plant of the genus *Sium*; particularly, *Sium sisarum*.

wa̤′tẽr pärt′ing, same as *watershed*.

wa̤′tẽr pär′tridġe (-trij), the ruddy duck, *Erismatura rubida*. [Dial.]

wa̤′tẽr pen′ny·wŏrt, the marsh pennywort.

wa̤′tẽr pep′pẽr, 1. the smartweed, *Polygonum Hydropiper*.
2. same as *waterwort*, sense 1.

wa̤′tẽr pē′wit, an aquatic pewit; a phoebe.

wa̤′tẽr pheas′ănt (fez′), 1. same as *pintail*, sense 1.
2. the Chinese jacana, *Hydrophasianus chirurgus*.
3. the goosander, *Mergus merganser*.
4. the hooded merganser, *Lophodytes cucullatus*.

wa̤′tẽr·phōne, *n.* an instrument for observing the flow of water or detecting leakage in underground pipes; a hydrophone.

wa̤′tẽr pī′et, the water ouzel. [Scot.]

wa̤′tẽr pig, 1. same as *capibara*.
2. a fish, the goramy.

wa̤′tẽr pil′lăr, a waterspout. [Obs.]

wa̤′tẽr pim′pẽr·nel, 1. a small plant with oblong leaves and white, pink, or blue flowers, generally found along the edge of brooks; brookline; brookweed.
2. the common pimpernel.

wa̤′tẽr pīpe, 1. a pipe for the conveyance of water.
2. a waterspout. [Obs.]
3. a kind of smoking pipe in which the smoke is drawn through water; a hookah.

wa̤′tẽr pip′it, the titlark, *Anthus aquaticus*.

wa̤′tẽr pitch′ẽr, 1. a pitcher for holding water.
2. any of a number of plants of the order *Sarraceniaceæ*, of which *Sarracenia purpurea*, or sidesaddle flower, a plant growing in marshy places in North America, is the type. They take their name from the form of their leaves, which somewhat resemble pitchers.

wa̤′tẽr plant, 1. any plant living entirely below water or sending up stems and leaves to or above the surface.
2. any plant able to grow either on land or in water.

wa̤′tẽr plan′tāin, an aquatic plant of the genus *Alisma*; particularly, *Alisma plantago*, the common water plantain, having large, heart-shaped leaves and small, usually white, flowers.

wa̤′tẽr plāte, a plate with a double bottom filled with hot water to keep food warm.

wa̤′tẽr plat′tẽr, same as *victoria* (the water lily).

wa̤′tẽr pō′ȧ, the reed meadow grass, *Glyceria aquatica*.

wa̤′tẽr pock′et, a small hollow or basin caused by the action of water, as a water hole in the bed of a stream which runs erratically or a bowl at the base of an embankment or bluff over which water rushes during a flood. [Dial.]

wa̤′tẽr poise, a hydrometer.

wa̤′tẽr pō′lō, a water game played with a round, partly inflated ball by two teams of swimmers, the object of the game being to pass or take the ball over the opponent's goal line.

wa̤′tẽr pōre, 1. in botany, a pore in the epidermis of some plants through which water is sometimes expelled.
2. in zoology, an orifice which constitutes the exterior mouth of a water tube.

wa̤′tẽr·pot, *n.* a vessel for holding or conveying water; a watering pot.

wa̤′tẽr pow′ẽr, 1. the power of running or falling water, used to drive machinery, etc., or capable of being so used.
2. a fall of water that can be so used.
3. a water right or privilege owned by a mill.

wa̤′tẽr pox, chicken pox; varicella.

wa̤′tẽr priv′i·leġe, the right to use running water to turn machinery.

wa̤′tẽr·pro͞of, *a.* impervious to water; so firm and compact as not to admit water; as, *waterproof* cloth, leather, or felt.

wa̤′tẽr·pro͞of, *n.* 1. waterproof cloth or other material.
2. a raincoat or other outer garment of waterproof material. [Chiefly Brit.]

wa̤′tẽr·pro͞of, *v.t.*; waterproofed (-pröft), *pt.*, *pp.*; waterproofing, *ppr.* to make waterproof, as cloth, leather, etc.

wa̤′tẽr·pro͞of″ing, *n.* 1. the process of making waterproof.
2. a composition for making articles waterproof.

wa̤′tẽr pũrs′lāne, a red-stemmed trailing plant found in watery or muddy places.

wa̤′tẽr quälm (kwäm), pyrosis.

wa̤′tẽr rab′bit, the swamp hare, *Lepus aquaticus*, found in the lower valley of the Mississippi.

wa̤′tẽr rad′ish, a species of water cress, *Nasturtium amphibium*.

wa̤′tẽr rāil, 1. the common European rail, *Rallus aquaticus*.
2. the European gallinule.

wa̤′tẽr ram, a hydraulic ram.

wa̤′tẽr rat, 1. any of several European voles that live on the banks of streams and ponds.
2. an American muskrat.
3. a water-front thief or tramp. [Slang.]

wa̤′tẽr rāte, a rate or tax for the supply of water.

wa̤′tẽr rat′tle, the water rattler.

wa̤′ter rat′tler, the diamond rattlesnake, *Crotalus adamanteus*, found in damp places near water.

wa̤′tẽr reed, a coarse kind of grass of the genus *Arundo*, growing in wet places.

wa̤′tẽr rē·sẽrve′, in Australia, land set apart to reinforce streams which serve as a source of water supply.

wa̤′tẽr-ret, *v.t.* same as *water-rot*.

wa̤′tẽr rīce, a kind of grass; Indian rice.

wa̤′tẽr rock′et, 1. a plant of the genus *Nasturtium*; water cress.
2. a kind of firework to be discharged in the water.

wa̤′tẽr-rōlled, *a.* smooth as from having been rolled in the water and worn by friction with gravel, etc.; as, *water-rolled* pebbles.

wa̤′tẽr rōse, the water lily.

wa̤′tẽr-rot, *v.t.*; water-rotted, *pt.*, *pp.*; water-rotting, *ppr.* to cause to rot by steeping in water; as, to *water-rot* hemp or flax.

wa̤′tẽr sāil, a small sail sometimes used under a studdingsail or driver boom.

wa̤′tẽr sap′phīre (saf′īr), [transl. of Fr. *saphir d'eau*.] a deep-blue, transparent variety of iolite, sometimes used as a gem.

wa̤′tẽr·scāpe, *n.* [from water, after *landscape*.] a view of a body of water; especially, a picture containing such a view; seascape.

wa̤′tẽr sco̤r′pi·ŏn, a voracious aquatic insect of the family *Nepidæ*; the scorpion bug, distinguished by a long breathing tube at the end of the abdomen.

wa̤′tẽr sc̤rew (skrü), a water elevator with spiral vanes placed on a slanting axis rotating inside of a casing: a modern application of the Archimedean screw.

wa̤′tẽr sēal, a body of water which serves to prevent the flow or escape of gas.

wa̤′tẽr sen′green, same as *water soldier*.

wa̤′tẽr sẽr′pent, a sea serpent. [Obs.]

wa̤′tẽr·shed, *n.* 1. a ridge or stretch of high land dividing the area drained by different rivers or river systems.
2. the area drained by a river or river system.

wa̤′tẽr·shiēld, *n.* 1. a purple-flowered water plant having floating leaves coated underneath with a jellylike substance.
2. any of a number of related water plants with roundish leaves on the water and finely cut leaves below.

wa̤′tẽr·sho͞ot, *n.* 1. a sprig or shoot from the root or stock of a tree.
2. a wooden trough for discharging water from a building.
3. in architecture, a dripstone.

wa̤′tẽr shrew (shrö), an aquatic shrew with oar-shaped feet: the common European species is *Crossopus fodiens*; the similar American species is *Neosorex palustris*.

wa̤′tẽr-sick″, *a.* not fertile or cultivable because of too much water: said of land which is irrigated to excess.

wa̤′tẽr·sīde, *n.* the margin or bank of a body of water, as a river, lake, etc.; the seashore.

wa̤′tẽr·sīde, *a.* 1. of or located on the waterside.
2. living or working along the shore.

wa̤′tẽr sil′vẽr·ing, silvering by a process similar to that used in wash gilding.

wa̤′tẽr·skin, a sack made of an animal's skin and used to hold drinking water.

wa̤′tẽr skip′pẽr, any long-legged aquatic bug which skips about on the surface of fresh water.

wa̤′tẽr skȳ, a dull, dark sky, caused by the reflection of the sea, thus indicating open water when observed above an ice-bound sea.

wa̧'tẽr slā'tẽr, an aquatic isopod of the genus *Asellus.*

wa̧'tẽr smärt'weed, a weed, *Polygonum acre*, growing in shallow water or wet soil, having acrid juice in the leaves.

wa̧'tẽr snāil, 1. one of a group of gastropodous mollusks living in water.

2. the Archimedean screw. [Rare.]

wa̧'tẽr snāke, any of various nonpoisonous snakes living in fresh-water streams and rivers, feeding on water animals, and found throughout the tropical and temperate zones.

wa̧'tẽr-sōak, *v.t.* to soak or fill the interstices of with water; to saturate.

wa̧'tẽr socks, the white water lily. [Obs.]

wa̧'tẽr sōl'diẽr (-jẽr), an aquatic plant, *Stratiotes aloides*, of the frogbit family, with long swordlike leaves, and flowers resembling plumes of white feathers.

wa̧'tẽr-sol"ū·ble, *a.* that can be dissolved in water: said especially of certain vitamins, and opposed to *fat-soluble.*

wa̧'tẽr söuch'y, a dish of small fish served in the water in which they were cooked.

wä'tẽr span'iel (-yel), either of two breeds of spaniel especially suited to retrieving game shot over water, and characterized by a curly, reddish-brown coat.

wa̧'tẽr speed'well, a low herb, *Veronica anagallis*, of the figwort family, growing in water.

wa̧'tẽr spī'dẽr, 1. an aquatic spider, *Argyroneta aquatica*, which builds its nest in the form of a silklike bag on plants below the surface of the water, with the opening downward. It fills this bag with air carried down in the form of bubbles attached to the legs.

2. any one of various spiders living on and near the surface of water and building their nests on overhanging plants at the surface of the water.

3. a water mite.

wa̧'tẽr spīke, a pondweed of the genus *Potamogeton.*

wa̧'tẽr spin'nẽr, same as *water spider.*

wa̧'tẽr·spout, *n.* 1. a hole, pipe, or spout from which water runs.

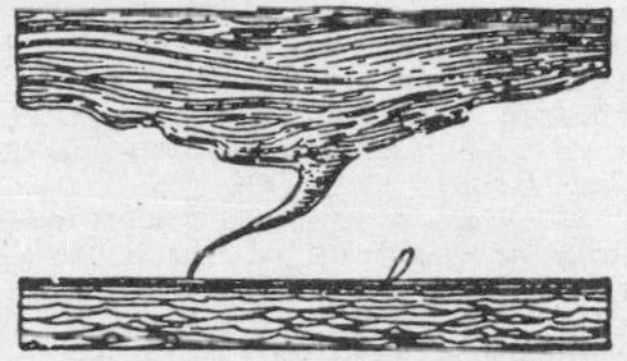

WATERSPOUT

2. a fast-moving, rapidly rotating, funnel-shaped or tubelike column of air full of mist and moisture, extending downward from a storm cloud to the surface of a body of water.

wa̧'tẽr sprīte, a sprite or spirit supposedly dwelling near or haunting the water; a water nymph.

wa̧'tẽr sprout, a water shoot.

wa̧'tẽr-stand'ing, *a.* filled with tears; as, a *water-standing* eye. [Rare.]

wa̧'tẽr stär, same as *star fruit.*

wa̧'tẽr stär grȧss, an aquatic herb of the genus *Schollera*, having star-shaped flowers and grasslike leaves.

wa̧'tẽr stär'wŏrt, an aquatic plant, *Callitriche verna*, of the water-milfoil family, having starlike scales on its leaves and bearing some resemblance to chickweed.

wa̧'tẽr stō'mȧ, same as *water pore.*

wa̧'tẽr strīd'ẽr, same as *water skipper.*

wa̧'tẽr sup·plȳ', 1. the water available for use of a community or in an area.

2. the system for storing and supplying such water, as the reservoirs, mains, etc.

wa̧'tẽr swäl'lōw, same as *water wagtail.*

wa̧'tẽr sys'tem, 1. a river with all its tributaries.

2. a water supply; plumbing system.

wa̧'tẽr tab'by, tabby having a wavelike sheen.

wa̧'tẽr tā'ble, 1. in architecture, a strong, coarse molding or other projection in the wall of a building to throw off rainwater.

2. a channel along a road for draining off water.

3. the level below which the ground is saturated with water.

wa̧'tẽr tär'get, same as *water shield.*

wa̧'tẽr tel'ē·sco̧pe, same as *water glass* (sense 3).

wa̧'tẽr thiēf, a pirate. [Rare.]

wa̧'tẽr thrush, 1. either of two North American warblers of the genus *Seiurus*, inhabiting the borders of swamps and streams; specifically, *Seiurus noveboracensis* of the North and *Seiurus motacilla* of the South: also called *water wagtail.*

2. the water ouzel.

wa̧'tẽr thȳme (tīm), the waterweed, *Elodea canadensis.*

wa̧'tẽr tick, a water mite.

wa̧'tẽr tī'gẽr, the larva of a water beetle.

wa̧'tẽr·tīght (-tīt), *a.* 1. so snugly put together that no water can get in or through.

2. so carefully stated that it cannot be misconstrued or misunderstood.

3. that cannot be defeated, nullified, etc.; as, a *watertight* plan.

wa̧'tẽr·tīght"ness, *n.* the quality of being watertight.

wa̧'tẽr to̧rch, the cattail, *Typha latifolia*: so called because its spike when soaked in oil burns like a torch.

wa̧'tẽr tow'ẽr, 1. an elevated tank used for water storage and for maintaining equalized pressure on a water system.

2. a firefighting apparatus that can be used to lift high pressure hose and nozzles to great heights.

wa̧'tẽr tree, an African vine of the genus *Tetracera*, containing a large quantity of watery sap.

wa̧'tẽr trē'foil, the buck bean.

wa̧'tẽr tūbe, one of a system of excretory tubes in many invertebrates.

wa̧'tẽr tū'pe·lō, a large species of tupelo, *Nyssa aquatica*, growing in swamps in the southern United States.

wa̧'tẽr tũr'key, the snakebird of America.

wa̧'tẽr tu·yère' (twē-yãr'), in metallurgy, a tuyère so constructed that cold water is made to flow in a continuous stream around the blast of air.

wa̧'tẽr twist, a kind of cotton twist made by the water frame.

wa̧'tẽr vā'pŏr, water in the form of mist or tiny diffused particles, especially when below the boiling point, as in the air: distinguished from *steam.*

wa̧'tẽr-vas'ço̧ū·lăr, *a.* in zoology, pertaining to a system of canals in many invertebrates, by which water circulates through the system.

wa̧'tẽr vīne, any climbing shrub of the genus *Phytocrene*, containing a watery sap sometimes used for drinking.

wa̧'tẽr vī'ō·let, an aquatic plant of the genus *Hottonia*; featherfoil.

wa̧'tẽr vī'pẽr, same as *water moccasin.*

wa̧'tẽr vōle, an aquatic European vole, *Arvicola amphibius*; a water rat.

wa̧'tẽr wag'ŏn, see under *wagon.*

wa̧'tẽr wag'tāil, 1. any of several species of wagtails of the genus *Motacilla.*

2. a water thrush of the genus *Seiurus.* [Dial.]

wa̧'tẽr-wāve, *v.t.*; water-waved, *pt., pp.*; water-waving, *ppr.* to make water waves in (hair).

wa̧'tẽr wāve, 1. a wave made in hair by moistening and setting it with a comb, and drying it with heat, usually from a drier.

2. a wave of water; a billow.

wa̧'tẽr·wāy, *n.* 1. a channel or runnel through or along which water runs.

2. any body of water wide enough and deep enough for boats, ships, etc., as a stream, canal, or channel; a water route.

3. in shipbuilding, the thick planking on the outside of a deck, wrought over the ends of the beams, and fitting against the inside of the top timbers to which they are bolted: the inner edge is hollowed out to form a channel for water to run off the deck.

wa̧'tẽr·weed, *n.* any water plant having inconspicuous flowers, as pondweed, etc.

wa̧'tẽr wee'vil, a weevil of the genus *Lissorhoptrus*, that feeds on growing rice.

wa̧'tẽr wheel (hwēl), 1. a wheel turned by running or falling water, usually for power.

2. a wheel with buckets on its rim, used for lifting water.

wa̧'tẽr wil'lōw, an aquatic plant, *Dianthera americana*, having willowlike leaves.

wa̧'tẽr wing, a wall erected on the bank of a river, next to a bridge, to secure the foundation from the action of the current.

wa̧'tẽr wings, a device, inflated with air, used to keep one afloat while learning to swim: it is shaped somewhat like a pair of wings, designed to be worn under the arms.

wa̧'tẽr witch, 1. a person who professes to have the power to find underground water with a divining rod, etc.

2. any of various diving birds, as the horned grebe.

wa̧'tẽr witch'ing, the supposed finding of underground water by the use of a divining rod.

wa̧'tẽr·wŏrk, *n.* 1. [*pl., often construed as sing.*] (a) a system of reservoirs, pumps, pipes, etc., used to bring a water supply to a town or city; a water system; (b) a pumping station in such a system, with its machinery, sediment basins, filters, etc.

2. the structure in which a spout, jet, or shower of water is produced; an ornamental fountain; also, an exhibition of the play of fountains.

3. cloth painted with water color, size, or distemper, formerly sometimes used for hangings instead of tapestry, and for tents. [Obs.]

4. a marine pageant or view. [Obs.]

5. [*pl.*] (a) the source of tears; (b) tears: usually in *to turn on the waterworks*, to shed tears.

wa̧'tẽr wŏrm, any of the *Naididæ*, a worm that lives in water.

wa̧'tẽr·wo̧rn, *a.* worn smooth by the action of running or falling water; as, *waterworn* stones.

wa̧'tẽr·wŏrt, *n.* 1. an aquatic plant of the genus *Elatine.*

2. any plant of the family *Philydraceæ.*

wa̧'tẽr·y, *a.* 1. of or connected with water.

2. containing or full of water; moist.

3. bringing rain, as clouds.

4. like water.

5. thin; diluted; as, *watery* tea.

6. tearful; weeping.

7. sweaty.

8. in or consisting of water; as, a *watery* grave.

9. weak; insipid; without force.

10. soft, soggy, or flabby.

11. full of, secreting, or giving off a morbid discharge resembling water.

wa̧'tẽr yam, a Madagascar plant, the latticeleaf or laceleaf, *Aponogeton fenestralis*, that grows in running streams.

WATS (wäts), *n.* [*w*ide *a*rea *t*elecommunications *s*ervice.] a telephone service that ties a customer into the long-distance network through special lines so that calls can be made to and received from a defined area or areas at a special rate.

wätt, *n.* [named after James *Watt*, Scot. inventor.] in electricity, a unit of electric power, equal to a current of one ampere under one volt of pressure, or one joule per second, or about 1/746 of one horsepower.

wätt'āġe, *n.* 1. in electricity, amount of electric power, expressed in watts, and arrived at by multiplying amperage by voltage.

2. the total number of watts needed to operate a given appliance or device.

Wat·teau' (-tō'), *a.* of or pertaining to Jean Antoine Watteau, early eighteenth-century French painter, or to the fashions, especially women's fashions, portrayed in his pictures.

wätt'-hour' (-our'), *n.* in electricity, a unit of electrical energy or work, equal to one watt acting for one hour.

wät'tle, *n.* [AS. *watel, watol*, a wattle, a hurdle, woven twigs.]

1. a sort of woven work made of sticks intertwined with twigs or branches, used for walls, fences, and roofs.

2. (a) a stick, rod, twig, or wand; (b) a hurdle or framework made of sticks, rods, etc. [Brit. Dial.]

3. [*pl.*] rods or poles used as the framework of a thatched roof.

4. in Australia, any of various acacias: so called because the flexible branches were much used by early settlers for making wattles.

5. a fleshy, wrinkled, often brightly colored piece of skin which hangs from the chin or throat of certain birds and reptiles, as cocks and turkeys.

6. a barbel of a fish.

wät'tle, *a.* made of or roofed with wattle or wattles.

wät'tle, *v.t.*; wattled, *pt., pp.*; wattling, *ppr.* [ME. *watelen*, from AS. *watel*, wattle.]

1. to twist or intertwine (sticks, twigs, branches, etc.) so as to form an interwoven structure or fabric.

2. to construct, as a fence, by intertwining sticks, twigs, etc.

3. to build of, or roof, fence, bind, etc. with, wattle or wattles.

4. to switch; to beat. [Brit. Dial.]

wät'tle and daub, a wattled network of twigs daubed over with clay and mud: used in making rude huts.

wät'tle bärk, a bark used for tanning, obtained from several species of *Acacia* growing in Australia and New Zealand.

wät'tle·bīrd, *n.* 1. an Australian bird, *Anthochæra carunculata*, belonging to the *Meliphagidæ*, or honey eaters, characterized by large, reddish wattles hanging from the ears.

2. the brush turkey; a wattle turkey.

3. a wattle crow.

wät'tle crōw, an Australian tree crow; especially, *Glaucopis cinerea* of the South Island of New Zealand.

wät'tled, *a.* 1. having wattles, as a cock or turkey.

2. built with wattles.

wät'tle gum, a gum derived from any of various Australian wattles.

wät'tle jaws, lantern jaws.

watt'less, *a.* in electricity, having no watts; wholly without power: said of an alternating current that differs in phase by 90 degrees from the electromotive force producing it, or of an electromotive force that differs in phase by 90 degrees from the current which it produces.

wät'tle tûr'kēy, same as *brush turkey.*

wät'tle·wŏrk, *n.* wickerwork.

wät'tling, *n.* the act of interweaving wattles together; also, the framework thus formed.

watt'mē"tēr, *n.* an instrument for measuring in watts the power in an electrical circuit.

waucht, waught, *n.* a large draught, as of liquor. [Scot. and N. Eng. Dial.]

wauff, *a.* same as *waff.*

wauk'en, *v.t.* and *v.i.* to waken. [Scot.]

waul, wawl, *v.i.*; wauled, *pt.*, *pp.*; wauling, *ppr.* to cry as a cat; to squall or howl.

waul, *n.* a wail or howl.

waur, *a.* and *adv.* worse: also *war.* [Scot. and N. Eng. Dial.]

Wāve, *n.* a member of the Women's Reserve of the United States Naval Reserve (WAVES): also written *WAVE.*

wāve, *v.i.*; waved, *pt.*, *pp.*; waving, *ppr.* [ME. *waven*, to wave in the wind; AS. *wafian*, to wave, fluctuate.]

1. to move up and down or back and forth in a curving or undulating motion; to swing, sway, or flutter to and fro: said of flexible things free at one end; as, the flag *waves.*

2. to signal by moving a hand, arm, light, etc. to and fro.

3. to have the form of a series of curves or undulations; as, her hair *waves* naturally.

4. to be in an unsettled state; to waver; to fluctuate; to hesitate. [Rare.]

wāve, *v.t.* 1. to cause to wave, undulate, or sway to and fro, as a flag.

2. to swing; to brandish, as a weapon.

3. (a) to move or swing (something) as a signal; (b) to signal (something) by doing this; as, we *waved* farewell; (c) to signal or signify something to (someone) by doing this; as, he *waved* us on.

4. to give an undulating form to; to make sinuous; as, she *waves* her hair.

5. to give a wavy, or watered, appearance to (silk, etc.).

wāve, *n.* [from the verb, taking the place of ME. *wawe*, a wave.]

1. a curving ridge or swell moving along the surface of a liquid, running in a more or less straight line at a right angle to the movement.

2. water; especially, the sea or other body of water. [Poetic.]

3. (a) an undulation or series of undulations in or on a surface, such as that caused by wind over a field of grain; (b) a curve or series of curves or curls, as in the hair; (c) a wavy or undulating line on a watered fabric.

4. a motion to and fro or up and down, such as that made by the hand in signaling.

5. something like a wave in action or effect; specifically, (a) an upsurge or rise, as to a crest, or a progressively swelling manifestation; as, a crime *wave*, heat *wave*, *wave* of emotion, etc.; (b) a movement of people, etc., in groups or masses, which recedes or grows smaller before subsiding or being followed by another; as, a *wave* of immigrants.

6. in electricity, a periodic variation of an electric current or voltage.

7. in physics, any of the series of advancing impulses set up by a vibration, pulsation, or disturbance in air or some other medium, as in the transmission of heat, light, sound, etc.

damped waves; in radiotelegraphy, a train of high-frequency oscillations of decreasing or varying amplitude.

undamped waves; in radiotelegraphy, a train of high-frequency oscillations of constant amplitude.

wave of contraction; in physiology, muscular contraction visible from the point of application of the stimulus.

Syn.—billow, breaker, swell, surge, undulation.

wāve, *v.t.* same as *waive.*

wāved, *a.* 1. in heraldry, same as *undé.*

2. variegated in luster; as, *waved* silk.

3. having the margin indented with a series or succession of arched segments or incisions.

4. wavy in form; undulated.

wāve frŏnt, in physics, an imaginary surface composed of all the points reached at any given instant by a wave or vibration in its advance.

wāve guīde (gīd), an electric conductor consisting of a metal tubing, usually circular or rectangular in cross section, used for the conduction or directional transmission of microwaves or ultra-high-frequency waves.

wāve length, 1. the distance between corresponding points on two successive waves.

2. in physics, the distance, measured in the direction of progression of a wave, from any given point to the next point characterized by the same phase.

wāve'less, *a.* without waves; not waving; undisturbed; unagitated; as, the *waveless* sea.

wāve'let, *n.* a small wave; a ripple.

wāve'-līne, *a.* designating a former principle of building ships with contours scientifically adapted to the curves of the sea waves they have to traverse.

wā'vel·līte, *n.* [named after William *Wavel*, Eng. discoverer.] a hydrous phosphate of aluminum, vitreous, translucent, and white, greenish-yellow, or brown.

wāve lōaf, *n.* a loaf for a wave offering: see Lev. xxiii. 17.

wāve mōld'ing, a molding of wavy outline.

wāve moth, a small geometrid moth of the genus *Acidalia.*

wāve mō'tion, motion in curves alternately concave and convex like that of waves; undulatory motion.

wāve of'fēr·ing, in the ancient Jewish ceremonial worship, an offering made with waving toward the four cardinal points: see Ex. xxix. 26.

wāve päth, in physics, any radial line along which wave motion is propagated from its origin.

wā'vēr, *v.i.*; wavered, *pt.*, *pp.*; wavering, *ppr.* [ME. *waveren*, from AS. *wæfre*, wandering, restless.]

1. to swing or sway to and fro; to move one way and the other; to flutter.

2. to show doubt or indecision; to be unsettled in opinion; to vacillate.

3. to be in danger of falling or failing; to begin to give way; to falter.

4. to quiver or flicker, as a light.

5. to tremble; to quaver: said of the voice, etc.

6. to fluctuate.

7. to totter.

Syn.—fluctuate, hesitate, scruple, vacillate.

wā'vēr, *n.* a wavering.

wā'vēr, *n.* [prob. from *wave*, v.i.] a sapling or young timber tree standing in a felled wood. [Brit.]

wā'vēr·ēr, *n.* one who wavers; one unsettled in doctrine, faith, or opinion.

wā'vēr·ing·ly, *adv.* in a wavering, doubtful, or fluctuating manner.

wā'vēr·ing·ness, *n.* the state or quality of being a waverer.

wāve'sŏn, *n.* [prob. from *waive*, by analogy with OFr. *floteson* (flotsam).] in early English law, goods which after shipwreck appear floating on the sea.

wāve sûr'fāce, the surface formed by an advancing wave front.

wāve trāin, in physics, a group of waves sent out on the same course and at regular intervals, as by a vibrating body.

wāve'worn, *a.* worn by the waves.

wā'vey, wā'vy, *n.*; *pl.* **wā'veys, wā'vies**, [from Am. Ind. *wawa.*] a snow goose.

wāv'i·ly, *adv.* in a wavy manner.

wāv'i·ness, *n.* the state or quality of being wavy.

wāv'y, *a.*; *comp.* wavier; *superl.* waviest, 1. having waves.

2. moving in a wavelike motion.

3. having undulating curves; forming waves and hollows; sinuous; undulatory.

4. like, characteristic of, or suggestive of waves.

5. wavering; fluctuating, tremulous, or unsteady.

6. in botany, undulating on the border or on the surface.

7. in heraldry, same as *undé.*

wȧ·wäs'keesh, *n.* [Am. Ind.] the wapiti.

wawl, *v.i.* and *n.* same as *waul.*

waw'-waw, *n.* the wild yam of the West Indies, *Rajania pleioneura.*

wax, *v.i.*; waxed (waxt), *pt.*, *pp.*; waxing, *ppr.* [ME. *waxen*, *wexen*; AS. *weaxan*, to grow. Of Teut. origin.]

1. to grow gradually larger, more numerous, etc.; to increase in strength, intensity, volume, etc.

2. to increase in the size of its lighted portion; to become gradually full; as, the *waxing* and the waning moon.

3. to pass from one state to another; to become; as, to *wax* strong; to *wax* old.

wax, *n.* [ME.; AS. *weax*, wax; akin to G. *wachs.*]

1. a plastic, dull-yellow substance secreted by bees for building cells; beeswax: it is hard when cold, easily molded when warm, melts at about 148°F., cannot be dissolved in water, and is used for candles, modeling, etc.

2. one of several substances resembling wax in appearance, consistency, plasticity, or other properties, as (a) any waxlike substance yielded by plants or animals; (b) a mineral product, one of certain hydrocarbons, the best-known being paraffin and ozocerite; (c) a thick, waxlike substance secreted in the ear; cerumen; earwax; (d) a waxy substance produced by scale insects; (e) a thick resinous substance used by shoemakers for rubbing their thread; (f) sealing wax.

3. any of a group of substances made up of esters, fatty acids, free alcohols, and hydrocarbons, as spermaceti.

4. a thick waxy substance made by boiling down maple sirup and cooling it. [Dial.]

5. in mining, wet clay used to seal crevices or leaks. [Brit.]

carnauba wax; a substance secreted by the carnauba, or wax palm, of Brazil: its chief use is in the making of candles: also called *Brazil wax.*

Japan wax; a hard wax obtained in Japan from certain wax trees, as *Rhus succedanea*, used in making candles: also called *Japanese wax.*

paraffin wax; same as *paraffin* (sense 1).

wax opal; a variety of opal having a luster resembling that of wax.

wax, *v.t.* to rub, polish, cover, smear, or treat with wax.

wax, *a.* made of wax.

wax, *n.* [prob. from phrase *wax angry*, etc.] a fit of anger or temper; a rage. [Chiefly Brit. Colloq.]

wax bēan, 1. a variety of the string-bean plant with long, narrow, yellow pods.

2. the seed pod of this, used for food. Also called *butter bean.*

wax'ber"ry, *n.*; *pl.* **wax'ber"ries**, 1. a shrub with showy white berries lasting into winter; snowberry.

2. the wax myrtle, *Myrica cerifera*, or its grayish-white fruit; bayberry.

wax'bill, *n.* any of numerous small Old World birds of the weaverbird family, and especially those of the genus *Estrelda*: so called because their pink, scarlet, or white bills resemble sealing wax. Many species are kept as cage birds, as the Java sparrow.

wax'bush, *n.* same as *waxweed.*

wax but'tēr, a white, buttery substance obtained from beeswax by distillation.

wax chan'dlēr, a maker or seller of wax candles.

wax cloth, oilcloth.

wax clus'tēr, a shrub, *Gaultheria hispida*, native to Tasmania and Australia, bearing an edible berrylike fruit of a white, waxy appearance.

wax dis'til·lāte, in chemistry, paraffin-bearing oils which have been obtained by distillation with steam of the paraffin-base petroleum after the second grade illuminating oil has been run off.

waxed end, a thread pointed with a bristle and covered with wax, used in sewing boots and shoes: also called *wax end.*

wax'en, *v.* poetic past participle of *wax* (to increase).

wax'en, *a.* 1. made of wax; as, *waxen* cells.

2. resembling wax, as in being white, soft, smooth, lustrous, pale, plastic, pliable, impressionable, etc.

Men have marble, women *waxen* minds. —Shak.

3. coated with wax; as, a *waxen* tablet.

wax end, same as *waxed end.*

wax'ẽr, *n.* one who or that which waxes; specifically, one who applies wax to anything; as, a *waxer* of a hardwood floor.

wax'flow''ẽr, *n.* 1. same as *wax plant.*

2. same as *stephanotis* (sense 2).

3. a shrub, *Clusia insignis,* of British Guiana, so called because it yields a vegetable wax.

wax gōurd, an East Indian plant, *Benincasa cerifera*; also, its fruit, which is covered with a waxy coating when ripe.

wax'i·ness, *n.* the quality or state of being waxy.

wax in'sect, any of various homopterous insects that secrete wax, as the Chinese wax insect, *Ericerus pela,* a small white insect of China, which deposits its wax as a coating on the branches of certain plants.

wax kẽr'nel, a small tumor caused by enlargement of a lymphatic gland, especially in children.

wax līght (līt), a taper or candle made of wax.

wax moth, a bee moth.

wax myr'tle (mẽr'), any of a number of related shrubs or trees, *Myrica cerifera,* having grayish berries covered with a waxy substance and leaves resembling those of the myrtle; the bayberry.

wax pāint'ing, same as *encaustic painting* under *encaustic.*

wax pälm (päm), 1. a species of palm, *Ceroxylon andicola,* native to the Andes, the stem of which is covered with a secretion consisting of two-thirds resin and one-third wax, used in making candles.

WAX PALM (*Ceroxylon andicola*)

2. a tree, *Copernicia cerifera,* native to Brazil, the leaves of which secrete a waxy substance.

wax pā'pẽr, a kind of paper made impermeable to moisture by a coating of wax, or paraffin: also called *waxed paper.*

wax pīne, any one of the coniferous trees of the genus *Agathis.*

wax plant, any plant of the genus *Hoya.*

wax pock'et, one of several cavities between the ventral segments of the abdomen of a honeybee, in which the wax scales are secreted.

wax sçāle, 1. a wax insect.

2. one of the small plates or scales of wax secreted by a honeybee.

wax tree, any one of various trees of different localities which yield wax, either as an exudation or as the deposit of insects, as (a) the Japan wax tree, *Rhus succedanea,* an evergreen tree cultivated for the wax it yields; (b) a Chinese wax tree, especially *Ligustrum lucidum,* on which a wax insect deposits wax; (c) the varnish tree, *Elæagia utilis*; (d) the wax myrtle.

wax'weed, *n.* an annual American herb, *Cuphea viscosissima,* bearing purple flowers and stems covered with viscid hairs.

wax'wing, *n.* any of a number of related birds of the genus *Ampelis,* found in many parts of the Northern Hemisphere, with silky-brown plumage, a showy crest, and distinctive scarlet spines, suggesting sealing wax, at the ends of the secondary quill feathers. The best known species are *Ampelis cedrorum,* the cedar waxwing, and *Ampelis garrula,* the Bohemian waxwing.

wax'wŏrk, *n.* 1. work in wax; figures, objects, etc. formed of wax; often, a single figure made of wax.

2. the American staff tree or bittersweet, *Celastrus scandens.*

wax'wŏrk''ẽr, *n.* 1. one who works in wax; a maker of waxwork.

2. a bee that makes wax.

wax'wŏrks, *n.pl.* [*construed as sing.*] an exhibition of wax figures, usually representations of well-known persons.

wax'y, *a.*; *comp.* waxier; *superl.* waxiest, 1. resembling wax in appearance, softness, plasticity, impressibility, adhesiveness, or other properties; hence, yielding; pliable; impressionable; soft.

2. made of, covered with, or full of wax.

3. in medicine, designating, of, or characterized by a degeneration resulting from the deposit of an insoluble, waxlike substance in an organ.

waxy degeneration; same as *amyloid degeneration* under *amyloid.*

wāy, *n.* [ME. *wei, way*; AS. *weg,* way.]

1. a track or path along or over which one passes, progresses, or journeys; a place for passing; a path, route, road, street, or passage of any kind.

2. length of space; distance; as, a long *way* off: also [Colloq.] *ways.*

3. a going, moving, or passing from one place to another; progression; transit; journey.

4. path or course in life; as, to fall into evil *ways.*

5. (a) room or space for passing; free area; an opening, as in a crowd; as, the police made *way* for him; (b) freedom of action or opportunity.

6. a route or course that is or may be used to go from one place to another; as, he knows the *way* to the kitchen.

7. means by which anything is reached, attained, or accomplished; method or manner of doing something; as, do it this *way.*

8. manner; mode; style; as, he had a pleasant *way.*

9. state; condition; as, he is in a bad *way.* [Colloq.]

10. vocation; business; calling. [Colloq.]

11. respect; point; view; particular; as, in some *ways* you are right.

12. usual or customary mode of acting, living, or being; method of life or action; regular or habitual course or scheme of life; as, the *way* of the world.

13. a characteristic plan or mode of action or conduct; as, that's just his *way.*

14. advancement; progress, as of a boat; as, under *way*: also spelled *weigh.*

15. direction of movement or action; as, go this *way*; look this *way.*

16. wish; desire; will; as, to have one's *way.*

17. range or scope, as of experience; as, that never came my *way.*

18. a district; locality; area; as, out our *way.* [Colloq.]

19. in law, the privilege that a person or group of persons, as residents in a village, have to go over certain ground; right of way.

20. in mechanics, a surface or slide on which the carriage of a lathe, etc. moves along its bed.

21. [*pl.*] in shipbuilding, a timber framework on which a ship is built and from which it slides in launching.

by the way; see under *by.*

by way of; (a) passing through; through; via; (b) as a way, method, mode, or means of; (c) [Chiefly Brit.] in the condition or position of; as, she is *by way of* being a fine pianist.

covered way; in fortification, a space of ground level with the field, on the edge of the counterscarp, having a parapet raised on a level, together with its banquets and glacis.

in the way; in a position or of such a nature as to obstruct, impede, hinder, or prevent; as, that meddling fellow is always *in the way.*

in the way of; (a) so as to meet or fall in with; in a favorable position for doing or getting; as, I can put you *in the way of* a good piece of business; (b) in respect of; as regards; as, *in the way of* the natural sciences.

on the way; in the course of construction, a journey, etc.; in progress.

out of the way; (a) in a position so as not to hinder or interfere; (b) disposed of; (c) out of existence; (put) to death; (d) not on the right or usual route or course; (e) improper; wrong; amiss; (f) unusual; uncommon; (g) lost.

to come one's way; (a) to come within one's scope or range; to come to one; (b) [Slang.] to turn out successfully for one.

to give way; see under *give.*

to give way to; to step aside for; to yield to.

to go one's way; to take one's departure; to set out; to depart; to be off.

to go out of one's way; to inconvenience oneself; to do something that one would not ordinarily do, or that requires extra effort or trouble.

to go the way of all flesh, etc; to die.

to make one's way; (a) to advance or proceed; (b) to advance in life by one's own exertions.

to make way; to make room; to clear a passage.

to see one's way (*clear*); (a) to be willing (to do something); (b) to find it convenient or possible.

to take one's way; to go.

under way; (a) moving; advancing; making progress; (b) in nautical usage, making headway: said of a boat: also *under weigh.*

way of the rounds; in fortification, a space left for passage between a rampart and the wall of a fortified town to allow a patrol to make the rounds.

Syn.—road, street, avenue, passage, path, track, trail, alley, channel, course, route, thoroughfare, highway.

wāy, *v.t.*; wayed, *pt., pp.*; waying, *ppr.* 1. to go in; to proceed along. [Rare.]

2. to teach to go in the way; to break to the road, as a horse.

wāy, *v.i.* to journey; to travel; to progress. [Obs.]

wāy, *adv.* away; far; at some distance; as, *way* down east. [Colloq.]

wä·yä'kä, *n.* [Polynesian.] the yam bean.

wāy bag'gȧġe, the baggage or effects of a way passenger.

wāy ben'net, wāy bent, same as *wall barley.*

wāy'bill, *n.* a description of goods and shipping instructions sent with or fastened to goods in transit.

wāy'bōard, *n.* in mining, a thin layer or band of rock, clay, etc. that separates or defines the boundaries of thicker strata.

wāy'bread (-bred), *n.* [AS. *wegbræde*; *weg,* a way, and *brad,* broad, from its being found on waysides, and from its broad leaves.] the common plantain, *Plantago major.* [Obs.]

wāy'bung, *n.* [Australian.] a large corvine bird, *Corcorax melanorhamphus,* native to Australia, and noted for the unusual actions of the male during breeding time.

wāy'fāre, *v.i.* to journey; to travel; particularly, to go on foot: used now only in the present participle or the verbal noun.

wāy'fār''ẽr, *n.* one who journeys or travels by road; a traveler; especially, one who travels on foot.

wāy'fār''ing, *a.* being on a journey; traveling, especially on foot.

wāy'fār''ing tree, a large European shrub, *Viburnum lantana,* having a great many branches and small white flowers in dense cymes; also, a similar shrub found in America; the hobble bush, *Viburnum lantanoides.*

wāy'gō''ing, *a.* 1. going away; departing.

2. of, pertaining to, or belonging to one who goes away.

3. in law, designating a crop that will not ripen until after a tenant's term of occupancy has expired, and in which he has an interest.

waygoing crops; same as *away-going crops* under *away-going.*

wāy·lāid', *v.* past tense and past participle of *waylay.*

Wāy'lȧnd, *n.* [AS. *Weland.*] in Germanic and English folklore, an invisible smith: also *Wayland* (*the*) *Smith.*

wāy·lāy', *v.t.*; waylaid, *pt., pp.*; waylaying, *ppr.* [*way* and *lay,* after M.L.G. *wegelagen,* to waylay.]

1. to lie in wait for and seize, rob, or slay; to ambush; as, to *waylay* a traveler.

2. to wait for and accost by surprise.

wāy·lāy′ẽr, *n.* one who waits for another in ambush; one who waylays.

wāy′less, *a.* having no way or path; pathless.

wāy′māk″ẽr, *n.* one who makes a way; a precursor.

wāy′märk, *n.* a mark to guide in traveling; a guidepost.

wāy′-out′, *a.* very unusual, unconventional, experimental, nonconformist, esoteric, etc. [Colloq.]

wāy pas′sen·ġẽr, a passenger picked up or set down at a way station.

-wāys, [*way*, and adv. genit. *-s*.] a suffix used to form adverbs from adjectives and nouns, meaning *in a* (specified) *direction, position,* or *manner*, as in end*ways*: it is usually equivalent to the adverbial suffix *-wise.*

wāys, *n.pl.* [*construed as sing.*] way (sense 2). [Colloq.]

wāys and mēans, 1. methods and resources at the disposal of a person, company, etc.

2. methods of raising money, as for government: in the British House of Commons, a committee of the whole house sits as a *Committee on Ways and Means* to consider all matters connected with revenue, etc. In the United States House of Representatives, the *Committee on Ways and Means* is a standing committee which deals with the raising of revenue.

wāy shăft, 1. in steam engines, the rocking shaft for working the slide valve from the eccentric.

2. in mining, an interior shaft. [Brit.]

wāy′sīde, *n.* the border or edge of a road; also, the area close to the side of the road.

wāy′sīde, *a.* of or pertaining to the wayside; growing, situated, etc. by or near the side of a road; as, *wayside* flowers; a *wayside* inn.

wāy stā′tion, a small railroad station between more important ones, where through trains stop only on signal.

wāy this′tle, the Canada thistle.

wāy trāin, a train which stops at all or nearly all of the stations on its line; a local.

wāy′wărd, *a.* [ME. *weiward*, short for *aweiward.*]

1. insistent upon having one's own way contrary to others' advice, wishes, or commands; headstrong, willful, disobedient, etc.

2. conforming to no fixed rule or pattern; unpredictable; irregular; capricious; erratic.

3. not expected or wanted; as, his *wayward* fate. [Archaic.]

wāy′ward″en, *n.* a supervisor of highways. [Brit.]

wāy′wărd·ly, *adv.* in a wayward manner; frowardly; perversely.

wāy′wărd·ness, *n.* frowardness; perverseness.

wāy′wīse, *a.* expert in finding or keeping the way; knowing the way or route.

wāy′wīs″ẽr, *n.* an instrument for measuring the distance traveled. [Obs.]

wāy′wōrn, *a.* wearied by traveling.

wāyz′goose, *n.* an annual banquet or picnic held by the employees of a printing establishment.

wē, *pron.* [ME. *we*; AS. *wē*.] the persons speaking or writing: sometimes used by a person in referring to several persons including himself, or by a king, author, editor, judge, etc. in referring to himself. *We* is the nominative case form, *us* the objective, *our* and *ours* the possessive, and *ourselves* (or, by a king, etc., *ourself*) the intensive and reflexive, of the first personal plural pronoun.

wēak, *a.*; *comp.* weaker; *superl.* weakest, [ME. *weik*; ON. *veikr, veykr*; Sw. *vek*, weak. The Scand. form has replaced the AS. *wac*.]

1. lacking or deficient in physical strength, as (a) deficient in strength of body or muscle; (b) not able to sustain a heavy weight, pressure, or strain; not having the parts firmly united or adhesive; easily broken, torn, or bent; fragile; as, a *weak* vessel; (c) not able to resist onset or attack; easily surmounted or overcome; as, a *weak* fortress.

2. unfit for purposes of attack or defense, from lack of numbers, training, courage, etc.; not strong in combat or competition; as, a *weak* force.

3. lacking in force or effectiveness; as, a *weak* authority.

4. deficient in force of utterance or sound; having little volume, loudness, or sonorousness; as, a *weak* voice.

5. lacking ability to perform in a well or normal manner; deficient in functional energy, activity, or force: said of a body organ or part; as, a *weak* stomach.

6. lacking in the full or proper strength of some ingredient or in stimulating or nourishing substances or properties; not of the usual strength; diluted; as, *weak* tea; *weak* ale.

7. not possessing moral strength, vigor, or energy; lacking will power.

8. having imperfect mental faculties or intelligence; foolish; silly; fatuous; stupid.

9. deficient in steadiness or firmness by reason of age, illness, etc.; lacking physical vitality.

10. not convincing; ineffective; controvertible; as, *weak* arguments.

11. lacking ruling power, or authority; incapable of issuing orders and seeing that they are carried out; as, a *weak* monarch.

12. indicating or suggesting moral or physical weakness; as, *weak* features.

13. lacking, poor, or deficient in something specified; as, *weak* in grammar; a baseball team *weak* in pitchers.

14. having a relatively low gluten content: said of a flour or wheat.

15. in finance, tending toward lower prices: said of a stock or stock market.

16 in grammar, (a) inflected by the addition of a suffix such as *-ed* or *-d* rather than by an internal vowel change: said of verbs popularly called *regular*; (b) inflected by the addition of a suffix originally belonging to a stem ending in *-n*: said of Germanic adjectives and nouns.

17. in phonetics, unstressed or lightly stressed.

18. in photography, lacking contrast; thin: said of a negative.

19. in prosody, designating or of a verse ending in which the stress falls on a word or syllable that is normally unstressed, often a preposition whose object occurs in the following line.

20. slight; inconsiderable; little. [Rare.]

Syn.—feeble, infirm, debilitated, enfeebled, enervated, invalid, sickly.

wēak, *v.t.* to make weak. [Rare.]

wēak, *v.i.* to become weak. [Rare.]

wēak′en, *v.t.* and *v.i.*; weakened, *pt., pp.*; weakening, *ppr.* to make or become weak or weaker; as, he *weakens* from day to day.

Syn.—enfeeble, debilitate, enervate, invalidate, dilute, impair, paralyze, attenuate, sap.

wēak′en·ẽr, *n.* one who or that which weakens.

wēak′fish, *n.*; *pl.* **wēak′fish** or **wēak′fish·es,** [from obs. D. *weekvisch*; *week*, soft and *visch*, a fish.] any of several ocean fishes used for food, especially the squeteague, a species common off the Atlantic coast of the United States.

wēak′heärt″ed, *a.* having little courage; fainthearted.

wēak′ish, *a.* somewhat weak; weakly.

wēak′ish·ness, *n.* the quality or condition of being weakish.

wēak′-kneed′ (-nēd′), *a.* 1. having weak knees.

2. lacking in resolution, courage, determination, or energy; timid.

wēak′li·ness, *n.* the state or quality of being weakly.

wēak′ling, *n.* 1. a person or animal low in physical strength or vitality.

2. a person of weak character or intellect.

wēak′ling, *a.* weak; feeble; without spirit, strength, or force.

wēak′ly, *adv.* in a weak manner.

wēak′ly, *a.*; *comp.* weaklier; *superl.* weakliest, sickly; feeble; weak; not strong; infirm; as, a man of a *weakly* constitution.

wēak′-mīnd′ed, *a.* 1. not firm of mind; indecisive; unable to refuse or deny.

2. having a weak mind; feeble-minded.

wēak′ness, *n.* 1. the state or quality of being weak.

2. a weak point; a fault; a defect, as in one's character.

3. a liking; especially, an unreasonable fondness (*for* something).

4. something of which one is unreasonably fond; as, candy is a *weakness* of mine.

Syn.—debility, failing, foible, feebleness, folly, frailty, imbecility, impotence, infirmity.

wēak′-sīght″ed (-sīt″), *a.* having weak sight.

wēak′-spir″it·ed, *a.* having a weak spirit.

wēal, *n.* [ME. *wele*; AS. *wela, weala, weola*, weal, opulence, prosperity.]

1. a sound or prosperous state; well-being; welfare; as, the common *weal*. [Archaic.]

2. wealth; riches. [Obs.]

wēal, *v.t.* to promote the weal of. [Obs.]

wēal, *n.* [form of *wale* (a ridge).] a mark, line, or ridge raised on the skin, as by a blow; a welt; a wale.

wēal, *v.t.* to mark with weals; to wale; to flog.

wēald, *n.* [readoption of AS. *weald* (ME. *weeld*), forest, wold, wilderness; var. of *wold* and akin to G. *wald*, forest.]

1. a wooded area; forest. [Poet.]

2. wild open country. [Poet.]

The Weald; a (former) woodland district in southeastern England, now mainly agricultural.

Wēald′en, *a.* of or pertaining to The Weald or the Wealden.

Wēald′en, *n.* in geology, a series of fresh-water strata belonging to the Lower Cretaceous Period and occurring between the uppermost beds of the oölite and the lower ones of the chalk formation.

wēald′ish, *a.* of or belonging to a weald, especially [W—] to The Weald. [Obs.]

wēal′fųl, *a.* happy; joyous; prosperous. [Obs.]

wēals′măn, *n.*; *pl.* **wēals′men,** a politician. [Obs.]

wealth (welth), *n.* [ME. *welthe*, wealth. Not in AS. An extended form of *weal*, by the addition of suffix *-th*, implying condition or state.]

1. much money or property; riches; large possessions of money, goods, or land; great abundance of worldly goods; affluence; opulence.

> Each day new *wealth* without their care provides. —Dryden.

2. a large amount (of something); an abundance; as, a *wealth* of ideas.

> Again the feast, the speech, the glee,
> The shade of passing thought, the *wealth*
> Of words and wit. —Tennyson

3. valuable products, contents, or derivatives; as, the *wealth* of the oceans.

4. weal; well-being. [Obs.]

5. in economics, (a) everything having economic value measurable in price; (b) any useful material thing capable of being bought, sold, or stocked for future disposition.

wealth′fųl, *a.* full of wealth or happiness; prosperous. [Obs.]

wealth′fųl·ly, *adv.* in prosperity. [Obs.]

wealth′i·ly, *adv.* richly; in a wealthy manner.

wealth′i·ness, *n.* the state or quality of being wealthy; richness.

wealth′y, *a.*; *comp.* wealthier; *superl.* wealthiest, 1. rich; having wealth; affluent.

2. of, characterized by, or suggestive of wealth.

3. rich (*in* something specified); abundant; as, a language *wealthy in* nuances.

4. well-fed. [Brit. Dial.]

wēan (wēn), *v.t.*; weaned, *pt., pp.*; weaning, *ppr.* [AS. *wenian*, to accustom, wean.]

1. to cause (a child or young animal) to become accustomed gradually to food other than its mother's milk; to stop suckling.

2. to withdraw (a person) by degrees (*from* a habit, object of affection, occupation, etc.), as by substituting some other interest.

wēan, *n.* [contr. of Scot. *wee ane*, little one.] a child or baby. [Scot.]

wēan′ed·ness, *n.* the state or condition of being weaned.

wēan′el, wēan′ell, *n.* a weanling. [Obs.]

wēan′ẽr, *n.* one who or that which weans.

wēan′ing brash, a form of diarrhea sometimes attacking infants after weaning.

wēan′ling, *n.* a child or young animal recently weaned.

wēan′ling, *a.* newly weaned.

weap′ŏn (wep′), *n.* [ME. *wepen*; AS. *wæpen*, a weapon; found only in Gmc.]

1. an instrument of any kind used for fighting.

2. any organ (of an animal or plant) so used.

3. any means of attack or defense; as, his best *weapon* was silence.

> Truth that is suppressed by friends is the readiest *weapon* of the enemy. —R. L. Stevenson.

weap′ŏned, *a.* armed; furnished with weapons or arms; equipped for defense or offense.

weap′ŏn·less, *a.* unarmed; having no weapon.

weap′ŏn·ry, *n.* 1. the design and production of weapons.

2. weapons collectively; especially, a nation's stockpile of weapons of war.

weap′ŏn sälve (säv), a salve which was supposed to cure a wound by being applied to the weapon that made it. [Obs.]

wēar, *n.* same as *weir.*

weãr, *v.t.*; wore, *pt.*; worn, *pp.*; wearing, *ppr.* [altered form of *veer* (to let out).] to turn or bring (a ship) about by swinging its bow away from the wind; to veer: opposed to *tack.*

weãr, *v.i.* to turn or come about by having the bow swung away from the wind: said of a ship.

weãr, *v.t.*; wore, *pt.*; worn, *pp.*; wearing, *ppr.* [ME. *weren*; AS. *werian*, to wear.]

1. to have on the body or carry on the person for covering, protection, ornament, defense, etc., as a dress, a suit, a hat, a ring, a pistol, etc.

On her white breast a sparkling cross she *wore.* —Pope.

2. to have or show in one's expression or appearance; as, she *wore* a smile; *wearing* an air of expectancy.

3. to have on the person habitually or as a general practice; as, does he *wear* glasses?

4. to have or bear as a characteristic or attribute; as, he *wears* a famous name.

5. to hold, keep, or arrange (a part of the body) in a specified way; as, she *wears* her hair curled; he *wore* his head high.

6. to fly or show (its flag): said of a ship.

7. to impair, consume, or diminish by constant use, handling, friction, etc. (often with *away*).

When waterdrops have *worn* the stones of Troy. —Shak.

8. to bring by use to a specified state; as, he *wore* his coat to rags.

9. to make, cause, or produce by the friction of rubbing, scraping, flowing, etc.; as, it will *wear* a hole in the floor.

10. to tire or exhaust (a person).

11. to pass (time) slowly or tediously (often with *away* or *out*).

12. to bring about gradually; to effect by degrees: often with *in* or *into.*

Trials *wear* us *into* a liking of what possibly in the first essay displeased us.—Locke.

to wear down; (a) to make or become worn; to lose or cause to lose thickness or height by use, friction, etc.; (b) to tire out; to weary; to exhaust (a person); (c) to overcome the resistance of by persistence.

to wear off; to diminish or pass away by degrees; to rub off; as, *to wear off* the nap.

to wear out; (a) to make or become useless from continued wear or use; (b) to waste, destroy, or consume by degrees; (c) to tire out; to exhaust; as, *worn out* with fatigue; (d) to efface.

Syn.—carry, bear, exhibit, sport, consume, don, waste, impair, rub, diminish.

weãr, *v.i.* 1. to become impaired, consumed, or diminished by constant use, friction, etc.; as, that cloth will *wear* soon.

2. to hold up in use; to bear continued use or handling; to last; as, that suit *wears* well.

3. to become in time; to gradually reach a specified state; as, my courage *wore* thin.

4. to pass away gradually (often with *away* or *on*): said of time; as, the year *wore on.*

5. to be commonly worn or used; to be in style. [Obs.]

weãr, *n.* 1. the act of wearing or the state of being worn, as on the person.

2. things, especially clothes, worn, or for wearing, on the body; as, men's *wear.*

3. the fashion or proper style of dress or the like.

4. (a) the gradual impairment, loss, or diminution from use, friction, etc.; (b) the amount of such loss.

5. the ability to resist impairment or loss from use, friction, etc.; as, there's much *wear* left in my coat.

wear and tear; the loss arising from wearing; the waste, diminution, decay, or injury which anything sustains by being used; as, an allowance for the *wear and tear* of the machinery.

weãr′ȧ·ble, *a.* capable of being worn; fit to be worn.

weãr′ȧ·bleṣ, *n.pl.* wearable things; garments; clothing.

weãr′ẽr, *n.* 1. one who wears or carries something on the body; as, the *wearer* of a cloak, a sword, a crown, etc.

2. that which wastes or diminishes.

wēa′ri·ȧ·ble, *a.* capable of being wearied. [Rare.]

wēa′ried, *v.* past tense and past participle of *weary.*

wēa′ri·fụl, *a.* that makes weary; tiresome; wearisome.

wēa′ri·less, *a.* unwearying; tireless.

wēa′ri·ly, *adv.* in a weary manner.

wēa′ri·ness, *n.* 1. the state or quality of being weary or tired; fatigue; lassitude; ennui.

2. something that wearies.

weãr′ing, *a.* 1. of or intended for wear; as, *wearing* apparel.

2. causing wear, or gradual impairment or diminution.

3. wearying; tiring.

weãr′ing, *n.* 1. clothes; garments. [Obs.]

2. the act of one who or that which wears.

weãr′ing ap·par′el, clothing; attire; garments.

weãr′ish, *a.* 1. insipid; tasteless. [Dial.]

2. shrunk; wizened. [Dial.]

wēa′ri·sŏme, *a.* causing weariness; tiresome; tedious; fatiguing; as, a *wearisome* day's work.

wēa′ri·sŏme·ly, *adv.* in a wearisome manner.

wēa′ri·sŏme·ness, *n.* the state or quality of being wearisome.

wēa′ry, *a.*; *comp.* wearier; *superl.* weariest, [ME. *weri, wēry*, AS. *wērig*, tired.]

1. having the strength much exhausted by toil or violent exertion; tired; fatigued; worn out.

2. without further liking, patience, tolerance, zeal, etc.; bored (with *of*); as, *weary of* singing.

3. tiring; as, *weary* work.

4. irksome; tedious; tiresome.

Syn.—fatigued, tired, exhausted, worn, jaded, debilitated, spent, toilworn, faint.

wēa′ry, *v.t.*; wearied, *pt., pp.*; wearying, *ppr.* 1. to reduce or exhaust the physical strength of; to tire; to fatigue; as, to *weary* oneself with labor or traveling.

2. to make impatient; to try the patience of.

to weary out; to subdue or exhaust by fatigue or tediousness.

wēa′ry, *v.i.* 1. to grow weary; to become tired.

2. to lose patience or pleasure in something; to be surfeited.

3. to long: with *for*; as, to *weary for* one's absent ones. [Chiefly Scot.]

wēa′ṣănd, *n.* [ME. *wesand*; AS. *wæsend*, the windpipe.]

1. the windpipe, or trachea. [Archaic.]

2. the esophagus, or the throat generally.

wēa′ṣel (-zl), *n.*; *pl.* **wēa′ṣelṣ** or **wēa′ṣel,** [ME. *wesel*; AS. *wesle.*]

1. any of a world-wide group of cunning, agile, flesh-eating mammals of the genus *Mustela*, related to the stoats and martens, with a long, slender body, short legs, and a long, bushy tail: they feed on rats, mice, birds, eggs, etc.

WEASEL
(15 in. long including tail)

2. a person likened to this animal, as in cunning or slyness.

Malacca weasel; same as *rasse.*

wēa′ṣel çat, the linsang.

wēa′ṣel çoot, a female or young male smew.

wēa′ṣel duck, same as *weasel coot.*

wēa′ṣel-fāced (-fāst), *a.* having a thin, sharp face, like a weasel's.

wēa′ṣel·fish, *n.* the whistlefish.

wēa′ṣel lē′mūr, a small short-tailed lemur, *Lepilemur mustelinus.*

wēa′ṣel·ling, *n.* a rockling. [Obs.]

wēa′ṣel·snout, *n.* the yellow dead nettle, *Lamium galeobdolon*: so called from the form of the corolla.

wēa′ṣel spī′dẽr, any one of the *Galeodidæ*, a family of arachnids having the abdomen long and segmented, and pedipalps simulating legs.

wēa′ṣel wŏrdṣ, words or remarks that are equivocal or deliberately ambiguous.

wēa′ṣẽr, *n.* the American merganser. [Dial.]

weath′ẽr (weth′), *n.* [ME. *weder*; AS. *weder*; akin to G. *wetter.*]

1. the state of the air or atmosphere at a given time or place, with respect to the temperature, pressure, humidity, cloudiness, or any other meteorological phenomena; as, warm or cold *weather*; wet or dry *weather*: distinguished from *climate.*

2. change of the state of the air; meteorological change; hence, figuratively, vicissitude; change of condition: usually in the plural.

3. disagreeable or harmful atmospheric conditions; storm, rain, etc.; as, for protection against the *weather.*

4. a light rain; a shower. [Obs.]

5. the inclination or obliquity of the sails of a windmill to the plane of revolution.

to make bad weather; in nautical usage, to roll and pitch violently in a storm: said of a ship.

to make fair weather; to make flattering representations to some one; to conciliate another by fair words and a show of friendship. [Obs.]

to make good weather; in nautical usage, to act well in a storm: said of a ship.

under the weather; (a) not feeling well; slightly ill; indisposed; (b) somewhat drunk.

weath′ẽr, *v.t.*; weathered, *pt., pp.*; weathering, *ppr.* 1. to expose to the action of weather or atmosphere, as for airing, drying, seasoning, etc.

2. to wear away, discolor, disintegrate, or otherwise change for the worse by exposure to the atmosphere.

3. to pass through safely or survive; as, they *weathered* the storm.

4. to slope (a roof, shingles, etc.) so as to throw off rain, etc.

5. in nautical usage, to pass to the windward of (a cape, reef, etc.).

to weather a point; (a) in nautical usage, to pass to the windward of a point of land: said of a ship; (b) to gain or accomplish anything against opposition.

to weather out; to endure; to hold out against to the end.

to weather through; to pass or go safely through a storm, peril, difficulty, etc.

weath′ẽr, *v.i.* 1. to change in some particular as a result of exposure to the weather or atmosphere.

2. to endure the effects of the weather in a specified manner; as, this canvas will *weather* well.

weath′ẽr, *a.* designating or of the side of a ship, etc. facing the wind; windward.

to keep one's weather eye open; see *weather eye.*

weath′ẽr bēam, in nautical usage, the side of a ship facing the wind.

weath′ẽr-bēat·en, *a.* showing the effect of exposure to weather, as, (a) stained, damaged, or worn down; (b) sunburned, roughened, hardened, etc.: said of a person, his face, etc.

weath′ẽr bitt, in nautical usage, an extra turn of the cable about the end of the bitts.

weath′ẽr-bitt, *v.t.* in nautical usage, to make an extra turn of (the cable) around the bitts.

weath′ẽr-bit·ten, *a.* worn, wasted away, or defaced by exposure to the weather; weather-beaten.

weath′ẽr-bōard, *n.* 1. a board so shaped that its thin upper edge is overlapped by the board above, and its thick lower edge covers the top edge of the one below, in order to shed water; clapboard.

2. in nautical usage, (a) that side of a ship which is toward the wind; the windward side; (b) a board so inclined as to keep water but not air out of a porthole.

weath′ẽr·bōard, *v.t.* to nail weatherboards on (a roof or wall).

weath′ẽr·bōard·ing, *n.* 1. the act of covering a roof or wall with weatherboards.

2. weatherboards collectively.

weath′ẽr-bound, *a.* delayed or halted by bad weather, as a ship, airplane, etc.

weath′ẽr box, a hygroscope, usually in the shape of a house, in which the weight or flexure of materials due to dampness is made to move a toy figure or figures, usually a man and a woman on a poised arm, advancing or retiring to indicate changes in atmospheric conditions: also *weather house.*

weath′ẽr breed′ẽr, a fine bright day which is believed to precede and presage a storm.

Weath′ẽr Bū′reau (-rō), a division of the Department of Agriculture that gathers and compiles data on weather conditions over the United States, on the basis of which weather forecasts are made.

weath′ẽr ċast, a weather forecast.

weath′ẽr ċast′ẽr, one who makes predictions concerning the weather.

weath′ẽr chärt, same as *weather map.*

weath′ẽr çloth, in nautical usage, a long piece of canvas or tarpaulin used to protect the hammocks from injury by the weather when stowed, or to protect persons from the wind and spray.

weath′ẽr·çock, *n.* 1. a vane in the form of a cock, which swings to point the direction of the wind; a weather vane.
2. any thing or person that turns easily and frequently; a fickle or changeable person or thing.

weath′ẽr çon′taçt, in electricity, a partial contact between wires owing to bad insulation in wet weather.

weath′ẽr çrọss, a cross connection between electric lines during wet weather, from a defective action of the insulators.

weath′ẽr dog, a broken or a fragmentary rainbow. [Brit. Dial.]

weath′ẽr dōor, a door which regulates ventilation in a mine: also called *trap door.*

weath′ẽred, *a.* 1. wasted, worn away, or discolored by exposure to the weather; seasoned by the weather.
2. given a stained or discolored finish intended to resemble that produced by exposure to the weather.
3. in architecture, designating or of surfaces which have a small slope or inclination given to them to prevent water lodging on them.

weath′ẽr eȳe (ī), jocularly, the eye that is supposed to watch the sky to forecast the weather; specifically, in the phrase, *to keep one's weather eye open,* to be vigilantly on one's guard; to have one's wits about one. [Colloq.]

weath′ẽr-fend, *v.t.* to shelter; to defend from the weather.

weath′ẽr·fish, *n.*; *pl.* **weath′ẽr·fish** or **weath′ẽr·fish·eș,** the thunderfish, *Misgurnus fossilis,* looked upon as a weather prophet, as it is supposed to come out of the mud, in which it burrows, at the approach of a storm.

weath′ẽr gạll, a secondary rainbow, said to be a sign of bad weather; a water gall.

weath′ẽr gāuġe, in nautical usage, the advantage of a windward position, or of receiving the wind first: said of one ship in relation to another; hence, a favorable position; the upper hand.

weath′ẽr gạw, same as *weather gall.*

weath′ẽr·glȧss, *n.* an instrument used to forecast the weather by showing changes in the pressure of the atmosphere; a barometer or similar device.

weath′ẽr·glēam, *n.* a clear sky near the horizon. [Scot. and Brit. Dial.]

weath′ẽr·head (-hed), *n.* a secondary rainbow. [Brit. Dial.]

weath′ẽr helm, in nautical usage, the act of keeping the helm slightly toward the windward or weather side.

weath′ẽr house, same as *weather box.*

weath′ẽr·ing, *n.* 1. in architecture, a slope built to shed water.
2. in geology, the erosive effects of the forces of weather on the surface of the earth, forming soil, sand, etc.

weath′ẽr·li·ness, *n.* the quality in a vessel of being weatherly.

weath′ẽr·ly, *a.* in nautical usage, that can sail close to the wind with very little drift to leeward.

weath′ẽr·man, *n.*; *pl.* **weath′ẽr·men,** a person who forecasts the weather, especially one employed by the Weather Bureau. [Colloq.]

weath′ẽr map, a map or chart showing the condition of the weather in a certain area at a given time by indicating the temperatures, atmospheric pressures, wind velocity and direction, and other meteorological phenomena: also called *weather chart.*

weath′ẽr mōld′ing, same as *drip* (*n.* sense 4).

weath′ẽr·mōst, *a.* farthest to windward.

weath·ẽr·ol′ō·ġy, *n.* meteorology. [Colloq.]

weath′ẽr plant, any plant whose leaves or flowers show sensitiveness to atmospheric changes; especially, *Abrus precatorius,* or Indian licorice.

weath′ẽr·prọọf, *a.* capable of withstanding exposure to wind, rain, snow, etc. without being damaged.

weath′ẽr·prọọf, *v.t.* to make weatherproof.

weath′ẽr proph′et, one who foretells weather; also, anything foretelling changes in the weather.

weath′ẽr rōll, the roll of a ship to windward.

weath′ẽr sig′năl, any signal used to announce the state of or change in the weather.

weath′ẽr·spȳ, *n.* one who foretells the weather; a weather prophet. [Rare.]

weath′ẽr stā′tion, a post or office where weather conditions are recorded and studied and forecasts are made.

weath′ẽr strip, a thin strip of metal, felt, wood, etc., used to cover the joint between a door or window sash and the jamb, casing, or sill, so as to keep out drafts, rain, etc.

weath′ẽr-strip, *v.t.*; weather-stripped (-stript), *pt., pp.*; weather-stripping, *ppr.* to fit or provide with weather strips.

weath′ẽr strip′ping, 1. a weather strip.
2. weather strips collectively.

weath′ẽr tīde, the tide which sets against the lee side of a ship, impelling her to the windward.

weath′ẽr vāne, a vane to indicate the direction of the wind; a weathercock.

weath′ẽr-wīșe, *a.* skillful in foreseeing the changes of the weather; hence, skilled in predicting shifts of opinion, feeling, etc.

weath′ẽr·wōrn, *a.* worn by the action of the weather; weather-beaten.

wēav′ȧ·ble, *a.* capable of being woven.

wēave, *v.t.*; wove *or rarely* weaved, *pt.*; woven *or* wove, *pp.*; weaving, *ppr.* [ME. *weven*; AS. *wefan,* to weave.]

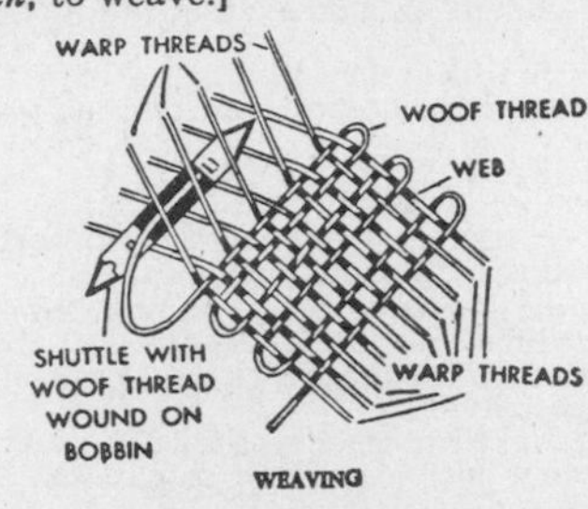

WEAVING

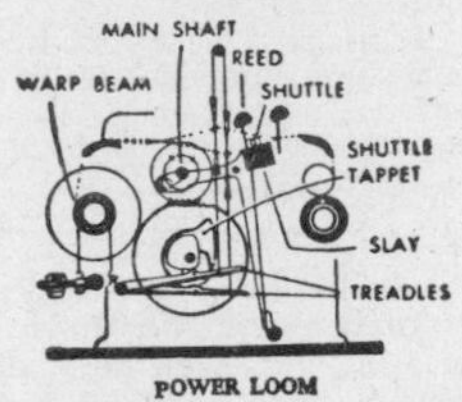

POWER LOOM

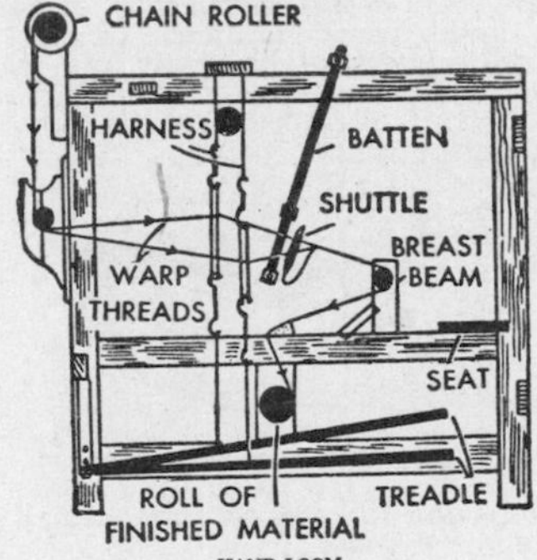

HAND LOOM

1. to make (a fabric) by interlacing threads, yarns, etc.; to make on a loom.
And now his *woven* girths he breaks asunder. —Shak.
2. to form (threads) into a fabric.
The spinsters and the knitters in the sun
And the free maids that *weave* their thread with bones
Do use to chant it. —Shak.
3. (a) to construct in the mind or imagination; (b) to form (details, incidents, etc.) into a story, poem, etc.
4. (a) to make by interlacing twigs, flowers, reeds, etc.; as, to *weave* a basket; (b) to twist or interlace (twigs, flowers, etc.) so as to form something.
5. to twist or interlace (something) into, through, or among; as, to *weave* flowers into one's hair.
6. to make or spin (a web): said of spiders, etc.
to weave one's way; to go by turning, twisting, and moving from side to side.
Syn.—interlace, braid, intertwine, intermix, plait, complicate, intersect.

wēave, *v.i.* 1. to do weaving; to work with a loom; to make cloth.
2. to become interlaced, woven, or interwoven.
3. to move from side to side or in and out.
4. to make a motion of the head, neck, and body from side to side like the shuttle of a weaver: said of a horse.

wēave, *n.* a specific pattern, method, or manner of weaving; as, a twill *weave.*

wēav′ẽr, *n.* 1. one who weaves; especially, one whose occupation is weaving.
2. a whirligig beetle.
3. a weaverbird.
4. a web-spinning spider.

YELLOW-CROWNED WEAVERBIRD AND NEST (*Ploceus icterocephalus*)

wēav′ẽr·bīrd, *n.* any of a number of insessorial birds of various genera, belonging to the family *Ploceinæ* and resembling the finches. They are so called from the structure of their nests, which are woven in an elaborate manner of various vegetable substances. Some species build single nests, but others build in companies, numerous nests suspended from the branches of a tree being under one roof, though each one forms a separate compartment and has a separate entrance. They are native to Asia, Africa, and Australia, none being found in Europe or America.

wēav′ẽr finch, a weaverbird.

wēav′ẽr shell, same as *weavers'-shuttle.*

wēav′ẽr's hitch (or **knot**) (not), a sheet bend, a type of knot: see *knot* illus.

wēav′ẽrș'-shut·tle, *n.* a gastropod, *Radius volva,* in which the aperture is extended into a long canal at each end: it belongs to the same family as the cowries: also called *weaver shell* and *shuttle shell.*

wēav′ing, *n.* the act or art of forming cloth, lacework, network, and the like by the interlacing of threads, etc.

wēa′zănd, *n.* same as *weasand.*

wēa′zen (-zn), *a.* same as *wizen.*

wēa′zen·y, *a.* somewhat wizened.

web, *n.* [ME. *web, webbe,* from AS. *webb, web,* a web.]
1. any woven fabric; especially, a length of cloth being woven on a loom or just taken off.
2. (a) the woven or spun network of a spider; a cobweb; (b) a similar network spun by the larvae of certain insects.
3. a carefully woven trap or snare.
4. anything like a web; a network.
5. in anatomy, (a) a tissue or membrane; (b) an abnormal membrane joining the fingers and toes at the base.
6. in architecture, the portion of a ribbed vault between the ribs.
7. a plain, flat surface, as (a) a sheet or thin plate of lead or other metal; (b) formerly, the blade of a sword; (c) the blade of a saw; (d) in mechanics, a thin plate between stiffeners, ribs, or other heavy structures; (e) the portion of a rail between the tread and foot; (f) the flat portion of a wheel, as of a railway carriage, between the hub and the rim; (g) the solid part of the bit of a key; (h) that portion of an anvil which is of reduced size below the head; (i) the thin, sharp part of the colter of a plow; (j) the arm of a crank extending from the wrist to the shaft.
8. anything carefully contrived and elaborately put together or woven by the mind, imagination, etc.; a plot; a scheme.
O, what a tangled *web* we weave,
When first we practise to deceive!—Scott.
9. (a) in zoology, the membrane partly or completely joining the toes of many water birds, water animals, etc.; (b) the series of

barbs on either side of the shaft of a feather; the vane.

10. in printing, a large roll of paper, especially newsprint.

web, *v.t.*; webbed, *pt., pp.*; webbing, *ppr.* 1. to cover with or as with a web; to envelop.

2. to join by a web.

3. to catch or snare in or as in a web.

webbed, *a.* 1. formed like a web or made of webbing.

2. joined by a web; as, *webbed* toes.

3. having the digits joined by a web; as, *webbed* foot.

web′bing, *n.* 1. a strong fabric of hemp, cotton, or other material woven in strips in various widths, used for supporting the seats of stuffed chairs, sofas, etc., for belts, etc.

2. the tapes on a printing machine.

3. a strong edging strip woven into a piece of fabric, as in rugs.

4. a membrane uniting the fingers or toes, as of a duck, goose, frog, etc.

web′by, *a.*; *comp.* webbier; *superl.* webbiest, 1. of, having the nature of, or like a web.

2. webbed or palmated.

we′bẽr (*or* vā′), *n.* [named after Wilhelm *Weber*, a German physicist.]

1. the practical unit of magnetic flux, equal to 10^8 maxwells.

2. formerly, a coulomb or ampere; later, a maxwell.

Web·ē′ri·ăn, *a.* in physiology, named after or pertaining to E. H. Weber, a German anatomist and physiologist (1795–1878).

Weberian apparatus; the system connecting the air bladder of a fish with its ear.

web′eÿe (-ī), *n.* pterygium (sense 1).

web′foot, *n.*; *pl.* **web′feet,** 1. a foot with two or more toes united by a web.

2. a person, animal, or bird with webbed feet.

web′-foot″ed, *a.* having webfeet, as a goose.

Web′foot″ẽr, *n.* a native or inhabitant of the State of Oregon. [Colloq.]

web mem′bẽr, in construction, a brace in a system of interlocking braces.

web press, a printing machine which uses a paper roll or rolls.

web saw, a frame saw.

web′stẽr, *n.* [AS. *webbestre*, f. of *webba*, weaver.] a weaver. [Obs.]

Web·stẽr′i·ăn, *adj.* pertaining to Noah Webster (1758–1843), American lexicographer, or Daniel Webster (1782—1852), American statesman.

web′stẽr·īte, *n.* [named after Thomas *Webster*, a Scottish geologist.] aluminite.

web′-tōed, *a.* web-footed.

web wheel (hwēl), a wheel in which the rim and the hub are connected by a thin plate or web.

web′wŏrm, *n.* any one of numerous lepidopterous insects whose gregarious larvae build large tentlike webs in which they live when not feeding; a tent caterpillar.

wecht, *n.* [AS. *wegan*, to lift.] an instrument in the form of a sieve but without holes, used for lifting grain, as in winnowing. [Scot.]

wed, *v.t.*; wedded, *pt.*; wedded *or* wed, *pp.*; wedding, *ppr.* [ME. *wedden*; AS. *weddian*, lit., to pledge, engage, from *wed*, a pledge.]

1. to marry; specifically, (a) to take for one's husband or wife; (b) to conduct the marriage ceremony for; to join in marriage.

2. to unite or join closely; to attach firmly; as, we are apt to be *wedded* to our own customs and opinions.

3. to espouse; to take part with. [Obs.]

wed, *v.i.* to become married; to take a husband or wife.

wē′d, (a) we had; (b) we should; (c) we would.

Wed′dȧh, *n.* same as *Veddah*.

wed′ded, *a.* 1. married; as, the *wedded* pair.

2. of or arising from marriage; as, *wedded* bliss.

3. devoted; as, *wedded* to one's work.

4. joined; as, *wedded* by common interests.

wed′dẽr, *n.* a wether. [Dial.]

wed′ding, *n.* [ME.; AS. *weddung*, from *weddian*, lit., to pledge, engage.]

1. (a) the act or ceremony of becoming married; marriage; (b) the marriage ceremony with its attendant festivities.

2. an anniversary of a marriage or the celebration of this.

Wedding anniversaries are named as follows, the qualifying word indicating the character of presents usually given on the occasion: first anniversary, paper *wedding*; fifth, wooden *wedding*; tenth, tin *wedding*; fifteenth, crystal *wedding*; twentieth, china *wedding*; twenty-fifth, silver *wedding*; fiftieth, golden *wedding*; sixtieth and seventy-fifth, diamond *wedding*.

wed′ding dress, the dress in which a woman is married.

wed′ding flow′ẽr, *Moræa* (*Iris*) *robinsoniana*, an iridaceous white-flowered plant of New South Wales; also, *Dombeya natalensis*, a bright-flowering tree of the cola nut family of South Africa.

wed′ding ring, a ring given by one of a married pair to the other at their wedding; usually, a plain gold circlet placed by the groom upon the third finger of the bride's left hand during the marriage ceremony.

wedġe (wej), *n.* [ME. *wegge*; AS. *wecg*, a mass of metal.]

1. a piece of wood, metal, etc., thick at one end and tapering to a thin edge at the other, used to split wood, rocks, etc., lift weights, reinforce structures, etc.

2. anything shaped like a wedge; as, a *wedge* of pie; specifically, (a) a wedge-shaped stroke in cuneiform writing; (b) a wedge-shaped tactical formation, as of troops or football players, used to penetrate a narrow front to a great depth.

3. any action or procedure that serves to open the way for a gradual change, disruption, intrusion, etc.

4. in geometry, a solid of five sides, viz., a rectangular base, two rhomboidal sides meeting in an edge, and two triangular ends, as in the figure, where the triangles A B E, D C F are the ends, the rectangles A D F E, B C F E the sides, and the rectangle A B C D the top.

WEDGE

spherical wedge; that part of a sphere included between two planes intersecting in a diameter.

the thin (or *small*) *end of the wedge*; an initiatory move of small apparent importance, but which is calculated to produce or lead to an ultimate important effect.

wedġe, *v.t.*; wedged, *pt., pp.*; wedging, *ppr.* 1. to split or force apart with or as with a wedge.

2. to fix solidly in place by driving a wedge or wedges under, beside, etc.

3. to force or pack in (often with *in*).

4. to force or crowd together in a narrow space.

5. to divide or shape into wedgelike masses and to knead until free from bubbles and made plastic; as, to *wedge* clay for pottery.

wedġe, *v.i.* to push or be forced as or like a wedge.

wedġe′bill, *n.* a hummingbird of South America of the genus *Schistes*, having a wedge-shaped bill.

wedġe mī·crom′e·tẽr, a graduated wedge of glass, metal, etc., to measure the distance between two points, edges, or surfaces.

wedġe phō·tom′e·tẽr, in astronomy, a wedge of tinted glass, used to measure the relative brightness of stars by being moved across the field of view, stars of equal brilliance being obscured by equal thickness of glass.

wedġe′-shāped (-shāpt), *a.* 1. having the shape of a wedge; cuneiform.

2. in botany, broad and truncate at the summit, and tapering down to the base.

wedġe shell, a bivalve of the genus *Donax*.

wedġe′-tāiled, *a.* in ornithology, having the tail feathers in the form of a wedge, growing longer from sides to center.

wedġe′wīṣe, *adv.* in the manner of a wedge.

wedġ′ie, *n.* a style of women's shoe having a wedge-shaped piece under the heel and forming a solid sole, flat from heel to toe. [Colloq.]

Wedġ′wood's sçāle, the scale of degrees of heat as shown by the pyrometer, invented by Josiah Wedgwood (1730–1795), a device to measure the temperature of pottery kilns. Zero is 580.5° C. or 1,077° F.

Wedġ′wood (**wāre**), [after Josiah *Wedgwood*.] a fine English pottery with delicately designed neoclassical figures which are applied in a white, cameolike relief on a tinted background, before the firing.

wedġ′y, *a.*; *comp.* wedgier; *superl.* wedgiest; shaped or used like a wedge.

wed′lock, *n.* [ME. *wedlak, wedloke*, from AS. *wedlac*, in the sense of a pledge; *wed*, a pledge, and *lac*, a sport, also a gift, in token of pleasure.]

1. marriage; matrimony; the married state.

2. a wife. [Obs.]

wed′lock, *v.t.* to marry. [Obs.]

Wednes′dāy (wenz′), *n.* [AS. *Wodnes dæg*, Woden's day. Woden is identified with Odin.] the fourth day of the week; the next day after Tuesday.

wee, *a.*; *comp.* weer (wē′ẽr); *superl.* weest (wē′ist), [ME. *we, wei*, small quantity (only in north Eng. and Scot. dial.); AS. (Anglian) *wege, weg*, from base of *weigh*.] very small; tiny.

wee, *n.* a little bit; especially, a short time; as, bide a *wee*. [Scot. and Brit. Dial.]

weech′-elm, *n.* the witch-elm. [Obs.]

weed, *n.* [ME. *weede*; AS. *weod*.]

1. any undesired, uncultivated plant that grows in profusion so as to crowd out a desired crop, disfigure a lawn, etc.

2. (a) tobacco: with *the*; (b) a cigar. [Colloq.]

3. something useless; specifically, a horse that is unfit for racing or breeding.

4. wild, luxuriant growth, as of underbrush. [Archaic.]

weed, *v.t.* 1. to remove the weeds from, as a garden.

2. to remove (a weed): often with *out*.

3. to remove or eliminate as useless, harmful, etc.: often with *out*.

4. to rid of elements regarded as useless or harmful.

weed, *v.i.* to remove weeds, etc.

weed, *n.* [ME. *wede*; AS. *wæde*, neut., *wæd* f., a garment.]

1. a garment or clothing. [Archaic.]

2. [*pl.*] black mourning clothes, especially those worn by a widow.

3. a black mourning band, as of crape, worn on a man's hat or sleeve.

weed, *n.* 1. any sudden illness from cold or relapse, usually accompanied by fever, especially one affecting women after childbirth or during nursing. [Scot.]

2. an inflammatory disease of the lymphatics in a horse, with swelling of the legs and fever.

weed′ẽr, *n.* 1. one who weeds.

2. a device for removing weeds.

weed′ẽr·y, *n.* weeds collectively; also, a place full of weeds. [Rare.]

weed′hook, weed′ing hook, a hook used for cutting away or extirpating weeds.

weed′i·ness, *n.* the state of being weedy.

weed′less, *a.* free from weeds.

weed′y, *a.*; *comp.* weedier; *superl.* weediest, 1. having weeds; full of weeds.

2. of or like a weed or weeds, as in rapid, rank growth.

3. lean, lanky, ungainly, etc.: said of persons or animals.

weed′y, *a.* wearing mourning weeds.

week, *n.* [ME. *weke, wike*; AS. *wicu*, a week.]

1. a period of seven days, especially one beginning with Sunday and ending with Saturday.

2. the hours or days of work in a seven-day period; as, he works a 40-hour *week*.

Passion Week; see under *passion*.

Sunday (or *Monday, Tuesday*, etc.) *week*; a week (counting backward or forward) from Sunday (or Monday, Tuesday, etc.). [Chiefly Brit.]

the Feast of Weeks; Shabuoth, a Jewish holiday.

this day (or *yesterday*, etc.) *week*; a week (counting backward or forward) from today (or yesterday, etc.). [Chiefly Brit.]

week after week; every week.

week and week about; every alternate week.

week in, week out; every week.

week by week; each week.

week′dāy, *n.* 1. any day of the week except Sunday (or, as in Judaism, Saturday).

2. any day not in the weekend.

week′end, week′-end, *n.* 1. the period from Friday night or Saturday to Monday morning; the end of the week.

2. a house party held over this period.

Also written *week end*.

long weekend; a weekend plus one or two days before or after.

week′end, week′-end, *a.* of or on a weekend: also written *week end*.

week′end, week′-end, *v.i.* to spend the weekend (*at* or *in* a specified place): also written *week end*.

week′ly, *a.* 1. continuing or lasting for a week.

2. done, happening, appearing, payable, etc. once a week, or every week; as, a *weekly* visit.

3. of a week, or each week; as, a *weekly* wage.

week'ly, *n.*; *pl.* **week'lieṣ,** a periodical, as a newspaper, issued once a week.

week'ly, *adv.* once a week; every week.

week'wäm, *n.* a wigwam. [Rare.]

weel, *a.* and *adv.* well. [Scot.]

weel, *n.* a whirlpool. [Scot. and Brit. Dial.]

weel, *n.* a kind of trap or snare for fish. [Brit.]

ween, *v.i.* and *v.t.* [ME. *wenen*; AS. *wenan*, to imagine, hope, expect, from *wen*, expectation, supposition, hope.] to think; to imagine; to fancy. [Archaic.]

ween'ie, ween'y, *n.*; *pl.* **ween'ieṣ,** a wiener. [Colloq.]

wee'nong, *n.* [Java.] an East Indian tree of the genus *Tetrameles*: also called *jungle bendy*.

weep, *v.i.*; wept, *pt., pp.*; weeping, *ppr.* [ME. *wepen*, from AS. *wepan* (for *wopjan*), lit., to cry aloud, to raise an outcry, lament loudly, from *wop*, a clamor, outcry, lament.]

1. to manifest or give expression to a strong emotion, usually grief or sorrow, by crying, wailing, or, especially, shedding tears.

Then they for sudden joy did *weep*. —Shak.

2. to lament; to mourn (with *for*).

3. to drop or flow as tears.

The blood *weeps* from my heart.—Shak.

4. to let fall drops of water or other liquid; especially, to drip moisture condensed from the air; as, cold pipes *weep* in hot weather.

5. to exude water or other liquid, as a wound, the stem of a plant, etc.

6. to have the branches drooping or hanging downward, as if in sorrow; to be pendent; to droop; as, the *weeping* willow.

weep, *v.t.* 1. to weep for; to mourn; to lament; to bewail; to bemoan.

And *weep* each other's woe. —Pope.

2. to shed or let fall drop by drop (tears or other drops of liquid); to pour forth in drops.

Groves whose rich trees *wept* odorous gums and balm. —Milton.

3. to bring to a specified condition by weeping; as, she *wept* herself to sleep.

weep, *n.* 1. [*often pl.*] a fit of weeping.

2. an exudation or dripping of moisture.

weep, *n.* [so called from its cry.] the lapwing.

weep'ẽr, *n.* 1. a person who weeps; especially, one who weeps habitually.

2. a hired mourner at a funeral.

3. a conventional badge of mourning, as, formerly, a white cuff band or, now, a black band of crape.

4. [*usually in pl.*] a widow's veil.

5. a species of monkey, the capuchin.

weep'fụl, *a.* full of weeping; grieving. [Obs.]

weep'ing, *n.* the act of one who or that which weeps; lamentation; mourning.

weep'ing, *a.* 1. having graceful, drooping branches.

2. that weeps; tearful; shedding tears; flowing.

3. overcharged with moisture.

weeping ash; a variety of ash, *Fraxinus pendula*, differing from the common ash only in its branches arching downward instead of upward.

weeping birch; a European variety of white birch, *Betula pendula*, with drooping branches.

weeping eczema; eczema accompanied by considerable exudation.

weeping grass; a perennial grass of Australia and New Zealand, *Microlæna* or *Ehrharta stipoides*, used for grazing.

weeping monkey; the capuchin.

weeping poplar; a variety of the soft poplar, *Populus grandidentata*.

weeping rock; a porous rock from which water exudes or trickles.

weeping sinew; in anatomy, an encysted ganglion, chiefly on the back of the hand, containing synovial fluid.

weeping spring; a spring that slowly discharges water.

weeping willow; see under *willow*.

weep'ing crọss, a cross, often of stone, erected on or by the side of a highway, for the devotions of penitents.

to return (or *come*) *home by weeping cross*; to suffer a defeat in some adventure; to meet with a repulse or failure. [Obs.]

weep'ing·ly, *adv.* in a weeping manner.

weep'ing-rīpe, *a.* ready for weeping.

weer'ish, *a.* wearish. [Obs.]

wee'ṣel, *n.* a weasel. [Obs.]

weet, *n.* [imitative.] the cry of several kinds of birds, as the European sandpiper and the wryneck; also, the bird itself.

weet, *v.i.* to utter a cry of or like a weet.

weet'bīrd, *n.* the wryneck. [Brit. Dial.]

weet'ing·ly, *adv.* wittingly. [Obs.]

weet'less, *a.* unknowing. [Obs.]

weet'weet, *n.* the European sandpiper. [Brit. Dial.]

weev'ẽr, *n.* [O.Norm. Fr. *wivre* (OFr. *guivre*), orig., serpent, dragon; L. *vipera*, viper.] any of a number of ocean fishes found at the bottom of temperate seas near shrimp beds, belonging to the genus *Trachinus* or family *Trachinidæ*, distinguished by long, soft, dorsal and anal fins, eyes near the top of the head, and several sharp spines. Several species are known, two of which are found in British seas, the greater weever, or stingbull, *Trachinus draco*, about ten or twelve inches long, and the lesser weaver, *Trachinus vipera*, about five inches long.

GREATER WEEVER (*Trachinus draco*)

wee'vil, *n.* [ME. *wevel, wivel, wevyl*; AS. *wifel, wibil*, from Teut. type *webila*, beetle.] any of a large number of beetles with the head ending in a projecting snout: the larvae are very destructive to many crops, the various species attacking cotton, fruits, grain, and nuts, and destroying plants and trees by boring.

wee'viled, wee'villed, *a.* infested with weevils, as grain.

wee'vil·y, wee'vil·ly, *a.* weeviled; infested with weevils.

weft, *v.* obsolete past tense and past participle of *wave*.

weft, *n.* [ME. *weft*, warp; AS. *weft, wefta*, lit., a thing woven.]

1. the woof of cloth; the threads that cross the warp from selvage to selvage.

2. something woven.

weft, *n.* a waif (sense 5).

weft'ȧġe, *n.* texture.

weft fọrk, in weaving, (a) an instrument used in certain kinds of looms, where the filling is laid in, one piece at a time; (b) a device formerly used for stopping the loom if the weft thread should break or fail.

wē'gō·tiṣm, *n.* the frequent use of the pronoun *we*; weism. [Slang.]

wēhr'geld, wēhr'gelt (wẽr'), *n.* same as *wergild*.

wẹhr'līte (vār'), *n.* [from A. *Wehrle*, an Austrian mineralogist.] a bright metallic, light steel-gray mineral related to tetradymite, consisting of bismuth, tellurium, silver, and sulfur.

Wehr'mächt (vār'mäkht), *n.* [G., lit., defense force.] the armed forces of Germany.

wēhr'wolf (wẽr'wulf), *n.* same as *werewolf*.

weī·ġē'lȧ (*or* -gē'), *n.* [Mod. L., after C. E. *Weigel* (1748–1831), G. physician.] any of a number of related shrubs of the honeysuckle family, with clusters of pink, red, or white bell-shaped flowers on drooping branches.

wẹigh (wā), *v.t.*; weighed, *pt., pp.*; weighing, *ppr.* [ME. *weghen, wezen, weyen, weien*, from AS. *wegan*, to carry, bear.]

1. to determine the weight of by means of a scale or balance.

2. to lift or balance (an object) in the hand or hands, in order to estimate its heaviness or weight.

3. to measure out, dole out, or apportion, by or as by weight (often with *out*).

They *weighed* for my price thirty pieces of silver. —Zech. xi. 12.

4. (a) to consider and choose carefully; as, *weigh* one's words; (b) to balance or ponder in the mind; to consider in order to make a choice; as, *weigh* one plan against another.

5. to burden; to bear or press down upon, as with heaviness or oppression (with *down*).

6. to hold in high regard; to esteem; to value. [Obs.]

7. in nautical usage, to hoist, or lift (an anchor).

to weigh in; to weigh (a boxer, jockey, etc.) before a contest in order to verify his declared weight.

wẹigh, *v.i.* 1. to have weight; to be heavy; especially, to have a specified weight; as, it *weighs* ten pounds.

2. to have significance, importance, or influence; as, his word *weighs* heavily with me.

3. to be a burden; to press or bear down (with *on* or *upon*); as, the theft *weighs on* his mind.

4. in nautical usage, (a) to hoist anchor; (b) to start to sail.

to weigh down; to sink by its own weight.

to weigh in; to be weighed in order to verify the declared weight: used of a boxer, jockey, etc.

wẹigh, *n.* [var. of *way*, in phr. *under way*, modified by the notion of "weighing anchor."] way: a popular variant in *under weigh*, progressing, advancing.

wẹigh'ȧ·ble, *a.* that can be weighed.

wẹigh'ȧġe, *n.* a duty or toll paid for weighing merchandise. [Obs.]

wẹigh bēam, a kind of steelyard supported in a frame for weighing merchandise.

wẹigh'bōard, *n.* same as *wayboard*.

wẹigh'bridġe, *n.* a large platform scale set flush with a road, for weighing cars, wagons, cattle, etc.

wẹigh'ẽr, *n.* one who weighs; specifically, an officer whose duty is to weigh commodities.

wẹigh'house, *n.* any building used primarily as a place for weighing commodities.

wẹigh'ing, *n.* 1. the act of ascertaining weight.

2. as much as is weighed at once; as, a *weighing* of beef.

wẹigh'ing house, same as *weighhouse*.

wẹigh'ing mȧ·ċhīne', any apparatus for weighing, especially for weighing heavy objects, as laden wagons, heavy boxes, etc.; a platform scale.

wẹigh'lock, *n.* a canal lock at which barges are weighed and their tonnage settled.

wẹigh'mȧs''tẽr, *n.* one who manages a weighhouse; especially, one who is licensed as public weigher.

wẹight (wāt), *n.* [ME. *weght, wight*; AS. *gewiht*, weight.]

1. a portion or quantity weighing a definite or specified amount; as, we had ten pounds *weight* of lead.

2. heaviness as a quality of things; attraction of a material body by gravitational pull toward the center of the earth: in physics, distinguished from *mass*.

3. quantity or amount of heaviness; how much a thing weighs; as, the *weight* of an egg.

4. (a) any unit of heaviness or mass; (b) any system of such units; as, troy *weight*, avoirdupois *weight*; (c) a piece of metal, wood, etc. of a specific standard heaviness, used on a balance or scale in weighing.

5. any block or mass of material used for its heaviness; specifically, (a) one used to hold light things down; as, a paper *weight*; (b) one used to drive a mechanism; as, the *weights* in a clock; (c) one used to maintain balance; as, *weights* placed on an automobile wheel; (d) one of a particular heaviness, lifted as an athletic exercise.

6. a burden or oppressiveness, as of responsibility or sorrow.

7. importance or consequence; as, a matter of great *weight*.

8. influence, power, or authority; as, he threw his *weight* to the losing side.

9. the relative thickness or heaviness of an article of clothing as proper to a particular season; as, a suit of summer *weight*.

10. any of the several classifications into which boxers and wrestlers are placed according to how much they weigh.

11. in statistics, (a) the frequency, hence relative importance, of a single item in a frequency list of related items; (b) the value or number used to express such frequency.

apothecaries' weight; see under *apothecary*.

avoirdupois weight; see *avoirdupois* (sense 1).

by weight; as determined by weighing.

combining weight; see under *combine* (to unite).

dead weight; see *dead weight* following *dead*.

fisherman's weight; estimated weight; weight guessed at.

gross weight; see under *gross*.

lazy weight; short weight. [Colloq.]

molecular weight; see under *molecular*.

net weight; the weight, as of a commodity, not including container and packing.

to pull one's weight; to do one's share.

weight of an observation; in physical science, the relative importance of a single observation when compared with others.

weight of metal; the total weight of the projectiles that can be fired by one discharge of a battery of guns. [Now Rare.]

weight of wind; the air pressure applied to or capable of being applied to a stop or a series of stops in an organ.

Syn.—burden, heaviness, gravity, pressure, importance, load, signification, influence, efficacy, consequence, moment.

wẹight, *v.t.*; weighted, *pt., pp.*; weighting, *ppr.*

1. to attach weights to; to load with more weight; to make heavy or heavier.

2. to burden; to load down; to oppress.

3. to treat (thread or fabric) with a solution of metallic salts, in order to increase its weight.

4. in statistics, to give a weight, or value, to (an item in a frequency list).

weight'i·ly, *adv.* in a weighty manner.

weight'i·ness, *n.* the state or quality of being weighty.

weight'less, *a.* having little or no apparent weight; specifically, lacking acceleration of gravity or other external force, as a satellite in earth orbit when the gravitational pull of the earth is counterbalanced by the centrifugal force imparted to the satellite by its initial rocket blast.

weight lift'ing, the athletic exercise or competitive sport of lifting weights.

weight'y, *a.*; *comp.* weightier; *superl.* weightiest, 1. having great weight; heavy; ponderous; as, a *weighty* body.

2. burdensome; oppressive; as, *weighty* responsibilities.

3. of great significance or moment; serious; as, *weighty* matters of state.

4. of great influence or importance; as, a *weighty* personage.

Wei'mä·rä·nẽr, *n.* [from *Weimar*, a city in East Germany, where the breed was developed.] a breed of lean, medium-sized hunting dog with a smooth, gray coat.

Wei'mär Rē·pub'lic (vī'), the German republic (1919–1933): its constitutional assembly met in Weimar in 1919.

weir, wear, *n.* [ME. *wer*, from AS. *wer*, a weir, a dam, lit., defense.]

1. a dam across a stream to back up or divert water, as for a mill; a milldam.

2. a brushwood or stake fence built in a stream, channel, etc., for catching fish.

3. an obstruction placed in a stream or channel, diverting the water through a prepared aperture for measuring the rate of flow.

weird, *n.* [ME. *wirde*, *werde*; AS. *wyrd*, *wird*, *wurd*, fate, from *weorthan*, to become.]

1. a spell or charm.

2. a prophecy.

3. one's allotted fate or fortune; destiny.

4. any of the Fates.

[Archaic or Scot. in all senses.]

weird, *a.* [from *weird*, *n.*]

1. of fate or destiny. [Archaic.]

2. suggestive of ghosts, evil spirits, or other supernatural things; mysterious; eerie.

3. queer; unusual; startlingly odd; as, he wore a *weird* costume. [Colloq.]

the Weird Sisters; the three Fates.

weird, *v.t.* to warn. [Scot.]

weird'ness, *n.* the state or quality of being weird.

Weis'mann·ism (vīs'), *n.* [after August *Weismann* (1834–1914), German biologist.] a theory of heredity in which the germ plasm is regarded as the vehicle of inheritance from generation to generation, no acquired characteristics being transmitted from parent to offspring.

weiss beer (vīs), [from G. *weissbier*, white beer.] an effervescent, light-colored beer, brewed especially from wheat.

weiss'wŭrst, *n.* [G., from *weiss*, white; and *wurst*, sausage: pork and veal whiten when cooked.] a variety of Bratwurst in which the meat is cooked, then stuffed into the casing.

wē'jack, *n.* [Am. Ind.] the pekan.

wē'kȧ, *n.* [Maori; from its cry.] any of several large, tawny-colored, flightless birds of the rail family, native to New Zealand.

Welch, *a.* and *n.* same as *Welsh.*

welch, *v.t.* and *v.i.* to welsh. [Slang.]

Welch'măn, *n.*; *pl.* **Welch'men,** a Welshman.

wel'cōme, *a.* [ME. *wilcome*, welcome, from AS. *wilcuma*, one who comes so as to please another; *wil-*, prefix, akin to *willa*, will, pleasure, and *cuma*, a comer, from *cuman*, to come.]

1. received with gladness and cordiality; as, a *welcome* guest.

2. producing gladness in its reception; agreeable or gratifying; as, *welcome* news.

3. freely and willingly permitted or invited (to use); as, you are *welcome* to (use) my car: also used in a conventional response to thanks ("you're welcome"), meaning *under no obligation for the favor given.*

wel'cōme, *n.* an act or expression of welcoming; as, a hearty (or cold) *welcome.*

to bid welcome; to receive with cordial expressions of hospitality.

to wear out one's welcome; to come so often or stay so long that one is no longer welcome.

wel'cōme, *interj.* you are welcome: an expression of cordial greeting.

wel'cōme, *v.t.*; welcomed, *pt.*, *pp.*; welcoming, *ppr.* 1. to receive and entertain hospitably and cheerfully.

2. to accept with pleasure or satisfaction; as, he always *welcomes* criticism.

wel'cōme·ly, *adv.* in a welcome manner.

wel'cōme mat, a doormat: chiefly in the phrase *to put out the welcome mat*, to give an enthusiastic reception.

wel'cōme·ness, *n.* gratefulness. [Archaic.]

wel'cōm·ẽr, *n.* one who welcomes.

weld, *n.* [ME. *welde*, *wolde.*]

1. a European mignonette, *Reseda luteola*, native to Great Britain and cultivated elsewhere: it yields a yellow dye.

2. the dye.

Also *wold*, *woald*, *would*, *wildwoad*, *dyer's weed.*

WELD (*Reseda luteola*)

weld, *v.t.* to wield. [Obs.]

weld, *v.t.*; welded, *pt.*, *pp.*; welding, *ppr.* [altered with unhistoric *-d* from *well*, to well up, boil.]

1. to unite (pieces of metal) by heating until molten and fused or until soft enough to hammer or press together.

2. to bring into close or intimate union; to unite in a single, compact whole.

weld, *v.i.* to be welded or capable of being welded; as, these alloys *weld* at different heats.

weld, *n.* 1. the act of welding.

2. the joint formed by welding; as, it broke at the *weld.*

weld·ȧ·bil'i·ty, *n.* capability of being welded.

weld'ȧ·ble, *a.* capable of union by welding.

weld'ẽr, *n.* one who or that which welds.

wel'fãre, *n.* [ME. *welfare*, from *wel*, well, and *fare*, from AS. *faru*, lit., a journey, from *faran*, to fare, go.]

1. the state of being or doing well; the condition of health, prosperity, and happiness; well-being.

2. a blessing. [Obs.]

3. welfare work.

on welfare; receiving government aid because of poverty, unemployment, etc.

wel'fãre stāte, a state in which the welfare of its citizens, with regard to employment, medical care, social security, etc. is considered to be the responsibility of the government.

wel'fãre wŏrk, the organized effort of a community or organization to improve the living conditions and standards of its members.

wel'fãr·ism, *n.* 1. the policies and practices of a welfare state or of public welfare agencies.

2. aid given or benefits made available by a welfare state or by public welfare agencies.

welk, *v.i.* to fade; to wane. [Obs.]

wel'kin, *n.* [ME. *welken*, *welkne*, from AS. *wolcnu*, pl. of *wolcen*, a cloud.] the curved vault of the sky, or the upper air: now chiefly in *to make the welkin ring*, to make a very loud sound. [Archaic or Poetic.]

well, *n.* [ME. *welle*; AS. *wella*, *well*, from *weallan*, to well up, boil.]

1. a flow of water from the earth; a natural spring and pool.

2. a deep hole or shaft sunk into the earth to tap an underground supply of water, gas, oil, etc.

3. a source of abundant supply; a fount; as, he was a *well* of information.

4. any of various shafts or deep enclosed spaces resembling a well; especially, (a) an open shaft in a building for a staircase; a stair well; (b) a shaft in a building or between buildings, open to the sky, for light and air; an airshaft; (c) an elevator shaft; (d) in English law courts, an open space before the bench, for solicitors.

5. any of various vessels, containers, etc. for holding liquid, as an inkwell.

6. the space between the seats of a jaunting car, used for holding luggage, etc.

7. a whirlpool or circular eddy in the sea.

8. in military mining, an excavation in the earth, with branches or galleries extending from it.

9. in nautical usage, (a) an enclosure in the hold of a ship for containing the pumps and protecting them from damage; (b) a compartment in a fishing vessel, with watertight sides and a bottom perforated with holes to give free admission to the water, so that fish may be kept alive therein; (c) [Rare.] the cockpit; (d) a shaft through which an auxiliary screw propeller may be raised and lowered.

artesian well; see under *artesian.*

driven well; a drive well.

well, *v.i.* [ME. *wellen*, to well up, bubble, boil, weld; AS. *wellan*, *wyllan*, to bubble, well up.] to flow or spring from or as from a well; to gush (often with *up*, *forth*, *down*, etc.).

well, *v.t.* to pour forth; to gush; as, her eyes *welled* tears.

well, *adv.*; *comp.* better; *superl.* best, [ME. wel; AS. *wel*, *well*, lit., agreeably, or suitably to one's will or wish.]

1. in a pleasing or desirable manner; satisfactorily; as, the affair ended *well.*

2. in a proper, friendly, or attentive manner; as, treat him *well.*

3. skillfully; expertly; as, she sings *well.*

4. in an appropriate manner; fittingly; as, spoken *well.*

5. prosperously; in comfort and plenty; as, they lived *well* in Paris.

6. with good reason; in justice; as, you may *well* ask.

7. satisfactorily in regard to health or physical condition; as, the patient is doing *well.*

8. to a considerable extent or degree; as, *well* advanced.

9. thoroughly; as, stir *well* before cooking.

10. with certainty; definitely; as, you know perfectly *well* that he was there.

11. intimately; familiarly; closely; as, I know him *well.*

12. in good spirits; with good grace; as, he took the news *well.*

13. conveniently; suitably; advantageously; easily; as, I cannot *well* go today.

Well is sometimes used in hyphenated compounds meaning *properly*, *satisfactorily*, *thoroughly*, etc., as in *well*-defined, *well*-able, *well*-worn.

as well; (a) besides; in addition; (b) with equal justification or propriety; equally.

as well as; (a) equally with; just as much or as good as; (b) in addition to.

well enough; in a moderate degree or manner; fairly; satisfactorily; sufficiently well; as, he acted *well* enough.

well, *a.* 1. suitable; proper; advisable; as, it is *well* that you came.

2. in good health; as, she is quite *well.*

3. in a good or satisfactory condition; favorable; comfortable; as, things are *well* with us these days.

4. in marine insurance, uninjured; safe; in good condition; as, a ship enters port *well.*

5. being in favor; favored. [Obs.]

well to live; having a competence; well-off. [Obs.]

His father is *well to live.* —Shak.

well, *n.* well-being; welfare; weal. [Obs.]

Well be with you, gentlemen. —Shak.

well, *interj.* an exclamation used to express surprise, acquiescence, agreement, resignation, expostulation, etc., or merely to preface or resume one's remarks.

wē'll, 1. we shall.

2. we will.

well'ȧ·dāy, *interj.* wellaway! alas! lackaday! [Archaic.]

well-ad·vīsed', *a.* showing or resulting from careful consideration or sound advice; wise; prudent.

well'-ap·poin'ted, *a.* excellently furnished or equipped; as, a *well-appointed* office.

well'ȧ·wāy', *interj.* [ME. *wei la wei*, lit., woe! lo! woe!; *wei* from O.N. *vei*, woe, and *la*, from AS. *la*, lo.] alas!: used as an exclamation of grief, regret, or sorrow. [Archaic.]

well'-bal'anced, *a.* 1. nicely or exactly balanced, adjusted, or regulated; evenly proportioned; as, a *well-balanced* formula.

2. of a steady, judicious temper; sane, sensible, and reliable.

well'-bē·hāved', *a.* behaving well; conducting oneself properly; displaying good manners.

well'-bē'ing, *n.* the state of being well; welfare; happiness; prosperity; as, virtue is essential to the *well-being* of men or of society.

Syn.—welfare, prosperity, happiness.

well bōat, a fishing boat having a well for keeping live fish.

well bōr'ẽr, one who or that which bores wells.

well'born', *a.* born of good family.

well'-bred', *a.* 1. having or manifesting good breeding; polite; courteous and considerate in manner or actions.

2. of good pedigree or breed, as a horse or other animal.

well buck'et, a vessel used in drawing water from a well, either single or one of a series on an endless band.

well chāin, a chain used in raising a bucket or buckets from a well.

well'-chō'sen, *a.* chosen with care and judgment; proper; appropriate.

well'-çŏn·tent', *a.* thoroughly pleased or satisfied.

well çūrb, the structure enclosing and rising above a well.

well'-dis·pōsed', *a.* 1. suitably or properly placed or arranged.

2. inclined to be friendly, kindly, or favorable (*toward* a person) or receptive (*to* an idea, etc.).

well'-dō'ēr, *n.* one who does well; especially, one who does good deeds.

well' dō'ing, *n.* good or benevolent action or conduct; a doing well.

well'-dŏne', *a.* 1. performed with skill and efficiency.

2. thoroughly cooked: said of meat: opposed to *rare*.

well'-dŏne', *interj.* an exclamation of approval of another's action.

well drāin, 1. a drain or vent for water, somewhat like a well or pit, serving to discharge the water of wet land.

2. a drain leading to a well.

well'-drāin, *v.t.*; well-drained, *pt., pp.*; well-draining, *ppr.* to drain (land) by means of wells or pits, which receive the water, and from which it is discharged by machinery.

well'fāre, *n.* welfare. [Obs.]

well'-fā'vŏred, *a.* handsome; well-formed; beautiful; pleasing to the eye.

well'-fed', *a.* showing the effect of much good food; plump; fat.

well'-found', *a.* properly and adequately equipped; as, a *well-found* ship.

well'-found'ed, *a.* based on facts, good evidence, or sound judgment; as, a *well-founded* suspicion.

well'-grọọmed', *a.* 1. carefully cared for; as, a *well-groomed* horse.

2. clean and neat; carefully washed, combed, dressed, etc.

well'-ground'ed, *a.* 1. having a thorough basic knowledge of a subject.

2. based on good reason; well-founded.

well'-han'dled, *a.* capably and efficiently managed.

well'head (-hed), *n.* 1. the source of a spring of water; a spring.

2. a source; a fountainhead.

well'-heeled', *a.* [*well*, adv. and pp. of *heel*.] having considerable money; rich; prosperous. [Slang.]

well'hōle, *n.* the cavity of a well; also, any similar opening, as (a) that which receives a counterbalancing weight in certain mechanical contrivances; (b) the central space within a flight of circular stairs, etc.

well'-in·fọrmed', *a.* 1. having thorough knowledge of a subject.

2. having considerable knowledge of many subjects, especially those of current interest.

Wel'ling·tŏn bọọt, a kind of boot formerly worn by military men: named after the Duke of Wellington.

Wel·ling·tō'ni·ȧ, *n.* the genus *Sequoia*. [Brit.]

Wel·ling·tō'ni·ăn, *a.* of or pertaining to Arthur Wellesley, first Duke of Wellington (1769–1852), British general and statesman.

well'-in·ten'tioned, *a.* having or showing good, kindly, or benevolent intentions: usually with the connotation of failure or miscarriage of intention.

well'-knit' (-nit'), *a.* strong; sturdy; close-knit.

well'-knōwn' (-nōn'), *a.* 1. thoroughly or fully known.

2. widely or generally known or acknowledged; famous or notorious; as, a *well-known* fact.

well'-līk'ing, *a.* being in admirable condition; of good appearance. [Archaic.]

well'-māde', *a.* 1. well-proportioned; strongly built; skillfully and soundly put together.

2. in literature and drama, (a) skillfully constructed or contrived, as a plot; (b) having a skillfully contrived plot; as, a *well-made* play or novel.

well'-man'nēred, *a.* having or showing good manners; courteous; polite; well-bred; complaisant.

well'-mēan'ēr, *n.* one whose intention is good.

well'-mēan'ing, *a.* having or showing good or kindly intentions: often used with slight contempt; as, a plain, *well-meaning* soul: see *well-intentioned*.

well'-meant' (-ment'), *a.* said or done with good intention; rightly intended; sincere; not feigned.

well'-mer'it·ed, *a.* well-deserved; just; fitting.

well'-nā'tūred, *a.* good-natured; kind.

well'-nīgh' (-nī'), *adv.* almost; nearly.

well'-off', *a.* 1. in a favorable or fortunate condition or circumstance.

2. prosperous; well-to-do.

Also *well off*.

well'-ọr'dēred, *a.* properly or carefully arranged or organized.

well pack'ing, in well sinking, a bag filled with flaxseed and placed around the tube in the bore hole.

well'-plīght'ed (-plīt'), *a.* 1. betrothed in a suitable manner; faithfully pledged.

2. well or properly folded. [Obs.]

well'-prē·ṣẽrved', *a.* in good condition or of good appearance, in spite of age.

well'-prō·pōr'tioned (-shund), *a.* symmetrical; of good proportions.

well'-read' (-red'), *a.* 1. having read a great deal; well-instructed in books; having a wide and appreciative knowledge of literature.

2. having read much (*in* a particular subject); as, *well-read in* philosophy.

well rọọm, 1. a room built over a mineral or other spring into which its waters are conducted, and where they are drunk.

2. in a boat, a place in the bottom where the water is collected, and whence it is bailed out. [Rare.]

well'-seen', *a.* well-informed from having traveled; accomplished; well-versed. [Archaic.]

well'-set', *a.* 1. firmly set; properly placed or arrayed.

2. having good symmetry of parts.

well sink'ēr, one who digs wells.

well'-sink''ing, *n.* the operation of sinking or digging wells; the act of boring for water, etc.

wells'īte, *n.* [after H. L. *Wells* (1855–1924), Am. chemist.] a colorless or white, crystalline silicate of aluminum, barium, calcium, and potassium, $(Ba, Ca, K_2)Al_2Si_3O_{10}\cdot 3H_2O$.

well'-sped', *a.* having good success.

well sphē·rom'e·tēr, a kind of spherometer for accurately measuring the radius of curvature of a lens.

well'-spō'ken, *a.* 1. courteous; civil; speaking with fitness or grace; speaking kindly.

2. spoken with propriety; properly or aptly spoken; as, *well-spoken* words.

3. speaking easily or fluently.

well'spring, *n.* 1. the source of a stream, spring, etc.; a fountainhead.

2. a source of abundant and continual supply; as, a *wellspring* of knowledge.

well sweep, a sweep for drawing water from a well.

well'-thought'-of (-thạt'), having a good reputation; of good repute.

well'-tīmed', *a.* 1. said or done at exactly the right moment; timely; opportune.

2. keeping accurate time; as, *well-timed* oars.

well'-tö-dö', *a.* well-off; prosperous; wealthy: also *well to do*.

well wạ'tēr, the water that flows into a well from subterranean springs; water drawn from a well.

well'-willed, *a.* kindly disposed; favorable. [Scot.]

well'-will'ēr, *n.* one who means kindly; a well-wisher. [Obs.]

well'-will'ing, *a.* friendly; well-willed. [Rare.]

well'-wish'', *n.* a wish of happiness.

well'wish'ēr, *n.* one who wishes success to a person or a cause.

well'-wish'ing, *a.* that wishes well to others; kindly disposed.

well'-wish'ing, *n.* the act, or an expression, of wishing well to others.

well'-wŏn, *a.* honestly gained.

well'-wọrn', *a.* 1. much worn; much used.

2. overused; trite; hackneyed; as, a *well-worn* joke.

3. worn or carried becomingly.

welṣ, *n.* the sheatfish, *Silurus glanis*.

Welṣ'bach (*or G.* vels'bäkh) **būrn'ēr**, [after Carl Auer von *Welsbach* (1858–1929), Austrian chemist, its inventor.] a gas burner with a gauze mantle impregnated with thorium oxide and about one per cent of cerium oxide: when lighted, the incombustible gauze becomes incandescent and gives off a bright, slightly greenish light.

Welsh, *a.* [from AS. *Welisc*, foreign, from *Wealh*, a foreigner.] of or pertaining to Wales, its people, their language, etc.; Cymric: also *Welch*.

Welsh flannel; a very fine flannel, chiefly handmade, from the wool of the flocks of the Welsh mountains.

Welsh glaive; same as *glaive*, sense 1.

Welsh groin; in architecture, a groin formed by the intersection of two cylindrical vaults, of which one is of less height than the other.

Welsh main; a match at cockfighting, where all must fight to death.

Welsh mortgage; a mortgage in which there is no proviso or condition for repayment at any time. The agreement is that the mortgagee to whom the estate is conveyed shall receive the rents till his debt is paid, and in such case the mortgagor is at liberty to redeem at any time.

Welsh mutton; a choice and delicate kind of mutton obtained from a breed of small sheep in Wales.

Welsh onion; the cibol, *Allium fistulosum*.

Welsh parsley; hemp or a hangman's rope made from it. [Obs.]

Welsh poppy; see under *poppy*.

Welsh rabbit; see under *rabbit*.

Welsh terrier; any of a breed of lean wire-haired terrier closely resembling the Airedale, but smaller: believed to have originated in Wales.

Welsh, *n.* the language of Wales or of the Welsh. Welsh is a member of the (Brythonic) Celtic family of languages. It is distinguished for its compounds, which it possesses the capacity of forming to an almost unlimited extent.

the Welsh; the natives or inhabitants of Wales: also called *the Cymry*.

welsh, *v.t.* and *v.i.* [19th-c. slang; prob. back-formation from *welsher*.]

1. to cheat or swindle by failing to pay a bet or other debt: often with *on*. [Slang.]

2. to evade or fail to fulfill (an obligation): often with *on*. [Slang.]

Also *welch*.

welsh'ēr, *n.* [prob. for *Welsher*, Welshman, with reference to supposed propensities.] a person who welshes; a cheat; a swindler: also *welcher*. [Slang.]

Welsh'măn, *n.*; *pl.* **Welsh'men**, 1. a native or inhabitant of Wales: also *Welchman*.

2. [w–] the squirrelfish.

3. [w–] the black bass. [Dial.]

wel'sŏme, *a.* well; prosperous. [Obs.]

wel'sŏme·ly, *adv.* prosperously. [Obs.]

welt, *n.* [ME. *welte, walt*.]

1. a strip of leather stitched into the seam between the sole and upper of a shoe to strengthen the joining.

2. a strip of material, often folded over a cord, placed at the edge or seam of a garment to reinforce or trim it.

3. (a) a raised ridge left on the skin by a slash or blow; a wale; a weal; (b) such a slash or blow.

4. a hem, fringe, border, or edging. [Obs.]

5. in shipbuilding, a back strip of wood forming an additional thickness laid over a flush seam or joint or placed in an angle to strengthen it.

6. in sheet-iron work and in steam boiler making, a strip riveted to two contiguous plates which form a butt joint.

7. in heraldry, a narrow border to an ordinary or charge.

8. in knitting, (a) a separate flap, as a heel-piece knitted on a stocking; (b) a finishing rib, as at the top of a stocking to prevent its rolling.

welt, *v.t.*; welted, *pt., pp.*; welting, *ppr.* 1. to furnish with a welt or welts; to sew a welt on, as a seam or border.

2. to beat or flog severely, especially in such a manner as to raise welts on the skin. [Colloq.]

Welt'än'schau·ung (velt'än'shou-ụng), *n.* [G., lit., world view.] one's philosophy or conception of the universe and of life.

Welt'än·sịcht (velt'än-zikht), *n.* [G.] a world view; a particular perspective of, or attitude toward, life and reality.

wel'tēr, *v.i.*; weltered, *pt., pp.*; weltering, *ppr.* [ME. *weltren*; M.D. *welteren*, freq. formation from base of AS. *wealtan*, to roll.]

1. to roll about or wallow, as a pig in mud: sometimes used figuratively, as, they *weltered* in sin.
2. to be soaked, stained, or bathed; as, the corpses *weltered* in their blood.
3. to rise and fall; to tumble; to toss about, as the sea.

wel'tẽr, *v.t.* 1. to make or force with or by wallowing. [Rare.]
2. to roll or roll over. [Obs.]

wel'tẽr, *n.* 1. the act of weltering or rolling about; hence, turmoil; confusion.
2. that in which weltering is done; slime; filth: often used figuratively, as, the *welter* of immorality.

wel'tẽr rāce, a race in which the horses carry welterweight.

wel'tẽr·weight (-wāt), *n.* [prob. from *welt*, to thrash, and *-er*.]
1. a weight of twenty-eight pounds carried by a horse in a race as a handicap.
2. a boxer or wrestler who weighs between 136 and 147 pounds.

wel'tẽr·weight, *a.* of welterweights.

welt'ing, *n.* 1. welt (material).
2. a severe flogging. [Colloq.]

Welt'po·li·tik' (velt'), *n.* [G.] world politics; international politics.

Welt'schmerz (velt'schmerts), *n.* [G., world pain.] a melancholy weariness of life; sentimental pessimism over the state of the world.

Wel·witsch'i·à (-wich'), *n.* [named after the discoverer, Dr. Friedrich *Welwitsch* (1806–1872), an Austrian botanist.] a genus of plants, growing in southern Africa in dry regions near the western coast. It has a stem or rhizome forming a woody mass, rising to a foot at most above the ground, and having a diameter of from four to five inches to as many feet, this mass bearing two cotyledonary leaves, which, when they reach their full development, become dry and split up into shreds but do not fall off. Every year several short flower stalks are developed at the base of these leaves, but no other leaves are produced. There seems to be but one species, *Welwitschia mirabilis*.

wem, *n.* the belly; the womb; the uterus. [Obs.]

wem, *n.* a spot; a scar; a fault; a blemish. [Archaic.]

wem, *v.t.* to corrupt; to vitiate. [Obs.]

wem'less, *a.* free from spot or blemish; spotless; immaculate. [Obs.]

wen, *n.* [ME. *wenne*, from AS. *wenn*; the original sense was probably pain or painful swelling.] a benign skin tumor consisting of a sebaceous cyst, most frequently occurring on the scalp.

wen, *n.* [ME. and AS.; var. of AS. *win, wyn*, joy, bliss.] an Old English rune (ƿ), replaced in the eleventh century by the letter *w*.

wench, *n.* [ME. *wenche*, from AS. *wencle*, maid, daughter, a word allied to *wencel*, weak.]
1. a girl or young woman; derogatory or facetious term.
2. a country girl; also, a female servant. [Archaic.]
3. a woman of loose character; a prostitute. [Archaic.]
4. a child. [Obs.]

wench, *v.i.*; wenched (wencht), *pt., pp.*; wenching, *ppr.* to associate with prostitutes or loose women. [Archaic.]

wench'ẽr, *n.* one who wenches.

wench'less, *a.* having no wench.

wend, *v.* obsolete past tense and past participle of *ween*.

wend, *v.i.*; wended, *pt., pp.*; wending, *ppr.* [ME. *wenden*, from AS. *wendan*, to turn, also, to turn oneself.]
1. to go; to pass to or from a place; to travel. [Archaic.]
2. to turn round. [Obs.]
3. to disappear; to vanish. [Obs].

wend, *v.t.* 1. to proceed on; to direct, as a course or way; to go; as, to *wend* one's way. [Now Chiefly Poet.]
2. to change; to turn. [Obs.]

wend, *n.* a certain quantity or circuit of ground. [Obs.]

Wend, *n.* [G. *Wende*.] one of a Slavic people of eastern Germany, descendants of the Sorbs.

wēnde, *v.* obsolete past tense of *ween*.

Wend'iç, *a.* and *n.* same as *Wendish*.

Wend'ish, *a.* of the Wends or their language.

Wend'ish, *n.* the West Slavic language of the Wends; Sorbian.

wēne, *v.i.* ween. [Obs.]

Wen'lock grŏup, in geology, the middle division of the Upper Silurian system in Great Britain: so called from being typically developed at Wenlock, in Shropshire.

wen'nel, *n.* a weanling. [Obs.]

wen'nish, *a.* of or pertaining to a wen or wens; having the nature of a wen; also, having wens.

wen'ny, *a.* wennish.

went, *v.* obsolete past tense and past participle of *wend*.

went, *v.* past tense of *go*.

went, *n.* 1. a change of course; a turning; a veering. [Obs.]
2. a way; a passage; a path. [Obs.]

wen'tle·trap, *n.* [D. *wenteltrap*, lit., a winding staircase; *wentel*, a winding, and *trap*, stair.] any of a group of sea mollusks of the family *Scalariidæ*, enclosed in a single, usually white, spiral shell crossed by numerous ridges.

wep'ŏn, *n.* a weapon.

wept, *v.* past tense and past participle of *weep*.

wẽr, *n.* 1. a man. [Obs.]
2. wergild. [Obs.]

wēre, *v.* to wear. [Obs.]

wēre, *n.* weir. [Obs.]

wēre, *n.* wer. [Obs.]

wẽre, *v.* [ME. *weren*; AS. *wæron*.] the plural and second person singular, past indicative, and the past subjunctive, of *be*.

wē're, we are.

wēre'gild, *n.* same as *wergild*.

wēre·n't (wẽrnt), were not.

wēre'wolf (-wu̇lf *or* wẽr'wu̇lf), *n.*; *pl.* **wēre'wolveș** (-wu̇lvz), [ME. *werwolf*; AS. *werwulf*; *wer*, a man, and *wulf*, a wolf.] in folklore, a person changed into a wolf, or one capable of assuming the form of a wolf at will: also spelled *werwolf*.

wẽr'gild, wēre'gild, *n.* [AS. *wergild*; *wer*, man, and *gild, geld*, a payment, recompense, compensation.] in early Germanic and Anglo-Saxon law, a price paid by the family of a manslayer to the family of the person killed, to atone for the killing and avoid reprisals.

wẽrk, wẽrke, *n.* work. [Obs.]

wẽrn, wẽrne, *v.* warn. [Obs.]

Wẽr·nē'ri·ăn, *a.* of or pertaining to Abraham Gottlob Werner (1750–1817), a German mineralogist and geologist, or to his theory of the earth's formation, called the Neptunian theory.

wẽr'nẽr·īte, *n.* [from A.G. *Werner*; and *-ite*.] a mineral, a silicate of aluminum and calcium; scapolite.

wẽrre, *n.* war. [Obs.]

wẽrst, *n.* verst. [Obs.]

wẽrt, *v.* archaic second person singular, past indicative and subjunctive, of *be*: used with *thou*.

wẽrt, *n.* wart. [Obs.]

wẽr'wolf (-wu̇lf), *n.*; *pl.* **wẽr'wolveș** (-wu̇lvz), a werewolf.

wē'sănd, *n.* same as *weasand*.

wesh, *v.* wash. [Dial.]

Wes'lēy·ăn, *a.* 1. pertaining to John Wesley (1703–1791) or the Methodist Church.
2. of or pertaining to the English family of which John and Charles Wesley were members; as, *Wesleyan* genealogy.

Wes'lēy·ăn, *n.* a follower of John Wesley; a Methodist.

Wes'lēy·ăn·ișm, *n.* the religious doctrines and method taught by John Wesley; Methodism.

west, *n.* [ME.; AS. *west*, adv., westward; *westan*, adv., from the west.]
1. the direction to the left of a person facing north; the direction in which sunset occurs: it is properly the point on the horizon at which the center of the sun sets at the equinox.
2. the point of the compass at 90°, midway between the north and south points and directly opposite the east.
3. a country or region toward this direction; as, to emigrate to the *west*.
4. [W–] the western half of the earth as distinguished from the eastern, or Orient; the Western Hemisphere or the Western Hemisphere and Europe; the Occident.
5. [W–] the western part of the United States, formerly, the region west of the Appalachian Mountains; now, the region west of the Mississippi River, especially the northern part of this region: with *the*.
6. [W–] the Western Roman Empire.
Empire of the West; same as *Western Empire* under *western*.

west, *a.* 1. in, of, to, toward, or facing the west.
2. coming or moving from the west or western region; as, a *west* wind.
3. [W–] designating the western part of a continent, country, etc.; as, *West* Africa, *West* Ohio.
4. in a church, opposite or pertaining to the part opposite the altar: from the conventional location of the altar at the eastern end.
West End; in London, England, the western part, especially the fashionable and aristocratic residential part embracing St. James's Park, Hyde Park, and Green Park.

west, *adv.* in or toward the west; in a westerly direction; westward; as, Ohio lies *west* of Pennsylvania.

west, *v.i.* to pass to the west.

west'bound, *a.* bound west; going westward.

west bȳ nọrth, the direction, or the point on a mariner's compass, halfway between due west and west-northwest; 11°15′ north of due west.

west bȳ south, the direction, or the point on a mariner's compass, halfway between due west and west-southwest; 11°15′ south of due west.

west'ẽr, *v.i.* to move, turn, or shift to the west.

west'ẽr·ing, *a.* passing to the west.

west'ẽr·ly, *a.* 1. in, of, or toward the west; situated in the western region; as, the *westerly* parts of England.
2. from the west; as, a *westerly* wind.

west'ẽr·ly, *adv.* 1. toward the west; as, a man traveling *westerly*.
2. from the west; as, the wind blew *westerly*.

west'ẽr·ly, *n.*; *pl.* **west'ẽr·lieș,** a wind blowing from the west.

west'ẽrn, *a.* [ME.; AS. *westerne*.]
1. in, of, toward, or facing the west.
2. from the west; as, a *western* wind.
3. [W–] of or characteristic of the West.
4. [W–] of the Western Church.
Western (*Roman*) *Empire*; the western portion of the Roman Empire as divided in 395 A.D. by Theodosius.

west'ẽrn, *n.* 1. a westerner.
2. a story, motion picture, etc. on the life of cowboys or frontiersmen in the western United States.

West'ẽrn Chũrch, 1. that part of the Catholic Church which recognizes the Pope as patriarch as well as pontiff and which follows the Latin Rite: it now comprises most of the Roman Catholic Church, excepting only certain Eastern churches.
2. broadly, all the Christian churches of Western Europe and America.

west'ẽrn·ẽr, *n.* one who is a native or inhabitant of the west; specifically [W–], a native or inhabitant of the western part of the United States.

West'ẽrn Hem'i·sphēre, that half of the earth which includes North and South America.

west'ẽrn·ișm, *n.* a word, expression, or practice peculiar to the west, especially one peculiar to the western United States.

west'ẽrn·īze, *v.t.*, westernized, *pt., pp.*; westernizing, *ppr.* to make western in character, habits, ideas, etc.

west'ẽrn·mōst, *a.* most western; farthest west.

West'ẽrn Ō'ceăn (-shun), the Atlantic: the ancient name.

West In'di·ăn, 1. pertaining to the West Indies.
2. a native or inhabitant of the West Indies.

west'ing, *n.* in nautical usage, the distance due west covered by a ship sailing in any westerly direction.

West'ing·house brāke, a railroad airbrake controlled by compressed air from a pump on the engine of a locomotive: it acts automatically when a coupling is disconnected.

West'min·stẽr Ab'bey, a Gothic church in Westminster where English kings are crowned: it is also the burial place of English kings, famous writers, etc.

West'min·stẽr As·sem'bly, an assembly of clergymen that met at Westminster, London (1643–1649), and formulated certain articles of faith now generally accepted as authoritative by Presbyterian churches.

west'mōst, *a.* farthest west.

west'-north·west', *n.* the direction, or the point on a mariner's compass, halfway between due west and northwest; 22°30′ north of due west.

west'-north·west', *a.* and *adv.* 1. in or toward west-northwest.
2. from west-northwest; as, a *west-northwest* wind.

West·phā'li·ăn, *a.* of Westphalia, its people, culture, etc.

West·phā'li·ăn, *n.* a native or inhabitant of Westphalia.

Wes·trā′li·ăn, *n.* a native or inhabitant of West Australia.

west′-south·west′, *n.* the direction, or the point on a mariner's compass, halfway between due west and southwest; 22°30′ south of due west.

west′-south·west′, *a.* and *adv.* 1. in or toward west-southwest.
 2. from west-southwest; as, a *west-southwest* wind.

West Vĭr·ġin′iăn (-yăn), 1. of West Virginia.
 2. a native or inhabitant of West Virginia.

west′wărd, *a.* and *adv.* [AS. *westeweard.*] toward the west; as, to ride or sail *westward.*

west′wărd, *n.* a westward direction, point, or region.

west′wărd·ly, *a.* and *adv.* 1. toward the west; as, to pass *westwardly.*
 2. from the west; as, a *westwardly* wind.

west′wărdș, *adv.* same as *westward.*

west′y, *a.* giddy; frivolous; dizzy. [Obs. exc. Brit. Dial.]

wet, *a.*; *comp.* wetter; *superl.* wettest, [ME. *wet, wete*; AS. *wæt,* wet.]
 1. moistened, saturated, or containing water or other liquid.
 2. rainy; foggy; misty; as, *wet* weather.
 3. not yet dry; as, *wet* paint.
 4. preserved or bottled in a liquid.
 5. using water; done with or in water or other liquid; as, *wet* sanding.
 6. permitting or favoring the manufacture or sale of alcoholic liquor; as, a *wet* candidate, *wet* town.
 7. in chemistry, treated with or analyzed by liquid reagents.
 8. tipsy; somewhat intoxicated. [Colloq.]
 all wet; wrong; mistaken; in error. [Slang.]
 wet bob; in Eton College slang, a boy who prefers boating to sports on land.
 wet goods; alcoholic beverages. [Colloq.]
 wet plate; in photography, a sensitized plate used while in a moist condition.
 wet provisions; in nautical usage, a class of provisions including meats in brine, vinegar, molasses, spirits, etc.
 wet steam; vaporized water.

wet, *n.* 1. that which moistens or makes wet; water or other liquid; moisture; as, wear thick shoes to keep your feet from the *wet.*
 2. rainy weather; foggy or misty weather.
 3. one who advocates the sale or manufacture of alcoholic liquors.

wet, *v.t.* and *v.i.*; wet *or* wetted, *pt., pp.*; wetting, *ppr.* to make or become wet (often with *through* or *down*); specifically, to make (a bed, oneself, etc.) wet by urination.
 to wet one's whistle; to take a drink. [Colloq.]

wet′back, *n.* [from the fact that many cross the border by swimming or wading the Rio Grande.] a Mexican agricultural laborer who illegally enters or is brought into the United States to work.

wet′bĭrd, *n.* the chaffinch: so called because it is said to give warning of rain by its cry. [Brit. Dial.]

wet blaǹ′ket, a person or thing that dampens, or discourages, activity, enthusiasm, or pleasure.

wet bulb, in a psychrometer, that bulb of one of the two thermometers which is kept moistened in measuring humidity.

wet cell, a voltaic cell in which the electrolyte is a liquid.

weth′ẽr, *n.* [ME.; AS. *wither.*] a castrated ram.

wet′land, *n.* [*usually pl.*] swamps or marshes, especially as an area preserved for wildlife.

wet′ness, *n.* the state or quality of being wet.

wet nŭrse, a woman hired to suckle a child not her own.

wet′-nŭrse, *v.t.*; wet-nursed, *pt., pp.*; wet-nursing, *ppr.* 1. to be a wet nurse for; to suckle.
 2. to treat tenderly; to coddle.

wet pack, in medicine, the wrapping of a patient in wet sheets to reduce fever.

wet′-shod, *a.* shod with wet shoes; having the shoes drenched with water. [Dial.]

wet′tẽr, *n.* one who or that which wets.

wet′tẽr-ọff, *n.* in glass blowing, one who with a wet tool detaches a bottle or other blown piece from the blower's tube.

wet′ting ā′ġent, any of a group of surface-active agents which, when added to a liquid, cause the liquid to spread more easily over, or penetrate into, a solid surface.

wet′tish, *a.* somewhat wet; moist; humid.

wet wăsh, 1. laundry returned while it is still damp or partly dry.
 2. a washing at a car wash in which the car is not wiped dry.

wet wind, a wind that is most frequently accompanied or followed by rain.

wē′ve, we have.

wex, wexe, *v.t.* and *v.i.* to wax.

wex, *n.* wax. [Dial.]

wẹy, *n.* [ME. *weye,* weight, from AS. *wæge,* a burden or weight, from *wegan,* to bear, carry, weigh.] a certain English weight, varying greatly with different commodities, as a wey of wool is six and one-half tods, or 182 pounds; of oats and barley, 48 bushels; of cheese, 224 pounds; of salt, 40 bushels.

whä (hwä) *pron.* who. [Obs.]

whạap, *n.* same as *whaup.*

whack (hwak), *v.t.*; whacked (hwakt), *pt., pp.*; whacking, *ppr.* [echoic.] 1. to beat; to strike with a sharp resounding blow; as he *whacked* him over the head with his billy. [Colloq.]
 2. to divide; to share; as, they *whacked* the booty. [Slang.]

whack, *v.i.* 1. to strike with sharp, resounding blows; as, he *whacked* away until the tree fell. [Colloq.]
 2. to settle; to divide; to square accounts: usually with *up.* [Slang.]

whack, *n.* 1. (a) a sharp, resounding blow; (b) the sound of this. [Colloq.]
 2. a share; a portion. [Slang.]
 3. a try; an attempt; as, let me have a *whack* at it. [Slang.]
 4. proper condition or adjustment; as, the motor is out of *whack.* [Slang.]

whack′ẽr, *n.* 1. one who whacks.
 2. one who or that which is of an unusually large size; as, that horse is a *whacker.* [Colloq.]

whack′ing, *a.* very large; whopping; as, a *whacking* lie. [Chiefly Brit. Colloq.]

whack′y, *a.*; *comp.* whackier; *superl.* whackiest, wacky. [Slang.]

whăd′die, *n.* waddie. [Obs.]

whāle (hwāl), *v.t.*; whaled, *pt., pp.*; whaling, *ppr.* [var. of *wale* (to ridge).] to thrash; to beat; to lash. [Colloq.]

whāle, *n.*; *pl.* **whāleș** or **whāle,** [ME. *whal*; AS. *hwæl.*] any of various large, warm-blooded, fishlike mammals of the order *Cetacea,* that breathe air, bear live young, and are found in all seas; specifically, any of the larger, toothless species (as distinguished from dolphins and porpoises) having sheets of baleen, or whalebone, suspended from the upper jaw. The whales are sometimes divided into two families, the *Balænidæ* and the

SPERM WHALE (63 ft. long)

Physeteridæ, or *Catodontidæ.* The *Balænidæ,* or whalebone whales, are distinguished by the absence of teeth, by the presence of baleen or whalebone, and by the nostrils being placed on the top of the head. The typical representative of this family is the common or Greenland right whale, *Balæna mysticetus,* valued for the oil and whalebone which it furnishes. It is principally found in the Arctic seas. Its length is usually about sixty feet, and its greatest circumference from thirty to forty feet. The razor-backed whale, or northern rorqual, is the *Balænoptera borealis.* It often measures a hundred feet in length, and thirty to thirty-five feet in circumference. The *Physeteridæ* or *Catodontidæ* are characterized by the fact that the upper jaw has no baleen, and the lower jaw possesses a series of pointed conical teeth. The best-known species of this family is the sperm whale or cachalot, *Physeter* or *Catodon macrocephalus,* which averages from fifty to seventy feet in length.
 a whale of a; an exceptionally large, fine, impressive, amusing, etc. example or specimen of a (class of things). [Colloq.]

whāle, *v.i.*; whaled, *pt., pp.*; whaling, *ppr.* to be engaged in the business of hunting whale.

whāle′back, *n.* something rounded on top like the back of a whale; specifically, a freight steamer with the bow and upper deck rounded so that heavy seas will wash right over: formerly used on the Great Lakes.

whāle bär′nȧ·cle (-kl), a cirriped that is parasitic on whales.

whāle′bĭrd, *n.* a bird that follows the whaling vessels to feed on the offal thrown into the sea; especially, an antarctic petrel of the genus *Prion* or *Pachytilla.*

whāle′bōat, *n.* a large, long rowboat, pointed at both ends to increase maneuverability: used by whalers, coastguards, etc., or as a ship's lifeboat.

whāle′bōne, *n.* 1. an elastic horny substance that adheres in thin parallel plates to the upper jaw of certain whales, especially the *Balænidæ*: it serves to strain the minute sea animals on which they feed. From its flexibility, strength, elasticity, and lightness, whalebone is employed for many purposes, as for the ribs of umbrellas and parasols, for stiffening stays, etc. Also called *baleen.*
 2. something made of whalebone as one of the stays of a corset, etc.

whāle′bōne *a.* made of or containing whalebone.

whāle′-built (-bilt), *a.* built in the form of a whaleboat.

whāle fin, whalebone. [Slang.]

whāle′fish, *n.* a whale. [Obs.]

whāle fish′ẽr, a person or vessel engaged in whale fishery; a whaler.

whāle fish′ẽr·y, 1. the hunting for whales or occupation of hunting for whales.
 2. a part of the ocean where whale fishing is carried on.

whāle fish′ing, the act or occupation of hunting whales.

whāle′head (-hed), *n.* the African shoebill of the stork and heron family.

whāle louse, a small crustacean, *Cyamus ceti,* found parasitic on the whale; also, any of various other species of the same genus.

whāle′măn, *n.*; *pl.* **whāle′men,** a man employed in whaling; a whaler.

whāle oil, the oil obtained from the blubber of the whale.

whāl′ẽr, *n.* 1. a whaling ship.
 2. a man whose work is whaling; whaleman.

whāl′ẽr, *n.* something unusually large of its kind; a whopper. [Slang.]

whāl′ẽr·y, *n.* whale fishery.

whāle shärk, 1. the basking shark.
 2. a very large harmless shark of the genus *Rhinodon,* found in tropical waters.

whāle shot, spermaceti. [Obs.]

whāle′ș′-tŏngue (-tung), *n.* a marine worm of the genus *Balanoglossus.*

whāl′ing, *a.* unusually large of its kind; whopping. [Slang.]

whāl′ing, *n.* the trade or occupation of hunting and killing whales for their blubber, whalebone, etc.

whāl′ing, *n.* [from *whale* (to beat), and *-ing.*] a sound thrashing; a whipping. [Colloq.]

whāl′ing gun, a harpoon gun.

whạll′y, *a.* having a light-colored iris, as the eyes of some horses. [Rare.]

whāme (hwām), *n.* the breeze fly.

wham′mel (hwam′), *v.t.* same as *whemmel.*

whăm·pee′ (hwăm-), *n.* same as *wampee.*

whăn (hwăn), *adv.* when. [Obs.]

whang (hwang), *n.* [a var. of *thong.*] a leather string; a thong. [Scot.]

whang, *v.t.* [of echoic origin.]
 1. to strike with a resounding blow; to whack.
 2. to beat or thrash. [Dial.]

whang, *v.i.* to make a whanging noise.

whang, *n.* a whack.

whang′dọọ·dle (-dl), *n.* [fanciful coinage.] a mythical creature with undefined characteristics: a humorous usage.

whang·ee′, *n.* [prob. from Chin. *huang-li*; *huang,* yellow, and *li,* bamboo, cane.]
 1. any of a number of related Chinese and Japanese bamboos.
 2. a walking stick made from any of these bamboos.

whang·hee′, *n.* same as *wangee.*

whăp (hwăp), *v.i.*; whapped (hwăpt), *pt., pp.*; whapping, *ppr.* to whop. [Dial. or Archaic.]

whăp′pẽr, *n.* a whopper. [Colloq.]

whä′rẹ (hwä′rā), *n.* [Maori.] a house; a dwelling.

whạrf (hwạrf), *n.*; *pl.* **whạrveș** or **whạrfs,** [ME. and AS. *hwerf,* a dam or bank to keep out water, lit., a turning, from *hwearf,* pt. of *hweorfan,* to turn.]
 1. a structure constructed of wood or stone, sometimes roofed over, on the margin of a harbor, river, etc., alongside of which ships are brought, as for being loaded or unloaded; a pier.
 2. the bank of a river or the shore of the sea. [Obs.]

whạrf, *v.t.*; wharfed (hwạrft), *pt., pp.*; wharfing, *ppr.* 1. to bring to a wharf; to moor at a wharf.
 2. to unload or store on a wharf.
 3. to furnish with a wharf or wharves.

whạrf′ȧġe, *n.* 1. the use of a wharf for mooring, loading, or unloading a ship, or for storing goods.

2. a fee charged for this.
3. port facilities; a wharf or wharves collectively; as, plenty of *wharfage*.

wharf bōat, in the United States, a kind of boat moored on a river and used as a substitute for a wharf, where the rise of the water is so variable as to make a fixed wharf unserviceable.

whärf'ing, *n.* 1. wharves collectively.
2. material for a wharf or wharves.
3. a protective facing for a shore or bank, consisting of planks driven in a row and fastened with tie beams; also, the process of making such a facing.

whärf'in·ġēr, *n.* [altered from earlier *wharfager*, from *wharfage*.] a person who owns or who has charge of a wharf.

whärf'măn, *n.*; *pl.* **whärf'men,** a man employed on or in connection with a wharf.

whärf rat, 1. a large brown rat, *Mus decumanus*, found around wharves.
2. a vagrant or petty criminal who haunts wharves.

whärl, *n.* a burr in pronunciation. [Rare.]

whärp, *n.* a fine sand from the valley of the river Trent, used in polishing. [Brit.]

whärve (hwärv), *n.* [ME. *wherve*; AS. *hweorfa*, from base of *hweorfan*, to turn.]
1. originally, a small flywheel on the lower end of the spindle of a spinning wheel, for giving momentum to the wheel.
2. a small drive pulley on a spindle of a modern spinning machine.

whärveṣ (hwärvz), *n.* alternative pl. of *wharf*.

whăt (hwot), *pron.* [ME. *hwat*, *hwet*; AS. *hwæt*, neut. of *hwā*, who.]
1. which thing, event, circumstance, etc.: used interrogatively in asking for the specification of an identity, quantity, quality, etc.; specifically, (a) in asking about the nature or class of a thing; as, *what* is that object?; (b) in asking for an explanation or repetition of something previously said; as, you told him *what?*; (c) in asking about the value, importance, or effect of something; as, *what* is life without Shirley? *What* is often used elliptically with the sense of 1(b), or, especially as a British colloquialism, to end a sentence with a general or rhetorical interrogative force; as, you're rather late, *what?*
2. that which or those which; as, I know *what* you want: used as a compound relative pronoun with the specific senses of (a) anything that; as, do *what* you will; (b) the exact person or thing that; as, as a swimmer, I am not *what* I was ten years ago; (c) that or who: now regarded as substandard (the man *what* gave it to me) except in *but what*, but that or but who; as, there is no one *but what* would approve this act: also used elliptically for *what it is*, *what to do*, etc. (I'll tell you *what*) and with an intensive force in exclamations (*what* I know about you!).
and what not; and other things of all sorts.
what for; (a) for what purpose? why?; (b) [Slang.] punishment; especially, a whipping; as, I'll give him *what for!*
what have you; anything else of a similar sort; as, he sells games, toys, or *what have you*. [Colloq.]
what if; what would happen if; suppose; supposing.
what it takes; whatever is necessary for success or popularity, as wealth, beauty, or intelligence.
what's what; the true state of affairs. [Colloq.]

whăt, *a.* 1. which or which kind of: used interrogatively or relatively in asking for or specifying the nature, identity, etc. of a person or thing; as, *what* man told you that? I know *what* books you will need.
2. as much, or as many, as; as, take *what* time (or men) you need.
3. how great, surprising, magnificent, disappointing, etc.: in exclamations, as, *what* a man! *what* nonsense!

whăt, *adv.* 1. in what respect? to what degree? how?; as, *what* does it help to complain?
2. in some manner or degree; in part; partly (usually followed by *with*); as, *what with* singing and joking, the time passed quickly.
3. how greatly, surprisingly, etc.: in exclamations, as, *what* tragic news!
What fine change is in the music.
—Shak.
4. why? [Obs.]

whăt, *conj.* 1. that: in *but what*, but that; as, never doubt *but what* he loves you.
2. so far as; as much as; as, we warned them *what* we could. [Dial.]

whăt, *interj.* an exclamation of surprise, anger, confusion, etc.; as, *what!* no dinner?

whăt, *n.* 1. something; a thing; stuff.
2. a certain quantity.

whăt·e'er' (hwot-âr'), *pron.* and *a.* whatever. [Poet.]

whăt·ev'ēr, *pron.* what: an emphatic variant; specifically, (a) which thing, event, circumstance, etc.?: used as an interrogative expressing perplexity or wonder; as, *whatever* can he mean by that?; (b) anything that; as, tell her *whatever* you like; (c) no matter what; as, *whatever* you may think, he's innocent.

whăt·ev'ēr, *a.* 1. of no matter what type, degree, quality, etc.; as, Don can make *whatever* repairs are needed.
2. being who it may be; as, *whatever* man told you that, it is not true.
Whatever is sometimes used following the word that it modifies; as, I have no plans *whatever*.

whăt hō! an exclamation used in calling.

whăt'not, *n.* 1. a set of open shelves used to hold papers, books, pictures, etc.
2. a nondescript or indescribable thing or, sometimes, person.

whăt's, what is.

whăt'sō, *pron.* whatever. [Archaic.]

whăt·sō·e'er' (-âr'), *pron.* and *a.* whatsoever. [Poet.]

whăt·sō·ev'ēr, *pron.* and *a.* whatever: an emphatic form.

whaup (hwäp), *n.* a curlew. [Scot. or Eng. Dial.]
little whaup; the whimbrel.

whēal (hwēl), *n.* [ME. *whele*, *whelle*, *wheel*, a wheal.]
1. a pustule; a pimple.
2. a small, itching elevation of the skin, as from the bite of an insect.

whēal, *n.* [altered from *weal*, a wale, by association with ME. *whele*, a pustule.] a raised stripe or ridge on the skin, as from a lash of a whip; a wale.

whēal, *n.* [Corn. *hwel*, a work, mine.] a mine. [Brit. Dial.]

whēal'wŏrm, *n.* an insect whose sting causes a wheal, as the harvest mite, itch mite, etc.

whēat (hwēt), *n.* [ME. *whete*; AS. *hwæte*, wheat.]
1. any of a number of related cereal grasses of the genus *Triticum*, especially *Triticum sativum* or *vulgare*, having spikes filled with seeds: the spikes in some species have awns (*bearded wheat*) and in others are bare (*beardless*, or *bald*, *wheat*).
2. the seed of any of these grasses, used for making flour, cereals, etc.: next to rice, the most widely used grain.
Guinea wheat; maize.
Indian wheat; (a) [Obs.] Indian corn; (b) Tatary wheat.
one-grained wheat; a wheat, *Triticum monococcum*, having a single seed to each spikelet.
Tatary wheat; a grain, *Fagopyrum tataricum*, somewhat resembling buckwheat.
Turkey or *Turkish wheat*; maize. [Obs.]
wheat bulb fly; a fly, *Hylemyia arctica*, of Europe, the larva of which eats wheat stems.
wheat bulb worm; the larva of a North American fly, *Meromyza americana*, which infests the stalks of wheat; also, the larva of the wheat bulb fly.
wheat eelworm; the wheatworm.
wheat gallfly; the adult of the jointworm.
wheat plant louse; an aphid which infests wheat, as *Siphonophora avenæ*.

whēat ā'phid, an aphid living upon growing wheat; a wheat plant louse.

whēat bee'tle, any beetle injurious to wheat, as *Sylvanus surinamensis*.

whēat'bīrd, *n.* the chaffinch. [Brit. Dial.]

whēat bug, a bug of the genus *Miris*, which is injurious to wheat.

whēat chăf'ēr, a European beetle of the genus *Anisoplia*, which infests growing wheat.

whēat çut'wŏrm, the larva of an American moth, *Laphygma frugiperda*.

whēat duck, the widgeon of America. [Dial.]

whēat'ēar, *n.* an ear of wheat.

whēat'ēar, *n.* [earlier *white ears*, from *white* and *erres*, *ers*, var. of *arse*: so named in reference to its white rump.] any of a group of small, long-legged, migrating birds, *Saxicola œnanthe*, of Northern Europe, Asia, and America, belonging to the family of chats: it is grayish-brown above, white below, with the wings and tip of the tail black.

whēat'en, *a.* 1. made of wheat or wheat flour; as, *wheaten* bread.
2. of the pale-yellow color of wheat.

whēat flȳ, any of various flies injurious or destructive to wheat, as (a) the frit fly, *Oscinis frit*; (b) the Hessian fly; (c) the wheat midge.

whēat grȧss, any wild grass of the genus *Triticum*; specifically, couch grass.

whēat'-head (-hed) **är'my wŏrm,** the larva of *Neleucania albilinea*, a moth of the family *Noctuidæ*: it is destructive to wheat.

whēat mag'gŏt, the larva of a wheat fly, destructive to growing wheat.

whēat midġe (mij), a two-winged gnat, *Diplosis tritici*, of England and the United States. The larvae hatch from eggs laid in the flowers of wheat and feed on the young kernels.

whēat mil'dew, *n.* a powdery fungus, *Erysiphe graminis*, attacking wheat.

whēat mīte, a flour mite.

whēat mŏth, any of various moths, the larvae of which subsist upon the grains of wheat.

whēat pest, the frit fly.

whēat'sel bīrd, the male wheatbird. [Brit. Dial.]

Whēat'stōne's bridġe (brij), see under *bridge*.

whēat thiēf, the bastard alkanet, *Lithospermum arvense*, introduced into the United States from Europe.

whēat thrips, a thrips injurious to wheat.

whēat wee'vil, the grain weevil; also, the rice weevil.

whēat'wŏrm, *n.* a small roundworm, *Tylenchus tritici*, that destroys wheat.

whed'ēr, *pron.* whether. [Obs.]

whee'dle (hwē'), *v.t.* and *v.i.*; wheedled, *pt.*, *pp.*; wheedling, *ppr.* [G. *wedeln*, to wag the tail, fan, hence to flatter, from *wedel*, a fan, tail.]
1. to flatter; to entice by soft words; to coax.
2. to get by coaxing or flattery; as, to *wheedle* a secret out of one.

wheel (hwēl), *n.* [ME. *whele*; AS. *hweol*, shortened from *hweowol*, a wheel.]
1. a solid disk, or a circular frame connected by spokes to a central hub, capable of turning on a central axis, and used to move vehicles or transmit power in machinery.
2. anything like a wheel in shape, movement, action, etc., as a firework that revolves in a circular orbit while burning.
3. a device or apparatus of which the principal element is a wheel or wheels; specifically, (a) in the Middle Ages, an instrument of torture consisting of a circular frame on which the victim's limbs were broken; (b) a wheel with projecting handles for controlling the rudder of a ship; (c) the steering wheel of a motor vehicle; (d) [Colloq.] a bicycle or, rarely, a tricycle; (e) a spinning wheel; (f) a potter's wheel.
4. [*usually pl.*] the moving, propelling, or controlling forces or agencies; as, the *wheels* of progress.
5. a turning about; rotation or revolution; specifically, in military usage, a turning movement of troops or ships in line, in which the line is maintained while one end makes a circular movement about the other as pivot.
6. a refrain of a song.
7. a dollar; a cart wheel. [Colloq.]
at the wheel; (a) steering or directing a ship or motor vehicle; at the steering wheel; (b) in charge; directing activities.
wheel and axle; a pulley fixed solidly to a shaft or drum, and used for lifting weights: the turning of the pulley by a rope or chain in the groove winds a rope on the shaft or drum: it is one of the simple machines. The common winch, the windlass, the capstan, and the treadmill are applications of the wheel and axle.
wheel of fortune; (a) the wheel which the goddess of fortune was believed to rotate to bring about the alternations or reverses in human affairs; (b) the changes or vicissitudes of life.
wheels within wheels; a series of involved circumstances, motives, etc. reacting upon one another.

wheel, *v.t.*; wheeled, *pt.*, *pp.*; wheeling, *ppr.* 1. to cause to turn on an axis, pivot, etc., or round a center; to cause to revolve or rotate.
2. (a) to move or roll on wheels; as, he *wheeled* the cart into the yard; (b) to convey in a vehicle mounted on wheels; as, to *wheel* a load of earth, hay, or timber.
3. to make or perform in a circular direction.

4. to provide with a wheel or wheels; as, to *wheel* a cart.

wheel, *v.i.* 1. to turn on an axis or as on an axis; to revolve; to rotate.

2. to reverse one's course of action, opinion, attitude, etc.: often with *about.*

3. to turn in a swooping circular motion: said of birds.

4. to move along on or as on wheels; specifically, to travel by means of a bicycle or, rarely, a tricycle.

wheel an'i·măl, wheel an·i·mal'çūle, a rotifer.

wheel'bar"rōw, *n.* [ME. *wilberwe.*] a shallow, open box for moving small loads, having a single wheel in front forming a tripod with the two legs in back, and two shafts with handles for raising the vehicle off its legs and pushing or pulling it.

wheel'bar"rōw, *v.t.* to move or transport in a wheelbarrow.

wheel'bāse, *n.* in a motor vehicle, the distance in inches from the center of the hub of a front wheel to the center of the hub of the corresponding back wheel: also *wheel base.*

wheel'bīrd, *n.* the common goatsucker. [Brit. Dial.]

wheel bug, an insect, *Prionidus cristatus,* which sucks the blood of other insects: so called from the shape of a saw-toothed crest on the prothorax, resembling a portion of a cog wheel.

wheel çar'riăģe (-rij), a carriage moved on wheels.

wheel chāin, a chain used to connect the wheel and the rudder of a ship or boat, in the manner of a wheel rope.

wheel chāir, a mobile chair or chairlike structure for invalids, mounted on large wheels; a Bath chair.

wheeled, *a.* furnished with a wheel or wheels: often used in hyphenated compounds, meaning *having a* (specified kind or number of) wheels; as, a two-*wheeled* carriage.

wheel'ēr, *n.* 1. one who or that which wheels.

2. one who makes wheels. [Obs.]

3. a wheel horse (sense 1).

4. something having a wheel or wheels: usually in hyphenated compounds, meaning *something having a* (specified kind or number of) *wheels,* as in side-*wheeler,* two-*wheeler.*

wheel hors̤e, 1. a horse hitched next to the fore wheel of a vehicle; one of a pair of horses next to the vehicle when more than one pair are used.

2. a person who works very hard and steadily in any enterprise.

wheel'house, *n.* a shelter built over the steering wheel of a ship; a pilothouse.

wheel'ie, *n.* a stunt performed on a motorcycle or bicycle, in which the front wheel is raised so that the vehicle is balanced for a moment on its rear wheel.

wheel'ing, *n.* 1. the act of a person who travels on wheels; especially, the act of one who cycles.

2. the condition of streets, highways, etc. in regard to traveling them on wheels; as, good *wheeling.*

3. a rotary movement, as of a body of soldiers; a circle; a revolution.

wheel lāthe, a lathe for turning metal wheels, as of a railway car.

wheel lock, 1. a firing mechanism on certain obsolete firearms, consisting of a rough wheel which spun on a flint when the trigger was pulled, throwing sparks into the pan and setting off the charge.

2. a device for locking a wheel; a sort of brake.

wheel'măn, *n.*; *pl.* **wheel'men,** 1. one who uses a bicycle, tricycle, or similar conveyance; a cyclist.

2. a wheelsman.

wheel ōre, [Corn. *wheel,* for *hwel,* a mine; and *ore.*] an opaque mineral of a steel-gray or black color and metallic luster, consisting chiefly of sulfur, antimony, lead, and copper; a variety of bournonite.

wheel plow, a plow with a wheel or wheels added to it for the purpose of regulating the depth of the furrow and rendering the movement of the implement more steady.

wheel'rāce, *n.* the part of a millrace in which the water wheel is fixed.

wheel rōpe, a rope reeved through a block on each side of the deck and led round the barrel of the steering wheel, to assist in moving the rudder.

wheel'-shāped (-shāpt), *a.* having a shape like a wheel.

wheelṣ'măn, *n.*; *pl.* **wheelṣ'men,** a person who steers a ship; a helmsman.

wheel stitch, an embroidery stitch resembling a spider's web.

wheel'swärf, *n.* a clayey cement or putty made from the dust of grindstones.

wheel'tree, *n.* same as *paddlewood.*

wheel win'dōw, same as *rose window.*

wheel'wŏrk, *n.* an arrangement of wheels or gears in a machine, or mechanical contrivance.

wheel'-wōrn, *a.* worn by the action of moving wheel tires.

wheel'wrīght (-rīt), *n.* a man whose occupation is to make and repair wheels and wheeled vehicles, as carts and wagons.

wheel'y, *a.* circular; suitable to rotation. [Colloq.]

wheen (hwēn), *n.* [ME. *qwheyn(e)*; AS. *hwēne, hwǣne,* somewhat, a little.] a few. [Scot. and Brit. Dial.]

wheeze (hwēz), *v.i.*; wheezed, *pt., pp.*; wheezing, *ppr.* [ME. *whesen*; AS. *hwēsan,* to wheeze.]

1. to breathe hard with a whistling, breathy sound, as persons affected with asthma.

2. to make a similar sound; as, the old organ *wheezed.*

wheeze, *v.t.* to utter with the sound of wheezing.

wheeze, *n.* 1. an act or sound of wheezing.

2. an overworked or trite remark, joke, or gag. [Slang.]

wheez'i·ly, *adv.* in a wheezy manner; with a whistling sound.

wheez'i·ness, *n.* the state or condition of being wheezy.

wheez'y, *a.*; *comp.* wheezier; *superl.* wheeziest, affected with or characterized by wheezing; as, a *wheezy* voice; a *wheezy* pump.

wheft (hweft), *n.* same as *waif* (signal flag).

whelk (hwelk), *n.* [ME. *whelke*; AS. *hwylca,* a pustule, from base of *hwelian,* to exude pus.] a pimple or pustule.

whelk, *n.* [ME. *wilke*; AS. *wiloc, wioluc*; so called from its convoluted shell; allied to AS. *wealcan,* to roll.] any of various large marine snails having a shell univalvular, spiral, and gibbous, with an oval aperture ending in a short canal or gutter, especially those used in Europe as food.

whelked (hwelkt), *a.* having the form of a whelk; ridged or twisted like the shell of a whelk.

whelk'y, *a.* protuberant; abounding in pustules or blisters.

whelm (hwelm), *v.t.*; whelmed, *pt., pp.*; whelming, *ppr.* [ME. *whelmen*; prob. a merging of AS. *-hwelfan,* to overwhelm, with *helmian,* to cover, and other words of like form.]

1. to cover, submerge, or engulf; as, to *whelm* a person or a company in the seas; to *whelm* a caravan in sand or dust.

2. to crush, ruin, or destroy; to overwhelm or overpower.

whelp (hwelp), *n.* [ME. *whelp*; AS. *hwelp,* whelp.]

1. a young dog; puppy.

2. the young of any of various flesh-eating animals, as of a lion, tiger, leopard, bear, wolf, etc.

3. a youth or child: a contemptuous usage.

4. [*usually in pl.*] in nautical usage, any of the upright pieces of wood placed round the barrel of the capstan of a ship to prevent it from being chafed and to afford resting points for the messenger or hawsers; also, any of the pieces of wood bolted on the main piece of a windlass or a winch for a similar purpose.

5. a tooth of a sprocket wheel.

whelp, *v.t.* and *v.i.* to bring forth (young); to give birth to: said of animals, and contemptuously of a woman; as, she has *whelped* thieves.

whem'mel, whem'mle (hwem'), *v.t.* and *v.i.* to whelm or turn over; to overturn. [Scot. and Brit. Dial.]

when (hwen), *adv.* [ME. *whan, whanne*; AS. *hwænne, hwonne.*] at what time? on what occasion?: used interrogatively and in indirect questions; as, *when* did he come? I do not know *when* he came (the latter being an indirect question).

when, *conj.* 1. at the time that; at or just after the moment that; as, he is most happy *when* most unselfish.

2. at which time; as, the time was *when* the land was new.

3. at the same time that; while; while instead; while on the contrary; whereas; as, you anger him *when* you should cheer him.

4. at what time; as, he told us *when* to eat.

5. at which; as, now is the time *when* we must fight.

6. as soon as; as, we will eat *when* father comes.

7. at whatever time; whenever; as, she cries *when* you criticize her.

8. if; considering the fact that; as, how can we finish, *when* you won't help?

when, *pron.* what or which time; as, until *when* will you remain? we came a week ago since *when* we've had no rest.

when, *n.* the time or moment (*of* an event); as, I know the *when* and where *of* his arrest.

when·aṣ', *conj.* 1. when.

2. whereas.

3. inasmuch as.

[Archaic in all senses.]

whence, *adv.* [ME. *whennes,* with genit. ending *-es* substituted for older form *whanene*; AS. *hwanan, hwanon, hwonan,* whence.]

1. from what place; where; as, *whence* do you come?

2. from what source or cause; as, *whence* does he get his strength?

3. to the place from which; as, return *whence* you came.

whence·fōrth', *adv.* whence. [Rare.]

whence·sō·ev'ēr, *adv.* and *conj.* from whatever place, cause, or source.

whenc·ev'ēr, *adv.* whencesoever.

when·e'er' (-ār'), *adv.* and *conj.* whenever. [Poet.]

when·ev'ēr, *adv.* when; an emphatic form expressing surprise or bewilderment; as, *whenever* will you learn? [Colloq.]

when·ev'ēr, *conj.* 1. at whatever time; as, I'll be here *whenever* he arrives.

2. on whatever occasion; as, visit us *whenever* you can.

when·sō·ev'ēr, *adv.* and *conj.* whenever: an emphatic form.

where (hwār), *adv.* [ME. *wher*; AS. *hwar, hwær,* where.]

1. at or in what place?; as, *where* is Athens?

2. to or toward which place or point? whither?; as, *where* are you going?

3. in what situation or position?; as, *where* will we be if we lose?

4. in what respect?; as, *where* do I come into the matter?

5. from what place or source? whence?; as, *where* did they get this grain?

where, *conj.* 1. in or at what place; as, I know *where* they are.

2. in or at which place; as, we came home, *where* we had dinner.

3. in or at the place or situation in which; as, I am *where* I should be.

4. in whatever place, situation, or respect in which; as, there is never peace *where* men are greedy.

5. (a) to or toward the place to which; as, I will take you *where* you're going; (b) to a place in which; as, I never go *where* I'm not wanted.

6. to or toward whatever place; as, I don't care *where* you go.

where, *pron.* 1. the place or situation in, at, or to which; as, I live just two miles from *where* I was born.

2. what or which place; as, *where* do you come from?

where, *n.* the place (*of* an event); as, I don't know the when and *where of* his arrest.

where'ȧ·bout, *adv.* whereabouts. [Rare.]

where'ȧ·bout, *n.* whereabouts. [Rare.]

where'ȧ·bouts, *adv.* 1. where? near or at what place?; as, *whereabouts* did you drop the coin?

2. concerning which; about which; on what purpose. [Obs.]

where'ȧ·bouts, *n.* the location of a person or thing; locality; approximate situation; as, do you know the *whereabouts* of that person?

where·aṣ', *conj.* 1. while on the contrary; the fact or the case really being that; when in fact; as, she is slender *whereas* he is stout.

2. the thing being so that; considering that things are so; in view of the fact that: used in the preamble to a formal document.

3. where. [Archaic.]

where·at', *adv.* 1. at which? [Archaic.]

2. at what?; as, *whereat* are you offended? [Rare or Archaic.]

where·at', *conj.* at which; upon which; as, he turned to leave, *whereat* she began to weep. [Rare or Archaic.]

where·bȳ', *adv.* 1. by which; by means of which; as, a device *whereby* to make money.

2. by what? how?; as, *whereby* did you expect to profit?

wher·e·er' (-ār'), *adv.* and *conj.* wherever. [Poet.]

where'fōre, *adv.* 1. for which.

Wherefore let us beseech him to grant us true repentance. —Book of Common Prayer.

2. why? for what reason or purpose?; as, *wherefore* did you go?

where'fōre, *conj.* on account of which; because of which; therefore; as, we ran out of water, *wherefore* we surrendered.

where'fōre, *n.* the cause; the reason; as, tell me the why and *wherefore*.

where·from', *adv.* from which; whence.

where·in', *adv.* 1. in which; in which thing, time, respect, book, etc.; as, the room *wherein* he lay.

2. in what thing, time, respect, etc.?; as, *wherein* was I wrong?

where·in'tö (*or* -in-tö'), *adv.* into which.

where'ness, *n.* the state or quality of having a place or position; ubiety.

where·of' (-ov'), *adv.* of which, what, or whom.

where·on', *adv.* 1. on which; as, the hill *whereon* we stand.

2. on what?; as, *whereon* do you rely?

where·out', *adv.* out of which. [Rare.]

where'sō, *adv.* wheresoever. [Obs.]

where·sō·e'er' (-ār'), *adv.* and *conj.* wheresoever. [Poetic.]

where·sō·ev'ẽr, *adv.* and *conj.* at, in, or to whatever place; wherever: an emphatic form.

where·thrōugh' (-thrů'), *adv.* through which; by reason of which.

where·tö', *adv.* 1. to which.

2. to what? toward what place, direction, or end?

where·un·til', *adv.* whereto. [Rare.]

where·un'tö (*or* -un-tö'), *adv.* whereto. [Archaic.]

where·up·on', *adv.* upon what or upon which? whereon?

where·up·on', *conj.* at which; upon which; as a consequence of which; as, I explained the matter, *whereupon* he laughed heartily.

wher·ev'ẽr, *adv.* where: an emphatic form expressing surprise or bewilderment, as, *wherever* did you hear that? [Colloq.]

wher·ev'ẽr, *conj.* in, at, or to whatever place or situation; as, he thinks of us, *wherever* he is.

where·with', *n.* wherewithal. [Rare.]

where·with', *adv.* 1. with what?; as, *wherewith* shall I clothe myself? [Archaic.]

2. with which; as, the care *wherewith* thou hast watched over me.

where·with', *pron.* that with which; as, they shall have *wherewith* to stock their larder.

where·with·al', *adv.* and *conj.* wherewith. [Archaic.]

where'with·al, *n.* the means necessary or required; especially, money (usually with *the*); as, he had not even *the wherewithal* to buy bread.

wher'ry (hwer'), *n.*; *pl.* **wher'ries,** [ME. *whyrry.*]

1. a light rowboat used on rivers.

2. a racing scull for one person.

3. a large, broad, but light barge, used for moving freight; a lighter. [Brit.]

wher'ry, *v.t.*; wherried, *pt., pp.*; wherrying, *ppr.* to carry or convey in or as in a wherry.

wher'ry·măn, *n.*; *pl.* **wher'ry·men,** one who rows a wherry.

wher'sō (hwär'), *conj.* whether. [Obs.]

whẽrve (hwẽrv), *n.* wharve. [Obs.]

whet (hwet), *v.t.*; whetted, *pt., pp.*; whetting, *ppr.* [AS. *hwettan*, to whet, from *hwæt*, sharp, keen, eager, bold.]

1. to sharpen by rubbing on a stone; to rub with a stone or other body for the purpose of sharpening; hence, to edge or sharpen in general.

Screen'd by such means, here Scandal *whets* her quill. —Crabbe.

2. to make sharp, keen, or eager; to excite; to stimulate; as, to *whet* the appetite.

to whet on or *whet forward*; to urge on; to instigate.

whet, *n.* 1. the act of whetting.

2. something that provokes or stimulates; especially, that which whets (the appetite, etc.).

He assisted at four hundred bowls of punch, not to mention sips, drams, and *whets*. —Spectator.

wheth'ẽr (hweth'), *pron.* [AS. *hwæther*, which of two.] which (especially of two): used interrogatively and relatively. [Archaic.]

They fell at words
Whether of them should be the lord of lords. —Spenser.

wheth'ẽr, *conj.* 1. if it be the case or fact that: used to introduce an indirect question. Example: He asked *whether* I would help.

2. in case; in either case that: used to introduce alternatives, the second of which is introduced by *or* or by *or whether*. Example: *Whether* he drives *or* (*whether* he) takes the train, he'll be on time. The second alternative is sometimes merely implied or understood. Example: I don't know *whether* he'll improve (or not).

3. either; as, he was completely ignored, *whether* by accident or design.

whether or no; no matter what the circumstances; in any case.

whet'ile, *n.* the green woodpecker, *Gecinus viridis*. [Brit. Dial.]

whet slāte, a fine-grained siliceous rock of a greenish-gray color, used for whetstones.

whet'stōne, *n.* [AS. *hwetstán.*] an abrasive stone for sharpening cutlery or tools by friction; sometimes used figuratively.

to give the whetstone; to acknowledge consummate skill in the art of lying. [Obs.]

whet'tẽr, *n.* 1. one who or that which whets or sharpens.

2. one who indulges in whets or tipples; a dram drinker. [Obs.]

whet'tle·bōnes, *n.pl.* the dorsal vertebrae.

whew (hwū), *interj.* [echoic.] an exclamation of surprise, contempt, dismay, relief, etc.

whew, *n.* the sound made in giving forth the interjection *whew.*

whew, *v.i.* 1. to utter the interjection *whew.*

2. to whistle; to pipe shrilly, as plovers.

whew, *v.i.* to move with great speed; to bustle about. [Brit. Dial.]

whew duck, the European widgeon, *Mareca penelope*. [Scot. and Brit. Dial.]

whew'ell·īte, *n.* [named after W. *Whewell*, of Trinity College, Cambridge, Eng.] a native oxalate of calcium, $CaC_2O_4 \cdot H_2O$.

whew'ẽr, *n.* the whew duck. [Brit. Dial.]

whey (hwā), *n.* [AS. *hwæg*, whey.] the thin, watery part of milk which separates from the thicker part (curds) after coagulation, as in cheesemaking.

alum whey; a whey prepared by boiling milk with a piece of alum and removing the curd by straining.

wine whey; a preparation of milk with white wine, the coagulated curd being strained off and the whey sweetened with sugar and flavored.

whey cūre, the treatment of disease by drinking and bathing in whey.

whey'ey, *a.* of, like, consisting of, or containing whey; wheyish.

whey'fāce, *n.* 1. a face white or pale, as from terror or fright.

2. a person having a white or pale face, or looking pale from fright.

whey'fāced (-fāst), *a.* having a white or pale face; pallid.

whey'ish, *a.* having the quality or character of whey.

whey'ish·ness, *n.* the state or quality of being wheyish.

which (hwich), *pron.* [AS. *hwilc, hwylc*, etc.]

1. what one (or ones) of the number of persons, things, or events mentioned or implied?; as, *which* of the men answered? *which* do you want?

2. the one (or ones) that; as, I know *which* you want.

3. who, whom, or that: used as a relative in a restrictive or nonrestrictive clause referring to the thing or event (or, archaically, person) specified in the antecedent word, phrase, or clause; as, my hat, *which* is on the table; the war *which* had just ended.

4. either, or any, of the persons, things, or events previously mentioned or implied; whichever; as, you may take *which* you prefer.

5. a thing or fact that; as, you are late—*which* reminds me, where were you yesterday?

which, *a.* 1. what one or ones (of the number mentioned or implied); as, *which* man (or men) answered? *which* books shall I choose?

2. whatever; no matter what; as, try *which* method you please, you cannot succeed.

3. being the one just mentioned; as, he is very old, *which* fact is important.

which is which; which is one and which the other?

which·ev'ẽr, *pron.* and *a.* 1. any one (of two or more); as, he may choose *whichever* (desk) he wishes.

2. no matter which; as, *whichever* (desk) he chooses, they won't be pleased.

which·sō·ev'ẽr, *pron.* and *a.* whichever: an emphatic form.

which wāy, where?; as, *which way* are you? [Dial.]

whic'kẽr (hwick'), *n.* [imitative.] a whinny. [Colloq. or Dial.]

whid (hwid *or* hwud), *v.i.*; whidded, *pt., pp.*; whidding, *ppr.* to move nimbly. [Scot.]

whid'ȧh bĩrd (hwid'), [altered from *widow* bird, by association with *Whidah*, a seaport in Dahomey, Africa.] any species of black weaverbird of the genus *Vidua*, native to West Africa, the males of which grow very long tail feathers during the breeding season: also known as *whidah finch, whydah bird, vidu finch*, and *widow bird.*

paradise whidah bird; a species of whidah bird, *Vidua paradisea*, native to western Africa, remarkable for its two long and prominent tail feathers: also called *broad-shafted whidah bird.*

whid'ȧh finch, a whidah bird.

whiff, *n.* a fish, the marysole.

whiff (hwif), *n.* [echoic.] 1. a light puff or gust of air or wind; a breath.

2. a slight wave or gust of odor; a faint momentary smell; as, a *whiff* of garlic.

3. a puff of smoke or vapor; especially, an exhaling of tobacco smoke.

4. an inhaling of tobacco smoke.

whiff, *v.t.*; whiffed (whift), *pt., pp.*; whiffing, *ppr.* 1. to blow or propel with a puff or gust; to waft.

2. to blow out (tobacco smoke) in puffs.

3. to smoke (a pipe, etc.).

whiff, *v.i.* 1. to blow or move in puffs; as, the wind *whiffed* through the trees.

2. to inhale or exhale whiffs, as in smoking.

whif'fet, *n.* 1. a little whiff, or puff.

2. a small dog.

3. an insignificant person: a term of contempt. [Colloq.]

whif'fle, *v.i.*; whiffled, *pt., pp.*; whiffling, *ppr.* [freq. of *whiff.*]

1. to blow fitfully; to blow in puffs or gusts: said of the wind.

2. to shift; veer; vacillate.

A person of a *whiffling* and unsteady turn of mind cannot keep close to a point of a controversy. —Watts.

whif'fle, *v.t.* to blow or scatter with or as with a puff of wind.

whif'flẽr, *n.* one who whiffles or frequently changes his opinion or course; one who uses shifts and evasions in argument.

whif'fle·tree, *n.* a whippletree.

whig (hwig), *n.* [AS. *hwæg*, whey.] acidulated whey, sometimes mixed with buttermilk and sweet herbs: used as a cooling beverage. [Scot. and Brit. Dial.]

Whig, *n.* [shortened form of *whiggamore*, applied to Scot. Covenanters who marched on Edinburgh in 1648; see *whiggamore.*]

1. in England, a political party (1697-c. 1832) which championed popular rights and change in the direction of democracy: it later became the Liberal Party: opposed to *Tory.*

2. in the American Revolution, a person who opposed continued allegiance to Great Britain and supported the Revolution.

3. an American political party (c. 1836–1856) opposing the Democratic Party and advocating protection of industry and limitation of the power of the executive branch of government.

Whig, *a.* 1. that is a Whig.

2. composed of Whigs.

3. adhering to, or characteristic of, Whiggism.

whig'gȧ·mōre, *n.* [an erratic form of W. Scot. *whiggamaire*, from *whig*, a cry to urge on horses, and *mare*, a horse.] in English history, (a) any of the Scottish Covenanters who marched on Edinburgh in 1648; (b) a Scottish Presbyterian opposed to the English court party: used in contempt.

Whig'găr·chy, *n.* government by Whigs. [Rare.]

Whig'gẽr·y, *n.* the principles and practices of the Whigs.

Whig"gi·fi·cā'tion, *n.* a rendering Whiggish.

Whig'gish, *a.* pertaining to or like Whigs or their doctrines.

Whig'gish·ly, *adv.* in a Whiggish manner.

Whig'gish·ness, *n.* the quality of being Whiggish.

Whig'gișm, *n.* the doctrines and principles of Whigs, especially of English Whigs.

Whig'ling, *n.* a petty Whig: used in contempt.

while (hwīl), *n.* [ME. *while,* while; AS. *hwil,* a time.]
 1. a period or space of time or continued duration; as, a short *while.*
 2. time or labor spent upon anything: now only in the phrases *worth-while, worth one's while.*
 between whiles; now and then; at intervals.
 once in a while; occasionally.
 the while; during the time that something else is going on; in the meantime.

while, *conj.* 1. during or throughout the time that; as, we waited *while* he dined.
 2. (a) at the same time that; although on the one hand; as, *while* he was not poor, he had no ready cash; (b) [Colloq.] whereas; and; as, the walls are green, *while* the ceiling is white.
 3. until. [Dial.]

while, *v.t.*; whiled, *pt., pp.*; whiling, *ppr.* to spend (time) pleasantly; to cause to pass idly (often with *away*); as, we *whiled* away the afternoon.

while, *v.i.* to pass away the time. [Dial.]

whil·ere' (-ār'), *adv.* erewhile. [Obs.]

whileș, *adv.* 1. sometimes. [Archaic or Dial.]
 2. meanwhile. [Archaic or Dial.]

whileș, *conj.* while. [Archaic.]

whilk (hwilk), *n.* 1. a kind of shell fish; a whelk.
 2. the scoter. [Brit. Dial.]

whilk, *pron.* which. [Obs.]

whī'lŏm (hwī'), *a.* former. [Archaic.]

whī'lŏm, *adv.* formerly; once; of old; at times. [Archaic.]

whilst, *conj.* while. [Chiefly Brit.]

whim (hwim), *n.* [short for *whim-wham,* a trinket.]
 1. a sudden turn or start of the mind; a freak; a fancy; a capricious notion; as, every man has his *whims.*

WHIM

 2. a hoisting device operated by horsepower, to wind a rope and draw a bucket from a mine. The rope is passed over a pulley and around a drum on a vertical shaft provided with a crossbar, to which a pair of traces is connected.
 Syn.—freak, caprice, fancy.

whim, *v.i.* to be subject to whims or capricious fancies; to be giddy.

whim, *n.* the widgeon. [Brit. Dial.]

whim'brel, *n.* [probably echoic, from its cry.] a European shore bird, *Numenius phæopus,* related to the curlew, and resembling it in its appearance, but smaller, with a pale stripe along its crown: they breed on the islands north of England: also called *half curlew, May whaup, little whaup,* etc.

whim ġin, in mining, same as *whim,* n. 2.

whim'ling, *n.* one who is childish, weak, or whimsical.

whim'my, *a.* given to whims; whimsical.

whim'pẽr, *v.i.*; whimpered, *pt., pp.*; whimpering, *ppr.* [freq. form from ME. *whimpe,* another form of *whine.*] to cry with a low whining broken voice; to whine; as, a child *whimpers.*

whim'pẽr, *v.t.* to utter in a low whining tone; as, to *whimper* out complaints.

whim'pẽr, *n.* a low whining cry, expressing complaint or sorrow; a whine.

whim'pẽr·ẽr, *n.* one who whimpers.

whim'pẽr·ing·ly, *adv.* in a whimpering manner.

whim'șey, *n.*; *pl.* **whim'șeyș,** whimsy.

whim'șey, *a.* and *v.* same as *whimsy.*

whim'și·căl, *a.* 1. full of whims; characterized by whimsy.
 2. fantastic; fanciful; odd.
 Syn.—fanciful, odd, capricious, freakish, crotchety.

whim·și·cal'i·ty, *n.* 1. the state or quality of being whimsical; whimsicalness; oddity.
 2. *pl.* **whim·și·cal'i·tieș,** a whimsical action or thought; a caprice.

whim'și·căl·ly, *adv.* in a whimsical manner; freakishly.

whim'și·căl·ness, *n.* the state or quality of being whimsical; whimsicality.

whim'șy, *n.*; *pl.* **whim'șieș,** 1. an odd fancy; an idle notion; a whim.
 2. curious, quaint, or fanciful humor; as, poems full of *whimsy.*
 3. in mining, a whim.
 Also spelled *whimsey.*

whim'șy, whim'șey, *a.* whimsical.

whim'șy, whim'șey, *v.t.* to fill with whims or whimsies. [Rare.]

whim'wham, *n.* a whimsical thing; a whim; a toy; a trinket.

whin (hwin), *n.* [ME. *whinne.*] gorse; furze, a low, spiny evergreen shrub of the genus *Ulex,* with yellow flowers, common on wastelands in Europe.
 petty whin; a European leguminous shrub, *Ononis arvensis*: also called *moor whin.*

whin, *n.* in mining, a whim.

whin, *n.* any hard, dark-colored rock, as basalt, chert, or any hard quartzose sandstone: also called *whinstone.*

whin'ber"ry, *n.* the bilberry. [Brit. Dial.]

whin'chat, *n.* [*whin* (shrub) and *chat,* a warbler (from *chat,* to chatter): so named from frequenting whins (furze).] any of a group of migrating songbirds which frequent the heaths and meadows of Europe and western Asia, with brown and buff plumage and white over each eye and on each side of the base of the tail.

whīne (hwīn), *v.i.*; whined, *pt., pp.*; whining, *ppr.* [ME. *whinen* (said of a horse), from AS. *hwinan,* to whine.]
 1. to utter a low, protracted, peevish, somewhat nasal sound, as in complaint, distress, fear, etc.
 2. to complain in a childish, undignified way.

whīne, *v.t.* to utter or express in a whining tone.

whīne, *n.* 1. an act of whining.
 2. the sound of whining.
 3. a complaint uttered in a whining tone.

whīn'ẽr, *n.* one who or that which whines.

whinġe (hwinj), *v.i.* to whine. [Scot.]

whing'ẽr (hwing'), *n.* a whinyard. [Archaic.]

whīn'ing·ly (hwīn'), *adv.* in a whining manner.

whin'nŏck (hwin'), *n.* a pail. [Brit. Dial.]

whin'ny, *a.*; *comp.* whinnier; *superl.* whinniest; covered with whin, or furze.

whin'ny, *v.i.*; whinnied, *pt., pp.*; whinnying, *ppr.* [a freq. of *whine.*] to neigh in a low and gentle way: said of a horse.

whin'ny, *n.*; *pl.* **whin'nieș,** the low and gentle neighing of a horse, or a similar sound.

whin spar'rōw, the hedge sparrow. [Scot.]

whin'stōne, *n.* any of various very hard, dark, especially basaltic rocks.

whīn'y (hwīn'), *a.*; *comp.* whinier; *superl.* whiniest; of, addicted to, or characterized by whining; as, a *whiny* child.

whin'yärd (hwin'), *n.* 1. a sword or hanger. [Obs.]
 2. the shoveler or shovelbill. [Brit. Dial.]
 3. the pochard. [Brit. Dial.]

whip (hwip), *v.t.*; whipped *or* whipt, *pt., pp.*; whipping, *ppr.* [ME. *whippen,* from M.D. *wippen,* to swing, move up and down.]
 1. to move, pull, jerk, snatch, throw, etc. suddenly and quickly (usually with *out, off, up,* etc.); as, he *whipped out* a knife.
 2. (a) to strike, as with a strap, rod, etc.; to lash; to beat; (b) to punish in this manner.
 3. to force, drive, compel, urge, etc. by or as by whipping.
 4. to strike as a whip does; as, the rain *whipped* her face.
 5. to attack with stinging words; to flay.
 6. to cover (a cord, rope, etc.) with cord or thread wound round and round, so as to prevent fraying.
 7. to wind or bind (cord, etc.) around something.
 8. to fish (a stream, etc.) by making repeated casts with a rod and line.
 9. to beat (eggs, cream, etc.) into a froth with a fork, egg beater, mixer, etc.
 10. to sew (a seam, etc.) with a loose overcasting or overhand stitch.
 11. to defeat or outdo, as in a contest. [Colloq.]
 12. in nautical usage, to hoist by means of a rope passing through an overhead pulley.
 to whip in; to bring together or assemble, as a party whip does.
 to whip up; (a) to rouse; excite; (b) [Colloq.] to cook or prepare quickly and easily.

whip, *v.i.* 1. to move, go, pass, etc. quickly and suddenly; as, he *whipped* down the stairs.
 2. to flap or thrash about in a whiplike manner; as, flags *whip* in high wind.
 3. to cast with a fishing rod, using a quick, whiplike motion.

whip, *n.* [ME. *whippe*; M.D. *wippe.*]
 1. an instrument for striking or flogging, consisting of a stiff rod with a long lash attached to one end or a long, flexible rod with a short lash attached to the tip.
 2. a blow, cut, etc. made with or as with a whip.
 3. a person who uses a whip, as a coachman, a huntsman who whips on the hounds, etc.
 4. (a) an officer of a political party in Congress, Parliament, etc. who maintains discipline, enforces attendance, etc.: also *party whip*; (b) a call issued to party members in a lawmaking body to be in attendance at a certain time.
 5. a whipping motion.
 6. a dessert made of fruit, sugar, and whipped cream or stiffly beaten egg whites.
 7. something resembling a whip in its action, as a windmill vane, mechanical part, etc.
 8. a hoisting apparatus consisting of a single rope passing through an overhead pulley.
 9. a life-saving apparatus, consisting of an endless line or rope from the shore to the wreck.
 10. a spring vibrating to and fro, used for opening and breaking circuits in electrical machines for testing capacity.
 11. the longest pennant flying at the masthead of a ship.
 whip and derry; a hoisting device used in mining.
 whip and spur; with the utmost haste.

whip'bīrd, *n.* same as *coachwhip bird* under *coachwhip.*

whip'çord, *n.* 1. a hard, twisted or braided cord used for whiplashes, etc.
 2. a strong worsted cloth with a hard, diagonally ribbed surface.
 3. a kind of catgut.

whip çrāne, a crane of simple construction used with a whip for rapid hoisting, usually in warehouses: also called *whip purchase.*

whip çrop, in botany, any of several trees of Great Britain and Europe, as the whitebeam, the guelder rose or snowball tree, etc., the wood of which is used for whipstocks.

whip'fish, *n.* a chaetodont fish, *Taurichthys macrolepidotus,* having one of the spines of the dorsal fin extended in the form of a whiplash.

whip ġin, same as *gin block.*

whip'grȧft, *v.t.* to graft by means of whip graftage.

whip grȧft'ăġe, a type of grafting in which the scion and stock, both cut on a long slant with a slit in each cut surface, are fitted together by inserting the tongue of one into the slot of the other: also *whip grafting, whip graft.*

whip grȧss, the American nut rush, *Scleria triglomerata.*

whip hand, 1. the hand in which a driver holds his whip.
 2. the position of advantage or control.
 to have (or *get*) *the whip hand of* (or *over*); to get the best of; to have or obtain the advantage over.

whip'han"dle, *n.* 1. the handle of a whip.
 2. an advantageous position; a whip hand.

whip'jack, *n.* a beggar of alms, particularly one pretending to be shipwrecked.

whip'lash, *n.* the lash of a whip.

whip'pẽr, *n.* 1. one who whips; particularly, an officer who inflicts the penalty of legal whipping.
 2. one who raises coal with a whip from a ship's hold: also called *coal whipper.*
 3. a thing or device that whips; specifically, in spinning, a simple kind of willow or willy.

whip·pẽr·ee', *n.* same as *whip ray.*

whip'pẽr-in', *n.*; *pl.* **whip'pẽrș-in',** 1. a huntsman's assistant who keeps the hounds from wandering and whips them in, if necessary, to the line of chase. [Chiefly Brit.]
 2. in politics, one who enforces party discipline; a party whip.
 3. in horse racing, a horse that comes in last or near the last. [Slang.]

whip'pẽr·snap"pẽr, *n.* [extended from *whip-*

snapper, one who snaps whips.] an insignificant, especially young, person who appears impertinent or presumptuous.

whip′pet, *n.* [dim., from *whip*.] a swift dog resembling a small greyhound, used in coursing and racing.

WHIPPET
(18 in. high at shoulder)

whip′ping, *n.* 1. the action of a person or thing that whips; especially, a flogging or beating, as in punishment.
2. cord, twine, etc. used to whip, or bind.

whip′ping boy, 1. originally, a boy who was brought up and educated together with a young prince and was required to take the punishment for the misdeeds of the latter.
2. a scapegoat (sense 2).

whip′ping pōst, a post to which offenders are tied when publicly whipped as a legal punishment.

whip′ping top, a whip top.

whip′ple·tree, *n.* [from *whip*.] the pivoted crossbar at the front of a wagon or carriage, to which the traces of the harness are attached: also *whiffletree*.

whip′pọọr·will′, *n.*; *pl.* **whip′pọọr·wills′** or **whip′pọọr·will′**, [echoic of its cry.] a nocturnal bird, *Antrostomus vociferus*, of the goatsucker family, common in the eastern part of the United States.

whip rāy, a sting ray; also, a ray of the *Myliobatidæ*, as the eagle ray.

whip rōll, in a loom, a roller or bar which supports the warp at a point between the beam and the harness.

whip rōw, in hoeing, the least difficult row: sometimes used figuratively indicating an advantage, as a task easier than that of a competitor. [Colloq.]

whip′saw, *n.* a long, narrow, tapering ripsaw, usually set in a frame and worked by one or two persons.

whip′saw, *v.t.*; whipsawed, *pt.*, whipsawed *or* whipsawn, *pp.*; whipsawing, *ppr.* 1. to saw with a whipsaw.
2. to get the advantage of (an opponent) two ways at once, as, in faro, by winning two different bets in a single play.

whip sçor′pi·ŏn, any one of numerous species of pedipalpate arachnids resembling scorpions but having a long slender abdomen and a bristly lashlike appendage instead of a sting.

whip′-shāped (-shāpt), *a.* shaped like the lash of a whip.

whip′snāke, *n.* a slender snake of whiplike form; specifically, (a) the coachwhip snake; (b) the emerald tree snake, *Philodryas viridissimus*, of South America.

whip′sock″et, *n.* a tube closed at the bottom and attached to the dashboard of a vehicle for holding the butt end of a whip.

whip′stȧff, *n.* 1. a bar by which a ship's rudder is turned; a tiller.
2. a whiphandle.

whip′stạlk (-stạk), *n.* a whipstock.

whip′stẽr, *n.* a nimble fellow; a sharp, shallow fellow. [Dial.]

> Every pitiful *whipster* that walks within a skin has his head filled with the notion that he is, shall be, or by human and divine laws ought to be "happy."—Carlyle.

whip′stick, *n.* a whipstock.

whip′stitch, *v.t.* and *v.i.*; whipstitched (-sticht), *pt.*, *pp.*; whipstitching, *ppr.* 1. in sewing, to cast, as a thread or thong, over and over again as in a spiral, and not through and back again.
2. in agriculture, to half-plow; to rafter. [Brit.]

whip′stitch, *n.* an overcast stitch.

whip′stock, *n.* the rod or staff to which the lash of a whip is fastened: also called *whipstick* and *whipstalk*.

whipt, *v.* alternate past tense and past participle of *whip*.

whip′-tom-kel′ly, *n.* a bird, *Vireo barbatulus*, of the West Indies and Florida: named in imitation of its note.

whip top, a top spun by whipping; a whipping top.

whip′wŏrm, *n.* the nematode worm, *Trichocephalus dispar*, which is found as a parasite in the human caecum.

whĩr (hwĩr), *v.i.* and *v.t.*; whirred, *pt.*, *pp.*; whirring, *ppr.* [perh. back-formation of *whirl*.] to revolve, fly, vibrate, or otherwise move quickly with a whizzing or buzzing sound; as, a quail flies with a *whirring* sound: also spelled *whirr*.

> *Whirring* me from my friends. —Shak.

whĩr, *n.* 1. the buzzing or whirring sound made by a quickly revolving wheel, a bird's wings, or the like.
2. hurry; bustle.
Also spelled *whirr*.

whĩrl (hwĩrl), *v.t.*; whirled, *pt.*, *pp.*; whirling, *ppr.* [ME. *whirlen*; ON. *hvirfla*.]
1. to cause to rotate, revolve, or spin rapidly.
2. to carry, move, drive, etc. by means of a rotating motion or something that revolves; as, he was *whirled* away in a carriage.
3. to hurl. [Obs.]

whĩrl, *v.i.* 1. to move rapidly in a circular manner or as in an orbit; to circle swiftly; as, they *whirled* round the dance floor.
2. to rotate or spin fast; to gyrate.
3. to move, go, drive, etc. swiftly.
4. to seem to spin; to reel; as, my head is *whirling*.

whĩrl, *n.* [G. *wirbel*; Dan. *hvirvel*.]
1. the act of whirling.
2. a whirling motion.
3. something whirling or being whirled; as, a *whirl* of dust.
4. a fast round of parties, etc.
5. a tumult; an uproar; a stir.
6. a confused or giddy condition; as, my head is in a *whirl*.

whĩrl′ȧ·bout, *n.* 1. a whirling about.
2. a whirligig or other contrivance that whirls rapidly.

whĩrl′bat, *n.* the cestus, an ancient weapon. [Obs.]

whĩrl′blȧst, *n.* a whirlwind.

whĩrl′bōne, *n.* the patella; the kneepan. [Brit. Dial.]

whĩrl′ẽr, *n.* 1. a person who or a thing that whirls.
2. a revolving hook used in ropemaking.

whĩrl′i·çōte, *n.* a heavy chariot or coach. [Obs.]

whĩrl′i·gig, *n.* [ME. *whirlygigge*.]
1. any of various child's toys that whirl or spin.
2. a merry-go-round.
3. something that seems to whirl, or revolve in a cycle; as, the *whirligig* of history.
4. a whirling motion.
5. a whirligig beetle.

whĩrl′i·gig bee′tle, a water beetle that moves swiftly about in circles on the surface of water.

whĩrl′ing tā′ble, whĩrl′ing mȧ·çhïne′, a whirling device, as (a) a machine contrived for the purpose of exhibiting the principal effects of centripetal or centrifugal forces; (b) a contrivance with horizontal arms attached to a vertical axle for experiments in aerodynamics; (c) a potters' wheel.

whĩrl′pit, *n.* a whirlpool. [Obs.]

whĩrl′pọọl, *n.* 1. water in rapid, violent, whirling motion caused by two meeting currents, by winds meeting tides, etc. and tending to form a vacuum at the center of the circle toward and into which floating objects are drawn; a vortex or eddy of water.
2. anything resembling a whirlpool, as in violent motion.
3. a kind of whale. [Obs.]

whĩrl′wig, *n.* a whirligig beetle.

whĩrl′wind, *n.* 1. a current of air whirling violently in spiral form around a more or less vertical axis that has a forward motion.
2. anything resembling a whirlwind, as in violent or destructive action, etc.
to reap the whirlwind; to suffer the consequences of evil or folly: see Hos. viii. 7.

whĩrr (hwĩr), *n.*, *v.t.* and *v.i.* same as *whir*.

whĩr′ret (hwĩr′), *n.* a slap; a blow. [Obs.]

whĩr′ret, *v.t.* 1. to tease; to annoy; also, to hurry. [Dial.]
2. to box the ear or ears of; to strike. [Dial.]

whĩr′ry, *v.t.* and *v.i.*; whirried, *pt.*, *pp.*; whirrying, *ppr.* to whirl. [Scot.]

whĩr′tle, *n.* a perforated steel plate through which pipe or wire is drawn to reduce its diameter.

whish (hwish), *v.i.* [echoic.] to move with a soft rushing or whizzing sound; to whiz; to swish.

whish, *n.* a soft rushing or whizzing sound; a swish.

whisht (hwisht; *Scot.* hwusht), *interj.* hush! quiet!: an exclamation ordering silence. [Chiefly Scot.]

whisht, *a.* still; silent; hushed; quiet. [Chiefly Scot.]

whisht, *v.t.* to silence. [Chiefly Scot.]

whisht, *v.i.* to be silent. [Chiefly Scot.]

whisht, *n.* 1. silence. [Chiefly Scot.]
2. a faint sound; a whisper. [Chiefly Scot.]

whisk (hwisk), *n.* a card game, whist. [Obs.]

whisk, *v.t.* whisked (hwiskt), *pt.*, *pp.*; whisking, *ppr.* [Dan. *viske*, to wipe, to rub, to sponge, from *visk*, a wisp; Sw. *viska*, to wipe, to wag the tail; G. *wischen*, to wipe.]
1. to move, remove, carry, brush, etc. with a quick sweeping motion (usually with *away*, *off*, *out*, etc.); as, she *whisked* out a handkerchief; I *whisked* off the crumbs.
2. to beat (eggs, cream, etc.) into a froth; to whip. [Chiefly Brit.]

whisk, *v.i.* to move nimbly and with velocity; as, the cat *whisked* around the corner.

whisk, *n.* [in part directly from verb, partly also from ON. *visk*, a wisp.]
1. the act of whisking; also, a quick, light, sweeping motion.
2. a small bunch of grass, straw, twigs, hair, etc. used for a brush; hence, a brush or small broom; a whisk broom.
3. a kitchen utensil for rapidly agitating or whipping cream, eggs, etc. [Chiefly Brit.]
4. part of a woman's dress; a kind of tippet or cape. [Obs.]
5. an impertinent fellow. [Obs.]
6. a coopers' plane for leveling the chimes of casks.

whisk brọọm, a small broom with a short handle, used for brushing clothes, upholstery, etc.

whisk′ẽr, *n.* [ME. *wisker*, something used for whisking.]
1. originally, anything that whisks.
2. [pl.] (a) formerly, a mustache; (b) the hair growing on a man's face; especially, the beard on the cheeks.
3. (a) a hair of a man's beard; (b) any of the long bristly hairs growing at each side on the upper lip of a cat or other animal; a vibrissa; (c) [*pl.*] any growth or formation of hair, feathers, etc. about the mouth of an animal; whiskerlike color markings, as maxillary stripes.
4. in nautical usage, either of two spars extending laterally one on each side of the bowsprit, for spreading the jib and flying jib guys: also *whisker boom*.
5. something grossly exaggerated; a palpable falsehood. [Obs.]

whisk′ẽred, *a.* 1. having whiskers; wearing whiskers.
2. formed into whiskers. [Rare.]

whisk′ẽr·less, *a.* without whiskers.

whis′ket, *n.* 1. a basket. [Brit. Dial.]
2. a dwarf lathe for turning wooden pins.

whis′key (hwis′), *n.* see *whisky*.

whis′ki·fīed, whis′key·fīed, *a.* intoxicated with whisky.

whisk′in, *n.* a shallow cup for beverages. [Obs.]

whisk′ing, *a.* moving swiftly or nimbly; as, the *whisking* winds.

whis′ky, whis′key, *n.* [so called because it *whisks* along swiftly.] a kind of one-horse chaise: also called *timwhiskey*.

whis′ky, whis′key, *n.*; *pl.* **whis′kieṣ, whis′keyṣ**, [Ir. and Gael. *uisgebeatha*; *uisge*, water, and *beatha*, life; lit., water of life.]
1. a strong alcoholic liquor distilled from the fermented mash of various grains, especially of rye, wheat, corn, or barley.
2. a drink of whisky.
bourbon whisky; same as *bourbon*.
rye whisky; a liquor prepared from rye or barley malt and unmalted rye.
whisky and soda; a drink made by combining whisky and soda water.
whisky sour; a mixed drink made with lemon juice, sugar, soda water, and whisky, shaken with cracked ice, and strained.

whisk′y, whisk′ey, *a.* of, for, or made with whisky.

whis′ky·fied, *a.* same as *whiskified.*

whis′ky jack, [Am. Ind. *wiss-ka-tjan.*] the common gray jay, native to the northern regions of North America; the moosebird, or Canada jay, *Perisoreus canadensis.*

whis′ky-jāy, *n.* same as *whisky jack.*

whisp (hwisp), *n.* a wisp. [Dial.]

whis′pẽr, *v.i.*; whispered, *pt., pp.*; whispering, *ppr.* [ME. *whisperen,* from AS. *hwisprian,* to whisper.]

1. to speak softly or in a low and not vocal tone; to speak without uttering voice or sonant breath.

2. to speak under the breath or furtively in order to plot, malign, or gossip.

3. to make a low sibilant sound; to rustle.

The trees began to *whisper,* and the wind began to roll. —Tennyson.

whis′pẽr, *v.t.* 1. to say very softly, especially without the resonance produced by the vibration of the vocal cords.

2. to tell privately or as a secret.

3. to tell or speak to (someone) in or as in a whisper. [Rare.]

whis′pẽr, *n.* 1. a low, soft, sibilant voice; the utterance of words with the breath but, usually, without voice.

2. a word uttered by whispering; hence, a secret or confidence.

3. a low sibilant sound, as of the wind.

4. a hint; a suggestion; an insinuation.

whis′pẽr·ẽr, *n.* 1. one who whispers.

2. one who tells secrets or who slanders secretly; a gossip or tattler.

whis′pẽr·ing, *a.* 1. speaking in a whisper.

2. resembling a whisper; nonvocal; sibilant.

3. making a low sibilant sound; rustling.

whis′pẽr·ing, *n.* 1. the act of one who whispers.

2. something whispered; whispered sound, speech, etc.

whis′pẽr·ing cam·pāign′ (-pān′), a campaign to defame a person, organization, etc. by spreading rumors to be passed around privately from person to person.

whis′pẽr·ing dōme, a whispering gallery.

whis′pẽr·ing gal′lẽr·y, a gallery formed of smooth walls having a continuous curved form. The voice of the speaker can be heard by reflection from the surface at great distances.

whis′pẽr·ing·ly, *adv.* in a whispering manner; in a low voice; with bated breath.

whis′pẽr·ous, *a.* characterized by or full of whispers; like a whisper.

whis′pẽr·ous·ly, *adv.* whisperingly.

whis′pẽr·y, *a.* whisperous.

whist (hwist), *v.t.* [echoic.] to silence. [Archaic or Dial.]

whist, *v.i.* to be silent. [Archaic or Dial.]

whist, *interj.* hush!: an exclamation ordering silence. [Archaic or Dial.]

whist, *n.* silence. [Archaic or Dial.]

whist, *a.* silent; mute; still. [Archaic or Dial.]

whist, *n.* [originally, *whisk,* probably from the habit of whisking the tricks from the table as soon as played.] a card game played with the full pack of fifty-two cards by four persons, two being partners against the other two, each player receiving thirteen cards dealt out one by one in rotation. Whist is similar to bridge, of which it is the forerunner.

duplicate whist; a form of whist in which the identity of the hands is preserved, so that after playing a series of deals, each side can exchange the hands as originally held by them with the other side, and replay the same deals under the conditions originally given to their adversaries, thus making the game one entirely of skill instead of chance.

long whist; an old form of whist in which the game was for ten points, the holding of the honor cards being counted.

short whist; a form of whist in which the game is for five points.

whis′tle (hwis′l), *v.i.*; whistled, *pt., pp.*; whistling, *ppr.* [ME. *whistlen*; AS. *hwistlan* or *hwistlian,* to whistle.]

1. to make a clear, shrill sound or note, or a series of these, by forcing breath between the teeth or through a narrow opening made by contracting the lips.

2. to make a clear, shrill cry: said of some birds and animals.

3. to move through the air with a high, shrill sound; as, the wind *whistled* past.

4. (a) to blow a whistle; as, the policeman *whistled*; (b) to have its whistle blown; as, the train *whistled.*

to go whistle; to leave without what one came for. [Colloq.]

to whistle down the wind; to talk or argue without avail. [Colloq.]

to whistle for; to seek or expect in vain; to fail to get.

to whistle for a wind; to whistle during a calm to obtain a breeze: an old superstitious practice among seamen.

whis′tle, *v.t.* 1. to form, utter, or modulate by whistling; as, to *whistle* a tune or air.

2. to call by a whistle; as, he *whistled* back his dog.

3. to move or cause to move with a whistling sound; as, to *whistle* a bullet through the air.

to whistle off; to send off by a whistle; to send from the fist in pursuit of prey: a term in falconry; hence, to dismiss or send away; to turn loose.

whis′tle, *n.* 1. an instrument for making whistling sounds, as by forcing the breath or steam into a cavity or against a thin edge.

2. a clear, shrill sound made by whistling or blowing a whistle.

3. the act of whistling.

4. a signal, summons, etc. made by whistling.

5. any whistling sound, as (a) the note of a bird; (b) the shrill sound of wind passing among trees or through crevices; (c) the sound produced by a mechanical whistle; as, the *whistle* of a steam engine; a factory *whistle*; (d) the sound made by an arrow, bullet, etc. flying through the air.

to wet one's whistle; see under *wet.*

whis′tle·fish, *n.* a rockling; specifically, a three-bearded rockling.

whis′tlẽr (hwis′lẽr), *n.* [AS. *hwistlere.*]

1. one who or that which whistles; specifically, (a) the whistlefish; (b) the hoary marmot, *Arctomys pruinosus,* of North America; (c) the whistlewing; (d) the lapwing or pewit; (e) the ring ouzel; (f) the widgeon.

2. a broken-winded horse.

3. a piper. [Obs.]

Whis·tle′ri·ăn (hwis-lêr′i-ăn), *a.* of or characteristic of James McNeill Whistler or his style of painting.

whis′tle stop, a small town, originally one at which a train stopped only upon signal, to which the engineer responded by tooting his whistle.

whis′tle·wing, *n.* the goldeneye.

whis′tle·wood, *n.* the striped maple: so called because the bark separates from the stems so that it can be used for whistles. The name is applied to various other trees having the same property.

whis′tling (-ling), *a.* that whistles.

whistling buoy; see under *buoy.*

whistling coot; the scoter. [Dial.]

whistling dick; (a) the song thrush or whistling thrush; (b) an Australian shrike thrush, especially *Colluricincla selbyi.*

whistling duck; (a) the widgeon; (b) the whistlewing; (c) a tree duck of India; (d) the scoter or whistling coot.

whistling eagle or *whistling hawk*; an eagle, *Haliastur sphenurus,* of Australia.

whistling marmot; the hoary marmot or whistler.

whistling plover; see under *plover.*

whistling snipe; a woodcock. [Dial.]

whistling swan; (a) the hooper, elk, or whooping swan; (b) the common American swan.

whistling thrush; the song thrush. [Brit. Dial.]

whis′tling·ly, *adv.* in a whistling manner; by means of a whistle.

whit (hwit), *n.* [from ME. *wight*; AS. *wiht,* a wight, person, a whit, bit.] the smallest part or particle imaginable; a jot; a point; an iota; a tittle: usually used in negative constructions; as, he doesn't seem a *whit* concerned.

whīte, *a.*; *comp.* whiter; *superl.* whitest, [ME. *whit, white*; AS. *hwit.*]

1. having the color of pure snow or milk; of the color of radiated, transmitted, or reflected light containing all of the visible rays of the spectrum: opposite to *black*: see *color.*

2. of a light or pale color: specifically, (a) gray; silvery; hoary; (b) very blond; (c) pale; wan; pallid; ashen; as, a face *white* with terror; (d) light-yellow or amber; as, *white* wines; (e) blank: said of a space unmarked by printing, writing, etc.; (f) of a light-gray color and lustrous appearance; unburnished: said of silver and other metals; (g) made of silver; (h) snowy; as, a *white* Christmas.

3. clothed in white; wearing a white habit; as, the *White* Friars.

4. morally or spiritually pure; spotless; innocent.

5. free from evil intent; harmless; as, *white* magic, a *white* lie.

6. happy; fortunate; auspicious: said of times and seasons. [Rare.]

7. (a) having a light-colored skin; Caucasian; (b) of or controlled by the white race; as, *white* supremacy; (c) [from notions of racial superiority.] [Slang.] honest; honorable; fair; dependable.

8. being at white heat.

9. reactionary, counterrevolutionary, or royalist, as opposed to *red* (radical or revolutionary).

10. favorite. [Obs.]

to bleed white; to drain (a person, country, etc.) completely of money, resources, etc.

white admiral; a butterfly of the northeastern United States, with showy white bands on its wings.

white alder; the pepper bush.

white alkali; (a) refined soda ash; (b) the white crust formed on some alkali soils, consisting of a mixture of sodium sulfate, magnesium sulfate, and sodium chloride.

white amber; see under *amber.*

white ant; a termite; any one of the *Termitidæ.*

white antimony; valentinite.

white arsenic; arsenic trioxide.

white bass; a fresh-water bass, *Roccus chrysops,* of the Great Lakes and the Mississippi Valley.

white bay; a fragrant magnolia, *Magnolia glauca*: also called *sweet bay* and *swamp sassafras.*

white bear; a polar bear.

white beech; the common beech of America.

white birch; either of two American birch trees, *Betula populifolia* and *Betula papyrifera*; also, the common birch of Europe.

white blood cell; a leucocyte.

white book; a publication issued by the government of Germany, Czechoslovakia, Japan, or certain other countries, containing an official report on certain political affairs: so called from the binding.

white brant; a snow goose.

white brass; an alloy of copper and zinc with a proportion of zinc predominating.

white bread; bread of a light color made from finely sifted wheat flour.

white bronze; a kind of bronze of a light color, due to a high proportion of tin.

white bryony; a variety of bryony with white fleshy roots, five-lobed leaves, clusters of greenish-white flowers, and red or black berries.

white campion; (a) a lychnis, *Lychnis vespertina,* of the Old World, bearing white flowers; (b) same as *starry campion* under *starry.*

white candlewood; the janca tree.

white cedar; any of various evergreen trees, as (a) the arborvitae, *Thuja occidentalis*; (b) a coniferous timber tree, *Chamæcyparis sphæroidea,* of North America; (c) a large Californian tree, *Libocedrus decurrens,* somewhat resembling arborvitae. Also, the wood of any of these trees.

white clover; a creeping variety of clover with small, round, white flowers.

white coal; water as a source of power.

white copper; a white alloy of copper.

white copperas; coquimbite.

white coral; an ornamental branched Mediterranean coral, *Amphihelia oculata.*

white corn; a variety of corn with long, compact ears and white kernels.

white corpuscle; a leucocyte.

white cricket; the tree cricket.

white crops; those crops, as wheat, barley, oats, and rye, which whiten or lose their color as they ripen: distinguished from *green crop, root crop,* etc.

white currant; see *currant,* sense 2.

white daisy; the oxeye daisy.

white damp; carbon monoxide, occurring as a poisonous gas in coal mines.

white dead nettle; a dead nettle, *Lamium album,* bearing white flowers.

white deal; the tough, white wood of the Norway spruce. [Brit.]

white elephant; (a) a rare, pale-gray variety of elephant, regarded as sacred by the Burmese, Siamese, etc.; (b) something from which little profit or use is derived; especially, such a possession acquired and maintained at much expense.

white elm; a North American timber tree, *Ulmus americana.*

white ensign; the distinguishing badge of ships of the British navy, consisting of a red cross on a white field, with the Union Jack in the upper quarter next to the mast.

white feather; [from the belief that a white feather in the tail of a gamecock indicates bad breeding, hence cowardice.] a symbol of cowardice: generally in the phrase *to show the white feather*, to behave like a coward.

white fir; see *fir*.

white flag; a white banner or cloth hoisted as a signal of truce or surrender.

white flesher; in Canada, the ruffed grouse. [Dial.]

White Friar; a Carmelite friar: so called from the white habit of the order.

white frost; hoarfrost.

white garnet; leucite. [Obs.]

white gasoline; gasoline without any tetraethyl lead additive: also called *white gas*.

white gold; see under *gold*.

white goods; (a) household linens, as sheets, pillowcases, towels, etc.; (b) large household appliances, as refrigerators, stoves, etc.

white goosefoot; a plant of the genus *Chenopodium*; lamb's quarters.

white grass; an American grass, *Leersia virginica*, with greenish-white glumes.

white grouse; (a) a white ptarmigan; (b) the prairie chicken.

white grub; the larva of the June bug and other related beetles.

white gum; (a) a variety of eucalyptus tree with light-colored bark; (b) a sweet gum tree.

white hake; a hake of the genus *Phycis*.

white heat; see under *heat*.

white heath; a heath, *Erica arborea*, of Europe; brierwood.

white hellebore; a plant, *Veratrum album*.

white hoarhound; the common hoarhound.

white horse; (a) a whitecap; (b) the tough, sinewy substance under the spermaceti case in a sperm whale; (c) a West Indian shrub bearing large, white flowers, *Portlandia grandiflora*.

White House; see under *house*.

white iron; see under *iron*.

white iron pyrites; see under *pyrites*.

white lark; the snow bunting. [Brit. Dial.]

white lead; (a) a poisonous heavy, white powder, basic lead carbonate, $2PbCO_3 \cdot Pb(OH)_2$, used in making paint; (b) native lead carbonate; cerussite.

white leather; leather tanned with alum and salt, a process which does not discolor the hide or give it the brown appearance due to tanning by oak bark, etc.

white leg; same as *milk leg*.

white lettuce; rattlesnake root.

white lie; a lie regarded as excusable because it concerns a trivial matter and is told out of politeness, etc. and without harmful intent.

white light; in physics, the light that comes directly from the sun, and that has not been decomposed by refraction in passing through a transparent prism.

white lime; a solution or preparation of lime used for whitewashing; a variety of whitewash.

white line; (a) in printing, a void space, broader than usual, left between lines; a blank line; (b) white rope.

white lupine; a plant with deeply cut leaves and spikes of white flowers, grown for fodder.

white man's burden; the alleged duty of the white, or Caucasian, peoples to bring their civilization to other peoples regarded as backward: phrase popularized by Kipling and other apologists for imperialism.

white matter; whitish nerve tissue of the brain and spinal cord, consisting chiefly of medullated nerve fibers: distinguished from *gray matter*.

white meat; (a) [Obs. or Dial.] any food composed of milk, cheese, butter, eggs, or the like; (b) any light-colored meat, as the breast of chicken or turkey, veal, etc.

white merganser; the smew. [Brit. Dial.]

white metal; any of various alloys containing large proportions of lead or tin, as pewter, plumber's solder, type metal, etc.

white miller; (a) the ordinary clothes moth; (b) a bombycid moth, *Spilosoma virginica*, of America, having a few black spots on its wings.

white mouse; an albino variety of the common mouse.

white mullet; a mullet, *Mugil curema*.

white nettle; the white dead nettle.

white nun; the smew.

white oak; see *oak*.

white owl; (a) the snowy owl; (b) the barn owl.

white paper; an official government report on some subject of less importance or less complete than that treated in a white book or blue book: so called from the binding, usually of the same white paper as that used for the text.

white pepper; pepper ground from the husked dried seeds of the pepper berry.

white perch; a small, silvery food fish found in coastal waters and streams of the eastern United States.

white pine; (a) a pine of eastern North America, with bluish-green or grayish-green needles in clusters of five, hanging brown cones, and soft, light wood; (b) the wood of this tree; (c) any of various closely related pines.

white plague; tuberculosis; particularly, tuberculosis of the lungs.

white poplar; a tree, *Populus alba*, or any of a number of similar trees, having lobed leaves with white or gray down on the undersides; also, the wood of the tulip tree.

white potato; the common potato; Irish potato: see *potato* (sense 2).

white precipitate; see under *precipitate*.

white primary; in some southern States of the United States, a direct primary election from which Negroes are excluded from voting.

white pudding; whitehass. [Scot. and Brit. Dial.]

white rabbit; (a) an albino rabbit; (b) the northern hare of America: so called in winter.

white race; loosely, the Caucasian division of mankind.

white rat; an albino rat; especially, one of a breed of albino Norway rats used in biological experiments.

white rhinoceros; (a) the common rhinoceros of India; (b) the African rhoniceros, *Rhinoceros simus*.

white ribbon; the badge of certain temperance organizations.

white room; a room from which all contaminants have been eliminated and in which temperature, humidity, and pressure are controlled: used for assembly and repair of precision mechanisms, in preventing infection, etc.

White Russian; (a) a Russian member of, or sympathizer with, a faction which fought the Bolsheviks (Reds) in the Russian civil war; (b) a Byelorussian.

white sage; a white North American shrub of the genus *Eurotia*.

white sale; a sale of household linens.

white sapphire; a precious stone of clear, colorless corundum.

white sauce; a sauce for vegetables, meat, fish, etc., made of fat or butter, flour, milk, and seasoning cooked together.

white scale; a scale insect of the genus *Aspidiotus*, that injures the orange tree, oleander, etc.

white slave; a woman unwillingly forced into or held in prostitution for the profit of others.

white slaver; a person engaged in white-slave traffic.

white slavery; (a) the business or practice of prostitution with white slaves; (b) the condition of white slaves.

white squall; a sudden squall at sea in the tropics, with no accompanying cloud formation.

white staff; the badge of office of the Lord High Treasurer of England.

white sturgeon; the shovelnose, *Scaphirhynchus platorhynchus*, of the Mississippi and Ohio rivers.

white tie; (a) a white bow tie, properly worn with a swallow-tailed coat; (b) a swallow-tailed coat and the proper accessories.

white trash; same as *poor white*.

white trout; a weakfish, *Cynoscion nothus*, of a silvery-white color.

white vitriol; hydrated zinc sulfate, $ZnSO_4 \cdot 7H_2O$, used as an antiseptic and emetic in medicine, as a mordant in dyeing, etc.

white wagtail; the common wagtail.

white wax; beeswax treated, as by bleaching, so as to make it white.

white whale; the beluga.

white widgeon; the smew. [Brit. Dial.]

white wine; wine from light-colored grapes, of a yellow color or colorless.

whīte, *n.* 1. the color of pure snow or milk; the color of radiated, transmitted, or reflected light containing all of the visible rays of the spectrum; achromatic color opposite to black.

2. whiteness; specifically, (a) fairness of complexion; (b) purity; innocence.

3. a white or light-colored part; specifically, (a) the albumen of an egg; (b) the white part of the eyeball; (c) a blank space in printing, writing, etc.; (d) the white or light-colored part of meat, wood, etc.

4. something white or nearly white in color; specifically, (a) white cloth; (b) [*pl.*] white garments or vestments; white uniform; (c) white wine; (d) white pigment; as, Chinese *white*; (e) a white breed, especially of pig; (f) a fine flour made from the whitest part of the wheat.

5. a person with a light-colored skin; a member of the Caucasian division of mankind.

6. a member of a reactionary or counterrevolutionary faction, party, etc. in certain European countries.

7. [*pl.*] leucorrhea.

8. in archery, (a) [Archaic.] a white target; (b) the outermost ring of a target; (c) a hit on this ring.

9. in checkers and chess, (a) the white or light-colored pieces; (b) the player who has them.

whīte, *v.t.*; whited, *pt., pp.*; whiting, *ppr.* 1. to make white; to whiten.

2. to leave blank spaces in (printed or written matter); as, *white* out this line.

whīte, *v.i.* to whiten; to become white.

whīte′back, *n.* the canvasback duck. [Brit. Dial.]

whīte′bāit, *n.* 1. the young of the herring and sprat, eaten as a delicacy.

2. any of various other very small fishes resembling these and used as food.

whīte′bēam, **whīte′bēam tree**, the common beam tree of England, *Pyrus aria*.

whīte′bēard, *n.* a man whose beard is white; an old man.

whīte′bel″ly, *n.* 1. the prairie chicken. [Dial.]

2. the American widgeon.

whīte′bill, *n.* the coot of North America. [Dial.]

whīte′blāze, *n.* see *whiteface*.

whīte′blōw, *n.* whitlow grass.

whīte′bot″tle (-tl), *n.* bladder campion.

Whīte′boy, *n.* 1. a member of an illegal association of peasants formed in Ireland about 1760 to resist tax and tithe collections and the extortion of their landlords: they made night raids during which they covered their usual attire with white shirts to enable them to distinguish each other.

2. [w–] a darling; a favorite. [Obs.]

Whīte′boy·ism, *n.* the principles and practices of the Whiteboys.

whīte′cap, *n.* 1. a wave with a crest of foam.

2. a bird with white upon the head, as (a) the whitethroat; (b) the European tree sparrow; (c) the European redstart.

3. a mushroom, *Agaricus arvensis*.

4. [W–] formerly, in the United States, a member of a lawless, secret organization that, under the pretext of protecting the community, committed crimes of terrorism and violence, especially against Negroes: they wore white hoods.

Whīte′chap″el cärt, a kind of spring cart with two wheels: originally used in Whitechapel, a district in London.

whīte′cōat, *n.* a young harp seal in its first coat: so called by Newfoundland sealers.

whīte′-col′lär, *a.* [from the formerly typical white shirts worn by such workers.] designating or of clerical or professional workers or the like: white-collar workers are usually salaried employees engaged in work not essentially manual.

white-collar crime; a crime, as fraud, embezzlement, etc., committed by a person in business, government, or a profession in the course of his occupational activities.

whīte′-crowned, *a.* having the crown of the head white.

white-crowned pigeon; a pigeon, *Columba leucocephala*, native to the West Indies and parts of Florida.

white-crowned sparrow; a sparrow, *Zonotrichia leucophrys*, native to eastern North America.

whīte′-ēar, *n.* a bird, the wheatear.

whīte′-eȳe (-ī), *n.* 1. any one of various birds of the genus *Zosterops*, small singing birds of India and Australia, which have a ring of white feathers around the eyes.

2. the white-eyed duck of Europe.

3. the white-eyed vireo or greenlet.

whīte′-eȳed (-īd), *a.* having the iris of the eye white or colorless.

whīte′fāce, *n.* a white mark in the forehead of a horse, descending almost to the nose: also called *whiteblaze.*

whīte′-fāced (-fāst), *a.* 1. having a white or pallid face; pale.
2. having a white facing or front.
3. having a white mark on the front of the head, as some animals.

White·fiēld′i·ăn (hwit-), *n.* in church history, a disciple of George Whitefield (1714–1770), English evangelist.

whīte′fish, *n.* 1. the menhaden.
2. a food fish of the salmon family, belonging to the genus *Coregonus,* inhabiting the lakes of North America and Europe. *Coregonus clupeiformis,* the largest and best-known American species, is the common whitefish of the Great Lakes.
3. the white whale or beluga.
4. the European whiting.
5. the yellowtail.
6. the young of the bluefish.

whīte′flaw, *n.* a whitlow. [Obs.]

whīte′foot, *n.* a white mark on a horse's foot, between the fetlock and the coffin.

whīte′-frŏnt″ed, *a.* having a white front, as a bird.
white-fronted goose; a European goose, *Anser albifrons,* a variety of which is known in America.

Whīte′hall, *n.* the British government: so called from the street in Westminster where several government offices are located.

whīte′-hand″ed, *a.* 1. having white hands.
2. having pure, unstained hands; not tainted with guilt.

whīte′häss, *n.* sausages stuffed with oatmeal and suet. [Scot.]

whīte′head (-hed), *n.* 1. the surf scoter. [Dial.]
2. the blue-winged snow goose.
3. a variety of pigeon having a white head.

whīte′-head′ed, *a.* 1. having white hair, feathers, etc. on the head.
2. having flaxen or very blond hair; fair-haired.
3. favorite; as, the *white-headed* boy. [Irish.]

whīte′heärt, *n.* a heart-shaped cherry of a white color.

whīte′-hot′, *a.* 1. glowing white with heat.
2. extremely angry, excited, enthusiastic, etc.

whīte′-līmed′, *a.* whitewashed. [Obs. or Dial.]

whīte′-liv′ēred, *a.* having a pale and sickly look; hence, cowardly.

whīte′ly, *adv.* so as to be white; with a white or pale appearance.

whīt′en, *v.i.*; whitened, *pt., pp.*; whitening, *ppr.* [ME. *hwiten,* to become white.] to turn or become white or whiter; to grow white; as, the sea *whitens* with foam; his face *whitened* with fear.

whīt′en, *v.t.* to make white or whiter; to bleach; to whitewash; as, to *whiten* cloth; to *whiten* a fence.

whīt′en·ēr, *n.* one who or that which bleaches or makes white; any agent used in bleaching.

whīte′ness, *n.* 1. the state or character of being white; white color, or freedom from any darkness or obscurity on the surface.
2. lack of color in the face; paleness, as from sickness, terror, grief, or the like.
3. purity; cleanness; freedom from stain or blemish.
4. moral pureness; innocence.
5. a white substance or part.

whīt′en·ing, *n.* 1. the act or process of making white.
2. the act, fact, or process of becoming white.
3. in tanning, the cleaning of the flesh side of a hide.
4. a preparation used for making something white; whiting.

whīt′en·ing stōne, a sharpening and polishing stone used by cutlers; also, a finishing grindstone of a finer texture than the ordinary large sandstones.

whīte′pot, *n.* a kind of pudding made of milk, cream, eggs, sugar, etc., baked in a pot.

whīte′root, *n.* a species of Solomon's seal, *Polygonatum multiflorum.*

whīte′rot, *n.* 1. the butterwort. [Obs.]
2. the common pennywort. [Obs.]
3. a disease of grapes.

whīte′rump, *n.* 1. the Hudsonian godwit or spotrump. [Dial.]
2. the wheatear. [Brit. Dial.]

whīte′sīde, *n.* a sea duck, the goldeneye. [Brit. Dial.]

whīte′-slāve′, *a.* 1. of white slaves; in white slavery; as, *white-slave* traffic: see *white slave* under *white,* a.
2. against white slavery; as *White-slave Act* (see *Mann Act*).

whīte′smith, *n.* 1. a tinsmith.
2. a worker in iron who finishes or polishes the work, in distinction from one who forges it.

whīte′stōne, *n.* a variety of granite composed essentially of feldspar, but containing mica and other minerals; granulite.

whīte′tāil, *n.* 1. the wheatear or stonechat. [Dial.]
2. the white-tailed deer.
3. a hummingbird of the genus *Urochroa.*

whīte′-tāiled, *a.* having a white tail.
white-tailed buzzard; a large hawk, *Buteo albocaudatus,* of the southern part of North America.
white-tailed deer; the common North American deer, *Cariacus virginianus*: also called *Virginia deer.*
white-tailed eagle; same as *bald eagle* under *bald.*
white-tailed gnu; the common gnu.
white-tailed ptarmigan; a ptarmigan, *Lagopus leucurus,* of the Rocky Mountain region.

whīte′thorn, *n.* the common hawthorn.

whīte′thrōat, *n.* 1. an Old World warbler of various species, especially *Sylvia cinerea,* the common whitethroat; *Sylvia curruca* is the lesser whitethroat.
2. a hummingbird of Brazil, *Loucochloris albicollis.*
3. the white-throated sparrow.

whīte′-thrōat″ed spăr′rōw, a common North American sparrow, *Zonotrichia albicollis,* having a square white patch on the throat.

whīte′tip, *n.* any hummingbird of the genus *Urosticte.*

whīte′wall, *n.* a bird, the spotted flycatcher. [Brit. Dial.]

whīte′wäsh (hwīt′wosh), *n.* 1. a mixture of lime, whiting, size, water, etc., for whitening walls, etc.
2. a toilet preparation for making the skin fair.
3. (a) a glossing over or concealing of faults or defects in an effort to exonerate or give the appearance of soundness; (b) something said or done for this purpose.
4. in sports, a defeat in which the loser scores no points at all. [Colloq.]

whīte′wäsh, *v.t.*; whitewashed, *pt., pp.*; whitewashing, *ppr.* 1. to whiten with whitewash; to cover with a white liquid composition; as, to *whitewash* a ceiling.
2. to gloss over or conceal the faults or defects of; to give a favorable interpretation of or a falsely virtuous appearance to.
3. in sports, to defeat (an opponent) without permitting him to score. [Colloq.]
4. to clear, as an insolvent or bankrupt of his debts, by going through a judicial process. [Brit.]

whīte′wäsh″ēr, *n.* one who whitewashes.

whīte′weed, *n.* [from the color of its flowers.] the oxeye daisy, *Chrysanthemum leucanthemum.*

whīte′wing, *n.* 1. the chaffinch. [Brit. Dial.]
2. the white-winged scoter.
3. a streetcleaner wearing a white uniform.

whīte′wood, *n.* any of numerous trees having white or whitish wood; also, their wood. The species common to North America are the tulip tree, the basswood, the cottonwood, and the wild cinnamon, which yields a bark known as whitewood bark.

whīte′wŏrt, *n.* a plant, feverfew; also, the Solomon's seal.

whith′ēr (hwith′), *adv.* [ME. *whider, whidir, whidur,* from AS. *hwider, hwyder,* whither.]
1. to what place, point, condition, result, etc.? where?: used to introduce questions.
Wither away so fast? —Shak.
2. to which place, point, condition, result, etc.: used relatively; as, the park *whither* we turned our footsteps.
3. to whatever place, point, condition, result, etc.; wherever; as, let them go *wither* they will.
Wither is now largely replaced by *where* except in poetical or rhetorical usage.

whith″ēr·sō·ev′ēr, *adv.* to whatever place; wherever: an emphatic usage.

whith′ēr·wärd, *adv.* in what or which direction: used relatively or interrogatively.

whīt′ing (hwīt′), *n.*; *pl.* **whīt′ings** or **whīt′ing,** [ME. *whytynge*; M.D. *wijting,* from *wit,* white.]
1. a European fish of the genus *Merlangus,* particularly *Merlangus vulgaris,* highly valued as a food fish.
2. any of various American fishes of the genus *Menticirrus.*
3. the silver hake; also, the menhaden.

whīt′ing, *n.* fine chalk pulverized and freed from impurities, used in fine whitewashing, the manufacture of putty, as a polish, etc.

whīt′ing-mop, *n.* 1. a young whiting. [Obs.]
2. figuratively, a fair lass; a pretty girl. [Obs.]

whīt′ing pol′lăck, the European pollack.

whīt′ing pout, a gadoid fish, *Gadus luscus.*

whīt′ish, *a.* somewhat white; white in a moderate degree.

whīt′ish·ness, *n.* the quality of being somewhat white.

whit′leath″ēr (hwit′leth″), *n.* same as *white leather* under *white.*

whit′ling, *n.* the young of the bull trout. [Scot. and Brit. Dial.]

whit′lōw, *n.* [corruption of *quick-flaw*; *flaw,* a flaw or flaking off of the skin near the *quick,* or sensitive part of the finger around the nail.] a painful, pus-producing inflammation at the end of a finger or toe, near or under the nail; a felon.

whit′lōw gràss, any of various plants regarded as a cure for whitlow. Vernal whitlow grass is *Draba verna.*

whit′lōw·wŏrt, *n.* whitlow grass of the genus *Paronychia.*

Whit′mŏn″dāy, *n.* [coined to match *Whitsunday.*] the Monday following Whitsunday. In England it is observed as a bank holiday: also called *Whitsun Monday.*

whit′ney·īte, *n.* in mineralogy, an arsenide of copper, mined in the Lake Superior district and named after an American geologist, J.D. Whitney.

Whit′sun, *a.* [abbrev. of *Whitsunday.*] of or observed on Whitsunday or Whitsuntide; as, *Whitsun* holidays.

Whit′sun″dāy, *n.* [ME. *hwitesunedei*; AS. *hwita sunnan-dæg,* White Sunday: so called from the white garments worn by candidates for baptism.]
1. the seventh Sunday (fiftieth day) after Easter: a festival of the church in commemoration of the descent of the Holy Spirit on the day of Pentecost.
2. in Scotland, one of the term days (May 15, or May 26, Old Style), in which rents, annuities, ministers' stipends, etc. are paid.

Whit′sun·tīde, *n.* Whitsunday and the week following, especially the first three days: also *Whitsun Tide.*

whit′ten, *n.* 1. the wayfaring tree. [Brit. Dial.]
2. the guelder rose. [Brit. Dial.]

whit′tēr·ick, *n.* the curlew. [Brit. Dial.]

whit′tle, *n.* [ME. *whitel,* from AS. *hwitel,* blanket, lit., a small white thing, from *hwit,* white.] a blanket worn over the shoulders like a cloak. [Brit. Dial.]

whit′tle, *n.* a knife; particularly, a large knife. [Now Dial.]

whit′tle, *v.t.*; whittled, *pt., pp.*; whittling, *ppr.* [ME. *thwitel,* dim. from AS. *thwītan,* to cut.]
1. (a) to cut or pare thin shavings from (wood) with a knife; (b) to make or fashion (an object) in this manner; as, he *whittled* a small dog for his grandson.
2. to reduce, destroy, or get rid of gradually, as if by whittling away with a knife: usually with *down, away,* etc., as, he *whittled down* the cost of the project.

whit′tle, *v.i.* to whittle wood; particularly, to shave or cut wood idly or to no purpose; as, to spend the time talking and *whittling.*

whit′tlings, *n.pl.* chips or shavings, made by one who whittles.

whit′tret, *n.* a weasel. [Scot.]

Whit′-Tūes″dāy, *n.* [coined to match Whitsunday.] the third day of Whitsuntide: also called *Whitsun Tuesday.*

whit′wall, *n.* same as *witwall.*

Whit′wŏrth gun, [after its English inventor, Sir Joseph Whitworth.] a rifled firearm having a hexagonal bore, with a twist more rapid than usual, shooting an elongated shot.

whīt′y (hwīt′), *a.*; *comp.* whitier; *superl.*

whitiest; whitish: often used [W–] as a nickname for a person with light blond hair.

whiz, whizz (hwiz), *v.i.*; whizzed, *pt.*, *pp.*; whizzing, *ppr.* [echoic.]

1. to make a whirring or hissing sound like that of an arrow or ball flying through the air.

2. to speed by with this sound; as, the bullet *whizzed* past him.

whiz, whizz, *v.t.* to cause to whizz, especially by rotating rapidly.

whiz, whizz, *n.* 1. the whirring or hissing sound of something rushing through the air.

2. (a) a person who is very quick, adroit, or skilled at something; as, he's a *whiz* at football; (b) a person or thing regarded as excellent, attractive, etc.; as, a *whiz* of an automobile; (c) an agreement; bargain; (d) a celebration. [Slang.]

whiz'-bang, whizz'-bang, *n.* 1. a high-explosive shell of great speed whose sound of explosion occurs immediately after its sound of flight. [Slang.]

2. a firework having an effect somewhat like this. [Slang.]

whiz'zẽr, *n.* one who or that which whizzes; specifically, any centrifugal machine, as a drier for sugar, grain, etc.

whiz'zing·ly, *adv.* with a whizzing sound.

whö (hö), *pron.*; *poss.* whose; *obj.* whom. [AS. *hwā*, who.]

1. what person or persons: used to introduce a question; as, *who* came?

2. which person or persons; as, I don't know *who* came.

3. (a) (the, or a, person or persons) that: used to introduce a relative clause; as, the man *who* came to dinner; (b) any person or persons that; whoever: used as an indefinite relative with an implied antecedent; as, "*who* steals my purse steals trash."

as who should say; as if one should say; as one might be supposed to say.

who all; all who. [Colloq.]

who's who; (a) who the important people are; (b) [*often* W– W–] a book or list containing the names and short biographies of the prominent contemporary persons of a country, city, profession, etc.

whōa (hwō), *interj.* [for *ho*, interj.] stop!: used especially in directing a horse to stand still.

whö·dun'it, *n.* [from *who* and *done* and *it*: coined in 1930 by D. Gordon in *American News of Books.*] a mystery novel, play, etc. in which a crime is solved at the end by the principal character, usually a detective, using clues scattered throughout the story. [Slang.]

whö·ev'ẽr, *pron.* 1. any person at all that; whatever person.

2. no matter what person; as, *whoever* did it, I didn't.

3. what person? who?: an emphatic usage; as, *whoever* told you that?

whōle (hōl), *a.* [ME. *hol, hool*, from AS. *hāl* whole, healthy.]

1. (a) in sound health; not diseased or injured; (b) [Archaic.] healed: said of a wound.

2. not broken, damaged, injured, defective, etc.; intact.

3. containing all of its elements or parts; entire, complete; as, a *whole* set of Dickens.

4. not divided up; in a single unit.

5. constituting the entire amount, extent, number, etc.; as, he slept through the *whole* night.

6. having both parents in common; as, a *whole* brother: distinguished from *half*.

7. in arithmetic, not a fraction; as, 28 is a *whole* number.

made out of whole cloth; completely fictitious or false; made up.

whole blood; blood for transfusion with no element extracted: distinguished from *blood plasma*.

whole milk; milk from which none of the elements has been removed: distinguished from *skim milk*.

whole note; in music, a note (○) having four times the duration of a quarter note: also called *semibreve*.

whole number; an integer as distinguished from a fraction or a mixed number; as, 28 is a *whole number*.

whole step; in music, an interval consisting of two adjacent half steps; a whole tone.

Syn.—all, undivided, uninjured, unimpaired, integral, unbroken, entire, total, complete.

whōle, *n.* 1. the entire amount, quantity, extent, or sum of something; totality or total assemblage of parts.

2. a complete organization of parts; a unity, entirety, or system.

as a whole; as a complete unit; altogether.

committee of the whole; see under *committee*.

on (or *upon*) the whole; all things considered; in general.

Syn.—total, totality, amount, aggregate, gross, entirety, sum.

whōle'heärt'ed, *a.* doing or done with all one's energy, enthusiasm, etc.; sincere; earnest.

whōle'-hoofed (-hooft), *a.* having undivided hoofs.

whōle'-length, *a.* 1. extending from end to end.

2. full-length; as, a *whole-length* portrait.

whōle'length, *n.* a statue or portrait exhibiting the entire figure.

whōle'ness, *n.* the state or quality of being whole, entire, or sound; completeness.

whōle'sāle, *n.* [ME. *holesale*, from phr. *by hole sale*, by wholesale.] the selling of goods in relatively large quantities; especially, the sale of such goods to retailers who then sell them to the consumer: opposed to *retail*.

by wholesale; (a) in large quantities and, usually, at a reduced price; hence, (b) extensively and generally, without singling out.

whōle'sāle, *a.* 1. of or engaged in selling at wholesale.

2. sold in relatively large quantities, usually at a lower cost per item; as, what is the *wholesale* price of these notebooks?

3. extensive and general; without singling out; as, modern warfare involves the *wholesale* destruction of peoples.

whōle'sāle, *adv.* in relatively large quantities; by wholesale; as, he bought (or sold) them *wholesale*.

whōle'sāle, *v.i.*; wholesaled, *pt.*, *pp.*; wholesaling, *ppr.* 1. to be engaged in wholesale selling.

2. to be sold in relatively large quantities; as, these pencils *wholesale* at $3.00 per gross.

whōle'sāle, *v.t.* to sell, as goods, in wholesale quantities.

whōle'sāl''ẽr, *n.* one who sells at wholesale.

whōle snīpe, the common snipe.

whōle'sōme, *a.* 1. promoting or conducive to good health or well-being; healthful; as, a *wholesome* climate.

2. tending to improve the mind or morals; as, a *wholesome* moving picture for children.

3. characterized by health and vigor; sound; as, a *wholesome* girl.

4. tending to suggest health, or soundness of body and mind; as, there was something *wholesome* about his smile.

Syn.—healthful, salubrious, salutary, beneficial, nutritious, healing.

whōle'sōme·ly, *adv.* in a wholesome manner; healthfully.

whōle'sōme·ness, *n.* the state or quality of being wholesome; salutariness.

whōle'-sōuled', *a.* noble; generous; wholehearted; doing or done with one's whole soul.

whōle'-whēat' (-hwēt'), *a.* 1. made of the entire grain of wheat, including a large part of the bran; as, *whole-wheat* flour.

2. made of whole-wheat flour; as, *whole-wheat* bread.

whö'll (höl), 1. who shall.

2. who will.

whōl'ly (hōl'), *adv.* [ME. *hooli, holi.*] entirely; completely; altogether.

whöm (höm), *pron.* [ME. *whom, hwom*; AS. *hwam*, dat. of *hwa.*] the objective case of *who*: in colloquial usage, now often replaced by *who*.

whöm·ev'ẽr, *pron.* the objective case of *whoever*.

whom'mle, whom'ble (hwom'l), *v.t.* to whemmel. [Scot.]

whöm·sō·ev'ẽr (höm-), *pron.* the objective case of *whosoever*.

whoop (höp), *n.* [ME. *houpen*, to call, shout; OFr. *houper*, to call afar off, cry out.] a loud shout, cry, or noise; specifically, (a) a shrill and prolonged cry, as of excitement, intense joy, ferocity, exultation, etc.; (b) a hoot, as of an owl; (c) the deep-sounding, convulsive intake of air immediately following a fit of coughing in whooping cough.

not worth a whoop; worth nothing at all. [Colloq.]

whoop, *v.t.*; whooped (höpt), *pt.*, *pp.*; whooping, *ppr.* 1. to utter with a whoop or whoops.

2. to call, drive, urge on, chase, etc. with a whoop or whoops; as, to *whoop* the hounds in a chase.

to whoop it (or *things*) *up*; (a) to create a noisy disturbance, as in celebrating; (b) to create enthusiasm (*for* something or someone); as, the boys *whooped it up for* Smith. [Slang.]

whoop, *v.i.* to utter a whoop or whoops.

whoop'ee (*or* hwoop'), *interj.* [from *whoop.*] an exclamation used to express great enjoyment, gay abandonment, etc.

whoop'ee, *n.* a shout of "whoopee!"

to make whoopee; to have a gay, noisy time. [Slang.]

whoop'ẽr, *n.* one who or that which whoops; specifically, an Old World swan with a characteristic whooping cry.

whoop'ing, *n.* a crying; a loud call or noise; specifically, the characteristic inspiration following the coughing in whooping cough.

whoop'ing cough (kof), an acute infectious disease, usually affecting children, caused by a bacillus and characterized by catarrh of the respiratory tract and repeated attacks of coughing that end in a forced inspiration, or whoop; pertussis.

whoop'ing crāne, a large white crane, *Grus americana*, native to North America and known for its whooping call: now extremely rare.

whoop'ing swän, a swan, *Olor cygnus*.

whoot (höt), *v.i.* and *v.t.* to hoot. [Obs.]

whop, whäp (hwop), *v.t.* and *v.i.*; whopped, whapped (hwopt), *pp.*, *pt*;. whopping, whapping, *ppr.* 1. to beat, thrash, or strike. [Archaic or Dial.]

2. to throw (oneself) down suddenly; to flop. [Archaic or Dial.]

whop, whäp, *n.* a heavy blow, a sudden fall or bump, etc., or the noise made by any of these. [Archaic or Dial.]

whop'pẽr, whäp'pẽr, *n.* anything unusually large; something astonishing; especially, a great lie; a palpable falsehood. [Colloq.]

whop'ping, whäp'ping, *a.* very large; thumping. [Colloq.]

whö're (hö'ẽr), who are.

whōre (hōr), *n.* [ME. and AS. *hore*; ON. *hora.*] a woman who engages in illegal sexual intercourse, especially one who engages in promiscuous sexual intercourse for pay; a prostitute; a harlot.

whōre, *v.i.*; whored, *pt.*, *pp.*; whoring, *ppr.* 1. to be a whore.

2. to fornicate with whores.

3. in the Bible, to worship false gods: see Deut. xxxi. 16.

whōre, *v.t.* to make a whore of (a woman). [Archaic.]

whōre'dŏm, *n.* [ME. *hordom*; O.N. *hórdómr.*]

1. prostitution or fornication.

2. in the Bible, the desertion of the worship of God for the worship of idols; idolatry.

whōre'house, *n.* a place where prostitutes are for hire; a brothel.

whōre'mȧs''tẽr, *n.* 1. one who keeps or procures whores for others; a pimp; a procurer.

2. a man who fornicates with whores; a lecher.

whōre'mȧs''tẽr·ly, *a.* having the character of a whoremaster; libidinous.

whōre'mŏn''gẽr, *n.* a whoremaster; a lecher.

whōre'sŏn, *n.* [ME. *hores son*, lit., son of a whore, bastard, after OFr. *fiz a putain.*]

1. a bastard. [Archaic.]

2. a scoundrel; knave: a general epithet of abuse. [Archaic.]

whōre'sŏn, *a.* vile; detestable; knavish, etc. [Archaic.]

whōr'ish, *a.* lewd; having the nature of a whore.

whōr'ish·ly, *adv.* in a whorish manner.

whōr'ish·ness, *n.* the character of being whorish.

whōrl (hwũrl *or* hworl), *n.* [ME. *whorwyl*, dial. var. of *whirl.*]

1. a small flywheel on a spindle, as for regulating the speed of a spinning wheel.

2. anything that whirls or appears to whirl like the whorl on a spindle; specifically, (a) [*usually in pl.*] any of the circular ridges that form the design of a fingerprint; (b) in botany, an arrangement of leaves, petals, etc. about the same point on a stem; (c) in zoology, any of the turns in a spiral shell; (d) in anatomy, a turn of the spiral cochlea in a man or any mammal; also, a turn of a turbinate bone.

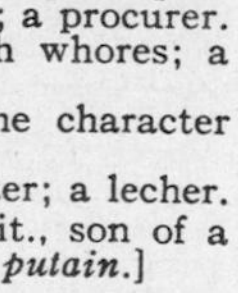

WHORLS

whŏrled, *a.* having, or arranged in, a whorl or whorls; verticillate.

whŏrt (hwŭrt), *n.* [AS. *horta,* a bilberry.] the fruit of the whortleberry or the shrub itself.

whŏr′tle, *n.* same as *whortleberry.*

whŏr′tle·ber·ry, *n.*; *pl.* **whŏr′tle·ber·ries,** [AS. *horta,* a bilberry.]

1. (a) a small European shrub, *Vaccinium myrtillus,* of the blueberry family, with pink flowers and blue or blackish edible berries; (b) any of these berries.

2. the huckleberry.

whö's (höz), who is.

whöse (höz), *pron.* [ME. *whos, hwas*; AS. *hwæs,* genit. of *hwa.*] the possessive case of *who,* and now, usually, of *which.*

whöse·sō·ev′ẽr, *pron.* the possessive case of *whosoever.*

whö′sō (hö′), *pron.* whosoever; whoever. [Archaic.]

whö·sō·ev′ẽr, *pron.* whoever; whatever person: an emphatic form.

whot (wot), *a.* hot. [Obs.]

whum′mle (hwum′), *v.t.* same as *whemmel.*

whŭrt (hwŭrt), *n.* same as *whort.*

whȳ (hwī), *adv.* [AS. *hwi, hwy,* the instrumental case of *hwa,* who.]

1. for what reason, cause, or purpose; with what motive: used interrogatively and relatively; as, *why* did he go? I'll tell you *why* he went.

2. because of which; on account of which: used relatively, often after *reason*; as, I can think of no reason *why* you shouldn't go.

3. the reason for which; as, this is *why* he went.

whȳ, *n.*; *pl.* **whȳs,** the reason, cause, motive, purpose, etc.; as, never mind the *why* and wherefore.

whȳ, *interj.* an exclamation used: (a) to express surprise, excitement, impatience, indignation, etc.; (b) to fill in while groping for what to say.

whȳ, *n.* a quey. [Brit. Dial.]

whyd′ȧh bīrd (hwid′), same as *whidah bird.*

Wich′i·tȧ, *n.*; *pl.* **Wich′i·tȧs,** one of a tribe of American Indians formerly located in the Middle Western States.

wick, *n.* [AS. *wic,* a village, town, from L. *vicus,* a village.] a village, town, or hamlet: now archaic except as compounded (often in the form *-wich*) in certain names, etc., as in War*wick,* Green*wich,* baili*wick.*

wick, *n.* [ME. *wicke, weyke*; AS. *weoca,* a wick.] a piece of cord or tape, or a thin bundle of threads, in a candle, oil lamp, cigarette lighter, etc., that absorbs the fuel by capillary attraction and, when lighted, burns with a small, steady flame.

wick, *n.* in Shetland, an open bay. [Archaic or Dial.]

wick, *n.* in the game of curling, a narrow port or passage in the rink or course flanked by the stones of those who have played before.

wick, *n.* a dairy house of small size. [Brit. Dial.]

wick, *n.* a corner; a corner of the mouth. [Dial.]

wick, *v.t.*; wicked (wikt), *pt., pp.*; wicking, *ppr.* to strike, as a stone, in an oblique direction: a term in curling.

wick, *a.* wicked. [Dial.]

wicked (wikt), *a.* having a wick, as a lamp.

wick′ed, *a.* [ME. *wikked, wicked,* from *wikke,* evil, from AS. *wicca,* a witch.]

1. having or resulting from bad moral character; evil; sinful; immoral; depraved; vicious; as, a *wicked* deed; a *wicked* heart.

2. generally bad, painful, etc., but without any moral considerations involved; as, it was a *wicked* blow on the head.

3. mischievous; roguish; naughty in a playful way; as, a *wicked* urchin.

4. cursed; baneful; pernicious. [Obs.]

wick′ed·ly, *adv.* in a wicked manner.

All that do *wickedly* shall be stubble.
—Mal. iv. 1.

wick′ed·ness, *n.* 1. the state or quality of being wicked.

2. a wicked thing or act; wicked conduct; as, to work *wickedness.*

wick′ẽr, *n.* [ME. *wiker, wikir*; prob. from O.N.]

1. a small, pliant twig; a withe; an osier.

2. (a) such twigs woven together, as in baskets or furniture; wickerwork; (b) something made of such twigs.

wick′ẽr, *a.* made of or covered with wicker; as, a *wicker* basket, a *wicker* chair.

wick′ẽred, *a.* made of or covered with wicker.

wick′ẽr·wŏrk, *n.* 1. thin, flexible twigs woven together; wicker.

2. things made of wicker.

wick′et, *n.* [ME. and Anglo-Fr. *wiket* (Fr. *guichet*).]

1. a small gate or doorway, especially a small door or gate near or forming part of a larger one.

2. a small window or opening, as for a bank teller or in a box office.

3. a small gate for regulating the flow of water to a water wheel or for emptying a canal lock.

4. [from orig. resemblance to a gate.] in cricket, (a) either of two sets of three vertical sticks (stumps) each, with two small pieces (bails) resting on top of them; (b) the playing space between the two wickets; (c) an unplayed or unfinished inning; (d) a player's turn at bat.

5. in croquet, any of the wire arches through which the balls must be hit; a hoop.

6. in mining, a heading or stall.

wick′et·keep·ẽr, *n.* in cricket, the fielder stationed immediately behind the wicket.

wick′ing, *n.* cord, yarn, or other material for making wicks.

wick′i·up, wik′i·up, *n.* [Am. Ind.] a kind of hut built by the Nomadic Indians of the southwestern United States, consisting of an oval-shaped frame covered with grass, brush, etc.: also spelled *wickyup.*

Wiç′lif·īte, Wick′liff·īte, *n.* and *a.* same as *Wycliffite.*

wiç′ō·py, *n.* [from Am. Ind.] any of various trees with strong, flexible shoots and tough bark, as the leatherwood, basswood, etc.

wid′dy, *n.* [a form of *withy.*] a rope; more properly, a rope made of withes or willows; hence, a halter; the gallows. [Scot. and Brit. Dial.]

wid′dy, *n.* a widow. [Dial.]

wīde, *a.*; *comp.* wider; *superl.* widest, [ME. *wid, wyd,* from AS. *wid.*]

1. extending over a large area; especially, extending over a larger area from side to side than is usual or normal; as, a *wide* bed: distinguished from *long* and opposed to *narrow.*

2. of a specified extent from side to side; as, three miles *wide.*

3. of great extent, range, or inclusiveness; as, a *wide* variety, *wide* reading.

4. roomy; ample; loose; full; as, a *wide* blouse.

5. open or extended to full width; as, her eyes grew *wide* with fear.

6. landing, striking, or ending far from the point, issue, etc. aimed at; usually with *of*; as, *wide of* the target.

7. in phonetics, pronounced with the tongue and other vocal organs in a more or less relaxed position; lax, as the *i* in *bit* or the *e* in *bed.*

wīde, *adv.* 1. over a relatively large area; afar; widely; extensively; as, his doctrines spread far and *wide.*

2. fully open or expanded to the greatest extent possible; as, the door swung *wide*; the graves yawned *wide.*

3. far from the mark or from the purpose; so as to miss the point, issue, etc. aimed at; astray; as, the bullet flew *wide* of the mark.

wīde, *n.* 1. a wide area or extent. [Rare or Poetic.]

Emptiness and the waste *wide*
Of that abyss. —Tennyson.

2. in cricket, a ball that is bowled out of the batsman's reach, counted as a run for the team at bat.

wīde′-an̄′gle, *a.* 1. designating or of a kind of camera lens that covers a wider angle of view than the ordinary lens.

2. designating or of any of several motion-picture systems (variously trade-marked, as *Cinerama, CinemaScope,* etc.) employing one or more cameras (and projectors) and an especially wide, curved screen to simulate normal panoramic vision.

wīde′-ȧ·wāke′, *a.* 1. completely awake.

2. alert; ready; prepared.

wīde′-ȧ·wāke′, *n.* 1. an obsolete kind of soft felt hat with a low crown and wide brim: also *wide-awake hat.*

2. a sooty tern.

wīde′-eyed (-īd), *a.* with the eyes opened widely.

wīde′gab, *n.* the angler: also called *widegap, widegut.*

wīde′ly, *adv.* 1. over a wide area; as, he's traveled *widely.*

2. to a wide distance or extent; as, *widely* different.

wīd′en, *v.t.* and *v.i.*; widened, *pt., pp.*; widening, *ppr.* to make or become wide or wider.

And arches *widen,* and long aisles extend.
—Pope.

wīde′ness, *n.* the character or state of being wide.

wīde′-ō′pen, *a.* 1. opened wide.

2. not enforcing, or careless in enforcing, laws prohibiting or regulating prostitution, gambling, the sale of liquor, etc.; as, a *wide-open* city.

wīde rē·ceīv′ẽr, in football, a player eligible to receive a pass who usually takes a position at some distance from the other members of the offensive team.

wīde′spread′ (-spred′), *a.* widely spread; covering a great distance; extending far; as, a *widespread* movement or belief.

widġ′eŏn (wij′un), *n.*; *pl.* **widġ′eŏns** or **widġ′eŏn,** [OFr. *vigeon,* a whistling duck.]

1. any of several wild, fresh-water ducks of the genus *Mareca.* The European widgeon, *Mareca penelope,* is numerous in the British Isles. The American widgeon, *Mareca* (*Anas*) *americana,* is most abundant in Carolina: also called *baldpate, baldhead, whew,* etc.

2. any wild duck, except the mallard: usually preceded by a qualifying word; as, the black *widgeon,* the tufted duck of Europe; the blue-billed *widgeon,* or American scaup; the spoon-billed *widgeon,* or shoveler, etc.

Also spelled *wigeon.*

widġ′eŏn ço͡ot, the ruddy duck. [Dial.]

wīd′ish, *a.* moderately wide; as, a *widish* gap.

Wid·măn·staet′ti·ăn (-stet′), *a.* of, discovered, or named by Aloys Beck von Widmanstätten (1753–1849), a Vienna physicist.

Widmanstaettian figures; the markings appearing on the smooth surface of certain meteoric irons when treated with acid.

wid′ōw, *n.* [ME. *widewe, widwe,* from AS. *widewe.*]

1. a woman who has outlived the man to whom she was married at the time of his death; especially, such a woman who has not remarried.

2. in certain card games, an extra hand dealt to the table.

3. in printing, an incomplete line, as that ending a paragraph, carried over to the top of a new page or column: it is generally avoided by rewriting copy to eliminate the line or fill it out.

4. a European moth, *Cidaria luctuata.*

wid′ow, *v.t.*; widowed, *pt., pp.*; widowing, *ppr.* 1. to cause to become a widow: usually in the past participle; as, she was *widowed* by the war.

2. to deprive of something valued; to bereave.

3. to survive as the widow of. [Rare.]

4. to endow with the rights of a widow. [Rare.]

wid′ōw-bench, *n.* that share which a widow is allowed of her husband's estate, besides her jointure. [Brit.]

wid′ōw bē·witch′ed, a grass widow or any woman who has been separated from her husband. [Colloq.]

wid′ōw bīrd, the whidah bird.

wid′ōw duck, *Dendrocygna viduata,* a tree duck of the West Indies.

wid′ōwed, *a.* of or pertaining to a widow or the state of being a widow; that has been deprived or bereaved of one's mate; alone; desolated.

wid′ōw·ẽr, *n.* a man who has outlived the woman to whom he was married at the time of her death; especially, such a man who has not remarried.

wid′ōw·ẽred, *a.* deprived or bereaved of one's mate, as a man who has been made a widower.

wid′ōw·ẽr·hood, *n.* the state of being a widower.

wid′ōw finch, same as *widow bird.*

wid′ōw fish, a rock fish of California.

wid′ōw·hood, *n.* 1. the condition or period of being a widow; rarely, the state of being a widower.

2. the estate settled on a widow. [Obs.]

wid′ōw·ly, *adv.* in the manner of a widow. [Rare.]

wid′ōw mŏn′key, a South American monkey, *Callithrix lugens,* having peculiar whitish markings on the arms, neck, and face.

wid'ōw's chām'bẽr, in English law, the furnishings of the bedchamber of a freeman's widow, to which she was formerly entitled.

wid'ōw's crụse, a supply that is apparently inexhaustible: 1 Kings xvii. 10–17; 2 Kings iv. 1–8.

wid'ōw's mīte, a small gift or contribution freely given by one who can scarcely afford it: Mark xii. 41–44.

wid'ōw's pēak, a point often formed by hair growing down in the middle of a forehead: formerly believed to be a foretelling of early widowhood.

wid'ōw-wāil", *n.* an evergreen shrub, *Cneorum tricoccon*, native to southern Europe.

width, *n.* [from *wide*, by analogy with *length*, *breadth*.]
1. the fact, quality, or condition of being wide; wideness.
2. the size of something in terms of how wide it is; distance from side to side.
3. a piece of something having a specified distance from side to side; as, sew two *widths* of cloth together.

wid'ū·ăl, *a.* of or pertaining to a widow; vidual. [Obs.]

wiē ġeht's? (vē gāts'), [G.] how goes it? how are you?

wiēld, *v.t.*; wielded, *pt.*, *pp.*; wielding, *ppr.* [ME. *welden*, to govern, from AS. *gweldan*, *gewyldan*, to have power over, a weak verb derived from the strong verb *wealdan*, to have power over, rule, possess.]
1. to handle and use (a tool or weapon), especially with skill and control.
2. to exercise (power, control, influence, etc.).
3. to govern, rule, or direct. [Obs.]
to wield the scepter; to govern with supreme command.
Syn.—govern, rule, keep, swing, employ, sway, handle, manage.

wiēld'ȧ·ble, *a.* adapted to wielding; fit to be wielded.

wiēld'ẽr, *n.* a person who rules or controls; a manager or keeper.

wiēld'ing, *n.* authority; power; government.

wiēld'less, *a.* unmanageable; unwieldy. [Obs.]

wiēld'y, *a.*; *comp.* wieldier; *superl.* wieldiest, manageable; wieldable.

wiē'nẽr, *n.* [short for G. *Wiener wurst*, Vienna sausage.] a smoked sausage of beef or beef and pork, usually enclosed in a membranous casing and made in links a few inches long; a frankfurter: also *weenie*, *weeny*.

Wiē'nẽr schnit'zel (vē'nẽr shnit'sel), [G.; *Wiener*, of Vienna, and *schnitzel*, dim. of *schnitz*, a little piece, cutlet, and *schneiden*, to cut.] a breaded veal cutlet served with various garnishings, as anchovy fillets, fried eggs, etc.

wiē'nẽr·wũrst, *n.* [G.] a wiener.

wiēr, *n.* weir. [Obs.]

wīfe, *n.*; *pl.* **wīveṣ,** [ME. *wif*, *wyf*; AS. *wif*, a woman, wife.]
1. a woman: still so used in certain compounds, as house*wife*. [Archaic or Rare.]
2. a married woman; specifically, a woman in her relationship to her husband.
to give to wife; to give a daughter's hand in marriage.
to take to wife; to marry (a specified woman).
wife's equity; in law, the obligation generally enforced by a court of equity obliging a husband to make a reasonable provision for his wife and children.

wīfe'hood, *n.* the state, character, or condition of being a wife.

wīfe'less, *a.* without a wife.

wīfe'līke, *a.* resembling, characteristic of, or suitable to a wife.

wīfe'ly, *a.*; *comp.* wifelier; *superl.* wifeliest, [ME. *wyfely*; AS. *wiflic*.] of, like, or suitable to a wife.

wig, *n.* [a shortened form of *periwig*.]
1. an artificial covering of hair for the head, used as part of a costume, to conceal baldness, etc. Wigs are usually made to imitate the natural hair, but formal curled wigs are worn professionally by judges and lawyers in Great Britain.
2. a full-grown male Alaskan seal.

wig, *v.t.*; wigged, *pt.*, *pp.*; wigging, *ppr.* 1. to rebuke or scold; to berate. [Brit. Colloq.]
2. to furnish with a wig or wigs.

wig, *n.* a kind of cake. [Dial.]

wig'ăn, *n.* [so called from *Wigan*, a town in Lancashire, Eng.] a cotton canvas fabric used to line and stiffen the hems, lapels, and other parts of garments.

wiġ'eŏn, *n.*; *pl.* **wiġ'eŏnṣ** or **wiġ'eŏn,** a widgeon.

wigged, *a.* having the head covered with a wig; wearing a wig.

wig'gẽr·y, *n.*; *pl.* **wig'gẽr·ieṣ,** 1. (a) a wig; (b) wigs collectively.
2. the practice of wearing a wig.

wig'ging, *n.* a scolding or reprimand. [Brit. Colloq.]

wig'gle, *v.t.* and *v.i.*; wiggled, *pt.*, *pp.*; wiggling, *ppr.* [ME. *wigelen*; prob. from M.D. and M.L.G. *wiggelen*, freq. of *wiggen*, to move from side to side.] to move or cause to move with short, jerky motions from side to side; to wriggle shakily or sinuously.
Syn.—wriggle, waggle, squirm, wabble.

wig'gle, *n.* the condition or act of wiggling.

wig'glẽr, *n.* 1. the aquatic larva or pupa of various insects, especially that of the mosquito.
2. a person or thing that wiggles.

WIGGLER (of mosquito)

wig'gly, *a.*; *comp.* wigglier; *superl.* wiggliest, 1. that wiggles; wiggling.
2. having a form that suggests wiggling; wavy; as, a *wiggly* line.

wīght (wīt), *n.* [ME. *wizt*, *wight*, from AS. *wiht*, creature, animal, person, thing.]
1. a human being; a person: now sometimes used humorously. [Archaic.]
The *wight* of all the world
who lov'd thee best.
—Dryden.
2. a preternatural or supernatural being; an unearthly creature. [Archaic.]
3. a moment; an instant; a bit. [Obs.]

wīght, *a.* [ME. *wihte*; ON. *vigr*, neut. *vigt*, warlike, fit for war.] strong, brisk, active, brave, etc. [Archaic.]
Thirty steeds both fleet and *wight*
Stood saddled in stable day and night.
—Scott.

wig'less, *a.* without a wig; not wigged.

wig'māk"ẽr, *n.* one who makes or supplies wigs.

wig'wag, *v.t.* and *v.i.*; wigwagged, *pt.*, *pp.*; wigwagging, *ppr.* [prob. short for *wigglewaggle*, redupl. of *wiggle*.]
1. to move back and forth; to wag.
2. to send (a message) by waving flags, lights, etc. back and forth in accordance with a code.

wig'wag, *n.* 1. the act or practice of sending messages in this way.
2. a message so sent.

wig'wag"gẽr, *n.* a person who sends messages by wigwagging.

wig'wąm, *n.* [from Am. Ind. (Algonquian) name.]
1. a more or less conical shelter made by Indians of eastern and central North America, consisting of a framework of poles covered with bark, hides, etc.
2. a building used by a political group; especially, a large, temporary structure for a political convention. [Colloq.]
the Wigwam; Tammany Hall. [Colloq.]

WIGWAMS

wik'i·up, *n.* a wickiup.

Wil'cox fọr·mā'tion, in geology, the uppermost of the two main parts of the Lower Eocene strata of the American Gulf Coastal region.

wīld, *a.* [ME. *wilde*, *wielde*, from AS. *wild*, wild, bewildered, confused.]
1. living or growing in its original, natural state; not domesticated or cultivated; as, *wild* flowers; a *wild* ox.
2. savage; uncivilized; primitive; not refined by culture; as, *wild* natives.
3. (a) dissipated, licentious, etc.; as, *wild* youth; (b) characterized by a lack of moral restraint; immoral; unbridled; orgiastic; as, a *wild* party.
4. turbulent; tempestuous; stormy; violently agitated; as, the *wild* winds.
5. angered; vexed; crazed; as, he was *wild* with desperation.
6. not easily restrained or regulated; not submitting to control; as, *wild* children.
I have been *wild* and wayward.
—Tennyson.
7. reckless; incautious; rash; not in accordance with reason or prudence; as, a *wild* adventure.
8. lacking order and regularity; in a state of disorder, disarrangement; etc.; as, *wild* hair.
9. indicating strong emotion or mental excitement; excited; roused; bewildered; distracted; as, a *wild* look.
10. eager or enthusiastic, as with desire or anticipation; as, *wild* with delight.
11. uncultivated; uninhabitated; desolate; as, *wild* land.
12. wide of the mark aimed at; missing the target; as, a *wild* throw.
13. fantastically impractical; visionary; as, a *wild* scheme.
14. in certain card games, having any value desired by the holder: said of a card, as, when deuces are *wild* in poker, they may be counted as aces, kings, etc.
the wild; the wilderness, nature, the out-of-doors, etc.; as, the call of *the wild*.
to run wild; to grow or exist without control or regulation.
to sow one's wild oats; see under *oat*.
wild allspice; a shrub with small, fragrant, yellowish flowers and red berries; the spicebush.
wild balsam apple; see under *balsam apple*.
wild basil; see under second *basil*.
wild bean; any of several leguminous plants of the pea family, especially those of the genera *Phaseolus*, *Apios*, etc.
wild bee; any undomesticated bee; also, any domesticated bee escaped into a wild state.
wild bergamot; the American horsemint, *Monarda punctata*, an aromatic plant of the mint family growing in dry grounds.
wild boar; a variety of hog (*Sus scrofa*) living wild in Europe and Asia, from which the domesticated hog was developed.
wild brier; any species of wild rose, especially the sweetbrier or dog rose.
wild bugloss; a very rough bristly weed, *Asperugo procumbens*, of the borage family, having a small blue corolla and growing in sandy fields.
wild card; (a) in card games, a card that has been declared wild; (b) in sports, any of the teams, other than those that finish in first and sometimes second place, that qualify for a championship play-off.
wild carrot; a weed, *Daucus carota*, with white, lacelike flowers, from which the cultivated carrot originated; Queen Anne's lace.
wild cherry; a large, uncultivated cherry tree, *Prunus* (*Cerasus*) *pennsylvanica*, bearing a small astringent fruit; also, the wild black cherry, *Prunus serotina*, which furnishes a wood much used in cabinetwork, being of a light-red color and a compact texture.
wild comfrey; a bristly hairy plant, *Cynoglossum virginicum*, of the borage family, growing in rich woods and bearing a few naked racemes of blue flowers.
wild cumin; see under *cumin*.

WILD DUCK (*Anas boscas*)

wild duck; any duck not domesticated; specifically, the mallard.
wild elder; a plant, *Aralia hispida*, of the ginseng family, having bristly stems: also called *bristly sarsaparilla*.
wild flower; any plant growing without cultivation in fields, woods, etc.; also, its flower.
wild fowl; wild birds; especially, game birds, as wild ducks, wild geese, partridges, pheasants, quail, etc.
wild ginger; a plant, *Asarum canadense*.
wild goose; any undomesticated goose; specifically, in North America, the Canada goose, *Branta canadensis*; in Great Britain, the graylag, *Anser ferus*.

wild-goose chase; 1. a useless search or pursuit: so called because of the futility of trying to catch a wild goose by chasing it.

2. any futile attempt or enterprise.

wild-goose plum; a variety of wild plum tree that has been domesticated and bears fruit of excellent quality.

wild heliotrope; any species of plant with blue or purple flowers belonging to the genus *Phacelia* of the waterleaf family.

wild honey; honey made by wild bees.

Wild Hunt; in European folklore, a nighttime ride of spectral huntsmen across the countryside or the sky.

Wild Huntsman; in European folklore, the leader of the Wild Hunt, originally probably Odin.

wild hyacinth; a variety of hyacinth with blue, bell-shaped flowers; the wood hyacinth; the bluebell.

wild indigo; any of a number of related plants with triangle-shaped leaflets, clusters of blue, yellow, or white flowers, and short pods.

wild Irishman; a shrub, *Discaria australis*, of the buckthorn family, having a twisting stem, small leaves, and very sharp spines, growing in Australia and New Zealand.

wild land; land that has never been cultivated; also, land that is unsuitable for cultivation.

wild lettuce; any species of uncultivated lettuce growing as a weed; especially, a species having prickly leaves, small yellow flowers, and milky juice.

wild madder; (a) madder (senses 1 and 2a); (b) either of two species of bedstraw.

wild mandrake; the May apple, a plant with shield-shaped leaves, white flowers, and lemon-shaped fruit.

wild marjoram; a labiate, somewhat aromatic plant, *Origanum vulgare*, which resembles sweet marjoram.

wild mustard; a yellow-flowered, rapid-spreading weed whose seeds are sometimes used to flavor food; charlock.

wild oat; (a) same as *oat* (sense 2a); (b) a tall oatlike grass, *Arrhenatherum avenaceum*, used for fodder.

wild pansy; an uncultivated pansy with small flowers in combinations of white, yellow, and purple.

wild parsley; (a) any of several perennial herbs of the carrot group, especially a nine-leaf variety used as forage; (b) lovage.

wild parsnip; the wild, original form of the cultivated parsnip, used as forage.

wild pear; a small tree or shrub, *Clethra tinifolia*, resembling the pear tree.

wild pieplant; an uncultivated American dock, *Rumex hymenosepalus*, the stalks of which are sometimes used in substitution for those of rhubarb.

wild pigeon; same as *rock dove*.

wild pink; a species of catchfly, *Silene pennsylvanica*, with lance-shaped leaves and flat clusters of pink or white flowers.

wild plantain; an arborescent bananalike herb, *Heliconia bihai*, the leaves and husks of which are used by West Indian merchants in wrapping goods for exportation.

wild plum; an uncultivated plum tree of any species; also, its fruit.

wild rice; same as *Indian rice* under *Indian*.

wild rose; any of many roses growing wild, as the sweetbrier.

wild rubber; rubber obtained from uncultivated trees.

wild rye; any of various tall related grasses of the genus *Elymus*, like rye.

wild sage; same as *sagebrush*.

wild sarsaparilla; a plant, *Aralia nudicaulis*, of the ginseng family, characterized by one long-stalked leaf: used as a substitute for sarsaparilla.

wild sensitive plant; any one of various species of *Mimosa* or of *Cassia*; specifically, *Mimosa strigillosa*, growing on river banks and bearing rose-colored flowers.

wild Spaniard; any one of several New Zealand plants of the genus *Aciphylla*, umbelliferous and characterized by spiny leaves.

wild turkey; the wild, original form of the North American domesticated turkey, now rare.

wild vanilla; a purple-flowered shrub whose leaves when bruised give off a vanilla scent.

Wild West, wild west; the western United States in its early frontier period of lawlessness.

Wild West show; a circuslike spectacle featuring horsemanship and other feats by cowboys, Indians, etc.

wild yam; see under *yam*.

Syn.—untamed, undomesticated, uncultivated, uninhabited, desert, savage, uncivilized, unrefined, rude, ferocious, untrained, violent, ferine, loose, disorderly, turbulent, ungoverned, inordinate, chimerical, visionary, incoherent, raving, distracted.

wīld, *n.* [*usually pl.*] a wilderness, waste, desert, etc.; as, the *wilds* of Africa; the sandy *wilds* of Arabia.

wīld, *adv.* in a wild manner; wildly; without aim or control; as, he fired *wild*.

wīld′cat, *n.*; *pl.* **wīld′cats** or **wīld′cat,** 1. (a) any of a group of fierce, medium-sized, undomesticated animals of the cat family, found throughout North America, as the bobcat, or lynx; (b) an undomesticated cat of Europe, *Felis catus*, similar to but slightly larger than the domestic cat.

2. any person considered like a wildcat in being fierce, aggressive, quick-tempered, etc.

3. an unsound or risky business scheme.

4. a productive oil well drilled in an area not previously known to have oil.

5. in railroading, a locomotive and tender without cars sent out on special tasks, as to help haul a train.

Also *wild cat*.

wīld′cat, *a.* 1. acting or carried on in a reckless manner; particularly, characterized by plunging, irresponsible speculation; unsound or financially risky; as, a *wildcat* venture.

2. designating a business, etc. that is illegal or unethical.

3. in railroading, running without authorization or on an irregular schedule; as, a *wildcat* train, a *wildcat* locomotive.

wīld′cat, *v.t.*; wildcatted, *pt., pp.*; wildcatting, *ppr.* to drill for oil in (an area previously considered unproductive).

wīld′cat bañk, in the period before the National Bank Act of 1863–1864, any bank that issued notes without sufficient capital to redeem them.

wīld′cat strīke, a labor strike without the authorization of the union representing the strikers.

wīld′cat″tẽr, *n.* 1. a person who drills for oil in territory not known to be oil-bearing.

2. a person who promotes very risky or fraudulent ventures.

wil′de·beest (*or D.* vil′de-bāst), *n.*; *pl.* **wil′de·beests** or **wil′de·beest,** [S.Afr. D., from D. *wild*, wild, and *beeste*, beast.] a gnu.

wil′dẽr, *v.i.* and *v.t.* [either aphetic from *bewilder* or formed from *bewilderness*.]

1. to lose or cause to lose one's way. [Archaic. or Poet.]

2. to bewilder or become bewildered. [Archaic or Poet.]

wīld′ẽr·ing, *n.* same as *wilding*.

wil′dẽr·ment, *n.* bewilderment; confusion. [Poet.]

wil′dẽr·ness, *n.* [ME. *wildernesse*; *wildern*, AS. *wilder*, a wild animal, and suffix *-nesse*.]

1. a region uncultivated and uninhabited; a waste; a wild.

A jug of wine, a loaf of bread and thou
Beside me singing in the *wilderness*.
—Omar Khayyám.

2. a barren, empty, or open area of any nature; as, a *wilderness* of sea.

3. a portion of a garden set apart for things to grow wild.

4. a large, confused mass or tangle of persons or things.

5. a wild condition or quality. [Obs.]

wīld′-eȳed (-īd), *a.* staring in a wild or distracted manner, as from fear.

wīld′fīre, *n.* 1. originally, (a) a highly destructive fire; (b) a composition of inflammable materials readily catching fire and difficult to extinguish, formerly used in warfare; Greek fire: now mainly in *to spread like wildfire*, to be disseminated widely and rapidly, as a rumor.

2. a kind of lightning unaccompanied by thunder; heat lightning.

3. formerly, in coal mining, fire damp.

4. the will-o'-the-wisp.

5. erysipelas. [Obs.]

6. a disease of sheep characterized by inflammation of the skin. [Obs.]

wīld′flow″ẽr, *n.* same as *wild flower* under *wild*.

wīld′fowl, *n.* same as *wild fowl* under *wild*.

wīld′grāve, *n.* [G. *wildgraf*, from *wild*, game, wild animals, and *graf*, commonly a title equivalent to count.] a head forest keeper in Germany in former times.

wīld′ing, *n.* 1. a wild plant; especially, a wild apple tree; also, its fruit.

2. a plant originally cultivated, but growing wild.

3. a person or thing that does not conform to type.

wīld′ing, *a.* wild; not cultivated or domesticated.

wīld′ish, *a.* somewhat wild.

wīld′ling, *n.* an uncultivated plant or undomesticated animal.

wīld′ly, *adv.* in a wild state or manner.

wīld′ness, *n.* 1. the state or character of being wild.

2. a wild region; a wilderness. [Obs.]

wīld pō·tā′tō, a low twining vine of the morning-glory family, having a very large, more or less bulbous root, cordate leaves, and large purplish flowers, with dark corollas; also, a kind of twining vine with a large tuberous root, which is native to the American tropics: it is regarded by some as the original of the sweet potato.

wīld tō·bac′cō, a species of tobacco, formerly cultivated by the Indians, but now growing wild in the eastern U. S. and Canada.

wīld′wood, *n.* an unfrequented wood or forest.

wīle, *n.* [ME. *wile*, from AS. *wil*, *wile*, wile.]

1. a sly trick; a deceitful artifice; a stratagem.

2. a beguiling or coquettish trick.

3. trickery; deceit.

wīle, *v.t.*; wiled, *pt., pp.*; wiling, *ppr.* 1. to deceive; to beguile; to lure.

2. to cause to pass, as the time, by some diversion; to while (*away*).

wīle′fu̇l, *a.* full of wiles; wily; tricky.

wil′fu̇l, *a.* same as *willful*.

wil′fu̇l·ly, *adv.* same as *willfully*.

wil′fu̇l·ness, *n.* same as *willfullness*.

wil′gȧ, *n.* [Australian.] a tree, *Geijera parviflora*, native to Australia.

wī′li·ly, *adv.* in a wily manner; by stratagem; with insidious art; craftily.

wī′li·ness, *n.* the quality or condition of being wily; cunning; guile.

wilk, *n.* same as *whelk*.

will, *n.* [ME. *wille*; AS. *willa*, will.]

1. the act or process of volition; specifically, (a) wish; desire; longing; (b) inclination; disposition; pleasure; (c) [Obs.] appetite; lust.

2. something wished by a person, especially by one with power or authority; specifically, (a) a request; as, it is his *will* that you appear; (b) a command; decree; as, His *will* be done.

3. strong purpose, intention, or determination; as, where there's a *will* there's a way.

4. energy or enthusiasm; as, he works with a *will*.

5. the power of self-direction or self-control; as, he has no strong *will*.

6. the power of conscious and deliberate action or choice; as, freedom of the *will*.

7. disposition or attitude toward others; as, I bear her no ill *will*.

8. (a) the legal statement of a person's wishes concerning the disposal of his property after death; (b) the document containing this.

at will; when one wishes; at one's discretion.

mystic, or *sealed, will*; in law, a will prepared by or under the direction of the testator, which is sealed in an envelope and acknowledged on the outside of the envelope.

to do the will of; to obey the wish or command of.

with a will; with willingness and pleasure; with all one's heart; heartily.

will, *v.t.*; willed, *pt., pp.*; willing, *ppr.* [ME. *willen*, from AS. *willan*, *wyllan*, to choose, select, prefer.]

1. to form a distinct volition of; to decide upon; to make a choice of.

A man that sits still is said to be at liberty,
because he can walk if he *wills* it.
—Locke.

2. to resolve firmly; to determine; as, he *willed* to survive.

3. to decree; to ordain.

4. to convey or express a command or authoritative instructions to; to command; to direct; to order. [Obs.]

They *willed* me to say so, madam. —Shak.

5. to long for; to desire. [Archaic.]

There, there, Hortensio, *will* you any wife?
—Shak.

6. to influence or control as by hypnotic power.

7. to dispose of by testament; to give as a legacy; to bequeath by a will.

will, *v.i.* to wish, prefer, or choose. [Archaic.]
As *will* the rest, so *willeth* Winchester.
—Shak.

will, *v. pt.* would; *archaic second pers. sing. pres. indic.*, wilt; *archaic second pers. sing., pt.*, wouldest *or* wouldst; *obs. pp.* wold *or* would; no other forms now in use. [ME. *willen*; AS. *willan*.]

1. an auxiliary used to express futurity, usually with implications of intention, determination, compulsion, obligation, or necessity: in this sense *will* is generally used instead of *shall* except in questions in the first person, singular or plural (e.g., *Shall* we go tomorrow?); *shall* and *will* are used interchangeably to express determination, compulsion, obligation, and necessity, but there is some tendency to prefer *shall* in all persons.

2. an auxiliary used in formal speech, (a) to express determination, compulsion, obligation, or necessity in the first person, and futurity in the second and third persons; (b) in a question expecting *will* in the answer; (c) in an indirect quotation, if *will* would be used in the direct form of the quotation. These formal conventions, however, do not reflect and have not reflected prevailing usage.

3. an auxiliary used to express willingness; as, *will* you go?

4. an auxiliary used to express ability, capability, or capacity; as, it *will* hold another quart.

5. an auxiliary used to express habit or customary practice; as, she *will* talk for hours on end.

6. an auxiliary used, colloquially, to express expectation, surmise, etc.; as, that *will* be his wife with him, I suppose.

will, *v.t.* and *v.i.* to wish; to desire; as, what *will* you, master? do as you *will*.

will'à·ble, *a.* that can be willed, wished, determined, etc.

will'-çall, *a.* designating or of that department in a large store at which a deposit may be made on a purchase to be called for when paid in full.

willed, *a.* having a will: used especially in hyphenated compounds, meaning *having a* (specified kind of) *will*, as in strong-*willed*.

wil'lem·ite, *n.* [after *Willem* (William) I., king of the Netherlands.] native silicate of zinc, Zn_2SiO_4, found in massive or crystalline form in various colors from pale yellow-green to red.

will'ẽr, *n.* one who wills.

wil'let, *n.*; *pl.* **wil'lets** or **wil'let**, [so named from its cry.] a long-legged wading bird of the snipe family, *Symphemia semipalmata*, a sandpiper native to central North America.

will'fụl, *a.* 1. said or done deliberately or intentionally.

2. following one's own will unreasoningly; obstinate; stubborn.

3. willing; ready. [Obs.]

Also spelled *wilful*.

will'fụl·ly, *adv.* in a willful manner: also spelled *wilfully*.

will'fụl·ness, *n.* the state or quality of being willful: also spelled *wilfulness*.

wil'li·ẽr, *n.* a willower.

wil'lieṣ, *n.pl.* [perh. from *willy-nilly* as orig. referring to a state of nervous indecision.] nervousness; jitters (with *the*). [Slang.]

will'ing, *a.* [ME.; AS. *willung*, from *willian*, to will.]

1. having the mind favorably disposed (to do something specified or implied); not choosing to refuse; not averse; desirous; fain; ready; consenting; complying.

Willing to wound, and yet afraid to strike.
—Pope.

2. accepted of choice or without reluctance; done, given, offered, etc. voluntarily; voluntary.

3. acting, giving, etc. readily and cheerfully; as, a *willing* assistant.

4. of the power of choice; volitional.

will'ing·ly, *adv.* in a willing manner.

will'ing·ness, *n.* the state or quality of being willing.

wil'li·wạw, wil'ly·wạw, *n.* [etym. obscure.] a violent windstorm; particularly, a sudden wind squall.

wil'lŏck, *n.* the common guillemot, *Uria troile* or *Lomvia troile*, found on the coasts of the North Atlantic. [Scot. and Brit. Dial.]

will'-ō'-the-wisp, *n.* [earlier *Will with the wisp*, from *Will* and *wisp*.]

1. the ignis fatuus; hence, any person or thing that misleads, eludes, or deceives.

2. a fresh-water alga, *Nostoc commune*, that makes sudden appearances.

wil'lōw, *n.* [ME. *wilow*; AS. *welig*, willow.]

1. any of a number of related trees of the genus *Salix*, with narrow leaves, tassellike spikes of flowers, and, usually, flexible twigs used in weaving baskets, etc.; also, the wood of any of these trees.

2. figuratively, an emblem of sorrow, defeat, or the like; as, to wear the *willow*, that is, to mourn the loss of one beloved.

3. something made of willow wood, as a baseball bat or cricket bat. [Colloq.]

4. a machine with revolving spikes for cleaning cotton or wool.

almond-leafed willow; same as *almond willow*.

Babylonian willow; the weeping willow.

bay willow; a European tree, *Salix pentandra*, cultivated for ornament.

bitter willow; same as *purple willow*.

crack willow or *brittle willow*; a tree, *Salix fragilis*, characterized by the brittleness of its branches.

desert willow; a small tree, *Chilopsis saligna*, growing in arid regions of North America.

French willow; the almond willow.

glaucous willow; same as *pussy willow*.

glossy willow; same as *shining willow*.

goat willow; the common sallow, *Salix caprea*, of the Old World.

golden willow; a variety of white willow, having yellow twigs that are used in basketmaking.

hedge willow; same as *goat willow*.

hoary willow; a shrub, *Salix candida*, forming a sparse undergrowth in woods in the north-central and northeastern parts of the United States.

Huntington willow; same as *white willow*.

purple willow; a large European shrub, *Salix purpurea*, having a bark rich in salicin.

ring willow; a cultivated species of weeping willow which has curled leaves.

rose willow; same as *purple willow*.

sandbar willow; a small tree, *Salix longifolia*, often growing in sandy places along rivers in the north central United States.

shining willow; a variety of willow, *Salix lucida*, whose leaves are shiny on both sides.

silky willow; the white willow.

weeping willow; one of the largest of the willows, *Salix Babylonica*, having graceful, drooping branches.

whipcord willow; same as *purple willow*.

white willow; a large tree, *Salix alba*, having both sides of the leaves of a light-grayish color, and furnishing a light wood much used in the arts, being burned as charcoal, made up in numerous articles, and having twigs utilized in basketmaking.

yellow willow; same as *golden willow*.

wil'lōw, *a.* of or covered with willows; also, made of willow wood.

wil'lōw, *v.t.*; willowed, *pt., pp.*; willowing, *ppr.* to clean (fibrous material) with a willow; to treat with a willowing machine.

wil'lōw beaū'ty, a geometrid moth, *Boarmia rhomboidaria*, common in England.

wil'lōw bee'tle, any of numerous kinds of beetle that feed on the willow; specifically, *Phyllodecta vitellinæ*, the larvae of which are destructive to willow leaves.

wil'lōw çaç'tus, a plant of the genus *Rhipsalis*.

wil'lōw çat'ẽr·pil·lăr, any of various larvae destructive to the willow.

wil'lōwed, *a.* abounding with willows. [Rare.]

wil'lōw·ẽr, *n.* a person or machine that willows (cotton, etc.).

wil'lōw flȳ a stone fly.

wil'lōw gạll, any of several varieties of gall, growing on the leaves or shoots of willow trees.

wil'lōw grouse, the willow ptarmigan.

wil'lōw hẽrb (ẽrb), any of a number of related plants of the genus *Epilobium*, particularly *Epilobium angustifolium*, with small, purplish, white, or yellow flowers, willowlike leaves, and long pods.

wil'lōw·ish, *a.* resembling a willow.

wil'lōw lärk, the sedge warbler. [Brit. Dial.]

wil'lōw lēaf, in astronomy, any of the small, irregularly shaped, gaseous clouds in the surface structure of the sun: they are very brilliant and measure many hundreds of miles across.

wil'lōw lēaf bee'tle, any of the various types of beetle that infest willow trees, especially *Lina scripta* and *Galerucella decora* of North America and *Phyllodecta vitellinæ* of Europe: they defoliate and often kill willows.

wil'lōw mọth, a European mouse-colored moth whose larvae are destructive to the willow tree.

wil'lōw myr'tle (mẽr'), an Australian tree, *Agonis flexuosa*, of the myrtle family, having slender, tapering leaves.

wil'lōw ōak, an oak, *Quercus phellos*, having leaves resembling those of the willow.

wil'lōw pat'tẽrn, a decorative design for china, originated in England (1780) by Thomas Turner, and picturing a river, pagodas, willow trees, etc., usually in blue on a white background.

wil'lōw ptär'mi·găn (tär'), see *ptarmigan*.

wil'lōw sạw'flȳ, any of various sawflies that infest the willow, as *Nematus ventralis*.

wil'lōw slug, the larva of a willow sawfly.

wil'lōw spar'rōw, *n.* the willow wren.

wil'lōw thorn, the sallow thorn.

wil'lōw thrush, a variety of veery.

wil'lōw wạr'blẽr, the willow wren.

wil'lōw·wāre, *n.* articles of china decorated with the willow pattern.

wil'lōw·weed, *n.* any of various plants having leaves resembling those of the willow, as the purple loosestrife and certain species of knotweed.

wil'lōw·wŏrt, *n.* 1. any plant of the willow family. [Obs.]

2. a variety of loosestrife. [Obs.]

wil'lōw wren (ren), 1. any of various European songbirds: also called *willow warbler*.

2. the chiff chaff.

wil'lōw·y, *a.* 1. covered or shaded with willows.

2. like a willow; flexible; drooping; graceful; swaying.

will pow'ẽr, strength of will, mind, or determination; self-control.

will'-wŏr''ship, *n.* worship that is instituted by man and thought not to be by divine authority.

will'-wŏr''ship·ẽr, *n.* one who favors or practices will-worship.

wil'ly, *n.* a machine, the willow (sense 4).

wil'ly, *a.* 1. willing. [Rare.]

2. willful. [Scot.]

will'yărd, *a.* 1. willful. [Scot.]

2. bewildered; shy. [Scot.]

will'yărt, *a.* willyard. [Scot.]

wil'ly·muf''ty, *n.* the willow wren. [Brit. Dial.]

wil'ly-nil'ly, *adv.* [contr. from *will I, nill I*.] whether one wishes it or not; willing or unwilling.

wil'ly-nil'ly, *a.* 1. willing or not willing; as, he always had his way, *willy-nilly*.

2. loosely, indecisive; vacillating; irresolute.

wil'ly-wag''tāil, *n.* the pied wagtail. [Brit. Dial.]

wil'ly-wil''ly, *n.* [Australian.] a severe windstorm.

wilnc, *v.t.* to wish; to consent to; to resolve. [Obs.]

wil'sŏme, *a.* willful. [Obs.]

wil'sŏme·ness, *n.* willfulness. [Obs.]

Wil'sŏn'ṣ thrush, a veery.

Wil'sŏn'ṣ wạr'blẽr, any of a group of small, yellow, North American warblers with black crowns.

wilt, *v.* archaic second pers. sing., pres. ind., of *will*.

wilt, *v.i.*; wilted, *pt., pp.*; wilting, *ppr.* [var. of obs. *welk*; ME. *welken*, to wither.]

1. to become limp, as from heat or lack of water; to wither; to lose freshness and become flaccid: said of plants.

2. to lose strength or vigor; to become faint or weak; to languish.

3. to lose courage; to quail.

wilt, *v.t.* to cause to wilt.

wilt, *n.* 1. a wilting or becoming wilted.

2. a state of weakness or faintness; languor.

3. (a) a highly infectious disease of some caterpillars, in which the carcasses liquefy; (b) any of several plant diseases caused by certain bacteria or fungi and characterized chiefly by wilting of the leaves. Also *wilt disease*.

Wil'tŏn, a variety of carpet, in which the loops are cut open into an elastic velvet pile: so called from being made originally at Wilton, England: also *Wilton carpet, Wilton rug*.

Wilt'shire (*or* -shẽr), *n.* any of an old breed of pure-white sheep originating in England and characterized by a long head and long curved horns.

wī'ly, *a.*; *comp.* wilier; *superl.* wiliest; cunning; sly; using craft or stratagem to accomplish a purpose; mischievously artful; subtle; as, a *wily* adversary.

Syn.—crafty, sly, guileful, artful, subtle, designing, fraudulent, cunning.

wim'ber"ry, *n.*; *pl.* **wim'ber"ries,** a winberry.

wim'ble, *n.* [ME. *wimbel*; M.D. *wimmel*, an auger.]

1. any of various tools for boring, as a gimlet, auger, etc.

2. a device for removing the rubble from a hole bored in mining.

wim'ble, *v.t.*; wimbled, *pt.*, *pp.*; wimbling, *ppr.* to bore with a wimble.

wim'ble, *a.* active; nimble. [Dial.]

wim'brel, *n.* same as *whimbrel.*

wim'ple, *n.* [ME. *wimpel*; AS. *wimpel*, that which binds around, a veil, streamer, pennant.]

1. a covering of silk, linen, or other material arranged about the head, chin, and neck, leaving only the face exposed: formerly worn by women out of doors, now only by certain orders of nuns.

2. a flag; a streamer. [Obs.]

3. (a) a fold; a plait; (b) a winding; a turn; a curve; (c) a ripple. [Scot.]

WIMPLE

wim'ple, *v.t.*; wimpled, *pt.*, *pp.*; wimpling, *ppr.* 1. to lay in folds; to draw down in folds.

2. to cover with or as with a wimple or veil.

3. to hoodwink. [Obs.]

4. to cause to ripple or undulate, as the surface of a lake.

wim'ple, *v.i.* 1. to lie in folds.

2. to resemble or suggest wimples; to undulate; to ripple.

3. to meander, as a brook. [Scot.]

win, *v.t.*; won *or obs.* wan, *pt.*; won, *pp.*; winning, *ppr.* [ME. *winnen*; AS. *winnan*, to fight, endure, struggle, hence, to gain by struggling.]

1. to get by effort, labor, struggle, etc.; specifically, (a) to gain; to acquire; as, he *won* distinctions; (b) to make, achieve, or cause to prevail; as, you've *won* your point; (c) to gain in competition, as a prize or award; (d) to obtain or earn (a livelihood, security, etc.).

2. to be successful or victorious in (a contest, game, dispute, etc.).

3. to prevail upon; to influence; persuade (also with *over*); as, I *won* him *over* to my side.

4. to persuade to marry one.

5. (a) to gain the affection, sympathy, regard, favor, respect, or love of; to attract; as, he *won* a supporter; (b) to gain (one's sympathy, affection, love, etc.).

6. to attain or reach, as a goal, usually by effort or struggle; to gain, as the end of one's journey.

7. (a) to extract (metal, minerals, etc.) from ore; (b) to prepare (a vein, shaft, etc.) for working; (c) to obtain (coal, ore, etc.) by mining.

8. to overtake. [Obs.]

Syn.—get, gain, procure, earn, attain, acquire, accomplish, reach.

win, *v.i.* 1. to succeed or prevail in a contest or effort; to triumph; to be victorious (sometimes with *out*).

2. to attain to or arrive at a specified state or degree; to become; to get (with *across, away, back, down, off, over, through*, etc. or with certain adverbs); as, to *win* loose.

to win on or *upon*; (a) to gain favor or influence with; as, *to win upon* the heart or affections; (b) to gain ground on.

win, *n.* 1. an act of winning; a victory, as in a contest. [Colloq.]

2. winnings or profit. [Colloq.]

win'ber"ry, *n.*; *pl.* **win'ber"ries,** [AS. *winberie, win-berige*, a grape; lit., wine berry.] a whortleberry.

wince, *v.i.*; winced (winst), *pt.*, *pp.*; wincing, *ppr.* [ME. *wincen, winsen, winchen*, from M.H.G. *wenken, wenchen*, to wince, flinch, from *vanc*, a flinch, from *wank*, pt. of *winken*, to move aside.]

1. to shrink, as from a blow or from pain; to start back suddenly; to flinch; as, he *winced* under her sarcasm.

2. to kick; to twist. [Obs.]

wince, *n.* the act or instance of one who winces; a start, as from pain.

wince, *n.* [variant of *winch.*] a reel or roller used between dyeing vats, etc. to facilitate the transfer of long pieces of cloth.

wince pit, wince pot, a vat or tank in which cloth is washed or dyed during the process of manufacture.

win'cẽr, *n.* one who winces.

win'cey, *n.* [probably altered contr. of *linsey-woolsey.*] a strong, durable cloth, plain or twilled, having a cotton warp and a woolen weft.

winch, *v.* and *n.* wince (flinch). [Obs. or Dial.]

winch, *n.* [ME. *winche*; AS. *wince*, a winch, lit., a bend; hence, a bent handle, from Teut. base *wank*, to bend sideways.]

1. a crank with a projecting handle or lever for transmitting motion, as to a grindstone.

2. any of various devices operated by turning a crank; specifically, a type of windlass for hoisting or hauling, having a crank connected by gears to a horizontal drum around which the rope or chain is wound.

WINCH

winch, *v.t.*; winched (wincht), *pt.*, *pp.*; winching, *ppr.* to move or hoist with or as with a winch.

Win'ches·tẽr (rī'fle), [after Oliver F. *Winchester*, the manufacturer.] a type of repeating rifle with a tubular magazine set horizontally under the barrel: a trade-mark.

win'cing mȧ·chïne', in dyeing, an arrangement of two or more wince pits and reels.

win̄'cō·pīpe, *n.* same as *wink-a-peep.*

wind (*also poetic* wīnd), *n.* [ME. *wind, wynd*; AS. *wind*, wind.]

1. a natural motion of the air; especially, a noticeable current of air moving in the atmosphere parallel to the earth's surface. Winds are caused by the tendency of heated air to ascend, and the subsequent inrush of a current of cold air to fill the void thus caused in the lower atmosphere.

2. a strong, fast-moving, or destructive natural current of air; a gale; a storm.

3. the direction from which a wind blows: now chiefly in *the four winds*, with reference to the cardinal points of the compass.

4. a natural current of air regarded as a bearer of odors or scents, as in hunting; as, the dogs are keeping the *wind.*

5. figuratively, air regarded as bearing information, indicating trends, etc.; intimation; a hint; as, get *wind* of something, what's in the *wind?*

6. air artificially put in motion, as by an air pump or fan.

7. breath or the power of breathing; as, he got the *wind* knocked out of him.

8. (a) idle or empty talk; nonsense; (b) bragging; pomposity; conceit.

9. gas in the stomach or intestines; flatulence.

10. [*pl.*] the wind instruments of an orchestra.

11. the solar plexus, where a blow may stop the breath temporarily by paralyzing the diaphragm. [Boxing Slang.]

12. in musical instruments or in voice production, the breath or air used to produce a sound, and regulated either by natural or artificial means.

13. a disease of sheep in which the intestines are inflamed and distended by gas.

14. the dotterel. [Brit. Dial.]

before the wind; see under *before.*

between wind and water; (a) close to the water line of a ship; (b) in a dangerous spot.

by the wind; see under *by.*

cardinal winds; see under *cardinal.*

down the wind; in the same direction as the wind.

how the wind blows or *lies*; what the trend of affairs, public opinion, etc. is.

in the teeth of the wind; toward the direct point from which the wind blows; straight against the wind: also *in the wind's eye.*

in the wind; happening or about to happen.

into the wind; in the direction from which the wind is blowing.

mountain and valley winds; diurnal winds that alternate, blowing up mountain sides during the day, and down during the night.

off the wind; with the wind coming from behind.

on the wind; approximately in the direction from which the wind is blowing.

second wind; (a) the return of relatively normal ease in breathing following the exhaustion that occurs during severe exertion or exercise, as in running: it is due to improved action of the heart; (b) the recovered capacity for continuing any sort of effort.

three sheets in the wind; see under *sheet.*

to break wind; to expel gas from the bowels.

to get (or *have*) *wind of*; to receive (or have) information concerning; to hear (or know) of.

to have a free wind; in nautical usage, to be able to sail free.

to sail close to the wind; (a) to sail as nearly as possible against the direction of the wind; (b) to be economical in one's affairs; (c) to border on indecency, foolhardiness.

to take or *have the wind*; to get to the windward of, as an advantageous position; hence, to have the advantage.

to take the wind out of one's sails; to remove one's advantage, nullify one's argument, etc. suddenly or unexpectedly.

up the wind; in a direction opposite to that of the wind.

wind, *v.t.* 1. to expose to the wind or air, as for drying; to air.

2. to get or follow the scent of; to scent.

3. to cause to be out of breath; as, the run *winded* him.

4. to rest (a horse, etc.) so as to allow recovery of breath.

wīnd, *v.t.*; wound *or rarely*, winded, *pt.*, *pp.*; winding, *ppr.* [Early Mod. Eng., from *wind*, *n.*]

1. to blow (a horn, etc.).

Wind the shrill horn. —Pope.

2. to sound (a signal, etc.), as on a horn.

wīnd, *v.t.*; wound *or rarely* winded, *pt.*, *pp.*; winding, *ppr.* [ME. *winden*; AS. *windan*, to wind.]

1. to turn; to make revolve; as, *wind* the crank.

2. to turn or coil (something) into a ball or around something else so as to encircle it closely; to twine; to wreathe; as, *wind* the bandage around your finger.

3. to wrap or cover by encircling with something turned in the manner of a coil; to entwine; as, *wind* the spool with thread.

4. to make (one's way) in a winding or twisting course.

5. to cause to move in a winding or twisting course.

6. to introduce deviously; insinuate; as, he *wound* his criticism into his argument.

7. to hoist or haul by or as by winding rope on a winch (often with *up*).

8. to tighten the operating spring of (a clock, etc.) by turning a stem or the like (often with *up*).

9. to contrive by shifts and expedients. [Obs.]

He endeavors to turn and *wind* himself every way to evade the force of this famous challenge. —Waterland.

10. to change or vary at will; to bend or turn to one's pleasure; to exercise complete control over.

Were our legislature vested in the prince he might *wind* and turn our constitution at his pleasure. —Addison.

to wind off; to unwind or remove by unwinding.

to wind out; to extricate.

to wind up; (a) to wind or roll into a ball or coil round a bobbin, reel, or the like; (b) to conclude; to end; to finish; to settle; (c) to tighten, as the strings of certain musical instruments, so as to bring them to the proper pitch; (d) to restore to harmony or concord; (e) to bring to a state of great tension; to excite greatly; (f) to bring into a state of renewed or continued motion, as a watch, clock, or the like, by winding the spring; (g) to prepare for continued movement, action, or activity; to restore to original vigor or order.

Is there a tongue, like Delia's o'er her cup,
That runs for ages without *winding up.*
—Young.

wīnd, *v.i.* 1. to turn; to change.

2. to move, go, or extend in a curving, zigzagging, or sinuous manner; to meander.

3. to double on one's track, so as to throw off pursuers.

4. to take a circuitous, devious, or subtle course in behavior, argument, etc.

5. to insinuate oneself.

6. to coil, twine, or spiral (*about* or *around* something).

7. to warp or twist: said of wood.

8. to walk with a defective gait in which one leg tends to twist around the other: said of a horse.

9. to undergo winding; as, this clock *winds* easily.

10. to make an indirect advance.

Spend but time
To *wind* about my love with circumstance.
—Shak.

to wind out; to be extricated; to escape. [Rare.]

to wind up; (a) to come to a conclusion, halt, or end; to conclude; to finish; (b) in baseball, to swing the arm preparatory to pitching.

wind, *n.* [ME. *winde* (in comp.) from the *v.*]
1. a winding.
2. a single turn of something wound.
3. a turn; a twist; a bend; a curve.

wind'age, *n.* 1. the disturbance of air around a moving projectile.
2. deflection of a projectile caused by the wind, or the degree of this.
3. the degree of deflection of the wind gauge necessary in firing a gun to compensate for displacement by the wind.
4. the space between the inside wall of the barrel of a firearm and its projectile, to allow for the expansion of gas in firing: it is measured by the difference in diameters of the bore and projectile.
5. the part of a ship's surface exposed to the wind.

wind'bag, *n.* a person who talks much and pretentiously but says little of importance. [Colloq.]

wind band, a band of wind instruments; also, the wind instruments of an orchestra collectively.

wind beam, a collar beam.

wind bill, an accommodation bill. [Brit.]

wind'-blown, *a.* 1. blown by the wind.
2. twisted in growth by the prevailing wind: said of a tree.
3. designating or of a woman's coiffure in which the hair is bobbed and brushed forward.

wind'bore, *n.* the end of the suction pipe of a pump, usually covered with a perforated plate to keep out foreign matter.

wind'-borne, *a.* transported by the wind, as certain pollen.

wind'bound, *a.* prevented from sailing by a contrary wind.

wind brace, in architecture, a brace, or strut.

wind'break, *n.* a hedge, fence, or row of trees that serves as a protection from wind.

wind'break·er, *n.* a warm sports jacket of leather, wool, etc., having a closefitting elastic waistband and cuffs: a trade-mark [*Windbreaker*].

wind'-bro''ken, *a.* having the heaves, a disease characterized by difficulty in breathing: said of a horse.

wind'chest, *n.* in music, the chest in an organ or harmonium for storing the wind produced by the bellows, which is thus prevented from acting by direct and intermittent currents on the pipes and reeds.

wind'chill fac'tor, same as *chill factor*.

wind chimes, a cluster of small chimes or pendants of glass, ceramic, etc., hung so that they strike one another and tinkle when blown by the wind: also called *wind bells*.

wind cone, a wind sock.

wind'dog, *n.* a fragment of a rainbow; a part of a rainbow seen on detached clouds and regarded by sailors as a sign of high winds.

wind drop'sy, a swelling of the abdomen from wind in the intestines; tympanites.

wind'ed, *a.* out of breath.

wind'ed, *v.* 1. rare past tense of *wind* (to blow).
2. rare past tense of *wind* (to turn).

wind egg, an imperfect and unproductive egg.

wind'er, *n.* 1. a person who winds material or operates a winding machine in textile and other industries.
2. an apparatus for winding or on which winding is done.
3. a key, knob, etc. for winding a spring-operated mechanism.
4. any of the steps in a winding staircase.
5. a plant that winds or twines.
6. one who blows or winds a horn.

wind'er, *n.* a blow that takes away one's breath. [Colloq.]

wind'fall, *n.* 1. something blown down by the wind, as fruit from a tree, or a number of trees in a forest.
2. a violent gust of wind rushing from coast ranges and mountains to the sea.
3. an unexpected legacy or any unexpected piece of good fortune.
4. the tract of fallen trees and the like which indicates the path of a tornado.
5. a sudden, large increase, as in profits due to price increases.

wind'fall''en, *a.* blown down by the wind.

wind'-fer''ti·lized, *a.* in botany, fertilized, as flowers, with wind-blown pollen; anemophilous.

wind'flaw, *n.* a gust of wind; a flaw.

wind'flow''er, *n.* any plant of the genus *Anemone*, with white, pink, red, or purplish, cup-shaped flowers; particularly, the wood anemone, *Anemone nemorosa*.

wind fur'nace, a natural-draft furnace; a furnace using the natural suction of a chimney without a blower or bellows.

wind'gall, *n.* a soft swelling on the fetlock joint of a horse.

wind gap, a notch in a mountain ridge, not deep enough to serve as the bed of a stream.

wind gauge, 1. an instrument for measuring the velocity and force of wind; an anemometer.
2. an apparatus for measuring the amount of the pressure of wind in the windchest of an organ.
3. a graduated attachment on a gunsight for indicating the degree of deflection necessary to counteract windage.

wind gun, an air gun.

wind herb (erb), a labiate plant, *Phlomis herbaventi*, of the mint family, native to southern Europe.

wind'hov·er, *n.* a species of hawk, the kestrel: so called from its ability to hover in the air.

wind'i·ly, *adv.* in a windy manner.

wind'i·ness, *n.* 1. the state of being windy or tempestuous.
2. flatulence.
3. tendency to cause flatulence; as, the *windiness* of vegetables.
4. puffiness; also, boastfulness.

wind'ing, *n.* 1. the action or effect of a person or thing that winds; specifically, (a) a sinuous path or course; (b) devious methods, actions, etc.; (c) a coiling, spiraling, or twining; (d) a single turn.
2. something that winds; specifically, (a) wire, thread, etc. wound around something; as, the *winding* on an electric coil; (b) a single turn of this; (c) the manner in which this is wound; as, a shunt *winding*.
3. the condition or fact of being warped or twisted; as, a board in *winding*.
4. a defective gait of horses in which one leg tends to twist around the other.
5. a call on a boatswain's whistle.

wind'ing, *a.* that winds, turns, coils, etc.

wind'ing en'gine, an engine that turns the drum around which a hoisting cable or rope is drawn.

wind'ing·ly, *adv.* in a winding manner.

wind'ing sheet, 1. a sheet in which a corpse is wrapped for burial; a shroud.

And in a *winding sheet* of vine leaf wrapt,
So bury me by some sweet garden side.
—Omar Khayyám.

2. a sheetlike dropping piece of tallow or wax from a burning candle: supposed to be an omen of death. [Obs.]

wind'ing tac'kle, a tackle consisting of one fixed triple block, and one double or triple movable block, used principally to hoist up heavy things.

wind in'stru·ment, a musical instrument played by blowing air through it, especially a portable one played with the breath, as a *wood wind* (flute, oboe, bassoon, clarinet, etc.) or a *brass wind* (trumpet, trombone, horn, tuba, etc.).

wind'jam''mer, *n.* 1. in nautical usage, (a) a sailing ship: so called originally in contempt by seamen on early steamships; (b) a crew member of such a ship.
2. a talkative person. [Slang.]

wind'lass, *n.* 1. a circular or circuitous path or course; a circle; a compass. [Obs.]
2. any indirect, artful course; art and contrivance. [Obs.]

wind'lass, *v.i.*; windlassed (-last), *pt.*, *pp.*; windlassing, *ppr.* 1. to adopt a circuitous, artful, or cunning course; to act indirectly or warily. [Obs.]
2. to take a circuitous path. [Obs.]

wind'lass, *v.t.* to twist; to bend; to bewilder. [Obs.]

wind'lass, *n.* [altered, after obs. *windle*, a wheel, winder (ME. *windel*, in comp., from *winden*, to wind) from ME. *windas*, windlass.]
1. an apparatus operated by hand or machine, for hauling or hoisting, consisting of a drum or cylinder upon which is wound the rope, cable, or chain which is attached to the object to be lifted.
2. a winchlike contrivance for bending the arbalist, or crossbow. [Obs.]

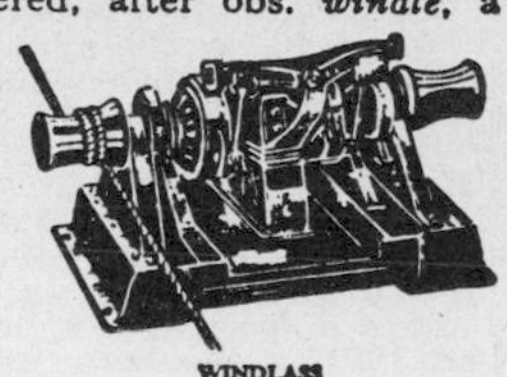
WINDLASS

wind'lass, *v.t.* and *v.i.* to hoist or haul with a windlass.

win'dle, (-dl), *n.* [AS. *windel*, a woven basket, from *windan*, to wind.]
1. a spindle. [Scot. and Brit. Dial.]
2. the windthrush. [Brit. Dial.]

wind'less, *a.* 1. without wind; calm.
2. out of breath.

win'dle·straw, *n.* 1. a reed; a stalk of grass, used in plaiting, etc. [Scot.]
2. a slender or weak person or thing. [Scot.]

wind'mill, *n.* 1. a mill operated by the wind's rotation of large, oblique sails or vanes radiating from a shaft: it is used as a cheap source of power for grinding grain, pumping water, etc.

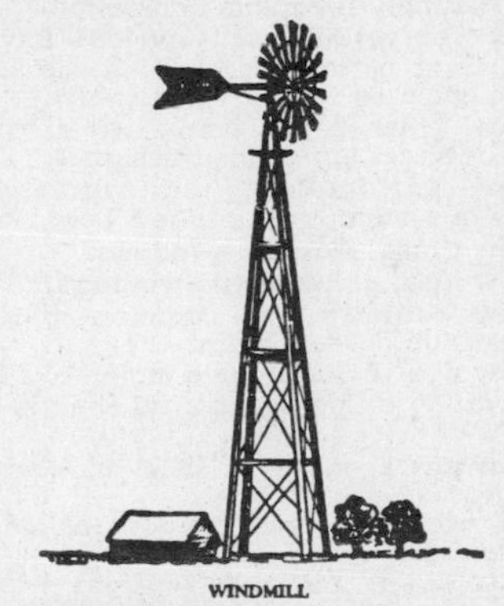
WINDMILL

2. anything like a windmill, as a propeller-like toy revolved by wind.

to fight (or *tilt at*) *windmills*; to fight imaginary evils or opponents: in allusion to Don Quixote's adventure with the windmills.

wind'mill grass, *Chloris truncata*, a grass of Australia, whose leaves bear a fancied resemblance to a windmill's vanes.

wind'mill plant, *Desmodium gyrans*, the telegraph plant.

win'dore, *n.* [from *window*, after *door*.] a window. [Obs.]

win'dow, *n.* [ME. *windoge*, from ON. *vindauga*, a window, lit., wind eye; *vindr*, wind, and *auga*, an eye.]
1. an opening in a building, vehicle, ship, etc. for admitting light and air, usually having a pane or panes of glass, etc. set in a frame or sash that is generally movable for opening or shutting it.
2. a windowpane; as, he broke the *window*.
3. a window with its sash and casement.
4. any opening resembling a window in shape, position, or use, as the transparent part of a window envelope.

The *window* of my heart, mine eye —Shak.

5. in anatomy, a fenestra.
6. any device put into the atmosphere to yield a perceptible radar echo, usually used for tracking an airborne object or as a tracer of wind.
7. same as *launch window*.
8. any portion of the frequency spectrum of the earth's atmosphere through which light, heat, or radio waves can penetrate to the earth's surface due to the low absorption or dissipation of electromagnetic energy in this particular portion.

clustered window; a window of three or more lights grouped together.

dormant window; a dormer.

false window; an imitation window built in a wall for symmetry in design: also called *blind* or *blank window*.

fan-shaped (or *fan*) *window*; same as *fanlight*.

French windows; see under *French*.

window tax or *window duty*; a tax formerly levied in Britain on all windows of houses above a specified number. It was abolished in 1851, a tax on houses above a certain rental being substituted.

win′dōw, *v.t.*; windowed, *pt., pp.*; windowing, *ppr.* 1. to furnish with a window or windows.

2. to set or place in or at a window. [Rare.]

win′dōw bär, 1. one of the bars of a window sash or lattice.

2. [*pl.*] latticework, as on a woman's stomacher. [Obs.]

3. a bar for securing a window or its shutters; also, a bar fitted in a window or doorway to prevent one from entering or escaping.

win′dōw blīnd, a blind, screen, or shade for a window.

win′dōw box, 1. a long, narrow box on or outside a window ledge, for growing plants.

2. any of the grooves along the sides of a window frame for containing the weights that counterbalance the sash.

win′dow dress′ing, 1. the arrangement or display of goods and trimmings in a store window to attract customers.

2. statements or actions intended to give a misleadingly favorable impression.

win′dōw en′vel·ōpe, an envelope having a transparent part through which the address on the enclosed matter can be seen.

win′dōw frāme, the frame of a window which receives and holds the sashes.

win′dōw gär′den·ing, the cultivation of plants in a window or window box.

win′dōw glȧss, glass for windows.

win′dōw·less, *a.* having no windows.

win′dōw mär′tin, the common martin of Europe; the house martin.

win′dōw oys′tẽr, a bivalve mollusk, *Placuna placenta*: so called because its shell is transparent.

win′dōw·pāne, *n.* 1. a sheet of glass in a window.

2. a fish, the daylight: also called *sand flounder*. [Dial.]

win′dōw sash, the sash or light frame in which panes of glass are set for windows.

win′dōw sēat, a long seat built in beneath a window or windows and usually containing storage space.

win′dōw shāde, a shade for a window, especially one consisting of a piece of stiffened cloth or heavy paper on a spring roller, with a pull to lower and raise it.

win′dōw shell, same as *window oyster*.

win′dōw-shop, *v.i.*; window-shopped, *pt., pp.*; window-shopping, *ppr.* to look at displays of goods in store windows without entering the stores to buy.

win′dōw sill, the sill of a window.

wind′pīpe, *n.* the trachea.

wind′plant, *n.* the windflower.

wind′-pol′li·nāt·ed, *a.* in botany, fertilized by pollen carried by the wind.

wind pump, a pump moved by the wind.

wind′-rōde, *a.* in nautical usage, riding with head to the wind instead of to the current: said of a ship.

wind rōṣe, a diagram that shows for a particular place the frequency and intensity of wind from different directions.

wind′rōw, *n.* 1. a row of hay raked together to dry before being rolled into cocks or heaps; also, sheaves of grain arranged in rows to let the wind blow between them.

2. a row of dry leaves, dust, etc. that has been swept together by the wind.

3. a deep furrow for planting cuttings of sugar cane.

4. the green border of a field, dug up in order to carry the earth on other land to improve it. [Brit.]

wind′rōw, *v.t.*; windrowed, *pt., pp.*; windrowing, *ppr.* 1. to rake or put into the form of a windrow.

2. to plant (sugar-cane cuttings) in windrows.

wind sāil, 1. a tube or funnel of canvas, used to convey air into the lower parts of a ship.

2. a sail on a windmill.

WIND SAIL

wind scāle, a scale used in meteorology to designate relative wind intensities, as the Beaufort scale in which wind velocities are graded from 0 to 12.

wind shȧft, the shaft from which the vanes of a windmill radiate.

wind shāke, a condition of timber in which there is separation of the concentric rings, supposedly due to strain from strong winds during growth.

wind′-shāk″en, *a.* 1. driven or agitated by the wind; tottering or trembling in the wind.

2. affected by wind shake: said of timber.

wind′shiēld, *n.* in automobiles, trucks, speedboats, motorcycles, etc., a transparent screen in front, as of glass, that protects the occupant or occupants from wind, etc. while riding.

wind sīde, the windward side.

wind sleeve, a wind sock.

wind sock, a long, cone-shaped cloth bag attached to the top of a mast, as at an airfield, to show the direction of the wind: also called *wind cone, wind sleeve.*

Wind′sọr (win′), *n.* the ruling family of England since 1917, when the name was officially changed from *Saxe-Coburg and Gotha.*

Wind′sọr bēan, the common broad bean.

Wind′sọr Cȧs′tle (kȧs′l), a residence of English sovereigns since the time of William the Conqueror.

Wind′sọr chāir, a style of wooden chair, especially popular in 18th-century England and America, with spreading legs, spindle back, and usually a saddle seat.

WINDSOR CHAIR

Wind′sọr Knight (nīt), one of a body of military pensioners, having their residence within the precincts of Windsor Castle.

Wind′sọr sōap, a kind of scented soap, the chief manufacture of which was once confined to Windsor.

Wind′sọr tīe, a wide necktie of silk cut on the bias, tied in a double bow.

wind stop, that part of a window frame which serves as a groove in which the sash moves.

wind′stọrm, *n.* a storm with a violent wind accompanied by little, if any, rain or snow.

wind′strōke, *n.* acute spinal paralysis in a horse.

wind′suck″ẽr, *n.* 1. the windhover or kestrel.

2. a horse addicted to wind sucking.

3. a person ready to find fault; a faultfinder. [Archaic.]

wind suck′ing, the habit that some horses have of swallowing air, as in crib biting.

wind′-swept, *a.* swept by or exposed to winds.

wind′thrush, *n.* the redwing. [Brit. Dial.]

wind′tīght (-tīt), *a.* impervious to wind or air; airtight.

wind tun′nel, a tunnellike chamber through which air is forced and in which scale models of airplanes, etc. are tested to determine the effects of wind pressure.

wīnd′up, *n.* 1. a winding up; conclusion; close; end.

2. in baseball, the loosening movements of the arm preparatory to pitching the ball.

wind′wărd, *n.* the direction or side from which the wind blows; as, to ply to the *windward*: opposed to *leeward.*

to lay or *cast an anchor to the windward*; to adopt measures for success or security.

to windward of; advantageously situated in respect to.

wind′wărd, *adv.* in the direction from which the wind blows; toward the wind.

wind′wărd, *a.* 1. moving windward.

2. on the side from which the wind blows.

wind wheel (hwēl), a wheel furnishing motive power and operated by the wind.

wind′y, *a.*; *comp.* windier; *superl.* windiest, 1. characterized or accompanied by wind; as, a *windy* day.

2. exposed to wind; as, a *windy* city.

3. like wind; stormy, changeable, gusty, etc.; as, *windy* anger.

4. produced by wind or compressed air; as, a *windy* tone.

5. airy; intangible.

6. that talks much and says little; verbose.

7. boastful; pompous.

8. (a) causing or apt to cause gas in the stomach or intestines; (b) caused by or troubled with flatulence; flatulent.

9. next the wind; windward. [Rare.]

wīne, *n.* [ME. *win*; AS. *wīn*, from L. *vinum*, wine.]

1. the fermented juice of grapes, used as an alcoholic beverage and in cooking, religious ceremonies, etc.; wines vary as to color (red or white) and sugar content (sweet or dry), may be effervescent (sparkling) or non-effervescent (still), and are sometimes strengthened with additional alcohol (fortified).

2. the fermented juice of other fruits or plants, used as a beverage; as, dandelion *wine.*

3. intoxication, as from wine.

Noah awoke from his *wine.* —Gen. ix. 24.

4. a wine party; specifically, a wine party at an English university. [Brit.]

5. a dark, purplish red resembling the color of red wines.

6. in pharmacy, a medicinal solution in which wine is the solvent.

birch wine; see under *birch.*

heavy oil of wine; see *ethereal oil of wine*, under *ethereal.*

new wine in old bottles; something new that is too potent to be confined in old forms: see Matt. ix. 17.

spirit of wine; alcohol.

to drink wine ape; to drink enough wine to make one silly. [Obs.]

wīne, *v.t.*; wined, *pt., pp.*; wining, *ppr.* to supply or entertain with wine; to treat to wine; as, his friends *wined* and dined him.

wīne, *v.i.* to drink wine.

wīne ac′id, tartaric acid: so called because often found in wine.

wīne bag, a wineskin.

wīne′ber″ry, *n.* 1. a Japanese species of the raspberry.

2. the whortleberry.

3. the currant; also, the gooseberry. [Brit. Dial.]

4. the tutu (plant).

wīne′bib″bẽr, *n.* one who drinks much wine; a tippler; a great drinker.

wīne′bib″bẽr·y, *n.* excessive drinking of wine.

wīne′bib″bing, *a.* given to the excessive drinking of wine.

wīne′bib″bing, *n.* the habit of drinking wine to excess.

wīne bis′çuit (-kit), a light biscuit served with wine.

Wīne·bren·nē′ri·ăn, *a.* pertaining to a Baptist sect founded in Pennsylvania in 1830, by the Rev. John Winebrenner.

Wīne·bren·nē′ri·ăn, *n.* a member of the Winebrennerian sect.

wīne çask, a strong, tight cask in which wine is or has been kept for ripening or transportation.

wīne cel′lăr, 1. an apartment or cellar for storing wine.

2. a stock of wine.

wīne′-cŏl″ŏred, *a.* having the color of red wine; dark purplish-red.

wīne çọọl′ẽr, a vessel for cooling wine before it is drunk.

wīne′flȳ, *n.* a fly of the genus *Piophila*, that lives in wine, cider, etc.

wīne gal′lŏn, an old English gallon of 231 cu. in., now the standard gallon in the United States.

wīne′glȧss, *n.* a small glass from which wine is drunk.

wīne′glȧss·fụl, *n.*; *pl.* **wīne′glȧss·fụls,** the measure or capacity of a wineglass, ordinarily two fluid ounces.

wīne grāpe, a grape cultivated for winemaking: distinguished from *raisin grape.*

wīne′grōw″ẽr, *n.* the proprietor of a vineyard; one who cultivates a vineyard and makes wine from the grapes.

wīne′grōw″ing, *n.* the art or process of cultivating grapes and making wine from them.

wīne'less, *a.* having no wine; as, a *wineless* dinner.

wīne märç, the refuse remaining after the juice has been pressed from the grape.

wīne meaṣ'ūre (mezh'), a former English system of measure by which wines and other spirits were sold. In this measure, the gallon contained 231 cubic inches.

wīne mēr'chănt, a merchant who deals in wines and other liquors, especially at wholesale.

wīne päլm (päm), a palm of any species from the sap of which palm wine can be made.

wīne press, a vat in which grapes are trodden, or a machine for pressing them, in order to extract the juice for making wine.

wīn'ēr·y, *n.*; *pl.* **wīn'ēr·ieṣ,** an establishment or place where wine is made.

Wīne'sap, *n.* a dark-red, medium-sized variety of winter apple grown in the United States.

wīne'skin, *n.* in Eastern countries, a large bag made of the skin of an animal, for containing or carrying wine.

wīne stōne, a deposit of tartar, or argol, on the interior of wine casks.

wīne vąult, 1. a vault in which wine is stored in casks.

2. a place where wine and other liquors are served.

wīne vin'ē·găr, any vinegar made from wine.

wīne whey (hwā), milk curdled with wine.

wing, *n.* [ME. *winge*; Ice. *vængr*; Dan. and Sw. *vinge*, wing.]

1. either of the two forelimbs of a bird, developed for flying, the lifting surface being formed by overlapping feathers

2. (a) either of the two forelimbs of a domesticated fowl, not sufficiently developed for use in flying; (b) such a forelimb used as food; as, a chicken *wing*.

3. either of the paired organs of flight of a bat, the lifting surface of which is formed of membranous skin connecting the long, modified digits of the forelimbs.

4. either of the paired organs of flight of insects, similar in appearance and use but structurally unrelated to the wings of vertebrates.

5. either of a pair of similar structures attributed to angels, demons, etc.

6. any of various winglike structures of certain animals, as of the flying fish, flying squirrel, etc.

7. something used as a wing or in the manner of a wing; specifically, (a) one of the main supporting structures of an airplane; a plane; (b) a float or other device attached to the shoulder; as, water *wings*.

8. something resembling a wing in position or in relation to the main part; specifically, (a) a part or extension of a building architecturally subordinate to the main part; hence, (b) a part of a large building of any shape, regarded as a separate section according to its use or to its location with relation to a central point; as, a surgical *wing*, the east *wing*; (c) an outlying area, as of an estate; (d) either of two side extensions of the back of a wing chair; (e) either part of a double door, screen, etc.; (f) in anatomy, an ala; (g) in botany, either lateral petal of a papilionaceous flower; also, a winglike extension on some stems, leafstalks, and seeds; (h) in the theater, any of the side-pieces in scenery; also, either side of the stage out of sight of the audience.

9. a group of persons or things having a winglike relation to another; specifically, (a) the right or left section of an army, fleet, etc.; (b) a group of political party members, legislators, etc. representing some specified shade of opinion or political doctrine; as, a right *wing*, agrarian *wing*; (c) an organization affiliated with or subsidiary to a parent organization; (d) a position or player on a team to the right or left of the center position or player.

10. (a) a unit of military aircraft and their personnel, larger than a group and smaller than a command; (b) [*pl.*] the insignia worn by pilots and crew members of military aircraft.

11. (a) a means of flying or traveling; (b) a flying or manner of flying; flight.

And the crow makes *wing* to the rooky wood. —Shak.

12. anything represented as flying or soaring, or as carrying one to soaring heights; as, on *wings* of song.

13. something that beats the air, as a vane.

14. either of the longer sides of an outwork in a fortification, extending back to the main work.

15. an arm of a human being: a humorous usage. [Colloq.]

16. the sail of a ship, etc. [Poet.]

17. in shipbuilding, that part of the hold or space between decks which is next to the ship's side, especially at the quarter; also, the overhang deck of a steamer before and abaft the paddle boxes, bounded by a thick plank called the *wing wale*, which extends from the extremity of the paddle beam to the ship's side.

18. the laterally extending portion of a plowshare which cuts the bottom of the furrow.

19. in engineering, (a) an extension from the end of a dam, sometimes at an angle with the main portion; (b) a side dam on a river shore for the purpose of contracting the channel; (c) a lateral extension of an abutment.

20. a shoulder knot or small epaulet.

21. a strip of leather or the like attached to the skirt of the runner in a grain mill to sweep the meal into the spout.

on the wing; in flight; continually moving about.

on the wings of the wind; with the greatest velocity.

to take wing; to take flight; to fly away.

to wing it; to act, speak, etc. with little or no planning or preparation; improvise. [Colloq.]

under the wing or *wings of*; under the guardianship, patronage, protection, etc. of.

wing, *v.t.*; winged, *pt., pp.*; winging, *ppr.*

1. to fly across, over, through, etc.

Wings the blue element, and borne sublime. —Rogers.

2. to provide with wings.

3. to enable to fly or hasten; to send flying; to speed; as, he *winged* his words.

4. to feather (an arrow).

5. to do, make, etc. by or as by means of wings.

6. to transport by or as by flight.

7. to furnish with side parts, as a building.

8. to wound (a bird) in the wing or (a person) in the arm, shoulder, etc.

wing, *v.i.* to fly.

wing and wing, in nautical usage, with sails extended on either side by booms.

wing back fọr·mā'tion, in football, either of two offensive formations, the *single wing formation*, in which one of the backs is placed behind and usually slightly beyond the end on his side, or the *double wing back formation*, in which both backs are so placed.

wing bōw, a mark of color on the bend of the wing of a domesticated fowl.

wing çāse, the case or shell which covers the wings of coleopterous insects, as the beetle, etc.; the elytrum: also called *wing cover*.

wing cell, one of the spaces enclosed by the veins of an insect's wing.

wing chāir, an upholstered armchair with a high back from each side of which extend high sides, or wings, to give additional head rest and protection from drafts.

wing çŏv'ēr (or **çāse**), an elytron.

wing çŏv'ērt, *n.* one of the smaller feathers covering the bases of the flight feathers in the wing of a bird.

winged (wingd *or* wing'ed), *a.* 1. having wings or winglike parts.

2. moving on or as if on wings.

3. (a) lofty; sublime; (b) swift; rapid.

4. (a) wounded in the wing; (b) [Colloq.] wounded in an arm or, sometimes, in any nonvital part.

5. swarming with flying creatures.

6. in heraldry, represented with wings; having wings of a different color from the body.

7. in botany and zoology, furnished with a winglike appendage or growth; as, a *winged* seed; a *winged* shell, etc.

winged elm; see under *elm*.

winged fly; an angler's artificial fly with wings.

winged horse; see under *horse*.

winged leaf; a pinnate or a pinnately divided leaf.

wing'er, *n.* 1. a small water cask stowed in the wing of a ship.

2. one who or that which wings.

wing'fish, *n.* a sea robin with large pectoral fins resembling wings; a gurnard.

wing'-foot"ed, *a.* 1. having winged feet; as, *wing-footed* Mercury.

2. swift; moving with rapidity; fleet.

3. in zoology, pteropod; as, a *wing-footed* mollusk.

wing'hand"ed, *a.* having the anterior limbs, or hands, adapted for flying, as bats and pterodactyls.

wing'lēaved (-lēvd), *a.* characterized by pinnate foliage or by leaves pinnately divided.

wing'less, *a.* having no wings or very rudimentary ones.

wing'let, *n.* 1. a little wing.

2. the bastard wing of a bird; an alula.

3. a pterygium (sense 3).

wing lōad'ing, the total weight of a loaded airplane divided by the area of the supporting surfaces, exclusive of stabilizer and elevators: also *wing load*.

wing'măn·ship, *n.* skill in flying. [Rare.]

wing pad, the undeveloped pupal wing of an insect, as a grasshopper.

wing'seed, *n.* any plant the seeds of which are characterized by wings or margins.

wing shell, any marine bivalve shell of various species of *Avicula*, which have projecting borders suggesting wings; also, any marine gastropod shell of the family *Strombidæ*, characterized by an extended lip; also, a pteropod shell of any species.

wing shot, 1. a shot made at a flying bird.

2. a person skilled in making these.

wing skid, a small protective runner under the tip of an airplane wing to keep it from touching the ground.

wing snāil, a pteropod.

wing'spread (-spred), *n.* the distance between the tips of a pair of wings when spread.

wing strōke, the stroke or sweep of the wings.

wing tran'sŏm, the uppermost or longest transom in a ship: also called *main transom*.

wing'y, *a.* 1. having wings; rapid.

2. flying on wings; soaring with or as if with wings; light; volatile.

wiṅk, *v.i.*; winked (wiṅkt), *pt., pp.*; winking, *ppr.* [ME. *winken*, from AS. *wincian*, to wink.]

1. to shut the eyes. [Obs.]

2. to close and open the eyelids quickly.

3. to close one eyelid and open it again quickly, as a signal, etc.

4. to shine intermittently; to twinkle.

to wink at; to pretend not to see, as in connivance.

wiṅk *v.t.* 1. to make (the eyes or an eye) wink.

2. to move, remove, etc. by winking; as, he *winked* back his tears.

3. to signal or express by winking.

wiṅk, *n.* 1. a winking.

2. the time occupied by this; an instant.

3. a nap: now only in *not a wink*.

4. a signal, hint, etc. given by winking.

5. a twinkle or twinkling.

forty winks; a brief period of sleep; a short nap. [Colloq.]

wiṅk'-à-peep, *n.* the scarlet pimpernel, *Anagallis arvensis*: so named because the flower closes or winks on damp days, and opens or peeps again when the weather becomes fine: also called *wincopipe*. [Brit. Dial.]

wiṅk'ēr, *n.* 1. one who or that which winks.

2. a horse's blinder.

3. an eye or eyelash. [Colloq.]

4. the nictitating membrane of a bird's eye.

5. the muscle employed in the act of winking.

6. a small bellows in an organ, attached to the main bellows and regulated by a spring in such a way as to render the tension of the compressed air uniform.

wiṅk'ing, *a.* that winks.

wiṅk'ing·ly, *adv.* in a winking manner.

wiṅ'kle, *n.* [shortened from *periwinkle*.] any of various edible sea snails; a periwinkle.

wiṅ'kle·hąwk, *n.* a rent in cloth having the form of a rectangle: also called *winklehole*. [Dial.]

win'nărd, *n.* the redwing. [Brit. Dial.]

Win·nē·bā'gō, *n.*; *pl.* **Win·nē·bā'gōṣ, Win·nē·bā'gōeṣ,** a member of a tribe of Siouan Indians that lived in eastern Wisconsin, where some still survive: others now live in Nebraska.

win'nēr, *n.* [from *win*.] one who or that which wins.

win'ning, *a.* 1. that wins; victorious.

2. attractive; adapted to gain favor; charming; as, a *winning* address.

win'ning, *n.* 1. the action of a person that wins; a victory.

2. [*pl.*] something won, especially money.

3. a shaft, bed, etc. in a coal mine, opened or ready for mining.

win'ning gal'lẽr·y, in court tennis, a netted opening opposite the spectator's gallery: a ball played into it is considered winning.

win'ning head'wāy (hed'), a headway that opens a seam of coal for exploration or mining.

win'ning·ly, *adv.* in a winning manner.

win'ning·ness, *n.* the state of being winning.

win'ning ō'pen·ing, in court tennis, any of various openings, as the dedans, winning gallery, etc.: a ball played into any of these is considered winning.

win'ning pōst, a post marking the end of a racecourse, the order of passing which determines the outcome of the race.

win'nin·ish, *n.* [Am. Ind.] the great lake trout.

win'nŏck, *n.* a window. [Scot.]

win'nōw, *v.t.*; winnowed, *pt., pp.*; winnowing, *ppr.* [ME. *wynewen, windewen*, from AS. *windwian, wyndwian*, to winnow, from *wind*, wind.]

1. to blow the chaff from (grain) by wind or a forced current of air.
2. to blow off (chaff) in this manner.
3. to blow away; to scatter; as, the wind *winnowed* the leaves.
4. to analyze or examine carefully in order to separate the various elements; to sift.
5. (a) to separate out or eliminate (the worthless part or parts of something); (b) to extract or select (the good part or parts of something).
6. (a) to fan with or as with the wings; (b) to flap (the wings); (c) to make (one's or its way) by or as by flying.

win'nōw, *v.i.* 1. to winnow grain.
2. to fly with or as with wings.

win'nōw, *n.* 1. a winnowing.
2. an apparatus for winnowing.

win'nōw·ẽr, *n.* one who or that which winnows; a machine for winnowing.

win'nōw·ing, *n.* the act of one who or that which winnows.

win'rōw, *n.* a windrow. [Dial.]

win'sŏme, *a.* [AS. *wynsum*, pleasant, delightful, from *wyn*, delight, joy, and *-sum*, later *-some.*]

1. attractive in appearance, character, manner, etc.; agreeable; engaging; charming; delightful; as, a *winsome* girl; a *winsome* face.
2. cheerful; merry; gay.

win'sŏme·ness, *n.* the quality or characteristic of being winsome.

win'tẽr, *n.* [AS. *winter*, winter, also, a year.]

1. the coldest season of the year, regarded in the North Temperate Zone as including the months of December, January, and February: in the astronomical year, that period between the winter solstice and the vernal equinox.
2. a year as reckoned by this season; as, a man of eighty *winters.*
3. any period regarded, like winter, as a time of decline, dreariness, adversity, etc.

Now is the *winter* of our discontent
Made glorious summer by this sun of
York. —Shak.

4. the last portion of grain brought home at the end of harvest, or the state of having all the grain on a farm reaped and stored; also, the rural feast held in celebration of the ingathering of the crop. [Obs. Scot.]

win'tẽr, *a.* 1. of or characteristic of the winter.
2. done, used, played, etc. during the winter; as, *winter* sports, quarters, etc.
3. that will keep during the winter; as, *winter* apples, pears, etc.
4. planted in the fall to be harvested in the spring; as, *winter* wheat, barley, rye, etc.

winter aconite; a small perennial herb having bright-yellow flowers that blossom early in spring.

winter barley; a kind of barley which is sown in autumn.

winter beer; schenk beer.

winter bonnet; the winter gull. [Brit. Dial.]

winter bud; in biology, a statoblast.

winter cherry; (a) a plant of the genus *Physalis*; also, its fruit, which is the size of a cherry; (b) heartseed.

winter chip bird; the tree sparrow of America.

winter clover; the partridgeberry.

winter cress; a plant of the mustard family, *Barbarea vulgaris*, bearing yellow flowers.

winter duck; the pintail duck. [Brit.]

winter egg; an egg with a thick shell laid by some invertebrates in the autumn and surviving the winter.

winter fallow; ground that is fallowed in winter.

winter fat; same as *white sage* under *white.*

winter fever; pneumonia. [Colloq.]

winter flounder; a flatfish of the genus *Pseudopleuronectes*, found along the eastern coast of North America, from Chesapeake Bay to Labrador.

winter flower; a fragrant Japanese shrub.

winter garden; an ornamental garden for winter.

winter gull; the common European gull, *Larus canus*; the winter mew. [Brit. Dial.]

winter hawk; a hen hawk, *Buteo lineatus.* [Dial.]

winter itch; a disorder of the skin, principally on the legs, prevalent in winter.

winter melon; (a) a large, mildly scented muskmelon that keeps through the cold season; (b) the plant it grows on.

winter mew; the winter gull. [Brit. Dial.]

winter midge; a tiny fly, *Trichocera hiemalis*, that sometimes appears in large numbers on mild days in winter.

winter shad; the gizzard shad.

winter sheldrake; the merganser.

winter sleep; hibernation.

winter snipe; see under *snipe.*

winter solstice; the time in the Northern Hemisphere when the sun is farthest south of the equator; December 21 or 22.

winter spore; a resting spore.

winter teal; the green-winged teal. [Dial.]

winter wagtail; the gray wagtail. [Brit. Dial.]

winter wren; a North American wren noted for its singing.

win'tẽr, *v.i.*; wintered, *pt., pp.*; wintering, *ppr.* to pass the winter; to hibernate; as, he *winters* in Mexico.

win'tẽr, *v.t.* to feed, keep, maintain, or manage during the winter; as, to *winter* young cattle on straw.

win'tẽr-bēat"en, *a.* harassed by the severe weather of winter.

win'tẽr·ber·ry, *n.*; *pl.* **win'tẽr·ber·rieṣ**, any of a number of related, North American evergreen trees or shrubs of the genus *Ilex* with glossy leaves and bright-red berries; holly.

win'tẽr·bloom, *n.* 1. a plant of the genus *Azalea.*
2. the witch hazel, *Hamamelis virginiana.*

win'tẽr·bōurne, *n.* [AS. *winter burna.*] a stream that flows only or principally in winter.

win'tẽr·ẽr *n.* one who winters.

win'tẽr·feed, *v.t.*; winterfed, *pt., pp.*; winter-feeding, *ppr.* to feed (animals) during the winter.

win'tẽr·green, *n.* [after G. *wintergrün*, D. *wintergroen*: so named because evergreen.]

1. a plant, *Gaultheria procumbens*, with egg-shaped leaves, white bell-shaped flowers, and red berries; checkerberry.
2. an oil (*oil of wintergreen*) made from the leaves of this plant and used as a flavor and in medicine.
3. its flavor or anything flavored with it.
4. any of a number of related plants of the genus *Pyrola* with white, greenish, or purple flowers on slender stalks; shinleaf.

chickweed wintergreen; the starflower, *Trientalis americana.*

false wintergreen; a plant, *Pyrola rotundifolia.*

flowering wintergreen; a plant, *Polygala paucifolia*, with prominent rose-purple flowers.

spotted wintergreen; a low plant of the genus *Chimaphila*, with spotted leaves.

win'tẽr-ground, *v.t.* to cover over during winter so as to preserve from the effects of frost; as, to *winter-ground* the roots of a plant.

win'tẽr·ish, *a.* somewhat wintry.

win'tẽr·īze, *v.t.*; winterized, *pt., pp.*; winterizing, *ppr.* to put into condition for or equip for winter, as an automotive vehicle.

win'tẽr·kill, *v.t.* and *v.i.*; winterkilled, *pt., pp.*; winterkilling, *ppr.* to kill or die by exposure to the cold weather in winter; as, to *winterkill* wheat or clover.

win'tẽr·less, *a.* not having any winter; free from winter, as a climate.

win'tẽr·ly, *a.* wintry.

win'tẽr-proud, *a.* too green and luxuriant in winter: applied to wheat or other crops.

win'tẽr-rig, *v.t.* to plow, as land, in ridges and let it lie fallow in winter. [Brit. Dial.]

Win'tẽr's bärk, [after Captain John *Winter*, 16th-c. Eng. explorer.] the bark of a small tree, *Drimys winteri*, of the magnolia family, found in Mexico and some parts of South America.

win'tẽr·tīde, *n.* [ME. *wintertid.*] wintertime; the winter season. [Archaic or Poet.]

win'tẽr·tīme, *n.* the season of winter.

win'tẽr·weed, *n.* any of various weeds that survive and flourish through the winter, especially the ivy-leaved speedwell, *Veronica hederæfolia.*

win'tẽr·y, *a.* wintry.

win'tle, *v.i.* to stagger; to writhe. [Scot.]

win'tri·ly, *adv.* in a wintry manner.

win'tri·ness, *n.* the quality of being wintry.

win'try, *a.*; *comp.* wintrier; *superl.* wintriest, of or pertaining to winter; appropriate to winter; cold; frosty; stormy; like winter; as, a *wintry* day; also, figuratively, cool; chilly; frosty; as, a *wintry* greeting.

wīn'y, *a.* like or having the qualities of wine in taste, smell, color, etc.; vinous.

winze, *n.* [prob. from *winds*, pl. of *wind*, winder, windlass.] a shaft or inclined passage from one level to another in a mine.

winze, *n.* a curse; an imprecation. [Scot.]

wīpe, *n.* wype. [Obs.]

wīpe, *v.t.*; wiped (wīpt), *pt., pp.*; wiping, *ppr.* [ME. *wipen*; AS. *wipian*, to wipe.]

1. to rub or pass over with a cloth, mop, etc., as for cleaning or drying.
2. to clean or dry in this manner; as, *wipe* the dishes.
3. to rub or pass (a cloth, etc.) over something.
4. to apply by wiping; as, *wipe* the oil into the surface.
5. to remove by or as by wiping (with *away, off, up, out*).
6. to form (a joint in lead pipe) by applying liquid solder and rubbing with a leather pad, greased cloth, etc.
7. figuratively, to cleanse, as from evil; to free, as of disadvantage or excess.
8. to cheat; to defraud. [Obs.]
9. to beat; to strike. [Slang.]

to wipe out; (a) to remove; to efface; to obliterate; to erase; as, *to wipe out* a blot; (b) to kill off; to annihilate; to ruin; to exterminate.

wīpe, *v.i.* to hit; to strike at; to beat off, with motions as if wiping; as, he kept *wiping* at the dogs with his huge paws. [Colloq.]

wīpe, *n.* 1. a wiping.
2. a blow; swipe.
3. a wiper (sense 4).
4. a gibe; jeer. [Dial. or Colloq.]
5. a handkerchief. [Slang.]
6. a mark of infamy; a brand; a scar. [Rare.]
7. [*pl.*] a brushwood fence. [Brit. Dial.]

wīp'ẽr, *n.* 1. one who or that which wipes.
2. something used for wiping, or that on which anything is wiped, as a handkerchief, towel, etc.
3. a moving electrical contact, as in a rheostat.
4. a projecting piece on a rotating or rocking part, which raises and lowers or trips another, usually reciprocating, part; a cam; an eccentric.
5. a handkerchief. [Slang.]
6. an implement used to hold a brush or rag for cleaning a gun barrel.

wīr'ble, *v.i.* to progress with a whirling movement; to eddy. [Rare.]

wīrche, *v.t.* and *v.i.* to work. [Obs.]

wīre, *n.* [ME. *wir, wyr*; AS. *wir*, wire.]

1. metal that has been drawn into a very long, thin thread or rod, usually circular in cross section.
2. a length of this, used for various purposes such as conducting electric current, stringing musical instruments, etc.
3. wire netting or other wirework.
4. anything made of wire or wirework, as a telephone cable, barbed wire fence, a snare, etc.
5. telegraph; as, reply by *wire.*
6. a telegram. [Colloq.]
7. in horse racing, the imaginary finish line of a race.
8. an expert pickpocket. [Slang.]
9. a fine metallic thread, a fiber of cobweb, or a minute line on glass, used in the focus of a telescope, etc.

to get under the wire; to manage to enter or achieve barely on time.

to pull wires; [from the wires used to operate puppets.] to use private influence to achieve a purpose.

wīre, *a.* made of wire or wirework.
wire bed; a bedspring or mattress of wire.
wire bridge; a suspension bridge.
wire cartridge; a cartridge for a shotgun, in which the charge of shot has a wire covering to prevent excessive scattering.
wire cloth; a type of fine wire netting, used for strainers, etc.
wire entanglement; a military defense consisting of rows of barbed wire twisted back and forth around stakes set in the ground.
wire gauze; a texture of finely interwoven wire netting resembling gauze.
wire glass; sheet glass containing wire netting.
wire lath; in plastering, wire netting used instead of wooden laths to make the plaster adhere to walls.
wire mattress; a mattress made with wire.
wire nail; a nail made by putting a point and a head on a piece of wire.
wire netting; netting of woven wire, used in various sizes for fences, guards, etc.
wire rod; a metal rod prepared to be made into wire.
wire rope; a rope made of wires twisted or bound together so as to act in unison in resisting a strain. They are extensively used in raising and lowering apparatus in coal mines, as standing rigging for ships, as substitutes for chains in suspension bridges, for telegraph cables, etc.

wīre, *v.t.*; wired, *pt., pp.*; wiring, *ppr.* 1. to bind, furnish, connect, attach, etc. with a wire or wires; to apply wire to, as corks in bottling liquors.
2. to string on a wire; as, to *wire* beads or buttons.
3. to install a system of wires for electric current in, as a telegraph or telephone system, or a house for electric lighting, etc.
4. to catch in a snare made of wire or wires.
5. to send by telegraph; as, to *wire* an acceptance. [Colloq.]
6. in croquet, to block (a ball) by placing it behind the wire of a wicket.

wīre, *v.i.* 1. to telegraph; to send a message by the telegraph. [Colloq.]
2. to flow in slender threadlike streams. [Rare.]

wīre bent, a matgrass of Europe.

wīre′bird, *n.* a plover, *Ægialites sanctæ-helenæ*, native to the island of St. Helena.

wīre cut′tẽr, a scissorlike tool for cutting wire.

wīre′dăn″cẽr, *n.* a person who performs acrobatic feats on a taut, high wire.

wīre′dra̤w, *v.t.*; wiredrew, *pt.*; wiredrawn, *pp.*; wiredrawing, *ppr.* 1. to draw (a metal) into wire by passing it through a hole in a plate of steel.
2. to draw by art or violence; to distort.
3. to draw out; to spin out; to protract; to prolong.
4. to reduce to the finest subtleties, as a point in argument; to overrefine; to strain.
5. in the steam engine, to draw off, as steam, through narrow ports, thus wasting part of its effect.

wīre′dra̤w″ẽr, *n.* 1. one who or that which draws metal into wire.
2. one who spins out an argument at great length; one who is subtle for the purpose of deceiving.

wīre edġe, a thin wirelike edge formed on a cutting tool by oversharpening it.

wīre fence, a fence made of parallel strands of wire, generally galvanized, or of wire netting attached to posts, suitably placed, and tightened.

wīre fīnd′ẽr, any form of galvanometer used to locate or find the corresponding ends of different wires in a bunched cable.

wīre fọrm′ẽr, a machine for shaping wire into desired forms.

wīre gāuġe, 1. a device for measuring the diameter of wire, thickness of sheet metal, etc.: it usually consists of a disk with notches of graduated sizes along its edge.
2. a standard system of measurement for wire.

wīre grȧss, any of several grasses with wiry stems, flat leaves, and umbrella-shaped groups of flower spikes.

wīre grub, a wireworm.

wīre′hāir, *n.* a wire-haired terrier.

wīre′-hāired, *a.* having short, stiff, and coarse, or wiry, hair.

wīre′-hāired tẽr′ri·ẽr, a fox terrier having short, wiry, slightly curly hair.

wīre′less, *a.* 1. without wire or wires; specifically, operating with electromagnetic waves and not with conducting wire.
2. radio. [Chiefly Brit.]
wireless telegraphy (or *telegraph*); telegraphy by radio-transmitted signals.
wireless telephone; a telephone operating by radio-transmitted signals.
wireless telephony; telephony by radio-transmitted signals.

wīre′less, *n.* 1. wireless telegraphy.
2. wireless telephony.
3. radio. [Chiefly Brit.]

wīre′less, *v.t.* and *v.i.* to communicate (with) by wireless.

wīre′măn, *n.*; *pl.* **wīre′men,** a man employed in putting up and looking after telegraph wires, electric-light wires, etc.

wīre mī·crom′e·tẽr, a micrometer in which very fine wires are drawn across the field and moved by means of screws with graduated heads, for the purpose of making minute measurements.

wīre pan, a baking pan, the bottom of which is made of wire cloth.

wīre peg′gẽr, a device used by shoemakers for driving small nails instead of wooden pegs into the soles of shoes.

wīre′phō″tō, *n.* 1. a system of reproducing photographs at a distance by means of electric impulses transmitted by wire.
2. a photograph so reproduced.
A trade-mark (*Wirephoto*).

wīre′phō·tō, *v.t.*; wirephotoed, *pt., pp.*; wirephotoing, *ppr.* to transmit a picture, diagram, or the like by means of wirephoto apparatus.

wīre point′ẽr, in wiredrawing, a machine for pointing the ends of wires so they can be started through the dies.

wīre′pụll″ẽr, *n.* 1. a person who pulls wires, as in working puppets.
2. a person who uses private influence to gain his ends.

wīre′pụll″ing, *n.* the action or practice of a wirepuller.

wīr′ẽr, *n.* 1. a person who wires; a wireman.
2. a person who uses wire to snare game.

wīre rē·cọrd′ẽr, a machine for recording sound electromagnetically on a thin wire: replaced by the tape recorder.

wīre rōad, same as *wireway.*

wīre′spun, *a.* 1. drawn out in the form of a wire.
2. figuratively, drawn out too fine; oversubtle; overrefined.

wīre′-stitched (-sticht), *a.* stitched with wire, as some bindings.

wīre′-tāiled, *a.* in zoology, having stiff, slender tail quills.

wīre′tap, *v.t.* and *v.i.*; wiretapped, *pt., pp.*; wiretapping, *ppr.* to tap (a telephone wire, etc.) to get information secretly or underhandedly.

wīre′tap, *n.* 1. the act or an instance of wiretapping.
2. a device used in wiretapping.

wīre′tap, *a.* of or relating to wiretapping.

wīre tāpe, a thin, flat, narrow band of steel wire, marked with inches, feet, etc., and wound on a reel, used as a measuring tape.

wīre tap′pẽr, a person who taps telephone wires, etc. to get information secretly or underhandedly.

wīre tram′wāy, same as *wireway.*

wīre twist, a very strong tube made of iron and steel bands twisted together, which can endure a great strain. It is used principally for the barrels of rifles, revolvers, etc.

wīre′wāy, *n.* 1. a ropeway using wires.
2. a railway for cash or parcels, especially in stores, traveling on wires.

wīre′wŏrk, *n.* any wirespun or wire-woven fabric or article, as netting, grilled work, etc.; any article in the manufacture of which wire is used wholly or to a great extent.

wīre′wŏrk″ẽr, *n.* 1. a person who makes articles out of wire.
2. a wirepuller.

wīre′wŏrks, *n.pl.* [*also construed as sing.*] a factory where wire is made or where things are made out of wire.

wīre′wŏrm, *n.* 1. a slender, hard-bodied larva of any of the click beetles, which often attacks the roots of crops.
2. a millipede.

wīre′-wōve, *a.* 1. designating or of a very fine grade of paper with a smooth surface, made in a frame of wire gauze.
2. made of woven wire.

wīr′i·ly, *adv.* in a wiry manner.

wīr′i·ness, *n.* the quality or condition of being wiry.

wīr′ing, *n.* 1. the action of a person or thing that wires.
2. a system of wires.
3. in surgery, the fastening of pieces of broken bone by means of wire sutures.
4. in taxidermy, the operation of fixing and keeping in place the parts of a specimen by means of wires.

wīr′ing, *a.* 1. that wires.
2. used in wiring.

wīr′ing mȧ·chīne′, a device (a) for preparing the rim of a tin vessel for receiving the wire which strengthens it; (b) for driving staples in the slats of a Venetian blind; (c) for shaping wire into a holder for the stopper of a bottle.

wīr′y, *a.*; *comp.* wirier; *superl.* wiriest. 1. of wire.
2. like wire in shape and substance; stiff; as, *wiry* hair.
3. lean, sinewy, and strong: said of persons and animals.
4. produced by or as if by a vibrating wire; as, a *wiry* sound.

wis, *adv.* truly; certainly. [Obs.]

wis, *v.t.* to think; to suppose; to imagine. [Archaic.]

wiş′ărd, *n.* a wizard. [Obs.]

Wis·çon′sin·īte, *n.* a native or inhabitant of Wisconsin.

wiş′dŏm, *n.* [ME.; AS. *wisdōm*, from *wīs*, wise, and the termination *-dōm*, judgment.]
1. the quality of being wise; the faculty of making the best use of knowledge, experience, understanding, etc.; good judgment; sagacity.

> We must act with *wisdom* or else our adherence to right will be mere sound without substance. —Theodore Roosevelt.

> Channing has the love of *wisdom* and the *wisdom* of love. —Coleridge.

2. learning; erudition; knowledge; as, the *wisdom* of the ages.
3. wise discourse or teaching.
4. a wise saying, action, etc. [Rare.]
Wisdom of Jesus, Son of Sirach; same as *Ecclesiasticus.*
Wisdom of Solomon; one of the books of the Old Testament Apocrypha: called *Wisdom* in the Douay Bible.
Word of Wisdom; a book used in the Mormon Church purporting to be one of the revelations made to Joseph Smith, the founder of that church. Instructions are given in it as to the proper kinds of food and drink, as well as other hygienic information.

Syn.—prudence, knowledge, sapience, understanding.

wiş′dŏm tọọth, [after Gr. *sōphronistēres*: so named from late appearance.] the back tooth on each side of each jaw in human beings, the third molar, appearing usually between the ages of 17 and 25.
to cut one's wisdom teeth; to arrive at the age of discretion.

wīşe, *a.*; *comp.* wiser; *superl.* wisest. [ME. *wis, wys*; AS. *wīs*, wise.]
1. having or showing good judgment; having the power of discerning and judging correctly or of discriminating between what is true and what is false, between what is proper and what is improper; sagacious; prudent; discreet; as, a *wise* leader; a *wise* magistrate.
2. informed; as, none the *wiser.*
3. learned; knowing; erudite; enlightened.

> 'Tis the wish to look *wise*, not knowing how. —Moore.

4. versed or skilled; experienced; dexterous; specifically, having knowledge of black magic, etc. [Obs. or Dial.]
5. calculating; crafty; cunning; subtle; wily.

> He taketh the *wise* in their own craftiness. —Job v. 13.

6. dictated or guided by wisdom; containing wisdom; judicious; sound; as, a *wise* saying; a *wise* scheme or plan.
7. (a) annoyingly self-assured, knowing, conceited, etc.; as, a *wise* guy; (b) impudent; fresh. [Slang.]
the seven wise men of Greece; seven philosophers, several of whom were legislators at an early period of Grecian history. They were Periander of Corinth, Pittacus of Mitylene, Thales of Miletus, Solon, Bias of Priene, Chilo of Sparta, and Cleobulus of Lindus.
to be (or *get*) *wise to*; to be (or become) aware of; to have (or attain) a proper understanding of. [Slang.]
to get wise; to become aware of the true facts or circumstances. [Slang.]

to put wise (*to*); to give (a person) information, explanation, etc. (about); to enlighten (concerning). [Slang.]

to wise up; to make or become informed. [Slang.]

wise woman; (a) a woman skilled in hidden arts; a fortune teller; a midwife; (b) a witch.

wīṣe, *n.* [ME. *wise*; AS. *wīse*, wise, lit., the way or mode of doing a thing.] manner; way of being or acting; mode: used chiefly in such phrases as *in any wise, in no wise, on this wise*, and the like.

Shall *in no wise* lose his reward. —Matt. x. 42.

-wīṣe, [from *wise, n.*] a suffix used to form adverbs meaning: (a) *in a* (specified) *direction, position*, or *manner*, as in side*wise*, any*wise*: in this sense, equivalent to *-ways*; (b) *in a manner characteristic of* (something specified), as in clock*wise*.

wīṣe′ā·cre (-kẽr), *n.* [D. *wijssegger*, altered from O.H.G. *wīzzago*, a prophet.] a person who thinks he knows everything; hence, a fool; a simpleton; a dunce.

wīṣe′çrack, *n.* a flippant or facetious remark, often a gibe or retort. [Slang.]

wīṣe′çrack, *v.i.* to make a wisecrack or wisecracks: also *crack wise*. [Slang.]

wīṣe′çrack, *v.t.* to say as a wisecrack. [Slang.]

wīṣe′like, *a.* resembling that which is wise; having a wise appearance; sensible. [Scot.]

wīṣe′ling, *n.* one who pretends to be wise; a wiseacre.

wīṣe′ly, *adv.* 1. in a wise manner; with wisdom or good judgment.

2. knowingly.

wīṣe′ness, *n.* wisdom.

wish, *v.i.*; wished (wisht), *pt., pp.*; wishing, *ppr.* [ME. *wisshen, wischen*; AS. *wȳscan*, to wish, from *wūsc*, a wish.]

1. to have a desire; to yearn; to long.

They cast four anchors out of the stern, and *wished* for the day. —Acts xxvii. 29.

2. to make a wish.

wish, *v.t.* 1. to desire; to long for; to want; to crave; as, I would not *wish* a better friend; I *wish* above all things that thou mayest prosper.

2. to have or express a desire concerning; as, I *wish* the week were over.

3. to have or express a desire concerning the fortune, circumstances, etc. of; as, I *wish* you good luck.

4. to give a (specified) greeting to; to bid; as, she *wished* me good morning.

5. to request or order; as, I *wish* you to leave.

6. to impose (with *on*); as, another duty *wished on* him.

7. to recommend. [Obs.]

wish, *n.* 1. a wishing; a felt or expressed desire for something.

2. something wished for; as, he got his *wish*.

3. a behest; request; as, it is her *wish* that you enter.

4. [*pl.*] expressed desire for a person's health, good fortune, etc.; as, they send their *wishes*.

wish′ȧ·ble, *a.* worthy or capable of being wished for; desirable.

wish′bōne, *n.* the forked bone in front of the breastbone of most birds: so called from the superstitious or joking custom of two persons breaking a dried wishbone by pulling the ends apart to see who will get the longer piece, the sign being that this person will be married first or will gain a wish.

wish′bōne bușh, a Californian four-o'clock, *Mirabilis lævis*, with red flowers.

wish′ẽr, *n.* one who desires; one who expresses a wish.

wish′fụl, *a.* 1. having or showing a wish; desirous; longing; as, *wishful* eyes.

2. desirable; exciting wishes. [Obs.]

wish′fụl·ly, *adv.* in a wishful manner; wistfully.

wish′fụl·ness, *n.* the state or quality of being wishful; longing.

wish′fụl thiṅk′ing, thinking in which one consciously or unconsciously interprets facts in terms of what he would like to believe.

wish′ing bōne, same as *wishbone*.

wish′ing çap, a fabled cap which insures its wearer the fulfillment of wishes and unlimited power.

wish′tŏn·wish, *n.* [Am. Ind.] the prairie dog.

wish′-wäsh, *n.* [a reduplicated form of *wash*.] a weak or insipid drink.

wish′y-wäsh″y, *a.* [a reduplicated form of *washy*.] very thin and weak; diluted; watery; insipid: said originally of liquid substances; hence, feeble; weak; not solid; unsubstantial; as, a *wishy-washy* speech.

wish′y-wäsh″y, *n.* wish-wash. [Dial.]

wis′ket, *n.* same as *whisket*.

wisp, *n.* [ME. *wisp, wips*; prob. from O.N.]

1. a small bundle or bunch of straw or other like substance; as, a *wisp* of hay; a *wisp* of herbs.

2. a slender, twisted piece; as, use a *wisp* of paper to light the fire.

3. a thin, slight, or filmy piece, portion, mass, etc.; a shred; as, a *wisp* of smoke.

4. a small broom; a whisk.

5. will-o'-the-wisp.

6. in falconry, a flight or flock of snipe.

wisp, *v.t.*; wisped (wispt), *pt., pp.*; wisping, *ppr.* 1. to brush, as with a whisk broom.

2. to roll or twist into a wisp.

wisp′en, *a.* made out of a wisp or wisps; as, a *wispen* broom. [Obs.]

wisp′y, *a.*; *comp.* wispier; *superl.* wispiest; like a wisp; slender, slight, filmy, etc.

wist, *v.* past tense and past participle of *wit* (to know).

Wis·tā′ri·ȧ, *n.* same as *Wisteria*.

Wis·tē′ri·ȧ, *n.* [named after Caspar *Wistar* (1761–1818), an American anatomist.]

1. a genus of woody climbing plants of the pea family, having pinnate leaves and full racemes of bluish, white, pink, or purplish flowers. The American species is *Wistaria frutescens*.

2. [w–] any plant of this genus.

wist′fụl, *a.* [altered (after *wishful*) from earlier *wistly*, closely attentive.]

1. earnestly or eagerly attentive; carefully or anxiously observant. [Obs.]

2. showing or expressing vague yearnings; longing pensively.

wist′fụl·ly, *adv.* in a wistful manner; pensively; thoughtfully.

wist′fụl·ness, *n.* the state or quality of being wistful.

wis′tit, *n.* [Fr. *ouistiti.*] a marmoset or monkey, native to South America: also called *ouistiti, wistiti*, etc.

wist′ly, *adv.* wistfully. [Obs.]

wis′tŏn·wish, *n.* same as *wishtonwish*.

wit, *v.t.* and *v.i.*; wist *or* wiste, *pt.*; wist, *pp.*; witing *or* witting, *ppr.* [ME. *witen*; AS. *witan*, to know.] to know or learn. *Wit* was conjugated, in the present indicative: (I) *wot*, (thou) *wost* or *wot(t)est*, (he, she, it) *wot* or *wot(t)eth*, (we, ye, they) *wite*, or *witen*.

And his sister stood afar off to *wit* what would be done to him. —Ex. ii. 4.

to wit; that is to say; namely.

wit, *n.* [ME. *witte*; AS. *wit*, knowledge, from *witan*, to know.]

1. originally, the mind.

2. [*pl.*] (a) powers of thinking and reasoning; intellectual and perceptive powers; (b) mental faculties with respect to their state of balance, especially in their normal condition of sanity.

3. a superior degree of intelligence or understanding; good sense; wisdom; sagacity. [Rare.]

I have the *wit* to think my master is a kind of knave. —Shak.

4. the ability to make clever, ironic, or satirical remarks, usually by perceiving the incongruous and expressing it in a surprising or epigrammatic manner.

5. a person having this ability.

6. any clever disparagement or raillery.

7. intellect; reason. [Archaic.]

at one's wit's end; see under *end*.

the five wits; the five senses; also, sometimes, five faculties: common wit, imagination, fantasy, estimation, and memory.

to keep (or ***have***) ***one's wits about one***; to remain mentally alert; to function with undiminished keenness of mental powers, as in an emergency.

to live by one's wits; to live by trickery or craftiness.

Syn.—humor, satire, irony, burlesque.

wit, *v.i.* to be witty; to act the part of a wit. [Rare.]

wit′ăn, *n.pl.* [AS., pl. of *wita*, one who knows, from wise man, councilor, from *witan*, to know.] in the Anglo-Saxon period of English history, the members of the king's council, or the council itself.

witch, *n.* [AS. *wicce*, f. of *wicca*, a magician, a wizard; prob. from *wiccian*, to use sorcery.]

1. a woman supposed to have supernatural power by a compact with the devil or evil spirits; a sorceress: the term was formerly also applied to men.

2. an old and ugly ill-tempered woman; a hag; a crone.

Foul wrinkled *witch*, what makest thou in my sight? —Shak.

3. a bewitching or charming young woman or girl. [Colloq.]

4. the stormy petrel. [Brit. Dial.]

5. in weaving, a dobby.

witch of Agnesi; in geometry, a versiera.

witch, *v.t.*; witched (wicht), *pt., pp.*; witching, *ppr.* 1. to put a magic spell on; to bewitch.

I'll *witch* sweet ladies with my words and looks. —Shak.

2. to cause, bring, effect, etc. by witchcraft.

3. to charm; fascinate.

witch, *n.* the wych-elm.

witch ạl′dẽr, a low-growing American shrub, *Fothergilla alnifolia*, of the witch-hazel family.

witch brọ̈om, a witches'-broom.

witch chick, a swallow.

witch′çrȧft, *n.* [ME. *wicchecrafte*; AS. *wicce-cræft*.]

1. the power or practices of witches; sorcery; black magic.

2. an instance of this.

3. bewitching attraction or charm; enchantment; irresistible influence; fascination.

O, father, what a hell of *witchcraft* lies
In the small orb of one particular tear. —Shak.

witch doç′tŏr, among primitive tribes, a person who professes to detect and counteract the effects of witchcraft; a medicine man.

witch′-elm, *n.* same as *wych-elm*.

witch′ẽr·y, *n.*; *pl.* **witch′ẽr·ieṣ**, 1. sorcery; enchantment; witchcraft.

2. fascination; entrancing charm.

witch′eṣ′-bē″ṣŏm, *n.* a witches'-broom.

witch′eṣ′-brọ̈om, *n.* an abnormal growth of shoots at the ends of branches, usually caused by the attack of a fungus, *Peridermium elatinum*; hexenbesen.

witch′eṣ′-but″tẽr, *n.* see *Nostoc*.

witch′eṣ′ Sab′băth, a midnight meeting of witches, sorcerers, and demons, supposed in medieval times to have been held annually as a demonic orgy.

witch′eṣ′-thim″ble, *n.* the sea campion.

witch grȧss, 1. a hairy grass with loosely flowered spikes; a panic grass, *Panicum capillare*.

2. couch grass.

witch hā′zel, 1. the wych-elm.

2. a North American shrub or small tree, *Hamamelis virginiana*, with large, alternate, obovate, acute, dentate leaves, axillary clustered yellow flowers, and woody fruit.

3. a lotion consisting of an alcoholic solution prepared from the bark and leaves of this plant, used medicinally and for toilet purposes.

witch hunt, [so named in allusion to persecutions of persons alleged to be witches.] an investigation usually conducted with much publicity, supposedly to uncover subversive political activity, disloyalty, etc., but really to harass and weaken the entire political opposition.

witch′ing, *n.* the action or practice of a person who witches; witchcraft or enchantment.

witch′ing, *a.* that witches; bewitching or enchanting.

witch′ing·ly, *adv.* in a bewitching manner.

witch mēal, the inflammable, powdery pollen of *Lycopodium clavatum*, a club moss.

witch mọth, any of several noctuid moths of the southern United States and the West Indies, having brightly colored wings marbled with dark markings.

witch′wood, *n.* 1. the wych-elm. [Brit. Dial.]

2. the mountain ash.

3. the pricktimber. [Brit. Dial.]

wit′-çrack″ẽr, *n.* a jester; a joker.

wit′çrȧft, *n.* 1. contrivance; invention. [Obs.]

2. the art of reasoning; logic. [Rare.]

wīte, *v.t.*; wited, *pt., pp.*; witing, [ME. *witen*; AS. *wītan*.] to censure; to impute wrong to; to reproach; to blame. [Obs. or Scot.]

wīte, *n.* 1. a punishment, penalty, or mulct. [Obs. exc. Scot. and Brit. Dial.]

2. blame; censure. [Obs. or Scot.]

wīt′less, *a.* blameless. [Obs.]

wit′en·ȧ·gē·mōt″, wit′en·ȧ·gē·mōte″, *n.* [AS. *witena-gemot*; *witena*, gen. pl. of *wita*, a wise man, and (*ge*)*mot*, a meeting, a moot, an assembly; lit., the assembly of the wise men.] among the Anglo-Saxons, the national council or parliament, consisting of athelings or princes, nobles or ealdormen, the large landholders, the principal ecclesiastics, etc.

wit′fụl, *a.* full of wisdom; wise. [Obs.]

with, (*or* with), *prep.* [AS. *with*, against, toward, near.]

1. in opposition to; against; as, to fight *with* an enemy.

2. (a) being together; in the company of; as, he remained *with* me during the day; (b) alongside of; close to; near to; (c) into; among; as, mix blue *with* yellow.

3. as an associate in action, purpose, thought, feeling, or the like.

With thee she talks, *with* thee she moans;
With thee she sighs, *with* thee she groans;
With thee she says: "Farewell, mine own."
—Surrey.

4. having as a possession, addition, accessory, accompaniments, etc.; as, a church *with* a spire, a horse *with* a driver.

5. at the same time as.

The world hath ending *with* thy life.
—Shak.

6. of the same opinions, belief, etc. as; as, do as you please, I am *with* you.

7. in the estimation, opinion, consideration, judgment, or thoughts of.

Such arguments had invincible force *with* those pagan philosophers who became Christians. —Addison.

8. by means of; as, to kill one *with* kindness.

9. as a result of; because of; as, his face became white *with* rage.

10. by the use, presence, etc. of; by.

Brought *with* armed men back to Messina.
—Shak.

11. as a member of; as, he plays *with* a string quartet.

12. concerning; specifically, (a) in terms of relationship to; as, friendly *with* strangers; (b) in regard to; as, pleased *with* her gift.

13. as well, completely, etc. as; as, he can jump *with* the best.

14. in support of; on the side of; as, he voted *with* the Tories.

15. in the region, sphere, circumstances, etc. of.

16. (a) accompanied by, attended by, circumstanced by, etc.; as, he entered *with* confidence; (b) having received; as, *with* your permission, I'll go.

17. exhibiting; as, he plays *with* skill.

18. in the keeping, care, etc. of; as, leave the children *with* grandmother.

19. added to; and; as, the woman, *with* her two daughters, arrived.

20. in spite of; notwithstanding; as, *with* all his boasting, he is a coward.

21. in the same direction as; as, travel *with* the sun.

22. to; onto; as, join this end *with* that one.

23. from; as, to part *with* one's gains.

in with; see under *in*, adv.

with that; after that; whereupon.

with, *n.* same as *withe* (sense 4).

with-, [AS. *with-*.] a combining form meaning: (a) *away, back*, as in *with*draw; (b) *against, from*, as in *with*hold.

with·ạl′, *adv.* [ME. *with alle.*]

1. besides.
2. thereby.
3. thereupon.
4. still.

[Archaic in all senses.]

with·ạl′, *prep.* with: used at the end of a sentence or clause; as, a staff to support himself *withal*. [Archaic.]

with′ăm·īte, *n.* [named after Dr. Henry *Witham*, of Glencoe, Scotland, its discoverer.] a red or yellow variety of epidote, found in Scotland.

with·drạw′, *v.t.*; withdrew, *pt.*; withdrawn, *pp.*; withdrawing, *ppr.* [ME. *withdrawen*; *with-*, against, opposite, and *draw*.]

1. to draw back; to take back; to remove.

2. to retract; to recall, as a promise, threat, statement, etc.

with·drạw′, *v.i.* 1. to move back; to go away; to retire; to retreat; as, he *withdrew* from the gathering.

2. in parliamentary procedure, to retract a motion, statement, etc.

with·drạw′ăl, *n.* the act of withdrawing; the act of taking back, as of money from the bank, a person or thing from its place or position, etc.

with·drạw′ẽr, *n.* a person who withdraws or retracts.

with·drạw′ing rọọm, a drawing room. [Archaic.]

with·drạw′ment, *n.* withdrawal. [Rare.]

with·drạwn′, *v.* past participle of *withdraw*.

with·drạwn′, *adj.* withdrawing within oneself; shy, reserved, abstracted, etc.

with·drew′ (-drụ′), *v.* past tense of *withdraw*.

withe, *n.* [ME. *wythe, witthe, wythth*, from AS. *withig*, willow, also, twig of a willow.]

1. a tough flexible branch or twig of willow, osier, etc., used in binding things; a withy.

2. a band made of twisted twigs.

3. in nautical usage, an iron instrument fitted to the end of a boom or mast, and having a ring through which another boom or mast is rigged or secured; a boom iron.

4. a wall dividing flues in a chimney.

withe, *v.t.*; withed (witht), *pt., pp.*; withing, *ppr.* to bind or tie with withes or twigs.

with′ẽr, *v.i.*; withered, *pt., pp.*; withering, *ppr.* [ME. *widren*, wither; a variant of *wederen*, lit., to weather, expose to the weather, from *weder*, weather.]

1. to dry and shrivel up, as from great heat; to wilt: said of plants.

Leaves have their time to fall,
And flowers to *wither* at the north wind's breath. —Hemans.

2. to become dry and wrinkled; to lose freshness, bloom, vigor, etc., as from age or disease; to become wasted or decayed.

A fair face will *wither*. —Shak.

3. to weaken; to decline; to languish.

The individual *withers* and the world is more and more. —Tennyson.

with′ẽr, *v.t.* 1. to cause to wither.

Like a blasted sapling, *withered* up.
—Shak.

2. to cause to quail or feel abashed; as, to *wither* a person by a scornful glance, reputations *withered* by scandal.

The love in a woman's heart is the one boon that time cannot *wither*.
—George Horton.

with′ẽr·band, *n.* a piece of iron under a saddle near a horse's withers, to strengthen the bow.

with′ẽred, *a.* faded; shriveled; dried up.

with′ẽred, *a.* having withers: used in compounds.

with′ẽred·ness, *n.* the condition of being withered.

with′ẽr·ing, *a.* tending to wither.

with′ẽr·ing·ly, *adv.* in a withering manner.

with′ẽr·īte, *n.* [after William *Withering* (1741–1799), Eng. scientist who discovered it.] native barium carbonate, $BaCO_3$, occurring in white, yellowish, or grayish crystals, often in columnar or granular masses: it is used in the sugar, glass, and pyrotechnic industries.

with′ẽr·ling, *n.* a withered thing or person. [Obs.]

with′ẽr·nam, *n.* in early English law, an unlawful distress or forbidden taking, as of a thing distrained, out of the country, so that the sheriff cannot upon the replevin make deliverance thereof to the party distrained; also, the reprisal of other cattle or goods in lieu of those that have been unjustly taken, eloigned, etc.

withe rod, a North American shrub of the genus *Viburnum*, with osierlike shoots, having clusters of white flowers in June, and heavy clusters of blue-black, pink, or yellowish-green berries in the fall.

with′ẽrṣ, *n.pl.* [ME. *wither*, resistance, lit., things that resist; that which the horse opposes to his load.] the juncture of the shoulder bones of a horse or other animal, forming the highest part of the back.

with′ẽr·shinṣ, *adv.* in a direction contrary to the apparent course of the sun. [Scot.]

with′ẽr-wrung (-rung), *a.* injured or hurt in the withers, as a horse.

with·held′, *v.* past tense and past participle of *withhold*.

with·hōld, *v.t.*; withheld, *pt., pp.*; withholding, *ppr.* [*with-*, back, away, and *hold*.]

1. to hold back; to restrain; to keep back.

2. to refrain from granting, permitting, etc.; to refuse; as, to *withhold* assent to a proposition.

3. to maintain; to keep. [Obs.]

with·hōld′, *v.i.* to refrain; to restrain oneself.

with·hōld′ăl, *n.* withholdment.

with·hōld′en, *v.* archaic past participle of *withhold*.

with·hōld′ẽr, *n.* one who withholds.

with·hōld′ing tax, the amount of income tax paid by employees through the employer's withholding of part of their wages or salaries.

with·hōld′ment, *n.* the act of withholding.

with·in′, *adv.* [ME. *withinne*; AS. *withinnan*, on the inside; *with*, against, toward, and *innan*, adv., from *in*, in.]

1. in the inner part; internally; on the inside.

2. indoors; as, he is not *within*.

3. inside the body, mind, heart, etc.; inwardly.

with·in′, *prep.* 1. in the inner part of; inside of: opposed to *without*; as, *within* the house.

2. in the limits or compass of; not beyond in distance, time, degree, etc.; as, *within* my sight, *within* one's income.

3. inside the limits of; not exceeding; not overstepping, etc.; as, *within* the law.

with·in′dōorṣ, *adv.* indoors. [Archaic.]

with·in′sīde, *adv.* inside. [Archaic.]

with′-it, *a.* 1. sophisticated, aware, up-to-date, etc. [Slang.]

2. fashionable; stylish. [Slang.]

with·out′, *adv.* [ME. *withuten, withouten*; AS. *withutan*, on the outside of; *with*, against, toward, and *utan*, adv., from *ūt*, out.]

1. not on the inside; not within; externally.

2. out of doors.

with·out′, *conj.* unless: often followed by *that*; as, I can't go, *without* (*that*) I get some money. [Dial.]

with·out′, *prep.* 1. at, on, to, or toward the outside of: opposed to *within*.

2. beyond; as, *without* his reach: opposed to *within*.

3. not with; lacking.

4. free from; as, *without* fear.

5. with avoidance of; as, he passed *without* speaking.

6. lacking or in the absence of (something previously mentioned): used with the object understood; as, we went *without*.

7. besides. [Obs.]

with·out′dōor, *a.* external; outside. [Obs.]

with·out′dōorṣ, *adv.* out-of-doors. [Archaic.]

with·out′en, *adv., prep.*, and *conj.* without. [Archaic.]

with·out′fōrth, *adv.* without. [Archaic.]

with·sāy′, *v.t.* to deny; to refuse. [Obs.]

with·set′, *v.t.* to oppose. [Obs.]

with·stand′, *v.t.* and *v.i.*; withstood, *pt., pp.*; withstanding, *ppr.* [ME. *withstonden*; AS. *withstandan*, to resist; *with*, against, and *standan*, to stand.] to oppose, resist, or endure.

with·stand′ẽr, *n.* one who resists.

with·stood′, *v.* past tense and past participle of *withstand*.

with′wīnd, *n.* a plant, the bindweed.

with′y, *n.*; *pl.* **with′ieṣ,** [ME. *wythe, witthe, wythth*, from AS. *withig*, a willow, also, a twig of a willow.]

1. a tough, flexible twig of willow, osier, etc., used for binding things; a withe.

2. a rope or leash made of withes.

with′y, *a.* 1. tough and flexible, as a withy.

2. wiry: said of people.

wit′ing, *n.* understanding; wit; knowledge. [Obs.]

wit′less, *a.* lacking wit or intelligence; foolish.

wit′less·ness, *n.* the state or quality of being witless.

wit′ling, *n.* one who fancies himself a wit.

wit′lōof, *n.* a large-rooted variety of chicory.

wit′ness, *n.* [ME. *witnesse*, from AS. *witnes*, testimony, from *witan*, to know.]

1. testimony; attestation of a fact or event; evidence.

2. a person who saw, or can give a firsthand account of, something.

3. a person who testifies in court.

4. a person called upon to observe a transaction, signing, etc. in order to testify concerning it if it is later held in question.

5. something providing or serving as evidence.

subscribing witness; a person who signs his name in attestation of the genuineness of the signature of the executor of a contract, etc.

to bear witness; to be or give evidence; to testify.

with a witness; to a great degree. [Obs.]

wit′ness, *v.t.*; witnessed (-nest), *pt., pp.*; witnessing, *ppr.* 1. to testify to.

2. to serve as evidence of.

3. to act as witness of, often by signing a statement to that effect.

4. to be present at; to see personally.

5. to be the scene or setting of; as, this field has *witnessed* many battles.

wit′ness, *v.i.* to bear testimony; to give evidence.

wit'ness·ẽr, *n.* one who gives or bears testimony.

wit'ness stand, the place from which a witness gives his testimony in a law court.

wit'-snap"pẽr, *n.* one who makes witty remarks. [Rare.]

wit'-stärved, *a.* barren of wit.

wit'ted, *a.* having wit: usually in hyphenated compounds, meaning *having* (a specified kind of) *wit*; as, a quick-*witted* boy.

wit'tiç·as·tẽr, *n.* a witling. [Rare.]

wit'ti·çişm, *n.* [from *witty*, after *Anglicism*, *criticism*, etc.] a witty remark.

wit'ti·fīed, *a.* having wit; clever; witty. [Obs.]

wit'ti·ly, *adv.* in a witty manner.

wit'ti·ness, *n.* the quality of being witty.

wit'ting, *a.* done or acting knowingly; deliberate.

wit'ting·ly, *adv.* consciously; intentionally.

wit'tŏl, *n.* [Late ME. *wetewold*, formed, after *cokewold*, cuckold, from *weten*, *witen*, to know.]
  1. a man who knows his wife's infidelity and is tolerant of it. [Archaic.]
  2. a bird, the wheatear or whitetail. [Brit. Dial.]

wit'tŏl·ly, *a.* like or characteristic of a wittol.

witts, *n.pl.* tin ore from which all earthy substance has been removed.

Witt's plan'et, the asteroid Eros, discovered by Dr. G. Witt in 1898.

wit'ty, *a.*; *comp.* wittier; *superl.* wittiest, [AS. *witig*, *wittig*, from *wit*, knowledge.]
  1. having, showing, or characterized by wit; cleverly amusing.
  2. intelligent; clever. [Obs. or Dial.]

wit'wall, *n.* [altered from *woodwale*, *woodewale*, an old name of various birds.]
  1. the green woodpecker or popinjay, *Gecinus viridis*.
  2. the greater spotted woodpecker, *Picus major*.
  3. the golden oriole.

wit'wŏrm, *n.* a wit. [Obs.]

wīve, *v.i.*; wived, *pt.*, *pp.*; wiving, *ppr.* [ME. *wiven*, from AS. *wifian*, to take a wife, from *wif*, a woman, wife.] to marry a woman; to take for a wife.

wīve, *v.t.* 1. to marry (a woman); to take for a wife.
  2. to provide with a wife.

wī'vẽrn, *n.* [ME. *wivere*, from OFr. *wivre*, a serpent.] in heraldry, a dragon with wings, two legs, and a barbed tail: also spelled *wyvern*.

WIVERN

wīveş, *n.* plural of *wife*.

wiz, *n.* [from *wizard*.] a person regarded as exceptionally clever or gifted at studies, etc.; as, he's a *wiz* at chemistry. [Slang.]

wiz'ärd, *n.* [ME. *wisard*, from OFr. *guischart*, from Ice. *viskr*, clever, knowing.]
  1. originally, a wise man; a sage.
  2. a magician; conjurer; sorcerer.
  3. a very skillful or clever person. [Colloq.]

wiz'ärd, *a.* 1. of wizards or wizardry.
  2. magic.

wiz'ärd·ly, *a.* resembling or characteristic of a wizard or wizardry.

wiz'ärd·ry, *n.* the art or practice of a wizard; sorcery.

wiz'en, *v.i.* and *v.t.* [ME. *wisenen*, from AS. *wisnian*, to become dry.] to wither; to shrivel; to dry up; to fade.

wiz'en, *a.* hard, dry, and shriveled; withered.

wiz'en, *n.* weasand. [Scot. and Brit. Dial.]

wiz'ened, *a.* withered; shrunken; shriveled.

wiz'en-fāced (-fāst), *a.* having a thin, shriveled face.

wlät'sŏme (lot'), *a.* disgusting; offensive; revolting. [Obs.]

wō, *n.* and *interj.* same as *woe*.

wōad, *n.* [ME. *wod*; AS. *wad*, *waad*, woad.]
  1. a cruciferous plant, *Isatis tinctoria*, formerly cultivated extensively in Great Britain for the blue dye extracted from its leaves.
  2. the dye itself.
  wild woad; an herb, *Reseda luteola*; dyer's weed; weld.

wōad'ed, *a.* 1. dyed or colored blue with woad.
  2. derived from woad; produced by woad or a woad mixture.

wōad mill, a mill for bruising and preparing woad.

wōad'wax"en, *n.* same as *woodwaxen*.

wōald, *n.* a weld (flower).

wob'bē·gong, wob'bi·gong, *n.* [Australian.] a broad-headed shark, *Crossorhinus barbatus*, native to Australia.

wob'ble, *v.i.*; wobbled, *pt.*, *pp.*; wobbling, *ppr.* [perh. from L.G. *wabbeln*, to wobble.]
  1. to move unsteadily from side to side, as in walking.
  2. to rotate unevenly so as to move from side to side.
  3. to shake; to tremble; as, jelly *wobbles*.
  4. to waver in one's opinions, etc.; to vacillate.
  Also *wabble*.

wob'ble, *v.t.* to cause to wobble: also *wabble*. [Colloq.]

wob'ble, *n.* wobbling motion: also *wabble*.

wob'bling, *a.* that wobbles: also *wabbling*.

wob'bly, *a.*; *comp.* wobblier; *super.* wobbliest, inclined to wobble; shaky: also *wabbly*.

wob'bly, *n.*; *pl.* **wob'blieș,** [said to be from Chin. mispronunciation of *I.W.W.* as *I. wobbly wobbly*.] [*also* W–] a member of the Industrial Workers of the World (I.W.W.). [Slang.]

wō'bē·gōne, *a.* same as *woebegone*.

Wō'den, Wō'dăn, *n.* [AS. *Woden*, the furious one, from the root of *wod*, mad.] the chief Germanic god, identified with the Norse Odin.

wōe, *n.* [ME. *wo*, from AS. *wa*, woe.]
  1. grief; sorrow; misery; a heavy calamity.
  2. a cause of sorrow; affliction; trouble.
  Also spelled *wo*.

wōe, *interj.* alas! an exclamation of misery, grief, calamity, or pain: also spelled *wo*.

wōe, *a.* sad; sorrowful; miserable; wretched. [Obs.]

wōe'bē·gōne", wō'bē·gōne", *a.* [ME. *wo begon*; *wo*, woe, and *begon*, to go around.]
  1. woeful. [Archaic.]
  2. of woeful appearance; showing woe; looking sorrowful, mournful, or wretched.

wōe'ful, wō'ful, *a.* 1. sorrowful; distressed with grief or calamity; mournful; full of woe.
  2. bringing calamity, distress, or affliction.
  3. wretched; pitiful; miserable.
  4. expressing woe; as, a *woeful* song.

wōe'ful·ly, wō'ful·ly, *adv.* in a woeful manner; sorrowfully.

wōe'ful·ness, wō'ful·ness, *n.* the state of being woeful; misery; calamity.

wōeh'lẽr·īte (vō'), *n.* a silicate and columbate of calcium, sodium, zirconium, etc. occurring in brown or yellow prismatic crystals: also spelled *wöhlerite*.

wōe'sŏme, *a.* woeful; sad.

wōe'vīne, *n.* *Cassytha americana*, a dodder laurel.

wok, *n.* [Chin.] a metal cooking pan with a convex bottom, for frying, braising, steaming, etc.: often used with a ringlike stand for holding it steady.

wōke, *v.* alternative past tense of *wake*.

wōk'en, *v.* rare past participle of *wake*.

wōl, *v.* obsolete form of *will*.

wōld, *n.* [AS. *weald*, *wald*, a wood, forest.]
  1. a forest. [Obs.]
  2. a treeless, rolling plain, especially a high one.

wōld, *n.* a weld (flower).

wōld, wōlde, *v.* alternative obsolete past participle of *will*.

wolf (wulf), *n.*; *pl.* **wolveș** (wulvz), [ME. *wolf*; AS. *wulf*, wolf: akin to G. *wolf*.]
  1. any of a large group of carnivorous, canine mammals of the genus *Canis*, the type genus of the dog family, widely distributed throughout the Northern Hemisphere: the best-known species are the common gray wolf, *Canis lupus*; the American timber wolf, *Canis occidentalis*; and the prairie wolf, *Canis latrans*.

COMMON WOLF (*Canis lupus*)

  2. a person or thing resembling a wolf in being cruel, fierce, or greedy.
  3. a man who flirts aggressively with many women; a philanderer. [Slang.]
  4. an eating ulcer. [Now Dial.]
  5. any of various destructive larvae of beetles or moths that infest grain, especially that of the wolf moth.
  6. in music, (a) the jarring discordant sound produced in playing certain chords on an organ or pianoforte when it has been tuned to unequal temperament; also, a chord in which such dissonance is heard; (b) a harsh tone often produced on a violin or other stringed instrument the intonation of which is not true.
  black wolf; a black variety of the common wolf.
  golden wolf; a wolf native to Tibet, *Canis laniger*.
  gray wolf; see under *gray*.
  Indian wolf; an Asiatic wolf, *Canis pallipes*, having the appearance of a jackal.
  to cry wolf; to give a false alarm.
  to keep the wolf from the door; to provide the necessities of life in sufficient quantity; to keep out hunger or want.
  to see a wolf; to lose one's voice.

wolf, *v.t.* to devour ravenously, as a wolf does; as, to *wolf* food, or *wolf down* food. [Slang.]

wolf, *v.i.* to hunt wolves; as, to go *wolfing*.

wolf'ber"ry, *n.*; *pl.* **wolf'ber"rieș,** a small shrub, *Symphoricarpos occidentalis*, of the honeysuckle family, having spikelike clusters of white berries.

wolf dog, 1. any of several breeds of large Irish dogs formerly trained to hunt wolves.
  2. a hybrid of a dog and a wolf.

Wolff'i·ȧ (wulf'), *n.* [after J. F. *Wolff* (1778–1806), German physician.] a genus of plants of about a dozen species, all aquatic. The plants are more or less globular bodies having no leaves and flowering from grooves in their surfaces. They are the smallest known flowering plants.

Wolff'i·ăn, *a.* relating to or discovered by Kaspar Friedrich Wolff (1733–1794), a German embryologist.
  Wolffian body; same as *Mesonephros*.
  Wolffian duct; the efferent duct of a mesonephros.

wolf fish, any of several large, savage sea fishes of the blenny group.

wolf'hound, *n.* a large dog of any of several breeds formerly used for hunting wolves.

wolf'ish, *a.* like a wolf; having the qualities of a wolf; rapacious; as, a *wolfish* visage; *wolfish* designs.

wolf'ish·ly, *adv.* in a wolfish manner.

wolf'kin, *n.* a small wolf.

wolf'ling, *n.* a wolfkin.

wolf moth, a small moth, *Tinea granella*, whose larvae infest grain.

wolf'răm, *n.* [G., from *wolf*, wolf, and M.H.G. *ram*, dirt, soot.]
  1. a hard, heavy, gray-white, metallic chemical element, found in wolframite, scheelite, and tungstite, and used in steel for high-speed tools, in electric lamp filaments, etc.: symbol, W; atomic weight, 183.85; atomic number, 74: the earlier name *tungsten* is preferred in the United States.
  2. wolframite.

wolf'răm·āte, *n.* a tungstate.

wolf'răm·īte, *n.* [G. *wolframit*, from *wolfram*.] a brownish or blackish mineral, (Fe, Mn)-WO_4, a tungstate of manganese and iron; the chief ore of tungsten.

wolf·rā'mi·um, *n.* wolfram.

wolfs'bāne, *n.* [trans. of L. *lycoctonum*, from Gr. *lykotonon*, from *lykos*, a wolf, and base of *kleinein*, to kill.] any of a number of related poisonous plants having large, showy, blue, white, or yellow flowers with hooded sepals; aconite; monkshood: also *wolf's-bane*.

WOLFSBANE (*Aconitum lycoctonum*)

wolfs'bẽrg·īte, *n.* [from *Wolfsberg*, in the Harz Mountains.] chalcostibite.

wolf's'-çlawș, *n.* a cryptogamous plant of the genus *Lycopodium*; club moss.

wolf's'-foot, *n.* club moss.

wolf's'-milk, *n.* any species of plant of the genus *Euphorbia*; specifically, the sun spurge,

 fāte, fär, fȧst, fall, fināl, cāre, at; mēte, prey, hẽr, met; pīne, marīne, bīrd, pin; nōte, mōve, fọr, atŏm, not; mọọn, book;

Euphorbia helioscopia, on account of its bitter milky juice.

wol'lăs·tōn·īte, *n.* [after William H. *Wollaston* (1766–1828), English physicist.] a white mineral, $CaSiO_3$, native silicate of calcium: also called *tabular spar*.

Wol'lăs·tŏn's doub'let (dub'), a combination lens in which two plano-convex lenses of unequal curvature are used to correct chromatic dispersion and spherical aberration in the microscope.

wolle, *n.* will. [Obs.]

wolve'boon (wulv'), *n.* [S. Afr. D.] a tree, the *Toxicodendron capense*, of South Africa, whose fruit is used as a poison.

wol'vẽr (wul'), *n.* a person who hunts wolves.

wol·vẽr·ine', *n.*; *pl.* **wol·vẽr·ines'** or **wol·vẽr·ine',** [a dim. formed from *wolf*, on account of its fierce, bloodthirsty disposition.]

1. a stocky, flesh-eating mammal, *Gulo luscus*, with thick fur, found in the northern United States and Canada and closely related to the European glutton.

WOLVERINE (3 ft. long)

2. [W-] a native or an inhabitant of Michigan, called the *Wolverine State*. [Colloq.]

Also spelled *wolverene*.

wolves (wulvz), *n.* plural of *wolf*.

wolv'ish, *a.* wolfish. [Obs.]

wom'ăn (woom'), *n.*; *pl.* **wom'en** (wim'), [ME. *wumman, wimmon, wifmon*; AS. *wifman*, later *wimman*, from *wif*, a wife, and *man*, in its primitive sense of human being, person.]

1. the female of the human race, or women collectively, as distinguished from man.

2. an adult female human being.

3. the characteristic qualities of a woman, as timidity, modesty, mildness, tenderness, etc.; womanliness; femininity.

4. a man who is effeminate, cowardly, emotional, weak, etc.; as, he seemed to me a very *woman*.

5. a female attendant or servant.

6. (a) a wife; (b) a sweetheart or mistress; as, she's my *woman*.

wom'ăn, *a.* 1. of or characteristic of a woman or women; feminine.

2. female.

wom'ăn, *v. i.* to play the woman in: with *it*; as, to *woman it*. [Obs.]

wom'ăn, *v.t.* 1. to cause to act like a woman. [Obs.]

2. to unite to or accompany by a woman. [Obs.]

3. to refer to (a person) as a woman, in an insulting manner; as, never *woman* me! [Obs.]

wom'ăn-hāt"ẽr, *n.* a man who dislikes women; a misogynist.

wom'ăn·head (-hed), *n.* womanhood. [Archaic.]

wom'ăn·hood, *n.* 1. the qualities of a woman; womanliness.

2. womankind; women.

3. the condition of being a woman.

wom'ăn·ish, *a.* pertaining to, characteristic of, or suitable to a woman; having the qualities of a woman; feminine; effeminate; as, *womanish* habits; a *womanish* voice.

wom'ăn·ish·ly, *adv.* in a womanish manner.

wom'ăn·ish·ness, *n.* the state or quality of being womanish.

wom'ăn·īze, *v.t.*; womanized, *pt., pp.*; womanizing, *ppr.* 1. to make effeminate.

2. to practice adultery with women. [Colloq.]

wom'ăn·kīnd, *n.* women in general.

wom'ăn·less, *a.* without women or a woman.

wom'ăn·līke, *a.* like a woman; womanly.

wom'ăn·li·ness, *n.* a womanly quality; the quality or nature of being womanly.

wom'ăn·ly, *a.* 1. characteristic of a woman; womanlike; as, *womanly* behavior.

2. like a woman; womanish.

3. suitable to a woman.

wom'ăn·ly, *adv.* in the manner of a woman.

wom'ăn-suf'frăġe, *a.* of woman suffrage.

wom'ăn suf'frăġe, the right of women to vote in governmental elections.

wom'ăn-suf'fră·ġist, *n.* a person who believes in or advocates woman suffrage.

wömb (wöm), *n.* [ME. *wombe, wambe*; AS. *wamb, womb*, the belly.]

1. the uterus.

2. any place or part that holds, envelops, generates, etc.; as, the *womb* of time.

3. the belly or stomach. [Obs.]

wömb, *v.t.* to enclose; to breed in secret. [Obs.]

wom'bat, *n.* [altered from the native Australian name *vomback* or *vombach*.] any of a group of burrowing marsupials, resembling small bears, as *Phascolomys wombat*, of the opossum family, found in Australia, Tasmania, and several Pacific islands. It is about the size of the badger.

wömb'y (wöm'), *a.* capacious. [Rare.]

wom'en (wim'), *n.* plural of *woman*.

wom'en·fōlk (-fōk), *n.pl.* women; womankind.

wom'en·fōlks (-fōks), *n.pl.* same as *womenfolk*.

wom'en's rīghts (rīts), the rights claimed by and for women of equal privileges and opportunities with men: also *woman's rights*.

wom'ẽr·ȧ (wom'), *n.* [Australian native name.] a spear-throwing device used by Australian aborigines: also *woomera*.

wŏn, *v.* past tense and past participle of *win*.

wŏn, *v.i.*; wonned, *pt., pp.*; wonning, *ppr.* to dwell; to abide. [Archaic or Dial.]

wŏn, wŏne, *n.* a dwelling. [Obs.]

wŏn'dẽr, *n.* [ME. *wunder, wonder*; AS. *wundor*, a portent. The original sense is *awe*, lit., *that from which one turns aside*.]

1. a person, thing, or event that excites surprise; a strange thing; a cause of astonishment or admiration; a prodigy or miracle.

2. the feeling of surprise, admiration, and awe which is excited by something new, unusual, strange, great, extraordinary, or not well understood.

3. a miracle.

4. a kind of cake; a cruller.

a nine days' wonder; see under *nine*.

for a wonder; surprisingly.

Seven Wonders of the World; seven remarkable objects of ancient times: the Egyptian pyramids, the Mausoleum erected at Halicarnassus, the temple of Artemis at Ephesus, the walls and hanging gardens of Babylon, the Colossus at Rhodes, the statue of Zeus by Phidias at Olympia, and the Pharos, or lighthouse, of Alexandria.

Syn.—admiration, appreciation, astonishment, reverence, surprise, amazement, prodigy.

wŏn'dẽr, *v.i.*; wondered, *pt., pp.*; wondering, *ppr.* [AS. *wundrian*, to wonder.]

1. to be seized or filled with wonder; to be amazed; to marvel.

We cease to *wonder* at what we understand.
—Johnson.

2. to have doubt mingled with curiosity.

wŏn'dẽr, *v.t.* 1. to have doubt and curiosity about; to want to know.

Like old acquaintance in a trance,
Met far from home, *wondering* each other's chance. —Shak.

2. to surprise; to amaze. [Rare.]

wŏn'dẽr, *a.* 1. wonderful. [Obs.]

2. of or like a wonder; seemingly miraculous; as, a *wonder* drug.

wŏn'dẽr, *adv.* wonderfully. [Archaic.]

wŏn'dẽr·ẽr, *n.* one who wonders.

wŏn'dẽr·ful, *a.* [ME.; AS. *wundorfull*.]

1. that causes wonder; marvelous.

2. very good; excellent; fine: generalized term of approval. [Colloq.]

Syn.—admirable, astonishing, curious, marvelous, strange, amazing, surprising.

wŏn'dẽr·ful·ly, *adv.* in a manner to excite wonder or surprise.

I am fearfully and *wonderfully* made.
—Ps. cxxxix. 14.

wŏn'dẽr·ful·ness, *n.* the state or quality of being wonderful.

wŏn'dẽr·ing, *a.* showing or feeling wonder.

wŏn'dẽr·ing·ly, *adv.* in a wondering manner.

wŏn'dẽr·land, *n.* 1. an imaginary land abounding in wonders.

2. any place of great beauty, etc.

wŏn'dẽr·ly, *adv.* wondrously. [Obs.]

wŏn'dẽr·ment, *n.* 1. a state or expression of wonder; amazement; astonishment.

2. something causing wonder; a marvel.

wŏn'dẽr-of-the-wŏrld', *n.* a plant, *Aralia ginseng*, the ginseng.

wŏn'dẽr-strick"en, wŏn'dẽr-struck, *a.* struck with wonder; feeling admiration, surprise, etc.

wŏn'dẽr·wŏrk, *n.* [ME. *wunder werk*; AS. *wundorweorc*.]

1. a wonderful work; a wonder.

2. a miraculous act; a miracle.

wŏn'dẽr-wŏrk"ẽr, *n.* one who performs miracles or any wonderful work; a magician.

wŏn'dẽr-wŏrk"ing, *a.* doing wonders or surprising things; performing miracles.

wŏn'drous, *a.* [alteration of ME. *wondres* wondrous.] wonderful: now only literary or rhetorical.

wŏn'drous, *adv.* to a wonderful or surprising degree; extraordinarily; surprisingly; as, *wondrous* fair to look upon: now only literary or historical.

wŏn'drous·ly, *adv.* in a strange or wonderful manner or degree.

wŏn'drous·ness, *n.* the quality of being wondrous.

wōne, *n.* won (dwelling). [Obs.]

wong, *n.* an open field: now obsolete except in place names.

woñ'gȧ-woñ'gȧ, *n.* an Australian variety of pigeon, *Leucosarcia picata*, noted for the whiteness of its flesh.

wŏn'ing, *n.* a dwelling; a habitation. [Obs.]

woñ'ky, *a.*; *comp.* wonkier; *superl.* wonkiest, [prob. from or suggested by dial. words based on AS. *wancol*, shaky, tottering.] shaky; tottery; feeble. [Brit. Slang.]

wŏn'nȧ, will not. [Scot.]

wŏn'nẽr, *n., v.i.* and *v.t.* wonder. [Dial.]

wŏn't, [contr. from ME. *wol not*, will not.] will not.

wŏnt, *a.* [ME. *wunt, woned*, pp. of *wunien*, to be accustomed; AS. *wunian*, to dwell, to be used to.] accustomed; habituated: used predicatively.

If the ox were *wont* to push with his horn.
—Ex. xxi. 29.

wŏnt, *n.* custom; habit; usual practice.

wŏnt, *v.i.*; wont, *pt.*; wont *or* wonted, *pp.*; wonting, *ppr.* 1. to be accustomed or habituated.

I *wont* to sit and watch the setting sun.
—Southey.

2. to dwell; to inhabit. [Obs.]

The king's fisher *wonts* commonly by the waterside and nestles in hollow banks.
—L'Estrange.

wŏnt, *v.t.* to accustom; to habituate.

wŏnt'ed, *a.* 1. accustomed; habituated.

Again his *wonted* weapon proved.
—Spenser.

2. customary; habitual.

wŏnt'ed·ness, *n.* the state or quality of being accustomed.

wŏnt'less, *a.* unaccustomed; unused. [Archaic.]

wọọ, *v.t.*; wooed, *pt., pp.*; wooing, *ppr.* [ME. *wozen, wowen*, from AS. *wogian*, to woo, from *woh*, bent, crooked, inclined (toward).]

1. to court; to make love to, usually with the intention of proposing marriage.

2. to entreat solicitously; to coax; to urge.

Thee, chantress, oft the woods among,
I *woo*, to hear thy evensong. —Milton.

3. to seek to gain or bring about; to court the presence or favor of; as, to *woo* sleep; to *woo* the muses.

wọọ, *v.i.* 1. to court; to make love; as, one *woos* by ceaseless attentions.

2. to make entreaty.

I pray thee, sing, and let me *woo* no more.
—Shak.

wọọd, *a.* [AS. *wod*.] 1. out of one's mind; insane. [Archaic or Dial.]

2. violently angry; enraged. [Archaic or Dial.]

wọọd, *v.i.* to act like a madman; to be furious. [Obs.]

wood, *n.* [ME. *wode*; AS. *wudu*, earlier *widu*, a wood.]

1. [*often pl.*] a thick growth of trees; a forest; a grove.

2. the substance of trees; the hard fibrous substance beneath the bark in the stems and branches of trees and shrubs; xylem.

3. trees cut and dressed for use in making things; lumber or timber; as, a bridge constructed wholly of *wood*.

4. firewood.

5. something made of wood; specifically, (a) the cask as a container for liquor, as opposed to the bottle; as, whisky aged in *wood*; (b) a wood block (sense 2); (c) a wooden wind instrument, or wood winds collectively.

diffuse-porous wood; wood in which pores are numerous but not visible without the use of a magnifier, as in beech, sycamore, and birch.

hard wood; same as *hardwood*.

Nicaragua wood; the wood of a South American tree used in dyeing, closely related to brazil wood.
plastic wood; see under *plastic*.
ring-porous wood; wood in which rings are distinct in cross section and the pores are visible without the use of a magnifier, as in white oak and hickory.
soft wood; same as *softwood*.

wood, *a.* 1. made of wood; wooden.
2. for cutting, shaping, or holding wood.
3. growing or living in woods.

wood, *v.i.*; wooded, *pt., pp.*; wooding, *ppr.* to get or take on a supply of wood; as, the vessel *wooded* twice during the voyage.

wood, *v.t.* 1. to furnish with wood, especially firewood; as, to *wood* a steamboat or a locomotive.
2. to plant trees thickly over.

wood ag′ăte, agate resulting from the petrifaction of wood, in which the structure of the wood is plainly shown.

wood al′ço·hol, methyl alcohol; methanol.

wood äl′mŏnd, *Hippocratea comosa*, a West Indian plant; also, its edible seed which yields a valuable oil.

wood ȧ·nem′ō·nē, any of a number of related anemones with airy, white flowers; especially, *Anemone nemorosa*.

wood ȧnt, a large ant living in woods and forests and constructing large nests; specifically, (a) a large red ant, *Formica rufa*; (b) a white ant, *Termes flavipes*.

wood ap′ple, same as *elephant apple*.

wood-ap′ple gum, an adulterant of gum arabic, obtained from the elephant apple.

wood as′tẽr, any one of several plants of the aster family, indigenous to eastern North American woods, and characterized by blue, white, or lavender flowers.

wood av′ens, *Geum urbanum*, a European plant having bright-yellow flowers and growing in Massachusetts.

wood ąwl, the green woodpecker. [Brit. Dial.]

wood bab·ọọn′, a baboon, *Cynocephalus leucophæus*, of western Africa, resembling the mandrill; the drill.

wood′bärk, *n.* a brown color, yellowish red in hue.

wood bass, the green sunfish.

wood bed′strąw, *Galium sylvaticum*, a perennial European herb.

wood bet′ō·ny, 1. the betony.
2. a variety of lousewort, *Pedicularis canadensis*, of eastern North America, with hairy, fernlike leaves and yellowish or reddish flowers.

wood′bin, *n.* a bin for firewood.

wood′bīnd, *n.* same as *woodbine*.

wood′bīne, *n.* [ME. *wodebinde*; AS. *wudubinde*; *wudu*, wood, and *binde*, from *bindan*, to bind.]
1. a European variety of climbing honeysuckle, *Lonicera periclymenum*, with fragrant, yellowish white flowers.
2. the Virginia creeper, a woody vine with greenish flowers and dark-blue berries; American ivy.
Spanish woodbine; same as *arbor-vine*.

wood′-block, *a.* made or printed from wood blocks.

wood block, 1. a block of wood.
2. a printing die cut on fine-grained wood.
3. a woodcut.

wood bōr′ẽr, anything that bores in wood, as a mollusk, a crustacean, or an insect.

wood′bound, *a.* encumbered with tall woody hedgerows.

wood brick, a block of wood of the shape and size of a brick, inserted in brickwork as a hold for the joinery.

wood brọọm, the wild teazel, *Dipsacus sylvestris*.

wood′bur·y·tȳpe (-ber-), *n.* [after Sir Walter *Woodbury*, 19th-c. Eng. photographer and its inventor.]
1. a process in photographic printing in which a relief image, obtained on gelatin hardened after certain operations, is made to produce an intaglio impression upon a plate of lead or other soft metal, from which prints are made in a press.
2. a picture produced by this process.

wood çal′ȧ·mint, a labiate herb, *Calamintha sylvatica*, of Europe.

wood′çärv·ing, *n.* 1. the art or craft of carving wood by hand to make art objects or decorative features.
2. an object so made.

wood cell, a fusiform fiber or cell forming part of the composition of the wood of plants.

wood′chat, *n.* 1. any of several small Asiatic birds of the thrush group.
2. a shrike, *Lanius senator*, found in Europe and Africa.

wood′chuck, *n.* [folk-etymologized form of *wejack*, Am. Ind. (Algonquian) name.] any of a group of common American burrowing and hibernating marmots, *Arctomys monax*, with coarse, red-brown fur: also called *ground hog*.
woodchuck day; same as *ground-hog* day.

WOODCHUCK (20 in. long)

wood′chuck, *n.* the green woodpecker. [Brit. Dial.]

wood çōal, 1. charcoal.
2. lignite.

wood′çock, *n.*; *pl.* **wood′cocks** or **wood′cock,** [ME. *wodekoc*; AS. *wuducoc*; *wudu*, wood, and *coc*, a cock.]
1. either of two birds of the snipe family: (a) a small, European migratory game bird, *Scolopax rusticula*, with short legs and a long bill; (b) a similar North American bird, *Philohela minor*.

WOODCOCK (*Scolopax rusticula*)

2. the pileated woodpecker. [Brit. Dial.]
3. a woodcock shell.
4. a simpleton; a fool: in allusion to the ease with which the woodcock is taken in springs or in nets. [Obs.]

wood′çock owl, the short-eared owl, *Asio accipitrinus*. [Scot and Brit. Dial.]

wood′çock pī′lŏt, the European kinglet, *Regulus cristatus*. [Brit. Dial.]

wood′çock shell, a shell of any mollusk of the genus *Murex*, with a long spout or beak.

wood′çock snīpe, the great snipe.

wood′çrack″ẽr, *n.* the nuthatch, *Sitta cæsia*. [Brit. Dial.]

wood′çrȧft, *n.* 1. anything which pertains to the woods or forest, as camping, trapping, hunting, etc.
2. woodworking.
3. skill in either of these.

wood′çrȧfts″măn, *n.*; *pl.* **wood′çrȧfts″men,** a person who practices, or has skill in, woodcraft.

wood çul′vẽr, the wood pigeon. [Brit. Dial.]

wood′çut, *n.* an engraving on wood, or a print or impression from such an engraving.

wood′çut″tẽr, *n.* 1. a person who cuts wood, fells trees, etc.
2. a maker of woodcuts; an engraver on wood.

wood′çut″ting, *n.* 1. the act or employment of cutting wood or felling trees.
2. wood engraving.

wood dŏve, the stock dove.

wood duck, 1. the summer duck, *Aix sponsa*.
2. the hooded merganser. [Dial.]

wood′ed, *a.* covered with woods or trees; as, land well *wooded* and watered.

wood′en, *a.* 1. made of wood; consisting of wood; as, a *wooden* box; a *wooden* leg.
2. stiff, lifeless, expressionless, etc., as if made of wood.
3. stupid; listless; dull; thickheaded.
4. of or pertaining to the woods. [Obs.]
wooden brick; a wood brick.
wooden horse; see *Trojan horse* under *Trojan*.
wooden Indian; (a) a wooden image of an American Indian in a standing position, formerly placed in front of cigar stores as an advertisement; (b) [Colloq.] a person who is dull, spiritless, or inarticulate.
wooden wedding; the fifth anniversary of a marriage.

wood en·grāv′ẽr, 1. a person who makes wood engravings.
2 any beetle of the family *Scolytidæ*, particularly some species of *Pityophthorus* or *Ips* which burrow beneath the bark of trees causing marks resembling engravings.

wood en·grāv′ing, 1. the art or process of engraving on wood, or of producing raised surfaces by excision on blocks of wood, from which impressions can be transferred by means of a colored pigment to paper or other suitable material.
2. a woodcut.

wood′en·head (-hed), *n.* a stupid person; a blockhead. [Colloq.]

wood′en·head·ed (-hed-), *a.* stupid; blockish. [Colloq.]

wood′en·ly, *adv.* in a wooden manner.

wood′en·ness, *n.* the state or quality of being wooden.

wood′en·wāre, *n.* dishes, bowls, platters, etc. made of wood.

wood fẽrn, 1. the common polypody.
2. any variety of *Aspidium*.

wood fī′bẽr, powdered wood.

wood fret′tẽr, an insect or worm that bores into wood.

wood frog, a North American frog, *Rana sylvatica*, found in damp woods.

wood ġẽr·man′dẽr, same as *wood sage*.

wood grȧss, 1. a kind of great wood rush, *Luzula sylvatica*. [Brit. Dial.]
2. Indian grass.

wood grouse, a grouse found in the woods, as the capercaillie.

wood′hack, *n.* the yaffle. [Brit. Dial.]

wood hen, 1. a bird of the genus *Ocydromus*, of New Zealand and other islands of the Pacific.
2. same as *woodcock* (sense 1).

wood hew′ẽr (hū′) 1. the woodpecker.
2. one who chops wood.

wood′hōle, *n.* a place where wood is stored.

wood họọp′ōe, an African hoopoe of the family *Irrisoridæ*.

wood′hörse, *n.* 1. a sawhorse.
2. a walking stick insect.

wood′house, *n.* a house or shed in which wood is deposited and sheltered from the weather.

wood hȳ′ȧ·cinth, the wild hyacinth; bluebell.

wood ī′bis, a large, white, heronlike stork, *Mycteria americana*, with a slender, downward curving bill and naked head, found in the wooded swamps of the southern United States and of Central and South America.

wood′i·ness, *n.* the state or quality of being woody.

wood′job″bẽr, *n.* a woodpecker.

wood′knack″ẽr (-nak″), *n.* the green woodpecker. [Brit. Dial.]

wood′land″ (*or* -lănd), *n.* land covered with woods or trees; a woods or forest.

wood′lănd, *a.* of, pertaining to, or inhabiting the woods; sylvan; as, *woodland* birds.
woodland caribou; the common North American caribou, *Rangifer caribou*, of wooded regions, as distinguished from the *barren-ground caribou*, which lives beyond the limits of trees.

wood′lănd·ẽr, *n.* one who lives in the woods.

wood lärk, a small European lark, *Lullula arborea*, which, like the skylark, utters its notes while on the wing, and which habitually perches on trees.

wood lau′rel, an Old World evergreen shrub, *Daphne laureola*, the spurge laurel.

wood leop′ărd (lep′), a white moth with black spots, *Zeuzera pyrina*, the larva of which lives in wood; a leopard moth.

wood′less, *a.* without wood.

wood′less·ness, *n.* the state or quality of being woodless.

wood lil′y, 1. the lily of the valley.
2. the wintergreen, *Pyrola minor*.
3. any species of *Trillium*.

wood lock, in nautical usage, a piece of elm or other hard wood, close fitted and sheathed with copper, in the throating or score of the pintle, to keep the rudder from rising.

wood lot, a piece of land on which trees are cultivated and cut.

wood louse, 1. any of a large number of crustaceans of the family *Oniscidæ*, with flattened, oval, segmented bodies, found in damp soil, under decaying wood, etc.
2. any one of the *Termitidæ*.
3. a book louse.

wọọd′ly, *adv.* madly; furiously. [Obs.]

wood′măn, *n.*; *pl.* **wood′men,** 1. a forest officer, appointed to take care of the king's woods; a forester. [Chiefly Brit.]
2. a sportsman; a hunter.
3. one who cuts down trees; a woodcutter.
4. a dweller in the forest.

wood mīte, any mite of the family *Oribatidæ,* having a horny integument.

wood'mŏn"gẽr, *n.* one who sells wood. [Rare.]

wood mouse, a mouse which lives in the woods; specifically, (a) the European field mouse, *Mus sylvaticus;* (b) any one of a number of white-footed mice.

wọọd'ness, *n.* anger; madness; rage. [Archaic.]

wood net'tle, a perennial nettle, *Laportea canadensis,* found in damp woods of the United States and Canada.

wood nīght'shāde (nīt'), the bittersweet; the woody nightshade.

wood'-nōte", *n.* a wild or natural note, like that of a forest bird or animal.

wood nut, the filbert.

wood nymph, 1. a goddess of the woods; a dryad.
2. any of several South American hummingbirds, as *Thalurania glaucopis.*
3. any one of several brilliantly colored moths of the genus *Eudryas,* the larvae of which feed on grapevines.
4. any of a group of brown and gray butterflies with eyespots on the wings.

wood of'fẽr·ing, wood burned on the altar.

wood'-ŏf-the-Hō"ly-Crọss' (-ŏv-), *n.* the mistletoe: so called because formerly believed to possess healing powers.

wood oil, any one of several resinous substances; specifically, (a) gurjun; (b) tung oil; (c) a product of the satinwood, *Chloroxylon swietenia.*

wood ō'păl, wood petrified with opal.

wood pā'pẽr, any paper made of wood pulp.

wood pēa, the heath pea.

wood'peck, *n.* the woodpecker. [Rare.]

wood'peck"ẽr, *n.* any bird of the genus *Picus,* or one of the allied genera of the large family *Picidæ.* They are climbing birds, comprising about 250 species found in nearly all parts of the world. The tail feathers are rigid and pointed at the tip, to assist in climbing, and the strong chisellike bill is adapted for boring into the bark and wood of trees in search of insects or insect larvae for food.
downy woodpecker; a small black and white woodpecker, *Dryobates pubescens,* very common in eastern North America.
golden-winged woodpecker; the common flicker, *Colaptes auratus.*
greater spotted woodpecker; a large woodpecker, *Dendrocopus major,* widely distributed through Europe and Asia.
green woodpecker; see under *green.*
hairy woodpecker; a black and white woodpecker, *Dryobates villosus,* of eastern North America.
ivory-billed woodpecker; same as *ivorybill.*
lesser spotted woodpecker; a small black and white woodpecker, *Dendrocopus minor,* widely distributed in Europe.
pileated woodpecker; see under *pileate.*

RED-HEADED WOODPECKER
(9 in. long)

red-bellied woodpecker; one of the commonest woodpeckers of the United States, *Melanerpes carolinus.*
three-toed woodpecker; any one of several American woodpeckers lacking the inner hind toe.
yellow-bellied woodpecker; a sapsucker.

wood pē'wee, a North American tyrant fly catcher of the genus *Contopus.*

wood pīe, the great or lesser spotted woodpecker; also, the green woodpecker. [Brit. Dial.]

wood pig'eŏn, 1. the ringdove, *Columba palumbus,* or any of several related pigeons; also, the stockdove.
2. a wild pigeon of western North America; the band-tailed pigeon, *Columba fasciata.* [Dial.]

wood'pīle, *n.* a pile of wood, especially of firewood.

wood pulp, pulp made from the fiber of wood, for use in the manufacture of paper.

wood quāil, an East Indian crested quail, *Rollulus roulroul,* or any other species of the same genus.

wood'-quēest, *n.* the ringdove. [Brit. Dial.]

wood rab'bit, the cottontail. [Dial.]

wood rat, a pack rat.

wood reed, 1. feather-top grass, *Calamagrostis epigeios.*
2. a tall sweet-scented grass, *Cinna arundinacea.*
Also called *wood reed grass.*

wood'reeve, *n.* in England, the steward or overseer of a wood.

wood rob'in, 1. the wood thrush. [Dial.]
2. an Australian warbler.

wood'rock, *n.* a compact variety of asbestos.

wood'ruff, wood'rọọf, *n.* [ME. *woderove;* AS. *wuderofe, wudurofe,* the first part being *wudu,* wood, the latter doubtful.] any of various related European plants, especially *Asperula odorata,* with an erect stem springing from a creeping rootstock, the lily-shaped flowers being white, pink, or blue with the leaves arranged in circles around the stem. The plant has an odor like that of sweet clover, and is commonly called *sweet woodruff.*

wood rush, a plant of the genus *Luzula.*

wood sāge, any of various plants of the genus *Teucrium,* as *Teucrium scorodonia,* having the smell of garlic, and a very bitter taste; wood germander.

wood sand'pī·pẽr, an Old World bird, *Totanus glareola,* resembling the redshank.

wood sąw, a bucksaw.

wood scręw (skrụ), the ordinary iron or steel screw having a conical point and spiral threads, for uniting pieces of wood.

wood'sēre, *n.* the time when there is no sap in a tree. [Obs.]

wood'sēre, *a.* dry; barren. [Obs.]

wood'shed, *n.* a shed for storing firewood.

wood shel'drāke, the hooded merganser. [Dial.]

wood'shock, *n.* the pekan, or fisher.

wood shrīke, an African bird of genus *Prionops.*

Wood'si·ȧ, *n.* [after Joseph *Woods* (1776–1864), a British botanist.] a genus of polypodiaceous ferns with wiry leafstalks, found chiefly on rock ledges; also, [w–] any plant of this genus.

wood slāve, a small lizard, *Mabouya agilis,* of Jamaica.

woodṣ'măn, *n.;* *pl.* **woodṣ'men,** 1. a person who lives or works in the woods, as a hunter, trapper, woodcutter, etc.
2. a person accustomed to the woods or skilled in woodcraft.

wood snīpe, the American woodcock. [Dial.]

wood sor'rel, [transl. of MFr. *sorrel de boys.*] any of a number of related plants of the genus *Oxalis,* especially *Oxalis acetosella,* having white, pink, red, yellow, or purplish flowers made up of five petals on a cone-shaped tube; oxalis.

wood spir'it, same as *methanol.*

wood'spīte, *n.* the green woodpecker. [Brit. Dial.]

wood stamp, an engraved or carved stamp or block of wood, to impress figures or colors on fabrics.

wood stär, any of certain hummingbirds of the genus *Calothorax.*

wood'stōne, *n.* petrified wood.

wood stork, a wood ibis.

wood swäl'lōw, any bird of the genus *Artamus,* or related genera, resembling the swallow.

woodṣ'y, *a.;* *comp.* woodsier; *superl.* woodsiest, of, characteristic of, or like the woods; as, a *woodsy* stream.

wood'tap"pẽr, *n.* a woodpecker. [Brit. Dial.]

wood tär, a dark sticky, siruplike substance obtained by the dry distillation of wood and used in the preservation of wood, etc.

wood thrush, 1. a large thrush, *Turdus mustelinus,* of eastern North America, having a rusty-brown mantle and a strong, clear song.
2. the European missel thrush.

wood tick, any tick of the family *Ixodidæ,* the young of which transfer themselves from the bushes where hatched to any animal coming in contact with them. They produce an itching and often a troublesome sore.

wood tin, a brown variety of oxide of tin, found in Cornwall and Mexico.

wood tit'mouse, the goldcrest.

wood tor'toise (-tis), a land tortoise, *Glyptemys insculpta.*

wood tũrn'ẽr, a person who turns wood on a lathe.

wood'-tũrn·ing, *a.* of or for wood turning.

wood tũrn'ing, the art or process of turning, or shaping, wood on a lathe.

wood vīne, the bryony.

wood vin'ē·gär, pyroligneous acid or crude acetic acid obtained by the distillation of wood.

wood'wąll, wood'wāle, *n.* the green woodpecker. [Brit. Dial.]

wood wąr'blẽr, a warbling bird frequenting the woods; as (a) any American bird of the warbler family; (b) the English wood wren.

wood'wąrd, *n.* an officer of the forest whose duty it is to guard the woods. [Brit.]

Wood·wąr'di·ȧ, *n.* a genus of ferns, named after Thomas J. Woodward, English botanist, comprising six species, three of which are American.

wood'wax"en, *n.* a plant of the pea family, with clusters of showy, yellow flowers and striped branches: also *woadwaxen, woodwax, woodwash.*

wood'-wind, *a.* designating or of wood winds.

wood wind, 1. [*pl.*] the wind instruments of an orchestra made, especially originally, of wood: the principal modern wood winds are the clarinet, oboe, bassoon, flute, and English horn.
2. any of these instruments.

wood wool, fine pine shavings treated for use in dressing wounds.

wood'wŏrk, *n.* 1. work done in wood.
2. things made of wood, especially the interior moldings, doors, stairs, etc. of a house.

wood'wŏrk·ẽr, *n.* a person who makes things out of wood.

wood'wŏrk·ing, *n.* the art or process of making things out of wood.

wood'wŏrk·ing, *a.* of woodworking.

wood'wŏrm, *n.* a worm that is bred in wood.

wood wren, (a) the wood warbler; (b) the willow warbler.

wood'y, *a.* 1. covered with trees; wooded; as, *woody* land; a *woody* region.
2. consisting of wood; ligneous; as, the *woody* parts of plants.
3. of a wood or woods. [Rare.]
4. like wood.
woody fiber; wood fiber; wood tissue.
woody nightshade; bittersweet.
woody pear; see *wooden pear* under *pear.*

wood'yärd, *n.* a yard for storing or sawing wood.

wood'y as'tẽr, a woody herb, *Xylorrhiza parryi,* family *Carduaceæ,* of the western United States, very poisonous to sheep.

wọọ'ẽr, *n.* one who courts, or woos; a suitor.

wọọf, *n.* [altered, by influence of *weave,* from ME. *oof.*]
1. the threads that cross the warp of a woven fabric; the weft.
2. texture; cloth; fabric; as, a pall of softest *woof.*

wọọ'fell, *n.* the blackbird of Europe.

wọọf'y, *a.* having a close texture; dense; as, a *woofy* cloud.

wọọ·họọ', *n.* the sailfish.

wọọ'ing, *n.* the act of one who woos.

wọọ'ing·ly, *adv.* in a wooing manner; enticingly.

wool, *n.* [ME. *wolle;* AS. *wull, wul,* wool.]
1. the soft, curly or crisped hair of sheep.
2. the hair of some other animals, as the goat, llama, or alpaca, having a similar texture.
3. woolen yarn used for knitting, etc.
4. cloth, clothing, etc. made of wool.
5. short, curly human hair: a humorous usage.
6. any material with a texture like wool; as, rock *wool.*
all wool and a yard wide; genuine or admirable.
dead-pulled wool; dead wool.
great cry and little wool; much ado about nothing.
mineral wool; a fibrous material made from melted slag and used as wall insulation in buildings: called also ***slag wool*** and ***mineral cotton.***

philosopher's wool; zinc oxide.
to pull the wool over one's eyes; to deceive or trick one.
wool, *a.* of wool or woolen goods.
wool, *v.t.* to rumple the hair of. [Slang.]
wool'-bear"ing, *a.* yielding wool.
wool bŭrl'ẽr, a person who removes the little knots or extraneous matter from wool and from woolen cloth.
wool clip, annual production of wool.
wool cŏmb'ẽr (kōm'), one who or that which combs wool.
woold, *v.t.*; woolded, *pt., pp.*; woolding, *ppr.* [D. *woelen*, to wind, wrap.] in nautical usage, to wind, particularly to wind (a rope or chain) round a mast or yard to strengthen it.
woold'ẽr, *n.* 1. a stick used as a lever in woolding.
2. in ropemaking, one of the pins passing through the top, forming a handle to it.
woold'ing, *n.* 1. the act of winding, as a rope round a mast.
2. a rope used for binding masts and spars.
wool'-dyed (-dīd), *a.* dyed in the form of wool or yarn before being made into cloth, as distinguished from *piece-dyed* or *yarn-dyed*.
wooled, *a.* having wool (of a specified grade or fineness): used in hyphenated compounds; as, this sheep is fine-*wooled*.
wool'en, wool'len, *a.* 1. made of wool; consisting of wool; as, *woolen* cloth.
2. pertaining to wool or woolen cloth; as, *woolen* manufactures; a *woolen* merchant.
wool'en, wool'len, *n.* [*pl.*] woolen goods or clothing.
wool·en·ette', wool·len·ette', *n.* a thin woolen fabric.
wool'en scrib'blẽr, a wool scribbler.
woo'lẽrt, *n.* the barn owl. [Brit. Dial.]
wool fat, 1. lanolin, a fatty oil found on sheep's wool: also *wool grease*.
2. same as *suint*.
wool'fell, *n.* the pelt of a wool-bearing animal with the wool still on it.
wool'gath"ẽr·ing, *n.* [used in reference to gathering tufts of wool caught on thorns and hedges.] absent-mindedness or daydreaming.
wool'gath"ẽr·ing, *a.* absent-minded or indulging in fancies.
wool grȧss, in botany, a woolly-spiked bulrush, *Scirpus eriophorum*, of eastern North America.
wool'grōw"ẽr, *n.* a person who raises sheep for wool.
wool'grōw"ing, *a.* producing sheep and wool; as, a *woolgrowing* region.
wool hall, a trade market in the woolen districts. [Brit.]
wool'head (-hed), *n.* the buffle duck.
wool'i·ness, *n.* woolliness.
wool'len, *a.* and *n.* woolen.
wool'li·ness, *n.* the state or quality of being woolly: also spelled *wooliness*.
wool'ly, *a.*; *comp.* woollier; *superl.* woolliest. 1. of or like wool.
2. bearing wool.
3. covered with wool or something resembling wool in texture.
4. having a soft, clinging consistency: said of some foods.
5. having characteristics of the early frontier life of the western United States; rough and uncivilized: used chiefly in *wild and woolly*.
woolly bear; the larva of several species of moths, covered with long soft hairs, as the salt-marsh caterpillar, the red and black woolly bear, or larva of the isabella moth.
woolly louse; an aphid, *Schizoneura lanigera*, which infests the apple tree.
woolly macaco; the Madagascar lemur, *Lemur mongoz*.
woolly maki; a Madagascar lemur, *Indris laniger*: also called *woolly lemur* and *woolly indris*.
woolly monkey; any South American monkey of the genus *Lagothrix*.
woolly rhinoceros; *Rhinoceros tichorhinus*, an extinct rhinoceros which lived in arctic regions.
wool'ly, *n.*; *pl.* **wool'lies**, 1. in the western United States, a sheep.
2. a woolen garment, especially one with a fleecelike surface.
Also spelled *wooly*.
wool'ly butt or **but**, either of two Australian timber trees of the genus *Eucalyptus*, *Eucalyptus longifolia* and *Eucalyptus viminalis*, attaining a height of from 100 to 150 feet. Their wood is used for work requiring strength and toughness.

wool'măn, *n.*; *pl.* **wool'men**, a dealer in wool.
wool'mŏn"gẽr, *n.* a woolman.
wool'pack, *n.* 1. a large bag of canvas, cotton, etc. into which wool or fleece is packed for carrying or sale.
2. a bale of wool so packed, usually weighing 240 pounds.
3. a fleecy cumulus cloud.
wool'sack, *n.* 1. a sack or bag of wool.
2. the seat of the British Lord Chancellor in the House of Lords, being a large, square cushion stuffed with wool.
wool'sey, *n.* same as *linsey-woolsey*, sense 1.
wool'sort"ẽr, *n.* a person who sorts wool according to its quality.
woolsorters' disease; pulmonary anthrax, an occupational disease of workers in unprocessed wool, contracted by inhaling the spores of the anthrax bacillus.
wool'sōw"ẽr, *n.* a woolly gall found on the twigs of the American white oak, produced by the gallfly, *Andricus seminator*.
wool stā'ple, a city or town where wool used to be brought for sale. [Brit.]
wool stā'plẽr, 1. one who deals in wool.
2. a woolsorter.
wool'stock, *n.* a heavy hammer used in fulling woolen cloth.
wool'wărd, *adv.* in wool or woolen underclothing. [Obs.]
I have no shirt; I go *woolward* for penance.
—Shak.
wool'wīnd"ẽr, *n.* one who winds wool into bundles to be packed for sale.
wool'y, *a.*; *comp.* woolier; *superl.* wooliest, same as *woolly*.
wool'y, *n.*; *pl.* **wool'ies**, same as *woolly*.
woom, *n.* [etym. obscure.] beaver fur. [Slang.]
woom'e·rȧ, *n.* a womera.
woon, *n.* [Burmese *wun*, a burden.] in Burma, a high official; a governor.
woo'rȧ·li, woo'rȧ·rȧ, woo'rȧ·ri, *n.* same as *curare*.
wootz (woots), *n.* [said to be a corruption of Canarese *ukku*, steel.] a kind of steel made in the East Indies by a process direct from the ore.
wooz'y, *a.*; *comp.* woozier; *superl.* wooziest, prob. coined after *wooze*, var. of *ooze*.] befuddled, as with liquor; muddled. [Slang.]
wop, *n.* a dark-skinned person of Latin, especially Italian, descent: vulgar term of prejudice and contempt. [Slang.]
wō'pen, *v.* obsolete past participle of *weep*.
Worces'tẽr chī'nȧ (woos'), a fine china or porcelain made at Worcester, England, from 1751: also *Worcester porcelain* and, by royal warrant, *Royal Worcester*.
Worces'tẽr·shire sauce, a spicy sauce for meats, poultry, etc., containing soy, vinegar, and other ingredients: originally made in Worcester, England.
wŏrd, *n.* [AS. *word*, a word; akin to G. *wort*.]
1. a brief expression; a remark; as, a *word* of advice.
2. a promise; affirmation; assurance; as, he gave his *word*.
3. news; information; tidings; as, no *word* from home.
4. (a) a password; signal; as, they gave the *word*; (b) a command; order.
5. [*usually pl.*] (a) talk; speech; (b) lyrics; text; libretto.
6. [*pl.*] a quarrel; dispute.
7. a speech sound or series of them, having meaning and used as a unit of language: words may consist of a single morpheme or of combinations of morphemes.
8. a letter or group of letters, written or printed, representing such a unit of language.
9. a saying; proverb. [Archaic.]
a good word; favorable mention; praise; commendation; as, speak *a good word* for me.
a man of his word; a person who keeps his promises.
a play upon words; see under *play*.
at a word; in quick response to a request or command; immediately.
a word and a blow; an angry word succeeded by a blow.
by word of mouth; see under *mouth*.
good word; favorable news; as, what's the *good word?* [Colloq.]
hard words; (a) words not easily written or spelled; (b) angry words; abuse.
household word; see under *household*.
in a word; briefly; in short; to sum up.
in so many words; precisely; succinctly.
in word; in declaration only; merely in profession.

Let us not love *in word*, but in deed and in truth. —1 John iii. 18.
of few words; untalkative; laconic.
of many words; wordy; talkative; garrulous.
the Word; (a) the Logos; (b) the Bible; Scriptures.
to be as good as one's word; see under *good*.
to break one's word; to fail to keep one's promise.
to eat one's words; see under *eat*.
to give one's word; to promise.
to hang on one's words; to listen to one eagerly.
to have a word with one; to have a conversation with one, usually in private.
to have no words for; to be incapable of describing.
to have words with; to argue angrily with.
to take one at one's word; to take one's words literally or seriously and, often, act accordingly.
to take the words out of one's mouth; to say what one was about to say oneself.
(*upon*) *my word*; indeed! really!: an exclamation of surprise, irritation, etc.
word for word; verbatim; in precisely the same words.
wŏrd, *v.i.* to use words; to speak. [Archaic or Dial.]
wŏrd, *v.t.* 1. to express in words; to phrase; as, take care to *word* ideas with propriety.
2. to flatter. [Obs.]
wŏrd'āġe, *n.* words collectively, or the number of words (of a novel, story, etc.).
wŏrd'-blīnd, *a.* affected by word blindness.
wŏrd blīnd'ness, a cerebral disorder characterized by the inability to read; alexia.
wŏrd'book, *n.* [modeled on G. *wörterbuch*, a dictionary, lit., a wordbook; *wörter*, pl. of *wort*, a word, and *buch*, a book.]
1. a vocabulary; a dictionary; a lexicon.
2. a libretto.
3. a book of song lyrics.
wŏrd'-bound, *a.* restrained or restricted in speech; unable or unwilling to express oneself; also, bound by one's word.
wŏrd'build"ing, *n.* the formation, construction, or composition of words; the process of forming or making words.
wŏrd'-catch"ẽr, *n.* one who cavils at words; a captious person.
wŏrd deaf'ness (def'), a cerebral disorder characterized by the loss of the ability to understand spoken words, though the ability to hear and to speak is unimpaired; auditory aphasia.
wŏrd'ẽr, *n.* one who puts something into words.
wŏrd'i·ly, *adv.* in a verbose or wordy manner.
wŏrd'i·ness, *n.* the state or quality of being wordy.
wŏrd'ing, *n.* 1. the act of expressing in words.
2. the manner of expressing in words; the choice and expression of words; phrasing; as, his *wording* of the idea is very judicious.
wŏrd'ish, *a.* verbose. [Rare.]
wŏrd'ish·ness, *n.* the quality or state of being wordy; wordiness. [Rare.]
wŏr'dle, *n.* one of the adjustable pieces in a drawplate which determines the cross section of wire or pipe as it is drawn through.
wŏrd'less, *a.* 1. without words; speechless.
2. unexpressed.
3. inexpressible.
Wŏrd ŏf God, the Bible.
wŏrd ŏf hon'ŏr (on'), pledged word; solemn promise.
wŏrd or'dẽr, the arrangement of words in a phrase, clause, or sentence.
wŏrd pāint'ing, the act of describing vividly by words only.
wŏrd piç'tūre, a vivid description of an object by means of words.
wŏrd'plāy, *n.* 1. a subtle or clever exchange of words; repartee.
2. punning or a pun.
wŏrd proc'ess·ing, an automated, computerized system, incorporating variously an electronic typewriter, video terminal, a printer, etc., used to prepare, edit, store, transmit, or duplicate letters, reports, records, etc., as for a business.
wŏrd'smith, *n.* a person, especially a professional writer, with a skillful, but often facile, use of language.
wŏrd squāre (skwãr), a square made of letters so arranged that if read either vertically or horizontally the letters form the same words:

t h e
h o e
e e l

wŏrd'y, *a.*; *comp.* wordier; *superl.* wordiest. 1. using or containing many or too many words; verbose; as, a *wordy* speaker; a *wordy* orator.
2. of words; verbal.

wōre, *v.* past tense of *wear.*

wŏrk, *v.i.*; worked (wŭrkt) *or* wrought (rąt), *pt., pp.*; working, *ppr.* [ME. *werchen, wirchen*; AS. *wyrcan, wircan, wercan,* to work, from *weorc,* work.]
1. to exert oneself in order to do or make something; to do work; to labor; to toil.
2. to be employed.
3. to perform its function; to operate; to act.
4. to ferment.
5. to operate effectively; to be effectual; as, the makeshift *works.*
6. to produce results or exert an influence; as, let it *work* in their minds.
7. to be manipulated, kneaded, etc.; as, this putty *works* easily.
8. to move, proceed, etc. slowly and with or as with difficulty.
9. to move, twitch, etc. as from agitation; as, his face *worked* with emotion.
10. to change into a specified condition, as by repeated movement; as, the door *worked* loose.
11. to make a passage; as, her elbow had *worked* through her sleeve.
12. in nautical usage, to strain so, as in a storm, that the fastenings become slack: said of a ship.
to work against; to strive against; to oppose.
to work and turn; in printing, to print a form on one side, reverse the sheet and print once more from the same form.
to work in; to be introduced or inserted.
to work on; (a) to influence; (b) to try to persuade.
to work out; (a) to make its way out, as from being embedded; (b) to result in some way; (c) to add up to a total (*at* a specified amount); (d) to develop.
to work to windward; in nautical usage, to sail or ply against the wind; to beat.
to work up; (a) to make one's (or its) way up; to advance; to rise; (b) to develop.

wŏrk, *v.t.* 1. to bestow labor, toil, or exertion upon; to convert to or prepare for use by labor or effort; as, to *work* land.
2. to extract useful materials or products from by labor; to operate; as, to *work* a mine.
3. to produce, accomplish, or acquire by labor, toil, or exertion; to effect; to perform.

The change shall please, nor shall it matter aught
Who *works* the wonder, if it be but wrought.
—Cowper.

4. to be the cause of; to effect; to bring about; as, to *work* a change; to *work* havoc.
5. to put or set in motion, action, or exertion; to keep busy, or in a state of activity; as, to *work* a team of horses.
6. to direct the action of; to manage; to handle; as, to *work* an engine or a ship.
7. to transact; to manage; to carry out.
8. to bring by action or motion to any state or condition.

So the pure limpid stream, when foul with stains
Works itself clear. —Addison.

9. to attain or make by continuous and severe labor, exertion, struggle, or striving; to force gradually and with labor or exertion; as, he *worked* his way through the crowd.
10. to solve; to work out; as, to *work* a problem.
11. to influence; to persuade; to induce; as, *work* him to your way of thinking.
12. to make into shape; to form; to fashion; to mold; as, to *work* clay.
13. to weave, knit, or embroider, etc.; as, she *worked* the sweater.
14. to operate upon, as a purgative or cathartic; to purge. [Obs. or Dial.]
15. to excite by degrees: to act upon so as to throw into a state of perturbation or agitation; to agitate violently; as, he *worked* himself into a passion.
16. to cause to ferment, as liquor.
17. to use artifice with (a person) to gain some profit or advantage. [Colloq.]
18. to draw, paint, or carve, etc. (a portrait or likeness).
19. to manipulate; to knead; as, *work* the butter well.
20. to carry on activity in; to cover; as, the salesman who *works* this region.
21. to make use of, especially by artful contriving; as, *work* your connections. [Colloq.]
to work double tides; in nautical usage, to perform the labor of three days in two.
to work in: to introduce or insert.
to work into; to insinuate into; as, *to work* oneself *into* favor or confidence.
to work off; to get rid of or dissipate, as by exertion; as, *to work off* a state of intoxication.
to work one's passage; in nautical usage, to pay for a passage by doing duty on board the ship.
to work out; (a) to exhaust (a mine, etc.); (b) to pay off (an obligation) by work instead of in money; (c) to bring about by work; to accomplish; (d) to solve; (e) to calculate; (f) to elaborate; (g) to put into practice.
to work up; (a) to manipulate, mix, etc. into a specified object or shape; (b) to elaborate; (c) to acquire knowledge of or skill at; (d) to arouse; to excite; (e) in nautical usage, to punish by keeping constantly employed at unnecessary work, as a crew.

wŏrk, *n.* [ME. *werk*; AS. *weorc, worc, werc,* work.]
1. bodily or mental effort exerted to do or make something; purposeful activity; labor; toil.
2. employment; as, out of *work.*
3. occupation; business; trade; craft; profession; as, his *work* is selling.
4. (a) something one is making, doing, or acting upon, especially as one's occupation or duty; a task; an undertaking; as, he laid out his *work*; (b) the amount of this: as, a day's *work.*
5. something that has been made or done; result of effort or activity; specifically, (a) [*usually pl.*] an act; a deed; as, a person of good *works*; (b) [*pl.*] collected writings; as, the *works* of Whitman; (c) [*pl.*] engineering structures, as bridges, dams, docks, etc.; (d) a fortification; (e) needlework; embroidery (f) a work of art.
6. material that is being or is to be processed, as in a machine tool, in some stage of manufacture.
7. [*pl.*] [*construed as sing.*] a place where work is done, as a factory, public utility plant, etc.
8. [*pl.*] the working parts of a watch, etc.; mechanism.
9. manner, style, quality, rate, etc. of working; workmanship.
10. foam due to fermentation, as in cider.
11. in mechanics, transference of force from one body or system to another, measured by the product of the force and the amount of displacement in the line of force.
12. [*pl.*] in theology, moral acts: distinguished from *faith.*
at work; working.
external work; in physics, work done against external forces as a result of heat imparted, as that resulting from the expansion of a body or from its diminution in volume.
internal work; in physics, work resulting from the introduction of heat among the molecules of a body, as in a change in condition or an increase in temperature.
out of work; not having any remunerative employment; unemployed.
to get the works; to be the victim of extreme measures. [Slang.]
to give one the works; (a) to murder one; (b) to subject one to an ordeal, either maliciously or jokingly. [Slang.]
to make short (or *quick*) *work of*; to do or dispose of quickly.
to shoot the works; (a) to risk everything on one chance or play; (b) to make a supreme effort or attempt. [Slang.]
Syn.—labor, toil, drudgery, employment, occupation, action, performance, feat, achievement.

wŏrk·ȧ·bil'i·ty, *n.* the state or quality of being workable.

wŏrk'ȧ·ble, *a.* 1. that can be worked; worth working; as, a *workable* mine; *workable* coal.
2. feasible; practicable, as a plan, method, etc.

wŏrk'ȧ·dāy, *a.* 1. of or suitable for working days; everyday.
2. commonplace; ordinary.

wŏrk''ȧ·hol'iç, *n.* [*work* and *-a-* and alco*holic.*] a person having a compulsive need to work.

wŏrk'-and-turn', *a.* of printing that is done all on one form, the sheet being turned over and printed upon once more from the same form. See *to work and turn,* under *work, v.i.*

wŏrk'bag, *n.* a bag for holding implements and materials for work, especially needlework.

wŏrk'bas''ket, *n.* a receptacle which contains implements and materials for work, or in which articles needing repair are deposited.

wŏrk'bench, *n.* a table at which work is done, as by a mechanic.

wŏrk'book, *n.* 1. a book for the use of students, containing questions and exercises based on a textbook or course of study.
2. a book containing instructions on the method of operation.
3. a book in which one keeps a record of work planned or done.

wŏrk'box, *n.* a box for holding implements and materials for work, especially those used in sewing, etc.

wŏrk'dāy, *n.* [ME. *werkdai,* prob. from *werk* and *dai*; AS. had *weorcdæg.*]
1. a day on which work is done; a working day.
2. the part of a day during which work is done; as, a 7-hour *workday.*

wŏrk'dāy, *a.* workaday.

wŏrk'ẽr, *n.* 1. a person, animal, or thing that works; specifically, (a) a person who works for a living, either with hand or brain; especially, one who does industrial or manual work for wages; (b) any of a class of sterile or sexually imperfect female ants, bees, wasps, etc. that do work for the colony.
2. in printing, an electrotype used to print from, as distinguished from one used as a mold for making duplicate electrotypes.
3. one of the urchins in a carding machine.
4. a tanners' tool for scraping hides.

wŏrk'ẽr cell, a cell for the larva of a worker bee.

wŏrk'ẽr çōmb (kōm), the part of a honeycomb containing the worker cells.

wŏrk'ẽrș' çom·pen·sā'tion, compensation to an employee for injury or occupational disease suffered in connection with employment, paid under a government-supervised insurance system contributed to by employers.

wŏrk'fel''lōw, *n.* one sharing the same employment with another; a fellow worker.

wŏrk'fōlk (-fōk), *n.pl.* working people.

wŏrk'fōlks, *n.pl.* workfolk.

wŏrk'fụl, *a.* industrious; diligent. [Obs.]

wŏrk'house, *n.* 1. originally, a workshop.
2. in England, formerly, a poorhouse.
3. a kind of prison where vagrants and petty offenders are confined and made to work.

wŏrk'ing, *a.* 1. that works.
2. of, for, used in, or taken up by work; as, a *working* day, *working* clothes.
3. sufficient to get work done; as, a *working* majority.
4. on which further work is or may be based; as, a *working* hypothesis.
5. moving or jerking convulsively, as from emotion: said of the face or facial features.

wŏrk'ing, *n.* 1. the act or process of a person or thing that works (in various senses).
2. convulsive movement or jerking, as of the face.
3. slow or gradual progress involving great effort or exertion.
4. [*usually pl.*] a part of a mine, quarry, etc. where work is or has been done.

wŏrk'ing cap'i·tăl, 1. in accounting, excess of readily convertible assets over current liabilities.
2. in finance, the part of a company's capital that remains readily convertible into cash.

wŏrk'ing-çlȧss, *a.* of or characteristic of the working class.

wŏrk'ing çlȧss, workers as a class; especially, industrial workers as a class; proletariat.

wŏrk'ing-dāy, *a.* same as *workaday.*

wŏrk'ing dāy, 1. a day on which work is ordinarily done, as distinguished from a Sunday, holiday, etc.; a workday.
2. the part of a day during which work is done; specifically, the number of hours constituting a day's work.

wŏrk'ing dra̤w'ing, a plan or sketch drawn to scale and used as a basis for actual work.

wŏrk'ing·man, *n.*; *pl.* **wŏrk'ing·men,** a worker; especially, an industrial or manual laborer.

wŏrk'ing mod'el, a miniature machine showing the operations to be performed by a machine when constructed for actual use.

wŏrk'ing pā'pẽrș, any official papers that legalize the employment of a minor.

wŏrk'ing pär'ty, a detail of soldiers, etc. doing a task, aside from their regular duties.

wŏrk'ing sub'stănce, the air, gas, or liquid that works the pistons, vanes, etc. of an engine.

wŏrk'ing·wom"ăn (-woom"), *n.*; *pl.* **wŏrk'ing·wom"en** (-wim"), a woman worker; especially, a woman industrial or manual worker.

wŏrk'less, *a.* 1. without work; not working.
2. without works; not carried out or exemplified in works; as, a *workless* faith. [Obs.]

wŏrk'lōad, *n.* the amount of work assigned for completion within a given period of time.

wŏrk'măn, *n.*; *pl.* **wŏrk'men,** 1. a laborer; a worker.
2. a person who accomplishes his work in a specified way; as, a careful *workman.*

wŏrk'măn·līke, *a.* resembling or characteristic of a skillful workman; well performed; skillful.

wŏrk'măn·līke, *adv.* in a workmanlike manner; skillfully.

wŏrk'măn·ly, *a.* workmanlike; expert.

wŏrk'măn·ly, *adv.* workmanlike.

wŏrk'măn·ship, *n.* 1. skill as a workman; craftsmanship; artistry.
2. evidence of this skill in something produced; execution; as, the vase has the highest *workmanship.*
3. something produced; as, the bookcases are my *workmanship.*

wŏrk'mas"tēr, *n.* the author, producer, performer, or designer of a work, especially of a great or important work; a skilled workman or artificer. [Rare.]

wŏrk of ärt, 1. something produced in one of the fine arts, especially in one of the plastic or graphic arts, as a painting, sculpture, carving, etc.
2. anything beautifully made, played, sung, acted, etc.

wŏrk'out, *n.* 1. a test, practice, etc. to develop, keep, or acquire proficiency, as for a competition.
2. any strenuous exercise, work, etc.

wŏrk'pēo·ple, *n.pl.* workers; especially, industrial or manual workers.

wŏrk'rọọm, *n.* a room in which work is done.

wŏrks çoun'cil, a committee of workers in a factory, business, etc., organized by an employer to discuss industrial relations.

wŏrk sheet, 1. any sheet of paper on which a record of work, working time, etc. is kept.
2. a sheet of paper printed with practice exercises, problems, etc. to be worked on directly by students.
3. a sheet of paper containing working notes, preliminary formulations, etc.

wŏrk'shop, *n.* a shop or building where work is done.

wŏrk sọng, a folk song sung by laborers, as in the fields, with a marked rhythm matching the rhythm of their work.

wŏrk'tā"ble, *n.* a table at which work is done; especially, a small table containing drawers, for needlework.

wŏrk'up, *n.* a complete medical study of a patient, including a thorough examination, laboratory tests, a survey of the patient's case history, etc.

wŏrk'-up, *n.* in printing, a mark on a printed page caused by the rising of spacing material.

wŏrk'week, *n.* the total number of hours worked in a week.

wŏrk'wom"ăn (-woom"), *n.*; *pl.* **wŏrk'wom"en** (-wim"), a woman engaged in any kind of work; especially, a woman industrial or manual worker.

wŏrld, *n.* [ME. *werld, world, worlde*; AS. *weoruld, weorold*, etc., world, lit., the age of man; AS. *wer*, man, and *yldo*, an age.]
1. the earth.
2. the universe.
3. the earth and its inhabitants.
4. [*also* W-] (a) some portion or division of the earth; as, the Old *World*, the New *World*; (b) any state or sphere of existence; any wide scene of life or action; as, the *world* to come; (c) some period of history, its society, etc.; as, the *ancient* world; (d) any sphere or domain; as, the dog *world*; the animal, vegetable, or mineral *world*; (e) any sphere of human activity; as, the *world* of music.
5. the inhabitants of the earth in general; humanity; mankind; the human race.
6. people generally; the public; society; as, what will the *world* say?
7. that which pertains to the earth or to the present state of existence only; the concerns of this life as distinguished from those of the life to come.

Love not the *world*, neither the things that are in the *world*. —1 John ii. 15.

8. that portion of mankind which is devoted to worldly or secular affairs.
9. the current of events, especially as affecting an individual; as, how goes the *world*?
10. any sphere of more or less complexity or development; individual experience, outlook, etc.; as, their home is their *world*.
11. [*often in pl.*] a large amount; a great deal; as, the rest did him a *world* (or *worlds*) of good.
12. a star or planet.

all the world; the entire world; specifically, (a) all the people in the world; everybody; mankind collectively; (b) everything that the world contains.

all the world and his wife; everybody; a large company. [Humorous.]

for all the world; (a) for any reason or consideration at all; (b) in every respect; exactly.

in the world; (a) on earth or in the universe; anywhere; (b) at all; ever.

man of the world; see under **man.**

New World; see under **new.**

Old World; see under *old.*

on top of the world; lifted up with joy, pride, success, etc.; elated; exultant. [Slang.]

out of this (or *the*) *world*; exceptionally fine; extraordinary; remarkable. [Slang.]

the other world; what is to come after death.

to bring into the world; to give birth to.

to come into the world; to be born.

World Bank; an agency (officially *International Bank for Reconstruction and Development*) of the United Nations, established in 1945 to make loans to member nations.

World Court; the Permanent Court of International Justice which was established by the League of Nations in December, 1920, to settle disputes between nations.

world power; [transl. of G. *weltmacht.*] a nation or organization large or powerful enough to have a world-wide influence.

world series; an annual series of games played in the autumn between the winning teams of the two major American baseball leagues to decide the championship: also *world's series.*

world's fair; an exhibition of the arts, crafts, industrial and agricultural products, scientific advances, etc. of various countries of the world.

world soul; the soul of the world, a universal animating principle analogous to the soul of the individual.

World War I; the war between the Allies (Great Britain, France, Russia, the United States, Italy, Japan, etc.) and the Central Powers (Germany, Austria-Hungary, etc.), fought from 1914 to 1918.

World War II; the war between the United Nations (Great Britain, France, the Soviet Union, the United States, etc.) and the Axis (Germany, Italy, Japan, etc.), fought from 1939 to 1945.

world without end; forever.

wŏrld'-çlass, *a.* of the highest class, as in international competition.

wŏrld'li·ness, *n.* the condition or quality of being worldly.

wŏrld'ling, *n.* a worldly person.

wŏrld'ly, *a.*; *comp.* worldlier; *superl.* worldliest, 1. secular; temporal; pertaining to this world or life: opposed to *heavenly, spiritual, ecclesiastical*, etc.; as, *worldly* pleasures.
2. devoted to this life and its enjoyments; bent on gain; as, a *worldly* man.
3. worldly-wise; as, *worldly* actions.
4. lay or secular, as opposed to clerical or monastic. [Rare.]

Syn.—terrestrial, mundane, temporal, secular, earthly, carnal.

wŏrld'ly, *adv.* with relation to this life.

wŏrld'ly-mīnd"ed, *a.* devoted to the acquisition of property and to temporal enjoyment.

wŏrld'ly-mīnd"ed·ness, *n.* the state of being worldly-minded.

wŏrld'ly-wīṣe, *a.* familiar with the affairs and practices of the world; sophisticated.

wŏrld'-shāk"ing, *a.* of great significance, effect, or influence; momentous.

wŏrld'-wēar"y, *a.* weary of the world or of living.

wŏrld'-wīde, *a.* pervading or extending throughout the entire world.

wŏrm, *n.* [AS. *wyrm*, a worm, dragon, snake.]
1. any of many long, slender, soft-bodied, creeping animals, some segmented, that live by burrowing underground or as parasites, as the earthworm, tapeworm, etc.
2. popularly, an insect larva, as a caterpillar, grub, or maggot.
3. an abject, wretched, or contemptible person.
4. something thought of as being wormlike because of its spiral shape, etc., as the thread of a screw or the coil of a still.
5. something that gnaws or distresses one inwardly, suggesting a parasitic worm; as, the *worm* of conscience.
6. a mechanical device thought of as resembling a worm; specifically, (a) an Archimedean screw or similar apparatus; (b) a short, rotating screw that meshes with the teeth of a worm wheel or a rack.
7. in anatomy, any organ or part resembling a worm, as the vermiform process.
8. [*pl.*] in medicine, any disease or disorder caused by the presence of parasitic worms in the intestines, etc.
9. in zoology, a lytta.

can of worms; a complex, usually unpleasant problem. [Colloq.]

wŏrm, *v.i.*; wormed, *pt., pp.*; worming, *ppr.* to move, proceed, etc. like a worm, in a winding, creeping, or devious manner.

wŏrm, *v.t.* 1. to bring about, make, etc. in a winding, creeping, or devious manner; as, he *wormed* his way in.
2. to insinuate (oneself) into a situation, conversation, etc.
3. to extract (information, secrets, etc.) by insinuation, cajolery, or subtle questioning.
4. to purge of intestinal worms.
5. to extract the lytta from the tongue of (a dog, etc.).
6. in nautical usage, to wind yarn or small rope in and around the strands of (a rope or cable) in order to smooth the surface.

wŏrm bärk, the bark of *Andira inermis* and similar trees, used as a narcotic and anthelmintic.

wŏrm'-ēat"en, *a.* 1. eaten into by worms, termites, etc.
2. worn-out, ragged, decrepit, out-of-date, etc.

wŏrm fence, a zigzag fence of rails; a snake fence.

wŏrm gēar, 1. a worm wheel.
2. a gear consisting of a worm and worm wheel.

WORM GEAR

wŏrm gráss, either of two plants: the Carolina pink, or pinkroot, or the English stonecrop, *Sedum album.*

wŏrm'hōle, *n.* a hole or track made by a worm, termite, etc.

Wọr'mi·ăn, *a.* pertaining to or named after Olaus Worm, a Danish physician.

Wormian bones; small bones found in the cranial sutures.

wọr'mil, *n.* a warble (larva).

wŏrm'ling, *n.* a small worm. [Rare.]

wŏrm oil, wormseed oil.

wŏrm pow'dēr, a powder used for expelling intestinal worms.

wŏrm'rọọt, *n.* an herb used in treating intestinal worms.

wŏrm'seed, *n.* any plant whose seeds are anthelmintic, as *Chenopodium ambrosoides*, the American wormseed, *Artemisia santonica*, or *Artemisia cina*, the Levant wormseed; also, the seeds of any of these plants.

wŏrm'seed mus'tărd, treacle mustard.

wŏrm'seed oil, a pale-yellow oil, obtained by distilling wormseed with water.

wŏrm'ṣ'-eye view, an outlook from very close range, but from an inferior or menial position.

wŏrm'-shāped (-shāpt), *a.* vermiform.

wŏrm shell, a gastropod of the genus *Vermetus.*

wŏrm snāke, an American snake, *Carphophis* or *Celuta amæna.*

wŏrm wheel (hwēl), a wheel designed to gear with the thread of a worm, either receiving or imparting motion.

wŏrm′wood, *n.* [altered by folk etym. from ME. and AS. *wermod*; akin to G. *wermut.*]

1. any of a number of related strong-smelling plants of the genus *Artemisia*, with white or yellow flowers; specifically, *Artemisia absinthium*, a species that yields a bitter-tasting, dark-green oil used in making absinthe.

2. any bitter, unpleasant, or mortifying experience; bitterness.

Roman wormwood; an American weed of the genus *Ambrosia*.

tree wormwood; a treelike species of wormwood, *Artemisia arborescens*, of the Mediterranean region.

wild wormwood; a plant of the genus *Parthenium*, of the aster family, of tropical America.

WORMWOOD (*Artemisia absinthium*)

wŏrm′y, *a.*; *comp.* wormier; *superl.* wormiest. 1. containing a worm or worms; full of worms.

2. infested with worms.

3. like a worm; hence, low; groveling; mean.

wōrn, *a.* 1. showing the effects of use, wear, etc.

2. damaged by use or wear.

3. showing the effects of worry or anxiety.

4. exhausted; enfeebled; spent.

wōrn, *v.* past participle of *wear*.

wor′nil, *n.* same as *warble* (larva of warble fly).

wōrn′-out, *a.* used until no longer effective, usable, or serviceable; as, a *worn-out* coat; also, fatigued; wearied; tired-out; as, he was quite *worn-out* after the journey.

wor′răl, *n.* [Ar. *waran.*] an animal of the lizard kind, with a forked tongue: it feeds on flies, and is harmless.

wŏr′ri·çow, *n.* a bugbear; a hobgoblin; specifically, the devil. [Scot.]

wŏr′ri·ẽr, *n.* one who worries.

wŏr′ri·less, *a.* not having worry.

wŏr′ri·ment, *n.* 1. a worrying or being worried; mental disturbance; anxiety.

2. a cause of worry.

wŏr′ri·sōme, *a.* 1. causing worry or anxiety.

2. having a tendency to worry.

wŏr′rit, *v.t.* to worry. [Dial.]

wŏr′rit, *n.* worry; annoyance; vexation. [Dial.]

wŏr′ry, *v.t.*; worried, *pt.*, *pp.*; worrying, *ppr.* [ME. *worowen*, *wirien*, etc., from AS. *wyrgan*, to choke or strangle, injure, violate.]

1. to harass or treat roughly with or as with continual biting or tearing with the teeth; as, the dog was *worrying* an old shoe.

2. to annoy; pester; bother.

3. to cause to feel troubled or uneasy; to make anxious; to distress.

wŏr′ry, *v.i.* 1. to bite, pull, or tear (*at* an object) with the teeth.

2. to feel distressed in the mind; to be anxious, troubled, or uneasy.

3. to manage to get (*along* or *through*) in the face of trials and difficulties.

wŏr′ry, *n.*; *pl.* **wŏr′rieṣ**, 1. the act of worrying.

2. a troubled state of mind; anxiety; distress; care; uneasiness.

3. something that causes anxiety or mental distress.

The cares and *worries* of life. —Lever.

wŏr′ry·ing·ly, *adv.* in a worrying manner.

wŏrse, *a.* [comparative of *bad* and *ill.*] [ME. *werse*, *worse*, adj., *wers*, *wors*, adv.; AS. *wyrsa*, adj., *wyrs*, adv.]

1. bad, evil, harmful, unpleasant, etc. in a greater degree; less good.

2. in poorer health or physical condition; more ill; less well.

3. in a less favorable condition; in a more unsatisfactory situation.

wŏrse, *adv.* [comparative of *badly* and *ill.*] in a worse manner or way; to a worse extent or degree.

We will deal *worse* with thee than with them. —Gen. xix. 9.

wŏrse, *n.* 1. discomfiture; defeat. [Rare.]

And Judah was put to the *worse* before Israel. —2 Kings xiv. 12.

2. that which is worse; something less good or desirable.

Thus bad begins and *worse* remains behind. —Shak.

wŏrse, *v.t.* to put to disadvantage; to defeat. [Obs.]

wŏrs′en, *v.t.* and *v.i.* to make or become worse.

wŏrs′ẽr, *a.* and *adv.* worse: a redundant form now considered a vulgarism.

wŏr′ship, *n.* [ME. *worschip*; AS. *weorthscipe*, *wyrthscipe*, honor; *weorth*, *wurth*, worthy, honorable, and suffix *-scipe*, -ship.]

1. the state or quality of being worthy; excellence of character; dignity; worth; worthiness. [Obs. or Archaic.]

2. a title of honor used in addresses to certain magistrates and others of rank or station; as, may it please your *worship*. [Chiefly Brit.]

My father desires your *worship's* company. —Shak.

3. a prayer, church service, or other rite showing reverence or devotion for a deity; religious homage or veneration.

4. honor; respect; civil deference.

5. unbounded admiration; intense love; extreme devotion.

6. that which is worshiped.

wŏr′ship, *v.t.*; worshiped *or* worshipped (-shipt), *pt.*, *pp.*; worshiping *or* worshipping, *ppr.* 1. to adore or pay divine honors to as a deity; to reverence with supreme respect and veneration; as, to *worship* God.

2. to respect; to honor; to treat with civil deference. [Rare.]

3. to have intense love or admiration for, as a lover; to idolize.

With bended knees I daily *worship* her. —Carew.

Syn.—honor, adore, revere, reverence.

wŏr′ship, *v.i.* to engage in worship; specifically, to perform religious service; to offer prayers, attend church services, etc.

Our fathers *worshiped* in this mountain. —John iv. 20.

wŏr′ship·ȧ·ble, *a.* capable of or worthy of being worshiped. [Rare.]

wŏr′ship·ẽr, **wŏr′ship·pẽr**, *n.* one who worships.

wŏr′ship·fụl, *a.* 1. feeling or offering great devotion or respect; worshiping.

2. worthy of being worshiped; honorable; respected: used as a title of respect for magistrates, certain lodge officials, etc.

wŏr′ship·fụl·ly, *adv.* respectfully; honorably.

wŏr′ship·fụl·ness, *n.* the state or quality of being worshipful.

wŏrst, *a.* [superl. of *bad* and *ill.*] [ME. *worst*, *werst*, adv., *worste*, *werste*, adj., from AS. *wyrst*, adv., *wyrsta*, adj., worst.] bad, evil, harmful, unpleasant, etc. in the highest degree; of the least value or worth; most inferior.

(*in*) *the worst way*; very much; greatly; intensely. [Slang.]

wŏrst, *n.* that which is worst; the most inferior, evil, severe, aggravated, etc.

at worst; under the worst circumstances; at the greatest disadvantage.

if worst comes to worst; if the worst possible thing happens.

to give one the worst of it; to defeat or get the better of one.

to make the worst of; to be pessimistic about; to consider only the least favorable aspects of.

wŏrst, *v.t.*; worsted, *pt.*, *pp.*; worsting, *ppr.* [AS. *wyrsian*, prop. intransitive, to grow worse, formed with excrescent *t*, as in amongs*t*, whils*t*, etc.] to get the better of; to defeat; to overthrow; as, he participated in the struggle and was *worsted*.

wŏrst, *v.i.* to grow worse; to worsen. [Rare.]

wŏrst, *adv.* [superl. of *badly* and *ill.*] in a degree, manner, or condition that is most bad, evil, unpleasant, etc.; as, when did you dislike it *worst*?

wŏrst′-çāse′, *a.* that is, or takes into account, the worst possible case, condition, situation, etc.

worst′ed (wụst′ed), *n.* [named from *Worsted*, now *Worstead*, in Norfolk, Eng., where it was first manufactured.]

1. a variety of smooth woolen yarn or thread, spun from long-staple wool which has been combed, and which, in the spinning, is twisted hard; also, a fabric made from this with a smooth, hard surface.

2. a woolen yarn used in ornamental needlework and knitting.

worst′ed, *a.* made of worsted; as, *worsted* socks.

wŏrt, *n.* [ME. *wort*; AS. *wyrt*, wort.]

1. a plant or herb: now used in compounds, as in mug*wort*, liver*wort*, spleen*wort*.

2. a plant of the cabbage kind. [Obs.]

wŏrt, *n.* [ME. *wort*, *worte*; AS. *wyrt-* (in compounds).] a liquid prepared with malt which, after fermenting, becomes beer, ale, etc.

wŏrth, *v.i.* [ME. *worthen*; AS. *weorthan*, to become.] to betide; to befall; to become; as, woe *worth* the day. [Archaic.]

wŏrth, *n.* [ME. *wurth*, *worth*, from AS. *weorth*, *wurth*, honorable.]

1. material value; that quality of a thing which renders it useful, or which will produce an equivalent in money or some other medium of exchange.

2. the amount or quantity of something that may be had for a given sum; as, a dollar's *worth* of nickels, fifty cents' *worth* of sugar.

3. the esteem in which a person or thing is held; importance, value, merit, excellence, etc.

As none but she, who in that court did dwell,
Could know such *worth*, or *worth* describe so well. —Waller.

4. the value of one's possessions; riches; wealth.

to put in one's two cents worth; to give one's own opinion, as in a discussion; to speak up.

Syn.—excellence, merit, price, virtue.

wŏrth, *a.* 1. equal in value or price to something specified.

If your arguments produce no conviction, they are *worth* nothing to me. —Beattie.

2. deserving or worthy of; meriting.

And to have added a little touch of joy and beauty to the land of one's living, this is *worth* a little effort, to be sure. —Andrew McNally.

3. equal in wealth or possessions amounting to; as, he is reputed to be *worth* a million dollars.

4. valuable; precious; worthy. [Obs.]

for all one is worth; to the extent of one's powers or ability; to the utmost.

wŏrth′fụl, *a.* same as *worthy*.

wŏr′thi·ly, *adv.* in a worthy manner; rightly; deservedly; according to merit; suitably.

You *worthily* succeed not only to the honors of your ancestors, but also to their virtues. —Dryden.

wŏr′thi·ness, *n.* the character or quality of being worthy.

wŏrth′less, *a.* having no worth or merit; useless, valueless, good-for-nothing, etc.

Syn.—cheap, valueless, useless.

wŏrth′less·ly, *adv.* in a worthless manner.

wŏrth′less·ness, *n.* the state or quality of being worthless.

wŏrth′-whīle′ (-hwīl′), *a.* important or valuable enough to repay time or effort spent; of true value, merit, or importance.

wŏrth′-whīle′, *n.* that which is worthy of the effort or time given.

wŏr′thy, *a.*; *comp.* worthier; *superl.* worthiest, 1. having worth, value, or merit; deserving praise; valuable; noble; estimable; virtuous.

2. deserving; having enough worth or merit; meriting: often followed by *of* or by an infinitive; as, a candidate *worthy of* support.

3. well-deserved; merited; as, *worthy* vengeance. [Obs.]

4. well-founded; justifiable; legitimate. [Archaic.]

5. fit; suitable; convenient; proper; fitting; having qualities suited to.

Foeman *worthy* of their steel. —Scott.

6. of high social station. [Obs.]

worthiest of blood; in English law, most worthy of those of the same blood in the succession to inheritances: applied to men as opposed to women.

wŏr′thy, *n.*; *pl.* **wŏr′thieṣ**, a person of outstanding worth or importance: often used humorously; as, the *worthies* of the church; political *worthies*; military *worthies*.

wŏr′thy, *v.t.* to render worthy; to exalt. [Obs.]

wōst, *v.* obsolete second person singular, present indicative, of *wit*, to know.

wot, *v.* archaic first and third persons singular, present indicative, of *wit*, to know.

would (wood), *v.* [ME. and AS. *wolde*, pt. of *willan*, to will, wish.] past tense and alternative obsolete past participle of *will*.

Would is also used: (a) to express condition; as, he *would* write if you *would* answer; (b) in indirect discourse to express futurity; as, he said he *would* bring it; (c) to express a wish; as, *would* that he were still living; (d) to soften somewhat the force of a statement or request; as, *would* you do this for me?

wōuld, *n.* a weld (flower).

would'-bē (wood'), *a.* [ME. (northern) *walde be.*]
1. that would be; wishing or pretending to be.
2. intended to be.

would'-bē, *n.* a vain pretender.

would'est, *v.* alternative archaic second person singular, past tense, of *will.*

would'ing, *n.* emotion of desire; inclination. [Obs.]

would'ing·ness, *n.* willingness. [Obs.]

would'n't, would not.

wouldst, *v.* alternative archaic second person singular, past tense, of *will.*

Woulfe bot'tle, [after Peter Woulfe (died 1803), Eng. chemist.] in chemistry, a bottle with two or more apertures, intended for the generation of gases or for cleansing them by allowing them to pass through certain solutions contained in the bottle.

wöund (*or, rarely, among surgeons* wound), *n.* [ME. *wounde*; AS. *wund*, a wound.]
1. an injury to the body in which the skin or other tissue is broken, cut, pierced, torn, etc.
2. a mark or scar resulting from this.
3. an injury to a plant caused by cutting, scraping, or other external force.
4. any hurt or injury to the feelings, honor, etc.

wöund, *v.i.*; wounded, *pt., pp.*; wounding, *ppr.* [ME. *wundien*; AS. *wundian*, from the n.] to inflict a wound or wounds; to harm.
Willing to *wound*, and yet afraid to strike. —Pope.

wöund, *v.t.* to inflict a wound or wounds on or upon; to hurt; to lacerate; to injure; to harm; as, to *wound* the head or the arm; to *wound* a tree; to *wound* the feelings.

wound, *v.* 1. past tense and past participle of *wind* (to twist).
2. past tense and past participle of *wind* (to blow).

wöund'à·ble, *a.* capable of being wounded.

wöund'ẽr, *n.* one who or that which wounds.

wöund gall, a gall produced on the branches of the grapevine by a weevil, *Ampeloglypter sesostris.*

wöund'i·ly, *adv.* excessively; woundy. [Obs.]

wöund'ing, *n.* hurt; injury.

wöund'less, *a.* 1. free from hurt or injury.
2. invulnerable; incapable of being wounded.
3. unwounding; harmless. [Obs.]
Not a dart fell *woundless* there. —Southey.

wöund'wŏrt, *n.* any of several British plants of the genus *Stachys*; especially, *Stachys palustris* and *Stachys germanica*; also, the kidney vetch.

wöund'y, *a.* causing or inflicting wounds. [Rare.]

wöund'y, *a.* excessive. [Obs.]

wöund'y, *adv.* excessively. [Obs.]

wöu'rà·li, wöu'rà·ri, *n.* [S. Am.] same as *curare.*

wöu'rà·li plant, a woody twining plant, *Strychnos toxifera*, covered with long, reddish hairs, having ovate leaves, rough and pointed, and large round fruit. From this plant is procured curare.

WOURALI PLANT (*Strychnos toxifera*)

woŭr'nil, *n.* the larva of the warble fly. [Obs.]

wou'-wou, *n.* same as *wow-wow.*

wōve, *v.* past tense and alternative past participle of *weave.*

wōv'en, *v.* alternative past participle of *weave.*

wōve pā'pẽr, paper made on a mold in which the wires are so closely woven together that the finished sheets do not show wire marks as on laid paper.

wow, *interj.* an expression of surprise, wonder, pleasure, pain, etc.

wow, *n.* 1. something very amusing. [Slang.]
2. a great success. [Slang.]

wow, *v.t.* to be a great success with. [Slang.]

wowe, *v.t.* and *v.i.* to woo. [Obs.]

wowf, *a.* wild; unreclaimed; disordered in intellect. [Scot.]

wow'sẽr, *n.* in Australia, a person who is rigorously puritanical, as in his objections to Sunday amusements or sports.

wow'-wow, *n.* [native name.] the agile gibbon, *Hylobates agilis*; also, the silvery gibbon, *Hylobates leuciscus.*

wox'en, *v.* obsolete past tense and past participle of *wax.*

wrack (rak), *n.* a rack of clouds or other vapor.

wrack, *v.t.* to rack or torture. [Obs.]

wrack, *n.* [ME. and M.D. *wrak.*]
1. ruin; destruction: now chiefly in the phrase *wrack and ruin.*
2. a wrecked ship.
3. wreckage.
4. seaweed or other marine plant life cast up on shore.
5. weeds. [Scot. and Dial.]

wrack, *v.t.* and *v.i.* to wreck or be wrecked. [Archaic.]

wrack'fụl, *a.* ruinous; destructive. [Obs.]

wrack gråss, same as *grass wrack.*

wrāin'bōlt (rān'), *n.* same as *wringbolt.*

wrāith (rāth), *n.* [Scot., earlier *warth*, guardian angel; O.N. *vörthr* (genit. *varthar*), a warden, guardian, from *vartha*, to guard.] an apparition or ghost; specifically, the spectral figure of a person in his exact likeness supposed to be seen just before death or a little after.
The ghastly *wraith* of one that I know. —Tennyson.

wramp (ramp), *n.* a sprain. [Brit. Dial.]

wrañ'gle (rañ'), *v.i.*; wrangled (-gld), *pt., pp.*; wrangling, *ppr.* [a freq. from *wring*, AS. *wringan*, pt. *wrang*, to press.]
1. to dispute angrily; to quarrel peevishly and noisily; to brawl; to altercate.
Others who had sparred and *wrangled* with him, who beheld him with no halo. —R. L. Stevenson.
2. to argue; to dispute.

wrañ'gle, *v.t.* 1. to argue (with *into, out of*, etc.).
2. to herd or round up (livestock).

wrañ'gle, *n.* an angry dispute; a noisy quarrel.

wrañ'glẽr, *n.* 1. a person who wrangles; specifically, (a) one who argues; (b) a cowboy who rounds up livestock.
2. a student in the highest class of honors in mathematics at Cambridge University.

wrañ'glẽr·ship, *n.* in Cambridge University, the honor or state of being a wrangler.

wrañ'gle·sŏme, *a.* contentious; quarrelsome. [Dial.]

wran'nŏck, wran'ny (ran'), *n.* the wren. [Brit. Dial.]

wrap (rap), *v.t.*; wrapped (rapt) *or* wrapt, *pt., pp.*; wrapping, *ppr.* [ME. *wrappen*, also *wlappen.*]
1. to wind or fold (a covering) around something; to arrange so as to cover something: generally with *about, round,* or the like.
Like one that *wraps* the drapery of his couch
About him, and lies down to pleasant dreams. —Bryant.
2. to envelop; to cover by winding something round; to cover completely: often with *up*; as, to *wrap up* a child in its blanket; to *wrap* the body well with flannel in winter.
3. to conceal by involving or enveloping; to hide in a mass of different character; to cover up or hide.
The evil which is here *wrapped* up. —Shak.
4. to enclose and fasten in a wrapper of paper, etc.; to do up in a package or wrapping.
5. to wind or fold; as, she *wrapped* her arms around him.
to be wrapped up in; (a) to be bound up with or in; to be comprised or involved in; to be entirely associated with or dependent on; (b) to be engrossed in or with; to be entirely devoted to; as, she is *wrapped up in* her son; he is *wrapped up in* his studies.

wrap, *v.i.* to twine, extend, coil, etc. (usually with *over, around,* etc.).

wrap, *n.* 1. an outer covering, especially a garment worn by being wrapped around the body: often in plural.
2. a blanket.

wrap'pă̤ġe, *n.* 1. that which wraps; a covering.
2. the act of wrapping.

wrap'pẽr, *n.* 1. a person or thing that wraps.
2. that in which something is wrapped; a covering; a cover; specifically, (a) the outer leaf of tobacco covering a cigar; (b) [Chiefly Brit.] the dust jacket of a book; (c) the paper wrapping in which a newspaper, magazine, etc. is enclosed for mailing.
3. a woman's dressing gown.

wrap'ping, *n.* [*usually in pl.*] the material, as paper, in which something is wrapped.

wrap'ping pā'pẽr, heavy paper specially adapted for wrapping up parcels.

wrap'ras"çăl, *n.* a loose overcoat worn formerly.

wrapt, *v.* alternative past tense and past participle of *wrap.*

wrasse (ras), *n.* [W. *gwrachen*, the wrasse.] any of various species of sea food fishes inhabiting the rocky parts of the coast of Europe and belonging to the family *Labridæ.* They are prickly-spined, hard-boned fishes, with oblong, scaly bodies and a single dorsal fin; their lips are large, double, and fleshy, and their teeth, strong, conical, and sharp. Many of the species have vivid colors, particularly in the spring just before the spawning season.

BALLAN WRASSE (*Labrus maculatus*)

Several species are native to British seas, as the ballan wrasse, *Labrus maculatus*, which attains a length of about eighteen inches, the green-streaked wrasse, *Labrus lineatus*, etc. *Labrus mixtus* is the red wrasse.

wras'tle (ras'l), *v.i.* to wrestle. [Now Dial.]

wrăth (răth *or* rath), *n.* [ME. *wraththe, wratthe*, from AS. *wrāth*, wroth.]
1. violent anger; vehement exasperation; indignation; fury.
By penitence the Eternal's *wrath's* appeased. —Shak.
2. any action carried out in great anger, especially for punishment or vengeance.
For he is the minister of God, a revenger to execute *wrath* upon him that doeth evil. —Rom. xiii.4.
Syn.—ire, fury, rage, vengeance, indignation, resentment, passion, anger.

wrăth, *a.* wrathful; wroth. [Rare or Archaic.]

wrăth, *v.t.* to cause wrath or anger in; to make angry. [Obs.]

wrăth'fụl, *a.* 1. very angry; greatly incensed.
2. resulting from, characterized by, or expressing wrath; as, *wrathful* passions; a *wrathful* countenance.
Syn.—exasperated, indignant, irate, furious, resentful.

wrăth'fụl·ly, *adv.* in a wrathful manner.

wrăth'fụl·ness, *n.* the state or quality of being wrathful.

wrăth'i·ly, *adv.* in a wrathful manner; very angrily. [Colloq.]

wrăth'i·ness, *n.* the state of being wrathful. [Colloq.]

wrăth'less, *a.* free from anger. [Obs.]

wrăth'y, *a.* very angry; wrathful. [Colloq.]

wrąw (rą), *a.* vexed; peevish; angry. [Obs.]

wrąw'fụl, *a.* having a bad temper. [Obs.]

wrąwl, *v.i.* to cry as a cat; to waul. [Obs.]

wrąw'ness, *n.* anger; peevishness. [Obs.]

wrāy (rā), *v.t.* to betray; to disclose; to reveal. [Obs.]

wrēak (rēk), *v.t.*; wreaked, *pt., pp.*; wreaking, *ppr.* [ME. *wreken*, from AS. *wrecan*, to wreak, revenge, punish.]
1. to give vent or free play to (anger, malice, range, etc.); as, he *wreaked* his anger on the students.
On me let Death *wreak* all his rage. —Milton.
2. to inflict (vengeance, etc.)
3. to avenge. [Archaic.]

wrēak, *n.* revenge; vengeance. [Archaic.]

wrēak, *v.i.* to reck. [Obs.]

wrēak'ẽr, *n.* one who wreaks. [Archaic.]

wrēak'fụl, *a.* revengeful; angry.

wrēak'fụl·ly, *adv.* in a wreakful manner. [Obs.]

wrēak′less, *a.* unrevenged. [Obs.]

wrēath (rēth), *n.*; *pl.* **wrēaths,** [ME. *wrethe,* from AS. *wræth,* a twisted band, bandage; formed (with vowel-change) from *wrāth,* pt. of *writhan,* to writhe, twist.]

1. a twisted band or ring of leaves, flowers, etc.; a chaplet worn as a mark of honor or victory, or a garland laid upon a grave, hung on a door, window, etc.

2. something suggesting or resembling this in shape; twisted or circular band; as, *wreaths* of smoke.

3. Corona Australis, a constellation.

4. in heraldry, the roll or chaplet above the helmet, on which the crest is usually borne. It is supposed to be composed of two bands of silk interwoven or twisted together, the one tinctured of the principal metal, the other of the principal color in the arms. If there is no metal, it must be of the two principal colors.

WREATHS

wrēathe, *v.t.*; wreathed, *pt.*; wreathed *or archaic* wreathen, *pp.*; wreathing, *ppr.* [from *wreath,* and also from ME. *wrethen,* pp. of *writhen,* to twist.]

1. to coil, twist, or entwine, especially so as to form a wreath.

Around her forehead that shines so bright
They *wreathe* a wreath of roses white.
—Praed.

2. to coil, twist, or entwine around; to encircle; as, clouds *wreathed* the mountains.

3. to decorate with wreaths.

And with thy winding ivy *wreathes* her lance. —Dryden.

4. to cover or envelop; as, a face *wreathed* in wrinkles, smiles, etc.

5. to writhe. [Obs.]

wrēathe, *v.i.* 1. to have a twisting or coiling movement.

2. to have or take the form of a wreath.

wrēath′en, *a.* wreathed; twisted; intertwined or intertwining. [Poet or Archaic.]

wrēath′less, *a.* without a wreath.

wrēath shell, a univalve shell of the genus *Turbo.*

wrēath′y, *a.* 1. covered with a wreath or wreaths; wreathed.

2. twisted; curled; spiral.

wrec′che (ret′), *n.* a wretch. [Obs.]

wrec′che, *a.* miserable; wretched. [Obs.]

wrēche (rēk), *n.* wreak. [Obs.]

wreck (rek), *v.t.* and *n.* wreak. [Obs.]

wreck, *n.* [ME. *wrak, wrecke;* Anglo-Fr. *wrec, wrech,* from Anglo-N. *wrek;* compare Ice. *rek,* Sw. *vrak,* anything driven ashore, wreck.]

1. the disabling or destruction of a ship by being driven ashore, dashed against rocks, foundered by stress of weather, or the like; shipwreck.

2. a ship that has been broken or otherwise destroyed by any disaster of navigation.

3. goods, etc. cast ashore after a shipwreck.

4. a wrecking or being wrecked; destruction or ruin; as, the *wreck* of a railway train.

5. the remains of anything destroyed, ruined, or badly damaged.

6. a person in very poor health.

wreck, *v.t.*; wrecked (rekt), *pt., pp.*; wrecking, *ppr.* 1. to cause the wreck of; to destroy or damage badly.

2. to tear down; to dismantle (a building, etc.).

3. to bring to ruin or disaster; to overthrow; thwart; defeat.

4. to destroy the health or physical soundness of.

wreck, *v.i.* 1. to suffer damage, destruction, or ruin; to be wrecked.

2. to be a wrecker.

wreck′āge, *n.* 1. the act of wrecking or the state of being wrecked.

2. the remains of something that has been wrecked; any wrecked material.

wreck′ẽr, *n.* 1. a person or thing that wrecks.

2. a person who causes ruin, obstruction, or disruption of any kind.

3. a person, car, train, boat, etc. that salvages or clears away wrecks.

4. a person who tears down and salvages old buildings, etc.

wreck′fish, *n.* a stone bass.

wreck′-free′, *a.* exempted from the forfeiture of shipwrecked goods and vessels.

wreck′fụl, *a.* causing wreck; producing or involving destruction or ruin. [Poet.]

wreck′ing, *a.* 1. pertaining to the act of causing wrecks.

2. engaged or used in dismantling, clearing, or salvaging wrecks; as, a *wrecking* crew.

wreck′ing, *n.* the act or work of a wrecker.

wreck′ing pump, a powerful pump for pumping water from the holds of wrecked vessels.

wreck mȧs′tẽr, a person appointed by law to take charge of goods, etc., cast ashore after a shipwreck.

Wren (ren), *n.* a member of the Women's Royal Naval Service, a British wartime service. [Brit. Colloq.]

wren, *n.* [AS. *wrenna, wrænna,* a wren.] any of a large number of small troglodytic songbirds of the Northern Hemisphere, characterized by a long bill, rounded wings, a stubby, erect tail, and a dark reddish-brown color varied with black; as, the European wren, *Troglodytes vulgaris;* the common house wren, *Troglodytes ædon;* the winter wren, *Troglodytes hiemalis;* the Carolina wren, *Troglodytes ludovicianus,* etc.

blue wren; same as *superb warbler* under *superb.*

wren bab′blẽr, any small species of babbler resembling a wren, especially of the genera *Alcippe, Stachyris,* and *Timelia.*

wrench (rench), *n.* [ME.; AS. *wrence, wrenc,* deceit, a trick, fraud.]

1. a sudden, violent twist or pull.

2. an injury caused by a twist or jerk, as to the back, a joint, etc.

3. a sudden feeling of anguish, grief, etc., as from separation; as, the *wrench* of saying good-by.

4. any of a number of tools used for holding and turning nuts, bolts, pipes, etc.

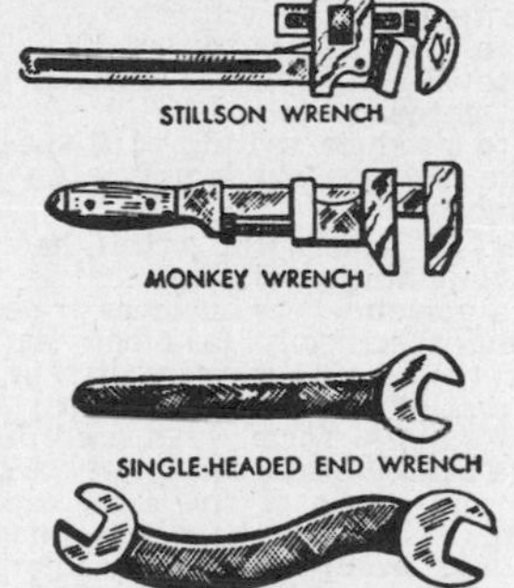

WRENCHES

5. a false or strained interpretation of an original meaning.

6. in physics, a combination of forces producing a twisting and a pulling or pushing motion at the same time.

wrench, *v.i.* to have or to undergo a wrenching motion; to turn or twist suddenly. [Obs.]

wrench, *v.t.* 1. to twist, pull, or jerk suddenly and violently.

2. to injure (a part of the body) with a twist or wrench.

3. to distort, strain, or give a false interpretation of (a meaning, statement, etc.).

Syn.—wrest, twist, distort, strain, extort, wring.

wrench ham′mẽr, a wrench that is also adapted for use as a hammer.

wren tit, a small bird, *Chamæa fasciata,* of the coastal region of California.

wren wạr′blẽr, any of various Old-World warblers related to the tailorbird.

wrest (rest), *v.t.*; wrested, *pt., pp.*; wresting, *ppr.* [ME. *wresten,* to wrestle, struggle, from AS. *wræstan,* to twist forcibly.]

1. to turn or twist; especially, to pull or force away violently with a twisting motion.

2. to take or extract by force; usurp; extort; wring.

3. to distort or change the true meaning, purpose, use, etc. of; to pervert; to twist.

wrest, *v.i.* to wrestle. [Obs.]

wrest, *n.* 1. the act of wresting; a twist; a wrench.

2. a wrenchlike key used for tuning pianos, harps, etc. by turning the pins around which the strings are coiled.

3. a partition in an overshot water wheel, which outlines the shape of the buckets.

wrest block, the wooden piece into which the wrest pins are driven.

wrest′ẽr, *n.* one who wrests or distorts.

wres′tle (res′l), *v.i.*; wrestled (-ld), *pt., pp.*; wrestling, *ppr.* [ME. *wrestlen, wrastlen,* to wrestle; AS. *wræstlian,* freq. of *wræstan,* to twist, wrestle.]

1. to struggle hand to hand with an opponent in an attempt to throw or force him to the ground without striking blows.

2. to struggle in opposition; to strive; to contend.

We *wrestle* not against flesh and blood.
—Eph. vi. 12.

wres′tle, *v.t.* 1. to struggle or fight with by wrestling; to wrestle with.

2. in the western United States, to throw (a calf, etc.) for the purpose of branding.

wres′tle, *n.* 1. the action of wrestling; a wrestling match.

2. a struggle or contest.

wres′tlẽr (-lẽr), *n.* one who wrestles, especially one who takes part in regular wrestling bouts.

wrest pin, either of two metal pins between which a single string of a piano, harp, etc. is stretched: the pins are turned to tune the instrument.

wrest plank, same as *wrest block.*

wretch (rech), *n.* [ME. *wrecche;* AS. *wrecca,* an outcast, exile, lit., one driven out, from *wrecan,* to drive out, also, to persecute, wreak, avenge.]

1. a miserable or unhappy person; one in deep distress or misfortune; as, a forlorn *wretch.*

2. a person who is despised and looked upon with contempt.

3. a person whose condition arouses sympathy. [Archaic.]

wretch′ed, *a.* [ME. *wrecched,* from *wrecche;* AS. *wræcc,* wretched, from *wrecan,* to drive out, wreak.]

1. deeply distressed or unhappy; miserable; unfortunate.

2. characterized by or causing distress or misery; woeful; depressing; dismal.

3. poor in quality; very inferior; unsatisfactory; as, he has done a *wretched* job.

4. contemptible; despicable; mean.

wretch′ed·ly, *adv.* in a wretched manner.

wretch′ed·ness, *n.* 1. the state or quality of being wretched.

2. that which is extremely wretched. [Obs.]

wretch′fụl, *a.* wretched. [Obs.]

wretch′less, *a.* reckless. [Obs.]

wretch′less·ly, *adv.* recklessly. [Rare.]

wretch′less·ness, *n.* recklessness. [Obs.]

wrey (rā), *v.t.* wray. [Obs.]

wrick (rik), *n.* [via S.W. dial., from ME. *wrikken,* to move jerkily.] a wrench or sprain.

wrick, *v.t.* to twist, wrench, or sprain.

wrig (rig), *v.t.* and *v.i.* to wriggle. [Obs.]

wrig′gle (rig′l), *v.i.*; wriggled (-gld), *pt., pp.*; wriggling, *ppr.* [M.L.G. *wriggeln.*]

1. to turn, twist, or move the body to and fro with a writhing, twisting motion; to twist and turn; to squirm.

2. to move along with a wriggling motion.

3. to make one's way by subtle or shifty means; to dodge; equivocate.

wrig′gle, *v.t.* 1. to cause to wriggle.

2. to bring into a specified condition, form, etc. by wriggling.

wrig′gle, *a.* wriggling.

wrig′gle, *n.* a wriggling movement or action.

wrig′glẽr, *n.* 1. one who or that which wriggles.

2. the larva of a mosquito.

wrig′gly, *a.*; *comp.* wrigglier; *superl.* wriggliest, wriggling; twisting; squirming.

wrīght (rīt), *n.* [ME. *wrighte,* from AS. *wyrhta,* a worker, workman, maker, creator, from *wyrcan,* to work.] one who makes or constructs; a workman; a mechanic: chiefly used in compounds, as in ship*wright,* wheel*wright,* etc.

wring (riñ), *v.t.*; wrung *or rare* wringed, *pt., pp.*; wringing, *ppr.* [ME. *wringen,* from AS. *wringan,* to press, compress, strain.]

1. to twist, squeeze, or compress, especially so as to force out water or other liquid; as, to *wring* a wet rag.

2. to torture; to torment; to afflict with anguish, distress, pity, etc.; as, her story *wrung* his heart.

3. to wrench or twist forcibly.

4. to extract or force out (water or other liquid) by twisting, pressing, or squeezing (usually with *out*); as, to *wring* water *out* of a wet garment.

5. to divert or turn from one's purpose or into a certain course of action. [Obs.]

6. to extort or draw out by force, violence, oppression, etc. or against one's will; to force from; as, to *wring* taxes from the people.

7. to wrest from the true or natural meaning or purpose; to pervert; to distort.

8. to bend or strain out of its proper position; as, to *wring* a mast.

wring (ring), *v.i.* to writhe, squirm, or twist with force or great effort.

wring, *n.* the action of wringing or twisting.

wring'bōlt, *n.* a bolt used by shipwrights, to bend and secure the planks against the timbers till they are fastened by bolts, spikes, etc.

wring'ẽr, *n.* 1. one who or that which wrings.
 2. a machine with opposed rollers used to squeeze out water from wet clothes in washing.
 3. an extortioner.

wring'ing-wet', *a.* so wet that liquid can be wrung out; as, his stockings were *wringing-wet.*

wring'stȧff, *n.* one of the strong bars of wood used in applying wringbolts.

wrĭn'kle (rĭn'), *n.* [ME. *wrinkel, wrinkil,* a wrinkle; from AS. *wringan,* to press, wring.]
 1. a small ridge or furrow in a normally smooth surface, caused by contraction, crumpling, folding, etc.
 2. a crease or pucker in the skin.

wrĭn'kle, *v.t.*; wrinkled (-kld), *pt., pp.*; wrinkling, *ppr.* to make a wrinkle or wrinkles in; to crease; as, to *wrinkle* the skin; to *wrinkle* the brow.

wrĭn'kle, *v.i.* to be or become wrinkled; to form wrinkles, as by contracting.

wrĭn'kle, *n.* [prob. dim. ult. from AS. *wrenc,* a trick.] a new or good idea; a clever device; a valuable hint; a trick; as, a new *wrinkle.* [Colloq.]

wrĭn'kly, *a.*; *comp.* wrinklier; *superl.* wrinkliest, having wrinkles; wrinkled.

wrist (rist), *n.* [ME. *wriste, wrist;* AS. *wrist,* from *wræstan,* to twist.]
 1. the joint or part of the arm between the hand and the forearm; the carpus.
 2. the corresponding part in an animal.
 3. the part of a sleeve, glove, etc. covering the wrist.
 4. a wrist pin.

wrist'band (*or* riz'bănd), *n.* the band or part of a full-length sleeve, especially of a shirtsleeve, which covers the wrist; a cuff, especially of a shirt.

wrist çlō'nus, a clonic spasm of the wrist.

wrist'-drop, *n.* paralysis of the extensor muscles of the hand, due to injury or, especially, lead poisoning: also *wrist drop.*

wrist'ẽr, *n.* a wrist covering; a wristlet. [Dial.]

wrist'let, *n.* 1. an elastic band worn round the wrist to confine the upper part of a glove, or for warmth; also, a bracelet.
 2. a handcuff. [Slang.]

wrist'lock, *n.* a wrestling hold in which one wrestler twists his opponent's arm from a hold at the wrist.

wrist pin, the stud or pin by which a connecting rod is attached to a wheel, crank, etc.

wrist plāte, an oscillating plate bearing two or more wrists for working the valves in a steam engine.

wrist wätch, a watch worn on a strap or band that fits around the wrist.

writ (rit), *n.* [AS. *writ, gewrit,* a writing, a writ, from *wrītan,* to write.]
 1. that which is written; writing; document. [Rare or Archaic.]
 2. a formal legal document ordering or prohibiting the performance of some action.
 Holy Writ; the Bible.
 writ of account; see under *account.*
 writ of prohibition; an order from a higher court to a lower one directing it to cease operating in some matter outside its jurisdiction.
 writ of right; a legal writ protecting or restoring title rights in freehold real estate.

writ, *v.* archaic past tense and past participle of *write.*

wrīt·ȧ·bil'i·ty (rīt-), *n.* ability or disposition to write. [Rare.]

wrīt'ȧ·ble, *a.* capable of or fit for being written.

wrīt'ȧ·tive, *a.* disposed or inclined to write; given to writing. [Rare.]

wrīte, *v.t.*; wrote, *pt.*; written, *pp.*; writ, *archaic pt.* and *pp.*; writing, *ppr.*, [ME. *writen,* from AS. *wrītan,* to engrave, write, compose; originally, to score, engrave.]
 1. to form or inscribe (words, letters, symbols, etc.) on a surface, as by cutting, carving, or, especially, marking with a pen or pencil.
 2. to form the words, letters, or symbols of with pencil, chalk, typewriter, etc.; to put down in writing; as, *write* your name; he *wrote* the formula on the blackboard.
 3. to produce (a literary or musical composition); to compose.
 4. to draw up or compose in legal form.
 5. to fill in (a check, printed form, etc.) with necessary writing.
 6. to cover with writing; as, he stopped after *writing* three pages.
 7. to communicate in writing; as, he *wrote* that he would be late.
 8. to communicate with in writing; to write a letter or note to; as, *write* me before you go.
 9. to call, entitle, or designate in writing; as, he *writes* himself "Judge."
 10. to underwrite.
 11. to leave marks, signs, or evidence of; to show clearly; as, greed was *written* on his face.

> There is *written* in your brow honesty and
> constancy. —Shak.

 to write down; (a) to put into written form; to write a record of; (b) to disparage or depreciate by writing.
 to write off; (a) to cancel or remove from accounts: said of bad debts, claims, etc., as in accounting or bookkeeping; (b) to drop from consideration.
 to write out; (a) to put into writing; (b) to write in full.
 to write up; (a) to write a record or account of; (b) to complete or bring up to date in writing; (c) to praise or make much of in writing; (d) in accounting, to set down an excessive value for (an asset).

wrīte, *v.i.* 1. to form or inscribe words, letters, symbols, etc. on a surface, especially by making marks with a pen or pencil.
 2. to write books or other literary matter; to be an author or writer.
 3. to write a letter or letters.
 4. to be employed at written work, as a clerk, copyist, etc.
 5. to produce writing of a specified kind; as, he *writes* very legibly; the pen *writes* scratchily.

wrīt'ẽr, *n.* 1. one who writes, has written, or is in the habit of writing.
 2. a person whose business or occupation is writing; specifically, (a) a copyist; a scribe or clerk; (b) an author, journalist, or the like.
 3. a solicitor or lawyer. [Scot.]
 ship's writer; formerly, a subordinate officer in the United States Navy, whose duty was to keep the books of the ship, especially the records relating to the watch-muster.
 writer's cramp; painful spasmodic contraction of the muscles of the hand and fingers, resulting from excessive use in writing.
 writer to the signet; in Scots law, one of a class of legal practitioners in Edinburgh who formerly had important privileges which are now nearly abolished. They acted generally as agents or attorneys in conducting causes before the Court of Session.
 Syn.—author, composer, scribe, copyist, clerk, correspondent, penman.

wrīte'-in, *n.* 1. the act of voting for some person whose name is not on the ballot by writing the name in.
 2. a name so written in.

wrīt'ẽr·ess, *n.* a woman writer or author.

wrīt'ẽr·ling, *n.* a petty, mean, or insignificant writer or author.

wrīt'ẽr·ship, *n.* the office or business of a writer.

wrīte'-up, *n.* 1. a written report or description, especially one that praises or is favorable to the subject written about, as in a newspaper, magazine, etc. [Colloq.]
 2. in finance, a statement of the alleged assets of a corporation in excess of the true value.

wrīthe (rīth), *v.t.*; writhed, *pt.*; writhed *or archaic or poet.* writhen (rith'n), *pp.*; writhing, *ppr.* [ME. *writhen,* from AS. *writhan,* to twist, wind about.]
 1. to twist with violence; to cause to twist or turn; to contort.
 2. to pervert; to misinterpret. [Obs.]
 Syn.—distort, contort, twist, wrest, wrench, wriggle, wring.

wrīthe, *v.i.* 1. to make twisting or turning movements; to contort the body, as in agony; to squirm.
 2. to suffer great emotional distress, as from embarrassment, revulsion, etc.

wrīthe, *n.* an act of writhing; writhing movement; contortion.

writh'en (rith'n), *a.* writhed; twisted; contorted. [Poet. or Archaic.]

wrīt'ing (rīt'), *n.* 1. the act of a person who writes.
 2. something written, as a letter, document, inscription, etc.
 3. written form.
 4. handwriting.
 5. a book, poem, article, or other literary work.
 6. the profession or occupation of a writer.
 7. the art, practice, style, or form of literary composition.

wrīt'ing, *a.* 1. that writes.
 2. used in writing.

wrīt'ing desk, a case or desk used for writing upon and for containing writing materials.

wrīt'ing lärk, the yellowhammer. [Brit. Dial.]

wrīt'ing mȧs'tẽr, one who teaches the art of penmanship.

wrīt'ing pā'pẽr, 1. paper for writing on.
 2. stationery.

wrīt'ing tā'ble, a table for writing on.

writ'ten (rit') *v.* past participle of *write.*

writ'ten law (or **laws**), law or laws enacted by a legislative body and written out in form, as distinguished from unwritten law.

wriz'zle (riz'), *v.t.* to wrinkle. [Obs.]

wrō'ken (rō'), *v.* obsolete past participle of *wreak.*

wrọng (rọng), *a.* [ME. *wrong;* AS. *wrang,* wrong, from *wrang,* pt. of *wringan,* to wring.]
 1. not morally right or just; sinful; wicked; immoral.
 2. not in accordance with an established standard, previous arrangement, given intention, etc.; as, this is the *wrong* method, he came on the *wrong* day.
 3. not suitable or appropriate; as, that was the *wrong* thing to say.
 4. (a) contrary to truth, fact, etc.; incorrect; inaccurate; (b) acting, judging, believing, etc. incorrectly; mistaken.
 5. unsatisfactory; in a bad state or condition.
 6. not functioning properly; out of order; as, something is *wrong* with my eyes.
 7. designed to be worn or placed inward or under and not displayed; as, the *wrong* side of a fabric.
 Syn.—unjust, immoral, inequitable, erroneous, inaccurate, incorrect, faulty, detrimental, injurious, hurtful, unfit, unsuitable.

wrọng, *adv.* amiss; incorrectly; in a wrong manner, direction, etc.; so as to be wrong.
 to get (someone) in wrong; to bring (someone) into disfavor. [Colloq.]
 to go wrong; (a) to turn out badly; (b) to change from good behavior to bad; to go astray.

wrọng, *n.* 1. the state or fact of being wrong; also, something that is wrong, especially a wicked or unjust act.
 2. in law, a violation of a legal right; a tort.
 in the wrong; wrong.

wrọng, *v.t.*; wronged, *pt., pp.*; wronging, *ppr.*
 1. to treat badly or unjustly; to do wrong to; to injure.
 2. to think badly of without real justification.
 3. to malign; dishonor.
 4. to seduce (a woman).

wrọng, *v.i.* to turn wrongside up; to be in the wrong position or attitude. [Rare.]

> Before one can say, Thank heaven, she (the
> ship) *wrongs* again. —Dickens.

wrọng'dö"ẽr, *n.* 1. one who injures another or does wrong.
 2. in law, one who commits a tort or trespass.

wrọng'dö"ing, *n.* any act or behavior that is wrong; the doing of wrong; transgression.

wrọng'ẽr, *n.* one who wrongs another.

wrọng font, in printing, the incorrect font: used to designate a type face of the wrong size or style.

wrọng'fụl, *a.* 1. full of wrong; unjust, unfair, or injurious.
 2. unlawful.

wrọng'fụl·ly, *adv.* unjustly; in a manner contrary to the moral law or to justice; as, to accuse one *wrongfully*; to suffer *wrongfully.*

wrọng'fụl·ness, *n.* the quality of being wrongful.

wrọng'head (-hed), *n.* a person of stubborn disposition; an obstinate individual. [Rare.]

wrọng'head, *a.* wrongheaded. [Rare.]

wrọng'head"ed, *a.* stubbornly refusing to yield, agree, etc. even when wrong; perverse.

wrọng'head"ed·ly, *adv.* in a wrongheaded manner.

wrọng'head"ed·ness, *n.* the character of being wrongheaded; perverseness.

wrong'less, *a.* void of wrong.
wrong'less·ly, *adv.* without injury to anyone.
wrong'ly, *adv.* in a wrong manner; unjustly; amiss; as, he judges *wrongly* of my motives.
wrong'ness, *n.* the condition or quality of being wrong; faultiness.
wron̄'gous (ron̄'), *a.* [ME. *wrongwis.*]
1. in Scottish law, not right; unjust; illegal; as, *wrongous* imprisonment.
2. wrongful; unjust. [Scot.]
wrong'-tīmed, *a.* done at an improper time.
wroot (rōt), *v.* obsolete past tense of *write.*
wrōte (rōt), *v.* past tense of *write.*
wrōte, *v.* obsolete past participle of *write.*
wrōte, *v.i.* and *v.t.* to root, as a pig. [Obs.]
wroth (roth), *a.* [AS. *wrath,* wroth, from *wrath,* pt. of *writhan,* to writhe.] very angry; irate; incensed.

Cain was very *wroth,* and his countenance fell. —Gen. iv. 5.

wrought (rat), *v.* alternative past tense and past participle of *work.*
wrought, *a.* 1. formed; fashioned; made.
2. shaped by hammering or beating: said of metals.
3. made with great care; elaborated.
4. decorated; ornamented.
wrought'-ī'ron (-ūrn), *a.* made of wrought iron.
wrought ī'ron, a kind of iron that contains some slag and very little carbon: it is tough and hard to break yet soft enough to be pounded into shape.
wrought'-ī'ron cast'ing, 1. the process of casting with mitis metal.
2. a casting made by this process.
wrought'-up', *a.* disturbed; excited.
wrung (run̄), *v.* past tense and past participle of *wring.*
wrȳ (rī), *v.t.* to cover; to clothe. [Obs.]
wrȳ, *v.t.* and *v.i.*; wried, *pt., pp.*; wrying, *ppr.* [ME. *wrien,* to twist, bend, from AS. *wrigian,* to drive, impel; also, to tend or bend toward.] to writhe or twist.
wrȳ, *a.*; *comp.* wrier; *superl.* wriest, 1. turned or bent to one side; twisted; distorted.
2. made by twisting or distorting the features; as, a *wry* face.
3. perverse; contrary.
4. distorted in meaning, interpretation, etc.

wrȳ'bill, *n.* a New Zealand plover, *Anarhynchus frontalis,* with the bill bent to one side.
wrȳ'ly, *adv.* in a wry or awkward manner.
wrȳ'mouth, *n.* any marine fish belonging to the genus *Cryptacanthodes*; especially, *Cryptacanthodes maculatus,* the common American wrymouth.
wrȳ'neck, *n.* 1. a condition in which the neck is twisted by a muscle spasm; torticollis.
2. a person afflicted with this. [Colloq.]
3. a small migratory scansorial bird of the genus *Iynx,* related to and resembling the woodpecker: so called from its habit of stretching and twisting its neck.

WRYNECK

wrȳ'-necked (-nekt), *a.* having a distorted neck.
wrȳ'ness, *n.* the state or quality of being wry or distorted.
wul'fen·īte, *n.* [named after Baron F. X. von *Wülfen* (1728–1805), an Austrian mineralogist.] a mineral, lead molybdate, $PbMoO_4$, having a high luster and occurring in various colors.
wull, *v.t.* and *v.i.* to will; to wish. [Obs. or Dial.]
wung'-out, *a.* in nautical slang, having the sails wing-and-wing.
wûr'ley, *n.* [Australian.] an Australian aboriginal hut.
wûr'măl, *n.* a warble (larva).

wůrst (*or* G. voorsht), *n.* [G.] sausage: used generally in combination, as in liver*wurst,* wiener*wurst.*
wûrtz'i·līte (wûrts'), *n.* [named after Dr. Henry *Wurtz,* Am. mineralogist.] a kind of asphalt found in the Uinta Mountains in Utah: it becomes plastic in boiling water.
wûrtz'īte (wûrts'), *n.* [named after C. A. *Wurtz,* a French chemist.] zinc sulfide, crystallizing in the hexagonal system.
wust, *v.* obsolete past tense of *wit.*
wuth'ĕr, *v.i.* (var. of *wither.*) to bluster, as wind among trees.
Wȳ'ăn·dot, *n.* 1. a member of the former Huron tribe or confederacy of North American Indians.
2. an Iroquoian language.
Also spelled *Wyandotte.*
Wȳ'ăn·dotte, *n.* any of a breed of American domestic fowls, a cross between the Brahma and the Hamburg.
wych'-elm, *n.* [from *witch,* as in *witch hazel*: so called because of the pliant branches.]
1. a small variety of elm found in Europe and northern Asia.
2. its wood.
Also spelled *witch-elm.*
wych'-hā"zel, *n.* 1. same as *witch-hazel.*
2. a wych-elm.
Wyc'liff·īte, Wyc'lif·īte, *n.* a follower of John Wycliffe, the English reformer: also called *Lollard.*
Wyc'liff·īte, Wyc'lif·īte, *a.* of or having to do with John Wycliffe or his followers.
wȳe, *n.*; *pl.* **wȳes,** 1. the letter Y.
2. something shaped like Y.
Wyke'hăm·ist, *n.* a present or past student of Winchester College, England, founded by William of Wykeham (1324–1404), Bishop of Winchester.
Wyke'hăm·ist, *a.* pertaining to Winchester College or Wykehamists.
wynd, *n.* a narrow lane or alley. [Scot. or Dial.]
wyn̄'kĕr·nel, *n.* the European water hen. [Brit. Dial.]
wynn, *n.* a kind of timber truck or carriage.
Wȳ·ō'ming·īte, *n.* a native or inhabitant of Wyoming.
wȳpe, *n.* the lapwing. [Obs.]
wȳs, wȳse, *a.* wise. [Obs.]
wythe, *n.* same as *withe.*
wȳ'vĕrn, *n.* same as *wivern.*

X

X, x (eks), *n.*; *pl.* **X's, x's, Xs, xs,** (eks'iz), 1. the twenty-fourth letter of the English alphabet: from a western Greek alphabet.
2. the sound of X or x.
3. a type or impression for X or x.
4. a symbol for the twenty-fourth in a sequence or group (or the twenty-third if J is omitted, or the twenty-first if V and W are also omitted).
X, x (eks), *a.* 1. of X or x.
2. twenty-fourth (or twenty-third if J is omitted, or twenty-first if V and W are also omitted) in a sequence or group.
X (eks), *n.* 1. an object shaped like X.
2. a mark shaped like an X used: (a) to represent the signature of a person who cannot write; (b) to indicate a particular point on a map, diagram, etc.; (c) as a symbol for a kiss in letters, etc.
3. the Roman numeral 10: with a superior bar ($\overline{X}$), 10,000: XX equals 20, XXX equals 30, and X before another Roman numeral expresses a number 10 less than that numeral.
4. a person or thing unknown or unrevealed.
5. Christ: used also in combination, as in Xmas.
6. in chemistry, a symbol for xenon.

X (eks), *a.* shaped like X.
x, in mathematics, (a) an unknown quantity; (b) a sign of multiplication; as, 3 x 3 = 9; (c) an abscissa.
xanth- (zanth-), same as *xantho-.*
xanth'ăl·ine, *n.* an alkaloid, $C_{20}H_{19}O_5N$, derived from opium.
xanth·am'ide, *n.* a white crystalline substance, C_3H_7NSO, derivable from xanthic acid.
xan'thāte (zan'), *n.* a salt or ester of xanthic acid.
xan'thē·in, *n.* [from *xanth-* and *-in.*] that portion of the yellow coloring matter in flowers which is soluble in water, as distinguished from *xanthin,* which is the insoluble part.
xan·thē·las'mȧ, *n.* same as *xanthoma.*
xan"thē·las·moi'dē·ȧ, *n.* [*xanthelasma,* and Gr. *eidos,* form.] a disease of infants characterized by the development of brownish wheals, followed by pigmentation.
Xan'thi·ăn (zan'), *a.* of or having to do with Xanthus, an ancient city of Asia Minor; as, the *Xanthian* sculptures in the British Museum.
xan'thic (zan'), *a.* [Fr. *xanthique.*]
1. yellow or yellowish in color.
2. of or having to do with xanthin or xanthine.
3. designating or of an unstable colorless acid, $C_3H_6OS_2$, that decomposes into ethyl alcohol and carbon disulfide at 24° C.
Xan·thid'i·um, *n.* [Gr. *xanthos,* yellow.] in botany, a genus of *Confervaceæ,* supposed to be sporangia of *Desmidiaceæ.* They are microscopic spherical bodies with radiating spines.
xan'thin, *n.* [*xanth-* and *-in.*] (a) that portion of the yellow coloring matter of flowers which is insoluble in water; (b) [Obs.] the yellow coloring matter contained in madder; (c) [Obs.] a gaseous product of the decomposition of xanthates; (d) xanthine.
xan'thine (*or* -thin), *n.* [*xanth-* and *-ine.*] a white, crystalline, nitrogenous compound, $C_5H_4N_4O_2$, resembling uric acid: it is present in blood, urine, and certain plants: also spelled *xanthin.*
xan·thin·ū'ri·ȧ, *n.* [*xanthin,* and Gr. *ouron,* urine.] excess of xanthin in the urine.
Xan'thi·um (zan'), *n.* [Gr. *xanthion,* a plant, said to have been used on the hair to turn it yellow, from *xanthos,* yellow.] a genus of plants of the *Compositæ. Xanthium struma-*

rium is a rank and weedlike plant, noted for the curious structure of its flowers and the prickly involucres which surround the fertile ones, enlarging and becoming part of the fruit.

xan·thi·ū'ri·ȧ (zan'), *n.* same as *xanthinuria.*

xan'thō- (zan'), [*from* Gr. *xanthos,* yellow.] a combining form meaning *yellow,* as in *xantho*chroid: also, before a vowel, *xanth-.*

xan·thō·căr'pous, *a.* [*xantho-* and *-carpous.*] in botany, having yellow fruit.

Xan·thoçh'rō·ī, *n.pl.* [*xantho-,* and Gr. *chroa,* skin, color.] in ethnology, one of the groups of Caucasian races, comprising the fair-haired whites.

xan·thō·çhroi'ȧ, *n.* in medicine, yellowish discoloration caused by changes in the pigmentary layer of the skin.

Xan·thō·çhrō'iç, *a.* of or relating to the *Xanthochroi.*

xan'thō·çhroid, *a.* [from *xantho-,* and Gr. *chroa;* and *-oid.*] having light-colored hair and complexion.

xan'thō·çhroid, *n.* a xanthochroid person.

xan·thō·çhrō'mi·ȧ, *n.* [*xantho-,* and Gr. *chrōma,* color.] in medicine, any yellowish discoloration, as of the skin.

xan·thoçh'rō·ous, *a.* [Gr. *xanthochroos,* yellow-skinned, from *xanthos,* yellow, and *chroa,* skin, color.] having a yellowish complexion; also, relating to the *Xanthochroi.*

xan'thō·çōne, *n.* [*xantho-,* and Gr. *konis,* powder.] a dull-red, clove-brown, orange-yellow, brittle, rhombohedral mineral occurring in small crystals and reniform groups. It is composed of silver, sulfur, and arsenic.

xan"thō·çrē·at'i·nine, *n.* a poisonous substance, $C_5H_{10}N_4O$, occurring in muscle tissue. It appears in the form of yellow crystals.

xan"thō·cy̆·an'op·sy, *n.* [*xantho-,* Gr. *kyanos,* blue, and *opsis,* appearance.] color blindness in which one can discern only yellow and blue: also written *xanthocyanopy.*

xan·thō·dẽr'mȧ, *n.* [*xantho-,* and Gr. *derma,* skin.] in medicine, a yellow discoloration of the skin.

xan'thō·dont, *a.* [*xantho-,* and Gr. *odous, odontos,* tooth.] having teeth of a yellowish color, as a rodent.

xan·thō·don'tous, *a.* same as *xanthodont.*

xan'thō·ġen, *n.* the hypothetical radical believed to be present in xanthic acid.

xan'thō·ġen·āte, *n.* a salt or ester of xanthic acid.

xan·thō·ġen'iç, *a.* xanthic.

xan·thō'mȧ, *n.* a disease attended with the formation of yellow neoplastic growths upon the skin, especially that of the eyelids The growths consist of flat patches or nodules, which are slightly raised above the surface, and vary in size from that of a pin's head to that of a bean.

xan·thom'ȧ·tous, *a.* of or pertaining to xanthoma.

xan·thō·mel'ȧ·nous, *a.* [*xantho-,* and Gr. *melas, melanos,* black.] pertaining to races of men with an olive, brown, or yellow complexion and black hair.

xan'thō·phāne, *n.* [*xantho-,* and Gr. *phainesthai,* to be seen, appear.] a yellow pigment of the retina.

xan'thō·phyll, xan'thō·phyl, *n.* [*xantho-* and *-phyll.*] a yellow crystalline pigment, $C_{40}H_{56}O_2$, found in plants: it is related to carotene and is the basis of the yellow seen in autumn leaves.

xan·thō·prō'tē·iç, *a.* designating an acid formed when protein is acted upon by hot nitric acid. It is of a yellow color.

xan·thō·prō'tē·in, *n.* a yellow pigment produced by heating proteins with nitric acid.

xan·thō·prō·tē·in'iç, *a.* same as *xanthoproteic.*

xan·thop'sin, *n.* [*xantho-,* and Gr. *opsis,* vision.] visual yellow.

xan·thop·sy·drā'ci·ȧ, *n.* [*xantho-,* and Gr. *psydrax,* a blister.] the occurrence on the skin of small yellow pustules.

xan·thō·rham'nine (-ram'), *n.* [*xantho-,* and Gr. *rhamnos,* buckthorn.] a yellow coloring in the ripe fruit of certain species of *Rhamnus,* as the Avignon berries.

Xan·thŏr·rhī'zȧ (-rī'), *n.* same as *Xanthorrhoea.*

Xan·thŏr·rhoe'ȧ, *n.* [*xantho-,* and Gr. *rhein,* to flow, from its yellow resinous exudation.] a genus of trees, family *Liliaceæ.* The species are called grass trees, and are found in Australia. They have thick trunks like those of palms, long wiry grasslike leaves, and long dense flower spikes.

xan·thō'sis, *n.* [Gr. *xanthos,* yellow.] in medicine, a yellow discoloration ofter occurring in cancerous tumors.

xan·thō·spẽr'mous, *a.* [*xantho-,* and Gr. *sperma,* seed.] in botany, having yellow seeds.

xan'thous, *a.* [Gr. *xanthos,* yellow.] yellow.

Xan·thox·yl'ē·ae, *n.pl.* same as *Rutaceae.*

xan·thox'y·lin, *n.* 1. a crystallizable compound, $C_{10}H_{12}O_4$, from *Xanthoxylum piperitum,* or Japanese pepper.

2. a concentration prepared from the bark of *Xanthoxylum fraxineum.*

Xan·thox'y·lum, *n.* [*xantho-,* and Gr. *xylon,* wood.] a genus of rutaceous plants, the species of which are trees or shrubs, with the petioles, leaves, and branches usually furnished with prickles.

xan·thū'ri·ȧ, *n.* same as *xanthinuria.*

X çhrō'mō·sōme (eks), a sex chromosome.

Xe, in chemistry, xenon.

xē'beç (zē'), *n.* [altered from earlier *chebec,* from Fr. *chébec;* Sp. *jabeque,* xebec, from Turk. *sumbeki,* a sort of ship.] a small three-masted vessel, formerly much used by corsairs in the Mediterranean: it has several square sails, as well as lateen sails, and an overhanging bow and stern.

XEBEC

xēme (zēm), *n.* an arctic gull, *Xema Sabinei;* the fork-tailed gull.

xen·ē·lā'si·ȧ (zen-), *n.* [Gr., the expulsion of strangers.] a Spartan institution which prohibited strangers from residing in Sparta without permission, and empowered magistrates to expel them if they saw fit to do so.

xē'ni·ȧ (zē'), *n.* [Gr. *xenia,* the rights of a guest, hospitality, from *xenos,* guest friend.] in botany, the immediate influence of pollen from one strain of a plant upon the seed of another strain, resulting in hybrid characteristics in the form, color, etc. of the resulting growth.

xē'ni·ăl, *a.* [Gr. *xenia,* the rights of a guest, hospitality, from *xenos,* guest friend.] pertaining to hospitable customs, especially as practiced in ancient Greece.

xē'ni·um, *n.; pl.* **xē'ni·ȧ,** [L., from Gr. *xenion,* usually in pl. *xenia,* a gift to a guest, from *xenos,* a guest.] in ancient Greece and Rome, a present given to a guest or stranger, or to a foreign ambassador.

xen'ō- (zen'), [from Gr. *xenos,* strange, foreign, a stranger.] a combining form meaning: (a) *stranger, foreigner,* as in *xeno*phobia; (b) *strange, foreign, extraneous,* as in *xeno*lith. Also, before a vowel, *xen-.*

xen"ō·bī·ō'sis, *n.* [Gr. *xenos,* guest friend, and *biosis,* from *bios,* life.] a form of communal life in which two colonies of different species live together on friendly terms but do not rear their young in common, as certain species of ants.

Xen·ō·crat'iç (zen-), *a.* pertaining to the doctrine or philosophy of Xenocrates (396–314 B.C.), which was a combination of Pythagoreanism and Platonism.

xen"ō·dō·çhē'um, xen"ō·dō·çhī'um, *n.; pl.* **xen"ō·dō·çhē'ȧ, xen"ō·dō·çhī'ȧ,** [Gr. *xenodocheion; xenos,* stranger, and *dechesthai,* to receive.] in the Middle Ages, a building for the reception of strangers, care of the sick, etc.

xē·nod'ō·çhy (zē-), *n.* [Gr. *xenodochia; xenos,* guest, stranger, and *dechesthai,* to receive.]

1. reception of strangers; hospitality.
2. same as *xenodocheum.*

xē·nog'ȧ·mous (zē-), *a.* of or having to do with xenogamy.

xē·nog'ȧ·my, *n.* [Gr. *xenos,* strange, and *gamos,* marriage.] in botany, cross-fertilization.

xen·ō·ġen'e·sis (zen-), *n.* [Mod. L.; see *xeno-* and *-genesis.*]

1. spontaneous generation; abiogenesis.
2. alternation of generations; metagenesis.
3. the supposed production of an individual completely different from either of its parents.

xen"ō·ġē·net'iç, *a.* of or pertaining to xenogenesis.

xen·ō·ġen'iç, *a.* xenogenetic.

xē·nog'ē·nous (zē-), *a.* caused by a foreign body or originating outside of the organism.

xē·nog'ē·ny, *n.* same as *xenogenesis.*

xen'ō·līte (zen'), *n.* [from Gr. *xenos,* stranger, and *lithos,* stone: so called because unrelated to the stones where it was found.] a variety of fibrolite with a high specific gravity.

xen'ō·lith, *n.* [*zeno-* and *-lith.*] a rock fragment embedded in the mass of another rock.

xen·ō·mā'ni·ȧ, *n.* [Gr. *xenos,* strange, and *mania,* madness, enthusiasm.] a mania for foreign institutions, customs, etc. [Rare.]

Xen'ō·mī (zen'), *n.pl.* [Gr. *xenos,* strange, and *ōmos,* shoulder.] an order of fishes of which the Alaskan blackfish, *Dallia pectoralis,* is the most important species.

xen·ō·mọr'phiç, *a.* [*xeno-* and *morphic.*] having a form not characteristic of its kind, but determined by the pressure of surrounding constituents: said of the granular constituents of crystalline rock.

xē'non (zē'), *n.* [Gr., neut. of *xenos,* strange.] a heavy, colorless, inert, gaseous chemical element present in the air in minute quantities; symbols, Xe, X; atomic weight, 131.3; atomic number, 54.

xen·ō·phō'bi·ȧ (zen-), *n.* [Mod. L.; see *xeno-* and *-phobia.*] fear or hatred of strangers or foreigners.

xē·nop·tē·ryġ'i·ăn (zē-), *a.* pertaining to the *Xenopterygii.*

xē·nop·tē·ryġ'i·ăn, *n.* one of the *Xenopterygii.*

Xē·nop·tē·ryġ'i·ī, *n.pl.* [Gr. *xenos,* strange, and *pteryx, pterygos,* a wing.] a suborder of small, scaleless, soft-rayed fishes inhabiting warm seas.

xen'ō·tīme (zen'-), *n.* a native phosphate of yttrium, having a yellowish-brown color.

xē·nū'rine (zē-), *n.* a kabassou.

xē·nū'rine, *a.* pertaining to *Xenurus,* a genus of armadillos, the kabassou.

xen'yl (zen'), *n.* [Gr. *xenos,* strange, and *-yl.*] the univalent radical, $C_6H_5C_6H_4$-, of xenylic compounds.

xē·nyl'iç (zē-), *a.* pertaining to or obtained from certain compounds of diphenyl.

xer'ȧ·fin (zer'), *n.* [Port. *xerafim,* from Ar. *ashrafī,* from *sharīf,* noble.] a silver coin formerly issued in India by the Portuguese. It was worth about 360 reis. [Obs.]

xē·ran'sis (zē-), *n.* [Gr. *xēros,* dry.] a dried-up or desiccated condition.

xē·ran'tiç, *a.* dried up; desiccated.

xē·rā'şi·ȧ (-zhi-), *n.* [Gr. *xērasia,* dryness, from *xēros,* dry.] in pathology, a disease of the hair, in which it becomes dry and ceases to grow.

xer'es (zer'), *n.* [Sp.] sherry: so called from the district of Spain, where it is produced.

xe·riff' (she-rēf'), *n.* a sherif.

xē'rō- (zē'), [from Gr. *xēros,* dry.] a combining form meaning *dry,* as in *xero*phyte: also, before a vowel, *xer-.*

xē·rō·dẽr'mȧ, xē·rō·dẽr'mi·ȧ, *n.* [*xero-,* and Gr. *derma,* skin.] same as *ichthyosis.*

xē·rog'rȧ·phy, *n.* [*xero-,* and *-graphy.*] a process for copying printed material, pictures, etc., in which the latent image of the original material is transferred by the action of light to an electrically charged surface to which the image attracts oppositely charged dry ink particles, which are then fused in place on the copy paper, reproducing the original image.

xē·rō'mȧ, *n.* [Gr. *xēros,* dry.] xerophthalmia.

xē·rom'y·rum, *n.* [*xero-,* and Gr. *muron,* ointment.] a dry ointment.

xē'rō·nāte, *n.* a salt of xeronic acid.

xē·ron'iç, *a.* [*xero-* and *citraconic.*] designating an acid, $C_8H_{12}O_4$, obtained from citraconic acid.

xē·rō·phā'ġi·ȧ, *n.* the eating of dry food; xerophagy.

xē·roph'ȧ·ġy, *n.* [*xero-,* and Gr. *phagein,* to eat.] the Christian rule of fasting; the act or habit of living on dry food or a meager diet: now observed chiefly in the Orthodox Eastern Church, particularly during Lent.

xē'rō·phil, *n.* a xerophyte.

xē·roph'i·lous, *a.* [*xero-* and *-philous.*] capable of or adapted to thriving in dry, hot climates, as certain plants or animals.

xē·roph·thal'mi·ȧ, *n.* [*xero-,* and Gr. *ophthalmia,* a disease of the eyes, from *ophthalmos,* the eye.] a form of conjunctivitis characterized by an abnormally dry and lusterless condition of the eyeball and caused by a deficiency of vitamin A.

xē·roph·thal′my, *n.* same as *xerophthalmia.*

xē′rō·phȳte, *n.* [*xero-* and *-phyte.*] a xerophilous plant.

xē·rō·phyt′iç, *a.* of, or having the nature of, a xerophyte; xerophilous.

xē″rō·rā″di·og′ra·phy, *n.* [*xero-*, and *radiography.*] an X-ray technique that quickly produces by xerography a detailed image of the X-rayed part: used especially for the early detection of breast tumors.

xē′rox, *n.* a device for copying graphic or printed material by xerography; a trade-mark (*Xerox*).

xē′rox, *v.t.* and *v.i.* to reproduce by xerography.

xē·rō′sis, *n.* [Gr., from *xēros*, dry.] abnormal dryness, as of the eye or skin; xeransis.

xē·rō·stō′mi·ȧ, *n.* [*xero-*, and Gr. *stoma*, mouth.] dryness of the mouth from lack of the normal secretion.

xē′rō·tēṣ, *n.* [Gr. *xērotēs*, dryness.] in medicine, a dry habit or disposition of the body.

xē·rot′iç, *a.* [Gr. *xērotēs*, dryness, and *-ic.*] characterized by xerosis; dry.

xē·rō·trip′sis, *n.* dry friction.

Xhō′sä (kō′sä, -zä; *the k is actually a click*), *n.* 1. *pl.* **Xhō′säṣ, Xhō′sä,** any member of a pastoral people living in Cape Province, South Africa.

2. their Bantu language, characterized by the use of clicks.

xi (zī, sī, *or* Gr. ksē), [Gr.] the fourteenth letter of the Greek alphabet, corresponding to English *X, x.*

-xion, (c)tion: British spelling, as in conne*xion* (connection).

xiph-, xiph′i-, xiph′ō-, (zif′), [from Gr. *xiphos*, a sword.] combining forms meaning *swordlike.*

Xiph′i·ȧs, *n.* [LL., from Gr. *xiphos*, a sword.]

1. the genus of fishes to which *Xyphias gladius*, or the common swordfish, belongs.

2. in astronomy, Dorado, a constellation in the southern hemisphere.

3. [x–] a sword-shaped comet. [Obs.]

xiph′i·oid, *a.* pertaining to the swordfish family.

xiph·i·plas′trăl, *a.* pertaining to the xiphiplastron.

xiph·i·plas′tron, *n.*; *pl.* **xiph·i·plas′trȧ,** the fourth lateral plate in the plastron of a turtle.

xiph·i·stẽr′năl, *a.* pertaining to the xiphisternum.

xiph·i·stẽr′num, *n.*; *pl.* **xiph·i·stẽr′nȧ,** [*xiphi-*, and Gr. *sternon*, a breastbone.]

1. in comparative anatomy, the inferior or posterior segment of the sternum; in man, the xiphoid process.

2. the xiphiplastron.

Xiph·i·sū′rȧ, Xiph·i·ū′rȧ, *n.pl.* same as *Xiphosura.*

xiph·i·sū′răn, *a.* same as *xiphosuran.*

xiph·i·sū′răn, *n.* same as *xiphosuran.*

Xiph′i·us, *n.* same as *Ziphius.*

Xiph′ō·don, *n.* [*xiph-*, and Gr. *odous, odontos*, a tooth.] a genus of fossil, small, two-toed artiodactyls.

xiph·ō·don′tid, *n.* a fossil mammal of the genus *Xiphodon.*

xiph·ō·dyn′i·ȧ, *n.* [*xipho-*, and Gr. *odynē*, pain.] pain in the xiphoid process.

xiph′oid, *a.* [Gr. *xiphoeides*, sword-shaped, from *xiphos*, sword, and *eidos*, a form.]

1. shaped like or resembling a sword; ensiform.

2. designating or of a cartilaginous process at the lower end of the sternum, or breastbone.

xiphoid cartilage; same as *xiphoid process.*

xiph′oid, *n.* the xiphoid process.

xiph·oid′i·ăn, *a.* xiphoid.

xiph·ō·phyl′lous, *a.* [*xipho-*, and Gr. *phyllon*, a leaf.] in botany, having ensiform leaves.

xiph·ō·stẽr′num, *n.* same as *xiphisternum.*

Xiph·ō·sū′rȧ, *n.pl.* [from Gr. *xiphos*, a sword, and *oura*, a tail.] an order of primitive arachnids made up of the king crabs.

xiph·ō·sū′răn, *a.* designating or of the *Xiphosura.*

xiph·ō·sū′răn, *n.* any member of the *Xiphosura.*

xiph′ō·sūre, *n.* a xiphosuran.

xiph·ō·sū′rous, *a.* same as *xiphosuran.*

Xi·phū′rȧ (zī-), *n.pl.* same as *xiphosura.*

xi·phū′rous, *a.* same as *xiphosuran.*

Xmas (kris′măs; *popularly* eks′măs), *n.* [see X (sense 5)], Christmas.

xō′ȧ·non (zō′), *n.*; *pl.* **xō′ȧ·nȧ,** [Gr., an image of wood, statue, from *xeein*, to carve.] in ancient Greece, a rude primitive statue, usually of wood and resembling the block it was cut from.

X pär′ti·çle, a mesotron.

X rāy, [so called by the discoverer because of its unknown character.]

1. a non-luminous electromagnetic ray or radiation of extremely short wave length, generally less than 2 angstroms, produced by the bombardment of a substance (usually one of the heavy metals) by a stream of electrons moving at great velocity, as in a vacuum tube. X rays are capable of penetrating opaque or solid substances, ionizing gases and tissues through which they pass, and affecting photographic plates and fluorescent screens. They are widely used in medicine for study, diagnosis, and treatment of certain organic disorders, especially of internal structures of the body.

2. a photograph made by means of X rays.

X′-rāy, *v.t.* to examine, treat, or photograph with X rays.

X′-rāy, *a.* of, by, or having to do with X rays.

xyl- (zil-), same as *xylo-.*

xȳ′lan (zī′), *n.* [from Gr. *xylon*, wood; and *-an.*] a yellow, gummy pentosan that is found in woody tissues and yields xylose upon hydrolysis.

xy·lan′thrax, *n.* [*xyl-*, and Gr. *anthrax*, coal.] woodcoal; charcoal. [Obs.]

xȳ′lāte, *n.* a salt or ester of xylic acid.

Xȳ·leb′ō·rus, *n.* [Gr. *xylēboros*, eating wood; *xylon*, wood, and *boros*, eating.] a genus of small beetles which bore into oak and other timber.

xȳ′lem, *n.* [G., from Gr. *xylon*, wood.] the woody tissue of a plant; especially, in higher forms, the part of the vascular bundle, consisting of tracheal tissue, parenchyma, etc., that gives firmness and conducts moisture.

xȳ′lēne, *n.* [*xyl-* and *-ene.*] any of three isomeric, colorless hydrocarbons, $C_6H_4(CH_3)_2$, having the characteristics of benzene and derived from coal tar and wood tar: used as solvents, antiseptics, etc.

xȳ′lē·nōl, *n.* any one of six white crystalline salts, C_8H_9OH, phenol derivatives of xylene.

xȳ·let′iç, *a.* designating an acid derived from xylenol by the action of sodium and carbon dioxide.

xȳ′liç, *a.* pertaining to or obtained from xylene; as, *xylic* acid.

xȳ′liç ac′id, any of six isomeric crystalline acids, $C_6H_3(CH_3)_2COOH$, carboxyl derivatives of xylene.

xȳ·lid′iç, *a.* pertaining to or obtained from xylic acid.

xylidic acid; a compound, $C_9H_8O_4$, obtained when xylic acid is oxidized.

xȳ′li·din, *n.* xylidine.

xȳ′li·dīne, *n.* [from *xyl*ene and *-ide* and *-ine.*]

1. any of the isomeric compounds having the formula $C_6H_3(CH_3)_2NH_2$, resembling aniline and derived from xylene.

2. a mixture of these isomeric compounds, used in making certain dyes.

xȳ·lin′id, *n.* [Gr. *xylinos*, of wood, wooden, from *xylon*, wood, and *-id.*] any moth of the family *Xylinidæ*, named from the genus *Xylina.* The larva of *Xylina cinerea* infests various trees in the United States.

xȳ′lō-, [from Gr. *xylon*, wood.] a combining form meaning *wood*, as in *xylo*graph: also, before a vowel, *xyl-.*

xȳ·lō·bal′sȧ·mum, *n.* [*xylo-*, and Gr. *balsamon*, balsam.] the wood of the oriental balsam tree; also, the balsam obtained from this wood.

xȳ′lō·çärp, *n.* [*xylo-*, and Gr. *karpos*, fruit.] a hard woody fruit.

xȳ·lō·çär′pous, *a.* [*xylo-*, and Gr. *karpos*, fruit.] having fruit which becomes hard or woody.

Xȳ·loç′ō·pȧ, *n.* [*xylo-*, and Gr. *koptein*, to cut.] the carpenter bees; a genus of hymenopterous insects with sharp-pointed mandibles which bore holes in wood.

xȳ′lō·ġen, *n.* same as *xylem.*

xȳ′lō·gràph, *n.* [*xylo-* and *-graph.*] an engraving on wood or an impression from such an engraving; a xylographic impression.

xȳ·log′rȧ·phẽr, *n.* one who engraves on wood.

xȳ·lō·graph′iç, xȳ·lō·graph′i·çăl, *a.* relating to or made by xylography.

xȳ·log′rȧ·phy, *n.* 1. wood engraving; the art of cutting figures or designs in wood or of taking printed impressions from such designs.

2. a process of decorative painting on wood.

xȳ′loid (zī′), *a.* of or like wood; ligneous.

xȳ·loid′ine, *n.* a white explosive substance, $C_6H_9NO_7$, prepared from starch by the action of nitric acid.

xȳ′lol, xȳ′lōle (zī′), *n.* same as *xylene.*

xȳ·lol′ō·ġy (zī-), *n.* a study of or treatise on the structure of wood.

xȳ·lō′mȧ (zī-), *n.*; *pl.* **xȳ·lom′ȧ·tȧ,** a woody tumor on a tree or plant.

xȳ′lōn·īte (zī′), *n.* same as *celluloid.*

Xȳ·loph′ȧ·gȧ (zī-) *n.pl.* [*xylo-*, and Gr. *phagein*, to eat.] a group of coleopterous insects identified by their habit of excavating wood. They resemble the weevils, but are distinguished from them by the absence of a proboscis.

xȳ·loph′ȧ·găn, *n.* an insect of the group or genus *Xylophaga.*

Xȳ·lō·phaġ′i·dae, *n.pl.* a family of *Diptera* or flies, having jointed antennae and a long ovipositor. The larva is cylindrical, with a scaly plate on the tail and the head ending in an acute point. They are very destructive to wood.

xȳ·loph′ȧ·gous, *a.* [*xylo-*, and Gr. *phagein*, to eat.] eating or boring into wood, as the larvae of certain insects.

Xȳ·loph′ȧ·gus, *n.* the typical genus of the family *Xylophagidæ.*

xȳ·loph′i·lous, *a.* [*xylo-*, and Gr. *philein*, to love.] growing or feeding on wood; also, living in wood.

xȳ′lō·phōne (zī′), *n.* [*xylo-*, and Gr. *phōnē*, voice.]

1. a musical percussion instrument consisting of a series of wooden bars graduated in length so as to sound the notes of the scale when struck with small wooden hammers.

2. an instrument for ascertaining the vibrative properties of different woods.

XYLOPHONE

xȳ·loph′ō·nist (*or* zī′lō-fō-nist), *n.* a person who plays the xylophone.

Xȳ·lō′pi·ȧ (zī-), *n.* from Gr. *xylon*, wood, and *pikros*, bitter.] a genus of trees and shrubs of the family *Anonaceæ*, chiefly native to South America.

xȳ″lō·pȳ·rog′rȧ·phy (zī″), *n.* [*xylo-*, Gr. *pyr, pyros*, fire, and *-graphy.*] the art or process of producing a picture on wood by burning it with a hot instrument of iron, platinum, or the like: formerly called *poker painting.*

xȳ·lō·quī′nōne, *n.* any of three quinone compounds, $C_8H_8O_2$, obtained by oxidizing xylene.

xȳ′lōse, *n.* [from *xylan* and *-ose.*] a colorless, crystalline pentose, $C_5H_{10}O_5$, formed by the hydrolysis of xylan.

xȳ′lō·tīle, *n.* [*xylo-*, and Gr. *tilos*, down.] a hydrous iron magnesium silicate, derived from asbestos.

xȳ·lot′ō·mous, *a.* [*xylo-*, and Gr. *tomos*, from *temnein*, to cut.] that can bore into or cut wood: said of certain insects.

xȳ·lot′ō·my, *n.* the preparing of sections of wood for microscopic examination.

xȳ′lyl, *n.* a univalent radical of xylene.

xȳ′lyl·ēne, *n.* a bivalent radical of xylene.

Xyr·i·dā′cē·ae (zir-), *n.pl.* a family of cotyledonous rushlike or sedgelike herbs, found in the tropics of both hemispheres: there are two genera, *Xyris* and *Abolboda.*

xyr·i·dā′ceous, *a.* pertaining or belonging to the *Xyridaceae.*

Xȳ′ris (zī′), *n.* [Gr. *xyris*, kind of iris, from *xyron*, razor, from *xyein*, to scrape.] the typical genus of the *Xyridaceae*, sedgelike plants, with narrow, radical leaves, and scapes bearing heads of yellow, fugacious flowers, chiefly found in tropical America, a few occurring in the hotter parts of the Eastern Hemisphere.

xyst (zist), *n.* [L. *xystus*; Gr. *xystos*, from *xyein*, to scrape, from its smooth and polished floor.] in Greek and Roman architecture, a long, covered portico or open court in which athletes performed their exercises: also *xystus, xystos.*

xys′tẽr, *n.* [Gr. *xystēr*, from *xyein*, to scrape.] a surgical instrument for scraping bones.

xys′tos, xys′tus, *n.* same as *xyst.*

Y

Y, y (wī), *n.*; *pl.* **Y's, y's, Ys, ys** (wīz), 1. the twenty-fifth letter of the English alphabet: from the Greek *upsilon.*
2. the sound of Y or y.
3. a type or impression for Y or y.
4. a symbol for the twenty-fifth in a sequence or group (or the twenty-fourth if J is omitted, or the twenty-second if V and W are also omitted).

Y, y (wī), *a.* 1. of Y or y.
2. twenty-fifth (or twenty-fourth if J is omitted, or twenty-second if V and W are also omitted) in a sequence or group.

Y (wī), *n.* 1. an object shaped like Y, as a branched piece of piping, a forked support for a telescope, etc.
2. a medieval Roman numeral for 150: with a superior bar ($\overline{Y}$), 150,000.
3. in chemistry, the symbol for yttrium.

Y (wī), *a.* shaped like Y.
Y cartilage; a cartilage in the acetabulum, shaped like the letter Y, joining the ilium, ischium, and pubes.
Y connector; in electricity, a connector resembling the letter Y in shape, for joining a conductor to two branch wires.
Y current; in electricity, the current between any wire of a three-phase system and the neutral point.
Y gun; a naval gun for firing depth bombs: it has two arms forming a Y, each holding a charge.
Y level; a form of level used in surveying, mounted in two Y-shaped holders.
Y ligament; in anatomy, the iliofemoral ligament.
Y potential; in electricity, the difference in potential between a terminal and the neutral point of an armature wound in three phases.

y, in mathematics, (a) the second of a set of unknown quantities, *x* usually being the first; (b) an ordinate.

y- (i), [ME. *y-*, *i-*; AS. *ge-*, perfective prefix; basic sense "together."] an obsolete or archaic prefix formerly used regularly with the past participles of verbs: its use, as a poetic archaism, survived until the end of the sixteenth century, as in *y*clept.

-y (i; *occas.* ē), [ME. *-y*, *-i*, *-ie*; prob. after OFr. *-i*, *-e*, in such familiar names as Davi (for *David*), *Mathe* (for *Matheu*), etc.] a suffix used in forming diminutives, nicknames, and terms of endearment or familiarity, as in kitt*y*, Bill*y*, dadd*y*: often spelled *-ie*, as in lass*ie*.

-y, [ME. *-y*, *-ie*; AS. *-ig.*] an adjective-forming suffix meaning: (a) *having*, *full of*, or *characterized by*, as in dirt*y*, health*y*; (b) *rather*, *somewhat*, as in yellow*y*, chill*y*, dusk*y*; (c) *inclined or tending to*, as in drows*y*, stick*y*; (d) *suggestive of*, *somewhat like*, as in wav*y*, hors*y*. Sometimes used with a slight intensive force that does not change the meaning of the root adjective, as in still*y*.

-y, [Fr. *-ie*; L. *-ia*, from or akin to Gr. *-ia*, *-eia.*] a suffix used to form abstract nouns, often corresponding to adjectives ending in *-ous* and *-ic*, meaning in general *quality* or *condition of* (*being*), as in allerg*y*, jealous*y*.

-y, [Anglo-Fr. *-ie*; L. *-ium.*] a noun-forming suffix meaning *action of*, as in inquir*y*, entreat*y*.

yä, *adv.* yea; yes. [Obs.]

yä, *pron.* you. [Brit. Dial.]

yä'bȧ, *n.* the bark of *Andira excelsa*, a tropical leguminous tree.

yab'bēr, *n.* and *v.i.* [from native Australian *yabba.*] talk; jabber. [Australian Colloq.]

yab'bēr, *n.* [native name.] an Australian crayfish of the genus *Astacoides*: also *yabby*, *yabbie.*

yab'bi, *n.* [prob. native name.] the thylacine of Tasmania.

yaç'ȧ·rę, *n.* same as *jacare.*

yaç'çȧ, *n.* either of two West Indian trees, *Podocarpus coriacea* and *Podocarpus purdieana*, belonging to the yew family and yielding a wood used in cabinetwork.

yäçh, *v.t.* [S. Afr.] to come upon suddenly; to encounter unexpectedly, as game.

yächt (yät), *n.* [D. *jagt*, *jacht*, a pursuit ship, from *jagen*, to hunt.] any of various relatively small ships for pleasure cruises, racing, etc.

yächt, *v.i.*; yachted, *pt.*, *pp.*; yachting, *ppr.* to sail or cruise in a yacht.

yächt'-built (-bilt), *a.* built like a yacht.

yächt'ēr, *n.* one owning or sailing a yacht; a yachtsman.

yächt'ing, *n.* the action or sport of sailing in a yacht.

yächts'măn, *n.*; *pl.* **yächts'men,** one owning or sailing a yacht.

yächts'măn·ship, *n.* the practice or skill of sailing or managing a yacht.

yächts'wom''ăn (-woom''), *n.*; *pl.* **yächts' wom''en** (-wim''), a woman who owns or sails a yacht.

yäf, *v.* obsolete past tense of *give.*

yaf'fle, yaf'fin·gāle, *n.* the green woodpecker, *Picus* or *Gecinus viridis.* [Dial.]

yaf'fle, *n.* [origin doubtful] an armful or handful. [Dial.]

yaf'fle, *v.t.* and *v.i.* to pile into yaffles, as codfish; to carry yaffles of codfish. [Dial.]

yä'gēr, *n.* a jäger.

yä·guȧ·run'di (-gwȧ-), *n.* same as *jaguarondi.*

yäh, *interj.* an exclamation of derision, defiance, or disgust.

Yȧ·hoọ', *n.* 1. in Swift's *Gulliver's Travels*, a race of brutes having the form and all the degrading passions of man.
2. [y–] a brutish, vicious person.
3. [y–] a crude or ill-mannered person; a bumpkin.

Yäh've, Yäh'veh (yä'vi), *n.* Yahweh.

Yäh'vist, *n.* same as *Yahwist.*

Yäh·vis'tiç, *a.* same as *Yahwistic.*

Yäh'weh, Yäh'we (yä'we), *n.* God: a modern form of the Hebrew name in the Old Testament commonly transliterated Jehovah.

Yäh'wiṣm, *n.* 1. the worship of Yahweh (Jehovah).
2. the use of *Yahweh* as a name for God.

Yäh'wist, *n.* the unidentified writer or writers of certain Old Testament passages in which *Yahweh* (Jehovah) instead of *Elohim* is used as the name for God.

Yäh·wist'iç, *a.* 1. of or written by the Yahwist(s).
2. using *Yahweh* (Jehovah) instead of *Elohim* as the name for God: said of certain Old Testament passages.

Yäj'ŭr-Vę'dȧ, *n.* [Sans.] see *Veda.*

yak, *n.*; *pl.* **yaks** or **yak,** [Tibetan *gyak.*] a ruminant mammal of the *Bos*, or *Poëphagus*, *grunniens*, a large species of ox, with horns curving outward, long, silky hair fringing its sides, a bushy mane of fine hair, and a horselike tail. It inhabits Tibet and the Himalayas, and is often domesticated as a beast of burden.

YAK
(5 ft. high at shoulder)

yak'ȧ·mik, *n.* [S. Am.] a bird that makes a trumpetlike sound; a trumpeter.

yȧ'kin, *n.* a large antelope, *Budorcas taxicolor*, that inhabits the Himalayas and other high mountains.

yak'shȧ, *n.* [Sans.] in Hindu mythology, a demigod who attends Kuvera, the god of riches, and guards his treasures.

Yä·kut', *n.* 1. any of a people living in the Yakutsk A.S.S.R.
2. their Altaic language: linguists are undecided whether it should be classified as Turkic or Mongolian.

Yąl'tȧ Con'fēr·ence, a conference of Roosevelt, Churchill, and Stalin at Yalta in February, 1945: also called *Crimea Conference.*

yam, *n.* [Port. *inhame*, of W. Afr. origin.]
1. a large, edible, starchy, tuberous root of any of various plants of the genus *Dioscorea*, growing in tropical climates. The common West Indian yam is produced by *Dioscorea alata*; the East Indian yams are produced by *Dioscorea globosa*, *rubella*, and *purpurea.*
2. any plant of the yam family, *Dioscoreaceæ.*
3. the common (or Irish) potato. [Scot.]
4. the sweet potato. [Dial.]
Chinese yam; a plant, *Dioscorea batatas*, growing in temperate climates.
common yam; a garden variety, *Dioscorea sativa.*
wild yam; (a) a North American plant, *Dioscorea villosa*, with a knotted rootstock; (b) an orchid, *Gastrodia sesamoides*, of Australia.

Yä'mȧ, *n.* [Sans. *yama*, twin.] a Hindu god, king of the underworld and the appointed judge and punisher of the dead. He is generally represented as crowned and seated on a buffalo, which he guides by the horns. He is four-armed and holds a mace in one hand, and in another a noose which is used to draw out of the bodies of men the souls which are doomed to appear before his judgment seat. His garments are red, his skin is a bluish-green.

YAMA

yam'ȧ·döu, *n.* an oil obtained from the tallow nutmeg.

yam'ȧ·maī', *n.* [Japan.] a large silkworm of Japan, *Antheræa jama mai*, that feeds on the oak.

yam bēan, a West Indian plant, *Pachyrrhizus tuberosus*, of the bean family, having edible tubers.

yä'men, *n.* [Chin.] formerly, in China, the office or residence of a mandarin or public official.

yam'mȧ, *n.* [S. Am.] the llama.

yam'mēr, *v.i.* [ME. *yameren*, from AS. *geomerian*, to lament, to groan, from *geomor*, sad, mournful, wretched.]
1. to complain; to whimper loudly; to whine. [Colloq. or Dial.]

2. to shout, yell, clamor, etc. [Colloq. or Dial.]

yam'mẽr, *v.t.* to say in a complaining tone.

yam'mẽr, *n.* the act of yammering.

yamp, *n.* [Am. Ind.] an umbelliferous plant, *Carum gairdneri,* growing in the western United States; also, its edible tuber.

yä'mun, *n.* same as *yamen.*

yang, *n.* [imitative.] the cry, or honk, of the wild goose.

yang, *v.i.* to make a cry like that of the wild goose.

yañk, *n.* [from New England Dial.] a jerk or twitch. [Colloq.]

yañk, *v.t.* and *v.i.;* yanked (yañkt), *pt., pp.;* yanking, *ppr.* to jerk. [Colloq.]

Yañk, *n.* a Yankee; especially, an American soldier in World Wars I and II. [Slang.]

Yañk, *a.* of or like a Yank or Yanks.

Yañ'kee, *n.* [prob. from D. *Jan Kees* (taken as pl.); *Jan,* John, and *Kees,* dial. form of *kaas,* cheese; orig. (*Jan Kaas*) used as disparaging nickname for a Hollander, later for Dutch freebooter; applied by colonial Dutch in New York to English settlers in Connecticut.]

1. a native or inhabitant of New England.

2. (a) a native or inhabitant of a Northern State; Northerner; (b) a Union soldier in the Civil War.

3. a native or inhabitant of the United States.

Yañ'kee, *a.* pertaining to, like, or characteristic of the Yankees; as, *Yankee* notions.

Yañ'kee·dŏm, *n.* 1. Yankees collectively.

2. the northern United States, especially New England.

3. the United States.

Yañ'kee-Dọọ'dle, *n.* 1. an early American song with several versions of humorous verses, popular during the Revolutionary War.

2. a Yankee. [Obs.]

Yañ'kee·fied, *a.* having Yankee characteristics. [Colloq.]

Yañ'kee·iṣm, *n.* 1. Yankee character or characteristics.

2. a particular Yankee mannerism, idiom, etc.

yan'ō·līte, *n.* same as *axinite.*

yaourt (yourt), *n.* yogurt.

yap, *v.i.;* yapped (yapt), *pt., pp.;* yapping, *ppr.* [echoic.]

1. to make a sharp, shrill yelp or bark.

2. to talk noisily and stupidly; jabber. [Slang.]

yap, *n.* 1. a sharp, shrill bark or yelp.

2. noisy, stupid talk; jabber. [Slang.]

3. a crude, noisy person. [Slang.]

4. a rowdy; hoodlum. [Slang.]

5. the mouth. [Slang.]

yȧ·pok', yȧ·pock', *n.* [named from the South American river *Oyapok,* between Brazil and Guiana.] a small, water-dwelling opossum, *Chironectes variegatus,* inhabiting the rivers of Brazil and Guiana. It closely resembles the otter, and differs from other opossums in its dentition, in having no opposable thumb, and in the toes of the hind feet being webbed.

yạ'pŏn, *n.* same as *yaupon.*

yap'ping, *n.* babbling; jabbering. [Slang.]

Yä'quï (-kē), *n.; pl.* **Yä'quï, Yä'quïṣ,** [after the *Yaqui* River in northwestern Mexico, where they formerly lived.] a member of a tribe of Uto-Aztecan Indians now settled in Sonora, Mexico.

yar'ăġe, *n.* manageability: said of a ship at sea. [Obs.]

yärb, *n.* an herb. [Dial.]

Yär'bŏr·ōugh (-bũr-ō), *n.* [said to be so named after an Earl of *Yarborough* who would bet 1,000 to 1 against its occurring.] a bridge or whist hand containing no card higher than a nine.

yärd, *n.* [ME. *yerde, gerde;* AS. *gyrd, gierd,* a rod, a staff, a yard measure.]

1. a measure of length, equal to 3 feet, or 36 inches: one yard is equivalent to .914 meter.

2. in nautical usage, a slender rod or spar, tapering toward the ends, fastened at right angles across a mast to support a sail.

3. a pole or rod three feet long for measuring a yard; a yardstick. [Rare.]

4. the penis. [Obs.]

5. a stick or staff; also, a twig. [Obs.]

6. a long piece of timber, as a rafter. [Obs.]

Yard and Ell; the three stars in the belt of Orion.

yärd, *n.* [ME. *yerd;* AS. *geard,* an enclosure, a yard, a court.]

1. the space or grounds surrounding or surrounded by a building or group of buildings: often in combination, as, church*yard,* farm*yard,* etc.

2. an enclosed place used for a particular purpose or business; as, a lumber *yard,* ship*yard.*

3. a place where wild deer, moose, etc. herd together for feeding during the winter.

4. a railroad center where trains are made up, serviced, switched from track to track, etc.

5. a garden; especially, a kitchen garden. [Dial.]

yärd, *v.t.* and *v.i.;* yarded, *pt., pp.;* yarding, *ppr.* to put, keep, or enclose in a yard (often with *up*).

yärd'ăġe, *n.* 1. measurement in yards.

2. the extent or amount of something so measured.

yärd'ăġe, *n.* 1. the use of a yard for storage, etc.

2. a charge made for such use.

yärd'ärm, *n.* either end of a ship's yard supporting a square sail.

yardarm and yardarm; so near as to touch or interlock yardarms: said of two ships.

yärd'fụl, *n.; pl.* **yärd'fụlṣ,** as much as will fill a yard; as, a *yardful* of cattle.

yärd gràss, a tough, coarse annual grass topped with long spikes, *Eleusine indica.*

yärd'keep, *n.* the yarwhelp. [Brit. Dial.]

yärd'land, *n.* a virgate, an old English measure of land.

yärd'măn, *n.; pl.* **yärd'men,** a man who works in a yard, especially a railroad yard.

yärd'màs"tẽr, *n.* a man in charge of a railroad yard.

yärd rōpe, in nautical usage, a rope passing through a block at a masthead, to lower or hoist a yard.

yärd sling, in nautical usage, a short chain from the middle of a lower yard to a lower masthead to aid in supporting the yard.

yärd'stick, *n.* 1. a graduated stick three feet in length, used in measuring.

2. anything that acts as a standard of measurement, judgment, or comparison; a gauge, test, or criterion; as, the court's ruling may be used as a *yardstick.*

yärd taç'kle, in nautical usage, a threefold tackle for lifting boats and other weights.

yärd'wänd, *n.* a yardstick.

yāre, *a.* 1. ready; prepared.

2. brisk; active; quick.

3. responding quickly and truly to the helm: said of a ship.

[Archaic or Dial. in all senses.]

yāre, *adv.* quickly; promptly. [Obs.]

yāre'ly, *adv.* readily; dexterously; promptly. [Obs.]

yärk, *v.t.* and *v.i.* to jerk. [Brit. Dial.]

yär'kē, *n.* a saki of the genus *Pithecia.*

Yär'mouth (-muth), *n.* in geology, a North American interglacial epoch.

Yär'mouth, *a.* pertaining to or characterized by the Yarmouth interglacial epoch.

Yär'mouth çā'pŏn, a red herring.

yärn, *n.* [ME. *yarn;* AS. *gearn,* yarn.]

1. any fiber, as wool, silk, flax, cotton, nylon, etc., spun into strands for weaving, knitting, or making thread.

2. a tale or story, especially one that seems exaggerated or hard to believe. [Colloq.]

3. any of the strands of which a rope is composed.

Saxony yarn; a kind of yarn made from wool produced in Saxony.

to spin a yarn; to tell a yarn or yarns. [Colloq.]

yärn, *v.i.* to tell stories or yarns. [Colloq.]

yärn'-dȳed, *a.* woven of yarn that was dyed before weaving.

yärn'en, *a.* made or consisting of yarn. [Rare.]

yär'ō·vīze, *v.t.;* yarovized, *pt., pp.;* yarovizing, *ppr.* to jarovize.

yärr, *n.* the spurry, *Spergula arvensis.* [Scot. and Brit. Dial.]

yärr, *v.i.* to growl or snarl, as a dog. [Obs.]

yar'rōw, *n.* [ME. *yarowe, yarwe,* from AS. *gæruwe, gearuwe,* yarrow, lit., healer, from *gearwian,* to prepare, *garwan,* to dress.] a plant, *Achillea millefolium,* having a strong smell and taste, finely divided leaves, and clusters of small, pink or white flowers.

yär'whelp (-hwelp), *n.* a godwit. [Brit. Dial.]

yär'whip (-hwip), *n.* same as *yarwhelp.*

yash'mak, yash'maç, *n.* [Ar.] the double veil worn by Moslem women in public.

yat'ȧ·ghan (-gan), *n.* [Turk.] a type of Turkish short saber with a double-curved blade, about two feet long and a handle without a cross-guard: also *yatagan, ataghan.*

YATAGHAN

yāte, *n.* a gate. [Obs.]

yāte tree, an Australian tree, *Eucalyptus cornuta,* which yields a tough wood; also, *Eucalyptus occidentalis,* a related species.

yạud, *n.* an old, worn-out mare; a jade. [Scot.]

yạul, *n.* a yawl. [Obs.]

yạuld, *a.* active, nimble, vigorous, etc. [Scot.]

yạup, *v.i.* to yawp.

yạup, *n.* 1. a yawp.

2. the blue titmouse. [Brit. Dial.]

yạu'pŏn, *n.* [Am. Ind. (Catawba) *yopûn,* dim. of *yop,* a shrub.] an evergreen of the holly family, native to the southern United States: its leaves are sometimes used as a substitute for tea.

yạw, *v.i.;* yawed, *pt., pp.;* yawing, *ppr.* [Ice. *jaga,* to hunt; also, to move to and fro.]

1. to turn or deviate unintentionally from the intended course or heading: said of a ship or boat.

2. to swing on the vertical axis to the right or left so that the longitudinal axis forms an angle with the line of flight: said of a projectile, aircraft, etc.

yạw, *v.t.* to cause to yaw.

yạw, *n.* 1. an act of yawing.

2. the angle formed by a yawing aircraft, etc.

yạw, *v.i.* to rise in blisters, breaking in white froth, as cane juice in the refining of sugar.

yạwd, *n.* a yaud. [Scot.]

yạw'ey, *a.* afflicted with yaws.

yạwl, *n.* [D. *jol;* Dan. *jolle;* Sw. *julle,* a yawl.]

1. a ship's boat; a jolly-boat.

2. a small sailboat rigged fore-and-aft, with a short mizzenmast astern of the cockpit: distinguished from *ketch.*

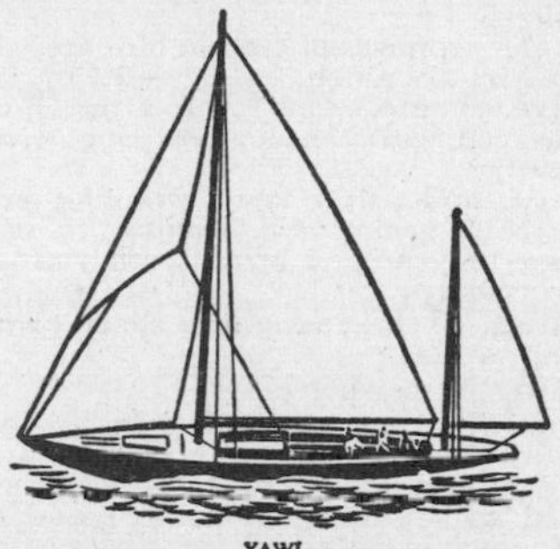

YAWL

yạwl, *v.i.* and *n.* yowl. [Dial.]

yạwl'-rigged", *a.* rigged like a yawl.

yạwn, *v.i.;* yawned, *pt., pp.;* yawning, *ppr.* [ME. *yanen;* AS. *ganian,* to yawn.]

1. to open the mouth wide, especially involuntarily, and with a deep inhalation, as a result of fatigue, drowsiness, or boredom.

The *yawning* audience nod beneath.
—Trumbull.

2. to be or become wide open; to gape; as, a *yawning* chasm.

3. to open the mouth as in surprise or bewilderment; to gape.

yạwn, *v.t.* to express or utter with a yawn.

yạwn, *n.* 1. an act of yawning or opening wide.

2. a wide opening; a chasm.

yạwn'ẽr, *n.* one who yawns.

yạwn'ing·ly, *adv.* in a yawning manner.

yạwp, *v.i.* [ME. *yolpen,* prob. an echoic var. of *yelpen,* to boast.]

1. to utter a loud, harsh call or cry.

2. to talk noisily and stupidly; to yap. [Slang.]

3. to yawn aloud; to gape. [Colloq.]

Also spelled *yaup.*

yạwp, *n.* the act or sound of yawping: also spelled *yaup.*

yạwṣ, *n.pl.* [prob. of W. Ind. origin.] a tropical infectious disease caused by a spirochete and characterized by raspberrylike skin eruptions followed by destructive lesions of the skin and bones (with *the*); frambesia.

yạw'weed, *n.* a West Indian shrub of the

genus *Morinda*: formerly used as a remedy for the yaws.

Yb, in chemistry, ytterbium.

y-bē′ (i-), *v.* obsolete past participle of *be*.

Y çhrō′mō·sōme (wī), a sex chromosome.

y-çlad′, *v.* archaic past participle of *clothe*.

y·çlept′, y-çlept′, *pp.* [ME. *ycleped*; AS. *geclypod*, pp. of *clipian*, to call; popularized by Spenser and Milton.] called; named; known as; as, a giant *yclept* Barbarossa: also spelled *ycleped*, *y-cleped*. [Archaic.]

y-dō′, *v.* obsolete past participle of *do*.

y-drad′, *v.* obsolete past participle of *dread*.

ye (yā), *adv.* yea. [Obs.]

yē, *n.* an eye. [Obs.]

yē, *pron.* [ME. *yhe*, *ge*; AS. *ge*, ye, nom. pl. corresponding to *thu*, thou; the genit. was *eower*, the dat. and acc. *eow*; so that *ye* is properly the nom. plural and *you* the obj.] you: originally used only as nominative plural, later as nominative singular, and still later, especially in dialectal speech, as accusative singular and plural. [Archaic.]

ye (thē, the, thi; yē *is incorrect*), *a.* the: Y was substituted by early printers for the thorn (þ), the Old and Middle English character representing the sound *th*: sometimes written *y*[e], as though a contraction.

yeā (yā), *adv.* [ME. *yo*, *ye*; AS. *geá*, yea, indeed.]
1. yes: used to express affirmation or assent; as, will you go? *Yea.*
Let your communication be *yea, yea*; nay, nay. —Matt. v. 37.
2. not this alone; not only so but also; furthermore; moreover; as, he was a good, *yea*, a fine man. [Archaic.]
I therein do rejoice; *yea*, and will rejoice. —Phil. i. 18.
3. indeed, verily, truly: used to introduce a question or statement.
Yea, mistress, are you so peremptory? —Shak.

yeā, *n.* 1. an affirmative statement or vote; also, one who votes in the affirmative or in favor of any question or motion; as, the decision was given to the *yeas*; there were more *yeas* than nays.
2. certainty, consistency, harmony, or stability.
All the promises of God in him are *yea*, and in him are amen. —2 Cor. i. 20.

yeah (ye, ya, etc.), *adv.* [prob. after D. and G. *ja*, merged with the cognate Eng. *yea*.] yes. [Colloq.]

yēan, *v.i.* and *v.t.*; yeaned, *pt.*, *pp.*; yeaning, *ppr.* [ME. *genen*; AS. *eánian*, to ean, *geeánian*, to yean.] to bring forth young, as a goat or sheep.

yēan′ling, *n.* the young of a sheep or a goat; a lamb; a kid.

yēan′ling, *a.* newborn.

yēar, *n.* [ME. *yeer*, *yer*; AS. *geár*, *gēr*, a year.]
1. (a) a period of 365 days (in leap year, 366 days) divided into 12 months and regarded as beginning January 1 and ending the following December 31; (b) a period of more or less the same length in other calendars.
2. the period of time, 365 days, 5 hours, 48 minutes, and 6 seconds, spent by the sun in making its apparent passage from vernal equinox to vernal equinox: also *astronomical*, *natural*, *equinoctial*, *solar*, or *tropical year*.
3. the period of time, 365 days, 6 hours, 9 minutes, and 9 seconds, spent by the sun in its apparent passage from a fixed star and back to the same position again: the difference in time between this and the astronomical year is due to the precession of the equinoxes: also *sidereal year*.
4. a period of 12 lunar months: also *lunar year*.
5. the period of time occupied by any planet in making one complete revolution around the sun.
6. a period of 12 calendar months reckoned from any date; as, we shall return one *year* from today.
7. a particular annual period of less than 365 days; as, a fisherman's work *year*, a short school *year*, etc.
8. [*pl.*] (a) age; as, he seems old for his *years*; (b) time; especially, a long time; as, he died *years* ago.
anomalistic year; see under *anomalistic*.
astronomical year; see under *astronomical*.
bissextile year; leap year.
calendar year; the civil or legal year. It covers a period of 365 days (366 days in the case of leap year) and is divided into twelve calendar months, beginning in January, and ending in December.
canicular year; see under *canicular*.
Christian year; the cycle of religious ceremonies commemorating events in the life of Christ: it begins with the season of Advent.
Church year; same as *Christian year*.
civil year; see under *civil*.
common year; any year of 365 days, as opposed to the bissextile or leap year.
ecclesiastical year; same as *Christian year*.
embolismic or *intercalary lunar year*; the period which consists of thirteen lunar months, or 384 days.
great year; same as *Platonic year* under *Platonic*.
Gregorian year; see under *Gregorian*.
Hebrew year; see *Jewish calendar*.
Julian year; see under *Julian*.
lunar year; see under *lunar*.
lunisolar year; see under *lunisolar*.
periodical year; same as *anomalistic year*.
Platonic year; see under *Platonic*.
sabbatical year; see under *sabbatical*.
sidereal year; see under *sidereal*.
solar year; see under *solar*.
tropical year; a solar year.
year after year; every year.
year by year; each year.
year in, year out, every year.
year of grace; any year of the Christian era.

ye·ä′rä, *n.* same as *poison oak* (b).

yēar′book, *n.* a book published every year, especially one giving statistics and data of the preceding year; an annual.

Yēar Book, a book containing annual reports of cases adjudged in the courts of England, from the time of Edward II to that of Henry VIII inclusive.

yēared, *a.* aged. [Obs.]

yēar′ling, *n.* 1. an animal one year old, or in the second year of its age.
2. in racing, a horse one year old, reckoned from January 1 of the year of its foaling.

yēar′ling, *a.* being a year old; as, a *yearling heifer*.

yēar′lọng, *a.* lasting or continuing a full year.

yēar′ly, *a.* 1. annual; happening, appearing, payable, etc. once a year, or every year; as, *yearly* rent or income.
2. continuing or lasting a year; as, a *yearly* plant.
3. of a year, or each year.

yēar′ly, *adv.* annually; once a year.

yēarn, *v.i.*; yearned, *pt.*, *pp.*; yearning, *ppr.* [ME. *yernen*; AS. *gyrnan*, to yearn, be desirous, from *georn*, desirous, eager.]
1. to be filled with longing or desire.
2. to be deeply moved, especially with pity or sympathy.

yēarn, *v.t.* to pain; to grieve. [Obs.]

yēarn, *v.t.* and *v.i.* to curdle or coagulate, as milk. [Scot.]

yēarn′fu̇l, *a.* mournful; longing.

yēarn′ing, *n.* rennet. [Scot.]

yēarn′ing, *n.* deep or anxious longing, desire, etc.

yēarn′ing·ly, *adv.* with yearning.

yēarth, *n.* earth. [Obs.]

yēast, *n.* [ME. *yest*; AS. *gist*, *gyst*, yeast.]
1. a yellow, frothy substance consisting of a mass of minute fungi which germinate and multiply in the presence of starch or sugar and form alcohol and carbon dioxide during a process of fermentation induced by an enzyme: used in making beer and as a leavening agent in baking.
2. any of the family of fungi, *Saccharomycetaceæ*, that form yeast; a yeast plant.
3. yeast mixed with flour or meal, usually made up in small cakes.
4. foam; froth.
5. (a) something that agitates or causes ferment; leaven; (b) ferment; agitation.

yēast, *v.i.* to froth or ferment. [Rare.]

yēast′-bit″ten, *a.* in brewing, too much affected by yeast.

yēast çāke, a small cake of a mixture of yeast and some substance, as meal or flour: sold commercially for use in baking, etc.

yēast cell, the yeast plant.

yēast′i·ness, *n.* a yeasty quality or state.

yēast plant, yeast (sense 2).

yēast pow′dẽr, baking powder.

yēast′y, *a.*; *comp.* yeastier; *superl.* yeastiest.
1. of, like, or containing yeast.
2. frothy; foamy.
3. light; superficial; frivolous.
4. in a ferment; unsettled; restless.

yed′ding, *n.* a song, as of a minstrel. [Obs.]

yegg, *n.* [said to be from name of famous safecracker.] a criminal; especially, a safecracker or burglar. [Slang.]

yegg′măn, *n.*; *pl.* **yegg′men,** a yegg. [Slang.]

yeld, *a.* [ME.; AS. *gelde*.]
1. barren. [Scot.]
2. not giving milk. [Scot.]

yel′drin, *n.* a yellowhammer. [Brit. Dial.]

yelk, *n.* a yolk. [Archaic or Dial.]

yell, *v.i.*; yelled, *pt.*, *pp.*; yelling, *ppr.* [ME. *yellen*; AS. *gellan*, *giellan*, *gyllan*, to yell, cry out, resound.] to utter a yell; to cry out loudly; to scream; to shriek.

yell, *v.t.* to declare, express, or utter in a yell, or by a yell; as, to *yell* out a warning.

yell, *n.* 1. a loud outcry or shout; a shriek; a scream.
2. a rhythmic cheer given in unison, as by college students at a football game.

yel′lōw, *a.*; *comp.* yellower; *superl.* yellowest. [ME. *yeiwe*, *zelu*, *zeoluh*; AS. *geolo*, *geolu* (f. acc. *geolwe*), yellow.]
1. of the color of gold, butter, or ripe lemons.
2. changed to a yellowish color as by age or illness, as old paper, jaundiced skin, etc.
3. having a yellowlike pigmentation of the skin, as that characteristic of the Mongolians.
4. cheaply sensational to an offensive degree: said of some newspapers.
5. cowardly or untrustworthy; lacking courage. [Colloq.]
6. jealous, envious or melancholy.
yellow adder's-tongue; *Erythronium americanum*, the dogtooth violet.
yellow alder; *Turnera ulmifolia*, a tropical American herb having a shrubby appearance and single, yellow flowers.
yellow angelfish; *Angelichthys ciliaris*, a bright-colored, teleost fish native to warm waters and valued as a food in the West Indies, Florida, etc.
yellow antimony; an allotropic form of antimony.
yellow apiol, in pharmacy, an oleoresin from which the chlorophyll has been removed: it is obtained from parsley fruit and is useful as an emmenagogue and antiperiodic.
yellow ash; same as *yellowwood* (sense 1a).
yellow asphodel; *Asphodeline lutea*, a plant supposed by some to be the asphodel of the Greek poets.
yellow aster; an American plant of the genus *Chrysopsis*; the golden aster.
yellow bass; a Mississippi River bass, *Morone interrupta*, yellow and marked with black.
yellow beak; same as *bejan*.
yellow berry; the Persian berry.
yellow box; an Australian timber tree, *Eucalyptus melliodora*.
yellow boy; (a) [Brit. Slang.] a gold coin; (b) [Colloq.] a mulatto.
yellow bugle; a plant of the mint family, *Ajuga chamæpytis*.
yellow bunting; the yellowhammer.
yellow cat; the yellow catfish, *Leptops olivaris*.
yellow cedar; the yellow cypress.
yellow centaury; the yellowwort.
yellow clover; (a) a species of clover, *Trifolium agrarium*, growing in dry places, and bearing yellow flowers; (b) *Trifolium procumbens*, a species of similar appearance and habit.
yellow copperas; same as *copiapite*.
yellow cress; any yellow-flowered species of cress, as the winter cress.
yellow cypress; a cypress of northwestern North America, especially Alaska, of the genus *Chamæcyparis*: its wood is yellow, and highly prized for cabinetwork.
yellow daisy; the black-eyed Susan or any of several similar flowers.
yellow dead nettle; weaselsnout.
yellow dock; a plant, *Rumex crispus*, with a yellow root which is used medicinally.
yellow-dog contract; an employer-employee contract, now illegal, by which a person being hired is first made to agree that he will join no labor union while employed.
yellow earth; yellow ocher.
yellow fever; an acute infectious disease chiefly of tropical America and Africa. It is due to a filterable virus which is transmitted to the human blood stream by the bite of certain mosquitoes: the disease is characterized by fever, jaundice, vomiting, etc.
yellow-fever mosquito; a mosquito, *Aëdes ægypti*, serving, usually, as the intermediate host of the parasite of yellow fever.
yellow flag; (a) see under *flag*; (b) the yellow iris.
yellow gold; the corn marigold.
yellow gum; (a) acaroid resin; (b) jaundice in infants.

yellow iris; the common iris, *Iris pseudacorus*, with yellow flowers.

yellow jack; (a) yellow fever; (b) a West Indian carangoid food fish having a gold and silver coloring; (c) same as *yellow flag* under *flag*.

yellow jacket; any of several social wasps and hornets of the genus *Vespa*, having bright-yellow markings.

yellow jasmine; see under *jasmine*.

yellow journalism; the use of cheaply sensational or unscrupulous methods in newspapers, etc. to attract or influence the readers.

yellow lead ore; same as *wulfenite*.

yellow lemur; the kinkajou.

yellow mackerel; the jurel.

yellow metal; (a) gold; (b) brass that is 60 parts copper and 40 parts zinc; Muntz's metal.

yellow ocher; an argillaceous earth, colored by an admixture of oxide of iron. When finely ground, it is used as a pigment.

yellow oxeye; the corn marigold, *Chrysanthemum segetum*.

yellow perch; the common perch of America.

yellow peril; the alleged danger to the world supremacy of the white, or Caucasian, peoples created by the vast numbers and potential political power of the yellow, or Mongolian, peoples.

yellow pike; the pike perch.

yellow pine; (a) any of several American pines having yellowish wood; (b) the wood of any of these.

yellow plover; a common plover of the genus *Pluvialis*: also called *golden plover*.

yellow poplar; the tulip tree.

yellow precipitate; yellow mercuric oxide, HgO.

yellow puccoon; orangeroot.

yellow race; loosely, the Mongolian division of mankind.

yellow rail; an American rail of the genus *Porzana*, of a yellow hue.

yellow rattle; same as *rattle*, n. 7b.

yellow Sally; a European stone fly of the genus *Chloroperla*.

yellow sculpin; same as *sculpin*.

yellow snake; a large West Indian boa, *Chilobothrus inornatus*, having an olive-green head and the front of the body covered with black lines, while the hinder part is black, spotted with yellowish-olive: it often attains a length of ten feet.

yellow spot; (a) the small, yellowish area in the retina where vision is most acute; (b) *Polites peckius*, an American butterfly marked with spots of yellow on the hind wings.

yellow streak; a tendency to be cowardly, craven, etc.

yellow tit; a yellow titmouse of India of the genus *Machlolophus*.

yellow viper; the fer-de-lance.

yellow warbler; a small bright-yellow North American warbler.

yellow wash; a solution of mercuric chloride and limewater.

yellow water lily; any of a number of water lilies having a yellow blossom.

yellow wren; (a) the willow warbler; (b) [Brit. Dial.] the wood warbler of Europe.

yel'lōw, *n.* 1. a yellow color; any color lying between red and green in the color spectrum.

2. a pigment or dye that is yellow or capable of producing yellow.

3. the yolk of an egg.

4. [*pl.*] any of several fungus or virus diseases of plants, causing yellowing of the leaves, stunting of growth, etc.

5. [*pl.*] jaundice, especially in farm animals.

6. [*pl.*] a bad humor; jealousy. [Obs.]

7. any one of a group of small yellow butterflies.

brilliant yellow; a dyestuff obtained from stilbene and phenol.

cassel yellow; patent yellow.

Chinese yellow; lemon yellow.

Indian yellow; see under *Indian*.

mineral yellow; patent yellow.

Naples yellow; a yellow pigment, a basic antimoniate of lead.

Paris yellow; a variety of chrome yellow.

patent yellow; a yellow pigment consisting of lead oxide and chloride.

Turner's yellow; patent yellow.

yel'lōw, *v.t.* and *v.i.*; yellowed, *pt.*, *pp.*; yellowing, *ppr.* to make or become yellow.

yel'lōw·am·mẽr, *n.* a yellowhammer. [Brit. Dial.]

yel'lōw·bill, *n.* the American scoter. [Dial.]

yel'lōw·bird, *n.* 1. the goldfinch of America.

2. the yellow warbler.

yel'lōw·crown, *n.* the myrtle bird, *Dendrœca coronata*.

yel'lōw-eyed (-īd), *a.* having yellow eyes.

yellow-eyed grass; an herb of the genus *Xyris*.

yel'lōw·fin, *n.* a kind of trout. [Scot.]

yel'lōw fish, *n.* a fish, *Pleurogrammus monopterygius*, native to Alaska: also called *Atka mackerel*.

yel'lōw-green', *n.* a color between yellow and green in the spectrum.

yel'lōw-green', *a.* of this color.

yel'lōw·ham"mẽr, *n.* [*yellow*, and AS. *amore* the name of a bird, same as G. *ammer*, the yellowhammer, called also *gold-ammer*, *gelb-ammer*, gold bunting, yellow bunting.]

1. a small European finch of the genus *Emberiza*, the *Emberiza citrinella*. The head, front of the neck, belly, and lower tail coverts are of a bright yellow; the upper surface is partly yellow, but chiefly brown, the feathers on the top of the back being blackish in the middle, and the tail feathers also blackish.

2. the golden-winged woodpecker, or flicker, of North America.

yel'lōw·head (-hed), *n.* the yellow-headed American blackbird.

yel'lōw·ing, *n.* the act of rendering or turning yellow.

yel'lōw·ish, *a.* somewhat yellow; tinged with yellow, as old ivory.

yel'low·ish·ness, *n.* the quality or state of being yellowish.

yel'lōw·legs, *n.*; *pl.* **yel'lōw·legs**, either of two sandpipers of the genus *Totanus*, having long legs of a bright yellow color and brown and white markings, native to North America.

yel'lōw·ly, *adv.* in a yellow manner.

yel'lōw·ness, *n.* the quality or condition of being yellow.

yel'lōw·pōll, *n.* 1. the European widgeon. [Brit. Dial.]

2. the yellow warbler. [Dial.]

yel'lōw·rọot, *n.* any of several species of plants having yellow roots; as, (a) *Xanthorrhiza apiifolia*; (b) orangeroot.

yel'lōw·rump, *n.* a passerine bird, *Dendrœca coronata*; the myrtle bird.

yel'lōws, *n.* 1. a kind of jaundice which affects horses, cattle, and sheep, causing yellowness of the eyes.

2. a disease of peach and other trees characterized by yellowing of the foliage.

3. jealousy. [Obs.]

yel'lōw·seed, *n.* a species of peppergrass, *Lepidum campestre*.

yel'lōw·shañk, yel'lōw·shañks, yel'lōw·shins, *n.* same as *yellowlegs*.

yel'lōw·tāil, *n.*; *pl.* **yel'lōw·tāils** or **yel'lōw·tāil**, any of several fishes having a yellowish tail; specifically, (a) any carangoid fish of the genus *Seriola*; especially, *Seriola dorsalis*, a valuable food fish, native to the California coast; (b) the silver perch; (c) *Elagatis pinnulatus*; the runner; (d) the menhaden; (e) a rockfish, *Sebastichthys flavidus*, native to California; (f) a pinfish, *Lagodon rhomboides*.

yel'lōw·thrōat, *n.* any of various American warblers of the genus *Geothlypis*; especially, *Geothlypis trichas*, the Maryland yellowthroat.

yel'lōw·top, *n.* a grass having yellow panicles.

yel'lōw·weed, *n.* 1. any of several species of goldenrod.

2. the European ragwort.

3. the bulbous crowfoot.

4. sneezeweed.

yel'lōw·wood, *n.* the yellow wood of various trees; also, any one of the trees themselves, as (a) *Cladrastis tinctoria*, a smooth-barked, white-flowering tree of the southern United States, source of a yellow dye; (b) any one of various trees of the genus *Podocarpus*, of the yew family, as *Podocarpus latifolia* of India, and *Podocarpus elongata*, a South African species; (c) the satinwood of the East Indies; (d) Osage orange; (e) the smoke tree; (f) any species of prickly ash.

yel'lōw·wŏrt, *n.* a European plant, *Chlora perfoliata*, of the gentian family, having bitter-tonic qualities.

yel'lōw·y, *a.* somewhat yellow; yellowish.

yelp, *v.i.*; yelped (yelpt), *pt.*, *pp.*; yelping, *ppr.* [ME. *yelpen*; AS. *gilpan*, *gielpan*, *gylpan*, to boast, originally, to talk noisily.]

1. to give out a sharp or shrill bark; to give a sharp, quick cry, as a dog.

2. to cry out sharply, as in pain.

3. to prate; to boast. [Obs.]

yelp, *v.t.* to utter or express by yelping.

yelp, *n.* a short, sharp bark or cry.

yelp'ẽr, *n.* an animal or bird that yelps or gives forth a yelping noise, as (a) [Brit. Dial.] the avoset; (b) [Dial.] the tattler.

ye̤'măn, *n.* a yeoman. [Obs.]

Yem'en·īte (*or* yā'), *a.* of Yemen, an Arab kingdom in southwestern Arabia, or its people.

Yem'en·īte, *n.* a native or inhabitant of Yemen.

yen, *n.*; *pl.* **yen**, [Japan., from Chin. *yüan*, round, dollar.] the monetary unit of Japan, a gold or silver coin equivalent to 100 sen.

yen, *n.* [Chin., opium smoke.] a strong desire; a nearly uncontrollable urge; an intense feeling or longing. [Colloq.]

yen, *v.i.*; yenned, *pt.*, *pp.*; yenning, *ppr.* to have a yen (for); to long; to yearn. [Colloq.]

yen'i, *n.* [S. Am.] a tanager of South America, *Calliste yeni*.

yen'īte, *n.* [from *Jena*, town in Germany.] same as *ilvaite*.

yeō'măn, *n.*; *pl.* **yeō'men**, [ME. *yeman*, *yoman*; not in AS.; prob. contr. from *yengman*, *young man*, young man.]

1. a man possessed of small estate in land; a gentleman farmer; a freeholder of a class below the gentry, who worked his own land. [Obs.]

2. an attendant or manservant in a royal or noble household. [Obs.]

3. an assistant or subordinate, as to a sheriff. [Obs.]

4. one not advanced to the rank of gentleman. [Obs.]

5. in the United States Navy, a petty officer who performs the duties of a clerk, typist, or stenographer.

6. a member of the yeomanry (sense 3); also, a yeoman of the guard. [Brit.]

yeoman of the (royal) guard; any of the 100 men forming a ceremonial guard for the English royal family: the guard was instituted in 1485 by Henry VII and still wears a traditional fifteenth-century uniform.

yeō·măn·ette', *n.* in World War I, a woman serving in the naval reserve force of the United States. The official designation is "Yeoman (F)."

yeō'măn·līke, *a.* of or relating to a yeoman.

yeō'măn·ly, *a.* 1. resembling or pertaining to a yeoman; suited to a yeoman.

2. brave; sturdy; faithful.

yeō'măn·ly, *adv.* in a yeomanly manner; bravely.

yeō'măn·ry, *n.* 1. the condition or rank of a yeoman. [Obs.]

2. the collective body of yeomen.

3. a volunteer cavalry force organized in 1761 in Great Britain as a home force, and consisting to a great extent of gentlemen or wealthy farmers: since 1907 it has been a part of the Territorial Army.

yeō'măn's sẽrv'ice, exceptionally good or loyal service or assistance: also *yeoman service*.

yeor'ling, *n.* the European yellowhammer. [Brit. Dial.]

yeō'wom'ăn (-woom'), *n.* same as *yeomanette*.

yep, *adv.* yes: an affirmative reply. [Slang.]

-yẽr, -ier: usually after *w*, as in *lawyer*.

yer'bȧ, *n.* [Sp., herb; the generic name for all the smaller plants.] a plant or herb; specifically, yerba maté, or maté.

yerba del oso; a species of buckthorn, *Rhamnus californica*.

yerba mansa; a plant, *Anemopsis californica*, having an aromatic root and used as a domestic remedy by Indians and Mexicans.

yerba maté; Paraguay tea, or maté.

yerba reuma; a small shrub, *Frankenia grandifolia*, native to California.

yerba santa; same as *Mountain balm*, sense 2.

yẽr'çum, *n.* [E. Ind.] either of two East Indian plants; also, the fiber from the bark of these plants.

yẽrd, *n.* a yard. [Obs.]

yẽrk, *v.t.*; yerked (yẽrkt), *pt.*, *pp.*; yerking, *ppr.* 1. to throw or thrust with a sudden smart spring or jerk; also, to jerk. [Obs.]

2. to lash; to strike; to beat. [Obs.]

yẽrk, *v.i.* 1. to jerk; to kick. [Obs.]

2. to move with sudden jerks. [Obs.]

yẽrk, *n.* a sudden or quick thrust or motion; a kick; a blow; a jerk. [Obs.]

yẽrn, *v.i.* to yearn. [Obs.]

yẽrn, *a.* eager; active; lively. [Obs.]

yẽrne, *adv.* quickly; briskly; soon. [Obs.]

yes, *adv.* [ME. *yus, yis*; AS. *gese, gise*, yes; prob. comp. from *gea*, yea, and *sī, sȳ*, be it so, let it be.]

1. aye; yea; it is so: the opposite of *no*, and used to express agreement, consent, affirmation, or confirmation.

2. not only that, but more; moreover; as, I shall be ready, *yes*, eager to help you.

Yes is sometimes used alone in inquiry to signify "What is it?," "Do you wish to say or add something?" or as a mere expression of interest equivalent to "Is it so?"

yes, *n.*; *pl.* **yes'es**, 1. the act of saying *yes*; agreement; concession.

2. an affirmative vote or a person voting this way: usually *aye*.

yes, *v.t.* and *v.i.*; yessed (yest), *pt., pp.*; yessing, *ppr.* to say *yes* (to).

ye·shi'vȧ, *n.*; *pl.* **ye·shi'vȧs**, Heb. **ye·shi·vōt'** [from Heb. *yeshīvāh*, lit., a sitting.]

1. a school or college for Talmudic studies; especially, a seminary for the training of orthodox rabbis.

2. a Jewish school combining religious and secular studies.

yes man, a person who agrees unconditionally with the opinions and suggestions of his superior; a servile sycophant. [Slang.]

yest, *n.* yeast. [Archaic.]

yes'tẽr, *a.* [first element of *yesterday* used as a combining form.] (a) of yesterday; (b) previous to this. Usually in combination; as, *yester*eve, *yester*year.

yes'tẽr·dāy, *n.* [ME. *yistredai*; AS. *geostrandæg*; *geostran*, yesterday, and *dæg*, day.]

1. the day just past; the day before today.
And all our *yesterdays* have lighted fools
The way to dusty death. —Shak.

2. time not long gone by; a recent day or time.

yes'tẽr·dāy, *adv.* 1. on the day preceding the present; on the day before today; as, the deed was signed *yesterday*.

2. recently.

yes'tẽr·dāy, *a.* of yesterday; as, *yesterday* morning.

yes'tẽr·ēve', *n.* and *adv.* yesterevening. [Archaic or Poet.]

yes'tẽr·ē'ven, *n.* and *adv.* yesterevening. [Archaic or Poet.]

yes'tẽr·ēve'ning, *n.* and *adv.* (on) the evening of yesterday. [Archaic or Poet.]

yes'tẽr·mọrn', *n.* and *adv.* yestermorning. [Archaic or Poet.]

yes'tẽr·mọrn'ing, *n.* and *adv.* (on) the morning of yesterday. [Archaic or Poet.]

yes'tẽrn, *a.* yester. [Archaic.]

yes'tẽr·nīght' (-nīt'), *n.* the night last past. [Archaic or Poet.]

yes'tẽr·nīght', *adv.* on the night last past. [Archaic or Poet.]

yes'tẽr·nọọn', *n.* the noon of yesterday. [Archaic or Poet.]

yes'tẽr·yēar', *n.* and *adv.* last year. [Poet.]

yes·treen', *n.* last evening. [Scot. or Poet.]

yest'y, *a.* yeasty. [Obs.]

yet, *adv.* [ME. *yit, yete*; AS. *giet, gieta*.]

1. up to now or to the time specified; thus far; as, they had not *yet* finished eating.

2. at the present time; now; as, we can't leave just *yet*.

3. still; even now; in the time still remaining; as, there is *yet* a chance for peace.

4. now or at a particular time, as continuing from a preceding time; as, I could hear him *yet*.

5. in addition; further; still; even (usually with a comparative); as, he was *yet* more kind.

6. as much as; even; as, he did not come, nor *yet* write.

7. now, after all the time that has elapsed; as, hasn't he finished *yet?*

8. nevertheless; as, she was lovely, *yet* stupid.

as yet; up to now.

yet, *conj.* nevertheless; however; as, she seems happy, *yet* she is troubled.
Yet I say unto you, that even Solomon, in all his glory, was not arrayed like one of these. —Matt. vi. 29.

yet, *v.t.* to cast, as metals. [Obs.]

yē'tï, *n.* [Tibetan.] [*often* Y–] a large, hairy, manlike animal reputed to live in the Himalayas: also called *Abominable Snowman*.

yev'en, *v.* obsolete past participle of *give*.

yew, *n.* [ME. *ew*; AS. *īw*, yew.]

1. a cone-bearing evergreen tree of the genus *Taxus*, related to the pines, having dark-green leaves and red berries. *Taxus baccata* is the common yew of the Old World.

2. the wood obtained from the yew. It is close-grained and elastic, and used especially for making archers' bows, etc.

3. a bow made of the wood of the yew. [Archaic.]

American yew; same as *ground hemlock*.

California yew; the short-leaved yew.

Irish yew; a hardy variety of the common yew having the branches erect.

YEW (*Taxus baccata*)

yew'en, *a.* made of yew. [Archaic.]

yé'yé, yé'-yé', *a.* [Fr., redupl. of Eng. exclamation *yeah*, used in lyrics of rock-and-roll songs.] fashionable, sophisticated, mod, etc. [Slang.]

yé'yé, yé'-yé', *n.* a person who is yéyé. [Slang.]

Yez'i·dï, Yez'i·dee, *n.* a member of a small sect of Kurdish-speaking tribes, living in Armenia and the Caucasus, whose religion is probably a mixture of the doctrines of the Magi, Mohammedans, and Christians.

y·fēre' (i-), *adv.* together. [Obs.]

Ygg'drȧ·sil (ig'), *n.* [O.N. *Yggdra Syll*, from *Yggr*, a name of Odin.] in Norse mythology, the ash tree whose roots and branches hold together the universe.

Y'gun (wī'), *n.* an antisubmarine gun, having two barrels in the form of the letter Y: used to fire a depth charge simultaneously on each side of the vessel.

YHVH, YHWH, Yahweh: see *Tetragrammaton*.

Yid'dish, *n.* [G. *jüdisch*, a short for *jüdischdeutsch*, Jewish-German; *jüdisch*, Jewish, from *Jude*, a Jew; L. *Judæus*.] a language spoken by many European Jews and their descendants on other continents: it is a dialect of High German written in characters of the Hebrew alphabet and containing elements of Hebrew, Russian, Polish, etc.

Yid'dish, *a.* designating or of Yiddish.

Yid'dish·ism, *n.* a Yiddish word, phrase, or idiom.

yiēld, *v.t.*; yielded, *pt., pp.*; yielding, *ppr.* [ME. *yelden*; AS. *gieldan, geldan, gildan*, to pay, restore, give up.]

1. to pay; to recompense. [Archaic.]

2. to give in return, or by way of recompense; to produce, as a reward or return for labor performed, capital invested, or the like.
Strabo tells us that the mines at Carthagena *yielded* the Romans per diem to the value of twenty-five thousand drachms. —Arbuthnot.

3. to produce generally; to bring forth; to give out; to bear; to furnish.
Nectarine fruits which the compliant boughs *yielded*. —Milton.

4. to afford; to confer; to grant; to permit.
Pray for my soul and *yield* me burial. —Tennyson.

5. to give up, as to a superior power, authority, or the like; to surrender: sometimes used reflexively with *up*.
We *yield* our town and lives to thy soft mercy. —Shak.

6. to give up or render generally; to emit.

7. to admit the force, justice, or truth of; to allow; to concede; to grant.
I *yield* it just, said Adam, and submit. —Milton.

Syn.—furnish, produce, afford, bear, render, relinquish, let go, forego, accede, resign, surrender, concede, allow, grant.

yiēld, *v.i.* 1. to give up; to submit; to surrender.

2. to give way to physical force; as, the gate would not *yield* to their blows.

3. to give place; to lose precedence, leadership, etc. (often with *to*).

4. to bear; to produce; as, the tree *yields* annually.

yiēld, *n.* 1. the act of yielding or producing.

2. the amount yielded or produced; return on labor, investment, taxes, etc.; product.

3. in finance, the ratio of the annual cash dividends or of the earnings per share of a stock to the market price.

4. in physics and chemistry, (a) the total products actually obtained from given raw materials, usually expressed as a percentage of the amount theoretically obtainable; (b) the force in tons of TNT of a nuclear or thermonuclear explosion.

yiēld'ȧ·ble, *a.* capable of yielding or of being yielded.

yiēld'ănce, *n.* the act of yielding or producing. [Rare.]

yiēld'ẽr, *n.* one who yields.

yiēld'ing, *a.* that yields; submissive; compliant.

yiēld'ing·ly, *adv.* in a yielding manner.

yiēld'ing·ness, *n.* the state or quality of being yielding.

yiēld'less, *a.* unyielding. [Obs.]

yiēld point, the point from which material quickly stretches without increase in stress.

yill, *n.* ale. [Scot.]

yin, *n.* [Chinese.] a Chinese measure of weight equal to about 2.67 pounds.

yin, *n., a., and pron.* one. [Scot.]

yince, *adv.* once. [Scot.]

yip, *n.* [echoic.] a yelp. [Colloq.]

yip, *v.i.*; yipped (yipt), *pt., pp.*; yipping, *ppr.* to yelp, as a young dog. [Colloq.]

yīpe, *interj.* an exclamation of pain, dismay, alarm, etc.

yip'pee, *interj.* an exclamation of joy, delight, etc.

yird, *n.* earth. [Scot.]

yīte, *n.* the yellowhammer. [Brit. Dial.]

-yl (il), [from Gr. *hylē*, wood.] a combining form used in chemistry to form the names of radicals, as in prop*yl*, but*yl*, am*yl*, etc.

y'läng-y'läng (ē'), *n.* same as *ilang-ilang*.

ȳ'lem, *n.* [ME., from MFr. *ilem*, perh. from ML. *hylem*, acc. of *hyle*, matter, orig., wood, from Gr. *hylē*.] in some theories of cosmogony, the primordial substance from which all the elements are supposed to have been derived.

Y'mīr (ē'), *n.* [O.N.] in Norse mythology, the giant from whose body the gods created the world.

Y mọth (wī), a moth, *Plusia gamma*: so called from a shining mark resembling the letter Y on its marbled upper wings.

y·näm'bú, *n.* [S. Am.] the great tinamou, *Rhynchotus rufescens*.

yōd, yōdh (yōd), *n.* [Heb., lit., hand.] the tenth letter of the Hebrew alphabet, corresponding to English initial *Y, y*.

yōde, *v.* obsolete past tense of *go*.

yō'del, *v.t.* and *v.i.*; yodeled *or* yodelled, *pt., pp.*; yodeling *or* yodelling, *ppr.* [G. dial. *jodeln*, to yodel.] to sing with abrupt, alternating changes between the normal chest voice and the falsetto.

yō'del, *n.* 1. the act or sound of yodeling.

2. a song or refrain sung in this way to meaningless syllables: popular among the mountain people of Switzerland and the Austrian Tyrol.

yō'del·ẽr, yō'del·lẽr (*or* -dlẽr), *n.* a person who yodels: also **yō'dlẽr**.

yō'dle, *n., v.t.* and *v.i.*; yodled, *pt., pp.*; yodling, *ppr.* yodel.

yō'gȧ, *n.* [Sans., union.] in Hindu philosophy, a practice involving intense and complete concentration upon something, especially the deity, in order to establish identity of consciousness with the object of concentration: it is a mystic and ascetic practice, usually involving the discipline of prescribed postures, controlled breathing, etc.

yōgh (yōkh), *n.* [ME.] the name of the Middle English character ȝ, representing: (a) a voiceless fricative, or guttural, similar to Modern German *ch*, as in *doch*: it is now written *gh* and is usually silent, as in *though*, or pronounced (f), as in *cough*; (b) a voiced palatal fricative, now represented by the *y* of *yes*.

yō'gï, *n.*; *pl.* **yō'gïs**, [Hind.] one who practices yoga: also **yō'gin**.

yō'gism, *n.* yoga.

yō'gụrt, yō'ghụrt (-goort), *n.* [Turk. *yōghurt*.] a thick, semisolid food made from milk fermented by a bacterium, originating in Turkey, Bulgaria, etc.: it is believed to have a beneficial effect on the intestines and is now sometimes prescribed dietetically: also *yohourt.*

yō'-hēave'-hō', *interj.* a chant formerly used by sailors while pulling or lifting together in rhythm.

yō·him'bin, *n.* an alkaloid, $(C_{21}H_{26}N_2O_3)_2H_2O$, obtained from a tropical African tree.

yōh'ourt (-oort), *n.* yogurt.

yoicks, *interj.* [earlier *hoik, hike,* also *yoaks;* prob. echoic.] a cry used for urging on the hounds in fox hunting. [Brit.]

yō'jȧ·nȧ, yō'jăn, *n.* [Hind.] a Hindu measure of distance varying in different places from four to ten miles, but generally reckoned as equivalent to five miles.

yōke, *n.* [ME. *zok, yok;* AS. *geoc, gioc, ioc,* yoke.]

1. a wooden frame or bar with loops or bows at either end, used for harnessing together a pair of oxen, etc.

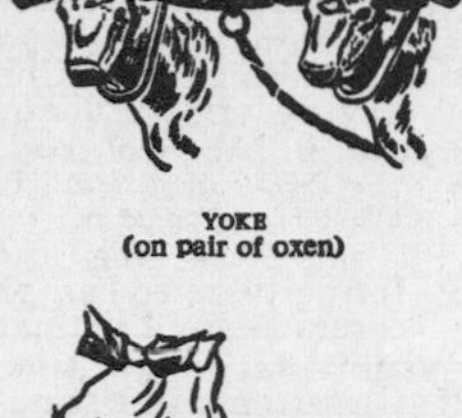

YOKE (on pair of oxen)

2. a pair of animals harnessed together; as, a *yoke* of oxen.

3. an ox yoke, arch of spears, etc. held over the shoulders of the conquered in ancient times.

4. any mark or symbol of bondage or servitude.

5. subjection; bondage; servitude.

6. something that binds, unites, or connects; as, the *yoke* of brotherhood.

YOKE

YOKE (on dress)

7. something like a yoke in shape or function; specifically, (a) a frame fitting over the shoulders for carrying pails, etc., one on either end; (b) a clamp, coupling, slotted piece, etc. used to hold a part in place, guide or control its movement, etc.; (c) the crosspiece to which the steering cables are attached on a ship's rudder; (d) the bar used in double harnessing to connect the horse's collar to the tongue of the wagon or carriage.

8. a part of a garment fitted closely to the shoulders or hips as a support for the gathered parts of the skirt, etc.

9. the usual amount of land plowed by a yoke of oxen in one day. [Obs.]

10. the time during which a yoke of oxen and the plowman work at a single, continuous stretch. [Scot.]

11. a part of the working day. [Scot.]

yōke, *v.t.;* yoked (yōkt), *pt., pp.;* yoking, *ppr.*
1. to put a yoke on.

2. (a) to harness an animal to (a plow, etc.); (b) to harness (an animal) to a plow, etc.

3. to join together; to link; to couple.

4. to marry.

5. to bring into bondage; to enslave. [Rare.]

Syn.—couple, conjoin, connect, link, enslave, subjugate.

yōke, *v.i.* to be joined together or closely united.

yōke'ăge, *n.* rockeage. [Dial.]

yōke elm, the European hornbeam.

yōke'fel″lōw, *n.* 1. one associated with another in a task, undertaking, or the like; a partner; a companion.

2. a husband or wife.

yō'kel, *n.* [prob. from *yokel, youkell,* dial. forms of *hickwall,* green woodpecker.] a person living in a rural area; a rustic; a country bumpkin: used contemptuously.

yōke'māte, *n.* a yokefellow.

yōke'-tōed, *a.* zygodactyl.

yōld, *v.* obsolete past tense and past participle of *yield.*

yōld'en, *v.* archaic past participle of *yield.*

yōlk (yōk; *now rarely* yōlk), *n.* [ME. *yolke, yelke;* AS. *geolca, gioleca,* yolk, lit., the yellow part, from *geolu,* yellow.]

1. the yellow, principal substance of an egg, as distinguished from the albumen, or white.

2. in biology, the contents of the ovum, including the protoplasm from which the embryo itself develops and, especially, the protoplasm that serves as nourishment for the growing embryo.

3. the oily secretion present in sheep's wool.

yōlk gland, same as *vitellarium.*

yōlk saç, the umbilical vesicle; the sac containing the food of the embryo.

yōlk'y, *a.; comp.* yolkier; *superl.* yolkiest; of, like, or full of yolk.

yōll, *v.i.* to yell. [Obs.]

yom, *n.; pl.* **yọm'im,** [Heb. *yōm.*] day: used in names of various Jewish holidays.

Yom Kip'pūr, [Heb. *yōm kipūr,* day of atonement.] a Jewish holiday, and day of fasting, the Day of Atonement: Lev. xvi. 29–34.

yon, *a.* and *adv.* [ME. *yone;* AS. *geon,* yon.] yonder. [Archaic or Dial.]

yon, *pron.* that or those at a distance. [Archaic or Dial.]

yoñ'çō·pin, *n.* the water chinkapin.

yond, *a.* and *adv.* yonder. [Archaic or Dial.]

yond, *a.* mad; furious. [Rare.]

yon'dẽr, *a.* [ME. *yonder, yender,* yonder.]

1. farther; more distant (with *the*).

2. being at a distance, but within, or as within, sight; that or those over there.

yon'dẽr, *adv.* at or in that (specified or relatively distant) place; over there; as, let us go *yonder.*

yō'nĭ, *n.* [Sans.] in Hindu mythology, the phallic symbol used in the worship of the supreme female energy of nature: usually associated with the lingam.

yoñ'kẽr, *n.* same as *younker.*

yōre, *adv.* [ME. *yore, youre;* AS. *geara,* from *gear,* year.] long ago. [Obs.]

yōre, *n.* time long past: now only in *of yore,* formerly.

But Satan now is wiser than *of yore.*—Pope.

York, *n.* the ruling family of England (1461–1485).

york'ẽr, *n.* [orig. *Yorker,* from the county of York, England; prob. a favorite bowl of Yorkshire teams.] in cricket, a bowled ball that hits the ground directly under or in front of the bat.

York'ist *n.* a member or supporter of the English royal house of York.

York'ist, *a.* of or supporting the house of York, especiay as opposed to the house of Lancaster in the Wars of the Roses.

York'shire pụd'ding, a batter pudding baked in the drippings of roasting meat.

York'shire ter'ri·ẽr, a small, long-haired terrier of a breed originating in Yorkshire, England.

Yō'rụ·bä, *n.; pl.* **Yō'rụ·bä, Yō'rụ·bäṣ,** 1. a member of a numerous Negro people and linguistic family along the coast of West Africa, chiefly between the Niger River and the Dahomey River.

2. the Sudanic lanaguge of the Yoruba.

yöu (ū), *pron.* [AS. *eow,* dat. and acc. pl. of *ge,* ye.]

1. the person or persons to whom one is speaking or writing: *you* is the nominative and objective form (sing. and pl.), *your* and *yours* the possessive (sing. and pl.), and *yourself* (sing.) and *yourselves* (pl.) the intensive and reflexive, of the second personal pronoun.

2. a person or people generally: equivalent in sense to indefinite *one,* as, *you* can never tell!

yöu'd, 1. you had.

2. you would.

youl, *v.t.* to yowl; to howl; to yell. [Obs.]

yöu'll, 1. you will.

2. you shall.

yŏung (yung), *a.; comp.* younger; *superl.* youngest, [ME. *yonge, yung;* AS. *geong,* young.]

1. being in an early period of life or growth; not old.

2. characteristic of youth in quality, appearance, or behavior; fresh; vigorous; strong; active.

3. representing or embodying a new tendency, social movement, progressivism, etc.; as, the *Young Turks.*

4. of or having to do with youth or early life.

5. lately begun; not advanced or developed; in an early stage.

6. lacking experience or practice; immature; raw; ignorant; green.

7. younger than another of the same name or family; as, they say *young* Jones is ill.

8. in geology, youthful.

yŏung, *n.* offspring, especially young offspring, collectively; as, the hen looks after its *young.*

the young; young people.

with young; pregnant.

yŏung'ber″ry, *n.; pl.* **yŏung'ber″rieṣ,** [after B. M. *Young,* Am. horticulturist.] a large, sweet, dark-red berry, a cross between a blackberry and a dewberry.

yŏung blood (blud), 1. young people; youth.

2. youthful strength, vigor, ideas, etc.

yŏung'ẽr (yung'gẽr), *n.* a young person; a junior.

yŏung'-eyed (-īd), *a.* 1. having the bright, clear, keen eyes associated with youth.

2. having a youthful or fresh outlook; enthusiastic, optimistic, etc.

yŏung'ish, *a.* somewhat young.

yŏung'ling, *n.* [ME. *yongling;* dim. from *young.*]

1. a young person; youth.

2. a young animal or plant.

3. an inexperienced person: a novice.

yŏung'ling, *a.* young.

yŏung'ly, *adv.* early in life. [Rare.]

yŏung'ly, *a.* young; youthful. [Obs.]

yŏung'ness, *n.* the state or quality of being young.

yŏung'stẽr, *n.* 1. a child.

2. a youth.

3. a young animal.

4. in the United States Naval Academy, a member of the second-year class.

yŏungth, *n.* youth. [Obs.]

yŏungth'ly, *a.* youthful. [Obs.]

yŏuñ'kẽr, *n.* [D. *jonker, jonkheer,* younker; *jong,* young, and *heer,* lord, gentleman.]

1. originally, a young nobleman or gentleman.

2. a young person; a stripling. [Rare.]

yöur, *pron.* [AS. *eōwer,* genit. of *gē,* ye.] possessive form of *you* (sing. and pl.).

yöur, *possessive pronominal a.* of, belonging to, or done by you: also used before some formal titles; as, *your* Honor, *your* Majesty.

yöu're, you are.

yöurṣ, *pron.* [ME. *youres; your* and genit. *-es;* hence, in form, a double possessive.] that or those belonging to you: the absolute form of *your,* used without a following noun, often after *of;* as, a friend of *yours,* that book is *yours, yours* are better.

O God, I fear thy justice will take hold
On me, and you, and mine, and *yours,* for this. —Shak.

yöur·self', *pron.; pl.* **yöur·selveṣ',** a form of the second person singular pronoun, used: (a) as an intensive; as, you *yourself* went; (b) as a reflexive; as, you hurt *yourself;* (c) as a quasi-noun meaning "your real, true, or actual self" (e.g., you are not *yourself* when you rage like that): in this construction *you* may be considered a possessive pronominal adjective and *self* a noun, and they may be separated; as, *your* own sweet *self.*

yöurṣ trụ'ly, 1. a phase or formula used before the signature in ending a letter.

2. I or me: used in humorous allusion to oneself. [Colloq.]

yöuṣe, *n.* [Hind.] the cheetah.

yöuth, *n.; pl.* **yöuths** (*or* ūthz), [ME. *youthe,* AS. *geōguth,* youth, from *geong,* young.]

1. the quality or state of being young; youngness.

2. the part of life coming between childhood and maturity; adolescence; also, an early stage of growth or existence.

3. a young person; especially, a young man.

4. young people generally or collectively.

5. freshness; novelty.

Syn.—adolescence, juvenility, childhood, juniority.

yöuth'fụl, *a.* 1. young; possessing youth; not yet old or mature.

2. of, characteristic of, or suitable for youth.

3. fresh; vigorous; active.

4. new; early; in an early stage.

5. in geology, having only begun to cause or undergo erosion.

Syn.—juvenile, boyish, puerile, young.

yöuth'fụl·ly, *adv.* in a youthful manner.

yöuth'fụl·ness, *n.* the quality or state of being youthful.

yöuth'hood, *n.* youth.

yöuth hos'tel, any of a system of supervised shelters providing cheap lodging on a co-operative basis for young people on bicycle tours, hikes, etc.

yöuth′ly, *a.* young; youthful. [Obs.]

yöuth′y, *a.* young. [Scot.]

yöu′ve, you have.

yōw, *n.* a ewe. [Obs. or Dial.]

yow, *interj.* an exclamation of pain, surprise, alarm, etc.

yowl, *v.i.*; yowled, *pt., pp.*; yowling, *ppr.* [O.N. *gaula,* to howl, yell.] to howl, as a dog; to utter a low mournful cry; to wail.

yowl, *n.* a protracted, wailing cry, as of a dog; a howl.

yow′ley, *n.* [Scot., from AS. *geolu,* yellow.] the yellowhammer. [Brit. Dial.]

yō′yō, *n.* [from Tagalog name: the toy came to the United States from the Philippines.]
1. a spoollike toy attached to one end of a string upon which it may be made to spin up and down by manipulating the string with the hand.
2. a dull, stupid, or gullible person. [Slang].

yō′yō, *v.i.*; yoyoed, *pt., pp.*; yoyoing, *ppr.* to move up and down; fluctuate; vary. [Colloq.]

y′pẽr·īte (ē′), *n.* [Fr. *ypérite,* after *Ypres,* Belgium.] mustard gas.

Y′-pō·ten·tiăl (wī′), *n.* same as *Y potential* under *Y.*

Y′pres lāce (ē′pr′), a kind of bobbin lace which is manufactured in Ypres, Belgium.

yp′sil·i·fọrm (ip′), *a.* [Gr. *upsilon,* the name of the letter *y,* and *-form.*] shaped like the Greek capital letter Y; Y-shaped.

Y′quem (ē′kem), *n.* [from the Château *Yquem,* an estate in southwestern France.] a fine variety of sauterne wine.

Y·seult′ (i-sọọlt′), *n.* Iseult (Isolde).

Yt, in chemistry, yttrium.

yt·tẽr′bi·ȧ (it-) [Mod. L., from *ytterbium.*] white ytterbium oxide, Yb_2O_3.

yt·tẽr′biç, *a.* of or containing ytterbium.

yt·tẽr′bi·um, *n.* [Mod. L., from *Ytterby,* in Sweden.] a rare, metallic chemical element of the rare-earth group, resembling and found with yttrium in gadolinite and certain other minerals: symbol, Yb; atomic weight, 173.04; atomic number, 70.

yt′tri·ȧ, [Mod. L., from *yttrium.*] yttrium oxide, Y_2O_3, a heavy, white, insoluble powder.

yt′tri·ăl·īte, *n.* an amorphous silicate of yttrium and thorium, of a vitreous luster.

yt′triç, *a.* of or containing yttrium.

yt·trif′ẽr·ous, *a.* yielding yttrium; containing yttrium.

yt′tri·um, *n.* [Mod. L., from *Ytterby,* Sweden.] a rare, metallic chemical element found in combination in gadolinite, samarskite, etc.: symbols, Y, Yt; atomic weight, 88.92; atomic number, 39.

yt′tri·um met′ăls, a series of closely related metals belonging, with the exception of yttrium, to the rare-earth group, including yttrium, dysprosium, holmium, erbium, thulium, ytterbium, lutetium, and, sometimes, terbium, and gadolinium.

yt″trō·çō·lum′bīte, *n.* yttrotantalite.

yt·trō·tan′tȧ·līte, *n.* a tantalate and columbate of yttrium, calcium, erbium, cerium, iron, etc., of a brown or black color.

Yū·än′, *n.* Mongol dynasty of China (1260–1368): founded by Kublai Khan.

yū·än′, *n.* [Chin.] the monetary unit of China.

yuç′çȧ, *n.* [Mod. L.; Sp. *yuca,* from W. Ind. (prob. Taino) native name.]
1. a plant of the lily family having stiff, sword-shaped leaves and white flowers in a single cluster, found in the southwestern United States and Latin America.
2. the flower of this plant.

YUCCA

yuç′çȧ bōr′ẽr, 1. a weevil common in California, *Yuccaborus frontalis.*
2. a North American moth of the genus *Megathymus,* that bores in yucca roots.

yuç′çȧ fẽr′ti·lī·zẽr, a moth of the genus *Pronuba,* the larvae of which infest yuccas: also called *yucca moth.*

yuck, *interj.* an expression of distaste, digust, etc.: also spelled *yuch.* [Slang.]

yuck′y, *a.*; *comp.* yuckier; *superl.* yuckiest; unpleasant, disgusting, etc. [Slang.]

Yụ′gȧ, *n.* [Sans. *yuga,* an age.] any of the four ages or eras of the world according to Hindu religious writings, each period being shorter, darker, and less righteous than the preceding: the first is the golden age (*Krita Yuga*), 1,728,000 years; the second (*Treta Yuga*), 1,296,000 years; the third (*Dvapara Yuga*), 864,000 years; the last, the present age (*Kali Yuga*), 432,000 years. The whole period is called *Maha Yuga.*

Yụ′gō·släv′ (*or* -slav′), *n.* [Serbo-Croatian, *jugo* or *jug,* south, and *Slav.*]
1. a member of a Slavic people, including Serbs, Croats, and Slovenes, that live in Yugoslavia: also spelled *Jugoslav.*
2. the language of Yugoslavia, or Serbo-Croatian.

Yụ′gō·släv′, *a.* of Yugoslavia or its people.

Yụ·gō·släv′i·ăn, *n.* and *a.* Yugoslav.

Yụ·gō·släv′ic, *a.* Yugoslav; Yugoslavian.

yuk, *n.* [echoic.] a loud laugh of amusement, or something evoking such a laugh. [Slang.]

yuk, *v.i.*; yukked, *pt., pp.*; yukking, *ppr.* to laugh loudly. [Slang.]

yụke, *v.i.* to itch. [Brit. Dial.]

yuk′kel, *n.* the green woodpecker. [Brit. Dial.]

yụ′lăn, *n.* [Chinese, *yu,* gem, and *lan,* plant.] a flowering tree of China, *Magnolia conspicua,* having large, brilliant, snow-white flowers.

yụle, *n.* [AS. *geol, giul, iul, geohol,* Christmas, the feast of the nativity.] Christmas or the Christmas season.
yule block, clog, or *log*; a large log of wood formerly used as the foundation for the ceremonial Christmas-Eve fire.

yụle′tīde, *n.* the time or season of yule, or Christmas; Christmas time.

yum, *interj.* [echoic: see *yummy.*] excellent; delicious: an expression of pleasure or enjoyment.

Yụ′mȧ, *n.*; *pl.* **Yụ′mȧ, Yụ′mȧṣ,** a Yuman Indian.

Yụ′măn, *a.* 1. of the Yumas or their language.
2. designating or of a North American Indian linguistic stock of the southwestern United States and northwestern Mexico, including Yuma and Mohave.

Yụ′măn, *n.* the Yuman linguistic stock.

yum′my, *a.*; *comp.* yummier; *superl.* yummiest, [echoic of a sound made in expressing pleasure at a taste.] very tasty; delectable; delicious: also used chiefly by women as a generalized term of approval. [Colloq.]

yum′-yum′, *interj.* same as *yum.*

yuñ′gan, *n.* [native name.] the dugong.

Yuñx, *n.* [Gr. *iynx.*] a genus of birds including the wrynecks.

yụrt, *n.* [Siberian.] a house or hut of the natives of northern Asia and Siberia.

y·wis′, *adv.* iwis. [Obs.]

Z

Z, z (zē; *Brit.* zed), *n.*; *pl.* **Z's, z's, Zs, zs** (zēz).
1. the twenty-sixth and last letter of the English alphabet: via Latin from the Greek *zeta.*
2. the sound of Z or z.
3. a type or impression for Z or z.
4. a symbol for the twenty-sixth in a sequence or group (or the twenty-fifth if J is omitted, or the twenty-third if V and W are also omitted.

Z, z (zē), *a.* 1. of Z or z.
2. twenty-sixth (or twenty-fifth if J is omitted, or twenty-third if V and W are also omitted) in a sequence or group.

Z (zē), *n.* 1. an object shaped like Z.
2. a medieval Roman numeral for 2,000: with a superior bar ($\bar{Z}$), 2,000,000.

Z (zē), *a.* shaped like Z.

z, in mathematics, an unknown quantity.

za-, [from Gr. *za-,* intensive and augmentative prefix.] a combining form meaning *very,* used in scientific terms to express a high degree of some quality.

za·bä·gliō′nē (za-băl-yō′nē), *n.* [It., augmentative of *zabaione,* ultimately from LL. *sabaia,* an Illyrian barley drink, beer.] a frothy dessert made of eggs, sugar, and wine, typically Marsala, beaten together over boiling water.

zä′brȧ, *n.* [Sp. and Port.] a small sailing vessel, formerly in use along the Spanish coast.

za·ca·tón′ (sä-kä-tōn′), *n.* [Sp.] a tough, wiry grass found in the Southwest and Mexico: it is used in making brushes, brooms, etc.

Zaçh·ȧ·rī′ăh, *n.* [LL. *Zacharias*; Gr. *Zacharias*; Heb. *zĕharyah,* lit., Jah remembers.] in the Bible, (a) the father of John the Baptist; (b) a man named as a martyr by Jesus: Matt. xxiii. 35.

Zaçh·ȧ·rī′ăs, *n.* Zachariah.

Zaçh′ȧ·ry, *n.* Zachariah.

zäd′dick (tsä′), *n.*; *pl.* **zäd·dik′im,** [Heb. *ṣaddiq,* righteous.]
1. in Judaism, a righteous and just man.
2. the spiritual leader of a Chassidic community.

zaf′fẽr, zaf′fre, *n.* [from Fr. *zafre* or It. *zaffera.*] unrefined oxide of cobalt, used in making smalt and by enamelers and porcelain manufacturers as a blue color.

zag, *n.* [see *zigzag.*]
1. any of the short, sharp angles or turns of a zigzag pattern, as alternating with a zig.
2. a sharp turning from a straight course.

zag, *v.i.*; zagged, *pt., pp.*; zagging, *ppr.* 1. to move in a zag.
2. to zigzag.

zaī′bä·tsụ, *n.*; *pl.* **zaī′bä·tsụ,** [Japan, *zai,* property, and *batsu,* family.] the few families that own and control most of the industry in Japan.

zāin, *n.* a dark-colored unspotted horse.

zä·ire′ (-ir′), *n.*; *pl.* **zä·ire′,** the monetary unit of Zaire.

zȧ·lamb′dō·dont (-lam′), *a.* [*za-,* Gr. *lambda,* the name for the letter *l,* and *odous, odontos.*] in zoology, pertaining to the *Zalambdodonta,* a group of insectivorous mammals which have the molars with a single V-shaped ridge.

zȧ·lamb′dō·dont, *n.* one of the *Zalambdodonta,* as the golden moles, tenrecs, etc.

Zā′mi·ȧ, *n.* [Mod. L.; L. *zamiæ* (pl.), false reading in Pliny for (*nuces*) *azaniæ,* pine (nuts).]
1. a genus of plants of the family *Cycadaceæ*: the typical member is a palmlike shrub

or tree having a thick, unbranched trunk, a crown of feather-shaped leaves, and oblong cones.

2. [z–] any plant of this genus.

zȧ·mïn·där′, *n.* [Hind. and Per. *zamīndār*, an occupant of land, landholder; *zamīn*, land, earth, and *-dār*, holding, possessing.]

1. in India, formerly, a collector of the revenue for land.

2. in India, a landowner, especially one paying revenue.

Also *zemindar*.

zȧ·mïn·dä′ri, *n.* the office or jurisdiction of a zamindar (sense 1); also, the land possessed by a zamindar (sense 2).

zȧ·möuse′, *n.* *Bos brachyceros*, a West African ox or buffalo, having the ears fringed with three rows of long hairs and lacking a dewlap.

zäm·pō′gnä (tsäm-pō′nyä), *n.* [It.] a bagpipe in use among Italian peasants.

zan′dẽr, *n.* [G.] the European pike perch, *Stizostedion lucioperca*.

zand′mōle, *n.* the sand mole, or coast rat.

Zan·ni·chel′li·ȧ, *n.* [named after J. J. *Zannichelli* (1662–1729), a Venetian botanist.] a genus of plants including *Zannichellia palustris*, the horned pondweed, native to ponds, ditches, and rivulets of both hemispheres. The leaves are opposite and very narrow, bearing the flowers at their base enclosed in a membranous sheath.

zan′tē, *n.* same as *zantewood*, sense 1.

Zan′tē çur′rănt, a small seedless grape from Zante, one of the Ionian group of islands.

Zan·tē·des′chi·ȧ, *n.* [after Francesco *Zantedeschi*, an Italian botanist.] the genus *Richardia*.

zan′tē·wood, *n.* [from *Zante*, one of the Ionian Islands.]

1. the smoke tree, *Rhus cotinus*: also called *zante fustic*.

2. the satinwood, *Chloroxylon swietenia*

Zan′ti·ōte, *n.* a native of Zante, one of the Ionian Islands.

zā′ny, *n.*; *pl.* **zā′nieș**, [Fr. *zani*, from It. *zanni*, *zane*, a zany or clown; originally, simply a familiar or abbreviated pronunciation of *Giovanni*, John.]

1. a clown or buffoon; specifically, a former stock character in comedies who clownishly aped the principal actors.

> Preacher at once, and *zany* of thy age. —Pope.

2. a fool; a dolt; a simpleton.

Syn.—buffoon, clown, harlequin, merry-andrew.

zā′ny, *v.t.* to mimic. [Obs.]

zā′ny·ișm, *n.* the state or character of a zany.

Zan·zȧ′li·ăn, *n.* [*Zanzalus*, a surname of Jacobus Baradaeus.] a Jacobite (sense 2).

zaph′ȧ·rȧ, *n.* same as *zaffer*.

Zȧ·phren′ti·dae, *n.pl.* a family of Paleozoic stone corals.

Zȧ·phren′tis, *n.* [LL.] 1. a genus of fossil cup-shaped corals of the Paleozoic formation, typical of the family *Zaphrentidæ*.

2. [z–] a coral of this genus.

zap·ō·til′lȧ, *n.* same as *sapodilla*.

zăp·ti′äh, *n.* [Turk. *ḍabṭīyah*; Ar. *ḍābiṭīyah*, from *ḍabṭ*, government.] a Turkish policeman.

zăp·ti′eh, *n.* a zaptiah.

zar·an′thăn, *n.* [Heb.] a hardening of the breast.

Zar·ȧ·thus′tri·ăn, Zar·ȧ·thus′triç, *a.* same as *Zoroastrian*.

Zar·ȧ·thus′tri·ăn·ișm, *n.* same as *Zoroastrianism*.

Zar·ȧ·thus′trișm, *n.* Zoroastrianism.

zär′ȧ·tīte, *n.* [Sp. *zaratita*, after a Señor *Zarate*.] a hydrated, basic carbonate of nickel, $NiCO_3 \cdot 2Ni(OH)_2 \cdot 4H_2O$, usually found as an emerald-green incrustation.

zȧ·rē′bȧ, zȧ·ree′bȧ, *n.* [Ar. *zarība*, a pen.] in the Sudan and surrounding territory, a camping place or enclosure formed by a palisade or thorn hedge: also *zariba*.

zärf, *n.* [Ar. *ẓarf*, a sheath.] a small, metal, cuplike stand, usually ornamented, used in the Levant for holding hot coffee cups.

zär′nich, *n.* [Ar. *zernikh*; Gr. *arsenikon*, arsenic.] native sulfide of arsenic, as sandarac, or realgar, and orpiment.

zas·trù′gȧ, *n.* same as *sastruga*.

zä′ti, [E. Ind.] the capped macaque, *Macacus pileolatus*, native to India and Ceylon.

Zau·schnē′ri·ȧ, *n.* [named after *Zauschner*, a German botanist.] a genus of flowering plants belonging to the evening primrose family; *Zauschneria californica* is known as the Californian fuchsia.

zax, *n.* [variant of *sax*; AS. *seax*, a knife.] an instrument for trimming roofing slates.

zä′yat, *n.* [Burmese.] a caravansary, or resting place for travelers in Burma.

zä′yin, *n.* [Heb. *zāyin*.] the seventh letter of the Hebrew alphabet, corresponding to English Z, z.

Zē′ȧ, *n.* [Gr. *zea*, a kind of grain, coarse wheat, used as fodder for horses.] a genus of annual grasses including the maize, or Indian corn, *Zea mays*, which is the only species known.

zēal, *n.* [Fr. *zèle*; L. *zelus*, zeal, from Gr. *zēlos*, zeal, ardor, lit., heat, from *zeein*, to boil.]

1. eager interest and enthusiasm; ardent endeavor or devotion; ardor; fervor.

2. a zealot. [Obs.]

Syn.—ardor, fervor, enthusiasm, fervency, earnestness, eagerness, vehemence.

zēal, *v.i.* to be zealous. [Obs.]

zeal′ănt (zel′), *n.* a zealot. [Obs.]

zēaled, *a.* characterized by zeal. [Obs.]

zēal′fụl, *a.* zealous; full of zeal.

zēal′less, *a.* lacking zeal.

zeal′ŏt (zel′), *n.* [Fr. *zelote*; LL. *zelotes*; Gr. *zēlōtēs*, zealot, from *zēlos*, zeal.]

1. one who is zealous or full of zeal, especially to an extreme or excessive degree; one carried away by excess of zeal; a fanatic.

> He was in truth not a man to be popular with the vindictive *zealots*. —Macaulay.

2. [Z–] one of a Jewish sect which struggled openly against the Roman rule in Palestine from about 6 A.D. till the fall of Jerusalem.

zēa·lot′iç·ăl, *a.* ardently zealous. [Rare.]

zeal′ŏt·ișm (zel′), *n.* the character or conduct of a zealot.

zeal′ŏt·ist, *n.* a zealot.

zeal′ŏt·ry, *n.* the conduct or behavior of a zealot; excessive or undue zeal; fanaticism.

zeal′ous, *a.* [LL. *zelosus*, from L. *zelus*; Gr. *zēlos*, zeal.] ardent in the pursuit of an object; enthusiastic; full of, characterized by, or showing zeal, ardor, or enthusiasm.

> *Zealous* in the salvation of souls. —Law.

zeal′ous·ly, *adv.* in a zealous manner.

zeal′ous·ness, *n.* the quality of being zealous.

zē′beç, zē′beck, *n.* same as *xebec*.

zē′brȧ, *n.*; *pl.* **zē′brăș** or **zē′brȧ**, [Port., from the native name in the Congo.] an African animal related to and resembling the horse and the ass: it has dark stripes on a white or tawny body.

ZEBRA
(4 1/2 ft. high at shoulder)

zē′brȧ çat′ẽr·pil·lăr, the larva of *Mamestra picta*, a noctuid moth of North America. It is of a yellow color and has three black stripes running lengthwise.

zē′brȧ ō·pos′sum, same as *zebra wolf*.

zē′brȧ par′rȧ·keet, the grass parrakeet.

zē′brȧ plant, a Brazilian plant of the genus *Calathea* or *Maranta*, of the ginger family, having striped leaves.

zē′brȧ poi′ṣōn, a South African euphorbiaceous tree, the milky juice of which is very poisonous. It is sometimes used as an arrow poison.

zē′brȧ shärk, a tiger shark.

zē′brȧ spī′dẽr, a hunting spider.

zē′brȧss, *n.* [from *zebra* and *ass*.] the offspring of a male zebra and a female ass.

zē′brȧ swäl′lōw·tāil, one of a species of swallow-tailed butterflies of the genus *Iphiclides*, having yellow wings with black stripes.

zē′brȧ wolf (wụlf), a carnivorous marsupial of the genus *Thylacinus*, the thylacine: also called *Tasmanian wolf*.

zē′brȧ·wood, *n.* 1. a hard, striped wood obtained from a South American tree of the genus *Connarus*, used in cabinetmaking; also, the tree itself.

2. the striped wood of various other trees.

3. any of several trees having striped wood.

zē′brïne, *a.* of or relating to a zebra; also, striped like a zebra.

zē′brù·lȧ, zē′brùle, *n.* the offspring of a male zebra and a female horse.

zē′bū, *n.*; *pl.* **zē′būș** or **zē′bū**, [Fr. *zébu*; of Tibet. origin.] a ruminant mammal of the genus *Bos*, found in India, China, and the northern part of Africa: it has a large hump over the shoulders, short, curving horns and a large dewlap.

ZEBU (4 1/2 ft. at shoulder)

zē′bub, *n.* [Ar. *zubāb*, a fly.] an Abyssinian fly, the zimb.

Zech·ȧ·rī′äh, *n.* in the Bible, (a) a Hebrew prophet of the sixth century B.C. who urged the rebuilding of the Temple; (b) a book of the Old Testament containing his prophecies.

zeç·chī′nō (tsek-), *n.*; *pl.* **zeç·chī′nī**, [It. *zecchino*.] a zechin.

zech′in, *n.* a sequin (gold coin).

Zech′stein, *n.* [G.] in geology, a subdivision of the Permian, constituting the upper of the two groups.

zed, *n.* [L. *zeta*; Gr. *zēta*, zed.] the British name for the letter Z, z.

zed′ō·ăr·y, *n.* [Fr. *zédoaire*; LL. *zedoaria*; Per. *zadwār*, *jadwar*, zedoary.] an aromatic substance obtained from the rootstocks of certain plants of the genus *Curcuma*, which are used in perfumes and medicines.

zee, *n.*; *pl.* **zees**, [D.] the letter Z, z.

zee′köe, *n.* [S. Afr.] the hippopotamus.

Zee′măn ef·fect′, [named after Pieter *Zeeman*, Du. physicist.] in physics, the effect produced upon the structure of the spectrum lines of light emitted or absorbed by atoms subjected to a moderately strong magnetic field, resulting in the splitting of each spectrum line into two or three lines (*normal Zeeman effect*) or into many lines (*anomalous Zeeman effect*).

zeh′nẽr (tsā′), *n.* [G., from *zehn*, ten.] a former Austrian silver coin, equivalent to ten kreutzers.

zē′in, *n.* [*zea* and *-in*.] a kind of protein obtained from maize.

zē′ișm, zē·is′mus, *n.* [*zea* and *-ism*.] a skin disease, said to be due to the too frequent use of maize as an article of food.

Zeit′geist (tsīt′), *n.* [G., from *zeit*, time, and *geist*, spirit.] the spirit of the time; the moral and intellectual trend of any age or period.

zel, *n* [Per.] a kind of Oriental cymbal.

Zē·lā′ni·ăn, *a.* of or relating to New Zealand.

zel′ănt, *n.* a zealot. [Obs.]

zel′ȧ·tŏr, *n.* a zealot. [Rare.]

zel·ō·typ′i·ȧ, *n.* [Gr. *zēlos*, zeal, and *typtein*, to strike.] morbid or insane zeal; also, insane jealousy. [Obs.]

zel·ō·typ′iç, *a.* pertaining to or showing zelotypia. [Obs.]

ze·mïn·där′, *n.* same as *zamindar*.

ze·mïn·dä′ri, *n.* same as *zamindari*.

zem′mi, zem′ni, *n.* a burrowing rodent, *Spalax typhlus*; the blind mole rat.

zemst′vō, *n.*; *pl.* **zemst′vōș**, [Russ.] a local administrative body in Czarist Russia.

Zem′zem, *n.* [Ar.] a fountain at Mecca which Mohammedans believe was the spring God made to slake the thirst of Ishmael when he and his mother Hagar were driven into the wilderness by Abraham.

Zen, *n.* [Japan., from Chin. *ch'an*, ult. from Sans. *dhyāna*, thinking meditation.]

1. an anti-rational Buddhist sect developed in India and now widespread in Japan: it differs from other Buddhist sects in seeking enlightenment through introspection and intuition rather than in Pali scripture.

2. the beliefs and practices of this sect.

zē·nä′nȧ, *n.* [Hind. *zenāna*, *zanāna*; Per. *zenāna*, belonging to women, from *zan*, woman.] in India and Persia, the portion of the house reserved exclusively for women.

Zend, *n.* [Per., interpretation.]

1. the Middle Persian translation of and

commentary on the Zoroastrian Avesta, or religious writings.

2. the original language of the Avesta, an ancient form of Persian or Iranian; Avestan.

Zend-A·ves'tȧ, *n.* [altered from *Avesta-va-Zend,* lit., (sacred) text and interpretation.] the sacred writings of the Zoroastrians.

Zend'iç, *a.* of or having to do with Zend or the Zend.

zē'nith, *n.* [ME. *senyth;* OFr. *cenith;* ML. *cenith,* from Ar. *semt,* way, road, path, as in *semt-ar-ras,* zenith, lit., way of the head.]

1. the vertical point of the heavens at any place, or the point right above a spectator's head; the upper pole of the celestial horizon: opposed to *nadir.*

2. the highest point; culmination; peak; summit.

zē'nith·ăl, *a.* pertaining to the zenith.

zē'nith dis'tănce, the angular distance of a heavenly body from the zenith.

zē'nith tel'ē·sçōpe, a geodetical instrument, having adjustments in altitude and azimuth, a graduated vertical semicircle, a level and a micrometer: used for measuring the difference of the zenith distances of two stars as a means of determining the latitude, the stars being such as pass the meridian about the same time, but on opposite sides of the zenith.

zē'nū, *n.* the dzeren.

zē'ō·līte, *n.* [Sw. *zeolit,* from Gr. *zeein,* to boil: so named by A. F. Cronstedt (1702?–1765), Sw. mineralogist, from its swelling up when heated.] any of a number of hydrous silicates of aluminum, sodium, or calcium found in the cavities of igneous rocks.

zē·ō·lit'iç, *a.* pertaining to zeolite; consisting of zeolite or resembling it.

zē·ō·lit·i·zā'tion, *n.* the act or process of changing a mineral into a zeolite.

zē·ol'i·tīze, *v.t.*; zeolitized, *pt., pp.*; zeoliting, *ppr.* to change into a zeolite.

Zeph"ȧ·nī'ăh, *n.* [Heb. *tsĕphanyāh,* lit., the Lord has hidden.]

1 a Hebrew prophet of the seventh century B.C.

2. the book in the Old Testament containing his prophecies.

zeph'yr (-ĭr), *n.* [L. *zephyrus,* from Gr. *zephyros,* the west wind.]

1. the west wind.

2. a soft, gentle breeze.

3. a fine, soft, lightweight yarn, cloth, or garment.

4. something light, airy, or unsubstantial.

zephyr cloth; a light cassimere for women's wear.

zephyr yarn or *worsted*; a fine yarn or worsted used in knitting, etc.

Zeph·yr·an'thēs̹, *n.* [Gr. *zephyros,* west wind, and *anthos,* flower.] a genus of chiefly American plants of the amaryllis family.

zeph'yr flow'ẽr, any plant of the genus *Zephyranthes.*

Zeph'y·rus, *n.* [L., from Gr. *Zephyros,* the west wind or zephyr.] the personification of the west wind, considered by the Greeks as the mildest and gentlest of all sylvan deities.

zep'pe·lin (*or* zep'lin), *n.* [*often* Z–] [after F. von *Zeppelin* (1838–1917), German general.] a dirigible airship of a type designed around 1900 by Count von Zeppelin.

zē'quin (-kwin), *n.* same as *sequin.*

zẽr'dȧ, *n* [Afr.] the fennec.

ze̤·rī'bȧ, *n.* same as *zareba.*

zē'rō, *n.*; *pl.* **zē'rōs̹** or **zē'rōes̹,** [Fr. *zéro;* It. and Sp. *zero,* from Ar. *sifr,* a cipher.]

1. the symbol or numeral 0; a cipher; a naught.

2. the point, marked 0, from which positive or negative quantities are reckoned on a graduated scale, as on thermometers; specifically, (a) on a centigrade thermometer, the freezing point of water; (b) on a Fahrenheit thermometer, a point 32° below the freezing point of water.

3. a temperature that causes a thermometer to register zero.

4. the point intermediate between positive and negative quantities.

5. nothing.

6. the lowest point; as, his chances of success sank to *zero.*

7. in gunnery, a sight setting for a range allowing for both elevation and windage.

absolute zero; see under *absolute.*

zero hour; (a) the time set for the beginning of an attack or other military operation; (b) any crucial or decisive moment; a critical point.

zero method; same as ***null method*** under ***null.***

zero point; same as *zero,* n. 2.

zero potential; see under *potential.*

zē'rō, *a.* 1. of or at zero.

2. without measurable value.

3. in aeronautics, (a) designating or of a ceiling that is at or near the ground, specifically one at a height of fifty feet or lower; (b) designating or of visibility along the ground regarded as within the limit of a few feet.

zē'rō, *v.t.* to adjust (an instrument, etc.) to a zero point or to an arbitrary point from which all positive and negative readings are to be measured.

to zero in; to adjust the sight settings of (a rifle) by calibrated firing on a standard range when there is no deflection due to wind.

to zero in on; (a) to adjust gunfire so as to be aiming directly at (a target); (b) to concentrate attention on; focus on.

zē'rō-bāse', *a.* [from the idea of starting at zero.] designating or of a technique for preparing a budget, in which each proposed item is evaluated on its merits without considering any previous budget.

zē'rō-bāsed', *a.* same as *zero-base.*

zē'rō pop·ū·lā'tion grōwth, a condition in a given population in which the birth rate equals the death rate so that the population remains constant.

zē'rō-sum', *a.* in a system of mathematical analysis, designating or of a situation, competition, etc. in which a gain for one must result in a loss for another or others.

zest, *n.* [Fr. *zeste,* one of the partitions in a walnut, hence, the peel of an orange or lemon used to give piquancy (*zest*) to.]

1. something that gives flavor, relish, or piquancy.

2. stimulating or exciting quality; flavor; relish; piquancy.

3. keen enjoyment or inclination; gusto (often with *for*); as, a *zest for* life.

4. peel of orange or lemon used as flavoring. [Rare.]

zest, *v.t.*; zested, *pt., pp.*; zesting, *ppr.* 1. to give a relish or flavor to; to heighten the taste or relish of.

2. to cut, as the peel of an orange or lemon, into thin slips; to squeeze, as peel, over the surface of anything.

zest'fụl, *a.* full of or characterized by zest.

zē'tȧ, *n.* [Gr.] the sixth letter of the Greek alphabet, corresponding to the English *Z, z.*

zē·tet'iç, *a.* [Gr. *zētētikos,* from *zētein,* to seek for, seek.] seeking; proceeding by inquiry.

Zeū'glō·don, *n.* [Gr. *zeuglē,* the strap of a yoke, and *odous, odontos,* a tooth, lit., yoke tooth: so called from the peculiar form of its molar teeth.]

1. an extinct genus of cetaceans found in the Eocene of the Gulf States.

2. [z–] a member of this genus.

zeū'glō·dont, *a.* pertaining to the *Zeuglodontia.*

zeū'glō·dont, *n.* any of the *Zeuglodontia*; a zeuglodon.

Zeū·glō·don'ti·ȧ (-shi-), *n.pl.* an extinct suborder of cetaceans of which the zeuglodons are the type.

zeū·glō·don'toid, *a.* and *n.* same as *zeuglodont.*

zeūg'mȧ, *n.* [L.; Gr., from *zeugnynai,* to join.] a figure of speech in which a single modifier, usually a verb or adjective, applies to two or more words, with only one of which it seems logically connected (e.g., The room was not light, but his fingers were.).

zeūg·mat'iç, *a.* pertaining to or resembling zeugma.

Zeū·gō·brañ'çhi·ȧ, *n.pl.* same as *Zygobranchiata.*

zeu'nẽr·īte, (zī'), *n.* [after G. *Zeuner,* of Freiburg.] a green hydrated arsenate of uranium, and protoxide of copper, crystallizing in the tetragonal system.

Zeūs, *n.* [Gr.] the supreme deity of the ancient Greeks, son of Cronus and Rhea and husband of Hera: identified by the Romans with Jupiter.

Zeū·zē'rȧ, *n.* a widely distributed genus of bombycid moths.

zeū·zē'ri·ăn, *n.* any species of the genus *Zeuzera,* some of which attain a large size. The larvae bore into wood.

zeū·zē'ri·ăn, *a.* pertaining to the genus *Zeuzera* or bombycid moths.

zib'el·ine, zib'el·line, *a.* [Fr. *zibeline;* It. *zibellino,* from Slavic base.] of or having to do with sables.

zib'el·ine, zib'el·line, *n.* the pelt or fur of a sable; also, a kind of soft woolen dress material, with a furlike nap.

zib'et, zib'eth, *n.* [from ML. or It.; ML. *zibethum;* It. *zibetto;* Ar. *zabād.*] a carnivorous mammal, *Viverra zibetha,* bearing a close resemblance to the civet, native to southern Asia and the East Indies, and often domesticated by the natives. It secretes a scent similar to that of the civet. Also called ***Indian*** or *Asiatic civet.*

ziē'gȧ, *n.* a kind of cheese made by treating milk with rennet and afterward with acetic acid.

ziē·tri·si'kīte, *n.* [named after *Zietrisika,* in Moldavia.] a member of the group of hydrocarbons resembling ozocerite.

Zif, *n.* [Heb. *Ziv.*] Iyar: the early Hebrew name: see *Jewish calendar.*

zig, *n.* [see *zigzag.*]

1. any of the short, sharp angles or turns of a zigzag pattern, alternating with a zag.

2. a sharp turning from a straight course.

zig, *v.i.*; zigged, *pt., pp.*; zigging, *ppr.* 1. to move in a zig.

2. to zigzag.

zig'gu̦·rat, *n.* [Assyr. *ziqquratu,* height, pinnacle.] a temple tower of the ancient Assyrians and Babylonians, in the form of a terraced pyramid with each story smaller than the one below it: also ***zikkurat, zikurat.***

zig'zag, *n.* [Fr. *zigzag,* from G. *zickzack,* perhaps reduplicated from *zacke,* a tooth or sharp prong or point, a dentil.]

1. any of a series of short, sharp turns or angles in alternate directions, as in a line; a number or series of short, sharp turns.

Cracks and *zigzags* of the head. —Pope.

2. something characterized by such a series, as a design, path, etc.

3. in architecture, a zigzag molding; a chevron or dancette.

4. in fortification, same as *boyau.*

zig'zag, *a.* having the form of or characterized by a zigzag.

zig'zag, *v.t.* and *v.i.*; zigzagged, *pt., pp.*; zigzagging, *ppr.* to move or form in a zigzag.

zig'zag, *adv.* in a zigzag course; so as to form a zigzag.

zig'zag·gẽr·y, *n.* a zigzag course. [Rare.]

zig'zag·gy, *a.* having sharp turns; zigzag.

zik'ku̦·rat, zik'u̦·rat, *n.* same as *ziggurat.*

zilch, *n.* [nonsense syllable, orig. used in the 1930's as name of a character in the magazine *Ballyhoo.*]

1. nothing; zero. [Slang.]

2. [Z–] a name used to refer to anyone whose name is unknown or to a nonentity. [Slang.]

Zil'lȧ, *n.* [Egypt.] a genus of shrubs of the mustard family. *Zilla myagroides* is native to Egyptian deserts: its leaves are boiled and eaten by Arabs.

zil'lăh (-lȧ), *n.* [Hind.] in India, an administrative district or division.

zil'liŏn, *n.* [arbitrary coinage, after ***million,*** *billion,* etc.] an indefinitely large number. [Colloq.]

Zil'päh, *n.* in the Bible, the mother of Gad: Gen. xxx. 10.

zimb, *n.* [Ar.] a dipterous insect of Ethiopia, of the genus *Pangonia,* related to the tsetse fly.

zi·moç'çȧ, *n.* a variety of sponge found in the Mediterranean.

ziñç, *n.* [G. *zink,* zinc.] a bluish-white, metallic chemical element, usually found in combination, used as a protective coating for iron, as a constituent in various alloys, as an electrode in electric batteries, and, in the form of salts, in medicines: symbol, Zn; atomic weight, 65.38; atomic number, 30.

flowers of zinc; same as ***zinc oxide.***

ziñç, *v.t.*; zincked *or* zinced (zingkt), *pt., pp.*; zincking *or* zincing, *ppr.* to coat or treat with zinc.

ziñç am'īde, a white amorphous substance, $Zn(NH_2)_2$, obtained from zinc ethyl by the action of ammonia.

ziñç'āte, *n.* a salt produced by the reaction of amphoteric zinc hydroxide as an acid.

ziñç blende, sphalerite.

ziñç blo̤om, an incrusting hydrous carbonate of zinc.

ziñç green, a green pigment composed of the oxides of zinc and cobalt.

ziñç'iç, *a.* of or containing zinc.

ziñç·if'ẽr·ous, *a.* yielding or containing zinc.

zinç″i·fi·çā′tion, *n.* the act or process of coating or impregnating with zinc.
zinç′i·fȳ, *v.t.*; zincified, *pt.*, *pp.*; zincifying, *ppr.* to coat or impregnate with zinc.
zinç′īte, *n.* native oxide of zinc, ZnO, a deep-red to yellowish mineral.
ziñck′en·īte, *n.* same as *zinkenite.*
ziñck′y, *a.* zincic: also spelled *zinky.*
zinç meth′yl, a volatile liquid, $Zn(CH_3)_2$, with a fetid smell and poisonous vapors: it ignites spontaneously on exposure to air.
ziñ′çō-, [from *zinc.*] a combining form indicating zinc as an element in specific double compounds.
zinç′ōde, *n.* in electricity, the zinc terminal or electrode of a voltaic cell. [Obs.]
ziñ′çō·grȧph, *n.* a zinc plate prepared by zincography; also, an impression taken from such a plate.
ziñ·çog′rȧ·phẽr, *n.* one who works in zincography.
ziñ·çō·graph′iç, ziñ·çō·graph′iç·ăl, *a.* of, or having the nature of, zincography.
ziñ·çog′rȧ·phy, *n.* the art or process of engraving or etching on zinc plates for printing.
zinç′oid, *a.* resembling zinc; pertaining to zinc. [Obs.]
zinç oint′ment, a salve or ointment containing zinc oxide.
zinç·ol′y·sis, *n.* [*zinco-*, and Gr. *lysis*, dissolving.] electrolysis. [Obs.]
zinç′ō·lȳte, *n.* an electrolyte. [Obs.]
ziñ′çō·tȳpe, *n.* same as *zincograph.*
zinç′ous, *a.* zincic.
zinç ox′īde, a white powder, ZnO, used as a pigment and in the manufacture of rubber articles, glass, cosmetics, ointments, etc.
zinç send′ẽr, a device used in telegraphic circuits which sends a momentary reverse current into the line after each signal in order to counteract retardation.
zinç spin′el, same as *gahnite.*
zinç sul′fīde, sulfide of zinc (ZnS), a white amorphous precipitate resulting from a zinc solution with an alkaline sulfide.
ziñ′cum, *n.* [L.] zinc. [Obs.]
zinç whīte, zinc oxide used as a white pigment.
zin′fan·del, *n.* [origin unknown.]
1. a dry, red wine like claret, made in California.
2. the dark grape from which it is made, originally imported from Hungary.
zing, *n.* [echoic.] a shrill, high-pitched sound, as of something moving at high speed. [Slang.]
zing, *v.i.* to make a shrill, high-pitched sound. [Slang.]
ziñ′gä·rä, *n.*; *pl.* **ziñ′gä·re,** [It.] a gypsy woman or girl.
ziñ′gä·rō, ziñ′gä·nō, *n.*; *pl.* **ziñ′gä·rī, ziñ′gä·nī,** [It.] a gipsy.
zing′el, *n.* [G.] a teleostean fish of the genus *Aspro*, closely related to the perch. The body is very elongated in form.
Zin′ġi·bẽr, *n.* [L. *zingiber*; Gr. *zingiberis*, ginger.] a genus of tropical plants, family *Zingiberaceæ*, widely cultivated in the East and West Indies, China, and Africa. *Zingiber officinale* is the common ginger.
Zin″ġi·bē·rā′cē·ae *n.pl.* [*Zingiber* and *-aceæ.*] a family of tropical monocotyledonous plants including the ginger, turmeric, etc., characterized by highly aromatic rootstocks.
zin″ġi·bē·rā′ceous, *a.* of or having to do with the *Zingiberaceæ*, or ginger family.
Zin·jan′thrō·pus, *n.* [Mod.L., from Ar. *Zinj*, East Africa, and Gr. *anthropus*, man.] a type of primitive man, *Australopithecus boisei*, who lived about 1,500,000 years ago, known from fossil remains found in Tanganyika in 1959.
ziñ′ke (tsing′), *n.* [G.] a musical wind instrument in the shape of a cornet. [Obs.]
ziñ′ken·īte, *n.* [G. *zinkenit*, after J.K.L. *Zinken*, director of mines in Anhalt, Germany.] a steel-gray metallic mineral, $PbSb_2S_4$.
ziñk′i·fȳ, *v.t.* same as *zincify.*
ziñk′y, *a.* zincky; zincic.
Zin′ni·ȧ, *n.* [named after J. G. *Zinn*, a German botanist.]
1. a genus of plants of the aster family, having colorful, composite flowers.
2. [z–] a plant of this genus.
zinn′wäld·īte (-vält-), *n.* [from *Zinnwald*, in Bohemia, where it occurs.] a monoclinic variety of lepidolite containing lithium and iron.
Zin′zi·bẽr, Zin″zi·bē·rā′cē·ae, etc. same as *Zingiber*, etc.

Zī′ŏn, *n.* [ME. *Syon*; AS. *Sion*; LL. *Sion*; Heb. *Tsīyōn*, orig., a hill.]
1. a hill in Jerusalem, site of the temple and of the royal residence of David and his successors: regarded by Jews as a symbol of the center of Jewish national life.
2. the theocracy of God.
3. heaven; the heavenly city.
4. the Jewish people.
Also *Sion.*
Zī′ŏn·iṣm, *n.* a movement formerly for re-establishing, now for advancing, the Jewish national state of Israel.
Zī′ŏn·ist, *n.* a supporter of Zionism.
Zī′ŏn·ist, *a.* of, supporting, or having to do with Zionism.
Zī·ŏn·is′tiç, *a.* Zionist.
Zī′ŏn·īte, *n.* 1. one who believes in the principles and practices advocated by John Alexander Dowie, who, in 1901, founded Zion City, Illinois, as an industrial community of his adherents.
2. a Zionist.
zip, *n.* [imitative.] 1. a sound as of a bullet whizzing through space.
2. energy; vim. [Colloq.]
zip, *v.i.*; zipped (zipt), *pt.*, *pp.*; zipping, *ppr.* 1. to make, or move with, a zip.
2. to act or move with speed or energy. [Colloq.]
zip, *v.t.* to fasten with a slide fastener.
ZIP çōde, [*z*oning *i*mprovement *p*lan.] a system devised to speed mail deliveries, under which the post office assigns a code number to individual areas and places.
ziph′i·oid, *a.* pertaining to the genus *Ziphius.*
ziph′i·oid, *n.* a member of the genus *Ziphius.*
Ziph′i·us, *n.* [from Gr. *xiphios*, swordfish, from *xiphos*, a sword.]
1. a genus of dolphinlike cetaceans, the toothed whales. The bottlenose is a species.
2. [z–] a cetacean of this genus.
zip′pē·īte, *n.* [after *Zippe*, a German mineralogist.] a yellow mineral occurring in Bohemia. It is essentially a sulfate of uranium.
zip′pẽr, *n.* 1. a boot or overshoe fitted with a slide fastener: a trade-mark (*Zipper*).
2. popularly, a slide fastener.
zip′py, *a.*; *comp.* zippier; *superl.* zippiest; full of vim and energy; brisk. [Colloq.]
zïr′çȧ·loy, *n.* [*zirc*onium and *alloy.*] a zirconium alloy that is resistant to corrosion and high temperatures, used to contain fuel in nuclear reactors, etc.
zïr′çīte, *n.* native zirconia, used for lining furnaces.
zïr′çon, *n.* [Fr., from Ar. *zarqūn*, cinnabar, from Per. *zargūn*, gold-colored.] a silicate of zirconium, $ZrSiO_4$, a mineral occurring in tetragonal crystals colored yellow, brown, red, etc.: transparent varieties are used as gems.
zïr′çŏn·āte, *n.* a salt produced by the reaction of zirconium hydroxide as an acid.
zïr·çō′ni·ȧ, *n.* zirconium dioxide, ZrO_2, a white, infusible powder used in making crucibles, furnace linings, and, because of its luminosity, in incandescent burners.
zïr·çon′iç, zïr·çō′ni·ăn, *a.* of, pertaining to, or containing zirconium.
zïr·çō′ni·um, *n.* a gray or black metallic chemical element found combined in zircon, etc., and used in alloys and in heat-resistant materials: symbol, Zr; atomic weight, 91.22; atomic number, 40.
zïr′çŏn·oid, *n.* in crystallography, a double eight-sided pyramid, of the tetragonal system. Zircon crystals are often in this form.
zit, *n.* [origin unknown.] a pimple, especially one on the face. [Slang.]
zith′ẽr, *n.* [G.; L. *cithera*; Gr. *kithara*, a lute.] a musical instrument having from thirty to forty strings stretched across a flat soundboard and played with a plectrum.

ZITHER

zith′ẽr·ist, *n.* one who plays on the zither.
zith′ẽrn, *n.* a zither.
zit′tẽrn, *n.* a cittern.
Zī·zā′ni·ȧ, *n.* [Gr. *zizanion*, darnel.] a genus of grasses, the best-known species of which is *Zizania aquatica*. It is common in all the waters of North America from Canada to Florida. The species are known as wild, water, or Indian rice.
ziz′el, *n.* the suslik.
zi′zith (tsē′tzith), *n.pl.* [Heb.] the fringes or tassels worn by orthodox Jews, formerly on the corners of the upper garment, now on the tallith: Deut. xxii. 12.
Ziz′y·phus, *n.* [L., from Gr. *zizyphos*, the jujube tree.] a genus of plants of the family *Rhamnaceæ*. The species are shrubs with alternate leaves and edible fruit. *Zizyphus vulgaris* or *sativa*, the common jujube, is native to Syria.
zlọ′ty, *n.*; *pl.* **zlọ′tys,** [Pol. *zloty*, golden.] the monetary unit of Poland, originally established to equal the gold franc.
Zn, in chemistry, zinc.
zō-, same as *zoo-.*
zō′ȧ, *n.* plural of *zoon.*
-zō′ȧ, [Mod. L., from Gr. *zōion*, an animal.] a combining form used in zoology to form the names of groups, as in Hydrozoa, Protozoa.
Zō·an·thā′cē·ȧ, *n.pl.* a suborder of actinarians, including the genus *Zoanthus.*
zō·an·thā′cē·ăn, *a.* pertaining to the *Zoanthacea.*
zō·an·thā′cē·ăn, *n.* one of the *Zoanthacea.*
Zō·an·thā′ri·ȧ, *n.pl.* [*zo-*, and Gr. *anthos*, a flower.] in zoology, a subclass of *Actinozoa* characterized by simple, usually numerous tentacles. They resemble flowers and are elongated and contractile. They are divided into three suborders, *Malacodermata, Sclerobasica*, and *Sclerodermata.*
zō·an·thãr′i·ăn, *a.* of or relating to the *Zoantharia.*
zō·an·thãr′i·ăn, *n.* one of the *Zoantharia.*
zō·an′thid, *n.* one of the *Zoanthidæ.*
Zō·an′thi·dae, *n.pl.* a family of polyps of the order *Zoantharia*. They form colonies united by a fleshy coenosare and have no power of locomotion.
zō·an′thō·dēme, *n.* [*zo-*, Gr. *anthos*, a flower, and *dema*, a bundle, from *deein*, to bind.] the zooids collectively of a compound zoantharian.
zō·an·thō·dem′iç, *a.* of or pertaining to a zoanthodeme.
zō·an′thoid, *a.* same as *zoanthid.*
zō·an·throp′iç, *a.* pertaining to or of the nature of zoanthropy.
zō·an′thrō·py, *n.* [*zo-*, and Gr. *anthrōpos*, man.] a form of mental disorder in which the patient imagines himself to be a beast.
Zō·an′thus, *n.* [*zo-*, and Gr. *anthos*, a flower.] a genus typical of *Zoanthidæ*. *Zoanthus couchi* is a species found on the coasts of Europe.
zō·ãr′i·ăl, *a.* of or relating to a zoarium.
zō·ãr′i·um, *n.*; *pl.* **zō·ãr′i·ȧ,** [Gr. *zōarion*, dim. of *zōon*, an animal.] polypary.
zō′bō, *n.* [Tibetan *mdzopo*, from *mdzo*, zobo.] a hybrid, supposedly, of the common zebu and the yak, reared in the western parts of the Himalayas for its flesh and milk. It is also used as a beast of burden.
zoç′çō, zō′çle, zoç′çō·lō, *n.* [It. *zoccolo*, from *zocco*, a socle, from L. *soccus*, a sock.] a socle.
zō′di·aç, *n.* [Fr. *zodiaque*; L. *zodiacus*, the zodiac, from Gr. *zōdiakos* (*kyklos*, circle, understood), from *zōdion*, dim. of *zōon*, an animal.]

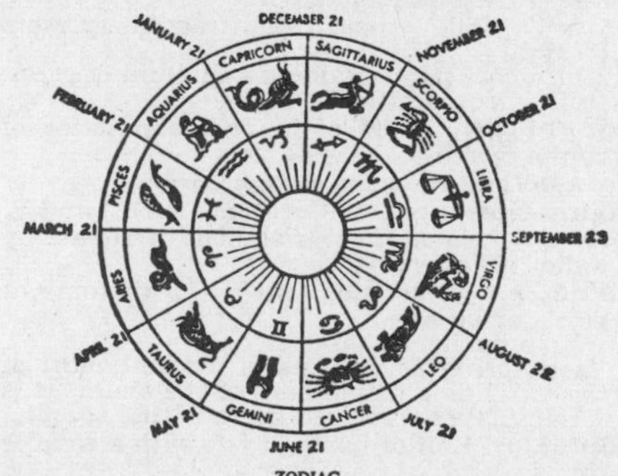

ZODIAC

1. an imaginary belt in the heavens extending for eight degrees on either side of the apparent path of the sun and including the paths of the moon and the principal planets: it is divided into twelve equal parts, or signs, each named for a different constellation.
2. a figure or diagram representing the zodiac and its signs: used in astrology.
3. a circle or circuit. [Rare.]
4. a girdle. [Rare.]
5. in heraldry, a bearing representing a portion of the zodiac.

zō·dī′ȧ·çăl, *a.* pertaining to the zodiac.
zodiacal light; a faint, elliptical disk of light around the sun, sometimes visible in the west during or after twilight and in the east before daybreak.

zō·di·oph′i·lous, *a.* [Gr. *zōdion*, dim. of *zōon*, an animal, and *philein*, to love.] same as *zoophilous.*

zō·ē′ȧ, zō·oe′ȧ, *n.*; *pl.* **zō·ē′ae, zō·oe′ae,** [Gr. *zōon*, an animal.] an early form of the larvae of some decapod crustaceans, having spiny projections on the cephalothorax, and lateral and median eyes.

zō·ē′ăl, zō·oe′ăl, *a.* of or relating to a zoea.

zō·et′iç, *a.* pertaining to life.

zō′ē·trōpe, *n.* [Gr. *zōē*, life, and *tropos*, a turning, from *trepein*, to turn.] an optical toy that shows figures as if alive and in action.

zō·ē·trop′iç, *a.* pertaining to the zoetrope.

Zō′här, *n.* [Heb. *zōhar*, splendor.] a Jewish book of cabalistic commentaries on Scripture.

zō·i·ā′tri·ȧ, *n.* [*zo-*, and Gr. *iatreia*, healing, from *iatros*, physician, from *iatreuein*, to heal.] veterinary surgery.

zō′iç, *a.* [Gr. *zōē*, life, and *-ic.*] pertaining to animals or living beings; characterized by animal life.

Zō·il′ē·ăn, *a.* pertaining or relating to Zoilus, a Greek critic and grammarian of Amphipolis, who severely criticized Homer, Plato, and Socrates: applied to bitter, severe, or malignant criticism or critics.

Zō′i·lişm, *n.* criticism resembling that of Zoilus; illiberal or carping criticism.

Zō′i·list, *n.* one who imitates Zoilus; an unjust critic.

zois′īte, *n.* [after Baron *Zois* von Edelstein (1747–1819), its discoverer.] a vitreous silicate of calcium and aluminum, $HCa_2Al_3Si_3O_{13}$, in which the aluminum is often replaced by iron.

zō′kor, *n.* a burrowing rodent that looks like the mole rat; the *Siphneus aspalax*, of the Altai Mountains.

Zöll′ner's līneş (tsĕl′nẽrz), [from J.K.F. *Zöllner* (1834–1882), a German physicist.] parallel lines made to seem unparallel by intersecting oblique lines.

Zoll′ve·reīn (tsōl′fĕr-īn), *n.* [G. *zoll*, toll, custom, duty, and *verein*, union or assocation.]
1. a union formed by the states of the German Empire during the nineteenth century to establish uniform tariff rates among themselves and between themselves and other countries.
2. any customs or tariff union among states.

zom′bi, zom′bie, *n.*; *pl.* **zom′biş, zom′bieş,** [of Afr. origin.]
1. in West African voodoo cults, the python deity.
2. any voodoo snake deity, as in Haiti and parts of southern United States.
3. in West Indian superstition, a supernatural power through which a corpse may be brought to a state of trancelike animation and made to obey the commands of the person exercising the power.
4. a corpse so animated.
5. a dull, stupid, unattractive person. [Slang.]
6. a cocktail containing a mixture of rums, fruit juices, and soda.

zom′bi·işm, *n.* belief in or the practice of zombi worship.

zom·bō′ruk, *n.* same as *zumbooruk.*

zō·mō·ther′ȧ·py, *n.* [Gr. *zōmos*, broth, and E. *therapy.*] the medical treatment of disease by a diet of raw meat.

zō′nȧ, *n.*; *pl.* **zō′nae,** [L.] 1. in anatomy, a girdle or belt.
2. in medicine, shingles.
zona pellucida or *radiata*; the innermost of the two lining membranes of the ovum. It is a thick layer traversed by radiating spores.

zōn′ăl, *a.* 1. of or having to do with a zone or zones.
2. formed or divided in zones; zoned.
zonal equation; in crystallography, an equation expressing the relation of all the planes of a zone and indicating their common position with regard to the axis.
zonal structure; in crystallography, a structure in which the bands and markings characteristic of a crystal are concentric and generally in harmony with its outline.
zonal view; in botany, that view of a diatom showing the overlapping edge of one valve.

zōn′ăl·ly, *adv.* in a zonal manner.

zō′när, *n.* [Gr. *zōnarion*, dim. of *zōnē*, a girdle.] a belt or girdle which native Christians and Jews in the East were obliged to wear to distinguish them from the Moslems.

Zō·nā′ri·ȧ, *n.pl.* [L. *zonarius*, from *zona*, a girdle, zone.] in Huxley's classification, a division of mammals characterized by a zonelike placenta.

zōn′ȧ·ry, *a.* [L. *zonarius*, from *zona*, zone.]
1. zonal.
2. like a zone, or girdle; beltlike.

zōn′āte, *a.* 1. marked with zones or bands; belted; striped.
2. in botany, arranged in one row, as the tetraspores of certain algae.

zō′nāt·ed, *a.* zonate.

zō·nā′tion, *n.* 1. the state of being zonal or arranged in zones.
2. arrangement in zones, or bands, as of color.

zon′dȧ, *n.* [from *Zonda*, a village in the Argentine Republic.] a scorching wind of the treeless plains of the Argentine Republic.

zōne, *n.* [Fr. *zone*; L. *zona*, from Gr. *zōnē*, a girdle, from *zōnnynai*, to gird.]
1. a belt or girdle. [Now Poet.]
2. an encircling band, stripe, course, etc. distinct in color, texture, structure, etc. from the surrounding medium.
3. any of the five great latitudinal divisions of the earth's surface, named according the the prevailing climate; specifically, the *torrid zone*, bounded by the Tropic of Cancer and the Tropic of Capricorn, two *temperate* (or *variable*) *zones* bounded by the Tropics and the polar circles, and two *frigid zones*, lying between the polar circles and the poles.

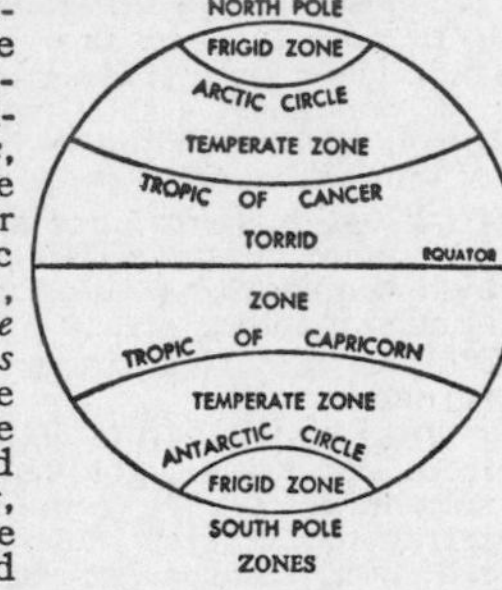

4. any area or region considered as separate or distinct from others because of its particular use, crops, plant or animal life, status in time of war, geological features, etc.; as, a canal *zone*, cotton *zone*, demilitarized *zone.*
5. any section or district in a city restricted by law for a particular use, as for homes, parks, businesses, etc.
6. (a) any of the sections into which a large metropolitan area is divided, each assigned a number to be added to the address on all postal matter to facilitate its delivery; (b) any of a series of ring-shaped areas concentric upon a given point, each having a different postage rate for goods shipped from that point.
7. any similar area used by railroads, telephone companies, etc. in determining the fare or tariff charged from one point to another.
8. the total number of railroad stations available in a given circumference about a particular shipping point.
9. in mathematics, a part of the surface of a sphere lying between two parallel planes that intersect the figure.
10. in anatomy, a region of the body formed by imaginary lines drawn around it transversely; as, an abdominal *zone.*
11. in crystallography, a series of planes the joint intersections of which are parallel.
zone axis; in crystallography, the line at which all the planes of a zone intersect, if supposed to pass through the same point.
zone of clouds; in meteorology, a belt of clouds above the sea near the equator.
zone of defense; the territory about a fortification under its fire.

zōne, *v.t.*; zoned, *pt., pp.*; zoning, *ppr.* 1. to mark off or divide into zones; specifically, to divide (a city, etc.) into areas determined by specific restrictions on types of construction, as into residential and business areas.
2. to surround with or as with a belt or girdle; to encircle.
3. to mark with bands or stripes.

zōne, *v.i.* to be or become zoned.

zōned, *a.* 1. wearing a zone; girt.
2. having zones or concentric bands; zonate.

zōne′less, *a.* without a zone or zones.

zōn·es·thē′şi·ȧ, zōn·aes·thē′şi·ȧ (-zhi-ȧ *or* -zhȧ *or* -zi-ȧ), *n.* [Gr. *zone*, zone, and *aisthesis*, sensation.] a sensation of constriction, as by a girdle.

zōn·if′ẽr·ous, *a.* zoned.

zō·nō·cil′i·āte, *a.* having a zone of cilia, as certain larvae.

zō″nō·plȧ·cen′tăl, *a.* of or pertaining to the *Zonoplacentalia.*

Zō·nō·plac·en·tā′li·ȧ, *n.pl.* the *Zonaria.*

zōn′ū·lȧ, *n.pl.* **zōn′ū·lae,** [L.] a zonule.

zōn′ū·lăr, *a.* pertaining to or resembling a zone or zonule: said of a cataract in which there are layers of opacity in the crystalline lens between the cortex and the nucleus, alternating with transparent layers.

zōn′ūle, *n.* [L. *zonula*, dim. of *zona*, a zone.] a little zone, or girdle.
zonule of Zinn; the suspensory ligament of the eye lens, consisting of a ring-shaped series of fibers extending from the ciliary body to the equator of the lens.

zōn′ū·let, *n.* a little zone; a zonule.

zōn′ūre, *n.* [Gr. *zōnē*, a belt, and *oura*, a tail.] an African lizard of the family *Zonuridæ.*

Zōn·ū′ri·dae, *n.pl.* a family of South African lizards, having a simple tongue and supratemporal fossae roofed over.

zọọ, *n.* [abbrev., from *zoological garden.*] a place where a collection of wild animals is kept for public showing; a menagerie.

zō′ō-, [from Gr. *zōion*, an animal.] a combining form meaning: (a) *animal, animals, the animal body*, etc., as in zoology; (b) *zoology and*, as in *zoogeography*. Words beginning with *zoo-* are also written *zoö-*; also, before a vowel, *zo-*.

zō′ō·blast, *n.* an animal cell.

zō·ō·çhem′iç·ăl, *a.* of or relating to zoochemistry.

zō·ō·çhem′is·try, *n.* [*zoo-* and *chemistry.*] the chemistry of the solids and fluids in the animal body.

zō′ō·çhem·y, *n.* zoochemistry.

zō″ō·çhlō·rel′lȧ, *n.*; *pl.* **zō″ō·çhlō·rel′lae,** [*zoo-*, Gr. *chlōros*, green, and dim. *-ella.*] one of the granular green particles found in the bodies of certain polyps and infusorians.

zō′ō·cyst, *n.* [*zoo-*, and Gr. *kystis*, the bladder.] a cyst which certain protophytes and protozoans form preparatory to spore formation.

zō·ō·cyst′iç, *a.* pertaining to a zoocyst.

zō·ō·cyt′i·ăl, *a.* relating to a zoocytium.

zō·ō·cyt′i·um, *n.*; *pl.* **zō·ō·cyt′i·ȧ,** [*zoo-*, and Gr. *kytos*, a cavity.] the gelatinous matrix excreted and inhabited by various colonial *Infusoria.*

zō·ō·den′dri·ăl, *a.* pertaining to a zoodendrium.

zō·ō·den′dri·um, *n.*; *pl.* **zō·ō·den′dri·ȧ,** [*zoo-*, and Gr. *dendron*, a tree.] the treelike colony stock of certain infusorians.

zō″ō·dȳ·nam′iç, *a.* relating to zoodynamics.

zō″ō·dȳ·nam′içs, *n.* animal physiology.

zō·oe′ci·ăl (-shi-), *a.* pertaining to a zooecium.

zō·oe′ci·um, *n.*; *pl.* **zō·oe′ci·ȧ,** [*zoo-*, and Gr. *oikia*, house.] one of the cells or chambers inhabited by the polypide of a polyzoan.

zō″ō·ē·ryth′rin, *n.* [*zoo-*, and Gr. *erythros*, red.] a red pigment found in the feathers of certain birds.

zō·ō·ful′vin, *n.* [*zoo-*, and L. *fulvus*, yellow.] a yellow coloring matter found in the feathers of the touracos.

zō′ō·gȧ·mēte″, *n.* [*zoo-*, and Gr. *gametē*, a wife.] a motile gamete; a planogamete.

zō·og′ȧ·mous, *a.* relating to zoogamy.

zō·og′ȧ·my, *n.* [*zoo-*, and Gr. *gamos*, marriage.] gamogenesis.

zō′ō·ġēne, *a.* [*zoo-*, and Gr. *-genēs*, producing.] due to or proceeding from animal life. [Rare.]

zō·ō·ġen′iç, *a.* relating to zoogeny.

zō·oġ′e·nous, *a.* acquired from animals.

zō·oġ′e·ny, zō·ō·ġen′e·sis, *n.* [*zoo-*, and Gr. *-geneia*, production.] the production or generation of animals.

zō″ō·ġē·og′rȧ·phẽr, *n.* a student of or expert in zoogeography.

zō·ō·ġē·ō·graph'iç, zō·ō·ġē·ō·graph'i·căl, *a.* relating to zoogeography.

zō"ō·ġē·og'rȧ·phy, *n.* [*zoo-* and *geography.*] the science dealing with the geographical distribution of animals; specifically, the study of the relationship between specific animal forms and the regions in which they live.

zō·ō·gloe'ȧ, *n.* [*zoo-,* and Gr. *gloios,* any glutinous substance.] a colony of bacteria embedded in a jellylike matrix as the result of the swelling of the cell walls through the absorption of water.

zō·ō·gloe'iç, *a.* pertaining to or characterized by the presence of zoogloea.

zō·ō·gloe'oid, *a.* resembling a zoogloea.

zō"ō·gō·nid'i·um, *n.*; *pl.* **zō"ō·gō·nid'i·ȧ,** a motile or locomotive gonidium.

zō·og'ō·ny, *n.* same as *zoogeny.*

zō'ō·gráft, *n.* a graft of tissue from one animal to another; a zooplastic graft.

zō·og'rȧ·phēr, *n.* a zographist.

zō·ō·graph'iç, zō·ō·graph'i·căl, *a.* pertaining to zoography.

zō·og'rȧ·phist, *n.* a student of or expert in zoography.

zō·og'rȧ·phy, *n.* [*zoo-* and *-graphy.*] the branch of zoology concerned with the description of animals, their forms and habits; descriptive zoology.

zō'oid, *a.* [*zo-* and *-oid.*] in biology, having an animal form or characteristics; like an animal.

zō'oid, *n.* in biology, (a) an independent animal organism produced by other than sexual methods, as by fission, gemination, etc.; (b) any of the distinct individuals or members of a colonial or compound organism, as the coral; (c) any organic body or cell having independent locomotion.

zō·oi'dăl, *a.* same as *zooid.*

zooks, *interj.* same as *gadzooks.*

zō·ol'ȧ·tēr, *n.* one who worships animals.

zō·ol'ȧ·trous, *a.* pertaining to zoolatry.

zō·ol'ȧ·try, *n.* [*zoo-,* and Gr. *latreia,* worship.] the worship of animals.

zō'ō·līte, *n.* a fossil animal substance.

zō'ō·lith, *n.* same as *zoolite.*

zō·ō·lith'iç, *a.* zoolitic.

zō·ō·lit'iç, *a.* pertaining to or resembling a zoolite.

zō·ol'ō·ġēr, *n.* a zoologist. [Rare.]

zō·ō·loġ'iç, *a.* zoological.

zō·ō·loġ'i·căl, *a.* of or having to do with zoology or with animals.

zō·ō·loġ'i·căl gär'den, a place where a collection of wild animals is kept for public showing; a zoo.

zō·ō·loġ'i·căl·ly, *adv.* according to the principles of zoology; in a zoological manner.

zō·ol'ō·ġist, *n.* a student of or expert in zoology.

zō·ol'ō·ġīze, *v.i.*; zoologized, *pt., pp.*; zoologizing, *ppr.* to collect or study zoological specimens: to study zoology.

zō·ol'ō·ġy, *n.* [*zoo-* and *-logy.*] 1. the science which deals with the classification of animals and the study of animal life: a division of biology, distinguished from *botany.*

2. a zoological treatise.

3. the animals collectively (*of* a particular region); as, the *zoology* of an island.

zōōm, *v.i.* [echoic.] 1. to make a loud, low-pitched, buzzing or humming sound.

2. to climb in an airplane suddenly and sharply at an angle greater than normal, using the energy of momentum.

zōōm, *v.t.* to cause to zoom.

zōōm, *n.* the act of zooming.

zō"ō·mag·net'iç, *a.* of zoomagnetism.

zō·ō·mag'net·ișm, *n.* animal magnetism.

zō'ō·man·cy, *n.* divination by observation of animals or the behavior of animals under certain conditions.

zō·ō·man'tiç, *a.* pertaining to zoomancy.

Zōō'mär, *n.* a system of lenses, as in a motion-picture camera, that can be rapidly adjusted for close-up shots or distance views while keeping the image in focus: a trade-mark.

zō"ō·me·çhan'içs, *n.pl.* zoodynamics.

zō·ō·mel'ȧ·nin, *n.* [*zoo-,* and Gr. *melas, melanos,* black.] a black coloring matter of the plumage of some birds.

zō·ō·met'riç, *a.* relating to zoometry.

zō·om'e·try, *n.* [*zoo-* and *-metry.*] the measurement and comparison of the relative sizes of the different parts of animals.

zō·ō·mọr'phiç, *a.* [*zoo-* and *-morphic.*] of, represented by, or having animal form: as, a *zoomorphic* deity.

zō·ō·mọr'phișm, *n.* [from *zoo-,* and Gr. *morphē,* form, shape; and *-ism.*]

1. the use or representation of animal forms in decorative art or symbolism.

2. the attributing of animal form or characteristics to God or the gods.

zō'ō·mọr·phy, *n.* zoomorphism.

zō'on, *n.*; *pl.* **zō'ȧ,** [Mod. L.; Gr. *zōion,* an animal, from *zaein,* to live.] any of the fully developed individual members of a compound animal.

zō·on'ăl, *a.* relating to or like a zoon.

zō"on·ē·ryth'rin, *n.* zooerythrin.

zō·on'iç, *a.* [Gr. *zōion,* an animal, and *-ic.*] derived from or contained in animal substances.

zō'ō·nīte, *n.* [Gr. *zōion,* an animal, and *-ite.*]

1. one of the theoretic transverse divisions of any segmented animal. [Rare.]

2. one of the segments of an articulated animal. [Rare.]

zō·ō·nit'iç, *a.* relating to a zoonite. [Rare.]

zō·ō·nō'mi·ȧ, *n.* zoonomy.

zō·ō·nom'iç, *a.* relating to zoonomy.

zō·on'ō·mist, *n.* one versed in zoonomy.

zō·on'ō·my, *n.* [Gr. *zōion,* an animal, and *nomos,* law.] the laws of animal life.

zō·on'ō'sis, *n.*; *pl.* **zō·on'ō'sēș,** [*zoo-,* and Gr. *nosos,* sickness, disease.] a disease produced by animal parasites.

zō"ō·nō·sol'ō·ġy, *n.* zoopathology. [Rare.]

zō·ō·not'iç, *a.* due to animal parasites: said of certain diseases.

zō'ō·nūle, *n.* a zoonite. [Rare.]

zō·ō·par'ȧ·sīte, *n.* any animal parasite.

zō·ō·par·ȧ·sit'iç, *a.* pertaining to or produced by animal parasites.

zō"ō·pȧ·thol'ō·ġy, *n.* animal pathology; the study of the diseases of animals.

zō·op'ȧ·thy, *n.* zoopathology.

zō·op'ēr·ăl, *a.* pertaining to zoopery.

zō·op'ēr·y, *n.* [*zoo-,* and Gr. *peirān,* to experiment.] the performing of experiments on the lower animals.

Zō·oph'ȧ·gȧ, *n.pl.* [*zoo-,* and Gr. *phagein,* to eat.] carnivorous animals collectively.

zō·oph'ȧ·găn, *n.* a carnivore.

zō·oph'ȧ·gous, *a.* subsisting on animal food; carnivorous; sarcophagous.

zō'ō·phīle, *n.* [*zoo-* and *-phile.*] a zoophilist; also, a zoophilous plant.

zō·oph'i·lișm, *n.* zoophily.

zō·oph'i·list, *n.* one who loves animals.

zō·oph'i·lous, *a.* [*zoo-* and *-philous.*]

1. loving animals.

2. adapted to pollination by animals: said of plants.

zō·oph'i·ly, *n.* [*zoo-,* and Gr. *philein,* to love.] a love of animals.

zō·ō·phō'bi·ȧ, *n.* [*zoo-,* and Gr. *phobos,* fear.] an abnormal fear of animals.

zō·ō·phor'iç, *a.* bearing or supporting a figure of an animal; as, a *zoophoric* column.

zō·oph'ō·rus, *n.* [Gr. *zōophoros*; *zōion,* an animal, and *-phoros,* from *pherein,* to bear.] in classical architecture, a frieze having figures of animals carved on it.

zō·ō·phyș'içs, *n.* the science including animal morphology and physiology.

zō·ō·phyș·i·ol'ō·ġy, *n.* the physiology of animals, as distinguished from that of human beings.

Zō·oph'y·tȧ, *n.pl.* [Fr. *zoophyte*; Gr. *zōophyton*; *zōion,* animal, and *phyton,* a plant, lit., that which has grown, from *phyein,* to produce, also, to grow.] a former division of animals which included the *Radiata,* but is now generally confined to the *Cœlentera.*

zō'ō·phȳte, *n.* 1. any of the *Zoophyta.*

2. any animal, as sponges, corals, etc., more or less resembling plants in appearance and character.

zō·ō·phyt'iç, zō·ō·phyt'iç·ăl, *a.* of, or having the nature of, zoophytes.

zō·oph'y·toid, *a.* like a zoophyte.

zō·ō·phȳ·tō·loġ'i·căl, *a.* pertaining to zoophytology.

zō"ō·phȳ·tol'ō·ġy, *n.* [Gr. *zōophyton,* a zoophyte, and *-logy.*] the branch of zoology dealing with zoophytes.

zō·ō·plas'tiç, *a.* of or having to do with zooplasty.

zō'ō·plas·ty, *n.* the surgical operation of grafting living tissue from a lower animal onto the human body.

zō·ō·prax'i·sçōpe, *n.* an early kind of moving-picture projector.

zō·op'si·ȧ, *n.* [*zoo-,* and Gr. *opsis,* vision.] a hallucination in which the person thinks he sees animals.

zō"ō·psȳ·çhō·loġ'iç·ăl (-sī-), *a.* pertaining to zoopsychology.

zō"ō·psȳ·çhol'ō·ġy, *n.* the psychology of animals other than man.

zō·ō·sçop'iç, *a.* pertaining to zooscopy.

zō·ŏs'çō·py, *n.* zoopsia.

zō'ō·spērm, *n.* [*zoo-,* and Gr. *sperma,* seed.]

1. same as *spermatozoon.*

2. a zoospore (sense 1).

zo"ō·spēr·mat'iç, *a.* of or having to do with a zoosperm.

zō·ō·spēr'mi·um, *n.*; *pl.* **zō·ō·spēr'mi·ȧ,** a spermatozoon.

zō'ō·spō·ranġe, *n.* a zoosporangium.

zō"ō·spō·ran'ġi·ăl, *a.* of or having to do with a zoosporangium.

zō"ō·spō·ran'ġi·um, *n.*; *pl.* **zō"ō·spō·ran'ġi·ȧ,** a sporangium producing zoospores.

zō'ō·spōre, *n.* 1. an asexual spore, especially of certain fungi or algae, capable of independent motion usually by means of cilia.

2. a motile flagellate or amoeboid cell or body in certain protozoa.

ZOOSPORES

zō·ō·spō'riç, *a.* of, pertaining to, or resembling a zoospore.

zō"ō·spō·rif'ēr·ous, *a.* producing zoospores.

zō·os'pō·rous, *a.* same as *zoosporic.*

zō'ō·tax·y, *n.* [*zoo-,* and Gr. *taxis,* arrangement.] zoological classification.

zō·ō·teçh'niç, *a.* relating to zootechny.

zō·ō·teçh'niçs, *n.* zootechny.

zō'ō·tech·ny, *n.* [*zoo-,* and Gr. *technē,* art, skill.] the branch of science dealing with the breeding and domestication of animals.

zō·ō·thē'ciăl (-shăl), *a.* pertaining to a zoothecium.

zō·ō·thē'ci·um (-shi-), *n.*; *pl.* **zō·ō·thē'ci·ȧ,** [*zoo-,* and Gr. *thēkion,* dim. of *thēkē,* a box, chest.] a zoocytium.

zō'ō·thē·ișm, *n.* the ascribing of divine attributes to animals.

zō'ō·thē·ist, *n.* a believer in zootheism.

zō"ō·thē·is'tiç, *a.* pertaining to zootheism.

zō·ō·ther'ȧ·py, *n.* animal therapeutics.

zō'ō·thōme, *n.* [*zoo-,* and Gr. *thōmos,* a heap.] a zooid colony of a compound polyp.

zō·ot'iç, *a.* containing the remains of organic life: said of soil, rock, etc. [Rare.]

Zō·ot'ō·çȧ, *n.pl.* [Gr. *zōotokos,* viviparous, from *zōion,* an animal, and *tiktein,* to bear, produce.] the *Vivipara.*

zō·ō·tom'iç, zō·ō·tom'iç·ăl, *a.* of or having to do with zootomy.

zō·ō·tom'iç·ăl·ly, *adv.* according to zootomy.

zō·ot'ō·mist, *n.* one who dissects animals.

zō·ot'ō·my, *n.* [*zoo-,* and Gr. *temnein,* to cut.] the dissection or anatomy of animals, especially those other than man.

zō·ō·troph'iç, *a.* [*zoo-,* Gr. *trophē,* food, from *trephein,* to feed, support, and *-ic.*] of or relating to the nourishment of animals.

zoot sūit, a former exaggerated style of man's suit with baggy trousers narrowing at the cuffs and a long, draped coat.

zō"ō·xan·thel'lȧ (-zan-), *n.*; *pl.* **zō"ō·xan·thel'lae,** [*zoo-,* Gr. *xanthos,* yellow, and dim. *-ella.*] any of the yellow pigmentary particles of some *Radiolaria.*

zō·ō·xan'thin, *n.* a yellow pigment from the feathers of certain birds, as the trogons.

zōō'zōō, *n.* [imitative.] a wood pigeon. [Brit. Dial.]

zō'pi·lōte, *n.* [Mex.] the urubu.

zōr'gīte, *n.* [named after *Zorge* in the Harz Mountains.] a metallic, lead-gray, massive granular mineral, a selenid of lead and copper.

zor'il, zor'ille, *n.* [Fr. *zorille*; Sp. *zorilla, zorillo,* dim. of *zorra, zorro,* a fox.] a small, South African animal, genus *Zorilla,* of the weasel family, resembling the skunk.

Zō·ril'lȧ, *n.* 1. a genus of carnivorous animals closely related to the weasels and skunks, of which a species, the zoril or mariput, *Zorilla striata,* or *Ictonyx zorilla,* is found in Africa. Like the skunk, it can eject an offensive-smelling liquid when molested.

2. [z–] a zoril.

Zō·rō·as'tri·ăn, *a.* of or pertaining to Zoroaster, founder of Zoroastrianism, or his religious system.

Zō·rō·as'tri·ăn, *n.* a follower of Zoroaster.

Zō·rō·as'tri·ăn·ișm, Zō·rō·as'trișm, *n.* the religious system of the Persians before their conversion to Islam: according to tradition, it was founded by Zoroaster, and its principles, contained in the Zend-Avesta, include belief in an afterlife and in the continuous struggle of the universal spirit of good (Ormazd) with the spirit of evil (Ahriman), the good ultimately to prevail.

zos'tēr, *n.* [L., from Gr. *zōstēr*, a girdle, from *zōnnynai*, to gird.]
1. in medicine, the shingles, or herpes zoster.
2. in ancient Greece, a belt or girdle.

Zos·tē'rȧ, *n.* [Gr. *zōstēr*, a girdle, from their ribbonlike leaves.] a genus of plants of the order *Naiadaceæ*, the pondweeds, marine algae, having ribbonlike leaves. *Zostera marina* is the sea wrack or eelgrass.

Zos·tēr'ops, *n.* [Gr. *zōstēr*, girdle, and *ōps*, eye.] a genus of birds, closely related to the warblers, with a ring of snow-white feathers encircling the eyes: also called *white-eyes.*

Zöu·äve', *n.* [Fr., from Ar. *Zouaoua*, the name of a tribe of Kabyles living among the Jurjura Mountains in Algeria.]
1. a soldier belonging to an infantry unit in the French army, organized in Algeria, and originally composed of Algerians, noted for their hardiness and courage and wearing a colorful oriental uniform.
2. a member of any military group having a similar uniform; specifically, a member of any of various volunteer regiments in the American Civil War.

zounds, *interj.* [altered from the oath *God's wounds.*] a mild oath used as an exclamation of surprise or anger. [Archaic.]

Zr, in chemistry, zirconium.

zụbr, *n.* [Polish.] the aurochs, the European bison.

zụç·chet'tō (tsụk-), *n.* [an erroneous var. of It. *zucchetta*, a cap, orig., dim. of *zucca*, a gourd.] in the Roman Catholic Church, the skull cap of an ecclesiastic: it is black for a priest, purple for a bishop, red for a cardinal, and white for a pope.

zụç·chi'nï, *n.* [It., pl. of *zucchino*, dim. of *zucca*, a squash.] a variety of green-skinned summer squash, shaped somewhat like a cucumber.

zūche, *n.* a tree stump. [Obs.]

zụ'fō·lō, zụf'fō·lō, *n.* [It. *zufolo*, from *zufolare*, to hiss or whistle.] a little flute or flageolet, especially one used to train singing birds.

zui'zin (zoi'), *n.* the American widgeon. [Dial.]

Zụ'lụ, *n.*; *pl.* **Zụ'lụs, Zụ'lụ,** 1. a member of a great Bantu nation of southeastern Africa.
2. their agglutinative Bantu language.

Zụ'lụ, *a.* pertaining to the Zulus, their culture, or their language.

Zụ'lụ-Kaf''fïr, *n.* the language spoken by the Zulus and Kaffirs.

zụm Beī'spiēl (tsụm bī'shpēl), [G.] for example.

zum·bọọ'ruk, *n.* [Turk. *zambūrak*, a small gun, dim. of Ar. *zambūr*, a hornet.] a small cannon usually supported by a swiveled rest on the back of a camel, from which it is fired.

zū'miç, *a.* same as *zymic.*

Zu'ñi (zụ'nyē), *n.*; *pl.* **Zu'ñis** (zu'nyēz), **Zu'ñi,** [Sp., from Am. Ind.] a member of a pueblo-dwelling tribe of North American Indians living in New Mexico and constituting a linguistic family.

Zu'ñi·an (zụ'nyi-ăn), *a.* of or pertaining to the Zuñis.

Zu'ñi·an (zụ'nyi-ăn), *n.* a Zuñi.

zū'ny·īte, *n.* a fluosilicate of aluminum, found crystallized in tetrahedrons.

zwan'zi·gēr (tsvän'tsi-), *n.* [G., from *zwansig*, twenty.] a former silver coin of Austria, equal to 20 kreutzers.

zwiē'bäck (tsvē'bäk), *n.* [G., from *zwie-*, two, twice, var. of *zwei*, two, and *backen*, to bake.] a kind of rusk or biscuit which is baked and then sliced and toasted.

Zwing'li·ăn (*or* tswing'), *a.* of or relating to Ulrich Zwingli (1484–1531), a Swiss patriot and Protestant reformer, or his doctrines, especially the doctrine that the body of Christ is not actually present in the Eucharist and that the ceremony is merely a commemorative one.

Zwing'li·ăn, *n.* a follower of Zwingli.

Zwing'li·ăn·iṣm, *n.* the doctrines of Zwingli.

zwisçh'en·spiēl (tsvish'en-shpēl), *n.* [G., from *zwischen*, between, and *spiel*, play, from *spielen*, to play.] in music, an interlude.

zwit'tēr·ī·ŏn (tsvit'), *n.* same as *zwitter ion.*

zwit'tēr ī'ŏn, in physical chemistry, an ion carrying both a positive and a negative charge, as in certain protein molecules.

zwit·tēr·ī·on'iç, *a.* of or having to do with a zwitter ion.

zyg-, see *zygo-*.

Zȳ·gad'ē·nus, *n.* [Gr. *zygon*, a yoke, and *adēn*, a gland.] a genus of liliaceous perennial herbs, native to North America and Asia, having linear leaves and greenish-white flowers. The root of *Zygadenus venenosus* has poisonous properties.

zȳ·gae'nid, *n.* [from Gr. *zygaina*, the hammer-headed shark.] a moth of the family *Zygænidæ*, as the wood nymph.

Zȳ·gae'ni·dae, *n.pl.* a family of moths having pectinate antennae and narrow wings rounded at the tip, found in Europe and America.

zȳ'găl, *a.* [Gr. *zygon*, a yoke.] shaped like a yoke; in anatomy, designating a fissure that consists of two portions united by a third portion.

zȳ·gan'trum, *n.*; *pl.* **zȳ·gan'trȧ,** [Gr. *zygon*, a yoke, and *antron*, a cave.] a hollow in the vertebrae of snakes and some lizards, by which an additional articulation is provided with the next vertebra.

zyg''ap·ō·phys'ē·ăl, zyg''ap·ō·phys'ī·ăl, *a.* pertaining to the zygapophysis.

zyg·ȧ·poph'y·sis, *n.*; *pl.* **zyg·ȧ·poph'y·sēṣ,** [Gr. *zygon*, a yoke, and *apophysis.*] any of the processes of the neural arch of a vertebra by which it articulates with the adjoining vertebrae.

zyġ'ī·ŏn, *n.* [Gr. *zygon*, a yoke.] a craniometric point at either end of the bregmatic diameter.

Zyg·nē'mȧ, *n.* [*zyg-*, and Gr. *nēma*, a thread.] a genus of fresh-water algae typical of the family *Zygnemaceæ.*

Zyg·nē·mā'cē·ae, *n.pl.* a family of fresh-water algae, the pond scums, with tubular cells united into jointed threads, which are at first distinct, and then brought into conjunction by the aid of transverse tubelets, which discharge a bright-green coloring matter.

zyg·nē·mā'ceous, *a.* pertaining to the *Zygnemaceæ.*

zȳ'gō-, [from Gr. *zygon*, a yoke.] a combining form meaning *yoke, articulation, pair*, as in *zygo*dactyl: also, before a vowel, *zyg-*.

zȳ'gō·brañçh, *n.* any member of the *Zygobranchiata.*

zȳ'gō·brañçh, *a.* same as *zygobranchiate.*

Zȳ'gō·brañ·çhi·ā'tȧ, Zȳ·gō·brañ'çhi·ȧ, *n.pl.* [*zygo-*, and Gr. *branchia*, gills.] a group of marine gastropods including the keyhole limpets and sea-ears.

zȳ·gō·brañ'çhi·āte, *a.* pertaining to the *Zygobranchiata.*

zȳ·gō·brañ'çhi·āte, *n.* any of the *Zygobranchiata.*

zȳ·gō·daç'tyl, zȳ·gō·daç'tyle, *a.* 1. of or belonging to the *Zygodactylæ*, a group of non-passerine birds including the parrots, woodpeckers, etc.
2. having the toes arranged in two opposed pairs, two in front and two behind; as, a *zygodactyl* foot.

zȳ·gō·daç'tyl, zȳ·gō·daç'tyle, *n.* a zygodactyl bird.

Zȳ·gō·daç'ty·lae, *n.pl.* [*zygo-*, and Gr. *daktylos*, a finger or toe.] same as *Scansores*: also written *Zygodactyli.*

zȳ''gō·daç·tyl'iç, zȳ·gō·daç'tyl·ous, *a.* same as *Zygodactyl.*

zȳ·gō·daç'tyl·iṣm, *n.* the quality or condition of being zygodactyl.

zȳ'gō·dont, *a.* having molar teeth with tubercles that are disposed in pairs.

zȳ·gō'mȧ, *n.*; *pl.* **zȳ·gō'mȧ·tȧ,** [Gr. *zygōma*, from *zygoun*, to yoke, from *zygon*, a yoke.]
1. the zygomatic arch.
2. the zygomatic bone.
3. the zygomatic process.

zȳ·gō·mat'ic, *a.* [from Mod. L. *zygoma*, and *-ic.*]
1. designating or of a bony arch on either side of the face just below the eye, consisting of the zygomatic bone and process.
2. designating either of a pair of quadrangular bones of the zygomatic arch forming the prominence of each cheek.
3. designating a process of the temporal bone forming part of the zygomatic arch.
zygomatic muscles; two muscles of the face that rise from the zygomatic bone and are inserted into the corner of the mouth.
zygomatic suture; the suture joining the zygomatic processes of the temporal and cheekbones.

zȳ·gō·mat'i·çō-, [from Gr. *zygon*, a yoke.] a combining form used in anatomy to mean *connection with or relation to the zygoma.*

zȳ·gō·mat''i·çō·ạu·riç'ū·lăr, *a.* pertaining to the zygoma and the auricle.

zȳ·gō·mat''i·çō·fā'ciăl, *a.* relating to the zygoma and the face.

zȳ·gō·mat''i·çō·tem'pō·răl, *a.* relating to the zygoma and the temporal bone.

zȳ·gō·mat'i·çus, *n.*; *pl.* **zȳ·gō·mat'i·cī,** a zygomatic muscle.

zȳ·gō·max·il·lā'rē, *n.* [L.] a craniometric point at the lower end of the zygomatic suture.

zȳ·gō·max'il·lăr·y, *a.* pertaining to the lower end of the zygomatic suture.

zȳ·gō·mọr'phiç, *a.* [*zygo-* and *-morphic.*] in biology, bilaterally symmetrical; that can be divided in two identical halves by a single plane passing through the axis: said of organisms, organs, or parts.

zȳ·gō·mọr'phiṣm, *n.* the quality or condition of being zygomorphic.

zȳ·gō·mọr'phous, *a.* zygomorphic.

zȳ·gō·mȳ'cēte, *n.* one of the *Zygomycetes.*

Zȳ''gō·mȳ·cē'tēṣ, *n.pl.* [Gr. *zygon*, a yoke, and *mykēs* (*-ētēs*), a mushroom.] a group of fungi including those in which reproduction takes place by conjugation. It includes the *Entomophthoreæ, Mucorini*, and others.

zȳ''gō·mȳ·cē'tous, *a.* pertaining to the *Zygomycetes.*

zȳ'gon, *n.* [Gr. *zygon*, a yoke.] in anatomy, the bar or stem connecting the two branches of a zygal fissure.

zȳ'gō·neūre, *n.* [*zygo-*, and Gr. *neuron*, a nerve.] a nerve cell connected with other nerve cells.

Zȳ''gō·phyl·lā'cē·ae, *n.pl.* [*zygo-*, and Gr. *phyllon*, leaf.] the bean caper family of herbs and shrubs.

zȳ''gō·phyl·lā'ceous, *a.* designating or of a number of herbs and shrubs of the caltrop or bean caper family, having jointed branches, stipulate leaves, and axillary flowers.

Zȳ·gō·phyl'lē·ae, *n.pl.* same as *Zygophyllaceæ.*

Zȳ·gō·phyl'lum, *n.* [*zygo-*, and Gr. *phyllon*, a leaf.] the typical genus of the family *Zygophyllaceae*; the bean caper of the East is *Zygophyllum fabago.*

zȳ'gō·phȳte, *n.* [*zygo-* and *-phyte.*] a plant that reproduces by means of zygospores.

zȳ'gōse, *a.* of or pertaining to zygosis.

zȳ·gō'sis, *n.* [Mod. L.; Gr. *zygosis*, a joining, balancing, from *zygoun*, to yoke, from *zygon*, a yoke.] in biology, conjugation; union of cells or gametes.

zȳ'gō·spērm, *n.* [*zygo-* and *sperm.*] same as *zygospore.*

zȳ'gō·sphēne, *n.* [*zygo-*, and Gr. *sphēn*, wedge.] a conical process on the front of the vertebrae of most snakes and some lizards, which fits into the zygantrum of that next in front.

zȳ'gō·spō·rañge'', *n.* same as *zygosporangium.*

zȳ''gō·spō·ran'ġi·um, *n.*; *pl.* **zȳ''gō·spō·ran'ġi·ȧ,** in botany, a sporangium producing zygospores.

zȳ'gō·spōre, *n.* [*zygo-* and *spore.*] a spore formed by conjugation of two similar gametes.

zȳ'gōte, *n.* [Gr. *zygōtos*, yoked, from *zygon*, a yoke.] any cell formed by the union of two gametes.

zȳ·gō·zō'ō·spōre, *n.* [*zygo-* and *zoospore.*] in botany, a motile zygospore.

zym-, same as *zymo-*.

zȳ'māse, *n.* [Fr. *zymase.*] an enzyme, present in yeast, which causes fermentation by breaking down glucose and some other carbohydrates into alcohol and carbon dioxide or into lactic acid.

zȳme, *n.* [Gr. *zymē*, a leaven.] 1. a ferment or enzyme.
2. the principal regarded as the specific cause of a zymotic disease.

zȳ'miç, *a.* in old chemistry, pertaining to fermentation.

zȳ'min, *n.* 1. same as *zyme.*
2. a pancreatic extract prepared for therapeutic use.

zym'īte, *n.* [Gr. *zymē*, leaven.] a priest who uses leavened bread in the Eucharist; also, one who receives such a Eucharist.

zȳ'mō-, [from Gr. *zymē*, a leaven.] a combining form meaning *fermentation*, as in *zymology*: also, before a vowel, *zym-*.

zȳ'mō·ġen, *n.* [Fr. *zymogène.*]
1. a substance capable of becoming an enzyme.
2. any bacteria capable of producing an enzyme.

zȳ'mō·ġēne, *n.* a zymogen.
zȳ·mō·gen'e·sis, *n.* [Mod. L.] the process by which a zymogen becomes an enzyme.
zȳ·mō·ġen'iç, zȳ·moġ'ē·nous, *a.* 1. of or having to do with a zymogen.
2. that can produce a ferment.
zymogenic organism; a yeast or other microorganism which causes fermentation.
zȳ'moid, *n.* any poison derived from a decaying tissue.
zȳ'moid, *a.* of, pertaining to, or resembling a zyme, or ferment.
zȳ·mō·loġ'iç, zȳ·mō·loġ'iç·ăl, *a.* pertaining to or having to do with zymology.
zȳ·mol'ō·ġist, *n.* a person skilled in zymology.
zȳ·mol'ō·ġy, *n.* 1. the science dealing with fermentation.
2. *pl.* **zȳ·mol'ō·ġies,** a treatise on fermentation.
zȳ·mol'y·sis, *n.* 1. the fermentative action of enzymes.
2. fermentation or other changes resulting from this.
zȳ·mō·lyt'iç, *a.* pertaining to or having to do with zymolysis.
zȳ'mōme, *n.* [Gr. *zymōma*, a fermented mass, from *zymē*, leaven.] in old chemistry, that part of gluten which is insoluble in alcohol.
zȳ·mom'e·tēr, zȳ·mō·sim'e·tēr, *n.* an instrument for measuring the degree of fermentation.
zȳ'mō·phȳte, *n.* [*zymo-*, and Gr. *phyton*, a plant.] a bacterium that causes fermentation.
zȳ·mō·plas'tiç, *a.* ferment-forming.
zȳ'mō·sçōpe, *n.* an instrument for testing the fermenting power of yeast by bringing it in contact with sugar-water and observing the quantity of carbonic anhydride evolved.
zȳ'mōse, *n.* a ferment produced by various yeast plants. It is found in the intestinal juice. Also called *invertin.*
zȳ·mō'sis, *n.* [Gr. *zymōsis*, fermentation, from *zymē*, a leaven.]
1. fermentation.
2. a process like fermentation by which infectious diseases were formerly believed to be developed.
3. any zymotic disease. [Rare.]
zȳ·mō·teçh'niç, *a.* pertaining to zymotechnics.
zȳ·mō·teçh'niçs, *n.* [*zymo-*, and Gr. *technē*, art, skill.] the technology of ferments.
zȳ·mot'iç, *a.* [Gr. *zymōtikos*, causing to ferment, from *zymoun*, to ferment, from *zymē*, ferment.]
1. of, causing, or caused by or as by fermentation.
2. designating or of any infectious disease, as smallpox, formerly believed to be caused by a fermentative process.
zȳ·mot'iç·ăl·ly, *adv.* in a zymotic manner.
zȳ'mūr·ġy, *n.* [*zymo-*, and Gr. *ergon*, work.] the chemistry of fermentation, as applied to wine making, brewing, etc.
zȳ'thum, *n.* [L., from Gr. *zythos*, beer.] a malt beverage brewed by the ancient Egyptians.

A PRONOUNCING DICTIONARY OF BIOGRAPHY

A

Aali Pasha (ä'lī pȧ-shä'), Turkish minister of state....1815—1871

Abauzit (ȧ-bō-zīt'), **Firmin**, French philosopher....1679—1767

Abbas (ȧ'bȧs, ȧ-bäs'), uncle of Mohammed and of Ali.... 566— 652

Abbas I (*the Great*), shah of Persia....1557—1628

Abbe (ab'ē), **Cleveland**, American meteorologist....1838—1916

A., Robert (*brother of C. A.*), American surgeon....1851—1928

Abbey (ab'ĭ), **Edwin Austin**, American artist....1852—1911

Abbot (ab'ŏt), **Charles Greeley**, American astrophysicist....1872—1973

Abbott (ab'ŏt), **Edwin**, English theologian....1838—1926

Abbott, Emma A., American singer....1849—1891

Abbott, Jacob, American pastor, writer of boys' books....1803—1879

A., Lyman (*son of J. A.*), Am. clergyman, author, editor....1835—1922

Abd-el-Kader (äb-del-kä'dẽr), Algerian emir....1808—1883

Abderhalden (äp'dẽr-häl-den), **Emil**, Swiss biochemist....1877—1950

Abdul-Aziz (äb-dul-ä-zīz'), sultan of Turkey....1830—1876

Abdul-Hamid (-hȧ-mīd') **II**, sultan of Turkey....1842—1918

Abdullah (äb-dul'ȧ), (*A. ibn Husein*), king of Jordan....1862—1951

Abdul-Mejid (-me-jīd'), sultan of Turkey....1823—1861

A Beckett (ȧ bek'et), **Gilbert Abbot**, English comic writer....1811—1856

Abel (ā'bel), **Sir Frederick Augustus**, English chemist....1826—1902

Abel, John Jacob, American pharmacologist....1857—1938

Abélard (ab'e-lärd), **Pierre**, French philosopher....1079—1142

Abercorn (ab'ẽr-corn), **James Albert Edward Hamilton, third Duke of**, governor of Northern Ireland (1922–45)....1869—1953

Abercrombie (ab'ẽr-crŏm-bi), **James**, British general....1706—1781

Abercrombie, Lascelles, English poet and critic....1881—1938

About (ȧ-bö'), **Edmond**, French novelist and misc. writer....1828—1885

Abramovich (ȧ-bräm'ō-vich), **Sholem Yacob** (pseud. *Mendele Mocher Sforim*), Yiddish novelist, b. Russia....1836—1917

Abruzzi (ä-brut'tsī), **Prince Luigi Amadeo Giuseppe, Duke of the**, Italian explorer....1873—1933

Abt (äpt), **Franz**, German composer....1819—1885

Abu Bakr (ȧ-bü' bak'ẽr), first caliph after Mohammed in Mecca; father of Aisha.... 573— 634

Acheson (ach'e-sŏn), **Dean Gooderham**, U. S. secretary of state (1949–53)....1893—1971

Acheson, Edward Goodrich, American inventor....1856—1931

Achilles Tatius (ȧ-chil'ēs tā'shi-us), Greek romance writer.... 5th cent.

Acton (ak'tăn), **Lord**, (*John Emerick Edward Dalberg-Acton, 1st Baron Acton*), English historian....1834—1902

Acuña, de (de ä-cün'yä), **Cristóbal**, Sp. Jesuit, explorer....1597—1676

Adam (ȧ-däñ'), **Juliette Lamber, Mme. Edmond**, Fr. author.1836—1936

Adam (ad'ăm), **Robert**, English architect....1728—1792

Adamic (ad'ȧ-mic), **Louis**, Am. author, b. Yugoslavia....1899—1951

Adams (ad'ămz), **Abigail**, wife of Pres. John Adams....1744—1818

Adams, Charles Francis (*son of J.Q.A.*), Am. diplomat....1807—1886

A., Charles Francis (*grandson of C.F.A.*), U. S. secretary of the navy (1929–33)....1866—1954

Adams, Charles Kendall, American historian....1835—1902

Adams, Franklin Pierce (pseud. *F.P.A.*), American journalist and humorist....1881—1960

Adams, George Burton, American educator and historian....1851—1925

Adams, Henry (*son of C.F.A.* [1807–86]), American historian....1838—1918

Adams, Herbert, American sculptor....1858—1945

Adams, James Truslow, American historian....1878—1949

Adams, John, second president of the United States....1735—1826

A., John Quincy (*son of J.A.*), sixth U. S. president....1767—1848

Adams, Maude (b. *Maude Kiskadden*), American actress....1872—1953

Adams, Samuel, American Revolutionary leader....1722—1803

Adams, Samuel Hopkins, American writer....1871—1958

Adams, William Taylor (pseud. *Oliver Optic*), American writer of children's stories....1822—1897

Adanson (ȧ-däñ-sôñ'), **Michel**, French naturalist....1727—1806

Addams (ad'ămz), **Jane**, American social worker....1860—1935

Addison (ad'i-sŏn), **Joseph**, English essayist and poet....1672—1719

Ade (ād), **George**, American humorist....1866—1944

Adenauer (ä'de-nou-ẽr), **Konrad**, German statesman; chancellor of the West German republic (1949–63)....1876—1967

Adler (äd'lẽr), **Alfred**, Austrian psychiatrist....1870—1937

Adler (ad'lẽr), **Cyrus**, American educator....1863—1940

Adler, Felix, American ethical reformer....1851—1933

Adrian (ā'dri-ăn), *see* Hadrian.

Adrian I, Pope.... ? — 795

Adrian IV (*Nicholas Breakspear*), the only English Pope....1100—1159

Adrian, Edgar Douglas, English physiologist....1889—1977

AE, *see* Russell, George William.

Aeschines (es'chi-nēs), Athenian orator....B.C. 389— 314

Aeschylus (es'chy-lus), Greek tragic poet....B.C. 525— 456

Aesop (ē'sop), Greek writer of fables....B.C. 620?—564?

Aesopus (ē-sō'pus), **Clodius**, Roman tragedian....fl.B.C. 1st cent.

Aethelstan, *see* Athelstan.

Aga Khan III (ä'gä kän), (*Aga Sultan Sir Mahomed Shah*), leader of the Ismailian Moslems in India....1877—1957

Agar (ā'găr), **Herbert**, American author....1897—1980

Agassiz (ag'ȧ-sī), **(Jean) Louis (Rodolphe)**, American naturalist, b. in Switzerland....1807—1873

A., Alexander (*son of J.L.R.A.*), American naturalist....1835—1910

Agathocles (ȧ-gath'ō-clēs), tyrant of Syracuse....B.C. 361?— 289

Agesilaus (ȧ-ges-i-lā'us) **II**, king of Sparta....B.C. 444?— 360

Agnew (ag'nū), **Cornelius Rea**, American surgeon....1830—1888

Agoult, d' (dȧ-gö'), **Marie Catherine Sophie de Flavigny, Countess** (pseud. *Daniel Stern*), French author....1805—1876

Agramonte (ä-grä-mōn'te), **Ignacio**, Cuban revolutionary....1841—1873

Agricola (ȧ-gri'cō-lȧ), **Gnaeus Julius**, Roman general.... 37— 93

Agricola, Georg (b. *Georg Bauer*), German mineralogist....1490?—1555

Agrippa (ȧ-grip'pȧ), **Marcus Vipsanius**, Roman statesman and general....B.C. 63— 12

Agrippina (ȧ-grip-pī'nȧ) **II**, mother of the emperor Nero.... 15?— 59

Aguilera (ä-gi-le'rä), **Ventura Ruiz**, Spanish poet....1820—1881

Aguinaldo (ä-gi-näl'dō), **Emilio**, Philippine insurgent....1870?–1964

Aidan (ā'dăn), **Saint**, Irish abbot of Lindisfarne.... ? — 651

Aidé (ä-i-dē'), **Charles Hamilton**, Eng. novelist, poet....1829—1906

Aiken (ā'ken), **Conrad**, American poet and novelist....1889—1973

Aimard (ā-mär'), **Gustave**, French novelist....1818—1883

Ainger (ān'gẽr), **Alfred**, English divine and writer....1837—1904

Ainslie (āns'lē), **Hew**, Scottish poet in America....1792—1878

Ainsworth (āns'wŏrth), **Robert**, English lexicographer (Latin)..1660—1743

Ainsworth, William Harrison, Eng. historical novelist....1805—1881

Aird (ārd), **Thomas**, English poet....1802—1876

Airy (ār'y), **Sir George Biddell**, English astronomer....1801—1892

Aisha (ä'i-shä) *or* **Ayesha** (*daughter of Abu Bakr*), favorite wife of Mohammed.... 611— 678

Aitken (āt'ken), **Robert Ingersoll**, American sculptor....1878—1949

Aiton (ā'tŏn), **William**, Scottish botanist....1731—1793

Akbar (äk'bär), emperor of Hindustan (1556–1605)....1542—1605

Akeley (āk'li), **Carl Ethan**, Am. naturalist, sculptor....1864—1926

Akenside (ā'ken-sīd), **Mark**, English poet....1721—1770

Akers (ā'kẽrs), **Benjamin Paul**, American sculptor....1825—1861

Akhenaten, Akhenaton (ä-ke-nä'tŏn), *see* Amenhotep IV.

Akins (ā'kins), **Zoë**, American poet and playwright....1886—1958

Alarcón, de (de ä-lär-cōn'), **Pedro Antonio**, Spanish novelist...1833—1891

Alarcón y Mendoza, de (ē men-dō'thä), **Don Juan Ruiz**, Spanish poet, b. in Mexico....1580—1639

Alaric (al'ȧ-ric), king of the Visigoths; conqueror of Rome....370?— 410

Alava, d' (dä'lä-vä), **Miguel Ricardo**, Sp. general, statesman....1771—1843

Alba (äl'bä), *see* Alva, Duke of.

Alban (al'băn), **Saint**, first Christian martyr of Great Britain.3d or 4th cent.

Albani (äl-bä'nī), **Francesco**, Italian painter....1578—1660

Albani, Madame (stage name of *Marie Louise Emma Cécile Lajeunesse, Mme. Ernest Gye*), Canadian soprano....1852—1930

Albee (al'bē), **Edward**, American playwright....1928—

Albeniz (äl-be-nīth'), **Isaac**, Spanish composer and pianist....1860—1909

Albert (al'bẽrt), **Francis Charles Augustus Emmanuel, Prince of Saxe-Coburg-Gotha**, consort of Queen Victoria....1819—1861

Albert I, king of the Belgians (1909–34)....1875—1934

Albert, d' (dal'bär), **Eugen**, Scottish pianist and composer....1864—1932

Albertus Magnus (al-bẽr'tus mag'nus), medieval scholar....1193?–1280

Alboin (al'boin), king of the Lombards (565?–573?).... ?—573?

Albuquerque, de (dē äl-bu-kẽr'kē), **Affonso**, Portuguese conqueror in the East Indies....1453—1515

Alcaeus (al-cē'us), Greek lyric poet....B.C. 620— 580

Alcibiades (al-ci-bī'ȧ-dēs), Athenian general and statesman..B.C. 450— 404

Alcman (alc'măn), lyric poet of Sparta....fl.B.C.—670?

Alcott (al'cŏt), **(Amos) Bronson**, American philosopher and educator....1799—1888

A., Louisa May (*daughter of A.B.A.*), American novelist....1833—1888

Alcuin (al'kwin), English theologian.... 735— 804

Alda (äl'dȧ), **Frances** (b. *Frances Davis*), Am. soprano....1885—1952

Alden (al'den), **John**, Pilgrim settler of Plymouth, Mass....1599?–1687

Alder (äl'dẽr), **Kurt**, German chemist....1902—1958

Aldington (al'ding-tŏn), **Richard**, English novelist, poet....1892—1962

Aldrich (al'drich), **Chester Holmes**, Am. architect....1871—1940

Aldrich, Thomas Bailey, American poet and novelist....1836—1907

Alegría (ä-le-grī'ȧ), **Ciro**, Peruvian novelist....1909—1967

Aleichem (ä-le'khem), **Sholem** (pseud. of *Solomon Rabinowitz*), Yiddish humorist, b. Russia, died in U.S....1859—1916

Alekhine (ȧ-lyekh'in), **Alexander**, French chess player, b. in Russia; world champion (1927–35, 1937–46)....1892—1946

Alemán (ä-le-män'), **Miguel**, pres. of Mexico (1946–52)....1902—

Alembert, d' (dä-läñ-ber'), **Jean le Rond**, French mathematician, philosopher, and encyclopedist....1717—1783

Alessandri (ä-les-sän'drī), **Arturo**, president of Chile....1868—1950

Alexander (al-eg-zan'dẽr) **I, Obrenovic**, king of Serbia (1889–1903).1876—1903

Alexander I (*son of Peter I of Serbia*), king of Yugoslavia (1921–34).1888—1934

Alexander I (*son of Paul I*), emperor of Russia (1801–25)....1777—1825?

A. II (*son of Nicholas I*), emperor of Russia (1855–81)....1818—1881

A. III (*son of A. II*), emperor of Russia (1881–94)....1845—1894

Alexander VI (*Rodrigo Lansol y Borgia*), Pope....1431—1503

Alexander, Francis, early American portrait painter....1800—1881

Alexander, Sir George (*George Alexander Gibb Samson*), English actor and theater manager....1858—1918

Alexander, Harold Rupert Leofric George, Earl of Tunis, British general in World War II....1891—1969

Alexander, John White, American painter....1856—1915

Alexander, Stephen, American astronomer....1806—1883

Alexander, William, Lord Stirling, major general in the American Revolutionary army....1726—1783

Alexander Nevski (nev'skī), Russian hero and saint....1220?–1263

Alexander Severus (sē-vẽr'us), Roman emperor.... 208?— 235

Alexander the Great, king of Macedonia....B.C. 356— 323

Alexandra (al-eg-zan'drȧ), queen of England; consort of Edward VII....1844—1925

Alexandra Feodorovna (fyō-dō-rōv'nȧ), consort of Nicholas II of Russia....1872—1918

Alexis Mikhailovich (ȧ-lek'sis mī-khī'lō-vich), (*father of Peter the Great*), czar of Russia (1645–76)....1629—1676

Alexis Petrovich (pye-trō'vich), (*son of Peter the Great*), prince of Russia....1690—1718

Alexius (ȧ-lek'si-us) **I**, (*A. Comnenus*), emperor of Byzantine Empire....1048—1118

Alfieri (äl-fi-e'rī), **Count Vittorio**, Italian poet, dramatist....1749—1803

Alfonso (al-fon'sō) **XIII**, king of Spain (deposed, 1931)....1886—1941

Alford (al'fŏrd), **Henry**, English scholar and poet....1810—1871

Alfred (al'fred) **the Great**, king of the West Saxons.... 849— 901

Algardi (äl-gär'dī), **Alessandro**, Italian sculptor....1602—1654

Algarotti (äl-gȧ-rot'tī), **Count Francesco**, It. philosopher....1712—1764

Alger (al'gẽr), **Horatio**, Am. writer of boys' stories....1834—1899

Ali (ä'lī), fourth caliph of Islam; son-in-law of Mohammed.... 600— 661

Ali Pasha (ä'lī pȧ-shä'), (*the Lion of Janina*) ruler of Albania....1741—1822

Alison, Sir Archibald, Scottish historian and essayist....1792—1867

Allan, Sir William, Scottish historical painter....1782—1850

Allegri (äl-le'grī), **Gregorio**, It. musician, composer....1582—1652

Allen (al'len), **Ethan**, Am. officer in Revolutionary War....1738—1789

Allen, Grant (*Charles Grant Blairfindie A.*), English scientist and novelist....1848—1899

Allen, Hervey, American novelist and poet....1889—1949

Allen, James Lane, American novelist....1849—1925

Allenby (al'len-by), **Edmund Henry Hynman, Viscount,** English general .... 1861—1936
Allibone (al'li-bōn), **Samuel Austin,** Am. bibliographer .... 1816—1889
Allingham (al'ling-hăm), **William,** Irish poet .... 1828—1889
Allison (al'li-sŏn), **William Boyd,** United States senator .... 1829—1908
Allori (äl-lō'rī), **Alessandro,** Italian painter .... 1535—1607
A., Cristofano (*son of A. A.*), Italian painter .... 1577—1621
Allouez (ȧl-lö-ẹ'), **Claude Jean,** French Jesuit missionary in America .... 1622—1689
Allston (ạl'stŏn), **Washington,** Am. painter and writer .... 1779—1843
Almagro, de (dẹ äl-mä'grō), **Diego,** explorer of Peru (with Pizarro). 1475—1538
Alma-Tadema (al'mȧ-tad'e-mȧ), **Sir Lawrence,** English painter, born in the Netherlands .... 1836—1912
Almeida-Garrett, de (dẹ äl-mẹ'i-dä-gär-ret'), **João Baptista Leitão,** Portuguese poet and dramatist .... 1799—1854
Almquist (älm'kvist), **Karl Jonas Ludwig,** Swedish poet and novelist .... 1793—1866
Alsop (ạl'sŏp), **Richard,** American poet and journalist .... 1761—1815
Altamira y Crevea (äl-tä-mī'rä ē crẹ-vẹ'ä), **Rafaél,** Sp. jurist, historian; World Court judge (1921–40) .... 1866—1951
Alten, von (fọn äl'ten), **Karl August, Graf,** Hanoverian general. 1764—1840
Altgeld (ạlt'geld), **John Peter,** American statesman .... 1847—1902
Altsheler (alt'shel-ẽr), **Joseph Alexander,** Am. novelist .... 1862—1919
Alva (äl'vä) *or* **Alba** (äl'bä), **Fernando Álvarez de Toledo, Duke of,** Spanish general in the Netherlands .... 1508—1582
Alvarado, de (dẹ äl-vä-rä'thō), **Pedro,** Spanish officer, companion of Cortez .... 1485?–1541
Álvarez (äl'vä-rẹth), **Juan,** Mexican general and president .... 1790?–1867
Álvarez Quintero (kīn-tẹ'rō), **Serafín,** Spanish dramatist .... 1871—1938
Á. Q., Joaquín (*brother of S.A.Q., and co-author*), dramatist .... 1873—1944
Amadeus (ä-mä-dẹ'us), **Ferdinando Maria, Duke of Aosta,** king of Spain (1870–73) .... 1845—1890
Amari (ä-mä'rī), **Michele,** Italian historian and politician .... 1806—1889
Amati (ä-mä'tī), **Nicola,** Italian violin maker .... 1596—1684
Amato (ä-mä'tō), **Pasquale,** Italian baritone .... 1879—1942
Amato, d' (dä-mä'tō), **Giovanni Antonio,** Neapolitan painter .. 1475—1555
Ambrose (am'brōs), **Saint,** bishop of Milan; Latin father .... 340?– 397
Amenhotep (ä-men-hō'tep) **III** *or* **Amenophis** (ä-men-ō'fis) **III,** king of Egypt .... fl.B.C. 1380
A. IV, Akhenaten (ä-ke-nä'tŏn) *or* **Ikhnaton** (ik-nä'tŏn), (*son of A.III*), king of Egypt .... B.C.1375—1358
Ames (āmș), **Fisher,** American orator and statesman .... 1758—1808
Ames, Oakes, American politician .... 1804—1873
Ames, Winthrop, American theatrical producer .... 1871—1937
Amherst (am'ẽrst), **Baron Jeffrey,** British field marshal .... 1717—1797
Amicis, de (dẹ ä-mī'chis), **Edmondo,** Italian misc. writer .... 1846—1908
Amiel (ȧ-myel'), **Henri Frédéric,** Swiss critic and poet .... 1821—1881
Ammianus Marcellinus (am-mi-ā'nus mär-cel-lī'nus), Roman historian .... 330— 395
Ampère (äṅ-per'), **André Marie,** French physicist .... 1775—1836
Amsdorf, von (fọn äms'dọrf), **Nikolaus,** German Lutheran reformer .... 1483—1565
Amundsen (ä'mun-sen), **Roald,** Norwegian explorer .... 1872—1928
Anacreon (ȧ-naç'rē-ŏn), Greek lyric poet .... B.C. 572?—488?
Ananda Mahidol (ȧ-nän'tä mä-hī-dŏn'), king of Siam (1935–46); assassinated .... 1925—1946
Anastasius (an-ȧs-tā'shi-us) **I,** Roman emperor of Eastern Roman Empire (491–518) .... 430?— 518
Anaxagoras (an-aks-a'gō-rȧs), Greek philosopher .... B.C. 500— 428
Anaximander (an-aks-i-man'dẽr), Greek philosopher .... B.C. 611— 547
Ancona, d' (dän-çō'nȧ), **Alessandro,** It. scholar, writer .... 1835—1914
Andersen (an'dẽr-sen), **Hans Christian,** Danish novelist, writer of fairy stories, and poet .... 1805—1875
Anderson (an'dẽr-sŏn), **Alexander,** Am. wood engraver .... 1775—1870
Anderson, Carl David, American physicist .... 1905—1975
Anderson, Clinton Presba, U. S. secretary of agriculture (1945–48); senator .... 1895—
Anderson, Marian, American contralto .... 1908—
Anderson, Mary, American actress .... 1859—1940
Anderson, Maxwell, American dramatist .... 1888—1959
Anderson, Robert, American general; defender of Fort Sumter .. 1805—1871
Anderson, Sherwood, Am. novelist and short-story writer .... 1876—1941
Andrássy (ŏn-dräs'sy), **Count Gyula,** Hungarian statesman .... 1823—1890
A., Count Gyula (*son of G.A.*), Hungarian statesman .... 1860—1929
André (an'drẹ), **Major John,** English officer, hanged as spy in American Revolution .... 1751—1780
Andrée (än-drẹ'), **Salomon Auguste,** Swedish aeronaut .... 1854—1897
Andrewes (an'drụș), **Lancelot,** English theologian .... 1555—1626
Andrews (an'drụș), **Charles McLean,** American historian .... 1863—1943
Andrews, Ethan Allen, American philologist .... 1787—1858
Andrews, Roy Chapman, American naturalist and explorer .... 1884—1960
Andreyev (än-drẹ'ef), **Leonid Nikolayevich,** Russ. novelist .... 1871—1919
Andronicus (an-drō-nī'çus), **I,** Byzantine emperor .... 1110?–1185
Andros (an'dros), **Sir Edmund,** English colonial governor in America .... 1637—1714
Angelico (än-ġel'i-çō), **Fra,** *see* Fiesole, da, Giovanni.
Angell (ān'ġel), **James Rowland,** American educator .... 1869—1949
Angell, Sir Norman (b. *Ralph Norman Angell Lane*), English author; received Nobel peace prize (1933) .... 1874—1967
Anglesey (aṅ'gl-si), **Henry William, Lord Paget,** British field marshal .... 1768—1854
Anglin (aṅ'glin), **Margaret Mary,** American actress, born in Canada .... 1876—1958
Angoulême, d' (däṅ-gö-lem'), **Marie Thérèse Charlotte, Duchess,** daughter of Louis XVI .... 1778—1851
Ångström (ŏng'strŭm), **Anders Jöns,** Swedish physicist .... 1814—1874
Å., Knut Johan (*son of A.J.A.*), Swedish physicist .... 1857—1910
Anne (an), queen of Great Britain and Ireland (1702–14) .... 1665—1714
Anne of Austria, wife of Louis XIII of France .... 1601—1666
Anne of Bohemia, wife of Richard II of England .... 1366—1394
Anne of Cleves, fourth wife of Henry VIII .... 1515—1557
Annunzio, Gabriele D', *see* D'Annunzio, Gabriele.
Anquetil-Duperron (äṅk-tīl'dụ-pe-rọṅ'), **Abraham Hyacinthe,** French Orientalist .... 1731—1805
Anselm (an'selm), **Saint,** archbishop of Canterbury .... 1033—1109
Anson (an'sŏn), **George, Lord,** English navigator .... 1697—1762
Anspacher (äns'päkh-ẽr), **Louis Kaufman,** American playwright .... 1878—1947
Antheil (än'tīl), **George,** American composer .... 1900—1959
Anthon (an'thŏn), **Charles,** American classical scholar .... 1797—1867

Anthony (an'to-ny, an'tho-ny), **Saint,** Egyptian founder of monasticism .... 251?—350?
Anthony, Saint, of Padua, Franciscan monk .... 1195—1231
Anthony (an'tho-ny), **Susan Brownell,** Am. suffragette .... 1820—1906
Antigonus (an-tig'ō-nus), general of Alexander the Great ... B.C. 382— 301
Antiochus (an-tī'ō-çhus) **III,** (*the Great*), king of Syria .... B.C. 242— 187
A. IV (*Epiphanes; son of A. III*), king of Syria .... B.C. ? — 163
Antipater (an-tip'ȧ-tẽr), regent of Macedonia .... B.C. ? — 319
Antisthenes (an-tis'the-nēș), Greek Cynic .... fl.B.C. ? — 400
Antonello (an-tō-nel'lō), **Antonio** (*da Messina*), Italian painter .. 1430–1479?
Antonescu (än-tō-ne'sçū), **Ion,** dictator of Romania (1940–44); executed .... 1882—1946
Antoninus (an-tō-nī'nus), **Marcus Aurelius,** *see* Marcus Aurelius.
Antoninus Pius (pī'us), Roman emperor (138–161) .... 86— 161
Antonius (an-tō'ni-us), **Marcus** (*Marc Anthony*), Roman general .... B.C. 83— 30
Anville, d' (däṅ-vīl'), **Jean Baptiste Bourguignon,** French geographer .... 1697—1782
Apelles (ȧ-pel'lēș), Greek painter .... fl. B.C. 330
Apollinaire (ȧ-pọ-lī-när'), **Guillaume,** French poet .... 1880—1918
Apollodorus (ȧ-pol-lō-dō'rus), (*the Shadower*), Athenian painter .... B.C. ? — 440
Apollodorus, grammarian of Athens .... fl. B.C. 140
Apollonius of Perga (ȧ-pol-lō'ni-us ov pẽr'gȧ), Greek mathematician .... fl. B.C. 240
Apollonius of Rhodes (rōdș), Greek poet, rhetorician .... fl. B.C. 230
Appiani (äp-pi-ä'nī), **Andrea,** Italian fresco painter .... 1754—1817
Appianus (ap-pi-ā'nus) *or* **Appian,** Roman historian .... fl. 2nd cent.
Apponyi (äp'pō-nyī'), **Albert Georg, Count,** Hungarian statesman .... 1846—1933
Apuleius (ȧp-ū-lē'us), **Lucius,** Roman philosopher .... fl. 150
Aquinas (ȧ-kwī'nȧs), **Saint Thomas** (*Angelic Doctor*), Italian scholastic philosopher .... 1225–1274?
Arabi Pasha (ä-rä'bī pȧ-shä'), Egyptian nationalist leader .... 1841—1911
Arago (ȧ-rȧ-gō'), **Dominique François Jean,** Fr. astronomer ... 1786—1853
Aragon (ȧ-rȧ-gọṅ'), **Louis,** French novelist and poet .... 1895—
Aram (ā'răm), **Eugene,** English scholar .... 1704—1759
Aranda (ä-rän'dä), **Peter P. A. de Bolea, Count of,** Spanish statesman .... 1718—1799
Arany (ŏ'rän-yu), **János,** Hungarian poet .... 1817—1882
Aratus (ȧ-rä'tus) **of Sicyon,** Achaean general .... B.C. 271— 213
Arblay, d' (där'blā), **Madame,** *see* Burney, Frances.
Arbuthnot (är'buth-not), **John,** Eng. physician, author .... 1675—1735
Arc, Joan of, Saint, *see* Joan of Arc.
Arcesilaus (är-ces-i-lā'us), Athenian philosopher .... B.C. 316— 241
Archer (ärch'ẽr), **William,** English drama critic, born in Scotland, translator of Ibsen .... 1856—1924
Archilocus (är-çhil'ō-çus) **of Paros,** Greek lyric poet .... B.C. 714?— 676
Archimedes (är-çhi-mē'dēș), Greek mathematician .... B.C. 287?— 212
Archipenko (är-çhi-peṅ'kō), **Aleksandr,** Russian sculptor and painter in America .... 1887—1964
Archytas (är-çhȳ'tȧs), philosopher of Tarentum .... B.C. 428—347?
Arensky (ȧ-ren'skē), **Anton Stepanovich,** Russ. composer .... 1861—1906
Areson (ä're-sŏn), **Jon,** Icelandic poet and bishop .... 1484—1550
Aretino (ä-rẹ-tī'nō), **Pietro,** Italian satirist .... 1492—1556?
Argelander (är'ge-lan-dẽr), **Friedrich Wilhelm August,** Prussian astronomer .... 1799—1875
Ariosto (ä-ri-ọs'tō), **Ludovico,** Italian poet .... 1474—1533
Arista (ä-rīs'tȧ), **Mariano,** Mexican general and president .... 1802—1855
Aristarchus (ar-is-tär'çhus), Greek astronomer .... B.C. 3d. cent.
Aristides (ar-is-tī'dēș), (*the Just*), Athenian statesman and general .... B.C. 530?—468?
Aristippus (ar-is-tip'us), Greek philosopher .... B.C. 435?—356?
Aristophanes (ar-is-tof'ȧ-nēș), Greek comic poet .... B.C. 448?—380?
Aristotle (ar'is-tot-l), Greek philosopher .... B.C. 384— 322
Arita (ä-rī'tȧ), **Hachiro,** Japanese statesman .... 1884—1945
Arius (ā'ri-us), Greek deacon at Alexandria; founder of Arianism. 280?— 336
Arkwright (ärk'rīt), **Sir Richard,** English inventor .... 1732—1792
Arlen (är'len), **Michael** (b. *Dikran Kuyumjian*), Armenian author. 1895—1956
Arliss (är'lis), **George,** English actor .... 1868—1946
Arminius (är-min'i-us), **Jacobus** (b. *Jacob Harmensen*), Dutch theologian .... 1560—1609
Armour (är'mŏr), **Norman,** American diplomat .... 1887—
Armstrong (ärm'strọng), **John,** Am. general and writer .... 1758—1843
Armstrong, William George, Baron, English inventor .... 1810—1900
Arnaud (ȧr-nō'), **Henri,** pastor and leader of Waldenses .... 1641—1721
Arnauld (ȧr-nō'), **Antoine,** French theologian .... 1612—1694
Arnault (ȧr-nō'), **Vincent Antoine,** French dramatist .... 1766—1834
Arndt (ärnt), **Ernest Moritz,** German poet .... 1769—1860
Arne (ärn), **Thomas Augustine,** English composer .... 1710—1778
Arnold (är'nŏld), **Benedict,** Am. Revolutionary War general; traitor 1741—1801
Arnold, Sir Edwin, English poet and Orientalist .... 1832—1904
Arnold, Henry Harley, American general in command of air forces in World War II .... 1886—1950
Arnold, Matthew (*son of T. A.*), English poet, critic .... 1822—1888
A., Thomas, English educator and historian .... 1795—1842
Arpad (är'päd), founder of the Hungarian monarchy .... 840?—907?
Arreboe (är-re-bō'ē), **Anders Christensen,** Danish poet .... 1587—1637
Arrhenius (är-rẹ'nī-us), **Svante August,** Swedish chemist .... 1859—1927
Arriaga, d' (dä-rī-ä'gä), **Manoel, José,** first president of the republic of Portugal .... 1839—1917
Arrian (ăr'ri-ăn), **Flavius,** Greek historian .... 100?—170?
Artaxerxes (är-tȧ-zẽrk'sēș) **I,** king of Persia .... B.C. ? — 425
A. II, king of Persia .... B.C. ? — 358
Artevelde, van (vän är'te-vel-de), **Jacob,** Flemish statesman .. 1290?–1345
A., Philip v. (*son of J.A.*), Flemish revolutionary leader .... 1340—1382
Arthur (är'thŭr), British king and hero of the Round Table .. 5th or 6th cent.
Arthur, Chester Alan, 21st U. S. president (1881–85) .... 1830—1886
Arthur, Timothy Shay, American moralist and writer .... 1809—1885
Artzybaschev (är-tsi-bä'shef), **Mikhail,** Russian novelist .... 1878—1927
Asbjörnsen (äs-byŏrn'sen), **Peter Christen,** Norwegian folklorist .... 1812—1885
Asbury (aș'bŭr-y), **Francis,** first Methodist bishop in United States, born in England .... 1745—1816
Asch (äsh), **Sholem,** Yiddish author, born in Poland, naturalized in U. S. .... 1880—1957
Ascham (as'çhăm), **Roger,** English scholar and author .... 1515—1568
Ashmole (ash'mōl), **Elias,** English antiquary .... 1617—1692
Ashton (ash'tŏn), **Winifred,** *see* Dane, Clemence.
Ashurbanipal (ä'shūr-bä-nī-päl'), king of Assyria .... B.C. ? — 626

Aspasia (as-pā'shi-ȧ), consort of Pericles................B.C. 470?— 410

Asquith (as'kwith), **Herbert Henry, first Earl of Oxford and Asquith**, British statesman; prime minister (1908–16)........1852—1928

Astaire (ȧ-stâr'), **Fred**, American dancer and actor............1900—

Aston (as'tŏn), **Francis William**, English chemist.............1877—1945

Astor (as'tŏr), **John Jacob**, American merchant...............1763—1848

Astor, Nancy Langhorne, Viscountess, first woman member of Brit. House of Commons, b. in U.S..........................1879—1964

Atahualpa (ä-tä-wäl'pä), last Inca of Peru......................1500?–1533

Ataturk, Kemal, *see* Kemal Ataturk, Mustafa.

Athanasius (ath-ȧ-nā'shi-us), **Saint**, Greek church father...... 296— 373

Athelstan *or* **Aethelstan** (ath'el-stăn), king of England........895?— 940

Athenaeus (ath-en-ē'us), Greek grammarian, rhetorician........ fl. c. 200

Atherton (ath'ẽr-tŏn), **Gertrude**, American novelist............1857—1948

Atkinson (at'kin-sŏn), **(Justin) Brooks**, Am. drama critic......1894—

Atterbom (at'tẽr-bom), **Peter Daniel Amadeus**, Swedish poet.1790—1855

Atterbury (at'tẽr-bũr-y), **Francis**, English bishop..............1662—1732

Atticus (at'ti-ḳus), **Titus Pomponius**, Roman philosopher, friend of Cicero...B.C. 109— 32

Attila (at'ti-lȧ), (*the Scourge of God*), king of the Huns.........406?— 453

Attlee (at'lē), **Clement Richard**, British Labour party leader; prime minister (1945–51)..................................1883—1967

Auber (ō-ber'), **Daniel François Esprit**, French composer......1782—1871

Aubrey (ą'bri), **John**, English antiquary..........................1626—1697

Auchinleck (ą'-ḳhin-lek), **Sir Claude John Eyre**, British field marshal..1884—1981

Auden (ą'den), **Wystan Hugh**, English poet in the U. S.........1907—1973

Audran (ō-drän'), **Gérard**, French historical engraver..........1640—1703

Audubon (ą'du-bon), **John James**, American naturalist..........1785—1851

Auer (ou'ẽr), **Leopold**, Hungarian violinist and teacher.........1845—1930

Auerbach (ou'ẽr-bäkh), **Berthold**, German novelist..............1812—1882

Auersperg, von (fọn ou'ẽrs-perk), **Anton Alexander, Graf** (pseud. *Anastasius Grün*), Austrian poet..............................1806—1876

Augier (ō-ẓyẹ'), **Guillaume Victor Émile**, Fr. dramatist.......1820—1889

Augustine (ą'gus-tīn), **Saint**, Latin church father, known for *Confessions* and *City of God*.................................. 354— 430

Augustine, Saint, first archbishop of Canterbury............ ? — 604

Augustus (ą-gus'tus), (*Gaius Julius Caesar Octavianus*), first emperor of Rome; grandnephew of Julius Caesar..........B.C. 63—14 A.D.

Augustus II, king of Poland and (as *Frederick Augustus I*) elector of Saxony...1670—1733

Aulard (ō-lär'), **Alphonse**, French historian.....................1849—1928

Aurangzeb (ą̈r'ăng-zeb), last Mogul emperor of Hindustan......1618—1707

Aurelian (ą-rē'li-ăn), (*Lucius Domitius Aurelianus*), Roman emperor (270–75)...212?– 275

Aurelius, Marcus, *see* Marcus Aurelius.

Auriol (ō-ryọl'), **Vincent**, president of France (1947–54)........1884—1966

Auslander (ous'lan-dẽr), **Joseph**, American poet..................1897—1965

Ausonius (ą-sō'ni-us), **Decimus Magnus**, Roman poet.........310?–395?

Austen (ąs'ten), **Jane**, English novelist............................1775—1817

Austin (ąs'tin), **Alfred**, English poet laureate.....................1835—1913

Austin, John, English jurist...1790—1859

Austin, Mary, American author..1868—1934

Austin, Stephen Fuller, founder of first American colony in Texas...1793—1836

Averroes (ȧ-ver'ō-ēṣ), (Arabic *Ibn Rushd*), Moslem philosopher and physician...1126—1198

Avicenna (av-i-cen'ȧ), (Arabic *Ibn Sina*), Arabian physician and philosopher... 980—1037

Avila Camacho (ä'vī-lä ḳä-mä'chō), **Manuel**, president of Mexico (1940–46)...1897?—1955

Avogadro (ä-vō-gä'drō), **Count Amadeo**, Italian physicist......1776—1856

Aydelotte (ā'de-lot), **Frank**, American educator..................1880—1956

Ayer (ā'ăr), **Alfred Jules**, British philosopher...................1910—

Ayesha (ä'ye-shä), *see* Aisha.

Ayres (ârṣ), **Leonard Porter**, American statistician..............1879—1946

Ayscough (as'ḳū), **Samuel**, English index-maker.................1745—1804

Ayton (ā'tŏn), **Sir Robert**, Scottish poet..........................1570—1638

Aytoun (ā'tụn; ā'tŏn), **William Edmondstoune**, Scottish poet and misc. writer...1813—1865

Azaña (ä-thä'nyä), **Manuel**, president of Spain (1936–39).......1880—1940

Azeglio, d' (däd-zel'yō), **Massimo Taparelli, Marchese**, Italian statesman, poet, and writer.................................1798—1866

B

Babbitt (bab'bit), **Irving**, American scholar and critic..........1865—1933

Babel (bä'băl), **Isaak (Emmanuilovich)**, Russian writer.........1894—1941

Baber *or* **Babur** (bä'bẽr), **Zahir ud-Din Mohammed**, founder of the Mogul empire in India.....................................1483—1530

Babeuf (bȧ-bũf'), **François Noël**, French revolutionist..........1760—1797

Babson (bab'sŏn), **Roger Ward**, American statistician...........1875—1967

Bach (bäkh), **Johann Sebastian**, German composer...............1685—1750

B., Johann Christian (*son of J.S.B.*), composer...................1735—1782

B., Karl Philipp Emanuel (*son of J.S.B.*), composer.............1714—1788

Bache (bāch), **Alexander Dallas**, American physicist..............1806—1867

Bacheller (bach'el-lẽr), **Irving**, American novelist...............1859—1950

Bachman (baḳh'măn), **John**, American naturalist...................1790—1874

Bacon (bā'ḳŏn), **Francis, Baron Verulam, Viscount St. Albans**, English philosopher, essayist, and statesman..........1561—1626

B., Sir Nicholas (*father of F.B.*), English statesman.............1509—1579

Bacon, Peggy, American artist and writer...........................1895—

Bacon, Roger, Friar, English philosopher and scientist..........1214?–1294

Baden-Powell (bā'den-pō'el), **Robert Stephenson Smyth, Baron**, British general; founder of Boy Scouts...............1857—1941

Badoglio (bä-dō'lyō), **Pietro, Marchese del Sabatino**, It. field marshal; premier (1943–44)..................................1871—1956

Baer, von (fọn bâr'), **Karl Ernst**, Estonian biologist..............1792—1876

Baffin (baf'fin), **William**, English navigator........................1584—1622

Bagehot (bag'ŏt), **Walter**, English economist and essayist.......1826—1877

Baggesen (bäg'ẹ-sen), **Jens Immanuel**, Danish poet..............1764—1826

Bagration (bȧ-grȧ-tī-on'), **Peter, Prince**, Russian general.......1765—1812

Baïf, de (dẽ bȧ-īf'), **Jean Antoine**, French poet...................1532—1589

Bailey (bā'li), **Gamaliel**, American journalist......................1807—1859

Bailey, Liberty Hyde, American botanist..............................1858—1954

Baillie (bā'li), **Joanna**, Scottish poet................................1762—1851

B., Matthew (*brother of J.B.*), Scottish physician..................1761—1823

Bailly (bȧ-yē'), **Jean Sylvain**, French astronomer..................1736—1793

Bain (bān), **Alexander**, Scottish psychologist........................1818—1903

Bainbridge (bān'briġ), **William**, American commodore............1774—1833

Bainville (baṅ-vīl'), **Jacques**, Fr. journalist, historian...........1879—1936

Bairnsfather (bârnṣ'fä-thẽr), **Bruce**, English author and illustrator..1888—1959

Baker (bā'kẽr), **Edward Dickinson**, Am. senator, soldier.........1811—1861

Baker, George Pierce, American professor of the drama...........1866—1935

Baker, Newton Diehl, U. S. secretary of war (1916–21)...........1871—1937

Baker, Ray Stannard (pseud. *David Grayson*), American biographer and essayist...1870—1946

Baker, Sir Samuel White, English explorer............................1821—1893

Bakst (bäkst), **Leon Nikolaievich**, Russian painter..................1866—1924

Bakunin (bȧ-kụ'nyin), **Mikhail**, Russian anarchist..................1814—1876

Balakirev (bä-lä-kī'ref), **Mili Alexeivich**, Russian composer and conductor...1837—1910

Balanchine (ba'lăn-chin), **George** (b. *Georgi Balinchinvadze*), Russ. ballet dancer and choreographer in U. S.........................1904—

Balbo (bäl'bō), **Cesare**, Italian writer and statesman...............1789—1853

Balbo, Italo, Italian Fascist leader and aviator.......................1896—1940

Balboa, de (dẹ bäl-bō'ȧ), **Vasco Nuñez**, Spanish discoverer of the Pacific Ocean..1475—1517

Balchen (bäl'ḳhen), **Bernt**, American aviator, b. in Norway......1899—1973

Baldovinetti (bäl″dō-vī-net'tī), **Alessio**, Florentine painter.....1425?–1499

Baldwin (bąld'win) **I**, king of Jerusalem (1100–1118)..............1058—1118

Baldwin I, a leader of the Fourth Crusade; emperor at Constantinople..1171?–1205

Baldwin, James Mark, American psychologist........................1861—1934

Baldwin, Stanley, Earl Baldwin of Bewdley, British statesman; prime minister (1923–24, 1924–29, 1935–37).....................1867—1947

Balfe (bälf), **Michael William**, Irish composer......................1808—1870

Balfour (bal'fur), **Arthur James, first Earl of Balfour**, British statesman; prime minister (1902–05)..........................1848—1930

Ball (bąl), **Sir Robert Stawell**, English astronomer.................1840—1913

Ball, John, English priest, hanged for participation in revolt led by Wat Tyler... ? —1381

Baltimore (bąl'ti-mọr), **Lord**, *see* Calvert, George.

Balzac, de (dẽ bál-zäḳ' *or* dẽ bal'zaḳ), **Honoré**, Fr. novelist.....1799—1850

Bancroft (ban'ḳrọft), **George**, Am. historian, statesman............1800—1891

Bancroft, Hubert Howe, Am. historian, publisher....................1832—1918

Bandinelli (bän-dī-nel'lī), **Baccio**, Italian sculptor...................1493—1560

Banér (bȧ-ner'), **Johan Gustavus**, Swedish general..................1596—1641

Bangs (bangṣ), **John Kendrick**, Am. humorist, editor..............1862—1922

Banim (bā'nim), **John**, Irish novelist...................................1798—1842

B., Michael (*brother of J.B.*), novelist.................................1796—1874

Bankhead (bank'hed), **John Hollis**, U.S. senator....................1872—1946

B., William Brockman (*brother of J.H.B.*), congressman; speaker of the House (1936–40)....................................1874—1940

B., Tallulah Brockman (*daughter of W.B.B.*), Am. actress.... 1903—1968

Banks (banks), **Sir Joseph**, English botanist..........................1743—1820

Banks, Nathaniel Prentiss, American statesman and general.....1816—1894

Banting (ban'ting), **Frederick Grant**, Canadian physician.........1891—1941

Banville, de (dẽ bäṅ-vīl'), **Théodore Faullain**, French poet.....1823—1891

Barbarossa (bär-bä-rọs'sȧ), *see* Frederick I of Germany.

Barbaroux (bȧr-bȧ-rō'), **Charles**, French revolutionist...........1767—1794

Barbauld (bär'bąld), **Anna Laetitia**, English poet, editor........1743—1825

Barber (bär'bẽr), **Samuel**, American composer......................1910—1981

Barbey d'Aurevilly (bȧr-bẹ'dōr-vī-yē'), **Jules Amédée**, French novelist...1809—1889

Barbier (bȧr-byẹ'), **Antoine Alexandre**, Fr. bibliographer.........1765—1825

Barbieri (bär-bī-ẹ'rī), **Giovanni Francesco**, *see* Guercino.

Barbirolli (bär-bi-rōl'i), **John**, English conductor....................1899—1970

Barbour (bär'bũr), **John**, Scottish poet..................................1316—1396

Barbusse (bȧr-bûs'), **Henri**, Fr. journalist and novelist...........1873—1935

Barclay (bär'ḳlā), **McClelland**, American illustrator...............1893—1943

Barham (bär'hăm), **Richard Harris** (pseud. *Thomas Ingoldsby*), English humorist..1788—1845

Baring (bâr'ing), **Maurice**, English writer............................1874—1945

Baring-Gould (bâr'ing-gōld'), **Sabine**, English divine, novelist, and miscellaneous writer.....................................1834—1924

Barkla (bär'klȧ), **Charles Glover**, English physicist................1877—1944

Barkley (bärk'li), **Alben William**, American statesman; U. S. vice president (1949–53)...1877—1956

Barlow (bär'lō), **Joel**, American patriot and poet....................1754—1812

Barnard (bär'nȧrd), **Edward Emerson**, Am. astronomer...........1857—1923

Barnard, Frederick Augustus Porter, Am. educator...................1809—1889

Barnard, George Grey, American sculptor..............................1863—1938

Barnave (bȧr-nȧv'), **Antoine Pierre Joseph Marie**, French revolutionist and orator...1761—1793

Barnes (bärnṣ), **Harry Elmer**, Am. historian, sociologist..........1889—1968

Barnes, Margaret Ayer, American novelist..............................1886—1967

Barneveldt (bär'ne-velt), **John van Olden**, Dutch statesman....1547—1619

Barney (bär'ni), **Joshua**, American naval officer.....................1759—1818

Barnum (bär'num), **Phineas Taylor**, American showman...........1810—1891

Barocchio (bä-rōḳ'ḳyō), **Giacomo**, *see* Vignola, Giacomo da.

Baroja (bä-rō'hä), **Pío**, Spanish novelist................................1872—1956

Baronius (bä-rō'ni-us), **Caesar**, It. cardinal and writer............1538—1607

Barras, de (dẽ bȧ-rä'), **Paul François Nicolas, Count**, French revolutionist..1755—1829

Barré (bȧ-rẹ'), **Isaac**, British statesman and soldier................1726—1802

Barrès (bȧ-res'), **Maurice**, French novelist and essayist............1862—1923

Barrett (bar'ret), **Lawrence**, American actor..........................1838—1891

Barrett, Wilson, English actor and theater manager..................1846—1904

Barrie (bar'i), **Sir James Matthew**, Scottish dramatist and novelist...1860—1937

Barros, de (dẽ bä'roosh), **João**, Portuguese historian..............1496?–1570

Barrow (bar'ō), **Isaac**, Eng. divine and mathematician..............1630—1677

Barry (bar'y), **Sir Charles**, English architect..........................1795—1860

Barry, Elizabeth, English actress..1658—1713

Barry, James, Irish painter...1741—1806

Barry, John, American naval commander................................1745—1803

Barry, Philip, American playwright.......................................1896—1949

Barry, Spranger, Irish actor..1719—1777

Barrymore (bar'y-mọr), **Maurice** (b. *Herbert Blythe*), American actor, born in England..1847—1905

B., Ethel (*daughter of M.B.*), American actress........................1879—1959

B., Georgiana Drew (*wife of M.B., sister of John Drew*), American actress...1856—1893

B., John (*son of M.B.*), American actor..................................1882—1942

B., Lionel (*son of M.B.*), American actor................................1878—1954

Barth (bärth), **Heinrich**, German explorer 1821—1865
Barthélemy (bår-tel-mē'), **Auguste Marseille**, French poet 1796—1867
Barthélemy, Jean Jacques, French writer, archaeologist 1716—1795
Bartholdi (bår-tōl-dī'), **Frédéric Auguste**, French sculptor 1834—1904
Barthou (bår-tö'), **Louis**, French statesman, biographer 1862—1934
Bartlett (bärt'let), **John**, American editor and publisher 1820—1905
Bartók (bär'tok), **Béla**, Hungarian composer 1881—1945
Bartolini (bär-tō-lī'nī), **Lorenzo**, Italian sculptor 1777—1850
Bartolommeo (bär"tō-lōm-me'ō), **Fra**, Italian painter 1475—1517
Barton, Clara, American philanthropist and organizer of American Red Cross 1821—1912
Baruch (bå-rųçh'), **Bernard Mannes**, Am. economist 1870—1965
Basedow (bä'se-dō), **Johann Bernhard**, German educator 1723—1790
Bashkirtseff (bäsh-kīrt'sef), **Maria Constantinova** (*Marie*) French painter and diarist, b. in Russia 1860—1884
Basil (bă'şil) **the Great, Saint**, bishop of Caesarea 330?— 379
Baskerville (bas'kẽr-vil), **John**, English typographer 1706—1775
Bassano (bäs-sä'nō), **Jacopo** (b. *Jacopo* or *Giacomo da Ponte*), Italian painter 1510—1592
B., Leandro (*son of J.B.*), Italian painter 1558—1623
Bassett (bas'set), **John Spencer**, American historian 1867—1928
Bassompierre, de (dē bä-soṅ-pyer'), **François, Baron**, marshal of France 1579—1646
Bastian (bäs'ti-ăn), **Adolf**, German anthropologist 1826—1905
Bastien-Lepage (bås-tyaṅ'lē-påẓ'), **Jules**, French painter 1848—1884
Bates (bāts), **Edward**, American statesman 1793—1869
Bates, Ernest Sutherland, American educator and writer 1879—1939
Bates, Henry Walter, English naturalist and geographer 1825—1887
Bates, Katharine Lee, American poet 1859—1929
Bathurst (bath'ürst), **Allen, first Earl**, English statesman 1684—1775
Batista (bä-tē'stà), **Fulgencio**, president of Cuba (1940–44; 1952–59) 1901—1973
Baudelaire (bō-dlâr'), **Charles**, French poet and critic 1821—1867
Baudouin (bō-dwaṅ), **I**, (*son of Leopold III*) king of the Belgians (1951–) 1930—
Bauer, Harold, English pianist 1873—1951
Baum (bąm), **Lyman Frank**, American writer of juveniles 1856—1919
Baum (boum), **Vicki**, American novelist, b. in Austria 1888—1960
Baumgarten (boum'gär-ten), **Alexander Gottlieb**, German philosopher 1714—1762
Bax (baks), **Sir Arnold**, English composer 1883—1953
Baxter (baks'tẽr), **Richard**, Eng. nonconformist divine 1615—1691
Bayard (bȳ'ärd), **Thomas Francis**, American statesman 1828—1898
Bayard, de (dē bå-yår'), **Pierre du Terrail, Seigneur**, French warrior-hero 1473?–1524
Bayle (bel), **Pierre**, French philosopher and historian 1647—1706
Bazaine (bå-zān'), **François Achille**, French general 1811—1888
Bazin (bå-zaṅ'), **René François**, French novelist 1853—1932
Beach (bēch), **Rex**, American novelist 1877—1949
Beaconsfield (bē'çōnş-fēld), **Earl of**, *see* Disraeli, B.
Beard (bērd), **Charles Austin**, American historian 1874—1948
Beard, Daniel Carter, American Boy Scout organizer and naturalist 1850—1941
Beardsley (bērdş'li), **Aubrey Vincent**, English artist 1872—1898
Beaton (bē'tŏn), **Cecil**, Eng. photographer, designer 1904—
Beaton, David, cardinal and primate of Scotland 1494—1546
Beatrice Portinari (bē'á-tric pǫr-tī-nä'rī; *It.* bę-ä-trī'chę), Florentine lady; inspiration of Dante 1266—1290
Beattie (bę'ti), **James**, Scottish poet and writer 1735—1803
Beatty (bē'ty), **David, first Earl**, British admiral 1871—1936
Beaumarchais, de (dē bō-mår-çhā'), **Pierre Augustin Caron**, French dramatist 1732—1799
Beaumont (bō'mont), **Francis**, English dramatist, collaborator with John Fletcher 1584—1616
Beaumont, William, American physician 1785—1853
Beauregard (bō're-gärd), **Pierre Gustave Toutant**, American Confederate general 1818—1893
Beaux (bō), **Cecelia**, American painter 1863—1942
Beaverbrook (bē'vẽr-brook), **William Maxwell Aitken, first Baron**, English statesman and newspaper publisher 1879—1964
Bebel (bę'bel), **August**, German socialist and writer 1840—1913
Beccaria, de (dę beç-çär-ī'ä), **Cesare Bonesana, Marchese**, Italian economist and criminologist 1738—1794
Beck (bek), **Christian Daniel**, German philologist, writer 1757—1832
Beck, Józef, Polish foreign minister (1932–39) 1894—1944
Becket, Thomas à, *see* Thomas à Becket.
Beckett (bek'et), **Samuel, Irish poet, novelist, playwright, in France, writing mostly in French 1906—**
Beckford (bek'fŏrd), **William**, English author 1759—1844
Becque (beç), **Henry François**, French dramatist 1837—1899
Becquerel (beç-rel'), **Antoine César**, Fr. physicist 1788—1878
B., Alexandre Edmond (*son of A.C.B.*), Fr. physicist 1820—1891
B., Antoine Henri (*son of A.E.B.*), Fr. physicist, discoverer of radioactivity 1852—1908
Beddoes (bed'dōş), **Thomas Lovell**, English poet 1803—1849
Bede (bēd), (*the Venerable*), English monk and ecclesiastical historian 673— 735
Bédier (bę-dyę'), **Joseph**, French literary historian 1864—1938
Beebe (bē'bē), **Charles William**, Am. biologist, author 1877—1962
Beecham (bēch'ăm), **Sir Thomas**, English conductor 1879—1961
Beecher (bēch'ẽr), **Henry Ward**, American preacher 1813—1887
B., Lyman (*father of H.W.B. and Harriet Beecher Stowe*), American clergyman and theologian 1775—1863
Beechey (bēch'i), **Frederick William**, Eng. navigator 1796—1856
Beechey, Sir William, English portrait painter 1753—1839
Beer (bēr), **George Louis**, American historian 1872—1920
Beer, Thomas, American author 1889—1940
Beerbohm (bēr'bōm), **Sir Max**, Eng. caricaturist, author 1872—1956
Beers, (bērş), **Clifford Whittingham**, Am. promoter of mental hygiene 1876—1943
Beethoven, van (vän be'tō-ven), **Ludwig**, German composer 1770—1827
Begin (bę'gin), **Menahem, Israeli prime minister (1977–), b. in Poland 1913—**
Behaim (bę'hīm), **Martin**, German navigator, geographer 1459?–1506
Beham (bę'häm), **Hans Sebald**, German painter, engraver 1500—1550
Behn (bęn), **Aphra**, Eng. dramatist, novelist, and poet 1640—1689
Behring, von (fǫn bę'ring), **Emil**, German physician 1854—1917
Behrman (bęr'măn), **Samuel Nathaniel**, Am. playwright 1893—1973
Beke (bēk), **Charles Tilstone**, English traveler and author 1800—1874

Belasco (bel-as'çō), **David**, American actor, theater manager, and playwright 1854—1931
Belcher (bel'chẽr), **Sir Edward**, Eng. explorer, admiral 1799—1877
Belinsky (bye-lyin'skē), **Vissarion Grigoryevich**, Russian literary critic 1810—1848
Belisarius (bel-i-sā'ri-us), Roman general 505?– 565
Belknap (bel'nap), **Jeremy**, American historian 1744—1798
Belknap, William Worth, U. S. sec. of war under Grant 1829—1890
Bell (bel), **Alexander Graham**, American scientist, inventor of the telephone, b. in Scotland 1847—1922
Bell, Sir Charles, British anatomist and physiologist 1774—1842
Bell, Clive, English art and literary critic 1881—
Bell, Gertrude, English explorer and writer 1868—1926
Bellamy (bel'lå-my), **Edward**, Am. author, political theorist 1850—1898
Bellini (bel-lī'nī), **Jacopo**, Venetian painter 1400?–1470?
B., Gentile (*son of J.B.*), Venetian painter 1429?–1507
B., Giovanni (*son of J.B.*), Venetian painter, teacher 1430?–1516
Bellini, Vincenzo, Sicilian composer 1801—1835
Bellman (bel'măn), **Carl Michael**, Swedish poet 1740—1795
Belloc (bel'loç), **Hilaire**, English author, born in France 1870—1953
Bellow (bel'ō), **Saul**, American author, born in Canada 1915—
Bellows (bel'lōş), **George Wesley**, American painter 1882—1925
Bellows, Henry Whitney, American Unitarian clergyman 1814—1882
Belmont (bel'mont), **August**, Am. financier, b. in Germany 1816—1890
Belmonte (bel-mōn'tę), **Juan**, Spanish bullfighter 1892—1962
Bemis (bē'mis), **Samuel Flagg**, American historian 1891—1954
Benavente (bę-nä-ven'tę), **Jacinto**, Spanish dramatist 1866—1954
Benbow (ben'bō), **John**, English admiral 1653—1702
Benchley (bench'li), **Robert Charles**, American humorist 1889—1945
Benedict (ben'e-diçt) **XIV**, (*Prospero Lambertini*), Pope 1675—1758
Benedict XV, (*Giacomo della Chiesa*), Pope (1914–22) 1854—1922
Benedict, Saint, Italian founder of the Benedictine order 480— 543
Benelli (bę-nel'lī), **Sem**, Italian dramatist 1875—1949
Beneš (ben'esh), **Eduard**, president of Czechoslovakia (1935–38, 1940–48) 1884—1948
Benét (be-nę'), **Stephen Vincent**, American poet, novelist 1898—1943
B., William Rose (*brother of S.V.B.*), poet, editor 1886—1950
Ben-Gurion (ben-gů'ri-ŏn), **David**, Israeli statesman, b. in Poland; first prime minister (1948–53, 1955–63) 1886—1973
Benjamin (ben'jå-min), **Judah Philip**, American statesman 1811—1884
Bennett (ben'net), **(Enoch) Arnold**, English novelist 1867—1931
Bennett, James Gordon, American journalist; founder of New York *Herald* 1795—1872
B., James Gordon (*Jr.*), newspaper publisher 1841—1918
Bennett, Richard Bedford, Viscount, Canadian statesman and prime minister (1930–35) 1870—1947
Bennett, Sir William Sterndale, Eng. pianist, composer 1816—1875
Benny (ben'ny), **Jack** (b. *Benjamin Kubelsky*), American comedian 1894—1974
Benoît (be-nwo'), **Pierre**, French novelist 1886—1962
Benson (ben'sŏn), **Edward Frederick**, English novelist 1867—1940
Benson, Ezra Taft, U.S. secretary of agriculture 1899—
Benson, Frank Weston, American artist 1862—1951
Bentham (ben'tăm *or* ben'thăm), **Jeremy**, English philosopher, theorist of utilitarianism 1748—1832
Bentley (bent'li), **Phyllis**, English novelist 1894—1977
Bentley, Richard, English classical scholar 1662—1742
Benton (ben'tŏn), **Thomas Hart**, American statesman 1782—1858
B., Thomas Hart (*grandnephew of T.H.B.*), Am. painter 1889—1975
Ben-Zvi (ben-tsvī'), **Itzhak**, second president of Israel (1952–63) 1884—1963
Béranger, de (dē bę-räṅ-zę') **Pierre Jean**, Fr. poet 1780—1857
Berchtold, von (fǫn berkh'tōlt), **Leopold, Count**, Austro-Hungarian foreign minister (1912–15) 1863—1942
Berenson (ber'en-sŏn), **Bernard**, American art critic 1865—1959
Beresford (ber'eş-fŏrd), **William Carr, Viscount**, Brit. general 1768—1854
Beresford, Charles William, Baron, English admiral 1846—1919
Berg (berk), **Alban**, Austrian composer 1885—1935
Bergerac, de (dē ber-zē-răç'), **Savinien Cyrano**, French dramatist, novelist, and duelist 1619—1655
Bergerat (ber-zē-rå'), **Auguste Emile**, French writer 1845—1923
Bergh (bẽrg), **Henry**, American philanthropist 1811—1888
Bergman (ber'ĭ-män), **Ingmar**, Swedish stage and film director 1918—
Bergner (berg'nẽr), **Elisabeth** (*Mrs. Paul Czinner*), English actress, born in Austria 1900?—
Bergson (berg-soṅ'), **Henri**, French philosopher 1859—1941
Beria (be'ryä), **Lavrenti Pavlovich**, Russian Communist leader, head of secret police, and vice premier; executed for treason 1899?–1953
Bering (bę'ring *or* ber'ing), **Vitus**, Danish navigator 1680—1741
Berkeley (bẽrk'li *or* bärk'li), **George**, Irish philosopher 1685—1753
Berkeley, Sir William, royal governor of Virginia 1606—1677
Berle (bẽr'lē), **Adolph August**, American lawyer 1895—1971
Berlichingen, von (fǫn ber'lich-ing-en), **Götz**, German warrior 1480—1562
Berlin (bẽr-lin'), **Irving** (b. *Irving Baline*), American composer, born in Russia 1888—
Berlioz (ber'lī-ōz), **Hector**, French composer 1803—1869
Bernadotte (bẽr-nå-dot'), **Folke, Count**, Swedish-born United Nations mediator in Palestine; assassinated 1895—1948
Bernadotte, Jean Baptiste Jules, Fr. marshal; as Charles XIV John, king of Sweden and Norway 1764—1844
Bernard (ber-når'), **Claude**, French physiologist 1813—1878
Bernard (bẽr'nård), **Sir Francis**, Am. colonial governor 1712—1779
Bernard (ber-når') **of Clairvaux, Saint**, Fr. churchman 1091—1153
Bernays (bẽr'nāş), **Edward L.**, American public relations counsel, b. in Austria 1891—
Bernhardt (bern'härt), **Sarah** (b. *Rosine Bernard*), French actress 1844—1923
Bernini (ber-nī'nī), **Giovanni Lorenzo**, Italian architect 1598—1680
Bernoulli (ber-nö-yī'), **Daniel**, Swiss mathematician 1700—1782
Bernstein (bern-staṅ'), **Henri Léon**, French dramatist 1876—1953
Bernstein (bẽrn'stīn), **Leonard**, Am. conductor, composer 1918—
Bernstorff, von (fǫn bern'stǫrf), **Johann Heinrich, Count**, German diplomat; ambassador to U.S. (1908–17) 1862—1939
Berthelot (bert-lō'), **Pierre Marcellin**, French chemist 1827—1907
Bertillon (ber-tī-yoṅ'), **Alphonse**, French criminologist 1853—1914
Berwick (bẽr'ik), **James Fitz-James, Duke of**, marshal of France 1670—1734
Berzelius (bẽr-zē'lī-us *or* ber-sę'lī-us), **Jons Jakob, Baron**, Swedish chemist 1779—1848
Besant (beş'ănt), **Annie (Wood)**, English theosophist 1847—1933
Besant (bē-şant'), **Sir Walter**, English novelist 1836—1901
Besnard (be-når'), **Paul Albert**, French painter 1849—1934

Bessemer (bes'se-mẽr), **Sir Henry,** English inventor...........1813—1898
Best (best), **Charles Herbert,** Canadian physiologist...........1899—1978
Bethe (bā'tē), **Hans Albrecht,** American theoretical physicist, b. in Germany...........1906—
Bethlen (beth'len), **Stephen, Count,** Hungarian statesman.....1874—1950
Bethmann-Hollweg, von (fọn bẹt'män-hōl'vẹk), **Theobald,** chancellor of Germany (1909–17)...........1856—1921
Betjeman (bech'e-măn), **John,** English poet...........1906—
Betterton (bet'ẽr-tŏn), **Thomas,** Eng. actor, theater manager...1635?–1710
Beveridge (bev'ẽr-ig), **Albert Jeremiah,** American historian, biographer, and senator...........1862—1927
Beveridge, William Henry, Baron, British economist...........1879—1963
Bevin (be'vin), **Ernest,** Brit. labor party leader; minister of labor (1940–45); foreign minister (1945–51)...........1881—1951
Beyle (bẹl), **Marie Henri,** *see* Stendhal.
Beza (bē'zȧ), **Théodore,** French reformer...........1519—1605
Bialik (byä'lik), **Chaim Nachman,** Hebrew poet, translator, and novelist, b. in Russia...........1873—1934
Bichat (bī-çhȧ'), **Marie François Xavier,** French physiologist and medical writer...........1771—1802
Bidault (bī-dō'), **Georges,** French statesman...........1899—
Biddle (bid'l), **Francis,** U.S. attorney general (1941–45)...........1886—1968
Biddle, John, father of English Unitarianism...........1615—1662
Biddle, Nicholas, American financier...........1786—1844
Biela, von (fọn bē'lȧ), **Wilhelm, Baron,** German astronomer....1782—1856
Bienville, de (dē byaṅ-vīl'), **Jean Baptiste Le Moyne, Sieur,** French governor of Louisiana...........1680—1768
Bierce (bẽrc), **Ambrose,** American writer...........1842–1914?
Bilderdijk (bil'dẽr-dīk), **Willem,** Dutch poet...........1756—1831
Billings (bil'lings), **Josh,** *see* Shaw, Henry W.
Binet (bī-ne'), **Alfred,** French psychologist...........1857—1911
Binns (binṣ), **Archie,** American novelist...........1899—
Binyon (bin'yŏn), **Laurence,** English poet, playwright, and critic.1869—1943
Bion (bī'ŏn) **of Smyrna,** Greek bucolic poet...........fl. 2d cent. B.C.
Biot (bī-ō'), **Jean Baptiste,** French physicist...........1774—1862
Birkenhead (bĩr'ken-hed), **Frederick Edwin Smith, first Earl of,** English lawyer, statesman, and author...........1872—1930
Birrell (bĩr'el), **Augustine,** English essayist, biographer...........1850—1933
Bishop (bish'ŏp), **Sir Henry Rowley,** English composer...........1786—1855
Bismarck, von (fọn bis'märk), **Otto Eduard Leopold, Prince,** Prussian statesman...........1815—1898
Bitter (bit'tẽr), **Karl Theodore Francis,** Am. sculptor...........1867—1915
Bizet (bī-zẹ'), **Georges** (b. *Alexander César Léopold B.*), French operatic composer...........1838—1875
Björnson (byŏrn'sŏn), **Björnstjerne,** Norwegian novelist, poet, and dramatist...........1832—1910
Black (blak), **Hugo La Fayette,** American jurist; associate justice of U.S. Supreme Court (1937–71)...........1886—1971
Black, Jeremiah, American statesman...........1810—1883
Black Hawk (blak hạk), Sac Indian chief...........1767—1838
Blackie (blak'i), **John Stuart,** Scot. classical scholar...........1809—1895
Blackmore (blak'mōr), **Richard Doddridge,** Eng. novelist...........1825—1900
Blackmun (blak'mun), **Harry Andrew,** associate justice of the U.S. Supreme Court (1970–)...........1908—
Blackstone (blak'stŏn), **Sir William,** English judge and law commentator...........1723—1780
Blackwood (blak'wood), **Algernon,** English novelist...........1869—1951
Blaine (blān), **James Gillespie,** American statesman...........1830—1893
Blair (blãr), **Francis Preston,** American politician...........1791—1876
  B., Francis Preston (*son of F.P.B.*), American soldier and politician...........1821—1875
  B., Montgomery (*son of F.P.B., Sr.*), American lawyer and politician...........1813—1883
Blair, Robert, English poet...........1699—1746
Blake (blāk), **Robert,** British admiral...........1599—1657
Blake, William, English poet and artist...........1757—1827
Blanc (blăṅ), **Jean Joseph Louis,** French socialist, publicist, and historian...........1811—1882
Blasco Ibáñez (bläs'çō ī-bän'yẹth), **Vicente,** Spanish novelist...1867—1928
Blashfield (blash'fēld), **Edwin Howland,** Am. painter...........1848—1936
Blavatsky (blȧ-vät'sky), **Helena Petrovna** (b. *Hahn*), Russian theosophist...........1831—1891
Blennerhassett (blen-nẽr-has'set), **Harman,** Irish accomplice of Aaron Burr...........1765—1831
Blériot (blẹ-rī-ō'), **Louis,** French aviator and inventor...........1872—1936
Bligh (blī), **William,** English naval officer: commander of the *Bounty,* whose crew mutinied...........1754—1817
Bliss (blis), **Tasker Howard,** American general...........1853—1930
Blixen (bliks'en), **Karen,** *see* Dinesen, Isak.
Bloch (bloçh), **Ernest,** Am. composer, b. in Switzerland...........1880—1959
Bloch, Felix, American physicist, b. in Switzerland...........1905—
Bloch, Jean Richard, French novelist...........1884—1947
Blok (blăk), **Alexandr Alexandrovich,** Russian poet...........1880—1921
Bloomer (bloom'ẽr), **Amelia Jenks,** American reformer...........1818—1894
Bloomfield (bloom'fēld), **Leonard,** American linguist...........1887—1949
Bloomgarden (bloom'gär-dn), **Solomon** (pseud. *Yehoash*), American writer in Yiddish, born in Lithuania...........1870—1927
Blücher, von (fọn blü'khẽr), **Gebhard Leberecht,** Prussian field marshal; helped defeat Napoleon at Waterloo...........1742—1819
Blum (blům), **Léon,** Fr. Socialist leader, premier, writer...........1872—1950
Blumenbach (blů'men-bäkh), **Johann Friedrich,** German physiologist and anthropologist...........1752—1840
Blunden (blun'den), **Edmund Charles,** Eng. poet, critic...........1896—1974
Blunt (blunt), **Wilfred Scawen,** English poet...........1840—1922
Boadicea (bō-ȧ-di-sē'ȧ), British queen...........?—A.D.62
Boas (bō'äs), **Franz,** Am. anthropologist, b. in Germany...........1858—1942
Boccaccio (boç-çät'chō), **Giovanni,** Italian author...........1313—1375
Boccherini (boç-çe-rī'nī), **Luigi,** Italian composer...........1743—1805
Boccioni (bot-cho'nē), **Umberto,** Italian futurist painter...........1882—1916
Bode (bō'de), **Johann Elert,** German astronomer...........1747—1826
Bodenheim (bō'den-hīm), **Maxwell,** Am. poet, novelist...........1893—1954
Bodin (bō-daṅ'), **Jean,** French political writer...........1530—1596
Bodoni (bō-dō'nī), **Giambattista,** Italian typographer...........1740—1813
Boem (bẹm), **Sir Joseph Edgar,** Eng. sculptor, b. in Austria....1834—1890
Boerhaave (bōr'hä-ve), **Hermann,** Dutch physician and chemist.1668—1738
Boethius (bō-ē'thi-us), **Anicius Manlius Severinus,** Roman philosopher and statesman...........475?–525?
Bogan (bō'găn), **Louise,** American poet...........1897—1970
Bohm (bōm), **Max,** American painter...........1868—1923
Böhme (bē'me), **Jakob,** German mystic and writer...........1575—1624
Bohr (bōr), **Niels Henrik David,** Danish physicist; researcher in quantum theory and atomic nuclei...........1885—1962
Boiardo (bō-yär'dō), **Matteo Maria,** Italian poet...........1434—1494
Boileau-Despréaux (bwȧ-lō'dẹ-pre-ō'), **Nicolas,** French poet, satirist, and critic...........1636—1711
Boisrobert, de (dē bwȧ-rō-ber'), **François le Metel,** French writer and wit...........1592—1662
Bojer (boi'ẽr), **Johan,** Norwegian novelist, dramatist...........1872—1959
Bok (bok), **Edward William,** Am. editor and author...........1863—1930
Boker (bō'kẽr), **George Henry,** Am. poet and playwright...........1823—1890
Boleyn (bool'in), **Anne,** wife of Henry VIII of England...........1507—1536
Bolingbroke (bol'ing-brook), **Henry St. John, Viscount,** English statesman and political writer...........1678—1751
Bolitho (bō-lī'thō), **William** (b. *W.B. Ryall*), Brit. author...........1890—1930
Bolívar (bol'i-vȧr *or Am. Sp.* bō-lī'vär), **Simón,** liberator of Venezuela, Colombia, Ecuador, and Peru...........1783—1830
Bologna, da (dä bō-lōn'yä), **Giovanni,** Flemish sculptor in Italy.1524—1608
Bonaparte (bō'nȧ-pärt) *or* **Buonaparte** (bwō-nä-pär'tẹ), family including the emperors Napoleon and the following (brothers of Napoleon I):
  B., Jérôme, king of Westphalia...........1784—1860
  B., Joseph, king of Naples and of Spain...........1768—1844
  B., Louis, king of Holland...........1778—1846
  B., Lucien, prince of Canino...........1775—1840
Bonar (bŏn'ȧr), **Horatius,** Scot. poet, hymn writer...........1808—1889
Bonaventura (bō-nä-ven-tū'rȧ), **Saint** (called the *Seraphic Doctor*), Italian scholastic theologian...........1221—1274
Bond (bond), **Carrie Jacobs,** American song writer...........1862—1946
Bond, George Phillips (*son of W.C.B.*), Am. astronomer...........1825—1865
  B., William Cranch, American astronomer...........1789—1859
Bone (bōn), **Sir Muirhead,** British etcher and painter...........1876—1953
Bonheur (bō-nũr'), **Rosa,** French painter of animals...........1822—1899
Boniface (bon'i-fāc) **VIII,** (*Benedetto Gaetano*), Pope...........1235?–1303
Boniface, Winfrid, Saint (*Apostle of Germany*), Eng. missionary...........680?— 755
Bonnard (bō-när'), **Pierre,** French impressionist painter...........1867—1947
Bonnat (bọ-nȧ'), **Léon Joseph Florentin,** French painter...........1833—1922
Bonnet (bọ-ne'), **Georges,** French politician...........1889—1973
Bonnivard, de (dē bō-nī-vär'), **François** (*Prisoner of Chillon*), Swiss nationalist leader...........1493?–1570
Bononcini (bō-nōn-chī'nī), **Giovanni Battista,** It. composer..1672? 1750?
Bonpland (bọṅ-pläṅ'), **Aimé,** French naturalist...........1773—1858
Boone (bọọn), **Daniel,** American explorer and colonizer...........1734—1820
Boorde (bōrd), **Andrew** (*Merry Andrew*), English physician and author...........1490?–1549
Booth (bọọth), **Barton,** English actor...........1681—1733
Booth, Charles, English sociologist...........1840—1916
Booth, Edwin (*son of J.B.B.*), American actor...........1833—1893
  B., John Wilkes (*son of J.B.B.*), actor; murderer of Lincoln....1838—1865
  B., Junius Brutus, English tragedian...........1796—1852
Booth, William, Eng. evangelist; founder of Salvation Army....1829—1912
  B., Ballington (*son of W.B.*), founder of Volunteers of America.1859—1940
  B., Evangeline Cory (*daughter of W.B.*), general of Salvation Army...........1865—1950
Boothe (bọọth), **Clare** (*Mrs. Henry R.Luce*), American playwright and politician...........1903—
Borah (bō'rȧ), **William Edgar,** American statesman...........1865—1940
Bordeaux (bōr-dō'), **Henri,** French novelist and critic...........1870—1963
Borden (bọr'den), **Gail,** American inventor...........1801—1874
Borden, Mary, American novelist...........1886—1968
Borden, Sir Robert Laird, Canadian premier...........1854—1937
Bordet (bōr-de'), **Jules,** Belgian immunologist...........1870—1961
Borgese (bōr-ġẹ'ṣẹ), **Giuseppe Antonio,** American author, b. in Italy...........1882—1952
Borgia (bọr'ġȧ), **Cesare** (*son of Pope Alexander VI*), Italian cardinal and military leader...........1476?–1507
  B., Lucrezia (*daughter of Pope Alexander VI*), duchess of Ferrara...........1480—1519
Borglum (bọr'glum), **John Gutzon,** American sculptor...........1867—1941
Borgognone (bọr-gōn-yō'nẹ), (*Ambrogio Stefani da Fossano*) Italian painter...........1445?–1523?
Bori (bō'rī), **Lucrezia,** Sp. operatic soprano in America...........1887—1960
Boris (bō'ris) **III,** (*son of Ferdinand I*), king of Bulgaria (1918–43).1894—1943
Born (bọrn), **Max,** German nuclear physicist...........1882—1970
Borodin (bō-rō-dīn'), **Aleksandr Porfirevich,** Russian scientist and composer...........1834—1887
Borrow (bor'rō), **George,** English writer and traveler...........1803—1881
Bosanquet (bō'ṣăn-ket), **Bernard,** English philosopher...........1848—1923
Boscán Almogaver (bōs-çăn' äl-mō-gä-ver'), **Juan,** Spanish poet.1495—1542
Bosch (bos), **Hieronymus,** Flemish painter...........1460?–1516?
Bose (bōs), **Sir Jagadis Chandra,** Indian physicist and plant physiologist...........1858—1937
Bossi (bos'sī), **Giuseppe,** It. painter and writer on art...........1777—1816
Bossuet (bọs-swe'), **Jacques Bénigne,** Fr. bishop, orator...........1627—1704
Boswell (boṣ'wel), **James,** Scottish biographer...........1740—1795
Botha (bō'tä), **Louis,** Boer commander...........1862—1919
Bothwell (both'wel), **James Hepburn, fourth Earl of,** third husband of Mary, Queen of Scots...........1536?–1578
Botticelli (bot-tī-chel'lī), **Sandro,** Italian painter...........1444?–1510
Bottome (bot-tōm'), **Phyllis,** English novelist...........1884—1963
Bouchardon (bö-çhär-dọṅ'), **Edmé,** French sculptor...........1698—1762
Boucher (bö-çhẹ'), **François,** French painter...........1703—1770
Boucher de Crèvecoeur de Perthes (bö-çhẹ' dē çrev-çũr' dē pert'), **Jacques,** French anthropologist, writer...........1788—1868
Boucicault (bö'ci-çạlt), **Dion,** Ir. dramatist, actor...........1822—1890
Boudinot (bö'dī-not), **Elias,** American statesman...........1740—1821
Bougainville, de (dē bö-gaṅ-vīl'), **Louis Antoine,** French navigator and colonizer...........1729—1811
Bouguereau (bö-ge-rō'), **Adolphe William,** French painter....1825—1905
Bouillé, de (dē bö-yẹ'), **François Claude Amour, Marquis,** French general and author...........1739—1800
Bouillon, de (dē bö-yọṅ'), **Henri de la Tour d'Auvergne, Duc,** French marshal...........1555—1623
Boulanger (bö-läṅ-zẹ'), **George Ernest,** Fr. general...........1837—1891
Bourbon, de (dē bör-bọṅ'), **Charles, Duc,** Fr. general...........1490—1527
Bourget (bör-zẹ'), **Paul Charles Joseph,** French writer...........1852—1935
Bourke-White (bũrk'hwīt'), **Margaret,** Am. photographer...........1905—1971
Bourne (bōrn), **Randolph Silliman,** American writer...........1886—1918
Bouvart (bö-vär'), **Alexis,** French astronomer...........1767—1843
Bouvier (bö-vẽr'), **John,** American jurist and law writer...........1787—1851

Bowditch (bou'dich), **Nathaniel**, American navigator and mathematician ....1773—1838
Bowdoin (bō'dn), **James**, Am. patriot and governor ....1726—1790
Bowen (bō'en), **Elizabeth**, British novelist ....1899—1973
Bowers (bou'ẽrș), **Claude Gernade**, American author, journalist, and ambassador ....1878—1958
Bowles (bōlș), **Chester Bliss**, U.S. ambassador ....1901—
Bowles, Samuel, American journalist ....1826—1878
Bowles, William Lisle, English poet and critic ....1762—1850
Bowman (bō'măn), **Isaiah**, American geographer ....1878—1950
Bowring (bou'ring), **Sir John**, Brit. statesman, translator ....1792—1872
Boyd (boid), **Ernest**, Am. essayist, critic, and translator ....1887—1946
Boyd, James, American novelist ....1888—1944
Boyle (boil), **Kay**, American novelist and short-story writer ....1903—
Boyle, Robert, English physicist and chemist ....1627—1691
Bozeman (bōz'măn), **John M.**, American pioneer ....1835—1867
Bozzaris (bō-zär'is), **Marcos**, Greek patriot and general ....1788—1823
Braddock (brad'dŏk), **Edward**, Brit. general in America ....1695—1755
Bradford (brad'fŏrd), **Gamaliel**, American biographer ....1863—1932
Bradford, Roark, American short-story writer ....1896—1948
Bradford, William, second governor of Plymouth colony ....1590—1657
Bradley (brad'li), **Omar Nelson**, American general in World War II; chairman of joint chiefs of staff ....1893—1981
Bradstreet (brad'strēt), **Anne**, American colonial poet ....1612?—1672
B., Simon (*husband of A.B.*), colonial governor ....1603—1697
Brady (brā'dy), **Mathew B.**, American photographer, notably of Lincoln and Civil War scenes ....1823—1896
Braga (brä'gä), **Teófilo**, president of Portugal (1910–11) ....1843—1924
Bragg (brag), **Braxton**, American Confederate general ....1817—1876
Bragg, Sir William Henry, English physicist ....1862—1942
B., Sir William Lawrence (*son of W.H.B.*), physicist ....1890—1971
Brahe (brä *or* brä'e), **Tycho**, Danish astronomer ....1546—1601
Brahms (brämș), **Johannes**, German composer ....1833—1897
Brainerd (brān'ẽrd), **David**, missionary to the American Indians; diarist ....1718—1747
Bramante (brä-män'tẹ), **Donato d'Agnolo**, It. architect ....1444—1514
Brancusi (brän'kọọsh), **Constantin**, Romanian sculptor ....1876—1957
Brandeis (bran'dīs), **Louis Dembitz**, associate justice of U.S. Supreme Court (1916–39) ....1856—1941
Brandes (brän'des), **Georg Morris** (b. *Cohen*), Dan. critic ....1842—1927
Brant (brant), **Joseph** (b. *Thayendanegea*), Mohawk chief ....1742—1807
Branting (bränt'ing), **Karl Hjalmar**, Swed. statesman ....1860—1925
Braque (bräk), **Georges**, French painter ....1881—1963
Braslau (bras'lạ), **Sophie**, American singer ....1892—1935
Bratianu (brä-ti-ä'nụ'), **John**, Romanian statesman ....1864—1927
Brauchitsch, von (fọn brou'khich), **Walther**, German field marshal; com. in chief at beginning of World War II ....1881—1948
Breasted (brest'ed), **James Henry**, Am. Egyptologist ....1865—1935
Brecht (brekht), **Bertolt**, German expressionist dramatist ....1898—1956
Breckinridge (brek'in-rij), **John Cabell**, U.S. vice-president (1857–61); Confederate secretary of war ....1821—1875
Bremer (brem'ẽr), **Fredrika**, Swedish novelist ....1801—1865
Brennan (bren'năn), **William Joseph, Jr.**, associate justice of U.S. Supreme Court (1956–) ....1906—
Brentano (bren-tän'ō), **Clemens**, German poet ....1778—1842
Breton (bre-tọṅ'), **André**, Fr. surrealist writer, critic ....1896—1966
Breton (bre'tŏn), **Nicholas**, English poet ....1545—1626
Breughel (brū'gel), **Pieter**, Flemish painter ....1525?—1569
B., Jan (*son of P.B.*), (*Velvet Breughel*) Flemish painter ....1568—1625
Brewster (brū'stẽr), **William**, Plymouth Pilgrim leader ....1567—1644
Brezhnev (brez-nọf'), **Leonid Ilich**, general secretary of the Communist Party of the U.S.S.R. (1964–) ....1906—
Brian Boroihme (brī'ăn bō'roim') *or* **Brian Boru** (bō-rö'), king of Ireland ....926—1014
Briand (brī-äṅ'), **Aristide**, French statesman and premier (1909–11, 1921–22, 1925–26, 1929) ....1862—1932
Bridger (brij'ẽr), **James**, Am. fur trader and guide ....1804—1881
Bridges (brij'eș), **Calvin Blackman**, American geneticist ....1889—1938
Bridges, Robert, English physician; poet laureate ....1844—1930
Bridget (brij'et), **Saint**, patroness of Ireland ....453— 523
Brieux (brī-ū'), **Eugène**, French dramatist ....1858—1932
Briggs (brigș), **Le Baron Russell**, American educator ....1855—1934
Bright (brīt), **John**, English statesman and orator ....1811—1889
Bright, Richard, English physician ....1789—1858
Brill (bril), **Abraham Arden**, American psychoanalyst, b. in Austria; translator and exponent of Freud ....1874—1948
Brill, Nathan Edwin, American physician ....1860—1925
Brillat-Savarin (brī-yä'sȧ-vȧ-raṅ'), **Anthelme**, French magistrate and gastronomist ....1755—1826
Brisbane (briș'bān), **Arthur**, American newspaper editor ....1864—1936
Brissot de Warville (brī-sō' dẽ vȧr-vīl'), **Jacques Pierre**, French lawyer and Girondist ....1754—1793
Britten (brit'ten), **(Edward) Benjamin**, Eng. composer ....1913—1976
Britton (brit'tŏn), **Nathaniel Lord**, American botanist ....1859—1934
Brock (brok), **Sir Isaac**, British general in War of 1812 ....1769—1812
Brodie (brō'di), **Sir Benjamin Collins**, English surgeon ....1783—1862
Broglie, de (dẽ brō'lyẹ), **Jacques Victor Albert, Duc**, French statesman and historian ....1821—1901
B., de, Louis Victor, Prince (*grandson of J.V.A.B.*), French physicist ....1892—
B., de, Maurice, Duke (*brother of L.V.B.*), physicist ....1875—1960
Brome (brōm), **Richard**, English dramatist ....? —1652
Bromfield (brom'fēld), **Louis**, American novelist ....1896—1956
Brongniart (bro-nyȧr'), **Alexandre**, French scientist ....1770—1847
Brontë (bron'ti), **Anne** (pseud. *Acton Bell*), (*sister of C.B. and E.B.*) English novelist and poet ....1820—1849
B., Charlotte (pseud. *Currer Bell*), English novelist and poet ....1816—1855
B., Emily (pseud. *Ellis Bell*), English novelist and poet ....1818—1848
Bronzino, Il (īl brŏn-tsī'nō), (b. *Agnolo di Cosimo Allori*), Italian painter ....1502?—1572
Brook (brook), **Alexander**, American painter ....1898—
Brooke (brook), **Alan Francis, Viscount Alanbrooke**, Brit. general; chief of imperial staff (1941–46) ....1883—
Brooke, Fulk Greville, first Baron, English poet ....1554—1628
Brooke, Henry, Irish author ....1703?—1783
Brooke, Rupert, English poet ....1887—1915
Brooke, Stopford Augustus, Eng. clergyman and writer ....1832—1916
Brooks (brooks), **Phillips**, American clergyman ....1835—1893
Brooks, Van Wyck, American critic and historian ....1886—1963

Broome (brọọm), **William**, English poet ....1689—1745
Brougham (brō'ăm), **Henry, Lord**, British statesman ....1778—1868
Broun (brōn), **Heywood Campbell**, American columnist ....1888—1939
Brouwer (brou'wẽr), **Adriaen**, Flemish painter ....1606?—1638
Browder (brou'dẽr), **Earl Russell**, American Communist leader ....1891—1973
Brown (broun), **Benjamin Gratz**, U.S. politician ....1826—1885
Brown, Charles Brockden, American novelist ....1771—1810
Brown, Ford Madox, English pre-Raphaelite painter ....1821—1893
Brown, Jacob Jennings, American major general ....1775—1828
Brown, John (*of Osawatomie*), American abolitionist ....1800—1859
Brown, Thomas, English humorist ....1663—1704
Browne (broun), **Charles Farrar** (pseud. *Artemus Ward*), American humorist ....1834—1867
Browne, Lewis, American rabbi and author, b. in England ....1897—1949
Browne, Sir Thomas, English physician and author ....1605—1682
Browne, William, English poet ....1591—1645?
Browning (broun'ing), **Elizabeth Barrett** (*wife of R.B.*), English poet ....1806—1861
Browning, John Moses, American inventor ....1855—1926
Browning, Robert (*husband of E.B.B.*), English poet ....1812—1889
Brownlow (broun'lō), **William G.**, Am. politician, preacher ....1805—1877
Brown-Séquard (broun-sẹ-kȧr'), **Charles Édouard**, physiologist, b. in Mauritius, of Am. and Fr. parents ....1817—1894
Bruce (brūc), **Robert the**, king of Scotland (1306–29) ....1274—1329
Bruce, Stanley Melbourne, Viscount, Australian statesman; prime minister (1923–29) ....1883—1967
Bruckner (brụk'nẽr), **Anton**, Austrian composer ....1824—1896
Brugsch (brụgsh), **Heinrich Karl**, German Egyptologist ....1827—1894
Brunelleschi (brū-nel-les'ḳhī), **Filippo**, Florentine architect ....1377—1446
Brunetière (brū-ne-tyer'), **Ferdinand**, French critic ....1849—1906
Brüning (brū'ning), **Heinrich**, German statesman; chancellor (1930–32); became (1937) Harvard U. professor ....1885—1970
Bruno (brū'nō), **Giordano**, Italian philosopher ....1548?—1600
Brush (brush), **Charles Francis**, American inventor ....1849—1929
Brusilov (brụ-sī'lọf), **Aleksey Alekseyevich**, Russian general ....1853—1926
Brutus (brū'tus), **Lucius Junius**, Roman statesman ....fl.500 B.C.
Brutus, Marcus Junius, Roman statesman; murderer of Caesar ....B.C. 85— 42
Bryan (brȳ'ăn), **William Jennings**, American statesman and orator; secretary of state (1913–15) ....1860—1925
Bryant (brȳ'ănt), **Jacob**, English antiquary ....1715—1804
Bryant, William Cullen, American journalist and poet ....1794—1878
Bryce (brȳc), **James, Viscount**, English statesman, diplomat, and historian ....1838—1922
Buchan (buḳh'ăn), **John, first Baron Tweedsmuir**, Scottish novelist and historian; governor general of Canada ....1875—1940
Buchanan (bū-ḳhan'ăn), **George**, Scot. historian, poet ....1506—1582
Buchanan, James, 15th U.S. president (1857–61) ....1791—1868
Buchanan, Robert William, Eng. poet, novelist, dramatist ....1841—1901
Buchman (bụḳh'măn), **Frank Nathan Daniel**, American clergyman; leader of Buchmanism ....1878—1961
Buck (buk), **Dudley**, American composer ....1839—1909
Buck, Pearl (Sydenstricker), (*Mrs. Richard J. Walsh*), American novelist ....1892—1973
Buckingham (buk'ing-hăm), **George Villiers, first Duke of**, English lord high admiral ....1592—1628
Buckle (buk'l), **George Earle**, English journalist and biographer ....1854—1935
Buckle, Henry Thomas, English historian ....1821—1862
Buckner (buk'nẽr), **Simon Bolivar**, Confederate general ....1823—1914
Buddha, *see* Gautama.
Budé (bū-dẹ') *or* **Budaeus** (bū-dē'us), **Guillaume**, French scholar 1467—1540
Budenny (bū-den'ny), **Semyon Mikhailovich**, Russ. marshal ....1883—1973
Buell (bū'el), **Don Carlos**, American general ....1818—1898
Buell, Raymond Leslie, American publicist ....1896—1946
Buffalo Bill, *see* Cody, William Frederick.
Buffon, de (dẽ bū-fọṅ'), **Georges Louis Leclerc, Comte**, French naturalist ....1707—1788
Bugeaud de la Piconnerie (bū-ẓō' dẽ lȧ pī-ḳọn-rē'), **Thomas Robert**, French marshal ....1784—1849
Bukharin (bụk-hä'rīn), **Nikolai Ivanovich**, Russian Communist leader and theoretician; executed ....1888—1938
Bulfinch (bụl'finch), **Charles**, American architect ....1763—1844
B., Thomas (*son of C.B.*), Am. author and mythologist ....1796—1867
Bulganin (bụl-gä'nīn), **Nikolai Aleksandrovich**, Russian Communist leader, marshal, and premier (1955–1958) ....1895?—1975
Bulgarin (bụl-gä'rīn), **Thaddeus**, Russian novelist ....1789—1859
Bull (bụl), **Ole Bornemann**, Norwegian violinist ....1810—1880
Bullet (bụl'let), **Gerald**, English novelist ....1893—1958
Bullitt (bụl'lit), **William Christian**, American diplomat ....1891—1967
Bülow, von (fọn bū'lō), **Friedrich Wilhelm, Count of Dennewitz**, Prussian general ....1755—1816
Bulow, von, Hans Guido, German pianist, composer ....1830—1894
Bulwer (bụl'wẽr), **William Henry Lytton Earle, Baron Dalling and Bulwer**, English author and diplomat ....1801—1872
Bulwer-Lytton (-lyt'tŏn), **Edward George Earle Lytton, Baron Lytton**, English novelist and playwright ....1803—1873
B.-L., Edward Robert, Earl of Lytton (*son of E.G.E.L.*), (pseud. *Owen Meredith*), English poet ....1831—1891
Bunche (bunch), **Ralph Johnson**, U.S. government official and U.N. mediator; awarded Nobel peace prize (1950) ....1904—1971
Bunin (bụ'nyīn), **Ivan Alekseyevich**, Russian poet and novelist ....1870—1953
Bunner (bun'nẽr), **Henry Cuyler**, Am. writer ....1855—1896
Bunsen, von (fọn bụn'sen), **Christian Karl Josias, Baron**, Prussian ambassador and philologist ....1791—1860
Bunsen, Robert Wilhelm, German chemist ....1811—1899
Buntline (bunt'lin), **Ned**, *see* Judson, E. Z. C.
Bunyan (bun'yăn), **John**, English preacher and author ....1628—1688
Buonaparte, *see* Bonaparte.
Burbage (bũr'băġ), **Richard**, English actor ....1567?—1619
Burbank (bũr'baṅk), **Luther**, American horticulturist ....1849—1926
Burchfield (bũrch'fēld), **Charles Ephraim**, Am. artist ....1893—1967
Burckhardt (bũrk'härt), **Jacob**, Swiss historian ....1818—1897
Burdett-Coutts (bũr-det'çōts'), **Angela Georgina, Baroness**, English philanthropist ....1814—1906
Burdette (bũr-det'), **Robert Jones**, American humorist ....1844—1914
Burger (bũr'gẽr), **Gottfried August**, German poet ....1748—1794
Burger, Warren Earl, U.S. jurist; chief justice of the U.S. Supreme Court (1969–) ....1907—
Burgess (bũr'ges), **(Frank) Gelett**, American humorist ....1866—1951
Burgess, Thornton W., American children's writer ....1874—1965

fāte, fär, fȧst, fạll, finăl, cāre, at; mēte, prẹy, hẽr, met; pīne, marine, bīrd, pin; nōte, mŏve, fọr, atŏm, not; mọọn, book;

Burghley *or* **Burleigh** (bûr'lē), **William Cecil, first Baron,** English statesman; adviser of Queen Elizabeth I .... 1520—1598
Burgoyne (bûr-goin'), **John,** Eng. general, dramatist .... 1722—1792
Burke (bûrk), **Edmund,** British statesman and orator .... 1729—1797
Burke, Thomas, English novelist .... 1887—1945
Burlingame (bûr'liñ-gām), **Anson,** American diplomat .... 1820—1870
Burne-Jones (bûrn'jōnẓ'), **Sir Edward,** English painter .... 1833—1898
Burnet (bûr-net'), **Gilbert,** British bishop, historian .... 1643—1715
Burnett (bûr-net'), **Frances Hodgson,** Am. author, b. in England . 1849—1924
Burnett, Whit, American editor and writer .... 1899—1973
Burney (bûrn'i), **Charles,** English musician and author .... 1726—1814
B., Frances (Fanny), (*Mme. D'Arblay; daughter of C.B.*) English novelist and diarist .... 1752—1840
Burnham (bûrn'ăm), **Sherburne W.,** Am. astronomer .... 1838—1921
Burns (bûrnẓ), **Robert,** Scottish poet .... 1759—1796
Burnside (bûrn'sīd), **Ambrose Everett,** American general .... 1824—1881
Burr (bûr), **Aaron,** 3d U.S. vice-president (1801–05) .... 1756—1836
Burritt (bûr'rit), **Elihu** (*the Learned Blacksmith*), American peace advocate and linguist .... 1810—1879
Burroughs (bûr'rōẓ), **Edgar Rice,** American novelist .... 1875—1950
Burroughs, John, American naturalist .... 1837—1921
Burt (bûrt), **(Maxwell) Struthers,** American novelist .... 1882—1954
Burton (bûr'tŏn), **Harold Hitz,** associate justice of U.S. Supreme Court (1945—58) .... 1888—1964
Burton, Sir Richard Francis, Eng. explorer and author .... 1821—1890
Burton, Robert, English philosopher and author .... 1577—1640
Bury (byūr'y), **John B.,** Irish classicist and historian .... 1861—1927
Bush (bụsh), **Vannevar,** Am. engineer, administrator .... 1890—1974
Busoni (bụ-sō'nī), **Ferruccio Benvenuto,** It. composer .... 1866—1924
Bustamante, de (dẹ bụ-stä-män'tẹ), **Antonio Sanchez,** Cuban jurist; member of the Hague Tribunal .... 1865—1951
Butler (but'lẽr), **Benjamin Franklin,** American lawyer, politician, and general .... 1818—1893
Butler, Ellis Parker, American humorist .... 1869—1937
Butler, Joseph, English bishop and author .... 1692—1752
Butler, Nicholas Murray, American educator and author .... 1862—1947
Butler, Pierce, associate justice of U.S. Supreme Court (1923–39) . 1866—1939
Butler, Samuel, English poet and satirist .... 1612—1680
Butler, Samuel, English novelist .... 1835—1902
Buxtehude (bụks-te-hū'de), **Dietrich,** German composer .... 1637—1707
Buxtorf (bụks'tọrf), **Johann,** German Hebraist .... 1564—1629
Byng (byng), **Julian Hedworth George, Viscount Byng of Vimy,** British general; governor general of Canada .... 1862—1935
Bynner (byn'nẽr), **Witter,** American poet .... 1881—1968
Byrd (bird), **Richard Evelyn,** American rear admiral, aviator, and polar explorer .... 1888—1957
Byrd, William, English composer .... 1542?–1623
Byrne (birn), **Donn,** American novelist .... 1889—1928
Byrnes (birns), **James Francis,** associate justice of U.S. Supreme Court (1941–42) .... 1879—1972
Byrom (bȳ'rŏm), **John,** English satiric poet .... 1692—1763
Byron (bȳ'rŏn), **George Noel Gordon, Lord,** Eng. poet .... 1788—1824

C

Caballero (çä-bäl-yẹ'rō), **Fernan** (pseud. of *Cecilia Böhl de Faber*), Spanish novelist .... 1797—1877
Cabell (çab'el), **James Branch,** American novelist .... 1879—1958
Cabeza de Vaca (çä-bẹ'thä dẹ vä'çä), **Álvar Núñez,** Spanish explorer in the Americas .... 1490?–1557?
Cable (çā'bl), **George Washington,** American novelist .... 1844—1925
Cabot (çab'ŏt), **John,** (b. *Giovanni Caboto*), Venetian pilot and navigator .... 1450? 1498
C., Sebastian (*son of J.C.*), English navigator .... 1474?–1557?
Cabrillo (çä-brē'yō), **Juan Rodriguez,** Sapnish navigator, b. in Portugal; explored California coast .... ? —1543
Cabrini (çä-brē'nē), **Saint Frances Xavier,** Roman Catholic educator; first U.S. citizen to be canonized (1946) .... 1850—1917
Cadalso Vázquez, de (dẹ çä-thäl'sō väth'kẹth), **José,** Spanish poet and satirist .... 1741—1782
Cade (çād), **John** (*Jack Cade*) English rebel .... ? —1450
Cadillac (ça'di-laç; *Fr.* çà-dī-yàç'), **Antoine de la Mothe, Sieur,** French colonial governor in America .... 1656?–1730
Cadman (çad'măn), **Charles Wakefield,** Am. composer .... 1881—1946
Cadman, Samuel Parkes, American Congregational clergyman . 1864—1936
Cadogan (çà-dŏg'ăn), **William, first Earl of,** English general . . 1675—1726
Cadorna (çä-dọr'nä), **Luigi, Count,** Italian general .... 1850—1928
Caedmon (çad'mŏn), (*father of English song*) Anglo-Saxon poet . . fl. 670
Caesar (cē'ṣãr), **Caius Julius,** Roman general and dictator . . B.C. 100— 44
Cagliari (çä'lyä-rī), **Paolo,** *see* Veronese, Paolo.
Cagliostro (çä-lyō'strō), **Alessandro, Count** (b. *Giuseppe Balsamo*), Sicilian alchemist and charlatan .... 1743—1795
Caillaux (çà-yō'), **Joseph,** French politician .... 1863—1944
Cain (çān), **James Mallahan,** Am. journalist, novelist .... 1892—
Caine (çān), **Hall** (*Sir Thomas Henry Hall Caine*), British novelist . 1853—1931
Caird (çãrd), **Edward,** Scottish philosopher .... 1835—1908
Cairnes (çãrnẓ), **John Elliot,** Irish political economist .... 1823—1875
Cairns (çãrnẓ), **Hugh McCalmont, Lord,** Irish jurist .... 1819—1885
Calder (çal'dẽr), **Alexander Stirling,** American sculptor .... 1870—1945
Calderón de la Barca (çäl-dẹ-rōn' dē lä bär'çä), **Pedro,** Spanish dramatist .... 1600—1681
Caldwell (çald'wel), **Erskine,** American fiction writer .... 1903—
Caldwell, (Janet) Taylor, Am. novelist, b. in England .... 1900—
Calhoun (çal-hōn'), **John Caldwell,** American statesman .... 1782—1850
Caligula (çà-lig'ū-là), **Caius Caesar,** Roman emperor .... 12— 41
Callaghan (cal'là-han), **(Leonard) James,** English politician; prime minister of the United Kingdom (1976–79) .... 1912—
Calles (çä'yẹs), **Plutarco Elías,** Mexican general and statesman; president (1924–28) .... 1877—1945
Callimachus (çal-lim'à-ḉhus), Greek poet and critic .... fl.B.C. 250
Callot (çà-lō'), **Jacques,** French artist and engraver .... 1592—1635
Calonne, de (dē çà-lọn'), **Charles Alexandre,** French statesman and financier .... 1734—1802
Calvaert (çäl'värt), **Denis,** Flemish painter in Italy .... 1540—1619
Calvé (çal-vẹ'), **Emma** (b. *Emma de Roquer*), Fr. soprano .... 1862?–1942
Calverley (çal'vẽr-li), **Charles Stuart,** English poet .... 1831—1884
Calvert (çal'vẽrt), **George, first Baron Baltimore,** English statesman; founder of Maryland .... 1580?–1632
Calvin (çal'vin), **John,** French Protestant reformer .... 1509—1564
Camacho, Manuel Ávila, *see* Ávila Camacho, Manuel.
Cambacérès, de (dē çañ-bà-cẹ-res'), **Jean Jacques Régis,** French statesman .... 1753—1824
Cambiaso (çäm-bi-ä'sō), **Luca,** Italian fresco painter .... 1527—1585
Cambon (çañ-bọñ'), **Jules Martin,** French diplomat .... 1845—1935
C., Pierre Paul (*brother of J.M.C.*), French diplomat .... 1843—1924
Cambon, Pierre Joseph, French statesman .... 1756—1820
Cambronne, de (dē çañ-brọn'), **Pierre, Count,** French general . 1770—1842
Cambyses (çam-by'sẽẓ), (*son of Cyrus the Great*), king of the Medes and Persians .... B.C. ? — 522
Camden (çam'den), **Charles Pratt, first Earl of,** English statesman .... 1714—1794
Camden, William, English antiquary and author .... 1551—1623
Cameron (çam'ẽr-ŏn), **Donald** (*the Gentle Lochiel*), Scottish chieftain .... 1695?–1748
Cameron, Richard, Scottish divine; founder of the Cameronians . ? —1680
Cameron, Simon, American politician .... 1799—1889
Cameron, Verney Lovett, British traveler and explorer .... 1844—1894
Cammaerts (çä'märts), **Émile,** Belgian poet in England .... 1878—1953
Camoëns (çäm'ō-enṣ), **Luis,** Portuguese poet .... 1524—1580
Camp (çamp), **Walter Chauncey,** American football coach .... 1859—1925
Campbell (çam'l *or* çam'bl), **Alexander,** founder of the Campbellites .... 1788—1866
Campbell (çam'bl), **Archibald, Marquis of Argyll,** Scottish Covenanter .... 1607—1661
Campbell, Colin, Baron Clyde, British general .... 1792—1863
Campbell, Mrs. Patrick, (b. *Beatrice Stella Tanner*), English actress .... 1865—1940
Campbell, Thomas, Scottish poet .... 1777—1844
Campbell, William Wallace, American astronomer .... 1862—1938
Campbell-Bannerman (çam'bl-ban'nẽr-măn), **Sir Henry,** British statesman; prime minister (1905 08) .... 1836—1908
Campion (çam'pī-ŏn), **Edmund,** English Jesuit martyr .... 1540?–1581
Campion, Thomas, English poet and composer .... 1567—1620
Camus (çà-mọọ'), **Albert,** French writer, b. in Algeria .... 1913—1960
Canal (çä-nal') *or* **Canaletto** (çan-à-let'tō), **Antonio,** Italian painter .... 1697—1768
Canby (çan'by), **Henry Seidel,** American critic and editor .... 1878—1961
Canning (çan'ing), **Charles John, Earl** (*son of G.C.*), English statesman .... 1812—1862
C., George, English statesman and wit .... 1770—1827
Cannon (çan'nŏn), **Annie Jump,** American astronomer .... 1863—1941
Cannon, Joseph Gurney, speaker of the U.S. House of Representatives (1903–11) .... 1836—1926
Cano (çä'nō), **Alonzo,** Spanish painter and sculptor .... 1601—1667
Cano, del (del çä'nō), **Juan Sebastián,** Spanish explorer .... 1460?–1526
Canonicus (çà-non'i-çus), Narragansett chief .... 1565?–1647
Canova (çä-nō'vä), **Antonio,** Italian sculptor .... 1757—1822
Canrobert (çañ-rō-ber'), **François Certain,** Fr. marshal .... 1809—1895
Cantemir (çän'tẹ-mir), **Demetrius,** Russian historian and Orientalist .... 1673—1723
Canute (çà-nūt'), Danish king of England .... 994?–1035
Capablanca (çä-pä-blañ'çä), **José,** Cuban chess player; world champion (1921–27) .... 1888—1942
Capek (chä'pek), **Joseph** (*brother of K.C.*), Czech playwright and painter .... 1887—1945
C., Karel, Czech dramatist and novelist .... 1890—1938
Capet (çā'pet *or* çà-pet'), **Hugh,** king of France .... 940?–996
Capote (çä-pō'tē), **Truman,** American author .... 1924—
Capra (çap'rà), **Frank,** American motion-picture director, b. in Sicily .... 1897—
Caracalla (ça-rà-çal'là), (*Marcus Aurelius Antoninus*), Roman emperor (211–17) .... 188— 217
Caravaggio, da (dä çä-rä-väd'gō), **Michelangelo Amerighi,** Italian painter .... 1569—1609
Cárdenas (çär'dẹ-näs), **Lázaro,** president of Mexico (1934–40) . . 1895—1970
Cardozo (çär-dō'zō), **Benjamin Nathan,** associate justice of U.S. Supreme Court (1932–38) .... 1870—1938
Carducci (çär-dūt'chī), **Giosuè,** Italian poet .... 1835—1907
Carew (çà-rū'), **Thomas,** English poet and courtier .... 1595?–1639?
Carey (çãr'i), **Henry,** English musician and poet .... 1690?–1743
Carleton (çärl'tŏn), **Guy, first Baron Dorchester,** British general in North America; governor of Quebec .... 1724—1808
Carleton, Will, American poet .... 1845—1912
Carleton, William, Irish novelist .... 1794—1869
Carlisle (çär-līl'), **John Griffin,** American politician; secretary of the treasury .... 1835—1910
Carlos (çär'lōs), **Don,** Spanish prince; pretender to the crown . . . 1788—1855
Carlyle (çär-lyl'), **Thomas,** Scot. essayist, historian .... 1795—1881
Carman (çär'măn), **(William) Bliss,** Canadian poet .... 1861—1929
Carmona (çär-mō'nà), **Antonio Oscar de Fragosa,** Portuguese general and president .... 1868—1951
Carneades (çär-nē'à-dēṣ), Greek philosopher .... B.C. 213— 129
Carnegie (çär-nẹ'gi), **Andrew,** Am. steel manufacturer and philanthropist, b. in Scotland .... 1837—1919
Carnot (çȧr-nō'), **Lazare Nicolas Marguerite,** French statesman and general (*father of N.L.S.C.*) .... 1753—1823
C., Nicolas Léonard Sadi, French physicist .... 1796—1832
Carol (çar'ŏl) **II,** king of Romania (1930–40) .... 1893—1953
Carossa (çä-rōs'sä), **Hans,** German novelist and poet .... 1878—1956
Carpenter (çär'pen-tẽr), **Edward Childs,** Am. author .... 1872—1950
Carpenter, John Alden, American composer .... 1876—1951
Carr (çär), **Eugene Asa,** American general .... 1830—1895
Carr, John Dickson (pseud. *Carter Dickson*), American writer of detective fiction .... 1905?–1977
Carranza (çär-rän'sä), **Venustiano,** president of Mexico (1915–20) .... 1859—1920
Carrel (çar-rel'), **Alexis,** French surgeon and biologist in America (1905–39); received Nobel prize in medicine (1912) .... 1873—1944
Carrera (çär-rẹ'rà), **José Miguel,** Chilean revolutionist .... 1785—1821
Carroll (çȧr'rŏl), **Charles** (*of Carrollton*), Am. patriot .... 1737—1832
Carroll, Gladys Hasty, American novelist .... 1904—
Carroll, Lewis (pseud. of *Charles Lutwidge Dodgson*), English writer and mathematician .... 1832—1898
Carson (çär'sŏn), **Christopher** (*Kit Carson*), American frontiersman .... 1809—1868
Carson, Edward Henry, Baron, Irish statesman .... 1854—1935
Carson, Rachel (Louise), American biologist and science writer . 1907—1964
Carstairs (çär'stãrẓ), **William,** Scottish divine .... 1649—1715

Carte (cärt), **Richard D'Oyly**, Eng. producer of operas....1844—1901
Carter (cär'tẽr), **Clarence Holbrook**, American artist....1904—
Carter, Elizabeth, English poet and scholar....1717—1806
Carter, Howard, English archaeologist....1873—1939
Carter, James Earl, Jr. (called "Jimmy"), 39th president of the United States (1977–81)....1924—
Carter, Mrs. Leslie, American actress....1862—1937
Carteret, John, *see* Granville, John Carteret, Earl.
Cartier (cȧr-tyẹ'), **Sir George Étienne**, Canad. statesman....1814—1873
Cartier, Jacques, French navigator and explorer....1491—1557
Cartwright (cärt'rīt), **Edmund**, English inventor....1743—1823
Cartwright, Peter, American Methodist preacher....1785—1872
Caruso (cȧ-rụ'sō), **Enrico**, Italian tenor in America....1873—1921
Carver (cär'vẽr), **George Washington**, American educator, scientist, and author....1864—1943
Cary (cā'ry), **Alice**, American poet....1820—1871
 C., Phoebe (*sister of A.C.*), American poet....1824—1871
Cary, Henry Francis, English poet and translator....1772—1844
Cary, Joyce (*Arthur Joyce Lunel C.*), English author....1888—1957
Casadesus (cäs-ȧ-dẹ-sụs'), **Robert Marcel**, French pianist and composer....1899—1972
Casals (cä-säls'), **Pablo**, Spanish cellist....1876—1973
Casanova de Seingalt (cä-sä-nō'vä dẽ sin'gält), **Giovanni Jacopo**, Venetian adventurer and author....1725—1798
Casaubon (cȧ-sō'bŏn), **Isaac**, German theologian, scholar....1559—1614
Casement (cās'ment), **Sir Roger**, Irish revolutionist....1864—1916
Casimir (cas'i-mir) **III** (*the Great*), king of Poland....1310—1370
Caslon (caş'lŏn), **William**, English typefounder....1692—1766
Cass (cas), **Lewis**, American statesman....1782—1866
Cassatt (cȧ-sat'), **Mary**, American painter....1845—1926
Cassin (cas'sin), **John**, American ornithologist....1813—1869
Cassini (cäs-sē'nē), **César François** (*Cassini de Thury*), French astronomer and topographer....1714—1784
Cassiodorus (cas-si-ō-dō'rus), **Flavius Magnus Aurelius**, Roman historian....480?—575?
Cassius Longinus (cash'i-us lon-gī'nus), **Caius**, Roman general and chief assassin of Julius Caesar....B.C.?—42
Castiglione (cäs-tēl-yō'nẹ), **Baldassare**, Italian statesman and author....1478—1529
Castilho, de (dẹ cäs-tēl'yō), **Antonio Feliciano**, Portuguese poet....1800—1875
Castilla (cäs-tē'yȧ), **Don Ramon**, president of Peru....1797—1867
Castlereagh (cas'l-rā), **Robert Stewart, Viscount**, British statesman....1769—1822
Castro, de (dẹ cäs'trō), **Guillén**, Spanish dramatist....1569—1631
Castro, de, João, Portuguese general and navigator....1500—1548
Castro (cas'trō), **Fidel**, Cuban revolutionary leader; prime minister (1959–1976); president (1976–)....1927?–
Cather (ca'thẽr), **Willa Sibert**, American novelist....1876—1947
Catherine (cath'ẽr-in) **of Aragon**, queen of England; first wife of Henry VIII....1485—1536
Catherine I, empress of Russia (1725–27); wife of Peter the Great....1684—1727
Catherine II (*the Great*), empress of Russia (1762–96); wife of Peter III....1729—1796
Catherwood (cath'ẽr-wood), **Mary Hartwell**, American novelist....1847—1902
Catiline (cat'i-līn), **Lucius Sergius**, Roman conspirator....B.C.108?— 62
Catlin (cat'lin), **George**, American artist and author....1796—1872
Cato (cā'tō), **Marcus Porcius** (*the Elder*), Roman statesman; champion of ancient Roman ideals....B.C. 234— 149
 C., Marcus Porcius (*the Younger; great-grandson of C. the Elder*), Roman Stoic philosopher and patriot....B.C. 95— 46
Cats (cäts), **Jacob**, Dutch statesman and poet....1577—1660
Catt (cat), **Carrie Chapman**, American suffragist....1859—1947
Cattermole (cat'tẽr-mōl), **George**, English painter....1800—1868
Catullus (cȧ-tul'lus), **Caius Valerius**, Roman lyric poet....B.C. 84?— 54
Catulus (cat'ū-lus), **Quintus Lutatius**, Roman general and scholar....B.C. 105— 87
Cavell (ca'vel), **Edith**, English nurse executed as a spy....1872—1915
Cavendish (cav'en-dish), **Henry**, English chemist....1731—1810
Cavendish *or* **Candish** (can'dish), **Thomas**, English navigator....1555?—1592
Caventou (cȧ-väṅ-tö'), **Joseph Bienaimé**, Fr. chemist....1795—1877
Cavour, di (dī cȧ-vör'), **Camillo Benso, Count**, Italian statesman....1810—1861
Caxton (caks'tŏn), **William**, earliest English printer....1422?—1491
Cecil (cec'il), **Edgar Algernon Robert, first Viscount Cecil of Chelwood**, English statesman and internationalist....1864—1958
Cecil, William, *see* Burghley, Baron.
Celestine (cel'es-tīn) **V, Saint**, Pope (1294)....1215—1296
Céline (cẹ-lin'), **Louis Ferdinand** (b. *Louis Ferdinand Destouches*), French physician and author....1894—1961
Cellini (chel-lē'nī), **Benvenuto**, Italian engraver, sculptor, and autobiographer....1500—1571
Celsius (cel'si-us), **Anders**, Swedish astronomer....1701—1744
Cenci (chẹn'chī), **Beatrice**, Roman beauty, famous for her tragic fate....1577—1599
Centlivre (cent-liv'ẽr), **Susanna**, English dramatist....1667?—1723
Cervantes Saavedra, de (dẹ cẽr-van'tēş sä-ä-vẹ'drȧ *or* ther-vän'tẹs), **Miguel**, Spanish novelist and dramatist....1547—1616
Cesari (chẹ'şä-rī), **Giuseppe** (*Cavaliere d'Arpino*), Italian historical painter....1568?—1640
Céspedes, de (dẹ çẹs'pẹ-thẹs), **Carlos Manuel**, Cuban revolutionist....1819—1874
Cézanne (cẹ-zän'), **Paul**, French painter....1839—1906
Chabannes, de (dẽ çhȧ-bän'), **Antoine, Comte de Dammartin**, French general....1411—1488
Chabas (çhȧ-bäs'), **Paul Émile Joseph**, French painter....1869—1937
Chabrier (çhȧ-bryẹ'), **Alexis Emmanuel**, Fr. composer....1841—1894
Chadwick (chad'wik), **George Whitefield**, Am. composer....1854—1931
Chadwick, Sir James, English physicist....1891—1974
Chaffee (chaf'ē), **Adna Romanza**, American general....1842—1914
Chagall (çhȧ-gäl'), **Marc**, Russian painter in France, U.S., etc....1887—
Chain (chān), **Ernst Boris**, Eng. biochemist, b. in Germany....1906—
Chaliapin (chäl-yä'pin), **Feodor Ivanovich**, Russ. basso....1873—1938
Chalmers (chä'mẽrş), **Thomas**, Scottish theologian....1780—1847
Chamberlain (chām'bẽr-lin), **Joseph**, English statesman....1836—1914
 C., (Arthur) Neville (*son of J.C.*), English statesman; prime minister (1937–40)....1869—1940
 C., Sir (Joseph) Austen (*son of J.C.*), Eng. statesman....1863—1937
Chambers (chām'bẽrs), **Robert W.**, Am. novelist, artist....1865—1933
Chaminade (çhȧ-mi-nȧd'), **Cécile**, French composer....1857?—1944
Chamisso, von (fọn chä-mis'sō), **Adelbert**, German poet....1781—1838
Chamorro (chä-mō'rō), **Emiliano**, president of Nicaragua....1871—1966
Champion (çhäṅ-pyọṅ'), **Pierre**, French historian....1880—1942
Champlain, de (dẽ çhaṅ-plaṅ' *or Eng.* çham-plān'), **Samuel**, French explorer; founder of Quebec and first governor of Canada....1567—1635
Champollion (çhäṅ-pọl-yọṅ'), **Jean François**, French Egyptologist (*brother of J.J. Champollion-Figeac*)....1790—1832
Champollion-Figeac (-fī-zȧç'), **Jean Jacques**, French archaeologist....1778—1867
Chandler (chand'lẽr), **Raymond T.**, American writer....1888—1959
Chandler, Zachariah, American statesman....1813—1879
Chang Tso-lin (chäng'tsō'lin'), Chinese general....1873—1928
Channing (chan'ing), **Edward**, American historian....1856—1931
Channing, William Ellery, Am. clergyman and author....1780—1842
Chapelain (çhȧ-plaṅ'), **Jean**, French poet and critic....1595—1674
Chaplin (chap'lin), **Sir Charles Spencer**, English motion-picture actor and producer in America and Europe....1889—1977
Chapman (chap'mȧn), **Frank Michler**, Am. ornithologist....1864—1945
Chapman, George, Eng. dramatic poet, and translator....1559?—1634
Charcot (çhȧr-çō'), **Jean Baptiste**, French physician and explorer (*son of J.M.C.*)....1867—1936
 C., Jean Martin, French neurologist....1825—1893
Chardin (çhȧr-daṅ'), **Jean Baptiste**, French painter....1699—1779
Charlemagne (çhär'lẽ-män), (*Charles the Great* or *Charles I*) king of the Franks and emperor of the West....742— 814
Charles (chärlş), prince of Wales, heir apparent to the British throne....1948—
Charles I (*Charles Stuart*), king of England; beheaded....1600—1649
 C. II (*son of C.I.*), king of England (1660–85)....1630—1685
Charles I king of Spain; Charles V of Germany....1500—1558
Charles I (*Charles Francis Joseph*), emperor of Austria and king (*Charles IV*) of Hungary (1916–18)....1887—1922
Charles III (*the Fat*), emperor of the Franks....839— 888
Charles IV, emperor of Germany and king of Bohemia....1316—1378
Charles V, emperor of Germany and king (*Charles I*) of Spain....1500—1558
Charles VI, emperor of Germany....1685—1740
Charles VII (*Charles Albert*), emperor of Germany....1697—1745
Charles Albert (al'bẽrt), king of Sardinia....1798—1849
Charles Edward Stuart (ed'wȧrd stū'ärt), (*the Young Pretender; Bonnie Prince Charlie*) English prince....1720—1788
Charles Martel (mär-tel'), ruler of the Franks (715–41)....688?— 741
Charles the Bold, duke of Burgundy....1433—1477
Charles, Jacques Alexandre César, French scientist....1746—1823
Charlevoix, de (dẽ çhȧr-lẽ-vwo'), **Pierre François Xavier**, French Jesuit missionary and explorer....1682—1761
Charlot (çhär-lō'), **Jean**, American painter, b. in France....1898—
Charnwood (chärn'wood), **Godfrey Rathbone Benson, Baron**, English biographer....1864—1945
Charpentier (çhȧr-päṅ-tyẹ'), **Alexandre**, Fr. sculptor....1856—1909
Charpentier, Gustave, French composer....1860—1956
Charron (çhȧ-rọṅ'), **Pierre**, Fr. preacher, theologian....1541—1603
Chase, Mary Ellen, American novelist....1887—1973
Chase, Salmon Portland, American statesman; chief justice of U.S. Supreme Court (1864–73)....1808—1873
Chase, Samuel, American Revolutionary leader and jurist....1741—1811
Chase, Stuart, American economist....1888—
Chase, William Merritt, American painter....1849—1916
Chateaubriand (çhȧ-tō-brī-äṅ'), **François René Auguste, Vicomte de**, French author and statesman....1768—1848
Chatham (chat'ăm), **first Earl of**, *see* Pitt, William.
Chatterton (chat'tẽr-tŏn), **Thomas**, English poet....1752—1770
Chaucer (chą'cẽr), **Geoffrey**, English poet....1340?-1400
Chausson (çhō-sọṅ'), **Ernest**, French composer....1855—1899
Chávez (chä'vẹs), **Carlos**, Mexican composer, conductor....1899—1978
Cheever (chē'vẽr), **John**, American novelist and short-story writer....1912—
Cheke (chēk), **Sir John**, English statesman and Hellenist....1514—1557
Chekhov (che'kọf), **Anton Pavlovich**, Russian novelist, dramatist, and short-story writer....1860—1904
Chelmsford (chemş'fŏrd), **Frederic John Napier Thesiger, first Viscount**, British statesman; viceroy of India....1868—1933
Cheney, Sheldon, Am. art and theater critic, historian....1886—
Chénier, de (dẽ çhẹ-nyẹ'), **André Marie**, French poet....1762—1794
Chennault (çhe-nąlt'), **Claire Lee**, American general; commander 14th air force in China in World War II....1890—1958
Cheops (çhē'ops), (*Khufu*) Egyptian king; builder of the Great Pyramid near Gizeh....fl. B.C.—2900
Cherbuliez (çher-bụ-lyẹ'), **Victor**, French novelist....1829—1899
Cherubini (çhẹ-rụ-bē'nī), **Maria Luigi Carlo Zenobio Salvatore**, Italian composer....1760—1842
Cheselden (ches'l-den), **William**, English surgeon....1688—1752
Chesney (ches'ni), **Francis Rawdon**, British explorer....1789—1872
Chesterfield (ches'tẽr-fēld), **Philip Dormer Stanhope, fourth Earl of**, English statesman and author....1694—1773
Chesterton (ches'tẽr-tŏn), **Gilbert Keith**, English essayist, critic, novelist, and short-story writer....1874—1936
Chettle (chet'l), **Henry**, English dramatist....1564?-1607?
Cheyne (chẹ'nē), **Thomas Kelly**, English biblical critic....1841—1915
Chiabrera (çhī-ȧ-brẹ'rȧ), **Gabriello**, Italian poet....1552—1637
Chiang Kai-shek (chī-äng' kī'shek'), (b. *Chiang Chungcheng*) Chinese generalissimo and president....1886—1975
 Chiang Kai-shek, Mme. (b. *Soong Mei-ling*), wife of Chiang; Chinese political leader....1896—
Chicherin (chī'che-rin), **Georgi Vassilyevich**, commissar for Soviet Russian foreign affairs (1918–30)....1872—1936
Chikamatsu (chi-kä'mät-sụ), **Monzaemon**, Japan. dramatist....1653—1724
Child (chīld), **Lydia Maria (Francis)**, American abolitionist and author....1802—1880
Child, Richard Washburn, Am. diplomat and author....1881—1935
Childeric (chil'dẽr-ic), **I**, king of the Franks....436?— 481
Chippendale (chip'pen-dāl), **Thomas**, English cabinetmaker....1718?—1779
Chirico, de (dẹ çhī-rī'çō), **Giorgio**, Italian modernist painter....1888—1978
Chladni (chlad'nī), **Ernst Florens Friedrich**, German inventor....1756—1827
Choate (chōt), **Rufus**, American lawyer and senator....1799—1859
 C., Joseph Hodges (*nephew of R.C.*), Am. diplomat....1832—1917
Choiseul, de (dẽ çhwo-şụl'), **Étienne François, Duc**, French statesman....1719—1785
Choisy, de (dẽ çhwo-şē'), **François Timoléon, Abbé**, French author....1644—1724
Chopin (çhō-paṅ'), **Frédéric François**, Polish pianist and composer in France....1810—1849

Chouan (çhö-äṅ'), **Jean** (b. *Cottereau*), French smuggler and chief of "La Chouannerie" .... 1767—1794

Chou En-lai (jō'en'lī'), Chinese Communist premier .... 1898—1976

Chrétien de Troyes (çhrę-tyaṅ' dẽ trwo'), French poet .... 1140?—1191

Christian (çhris'chăn) **X**, king of Denmark (1912–47) and Iceland (1912–44) .... 1870—1947

Christiansen (çhrĭs'tyän-sen), **Sigurd**, Norw. author .... 1891—1947

Christie (çhris'tē), **Dame Agatha**, Eng. detective-story writer .... 1890—1976

Christina (çhris-tī-na), (*daughter of Gustavus Adolphus*), queen of Sweden .... 1626—1689

Christophe (çhris-tọf'), **Henri**, king of Haiti .... 1767—1820

Christy (çhrist'y), **Howard Chandler**, American painter .... 1873—1952

Chrysostom (çhris'ŏs-tŏm), **Saint John**, Greek church father, b. in Antioch .... 345?— 407

Chulalonkhorn (chụ-lä-lọn'kọrn) **I**, (*Phra Paramindr Maha*) king of Siam .... 1853—1910

Church (chûrch), **Frederic Edwin**, Am. landscape painter .... 1826—1900

Churchill (chûrch'il), **Charles**, Eng. poet and satirist .... 1731—1764

Churchill, John, *see* Marlborough, Duke of.

Churchill, Randolph Henry Spencer, Lord, Brit. statesman .... 1849—1895

Churchill, Winston, American novelist .... 1871—1947

Churchill, Sir Winston Leonard Spencer (*son of R.H.S.C.*), British statesman, orator, and historian; prime minister (1940–45, 1951–55) .... 1874—1965

Churchyard (chûrch'yärd), **Thomas**, English poet .... 1520—1604

Churriguera (chụ-rī-ge'rä), **José**, Spanish architect .... 1650—1725

Chu Teh (jụ du), Chinese Communist general .... 1886—

Ciano (chä'nō), **Galeazzo, Count** (*son-in-law of Mussolini*), Italian Fascist leader; foreign minister .... 1903—1943

Cibber (cib'bẽr), **Colley**, English dramatist and actor .... 1671—1757

Cicero (cic'e-rō), **Marcus Tullius**, Roman orator, statesman, and philosopher .... B.C. 106— 43

Cicognara, da (dä chī-çōn-yä'rä), **Leopoldo, Count**, Italian diplomat; writer on art .... 1767—1834

Cid (cid), **the** (*Ruy* or *Rodrigo Diaz de Bivar*), Castilian hero, celebrated in literature .... 1040—1099

Cimabue (chī-mä-bụ'ę), **Giovanni**, Florentine painter .... 1240?—1302?

Cimon (cī'mŏn), Athenian general .... B.C. 510— 449

Cincinnatus (cin-cin-nā'tus), **Lucius Quinctius**, Roman dictator and legendary hero .... B.C. 519?–439?

Clair (çlãr), **René**, French film director and writer .... 1898—

Clare (çlãr), **John**, English poet .... 1793—1864

Clarendon (çlăr'en-dŏn), **Edward Hyde, Earl of**, English statesman and historian .... 1609—1674

Clark (çlärk), **Alvan**, American optician and astronomer .... 1804—1887

Clark, Champ (b. *James Beauchamp Clark*), speaker of the U.S. House of Representatives (1911–19) .... 1850—1921

Clark, Francis Edward, Am. Congregational clergyman .... 1851—1927

Clark, George Rogers (*brother of William C.*), American frontiersman and Revolutionary general .... 1752—1818

Clark, John Bates, American political economist .... 1847—1938

Clark, Mark Wayne, American general in World War II; U.N. supreme commander in Korea (1952–53) .... 1896—

Clark, Thomas Campbell, U.S. attorney general (1945–49); associate justice of U.S. Supreme Court (1949–67) .... 1899—1977

Clark, William (*brother of G.R.C.*), American explorer; co-leader in Lewis and Clark expedition (1804–06) .... 1770—1838

Clarke (çlärk), **Samuel**, English divine and philosopher .... 1675—1729

Clarkson (çlärk'sŏn), **Thomas**, English abolitionist .... 1760—1846

Claudel (çlō-del'), **Paul**, French diplomat and author .... 1868—1955

Claude Lorrain (çlōd'lō-raṅ'), (b. *Claude Gelée*), French painter in Italy .... 1600—1682

Claudian (çla'di-ăn), (*Claudius Claudianus*) Latin poet .... 365?— 408?

Claudius (çla'di-us) **I** (*Tiberius Claudius Drusus Nero Germanicus*), emperor of Rome (41–54) .... B.C. 10–A.D.54

Claudius II (*Marcus Aurelius Claudius*), emperor of Rome (268–70) .... 214— 270

Clausewitz, von (fọn çlou'ṣĕ-vits), **Karl**, Prussian general; writer on strategy of total war .... 1780—1831

Clay (çlā), **Cassius M.**, Am. abolitionist and diplomat .... 1810—1903

Clay, Henry, American statesman and orator .... 1777—1852

Clay, Lucius DuBignon, Am. general; U.S. military governor in Germany (1947–49) .... 1897—1978

Clayton (çlā'tŏn), **Henry De Lamar**, Am. congressman .... 1857—1929

Clayton, Henry Helm, American meteorologist .... 1861—1946

Clayton, John Middleton, American statesman .... 1796—1856

Cleanthes (çlē-an'thēṣ), Greek Stoic philosopher .... B.C. 300?–220?

Clearchus (çlē-är'çhus), Lacedaemonian general .... fl. B.C.401?

Cleef, van (vän çlef'), **Jan**, Flemish painter .... 1646—1716

Cleisthenes (çlis'the-nēṣ), Athenian statesman .... fl.B.C. 507

Clemenceau (çlē-mäṅ-cō'), **Georges** (*the Tiger*), French statesman and writer; premier (1906–09, 1917–20) .... 1841—1929

Clemens (çlem'enṣ), **Samuel Langhorne** (pseud. *Mark Twain*), American humorist .... 1835—1910

Clement (çlem'ent) **I, Saint** *or* **Clemens Romanus** (rō-mā'nus), Pope; first of the Apostolic Fathers .... 30?— 100?

Clement VII (*Giulio de'Medici*), Pope (1523–34) .... 1478—1534

Clement of Alexandria, Greek Christian theologian .... 150?—220?

Clementi (çlę-men'tī), **Muzio**, Italian composer, pianist .... 1752—1832

Cleomenes (çlē-ŏm'ē-nēṣ) **III**, Spartan king .... B.C.?— 220

Cleopatra (çlē-ō-pā'trȧ), queen of Egypt .... B.C. 69— 30

Clerk (çlärk), **Sir Dugald**, Scottish inventor .... 1854—1932

Clerk-Maxwell, James, *see* Maxwell, James Clerk.

Cleveland (çlēv'lănd), **(Stephen) Grover**, 22nd and 24th U.S. president (1885–89, 1893–97) .... 1837—1908

Clinedinst (çlīn'dinst), **Benjamin**, American illustrator .... 1860—1931

Clinton (çlin'tŏn), **De Witt**, American statesman .... 1769—1828

C., George, (*brother of J.C.*), American statesman; U.S. vice-president (1805–12) .... 1739—1812

C., James, (*father of De W.C.*), American general .... 1733—1812

Clinton, Sir Henry, Brit. commander in Am. Revolution .... 1738?—1795

Clive (çlīv), **Robert, Baron Clive of Plassey**, British general and statesman; founder of the empire of British India .... 1725—1774

Clootz (çlōts), **Jean Baptiste, Baron** (*Anacharsis Cloots*), Prussian active in the French Revolution .... 1755—1794

Clouet (çlọọ-ā'), **Francois**, French portrait painter .... 1516?—1572

C., Jean, (*father of Francois*), Flemish portrait painter .... 1485?—1540?

Clough (çluf), **Arthur Hugh**, English poet .... 1819—1861

Clovis (çlō'vis) **I**, founder of the Frankish monarchy .... 466?— 511

Coates (çōts), **Albert**, English conductor and composer, born in Russia .... 1882—1953

Coates, Eric, English composer and conductor .... 1886—1957

Coates, Joseph Gordon, New Zealand statesman .... 1878—1943

Cobb (çob), **Howell**, American statesman .... 1815—1868

Cobb, Irvin Shrewsbury, American humorist .... 1876—1944

Cobb, Tyrus Raymond (*Ty Cobb*), American baseball player .... 1886—1961

Cobbett (çob'bet), **William**, English writer and reformer .... 1763—1835

Cobden (çob'den), **Richard**, Eng. statesman, economist .... 1804—1865

Cobham (çob'ăm), **John Oldcastle, Lord**, English leader of the Lollards; hanged for heresy and treason .... ? —1417

Cockburn (çō'bûrn), **Sir George**, British admiral .... 1772—1853

Cockcroft (çok'crọft), **Sir John Douglas**, British physicist; director of atomic energy research .... 1897—1967

Cocteau (çọç-tō'), **Jean**, French writer, artist, stage designer, and producer .... 1891—1963

Cody (çō'dy), **William Frederick** (*Buffalo Bill*), American Indian fighter, army scout, and showman .... 1846—1917

Coeur de Lion (çûr dẽ lī-ọṅ'), *see* Richard I.

Coffin (çọf'fin), **Henry Sloane**, American clergyman and author .... 1877—1954

Coffin, Robert Peter Tristram, Am. poet and author .... 1892—1955

Cohan (çō-han'), **George Michael**, American actor, theatrical manager, and playwright .... 1878—1942

Cohen (çō'en), **Morris Raphael**, Am. philosopher, b. Russia .... 1880—1947

Cohn (çōn), **Ferdinand Julius**, German plant bacteriologist .... 1828—1898

Coke (çōk), **Sir Edward**, lord chief justice of England .... 1552—1634

Colbert (çol-ber'), **Jean Baptiste, Marquis de Seignelay**, French statesman and economist .... 1619—1683

Cole (çōl), **George Douglas Howard**, English economist, sociologist, and author .... 1889—1959

Coleridge (çōl'rig), **Samuel Taylor**, English poet and philosopher .... 1772—1834

Coleridge-Taylor (-tā'lōr), **Samuel**, English composer .... 1875—1912

Colet (çol'et), **John**, English clergyman and humanist .... 1467?—1519

Colet (çō-le'), **Louise Révoil**, French poet and novelist .... 1810—1876

Colette (çō-let'), (*Sidonie Gabrielle Claudine Collete*), French novelist .... 1873—1954

Colfax (çol'faks), **Schuyler**, U.S. vice-president (1869–73) .... 1823—1885

Coligny, de (dẽ çō-lī-nyē'), **Gaspard**, Huguenot leader .... 1519—1572

Collier (çol'li-ẽr), **Jeremy**, English divine .... 1650—1726

Collins (çol'lınṣ), **Anthony**, English theologian .... 1676—1729

Collins, Joseph, American neurologist and author .... 1866—1950

Collins, Michael, Irish Sinn Fein leader; assassinated .... 1890—1922

Collins, William, English poet .... 1721—1759

Collins, (William) Wilkie, English novelist .... 1824—1889

Collodi (çōl-lō'dī), **Carlo** (pseud. of *Carlo Lorenzini*), Italian journalist and children's writer .... 1826—1890

Colonna (çọ-lōn'nȧ), **Vittoria**, Italian poet .... 1492—1547

Colt (çōlt), **Samuel**, American inventor .... 1814—1862

Colum (çol'um), **Padraic**, Irish poet and playwright .... 1881—1972

Columba (çō-lum'bȧ), **Saint**, Irish apostle to Scotland .... 521— 597

Columbus (çō-lum'bus), **Christopher** (It. *Cristoforo Colombo*), Genoese discoverer of America (1492) .... 1446?–1506

Colvin (çol'vin), **Sir Sidney**, English author .... 1845—1927

Combe (çōm), **George**, Scottish phrenologist .... 1788—1858

Comenius (çō-mēn'i-us), **John Amos** (*Jan Amos Komensky*), Moravian bishop and educator .... 1592—1670

Comines, de (dẽ çō-mīn'), **Philippe**, French historian .... 1445?—1509?

Commodus (çom'mō-dus), **Lucius Aelius Aurelius**, Roman emperor (180–92) .... 161— 192

Compton (çomp'tŏn), **Arthur Holly**, American physicist .... 1892—1962

C., Karl Taylor (*brother of A.H.C.*), Am. physicist .... 1887—1954

Comstock (çom'stok), **Ada Louise**, American educator .... 1876—

Comstock, Anthony, American crusader against vice .... 1844—1915

Comte (çoṅt), **Auguste**, French positivist philosopher .... 1798—1857

Conant (çō'nănt), **James Bryant**, American chemist and educator .... 1893—1978

Condé, de (dẽ çoṅ-dę'), **Louis II de Bourbon, Prince, Duc d'Enghien** (*the Great Condé*), French general .... 1621—1686

Condillac, de (dẽ çoṅ-dī-yaç'), **Étienne Bonnot**, French philosopher .... 1715—1780

Condon (çon'dŏn), **Edward Uhler**, American physicist .... 1902—1974

Condorcet, de (dẽ çoṅ-dọr-ce'), **Marie Jean Antoine Nicolas Caritat, Marquis**, French mathematician and philosopher .... 1743—1794

Confucius (çŏn-fū'shi-us), Chinese philosopher .... B.C.551?—479?

Congreve (çon'grēv), **William**, English dramatist .... 1670—1729

Conklin (çoṅk'lin), **Edwin Grant**, American biologist .... 1863—1952

Conkling (çonk'ling), **Roscoe**, U.S. senator .... 1829—1888

Connally (çon'năl-ly), **Tom** (*Thomas Terry C.*), U.S. senator; delegate to U.N. General Assembly (1945–47) .... 1877—1963

Connelly (çon'nel-ly), **Marc** (*Marcus Cook Connelly*), American playwright .... 1890—

Conrad (çon'rad) *or* **Konrad** (kōn'rät) **I**, duke of Franconia and king of Germany .... ? — 918

Conrad III, king of Germany .... 1093—1152

Conrad, Joseph (b. *Teodor Jozef Konrad Korzeniowski*), English novelist, born in Poland .... 1857—1924

Conscience (çoṅ-syäṅç'), **Hendrik**, Flemish novelist .... 1812—1883

Constable (çon'stȧ-bl), **Henry**, English poet .... 1562—1613

Constable, John, English painter .... 1776—1837

Constans (çon'stanṣ) **I, Flavius Julius**, emperor of Rome .... 320?– 350

Constant (çoṅ-stäṅ'), **Jean Joseph Benjamin**, Fr. painter .... 1845—1902

Constant de Rebecque (çoṅ-stäṅ' dẽ rē-beç'), **Henri Benjamin**, French statesman and writer .... 1767—1830

Constantine (çon'stăn-tīn) **I** (*the Great*), first Christian emperor of Rome .... 272— 337

Constantine Nikolayevich (ni-kō-ly'e-vich), grand duke of Russia .... 1827—1892

Contarini (çon-tȧ-rī'nī), **Andrea**, doge of Venice .... 1300?—1382

Converse (çon'vẽrs), **Frederick Shepherd**, American composer .... 1871—1940

Conway (çon'wā), **Moncure Daniel**, Am. clergyman .... 1832—1907

Conway of Allington, William Martin, Baron, English explorer and author .... 1856—1937

Cook (çook), **Frederick Albert**, American explorer .... 1865—1940

Cook, George Cram, American playwright .... 1873—1924

Cook, James, English sea captain and explorer .... 1728—1779

Cook, Sir Joseph, Australian statesman and premier .... 1860—1947

Cooke (çook), **Jay**, American financier .... 1821—1905

Cooke, John Esten, American novelist .... 1830—1886

Coolidge (çọọl'ig), **Archibald Cary**, American historian .... 1866—1928

Coolidge, Calvin, 30th U.S. president (1923–29) .... 1872—1933

Coolidge, William David, American physicist .... 1875—1976
Coomaraswamy (ço͞om-ȧ-rȧs-wäm'y), **Ananda Kentish,** Ceylonese art critic in the United States .... 1877—1947
Cooper (ço͞o'pẽr), **Alfred Duff, Viscount Norwich,** British statesman .... 1890—1954
Cooper, James Fenimore, American novelist .... 1789—1851
Cooper, Peter, American philanthropist .... 1791—1883
Cope (çōp), **Edward Drinker,** American naturalist .... 1840—1897
Copeau (ço-pō'), **Jacques,** French dramatist and critic .... 1879—1949
Copeland (çōp'lănd), **Charles Townsend,** American educator and author .... 1860—1952
Copeland, Royal Samuel, Am. physician, senator .... 1868—1938
Copernicus (çō-pẽr'ni-çus), **Nicholaus** (Pol. *Kopernik*), Polish astronomer .... 1473—1543
Copland (çōp'land), **Aaron,** American composer .... 1900—
Copley (çop'lē), **John Singleton,** American painter .... 1738—1815
Coppard (çop'pärd), **Alfred Edgar,** English poet and short-story writer .... 1878—1957
Coppée (ço-pe'), **François,** French poet and playwright .... 1842—1908
Coquelin (çok-lan'), **Benoît Constant,** French actor .... 1841—1909
C., Ernest Alexandre (*brother of B.C.C.*) Fr. actor .... 1848—1909
Corbett (çor'bet), **James J.** (*Gentleman Jim*), Am. prize fighter; world heavyweight champion (1892–97) .... 1866—1933
Corday (çor-dā'), **Charlotte** (*Marie Anne Charlotte Corday d'Armont*), Fr. patriot; assassin of Marat .... 1768—1793
Corelli (çō-rel'li), **Arcangelo,** It. violinist, composer .... 1653—1713
Corelli, Marie, English novelist .... 1855—1924
Corinna (çō-rin'ȧ) **of Tanagra,** Greek lyric poetess .... fl.5th cent.B.C.
Coriolanus (çor''i-ō-lā'nus), **Caius** (*or* **Gnaeus**) **Marcius,** Roman legendary hero .... fl.B.C. 489
Corneille (çor-ne'y'), **Pierre,** French dramatist .... 1606—1684
C., Thomas (*brother of P.C.*), French dramatist .... 1625—1709
Cornelia (çor-nē'li-ȧ), Roman matron; mother of the Gracchi . fl.2nd cent.B.C.
Cornelius, von (fon çor-ne'li-us), **Peter,** German painter .... 1783—1867
Cornell (çor-nel'), **Ezra,** American financier .... 1807—1874
Cornell, Katherine, American actress .... 1898—1974
Cornwallis (çorn-wąl'lis), **Charles, first Marquis,** Brit. general, statesman; Brit. commander in Am. Revolution .... 1738—1805
Coronado, de (de çō-rō-nä'thō), **Francisco Vasquez,** Spanish explorer in southwestern North America .... c.1500—1554
Corot (çō-rō'), **Jean Baptiste Camille,** Fr. landscapist .... 1796—1875
Correggio, da (dä çō-red'gō), **Antonio Allegri,** Italian painter . . 1494—1534
Cortelyou (çor-tel'yū), **George Bruce,** Am. statesman .... 1862—1940
Cortés *or* **Cortez** (çor'teṣ *or Sp.* çor-teṣ'), **Hernando** *or* **Hernán,** Spanish conqueror of Mexico .... 1485—1547?
Cortissoz (çor-tis'sŏz), **Royal,** American art critic .... 1869—1948
Cortona, da (dä çōr-tō'nȧ), **Pietro** (b. *Pietro Berrettini*), Italian painter .... 1596—1669
Cortot (çor-tō'), **Alfred Denis,** Fr. pianist, conductor .... 1877—1962
Corwin (çor'win), **Thomas,** American statesman .... 1794—1865
Coryate (çor-i-ăt), **Thomas,** Eng. traveler and writer .... 1577?—1617
Cosgrave (çoṣ'grāv), **William Thomas,** Irish statesman; president of the executive council of Irish Free State (1922–32) .... 1880—1965
Costanzo, di (dī çōs-tän'tsō), **Angelo,** Neapolitan poet and historian .... 1507—1591
Cotton (çot'tŏn), **Charles,** English poet .... 1630—1687
Cotton, John, English Puritan minister in Boston .... 1584—1652
Cotton, Sir Robert Bruce, English antiquarian .... 1571—1631
Cottrell (çot'rel), **Frederick Gardner,** American chemist .... 1877—1948
Coty (ço-tē'), **René,** president of France (1954–59) .... 1883—1962
Coué (çō-e'), **Émile,** French psychotherapist .... 1857—1926
Coues (çouṣ), **Elliott,** American naturalist .... 1842—1899
Coulomb, de (dē çō-lon'), **Charles Auguste,** French physicist . 1736—1806
Coulter (çōl'tẽr), **John Merle,** American botanist .... 1851—1928
Couperin (çö-pē-ran'), **François,** French composer .... 1668—1733
Courbet (çōr-be'), **Gustave,** French painter .... 1819—1877
Courier de Méré (çōr-ye' dē me-re'), **Paul Louis,** French Hellenist and political writer .... 1772—1825
Cournot (çōr-nō'), **Antoine Augustin,** French mathematician and economist .... 1801—1877
Cousin (çō-ṣan'), **Jean,** French painter and sculptor .... 1501?—1589?
Cousin, Victor, French educator and philosopher .... 1792—1867
Couzens (çuz'enṣ), **James,** U.S. senator .... 1872—1936
Covarrubias (çō-vär-rū'bĭ-ăs), **Miguel,** American artist and illustrator, born in Mexico .... 1902—1957
Coverdale (çŏv'ẽr-dăl), **Miles,** Eng. translator of Bible .... 1488—1569
Coward (çou'ărd), **Sir Noel, English playwright and actor** .... 1889—1973
Cowl (çoul), **Jane,** American actress .... 1890—1950
Cowley (çou'li), **Abraham,** English poet .... 1618—1667
Cowper (çöp'ẽr *or* çou'pẽr), **William,** English poet .... 1731—1800
Cowper (çou'pẽr *or* çö'pẽr), **William,** English anatomist .... 1666—1709
Cowper, William, Earl, lord chancellor of England .... 1664—1723
Cox (çoks), **James Middleton,** U.S. governor (Ohio); Democratic presidential nominee in 1920 .... 1870—1957
Cox, Palmer, American artist and writer of children's stories, b. in Canada .... 1840—1924
Coxey (çok'si), **Jacob Sechler,** Am. social reformer; leader of a march to Washington by unemployed men petitioning for relief . 1854—1951
Cozzens (çŏz'zenṣ), **James Gould,** American novelist .... 1903—1978
Crabb (çrab), **George,** English philologist .... 1778—1851
Crabbe (çrab), **George,** English poet .... 1754—1832
Crabtree (çrab'trē), **Lotta,** American actress .... 1847—1924
Craddock (çrad'dŏk), **Charles Egbert** (pseud. of *Mary Noailles Murfree*), American novelist .... 1850—1922
Craig (çrāg), **Edward Gordon** (*son of Ellen Terry*), English actor, theatrical designer and producer .... 1872—1966
Craig, Malin, U.S. general; chief of staff (1935–39) .... 1875—1945
Craigavon (çrăg-ăv'ŏn), **James Craig, first Viscount,** prime minister of Northern Ireland (1921–40) .... 1871—1940
Craigie (çrāg'i), **Pearl Mary Teresa Richards** (pseud. *John Oliver Hoddes*), American novelist and playwright .... 1867—1906
Craigie, Sir William A., Scottish lexicographer .... 1867—1957
Craik (çrāk), **Dinah Maria Mulock,** English novelist .... 1826—1887
Cram (çram), **Ralph Adams,** American architect .... 1863—1942
Cranach (çra'näçh), **Lucas,** German painter and engraver .... 1472—1553
Cranch (çranch), **Christopher Pearse,** American painter and poet .... 1813—1892
Crane (çrān), **Hart,** American poet .... 1899—1932
Crane, Stephen, American novelist, poet, journalist .... 1871—1900
Crane, Walter, English painter and designer .... 1845—1915
Crane, William Henry, American actor .... 1845—1928
Cranmer (çran'mẽr), **Thomas,** English reformer; archbishop of Canterbury .... 1489—1556
Crashaw (çrā'shą), **Richard,** English poet .... 1613?—1649
Crassus (çras'sus), **Lucius Licinius,** Roman orator and statesman .... B.C. 140— 91
Crassus, Marcus Licinius, Roman statesman and financier . B.C.115?— 53
Crawford (çrą'fŏrd), **Francis Marion,** American novelist .... 1854—1909
Crawford, Thomas, American sculptor .... 1814—1857
Crazy Horse (çrā'zy hors), chief of Oglala Sioux .... 1849?—1877
Creasy (çrē'sy), **Sir Edward Shepherd,** English historian .... 1812—1878
Crébillon, de (dē çre-bī-yon'), **Claude Prosper Jolyot,** French novelist (*son of P.J.C.*) .... 1707—1777
C., de, Prosper Jolyot, French dramatist .... 1674—1762
Creighton (çre'tŏn), **Mandell,** Eng. bishop, historian .... 1843—1901
Crerar (çrē'rär), **Henry Duncan Graham,** Canadian general in World War II, commanding Canadian forces in W. Europe .... 1888—1965
Crèvecoeur (çrev-çûr'), **Jean Hector St. John,** American farmer and author, b. in France .... 1735—1813
Crewe (çro͞o), **Robert Offley Ashburton Crewe-Milnes, first Marquis of,** British statesman .... 1858—1945
Crichton (çrī'tŏn), **James** (*the Admirable Crichton*), Scottish savant .... 1560?—1582
Crile (çrīl), **George Washington,** American surgeon .... 1864—1943
Crillon, de (dē çri-yon'), **Louis des Balbes de Berton,** French general .... 1541—1615
Cripps (çrips), **Sir (Richard) Stafford,** British statesman .... 1889—1952
Crispi (çris'pi), **Francesco,** Italian statesman .... 1819—1901
Crittenden (çrit'ten-den), **John Jordan,** Am. statesman .... 1787—1863
Croce (çrō'çhe), **Benedetto,** Italian philosopher, historian .... 1866—1952
Crockett (çrok'et), **David,** American frontiersman .... 1786—1836
Crockett, Samuel Rutherford, Scottish novelist .... 1860—1914
Croesus (çrē'sus), fabulously wealthy king of Lydia fl.B.C.560
Croker (çrō'kẽr), **John Wilson,** Brit. statesman, critic .... 1780—1857
Croker, Richard, American politician, b. in Ireland; leader of Tammany Hall (1886–1901) .... 1841—1922
Croker, Thomas Crofton, Irish writer on folklore .... 1798—1854
Cromer (çrō'mẽr), **Evelyn Baring, first Earl,** British agent in and administrator of Egypt (1883–1907) .... 1841—1917
Crompton (çromp'tŏn), **Samuel,** English inventor .... 1753—1827
Cromwell (çrom'wel), **Oliver,** lord protector of the English commonwealth .... 1599—1658
Cromwell, Thomas, Earl of Essex, English statesman .... 1485?—1540
Cronin (çrō'nin), **Archibald Joseph,** Scottish novelist .... 1896—1981
Cronje (çrŏn'ye), **Piet,** Boer commander .... 1835?—1911
Crookes (çrooks), **William,** English physicist .... 1832—1919
Crosby (çroṣ'bē), **Bing** (*Harry Lillis Crosby*), American singer and comedian .... 1904—1977
Crosman (çroṣ'măn), **Henrietta,** American actress .... 1870—1944
Cross (çroṣ), **Wilbur Lucius,** Am. educator, literary critic and historian, and governor (Conn.) .... 1862—1943
Crothers (çrŏ'thẽrṣ), **Rachel,** American playwright .... 1878—1958
Crothers, Samuel McChord, Am. essayist and clergyman .... 1857—1927
Crowder (çrou'dẽr), **Enoch Herbert,** American statesman; provost marshal general in World War I .... 1859—1932
Crowe (çrō), **Sir Joseph Archer,** English art historian .... 1825—1896
Cruikshank (çruk'shank), **George,** English caricaturist .... 1792—1878
Cruz, de la (de lä çro͞oth'), **Juana Inés,** Mexican poet .... 1651—1695
Csokonai (chō'kō-noi), **Vitéz Mihály,** Hungarian poet .... 1773—1805
Cudworth (çud'wŏrth), **Ralph,** English philosopher .... 1617—1688
Cui (çü-i'), **César Antonovich,** Russian composer .... 1835—1918
Culbertson (çul'bẽrt-sŏn), **Ely,** American expert and writer on contract bridge, b. in Romania .... 1893—1955
Cullen (çul'len), **Countee,** American poet .... 1903—1946
Culpeper (çul'pep-ẽr), **Thomas, second Baron,** English colonial governor of Virginia .... 1635—1689
Cumberland (çum'bẽr-lănd), **Richard,** English dramatist .... 1732—1811
Cummings (çum'mingṣ), **Edward Estlin,** American poet .... 1894—1962
Cummings, Homer Stillé, U.S. attorney-gen. (1933–38) .... 1870—1956
Cummins (çum'minṣ), **Albert Baird,** U.S. senator .... 1850—1926
Cunningham (çun'ning-hăm), **Sir Alan Gordon** (*brother of A.B.C.*), Brit. general, high commissioner for Palestine .... 1887—
C., Andrew Browne, first Viscount Cunningham of Hyndhope, Brit. admiral; commander in Mediterranean in World War II; chief of naval staff (1943–46) .... 1883—1963
Curel, de (dē çü-rel'), **François,** French dramatist .... 1854—1928
Curie (çü-rē'), **Pierre,** French physicist and chemist; for work on radioactivity, shared Nobel prize (1903) .... 1859—1906
C., Marie Sklodowska (*wife of P.C.*), Polish chemist and physicist in France; Nobel awards (1903, 1911) .... 1867—1934
C., Ève Denise (*daughter*), Fr. writer and lecturer .... 1904 –
Curran (çûr'răn), **John Philpot,** Irish orator, statesman .... 1750—1817
Currie (çûr'ri), **Sir Arthur William,** Canadian general .... 1875—1933
Currier (çûr'i-ẽr), **Nathaniel,** Am. lithographer, collaborated with James M. Ives (1824–95) .... 1813—1895
Curry (çûr'ri), **John Steuart,** American painter .... 1897—1946
Curti (çûr'ti), **Merle (Eugene),** American historian .... 1897—
Curtis (çûr'tis), **Charles,** U.S. vice-president (1929–33) .... 1860—1936
Curtis, Cyrus, Am. newspaper and magazine publisher .... 1850—1933
Curtis, George William, American publicist and author .... 1824—1892
Curtiss (çûr'tis), **Glenn Hammond,** Am. aviator, inventor .... 1878—1930
Curwood (çûr'wood), **James Oliver,** American novelist .... 1878—1927
Curzon of Kedleston (çûr'zŏn ov ked'l-stŏn), **George Nathaniel Curzon, first Marquis,** English statesman, author, and viceroy of India (1899–1905) .... 1859—1925
Cushing (çush'ing), **Caleb,** American statesman .... 1800—1879
Cushing, Harvey Williams, Am. surgeon and author .... 1869—1939
Cushman (çush'măn), **Charlotte Saunders,** Am. actress .... 1816—1876
Custer (çus'tẽr), **George Armstrong,** American general .... 1839—1876
Cutter (çut'tẽr), **Charles Ammi,** American librarian .... 1837—1903
Cuvier (çū-vi-e'), **Georges, Baron,** French naturalist .... 1769—1832
Cuyp (çoip), **Albert,** Dutch landscape painter .... 1620—1691
Cynewulf (çyn'e-wulf), Anglo-Saxon poet .... fl.750?
Cyrano (cē-rȧ-nō') **de Bergerac,** *see* Bergerac, de.
Cyrus (cy'rus), (*the Great*), king of Persia .... ?–B.C.529
Czajkowski (chī-kof'skī), **Michael,** Polish novelist .... 1804—1886
Czerny (cher'nē), **Karl,** Austrian composer .... 1791—1857

D

Da Costa (dä ços'tȧ), **Isaäk**, Dutch historian and poet..........1798—1860
Dafoe (dā'fō), **Allan Roy**, Canadian physician who delivered the Dionne quintuplets in 1934..........1883—1943
Dagobert (dag'ō-bẽrt) **I**, king of the Franks..........600—638?
Daguerre (dȧ-ger'), **Louis Jacques Mandé**, French physicist and inventor..........1789—1851
Daimler (dām'lẽr *or Ger.* dīm'lẽr), **Gottlieb**, German inventor and pioneer automobile manufacturer..........1834—1900
Dakin (dā'kin), **Henry Drysdale**, American chemist, born in England..........1880—1952
Daladier (dȧ-lȧ-dyę'), **Édouard**, French statesman; premier (1933, 1934, 1938–40)..........1884—1970
Dale (dāl), **Sir Henry Hallett**, English research scientist..........1875—1968
Dale, Sir Thomas, Eng. colonial governor of Virginia.......... ? —1619
Dalén (dä-lān'), **Nils Gustaf**, Sw. physicist, inventor..........1869—1937
Dalhousie (dal-hǫǫ'ʂi), **James Andrew Broun Ramsay, Marquis of**, Brit. governor general of India (1847–56)..........1812—1860
Dali (dä'lī), **Salvador**, Sp. surrealist painter, author..........1904—
Dalin, von (fǫn dä'līn), **Olof**, Swedish historian and poet..........1708—1763
Dallas (dal'lȧs), **Alexander James**, American statesman..........1759—1817
D., George Mifflin (*son of A.J.D.*), vice-president of the United States (1845–49)..........1792—1864
Dallin (dal'lin), **Cyrus Edwin**, American sculptor..........1861—1944
Dalton (dạl'tŏn), **Hugh**, British political leader..........1887—1962
Dalton, John, English chemist and natural philosopher..........1766—1844
Daly (dā'ly), **Arnold**, American actor..........1875—1927
Daly, Augustin, Am. theatrical manager and playwright..........1838—1899
Damien de Veuster (dȧ-myaṅ' dẽ vu'ster), **Joseph** (*Father Damien*), Belgian Catholic missionary to leper colony at Molokai..........1840—1889
Dampier (dăm'pẽr), **William**, English navigator..........1652—1715
Damrosch (dam'rosh), **Walter Johannes**, American conductor and composer, born in Germany..........1862—1950
Dana (dā'nȧ), **Charles Anderson**, American journalist..........1819—1897
Dana, James Dwight, American geologist..........1813—1895
Dana, Richard Henry, American lawyer and author..........1815—1882
Dane (dān), **Clemence** (pseud. of *Winifred Ashton*), English novelist and playwright..........1888?—1965
Daniel (dan'yel), **Samuel**, English poet..........1562—1619
Daniels (dan'yelʂ), **Josephus**, U.S. secretary of the navy (1913–21); ambassador to Mexico (1933–41)..........1862—1948
Dannay (dan'nā), **Frederic**, *see* Queen, Ellery.
D'Annunzio (dän-nün'tsyō), **Gabriele**, Italian poet, playwright, novelist, and patriot..........1863—1938
Dante Alighieri (dän'tę ä-lï-gyę'rï), (b. *Durante Alighieri*) Italian poet; wrote *The Divine Comedy*..........1265—1321
Danton (dan'tŏn *or Fr.* däṅ-tǫṅ'), **Georges Jacques**, orator and leader in French Revolution..........1759—1794
Darius (dȧ-rī'us) **I** (*the Great*), king of Persia.......... ?–B.C.486
Darlan (dȧr'läṅ), **Jean**, French admiral and politician..........1881—1942
Darling (där'ling), **Jay Norwood** (*Ding*), American cartoonist..........1876—1962
Darnley (därn'li), **Henry Stewart, Lord**, second husband of Mary, Queen of Scots..........1545—1567
Darrow (dar'rō), **Clarence Seward**, American lawyer..........1857—1938
Daru (dȧ-rü'), **Pierre Antoine Noël Bruno, Count**, French statesman and poet..........1767—1829
Darwin (där'win), **Charles Robert**, English evolutionist..........1809—1882
D., Erasmus (*grandfather of C.R.D.*), English physician and poet..........1731—1802
Daubigny (dō-bï-nyē'), **Charles François**, Fr. painter..........1817—1878
Daudet (dō-de'), **Alphonse**, French novelist and dramatist..........1840—1897
D., Léon (*son of A.D.*), French journalist and politician..........1867—1942
Daumier (dō-myę'), **Honoré**, French caricaturist and artist..........1808—1879
Davenant (dav'en-ănt), **Sir William**, English poet laureate and dramatist..........1606—1668
Davenport (dav'en-pōrt), **Charles Benedict**, American zoologist..1866—1944
Davenport, Edward Loomis, American actor..........1815—1877
D., Fanny Lily (*daughter of E.L.D.*), actress, b. in Eng..........1850—1898
David (dȧ-vïd'), **Jacques Louis**, French painter..........1748—1825
David, Pierre Jean (*David d'Angers*), French sculptor..........1788—1856
Davids (dā'vidʂ), **Thomas William Rhys**, English Orientalist..........1843—1922
Davidson (dā'vid-sŏn), **Jo**, American sculptor..........1883—1952
Davies (dā'vēʂ), **Arthur Bowen**, American painter..........1862—1928
Davies, Hubert Henry, English dramatist..........1876—1917
Davies, Joseph Edward, American diplomat; ambassador to Russia (1936–38) and to Belgium (1938–40)..........1876—1958
da Vinci, Leonardo, *see* Vinci, da.
Davis (dā'vis), **Clyde Brion**, American novelist..........1894—1962
Davis, David, American jurist and senator..........1815—1886
Davis, Dwight F., U.S. sec. of war (1925–29); gov. gen. of Philippines (1929–32); donor of tennis trophy..........1879—1945
Davis, H. L., (*Harold Lenoir D.*), Am. novelist, poet..........1896—1960
Davis, Jefferson, president of the Confederacy..........1808—1889
Davis, Norman Hezekiah, American diplomat..........1878—1944
Davis, Owen, American playwright..........1874—1956
Davis, Richard Harding, Am. journalist and author..........1864—1916
Davis, William Morris, American geologist and educator..........1850—1934
Davitt (da'vit), **Michael**, Irish nationalist..........1846—1906
Davout (dȧ-vö'), **Louis Nicholas, Duke of Auerstädt and Prince of Eckmühl**, marshal of France..........1770—1823
Davy (dā'vy), **Sir Humphry**, English chemist..........1778—1829
Dawes (dạʂ), **Charles Gates**, U.S. vice president (1925–29); ambassador to Great Britain (1929–32)..........1865—1951
Dawkins (dạ'kinʂ), **Sir William Boyd**, Welsh geologist..........1837—1929
Dawson (dạ'sŏn), **Sir John William**, Canadian geologist..........1820—1899
Day (dā), **Clarence Shepard**, American poet and essayist..........1874—1935
Day, John, English dramatist..........1574?–1640?
Day *or* **Daye, Stephen**, Eng. settler in Am. who operated first printing plant in the Eng. colonies..........1594?—1668
Day, Thomas, English philanthropist and author..........1748—1789
Day, William Rufus, American statesman and associate justice of the U.S. Supreme Court (1903–22)..........1849—1923
Day Lewis, C(ecil), British poet and (under pseud. *Nicholas Blake*) novelist, b. in Ireland; poet laureate (1968–72)..........1904—1972
Deák (dę'äk), **Ferencz**, Hungarian statesman..........1803—1876
Deane (dēn), **Silas**, American diplomat..........1737—1789
Dearborn (dẽr'bŏrn), **Henry**, American general..........1751—1829
Debierne (dē-byern'), **André Louis**, French chemist..........1874—1949
Debs (debʂ), **Eugene Victor**, Am. Socialist leader..........1855—1926
Debussy (dē-bü-sē'), **Claude**, French composer..........1862—1918
Decatur (dē-çā'tũr), **Stephen**, American commodore..........1779—1820
Deeping (dēp'ing), **Warwick**, English novelist..........1877—1950
Defoe *or* **De Foe** (dē-fō'), **Daniel**, English author..........1659—1731
De Forest (dē for'est), **Lee**, American inventor..........1873—1961
Degas (dē-gä'), **Hilaire Germain Edgar**, French painter..........1834—1917
De Gasperi (dę gä'spę-rï), **Alcide**, Italian statesman; premier (1945–53)..........1881—1954
DeGaulle (dē-gōl'), **Charles**, French general, statesman; premier (1958–59); president (1959–69)..........1890—1970
De Kalb (dē kälb'), **Johann** (*Baron de Kalb*), Am. general in the Revolutionary Army, b. in Germany..........1721—1780
Dekker (dek'kẽr), **Thomas**, English dramatist..........1572?–1632?
Dekobra (dē kō'brȧ), **Maurice**, French novelist..........1885—1973
de Kooning (dē kō'ning), **Willem**, American painter, b. in Netherlands..........1904—
de Koven (dē kō'ven), **Reginald**, American composer..........1859—1920
de Kruif (dē krīf'), **Paul**, Am. bacteriologist, author..........1890—1971
Delacroix (dē-lȧ-ḉrwo'), **Ferdinand Victor Eugène**, French painter..........1799—1863
Delafield (del'ȧ-fēld), **E. M.** (pseud. of *Mrs. Arthur Paul Dashwood*), English novelist..........1890—1943
de la Mare (dē lȧ mãr'), **Walter**, Eng. poet, novelist..........1873—1956
Deland (dē-land'), **Margaret Campbell**, American novelist..........1857—1945
De la Ramée (dē lȧ rȧ-mę'), **Louise**, *see* Ouida.
Delaroche (dē-lȧ-rǫçh'), **Hippolyte**, French painter..........1797—1856
de la Roche (rǫçh'), **Mazo**, Canadian novelist..........1885—1961
Delavigne (dē-lȧ-vïn'y), **Jean François Casimir**, French poet and dramatist..........1793—1843
De la Warr *or* **Delaware** (del'ȧ-wãr), **Thomas West, Baron**, English colonial governor of Virginia..........1577—1618
Delcassé (del-çȧ-sę'), **Théophile**, French statesman..........1852—1923
Deledda (dę-led'dȧ), **Grazia**, Italian novelist..........1875—1936
Delibes (dē-lïb'), **Léo**, French composer..........1836—1891
Delius (dē'li-us), **Frederick**, English composer..........1862—1934
Dell (del), **Floyd**, American author..........1887—1969
Dellinger (del'lin-gẽr), **John Howard**, American physicist..........1886—1962
De Long (dē lǫng'), **George Washington**, Am. explorer..........1844—1881
Delorme (dē-lǫrm'), **Philibert**, French architect..........1515—1570
Delsarte (del-särt'), **François**, Fr. teacher of elocution..........1811—1871
Demetrius Poliorcetes (dē-mē'tri-us pol-i-ǫr'cē-tēʂ), king of Macedonia..........B.C. 337— 283
De Mille (dē mil'), **Agnes (George)**, American dancer and choreographer..........1905?–
D., Cecil B(lount), (*uncle of A.*), American motion-picture producer..........1881—1959
Democritus (dem-oç'ri-tus), Greek philosopher..........B.C. 460?–362?
De Morgan (dē mǫr'găn), **William**, English novelist..........1839—1917
Demosthenes (dē-mos'the-nēʂ), Athenian orator..........B.C. 384?– 322
Dempsey (demp'si), **William H.** (*Jack*), (*Manassa Mauler*) Am. prize fighter; world heavyweight champion (1919–26)..........1895—
Demuth (dē-muth'), **Charles Henry**, American painter..........1883—1935
Denby (den'by), **Edwin**, U.S. sec. of navy (1921–24)..........1870—1929
Denham (den'ăm), **Sir John**, British poet..........1615—1669
Denis (dē-nï' *or* den'is), **Saint**, first bishop of Paris..........fl.3rd cent.
Dennett (den'net), **Tyler**, Am. educator and historian..........1883—1949
Dennis (den'nis), **John**, English writer and critic..........1657—1734
Denver (den'vẽr), **James W.**, Am. territorial governor..........1817—1892
Depew (dē-pū'), **Chauncey Mitchell**, American railroad president, senator, and orator..........1834—1928
De Quincey (dē kwin'ci), **Thomas**, English author..........1785—1859
Derain (dē-raṅ'), **André**, French painter..........1880—1954
Derby (där'by), **Edward George Stanley, Earl of**, English statesman and premier..........1799—1869
De Sanctis (dę säṅç'tïs), **Francesco**, Italian critic..........1818—1883
Descartes (dę-çärt'), **René**, French philosopher..........1596—1650
Deschanel (dę-shȧ-nel'), **Paul Eugène Louis**, French statesman 1856—1922
de Seversky (de se-vẽr'ski), **Alexander Procofieff**, U.S. aeronautical engineer, born in Russia..........1894—1974
Desfontaines (dę-fǫṅ-tān'), **René Louiche**, French botanist..........1750—1833
Deshoulières (dę-ṣö-lyer'), **Antoinette**, French poet..........1638—1694
de Sitter (dē sit'tẽr), **Willem**, Dutch astronomer..........1872—1934
Desmoulins (de-mö-laṅ'), **Camille**, French revolutionist..........1760—1794
De Soto (dē sō'tō), **Hernando**, Spanish explorer..........1499?–1542
Deutsch (doitch), **Babette**, American poet and translator..........1895—
Deval (dē-väl'), **Jacques**, French playwright..........1894—
De Valera (dę vä-ler'ȧ), **Eamon**, Irish statesman, born in U.S.; prime minister of Eire (1937–48), of Ireland (1951–54, 1957–59); president of Ireland (1959–73)..........1882- 1975
De Vere (dē vẽr'), **Aubrey Thomas**, Irish poet..........1814—1902
Devereux (dev'ẽr-ü), *see* Essex, Earl of.
De Voto (dē vō'tō), **Bernard Augustine**, American author..........1897—1955
De Vries (dē vrēs'), **Hugo**, Dutch botanist..........1848—1935
Dewar (dū'ăr), **Sir James**, Scot. chemist, physicist..........1842—1923
De Wet (dē vet'), **Christian Rudolph**, Boer general..........1854—1922
Dewey (dū'i), **George**, American admiral..........1837—1917
Dewey, John, American philosopher and educator..........1859—1952
Dewey, Melvil, American librarian..........1851—1931
Dewey, Thomas Edmund, American lawyer, governor (N.Y.), and Rep. presidential nominee (1944, 1948)..........1902—1971
Dewing (dū'ing), **Thomas Wilmer**, American painter..........1851—1938
De Witt (dē vit'), **Jan**, Dutch statesman..........1625—1672
Diaghilev (dyä'gi-lyef), **Sergei Pavlovich**, Russian ballet producer and art critic..........1872—1929
Dias (dï'ăsh), **António Gonçalves**, Brazilian poet..........1823—1864
Dias, Bartholomeu, Portuguese navigator; discovered Cape of Good Hope in 1488..........1450?–1500
Diaz (dï'äs), **Porfirio**, president of Mexico (1877–80, 1884–1911)..1830—1915
Dick (dik), **George Frederick**, American physician..........1881—1967
Dickens (dik'enʂ), **Charles** (pseud. *Boz*), Eng. novelist..........1812—1870
Dickinson (dik'in-sŏn), **Emily**, American poet..........1830—1886
Dickinson, Goldsworthy Lowes, English writer..........1862—1932
Dickinson, John, American statesman..........1732—1808
Diderot (dï-dē-rō'), **Denis**, Fr. author, encyclopedist..........1713—1784
Diels (dēls), **Otto**, German chemist..........1876—1954
Diemen, van (vän dē'men), **Anthony**, Dutch East Indies governor..........1593—1645
Diesel (dēʂ'l), **Rudolf**, German inventor, born in Paris..........1858—1913
Diez (dēts), **Friedrich Christian**, German philologist..........1794—1876

Dillon (dil'lŏn), **George**, American poet....1906—1968

Dillon, John, Irish political leader....1851—1927

Dimitrov (di-mī'trọf), **Georgi**, Bulg. Communist leader....1882—1949

Dimnet (dĭm-ne'), **Ernest, Abbé**, French author....1866—1954

Dinesen (dĭn'e-sen), **Isak** (pseud. of *Baroness Karen Blixen*), Danish writer....1885—1962

Dinwiddie (din-wid'i *or* din'wid-i), **Robert**, British lieutenant governor of colonial Virginia (1751–58)....1693—1770

Diocletian (dī-ō-çlē'shăn), Roman emperor (284–305)....245— 313

Diogenes (dī-og'en-ēş), Greek Cynic philosopher....B.C. 412?–323?

Diogenes Laertius (lā-er'shi-us), Greek biographer....fl.222

Dionysius (dī-ō-nysh'i-us), (*the Elder*), tyrant of Syracuse...B.C. 430— 367

Dionysius of Halicarnassus (ov hal''i-çär-nas'sus), Greek historian and rhetorician....B.C. 54?— 7?

Dirac (di-raç'), **Paul Adrien Maurice**, Eng. physicist....1902—

Disney (diş'ni), **Walt** (*Walter Elias Disney*), American artist; producer of animated sound cartoons....1901—1966

Disraeli (diş-rā'li), **Benjamin, Earl of Beaconsfield**, English statesman and author....1804—1881

D'Israeli, Isaac (*father of B.D.*), English littérateur....1761—1848

Ditmars (dit'märş), **Raymond Lee**, Am. herpetologist....1876—1942

Dix (diks), **Dorothea Lynde**, American philanthropist....1802—1887

Dix, John Adams, American general and governor....1798—1879

Dixon (diks'ŏn), **Roland Burrage**, American anthropologist....1875—1934

Dixon, Thomas, American novelist and playwright....1864—1946

Dobell (dō-bel'), **Sydney Thompson**, English poet....1824—1874

Döblin (dẽp'lin), **Alfred**, German expressionist writer....1878—1957

Dobson (dob'sŏn), **(Henry) Austin**, Eng. poet and critic....1840—1921

Doddridge (dod'riġ), **Philip**, English dissenting divine....1702—1751

Dodds (dodş), **Harold Willis**, American educator....1889—

Dodge (doġ), **Mary Mapes**, Am. writer of juveniles....1831—1905

Dodgson (doġ'sŏn), **Charles**, *see* Carroll, Lewis.

Dohnányi, von (fọn dō'nän-yī), **Ernst**, Hungarian composer, pianist, and conductor....1877—1959

Doisy (doi'şē), **Edward Adelbert**, American biochemist....1893—

Dole (dōl), **Sanford Ballard**, Hawaiian statesman....1844—1926

Dolin (dō'lin), **Anton** (b. *Patrick Healey-Kay*), English choreographer and ballet dancer....1904—

Dollfuss (dol'fụs), **Engelbert**, Austrian statesman....1892—1934

Dominic (dom'in-iç), **Saint** *or* **Domingo de Guzmán** (dō-mĭng'-gō dẹ göth-män'), Spanish founder of the order of Dominicans..1170—1221

Domitian (dō-mish'i-ăn), Roman emperor (81–96)....51— 96

Donatello (don-ȧ-tel'lō), Italian sculptor....1386—1466

Donati (dō-nä'tī), **Giovanni Battista**, Italian astronomer....1826—1873

Donatus (dō-nā'tus), **Aelius**, Roman grammarian....fl.350

Donizetti (dō-nī-dzet'tī), **Gaetano**, Italian composer....1797—1848

Donne (dŏn *or* don), **John**, English divine and poet....1573—1631

Donnelly (don'nel-ly), **Ignatius**, American author and politician..1831—1901

Doolittle (dö'lit-l), **James H.**, Am. air force general....1896—

Doré (dō-re'), **Paul Gustave**, French illustrator, painter, and sculptor....1833—1883

Dornier (dŏr-nye'), **Claude**, German aircraft mfr....1884—1969

Dorsey (dọr'si), **George Amos**, American anthropologist and author....1868—1931

Dos Passos (dŏs pas'sŏs), **John**, American novelist....1896—1970

Dostoevski (dọs-to-yef'skĭ), **Feodor Mikhailovich**, Russian novelist....1821—1881

Dou *or* **?** (dou), **Gerard**, Dutch painter....1613—1675

Doubleday (dub'l-dā), **Abner**, American general; reputed inventor of baseball....1819—1893

Dougherty (dō'hẽr-ty), **Denis J.**, American Roman Catholic cardinal (1921–51)....1865—1951

Doughty (dö'ty), **Charles Montagu**, English writer....1843—1926

Douglas (dug'lăs), **Gavin**, Scottish poet....1474?–1522

Douglas, Lloyd C., American clergyman and novelist....1877—1951

Douglas, Norman, British novelist....1868—1952

Douglas, Stephen Arnold, American statesman....1813—1861

Douglas, William Orville, associate justice of U.S. Supreme Court (1939–75)....1898—1980

Douglass (dug'lăs), **Frederick**, Am. Negro leader, statesman....1817?–1895

Doumer (dö-mer'), **Paul**, Fr. statesman and president (1931–32)..1857—1932

Doumergue (dö-merg'), **Gaston**, French statesman; president of France (1924–31)....1863—1937

Doumic (dö-mīç'), **René**, French literary critic....1860—1937

Dow (dow), **Herbert Henry**, Am. chemist, manufacturer....1866—1930

Dow, Lorenzo, American Methodist preacher....1777—1834

Dow, Neal, American soldier and temperance advocate....1804—1897

Dowden (dou'den), **Edward**, Irish literary critic....1843—1913

Dowson (dou'sŏn), **Ernest Christopher**, English poet....1867—1900

Doyle (doil), **Sir Arthur Conan**, Scottish physician and novelist; famous for his *Sherlock Holmes* stories....1859—1930

Drake (drāk), **Sir Francis**, English navigator and buccaneer; first Englishman to circumnavigate the globe....1540?–1596

Drake, Joseph Rodman, American poet and satirist....1795—1820

Draper (drāp'ẽr), **John William**, American chemist, physiologist, and historian....1811—1882

D., Henry (*son of J.W.D.*), American astronomer....1837—1882

Draper, Ruth, American diseuse....1884—1956

Drayton (drā'tŏn), **Michael**, English poet....1563—1631

Dreiser (drī'sẽr), **Theodore**, American novelist....1871—1945

Dressler (dres'lẽr), **Marie**, Am. stage, screen actress....1869—1934

Drew (drů), **Daniel**, American financier....1797—1879

Dreyfus (drẹ'fus *or Fr.* drẹ-fůs'), **Alfred**, French officer unjustly imprisoned for treason....1859—1935

Drinkwater (drink'wạ-tẽr), **John**, English poet, dramatist, and biographer....1882—1937

Drummond (drum'mŏnd), **Sir Eric**, English diplomat; first secretary-general of League of Nations (1919–33)....1876—1951

Drummond, Henry, Scottish clergyman and author....1851—1897

Drummond, William, Scottish poet....1585—1649

Drusus (drů'sus), (*Nero Claudius Drusus Germanicus*), Roman general....B.C. 38— 9

Dryden (drȳ'den), **John**, Eng. poet laureate, dramatist....1631—1700

Du Barry (dů bȧ-rē' *or Eng.* bar'ē), **Jeanne Bécu, Comtesse**, French courtesan; mistress of Louis XV....1746—1793

Du Bois (dů bois'), **William Edward Burghardt**, American editor and author....1868—1963

Du Cange (dů çänz'), **Charles du Fresne**, French medievalist..1610—1688

Du Chaillu (dů çhȧ-yů'), **Paul Belloni**, American explorer in Africa, b. in France....1831?–1903

Duchamp (dů-çhäṅ'), **Marcel**, French painter....1887—1968

Duclos (dů-çlō'), **Charles Pinot**, French historiographer....1704—1772

Dudevant (důd-väṅ'), **Baronne**, *see* Sand, George.

Dudley (dud'li), **Joseph**, colonial governor of Massachusetts....1647—1720

Dudley, Robert, Earl of Leicester, *see* Leicester.

Duffy (duf'fy), **Francis Patrick**, U.S. army chaplain....1871—1932

Dufy (dů-fē'), **Raoul**, French painter....1878—1953

Duguay-Trouin (dů-gā'trö-aṅ'), **René**, French admiral....1673—1736

Du Guesclin (dů ge-çlaṅ'), **Bertrand**, constable of France....1320?–1380

Duhamel (dů-ȧ-mel'), **Georges**, Fr. novelist, dramatist....1884—1966

Dukas (dů-kä'), **Paul Abraham**, French composer....1865—1935

Duke (dūk), **James Buchanan**, Am. tobacco processor....1856—1925

Dulles (dul'les), **John Foster**, American statesman and diplomat; secretary of state (1953–59)....1888—1959

Dumas (dů-mä'), **Alexandre**, Fr. novelist, dramatist....1802—1870

D., Alexandre (*son of A.D.*), Fr. dramatist, novelist....1824—1895

Du Maurier (dů mō-rye'), **George**, Eng. artist, novelist....1834—1896

Du M., Daphne (*granddaughter of G.D.M.*), English novelist...1907—

Dumouriez (dů-mö-rye'), **Charles François**, French general....1739—1823

Dunant (dů-näṅ'), **Jean Henri**, Swiss philanthropist; founder of the Red Cross society....1828—1910

Dunbar (dun'bär), **Paul Laurence**, American poet....1872—1906

Dunbar, William, Scottish poet....1460?–1520?

Duncan (dun'çăn) **I**, king of Scotland (1034–40?); murdered by Macbeth....? –1040?

Duncan, Isadora, American dancer....1878—1927

Dundonald (dun'don-ăld), **Thomas Cochrane, tenth Earl of**, British admiral....1775—1860

Dunne (dun), **Finley Peter**, American humorist....1867—1936

Dunning (dun'ing), **John Ray**, American physicist....1907—1975

Dunois, de (dẽ dů-nwo'), **Jean, Count** (*the Bastard of Orléans*), French general and national hero....1403?–1468

Dunsany (dun-sā'ny), **Edward John Plunkett, Lord**, Irish dramatist and writer....1878—1957

Duns Scotus (dunş sçō'tus), **John** (*the Subtle Doctor*), Scottish scholar and theologian....1265—1308

Dunstan (dun'stăn), **Saint**, archbishop of Canterbury....925?— 988

Du Pont (dů-pọṅ' *or Eng.* dů-pont'), **Eleuthère Irénée**, American gunpowder manufacturer, born in Paris....1771—1834

Dupré (dů-prẹ'), **Jules**, French landscapist....1811?–1889

Duquesne (dů-kẹn'), **Abraham, Marquis**, Fr. naval hero....1610—1688

Duquesnoy (dů-kẹ-nwo'), **François**, Flemish sculptor....1594–1643?

Durand (dů-rand'), **Asher Brown**, Am. painter, engraver....1796—1886

Durant (dů-rant'), **Will** (*William James D.*), Am. writer....1885—1981

Duranty (dů-rant'y), **Walter**, Am. journalist, b. in England....1884—1957

Dürer (dür'ẽr), **Albrecht**, German painter and engraver....1471—1528

D'Urfey (dũr'fi), **Thomas**, Eng. dramatist and song writer....1653—1723

Duroc (dů-roç), **Gérard Christophe Michel, Duke of Friuli**, French general....1772—1813

Duruy (dů-rů-ē'), **Victor**, French historian....1811—1894

Duse (dů'şẹ), **Eleonora**, Italian actress....1859—1924

Dutra (dů'trȧ), **Enrico Gaspar**, Brazilian army officer; president of Brazil (1946–51)....1885—1974

Dutt (dut), **Rajani Palme**, English writer....1896—1974

Duveen (dů-vēn'), **Joseph, first Baron Duveen of Millbank**, English art dealer and collector....1869—1939

Duveneck (dů've-nek), **Frank**, Am. painter and teacher....1848—1919

Duyckinck (dȳ'kiňk), **Evert A.**, Am. author and editor....1816—1878

Dvořák (dvọr'zäk), **Anton**, Bohemian composer....1841—1904

Dwight (dwīt), **Timothy**, American divine and educator....1752—1817

E

Eads (ēdş), **James Buchanan**, American engineer....1820—1887

Eaker (ẹ'kẽr), **Ira Clarence**, U.S. air force general....1896—

Eakins (ẹ'kinş), **Thomas**, American painter....1844—1916

Eames (ẹmş), **Emma**, American soprano....1865—1952

Earhart (er'härt), **Amelia** (*Mrs. George Palmer Putnam*), American aviator; first woman to fly across Atlantic; lost in trans-Pacific flight....1898—1937

Early (ẽr'ly), **Jubal Anderson**, Confederate general....1816—1894

Eastman (ēst'măn), **George**, American inventor (photographic equipment) and philanthropist....1854—1932

Eastman, Joseph Bartlett, U.S. govt. administrator....1882—1944

Eastman, Max (Forrester), American author and editor....1883—1969

Eaton (ē'tŏn), **Cyrus S(tephen)**, American industrialist and financier, b. in Canada....1883—1979

Eaton, John Henry, U.S. sec. of war (1829–31)....1790—1856

E., Margaret O'Neale (*Peggy*), second wife of J.H.E....1796—1879

Eaton, Walter Pritchard, Am. critic, writer on drama....1878—1957

Ebers (ẹ'bẽrs), **Georg Moritz**, German Egyptologist and novelist..1837—1898

Ebert (ẹ'bẽrt), **Friedrich**, German statesman (Social Dem.); first president of German republic (1919–25)....1871—1925

Eccles (ek'lz), **Marriner Stoddard**, American banker; chairman of the Federal Reserve Board (1936–48)....1890—1977

Echegaray (e-che-gä-rä'ē), **José**, Spanish dramatist....1832—1916

Eck (ek), **Johann Maier von**, German Catholic theologian....1486—1543

Eckhart (ek'härt), **Johannes** (*Meister Eckhart*), German theologian and mystic....1260?–1328?

Eddington (ed'ding-tŏn), **Sir Arthur Stanley**, English astronomer and physicist....1882—1944

Eddy (ed'dy), **Mary Baker Glover**, Am. religious leader; founder of Christian Science....1821—1910

Eden (ē'den), **Sir (Robert) Anthony**, British statesman; prime minister (1955–57)....1897—1977

Edgeworth (eġ'wŏrth), **Maria**, Irish novelist....1767—1849

Edison (ed'i-sŏn), **Thomas Alva**, American inventor (phonograph, incandescent lamp, etc.)....1847—1931

E., Charles (*son of T.A.E.*), U.S. sec. of navy (1939–40)....1890—1969

Edman (ed'măn), **Irwin**, American philosopher, author....1896—1954

Edward (ed'wărd), (*the Black Prince*), prince of Wales....1330—1376

Edward I (*Longshanks*), king of England (1272–1307)....1239—1307

E. II (*son of E.I.*), king of England (1307–27)....1284—1327

E. III (*son of E.II*), king of England (1327–77)....1312—1377

E. IV, king of England (1461–70, 1471–83)....1442—1483

E. V (*son of E.IV*), king of England (1483); murdered in the Tower....1470—1483

E. VI (*son of Henry VIII and Jane Seymour*), king of England (1547–53)....1537—1553

E. VII (*Albert Edward*), (*son of queen Victoria*) king of England (1901–10) . . . 1841—1910
E. VIII (*son of George V*), king of England (1936); abdicated; thereafter, duke of Windsor . . . 1894—1972
Edwards (ed'wärds), **Jonathan**, American theologian and philosopher . . . 1703—1758
Edward the Confessor, king of England (1042–66) . . . 1002?–1066
Egan (ē'găn), **Maurice Francis**, Am. author, diplomat . . . 1852—1924
Egbert (eg'bĕrt), (*the Great*) king of the West Saxons . . . 775?— 839
Eggleston (eg'l-stŏn), **Edward**, American novelist . . . 1837—1902
Egmont (eg-mọń'), **Lamoral, Count of**, Flemish soldier and statesman . . . 1522—1568
Ehrenburg (ẹ'ren-bụrk), **Ilya Grigoryevich**, Russian novelist and journalist . . . 1891—1967
Ehrlich (er'likh), **Paul**, German bacteriologist . . . 1854—1915
Eichendorf, von (fọn ī'khen-dọrf), **Josef, Baron**, German lyric poet and author . . . 1788—1857
Eichhorn (īkh'họrn), **Johann Gottfried**, German theologian and Orientalist . . . 1752—1827
Eijkman (ik'män), **Christiaan**, Dutch pathologist . . . 1858—1930
Einhard (īn'härd) *or* **Eginhard** (ẹ'gin-härd), Frankish biographer. 770— 840
Einstein (īn'stīn), **Albert**, German-born physicist, became Am. citizen (1940); received Nobel prize (1921) . . . 1879—1955
Einthoven (īnt'hō-ven), **Willem**, Dutch physiologist . . . 1860—1927
Eisenhower (ī'sẹn-hou-ĕr), **Dwight David**, American general and 34th U.S. president (1953–61); supreme Allied commander in Europe in World War II . . . 1890—1969
Eisenstein (i-sẹn-shtyĕn'), **Sergei Mikhailovich**, Russian motion-picture director . . . 1898—1948
Elgar (el'gär), **Sir Edward**, English composer . . . 1857—1934
El Greco (el greç'ō), (b. *Domenico Theotocopoulos*) Greek painter and sculptor in Spain . . . 1548?–1614?
Eliot (el'i-ŏt), **Charles William**, American educator . . . 1834—1926
Eliot, George (pseud. of *Mary Ann Evans*), English novelist . . . 1819—1880
Eliot, John (*Apostle of the Indians*), English evangelist in colonial America . . . 1604—1690
Eliot, Sir John, English statesman and orator . . . 1592—1632
Eliot, T.S. (*Thomas Stearns E.*), Eng. poet, critic, and dramatist, b. in U.S.; received Nobel prize (1948) . . . 1888—1965
Elizabeth (ē-liz'ȧ-beth) **I** (*daughter of Henry VIII and Anne Boleyn*), queen of England (1558–1603) . . . 1533—1603
Elizabeth II (*daughter of George VI*), queen of England (1952–) . 1926—
Elizabeth (*daughter of Peter the Great*), empress of Russia (1741–62). 1709—1762
Elizabeth (pseud. *Carmen Sylva*), queen of Romania and author . 1843—1916
Ellery (el'lĕr-y), **William**, Am. Revolutionary patriot . . . 1727—1820
Ellicott (el'li-çot), **Andrew**, American surveyor general . . . 1754—1820
Ellington (el'ing-tŏn), **Duke** (b. *Edward Kennedy E.*) American jazz musician and composer . . . 1899—1974
Ellis (el'lis), **(Henry) Havelock**, English psychologist, editor, and author . . . 1859—1939
Elman (el'măn), **Mischa**, American violinist, b. in Russia . . . 1891—1967
Ellsworth (els'wŏrth), **Lincoln**, Am. polar explorer . . . 1880—1951
Ellsworth, Oliver, chief justice U.S. Supreme Court (1796–99) . . . 1745—1807
Éluard (ā-lü-är'), **Paul**, (pseud. of *Eugène Grindel*), French poet . . 1895—1952
Ely (ē'ly), **Richard Theodore**, American economist . . . 1854—1943
Elyot (el'yŏt), **Sir Thomas**, English scholar, diplomat . . . 1490?–1546
Elytis (e-lē'tis), **Odysseus** (b. *Odysseus Alepoudhelis*), Greek poet . 1911—
Elzevir (el'ze-vir *or* -vīr), **Louis**, Dutch printer . . . 1540—1617
E., **Bonaventure** (*son of L.E.*), Dutch printer . . . 1583—1652
Emerson (em'ĕr-sŏn), **Ralph Waldo**, American essayist, poet, and philosopher . . . 1803—1882
Emmet (em'met), **Robert**, Irish patriot . . . 1778—1803
Emmett (em'met), **Daniel Decatur**, Am. song writer . . . 1815—1904
Empedocles (em-ped'ō-çlēş), Greek philosopher . . . B.C. 5th cent.
Encke (en'ke), **Johann Franz**, German astronomer . . . 1791—1865
Endecott *or* **Endicott** (en'di-çot), **John**, colonial governor of Massachusetts . . . 1588?–1665
Enesco (en-es'çō), **Georges**, Romanian violinist, composer, and conductor . . . 1881—1955
Engels (eng'els), **Friedrich**, German socialist . . . 1820—1895
Engle (en'gl), **Paul Hamilton**, American poet . . . 1908—
Ennius (en'ni-us), **Quintus**, Roman epic poet . . . B.C. 239?—169
Enzina *or* **Encina, del** (del ẹn-thī'nä), **Juan**, Spanish poet and dramatist . . . 1446?–1516?
Epaminondas (ē-păm-i-non'dăs), Theban statesman and general . . . B.C. 418?—362
Epictetus (ep-iç-tē'tus), Greek Stoic philosopher . . . 60?—120?
Epicurus (ep-i-çūr'us), Greek philosopher . . . B.C. 342?—270
Epimenides (ep-i-men'i-dēş), Cretan poet, prophet . . . B.C. 6th cent.
Épinay, d' (dẹ-pī-nā'), **Louise Florence**, French author; friend of Rousseau, F. M. Grimm, Diderot, Voltaire . . . 1726—1783
Epstein (ep'stīn), **Jacob**, British sculptor, b. in U.S. . . . 1880—1959
Erasmus (ē-raş'mus), **Desiderius**, Dutch humanist, scholar, and author . . . 1466?–1536
Erastus (ē-ras'tus), **Thomas**, German-Swiss theologian . . . 1524—1583
Eratosthenes (er-ȧ-tos'the-nēş), Greek astronomer . . . B.C. 276?—195
Ercilla y Zúñiga, de (dẹ er-thīl'yä ē thü'nyī-gä), **Alonzo**, Spanish epic poet . . . 1533–1594?
Erckmann-Chatrian (erk-män'chä-trī-äṅ'), [pen name of *Emile Erckmann* (1822–99) and *Alexandre Chatrian* (1826–90)], Fr. novelists and dramatists in collaboration.
Ericsson (er'iç-sŏn), **John**, Swedish inventor in America . . . 1803—1889
Ericsson, Leif (*son of Eric the Red*), Norwegian discoverer of North America . . . fl. 1000
Eric the Red, Norwegian navigator; discovered and colonized Greenland . . . fl.10th cent.
Erigena (er-i'ġen-ȧ), **Johannes Scotus**, Scottish philosopher, b. in Ireland . . . ? —880
Ernst (ernst), **Max**, German surrealist painter . . . 1891—1976
Ersch (ersh), **Johann Samuel**, German encyclopedist . . . 1766—1828
Erskine (ĕr'skin), **Ebenezer**, Scottish preacher . . . 1680—1754
Erskine, John, Am. educator, musician, and author . . . 1879—1951
Erskine, Thomas, Baron, lord chancellor of England . . . 1750—1823
Ervine (ĕr'vin), **St. John Greer**, Irish novelist, critic, and dramatist . . . 1883—1971
Escoffier (es-ço-fyā'), **Auguste**, French chef and writer on cooking . 1847—1935
Espartero (es-pär-tẹ'rō), **Baldomero, Duque de la Victoria**, Spanish general and statesman . . . 1792—1879
Espiña (es-pīn'yä), **Concha**, Spanish novelist . . . 1877—1955
Essex (es'seks), **Robert Devereux, second Earl of**, Eng. soldier; favorite of Queen Elizabeth I; executed . . . 1567—1601
Estaing, d' (des-taṅ'), **Charles Hector, Count**, French admiral . 1729—1794
Esterhazy (es'tĕr-hä-zy), family of Hungarian nobles.
Estienne (es-tyen'), **Henri**, French printer . . . 1460—1520
Estrades, d' (des-trȧd'), **Godefroi, Comte**, marshal of France . . 1607—1686
Ethelred (eth'el-red) *or* **Ethelred I**, king of Wessex . . . ? — 871
Ethelred II (*the Unready*), king of England (978–1016) . . . 968?–1016
Etherege (eth'ĕr-eġ), **Sir George**, English dramatist . . . 1635—1691
Eucken (oik'en), **Rudolf Christoph**, German philosopher . . . 1846—1926
Euclid (ū'çlid) **of Alexandria**, Greek geometrician . . . fl. B.C. 300
Euclid of Megara, Greek philosopher . . . fl. B.C. 400
Eugene (ū-ġēn' *or Fr.* ü-zen') **of Savoy, Prince**, Austrian general . 1663—1736
Eugénie (ü-zẹ-nē') *or* **Marie Eugénie de Montijo**, wife of Napoleon III and empress of France . . . 1826—1920
Euler (oil'ĕr *or* ū'lĕr), **Leonhard**, Swiss geometrician . . . 1707—1783
Euripides (ū-rip'i-dēş), Athenian tragic dramatist . . . B.C. 480— 406
Eusebius (ū-sē'bi-us), **Pamphili**, Gr. church historian . . . 260?–340?
Evans (ev'ănş), **Sir Arthur John**, Eng. archaeologist . . . 1851—1941
Evans, Augusta Jane, American novelist . . . 1835—1909
Evans, Caradoc, Welsh short-story writer, novelist . . . 1883—1945
Evans, Sir John, Eng. archaeologist and numismatist . . . 1823—1908
Evans, Mary Ann, *see* Eliot, George.
Evans, Maurice, English actor . . . 1901—
Evarts (ev'ărts), **William Maxwell**, American lawyer and statesman . . . 1818—1901
Evatt (ev'ăt), **Herbert Vere**, Australian statesman; president of U.N. General Assembly (1948–49) . . . 1894—1965
Evelyn (ēv'lin), **John**, English diarist . . . 1620—1706
Everett (ev'ĕr-et), **Edward**, Am. orator and statesman . . . 1794—1865
Ewald, von (fọn ẹ'vȧlt), **Georg Heinrich August**, German Orientalist . . . 1803—1875
Ewald, Johannes, Danish poet . . . 1743—1781
Ewell (ū'el), **Richard Stoddert**, Confederate general . . . 1817—1872
Eyck, van (vän īk'), **Hubert**, Flemish painter . . . 1370?–1426
E.,v., Jan (*brother of H.v.E.*), Flemish painter . . . 1390?–1440
Ezekiel (ē-zē'ki-el), **Moses Jacob**, American sculptor . . . 1844—1917

F

Faber (fā'bĕr), **Frederick William**, English theologian and poet . 1814—1863
Fabius (fā'bi-us), (*Quintus Fabius Maximus*, called *Cunctator* [*Delayer*]) Roman general; opposed Hannibal . . . B.C. ? — 203
Fabre (fä'br), **Jean Henri**, Fr. entomologist, author . . . 1823—1915
Fabricius (fȧ-brish'i-us), (*Caius Fabricius Luscinus*) Roman general and statesman . . . fl.B.C.280
Fabricius (fä-bri'ci-ụs), **Johan Christian**, Danish entomologist . 1745—1808
Fabyan (fā'bi-ăn), **Robert**, English chronicler . . . 1450—1513
Fadiman (fad'i-măn), **Clifton**, Am. critic, entertainer . . . 1904—
Faguet (fȧ-ge'), **Émile**, Fr. literary critic, historian . . . 1847—1916
Fahrenheit (fä'ren-hīt), **Gabriel Daniel**, German physicist . . . 1686—1736
Fairbairn (fār'bărn), **Sir William**, Scot. civil engineer . . . 1789—1874
Fairbanks (fär'banks), **Charles Warren**, vice-president of the United States (1905–09) . . . 1852—1918
Fairbanks, Douglas, American motion-picture actor . . . 1883—1939
Fairfax (fär'faks), **Edward**, English poet and translator . . . ? —1635
Fairfax, Thomas, Lord, English parliamentary general . . . 1612—1671
Falconer (fạ'çŏn-ĕr), **Hugh**, Scottish palaeontologist . . . 1808—1865
Falconer, Sir Robert Alexander, Canadian educator . . . 1867—1943
Falconer, William, Scottish poet and lexicographer . . . 1732—1769
Falconet (fȧl-çō-ne'), **Étienne Maurice**, French sculptor . . . 1716—1791
Falguière (fȧl-gyẹr'), **Jean Alexandre Joseph**, French sculptor and painter . . . 1831—1900
Faliero (fä-lyẹ'rō), **Marino**, doge of Venice . . . 1274?–1355
Falkenhayn, von (fọn fäl'ken-hȳn), **Erich**, German general . . . 1861—1922
Fall (fạl), **Albert B.**, U.S. sec. of interior (1921–23) . . . 1861—1944
Falla, de (dẹ fäl'yä), **Manuel**, Spanish composer . . . 1876—1946
Fallada (fäl'lä-dä), **Hans** (pseud. of *Rudolf Ditzen*), German novelist . . . 1893—1947
Fallières (fȧl-yẹr'), **Clément Armand**, French statesman and president (1906–13) . . . 1841—1931
Fallopio (fäl-lō-pyō), **Gabriello**, Italian anatomist . . . 1523—1562
Falstaff (fạl'staf), **Jake** (pseud. of *Herman Fetzer*), American author and poet . . . 1899—1935
Fantin-Latour (fäṅ-taṅ'lȧ-tör'), **Ignace Théodore**, French painter and lithographer . . . 1836—1904
Faraday (far'ȧ-dā), **Michael**, Eng. physicist, chemist . . . 1791—1867
Farel (fä-rel'), **Guillaume**, French Protestant reformer . . . 1489—1565
Fargo (fär'gō), **William George**, American express owner . . . 1818—1881
Farina (fä-rī'nä), **Salvatore**, Italian novelist . . . 1846—1918
Farinato (fä-rī-nä'tō), **Paolo**, Italian painter . . . 1525—1606
Farinelli (fär-ī-nel'lī), **Carlo** (b. *Carlo Broschi*), Neapolitan singer . 1705—1782
Farini (fä-rī'nī), **Luigi Carlo**, It. statesman, author . . . 1812—1866
Farley (fär'li), **James Aloysius**, Am. political leader; U.S. postmaster general (1933–36, 1937–40) . . . 1888—1976
Farmer (fär'mĕr), **Fannie Merritt**, Am. cookery expert . . . 1857—1915
Farnol (fär'nŏl), **(John) Jeffery**, English novelist . . . 1878—1952
Farouk (fä-rök') **I**, king of Egypt (1936–52); abdicated . . . 1920—1965
Farquhar (fär'kwăr), **George**, Irish dramatist . . . 1678—1707
Farragut (far'ȧ-gut), **David Glasgow**, American admiral . . . 1801—1870
Farrar (far'răr), **Frederick William**, English clergyman and author . . . 1831—1903
Farrar (fȧ-rär'), **Geraldine**, American operatic soprano . . . 1882—1967
Farrell (fä-rel'), **Edelmiro J.**, president of Argentina (1944–46) . . 1887?–1980
Farrell (fa'rel), **James Thomas**, American novelist . . . 1904—1979
Farson (fär'sŏn), **(James) Negley**, American author . . . 1890—1960
Fast (fȧst), **Howard**, American novelist . . . 1914—
Fatima (fat'i-mȧ), daughter of Mohammed . . . 606?– 632
Faulhaber, von (fọn foul'hä-bĕr), **Michael, Cardinal**, German ecclesiastic and cardinal . . . 1869—1952
Faulkner (fạk'nĕr), **William**, American novelist and short-story writer; received Nobel prize (1949) . . . 1897—1962
Faure (fōr), **Élie**, French art critic . . . 1873—1937
Faure, François Félix, president of France (1895–99) . . . 1841—1899
Fauré (fō-rẹ'), **Gabriel**, French composer and organist . . . 1845—1924
Faust (foust) *or* **Faustus** (fous'tus), **Johann**, German alchemist . 1480?–1541
Faversham (fav'ĕr-shăm), **William**, American actor, born in London . . . 1868—1940

Fawcett (fa̤'cet), **Edgar**, American novelist....................1847—1904
Fawcett, George, American actor..........................1861—1939
Fawkes (fa̤ks), **Guy**, English conspirator; executed...........1570—1606
Fay (fä-ē'), **Bernard**, French historian and biographer.........1893—
Fay (fā), **Sidney Bradshaw**, American historian...............1876—1967
Fechner (fekh'nēr), **Gustav Theodor**, German philosopher, physicist, and psychologist..................................1801—1887
Feininger (fī'ning-ēr), **Lyonel (Charles Adrian)**, Am. painter. 1871—1956
Feisal (fī'sa̤l), **I**, king of Syria (1920) and Iraq (1921–33)........1885—1933
F.II (*grandson of F.I.*), king of Iraq (from 1939); ascended the throne in 1953, ending a regency; assassinated...............1935—1958
Feith (fīt), **Rhijnvis**, Dutch poet and writer..................1753—1824
Fellows (fel'ōs), **Sir Charles**, English archaeologist...........1799—1860
Fénelon (fe̤-ne-lo̤ṅ'), **François de Salignac de la Mothe**, French prelate and author; archbishop of Cambrai....................1651—1715
Fenton (fen'tŏn), **Elijah**, English poet and writer..............1683—1730
Feodor (fyo̤'do̤r) **I**, (*Feodor Ivanovich*), czar of Russia...........1557—1598
Ferber (fēr'bēr), **Edna**, American novelist.....................1887—1968
Ferdinand (fēr'di-nand) **I**, emperor of Germany.................1503—1564
Ferdinand, king of Romania (1914–27)..........................1865—1927
Ferdinand V (*the Catholic*), king of Castile and Spain...........1452—1516
Ferdinand VI (*the Wise*), king of Spain (1746–59)................1713—1759
Ferdinand VII, king of Spain (1808–33).........................1784—1833
Ferguson (fēr'gu-sŏn), **Adam**, Scottish philosopher and historian.1723—1816
Ferguson, Sir Samuel, Irish poet and antiquary..................1810—1886
Fermi (fer'mī), **Enrico**, Am. physicist, b. Italy; furthered atomic bomb project; received 1938 Nobel prize........................1901—1954
Fernández (fēr-nän'de̤th), **Juan**, Spanish navigator...........1536?–1602?
Ferrari (fer-rär'ī), **Giuseppe**, Italian philosopher and historian..1812—1876
Ferreira (fer-re̤'i-rä), **Antonio**, Port. poet, dramatist..........1528—1569
Ferrero (fer-re̤'rō), **Guglielmo**, It. historian, writer...........1871—1942
Ferrier (fer'i-ēr), **Sir David**, Scottish neurologist..............1843—1928
Ferry (fe-rē'), **Jules François Camille**, French statesman......1832—1893
Fersen, von (fo̤n fer'sen), **Axel, Count**, Swedish marshal.........1755—1810
Fessenden (fes'sen-den), **Reginal Aubrey**, American inventor and physicist..1866—1932
Fessenden, William Pitt, American statesman....................1806—1869
Fetzer (fet'sēr), **Herman**, *see* Falstaff, Jake.
Feuchtwanger (foikht'väng-ēr), **Lion**, German novelist.........1884—1958
Feuerbach (foi'ēr-bakh), **Ludwig Andreas**, German philosopher.1804—1872
Feuillet (fū-ye'), **Octave**, French novelist.....................1821—1890
Fewkes (fūks), **Jesse Walter**, American ethnologist..............1850—1930
Fibiger (fī'bi-gēr), **Johannes**, Danish pathologist..............1867—1928
Fichte (fikh'te), **Johann Gottlieb**, German philosopher.........1762—1814
Fiedler (fēd'lēr), **Max**, German orchestra conductor.............1859—1939
Field (fēld), **Charles W.**, American Confederate general.........1828—1892
Field, Cyrus West, American merchant; sponsor of first Atlantic submarine telegraph..1819—1892
Field, David Dudley, American jurist..........................1805—1894
Field, Eugene, American poet and journalist.....................1850—1895
Field, Marshall, American merchant............................1834—1906
Field, Rachel Lyman, American novelist........................1894—1942
Fielding (fēld'ing), **Henry**, English novelist....................1707—1754
Fiesole, da (dä fye'so̤-le̤), **Giovanni** (*Fra Angelico*), Italian painter.1387—1455
Figueroa, de (de̤ fī-ge̤-rō'ä), **Francisco** (*the Divine*), Spanish poet.1536–1617?
Fillmore (fil'mōr), **Millard**, thirteenth president of the United States (1850–53)...1800—1874
Finley (fin'li), **John Huston**, Am. educator, editor...............1863—1940
Finley, Martha Farquharson, American children's writer......1828—1909
Finsen (fin'sin), **Niels Ryberg**, Danish physician; founder of phototherapy..1860—1904
Firdausi (fir-dou'sī), (b. *Abul Kasim Mansur*) Persian epic poet.940?–1020?
Firestone (fīr'stōn), **Harvey Samuel**, Am. industrialist........1868—1938
Fischer (fish'ēr), **Kuno** (*Ernest Kuno Berthold F.*), German philosopher...1824—1907
Fish (fish), **Hamilton**, U.S. sec. of state (1869–77)..............1808—1893
Fisher (fish'ēr), **Dorothy Canfield**, American novelist.........1879—1958
Fisher, Irving, American economist.............................1867—1947
Fisher, John Arbuthnot, first Baron Fisher of Kilverstone, British admiral.....................................1841—1920
Fiske (fisk), **John**, American historian and philosopher.........1842—1901
Fiske, Minnie Maddern Davey, American actress...............1865—1932
Fitch (fich), **Clyde** (*William Clyde F.*), Am. playwright..........1865—1909
Fitch, John, American steamboat inventor......................1743—1798
FitzGerald (fits-ġer'ăld), **Edward**, English poet and translator..1809—1883
Fitzgerald, Francis Scott Key, American novelist.................1896—1940
Flagg (flag), **James Montgomery**, American painter and illustrator..1877—1960
Flagstad (fläg'stät), **Kirsten**, Norwegian soprano..............1895—1962
Flamininus (fla-mi-nī'nus), **Titus Quinctius** (*Liberator of the Greeks*), Roman general and statesman.....................B.C. 230?–175?
Flammarion (flȧ-mȧ-ryo̤ṅ'), **Camille**, Fr. astronomer.............1842—1925
Flanagan (flan'ȧ-găn), **Edward Joseph**, Am. R.C. priest, b. Ireland; director Father Flanagan's Boys' Home...............1886—1948
Flandin (fläṅ-daṅ'), **Pierre Étienne**, French politician; premier (1934–35); member of Vichy government......................1889—1958
Flaubert (flō-ber'), **Gustave**, French novelist...................1821—1880
Flecker (flek'ēr), **James Elroy**, Eng. poet, dramatist............1884—1915
Fleming (flem'ing), **Sir Alexander**, Scottish bacteriologist; discovered penicillin; shared 1945 Nobel prize with H. W. Florey and E. B. Chain..1881—1955
Fletcher (flech'ēr), **John**, English dramatist; colleague of Beaumont..1579—1625
Fletcher, John Gould, American poet............................1886—1950
Fleury (flē-rē'), **Claude**, French ecclesiastical historian...........1640—1723
Flexner (fleks'nēr), **Abraham**, American educator...............1866—1959
F., Simon (*brother of A.F.*), American pathologist................1863—1946
Flint (flint), **Austin**, Am. physician, medical writer............1812—1886
F., Austin (*son of A.F.*), Am. physiologist, medical writer.......1836—1915
Florey (flōr'i), **Sir Howard Walter**, Australian pathologist in England; shared 1945 Nobel prize with A. Fleming, E. B. Chain..1898—1968
Florian, de (dē flō-ryäṅ'), **Jean Pierre Claris**, French novelist..1755—1794
Florio (flō'ri-ō), **John**, Eng. philologist, translator..............1553?–1625
Flotow, von (fo̤n flō'tō), **Friedrich Ferdinand Adolf, Count**, German composer..1812—1883
Foch (fo̤ch), **Ferdinand**, marshal of France; generalissimo of Allied armies in France (1918)..................................1851—1929
Fokine (fō-kīn'), **Michel**, Am. choreographer, b. in Russia......1880—1942
Fokker (fōk'kēr), **Anthony Herman Gerard**, Dutch aircraft designer, constructor, in Germany and U.S......................1890—1939
Fonseca, da (dä fo̤n-se̤'ça̤), **Manuel Deodoro**, Brazilian general and first president of the republic (1891)......................1827—1892
Fontana (fōn-tä'nä), **Domenico**, Italian architect...............1543—1607
Fontanne (fon-tan'), **Lynn** (*Mrs. Alfred Lunt*) American actress, born in England.....................................1887?–
Foote (foot), **Andrew Hull**, American rear admiral................1806—1863
Foote, Henry Stuart, American politician.......................1804—1880
Foote, Samuel, English dramatist and wit.......................1720—1777
Forbes (fo̤rbs̤), **Archibald**, English journalist...................1838—1900
Forbes, Edward, British naturalist.............................1815—1854
Forbes, James David, Scottish physicist.........................1809—1868
Forbes-Robertson (-rob'ērt-sŏn), **Sir Johnston**, English actor..1853—1937
Ford (fo̤rd), **Ford Madox** (b. *Ford Madox Hueffer*), English novelist and critic...1873—1939
Ford, Gerald R(udolph), Jr., 38th president of the United States (1974–77)......................................1913—
Ford, Henry, American automobile manufacturer.................1863—1947
Ford, John, English dramatist.................................1586–1639?
Ford, Paul Leicester, Am. novelist and historian.................1865—1902
Ford, Worthington Chauncey, Am. editor and historian.........1858—1941
Forester (fo̤r'is-tēr), **Cecil Scott**, English novelist...............1899—1966
Forrest (for'rest), **Edwin**, American tragedian...................1806—1872
Forrest, Nathan Bedford, Am. Confederate general..............1821—1877
Forrestal (for'res-tăl), **James Vincent**, U.S. secretary of navy (1944–47) and secretary of defense (1947–49).....................1892—1949
Forster (fo̤r'stēr), **Edward Morgan**, English novelist..........1879—1970
Forster, John, English biographer..............................1812—1876
Forsyth (fo̤r'sȳth), **John**, American statesman..................1780—1841
Foscolo (fo̤s-ço̤'lō), **Ugo**, Italian poet and writer................1778—1827
Fosdick (fo̤s̤'dik), **Harry Emerson**, American clergyman.........1878—1969
Foster, John Watson, American diplomat........................1836—1917
Foster, Stephen Collins, American song writer..................1826—1864
Foster, William Zebulon, Am. Communist party leader..........1881—1961
Foucault (fö-ço̤'), **Jean Bernard Léon**, Fr. physicist............1819—1868
Fouché (fö-ch̤e̤'), **Joseph, Duke of Otranto**, French Jacobin and minister of police.....................................1759—1820
Fouqué (fö-ke̤'), **Friedrich Heinrich Karl, Baron de la Motte**, German poet and novelist.....................................1777—1843
Fourier (fö-rye̤'), **François Marie Charles**, French socialist....1772—1837
Fourier, Jean Baptiste Joseph, Baron, French mathematician and physicist......................................1768—1830
Fox (foks), **Charles James**, Eng. orator and statesman...........1749—1806
Fox, Dixon Ryan, American historian and educator..............1887—1945
Fox, George, English founder of the Society of Friends...........1624—1691
Fox, John, Jr., American novelist..............................1862—1919
Foxe *or* **Fox** (foks), **John**, English reformer and author..........1516—1587
Fragonard (frȧ-gō-nȧr'), **Jean Honoré**, French painter..........1732—1806
France (fräṅc), **Anatole** (pseud. of *Jacques Anatole Thibault*), French novelist; received 1921 Nobel prize.......................1844—1924
Francesca (frän-ches'çä), **Piero della**, Italian painter.........1420?–1492
Francis (fran'cis) **I**, king of France............................1494—1547
Francis II, last Holy Roman emperor (1792–1806) and (as Francis I) first emperor of Austria (1804–35)...........................1768—1835
Francis Ferdinand (fēr'di-nand), **Archduke**, heir to crown of Austria; assassinated at Serajevo.................................1863—1914
Francis Joseph (jō'ṣef) **I** (*Franz Josef*), emperor of Austria (1848–1916) and king of Hungary (1867–1916).......................1830—1916
Francis of Assisi, Saint, Italian friar; founder of the Order of Franciscans.......................................1182—1226
Francis, Sir Philip, British statesman and writer...............1740—1818
Franck (fräṅk), **César Auguste**, French composer..............1822—1890
Franco (fräṅ'ço̤), **Francisco**, Spanish general, dictator (1939–75), and chief of state.......................................1892—1975
François-Poncet (fräṅ'cwo-po̤ṅ-ce̤'), **André**, French politician and diplomat...1887—
Frank (fräṅk), **Bruno**, German novelist and dramatist...........1887—1945
Frank (frank), **Glenn**, American educator and author...........1887—1940
Frank (fräṅk), **Leonhard**, German novelist....................1882—1961
Frank (frank), **Tenney**, American historian....................1876—1939
Frankau (fran'ka̤), **Gilbert**, English novelist...................1884—1952
Frankfurter (frank'fūr-tēr), **Felix**, American jurist, b. in Austria; associate justice of U.S. Supreme Court (1939–62)...............1882—1965
Franklin (frank'lin), **Benjamin**, American statesman, scientist, inventor, and author.....................................1706—1790
Franklin, Christine Ladd, American psychologist................1847—1930
Franklin, Sir John, English arctic explorer......................1786—1847
Franklin, William Buel, American general......................1823—1903
Franz (fränts), **Robert**, German song writer....................1815—1892
Fraser (frā'ṣēr), **Alexander Campbell**, Scottish philosopher and educator...1819—1914
Fraser, James Baillie, Scottish traveler and writer..............1783—1856
Fraser, James Earle, American sculptor........................1876—1953
Fraunhofer, von (fo̤n froun'hō-fēr), **Joseph**, Bavarian optician..1787—1826
Frazee (frȧ-zē'), **John**, American sculptor......................1790—1852
Frazer (frā'zēr), **Sir James George**, Scottish anthropologist.....1854—1941
Frazer, Joseph Washington, American automobile mfr..........1892—
Fréchette (fre̤-ch̤et'), **Louis Honoré**, Fr.-Can. poet..............1839—1908
Frederick (fred'ēr-ik) **I**, (*Barbarossa*), German emperor........1123?–1190
Frederick II, German emperor................................1194—1250
Frederick I, first king of Prussia..............................1657—1713
Frederick II (*Frederick the Great*), king of Prussia (1740–86).......1712—1786
Frederick William (wil'yăm), (*the Great Elector*) elector of Brandenburg and founder of the Prussian monarchy.....................1620—1688
F.W. I (*father of Frederick the Great*), king of Prussia (1713–40).1638—1740
F.W. II (*nephew of Frederick the Great*), king of Prussia (1786–97).1744—1797
F.W. III (*son of F.W. II*), king of Prussia (1797–1840)...........1770—1840
F.W. IV (*son of F.W. III*), king of Prussia (1840–61)............1795—1861
Freeman (frē'măn), **Douglas Southall**, Am. biographer..........1886—1953
Freeman, Edward Augustus, English historian..................1823—1892
Freeman, Mary E. Wilkins, Am. novelist........................1852—1930
Freiligrath (frī'likh-rät), **Ferdinand**, German poet..............1810—1876
Frelinghuysen (frē'ling-hȳ-ṣen), **Frederick Theodore**, American statesman; secretary of state (1881–85)..........................1817—1885
Frémont (frē-mont'), **John Charles**, American explorer and general; Rep. presidential nominee (1856).........................1813—1890
Fremstad (frem'städ), **Olive**, Am. soprano, b. in Sweden.........1870—1951
French (french), **Daniel Chester**, American sculptor...........1850—1931
French, John Denton Pinkstone, first Earl of Ypres, British field marshal..1852—1925
Freneau (frē-nō'), **Philip**, American poet and journalist..........1752—1832

Frenssen (fren'sen), **Gustav,** German pastor, novelist ....1863—1945?

Fréron (frẹ-roṅ'), **Élie Catherine,** French critic ....1719—1776

F., Louis Marie Stanislas (*son of E.C.F.*), French revolutionist 1754—1802

Frescobaldi (frẹs-cō-bäl'dī), **Girolamo,** Italian composer ..... 1583—1643

Freud (froit), **Sigmund,** Austrian psychiatrist and author; founder of psychoanalysis ....1856—1939

Freytag (frȳ'täk), **Gustav,** German novelist, playwright ....1816—1895

Frick (frik), **Henry Clay,** American industrialist ....1849—1919

Frick, Wilhelm, German Nazi politician; minister of interior.1877—1946

Fries (frēs), **Elias Magnus,** Swedish botanist ....1794—1878

Friml (frim'l), **Rudolf,** Am. composer, b. in Bohemia ....1879—1972

Frobenius (frō-bẹ'ni-ụs), **Leo,** German ethnologist ....1873—1938

Frobisher (frō'bish-ẽr), **Sir Martin,** English navigator ....1535?-1594

Froebel (frē'bel), **Friedrich Wilhelm August,** German educator; originator of the kindergarten ....1782—1852

Frohman (frō'măn), **Charles,** Am. theatrical producer ....1860—1915

F., Daniel (*brother of C.F.*), Am. stage producer ....1851—1940

Froissart (frwo-sȧr'), **Jean,** French chronicler and poet ....1333?-1400?

Fromentin (frō-mäṅ-taṅ'), **Eugène,** French painter ....1820—1876

Frontenac, de (dẽ froṅ-te-näç'), **Louis de Buade, Comte,** French colonial governor of Canada ....1620—1698

Frost (frọst), **Edwin Brant,** American astronomer ....1866—1935

Frost, Robert, American poet ....1874—1963

Froude (fröd), **James Anthony,** English historian ....1818—1894

Frunze (frun'ze), **Mikhail Vassilyevich,** Soviet Russian army commander ....1885—1925

Fry (frȳ), **Christopher,** English playwright ....1907—

Fuad (fụ-äd') **I,** (*Ahmed Fuad Pasha*), king of Egypt (1922–36) . . 1868—1936

Fuad Pasha (pȧ-shä'), Turkish general and statesman ....1815—1869

Fulda (fụl'dȧ), **Ludwig,** German poet and playwright ....1862—1939

Fuller (fụl'lẽr), **Margaret, Marchioness Ossoli,** Am. author. . . . 1810—1850

Fuller, Melville Weston, chief justice of the U.S. Supreme Court (1888–1910) ....1833—1910

Fuller, Thomas, English clergyman and author ....1608—1661

Fülöp-Miller (fü'lẽp-mil'lẽr), **René,** Austrian writer ....1891—1963

Fulton (fụl'tŏn), **Robert,** American engineer and inventor ......1765—1815

Funk (fuṅk), **Casimir,** American biochemist, b. in Poland ......1884—1967

Funston (fun'stŏn), **Frederick,** American general ....1865—1917

Furness (fũr'nes), **Horace Howard,** American Shakespearean scholar ....1833—1912

Furniss (fũr'nis), **Harry,** Irish caricaturist ....1854—1925

Furtwängler (fụrt'veng-lẽr), **Adolf,** German archaeologist ....1853—1907

Furtwängler, Wilhelm, German orchestra conductor ....1886—1954

G

Gable (gā'b'l), **Clark,** American motion-picture actor ....1901—1960

Gaboriau (gȧ-bō-ryō'), **Émile,** French author ....1835—1873

Gabrilowitsch (gä-bri-lŏv'ich), **Ossip,** American pianist and orchestra conductor, born in Russia ....1878—1936

Gaddi (gäd'di), **Taddeo,** Florentine painter ....1300?-1366

Gade (gä'de), **Niels Wilhelm,** Danish musician ....1817—1890

Gadsden (gadṣ'den), **James,** Am. soldier and diplomat ....1788—1858

Gage (gāġ), **Thomas,** British general in America ....1721—1787

Gainsborough (gānṣ'bu-ru *or* -bŏr-ō), **Thomas,** English painter . . 1727—1788

Galba (gal'bȧ), **Servius Sulpicius,** Roman emperor ........B.C. 3–A.D.69

Gale (gāl), **Zona** (*Mrs. William Breese*), American novelist and playwright ....1874—1938

Galen (gā'len), **Claudius,** Greek physician and writer.......... 130—200?

Galileo (gal-i-lē'ō), (*Galileo Galilei*), It. astronomer, physicist .....1564—1642

Gall (gạl), **Franz Joseph,** German physician; founder of phrenology ....1758—1828

Gallatin (gal'ȧ-tin), **Albert,** American statesman ....1761—1849

Gallaudet (gal-ạ-det'), **Thomas Hopkins,** American philanthropist ....1787—1851

Galle (gäl'e), **Johann Gottfried,** German astronomer ....1812—1910

Galli-Curci (gäl'lī-ċụr'chī), **Amelita,** American coloratura soprano, born in Italy ....1889—1963

Gallieni (gȧ-lyẹ-nī'), **Joseph Simon,** French general ....1849—1916

Gallitzin (gȧ-lit'sin), **Mikhail Mikhailovich, Prince,** Russian general ....1675—1730

Gallup (gal'up), **George Horace,** American public opinion statistician ....1901—

Galsworthy (gạlṣ'wŏr-thy), **John,** English novelist and dramatist; received Nobel prize in literature (1932) ....1867—1933

Galt (gạlt), **John,** Scottish author ....1779—1839

G., Sir Alexander Tilloch (*son of J.G.*), Canadian statesman, born in England ....1817—1893

Galton (gạl'tŏn), **Sir Francis,** English scientist; pioneer in eugenics ....1822—1911

Galvani (gäl-vä'nī), **Luigi,** Italian physician; discoverer of galvanism ....1737—1798

Gama, da (dä gä'mä), **Vasco,** Portuguese navigator ....1469?-1524

Gambetta (gam-bet'tȧ), **Léon,** French statesman ....1838—1882

Gamelin (gȧ-me-laṅ'), **Maurice Gustave,** French general; Allied generalissimo at beginning of World War II ....1872—1958

Gandhi (gän'di), **Mrs. Indira,** prime minister of India (1966–77); daughter of Jawaharlal Nehru ....1917—

Gandhi, Mohandas Karamchand (*Mahatma Gandhi*), Hindu nationalist leader; assassinated ....1869—1948

Ganso (gan'sō), **Emil,** American painter, b. in Germany ....1895—1941

Garand (ga'rănd), **John C.,** Am. inventor of semiautomatic rifle adopted (1936) by U.S. army; b. in Canada ....1888—1974

Garbo (gär'bō), **Greta** (b. *Greta Lovisa Gustafsson*), American motion-picture actress, b. in Sweden ....1905—

García (gär-cī'ȧ), **Calixto,** Cuban patriot ....1836—1898

Garcilaso de la Vega (gär-thī-lä'sō dẹ lä vẹ'gä), Sp. poet..........1503—1536

Garden (gär'den), **Mary,** Am. opera singer, b. in Scotland.......1877—1967

Gardiner (gär'di-nẽr), **Samuel Rawson,** English historian.......1829—1902

Gardner (gärd'nẽr), **Erle Stanley** (pseud. *A.A.Fair,* etc.), American writer of detective fiction ....1889—1970

Gardner, Percy, English archaeologist ....1846—1937

Garfield (gär'fēld), **James Abram,** twentieth president of the United States (1881); assassinated ....1831—1881

Garibaldi (gär-ī-bäl'dī), **Giuseppe,** Italian patriot ....1807—1882

Garland (gär'lănd), **Hamlin,** American novelist ....1860—1940

Garneau (gȧr-nō'), **François Xavier,** Fr.-Can. historian..........1809—1866

Garner (gär'nẽr), **John Nance,** vice-president of the United States (1933–41) ....1869—1967

Garnett (gär'net), **Richard,** Eng. librarian and author ....1835—1906

G., Edward (*son of R.G.*), Eng. critic and writer ....1868—1937

G., Constance (*wife of E.G.*), English translator ....1862—1946

G., David (*son of E. and C.G.*), English novelist ....1892—

Garrick (gar'rik), **David,** English actor and dramatist ....1717—1779

Garrison (gar'ri-sŏn), **William Lloyd,** Am. abolitionist ....1804—1879

Garth (gärth), **Sir Samuel,** English poet ....1661—1719

Garvey (gär'vē), **Marcus,** American Negro leader, b. in Jamaica, W. Indies ....1887—1940

Gascoigne (gas-ċoin'), **George,** English poet ....1539?-1577

Gascoigne, Sir William, English judge ....1350?-1419

Gaskell (gas'kel), **Elizabeth Cleghorn,** English novelist ....1810—1865

Gassendi (gȧ-säṅ-dī'), **Pierre,** French philosopher ....1592—1655

Gates (gāts), **Horatio,** American general in the Revolutionary War, b. in England ....1728?-1806

Gates, Sir Thomas, English colonizer of Virginia .... ? —1621

Gatling (gat'ling), **Richard Jordan,** American inventor ....1818—1903

Gatti-Casazza (gät'tī-çȧ-sät'sä), **Giulio,** Italian opera director. . 1869—1940

Gauguin (gō-gaṅ'), **Paul,** French painter ....1848—1903

Gauss (gous), **Karl Friedrich,** German mathematician ....1777—1855

Gautama (gạ'tȧ-mȧ) *or* **Gotama** (gō'tȧ-mȧ), Indian religious teacher; founder of Buddhism ..........B.C.563?-483?

Gautier (gō-tyẹ'), **Théophile,** French poet and novelist ....1811—1872

Gay (gā), **John,** English dramatist and poet ....1685—1732

Gay-Lussac (gā-lụ-säç'), **Joseph Louis,** French chemist and physicist ....1778—1850

Gaynor (gā'nŏr), **William Jay,** American politician ....1849—1913

Geary (gē'ry), **John White,** Am. general and politician ....1819—1873

Geddes (ged'des), **Auckland Campbell, Baron,** British statesman; ambassador to the U.S. (1920–24) ....1879—1954

G., Sir Eric Campbell (*brother of A.C.G.*), British transportation expert; first lord of admiralty (1917–18) ....1875—1937

Geddes, Norman Bel, Am. stage producer and designer ....1893—1958

Geddes, Sir Patrick, Scottish sociologist and biologist ....1854—1932

Geikie (gē'ki), **Sir Archibald,** Scottish geologist ....1835—1924

G., James (*brother of A.G.*), Scottish geologist ....1839—1915

Gell (ġel), **Sir William,** English archaeologist ....1777—1836

Gellert (gel'ẽrt), **Christian Fürchtegott,** German poet and novelist ....1715—1769

Genêt (ẑe-nẹ'), **Edmond Charles Édouard,** Fr. diplomat ....1763—1834

Genghis Khan (ġen'gis kän'), Mongol conqueror ....1167?-1227

Genlis, de (dẽ ẑaṅ-lis'), **Stéphanie-Félicité,** Fr. writer 1746 1830

Genovesi (ġe-nō-vẹ'sī), **Antonio,** Italian philosopher ....1712—1769

Genseric (ġen'sẽr-iç), king of the Vandals .... 390?- 477

Gentile (ġẹn-tī'lẹ), **Giovanni,** Italian philosopher ....1875—1944

Gentile da Fabriano (dä fä-brī-ä'nō), Italian painter ....1370?-1427?

Geoffrey (ġef'ri) **of Monmouth,** English historian ....1100?-1154

George (ġọrġ) **I,** king of Great Britain (1714–27) ....1660—1727

G. II (*son of G. I*), king of Great Britain (1727–60) ....1683—1760

G. III (*grandson of G. II*), king of Great Britain (1760–1820) . . . 1738—1820

G. IV (*son os G. III*), king of Great Britain (1820–30) ....1762—1830

G. V (*son of Edward VII*), king of Great Britain (1910–36) ......1865—1936

G. VI (*son of G. V; succeeded his brother Edward VIII*), king of Great Britain (1936–52) ....1895—1952

George I, king of Greece (1863–1913); assassinated ....1845—1913

G. II (*son of Constantine I*), king of Greece (1922–23, 1935–47) . 1890—1947

George, Henry, American political economist ....1839—1897

George, Saint, patron saint of England .... ? —303?

George (ġẹ-ọr'ġe), **Stefan,** German poet ....1868—1933

Gérard (ẑẹ-rȧr'), **Étienne Maurice, Count,** marshal of France . 1773—1855

Gérard, François, Baron, French painter ....1770—1837

Gerard (ġẽr-ärd'), **James Watson,** American lawyer and diplomat; ambassador to Germany (1913–17) ....1867—1951

Gérard (ẑẹ-rȧr'), **Jean Ignace Isidore** (pseud. *Grandville*), French caricaturist ....1803—1847

Géricault (ẑẹ-rī-çō'), **Jean Louis Théodore André,** French painter 1791 1824

Germanicus (ġẽr-man'i-çus) **Caesar,** Roman general ........B.C. 15–A.D.19

Gérôme (ẑẹ-rōm'), **Jean Léon,** French painter ....1824—1904

Geronimo (ġē ron'i-mō), chief of an American Apache Indian tribe ....1829?-1909

Gerould (ġer'uld), **Katharine Fullerton,** Am. writer ....1879—1944

Gerry (ger'ry), **Elbridge,** U.S. vice-pres. (1813–14) ....1744—1814

Gershwin (gẽrsh'win), **George,** American composer ....1898—1937

Gervinus (ger-vī'nụs), **Georg Gottfried,** German historian ....1805—1871

Gesenius (ġẹ-sẹ'ni-ụs), **Wilhelm,** German Orientalist ....1786—1842

Gessner (ges'nẽr), **Salomon,** Swiss painter and poet ....1730—1788

Gest (gest), **Maurice,** Russian theatrical producer ....1881—1942

Geulincx (gē'liṅks), **Arnold,** Belgian philosopher ....1624—1669

Ghiberti (gī-ber'tī), **Lorenzo,** Italian sculptor ....1378—1455

Ghirlandaio (gẽr-län-dä'yō), **Domenico,** Italian painter ....1449—1494

Gibbon (gib'bŏn), **Edward,** English historian ....1737—1794

Gibbons (gib'bŏnṣ), **James, Cardinal,** Am. R.C. cardinal ....1834—1921

Gibbons, Orlando, English composer ....1583—1625

Gibbs (gibṣ), **A. Hamilton,** English novelist ....1888—1964

G., Sir Philip (Hamilton), Eng. journalist and novelist (*brother of A.H.G. and Cosmo Hamilton*) ....1877—1962

Gibson (gib'sŏn), **Charles Dana,** American illustrator ....1867—1944

Gibson, Hugh, American diplomat ....1883—1954

Giddings (gid'dingṣ), **Franklin Henry,** Am. sociologist ....1855—1931

Giddings, Joshua Reed, American antislavery leader ....1795—1864

Gide (ẑid), **André,** French novelist; recd. Nobel prize (1947) ......1869—1951

Gieseking (gī'ṣe-king), **Walter,** German pianist ....1895—1956

Gifford (gif'fŏrd), **William,** English critic and editor ....1756—1826

Gigli (ġī'lyi), **Beniamino,** Italian operatic tenor ....1890—1957

Gilbert (gil'bẽrt), **Cass,** American architect ....1859—1934

Gilbert, Sir Humphrey, English navigator ....1539—1583

Gilbert, Sir John, English historical painter ....1817—1897

Gilbert, Sir John Thomas, Irish historian ....1829—1898

Gilbert, William Schwenck, English light opera librettist; collaborated with A. S. Sullivan ....1836—1911

Gilder (gil'dẽr), **Richard Watson,** Am. editor and poet ....1844—1909

Gillette (ġil-let'), **William,** Am. actor and playwright ....1855—1937

Gillmore (gil'mōr), **Quincy Adams,** American military engineer . 1825—1888

Gilman (gil'măn), **Lawrence,** American music critic ....1878—1939

Gilpin (gil'pin), **Charles Sidney,** Am. Negro actor ....1878—1930

Ginsburg (ginṣ'bũrg), **Christian David,** English biblical and rabbinical scholar ....1831—1914

Giordano (ġōr-dä'nō), **Luca** (*Fa Presto*), It. painter ....1632—1705

Giorgione (ġọr-ġō'nẹ), (*Giorgio Barbarelli*) It. painter ....1478?-1511

Giotto (ġot'tō), Florentine painter and architect....1276?–1337?
Girard (ġi-rärd'), **Stephen**, American financier....1750—1831
Giraud (zhē-rō'), **Henri Honoré**, Fr. general, anti-Vichy leader...1879—1949
Giraudoux (zhī-rō-dö'), **Jean**, Fr. diplomat and author....1882—1944
Gish (gish), **Lillian**, American actress....1896—
G., Dorothy (*sister of L.G.*), American actress....1898—1968
Gissing (gis'sing), **George Robert**, English novelist....1857—1903
Giulio Romano (ġůl'yō rō-mä'nō), Italian painter and architect.1492—1546
Giusti (ġůs'tī), **Giuseppe**, Italian satirical poet....1809—1850
Gjellerup (yel'ē-rụp), **Karl Adolf**, Danish novelist....1857—1919
Glackens (glak'ens), **William James**, American artist....1870—1938
Gladstone (glad'stǒn), **William Ewart**, British statesman and premier....1809—1898
Glasgow (glas'gō), **Ellen**, American novelist....1874—1945
Glaspell (glas'pel), **Susan**, Am. novelist, playwright....1882—1948
Glass (glȧs), **Carter**, American statesman; secretary of the treasury (1918–20)....1858—1946
Glass, Montague, American author, b. in England....1877—1934
Glazunov (glä-zụ-nọf'), **Aleksandr Konstantinovich**, Russian composer....1865—1936
Glennon (glen'nǒn), **John Joseph, Cardinal**, Am. R.C. archbishop and cardinal....1862—1946
Glinka (gliṅ'kȧ), **Mikhail Ivanovich**, Russian composer....1803—1857
Gloucester (glos'tẽr), **Duke of** (*Prince Henry William Frederick Albert*), son of George V of England....1900—1974
Gluck (glụk), **Alma** (*Reba Fiersohn Gluck Zimbalist*), American soprano, b. in Romania....1884—1938
Gluck, von (fọn), **Christoph Willibald**, German composer....1714—1787
Godard (gō-dȧr'), **Benjamin Louis Paul**, Fr. composer....1849—1895
Goddard (god'dȧrd), **Henry Herbert**, Am. psychologist....1866—1957
Godkin (god'kin), **Edwin Lawrence**, American journalist....1831—1902
Godowsky (gō-dọf'skē), **Leopold**, American pianist and composer, b. in Russia....1870—1938
Godunov (go-dụ-nọf'), **Boris**, czar of Russia (1598–1605)....1551?–1605
Godwin (god'win), **Parke**, American journalist....1816—1904
Godwin, William, English novelist (*husband of Mary Wollstonecraft, father of M.W. Shelley*)....1756—1836
Goebbels (gẽ'bels), **Paul Joseph**, German politician; Nazi minister of propaganda (1933–45)....1897—1945
Goering *or* **Göring** (gẽ'ring), **Hermann Wilhelm**, German Nazi leader; sentenced to hang for war crimes, committed suicide....1893—1946
Goethals (gō'thȧls), **George Washington**, American army engineer in charge of building Panama Canal....1858—1928
Goethe *or* **Göthe, von** (fọn gẽ'te), **Johann Wolfgang**, German poet, dramatist, and novelist....1749—1832
Goffe (gof), **William**, English Puritan and Regicide....1605?–1679?
Gogh, van (vän gokh' *or Eng.* van gō'), **Vincent**, Dutch painter.1853—1890
Gogol (gọ'gọl), **Nikolai Vassilievich**, Russian author....1809—1852
Goldberg (gōld'bẽrg), **Rube** (*Reuben Lucius G.*), American cartoonist....1883—1970
Golding (gōld'ing), **Louis**, English novelist and poet....1895—1958
Goldman (gōld'mȧn), **Emma**, Am. anarchist, b. in Russia....1869—1940
Goldmark (gōld'märk), **Karl**, Hungarian composer....1830—1915
Goldoni (gōl-dō'nī), **Carlo**, Italian comic dramatist....1707—1793
Goldsborough (gōlds'bör-ō), **Louis Malesherbes**, American rear admiral....1805—1877
Goldsmith (gōld'smith), **Oliver**, British poet, dramatist, and novelist....1728—1774
Goldwyn (gōld'win), **Samuel**, Am. motion-picture producer....1882—1974
Gómez (gō'mes), **Juan Vicente**, Venezuelan general and dictator (1908–35)....1857?–1935
Gompers (gom'pẽrs), **Samuel**, American labor leader, b. in England; pres. of A.F. of L. (1886–1924, except 1895)....1850—1924
Goncourt, de (dē gọṅ-çör'), **Edmond** (1822–96) and **Jules** (1830–70), (*brothers*), Fr. novelists in collaboration.
Gonsalvo de Córdova (gōn-säl'vō dẹ çọr'dō-vä), (*the Great Captain*) Spanish warrior....1453—1515
Gooch (gọọch), **George Peabody**, English historian....1873—1968
Goodhue (good'hū), **Bertram Grosvenor**, Am. architect....1869—1924
Goodrich (good'rich), **Samuel Griswold** (pseud. *Peter Parley*), American writer of children's books....1793—1860
Goodwin (good'win), **Nathaniel Carl** (*Nat*), Am. actor....1857—1919
Goodyear (good'yẽr), **Charles**, American inventor....1800—1860
Googe (gọọġ), **Barnabe**, English poet....1540—1594
Goossens (gọọs'sens), **Eugene**, English composer and conductor.1893—1962
Gorchakov (gọr-chȧ-kọf'), **Aleksandr Mikhailovich, Prince**, Russian diplomat and statesman....1798—1883
Gordon (gọr'dǒn), **Adam Lindsay**, Australian poet....1833—1870
Gordon, Charles George (*Chinese Gordon*), British general and administrator....1833—1885
Gordon, Charles William (pseud. *Ralph Connor*), Canadian clergyman and novelist....1860—1937
Gordon, John Brown, American Confederate general....1832—1904
Gorgas (gọr'gȧs), **William Crawford**, American surgeon general and sanitation expert....1854—1920
Göring, *see* Goering.
Gorki (gọr'ki), **Maxim** (pseud. of *Aleksei Maksimovich Pyeshkov*), Russian novelist and dramatist....1868—1936
Gort (gọrt), **John Standish Vereker, sixth Viscount**, Br. general; commander British field force (1939–40)....1886—1946
Gosse (gos), **Sir Edmund William**, Eng. poet and critic....1849—1928
Gotama, *see* Gautama.
Göthe, *see* Goethe.
Gottwald (gọt'väld), **Klement**, Czechoslovakian statesman and Communist leader; president (1948–53)....1896—1953
Goudy (gou'dy), **Frederic William**, American type designer....1865—1947
Gould (gōld), **Jay**, American stockbroker and speculator....1836—1892
Gounod (gö-nō'), **Charles François**, French composer....1818—1893
Gourgaud (gör-gō'), **Gaspard, Baron**, French general....1783—1852
Gourmont, de (dē gör-mọṅ'), **Rémy**, French novelist, playwright, and critic....1858—1915
Gower (gou'ẽr), **John**, English poet....1325?–1408
Goya y Lucientes, de (dẹ gō'yä ē lů-thi-en'tẹs), **Francisco**, Spanish painter....1746—1828
Gracchus (graç'ḉhus), **Caius Sempronius**, Roman statesman (*brother of T.S.G.*)....B.C. 153?– 121
G., Tiberius Sempronius, Roman statesman....B.C. 162?– 133
Grady (grā'dy), **Henry Woodfin**, Am. journalist, orator....1850—1889
Grafton (graf'tǒn), **Richard**, English chronicler.... ? –1572?
Graham (grā'ȧm), **Sylvester**, American dietician....1794—1851
Graham, Thomas, Scottish chemist....1805—1869
Graham, William Alexander, U.S. secretary of the navy (1850–52)....1804—1875
Grahame (grā'ȧm), **Kenneth**, Scottish author....1859—1932
Grainger (grān'gẽr), **Percy Aldridge**, American composer and pianist, born in Australia....1882—1961
Grandi (grän'di), **Dino, Count**, Italian Fascist politician....1895—
Grant (grant), **James**, Scottish novelist....1822—1887
Grant, Ulysses Simpson, American general and eighteenth president of the United States (1869–77)....1822—1885
Granvelle, de (dē gran'vel *or Fr.* dē gräṅ-vel'), **Antoine Perrenot, Cardinal**, Spanish statesman....1517—1586
Granville (gran'vil), **Granville George Leveson-Gower, Earl**, English statesman....1815—1891
Granville, John Carteret, Earl, English statesman....1690—1763
Granville-Barker (-bär'kẽr), **Harley**, English playwright, producer, and translator....1877—1946
Grasse, de (dē grȧs'), **François Joseph Paul, Comte**, French admiral....1723—1788
Gratian (grā'shi-ȧn), (*Flavius Gratianus*) Roman emperor.... 359— 383
Grattan (grat'tȧn), **Henry**, Irish statesman and orator....1746—1820
Grau San Martín (grou sän mär-tīn'), **Ramon**, president of Cuba (Sept., 1933–Jan., 1934 and 1944–48)....1887—1969
Graves (grāvs), **Robert**, English poet and novelist....1895—
Gray (grā), **Asa**, American botanist and writer....1810—1888
Gray, Elisha, American inventor and electrician....1835—1901
Gray, Horace, associate justice of the U.S. Supreme Court (1881–1902)....1828—1902
Gray, Thomas, English poet and prose writer....1716—1771
Grayson (grā'sǒn), **Cary Travers**, American rear admiral....1878—1938
Grayson, David, *see* Baker, Ray Stannard.
Graziani (grät-tsī-ä'nī), **Rodolfo, Marchese di Neghelli**, Italian marshal; viceroy of Ethiopia (1936–37)....1882—1955
Greeley (grē'li), **Horace**, Am. journalist, politician....1811—1872
Greely (grē'ly), **Adolphus Washington**, American arctic explorer.1844—1935
Green (grēn), **Anna Katharine** (*Mrs. Charles Rohlfs*), American writer of detective novels....1846—1935
Green, Henry (pseud. of *Henry Vincent Yorke*), English novelist.1905—
Green, Hetty (*Henrietta Howland G.*), Am. financier....1834—1916
Green, John Richard, English historian....1837—1883
Green, Julian Hartridge, American novelist in France....1900—
Green, Paul, American playwright....1894—
Green, Seth, American zoologist....1817—1888
Green, Thomas Hill, English philosopher....1836—1882
Green, William, American labor leader; president of A.F. of L. (1924–52)....1873—1952
Greenaway (grēn'ȧ-wā), **Kate**, English illustrator....1846—1901
Greene (grēn), **Graham**, English writer, novelist....1904—
Greene, Nathanael, Am. Revolutionary general....1742—1786
Greene, Robert, English dramatist and writer....1560?–1592
Greenleaf (grēn'lēf), **Simon**, American writer on law....1783—1853
Greenough (grē'nō), **Horatio**, American sculptor....1805—1852
Gregory (greg'ō-ry) **I, Saint** (*the Great*), Pope.... 540?– 604
Gregory VII (*Saint Hildebrand*), Pope....1020?–1085
Gregory XIII (*Ugo Buoncompagni*), Pope....1502—1585
Gregory XVI (*Bartolommeo Alberto Capellari*), Pope....1765—1846
Gregory of Tours (ov tör'), **Saint**, French historian.... 538— 593
Gregory, Augusta (**Persse**), **Lady**, Irish playwright....1859—1932
Grenfell (gren'fel), **Sir Wilfred Thomason**, English surgeon and missionary to Labrador....1865—1940
Grenville (gren'vil), **George**, English statesman....1712—1770
Grenville, Sir Richard, British naval hero....1541? 1591
Gresham (gresh'ȧm), **Sir Thomas**, English merchant, financier, and diplomat....1519?–1579
Gresham, Walter Quintin, American soldier, jurist, and secretary of state (1893–95)....1832—1895
Greuze (grēz), **Jean Baptiste**, French painter....1725—1805
Grew (grů), **Joseph Clark**, American diplomat; ambassador to Japan (1932–41)....1880—1965
Grey (grẹ), **Charles, Earl**, British premier (1830–34)....1764—1845
Grey, Edward, Viscount of Fallodon, English statesman; ambassador to the U.S. (1919–20)....1862—1933
Grey, Jane, Lady, nominal queen of England (July 10–19, 1553); executed....1537—1554
Grey, Zane, American novelist....1875—1939
Gridley (grid'li), **Charles Vernon**, American naval officer....1844—1898
Gridley, Richard, American general....1711—1796
Grieg (grẽg), **Edvard**, Norwegian composer....1843—1907
Griffes (grif'fes), **Charles Tomlinson**, Am. composer....1884—1920
Griffith (grif'fith), **David Wark**, American motion-picture director and producer....1875—1948
Grillparzer (gril'pär-tsẽr), **Franz**, German dramatist....1791—1872
Grimaldi (gri-mäl'dī), **Giovanni Francesco** (*Il Bolognese*), Italian painter and architect....1606—1680
Grimm (grim), **Friedrich Melchior, Baron**, German littérateur in France....1723—1807
Grimm, Jakob, German philologist; collected fairy tales in collaboration with his brother Wilhelm....1785—1863
G., Wilhelm, German philologist and mythologist....1786—1859
Grinnell (grin-nel'), **George Bird**, American naturalist and educator....1849—1938
Gris (grēs), **Juan** (b. *José Victoriano Gonzáles*), Spanish cubist painter....1887—1927
Grolier de Servières (grō-lyā' dē ser-vyer'), **Jean**, French bibliophile....1479—1565
Gromyko (grō-mē'kō), **Andrei A.**, Russian diplomat....1909—
Gropius (grō'pē-us), **Walter**, German architect, in the U.S. after 1937; founder of the Bauhaus....1883—1969
Gropper (grop'ẽr), **William**, Am. artist, cartoonist....1897—
Gros (grō), **Antoine Jean, Baron**, French painter....1771—1835
Grosseteste (grōs'test), **Robert**, English theologian....1175—1253
Grosz (grōs), **George**, German painter in America....1893—1959
Grote (grōt), **George**, English historian....1794—1871
Grotius (grō'shi-us), **Hugo**, Dutch statesman and jurist....1583—1645
Grove (grōv), **Sir George**, English writer on music....1820—1900
Gruenberg (grů'en-bẽrg), **Louis**, Am. composer, b. Russia....1884—1964
Gruenther (grun'thẽr), **Alfred Maximilian**, Am. general....1899—
Gryphius (grů'fi-ụs), **Andreas**, German poet and dramatist....1616—1664
Guardi (gwär'dī), **Francesco**, Italian painter....1712—1793

Guarneri (gwär-ne'rī), **Giuseppe Antonio** (*Guarnerius*), Italian violinmaker....1687?–1745
Guedalla (gwē-dal'lȧ), **Philip**, English biographer and historian..1889—1944
Guercino (gwer-chī'nō), (b. *Giovanni Francesco Barbieri*), Italian painter....1591?–1666
Guericke, von (fọn ge'rik-e), **Otto**, German natural philosopher; inventor of the air pump....1602—1686
Guggenheim (gụg'en-hīm), **Daniel**, American capitalist....1856—1930
Guicciardini (gwīt-chär-dī'nī), **Francesco**, It. historian....1483—1540
Guido d'Arezzo (gwī'dō dä-ret'tsō), Italian musician....995?–1050?
Guido Reni (re'nī), Italian painter....1575—1642
Guilbert (gīl-ber'), **Yvette**, French singer....1869—1944
Guise, de (dē gis'), **François de Lorraine, Duc**, French general and statesman (*father of Henri*)....1519—1563
G., de, Henri de Lorraine, Duc, Fr. gen., statesman....1550—1588
Guiterman (git'ēr-mȧn), **Arthur**, Am. poet, b. in Austria....1871—1943
Guitry (gī-trē'), **Lucien**, French actor....1860—1925
G., Sacha (*son of L.G.*), French actor, playwright....1885—1957
Guizot (gī-zō'), **François Pierre Guillaume**, French statesman and historian....1787—1874
Gunther (gun'thēr), **John**, Am. journalist and author....1901—1970
Gustav (gus'tȧv) **V**, king of Sweden (1907–50)....1858—1950
G. VI (*Gustavus Adolphus*), (*son of G. V*) king of Sweden(1950–73).1882—1973
Gustavus Adolphus (gus-tā'vus ȧ-dol'fus) *or* **Gustavus II**, king of Sweden (1611–32)....1594—1632
Gutenberg (gụt'en-berk), **Johann**, German printer, reputedly first printer in Europe to use movable type....1397?–1468
Guthrie (guth'ri), **Alfred Bertram, Jr.**, Am. novelist....1901—
Guyon (gụē-yọn'), **Jeanne Marie Bouvier de la Mothe**, French mystic....1648—1717
Guyot (gē-yō'), **Arnold Henry**, Swiss naturalist in U.S....1807—1884
Guzmán Blanco (gụs-män' bläñ'çō), **Antonio**, president of Venezuela....1829—1899
Gwinnett (gwin'net), **Button**, American patriot; signer of Declaration of Independence....1735?–1777
Gwyn (gwyn), **Eleanor** (*Nell*), English actress; mistress of Charles II....1650—1687

H

Haakon (hạ'koon) **VII**, king of Norway (1905–57)....1872—1957
Hácha (hä'chä), **Emil**, Czech jurist; puppet president of Bohemia-Moravia during Nazi control (1939–45)....1872—1945
Hackett (hak'et), **Francis**, American author, b. in Ireland....1883—1962
Hackett, James Henry, American actor and author....1800—1871
H., James Keteltas (*son of J.H.H.*), American actor....1869—1926
Hadley (had'li), **Arthur Twining**, Am. economist, educator....1856—1930
Hadley, Henry Kimball, Am. composer and conductor....1871—1937
Hadrian (hā'dri-an) *or* **Adrian**, Roman emperor.... 76— 138
Haeckel (hek'el), **Ernst Heinrich**, German biologist....1834—1919
Hafiz (hä'fiz), (*Shams-ud-Din Mohammed*) Persian poet.... ? –1389?
Hagen (hā'gen), **Walter**, American golfer....1892—1969
Haggard (hag'gȧrd), **Sir Henry Rider**, English novelist....1856—1925
Hahn (hän), **Otto**, German nuclear physicist....1879—1968
Hahnemann (hä'ne-män), **Samuel Christian Friedrich**, German physician; founder of homeopathy....1755—1843
Hahn-Hahn, von (fọn hän'hän), **Ida, Countess**, German novelist and poet....1805—1880
Haig (hāg), **Douglas, first Earl**, British commander in chief in World War I....1861—1928
Haile Selassie (hī'lē se-lä'sē) **I**, emperor of Ethiopia (1930–74)...1891—1975
Hakluyt (hak'lụt), **Richard**, English geographer....1552?–1616
Haldane (hạl'dān), **John Burdon Sanderson**, British biologist (*son of J.S.H.*)....1892—1964
H., John Scott, English physiologist....1860—1936
H., Richard Burdon, Viscount (*brother of J.S.H.*), British statesman and philosopher....1856—1928
Hale (hāl), **Edward Everett**, Am. clergyman, author....1822—1909
Hale, George Ellery, American astronomer....1868—1938
Hale, John Parker, American statesman....1806—1873
Hale, Sir Matthew, English jurist and author....1609—1676
Hale, Nathan, Am. Revolutionary patriot; hanged as spy by the British....1755—1776
Hale, Sarah Josepha (Buell), Am. writer and editor....1788—1879
Halévy (ȧ-le-vē'), **Jacques François Fromental Élie**, French composer (*uncle of L.H.*)....1799—1862
H., Ludovic, French librettist and novelist....1834—1908
Halévy, Joseph, French Orientalist, born in Turkey....1827—1917
Haliburton (hal'i-būr-tŏn), **Thomas Chandler** (pseud. *Sam Slick*), Nova Scotian judge and humorous writer....1796—1865
Halifax (hal'i-faks), **Charles Montagu, Earl of**, English poet and statesman....1661—1715
Halifax, Edward Frederick Lindley Wood, Earl of, British statesman and cabinet member; gov. gen. of India (1926–31); ambassador to U.S. (1941–46)....1881—1959
Hall (hạl), **Asaph**, American astronomer....1829—1907
Hall, Charles Francis, American arctic explorer....1821—1871
Hall, Charles Martin, American chemist....1863—1914
Hall, Granville Stanley, American psychologist....1846—1924
Hall, Joseph, English divine and satirist....1574—1656
Hall, Marshall, English physiologist....1790—1857
Hallam (hal'ȧm), **Henry**, English historian....1777—1859
Halleck (hal'ek), **Fitz-Greene**, Am. poet and satirist....1790—1867
Halleck, Henry Wager, Am. general, military writer....1815—1872
Halley (hal'i), **Edmund**, English astronomer....1656—1742
Halliburton (hal'i-būr-tŏn), **Richard**, American author....1900–1939?
Halper (hal'pēr), **Albert**, American novelist....1904—
Hals (häls), **Franz**, Dutch painter....1580?–1666
Halsey (hạl'sẹ), **William Frederick**, American admiral in World War II....1882—1959
Hamilcar Barca (hȧ-mil'çär bär'çȧ), (*father of Hannibal*) Carthaginian general....B.C.270?– 228
Hamilton (ham'il-tŏn), **Alexander**, American statesman; first secretary of the treasury (1789–95)....1757—1804
Hamilton, Cosmo, English novelist and dramatist....1879—1942
Hamilton, Sir Ian Standish Monteith, British general....1853—1947
Hamilton, Sir William, Scottish philosopher....1788—1856
Hamilton, Sir William Rowan, Irish mathematician and astronomer....1805—1865

Hamlin (ham'lin), **Hannibal**, vice-president of the United States (1861–65)....1809—1891
Hammarskjold (häm'ar-shöld), **Dag**, Swedish statesman; secretary general of the United Nations (1953–61)....1905—1961
Hammerstein (ham'ēr-stīn), **Oscar, II**, American librettist....1895—1960
Hammett (ham'met), **Dashiell**, American writer of detective fiction....1894—1961
Hammond (ham'mŏnd), **John Hays**, American inventor....1888—1965
Hammurabi (häm-ū-rä'bi), king of Babylon....fl.B.C.1925
Hampden (ham'den), **John**, English statesman....1594—1643
Hampden, Walter (b. *Walter Hampden Dougherty*), American actor....1879—1955
Hampton (hamp'tŏn), **Wade**, American general....1752?–1835
H., Wade (*grandson of W.H.*), Am. Confederate general....1818—1902
Hamsun (ham'sun), **Knut**, Norwegian novelist....1859—1952
Hancock (han'çok), **John**, American statesman....1737—1793
Hancock, Winfield Scott, Union general in Civil War....1824—1886
Hand (hand), **Learned**, American jurist....1872—1961
Handel (han'del), **George Frederick** (b. *Georg Friedrich Händel*), English composer, born in Germany....1685—1759
Handy (han'dē), **W(illiam) C(hristopher)**, American jazz musician and composer....1873—1958
Hanna (han'nȧ), **Marcus Alonzo**, American statesman....1837—1904
Hannibal (han'ni-bȧl), Carthaginian general....B.C. 247— 183
Hanotaux (ȧ-nō-tō'), **Gabriel Albert Auguste**, French historian and statesman....1853—1944
Hanson (han'sŏn), **Howard**, American composer....1896—1981
Hardee (här'dē), **William J.**, Am. Confederate general....1815—1873
Hardenberg von (fọn här'den-berk), **Karl August, Prince**, Prussian chancellor....1750—1822
Hardie (här'dē), **James Keir**, British labor leader....1856—1915
Harding (härd'ing), **Warren Gamaliel**, twenty-ninth president of the United States (1921–23)....1865—1923
Hardwicke (härd'wik), **Sir Cedric Webster**, British actor....1893—1964
Hardy (här'dy), **Thomas**, English novelist and poet....1840—1928
Hardyng (här'dyng), **John**, English chronicler....1378—1465
Hargreaves (här'grēvs), **James**, English inventor of the spinning jenny.... ? —1778
Harington (har'ing-tŏn), **Sir John**, English poet....1561—1612
Harlan (här'lȧn), **John Marshall**, associate justice of U.S. Supreme Court (1955–71)....1899—
Harley (här'li), **Robert, first Earl of Oxford**, Eng. statesman...1661—1724
Harney (här'ni), **William Selby**, American general....1800—1889
Harold (har'öld) **I**, (*Harefoot*) king of England.... ? —1040
Harold II, last Saxon king of England....1022?–1066
Harper (här'pēr), **William Rainey**, American educator....1856—1906
Harriman (har'ri-mȧn), **Edward Henry**, American railroad financier (*father of W.A.H.*)....1848—1909
H., William Averell, Am. financier and govt. administrator; ambassador to Russia (1943–46); sec. of commerce (1946–48)....1891—
Harrington (har'ring-tŏn), **James**, English political economist..1611—1677
Harris (har'ris), **Frank**, American author, b. in Ireland....1856—1931
Harris, James, English grammarian....1709—1780
Harris, Joel Chandler, American journalist and writer....1848—1908
Harris, Roy, American composer....1898—1979
Harrison (har'ri-sŏn), **Benjamin**, signer of the Declaration of Independence (*father of W.H.H.*)....1726?–1791
H., Benjamin (*grandson of W.H.H.*) twenty-third president of the United States (1889–93)....1833—1901
H., William Henry, American general and ninth president of the United States (1841)....1773—1841
Hart (härt), **Albert Bushnell**, American historian....1854—1943
Hart, Lorenz, American lyricist....1895—1943
Hart, Moss, American playwright....1904—1961
Hart, William S., American stage and screen actor....1870—1946
Harte (härt), **Bret** (*Francis Bret H.*), Am. author....1839—1902
Hartley (härt'li), **David**, English philosopher and physician....1705—1757
Hartlib (härt'lib), **Samuel**, English miscellaneous writer.... ? —1670
Hartmann, von (fọn härt'man), **Karl Robert Eduard**, German philosopher....1842—1906
Hartmann, Moritz, German poet....1821—1872
Harun al-Rashid (hä-rụn' är-rȧ-shīd'), caliph of Bagdad (786–809)....764?— 809
Harvard (här'vȧrd), **John**, English clergyman in America; founder of Harvard College....1607—1638
Harvey (här'vi), **Gabriel**, English poet....1545—1630
Harvey, William, English anatomist; discoverer of the circulation of the blood....1578—1657
Hasdrubal (has'drụ-bȧl), (*brother of Hannibal*) Carthaginian general....?B.C.207
Haskins (has'kins), **Charles Homer**, American medievalist....1870—1937
Hassam (has'ȧm), **Childe**, American painter....1859—1935
Hastings (hāst'ings), **Francis Rawdon-Hastings, Marquis of**, Eng. general; governor-general of India (1813–22)....1754—1826
Hastings, Warren, English statesman; first governor-general of India (1773–85)....1732—1818
Hatshepsut (hȧ-chep'sut), Egyptian queen of 18th dynasty..B.C.1516—1481
Hauptmann (houpt'män), **Gerhardt**, German poet and dramatist; received Nobel prize in literature (1912)....1862—1946
Hauptmann, Moritz, German composer and writer....1792—1868
Hawkesworth (hạks'wŏrth), **John**, English essayist....1715?–1773
Hawkins (hạk'ins), **Sir Anthony Hope**, *see* Hope, Anthony.
Hawkins *or* **Hawkyns, Sir John**, English admiral....1532—1595
Hawthorne (hạ'thọrn), **Nathaniel**, American author....1804—1864
H., Julian (*son of N.H.*), American novelist....1846—1934
Hay (hā), **Ian** (pseud. of *John Hay Beith*), English officer, author, and lecturer....1876—1952
Hay, John Milton, American author, diplomat; secretary to President Lincoln; secretary of state (1898–1905)....1838—1905
Hayden (hā'den), **Ferdinand Vandiveer**, Am. geologist....1829—1887
Haydn (hȳ'dn), **(Franz) Joseph**, German composer....1732—1809
Haydon (hā'dŏn), **Benjamin Robert**, English painter....1786—1846
Hayes (hās), **Helen** (*Mrs. Charles MacArthur*), Am. actress....1900—
Hayes, Isaac Israel, American arctic explorer....1832—1881
Hayes, Patrick Joseph, Cardinal, American R. C. cardinal (1924–38)....1867—1938
Hayes, Rutherford Birchard, nineteenth president of the United States (1877–81)....1822—1893
Hayne (hān), **Isaac**, American Revolutionary officer; hanged as a spy by the British....1745—1781

Hayne, Robert Young, American senator and orator . . . 1791—1839
Haywood (hā'wood), **William Dudley,** Am. labor leader . . . 1869—1928
Hazard (ȧ-zȧr'), **Paul,** Fr. scholar, author, professor . . . 1878—1944
Hazen (hāz'en), **Charles Downer,** American historian . . . 1868—1941
Hazen, William Babcock, American general . . . 1830—1887
Hazlitt (haz'lit), **William,** English critic and essayist . . . 1778—1830
Headley (hed'li), **Joel Tyler,** American historical writer . . . 1813—1897
Healy (hē'ly), **George Peter Alexander,** Am. painter . . . 1813—1894
Healy, Timothy Michael, Irish statesman; first governor general of Irish Free State (1922–27) . . . 1855—1931
Heard (hẽrd), **Gerald,** English writer in America . . . 1889—1971
Hearn (hẽrn), **Lafcadio,** author, of European-American antecedents, who became a naturalized Japanese . . . 1850—1904
Hearne (hẽrn), **Samuel,** English explorer in Canada . . . 1745—1792
Hearst (hẽrst), **William Randolph,** American journalist, publisher, and politician . . . 1863—1951
Heath (hēth), **Edward Richard George,** British statesman; prime minister (1970–74) . . . 1916—
Heaviside (hev'i-sīd), **Oliver,** English physicist . . . 1850—1925
Hebbel (heb'el), **Friedrich,** German poet and dramatist . . . 1813—1863
Heber (hē'bẽr), **Reginald,** Eng. bishop and hymn writer . . . 1783—1826
Hébert (ẹ-ber'), **Jacques René,** French revolutionist . . . 1757—1794
Hecht (hekt), **Ben,** American playwright and novelist . . . 1894—1964
Hedin (he-dēn'), **Sven Anders,** Swedish explorer in Asia . . . 1865—1952
Hegel (hẹ'gel), **Georg Wilhelm Friedrich,** German philosopher . 1770—1831
Heidegger (hī'de-gẽr), **Martin,** German philosopher . . . 1889—1976
Heidenstam, von (fọn hẹ'den-stäm), **Karl Gustav Verner,** Swedish poet and novelist; recd. Nobel prize (1916) . . . 1859—1940
Heifetz (hī'fets), **Jascha,** Russian violinist in America . . . 1901—
Heine (hī'ne), **Heinrich,** German poet and writer . . . 1797—1856
Heiser (hī'ṣẽr), **Victor George,** Am. physician, writer . . . 1873—1972
Held (held), **Anna,** American musical comedy star, born in Paris . 1873?—1918
Heliodorus (hē''li-ō-dō'rus), Greek romance writer . . . fl. 3rd cent.?
Heliogabalus (hē''li-ō-gab'ȧ-lus), Roman emperor . . . 204— 222
Hellman (hel'măn), **Lillian,** American playwright . . . 1905—
Helmholtz, von (fọn helm'hōlts), **Hermann Ludwig Ferdinand,** German physiologist and natural philosopher . . . 1821—1894
Héloïse (ẹ-lo-īṣ'), abbess of the Paraclete; mistress and wife of Abélard . . . 1101?-1164?
Helvétius (hel-vē'shi-us), **Claude Adrien,** French philosopher . . . 1715—1771
Hemans (hē'mănṣ), **Felicia Dorothea,** English poet . . . 1793—1835
Hemingway (hem'ing-wā), **Ernest,** American novelist . . . 1898—1961
Hémon (ẹ-mọṅ'), **Louis,** French novelist . . . 1880—1913
Hench (hench), **Philip Showalter,** American physician . . . 1896—1965
Henderson (hen'dẽr-sŏn), **Arthur,** English statesman and labor leader; received Nobel peace prize (1934) . . . 1863—1935
Henderson, David Bremner, American statesman . . . 1840—1906
Henderson, Leon, Am. economist and administrator . . . 1895—
Henderson, Sir Nevile, British ambassador to Germany (1937–39) . . . 1882—1942
Hendricks (hen'driks), **Thomas Andrews,** vice-president of the United States (1885) . . . 1819—1885
Hengist (heṅ'gist), Jute leader; reputed, with his brother Horsa, to have founded the kingdom of Kent . . . ? — 488
Henlein (hen'līn), **Konrad,** Sudeten German Nazi leader in Czechoslovakia . . . 1898—1945
Henley (hen'li), **William Ernest,** English poet, dramatist, and critic . . . 1849—1903
Hennepin (hen'ne-pin *or Fr.* en-paṅ'), **Louis,** Flemish missionary and explorer in North America . . . 1640–1701?
Henri (hen'ri), **Robert,** American artist . . . 1865—1929
Henry (hen'ry), **I** (*the Fowler*), German king . . . 876?— 936
Henry VII, German king and Holy Roman emperor . . . 1275?-1313
Henry IV, first Bourbon king of France . . . 1553—1610
Henry I (*son of William I*), king of England . . . 1068—1135
  H. II (*grandson of H. I*), king of England . . . 1133—1189
  H. III (*of Winchester*), king of England . . . 1207—1272
  H. IV (*Bolingbroke*), king of England . . . 1367—1413
  H. V (*son of H. IV*), king of England . . . 1387—1422
  H. VI (*son of H. V*), king of England . . . 1421—1471
  H. VII, king of England . . . 1457—1509
  H. VIII (*son of H. VII*), king of England . . . 1491—1547
Henry, Joseph, American physicist . . . 1797—1878
Henry, O. (pseud. of *William Sydney Porter*), American short-story writer . . . 1862—1910
Henry, Patrick, American orator and patriot . . . 1736—1799
Henryson (hen'ry-sŏn), **Robert,** Scottish poet . . . 1425?-1506
Henschel (hen'shel), **Sir George,** English conductor and composer . . . 1850—1934
Henslowe (henṣ'lō), **Philip,** Eng. theater manager . . . ? —1616
Henty (hen'ty), **George A.,** Eng. novelist and journalist . . . 1832—1902
Hepplewhite (hep'l-hwīt), **George,** English cabinetmaker . . . ? —1786
Heraclitus (her-ȧ-ḉlī'tus), (*the Dark Philosopher*) Greek philosopher . . . fl.B.C.500
Heraclius (her-ȧ-ḉlī'us), Eastern Roman emperor . . . 575?— 641
Herbart (her'bärt), **Johann Friedrich,** German philosopher . . . 1776—1841
Herbert (hẽr'bẽrt), **Alan Patrick,** English humorist . . . 1890—1971
Herbert, George, English poet . . . 1593—1633
Herbert, Victor, American conductor and composer, born in Ireland . . . 1859—1924
Herder, von (fọn her'dẽr), **Johann Gottfried,** German philosopher, critic, and poet . . . 1744—1803
Heredia (ẹ-rẹ'thī-ä), **José María,** Cuban poet . . . 1803—1839
  H., de, José Maria (*cousin of J.M.H.*), French poet . . . 1842—1905
Hergesheimer (hẽr'ges-hī-mẽr), **Joseph,** Am. novelist . . . 1880—1954
Herkimer (hẽr'ki-mẽr), **Nicholas,** American general . . . 1728—1777
Herndon (hẽrn'dŏn), **William Henry,** American lawyer; partner and biographer of Abraham Lincoln . . . 1818—1891
Herne (hẽrn), **James A.,** American playwright and actor . . . 1839—1901
Herod (her'ŏd), (*the Great*) king of the Jews . . . B.C. 62?—A.D. 4
Herod Antipas (an'ti-pas), (*son of H.*) ruler of Galilee . . . B.C. 4—A.D. 39
Herodotus (he-rod'ō-tus), (*Father of History*) Greek historian . B.C. 484?-425?
Heron (hē'ron) *or* **Hero** (hē'rō), Greek philosopher and mathematician . . . fl. B.C. 3rd cent.
Herrera, de (dẹ e-rẹ'rä), **Fernando** (*the Divine*), Spanish poet . . . 1534?-1597
Herrera, de, Francisco (*the Elder*), Spanish painter . . . 1576—1656
Herrera, José Joaquín, president of Mexico (1844–45, 1848–51) . 1792—1854
Herrick (her'rik), **Myron Timothy,** American ambassador to France (1912–14, 1921–29) . . . 1854—1929
Herrick, Robert, English poet . . . 1591—1674
Herrick, Robert, American novelist and educator . . . 1868—1938
Herriot (e-rī-ō'), **Édouard,** Fr. statesman and premier . . . 1872—1957
Herschel (hẽr'shel), **Caroline Lucretia,** German astronomer (*sister of Sir W.H.*) . . . 1750—1848
  H., Sir John Frederick William (*son of Sir W.H.*), English astronomer and chemist . . . 1792—1871
  H., Sir William, English astronomer, b. in Germany . . . 1738—1822
Hersey (hẽr'sē), **John,** American writer . . . 1914—
Hertz (herts), **Gustav,** German physicist . . . 1887—1975
Hertz, Heinrich Rudolph, German physicist . . . 1857—1894
Hertzog (her'tsokh), **James Barry Munnik,** South African general; prime minister of Union of South Africa (1924–39) . . . 1866—1942
Hervieu (er-vyū'), **Paul,** Fr. novelist and dramatist . . . 1857—1915
Herzl (her'tsl), **Theodor,** Austrian-Jewish journalist and writer, born in Hungary; founder of Zionism . . . 1860—1904
Hesiod (hē'si-ŏd), Greek didactic poet . . . fl. B.C. 800?
Hess (hes), **Myra, Dame,** English pianist . . . 1890—1965
Hess, Rudolf, German Nazi leader; sentenced to life imprisonment for war crimes . . . 1894—
Hess, Victor Francis, American physicist, b. in Austria . . . 1883—1964
Hewlett (hū'let), **Maurice Henry,** English novelist . . . 1861—1923
Heyden, van der (vän dẽr hȳ'den), **Jan,** Dutch painter . . . 1637—1712
Heydrich (hȳ'drikh), **Reinhard** (*the Hangman*), German police official and administrator; shot by Czech patriots, in reprisal for which Lidice was razed . . . 1904—1942
Heyse (hȳ'ṣe), **Karl Wilhelm Ludwig,** German philologist . . . 1797—1855
Heyse, Paul Johann Ludwig, German poet and novelist . . . 1830—1914
Heyward (hẹ'wȧrd), **Du Bose,** Am. poet and playwright . . . 1885—1940
Heywood (hẹ'wood), **John,** English dramatist . . . 1497?-1580?
Heywood, Thomas, English dramatist and actor . . . ? —1650?
Hibben (hib'ben), **John Grier,** American educator . . . 1861—1933
Hickok (hik'ok), **James Butler** (*Wild Bill Hickok*), American scout and frontier marshal . . . 1837—1876
Hicks (hiks), **Granville,** American writer . . . 1901—
Higginson (hig'gin-sŏn), **Thomas Wentworth,** American author and social reformer . . . 1823—1911
Hilary (hil'ȧ-ry), **Saint,** bishop of Poitiers . . . 315?— 367
Hildreth (hil'dreth), **Richard,** American historian . . . 1807—1865
Hill (hil), **Ambrose Powell,** American Confederate general . . . 1825—1865
Hill, Benjamin Harvey, Am. orator and senator . . . 1823—1882
Hill, James Jerome, American railroad builder . . . 1838—1916
Hillman (hil'măn), **Sidney,** American labor leader . . . 1887—1946
Hillyer (hil'yẽr), **Robert Silliman,** American poet . . . 1895—1961
Hilton (hil'tŏn), **James,** English novelist . . . 1900—1954
Himmler (him'lẽr), **Heinrich,** German Nazi leader; Gestapo chief (1936–45); committed suicide . . . 1900—1945
Hindemith (hin'de-mith), **Paul,** German composer in America . . 1895—1963
Hindenburg, von (fọn hin'den-burk), **Paul,** German field marshal; president of Germany (1925–34) . . . 1847—1934
Hines (hīnṣ), **John L.,** Am. general and chief of staff . . . 1868—1968
Hipparchus (hip-pär'ḉhus), Greek astronomer . . . B.C. 2nd cent.
Hippocrates (hip-poḉ'rȧ-tēṣ), (*Father of Medicine*) Greek physician . . . B.C. 460?—377?
Hiranuma (hī-rä'nu̇-mä), **Kiichiro, Baron,** Japanese statesman; sentenced (1948) to prison as a war criminal . . . 1865—1952
Hirohito (hī-rō-hī'tō), emperor of Japan (1926–) . . . 1901—
Hiroshige (hī-rō-shī'ge), Japanese painter . . . 1797—1858
Hirota (hī'rō-tä), **Koki,** Japanese statesman and diplomat; convicted as a war criminal and hanged . . . 1878—1948
Hiss (his), **Alger,** Am. public official, imprisoned after a trial involving Communist spying in the U.S. . . . 1904—
Hitchcock (hich'ḉok), **Ethan Allen,** American statesman . . . 1835—1909
Hitler (hit'lẽr), **Adolf** (*Der Führer*), German dictator and chancellor (1933–45) and Nazi leader, b. Austria; on defeat in World War II, apparently shot himself . . . 1889—1945
Hoadly (hōd'ly), **Benjamin,** Eng. bishop and theologian . . . 1676—1761
Hoare (hōr), **Sir Samuel,** *see* Templewood, Viscount.
Hobart (hō'bȧrt), **Garret Augustus,** vice-president of the United States (1897–99) . . . 1844—1899
Hobbema (hob'be-mä), **Meyndert,** Dutch landscapist . . . 1638—1709
Hobbes (hobṣ), **Thomas,** English philosopher . . . 1588—1679
Hobby (hob'by), **Oveta Culp** (*Mrs. William Pettus H.*), U.S. secretary of health, education, and welfare (1953–55) . . . 1905—
Hobson (hob'sŏn), **John Atkinson,** English economist . . . 1858—1940
Hobson, Richmond Pearson, American naval officer . . . 1870—1937
Ho Chi Minh (hō' chē' min'), (b. *Nguyen Van,* or *That, Thanh*), president of North Vietnam (1954–69) . . . 1890—1969
Hodge (hoġ), **Charles,** American theologian . . . 1797—1878
Hodges (hoġ'eṣ), **Courtney H.,** American general in World War II . . . 1887—1966
Hodža (hōd'jȧ), **Milan,** Czechoslovakian politician . . . 1878—1944
Hoe (hō), **Richard March,** American inventor . . . 1812—1886
Hofer (hō'fẽr), **Andreas,** Tirolean leader and patriot . . . 1767—1810
Hoffman (hof'măn), **Charles Fenno,** American author . . . 1806—1884
Hoffman (họf'män), **Ernst Theodor Amadeus,** German novelist, composer, and painter . . . 1776—1822
Hofmann (hof'măn), **Josef,** American pianist, b. in Poland . . . 1876—1957
Hofmannsthal, von (fọn hōf'män-stäl), **Hugo,** Austrian dramatist and poet . . . 1874—1929
Hogan (hō'găn), **Ben,** American golfer . . . 1912—
Hogarth (hō'gärth), **William,** English satirical artist . . . 1697—1764
Hogg (hog), **James** (*the Ettrick Shepherd*), Scot. poet . . . 1770—1835
Hokusai (hō'ku̧-sä-ī), **Katsuhika,** Japanese painter . . . 1760—1849
Holbein (hōl'bīn), **Hans** (*the Elder*), German painter . . . 1465?-1524
  H., Hans (*the Younger*), German painter . . . 1497—1543
Holberg, von (fọn hōl'berk), **Ludwig, Baron,** Danish author . . . 1684—1754
Holden (hōl'den), **Edward Singleton,** Am. astronomer . . . 1846—1914
Holinshed (hol'inṣ-hed), **Raphael,** English chronicler . . . ? -1580?
Holman-Hunt (hōl'măn-hunt'), **William,** Eng. painter . . . 1827—1910
Holmes (hōmṣ), **John Haynes,** Am. clergyman and liberal . . . 1879—1964
Holmes, Oliver Wendell, American physician, author, and wit . 1809—1894
  H., Oliver Wendell (*son of O.W.H.*), associate justice of the U.S. Supreme Court (1902–32) . . . 1841—1935
Holst (hōlst), **Gustav,** English composer . . . 1874—1934
Holst, von (fọn), **Hermann Eduard,** American historian, of German-Russian antecedents . . . 1841—1904
Holtby (hōlt'by), **Winifred,** English novelist . . . 1898—1935
Holz (hōlts), **Arno,** German poet and critic . . . 1863—1929
Home (hōm), **Daniel Dunglas,** Am. medium, b. in Scotland . . . 1833—1886
Home, John, Scottish dramatist . . . 1722—1808

Homer (hōm'ẽr), Greek epic poet .... B.C. 9th cent.?
Homer, Louise Beatty, American contralto .... 1871?–1947
Homer, Winslow, American painter .... 1836—1910
Homma (hō-mä'), **Masaharu**, Japanese general in World War II; executed for war crimes .... 1888?–1946
Hone (hōn), **Philip**, American businessman and diarist .... 1780—1851
Honegger (hōn'eg-ẽr), **Arthur**, French composer .... 1892—1955
Honorius (hō-nō'ri-us), **Flavius**, Roman emperor .... 384— 423
Honorius III (*Cencio Savelli*), Pope .... ? —1227
Hooch, de (dē hōkh) *or* **Hoogh, Pieter**, Dutch painter .... 1629—1677?
Hood (hood), **John Bell**, American Confederate general .... 1831—1879
Hood, Samuel, Viscount, English admiral .... 1724—1816
Hood, Thomas, English poet, wit, and writer .... 1799—1845
Hooft *or* **Hoofft** (hōft), **Pieter Corneliszoon**, Dutch poet and historian .... 1581—1647
Hooke (hook), **Robert**, Eng. mathematician, inventor .... 1635—1703
Hooker (hook'ẽr), **Joseph**, Union general in Civil War .... 1814—1879
Hooker, Sir Joseph Dalton, English botanist and traveler ...... 1817—1911
Hooker, Richard, English clergyman and theologian .... 1554?–1600
Hooker, Thomas, American colonist and clergyman .... 1586?–1647
Hooton (hoo'tŏn), **Earnest Albert**, Am. anthropologist .... 1887—1954
Hoover (hoo'vẽr), **Herbert Clark**, thirty-first president of the United States (1929–33) .... 1874—1964
Hoover, John Edgar, American administrator; director of Federal Bureau of Investigation .... 1895—1972
Hope (hōp), **Anthony** (pseud. of *Sir Anthony Hope Hawkins*), English novelist .... 1863—1933
Hope, Bob (*Leslie Townes Hope*), American comedian .... 1903—
Hopkins (hop'kinş), **Esek**, American naval hero .... 1718—1802
Hopkins, Sir Frederick Gowland, English biochemist .... 1861—1947
Hopkins, Gerard Manley, English poet and Jesuit .... 1844—1889
Hopkins, Harry Lloyd, Am. statesman; adviser to Pres. F. D. Roosevelt; secretary of commerce (1938–40) .... 1890—1946
Hopkins, Mark, American theologian and educator .... 1802—1887
Hopkinson (hop'kin-sŏn), **Francis**, Am. poet and jurist .... 1737—1791
  H., Joseph (*son of F.H.*), American jurist .... 1770—1842
Hoppe (hop'ē), **William Frederick** (*Willie Hoppe*), American billiards champion .... 1887—1959
Hopper (hop'pẽr), **(William) De Wolf**, American actor .... 1858—1935
Horace (hor'āc), (*Quintus Horatius Flaccus*), Latin poet ..... B.C. 65— 8
Hore-Belisha (hōr'be-lish'á), **Leslie**, British politician .... 1894—1957
Horgan (hor'găn), **Paul**, American novelist .... 1903—
Hornaday (horn'á-dā), **William Temple**, American naturalist .. 1854—1937
Horne (horn), **Richard Hengist**, English poet .... 1803—1884
Hornung (hor'nung), **Ernest William**, English novelist .... 1866—1921
Horowitz (hor'ō-wits), **Vladimir**, Am. pianist, b. in Russia ..... 1904—
Horsa (hor'sá), Jute leader; *see* Hengist .... ? — 455
Horthy, von (fon hōr'tē), **Miklós**, Hungarian admiral; regent of Hungary (1920–44) .... 1869—1957
Hosack (hō'sak), **David**, American physician and writer .... 1769—1835
Hosmer (hoş'mẽr), **Harriet Goodhue**, American sculptor .... 1830—1908
Houdin (ö-dañ'), **Jean Eugène Robert**, French conjurer .... 1805—1871
Houdini (hö-dī'nī), **Harry** (b. *Erich Weiss*), American magician, famous for escape feats .... 1874— 1926
Houdon (ö-doñ'), **Jean Antoine**, French sculptor .... 1741—1828
Hough (huf), **Emerson**, American novelist .... 1857—1923
Houghton (ho'tŏn *or* hou'), **Richard Monckton Milnes, Baron**, English poet .... 1809—1885
House (hous), **Edward Mandell**, American diplomat .... 1858—1938
Housman (hous'măn), **Alfred Edward**, English poet and classicist (*brother of L.H.*) .... 1859—1936
  H., Laurence, English writer and artist .... 1865—1959
Houston (hūs'tŏn), **Samuel**, American general and statesman; president of the Republic of Texas .... 1793—1863
Hovey (hŏv'ē), **Richard**, American poet .... 1864—1900
Howard (hou'ărd), **Bronson**, American dramatist .... 1842—1908
Howard, Catherine, fifth wife of Henry VIII; beheaded .... ? —1542
Howard, Roy Wilson, Am. editor and newspaper magnate .... 1883—1964
Howard, Sidney Coe, American dramatist .... 1891—1939
Howe (hou), **Elias**, American inventor of the sewing machine .... 1819—1867
Howe, Julia Ward, American poet .... 1819—1910
Howe, Richard Earl, British admiral (*Brother of W. H.*) .... 1726—1799
  H., William, Viscount, British commander in chief in the American Revolution .... 1729—1814
Howells (hou'elş), **William Dean**, American author .... 1837—1920
Hoyle (hoil), **Edmund**, English writer on games .... 1672—1769
Hrdlicka (hûr'dlich-kä), **Ales**, American anthropologist, born in Czechoslovakia .... 1869—1943
Hrolf, *see* Rollo.
Hubbard (hub'bărd), **Elbert**, American editor and writer .... 1856—1915
Hudson (hud'sŏn), **Henry**, Eng. navigator and explorer .... ? —1611
Hudson, William Henry, English naturalist and author .... 1841—1922
Huerta (wer'tä), **Victoriano**, Mexican general and president (1913–14) .... 1854—1916
Huggins (hug'ginş), **Sir William**, English astronomer .... 1824—1910
Hughes (hūş), **Charles Evans**, Am. statesman and jurist; Rep. presidential nominee (1916); secretary of state (1921–25); chief justice of the U.S. Supreme Court (1930–41) .... 1862—1948
Hughes, Hatcher, American playwright .... 1881—1945
Hughes, Howard Robard, American capitalist, aviator, and motion-picture producer .... 1905—1976
Hughes, (James) Langston, American poet .... 1902—1967
Hughes, Rupert, American novelist and biographer .... 1872—1956
Hughes, Thomas, English author .... 1822—1896
Hugo (hū'gō *or Fr.* ü-gō'), **Victor Marie, Vicomte**, French novelist, dramatist, and poet .... 1802—1885
Huizinga (hī'zing-á), **Johan**, Dutch historian .... 1872—1945
Hull (hul), **Cordell**, U.S. secretary of state (1933–44) .... 1871—1955
Hull, Isaac, American naval officer .... 1773—1843
Hull, William, American general .... 1753—1825
Humbert (hum'bẽrt) **I** *or It.* **Umberto** (ûm-ber'tō), king of Italy; succeeded by his son, Victor Emmanuel III .... 1844—1900
  H. II, successor to Italian throne on abdication (1946) of his father (V.E. III), went into exile .... 1904—
Humboldt, von (fon hum'bōlt), **Friedrich Heinrich Alexander, Baron**, German naturalist and explorer .... 1769—1859
  H., von, Karl Wilhelm, Baron (*brother of F.H.A.v.H.*), German philologist and statesman .... 1767—1835
Hume (hūm), **David**, Scottish historian and philosopher .... 1711—1776
Humperdinck (hum'pẽr-dink), **Engelbert**, German composer ... 1854—1921
Humphrey, Hubert Horatio, vice-president of the U.S. (1965–69) . 1911—1978
Humphreys (hump'frīs), **Andrew Atkinson**, Union general in the Civil War .... 1810—1883
Humphreys, David, American poet and soldier .... 1752—1818
Huneker (hun'ek-ẽr), **James**, Am. novelist and critic .... 1860—1921
Hunt (hunt), **Alfred William**, English painter .... 1830—1896
Hunt, (James Henry) Leigh, English poet and essayist .... 1784—1859
Hunt, William Holman, *see* Holman-Hunt.
Hunter (hunt'ẽr), **John**, Scot. anatomist, physiologist .... 1728—1793
Hunter, Robert Mercer Taliafero, American Confederate secretary of state .... 1809—1887
Hunyady (hun'yä-dy), **János**, Hungarian general and hero ..... 1395—1456
Hurley (hûr'li), **Patrick Jay**, U.S. secretary of war (1929–33); ambassador to China (1944–45) .... 1883—1963
Hurok (hûr'ok), **Solomon** (*S. Hurok*), Am. impresario .... 1888—1974
Hurst (hûrst), **Fannie**, American novelist .... 1889—1968
Huskisson (hus'kis-sŏn), **William**, English statesman .... 1770—1830
Huss (hus), **John**, Bohemian religious reformer .... 1369—1415
Hussein (hụs-sīn') **I**, king of Jordan (1952–) .... 1935—
Hutcheson (huch'e-sŏn), **Ernest**, American composer and pianist, b. in Australia .... 1871—1951
Hutcheson, Francis, Irish metaphysician .... 1694—1746
Hutchins (huch'inş), **Robert Maynard**, Am. educator .... 1899—1977
Hutchinson (huch'in-sŏn), **Anne**, Am. religious leader .... 1591—1643
Hutchinson, Arthur Stuart Mentieth, English novelist .... 1879—1971
Hutchinson, Thomas, governor of colonial Massachusetts ...... 1711—1780
Hutten, von (fon hut'ten), **Ulrich**, German poet and humanist . 1488—1523
Huxley (huks'lī), **Aldous**, English novelist, essayist, and poet (*son of L. H.*) .... 1894—1963
  H., Julian Sorrell (*son of L.H.*), English biologist .... 1887—1975
  H., Leonard (*son of T.H.H.*), Eng. editor, author .... 1860—1933
  H., Thomas Henry, English biologist and writer .... 1825—1895
Huygens *or* **Huyghens** (hy'genş *or* hoi'), **Christian**, Dutch astronomer .... 1629—1695
Huysmans (ü-ēs-mäñs'), **Joris Karl**, French novelist .... 1848—1907
Huysum, van (vän hoi'sum), **Jan**, Dutch painter .... 1682—1749
Hyde (hȳd), **Douglas**, Irish poet and philologist; first president of Eire (1938–45) .... 1860—1949
Hyder Ali (hȳ'dẽr ä'lī), sultan of Mysore .... 1728?–1782
Hyperides (hȳ-per'i-dēş), Greek orator .... ?—B.C.322

I

Ibáñez, Vicente Blasco, *see* Blasco Ibáñez.
Ibn-Saud (ib'n-sä-ūd'), **Abdul-Aziz**, king of Saudi Arabia (1932–53) .... 1880—1953
Ibsen (ib'sen), **Henrik**, Norwegian poet and dramatist .... 1828—1906
Ickes (ik'es), **Harold LeClaire**, U.S. secretary of the interior (1933–46) .... 1874—1952
Ignatius (ig-nā'shus), **Saint** (*Theophorus*), bishop of Antioch and Christian martyr .... ? —107?
Ignatius, Saint, patriarch of Constantinople .... 798?— 878
Ignatius of Loyola (loi-ō'lá), **Saint**, Spanish founder of the Jesuit order .... 1491—1556
Ikhnaton, *see* Amenhotep IV.
Indy, d' (dañ-dē'), **Vincent**, French composer .... 1851—1931
Inge (ing), **William Ralph**, Eng. clergyman and author .... 1860—1954
Ingelow (in'ge-lō), **Jean**, English poet and novelist .... 1820—1897
Ingemann (ing'e-män), **Bernard Severin**, Danish poet and novelist .... 1789—1862
Ingersoll (iñ'gẽr-sol), **Robert Green**, American lawyer, orator, and antitheist .... 1833—1899
Ingoldsby (iñ'gōlş-by), **Thomas**, *see* Barham, Richard H.
Ingres (añ'gr), **Jean Auguste Dominique**, French painter ...... 1780—1867
Inness (in'neş), **George**, American landscape painter .... 1825—1894
Innocent (in'nō-cent), **II** (*Gregorio Papareschi*), Pope .... ? —1143
Innocent III (*Lotario di Segni*), Pope .... 1161—1216
Innocent IV (*Sinivaldo de' Fieschi*), Pope .... ? —1254
Innocent XI (*Benedetto Odescalchi*), Pope .... 1611—1689
Innocent XII (*Antonio Pignatelli*), Pope .... 1615—1700
Inönü (i-nū-nū'), **Ismet**, pres. of Turkey (1938–50) .... 1884—1973
Insull (in'sul), **Samuel**, Am. public-utilities magnate .... 1859—1938
Inverchapel (in'vẽr-chăp-el), **Archibald Clark Kerr, first Baron**, British diplomat; ambassador to Soviet Union (1942–45); to the United States (1946–48) .... 1882—1951
Ionesco (yō-nes'cō), **Eugene**, French playwright, b. in Romania .. 1912—
Ippolitov-Ivanov (ī-pō-lyī'tof-ī-vän'of), **Mikhail Mikhailovich**, Russian composer and conductor .... 1859—1935
Ireland (īr'lănd), **John**, archbishop of St. Paul, Minn. .... 1838—1918
Irenaeus (ī-re-nē'us), **Saint**, Greek bishop of Lyons .... 130?– 202?
Irigoyen (ī-rī-gō'yen), **Hipólito**, Argentine president .... 1850?–1933
Ironside (ī'ẽrn-sīd), **William Edmund, first Baron**, British general .... 1880—1959
Irving (ẽr'ving), **Sir Henry** (b. *John Henry Brodribb*), English actor .... 1838—1905
Irving, Washington, American author and humorist .... 1783—1859
Irwin (ẽr'win), **Wallace**, Am. writer (*brother of Will*) .... 1876—1959
  I., Will (*William Henry I.*), Am. author, journalist .... 1873—1948
Isaacs (ī'şaçs), **Sir Isaac Alfred**, Australian jurist and statesman; governor-general (1931–36) .... 1855—1948
Isabella (iş-â-bel'lá), **I** (*the Catholic*), queen of Castile and Leon; patron of Columbus .... 1451—1504
Isherwood (ī'shẽr-wood), **Christopher**, English novelist .... 1904—
Ishii (ī'shī-ī), **Kikujiro, Viscount**, Japanese diplomat .... 1866— 1945
Ismail Pasha (is-mä-il' på-shä') *or* **Ismail I**, khedive of Egypt (1863–79) .... 1830—1895
Isocrates (ī-soç'rá-tēş), Athenian orator .... B.C. 436— 338
Ito (ī'tō), **Hirobumi, Prince**, Japanese statesman .... 1841—1909
Iturbi (ī-tûr'bī), **José**, Am. pianist, conductor, b. in Spain .... 1895—1980
Iturbide, de (dē ī-tûr-bī'the), **Agustín**, emperor of Mexico (1822–23) .... 1783—1824
Ivan (ī-vän') **III** (*the Great*), grand duke of Muscovy .... 1440—1505
  I. IV (*grandson of I. III*), (*the Terrible*) first Czar of Russia (1547–84) .... 1530—1584
Ives, (īvş), **Charles Edward**, American composer .... 1874—1954
Ives, James M., *see* Currier.

J

Jackson (jak'sŏn), **Andrew** (*Old Hickory*), American general and 7th U.S. president (1829–37)........1767—1845
Jackson, Helen Maria Fiske Hunt, Am. novelist, poet........1830—1885
Jackson, Robert Houghwout, associate justice of U.S. Supreme Court (1941–54)........1892—1954
Jackson, Thomas Jonathan (*Stonewall*), Am. Confederate general in the Civil War........1824—1863
Jacobs, William Wymark, English writer........1863—1943
James (jāmẓ) **I**, king of Scotland and poet........1394—1437
James I (*son of Mary Stuart*), king of England (1603–25) and, as James VI, king of Scotland (1567—1625)........1566—1625
James II (*son of Charles I*), king of England (1685–88)........1633—1701
James, Henry (*brother of William*), American novelist........1843—1916
James, Jesse, American outlaw........1847—1882
James, William, American philosopher and psychologist........1842—1910
Jameson (jām'sŏn), **Sir Leander Starr**, British statesman in South Africa........1853—1917
Jammes (ẓȧm), **Francis**, French poet........1868—1938
Janáček (yä'nä-chek), **Leoš**, Czech composer........1854—1928
Janet (ẓȧ-ne'), **Pierre**, French psychologist........1859—1947
Jansen (jan'sen *or* yän'), **Cornelis**, Dutch theologian........1585—1638
Janssen (jan'sen), **Werner**, Am. composer, conductor........1900—
Jaques-Dalcroze (ẓȧk-dȧl-ḵrōz'), **Émile**, Swiss composer and educator; originator of eurythmics........1865—1950
Jaspers (yäs'pẽrz), **Karl**, German philosopher........1883—1969
Jastrow (jas'trō), **Joseph**, Am. psychologist, b. in Poland........1863—1944
Jaurès (ẓō-res'), **Jean Léon**, Fr. socialist and author........1859—1914
Jay (jā), **John**, American jurist and statesman; first chief justice, U.S. Supreme Court........1745—1829
Jean de Meung (ẓäṅ dẽ mūṅ'), French author........1250?–1305
Jeanne d'Arc, *see* Joan of Arc.
Jeans (jēnṣ), **Sir James Hopwood**, English astronomer, physicist, and writer........1877—1946
Jebb (jeb), **Sir Richard Claverhouse**, Scottish classicist........1841—1905
Jeffers (jef'fẽrṣ), **Robinson**, American poet........1887—1962
Jefferson (jef'fẽr-sŏn), **Joseph**, American actor........1829—1905
Jefferson, Thomas, 3rd U.S. president (1801–09)........1743—1826
Jeffrey (jef'ri), **Francis, Lord**, Scottish critic and editor........1773—1850
Jeffreys (jef'riṣ), **George, Baron**, English judge........1648—1689
Jeffries (jef'friṣ), **James J.**, American prize fighter; world heavyweight champion (1899–1905)........1875—1953
Jellicoe (jel'i-cō), **John Rushworth, Earl**, English admiral........1859—1935
Jenner (jen'nẽr), **Edward**, English physician; demonstrated efficacy of vaccination........1749—1823
Jenner, Sir William, English physician........1815—1898
Jennings (jen'ningṣ), **Herbert Spencer**, Am. biologist........1868—1947
Jeritza (ye'rit-sä), **Maria**, Austrian operatic soprano........1887—
Jerome (je-rōm'), **Jerome Klapka**, English novelist and dramatist........1859—1927
Jerome, Saint (*Eusebius Sophronius Hieronymus*), Latin church father........340?— 420
Jesperson (yes'pẽr-sen), **Otto**, Danish linguist........1860—1943
Jessup (jes'sup), **Philip Caryl**, Am. jurist, diplomat........1897—
Jesus Christ (jē'sus ḵhrist), founder of Christianity........B.C.4?–A.D.29?
Jewett (jū'et), **Sarah Orne**, American writer........1849—1909
Joachim (yō'ȧ-ḵhim), **Joseph**, Hungarian violinist........1831—1907
Joad (jō'ad), **Cyril Edwin Mitchinson**, Eng. philosopher........1891—1953
Joan of Arc (jōn ov ärḵ) *or Fr.* **Jeanne d'Arc** (ẓän' därḵ), (*the Maid of Orleans*), French heroine and saint........1412—1431
Joffre (ẓof'r), **Joseph Jacques Césaire**, Fr. marshal........1852—1931
Jogues (ẓog), **Isaac**, French Jesuit missionary........1607—1646
John (jon), (*son of Henry II*) king of England........1167?–1216
John III (*John Sobieski*), king of Poland (1674–96)........1624—1696
John XXIII (*Angelo Guiseppe Roncalli*), Pope (1958–63)........1881—1963
John, Augustus Edwin, English painter........1879—1961
John of Austria, Don, Spanish general and admiral........1547—1578
John Paul I (jon pạl) (*Albino Luciani*), Pope (1978)........1912—1978
John Paul II (*Karol Wojtyla*), Pope (1978–)........1920—
Johnson (jon'sŏn), **Andrew**, seventeenth president of the United States (1865–69)........1808—1875
Johnson, Hiram Warren, American political leader........1866—1945
Johnson, Hugh Samuel, Am. soldier, govt. administrator........1882—1942
Johnson, Jack (*John Arthur J.*), American prize fighter; world heavyweight champion (1908–15)........1876—1946
Johnson, James Weldon, American writer........1871—1938
Johnson, Josephine Winslow, American novelist........1910—
Johnson, Lyndon B., 36th president of the United States (1963–69)........1908—1973
Johnson, Martin Elmer, American explorer........1884—1937
Johnson, Reverdy, American lawyer and statesman........1796—1876
Johnson, Richard Mentor, vice-president of the United States (1837–41)........1780—1850
Johnson, Robert Underwood, Am. diplomat and author........1853—1937
Johnson, Samuel, English lexicographer and author........1709—1784
Johnson, Sir William, Br. colonial statesman in America........1715—1774
Johnston (jon'stŏn), **Albert Sidney**, Am. Confederate general........1803—1862
Johnston, Joseph Eggleston, Am. Confederate general........1807—1891
Johnston, Mary, American novelist........1870—1936
Joinville, de (dẽ ẓwaṅ-vil'), **Jean**, Fr. chronicler........1224—1317
Jókai (yō'koi), **Maurus** *or* **Mór**, Hungarian novelist........1825—1904
Joliet (ẓō-lye'), **Louis**, French explorer of the Mississippi........1645—1700
Joliot-Curie (ẓō-lyō'ḵū-rē'), **Frédéric**, Fr. chemist; shared Nobel prize (1935) with his wife *Irène*........1900—1958
J.-C., Irène (*daughter of Pierre and Marie Curie*), French chemist........1897—1956
Jones (jōnṣ), **Henry Arthur**, English dramatist........1851—1929
Jones, Inigo, English architect........1573—1652
Jones, Jesse Holman, U.S. sec. of commerce (1940–45)........1874—1956
Jones, John Paul, American naval officer, b. in Scotland........1747—1792
Jones, Robert Tyre, Jr. (*Bobby J.*), American golfer........1902—1971
Jones, Sir William, English Orientalist and jurist........1746—1794
Jonson (jon'sŏn), **Ben**, English dramatist........1573?–1637
Joplin (jop'lin), **Scott**, American ragtime pianist and composer........1868—1917
Jordan (jọr'dăn), **David Starr**, Am. biologist, educator........1851—1931
Joseph (jō'ṣef) **II**, Holy Roman emperor (1765–90)........1741—1790
Josephine (jō'ṣe-fīn) **de Beauharnais**, empress of France; first wife of Napoleon........1763—1814
Josephus (jō-sē'fus), **Flavius**, Jewish historian........37?— 95?
Joubert (ẓö-ber'), **Barthélemy Catherine**, Fr. general........1769—1799
Joubert (you'bert), **Petrus Jacobus**, Boer commander........1831—1900
Jouhaux (ẓö-ō'), **Léon**, Fr. socialist labor leader........1879—1954
Joule (jōl *or* joul), **James Prescott**, English physicist........1818—1889
Jourdan (ẓör-däṅ'), **Jean Baptiste, Count**, Fr. marshal........1762—1833
Jovian (jō'vi-ăn), emperor of Rome........331— 364
Jowett (jou'et), **Benjamin**, English Greek scholar........1817—1893
Joyce (joic), **James**, Irish novelist and poet........1882—1941
Juan Carlos I (hwän ḉär'lōs) (*grandson of Alfonso XIII*) king of Spain (1975–)........1938—
Juárez (hwä'reṣ), **Benito**, president of Mexico (1857–63, 1867–72)........1806—1872
Judas Maccabaeus (jū'dȧs maç-ȧ-bē'us), Jewish patriot........?–B.C.160
Judd (jud), **Charles Hubbard**, American psychologist........1873—1946
Judson (jud'sŏn), **Edward Zane Carroll** (pseud. *Ned Buntline*), Am. adventurer and writer of dime novels........1823?–1886
Jugurtha (jū-gūr'thȧ), king of Numidia........?–B.C.104
Juin (ẓwaṅ), **Alphonse Pierre**, marshal of France........1888—1967
Julia (jū'li-ȧ), daughter of Julius Caesar, wife of Pompey........?–B.C.54
Julian (jūl'yăn), (*the Apostate*) emperor of Rome........331— 363
Juliana (yū-li-ä'nä *or Eng.* jū-li-an'ȧ), (*daughter of Wilhelmina*) queen of the Netherlands (1948–)........1909—
Jung (yụng), **Carl Gustav**, Swiss psychiatrist........1875—1961
Junius (jūn'yus), the assumed name of an unknown English writer........fl.1769—1772
Junot (ẓū-nō'), **Andoche, Duc d'Abrantes**, Fr. marshal........1771—1813
Jusserand (ẓū-sräṅ'), **Jean Jules**, French diplomat and author........1855—1932
Justin Martyr (jus'tin), **Saint**, Christian apologist........100?–165?
Justinian (jus-tin'i-ăn) **I** *or* **Justinianus** (jus-tin-i-an'us), **Flavius Anicius** (*the Great*), Byzantine emperor........483— 565
Juvenal (jū've-năl) *or* **Juvenalis** (jū-ven-al'is), **Decimus Junius**, Roman satirical poet........60?– 140?

K

Kafka (käf'kȧ), **Franz**, Austrian writer........1883—1924
Kaiser (kīs'ẽr), **Georg**, German playwright........1878—1945
Kaiser, Henry J., American industrialist........1882—1967
Kalidasa (kä-li-dä'sä), (*the Shakespeare of India*), Hindu poet........5th cent.?
Kalinin (kä-lyī'nyin), **Mikhail Ivanovich**, president of the Soviet Union (1923–46)........1875—1946
Kallio (käl'i-ō), **Kyosti**, president of Finland (1937–40)........1873—1940
Kamehameha (kä-mẹ'hä-mẹ'hä) **IV**, king of the Hawaiian Islands........1834—1863
Kamenev (kä'myen-yef), **Lev B.** (b. *Rosenfeld*), Russian Communist leader; executed........1883—1936
Kamerlingh Onnes (kä'mẽr-ling ōn'es), **Heike**, Dutch physicist; received Nobel prize (1913)........1853—1926
Kames (kāmṣ), **Henry Home, Lord**, Scottish jurist and philosopher........1696—1782
Kandinsky (kän-dyīn'skē), **Vassily**, Russian painter........1866—1944
Kane (kān), **Elisha Kent**, American arctic explorer........1820—1857
Kant (känt), **Immanuel**, German philosopher........1724—1804
Kapitza (kä'pi-tsä), **Pëtr Leonidovich**, Russian nuclear physicist........1894—
Karamzin (kȧ-räm-zin'), **Nicolai M.**, Russian historian, novelist, and poet........1766—1826
Karlfeldt (kärl'felt), **Erik Axel**, Swedish poet........1864—1931
Karloff (kȧr'lọf), **Boris** (b. *William Henry Pratt*), American stage and screen actor, b. in England........1887—1969
Károlyi (kä'rōl-yī), **Michael, Count**, Hung. statesman........1875—1955
Katayev (kȧ-tȳ'ef), **Valentin P.**, Russian novelist........1897—
Kato (kä'tō), **Takaakira, Viscount**, Japanese statesman........1859—1926
Kaufman (kạf'măn), **George S.**, American playwright........1889—1961
Kautsky (kout'sky), **Karl**, Austrian socialist and author........1854—1938
Kay (kā), **John**, English inventor........1704—1764
Kaye-Smith (-smith), **Sheila**, English novelist........1887—1956
Kazinczy (käz'in-tsē), **Ferencz**, Hungarian author and translator........1759—1831
Kean (kēn), **Charles John** (*son of E.K.*), English actor........1811?–1868
K., Edmund, English tragedian........1787?–1833
K., Ellen Tree (*wife of C.J.K.*), English actress........1808—1880
Kearny (kär'ny), **Lawrence**, American naval officer........1789—1868
Kearny, Philip, Union general in the Civil War........1814—1862
Kearny, Stephen Watts, Am. general in the Mexican War........1794—1848
Keats (kēts), **John**, English poet........1795—1821
Keble (kē'bl), **John**, English poet and clergyman........1792—1866
Keene (kēn), **Laura**, American actress........1826?–1873
Kefauver (kē-fō'vẽr), **Carey Estes**, U.S. senator........1903—1963
Keith (kēth), **Sir Arthur**, British anthropologist........1866—1955
Kekulé von Stradonitz (kẹ'kū-lẹ fọn shträ'dō-nits), **Friedrich August**, German chemist........1829—1896
Keller (kel'lẽr), **Helen Adams**, American blind and deaf author and lecturer........1880—1968
Kelley (kel'li), **Edgar Stillman**, American composer........1857—1944
Kellogg (kel'lŏg), **Clara Louisa**, American singer........1842—1916
Kellogg, Frank Billings, American lawyer, diplomat, and statesman; secretary of state (1925–29)........1856—1937
Kelly (kel'ly), **George**, American playwright........1887—1974
Kelly, William, American inventor........1811—1888
Kelvin (kel'vin), **William Thomson, first Baron**, English physicist and mathematician........1824—1907
Kemal Ataturk (ke-mäl' ä-tä-tūrk'), **Mustafa**, Turkish statesman and president (1923–38)........1881—1938
Kemble (kem'bl), **Charles**, English actor........1775—1854
K., Frances Anne (*daughter of C.K.*), (*Fanny Kemble*), English actress........1809—1893
K., John Philip (*brother of C.K.*), English tragedian........1757—1823
Kempis, Thomas à, *see* Thomas à Kempis.
Ken (ken), **Thomas**, English bishop and hymn writer........1637—1711
Kendal (ken'dăl), **Madge, Dame** (b. *Margaret Robertson*), English actress........1849—1935
Kendall (ken'dăl), **Amos**, American statesman........1789—1869
Kendall, Edward Calvin, American biochemist........1886—1972
Kennan (ken'năn), **George Frost**, American diplomat........1904—
Kennedy (ken'ne-dy), **Charles Rann**, Am. playwright, b. in England........1871—1950
Kennedy, John Fitzgerald, 35th president of the United States (1961–63); assassinated........1917—1963
Kennedy, Margaret, English novelist........1896—1967

Kenny (ken'ny), **Elizabeth** (*Sister Kenny*), Australian nurse; developed a treatment for infantile paralysis .... 1886—1952
Kensett (ken'set), **John Frederick**, Am. landscapist .... 1818—1872
Kent (kent), **James**, Am. jurist and law commentator .... 1763—1847
Kent, Rockwell, American painter and illustrator .... 1882—1971
Kenyatta (ken-yät'ȧ), **Jomo**, African political leader; president of Kenya (1964–78) .... 1893?–1978
Kenyon (ken'yŏn), **John Samuel**, American phonetician .... 1874—1959
Keokuk (kē'ō-kuk), chief of the Sacs and Foxes .... 1780—1848
Kepler (kep'lẽr), **Johann**, German astronomer .... 1571—1630
Kerensky (ke-ren'sky), **Aleksandr Feodorovich**, Russian premier during the 1917 revolution, overthrown by the Bolsheviks .... 1881—1970
Kern (kẽrn), **Jerome David**, American composer .... 1885—1945
Kesselring (kes'el-ring), **Albert**, German field marshal .... 1887—1960
Key (kē), **Francis Scott**, American lawyer; author of *The Star-Spangled Banner* .... 1780—1843
Keyes (kēș), **Roger John Browlow, Baron**, Brit. admiral .... 1872—1945
Keynes (kęnș), **John Maynard, Baron**, Eng. economist .... 1883—1946
Keyserling (kȳ'șẽr-ling), **Hermann, Count**, German philosopher and author .... 1880—1946
Khachaturian (kä-chȧ-tụ-ryän'), **Aram Ilich**, Russ. composer .... 1904?–1978
Khrushchev (krōōs'chev), **Nikita Sergeyevich**, premier of the U.S.S.R. (1958–64) .... 1894—1971
Kidd (kid), **William** (*Captain Kidd*), Scottish privateer and reputed pirate; hanged .... 1645?–1701
Kierkegaard (kẽr'ke-gōr), **Soren Aabye**, Danish philosopher and theologian .... 1813—1855
Kilmer (kil'mẽr), **Joyce**, American poet .... 1886—1918
King (king), **Ernest Joseph**, Am. admiral of the fleet; com. in chief of U.S. naval forces in World War II .... 1878—1956
King, Grace Elizabeth, American author .... 1852—1932
King, Henry, English poet .... 1592—1669
King, Martin Luther, Jr., American clergyman and leader in Negro civil rights movement; assassinated .... 1929—1968
King, Rufus, American statesman .... 1755—1827
King, William Lyon MacKenzie, Canadian statesman and premier (1921–30, 1935–48) .... 1874—1950
Kingsley (kingș'li), **Charles**, Eng. clergyman and author .... 1819—1875
Kingsley, Sidney, American playwright .... 1906—
Kinsey (kin'și), **Alfred Charles**, Am. zoologist; prepared statistical surveys of human sexual behavior in U.S. .... 1894—1956
Kipling (kip'ling), **Rudyard**, English novelist and poet .... 1865—1936
Kirby (kẽr'by), **William**, English entomologist .... 1759—1850
Kirchhoff (kirkh'hōf), **Gustav Robert**, German physicist .... 1824—1887
Kirke (kẽrk), **Sir David**, English colonial adventurer .... 1596—1654
Kirov (kī'rǫf), **Sergei Mironovich**, Russian Communist leader; assassinated .... 1888—1934
Kirshon (kir'shŏn), **Vladimir Mikhailovich**, Russian playwright .... 1902—1937
Kissinger, Henry Alfred, U.S. secretary of state (1973–77), b. in Germany .... 1923—
Kitchener (kich'en-ẽr), **Horatio Herbert, first Earl**, British general and statesman .... 1850—1916
Kittredge (kit'reġ), **George Lyman**, American scholar .... 1860—1941
Klee (klā), **Paul**, Swiss abstract painter .... 1879—1940
Klein (klīn), **Felix**, German mathematician .... 1849—1925
Kleist, von (fǫn klist), **Heinrich**, German dramatist .... 1777—1811
Klopstock (klop'stok), **Friedrich Gottlieb**, German poet .... 1724—1803
Kneller (nel'ẽr), **Sir Godfrey**, English painter .... 1646—1723
Knight (nīt), **Eric**, English novelist .... 1897—1942
Knoblock (nob'lok), **Edward**, Eng. playwright, novelist .... 1874—1945
Knowles (nōlș), **James Sheridan**, Irish dramatist .... 1784—1862
Knowlton (nōl'tŏn), **Frank Hall**, American paleobotanist .... 1860—1926
Knox (noks), **Frank** (*William Franklin Knox*), Am. newspaper publisher; secretary of the navy (1940–44) .... 1874—1944
Knox, Henry, American Revolutionary general .... 1750—1806
Knox, John, Scottish religious reformer .... 1505—1572
Knudsen (nǫǫd'sen), **William S.**, American industrialist and production expert, born in Denmark .... 1879—1948
Koch (kōkh), **Robert**, German bacteriologist .... 1843—1910
Kock, de (dē kōk), **Charles Paul**, French novelist and dramatist .... 1794—1871
  K., de, Henri (*son of C.P. de K.*), French novelist .... 1819—1892
Kodály (kō'dä-yȧ), **Zoltán**, Hungarian composer .... 1882—1967
Koestler (kest'lẽr), **Arthur**, Hung. author in England .... 1905—
Koffka (kof'kȧ), **Kurt**, Am. psychologist, b. in Germany .... 1886—1941
Köhler (kö'lẽr), **Wolfgang**, German psychologist in the U.S. .... 1887—1967
Kokoschka (kō-kosh'kȧ), **Oskar**, British painter, b. in Austria .... 1886—1980
Kolchak (kŏl-chäk'), **Aleksandr Vassilyevich**, Russian anti-Bolshevik leader .... 1874—1920
Kollwitz (kol'vits), **Käthe** (b. *Käthe Schmidt*), German painter, etcher, and lithographer .... 1867—1945
Komroff (kŏm'rǫf), **Manuel**, American novelist .... 1890—
Kondylis (kŏn-dȳ'lis), **George**, Greek general, premier .... 1880—1936
Konoye (kŏ-nō'ye), **Fumimaro, Prince**, Japanese premier .... 1891—1945
Konrad (kōn'rät) **I** *see* Conrad I.
Koo (kǫǫ), **Wellington**, Chinese statesman and diplomat .... 1887—
Körner (kẽr'nẽr), **Karl Theodor**, German poet .... 1791—1813
Korzybski (kǫr-zyb'skī), **Alfred Habdank**, American expert in semantics, b. in Poland .... 1879—1950
Kosciusko (kos-ci-us'kō), **Thaddeus**, Polish patriot .... 1746—1817
Kossuth (ko-sụth'), **Louis**, Hungarian statesman .... 1802—1894
Kosygin (kō-sē'gin), **Aleksei Nikolaevich**, premier of the U.S.S.R. (1964–80) .... 1904—1980
Kotzebue, von (fǫn kōt'se-bụ), **August Friedrich Ferdinand**, German dramatist .... 1761—1819
Koussevitzky (kö-se-vit'skē), **Serge Alexandrovich**, Russian orchestral conductor in the U.S. .... 1874—1951
Kraepelin (krā-pe-lin'), **Emil**, German psychiatrist .... 1856—1926
Krafft-Ebing, von (fǫn kräft'ġ-bing), **Richard, Baron**, German neurologist .... 1840—1902
Kreisler (kris'lẽr), **Fritz**, Austrian violinist in the U.S. .... 1875—1962
Krenek (kren'ek), **Ernst**, American composer, b. in Austria .... 1900—
Kreutzer (kroit'sẽr), **Rodolphe**, French violinist and composer .... 1766—1831
Kreymborg (krem'bǫrg), **Alfred**, Am. poet and writer .... 1883—1966
Krilof (krī'lǫf), **Ivan Andreyevich**, Russian dramatist .... 1768—1844
Kropotkin (krō-pōt'kin), **Peter Alekseyevich, Prince**, Russian author and revolutionist .... 1842—1921
Kruger (krụ'gẽr), **Paul** (*Stephanus Johannes Paulus K.*), (*Oom Paul*) president of Transvaal (1883–1900) .... 1825—1904
Krupp (krụp), **Alfred**, German gunmaker .... 1812—1887
Krupp von Bohlen und Halbach (fǫn bō'len ụnt häl'bäkh), **Gustav, Count**, German munitions manufacturer .... 1870—1950
Krutch (krụtch), **Joseph Wood**, American critic .... 1893—1970
Kubelik (kụ'be-lik), **Jan**, Bohemian violinist .... 1880—1940
Kublai Khan (kụ'blī kän'), founder of the Mongol dynasty of China .... 1216?–1294
Kun (kůn), **Béla**, Hungarian Communist leader .... 1885—1937
Kung (kůng), **H. H.** (*Kung Hsiang-hsi*), Chinese statesman and minister of finance .... 1881—1967
Kuprin (kụ-prīn'), **Aleksandr Ivanovich**, Russ. novelist .... 1870—1938
Kutuzov (kụ-tụ'zǫf), **Mikhail**, Russian field marshal .... 1745—1813
Kyd (kyd), **Thomas**, English dramatist .... 1558—1594

L

Labiche (lȧ-bĭçh'), **Eugène Marin**, French dramatist .... 1815—1888
La Bruyère, de (dē lȧ brụ-yer'), **Jean**, French scholar and moralist .... 1645—1696
Ladd (lad), **George Trumbull**, American philosopher .... 1842—1921
La Farge (lȧ färẓ'), **John**, American artist and writer .... 1835—1910
  La F., Oliver (*grandson of J. La F.*), Am. novelist .... 1901—1963
Lafayette *or* **La Fayette, de** (dē lȧ-fȧ-yet'), **Marie Joseph Paul Yves Roch Gilbert du Motier, Marquis**, French statesman and general; fought in Am. Revolution .... 1757—1834
Lafitte *or* **Laffite** (lȧ-fīt'), **Jean**, French privateer in the Gulf of Mexico .... 1780?–1825?
La Follette (lä fol'let), **Robert Marion**, American statesman; Progressive presidential nominee (1924) .... 1855—1925
La Fontaine, de (dē lȧ fọṅ-tān'), **Jean**, French fabulist and poet .... 1621—1695
Lagerkvist (lä'gẽr-kvist), **Pär Fabian**, Swedish author .... 1891—1974
Lagerlöf (lä'gẽr-lüf), **Selma**, Swedish novelist .... 1858—1940
Lagrange (lȧ-gräṅẓ'), **Joseph Louis, Comte**, French astronomer .... 1736—1813
La Guardia (lȧ gwär'dī-ȧ), **Fiorello**, American politician .... 1882—1947
Lake (lāk), **Kirsopp**, Am. biblical scholar, b. in England .... 1872—1946
Lalique (lȧ-lĭk'), **René**, French artist .... 1860—1945
Lalo (lȧ-lō'), **Édouard Victor**, French composer .... 1823—1892
Lamarck, de (dē lȧ-märk'), **Jean Baptiste Pierre Antoine de Monet, Chevalier**, French naturalist .... 1744—1829
Lamartine, de (dē lȧ-mȧr-tīn'), **Alphonse Marie Louis**, French author and statesman .... 1790—1869
Lamb (lam), **Charles**, English essayist and humorist .... 1775—1834
  L., Mary (*sister of C.L.*), English poet and writer .... 1764—1847
La Mettrie, de (dē lȧ me-trē'), **Julien Offray**, French philosopher .... 1709—1751
La Motte-Fouqué, de (dē lȧ mọt'fö-kę'), *see* Fouqué.
Landis (lan'dis), **Kenesaw Mountain**, American jurist and baseball commissioner .... 1866—1944
Landon (lan'dŏn), **Alfred Mossman**, American politician .... 1887—
Landor (lan'dǫr), **Walter Savage**, Eng. poet and writer .... 1775—1864
Landowska (lan-dǫf'skȧ), **Wanda**, Polish pianist and harpsichordist in France .... 1877—1959
Landseer (land'sẽr), **Sir Edwin Henry**, English animal painter .... 1802—1873
Landsteiner (länt'shtīn-ẽr), **Karl**, American pathologist, born in Austria; received Nobel prize (1930) .... 1868—1943
Lane (lān), **Edward William**, English Orientalist .... 1801—1876
Lane, Franklin Knight, U.S. secretary of the interior (1913–20) .... 1864—1921
Lane, James Henry, American antislavery politician, soldier, and senator .... 1814—1866
Lang (lang), **Andrew**, Scottish scholar and writer .... 1844—1912
Lang, Cosmo Gordon, archbishop of Canterbury (1928–42) .... 1864—1945
Langdon (lang'dŏn), **John**, American statesman .... 1741—1819
Langland (lang'lȧnd), **William**, English poet .... 1332?–1400?
Langley (lang'li), **Samuel Pierpont**, American astronomer, physicist, and pioneer in aviation .... 1834—1906
Langmuir (lang'mūr), **Irving**, American chemist .... 1881—1957
Langtry (lang'try), **Lillie**, English actress .... 1852—1929
Lanier (lȧ-nēr'), **Sidney**, American poet .... 1842—1881
Lankester (lañ'kes-tẽr), **Sir Edwin Ray**, Eng. biologist .... 1847—1929
Lansing (lan'sing), **Robert**, U.S. secretary of state (1915–20) .... 1864—1928
Lanson (läṅ-sǫṅ'), **Gustave**, French literary historian .... 1857—1934
Lao-tse *or* **Lao-tzu** (lou'dzu'), Chinese philosopher; founder of Taoism .... B.C. 604— 531
Laplace, de (dē lȧ-plȧç'), **Pierre Simon, Marquis**, French astronomer and mathematician .... 1749—1827
Larcom (lär'çom), **Lucy**, American poet .... 1824—1893
Lardner (lärd'nẽr), **Ring** (*Ringgold Wilmer L.*), American humorist and short-story writer .... 1885—1933
La Rochefoucauld, de (dē lȧ rǫçh-fö-çō'), **François, Duc, Prince of Marsillac**, French moralist and writer .... 1613—1680
Larousse (lȧ-rös'), **Pierre Athanase**, Fr. lexicographer .... 1817—1875
La Salle, de (dē lȧ sȧl'), **Robert Cavelier, Sieur**, French explorer .... 1643—1687
Lasca, Il (īl läs'çȧ), (pseud. of *Antonio Francesco Grazzini*), Italian author .... 1503—1584
Lasker (las'kẽr), **Eduard**, German statesman .... 1829—1884
Lasker, Emanuel, German mathematician and chess player (world champion 1894–1921) .... 1868—1941
Laski (las'kē), **Harold Joseph**, British labor party leader and political economist .... 1893—1950
Lassalle (lȧ-sȧl'), **Ferdinand**, German socialist .... 1825—1864
Lasso, di (dī lä'sō), **Orlando**, Belgian composer .... 1532?–1594
Latané (la'tȧ-nę), **John Holladay**, American historian .... 1869—1932
Lathrop (lāth'rǫp), **George Parsons**, American author .... 1851—1898
Latimer (lat'i-mẽr), **Hugh**, English bishop and reformer .... 1485?–1555
Latourette (lä-tụ-ret'), **Kenneth Scott**, American clergyman and educator .... 1884—1969
Laube (lou'be), **Heinrich**, German novelist and poet .... 1806—1884
Laud (lạd), **William**, archbishop of Canterbury; executed .... 1573—1645
Lauder (lạ'dẽr), **Sir Harry** (*Harry MacLennan*), Scottish singer and comedian .... 1870—1950
Lauderdale (lạ'dẽr-dāl), **James Maitland, Earl of**, Scottish statesman .... 1759—1839
Lauderdale, John Maitland, Duke of, cabal minister in England .... 1616—1682
Laughton (lạ'tŏn), **Charles**, English actor .... 1899—1962
Laurence (lạ'renc), **William Leonard**, Am. journalist .... 1888—1977
Laurencin (lō-räṅ-caṅ'), **Marie**, French painter .... 1885—1956
Laurens (lạ'rens), **Henry**, Am. Revolutionary statesman .... 1724—1792
  L., John (*son of H.L.*), Am. Revolutionary soldier .... 1754—1782

Laurier (lō′ri-ẹ), **Sir Wilfrid**, Canadian statesman and prime minister (1896–1911)....1841—1919

Laval (lȧ-vȧl′), **Pierre**, French politician; premier (1931–32, 1935–36); leader of Vichy regime; executed for treason....1883—1945

La Vallière, de (dẽ lȧ vȧ-lyer′), **Louise Françoise, Duchesse**, French beauty; mistress of Louis XIV....1644—1710

Lavedan (lȧ-ve-däṅ′), **Henri Léon Émile**, Fr. dramatist....1859—1940

Lavisse (lȧ-vēs′), **Ernest**, French historian....1842—1922

Lavoisier (lȧ-vwȧ-ẓyẹ′), **Antoine Laurent**, French chemist....1743—1794

Law (lạ), **Andrew Bonar**, British statesman, b. in Canada....1858—1923

Law, John, Scottish economist in France....1671—1729

Lawes (lạs), **Henry**, English composer....1596—1662

Lawes, Lewis Edward, American penologist; warden of Sing Sing Prison, Ossining, N.Y. (1920–41)....1883—1947

Lawrence (lạ′renc), **Saint**, Roman Christian martyr.... ? — 258

Lawrence, Abbott, American merchant and diplomat....1792—1855

Lawrence, David Herbert, English novelist....1885—1930

Lawrence, Ernest Orlando, American physicist....1901—1958

Lawrence, Gertrude, English actress in America....1901—1952

Lawrence, James, American naval officer....1781—1813

Lawrence, Josephine, American novelist....1897—

Lawrence, Sir Thomas, English portrait painter....1769—1830

Lawrence, Thomas Edward (*Lawrence of Arabia*), (changed name, 1927, to *T.E. Shaw*) British archaeologist, adventurer, and author.1888—1935

Layamon (lā′ȧ-mŏn), English chronicler.... fl.1200

Layard (lā′ärd), **Sir Austen Henry**, English traveler, archaeologist, and diplomat....1817—1894

Lazarus (la′zȧ-rus), **Emma**, Am. writer and poet....1849—1887

Lazear (lä-zēr′), **Jesse Williams**, American physician....1866—1900

Lea (lē), **Henry Charles**, American historian....1825—1909

Lea, Homer, Am. writer; general in Chinese army; friend of Sun Yat-sen; warned against Japanese militarism....1876—1912

Leacock (lē′çok), **Stephen Butler**, Canadian humorist....1869—1944

Leaf (lēf), **Munro**, American children's writer....1905—

Leahy (lā′hē), **William Daniel**, Am. admiral, diplomat....1875—1959

Leake (lēk), **William Martin**, English topographer....1777—1860

Leakey (lē′kē), **L(ouis) S(eymour) B(azett)**, British anthropologist....1903—1972

Lear (lēr), **Edward**, English traveler, artist, and writer....1812—1888

Lebrun (lẽ-brüṅ′), **Albert**, French statesman; president of France (1932–40)....1871—1950

Le Brun *or* **Lebrun** (lẽ-brüṅ′), **Charles**, French painter....1619—1690

Lebrun, Charles François, Duke of Piacenza, French statesman and author....1739—1824

Lecky (lek′y), **William Edward Hartpole**, Irish historian and philosopher....1838—1903

Leconte de Lisle (lẽ-çoṅt′ dẽ lēl′), **Charles Marie**, French poet.1818—1894

Le Corbusier (lẽ çor-bü-zyẹ′), (b. *Charles Édouard Jeanneret*) Swiss architect in France.... 1887—1965

Ledyard (led′yärd), **John**, American traveler....1751—1789

Lee (lē), **Ann** (*Mother Ann*), founder of the Shakers in America.1736—1784

Lee, Arthur (*brother of Francis, Richard, and William*), American Revolutionary diplomat....1740—1792

Lee, Charles, Am. Revolutionary general, b. in England....1731—1782

Lee, Fitzhugh (*nephew of R.E.L.*), Am. Confederate cavalry leader; U.S. general in Spanish-American War....1835—1905

Lee, Francis Lightfoot (*brother of Arthur, Richard, and William*), American Revolutionary patriot....1734—1797

Lee, Henry (*Light-Horse Harry*), (*father of R.E.L.*) American Revolutionary cavalry officer; governor of Virginia....1756—1818

Lee, Ivy Ledbetter, American public relations advisor....1877—1934

Lee, Manfred B., *see* Queen, Ellery.

Lee, Nathaniel, English dramatist....1653?–1692

Lee, Richard Henry (*brother of Arthur, Francis, and William*), American Revolutionary statesman....1732—1794

Lee, Robert Edward (*son of H.L.*), commander in chief of Confederate army in the Civil War....1807—1870

Lee, Sir Sidney, English editor and writer....1859—1926

Lee, William (*brother of Arthur, Francis, and Richard*), American Revolutionary diplomat....1739—1795

Leeuwenhoek, van (vän lẹ′ven-hook), **Anton**, Dutch microscopist and scientist....1632—1723

Le Gallienne (lẽ gal′yen), **Eva**, American actress and theatrical producer (*daughter of R. Le G.*)....1899—

  Le G., Richard, English poet and essayist....1866—1947

Léger (lā-zhā′), **Fernand**, French painter....1881—1955

Leginska (lē-gin′skȧ), **Ethel**, Eng. pianist and conductor....1890—

Legouis (lẽ-gö-ī′), **Émile**, French literary critic....1861—1937

Legros (lẽ-grō′), **Alphonse**, French painter and engraver....1837—1911

Lehár (le′här), **Franz**, Hungarian composer....1870—1948

Lehman (lē′măn), **Herbert Henry**, American statesman....1878—1963

Lehmann (lẹ′män), **Lilli**, German soprano....1848—1929

Lehmann, Lotte, Am. soprano, b. in Germany....1888—1976

Lehmann, Rosamund, English novelist....1904?—

Leibnitz, von (fọn līp′nits), **Gottfried Wilhelm, Baron**, German philosopher and mathematician....1646—1716

Leicester (les′tẽr), **Robert Dudley, Earl of**, favorite of Queen Elizabeth I....1532?–1588

Leighton (lẹ′tŏn), **Frederick, Lord**, English painter....1830—1896

Leighton, Robert, Scottish archbishop and theologian....1611—1684

Leland (lē′lănd), **Charles Godfrey**, American author....1824—1903

Leland, John, English antiquarian....1506—1552

Lely (lē′ly), **Sir Peter**, Dutch painter in England....1618—1680

Lemaître (lẽ-mā′tr), **Georges Édouard, Abbé**, Belgian astrophysicist....1894—1966

Lemaître, Jules, French literary critic....1853—1914

LeMay (lẽ-mā′), **Curtis**, American air force general....1906—

Lemonnier (lẽ-mọ-nyẹ′), **Pierre**, French astronomer....1715—1799

Lemoyne (lẽ-mwȧn′), **François**, French historical painter....1688—1737

Lenard (lẹ′närt), **Philipp**, German physicist....1862—1947

Lenclos, de (dẽ läṅ-çlō′), **Ninon**, Fr. beauty and wit....1620?–1706?

L'Enfant (läṅ-fäṅ′), **Pierre Charles**, French architect and city planner; officer in the American Revolution....1754—1825

Lenin (len′in *or Russ.* lye′nin), **Vladimir Ilich** (b. *Ulianov*), Soviet Russian statesman and Communist leader; Com. party chairman and virtual dictator (1917–24)....1870—1924

Lennox (len′ŏks), **Charlotte**, Am. novelist in England....1720—1804

Lenôtre (lẽ-nō′tr), **André**, French architect....1613—1700

Leo (lē′ō) **I** (*the Thracian*), Eastern Roman emperor.... 400— 474

Leo I, Saint (*the Great*), Pope....390?— 461

Leo III, Saint, Pope who crowned Charlemagne....750?— 816

Leo X (*Giovanni de' Medici*), Pope; art patron....1475—1521

Leo XIII (*Gioacchino Pecci*), Pope....1810—1903

Leonard (len′ărd), **William Ellery**, American poet....1876—1944

Leoncavallo (lẹ-ōn-çä-väl′lō), **Ruggiero**, It. composer....1858—1919

Leonidas (lē-on′i-dăs), heroic king of Sparta.... ?–B.C.480

Leonov (lyẹ-ọ′nọf), **Leonid**, Russian novelist....1899—

Leopardi (lẹ-ō-pär′dī), **Giacomo, Count**, Italian poet....1798—1837

Leopold (lē′ō-pōld) **I**, (*the Great*), Holy Roman emperor....1640—1705

Leopold II, Holy Roman emperor....1747—1792

Leopold I, king of the Belgians (1831–65)....1790—1865

  L. II (*son of L. I*), king of the Belgians (1865–1909)....1835—1909

  L. III (*son of Albert I*), king of the Belgians (1934–51); abdicated in favor of his son, Baudouin....1901—

Lepidus (lep′i-dus), **Marcus Aemilius**, Roman triumvir.... ?–B.C.13

Lepsius (lep′si-us), **Karl Richard**, German Egyptologist....1810—1884

Lermontov (lyer′mon-tọf), **Mikhail Yurevich**, Russian poet and novelist....1814—1841

Le Sage (lẽ säz′), **Alain René**, French dramatist and novelist...1668—1747

Leschetizky (le-she-tit′ski), **Theodore**, Polish pianist, composer, and teacher....1830—1915

Leslie (les′li), **Alexander, Earl of Leven**, Scottish general....1580?–1661

Leslie, Frank (b. *Henry Carter*), American publisher and engraver, born in England....1821—1880

Leslie, John, English bishop and historian....1527—1596

Leslie, Sir John, English physicist....1766—1832

Lesseps, de (dẽ le-seps′ *or Eng.* les′seps), **Ferdinand, Viscount**, French diplomat and engineer; builder of Suez Canal....1805—1894

Lessing (les′ing), **Gotthold Ephraim**, German dramatist and critic....1729—1781

Lesueur (lẽ-sü-ẽr′), **Eustache**, French historical painter....1617—1655

Lever (lē′vẽr), **Charles James**, Irish novelist....1806—1872

Leverett (lev′ẽr-et), **John**, governor of the colony of Massachusetts....1616—1679

Leverrier (lẽ-ve-ryẹ′), **Urbain Jean Joseph**, French astronomer.1811—1877

Levitzki (le-vit′skī), **Mischa**, Russian pianist and composer....1898—1941

Lewes (lů′is), **George Henry**, English scientist and author....1817—1878

Lewis (lů′is), **Andrew**, Am. frontiersman, soldier....1720—1781

Lewis, D. B. Wyndham, British biographer....1894—1969

Lewis, John Llewellyn, Am. labor leader; pres. of United Mine Workers (1920–60) and C.I.O. (1935–41)....1880—1969

Lewis, Matthew Gregory (*Monk Lewis*), English novelist....1775—1818

Lewis, Meriwether, American explorer....1774—1809

Lewis, Sinclair, American novelist....1885—1951

Lewisohn (lü′i-sọn), **Ludwig**, Am. author, b. in Germany....1883—1955

Lhévinne (lẹ-vīn′), **Joseph**, Russian pianist....1874—1944

Liadov (lyȧ′dọf), **Anatoli K.**, Russian composer....1855—1914

Liddell (lid′l), **Henry George**, English classical scholar....1811—1898

Liddell Hart (härt′), **Basil Henry**, English military strategist and writer....1895—1970

Lie (lē), **Jonas**, Norwegian novelist....1833—1908

Lie, Jonas, Norwegian-born American painter....1880—1940

Lie, Trygve, Norwegian statesman; foreign minister (1941–45); secretary general of the U.N. (1945–53)....1896—1968

Lieber (lē′bẽr), **Francis**, American political scientist, born in Germany....1800—1872

Liebermann (lē′bẽr-män), **Max**, German painter, etcher....1847—1935

Liebig, von (fọn lē′bikh), **Justus, Baron**, Ger. chemist....1803—1873

Liebknecht (lēp′knekht), **Karl**, German socialist leader; creator of the Spartacans (*son of W.L.*)....1871—1919

  L., Wilhelm, German social democrat....1826—1900

Li Hung Chang (lī′hụng′chäng′), Chinese statesman....1823—1901

Lilienthal (lil′yen-thạl), **David Eli**, Am. administrator; chairman U.S. Atomic Energy Commission (1947–50)....1899—

Lilienthal (lil′yen-täl), **Otto**, German pioneer experimenter with aircraft....1848—1896

Liliuokalani (lī′lī-ụ-ō-kä-lä′nī), **Lydia Kamekeha**, last Hawaiian ruler....1838—1917

Lillo (lil′lō), **George**, English dramatist....1693—1739

Lilly (lil′y), **John**, *see* Lyly, John.

Lincoln (liṅ′çŏn), **Abraham** (*the Great Emancipator*), 16th U.S. president (1861–65); assassinated....1809—1865

Lincoln, Benjamin, American Revolutionary general....1733—1810

Lincoln, Joseph Crosby, American novelist....1870—1944

Lincoln, Levi, American lawyer and statesman....1749—1820

Lind (lind), **Jenny** (*Swedish Nightingale*), Swedish soprano....1820—1887

Lindbergh (lind′bẽrg), **Charles Augustus**, Am. aviator; made first solo nonstop flight N.Y.–Paris (1927)....1902—1974

Lindley (lind′li), **John**, English botanist....1799—1865

Lindsay (lind′sy), **Sir David**, Scottish poet....1490?–1555?

Lindsay, Vachel (*Nicholas Vachel L.*), American poet....1879—1931

Lindsey (lind′sy), **Benjamin Barr**, Am. judge, reformer....1869—1943

Ling (ling), **Per Henrik**, Swedish founder of a medical-gymnastic system....1776—1839

Linlithgow (lin-lith′gō), **Victor Alexander John Hope, second Marquess of**, British viceroy of India (1936–43)....1887—1952

Linnaeus, von (fọn lin-nē′us) *or Sw.* **Linné, von** (fọn lin′ẹ), **Carl** *or* **Charles**, Swedish botanist....1707—1778

Lipchitz (lip′shits), **Jacques** (b. *Chaim Jacob L.*), American sculptor, b. in Lithuania....1891—1973

Li Po (lī pō), Chinese poet....700?— 762

Lippi (lēp′pī *or Eng.* lip′i), **Fra Filippo**, Italian painter....1406?–1469

  L., Filippino (*son of F.F.L.*), Italian painter....1457?–1504?

Lippmann (lip′măn), **Walter**, Am. journalist and author....1889—1974

Lipsius (lip′si-ụs), **Justus**, Flemish critic and philologist....1547—1606

Lipton (lip′tŏn), **Sir Thomas Johnstone**, British merchant and yachtsman....1850—1931

Lisa (lī′sȧ), **Manuel**, American fur trader....1772—1820

List (list), **Friedrich**, German political economist....1789—1846

Lister (lis′tẽr), **Joseph, first Baron**, English surgeon; introduced antisepsis in surgery....1827—1912

Liszt (list), **Franz**, Hungarian composer and pianist....1811—1886

Littré (lī-trẹ′), **Maximilien Paul Émile**, French philologist....1801—1881

Litvinov (lit-vī′nŏf), **Maxim**, Soviet Russian foreign commissar (1930–39); ambassador to U.S. (1941–43)....1876—1951

Livingston (liv′ing-stŏn), **Edward**, American statesman and jurist (*brother of R.R.L.*)....1764—1836

  L., Robert R., American statesman and diplomat....1746—1813

Livingstone (liv′ing-stŏn), **David**, Scottish explorer in Africa....1813—1873

Livy (liv′y), (*Titus Livius*), Roman historian....B.C. 59–A.D.17

Lloyd George (loid ġorġ), **David, Earl of Dwyfor,** British statesman and premier (1916–22)....1863—1945

Locke (lok), **David Ross** (pseud. *Petroleum V. Nasby*), American humorist....1833—1888

Locke, John, English philosopher....1632—1704

Locke, William John, English novelist....1863—1930

Locker-Lampson (lok'ẽr-lamp'sŏn), **Frederick,** English poet....1821—1895

Lockhart (lok'härt), **John Gibson,** Scot. critic, poet; son-in-law and biographer of Sir Walter Scott....1794—1854

Lockyer (lok'yẽr), **Sir Joseph Norman,** Eng. astronomer....1836—1920

Lodge (loġ), **Henry Cabot,** Am. statesman and author....1850—1924

L., Henry Cabot, Jr. (*grandson*), U.S. senator; U.S. representative to the U.N. (1953–60)....1902—

Lodge, Sir Oliver Joseph, English scientist....1851—1940

Lodge, Thomas, English dramatist....1558?–1625

Loeb (lōb), **Jacques,** American physiologist, b. in Germany....1859—1924

Loeffler (lef'lẽr), **Charles Martin Tornov,** American violinist and composer....1861—1935

Loewi (lō'ī), **Otto,** German pharmacologist in America....1873—1961

Löffler (lẽf'lẽr), **Friedrich,** German bacteriologist....1852—1915

Logan (lō'găn), (*Tah-gah-jute*), American Indian chief....1725?–1780

Logan, Benjamin, American pioneer in Kentucky....1752—1802

Logan, James, Am. colonial statesman and writer....1674—1751

Logan, John Alexander, American general and statesman....1826—1886

Lombroso (lōm-brō'ṣō), **Cesare,** Italian criminologist....1836—1909

London (lŏn'dŏn), **Jack** (*John Griffith L.*), American novelist and short-story writer....1876—1916

Long (lọng), **Crawford Williamson,** American surgeon....1815—1878

Long, Huey Pierce (*the Kingfish*), American governor (Louisiana) and senator; assassinated....1893—1935

Longfellow (lọng'fel-ō), **Henry Wadsworth,** American poet....1807—1882

Longinus (lon-gī'nus), **Dionysius Cassius,** Greek philosopher and critic....213— 273

Longstreet (lọng'strēt), **James,** Am. Confederate general....1821—1904

Longworth (lọng'wŏrth), **Nicholas,** American politician; speaker of U.S. House of Representatives (1925–31)....1869—1931

Lönnrot (lūn'rōt), **Elias,** Finnish philologist and folklorist....1802—1884

Lonsdale (lonṣ'dāl), **Frederick,** British playwright....1881—1954

López (lō'pẹs *or Sp.* lō'pẹth), **Narcisco,** Cuban revolutionist....1799—1851

Lorentz (lō'rents), **Hendrik Antoon,** Dutch physicist....1853—1928

Lorenz (lō'rents), **Adolf,** Austrian surgeon....1854—1946

Lorimer (lor'i-mẽr), **George Horace,** American editor....1868—1937

Lossing (los'sing), **Benson John,** American engraver and historian....1813—1891

Lothaire (lō-thăr') **I,** Holy Roman emperor....795?— 855

Lothaire II *or* **III** (*the Saxon*), emperor of Germany....1060?–1137

Lothian (lō'thi-ăn), **Philip Henry Kerr, Marquess of,** British statesman and diplomat....1882—1940

Loti (lō-tī'), **Pierre** (pseud. of *Louis Marie Julien Viaud*), French novelist....1850—1923

Lotze (lō'tse), **Rudolf Hermann,** German philosopher....1817—1881

Loubet (lů-be'), **Émile,** president of France (1899–1906)....1838—1929

Loudon (lou'dŏn), **John Claudius,** Scottish botanist....1783—1843

Louis (lō'is *or* lö'ī; *Fr.* lö-ī') **I,** (*le Debonnaire* or *the Pious*), (*son of Charlemagne*) Holy Roman emperor and king of France....778— 840

L. VI (*the Fat*), king of France (1108–37)....1081—1137

L. IX (*St. Louis*), king of France (1226–70)....1214—1270

L. XI (*son of Charles VII*), king of France (1461–83)....1423—1483

L. XII, king of France (1498–1515)....1462—1515

L. XIII (*son of Henry IV*), king of France (1610–1643)....1601—1643

L. XIV (*the Great*), (*son of L. XIII*) king of France (1643–1715)....1638—1715

L. XVI, king of France (1774–93); guillotined....1754—1793

L. XVII (*son of L. XVI and Marie Antoinette*), nominal king of France (1793–95)....1785–1795?

L. XVIII (*Monsieur*), (*brother of L. XVI*), king of France (1814–24)....1755—1824

Louis (lö'is), **Joe** (*Joseph Louis Barrow*), American prize fighter; world heavyweight champion (1937–49)....1914—1981

Louis Napoleon, *see* Napoleon III.

Louis Philippe (lö-ī' fī-lip'), king of France (1830–48)....1773—1850

Louÿs (lwē), **Pierre** (pseud. of *Pierre Louis*), French novelist and poet....1870—1925

Lovejoy (lŏv'joi), **Elijah Parish,** American abolitionist....1802—1837

Lovelace (lŏv'lāc), **Richard,** English poet....1618—1658

Lovell (luv'ăl), **Sir (Alfred Charles) Bernard,** English astronomer....1913—

Lover (lŏv'ẽr), **Samuel,** Irish novelist and poet....1797—1868

Lovett (lŏv'et), **Robert Morss,** Am. author, educator....1870—1956

Low (lō), **Seth,** American educator and political reformer....1850—1916

Lowell (lō'el), **Abbott Lawrence,** American educator....1856—1943

L., Amy (*sister of A.L.L. and P.L.*), American poet and critic....1874—1925

L., Percival, American astronomer....1855—1916

Lowell, James Russell, Am. poet, editor, diplomat....1819—1891

Lowell, Robert (Traill Spence, Jr.), American poet....1917—1977

Lowes (lōṣ), **John Livingston,** Am. literary scholar....1867—1945

Loyola, Ignatius of, *see* Ignatius of Loyola.

Lucan (lū'căn), (*Marcus Annaeus Lucanus*), Roman poet, born in Spain....39— 65

Lucas (lū'căs), **Edward Verrall,** English essayist....1868—1938

Luce (lūc), **Henry Robinson,** American editor and publisher, born in China....1898—1967

Lucian (lū'shăn), Greek satirical author....120?–200?

Luckner, von (fọn lụk'nẽr), **Felix, Count** (*the Sea Devil*), German naval officer in World War I....1886—1966

Lucretia (lū-ҫrē'shi-å), Roman woman illustrious for her virtue...?–B.C.510?

Lucretius (lū-ҫrē'shi-us), (*Titus Lucretius Carus*), Roman poet....B.C. 96?— 55

Lucullus (lū-ҫul'us), **Lucius Licinius,** Roman consul and general....B.C. 110?— 57

Ludendorff (lů'den-dọrf), **Erich,** German general and politician; Hindenburg's chief of staff in World War I....1865—1937

Ludwig (lůt'vikh), **Emil** (b. *Cohn*), German biographer....1881—1948

Ludwig, Otto, German novelist and playwright....1813—1865

Luini (lů-ī'nī), **Bernardino,** Italian painter....1480?–1533?

Luks (lůks), **George Benjamin,** American painter....1867—1933

Lully (lū-lē'), **Jean Baptiste,** Fr. composer, b. in Italy....1632—1687

Lully (lul'y), **Raymond** (*the Enlightened Doctor*), Spanish philosopher....1235?–1315

Lundy (lun'dy), **Benjamin,** American abolitionist....1789—1839

Lunt (lunt), **Alfred,** American actor....1893—1977

Luther (lū'thẽr *or Ger.* lů'tẽr), **Martin,** leader of the German Reformation; founder of Lutheran Church....1483—1546

Luxemburg (lụk'sem-bụrk), **Rosa,** German socialist....1870?–1919

Lyautey (lē-ō-tẹ'), **Louis Hubert Gonzalve,** Fr. marshal....1854—1934

Lycurgus (lȳ-ҫūr'gus), Spartan lawgiver....fl.B.C.9th cent.

Lydgate (lyd'găt), **John,** English poet....1370—1451

Lyell (lȳ'el), **Sir Charles,** British geologist....1797—1875

Lyly (ly'ly), **John,** English dramatist and author....1554?–1606

Lynd (lynd), **Robert Staughton,** American sociologist....1892—1970

Lyon (lȳ'ŏn), **Mary,** American educator....1797—1849

Lyons (lȳ'ŏnṣ), **Joseph Aloysius,** prime minister of Australia (1932–39)....1879—1939

Lysander (lȳ-san'dẽr), Spartan general and statesman.... ?–B.C.395

Lysias (lys'i-ăs), Athenian orator....B.C.450?—380?

Lysimachus (lȳ-sim'å-ҫhus), Greek general and king of Thrace B.C. 361?–281

Lysippus (lȳ-sip'pus), Greek sculptor....B.C. 4th cent.

Lytton (lyt'tŏn), *see* Bulwer-Lytton.

M

Mabillon (må-bī-yọṅ'), **Jean,** French Benedictine historian....1632—1707

Mabuse, de (dẽ må-bůṣ'), **Jan,** Flemish painter....1478?–1532?

MacArthur (măҫ-är'thūr), **Arthur,** American general....1845—1912

M., Douglas (*son of A.M.*), American general in S.W. Pacific in World War II....1880—1964

Macaulay (må-ҫa'li), **Rose,** English novelist....1889?–1958

Macaulay, Thomas Babington, Baron of Rothley, English historian, poet, essayist, and statesman....1800—1859

Macbeth (maҫ-beth'), king of Scotland.... ? —1057

MacCracken (må-ҫrak'en), **Henry Mitchell,** American educator.1840—1918

MacDonald (măҫ-don'ăld), **Flora,** Scottish heroine....1722—1790

MacDonald, George, Scottish novelist....1824—1905

Macdonald, Sir John Alexander, Canadian statesman, born in Scotland....1815—1891

MacDonald, James Ramsay, British statesman and Labor leader; premier (1924, 1929–35)....1866—1937

Macdonough (măҫ-do'nu), **Thomas,** Am. naval officer....1783—1825

MacDowell (măҫ-dou'el), **Edward Alexander,** American composer....1861—1908

MacGrath (må-grath'), **Harold,** American novelist....1871—1932

Mach (mäkh), **Ernst,** Austrian philosopher and physicist....1838—1916

Machado (må-chä'dō), **Gerardo,** Cuban president....1871—1939

Machiavelli (maҫh-i-å-vel'i), **Niccolò,** Florentine statesman and writer....1469—1527

Mack (mak), **Connie** (*Cornelius McGillicuddy*), American baseball manager....1862—1956

Mackay (mak'y), **John William,** Am. financier, b. in Ireland....1831—1902

MacKaye (må-kȳ'), **Percy,** Am. poet and playwright....1875—1956

M., Steele (*father of P.M.*), Am. dramatist, actor....1842—1894

Mackensen, von (fọn mäk'en-sen), **August,** German field marshal.1849—1945

Mackenzie (må-ken'zi), **Sir Alexander,** Scottish explorer....1755?–1820

Mackenzie, Sir Compton, English novelist....1883—1972

Mackenzie, Henry, Scottish essayist and novelist....1745 1831

Mackintosh (mak'in-tosh), **Sir James,** British historian....1765—1832

Macklin (mak'lin), **Charles** (b. *Charles McLaughlin*), English actor and dramatist....1697?–1797

Maclean (măҫ-lān'), **John,** Am. jurist and statesman....1785—1861

MacLeish (măҫ-lēsh'), **Archibald,** American poet....1892—

Macleod (măҫ-loud'), **John James Rickard,** Scottish physiologist; co-discoverer of insulin....1876—1935

Macleod, Norman, Scottish clergyman and writer....1812—1872

MacMahon (măҫ-må-ọṅ'), **Marie Edmé Patrice Maurice, Duc de Magenta,** president of France (1873–79)....1808—1893

MacMillan (măҫ-mil'lăn), **Donald Baxter,** American arctic explorer....1874—1970

MacMonnies (măҫ-mŏn'ēṣ), **Frederick William,** Am. sculptor....1863—1937

MacNarney (măc-när'nē), **Joseph Taggart,** Am. general....1893—1972

MacNaughton (măc-nạ'tŏn), **Andrew George Latta,** Canadian general and statesman; representative to U.N....1887—1966

MacNeil (măҫ-nēl'), **Hermon Atkins,** American sculptor....1866—1947

Macpherson (măҫ-fẽr'sŏn), **James,** Scottish poet....1736—1796

MacPherson, James Birdseye, Union general in Civil War....1828—1864

Macready (măҫ-rē'dy), **William Charles,** English actor....1793—1873

Macrobius (măҫ-rō'bi-us), **Ambrosius Theodosius,** Roman philosopher....fl.5th cent.

Madariaga, de (dẹ mä-thä-ryä'gä), **Salvador,** Spanish diplomat and author....1886—

Madero (mä-thẹ'rō), **Francisco,** Mexican statesman and president (1911–13)....1873—1913

Madison (mad'i-sŏn), **James,** fourth president of the United States (1809–17)....1751—1836

Maecenas (mi-cē'năs), **Caius Cilnius,** Roman patron of literature....B.C. 70?— 8

Maerlant, van (vän mär'länt), **Jacob,** Flemish poet....1235?–1300

Maeterlinck (mā'tẽr-link *or* met'ẽr-), **Maurice,** Belgian poet and dramatist; received Nobel prize (1911)....1862—1949

Maffei, di (dī mäf-fẹ'ī), **Francesco Scipione, Marchese,** Italian dramatist and antiquary....1675—1755

Magellan (må-ġel'lăn), **Fernando,** Portuguese navigator....1480—1521

Magendie (må-ẑäṅ-dē'), **François,** French physiologist....1783—1855

Magruder (må-grū'dẽr), **John Bankhead,** Am. Confederate general....1810—1871

Mahaffy (må-haf'fy), **Sir John Pentland,** Irish classicist....1839—1919

Mahan (må-han'), **Alfred Thayer,** Am. naval officer, author....1840—1914

Mahler (mä'lẽr), **Gustav,** Austrian composer, conductor....1860—1911

Mahmud *or* **Mahmoud** (mä-mūd') **I,** sultan of Turkey....1696?–1754

Mahmud *or* **Mahmoud II,** sultan of Turkey....1784—1839

Mahomet (må-hom'et), *see* Mohammed.

Mahone (må-hōn'), **William,** Am. Confederate general and United States senator....1826—1895

Mailer (māl'ẽr), **Norman,** American writer, especially of novels....1923—

Maimonides (mī-mon'i-dēṣ), (*Moses ben Maimon*) Spanish rabbi, philosopher, and writer....1135—1204

Maine (mān), **Sir Henry James Sumner,** English legal and political writer....1822—1888

Maintenon, de (dẽ maṅt-nọṅ'), **Françoise d'Aubigné, Marquise,** second wife of Louis XIV....1635—1719

Maistre, de (dē mā'str), **Joseph Marie, Count,** French diplomat and writer....1754—1821
M., de, Xavier, Count (*brother of J. de M.*), Fr. writer....1763—1852
Maitland (māt'lănd), **Frederic William,** English jurist....1850—1906
Major (mā'jŏr), **Charles,** American novelist....1856—1913
Malan (ma-län'), **Daniel François,** S. African premier....1874—1959
Malcolm (mal'cŏm) **III** (*Canmore*), king of Scotland.... ? —1093
Malebranche (mȧl-brăṅch'), **Nicolas,** French philosopher....1638—1715
Malenkov (mä'lyen-kọf), **Georgi M.,** Russian Communist leader and statesman; premier (1953–55)....1901—
Malherbe, de (dē mȧl-erb'), **François,** Fr. poet, critic....1555—1628
Malik (mä'lik), **Yakov A.,** Russian diplomat....1906—
Malinowski (mä-li-nọf'ski), **Bronislaw Kasper,** Polish anthropologist in England and the U.S....1884—1942
Mallarmé (mȧ-lȧr-mẹ'), **Stéphane,** Fr. symbolist poet....1842—1898
Mallet (mal'let), **David,** Scottish poet....1705?–1765
Malone (mȧ-lōn'), **Edmond,** Irish Shakespearean expert....1741—1812
Malory (mal'ō-ry), **Sir Thomas,** English author.... ? —1471
Malot (mȧ-lō'), **Hector Henri,** French author....1830—1907
Malpighi (mäl-pī'gī), **Marcello,** Italian anatomist....1628—1694
Malraux (mȧl-rō'), **André,** French novelist....1901—1976
Malte-Brun (mäl'te-brụn), **Conrad** (b. *Malthe Conrad Bruun*), Danish geographer....1775—1826
Malthus (mal'thus), **Thomas Robert,** English political economist.1766—1834
Manco Capac (măñ'çō çä-päç'), founder of Inca dynasty of Peru. fl.c.1000
Mandeville (man'de-vil), **Bernard,** English satirist and philosopher, born in the Netherlands....1670—1733
Mandeville, Sir John, fictitious author of a narrative of travels, real and fictional, probably compiled by a French physician, John de Bourgogne.... ? —1372
Manet (mȧ-ne'), **Édouard,** Fr. impressionist painter....1832—1883
Mangan (mañ'găn), **James Clarence,** Irish poet....1803—1849
Mann (män), **Heinrich** (*brother of T.M.*), German novelist....1871—1950
Mann (man), **Horace,** American educator....1796—1859
Mann (män), **Thomas,** German novelist in America; recd. Nobel prize (1929)....1875—1955
M., Erika (*daughter of T.M.*), writer, actress in America....1905—1969
M., Klaus (*son of T.M.*), writer in America....1906—1949
Mannerheim (män'ĕr-hīm), **Carl Gustaf Emil, Baron,** Finnish field marshal and statesman....1867—1951
Manning (man'ing), **Henry Edward,** Eng. R.C. cardinal....1808—1892
Mansart *or* **Mansard** (mäñ-sȧr'), **François,** Fr. architect....1598—1666
Mansel (man'sel), **Henry Longueville,** Eng. philosopher....1820—1871
Mansfeld, von (fọn mäns'felt), **Ernst, Count,** German general.1580?–1626
Mansfield (manş'fēld), **Katherine** (pseud. of *Kathleen Beauchamp; Mrs. J.M. Murry*), British short-story writer....1888—1923
Mansfield, Richard, English actor in the U.S....1857—1907
Mansfield, William Murray, Earl of, lord chief justice of England....1705—1793
Manship (man'ship), **Paul,** American sculptor....1885—1966
Mantegna (män-tẹn'yȧ), **Andrea,** Italian painter....1431—1506
Manuel (mä-nụ-el') **II,** king of Portugal (1908–10)....1889—1932
Manutius (mȧ-nū'shi-us) *or It.* **Manuzio** (mä-nụt'syō), **Aldus,** Italian printer; inventor of italic type....1450—1515
Manzoni (män-dzō'nī), **Alessandro, Count,** Italian novelist and poet....1785—1873
Mao Tse-tung (mä'ō dṣu-doong'), Chinese Communist leader; chairman of Chinese People's Republic (1949–59)....1893—1976
Marat (mȧ-rȧ'), **Jean Paul,** French revolutionary leader....1743—1793
Marble (mär'bl), **Alice,** American tennis player....1913—
Marc (märç), **Franz,** German painter....1880—1916
Marc Antony (märç an'tō-ny), *see* Antonius, Marcus.
Marceau (mȧr-cō'), **François, Séverin,** French general....1769—1796
Marceau, Marcel, French pantomimist....1923—
Marcel (mär-sel'), **Gabriel,** French philosopher....1889—1973
Marcellus (mär-cel'lus), **Marcus Claudius,** Roman consul and conqueror of Syracuse....B.C.268?— 208
March (märch), **Fredric** (b. *Frederick Bickel*), American actor....1897—1975
March, Peyton Conway, American general....1864—1955
Marciano (mär-cī-ä'nō), **Rocky** (*Rocco Francis Marchegiano*), American prize fighter; world heavyweight champion (1952–56).1924—1969
Marconi (mär-çō'nī), **Guglielmo, Marchese,** It. physicist, famous for development of wireless telegraphy....1874—1937
Marco Polo, *see* Polo, Marco.
Marcus Aurelius (mär'çus ą-rē'li-us), (*Marcus Aurelius Antoninus*) Roman emperor (161–80) and Stoic.... 121— 180
Marcy (mär'cy), **William Learned,** American statesman....1786—1857
Margaret (mär'gȧ-ret), (*Margaret of Angouleme*) queen of Navarre.1492—1549
Marggraf (märk'gräf), **Andreas Sigismund,** German chemist....1709—1782
Margueritte (mär-ge-rīt'), **Paul,** French novelist....1860—1918
M., Victor (*brother of P.M.*), French novelist....1866—1942
Mariana, de (dẹ mär-ī-än'ȧ), **Juan,** Spanish historian....1536?–1623
Maria Theresa (mȧ-rī'ȧ te-rē'sȧ), empress of Germany and queen of Hungary and Bohemia....1717—1780
Marie (mȧ-rē'), (*wife of Ferdinand I*) queen of Romania (1914–27).1875—1938
Marie Antoinette (än-twȧ-net'), (*wife of Louis XVI*) queen of France; guillotined....1755—1793
Marie de Médicis (dē mẹ-dī-cīs'), queen of France....1573—1642
Marie Louise (lụ-īş'), second wife of Napoleon I....1791—1847
Mariette (mȧ-rī-et'), **Auguste Édouard,** French archaeologist....1821—1881
Marin (mar'in), **John,** American painter....1872—1953
Marini (mȧ-rī'nī) *or* **Marino** (mȧ-rī'nō), **Giambattista,** Italian poet....1569—1625
Marion (mar'i-ŏn), **Francis** (*the Swamp Fox*), American general in the Revolutionary War....1732—1795
Mariotte (mȧ-rī-ọt'), **Edme,** French physicist....1620?–1684
Maris (mä'ris), **Jacob,** Dutch landscape painter....1837—1899
Maritain (mȧ-rī-tañ'), **Jacques,** French philosopher....1882—1973
Marius (mar'i-us), **Caius,** Roman general and consul....B.C.155?— 86
Marivaux, de (dē mȧ-rī-vō'), **Pierre Carlet de Chamblain,** French playwright and novelist....1688—1763
Markham (märk'hăm), **Sir Clements Robert,** English geographer.1830—1916
Markham, Edwin, American poet....1852—1940
Marlborough (mąl'bu-ru *or Brit.* mąl'br-ru, mąl'bru), **John Churchill, Duke of,** English general and statesman....1650—1722
Marlowe (mär'lō), **Christopher,** English dramatist....1564—1593
Marlowe, Julia (*Mrs. E.H. Sothern*), American actress, born in England....1866—1950
Marmont, de (dē mȧr-moṅ'), **Auguste Frédéric Louis Viesse, Duke of Ragusa,** marshal of France....1774—1852
Marmontel (mȧr-moṅ-tel'), **Jean François,** French historiographer, playwright, and critic....1723—1799
Marquand (mär-kwänd'), **John Phillips,** Am. novelist....1893—1960
Marquette (mär-ket'), **Jacques,** French explorer of the Mississippi....1637—1675
Marquis (mär'kwis), **Don** (*Donald Robert Perry M.*), American humorist....1878—1937
Marryat (mar'ry-at), **Frederick,** English naval officer and novelist....1792—1848
Marsh (märsh), **Othniel Charles,** Am. paleontologist....1831—1899
Marsh, Reginald, American painter....1898—1954
Marshall (mär'shăl), **Alfred,** English political economist....1842—1924
Marshall, George Catlett, American general and statesman; chief of staff (1939–45); secretary of state (1947–49)....1880—1959
Marshall, John, chief justice of the U.S. Supreme Court (1801–35)....1755—1835
Marshall, Thurgood, associate justice of the U.S. Supreme Court (1967–)....1908—
Marston (mär'stŏn), **John,** English dramatist and poet....1576—1634
Martial (mär'shăl), (*Marcus Valerius Martialis*), Roman epigrammatist, b. in Spain.... 40—102?
Martin (mär'tin), **Homer Dodge,** American painter....1836—1897
Martin du Gard (mȧr-tañ' dụ gär'), **Roger,** French novelist; received Nobel prize (1937)....1881—1958
Martineau (mär'tin-ō), **Harriet,** English author....1802—1876
M., James (*brother of H.M.*), Unitarian divine and author....1805—1900
Martinelli (mär-tī-nel'lī), **Giovanni,** Am. tenor, b. in Italy....1885—1969
Martínez de la Rosa (mär-tī'nẹth dẹ lä rō'sä), **Francisco,** Spanish orator, poet, and statesman....1787—1862
Martínez Sierra (mär-tī'nẹth sye'rä), **Gregorio,** Spanish playwright, novelist, and poet....1881—1947
Martini (mär-tī'nī), **Simone,** Italian painter....1283—1344
Marvell (mär'vel), **Andrew,** English author....1621—1678
Marx (märks), **Karl,** German journalist and socialist....1818—1883
Mary (mār'y), (*wife of George V*) queen of England....1867 —1953
Mary I (*Bloody Mary*), queen of England....1516—1558
Mary II (*wife of William III*), queen of England....1662—1694
Mary, Queen of Scots (*Mary Stuart*), queen of Scotland (1542–67); beheaded....1542—1587
Masaccio (mä-ṣät'chō), (*Tommaso Guidi*) Italian painter....1401—1428
Masaryk (mä'sȧ-ryk), **Thomas Garrigue,** Czech patriot and first president of Czechoslovakia (1918–35)....1850—1937
M., Jan (*son of T.G.M.*), Czech statesman; allegedly a suicide after Communist coup d'état of 1948....1886—1948
Mascagni (mäs-çän'yī), **Pietro,** Italian composer....1863—1945
Masefield (mās'fēld), **John,** English poet laureate, novelist, and playwright....1878—1967
Masinissa *or* **Massinissa** (mas-i-nis'sȧ), Numidian king; fought on side of Romans against Hannibal....B.C.238?— 149
Mason (mā'sŏn), **Alfred Edward Woodley,** English novelist and playwright....1865—1948
Mason, Daniel Gregory, Am. composer and writer....1873—1953
Mason, George, American statesman....1725—1792
Mason, James Murray, Am. Confederate commissioner to England....1798—1871
Mason, John Young, secretary of the U.S. navy....1799—1859
Maspero (mȧ-spe-rō'), **Gaston Camille Charles,** French Egyptologist....1846—1916
Massasoit (mas'ȧ-soit), (*father of King Philip*) chief of the Wampanoag Indians....1580?–1661
Masséna (mȧ-sẹ-nȧ'), **André, Prince d'Essling,** French marshal under Napoleon I....1758—1817
Massenet (mȧs-ne'), **Jules Émile Frédéric,** French composer....1842—1912
Massey (mas'si), **Vincent,** Canadian statesman and diplomat; governor general of Canada (1952–59)....1887—1967
Massillon (mȧ-sī-yọñ'), **Jean Baptiste,** French pulpit orator....1663—1742
Massine (mas-sin'), **Leonide,** Russian choreographer and dancer.1896—
Massinger (mas'sin-ġēr), **Philip,** English dramatist....1583—1640
Masters (mas'tẽrş), **Edgar Lee,** Am. poet, biographer....1869—1950
Mather (maŧh'ẽr), **Cotton,** Am. theologian and writer....1663—1728
M., Increase (*father of C.M.*), American theologian....1639—1723
Mather, Frank Jewett, Jr., American art critic....1868—1953
Matisse (mȧ-tīs'), **Henri,** French painter....1869—1954
Matsudaira (mä-tsụ-dī'rä), **Tsuneo,** Japanese diplomat....1877—1949
Matsukata (mä'tsụ-kä'tä), **Masayoshi, Prince,** Japanese financier and statesman....1835—1924
Matsuoka (mät-sụ-ō'kȧ), **Yosuke,** Japanese politician and foreign minister....1880—1946
Matthew of Paris (math'ū ov par'is), English historian.... ? —1259
Matthews (math'ūş), **(James) Brander,** Am. author....1852—1929
Matthews, Stanley, U.S. senator and jurist....1824—1889
Matthias (mat-tī'ȧs), Holy Roman emperor....1557—1619
Maturin (mat'ū-rin), **Charles Robert,** Irish novelist....1782—1824
Maude (mąd), **Cyril,** English actor and theatrical manager....1862—1951
Maude, Sir Frederick Stanley, British general....1864—1917
Maugham (mąm), **William Somerset,** English novelist, dramatist, and short-story writer....1874—1965
Mauldin (mąl'din), **William Henry,** American cartoonist....1921—
Maupassant, de (dē mō-pȧ-sän'), **Guy,** French novelist and short-story writer....1850—1893
Mauriac (mō-ryȧç'), **François,** French novelist....1885—1970
Maurois (mō-rwo'), **André** (b. *Émile Herzog*), French novelist and biographer....1885—1967
Maury (mą'ry), **Matthew Fontaine,** Am. hydrographer....1806—1873
Mavrocordatos (mäv'rō-çọr-dä'tōs), **Alexander,** Greek statesman.1791—1865
Mawson (mą'sŏn), **Sir Douglas,** Brit. antarctic explorer....1882—1958
Maxim (maks'im), **Hiram Percy** (*son of H.S.M.*), American inventor....1869—1936
M., Sir Hiram Stevens, Am. inventor in England....1840—1916
M., Hudson (*brother of H.S.M.*), American inventor and author.1853—1927
Maximilian (maks-i-mil'i-ăn), (*Ferdinand Maximilian Joseph*) archduke of Austria and emperor of Mexico; executed in Mexico.1832—1867
Maximilian I, Holy Roman emperor....1459—1519
Maxwell (maks'wel), **James Clerk,** Scottish physicist....1831—1879
May (mā), **Thomas,** English poet and historian....1595—1650
Mayakovski (mä-yȧ-kọf'ski), **Vladimir,** Russian poet....1894—1930
Mayo (mā'ō), **Charles Horace,** American surgeon....1865—1939
M., William James (*brother of C.H.M.*), Am. surgeon....1861—1939
Mazarin (mȧ-zȧ-rañ'), **Jules,** French cardinal, born in Italy; prime minister of Louis XIV....1602—1661

Mazzini (mät-sē'nē), **Giuseppe,** Italian patriot and author......1805—1872
Mc-, *see also* Mac-.
McAdoo (mac'å-doo), **William Gibbs, U.S.** secretary of the treasury (1913–18)....................1863—1941
McBain (măc-bān'), **Howard Lee,** Am. political scientist.......1880—1936
McBurney (măc-bûr'ni), **Charles,** American surgeon...........1845—1913
McCarthy (må-cär'thy), **Joseph Raymond,** U.S. senator.......1909—1957
McCarthy, Justin, Irish politician and author................1830—1912
M., Justin Huntley, (*son of J. M.*), British writer..........1860—1936
McClellan (må-clel'ăn), **George Brinton,** Union general in the Civil War....................1826—1885
McClernand (må-clẽr'nand), **John Alexander,** Union general in the Civil War....................1812—1900
McClintock (må-clin'tŏk), **Sir Francis Leopold,** British arctic explorer....................1819—1907
McCollum (må-col'um), **Elmer Verner,** American chemist......1879—1967
McCormack (må-cor'măk), **John,** Am. tenor, b. in Ireland........1884—1945
McCormick (må-cor'mik), **Cyrus Hall,** American inventor of the reaper....................1809—1884
McCosh (må-cosh'), **James,** American philosopher and educator, b. in Scotland....................1811—1894
McCrae (må-crā'), **John,** Canadian surgeon and poet...........1872—1918
McCutcheon (må-cut'chŏn), **George Barr,** American novelist..1866—1928
McDougall (măc-dö'găl), **Alexander,** American general.........1731—1786
McDougall, William, Am. psychologist, b. in England........1871—1938
McDowell (măc-dou'el), **Irvin,** Union gen. in Civil War........1818—1885
McFee (măc-fē'), **William,** English novelist.................1881—1966
McGee (må-gē'), **Thomas D'Arcy,** Irish journalist............1825—1868
McGraw (măc-gra'), **John Joseph,** Am. baseball manager......1873—1934
McGuffey (må-guf'fi), **William Holmes,** Am. educator.........1800—1873
McIntyre (mac'in-tȳr), **James Francis Aloysius,** American Roman Catholic prelate; created cardinal (1953)................1886—1979
McIntyre, Oscar Odd, American newspaper columnist.........1884—1938
McKean (må-kēn'), **Thomas,** American patriot and jurist......1734—1817
McKinley (må-kin'li), **William,** 25th U.S. president (1897–1901); assassinated....................1843—1901
McLaughlin (măc-laf'lin), **Andrew Cunningham,** American historian....................1861—1947
McLuhan (măc-lü'ăn), **(Herbert) Marshall,** Canadian educator 1911—1980
McMaster (măc-mås'tẽr), **John Bach,** American historian......1852—1932
McMillan (măc-mil'lăn), **Edwin Mattison,** Am. physicist......1907—
McNary (măc-năr'y), **Charles Linza,** U.S. senator.........1874—1944
McNutt (măc-nut'), **Paul Vories,** Am. govt. administrator; commissioner to Philippines (1937–39, 1945–46)................1891—1955
McReynolds (măc-ren'ŏlds), **James Clark,** associate justice of the U.S. Supreme Court (1914–41)....................1862—1946
Mead (mēd), **George Herbert,** American philosopher...........1863—1931
Mead, Larkin Goldsmith, American sculptor...................1835—1910
Mead, Margaret, American anthropologist....................1901—1978
Meade (mēd), **George Gordon,** Union general in the Civil War..1815—1872
Meagher (mär), **Thomas Francis,** Irish revolutionist and Union general in the Civil War....................1823—1867
Meany (mē'ny), **George,** American labor leader; president of the AFL-CIO (1955–79)....................1894—1980
Medici, de' (de med'ī-chī), **Alessandro,** duke of Florence; assassinated....................1511—1537
Medici, de', Cosimo (*the Elder*), chief of the Florentine republic....................1389—1464
Medici, de', Cosimo I (*the Great*), duke of Florence; first grand duke of Tuscany....................1519—1574
Medici, de', Lorenzo I (*the Magnificent*), Florentine ruler and patron of art....................1449—1492
Medill (me-dil'), **Joseph,** American journalist...............1823—1899
Meer, van der (vän dẽr mer'), **Jan,** Dutch painter...........1628—1691
M., v.d., Jan (*son of J.v.d.M.*), Dutch painter...............1656—1705
Meer van Delft (delft), **Jan van der,** *see* Vermeer, Jan.
Mehemet Ali (me'he-met ä-lī') *or* **Mohammed Ali,** viceroy of Egypt (1805–48)....................1769—1849
Méhul (me-ül'), **Étienne Henri,** French composer.............1763—1817
Meier-Graefe (mī'ẽr-gre'fe), **Julius,** German author..........1867—1935
Meiklejohn (mik'l-jon), **Alexander,** American educator........1872—1964
Meilhac (me-yȧc'), **Henri,** French playwright................1831—1897
Meissonier (me-sō-nye'), **Jean Louis Ernst,** French painter....1815—1891
Meitner (mīt'nẽr), **Lise,** Austrian physicist in Sweden.........1878—1968
Melancthon (me-lañc'thŏn), **Philipp,** German Lutheran reformer....................1497—1560
Melba (mel'bȧ), **Dame Nellie** (*Mrs. Helen Mitchell Armstrong*), Australian soprano....................1861—1931
Melbourne (mel'bŭrn), **William Lamb, second Viscount,** English statesman....................1779—1848
Melchers (mel'chẽrs), **Gari,** American painter...............1860—1932
Melchior (mel'chi-or), **Lauritz,** Danish tenor in U.S..........1890—1973
Mellon (mel'lŏn), **Andrew William,** American capitalist and diplomat; U.S. secretary of treasury (1921–32)................1855—1937
Melville (mel'vil), **Herman,** American novelist...............1819—1891
Memlinc (mem'liñc), **Hans,** *or* **Memling** (mem'ling), Flemish painter....................1430?—1495
Menander (me-nan'dẽr), Greek poet and dramatist..........B.C.343?—291?
Mencius (men'shi-us), Chinese philosopher...............B.C.372?—289?
Mencken (meñk'en), **H. L.** (*Henry Louis M.*), Am. critic......1880—1956
Mendel (men'del), **Gregor Johann,** Austrian botanist.........1822—1884
Mendele Mocher Sforim (men'dē-lē mokh'ẽr sfor'im), *see* Abramovich, Sholem Yakob.
Mendelssohn (men'del-sŏn *or* -sŏn), **Felix** (*Jakob Ludwig Felix Mendelssohn-Bartholdy*), German composer.................1809—1847
M., Moses (*grandfather of F.M.*), German philosopher.........1729—1786
Mendelyeev (men-dye-lye'ef), **Dmitri Ivanovich,** Russian chemist....................1834—1907
Mendes (mäñ-des'), **Catulle,** French poet and novelist.........1841—1909
Menelik (men'e-lik) **II,** emperor of Abyssinia...............1844—1913
Menninger (men'nin-gẽr), **Karl Augustus,** American psychiatrist....................1893—
Menocal (me-nō-cäl'), **Mario Garcia,** president of Cuba (1913–21)....................1866—1941
Menotti (me-not'tī), **Gian-Carlo,** Italian composer in U.S......1911—
Menuhin (men'ū-in), **Yehudi,** American violinist..............1917—
Menzies (men'zēs), **Sir Robert Gordon,** Australian prime minister (1939–41; 1949–66)....................1894—1978
Mercator (mẽr-cā'tŏr), **Gerardus** (Latinized from *Gerhard Kremer*), Flemish geographer and cartographer.................1512—1594
Mercier (mer-cye'), **Désiré Joseph,** Belgian cardinal..........1851—1926
Meredith (mer'e-dith), **George,** Eng. novelist and poet........1828—1909
Meredith, Owen, *see* Bulwer-Lytton, Edward Robert.
Merezhkovsky (me-resh-kof'skē), **Dmitri,** Russ. novelist.......1865—1941
Mergenthaler (mer'gen-tä-lẽr), **Ottmar,** American inventor of the linotype, born in Germany....................1854—1899
Mérimée (me-rī-me'), **Prosper,** French novelist, essayist and historian....................1803—1870
Merrick (mer'rik), **Leonard,** English novelist...............1864—1939
Mesmer (mes'mẽr), **Friedrich Anton,** German originator of mesmerism....................1733—1815
Messalina (mes-sȧ-lī'nȧ), **Valeria,** profligate Roman empress, third wife of Claudius I; executed....................? — 48
Meštrović (mesh'trō-vich), **Ivan,** Yugoslav sculptor............1883—1962
Metaxas (me-täk-säs'), **Joannes,** Gr. general, premier..........1871—1941
Metchnikoff (mech'ni-kof), **Élie,** Russian biologist...........1845—1916
Metternich, von (fon met'tẽr-nikh), **Klemens Wenzel, Prince,** Austrian statesman....................1773—1859
Meunier (mē-nye'), **Constantin,** Belgian painter, sculptor.....1831—1905
Meyerbeer (mȳ'ẽr-ber), **Giacomo** (b. *Jakob Liebmann Beer*), German composer....................1791—1864
Meyerhof (mȳ'ẽr-hōf), **Otto,** German physiologist............1884—1951
Meynell (me'nel), **Alice Thompson,** Eng. poet, essayist.......1847?—1922
Michael (mī'chel) **I** (*son of Carol II*), king of Romania (1927–30, 1940–47); abdicated....................1921—
Michaud (mī-chō'), **Joseph François,** French historian.........1767—1839
Michelangelo Buonarroti (mī'chel-an'ge-lō bwo-när-ro'tī), Italian painter and sculptor....................1475—1564
Michelet (mich-le'), **Jules,** French historian................1798—1874
Michelson (mī-chel'sŏn), **Albert Abraham,** American physicist, b. in Germany; received Nobel prize (1907)................1852—1931
Michener (mich'en-ẽr), **James Albert,** American author.......1907—
Mickiewicz (mits-kye'vich), **Adam,** Polish poet...............1798—1855
Middleton (mid'l-tŏn), **Thomas,** English dramatist...........1570?—1627
Mielziner (mel-zī'nẽr), **Jo,** American stage designer..........1901—1976
Mieris, van (vän mē'ris), **Frans,** Dutch painter..............1635—1681
Mies van der Rohe (mēz'van der rō'ä), **Ludwig,** American architect, b. in Germany....................1886—1969
Mifflin (mif'lin), **Thomas,** American patriot and general......1744—1800
Mikhailovitch (mik-hīl'ō-vich), **Draja,** Yugoslav general; war minister in government-in-exile; Chetnik leader; executed......1893—1946
Milburn (mil'bŭrn), **George,** Am. writer....................1906—
Miles (mīls), **Nelson Appleton,** American general............1839—1925
Milhaud (mī-yō'), **Darius,** French composer in America........1892—1974
Mill (mil), **James,** British historian and philosopher..........1773—1836
M., John Stuart (*son of J.M.*), English philosopher and political economist....................1806—1873
Millais (mil-lā'), **Sir John Everett,** English painter..........1829—1896
Millay (mil-ā'), **Edna St. Vincent,** American poet.............1892—1950
Miller (mil'lẽr), **Arthur,** American dramatist................1915—
Miller, Dayton Clarence, American physicist.................1866—1941
Miller, Henry, American writer...............................1891—1980
Miller, Hugh, Scottish geologist and writer...................1802—1856
Miller, Joaquin (pesud. of *Cincinnatus Heine Miller*), American poet....................1841—1913
Miller, William, American founder of the Millerites............1782—1849
Millerand (mil-räñ'), **Alexandre,** French statesman and president (1920–24)....................1859—1943
Milles (mil'ăs), **Carl** (b. *Carl Wilhelm Emil Anderson*), American sculptor, b. in Sweden....................1875—1955
Millet (mi-le'), **Jean François,** French painter...............1814—1875
Millikan (mil'li-kăn), **Robert Andrews,** Am. physicist.........1868—1953
Millin (mil'lin), **Sarah Gertrude,** S. African novelist..........1889—1968
Mills (mils), **Ogden Livingston,** Am. political leader..........1884—1937
Milman (mil'măn), **Henry Hart,** English historian.............1791—1868
Milmore (mil'mōr), **Martin,** Am. sculptor, b. in Ireland.......1844—1883
Milne (miln), **A. A.** (*Alan Alexander M.*), English playwright, and children's writer....................1882—1956
Milstein (mil'stin), **Nathan,** American violinist, b. in Russia....1904—
Miltiades (mil-ti'ȧ-dēs), Athenian general and statesman..........fl.B.C.500
Milton (mil'tŏn), **John,** English poet.......................1608—1674
Milyukow (mil-yu-kof'), **Paul Nikolaievich,** Russian historian..1859—1943
Mindszenty (mind'sen-ty), **Joseph,** Hungarian R.C. cardinal; sentenced to prison for treason (1949–56); his prosecutors were excommunicated by Pope Pius XII....................1892—1975
Minot (mī'not), **George Richards,** Am. pathologist............1885—1950
Minuit (min'ū-it), **Peter,** first governor of New Netherland (New York); colonizer of New Sweden....................1580—1638
Mirabeau, de (dē mī-rȧ-bō' *or* mir'ȧ-bō), **Gabriel Honoré Riquetti, Count,** French orator and revolutionist..................1749—1791
Miró (mī-rō'), **Joan,** Spanish surrealist painter..............1893—
Mistral (mis-trȧl'), **Frédéric,** French Provencal poet..........1830—1914
Mitchel (mich'el), **John,** Irish journalist and revolutionist.....1815—1875
Mitchel, Ormsby MacKnight, Am. astronomer and general....1809—1862
Mitchell (mich'el), **Donald Grant** (pseud. *Ik Marvel*), American author....................1822—1908
Mitchell, John, American labor leader......................1870—1919
Mitchell, Margaret (*Mrs. John R. Marsh*), Am. novelist.......1900—1949
Mitchell, Maria, American astronomer.....................1818—1889
Mitchell, Silas Weir, American physician and author.........1829—1914
Mitchell, William, American general; an outspoken advocate of a stronger air force....................1879—1936
Mitford (mit'ford), **Mary Russell,** English author.............1787—1855
Mithridates (mith-ri-dā'tēs) **VI** (*the Great*), king of Pontus (120–63 B.C.)....................B.C.132?— 63
Mitropoulos (mī-tro'poo-los), **Dimitri,** Greek conductor and composer in America....................1896—1960
Modigliani (mō-di-lyä'nī), **Amedeo,** Italian painter...........1884—1920
Mohammed (mō-ham'ed), *or* **Mahomet** *or* **Muhammad,** Arabian prophet; founder of the Moslem religion....................570— 632
Mohammed Ali, *see* Mehemet Ali.
Mohammed VI, last Ottoman sultan (1918–22); deposed.......1861—1926
Mohammed Riza Pahlavi (rī-zä' pä'lȧ-vī), (*son of Riza Shah Pahlavi*) shah of Iran (1941–80)....................1919—1980
Molière (mō-lyer'), (pseud. of *Jean Baptiste Poquelin*) French dramatist....................1622—1673
Molnár (mōl'när), **Ferenc,** Hungarian dramatist..............1878—1952
Molotov (mo'lo-tof); **Vyacheslav Mikhailovich,** Russian statesman; foreign minister (1939–49, 1953–56)....................1890—

Moltke, von (fọn mōlt'ke), **Helmuth Karl Bernhard, Count,** Prussian field marshal.......1800—1891
Mommsen (mom'sen), **Theodor,** German historian.......1817—1903
Monboddo (mon-bod'dō), **James Burnet, Lord,** Scottish jurist.1714—1799
Monckton (mŏnk'tŏn), **Robert,** Brit. general in America.......1726—1782
Monet (mō-ne'), **Claude,** Fr. impressionist painter.......1840—1926
Monier-Williams (mŏn'i-ēr-wil'yămṣ), **Sir Monier,** English Sanskrit scholar.......1819—1899
Monk *or* **Monck** (mŏnk), **George, Duke of Albemarle,** English general; helped effect the Restoration (1660).......1608—1670
Monmouth (mon'muth), **James Scott, Duke of,** English political leader and rebel.......1649—1685
Monroe (mŏn-rō'), **Harriet,** American poet and editor.......1860—1936
Monroe, James, 5th U.S. president (1817–25).......1758—1831
Montagu (mon'tȧ-gū), **Lady Mary Wortley,** Eng. writer.......1689—1762
Montaigne, de (dē mon-tān'), **Michel Eyquem, Seigneur,** French philosopher and essayist.......1533—1592
Montcalm de Saint-Véran, de (dē mọn-çȧlm' dē saṅ-vē-räṅ' *or Eng.* mont-çäm'), **Louis Joseph, Marquis,** French general; defeated by Wolfe at Quebec (1759).......1712—1759
Montecuccoli, de (dē mōn-tē-çŭç'çū-lī), **Raimondo, Count,** Austrian general.......1609—1681
Montespan, de (dē mọṅ-tes-päṅ'), **Françoise Athénaïs Rochechouart, Marquise,** mistress of Louis XIV of France.......1641—1707
Montesquieu, de (dē mọṅ-tes-kyū' *or Eng.* mon-tes-kū'), **Charles de Secondat, Baron,** French jurist and philosopher.......1689—1755
Montessori (mōn-tes-sō'rī), **Maria,** Italian educator.......1870—1952
Monteux (mọṅ-tū'), **Pierre,** French conductor in U.S.......1875—1964
Monteverdi (mōn-tē-ver'dī), **Claudio,** Italian composer.......1567—1643
Montezuma (mon-te-zū'mȧ) **II,** last Aztec emperor of Mexico (1502–20).......1480?–1520
Montfort, de (dē mọṅ-fọr'), **Simon,** French crusader.......1160?–1218
M., de, Simon, Earl of Leicester (*son of S. de M.*), English soldier and statesman.......1208?–1265
Montgomery (mont-gŏm'ēr-y), **Bernard Law, Viscount of Alamein,** British field marshal; commander of British ground forces in World War II.......1887—1976
Montgomery, Lucy Maud, Canadian author.......1874—1942
Montgomery, Richard, American general.......1738—1775
Montherlant (mōṅ-tĕr-läṅ'), **Henri Millon de,** Fr. novelist.......1896—1972
Monti (mŏn'tī), **Vincenzo,** Italian poet.......1754—1828
Montmorency, de (dē mọṅ-mō-räṅ-cē' *or Eng.* mont-mō-ren'cy), **Anne, Duc,** constable of France.......1493—1567
Montrose (mont-rōṣ'), **James Graham, Marquis of,** Scottish general and Royalist; executed.......1612—1650
Moody (mọọd'y), **Dwight Lyman,** American evangelist.......1837—1899
Moody, William Vaughan, American poet and playwright.......1869—1910
Mooney (mọọn'i), **Edward Francis,** Am. R.C. cardinal.......1882—1958
Mooney, Thomas J., Am. labor leader; imprisoned for bomb killings (San Francisco, 1916); pardoned (1939).......1883—1942
Moore (moor *or* mōr), **Douglas Stuart,** American composer.......1893—1969
Moore, George, Irish novelist and playwright.......1852—1933
Moore, G(eorge) E(dward), English philosopher.......1873—1958
Moore, Grace, American opera singer.......1901—1947
Moore, Henry, English sculptor.......1898—
Moore, Sir John, British general.......1761—1809
Moore, John Bassett, American authority on international law..1860—1947
Moore, Marianne (Craig), American poet.......1887—1972
Moore, Thomas, Irish poet.......1779—1852
Morales, de (dē mō-rä'lēs), **Luis** (*El Divino*), Spanish painter....1509?–1586?
Moran (mō-ran'), **Thomas,** American painter and etcher.......1837—1926
Morand (mō-räṅ'), **Paul,** French author.......1888—1976
Mordaunt (mọr'dănt), **Charles, third Earl of Peterborough,** English general.......1658—1735
More (mōr), **Hannah,** English writer.......1745—1833
More, Henry, English Platonist.......1614—1687
More, Paul Elmer, American critic and essayist.......1864—1937
More, Sir Thomas, English chancellor and writer; canonized in 1935.......1478—1535
Moreau (mō-rō'), **Gustave,** French painter and teacher.......1826—1898
Moreau, Jean Victor, French general.......1763—1813
Morgan (mọr'găn), **Arthur Ernest,** Am. engineer and educator..1878—1975
Morgan, Charles Langbridge, English author.......1894—1958
Morgan, Daniel, American Revolutionary general.......1736—1802
Morgan, Harcourt Alexander, Am. entomologist and educator..1867—1950
Morgan, Sir Henry, Welsh buccaneer.......1635?–1688
Morgan, John Hunt, Am. Confederate guerilla chief.......1825—1864
Morgan, John Pierpont, American capitalist.......1837—1913
M., John Pierpont (*son of J.P.M.*), American capitalist.......1867—1943
Morgan, Lady Sydney Owenson, Irish novelist.......1783?–1859
Morgan, Thomas Hunt, American zoologist.......1866—1945
Morgenthau (mọr'gen-thạ), **Henry,** American diplomat.......1856—1946
M., Henry, Jr. (*son of H.M.*), U.S. sec. of treasury (1934–45)..1891—1967
Morison (mọr'i-sŏn), **Samuel Eliot,** American historian.......1887—1976
Morley (mọr'li), **Christopher,** American novelist, poet, and essayist.......1890—1957
Morley, Henry, English author and editor.......1822—1894
Morley, John, Viscount, English statesman and author.......1838—1923
Moroni (mō-rō'nī), **Giambattista,** Italian painter.......1525—1578
Morosini (mō-rō-sī'nī), **Francesco,** doge of Venice.......1618—1694
Morphy (mọr'fē), **Paul Charles,** American chess player; world champion (1858–62).......1837—1884
Morrill (mor'ril), **Justin Smith,** U.S. senator.......1810—1898
Morris (mọr'ris), **Clara,** American actress.......1849—1925
Morris, Gouverneur, American patriot and statesman.......1752—1816
Morris, Robert, American patriot and financier.......1734—1806
Morris, William, English poet, artist, and socialist.......1834—1896
Morrison (mọr'ri-sŏn), **Arthur,** English novelist.......1863—1945
Morrison, Herbert Stanley, Brit. statesman and Labor party leader.......1888—1965
Morrow (mor'rō), **Dwight Whitney,** Am. banker, diplomat.......1873—1931
Morrow, Honoré Willsie, Am. novelist and biographer.......1880—1940
Morse (mọrs), **Samuel Finley Breese,** American inventor of electric telegraph and artist.......1791—1872
Morton (mọr'tŏn), **Levi Parsons,** vice-president of the United States (1889–93).......1824—1920
Morton, William Thomas Green, American dentist; introduced use of ether for anesthesia.......1819—1868
Mosby (mọṣ'by), **John Singleton,** Am. Confederate cavalry officer1833—1916
Moschus (mos'çhus), Greek pastoral poet.......fl.B.C.2nd cent.
Mossadegh (mō-sä-dekh'), **Mohammed,** Iranian premier (1951–53); nationalized British-owned oil industry.......1880—1967
Moszkowski (mōsh-kọf'skī), **Moritz,** Polish composer.......1854—1925
Motley (mot'li), **John Lothrop,** Am. historian, diplomat.......1814—1877
Moton (mō'tŏn), **Robert Russa,** American educator.......1867—1940
Mott (mot), **Lucretia Coffin,** American reformer.......1793—1880
Mott, Valentine, American surgeon.......1785—1865
Moulton (mōl'tŏn), **Forest Ray,** American astronomer.......1872—1952
Mountbatten (mount-bat'en), **Louis, first Earl Mountbatten of Burma,** British admiral in World War II.......1900—1979
Moussorgsky (mŭs-sọrg'skē), **Modest Petrovich,** Russian composer.......1839—1881
Mozart (mō'tsärt), **Wolfgang Amadeus,** Austrian composer....1756—1791
Muck (mụk), **Karl,** German orchestral conductor.......1859—1940
Muhammad (mu-häm'mȧd), *see* Mohammed.
Muhammad Ali (b. *Cassius Clay*) American prize fighter; world heavyweight champion (1964–67; 1974–).......1942—
Mühlbach (mül'bäkh), **Luise** (pseud. of *Klara Müller Mundt*), German novelist.......1814—1873
Muir (mūr), **John,** American naturalist.......1838—1914
Mukerji (mụ-kēr'jī), **Dhan Gopal,** Indian novelist.......1890—1936
Müller (mül'ĕr), **Hermann,** German statesman and chancellor (1920, 1928–30).......1876—1931
Müller (mul'ĕr), **Hermann Joseph,** American geneticist.......1890—1967
Müller (mül'ĕr), **Johannes Peter,** German physiologist.......1801—1858
Müller, Karl Otfried, German classical archaeologist.......1797—1840
Müller, Max (*Friedrich Max M.*), English philologist and mythologist, born in Germany.......1823—1900
M., Wilhelm (*father of M.M.*), German lyric poet.......1794—1827
Mulock (mū'lok), **Dinah Maria,** *see* Craik, D. M. M.
Mulready (mul'red-y), **William,** Irish painter.......1786—1863
Mumford (mum'fŏrd), **Lewis,** Am. critic and author.......1895—
Münch (münsh), **Charles,** French conductor in America.......1891—
Munch (mụngk), **Edvard,** Norwegian painter.......1863—1944
Münchhausen, von (fọn müṅkh'hou-ṣen) *or Eng.* **Munchausen** (mun-chạ'ṣen), **Karl Friedrich Hieronymus, Baron,** German adventurer and teller of tall tales.......1720—1797
Munday (mun'dy), **Anthony,** English dramatist.......1553—1633
Mundelein (mun'de-līn), **George William,** American Roman Catholic cardinal.......1872—1939
Muni (mū'nī), **Paul** (b. *Muni Weisenfreund*), American actor, born in Austria.......1895—1967
Munkácsy (mụn'kä-chi), **Mikhail** (b. *Michael Lieb*), Hungarian painter.......1844—1900
Munro (mun-rō'), **Dana Carleton,** American historian.......1866—1933
Munro, Hector Hugh (pseud. *Saki*), British short-story writer and novelist, born in Burma.......1870—1916
Munsey (mun'si), **Frank Andrew,** American publisher.......1854—1925
Münsterberg (mun'stēr-bērg *or* min'), **Hugo,** American psychologist, born in Danzig.......1863—1916
Munthe (mun'te), **Axel,** Swedish psychiatrist and author.......1857—1949
Murasaki (mû'rä-sä'kī), **Baroness** (*Murasaki Shikibu*), Japanese novelist.......fl.11th cent.
Murat (mü-rȧ'), **Joachim,** marshal of France; king of Naples (1808–15).......1767—1815
Muratori (mû-rä-tō'rī), **Ludovico Antonio,** Italian antiquary and historian.......1672—1750
Murchison (mūr'chi-sŏn), **Sir Roderick,** Eng. geologist.......1792—1871
Murdoch (mūr'doçh); **James Edward,** American actor.......1811—1893
Murfree (mūr'frē), **Mary Noailles,** *see* Craddock, C. E.
Murger (mür-ẓer'), **Henri,** French novelist and poet.......1822—1861
Murillo (mū-ril'lō *or Sp.* mụ-rīl'yō), **Bartolomé Estéban,** Spanish painter.......1618—1682
Murner (mụr'nēr), **Thomas,** German satirist.......1475—1537
Murphy (mūr'fy), **Frank,** associate justice of the U.S. Supreme Court (1940–49).......1890—1949
Murphy, William Parry, American physician.......1892—
Murray (mūr'ry), **Gilbert,** British classicist.......1866—1957
Murray, Sir James Augustus Henry, Brit. lexicographer.......1837—1915
Murray, Lindley, American grammarian in England.......1745—1826
Murray, Philip, American labor leader, born in Scotland; president of the C.I.O. (1940–52).......1886—1952
Murry (mūr'ry), **John Middleton,** English critic.......1889—1957
Musil (mū'ṣil), **Robert,** Austrian novelist.......1880—1939
Musset, de (dē mü-se'), **Alfred** (*Louis Charles Alfred de M.*), French poet, dramatist, and novelist.......1810—1857
Mussolini (mụs-sō-lī'nī), **Benito** (*Il Duce*), Italian Fascist leader; premier and dictator (1922–43); executed.......1883—1945
Mustafa Kemal (mụs-tō-fä'), *see* Kemal Ataturk.
Mutsuhito (mụt'sụ-hī'tō), emperor of Japan (1867–1912).......1852—1912
Myron (mȳ'rŏn), Greek sculptor.......fl.B.C.450

N

Nader (nā'dēr), **Ralph,** U.S. lawyer and reformer.......1934—
Nadir Shah (nä'dīr shä), Persian conqueror.......1688—1747
Nairne (nārn), **Carolina Oliphant, Baroness,** Scot. poet.......1766—1845
Naismith (nā'smith), **James,** American inventor of basketball, b. in Canada.......1861—1939
Nansen (nän'sen), **Fridtjof,** Norwegian arctic explorer, author, and statesman.......1861—1930
Napier (nā'pi-ēr), **Sir Charles James,** British general.......1782—1853
Napier, John, Laird of Merchiston, Scottish inventor of logarithms.......1550—1617
Napier of Magdala, Robert Cornelis Napier, Baron, British general.......1810—1890
Napoleon (nȧ-pō'lē-ŏn) **I** (*Napoléon Bonaparte*), (*the Little Corporal*) emperor of the French (1804–15).......1769—1821
N. II (*François Charles Joseph Bonaparte*), (*son of N. I and Marie Louise*) nominal emperor of France.......1811—1832
N. III (*Louis Napoléon Bonaparte*), (*nephew of N.I*) emperor of the French (1852–70); deposed.......1808—1873
Narváez, de (dē när-vä'ēth), **Pánfilo,** Spanish commander in America.......1470?–1528
Nasby (naṣ'by), **Petroleum V.** *see* Locke, David Ross.
Nash (nash), **Ogden,** American humorous poet.......1902—1971
Nash, Richard (*Beau Nash*), Eng. dandy and gambler.......1674—1762
Nash *or* **Nashe** (nash), **Thomas,** English dramatist.......1567—1601

Nasser (nas'ẽr), **Gamal Abdel**, Egyptian president of the United Arab Republic (1958–70) .... 1918—1970

Nast (nast), **Thomas**, American caricaturist, born in Bavaria .... 1840—1902

Nathan (nā'thăn), **George Jean**, American drama critic .... 1882—1958

Nathan, Robert, American novelist .... 1894—

Nation (nā'shŏn), **Carry** (b. *Carry Amelia Moore*), American temperance agitator .... 1846—1911

Nattier (nȧ-tyę'), **Jean Marc**, French painter .... 1685—1766

Naville (nȧ-vīl'), **Édouard Henri**, Swiss Egyptologist .... 1844—1926

Nazimova (nȧ-zim'ō-vȧ), **Alla**, Russian actress in U.S. .... 1879—1945

Nebuchadnezzar (neb"ū-ķhăd-nez'zăr), Chaldean king of Babylon . ? B.C.562

Necker (nek'ẽr), **Jacques**, French statesman and financier; father of Mme. de Staël .... 1732—1804

Nehru (nę'rụ̈), **Jawaharlal**, Indian statesman and leader of National Congress party; prime minister (1947–64) .... 1889—1964

N., Motilal (*father of J.N.*), Indian nationalist leader .... 1861—1931

Neihardt (nī'härt), **John Gneisenau**, American poet .... 1881—1973

Neilson (nēl'sŏn), **William Allen**, American educator, author, and editor, born in Scotland .... 1869—1946

Nekrasov (nye-krä'sọf), **Nicolai A.**, Russian poet .... 1821—1877

Nelson (nel'sŏn), **Donald Marr**, American administrator; chairman of War Production Board (1942–44) .... 1888—1959

Nelson, Horatio, Viscount, English admiral; broke Napoleon's sea power in battle of Trafalgar (1805) .... 1758—1805

Nepos (nē'pos), **Cornelius**, Roman historian .... fl.B.C. 40

Nernst (nernst), **Walter**, German chemist and physicist .... 1864—1941

Nero (nē'rō), (*Nero Claudius Caesar*) Roman emperor .... 37— 68

Néruda (nye'rụ-dä), **Ján**, Bohemian journalist and poet .... 1834—1891

Neruda (nā-rụ̈'dȧ), **Pablo** (b. *Ricardo Eliezer Neftali Reyes Basoalto*), Chilean poet .... 1904—1973

Nerva (nẽr'vȧ), **Marcus Cocceius**, Roman emperor .... 32— 98

Nerval, de (dẽ ner-vȧl'), **Gérard** (b. *Gérard Labrunie*), French poet and author .... 1808—1855

Nesselrode (nyes-sel-rọ'dye), **Karl Robert, Count**, Russian statesman .... 1780—1862

Nestorius (nes-tō'ri-us), Syrian bishop .... ? —451?

Nethersole (ne'thẽr-sōl), **Dame Olga**, English actress .... 1870—1951

Neumann (noi'män), **Alfred**, German novelist .... 1895—1952

Nevin (nev'in), **Ethelbert Woodbridge**, Am. composer .... 1862—1901

Nevins (nev'inș), **Allan**, American historian .... 1890—1971

Newbolt (nū'bōlt), **Sir Henry John**, English naval historian and poet .... 1862—1938

Newcomb (nū'ķŏm), **Simon**, American astronomer .... 1835—1909

Newcomen (nū-ķŏm'en), **Thomas**, English inventor of the steam engine .... 1663—1729

Newman (nū'măn), **Ernest**, English music critic .... 1868—1959

Newman, John Henry, Cardinal, English theologian and writer . 1801—1890

Newton (nū'tŏn), **Sir Isaac**, English philosopher and mathematician .... 1642—1727

Nexö (neks'ū), **Martin Andersen**, Danish novelist .... 1869—1954

Ney (nę), **Michel**, duke of Elchingen, prince of the Moskowa, and marshal of France; executed .... 1769—1815

Niccolini (niķ-ķō-lī'nī), **Giovanni Battista**, Italian poet .... 1782—1861

Nicholas (niķh'ō-lȧs) **I** (*Nikolai Pavlovich*), czar of Russia (1825–55) .... 1796—1855

Nicholas I, Saint (*the Great*), Pope .... 800?— 867

Nicholas II, czar of Russia (1894–1917); executed .... 1868—1918

Nicholas, Saint, bishop of Myra; patron of children .... ? —345?

Nicholson (niķh'ŏl-sŏn), **Meredith**, American novelist and diplomat .... 1866—1947

Nicias (ni'shi-ȧs), Athenian statesman and general .... B.C. ? — 413

Nicolle (nī-ķọl'), **Charles**, French bacteriologist .... 1866—1936

Nicolson (niķ'ŏl-sŏn), **Harold**, English biographer, historian, and diplomat, born in Persia .... 1886—1968

Niebuhr (nē'bụ̈r), **Barthold Georg**, German historian .... 1776—1831

Niebuhr, Reinhold, American theologian and writer .... 1892—1971

Niemcewicz (nyem-tcę'vich), **Julian Ursyn**, Polish statesman and writer .... 1758—1841

Niemoeller (nē'mē-lẽr), **Martin**, German Protestant clergyman, opposed to Nazis .... 1892—

Niepce (nyepc), **Joseph Nicéphore**, French chemist and inventor of a method of photography .... 1765—1833

Nietzsche (nē'tshe), **Friedrich Wilhelm**, German philosopher . 1844—1900

Nightingale (nit'in-gāl), **Florence** (*the Lady of the Lamp*), English nurse .... 1820—1910

Nijinsky (ni-jin'sky), **Vaslav**, Russian ballet dancer .... 1890—1950

Nimitz (nim'its), **Chester William**, American admiral; commander of U.S. Pacific fleet in World War II .... 1885—1966

Nitti (nit'tī), **Francesco Saverio**, Italian statesman .... 1868—1953

Nixon (nik'sŏn), **Richard Milhous**, president of the United States (1969–74); resigned .... 1913—

Noailles, de (dẽ nọ-ä'y), **Adrien Maurice, Duc**, marshal of France .... 1678—1766

Nobel (nō-bel'), **Alfred Bernhard**, Swedish industrialist; inventor of dynamite; founded Nobel prizes .... 1833—1896

Nobile (nō'bī-lę), **Umberto**, Italian arctic explorer .... 1885—1978

Noguchi (nō-gụ̈'chī), **Hideyo**, Japanese bacteriologist in the United States .... 1876—1928

Nomura (nō'mụ̈-rä), **Kichisaburo**, Japanese admiral; ambassador to the United States (1940–41) .... 1877—1964

Nordau (nọr'dou), **Max Simon** (*Max Simon Südfeld*), German author and Zionist, born in Hungary .... 1849—1923

Nordenskjöld (nör'den-shēld), **Nils Adolf Erik, Baron**, Swedish geologist and navigator .... 1832—1901

Nordhoff (nọrd'họf), **Charles**, Am. author, b. in Germany .... 1830—1901

N., Charles (*grandson of C.N.*), American author .... 1887—1947

Nordica (nọr'di-ķȧ), **Lillian** (b. *Lillian Norton*), American operatic soprano .... 1859—1914

Norris (nọr'ris), **Frank** (*Benjamin Frankin N.*), Am. novelist .... 1870—1902

N., Charles Gilman (*brother of F.N.*), Am. novelist .... 1881—1945

N., Kathleen (*wife of C.G.N.*), American novelist .... 1880—1966

Norris, George William, U.S. senator .... 1861—1944

Norris, John, English clergyman and philosopher .... 1657—1711

North (nọrth) **Frederick, second Earl of Guilford, eighth Baron North** (*Lord North*), English statesman; prime minister (1770–82) .... 1732—1792

North, Sir Thomas, English translator .... 1535?–1601?

Northcliffe (nọrth'ķlif), **Alfred Charles William Harmsworth, first Viscount**, English newspaper publisher .... 1865—1922

Northrop (nọr'thrŏp), **John Howard**, Am. biochemist .... 1891—

Norton (nọr'tŏn), **Charles Eliot**, American art historian and editor .... 1827—1908

Nostradamus (nos-trȧ-dā'mus), (*Michel de Notredame*) French astrologer .... 1503—1566

Novalis (nō-vä'lis), (pseud. of *Friedrich von Hardenberg*) German poet and novelist .... 1772—1801

Noyes (noiș), **Alfred**, English poet .... 1880—1958

Noyes, John Humphrey, American founder of communist community at Oneida, N. Y. .... 1811—1886

Núñez (nụ̈'nyęth), **Alvar**, *see* Cabeza de Vaca.

Nuttall (nut'ạl), **Thomas**, Am. nautralist, b. in England .... 1786—1859

Nye (nȳ), **Edgar Wilson** (*Bill Nye*), American humorist .... 1850—1896

O

Oates (ōts), **Titus**, English contriver of the "Popish Plot" .... 1649—1705

O'Brien (ō-brī'en), **Fitz-James**, Irish author in America .... 1828—1862

O'Brien, William Smith, Irish patriot .... 1803—1864

O'Casey (ō-ķā'si), **Sean**, Irish dramatist .... 1880—1964

Occam *or* **Ockham** (oķ'ăm), **William of** (*the Invincible Doctor*), English scholastic philosopher .... 1300?–1349?

Ochs (oķhs), **Adolph Simon**, Am. newspaper publisher .... 1858—1935

O'Connell (ō-ķon'nel), **Daniel**, Irish orator and political leader . 1775—1847

O'Connor (ō-ķon'nŏr), **Feargus Edward**, Irish leader of the English Chartists .... 1794—1855

O'Connor, Sandra Day, associate justice of the U.S. Supreme Court (1981–) .... 1930—

O'Connor, Thomas Power (*Tay Pay O'Connor*), Irish journalist, critic, and politician .... 1848—1929

Octavia (oķ-tā'vi-ȧ), sister of Augustus and wife of Marc Antony .... B.C. 70?— 11

Odets (ō-dets'), **Clifford**, American playwright .... 1906—1963

Odoacer (ō-dō-ā'cẽr), first barbarian ruler of Italy .... 434— 493

Odum (ō'dum), **Howard Washington**, American sociologist .... 1884—1954

Oehlenschläger (ẽ'len-shlā-gẽr), **Adam Gottlob**, Danish poet . 1779—1850

Oersted (ẽr'steth), **Hans Christian**, Danish physicist .... 1777—1851

O'Faoláin (ō-fa'lin), **Seán**, Irish author .... 1900—

Offenbach (ọf'fen-bäkh), **Jacques**, French composer of comic operas, born in Germany .... 1819—1880

O'Flaherty (ō-fla'hẽr-ty), **Liam**, Irish playwright and short-story writer .... 1896—

Ogilvie (ō'gil-vi), **John**, Scottish lexicographer .... 1797—1867

Oglethorpe (ō'gl-thọrp), **James Edward**, English general; founder of Georgia .... 1696—1785

O'Hara (ō-har'ȧ), **John (Henry)**, American novelist .... 1905—1970

Ohm (ōm), **Georg Simon**, German physicist .... 1787—1854

O'Higgins (ō-hig'inș), **Bernardo**, South American revolutionary leader; 1st president of Chile (1817–1823) .... 1778—1842

Oistrakh (oi'sträkh), **David (Fyodorovich)**, Russian violinist .... 1908—1974

O'Keefe, John, Irish dramatist .... 1747—1833

O'Keeffe (ō-kēf'), **Georgia**, American painter .... 1887—

O'Kelly (ō-kel'li), **Sean Thomas**, pres. of Eire (1945–49) and Ireland (1949–59) .... 1883—1966

Okuma (ō'kụ̈-mä), **Shigenobu, Marquis**, Japanese statesman .... 1838—1922

Olaf (ō'läf) **I** (*Olaf Tryggvesson*), king of Norway .... 969—1000

Olaf II (*Saint Olaf Olaf the Fat*), king of Norway .... 995—1030

Olaf V, king of Norway (1957–) .... 1903—

Olcott (ol'ķŏt), **Chauncey**, American actor .... 1860—1932

Oldcastle (ōld'ķasl), **John, Lord Cobham**, English Lollard leader and martyr .... ? —1417

Oldham (ōld'ăm), **John**, English satirical poet .... 1653—1683

Olivares (ō-lī-vä'ręs), **Gaspar de Guzmán, third Count of, and Duke of San Lucar**, Spanish statesman .... 1587—1645

Olivier (ō-liv'i-ā), **Sir Laurence Kerr**, English actor .... 1907—

Olmsted, Frederick Law, American landscape gardener .... 1822—1903

Olney (ōl'ni), **Jesse**, American geographer .... 1798—1872

Olney, Richard, U.S. secretary of state (1895–97) .... 1835—1917

O'Malley (ō-mai'li), **Frank Ward**, American journalist .... 1875—1932

Omar (ō'mȧr) **I**, second caliph, successor of Abu Bakr .... 581?— 644

Omar Khayyám (kȳ-yäm'), Persian poet .... ? —1123

O'Neill (ō-nēl'), **Eugene (Gladstone)**, Am. dramatist .... 1888—1953

Onsager (ọn-säg'ẽr), **Lars**, American chemist, born in Norway . 1903—1976

Oost, van (vän ōst'), **Jacob** (*the Elder*), Flemish painter .... 1600—1671

Oppenheim (op'pen-hīm), **E. Phillips**, English novelist .... 1866—1946

Oppenheimer (op'pen-him-ẽr), **J. Robert**, American physicist; furthered atomic energy programs .... 1904—1967

Orcagna (ọr-ķä'nyä), (*Andrea di Cione*) Italian painter, sculptor, and architect .... 1308?-1368?

Orff (ọrf), **Carl**, German composer .... 1895—

Origen (ọr'i-ġen), (*Origenes Adamantius*) Christian scholar and writer of Alexandria .... 185?—254?

Orlando (ọr-län'dō), **Vittorio Emanuele**, Italian statesman; premier (1917–19) .... 1860—1952

Orléans, d' (dọr-lę-äṅ'), **Ferdinand Philippe Louis Charles Henri, Duc**, eldest son of King Louis Philippe .... 1810—1842

Orléans, d', Louis Philippe Joseph, Duc (*Philippe Égalité*), French political leader; guillotined .... 1747—1793

Orlov (ọr'lọf), **Alexei, Count**, Russian admiral .... 1737—1808

Ormandy (ọr'măn-dy), **Eugene**, American orchestra conductor, born in Hungary .... 1899—

Orosius (ō-rō'shi-us), **Paulus**, Spanish theologian and historian . . fl.5th cent.

Orozco (ō-rōs'ķō), **José Clemente**, Mexican painter .... 1883—1949

Orpen (ọr'pen), **Sir William**, Brit. painter, b. in Ireland .... 1878—1931

Orsay, d' (dọr-sā'), **Alfred Guillaume Gabriel, Count**, French artist .... 1801—1852

Ortega y Gasset (ōr-tę'gä ē gäs'set), **José**, Spanish philosopher and author .... 1883—1955

Orwell (ọr'wel), **George** (b. *Eric Blair*), Eng. satirist .... 1903—1950

Osborn (oș'bŏrn), **Henry Fairfield**, Am. paleontologist .... 1857—1935

Osborne (oș'bŏrn), **John (James)**, English playwright .... 1929—

Osborne, Thomas Mott, American penologist .... 1859—1926

Oscar (os'ķär) **I**, king of Sweden and Norway (1844–59) .... 1799—1859

O. II, (*son of O. I*), king of Sweden (1872–1907) and Norway (1872–1905) .... 1829—1907

Osceola (os-cē-ō'lȧ), (*Asseheholar*) chief of the Seminoles .... 1804—1838

Osiander (ō-și-än'dẽr), **Andreas** (b. *Hosemann*), German reformer .... 1498—1552

Osler (ōs'lẽr), **Sir William**, Canadian physician and writer .... 1849—1919

Osmeña (os-mā'nyä), **Sergio**, Philippine statesman; vice president of the Philippine Commonwealth (1935–44); president (1944–46). 1878—1961
Ossian (osh'ăn), legendary Celtic bard ... fl.3rd cent.?
Ossietzky, von (fon os-i-et'sky), **Carl**, German pacifist ... 1889—1938
Ossoli (os'sō-lī), *see* Fuller, Margaret.
Ostenso (os-ten'sō), **Martha**, American novelist ... 1900—1963
Ostwald (ōst'vält), **Wilhelm**, German chemist ... 1853—1932
Othman (ŏth'män) *or* **Osman** (os'man), (*the Conqueror*) founder of the Ottoman empire ... 1259—1326
Otho (ō'thō), **Marcus Salvius**, Roman emperor (69) ... 32— 69
Otis (ō'tis), **James**, American orator and patriot ... 1725—1783
Otto (ot'tō) **I** (*the Great*), Holy Roman emperor (962–73) ... 912— 973
Otway (ot'wā), **Thomas**, English dramatist and poet ... 1652—1685
Ouida (wī'dȧ), (pseud. of *Louise de la Ramée*) English novelist and writer of children's stories ... 1839—1908
Overbeck (ō'vẽr-bek), **Friedrich**, German painter ... 1789—1869
Overbury (ō'vẽr-bŭr-y), **Sir Thomas**, Eng. poet, writer ... 1581—1613
Ovid (ov'id), (*Publius Ovidius Naso*) Roman poet ... B.C. 43–A.D.17
Owen (ō'wen), **Robert**, British socialist and philanthropist ... 1771—1858
O., Robert Dale (*son of R.O.*), American politician and author, born in Scotland ... 1801—1877
Owen Glendower (glen-dou'ẽr), Welsh chieftain ... 1359?–1416
Oxenstierna (ok'sen-stẽr-nȧ), **Axel Gustafsson, Count**, Swedish statesman ... 1583—1654
Oxford (oks'fŏrd), **Edward de Vere, seventeenth Earl of**, English politician and poet ... 1550—1604
Oxford, Robert Harley, first Earl of, *see* Harley.
Oxnam (oks'năm), **Garfield Bromley**, American Methodist bishop ... 1891—1963
Oyama (ō'yä-mä), **Iwao, Prince**, Japanese field marshal ... 1842—1916
Ozanam (ō-zȧ-nȧm'), **Antoine Frédéric**, French scholar ... 1813—1853

P

Pachmann, de (dẽ päkh'män), **Vladimir**, Russian pianist ... 1848—1933
Packer (pak'ẽr), **Asa**, American capitalist ... 1805—1879
Paderewski (pȧ-de-ref'skī), **Ignace Jan**, Polish pianist and composer; prime minister of Poland (1919) ... 1860—1941
Padilla (pä-dē'yȧ), **Ezequiel**, Mexican foreign minister ... 1890—1971
Paganini (pä-gä-nī'nī), **Nicolò**, Italian violinist ... 1782—1840
Page (pāģ), **Thomas Nelson**, Am. novelist and diplomat ... 1853—1922
Page, Walter Hines, American editor and diplomat ... 1855—1918
Page, William, American painter ... 1811—1885
Paine (pān), **Albert Bigelow**, American editor and author ... 1861—1937
Paine, Robert Treat, American lawyer and patriot ... 1731—1814
Paine, Thomas, American Revolutionary patriot, writer, and political thinker, born in England ... 1737—1809
Painlevé (pan-lē-vę'), **Paul**, French statesman and mathematician. 1863—1933
Pakenham (pak'en-ăm), **Sir Edward Michael**, Brit. general ... 1778—1815
Palacio Valdés (pä-lä'thyō väl-dęs'), **Armando**, Spanish novelist. 1853—1938
Palacký (pä'läts-ky), **František**, Bohemian historian ... 1798—1876
Palestrina, da (dä pä-lęs-trī'nä), **Giovanni Pierluigi**, Italian composer of church music ... 1526?–1594
Paley (pā'li), **William**, English moralist and writer ... 1743—1805
Palfrey (pąl'fri), **John Gorham**, American theologian and historian ... 1796—1881
Palgrave (pąl'grāv), **Sir Francis** (b. *Cohen*), English historian ... 1788—1861
P., Francis Turner (*son of F.P.*), English poet, critic, and anthologist ... 1824—1897
Palikao, de (dẽ pȧ-lī-kȧ-ō'), **Charles Guillaume Cousin-Montauban, Count**, French general and statesman ... 1796—1878
Palissy (pȧ-lī-sē'), **Bernard**, French potter and enameler ... 1510?–1589
Palladio (päl-lä'dyō), **Andrea**, Italian architect ... 1518—1580
Palma (päl'mä), **Jacopo** (*the Elder*), Italian painter ... 1480?–1528
P., Jacopo (*the Younger*), (*grandnephew of J.P.*) It. painter ... 1544—1628
Palma, Tomás Estrada, first president of the Cuban republic (1902–06) ... 1835—1908
Palmer (pä'mẽr), **Alice Freeman** (*wife of G.H.P.*), American educator ... 1855—1902
P., George Herbert, American educator and author ... 1842—1933
Palmer, John McAuley, American general and statesman ... 1817—1900
Palmerston (päm'ẽr-stŏn), **Henry John Temple, third Viscount**, British prime minister (1855–58, 1859–65) ... 1784—1865
Palomino de Velasco (pä-lō-mī'nō dę vę-läs'çō) *or* **Palomino de Castro y Velasco, Acislo Antonio**, Spanish painter ... 1653—1726
Paludan-Müller (pä'lų-dän-mül'lẽr), **Frederik**, Danish poet ... 1809—1876
Pandit (păn'dit), **Vijaya Lakshmi** (*sister of J. Nehru*), Indian diplomat; president U.N. Assembly (1953–54) ... 1900—
Pankhurst (pañk'hŭrst), **Emmeline**, English suffragist ... 1857—1928
Papen, von (fon pä'pen), **Franz**, German diplomat and politician. 1879—1969
Papin (pȧ-pan'), **Denis**, French physicist and inventor ... 1647—1714?
Papineau (pȧ-pi-nō'), **Louis Joseph**, Canadian revolutionist ... 1786—1871
Papini (pä-pī'nī), **Giovanni**, It. philosopher, author ... 1881—1956
Paracelsus (par-ȧ-cel'sus), **Philippus Aureolus** (b. *Theophrastus Bombastus von Hohenheim*), Swiss alchemist and physician ... 1493—1541
Paré (pȧ-rę'), **Ambroise**, French surgeon ... 1517—1590
Pares (pârş), **Sir Bernard**, British writer on Russia ... 1867—1949
Pareto (pä-rę'tō), **Vilfredo**, Italian sociologist and economist ... 1848—1923
Paris (pȧ-rīs'), **Gaston**, French philologist ... 1839—1903
Paris (par'is), **Matthew**, *see* Matthew of Paris.
Park (pärk), **Mungo**, Scottish explorer in Africa ... 1771—1806
Parker (pär'kẽr), **Alton Brooks**, American jurist ... 1852—1926
Parker, Charley (b. *Charles Christopher Parker, Jr.*), American jazz musician ... 1920—1955
Parker, Dorothy (Rothschild), American humorist ... 1893—1967
Parker, Sir Gilbert, Canadian novelist in England ... 1862—1932
Parker, Sir Hyde, British admiral ... 1739—1807
Parker, Theodore, American preacher and reformer ... 1810—1860
Parkes (pärks), **Sir Henry**, Australian statesman ... 1815—1896
Parkhurst (pärk'hŭrst), **Charles Henry**, American clergyman and reformer ... 1842—1933
Parkman (pärk'măn), **Francis**, American historian ... 1823—1893
Parmenides (pär-men'i-dēş), Greek Eleatic philosopher ... fl.B.C.500
Parnell (pär-nel'), **Charles Stewart**, Irish statesman ... 1846—1891
Parnell, Thomas, Irish poet ... 1679—1718
Parr (pär), **Catherine**, sixth wife of Henry VIII ... 1512—1548
Parrhasius (pa-rā'shi-us), Greek painter ... fl.B.C.400
Parrington (par'ring-tŏn), **Vernon Lewis**, American literary critic ... 1871—1929
Parrish (par'rish), **Anne**, American novelist ... 1888—1957
Parrish, Maxfield, American painter ... 1870—1966
Parry (par'ry), **Sir William Edward**, English arctic explorer ... 1790—1855
Parton (pär'tŏn), **James**, American biographer ... 1822—1891
P., Sara Payson Willis (pseud. *Fanny Fern*), (*wife of J.P.*) American author ... 1811—1872
Pascal (pas'çăl *or Fr.* pȧs-çȧl'), **Blaise**, French philosopher and mathematician ... 1623—1662
Paskevich (pas-kye'vich), **Ivan Feodorovich, Prince of Warsaw**, Russian general ... 1782—1856
Passy (pȧ-sē'), **Paul Édouard**, French phonetician ... 1859—1940
Pasteur (pȧs-tŭr'), **Louis**, French chemist and biologist ... 1822—1895
Pastor (pas'tŏr), **Antonio** (*Tony P.*), Am. theater operator ... 1837?–1908
Pater (pā'tẽr), **Walter (Horatio)**, English critic, essayist, and novelist ... 1839—1894
Patmore (pat'mōr), **Coventry**, English poet ... 1823—1896
Patrick (pat'rik), **Saint**, apostle and patron saint of Ireland ... 389?–461?
Pattee (pat-tē'), **Fred Lewis**, Am. literary historian ... 1863—1950
Patterson (pat'tẽr-sŏn), **Joseph Medill**, American journalist and publisher ... 1879—1946
Patterson, Robert Porter, U.S. sec. of war (1945–47) ... 1891—1952
Patti (pat'tī), **Adelina** (*Baroness Cederström*), Italian soprano, born in Spain ... 1843—1919
Pattison (pat'ti-sŏn), **Mark**, English author ... 1813—1884
Patton (pat'tŏn), **George Smith, Jr.**, American general in World War II ... 1885—1945
Paul (pąl), **Saint** (*the Apostle to the Gentiles*), a Jew of Tarsus, first great Christian missionary ... ? — 67?
Paul I (*son of Catherine II and Peter III*), czar of Russia (1796–1801); assassinated ... 1754—1801
Paul III (*Alessandro Farnese*), Pope ... 1468—1549
Paul V (*Camillo Borghese*), Pope ... 1552—1621
Paul VI (*Giovanni Battista Montini*), Pope (1963–78) ... 1897—1978
Paul-Boncour (pōl-boṅ-çōr'), **Joseph**, French statesman and premier (1932–33) ... 1873—1972
Paulding (pąl'ding), **Hiram**, American rear admiral ... 1797—1878
Paulding, James Kirke, American author and politician ... 1779—1860
Pauli (pou'lē), **Wolfgang**, Austrian physicist ... 1900—1958
Pauling (pąl'ing), **Linus (Carl)**, American chemist ... 1901—
Paulsen (poul'şen), **Friedrich**, German philosopher ... 1846—1908
Pausanias (pą-sā'ni-ȧs), Greek traveler ... fl.180
Pavlov (päv'lọf), **Ivan Petrovich**, Russian physiologist ... 1849—1936
Pavlova (päv-lō'vȧ), **Anna**, Russian ballet dancer ... 1885—1931
Paxson (pak'sŏn), **Frederic Logan**, American historian ... 1877—1948
Payne (pān), **John**, English poet and translator ... 1842—1916
Payne, John Howard, American actor and playwright ... 1791—1852
Peabody (pē'bod-y), **George**, American banker and philanthropist in London ... 1795—1869
Peabody, Josephine Preston, Am. poet and playwright ... 1874—1922
Peacock (pē'çok), **Thomas Love**, Eng. poet and novelist ... 1785—1866
Peale (pēl), **Charles Willson**, Am. portrait painter ... 1741—1827
Pearl (pẽrl), **Raymond**, American biologist ... 1879—1940
Pearson (pẽr'sŏn), **John**, English bishop and theologian ... 1613—1686
Pearson, Lester Bowles, Canadian diplomat; president of U.N. General Assembly (1952–53); prime minister of Canada (1963–68). 1897—1972
Peary (pẽr'y), **Robert Edwin**, American arctic explorer; discovered the North Pole (1909) ... 1856—1920
Peck (pek), **Harry Thurston**, Am. scholar and editor ... 1856—1914
Pedro (pę'drō) **II**, last emperor of Brazil (1831–89) ... 1825—1891
Peel (pēl), **Sir Robert**, English statesman; prime minister (1834–35, 1341–46) ... 1788—1850
Peele (pēl), **George**, English dramatist ... 1558—1597?
Peirce (pẽrc), **Benjamin**, American mathematician ... 1809—1880
P., Charles Sanders (*son of B.P.*), Am. philosopher ... 1839—1914
Pelagius (pe-lā'gi-us), founder of Pelagianism ... fl.400
Pelletier (pel-tyę'), **Pierre Joseph**, French chemist ... 1788—1842
Pellico (pel'lī-çō), **Silvio**, Italian poet and patriot ... 1789—1854
Pelopidas (pe-lop'i-dȧs), Theban general ... B.C. ? — 364
Pendleton (pen'dl-tŏn), **Edmund**, American statesman ... 1721—1803
Penn (pen), **William**, English Quaker; founder of Pennsylvania ... 1644—1718
Pennell (pen'nel), **Joseph**, American etcher and author ... 1860—1926
P., Elizabeth Robins (*wife of J.P.*), Am. author ... 1855—1936
Pepin (pep'in), (*the Short*) king of the Franks ... 714?— 768
Pepperell (pep'ẽr-el), **Sir William**, American general ... 1696—1759
Pepys (pēps), **Samuel**, Eng. diarist and govt. official ... 1633—1703
Percy (pẽr'cy), **Sir Henry** (*Hotspur*), English warrior ... 1364—1403
Percy, Thomas, English bishop, scholar, and writer ... 1729—1811
Perez (pe'rets), **Isaac Loeb**, Jewish author, b. Poland ... 1851—1915
Pérez Galdós (pę'ręth gäl-dōs'), **Benito**, Spanish novelist ... 1845—1920
Pericles (per'i-çlēş), Athenian statesman ... B.C.495?— 429
Perkins (pẽr'kinş), **Frances** (*Mrs. P.C. Wilson*), U.S. secretary of labor (1933–45) ... 1882—1965
Perón (pę-rōn'), **Juan Domingo**, president of Argentina (1946–55, 1973–74) ... 1895—1974
P., de, Eva Duarte (*Evita Perón*), wife of J.D.P. ... 1919?–1952
Perrault (pe-rō'), **Charles**, French poet and compiler of fairy tales. 1628—1703
Perrin (pe-ran'), **Jean Baptiste**, French physicist ... 1870—1942
Perry (per'ry), **Bliss**, American educator and author ... 1860—1954
Perry, Matthew Calbraith, American commodore; negotiated first treaty between Japan and U.S. (1854) ... 1794—1858
P., Oliver Hazard (*brother of M.C.P.*), Am. naval officer; defeated British in Battle of Lake Erie ... 1785—1819
Perry, Ralph Barton, Am. philosopher and educator ... 1876—1957
Pershing (pẽr'shing), **John Joseph**, American general; commander in chief of American Expeditionary Force in World War I ... 1860—1948
Perugino (pę-rų-gī'nō), (*Pietro Vannucci*), It. painter ... 1446—1523?
Peruzzi (pę-rūt'tsī), **Baldassare**, Italian architect ... 1481—1536
Pestalozzi (pes-tȧ-lōt'sī), **Johann Heinrich**, Swiss educational reformer ... 1746—1827
Pétain (pę-tan'), **Henri Philippe**, marshal of France; chief of state in Vichy government; convicted of treason (1945) ... 1856—1951
Peter (*the Cruel*), king of Castile (1350–69) ... 1334—1369
Peter (pē'tẽr) **I**, king of Aragon ... ? —1104
Peter I (*the Great*), czar of Russia (1682–1725) ... 1672—1725
Peter I (*the Severe*), king of Portugal (1357–67) ... 1320—1367
Peter II (*son of Alexander I*), king of Yugoslavia (1934–45) ... 1923—1970
Peter III (*Pëtr Feodorovich*), czar of Russia (1762); assassinated ... 1728—1762

Peter the Hermit, preacher of the first crusade....1050?–1115
Peterkin (pē'tēr-kin), **Julia**, American novelist....1880—1961
Pétion de Villeneuve (pe-syoṅ' dē vil-nûv'), **Jérôme**, French revolutionist....1753?–1794
Petitot (pē-ti-tō'), **Jean**, Genevese enamel painter....1607—1691
Petöfi (pe'tē-fi), **Sándor**, Hungarian patriot and poet....1822—1849
Petrarch (pē'trärch) *or It.* **Petrarca** (pe-trär'cä), **Francesco**, Italian poet....1304—1374
Petrie (pē'tri), **Sir William Matthew Flinders**, English Egyptologist....1853—1942
Petronius (pe-trō'ni-us), **Gaius** (*Arbiter Elegantiae*), Roman satirist....?–66A.D.
Petty (pet'ty), **Sir William**, English political economist....1623—1687
Phaedrus (fē'drus), Roman fabulist....fl.1st cent.
Phelps (felps), **William Lyon**, Am. critic and educator....1865—1943
Phidias (fid'i-ås), Greek sculptor....B.C. 500?–432?
Philip (fil'ip), (*King Philip*), (*son of Massasoit*) sachem of Wampanoag Indians....? —1676
Philip II (*father of Alexander*), king of Macedonia....B.C. 382— 336
Philip II (*Augustus*), king of France....1165—1223
Philip II, king of Spain....1527—1598
Philip IV (*the Fair*), king of France....1268—1314
Philip V, king of Spain; first of the House of Bourbon....1683—1746
Philip the Bold, duke of Burgundy....1342—1404
Philip the Good, duke of Burgundy....1396—1467
Philips (fil'ips), **Ambrose**, English dramatist and poet....1675?–1749
Philips, John, English poet....1676—1708
Phillips, David Graham, American novelist....1867—1911
Phillips, Stephen, English poet and playwright....1868—1915
Phillips, Wendell, American orator and abolitionist....1811—1884
Phillips, William, American diplomat....1878—1968
Phillpotts (fil'pots), **Eden**, English novelist....1862—1960
Philopaemen (fil-ō-pē'men), Greek general and statesman....B.C. 252?—183
Philo Judaeus (fī'lō jů-dē'us), Jewish philosopher of Alexandria....B.C.20?–A.D.50?
Phocion (fō'shi-ŏn), Athenian statesman and general....B.C.402?—317
Phumiphon Aduldet (pům'i-pōn ä-důl'det), king of Siam (1946–49) and Thailand (1949–)....1927—
Phyfe (fȳf), **Duncan**, American furniture designer and cabinetmaker, born in Scotland....1768—1854
Piatigorsky (pyät-i-gor'skē), **Gregor**, Am. cellist, b. in Russia...1903—
Picasso (pi-çäs'sō), **Pablo**, Spanish painter and sculptor....1881—1973
Piccard (pī-çär'), **Auguste**, Swiss physicist....1884—1962
P., Jean Felix, American chemist and aeronautical engineer (*twin brother of A.*)....1884—1963
Pickens (pik'enș), **Andrew**, Am. Revolutionary general....1739—1817
Pickering (pik'ēr-ing), **Edward Charles**, American physicist and astronomer (*brother of W.H.P.*)....1846—1919
P., William Henry, American astronomer....1858—1938
Pickering, Timothy, American statesman....1745—1829
Pickett (pik'et), **George Edward**, Am. Confederate general....1825—1875
Pickford (pik'fŏrd), **Mary** (b. *Gladys Smith*), American motion-picture actress, born in Canada....1893—1979
Pico della Mirandola (pī'çō del'lä mī-rän'dō-lä), **Giovanni, Count**, Italian theologian and philosopher....1463—1494
Pierce (pērc), **Franklin**, fourteenth president of the United States (1853–57)....1804—1869
Pierné (pyer-ne'), **Henri Constant Gabriel**, French composer..1863—1937
Pike (pīk), **Zebulon Montgomery**, American general and explorer....1779—1813
Pilnyak (pīl-nyäk'), **Boris** (pseud. of *Boris Andreievich Vogau*), Russian novelist....1894—
Pilon (pī-loṅ'), **Germain**, French sculptor....1535—1590
Piloty, von (fon pi-lō'ty), **Karl Theodor**, German painter....1826—1886
Pilsudski (pil-sut'skĭ), **Josef**, Polish marshal; president (1918–22); premier (1926–28, 1930)....1867—1935
Pinchot (pin'chō), **Gifford**, American politician and forester....1865—1946
Pinckney (piñk'ni), **Charles**, American statesman....1757—1824
P., Charles Cotesworth, American soldier and statesman (*cousin of C.P. and brother of T.P.*)....1746—1825
P., Thomas, American general and diplomat....1750—1828
Pindar (pin'dår), Greek lyric poet....B.C. 522?–443?
Pinero (pi-ner'ō), **Sir Arthur Wing**, English dramatist....1855—1934
Pinkerton (piñk'ēr-tŏn), **Allan**, American detective, born in Scotland....1819—1884
Pinski (pin'ski), **David**, Am.-Yiddish writer, b. in Russia....1872—1959
Pinter (pin'tēr), **Harold**, English playwright, director, and screenplay writer....1930—
Pinzón (pīn-thōn'), **Martin Alonso**, Spanish navigator with Columbus, in command of the *Pinta*....1440?–1493
P., Vicente Yáñez (*brother of M.A.P.*), Spanish navigator with Columbus, in command of the *Niña*....1460?–1524?
Pirandello (pi-rän-del'lō), **Luigi**, Italian dramatist and novelist; received Nobel prize (1934)....1867—1936
Pisano (pī-sän'ō), **Andrea**, Italian architect and sculptor....1270?–1348
Pisano, Giovanni (*son of N.P.*), Italian sculptor and architect..1245–1320?
P., Niccola, Italian sculptor and architect....1225?–1278?
Pisistratus (pis-is'trå-tus), Athenian ruler and tyrant....B.C. 605?– 527
Pissaro (pī-sà-rō'), **Camille**, Fr. impressionist painter....1831—1903
Piston (pis'tŏn), **Walter**, American composer....1894—1976
Pitman (pit'măn), **Isaac**, English phonographer....1813—1897
Pitt (pit), **William, first Earl of Chatham** (*the Great Commoner*), English statesman and orator....1708—1778
P., William (*son of W.P.*), English statesman; prime minister (1783–1801, 1804–06)....1759—1806
Pius (pī'us), **I**, (It. *Pio I*), **Saint**, Pope....90?– 157
Pius X (*Giuseppe Sarto*), **Saint**, Pope....1835—1914
Pius XI (*Achille Ratti*), Pope (1922–39)....1857—1936
Pius XII (*Eugenio Pacelli*), Pope (1939–58)....1876—1958
Pizarro (pi-zär'ō *or Sp.* pi-thä'rō), **Francisco**, Spanish conqueror of Peru....1475?–1541
Planck (pläñk), **Max**, German physicist; devised the quantum theory; received Nobel prize (1918)....1858—1947
Plantagenet (plan-tag'e-net), family of English kings....1154—1485
Plato (plā'tō), Greek philosopher....B.C. 427?–347?
Plautus (pla'tus), **Titus Maccius**, Roman comic dramatist.B.C. 254?– 184
Plekhanov (ple-kä'nof), **Georgi Valentinovich**, Russian socialist philosopher....1857—1918
Pliny (plin'y), (*Caius Plinius Secundus*), (*the Elder*) Roman naturalist....23— 79
Pliny (*Caius Plinius Caecilius Secundus*), (*the Younger*) (*nephew of P.*), Latin author and orator....62?–114?
Plotinus (plō-tī'nus), Egyptian Neoplatonist....205?–270?
Plunkett (pluñ'ket), **Sir Horace Curzon**, Ir. statesman....1854—1932
Plutarch (plů'tärch), Greek biographer and moralist....46?–120?
Pocahontas (pō-çà-hon'tås), daughter of Powhatan....1595?–1617
Poe (pō), **Edgar Allan**, American poet, critic, and writer....1809—1849
Poincaré (pwan çà-re'), **Jules Henri**, French mathematician and physicist (*cousin of R.P.*)....1854—1912
P., Raymond, president of France (1913–20)....1860—1934
Pole (pōl), **Reginald**, English Roman Catholic cardinal and archbishop of Canterbury....1500—1558
Polk (pōk), **James Knox**, eleventh president of the United States (1845–49)....1795—1849
Polk, Leonidas, Am. bishop and Confederate general....1806—1864
Pollard (pol'lård), **Albert Frederick**, English historian....1869—1948
Pollock (pol'lŏk), **Channing**, American playwright....1880—1946
Pollock, Sir Frederick, English writer on jurisprudence....1845—1937
Polo (pō'lō), **Marco**, Venetian traveler in China....1254?–1324?
Polybius (pō-lyb'i-us), Greek historian....B.C. 205?–123?
Polycarp (pol'y-çärp), **Saint**, bishop of Smyrna and martyr....69?–155?
Polycleitus (pol-y-çlī'tus), Greek sculptor....fl. B.C. 430
Polycrates (pō-lyç'rå-tēș), tyrant of Samos....B.C. ? —522?
Polydorus (pol-y-dō'rus), Greek sculptor....B.C. 1st cent.
Pomfret (pom'fret), **John**, English poet....1667—1702
Pompadour, de (dē poṅ-pà-dōr'), **Jeanne Antoinette Poisson, Marquise**, mistress of Louis XV....1721—1764
Pompey (pom'pi) **the Great** (*Gnaeus Pompeius Magnus*), Roman general and statesman....B.C. 106— 48
Ponce de Leon (pōn'the de le-ōn' *or Eng.* pons dē lē'ŏn), **Juan**, Spanish discoverer of Florida....1460?–1521
Ponchielli (pōñ-chi-el'lī), **Amilcare**, It. opera composer....1834—1886
Poniatowski (pō-nyä-tof'skĭ), **Jozef Anton, Prince**, Polish general and marshal of France....1762—1813
Pons (poṅs), **Jean Louis**, French astronomer....1761—1831
Pons (pons *or Fr.* poṅș), **Lily**, French opera singer in U.S....1904—1976
Ponselle (pon-sel'), **Rosa**, American soprano....1894—1981
Pontiac (pon'ti-aç), chief of the Ottawa Indians....1720?–1769
Pontoppidan (pon-top'i-dän), **Henrik**, Danish novelist....1857—1943
Pontormo, da (dä pōn-tor'mō), **Jacopo** (b. *Carucci*), Florentine painter....1494—1557
Poole (pool), **Ernest**, American novelist....1880—1950
Poole, Reginald Lane, English historian....1857—1939
Poole, William Frederick, American librarian....1821—1894
Poore (poor), **Benjamin Perley**, American journalist....1820—1887
Pope (pōp), **Alexander**, English poet and critic....1688—1744
Pope, John, Union general in the Civil War....1822—1892
Poppaea Sabina (pop-pē'à sà-bī'nà), a wife of Nero....? — 65?
Porphyry (por'fy-ry), Greek philosopher and writer....233— 304
Porpora (por'pō-rä), **Niccolo**, Italian composer....1686—1766
Porson (por'sŏn), **Richard**, English classicist and critic....1759—1808
Porta, della (del'lä por'tä), **Giambattista**, It. physicist....1541?–1615
Porter (por'tēr), **Cole**, American composer and lyricist....1893—1964
Porter, David, American naval officer and diplomat....1780—1843
P., David Dixon (*son of D.P.*), American admiral....1813—1891
P., Fitz-John (*nephew of D.P.*), American general....1822—1901
Porter, Gene Stratton, American novelist....1868—1924
Porter, Horace, American general and diplomat....1837—1921
Porter, Jane, Scottish novelist....1776—1850
Porter, Katherine Anne, American writer....1890—1980
Porter, Noah, American philosopher and educator....1811—1892
Porter, William Sydney, *see* Henry, O.
Post (pōst), **Emily** (**Price**), American writer on etiquette....1873—1960
Potemkin (pō-tem'kin), **Grigori Aleksandrovich, Prince**, Russian field marshal; favorite of Catherine II....1739—1791
Potter (pot'tēr), **Paulus**, Dutch painter of animals....1625—1654
Poulenc (pō-läñç'), **Francis**, French composer....1899—1963
Pound (pound), **Ezra** (**Loomis**), Am. poet and critic....1885—1972
Pound, Louise, American linguist and folklorist....1872—1958
P., Roscoe, Am. educator and writer on law (*brother of L.*)....1870—1964
Poussin (pö-saṅ'), **Nicolas**, French painter....1594—1665
Powell (pou'el), **Cecil Frank**, English physicist....1903—1969
Powell, John Wesley, Am. geologist and ethnologist....1834—1902
Powell, Lewis Franklin, associate justice of the U.S. Supreme Court (1972–)....1907—
Power (pou'ēr), (**Frederic**) **Tyrone**, Am. actor, b. in England....1869—1931
Powers (pou'ērș), **Hiram**, American sculptor....1805—1873
Powhatan (pou-hà-tan'), (*father of Pocahontas*) Indian chief in Virginia....1550?–1618
Powys (pō'ys), **John Cowper**, English novelist, poet, and critic (*brother of L.P. and T.F.P.*)....1872—1963
P., Llewelyn, English novelist and essayist....1884—1939
P., Theodore Francis, English novelist....1875—1953
Prajadhipok (prà-chä'ti-pok), king of Siam (1925–35)....1893—1941
Prasad (prà-säd'), **Rajendra**, Indian nationalist leader and the first president of India (1950–62)....1884—1963
Pratt (prat), **Orson**, Mormon apostle and scholar....1811—1881
Praxiteles (praks-it'e-lēș), Greek sculptor....fl. B.C. 340
Preble (preb'l), **Edward**, American commodore....1761—1807
Prescott (pres'çot), **William**, American colonel in Revolutionary war (*grandfather of W.H.P.*)....1726—1795
P., William Hickling, American historian....1796—1859
Pretorius (pre-to'ri-us), **Andries**, Boer leader....1799—1853
P., Martinus Wessel (*son of A.P.*), Boer statesman....1819?–1901
Prevost (pre'vō), **Sir George**, English general....1767—1816
Prévost (pre-vō'), **Marcel**, French novelist....1862—1941
Prévost d'Exiles (deg-zēl'), **Antoine François** (called *Abbé Prévost*), French novelist....1697—1763
Prichard (prich'ård), **James Cowles**, English ethnologist....1786—1848
Priestley (prēst'li), **J. B.** (*John Boynton P.*), English novelist, dramatist, and critic....1894—
Priestley, Joseph, English clergyman and chemist....1733—1804
Prim (prīm), **Juan, Count of Reus and Marquis de los Castillejos**, Spanish general and statesman....1814—1870
Primaticcio (prī-mä-tīt'chō), **Francesco**, It. painter....1504—1570
Primo de Rivera (prī'mō de rī-ve'rä), **Miguel, Marquis of Estella**, Spanish general and dictator (1923–30)....1870—1930
Primrose (prim'rōș), **William**, Scottish violist in U.S....1904—
Prince (princ), **Morton**, American neurologist....1854—1929
Prior (prī'ŏr), **Matthew**, English poet and diplomat....1664—1721

Priscian (prish'i-ăn), Latin grammarian....................... fl.525?
Probus (prō'bus), **Marcus Aurelius**, Roman emperor..........235?— 282
Procaccini (prō-çät-chī'nī), **Giulio Cesare**, Bolognese painter..1570?–1625?
Proclus (prō'çlus), Greek philosopher......................411?— 485
Procopius (prō-çō'pi-us), Byzantine historian..............490?—562?
Prokofiev (prọ-kọf'yef), **Sergei**, Russian composer.........1891—1953
Prokosch (prō'kosh), **Frederic**, Am. novelist and poet.........1909—
Propertius (prō-pẽr'shi-us), **Sextus**, Roman poet..........B.C. 50?—15?
Protagoras (prō-tag'ō-răs), Greek Sophist..................B.C.480?—410?
Protogenes (prō-toġ'e-nēṣ), painter of Rhodes..................fl. B.C. 300
Proudhon (prö-doṅ'), **Pierre Joseph**, French scholar and socialist.1809—1865
Proust (pröst), **Marcel**, French novelist....................1871—1922
Prout (prout), **William**, English chemist....................1785—1850
Prudentius (prụ-den'shi-us), **Aurelius Clemens**, Christian Latin poet...fl.4th cent.
Prud'hon (prụ-doṅ'), **Pierre Paul**, French painter.............1758—1823
Prynne (pryn), **William**, English polemical writer.............1600—1669
Ptolemy (tol'e-my), (*Claudius Ptolemaeus*), Alexandrian astronomer and geographer... fl. 150
Ptolemy I (*Soter*), founder of the dynasty of Greek kings of Egypt...B.C.367?— 283
Puccini (pụt-chī'nī), **Giacomo**, Italian opera composer.........1858—1924
Pugatchef (pụ-gät'chef), **Yemelyan**, Russian adventurer.......1726?–1775
Pulaski (pū-las'ki), **Casimir, Count**, Polish patriot and American Revolutionary general................................1748—1779
Pulci (pụl'chī), **Luigi**, Florentine poet......................1432—1484
Pulitzer (pū'lit-sẽr), **Joseph**, American journalist and newspaper owner, born in Hungary......................................1847—1911
Pupin (pụ-pīn'), **Michael Idvorsky**, American physicist and inventor, born in Yugoslavia..................................1858—1935
Purcell (pũr-cel'), **Edward Mills**, American physicist.........1912—
Purcell (pũr'cel), **Henry**, English composer...................1659—1695
Purchas (pũr'chăs), **Samuel**, English compiler of travel literature.1577—1626
Purkinje (pụr'kin-ye), **Johannes Evangelista**, Czech physiologist...1787—1869
Pusey (pū'ṣē), **Edward Bouverie**, English theologian...........1800—1882
Pushkin (pụsh'kin), **Aleksandr Sergeyevich**, Russian poet....1799—1837
Putnam (put'năm), **Frederick Ward**, American archaeologist and anthropologist...1839—1915
Putnam, Israel, American general and Indian fighter.........1718—1790
Putnam, Rufus, American Revolutionary general..............1738—1824
Puvis de Chavannes (pụ-vīs' dē çhá-văṅ'), **Pierre Cécile**, French painter..1824—1898
Pu-yi (pụ-yī'), **Henry**, emperor of China (1908–12) and ruler of Manchukuo (1932–45)....................................1906—1967
Pyle (pȳl), **Ernie** (*Ernest Taylor P.*), Am. journalist..........1900—1945
Pyle, Howard, American writer and illustrator.................1853—1911
Pym (pym), **John**, British orator and statesman..............1584?–1643
Pyrrhus (pyr'rus), king of Epirus.......................B.C. 318?—272
Pythagoras (py-thag'ō-răs), founder of the Pythagorean system of philosophy, born in Samos.......................B.C. 582—507?

Q

Quantrill (kwän'tril), **William Clarke**, Am. Confederate guerrilla leader; killed by Federal troops..............................1837—1865
Quantz (kvänts), **Johann Joachim**, German composer.........1697—1773
Quarles (kwärlṣ), **Francis**, English poet.....................1592—1644
Quay (kwā), **Matthew Stanley**, Am. political leader.........1833—1904
Queen (kwēn), **Ellery**, pseudonym of *Frederic Dannay* (1905–) and *Manfred B. Lee* (1905–), American writers of detective fiction in collaboration.
Quesnay (ke-ne'), **François**, French physician and political economist..1694—1774
Quesnel (ke-nel'), **Pasquier**, French Jansenist author.........1634—1719
Quételet (ket-le'), **Lambert Adolphe Jacques**, Belgian statistician...1796—1874
Quevedo y Villegas, de (dẹ kẹ-vẹ'thō ē vīl-yẹ'gäs), **Francisco Gómez**, Spanish poet and author.............................1580—1645
Quezon (kẹ-sōn'), **Manuel Luis**, first president of the Philippine Commonwealth (1935–44)...................................1878—1944
Quick (kwik), **Herbert**, American novelist and editor.........1861—1925
Quiller-Couch (kwil'lẽr-çöch'), **Sir Arthur Thomas**, English critic and novelist.......................................1863—1944
Quincy (kwin'cy), **Josiah**, Am. lawyer and patriot............1744—1775
Quinet (kī-ne'), **Edgar**, French poet and scholar...............1803—1875
Quintero, Joaquín *and* **Serafín Álvarez**, *see* Álvarez Quintero.
Quintilian (kwin-til'i-ăn), (*Marcus Fabius Quintilianus*) Roman rhetorician... 35?—100?
Quirino (kī-rī'nō), **Elpidio**, Filipino statesman; president of the Philippine republic (1948–53)................................1890—1956
Quisling (kwiz'ling), **Vidkun**, Norwegian Nazi leader; puppet ruler (1940–45); executed for treason.........................1887—1945

R

Rabelais (răb-lā'), **François**, French physician and humorist....1490?–1553
Rabinowitz (rá-bin'ō-wits), **Solomon**, *see* Aleicham, Sholem.
Rachel (rá-çhel'), (b. *Élisa Félix*) Fr. tragedienne...............1821—1858
Rachmaninov (räçh-mä'nī-nọf), **Sergei Vassilievich**, Russian composer, pianist, and conductor.............................1873—1943
Racine (rá-cīn'), **Jean**, French dramatic poet..................1639—1699
Rackham (rak'ăm), **Arthur**, Eng. painter, illustrator..........1867—1939
Radcliffe (rad'çlif), **Ann (Ward)**, English novelist.............1764—1823
Radek (rä'dek), **Karl**, Soviet Russian politician and writer; convicted of treason (1937)......................................1885—
Raeburn (rā'bũrn), **Sir Henry**, Scottish painter..............1756—1823
Raleigh *or* **Ralegh** (rạ'li), **Sir Walter**, English courtier, navigator, statesman, and writer; executed.............................1552—1618
Rameau (rá-mō'), **Jean Philippe**, French composer.............1683—1764
Ramirez (rä-mī'rẹth), **Pedro Pablo**, president of Argentina (1943–44)..1884—1962
Ramsay (ram'ṣy), **Allan**, Scottish poet.........................1686—1758
Ramsay, Sir William, Scottish chemist.........................1852—1916
Ramses (ram'sēṣ) **II**, Egyptian king.......................B.C.1324—1258
Ramses III, Egyptian king..................................fl. B.C.1230
Ramus (rā'mus), **Peter** *or* **Pierre de la Ramée** (pyer' dē lá rá-mẹ'), French philosopher and classical scholar...................1515—1572
Randall (ran'dăl), **James Garfield**, American historian........1881—1953
Randolph (ran'dolf), **Edmund**, American statesman...........1753—1813
Randolph, John (*of Roanoke*), American orator and statesman...1773—1833
Randolph, Peyton, American patriot and statesman...........1721?–1775
Randolph, Thomas, English poet and playwright..............1605—1635
Ranjit Singh (rǎn'jit sing), maharajah of the Punjab...........1780—1839
Ranke, von (fọn räṅ'ke), **Leopold**, German historian...........1795—1886
Raphael (raf'ā-el) (It. *Sanzio* or *Santi Raffaello*), Italian painter..1483—1520
Rask (räsk), **Rasmus Christian**, Danish philologist...........1787—1832
Rasmussen (räs'mụs-en), **Knud**, Danish arctic explorer........1879—1933
Raspe (räs'pe), **Rudolph Erich**, German writer................1737—1794
Rasputin (rás-pụ'tyin), **Grigori Efimovich**, Russian mystic; adviser to Czarina Alexandra; assassinated.........................1871—1916
Rathenau (rä'te-nou), **Walter**, German industrialist and foreign minister; assassinated..1867—1922
Rauch (roukh), **Christian Daniel**, German sculptor.............1777—1857
Ravel (rá-vel'), **Maurice**, French composer.....................1875—1937
Rawlings (rạ'lingṣ), **Marjorie Kinnan**, Am. novelist...........1896—1953
Rawlins (rạ'linṣ), **John Aaron**, Union general in the Civil War and adviser to Grant...1831—1869
Rawlinson (rạ'lin-sŏn), **George**, English historian..............1812—1902
Rawlinson, Sir Henry Creswicke, English Orientalist..........1810—1895
Ray (rā), **John**, English naturalist..............................1627—1705
Rayburn (rā'bũrn), **Sam** (*Samuel Taliaferro R.*), speaker of the U.S. House of Representatives (1940–46, 1949–52, 1955–61)....1882—1961
Rayleigh (rā'li), **John William Strutt, third Baron**, English physicist; received Nobel prize (1904)............................1842—1919
Reade (rēd), **Charles**, English novelist.........................1814—1884
Reading (red'ing), **Rufus Daniel Isaacs, Marquis of**, English jurist; viceroy and gov. gen. of India (1921–26)...........1860—1935
Reagan (rẹ'găn), **Ronald Wilson**, fortieth president of the United States (1981–)...1911—
Réaumur, de (dē rẹ-ō-mụr'), **René Antoine Ferchault**, French physicist and inventor of a thermometer.......................1683—1757
Récamier (rẹ-çá-myẹ'), **Jeanne Françoise Julie Adélaïde (Bernard)**, Fr. beauty; friend of literary notables.....................1777—1849
Reclus (rē-çlü'), **Jean Jacques Élisée**, Fr. geographer..........1830—1905
Red Cloud (red çloud), chief of the Oglala Sioux.................1822?–1909
Redi (rẹ'dī), **Francesco**, Italian naturalist and poet............1626?–1698
Red Jacket (red jak'et) *or* **Sagoyewatha** (sá-gō-yē-wät'hä), chief of the Senecas...1758?–1830
Redmond (red'mŏnd), **John Edward**, Irish statesman..........1856—1918
Redon (rē-doṅ'), **Odilon**, French painter.......................1840—1916
Reed (rēd), **John**, American journalist and writer..............1887—1920
Reed, Stanley Forman, associate justice of the U.S. Supreme Court (1938–1957)..1884—1980
Reed, Thomas Brackett, speaker of the U.S. House of Representatives (1889–91, 1895–99)......................................1839—1902
Reed, Walter, American surgeon and bacteriologist.............1851—1902
Reese (rēs), **Lizette Woodworth**, American poet...............1856—1935
Reeve (rēv), **Clara**, English novelist............................1729—1807
Regnard (re-nyär'), **Jean François**, French comic poet and dramatist..1655—1709
Régnier, de (dē rẹ-nyẹ'), **Henri**, Fr. poet, novelist..............1864—1936
Régnier, Mathurin, French satirical poet.......................1573—1613
Regulus (reg'ū-lus), **Marcus Atilius**, Roman general.......B.C. ? —250?
Rehnquist (ren'kwist), **William Hubbs**, associate justice of the U.S. Supreme Court (1972–)...................................1924—
Reid (rēd), **Thomas**, Scottish philosopher......................1710—1796
Reid, Whitelaw, American journalist and politician............1837—1912
Reinach (re-näçh'), **Salomon**, Fr. archaeologist and author.....1858—1932
Reinhardt (rīn'härt), **Max**, German theater director...........1873—1943
Réjane (rẹ-zăn'), (b. *Gabrielle Réju*) French actress.............1857—1920
Remarque (rē-märk'), **Erich Maria**, German novelist...........1897—1970
Rembrandt (rem'bränt), (*Rembrandt Harmenszoon van Rijn* or *Ryn*) Dutch painter..1606—1669
Remington (rem'ing-tŏn), **Frederic**, American painter and illustrator of Western scenes..1861—1909
Remington, Philo, American inventor...........................1816—1889
Remsen (rem'sen), **Ira**, American chemist and educator.........1846—1927
Rémusat, de (dē rẹ-mụ-ṣä'), **Charles François Marie, Count**, French philosopher and minister of state............................1797—1875
Renan (rē-näṅ'), **Ernest**, French Orientalist and critic.........1823—1892
Reni (rẹ'nī), **Guido**, Italian painter............................1575—1642
Renner (ren'ẽr), **Karl**, president of Austria (1945–50)..........1870—1950
Renoir (rē-nwär'), **Pierre Auguste**, French painter..............1841—1919
Renwick (ren'wik), **James**, American architect..................1818—1895
Repplier (rep'lẽr), **Agnes**, American essayist....................1855—1950
Respighi (res-pī'gī), **Ottorino**, Italian composer.................1879—1936
Reszke, de (dẹ resh'ke), **Jean**, Polish tenor.....................1850—1925
Retz, de (dē rets), **Jean François Paul de Gondi, Cardinal**, French churchman and politician...............................1613—1679
Reuchlin (roikh'lin), **Johann**, German humanist.................1455—1522
Reuter (roi'tẽr), **Fritz**, German poet and novelist...............1810—1874
Reuter, Paul Julius, Baron, German founder of telegraphic system..1821—1899
Reuther (rụ'thẽr), **Walter Philip**, American labor leader; vice-president of the AFL-CIO (1955–70)...............................1907—1970
Revere (rē-vẽr'), **Paul**, American patriot.......................1735—1818
Reymont (rẹ'mont), **Wladyslaw**, Polish novelist..................1868—1925
Reynaud (rẹ-nō'), **Paul**, Fr. statesman; premier (1940)..........1878—1966
Reynolds (ren'ŏlds), **Sir Joshua**, English portrait painter.......1723—1792
Rhee (rē), **Syngman**, president of the Republic of Korea (1948–60).1875—1965
Rhodes (rōds), **Cecil John**, British administrator in South Africa; founder of Rhodes scholarships...................................1853—1902
Rhodes, James Ford, American historian.........................1848—1927
Rhys (rēs), **Ernest**, British editor and author....................1859—1946
Ribault *or* **Ribaut** (rī-bō'), **Jean**, French explorer in America....1520?–1565
Ribbentrop, von (fọn rib'ben-trōp), **Joachim**, German Nazi leader; foreign minister (1938–45); hanged as a war criminal....1893—1946
Ribera (rī-bẹ'rä), **José** (*Lo Spagnoletto*), Sp. painter.............1588—1656
Ricardo (ri-çär'dō), **David**, English political economist..........1772—1823
Rice (rīc), **Alice Caldwell Hegan**, American novelist..............1870—1942
Rice, Elmer, American dramatist..................................1892—1967
Richard (rich'ărd) **I** (*Coeur de Lion*), king of England...........1157—1199
Richard II (*son of Edward, the Black Prince*), king of England.......1367—1400

Richard III (*duke of Gloucester*), king of England .... 1452—1485
Richards (rich'ărds), **I(vor) A(rmstrong)**, English literary critic in the United States .... 1893—1979
Richards, Theodore William, Am. chemist .... 1868—1928
Richardson (rich'ărd-sŏn), **Dorothy**, English novelist .... 1882—1957
Richardson, Henry Handel (pseud. of *Henrietta Richardson Robertson*), Australian novelist .... 1880?–1946
Richardson, Henry Hobson, American architect .... 1838—1886
Richardson, Sir Owen Willans, English physicist .... 1879—1959
Richardson, Sir Ralph David, English actor .... 1902—
Richardson, Samuel, English novelist .... 1689—1761
Richelieu, de (dē rī-çhē-lyū' *or Eng.* riçh'ē-lü), **Armand Jean du Plessis, Cardinal and Duke**, Fr. statesman .... 1585—1642
Richter (rikh'tẽr), **Johann Paul Friedrich** (pseud. *Jean Paul*), German author .... 1763—1825
Richthofen, von (fọn rikht'hō-fen), **Manfred, Baron**, German aviator; ace in World War I .... 1892—1918
Rickenbacker (rik'en-bak-ẽr), **Edward Vernon**, American aviation executive; ace in World War I .... 1890—1973
Ridgway (riġ'wā), **Matthew Bunker**, American general .... 1895—
Ridley (rid'li), **Nicholas**, English bishop and martyr .... 1500?–1555
Ridpath (rid'path), **John Clark**, American historian .... 1840—1900
Riemann (rē'män), **Georg Friedrich Bernhard**, German mathematician .... 1826—1866
Rienzi (rī-en'tsī) *or* **Rienzo** (rī-en'tsō), **Niccolo Gabrini** (*Cola di Rienzi*), Roman tribune .... 1313?–1354
Riggs (rigṣ), **Lynn**, American playwright .... 1899—1954
Riis (rēs), **Jacob August**, Am. social worker, b. in Denmark .... 1849—1914
Riley (rī'li), **James Whitcomb** (*the Hoosier Poet*), American poet .. 1849—1916
Rilke (ril'ke), **Rainer Maria**, German poet, b. Prague .... 1875—1926
Rimbaud (raṅ-bō'), **Arthur**, French poet .... 1854—1891
Rimsky-Korsakov (rim'skē-kọr'sȧ-kọf), **Nikolai Andreevich**, Russian composer .... 1844—1908
Rinehart (rīn'härt), **Mary Roberts**, American novelist .... 1876—1958
Ristori (ris-tō'rī), **Adelaide, Marchioness del Grillo**, Italian actress .... 1822—1906
Ritter (rit'tẽr), **Karl**, German geographer .... 1779—1859
Rivera (rī-ve'rä), **Diego**, Mexican painter .... 1886—1957
Rivera, Miguel Primo de, *see* Primo de Rivera, Miguel.
Rizal (rī-ṣäl'), **José**, Filipino patriot and author .... 1861—1896
Riza Shah Pahlavi (rī-zä' sha pä'lȧ-vī), shah of Iran (1925–41); abdicated in favor of son, Mohammed Riza .... 1877—1944
Rizzio (rīt'tsyō) *or* **Riccio** (rīt'chō), **David**, It. musician; favorite of Mary, Queen of Scots; assassinated .... 1533?–1566
Robbia, della (del'lä rōb'byä), **Luca**, Florentine sculptor .... 1400?–1482
Robert (rob'ẽrt *or Fr.* rō-ber') **I** (*le Diable*), duke of Normandy ... ? —1035
Robert I, *see* Bruce, Robert the.
Roberts (rob'ẽrts), **David**, Scottish landscape painter .... 1796—1864
Roberts, Elizabeth Madox, American novelist and poet .... 1885—1941
Roberts, Frederick Sleigh, Earl of Kandahar, British field marshal .... 1832—1914
Roberts, Kenneth Lewis, American novelist .... 1885—1957
Roberts, Owen Josephus, associate justice of the United States Supreme Court (1930–45) .... 1875—1955
Robertson (rob'ẽrt-sŏn), **Thomas William**, Eng. dramatist .... 1829—1871
Robertson, William, Scottish historian .... 1721—1793
Robertson, Sir William, British field marshal; chief of staff (1915–18) .... 1860—1933
Robeson (rōb'sŏn), **Paul**, Am. singer and actor .... 1898—1976
Robespierre, de (dē rō-bes-pyer'), **Maximilien Marie Isidore**, French revolutionist; guillotined .... 1758—1794
Robinson (rob'in-sŏn), **Charles**, American free soil leader .... 1818—1894
Robinson, Edwin Arlington, American poet .... 1869—1935
Robinson, James Harvey, American historian .... 1863—1936
Robinson, Joseph Taylor, U.S. senator .... 1872—1937
Robinson, Lennox, Irish dramatist .... 1886—1958
Rob Roy (rob roi'), (b. *Robert Macgregor*) Scottish freebooter .... 1671—1734
Rochambeau, de (dē rō-çhäṅ-bō'), **Jean Baptiste Donatien de Vimeur, Count**, French marshal; commanded French troops supporting Washington in Am. Revolution .... 1725—1807
Rochester (roch'es-tẽr), **John Wilmot, second Earl of**, English poet .... 1647—1680
Rockefeller (rok'e-fel-lẽr), **John Davison**, American capitalist and philanthropist .... 1839—1937
Rockne (rok'nē), **Knute Kenneth**, Am. football coach .... 1888—1931
Roderick (rod'ẽr-ik), last king of the Visigoths in Spain .... ? —713?
Rodgers (rod'ġẽrṣ), **Richard**, American composer .... 1902—1979
Rodin (rō-daṅ'), **Auguste**, French sculptor .... 1840—1917
Rodney (rod'nī), **Caesar Augustus**, signer of the Declaration of Independence .... 1728—1784
Rodney, George Brydges, Baron, British admiral .... 1718—1792
Rodzinski (rod-jin'skī), **Artur**, American conductor, born in Dalmatia .... 1892—1958
Roe (rō), **Edward Payson**, American novelist .... 1838—1888
Roebling (rōb'ling), **John Augustus**, American civil engineer, born in Germany .... 1806—1869
R., Washington Augustus (*son of J.A.R.*), American engineer .. 1837—1926
Roentgen *or* **Röntgen** (rẽnt'gen), **Wilhelm Konrad**, German physicist; discovered X rays .... 1845—1923
Roerich (rẽr'ikh), **Nicholas**, Russian painter and explorer .... 1874—1947
Roethke (ret'ke), **Theodore**, American poet .... 1908—1963
Rogers (roġ'ẽrṣ), **Will** (*William Penn Adair R.*), American actor and humorist .... 1879—1935
Roget (rō-ẓe'), **Peter Mark**, English physician and lexicographer .. 1779—1869
Rohmer (rō'mẽr), **Sax** (pseud. of *Arthur Sarsfield Warde*), English writer of mystery stories .... 1883—1959
Roland de la Platière (rō-läṅ' dē lȧ plȧ-tyer'), **Manon Jeanne Philipon**, French Girondist; guillotined .... 1754—1793
Rolland (rō-läṅ'), **Romain**, French novelist, biographer, and music critic; received Nobel prize (1915) .... 1866—1944
Rollo (rol'lō) *or* **Hrolf** (hrolf), Norwegian viking; first duke of Normandy .... 860?— 931
Rölvaag (rūl'vạg), **Ole Edvart**, Am. novelist, b. in Norway .... 1876–1931?
Romains (rō-maṅ'), **Jules** (pseud. of *Louis Farigoule*), French novelist, playwright, and poet .... 1885—1972
Romanov (rō-mä'nọf), **Mikhail Feodorovich**, founder of the Russian Romanov dynasty .... 1596—1645
Romberg (rom'bẽrg), **Sigmund**, Am. composer, b. in Hungary .. 1887—1951
Römer (rẽ'mẽr), **Olaus**, Danish astronomer .... 1644—1710
Romilly (rom'il-ly), **Sir Samuel**, Eng. law reformer .... 1757—1818
Rommel (rọm'el), **Erwin**, German field marshal in World War II. 1891—1944
Romney (rom'ni), **George**, English portrait painter .... 1734—1802
Romulo (rō'mū-lō), **Carlos Pena**, Filipino statesman .... 1900—
Ronsard, de (dē rọṅ-sȧr'), **Pierre**, French poet .... 1524—1585
Röntgen, Wilhelm Konrad, *see* Roentgen.
Rooke (rook), **Sir George**, English admiral .... 1650—1709
Roon, von (fọn rōn'), **Albrecht Theodor Emil, Graf**, German general .... 1803—1879
Roosevelt (rō'ẓe-velt), **Franklin Delano**, thirty-second president of the United States (1933–45) .... 1882—1945
R., Eleanor (b. *Anna Eleanor Roosevelt*), wife of F.D.R.; newspaper columnist; delegate to U.N. 1884 1962
Roosevelt, Theodore, twenty-sixth president of the United States (1901–09) .... 1858—1919
Root (rọọt *or* root), **Elihu**, American lawyer and statesman; secretary of state (1905–09) .... 1845—1937
Root, George Frederick, American composer .... 1820—1895
Rosas, de (dẹ rō'säs), **Juan Manuel**, Argentine despot .... 1793—1877
Roscius (rosh'i-us), **Quintus**, Roman actor .... fl. B.C. 60?
Roscommon (ros'çom-mŏn), **Wentworth Dillon, Earl of**, English poet .... 1663?–1685
Rosebery (rōṣ'bẽr-y), **Archibald Philip Primrose, Earl of**, English statesman; prime minister (1894–95) .... 1847—1929
Rosecrans (rōṣ'çranṣ *or* rō'ṣē-çranṣ), **William Starke**, Union general in the Civil War .... 1819—1898
Rosenberg (rōṣ'en-berk), **Alfred**, German Nazi theoretician and politician; hanged as a war criminal .... 1893—1946
Rosenthal (rō'ṣen-täl), **Moriz**, Polish pianist .... 1862—1946
Rosenwald (rō'ṣen-wạld), **Julius**, Am. philanthropist .... 1862—1932
Ross (rọs), **Betsy** (*Elizabeth Griscom R.*), reputed maker of the first American flag .... 1752—1836
Ross, Sir James Clark, English arctic navigator and rear admiral (*nephew of J.R.*) .... 1800—1862
R., Sir John, Eng. arctic navigator and rear admiral .... 1777—1856
Ross, Sir Ronald, English physician .... 1857—1932
Rossetti (rō-set'ti), **Christina Georgina** (*sister of D.G.R.*), English poet .... 1830—1894
R., Dante Gabriel, English Pre-Raphaelite poet and painter .. 1828—1882
Rossini (rōs-sī'nī), **Gioacchino Antonio**, It. composer .... 1792—1868
Rostand (rọs-täṅ'), **Edmond**, French dramatic poet .... 1868—1918
Rostovtzeff (rō-stọf'tsef), **Michael Ivanovich**, American historian, born in Russia .... 1870—1952
Rothschild (roths'child *or Ger.* rōt'shilt), **Meyer Anselm**, German banker; founder of important banking house .... 1743—1812
R., Nathan Meyer (*son of M.A.R.*), English financier, born in Germany .... 1777—1836
Rotrou, de (dē rō-trō'), **Jean**, French dramatist .... 1609—1650
Rouault (rō-ō'), **Georges**, French artist .... 1871— 1958
Rouget de Lisle *or* **de l'Isle** (rö-ẓe' dē lil), **Claude Joseph**, French poet and soldier; wrote the *Marseillaise* .... 1760—1836
Rousseau (rō-sō'), **Henri**, French primitive painter .... 1844—1910
Rousseau, Jean Jacques, French philosopher, social theorist, and author, born in Geneva .... 1712—1778
Rousseau, Théodore, French landscape painter .... 1812—1867
Rowe (rō), **Nicholas**, Eng. dramatist and poet laureate .... 1674—1718
Rowley (rou'li), **William**, English dramatist and actor .... 1585?–1642?
Roxas (rō'hȧs), **Manuel**, first president of the republic of the Philippines (1946–48) .... 1892—1948
Royce (roic), **Josiah**, Am. philosopher and educator .... 1855—1916
Rubens (rụ'benṣ), **Peter Paul**, Flemish painter .... 1577—1640
Rubinstein (rụ'bin-stīn), **Anton**, Russian pianist and composer . 1829—1894
Rubinstein, Artur, Polish pianist in America .... 1889?—
Rückert (rük'ẽrt), **Friedrich**, German poet and Orientalist .... 1788—1866
Rudolph (rụ'dọlf) **I** (*of Hapsburg*), Holy Roman emperor; founder of the House of Hapsburg .... 1218—1291
Rumford (rum'fŏrd), **Benjamin Thompson, Count**, British physicist and executive in Bavaria, b. in America .... 1753—1814
Rundstedt, von (fọn rụnt'shtet), **Karl Rudolf Gerd**, German field marshal in World War II .... 1875—1953
Runeberg (rụ'ne-ber-y), **Johan Ludvig**, Finnish poet .... 1804—1877
Rupert (rụ'pẽrt), **Prince**, count palatine of the Rhine and duke of Bavaria; soldier and admiral, b. in Prague .... 1619—1682
Rurik (rụr'ik), Scandinavian leader, considered founder of the Russian monarchy .... ? — 879
Rush (rush), **Benjamin**, Am. physician and patriot .... 1745—1813
Ruskin (rus'kin), **John**, English art critic, author, and social theorist .... 1819—1900
Russell (rus'sel), **Bertrand, third Earl**, English philosopher and mathematician .... 1872—1970
Russell, Elizabeth Mary, Countess (pseud. *Elizabeth*). (b. *Mary Annette Beauchamp*) English novelist .... 1866—1941
Russell, George William (pseud. *A.E.*), Irish poet .... 1867—1935
Russell, John, first Earl, English statesman; prime minister (1846–52, 1865–66) .... 1792—1878
Russell, Lillian (b. *Helen Louise Leonard*), American singer and actress .... 1861—1922
Ruth (rụth), **George Herman** (*Babe Ruth*), American baseball player .... 1895—1948
Rutherford (ruth'ẽr-fŏrd), **Ernest, Baron**, Brit. physicist .... 1871—1937
Rutherford, Samuel, Scottish theologian .... 1600—1661
Rutledge (rut'leġ), **John**, American jurist and statesman .... 1739—1800
Rutledge, Wiley Blount, associate justice of the U.S. Supreme Court (1943–49) .... 1894—1949
Ruysdael (rois'däl), **Jacob**, Dutch painter .... 1628—1681
Ruyter, de (dē roi'tẽr), **Michel A.**, Dutch admiral .... 1607—1676
Ryder (rȳ'dẽr), **Albert Pinkham**, American painter .... 1847—1917
Rykov (rē'kọf), **Aleksey Ivanovich**, Russian political leader; executed for treason .... 1881—1938
Rymer (rȳ-mẽr), **Thomas**, English critic and historian .... 1638—1714

S

Saadia ben Joseph (sä'dyä ben jō'ṣef), Jewish theologian and philosopher in Babylonia .... 892?— 942
Saarinen (sär'i-nen), **Eero**, American architect, b. in Finland .. 1910—1961
S., (Gottlieb) Eliel, Finnish architect (*father of E.S.*) .... 1873—1950
Saavedra Lamas (sä-vẹ'thrä lä'mäs), **Carlos**, Argentine statesman; received Nobel peace prize (1936) .... 1880—1959

Sabatini (säb-ä-tē'nē), **Rafael**, English novelist, b. in Italy......1875—1950
Sabin (sā'bin), **Albert B(ruce)**, American physician and bacteriologist, b. in Russia......1906—
Sabin, Florence Rena, American anatomist......1871—1953
Sacchetti (säc-ḳhet'tē), **Franco**, It. poet and novelist......1335?–1400
Sacchini (säc-ḳhē'nē), **Antonio Maria Gasparo**, Italian composer.1734—1786
Sacco (saç'cō), **Nicola**, It. anarchist in U.S.; together with B. Vanzetti, executed for murder despite international protest that they were victims of political bias......1891—1927
Sachs (säḳhs), **Hans** (*Shoemaker of Nuremberg*), German poet....1494—1576
Sackville (sak'vil), **Charles, sixth Earl of Dorset**, English wit and poet......1638—1706
Sackville, Thomas, Baron Buckhurst and Earl of Dorset, English statesman and poet......1536—1608
Sackville-West (-west'), **Victoria** (*Mrs. Harold Nicolson*), English novelist and poet......1892—1962
Sacy, de (dē sȧ-sē'), **Antoine Isaac, Baron Sylvestre**, French Orientalist......1758—1838
Sadat (sä-dät'), **Anwar el-**, Egyptian president (1970–81)......1918—1981
Sade, de (dē sȧd'), **Donatien Alphonse François, Count** (*the Marquis de Sade*), French libertine and novelist......1740—1814
Sadi *or* **Saadi** (sä-dē'), Persian poet......1184?–1291
Sage (sāj), **Russell**, American capitalist......1816—1906
Saint Clair (sānt ḳlãr'), **Arthur**, American general......1734—1818
Sainte-Beuve (sant-bųv'), **Charles Augustin**, French critic......1804—1869
Saint-Évremond, de (dē san-tevr-mǫn'), **Charles de Marguetel de Saint-Denis, Seigneur**, French critic......1613?–1703
Saint Exupéry, de (dē sant eg-zū-pẹ-rē'), **Antoine**, French aviator and writer......1900—1944
Saint-Gaudens (sānt'gą'denṣ), **Augustus**, American sculptor...1848—1907
Saint Just, de (dē san-zūst'), **Louis**, Fr. revolutionist......1767—1794
Saint Laurent (san lǫ-rän'), **Louis Stephen**, Canadian statesman; prime minister (1948–57)......1882—1973
Saint-Martin, de (dē san-mȧr-tan'), **Louis Claude, Marquis** (pseud. *Unknown Philosopher*), French mystic......1743—1803
Saint-Pierre, de (-pyer'), **Jacques Henri Bernadin**, French author......1737—1814
Saint-Saëns (-säns'), **Charles Camille**, Fr. composer......1835—1921
Saintsbury (sānts'bũr-y), **George Edward Bateman**, English literary critic......1845—1933
Saint-Simon, de (dē san-sē-mǫn'), **Claude Henri de Rouvroy, Comte**, French socialist......1760—1825
Saint-Simon, de, Louis de Rouvroy, Duc, French writer of memoirs......1675—1755
Saionji (sī-ōn'jē), **Kimmochi, Prince**, Japanese statesman......1850—1940
Saki (sä'ki), *see* Munro, Hector Hugh.
Saladin (sal'ȧ-din), sultan of Egypt; withstood the Crusaders....1137—1193
Salazar (sȧ-lä-zär'), **Antonio de Oliveira**, Portuguese statesman; prime minister and dictator (1932–68)......1889—1970
Salieri (sä-lē-ẹ'rē), **Antonio**, Italian composer......1750—1825
Salinas (sä-lē'näs), **Pedro**, Spanish poet and critic......1892—1951
Salinger (sal'in-jẽr), **J(erome) D(avid)**, American novelist and short-story writer......1919—
Salisbury (sąlṣ'bũr-y), **Robert Arthur Talbot Gascoyne-Cecil, third Marquis of**, English statesman......1830—1903
Salk (salk), **Jonas Edward**, American epidemiologist and physician: discovered anti-polio vaccine......1914—
Sallust (sal'lust), (*Caius Sallustius Crispus*) Roman historian.B.C. 86— 34
Salmasius (sal-mā'shi-us), **Claudius** (Latin form of *Claude de Saumaise*), French scholar......1588—1653
Salten (ṣäl'ten), **Felix**, Austrian novelist......1869—1945
Saltus (sąl'tus), **Edgar Evertson**, American author......1858—1921
Salvini (säl-vē'nē), **Tommasco**, Italian tragedian......1829—1915
Sampson (samp'sŏn), **William T.**, American rear admiral......1840—1902
Sand (sän *or Eng.* sand), **George** (pseud. of *Amantine Lucile Aurore Dupin, Baronne Dudevant*), French novelist......1804—1876
Sandburg (sand'bũrg), **Carl**, Am. poet and biographer......1878—1967
Sandeau (sän-dō'), **Jules** (*Léonard Sylvain Jules S.*), French novelist......1811—1883
Sandys (sandṣ), **George**, English traveler and poet......1578—1644
Sanger (sañ'gẽr), **Margaret**, American birth-control advocate....1883—1966
Sankey (sañk'i), **Ira David**, American evangelist and singer....1840—1908
San Martín, de (dẹ sän mär-tēn'), **José**, South American revolutionary leader......1778—1850
Santa Anna *or* **Ana, de** (dẹ sän'tä ä'nä), **Antonio López**, Mexican president and general......1795?–1876
Santayana (sän-tä-yä'nä), **George**, American philosopher and poet, born in Spain; moved to Italy (1923)......1863—1952
Santos-Dumont (sän-tōs'dū-mǫn'), **Alberto**, Brazilian aeronaut in France......1873—1932
Sappho (saf'ō), Greek lyric poetess, born in Lesbos......fl. B.C. 600?
Sarasate, de (dẹ sä-rä-sä'tẹ), **Pablo Martin Meliton**, Spanish violinist......1844—1908
Sardanapalus (sär-dȧ-na'pȧ-lus), king of Assyria......fl. B.C. 900?
Sardou (sär-dö'), **Victorien**, French dramatist......1831—1908
Sargent (sär'ġent), **John Singer**, American painter......1856—1925
Sargon (sär'gŏn) **II**, king of Assyria......B.C. ? — 705
Saroyan (sȧ-roi'ăn), **William**, American short-story writer, playwright, and novelist......1908—1981
Sarpi (sär'pē), **Paolo**, Italian ecclesiastic and historian......1552—1623
Sarto, del (del sär'tō), **Andrea**, Florentine painter......1486—1531
Sarton (sär'tŏn), **George**, Am. historian of science, b. in Belgium.1884—1956
Sartre (sȧr'tr), **Jean Paul**, Fr. philosopher and author......1905—1980
Sassoon (sas-sǫǫn'), **Siegfried**, Eng. poet and novelist......1886—1967
Satie (sȧ-tē'), **Erik**, French composer......1866—1925
Savage (sav'āġ), **Richard**, English poet......1697?–1743
Savary (sȧ-vȧ-rē'), **Anne Jean Marie René, Duc de Rovigo**, French general and diplomat......1774—1833
Savigny, von (fǫn sȧ-vē-nyē'), **Friedrich Karl**, German jurist...1779—1861
Savile (sav'il), **Sir Henry**, English mathematician and scholar. 1549—1622
Savonarola (sav"ō-nȧ-rō'lȧ), **Girolamo**, Italian reformer and pulpit orator; executed for heresy......1452—1498
Saxe, de (dē saks), **Maurice, Count**, marshal of France......1696—1750
Saxo Grammaticus (sak'sō grȧ-ma'ti-ḳus), Danish historian...1150?–1220?
Say (sā), **Jean Baptiste**, French economist......1767—1832
Sayers (sā'ẽrṣ), **Dorothy Leigh**, English writer of detective fiction.1893—1957
Scaevola (sēv'ō-lȧ), **Caius Mucius**, legendary Roman hero.fl.B.C. 6th cent.?
Scaliger (sḳal'i-ġẽr), **Joseph Justus**, French scholar......1540—1609
S., Julius Caesar (*father of J.J.S.*), Italian Latin critic and philologist in France......1484—1558

Scanderbeg (sḳan'dẽr-beg), (b. *George Castriota*) Albanian patriot and leader......1403?–1468
Scarlatti (sḳär-lät'tē), **Alessandro**, Italian composer......1659—1725
S., Domenico (*son of A.S.*), Italian composer......1685—1757
Scarron (sḳȧ-rǫn'), **Paul**, French dramatist and comic writer....1610—1660
Schacht (shäḳht), **Hjalmar**, German financier; president of the Reichsbank (1923–30, 1934–39)......1877—1970
Schadow (shä'dō), **Johann Gottfried**, German sculptor......1764—1850
Schaff (shäf), **Philip**, Am. biblical scholar, b. in Switzerland......1819—1893
Scharwenka (shär-veñ'kä), **Franz Xaver**, German composer and pianist (*brother of L.P.S.*)......1850—1924
S., Ludwig Philipp, German composer and teacher......1847—1917
Scheele (shẹ'le), **Karl Wilhelm**, Swedish chemist......1742—1786
Scheffel, von (fǫn shef'fel), **Joseph Viktor**, German poet and novelist......1826—1886
Scheffer (she-fer'), **Ary**, Dutch painter in Paris......1795—1858
Scheiner (shīn'ẽr), **Christoph**, German Jesuit and astronomer..1575?–1650
Schelling (shel'ling), **Ernest Henry**, American composer......1876—1939
Schelling, von (fǫn), **Friedrich Wilhelm Joseph**, German philosopher......1775—1854
Scherer (sher'ẽr), **Edmond Henri Adolphe**, French literary critic......1815—1889
Schiaparelli (sḳhyä-pä-rel'lē), **Giovanni Virginio**, Italian astronomer......1835—1910
Schick (shik), **Béla**, American pediatrician, b. in Hungary......1877—1967
Schiller, von (fǫn shil'ẽr), **Johann Christoph Friedrich**, German poet and dramatist......1759—1805
Schinkel (shink'el), **Karl Friedrich**, German architect......1781—1841
Schlegel, von (fǫn shlẹ'gel), **August Wilhelm**, German critic and poet......1767—1845
S., v., Friedrich (*brother of A.W.v.S.*), German philosopher and author......1772—1829
Schleiermacher (shlī'ẽr-mäkh-ẽr), **Friedrich Ernst Daniel**, German theologian......1768—1834
Schlesinger (shlẹ'siñ-gẽr), **Arthur Meier**, Am. historian......1888—1965
S., Arthur Meier, Jr. (*son of A.M.S.*), American historian....1917—
Schley (slȳ), **Winfield Scott**, American rear admiral......1839—1911
Schliemann (shlē'män), **Heinrich**, German archaeologist......1822—1890
Schmeling (shmẹ'ling), **Max**, German prize fighter; world heavyweight champion (1930–32)......1905—
Schnabel (shnä'bel), **Artur**, Austrian pianist......1882—1951
Schnitzler (shnits'lẽr), **Arthur**, Austrian novelist and playwright.1862—1931
Schofield (sḳō'fēld), **John McAllister**, American general......1831—1906
Schomberg (shom'bẽrg), **Friedrich Armand Hermann, Duke of**, German soldier of fortune in England and elsewhere......1615—1690
Schomburgk (shom'bũrk), **Sir Robert Hermann**, English traveler, born in Germany......1804—1865
Schönberg (shẽn'bẽrk), **Arnold**, Austrian composer......1874—1951
Schongauer (shōn'gou-ẽr), **Martin**, German engraver......1445—1491
Schopenhauer (shō'pen-hou-ẽr), **Arthur**, German philosopher..1788—1860
Schreiner (shrīn'ẽr), **Olive** (*Mrs. Cronwright*), South African author......1855—1920
Schröder (shrẽd'ẽr), **Friedrich Ludwig**, German dramatist......1744—1816
Schrödinger (shrẽ'ding-ẽr), **Erwin**, Austrian physicist......1887—1961
Schubert (shů'bert), **Franz**, Austrian composer......1797—1828
Schuman (shů-män'), **Robert**, French statesman......1886—1963
Schuman (shů'măn), **William**, American composer......1910—
Schumann (shů'män), **Robert**, German composer......1810—1856
Schumann-Heink (-hīnk'), **Ernestine**, American contralto, born in Austria......1861—1936
Schurman (shųr'măn), **Jacob Gould**, American educator and diplomat......1854—1942
Schurz (shųrts), **Carl**, Am. general, statesman, b. in Germany...1829—1906
Schuschnigg, von (fǫn shųsh'nik), **Kurt**, Austrian statesman; chancellor (1934–38)......1897—1977
Schütz (shǫǫts), **Heinrich**, German composer......1585—1672
Schuyler (sḳhȳ'lẽr), **Philip**, Am. general and statesman......1733—1804
Schwab (shwäb), **Charles Michael**, American steel mfr......1862—1939
Schwanthaler (shvän'tä-lẽr), **Ludwig Michael**, German sculptor.1802—1848
Schwartz (shwąrts), **Maurice**, American Yiddish actor and producer, born in Russia......1889—1960
Schweitzer (shvī'tsẽr), **Albert**, Alsatian physician, philosopher, theologian, and musician, in Fr. Africa......1875—1965
Scipio (sip'i-ō), **Publius Cornelius** (*Scipio Africanus Major*), Roman general......B.C.237?— 183
S., Publius Cornelius (*Scipio Aemilianus Africanus Minor*), (*grandson, through adoption*) Roman general......B.C.185?— 129
Scopas (sḳō'pȧs), Greek sculptor......fl. B.C. 4th cent.
Scott (sḳot), **Cyril Meir**, English composer and writer......1879—1970
Scott, Robert Falcon, English naval officer and explorer; reached South Pole on Jan. 18, 1912......1868—1912
Scott, Thomas, English theologian......1747—1821
Scott, Sir Walter, Scottish novelist and poet......1771—1832
Scott, Winfield, American lieutenant general......1786—1866
Scriabin (sḳryä'bĭn), **Aleksandr Nikolayevich**, Russian composer......1872—1915
Scribe (sḳrīb), **Augustin, Eugène**, French dramatist......1791—1861
Scripps (sḳrips), **Edward Wyllis**, American newspaper publisher.1854—1926
Scudéry, de (dē sḳů-dẹ-rē'), **Madeleine**, French author......1607—1701
Seaborg (sē'bǫrg), **Glenn T(heodore)**, American nuclear chemist.1912—
Sebastian (se-bas'chăn), **Saint**, Roman Christian martyr......255? —288
Sebastian, king of Portugal......1554—1578
Secchi (seç'ḳhē), **Pietro Angelo**, Italian astronomer......1818—1878
Sedgwick (seġ'wik), **Anne Douglas**, American novelist......1873—1935
Sedgwick, Catharine Maria, American novelist......1789—1867
Sedgwick, John, Union general in the Civil War......1813—1864
Sedley (sed'li), **Sir Charles**, English dramatist......1639—1701
Seeger (sē'gẽr), **Alan**, American poet......1888—1916
Seeley (sē'li), **Sir John Robert**, English historian......1834—1895
Segovia (sẹ-gō'vyä), **Andrés**, Sp. concert guitarist......1894—
Ségur, de (dē sẹ-gůr'), **Louis Philippe, Comte**, French diplomat and historian (*son of P.H. de S.*)......1753—1830
S., de, Philippe Henri, Marquis, marshal of France......1724—1801
S., de, Philippe Paul, Comte (*son of L.P. de S.*), French general and historian......1780—1873
Seitz (sīts), **Don Carlos**, Am. journalist, biographer......1862—1935
Selden (sel'den), **John**, English lawyer and scholar......1584—1654
Seldes (sel'des), **George**, Am. journalist and writer......1890—1970
S., Gilbert (*brother of G.S.*), Am. critic, author......1893—1970
Seleucus (sē-lū'ḳus) **I** (*Nicator*), first king of Syria......B.C.365?—281?

Seleucus II (*Callinicus*), king of Syria ....?—B.C.226
Seligman (sel'ig-măn), **Edwin Robert Anderson,** American political economist ....1861—1939
Selim (sē'lim) **III,** sultan of Turkey ....1761—1808
Selkirk (sel'kirk), **Alexander,** Scottish sailor; the original Robinson Crusoe ....1676—1721
Sembrich (şem'brikh), **Marcella,** Am. soprano, b. in Austria ....1858—1935
Semiramis (se-mir'á-mis), queen of Assyria ....fl. B.C. 1250?
Semmes (semş), **Raphael,** Am. Confederate naval officer ....1809—1877
Sénancour, de (dē se-nän-çör'), **Étienne Pivert,** French author .1770—1846
Seneca (sen'e-çá), **Lucius Annaeus,** Roman Stoic, dramatist, and statesman ....B.C. 4?–A.D.65
Senefelder (şe'ne-fel-dēr), **Aloys,** German inventor of lithography .1771—1834
Senior (sēn'yōr), **Nassau,** English political economist ....1790—1864
Sennacherib (se-naçh'ēr-ib), king of Assyria ....?—B.C. 681
Serao (se-rä'ō), **Matilde,** Italian novelist ....1856—1927
Serkin (sūr'kin), **Rudolf,** American pianist, b. in Bohemia ....1903—
Sertorius (sēr-tō'ri-us), **Quintus,** Roman general ....?—B.C. 72
Servetus (sēr-vē'tus), **Michael,** Spanish physician and theologian; burned at the stake ....1511—1553
Service (sēr'vic), **Robert William,** Canadian poet ....1874—1958
Sessions (sesh'ōnş), **Roger Huntington,** Am. composer ....1896—
Seton (sē'tōn), **Saint Elizabeth Ann** (*Mother Seton*), Roman Catholic educator; first native-born American saint (1974) ....1774—1821
Seton, Ernest Thompson, Am. writer and painter ....1860—1946
Seurat (sū-rá'), **Georges,** French painter ....1859—1891
Severus (sē-vē'rus), **Lucius Septimius,** Roman emperor ....146— 211
Sevier (sē-vēr'), **John,** American soldier and governor ....1745—1815
Sévigné, de (dē sā-vē-nyā'), **Marie de Rabutin-Chantal, Marquise,** French beauty and letter writer ....1626—1696
Sewall (sū'ál), **Samuel,** American judge, born in England; sat in Salem witchcraft trials (1692) ....1652—1730
Seward (sū'ārd), **Anna,** English poet ....1742—1809
Seward, William Henry, American statesman; secretary of state (1861–69) ....1801—1872
Seydlitz, von (fon şyd'lits), **Friedrich Wilhelm,** Prussian general .1721—1773
Seymour (sē'mōr), **Horatio,** American political leader ....1810—1886
Seymour, Jane, third wife of Henry VIII ....1509—1537
Sforza (sfor'tsä), **Carlo, Count,** Italian anti-Fascist statesman ..1873—1952
Shackleton (shak'l-tōn), **Sir Ernest Henry,** British antarctic explorer ....1874—1922
Shadwell (shad'wel), **Thomas,** English dramatist and poet laureate ....1642?–1692
Shafter (shaf'tēr), **William Rufus,** American general ....1835—1906
Shaftesbury (shafts'būr-y), **Anthony Ashley Cooper, first Earl of,** English statesman ....1621—1683
S., Anthony Ashley Cooper, third Earl of (*grandson of A.A.C.S.*), English moral philosopher and writer ....1671—1713
Shahn (shän), **Ben(jamin),** American painter, b. in Lithuania ..1898—1969
Shakespeare *or* **Shakspere** (shāk'spēr), **William** (*the Bard of Avon*), English dramatist and poet ....1564—1616
Shaler (shāl'ēr), **Nathaniel Southgate,** Am. geologist ....1841—1906
Shapley (shap'li), **Harlow,** American astronomer ....1885—1972
Sharp (shärp), **Dallas Lore,** Am. educator and author ....1870—1929
Sharp, Granville, Eng. abolitionist and philanthropist ....1735—1813
Sharp, William (pseud. *Fiona Macleod*), Scottish poet and author .1855—1905
Shaw (sha), **Albert,** American editor and writer ....1857—1947
Shaw, Anna Howard, American suffragist, b. in England ....1847—1919
Shaw, George Bernard, Irish dramatist; received Nobel prize (1925) ....1856—1950
Shaw, Henry Wheeler (pseud. *Josh Billings*), American humorist .1818—1885
Shaw, Irwin, American playwright and novelist ....1913—
Shaw, Thomas Edward, *see* Lawrence, Thomas Edward.
Shays (shāş), **Daniel,** American soldier; leader in Shays' rebellion (1786–87) ....1747—1825
Sheean (shē'ăn), **Vincent,** Am. journalist and author ....1899—
Sheen (shēn), **Fulton John,** American Roman Catholic clergyman, orator, and writer ....1895—
Sheldon (shel'dōn), **Edward Brewster,** Am. dramatist ....1886—1946
Shelley (shel'li), **Mary Wollstonecraft** (b. *Godwin; wife of P.B.S.*), English author ....1797—1851
S., Percy Bysshe, English poet ....1792—1822
Shenstone (shen'stōn), **William,** English poet ....1714—1763
Sheraton (sher'á-tōn), **Thomas,** English furniture designer and cabinetmaker ....1751—1806
Sheridan (sher'i-dăn), **Philip Henry,** Union general in the Civil War ....1831—1888
Sheridan, Richard Brinsley Butler, Irish dramatist and politician ....1751—1816
Sherman (shēr'măn), **John** (*brother of W.T.S.*), Am. statesman ..1823—1900
Sherman, Roger, American statesman; signer of the Declaration of Independence ....1721—1793
Sherman, Stuart Pratt, American critic and editor ....1881—1926
Sherman, William Tecumseh (*brother of J.S.*), Union general in the Civil War ....1820—1891
Sherriff (sher'rif), **Robert Cedric,** English playwright ....1896—
Sherrington (sher'ring-tōn), **Sir Charles Scott,** English physiologist; shared Nobel prize (1932) ....1857—1952
Sherwood (shēr'wood), **Robert Emmet,** American dramatist and biographer ....1896—1955
Shillaber (shil'á-bēr), **Benjamin Penhallow,** American humorist .1814—1890
Shirley (shir'li), **James,** English dramatist ....1596—1666
Sholokhov (shol'ō-khōf), **Mikhail,** Russian novelist ....1905—
Shostakovich (shos-tá-kō'vich), **Dmitri,** Russian composer ....1906—1975
Shotwell (shot'wel), **James Thomson,** American historian ....1874—1965
Sibelius (si-be'li-us), **Jean Julius Christian,** Finnish composer .1865—1957
Sickles (sik'lş), **Daniel Edgar,** Am. general and politician ....1825—1914
Siddons (sid'dōnş), **Sarah Kemble,** English actress ....1755—1831
Sidney (sid'ni), **Algernon,** English republican; beheaded ....1622—1683
Sidney, Sir Philip, Eng. author, statesman, and soldier ....1554—1586
Siemens (sē'mens *or Eng.* sē'menş), **Sir William** (b. *Karl Wilhelm von S.*), English inventor, born in Germany ....1823—1883
Sienkiewicz (shen-kye'vich), **Henryk,** Polish author ....1846—1916
Sigel (sī'gel), **Franz,** Baden revolutionist and Union general in the Civil War ....1824—1902
Sigismund (sig'is-mund *or G.* şi'gis-munt), Holy Roman emperor .1368—1437
Signorelli (sī-nyō-rel'li), **Luca,** Italian painter ....1441—1523
Sigourney (sig'ūr-ni), **Lydia Huntley,** American author ....1791—1865
Sigsbee (sigs'bi), **Charles Dwight,** American naval officer ....1845—1923
Sikorsky (si-kor'sky), **Igor,** American aeronautical engineer, born in Russia ....1889—1972
Silliman (sil'li-măn), **Benjamin,** American scientist ....1779—1864
Silone (sī-lō'ne), **Ignazio** (pseud. of *Secondo Tranquilli*), Italian novelist and anti-Fascist writer ....1900—1978
Silverius (sil-ver'i-us), **Saint,** Pope ....? — 537
Simenon (sī-me-noṅ'), **Georges,** Belgian novelist and short-story writer ....1903—
Simeon (sĭm'e-ŏn), **II,** king of Bulgaria (1943–46) ....1937—
Simmel (şim'el), **Georg,** German sociologist and philosopher ....1858—1918
Simms (simş), **William Gilmore,** American novelist ....1806—1870
Simon (sī'mōn), **John Allsebrook, first Viscount,** English lawyer and statesman ....1873—1954
Simon (sī-moṅ'), **Jules François Suisse,** French philosopher and statesman ....1814—1896
Simon Maccabaeus (sī'mōn maç-çá-bē'us), high priest of the Jews .?—B.C.135
Simonds (sī'mŏndş), **Frank Herbert,** Am. journalist ....1878—1936
Simonides (sī-mon'i-dēş) **of Amorgus,** Greek poet ....fl. B.C. 660?
Simonides of Ceos Greek lyric poet ....B.C.556?—468?
Sims, William Snowden, Am. admiral in World War I ....1858—1936
Sinclair (siṅ'çlâr), **May,** English novelist ....1865?–1946
Sinclair, Upton Beall, American novelist and socialist ....1878—1968
Sinding (sin'ding), **Christian,** Norwegian composer ....1856—1941
Singer (sing'ēr), **Isaac Bashevis,** Polish writer in Yiddish, in the United States ....1904—
Singer, Isaac Merritt, American inventor and manufacturer; improved the sewing machine ....1811—1875
Siqueiros (sē-kā'rōs), **(José) David Alfaro,** Mexican painter ....1896—1974
Sismondi, de (dē sis-moṅ-dī' *or Eng.* sis-mon'di), **Jean Charles Leonard Simonde,** Swiss historian and economist ....1773—1842
Sitting Bull (sit'ing bul'), chief of the Sioux Indians of Dakota; defeated General Custer (1876) ....1837—1890
Sitwell (sit'wel), **Edith** (*sister of O.S. and S.S.*), English poet and critic ....1887—1964
S., Sir Osbert, English poet and author ....1892—1969
S., Sacheverell, English poet and critic ....1897—
Sixtus (siks'tus) **IV,** (*Francesco della Rovere*), Pope ....1414—1484
Skeat (skēt), **Walter William,** English philologist ....1835—1912
Skelton (skel'tōn), **John,** English poet and satirist ....1460?–1529
Skinner (skin'nēr), **Cornelia Otis** (*daughter of O.S.*), American actress, disease, and writer ....1901—1979
S., Otis, American actor ....1858—1942
Slidell (slī-del'), **John,** Am. diplomat and politician ....1793—1871
Sloan (slōn), **John,** American painter and etcher ....1871—1951
Slocum (slō'cum), **Henry Warner,** American general ....1827?—1894
Slosson, (slos'sōn), **Edwin Emery,** Am. scientist and writer ....1865—1929
Smart (smärt), **Charles Allen,** American novelist ....1904—
Smart, Christopher, English poet ....1722—1771
Smetana (sme'tä-nä), **Friedrich,** Bohemian composer ....1824—1884
Smigly-Rydz (smig'ly-rydz), **Edward,** Polish statesman ....1886—1943?
Smiles (smīlş), **Samuel,** Scottish biographer and writer ....1812—1904
Smith (smith), **Adam,** Scottish political economist ....1723—1790
Smith, Alfred Emanuel, Am. political leader; governor of New York; Democratic presidential nominee (1928) ....1873—1944
Smith, Edmund Kirby, Am. Confederate general ....1824—1893
Smith, Francis Hopkinson, American painter and author ....1838—1915
Smith, George, English Assyriologist ....1840—1876
Smith, Gerrit, American antislavery agitator ....1797—1874
Smith, Goldwin, English historian ....1823—1910
Smith, Horace, English parodist and novelist ....1779—1849
S., James (*brother of H.S.*), English parodist ....1775—1839
Smith, Jedediah Strong, American explorer and trader ....1799—1831
Smith, John, Eng. adventurer and colonist in America ....1580—1631
Smith, Joseph, American founder of the Mormon sect ....1805—1844
Smith, Lillian, American writer ....1897—1966
Smith, Logan Pearsall, American author in England ....1865—1946
Smith, Melancton, American rear admiral ....1810—1893
Smith, Preserved, American historian ....1880—1941
Smith, Seba (pseud. *Major Jack Downing*), American humorist ....1792—1868
Smith, Sydney, English clergyman and satirical writer ....1771—1845
Smith, Thorne, American humorous novelist ....1892—1934
Smith, Walter Bedell, American general; chief of staff for General Eisenhower (1942–45); ambassador to Soviet Union (1946–49) ..1895—1961
Smith, William, English geologist ....1769—1839
Smith, Sir William, English classical scholar ....1813—1894
Smith, William Robertson, Scottish biblical critic ....1846—1894
Smithson (smith'sōn), **James,** English chemist; founder of the Smithsonian Institution at Washington ....1765—1829
Smollett (smol'let), **Tobias,** Scottish novelist ....1721—1771
Smoot (smoot), **Reed,** U.S. senator ....1862—1941
Smuts (smuts), **Jan Christiaan,** South African general and statesman; prime minister (1919–24, 1939–48) ....1870—1950
Snowden (snō'den), **Philip, first Viscount,** Brit. statesman ....1864—1937
Sobieski (sō-byes'ki), **John,** *see* John III.
Socinus (sō-cī'nus), **Faustus** (b. *Fausto Sozzini*), It. religious reformer and promoter of Socinianism ....1539—1604
S., Laelius (b. *Lelio Sozzini*), (*uncle of F.S.*) It. religious reformer and originator of Socinianism ....1525—1562
Socrates (soç'rá-tēş), Athenian philosopher ....B.C. 469— 399
Sodoma, Il (il so-dō'mä), (*Giovanni Antonio Bazzi*) Italian painter .1477?–1549
Solís, de (de sō-līs'), **Antonio,** Spanish historian and poet ....1610—1686
Solís, de, Juan Díaz, Spanish navigator ....? —1516
Solomon (sol'ō-mōn), king of Israel ....B.C.10th cent.
Solon (sō'lōn), Athenian statesman and lawgiver ....B.C.639?— 559
Solvay (sol'vā *or* sol-vā'), **Ernest,** Belgian chemist ....1838—1922
Solyman (sol'y-măn), *see* Suleiman.
Solzhenitsyn (sôl-zhe-nēt'sin), **Aleksandr Isayevich,** Russian author; exiled 1974 ....1918—
Somervell (sŏm'ēr-vel), **Brehon Burke,** American general ....1892—1955
Somerville (sŏm'ēr-vil), **William,** English poet ....1675—1742
Somoza (sō-mō'sä), **Anastasio,** president of Nicaragua (1937–47, 1950–56) ....1896—1956
Sontag (şon'täk), **Henrietta, Countess Rossi,** German singer ..1806—1854
Soong (sooṅg), a prominent Chinese family, including Mme. Sun Yat-sen, Mme. Chiang Kai-shek, and Mme. H. H. Kung, sisters, and their brother (*following*):
S., T. V. (*Soong Tse-vung*), Chinese statesman ....1894—1971
Sophia (sō-fī'á), **Princess,** regent of Russia (1682–89) ....1657—1704
Sophocles (sof'ō-çlēş), Greek tragic dramatist ....B.C.496?— 406
Sorel (sō-rel'), **Albert,** French historian ....1842—1906
Sorokin (sō-rō'kin), **Pitirim Alexandrovitch,** American sociologist, born in Russia ....1889—1968

Sothern (sŏth'ērn), **Edward Askew**, English actor ... 1826—1881
S., E. H. (*Edward Hugh Sothern*), (*son of E.A.S.*) American actor. 1859—1933
Sousa (sö'sȧ), **John Philip**, American bandmaster and composer. 1854—1932
South (south), **Robert**, English clergyman ... 1634—1716
Southerne (suth'ērn), **Thomas**, English dramatist ... 1660—1746
Southey (south'i *or* suth'i), **Robert**, English poet laureate and author ... 1774—1843
Southwell (south'wel), **Robert**, English poet ... 1561?–1595
Spaak (späk), **Paul Henri**, Belgian statesman; prime minister (1938–39, 1947–49); foreign minister (1938–49) ... 1899—1972
Spaatz (späts), **Carl**, Am. general; commanded U.S. air forces bombing Germany (1944) and Japan (1945) ... 1891—1974
Spada (spä'dä), **Lionello**, Italian painter ... 1576—1622
Spagnoletto, Lo (lō spän-yō-let'tō), *see* Ribera, José.
Spalding (spạld'ing), **Albert**, American violinist ... 1888—1953
Sparks (spärks), **Jared**, American biographer, historian, and educator ... 1789—1866
Spartacus (spär'tȧ-çus), Roman gladiator; leader of a rebellion of slaves against Rome ... ? —B.C.71
Spee, von (fọn shpę'), **Maximilian, Count**, German admiral in World War I ... 1861—1914
Speed (spēd), **John**, English historian ... 1550?–1629
Speke (spēk), **John Hanning**, English African explorer; discoverer of the source of the Nile ... 1827—1864
Spellman (spel'măn), **Francis Joseph, Cardinal**, American Roman Catholic archbishop of New York ... 1889—1967
Spencer (spen'cēr), **Herbert**, English philosopher ... 1820—1903
Spender (spend'ēr), **Stephen**, English poet and critic ... 1909—
Spengler (shpeṅ'lēr), **Oswald**, German philosopher ... 1880—1936
Spenser (spen'sēr), **Edmund**, English poet ... 1552?–1599
Sperry (sper'ry), **Elmer Ambrose**, American inventor ... 1860—1930
Spielhagen (shpēl'häg-en), **Friedrich**, German novelist ... 1829—1911
Spingarn (spin'gärn), **Joel Elias**, Am. literary critic ... 1875—1939
Spinola, de (dę spī'nō-lȧ), **Ambrosio, Marquis**, Spanish general. 1569—1630
Spinoza (spi-nō'zȧ), **Baruch** *or* **Benedict**, Dutch philosopher ... 1632—1677
Spitteler (shpit'te-lēr), **Carl**, Swiss poet ... 1845—1924
Spock (späk), **Benjamin (McLane)**, American pediatrician, ęducator, and writer of books on child care ... 1903—
Spofford (spof'fŏrd), **Ainsworth Rand**, Am. librarian ... 1825—1908
Spofford, Harriet Elizabeth, American novelist ... 1835—1921
Spohr (shpōr), **Ludwig**, German composer and violinist ... 1784—1859
Spottiswoode (spot'tis-wood), **John**, Scot. archbishop ... 1565—1639
Spurgeon (spŭr'gŏn), **Charles Haddon**, English Baptist preacher. 1834—1892
Staël-Holstein, de (dē stäl'ōl-stań' *or Eng.* stä'el-hōl'stin), **Anne Louise Germaine Necker, Baronne** (*Madame de Staël*), French author ... 1766—1817
Stafford (staf'fŏrd), **William Howard, Viscount**, English statesman; executed ... 1614—1680
Stalin (stä'lin), **Joseph Vissarionovich** (b. *Dzugashvili*) Soviet statesman; secretary of the Communist party; premier (1941–53) .. 1879—1953
Stallings (stạl'lings), **Laurence**, American playwright ... 1894—1968
Standish (stan'dish), **Miles**, military leader at Plymouth, Mass., born in England ... 1584?–1656
Stanford (stan'fŏrd), **Leland**, American railroad builder, senator, and founder of Stanford University ... 1824—1893
Stanhope (stan'hōp), **Charles, third Earl**, English inventor ... 1753—1816
S., James, first Earl, Eng. general and statesman ... 1673—1721
S., Philip Henry, fifth Earl (*Lord Mahon*), English historian. 1805—1875
Stanislavsky (stȧ-nyi-släf'skē), **Konstantin** (b. *Konstantin S. Alekseyev*), Russian director and actor ... 1863—1938
Stanley (stan'li), **Arthur Penrhyn** (*Dean Stanley*), English clergyman and author; dean of Westminster ... 1815—1881
Stanley, Sir Henry Morton (b. *John Rowlands*), British explorer in Africa ... 1841—1904
Stanton (stan'tŏn), **Edwin McMasters**, American statesman; secretary of war (1862–67) ... 1814—1869
Stanton, Elizabeth Cady, American woman's rights advocate .. 1815—1902
Stark (stärk), **Harold Raynsford**, American admiral in World War II ... 1880—1972
Stark, John, American Revolutionary general ... 1728—1822
Stassen (stas'sen), **Harold Edward**, American political leader .. 1907—
Statius (stā'shi-us), **Publius Papinius**, Roman epic poet ... 40?— 96?
Stead (sted), **William Thomas**, English journalist ... 1849—1912
Stedman (sted'măn), **Edmund Clarence**, American poet ... 1833—1908
Steele (stēl), **Sir Richard**, Eng. essayist and playwright ... 1672—1729
Steele, Wilbur Daniel, American novelist and short-story writer. 1886—1970
Steen (stęn), **Jan**, Dutch painter ... 1626—1679
Stefansson (stef'ăn-sŏn), **Vilhjalmur**, Canadian arctic explorer. 1879—1962
Steffens (stef'ens), **(Joseph) Lincoln**, American author ... 1866—1936
Steichen (stī'ḉhen), **Edward**, American photographer ... 1879—1973
Stein (stīn), **Gertrude**, American poet and writer ... 1874—1946
Steinbeck (stīn'bek), **John Ernst**, American novelist and short-story writer ... 1902—1968
Steinmetz (stīn'mets), **Charles Proteus**, American electrical engineer, born in Germany ... 1865—1923
Stendhal (stäṅ-dȧl'), (pseud. of *Marie Henri Beyle*) French novelist ... 1783—1842
Stephen (stē'ven), **Sir Leslie**, English critic, biographer, and editor ... 1832—1904
Stephens (stē'vens), **Alexander Hamilton**, American statesman; vice president of the Confederate States ... 1812—1883
Stephens, James, Irish poet and novelist ... 1882—1950
Stephenson (stē'ven-sŏn), **George**, English engineer and one of the first locomotive builders ... 1781—1848
Sterling (stēr'ling), **John**, English critic and writer ... 1806—1844
Stern (stērn), **Gladys Bronwyn**, English novelist ... 1890—1973
Sterne (stērn), **Laurence**, Eng. novelist and clergyman ... 1713—1768
Stettinius (ste-tin'i-us), **Edward R.**, American industrialist and financier; secretary of state (1944–45) ... 1900—1949
Steuben, von (von stū'ben *or G.* fọn shtoi'ben), **Frederick William Augustus, Baron**, American Revolutionary general, born in Prussia ... 1730—1794
Stevens (stē'vens), **John Paul**, associate justice of U.S. Supreme Court (1975–) ... 1920—
Stevens, Thaddeus, American statesman and abolitionist ... 1792—1868
Stevens, Wallace, American poet ... 1879—1955
Stevenson (stē'ven-sŏn), **Adlai Ewing**, American lawyer and vice-president of the United States (1893–97) ... 1835—1914
S., Adlai Ewing (*grandson of A.E.S.*), American political leader; Democratic presidential nominee (1952) ... 1900—1965
Stevenson, Robert Louis, Scottish author ... 1850—1894
Stewart (stū'ărt), **Charles**, American rear admiral ... 1778—1869
Stewart, Dugald, Scottish philosopher ... 1753—1828
Stewart, Potter, associate justice of the U.S. Supreme Court (1958–81) ... 1915—
Stieglitz (stēg'lits), **Alfred**, American photographer ... 1864—1946
Stiles (stīls), **Charles Wardell**, American zoologist ... 1867—1941
Stiles, Ezra, American theologian and educator ... 1727—1795
Stilicho (stil'i-ḉhō), **Flavius**, Roman general ... ? — 408
Still (stil), **John**, English bishop and dramatist ... 1543?–1608
Stilwell (stil'wel), **Joseph Warren**, Am. general, commanding in China-India-Burma theater (1942–44) ... 1883—1946
Stimson (stim'sŏn), **Henry Lewis**, American statesman; secretary of state (1929–33), of war (1911–13, 1940–45) ... 1867—1950
Stock (stok), **Fredrick August**, American conductor and composer, born in Germany ... 1872—1942
Stockton (stok'tŏn), **Frank R.** (*Francis Richard S.*), American novelist and short-story writer ... 1834—1902
Stoddard (stod'ărd), **Richard Henry**, American poet ... 1825—1903
Stoessel (stes'el), **Albert**, Am. conductor, composer ... 1894—1943
Stoker (stōk'ēr), **Bram** (*Abraham Stoker*), Brit. novelist ... 1847—1912
Stokowski (stŏ-kọf'skī), **Leopold**, American conductor, b. in England ... 1882—1977
Stone (stōn), **Edward Durell**, American architect ... 1902—1978
Stone, Harlan Fiske, chief justice of the United States Supreme Court (1941–46) ... 1872—1946
Stone, Lucy (*Mrs. Henry Brown Blackwell*), American suffragist. 1818—1893
Stoneman (stōn'măn), **George**, Union general in the Civil War and governor of California ... 1822—1894
Stopes (stōps), **Marie Carmichael**, English scientist and advocate of birth control ... 1880—1958
Storm (shtọrm), **Theodor**, German novelist and poet ... 1817—1888
Story (stō'ry), **Joseph**, American jurist ... 1779—1845
S., William Wetmore (*son of J.S.*), American sculptor and poet. 1819—1895
Stout (stout), **Rex (Todhunter)**, American writer of detective fiction ... 1886—1975
Stow (stō), **John**, English antiquarian ... 1525—1605
Stowe (stō), **Harriet Beecher** (*daughter of Lyman Beecher*), American author ... 1811—1896
Strabo (strā'bō), Greek geographer ... B.C.63?—A.D.24?
Strachey (strā'chi), **John** (*Evelyn John St. Loe S.*), British radical political leader and author ... 1901—1963
Strachey, (Giles) Lytton, English biographer ... 1880—1932
Stradivarius (strad-i-vär'i-us), **Antonius** (Latin form of *Antonio Stradivari*), Italian violin maker ... 1644—1737
Strafford (straf'ŏrd), **Thomas Wentworth, Earl of**, English statesman; adviser of Charles I; beheaded ... 1593—1641
Straparola (sträp-ä-rō'lä), **Giovanni Francesco**, Italian author .. ? —1577?
Strathcona (strath-çō'nȧ) **and Mount Royal, Donald Alexander Smith, Baron**, Canadian railroad builder ... 1820—1914
Straus (shtrous), **Oskar**, Austrian composer ... 1870—1954
Strauss (shtrous), **David Friedrich**, German rationalistic theologian ... 1808—1874
Strauss, Johann, Austrian composer ... 1804—1849
S., Johann (*son of J.S.*), Austrian composer ... 1825—1899
Strauss (strous), **Lewis Lichtenstein**, Am. public official; chairman of Atomic Energy Commission (1953–58) ... 1896—1974
Strauss (shtrous), **Richard**, German composer, conductor ... 1864—1949
Stravinsky (strȧ-vin'skē), **Igor Feodorovich**, Russian composer in France and America ... 1882—1971
Street (strēt), **George Edmund**, English architect ... 1824—1881
Street, Julian, American author ... 1879—1947
Stresemann (shtrę'sę-män), **Gustav**, German statesman; foreign minister (1923–29) ... 1878—1929
Stribling (strib'ling), **T. S.** (*Thomas Sigismund S.*), American novelist ... 1881—1965
Strickland (strik'lănd), **Agnes**, English historian ... 1796—1874
Strickland, William, American architect ... 1787—1854
Strindberg (strin'ber-y *or Eng.* strin'bērg), **Johan August**, Swedish author and dramatist ... 1849—1912
Stritch (strich), **Samuel Alphonsus, Cardinal**, American Roman Catholic archbishop of Chicago ... 1887—1958
Strong (strọng), **Anna Louise**, American author ... 1885—1970
Strong, Leonard Alfred George, British novelist ... 1896—1958
Strother (strŏth'ēr), **David Hunter** (pseud. *Porte Crayon*), American artist, soldier, and author ... 1816—1888
Struther (struth'ēr), **Jan** (b. *Joyce Anstruther; Mrs. Maxtone-Graham*), English author ... 1901—1953
Struve (strụ'vē), **Otto**, Am. astronomer, b. in Russia ... 1819—1905
Stuart (stū'ărt), ruling family in Scotland (1371–1603) and in England and Scotland (1603–1714, except 1649–1660).
Stuart, Gilbert (Charles), American portrait painter ... 1755—1828
Stuart, James Ewell Brown (*Jeb Stuart*), Am. Confederate cavalry general ... 1833—1864
Stubbs (stubs), **William**, English bishop and historian ... 1825—1901
Stuyvesant (stȳ've-sănt), **Peter**, last Dutch governor of New Netherland (New York) ... 1592—1672
Suckling (suk'ling), **Sir John**, English courtier and poet ... 1609—1642
Suckow (sụ'kō), **Ruth**, American novelist ... 1892—1960
Sucre, de (dę sụ'çrę), **Antonio José**, South American patriot and general, born in Venezuela ... 1795—1830
Sudermann (sụ'dēr-män), **Hermann**, German dramatist and novelist ... 1857—1928
Sue (sụ), **Eugène** (b. *Marie Joseph Sue*), French novelist ... 1804—1857
Suetonius (swē-tō'ni-us), (*Caius Suetonius Tranquillus*) Roman biographer ... fl. 2nd. cent.
Sukarno (sụ-kär'nō), president of Indonesia (1945–67) ... 1902?–1970
Suleiman (sụ'lę-män) *or* **Solyman** (*the Magnificent*) Ottoman sultan (1520–66) ... 1496?–1566
Sulla (sul'lȧ) *or* **Sylla, Lucius Cornelius (Felix)**, Roman dictator ... B.C. 138— 78
Sullivan (sul'li-văn), **Sir Arthur Seymour**, English composer; collaborated with W. S. Gilbert on comic operas ... 1842—1900
Sullivan, Harry Stack, American psychiatrist ... 1892—1949
Sullivan, John, American Revolutionary general ... 1740—1795
Sullivan, John Lawrence (*the Boston Strong Boy*), Am. prize fighter; world heavyweight champion (1882–92) ... 1858—1918
Sullivan, Louis Henri, American architect ... 1856—1924
Sully, de (dē sụ-lē'), **Maximilien de Béthune, Duc**, French statesman and writer ... 1560—1641
Sully (sul'ly), **Thomas**, Am. portrait painter, b. in England ... 1783—1872

Sully-Prudhomme (sü-lē'prü-dọm'), **René François Armand,** French poet; received Nobel prize (1901)....1839—1907
Sumner (sụm'nẽr), **Charles,** American statesman and abolitionist..1811—1874
Sumner, William Graham, Am. economist and sociologist....1840—1910
Sumter (sụm'tẽr), **Thomas,** American Revolutionary general....1734—1832
Sunday (sun'dā), **William Ashley** (*Billy Sunday*), American evangelist....1863—1935
Sunderland (sun'dẽr-lȧnd), **Charles Spencer, third Earl of,** English statesman....1674—1722
Sun Yat-sen (sün' yät'sen'), Chinese revolutionist; president of Southern Chinese Republic (1921–22)....1866—1925
Sun Yat-sen, Mme. (*wife of Y.S.*), (b. *Soong Ching-ling*) Chinese political leader....1890—
Suppé, von (fọn sü-pẹ'), **Franz,** (b. *Francesco Suppè-Demelli*), Austrian composer....1820—1895
Surrey (sûr'ri), **Henry Howard, Earl of,** English poet....1517?—1547
Surtees (sûr'tēṣ), **Robert Smith,** Eng. humorous writer....1803—1864
Sutherland (suth'ẽr-lȧnd), **George,** associate justice of the U.S. Supreme Court (1922–38)....1862—1942
Sutro (sü'trō), **Alfred,** British dramatist....1863—1933
Suttner, von (fọn ṣụt'nẽr), **Bertha, Baroness,** Austrian novelist; received Nobel peace prize (1905)....1843—1914
Suvarov (sụ-vä'rọf), **Aleksandr Vasilyevich, Count, and Prince Italiski,** Russian field marshal....1729—1800
Swan (swän), **Sir Joseph Wilson,** English electrician and inventor.1828—1914
Swanson (swän'sŏn), **Claude Augustus,** American secretary of the navy (1933–39)....1862—1939
Swasey (swā'ṣi), **Ambrose,** American manufacturer....1846—1937
Swedenborg (svẹ'den-bọr-y *or Eng.* swē'den-bọrg), **Emanuel,** Swedish scientist, seer, and founder of "New Church"....1688—1772
Sweet (swēt), **Henry,** Eng. philologist and phonetician....1845—1912
Swift (swift), **Jonathan,** English satirist, b. in Ireland....1667—1745
Swift, Lewis, American astronomer....1820—1913
Swinburne (swin'bûrn) **Algernon Charles,** English poet....1837—1909
Swinnerton (swin'nẽr'tŏn), **Frank,** English novelist and critic...1884—
Swope (swōp), **Herbert Bayard,** American publicist....1882—1958
Sybel, von (fọn ṣē'bel), **Heinrich,** German historian....1817—1895
Sylla (syl'lȧ), *see* Sulla.
Symonds (sym'ŏnṣ), **John Addington,** English scholar, critic, and poet....1840—1893
Symons (sȳ'mŏnṣ), **Arthur,** English poet and critic....1865—1945
Synge (syng), **John Millington,** Irish dramatist....1871—1909
Szell (sel), **George,** Am. conductor, born in Budapest....1897—1970
Szigeti (si-get'i), **Joseph,** Hungarian violinist....1892—1973
Szold (zōld), **Henrietta,** Am. Jewish leader; translator....1860—1945

T

Tacitus (tac'i-tus), **Publius Cornelius,** Roman historian....55?—117?
Taft (taft), **Lorado,** American sculptor....1860—1936
Taft, William Howard, 27th U.S. president (1909–13); U.S. chief justice (1921–30)....1857—1930
T., Robert Alphonso (*son of W.H.T.*), U.S. senator....1889—1953
Taggard (tag'gärd), **Genevieve,** American poet....1894—1948
Taglioni (täl-yō'nī), **Maria,** Swedish ballet dancer....1804—1884
Tagore (tȧ-gōr'), **Sir Rabindranath,** Hindu poet....1861—1941
Taine (tān), **Hippolyte Adolphe,** Fr. critic and historian....1828—1893
Tallemant des Réaux (tȧl-mäṅ' dẹ rẹ-ō'), **Gédéon,** French biographer and anecdotist....1619—1692
Talleyrand-Périgord, de (dẽ tȧ-le-räṅ' pẹ-rī-gōr' *or Eng.* tal'i-rand), **Charles Maurice, Prince,** French statesman....1754—1838
Tallien (tȧ-lyaṅ'), **Jean Lambert,** French revolutionist....1767—1820
Tallis (tal'lis), **Thomas,** English composer....1510—1585
Talma (tȧl-mȧ'), **François Joseph,** French tragedian....1763—1826
Talmage (tal'mȧg), **Thomas De Witt,** Am. clergyman....1832—1902
Tamayo (tä-mä'yō), **Rufino,** Mexican painter....1899—
Tamerlane (tam'ẽr-lān) *or* **Timour** (ti-moor'), Mongol conqueror.1333?—1405
Tamm (täm), **Igor Evgenyevich,** Soviet physicist....1895—1971
Tammany (tam'mȧn-y), chief of the Delaware Indians....fl. 1680
Tancred (tan'cred), Norman leader in the first crusade....1078?—1112
Taney (tą'ni), **Roger Brooke,** chief justice of the United States Supreme Court (1836–64)....1777—1864
Tappan (tap'pȧn), **Arthur,** American abolitionist....1786—1865
Tarbell (tär'bel), **Ida,** American biographer....1857—1944
Tarde, de (dẽ tȧrd), **Gabriel,** French criminologist....1843—1904
Tardieu (tȧr-dyü'), **André,** French statesman and journalist; premier (1929–30, 1932)....1876—1945
Tarkington (tärk'ing-tŏn), **(Newton) Booth,** American novelist.1869—1946
Tarleton (tärl'tŏn), **Sir Banastre,** British officer in the American Revolution....1754—1833
Tarquin (tär'kwin), (*the Proud*), (*Lucius Tarquinius Superbus*) seventh and last king of Rome....?—B.C.495?
Tartini (tär-tī'nī), **Giuseppe,** It. violinist, composer....1692—1770
Tasman (täs'män), **Abel Janszoon,** Dutch navigator....1603—1659
Tasso (tas'sō), **Torquato,** Italian epic poet....1544—1595
Tate (tāt), **Allen,** Am. poet, critic, and biographer....1899—1979
Tate, Nahum, British dramatist and poet laureate....1652—1715
Tattnall (tat'nạl), **Josiah,** American naval officer....1795—1871
Tauler (tou'lẽr), **Johannes,** German mystic....1300—1361
Taussig (tous'sig), **Frank William,** American economist....1859—1940
Tavernier (tȧ-ver-nyẹ'), **Jean Baptiste,** French traveler....1605—1689
Taylor (tā'lŏr), **Bayard,** Am. traveler, poet, and writer....1825—1878
Taylor, Bert Leston (*B.L.T.*), American columnist....1866—1921
Taylor, Brook, English mathematician....1685—1731
Taylor, (Joseph) Deems, American composer and critic....1885—1966
Taylor, Henry Osborn, American medievalist....1856—1941
Taylor, Jeremy, English bishop and author....1613—1667
Taylor, John (*the Water Poet*), English poet....1578—1653
Taylor, John, U.S. senator, expounder of States' rights....1753—1824
Taylor, Tom, English dramatist and editor....1817—1880
Taylor, Zachary, American general and twelfth president of the United States (1849–50)....1784—1850
Tchaikowsky (chī-kọf'skē), **Pëtr Ilich,** Russian composer....1840—1893
Tchekhoff (che'kọf), **Anton Pavlovich,** *see* Chekhov.
Teasdale (tēṣ'dāl), **Sara,** American poet....1884—1933
Tecumseh (tē-çum'se) *or* **Tecumtha** (-thȧ), Shawnee chief and British general....1768?—1813
Tedder (ted'ẽr), **Arthur William, first Baron,** British air force chief in World War II....1890—1967
Tegnér (teng nẹr'), **Esaias,** Swedish poet....1782—1846
Teilhard de Chardin (te-yär' dẽ shär-daṅ'), **Pierre,** French paleontologist, geologist, and philosopher....1881—1955
Telemann (te'lȧ-män), **Georg Philipp,** German composer....1681—1767
Teller (tel'ẽr), **Edward,** American nuclear physicist, b. in Hungary.1908—
Téllez (tel'yẹth), **Gabriel** (pseud. *Tirso de Molina*), Spanish dramatist....1571?—1648
Temple (tem'pl), **Sir William,** English diplomat, statesman, and author....1628—1699
Teniers (ten'yẽrṣ *or Fl.* te-nērs'), **David,** (*the Younger*), Flemish painter....1610—1690
Tenniel (ten'yel), **Sir John,** English artist and cartoonist....1820—1914
Tennyson (ten'y-sŏn), **Alfred, first Baron,** English poet laureate.1809—1892
Ter Borch (tẽr bōrkh'), **Gerard,** Dutch painter....1617—1681
Terence (ter'enc), (*Publius Terentius Afer*) Roman comic dramatist....B.C. 190?- 159
Terhune (tẽr-hūn'), **Albert Payson** (*son of M.V.T.*), American author (notably of stories of dogs)....1872—1942
Terry (ter'ry), **Dame Ellen Alicia,** English actress....1848—1928
Tertullian (tẽr-tụl'li-ȧn), (*Quintus Septimius Florens*) Latin church father....150?—230?
Tesla (tes'lȧ), **Nikola,** Am. physicist, b. in Yugoslavia....1856—1943
Tetrazzini (tẹ-trät-tsī'nī), **Luisa,** Italian soprano....1874—1940
Tetzel (tet'sel), **Johann,** German Dominican preacher, castigated by Luther for his selling of indulgences....1465?—1519
Tewfik Pasha (tü'fik pȧ-shä'), (*Mohammed Tewfik*) khedive of Egypt (1879–92)....1852—1892
Thackeray (thak'ẽr-y), **William Makepeace,** English novelist...1811—1863
Thaïs (thā'is), courtesan of Corinth; mistress of Alexander....fl.B.C. 4th cent.
Thales (thā'lēṣ), Greek philosopher; one of the Seven Sages of Greece....B.C. 640?—546?
Thant (thänt), **U,** Burmese diplomat; secretary-general of the United Nations (1962–71)....1909—1974
Thatcher (thach'ẽr), **Margaret Hilda** (b. *Margaret Hilda Roberts*), English politician; prime minister (1979–)....1925—
Themistocles (the-mis'tō-çlēṣ), Athenian general and statesman....B.C. 527?—460?
Theocritus (thē-oç'ri-tus), Greek pastoral poet....fl.B.C. 283?—263?
Theodora (thē-ō-dō'rȧ), Byzantine empress; wife of Justinian I...508?- 548
Theodoret (thē-od'ō-ret), bishop of Cyrus and ecclesiastical historian....390?—457?
Theodoric (thē-od'ō-riç), (*the Great*) king of the Ostrogoths....454— 526
Theodosius (thē-ō-dō'shi-us) **I,** (*the Great*), Roman emperor....346?- 395
Theophrastus (thē-ō-fras'tus), Greek philosopher....B.C. 370?—287?
Theotocopoulos (thẹ"ō-tō-çō-pụ'lōs), **Domenico,** *see* El Greco.
Theresa (te-rē'sȧ), **Saint,** Sp. Carmelite nun and mystic....1515—1582
Theresa, Saint (*the Little Flower of Jesus*), Fr. nun....1873—1897
Thierry (tye-rē'), **Augustin,** French historian....1795—1856
Thiers (tyer), **Louis Adolphe,** French historian, and president of the French republic (1871–73)....1797—1877
Thomas (tō-mä'), **Ambroise,** French opera composer....1811—1896
Thomas, Dylan (Marlais), British poet, born in Wales....1914—1953
Thomas, George Henry, Union general in the Civil War....1816—1870
Thomas, Lowell, American author and radio commentator....1892—1981
Thomas, Martha Carey, American educator....1857—1935
Thomas, Norman Mattoon, American socialist leader....1884—1968
Thomas, Seth, American clock manufacturer....1785—1859
Thomas à Becket (ȧ bek'et), **Saint,** archbishop of Canterbury; martyr....1118?—1170
Thomas à Kempis (ȧ kem'pis), German abbot, ascetic, and writer....1380—1471
Thompson (tomp'sŏn), **Francis,** English poet....1859—1907
Thomson (tom'sŏn), **Sir Charles Wyville,** Scottish biologist....1830—1882
Thomson, Sir George Paget (*son of Sir J.J.T.*), English physicist; shared Nobel prize (1937)....1892—1975
Thomson, James, Scottish poet....1700—1748
Thomson, James, Scottish poet....1834—1882
Thomson, Sir John Arthur, Scot. naturalist and writer....1861—1933
Thomson, Joseph, Scottish explorer in Africa....1858—1895
Thomson, Sir Joseph John, English physicist....1856—1940
Thomson, Virgil, American composer and critic....1896—
Thomson, William, *see* Kelvin, William Thomson.
Thoreau (thọr'ō *or* thō-rō'), **Henry David,** American essayist, poet, and naturalist....1817—1862
Thorndike (thọrn'dīk), **Ashley Horace,** Am. literary scholar and educator (*brother of E.L.T. and L.T.*)....1871—1933
T., Edward Lee, American psychologist and educator....1874—1949
T., Lynn, American historian and educator....1882—1965
Thorndike, Dame Sybil, English actress....1882—1976
Thorpe (thọrp), **James,** American athlete....1888—1953
Thou, de (dẽ tö), **Jacques Auguste,** French historian....1553—1617
Thucydides (thū-cyd'i-dēṣ), Athenian historian....B.C. 471?—400?
Thurber (thûr'bẽr), **James (Grover),** American humorist....1894—1961
Thutmose (thut'mōṣ *or* tut') **III** *or* **Thothmes** (thoth'mēṣ) **III,** king of Egypt....B.C. ? —1447
Tiberius (tī-bē'ri-us), (*Tiberius Claudius Nero Caesar*) Roman emperor (14–37)....B.C.42—A.D.37
Tibullus (ti-bul'lus), **Albius,** Roman poet....B.C. 54?— 18?
Tickell (tik'el), **Thomas,** English poet and essayist....1686—1740
Tieck (tēk), **Johann Ludwig,** German poet, dramatist, and novelist....1773—1853
Tiepolo (tyẹ'pō-lō), **Giovanni Battista,** Italian painter....1696—1770
Tiffany (tif'fȧ-ny), **Charles Lewis,** American jeweler....1812—1902
T., Louis Comfort (*son of C.L.T.*), American artist....1848—1933
Tiglath-pileser (tig'lath-pi-lē'sẽr) **III,** king of Assyria (B.C. 745–27)....B.C. ? — 727
Tikhonov (tyē'khọ-nọf), **Nikolai A.,** premier of the U.S.S.R. (1980–)....1905—
Tilden (til'den), **Samuel Jones,** American lawyer and statesman.1814—1886
Tilden, William Tatem, II, American tennis player....1893—1953
Tillich (til'ik), **Paul (Johannes),** American theologian, b. in Germany....1886—1965
Tilly, von (fọn til'i *or Fr.* tī-yē'), **Johann Tserklaes, Count,** Bavarian general....1559—1632
Timoleon (tī-mō'lē-ŏn), Greek general and statesman....B.C. 400?- 337
Timoshenko (tyi-mō-sheṅ'kō), **Semyon,** Russian marshal in World War II....1895—1970
Timour, *see* Tamerlane.
Tindal (tin'dȧl), **Matthew,** English deist....1653?—1733
Tindal *or* **Tindale, William,** *see* Tyndale, William.
Tintoretto, Il (ïl tin-tō-ret'tō), (*Jacopo Robusti*) Italian painter..1518—1594

Tiraboschi (tī-rä-bọs′ḳhī), **Girolamo**, Italian Jesuit and literary historian ....1731—1794
Tirpitz, von (fọn tir′pits), **Alfred**, German admiral ....1849—1930
Tissot (tī-sō′), **James Joseph Jacques**, French painter ....1836—1902
Tisza (tī′sä), **István, Count**, Hungarian statesman ....1861—1918
Titian (tish′ăn), (*Tiziano Vecellio*) Venetian painter ....1477—1576
Titiens (tīt-yens′), **Teresa**, Hungarian operatic singer ....1831?—1877
Tito (tī′tō), **Josip Broz**, Yugoslav marshal and Communist leader; led liberation movement (1941–45); thereafter, dictator, as premier and (1953–80) president ....1892—1980
Titus (tī′tus), (*Titus Flavius Sabinus Vespasianus*) Roman emperor (79–81) ....40?— 81
Tocqueville, de (dē tọk-vīl′), **Alexis Charles Henri Clérel**, French statesman and author ....1805—1859
Todleben (tōt′lẹ-ben), **Franz Eduard**, Russian general ....1818—1884
Togo (tō′gō), **Heihachiro, Count**, Japanese admiral ....1847—1934
Tojo (tō′jō), **Hideki**, Japanese general and prime minister (1941–44); executed as a war criminal ....1885—1948
Toland (tō′lănd), **John**, British deist, born in Ireland ....1670—1722
Toledo, de (dẹ tō-lẹ′thō), **Francisco**, Spanish viceroy of Peru ....? —1584
Tollens (tol′lens), **Hendrik**, Dutch poet ....1780—1856
Toller (tōl′lẽr), **Ernst**, German playwright and poet ....1893—1939
Tolstoy (tol′stoi *or Russ.* tọl-stoi′), **Aleksey Konstantinovich, Count**, Russian dramatist, novelist, and poet ....1817—1875
Tolstoy, Aleksey Nicolayevich, Soviet Russian novelist ....1882—1945
Tolstoy, Leo, Count (*Lev Nikolayevich Tolstoi*), Russian author and social reformer ....1828—1910
Tomlinson (tom′lin-sŏn), **H. M.** (*Henry Major T.*), English novelist ....1873—1958
Tone (tōn), **(Theobald) Wolfe**, Irish revolutionist ....1763—1798
Tonti (ton′tī), **Lorenzo**, Italian banker; originator of *tontines* .... fl. 1653
Toole (tọọl), **John Lawrence**, English comedian ....1830?—1906
Toombs (tọọmẓ), **Robert**, American politician and Confederate general ....1810—1885
Töpffer (tẽp′fẽr), **Rodolphe**, Swiss author and caricaturist ....1799—1846
Torquemada, de (dẹ tọr-kẹ-mä′thä), **Tomás**, Spanish inquisitor general ....1420—1498
Torrence (tọr′renc), **Ridgely**, American poet ....1875—1950
Torrey (tor′ĭ), **John**, American botanist and chemist ....1796—1873
Torricelli (tōr-rī-chel′lī), **Evangelista**, Italian physicist ....1608—1647
Torrigiano (tōr-rī-gä′nō), **Pietro**, Italian sculptor ....1472—1528
Torstensson (tōr′sten-sōn), **Lennart, Count of Ortola**, Swedish general ....1603—1651
Toscanini (tōs-çä-nī′nī), **Arturo**, It. conductor in U.S. ....1867—1957
Totila (tot′i-lȧ), (*Baduila*) last king of Ostrogoths .... ? — 552
Toulouse-Lautrec, de (dē tọọ-lọọs′lō-treç′), **Henri**, French painter and lithographer ....1864—1901
Tourneur (tûr′nûr), **Cyril**, English dramatist ....1580?—1626
Toussaint L'Ouverture (tö-saṅ′ lö-ver-tůr′), **François Dominique**, Haitian Negro general and liberator ....1743—1803
Townsend (toun′ẓend), **Francis Everett**, American physician and promoter of an old-age pension plan ....1867—1960
Toynbee (toin′bē), **Arnold Joseph**, English historian ....1889—1975
Tracy (trā′cy), **Benjamin Franklin**, American general, lawyer, and secretary of the navy (1889–93) ....1830—1915
Train (trān), **Arthur**, American lawyer and novelist ....1875—1945
Trajan (trā′jăn), (*Marcus Ulpius Trajanus*) Roman emperor (98–117) ....52?— 117
Tree (trē), **Sir Herbert Beerbohm** (b. *Herbert Beerbohm*), English actor and theatrical producer ....1853—1917
Treitschke, von (fon trīch′ke), **Heinrich**, German historian ....1834—1896
Trench (trench), **Richard Chenevix**, British archbishop and author ....1807—1886
Trevelyan (trē-vel′yăn), **George Macaulay** (*son of G.O.T.*), English historian ....1876—1962
T., Sir George Otto, English politician and historian ....1838—1928
Trochu (trō-çhů′), **Louis Jules**, French general ....1815—1896
Trollope (trol′ŏp), **Anthony**, English novelist ....1815—1882
T., Frances (*mother of A.T. and T.T.*), Eng. novelist ....1780—1863
T., Thomas, English novelist ....1810—1892
Trotsky (trọt′skē), **Leon** (b. *Lev Bronstein*), Russian revolutionary leader; exiled; assassinated ....1877—1940
Troyon (trwo-yọṅ′), **Constant**, French painter ....1810—1865
Trudeau (trů′dō), **Edward Livingston**, Am. physician ....1848—1915
Trudeau, Pierre Elliott, prime minister of Canada (1968–79; 1980–) ....1921—
Trujillo Molina (trů-hī′yō mō-lī′nä), **Rafael Leonidas**, president of Dominican Republic (1930–38, 1942–52) ....1891—1961
Truman (trů′măn), **Harry S.**, 33rd president of the United States (1945–53) ....1884—1972
Trumbull (trum′bul), **John**, Am. jurist and satirist ....1750—1831
Trumbull, John (*son of Jonathan*), American painter ....1756—1843
T., Jonathan, American statesman ....1710—1785
Truxton (truks′tŏn), **Thomas**, American commodore ....1755—1822
Tucker (tuk′ẽr), **John Randolph**, American naval officer ....1812—1883
Tunney (tun′ni), **James Joseph** (*Gene Tunney*), Am. prize fighter; world heavyweight champion (1926–28) ....1897—1978
Tupper (tup′pẽr), **Sir Charles**, Canadian statesman ....1821—1915
Turenne, de (dē tů-ren′), **Henri de la Tour d'Auvergne, Vicomte**, marshal of France ....1611—1675
Turgenev *or* **Turgenieff** (tůr-gẹ′nyef), **Ivan Sergeyevich**, Russian novelist ....1818—1883
Turgot (tůr-gō′), **Anne Robert Jacques, Baron de l'Aulne**, French financier and statesman ....1727—1781
Turner (tûrn′ẽr), **Frederick Jackson**, Am. historian ....1861—1932
Turner, Joseph Mallord William, Eng. landscapist ....1775—1851
Tusser (tus′sẽr), **Thomas**, English poet ....1524?—1580?
Tutankhamen (tůt-äṅk-ä′men), Egyptian king of the 18th dynasty .... fl. B.C. 1358
Twain (twān), **Mark**, *see* Clemens, Samuel Langhorne.
Tweed (twēd), **William Marcy** (*Boss Tweed*), New York City politician ....1823—1878
Twiggs (twigẓ), **David Emanuel**, American general ....1790—1862
Tyler (tȳ′lẽr), **John**, tenth U.S. president (1841–45) ....1790—1862
Tyler, Moses Coit, American literary historian ....1835—1900
Tyler, Royall, American jurist, writer, and playwright ....1757—1826
Tyler, Wat, English rebel; killed by mayor of London .... ? —1381
Tylor (tȳ′lŏr), **Sir Edward B.**, English anthropologist ....1832—1917
Tyndale (tyn′dăl) *or* **Tindal, William**, English reformer, biblical translator, and martyr ....1492?—1536
Tyndall (tyn′dăl), **John**, British scientist, b. in Ireland ....1820—1893
Tyrtaeus (tīr-tẹ′us), Greek lyric poet .... fl.B.C. 684
Tytler (tȳt′lẽr), **Patrick Fraser**, Scottish historian ....1791—1849

U

Uccello (ůt-chel′lō), **Paolo** (b. *di Dono*) It. painter ....1396?—1475
Udall (ū′dăl), **Nicholas**, English teacher and dramatist ....1505—1556
Uhland (ů′länt), **Johann Ludwig**, German lyric poet ....1787—1862
Umberto, *see* Humbert I.
Unamuno, de (dẹ ů-nä-mů′nō), **Miguel**, Spanish scholar, philosopher, and author ....1864—1936
Underwood (un′dẽr-wood), **Oscar Wilder**, American political leader ....1862—1929
Undset (ụn′set), **Sigrid**, Norwegian novelist ....1882—1949
Unruh, von (fon un′rů), **Fritz**, German dramatist ....1885—1970
Untermeyer (un′tẽr-my-ẽr), **Louis**, American poet and critic ....1885—1977
Untermeyer, Samuel, American lawyer ....1858—1940
Upshur (up′shūr), **Abel Parker**, U.S. secretary of the navy (1841–43); secretary of state (1843–44) ....1791—1844
Urban (ūr′băn) **II** (*Otho*, or *Eudes, de Lagery*), Pope ....1042?—1099
Urban VIII (*Maffeo Barberini*), Pope ....1568—1644
Ure (ūr), **Andrew**, Scottish chemist and author ....1778—1857
Urey (ū′ri), **Harold Clayton**, American chemist ....1893—1981
Urfé, d' (důr-fẹ′), **Honoré**, French novelist ....1567—1625
Urquhart (ūr′kärt), **David**, Brit. diplomat, b. in Scotland ....1805—1877
Urquhart, Sir Thomas, Scottish translator and writer ....1611—1660
Ussher (ush′ẽr), **James**, Irish archbishop and historian ....1581—1656
Utamaro (ů-tä′mä-rō), Japanese color-print maker ....1754—1806
Utrillo (ů-trī-lō′), **Maurice**, French painter ....1883—1955

V

Vaihinger (fī′hing-ẽr), **Hans**, German philosopher ....1852—1933
Vail (vāl), **Alfred**, American electrician and inventor ....1807—1859
Valdemar I, *see* Waldemar I.
Valdivia, de (dẹ väl-dī′vyä), **Don Pedro**, Sp. conqueror of Chile ..1500?—1554?
Valentine (val′en-tīn), **Saint**, Roman Christian martyr .... 3rd cent.
Valentinian (val-en-tin′i-ăn) **I**, Roman emperor ....321— 375
Valera, Eamon De, *see* De Valera, Eamon.
Valera y Alcala Galiano (vä-lẹ′rä ē äl-çä-lä′ gäl-yä′nō), **Juan**, Spanish author and diplomat ....1824—1905
Valerian (vȧ-lē′ri-ăn), (*Publius Licinius Valerianus*) Roman emperor (253–60) .... ? —269?
Valéry (vȧ-lẹ-rē′), **Paul**, French poet and essayist ....1871—1945
Vámbéry (väm′bẹ-rē), **Ármin**, Hungarian traveler and scholar ....1832—1913
Vanbrugh (van′bru *or* van-brů′), **Sir John**, English dramatist and architect ....1664—1726
Van Buren (van bū′ren), **Martin**, eighth president of the United States (1837–41) ....1782—1862
Vancouver (van-çö′vẽr), **George**, English navigator ....1758—1798
Vandegrift (van′de-grift), **Alexander Archer**, American Marine Corps general in World War II ....1887—1973
Vandenberg (van′den-bẽrg), **Arthur H.**, U.S. senator ....1884—1951
V., Hoyt Sanford (*nephew of A.H.V.*), U.S. Air Force chief ....1899—1954
Vanderbilt (van′dẽr-bilt), **Cornelius**, Am. capitalist ....1794—1877
Van Devanter (van de-van′tẽr), **Willis**, associate justice of the U.S. Supreme Court (1910–37) ....1859—1941
Vandevelde (vän-dē-vel′de), **Willem** (*the Younger*), Dutch marine painter ....1633—1707
Van Dine (van dīn′), **S. S.**, *see* Wright, Willard H.
Van Doren (dō′ren), **Carl**, Am. critic, author, and editor ....1885—1950
V., Mark (*brother of C.V.*), Am. poet and author ....1894—1972
Van Druten (drů′ten), **John**, Eng. dramatist in U.S. ....1901—1957
Van Dyck *or* **Vandyke** (-dyk′), **Sir Anthony**, Flemish portrait painter ....1599—1641
van Dyke (dȳk), **Henry**, Am. clergyman and author ....1852—1933
Vane (vān), **Sir Henry**, English statesman and writer ....1613—1662
Van Gogh, Vincent, *see* Gogh, Vincent van.
Vanloo (vän-lō′), **Charles André** (*Carle V.*), French painter ....1705—1765
V., Jean Baptiste (*brother of C.A.V.*), Fr. painter ....1684—1745
van Loon (van lōn), **Hendrik Willem**, American author, born in the Netherlands ....1882—1944
Van Rensselaer (van ren′sel-ẽr), **Stephen** (*the Patroon*), American statesman ....1764—1839
Vansittart (van-sit′ärt), **Robert Gilbert, first Baron**, British diplomat ....1881—1957
Van Tyne (van tȳn), **Claude Halstead**, Am. historian ....1869—1930
Van Vechten (van veçh′ten), **Carl**, Am. music critic, novelist ....1880—1964
Vanzetti (van-zet′tī), **Bartolomeo**, *see* Sacco, Nicola ....1888—1927
Varen (vä′ren) *or* **Varenius** (vä-rẹ′ni-ụs), **Bernhard**, Dutch geographer ....1622—1650
Vargas (vär′gȧs), **Getulio Dornelles**, Brazilian general; president of Brazil (1930–45, 1951–54) ....1883—1954
Varnhagen von Ense (färn′hä-gen fọn en′ẓe), **Karl August**, German biographer ....1785—1858
Varro (var′ō), **Marcus Terentius**, Roman scholar, writer .... B.C. 116— 27
Vasari (vä-ṣä′rī), **Giorgio**, Italian painter, architect, and art historian ....1511—1574
Vassar (vas′săr), **Matthew**, American philanthropist ....1792—1868
Vattel, de (dē vȧ-tel′), **Emheric**, Swiss jurist and writer ....1714—1767
Vauban, de (dē vō-bäṅ′), **Sébastien Le Prestre, Marquis**, French military engineer and marshal ....1633—1707
Vaughan (vȧn) **Henry**, British poet ....1622—1695
Vaughan Williams (wil′yămẓ), **Ralph**, English composer ....1872—1958
Veblen (veb′len), **Thorstein**, American economist ....1857—1929
Vedder (ved′dẽr), **Elihu**, Am. painter and illustrator ....1836—1923
Vega Carpio, de (dẹ vẹ′gä çär′pī-ō), **Lope Félix** (*Lope de Vega*), Spanish poet and dramatist ....1562—1635
Velázquez (vẹ-läth′kẹth), **Diego Rodríguez de Silva y**, Spanish painter ....1599—1660
Vendôme, de (dē väṅ-dōm′), **Louis Joseph, Duc**, French marshal ....1654—1712
Venizelos (ven-ī-zẹ′lōs), **Eleutherios**, Greek statesman ....1864—1936
Verboeckhoven (vẽr-bök-hō′ven), **Eugène Joseph**, Belgian animal painter ....1798—1881
Verdi (ver′dī), **Giuseppe**, Italian composer of operas ....1814—1901
Vereshchagin (vye-resh-chä′gin), **Vasili**, Russian painter ....1842—1904
Verga (ver′gä), **Giovanni**, Italian novelist ....1840—1922

Vergennes, de (dẽ ver-zen'), **Charles Gravier, Count,** French statesman....1717—1787
Vergil (vẽr'ġil), *see* Virgil
Verhaeren (vẽr-hä'ren), **Émile,** Belg. poet and playwright....1855—1916
Verlaine (ver-lãn'), **Paul,** French symbolist poet....1844—1896
Vermeer (vẽr-mẹr'), **Jan** (*Jan van der Meer van Delft*), Dutch painter....1632—1675
Verne (vern *or Eng.* vẽrn), **Jules,** French novelist....1828—1905
Verner (ver'nẽr), **Karl Adolf,** Danish philologist....1846—1896
Vernet (ver-ne'), **Antoine Charles Horace** (*Carle*), French painter (*son of Joseph; father of Horace*)....1758—1835
V., Claude Joseph (*Joseph*), Fr. marine painter....1714—1789
V., Émile Jean Horace (*Horace*), Fr. military painter....1789—1863
Vernon (vẽr'nŏn), **Edward** (*Old Grog*), English admiral....1684—1757
Veronese (vẹ-rō-nẹ'ṣẹ), **Paolo** (b. *Paolo Cagliari*), Italian painter.1528—1588
Verrazano, da (dä ver-rä-tsä'nō), **Giovanni,** Italian navigator in the service of France....1485?–1528?
Verres (ver'rẽṣ), **Caius,** Roman governor....B.C.120?— 43?
Verrocchio, del (del ver-rŏç'çyō), **Andrea,** It. painter....1435—1488
Vesalius (ve-sā'li-us), **Andreas,** Flemish anatomist....1514—1564
Vespasian (ves-pā'ẓi-ăn), (*Titus Flavius Sabinus Vespasianus*), Roman emperor (69–79)....9— 79
Vespucci (ves-pût'chi), **Amerigo** (L. *Americus Vespucius*), It. navigator, after whom America was named....1451—1512
Viaud (vyō), **Louis Marie Julien,** *see* Loti, Pierre.
Vico (vī'çō), **Giovanni Battista,** Italian philosopher....1668—1744
Victor Emmanuel (viç'tọr em-man'ū-el) **I,** king of Sardinia (1802–21)....1759—1824
Victor Emmanuel II, king of Sardinia (1849–61), and first king of modern Italy (1861–78)....1820—1878
Victor Emmanuel III (*son of Humbert I*), king of Italy (1900–46); abdicated in favor of son, Humbert II....1869—1947
Victoria (viç-tō'ri-ȧ), queen of Great Britain (1837–1901) and empress of India (1876–1901)....1819—1901
Vicuña (vī-çūn'yä), **Benjamin Mackenna,** Chilean historian...1831—1886
Vida (vī'dä), **Marco Girolamo,** Italian Latin poet....1485?–1566
Vidocq (vī-dọk'), **Eugène François,** French convict and detective.1775—1857
Vien (vī-aṅ'), **Joseph Marie,** French historical painter....1716—1809
Vieuxtemps (vyū-täṅ'), **Henri,** Belgian violinist and composer..1820—1881
Vignola, da (dä vī-nyō'lä), **Giacomo** (b. *Giacomo Barocchio*), Italian architect....1507—1573
Vigny, de (dẽ vē-nyē'), **Alfred Victor, Count,** French poet, novelist, and playwright....1797—1863
Villa (vī'yä), **Francisco** (*Pancho Villa*), Mexican revolutionary leader....1877—1923
Villa-Lobos (vīl'lä-lọ'boosh), **Heitor,** Brazilian composer....1881—1959
Villani (vil-lä'nī), **Giovanni,** Florentine historian....1275?–1348
Villard (vi-lärd'), **Oswald Garrison,** Am. journalist....1872—1949
Villars (vī-lȧr'), **Claude Louis Hector, Duke of,** marshal of France....1653—1734
Villemain (vīl-maṅ'), **Abel François,** French scholar....1790—1870
Villeneuve, de (dẽ vīl-nūv'), **Pierre,** French admiral; defeated at Trafalgar by Nelson....1763—1806
Villiers (vil'yẽrṣ), **George,** *see* Buckingham, Duke of.
Villiers de l'Isle-Adam, de (dẽ vī-yç' dẽ līl-ȧ-däṅ'), **Philippe Auguste Mathias, Count,** Fr. poet and author....1838—1889
Villon (vī-yọṅ'), **François** (b. *François de Montcorbier*), French poet....1431— ?
Vincent de Paul (vin'cent dẽ pạl'), **Saint,** French founder of the R. C. Sisters of Charity....1576—1660
Vincent of Beauvais (ŏv bō-vā'), French encyclopedist....1190—1264
Vinci, da (dä vīn'chī), **Leonardo,** Italian painter, sculptor, architect, and scientist....1452—1519
Vinet (vī-ne'), **Alexandre Rodolphe,** Swiss theologian and literary critic....1797—1847
Vinogradoff (vī-nọ-grä'dọf), **Sir Paul,** English historian, born in Russia....1854—1925
Vinson (vin'sŏn), **Frederick Moore,** chief justice of the United States Supreme Court (1946–53)....1890—1953
Virchow (fīr'khō), **Rudolf,** German pathologist....1821—1902
Virgil (vīr'ġil), (*Publius Virgilius Maro*) Latin poet....B.C. 70— 19
Vishinsky (vi-shin'sky), **Andrei Yanuarievich,** Russian lawyer and statesman; foreign minister (1949–53)....1883—1954
Vitellius (vi-tel'li-us), **Aulus,** emperor of Rome (69)....15— 69
Vitruvius (vi trū'vi-us), (*Marcus Vitruvius Pollio*) Roman authority on architecture....B.C. 1st cent.
Vivaldi (vī-väl'dī), **Antonio,** Italian composer....1675?–1743
Vives (vī'vẹs), **Juan Luis,** Spanish scholar and writer....1492—1540
Viviani (vī-vyȧ'nī), **René,** French statesman....1863—1925
Vizetelly (viz-e-tel'ly), **Frank Horace,** American lexicographer, editor, and author, born in England....1864—1938
Vladimir (vlad'i-mir *or Russ.* vlȧ-dyī'mīr), (*the Great*) grand duke of Russia....? —1015
Volstead (vol'sted), **Andrew Joseph,** U.S. congressman....1860—1947
Volta (vōl'tä), **Alessandro, Count,** Italian physicist....1745—1827
Voltaire, de (dẽ vọl-tãr'), **François Marie Arouet,** French philosopher, historian, dramatist, and poet....1694—1778
von Braun (fọn broun'), **Wernher,** U.S. rocket engineer, born in Germany....1912—1977
Vondel, van den (vän den vọn'del), **Joost,** Dutch poet....1587—1679
Voroshilov (vọ-rọ-shī'lọf), **Klement Efremovich,** Russian general; president of U.S.S.R. (1953–60)....1881—1969
Vries, De, Hugo, *see* De Vries, Hugo.

W

Waals, van der (vän dẽr väls), **Johannes Diderik,** Dutch physicist....1837—1923
Wace (wāc *or* wäc), Anglo-Norman poet and chronicler....fl. 12th cen.
Wade (wād), **Benjamin Franklin,** American statesman....1800—1878
Wagner (väg'nẽr), **Richard,** German composer....1813—1883
Wagner (wag'nẽr), **Robert Ferdinand,** United States senator, born in Germany....1877—1953
Wainwright (wān'rīt), **Jonathan Mayhew,** Am. general in command in Philippines (1942); prisoner of war....1883—1953
Waite (wāt), **Morrison Remick,** chief justice of the United States Supreme Court (1874–88)....1816—1888
Waksman (waks'măn), **Selman Abraham,** American microbiologist, born in Russia; won Nobel prize (1952)....1888—1973
Waldeck-Rousseau (vȧl-dek'rö-sō'), **René,** French statesman...1846—1904
Waldemar *or* **Valdemar** (väl'de-mär) **I** (*the Great*), king of Denmark (1157–82)....1131—1182
Waldheim (vält'hīm), **Kurt,** Austrian diplomat; secretary general of the U.N. (1972–)....1918—
Walker (wạk'ẽr), **James John,** mayor of N.Y. (1925–32)....1881—1946
Walker, Robert J., American statesman; secretary of the treasury (1845–49)....1801—1869
Walker, William, American filibusterer; shot at Trujillo....1824—1860
Wallace (wäl'lăc), **Alfred Russell,** English naturalist....1823—1913
Wallace, Edgar, English novelist and playwright....1875—1932
Wallace, Henry Agard, U.S. vice president (1941–45); secretary of agriculture (1933–41), of commerce (1945–46); Progressive presidential nominee (1948)....1888—1965
Wallace, Lewis (*Lew*), American general and novelist....1827—1905
Wallace, Sir William, Scottish hero and patriot....1272?–1305
Wallenstein, von (fọn väl'len-shtīn *or Eng.* wäl'en-stīn), **Albrecht Wenzel Eusebius, Duke of Friedland,** German general....1583—1634
Waller (wạl'lẽr), **Edmund,** English poet....1606—1687
Walpole (wạl'pōl), **Horace, fourth Earl of Orford** (*son of R.W.*), English author and wit....1717—1797
Walpole, Sir Hugh (Seymour), English novelist....1884—1941
Walpole, Robert, first Earl of Orford, Eng. statesman....1676—1745
Walter (väl'tẽr), **Bruno** (b. *Bruno Schlesinger*), German orchestral conductor in the United States....1876—1962
Walter (wạl'tẽr), **Eugene,** American dramatist....1874—1941
Walton (wạl'tŏn), **Ernest Thomas Sinston,** Ir. physicist....1903—
Walton, Izaak, Eng. author; wrote *The Compleat Angler*....1593—1683
Walton, Sir William Turner, English composer....1902—
Wanamaker (wän'ȧ-mā-kẽr), **John,** American merchant; postmaster-general (1889–93)....1838—1922
Warburg (vär'bụrk), **Otto Heinrich,** German physiologist....1883—1970
Warburton (wạr'bũr-tŏn), **William,** Eng. bishop and author....1698—1779
Ward (wạrd), **Artemas,** American Revolutionary general....1727—1800
Ward, Artemus, *see* Browne, Charles Farrar.
Ward, Mrs. Humphry (b. *Mary Augusta Arnold*), English novelist....1851—1920
Ward, John Quincy Adams, American sculptor....1830—1910
Ward, Lynd Kendall, American artist....1905—
Warfield (wạr'fēld), **David,** American actor....1866—1951
Warner (wạr'nẽr), **Charles Dudley,** Am. author, editor....1829—1900
Warner, Glenn Scobey (*Pop Warner*), Am. football coach....1871—1954
Warner, Sylvia Townsend, English novelist and poet....1893—1978
Warren (wạr'ren), **Charles,** Am. jurist and historian....1868—1954
Warren, Earl, chief justice of the U.S. Supreme Court (1953–69).1891—1974
Warren, Joseph, American Revolutionary patriot....1741—1775
Warren, Robert Penn, American novelist and poet....1905—
Warton (wạr'tŏn), **Joseph,** English poet and critic....1722—1800
W., Thomas (*brother of J.W.*), English poet laureate....1728—1790
Warwick (wär'ik), **Richard Neville, Earl of** (*the Kingmaker*), English warrior....1428—1471
Washburn (wäsh'bũrn), **Elihu Benjamin,** American diplomat..1816—1887
Washington (wäsh'ing-tŏn), **Booker Taliaferro,** American Negro educator....1856—1915
Washington, George, American general and first president of the United States (1789–97)....1732—1799
W., Martha (b. *Martha Dandridge; widow of D.P. Custis*), wife of G. W....1732—1802
Wassermann, von (fọn väs'ẽr-män), **August,** German physician.1866—1925
Wassermann, Jakob, German novelist....1873—1934
Watson (wät'sŏn), **John Broadus,** American psychologist....1878—1958
Watson, Sir William, English poet....1858—1935
Watt (wät), **James,** Scottish inventor....1736—1819
Watteau (vȧ-tō'), **Antoine,** French painter....1684—1721
Watterson (wät'tẽr-sŏn), **Henry,** American journalist....1840—1921
Watts (wäts), **George Frederick,** English painter....1817—1904
Watts, Isaac, English clergyman and writer of hymns....1674—1748
Watts-Dunton (-dun'tŏn), **Walter Theodore,** English critic, poet, and novelist....1832—1914
Waugh (wạ), **Evelyn,** English novelist and critic....1903—1966
Wavell (wā'vel), **Archibald Percival, Viscount,** British field marshal; viceroy of India (1943–47)....1883—1950
Wayne (wān), **Anthony** (*Mad Anthony Wayne*), American Revolutionary general....1745—1796
Webb (web), **Beatrice Potter** (*wife of S.J.W.*), English economist, sociologist, and author....1858—1943
W., Sidney James, first Baron Passfield, English economist, sociologist, and statesman....1859—1947
Weber, von (fọn vẹ'bẽr), **Carl Maria, Baron,** German composer.1786—1826
Weber, Ernst Heinrich, German physiologist....1795—1878
W., Wilhelm Eduard (*brother of E.H.W.*), German physicist..1804—1891
Webster (web'stẽr), **Daniel,** American orator and statesman; secretary of state (1841–43, 1850–52)....1782—1852
Webster, John, English dramatist....1580?–1625?
Webster, Noah, American lexicographer....1758—1843
Wedekind (vẹ'de-kint), **Frank,** German dramatist....1864—1918
Wedgwood (weġ'wood), **Josiah,** English potter....1730—1795
Weed (wēd), **Thurlow,** Am. journalist and politician....1797—1882
Weems (wēmṣ), **Mason Locke** (*Parson Weems*), American writer and preacher....1759—1825
Weigall (wī'gạl), **Arthur Edward Pearse Brome,** English Egyptologist and author....1880—1934
Weill (vīl), **Kurt,** German composer in America....1900—1950
Weinberger (wīn'bẽrg-ẽr), **Jaromir,** Czech composer in the United States....1896—1967
Weingartner (vīn'gärt-nẽr), **Felix,** Austrian conductor and composer....1863—1942
Weismann (vīs'män), **August,** German biologist....1834—1914
Weizmann (vīts'män), **Chaim,** Israeli Zionist leader and chemist, born in Russia; first president of Israel (1948–52)....1874—1952
Welles (welṣ), **Gideon,** U.S. secretary of navy (1861–69)....1802—1878
Welles, Sumner, American statesman....1892—1961
Wellhausen (vel'hou-ṣen), **Julius,** German biblical critic....1844—1918
Wellington (wel'ling-tŏn), **Arthur Wellesley, first Duke of,** British general; defeated Napoleon at Waterloo (1815); prime minister (1828–30)....1769—1852
Wells (welṣ), **H. G.** (*Herbert George W.*), English novelist and historian....1866—1946
Wells, Horace, American dentist; experimented in use of laughing gas in anesthesia....1815—1848
Welsbach, von (fọn vels'bäkh), **Carl Auer, Baron,** Austrian chemist and inventor....1858—1929

Wenceslaus (wen'ces-lọs), Holy Roman emperor and king of Bohemia....1361—1419
Wenceslaus, Saint, Christian martyr and patron saint of Bohemia....903—935?
Wendell (wen'del), **Barrett**, Am. educator and author....1855—1921
Werfel (ver'fel), **Franz**, Austrian poet, dramatist, and novelist, born in Prague....1890—1945
Werner (ver'nẽr), **Abraham Gottlob**, German geologist....1750—1817
Werner, Friedrich Ludwig Zacharias, German dramatist....1768—1823
Wertheimer (vert'hī-mẽr), **Max**, German psychologist....1880—1943
Wescott (wes'ç̄ŏt), **Glenway**, American novelist....1901—
Wesley (wes'li), **Charles** (*brother of J.W.*), English Methodist clergyman and hymn writer....1707—1788
W., John, English founder of Methodism....1703—1791
West (west), **Benjamin**, American painter; president of the Royal Academy, England....1738—1820
West, Rebecca, English critic and novelist....1892—
Westcott (west'ç̄ŏt), **Edward Noyes**, American novelist....1846—1898
Westermarck (ve'stẽr-märk), **Edward Alexander**, Finnish anthropologist....1862—1939
Westinghouse (west'ing-hous), **George**, Am. inventor....1846—1914
Weygand (vẹ-gäṅ'), **Maxime**, French general....1867—1965
Weyman (wȳ'măn), **Stanley John**, English novelist....1855—1928
Wharton (hwạr'tŏn), **Edith** (b. *Edith Newbold Jones*), American novelist....1862—1937
Wheatley (hwēt'li), **Phillis**, American Negro poet, born in Africa and brought to Boston as a slave....1753?—1784
Wheatstone (hwēt'stŏn), **Sir Charles**, English physicist....1802—1875
Wheeler (hwēl'ẽr), **Benjamin Ide**, American educator....1854—1927
Wheeler, Joseph, American cavalry leader and general....1836—1906
Wheeler, Wayne Bidwell, American prohibitionist....1869—1927
Wheelock (hwē'lŏk), **Eleazar**, American preacher; founder and first president of Dartmouth College....1711—1779
Whipple (hwip'l), **Abraham**, American naval officer....1733—1819
Whipple, Edwin Percy, American essayist and critic....1819—1886
Whipple, George Hoyt, American pathologist....1878—1976
Whistler (hwis'lẽr), **James Abbot McNeill**, American painter and etcher in England....1834—1903
Whiston (hwis'tŏn), **William**, English theologian....1667—1752
White (hwīt), **Andrew Dickson**, American educator and diplomat; first president of Cornell University....1832—1918
White, Byron Raymond, associate justice, U.S. Supreme Court (1962–)....1917—
White, Edward Douglass, chief justice of the United States Supreme Court (1910–21)....1845—1921
White, Elwyn Brooks (*E.B. White*), American author and humorist....1899—
White, Gilbert, English naturalist....1720—1793
White, Henry Kirke, English poet....1785—1806
White, Horace, American journalist and writer....1834—1916
White, Richard Grant, American scholar and writer....1821—1885
W., Stanford (*son of R.G.W.*), American architect....1853—1906
White, Stewart Edward, American novelist....1873—1946
White, Walter (Francis), American Negro leader....1893—1955
White, William Alanson, American psychiatrist....1870—1937
White, William Allen, American journalist and author....1868—1944
Whitefield (hwīt'fēld), **George**, English Methodist-Calvinistic preacher....1714—1770
Whitehead (hwīt'hed), **Alfred North**, English mathematician and philosopher....1861—1947
Whitehead, William, Eng. dramatist and poet laureate....1715—1785
Whiteman (hwīt'măn), **Paul**, Am. musician and conductor....1891—1967
Whitlock (hwit'lok), **Brand**, Am. diplomat and author....1869—1934
Whitman (hwit'măn), **Marcus**, American missionary....1802—1847
Whitman, Walt (*Walter Whitman*), American poet....1819—1892
Whitney (hwit'ni), **Eli**, Am. inventor of the cotton gin....1765—1825
Whitney, Josiah Dwight, American geologist....1819—1896
W., William Dwight (*brother of J.D.W.*), American philologist....1827—1894
Whittier (hwit'i-ẽr), **John Greenleaf**, American poet....1807—1892
Whittington (hwit'ing-tŏn), **Richard**, mayor of London....1358?—1423
Whyte-Melville (hwȳt'mel'vil), **George John**, English novelist and sportsman....1821—1878
Wickard (wik'ărd), **Claude Raymond**, U.S. secretary of agriculture (1940–45)....1893—1967
Wickliffe (wik'lif), **John**, *see* Wyclif, John.
Wieland (vē'länt), **Christoph Martin**, German poet and novelist....1733—1813
Wieland, Heinrich, German chemist....1877—1957
Wien (vēn), **Wilhelm**, German physicist....1864—1928
Wiener (wē'nẽr), **Norbert**, American mathematician and pioneer in cybernetics....1894—1964
Wieniawski (vye-nyäf'skī), **Henri**, Polish violinist....1835—1880
Wiggin (wig'gin), **Kate Douglas**, American novelist....1856—1923
Wilberforce (wil'bẽr-fọrc), **William**, English philanthropist, devoted to the abolition of slavery....1759—1833
Wilbur (wil'bŭr), **Ray Lyman**, American educator and secretary of the interior (1929–33)....1875—1949
Wilcox (wil'ç̄oks), **Ella Wheeler**, American poet....1855—1919
Wilde (wīld), **Oscar** (*Oscar Fingall O'Flahertie Wills Wilde*), Irish poet, dramatist, and novelist....1854—1900
Wilder (wīld'ẽr), **Thornton (Niven)**, American novelist and playwright....1897—1975
Wilhelmina (vil-hel-mī'nä) **I**, queen of the Netherlands (1890–1948)....1880—1962
Wilkes (wilks), **Charles**, Am. naval officer and explorer....1798—1877
Wilkes, John, English politician and reformer....1727—1797
Wilkie (wil'ki), **Sir David**, Scottish painter....1785—1841
Wilkins (wil'kinș), **Sir George Hubert**, Australian explorer of the Arctic and Antarctic....1888—1958
Wilkins, Mary Eleanor, *see* Freeman, Mary E. Wilkins.
Wilkinson (wil'kin-sŏn), **Sir John Gardner**, English Egyptologist....1797—1875
Willard (wil'lărd), **Emma Hart**, American educator....1787—1870
Willard, Frances Elizabeth, American educator and temperance advocate....1839—1898
Willard, Jess, American prize fighter; world heavyweight champion (1915–19)....1883—1968
William (wil'yăm) **I** (*the Conqueror*), king of England (1066–87)....1027—1087
W. II (*Rufus*), (*son of W. I*), king of England (1087-1100)....1056—1100
W. III (*William of Nassau, Prince of Orange*), king of England (1689–1702)....1650—1702
W. IV (*son of George III*), king of England (1830–37)....1765—1837
William I, first king of the Netherlands (1815–40)....1772—1843
W. II (*son of W.I*), king of Netherlands (1840–49)....1792—1849
W. III (*son of W.II*), king of Netherlands (1849–90)....1817—1890
William I (*Wilhelm Friedrich Ludwig*), king of Prussia (1861–88) and emperor of Germany (1871–88)....1797—1888
W. II (*Friedrich Wilhelm Viktor Albert*), (*son of Frederick III*) king of Prussia and emperor of Germany (1888–1918); abdicated....1859—1941
William of Malmesbury (ov mämș'bŭr-y), English historian....1095?—1143
William of Nassau (nä'sou), (*the Silent*) prince of Orange....1533—1584
Williams (wil'yămș), **Ben Ames**, American novelist....1889—1953
Williams, Ephraim, American colonial soldier....1715—1755
Williams, Sir Monier Monier-, *see* Monier-Williams.
Williams, Roger, Puritan reformer and founder of Rhode Island, born in England....1603?—1683
Williams, Tennessee, American dramatist....1914—
Williams, William Carlos, American novelist and poet....1883—1963
Willis (wil'lis), **Nathaniel Parker**, American poet and journalist....1806—1867
Willis, Robert, English physicist and mechanician....1800—1875
Willis, Thomas, English anatomist and physician....1621—1675
Willkie (wil'kē), **Wendell Lewis**, Am. lawyer and industrialist; Rep. presidential candidate (1940)....1892—1944
Wills (wilș), **Helen Newington**, American tennis player....1906—
Wills, William Gorman, Irish dramatist....1828—1891
Willstätter (vil'shtāt-ẽr), **Richard**, German chemist....1872—1942
Wilmot (wil'mot), **David**, American political leader....1814—1868
Wilson (wil'sŏn), **Alexander**, American ornithologist, born in Scotland....1766—1813
Wilson, Charles Erwin, U.S. sec. of defense (1953–59)....1890—1961
Wilson, Charles Thomson Rees, English physicist....1869—1959
Wilson, Edmund, American critic and writer....1895—1972
Wilson, Harry Leon, American novelist....1867—1939
Wilson, Henry, U.S. vice-president (1873–75)....1812—1875
Wilson, Horace Hayman, English Orientalist....1786—1860
Wilson, James, American jurist; signer of the Declaration of Independence....1742—1798
Wilson, (James) Harold, English politician; prime minister of the United Kingdom (1964–70, 1974–76)....1916—
Wilson, John (pseud. *Christopher North*), Scot. author....1785—1854
Wilson, Margaret, American novelist....1882—
Wilson, Richard, English landscape painter....1714—1782
Wilson, William Lyne, Am. politician and educator....1843—1900
Wilson, Woodrow (*Thomas Woodrow W.*), 28th president of the United States (1913–21)....1856—1924
Winant (wī'nănt), **John Gilbert**, American statesman; ambassador to Great Britain (1941–46)....1889—1947
Winchell (win'chel), **Walter**, American columnist....1897—1972
Winckelmann (viñ'kel-män), **Johann Joachim**, German archaeologist and art historian....1717—1768
Windaus (vin'dous), **Adolf**, German chemist....1876—1959
Windham (wind'ăm), **William**, English statesman....1750—1810
Windsor (wind'șŏr), **Edward, Duke of**, *see* Edward VIII.
W., Wallis Warfield, Duchess of, Am.-born wife of W....1894—
Winslow (winș'lō), **Edward**, gov. of Plymouth colony....1595—1655
Winslow, John Ancrum, American commodore....1811—1873
Winsor (win'șŏr), **Justin**, Am. historian and librarian....1831—1897
Winter (win'tẽr), **William**, American poet and drama critic....1836—1917
Winthrop (win'thrŏp), **John**, governor of Massachusetts Bay colony....1588—1649
W., John (*son of J.W.*), governor of Connecticut colony....1606—1676
Winthrop, Robert Charles, American statesman....1809—1894
Winthrop, Theodore, American soldier and novelist....1828—1861
Wirt (wirt), **William**, American lawyer and writer....1772—1834
Wise (wīș), **Henry Alexander**, American politician and Confederate general....1806—1876
Wise, Stephen Samuel, American rabbi and author....1874—1949
Wiseman (wīș'măn), **Nicholas Patrick**, English cardinal....1802—1865
Wister (wis'tẽr), **Owen**, American novelist....1860—1938
Wither (with'ẽr), **George**, English poet....1588—1667
Witte (vit'e), **Sergei Yulievich, Count**, Russian statesman....1849—1915
Wittgenstein (vit'găn-shtīn), **Ludwig Josef Johann**, British philosopher, b. in Austria....1889—1951
Wodehouse (wŏd'hous), **Sir Pelham Grenville** (*P. G. Wodehouse*), English novelist....1881—1975
Woffington (wof'ing-tŏn), **Margaret** (*Peg*), Ir. actress....1714?—1760
Wolcot (wool'ç̄ŏt), **John** (pseud. *Peter Pindar*), English satiric poet....1738—1819
Wolcott (wool'ç̄ŏt), **Oliver**, American Revolutionary patriot and statesman....1726—1797
W., Oliver (*son of O.W.*), U.S. sec. of treasury (1795–1801)....1760—1833
Wolf (vōlf), **Friedrich August**, German classical scholar and critic....1759—1824
Wolf, Hugo, Austrian composer of songs....1860—1903
Wolfe (woolf), **Charles**, Irish poet....1791—1823
Wolfe, Humbert, English poet and biographer....1885—1940
Wolfe, James, Eng. general; defeated Montcalm; killed at Quebec....1727—1759
Wolfe, Thomas (Clayton), American novelist....1900—1938
Wolf-Ferrari (vọlf-fẹr-rä'ri), **Ermanno**, Italian composer....1876—1948
Wolfram von Eschenbach (vọl'främ fọn esh'en-bäkh), German poet....? —1220?
Wollstonecraft (wool'stŏn-ç̄raft), **Mary** (*Mrs. William Godwin*), English social theorist and author....1759—1797
Wolseley (woolș'li), **Garnet Joseph, Viscount**, British general....1833—1913
Wolsey (wool'și), **Thomas**, Eng. cardinal and statesman....1475?—1530
Wood (wood), **Anthony à**, English antiquarian....1632—1695
Wood, Mrs. Henry (b. *Ellen Price*), English novelist....1820—1887
Wood, Grant, American painter....1892—1942
Wood, Leonard, American general; governor general of the Philippines (1921–27)....1860—1927
Woodworth (wood'wŏrth), **Robert Sessions**, American psychologist....1869—1962
Wool (wool), **John Ellis**, American general....1784—1869
Woolf (woolf), **Virginia (Stephen)**, English novelist....1882—1941
Woollcott (wool'ç̄ŏt), **Alexander**, Am. critic and essayist....1887—1944
Woolsey (wool'și), **Sarah Chauncey** (pseud. *Susan Coolidge*), American writer of children's books....1835—1905
Woolson (wool'sŏn), **Constance Fenimore**, Am. author....1840—1894
Woolworth (wool'wŏrth), **Frank Winfield**, Am. merchant....1852—1919
Wooster (woos'tẽr), **David**, Am. Revolutionary general....1711—1777
Worcester (woos'tẽr), **Edward Somerset, Marquis of**, English peer and inventor....1601—1667
Worcester, Joseph Emerson, American lexicographer....1784—1865

Worden (wọr'den), **John Lorimer**, American naval officer; commander of the *Monitor*....1818—1897
Wordsworth (wŏrdṣ'wŏrth), **William**, Eng. poet laureate....1770—1850
Worth (wŏrth), **William Jenkins**, American general....1794—1849
Wotton (wot'tŏn), **Sir Henry**, English poet....1568—1639
Wouk (wōk), **Herman**, American novelist....1915—
Wrangell, von (vọn vrän'gel), **Ferdinand Petrovich, Baron**, Russian explorer and governor of Russian America....1794—1870
Wren (ren), **Sir Christopher**, English architect....1632—1723
Wren, Percival Christopher, English novelist....1885—1941
Wright (rīt), **Frank Lloyd**, American architect....1869—1959
Wright, Harold Bell, American novelist....1872—1944
Wright, Joseph, English lexicographer and grammarian....1855—1930
Wright, Orville, Am. airplane inventor, working with his brother *Wilbur*; they made the first successful airplane flights (at Kitty Hawk, N.C., Dec. 17, 1903)....1871—1948
Wright, Richard, American author....1908—1960
Wright, Silas, American statesman....1795—1847
Wright, Wilbur, Am. airplane inventor, working with his brother *Orville*....1869—1912
Wright, Willard Huntington (pseud. *S.S. Van Dine*), American art critic and writer of detective novels....1888—1939
Wundt (vụnt), **Wilhelm Max**, German psychologist and physiologist....1832—1920
Wurdemann (wūr'de-măn), **Audrey May** (*Mrs. Joseph Auslander*), American poet....1911—1960
Wyant (wȳ'ănt), **Alexander Helwig**, American painter....1836—1892
Wyatt (wȳ'ăt), **Sir Thomas**, English poet and courtier....1503—1542
Wycherley (wych'ĕr-li), **William**, English dramatist....1640?–1716
Wyclif, Wycliffe *or* **Wickliffe** (wyç'lif), **John**, English ecclesiastical reformer; first translator of Bible into English....1324?-1384
Wylie (wȳ'li), **Elinor** (*Mrs. W.R. Benét*), American poet and novelist....1885—1928
Wylie, Ida Alexa Ross, British novelist....1885—1959
Wyndham (wynd'ăm), **Sir Charles**, English actor and theatrical manager....1837—1919
Wyss (vēs), **Johann David**, Swiss writer....1743—1818
Wythe (wyth), **George**, American jurist; signer of the Declaration of Independence....1726—1806

X

Xavier (zav'i-ĕr), **Saint Francis** (*the Apostle of the Indies*), Spanish Jesuit missionary....1506—1552
Xenocrates (ze-noç'rȧ-tēṣ), Greek philosopher....B.C. 396— 314
Xenophanes (ze-nof'ȧ-nēṣ), Greek philosopher....fl.B.C. 6th cent.
Xenophon (zen'ō-fŏn), Athenian historian and general....B.C. 434?–355?
Xerxes (zĕrk'sēṣ) **I** (*the Great*), (*son of Darius I*) king of Persia. B.C. ? — 465

Y

Yale (yāl), **Elihu**, patron of Yale College, b. Boston....1649—1721
Yale, Linus, American inventor....1821—1868
Yamagata (yä'mä ga'tä), **Aritomo, Prince**, Japanese marshal and statesman....1838—1922
Yamamoto (yä'mä-mō'tō), **Isoroku**, commander of the Japanese fleet (1939–43); killed in action....1884—1943
Yamashita (yä'mä-shĭ'tä), **Tomoyuki** (*the Tiger of Malaya*), Japanese general; conqueror of Malaya and Luzon; executed for war crimes....1885—1946
Yancey (yan'ci), **William Lowndes**, American politician....1814—1863
Yeats (yāts), **William Butler**, Irish poet and dramatist....1865—1939
Yerkes (yĕr'kēṣ), **Robert Mearns**, Am. psychologist....1876—1956
Yonge (yung), **Charlotte Mary**, English novelist....1823—1901
Yoshihito (yō'shĭ-hĭ'tō), emperor of Japan (1912–26)....1879—1926
Youmans (yŏ'mănṣ), **Edward Livingston**, American scientist and editor....1821—1887
Young (yung), **Art** (*Arthur Henry Y.*), Am. cartoonist....1866—1943
Young, Brigham, American leader of the Mormons....1801—1877
Young, Charles Augustus, American astronomer....1834—1908
Young, Edward, English poet....1683—1765
Young, Francis Brett, English novelist and playwright....1884—1954
Young, Mahonri Mackintosh, American painter and sculptor.1877—1957
Young, Owen D., American lawyer and financier....1874—1962
Young, Stark, American novelist and playwright....1881—1963
Young, Thomas, English physicist and Egyptologist....1773—1829
Ypsilanti (ēp-sĭ-län'tĭ), **Alexander, Prince**, Greek patriot and general....1792—1828
Ysaye (ē-ṣȧ-ē'), **Eugène**, Belgian violinist....1858—1931
Yüan Shi-kai (yụ-än' shĭ'kī'), pres. of China (1912–16)....1859—1916

Z

Zaharoff (za'hȧ-rof), **Sir Basil** (b. *Basileios Zacharias*), (*the Mystery Man of Europe*) munitions magnate, born in Turkey of Greek parents....1850—1936
Zaïmis (zä'ī-mis), **Alexander**, Greek statesman....1855—1936
Zamojski *or* **Zamoyski** (zä-moi'skĭ), **Jan**, Polish statesman, general, and scholar....1541—1605
Zamora y Torres (thä-mō'rä ē tō'rẹs), **Niceto Alcalá**, first president of the Spanish Republic (1931–36)....1877—1949
Zangwill (zang'wil), **Israel**, English novelist and poet....1864—1926
Zaturenska (zä-tûr-en'skȧ), **Marya** (*Mrs. Horace Gregory*), American poet....1902—
Zeeland, van (vän zẹ'länt), **Paul**, Belgian economist and prime minister (1935–37)....1893—
Zeeman (zẹ'män), **Pieter**, Dutch physicist....1865—1943
Zeiss (tsīs), **Carl**, German optician....1816—1888
Zeno (zē'nō), Greek philosopher; founder of the Stoic school. B.C. 336?–264?
Zeno (*the Isaurian*), emperor of Eastern Roman Empire.... 426?– 491
Zeno (dzẹ'nō), **Apostolo**, Italian poet and biographer....1668—1750
Zeno of Elea, Greek philosopher....fl.B.C.475?
Zenobia (ze-nō'bi-ȧ), **Septimia**, queen of Palmyra.... ? –aft. 272
Zeppelin, von (fọn tsep-e-lĭn'), **Ferdinand, Count**, German general and aircraft inventor....1838—1917
Zeuxis (zūk'sis), Greek painter....fl.B.C.450?
Zhukov (zụ'kọf), **Georgi Konstantinovich**, Russ. marshal....1896—1974
Ziegfeld (zēg'feld), **Florenz**, Am. theatrical producer....1869—1932
Zieten, von (fọn tsē'ten), **Hans Joachim**, Prussian general....1699—1786
Zimbalist (zim'bȧ-list), **Efrem**, Russian violinist in U.S....1889—
Zinoviev (zi-nọ'vyef), **Grigori Evseyevich**, Russian Communist leader; executed....1883—1936
Zinsser (zin'sẽr), **Hans**, American bacteriologist....1878—1940
Ziska (zis'kä) *or* **Žižka** (zish'kä), **Jan**, Bohemian general; leader of the Hussites....1360?–1424
Zola (zō-lȧ'), **Émile**, French novelist....1840—1902
Zorach (zọr'äçh), **William**, American painter and sculptor, born in Lithuania....1887—1966
Zorn (sọrn), **Anders Leonhard**, Swedish etcher and painter....1860—1920
Zoroaster (zō-rō-as'tẽr), (*Zarathustra*) philosopher and founder of the ancient Persian religion....fl.c.B.C.1000
Zorrilla y Moral (thō-rĭl'yä ē mō-räl'), **José**, Spanish poet and dramatist....1817—1893
Zsigmondy (shig'mŏn-dē), **Richard**, Austrian chemist....1865—1929
Zuccarelli (tsụç-çä-rel'lĭ), **Francesco**, It. landscapist....1702—1788
Zuccaro (tsụç'çä-rō) *or* **Zucchero** (tsụç'çhẹ-rō), **Federigo**, Italian painter....1543—1609
Zuloaga (thụ-lō-ä'gä), **Ignacio**, Spanish painter....1870—1945
Zweig (tsvīkh), **Arnold**, German novelist in Israel....1887—1968
Zweig, Stefan, German novelist, biographer, and playwright....1881—1942
Zwingli (tsving'lĭ), **Ulrich** *or* **Huldreich**, Swiss patriot and Protestant reformer....1484—1531

A DICTIONARY OF GEOGRAPHY

Including areas and population figures for countries, provinces, states, counties.

A

Abkhazian Autonomous Soviet Socialist Republic, a division of Georgian S.S.R., on Black Sea: 3,358 sq. mi.; pop., 487,000; cap., Sukhumi.

Abruzzi e Molise, a region of central Italy, on the Adriatic.

Abu Dhabi, the largest sheikdom of the United Arab Emirates, on the Persian Gulf: area, c.4,000 sq. mi.

Abu Simbel, village in S. Egypt, on the Nile: site of two temples built in a cliff for Ramses II.

Abydos, 1. an ancient Egyptian city. **2.** an ancient city in Asia Minor.

Abyssinia, same as *Ethiopia.*

Accad, same as *Akkad.*

Achaia, Achaea, a province of ancient Greece, in the Peloponnesus.

Aden, a former British state in S.W. Arabia: now part of People's Democratic Republic of Yemen.

Admiralty Islands, a group of small islands in the Bismarck Archipelago: pop., 19,000.

Adygei Autonomous Region, a division of the R.S.F.S.R., in N.W. Caucasus: area, 1,505 sq. mi.; pop., 386,000; cap., Maikop.

Adzhar Autonomous Soviet Socialist Republic, a division of Georgian S.S.R., in Transcaucasus: area, 1,080 sq. mi.; pop., 310,000; cap., Batumi.

Aegean Islands, a group of islands in the Aegean Sea.

Aegina, an island off S.E. coast of Greece: area, 41 sq. mi.; pop., 6,500.

Aeolis, Aeolia, a region in N.W. Asia Minor.

Aetolia, a region in W. part of ancient Greece.

Afghanistan, a country in S.W. Asia, between Iran and India: area, 245,000 sq. mi.; pop., 18,294,000; cap., Kabul.

Afrasia, N. Africa E. of the Sahara, and S.W. Asia, considered together.

Africa, the second largest continent, situated in Eastern Hemisphere, S. of Europe, between Atlantic and Indian Oceans: area, 11,500,000 sq. mi.; pop., 412,000,000.

Agrigentum, an ancient city in S. Sicily.

Aguascalientes, a state of central Mexico: area, 2,499 sq. mi.; pop., 335,000; also, its capital.

Aïr, a region and native kingdom in Niger: area, c.30,000 sq. mi.: also called *Asben.*

Ajmer, a former state of N.W. India: area, 2,400 sq. mi.

Ajmer–Merwara, a former province of N.W. central India: since 1950, included in Rajasthan state: area, 2,400 sq. mi.

Akkad, an ancient country N. of Babylonia; also, its chief city: also spelled *Accad.*

Aksum, an ancient capital of Ethiopia: also spelled *Axum.*

Alabama, a Southern State of the United States: area, 51,609 sq. mi.; pop., 3,444,000; cap., Montgomery.

Aland Islands, a group of Finnish islands at the entrance to the Gulf of Bothnia: area, 572 sq. mi.; pop., 22,000.

Alaska, a State of the U.S. in N.W. North America, separated from Asia by Bering Strait: area, 586,400 sq. mi.; pop., 302,000; cap. Juneau.

Alba Longa, an ancient city in Italy, near Rome.

Albania, a country in W. Balkan Peninsula: area, 10,629 sq. mi.; pop., 2,188,000; cap., Tirana.

Alberta, a province of S.W. Canada: area, 255,285 sq. mi.; pop., 1,838,000; cap., Edmonton.

Alcatraz, a small island in San Francisco Bay: formerly, the site of a Federal prison.

Alderney, one of the Channel Islands of Great Britain: area, 3 sq. mi.; pop., 1,500.

Aleutian Islands, a chain of islands extending c.1,200 miles S.W. from Alaska: pop., 8,000: a part of the State of Alaska.

Alexander Archipelago, a chain of islands off the S.E. coast of Alaska.

Algeria, a country in N. Africa, formerly under French control: area, 847,552 sq. mi.; pop., 16,776,000; cap., Algiers.

Algiers, a former Barbary State in North Africa: now *Algeria.*

Alsace, a former province of N.E. France.

Alsace–Lorraine, a region in N.E. France, consisting of former provinces of Alsace and Lorraine: seized by Germany in 1871; restored to France by Versailles Treaty; again regained by France in 1944 after German occupation in 1940.

Amboina, one of the Molucca Islands, in Indonesia: area, 384 sq. mi.; pop., 400,000; also, its capital.

Amchitka, an island in the Aleutians.

America, 1. North America. **2.** South America. **3.** North America, South America, and Central America considered together. **4.** the United States.

American Samoa, a possession of the U.S. since 1899, consisting of 6 Samoan islands in South Pacific: area, 76 sq. mi.; pop., 20,000; cap., Pago Pago on Tutuila Island.

Amhara, a district of N. Ethiopia, formerly a kingdom.

Amoy, an island of China, in Taiwan Strait.

Anam, same as *Annam.*

Anatolia, Asia Minor: ancient name; also, the Asiatic part of modern Turkey.

Andalusia, an old province of S. Spain.

Andaman Islands, a group of islands in Bay of Bengal, S.W. of Burma: with Nicobar Islands, a union territory of India. See *Nicobar Islands.*

Andorra, a republic in the Pyrenees Mountains, between Spain and France: area, 191 sq. mi.; pop., 27,000; also, its capital.

Andreanof Islands, a group of the Aleutian Islands.

Angkor, an ancient city in Cambodia, now in ruins.

Anglesey, an island of Wales: area, 276 sq. mi.; pop., 52,000.

Anglia, England: ancient Latin name.

Anglo–Egyptian Sudan, Sudan (sense 1): the former name.

Angola, a country on the S.W. coast of Africa: a former overseas province of Portugal: area, 481,351 sq. mi.; pop., 6,761,000; cap., Luanda.

Angus, a former county of E. Scotland.

Anhalt, a former state of central Germany: area, 893 sq. mi.; cap., Dessau.

Anhwei, a province of E. China: area, 57,440 sq. mi.; pop., 35,000,000; cap., Hofei: also called *Nganhui.*

Anjou, an old province of W. France about the city of Angers: name used by several royal houses, notably by the Plantagenets.

Annam, a former state of French Indochina, now part of Vietnam: also spelled *Anam.*

Antarctica, a region, mainly of ice fields, about the South Pole. area, c.5,000,000 sq. mi.: claims to parts of it have been made by various countries: sometimes called *Antarctic Continent.*

Antarctic Archipelago, a group of islands between South America and Antarctica.

Antarctic Circle, an imaginary circle parallel to the equator, 23°30′ from the South Pole.

Antarctic Zone, all of the region S. of the Antarctic Circle.

Anticosti, an island at mouth of St. Lawrence River, Quebec, Canada: area, c.3,000 sq. mi.

Antigua, a self-governing island of the Leeward group in the West Indies: it is an associated state of Great Britain: area, 108 sq. mi.; pop., 70,000; chief town, St. John's.

Antilles, a group of islands in West Indies.

Antioch, the capital of ancient Syria, in N.W. part: now a city in S. Turkey; also, an ancient city in Pisidia, Asia Minor.

Antipodes, a group of islands S.E. of New Zealand.

Antrim, a former county of Northern Ireland: chief city, Belfast.

Antung, a former province of China, in Manchuria: area, 22,468 sq. mi.

Antwerp, a province of N. Belgium; area, 1,104 sq. mi.; pop., 1,530,000; also, its capital.

Aquileia, an ancient town in Italy, at N. end of the Adriatic.

Aquitaine, a former district of S.W. France: later called *Guyenne.*

Aquitania, the S.W. division of ancient Gaul.

Arabia, a peninsula in S.W. Asia, largely a desert region: area, 1,000,000 sq. mi.

Arabia Felix, 1. the fertile region of Yemen, S.W. Arabia: the ancient Latin name. **2.** all of ancient Arabia except the northern parts.

Araby, same as *Arabia.*

Aragon, a N.E. region in Spain, formerly a separate kingdom.

Aram, ancient Syria: the Hebrew name.

Arbela, an ancient Persian city, now in N. Iraq: modern name, *Erbil.*

Arcadia, an ancient pastoral district of central Peloponnesus, Greece.

Archangel, a region in the R.S.F.S.R., on Arctic Ocean: pop., 1,199,000; also, its capital.

Arctic Circle, an imaginary circle parallel to the equator, 23°30′ from the North Pole.

Arctic Zone, all the region north of the Arctic Circle.

Argentina, a country in S. South America: area, 1,079,965 sq. mi.; pop., 25,383,000; cap., Buenos Aires.

Argolis, a district of ancient Greece, on E. coast of the Peloponnesus: ancient name.

Argyll, a former county of W. Scotland, including many islands of the Hebrides.

Arica, a region of N. Chile: formerly part of Tacna-Arica.

Arimathea, Arimathaea, a town in ancient Palestine.

Arizona, a Southwestern State of the U.S., on Mexican border: area, 113,909 sq. mi.; pop., 1,772,000; cap., Phoenix.

Arkansas, a Southern State of the south central U.S.: area, 53,102 sq. mi.; pop., 1,923,000; cap., Little Rock.

Armenia, 1. a former country in S.W. Asia, S. of Caucasus Mountains. **2.** the Armenian S.S.R.

Armenian Soviet Socialist Republic, a republic of the U.S.S.R., in the Transcaucasus: area, 11,580 sq. mi.; pop., 2,500,000; cap., Yerevan: sometimes called *Armenia.*

Armorica, an ancient region in N.W. France, corresponding to Brittany.

Arran, a Scottish island in Firth of Clyde: area, 165 sq. mi.; pop., 8,000.

Arru Islands, same as *Aru Islands.*

Artois, a former province of N. France.

Aruba, an island of the Netherlands Antilles, off W. Venezuela: area, 70 sq. mi.; pop., 59,000.

Aru Islands, a group of islands in Indonesia, S.W. of New Guinea: area, 3,326 sq. mi.: also spelled *Arru Islands.*

Asben, same as *Aïr.*

Ashanti, a region in central Ghana: area, 24,380 sq. mi.; pop., 1,447,000; cap., Kumasi.

Asia, the largest continent: situated in the Eastern Hemisphere and separated from N. Europe by Ural Mountains: area, 16,990,000 sq. mi.; pop., 2,366,000,000.

Asia Minor, a peninsula in W. Asia, between Black Sea and Mediterranean, including most of Asiatic Turkey: formerly called *Anatolia.*

Asir, a S.W. district of Saudi Arabia: formerly a principality.

Assam, a state of N.E. India, on borders of Burma and Tibet: area, 58,739 sq. mi.; pop., 11,873,000; cap., Shillong.

Assam States, a group of individual states in Assam, including Manipur and those of Khasi Hills.

Assyria, an ancient empire in W. Asia in region of upper Tigris River: capital, Nineveh.

Asturias, an old province of N.W. Spain.

Attica, a state of ancient Greece: cap., Athens.

Attu, an island in W. Aleutians.

Australasia, 1. the part of the earth including Australia, Tasmania, New Zealand, Malaysia, Melanesia, Micronesia, and Polynesia. **2.** Australia, Tasmania, New Zealand, and British possessions of Melanesia.

Australia, 1. a continent in the Southern Hemisphere, between South Pacific and Indian Oceans. **2.** a country comprising this continent and Tasmania: area, 2,974,581 sq. mi.; pop., 13,601,000; cap., Canberra: official name, *the Commonwealth of Australia.*

Australian Capital Territory, a federal territory in New South Wales: seat of Australian government: area, 939 sq. mi.; pop., 96,000: formerly called *Federal Capital Territory.*

Austrasia, the eastern territory of the Franks (5th-9th centuries) composed of what is now N.E. France, Belgium, and W. Germany.

Austria, a country in central Europe: area, 32,375 sq. mi.; pop., 7,523,000; cap., Vienna.

Austria–Hungary, a former monarchy in central Europe: included territory that became Austria, Czechoslovakia, and Hungary, and parts of Poland, Romania, Yugoslavia, and Italy: broken up by the Versailles Treaty: area, 240,000 sq. mi.

Austronesia, the islands in the central and S. Pacific.

Auvergne, an old province of central France.

Avon, a county of S.W. England, on the Severn estuary: area, 520 sq. mi.; pop., 915,000.

Axum, same as *Aksum.*

Azerbaijan, 1. a province of N.W. Iran: capital, Tabriz. **2.** the Azerbaijan S.S.R.
Azerbaijan Soviet Socialist Republic, a republic of the U.S.S.R., on the Caspian Sea, in Transcaucasia: area, 33,200 sq. mi.; pop., 5,100,000; cap., Baku.
Azores, a group of islands W. of Portugal and constituting three districts of Portugal: area, 922 sq. mi.; pop., 596,000.

B

Babuyan Islands, a small group of islands in the Philippines, off N. coast of Luzon.
Babylon, an ancient city on Euphrates River, capital of Babylonia and later of Chaldea.
Babylonia, an ancient empire of S.W. Asia, in lower valley of Tigris and Euphrates Rivers.
Bactria, an ancient country in N.E. part of modern Afghanistan: also called *Balkh.*
Baden, a region of S.W. Germany: formerly a duchy: area, 5,818 sq. mi.
Baffin Island, an island in Northwest Territories, Canada, N.E. of mainland: area, 211,000 sq. mi.; pop., 2,000.
Bagdad, Baghdad, a former caliphate in region of Tigris and Euphrates Rivers.
Bahamas, a country on a group of islands in West Indies, S.E. of Florida and N. of Cuba: area, 4,404 sq. mi.; pop., 204,000; cap., Nassau: official name, *Commonwealth of the Bahamas.*
Bahrein, a group of islands in Persian Gulf, off Arabian coast, constituting an independent Arab sheikdom: area, 250 sq. mi.; pop., 256,000; cap., Manama.
Baja California, Lower California: Mexican name.
Baker Island, a small island in Pacific, near the equator.
Balearic Islands, a group of Spanish islands, including Majorca and Minorca, in Mediterranean, E. of Spain: area, 1,935 sq. mi.; pop., 443,000; cap., Palma.
Bali, an island in Indonesia, E. of Java: area, 2,168 sq. mi.
Balkan Peninsula, a peninsula in S. Europe, E. of Italy and W. of Black Sea.
Balkans, the countries of the Balkan Peninsula: Yugoslavia, Romania, Bulgaria, Albania, Greece, and European Turkey: also called *Balkan States.*
Balkh, same as *Bactria.*
Baltic States, Lithuania, Latvia, and Estonia: Finland is sometimes included.
Baluchistan, a former province of Pakistan, which included a union of native states (the *Baluchistan States*): two divisions of Pakistan now comprise this area.
Banat, an agricultural region formerly in S.E. Hungary, now in S.W. Romania and N.E. Yugoslavia.
Banff, a former county of N.E. Scotland: also *Banffshire.*
Bangka, Banka, an island of Indonesia, E. of Sumatra: area, 4,611 sq. mi.
Bangladesh, a country in S. Asia, on the Bay of Bengal: area, 55,134 sq. mi.; pop., 76,815,000; cap., Dacca.
Barbados, a country on an island of the West Indies, east of the Windward Islands: area, 166 sq. mi.; pop., 245,000; cap., Bridgetown.
Barbary Coast, the coastal region in N. Africa, from Tripoli to Morocco.
Barbary States, the former countries of Morocco, Algiers, Tunis, and Tripoli in N. Africa.
Barbuda, a British island dependency in the West Indies: area, 62 sq. mi.; pop., 1,000.
Barca, same as *Cyrenaica.*
Barotseland, a province of W. Zambia: area, 44,920 sq. mi.; pop., 399,000.
Barren Grounds, Barren Lands, a region of bare tundras in Canada, northwest of Hudson Bay.
Bashan, a region E. and N.E. of the Sea of Galilee, Palestine.
Bashkir Autonomous Soviet Socialist Republic, a division of the R.S.F.S.R., W. of the South Ural Mountains: area, 54,233 sq. mi.; pop., 3,819,000; cap., Ufa.
Basque Provinces, a region in N. Spain.
Bas-Rhin, a department of France, on the Rhine: formerly Lower Alsace: area, 1,484 sq. mi.; pop., 827,000; cap., Strasbourg.
Basutoland, a former British protectorate in S. Africa: now the country of Lesotho.
Bataan, a peninsula W. of Manila Bay in the Philippines: famous for stand made by American soldiers against numerically superior Japanese forces in 1942.
Batan Islands, the northernmost group of islands in the Philippines: area, 74 sq. mi.
Bavaria, a division of S. Germany, formerly a duchy, kingdom, and republic: area, 30,054 sq. mi.; pop., 10,569,000; cap., Munich.
Bayern, Bavaria: German name.
Bechuanaland, a former British protectorate in S. Africa: now the country of Botswana.
Bedfordshire, Bedford, a county of central England: pop., 484,000; county seat, Bedford.
Bedloe Island, an island in New York Bay; site of Statue of Liberty: now called *Liberty Island.*
Beersheba, an ancient city in S.W. Palestine.
Belgian Congo, a former Belgian colony in central Africa, on the Atlantic: now the independent country of Zaire.
Belgium, a country in W. Europe, on the North Sea: area, 11,775 sq. mi.; pop., 9,804,000; cap., Brussels.
Belize, a self-governing British territory in Central America, on the Caribbean: area, 8,866 sq. mi.; pop., 127,000; cap., Belmopan.
Belorussia, same as *Byelorussia.*
Bengal, a former province of British India divided (1948) between Pakistan and India.
Benin, a country in W. central Africa, on the Gulf of Guinea: a former French colony: area, 44,696 sq. mi.; pop., 3,112,000; cap., Porto Novo.
Berar, formerly, a division of Central Provinces, India: since 1950, part of Madhya Pradesh.
Berkshire, a county of S. central England: pop., 653,000; county seat, Reading.
Bermuda, a group of British islands in the Atlantic, 677 mi. S.E. of New York: area, 20 sq. mi.; pop., 52,000; cap., Hamilton.
Berwick, a former county of S.E. Scotland.
Bessarabia, a district ceded to the U.S.S.R. by Romania in 1940, made part of Moldavian S.S.R.
Bethany, an ancient town near Jerusalem, on Mount of Olives.
Bethel, an ancient village in central Palestine, near Jerusalem.
Bethlehem, an ancient town in Judea: birthplace of Jesus; also a modern town in Palestine on the same site.
Bharat, Republic of India: Hindi name.
Bhopal, Bhopol, a former state of central India.
Bhutan, a state in the Himalaya Mountains, N. of India: area, 18,000 sq. mi.; pop., 1,035,000.
Bihar, a state of N.E. India: area, 70,368 sq. mi.; pop., 36,548,000; cap., Patna: also spelled *Behar.*
Bikaner, a former princely state in N.W. India: area, 23,181 sq. mi.
Bikini, an atoll in the Marshall Islands: site of atomic bomb tests in 1946.
Billiton, an island of Indonesia, between Sumatra and Borneo: area, 1,866 sq. mi.
Birobijan, Birobidzhan, the Jewish National Autonomous Region, an autonomous region of the R.S.F.S.R.: also, its capital.
Bismarck Archipelago, a group of islands N.E. of New Guinea: part of Papua New Guinea: area, 19,200 sq. mi.; pop., 183,000.
Black Forest, a mountainous district, about 100 mi. long, in S.W. Germany.
Blackwells Island, Welfare Island: former name.
Block Island, an island off coast of Rhode Island: pop., 500.
Boeotia, an ancient Greek state, N.W. of Attica: cap., Thebes.
Bohemia, a region of Czechoslovakia: formerly a kingdom and province of Austria-Hungary; area, 20,102 sq. mi.
Bohemian Forest, a wooded mountain region between Bavaria and Bohemia.
Böhmerwald, Böhmer Wald, the Bohemian Forest: German name.
Bohol, an island in the Philippines, between Cebu and Leyte: area, 1,534 sq. mi.
Bokhara, a part of the Uzbek Republic, U.S.S.R.: formerly a state of W. Asia.
Bolivia, an inland country of W. central South America: area, 420,000 sq. mi.; pop., 5,634,000; caps., La Paz and Sucre.
Bombay, a former state of W. India.
Bonin Islands, a group of islands in the Pacific, 500 mi. S.E. of Honshu Island, Japan: area, 30 sq. mi.; pop., 200.
Borders, a region of S. Scotland, on the border of England: area, 1,736 sq. mi.; pop., 99,000.
Border States, the States having Negro slavery and bordering on free territory in the U.S. before the Civil War: Missouri, Kentucky, Virginia, Maryland, and Delaware.
Borneo, 1. a large island in East Indies, S.W. of the Philippines, partly in Indonesia and partly composed of Brunei and the Malaysian states of Sabah and Sarawak: area, c.287,000 sq. mi. **2.** the S. (Indonesian) part of this island: area, c.208,000 sq. mi.; pop., 4,101,000: Indonesian name, *Kalimantan.*
Bornholm, a Danish island in Baltic Sea, S. of Sweden: area, 227 sq. mi.; pop., 47,000.
Bornu, a former sultanate: now part of Nigeria: area, c.50,000 sq. mi.
Bosnia, a part of Yugoslavia: formerly a kingdom in W. Balkan Peninsula.
Bosnia-Herzegovena, a federated republic of Yugoslavia: area, 19,678 sq. mi.; pop., 3,278,000; cap., Sarajevo.
Botswana, a country in S. Africa, north of South Africa: area, 222,000 sq. mi.; pop., 691,000; cap., Gaborone.
Bougainville, one of the Solomon Islands: part of Papua New Guinea: area, 3,880 sq. mi.
Brasil, Brazil: Spanish and Portuguese name.
Brazil, a country in central and N.E. South America on the Atlantic: area, 3,275,510 sq. mi.; pop., 107,145,000; cap., Brasilia.
Brecknockshire, a former county of Wales.
Bretagne, Brittany: French name.
Britain, England, Wales, and Scotland.
Britannia, 1. Britain: ancient Latin name. **2.** Great Britain, including Ireland and the Dominions. **3.** the British Empire.
British America, the British possessions in or adjacent to the Americas; also, Canada.
British Borneo, the former name for the N. part of the island of Borneo, comprising the British territories of Sarawak and North Borneo, and the sultanate of Brunei.
British Columbia, a province of S.W. Canada: area, 366,255 sq. mi.; pop., 2,467,000; cap., Victoria.
British Commonwealth of Nations, the British Empire; political aggregate comprising: (a) the United Kingdom (Great Britain and Northern Ireland); the Channel Islands; the Isle of Man; the British colonies, protectorates, and dependencies; and (b) Australia, Bahamas, Bangladesh, Barbados, Botswana, Canada, Cyprus, Fiji, Gambia, Ghana, Grenada, Guyana, India, Jamaica, Kenya, Lesotho, Malawi, Malaysia, Malta, Mauritius, Nauru, Nigeria, New Zealand, Papua New Guinea, Sierra Leone, Singapore, Sri Lanka, Swaziland, Tanzania, Tonga, Trinidad and Tobago, Uganda, Western Samoa, and Zambia: official name, **the Commonwealth.**
British East Africa, formerly, the British territories in E. Africa, including Kenya, Tanzania, and Uganda.
British Empire, the British Commonwealth of Nations; also, occasionally, the United Kingdom and its dependencies.
British Guiana, a former British colony in N. South America: now the country of Guyana.
British Honduras, Belize: the former name.
British India, the part of India formerly under British rule.
British Isles, Great Britain, Ireland, the Isle of Man, and the Channel Islands.
British Malaya, the former name for the British territories in the Malay Peninsula and the Malay Archipelago.
British New Guinea, Territory of Papua: former name.
British North America, Canada: former name.
British Somaliland, a former British protectorate in E. Africa: merged with Italian Somaliland to form the independent republic of Somalia.
British Virgin Islands, those of the Virgin Islands that are part of the Leeward Islands and constitute a colony of Great Britain: area, 58 sq. mi.; pop., 11,000; cap., Road Town.
British West Africa, the former British possessions in W. Africa.
British West Indies, the British colonies of the Lesser Antilles of the West Indies.
Brittany, a former province on N.W. coast of France.
Brunei, a sultanate on the N. coast of Borneo, under British protection: area, 2,226 sq. mi.; pop., 142,000.
Brunswick, a former division of central Germany: earlier, a duchy.
Buckinghamshire, a county in S. central England: pop., 498,000; county seat, Aylesbury.
Bucovina, a division of N. Romania, part of which was ceded to the U.S.S.R. in 1940.
Buenos Aires, a province in Argentina: pop., 8,733,000.
Bulgaria, a country in the Balkans, on the Black Sea: area, 42,796 sq. mi.; pop., 8,722,000; cap., Sofia.
Bundelkhand, a former agency of British India, in E. central India: area, 10,081 sq. mi.
Burgundy, a former duchy, kingdom, and province of E. France.
Burma, a country in S.E. Asia, on Bay of Bengal: formerly, a British colony: area, 261,610 sq. mi.; pop., 29,563,000; cap., Rangoon.
Burundi, a country in E. central Africa, E. of Zaire: area, 10,745 sq. mi.; pop., 3,763,000; cap., Bujumbura.
Bute, 1. a Scottish island in Firth of Clyde: area, 46 sq. mi. **2.** a former county of Scotland, including this island, Arran, and other islands in Firth of Clyde: also called *Buteshire.*
Byelorussia, 1. the W. part of European Russia. **2.** the Byelorussian S.S.R. Also spelled *Belorussia.*
Byelorussian Soviet Socialist Republic, a republic of the U.S.S.R., in W. European Russia: area, 89,300 sq. mi.; pop., 9,000,000; cap., Minsk: also called *White Russian S.S.R.*
Byzantine Empire, the E. division of the later Roman Empire (395–1453 A.D.): cap., Byzantium (Constantinople): also called *Eastern Empire.*
Byzantium, an ancient city on the Bosporus: cap. of Roman Empire 330 A.D.: site of modern Istanbul.

C

Caernarvonshire, Caernarvon, a former county of N.W. Wales: also *Carnarvon.*
Caird Coast, a region in Antarctica, E. of Weddell Sea: part of Falkland Islands dependency.
Caithness, a former county of N. Scotland.
Calabria, a region of S.W. Italy, opposite Sicily.
Calakmul, a ruined Mayan city in Campeche, Mexico.
California, a Western State of the U.S., on the Pacific Coast: area, 158,693 sq. mi.; pop., 19,953,000; cap., Sacramento.
Calydon, an ancient Greek city in Aetolia.
Cambodia, a country in the S. part of the Indochinese peninsula: area, 66,606 sq. mi.; pop., 6,701,000; cap., Pnom-Penh: official name, *Democratic Kampuchea.*
Cambridgeshire, Cambridge, a county of E. central England: pop., 541,000; county seat, Cambridge.
Cameroons, a former British trust territory in W. Africa: see *Cameroun and Nigeria.*
Cameroun, Cameroon, a country in W. central Africa: the S.

section of Cameroons joined Cameroun by plebescite in 1961: area, 183,576 sq. mi.; pop., 5,836,000; cap., Yaoundé.
Campania, a region of S.W. Italy: chief city, Naples.
Campeche, a state of Mexico, on Yucatan peninsula: area, 19,670 sq. mi.; pop., 250,000; also, its capital.
Campobello, an island in Bay of Fundy: part of New Brunswick.
Canaan, the Promised Land of the Israelites, a region roughly corresponding to modern Palestine.
Canada, a country in N. North America: a member of the British Commonwealth of Nations: area, 3,852,000 sq. mi.; pop., 22,598,000; cap., Ottawa.
Canal Zone, a military reservation of the U.S., consisting of a strip of land extending c.5 mi. on either side of the Panama Canal, excluding cities of Panama and Colón: area, 362 sq. mi.; pop., 45,000: ceded by Panama (1904) as perpetual lease.
Canara, same as *Kanara.*
Canary Islands, a group of islands off N.W. Africa, forming 2 provinces of Spain: area, 2,807 sq. mi.; pop., 944,000.
Candia, same as *Crete.*
Cannae, an ancient city in S.E. Italy: in a famous battle fought near Cannae (216 B.C.) Hannibal defeated the Romans by tactics of encirclement and annihilation now classical in military science.
Canopus, an ancient city in Lower Egypt, E. of Alexandria.
Canossa, an ancient town in N. Italy.
Cape Breton Island, an island at the mouth of the Gulf of St. Lawrence, constituting the N.E. part of Nova Scotia, Canada: area, 3,120 sq. mi.; pop., 166,000.
Cape Colony, Cape of Good Hope: former name.
Cape Province, same as *Cape of Good Hope.*
Capernaum, an ancient city in Palestine, on the Sea of Galilee.
Cape Verde, a country on a group of islands in the Atlantic, W. of the coast of Senegal: formerly an overseas territory of Portugal: area, 1,557 sq. mi.; pop., 294,000; cap., Praia.
Cappadocia, an ancient kingdom and Roman province of S. central Asia Minor.
Capri, an island in the Bay of Naples: area, 4 sq. mi.; pop., 6,000.
Capua, an ancient city in Italy, near Naples.
Cardiganshire, Cardigan, a former county of S. Wales.
Caria, an ancient country in S.W. Asia Minor.
Caribees, same as *Lesser Antilles.*
Carinthia, a province of S. Austria: pop., 495,000.
Carmarthenshire, Carmarthen, a former county of S. Wales.
Carnarvon, same as *Caernarvonshire.*
Carnatic, a region in S. India: part of Madras.
Carolina, an American colony on Atlantic coast, first settled in 1653: divided into North Carolina and South Carolina in 1729.
Carolinas, the, North Carolina and South Carolina.
Caroline Islands, a chain of c.550 small coral islands in Micronesia: area, 380 sq. mi.: former Japanese mandate; after World War II under U.S. trusteeship.
Carpatho-Ukraine, a region in Ukrainian S.S.R.: area, c.4,870 sq. mi.; former province of Czechoslovakia called *Ruthenia.*
Carthage, an ancient city and state in N. Africa, founded by the Phoenicians near present site of Tunis: destroyed by the Romans (146 B.C.).
Cashmere, same as *Kashmir.*
Castile, a former kingdom of central Spain.
Castilla la Nueva, a former province of central Spain: English name, *New Castile.*
Castilla la Vieja, a former province of central Spain: English name, *Old Castile.*
Catalina, same as *Santa Catalina.*
Catalonia, an old province of N.E. Spain.
Cataluña, Catalonia: Spanish name.
Caucasia, a region of the U.S.S.R., on either side of the Caucasus, between Black Sea and Caspian: also called *the Caucasus.*
Cayman Islands, three British islands S. of Cuba: area, 100 sq. mi.; pop., 7,600.
Cebu, an island in the Philippines, between Negros and Leyte: area, 1,703 sq. mi.; pop., 947,000; also, a province consisting of this island and adjacent small islands: pop., 1,350,000.
Celebes, an island of Indonesia, E. of Borneo: area, 69,255 sq. mi.; also, this island and several small adjacent island dependencies: area, 72,986 sq. mi.; pop., 7,079,000: Indonesian name, *Sulawesi.*
Central, a region of S. central Scotland.
Central African Empire, a country in central Africa, N. of the Congo and Zaire: a former French colony: area, 241,700 sq. mi.; pop., 2,370,000; cap., Bangui.
Central America, the part of North America between Mexico and South America: area, 226,881 sq. mi.
Central Provinces and Berar, Madhya Pradesh: former name.
Cephalonia, one of the Ionian Islands, off W. Greece: area, 277 sq. mi.; pop., 66,000.
Ceram, one of the Molucca Islands, in Indonesia: area, 6,621 sq. mi.; pop., 83,000: also called *Serang.*
Cerigo, one of the Ionian Islands, S. of Greece: area, 110 sq. mi.; pop., 9,000.
Cévennes, a former district of France, in N.E. Languedoc.
Ceylon, a country on an island off the S. tip of India: it is a member of the British Commonwealth of Nations: area, 25,332 sq. mi.; pop., 13,249,000; cap., Colombo: official name, *Sri Lanka.*
Chaco, a region in South America between the Pilcomayo River and Paraguay River, in dispute until 1938, when it was divided between Bolivia and Paraguay: area, 100,000 sq. mi.
Chad, a country in central Africa, south of Libya: a former French colony: area, 495,750 sq. mi.; pop., 4,030,000; cap., N'Djamena.
Chaeronea, an ancient Greek city in Boeotia, on the Attic border.
Chahar, a former province of Inner Mongolia.
Chalcedon, an ancient city in Asia Minor.
Chalcidice, a peninsula in N.E. Greece.
Chaldea, an ancient region in S.W. Asia, on Euphrates River and Persian Gulf.
Champagne, a former province of N.E. France.
Chandernagor, Chandarnagar, a former dependency of French India, N. of Calcutta: since 1950, a part of India: area, c.4 sq. mi.
Channel Islands, a group of British islands in the English Channel, off coast of Normandy, including Alderney, Jersey, and Guernsey: area, 75 sq. mi.; pop., 122,000.
Chatham Islands, a group of islands forming part of New Zealand: c.500 mi. E. of South Island: area, 372 sq. mi.; pop., 560.
Checheno-Ingush Autonomous Soviet Socialist Republic, a division of the R.S.F.S.R., in the Caucasus: area, 6,060 sq. mi.; pop., 1,065,000; cap., Grozny.
Chekiang, a province of China, on East China Sea: area, 39,750 sq. mi.; pop., 31,000,000; cap., Hangchow.
Chelyabinsk, a region of the R.S.F.S.R., in W. Siberia, E. of Ural Mountains: pop., 2,982,000; also, its capital.
Cherkessk Autonomous Region, a division of the R.S.F.S.R., in the Caucasus: area, 1,273 sq. mi.; pop., 97,000; cap., Sulimov.
Cheshire, Chester, a county of W. England: pop., 902,000; county seat, Chester.
Chiapas, a state of S. Mexico: area, 28,729 sq. mi.; pop., 1,578,000; cap., Tuxtla.
Chihli, Hopei: former name.
Chihuahua, a state of N. Mexico: area, 94,822 sq. mi.; pop., 1,730,000; also, its capital.
Chile, a country on S.W. coast of South America: area, 286,396 sq. mi.; pop., 10,253,000; cap., Santiago.
China, a country in E. Asia: area, 3,760,000 sq. mi.; pop., 700,000,000; Peking is the capital of the People's Republic of China (*Communist China,* established in 1949): the Kuomintang government (*National Republic of China*) in 1970 controlled only Taiwan and near-by islands.
Chinghai, a province of N.W. China, N.E. of Tibet: area, 258,000 sq. mi.; pop., 2,000,000; cap., Sining: also called *Koko Nor.*
Chin Hills, a mountainous district of N.W. Burma.
Chios, a Greek island off W. coast of Asia Minor: area, 350 sq. mi.; pop., 67,000.
Chishima, Kurile Islands, Japan: Japanese name.
Chita, a territory of the U.S.S.R., in S.E. Siberia: pop., 1,159,000; also, its capital.
Chkalov, a region of the R.S.F.S.R., in E. European Russia: pop., 1,677,000; also, its capital.
Choiseul, one of the Solomon Islands, in South Pacific, E. of Bougainville: area, 1,500 sq. mi.; pop., 4,000.
Chosen, Korea: Japanese name.
Christmas Island, 1. an island in the Indian Ocean, S. of Java: area, 62 sq. mi.; pop., 3,000: under Australian administration. **2.** a British island in the Pacific, near the equator: area, 235 sq. mi.; pop., 300.
Chuvash Autonomous Soviet Socialist Republic, a division of the R.S.F.S.R., in region of the middle Volga: area, 6,909 sq. mi.; pop., 1,224,000.
Circassia, a region of the U.S.S.R., N. of Caucasus Mountains, on Black Sea.
Cirenaica, a district of N.E. Libya: area, 212,000 sq. mi.: also spelled *Cyrenaica.*
Ciscaucasia, the part of Caucasia N. of the Caucasus.
Clackmannan, a former county of Scotland, on Firth of Forth.
Cleveland, a county of N. England, on the North Sea: pop., 566,000.
Clwyd, a county of N. Wales, on the Irish Sea: pop., 369,000.
Cnidus, an ancient town in S.W. Asia Minor.
Cnossus, same as *Knossos.*
Coahuila, a state of N. Mexico: area, 58,062 sq. mi.; pop., 1,041,000; cap., Saltillo.
Cochin, a former native state of S.W. India.
Cochin-China, a former state of S. French Indochina, on South China Sea: in 1949, became part of Vietnam.
Cochinchine, Cochin-China: French name.
Cocos Islands, a group of islands in the Indian Ocean, S. of Sumatra: area, 9 sq. mi.; pop., 600: a territory belonging to Australia: also called *Keeling Islands.*
Colchis, an ancient country in Transcaucasia, on E. shore of Black Sea.
Colima, a state of S. Mexico, on the Pacific: area, 2,009 sq. mi.; pop., 240,000; also, its capital.
Colombia, a country in N.W. South America: area, 439,920 sq. mi.; pop., 23,542,000; cap., Bogotá.
Colón Archipelago, same as *Galápagos Islands.*
Colophon, an ancient Ionian city.
Colorado, a Western State of the U.S.: area, 104,247 sq. mi.; pop., 2,207,000; cap., Denver.
Colossae, a city in ancient Phrygia.
Comores, Comoros: French name.
Comoros, a country on a group of islands in the Indian Ocean, between Mozambique and Madagascar: formerly a French colony: area, 838 sq. mi.; pop., 292,000; cap., Moroni.
Coney Island, a peninsula, formerly an island, in Brooklyn, New York, at S.W. end of Long Island, famous for its beach and amusement park.
Congo, 1. a country in W. central Africa, on the equator, N.W. of Zaire: formerly a territory (called *Middle Congo*) in French Equatorial Africa: area, 134,750 sq. mi.; pop., 1,300,000; cap., Brazzaville. **2.** Zaire: a former name.
Connaught, a province of W. Ireland: area, 6,610 sq. mi.; pop., 402,000.
Connecticut, a New England State of the U.S.: area, 5,009 sq. mi.; pop., 3,032,000; cap., Hartford.
Cooch Behar, a former state of N.E. India: in 1950, became part of West Bengal: area, 1,318 sq. mi.
Cook Islands, a group of Polynesian islands, belonging to New Zealand: area, 140 sq. mi.; pop., 21,000.
Corea, same as *Korea.*
Corfu, one of the Ionian Islands W. of Greece: area, 227 sq. mi.; pop., 106,000.
Corinth, an ancient city in S. Greece.
Cork, a county on S. coast of Ireland: pop., 340,000.
Cornwall, a county of S.W. England: pop., 399,000; county seat, Bodmin.
Coromandel Coast, a coastal region in S.E. India, extending inland to Eastern Ghats.
Corregidor, a small, fortified island in the Philippines, at entrance to Manila Bay: surrendered to Japan, but recaptured by U.S. forces, in World War II.
Corse, Corsica: French name.
Corsica, a French island in the Mediterranean, N. of Sardinia: area, 3,367 sq. mi.; pop., 270,000; cap., Ajaccio.
Costa Rica, a country in Central America, N.W. of Panama: area, 23,000 sq. mi.; pop., 1,968,000; cap., San José.
Cosyra, Pantelleria: ancient name.
Côte d'Azure, the S.E. coast of France, along the Riviera.
Crete, a Greek island in E. Mediterranean: area, 3,199 sq. mi.; pop., 483,000; cap., Canea: also called *Candia.*
Crimea, a peninsula in Soviet Russia, extendng into the Black Sea.
Crimean Autonomous Soviet Socialist Republic, a former division of the R.S.F.S.R., in the Crimea: area, 10,036 sq. mi.: abolished in 1945.
Croatia, an ancient kingdom: now federated republic of Yugoslavia, in N.W. part; cap., Zagreb.
Ctesiphon, an ancient city in Babylonia, on Tigris River, near modern Bagdad.
Cuba, a country on an island in West Indies, S. of Florida: area, 44,164 sq. mi.; pop., 9,090,000; cap., Havana.
Culion, a small island in W. Philippines.
Cumberland, a former county of N.W. England.
Cumbria, a county of N.W. England, on the border of Scotland: pop., 476,000.
Cunaxa, an ancient town near Babylon.
Curaçao, 1. the Netherlands Antilles: so called before 1949. **2.** the largest island of this state: area, 210 sq. mi.; pop., 132,000; cap., Willemstad.
Cutch, a former state of W. India: area, 8,461 sq. mi.
Cyclades, a group of Greek islands in the Aegean: area, 1,023 sq. mi.; pop., 100,000.
Cyprus, a country on an island in the E. Mediterranean, S. of Turkey: a former British crown colony, it is now a member of the British Commonwealth of Nations: area, 3,572 sq. mi.; pop., 639,000; cap., Nicosia.
Cyrenaica, an ancient land in N. Africa, in region of modern Cirenaica, Libya: also called *Barca.*
Cyrene, an ancient Greek city in N. Africa: capital of Cyrenaica.
Cyzicus, an ancient peninsular city on S. shore of Sea of Marmara.
Czechoslovakia, Czecho-Slovakia, a country in central Europe, formed after World War I, consisting of Bohemia, Moravia and Silesia, and Slovakia: area, 54,244 sq. mi.; pop., 14,862,000; cap., Prague.

D

Dacia, an ancient Roman province between the Danube and Carpathian Mountains.
Daghestan Autonomous Soviet Socialist Republic, a division of the R.S.F.S.R. in the Caucasus, on the Caspian: area, 13,124 sq. mi.; pop. 1,429,000; cap., Makhachkala: also spelled *Dagestan.*
Dahomey, Benin: the former name.
Dakota, a former Territory of the U.S., which now forms North Dakota and South Dakota.
Dakotas, the, North Dakota and South Dakota.
Dalmatia, a region of S.W. Yugoslavia.
Danish West Indies, the Virgin Islands, now belonging to the U.S.: former name.
Darfur, a province of Sudan: area, 144,100 sq. mi.; pop., 1,539,000.
Death Valley, a dry, hot region in E. California: 276 ft. below sea level.
Deccan, 1. that part of India S. of Narbada River. **2.** sometimes, the region between Narbada and Kistna Rivers.

Delaware, an Eastern State of the U.S.: area, 2,057 sq. mi.; pop., 548,000; cap., Dover.
Delhi, a small union territory of N. India: area, 574 sq. mi.; pop., 2,659,000; also, its capital.
Delos, one of the small islands of the Cyclades in the Aegean.
Delphi, a city in ancient Phocis, Greece.
Denbighshire, Denbigh, a former county of N. Wales.
Denmark, a country in Europe, N. of Germany, between the North and Baltic Seas: area, 16,576 sq. mi.; pop., 5,059,000; cap., Copenhagen.
D'Entrecasteaux Islands, a group of islands off S.E. New Guinea: part of the country of Papua New Guinea: area, 1,200 sq. mi.
Derbyshire, Derby, a county of central England: pop., 892,000; county seat, Derby.
Devil's Island, an island off coast of French Guiana: site of former French penal colony.
Devon, an island in Northwest Territories, Canada, S. of Ellesmere Island: area, 20,484 sq. mi.
Devonshire, Devon, a county of S.W. England: pop., 929,000; county seat, Exeter.
District of Columbia, a federal district of the U.S. on the N. bank of Potomac River: area, 69 sq. mi.; pop., 757,000: occupied by city of Washington.
Diu, 1. a district of the former Portuguese India, consisting of a small island and a section of the adjacent mainland in N.W. India: area, 14 sq. mi.: with Goa and Daman (another small coastal region) it forms a union territory of India. **2.** the island of this district.
Djebel Druze, a region of S. Syria: area, 2,400 sq. mi.
Djibouti, a country in E. Africa, on the Gulf of Aden: area, 8,500 sq. mi.; pop., 175,000; cap., Djibouti.
Dobruja, Dobrudja, a district of S.E. Romania, along the Black Sea.
Dodecanese, a group of islands in the Aegean, off S.W. Turkey: area, 974 sq. mi.; pop., 122,000.
Dominican Republic, a country in E. part of Hispaniola, in West Indies: area, 18,700 sq. mi.; pop., 4,697,000; cap., Santo Domingo: former name, *Santo Domingo*.
Donegal, a county on N. coast of Ireland, in Ulster province: pop., 109,000; county seat, Lifford.
Dongola, a province of N. Sudan: area, 120,100 sq. mi.
Dorsetshire, Dorset, a county on S. coast of England: pop., 571,000; county seat, Dorchester.
Dry Tortugas, a group of small islands in Gulf of Mexico, W. of Florida Keys, belonging to Florida.
Dumbarton, a former county of W. Scotland.
Durango, a state of N. Mexico: area, 42,272 sq. mi.; pop., 919,000; also, its capital.
Durham, a county of N. England: pop., 611,000; county seat, Durham.
Dutch Borneo, formerly, that part of Borneo belonging to the Netherlands.
Dutch East Indies, same as *Netherlands Indies*.
Dutch Guiana, same as *Surinam*.
Dutch New Guinea, same as *Netherlands New Guinea*.
Dutch West Indies, same as *Netherlands Antilles*.
Dyfed, a county of S.W. Wales, on Bristol Channel: pop., 320,000.
Dzungaria, a district of N. Sinkiang, China.

E

East Anglia, 1. a former Anglo-Saxon kingdom of E. England. **2.** the district of E. England comprising Norfolk and Suffolk.
East Bengal, the E. territories of Bengal: now part of Bangladesh.
Easter Island, a Chilean island in South Pacific.
Eastern Empire, same as *Byzantine Empire*.
Eastern Hemisphere, that half of the earth which includes Europe, Africa, Asia, and Australia.
East Flanders, a province of W. Belgium: area, 1,147 sq. mi.; pop., 1,311,000; cap., Ghent.
East Indies, East India, 1. the islands S.E. of Asia; the Malay Archipelago. **2.** the Malay Archipelago, the Malay Peninsula, the Indochinese peninsula, and India.
East Lothian, a former county of S.E. Scotland.
East Prussia, a former province of Prussia, Germany, on Baltic Sea, separated from Germany proper by Polish Corridor: cap., Königsberg: now divided between the R.S.F.S.R. and Poland.
Eboracum, York, England: ancient name.
Ecbatana, the capital of ancient Media, on site of modern Hamadan.
Ecuador, a country on the N.W. coast of South America: area, 275,000 sq. mi.; pop., 6,733,000; cap., Quito.
Edessa, an ancient city in Mesopotamia, on site of modern Urfa, Turkey.
Edinburgh, Midlothian, Scotland: former name.
Egypt, a country in N.E. Africa, on the Mediterranean and Red Seas: area, 386,000 sq. mi.; pop., 37,233,000; cap., Cairo: former name, *United Arab Republic*.
Eire, Republic of Ireland: the Gaelic name.
Elam, an ancient kingdom in region of modern Khuzistan, Iran.
Elba, an Italian island between Corsica and Italy: area, 86 sq. mi.; pop., 30,000.
Eleusis, a city in ancient Greece, N.W. of Athens.
Ellesmere Island, an island in Northwest Territories, Canada, W. of N.W. Greenland: area, 76,000 sq. mi.
Ellice Islands, Tuvalu: the former name.
Ellis Island, a small island in New York harbor: immigrants were formerly examined there before being allowed into the U.S.
El Salvador, a country in W. Central America, on the Pacific: area, 8,259 sq. mi.; pop., 4,007,000; cap., San Salvador.
Ely, Isle of, a former administrative county in Cambridgeshire, England.
Emilia, a department of N. Italy.
Enderby Land, a region in Antarctica, S. of Africa.
England, a division of Great Britain, bounded by Wales and Scotland: area, 50,874 sq. mi.; pop., 46,018,000; cap., London.
Ephesus, an ancient city in Asia Minor.
Epirus, a former country in N.W. part of ancient Greece.
Equatorial Guinea, a country in central Africa, consisting of Fernando Po and Rio Muni: formerly (until 1968) a Spanish possession: area, 10,832 sq. mi.; pop., 286,000; cap., Malabo.
Eritrea, an autonomous unit of Ethiopia, in E. Africa, on the Red Sea: it is a former Italian colony: area, 48,000 sq. mi.; pop., 1,100,000; cap., Asmara.
España, Spain: Spanish name.
Essex, 1. a former Anglo-Saxon kingdom of E. England. **2.** a county on E. coast of England: pop., 1,408,000; county seat, Chelmsford.
Estonia, Esthonia, a country in N.E. Europe that became the Estonian S.S.R. in 1940.
Estonian Soviet Socialist Republic, a republic of the U.S.S.R., on the Baltic Sea: area, 18,050 sq. mi.; pop., 1,400,000; cap., Tallinn.
Estremadura, 1. a former province of S.W. Spain. **2.** a province of W. Portugal.
Ethiopia, 1. an ancient region in N.E. Africa, S. of Egypt. **2.** a country in E. Africa, on the Red Sea: area, 395,000 sq. mi.; pop., 27,946,000; cap., Addis Ababa: Eritrea became federated with Ethiopia in 1952: also called *Abyssinia*.
Etruria, an ancient country in central part of W. Italy, now forming Tuscany and part of Umbria.
Euboea, Evvoia: ancient name.
Eurasia, Europe and Asia, considered as a unit.
Europe, the continent W. of Asia: area, 3,872,000 sq. mi.; pop., c.658,000,000.
Everglades, the a large tract of swampland in S. Florida: length, 140 mi.; width, 50 mi.: the S. part constitutes a national park.
Evvoia, a large Greek island in the Aegean: area, 1,585 sq. mi.; pop., 166,000.
Eyre's Peninsula, a peninsula in South Australia.

F

Faeroe Islands, Faeroes, a group of Danish islands between Great Britain and Iceland: area, 540 sq. mi.; pop., 35,000: also spelled *Faroe*.
Faiyûm, a division of N. Egypt: area, 670 sq. mi.; pop., 839,000: also spelled *Fayum, Fayoum*.
Falkland Islands, a group of British islands, E. of S. tip of South America: area, 4,618 sq. mi.; pop., 2,400; cap., Port Stanley.
Falster, one of the islands of Denmark: area, 199 sq. mi.; pop., 46,000.
Far East, E. Asia, including China, Japan, etc.
Faroe Islands, same as *Faeroe Islands*.
Fars, a province of S. Iran: pop., 1,500,000; cap., Shiraz.
Farther India, same as *Indochina*.
Fayal, one of the islands forming the Azores: area, 64 sq. mi.
Fayum, Fayoum, same as *Faiyûm*.
Federated Malay States, a former division of Malay Peninsula, including native states of Pahang, Perak, Negri Sembilan, and Selangor: area, 27,540 sq. mi.: now part of Malaysia.
Fengtien, Liaoning: former name.
Fernando de Noronha, an island in South Atlantic, N.E. of Natal, Brazil: Brazilian penal colony: area, 10 sq. mi.
Fernando Po, an island in Gulf of Guinea, part of Equatorial Guinea: area, 786 sq. mi.; pop., 72,000; cap., Santa Isabel.
Fernando Poo, Fernando Po: Spanish name.
Fife, Fifeshire, a former county of E. Scotland, on Firth of Forth.
Fiji, a country on a group of islands (*Fiji Islands*) in the S.W. Pacific, N. of New Zealand: area, 7,000 sq. mi.; pop., 573,000; cap., Suva.
Finland, a country in N. Europe, N.E. of Baltic Sea: area, 119,113 sq. mi.; pop., 4,729,000; cap., Helsinki.
Flanders, a former country in Europe, on coast of North Sea: now the Belgian provinces of East Flanders and West Flanders, and part of N. France.
Flintshire, Flint, a former county of N.E. Wales.
Flores, 1. an island of Indonesia, W. of Timor: area, 5,509 sq. mi. **2.** a W. island in the Azores: area, 57 sq. mi.
Florida, a State on a peninsula in the S.E. U.S.: area, 58,560 sq. mi.; pop., 6,789,000; cap. Tallahassee.
Florida Keys, a chain of islands extending S.W. from the S. tip of Florida.
Formosa, Taiwan, an island province off S.E. China: see *Taiwan*.
France, a country in W. Europe: area, 212,737 sq. mi.; pop., 52,544,000; cap., Paris.
Franche-Comté, a former province of E. France.
Franconia, a former duchy of S.W. Germany.
Franz Josef Land, same as *Fridtjof Nansen Land*.
Freiburg, same as *Fribourg*.
French Equatorial Africa, a former federation of French colonies in W. central Africa.
French Guiana, a French overseas department in N. South America, on the Atlantic: area, 34,740 sq. mi.; pop., 51,000; cap., Cayenne.
French Guinea, a former French colony in W. Africa: now, the independent country of Guinea.
French India, formerly, five small dependencies of France along coast of India: incorporated into India since 1954.
French Indochina, former French federation in S.E. Asia, on South China Sea, including Vietnam, Cambodia, and Laos.
French Morocco, formerly, the French zone of sultanate of Morocco: in 1956 it became, with Spanish Morocco and Tangier, the independent state of Morocco.
French Polynesia, a French overseas territory in the South Pacific, consisting of five scattered island groups: area, 1,544 sq. mi.; pop., 119,000; cap., Papeete. Former name, *French Oceania*.
French Somaliland, a former French territory, called the *French Territory of the Afars and the Issas* from 1967 to 1977, when it became the independent country of Djibouti.
French Sudan, a former French colony in W. Africa: since 1960, the independent republic of Mali.
French West Africa, a former group of French colonies in W. Africa, consisting of Senegal, Ivory Coast, Dahomey, French Sudan, Mauritania, Upper Volta, and Niger.
French West Indies, French overseas departments in the West Indies, including Guadeloupe and Martinique.
Fribourg, a canton of W. Switzerland: pop., 159,000; also, its capital.
Fridtjof Nansen Land, islands of the U.S.S.R., N. of Novaya Zemlya, in the Arctic Ocean: also called *Franz Josef Land*.
Friendly Islands, same as *Tonga Islands*.
Friesland, a province of N. Netherlands: cap., Leeuwarden.
Frigid Zone, the Arctic Zone; also, the Antarctic Zone.
Frisian Islands, a chain of islands in the North Sea off coast of the Netherlands and Germany.
Friuli-Venezia Giulia, a semi-autonomous region of N.E. Italy, on the Adriatic.
Fukien, a province of S.E. China: area, 46,514 sq. mi.; pop., 18,000,000; cap., Foochow.
Fünen, Fyn: German name.
Fyn, a Danish island, between Jutland and Zealand islands: area, 1,150 sq. mi.; pop., 431,000.

G

Gabon, Gabun, a country in W. central Africa, on the Gulf of Guinea: a former French colony: area, 102,300 sq. mi.; pop., 500,000; cap., Libreville.
Galapagos Islands, a group of islands in the Pacific, on the equator: possession of Ecuador: area, 2,868 sq. mi.; pop., 2,400: also called *Colón Archipelago*.
Galatia, an ancient kingdom, and later a Roman province, in central Asia Minor.
Galicia, 1. a former province of N.W. Spain. **2.** a former province of Poland, in the S. part: now divided between Poland and the Ukrainian S.S.R.
Galilee, an ancient division of N. Palestine.
Gallia, Gaul: Latin name.
Galloway, a district of Scotland, consisting of the former counties of Wigtown, Kircudbright, and Dumfries.
Galway, a county of Connaught province, Ireland: pop., 148,000; also, its capital.
Gambia, a country on the W. coast of Africa, surrounded on three sides by Senegal: formerly a British colony, it is now independent and a member of the British Commonwealth of Nations: area, c.4,000 sq. mi.; pop., 524,000; cap., Banjul.
Gambier Islands, a group of French islands in Tuamotu Archipelago, South Pacific: area, 12 sq. mi.; pop., 7,000.
Gascony, a former province of S.W. France.
Gaspé Peninsula, a peninsula in Quebec, Canada, between the St. Lawrence River and Gulf of St. Lawrence.
Gaul, an ancient division of the Roman Empire, consisting of France and Belgium, N. Italy, and parts of the Netherlands, Germany, and Switzerland.
Gaza, an ancient city in Asia Minor.
Gelderland, a province of E. Netherlands: area, 1,940 sq. mi.; pop., 1,506,000; cap., Arnhem.
Genoa, a former republic of Italy.
Georgia, 1. a Southern State of the U.S.: area, 58,876 sq. mi.; pop., 4,590,000; cap., Atlanta. **2.** same as *Georgian S.S.R.*
Georgian Soviet Socialist Republic, a republic of the U.S.S.R., in the Transcaucasus, on the Black Sea: area,

26,875 sq. mi.; pop., 4,700,000; cap., Tiflis: also called *Georgia*.

German East Africa, a former German colony in E. Africa: now mostly in Tanzania.

German Southwest Africa, a former German colony, now South West Africa.

German Volga Autonomous Soviet Socialist Republic, a former division of the R.S.F.S.R., on the lower Volga: abolished in 1941.

Germany, a country in N. central Europe, on the North and Baltic Seas: area, 137,555 sq. mi.; pop., 78,596,000: in 1945, Germany was divided into 4 zones of occupation, administered respectively by France, Great Britain, the Soviet Union, and the U.S.; in 1949, it was divided into (a) the Federal Republic of Germany (*West Germany*), comprising the U.S., British, and French zones: area, 95,734 sq. mi.; pop., 61,746,000; cap., Bonn, and (b) the German Democratic Republic (*East Germany*), comprising the Soviet zone: area, 41,635 sq. mi.; pop., 16,850,000; cap., East Berlin.

Ghana, a country in W. Africa, on the Gulf of Guinea: formed (1957) by a merger of the Gold Coast and British Togoland, it is a member of the British Commonwealth of Nations: area, 91,843 sq. mi.; pop., 9,866,000; cap., Accra.

Gibraltar, a British colony and fortress on the Rock of Gibraltar: area, 1 7/8 sq. mi.; pop., 27,000.

Gibraltar, Rock of, a large rock forming a peninsula in S. Spain, at entrance to the Mediterranean.

Gilbert Islands, a group of British islands on the equator, in the Pacific between the Marshall Islands and Tuvalu: area, 116 sq. mi.; pop., 44,000.

Gilead, a region in ancient Palestine, E. of the Jordan: also, a city in this region.

Glamorganshire, Glamorgan, a former county in S.E. Wales, on Bristol Channel: now divided into three counties (a) *Mid Glamorgan*, pop., 539,000, (b) *South Glamorgan*, pop., 391,000, (c) *West Glamorgan*, pop., 371,000.

Gloucestershire, a county of S.W. England: pop., 485,000; county seat, Gloucester.

Goa, a former Portuguese colony on S.W. coast of India: since 1962, a part of a union territory of India (see *Diu*): area, 1,426 sq. mi.; pop., 627,000: official name, *Goa, Daman, and Diu*.

Golconda, an ancient city in Hyderabad, India.

Gold Coast, formerly, a British territory in W. Africa: it merged with British Togoland (1957) to form Ghana.

Good Hope, Cape of, **1.** a cape at S. tip of Africa. **2.** a province of South Africa: area, 276,966 sq. mi.; pop., 5,363,000; cap., Cape Town: former name, *Cape Colony*: also called *Cape Province*.

Gorno-Badakhshan Autonomous Region, an autonomous area of Tadzhik S.S.R., in S.W. Asiatic Russia: area, 25,784 sq. mi.; pop., 98,800; cap., Khorog.

Gotland, a Swedish island, and county, in the Baltic: area, 1,224 sq. mi.; pop., 59,000; cap., Visby.

Governors Island, an island in New York Bay at entrance to East River.

Grampian, a region of E. Scotland, on the North Sea: pop., 441,000.

Granada, a district of S. Spain; also, its capital.

Gran Chaco, plains in Argentina, Paraguay, and Bolivia: area, 300,000 sq. mi.

Grand Manan, an island in Bay of Fundy: part of New Brunswick: pop., 2,000.

Great Britain, England, Wales, and Scotland: a division of the United Kingdom and the British Commonwealth of Nations: area, 89,041 sq. mi.; pop., 53,979,000; cap., London.

Greater Antilles, a group of islands in West Indies, including islands of Cuba, Jamaica, Hispaniola, and Puerto Rico.

Great Plains, the large area of low valleys and plains E. of Rocky Mountains in the U.S. and Canada.

Greece, a country in S. Balkan Peninsula, on the Mediterranean: area, 50,147 sq. mi.; pop., 9,046,000; cap., Athens.

Greenland, a Danish island N.E. of North America: the world's largest island: area, 736,518 sq. mi. (ice-free land, 31,284 sq. mi.); pop., 40,000; cap., Godthaab.

Grenada, a country consisting of the southernmost island of the Windward group, West Indies, and part of the Grenadines: area, 133 sq. mi.; pop., 95,000; cap., St. George's.

Grenadines, a group of small islands of the Windward group, West Indies, divided between Grenada and St. Vincent: area, 30 sq. mi.

Grisons, a canton of E. Switzerland: pop., 147,000.

Groningen, a province of N.E. Netherlands; also, its capital.

Guadalcanal, one of the Solomon Islands, in South Pacific: part of the independent country of the Solomon Islands: area, 2,500 sq. mi.: scene of heavy fighting in World War II.

Guadeloupe, an overseas department of France consisting of two main islands and five small islands of the Leeward group in the West Indies: area, 688 sq. mi.; pop., 341,000; cap., Basse-Terre.

Guam, one of the Marianas Islands, in Western Pacific: naval station belonging to U.S.: area, 209 sq. mi.; pop., 87,000; cap., Agana.

Guanajuato, a state of central Mexico: pop., 2,285,000; also, its capital.

Guatemala, a country in Central America, S. and E. of Mexico: area, 45,452 sq. mi.; pop., 5,540,000; also, its capital.

Guernsey, a British island in the English Channel: area, 25 sq. mi.; pop., 46,000.

Guiana, a region in N. South America, including Guyana, French Guiana, and Surinam.

Guinea, **1.** a country in W. Africa, on the Atlantic: area, 94,925 sq. mi.; pop., 3,702,000; cap., Conakry: formerly *French Guinea*. **2.** a region along W. coast of Africa, extending from S. Senegal to E. Nigeria.

Guinea-Bissau, a country in W. Africa, S. of Senegal: area, 15,505 sq. mi.; pop., 759,000; cap., Madina do Boe: formerly *Portuguese Guinea*.

Gujarat, a state of W. India: area, 72,138 sq. mi.; pop., 20,633,000.

Gulf States, the States of the U.S. on the Gulf of Mexico: Florida, Alabama, Mississippi, Louisiana, Texas.

Guyana, a country in N.E. South America: formerly a British colony: area, 83,000 sq. mi.; pop., 758,000; cap., Georgetown.

Guyenne, a former province of S.W. France: previously district of Aquitaine.

Gwent, a county of S.E. Wales, on the Severn estuary: pop., 441,000.

Gwynedd, a county of N.W. Wales, on the Irish Sea: pop., 224,000.

H

Hadhramaut, Hadramaut, a district of S. Arabia, on Arabian Sea: part of People's Democratic Republic of Yemen.

Hainan, an island off S. China: part of Kwantung province: area, 13,500 sq. mi.

Hainaut, a province of S.W. Belgium: pop., 1,332,000; cap., Mons.

Haiti, **1.** a republic on Hispaniola island, West Indies: area, 10,204 sq. mi.; pop., 4,584,000; cap., Port-au-Prince. **2.** Hispaniola: former name.

Halicarnassus, an ancient city in S.W. Asia Minor.

Halmahera, Halmaheira, one of the Molucca islands in Indonesia: area, 6,500 sq. mi.

Hampshire, a county on S. coast of England, consisting of administrative divisions of Southampton and Isle of Wight: pop., 1,435,000; also called *Hants*.

Hanover, Hannover, a former kingdom and duchy in N. Germany and, later, a province of Prussia: now part of West Germany.

Hasa, El, a region in Saudi Arabia, on Persian Gulf: area, 25,000 sq. mi.

Haut-Rhin, a department of France, on the Rhine: area, 1,354 sq. mi.; pop., 585,000; cap., Colmar.

Hawaii, **1.** a State of the United States, consisting of a group of islands in the North Pacific: area, 6,415 sq. mi.; pop., 770,000; capital, Honolulu. **2.** the largest of the islands of Hawaii: area, 4,030 sq. mi.; pop., 63,000; chief city, Hilo.

Hawaiian Islands, the islands comprising the State of Hawaii: formerly called *Sandwich Islands*.

Hayti, same as *Haiti*.

Hebrides, a group of Scottish islands W. of Scotland, divided into two groups (*Inner Hebrides* and *Outer Hebrides*): area, 2,900 sq. mi.; pop., 80,000.

Hedjaz, same as *Hejaz*.

Heilungkiang, a province of N.E. China: pop., 25,000,000.

Hejaz, a former country in W. Arabia, along the Red Sea: now a province of Saudi Arabia: area, 150,000 sq. mi.; pop., c.2,000,000; cap., Mecca.

Helgoland, a small German island in North Sea: British defeated Germans in naval battle near here in 1914.

Heligoland, Helgoland: English name.

Heliopolis, **1.** the ruins of an ancient holy city in Egypt, N. of Cairo. **2.** an ancient city in Syria, near Damascus.

Helvetia, **1.** an ancient country in Europe: it included most of what is now Switzerland. **2.** Switzerland: Latin name.

Heraclea, an ancient city in Italy, near Gulf of Taranto.

Hercegovina, same as *Herzegovina*.

Herculaneum, an ancient city in Italy, on Bay of Naples: destroyed by eruption of Mt. Vesuvius (79 A.D.).

Herefordshire, Hereford, a former county of W. central England.

Hereford and Worcester, a county of W. central England, formed of the former counties of Hereford and Worcester: pop., 586,000.

Hertfordshire, Hertford, a county of S.E. England: pop., 942,000; county seat, Hertford.

Herzegovena, a former province of Austria-Hungary: now part of Yugoslavia.

Hesse, a former kingdom and duchy of W. central Germany: now, a state of W. Germany: area, 2,969 sq. mi.; pop., 5,423,000; cap., Darmstadt.

Hessen, Hesse: German name.

Hesse-Nassau, a former province of Prussia: cap., Kassel.

Hidalgo, a state of central Mexico: pop., 1,156,000; cap., Pachuca.

Highlands, the, the elevated mountainous region in N. and W. Scotland.

Hiiumaa, an Estonian island in the Baltic Sea, W. of Estonian S.S.R.: area, 371 sq. mi.: also called *Dagö*.

Himachal Pradesh, a union territory of N. India: area, 10,904 sq. mi.; pop., 1,351,000; cap., Simla.

Hindustan, **1.** the N. part of India, where chiefly Hindi is spoken, including the states of Rajasthan, Punjab, and Uttar Pradesh. **2.** the Indian peninsula N. of Deccan. **3.** popularly, India.

Hispania, a division of ancient Roman Empire, including what is now Spain and Portugal.

Hispaniola, an island in West Indies, between Cuba and Puerto Rico: area, 28,242 sq. mi.; divided between Haiti and Dominican Republic: former name, *Haiti*.

Hohenzolern, a former province of Prussia, Germany: area, 440 sq. mi.; cap., Sigmaringen.

Hokkaido, one of the islands forming Japan, N. of Honshu: area, 34,084 sq. mi.; pop., 5,039,000; cap., Hakodate: former name, *Yezo*.

Hoko Gunto, same as *Pescadores Islands*.

Holland, same as *Netherlands*.

Holstein, a former duchy of Denmark: now part of Schleswig-Holstein.

Honan, a province of E. China: area, 63,843 sq. mi.; pop., 50,000,000; cap., Chengchow.

Hondo, same as *Honshu*.

Honduras, a country in Central America, on the Caribbean and Pacific: area, 59,160 sq. mi.; pop., 2,654,000; cap., Tegucigala.

Hong Kong, Hongkong, a British crown colony in S.E. China, on South China Sea, including Hong Kong island, Kowloon peninsula, and a section of the Chinese mainland: area, 391 sq. mi.; pop., 3,948,000.

Honshu, the largest of the islands forming Japan: area, 91,278 sq. mi.; pop., 71,354,000; chief city, Tokyo: also called *Hondo*.

Hopei, Hopeh, a province on E. coast of China: area, 56,116 sq. mi.; pop., 43,000,000; cap., Tientsin: former name, *Chihli*.

Howland Island, a small equatorial island in the mid-Pacific belonging to the U.S.

Humberside, a county of N.E. England, on the North Sea: pop., 849,000.

Hunan, a province of S.E. China: area, 83,921 sq. mi.; pop., 38,000,000; cap., Changsha.

Hungary, a country in central Europe: area, 35,872 sq. mi.; pop., 10,596,000; cap., Budapest.

Huntingdonshire, Huntingdon, a former county of E. central England.

Hupeh, a province of E. central China: area, 71,234 sq. mi.; pop., 32,000,000; cap., Wuhan.

Hyderabad, a former state of S. central India; also, its capital.

Hyrcania, an ancient district of Asia, on S. shores of the Caspian.

I

Iberia, **1.** the Spanish-Portuguese peninsula: ancient Latin name. **2.** an ancient region in the Caucasus, between Black Sea and Caspian.

Iceland, an island republic in the North Atlantic, between Norway and Greenland: area, 39,709 sq. mi.; pop., 218,000; cap., Reykjavik.

Idaho, a Northwestern State of the U.S.: area, 83,557 sq. mi.; pop., 713,000; cap., Boise.

Ifni, a former Spanish province on N.W. coast of Africa: ceded to Morocco in 1969.

Île de France, a former province in N. France, surrounding Paris.

Île du Diable, Devil's Island: French name.

Ilium, ancient Troy.

Illinois, a Middle Western State of the U.S.: area, 56,400 sq. mi.; pop., 11,114,000; cap., Springfield.

Illyria, an ancient country on E. coast of the Adriatic.

Illyricum, a Roman province in ancient Illyria.

India, **1.** a large peninsula of S. Asia, between Bay of Bengal and Arabian Sea: area, c.1,500,000 sq. mi.; formerly divided into British India and the Indian States and Agencies, it now contains India (sense 2), Pakistan, Nepal, Bangladesh, and Bhutan. **2.** a republic in central and S. India, a member of the British Commonwealth of Nations: formerly a dominion (1947–1950): area, 1,260,000 sq. mi.; pop. (including the Indian-held section of Jammu and Kashmir), 598,097,000; cap., New Delhi.

Indiana, a Middle Western State of the U.S.: area, 36,291 sq. mi.; pop., 5,194,000; cap., Indianapolis.

Indian Empire, a former federation in India, which included British India and a number of dependent and semidependent states and agencies: area, 1,575,187 sq. mi.; cap., New Delhi.

Indian States and Agencies, formerly a number of semidependent native states and agencies of India: in 1947, became independent states or affiliated with republics of India or Pakistan.

Indian Territory, a former territory of the U.S., reserved for settlement of Indians: now part of Oklahoma.

Indies, **1.** the East Indies **2.** the East Indies, India, and the Indochinese peninsula. **3.** the West Indies.

Indochina, Indo-China, **1.** the large peninsula S. of China, including Burma, Thailand, Malaya, Vietnam, Laos, and Cambodia. **2.** a former region in the E. part of this peninsula, consisting of Vietnam, Laos, and Cambodia: also *French Indochina*.

Indonesia, **1.** the Malay Archipelago; East Indies. **2.** a republic, established in 1949 (1946–49, an independent commonwealth under the Netherlands crown), consisting of Java, Sumatra, Borneo (the S. part), Celebes, West Irian, and other islands in the Malay Archipelago: area, c.734,000 sq. mi.; pop., 130,597,000; cap., Jakarta: these islands formerly constituted the Netherlands Indies.

Indore, a former state in central India.

Inner Mongolia, an autonomous region in N. China, S. and S.E. of the Mongolian People's Republic: it is made up of parts of the former provinces of Jehol, Chahar, and Suiyan and part of Manchuria: area, 450,000 sq. mi.; pop., 6,240,000; cap., Huhehot.

Inverness-shire, Inverness, a former county of N. Scotland.

Ionian Islands, a group of 7 Greek islands along W. coast of Greece: area, 963 sq. mi.; pop., 229,000.

Iowa, a Middle Western State of the U.S.: area, 56,280 sq. mi.; pop., 2,824,000; cap., Des Moines.

Iran, a country in S.W. Asia, S. of the Caspian: area, 628,000 sq. mi.; pop., 33,744,000; cap., Teheran: former name, *Persia.*

Iraq, Irak, a country in S.W. Asia, on the Persian Gulf: area, 116,600 sq. mi.; pop., 11,124,000; cap., Bagdad: former name, *Mesopotamia.*

Ireland, **1.** one of the British Isles, comprising Ireland (sense 2) and Northern Ireland: formerly part of the United Kingdom: area, 31,839 sq. mi.; pop., 4,655,000; chief cities, Dublin and Belfast. **2.** a country comprising S. provinces of Ireland (Leinster, Munster, and Connaught) and 3 counties (Cavan, Donegal, and Monaghan) of Ulster province: established as a republic in December, 1925, associated (until 1949) with the British Commonwealth of Nations: area, 26,601 sq. mi.; pop., 3,127,000; cap., Dublin: former names, *Irish Free State, Eire.*

Isle Royale, an island in N. Lake Superior; part of State of Michigan: area, 209 sq. mi.

Israel, **1.** the Kingdom in N. part of ancient Palestine formed by the 10 tribes of Israel that broke with Judah and Benjamin. **2.** a republic comprising parts of Palestine, established as a Jewish state in 1948, in conformity with United Nations plan of 1947 to partition Palestine into separate Jewish and Arab states: area, 7,993 sq. mi.; pop., 3,459,000; cap., Jerusalem.

Issus, an ancient town in S.E. Asia Minor.

Istria, a peninsula mostly in N.W. Yugoslavia: Italy shares the N. coast.

Italian East Africa, a former Italian colony in E. Africa, consisting of Ethiopia, Eritrea, and Italian Somaliland.

Italian Somaliland, a former Italian colony in E. Africa: a United Nations trust territory from 1950 to 1960 when it merged with British Somaliland to form the independent country of Somalia.

Italy, a country in S. Europe, including islands of Sicily and Sardinia: area, 119,768 sq. mi.; pop., 56,110,000; cap., Rome.

Ithaca, one of the Ionian Islands, off W. coast of Greece.

Ivanovo, a region of the R.S.F.S.R., in central European Russia: pop., 1,306,000; also, its capital.

Ivory Coast, **1.** a country in W. central Africa, on the Gulf of Guinea: a former French colony: area, 124,500 sq. mi.; pop., 6,673,000; cap., Abidjan. **2.** formerly, the African coast in this region.

Iwo Jima, a small island of the Volcano Islands in the W. Pacific: scene of heavy fighting in World War II, in which the Americans captured the island from the Japanese.

J

Jaén, a province of S. Spain: pop., 764,000; also, its capital.

Jaipur, a former native Indian state, attached to the Rajputana agency until 1948: since 1950, included in Rajasthan state.

Jalisco, a state of W. Mexico, on the Pacific: area, 31,149 sq. mi.; pop., 3,323,000; cap., Guadalajara.

Jamaica, a country on an island in the West Indies, S. of Cuba: it is a member of the British Commonwealth of Nations: area, 4,400 sq. mi.; pop., 2,025,000; cap., Kingston.

Jammu and Kashmir, see **Kashmir.**

Japan, an island country E. of Asia, including Hokkaido, Honshu, Shikoku, Kyushu, and smaller islands: area, 147,700 sq. mi.; pop., 111,934,000; cap., Tokyo.

Java, a large island of Indonesia, between Malay Peninsula and Australia: area, 48,504 sq. mi.; pop., with Madura, 63,000,000.

Jehol, a former province of N.E. China.

Jersey, one of the Channel Islands off French coast: area, 45 sq. mi.; pop., 72,000.

Jewish National Autonomous Region, an autonomous region of the R.S.F.S.R., in far E. Siberia N. of Amur River, set aside for Jewish colonization: area, 14,204 sq. mi.; pop., 173,000: also called *Birobijan.*

Jodhpur, a former state of N.W. India, now in Rajputana.

Johore, a state of Malaya, at tip of Malay Peninsula: area, 7,330 sq. mi.; pop., 1,353,000.

Jolo, the largest island of Sulu Archipelago, Philippine Islands: area, 326 sq. mi.

Jordan an Arab kingdom in the Near East, E. of Israel: British mandate (1921–1946): area, c.37,000 sq. mi.: pop., 2,702,000; cap., Amman: official name *Hashemite Kingdom of Jordan.*

Juan Fernández Islands, two islands in the South Pacific, c.500 mi. W. of, and belonging to, Chile: area, 70 sq. mi.

Judea, Judaea, a part of S. Palestine that was under Roman rule.

Jugoslavia, Jugo-Slavia, same as *Yugoslavia.*

Jutland, the peninsula of N. Europe which forms mainland of Denmark: naval battle between the Germans and British was fought in the Skagerrak, a strait near Jutland, in 1916.

K

Kabardino-Balkar Autonomous Soviet Socialist Republic, a division of the R.S.F.S.R., in the Caucasus: area, 4,747 sq. mi.; pop., 589,000; cap., Nalchik.

Kaffraria, the region of the Kaffirs, in E. Cape Province, South Africa.

Kafiristan a mountainous region in E. Afghanistan, S. of Hindu Kush Mountains.

Kahoolawe, one of the Hawaiian Islands, S.W. of Maui: area, 45 sq. mi.

Kalahari, a desert plateau in Botswana, S. Africa: area, c.400,000 sq. mi.

Kalat, a former state in W. India and Pakistan: now a part of Pakistan.

Kalinin, a region of the R.S.F.S.R., in W. European Russia: pop., 1,802,000; also, its capital.

Kalmuck Autonomous Soviet Socialist Republic, a division of the R.S.F.S.R., in N.E. Caucasus: area, 28,641 sq. mi.; pop., 268,000; cap., Elista.

Kamchatka, a peninsula in N.E. Siberia, between the Sea of Okhotsk and the Bering Sea: area, c.105,000 sq. mi.

Kampuchea, Democratic, Cambodia: the official name.

Kanara, a region in W. and S. India, divided into North Kanara and South Kanara: area, c.8,000 sq. mi.: also spelled *Canara.*

Kansas, a Middle Western State of the U.S.: area, 82,276 sq. mi.; pop., 2,249,000; cap., Topeka.

Kansu, a province of N.W. China: area, c.250,000 sq. mi.; pop., 12,928,000; cap., Lanchow.

Karafuto, **1.** Sakhalin Island: Japanese name. **2.** the S. part of this island: annexed by Japan, 1905; returned to U.S.S.R., 1945.

Kara-Kalpak Autonomous Soviet Socialist Republic, a division of the Uzbek S.S.R., in central Asia: area, 79,631 sq. mi.; pop., 702,000; cap., Nukus.

Karelia, an autonomous republic of the R.S.F.S.R., in the N.W. part, E. of Finland: area, 66,500 sq. mi.; pop., 714,000; cap., Petrozavodsk: officially, *Karelian Autonomous Soviet Socialist Republic.*

Karelo-Finnish Soviet Socialist Republic, a former republic of the U.S.S.R., E. of Finland, composed of Karelia and territory ceded by Finland.

Kashmir, a state of N. India: area, 85,861 sq. mi.; pop., 4,617,000; cap., Srinagar: control of this region is disputed by Pakistan which occupies c.31,000 sq. mi. in the N.W. part: also spelled *Cashmere:* name in full, *Jammu and Kashmir.*

Kauai, one of the Hawaiian Islands, N.W. of Oahu: area, 551 sq. mi.; pop., 30,000.

Kazak Soviet Socialist Republic, Kazakstan, a republic of the U.S.S.R., in W. Asia: area, 1,059,700 sq. mi.; pop., 12,900,000; cap., Alma-Ata.

Kedah, a state of Malaya: area, 3,660 sq. mi.; pop., 964,000.

Keeling Islands, same as *Cocos Islands.*

Kelantan, a state of Malaya: area, 5,720 sq. mi.; pop., 703,000.

Kent, **1.** a former Anglo-Saxon kingdom. **2.** a county of S.E. England, on the English Channel: pop., 1,435,000; county seat, Maidstone.

Kentucky, an East Central State of the U.S.: area, 40,395 sq. mi.; pop., 3,219,000; cap., Frankfort.

Kenya, a country in E. Africa, on the Indian Ocean: formerly a British colony and protectorate, it is now independent and a member of the British Commonwealth of Nations: area, 224,960 sq. mi.; pop., 13,399,000; cap., Nairobi.

Keos, one of the Cyclades Islands, in the Aegean: area, 67 sq. mi.: also called *Zea.*

Kephallenia, Cephalonia: Greek name.

Kerguelen, an uninhabited island in S. Indian Ocean, belonging to France: area, 1,400 sq. mi.

Kerry, a county in S.W. Ireland, in Munster province: pop., 113,000.

Key Largo, a large island in Florida Keys, off coast of S.E. Florida.

Key West, the westernmost island in Florida Keys.

Khabarovsk Territory, a territory of the R.S.F.S.R., in E. Siberia, extending from China to Arctic Ocean: area, 901,000 sq. mi.; pop., 1,143,000; cap., Khabarovsk.

Khakass Autonomous Region, a division of the R.S.F.S.R., in S. central Siberia: area, 19,161 sq. mi.; pop., 446,000; cap., Abakan.

Khalkidike, same as *Chalcidice.*

Khios, Chios: Greek name.

Khiva, a former khanate in W. Asia: now divided between Uzbek S.S.R. and Turkmen S.S.R.

Khuzistan, a province of Iran, N. of Persian Gulf: area, 38,500 sq. mi.; pop., 1,800,000.

Kiangsi, a province of S.E. China: area, 67,300 sq. mi.; pop., 23,000,000; cap., Nanchang.

Kiangsu, a province on coast of E. China: area, 39,100 sq. mi.; pop., 47,000,000; cap., Nanking.

Kiaochow, a district of Shantung province, in E. China: area, 200 sq. mi.

Kildare, a county of E. Ireland, Leinster province: pop., 66,000.

Kilkenny, a county of S. Ireland, Leinster province: pop., 60,000; also, its county seat.

Kincardine, Kincardineshire, a former county on E. coast of Scotland.

Kinross-shire, Kinross, a former county of central Scotland.

Kirghiz Soviet Socialist Republic, a republic of the U.S.S.R., in S. central Asia: area, 75,950 sq. mi.; pop., 2,900,000; cap., Frunze.

Kirin, a province of N.E. China: area, 105,000 sq. mi.; pop., 20,000,000; cap., Changchun.

Kirkcudbrightshire, Kirkcudbright, a former county of S.W. Scotland.

Kirov, a region of the R.S.F.S.R., in E. central European Russia; also, its capital.

Kiska, one of the W. Aleutian Islands.

Kiushu, same as *Kyushu.*

Klondike, a region in the Yukon Territory, N.W. Canada, celebrated for its gold fields.

Knossos, the chief city of ancient Crete: also *Cnossus, Gnossus.*

Kodiak Island, an island off S.W. coast of Alaska, a district of Alaska: pop., 9,000.

Koko Nor, same as *Chinghai.*

Kola Peninsula, a peninsula in N.W. U.S.S.R., between the White and Barents Seas.

Kolhapur and Deccan States, formerly, a group of individual Indian states: area, 10,870 sq. mi.

Komi Autonomous Soviet Socialist Republic, a division of the R.S.F.S.R., in N.W. Urals: area, 145,221 sq. mi.; pop., 965,000; cap., Syktyvka.

Kongo, same as *Congo.*

Kordofan, a province of central Sudan: formerly a country: area, 147,100 sq. mi.; pop., 2,052,000; cap., El Obeid.

Korea, a country on a peninsula in E. Asia, W. of Japan: area, 85,228 sq. mi.; pop., 50,540,000; occupied by Japan (1910–1945): since 1948 divided into two republics, *People's Republic of Korea* (North), cap., Pyongyang, and *Republic of Korea* (South), cap., Seoul: war between North and South (June, 1950) with the UN supporting South Korea: truce signed (July, 1953).

Kowloon, a peninsula opposite Hong Kong island: part of British colony of Hong Kong.

Krakatao, an island in Indonesia, between Java and Sumatra.

Krasnodar Territory, a division of the R.S.F.S.R., in N. Caucasus: pop., 3,766,000.

Krasnoyarsk Territory, a division of the R.S.F.S.R., extending from S. border of Siberia to the Arctic: pop., 2,614,000.

Kuibyshev, a region of the R.S.F.S.R., in E. central European Russia: pop., 2,257,000; also, its capital.

Kurdistan, a region in S.E. Turkey, N. Iraq, and N.W. Iran.

Kurile Islands, one of the chains of islands, N. of Hokkaido, between Japan and Kamchatka: ceded to the U.S.S.R. in 1945: area, 6,150 sq. mi.

Kurland, a former Russian Province, on Baltic Sea: now part of Latvian S.S.R.: also spelled *Courland.*

Kursk, a region of the R.S.F.S.R., in S. central European Russia: pop., 1,481,000; also, its capital.

Kuwait, an independent Arab skeikdom in E. Arabia, on the Persian Gulf: under British protection until 1961: area, 6,000 sq. mi.; pop., 996,000; also, its capital.

Kwangchowan, a former territory on coast of Kwangtung province, China, leased to France (1898–1945): area, 325 sq. mi.

Kwangsi-Chuang, an autonomous region of S. China: area, 85,097 sq. mi.; pop., 24,000,000; cap., Nanning.

Kwangtung, a province of S. China, on South China Sea: area, 90,247 sq. mi.; pop., 40,000,000; cap., Kwangchow.

Kweichow, a province of S. China: area, 72,058 sq. mi.; pop., 20,000,000; cap., Kweiyang.

Kythera, Cerigo Island: Greek name.

Kyushu, one of the islands forming Japan: area, 14,719 sq. mi.; pop., 12,937,000; chief city, Nagasaki: also spelled *Kiushu.*

L

Labrador, **1.** a peninsula in N.E. North America, between the Atlantic and Hudson Bay: area, c.530,000 sq. mi. **2.** the E. part of this peninsula, constituting part of Newfoundland: area, 112,400 sq. mi.

Labuan, an island N. of Borneo: area, 29 sq. mi.: see *Sabah.*

Laccadive Islands, a group of Indian islands off S.W. coast of India.

Lacadaemon, ancient Sparta.

Laconia, an ancient country in S.E. Peloponnesus: cap., Sparta.
Ladrone Islands, Marianas Islands: former name.
Lagoon Islands, old name of *Ellice Islands.*
Lake District, Lake Country, a section of mountain and lake country in counties of Cumbria and Lancashire, England.
Lampedusa, an Italian island in the Mediterranean, between Malta and Tunisia.
Lanai, one of the Hawaiian Islands, W. of Maui: area, 141 sq. mi.; pop., 2,200.
Lanarkshire, Lanark, a former county of S. central Scotland.
Lancashire, a county on N.W. coast of England: pop., 1,370,000; county seat, Lancaster.
Languedoc, a former province of S. France, between the Pyrenees and Loire River.
Laos, a country in the N.W. part of the Indochinese peninsula: area, 91,500 sq. mi.; pop., 3,257,000; cap., Vientiane.
Lapland, a region in N. Norway, Sweden, Finland, and the U.S.S.R.
Latakia, a district of Syria, on the Mediterranean: area, 2,800 sq. mi.; pop., 520,000.
Latin America, the countries in North America, South America, Central America, and West Indies where Spanish, Portuguese, and French are spoken.
Latium, an ancient country in central Italy, S.E. of Rome.
Latvia, a country in N.E. Europe that became the Latvian S.S.R. in August, 1940.
Latvian Soviet Socialist Republic, a republic of the U.S.S.R., on Baltic Sea: area, 24,700 sq. mi.; pop., 2,400,000; cap., Riga.
Lauenburg, a former duchy of Denmark, now part of Schleswig-Holstein.
Lebanon, a country in W. Asia, on the Mediterranean: area, 3,600 sq. mi.; pop., 2,869,000; cap., Beirut.
Leeward Islands, 1. the N. group of islands in the Lesser Antilles, in West Indies. **2.** a former British colony made up of some of these islands, constituted as four separate colonies in 1960.
Leicestershire, Leicester, a county of central England: pop., 830,000; county seat, Leicester.
Leinster, a province of E. Ireland: area, 7,580 sq. mi.; pop., 1,414,000.
Leith, a former burgh in Scotland: now part of Edinburgh.
Lemnos, a Greek island in the Aegean: area, 175 sq. mi.
Leningrad, a region of the R.S.F.S.R., in N.W. European Russia: pop., 4,561,000; also, its capital.
León, a former province of N.W. Spain.
Lesbos, Mytilene: ancient name.
Lesotho, a country in S.E. Africa, surrounded by South Africa: area, 11,716 sq. mi.; pop., 1,039,000; cap., Maseru.
Lesser Antilles, a group of islands in West Indies, S.E. of Puerto Rico, including the Leeward Islands, the Windward Islands, and islands N. of Venezuela.
Leucas, Leukas, same as *Levkas.*
Levant, the regions on the E. Mediterranean and the Aegean, from Greece to Egypt.
Levkas, one of the Ionian Islands, off W. coast of Greece: also *Leucas, Leukas.*
Leyte, one of the Philippine Islands, between Samar and Cebu: area, 2,799 sq. mi.; pop., 1,210,000.
Liaoning, a province of N.E. China: pop., 28,000,000.
Liaotung Peninsula, a peninsula in N.E. China.
Liberia, a country on W. coast of Africa, founded in 1847 by freed American Negro slaves: area, 43,000 sq. mi.; pop., 1,571,000; cap., Monrovia.
Libia, Libya: Italian name.
Libya, 1. N. Africa W. of Egypt: ancient Greek and Roman name. **2.** a country in N. Africa, on the Mediterranean: area, 679,358 sq. mi.; pop., 2,444,000; cap., Tripoli.
Liechtenstein, a country in W. central Europe, between Switzerland and Austria: area, 65 sq. mi.; pop., 24,000; cap., Vaduz.
Liège, a province of E. Belgium: pop., 1,016,000; also, its capital.
Liguria, a region of Italy, along N.W. coast: chief city, Genoa.
Ligurian Republic, a republic set up by Napoleon in 1797: under French control until 1815: now the region of Liguria.
Limbourg, Limburg, a province of N.E. Belgium: pop., 650,000; cap., Hasselt.
Limburg, a province of S.E. Netherlands: pop., 999,000; cap., Maastricht.
Limerick, a county of central Munster province, Ireland: pop., 138,000; also, its capital.
Limousin, a former province of central France.
Lincolnshire, Lincoln, a county on E. coast of England: pop., 520,000; county seat, Lincoln.
Linlithgow, West Lothian: former name.
Lipari Islands, a group of volcanic islands N. of Sicily: area, 45 sq. mi.; pop., 14,000.
Lippe, a former division of N.W. Germany: at one time, also, a principality, duchy, and republic.
Lithuania, a country in N.E. Europe that became the Lithuanian S.S.R. in August, 1940.
Lithuanian Soviet Socialist Republic, a republic of the U.S.S.R., on Baltic Sea: area, 22,800 sq. mi.; pop., 3,100,000; cap., Vilna.
Little Russia, S.W. European Russia; the Ukraine and regions near it.
Livonia, a former province of the Russian Empire, on Gulf of Riga: now part of Latvian and Estonian republics of the U.S.S.R.
Llano Estacado, a large plateau in S.E. New Mexico and W. Texas: height, 1,000 to 5,000 ft.
Locris, a district of ancient Greece, on Gulf of Corinth.
Lofoten Islands, a group of Norwegian islands N.W. of Norway: area, 475 sq. mi.
Lolland, a Danish island, S. of Zealand Island.
Lombok, an island of Indonesia, between Bali and Sumbawa: area, 1,811 sq. mi.
Long Island, an island in New York State, between Long Island Sound and the Atlantic: it includes Kings, Queens, Nassau, and Suffolk Counties: area, 1,411 sq. mi.; pop., 7,115,000.
Lorraine, a former province of N.E. France.
Lothian, a region in S.E. Scotland, made up of three former counties: pop., 679,000.
Louisiana, a Southern State of the U.S., on Gulf of Mexico: area, 48,523 sq. mi.; pop., 3,643,000; cap., Baton Rouge.
Louisiana Purchase, the land bought by the U.S. from France in 1803: it extended from Gulf of Mexico to Canada and from the Mississippi to Rocky Mountains.
Low Archipelago, same as *Tuamotu Archipelago.*
Low Countries, the Netherlands, Belgium, and Luxemburg.
Lower Austria, a province of N.E. Austria: pop., 1,400,000.
Lower California, a peninsula in Mexico, between the Pacific and Gulf of California: area, 55,629 sq. mi.; pop., 981,000; cap. of N. territory, Mexicali; of S. territory, La Paz.
Lower Canada, Quebec province: former name.
Lowlands, the, lowlands of S. and E. Scotland.
Lubang Islands, a small group of islands in the Philippines, near Manila Bay.
Lucania, 1. an ancient region in S. Italy. **2.** a department of S. Italy.
Lucerne, a canton of central Switzerland: pop., 253,000; also, its capital.
Lusatia, a former region in E. Germany, between the Elbe and Oder Rivers.
Lusitania, an ancient region in the Iberian Peninsula, corresponding to what is now Portugal.
Luxembourg, Luxemburg, a province of S.E. Belgium: area, 1,706 sq. mi.; pop., 219,000; cap., Arlon.
Luxembourg, Luxembourg, a grand duchy in W. Europe, bounded by Belgium, Germany, and France: area, 999 sq. mi.; pop., 357,000; also, its capital.
Luzon, the main island of the Philippine Islands: area, 40,420 sq. mi.; chief city, Manila.
Lycaonia, an ancient province of central Asia Minor.
Lycia, an ancient country in S. Asia Minor.
Lydia, an ancient country in W. Asia Minor.
Lyonnais, Lyonais, a former province of E. central France

M

Macao, 1. an island at mouth of Canton (*or* Chu Kiang) River, in S.E. China, opposite Hong Kong. **2.** a Portuguese overseas territory including Macao Island and 2 near-by islands: area, 6 sq. mi.; pop., 249,000.
Macedon, ancient Macedonia.
Macedonia, 1. an ancient kingdom N. of Greece: now part of Greece, Bulgaria, and Yugoslavia. **2.** a district of N. Greece.
Mackinac Island, a small island in Strait of Mackinac.
Madagascar, a country that is a large island in the Indian Ocean, off the S.E. coast of Africa: formerly a French colony: area, 228,000 sq. mi.; pop., 6,750,000; cap., Tananarive.
Madeira, a group of 5 Portuguese islands off coast of Morocco: area, 314 sq. mi.; pop., 267,000; cap., Funchal; also, the chief island of this group.
Madhya Bharat, a former state of W. central India: now in Madhya Pradesh.
Madhya Pradesh, a state of central India: area, 171,200 sq. mi.; pop., 32,372,000; cap., Bhopal.
Madras, a former state of S.E. India: area, 50,172 sq. mi.
Madura, an island of Indonesia, N.E. of Java: area, 1,726 sq. mi.
Maine, a New England State of the U.S.: area, 33,215 sq. mi.; pop., 994,000; cap., Augusta.
Mainland, 1. same as *Pomona.* **2.** the largest of the Shetland Islands: area, 407 sq. mi.
Majorca, the largest of the Balearic Islands: area, 1,352 sq. mi.; pop., 290,000.
Malabar, Malabar Coast, a coastal region in S.W. India, extending inland to Western Ghats.
Malacca, a state of Malaya, on W. coast of Malay Peninsula: area, 640 sq. mi.; pop., 428,000; also, its chief city.
Malaga, a province of S. Spain.
Malagasy, Madagascar: the former name.
Malawi, a country in S.E. Africa, on Lake Nyasa: formerly the British protectorate of Nyasaland, it is a member of the British Commonwealth of Nations: area, 46,066 sq. mi.; pop., 5,044,000; cap., Lilongwe.
Malaya, 1. same as *Malay Peninsula.* **2.** a part of Malaysia (called *West Malaysia*) consisting of eleven states in the lower part of the Malay Peninsula: area, 50,700 sq. mi.; pop., 8,899,000: former name, *Federation of Malaya.*
Malay Archipelago, a chain of islands extending from Malay Peninsula to a point N. of E. Australia: also called *East Indies, Indonesia, Malaysia.*
Malay Peninsula, a peninsula in S.E. Asia, including Malaya (sense 2) and part of Thailand.
Malaysia, 1. the Malay Archipelago (and, sometimes, the Malay Peninsula). **2.** a country in S.E. Asia, consisting of Malaya, Sarawak, and Sabah: it is a member of the British Commonwealth of Nations: area, 128,429 sq. mi.; pop., 11,900,000; cap., Kuala Lumpur.
Malay States, the former Federated Malay States and Unfederated Malay States.
Maldives, an independent sultanate on a group of islands, S.W. of India: formerly under British protection: area, 115 sq. mi.; pop., 129,000; cap., Malé.
Mali, a country in W. Africa, S. and E. of Mauritania: area, 590,966 sq. mi.; pop., 5,376,000; cap., Bamako: formerly, *French Sudan.*
Mallorca, Majorca: Spanish name.
Malta, 1. an island in the Mediterranean, S. of Sicily. **2.** a country consisting of this island and two others: formerly a British colony, it is now independent and a member of the British Commonwealth of Nations: area, 122 sq. mi.; pop., 319,000; cap., Valletta.
Man, Isle of, one of the British Isles, between Northern Ireland and England: area, 211 sq. mi.; pop., 56,000; cap., Douglas.
Manchester, a county in N.W. England, surrounding the city of Manchester: pop., 2,718,000: also called *Greater Manchester.*
Manchukuo, Manchoukuo, a former state in E. Asia, including Manchuria, Jehol province, and part of Chahar, set up by Japan in 1932, abolished in 1945 as result of World War II.
Manchuria, a region in N.E. China, on the Yellow Sea: formerly an administrative unit, it is now divided into the provinces of Heilungkiang, Kirin, and Liaoning: area, c.364,000 sq. mi.
Manhattan, an island between the Hudson and East Rivers, forming part of New York City: length, 13 mi.; area, with small near-by islands, 22 sq. mi.
Manipur, a union territory of E. India: area, 8,620 sq. mi.; pop., 780,000; cap., Imphal.
Manitoba, a province of S. central Canada: area, 251,000 sq. mi.; pop., 1,022,000; cap., Winnipeg.
Manitoulin Island, a Canadian island in Lake Huron, S. of Ontario, Canada: length, 80 mi.
Marajó, an island between the estuaries of Amazon and Pará Rivers, Brazil: area, 16,000 sq. mi.
Marathon, an ancient Greek village on E. coast of Attica.
Marche, Le, a former department of central Italy, on the Adriatic.
Mare Island, an island in San Pablo Bay, N. California.
Mariana Islands, a chain of islands in the Pacific, E. of the Philippines: area, c.450 sq. mi.; pop., 12,000; (except Guam), formerly a Japanese mandate, now under U.S. trusteeship: also called *Ladrone Islands, Ladrones.*
Mari Autonomous Soviet Socialist Republic, a division of the R.S.F.S.R., in the middle Volga region: area, 8,994 sq. mi.; pop., 685,000; cap., Ioshkar-Ola.
Marie Byrd Land, a region in Antarctica, S.E. of Ross Sea.
Marie Galante, a French island of the Leeward group, in West Indies: area, 60 sq. mi.; pop., 16,000.
Marinduque, one of the Philippine Islands, S. of Luzon: area, 356 sq. mi.
Maritime Provinces, the Canadian provinces of Nova Scotia, New Brunswick, and Prince Edward Island.
Maroc, Morocco: French name.
Marquesas Islands, a group of French islands in the South Pacific: area, 480 sq. mi.; pop., 4,200.
Marshall Islands, a group of coral atolls in the North Pacific, E. of Caroline Islands: area, 160 sq. mi.; pop., 18,000; chief island, Jaluit: formerly Japanese mandate, now under U.S. trusteeship.
Martha's Vineyard, an island off S.E. coast of Massachusetts, S. of Cape Cod: area, c.100 sq. mi.; pop., c.5,800.
Martinique, an island off the Windward group, in West Indies, constituting an overseas department of France: area, 385 sq. mi.; pop., 343,000; cap., Fort-de-France.
Maryland, an Eastern State of the U.S.: area, 10,577 sq. mi.; pop., 3,922,000; cap., Annapolis.
Masbate, one of the Philippine Islands, W. of Samar: area, 1,255 sq. mi.
Massachusetts, a New England State of the U.S.: area, 8,257 sq. mi.; pop., 5,689,000; cap., Boston.
Masuren, Masuria: German name.
Masuria, a region in N.E. Poland, formerly in East Prussia.
Matabeleland, a district of Rhodesia, formerly under British control.
Matto Grosso, a state of W. Brazil, bordering Bolivia and Paraguay: area, 532,210 sq. mi.; pop., 1,475,000; cap., Cuyabá.
Maui, one of the Hawaiian Islands, N.W. of Hawaii: area, 728 sq. mi.; pop., 39,000.
Mauretania, Mauritania, an ancient kingdom, and later a Roman province, in N.W. Africa.
Mauritania, Mauretania, a country in W. Africa, on the Atlantic: a former French colony: area, c.450,000 sq. mi.; pop., 1,318,000; cap., Nouakchott: official name, *Islamic Republic of Mauritania.*
Mauritius, an island country in the Indian Ocean, E. of Madagascar: formerly a British colony, it is now independent and a member of the British Commonwealth of Na-

tions: area, 809 sq. mi.; pop., 872,000; cap., Port Louis.
Mayo, a maritime county of Connaught province, Ireland: pop., 116,000.
Mecklenburg, a former division of N. Germany: earlier a kingdom and duchy.
Media, an ancient country in the part of Asia that is now N.W. Iran.
Megaris, a district of ancient Greece, on Isthmus of Corinth.
Megiddo, an ancient city in N. Palestine, near Nazareth.
Melanesia, a group of islands in the South Pacific, extending from the Admiralty to the Fiji Islands.
Melos, one of the Cyclades Islands, in the Aegean: area, 57 sq. mi.; pop., 5,000.
Melville Island, 1. an island in Northwest Territories, Canada, N. of Victoria Island: area, 16,164 sq. mi. **2.** an island in Northern Territory, Australia: area, 2,400 sq. mi.
Memel, a territory of Lithuania: now part of the Lithuanian S.S.R.
Memphis, an ancient city in Egypt, near mouth of Nile: former cap. of Egypt.
Menorca, Minorca: Spanish spelling.
Mercia, a former Anglo-Saxon kingdom of central England.
Merionethshire, a former county of Wales.
Meroë, a ruined city on the Nile: ancient cap. of Ethiopia.
Mersyside, a county of N.W. England, on the Irish Sea: pop., 1,603,000.
Mesopotamia, 1. an ancient country in S.W. Asia, between Tigris and Euphrates rivers. **2.** Iraq: former name.
Messene, an ancient city in S.W. Peloponnesus.
Mexico, 1. a country in North America, S. of the U.S.: area, 760,290 sq. mi.; pop., 60,145,000; cap., Mexico City. **2.** a state of S. Mexico: area, 8,267 sq. mi.; pop., 3,798,000; cap., Toluca.
Michigan, a Middle Western State of the U.S.: area, 58,216 sq. mi.; pop., 8,875,000; cap., Lansing.
Micronesia, the groups of islands in the Pacific N. of the Equator and E. of the Philippines.
Middle America, the part of Latin America S. of the U.S. and N. of South America.
Middle Atlantic States, New York, New Jersey, and Pennsylvania.
Middle Congo, a French colony in French Equatorial Africa: see *Congo* (sense 1).
Middle East, the area including Iraq, Iran, Afghanistan, and, sometimes, India, Tibet, and Burma.
Middle Kingdom, Middle Empire, a kingdom of ancient Egypt, c.2400–1580 B.C., with its cap. at Heracleopolis and, later, at Thebes.
Middlesex, a former county of England.
Middle States, those eastern States between the New England States and the South: New York, New Jersey, Pennsylvania, Delaware, and Maryland.
Middle West, that part of the U.S. between the Rocky Mountains and the Allegheny Mountains, N. of the Ohio River and S. borders of Kansas and Missouri: also *Midwest.*
Midlands, the, the middle counties of England.
Midlothian, a former county of S.E. Scotland.
Midway Islands, a group of islands in the North Pacific, part of Hawaiian group, about halfway between the U.S. and the Philippines: area, 28 sq. mi.; pop., 416.
Midwest, same as *Middle West.*
Miletus, an ancient Greek city in W. Asia Minor, now in ruins.
Milo, Melos: Italian name.
Minas Geraes, a state of E. central Brazil: area, 221,894 sq. mi.; pop., 11,280,000; cap., Belo Horizonte.
Mindanao, the southernmost large island of the Philippines: area, 36,906 sq. mi.; chief city, Zamboanga.
Mindoro, one of the Philippine Islands, S. of Luzon: area, 3,794 sq. mi.
Minnesota, a Middle Western State of the U.S., adjoining the Canadian border: area, 84,068 sq. mi.; pop., 3,805,000; cap., St. Paul.
Minorca, one of the Balearic Islands, E. of Majorca: area, 271 sq. mi.; pop., 43,000.
Miquelon, a French island off S. coast of Newfoundland: area, 83 sq. mi.; pop., 600.
Mississippi, a Southern State of the U.S., on Gulf of Mexico: area, 47,716 sq. mi.; pop., 2,217,000, cap., Jackson.
Missouri, a Middle Western State of the U.S.: area, 69,674 sq. mi.; pop., 4,677,000; cap., Jefferson City.
Moldavia, a former principality and district of Romania, now part of Moldavian S.S.R.
Moldavian Soviet Socialist Republic, a republic of the U.S.S.R. in S.W. European Russia, on the Black Sea: formed (1940) from former Moldavian A.S.S.R (in the Ukraine) and Bessarabia: area, 13,680 sq. mi.; pop., 3,600,000; cap., Kishinev.
Molokai, one of the Hawaiian Islands, N.W. of Maui: area, 259 sq. mi.; pop., 5,000.
Molotov, Perm, a region of the R.S.F.S.R. in W. Siberia: the former name.
Molucca Islands, Moluccas, a group of islands in Indonesia, between Celebes and New Guinea: area, 30,168 sq. mi.; pop., 893,000: also called *Spice Islands.*
Monaco, a principality on the Mediterranean, surrounded on three sides by S.E. France: area, 1/2 sq. mi.; pop., 24,000.
Monaghan, a county of N.E. Ireland: pop., 46,000; also, its county seat.
Mongolia, a region in central Asia, consisting of Mongolian People's Republic and Inner Mongolia.
Mongolian People's Republic, a country in central Asia, N. of China and S. of the U.S.S.R.: area, 600,000 sq. mi.; pop., 1,444,000; cap., Ulan Bator: formerly called *Outer Mongolia.*
Monmouthshire, Monmouth, a former county in S.E. Wales.
Montana, a Western State of the U.S., bordering Canada: area, 147,138 sq. mi.; pop., 694,000; cap., Helena.
Montenegro, a former kingdom N. of Albania, now a federated republic of Yugoslavia: area, 5,345 sq. mi.
Montgomeryshire, Montgomery, a former county of Wales.
Montserrat, a British island of the Leeward group in West Indies: area, 32 sq. mi.; pop., 14,000.
Mont St. Michel, a small island off N.W. coast of France, noted for its fortress and abbey: also *Mont-Saint-Michel, Mont Saint Michel.*
Moravia, a former province of Austria: now part of Czechoslovakia.
Moray, a former county on coast of N.E. Scotland.
Mordovian Autonomous Soviet Socialist Republic, a division of the R.S.F.S.R., in E. central European Russia: area, 9,843 sq. mi.; pop., 1,030,000; cap., Saransk.
Morea, the Peloponnesus: the former name.
Morocco, a kingdom in N.W. Africa: until 1956, divided into the French zone, Spanish zone, and Tangier: area, 174,471 sq. mi.; pop., 17,305,000; cap., Rabat.
Moscow, a region of the R.S.F.S.R., in central European Russia: pop., 10,938,000.
Moskva, Moscow: Russian name.
Mozambique, a country in S.E. Africa, on the Mozambique Channel of the Indian Ocean: formerly a Portuguese overseas territory: area, 302,300 sq. mi.; pop., 9,239,000; cap., Maputo.
Mull, the largest island in the Hebrides.
Munster, a province of S.W. Ireland: area, 9,316 sq. mi.; pop., 849,000.
Murman Coast, the coast of Kola Peninsula, U.S.S.R., on the Arctic Ocean.
Murmansk, a region in the R.S.F.S.R., on Kola Peninsula: pop., 291,000; also, its capital.
Muscat and Oman, Oman: the former name.
Muscovy, Russia: ancient name.
Mycenae, an ancient Greek city in N.E. Peloponnesus.
Myra, a city in ancient Lycia, Asia Minor.
Mysia, an ancient country in N.W. Asia Minor.
Mysore, a state of S. India: area, 29,458 sq. mi.; pop., 23,587,000; also, its capital.
Mytilene Mytileni, a Greek island in the Aegean, off coast of Asia Minor: area, 675 sq. mi.; pop., 26,000.

N

Nairnshire, Nairn, a former county of N. Scotland.
Nakhichevan, Autonomous Soviet Socialist Republic, a division of the Azerbaijan S.S.R., in the Transcaucasus: area, 2,277 sq. mi.; pop., 202,000; cap., Nakhichevan.
Namaqua Land, Nama Land, a region in South West Africa: also *Great Namaqua Land.*
Namibia, South West Africa: the official (U.N.) name.
Namur, a province of S. Belgium; also, its capital.
Nantucket, an island off Massachusetts: area, 51 sq. mi.
Nassau, a former duchy in W. Germany: now in Hesse.
Natal, a province of South Africa, on Indian Ocean: area, 33,578 sq. mi.; pop., 2,933,000; cap., Pietermaritzburg.
Naucratis, an ancient Greek city in the Nile delta, Egypt.
Nauru, a country on an island in Micronesia: formerly a UN trust territory administered by Australia: area, 8 sq. mi.; pop., 7,000.
Navarra, Navarre: Spanish name.
Navarre, a former kingdom of N. Spain and S.W. France.
Navigators Islands, Samoa: former name.
Naxos, the largest of the Cyclades Islands, in the Aegean: area, 171 sq. mi.; pop., 17,000.
Near East, variously, the countries near or E. of E. Mediterranean, including S.W. Asia (Turkey, Syria, Lebanon, Israel, Jordan, Saudi Arabia, etc.) and, sometimes, the Balkans and Egypt.
Nearer Tibet, the E. part of Tibet: now part of Chinghai and Szechwan provinces, China.
Nebraska, a Middle Western State of the U.S.: area, 77,273 sq. mi.; pop., 1,483,000; cap., Lincoln.
Negev, Negeb, a region in S. Israel, of partially reclaimed desert.
Negri Sembilan, a native state of Malaya: area, 2,580 sq. mi.; pop., 531,000; cap., Seremban.
Negros, one of the Philippine Islands, between Panay and Cebu: area, 4,903 sq. mi.
Nejd, an inland state of Saudi Arabia: area, c.170,000 sq. mi.; pop., 3,000,000; cap., Riyadh.
Nepal, a country in the Himalaya Mountains, between India and Tibet: area, 54,000 sq. mi.; pop., 12,321,000; cap., Katmandu.
Netherlands, 1. a country in W. Europe, on North Sea: area, 12,868 sq. mi.; pop., 13,763,000; commercial cap., Amsterdam; political cap., The Hague: also called *Holland.* **2.** a kingdom consisting of the independent states of the Netherlands and Netherlands Antilles.
Netherlands Antilles, a group of islands in the West Indies constituting two of the Windward Islands and part of another and three of the Leeward Islands: total area, 394 sq. mi.; pop., 228,000; cap., Willemstad.
Netherlands Guiana, same as *Surinam.*
Netherlands Indies, formerly, islands in the East Indies belonging to the Netherlands: also called *Dutch East Indies:* see *Indonesia.*
Netherlands New Guinea, the W. part of New Guinea: since 1963, a part of Indonesia called *West Irian.*
Neustria, the W. part of the empire of the Franks, now included in N. and N.W. France.
Nevada, a Western State of the U.S.: area, 110,540 sq. mi.; pop., 489,000; cap., Carson City.
Nevis, a British island of the Leeward group, West Indies: area, 50 sq. mi.: see *St. Kitts.*
New Amsterdam, a Dutch colonial town on Manhattan Island: later became New York City.
New Britain, an island in Bismarck Archipelago: area, 14,500 sq. mi.; pop., 115,000; chief city, Rabaul.
New Brunswick, a province of Canada, on S.E. coast: area, 28,354 sq. mi.; pop., 677,000; cap., Fredericton.
New Caledonia, 1. a French island in Melanesia, in Coral Sea: area, 6,296 sq. mi.; pop., 117,000; cap., Nouméa. **2.** a French territory including New Caledonia and adjacent islands.
New England, the 6 N.E. States of the U.S.; Maine, Vermont, New Hampshire, Massachusetts, Rhode Island, and Connecticut.
Newfoundland, 1. an island off E. coast of Canada: area, 42,734 sq. mi. **2.** a province of Canada comprising Newfoundland and Labrador: area, 156,185 sq. mi.; pop., 558,000; cap., St. John's.
New France a French territory (1609–1763) in North America, including Canada and Mississippi Valley.
New Georgia, one of the British Solomon Islands.
New Granada, 1. Panama and Colombia when owned by Spain. **2.** the former Spanish possessions in N.W. South America and Central America, including New Granada, Ecuador, and Venezuela.
New Guinea, a large island in East Indies, N. of Australia: divided between West Irian, in the W. half, and the independent country of Papua New Guinea, in the E. half.
New Guinea, Territory of, a former Australian trust territory including N.E. New Guinea, the Bismarck Archipelago, Bougainville, Buka, and smaller adjacent islands of the Solomons: now part of Papua New Guinea.
New Hampshire, a New England State of the U.S.: area, 9,304 sq. mi.; pop., 738,000; cap., Concord.
New Hebrides, a group of Melanesian islands in the South Pacific, under joint control of Britain and France: area, 5,700 sq. mi.; pop., 84,000; cap., Vila.
New Ireland, an island in Bismarck Archipelago: area, 3,800 sq. mi.; pop., 41,000.
New Jersey, an Eastern State of the U.S.: area, 7,836 sq. mi.; pop., 7,168,000; cap., Trenton.
New Mexico, a Southwestern State of the U.S., on the Mexican border: area, 121,666 sq. mi.; pop., 1,016,000; cap., Santa Fe.
New Netherland, a former Dutch colony (1613–1665) in North America, later comprising British colonies of New York, New Jersey, and Delaware.
New Siberian Islands, a group of islands in the U.S.S.R., in Arctic Ocean, N. of E. Siberia.
New South Wales, a state of S.E. Australia: area, 309,433 sq. mi.; pop., 4,567,000; cap., Sydney.
New Spain, the former Spanish possessions in Mexico, S.W. U.S., Central America (excluding Panama), West Indies, and the Philippines.
New World, the Western Hemisphere.
New York, as Eastern State of the U.S.: area, 49,576 sq. mi.; pop., 18,241,000; cap., Albany.
New Zealand, a country made up of 2 large and several small islands in the Pacific, S.E. of Australia: it is a member of the British Commonwealth of Nations: total area, 103,934 sq. mi.; pop., 3,148,000; cap., Wellington.
Nicaragua, a country in Central America, on the Caribbean and Pacific: area, 57,143 sq. mi.; pop., 2,155,000; cap., Managua.
Nicobar Islands, a group of islands in Bay of Bengal, S.W. of Burma: with the Andaman Islands, constituting a union territory of India (*Andaman and Nicobar Islands*): area (of the territory), 3,215 sq. mi.; pop. (of the state), 64,000.
Niger, a country in central Africa, N. of Nigeria: a former French colony: area, 459,000 sq. mi.; pop., 4,600,000; cap., Niamey.
Nigeria, a country in W. central Africa, on the Gulf of Guinea: a former British colony and protectorate, it is now independent and a member of the British Commonwealth of Nations: the N. section of the Cameroons joined Nigeria by plebescite in 1961: area, 356,670 sq. mi.; pop., 74,870,000; cap., Lagos.
Niihau, one of the Hawaiian Islands, W. of Kauai: area, 72 sq. mi.; pop., 250.
Nineveh, a city in ancient Assyria, on the Tigris, near modern Mosul.
Ningsia–Hui, an autonomous region in N.E. China: area, 26,600 sq. mi.; pop., 2,000,000; cap., Yinchuan.
Nippon, Japan: Japanese name.
Norfolk, a county on E. coast of England: pop., 650,000; county seat, Norwich.

Norfolk Island, an Australian island, 930 mi. N.E. of Sydney: area, 13 1/2 sq. mi.; pop., 1,000.
Noricum, a Roman province S. of the Danube, in region of modern Austria.
Normandy, 1. a former province of France, on English Channel: cap., Rouen. **2.** a district on N. coast of France, between Dieppe and Mont St. Michel.
North America, the northern continent in the Western Hemisphere: including adjacent islands, area, 9,330,000 sq. mi.; pop., 348,000,000.
Northamptonshire, Northampton, a county of central England: pop., 496,000; county seat, Northampton.
North Borneo, a former British colony in N. Borneo: see *Sabah.*
North Carolina, a Southern State of the U.S.: area, 52,712 sq. mi.; pop., 5,082,000; cap., Raleigh.
North Dakota, a Middle Western State of the U.S.: area, 70,665 sq. mi.; pop., 618,000; cap., Bismarck.
North Eastern New Guinea, formerly, the N.E. part of New Guinea.
North East Frontier Agency (or **Tract**), a territory of N.E. India, on the border of Tibet, administered as part of Assam state: area, 31,438 sq. mi.; pop., 337,000.
Northern Hemisphere, that half of the earth N. of equator.
Northern Ireland, a division of the United Kingdom, in N.E. Ireland: it consists of major part of former province of Ulster: area, 5,241 sq. mi.; pop., 1,537,000; cap., Belfast.
Northern Rhodesia, a former British protectorate in S. Africa: see *Zambia.*
Northern Sporades, a group of Greek islands in the Aegean, E. of Thessaly, Greece.
Northern Territories, a region in N. Ghana: it was a British protectorate in the Gold Coast from 1901 to 1957: area, 27,122 sq. mi.
Northern Territory, a territory of N. Australia: area, 523,620 sq. mi.; pop., 71,000; cap., Darwin: also called *North Australia.*
North Holland, a province of N.W. Netherlands, on North Sea: area, 1,058 sq. mi.; pop., 2,244,000; cap., Haarlem.
North Island, the northern of the 2 chief islands of New Zealand: area, 44,281 sq. mi.
North Ossetian Autonomous Soviet Socialist Republic, a division of the R.S.F.S.R., in the Caucasus: area, 2,393 sq. mi.; pop., 533,000; cap., Ordzhonikidze.
Northumberland, the northernmost county of England: pop., 286,000; county seat, Newcastle.
Northumbria, a former Anglo-Saxon kingdom of N.E. England, N. of River Humber.
North-West Frontier Agencies and Tribal Areas, a group of native agencies and tribal areas of British India.
Northwest Territories, a division of N. Canada, on the Arctic Ocean: area, 1,309,600 sq. mi.; pop., 43,000; cap., Yellowknife.
Northwest Territory, a region N. of the Ohio, between Pennsylvania and the Mississippi, ceded (1783) by England to the U.S.: now forms Ohio, Indiana, Illinois, Michigan, Wisconsin, and part of Minnesota.
Norway, a country in N. Europe, in W. part of Scandinavian Peninsula: area, 124,556 sq. mi.; pop., 3,948,000; cap., Oslo.
Nottinghamshire, Nottingham, a county of central England: pop., 981,000; county seat, Nottingham.
Nova Scotia, a peninsular maritime province of S.E. Canada: area, 21,425 sq. mi.; pop., 829,000; cap., Halifax: formerly called *Acadia.*
Novaya Zemlya, two large islands in the European U.S.S.R., in the Arctic Ocean: area, 36,000 sq. mi.
Novosibirsk, a territory of the U.S.S.R., in W. Siberia: pop., 2,299,000; also, its capital.
Nubia, a former kingdom of N.E. Africa, between Red Sea and Sahara Desert: now part of Egypt and Sudan.
Nuevo Leon, a state of N.E. Mexico: area, 25,134 sq. mi.; pop., 1,654,000; cap., Monterrey.
Numantia, an ancient Celtic city in N. Spain.
Numidia, an ancient kingdom, and later a Roman province, on N. coast of Africa.
Nyasaland, a former British protectorate in S.E. Africa: see *Malawi.*

O

Oahu, the chief island of the Hawaiian Islands: area, 595 sq. mi.; pop. 629,000; chief city, Honolulu.
Oaxaca, a state of S. Mexico, on the Pacific: area, 36,371 sq. mi.; pop., 2,012,000; also, its capital.
Oberland, a mountainous district in central Switzerland.
Occident, the countries W. of Asia: formerly, Europe; now, also the Western Hemisphere.
Oceania, Oceanica, the islands in the Pacific, including Melanesia, Micronesia, and Polynesia, and sometimes New Zealand, Australia, and Malay Archipelago.
Oesel, an Estonian island in Gulf of Riga: area, 1,010 sq. mi.
Ohio, a Middle Western State of the U.S.: area, 41,222 sq. mi.; pop., 10,652,000; cap., Columbus.
Oil Rivers, the region surrounding the rivers of the Niger Delta, formerly a British protectorate, now part of Nigeria.
Oirot Autonomous Region, a former division of the R.S.F.S.R., in S. central Siberia: area, 35,936 sq. mi.
Okinawa, one of the Ryukyu Islands, in the North Pacific, between Taiwan and Kyushu: captured by American forces (1945) in World War II: area, 454 sq. mi.; pop., 759,000; cap., Naha City.
Oklahoma, a Southern State of the U.S.: area, 69,919 sq. mi.; pop., 2,559,000; cap., Oklahoma City.
Old Castile, a former province of central Spain.
Oldenburg, a former division of N.W. Germany: earlier, a duchy.
Old Northwest, same as *Northwest Territory.*
Old World, the Eastern Hemisphere; Europe, Asia, and Africa.
Olympia, a plain in ancient Elis, Greece.
Olynthus, a city in ancient Greece, on Chalcidice Peninsula.
Oman, a country in S.E. Arabia on the Arabian Sea and the Gulf of Oman: area, 82,000 sq. mi.; pop., 766,000; cap., Muscat: formerly called *Muscat and Oman.*
Omsk, a region of the U.S.S.R., in N.W. Siberia: pop., 1,646,000; also, its capital.
Ontario, a province of S. central Canada, on the Great Lakes: area, 412,582 sq. mi.; pop., 8,264,000; cap., Toronto.
Orange, a former principality of W. Europe: now part of S.E. France.
Orange Free State, a province of South Africa: area, 49,647 sq. mi.; pop., 1,387,000; cap., Bloemfontein: formerly a Boer republic (1854–1900), later a British colony (*Orange River Colony,* 1900–1910).
Oregon, a Northwestern State of the U.S.: area, 96,981 sq. mi.; pop., 2,091,000; cap., Salem.
Orel, a region of the R.S.F.S.R., in central European Russia: pop., 3,482,000; also, its capital.
Orient, 1. the East; Asia. **2.** the Far East; E. Asia.
Oriente, a province of E. Cuba: area, 14,211 sq. mi.; pop., 2,600,000; cap., Santiago de Cuba; former name, *Santiago de Cuba.*
Orissa, a state of E. India, on Bay of Bengal: area, 60,136 sq. mi.; pop., 17,549,000; cap., Cuttack.
Orkney Islands, a group of islands N. of Scotland, constituting a region (called *Orkney*): area, 376 sq. mi.; pop., 18,000.
Ossetia, a region in the Caucasus, U.S.S.R.
Ostpreussen, East Prussia: German name.
Otaheiti, Tahiti: former name.
Ottoman Empire, the empire (c.1300–1919) of the Turks in S.E. Europe, S.W. Asia, and N.E. Africa: cap., Constantinople: also called *Turkish Empire.*
Oubangui Chare, Ubangi-Shari: French spelling.
Outer Mongolia, Mongolian People's Republic: former name.
Oxfordshire, Oxford, Oxon, a county of S. central England: pop., 535,000; county seat, Oxford.

P

Paestum, an ancient Greek city in S. Italy.
Pahang, a state of Malaya: area, 13,820 sq. mi.; pop., 445,000.
Pakistan, a country on the peninsula of India, in the N.W. part: area, 310,403 sq. mi.; pop., 70,260,000; cap., Islamabad. See also *Kashmir.*
Palatinate, the (Rhine), a district W. of the Rhine, formerly a state of German Empire: in 1945, it was incorporated into a state of West Germany (*Rhineland-Palatinate*): German name, *Pfalz.*
Palau Islands, a group of islands in the Pacific, between Mindanao and Caroline Islands: they are under U.S. trusteeship: area, 175 sq. mi.; pop., 11,000: also called *Pelew Islands.*
Palawan, one of the Philippine Islands, near Mindoro: area, 4,500 sq. mi.
Palestine, 1. a territory on E. coast of the Mediterranean, the country of the Jews in Biblical times. **2.** part of this territory under a British mandate after World War I: divided into Israel and Jordan by action of UN in 1947.
Palma, one of the Canary Islands: area, 280 sq. mi.; cap., Santa Cruz de la Palma.
Palmyra, an ancient city in Syria.
Palmyra Island, an atoll in the central Pacific, belonging to the U.S.
Pamphylia, an ancient land in S. Asia Minor.
Panama, a republic of Central America, on Isthmus of Panama: area, 32,001 sq. mi.; pop., 1,668,000; also, its capital.
Panama Canal Zone, same as *Canal Zone.*
Panay, one of the Philippine Islands, between Mindoro and Negros: area, 4,448 sq. mi.; chief city, Iloilo.
Pannonia, an ancient Roman province, between the Danube and Sava Rivers.
Pantelleria, an Italian island between Sicily and Tunisia: area, 32 sq. mi.; pop., 9,800.
Paphlagonia, an ancient country and Roman province in Asia Minor, on Black Sea.
Paphos, an ancient city in Cyprus.
Papua, same as *New Guinea.*
Papua New Guinea, a country occupying the E. half of the island of New Guinea: formerly made up of two territories (*Territory of Papua* and *Trust Territory of New Guinea*) jointly administered by Australia: area, 183,540 sq. mi.; pop., 2,756,000; cap., Port Moresby.
Para, a state of N. Brazil: area, 443,789 sq. mi.; pop., 1,985,000; cap., Belém.
Paraguay, a country in central South America: area, 151,570 sq. mi.; pop., 2,647,000; cap., Asunción.
Parma, a former duchy of Italy.
Paros, an island of Greece in the Aegean: area, 80 sq. mi.; pop., 7,700.
Parthia, an ancient kingdom S.E. of the Caspian.
Patagonia, a region in S. Argentina and Chile.
Patiala and East Punjab, a former state of N.W. India: now part of the state of Punjab.
Patmos, a Greek island in the Aegean: area, 22 sq. mi.; pop., 3,000.
Paumoto Archipelago, same as *Tuamotu Archipelago.*
Peebles, Peeblesshire, a former county of S. Scotland.
Pelew Islands, same as *Palau Islands.*
Peloponnesus, Peloponnesos, the peninsula of S. Greece: seat of early Mycenaean civilization and of Sparta.
Pemba, an island off E. coast of Africa: formerly in the British protectorate of Zanzibar, it is now part of Tanzania: area, 380 sq. mi.
Pembrokeshire, Pembroke, a former county of S.W. Wales.
Penang, 1. an island N.W. of Malay Peninsula: area, 110 sq. mi.; pop., 240,000. **2.** a state of Malaya, including this island and part of Malay Peninsula: area, 290 sq. mi.; pop., 779,000.
Pennsylvania, an Eastern State of the U.S.: area, 45,333 sq. mi.; pop., 11,794,000; cap., Harrisburg.
Penza, a region of the R.S.F.S.R., in central European Russia: pop., 1,510,000; also, its capital.
Peraea, an ancient division of Palestine, beyond the Jordan.
Perak, a native state of Malaya: area, 7,980 sq. mi.; pop., 1,702,000.
Perche, a former division in N. France.
Pergamum, Pergamus, an ancient Greek city in Mysia, on site of modern Bergama, Turkey.
Perm, a region of the U.S.S.R., in W. Siberia: pop., 2,998,000: former name, *Molotov.*
Persia, 1. same as *Persian Empire.* **2.** Iran: former name.
Persian Empire, an empire of S.W. Asia, from the Indus River to the Mediterranean: founded by Cyrus the Great (6th century B.C.) and destroyed by Alexander the Great (331 B.C.).
Perth, Perthshire, a former county of N. central Scotland.
Peru, a country in South America, on the Pacific: area, 482,133 sq. mi.; pop., 15,615,000; cap., Lima.
Pescadores, a group of islands in Formosa Strait, belonging to Taiwan: area, 50 sq. mi.
Pesto, Paestum: modern name.
Peterborough, Soke of, a former county of E. central England.
Petra, an ancient city in modern Jordan.
Pfalz, the Palatinate: German name.
Pharos, a small peninsula at Alexandria, in N. Egypt: in ancient times it was an island.
Pharsalia, an ancient Greek district of Thessaly, surrounding the city of Pharsalus.
Pharsalus, an ancient city in Thessaly, Greece.
Phenicia, same as *Phoenicia.*
Philippi, an ancient city in Macedonia.
Philippine Islands, a group of 7,083 islands in the Pacific, N.E. of Borneo, comprising a republic (*Republic of the Philippines*): under the jurisdiction of the U.S. until 1946, and called the Commonwealth of the Philippines from 1935 to 1946; area, 114,830 sq. mi.; pop., 43,751,000; cap., Manila: also called *Philippines.*
Philistia, an ancient country on S. coast of Palestine.
Phocaea, an ancient Ionian city in Asia Minor.
Phocis, an ancient region in central Greece, on the Gulf of Corinth.
Phoenicia, an ancient kingdom on the Mediterranean in region of modern Syria and Palestine: also spelled *Phenicia.*
Phrygia, an ancient country in central Asia Minor.
Picardy, a region and former province of N. France, once part of Flanders.
Piedmont, 1. a plateau between Atlantic coast and the Appalachians, covering parts of Alabama, Georgia, South Carolina, North Carolina, and Virginia. **2.** a former principality, now a department of N.W. Italy.
Piemonte, Piedmont, Italy: Italian name.
Pieria, a region in ancient Macedonia.
Pines, Isle of, a Cuban island, S. of W. Cuba: area, 1,180 sq. mi.
Pisidia, an ancient country in S. Asia Minor: later a Roman province.
Pitcairn Island, a British island in Polynesia in the South Pacific: area, 2 sq. mi.; pop., 92.
Plataea, an ancient city in Boeotia, Greece.
Pleasant Island, Nauru: former name.
Plymouth Colony, the colony founded by the Pilgrims in 1620 on Massachusetts Bay.
Poitou, a former province of W. central France.
Poland, a country in central Europe, on Baltic Sea: area, 150,470 sq. mi.; pop., 34,364,000; cap., Warsaw.
Polish Corridor, the narrow strip of Poland between Germany and East Prussia, extending to Baltic Sea (1919–1945).
Polska, Poland: Polish name.
Polynesia, a scattered group of islands in the Pacific, E. of Micronesia and Melanesia, including the Hawaiian Islands, Samoa, Tonga, etc.

Pomerania, a former province of Prussia, on Baltic Sea: divided between Germany and Poland (1945).
Pommern, Pomerania: German name.
Pomona, the largest of the Orkney Islands: area, 190 sq. mi.: also called *Mainland.*
Pompeii, an ancient city on Bay of Naples: destoryed by eruption of Mount Vesuvius (79 A.D.).
Pondichéry, a former province of French India, on Coromandel Coast: area, 196 sq. mi.
Pontus, an ancient kingdom in Asia Minor, on Black Sea.
Porto Rico, Puerto Rico: former name.
Portugal, a country in S.W. Europe, on the Atlantic: area, 35,490 sq. mi.; pop., 9,228,000; cap., Lisbon.
Portuguese East Africa, a former Portuguese overseas territory on the E. coast of Africa: now the country of Mozambique.
Portuguese Guinea, a former Portuguese overseas territory on coast of W. Africa: now the country of Guinea-Bissau.
Portuguese India, the former Portuguese overseas territory consisting of Goa, Daman, and Diu, on W. coast of India.
Portuguese Timor, a former Portuguese overseas territory on E. Timor Island, in East Indies: now part of Indonesia.
Portuguese West Africa, a former Portuguese overseas territory on the W. coast of Africa: now the country of Angola.
Potidaea, a city in ancient Macedonia.
Powys, a county of central Wales: pop., 100,000.
Preussen, Prussia: German name.
Pribilof Islands, a group of Alaskan islands in Bering Sea, N. of Aleutians.
Prince Edward Island, an island province of Canada, in Gulf of St. Lawrence: area, 2,184 sq. mi.; pop., 118,000; cap., Charlottetown.
Prince of Wales Island, 1. an island of Alexander Archipelago, S.E. Alaska. **2.** an island between Victoria Island and Somerset Island, Northwest Territories, Canada: area, 14,004 sq. mi.
Provence, a former province of S.E. France, on the Mediterranean.
Prussia, a former division of Germany: earlier, a kingdom.
Puebla, a state of S. Mexico: area, 13,124 sq. mi.; pop., 2,484,000; also, its capital.
Puerto Rico, an island commonwealth in the West Indies, associated with the U.S.: area, 3,421 sq. mi.; pop., 2,712,000; cap., San Juan: ceded by Spain in Treaty of Paris (1898): formerly *Porto Rico.*
Punjab, a former province of British India: in 1947, divided between India and Pakistan: the part in India is a state, called *Punjab:* area, 47,084 sq. mi.; pop., 20,307,000; cap., Chandigarh.
Pydna, an ancient city in Macedonia.

Q

Qatar, an independent Arab sheikdom occupying a peninsula on the E. coast of Arabia: formerly under British protection: area, 4,000 sq. mi.; pop., 180,000.
Qishm, an island of Iran, in Strait of Hormuz: area, 516 sq. mi.
Quebec, a province of E. Canada: area, 594,860 sq. mi.; pop., 6,234,000; also, its capital: former name, *Lower Canada.*
Queen Charlotte Islands, a group of islands in the Pacific, off coast of British Columbia, Canada.
Queensland, a state of E. Australia: area, 667,000 sq. mi.; pop., 1,799,000; cap., Brisbane.
Quelpart Island, Saishu: English name.
Queretaro, a state of central Mexico: area, 4,432 sq. mi.; pop., 464,000; also, its capital.

R

Radnorshire, Radnor, a former county of E. Wales.
Rajasthan, a state of N.W. central India, including the Rajputana region and the former Ajmer-Merwara province: area, 132,227 sq. mi.; pop., 20,156,000; cap., Jaipur.
Rajputana, a region in N.W. central India: since 1950, included in Rajasthan.
Rapa Nui, Easter Island: native name.
Rarotonga, one of the Cook Islands, in the South Pacific: pop., 10,000.
Renfrew, Renfrewshire, a former county of W. Scotland, on the Clyde.
Réunion, a French island in the Indian Ocean, E. of Madagascar: area, 970 sq. mi.; pop., 466,000; cap., St. Denis: former name, *Bourbon.*
Rhaetia, an ancient Roman province in region of modern E. Switzerland and W. Austria.
Rhineland, 1. same as *Rhine Province.* **2.** that part of Germany W. of the Rhine.
Rhine Province, a former province of Prussia, Germany, W. of the Rhine: area, 9,459 sq. mi.: also called *Rhineland.*
Rhode Island, a New England State of the U.S.: area, 1,214 sq. mi.; pop., 950,000; cap., Providence.
Rhodes, one of the Dodecanese Islands, S.W. of Turkey: area, 545 sq. mi.; pop., 55,000; also, its capital.
Rhodesia, a country, formerly a British territory, in S. Africa: area, 150,333 sq. mi.; pop., 6,310,000; cap. Salisbury: former name, *Southern Rhodesia:* Bantu name, *Zimbabwe.*
Rialto, an island in Venice.
Rif, Riff, a hilly region along the Mediterranean coast of Morocco: also *Er Rif.*
Rio de Oro, a former Spanish territory on the N.W. coast of Africa: it was once part of Spanish Sahara.
Rio Muni, a province of Equatorial Guinea, on W. central African mainland: area, 9,470 sq. mi.; pop., 201,000; chief city, Bata.
Riviera, the Mediterranean coast of France and Italy, from Nice to La Spezia.
Roanoke, an island off N.E. coast of North Carolina, between Albemarle and Pamlico Sounds.
Roman Empire, the empire of ancient Rome, established by Augustus in 27 B.C.: it continued until 395 A.D.
Romania, a country in S. central Europe, on Black Sea: area, 91,669 sq. mi.; pop., 21,245,000; cap., Bucharest: also *România, Rumania, Roumania.*
Ross and Cromarty, a former county of N. Scotland, on Moray Firth.
Ross Dependency, a region in Antarctica, including coasts of Ross Sea and a number of islands, claimed by Great Britain and administered by New Zealand: area, c.175,000 sq. mi.
Roumania, same as *Romania.*
Roxburgh, Roxburghshire, a former county of Scotland, on the English border.
Ruanda-Urundi, a former Belgian administered trust territory in central Africa: since 1962, divided between the independent countries of Rwanda and Burundi.
Ruhr, a mining and industrial region centered in valley of Ruhr River in W. Germany.
Rumania, same as *Romania.*
Rumelia, the area of the former Turkish empire in the Balkans, including Macedonia, Thrace, and Albania: also spelled *Roumelia.*
Russia, 1. before 1917, an empire (*Russian Empire*) in E. Europe and N. Asia, ruled by a czar: cap., St. Petersburg (Petrograd). **2.** now, (a) the Union of Soviet Socialist Republics: Soviet Union: popularly so called; (b) the Russian Soviet Federated Socialist Republic, a part of the Soviet Union.
Russian Soviet Federated Socialist Republic, a republic in Europe and Asia, forming the largest division of the Soviet Union: a federation of Regions, Territories, Autonomous Soviet Socialist Republics, and Autonomous Regions: area, 6,322,350 sq. mi.; pop., 130,100,000; cap., Moscow: also called (*Soviet*) *Russia.*
Rutlandshire, Rutland, a former county of E. central England.
Rwanda, a country in E. central Africa, E. of Zaire: area, 10,169 sq. mi.; pop., 4,198,000; cap., Kigali.
Ryukyu, a chain of Japanese islands in W. Pacific, between Kyushu and Taiwan: area, 921 sq. mi.; pop., 952,000.

S

Saarland, Saar, a state of West Germany, in valley of Saar River, it was administered by France under League of Nations supervision (1919–1935), returned to Germany by plebiscite: from 1947 to 1957, an autonomous government having a customs union with France: area, 743 sq. mi.; pop., 2,134,000.
Sabah, a state of Malaysia, including part of N. Borneo and the island of Labuan: area, 29,388 sq. mi.; pop., 454,000; formerly, the British colony of North Borneo.
Safety Islands, a group of 3 islands off coast of French Guiana.
Sahara, a vast desert region of plateaus and lowlands extending over N. Africa: area, 3,500,000 sq. mi.
Saipan, one of the Mariana Islands, in W. Pacific: formerly a Japanese mandate, in 1946 became a trust territory of the U.S.
Saïs, an ancient city in the Nile delta.
Saishu Island, a Japanese island in Yellow Sea, S. of Korea: area, 710 sq. mi.
Sakhalin, an island off E. Siberia, N. of Japan: area, 24,560 sq. mi.: formerly, the northern part belonged to the U.S.S.R., the southern, to Japan; in 1946, the entire island was granted to the U.S.S.R.: also *Saghalien.*
Salamis, 1. a Greek island in Gulf of Aegina, near Athens: area, 36 sq. mi.; pop., 15,000. **2.** an ancient city of Cyprus.
Salop, a county of W. England, on the border of Wales: pop., 354,000.
Samar, one of the Philippine Islands, S.E. of Luzon: area, 5,124 sq. mi.
Samaria, 1. an ancient kingdom of Palestine, between Judea and Galilee. **2.** a city in Samaria: ancient cap. of Israel.
Samoa, a group of islands in South Pacific, N. of Tonga, divided into two groups, *American Samoa* and *Western Samoa:* former name, *Navigators Islands.*
Samos, a Greek island off Asia Minor: area, 180 sq. mi.; pop., 60,000.
Samothrace, Samothracia, a Greek island in N. Aegean: area, 68 sq. mi.; pop., 4,000.
Samothrake, Samothrace: Greek name.
Sandalwood Island, Sumba: English name.
Sandwich Islands, Hawaiian Islands: former name.
San Juan Islands, a group of islands off N.W. Washington.
San Luis Potosí, a state in E. central Mexico: area, 24,415 sq. mi.; pop., 1,257,000; also, its capital.
San Marino, an independent republic within E. Italy: area, 38 sq. mi.; pop., 20,000; also, its capital.
San Salvador, one of the E. Bahama Islands: area, 60 sq. mi.: also called *Watling Island.*
Santa Barbara Islands, a chain of islands off coast of S. California.
Santa Catalina, an island off coast of S. California: area, 70 sq. mi.: also *Catalina.*
Santa Clara, a province of central Cuba: area, 8,257 sq. mi.; pop., 1,235,000 (now called *Las Villas*); also, its capital.
Santa Cruz, 1. same as *St. Croix.* **2.** one of the Santa Barbara Islands.
Santiago de Cuba, Oriente: former name.
Santo Domingo, Dominican Republic: former name.
São Miguel, the largest island of the Azores: area, 297 sq. mi.
São Paulo, a state of S.E. Brazil: area, 91,310 sq. mi.; pop., 17,716,000; also, its capital.
São Tomé and Príncipe, a country consisting of two islands in the Gulf of Guinea, off the W. coast of Africa: formerly an overseas territory of Portugal: area, 372 sq. mi.; pop., 75,000; cap., São Tomé.
Saratov, a region of the R.S.F.S.R., in S.E. central European Russia: pop., 2,167,000; also, its capital.
Sarawak, a state of Malaysia, occupying the N.W. coast of Borneo: area, 47,000 sq. mi.; pop., 924,000; cap., Kuching.
Sardinia, 1. an Italian island in the Mediterranean, S. of Corsica: area, 9,300 sq. mi.; pop., 1,419,000; chief city, Cagliari. **2.** a former kingdom, including this island, Piedmont, Savoy, and Genoa, ruled by the House of Savoy.
Sardis, the capital of ancient Lydia.
Sarmatia, the region between the Vistula and the Volga, now part of Poland and the Soviet Union: ancient name.
Saskatchewan, a province of S. central Canada: area, 251,700 sq. mi.; pop., 921,000; cap., Regina.
Saudi Arabia, a kingdom in central Arabia: area, c.597,000 sq. mi.; pop., c.7,031,000; caps., Riyadh and Mecca.
Saurashtra, a former state of W. India: merged into the State of Bombay, 1956: area, 21,742 sq. mi.
Savage Island, same as *Niue.*
Savaii, an island of Western Samoa, in the South Pacific: area, 703 sq. mi.; pop., 36,000.
Savoie, Savoy: French name.
Savoy, a former duchy of the kingdom of Sardinia, ceded to France (1860).
Saxe-Altenburg, a former duchy of central Germany: now part of Thuringia, Germany.
Saxe-Coburg-Gotha, a former duchy of central Germany: now divided between Bavaria and Thuringia, Germany.
Saxe-Meiningen, a former duchy of central Germany: now part of Thuringia, Germany.
Saxe-Weimar-Eisenach, a former grand duchy of central Germany: now part of Thuringia, Germany.
Saxony, 1. a former kingdom of Germany. **2.** a former division of S. Germany. **3.** a former province of Prussia: this area is now a state of West Germany called *Lower Saxony:* area, 9,755 sq. mi.; pop., 7,100,000; cap., Hanover.
Scandinavia, the ancient Norse lands: now, Sweden, Norway, Denmark, and Iceland.
Scandinavian Peninsula, Scandinavia, a large peninsula of N. Europe, containing Norway and Sweden.
Schaumburg-Lippe, a former division of N.W. Germany: earlier, a principality.
Schlesien, Silesia: German name.
Schleswig, a former duchy of Denmark: now part of Schleswig-Holstein.
Schleswig-Holstein, a state of West Germany, on border of Denmark: area, 5,420 sq. mi.; pop., 2,557,000; cap., Kiel: formed from former Danish duchies of Lauenburg, Holstein, and part of Schleswig.
Schwaben, Swabia: German name.
Schwarzwald, the Black Forest: German name.
Schweiz, Switzerland: German name.
Schwyz, a canton of central Switzerland: pop., 78,000; also, its capital.
Scilly Isles, a group of numerous small islands off Cornwall, England: pop., 1,700.
Scotland, a division of Great Britain, N. of England: area, 30,405 sq. mi.; pop., 5,206,000; cap., Edinburgh.
Scythia, an ancient region in S.E. Europe and Asia.
Sea Islands, a chain of islands off coasts of South Carolina, Georgia, and Florida.
Seeland, same as *Zealand.*
Selangor, a state of Malaya: area, 3,160 sq. mi.; pop., 1,478,000.
Seleucia, an ancient city in Babylonia, on Tigris River.
Selkirk, Selkirkshire, a former county of S. Scotland.
Senegal, a country in W. Africa, on the Atlantic: a former French colony: area, 76,124 sq. mi.; pop., 3,780,000; cap., Dakar: also written *Sénégal.*
Senegambia, a region in W. Africa between the Senegal and Gambia Rivers, in Senegal, Mali, and Gambia.

Serang, same as *Ceram.*
Serbia, a former kingdom in the Balkans: now federated republic of Yugoslavia, in E. part: cap., Belgrade.
Servia, Serbia: former name.
Seward Peninsula, an Alaskan peninsula, on Bering Strait.
Seychelles, a country on a group of islands in the Indian Ocean, N.E. of Madagascar: formerly a British colony, it is now a member of the British Commonwealth of Nations: area, 156 sq. mi.; pop., 58,000; cap., Victoria.
Shansi, a province of N.E. China: area, 66,265 sq. mi.; pop., 18,000,000; cap., Taiyuan.
Shan States, native states of N.E. Burma, including the *Northern* and *Southern Shan States:* area, c.60,000 sq. mi.
Shantung, 1. a province of N.E. China, on Yellow Sea: area, 57,851 sq. mi.; pop., 57,000,000; cap., Tsinan. **2.** a peninsula in E. part of this province.
Shensi, a province of N. central China: area, 76,382 sq. mi.; pop., 21,000,000; cap., Sian.
Shetland Islands, Shetland, a group of islands N.E. of Orkney Islands, constituting a region (called *Shetland*) of Scotland: area, 551 sq. mi.; pop., 18,000; also called *Zetland Islands.*
Shikoku, an island of Japan, S. of Honshu: area, 7,246 sq. mi.; pop., 4,022,000.
Shinar, Babylonia or its southern division, Sumer: Biblical name.
Shropshire, same as *Salop.*
Shushan, Susa: Biblical name.
Siam, Thailand: official name until 1939, and from 1945 to 1949.
Siberia, the region of the Soviet Union in N. Asia, extending from Ural Mountains to the Pacific.
Sicilia, Sicily: Italian name.
Sicily, an island of Italy, off its S.W. tip: area, 9,926 sq. mi.; pop., 4,721,000; chief city, Palermo.
Sicyon, a city of ancient Greece, in N. Peloponnesus.
Sidon, the capital of ancient Phoenicia: site of modern Saida.
Siena, a former republic surrounding the city of Siena in W. central Italy: annexed to Tuscany in 1557.
Sierra Leone, a country in W. Africa, on the Atlantic, between Guinea and Liberia: a former British colony and protectorate, it is now a member of the British Commonwealth of Nations: area, 27,925 sq. mi.; pop., 2,729,000; cap., Freetown.
Sikang, a former province of W. China.
Sikkim, a state of India in the N.E. part: area, 2,818 sq. mi.; pop., 202,000; cap., Gangtok.
Silesia, a region of central Europe, in upper valley of Oder River, divided before World War II among Germany (which held the largest part), Czechoslovakia, and Poland: in 1945, by terms of Potsdam agreement, German Silesia was given to Poland.
Sinai Peninsula, a peninsula in N.E. Egypt, projecting into Red Sea; it is E. of Suez Canal and W. of Israel.
Sinaloa, a state of W. Mexico: area, 22,580 sq. mi.; pop., 1,273,000; cap., Culiacán.
Sind, a former province of Pakistan.
Singapore, 1. an island off tip of Malay Peninsula. **2.** a country on this island and near-by islets: formerly a state of Malaysia (1963–65) and a British colony: area, 225 sq. mi.; pop., 2,250,000.
Sinkiang, an autonomous region in N.W. China: area, 635,830 sq. mi.; pop., 8,000,000; cap., Urumchi.
Sitsang, Tibet: Chinese name.
Sjaelland, Zealand island: Danish name.
Skye, an island in the Hebrides, Scotland: area, 670 sq. mi.; pop., 9,900.
Skyros, an island in Northern Sporades, in the Aegean: area, 80 sq. mi.; pop., 3,000.
Ślask, Silesia: Polish name.
Slave Coast, the W. African coast between Volta and Benin rivers, on Gulf of Guinea: former center of African slave trade.
Slavonia, a region of the Balkans, now in N. Yugoslavia.
Slesvig, Schleswig: Danish name.
Sligo, a county in N.W. Ireland, in Connaught province: area, 694 sq. mi.; pop., 51,000; also, its county seat.
Slovakia, a region in E. Czechoslovakia: area, 18,921 sq. mi.; chief city, Bratislava.
Slovenia, a federated republic of Yugoslavia, in N.W. part: area, 6,265 sq. mi.; pop., 1,592,000; cap., Ljubljana.
Smolensk, a region of the R.S.F.S.R., in W. central European Russia: pop., 2,691,000; also, its capital.
Society Islands, a group of islands of French Polynesia, in the South Pacific: area, 650 sq. mi.; pop., 75,000; cap., Papeete, on Tahiti.
Socotra, an island in Indian Ocean, S. of Arabia: part of People's Democratic Republic of Yemen: area, 1,400 sq. mi.; pop., 12,000: also spelled *Sokotra.*
Soemba, same as *Sumba.*
Soembawa, same as *Sumbawa.*
Soenda Islands, same as *Sunda Islands.*
Sogdiana, an ancient land in region of modern Uzbekistan, between Oxus River and the Syr Darya: part of Persian Empire: cap., Samarkand.
Sokoto, a former kingdom, now a region in N. Nigeria.
Solomon Islands, a group of islands in the Pacific, E. of New Guinea: area, 14,800 sq. mi.; pop., 298,000; Bougainville, Buka, and small adjacent islands form part of Papua New Guinea; other islands, which were once a British territory, became an independent nation in 1978.
Somalia, a country in E. Africa, on the Indian Ocean and the Gulf of Aden: formed by the merger of British Somaliland and Italian Somaliland: area, 246,201 sq. mi.; pop., 2,941,000; cap., Mogadishu.
Somaliland, a region in E. Africa, on Gulf of Aden and Indian Ocean: see *French Somililand* and *Somalia.*
Somaliland Protectorate, a former British protectorate in E. Africa, on Gulf of Aden: merged with Italian Somaliland to form Somalia: also called *British Somaliland.*
Somersetshire, Somerset, a county of S.W. England, on Bristol Channel: pop., 400,000; county seat, Taunton.
Sonora, a state of N.W. Mexico, on Gulf of California: area, 70,477 sq. mi.; pop., 1,092,000; cap., Hermosillo.
Soudan, Sudan: French spelling.
South Africa, a country in southernmost Africa: it was a British dominion until 1961 when it became a republic: area, 472,359 sq. mi.; pop., 25,471,000; caps., Cape Town and Pretoria: former name, *Union of South Africa.*
South America, a continent in the Western Hemisphere: area, 6,814,000 sq. mi.; pop., 224,000,000.
Southampton, the mainland division of Hampshire county, in S. England.
Southampton Island, an island in N. Hudson Bay, Canada: area, 16,114 sq. mi.
South Australia, a state of S. central Australia: area, 380,070 sq. mi.; pop., 1,165,000; cap., Adelaide.
South Carolina, a Southern State of the U.S.: area, 31,055 sq. mi.; pop., 2,591,000; cap., Columbia.
South Dakota, a Middle Western State of the U.S.: area, 77,047 sq. mi.; pop., 666,000; cap., Pierre.
Southern Hemisphere, that half of the earth south of the equator.
Southern Rhodesia, Rhodesia: the former name.
Southern Sporades, a group of Greek islands in the Aegean, S.W. of Turkey: belonged to Italy (1912–1947).
Southern Yemen, People's Democratic Republic of Yemen: the former name.
South Holland, a province of W. Netherlands, on North Sea: pop., 2,969,000; cap., The Hague.
South Island, the larger of the 2 large islands of New Zealand: area, 58,092 sq. mi.
South Ossetian Autonomous Region, an autonomous region of Georgian S.S.R., in the Caucasus: area, 1,428 sq. mi.; pop., 100,000; cap., Tskhinvali.
South Sea Islands, the islands in the temperate and tropical parts of the South Pacific.
South West Africa, a territory in S.W. Africa, on the Atlantic: administered by South Africa: area, 317,887 sq. mi.; pop., 574,000; cap., Windhoek: formerly, *German Southwest Africa;* official (U.N.) name, *Namibia.*
Soviet Russia, 1. same as *Union of Soviet Socialist Republics.* **2.** same as *Russian Soviet Federated Socialist Republic.*
Soviet Union, same as *Union of Soviet Socialist Republics.*
Spain, a country in S.W. Europe, on Iberian Peninsula: area, 190,050 sq. mi.; pop., 35,472,000; cap., Madrid: declared a monarchy in 1947.
Spanish America, those countries in Central and South America and those islands in the Caribbean in which Spanish is the chief language.
Spanish Equatorial Guinea, a former Spanish territory in W. Central Africa, including Río Muni on the mainland, the island of Fernando Po, and other small islands in Gulf of Guinea: since 1968, the independent Equatorial Guinea.
Spanish Main, formerly, the mainland of America adjacent to the Caribbean; especially, the N. coast of South America, from Isthmus of Panama to mouth of Orinoco.
Spanish Morocco, formerly, the Spanish zone of the sultanate of Morocco: see *Morocco.*
Spanish Sahara, a former Spanish province on the N.W. coast of Africa: area, 102,702 sq. mi.: in 1976, divided between Morocco and Mauritania.
Sparta, in ancient Greece, the chief city of the Peloponnesus, in Laconia: also called *Lacedaemon.*
Spice Islands, same as *Molucca Islands.*
Spitsbergen, same as *Svalbard.*
Sporades, two groups of Greek islands (Northern Sporades and Southern Sporades) in the Aegean, off S.W. coast of Asia Minor.
Sri Lanka, Ceylon: the official name.
Staffordshire, Stafford, a county of central England: pop., 991,000; county seat, Stafford.
St. Christopher, same as *St. Kitts.*
St. Croix, an island of the U.S., part of Virgin Islands: area, 82 sq. mi.; pop., 32,000: also called *Santa Cruz.*
St. Helena, 1. a British island in the Atlantic, off S. Africa: area, 47 sq. mi.; pop., 5,000: place of Napoleon's exile. **2.** a British colony including St. Helena, Ascension, and the Tristan da Cunha islands: area, 119 sq. mi.; pop., 7,000.
Stirling, Stirlingshire, a former county in central Scotland.
St. Kitts, a British island of the Leeward group, in West Indies: area, 68 sq. mi.; pop. (with Nevis), 64,000: also called *St. Christopher.*
St. Lucia, a British island of the Windward group, in West Indies: area, 233 sq. mi.; pop., 101,000.
St. Pierre and Miquelon Islands, a French colony in the Atlantic, off S. coast of Newfoundland: area, 93 sq. mi.; pop., 6,000; cap., St. Pierre.
Straits Settlements, a former British colony in Malay Peninsula, including the settlements of Penang and Malacca, Cocos Island, Christmas Island, and Singapore.
Strathclyde, a region of S.W. Scotland, on the Firth of Clyde.
Stromboli, one of the Lipari Islands in the Mediterranean, N. of Sicily.
St. Thomas, an island of the U.S. in Virgin Islands, West Indies: area, 32 sq. mi.; pop., 30,000.
St. Vincent, a British island of the Windward group, in West Indies: area, 150 sq. mi.; pop., 89,000.
Styria, a province of S.E. Austria: area, 6,326 sq. mi.; pop., 1,138,000; cap., Graz.
Sudan, 1. a country S. of Egypt: formerly under British and Egyptian control, it was proclaimed an independent republic in 1956: area, 967,500 sq. mi.; pop., 17,757,000; cap., Khartoum: former name, *Anglo-Egyptian Sudan.* **2.** a vast plains region extending across central Africa.
Sudetenland, Sudeten, a mountainous region in N. Czechoslovakia, including the Sudetes Mountains, annexed by Nazi Germany in October, 1938, after the Munich Pact and returned to Czechoslovakia in 1945.
Suffolk, a county on E. coast of England: pop., 567,000.
Suiyuan, a former province of Inner Mongolia: area, 113,758 sq. mi.; cap., Kweihsui.
Sulu Archipelago, a group of islands in the Philippines, S.W. of Mindanao: area, 1,086 sq. mi.; pop., 390,000.
Sumatra, a large island of Indonesia, S. of Malay Peninsula: area, 163,145 sq. mi.; pop., 15,739,000; chief cities, Medan and Padang.
Sumba, an island of Indonesia, W. of Timor: area, 4,272 sq. mi.: also spelled *Soemba.*
Sumbawa, an island of Indonesia, between Lombok and Flores: area, 5,129 sq. mi.: also spelled *Soembawa.*
Sumer, an ancient region in lower Euphrates River valley.
Sunda Islands, a chain of islands in Indonesia, including Sumatra, Java, Bali, Lombok, Sumbawa, and Flores.
Sungkiang, a former province of central Manchuria: area, 30,703 sq. mi.; cap., Harbin.
Suomi, Finland: Finnish name.
Surinam, a country in N. South America, on the Atlantic: formerly part of the Netherlands: area, 54,291 sq. mi.; pop., 385,000; cap., Paramaribo: formerly called *Netherlands Guiana, Dutch Guiana.*
Surrey, a county of S.E. England: pop., 1,006,000; county seat, Guildford.
Susa, a ruined city in W. Iran.
Sussex, 1. a former Anglo-Saxon kingdom of S. England. **2.** a former county on S. coast of England: now divided into two countries, (a) *East Sussex,* pop., 659,000, and (b) *West Sussex,* pop., 615,000.
Sutherland, Sutherlandshire, a county on N. coast of Scotland; pop., 13,000, county seat, Dornoch.
Svalbard, a group of Norwegian islands in the Arctic Ocean: area, 24,294 sq. mi.; pop., 3,000: also called *Spitsbergen.*
Sverdlovsk, a region of the R.S.F.S.R., in the Ural Mountains of W. Siberia: pop., 4,048,000.
Swabia, a former duchy in S.W. Germany: now district of S.W. Bavaria.
Swat, a district in N.W. Pakistan, on the Indus River.
Swaziland, a country in S.E. Africa: area, 6,705 sq. mi.; pop., 494,000; cap., Mbabane.
Sweden, a country in N. Europe, on Scandinavian Peninsula: area, 173,143 sq. mi.; pop., 8,219,000; cap., Stockholm.
Switzerland, a country in W. central Europe, in the Alps: area, 15,940 sq. mi.; pop., 6,333,000; cap., Bern.
Sybaris, an ancient Greek city in S. Italy: destroyed in 510 B.C.
Syracuse, an ancient city on E. coast of Sicily.
Syria, 1. an ancient country in Asia, along E. coast of the Mediterranean. **2.** a former territory comprising modern Syria and Lebanon: French mandate (1922–1941): also called *Levant States.* **3.** a republic in W. Asia, S. of Turkey, established 1941 and, since 1942, including territories of Djebel Druze and Latakia: area, 72,000 sq. mi.; pop., 7,585,000; cap., Damascus.
Szechwan, a province of central China: area, 156,675 sq. mi.; pop., 70,000,000; cap., Chengtu.

T

Tabasco, a state of S.E. Mexico, on Gulf of Campeche: area, 9,782 sq. mi.; pop., 766,000; cap., Villahermosa.
Tacna, a department of S. Peru: pop., 94,000.
Tacna–Arica, a disputed region in W. South America: divided (1929) into 2 departments, Tacna, Peru and Arica, Chile.
Tadzhikistan, same as *Tadzhik S.S.R.*
Tadzhik Soviet Socialist Republic, a republic of the U.S.S.R. in central Asia: area, 55,584 sq. mi.; pop., 2,900,000; cap., Dushanbe.
Tahiti, one of the Society Islands of French Polynesia, in the South Pacific: area, 600 sq. mi.; chief town, Papeete.
Taimyr Peninsula, a large peninsula in N. Siberia, between Yenisei and Khatanga rivers.
Taiwan, an island province off the S.E. coast of China: seat of the Kuomintang (Nationalist) government: area, 13,890 sq. mi.; pop., 16,172,000; cap., Taipei: formerly called *Formosa.*
Tajik Soviet Socialist Republic, same as *Tadzhik S.S.R.*
Tamaulipas, a state of N.E. Mexico, on Gulf of Mexico: area, 30,731 sq. mi.; pop., 1,438,000; cap., Ciudad Victoria.

Tambov, a region of central European R.S.F.S.R.: pop., 1,547,000; also, its capital.
Tanagra, an ancient Greek town in Boeotia.
Tanganyika, a former country in E. Africa, on the Indian Ocean: merged with Zanzibar (1964) to form Tanzania: before 1961, a British territory.
Tangier, a former province in the sultanate of Morocco: it was an international zone until 1956.
Tanis, an ancient city in Egypt, in Nile delta.
Tannu Tuva, the Tuvinian Autonomous Region: former name.
Tanzania, a country in E. Africa, formed by the merger (1964) of Tanganyika and Zanzibar: it is a member of the British Commonwealth of Nations: area, 362,280 sq. mi.; pop., 15,300,000; cap., Dar es Salaam.
Tarawa, one of the Gilbert Islands in the Pacific, near the equator: site of a battle (1943) in World War II.
Tarsus, an ancient city, now in S. Turkey.
Tartary, same as *Tatary*.
Tasmania, an island off S.E. Australia: a state of Commonwealth of Australia: area, 26,215 sq. mi.; pop., 393,000; cap., Hobart: former name, *Van Diemen's Land*.
Tatar Autonomous Soviet Socialist Republic, a division of the R.S.F.S.R., in E. central European Russia: area, 26,200 sq. mi.; pop., 3,131,000; cap., Kazan.
Tatary, a vast region of central and W. Siberia and S. Russia, invaded and inhabited by Tatars.
Tayside, a region of central Scotland.
Tchad, Chad: French spelling.
Tenedos, a Turkish island in the Aegean, near the Dardanelles.
Tenerife, Teneriffe, the largest of the Canary Islands, off N.W. Africa: area, 782 sq. mi.
Tennessee, a South Central State of the U.S.: area, 42,246 sq. mi.; pop., 3,924,000; cap., Nashville.
Terceira, a Portuguese island in the Azores: area, 223 sq. mi.
Ternate, one of the Molucca Islands, in Indonesia: area, 53 sq. mi.
Texas, a Southern State of the U.S., on Gulf of Mexico and the Mexican border: area, 267,339 sq. mi.; pop., 11,197,000; cap., Austin.
Thailand, a country in S.E. Asia, on Gulf of Siam and Bay of Bengal: area, 200,234 sq. mi.; pop., 41,869,000; cap., Bangkok: former name, *Siam* (until 1939, and from 1945 to 1949).
Thapsus, an ancient town in N. Africa, on E. coast of present Tunisia.
Thasos, a Greek island in N. Aegean: area, 150 sq. mi.
Thebes, 1. an ancient city in Egypt on the Nile, near modern Luxor. **2.** an ancient city of Greece in Boeotia.
Thessaly, an ancient region in N.E. Greece.
Thibet, same as *Tibet*.
Thousand Islands, a group of islands in upper St. Lawrence River, belonging to New York State and Ontario, Canada.
Thrace, an ancient region in E. Balkan Peninsula.
Thurgau, a canton of N.E. Switzerland: pop., 166,000.
Thuringen, Thuringia: German name.
Thuringia, a former region of central Germany, including duchies and principalities.
Thursday Island, an Australian island in Torres Strait: pop., 2,200.
Tibet, an autonomous region of S.W. China: area, 469,194 sq. mi.; pop., c.1,000,000; cap., Lhasa: also spelled *Thibet*.
Ticino, a canton of S. Switzerland: pop., 196,000.
Tierra del Fuego, 1. a group of islands belonging to Chile and Argentina, S. of Strait of Magellan: area, 27,600 sq. mi. **2.** the chief island in the group: area, 18,530 sq. mi.
Tigré, a province of Ethiopia: formerly a kingdom of E. Africa.
Timor, an Indonesian island of East Indies, N. of Australia: area, 13,700 sq. mi.
Timor Archipelago, a group of islands of Indonesia, including W. Timor, Sumbawa, Sumba, Flores, and smaller adjacent islands: area, 24,449 sq. mi.: Indonesian name, *Nusa Tenggara*.
Tipperary, a county of Munster province in S. central Ireland: pop., 123,000.
Tirol, same as *Tyrol*.
Tlaxkala, a state of S. Mexico, nearly surrounded by the state of Puebla: area, 1,555 sq. mi.; pop., 418,000; also, its capital.
Tobago, an island in the West Indies, N.E. of Trinidad: part of Trinidad and Tobago: area, 116 sq. mi.
Togo, a country in W. Africa, on the Gulf of Guinea, E. of Ghana; formerly, a French mandate (1922–1946) and trust territory (1946–1960): area, 22,000 sq. mi.; pop., 2,222,000; cap., Lomé: former name, *Togoland*.
Togoland, 1. a former British mandate (1922–1946) and trust territory (1946–1957) in N.W. Africa; merged with the Gold Coast (1957) to form Ghana: area, 13,041 sq. mi. **2.** Togo: the former name.
Tonga, an independent kingdom occupying a group of islands (*Tonga Islands*) in the South Pacific, E. of Fiji: a member of the British Commonwealth: area, 270 sq. mi.; pop., 102,000; cap., Nuku'alofa.
Tonkin, Tongking, a former state of French Indochina, on Gulf of Tonkin: in 1946, became part of Vietnam: area, 40,530 sq. mi.; cap., Hanoi.
Tortuga, an island in West Indies, belonging to Haiti: area, 117 sq. mi.
Toscana, Tuscany: Italian name.
Touraine, a former province of W. France.
Transcaucasia, the region S of Caucasus Mountains, U.S.S.R., containing the republics of Georgia, Armenia, and Azerbaijan: former name, *Transcaucasian Socialist Federated Soviet Republic*.
Trans–Jordan, Jordan: former name.
Transjordania, Jordan: former name.
Transvaal, a province of South Africa, in N.E. part: area, 110,450 sq. mi.; pop., 6,273,000; cap., Pretoria.
Transylvania, a plateau region in central Romania, N. of the Transylvanian Alps: area, 24,020 sq. mi.
Travancore, a former native state of S.W. India.
Travancore and Cochin, a former state of S.W. India, formed by merging of 2 native states, Travancore and Cochin.
Trebizond, a medieval empire around Black Sea and in the Caucasus.
Trengganu, a state of Malaya: area, 5,050 sq. mi.; pop., 395,000; cap., Kuala Trengganu.
Trentino–Alto Adige, a region of N. Italy, a part of the Tyrol.
Trinidad, an island in the West Indies, off coast of Venezuela: part of Trinidad and Tobago: area, 1,864 sq. mi.
Trinidad and Tobago, a country consisting of two islands (*Trinidad* and *Tobago*) in the West Indies: it is a member of the British Commonwealth of Nations: area, 1,980 sq. mi.; pop., 1,074,000; cap., Port of Spain, on Trinidad.
Tripoli, a former Barbary State, now part of Libya.
Tripolitania, a region of N.W. Libya: area, 350,000 sq. mi.; chief city, Tripoli.
Tripura, a union territory of N.E. India: area, 4,116 sq. mi.; pop., 1,142,000.
Tristan da Cunha, a group of British islands in the South Atlantic.
Troas, the ancient region in Asia Minor in which Troy was located: also called **the Troad.**
Troy, an ancient city in N.W. Asia Minor: also called *Ilium*.
Trucial States, a former group of seven British-protected Arab sheikdoms on E. coast of Arabia, on the Persian Gulf: area, c.32,300 sq. mi.: now an independent country called *United Arab Emirates*.
Truk Islands, a group of islands in the Caroline Islands: area, c.50 sq. mi.
Tsushima, a Japanese island between Korea and Japan: area, 271 sq. mi.
Tuamotu Archipelago, a group of French islands in Polynesia, South Pacific: area, 330 sq. mi.; pop., 7,000: also called *Low Archipelago*.
Tula, a region of the R.S.F.S.R., in central European Russia: pop., 1,912,000; also, its capital.
Tunis, a former Barbary State in N. Africa, now Tunisia.
Tunisia, a country in N. Africa, on the Mediterranean: French protectorate (1881–1946): an associated state of the French Union (1946–1956): area, 48,300 sq. mi.; pop., 5,772,000; cap., Tunis.
Turkestan, a region in central Asia, including parts of the U.S.S.R., Sinkiang, and Afghanistan.
Turkey, a republic occupying Asia Minor and part of Balkan Peninsula: area, 296,380 sq. mi.; pop., 39,180,000; cap., Ankara.
Turkish Empire, same as *Ottoman Empire*.
Turkmen Soviet Socialist Republic, a republic of the U.S.S.R., in central Asia, N. of Iran: area, 189,370 sq. mi.; pop., 2,200,000; cap., Ashkhabad.
Turks and Caicos Islands, a group of British islands in the Bahamas, N. of Haiti: area, 166 sq. mi.; pop., 7,000; cap., Grand Turk.
Tuscany, formerly a grand duchy, later a region, of W. Italy: area, 8,861 sq. mi.; pop., 3,286,000; chief city, Florence.
Tutuila, an island of American Samoa, in the South Pacific: area, 52 sq. mi.; pop., 25,000; chief city, Pago Pago.
Tuva Autonomous Soviet Socialist Republic, a division of the R.S.F.S.R., N.W. of Mongolian People's Republic: area, 65,000 sq. mi.; pop., 231,000; cap., Kyzyl.
Tuvalu, a group of British islands in the South Pacific, between the Gilbert Islands and Fiji: area, 9 1/2 sq. mi.; pop., 6,000: former name *Ellice Islands*.
Two Sicilies, a former kingdom including Naples (with lower Italy) and Sicily: united with Kingdom of Italy (1860).
Tyne and Wear, a county of N. England, on the North Sea: pop., 190,000.
Tyre, an important seaport in ancient Phoenicia, now in Lebanon.
Tyrol, a region in the Alps of W. Austria and N. Italy: also spelled *Tirol*.
Tyrone, a former county of Northern Ireland.

U

Ubangi–Shari, a former French colony in central Africa: now, the independent Central African Empire.
Udmurt Autonomous Soviet Socialist Republic, a division of the R.S.F.S.R., in E. central European Russia: area, 14,494 sq. mi.; pop., 1,417,000; cap., Izhevsk.
Uganda, a country in E. central Africa, W. of Kenya: it is a member of the British Commonwealth of Nations: area, 93,981 sq. mi.; pop., 11,549,000; cap., Kampala.
Ukrainian Soviet Socialist Republic, a republic of the U.S.S.R., in S.W. European part, on Black Sea: area, 202,540 sq. mi.; pop., 47,100,000; cap., Kiev: also called *the Ukraine*.
Ulster, 1. a former province of N. Ireland, now divided beteen Northern Ireland and Ireland. **2.** a province of N. Ireland: area, 3,093 sq. mi.; pop., 208,000.
Umbria, a region of central Italy: area, 3,270 sq. mi.; pop., 795,000; chief city, Perugia.
Unalaska, an Alaskan island in E. Aleutians: c.75 mi. long.
Unfederated Malay States, a former division of Malay Peninsula, including native states of Kelantan, Kedah, Johore, Perlis, and Trengganu: now part of Malaya.
Ungava, a former region in N.E. Canada, including most of Labrador: now part of Quebec.
Union of South Africa, South Africa: the former name.
Union of Soviet Socialist Republics, a federation of 15 republics of E. Europe and N. Asia, extending from Arctic Ocean to Black Sea and E. to the Pacific, including most of former Russian Empire: area, 8,518,000 sq. mi.; pop., 254,382,000; cap., Moscow: also called *Soviet Union, Soviet Russia;* former name (still loosely used), *Russia*.
United Arab Emirates, a country in E. Arabia, on the Persian Gulf, consisting of seven Arab sheikdoms (formerly called *Trucial States*): area, 32,000 sq. mi.; pop., 335,000; cap., Abu Zaby.
Unitd Arab Republic, a republic in the Middle East formed (1958) by the union of Egypt and Syria: in 1961, Syria withdrew: Egypt retained the name until 1971.
United Kingdom, 1. Great Britain and Northern Ireland: area, 94,279 sq. mi.; pop., 55,962,000; cap., London: official name, *United Kingdom of Great Britain and Northern Ireland*. **2.** formerly (1801–1922), Great Britain and Ireland.
United Provinces, Uttar Pradesh: former name.
United States of America, a country in North America made up of 50 States and the District of Columbia: the main body extends from the Atlantic to the Pacific and from Mexico and Gulf of Mexico to Canada; its possessions include the Virgin Islands, Guam, Wake Island, the Panama Canal Zone, Midway, American Samoa, etc.: (of the U.S. proper) area, 3,615,211 sq. mi.; pop., 216,452,000; (of possessions) area, 4,455 sq. mi.; pop., 3,300,000; cap., Washington, D.C.: also called *United States, America*.
Unterwalden, a canton of central Switzerland: pop., 48,000.
Upolu, an island of Western Samoa, in South Pacific: area, 430 sq. mi.; pop., 95,000; chief town, Apia.
Upper Austria, a province in N. Austria: area, 4,626 sq. mi.; pop., 1,132,000; cap., Linz.
Upper Canada, a former province of Canada: now part of province of Ontario.
Upper Silesia, a former province of Prussia (part of Silesia) divided between Germany and Poland after World War I and again after World War II.
Upper Volta, a country in W. Africa, N. of Ghana: a former French colony: area, 105,800 sq. mi.; pop., 6,144,000; cap., Ouagadougou.
Ur, an ancient city of the Sumerians, on Euphrates River; also, the district surrounding this city.
Uri, a canton of E. Switzerland: pop., 32,000.
Uruguay, a country in S. South America, on the Atlantic: area, 72,153 sq. mi.; pop., 3,064,000; cap., Montevideo.
Utah, a Western State of the U.S.: area, 84,916 sq. mi.; pop., 1,059,000; cap., Salt Lake City.
Utrecht, a province of the Netherlands, in central part: pop., 801,000; also, its capital.
Uttar Pradesh, a state of N. India: area, 112,523 sq. mi.; pop., 73,746,000; cap., Allahabad: former name, *United Provinces*.
Uxmal, a ruined Mayan city in Yucatan state, Mexico.
Uzbek Soviet Socialist Republic, a republic of the U.S.S.R., in central Asia: area, 146,000 sq. mi.; pop., 12,000,000; cap., Tashkent.

V

Valais, a canton of S.W. Switzerland: pop., 178,000.
Valencia, a province in E. Spain: formerly a kingdom: area, 4,239 sq. mi.; pop., 1,430,000.
Valois, a duchy of N. France in the Middle Ages.
Vancouver, an island of British Columbia, off S.W. coast: area, 12,408 sq. mi.; chief city, Victoria.
Vanua Levu, one of the Fiji Islands: area, 2,130 sq. mi.
Vatican City, the papal state within Rome, established in 1929: it includes the Vatican and St. Peter's Church: area, 1/6 sq. mi.; pop., 1,000: Italian name, *Città del Vaticano*.
Vaud, a canton of W. Switzerland: area, 1,239 sq. mi.; pop., 430,000; cap., Lausanne.
Veii, an ancient Etruscan town, destroyed by the Romans.
Vendée, a department in W. France.
Venetia, an ancient Roman province in what is now N.E. Italy and N.W. Yugoslavia.
Veneto, a region in N.E. Italy: area, 9,856 sq. mi.; pop., 3,847,000.
Venezia, 1. a province in Veneto, Italy. **2.** a former region in Italy, generally corresponding to ancient Venetia.
Venezia Giulia, a former region in N.E. Italy, most of which was ceded to Yugoslavia in 1947; the part remaining in Italy is the region called *Friuli-Venezia Giulia*.

Venezia Tridentina, a region in N. Italy: area, 5,252 sq. mi.; pop., 786,000: the former name: now called *Trentino-Alto Adige.*

Venezuela, a country in N. South America, on the Caribbean: area, 352,051 sq. mi.; pop., 11,993,000; cap., Caracas.

Veracruz, a state of Mexico, on E. coast: area, 27,736 sq. mi.; pop., 3,814,000; cap., Jalapa: formerly written *Vera Cruz.*

Vermont, a New England State of the U.S.: area, 9,609 sq. mi.; pop., 444,000; cap., Montpelier.

Victoria, a state of the Commonwealth of Australia: area, 87,884 sq. mi.; pop., 3,444,000; cap., Melbourne.

Victoria Island, an island of Northwest Territories, Canada, N. of the mainland: area, 74,000 sq. mi.

Victoria Land, a region in Antarctia, W. of Ross Sea.

Vietnam, Viet-Nam, Viet Nam, a country in S.E. Asia, on the Indochinese peninsula: formerly a part of French Indochina and, from 1954 to 1975, divided into two republics (*North Vietnam* and *South Vietnam*): area, 129,607 sq. mi.; pop., 45,211,000; cap., Hanoi.

Vindhya Pradesh, a former state of central India: now part of Madhya Pradesh.

Virginia, a Southern State of the U.S.: area, 40,815 sq. mi.; pop., 4,648,000; cap., Richmond.

Virgin Islands, a group of islands in West Indies, E. of Puerto Rico: some belong to the U.S. and some to Great Britain.

Virgin Islands of the United States, those of the Virgin Islands that the U.S. bought from Denmark in 1917: area, 132 sq. mi.; pop., 63,000; cap., Charlotte Amalie: former name, *Danish West Indies.*

Visayan Islands, a group of islands in the central Philippines: also *Bisayas.*

Viti Levu, one of the Fiji Islands: area, 4.053 sq. mi.; chief town, Suva.

Volcano Islands, three Japanese islands in W. Pacific, including Iwo Jima.

Voronezh, a region in the R.S.F.S.R., in S. central European Russia: pop., 3,363,000; also, its capital.

Votyak Autonomous Soviet Socialist Republic, Udmurt A.S.S.R.: former name.

Waadt, Vaud: German name.

Wadai, a former independent sultanate of the Sudan: now E. part of Chad.

Wake Island, a small island in N. Pacific between Midway and Guam, belonging to the U.S.: area, 4 sq. mi.

Walachia, a former principality in S.E. Europe: now part of Romania: also spelled *Wallachia.*

Walcheren, an island of the Netherlands, in Zeeland province, off S.W. coast.

Wales, a division of Great Britain, bounded on the E. by England: area, 7,466 sq. mi.; pop., 2,759,000; chief cities, Cardiff, Swansea.

Warwickshire, Warwick, a county in central England: pop., 470,000; county seat, Warwick.

Washington, a Western State of the U.S.: area, 68,192 sq. mi.; pop., 3,409,000; cap., Olympia.

Waterford, a county of Munster province, Ireland: pop., 74,000; also, its county seat.

Watling, same as *San Salvador.*

Welfare Island, an island in the East River, in New York City: former name, *Blackwells Island.*

Wessex, 1. a former Anglo-Saxon kingdom in S. England. **2.** a corresponding section in modern England, chiefly in Dorsetshire.

West Bengal, a state of N.E. India: until 1948, part of Bengal, British India: area, 34,945 sq. mi.; pop., 34,926,000; cap., Calcutta.

Western Australia, a state of Australia: area, 975,920 sq. mi.; pop., 980,000; cap., Perth.

Western Hemisphere, that half of the earth which includes North and South America.

Western India States, a former agency of British India including a number of native states in W. India.

Western Islands, 1. same as *Azores.* **2.** same as *Hebrides.*

Western Reserve, a section of land in N.E. Ohio, on Lake Erie, which Connecticut reserved for settlers when its western lands were ceded to the Federal Government in 1786.

Western (Roman) Empire, the W. part of the Roman Empire after it was divided in 395 A.D. by Theodosius.

Western Samoa, a country in the South Pacific, consisting of two large islands and several small ones: it was formerly a New Zealand trust territory: area, 1,130 sq. mi.; pop., 152,000; cap., Apia.

West Flanders, a province of W. Belgium, on North Sea: pop., 1,051,000; cap., Bruges.

West Indies, a large group of islands between the U.S. and South America: divided into the Bahamas, Greater Antilles, and Lesser Antilles.

West Irian, the W. part of the island of New Guinea, belonging to Indonesia: area, 160,000 sq. mi.; pop., 750,000; cap., Kotabaru: formerly a territory of the Netherlands.

West Lothian, a former county of Scotland, on Firth of Forth.

West Midlands, a county of central England: pop., 2,780,000.

Westmorland, a former county of N.W. England.

Westphalia, a province of Prussia: the area is now in W. Germany.

West Prussia, a former province of Prussia: since 1945, part of Poland.

West Virginia, an Eastern State of the U.S.: area, 24,181 sq. mi.; pop., 1,744,000; cap., Charleston.

Wexford, a county of Leinster province, Ireland: pop., 83,000; also, its county seat.

White Russia, same as *Byelorussia.*

White Russian Soviet Socialist Republic, same as *Byelorussian S.S.R.*

Wicklow, a county of Leinster province, Ireland: pop., 60,000; also, its county seat.

Wight, Isle of, an island in English Channel, off coast of Hampshire, constituting a county of England: area, 147 sq. mi.; pop., 111,000; cap., Newport.

Wigtown, Wigtownshire, a former county on S.W. coast of Scotland.

Wilderness, a region in N.E. Virginia, S. of the Rapidan River.

Wiltshire, Wilts, a county of S. England: pop., 507,000; county seat, Salisbury.

Windward Islands, 1. the S. group of islands in Lesser Antilles, in West Indies: all except Martinique belong to Great Britain. **2.** a former British colony in West Indies, comprising St. Lucia, St. Vincent, Grenada, and Dominica: St. Lucia, St. Vincent, and Dominica are now self-governing territories under British protection and Grenada is an independent country.

Wisconsin, a Middle Western State of the U.S.: area, 56,154 sq. mi.; pop., 4,418,000; cap., Madison.

Worcestershire, Worcester, a former county of W. central England.

Württemberg, a former division of S.W. Germany: earlier, a kingdom: now part of West Germany.

Wyoming, a Western State of the U.S.: area, 97,914 sq. mi.; pop., 332,000; cap., Cheyenne.

XYZ

Xanthus, an ancient city in Asia Minor.

Yakutsk Autonomous Soviet Socialist Republic, a division of the R.S.F.S.R., in N.E. Siberia: area, 1,169,927 sq. mi.; pop., 664,000; cap., Yakutsk.

Yaroslavl, a region of the R.S.F.S.R., in N. central European Russia: pop., 1,395,000.

Yemen, People's Democratic Republic of, a country in the S. Arabian Peninsula, on the Gulf of Aden: area, 112,000; pop., 1,690,000; cap., Aden.

Yemen Arab Republic, a country in the S. Arabian Peninsula, on the Red Sea: area, 75,000 sq. mi.; pop., 5,238,000; cap., San'a.

Yerba Buena, an island in San Francisco Bay, between San Francisco and Oakland.

Yezo, Hokkaido: former name.

Yorkshire, York, a former county of England, on N.E. coast: now divided into three counties, (a) *North Yorkshire,* pop., 649,000, (b) *South Yorkshire,* pop., 1,317,000, and (c) *West Yorkshire,* pop., 2,082,000.

Yorubaland, a region of Nigeria, Africa: formerly a kingdom.

Yucatan, 1. a peninsula of S. North America extending into Gulf of Mexico. **2.** a state of Mexico on tip of this peninsula: area, 23,926 sq. mi.; pop., 774,000; cap., Mérida. Also written *Yucatán.*

Yugoslavia, a republic on Balkan Peninsula, bordering the Adriatic, established as a nation in 1918: area, 95,576 sq. mi.; pop., 21,559,000; cap., Belgrade: former name (1918–1929), *Kingdom of the Serbs, Croats, and Slovenes:* also spelled *Jugoslavia.*

Yukon, a territory of N.W. Canada, E. of Alaska: area, 207,076 sq. mi.; pop., 22,000; cap., Whitehorse.

Yunnan, a province of S. China: area, 147,849 sq. mi.; pop., 23,000,000; cap., Kunming.

Zacatecas, a state of central Mexico: area, 24,471 sq. mi.; pop., 950,000; also, its capital.

Zaire, a country in central Africa, on the equator: area, 905,563 sq. mi.; pop., 24,902,000; cap., Kinshasa: formerly, *Belgian Congo.*

Zakynthos, Zante: Greek name.

Zama, an ancient town in Numidia, Africa.

Zambia, a country in S. Africa, S. of Zaire: formerly the British protectorate of Northern Rhodesia, it is now independent and a member of the British Commonwealth of Nations: area, 290,323 sq. mi.; pop., 4,896,000; cap., Lusaka.

Zante, one of the Ionian Islands off W. Greece: area, 156 sq. mi.; pop., 38,000: Greek name, *Zakynthos.*

Zanzibar, 1. an island off E. coast of Africa: area, 640 sq. mi. **2.** a former country including this island and the island of Pemba: merged with Tanganyika (1964) to form the country of Tanzania: before 1963, a British protectorate.

Zea, same as *Keos.*

Zealand, an island of Denmark, between Jutland and Sweden: area, 2,710 sq. mi.; chief city, Copenhagen: also *Seeland.*

Zeeland, a province of S.W. Netherlands: area, 1,040 sq. mi.; pop., 306,000; cap., Middleburg.

Zetland, same as *Shetland Islands.*

Zipangu, Japan: name used by Marco Polo.

Zoan, Tanis: Biblical name.

Zug, a canton of central Switzerland: pop., 52,000; also, its capital.

Zululand, a region of Natal province, South Africa: area, 10,427 sq. mi.: it was formerly a Zulu kingdom.

Zurich, a canton in N. Switzerland: area, 668 sq. mi.; pop., 952,000; also, its capital: also written *Zürich.*

A DICTIONARY OF NOTED NAMES IN FICTION, MYTHOLOGY, LEGEND

A

Abaris (ab'ȧ-ris). In Greek legend, a Scythian, a priest of Apollo, who gave him a golden arrow on which he could ride through the air, and by which he worked miracles.

Abdiel (ab'di-el). A seraph in Milton's *Paradise Lost* who withstood the revolt of Satan, 'faithful found among the faithless, faithful only he.'

Abessa (ȧ-bes'ȧ). The impersonation of conventual life in Spenser's *Faerie Queene*.

Abou Hassan (ä'bö has'an). A young man of Bagdad in the *Arabian Nights* who is carried while asleep to the bed of the Caliph Harun-al-Rashid, and next morning is persuaded that he really is the caliph.

Absalom and Achitophel (ab'sȧ-lom and ȧ-ḳit'ō-fel). A satiric poem by Dryden, in which Absalom represents the Duke of Monmouth and Achitophel the Earl of Shaftesbury.

Absolute (ab'sō-lūt), **Sir Anthony.** A hot-tempered and domineering but good-hearted and generous old gentleman, in Sheridan's comedy *The Rivals*. His son, the gallant and spirited Captain Absolute, is in love with Lydia Languish, to whom he passes himself off as a penniless ensign named Beverley. See **Acres, Bob.**

Achates (ȧ-ḳā'tēṣ). The faithful companion of Aeneas in Virgil's *Aeneid*, an archetype of the stalwart comrade.

Acheron (aḳ'ẽr-on). In classical fable, a river of the infernal regions (Hades).

Achilles (ȧ-ḳil'ēṣ). The chief Greek hero in the siege of Troy as told in Homer's *Iliad*, son of Peleus and the sea goddess Thetis, and leader of the Myrmidons. He slew Hector, but according to later writers was himself slain by Paris, who wounded him in the right heel, where alone he was vulnerable. His bosom friend was Patroclus, who was killed by Hector. See **Ilium, Hector, Philoctetes,** etc.

Acres (ā'ḳẽrṣ), **Bob.** A blustering, swearing, but cowardly character, albeit amusing, in Sheridan's comedy *The Rivals*. He challenges his rival, Ensign Beverley (Captain Absolute), but has no stomach for fighting. See **Absolute.**

Actaeon (aç-tē'on). In classical mythology, a huntsman, who, having surprised Diana bathing, was turned by her into a stag and torn by his own dogs.

Adam (ad'ăm). A loyal, aged servant in Shakespeare's *As You Like It*, who accompanies Orlando into exile.

Adams (ad'ămṣ), **Alice.** The heroine of a novel of the same name by Booth Tarkington. She is an ambitious small-town girl of the lower middle class, whose attempt to marry Arthur Russell, one of the town's socialites, fails.

Adams, Parson Abraham. A country curate in Fielding's *Joseph Andrews*—poor, pious, learned, absent-minded, and extremely ignorant of the world.

Admetus (ad-mē'tus). A mythological king of Thessaly under whom, for a year, Apollo served as a shepherd. See **Alcestis.**

Adonais (ad-ō-nā'is). In Shelley's elegy of this name, Keats. Probably comparisons between Keats' early death and that of Adonis were intended by the coined name.

Adonis (ȧ-dō'nis). In Greek mythology, a beautiful youth beloved by Venus and killed by a wild boar. The myths connected with Adonis are of Eastern origin, and he himself appears to be a personification of the sun.

Adriana (ā-dri-ā'nȧ). One of the two chief female characters in Shakespeare's *Comedy of Errors*, wife of Antipholus of Ephesus, very suspicious of her husband.

Adverse (ad'vẽrs), **Anthony.** The hero of Hervey Allen's novel of the same name, a foundling who roams over three continents, achieves success as a businessman and a slave trader, suffers imprisonment, and at last finds contentment.

Aegeus (ē'ḡūs). A legendary king of Athens, the father of Theseus.

Aegisthus (ē-ḡis'thus). A son of Thyestes, he killed the latter's brother Atreus. He became the paramour of Clytemnestra, and helped her murder her husband Agamemnon; and in revenge was slain by Orestes.

Aeneas (ē-nē'ăs). The hero of Virgil's poem the *Aeneid*, a Trojan warrior, who came to Italy after the fall of Troy, having passed through various adventures by the way, and was regarded as the remote founder of Rome. He was said to be the son of Anchises and Venus. See also **Dido.**

Aeolus (ē'ō-lus). God of the winds among the Greeks and Romans. He kept the winds confined in a cave in the Aeolian Islands.

Aesculapius (es-ḳū-lā'pi-us). The god of medicine among the Greeks and Romans.

Agamemnon (ag-ȧ-mem'non). Leader of the Greeks in the war against Troy, after his return home slain by his wife Clytemnestra and her paramour Aegisthus. His brother was Menelaus, his son Orestes, and his daughters Iphigenia and Electra.

Aguecheek (ā'gū-chēk), **Sir Andrew.** A silly and ridiculous character in Shakespeare's *Twelfth Night*, a crony of Sir Toby Belch.

Ahab (ā'hab), **Captain.** In Melville's novel *Moby Dick*, the whaler who fiercely pursues Moby Dick, the whale that bit off his leg.

Ahriman *or* **Ahrimanes** (ä'ri-man; ä-ri-mā'nēṣ). The evil principle or deity in the religious system of Zoroaster.

Ah Sin (ä sin). The subject of Bret Harte's humorous poem *Heathen Chinee*, and of a play by Harte and Mark Twain. His chief characteristic is his apparent innocence, which masks his cunning and guile.

Aimwell (ām'wel), **Viscount Thomas.** One of the two beaux in Farquhar's comedy *The Beaux' Stratagem*. An impoverished fortune-hunter, he falls in love with and marries the daughter of Lady Bountiful.

Ajax (ā'jaks). A Greek hero of the war against Troy and of a tragedy by Sophocles, who became frenzied and killed himself when the armor of Achilles was awarded to Ulysses.

Aladdin (ȧ-lad'din). A well-known character in the *Arabian Nights*, son of a poor tailor in China. He gains possession of a magic ring and lamp and thus has at his beck and call the genii (jinn) who are attached to them as slaves.

Alasnam (ȧ-las'năm). A prince in the *Arabian Nights* who possessed eight precious statues, but was led to seek one still more precious, and found it in the person of a pure and beautiful woman. He received a magic mirror, which became dimmed when it reflected any damsel sullied with impurity.

Alastor (ȧ-las'tọr). In Greek, a name for an avenging deity, adopted by Shelley as that of the Spirit of Solitude in his poem *Alastor*.

Alborak (al-bō-rak'). A celestial animal of wondrous form that carried Mohammed to the seventh heaven.

Alceste (ȧl-cest'). The misanthropic hero of Molière's comedy *Le Misanthrope*.

Alcestis (al-ces'tis). The heroine of a drama of Euripides. The wife of Admetus, she gave herself up to death in his stead, but was brought back from the grave alive by Hercules.

Alcides (al-cī'dēṣ). A name of Hercules, applied to him as a descendant of Alcaeus.

Alcinoüs (al-cin'ō-us). In Homer's *Odyssey*, king of the Phaeacians and father of Nausicaä, who hospitably entertained Ulysses.

Alcmena *or* **Alcmene** (alç-mē'nȧ; -nē). The mother of Hercules by Jupiter. See **Amphitryon.**

Alden (ạl'den), **John.** The lover of Priscilla, the Puritan maiden, in Longfellow's *Courtship of Miles Standish*.

Alden, Roberta. A factory girl who is seduced and drowned by Clyde Giffiths, in Theodore Dreiser's *American Tragedy*.

Aldiborontephoscophornio (ạl'di-bō-ron'tē-fos'ḳō-fọr'ni-ō). A character in Henry Carey's burlesque *Chrononhotonthologos* (1734), the name being humorously given by Sir Walter Scott to his friend and printer, James Ballantyne.

Alecto (ȧ-leç'tō). In classical mythology, one of the three Furies.

Alexander of the North (al'eg-zan'dẽr ov thē nọrth). A name for Charles XII of Sweden.

Ali Baba (ä'lï bä'bä). The hero of the story of *The Forty Thieves* (in the *Arabian Nights*), whose treasure cave he is enabled to enter after overhearing their magic password, 'Open, Sesame!' ('sesame' being the herb of that name). His brother is Cassim Baba, his female slave Morgiana.

Alice (al'ic). The heroine of Meyerbeer's opera *Robert the Devil*.—The heroine of Tennyson's *Miller's Daughter*.—The heroine of Lewis Carroll's famous stories *Alice in Wonderland* and *Through the Looking-Glass*.

Allen (al'en), **Arabella.** A young lady in Dickens' *Pickwick*, married to Mr. Winkle. Her brother Ben Allen, an unsteady young man, is the bosom friend of Bob Sawyer.

Allworthy (ạl'wŏr-thy), **Mr.** A country gentleman in Fielding's *Tom Jones*, distinguished for benevolence, charity, rectitude, and modesty. He brings up Jones, who turns out to be the natural son of his sister.

Almaviva (al-mȧ-vī'vȧ), **Count.** A nobleman of somewhat loose principles who figures prominently in Beaumarchais' comedies *The Barber of Seville* and *The Marriage of Figaro*. See **Figaro.**

Almeria (al-me-rī'ȧ). See **Mourning Bride.**

Alpheus (al-fē'us). A river-god of Greek mythology. See **Arethusa.**

Alsatia (al-sā'shi-ȧ). A popular name formerly given to the district of Whitefriars in London, a sanctuary for debtors and lawbreakers. It figures in Scott's *Fortunes of Nigel*.

Al Sirat (al sï-rät'). In Mohammedan belief a bridge of incredible slenderness and sharpness, leading over the abyss of hell, which all must cross to get into paradise.

Alton Locke (lok). See **Locke, Alton.**

Amadis of Gaul (am'ȧ-dis ov gạl). The hero of a famous romance of chivalry, supposed to have been originally written in Portugal. *Gaul* stands for Wales. After many knightly exploits and adventures, Amadis weds the heroine, Oriana. Reading this romance unhinged the mind of Don Quixote.

Amalthea (am-ăl-thē'ȧ). In classic fable, the nurse of Zeus, variously accounted a nymph or a she-goat. In the latter version Zeus in gratitude broke off one of the goat's horns and endowed it with power to become filled with whatever its possessor desired: hence the 'horn of Amalthea' or cornucopia.

Amaryllis (am-ȧ-ryl'is). A country girl in ancient pastoral poetry; hence, a rustic beauty in general.

Amberson (am'bẽr-sŏn) **Family.** A family—the most prominent in a small midwestern town—depicted in Booth Tarkington's novel *The Magnificent Ambersons*. The story is concerned chiefly with George Amberson Minafer, Major Amberson's grandson, who does not live up to family traditions.

Amelia (ȧ-mēl'yȧ). The heroine of Fielding's novel of same name, wife of the profligate Captain Booth, and a most perfect specimen of wifehood.

Amina (ä-mï'nä). The heroine of Bellini's opera *La Sonnambula*, whose nocturnal wandering alienates her fiancé, until it is discovered that she is a sleepwalker.

Ammon (am'ŏn). An ancient Egyptian deity, identified by the Greeks and Romans with Zeus and Jupiter, represented with the head or horns of a ram.

Amory (ā'mọr-y), **Blanche.** A young lady in Thackeray's novel *Pendennis*, good-looking, clever, and pretending to sentiment, but shallow, selfish, and a vixen. She was at one time engaged to Pendennis, but she marries Henry Foker.

Amphion (am-fī'on). A son of Zeus or Jupiter, at the sound of whose lyre the stones moved into their places so as to form the walls of Thebes in Greece.

Amphitrite (am-fi-trī'tē). A goddess of the sea, the wife of Poseidon.

Amphitryon (am-fit'ry-on). In Greek mythology, a king of Thebes, husband of Alcmena, who became mother of Hercules by Jupiter when he assumed Amphitryon's form. There are comedies by Plautus, Dryden, Molière, and Giraudoux on the incidents connected with this story.

Anchises (an-ḳī'sēṣ). The father of Aeneas by Venus.

Ancient Mariner (ān'shent mar'in-ẽr). Hero of a famous poem by Coleridge, turning on the shooting of an albatross by the mariner.

Andrews (an'drůṣ), **Joseph.** A novel by Fielding, written to ridicule Richardson's *Pamela*, and named after the hero, a virtuous footman who overcomes temptations.

Androcles *or* **Androclus** (an'drō-ḳlēṣ; -ḳlus). A runaway Roman slave who extracted a thorn from a lion's paw. Subsequently doomed to fight a lion in the arena, he was confronted, by chance, with the beast he had befriended. The lion fawned upon him in gratitude, so he was freed.

Andromache (an-drom'ȧ-ḳē). The wife of Hector, a beautiful and touching figure in Homer's *Iliad*. See **Hector, Ilium.**

Andromeda (an-drom'e-dȧ). In Greek fable, the fair daughter of an Ethiopian queen, exposed to a sea monster at the command of an oracle, but rescued by Perseus.

Angelica (an-ġel'i-çȧ). In Ariosto's *Orlando Furioso*, a princess of great beauty beloved by Orlando.

Angelo (an'ġe-lō). In Shakespeare's *Measure for Measure*, the hypocritical deputy of Vincentio, Duke of Vienna, who, stringent in executing the law against others, yet violates it himself.

Anna Livia Plurabelle (an'ȧ liv'i-ȧ plụr'ȧ-bel). A personification of the river Liffey, and the wife of Earwicker, in Joyce's *Finnegans Wake*. See **Earwicker.**

Anne (an). The heroine of *Anne of Green Gables*, a book for girls by L. M. Montgomery.

Anne, Sister. The sister of Fatima, Bluebeard's last wife, who watches on a tower for the arrival of her brothers to save her sister from the results of her fatal curiosity.

Antaeus (an-tē'us). A giant invincible so long as he touched the earth, killed by Hercules, who held him up in the air and crushed him.

Anteros (an'te-ros). The god of mutual love in Greek mythology, who punished those that did not reciprocate love.

Antigone (an-tig'ō-nē). The heroine of Sophocles,

tragedy of this name, daughter of Oedipus. Creon, regent of Thebes, had forbidden anyone to bury the body of her brother Polynices, but she defied this order and performed what she deemed her duty. Creon thereupon had her confined in an underground vault, where she died by her own hand.

Antipholus (an-tif'ō-lus). The name of the twin brothers who are the chief characters in Shakespeare's *Comedy of Errors.*

Antiquary (an'ti-kwăr-y). See **Oldbuck.**

Ántonia (än'tō-nyä). See **Shimerda, Ántonias.**

Antonio (an-tō'ni-ō). The name of the merchant in Shakespeare's *Merchant of Venice.*

Anu (ä'nů). An ancient Assyro-Babylonian deity, worshiped as 'lord of heaven' and 'father of the universe.'

Anubis (ȧ-nū'bis). A jackal-headed divinity of ancient Egypt, who led the souls of the dead to the judge of the infernal regions.

Aphrodite (af-rō-dī'tē). The Greek goddess of love and beauty, identified by the Romans with Venus. She was of extreme beauty, and was fabled to have risen from the sea near the island of Cyprus. Hephaestus (Vulcan) was her husband, and she was attended by the Graces and Eros (Cupid), and often accompanied by doves. She had a notorious intrigue with Ares or Mars.

Apis (ā'pis). The sacred bull of ancient Egypt, worshiped as a symbol of the god Osiris.

Apley (ap'li), **George.** A Boston Brahmin in *The Late George Apley*, a satirical study of a conservative Bostonian by J. P. Marquand.

Apollo (ȧ-pol'ō). The Greek and Roman god of music and prophecy, the averter of disease and suffering, originally a sun-god (hence his epithet Phoebus, meaning 'bright' or 'radiant'). He was a son of Zeus and Latona, and brother of Artemis (Diana).

Apollonius of Tyre (ap-o-lō'ni-us ov tȳr). The hero of a tale which was very popular in the middle ages, and furnished the plot for Shakespeare's *Pericles, Prince of Tyre.*

Apollyon (ȧ-pol'yŏn). King of the bottomless pit, introduced in Bunyan's *Pilgrim's Progress.*

Arabian Nights (ȧ-rā'bi-ȧn nīts) *or* **Thousand and One Nights.** A collection of Eastern tales, written in Arabic and many times translated. A framework for the series is provided in the story of Scheherazade (which see). Other famous tales include those of Ali Baba, Aladdin, and Sinbad.

Arachne (ȧ-raḉh'nē). In classical mythology, a maiden who, having surpassed Minerva in weaving, was transformed by the goddess into a spider.

Aram (ā'răm), **Eugene.** An English philologist and murderer, the subject of a semihistorical novel of the same name by Bulwer-Lytton and of Thomas Hood's poem *The Dream of Eugene Aram.*

Aramis (ȧ-rȧ-mīs'). Comrade of **d'Artagnan.**

Archimago *or* **Archimage** (är-ḉhi-mā'gō; är'ḉhi-māġ). An enchanter in Spenser's *Faërie Queene* who was a hypocrite.

archy (är'chy). In Don Marquis' satirical book *archy and mehitabel*, a cockroach with the soul of a poet; and mehitabel is an alley cat.

Arden (är'den), **Enoch.** Hero of Tennyson's poem of this name, a seaman, supposedly dead, who returns home and finds his wife happily married to another man. To spare her he leaves without revealing himself, and dies broken-hearted.

Ares (ā'rēṣ). The Greek god of war, son of Zeus and Hera, identified with the Roman Mars.

Arethusa (a-re-thū'ṣȧ). One of the Nereids, changed by Artemis into a fountain near Syracuse, to free her from the pursuit of the river-god Alpheus, whose waters, however, flowed under the sea from Greece to mingle with those of the nymph.

Argo (är'gō). In Greek legend, the ship in which Jason and his companion heroes, the Argonauts, sailed to bring back the golden fleece from Colchis, at the eastern extremity of the Euxine. Jason obtained the fleece with the aid of Medea, daughter of the king of Colchis. See **Jason, Medea.**

Argus (är'gus). A creature of Greek mythology who had a hundred eyes and was ever watchful (hence his epithet Panoptes: 'all eyes').

Ariadne (a-ri-ad'nē). In Greek mythology, the daughter of Minos, king of Crete. She gave Theseus a clew of thread to guide him out of the labyrinth after killing the Minotaur. Theseus deserted her in the isle of Naxos, and according to some accounts she became the wife of Bacchus.

Ariel (ā'ri-el). A spirit of Jewish and Middle-Ages fable, adopted by Shakespeare in *The Tempest* and by Pope in *The Rape of the Lock.*

Arion (ȧ-rī'ŏn). An ancient Greek poet and musician (*c.* 700 B.C.), fabled to have been flung into the sea by sailors who coveted his treasure, but carried safe to land by a dolphin.

Armado (är-mä'dō). A vain, bombastic Spaniard in Shakespeare's *Love's Labour's Lost.*

Arnold (är'nŏld). The hero of Byron's unfinished drama *The Deformed Transformed.*

Arrowsmith (ar'ō-smith), **Martin.** A doctor in the novel of the same name by Sinclair Lewis, who is disillusioned by the conditions he encounters in a large research institute. He later dedicates himself to the relief of human suffering by studying the control of yellow fever in the tropics, and his wife dies of the malady.

Artagnan, d' (dȧr-tȧ-nyän'), **Charles de Baatz, Seigneur.** The chief character in Dumas' *The Three Musketeers*, who takes part in stirring adventures, in company with his guardsmen friends Athos, Porthos, and Aramis. All four appear also in the sequels *Twenty Years After* and *The Vicomte de Bragelonne.*

Artegal (är'tē-găl). A character in Spenser's *Faërie Queene*, typifying justice.

Artemis (är'te-mis). The Greek goddess identified by the Romans with Diana.

Artful Dodger (ärt'fu̇l doġ'ẽr), **the.** A youthful pickpocket in Dickens' *Oliver Twist.*

Arthur (är'thūr). A British king at the time of the settlement of the Anglo-Saxons in Britain. Nothing is really known of him, but he became the center of a vast upgrowth of legend or fable, especially in regard to the exploits of his knights of the Round Table.

Arviragus (är-vir'ȧ-gus). See **Guiderius.**

Ascanius (as-ḉā'ni-us). In Virgil's *Aeneid*, the son of Aeneas and his wife Creusa.

Asgard (äs'gärd). In Scandinavian mythology, the abode of the gods, rising above Midgard, that is, the earth.

Ashfield (ash'fēld), **Farmer, and his wife.** See **Grundy** (Mrs.).

Ashley (ash'li), **Brett.** A promiscuous divorcee who is the heroine in *The Sun Also Rises* by Ernest Hemingway, a novel concerning postwar American expatriates.

Ashton (ash'tŏn), **Lucy.** The heroine of Scott's novel *The Bride of Lammermoor*, loving and loved by Edgar Ravenswood. Married against her inclination to Frank Hayston of Bucklaw, she goes mad on her marriage night.

Ashtoreth (ash'tō-reth). The Phoenician goddess of fertility and love, also regarded as goddess of the moon; equivalent to the Greek Astarte and corresponding to the Babylonian Ishtar.

Ashur (ä'shůr). The national god of the ancient Assyrians, the king of the gods and ruler over heaven and earth.

Asmodeus (aṣ'mō-dē'us). An evil spirit of the ancient Jews mentioned in the book of Tobit, and introduced by Le Sage in his *Devil on Two Sticks* (*Le Diable boiteux*).

Aspasia (as-pā'shi-ȧ). The unfortunate heroine of Beaumont and Fletcher's *The Maid's Tragedy.*

Astarte (as-tär'tē). The Greek name for Ashtoreth. She in some respects corresponds with the Greek goddess Aphrodite and the Roman Venus.

Astolpho (as-tol'fō). A generous but boastful knight in Ariosto's *Orlando Furioso.*

Astraea (as-trē'ȧ). A goddess of justice of classical mythology, who was the last of the deities to leave the earth at the close of the Golden Age.

Astrophel (as'trō-fel). Spenser's name for Sir Philip Sidney.

Atalanta (at-ȧ-lan'tȧ). A famous huntress of Greek mythology who agreed to marry anyone who could outrun her, the penalty of failure being death to the wooer. She was vanquished by Hippomenes, who dropped successively three golden apples as he ran, which she stopped to pick from the ground.

Ate (ā'tē). A Greek goddess of hatred, crime, and retribution.

Athelny (ath'el-ny), **Sally.** The girl whom Philip Carey ultimately marries in Somerset Maugham's *Of Human Bondage.*

Athelstane (ath'el-stān). The sluggish Saxon thane of royal lineage in Scott's *Ivanhoe*, a somewhat backward rival of the hero.

Athene *or* **Athena** (ȧ-thē'nē; -nȧ). The Greek goddess of wisdom, usually identified with the Roman Minerva and also called Pallas or Pallas Athene.

Athos (ȧ-tọṣ'). Comrade of **d'Artagnan.**

Atlantis (at-lan'tis). A large island believed by the ancients to have existed in the Atlantic westward of the Straits of Gibraltar and to have sunk under the ocean. In his allegory *The New Atlantis*, Bacon represents himself as having been wrecked on such an island and having found there an ideal community.

Atlas (at'lăs). In Greek mythology, a Titan compelled to support the vault of heaven.

Atreus (ā'trůs; ā'trē-us). In Greek mythology, the father of Agamemnon and Menelaus, who are hence called Atridae (ȧ-trī'dē). See **Thyestes.**

Atropos (at'rō-pos). One of the three Fates among the Greeks and Romans: it was she who cut the thread of life. The others were **Clotho** and **Lachesis.**

Auburn (ạ'būrn). The name of the 'deserted village' of Goldsmith's poem of this name. See **Deserted Village.**

Audrey (ạ'dri). A country wench in Shakespeare's *As You Like It.*

Aunt Polly (ant pol'y). See **Polly, Aunt.**

Aurora (ạ-rō'rȧ). In Roman mythology, the goddess of the dawn, in Greek called Eos. See **Tithonus.**

Auster (ạs'tẽr). God of the south wind.

Autolycus (ạ-tol'y-ḉus). A roguish peddler in Shakespeare's *Winter's Tale.* The name originally belongs to a robber in Greek fable.

Avalon *or* **Avallon** (av'ȧ-lon). A sort of fairyland or elysium mentioned in connection with the legends of King Arthur.

Avenel (av'e-nel), **the White Lady of.** A supernatural being connected with the family of Avenel in Scott's novels *The Monastery* and *The Abbot.*

Avernus ((ȧ-vẽr'nus). A name for the lower world among the Romans, originally given to a gloomy lake about 9 miles west of Naples, regarded as the entrance to the lower regions.

Ayacanora (ä'yä-ḉä-nō'rȧ). The half-Indian bride of Amyas Leigh in C. Kingsley's *Westward Ho!*

Azrael (az'rā-el). The angel of death in Jewish and Mohammedan mythology

B

Baal (bā'ăl). Any of a number of local ancient Semitic deities, usually of agriculture.

Babbie (bab'i). The entrancing gypsy with whom Gavin Dishart falls in love in James Barrie's *Little Minister.*

Babbitt, (bab'it), **George.** The hero of Sinclair Lewis' *Babbitt*, a pompous, vulgar realtor who has come to symbolize stupid, materialistic, middle-class conformity to arbitrary standards.

Bacchus (baḉ'us). The Greek and Roman god of wine, son of Zeus (Jupiter) and Semele, in Greek commonly called Dionysus.

Backbite (bak'bīt), **Sir Benjamin.** A spiteful scandalmonger in Sheridan's *School for Scandal.*

Bagstock (bag'stok), **Major.** A purple-faced, pompous, and irascible retired officer in Dickens' *Dombey and Son*, always swaggering and boasting about himself as 'Joey B,' 'Old Joe B,' etc.

Bailey (bā'li). A diminutive lad in Dickens' *Martin Chuzzlewit*, who, after becoming 'tiger' to Montague Tigg, poses as a wide-awake and rather sporting character.

Baines (bānṣ), **Constance.** A leading character in Arnold Bennett's *Old Wives' Tale*, whose life resolves itself into intensive concern with the trivialities of respectable living. Her sister Sophia represents a tragic waste of a woman of splendid promise. Unlike Constance, she brushes with reality, but her unhappy marriage and subsequent running of a Paris boardinghouse merely accentuate her frustration.

Balafré, Le (bȧ-lȧ-frẹ', lẽ). Ludovic Lesly, a Scottish archer under Louis XI in Scott's novel *Quentin Durward*, uncle of the hero.

Balder *or* **Baldr** (bạl'dẽr). The Scandinavian deity of light, son of Odin and Frigga, beautiful, wise, and beloved of all the gods; slain through the guile of the evil god Loki.

Balderstone (bạl'dẽr-stōn), **Caleb.** A devoted but ridiculous old domestic in Scott's *Bride of Lammermoor*, who thinks it his duty by all shifts to uphold the dignity of the house.

Baldy of Nome (bạl'dy ov nōm). The dog hero of a tale of Alaska dog-racing by Esther Darling.

Balfour (bal'fu̇r), **David.** The hero of a novel of this name by Robert Louis Stevenson, the sequel to *Kidnapped.*

Baliverso (bal-i-vẽr'sō). The basest knight in the Saracen army, in Ariosto's *Orlando Furioso.*

Balkis (bal'kis). The Arabian name said to be that of the Queen of Sheba.

Balthazar (bal-thā'zăr). See **Magi.**

Banquo (baṅ'kwō). A thane in Shakespeare's *Macbeth*, whom Macbeth causes to be murdered, and whose ghost haunts him.

Barabas (bȧ-rab'ȧs). A Jew in Marlowe's play *The Jew of Malta*, a monster of wickedness.

Barataria (bä-rȧ-tä'ri-ȧ). In Cervantes' *Don Quixote*, the island-city of which Sancho Panza is appointed governor.

Bard of Avon (bärd ov ā'vŏn). Shakespeare.—**of Ayrshire** (ār'shir), Burns.—**of Hope,** Campbell (*The Pleasures of Hope*).—**of Memory,** Rogers (*The Pleasures of Memory*).—**of Olney** (ōl'ni), Cowper (from his residence).—**of Twickenham** (twik'n-ăm), Pope.

Bardell (bär-del'), **Mrs.** Mr. Pickwick's landlady in Dickens' *Pickwick Papers*, who wins damages against him in a trumped-up case of breach of promise.

Bardolph (bär'dŏlf). The red-nosed follower of Falstaff in Shakespeare's *Merry Wives* and *Henry IV*, appearing also in *Henry V*—a swaggering, drunken, but amusing rascal.

Barkis (bär'kis). A carrier in Dickens' *David Copperfield*, who marries David's old nurse Peggotty, expressing his proposal to do so by the words, 'Barkis is willin'.'

Barkley (bärk'li), **Catherine.** A nurse in Ernest Hemingway's *Farewell to Arms*, who is the mistress of Frederic Henry, an American fighting on the Italian front in the first World War, and who dies in childbirth.

Barmecide (bär'me-cīd). In the *Arabian Nights*, a prince of the Barmecide family, who at first pretended to treat a beggar named Schacabac to a sumptuous feast, pressing him to eat, though no dishes were on the table.

Barnaby (bär'nȧ-by), **Widow.** The vulgar heroine of a novel by Mrs. Trollope, so named, and of its sequel, *The Widow Married.*

Barnacle (bär'nȧ-ḉl) **Family.** A family in Dickens' *Little Dorrit* through whom the author satirizes the way in which noble families formerly monopolized offices in the public service, and, through Mr. Tite Barnacle, head of the 'Circumlocution Office,' governmental red tape.

Barnes (bärnṣ), **Jake.** An American newspaperman, one of the expatriates in Hemingway's *The Sun Also Rises.*

Barsetshire (bär'set-shir). A fictitious county in southern England, including the cathedral town of Barchester, which is the scene of a series of novels by Anthony Trollope, and of a later series by Angela Thirkell.

Basil the Blacksmith (baṣ'il thē blak'smith). The father of Gabriel, lover of Evangeline (which see).

Bassanio (bȧ-sä'ni-ō). The lover of Portia in Shakespeare's *Merchant of Venice.* See **Portia.**

Bates (bāts), **Charley.** A merry young pickpocket in Dickens' *Oliver Twist.*

Battle (bat'l), **Sarah.** A character in one of Lamb's

Essays of Elia, who considers that whist is 'her life business, her duty,' and literature one of the relaxations.

Baucis and Philemon (bạ'cis; fi-lē'mŏn). An aged and affectionate couple, who, having hospitably entertained the gods Jupiter and Mercury, had their humble abode changed into a splendid temple; and they, in response to their wish that they might die together, were changed into two trees.

Bazarov (bä-zä'rọf). The chief character in Turgenev's novel *Fathers and Sons*, a young radical who vainly tries to bridge the gap between the generations and win his father to his social views.

Beatrice (bē'ȧ-tric; bẹ-ä-trī'chẹ). A young lady beloved by Dante and celebrated in his *Divine Comedy*. —The heroine of Shakespeare's *Much Ado About Nothing*. See **Benedick.**

Beaucaire (bō-cãr'), **Monsieur.** In Booth Tarkington's short story of this name, a nobleman who seeks adventure in the guise of a barber.

Beau Geste (bō ẓest). See **Geste, Beau.**

Beau Tibbs (tibṣ). See **Tibbs, Beau.**

Beauty and the Beast (bū'ty and thē bēst). An old fairy tale which illustrates the triumph of love over externals.

Bede (bēd), **Adam.** The hero of a novel by George Eliot, a manly and straightforward artisan, in love with Hetty Sorrel, who is seduced by the young squire Arthur Donnithorne. He marries Dinah Morris, a Methodist preacher.

Bedivere (bed'i-vēr), **Sir.** One of King Arthur's knights, the last who remained to him at his death, and the one who threw his famous sword Excalibur into the mere, as described in Tennyson's *Morte d'Arthur.*

Bel (bẹl). One of the principal Babylonian gods, sometimes called the 'father of the gods,' considered creator of the world, especially of mankind. Under the title of Bel-Merodach he was worshiped as the patron god of Babylon. He corresponded in many respects with the Phoenician Baal.

Belch (belch), **Sir Toby.** A jolly toper, the uncle of Olivia in Shakespeare's *Twelfth Night*, who plays on the folly of Sir Andrew Aguecheek.

Belial (bē'li-ăl). A biblical word meaning worthlessness or wickedness, often treated as a proper name, and by Milton made one of the fallen angels.

Belinda (bel-in'dȧ). The heroine of Pope's *Rape of the Lock*, and of a novel by Maria Edgeworth.

Bell (bel), **Adam.** An archer and outlaw of northern England, a hero of ballad romance in association with Clym of the Clough and William of Cloudesley.

Bellaston (bel'ăs-tŏn), **Lady.** An abandoned woman of rank in Fielding's *Tom Jones.*

Bellenden (bel'en-den), **Lady Margaret.** The mistress of Tillietudlem Castle in Scott's *Old Mortality*, a strong adherent of the Stuarts. Her granddaughter Edith Bellenden, marries Henry Morton, who belongs to the Covenanting party.

Bellerophon (be-ler'ō-fon). A hero of Greek mythology, who, mounted on the winged horse Pegasus, killed the Chimaera. He tried to fly to heaven on Pegasus, but fell and wandered about blind till his death.

Bellona (be-lō'nȧ). The goddess of war among the Romans.

Belphoebe (bel-fē'bē). A huntress in Spenser's *Faërie Queene*, intended to portray Queen Elizabeth.

Benedick (ben'e-dik). One of the chief characters in Shakespeare's *Much Ado About Nothing*, who has many an encounter of wit with Beatrice, whom he at last marries. His name, usually spelled 'benedict,' is applicable to a man recently married, especially after long bachelorhood.

Ben Hur (ben hũr). The hero of the historical novel of that name by Lew Wallace. After many vicissitudes, he triumphs over his enemy in a spectacular chariot race.

Bennet (ben'et) **Family.** A middle-class English family whose lives are depicted in Jane Austen's novel *Pride and Prejudice.* The easy-going father is continually prodded by the scheming mother, who is anxious to marry off her five daughters. Elizabeth, the heroine, is blinded by prejudice against her lover, Darcy, whose pride in his superior birth and interference in the affairs of her sister Jane, irritate her. His devotion finally overcomes her objections.

Beowulf (bẹ'ō-wụlf). The hero of a celebrated Anglo-Saxon epic, who kills two man-eating semihuman monsters (Grendel and his mother), and at last slays a fiery dragon, but dies from its poisonous bite.

Berenice (ber-e-nī'cē). Wife of Ptolemy III, king of Egypt, who vowed to sacrifice her beautiful hair to the gods if her husband returned safe from the war in Syria. She suspended it in the temple of the war god, from which it disappeared, and according to legend it was transferred to the skies as the constellation Coma Berenices ('Berenice's Hair').

Berling (bẽr'ling), **Gösta.** The fascinating but erratic hero of Selma Lagerlöf's novel *The Story of Gösta Berling.* Attractive to women, he involves them and himself in many difficulties. He marries Countess Elizabeth Dohna, a divorcee, who influences him to lead a better life.

Bern (bẽrn), **Julien.** The protagonist in Robert Briffault's *Europa* and *Europa in Limbo*, novels depicting the decadence of the upper classes in Europe.

Bertha the Spinner (bẽr'thȧ thē spin'ẽr). Wife of Rudolph II, king of Burgundy, famous for her industry and goodness.

Bertram (bẽr'trăm). Count of Rousillon, the unworthy husband of Helena in Shakespeare's *All's Well that Ends Well.*—The name of the family to which belongs the hero, Harry Bertram, of Scott's *Guy Mannering.*

Bess (bes). Daughter of the Blind Beggar of Bethnal Green.—The landlord's daughter who is loved by The Highwayman, in the poem of this name by Alfred Noyes.—A Charleston Negress, the sweetheart of Porgy, in the novel by Du Bose Heyward.

Bett (bet), **Miss Lulu.** In the novel and play of this name by Zona Gale, an old maid who is treated as the maid of all work in her brother-in-law's home. She escapes briefly through a marriage which does not work out, but on her return, evinces a new spirit of independence and courage.

Beulah (bū'lȧ). In Bunyan's *Pilgrim's Progress*, the land of sunshine and all delight, in which the pilgrims rest till called upon to cross the river to the Celestial City.

Bevis of Hampton (bē'vis ov hamp'tŏn). A famous hero of medieval romance, in English, French, and Italian versions.

Bickerstaff (bik'ẽr-stȧf), **Isaac.** A pseudonym used by Jonathan Swift in predicting the death of an astrologer named Partridge and in subsequently announcing that the event had occurred—even though Partridge protested that he was still alive and well. The popularity of the joke led Richard Steele to adopt the pseudonym, in *The Tatler.*

Bifrost (bĭf-rost). In Scandinavian mythology, the rainbow bridge connecting Asgard and Midgard (heaven and earth).

Big-endians (big'en'di-ănṣ). In Swift's *Gulliver's Travels*, a Lilliputian party (satirizing the English Catholics) who break their eggs at the big end, which is regarded as heretical by the party of Little-endians (Protestants), who break theirs at the little end.

Biglow (big'lō), **Hosea.** The professed writer of several satirical poems on public affairs in the United States, the real author being James Russell Lowell.

Biron (bi-rōn'; *Fr.* bī-rọṅ'). A 'merry madcap' young lord in the court of the king of Navarre, in Shakespeare's *Love's Labour's Lost.*

Black Agnes (blak ag'nes). Countess of March, famous for her defense of Dunbar Castle against the English in the time of Edward III.

Black Beauty (bū'ti). A horse in the children's classic of the same name, who, after being a family pet, is sold and becomes an abused dray horse, but is later rescued and retired to pasture. The story is credited with initiating the Society for Prevention of Cruelty to Animals.

Black Bess (bes). The famous mare of Dick Turpin, the highwayman, in W. H. Ainsworth's novel *Rookwood.*

Black Death (deth). A form of pestilence, chiefly bubonic plague, which came from Asia and carried off from one-fourth to three-fourths of the population of Europe in the fourteenth century.

Black Flag (flag). The flag of a pirate ship, usually adorned with skull and crossbones, called the 'Jolly Roger.'

Black George (ġọrġ). A gamekeeper in Fielding's *Tom Jones.*

Black Knight (nīt). A character in Tennyson's *Gareth and Lynette*; also, King Richard, when wandering incognito, in Scott's *Ivanhoe.*

Blackpool (blak'pọọl), **Stephen.** A striking character in Dickens' *Hard Times*, a workingman of high principle but unfortunate.

Black Prince (princ), **the.** Edward, prince of Wales, son of Edward III, so called from his black armor, though Froissart says 'by terror of his arms.'

Blanchard (blan'chȧrd), **Jennie.** The heroine of Frank Swinnerton's *Nocturne*, who sacrifices her love to her duty toward her paralyzed father.

Blanchefleur (blänçh'flũr). A heroine of medieval story, beloved by Flores.

Blandamour (bland'ȧ-mör). A brave but vainglorious knight in Spenser's *Faërie Queene.*

Blandina (blan-dī'nȧ). A persuasive but perfidious character in the *Faërie Queene*, wife of the knight Turpin.

Blandish (blan'dish), **Serena.** The beautiful heroine of the satirical novel of the same name by Enid Bagnold (pseud. *A Lady of Quality*), and of the dramatization by S. N. Behrman. After several unsuccessful romances she marries a half-caste.

Blarney (blär'ni), **Lady.** In Goldsmith's *Vicar of Wakefield*, one of the two women of loose character introduced to the Primrose family as ladies of fashion.

Blatant Beast (blā'tănt bēst). A monster in Spenser's *Faerie Queene*, supposed to typify the voice of the mob or popular outcry.

Bleeding-heart Yard (blēd'ing-härt yärd). In Dickens' *Little Dorrit*, a real place so called from a legend about Lady Hatton, wife of Queen Elizabeth's chancellor.

Blefuscu (blē-fus'çū). In *Gulliver's Travels*, an island typifying France.

Blifil (blĭ'fil). A hypocritical and sneaking character in Fielding's *Tom Jones.*

Blimber (blim'bẽr), **Dr.** In Dickens' *Dombey and Son*, the proprietor of a select academy at Brighton, where a few boys are crammed with knowledge, one of these being young Paul Dombey. His daughter Cornelia is an exceedingly learned young lady, who wears spectacles and despises sentiment.

Blimp (blimp), **Colonel.** An imaginary hidebound and finicky British officer.

Blind Beggar of Bethnal Green (blīnd beg'ăr ov beth'năl grēn). A hero of ballad and drama, son and heir of Simon de Montfort, living in disguise.

Bloom (blọọm), **Leopold.** Principal character in James Joyce's *Ulysses*, a stream-of-consciousness novel, in which are related in minutiae the thoughts and actions of the central characters in one day of their lives. Bloom is essentially an average man, portrayed in mythological and symbolic terms. Thus, he is comparable variously with Ulysses and the Wandering Jew. Molly, his unfaithful wife, is a sensual woman, in some respects an ironic counterpart of Penelope. To Stephen Dedalus, who corresponds somewhat to Telemachus, he is a father symbol.

Blouzelinda (blou-ze-lin'dȧ). A country girl in Gay's pastoral poems, natural and uncultivated, such as one might really meet, and not a figure from an ideal Arcadia.

Bluebeard (blụ'bẽrd'). The bloody ogre of a fairy tale, translated from the French of Charles Perrault. His handsome young wife Fatima received all the keys of the castle, but was forbidden on pain of death to unlock one particular room. In the absence of her husband, however, she opened the mysterious room and found in it the dead bodies of his former wives. Betrayed by an indelible bloodstain on the key, she was about to be put to death, but was saved by the arrival of her brothers, and Bluebeard was slain. Some find the original of Bluebeard in a marshal of France, Gilles de Retz, who was notorious for his cruelty and licentiousness.

Blunderbore (blun'dẽr-bōr). A giant killed by Jack the Giant-killer, who scuttled his boat.

Bluntschli (blunt'shli), **Captain.** A Swiss officer in the Serbian army in Shaw's play *Arms and the Man*, a realistic soldier more concerned for his chocolate rations than for bravado. The light opera *The Chocolate Soldier*, by Oscar Straus, was based on the play.

Boanerges (bō-ȧ-nẽr'ġēṣ). A loud-voiced dissenting minister in Mrs. Oliphant's *Salem Chapel*, a vigorous exponent of the doctrines of election and reprobation. The name was taken from the Apostles James and John, surnamed Boanerges (sons of thunder).

Bobadil (bob'ȧ-dil), **Captain.** A cowardly braggart in Ben Jonson's *Every Man in his Humour.* He proposes to annihilate a hostile army by selecting nineteen other warriors like himself, and challenging and killing the enemy by successive twenties.

Boffin (bof'in), **Nicodemus.** The 'Golden Dustman' in Dickens' novel *Our Mutual Friend*, a man of no education, but shrewd, kind, and unselfish. On the death of his employer, John Harmon, dustman and miser, he came in for his property but gave it up to his son, young John Harmon.

Bois-Guilbert, de. (dē bwä'gĭl-ber'), **Brian.** A brave but cruel and irreligious leader of the Knights Templars in Scott's *Ivanhoe*, inspired with an evil passion for the Jewish maiden Rebecca. He falls dead when about to encounter Ivanhoe.

Bombastes Furioso (bom-bas'tēṣ fū-ri-ō'sō). The hero of a burlesque tragic opera, parodying *Orlando Furioso*, by William Barnes Rhodes.

Bona Dea (bō'nȧ dē'ȧ). A Roman female deity of fertility and chastity, whose worship was confined to women.

Bonnard (bọ-nȧr'), **Sylvestre.** A kindly old scientist, the hero of Anatole France's novel *The Crime of Sylvestre Bonnard.* His 'crime' consisted in kidnaping a minor, Jeanne Alexandre, from a boarding school where she had been abused and miserable. After many complications, he is allowed to make the girl his legal ward.

Bontemps (bọṅ-täṅ'), **Roger.** The French impersonation of contentment, in a song of Béranger, one always hopeful and inclined to make the best of things.

Booby (bọọ'by), **Lady.** A lady of loose morals in Fielding's *Joseph Andrews*, who tries to lead Joseph astray.

Booth (bọọth), **Captain.** The husband of Amelia in Fielding's novel *Amelia*, dissipated but good-natured.

Border Minstrel (bọr'dẽr min'strel). Sir Walter Scott.

Boreas (bō'rē-ăs). In Greek mythology, a personification of the north wind.

Borrioboola-Gha (bor'i-ō-bọọ'lȧ-gä'). See **Jellyby.**

Bottom (bot'ŏm), **Nick.** The Athenian weaver in Shakespeare's *Midsummer Night's Dream*, upon whom the fairy queen Titania is made to dote, and whose head is changed by Puck into that of an ass.

Bounderby (boun'dẽr-by). A banker at Coketown in Dickens' *Hard Times*, who boasts that he has raised himself from the gutter, though his real origin was respectable.

Bountiful (boun'ti-ful), **Lady.** A benevolent country lady in Färquhar's *Beaus' Stratagem.* See **Aimwell.**

Bovary (bō-vȧ-rī'), **Emma.** The immoral heroine of Gustave Flaubert's novel *Madame Bovary*, who had a romantic conception of herself, but who married a plodding husband. Her horrible suicide remains a classic of deathbed scenes.

Bowley (bou'li), **Sir Joseph.** In Dickens' *Chimes*, a pompous, narrow-minded member of parliament who poses as 'the poor man's friend.'

Bowzybeus (bou-zy-bē'us). A drunken ballad-singer in Gay's *Pastorals.*

Box and Cox (boks and çoks). Characters in J. M. Morton's farce of that name, who unknowingly tenant the same room, for one works at night, the other in the day.

Boythorn (boi'thọrn), **Lawrence.** A gentleman in Dickens' *Bleak House*, who expresses ferocious sentiments in a stentorian voice but is really gentle and kindhearted; a fictional portrayal of Walter Savage Landor.

Boz (boz). The pseudonym used by Dickens in early life.

Bozzy (boz'y). The familiar abbreviation of the name of Boswell, the biographer of Dr. Johnson.

Bracy (brā'cy), **Sir Maurice de.** A knight who was determined, though unsuccessfully, to marry Rowena in Scott's *Ivanhoe.*

Bradamante *or* **Bradamant** (brä-dä-män'te; brad'-ȧ-mănt). The sister of Rinaldo and cousin of Orlando in Ariosto's *Orlando Furioso.* She was called the Virgin Knight, wore white armor, and was armed with an irresistible spear.

Bradwardine (brad'wär-dīn), **Baron.** A Scottish nobleman in Scott's *Waverley*, brave, pedantic, and a devoted adherent of the exiled Stuarts. His daughter Rose is in love with, and latterly married to, Waverley.

Bragi (brä'gī). A Scandinavian deity, son of Odin and Frigga, the god of eloquence and poetry.

Brahma (brä'mȧ). The supreme god of the Hindu trinity, the creator, as opposed to Vishnu the preserver, and Siva the destroyer.

Brainworm (brān'wŏrm). A character in Ben Jonson's comedy *Every Man in his Humour*, who tricks various persons by assuming different characters.

Bramble (bram'bl), **Matthew.** An elderly gentleman in Smollett's *Humphry Clinker*, shrewd, cynical, and irascible, but generous and benevolent. His sister Tabitha is a niggardly, malicious, vain, and ridiculous old maid, who finally weds Lismahago.

Bramble, Sir Robert. The gouty, testy, but kindhearted country squire in Colman's play *The Poor Gentleman.*

Brand (brand). In Ibsen's drama of the same name, a young priest whose uncompromising idealism results in his personal ruin.

Brandan (bran'dăn), **St., Island of.** A wonderful flying or floating island, which legend placed in the Atlantic west of the Canaries.

Brandon (bran'dŏn), **Adam.** The chief figure in Hugh Walpole's novel *The Cathedral.* Archdeacon of a cathedral, he is a pompous figure who is humiliated.

Brandon, Charles. The hero of Charles Major's historical novel *When Knighthood Was in Flower*, who married Mary Tudor, sister of Henry VIII.

Brandon, Kit. The heroine in the novel of the same name by Sherwood Anderson, the daughter of a ne'er-do-well mountaineer family who marries for money, becomes a driver for a bootlegger, and then settles down to simple life.

Brandt (brant), **Margaret.** The heroine of Charles Reade's historical novel *The Cloister and the Hearth*, mother of Erasmus. See **Gerard.**

Brass (brȧs), **Sampson.** In Dickens' *Old Curiosity Shop*, a knavish attorney who fleeces his clients. His sister Sally is of similar temperament.

Bray (brā). The selfish father of Madeline Bray in Dickens' *Nicholas Nickleby.* He is eager for her to marry the wretched old miser Gride, but she becomes the wife of Nicholas.

Bray, Vicar of. See **Vicar of Bray.**

Brer Rabbit, Brer Fox (brer rab'it; foks). Characters in tales told by Uncle Remus.

Briareus (brī-âr'ē-us). In Greek fable, a giant with a hundred arms and fifty heads.

Brick (brik), **Jefferson.** An American journalist in Dickens' *Martin Chuzzlewit*, a slight, pale young man, giving utterance to warlike and bombastic sentiments.

Bridehead (brīd'hed), **Sue.** A principal character in Thomas Hardy's *Jude the Obscure*, who is in love with Jude (Fawley).

Bride of Lammermoor (brīd ov lam'ẽr-mo͝or). Lucy Ashton in Scott's novel so called. See **Ashton.**

Bride of the Sea (ov thē sē). Venice, thus named from the ancient ceremony of the doge, who threw a ring into the sea with the words: 'We wed thee, O sea, in token of perpetual domination.'

Brigadoon (brig-ȧ-do͝on'). In the musical play of the same name by A. J. Lerner, a Scottish village which comes to life once every hundred years.

Brinker (brink'ẽr), **Hans.** The hero of a well-known children's book, *Hans Brinker, or the Silver Skates.* He is a Dutch boy who wins the great race of the year and a pair of silver skates as the prize.

Brisk (brisk). A fantastic fop in Ben Jonson's comedy *Every Man out of his Humour.*

Britling (brit'ling), **Mr.** A literary man in H. G. Wells's novel *Mr. Britling Sees It Through*, whose pleasant life is devastated by the outbreak of the first World War. His son Hugh, his old aunt, and a young German tutor who had lived in his home, are all killed, and Mr. Britling is forced to adopt a new outlook on life to see him through.

Britomart (brit'ō-märt). A 'lady knight,' daughter of King Ryence of Wales, in Spenser's *Faërie Queene*, typifying chastity, and armed with an irresistible magic spear.

Britomartis (brit-ō-mär'tis). In classical mythology, a nymph and huntress of Crete. To escape the advances of King Minos, who had fallen in love with her, she cast herself into the sea.

Brobdingnag (brob'ding-nag). The country of the giants in Swift's *Gulliver's Travels;* often written Brobdignag.

Brooke (brook), **Dorothea.** Heroine of George Eliot's novel *Middlemarch*, full of benevolent enthusiasm but not very practical. She is married first to Mr. Casaubon, and after his death to Will Ladislaw.

Brother Jonathan (brŏth'ẽr jon'ȧ-thăn). A playful personification of the people of the United States collectively.

Browdie (brou'di), **John.** A brawny Yorkshireman in Dickens' *Nicholas Nickleby*, who befriends Nicholas and Smike.

Brown (broun), **Father.** A Catholic priest who is a shrewd detective, in numerous stories by G. K. Chesterton.

Brown, Tom. The hero of Thomas Hughes' stories *Tom Brown's School Days* and *Tom Brown at Oxford*, a merry, natural fellow, but not overfond of books.

Brunhild *or* **Brünnehilde** (bru̇n'hilt; brůn-e-hil'de). A princess of extraordinary strength and prowess in the German epic the *Nibelungenlied*, overcome by the devices of Siegfried and married to Gunther, king of Burgundy. Her vengeance on Siegfried, when she discovers how she has been tricked, leads to many important incidents in the poem.

Brut *or* **Brutus** (brůt; brů'tus). The mythical first king of Britain, great-grandson of Aeneas, named in the old chronicles, in Drayton's *Polyolbion*, and in Spenser's *Faërie Queene.*

Brute (brůt), **Sir John and Lady.** Characters in Vanbrugh's comedy *The Provoked Wife.*

Bubastis (bū-bas'tis). The Diana of Egyptian mythology, whose real name was properly Bast (Bubastis being a city sacred to her).

Bucephalus (bū-cef'ȧ-lus). The famous horse of Alexander the Great.

Buck (buk). The dog hero of Jack London's *Call of the Wild.*

Budd (bud), **Lanny.** The protagonist in a ten-volume series of novels by Upton Sinclair, reflecting momentous historical events of the first and second World Wars and the years between.

Buddenbrook (bud'den-brook) **Family.** The members of the family in Thomas Mann's *Buddenbrooks*, which traces the rise and decline of a bourgeois German family through four generations, and shows the conflict between the artists and businessmen. It is autobiographical to a large extent. The head of the family is Consul Thomas Buddenbrook; Christian is the frustrated artist; Toni, the favorite daughter; and little Hanno, who dies, a musician of great promise.

Buddha (bu̇d'ȧ). The title (the Enlightened) of Gautama, the founder of Buddhism, an Indian sage of whom various mythical stories are related.

Bull (bu̇l), **John.** The English nation personified, originally used in Arbuthnot's political satire *The History of John Bull.*

Bumble (bum'bl). The celebrated pompous parish beadle in Dickens' *Oliver Twist.*

Bumppo (bum'pō), **Natty.** See **Leatherstocking.**

Bunch (bunch), **Mother.** An alewife of Elizabethan London, around whose name many anecdotes and jokes sprang up.

Bunsby (bunṣ'by), **Jack.** In Dickens' *Dombey and Son*, the skipper of a trading vessel, friend of Captain Cuttle, who regards him as an oracle; his words are few and hazy, and his ideas seem to be equally so.

Bunyan (bun'yăn), **Paul.** A legendary hero of the lumber camps of northwestern United States. A collection of stories concerning him are contained in a chapbook called *Paul Bunyan Comes West.*

Burchell (bûr'chel), **Mr.** A chief character in Goldsmith's *Vicar of Wakefield*, who appears as a plain man of abrupt manners and no position in life, but is really the baronet Sir William Thornhill.

Busiris (bū-sī'ris). A king of Egypt, supposed by Milton to be the Pharaoh drowned in the Red Sea.—One king of this name is said to have sacrificed to the gods all foreigners who entered Egypt, in order to prevent a famine, until he was slain by Hercules.

Butler (but'lẽr), **Rhett.** One of the chief characters in Margaret Mitchell's *Gone With the Wind*; amoral, unethical, vital and fascinating. A blockade runner for profit during the Civil War, he is Scarlett O'Hara's third husband, and the only man who sees through her.

Buttercup (but'ẽr-c̹up), **Little.** In Gilbert and Sullivan's comic opera *H. M. S. Pinafore*, a 'bumboat woman.' She interchanged the babies who grew up to be Ralph Rackstraw and the captain of the *Pinafore.*

Buzfuz (buz'fuz), **Serjeant.** A bullying lawyer in the famous breach of promise trial in Dickens' *Pickwick.* See **Bardell, Mrs.**

Byron (bȳrŏn), **Miss Harriet.** In Richardson's novel *Sir Charles Grandison*, a beautiful and accomplished lady, who finally marries Sir Charles.

C

Cabot (c̹ab'ŏt), **Ephraim.** A bigoted old New England farmer, one of the leading characters in Eugene O'Neill's play *Desire Under the Elms.* He marries Abbie Putnam (his third wife), a woman half his age. She seduces his son Eben, and tells Ephraim that her baby is his.

Cacus (c̹ā'c̹us). A mythical robber and giant of ancient Italy, slain by Hercules for stealing his cattle.

Cadmus (c̹ad'mus). In Greek mythology, a Phoenician prince who slew a dragon and sowed its teeth, from which sprang up armed warriors who fought one another until all but five were killed. He and these five founded Thebes in Boeotia. He was the reputed introducer of the alphabet into Greece.

Caduceus (c̹ȧ-dū'cē-us). The winged wand of Mercury, usually represented with two serpents twined around it; a symbol of a doctor or a medical corps.

Cadwallader (c̹ad-wäl'ȧ-dẽr), **Rev. Mr. and Mrs.** The easygoing clergyman and his shrewd wife in George Eliot's *Middlemarch.*

Caerleon (c̹är-lē'ŏn). King Arthur's royal residence, the site of which is not certain. The battle of that name was one of King Arthur's twelve victories.

Caius (c̹ā'yus). A French doctor in Shakespeare's *The Merry Wives of Windsor.*

Calandrino (c̹al-ăn-drī'nō). The name of a simpleton and butt for merriment introduced in Boccaccio's *Decameron.*

Calenders (c̹al'en-dẽrṣ). A sect of dervishes in Turkey and Persia similar to friars and hermits.

Caliban (c̹al'i-ban). A deformed, brutal, and malignant creature in Shakespeare's *Tempest*, offspring of the hag Sycorax, and servant of Prospero.

Caliburn (c̹al'i-bûrn). Another name for Excalibur, the famous sword of King Arthur.

Calidore (c̹al'i-dŏr), **Sir.** A knight who typifies courtesy in Spenser's *Faërie Queene.*

Calista (c̹ȧ-lis'tȧ). The haughty heroine of Rowe's tragedy *The Fair Penitent*, seduced by Lothario. Her guilt is disclosed, unhappy events ensue, and she stabs herself.

Calliope (c̹a-lī'ō-pē). The Muse who presided over eloquence and heroic poetry.

Callisto (c̹ȧ-lis'tō). In Greek mythology, an Arcadian nymph, changed into a bear, and with her son afterwards transformed into the constellations Ursa Major and Ursa Minor.

Caloveglia (c̹ä-lō-ve̱l'yä), **Count.** A philosopher in Norman Douglas' *South Wind*, one of the individualistic members of the island of Nepenthe in the Mediterranean.

Calydonian Boar (c̹al'y-dō'ni-ăn bōr). A fabulous monster of ancient Greece, which ravaged the district of Calydon, and was slain by Meleager.

Calypso (c̹ȧ-lyp'sō). An ocean nymph who lived in the island of Ogygia, where she detained Ulysses for seven years, delaying his return to Ithaca.

Camaralzaman (c̹am-ȧ-ral'zȧ-măn). A prince in the *Arabian Nights*, who marries the Princess Badoura.

Cambuscan (c̹am-bus-c̹an'; c̹am-bus'c̹ăn). A king of Tartary in Chaucer's *Squire's Tale.*

Camelot (c̹am'e-lot). King Arthur's city or residence, the site of which is doubtful.

Camilla (c̹ȧ-mil'ȧ). In Virgil's *Aeneid*, queen of the Volscians, so swift of foot that she could run over standing grain without causing it to bend.

Camille (c̹ȧ-mīl'). The English version of the title of *La Dame aux camélias*, a highly successful play by Dumas *fils*, based on a novel, concerning a beautiful courtesan who gives up the man she loves rather than ruin him.—The heroine of Corneille's tragedy *Horace.*

Candida (c̹an'di-dȧ). The heroine of Bernard Shaw's play of the same name, a cultured, intelligent woman who represents Shaw's ideal. Her rather stuffy husband, the Rev. James Morell, does not fully appreciate her, but she adheres to him despite the aspirations of Marchbanks, a young poet in love with her.

Candide (c̹äṅ-dīd'). The hero of Voltaire's novel of the same name, which satirizes the optimistic view that all is for the best (see **Pangloss**). After calamitous misadventures, he settles down to the practical and modest project of cultivating his garden.

Candour (c̹an'dŏr), **Mrs.** A backbiting lady in Sheridan's *School for Scandal.*

Canty (c̹an'ty), **Tom.** The beggar boy who changes places with Prince Edward in Mark Twain's novel *The Prince and the Pauper.*

Caora (c̹ä'ō-rä). A river near which dwelled people who were said to have their eyes in their shoulders and their mouths in the middle of their breasts, as described in Hakluyt's *Voyages.*

Capaneus (c̹ap'ȧ-nūs). A hero of Greek mythology, killed by Jove with a thunderbolt; one of the Seven against Thebes.

Capulet (c̹ap'ū-let). The noble family in Verona to which Juliet belonged in Shakespeare's *Romeo and Juliet.*

Carabas (c̹ar'ȧ-bas), **Marquis of.** A fanciful title standing for a great nobleman or grandee; familiar from its occurrence in the story of *Puss in Boots.*

Caradoc *or* **Cradock** (c̹ar'ȧ-doc̹; c̹ra'dŏk). One of Arthur's knights, the only one whose wife was not unfaithful.

Carey (c̹âr'i), **Philip.** The leading character in Somerset Maugham's *Of Human Bondage*, a partly autobiographical novel. As a boy and youth his shyness and sensitivity are heightened by consciousness of his clubfoot. After abandoning hope of becoming a painter, he undergoes numerous misfortunes, including an unhappy love affair (see **Mildred**), studies medicine, and ultimately settles down as a married country doctor.

Carker (c̹är'kẽr), **James.** In Dickens' *Dombey and Son*, Mr. Dombey's manager, conspicuous for his white teeth and snarling smile, treacherous to his employer, whose wife he induces to run away with him.

Carmen (c̹är'men). A voluptuous gypsy coquette in Mérimée's story of the same name, which has furnished the basis for Bizet's opera and other adaptations. After stabbing a girl in the cigar factory where she works, Carmen persuades Don José, a young Spanish officer, to let her escape punishment. He becomes infatuated with her, kills a man for her, and turns outlaw. When her love for him cools, he stabs her.

Carol Bird (ça̤r'ŏl bĩrd). The child invalid in *Birds' Christmas Carol* by Kate Douglas Wiggin.

Carton (çär'tŏn), **Sydney.** The hero of Dickens' *Tale of Two Cities*, a young man whose latent nobility is evoked by his love for Lucie Manette and friendship for Charles Darnay. Utilizing physical resemblance, he takes Darnay's place and dies on the guillotine in his stead.

Casabianca (çä-sȧ-byäṅ'çȧ). Son of the captain of *L'Orient*, a ship blown up in the battle of the Nile. The boy kept his post on deck to the last, as told in Felicia Hemans' well-known poem.

Casaubon (çȧ-sa̤'bŏn), **Rev. Mr.** A wealthy and learned scholar, but narrow-minded and without any originality, in George Eliot's *Middlemarch*. See **Brooke, Dorothea.**

Cassandra (çȧ-san'drȧ). Daughter of King Priam of Troy, gifted with the power of prophecy, but condemned by Apollo to be always disbelieved.

Cassim (ças'im). Brother of Ali Baba in the *Arabian Nights*, killed by the Forty Thieves.

Cassio (çash'i-ō). A lieutenant under Othello's command in Shakespeare's *Othello*, against whom Iago stirs up the Moor's jealousy.

Cassiopeia (ças-i-ō-pē'yȧ). In Greek fable, a queen of Ethiopia, mother of Andromeda, made a constellation after her death.

Castalia or **Castaly** (ças-tā'li-ȧ; ças'tȧ-ly). A fountain of Parnassus, sacred to the Muses.

Castle Dangerous (çȧs'l dān'gẽr-us). Title of Scott's last novel, referring to Castle Douglas, which is also termed Castle Perilous.

Castle of Indolence (ov in'dō-lenc). In the poem of this name by Thomson, the castle is a luxurious abode in the land of Drowsiness. It is owned by an enchanter, who deprives all visitors of their strength and will power.

Castle of Otranto (ō-tran'tō). A novel by Horace Walpole, abounding in mystery, horror, and supernatural incidents.

Castle Perilous (per'i-lus). Abode of Lyonors in Tennyson's *Gareth and Lynette*.

Castlewood (çȧs'l-wood). The title of a family in Thackeray's *Henry Esmond*. See **Esmond.**

Castor and Pollux (ças'tŏr and pol'uks). Twin deities among the Greeks and Romans, sons of Jupiter, latterly placed among the stars as Gemini or the Twins.

Castorp (çäs'to̤rp), **Hans.** In Thomas Mann's *Magic Mountain*, a young engineer from Hamburg whose whole life is changed for the better by a sojourn in a Swiss sanitarium, but from which he goes to war, presumably to be killed.

Catherine (çath'ẽr-in), **St., of Alexandria.** Patron saint of unmarried women and girls, whose symbol is the wheel. Legend has it that she escaped death at the wheel, to which she had been condemned for professing Christianity, but was beheaded.

Cato (çā'tō). The hero and title of a tragedy by Addison, based on the story of the ancient Roman who committed suicide to avoid falling into Caesar's hands.

Caudle (ça̤'dl), **Mrs.** A lady who figures in a series of humorous papers by Douglas Jerrold, professing to give the *Curtain Lectures* she delivered to her patient spouse.

Cauline (ça̤'lin), **Sir.** See **Christabelle.**

Cawther (ça̤'thẽr). The lake of paradise in the Koran, with sweet and cool waters. He who drinks from it never thirsts again.

Cecilia (ce-cil'i-ȧ). The heroine of a novel by Fanny Burney.—**St.** Patroness of music.

Cedric (ced'riç). The wealthy Saxon thane in Scott's *Ivanhoe*, father of the hero. The name appears to be borrowed from a historic king, Cerdic.

Celestial City (ce-les'chăl cit'y). Name for heaven in Bunyan's *Pilgrim's Progress*, to which Christian makes his pilgrimage from the City of Destruction. —A name for Peking, China.

Celia (cēl'yȧ). Daughter of Frederick, the usurping duke in Shakespeare's *As You Like It*, and bosom friend of Rosalind, with whom she goes, both in disguise, to the forest of Arden.

Cenci (chen'chī) **Family.** A historical family, which included Beatrice Cenci (1577–99), 'the beautiful parricide.' With her brothers, stepmother, and others she arranged the murder of her father because of his cruelty to his wife and children. The conspirators were executed after a famous trial. Among many treatments, Shelley's tragedy *The Cenci* is notable.

Ceres (cē'rēş). The Roman goddess of agriculture and the fruits of the harvest, identified with the Greek Demeter.

Chadband (chad'band), **Rev. Mr.** A hypocritical clergyman in Dickens' *Bleak House*.

Charlus, de (dē chär-lů'), **Baron.** A sinister figure, a homosexual, who dominates the later volumes of Marcel Proust's *Remembrance of Things Past*. He is a member of the Guermantes family.

Charmaine (çhär-mān'). The promiscuous innkeeper's daughter in *What Price Glory*, a play by Maxwell Anderson and Lawrence Stallings, for whose affections Captain Flagg and Sergeant Quirt are rivals.

Charon (çā'ron; çâr'ŏn). The Greek and Roman deity of the lower world who ferried the souls of the dead across the Styx to Hades.

Charybdis (çȧ-ryb'dis). See **Scylla.**

Chatterley (chat'ẽr-ly), **Lady Constance.** The neurotic wife of a semiparalyzed old aristocrat in D. H. Lawrence's *Lady Chatterley's Lover*. The frankness with which her love affair with her lodgekeeper is delineated caused the book to be banned.

Chauchat (çhō-çhȧ'), **Clavdia.** A beautiful Russian woman with whom Hans Castorp is in love in Mann's *Magic Mountain*.

Cheeryble Brothers (chēr'y-bl brŏth'ẽrş). Two merchants in Dickens' *Nicholas Nickleby*, alike in their kind and benevolent characters.

Chester (ches'tẽr), **Sir John.** A villainous fine gentleman in Dickens' *Barnaby Rudge*, supposed to be intended as a portrait of Lord Chesterfield.

Chevalier (çhev-ȧ-lēr'), **the Young.** Charles Edward Stuart (1720–88), usually called the Young Pretender.

Chevy Chase (chev'y chās). A famous old ballad describing a contest near the Cheviot Hills between Percy and Douglas and their followers, supposed to stand for the battle of Otterburn.

Cheyne (che̤'nē), **Harvey.** A millionaire's spoiled son in Kipling's novel *Captains Courageous*, who falls from the deck of an Atlantic liner and is picked up by a dory from a Gloucester fishing schooner. The captain, Disko Troop, does not believe Harvey's story of his wealth, and the boy has to stay with the schooner until the fishing season is over. The wholesome discipline and hard work remake Harvey, to his father's delight.

Chichikov (chī'chi-ko̤f). A crafty and ambitious petty official in Gogol's humorous novel *Dead Souls*, who sees a way to become a wealthy landowner through the technical acquisition of numerous serfs. He accordingly travels around Russia buying up 'dead souls,' that is, serfs who have died since the last census and therefore are not yet officially dead. The scheme goes well until he is detected.

Chick (chik), **Mr. and Mrs.** Brother-in-law and sister of Mr. Dombey in Dickens' *Dombey and Son*. Mrs. Chick was convinced that the first Mrs. Dombey might have recovered from her last illness if she had only 'made an effort.'

Chicken (chik'en), **the Game.** A low fellow taken up by Mr. Toots to instruct him in the noble art of self-defense in Dickens' *Dombey and Son*.

Childe Harold (chīld här'ŏld). See **Harold.**

Chillon (çhi-lon'; *Fr.* çhī-yoṅ'), **Prisoner of.** Bonnivard, the Genevese patriot, imprisoned for his republican principles by the duke-bishop of Savoy. Lord Byron has a poem on the subject, in which, however, fictitious matter is introduced.

Chingachgook (chin-gach'gook). Chief of the Mohicans and father of Uncas, in Cooper's *Leatherstocking Tales*.

Chips (chips), **Mr.** A popular and kindly English schoolmaster in James Hilton's novel *Goodbye, Mr. Chips*.

Chiron (çhī'ron). In Greek mythology, one of the centaurs, famed for his knowledge of medicine, music, and other arts, the preceptor of Achilles and other heroes of ancient Greece.

Chloë (çhlō'ē). A shepherdess in the famous pastoral romance of *Daphnis and Chloë*, attributed to the Greek writer Longus (3rd century after Christ). Often used generally for a rustic beauty or sweetheart.

Chocolate Soldier (cho̤ç'ō-lăt sōl'jẽr). A character in the light opera of the same name by Oscar Straus. See **Bluntschli.**

Chriemhild (çhrēm'hilt). See **Kriemhild.**

Christabel (çhris'tȧ-bel). The heroine of a beautiful but unfinished romantic poem by Coleridge.

Christabelle (çhris'tȧ-bel). An Irish princess, daughter of a 'bonnye kinge,' who fell in love with Sir Cauline, the hero of an old English ballad, extant in the Percy *Reliques*.

Christian (çhris'chăn). The hero of Bunyan's *Pilgrim's Progress*, an allegory of the experiences and vicissitudes of Christian life.

Christiana (çhris-ti-an'ȧ). The wife of Christian in Bunyan's *Pilgrim's Progress*, who leaves her home with her children, under the guidance of Mr. Greatheart, to join her husband in the Celestial City.

Christian King (king), **Most.** A title bestowed on the kings of France by the popes from early times.

Christie (çhris'ti), **Anna.** A prostitute who is the leading character in Eugene O'Neill's play of the same name.

Christophe (çhrīs-to̤f)', **Jean.** The hero of Romain Rolland's novel of the same name, a musician who is concerned with the social order.

Christopher Robin (çhris'tō-fẽr rob'in). A child (the son of the author) who figures in the poems of A. A. Milne, *When We Were Very Young*, *Now We Are Six*, etc.

Chrononhotonthologos (çhrō-non'hō-ton-thol'ō-gos). The hero of the burlesque of same name. See **Aldiborontephoscophornio.**

Chuzzlewit (chuz'l-wit), **Martin.** The hero of Dickens' novel of same name.

Cid (cid), **the.** A famous Spaniard, Rodrigo or Ruy Diaz de Bivar (*c.* 1040–99), who was always victorious in battle, and of whom many colorful accounts, based on fact and legend, have been written. Noteworthy is Corneille's *Le Cid*.

Cimmerians (ci-mēr'i-ănş). A people fabled by Homer to live in a land of darkness.

Cinderella (cin'dẽr-el'ȧ). The heroine of a well-known and widely-spread fairy tale.

Circe (cĩr'cē). A sorceress of Greek mythology. She converted the companions of Ulysses into swine, but he overcame her enchantment by means of the herb called moly, given to him by Hermes.

Circumlocution Office (cĩr-çum-lō-çū'shun of'ic). The name applied by Dickens in *Little Dorrit* to one of the government offices, in satire of the inefficiency and red tape of public departments.

Clarice (çlar'ic; çlä-rī'çhe). Wife of Rinaldo in some of the old romances of the Orlando cycle.

Claudio (çla̤'di-ō). The lover of Hero in Shakespeare's *Much Ado About Nothing*.—The brother of Isabella in Shakespeare's *Measure for Measure*.

Claudius (çla̤'di-us). Hamlet's uncle, in Shakespeare's *Hamlet*, who poisoned his brother, married the widowed Gertrude, and became king.

Clayhanger (çlā'hang-ẽr), **Edwin.** The hero of Arnold Bennett's novel *Clayhanger*, one of a trilogy. He is a poor boy of Bursley, one of Bennett's Five Towns, who becomes successful, loves and loses Hilda Lessways, and then is reunited with her.

Claypole (çlā'pōl), **Noah.** A mean and dishonest charity boy in Dickens' *Oliver Twist*.

Clélie (çle̤-lē'). Heroine and title of an old French novel of the high-flown school, by Mlle. de Scudéry, founded on the legendary maiden of ancient Rome who swam the Tiber to escape from the Etruscans.

Clementina (çlem'en-tī'nȧ). A lady in Richardson's *Sir Charles Grandison*, who loses her reason through her love for the hero.

Cleon (çlē'ŏn). Governor of Tarsus in Shakespeare's *Pericles*.

Cleopatra (çlē'ō-pat'rȧ). Queen of Egypt in the time of Julius Caesar and Augustus, and heroine of many plays and novels, including several French tragedies, Shakespeare's *Antony and Cleopatra*, Dryden's *All for Love*, and Shaw's *Caesar and Cleopatra*.

Clifford (çlif'ŏrd), **Paul.** A romantic highwayman, the hero of Bulwer-Lytton's novel of same name, reformed by virtuous love.

Clim of the Clough (çlim). See **Clym.**

Clinker (çliṅk'ẽr), **Humph: y.** The hero of a novel of the same name by Smollett, brought up in the workhouse, and latterly employed as a servant by Matthew Bramble. He turns out to be a natural son of his employer, and marries his fellow servant, Winifred Jenkins.

Clio (çlī'ō). One of the nine Muses, having history as her province.

Clotho (çlō'thō). One of the three Fates or Parcae among the Greeks and Romans, the one who spun the thread of life. The other two were Atropos and Lachesis.

Cloudesley (çloudş'li), **William of.** A famous north-country archer and outlaw in English legend, whose companions were Clym of the Clough and Adam Bell.

Clout (çlout), **Colin.** See **Colin Clout.**

Clym of the Clough (çlym ov the çluf). A noted outlaw of legend, who, with Adam Bell and William of Cloudesley, was a famous bowman of the north of England. The chief resort of these outlaws was Englewood Forest, near Carlisle.

Clytemnestra (çly̆-tem-nes'trȧ). The wife of Agamemnon, whom she and her paramour Aegisthus murdered on his return from Troy. She was slain by her son Orestes.

Clytie (çly̆'ti-ē). A nymph of classical story who fell in love with Apollo, and was changed into a sunflower.

Cockaigne (ço̤ç-ān'), **Land of.** An imaginary country where all sorts of good things are to be had for the taking, and exist in overflowing abundance, celebrated both in French and English literature.

Cocytus (çō-çy̆'tus). In classical mythology, a river of the infernal regions.

Coignard (çwo-nyär'), **Jerome.** A licentious but philosophical abbé in Anatole France's novels *At the Sign of the Reine Pédauque* and *The Opinions of Monsieur Jerome Coignard*. He is kindly and moral after his own fashion. Many of the opinions he expresses are presumably those of the author.

Cole (çōl), **King.** A legendary British king, noted for his jovial disposition.

Colin Clout (çō'lin çlout). The pastoral name assumed by the poet Spenser in *The Shepherd's Calendar* and *Colin Clout's Come Home Again*.

Colleen Bawn (ço̤l'ēn ba̤n). The fair-haired heroine of a drama by Dion Boucicault so named.

Collin (çō-laṅ') **Jacques.** A villainous and criminal character who appears in several of Balzac's novels, under various disguises and names; thus, as 'Vautrin' in *Le Père Goriot* and elsewhere.

Colossus of Rhodes (çō-los'us ov rōdş). A huge brazen statue of Apollo, esteemed as one of the wonders of the world.

Comedy of Errors (ço̤m'e-dy ov er'ŏrş). One of Shakespeare's plays, involving, with considerable resultant confusion, the identities of two pairs of twin brothers. See **Antipholus, Dromio.**

Comus (çō'mus). A god of revelry among the ancients; in Milton's masque of same name, a lewd enchanter.

Coningsby (ço̤n'ingş-by). The hero of a novel by Disraeli (Earl of Beaconsfield), standing as a type of the Young England party.

Conrad (ço̤n'rad). The hero of Byron's *Corsair*, and of *Lara* also.

Cophetua (çō-fet'ū-ȧ). A legendary king of Africa, celebrated in a ballad as having loved and married a beggar maid.

Copperfield (ço̤p'ẽr-fēld), **David.** The hero of Dickens' novel of same name, in which are introduced also Mr. Micawber, David's great-aunt Betsy Trotwood, the Peggottys, Mrs. Gummidge, Steerforth, Uriah Heep, Agnes Wickfield, Mr. Dick, etc. Experiences of Dickens' own early life are embodied in the novel.

Cordelia (çor-dēl'yȧ). In Shakespeare's *King Lear*, the youngest and only loyal daughter of the king, whose mind, however, is turned against her, so that he disinherits her and divides his kingdom between her two sisters. See **Lear.**

Corinne (çō-rin'). The heroine of a novel by Madame de Staël, caused to pine away by the falsity of her lover.

Coriolanus (çor'i-ō-lā'nus), **Caius Marcius.** A noble Roman on whose legendary history Shakespeare based his *Coriolanus*.

Corydon (çor'y-dŏn). The name of a shepherd in the poems of Theocritus and Virgil; hence a shepherd or rustic in general.

Cosette (çō-şet'). The daughter of Fantine in Victor Hugo's *Les Misérables*. She is protected by Jean Valjean and loved by Marius.

Costard (ços'tärd). A clown in Shakespeare's *Love's Labour's Lost*.

Count of Monte Cristo (çount ov mon'tē çris'tō). See **Dantès, Edmond.**

Coverley (çŏv'ẽr-li), **Sir Roger de.** An old knight and country gentleman pictured by Steele and Addison in the pages of the *Spectator*, a delightful compound of simplicity, modesty, benevolence, harmless pomposity, eccentricity, and whim.

Cowperwood (çou'pẽr-wood), **Frank.** The central figure in Theodore Dreiser's novels *The Financier*, *The Titan*, and *The Stoic*. He is a magnetic, ruthless personality, whose brilliant career is interrupted by a prison sentence for illegal dealings. In *The Titan* he comes out of prison and rebuilds his fortune.

Crabtree (çrab'trē), **Cadwallader.** A character in Smollett's *Peregrine Pickle*, a cynical old man who delights in exposing the weaknesses and follies of society.

Crane (çrān), **Dame Alison and her husband.** Characters in Scott's *Kenilworth*, who kept the Crane Inn.

Crane, Ichabod. A character in Washington Irving's *Legend of Sleepy Hollow*, an awkward and credulous schoolmaster.

Cratchit (çrach'it), **Bob.** Father of Tiny Tim in Dickens' *Christmas Carol*, clerk to Scrooge, impecunious but far happier than his miserly employer.

Crawley (çrą'li). The name of an aristocratic family in Thackeray's *Vanity Fair*. Old Sir Pitt is a sad reprobate, miserly, ignorant, coarse, and drunken, but not devoid of shrewdness. His son Pitt, latterly Sir Pitt, is the very reverse of this, but pompous, priggish, and dull. His other son, Rawdon, a heavy dragoon, is a careless spendthrift, always in debt. Rawdon marries Becky Sharp, but her intimacy with Lord Steyne makes him throw her off. The Rev. Bute Crawley, brother of old Sir Pitt, is a sport-loving, easygoing parson, with a clever wife.

Cressida (çres'i-dȧ). The fair but frail heroine of Shakespeare's *Troilus and Cressida*, sung also by Chaucer. See **Troilus.**

Crichton (çrī'tŏn), **the Admirable.** A butler in J. M. Barrie's play of the same name, whose personal superiority makes him the leader of a shipwrecked group on a desert island, and who becomes engaged to Lady Mary, daughter of his employer, the Earl of Loam.

Crispin (çris'pin). The patron saint of shoemakers. He and his brother Crispian are said to have preached the gospel in Gaul, and supported themselves by making shoes.

Croaker (çrōk'ẽr), **Mr. and Mrs.** Characters in Goldsmith's comedy *The Good-Natured Man*, the former a perpetual grumbler, the latter, gay and lighthearted.

Croftangry (çroft'añ-gry), **Chrystal.** One of Scott's fictitious characters, represented as having written two of the Waverley novels. His history is related in the introduction to *The Highland Widow*.

Cronus (çrō'nus). A Greek deity, son of Uranus and Ge (Heaven and Earth), corresponding to the Roman Saturn.

Cronshaw (çron'shą). A poet of the Montparnasse cafés in Somerset Maugham's *Of Human Bondage*, who dies miserably in a London slum.

Crook-fingered Jack ((çrook'fiñ'gẽrd jak). One of the light-fingered gentry in Gay's *Beggar's Opera*.

Crosby (çroş'by), **Jane.** Heroine of Owen Davis' play *Icebound*. See **Jordans.**

Croye (croi), **Isabelle, Countess de.** Heroine of Scott's *Quentin Durward*, a Burgundian heiress who ultimately marries the novel's hero.

Crummles (çrum'lz), **Mr. Vincent.** In Dickens' *Nicholas Nickleby*, a kindhearted, eccentric theatrical manager, in whose theatrical company Nicholas is engaged for a time.

Cruncher (çrun'chẽr), **Jerry.** A character in Dickens' *Tale of Two Cities*.

Crupp (çrup), **Mrs.** David's landlady in Dickens' *David Copperfield*.

Crusoe (çrū'sō), **Robinson.** The hero of Defoe's famous story of life as a castaway.

Cupid (çū'pid). The Roman god of love, son of Venus, the goddess of beauty. He is usually depicted as a naked infant with wings, armed with a bow and a quiver full of arrows. Identified with the Greek Eros.

Custance (çus'tănc). Daughter of a Roman emperor, married to King Alla of Northumberland. See Chaucer's *Canterbury Tales: Man of Law's Tale.*—A character in the first English comedy, *Ralph Roister Doister*, by Udall.

Cuttle (çut'l), **Captain.** A retired sea captain in Dickens' *Dombey and Son*, simple, credulous, warmhearted, and generous. He has an iron hook in place of one of his hands, and a favorite saying of his is, 'When found make a note of.'

Cybele (cyb'e-lē). A goddess of agriculture and settled life among the Greeks and Romans, represented with a sort of towered crown on her head.

Cyclops *or* **Cyclopes** (cȳ'çlops; cȳ'çlō-pēş). Three giants of the race of Titans, according to Greek mythology sons of Uranus (Heaven) and Ge (Earth), who forged the thunderbolts of Zeus, and were the patrons of smiths.—Also a fabled race of one-eyed giants, Polyphemus their chief, described in the *Odyssey* as inhabiting Sicily.

Cymbeline (cym'be-līn). A semimythical king of Britain, standing for the historical Cunobelinus, whose name occurs on coins.—Character in Shakespeare's play so named.

Cynthia (cyn'thi-ȧ). A name for Diana or the moon. —In Fletcher's *Purple Island*, and Spenser's *Colin Clout's Come Home Again*, a name for Queen Elizabeth.

Cyrano de Bergerac (cē-rȧ-nō'dē ber-zē-răç'). The huge-nosed hero of the drama of the same name by Edmond Rostand, a witty Gascon soldier who woos and wins Roxane for a handsome but stupid friend, and tells of his love for her only when he is dying.

Cytherea (cyth-e-rē'ȧ). An epithet of Aphrodite or Venus, from the island of Cythera.

Czepanek (tchē-pan'ek), **Lily.** The talented but immoral heroine of Hermann Sudermann's *Song of Songs*, whose gradual degeneration is traced in the novel.

D

Daedalus (ded'ȧ-lus). A mythical Greek sculptor and artificer, architect of the Cretan labyrinth, from imprisonment in which he escaped by means of wings invented by himself. His son Icarus accompanied him, but was drowned.

Dagon (dā'gon). The chief deity of the Philistines, represented as half man, half fish, by Milton made one of the fallen angels.

Dagonet (dag'ō-net), **Sir.** The court fool of the famous King Arthur.

Dalloway (dal'ō-wā), **Clarissa.** The central character in Virginia Woolf's *Mrs. Dalloway*, an English society woman whose activities during one day serve as the novel's framework.

Damocles (dam'ō-çlēş). A courtier, envious of pomp and power, whom Dionysius, ruler of Syracuse, treated to a splendid feast, but over whose head a naked sword was suspended by a hair, as a lesson that danger may overhang greatness and outward felicity.

Damon (dā'mŏn). A goatherd in Virgil's *Eclogues*; hence, any rustic swain.

Damon and Pythias (pyth'i-ăs). Two Syracusans, whose names have become a symbol of friendship. When Pythias was condemned to death, but was allowed to go home to settle his affairs, Damon took his place as surety. Pythias returned in the nick of time, saving Damon from execution. In reward for this impressive display of mutual friendship, both were pardoned.

Danaë (dan'ā-ē). In Greek legend, a princess shut up in a brazen tower, to which Jove gained access in the form of a golden shower, and thus became by her the father of Perseus.

Danaides *or* **Danaids** (dȧ-nā'i-dēş; dan'ā-idş). In Greek legend, the fifty daughters of Danaüs, king of Argos, who married the fifty sons of Aegyptus. At their father's command, all but one killed their husbands on their wedding night. The forty-nine were condemned to draw water in sieves interminably in Hades.

Dandin (dän-dań'), **George.** The hero of a comedy of same name by Molière, a wealthy plebeian who marries a highborn wife, and realizes too late that he has brought on himself countless burdens and humiliations.

Dangle (dañ'gl). A character in Sheridan's *The Critic*, who pesters a theatrical manager with advice and criticism.

Danny Deever (dan'y dēv'ẽr). In the popular ballad of that name by Rudyard Kipling, a soldier hanged for murder.

Dantès (dän-tes'), **Edmond.** The hero of *The Count of Monte Cristo*, by Alexandre Dumas, who is sentenced on a false charge to life imprisonment in the Chateau d'If. After many years, during which he has laboriously dug through thick walls, he manages to escape. He finds buried treasure on the island of Monte Cristo, the whereabouts of which he has learned in prison, and becomes a powerful and vengeful figure.

Daphne (daf'nē). A nymph pursued by Apollo, whom she escaped by being changed into a laurel.

Daphnis (daf'nis). In Greek mythology, a Sicilian shepherd, son of Mercury and inventor of pastoral poetry.—A goatherd in love with Chloë. See **Chloë.**

Darby and Joan (där'by and jōn). A married couple, typical of simple domestic happiness, celebrated in an old ballad.

Darcy (där'cy). The hero of Jane Austen's *Pride and Prejudice*, who finally manages to surmount his own pride and Elizabeth's prejudice. See **Bennet Family.**

Darnay (där-nā'), **Charles.** In Dickens' *Tale of Two Cities*, the lover and ultimately the husband of Lucie Manette, saved from the guillotine by Sydney Carton, whom he resembles physically.

Darrell (dar'el), **Ned.** The doctor who is father of Nina's son Gordon in Eugene O'Neill's play *Strange Interlude*.

D'Artagnan (dár-tá-nyän'). See **Artagnan, d'.**

Dartle (därt'l), **Rosa.** Companion to Mrs. Steerforth in Dickens' *David Copperfield*, an intensely passionate woman, cherishing a fierce but vain love for Steerforth.

Davidson (dā'vid-sŏn), **Reverend.** The missionary in the short story *Miss Thompson*, by Somerset Maugham, and its dramatization entitled *Rain*. He attempts to regenerate Sadie Thompson, but then disillusions her by evincing the same lusts as other men she has known.

Davus (dā'vus). A common name for a slave in Latin comedy.

Daw (dą), **Majorie.** A supposititious character in the short story of the same name by T. B. Aldrich. Though only imaginary, she is described as real in letters written by one character in the story to another, and the latter falls in love with her.

Deans (dēnş), **Jeanie and Effie.** The heroines of Scott's *Heart of Midlothian*, daughters of the cowfeeder or dairyman Davie Deans. Effie is seduced by George Staunton and is (wrongly) condemned for child murder, but Jeanie trudges all the way to London and obtains her pardon. Their father is very strict in religious matters and strong in theological controversy.

Dedalus (ded'ȧ-lus), **Stephen.** A leading character, largely autobiographical, in James Joyce's *Portrait of the Artist as a Young Man* and *Ulysses*. In the latter he is a disillusioned young writer befriended by Leopold Bloom; and his quest of a spiritual father parallels Telemachus' search for Ulysses.

Dedlock (ded'lok), **Lady.** The wife of Sir Leicester Dedlock in Dickens' *Bleak House*, mother out of wedlock to Esther Summerson.

Deerslayer (dēr'slā'ẽr). See **Leatherstocking.**

Deever (dēv'ẽr), **Danny.** See **Danny Deever.**

Defarge (dē-färz'), **Madame.** One of the bloodthirsty women of the French Revolution in Dickens' *Tale of Two Cities*, a hater of all aristocrats.

Deianira (dē-yȧ-nī'rȧ). The wife of Hercules, she was carried off by the centaur Nessus, who was stopped by a poisoned arrow shot by Hercules. Deianira, deceived by the dying Nessus into believing that his blood would serve as a love charm, later gave Hercules (sending it by Lichas) a shirt which she had steeped in the blood. The residual poison had so agonizing an effect that Hercules put an end to his life, and Deianira hanged herself in remorse.

Delectable Mountains (de-leç'tȧ-bl moun'tiṇş). In Bunyan's *Pilgrim's Progress*, a delightful range from which the Celestial City can be seen.

Delia (dē'li-ȧ). In classical literature, a name of Diana, from the island of Delos. Also a poetical name for a young woman generally.

Delphine (del-fīn'). Heroine of a novel by Madame de Staël, who dies of a broken heart from disappointment in love.

Demeter (de-mē'tẽr). The Greek goddess corresponding with the Roman Ceres.

Demogorgon (dē-mō-gor'gŏn; dem-ō-). A mysterious evil divinity, holding powerful sway in the unseen world.

Dennis the Hangman (den'is thē hang'măn). A despicable character in Dickens' *Barnaby Rudge*.

Deronda (de-ron'dȧ), **Daniel.** The hero of a novel of same name by George Eliot.

Desborough (deş'bŏr-ō), **Lucy.** The heroine of George Meredith's novel *The Ordeal of Richard Feverel*. See **Feverel, Richard.**

Desdemona (deş-de-mō'nȧ). The heroine of Shakespeare's *Othello*, killed by her husband Othello, who is led by the devilish malice of Iago to believe her unfaithful.

Deserted Village (de-şẽr'ted vil'āğ), **The.** 'Sweet Auburn,' the village described by Goldsmith in his well-known poem, ruined by the growth of luxury—probably not to be identified with any single real village.

Des Esseintes (dę-şe-sań'). The hero of the novel *Against the Grain* (*À rebours*) by J. K. Huysmans, a typical example of literary 'decadence.' Neurasthenic and hypersensitive, he resorts to esoteric practices to escape ennui.

Despair (de-spãr'), **Giant.** See **Giant Despair, Doubting Castle.**

Deucalion and Pyrrha (dū-çā'li-ŏn, pyr'ȧ). In Greek mythology, a man and wife who alone survived a deluge and became originators of a new race of men.

Dhu, Roderick (dū). See **Roderick Dhu.**

Diana (dī-an'ȧ). The Roman goddess corresponding to the Greek Artemis, the sister of Apollo, a virgin, goddess of hunting and of the moon.

Diana Merion (mer'i-ŏn). See **Diana of the Crossways.**

Diana of the Crossways (çroş'wāş). The Irish heroine of George Meredith's novel *Diana of the Crossways*. She is the author's conception of an ideal woman, beautiful and intelligent. Her unfortunate marriage to Mr. Warwick ends in separation because of his unjust suspicion of her relations with Lord Dannisburgh. Diana is drawn from Lady Caroline Norton, granddaughter of Richard Brinsley Sheridan.

Dick (dik), **Mr.** An amiable, half-witted gentleman in Dickens' *David Copperfield*, who thinks he is bound to prepare a certain 'memorial,' but cannot keep himself from putting into it something about the head of Charles I.

Dido (dī'dō). The mythical founder and queen of Carthage, described by Virgil in the *Aeneid* as hospitably entertaining Aeneas, falling in love with him, and putting an end to her life when he deserts her.

Diggory (dig'ō-ry). In Goldsmith's comedy *She Stoops to Conquer*, a farm laborer, called in to wait on table, who makes himself as familiar as he is awkward.

Dimmesdale (dimȩ'dāl), **Arthur.** A minister, the lover of Hester Prynne, in Nathaniel Hawthorne's *Scarlet Letter*, who confesses publicly that he is the father of her child long after she has been doomed to wear the scarlet 'A'.

Dinarzade (dī-när-zäd'e). Sister of Scheherazade in the *Arabian Nights.*

Dinmont (din'mont), **Dandie** (that is, Andrew). A farmer in Scott's *Guy Mannering*, brawny, pugnacious, genuinely hospitable, and kindhearted.

Diomedes *or* **Diomede** (dī-ō-mē'dēș; dī'ō-mēd). A renowned Grecian chief at the siege of Troy, son of Tydeus, and hence called Tydides.

Dionysus (dī-ō-nȳ'sus). A Greek name of the god Bacchus.

Dioscuri (dī-os-çū'rī). A name of the twins Castor and Pollux.

Dishart (dish'ärt), **Gavin.** The Scottish minister in Barrie's *Little Minister*, who loves Babbie, the gypsy, at whom his parishioners look askance, while his mother, Margaret, is dismayed at the whole affair.

Distaffina (dis-tȧ-fī'nȧ). Heroine of Rhodes' burlesque *Bombastes Furioso*, beloved by Bombastes, whom she jilts.

Ditte (dit). A Danish peasant girl in Martin Andersen Nexö's book of the same name.

Dives (dī'vēș). The Latin word for a rich man, which came to be used as a sort of proper name for the rich man of the parable of Lazarus, and hence for a luxurious rich man generally.

Dobbin (dob'in), **Colonel.** One of the chief characters in Thackeray's *Vanity Fair*, an excellent soldier and thorough gentleman, but somewhat shy and awkward. He is a faithful friend of George Osborne and in love with Amelia Sedley, whom he ultimately marries.

Dodson and Fogg (dod'sŏn and fog). The pettifogging lawyers who carry on the breach-of-promise action against Mr. Pickwick in Dickens' *Pickwick Papers.*

Dodsworth (dodș'wŏrth), **Samuel.** The chief character in Sinclair Lewis' novel *Dodsworth*, a wealthy American automobile manufacturer who visits Europe with his frivolous wife and achieves a new stability.

Doe (dō), **John.** An imaginary person whose name used to appear in certain English actions at law, along with that of Richard Roe, an equally fictitious personage. Hence, in common usage, an anonymous person.

Dogberry and Verges (dog'ber-y and vẽr'ġeș). Two ridiculous constables in Shakespeare's *Much Ado about Nothing.*

Dollalolla (dol-ȧ-lol'ȧ). Wife of King Arthur in Fielding's burlesque *Tom Thumb*, in love with the little hero.

Doll Common (dol çom'ŏn). A young woman who helps Subtle in Ben Jonson's *Alchemist.*

Doll Tearsheet (dol tãr'shēt). A strumpet in Shakespeare's *Henry IV.*

Dolon (dō'lŏn). In Homer's *Iliad*, a spy from Troy, detected by Ulysses.

Dombey (dom'bi), **Mr.** In Dickens' *Dombey and Son*, a wealthy London merchant, full of pride and self-importance. His son Paul, a sensitive and delicate boy, is not equal to the rigors of Dr. Blimber's school. Paul's death is a hard blow to his father, who had had great hopes for him and has no love, but indeed only resentment, for his daughter Florence.

Donatello (don-ȧ-tel'ō), **Count.** A young Italian in Nathaniel Hawthorne's *Marble Faun*, who resembles the Faun of Praxiteles. He leads a simple animal life until crime changes him.

Don Juan (don jụ'ăn *or Sp.* dōn hwän'). The legendary Spanish hero of many peoms and dramas, a typical libertine who made innumerable conquests, killed the father of one of his victims, and was at last carried off to the infernal regions. The material has been used, among others, by Gabriel Téllez, Molière, Corneille, Rostand, Shaw, and Mozart (the opera *Don Giovanni*). Byron's poem of this name makes almost no use of the legend.

Don Quixote (don kwik'sŏt *or Sp.* dōn kī-hō'tȩ). The hero of the great Spanish romance of Cervantes, a Castilian country gentleman so crazed by reading books of chivalry that he sallies forth as a knight-errant to succor the oppressed and redress wrongs. As his squire he takes along with him Sancho Panza, a pot-bellied peasant, ignorant but shrewd, selfish but faithful to his master. The knight, mounted on his steed Rosinante, as gaunt as its rider, and the squire on his ass Dapple, have various amusing experiences, since the don looks upon flocks of sheep as armies, windmills as giants, and galley slaves as oppressed gentlemen. See **Dulcinea.**

Dooley (dọọ'li), **Mr.** A fictitious Irish-American character, humorous and politically astute, appearing in several volumes, bearing his name in the titles, by F. P. Dunne.

Doolittle(dọọ'lit-l), **Eliza.** The heroine of G. B. Shaw's play *Pygmalion*. She is a cockney flower-seller, who is transformed into a 'lady' by Henry Higgins, a professor of phonetics. Her changed status at first makes her miserable, but the professor eventually falls in love with his 'Galatea.' Her father, Mr. Doolittle, is a dustman who champions the 'undeserving poor.'

Doone (dọọn), **Lorna.** The heroine of the novel of the same name by R. D. Blackmore, who saves John Ridd from her outlaw relatives and ultimately marries him.

Dorinda (dọr-in'dȧ). Daughter of Lady Bountiful. See **Aimwell.**

Dorothea (dọr-ō-thē'ȧ). The heroine of Massinger's *Virgin Martyr.*—Heroine of Goethe's poem *Hermann and Dorothea.*

Dorothy la Désirée (dọr'ō-thy lä dę'și-rę'). A daughter of Count Manuel in Cabell's *Jurgen*, the beautiful girl whom Jurgen loved in his youth.

Dorrit (dọr'it), **Little.** See **Little Dorrit.**

Dot (dot). The pet name of Mrs. Peerybingle, in Dickens' *Cricket on the Hearth.*

Dotheboys Hall (dö-the-boiș) (that is, 'do the boys,' cheat them). The famous academy of the ignorant and brutal schoolmaster Squeers in Dickens' *Nicholas Nickleby.*

Double Dealer (dub'l dē'lẽr). See **Maskwell.**

Doubting Castle (dout'ing çȧs'l). The castle of Giant Despair in *Pilgrim's Progress.*

Douglas (dug'lȧs). A great Scottish family, famous in history and legend, many members of which figure, notably, in Scott's novels and poems.

Douglas, Ellen. Heroine of Scott's *Lady of the Lake.*

Dromio (drō'mi-ō). The name of the twin brothers in Shakespeare's *Comedy of Errors* who serve the twin brothers Antipholus.

Dryasdust (drȳ'aș-dust), **Rev. Dr.** A fictitious personage brought forward by Scott to introduce some of his novels. The name, hence, applies to a historical writer or investigator of the driest and most matter-of-fact kind.

Dryope (drȳ'ō-pē.) A nymph of Greek mythology changed into a poplar.

Duenna (dū-en'ȧ), **the.** Margaret, in Sheridan's comic opera *The Duenna*, who assists her charge Louisa in marrying her lover Don Antonio.

Duessa (dū-es'ȧ). A witch in Spenser's *Faërie Queene*, who deceives the Red Cross Knight and becomes the leman of the giant Orgoglio, but she and her paramour are overthrown by Prince Arthur.

Duke (dūk), **the Iron.** The first duke of Wellington, also called the Great Duke.

Dulcinea del Toboso (dul-cin'ē-ȧ del tō-bō'sō). The country girl whom Don Quixote selects as the lady of his knightly devotion.

Dumain (dū-mān'). A French lord in Shakespeare's *Love's Labour's Lost.*

Dumbiedikes (dum'bi-dīks). A bashful young laird in Scott's *Heart of Midlothian*, fond of money and also of Jeanie Deans, to whom he pays his addresses (without effect) in the most silent and undemonstrative way. His father, the old laird, is a stubborn and exacting landlord.

Duncan (duñ'çăn). The king of Scotland, murdered by Macbeth, in Shakespeare's tragedy *Macbeth.*

Dundreary (dun-drē'ry), **Lord.** The chief character in Tom Taylor's play *Our American Cousin*, an amusing portrait of a nobleman whose head is full of trivialities and whimsicalities.

Dupin (dụ-pañ'), **C. Auguste.** A keen amateur detective in Poe's stories *The Murders in the Rue Morgue, The Mystery of Marie Rogêt*, and *The Purloined Letter.*

Durandana *or* **Durandal** (dū-răn-dä'nȧ; dū'răn-däl). The wonderful sword of Orlando, the hero of Italian romance.

Durbeyfield (dũr'bi-fēld), **Tess.** The heroine of Hardy's *Tess of the D' Urbervilles*, who is betrayed by Alec D'Urberville. Hardy arraigns society for its cruel treatment of her.

Durden (dũr'den), **Dame.** A lady of the country, named in an old glee. The name is given playfully to Esther Summerson in Dickens' *Bleak House.*

Durward (dũr'wȧrd), **Quentin.** The hero of Scott's novel of same name, an archer in the Scottish Guard of Louis XI of France, who finally wins the hand of the young Countess Isabelle de Croye.

Duval (dū-val'), **Denis.** The hero of Thackeray's unfinished novel *Denis Duval.*

E

Ea (ę'ä). In Babylonian mythology, the god of the atmospheric deep on which the world floated, and of the ocean, rivers, and streams, whose commands were carried into effect by his son Merodach.

Earnshaw (ẽrn'shạ), **Catherine.** The heroine of Emily Brontë's *Wuthering Heights*, who loves Heathcliff, and reaches out to him even after her death.

Earwicker (ẽr'wik-ẽr), **Humphrey Chimpden.** The principal character in James Joyce's *Finnegans Wake*, the keeper of a public-house in Dublin, whose memories, fantasies, and even unconscious personality are portrayed. He is also numerous other characters, fictitious, legendary, and historical, and in general represents the masculine principle of the universe. His wife Maggie represents the feminine principle, especially in her form as Anna Livia Plurabelle, a personification of the river Liffey.

Eastward Ho (ēst'wȧrd hō). The name of a drama (1605) by Ben Jonson, Chapman, and Marston. For its satire of the Scots, the authors were briefly imprisoned.

Easy (ē'șy), **Sir Charles and Lady.** A lazy gentleman of loose morals and his wife in Cibber's *Careless Husband.*

Easy, Jack. The hero of Captain Marryat's novel *Mr. Midshipman Easy.*

Eblis *or* **Iblis** (eb'lis; ib'lis). In Mohammedan mythology, the chief of the evil angels.

Edgar (ed'gär). Son of Gloucester and half-brother of Edmund in Shakespeare's *King Lear.*

Edgar, Master of Ravenswood. See **Ravenswood.**

Edmund (ed'mund). The wicked natural son of Gloucester in Shakespeare's *King Lear*, with whom both Goneril and Regan are in love.

Edyrn (ed'ĭrn). An evil character reformed at King Arthur's court in Tennyson's *Idylls of the King.*

Egeria (ē-ġē'ri-ȧ). In Roman legend, a nymph from whom King Numa Pompilius is said to have received instructions in regard to religious institutions.

Egeus (ē-ġē'us). Father of Hermia in Shakespeare's *Midsummer Night's Dream.*

Eglamour (eg'lȧ-mör), **Sir.** A knight of King Arthur who slew a dragon.

Eglantine (eg'lăn-tīn). The prioress in Chaucer's *Canterbury Tales.*

Elaine (ē-lān'). A damsel of the time of King Arthur, who pines and dies of love for Lancelot; the heroine of one of Tennyson's *Idylls.*

Eldorado (el-dō-rä'dō). The name of a country, exceedingly rich in gold, once imagined to exist in the Orinoco region of S. America.

Electra (ē-leç'trȧ). The daughter of Agamemnon and Clytemnestra, and sister of Orestes, whom she abetted in the murder of their mother, to avenge the death of their father. Her story was treated by the Greek tragedians Aeschylus, Sophocles, and Euripides.

Elmo (el'mō), **St.** The patron saint of sailors. He is invoked by Italian sailors during storms.

Elsie (el'si). The heroine of Longfellow's *Golden Legend*, who offers to give her life to cure Prince Henry, but instead becomes his bride.

Elton (el'tŏn), **Mr. and Mrs.** A young clergyman and his wife in Jane Austen's *Emma.*

Elvira (el-vī'rȧ). A character in Sheridan's *Pizarro;* in Mozart's opera *Don Giovanni* (wife of the don); in Bellini's opera *I Puritani;* in Verdi's opera *Ernani.*

Emelie (em'e-lē). Sister-in-law of Theseus, and married to Palamon in Chaucer's *Knight's Tale*. Called Emilia in other versions of the story.

Emerald Isle (em'ẽr-ăld īl). Ireland, so called from the vivid green of the verdure of that country.

Émile (ę-mīl'). In Rousseau's didactic romance of this name, a boy who is brought up in conformity with the author's concept of proper education.

Emilia (e-mil'yä). Wife of Iago, and the waiting woman to Desdemona, in Shakespeare's *Othello*, misled by her husband so as to bring about the catastrophe.—Hermione's friend in Shakespeare's *Winter's Tale.*—Lady-love of the titular hero of Smollett's *Peregrine Pickle*. See also **Emelie.**

Emilia (ę-mil'yä), **Doña.** The gracious but neglected wife of Charles Gould in Joseph Conrad's novel *Nostromo*. She has been called the 'most moving figure in all Conrad's books.'

Emily (em'i-ly). 'Little Em'ly,' niece of Daniel Peggotty in Dickens' *David Copperfield*, betrothed to Ham Peggotty but seduced by Steerforth.

Emma (em'ȧ). See **Woodhouse, Emma.**

Empedocles (em-ped'ō-çlēș). One of Pythagoras' scholars, who, according to the legend, threw himself into the crater of Etna, as told in Matthew Arnold's poem.

Emperor Jones (em'pẽr-ŏr jōnș). The leading character in the play of that name by Eugene O'Neill. He is an American Negro who sets up an empire in Africa. He is finally exposed, and pursued through the jungle by the infuriated natives.

Enceladus (en-cel'ȧ-dus). A giant overthrown by the thunderbolts of Jove and cast under Etna; when he turned from one side to the other he shook the whole island.

Endymion (en-dym'i-ŏn). A beautiful shepherd, kissed by Diana as he lay asleep on Mount Latmus. Keats has a celebrated poem of this name.

English Opium Eater (iñ'glish ō'pi-um ēt'ẽr). A designation of Thomas De Quincey (1785–1859), author of *Confessions of an English Opium Eater.*

English Rabelais (rab-e-lā'). A designation of Dean Swift, from the resemblance of his writings to those of the great French writer.

Enid (ē'nid). The heroine of one of Tennyson's *Idylls*, the wife of Geraint and a perfect example of conjugal love and patience.

Eos (ē'os). In Greek mythology, the goddess of dawn, equivalent to Aurora.

Epicene (ep'i-cēn). In Ben Jonson's comedy *Epicene, or The Silent Woman*, a lad who impersonates a 'silent woman' and is married to Morose, a miserly old man who is greatly afraid of noise. Continuing the stratagem, which has been engineered by a nephew of Morose, the supposed wife immediately becomes a vociferous virago, who drives Morose to distraction. The nephew finally ends the deception in consideration of a handsome sum of money.

Epigoni (ē-pig'ō-nī) (*Gr.*, 'descendants'). Legendary Greek heroes who avenged their fathers and conquered Thebes. See **Seven against Thebes.**

Epimenides (ep-i-men'i-dēș). A sage and prophet of ancient Greece, who, according to legend, slept in a cave for fifty-seven years, and on awaking found himself possessed of prodigious wisdom.

Epimetheus (ep-i-mē'thūs). The brother of Prometheus and husband of Pandora.

Eppie (ep'i). The adopted child of Marner in George Eliot's novel *Silas Marner.*

Erato (er'ȧ-tō). One of the Muses: she presided over lyric and, especially, amatory poetry.

Erceldoune (ẽr'cel-dōn), **Thomas of.** See **Thomas the Rhymer.**
Erewhon (er'e-won). The name (an anagram on 'nowhere') of a utopian novel by Samuel Butler.
Eris (ē'ris). A Greek goddess of strife or discord.
Erlking (ẽrl'king). An evil elf or goblin of German folklore, harmful especially to children.
Erlynne (ẽr'lyn), **Mrs.** A character in Oscar Wilde's drama *Lady Windermere's Fan*, who saves the reputation of her daughter, Lady Windermere, at the expense of her own.
Erminia (ẽr-min'i-ȧ). The heroine of Tasso's *Jerusalem Delivered*.
Ernani (er-nä'nī). A robber captain in Verdi's opera of the same name.
Eros (ē'ros). The Greek name of the god of love; Cupid.
Escalus (es'çȧ-lus). A kindhearted lord associated with Angelo in Shakespeare's *Measure for Measure*.
Esmeralda (eş-mẽr-al'dȧ). A beautiful dancing girl in Victor Hugo's novel *Notre-Dame de Paris*, put to death as a witch.
Esmond (eş'mŏnd), **Col. Henry.** The hero of Thackeray's novel *The History of Henry Esmond*, a chivalrous soldier and man of taste. He is on the Jacobite side, and assists in a plan for bringing back the Stuarts. For a time he is attracted by his kinswoman, the imperious and ambitious beauty Beatrix Esmond, but later marries her mother and retires to America. He is grandfather of the two Warrington brothers who figure in *The Virginians*.
Estella (es-tel'ȧ). The heroine of Dickens' *Great Expectations*, adopted by Miss Havisham. See **Pip.**
Eteocles and Polynices (ē-tē'ō-çlēş and pol-y-nī'çēş). In Greek mythology, sons of Oedipus, who, after their father's expulsion, agreed to reign over Thebes in alternate years. When Eteocles, the elder brother, refused to yield the throne at the end of the first year, Polynices led an expedition against him (see **Seven against Thebes**), and the two brothers, meeting in single combat, killed each other. See also **Antigone.**
Ettarre (e-tär'). The false love of Pelleas in Tennyson's *Pelleas and Ettarre*, one of the *Idylls of the King*.—The heroine of Cabell's *Cream of the Jest*, a daughter of Count Manuel.
Eugenio (ū-ġē'ni-ō). A character in *Don Quixote*, who turns goatherd when jilted.
Eugenius (ū-ġē'ni-us). The friend of Yorick in Sterne's *Tristram Shandy*.
Eulenspiegel (oi'len-spē'gel), **Till.** A 14th-century Brunswick peasant whose pranks and drolleries were the subject of widesperad tales, and inspired a tone-poem by Richard Strauss.
Eumaeus (ū-mē'us). In Homer's *Odyssey*, the faithful swineherd of Ulysses; hence, a swineherd.
Euphrosyne (ū-fros'y-nē). In Greek mythology, one of the three Graces, the others being Aglaia and Thalia.
Europa (ū-rō'pȧ). A nymph of Greek fable, carried off by Jove, who assumed the form of a white bull. Mother, by him, of Minos, Rhadamanthus, and Sarpedon.
Europa, Dame. A name for the continent of Europe.
Eurus (ū'rus). The southeast or east wind.
Euryalus (ū-rȳ'ȧ-lus). See **Nisus.**
Eurydice (ū-ryd'i-çē). The wife of the poet Orpheus. See **Orpheus.**
Eurytion (ū-ryt'i-on). A sleepless herdsman in Spenser's *Faërie Queene*.
Euterpe (ū-tẽr'pē). The Muse of music.
Eva (ē'vȧ), **Little.** The youthful heroine in *Uncle Tom's Cabin*, by Harriet Beecher Stowe.
Evangeline (ē-van'ġe-lin). The heroine of Longfellow's well-known poem, founded on the expulsion of the French colonists from Acadia (Nova Scotia) in 1756. She and her lover Gabriel are parted, and do not meet until a great many years later, when he is dying in a Philadelphia hospital, where she is a nurse.
Evans (ev'ănş), **Sir Hugh.** A laughable Welsh schoolmaster in Shakespeare's *Merry Wives*.
Evans, Sam. The husband of Nina Leeds in O'Neill's play *Strange Interlude*, in whose family, unknown to him, there is insanity. He dies of a heart attack while watching a race in which his supposed son Gordon is competing.
Evelina (ev-e-lī'nȧ). The heroine of a novel so named by Fanny Burney (Mme. d'Arblay).
Everdene (ev'ẽr-dēn), **Bathsheba.** The heroine of Hardy's *Far from the Madding Crowd*, who ultimately marries Gabriel Oak.
Excalibur (eks-çal'i-bũr). The famous sword of King Arthur.
Eyre (ẹr), **Jane.** The heroine of a novel by Charlotte Brontë, governess to a gentleman called Rochester, to whom she is married after the death of his insane wife.

F

Face (fāc). A character in Ben Jonson's *Alchemist* assistant of Subtle the 'alchemist.'
Fadladeen (fad-lȧ-dēn'). A conceited grand chamberlain in Moore's *Lalla Rookh*, an infallible judge of everything.
Fag (fag). The lying servant of Captain Absolute in Sheridan's comedy *The Rivals*.
Fagin (fā'gin). The receiver of stolen goods in Dickens' *Oliver Twist*, who trains boys to steal.
Fairservice (fãr'sẽr-vic), **Andrew.** In Scott's *Rob Roy*, the cunning and conceited Scottish gardener at Osbaldistone Hall.
Faithful (fāth'fụl). A companion of Christian in Bunyan's *Pilgrim's Progress*, burned alive at Vanity Fair.
Falkland (fạk'lănd). The central character in William Godwin's *Caleb Williams*, who commits a murder and is ultimately found out.
Falstaff (fạl'ståf), **Sir John.** The fat 'knight,' the finest comic character of Shakespeare and of literature, appearing in *Henry IV* (both parts) and the *Merry Wives*. Gross, profligate, dishonest, and utterly unprincipled, he would be despicable were it not for his overflowing wit and humor, his gaiety and good sense.
Fang (fang), **Mr.** A course, bullying magistrate in Dickens' *Oliver Twist*.
Fantine (fäṅ-tīn'). The mother of little Cosette in Victor Hugo's *Les Misérables*.
Farintosh (fär'in-tosh), **Marquis of.** A Scottish nobleman in Thackeray's *Newcomes*, who has neither abilities, character, nor breeding to recommend him, but is a great catch in the marriage market, and is expected to become the husband of Ethel Newcome.
Fata Morgana (fä'tä mọr-gä'nä). A celebrated fairy in medieval romantic poems of Italy.—A mirage sometimes seen at the Strait of Messina.
Fat Boy (fat boi). In Dickens' *Pickwick Papers*, a boy named Joe, always either eating or sleeping.
Fates *or* **Parcae** (fāţş; pär'çē). In classical mythology, three goddesses who controlled human destiny: **Atropos, Clotho, Lachesis.**
Father of Comedy (fä'ŧher ov çom'e-dy). Aristophanes.—**of English Poetry,** Chaucer.—**of Epic Poetry,** Homer.—**of History,** Herodotus.—**of Tragedy,** Aeschylus.
Fatima (fä'tī-mä). A holy woman in the story of *Aladdin or the Wonderful Lamp* in the *Arabian Nights*; also in the same work the mother of Prince Camaralzaman.—The last of Bluebeard's wives. See **Bluebeard.**
Faulconbridge (fạ'çŏn-briġ), **Philip.** In Shakespeare's *King John*, a natural son of Richard I, an outspoken and daring soldier, true as steel to his friends.
Faulkland (fạk'lănd). In Sheridan's *The Rivals*, the jealous lover of Julia Melville.
Faust (foust). The hero of Goethe's celebrated dramatic poem *Faust* and of Marlowe's tragedy *Dr. Faustus*. In popular German legend (deriving, with embellishments, from the life of a Dr. Johann Faust who died *c.* 1541), Faust was a magician and astrologer who sold his soul to the devil in return for youth, knowledge, and all pleasures. Goethe treats the subject with a philosophic depth and a symbolic scope which transcend the old legend. He effects the salvation of Faust. He introduces the tragic episode of Margaret, who is seduced by Faust and is condemned for murdering her infant. His Mephistopheles, the demonic being who fulfills all Faust's wishes, is a richer and more provocative figure than the vulgar fiend of the older stories. Several operas are based on the legend, among them *The Damnation of Faust* by Berlioz and Gounod's *Faust*.
Fawley (fạ'li), **Jude.** The hero of Hardy's *Jude the Obscure*, whose unhappy marriage, and love for Sue Bridehead, lead to a series of tragedies.
Fay (fā), **Felix.** The leading character, seen in adolescence and early manhood, in Floyd Dell's *Moon-Calf* and *The Briary-Bush*, novels largely autobiographical.
Feeble (fēb'l), Jestingly called by Falstaff 'most forcible Feeble,' one of the knight's 'ragged regiment' in *Henry IV*, part ii.; a puny, timid creature.
Fell (fel), **Dr. Gideon.** The fictional detective of John Dickson Carr.
Fenton (fen'tŏn). The lover of Anne Page in Shakespeare's *Merry Wives of Windsor*.
Feramorz (fer'ȧ-mōrz). A poet (in reality the sultan in disguise) in Moore's *Lalla Rookh*. See **Lalla Rookh.**
Ferdinand (fẽr'di-nand). King of Navarre in Shakespeare's *Love's Labour's Lost*.—Prince of Naples in Shakespeare's *Tempest*.
Ferdinand the Bull. A bull who refuses to fight, but who likes to smell flowers, in Munro Leaf's story for children.
Ferrex and Porrex (fer'eks; pọr'eks). Sons of Gorboduc, a mythical British king, who divided his kingdom between them. Ferrex, driven from Britain by his brother, returned with an army and was slain; and Porrex soon afterwards was killed by their mother, who loved Ferrex more. See **Gorboduc.**
Feverel (fev'ẽr-el), **Richard.** The hero of the novel *The Ordeal of Richard Feverel*, by George Meredith. Sir Austin, Richard's father, has evolved his own educational system, which excludes almost all natural interests. Richard falls in love with Lucy Desborough, a farmer's niece, and marries her against his father's wish. Richard's uncle reconciles Sir Austin and Lucy. Richard fights a duel with an admirer of Lucy, is wounded, and on his recovery learns that Lucy has died of brain fever.
Fielding (fēl'ding), **Mrs., and her daughter May.** Characters in Dickens' *Cricket on the Hearth*, the latter the sweetheart of Edward Plummer.
Field of the Forty Footsteps (fēld, fọr'ty foot'-steps). At the back of the British Museum, where tradition says two brothers fought together and were killed, leaving forty impressions of their feet.
Figaro (fig'ȧ-rō). A sharp-witted barber and valet, the hero of Beaumarchais' comedies *The Barber of Seville* and *The Marriage of Figaro*, on which are based operas respectively by Rossini and Mozart.
Fingal (fiṅ'găl). A hero of Celtic tradition, **king** of Morven, on the west coast of Scotland.
Finn (fin), **Huckleberry.** A small-town waif in Mark Twain's *Tom Sawyer* and its sequel *Huckleberry Finn*, two classic stories of American boyhood. He and his friend Tom share many adventures. Huck assists a runaway slave (Jim) to escape down the Mississippi River on a raft.
Fitz-Boodle (fits-bọọd'l), **George Savage.** In Thackeray's *The Fitz-Boodle Papers*, a young nobleman with a taste for Bohemianism.
Flagg (flag), **Captain.** In *What Price Glory*, by Anderson and Stallings, a hard-boiled A.E.F. captain who feuds with Sergeant Quirt over Charmaine.
Flamborough (flam'bŏr-ō). A farmer and his daughters in Goldsmith's *Vicar of Wakefield*.
Flanders (flan'dẽrş), **Moll.** In Defoe's novel named after her, a reformed thief and strumpet.
Fledgeby (fleġ'by). A mean and cowardly sneak in Dickens' *Our Mutual Friend*.
Fleming (flem'ing), **Henry.** A soldier in Stephen Crane's *Red Badge of Courage*, whose impulse is to flee from the horrors of war, though he is also ashamed that he does not have a wound (the red badge of courage). He later is distinguished for bravery under fire.
Fleming, Rhoda. The heroine of Meredith's novel of the same name.
Flibbertigibbet (flib'ẽr-ti-ġib-et). A malicious fiend named in Shakespeare's *King Lear*.—A dwarfish boy in Scott's *Kenilworth*.
Flite (flīt), **Miss.** A pathetic, half-crazy woman in Dickens' *Bleak House*, waiting for a decision of the court of chancery.
Flora (flō'rȧ). In Roman mythology, the goddess of flowers and spring. An annual festival in her honor, the Floralia (April 28–May 1), was accompanied with much licentiousness.
Florac (flō'raç), **Paul de.** In Thackeray's *Newcomes*, a French nobleman with an English wife. A kindhearted prodigal, he presently settles in England and assumes the character of an English country gentleman, while remaining as thoroughly French as ever. Colonel Newcome was passionately in love with Florac's mother in early life.
Florimel (flọr'i-mel). A virtuous lady in Spenser's *Faërie Queene*. By sorcery a witch has made a figure that is mistaken for her, but the false Florimel vanishes when the real one is brought to her side.
Florinda (flō-rin'dȧ). Daughter of Count Julian, seduced, according to legend, by Roderick, last king of the Goths in Spain.
Florismart (flọr'is-märt). One of the paladins of Charlemagne, and the devoted friend of Orlando.
Florizel (flọr'i-zel). The prince of Bohemia in Shakespeare's *Winter's Tale*, in love with Perdita.
Fluellen (flū-el'en). A brave but pedantic Welsh captain in Shakespeare's *Henry V*.
Flying Dutchman (flȳ'ing duch'măn). A phantom ship seen in the neighborhood of the Cape of Good Hope, and said to be commanded by a Dutch captain (Vanderdecken) who for his impiety has to sail till the day of judgment.
Foker (fō'kẽr), **Henry.** In Thackeray's *Pendennis*, the son of a wealthy brewer, a sporting, slangy, wide-awake young sybarite, who is enthralled by the siren Blanche Amory.
Ford (fọrd), **Mrs.** One of Shakespeare's *Merry Wives of Windsor*, who befools Falstaff for his evil intentions.
Fornarina (fọr-nä-rī'nä), **La.** The baker's daughter to whom Raphael is said to have been devoted, and whose portrait appears in some of his pictures.
Forsyte (fọr'sȳt) **Family.** The members of the family in John Galsworthy's novels which make up the *Forsyte Saga*, chronicling the ripeness and decay of a middle-class family of the Victorian era. Soames and Jolyon are shrewd, cautious, and tenacious. The younger generation is embittered and futile; Jon and Fleur love hopelessly.
Fortinbras (fọr'tin-bras). In Shakespeare's *Hamlet*, the prince of Norway.
Fortunatus (fọr-tū-nā'tus). The hero of a popular tale who obtained an inexhaustible purse and a cap that would carry him wherever he pleased.
Forty Thieves (fọr'ty thēvş), **the.** A band of robbers in the *Arabian Nights* who occupy a secret forest cave, the door of which responds to the commands, 'Open, Sesame!' and 'Close, Sesame!' See **Ali Baba, Cassim,** and **Morgiana.**
Foscari (fōs'çä-ri). **Francis.** Doge of Venice, who, with his son, figures in Byron's drama *The Two Foscari*.
Fra Diavolo (frä dī-äv'ō-lō). A brigand chief of S. Italy who has given name to a comic opera by Auber, with words by Scribe.
Fradubio (frä-dū'bi-ō). Husband of Duessa in Spenser's *Faërie Queene*, metamorphosed by her into a tree.
Francesca (fran-ces'çȧ *or It.* frän-cheş'çä). A Venetian maiden in Byron's *Siege of Corinth;* loved by Alp, she dies of a broken heart.
Francesca da Rimini (dä rī'mī-nī). Daughter of Guido da Polenta, lord of Ravenna, and married to Giovanni Malatesta, the Lame, lord of Rimini. The latter, discovering her love affair with his brother Paolo, the Handsome, killed them both (*c.* 1285). The subject has been treated, notably, by Dante in the *Divine Comedy* and by Silvio Pellico, Leigh Hunt, Stephen Phillips, and D'Annunzio.
Frankenstein (frank'en-stīn). A student of physiology in Mrs. Shelley's romance of the same name, who attains profound knowledge and constructs a

hideous monster endowed with some human attributes. The monster, though craving sympathy and love, proves the curse and ruin of its creator.

Frederick (fred'ēr-ik). The usurping duke in Shakespeare's *As You Like It*, father of Celia and uncle of Rosalind. Undergoing a change of heart, he finally restores his brother to his dukedom.

Freeport (frē'pǫrt), **Sir Andrew.** One of the members of the club which figures in Addison and Steele's *Spectator*, a London merchant distinguished for common sense and generous nature.

Freischütz (frī'shüts). A marksman of German legend who obtains seven magic balls, six of which hit whatever he aims at, but the seventh goes as the fiend directs.

Freya (frȳ'ȧ). A Scandinavian goddess of love and youth, often confounded with Frigga.

Friar John (frī'ăr jon). In Rabelais' romance of *Gargantua and Pantagruel*, a profane and debauched but bold and amusing character, always in the heart of everything going on.

Friar Tuck (tuk). The paunchy, humorous, and pugnacious friar who is said to have been among Robin Hood's merry men, and who figures in Scott's *Ivanhoe.*

Frome (frōm), **Ethan.** A New England farmer in Edith Wharton's novel of the same name, who is married to a petulant invalid. When he and his wife's cousin are faced with the termination of their companionship, important to both of them, they yield to a suicidal impulse which results only in their being crippled for life.

Frigga (frig'ȧ). The supreme Scandinavian goddess, wife of Odin, though corresponding in some respects to Venus.

Fudge (fuġ) **Family.** An English family whose adventures abroad are amusingly chronicled by the poet Thomas Moore in a series of letters in verse, ostensibly written by them.

Fusbos (fus'bos). Minister of state in Rhodes' burlesque *Bombastes Furioso.*

G

Gabler (gab'lẽr), **Hedda.** The heroine of a drama of the same name by Henrik Ibsen, married to an ineffectual professor who bores her. She exerts a destructive influence over a former lover of hers, who is killed ignominiously in a brawl, and to avoid exposure, shoots herself.

Gabriel (gā'bri-el). Chief of the angelic host, in Milton's *Paradise Lost.* He figures in Jewish and Mohammedan mythology, and is said to have dictated the Koran to Mohammed.—In Longfellow's *Evangeline*, Evangeline's lover.

Gaea *or* Ge (ġē'ȧ; ġē). In Greek mythology, the earth regarded as a goddess.

Galahad (gal'ȧ-had), **Sir.** One of the knights of King Arthur's Round Table, the son of Lancelot, celebrated for his chastity.

Galatea (gal-ȧ-tē'ȧ). A nymph of Greek fable, beloved by and loving Acis. The latter was killed by the Cyclops Polyphemus from jealousy.—An ivory statue made by Pygmalion, who fell in love with it, and which, in response to his prayer to Aphrodite, became alive. See **Pygmalion.**

Gallegher (gal'e-gẽr). An Irish-American newsboy in the short story of the same name by Richard Harding Davis, who helps 'break' a murder story.

Gammer Gurton's Needle (gam'ẽr gũr'tǒnş nēd'l). See **Gurton, Gammer.**

Gamp (gamp), **Sarah.** A monthly nurse in Dickens' *Martin Chuzzlewit*, fond of liquor, carrying a big, baggy umbrella, and making frequent references to a purely imaginary friend of hers named Mrs. Harris.

Ganelon (gan'e-lon). One of Charlemagne's knights, celebrated for malevolence and treachery.

Ganem (gā'nem). The 'slave of love' in the *Arabian Nights.*

Gant (gant), **Eugene.** The autobiographical hero of Thomas Wolfe's *Look Homeward, Angel* and its sequel *Of Time and the River*, an intense young man, abounding in energies and imaginings, who comes from a quarreling, striving family, headed by a drunken father.

Gantry (gan'try), **Elmer.** A religious racketeer posing as an evangelist in Sinclair Lewis' novel of the same name.

Ganymede (gan'y-mēd). A beautiful youth of Greek fable, carried to heaven from Mount Ida by an eagle, and made cupbearer to the gods.

Gareth (gar'eth). One of King Arthur's knights, who served as a scullion for a year before being knighted. His expedition in the company of Lynette to liberate her sister Lyonors is the subject of one of Tennyson's *Idylls.*

Gargantua (gär-gan'tū-ȧ). The hero of the humorous and fantastic romance of the same name (also called *Gargantua and Pantagruel*) by Rabelais. He is a giant of tremendous size who has a son equally wonderful, named Pantagruel. Rabelais borrowed his Gargantua from the popular mythology of France.

Gargery (gär'ġẽr-y), **Joe.** A simple, ignorant, warm-hearted blacksmith in Dickens' *Great Expectations*, married to Pip's sister.

Gashford (gash'fõrd). Secretary to Lord George Gordon in Dickens' *Barnaby Rudge.*

Gatsby (gats'by), **Jay.** The central character in F. Scott Fitzgerald's novel *The Great Gatsby*, a wealthy racketeer whose attempt to revive an old romance ends in disaster.

Gawain (gä'wān). One of the knights of the Round Table, a nephew of King Arthur, renowned for strength as well as courtesy.

Gebir (ġē'bīr; ge'bir). A prince in Eastern legend who invaded Africa. Gibraltar is said to have been named from him.

Gelert (gel'ẽrt). The faithful hound of Llewellyn, which kills a wolf that would have devoured its master's infant, and is rashly slain by Llewellyn before he sees how matters really stand. Similar stories are of almost world-wide currency.

Gellatley (gel'ăt-li), **Davie.** In Scott's *Waverley*, a feeble-minded servant of the Baron Bradwardine, given to answering questions with snatches of song.

Genevieve (ġen'e-vēv). Heroine of a poem by Coleridge.

Genevieve, St. An apocryphal saint, a lady who, according to legend, was falsely accused of adultery and condemned to death, but escaped and lived six years in a forest until her husband found her and took her home, convinced of her innocence.

Geoffrey Crayon (ġef'ri çrā'ǒn). The pseudonym of the author of *The Sketch Book*, Washington Irving.

George (ġǫrġ). See **Milton, George.**

George, St. The patron saint of England, by some identified with a Cappadocian prince martyred under Diocletian. The killing of a dragon is one of the legendary feats attributed to him.

George-a-Green (-ȧ-grēn'). The pinner or pound-keeper of Wakefield, one of the associates of Robin Hood.

Geraint (ġe-rānt'). A knight of the Round Table, married to Enid, and celebrated in one of Tennyson's *Idylls of the King.* See **Enid.**

Gerard (ġer'ărd). The chief figure in Charles Reade's historical novel *The Cloister and the Hearth*, depicting life in 15th-century Europe and revolving around the parents of Erasmus. Separated from Margaret Brandt, with whom he is in love, Gerard has many adventures. After a false report that Margaret has died, he becomes a monk; but years later he is amazed to find her alive and to learn that he is the father of a son (Erasmus).

Gerhardt (ger'härt), **Jennie.** The tragic heroine of Theodore Dreiser's novel of same name.

Gertrude (gẽr'trůd). The queen in Shakespeare's *Hamlet*, mother of Hamlet.

Geryon (ġē'ry-ǒn). In ancient classical legend, a monstrous king of Hesperia, who fed his oxen on human flesh and was slain by Hercules.

Geste (ẓest), **Beau.** One of the leading characters in the romantic novel of the same name by Percival Christopher Wren.

Giafar (ġä'fär). Vizier of the Caliph Harun-al-Rashid in the *Arabian Nights.*

Giaffir (ġaf'īr). Father of Zuleika in Byron's *Bride of Abydos.*

Giant Despair (ġī'ănt de-spãr'). A formidable giant in Bunyan's *Pilgrim's Progress*, who lives in Doubting Castle, where he keeps Christian and Hopeful prisoners until they escape by means of the key Promise.

Giaour (ġour). Turkish name for an infidel, especially a Christian. Byron wrote a poem so titled.

Gilberte (ġil-bert'). The daughter of Swann and Odette in Proust's *Remembrance of Things Past.* In his youth Marcel is in love with her. She marries Saint-Loup.

Gil Blas (ẓīl bläs). The hero of a picaresque novel by Le Sage, a gay rascal who participates in many diverting and instructive incidents.

Gilderoy (gil'de-roi). A famous highwayman of ballad fame, reputedly handsome, who was hanged in 1636.

Gill (gil), **Harry.** A farmer in Wordsworth's poem *Goody Blake and Harry Gill.* See **Goody Blake.**

Gilpin (gil'pin), **John.** A London linendraper whose exploits on horseback are celebrated in Cowper's humorous poem *John Gilpin's Ride.*

Ginevra (ġi-nev'rȧ). The bride who, according to a well-known story, playfully hid in a trunk on her wedding day. The lid fell, burying her alive; and eventually her skeleton was discovered.

Giovanni (ġō-vän'nī), **Don.** The Italian form of the name *Don Juan* and the title of an opera by Mozart based on the Don Juan legend. See **Don Juan.**

Glasse (glȧs), **Mrs. Hannah.** Author of a famous cookery book of 1747, in which the recipe for cooking a hare is (mistakenly) said to begin with the direction, 'First catch your hare.' Actually, the book's text meant *skin*, not *catch.*

Glaucus (glạ'çus). A Greek divinity of the sea.

Gloriana (glō-ri-ā'nȧ). The queen of fairyland in Spenser's *Faërie Queene*, intended to stand for Queen Elizabeth.

Glossin (glos'in), **Gilbert.** A rascally lawyer in Scott's *Guy Mannering*, killed by Dirk Hatteraick, his accomplice in kidnaping Harry Bertram.

Gloucester (glos'tẽr), **Earl of.** In Shakespeare's *King Lear*, a tragic figure, who is blinded.

Glubdubdrib (glub-dub'drib). In Swift's *Gulliver's Travels*, an island inhabited by sorcerers and magicians, who call up at Gulliver's desire the spirits of many personages of former times.

Glumdalca (glum-dal'çȧ). A giantess in Fielding's burlesque *Tom Thumb.*

Glumdalclitch (glum-dal'çlich). An amiable nine-year-old girl, only forty feet tall, who has charge of Gulliver in Brobdingnag.

Gobbo (gob'ō), **Launcelot.** An amusing clown in Shakespeare's *Merchant of Venice*, at one time servant to Shylock.

Godden (god'en), **Joanna.** A Sussex woman in Sheila Kaye-Smith's novel of the same name, who runs her father's farm after his death, educates her younger sister Ellen as a lady, and bears an illegitimate child by one of her farm hands.

Godiva (gō-dī'vȧ) **Lady.** The wife of Leofric, earl of Mercia and lord of Coventry, in the eleventh century, who, according to the story, obtained relief from burdensome taxes for the people of Coventry by riding naked through the town, as her husband had challenged her to do before he would grant the favor. Everyone withdrew from the streets and kept closely within doors; but one wretch, hence called 'Peeping Tom,' ventured to look out, and was immediately stricken blind. The story has been versified by Tennyson.

Gog and Magog (gog and mā'gog). Names of doubtful application occurring in the Bible. The names are applied to giants in old legends of Britain, and to two enormous figures in the Guildhall of London.

Golden Ass (gōl'den ȧs). The name of a tale by the Latin writer Apuleius, relating the adventures of a young man who for a time has been made to assume the form of an ass. The story of Cupid and Psyche occurs in it.

Golden Bells (gōl'den belş). The daughter of Kubla Khan in Donn Byrne's *Messer Marco Polo*, who is loved by Marco Polo.

Golden Fleece (flēc). In classical mythology, the fleece of a famous ram hung in a grove in Colchis, and guarded by a dragon. It was carried off by the Argonauts, with Jason at their head. See **Argo.**

Goneril (gon'ẽr-il). One of the two evil daughters of King Lear. See **Lear.**

Goodfellow (good'fel-ō), **Robin.** A tricksy imp or sprite of popular English tales, called also Puck.

Goody Blake (good'y blāk). In Wordsworth's poem *Goody Blake and Harry Gill*, a poor old dame who pilfers a few sticks from her neighbor during the severe cold, and is forced by him to restore the property. In doing so she invokes a curse upon him that he may 'never more be warm,' and his teeth have chattered ever since.

Gopher Prairie (gō'fẽr prãr'i). A fictitious town in Minnesota, the scene of Sinclair Lewis' novel *Main Street* and typical of a hidebound small town of petty character.

Gorboduc (gǫr'bō-duç). A legendary British king who figures in a play of the same name, the first English tragedy (1562), by Thomas Sackville and Thomas Norton. See **Ferrex and Porrex.**

Goriot (gōr-yō'), **Père.** The hero of Balzac's novel of that name. He sacrifices his wealth, comfort, and self-respect and lives in utter poverty for the sake of his two ungrateful daughters, Mme. de Nucingen (Delphine) and Mme. de Restaud (Anastasie).

Gösta Berling. See **Berling, Gösta.**

Gould (gōld), **Charles.** An engineer in Joseph Conrad's *Nostromo* who is obsessed with a silver mine he owns in a South American republic, and which causes a revolution.

Gradgrind (grad'grīnd), **Thomas.** A successful businessman connected with the iron trade, in Dickens' *Hard Times*, who is above all sentiment and cares only for what is practical and matter-of-fact.

Grandet (grän-de') **Family.** In Balzac's *Eugénie Grandet*, a French family which includes **Félix**, a miser and household tyrant, and his daughter Eugénie, the heroine of the novel. She is in love with her spoiled cousin Charles, but he marries another.

Grandison (gran'di-sǒn), **Sir Charles.** The hero of Richardson's novel *The History of Sir Charles Grandison*, a somewhat tiresome character intended to exemplify the perfect Christian gentleman.

Graveairs (grāv'ãrş), **Lady.** A lady of doubtful virtue in Colley Cibber's comedy *The Careless Husband.*

Gray (grā), **Auld Robin.** The title of a popular Scotch ballad by Lady Anne Lindsay (afterward Lady Barnard). To rescue her parents from ruin Jennie marries Auld Robin, her suitor, while her lover Jamie is absent at sea.

Great Commoner (grāt çom'ǒn-ẽr). William Pitt, the Elder.—**Great Duke,** the duke of Wellington. —**Great Magician,** Sir Walter Scott.—**Great Moralist,** Dr. Johnson.—**Great Unknown,** a designation for the anonymous writer of the *Waverley Novels* before the real author (Scott) was known.

Greatheart (grāt'härt). In the *Pilgrim's Progress*, the guide of Christiana and her children to the Celestial City.

Greaves (grēvş), **Sir Launcelot.** A sort of English *Don Quixote*, the hero of a novel by Smollett.

Greedy (grē'dy), **Justice.** In Massinger's *A New Way to Pay Old Debts*, a venal magistrate whose character corresponds to his name.

Grendel (grend'l). See **Beowulf.**

Gretchen (grech'en). A German diminutive of Margaret, often used of the heroine of Goethe's *Faust.*

Gride (grīd), **Arthur.** An old miser in Dickens' *Nicholas Nickleby* who wishes to marry Madeline Bray.

Grieux, des (dẹ grī-ū'), **Chevalier.** A young man ruined by his love for Manon in the novel *Manon Lescaut* by the Abbé Prévost.

Griffiths (grif'iths), **Clyde.** The chief character, the son of an evangelist, in Theodore Dreiser's *American Tragedy*, who seduces a factory girl and then drowns her when he falls in love with the factory-owner's daughter. He is electrocuted for the crime.

Griselda (gri-ẓel'dȧ). The heroine of one of Chaucer's *Canterbury Tales*, borrowed from the Italian. She is subjected to the cruelest trials by her husband in order to test her patience and obedience, but never complains or murmurs.

Grizel (gris'el). The patient and forgiving wife of Tommy Sandys in Barrie's *Sentimental Tommy* and its sequel *Tommy and Grizel*.

Grub Street (grub strēt). A name, once that of a street in London, which has become applicable to hack writers and poor literature.

Grueby (grụ'by), **John.** Servant to Lord George Gordon in Dickens' *Barnaby Rudge*.

Grundy (grun'dy), **Mrs.** A farmer's wife frequently spoken of by Mrs. Ashfield, another farmer's wife, in Morton's comedy *Speed the Plough* (1798). Mrs. Ashfield is much given to speculating about 'what Mrs. Grundy will say' in such and such circumstances.

Grushenka (grụ-sheñ'kȧ). The girl loved by Dmitri Karamazov and his father in *The Brothers Karamazov*, by Feodor Dostoevski.

Gudrun (gụd'rụn). The heroine of an old German epic, a princess who is carried off and is kept for years at servile drudgery, because she refuses to marry against her inclinations.

Guermantes, de (dē ger-mäṅt'). In Proust's *Remembrance of Things Past*, a French noble family, including an arrogant prince, a haughty duke, their wives, Baron de Charlus, and Robert Saint-Loup.

Guiderius (gwi-dē'ri-us). In Shakespeare's *Cymbeline*, the elder son of Cymbeline, a legendary king of Britain. He and his brother Arviragus were stolen during infancy by Belarius, a disgraced nobleman. When grown up they distinguished themselves against the Romans, and subsequently were made known to the king.

Guildenstern (gil'den-stẽrn). A courtier in Shakespeare's *Hamlet*.

Guinevere (gwin'e-vẽr). The wife of King Arthur, notorious for her guilty attachment to Sir Lancelot. She later retired to a nunnery. She is best known from Tennyson's *Idylls*.

Gulbeyaz (gul-be'äz). The sultana in Byron's *Don Juan*.

Gulliver (gul'i-vẽr), **Lemuel.** The hero of Swift's famous *Gulliver's Travels*, who makes various voyages and in one way or another visits some remarkable countries, especially Lilliput, Brobdingnag, Laputa, and the land of the Houyhnhnms. See these entries, also **Glubdubdrib, Glumdalclitch, Struldbrugs.**

Gummidge (gum'ig), **Mrs.** The widow who keeps house for Daniel Peggotty in Dickens' *David Copperfield*, always in the depths of melancholy as 'a poor, lone, lorn creetur.'

Gunther (gụn'tẽr), **King.** In the *Nibelungenlied*, a king of the Burgundians, brother of Kriemhild and husband of Brunhild.

Guppy (gup'y), **William.** A silly young law clerk in Dickens' *Bleak House*.

Gurth (gũrth). The faithful and sturdy swineherd of Cedric in Scott's *Ivanhoe*.

Gurton (gũr'tŏn), **Gammer.** The heroine of the second English comedy, *Gammer Gurton's Needle* (printed in 1575), which turns on the loss of this useful article and the finding of it sticking in her man Hodge's breeches.

Guy of Warwick (gȳ ov wạr'ik). A hero of English legend who, among many knightly exploits, saved England from the Danes by slaying a giant.

Guyon (gȳ'ŏn), **Sir.** A knight in Spenser's *Faërie Queene*, the personification of temperance and self-restraint.

Gyges (ġȳ'ġēs). A king of ancient Lydia fabled to have had a magic ring that rendered him invisible, and thus helped him to slay his predecessor Candaules.

Gynt (gynt), **Peer.** The hero of Henrik Ibsen's drama of the same name, an irresponsible youth who breaks his mother's and his wife's heart.

H

Hagen (hä'gen). A warrior in the *Nibelungenlied* who kills Siegfried, and is himself killed by Kriemhild.

Haidee (hī-dē'). In Byron's *Don Juan*, the daughter of the pirate Lambro, a beautiful girl who rescues Juan when cast ashore, and dies when her father drags him off to slavery.

Halcyone (hal-cȳ'ō-nē). In Greek mythology, daughter of Aeolus and wife of Ceyx, at whose death she threw herself into the sea and became a kingfisher.

Halifax (hal'i-faks), **John.** The central figure in Dinah Mulock Craik's novel *John Halifax, Gentleman*, who rises from poverty to the status of mid-Victorian gentleman, and marries the well-bred Ursula March.

Hamilton (ham'il-tŏn), **Melanie.** The gentle, ladylike Southern girl who marries Ashley Wilkes in Margaret Mitchell's *Gone With the Wind*.

Hamlet (ham'let). The prince of Denmark, hero of Shakespeare's great tragedy *Hamlet*, the substance of which is contained in old chronicles.

Handy Andy (han'dy an'dy). The Irish hero of a novel of that name by Samuel Lover, an awkward but amusing fellow.

Hardcastle (härd'cȧs-l), **Squire.** In Goldsmith's comedy *She Stoops to Conquer*, an English country gentleman whose house young Marlow mistakes for an inn, and whose daughter 'stoops to conquer' him, pretending to be the chambermaid. The squire is a jovial old gentleman, fond of telling stories, and has one special favorite of 'grouse in the gunroom.' Mrs. Hardcastle is a lady who is devoted to what is 'genteel.' Tony Lumpkin is her son by a former marriage. See **Lumpkin.**

Haredale (hãr'dāl), **Mr., and his daughter Emma.** Characters in Dickens' *Barnaby Rudge*.

Harlowe (här'lō), **Clarissa.** The heroine of Richardson's novel of this name, a girl of great sweetness, purity, and moral dignity, who is overcome by drugs and betrayed by the man she loves, the libertine Lovelace, and later, scorning his offered reparation of marriage, dies of grief and shame.

Harmon (här'mŏn), **John.** The hero of Dickens' *Our Mutual Friend*, son of a rich and miserly dustman. He marries Bella Wilfer under the guise of secretary to Mr. Boffin. See **Boffin, Wilfer.**

Harmonia (här-mō'ni-ȧ). In classical mythology, a daughter of Mars and Venus and wife of Cadmus. On her marriage day she received a necklace which proved unlucky to everyone that came into possession of it.

Harold (har'ŏld), **Childe.** The hero of Byron's poem *Childe Harold's Pilgrimage*, the Childe being a man of birth, wealth, and intellect, who, while still young, has become sated with pleasure and resolves to travel, thus giving the poet an opportunity for much fine descriptive and reflective writing.

Harold the Dauntless (thē dạnt'les). A Danish hero in Scott's poem of that name.

Harpagon (ȧr-pȧ-goṅ'). A wretched miser, the hero of Molière's comedy *L'Avare* (The Miser).

Harpocrates (här-poc'rȧ-tēs). God of silence among the Greeks and Romans.

Harris (har'is), **Mrs.** Mrs. Gamp's oft-quoted but imaginary friend. See **Gamp.**

Harum (har'um), **David.** The hero of a novel so titled by Edward Noyes Westcott. He is a shrewd banker and horse-trader in a small town in New York State.

Harun-al-Rashid (hä-rụn' är-rȧ-shīd'). Caliph of Bagdad (786–809), celebrated in tradition and, most notably, in stories of the *Arabian Nights*. He was accustomed, it is said, in company with his vizier, Giafar, to visit the different quarters of his capital at night in disguise.

Harvey (här'vi). An invisible rabbit in the play of the same name by Mary Coyle Chase.

Hastings (hāst'ings), **Mr.** The friend and companion of young Marlow in Goldsmith's *She Stoops to Conquer*, in love with Miss Neville.

Hatchway (hach'wā), **Lieutenant Jack.** An amusing half-pay naval officer, the companion of Commodore Trunnion in Smollett's *Peregrine Pickle*.

Hatteraick (hat'ẽr-āk), **Dirk.** A smuggler in Scott's *Guy Mannering*, who finally, in prison, kills Glossin, then hangs himself.

Hatto (hat'ō). In German legend, an archbishop of Mainz, devoured by an army of mice (or rats) as a judgment upon him for having, during a severe famine, shut up a number of poor people in a barn and burned them. The Mouse Tower, on an island of the Rhine near Bingen, is said to have been the scene of the bishop's death.

Hauser (hou'sẽr), **Kaspar.** A mysterious German youth (1812?–33) who showed up in Nuremberg in 1828 in a state of almost native ignorance, the result, according to his vague account, of imprisonment. His brief career, ended perhaps by murder, aroused much interest and conjecture. He is the subject of Jakob Wassermann's novel *Caspar Hauser*.

Havelok (hav'e-lok) **the Dane.** The hero of a medieval English romance, the orphan son of a king of Denmark. Through the treachery of his guardians he was cast adrift on a raft, which reached the Lincolnshire coast. Here he was adopted by the fisherman who picked him up. He subsequently married an English princess and became king of Denmark.

Havisham (hav'i-shăm), **Miss.** In Dickens' *Great Expectations*, an eccentric lady who, having been deserted on her wedding morning, continues to wear her bride's dress for the rest of her life. She adopts Estella.

Hawk (hạk), **Sir Mulberry.** In Dickens' *Nicholas Nickleby*, a worthless roué who insults Kate Nickleby and kills in a duel the young Lord Verisopht, who has been his associate and admirer.

Hawkeye (hạk'ȳ). The trapper in several of Cooper's novels; also called Leatherstocking.

Hawksbee (hạks'bē), **Mrs. Lucy.** A character in Kipling's stories about Simla, who is witty and malicious, and a leader in fashionable British India.

Headstone (hed'stōn), **Bradley.** A schoolmaster in Dickens' *Our Mutual Friend*, who, being passionately in love with Lizzie Hexam, tries to murder Eugene Wrayburn out of jealousy.

Heard (hẽrd), **Bishop.** A writer in Norman Douglas' *South Wind*.

Heart of Midlothian (härt ov mid-lō'thi-ăn). A name for the old tolbooth or jail of Edinburgh, adopted by Sir Walter Scott as the title of one of his novels, in which it figures. Jeanie Deans is the chief character in the novel. See **Deans.**

Heathcliff (hēth'clif). The hero of Emily Brontë's *Wuthering Heights*, a strange, truculent, and passionate creature, in love with Catherine Earnshaw.

Hebe (hē'bē). The Greek goddess of youth, and cupbearer to the gods (before Ganymede), represented as a beautiful young girl.

Hecate (hec'ȧ-tē). A Greek goddess whose powers were various, and who was sometimes confounded with Artemis (Diana) and Proserpine, but later became especially a goddess of the infernal regions and patroness of magicians and witches.

Hector (hec'tŏr). The son of Priam, king of Troy, and husband of Andromache, the most valiant among the Trojans, and the noblest hero described in the *Iliad*. He was slain by Achilles, and his body dragged round the city walls in revenge for his having killed Patroclus, the friend of Achilles. See **Ilium.**

Hecuba (hec'ū-bȧ). The wife of King Priam of Troy, and mother of Hector, Paris, and Cassandra. After the fall of Troy she was given to Ulysses as a slave, and some say she drowned herself in despair.

Heep (hēp), **Uriah.** Clerk to Mr. Wickfield, the lawyer, in Dickens' *David Copperfield*, a sneaking and malignant character, always proclaiming how ''umble' he is, but trying to ruin his employer and marry his daughter Agnes.

Heidi (hī'di). A Swiss orphan in the children's novel of the same name by Johanna Spyri. She is reared in the Alps by her grandfather, who was at first unwilling to take her, but who grew to love her. She and Peter the goatherd enjoy busy, happy days together.

Hel *or* **Hela** (hel; hē'lȧ). The Scandinavian goddess of the dead, daughter of Loki; a frightful being, half blue and half of fair complexion.

Helen (hel'en). The wife of Menelaus, king of Sparta, and daughter of Jupiter and Leda, the most beautiful woman of her time. She was carried off to Troy by Paris, and thus caused the Trojan war, by which the Greek princes purposed to recover her and avenge Menelaus.

Helena (hel'e-nȧ). The heroine of Shakespeare's *All's Well that Ends Well*, married to Bertram, count of Rousillon, who neglects and despises her until brought to a better frame of mind.

Helicon (hel'i-con). A mountain of Greece anciently sacred to Apollo and the Muses.

Helios (hē'li-os). The Greek name for the sun and sun-god, in the latter sense identified with Phoebus or Apollo.

Helmer (hel'mẽr), **Nora.** The heroine of Henrik Ibsen's *A Doll's House*, who resents being treated as a plaything by her husband rather than as an intelligent being, and finally leaves his house to make her own life.

Henry (hen'ry), **Frederic.** An American in Ernest Hemingway's *Farewell to Arms*, who enlists in an Italian ambulance unit, is wounded, and takes part in the retreat from Caporetto. He is the lover of an English nurse, Catherine Barkley, who dies in childbirth.

Henry, John. A legendary American Negro of amazing strength, variously described as a railroad steel-driller and a roustabout on the Mississippi, and celebrated in ballads and tales. Consult Roark Bradford's *John Henry*.

Hephaestus (hē-fes'tus). The Greek equivalent of Vulcan.

Hera (hē'rȧ). Greek equivalent of Juno.

Hercules *or* **Heracles** (hẽr'cū-lēs; her-ȧ-clēs). In classical mythology, a hero or demigod, son of Jupiter and Alcmena, renowned for his prodigious strength and for his wonderful exploits, which included the hard and dangerous tasks known as the twelve labors of Hercules. He was for a time slave to Omphale, queen of Lydia, and later married to Deianira. Being mortally poisoned by the blood of Nessus, he voluntarily ascended his funeral pile, and was received among the gods.

Hereward (her'e-wărd) **the Wake.** Hero of Kingsley's novel of that name, one of the English who long resisted the power of William the Conqueror.

Hermes (hẽr'mēs). The Greek deity regarded as equivalent to the Roman Mercury, the messenger of the gods, the inventor of the lyre (which he resigned to Apollo), the god of commerce, and also of fraud and cunning. He is generally represented with small wings attached to his head and ankles, and with a winged rod—the caduceus.

Hermes Trismegistus (tris-mē-gis'tus). A mythical personage, the same as the Egyptian god Thoth, considered the author of a great number of ancient occult writings.

Hermia (hẽr'mi-ȧ). One of the heroines of Shakespeare's *Midsummer Nights' Dream*.

Hermione (hẽr-mī'ō-nē). In Shakespeare's *Winter's Tale*, the wife of King Leontes of Sicily, unjustly suspected by her husband. She is an example of 'dignity without pride, love without passion, and tenderness without weakness.'

Hero (hē'rō). The beautiful priestess of Venus at Sestos, to visit whom Leander used to swim the Hellespont nightly. On his death she drowned herself.—The quiet and serious daughter of Leonato in Shakespeare's *Much Ado About Nothing*.

Hesperides (hes-per'i-dēs). In Greek mythology, three nymphs who lived in pleasant gardens in an island of the western ocean, and had charge of a tree which produced golden apples. One of the labors of Hercules was to fetch apples from this tree, which was watched by a dragon.

Hesperus (hes'pẽr-us). In classical literature a personification of the evening star (the planet Venus).

Hestia (hes'tyȧ). The Greek name of the goddess Vesta.

Hexam (heks'ăm), **Lizzie.** The heroine of Dickens' *Our Mutual Friend*, a beautiful, intelligent girl of humble birth, who saves Eugene Wrayburn's life, when he is all but killed by the jealous Bradley Headstone, and becomes his wife.

Heythorp (hē'thorp), **Sylvanus.** In Galsworthy's story *A Stoic*, dramatized as *Old English*, a resolute octogenarian who has lived richly though not scrupulously, and eludes imminent ignominy.

Hiawatha (hī-ȧ-wä'thȧ). A mythical hero of the North American Indians, subject of a poem by Longfellow.

Higgins (hig'inṣ), **Henry.** The professor of phonetics in G. B. Shaw's play *Pygmalion.* See **Doolittle, Eliza.**

Hippocrene (hip'ō-ç̄rēn; hip-ō-ç̄rē'nē). A fountain of the Muses in ancient Greece, on Mount Helicon.

Hippolyta (hip-pol'y-tȧ). In classical literature, a queen of the Amazons, according to some accounts married to Theseus. One of Hercules' twelve labors was to capture her girdle, which she had received from Mars, her father.

Hippolytus (hip-pol'y-tus). In Greek fable, a chaste youth, son of Theseus. After his stepmother Phaedra had vainly tried to seduce him, she accused him to his father of attempting her virtue, thus bringing about his death.

Hippomenes (hip-pom'e-nēṣ). See **Atalanta.**

Hodge (hoġ). The servant of Gammer Gurton in the old comedy (see **Gurton**), and also a name typical of a rustic or a farm laborer.

Holmes (hōmṣ), **Sherlock.** A shrewd detective who is the hero of many tales by A. Conan Doyle. The stories are related in the first person by Holmes' assistant, Dr. Watson.

Holofernes (hol-ō-fẽr'nēṣ). A pedant in Shakespeare's *Love's Labour's Lost*

Honeycomb (hŏn'i-ç̄ōm), **Will.** One of the members of the club described in the *Spectator*, an oracle on matters of fashion.

Honeyman (hŏn'i-măn), **Charles.** A lackadaisical High Church clergyman in Thackeray's *Newcomes*, an uncle to Clive Newcome, smacking of the humbug and sybarite.

Hood (hood), **Robin.** See **Robin Hood.**

Hopeful (hōp'ful). A companion of Christian in *Pilgrim's Progress*, who, after Faithful's death, accompanies him to the end of his journey.

Horae (hō'rē). Ancient deities personifying the changes of the seasons, usually called in English the Hours.

Horatio (hō-rā'shi-ō). In Shakespeare's *Hamlet*, the friend and intimate of Hamlet.

Horatius Cocles (hō-rā'shus ç̄oç'lēṣ). The hero of an ancient Roman legend, which tells how he held the wooden bridge leading into Rome against Lars Porsena's men until the Romans had time to cut it. See Lord Macaulay's *Lays of Ancient Rome.*

Hortensio (hor-ten'shi-ō). In Shakespeare's *Taming of the Shrew*, lover of Bianca.

Horus (hō'rus). An ancient Egyptian deity personifying the sun.

Hotspur (hot'spũr). Name of Harry Percy in Shakespeare's *Henry IV.*

Houyhnhnms (hö-yn'umṣ). In Swift's *Gulliver's Travels*, the race of wonderful horses among whom his hero is thrown. They are endowed with reason and form a civilized community, their servants being the Yahoos.

Hubberd (hub'ẽrd), **Mother.** The supposed teller of a story in *Mother Hubberd's Tale*, a satirical fable by Spenser.

Hubert (hū'bẽrt). **St.** Patron saint of huntsmen.

Hudibras (hū'di-bras). The hero of the famous satire in verse by Samuel Butler directed against the Puritans. Hudibras is a ridiculous Presbyterian knight-errant with a squire named Ralpho.

Hudson (hud'sŏn), **Roderick.** In Henry James' novel of the same name, a young American sculptor who goes to Rome to study, has a love affair, and loses sight of his objectives.

Hugh (hū). An ostler in Dickens' *Barnaby Rudge*, illegitimate son of Sir John Chester, a rude, kindhearted giant, executed for the part he took in the Gordon riots.

Hugh of Lincoln (ov liñ'ç̄ŏn). A young boy who, according to an old English legend, the subject of Chaucer's *Prioress's Tale*, was murdered by the Jews of Lincoln.

Hugo (hū'gō). Son of Azo, in Byron's *Parisina*, put to death by his father because he loved and was beloved by Parisina, who had been betrothed to him before his father took her as his wife.

Humphrey (hum'fri), **Master.** The imaginary compiler of the tales by Dickens in *Master Humphrey's Clock*, including *Barnaby Rudge.*

Huncamunca (huñ'ç̄ȧ-muñ'ç̄ȧ), **Princess.** Heroine of Fielding's burlesque *Tom Thumb*, daughter of King Arthur.

Hunchback (hunch'bak), **the Little.** Subject of a story in the *Arabian Nights.*

Hunchback of Notre-Dame. See **Quasimodo.**

Hunter (hunt'ẽr), **Mrs. Leo.** A ridiculous matron in Dickens' *Pickwick Papers*, who courts any social 'lion' within reach.

Hunter, Vridar. The hero, largely autobiographical, of a realistic tetralogy of novels by Vardis Fisher. He is an Idaho youth whose first wife commits suicide, who remarries and becomes a college professor, and then returns to his early home to write of his inner struggles and his discovery of moral freedom.

Hyacinthus (hȳ-ȧ-cin'thus). A beautiful boy beloved by Apollo and, according to one version, accidentally killed by a discus thrown by the latter; from his blood sprang the flower hyacinth.

Hydra (hȳ'drȧ). A nine-headed monster slain by Hercules, fulfilling one of his twelve labors. Since for each head that he cut off two new heads sprang up, he finished the task with fire.

Hylas (hȳ'lăs). A youth beloved by Hercules and carried off by water nymphs charmed with his beauty.

Hymen (hȳ'men). God of marriage among the Greeks and Romans.

Hyperion (hȳ-pē'ri-ŏn). In ancient mythology, one of the Titans; sometimes a name equivalent to the sun.

Hypnos (hyp'nos). God of sleep among the ancient Greeks.

I

Iachimo (yäç̄h'ī-mō). An Italian libertine in Shakespeare's *Cymbeline*, who leads Posthumus to believe that his wife Imogen has been unfaithful to him.

Iago (ī-ä'gō). The 'ancient' or ensign of Othello in Shakespeare's *Othello*, who, out of jealousy and devilish malignity, persuades the Moor of Desdemona's unfaithfulness.

Ibbetson (ib'et-sŏn), **Peter.** In the novel of the same name by George du Maurier, a prisoner who shares a dream existence with his beloved.

Icarus (iç'ȧ-rus). The son of Daedalus, who fled with his father, but soared too high. The sun melted the wax attachments of his wings, so that he fell into the sea and was drowned. See **Daedalus.**

Idalia (ī-dā'li-ȧ). A name for Venus, from Idalium in Cyprus.

Idomeneus (ī-dom'ē-nūs). A king of ancient Crete, who sacrificed his own son in fulfillment of a rash vow similar to that of Jephthah.

Ignaro (ig-nä'rō). Foster father of Orgoglio in Spenser's *Faërie Queene*, who always answers, 'I cannot tell' to questions.

Iliad (il'i-ăd), **The.** Poem by Homer. See **Ilium.**

Ilium *or* **Ilion** (il'i-um; il'i-ŏn). A poetic name of Troy, whence the name of Homer's Greek epic the *Iliad*. This poem (in twenty-four books) describes incidents that take place during part of the ten years' war waged by the Greeks against Troy, the cause of which was the abduction of Helen, wife of the Greek prince Menelaus, by Paris, son of Priam, king of Troy. The *Iliad* begins with a quarrel and its important consequences between Achilles, the chief Grecian warrior, and Agamemnon, the generalissimo of the Greek host. It ends with the funeral of Hector, who is slain by Achilles, and whose parting with his wife Andromache before the fatal contest is one of the most famous passages in the epic. Gods as well as heroes are freely introduced, and the whole sets before us a varied, richly colored, and impressive picture of ancient life.

Imlac (im'laç). A poet and traveler, the friend of Rasselas in Samuel Johnson's novel *Rasselas.*

Imogen (im'ō-ġen). The wife of Posthumus and heroine of Shakespeare's *Cymbeline*. She suffers sorrow and hardship through her husband's belief in her infidelity (see **Iachimo**), but is finally made happy.

Inchcape Rock (inch'ç̄āp rok). The Bell Rock, in the North Sea, upon which a warning bell was fixed. Southey wrote a ballad with this name, telling how Ralph the Rover removed the bell and was wrecked on the rock himself.

Indra (in'drȧ). A Hindu god of the heavens.

Inez (ī'nez), **Donna.** Mother of Byron's Don Juan, a learned lady whose strict training of her son hardly succeeded as she desired.

Inger (iñ'gẽr). The wife of Isak in Hamsun's *Growth of the Soil*, who is a symbol for childbearing farm women.

Io (ī'ō). In classical mythology, a princess beloved by Jupiter, and temporarily changed into a cow to avoid the enmity of Juno.

Ion (ī'on). A son of Apollo, and ancestor of the Ionians or Athenian Greeks.—A king of Argos, who offered himself as a victim to appease the wrath of the gods.

Iphigenia (if-i-ġe-nī'ȧ). A daughter of Agamemnon and Clytemnestra, who was about to be sacrificed by her father to avert the wrath of Artemis, when, at the last moment, Artemis saved her life and made her a priestess. She is the subject of tragedies by Aeschylus, Euripides, Racine, and Goethe, and operas by Gluck.

Iris (ī'ris). A Greek and Roman goddess of the rainbow; also, a messenger of the gods, especially of Juno.

Irus (ī'rus). A beggar of Ithaca who provoked the ire of Ulysses, who was himself acting the beggar on his return from Troy.

Isaac of York (ī'ṣȧç ov york). A wealthy Jew, father of Rebecca, in Scott's *Ivanhoe.*

Isabella (iṣ-ȧ-bel'ȧ). The heroine of Shakespeare's *Measure for Measure*, for whom Angelo, the deputy of the duke of Vienna, has an evil passion, and whose brother Claudio is willing to sacrifice her virtue in return for his own safety.—Heroine of Keats' poem *Isabella or, the Pot of Basil.*

Isak (ī'ṣăk). The peasant in Knut Hamsun's *Growth of the Soil*, husband of Inger, who epitomizes the ancient traditional struggle of man with the soil.

Isengrim (ī'ṣn-grim). The wolf, uncle of Reynard, in the famous story of *Reynard the Fox.*

Isis (ī'sis). An Egyptian goddess of the moon, wife of Osiris and mother of Horus, often represented as veiled.

Islands of the Blest *or* **Fortunate Islands.** Islands believed by the Greeks to lie far out in the Atlantic and to form a sort of Elysium.

Isolde (i-sōld'; i-sōl'de), **Iseult** *or* **Yseult** (i-sûlt'), *or* **Isolt** (i-sōlt'; is'ōlt). The name of two heroines of medieval romance belonging to the Arthurian cycle. Isolde the Fair was the wife of King Mark and the lover of Tristram. In one version of the story, Mark killed Tristram. In another, Tristram fled from Mark and married Isolde of the White Hands, also called Isolde of Brittany, through whose treachery both he and Isolde the Fair died.

Israfil *or* **Israfel** (is'rȧ-fil; -fel). In Mohammedan mythology, the angel who will blow the trump at the resurrection, and who himself has 'the sweetest voice of all God's creatures.'

Ishtar (ish'tär). In early Babylonian mythology, the goddess of the evening star, in later times the fruitful goddess of the earth and the patroness of love, whose cult was associated with voluptuousness and abominable rites: equivalent to the Ashtoreth of the Phoenicians and of the Old Testament, and to the Astarte of the Greeks.

Ithuriel (i-thū'ri-el). An angel in Milton's *Paradise Lost* who, when he found Satan in the shape of ' toad, 'close at the ear of Eve,' touched him wit his spear and thus made him at once return to his proper form.

Ivanhoe (ī'văn-hō). The hero of Scott's well-known novel, son of Cedric the Saxon, and a favorite of Richard I. He loves and ultimately marries Rowena, the Saxon beauty.

Ixion (ik-sī'on). In classical mythology, a Thessalian king who for his wickedness was punished in the infernal regions by being bound to a perpetually revolving fiery wheel.

J

Jack (jak), **Colonel.** The hero of a fictitious biography by Defoe, who from a pickpocket becomes a slave-owner in America.

Jaffier (jaf'yẽr). Hero of Otway's tragedy *Venice Preserved*, which revolves upon a conspiracy to assassinate the Venetian senate. He is induced by his friend Pierre to participate in the plot; and by his wife Belvidera to reveal it on condition of a general amnesty. Deceived in the latter regard, though spared himself, he stabs Pierre to save him from the wheel, then kills himself; and Belvidera goes mad and dies.

Jaggers (jag'ẽrṣ). A criminal lawyer in Dickens' *Great Expectations*, a dark, stern man, who serves as Pip's guardian.

Jalna (jäl'nȧ). The home of the Whiteoak family.

Janus (jā'nus). A Roman deity represented with two faces looking in opposite directions, and whose temple was closed in time of peace, but open during war.

Jaques (jāk'wēṣ; zäk). A melancholy and contemplative lord in Shakespeare's *As You Like It.*

Jarley (jär'li), **Mrs.** The proprietress of a traveling waxworks in Dickens' *Old Curiosity Shop*, who employs little Nell in showing off the figures.

Jarndyce (järn'dyç), **Mr.** A character in Dickens' *Bleak House*, good-natured and shrewd, who is given to remarking when anything annoying happens to him, 'The wind is in the east.' In the law suit, Jarndyce v. Jarndyce, Dickens caricatures the court of chancery.

Jarvie (jär'vi), **Bailie Nicol.** A Glasgow magistrate in Scott's *Rob Roy*, conceited and prejudiced, but kindhearted.

Jason (jā'sŏn). An ancient Greek hero, the leader of the Argonauts and husband of Medea. See **Argo, Medea.**

Javert (ẓȧ-ver'). A police officer in Victor Hugo's *Les Misérables*, the personification of devotion to duty. See **Valjean.**

Jeames (jēmṣ). Jeames de la Pluche, the professed writer of an amusing diary, one of Thackeray's contributions to *Punch*; a footman who makes money by railway speculation and for a time is a man of consequence.

Jeddler (jed'lẽr), **Dr., and his daughters Grace and Marion.** Characters in Dickens' *Battle of Life.*

Jekyll (jēk'l; jek'l), **Dr.** Character in a romance of R. L. Stevenson's called *The Strange Case of Dr. Jekyll and Mr. Hyde*. Dr. Jekyll is a man of excellent character and principles, who by means of a drug can change his personality so that he becomes the debased and sensual being known as Mr. Hyde.

Jellyby (jel'y-by), **Mrs.** In Dickens' *Bleak House*, a lady so immersed in missionary matters, and so much concerned for the poor heathens in Africa, especially those of Borrioboo[illegible]-Gha, that she neglects her own household.

Jenkins (jeñ'kinṣ), **Winifred.** In Smollett's *Humphry Clinker*, Miss Tabitha Bramble's maid, who writes letters amusing for their blunders, and becomes the wife of Humphry.

Jenkinson (jeñ'kin-sŏn), **Ephraim.** A swindler in Goldsmith's *Vicar of Wakefield*, who cheats the vicar and his son Moses and talks learnedly about the 'cosmogony of the world.'

Jeremy (jer'e-my). A little English boy, whose adventures, and those of his dog, are told in *Jeremy* and *Jeremy and Hamlet*, by Hugh Walpole.

Jerome (jer'ŏm), **Don.** In Sheridan's play *The Duenna*, the father of the heroine, Louisa.

Jessica (jes'i-ç̄ȧ). The charming daughter of Shylock, the Jew, in Shakespeare's *Merchant of Venice*. She elopes with Lorenzo, leaving the old man distracted between the loss of 'his ducats and his daughter.'

Jew (jû), **the Wandering.** See **Wandering Jew.**

Jingle (jiñ'gl), **Alfred.** An amusing strolling player and swindler in Dickens' *Pickwick Papers*, who talks in a peculiar elliptical style. Though cheated by him, Mr. Pickwick rescues him from debtor's prison. His henchman is Job Trotter.

Jiniwin (jin'i-win), **Mrs.** Quilp's mother-in-law in Dickens' *Old Curiosity Shop.*

Jo (jō). A poor outcast in Dickens' *Bleak House.*

Joad (jōd) **Family.** A family of Oklahoma sharecroppers of old American stock who are the central figures in John Steinbeck's novel *The Grapes of Wrath.* Driven from their farm by dust and drought, they drive to California, where they have heard that jobs are available in the orchards. Included are Ma, the granitelike character who manages to keep the family together; Pa, the eternal searcher for the land of Canaan; Tom, their son, who becomes a fugitive after killing a vigilante; and their daughter Rosasharn, who gives birth to a baby under harrowing conditions.

Joan (jōn). See **Darby and Joan.**

Jocasta (jō-ças'tȧ). See **Oedipus.**

Joe, the Fat Boy (jō thē fat boi). See **Fat Boy.**

John (jon), **Don.** The bastard brother of Don Pedro in Shakespeare's *Much Ado about Nothing.*

John, Friar. See **Friar John.**

John, Prester. See **Prester John.**

Johnson (jon'sŏn), **Maggie.** The heroine of Stephen Crane's *Maggie: A Girl of the Streets,* who is seduced by Pete the bartender, turns prostitute, and commits suicide.

Jolly Roger (jol'y roġ'ẽr). See **Black Flag.**

Jones (jōnṣ), **Tom.** The hero of a novel by Fielding, manly and goodhearted but dissipated and wanting in self-respect. He marries Sophia, daughter of Squire Western.

Jordan (jọr'dăn), **Robert.** The hero of Hemingway's novel *For Whom the Bell Tolls,* a young American liberal who joins the Loyalist cause in the Spanish civil war of 1936–39 and executes a fateful assignment to blow up a key bridge. See **Maria, Pilar.**

Jordan, Ruth. The heroine of William Vaughn Moody's play *The Great Divide,* which reflects differences of attitude between New England and the West.

Jordans (jọr'dănṣ), **the.** The members of a New England family in Owen Davis' play *Icebound.* Most of them are selfishly awaiting inheritance from their mother, but she has left her money to Jane Crosby, who has befriended her, to hold for Ben Jordan, the black sheep of the family, whom Jane loves.

Jorkins (jọrk'inṣ). Partner of Mr. Spenlow, in Dickens' *David Copperfield.* See **Spenlow.**

José (hō-sẹ'), **Don.** A young Spanish officer in Mérimée's *Carmen,* in love with the fickle Carmen, whom he finally kills.

Joseph Andrews. See **Andrews.**

Jotunheim (yọ'tụn-hẹm). The abode of the frost giants in Scandinavian mythology.

Jourdain (z̄ör-dañ'), **Monsieur.** The hero of Molière's comedy *Le Bourgeois Gentilhomme,* representing a worthy but ignorant bourgeois placed by his wealth among gentlemen, but who renders himself ridiculous in his attempts to acquire all the accomplishments necessary to fashionable life.

Jove (jōv). Alternative name of Jupiter.

Juan (hwän), **Don.** See **Don Juan.**

Juba (jṳ'bȧ). Prince of Numidia in Addison's *Cato.*

Jude (jṳd). See **Fawley, Jude.**

Julia (jṳl'i-ȧ). A lady in Shakespeare's *Two Gentlemen of Verona,* beloved but for a time left by Proteus.

Julia, Donna. A married woman in Byron's *Don Juan,* sent to a convent because of her liaison with the young don.

Julian (jṳl'i-ăn), **Count.** A nobleman of Spanish legend whose daughter Florinda was debauched by Roderick, the Gothic king, and who in revenge brought in the Moors.

Julie (z̄ü-lē'). The heroine of Rousseau's *Nouvelle Héloïse.*

Juliet (jṳ'li-et). The heroine of Shakespeare's famous tragedy *Romeo and Juliet,* a member of the Capulet family, while Romeo is one of the Montagues.

Juno (jṳ'nō). The supreme goddess among the Romans, wife of Jupiter and queen of heaven; identified with the Greek Hera.

Jupiter (jṳ'pi-tẽr). The supreme Roman deity, also called Jove; son of Saturn; identified with the Greek Zeus.

Jurgen (jũr'gen). A middle-aged pawnbroker, the leading character in the allegorical novel of the same name by James Branch Cabell. Given a year of youth, he leaves his wife, Dame Lisa, and has numerous erotic adventures in the imaginary realm of Poictesme.

K

K. (kā). The hero of Franz Kafka's *The Castle,* a land surveyor whose fruitless efforts to enter the Castle in the novel are probably symbolic of man's striving for divine grace.

K., Joseph. A bank assessor who is arrested for a crime about which he knows nothing, in Franz Kafka's novel *The Trial.* His vain attempt to defend himself probably symbolizes man's quest of an essentially inscrutable divine justice.

Kaf (kaf). In Mohammedan mythology, a mountain that surrounds and walls in the earth.

Kama (kä'mä). The Hindu god of love.

Karamazov (ka-rȧ-mä'zọf) **Family.** The leading characters in Dostoevski's novel *The Brothers Karamazov.* The elder Karamazov, a miserly, drunken roué, has three legitimate sons: Dmitri, a hot-tempered roisterer, of military education; Ivan, a self-doubting intellectual and nihilist; and Alexey, a gentle religious mystic. When the father is murdered by his other, illegitimate son Smerdyakov, an epileptic, Dmitri is charged with the crime on circumstantial evidence. Ivan, who discovers that he has unwittingly inspired Smerdyakov's deed, vainly tries to save Dmitri.

Karenina (kä-rẹ'nyi-nȧ), **Anna.** The heroine of Leo Tolstoy's novel of the same name. She leaves her husband and son for the dashing Russian officer Vronsky, and when she loses his love, commits suicide by throwing herself under a train.

Katharina *or* **Katharine,** (kath-ȧ-rī'nȧ; kath'ȧ-rin). Heroine of Shakespeare's *Taming of the Shrew,* the elder daughter of Baptista, a wealthy gentleman of Padua. She is noted for both her beauty and her shrewish temper, until Petruchio of Verona, who marries her, so 'tames' her by his stronger will that she becomes the most submissive of wives and a model for all others.

Kay (kā), **Sir.** A rude, boastful, and mannerless knight at King Arthur's court.

Kehama (kē-hä'mȧ). A great Indian rajah who obtains supernatural powers but meets a wretched doom, the subject of Southey's poem *The Curse of Kehama.*

Kenilworth (ken'il-wŏrth). A castle in Warwickshire, the scene of Scott's novel of that name in which are introduced Queen Elizabeth, the Earl of Leicester, Amy Robsart, etc.

Kennaquhair (ken'ȧ-kwãr). Scottish for a place which does not exist; a name for some imaginary place.

Kennaston (ken'ăs-tŏn), **Felix.** The hero of Cabell's *Cream of the Jest,* by day a sedate writer but at night a visitor in the magic world of Poictesme, where he is in love with the beautiful Ettarre; but he finds that dreams are not a satisfying escape from reality.

Kennicott (ken'i-çot), **Carol.** The dissatisfied heroine of Sinclair Lewis' novel *Main Street.*

Kenwigs' (ken'wigṣ). Members of an artisan's family aiming at a measure of gentility, in Dickens' *Nickolas Nickleby.* Mrs. Kenwigs' uncle, Mr. Lillyvick, is a rate collector of some means and is worshiped accordingly by the family. There are also several little girls, who wear their hair in flaxen pigtails fastened by bows of blue ribbon.

Kew (kū), **Lady.** In Thackeray's *Newcomes,* an aristocratic dowager, grandmother of Ethel Newcome, given to domineering over all the members of her family, though Ethel is disposed to rebel. Her grandson Lord Kew, an amiable young nobleman, was at one time engaged to Ethel.

Keyne (kēn), **St.** A Celtic saint, noted for her well, near Liskeard, Cornwall. According to folklore, whoever—of a bridegroom and his bride—drinks from it first, will be 'boss' of the house. Southey wrote a ballad on the legend.

Kim (kim). An Irish boy (full name, Kimball O'Hara) who lives adventurously in India, in Kipling's novel *Kim,* and wins fame for counterespionage.

Kit Nubbles (kit nub'lṣ). See **Nubbles, Kit.**

Knickerbocker (nik'ẽr-bok-ẽr), **Diedrich.** An imaginary Dutchman put forward as the author of a fictitious history of New York written by Washington Irving.

Kriemhild (krēm'hilt). In the *Nibelungenlied,* the wife of Siegfried and sister of Gunther.

Krishna (krish'nȧ). In Hindu mythology, the eighth avatar of Vishnu. According to one story he was the son of Vasudeva and Devaki, and his uncle Kansa, the demon-king of Mathura, sought to kill him while a child because of a divine warning that this nephew would some day slay him. With divine help the child escaped, was brought up by shepherds, and after numerous heroic and amorous exploits he slew Kansa and occupied the throne. Krishna was ultimately killed by an arrow shot by a huntsman.

Krook (krook). In Dickens' *Bleak House,* a drunken old dealer in rags and bones, who dies of spontaneous combustion.

Kuvera (kṳ-vẹ'rȧ). The Hindu god of wealth.

Kwasind (kwä'sind). In Longfellow's *Hiawatha,* the strongest man who ever lived.

L

Lachesis (laçh'ē-sis). One of the three classic Fates: the one who measured the length of the thread of life. See **Atropos, Clotho.**

Ladas (lā'dăs). A famous runner of ancient Greece, whose swiftness became proverbial.

Ladislaw (lad'is-lạ), **Will.** A gay and likable character in George Eliot's novel *Middlemarch,* ultimately married to Dorothea Brooke.

Lady Bountiful (lā'dy boun'ti-fụl). See **Bountiful.**

Lady of Shalott (ov shȧ-lot'). The title of a poem by Tennyson; the lady's fate is similar to that of Elaine.

Lady of the Lake (thē lāk). A female of supernatural powers who figures in the legend of King Arthur.—Also the name of a poem by Sir Walter Scott, from its heroine Ellen Douglas, whose father has been banished from court by James V of Scotland, and with whom she lives near Loch Katrine.

Laertes (lā-ẽr'tēṣ). In Greek story the father of Ulysses.—In Shakespeare's *Hamlet,* son of Polonius and brother of Ophelia.

Lafeu (lȧ-fū'). An old lord in Shakespeare's *All's Well that Ends Well.*

Lagado (lȧ-gä'dō). In Swift's *Gulliver's Travels,* the capital of Balnibarbi, visited by Gulliver in his Laputa journey. It is famous for its academy of projectors, in which the scholars assiduously work on schemes for extracting sunbeams from cucumbers, converting ice into gunpowder, etc.

Lalla Rookh (lȧ'lä rọọk). The heroine of Thomas Moore's poem of this name, represented as a daughter of the emperor Aurungzebe, and as going to Cashmere to marry the sultan of Bucharia. On the way she is entertained by a series of tales told by a young Persian poet named Feramorz, with whom she falls in love, and who turns out to be the sultan in disguise.

Lambro (lam'brō). In Byron's *Don Juan,* a Greek pirate, father of Haidee, represented as having his headquarters in a small island of the Aegean, and as being 'the mildest-mannered man that ever scuttled ship or cut a throat.'

Lamia (lā'mi-ȧ). A kind of female demon of the nature of a serpent, who, in guise of a beautiful woman, marries a young man, as told in a poem by Keats so named.

Lammermoor (lam'ẽr-mọọr), **Bride of.** Lucy Ashton, heroine of a tragic novel by Scott. See **Ashton, Ravenswood.**

Lancelot *or* **Launcelot** (lan'ce-lot; lanc'lot; lạn'). The most famous of King Arthur's knights, paramour of Queen Guinevere.

Languish (lañ'gwish), **Lydia.** A very romantic young lady, the heroine of Sheridan's comedy *The Rivals.* See **Absolute.**

Lantier (läñ-tyẹ'), **Étienne.** The leading character in Émile Zola's social novel *Germinal,* a coal miner and labor agitator.

Laocoön (lā-oç'ō-on). In Greek legend, a Trojan priest who along with his two sons was killed by two enormous serpents—an incident represented in sculpture.

Laodamia (lā'o-dȧ-mī'ȧ). In classic fable, the wife of Protesilaus, whom she followed to Hades after his death.

Lapham (lap'ăm), **Silas.** The central character in Howells' novel *The Rise of Silas Lapham,* a man who has made a fortune and would like to see his daughters accepted by Boston's social aristocracy. When his finances collapse, his essential worthiness becomes apparent.

Laputa (lȧ-pū'tȧ). A sort of flying island visited by Gulliver, raised above the earth by means of a huge lodestone, and inhabited by persons engaged in the most abstruse studies. These philosophers become so deeply immersed in study as to be quite oblivious of everything else, and therefore they have attendants called 'flappers,' whose duty is to rouse their attention by striking them with a blown bladder attached to a handle.

Lara (lär'ȧ). A name of Conrad the Corsair, under which he appears as the hero of Byron's poem *Lara.*

Larsen (lär'sen), **Wolf.** The brutal captain of a tramp steamer in Jack London's novel *The Sea-Wolf.* A pair of lovers manage to escape from his power only after some harrowing adventures.

Las Casas (läs çä'säs). A noble old Spaniard in Sheridan's *Pizarro.*

Last of the Goths (låst ov thē gọths). Don Roderick, last of the Gothic kings of Spain.—**of the knights,** Maximilian I, emperor of Germany (1459–1519).—**of the Mohicans,** Uncas in Cooper's novel.—**of the Romans,** Cassius, one of the murderers of Caesar, was so called by his fellow-assassin Brutus; and Congreve, Dr. Johnson, and others have been called *ultimus Romanorum.*—**of the Tribunes,** Cola di Rienzi, hero of Bulwer-Lytton's novel named for him.—**of the Troubadours,** Jacques Jasmin, the Gascon.

Latona (lȧ-tō'nȧ). The mother of Apollo and Diana by Jupiter.

Launce (lạnc). An amusing clown in Shakespeare's *Two Gentlemen of Verona,* who has a dog named Crab.

Launfal (lạn'fạl), **Sir.** King Arthur's steward, possessed of a never-failing purse. See also Lowell's poem *The Vision of Sir Launfal.*

Laurence (lạr'enc), **Friar.** The Franciscan friar in Shakespeare's *Romeo and Juliet.* To the latter he gave a sleeping draught, and when Romeo found her apparently dead he killed himself.

Lavaine (lȧ-vān'), **Sir.** A brave young knight and brother of Elaine in Tennyson's *Idylls of the King.*

Lavendar (lav'en-dăr), **Dr.** The best-known character in Margaret Deland's Old Chester novels. He is a kindly old clergyman who acts as friend and advisor to his parishioners.

Lavinia (lȧ-vin'i-ȧ). In Virgil's *Aeneid,* the second wife of Aeneas, previously betrothed to Turnus, king of the Rutuli, a people of Latium.—The hapless heroine of Shakespeare's *Titus Andronicus.*

Lavransdatter (läv'räns-dạt-ẽr). **Kristin.** The heroine of a trilogy of the same name, by Sigrid Undset, who lived in 13th-century Norway. She rejects her faithful suitor, Simon Andressön to marry the fascinating scoundrel Erlend Nikulaussön, the master of Husaby. Her life thereafter is marked by happiness, adversity, and disaster.

Lazenby (lā'zen-by), **Lady Sybil.** A character in J. M. Barrie's play *What Every Woman Knows.* After John Shand, the husband of Maggie Wylie, becomes a successful politician, he falls in love with Lady Sybil; but Maggie throws them together so much that he becomes surfeited and returns to his wife.

Leander (lē-an'dẽr). In Greek story a young man of Abydos who used to swim the Hellespont to visit Hero of Sestos. See **Hero.**

Leandro the Fair (lē-an'drō thē fãr). A knight whose adventures are narrated in the Spanish romance *Amadis de Gaul.*

Lear (lẽr). A mythical king of Britain, the subject of Shakespeare's tragedy *King Lear.* Confident of the love of his daughters Goneril and Regan, he divides his kingdom between them, believing that his other daughter, Cordelia, is undutiful; but the former drive him mad by ingratitude, and he learns the worth of Cordelia only too late.

Leatherstocking (leth'ẽr-stok'ing). A famous character in several of James Fenimore Cooper's novels, whose real name is Natty Bumppo. He appears also as Hawkeye, the Pathfinder, the Trapper, and the Deerslayer.

Lecoq (lē-çok'), **Monsieur.** The fictional detective of Émile Gaboriau.

Leda (lē'dȧ). In Greek mythology, the mother of Castor and Pollux, Helen, and Clytemnestra. She was visited by Jupiter in the form of a swan.

Leeds (lēdş), **Nina.** A neurotic woman in Eugene O'Neill's drama *Strange Interlude*, in love with her fiancé, Gordon, who has died in the war. She marries Sam Evans, discovers there is insanity in his family, and bears a son by Dr. Darrell. Ultimately she marries a writer, Marsden, who has always followed her with doglike devotion. The secret thoughts of the characters are revealed by the use of asides.

Leerie (lẽr'i). A lamplighter beloved of children in Robert Louis Stevenson's poem *The Lamplighter*.

Legree (lē-grē'). **Simon.** A brutal slave owner in Mrs. Stowe's *Uncle Tom's Cabin*.

Leigh (lē), **Amyas.** Hero of Kingsley's novel *Westward Ho!*, a tale of Elizabethan times, and of the war between England and Spain.

Leigh, Aurora. Heroine of Mrs. Browning's poem of that name, the story of a poetess and her love.

Lennie (len'i). See **Small, Lennie.**

Lenore (lē-nọr'). A heroine of German ballad whose dead lover in spectral form carries her on horseback with him to the graveyard.

Leonato (lē-ō-nä'tō). Father of Hero in Shakespeare's *Much Ado About Nothing*.

Leonora (lē-ō-nō'rȧ). In Beethoven's opera *Fidelio*, the wife of Fernando Florestan, who is confined as a state prisoner at Seville. To save her husband she enters into the service of Rocco, the jailer, disguised as a young man, and under the name of Fidelio.—The heroine of Verdi's opera *Il Trovatore*. She is enamoured of Manrico, the troubadour, reputed son of Azucena, a gypsy. The two latter fall into the power of Count di Luna, who loves Leonora, and puts Manrico to death, not knowing he is actually his brother, while Leonora falls victim to a poisoned ring she has sucked.

Leontes (lē-on'tēş). In Shakespeare's *Winter's Tale*, king of Sicily, husband of Hermione and father of Perdita. The action of the play derives from his jealous suspicion of his wife.

Lesly (les'ly), **Ludovic, le Balafré.** A character in Scott's *Quentin Durward*. See **Balafré.**

Lessways (les'wāş), **Hilda.** The girl whom Clayhanger loves in Bennett's trilogy. She marries Cannon, discovers he is a bigamist, and is finally reunited with Clayhanger.

Lester (les'tẽr), **Jeeter.** A degenerate Georgia cracker, the leading character in Erskine Caldwell's novel and play *Tobacco Road*.

Lethe (lē'thē). One of the rivers of the infernal regions in Greek mythology, which caused those who drank its water to lose all recollection of their past existence.

Libitina (lib-i-tī'nȧ). An ancient Roman goddess presiding over deaths and funerals.

Lichas (lī'ҫhȧs). The friend of Hercules, who brought him the fatal garment prepared by Deianira. Hercules, frenzied with pain, threw him into the sea.

Ligea (li-ġē'ȧ). One of the three Sirens. The others were Parthenope and Leucosia.

Light of the Harem, the. Nourmahal, the bride of Selim, in Moore's *Lalla Rookh*.

Liliom (lil'yŏm). A swaggering but likable barker in Ferenc Molnár's drama of the same name, who marries a servant girl and ill-treats her. For the sake of their child he commits a crime. He dies; is tried in heaven and sent to hell, from which after sixteen years he is sent back to earth for one day, to see whether he can do one good deed. He does not learn humility even in hell.

Lilith (lil'ith). In Jewish mythology, a sort of female demon who was Adam's wife before Eve was created.

Lilliput (lil'i-put). The land of the Lilliputians, pygmies about six inches tall, in Swift's *Gulliver's Travels*.

Lilyvick (lil'y-vik), **Mr.** A pompous collector of water rates in Dickens' *Nicholas Nickleby*, uncle of Mrs. Kenwigs.

Lily Maid of Astolat (lil'y mād ov as'tō-lät). A name of Elaine.

Linkinwater (liṅ'kin-wä-tẽr), **Tim.** The devoted head clerk of the brothers Cheeryble in Dickens' *Nicholas Nickleby*.

Li Po (lī pō). A poet in Donn Byrne's *Messer Marco Polo*.

Lirriper (lir'i-pẽr), **Mrs.** A kindhearted and voluble London lodginghouse-keeper who is the chief character in two of Dickens' Christmas stories.

Lisa (lī'sȧ), **Dame.** The prosaic wife of Jurgen in Cabell's novel *Jurgen*, to whom he rather thankfully returns after his adventures.

Lismahago (lis-mȧ-hā'gō), **Captain.** In Smollett's *Humphry Clinker*, a superannuated Scottish officer, dour, eccentric, and conceited, who marries Tabitha Bramble for her money.

Little Black Sambo (lit'l blak sam'bō). A little colored boy in a popular children's tale, who meets with tigers in the jungle, and escapes when they all pursue each other, finally melting into a pool of butter which his mother, Black Mumbo, makes into pancakes.

Little Corporal (çọr'pō-rȧl). A nickname of Napoleon Bonaparte, given to him after the battle of Lodi (1796) by his soldiers, from his youthful appearance.

Little Dorrit (dọr'it). The heroine of a novel of the same name by Dickens, born and brought up in the Marshalsea prison.

Little Em'ly (em'ly). See *Emily*.

Little-endians (-en'di-ȧnş). See **Big-endians.**

Little John (jon). Robin Hood's lieutenant, a man of great stature and strength.

Lochinvar (loḉh-in-vär'). A young Scottish gallant, the hero of a song in Scott's *Marmion*.

Locke (lok), **Alton.** The hero of a novel of the same name by Charles Kingsley. He is a tailor and a Chartist.

Lockit (lok'it). An inhuman jailer in Gay's *Beggar's Opera*. His daughter Lucy is in love with Macheath, the dashing highwayman. See **Macheath, Peachum.**

Locksley (loks'li). Name used by Robin Hood, who appears as an archer at the tournament in Scott's *Ivanhoe*.

Lodona (lō-dō'nȧ). A nymph changed into a river on her attempting to escape from the embraces of Pan.

Log (log), **King.** The subject of Aesop's fable *The Frogs Choosing a King*.

Lohengrin (lō'en-grin). Knight of the Swan, hero of a 13th-century romance by Wolfram von Eschenbach, and the theme of an opera by Richard Wagner.

Loki (lō'ki). In Scandinavian mythology, the evil god who brought about the death of Balder.

Long John Silver (lọng jon sil'vẽr). See **Silver, Long John.**

Lonigan (lon'i-gȧn), **Studs.** The central character in James Farrell's *Studs Lonigan* trilogy, a boy of the Chicago slums who is a tough, and whom Farrell presents as never having had a chance to be anything else.

Lorelei (lō're-lī). In German legend, a siren of the Rhine who lures men to destruction.

Lorenzo (lō-ren'zō). The gallant with whom Jessica elopes in Shakespeare's *Merchant of Venice*.

Lost Lady (lọst lā'dy). Marian Forrester, the chief character in the novel of that name by Willa Cather. Niel Herbert, the boy who tells the story, admires her greatly as a symbol of loveliness in a harsh frontier town, but has his faith shattered when he learns that she is not true to her husband, Captain Forrester.

Lothair (lō-thãr'). The hero of a novel by Disraeli, a young nobleman who shows some favor for the Roman Catholic religion, but ultimately marries Lady Corisande and attaches himself to the English Church.

Lothario (lō-thã'ri-ō). Original of 'a gay Lothario,' a libertine in Rowe's *Fair Penitent*, seducer of Calista, the heroine.

Lotus- *or* **Lotos-Eaters** (lō'tus-ēt'ẽrş), **the.** A dreamy, indolent race mentioned in Homer's *Odyssey*, and about whom Tennyson has written a poem so named.

Louisa (lụ-ī'şȧ). Heroine of Sheridan's *Duenna*, who is enabled to marry her lover when her father is outwitted and led to mistake the duenna for her.

Lovelace (lŏv'lāc). The libertine hero of Richardson's novel *Clarissa Harlowe*.

Lubberland (lub'ẽr-land). A burlesque name for a fabulous country such as the land of Cockaigne.

Lucentio (lū-cen'shi-ō). In Shakespeare's *Taming of the Shrew*, the wooer of Bianca.

Lucia di Lammermoor (lụ-chī'ä dī läm-mer-mọọr'). The heroine of Donizetti's opera of that name, based on Scott's *Bride of Lammermoor*.

Luciana (lụ-çhi-än'ȧ). Sister of Adriana in Shakespeare's *Comedy of Errors*.

Lucina (lū-cī'nȧ). The goddess who presided over childbirth among the Romans, often identified with Juno or Diana.

Lucinde (lụ-cand'). The heroine of Molière's *Le Médecin malgré lui*, who pretends dumbness, and is cured by her lover, who visits her in company with a mock doctor.—In Molière's *L'Amour médecin*, the ailing heroine, cured by her lover, who, for the benefit of her father, pretends to be a doctor.

Lucio (lū'çhi-o). A fantastic and vicious character in Shakespeare's *Measure for Measure*.

Lucrece (lū-çrēs'). Same as **Lucretia.**

Lucretia (lū-çrē'shi-ȧ). The heroine of a legendary tale of early Rome, who stabbed herself after being defiled by Sextus Tarquinius. Her story has been the basis of numerous poems and dramas.

Lucrezia Borgia (lụ-çret'sī-ä bọr'ġȧ). Daughter of Pope Alexander VI, heroine of an opera by Donizetti, based on a drama by Victor Hugo. The stories current regarding her are mostly fictions.

Lud (lud). A fabulous king of Britain.

Lufra (luf'rȧ). The hound belonging to Douglas in Scott's *Lady of the Lake*.

Luggnagg (lug'nag). An island in Swift's *Gulliver's Travels*. See **Struldbrugs.**

Lumpkin (lump'kin), **Tony.** The son of Mrs. Hardcastle by her first marriage, in Goldsmith's comedy *She Stoops to Conquer*; an ignorant, idle, mischievous, but good-natured young booby.

Lupin (lū'pin), **Mrs.** The kindly and buxom hostess in Dickens' *Martin Chuzzlewit*, who marries Mark Tapley.

Lycidas (lyc'i-dȧs). A poetic name under which Milton in a celebrated elegy laments his deceased friend Edward King.

Lynceus (lyn'cūs). One of the Argonauts of Greek legend, famed for his extraordinary sharpness of sight.

Lynette (ly-net'). Sister of Lady Lyonors in Tennyson's *Gareth and Lynette*.

Lyonnesse (lȳ-on-nes'). A tract in the southwest of England, said to be now covered by the sea.

Lyonors (lȳ'ō-nōrş). Lady of Castle Perilous in Tennyson's *Idylls*.

Lysander (lȳ-san'dẽr). Lover of Hermia in Shakespeare's *Midsummer Night's Dream*.

Lysimachus (lȳ-sim'ȧ-çhus). A character in Shakespeare's *Pericles*, married to Marina.

M

Ma (mä). In Egyptian mythology, the goddess of truth and justice.

Mab (mab). The queen of the fairies, according to Shakespeare and other English poets.

Macaire (mȧ-çãr'), **Robert.** The name for a villainous character in certain French plays. The name Macaire is also that of a legendary French murderer whose guilt was brought to light by his victim's dog.

Macbeth (maç-beth'). A historic personage who raised himself to be king of Scotland, and is celebrated along with his wife, Lady Macbeth, in Shakespeare's famous tragedy, the events of which, however, are almost entirely fictitious.

McChesney (maç-ches'ni), **Emma.** A traveling saleswoman, the chief character in many short stories by Edna Ferber, the best known being *Personality Plus*. She is a hearty, energetic person, whose chief interest, aside from her business of selling skirts and petticoats, is her son Jock.

Macgregor (mȧ-greg'ŏr), **Rob Roy.** The Highland outlaw and freebooter, hero of Scott's *Rob Roy*, in which also appear his wife Helen and two sons, the period being that of the Jacobite rising of **1715.** Rob himself was a real enough character, but the incidents and details of the novel are mainly fictitious. Frank Osbaldistone and other Osbaldistones, Diana Vernon, Bailie Nicol Jarvie, and Andrew Fairservice are among the characters.

Macheath (maç-hēth'), **Captain.** The highwayman hero of Gay's *Beggar's Opera*, who declares he could be so happy with either Polly Peachum or Lucy Lockit. Though actually married to the former, he promises to wed the latter, and is assisted by her to escape from jail.

MacIvor (maç-ī'vŏr), **Fergus and Flora.** In Scott's *Waverley*, a Highland chief and his sister, both devoted to the cause of Charles Edward Stuart. To the beautiful and high-minded Flora, Waverley proposes marriage, but is not accepted. Fergus is executed; and Flora retires to a convent.

MacStinger (maç-stiṅg'ẽr), **Mrs.** In Dickens' *Dombey and Son*, the landlady of Captain Cuttle and a perfect terror and tyrant to him; married later to his friend Bunsby.

MacWheeble (maç-hwē'bl), **Duncan.** A character in Scott's *Waverley*, 'bailie' or agent for Baron Bradwardine.

Mad Hatter (mad hat'ẽr). A character in Lewis Carroll's *Alice in Wonderland*.

Madoc (mad'oç). A prince or king of Welsh tradition, who is said to have discovered America long before Columbus; the subject of a poem by Southey.

Maeonides (mē-on'i-dēş). A poetical designation of Homer.

Maggie (mag'i). See **Johnson, Maggie; Tulliver, Maggie; Wylie, Maggie.**

Maggy (mag'y). A half-witted character in Dickens' *Little Dorrit*.

Magi (mā'ġī). The three wise men from the East who brought presents of gold, frankincense, and myrrh to the infant Christ (Matt. ii.). According to tradition they were Eastern kings, and were named respectively Melchior, Gaspar, and Balthazar. It is said that their bodies were brought by the Empress Helena to Constantinople, but that they were subsequently interred at Milan and Cologne. From this last circumstance they were called the Three Kings of Cologne.

Magog (mā'gog). See **Gog.**

Magwitch (mag'wich), **Abel.** A transported convict in Dickens' *Great Expectations*, who makes money in Australia and sends home funds to keep Pip like a gentleman, though for a long time Pip does not know who his benefactor is.

Maid Marian (mād mā'ri-ȧn). The wife of Robin Hood.

Maigret (mā-gre'), **Inspector.** The fictional detective of Georges Simenon.

Major Barbara (bär'bȧ-rȧ). The heroine of G. B. Shaw's play of the same name. The theme of the drama is that poverty is the worst of crimes. Barbara, the daughter of an earl, becomes a Salvation Army major. Undershaft, the male protagonist, is the head of a munitions factory, and Shaw disserts in typical fashion on morals and social problems arising from the situations.

Malambruno (mal-ȧm-brụ'nō). A giant in Cervantes' *Don Quixote* who by enchantment transforms Antonomasia and her husband respectively into a brazen monkey and a crocodile. Their disenchantment is accomplished by Don Quixote.

Malaprop (mal'ȧ-prop), **Mrs.** A lady in Sheridan's comedy *The Rivals*, notorious for her amusing blunders in the use of words; aunt and guardian to Lydia Languish.

Malbecco (mal-beç'ō). In Spenser's *Faërie Queene*, the wealthy but mean and miserly husband of a young wife, Helenore, who, after setting fire to the house, elopes with Sir Paridel. In his despair

Malbecco throws himself from a rock, leaving nothing but his ghost behind, which is metamorphosed into Jealousy.

Malebolge (mä-le-bōl'gē). The eighth circle of punishment in Dante's *Inferno*, containing ten bolgi or pits.

Malvolio (mal-vō'li-ō). The pompous and conceited steward or major-domo of Olivia in Shakespeare's *Twelfth Night*.

Mambrino's Helmet (mam-brī'nōş hel'met). A wonderful helmet of medieval romance, which Don Quixote claimed to have found although his was merely a barber's basin.

Manette (mȧ-net'), **Dr., and his daughter Lucie.** Characters in Dickens' *Tale of Two Cities*. Dr. Manette's mental faculties have been somewhat impaired by a long period of unjust imprisonment, during which he made shoes. Lucie, heroine of the novel, is loved by Sydney Carton and Charles Darnay.

Manfred (man'fred), **Count.** Hero of Byron's drama so named, a man who has dealings with elemental spirits and has lost all sympathy for his fellows.

Manly (man'ly). A fine character in Vanbrugh and Cibber's *Provoked Husband*.—A blunt, straightforward sea captain, the hero of Wycherley's *Plain Dealer*.

Mannering (man'ēr-ing), **Guy.** The English officer and gentleman who gives name to Scott's well-known novel, and whose daughter Julia is married to its hero, Harry Bertram. Julia is beautiful, sprightly, and clever, but somewhat lightheaded and romantic.

Man of Brass (man ov brȧs). See **Talus.**

Man of Destiny (des'ti-ny). Napoleon I, who professed to regard himself as under a special destiny.

Manon Lescaut (mȧ-noṇ' les-ḉō'). Title and heroine of a French romance by the Abbé Prévost, telling of the passionate love of the Chevalier des Grieux for the harlot Manon, with whom he elopes. She soon proves unfaithful, but he cannot give her up, and he loses fortune, friends, and moral standards.

Mantalini (man-tȧ-lī'nī). A dissipated fop in Dickens' *Nicholas Nickleby*, husband of a fashionable milliner, reduced to turning his wife's mangle.

Manuel (mä-nų-el'), **Count.** The hero of Cabell's satiric romance *Figures of Earth*, who has several love affairs. He is the ruler of Poictesme and the father of Dorothy la Désirée, Ettarre, and Melicent.

Marcel (mȧr-cel'). The narrator and a central character in Marcel Proust's *Remembrance of Things Past*. See **Swann, Guermantes.**

Marcella (mär-cel'ȧ). A fair but cruel shepherdess in *Don Quixote*.

Marcellus (mär-cel'us). A character in Shakespeare's *Hamlet*, who sees the ghost of Hamlet's father before the prince himself.

March (märch), **Iris.** The promiscuous heroine of Michael Arlen's *Green Hat*. She loved her husband, who killed himself on his wedding night, and her dissolute twin brother, who also committed suicide. She kills herself by driving her roadster into a tree.

Marchbanks (märch'baṅks). The poet who is in love with Candida in Shaw's *Candida*.

March (märch) **Family.** A delightful family of girls, Meg, Jo, Beth, and Amy, who figure in Louisa May Alcott's *Little Women*, a story of Civil War days. Jo, the tomboy, is the strongest of the characters.

Marchioness (mär'chǒn-es), **the.** A half-starved girl, maid of all work to Sampson Brass in Dickens' *Old Curiosity Shop*, later married to Dick Swiveller.

Marduk (mär'dųk). See **Merodach.**

Margaret (mär'gȧ-ret). The heroine of Goethe's *Faust*. See **Faust.**—Lady Margaret of Branksome Hall, the heroine of Scott's *Lay of the Last Minstrel*.

Margarete (mär-gȧ-re'te). See **Ugly Duchess.**

Margarita (mär-gȧ-rī'tȧ). In John Fletcher's *Rule a Wife and Have a Wife*, a rich young Spanish widow who marries again with the idea that she may indulge in pleasure at her will, believing her husband to be a weakling, but finds that she has met her master.

Maria (mȧ-rī'ȧ). A lady attending on the French princess in Shakespeare's *Love's Labour's Lost*.—Waiting maid of the Countess Olivia in Shakespeare's *Twelfth Night*, who assists in making a fool of Malvolio.—An unfortunate half-witted maiden in Sterne's *Sentimental Journey*.—A Spanish girl in Hemingway's *For Whom the Bell Tolls* who, after terrible experiences in the civil war, falls in love with Robert Jordan.

Mariana (mãr-i-an'ȧ). A lady in Shakespeare's *Measure for Measure* who, after having been abandoned by Angelo, is ultimately married to him.—A lady called Mariana is also the subject of *Mariana* and *Mariana in the South*, poems by Tennyson.

Marigold (mar'i-gōld), **'Doctor.'** The itinerant hero of Dickens' Christmas tale *Doctor Marigold's Prescriptions*.

Marina (mȧ-rī'nȧ). Daughter of Pericles in Shakespeare's *Pericles, Prince of Tyre*.

Marinel (mãr-i-nel'). Lover of Florimel in Spenser's *Faërie Queene*.

Maritornes (mãr-i-tọr'nęs). A humpbacked, ugly inn servant in *Don Quixote*, regarded by the knight as the beauteous daughter of the lord of the castle (the inn).

Mark (märk), **King.** In the Arthurian legends, a king of Cornwall, cowardly, treacherous, and despicable. His wife was Isolde, beloved by Sir Tristram, his nephew.

Markleham (märk'lăm), **Mrs.** The foolish and meddlesome mother of Mrs. Strong in Dickens' *David Copperfield*.

Marlow (mär'lō), **Young.** The hero of Goldsmith's comedy *She Stoops to Conquer*, bashful with ladies, but by no means so with chambermaids. See **Hardcastle.**

Marmion (mär'mi-ŏn). A brave but profligate English lord, hero of Scott's poem of same name, the scene of which is partly in Scotland; slain at Flodden.

Marner (mär'nẽr), **Silas.** The character who gives name to a novel by George Eliot, a weaver who believes himself deserted by God and has his small store of gold stolen, but is restored to heart and hope by a little foundling child (Eppie) who comes to him.

Mars (märş). The Roman god of war, corresponding to the Greek god Ares.

Marsden (märs'den), **Charles.** The novelist in O'Neill's *Strange Interlude*, in love with Nina Leeds, whom he finally marries.

Marsyas (mär'sy-ȧs). A satyr fabled to have been conquered by Apollo in a musical contest, and to have been flayed alive by the victor.

Martext (mär'tekst), **Sir Oliver.** A clergyman in Shakespeare's *As You Like It*.

Martha (mär'thȧ). A friend of Margaret in Goethe's *Faust*, who boldly 'sets her cap' for Mephistopheles, while Faust is engaged with Margaret.—Also, the heroine of Flotow's opera of this name.

Martin (mär'tin). In Swift's *Tale of a Tub*, and in Dryden's *Hind and Panther*, a character representing Luther.

Mary Rose (mâr'y rōş). See **Morland, Mary Rose.**

Maskwell (mȧsk'wel). The 'Double Dealer' of Congreve's play of this name, a model of duplicity and cunning.

Mason (mā'sŏn), **Perry.** An ingenious lawyer who is a principal character in numerous detective novels by Erle Stanley Gardner.

Master Humphrey (mȧs'tẽr hum'fri). See **Humphrey.**

Mat o' the Mint (mat ō thē mint). A highwayman in Gay's *Beggar's Opera*.

Mattie (mat'i). The maid of Bailie Nicol Jarvie in Scott's *Rob Roy*, afterward married to her master.

Maul (mạl). A giant in Bunyan's *Pilgrim's Progress*.

Maylie (mā'li), **Mrs., and her son Harry.** Characters in Dickens' *Oliver Twist*, by whom Oliver is befriended.

Maypole (mā'pōl), **the.** An inn in Dickens' *Barnaby Rudge*, kept by Joe Willet and his wife, the former Dolly Varden.

May Queen (mā kwēn), **the.** The subject of a pathetic poem by Tennyson.

Mazeppa (mȧ-zep'ȧ). Hetman of the Cossacks, the hero of Byron's poem *Mazeppa*. He belonged to a noble Polish family, and while serving as a page at the court of the king of Poland, engaged in a love intrigue with the young wife of a count. By order of her husband Mazeppa was fastened to a wild horse, which was then turned loose. The page was rescued by some Cossacks, and became, by favor of Peter I of Russia, prince of the Ukraine. He afterward fought against the Russians.

Medamothi (me-dȧ-mō-tī'). An island in Rabelais' *Pantagruel*: from Greek word meaning nowhere.

Medea (mē-dē'ȧ). The daughter of a king of Colchis in Greek legend, a famous sorceress, who helped Jason to carry off the golden fleece. After ten years of marriage to him, Jason deserted her, and in revenge she murdered their two children.

Medora (mę-dō'rȧ). Heroine of Byron's *Corsair*, who pines away in the absence of her husband, the corsair, who has been taken prisoner.

Medusa (mē-dū'sȧ). A Gorgon, whose head was cut off by Perseus, and placed upon Minerva's shield. The head turned to stone all who looked at it.

Meg Merrilies (meg mer'i-lēş). See **Merrilies.**

Megaera (me-ġē'rȧ). In classical mythology, one of the three Furies.

Meister (mīs'tẽr), **Wilhelm.** Hero and title of a novel by Goethe, showing how the character of a somewhat uninteresting young man is molded by his experiences in life.

Melanie (mel'ȧ-ni). See **Hamilton, Melanie.**

Melchior (mel'ḉhi-ọr). See **Magi.**

Meleager (mel-ē-ā'ġẽr). A Greek legendary hero, slayer of the formidable Calydonian boar and lover of Atalanta; his life depended on how long a firebrand remained unconsumed

Melema (me-lę'mä), **Tito.** The unworthy husband of Romola in George Eliot's novel *Rom ola*. Selfish and deceitful, though attractive, he resorts to base acts which finally bring retribution upon him.

Melisignes (mel-e-siġ'e-nēş). A poetic name for Homer.

Melicent (mel'i-cent). The heroine of Cabell's novel *Domnei*, a daughter of Count Manuel.

Mellors (mel'ọrş). A miner, groom, and poacher, who is Lady Constance's lover in D. H. Lawrence's *Lady Chatterley's Lover*.

Melmoth (mel'mŏth). A man who sells his soul to the devil in exchange for everlasting life in Charles Maturin's gothic novel *Melmoth the Wanderer*.—A pseudonym (Sebastian Melmoth) of Oscar Wilde.

Melpomene (mel-pom'e-nē). The Muse who presided over tragedy.

Melusina (mel-ū-sī'nȧ). A fairy of French legend, who was condemned to become every Saturday a serpent from the waist downward. She married and lived happily until her husband discovered her in her deformed state, whereupon, with a scream of despair, she left him and became a ghost destined to roam the world until doomsday.

Melville (mel'vil), **Julia.** A character in Sheridan's *Rivals*, in love with Faulkland, who is causelessly jealous of her.

Memnon (mem'non). A king of Ethiopia slain in the Trojan war, where he fought on the Trojan side.—The colossal statue of Amenophis III at Thebes received this name.

Menelaus (men-e-lā'us). A mythical king of Sparta, husband of Helen and brother of Agamemnon, a prominent figure in Greek legend.

Mentor (men'tŏr). A friend of Ulysses and the tutor of Telemachus. Occasionally, in order to advise either of the latter two, Athena assumed his form. His name, hence, stands for a trusty counselor.

Mephistopheles (mef-i-stof'e-lēş). A fiend or spirit of evil who figures in the Faust story, and is made a striking personage by Goethe. See **Faust.**

Merchant of Venice (mẽr'chănt ov ven'ic), **the.** See **Antonio.**

Mercury (mẽr'ḉū-ry). See **Hermes.**

Mercutio (mẽr-ḉū'shi-ō). The witty and elegant friend of Romeo in Shakespeare's *Romeo and Juliet*.

Mercy (mẽr'cy). A young pilgrim in Bunyan's *Pilgrim's Progress*.

Merdle (mẽr'dl), **Mr.** A great financial magnate in Dickens' *Little Dorrit*, who becomes insolvent and commits suicide after being found guilty of forgery and swindling.

Merlin (mẽr'lin). The famous enchanter in the legends connected with King Arthur.

Merodach *or* **Marduk** (mē-rō'daḉh; mär'dųk). In Babylonian mythology, the first-born of Ea and Bel or Baal, the god of life and benefactor of men. Subsequently, under Semitic influence, the great sun-god and the lord of the gods.

Merrilies (mer'i-lēş), **Meg.** An old gypsy woman who is a striking character in Scott's *Guy Mannering*.

Merrivale (mer'i-vāl), **Sir Henry.** The fictional detective of Carter Dickson (pseud. of J. D. Carr).

Merrylegs (mer'y-legş). A performing dog, in Dickens' *Hard Times*.

Mezentius (mē-zen'shi-us). A tyrant of ancient Roman legend, noted for his cruelties.

Micawber (mi-ḉạ'bẽr). **Mr. Wilkins.** A delightfully humorous character in Dickens' *David Copperfield*, of no particular profession, given to high-flown language, fond of good living, and carelessly improvident; often, if one could believe him, in the deepest gloom, but generally hopeful and waiting 'for something to turn up.' Mrs. Micawber is a lady of very similar character, and a firm believer in her husband's abilities.

Michael (mī'ḉhel). An archangel mentioned several times in the Bible and introduced in Milton's *Paradise Lost*.

Midas (mī'dȧs). A legendary king of Phrygia, who, having obtained from the gods the gift of turning everything he touched into gold, found it a curse. Apollo gave him ass's ears for deciding a musical contest against him.

Midgard (mid'gärd). In Scandinavian mythology, the abode of human beings, or the earth.

Miggs (migş). In Dickens' *Barnaby Rudge*, the shrewish maidservant of Mrs. Varden, the toady of her mistress, and the admirer of the conceited apprentice Sim Tappertit, who, however, having an eye to his master's daughter, pronounces her 'scraggy.'

Mignon (mī-nyọṇ). The Italian girl protected by Wilhelm Meister in Goethe's *Wilhelm Meister's Apprenticeship*. She falls in love with her protector, but since her affection is not requited she loses her mind, and dies. Ambroise Thomas' opera *Mignon* is based on her story.

Mildendo (mil-den'dō). The capital of Lilliput in Swift's *Gulliver's Travels*.

Mildred (mil'dred). The cheap little waitress and prostitute who breaks Philip Carey's heart in Maugham's *Of Human Bondage*, using him for her own purposes.

Miletus (mī-lē'tus), **Tales of.** Fabulous stories of Greece and Rome. Bulwer-Lytton published certain stories under the title of *Lost Tales of Miletus*.

Millamant (mil'ȧ-mănt). A brilliant and beautiful coquette in Congreve's *Way of the World*, wooed and won by Mirabell.

Miller (mil'ẽr), **Daisy.** A young American girl in the story of the same name by Henry James. She and her young brother travel in Europe with their newly-rich and complacent mother. Her innocence and her ignorance and disregard of European customs and standards of propriety lead her into situations which are capable of misconstruction, and have untoward results.

Miller (mil'ẽr), **Joe.** An English comedian (1684–1738) to whom was ascribed the authorship of a jestbook (1739) actually compiled by John Mottley.

Mills (milş), **Julia.** The bosom friend of Dora Spenlow in Dickens' *David Copperfield*, a young lady who sympathizes with the fond pair, David and Dora, but regards herself as one for whom love is only a dream of the past. She marries a rich East Indian.

Milton (mil'tŏn), **George.** A matter-of-fact, earthy laborer in John Steinbeck's *Of Mice and Men*, who tries to care for his huge, half-witted friend Lennie Small.

Minerva (mi-nẽr'vȧ). The Roman goddess of wisdom, fabled to have sprung from the brow of Jove; identified with Athene.

Minnehaha (min-ē-hä'hä). The wife of Hiawatha in Longfellow's *Hiawatha*.

Minos (mī'nos). A legendary king and lawgiver of Crete, made after death one of the judges of the lower world.

Minotaur (min'ō-tạr). A monster of Greek fable, half man, half bull, which lived in the Cretan labyrinth, and was slain by Theseus.

Mio (mī'ō). The hero of Maxwell Anderson's verse drama *Winterset*, who seeks to avenge the death of his father, unjustly executed for a murder. He finds the real murderer, a gang leader, but is killed, along with Miriamne, a girl with whom he is in love.

Mirabel (mir'ȧ-bel). A gallant in John Fletcher's *The Wild-Goose Chase*, ultimately married to Oriana, though a professed enemy to marriage.

Mirabell (mir'ȧ-bel). A handsome and attractive gentleman in love with Millamant in Congreve's *Way of the World*.

Miranda (mi-ran'dȧ). The daughter of Prospero in Shakespeare's *Tempest*.

Miriamne (mir-i-am'nē). A lonely girl who falls in love with Mio, in Maxwell Anderson's play *Winterset*.

Mirza (mĭr'zä). A fictitious personage described in *The Spectator* (No. 159) as seeing a noble allegorical vision of human life.

Mithras (mith'răs). A deity of the ancient Persians, the benefactor of mankind and supporter of Ormuzd, generally regarded as a personification of the sun.

Moby Dick (mō'by dik). A savage white whale that bit off Captain Ahab's leg, in Herman Melville's novel *Moby Dick*, and symbolizes the terrific and malignant forces of the universe.

Modish (mō'dish), **Lady Betty.** A wayward, coquettish woman in Cibber's *Careless Husband*.

Modo (mō'dō). A fiend, named in Shakespeare's *King Lear*, that impels to murder.

Modred *or* **Mordred** (mō'dred; mọr'dred). The treacherous nephew of King Arthur, against whom he rebelled; he was slain in the battle that ensued, and in it King Arthur also received his death wound.

Mokanna (mō-kan'ȧ). The Veiled Prophet in Moore's *Lalla Rookh*. See **Veiled Prophet.**

Mommur (mom'ūr). The name of an imaginary city, the residence of Oberon, king of the fairies.

Momus (mō'mus). The Greek god of laughter and ridicule.

Montague (mon'tȧ-gū). The family name of the noble house of Verona to which Romeo belonged in Shakespeare's *Romeo and Juliet*.

Mordred (mọr'dred). See **Modred.**

More of More Hall (mōr ov mōr hạl). A legendary hero, who killed the Dragon of Wantley.

Morel (mọr-el'), **Paul.** The sensitive and largely autobiographical hero of D. H. Lawrence's novel *Sons and Lovers*. Hatred of his father has led him to an excessive attachment to his mother, which has an inhibiting effect on his love for other women and his general adaptation.

Morell (mō-rel'), **Rev. James.** The husband of Candida in Shaw's play *Candida*.

Morgan le Fay (mọr'găn lē fā). The wicked fairy sister of King Arthur, who tried to have him murdered.

Morgiana (mọr-ġi-an'ȧ). The clever female slave of Ali Baba in the famous story of *The Forty Thieves*.

Morland (mọr'lănd), **Mary Rose.** The chief character in Barrie's play *Mary Rose*, a young wife and mother who revisits an island in the Hebrides, where she disappears for twenty-five years. Returning as young as ever, she dies from the shock of seeing her family aged. She then haunts her house, calling for her baby.

Morning Star of the Reformation (mọr-ning stär ov thē ref-ọr-mā'shun). A name given to John Wyclif (1324–84).

Morose (mō-rōs'). See **Epicene.**

Morris (mọr'is), **Dinah.** A Methodist preacher who marries Adam Bede in George Eliot's novel *Adam Bede*.

Mortality (mọr-tal'i-ty), **Old.** See **Old Mortality.**

Moth (mọth). A page in Shakespeare's *Love's Labour's Lost*.—A fairy in Shakespeare's *Midsummer Night's Dream*.

Mouldy (mōl'dy), **Ralph.** A character in Shakespeare's *Henry IV*, one of Falstaff's recruits.

Mourning Bride (mōr'ning brīd), **the.** Almeria, daughter of the king of Granada, in Congreve's drama *The Mourning Bride*, separated from her husband on their wedding day, but afterward happily reunited with him.

Mowcher (mou'chẽr), **Miss.** A kindhearted and amusing dwarf who dresses gentlemen's hair in Dickens' *David Copperfield*.

Mowgli (mou'gli). An infant boy lost in a forest and brought up by Mother Wolf, in Kipling's *Jungle Books*. When he finally joins human society, he is possessed of wisdom gained from the jungle animals.

Mucklewrath (muk'l-rath), **John.** In Scott's *Waverley*, the smith at the village of Cairnvreckan, whose wife is a virago and enthusiastic Jacobite.

Mumblazon (mum-blā'zŏn), **Master.** A character in Scott's *Kenilworth*, a connection of the Robsart family, and a great authority on heraldry and genealogy.

Munchausen (mun-chạ'sen), **Baron.** The name attached to a collection (compiled by R. E. Raspe) of most extravagant and amusing fictions, corrupted from the real name of a German officer in the Russian army, Baron von Münchhausen.

Mylitta (mȳ-lit'ȧ). The Assyrian goddess of the moon, and the representative of the female principle of generation.

Myrrha (myr'ȧ). In Byron's drama *Sardanapalus*, an Ionian slave and concubine of Sardanapalus, king of Assyria. She incites him to oppose Arbaces the Mede, and when defeated, expires with her lord on a funeral pyre, which she has lighted with her own hand.

Myshkin (mysh'kin), **Prince.** The hero of Dostoevski's novel *The Idiot*. He is an epileptic, but gentle and sincere.

N

Nadgett (naġ'et), **Mr.** In Dickens' *Martin Chuzzlewit*, a man of the most secretive habits, who acts as a private detective and ultimately brings Jonas Chuzzlewit to his doom.

Namtar (nam'tär). In Babylonian mythology, the plague-god and arbiter of human destiny, servant of Nergal.

Nana (nȧ-nȧ'). A Parisian prostitute in Émile Zola's novel of the same name, whose rise and fall are realistically portrayed.

Nancy (nan'cy). An unfortunate girl in Dickens' *Oliver Twist*, kindhearted and faithful to Bill Sikes, who brutally murdered her.

Nanki-Poo (nañk-i-pọọ'). In Gilbert and Sullivan's comic opera *The Mikado*, the son of the mikado, in love with Yum-Yum, ward of Ko-Ko, the lord high executioner.

Nanna (nan'ȧ). In Scandinavian mythology, the wife of Balder, on whose funeral pile she threw herself and died when her husband was unwittingly slain by the god Hoder.

Naphta (näf'tȧ), **Leo.** A Jesuit in Mann's *Magic Mountain*, who refuses to fire in a duel he fights with Settembrini.

Naraka (nŭr'ȧ-kȧ). In Hindu mythology, hell, which has twenty-eight divisions designed for the punishment of different degrees of wickedness.

Narcissus (när-cis'us). A youth of Greek fable, who fell in love with his own image as he saw it reflected in a fountain, and pined away and died.

Nathaniel (nȧ-than'yel), **Sir.** A curate in Shakespeare's *Love's Labour's Lost*.

Natty Bumppo (nat'y bum'pō). A character in five of Cooper's novels. See **Leatherstocking.**

Nausicaä (nạ-siç'ā-ȧ). A princess of the Phaeacians in Homer's *Odyssey*, who takes compassion on Ulysses when shipwrecked.

Nebo (nē'bō). In Babylonian mythology, the prophet-god who proclaimed the mind and will of Merodach, and the god of science and literature.

Neith (nē'ith). In Egyptian mythology, the goddess of wisdom, identified with the Greek Athene and the Roman Minerva.

Nekayah (nek'ȧ-yȧ). Sister of Rasselas, in Dr. Johnson's tale *Rasselas*.

Nell (nel), **Little.** The child heroine of Dickens' *Old Curiosity Shop*, living with her grandfather, who has a passion for gambling, and at last wanders away with her into the country, where both die.

Nemo (nē'mō), **Captain.** The hero of Jules Verne's *Twenty Thousand Leagues under the Sea*.

Neptune (nep'tūn). The Roman god of the sea, equivalent to the Greek Poseidon.

Nereus (nēr'ūs). In classical mythology, father of the water nymphs, or Nereids.

Nergal (ner'gl). In Babylonian mythology, the god of the dead.

Nerissa (ner-is'ȧ). Portia's maid in Shakespeare's *Merchant of Venice*.

Nessus (nes'us). A centaur who brought about the death of Hercules. See **Deianira.**

Nestor (nes'tŏr). A legendary king in southern Greece, noted for his wisdom. He was the oldest chieftain at the siege of Troy, where his advice was constantly solicited.

Neville (nev'il), **Miss.** The friend and confidante of Miss Hardcastle, in Goldsmith's *She Stoops to Conquer*, married to Mr. Hastings.

Newcome (nū'cŏm), **Colonel.** One of the most prominent characters in Thackeray's novel *The Newcomes*, brave, simple, and good, though not overwise. He loses his fortune and retires to an almshouse, where he dies. His son Clive, a fine, handsome young fellow, who adopts the profession of an artist, long hankers in vain after his beautiful, clever, and spirited cousin Ethel Newcome, who is the daughter of a wealthy banker, and is intended to marry into the nobility. She is brought up to love wealth and title, but later is married to Clive. Other members of the Newcome family are introduced, such as the odious Sir Barnes, whose ill-treatment causes his wife to run away from him. See also **Florac, Honeyman, Kew.**

Nibelungen (nī'be-lụng-en). A race or family in German legend possessed of a great treasure, and whose name is attached to the old German epic the *Nibelungenlied*, or song of the Nibelungs. See **Siegfried, Kriemhild, Brunhild.**

Nickleby (nik'l-by), **Nicholas.** The hero of the novel of the same name by Dickens, who teaches under Squeers at Dotheboys Hall, joins the theatrical company of Mr. Crummles, and is befriended by the brothers Cheeryble. His mother, with her rambling and inconsequent style of speaking, is very amusing. His sister Kate is a charming young lady; his uncle Ralph is a hardhearted and miserly moneylender, who hangs himself when his schemes fail. Madeline Bray, Smike, Newman Noggs, Mr. Mantalini, John Browdie, the Kenwigs', etc., also appear in the story.

Niflheim (niv'l-hęm). A region of cold and darkness in Scandinavian mythology.

Nikulaussön (nik-ul-ou'sön), **Erlend.** The master of Husaby in Sigrid Undset's novel *Kristin Lavransdatter*, who marries Kristin. A hard-drinking, sports-loving, feudal Norwegian of the thirteenth century, he lets his property run down and abuses Kristin.

Niobe (nī'ō-bē). A queen of classic story, wife of Amphion of Thebes and daughter of Tantalus. Because she exulted over Latona on account of her own numerous offspring, her children were all slain by the children of Latona, Diana and Apollo, and she herself turned to stone. She is the symbol of grief.

Nipper (nip'ẽr), **Susan.** An attendant on Florence Dombey in Dickens' *Dombey and Son*, good-looking, shrewd, and sharp-tongued, but faithful and affectionate; married to Mr. Toots.

Nisus (nī'sus). In Virgil's *Aeneid*, a Trojan youth who accompanied Aeneas to Italy, and was killed in attempting to rescue his intimate friend Euryalus. The two are a proverbial example of friendship.

Noggs (nogṣ), **Newman.** In Dickens' *Nicholas Nickleby*, an extremely odd but kindhearted character, clerk to Ralph Nickleby, and once a country gentleman.

Nora (nō'rȧ). The heroine of Ibsen's *A Doll's House*. See **Helmer, Nora.**

Norns (nọrnṣ). The three Fates in Scandinavian mythology, representing the Past, the Present, and the Future.

Norris (nọr'is). A family in America described in Dickens' *Martin Chuzzlewit*, professing to despise distinctions of rank and title, but deeply interested in members of the British aristocracy.

Nostromo (nos-trō'mō). An Italian sailor in Joseph Conrad's novel of the same name, who is foreman of a wharf and is entrusted with the silver from Gould's mine, but he steals it. He is shot by his sweetheart's father and dies.

Notus (nō'tus). The Latin name of the south wind.

Noureddin (nọọ-red-in'). A character in the *Arabian Nights*, in the story *Noureddin and the Beautiful Persian*.

Nourmahal (nọọr-mȧ-häl'). The Light of the Harem (namely, that of Harun-al-Rashid) in Moore's *Lalla Rookh*.

Nubbles (nub'lṣ), **Kit.** In Dickens' *Old Curiosity Shop*, a boy who attends little Nell and is hated by Quilp.

Number Nip (num'bẽr nip). A gnome king or mountain goblin in German tales.

Nupkins (nup'kinṣ), **Mr.** A pompous, ignorant mayor of Ipswich in Dickens' *Pickwick Papers*.

Nut-brown Maid (nut-broun mād), **the.** Heroine and title of a very old ballad.

Nydia (nyd'i-ȧ). A blind girl in Bulwer-Lytton's *Last Days of Pompeii*.

Nym (nym). A follower of Falstaff's in Shakespeare's *Merry Wives* and *Henry V*, an amusing rogue, who gets hanged.

O

Obadiah (ō-bȧ-dī'ȧ). A domestic servant of the Shandy family in Sterne's *Tristram Shandy*.

Oberon (ō'bẽr-on). The king of the fairies, familiar to us from Shakespeare's *Midsummer Night's Dream*, celebrated also in a poem by Wieland and an opera by Weber.

Obstinate (ob'sti-nāt). A character in Bunyan's *Pilgrim's Progress*.

Odette (ō-det'). See **Swann.**

Odin (ō'din). The supreme Scandinavian deity, king of gods and men. As god of war he holds his court in Valhalla, surrounded by warriors who have fallen in battle. He has two ravens that sit on his shoulders and bring him tidings of all that goes on in the world. His wife is Frigga; one of his sons is Balder the Beautiful.

Odysseus (ō-dys'ūs). The Greek form of Ulysses; hence the name of the great Homeric epic the *Odyssey*, which narrates the wanderings and adventures of Ulysses on his way home from the Trojan war. The poem, like the *Iliad*, is in twenty-four books, and in it we read of the Lotus-eaters, the Cyclops Polyphemus, the enchantress Circe, the nymph Calypso, the descent of Ulysses to Hades, Scylla and Charybdis, the Sirens, the return of Ulysses to Ithaca, and his slaughter of the wooers who harassed his wife Penelope and wasted his substance.

Oedipus (ed'i-pus). A legendary king of Thebes in Greece, son of Laius and Jocasta, celebrated in tragedy. Unaware of his parentage, he unwittingly killed his own father, and, having answered the riddle of the Sphinx, obtained the throne of Thebes and his own mother as his wife. When the real state of matters became known Jocasta hanged herself, and Oedipus put out his eyes and left Thebes as a poor wanderer, attended by his daughter Antigone. Oedipus is the subject of tragedies by Sophocles, Corneille, and Voltaire. See **Eteocles and Polynices.**

Oenone (ē-nō'nē). A nymph of classic fable, married to Paris, who deserted her for Helen, the famous beauty.

Ogier (ōẓ'i-ẽr), **the Dane.** One of the paladins or mighty warriors of the Charlemagne romances.

O'Hara (ō-hăr'ȧ), **Scarlett.** The dynamic heroine of Margaret Mitchell's *Gone With the Wind*, the daughter of a plantation owner at the time of the Civil War, who is selfish and ruthless in obtaining her ends, but who keeps the family together (what is left of it) after the war is over, and remakes their fortunes. After the death of her first two husbands, one of whom she married for spite, the other by chicanery, she marries Rhett Butler, who is more than a match for her. See **Hamilton.**

Oldbuck (ōld′buk), **Jonathan.** The 'laird' of Monkbarns, an elderly country gentleman of antiquarian tastes, from whom Scott's novel *The Antiquary* takes its name, a confirmed bachelor and hater of women, hasty, sarcastic, and whimsical, but shrewd and kindhearted; an admirably humorous portrait.

Old Curiosity Shop (ōld cū-ri-os′i-ty shop). The shop, which gives title to one of Dickens' novels, kept by the grandfather of Little Nell, a weak old man who has an infatuation for gaming, believing that he will make a fortune for his grandchild. See **Marchioness, Nell, Nubbles.**

Old English (ōld iṅ′glish). See **Heythorp.**

Old Man of the Mountain (man ov the moun′tin). A name applied to Hassan ben Sabbah (and his successors), the chief of a Mohammedan sect which he founded in Persia (*c.* 1090). In the west, members of this murderous order were known by the title of Assassins.

Old Man of the Sea (sē). In the *Arabian Nights*, a malignant old wretch who managed to get himself planted on the shoulders of Sinbad, who only got rid of him by intoxicating him.

Old Mortality (mọr-tal′i-ty). A novel by Scott dealing with the persecution of the Covenanters. The real Old Mortality was an old man who made it his task to keep fresh the tombstones of the Covenanters in country churchyards.

Oliver (ol′i-vẽr). One of the twelve peers of Charlemagne. See **Roland.**

Olivia (ō-liv′i-ȧ). In Shakespeare's *Twelfth Night*, a rich countess whose love is sought by the duke of Illyria. She, however, falls in love with Viola, who is dressed as a page, and marries her twin brother and counterpart Sebastian.

Olivia Primrose (prim′rōṣ). See **Primrose.**

Olivier (ō-liv′i-ẽr), **Mary.** In May Sinclair's novel of the same name, an intelligent and sensitive woman whose life is largely taken up with caring for her mother. She finds happiness in a love affair, however, and eventually becomes an author.

Olympus (ō-lym′pus). A mountain of northern Greece, in ancient times believed to be the abode of the gods.

Omphale (om′fȧ-lē). A queen of Lydia whom Hercules served for three years as a slave, spinning among her women and dressed in women's clothes, while Omphale kept his club and his lion's skin.

Ophelia (ō-fē′lyȧ). The daughter of Polonius in Shakespeare's *Hamlet*, loving and loved by Hamlet, but driven mad by his treatment of her and her father's death.

Orestes (ō-res′tēṣ). A hero of Greek tragedy, the son of Agamemnon and Clytemnestra. He killed his mother and Aegisthus in punishment of his father's murder; and for the crime of matricide he was pursued by the Furies. His friendship with Pylades, who married his sister Electra, is proverbial.

Orgoglio (ọr-gōl′yō). A hideous giant in Spenser's *Faërie Queene*, the personification of Arrogance, who overcomes the Red Cross Knight and imprisons him in one of the dungeons of his castle. Una, hearing of the knight's misfortune, informs Prince Arthur, who slays the giant and sets free the captive.

Oriana (ọ-ri-an′ȧ). A name applied to Queen Elizabeth in certain poems in her honor.—A lady in Tennyson's ballad of that name.—The beloved of Amadis of Gaul.

Orion (ō-rī′on). A giant and mighty hunter of Greek fable, who was blinded as a punishment, but recovered his sight by traveling eastward and exposing his eyes to the rays of the rising sun. After death he became a constellation.

Orlando (ọr-lan′dō). One of the paladins of Charlemagne, a hero of romance and Italian epic. Roland (which see) is another form of the name.—The hero of Shakespeare's *As You Like It*, and Rosalind's lover.

Orlando Furioso (fū-ri-ō′sō). 'Orlando Mad,' an epic poem so named, by Ariosto. It continues the *Orlando Innamorato* of Boiardo, and is descriptive of the gallant deeds and adventures of the paladins of the time of Charlemagne, whose nephew Orlando figures as the hero.

Orlick (ọr′lik). In Dickens' *Great Expectations*, the journeyman blacksmith employed by Joe Gargery; the enemy of Pip, whom he tries to murder.

Ormuzd (ọr′muzd). The supreme deity of the ancient Persians and the modern Parsees, the good spirit who is opposed by the evil spirit Ahriman. The antagonism of these two is a leading principle in the Zoroastrian religion.

Orpheus (ôr′fūs; ọr′fē-us). A mythical musician of Greece, who could charm beasts and make rocks and woods move to his melody. After the death of his wife Eurydice, he went to Hades in quest of her, and his music so charmed the infernal deities that they consented to let her follow him, provided that he did not look behind him until he and she had quite reached the upper world. But Orpheus looked a moment too soon, and thus lost her forever.

Orsino (ọr-sī′nō). In Shakespeare's *Twelfth Night*, the duke of Illyria, who sues for the love of the Countess Olivia. He finally marries Viola.

Orson (ôr′sŏn). See **Valentine.**

Orville (ọr′vil), **Lord.** Lover of Evelina in Fanny Burney's novel *Evelina*.

Osbaldistone (oṣ-bạld′is-tōn). A family in Scott's *Rob Roy*, the hero of which is Frank Osbaldistone, who is in love with and ultimately marries Diana Vernon. Rashleigh Osbaldistone, the villian of the novel, is killed by Rob Roy.

Osborne (oṣ′bọrn), **Capt. George.** In Thackeray's *Vanity Fair*, a dandified, selfish, and shallowhearted young officer, who marries Amelia Sedley. He is killed at Waterloo, after proposing an elopement with Becky Sharp. His father, a harsh, purse-proud, and domineering merchant, had previously cast him off because he objected to the marriage, for Amelia's father had become bankrupt. See **Dobbin.**

O'Shanter (ō-shan′tẽr), **Tam.** The hero of a narrative poem by Burns, who sees a dance of witches—with the devil as their musician—in old Alloway Church. He is chased by them to the river Doom, and one of them tears the tail from his mare Maggie.

Osiris (ō-sī′ris). In Egyptian mythology, one of the chief gods, the source of life and fruitfulness, the sum of all beneficent agencies, the Creator, and the god of the Nile. He was the father of Horus and the husband of Isis. After he had been slain by his brother Set, the personification of all evil, Osiris became the judge of the dead, and his soul animated the sacred bull Apis. Thus, under this form, Osiris continued to be present among men.

Osrick (oṣ′rik). A court dandy in Shakespeare's *Hamlet*.

Ossian (osh′ăn). A hero of Gaelic and Irish tradition.

Oswald (oṣ′wạld). Steward to Goneril in Shakespeare's *King Lear*.—Cupbearer to Cedric in Scott's *Ivanhoe*.

Othello (ō-thel′ō). In Shakespeare's tragedy *Othello*, a Moor who commands the Venetian forces, marries Desdemona, the daughter of a Venetian senator, smothers her when led by the devilish Iago to believe her unfaithful to him, and then kills himself.

Otranto (ō-tran′tō), **Castle of.** The name of a romance by Horace Walpole. See **Castle.**

O'Trigger (ō-trig′ẽr), **Sir Lucius.** A fighting Irishman in Sheridan's comedy *The Rivals*. 'A very pretty quarrel as it stands' is a phrase of Sir Lucius.

Overreach (ō′vẽr-rēch), **Sir Giles.** A proud and unscrupulous rascal in Massinger's comedy *A New Way to Pay Old Debts*.

Oz (oz). A fictitious kingdom which is the scene of *The Wonderful Wizard of Oz* and other juvenile stories by Lyman Frank Baum.

P

Page (pāġ), **Mrs.** In Shakespeare's *Merry Wives of Windsor*, a lady who joins with Mrs. Ford in making sport of Falstaff. Her daughter Anne is desired in marriage by Slender, but marries Fenton.

Palamon (pal′ȧ-mon). A knight who wins and weds Emelie in Chaucer's *Knight's Tale*.

Palinode (pal′i-nōd). A shepherd in Spenser's *Eclo ues* representing the Roman Catholic priests.

Palinurus (pal-in-ū′rus). The name of Aeneas' pilot in Virgil's *Aeneid*, often used as a general term for a pilot or steersman.

Pallas (pal′ăs). A name of Athena.

Pallet (pal′et). A ridiculous painter in Smollett's novel *Peregrine Pickle*.

Pamela (pam′e-lȧ). The heroine of a novel of that name by Richardson, a servant who resists her master's attempts to seduce her, and becomes his wife.

Pan (pan). Among the Greeks and Romans a god of flocks and herds, represented with two horns, pointed ears, and goat's legs.

Pancks (paṅks). A character in Dickens' *Little Dorrit*, a shabby, dirty little man employed to collect rents and exact the utmost farthing from the tenants.

Pandarus (pan′dȧ-rus). In Homer's *Iliad*, a Lycian who fought on the Trojan side, and was a distinguished archer. In the medieval story of *Troilus and Cressida* he is represented as assisting in bringing the two lovers together, and in Shakespeare's play his part is the well-known one which has given rise to the word *pander*.

Pandemonium (pan-de-mō′ni-um). The capital of Satan in Milton's *Paradise Lost*.

Pandora (pan-dō′rȧ). In classical mythology, a woman sent by the gods to bring evil upon men as a punishment of the theft of fire by Prometheus. Prometheus would not have anything to do with her, but his brother Epimetheus married her. Later accounts say that she had a box of blessings, which she opened out of curiosity, whereupon all escaped except Hope. Another version states that the box contained all the ills of mankind, which were released throughout the world.

Pangloss (pan′glos). A philosopher in Voltaire's *Candide* who believes that all is for the best in this the best of all possible worlds.

Panope (pan′ō-pē). One of the Nereids.

Pantagruel (pan-tag′rụ-el). An enormous giant, son of Gargantua in Rabelais' famous romance. See **Gargantua.**

Panurge (pa-nūrġ′). An important character in Rabelais' romance of *Gargantua and Pantagruel*, a great friend of the latter, a drunkard, rogue, and coward, but remarkably clever and amusing.

Panza (pan′zȧ), **Sancho.** See **Don Quixote.**

Parcae (pär′cē). Latin name of the **Fates.**

Paridel (par′i-del), **Sir.** A character in Spenser's *Faërie Queene*, a betrayer of women.

Paris (par′is). The son of Priam of Troy, celebrated for passing judgment as to the comparative beauty of the three goddesses Juno, Venus, and Minerva. Each offered him a bribe: regal power, the most beautiful woman in the world, martial glory. He decided for Venus, who helped him carry off Helen, the wife of Menelaus, thus causing the Trojan war. See **Achilles, Philoctetes.**—A character in Shakespeare's *Romeo and Juliet*, cousin and wooer of Juliet.

Parisina (par-i-sī′nȧ). Heroine and title of a poem by Lord Byron. See **Hugo.**

Parizade (pä-ri-zä′de). Heroine of a story in the *Arabian Nights*, a daughter of the sultan of Persia, by the machination of her two aunts brought up in ignorance of her birth. She succeeded in obtaining the talking bird, the singing tree, and the yellow water, and later became known to her father as his daughter.

Parsifal (pär′si-fäl). A hero of German legend belonging to the cycle of King Arthur and the Grail.

Parthenope (pär-then′ō-pē). One of the three Sirens in Greek mythology. The other two were Ligea and Leucosia. She was buried at Naples, which is poetically known by her name.

Partington (pärt′ing-tŏn), **Mrs.** An imaginary old lady to whom are assigned many laughable blunders in the use of words. An anecdote was told by Sydney Smith of a Mrs. Partington who, during a tempest and high tide, was seen with her mop trying to keep the Atlantic out of her house.

Partlet (pär′let), **Dame.** The hen in Chaucer's *Nun's Tale* and also in *Reynard the Fox*.

Partridge (pärt′riġ). The attendant of Tom Jones in Fielding's novel *Tom Jones*, faithful, simple, and ignorant of the world, but naturally shrewd.

Pastorella (pas-tọr-el′ȧ). A shepherdess in Spenser's *Faërie Queene* beloved by Sir Calidore.

Pathfinder (path′fīnder), **the.** See **Leatherstocking.**

Patrocius (pȧ-trō′clus). The bosom friend of Achilles in Homer's *Iliad*, slain by Hector.

Patterne (pat′ẽrn), **Sir Willoughby.** The central character in *The Egoist*, a novel by George Meredith. A wealthy, smug, humorless man, he searches unsuccessfully for a wife whose qualities he feels will match his own perfection.

Paul and Virginia (pạl and vĩr-ġin′i-ȧ). A pair of youthful lovers, whose history is told in St. Pierre's popular story of the same name.

Paulina (pạ-lī′nȧ). Character in Shakespeare's *Winter's Tale*, the clever and warmhearted friend of Hermione.

Pawkins (pạ′kinṣ), **Major.** An American character in Dickens' *Martin Chuzzlewit*, an unscrupulous speculator and great patriot.

Peachum (pēch′um). A harborer of thieves in Gay's *Beggar's Opera*. His daughter Polly is married to Macheath, and is virtuous in the midst of depravity. See **Macheath.**

Peake (pēk), **Selina.** The chief character in Edna Ferber's novel *So Big*, a widow who becomes a successful businesswoman against great odds and sees her son Dirk become successful in his turn.

Pecksniff (pek′snif). In Dickens' *Martin Chuzzlewit*, a sleek, unctuous humbug, an architect by profession, so thoroughly imbued with hypocrisy that it has become second nature with him. His daughters are named Charity and Mercy. The former is a shrew, the latter giddy and thoughtless, but sobered by marriage with her scoundrel cousin Jonas Chuzzlewit.

Pedro (pē′drō), **Dr.** A character in *Don Quixote*, the court physician of Barataria, who supervises Sancho Panza's food and causes the dishes set before him to be removed for various specious reasons.

Pedro, Don. The prince of Aragon in Shakespeare's *Much Ado About Nothing*.

Peecher (pēch′ẽr), **Miss.** A schoolmistress in Dickens' *Our Mutual Friend*, a neat, precise little woman, hopelessly attached to the teacher Bradley Headstone.

Peeperkorn (pe′pẽr-kọrn), **Mynheer.** Hans Castorp's rival for the affections of Clavdia Chauchat in Mann's *Magic Mountain*.

Peerybingle (pẽr′y-biṅ-gl), **John, and his wife.** In Dickens' *Cricket on the Hearth*, a big, honest, warmhearted carrier, married to a wife considerably younger, whose pet name is Dot.

Pegasus (peg′ȧ-sus). The winged horse of the Muses.

Peggotty (peg′ŏt-y), **Clara.** Nurse of David Copperfield in Dickens' novel *David Copperfield*, finally married to Barkis. Her brother Daniel is a Yarmouth fisherman, with whom live his nephew Ham Peggotty and niece 'Little Em'ly.'

Pelham (pel′ăm). The hero of the novel of this name by Bulwer-Lytton, in which is depicted a man of fashion—a Charles Surface of the nineteenth century.

Pelides (pe-lī′dēṣ). A name of Achilles, from his father Peleus.

Pell (pel), **Solomon.** An attorney in Dickens' *Pickwick Papers* with a rather poor practice, though he boasts of his intimacy with the lord chancellor.

Pelle (pel′ē). The proletarian hero of Martin Nexö's novel *Pelle the Conqueror*, who starts life as a peasant, and becomes interested in co-operatives. He is imprisoned on a trumped-up charge, and on his release, wins back his estranged wife and renews his struggle to further social justice.

Pelleas (pel′ē-ȧs). One of the knights of the Round Table, who is depicted, in one of Tennyson's *Idylls of the King*, as a noble youth in love with Ettarre, who scorns him.

Pelops (pē′lops). In Greek mythology, the son of

Tantalus, killed and served as food to the gods by his father, who wished to test their divine powers. He was restored to life, and received an ivory shoulder in place of the one eaten by Demeter. His sons were Atreus and Thyestes, and the tragic events connected with Pelops' line were famous in antiquity.

Pendennis (pen-den'is), **Arthur.** The hero of Thackeray's novel *Pendennis*, a young man of middle-class rank, somewhat conceited, but clever, honorable, and goodhearted. He makes his way as a novelist and man of letters, and after being engaged to Blanche Amory marries his cousin Laura Bell. His mother, greatly devoted to him, is a singularly sweet and good woman. His uncle, Major Pendennis, is a diner-out and man about town who sincerely worships rank and wealth. Pendennis' chief friend is the barrister and publicist George Warrington. It is Pendennis who is supposed to write Thackeray's novel *The Newcomes*.

Penelope (pe-nel'ō-pē). The wife of Ulysses, during whose long absence from home she is pestered with wooers. Faithful to her husband, she puts them off by saying she will wed no one till the web she has in hand is finished, and at night unweaves what she has woven by day.

Penrod (pen'rod). The central character in Booth Tarkington's novel of the same name. Penrod Schofield typifies small-town boyhood in America at the turn of the century, and his escapades, with those of his friend Sam Williams (in the sequel *Penrod and Sam*), have become part of American folklore.

Penthesilea (pen-thes-i-lē'á). In Homeric commentaries and Virgil, a queen of the Amazons.

Percival (pẽr'ci-văl), **Sir.** One of King Arthur's knights.

Perdita (pẽr'di-tȧ). The heroine of Shakespeare's *Winter's Tale*, daughter of Leontes, king of Sicily, abandoned as a child and brought up as a shepherdess, beloved by Florizel.

Peread (pẽr'ē-ad), **Sir.** The Black Knight in Tennyson's *Gareth and Lynette*.

Pericles (per'i-clēs). The hero of Shakespeare's *Pericles, Prince of Tyre*, and of a popular tale of the middle ages.

Perker (pẽrk'ẽr). A lawyer in Dickens' *Pickwick Papers*, a dapper little man who acts as Mr. Pickwick's agent.

Persephone (pẽr-sef'ō-nē). The Greek equivalent of the Roman Proserpina or Proserpine.

Perseus (pẽr'sūs). In Greek mythology, the son of Zeus and Danaë. With the aid of equipment given to him by the gods, he slew Medusa; and he rescued Andromeda by killing the sea monster that threatened her, and married her.

Pertolope (pẽr'tō-lōp), **Sir.** The Green Knight in Tennyson's *Gareth and Lynette*.

Peter (pē'tẽr), **Lord.** The name under which Swift satirizes the Pope and the Roman Catholic Church in his *Tale of a Tub*.

Peter Pan (pan). The little lost boy who never grew up, in Barrie's children's story of the same name. He entices the Darling children to go on adventures with him in Never-Never Land, and Wendy Darling mothers him.

Peter the Hermit (thē hẽr'mit). The personage who led the first Crusade. Introduced in Tasso's *Jerusalem Delivered* and Scott's *Count Robert of Paris*.

Peto (pē'tō). A follower of Falstaff in Shakespeare's *Henry IV*.

Petruchio (pe-trū'chi-ō). The hero of Shakespeare's *Taming of the Shrew*, husband of the shrew Katharina.

Phaeacians (fē-ā'shi-ăns). An island people with whom Ulysses came in contact in his wanderings. See **Alcinous, Nausicaä.**

Phaedra (fē'drȧ). Wife of Theseus, who fell in love with her stepson Hippolytus. After causing the latter's death, she strangled herself in remorse.

Phaedria (fē'dri-ȧ). A female wanton in Spenser's *Faerie Queene* attending on Acrasia.

Phantom Ship (fan'tŏm ship). See **Flying Dutchman.**

Philander (fil-an'dẽr). A male flirt in Ariosto's *Orlando Furioso*.

Philaster (fil-as'tẽr), **Prince.** The hero of Beaumont and Fletcher's play *Philaster*, who is in love with and ultimately marries Princess Arethusa. Affairs are complicated by Euphrasia, whose love for Philaster leads her to enter his service in the guise of a page.

Philemon (fil-ē'mŏn). See **Baucis.**

Philoctetes (fil-oc-tē'tēs). A Greek hero and friend of Hercules, whose bow and poisoned arrows he inherited. After an oracle had declared that Troy could not be captured without Hercules' weapons, Philoctetes was brought to Troy, where he mortally wounded Paris with a poisoned arrow. He is the subject of a tragedy by Sophocles.

Philomela (fil-ō-mē'lȧ). A legendary princess of Athens, violated by her sister Procne's husband Tereus, who cut out her tongue to keep her from telling of the deed. However, she informed Procne through writing, and the two sisters in revenge killed the son of Procne and Tereus and served the flesh to Tereus. When he prepared to kill the sisters, the gods transformed all three into birds: Tereus became the hawk, Procne the swallow, and Philomela the nightingale.

Philosophers (fi-los'ō-fẽrs), **the.** The two wise men in James Stephens' *Crock of Gold*, an allegorical novel which satirizes present-day civilization.

Phipps (fips), **Denis.** One of the expatriates in Norman Douglas' *South Wind*.

Phiz (fiz). Pseudonym of Hablot K. Browne, who illustrated Dickens' works.

Phoebus (fē'bus). An appellation of Apollo, especially in his quality of sun-god.

Phoebus, Captain. In Victor Hugo's *Notre-Dame de Paris*, an aristocrat who cherishes a base love for Esmeralda.

Phosphor (fos'for). The morning star.

Pickle (pik'l), **Peregrine.** The hero of an amusing novel of the same name by Smollett, a young gentleman of profligate and debased character. See **Hatchway, Pipes, Trunnion.**

Pickwick (pik'wik), **Samuel.** The hero of Dickens' *Pickwick Papers*, in which are narrated the diverting experiences of Mr. Pickwick and certain members of a club named after him, especially Messrs. **Winkle, Tupman,** and **Snodgrass.** See also **Bardell, Weller.**

Pied Piper of Hamelin (pīd pī'pẽr ov ham'lin). A wonderful musician of German legend who pipes away all the rats from the town of Hamelin, but is defrauded of his reward, and thereupon pipes away the children of the town, who with him enter a neighboring hill and are nevermore seen.

Pilar (pī-lär'). A strong-willed but warmhearted peasant woman, the dominant member of a guerrilla band helping Robert Jordan in Hemingway's *For Whom the Bell Tolls*.

Pim (pim), **Mr.** An old gentleman in A. A. Milne's play *Mr. Pim Passes By*, who by his mistake in a name causes a couple to wonder whether their marriage is actually bigamous.

Pinch (pinch), **Tom.** In Dickens' *Martin Chuzzlewit*, an assistant to Pecksniff the architect, who takes advantage of his simplicity and unselfishness, and treats him as a drudge. At last realizing Pecksniff's baseness, Tom leaves him, and is afterwards befriended by old Martin Chuzzlewit. Tom is a great performer on the organ. His sister Ruth becomes the wife of his friend John Westlock.

Pinchbeck (pinch'bek), **Lady.** In Lord Byron's *Don Juan*, the lady to whom Juan gives Leila in charge.

Pinchwife (pinch'wīf), **Mr. and Mrs.** In Wycherley's *Country Wife*, a husband and his unsophisticated young wife, whom he introduces to town society and jealously watches.

Pinkerton (piñk'ẽr-tŏn), **Miss.** In Thackeray's *Vanity Fair*, a very majestic lady who keeps a boarding school, attended by Amelia Sedley and Becky Sharp.

Pinocchio (pin-ō'çī-ō). A wooden marionet whose adventures are narrated in the children's book of the same name.

Pip (pip). The hero of Dickens' *Great Expectations*, whose real name is Philip Pirrip, born in humble life and apprenticed to the blacksmith Joe Gargery. The 'great expectations' are based on the prospect of an inheritance from an unknown benefactor, who turns out to be Magwitch, the convict. Pip is in love with Estella, who marries another man; but he is united with her after she is widowed.

Pipchin (pip'chin), **Mrs.** The keeper of an establishment for training children, at Brighton, in Dickens' *Dombey and Son*.

Pipes (pīps), **Tom.** A taciturn retired boatswain's mate living with Commodore Trunnion in Smollett's *Peregrine Pickle*.

Pippa (pip'ȧ). A little Italian silk-factory girl in Browning's poem *Pippa Passes*, who influences unknowingly everyone she meets when she is singing happily on her way to work.

Pisanio (pi-sä'ni-ō). In Shakespeare's *Cymbeline*, a servant of Posthumus. Though sent to murder Imogen, he assists her to escape.

Pistol (pis'tŏl). A follower of Falstaff in Shakespeare's plays, a ranting, swaggering bully and coward. He marries Mistress Quickly.

Pleydell (plę'del), **Mr.** An advocate in Scott's *Guy Mannering*, shrewd in business, but fond of fun.

Pliable (plī'ȧ-bl). A character in Bunyan's *Pilgrim's Progress*, who starts out with Christian but turns back at the Slough of Despond.

Pliant (plī'ănt), **Sir Paul and Lady.** In Congreve's *Double Dealer*, an old husband ruled by his wife, whose virtue is not irreproachable.

Plornish (plor'nish). A plasterer in Dickens' *Little Dorrit*, who has the habit of repeating the last words of any person speaking.

Plowman (plou'măn), **Piers.** The dreamer in a poetical religious satire commonly attributed, though questionably, to William Langland, called *The Vision of Piers Plowman*.

Plume (plūm), **Sir.** A fop in Pope's *Rape of the Lock*, 'of amber snuffbox justly vain, and the nice conduct of a clouded cane.'

Plummer (plum'ẽr), **Caleb.** In Dickens' *Cricket on the Hearth*, a poor old toymaker with a blind daughter, for whom he makes believe that they are quite well off and living in good style—a pathetic yet humorous portrait. His son Edward marries May Fielding.

Pocket (pok'et), **Herbert, with his father, mother, and aunt.** Characters in Dickens' *Great Expectations* with whom Pip, the hero, is associated.

Podsnap (pod'snap), **Mr., Mrs., and Georgiana.** Characters in Dickens' *Our Mutual Friend*. Mr. Podsnap is very wealthy and respectable, and a profound believer in respectability and wealth.

Pogram (pō'grăm), **Elijah.** A bombastic and ridiculous American character in Dickens' *Martin Chuzzlewit*.

Poictesme (pwȧ-teş'm). The imaginary medieval country in the south of France where many of James Branch Cabell's novels are set.

Poins (poins). Companion of Prince Hal and Falstaff in Shakespeare's *Henry IV*.

Poirot (pwȧ-rō'), **Hercule.** A Belgian detective appearing in many novels and stories by Agatha Christie.

Polixenes (po-lik'sē-nēs). King of Bohemia in Shakespeare's *Winter's Tale*, and father of Florizel.

Polly (pol'y), **Aunt.** The aunt of Tom Sawyer in Mark Twain's *The Adventures of Tom Sawyer*.

Polly, Mr. A philosophical character in H. G. Wells' novel of the same name.

Pollyanna (pol'y-an'ȧ). A little girl, known as the Glad Girl, who finds good in everything, in a novel of the same name by Eleanor H. Porter.

Polonius (pō-lō'ni-us). Lord chamberlain of Denmark in Shakespeare's *Hamlet*, father of Laertes and Ophelia, garrulous and not without worldly wisdom, but not so wise as he thinks.

Polynices (pol-y-nī'cēs). See **Eteocles.**

Polyolbion (pol-y-ol'bi-ŏn). Name of a great poem by Michael Drayton, in thirty songs or books, descriptive of England (1612–22).

Polyphemus (pol-y-fē'mus). A Cyclops or one-eyed giant in Homer's *Odyssey*, who imprisoned Ulysses and his companions in his cave and devoured some of them; but the rest blinded him when he was in a drunken sleep and escaped.

Pomona (pō-mō'nȧ). The Roman goddess of fruits and fruit trees, wife of Vertumnus.

Pompilia (pom-pil'i-ȧ). The unfortunate heroine of Browning's poem *The Ring and the Book*.

Pontifex (pon'ti-feks), **Ernest.** The hero of Samuel Butler's *Way of All Flesh*, who achieves happiness by throwing off all the shackles of convention.

Ponto (pon'tō), **Major.** One of the chief figures in Thackeray's *Book of Snobs*, a retired officer and country gentleman of small estate, who is forced into the ranks of the snobs through his wife's ambition to mix only with 'the county families.'

Ponza (pon'zȧ), **Signor.** A leading character in Luigi Pirandello's comedy, *Right You Are If You Think You Are*, in which his mother-in-law and he accuse each other of insanity, each with various witnesses. It is never clear who is or is not crazy.

Pooh-Bah (pọọ'bä'). The Lord High Everything Else in Gilbert and Sullivan's comic opera *The Mikado*.

Porgy (por'gy). A crippled Negro beggar of Catfish Row, Charleston, in the novel *Porgy*, by DuBose Heyward, later made into a play and, under the title *Porgy and Bess*, an opera (music by Gershwin). Porgy loves Bess, the sweetheart of Crown, a fugitive murderer. Bess goes to live with Porgy, and becomes fairly respectable through his kindness and love. When Crown returns to claim her, Porgy kills him, and is arrested. Released, he again seeks Bess.

Porter (por'tẽr), **Sir Joseph, K. C. B.** The admiral in the comic opera *H. M. S. Pinafore*, by Gilbert and Sullivan, who 'never went to sea,' and was rewarded by becoming ruler of the 'queen's navee.'

Porthos (por-tos'). Comrade of **d'Artagnan.**

Portia (por'shi-ȧ). A rich heiress in Shakespeare's *Merchant of Venice*, whose father has settled that the suitor whom she will marry must first select from three sealed caskets the one which contains her picture. Fortunately her lover, Bassanio, chooses correctly. Disguised as a learned doctor of law, she afterward wins judgment against Shylock. See **Shylock.**

Poseidon (pō-sī'dŏn). The Greek sea-god corresponding with the Roman Neptune.

Posthumus (post'hū-mus), **Leonatus.** The husband of Imogen in Shakespeare's *Cymbeline*, who too rashly believes in the infidelity of his wife.

Pott (pot), **Mr.** The editor of the *Eatanswill Gazette* in Dickens' *Pickwick Papers*.

Poyser (poi'sẽr), **Mrs.** In George Eliot's *Adam Bede*, a farmer's wife, remarkable for the sharpness of her tongue, and her pithy and epigrammatic sayings.

Prester John (pres'tẽr jon). A fabulous king of the interior of Asia. According to Mandeville's *Travels* he was a descendant of Ogier the Dane, who, with certain of his barons, penetrated into Asia. John received the name of Prester (priest) from having converted the natives. Some writers make him a ruler in Ethiopia.

Priam (prī'ăm). The king of Troy in the classical story of the Trojan war, father of Hector and Paris, and husband of Hecuba, slain by Pyrrhus.

Price (prīc), **Fanny.** The heroine of Jane Austen's novel *Mansfield Park*. Fanny is a poor relation adopted by her rich uncle Sir Thomas Bertram, and is patronized by the family. She falls in love with her cousin Edmund Bertram, a clergyman. He is fond of Fanny but loves Mary Crawford, a worldly girl. Mary's brother Harry courts Fanny but elopes with Edmund's sister Maria, which breaks off the relations between Edmund and Mary, leaving Edmund free to marry Fanny.

Priest (prēst), **Judge.** A kindly Kentucky judge in various stories by Irvin Cobb.

Prig (prig), **Betsy.** A coarse, liquor-loving monthly nurse in Dickens' *Martin Chuzzlewit*, friend and 'pardner' of Mrs. Gamp, with whom, however, she has a famous quarrel.

Primrose (prim'rōs) **Family.** Related characters in

Goldsmith's *Vicar of Wakefield*. The Rev. Dr. Charles Primrose, the vicar in the novel, is a good and simple man with amiable weaknesses and vanities. His wife is a great housekeeper and stickler for gentility. His daughters are Olivia and Sophia, his sons George and Moses, the latter of whom is naive and pedantic, and foolishly barters a horse for a gross of green spectacles. Olivia elopes with young Squire Thornhill, who thinks he deceives her by a mock marriage, which is found to be real after all.

Priscilla (pris-il'ȧ). The Puritan maiden in Longfellow's *Courtship of Miles Standish*.

Prisoner of Chillon (priṣ'nẽr ov chi-lon'), **the.** Bonnivard, in a poem by Lord Byron so called. See **Chillon.**

Procne (proç'nē). See **Philomela.**

Procrustes (prō-çrus'tēṣ). An Attican highwayman who tied his victims to a bed, and adapted them to its length by stretching or amputating their legs.

Prometheus (pro-mē'thūs). A divine personage of Greek mythology, who brought fire from heaven to man, and was punished by Zeus (Jupiter), who had him chained to a rock on Mount Caucasus, where an eagle or vulture fed constantly on his liver, which was ever reproduced.

Proserpina *or* **Proserpine** (prō-sẽr'pi-nȧ; -ē). The daughter of Ceres and wife of Pluto, who carried her off to the lower world while she was gathering flowers in Sicily.

Prospero (pros'pẽr-ō). The magician and exiled duke of Milan in Shakespeare's *Tempest*, father of Miranda, and master of Ariel and Caliban.

Pross (pros), **Miss.** In Dickens' *Tale of Two Cities*, a domestic in the Manette family, who justly causes the death of Madame Defarge.

Protesilaus (prō'tes-i-lā'us). A legendary Greek hero of the Trojan war, the first man to land from the Greek fleet. An oracle had foretold that the first to step on Trojan soil would be killed; and Protesilous was slain by Hector. See **Laodamia.**

Provincial Lady (prō-vin'shăl lā'dy). The name for herself used by E. M. Delafield in books about her trips away from her English country home.

Pry (prȳ), **Paul.** A busybody in John Poole's comedy of the same name.

Prynne (pryn), **Hester.** The heroine of Nathaniel Hawthorne's *Scarlet Letter*, condemned to wear an embroidered scarlet 'A,' symbol of adultery. She does not disclose the name of her companion in guilt, even under the public urging of the young minister Arthur Dimmesdale.

Psyche (sȳ'çhē). An allegorical personification of the soul, a beautiful maiden whose charming story is given by the Latin writer Appuleius. Cupid fell in love with her, but Psyche had to undergo many trials, partly because of the jealousy of Venus, before the lovers were finally united.

Puck (puk). See **Goodfellow.**

Pumblechook (pum'bl-chook). Uncle of Joe Gargery in Dickens' *Great Expectations*, a bully or a toady as occasion seems to require.

Pure (pūr), **Simon.** A Quaker in *A Bold Stroke for a Wife* by Mrs. Centlivre. A Colonel Feignwell represents himself as Simon Pure in order to win Miss Lovely, the heroine. He obtains her guardian's consent to marry her, but at this point the real Simon Pure appears and conclusively identifies himself.

Pygmalion (pyg-mā'li-ŏn). A Greek sculptor who is said to have fallen in love with the statue of a beautiful woman he had made, and to have had his prayer granted that she should be endowed with life. The story has been used, among others, by Bernard Shaw. See **Galatea** and **Doolittle, Eliza.**

Pyramus and Thisbe (pyr'ȧ-mus, thiṣ'bē). In Ovid's *Metamorphoses*, two lovers of Babylon, whose parents were against their marriage, and who conversed through a chink in a wall. Having agreed to meet at the tomb of Ninus, Thisbe arrived first, but ran away at the sight of a lioness all bloody, leaving her robe, which Pyramus found stained with blood. Thinking her dead, he killed himself; and finding his dead body, Thisbe did likewise. Shakespeare included a travesty on the legend in *Midsummer Night's Dream*.

Pyrrha (pyr'ȧ). Wife of **Deucalion.**

Pythias (pyth'i-ăs). See **Damon.**

Q

Quasimodo (kwä-si-mō'dō). The hunchback in Victor Hugo's *Notre-Dame de Paris*, hopelessly in love with Esmeralda.

Quarles (kwärlṣ), **Philip.** An author, the chief character in *Point Counter Point*, by Aldous Huxley, who is too self-conscious and skeptical to keep alive the love between him and his wife Elinor.

Queeg (kwēg), **Lt. Commander.** In Herman Wouk's novel *The Caine Mutiny* and its dramatization, an American naval officer in World War II whose questionable competence and courage lead to the 'mutiny' and a court-martial.

Queen (kwēn), **Ellery.** The fictional detective of F. Dannay and M. B. Lee, and also their joint pseudonym.

Quickly (kwik'ly), **Mrs.** The hostess of a London inn frequented by Falstaff in Shakespeare's *Henry IV*, garrulous and foolish, and taken advantage of by Falstaff, who runs in debt to her. In *Henry V* she describes the death of Falstaff, and is represented as having become the wife of Pistol.

Quilp (kwilp). A hideous and malignant dwarf in Dickens' *Old Curiosity Shop*, drowned in the Thames.

Quinapalus (kwin-ap'ȧ-lus). An imaginary author quoted by Shakespeare in *Twelfth Night*.

Quince (kwinc), **Peter.** A carpenter in Shakespeare's *Midsummer Night's Dream*, who assists in the interlude of Pyramus and Thisbe.

Quirt (kwĩrt), **Sergeant.** A member of the A. E. F. in France who is the rival of Captain Flagg for the affections of Charmaine, in Anderson and Stallings' play *What Price Glory*.

Quixote(kwik'sŏt;kī-hō'tā), **Don.** See **Don Quixote.**

R

Rab (rab). A dog in a story called *Rab and His Friends*, by Dr. John Brown.

Rackrent (rak'rent), **Sir Condy.** A character in Miss Edgeworth's story *Castle Rackrent*.

Raddle (rad'l), **Mrs.** Bob Sawyer's landlady in Dickens' *Pickwick Papers*.

Radigund (rad'i-gund). Queen of the Amazons, in Spenser's *Faërie Queene*, who makes every man that falls into her hands dress himself like a woman, and work at sewing, spinning, etc.

Raffles (raf'elṣ). The burglar hero of *The Amateur Cracksman* and other stories by E. W. Hornung.

Rakonitz (rak'ō-nits) **Family.** A fictitious international Jewish family created by G. B. Stern in the *Matriarch* series. Founders of the family were Babette Weinberg and Simon Rakonitz, obscure Viennese, whose progeny made fortunes in jewel mines. The outstanding character is Anastasia, the matriarch. The rise and fall of family fortunes, loves and marriages, are chronicled.

Ralph Roister Doister (rȧlf rois'tẽr dois'tẽr). See **Roister Doister.**

Rampion (ramp'i-ŏn), **Mark.** A philosopher in *Point Counter Point* by Aldous Huxley.

Random (ran'dŏm), **Roderick.** The hero of a novel by Smollett, a worthless young fellow who has many amusing adventures in different parts of the world.

Raphael (raf'ȧ-el). An archangel who is introduced in the apocryphal book of Tobit, and who takes a considerable place in Milton's *Paradise Lost*.

Rarahu (rär'ȧ-hū). The native wife of Loti in Pierre Loti's idyll of the South Seas, *The Marriage of Loti*.

Raskolnikov (rȧs-kol'nyi-kǫf). The hero of Dostoevski's novel *Crime and Punishment*, a student who, under stress of poverty and ill-health, plans and commits murder, having convinced himself that the deed is justifiable. Remorse, confession, and punishment follow, and ultimately, a struggle for regeneration.

Rasselas (ras'e-lăs). A prince of Abyssinia, in a moral tale by Dr. Johnson, detained in delightful captivity in a certain 'happy valley.' From this he escapes and wanders over the world, but finding no greater happiness elsewhere, returns to his old abode.

Rastignac, de (dē rȧs-tī-nyȧç'), **Eugène.** An opportunist who appears in various stages of striving and success in several of Balzac's novels.

Ravenswood (rā'venṣ-wood), **Edgar.** The hero of Scott's tragic romance *The Bride of Lammermoor*, who is separated by her friends from his betrothed, Lucy Ashton, the heroine of the novel, and who, in accordance with an ancient prophecy, perishes in quicksand.

Raymond (rā'mŏnd), **Count of Toulouse.** A crusader introduced in Tasso's *Jerusalem Delivered*, and in Scott's *Count Robert of Paris*.

Rebecca (rē beç'ȧ). In Scott's *Ivanhoe*, the daughter of Isaac the Jew, the real heroine of the novel, beautiful, high-principled, benevolent, loving Ivanhoe and persecuted by Bois-Guilbert. In Thackeray's humorous continuation of the novel, *Rebecca and Rowena*, Rebecca is married to Ivanhoe.

Rebecca of Sunnybrook Farm (rē-beç'ȧ ov sun'y-brook färm). The ten-year-old heroine of a children's novel of the same name by Kate Douglas Wiggin. Rebecca Randall goes to live with two strict maiden aunts, Miranda and Jane. The book deals with her childish adventures, and ends with her graduation. A sequel is *New Chronicles of Rebecca*.

Red Cross Knight (red çrǫs nīt). A knight in Spenser's *Faerie Queene*, who slays a dreadful dragon and marries Una.

Reeve's Tale (rēvṣ tāl), **The.** One of Chaucer's *Canterbury Tales*, about a miller who is tricked by two students.

Regan (rē'găn). One of King Lear's unnatural daughters.

Reini Kugel (rī'nī kų'gel). The Rabelaisian hero and strong man of Jake Falstaff's satirical extravaganza of the same name.

Remus (rē'mus). See **Romulus, Uncle Remus.**

Reynard the Fox (ren'ärd; rā'närd thē foks). The hero of the old German beast epic, in which animals are introduced speaking and acting like human beings. The fox, who is the cleverest of all, represents the church. He tricks his uncle Isengrim, the wolf, who represents the baronial class.

Rhadamanthus (rad'ȧ-man'thus). A legendary king of Lycia, who for his justice was made after death a judge in the other world.

Rhea (rē'ȧ). A goddess of the Greeks and Romans, also known as Cybele.

Richie (rich'i), **Helena.** The heroine of Margaret Deland's novel *The Awakening of Helena Richie*. Called upon to choose between her adopted son David and her lover, she chooses David. The story takes place in Old Chester, the village around which most of Margaret Deland's stories are woven.

Ridd (rid), **John.** The hero of R. D. Blackmore's novel *Lorna Doone*, in love with Lorna.

Riderhood (rī'dẽr-hood), **Rogue.** In Dickens' *Our Mutual Friend*, a 'waterside character' engaged in drugging and robbing seamen and such work, drowned by Bradley Headstone, who shares his fate.

Rienzi (rī-en'tsī), **Cola di.** The Roman tribune, introduced in Bulwer-Lytton's novel so named, and in Wagner's opera.

Rigoletto (rig-ō-let'ō). The name of an opera by Verdi, and of a buffoon who figures in it, and who unwittingly assists in the abduction and murder of his own daughter.

Rima (rī'mȧ). The bird girl in W. H. Hudson's *Green Mansions*, who lives in the wilds of Venezuela, in South America. She is loved by a Mr. Abel, who writes in the first person, and who plans to take her to civilization; but she is burned at the stake by savages who think her an evil spirit.

Rimini (rī'mī-nī), **Francesca da.** See **Francesca da Rimini.**

Rinaldo (rī-näl'dō). A famous hero in Ariosto's *Orlando Furioso*, one of Charlemagne's paladins, and cousin of Roland or Orlando.

Rip Van Winkle (rip van win̄'kl). See **Winkle.**

Rivals (rī'vălṣ), **The.** Title of a comedy by R. B. Sheridan, in which the rivals are Captain Absolute and Bob Acres, and Lydia Languish is the lady of whom both are suitors. Sir Lucius O'Trigger is another character.

Robert le Diable (rō-ber' lē dī-ȧb'l'). Duke of Normandy, introduced in Meyerbeer's opera *Robert le Diable*: but the Robert of opera and legend has little in common with the historical Robert.

Robert of Paris (rob'ẽrt ov par'is), **Count.** A crusader in Scott's novel so called, the scene of which is chiefly laid at Constantinople.

Robin Hood (rob'in hood). The famous archer and outlaw of medieval England, a popular legendary hero.

Robinson Crusoe (rob'in-sŏn çrū'sō). The hero and title of Defoe's famous novel.

Rob Roy (rob roi). See **Macgregor, Rob Roy.**

Robsart (rob'särt), **Amy.** Countess of Leicester, heroine of Scott's *Kenilworth*, which is founded on history but makes no pretense to historical accuracy.

Rochester (roch'es-tẽr), **Mr.** The principal male character in Charlotte Bronte's *Jane Eyre*.

Roderick (rod'ẽr-ik), **Last of the Goths.** The hero of Southey's poem, and of Scott's *Vision of Don Roderick*.

Roderick Dhu (dū). 'Black Roderick,' an outlawed Highland chief in Scott's *Lady of the Lake*, who is defeated in a desperate hand-to-hand conflict with Fitz-James, that is, the king of Scotland, James V.

Roderigo (rod-ẽr-ī'gō). A character in Shakespeare's *Othello*, a gentleman in love with Desdemona, a dupe and tool of Iago, who later kills him.

Roe (rō), **Richard.** A fictitious character whose name formerly appeared in certain English legal proceedings along with that of John Doe.

Roger de Coverley (roġ'ẽr dē çŏv'ẽr-li), **Sir.** See **Coverley.**

Roister Doister (rois'tẽr dois'tẽr), **Ralph.** The hero of the earliest English comedy, by Nicholas Udall, printed in 1566.

Rokesmith (rōk'smith). Assumed name of John Harmon in Dickens' *Our Mutual Friend*. See **Harmon.**

Roland (rō'lănd). A hero of tales connected with Charlemagne, whose nephew he was, said to have been killed in the rout of Charlemagne's rear guard at Roncesvalles. Orlando is another form of his name. Some of his exploits involve his friend Oliver. He is celebrated, notably, in the *Chanson de Roland*, Boiardo's *Orlando Innamorato*, and Ariosto's *Orlando Furioso*.

Roman Father (rō'măn fäth'ẽr), **the.** Horatius, the father of the Horatii in the ancient Roman legend of the Horatii and Curiatii, dealt with in Whitehead's tragedy.

Romeo (rō'mē-ō). The hero of Shakespeare's well-known tragedy *Romeo and Juliet*, one of the Montague family, while Juliet is a Capulet.

Romola (rom'ō-lȧ). The heroine of a novel of the same name by George Eliot, the scene of which is Florence in the time of Savonarola and the revival of learning in Italy. Romola is a patrician maiden, the daughter of a learned man, and marries a handsome young Greek scholar, Tito Melema, who turns out to be self-seeking, unprincipled, and altogether unworthy of his wife.

Romulus (rom'ū-lus). The legendary founder and first king of Rome, twin brother of Remus.

Rosalind (roṣ'ȧ-lind). The sprightly and charming daughter of the banished duke in Shakespeare's *As You Like It*, beloved by Orlando. Dressed in male attire, and accompanied by her cousin Celia and Touchstone the jester, she seeks her exiled father in the forest of Arden.

Rosamond Clifford (roṣ'ȧ-mŏnd çlif'ŏrd) *or* **Fair Rosamond.** Introduced in many poems and dramas, among the rest in Tennyson's *Becket*. The romantic incidents and surroundings of her life are almost all fictitious.

Rosencrantz (rō'ṣen-çrants). A courtier in Shakespeare's *Hamlet*.

Rosinante (rōṣ-i-nan'tē). Don Quixote's famous steed. See **Don Quixote.**

Rouncewell (rounc'wel), **Mrs.** Lady Dedlock's housekeeper in Dickens' *Bleak House*.

Round Table (round tā'bl). The large circular table at which King Arthur and his knights used to sit, giving its name to an order of knighthood instituted by the king.

Rowena (rō-ē'nȧ). In Scott's *Ivanhoe*, the fair Saxon lady whom the hero marries. See **Rebecca.**

Roxane (rọk-sȧn'). The heroine of Rostand's *Cyrano de Bergerac.*

Rubrick (rụ'brik), **the Rev. Mr.** The Episcopal chaplain to the Baron Bradwardine in Scott's *Waverley.*

Rudge (ruġ), **Barnaby.** The hero of the novel of the same name by Dickens, a half-witted young man, always accompanied by a tame raven called Grip. He takes an innocent part in the Gordon 'No Popery!' riots, and is condemned to death, but pardoned. His mother's life is overshadowed by the knowledge that her husband, Barnaby's father, is a murderer, skulking about the country in danger of his life.

Ruggles of Red Gap (rug'ḷṣ ov red gap). A butler in a humorous novel by Harry Leon Wilson, who, when given an opportunity to be a gentleman by his master, decides he prefers to be a butler.

Rustam *or* **Rustum** (rus'tăm; -tum). A hero of Persian legend and epic poetry. In Matthew Arnold's poem *Sohrab and Rustum*, Rustum fights and kills Sohrab, and learns only afterwards that the latter was his son.

Ryecroft (rȳ'ǥrọft), **Henry.** The hero of George Gissing's novel *The Private Papers of Henry Ryecroft*, a largely autobiographical story, dealing with a struggling author.

S

Sabrina (sȧ-brī'nȧ). A fabulous princess of ancient Britain, said to have become the nymph of the river Severn.

Saint-Loup (saṅ-lö'), **Robert.** In Proust's *Remembrance of Things Past*, the heir of the Guermantes family, and the husband of Gilberte. His mistress is a Jewish actress, Rachel. He is killed in the first World War.

Sampson (samp'sŏn), **Dominie.** The profoundly learned tutor at Ellangowan in Scott's *Guy Mannering*, exceedingly awkward and utterly ignorant of the world.

Sandalphon (san-dal'fŏn). According to an old Jewish belief, one of three angels who receive the prayers of the faithful and weave them into crowns.

Sandys (sandṣ) **Thomas.** The hero of Barrie's *Sentimental Tommy* and *Tommy and Grizel*, a conceited, likable, contradictory character, who is a writer in London. He meets an accidental death while pursuing an amour he has told his wife Grizel he will give up.

Sanger (saṅg'ẽr) **Family.** A family whose history is related in *The Constant Nymph* by Margaret Kennedy. The eccentric father, Albert, is a musical genius and has seven undisciplined children by two wives and a mistress. Known as the Sanger Circus, they wander all over the Continent, and have a home in the Austrian Tyrol, headquarters for an assortment of guests.

Sangrado (san-grä'dō), **Dr.** A doctor in Le Sage's novel *Gil Blas*, who prescribes copious bleeding and the drinking of ho. water for every sort of ailment.

Sangrail (san'grāl), **Clovis.** The chief character in many of the humorous short stories by H. H. Munro (Saki), particularly *The Chronicles of Clovis.*

Sans-Gêne (säṅ-ẓen'), **Madame.** The heroine of a drama by Sardou and Moreau, a vivacious French washerwoman who becomes the duchess of Danzig and a prominent member of the court of Napoleon I, where she keeps her simple, free manners.

Santa Claus (san'tȧ ǥlạṣ). A personage of popular mythology, represented as bringing presents to the young on Christmas eve. The name is equivalent to St. Nicholas, being based on the Dutch form Sant Nikolaas.

Sapho (sȧ-fō'). The heroine, a French courtesan, in the novel of the same name by Daudet

Sarpedon (sär-pē'dŏn). A king of Lycia in Homer's *Iliad*, who went to the Trojan war as an ally of Priam and was slain by Patroclus.

Saturn (sat'ûrn). A Roman deity equivalent to the Greek Cronus, dethroned as ruler of the world by his son Jupiter (Zeus).

Sawyer (sạ'yẽr), **Bob.** A roistering young doctor in Dickens' *Pickwick*, close friend of Ben Allen, another medical student.—**Tom,** the boy hero of the story of the same name by Mark Twain, an inhabitant of a small Missouri town in the middle of the last century. His companion is Huckleberry Finn, with whom he shares many adventures in this novel and its sequel *Huckleberry Finn*. Two more books followed: *Tom Sawyer Abroad* and *Tom Sawyer, Detective.*

Scadder (sǥad'ẽr). An American land agent in Dickens' *Martin Chuzzlewit*, by whose misrepresentations Martin is led to purchase land at the wretched settlement of Eden.

Scales (sǥālṣ), **Gerald.** The husband of Sophia in Arnold Bennett's *Old Wives' Tale.*

Schacabac (shaǥ'ȧ-baǥ). In the *Arabian Nights*, a starveling who is invited to a feast. See **Barmecide.**

Scheherazade (she-hẹ'rȧ-zä'de). The bride of the sultan of the Indies, and the narrator of the stories that form the *Arabian Nights*. The sultan, after executing his unfaithful first wife, had resolved to take a new bride nightly and have her beheaded in the morning. Scheherazade marries him nevertheless, and undertakes to let him hear stories, which she interrupts at the climax, of enough interest to make him postpone her execution so that he can learn how they end. After a thousand and one nights the sultan relents and abandons his resolve.

Schlemihl (shlẹ-mīl'). **Peter.** In the story titled with his name, by Chamisso, a man who sells his shadow to the devil for an inexhaustible purse of gold, but then regrets the bargain.

Schofield (sǥhō'fēld), **Penrod.** See **Penrod.**

Scrooge (sǥrọọġ), **Ebenezer.** In Dickens' *Christmas Carol*, a 'grasping, covetous old hunks' of a London merchant, who is converted to an entirely different disposition by a series of visions or dream pictures he sees at Christmas.

Scylla (syl'ȧ). In ancient geography, a rock in the Strait of Messina which, with the adjacent whirlpool **Charybdis** (ǥhȧ-ryb'dis), was proverbial as a source of danger to mariners, since in trying to avoid the one they were liable to encounter the other. Scylla was also represented as a hideous monster.

Sebastian (sē-bas'chăn). In Shakespeare's *Twelfth Night*, the twin brother of Viola, ultimately married to the lady Olivia. See **Olivia, Viola.**—A character in Shakespeare's *Tempest.*

Sedley (sed'li), **Amelia.** One of the two chief female characters of Thackeray's *Vanity Fair*, amiable and affectionate, but not clever, and thus very different from Becky Sharp. She marries George Osborne, and cherishes his memory until she finds how unworthy he was, and then marries Colonel Dobbin, who had long wooed her in vain. Her father, at one time wealthy, becomes a poor, broken-down creature, fruitlessly trying to sell wine, coal, etc. Her brother Jos (Joseph), an Indian civilian, is a fat and cowardly dandy, latterly victimized by Becky Sharp.

Semele (sem'e-lē). In ancient mythology, the mother of Bacchus by Jupiter.

Sentry (sen'try), **Captain.** A member of the Spectator Club. See **Mr. Spectator.**

Serapis (sē-rā'pis). A deity worshiped in Egypt, chiefly by Greek and Roman residents there.

Serena (sẽr-ē'nȧ). A maiden in Spenser's *Faërie Queene* attacked by the Blatant Beast and rescued by Sir Calidore.

Set (set). The god of evil in Egyptian mythology, brother and deadly enemy of **Osiris.**

Setebos (set'e-bos). A god of the Patagonians mentioned in Shakespeare's *Tempest.*

Settembrini (set-em-brī'nī). An Italian liberal democrat in Mann's *Magic Mountain.*

Seven against Thebes (sev'en ȧ-genst' thēbṣ). Seven legendary Greek heroes who laid siege to Thebes unsuccessfully, and, except for one, perished in the attempt. They were led by Polynices, who sought to obtain from his brother Eteocles his rightful share of power in Thebes. Ten years later their sons, the Epigoni, determined to avenge their fathers, marched against the city and captured it. The legend was treated by Aeschylus and Euripides. See **Eteocles and Polynices.**

Seven Champions of Christendom (cham'pionṣ ov ǥhris'n-dŏm). St. George of England, St. Andrew of Scotland, St. Patrick of Ireland, St. David of Wales, St. Denis of France, St. James of Spain, St. Anthony of Italy.

Seven Sleepers (slēp'ẽrṣ). The subject of a legend which tells how seven Christian youths of Ephesus, having taken refuge from persecution in a cave, were there walled up, but were miraculously made to sleep for two or three hundred years.

Seven Vices (vīc'eṣ). **the.** Pride, wrath, envy, lust, gluttony, avarice, and sloth.

Seven Virtues (vẽr'tūṣ), **the.** Faith, hope, charity, prudence, justice, fortitude, and temperance.

Seven Wise Men of Greece (wīṣ men ov grēc). Bias, Chilo, Cleobulus, Periander, Pittacus, Solon, and Thales.

Seven Wonders of the World (wŏn'dẽrṣ ov thē wŏrld) (the ancient world). The Pyramids of Egypt, Hanging Gardens of Babylon, Tomb of Mausolus at Halicarnassus, Temple of Diana at Ephesus, Colossus of Rhodes, Statue of Zeus at Olympia, Pharos or Lighthouse of Alexandria.

Shaddai (shad'ā-ī), **King.** The name under which God is typified in Bunyan's *Holy War.*

Shafton (shaf'tŏn), **Sir Piercie.** A character in Scott's *Monastery* whose language is marked by the affectation called euphuism.

Shallow (shal'ō), **Justice.** A foolish justice in Shakespeare's *Merry Wives* and *Henry IV.*

Shalott (shȧ-lot'), **The Lady of.** A ballad by Tennyson, the conclusion of which resembles that of the Idyll called *Elaine.*

Shand (shand), **John.** The husband of Maggie Wylie in J. M. Barrie's play *What Every Woman Knows.* He breaks into the Wylie library when he is a struggling student to investigate their books; he is pledged to marry Maggie, who has 'no charm' according to her father and brother, in return for money to complete his education. Although he never truly appreciates the fact, his wife makes his successful career as a politician possible.

Shandon (shan'dŏn), **Captain.** A literary man in Thackeray's *Pendennis*, with excellent abilities but easy and self-indulgent, spending much of his time in debtor's prison.

Shandy (shan'dy), **Tristram.** The titular hero of Sterne's *Life and Opinions of Tristram Shandy*, in which, however, his father and uncle, 'Uncle Toby,' take the chief place. The former (Walter Shandy), a retired merchant, is a man of much reading, but a strange embodiment of whims and fantastic notions. Uncle Toby, who has been an officer in the army in Flanders, and has been wounded, in his childlike simplicity and his all-embracing humanity—with the mimic sieges that he carries on in his garden, and the attempts of Widow Wadman to hook him—is one of the finest and most genuinely humorous characters in literature.

Shane (shān), **Lily.** The beautiful heroine of Louis Bromfield's *Green Bay Tree* and other books, who has an illegitimate child by the governor of her state, but does not wish to marry him. She leaves America for a while, and on her return, falls in love with a labor leader in her father's employ, her sister Irene's protégé. She finally marries a French cabinet minister, and flourishes like 'the green bay tree,' while others her life has touched suffer.

Sharp (shärp), **Becky.** The principal character in Thackeray's *Vanity Fair*—clever, good-looking, heartless, ambitious, and utterly unscrupulous. She marries Rawdon Crawley, is justly discarded by him because of her intrigue with Lord Steyne, turns adventuress, cheats Jos Sedley out of his money, and then becomes respectable. See **Sedley, Amelia; Osborne, George.**

Shibboleth (shib'ō-leth). A test word used by Jephthah to distinguish the Ephraimites from the Gileadites at the fords of the Jordan: the former, unable to prounce *sh*, said *sibboleth* (Judges xii.). Hence, a password or a criterion.

Shimerda (shī'mer-dä). **Ántonia.** A Bohemian immigrant domestic in Willa Cather's *My Ántonia*, a story of early days in Nebraska. She is betrayed by an Irish neighbor, but eventually marries a man of her own nationality and has a large family on a Nebraska farm, her manifest destiny.

Shipton (ship'tŏn). **Mother.** The supposititious author of certain ancient prophecies.

Shylock (shȳ'lok). The famous Jew in Shakespeare's *Merchant of Venice*, who lends money to Antonio, 'the merchant,' stipulating that if it is not paid at a certain date he may take a pound of his debtor's flesh instead.

Siegfried (sēk'frēt). A hero of Teutonic legend, who is celebrated in the German epic the *Nibelungenlied.* Sigurd is another form of the name.

Sigismonda (siġ-is-mon'dȧ). In a story by Boccaccio, retold by Dryden, the daughter of a king of Salerno, who poisons herself when her father sends to her the heart of her lover, a page named Guiscardo.

Sikes (sīks), **Bill.** A brutal housebreaker in Dickens' *Oliver Twist*, who murders the girl Nancy, who lives with him, and gets hanged by a rope in trying to escape.

Silas Marner (mär'nẽr). See **Marner, Silas.**

Silence (sī'lenc). A country justice, friend of Justice Shallow, in Shakespeare's *Henry IV.*

Silenus (sī-lē'nus). In classical mythology, the companion of Bacchus, represented as a jovial, drunken, sensual old man.

Silver (sil'vẽr), **Long John.** A treacherous one-legged buccaneer in Robert Louis Stevenson's novel *Treasure Island.*

Silvia (sil'vi-ȧ). The lady in Shakespeare's *Two Gentlemen of Verona* who is beloved by Valentine and for a time is persecuted by Proteus.

Simeon Stylites (sim'ē-ŏn stȳ-lī'tēṣ), **St.** The subject of a poem by Tennyson, Simeon being one of those fanatics known as 'pillar saints' from spending years on the top of a pillar.

Simon Pure (sī'mŏn pūr). A character in Mrs. Centlivre's *Bold Stroke for a Wife.* See **Pure, Simon.**

Simple (sim'pl). A character in Shakespeare's *Merry Wives of Windsor.*

Sinbad *or* **Sindbad the Sailor** (sin'bad; sind'bad thē sā'lŏr). A merchant and mariner in the *Arabian Nights* who makes several wonderful voyages.

Sirens (sī'renṣ). Sea nymphs of Greek mythology, named Parthenope, Ligea, and Leucosia.

Sister Anne (sis'tẽr an). See **Anne, Sister.**

Skeggs (skegṣ), **Miss Carolina Wilhelmina Amelia.** The companion of Lady Blarney in Goldsmith's *Vicar of Wakefield.* See **Blarney.**

Skewton (skū'tŏn), **Hon. Mrs., and her daughter Edith.** Characters in Dickens' *Dombey and Son.* Edith became the second wife of Mr. Dombey.

Skimpole (skim'pōl), **Harold.** In Dickens' *Bleak House*, an utterly selfish character, who poses as a man of artistic tastes and a child in money matters, and takes advantage of his friends' good nature.

Slawkenbergius (slạ'ken-bẽr'ġi-us). An imaginary author quoted in Sterne's *Tristram Shandy*, and represented as having a huge nose.

Slaygood (slā'good), **Giant.** In Bunyan's *Pilgrim's Progress*, an evil giant slain by Greatheart.

Sleary (slē'ry). A circus proprietor in Dickens' *Hard Times*, a bibulous, kindhearted fellow who assists the scamp Tom Gradgrind.

Sleeping Beauty (slēp'ing bū'ty), **The.** A well-known fairy tale, poetized by Tennyson as *The Dream.*

Slender (slen'dẽr). A country lout in love with 'sweet Anne Page' in Shakespeare's *Merry Wives of Windsor.*

Sliderskew (slī'dẽr-skū), **Peg.** An old hag who acts as housekeeper to Arthur Gride in Dickens' *Nicholas Nickleby.*

Slop (slop), **Dr.** A narrow-minded and irritable medical man in Sterne's *Tristram Shandy.*

Slough of Despond (slou ov dē-spond′), **the.** The deep bog in Bunyan's *Pilgrim's Progress.*
Slowboy (slō′boi), **Tilly.** An awkward, odd-looking girl, servant of Mrs. Peerybingle in Dickens' *Cricket on the Hearth.*
Slum (slum), **Mr.** A poet in Dickens' *Old Curiosity Shop* who writes to order and for advertising purposes.
Slumkey (slum′ki), **Mr.** A candidate for Parliament in Dickens' *Pickwick Papers.*
Sly (slȳ), **Christopher.** A tinker in the 'Induction' to Shakespeare's *Taming of the Shrew,* who is taken when dead drunk, dressed up, and made to fancy himself a lord.
Slyme (slȳm), **Chevy.** In Dickens' *Martin Chuzzlewit,* one of the Chuzzlewit family, a disreputable loafer who affects to despise those on whom he sponges, and ends by becoming a police officer.
Small (smạl), **Lennie.** A huge half-wit of great strength in John Steinbeck's *Of Mice and Men,* an itinerant farm hand who adores his friend George Milton, with whom he wants to settle down on a farm. He kills the wife of his boss, led by instincts he does not understand, when she tries to seduce him. A posse tracks him down, and his friend George shoots him to save him from being lynched.
Smike (smīk). An ill-used boy in Dickens' *Nicholas Nickleby,* befriended by Nicholas, and discovered to be the son of his uncle Ralph.
Smith (smith), **Wayland.** In Scott's *Kenilworth,* a sort of blacksmith and juggler with a knowledge of chemistry. The name and character are based on a personage of Northern mythology. See **Wayland.**
Snake (snāk), **Mr.** A base scandalmonger in Sheridan's *School for Scandal* who lives 'by the baseness of his character.'
Sneer (snēr), **Mr.** A malicious critic in Sheridan's comedy *The Critic.*
Sneerwell (snēr′wel), **Lady.** A scandal-loving dame in Sheridan's *School for Scandal.*
Snevellicci (snev-e-lī′chī), **Mr., Mrs., and Miss.** A theatrical family in Dickens' *Nicholas Nickleby.*
Snodgrass (snod′gràs), **Augustus.** A poetical young man, one of the companions of Mr. Pickwick.
Snout (snout), **Tom.** The tinker in Shakespeare's *Midsummer Night's Dream.*
Snow White (snō hwīt). A fairy-tale character who is abused by her jealous stepmother, the Queen, and who is driven to seek refuge with seven little dwarfs who live on the mountainside. The Queen disguises herself as a witch and tries to poison Snow White, but she is restored by the kiss of Prince Charming, whom she marries.
Snubbin (snub′in), **Sergeant.** A legal luminary on the side of the defense in the famous case Bardell against Pickwick, in Dickens' *Pickwick Papers.*
Snug (snug). The joiner in Shakespeare's *Midsummer Night's Dream.*
Sohrab (sō′räb). See **Rustum.**
Sonnambula (sōn-näm′bụ-lä), **La.** Amina, the heroine of Bellini's opera so named. See **Amina.**
Sparsit (spär′sit), **Mrs.** An aristocratic lady, housekeeper to Mr. Bounderby in Dickens' *Hard Times.*
Spectator (spek-tā′tŏr), **Mr.** One of the characters appearing in the essays of *The Spectator,* a periodical written chiefly by Addison and Steele, and a member of the 'Spectator Club,' therein described, which also included Sir Roger de Coverley, Sir Andrew Freeport, Will Honeycomb, and Captain Sentry.
Spenlow and Jorkins (spen′lō and jọr′kinş). In Dickens' *David Copperfield,* a firm of proctors to whom David is articled. Jorkins has little share in the business, but is represented by Spenlow as very strict and stern, and as setting his face against any lenient or indulgent course that he himself would otherwise be disposed to adopt. Spenlow's daughter Dora marries David. A pretty, affectionate girl, she dies young.
Spens *or* **Spence** (spens), **Sir Patrick.** The subject of a famous old Scotch ballad which relates how Sir Patrick and all on board his ship were wrecked and drowned on their way home from Norway.
Spoon River (spọọn riv′ẽr). A midwestern American town which is the scene of Edgar Lee Masters' *Spoon River Anthology,* a volume of free verse containing posthumous confessions, or epitaphs, of the townspeople.
Square (skwâr), **Mr.** See **Thwackum and Square.**
Squeers (skwērş). In Dickens' *Nicholas Nickleby,* the ignorant and brutal Yorkshire schoolmaster of Dotheboys Hall. His wife is as bad as he, and his daughter and son are worthy of their parents.
Squint (skwint). A lawyer in Goldsmith's *Citizen of the World,* who writes speeches for members of parliament and can speak upon every topic.
Standish (stan′dish), **Miles.** The 'puritan captain' in Longfellow's *Courtship of Miles Standish,* who woos the maiden Priscilla by proxy, but his proxy, John Alden, gains her favor for himself.
Statira (stȧ-tī′rȧ). Daughter of Darius and wife of Alexander the Great, introduced in many plays and romances.
Steerforth (stēr′fọrth), **James.** A young man of wealth who leads 'little Em'ly' astray, in Dickens' *David Copperfield,* and is drowned in a shipwreck at Yarmouth, where Ham Peggotty is also drowned trying to rescue him.
Stella (stel′ȧ). A poetical name given by Swift to Esther Johnson, a young lady with whom he was long on most intimate terms.
Stentor (sten′tọr). A Greek herald with a loud voice, who took part in the siege of Troy.
Stephano (stef′ȧ-nō). A drunken butler in Shakespeare's *Tempest.*
Steyne (stȳn), **Marquis of.** A great English nobleman, who figures in Thackeray's *Vanity Fair,* and also appears in *Pendennis*—proud, sarcastic, irreligious, sensual, despising his toadies, yet accepting their attentions, heartless in pursuit of pleasure, yet maintaining a reputable position in society and the world at large. His intrigue with Becky Sharp causes her husband to discard her.
Stiggins (stig′inş). A hypocritical dissenting preacher in Dickens' *Pickwick,* given to the consumption of strong waters, and dipped in the horse trough by Old Weller.
Strap (strap). The faithful friend and attendant of Roderick Random, who shows him but little gratitude for many services rendered.
Strephon (stref′ŏn). The name of a shepherd in Sir Philip Sidney's *Arcadia;* often used in a general sense for a rural swain, as in Pope's *Pastorals.*
Strickland (strik′lănd), **Charles.** The artist in *Moon and Sixpence,* by Somerset Maugham, who abandons his family and goes to the South Seas to paint, and 'go native.' He dies in diseased poverty, but after his death his paintings become famous. He is supposed to be modeled on the character of the French painter Gauguin.
Strong (strọng), **Dr., and his young wife.** Characters in Dickens' *David Copperfield.* David was a pupil of the doctor, who is a schoolmaster and a great scholar.
Struldbrugs (struld′brugş). Wretched beings described in Swift's *Gulliver's Travels,* living in Luggnagg, who cannot die, but suffer from the infirmities of old age.
Stryver (strȳ′vẽr). A pushing, vulgar barrister in Dickens' *Tale of Two Cities.*
Subtle (sut′l). The alchemist in Ben Jonson's play *The Alchemist,* a quack who swindles Sir Epicure Mammon and others through pretenses of discovering the philosopher's stone.
Sullen (sul′en), **Squire, and his wife.** An ill-mated couple in Farquhar's *Beaux' Stratagem.* The squire is a son of Lady Bountiful.
Summerson (sum′ẽr-sŏn), **Esther.** The sweet and lovable heroine of Dickens' *Bleak House,* who, it transpires, is the illegitimate daughter of Lady Dedlock.
Surface (sûr′fāc), **Charles.** A spendthrift but a good-hearted fellow in Sheridan's *School for Scandal.* His brother Joseph is a plausible hypocrite who professes much prudence and benevolence.
Surly (sûr′ly). A character in Ben Jonson's *Alchemist* who does not believe in the quack Subtle.
Susanna (sū-şan′ȧ). A servant in the Shandy family in Sterne's *Tristram Shandy.*
Sutphen (sut′fen), **Thomas.** A southern plantation owner in William Faulkner's *Absalom, Absalom!* who rears a family composed of children by his wife Ellen and half-caste children borne by colored women on his plantation. The grandfather of one of his mistresses kills him.
Svengali (sven-gä′li). See **Trilby.**
Swann (swän), **Charles.** The hero of the boy Marcel in Proust's *Remembrance of Things Past,* who marries his mistress, Odette, and is the father of Gilberte.
Swiveller (swiv′e-lẽr), **Dick.** The lighthearted and amusing shabby-genteel clerk to Sampson Brass in Dickens' *Old Curiosity Shop,* who later comes into a small annuity and marries 'the marchioness.'
Sycorax (syc̦′ō-raks). A foul witch mentioned in Shakespeare's *Tempest,* mother of Caliban.
Syntax (syn′taks), **Dr.** The hero of Coombe's humorous *Tour of Dr. Syntax in Search of the Picturesque* (1812) and of two other *Tours*—a simple, inexperienced clergyman.
Syphax (sȳ′faks). A soldier in Addison's **Cato** who went over in battle to Caesar's side.
Syrinx (syr′iñks). A nymph beloved by Pan.

T

Tackleton (tak′l-tŏn). A surly, hardhearted toyseller for whom Caleb Plummer works, in Dickens' *Cricket on the Health.*
Talisman (tal′is-măn), **The.** The title of a novel by Sir Walter Scott, the scene of which is laid in the Holy Land. Richard Coeur de Lion and other crusaders are introduced (including Kenneth, prince of Scotland), as well as Saladin, etc. The talisman is a precious stone or pebble which imparts healing properties to water in which it is dipped.
Talus (tā′lus). A wonderful man of iron in Spenser's *Faërie Queene,* who has an iron flail with which he executes summary justice. (Spenser's Talus is based on the classical Talos, a brazen man made by Vulcan.)
Tamerlane (tam′ẽr-lān). The great Asiatic conqueror, hero of Rowe's tragedy so named. *Tamburlaine the Great* is also the title of a tragedy by Marlowe (in part at least).
Tammuz *or* **Thammuz** (tȧm′mụz; thȧm′). A Babylonian god of agriculture, the Syrian counterpart of Adonis.
Tamora (tam′ō-rȧ). Queen of the Goths in Shakespeare's *Titus Andronicus.*
Tancred (tañ′c̦red). A crusader in Tasso's *Jerusalem Delivered,* beloved by Erminia, by whom he is tenderly nursed when wounded.
Tanner (tan′ẽr), **John.** Hero of G. B. Shaw's play *Man and Superman.* See **Whitefield, Ann.**
Tannhäuser (tän′hoi-şẽr). In German legend a knight who gains admission into a hill where Venus holds her court, and there remains for years sunk in sensual delights. Being at last allowed to depart, he repairs to Rome to seek absolution from the Pope, but is refused, and thereupon returns to Venus and is no more seen.
Tanqueray (tañ′kẽr-ā), **Paula.** A woman with a discreditable past in Pinero's play *The Second Mrs. Tanqueray,* who becomes the second wife of Charles Tanqueray, a man of good social position. When his daughter refuses to accept her as a stepmother, and his friends ignore her, she commits suicide.
Tapley (tap′li), **Mark.** In Dickens' *Martin Chuzzlewit,* the humble friend who accompanies young Martin to America, and whose pride in life it is to keep 'jolly' in the most depressing circumstances.
Tappertit (tap′ẽr-tit), **Simon.** A conceited and ridiculous shrimp of an apprentice in Dickens' *Barnaby Rudge,* employed by Varden, the locksmith, and having designs on his daughter Dolly.
Tara (tä′rȧ). The plantation home of Scarlett O'Hara in *Gone With the Wind,* by Margaret Mitchell, which is burned in the Civil War.
Tartuffe (tär-tûf′). A religious impostor and hypocrite in Molière's comedy of the same name; hence, anyone who uses religion as a cloak. From this comedy Bickerstaff modeled *The Hypocrite.*
Tarzan (tär′zăn). The hero of a series of stories by Edgar Rice Burroughs. He was adopted and reared by apes in the forest, and became remarkably strong and agile.
Tattycoram (tat′y-c̦ō′răm). A passionate girl in Dickens' *Little Dorrit.*
Teazle (tē′zl), **Lady.** The heroine of Sheridan's *School for Scandal,* wife of Sir Peter Teazle, who is much her senior. She is ignorant of the world, thoughtless and imprudent, and thus gives rise to scandal, though she is really fond of her husband.
Telemachus (tē-lem′ȧ-c̦hus). Son of Ulysses, of whom, when he had been long absent after the fall of Troy, Telemachus went in quest, accompanied by Minerva in the form of Mentor.
Tempest (tem′pest), **Lady Betty.** A character in Goldsmith's *Citizen of the World,* a lady who is left an old maid owing to her high-flown notions regarding a suitable husband.
Tempest, The. A play of Shakespeare's in which Prospero, Miranda, Caliban, Ariel, etc., appear.
Tereus (tẽr′ūs; tē′rē-us). See **Philomela.**
Terpsichore (tẽrp-sic̱h′ō-rē). The Muse of dancing and choral song.
Tethys (tē′thys). In Greek mythology, a daughter of Uranus and wife of Oceanus; sometimes used figuratively for the sea.
Teucer (tū′cẽr). A Greek warrior in the Trojan war, the best archer among the Greeks.
Teufelsdrockh (toi′felş-drekh). **Herr.** The hero of Carlyle's *Sartor Resartus,* a learned German professor of things in general, who expounds a new philosophy—the philosophy of clothes.
Thaddeus of Warsaw (thad′ē-us ov wạr′sạ). The hero of Jane Porter's novel of that name.
Thaïs (thā′is). An Athenian courtesan introduced in Dryden's *Alexander's Feast.* Also (tä-īs′), the heroine of a novel by Anatole France and an opera by Massenet, a Greek courtesan reformed by a monk.
Thalia (thȧ-lī′ȧ). The Muse of comedy and bucolic poetry.—One of the three Graces.
Thammuz (thȧm′mụz). See **Tammuz.**
Thélème (tẹ-lem′), **Abbey of.** An institution in Rabelais' romance *Gargantua,* where all good things may be enjoyed, and whose motto is 'Do what you will.'
Thersites (thẽr-sī′tēş). The ugliest and most scurrilous of the Greeks in the Trojan war.
Theseus (thē′sūs). A famous legendary king of Athens, son of Aegeus. He killed Procrustes; and slew the Minotaur with the assistance of Ariadne, whom he afterwards deserted. He conquered the Amazons and, according to some accounts, married their queen Hippolyta, after whose death Phaedra became his wife. He also took part in the expedition of the Argonauts and in the Calydonian boar hunt. See **Hippolytus.**
Thetis (thē′tis). A sea-nymph of Greek mythology, mother of Achilles by Peleus.
Thibault (tī-bō′) **Family.** A French family portrayed in the novel cycle *Les Thibaults,* by Roger Martin du Gard.
Thisbe (thiş′bē). See **Pyramus.**
Thomas the Rhymer (tom′ăs thĕ rȳ′mẽr) *or* **Thomas of Erceldoune** (ẽr′cel-dōn). A celebrated Scottish character of the 13th century, popularly regarded as a prophet and wizard. He lived for seven years in fairyland, according to legend, and ultimately disappeared in a mysterious manner.
Thompson (tomp′sŏn), **Sadie.** The heroine in Somerset Maugham's short story *Miss Thompson* in the play *Rain,* who entertains the sailors at Pago-Pago. The Reverend Davidson reforms her, but reveals himself subject to the same lusts as other men, disillusioning her.
Thor (thọr). In Norse mythology, the god of thunder.
Thorndyke (thọrn′dȳk), **Dr.** The fictional detective, expert in scientific methods, of Richard Austin Freeman.
Thornhill (thọrn′hil), **Squire.** A dissolute young man in Goldsmith's *Vicar of Wakefield,* who abducts the vicar's daughter Olivia, and goes through what he thinks is a mock marriage with her, but it turns out to be binding. His uncle, on whom he is dependent, passes himself off as Mr. Burchell (which see).

Thoth (thoth; tōt). The ancient Egyptian god of wisdom and magic, patron of the arts and of learning, the scribe of the gods, represented with the head of an ibis and a human body; corresponding to Hermes.

Thousand and One Nights. See **Arabian Nights.**

Thumb (thum), **Tom.** A minute dwarf of popular legend, said to have lived in King Arthur's time. He is known in the popular tales of France and Germany as well as England. There is an English history of him dated 1621. Fielding wrote a burlesque on the subject.

Thurio (thū'ri-ō). In Shakespeare's *Two Gentlemen of Verona*, a foolish rival of Valentine.

Thwackum and Square (thwak'um and skwãr). In Fielding's *Tom Jones*, two members of Mr. Allworthy's household, the former engaged as tutor to young Jones and Blifil. The Rev. Mr. Thwackum's moral system is based entirely upon the precepts of revealed religion and the 'divine power of grace'; whereas Square is a philosopher, and his morality is derived from 'the natural beauty of virtue, and the eternal fitness of things.' They are alike in being narrow-minded pedants, without a spark of real goodness between them.

Thyestes (thȳ-es'tēs). Son of Pelops and brother of Atreus, whose wife he seduced. In revenge Atreus killed three sons of Thyestes and served them to the father at a banquet. See **Aegisthus.**

Thyrsis (thĩr'sis). A herdsman in the *Idylls* of Theocritus, and in Virgil's *Eclogues*. Matthew Arnold wrote a poem of this name to the memory of his friend Arthur Hugh Clough.

Tibbs (tibs), **Beau.** A vain, foppish, hard-up character in Goldsmith's *Citizen of the World*. His wife is a slattern and would-be fine lady.

Tibert (tib'ẽrt). The cat in the beast epic *Reynard the Fox*.

Tigg (tig), **Montague.** A shabby-genteel and amusing character in Dickens' *Martin Chuzzlewit*, who blossoms out into a man of fashion and wealth. These pretensions are supported by his carrying on a bogus insurance company. He is murdered by Jonas Chuzzlewit.

Timon (tī'mŏn). A misanthropic Athenian, the hero of Shakespeare's *Timon of Athens*.

Tintagel (tin-tag'el). The legendary birthplace of King Arthur, a strong castle on the cliffs of Cornwall, still represented by extensive ruins.

Tippins (tip'ins), **Lady.** A ridiculous old lady posing as something of a belle in Dickens' *Our Mutual Friend*

Tisiphone (ti-sif'ō-nē). In classical mythology, one of the three Furies.

Titania (ti-tā'ni-à). The queen of the fairies and wife of Oberon.

Titans (tī'tăns). A race of giant Greek deities who warred against Saturn and Jupiter, and were thrown into Tartarus.

Tithonus (ti-thō'nus). A young man of whom Aurora is fabled to have been enamored and whom Jupiter made immortal, but as he was not also endowed with perpetual youth he withered away and was changed into a cicada.

Tito Melema (tī'tō me-le'mä). See **Melema.**

Toby (tō'by), **Uncle.** A character in Sterne's *Tristram Shandy*. See **Shandy.**

Todgers (tog'ẽrs), **Mrs.** Keeper of a London boardinghouse for commercial gentlemen in Dickens' *Martin Chuzzlewit*.

Tom Jones (tom jōns). The hero and title of a novel by Fielding. See **Jones.**

Tony Lumpkin (tō'ny lump'kin). A character in Goldsmith's *She Stoops to Conquer*. See **Lumpkin.**

Toodle (tọọ'dl). A fireman to an engine in Dickens' *Dombey and Son*. His wife was wet nurse to young Paul Dombey.

Toots (toots), **Mr.** In Dickens' *Dombey and Son*, a well-to-do young man, warmhearted and unselfish, but rather scatterbrained, who thinks himself dreadfully in love with Florence Dombey; but this, to use his favorite expression, 'is of no consequence.'

Topsy (top'sy). An amusing young slave girl in Mrs. Stowe's *Uncle Ton's Cabin*.

Touchstone (tuch'stōn). A wise and witty clown in Shakespeare's *As You Like It*.

Tox (toks), **Lucretia.** An old maid in Dickens' *Dombey and Son* who has hopes of an offer both from Mr. Dombey and Major Bagstock.

Traddles (trad'ls), **Thomas.** A friend of David's in Dickens' *David Copperfield*, distinguished when at school by his fondness for drawing skeletons. He takes a high position in the legal profession.

Tranio (trā'ni-ō). A character in Shakespeare's *Taming of the Shrew*.

Trapper (trap'ẽr), **the.** Natty Bumppo's name in Cooper's *Prairie*. See **Leatherstocking.**

Trenchard (tren'chărd) **Family.** An upper middle-class English family in Hugh Walpole's *Green Mirror*, who do not understand the sensitive Henry Trenchard, the strange duckling.

Trent (trent), **Nelly.** See **Nell.**

Tressilian (tres'sil-yăn), **Edmund.** The rejected lover of Amy Robsart in Scott's *Kenilworth*, a man of high character.

Trilby (tril'by). The heroine of the novel of that name by Du Maurier. She is an artist's model, who, under the hypnotic influence of Svengali, a Hungarian musician, becomes the greatest singer in the world. When Svengali dies of a heart attack, she loses her voice.

Trim (trim), **Corporal.** An old soldier acting as servant to Uncle Toby in Sterne's *Tristram Shandy*, simple, ignorant, honest, and affectionate.

Triptolemus (trip-tol'ē-mus). An ancient Greek patron of agriculture, considered the inventor of the plow, a special favorite of Demeter.

Trismegistus (tris-mē-gis'tus). See **Hermes Trismegistus.**

Tristram (tris'trăm), **Sir.** A knight of King Arthur's court and a famous hero of medieval romance; lover of Isolde, wife of his uncle, King Mark of Cornwall. He appears in Tennyson's *Idylls of the King*, in Matthew Arnold's poem *Tristram and Iseult*, in E. A. Robinson's poem *Tristram*, and in Wagner's opera *Tristan und Isolde*. See **Isolde.**

Trivia (triv'i-à). A name of Diana.—The title of a poem by Gay, his name for a goddess, of his invention, of streets and ways.

Troilus (trō'i-lus; troi'lus). A son of Priam of Troy, represented in postclassical times as in love with Cressida. Chaucer in his poem *Troilus and Criseyde*, and Shakespeare in *Troilus and Cressida*, deal with this story.

Trotter (trot'ẽr), **Job.** A sly, hypocritical character in Dickens' *Pickwick Papers*, the friend and henchman of Jingle.

Trotty Veck (trot'y vek). See **Veck, Toby.**

Trotwood (trot'wood), **Mrs. Betsy.** David's great-aunt in Dickens' *David Copperfield*, kindhearted and strong-minded.

Troy (troi). See **Ilium.**

Trunnion (trun'yŏn), **Commodore.** A retired old sea dog in Smollett's *Peregrine Pickle*, whose household arrangements are made to coincide as far as possible with those on board ship. His servants, thus, are obliged to keep the watches and sleep in hammocks. See **Hatchway, Pipes.**

Tubal (tū'băl). A Jew in Shakespeare's *Merchant of Venice*, friend of Shylock.

Tuck (tuk), **Friar.** See **Friar Tuck.**

Tulkinghorn (tul'king-hǫrn), **Mr.** A lawyer in Dickens' *Bleak House*, murdered by a French lady's maid.

Tulliver (tul'i-vẽr). The name of a family with whose fortunes George Eliot's *Mill on the Floss* deals. The chief characters are the brother and sister, Tom and Maggie Tulliver, who at the close of the book are drowned together in the Floss.

Tupman (tup'măn), **Tracy.** One of the companions of Mr. Pickwick, rather fat, but a bit of a dandy and an admirer of the ladies.

Turpin (tũr'pin). A base knight in Spenser's *Faërie Queene*.

Turveydrop (tũr'vi-drop), **Mr.** In Dickens' *Bleak House*, a vain and selfish dancing master who apes the prince regent, poses as a master of deportment, and selfishly lives on his son's earnings.

Tutt (tut), **Ephraim.** A learned and shrewd American lawyer in numerous stories by Arthur Train.

Twemlow (twem'lō), **Mr.** A mild, inoffensive old gentleman with some aristocratic connections, on which account he is often invited to dinner by the Veneerings, in *Our Mutual Friend*, by Dickens.

Twist (twist), **Oliver.** Hero of Dickens' novel of the same name, a boy of good parentage brought up in a workhouse and thrown among thieves in London, but always gentle and innocent.

Twitcher (twich'ẽr), **Jemmy.** A scoundrelly highwayman in Gay's *Beggar's Opera*, who at last 'peaches' on the more gentlemanly rogue, 'Captain' Macheath.

Tybalt (tyb'ălt). A fiery young Capulet in Shakespeare's *Romeo and Juliet*, who slays Mercutio and is slain by Romeo.

Tyler (tȳ'lẽr), **Toby.** The hero of a children's story of that name by James Otis. Toby runs away to join a circus, and the story deals with his disillusioning adventures there.

Tyr (tûr). In Scandinavian mythology, the god of war, son of Odin and brother of **Thor.**

U

Ugly (ug'ly) **Duchess, the.** Margarete, in the book of the same name by Lion Feuchtwanger, a novel of 14th-century Central Europe. She was heiress of Carinthia and the Tyrol. Her life is a series of frustrations, plots, and counterplots. Almost all her associates meet violent deaths, and she is forced to give her country to Austria, and live in exile.

Ugolino (ū-gō-lī'nō). A nobleman of Pisa who, being defeated by his political opponents, was starved to death along with two sons and two grandsons; a dreadful story treated by Dante and other writers.

Ullin (ul'in), **Lord.** The father of the young lady who was drowned when eloping with 'the chief of Ulva's Isle' in *Lord Ullin's Daughter*, a poem by Campbell.

Ulrica (ul'ri-cà). An old beldame, daughter of a Saxon thane in Scott's *Ivanhoe*.

Ulysses (ū-lys'ēs), in Greek **Odysseus** (ō-dys'ūs). King of Ithaca, one of the heroes of the Trojan war, husband of Penelope and father of Telemachus; his wanderings after the war form the subject of the *Odyssey*. See **Odysseus.**

Umbriel (um'bri-el). A sprite in Pope's *Rape of the Lock*.

Una (ū'nà). A lovely damsel in Spenser's *Faërie Queene*, a personification of truth. She is introduced as riding on a white ass, and leading a lamb; and she comes to the court of the fairy queen Gloriana to get a champion to slay a destructive dragon. The Red Cross Knight is accordingly sent with her. When she is separated from him, a lion fawns on her and becomes her attendant. She is finally married to the Red Cross Knight.

Uncas (uñ'căs). The Indian name of Deerfoot, 'the Last of the Mohicans' in Cooper's novel of this title.

Uncle Remus (uñ'cl rē'mus). The central character in several books, containing his name in the titles, by Joel Chandler Harris. An old Negro, a former slave, Uncle Remus tells his humorous tales and verses in dialect. They concern the doings of animals with human characteristics, such as Brer Rabbit, Brer Fox, etc.

Uncle Toby (uñ'cl tō'by). See **Shandy.**

Uncle Tom (tom). A Negro slave, the hero of Harriet Beecher Stowe's novel *Uncle Tom's Cabin*, depicting the evils of slavery in the United States.

Undine (un'dīn). A water nymph or sylph, heroine of a charming German story by Fouqué.

Urania (ū-rā'ni-à). The Muse who presided over astronomy.

Uranus (ū'rà-nus). A Greek deity, the first ruler of the universe, son and husband of Gaea, and father of the Titans, the Cyclops, the Furies, etc.; dethroned by his son Cronus. The name means literally heaven.

Uriel (u'ri-el). An archangel in Milton's *Paradise Lost*, one of the seven who stand nearest God's throne, regent of the sun, and sharpest-sighted of all the angels.

Ursula (ũr'sū-là). An attendant of Hero in Shakespeare's *Much Ado About Nothing*.—The mother of Elsie in Longfellow's *Golden Legend*.

Uther (ū'thẽr). A legendary king of Britain, father of King Arthur.

Uzziel (u-zī'el; uz'i-el). An archangel in Millton's *Paradise Lost*

V

Valentine (val'en-tīn). One of Shakespeare's *Two Gentlemen of Verona*, a gallant young fellow who marries Silvia.—The brother of Margaret in Goethe's *Faust*, who, being enraged at his sister's shame, attacks Faust and is stabbed by Mephistopheles.

Valentine and Orson (ǫr'sŏn). The heroes of an old romance, twin brothers born in a forest, the latter suckled and brought up by a bear, the former reared at the king's court. Orson becomes a wild man of the forest, but is ultimately reclaimed from savagery by his brother.

Valjean (vàl-zäñ'; val'jēn), **Jean.** The hero of Victor Hugo's *Les Misérables*. After imprisonment for a small offense, protracted by his attempts to escape, he builds a new and honorable life for himself under a different name; but an event involving his past again embroils him with the law, and he is relentlessly pursued by the police officer Javert.

Vance (vanc), **Philo.** An erudite detective of keen perceptive powers in several detective novels by S. S. Van Dyne (pseud. of W. H. Wright).

Vanity Fair (van'i-ty fãr). A famous fair in Bunyan's *Pilgrim's Progress*, held in the town of Vanity, where Christian and Faithful are maltreated, and the latter condemned to be burned.—The name of one of the chief of Thackeray's novels. See **Crawley, Dobbin, Osborne, Sedley, Sharp, Steyne.**

Van Weyden (van wȳ'den), **Humphrey.** The narrator in the *Sea-Wolf*, by Jack London, who is tossed overboard by a collision, picked up and pressed into service by Wolf Larsen, the brutal captain of a sealing ship.

Varden (vär'den), **Gabriel, and his family.** An honest locksmith in Dickens' *Barnaby Rudge*, with a charming daughter named Dolly, who marries young Joe Willet. Mrs. Varden is a religious shrew, a martyr in her own eyes, and in those of her sycophantic servant Miggs.

Varney (vär'ni). A treacherous character in Scott's *Kenilworth*, who murders Amy Robsart.

Vathek (vath'ek). In William Beckford's Oriental fantasy of the same name, a caliph who commits innumerable crimes and whose search for treasure leads to his eternal damnation.

Vautrin (vō-trañ'). An assumed name of **Collin.**

Veck (vek), **Toby.** In Dickens' *Chimes*, a ticket porter nicknamed 'Trotty' because he is always on the trot, a kindly old man who has a dream on New Year's Eve in which the church bells take a part.

Veiled Prophet of Khorassan (vēld prof'et ov kō-rà-sän'). One of the metrical tales forming Moore's *Lalla Rookh*, founded upon the story of a real personage. The prophet claims to have supernatural powers, and pretends to wear a veil to hide the excessive brightness of his countenance, but really to conceal his deformed features.

Veneering (ve-nē'ring), **Mr. and Mrs.** Characters in Dickens' novel *Our Mutual Friend*, 'bran-new people, in a bran-new house, in a bran-new quarter of London,' giving dinners and eager to mingle in society superior to their own. Mr. Veneering is partner in a drug business.

Ventidius (ven-tid'i-us). A character in Shakespeare's *Timon of Athens*, a false friend of Timon.

Venus (vē'nus). The Roman goddess of love and beauty.

Verges (vẽr'ges). See **Dogberry and Verges.**

Verinder (vẽr-in'dẽr), **Rachel.** The heroine of Wilkie Collins' *Moonstone*. The moonstone was a diamond in the forehead of the Brahmin moon-god, which had been stolen during the Mohammedan conquest.

and had been acquired by an unscrupulous uncle of Rachel who gave it to her, but it brought bad luck.
Verisopht (ver'i-sǫft), **Lord.** A young nobleman in Dickens' *Nicholas Nickleby*, the admirer and pupil of Sir Mulberry Hawk, by whom he is shot in a duel.
Vernon (vĕr'nŏn), **Diana.** The heroine of Scott's *Rob Roy*, perhaps the most charming of all his female characters—beautiful, well-read, and well-educated, fond of field sports, spirited, and self-reliant. We meet her at Osbaldistone Hall and in the Highlands, and are told that she became the wife of Frank Osbaldistone. Her father is a gentleman who intrigues in favor of the exiled Stuarts.
Vertumnus (vĕr-tum'nus). A Roman god of the crops and orchards.
Vicar of Bray (viç'ăr ov brā). An English vicar said to have lived in the reign of Henry VIII, Edward VI, Mary, and Elizabeth, and to have been twice a Roman Catholic and twice a Protestant, the subject of an old humorous song.
Vicar of Wakefield (wāk'fēld). See **Primrose.**
Vincentio (vin-cen'shi-ō). Duke of Vienna in Shakespeare's *Measure for Measure*, who leaves the city for a time and appoints Angelo his deputy.
Viola (vī'ō-lȧ). The heroine of Shakespeare's *Twelfth Night*, sister of Sebastian, in love with the Duke Orsino, between whom and the Lady Olivia she acts as intermediary, dressed as a page. The duke ultimately marries her.
Virgilia (vĭr-ġil'i-ȧ). Wife of Coriolanus in Shakespeare's play *Coriolanus.*
Virginia (vir-ġin'i-ȧ). A beautiful Roman girl whom the lustful decemvir Appius Claudius wished to get into his power, claiming her as his slave, but who was stabbed by her own father to preserve her from such a fate; the subject of Knowles' play *Virginius*, and one of Macaulay's *Lays of Ancient Rome*. See also **Paul and Virginia.**
Vivien *or* **Vivian** (viv'i-ăn). A wanton connected with the story of King Arthur, whose charms overcame the enchanter Merlin, so that she enclosed him in a hollow oak for all time coming.
Volpone (vol-pō'nē). The hero of Ben Jonson's play so named, otherwise 'the Fox.' He is rich but greedy, and after a career of successful knavery is at last laid by the heels.
Volumnia (vō-lum'ni-ȧ). Mother of Coriolanus in Shakespeare's *Coriolanus.*
Vortigern (vǫr'ti-gĕrn). A mythical or semimythical British king, said to have married Rowena, daughter of Hengist.
Vronsky (vron'sky), **Count.** The lover of Anna Karenina, in Tolstoy's novel *Anna Karenina.*
Vulcan (vul'căn). The Roman deity who presided over fire and the working of metals, identified with the similar Greek deity Hephaestus. He made thunderbolts for Jupiter, arms for gods and heroes, and many wonderful contrivances; and had forges in Olympus as well as under Etna, where the Cyclops were his workmen. He is always represented as lame.

W

Wackles (wak'lz), **Mrs. and the Misses.** The keepers of a 'ladies' seminary' in Dickens' *Old Curiosity Shop.*
Wade (wād), **Miss.** A handsome woman, whose prevailing feeling is hatred of everybody, in Dickens' *Little Dorrit.*
Wadman (wad'măn), **Widow.** A buxom lady in Sterne's *Tristram Shandy*, whose wiles nearly captivate Uncle Toby.
Wagg and Wenham (wag and wen'ăm). Two sycophants and doers of dirty work for the Marquis of Steyne in Thackeray's *Vanity Fair* and *Pendennis.*
Wamba (wäm'bȧ). The jester of Cedric the Saxon in Scott's *Ivanhoe.*
Wandering Jew (wän'dĕr-ing jů). A Jew who, according to a legend that arose in the Middle Ages, was condemned for harsh treatment of Christ to wander over the world until His second coming.
Ward (wąrd), **Artemus.** A fictitious itinerant showman, whose name was used by his creator, Charles Farrar Browne, as a pen name.
Wardle (wąr'dl), **Mr., and his family.** Characters in Dickens' *Pickwick Papers*, living at Dingley Dell, where Mr. Pickwick and his friends are hospitably entertained.
Warrington (wąr'ing-tŏn), **George.** In Thackeray's *Pendennis*, a young man of good family, a barrister and writer for the press, whose prospects have been blasted by an unfortunate early marriage. He is a great friend of Arthur Pendennis. Members of the same family, but of an earlier generation, figure in Thackeray's novel *The Virginians.*
Waters (wą'tĕrș), **Esther.** An illiterate servant in George Moore's novel of that title, who has a desperate struggle to care for an illegitimate son but who finally finds a subdued happiness.
Watson (wät'sŏn), **Dr.** The assistant of Sherlock Holmes. See **Holmes, Sherlock.**
Waverley (wā'vĕr-li). The first of Scott's great series of historical novels, to which it gives name. The hero is Edward Waverley, a young English gentleman, and the scene is chiefly Scotland during the rebellion of 1745. The characters include the Baron Bradwardine and his daughter Rose, Fergus and Flora MacIvor, Prince Charles Edward himself, Davie Gellatley, etc.
Wayland (wā'lănd), **the Smith.** A supernatural smith of English and Scandinavian mythology. See also **Smith, Wayland.**
Wegg (weg), **Silas.** In Dickens' *Our Mutual Friend*, a wooden-legged man with a street stall, whom Mr. Boffin engages to read to him, and finds him to be an ungrateful old scoundrel. Good Mr. Boffin admires the way in which this ignorant pretender can 'drop into poetry,' that is, repeat some scraps of hackneyed verse at times.
Weissnichtwo (vīs'nikht-vō). That is, 'know-not-where,' the place in which was situated the university of Professor Teufelsdröckh in Carlyle's *Sartor Resartus.*
Weller (wel'ĕr), **Sam.** The valet or personal attendant of Mr. Pickwick in Dickens' *Pickwick Papers*, a genuine Londoner, uneducated, ready-witted, full of humor, and devoted to his master's interests. His father, Tony Weller, is a fat old coachman ignorant of almost everything except what belongs to his business. Having married a widow (landlady of the Marquis of Granby Inn, and painfully religious), he holds strong opinions about widows and their artfulness.
Wemmick (wem'ik), **John.** Clerk to the lawyer Mr. Jaggers in Dickens' *Great Expectations.* He lives with his old father in a little house which he has converted into a sort of miniature fortress.
Wendy (wen'dy). The daughter of the Darling family, in Barrie's *Peter Pan* and *Peter and Wendy*, who journey with Peter to Never-Never Land.
Wenham (wen'ăm). See **Wagg and Wenham.**
Werther (ver'tĕr). A young German student, the sickly sentimental hero of Goethe's *Sorrows of Werther*, who puts an end to himself because of his unrequited love for his friend's wife. Thackeray compressed the story into a few humorous verses more pithy than complimentary to the hero.
Western (wes'tĕrn), **Squire.** A jolly, ignorant, coarse, hot-tempered, and intensely prejudiced English squire in Fielding's *Tom Jones.* His charming daughter Sophia is in love with and marries Tom Jones.
Westlock (west'lok), **John.** In Dickens' *Martin Chuzzlewit*, a fine young man who studies architecture under Pecksniff, and marries Ruth Pinch.
Westward Ho! (west'wărd hō). The name of a novel by Charles Kingsley. See **Leigh, Amyas.**
Whang (hwang). A character in Goldsmith's *Citizen of the World*, an avaricious miller who undermined his mill in digging for a treasure.
White Cat (hwīt ęat). Name of a fairy tale by Madame d'Aulnoy, telling of a beautiful princess turned into a cat by fairy power.
Whitefield (hwīt'fēld), **Ann.** The heroine of G. B. Shaw's comedy *Man and Superman*, who takes the initiative in a sex duel with the conventional John Tanner. She pursues him to the mountains of Spain, triumphs as Everywoman, and makes him submit to the Life Force.
Whiteoak (hwīt'ōk) **Family.** An extremely individualistic Canadian family created by Mazo de la Roche in the *Jalna* books, headed by Adeline, the old matriarch, who lives to celebrate her hundredth birthday. Other Whiteoaks are Renny, Piers, Ernest, Meg, Wakefield, Eden, and Finch.
Whittington (hwit'ing-tŏn), **Dick.** The hero of a story known to everyone, and which seems to have been at least founded on fact.
Wickfield (wik'fēld), **Agnes.** A beautiful, amiable, and sensible young lady in Dickens' *David Copperfield*, daughter of Mr. Wickfield, a lawyer. She becomes David Copperfield's second wife. Uriah Heep is clerk to her father, and nearly brings ruin upon him.
Wilberforce (wil'bĕr-fǫrc), **Miss.** An alcoholic aristocrat who drifts to the island of Nepenthe in Douglas' *South Wind*, and lives there far from her native English Midlands.
Wild (wīld), **Jonathan.** A notorious English robber who is the hero of Fielding's satiric novel *The Adventures of Jonathan Wild the Great.*
Wildair (wīld'ãr), **Sir Harry.** The hero and title of a comedy by Farquhar, a rakish young fellow not devoid of good feeling.
Wild Huntsman (hunts'măn). A spectral huntsman of German legend, who goes careering along at night with a noisy train of men and dogs; the subject of a ballad by Bürger, translated by Sir Walter Scott.
Wilfer (wil'fĕr), **Bella.** The heroine of *Our Mutual Friend*, by Dickens, a pretty girl somewhat willful and giddy, married by John Harmon under an assumed name. Her mother is oppressively dignified and majestic, her father, not at all so.
Wilkes (wilks), **Ashley.** The great love of Scarlett O'Hara's life until the realization of her love for Rhett Butler, in Margaret Mitchell's *Gone With the Wind.* See **Hamilton.**
Willet (wil'et), **John.** The ignorant, pig-headed landlord of the Maypole in Dickens' *Barnaby Rudge*, who tyrannizes over his son Joe in such a way as to make him run away and enlist. Joe afterwards marries Dolly Varden and becomes landlord himself.
Wilmot (wil'mŏt). **Family.** A married couple and their son in Lillo's tragedy *Fatal Curiosity.* Young Wilmot goes to India and makes a fortune, and, having returned, visits his father and mother in disguise and leaves with them a casket. This they open, and, finding that it contains jewels, murder their son—not knowing his identity until too late—to obtain them.
Wilton (wil'tŏn), **Ralph de.** A gallant young man in Scott's *Marmion*, loving and loved by the Lady Clare, who is also wooed by Marmion.
Wimble (wim'bl), **Will.** An amusing character in the *Spectator*, a member of the club to which Sir Roger de Coverley and others belong.
Wimsey (wim'și), **Lord Peter.** The fictional detective of Dorothy L. Sayers.
Windermere (win'dĕr-mĕr), **Lady.** In Wilde's social comedy *Lady Windermere's Fan*, a young woman who, resentful of her husband's interest in a Mrs. Erlynne, decides to run away with a lover. She does not know that Mrs. Erlynne is actually her mother; but she is saved from a compromising situation by the latter, who forfeits her own reputation.
Winesburg (wīns'bŭrg), **Ohio.** A fictitious small town which is the scene of, and gives title to, a collection of short stories by Sherwood Anderson.
Winkle (wiñ'kl), **Mr. Nathaniel.** One of the companions of the immortal Pickwick, represented as the would-be sportsman of the party, but knowing as little of shooting as he does of skating. He marries Arabella Allen.
Winkle, Rip Van. A Dutch colonist in New York, hero of a story by Washington Irving, a good-humored, indolent sort of fellow, who encounters a strange company playing at ninepins in the Catskill Mountains. After he has drunk some of their liquor, he falls asleep and does not awake for twenty years.
Witwould (wit'wood), **Sir Wilful.** In Congreve's *Way of the World*, 'a superannuated old bachelor' who is inclined to marry Millamant but gets little encouragement.
Woden (wō'den). Same as **Odin.**
Woodcock (wood'çok), **Adam.** A falconer at Avenel Castle in Scott's *Abbot.*
Wooden Horse (wood'en hǫrs). A huge figure of a horse, made of wood and containing armed Greeks, which the Trojans were induced by the Greeks to admit into Troy, thus leading to the capture of the city.
Woodhouse (wood'hous), **Emma.** The wealthy and unoccupied heroine of Jane Austen's novel *Emma*, whose friendly interference with others' affairs causes trouble. She finally marries her brother-in-law, Mr. Knightley, whose excellent qualities are revealed to her as her character develops.
Wrayburn (rā'bŭrn), **Eugene.** An indolent, aimless barrister in *Our Mutual Friend*, by Dickens, in love with Lizzie Hexam, and nearly murdered by Bradley Headstone in consequence.
Wren (rĕn), **Jenny.** A girl with a rickety body and beautiful head of hair, who works as a 'doll's dressmaker' in Dickens' *Our Mutual Friend.* Her real name is Fanny Cleaver.
Wronghead (rǫng'hed), **Sir Francis and Lady.** A country couple who come to London and nearly ruin themselves by their follies, in Vanbrugh and Cibber's *Provoked Husband.*
Wylie (wȳ'li), **Maggie.** The wife of John Shand in J. M. Barrie's play *What Every Woman Knows.* A plain but wise woman, she assists her husband in his political carreer without his realizing that his success is due to anything but his own efforts.

X

Xanadu (zan'ȧ-dů). A city of Asia named in Coleridge's poem *Kubla Khan.*
Xanthus (zan'thus). The horse of Achilles, that could speak with a human voice.
Xantippe (zan-tip'ē). The wife of Socrates, proverbial as a shrew.
Xury (zů'ry). A Morisco boy in Defoe's *Robinson Crusoe*, companion of Crusoe when he escaped from the Moors of Sallee.

Y

Yahoo (yä'hǫǫ; yā'). In Swift's *Gulliver's Travels*, a race of brutes having both the form and the vices of man, and subject to the Houyhnhnms.
Yama (yam'ȧ; yum'ȧ). An Indian deity, lord of hell, fierce and terrible.
Yank (yank). A crude stoker on an ocean liner in O'Neill's drama *The Hairy Ape.* His pride in his place in life is shattered when a society girl, seeing him at work, shows her revulsion, and he turns against humanity.
Yellow Dwarf (yel'ō dwąrf). A malignant imp in the fairy tale so named, by the Countess d'Aulnoy.
Yggdrasil (yg'drȧ-sil). The tree of the universe, a huge ash which holds an important place in Scandinavian mythology and cosmogony.
Yniol (yn'i-ol). The father of Enid, in Tennyson's *Idylls of the King.*
Yorick (yǫr'ik). Jester to the king of Denmark in Shakespeare's *Hamlet.* Sterne introduced a personage of this name into his *Tristram Shandy*—simple, lighthearted, and humorous—intended as a portrait of himself.
Young (yung), **Bertha.** The heroine of Katherine Mansfield's *Bliss*, who in the instant of realization that she is in love with her husband as never before, discovers that he loves another woman. The moment before the discovery represented bliss.
Ysolde (y-sōld'). See **Isolde.**

Z

Zadig (zä-dīg'). The hero and title of a novel by Voltaire—a Babylonian tale showing that the ways of providence are inscrutable.
Zanga (zañ'gȧ). A revengeful Moor in Young's *Revenge.*

Zanoni (zȧ-nō'ni). The hero of a novel of the same name by Bulwer-Lytton; a man who can communicate with spirits, produced gold and gems, etc.
Zelica (zel'i-çȧ). The heroine in Moore's *Veiled Prophet.*
Zenelophon (zē-nel'ō-fon). The 'beggar maid,' married by King Cophetua.
Zecia (zē'ni-ȧ). In Edith Wharton's *Ethan Frome,* Ethan's wife, a petulant, self-centered invalid.
Zephon (zē'fon). A cherub in Milton's *Paradise Lost,* sent with Ithuriel to seek for Satan in Eden.
Zephyr (zef'ẽr). In classical mythology, a personification of the west wind.
Zeus (zūs). The Greek name of Jupiter.

A DICTIONARY OF FOREIGN WORDS AND PHRASES

A

à bas [Fr.], down, down with.
à beau jeu, beau retour [Fr.], one good turn deserves another; tit for tat.
ab extra [L.], from without.
ab imo pectore [L.], from the bottom of the heart.
ab incunabulis [L.], from the cradle.
ab initio [L.], from the beginning.
ab intra [L.], from within.
a bisogni si conoscono gli amici [It.], a friend in need is a friend indeed.
à bon chat, bon rat [Fr.], to a good cat, a good rat; tit for tat.
à bon marché [Fr.], cheap; a good bargain.
ab origine [L.], from the origin.
ab ovo [L.], from the egg; from the beginning.
ab ovo usque ad mala [L.], from the egg to the apples (as in Roman banquets); from beginning to end.
à bras ouverts [Fr.], with open arms.
abrégé [Fr.], an abridgment.
absens hæres non erit [L.], the absent one will not be heir; out of sight, out of mind.
absente reo [L.], the accused being absent.
absit invidia [L.], let there be no ill-will; envy apart.
absit omen [L.], may this not prove of (evil) omen.
ab uno disce omnes [L.], from one specimen judge of all the rest.
a buon vino non bisogna frasca [It.], good wine needs no bush.
ab urbe condita [L.], from the founding of the city, i.e. Rome (753 B. C.).
a capite ad calcem [L.], from head to heel.
à chaque saint sa chandelle [Fr.], to each saint his candle; honor to whom honor is due.
à cheval [Fr.], on horseback.
a che vuole, non mancano modi [It.], where there's a will there's a way.
à compte [Fr.], on account.
à corps perdu [Fr.], with breakneck speed.
à coup sûr [Fr.], of a certainty; without fail.
à couvert [Fr.], under cover.
a cruce salus [L.], salvation by the cross.
actionnaire [Fr.], shareholder in a company.
ad aperturam (libri) [L.], at the opening of the book; wherever the book opens.
ad arbitrium [L.], at will.
ad astra per aspera [L.], to the stars through hardship.
ad calendas Græcas [L.], at the Greek calends; i.e. never, as the Greeks had no calends in their mode of reckoning.
ad captandum vulgus [L.], to attract or please the rabble.
a Deo et rege [L.], from God and the king.
à dessein [Fr.], on purpose; intentionally.
à deux mains [Fr.], for two hands; two-handed; having a double office.
ad extremum [L.], to the last, or extremity.
ad finem [L.], to the end; at or near the end.
ad gustum [L.], to one's taste.
ad hominem [L.], to the man; to an individual's interests or passions.
adhuc sub judice lis est [L.], the case is still before the judge; the controversy is not yet settled.
a die [L.], from that day.
ad infinitum [L.], to infinity.
ad instar [L.], after the fashion of.
ad interim [L.], in the meanwhile.
ad internecionem [L.], to extermination.
à discrétion [Fr.], at discretion; without restriction.
ad libitum [L.], at pleasure.
ad majorem Dei gloriam [L.], for the greater glory of God.
ad modum [L.], in the manner of.
ad multos annos [L.], for many years.
ad nauseam [L.], to disgust or satiety.
adorer le veau d'or [Fr.], to worship the golden calf.
ad patres [L.], gathered to his fathers.
ad referendum [L.], for further consideration.
ad rem [L.], to the purpose; to the point.
à droite [Fr.], to the right.
adscriptus glebæ [L.], attached to the soil.
adsum [L.], I am present; here!
ad summum [L.], to the highest point.
ad unguem [L.], to the nail; to a nicety; exactly; perfectly.
ad unum omnes [L.], all to a man.
ad utrumque paratus [L.], prepared for either case or alternative.
ad valorem [L.], according to the value.
ad vitam aut culpam [L.], for life or fault; i.e. till some misconduct be proved.
ad vivum [L.], to the life; portrayed in a lifelike manner.
ægrescit medendo [L.], he becomes worse by the remedies used.
æquabiliter et diligenter [L.], equably and diligently.
æquo animo [L.], with an equal mind; with equanimity.
ære perennius [L.], more lasting than brass.
æs triplex [L.], triple brass; armor of adamant.
ætatis suæ [L.], of his (or her) age.
affaire d'amour [Fr.], a love affair.
affaire d'honneur [Fr.], an affair of honor; a duel.
affaire du cœur [Fr.], an affair of the heart.
affreux [Fr.], frightful; shocking.
à fleur d'eau [Fr.], on a level with the water.
à fond [Fr.], to the bottom; thoroughly; heartily.
a fortiori [L.], with stronger reason. See in Dict.
à gauche [Fr.], to the left.
à genoux [Fr.], on the knees.
age quod agis [L.], attend to what you are about.
à grands frais [Fr.], at great expense.
à haute voix [Fr.], aloud.
à huis clos [Fr.], with closed doors; secretly.
aide toi, et le ciel t'aidera [Fr.], help yourself, and Heaven will help you.
à la belle étoile [Fr.], under the stars; in the open air.
à la bonne heure [Fr.], in good time; very well, all right, as you please.
à l'abri [Fr.], under shelter.
à la campagne [Fr.], in the country.
à la carte [Fr.], according to the bill of fare at table.
à la dérobée [Fr.], by stealth.
à la française [Fr.], after the French mode.
à la mode [Fr.], according to the custom or fashion.
à la Tartuffe [Fr.], like Tartuffe, i.e. hypocritically.
al bisogno si conoscono gli amici [It.], friends are known in time of need.
à l'envi [Fr.], emulously; so as to vie.
alere flammam [L.], to feed the flame.
al fresco [It.], in the open air; cool.
alieni appetens, sui profusus [L.], greedy of other people's possessions, lavish of his own.
à l'improviste [Fr.], on the sudden.
alla vostra salute [It.], to your health.
allez-vous-en! [Fr.], away with you!
allons [Fr.], let us go; come on; come.
al piu [It.], at most.
alter ego [L.], another self.
alter idem [L.], another exactly similar.
alter ipse amicus [L.], a friend is the counterpart of oneself.
alterum tantum [L.], as much more.
à main armée [Fr.], by force of arms.
amantium iræ amoris integratio [L.], the quarrels of lovers are the renewal of love.
à ma puissance [Fr.], to the best of my power.
amar y saber no puede ser [Sp.], no one can love and also be wise.
a maximis ad minima [L.], from the greatest to the least.
âme de boue [Fr.], a soul of mud.
amende honorable [Fr.], satisfactory apology; reparation.
à merveille [Fr.], to a wonder; marvellously.
amici probantur rebus adversis [L.], friends are tested in adversity.
amicus humani generis [L.], a friend of the human race.
amicus Plato, sed magis amica veritas [L.], Plato is my friend, but truth is still more a friend to me.
amicus usque ad aras [L.], a friend even to the sacrificial altar, i.e. to the utmost extremity.
ami de cour [Fr.], a court friend; a false or unreliable friend.
à mon avis [Fr.], in my opinion.
amor patriæ [L.], love of country.
amour propre [Fr.], self-love; vanity.
ancient régime [Fr.], the ancient or former order of things.
anglicé [Fr.], in English; in the English language.
anguis in herba [L.], a snake in the grass; an unsuspected danger; a false friend.
animo et fide [L.], with courage and confidence.
anno ætatis suæ [L.], in the year of his or her age.
anno Christi [L.], in the year of Christ.
anno Domini [L.], in the year of our Lord.
anno humanæ salutis [L.], in the year of man's redemption.
anno mundi [L.], in the year of the world.
anno urbis conditæ [L.], in the year from the time the city (Rome) was founded (753 B. C.).
annuit cœptis [L.], He (God) has smiled on our undertakings: motto, adapted from Virgil, on the reverse of the great seal of the United States.
annus mirabilis [L.], year of wonders; especially used in reference to the year 1666, in which occurred the great plague, and the great fire of London.
ante lucem [L.], before the dawn.
ante meridiem [L.], before noon.
à outrance [Fr.], to extremities.
à pas de géant [Fr.], with a giant's stride; with gigantic steps.
à peindre [Fr.], to be painted; worthy of the painter's art.
aperçu [Fr.], a general sketch or survey.
à perte de vue [Fr.], till beyond one's view.
à peu près [Fr.], nearly.
à pied [Fr.], on foot.
à point [Fr.], to a point; just in time; perfectly right.
a posse ad esse [L.], from possibility to reality.
appartement [Fr.], set of rooms on the same floor.
aprés moi le déluge [Fr.], after me the deluge.
a prima vista [It.], at first sight.
à propos de bottes [Fr.], apropos of boots; in an irrelevant manner; without rhyme or reason.
à propos de rien [Fr.], apropos of nothing; without reference to anything in particular; without a motive.
aquila non capit muscas [L.], an eagle does not catch flies.
arbiter bibendi [L.], ruler of the symposium; toastmaster.
arbiter elegantiarum [L.], a judge or supreme authority in matters of taste.
arcades ambo [L.], Arcadians both; fellows of the same stamp.
arcana cælestia [L.], celestial mysteries.
arcana imperii [L.], state secrets.
ardentia verba [L.], glowing language.
argent comptant [Fr.], ready money.
argumentum ad crumenam [L.], an argument to the purse, i.e. to one's interests.
argumentum ad hominem [L.], an argument to the individual man, i.e. to his interests and prejudices.
argumentum ad ignorantiam [L.], an argument intended to work on a person's ignorance.
argumentum ad judicium [L.], argument appealing to the judgment.
argumentum ad verecundiam [L.], argument appealing to modesty.
argumentum baculinum [L.], the argument of the cudgel; brute force.
ariston metron [Gr.], moderation is best.
arrectis auribus [L.], with ears pricked up; all attention.
arrière pensée [Fr.], mental reservation.
ars est celare artem [L.], it is true art to conceal art.
ars longa, vita brevis [L.], art is long, life is short.
Artium Magister [L.], Master of Arts.
asinus ad lyram [L.], an ass at the lyre; a stupid awkward fellow.
Athanasius contra mundum [L.], Athanasius against the world.
à tort et à travers [Fr.], at random; without consideration.
à toute force [Fr.], with all one's might.
à tout hasard [Fr.], at all hazards.
à tout prix [Fr.], at any price; at all costs.
at spes non fracta [L.], but hope is not crushed.
au bout de son Latin [Fr.], at the end of his Latin, at his wit's end; in a fix or quandary.
au contraire [Fr.], on the contrary.
au courant [Fr.], fully acquainted with matters; up to date.
audaces (or audentes) fortuna juvat [L.], fortune aids the bold.
au désespoir [Fr.], in despair.
audi alteram partem [L.], hear the other side.
audiatur et altera pars [L.], let the other side also be heard.
au fait [Fr.], well acquainted with; expert.
au fond [Fr.], at bottom; in reality.
auf Wiedersehen [G.], till we meet again; **au revoir.**
au grand sérieux [Fr.], in all seriousness.
au jour le jour [Fr.], from day to day; without thought of tomorrow; from hand to mouth.
au naturel [Fr.], in the natural state.
au pis aller [Fr.], at the worst.
aurea mediocritas [L.], the golden or happy mean.
au reste [Fr.], as for the rest.
au revoir [Fr.], adieu; until we meet again.
auri sacra fames [L.], the accursed craving for gold.
au sérieux [Fr.], seriously.
auspicium melioris ævi [L.], an auspice (or augury) of a better age (to come).
aussitôt dit, aussitôt fait [Fr.], no sooner said than done.
autant d'hommes, autant d'avis [Fr.], so many men, so many minds.
aut Cæsar aut nullus [L.], either Cæsar or nobody.
aut inveniam viam aut faciam [L.], I shall either find a way or make one.
autrefois acquit [Fr.], formerly acquitted; previously tried for the same offense and acquitted.
autre temps, autres mœurs [Fr.], other times, other manners.
au troisième [Fr.], on the third story.

aut vincere aut mori [L.], either to conquer or to die; victory or death.

aux armes! [Fr.], to arms!

auxilium ab alto [L.], help from on high.

avant-propos [Fr.], preliminary matter; preface.

avec permission [Fr.], with permission.

ave, Imperator! morituri te salutant [L.], hail, Emperor! those about to die (gladiators) salute thee.

a verbis ad verbera [L.], from words to blows.

avito viret honore [L.], flourishes on his ancestral honors.

à volonté [Fr.], at pleasure.

a vostra salute [It.]
à votre santé [Fr.]
a vuestra salud [Sp.] } to your health.

B

badaud [Fr.], a lounger in the streets; an idler.

badinage [Fr.], jocularity; chaff.

ballon d'essai [Fr.], a balloon sent up to ascertain the direction of the air-currents; hence, a device to test public opinion on any subject.

bas bleu [Fr.], a blue-stocking; a literary woman.

beatæ memoriæ [L.], of blessed memory.

beau idéal [Fr.], the ideal of perfection.

beauté du diable [Fr.], the devil's good looks; youthful freshness.

beaux esprits [Fr.], men of wit.

beaux yeux [Fr.], fine eyes; good looks.

bel esprit [Fr.], a person of wit or genius; a brilliant mind.

bella! horrida bella! [L.], wars! horrid wars!

bella matribus detestata [L.], wars hated by mothers.

bellum internecinum [L.], a war of extermination.

benedetto è quel male che vien solo [It.], blessed the misfortune that comes singly.

bene orasse est bene studuisse [L.], to have prayed well is to have striven well.

ben trovato [It.], well invented; cleverly fabricated or concocted.

bête noire [Fr.], a black beast; a bugbear.

bêtise [Fr.], a piece of stupidity; stupidity.

billet d'amour [Fr.], a love-letter.

bis dat qui cito dat [L.], he gives twice who gives quickly.

bis peccare in bello non licet [L.], it is not permissible to blunder twice in war.

bis pueri sens [L.], old men are twice boys.

bona fide [L.], in good faith.

bona fides [L.], good faith.

bon ami [Fr.], good friend.

bon avocat, mauvais voisin [Fr.], a good lawyer is a bad neighbor.

bon diable [Fr.], a good-natured fellow.

bon gré, mal gré [Fr.], with good or ill grace; willing or unwilling.

bon jour [Fr.], good day; good morning.

bon jour, bonne œuvre [Fr.], a good day, a good work; i.e. the better the day, the better the deed.

bonne bouche [Fr.], a delicate morsel, titbit.

bonne et belle [Fr.], good and handsome.

bonne foi [Fr.], good faith.

bon soir [Fr.], good evening.

bon vivant [Fr.], one fond of luxury and good living; a gourmet.

bon voyage! [Fr.], a good voyage (or journey) to you!

Borgen macht Sorgen [G.], borrowing makes sorrowing; who goes a-borrowing goes a-sorrowing.

breveté [Fr.], patented.

brevi manu [L.], with a short hand; extemporaneously.

brevis esse laboro obscurus fio [L.], if I labor to be brief, I become obscure.

brutum fulmen [L.], a senseless thunderbolt; striking blindly.

C

cadit quæstio [L.], the question falls; there is no further discussion.

cæca est invidia [L.], envy is blind.

cælum non animum mutant qui trans mare currunt [L.], they who cross the sea change their sky but not their feelings.

cætera desunt [L.], the rest is wanting.

cæteris paribus [L.], other things being equal.

campo santo [It.], a burying-ground—lit. 'holy field'.

candida Pax [L.], white-robed Peace.

cantabit vacuus coram latrone viator [L.], the penniless traveler will sing in the presence of the highwayman; i.e. a penniless man has nothing to lose.

cantate Domino [L.], sing unto the Lord.

cap à pié [Fr.], from head to foot.

caput mortuum [L.], lit. 'dead head'; worthless residue.

cara sposa [It.], dear wife.

carent quia vate sacro [L.], because they have no sacred bard (to celebrate their praise).

carpe diem [L.], enjoy the present day; improve the time.

castello che dà orecchia si vuol rendere [It.], the fortress that parleys speedily surrenders.

casus belli [L.], that which causes or justifies war.

catalogue raisonné [Fr.], a catalogue arranged according to the subjects.

causa sine qua non [L.], an indispensable cause or condition.

cause célèbre [Fr.], a celebrated law case or trial.

caveat emptor [L.], let the buyer beware.

cave canem [L.], beware of the dog.

cavendo tutus [L.], safe by using caution.

cedant arma togæ [L.], let arms yield to the gown, that is, military authority to the civil power.

cela va sans dire [Fr.], that goes without saying; needless to say; that is a matter of course.

cela viendra [Fr.], that will come.

ce n'est pas être bien aise que de rire [Fr.], laughing is not always a sign that the mind is at ease.

ce n'est que le premier pas qui coute [Fr.], it is only the first step that is difficult.

censor morum [L.], a censor of morals.

c'est à dire [Fr.], that is to say.

c'est le commencement de la fin [Fr.], it is the beginning of the end.

c'est magnifique, mais ce n'est pas la guerre [Fr.], it is magnificent, but it is not war; said by a French officer as he watched the Charge of the Light Brigade at Balaklava.

c'est selon [Fr.], that is according to circumstances; that is as may be.

c'est un autre chose [Fr.], that's quite another thing.

cetera desunt [L.], the rest is wanting; here there is a break.

ceteris paribus [L.], see cæteris.

chacun à son goût [Fr.], every one to his taste.

chacun tire de son coté [Fr.], every one inclines to his own side.

chapeau bras [Fr.], a cocked hat.

chapelle ardente [Fr.], the chamber in which a dead body lies in state.

chemin de fer [Fr.], iron road; a railway.

cherchez la femme [Fr.], look for the woman (to find where she has had a hand in the matter).

chère amie [Fr.], a dear (female) friend.

che sarà, sarà [It.], what will be, will be.

cheval de bataille [Fr.], a war-horse; what one chiefly relies on.

chevalier d'industrie [Fr.], lit. a knight of industry; a swindling or cheating rogue; one who lives by his wits.

chi tace confessa [It.], he who keeps silence confesses.

ci git [Fr.], here lies.

clarior e tenebris [L.], brighter from darkness or obscurity.

clarum et venerabile nomen [L.], an illustrious and venerable name.

cogito, ergo sum [L.], I think, therefore I exist.

comitas inter gentes [L.], politeness between nations.

comme il faut [Fr.], as it should be.

commune bonum [L.], a common good.

commune periculum concordiam parit [L.], common danger begets concord.

communibus annis [L.], on the annual average.

communi consensu [L.], by common consent.

compagnon de voyage [Fr.], a traveling companion.

componere lites [L.], to settle disputes.

compos voti [L.], having obtained one's wish.

compte rendu [Fr.], an account rendered; a report.

con amore [It.], with love; very earnestly.

conciergerie [Fr.], a doorkeeper's lodge; also name of an ancient prison at Paris.

concio ad clerum [L.], a discourse to the clergy.

concordia discors [L.], discordant concord.

concours [Fr.], a competition, as for a prize.

con diligenza [It.], with diligence.

conditio sine qua non [L.], a necessary condition.

con dolore [It.], with grief; sorrowfully.

confido et conquiesco [L.], I trust and am at peace.

conjunctis viribus [L.], with united powers.

conseil d'état [Fr.], a council of state; a privy-council.

consensus facit legem [L.], consent makes the law.

consilio et animis [L.], by wisdom and courage.

consilio et prudentia [L.], by wisdom and prudence.

constantia et virtute [L.], by constancy and virtue (or bravery).

consuetudo pro lege servatur [L.], custom or usage is held as law.

consule Planco [L.], when Plancus was consul; when I was a young fellow.

contra bonos mores [L.], against good manners or morals.

copia verborum [L.], rich supply of words.

coram nobis [L.], before us; in our presence.

coram non judice [L.], before one who is not a proper judge.

coram populo [L.], in presence of the people.

cordon bleu [Fr.], blue-ribbon; a cook of the highest excellence.

cordon sanitaire [Fr.], a line of guards to prevent the spreading of contagion or pestilence; a quarantine.

corps d'armée [Fr.], the body of an army; an army corps.

corps de garde [Fr.], a body of men in a guardroom; the room itself.

corps diplomatique [Fr.], a diplomatic body; a body of ambassadors and similar representatives.

corrigenda [L.], things to be corrected; a list of errors or imperfections.

corruptio optimi pessima [L.], a corruption of what is best is worst.

cos ingeniorum [L.], a whetstone for wits.

couleur de rose [Fr.], rose-color; an alluring aspect of circumstances.

coup [Fr.], a stroke.

coup de grâce [Fr.], a finishing stroke.

coup de main [Fr.], a sudden attack or enterprise.

coup de maître [Fr.], a master stroke.

coup de pied [Fr.], a kick.

coup de soleil [Fr.], sunstroke.

coup d'essai [Fr.], a first attempt.

coup d'état [Fr.], a sudden decisive blow in politics; a stroke of policy.

coup de théâtre [Fr.], a theatrical effect.

coup d'œil [Fr.], a rapid glance of the eye.

courage sans peur [Fr.], fearless courage.

coûte que coûte [Fr.], cost what it may.

crambe repetita [L.], cabbage warmed up a second time; i.e. the repetition of an old joke, a truism, etc.

credat Judæus Apella [L.], let Apella, the superstitious Jew, believe it, I won't; 'tell that to the marines.'

crede quod habes, et habes [L.], believe that you have it, and you have it.

credo quia absurdum [L.], I believe because it is absurd.

credo quia impossibele est [L.], I believe it because it is impossible.

crême de la crême [Fr.], cream of the cream; the very best or most select.

crescit amor nummi, quantum ipsa pecunia crescit [L.], the love of money increases as wealth grows.

crescit eundo [L.], it increases as it goes.

crescit sub pondere virtus [L.], virtue increases beneath oppression.

crimen falsi [L.], the crime of perjury.

crimen læsæ majestatis [L.], the crime of high treason; lese-majesty.

Croix rouge [Fr.], Red Cross.

crux [L.], a cross; puzzle; difficulty.

crux criticorum [L.], the puzzle of critics.

crux medicorum [L.], the puzzle of the doctors.

cucullus non facit monachum [L.], the cowl does not make the friar; i.e. don't trust to appearances.

cui bono? [L.], for whose advantage? to what end?

cui Fortuna ipsa cedit [L.], to whom Fortune herself yields.

cuilibet in arte sua credendum est [L.], everyone is to be trusted in his own special art.

culpam pœna premit comes [L.], punishment follows hard on crime.

cum bona venia [L.], with your good leave.

cum grano salis [L.], with a grain of salt; with some allowance.

cum multis aliis [L.], with many others.

cum notis variorum [L.], with the notes of various commentators.

cum privilegio [L.], with privilege or license from the authorities.

curiosa felicitas [L.], nice felicity of expression.

currente calamo [L.], with a running or rapid pen.

custus morum [L.], guardian of manners (or morals).

D

d'accord [Fr.], in agreement.

da locum melioribus [L.], give place to your betters.

dame d'honneur [Fr.], matron of honor.

dames de la halle [Fr.], women who sell articles in a market; market-women.

damnant quod non intelligunt [L.], they condemn what they do not understand.

dare pondus fumo [L.], to give weight to smoke; i.e. attach importance to matters of no consequence.

das Beste ist gut genug [G.], the best is good enough.

das Ewig-Weibliche zieht uns hinan [G.], the eternal-feminine draws us upwards.

data et accepta [L.], expenses and receipts.

data obolum Belisario [L.], give an obolus to Belisarius (a general of Justinian, said to have been neglected in his old age by that emperor and compelled to beg).

Davus sum non Œdipus [L.], I am Davus not Œdipus (who solved the riddle of the Sphinx); I am a bad hand at riddles.

de bon augure [Fr.], of good augury or omen.

de bonne grâce [Fr.], with good grace; willingly.

deceptio visus [L.], an optical illusion.

decet verecundum esse adolescentem [L.], it becomes a young man to be modest.

decies repetita placebit [L.], when ten times repeated it will still please.

decipimur specie recti [L.], we are deceived by the show of rectitude.

decori decus addit avito [L.], he adds distinction to his ancestral honors.

de die in diem [L.], from day to day.

de facto [L.], in point of fact; actual; actually.

dégagé [Fr.], free; easy; unconstrained.

de gustibus non est disputandum [L.], there is no disputing about tastes.

de haut en bas [Fr.], in a contemptuous or supercilious manner.

dei gratia [L.], by the grace of God.

de integro [L.], anew; over again from beginning to end.

déjeuner à la fourchette [Fr.], breakfast with a fork; a breakfast or luncheon with meat.

de jure [L.], from the law; by right.

de l'audace, encore de l'audace, et toujours de l'audace [Fr.], audacity, more audacity, and always audacity.

delenda est Carthago [L.], Carthage must be blotted out, or destroyed.

de luxe [Fr.], of luxury; made with unusual elegance.

de mal en pis [Fr.], from bad to worse.

de minimis non curat lex [L.], the law does not concern itself with trifles.

de mortuis nil nisi bonum [L.], (say) nothing but good of the dead.

de nihilo nihil fit [L.], from nothing nothing is made.

dénouement [Fr.], issue; solution.

de novo [L.], anew.

Deo adjuvante [L.], God assisting.

Deo duce [L.], God being the leader.

Deo favente [L.], God favoring.
Deo gratias [L.], thanks to God.
Deo juvante [L.], with God's help.
de omnibus rebus et quibusdam aliis [L.], concerning all things and certain others.
Deo non fortuna [L.], from God, not by chance.
Deo volente [L.], God willing.
de pis en pis [Fr.], from worse to worse.
de profundis [L.], out of the depths.
de retour [Fr.], having come back; returned.
de rigueur [Fr.], imperatively necessary; not to be dispensed with.
dernier ressort [Fr.], a last resource.
désagrément [Fr.], something disagreeable.
desipere in loco [L.], to jest or be jolly at the proper time.
désorienté [Fr.], having lost one's way; not knowing where to turn.
desunt cætera [L.], the remainder is wanting.
de trop [Fr.], too much; more than is wanted.
detur digniori [L.], let it be given to the more worthy.
detur pulchriori [L.], let it be given to the more (or most) beautiful.
Deus avertat! [L.], God forbid!
deus ex machina [L.], a god out of the machine; a deity introduced to bring about the dénouement of a drama; referring to the machinery and practice of the Greek and Roman stage.
Deus vobiscum! [L.], God be with you!
Deus vult [L.], God wills it.
di buona volontà sta pieno l'inferno [It.], hell is full of good intentions.
Dichtung und Wahrheit [G.], fiction and fact; poetry and truth.
dictum factum [L.], no sooner said than done.
dies non [L.], a day on which a law-court is not held.
Dieu est toujours pour les plus gros bataillons [Fr.], God is always on the side of the largest battalions; the leader with the largest army has the best chance of victory.
Dieu et mon droit [Fr.], God and my right.
Dieu vous garde [Fr.], God protect you.
digito monstrari [L.], to be pointed out with the finger (as a person of note).
dignus vindice nodus [L.], a difficulty worthy of powerful intervention.
dii majorum gentium [L.], gods of the superior class; the twelve higher gods of the Romans.
dii penates [L.], household gods.
diis aliter visum [L.], the gods decided otherwise; fate willed differently.
Dios me libre de hombre de un libro [Sp.], God deliver me from a man of one book.
di salto [It.], by leaps.
diseur de bons mots [Fr.], a sayer of good things; one noted for witty sayings.
disjecta membra [L.], scattered remains.
divide et impera [L.], divide and rule.
docendo discimus [L.], we learn by teaching.
dolce far niente [It.], sweet doing-nothing; sweet idleness.
Dominus vobiscum [L.], the Lord be with you.
domus et placens uxor [L.], home and a pleasing wife.
dorer la pilule [Fr.], to gild the pill.
double entendre [Fr.], incorrect for next:
double entente [Fr.], a double or equivocal meaning; a play on words.
do ut des [L.], I give that you may give; reciprocity.
doux yeux [Fr.], soft glances.
dramatis personæ [L.], the characters in the play.
droit au travail [Fr.], the right to live by labor.
droit des gens [Fr.], the law of nations.
drôle [Fr.], funny; a comic actor.
ducit amor patriæ [L.], love of country draws me.
dulce domum [L.], sweet home (or rather homeward).
dulce est desipere in loco [L.], it is pleasant to play the fool at times.
dulce et decorum est pro patria mori [L.], it is sweet and glorious to die for one's country.
dum spiro, spero [L.], while I breathe, I hope.
dum vivimus, vivamus [L.], while we live, let us live.
duomo [It.], a cathedral.
durante bene placito [L.], during good pleasure.
durante vita [L.], during life.

E

eau sucrée [Fr.], sweetened water: a French beverage.
ébauche [Fr.], a preliminary sketch; a rough outline.
ecce homo! [L.], behold the man!
ecce signum! [L.], behold the sign!
école [Fr.], a school.
e contra [L.], on the other hand.
édition de luxe [Fr.], a splendid and expensive edition of a book.
editio princeps [L.], the first printed edition of a book.
égarement [Fr.], bewilderment, mental confusion.
ego et rex meus [L.], I and my king.
eheu! fugaces labuntur anni [L.], alas! the fleeting years glide by.
elapso tempore [L.], the time having elapsed.
élève [Fr.], a pupil or student.
embarras de richesses [Fr.], an embarrassment of riches; an over-supply.
emeritus [L.], retired or superannuated after long service.
empressement [Fr.], promptitude; eagerness.
en ami [Fr.], as a friend.
en arrière [Fr.], in the rear; behind; back.
en attendant [Fr.], in the meantime.
en avant [Fr.], forward.
en badinant [Fr.], in sport; jestingly.
en cueros [Sp.], naked; unclothed.
en déshabillé [Fr.], in undress.
en Dieu est ma fiance [Fr.], my trust is in God.
en Dieu est tout [Fr.], in God are all things.
en effet [Fr.], in effect; substantially; really.
en famille [Fr.], with one's family; in a domestic state.
enfant gâté [Fr.], a spoiled child.
enfants perdus [Fr.], lost children; the soldiers forming a forlorn hope.
enfant terrible [Fr.], a terrible child, or one that makes disconcerting remarks.
enfant trouvé [Fr.], a foundling.
enfin [Fr.], in short; at last; finally.
en grand seigneur [Fr.], like a grandee or magnate.
en grande tenue [Fr.], in full dress, either official or evening.
en masse [Fr.], in a mass.
en passant [Fr.], in passing.
en pension [Fr.], in a boarding-house.
en plein jour [Fr.], in broad day.
en queue [Fr.], standing one behind another.
en rapport [Fr.], in harmony; in agreement.
en règle [Fr.], according to rules; in order.
en revanche [Fr.], in requital; in return.
en route [Fr.], on the way.
en suite [Fr.], in company; in a set.
entente cordiale [Fr.], cordial understanding, especially between two states.
entêté [Fr.], obstinate; self-willed.
entourage [Fr.], surroundings; adjuncts.
entr'acte [Fr.], the interval between the acts of a play.
entre deux feux [Fr.], between two fires.
entre deux vins [Fr.], between two wines; half-drunk.
entremets [Fr.], side dishes of dainties to be eaten between the serving of the joints.
entre nous [Fr.], between ourselves.
en vérité [Fr.], in truth; verily.
en vieillissant on devient plus fou et plus sage [Fr.], in growing old, men become more foolish and more wise.
eo animo [L.], with that mind or design.
eo nomine [L.], by that name.
epea pteroenta [Gr.], winged words.
Epicuri de grege porcus [L.], a swine from the herd of Epicurus; an Epicurean.
e pluribus unum [L.], one out of many; one composed of many.
epulis accumbere divum [L.], to sit down at the banquets of the gods.
e re nata [L.], according to the exigency.
errare humanum est [L.], to err is human.
esprit borné [Fr.], a narrow or contracted spirit.
esprit de corps [Fr.], the animating spirit of a collective body, as a regiment.
essayez [Fr.], try; make the attempt.
esse quam videri [L.], to be, rather than to seem.
est modus in rebus [L.], there is a method in all things.
esto quod esse videris [L.], be what you seem to be.
et cætera (or **et cetera**) [L.], and the rest.
et hoc genus omne [L.], and everything of the sort.
et id genus omne [L.], and everything of the kind.
et sequentes or **et sequentia** [L.], and those that follow.
et sic de cæteris [L.], and so of the rest.
et sic de similibus [L.], and so of the like.
et tu, Brute! [L.], thou also, Brutus!
eureka [Gr.], I have found it.
événement [Fr.], an event.
eventus stultorum magister [L.], fools must be taught by the result.
Ewigkeit [G.], eternity.
ex abrupto [L.], suddenly.
ex abundantia [L.], out of the abundance.
ex adverso [L.], on the opposite side; over against.
exæquo et bono [L.], agreeably to what is good and right.
ex animo [L.], heartily; sincerely.
ex auctoritate mihi commissa [L.], by virtue of the authority intrusted to me.
ex capite [L.], from the head; from memory.
ex cathedra [L.], from the chair or seat of authority; with high authority.
excelsior [L.], higher; that is, loftier or taller; not correctly used as an adverb.
exceptio probat regulam [L.], the exception proves (or tests) the rule.
exceptis excipiendis [L.], the due exceptions being made.
excerpta [L.], extracts.
ex concesso [L.], from what has been conceded or granted in argument.
ex curia [L.], out of court.
ex delicto [L.], from the crime.
ex dono [L.], by the gift.
exegi monumentum ære perennius [L.], I have reared a monument more lasting than brass.
exempla sunt odiosa [L.], examples are offensive.
exempli gratia [L.], by way of example.
ex facto jus oritur [L.], the law springs from the fact.
excitus acta probat [L.], the event justifies the deed.
ex mera gratia [L.], through mere favor.
ex mero motu [L.], from his own impulse; from his own free-will.
ex more [L.], according to custom.
ex necessitate rei [L.], from the necessity of the case.
ex nihilo nihil fit [L.], from, or out of, nothing, nothing comes; nothing produces nothing.
ex officio [L.], by virtue of office.
ex opere operato [L.], by outward acts.
ex pede Herculem [L.], from the foot (we recognize) a Hercules; we judge of the whole from the specimen.
experientia docet stultos [L.], experience instructs fools.
experimentum crucis [L.], the trial or experiment of the cross; an experiment of a most searching nature.
experto crede [L.], trust one who has had experience.
expertus metuit [L.], having experience, he fears it.
exposé [Fr.], statement; showing up.
ex post facto [L.], after the deed is done; retrospective.
expressis verbis [L.], in express terms.
ex professo [L.], professedly.
ex propriis [L.], from one's own resources.
ex quocunque capite [L.], for whatever reason.
ex tacito [L.], tacitly.
extinctus amabitur idem [L.], the same man when dead will be loved.
extrait [Fr.], extract.
extra muros [L.], beyond the walls.
ex ungue leonem [L.], from a claw (we may know) the lion.
ex uno disce omnes [L.], from one learn all; from this specimen judge of the rest.
ex usu [L.], by use.
ex vi termini [L.], by the force or meaning of the term or word.
ex voto [L.], according to one's prayer or vow.

F

faber suæ fortunæ [L.], the architect of his own fortune, a self-made man.
fâcheux [Fr.], vexatious; annoying; troublesome.
facies non omnibus una [L.], all have not the same face or features.
facile est inventis addere [L.], it is easy to add to things already invented.
facile princeps [L.], easily preëminent; indisputably the first; the admitted chief.
facilis descensus Averni [L.], the descent to the lower world is easy; the road to evil is easy.
facit indignatio versum [L.], indignation instigates the verse.
façon [Fr.], manner, style.
façon de parler [Fr.], manner of speaking.
facta non verba [L.], deeds not words.
fade [Fr.], insipid; tasteless.
fænum habet in cornu, longe fuge [L.], he has hay upon his horn (of old the sign of a dangerous bull), beware of him.
fæx populi [L.], the dregs of the people.
faire bonne mine [Fr.], to put a good face upon the matter.
faire l'homme d'importance [Fr.], to assume an air of importance.
faire mon devoir [Fr.], to do my duty.
faire sans dire [Fr.], to do, not to say; to act without ostentation.
fait accompli [Fr.], a thing already done.
falsi crimen [L.], the crime of forgery.
falsus in uno, falsus in omnibus [L.], false in one thing, false in all.
fama clamosa [L.], a current scandal; a prevailing report.
fama nihil est celerius [L.], nothing travels swifter than scandal.
fama semper vivat [L.], may his fame endure forever.
far niente [It.], the doing of nothing.
fas est et ab hoste doceri [L.], it is right to be taught even by an enemy.
Fata obstant [L.], the Fates oppose it.
Fata viam invenient [L.], the Fates will find a way.
faux pas [Fr.], a false step; a slip in behavior; a lapse from virtue.
fax mentis incendium gloriæ [L.], the passion for glory is the torch of the mind.
felicitas multos habet amicos [L.], prosperity has many friends.
femme couverte [Fr.], a married woman.
femme de chambre [Fr.], a chamber-maid.
femme galante [Fr.], a gay woman; a courtesan.
femme seule (as a law term, **femme sole**) [Fr.], an unmarried woman.
fendre un cheveu en quatre [Fr.], to split a hair in four; to make a very subtle distinction.
festina lente [L.], hasten slowly.
fête champêtre [Fr.], an open-air festival or entertainment; a rural festival.
feu de joie [Fr.], a fire of joy; a bonfire; a fusillade as a sign of rejoicing.
feuilleton [Fr.], a fly-sheet; a novel or a story appearing in a newspaper.
fiat experimentum in corpore vili [L.], let the trial (or experiment) be made on a worthless subject.
fiat justitia, ruat cælum [L.], let justice be done though the heavens should fall.
fiat lux [L.], let there be light.
fide et amore [L.], by faith and love.
fide et fiducia [L.], by fidelity and confidence.
fide et fortitudine [L.], with faith and fortitude.
fidei coticula crux [L.], the cross is the touchstone of faith.
fidei defensor [L.], defender of the faith.
fideli certa merces [L.], to the faithful one reward is certain.
fide non armis [L.], by faith, not by arms.
fide, sed cui vide [L.], trust, but see whom.
fides et justitia [L.], fidelity and justice.
fides Punica [L.], Punic faith; treachery.
fidus Achates [L.], faithful Achates; i.e. a true friend.
fidus et audax [L.], faithful and bold.
filius nullius [L.], a son of nobody.
filius populi [L.], a son of the people.
filius terræ [L.], a son of the earth; one of low birth.
fille de chambre [Fr.], a chamber-maid.

fille de joie [Fr.], a woman of licentious pleasure; a prostitute.
fille d'honneur [Fr.], a maid of honor.
fin de siècle [Fr.], end of the (nineteenth) century.
finem respice [L.], look to the end.
finis coronat opus [L.], the end crowns the work.
flagrante bello [L.], during hostilities.
flagrante delicto [L.], in the actual commission of the crime.
flamma fumo est proxima [L.], flame is akin to smoke; where there is smoke there is fire.
flâneur [Fr.], a lounger.
flecti, non frangi [L.], to be bent, not broken.
flosculi sententiarum [L.], flowers of fine thoughts.
flux de bouche [Fr.], an inordinate flow of words; garrulity.
foi en tout [Fr.], faith in everything.
foi pour devoir [Fr.], faith for duty.
fons et origo [L.], the source and origin.
forensis strepitus [L.], the clamor of the forum.
forte scutum salus ducum [L.], a strong shield is the safety of leaders.
fortes fortuna juvat [L.], fortune helps the brave.
forti et fideli nihil difficile [L.], nothing is difficult to the brave and faithful.
fortiter et recte [L.], with fortitude and rectitude.
fortiter, fideliter, feliciter [L.], boldly, faithfully, successfully.
fortiter in re [L.], with firmness or resolution in acting.
fortunæ filius [L.], a spoiled child of fortune.
fortuna favet fortibus [L.], fortune favors the bold.
frangas, non flectes [L.], you may break but not bend (me).
fraus pia [L.], a pious fraud.
fripon [Fr.], a rogue; a knave; a cheat.
froides mains, chaud amour [Fr.], cold hands, warm heart.
front à front [Fr.], face to face.
fronti nulla fides [L.], there is no trusting to appearances.
fruges consumere nati [L.], born to consume fruits; born only to eat.
fugit irreparabile tempus [L.], irrecoverable time flies on.
fuimus Troes [L.], we were once Trojans (but Troy has been overthrown).
fuit Ilium [L.], Troy has been (but is now no more).
fulmen brutum [L.], a senseless thunderbolt; striking blindly.
fumum et opes, strepitumque Romæ [L.], the smoke, the show, and the noise of Rome.
functus officio [L.], having performed one's office or duty; hence, out of office.
furor arma ministrat [L.], rage provides arms.
furor loquendi [L.], a rage for speaking.
furor poeticus [L.], poetic fire.
furor scribendi [L.], a rage for writing.
fuyez les dangers de loisir [Fr.], avoid the dangers of leisure.

G

gage d'amour [Fr.], a pledge of love.
gaieté de cœur [Fr.], gaiety of heart.
Gallice [L.], in French.
garçon [Fr.], a boy; a waiter.
garde à cheval [Fr.], a mounted guard.
garde du corps [Fr.], a body-guard.
garde mobile [Fr.], a guard liable to general service.
gardez [Fr.], be on your guard; take care.
gardez bien [Fr.], take good care.
garde la foi [Fr.], keep the faith.
gaudeamus igitur [L.], therefore let us be joyful.
gaudet tentamine virtus [L.], virtue rejoices in temptation.
gaudium certaminis [L.], the joy of conflict.
genius loci [L.], the presiding spirit or genius of the place.
gens d'armes [Fr.], men at arms.
gens de condition [Fr.], people of standing.
gens d'église [Fr.], churchmen.
gens de guerre [Fr.], military men.
gens de lettres [Fr.], literary men.
gens de loi [Fr.], lawyers.
gens de même famille [Fr.], persons of the same family; birds of a feather.
gens de peu [Fr.], the meaner class of people.
gens togata [L.], civilians.
gentilhomme [Fr.], a gentleman.
genus irritabile vatum [L.], the irritable race of poets.
Germanice [L.], in German.
gibier de potence [Fr.], a gallowsbird.
giovine santo, diavolo vecchio [It.], a young saint, an old devil.
gitano [Sp.], a gypsy.
gli assenti hanno torto [It.], the absent are in the wrong.
gloria in excelsis [L.], glory to God in the highest.
gloria Patri [L.], glory be to the Father.
glückliche Reise! [G.], a pleasant journey!
gnothi seauton [Gr.], know thyself.
gobe-mouche [Fr.], a person who has no ideas of his own; a ninny; a trifler.
goût [Fr.], taste; relish.
goutte à goutte [Fr.], drop by drop.
grâce à Dieu [Fr.], thanks to God.
gradu diverso, via una [L.], the same road by different steps.
gradus ad Parnassum [L.], a step to Parnassus; aid in writing Greek or Latin verse.
grande chère et beau feu [Fr.], good cheer and a good fire; comfortable quarters.
grande fortune, grande servitude [Fr.], a great fortune is a great slavery.
grande parure / **grande toilette** [Fr.], full dress.
grand merci [Fr.], many thanks.
gratia placendi [L.], the delight of pleasing.
gratis dictum [L.], mere assertion.
graviora manent [L.], greater afflictions await us, more serious matters remain.
graviora quædam sunt remedia periculis [L.], some remedies are worse than the disease.
grex venalium [L.], a venal rabble.
grosse tête et peu de sens [Fr.], a large head and little sense.
grossièreté [Fr.], coarseness; vulgarity in conversation.
guerra al cuchillo [Sp.], war to the knife.
guerra cominciata, inferno scatenato [It.], war begun, hell unchained.
guerre à mort [Fr.], war to the death.
guerre à outrance [Fr.], war to the uttermost.
gutta cavat lapidem non vi, sed sæpe cadendo [L.], the drop hollows the stone by frequent falling, not by force.

H

habitué [Fr.], one who is in the habit of frequenting a place.
hac lege [L.], on this condition; with this restriction.
hæc olim meminisse juvabit [L.], it will delight us to remember this some day.
Hannibal ad portas [L.], Hannibal before the gates; the enemy close at hand.
hapax legomenon [Gr.], a word or expression occurring once only.
hardi comme un coq sur son fumier [Fr.], bold as a cock on his own dunghill.
haud longis intervallis [L.], at intervals of no great length.
haud passibus æquis [L.], not with equal steps.
haut goût [Fr.], high flavor; elegant taste.
helluo librorum [L.], a devourer of books; a bookworm.
heu pietas! heu prisca fides! [L.], alas for piety! alas for the ancient faith!
hiatus valde deflendus [L.], a hiatus or deficiency much to be regretted.
hic et nunc [L.], here and now.
hic et ubique [L.], here and everywhere.
hic jacet [L.], here lies.
hic labor, hoc opus est [L.], this is a laborious task; this is a toil.
hic sepultus [L.], here buried.
hinc illæ lacrimæ [L.], hence these tears.
hoc opus, hic labor est [L.], same as **hic labor, hoc opus est.**
hodie mihi, cras tibi [L.], mine today, yours tomorrow.
hoi polloi [Gr.], the many; the vulgar; the rabble.
hombre de un libro [Sp.], a man of one book.
hominis est errare [L.], to err is human.
homme d'affaires [Fr.], a businessman.
homme de bien [Fr.], a good man.
homme de lettres [Fr.], a man of letters.
homme d'épée [Fr.], a man of the sword; a soldier.
homme de robe [Fr.], a man in civil office; magistrate.
homme d'esprit [Fr.], a man of wit or genius.
homme d'état [Fr.], a statesman.
homo factus ad unguem [L.], a highly polished man; one finished to the highest degree.
homo homini lupus [L.], man is a wolf to man.
homo multarum litterarum [L.], a man of great learning.
homo sui juris [L.], a man who is his own master.
homo sum; humani nihil a me alienum puto [L.], I am a man; I count nothing that is human indifferent to me.
honi soit qui mal y pense [O. Fr.], shame to him who thinks evil of it; evil to him who evil thinks.
honores mutant mores [L.], honors change men's manners or characters.
honos habet onus [L.], honor brings responsibility.
horæ canonicæ [L.], prescribed hours for prayer; canonical hours.
horas non numero nisi serenas [L.], I number only hours of sunshine. (Motto for a sun dial.)
horresco referens [L.], I shudder as I relate.
horribile dictu [L.], horrible to relate.
hors de combat [Fr.], rendered unable any longer to fight.
hors de concours [Fr.], out of the competition.
hors de la loi [Fr.], in the condition of an outlaw.
hors de propos [Fr.], not to the point or purpose.
hors de saison [Fr.], out of season.
hors d'œuvre [Fr.], out of course; out of order.
hos ego versiculos feci, tulit alter honores [L.], I wrote these lines, another has borne away the honor.
hôtel de ville [Fr.], a townhall; municipal building of a town.
hôtel Dieu [Fr.], a hospital.
hôtel garni [Fr.], a furnished lodging.
humanum est errare [L.], to err is human.
hunc tu Romane caveto [L.], Roman, beware of that man.
hurtar para dar por Dios [Sp.], to steal for the purpose of giving to God (in alms).

I

ich dien [G.], I serve.
ici on parle Français [Fr.], French is spoken here.
idée fixe [Fr.], a fixed idea.
id genus omne [L.], all of that sort or description.
ignorantia legis neminem excusat [L.], ignorance of the law excuses no one.
ignorantio elenchi [L.], ignorance of the point in question; the logical fallacy of arguing to the wrong point.
ignoscito sæpe alteri, nunquam tibi [L.], forgive others often, yourself never.
ignoti nulla cupido [L.], no desire is felt for a thing unknown.
ignotum per ignotius [L.], the unknown (explained) by the still more unknown.
i gran dolori sono muti [It.], great griefs are silent.
il aboie après tout le monde [Fr.], he snarls at everybody.
il a la mer à boire [Fr.], he has the sea to drink up; i.e. all his powers will be taxed to succeed.
il a le diable au corps [Fr.], the devil is in him.
il conduit bien sa barque [Fr.], he steers his boat well; he knows how to get on.
il est plus aisé d'être sage pour les autres, que pour soi-même [Fr.], it is easier to be wise for others than for oneself.
il est plus honteux de se défier de ses amis, que d'en être trompé [Fr.], it is more disgraceful to suspect one's friends than to be deceived by them.
il faut attendre le boiteux [Fr.], it is necessary to wait for the lame man; we must wait for the truth.
il faut de l'argent [Fr.], money is needful.
Ilias malorum [L.], an Iliad of ills; a host of evils.
il n'a ni bouche ni éperon [Fr.], he has neither mouth nor spur; neither wit nor courage.
il n'appartient qu'aux grands hommes d'avoir de grands défauts [Fr.], only great men may have great faults.
il ne faut jamais défier un fou [Fr.], never defy a fool.
il ne faut pas éveiller le chat qui dort [Fr.], it is not wise to awake the cat that sleeps; let sleeping dogs lie.
il n'y a pas de héros pour son valet de chambre [Fr.], no man is a hero in the eyes of his valet.
il penseroso [It.], the pensive man.
il rit bien qui rit le dernier [Fr.], he laughs best who laughs last.
il sent le fagot [Fr.], he smells of the faggot; he is suspected of heresy.
il vaut mieux tâcher d'oublier ses malheurs, que d'en parler [Fr.], it is better to try to forget one's misfortunes, than to talk of them.
imitatores, servum pecus [L.], imitators, a servile herd.
immedicabile vulnus [L.], an incurable wound; irreparable injury.
imo pectore [L.], from the bottom of the breast.
impari Marte [L.], with unequal military strength.
impedimenta [L.], travelers' luggage; the baggage of an army.
imperium in imperio [L.], a state within a state, a government within another.
implicite [Fr.], by implication.
impos animi [L.], of weak mind.
in actu [L.], in act or reality.
in æternum [L.], forever.
in ambiguo [L.], in doubt.
in articulo mortis [L.], at the point of death; in the last struggle.
in bianco [It.], in blank; in white.
in camera [L.], in the chamber of the judge; in secret.
in capite [L.], in chief.
in cælo quies [L.], there is rest in heaven.
incredulus odi [L.], being incredulous I cannot endure it.
in curia [L.], in court.
inde iræ [L.], hence these resentments.
Index Expurgatorius [L.], a list of expurgated books (compiled by the Roman Catholic authorities).
Index Prohibitorius [L.], a list of prohibited books (prohibited to Roman Catholics).
in dubio [L.], in doubt.
in equilibrio [L.], in equilibrium; equally balanced.
in esse [L.], in being; in actuality.
in extenso [L.], at full length.
in extremis [L.], at the point of death.
infandum renovare dolorem [L.], to revive unspeakable grief.
in forma pauperis [L.], as a poor man or pauper.
in foro conscientiæ [L.], before the tribunal of conscience.
infra dignitatem [L.], below one's dignity.
in futuro [L.], in future; henceforth.
in hoc signo spes mea [L.], in this sign is my hope.
in hoc signo vinces [L.], under this sign or standard thou shalt conquer.
in limine [L.], at the threshold.
in loco [L.], in the place; in the passage mentioned; in the natural or proper place.
in loco parentis [L.], in the place of a parent.
in medias res [L.], into the midst of things.
in medio tutissimus ibis [L.], you will go safest in a middle course.
in memoriam [L.], to the memory of; in memory.
in necessariis unitas, in dubiis libertas, in omnibus caritas [L.], in things essential unity, in things doubtful liberty, in all things charity.
in nomine [L.], in the name of.
in nubibus [L.], in the clouds.
in nuce [L.], in a nutshell.
in omnia paratus [L.], prepared for all things.
inopem copia fecit [L.], abundance made him poor.
in ovo [L.], in the egg.
in pace [L.], in peace.
in partibus infidelium [L.], in parts belonging to infidels, or countries not adhering to the Roman Catholic faith.
in perpetuam rei memoriam [L.], in perpetual memory of the thing.
in perpetuum [L.], forever.
in petto [It.], within the breast; in reserve.
in pleno [L.], in full.

in posse [L.], in possible existence; in possibility.

in præsenti [L.], at the present moment.

in propria persona [L.], in one's own person.

in puris naturalibus [L.], purely in a state of nature; quite naked.

in re [L.], in the matter of.

in rerum natura [L.], in the nature of things.

in sæcula sæculorum [L.], for ages on ages.

in sano sensu [L.], in a proper sense.

in situ [L.], in its original situation.

in solo Deo salus [L.], in God alone is safety.

insouciance [Fr.], unconcern; careless indifference.

insouciant [Fr.], unconcerned; indifferent.

instar omnium [L.], equivalent to them all.

in statu quo [L.], in the former state, in the same state as before (some event).

in te, Domine, speravi [L.], in thee, Lord, have I put my trust.

inter alia [L.], among other things.

inter arma silent leges [L.], laws are silent in the midst of arms.

inter canem et lupum [L.], between dog and wolf; at twilight.

interdum vulgus rectum videt [L.], the rabble sometimes see what is right.

inter nos [L.], between ourselves.

inter pocula [L.], at one's cups.

in terrorem [L.], as a means of terrifying; by way of warning.

inter se [L.], among themselves.

inter spem et metum [L.], between hope and fear.

in totidem verbis [L.], in so many words.

in toto [L.], in whole; entirely.

intra muros [L.], within the walls.

in transitu [L.], in course of transit or passage.

intra parietes [L.], within walls; in private.

in usum Delphini [L.], for the use of the Dauphin; applied to editions of the classical authors.

in utramque fortunam paratus [L.], prepared for either fortune (or result).

in utroque fidelis [L.], faithful in both or each (of two).

in vacuo [L.], in empty space; in a vacuum.

inverso ordine [L.], in an inverse order.

in vino veritas [L.], there is truth in wine; truth is told under the influence of intoxicants.

invita Minerva [L.], against the will of Minerva; at variance with one's mental capacity; without genius.

ipse dixit [L.], he himself said it; a dogmatic saying or assertion.

ipsissima verba [L.], the very words.

ipso facto [L.], by the fact itself.

ipso jure [L.], by the law itself.

ira furor brevis est [L.], anger is a short madness.

ir por lana y volver trasquilado [Sp.], to go for wool, and come back shorn.

ita est [L.], it is so.

ita lex scripta [L.], thus the law stands written.

Italice [L.], in the Italian language.

J—K

Jacquerie [Fr.], French peasantry; a revolt of peasants.

jacta est alea [L.], the die is cast.

j'ai bonne cause [Fr.], I have a good cause.

jamais arrière [Fr.], never behind.

jamais bon coureur ne fut pris [Fr.], a good runner is never caught; an old bird is not to be caught with chaff.

januis clausis [L.], with closed doors.

je maintiendrai le droit [Fr.], I will maintain the right.

je me fie en Dieu [Fr.], I trust in God.

je ne sais quoi [Fr.], I know not what; a something or other.

je n'oublierai jamais [Fr.], I shall never forget.

je suis prêt [Fr.], I am ready.

jet d'eau [Fr.], a jet of water; a fountain.

jeu de main [Fr.], horseplay, practical joke.

jeu de mots [Fr.], a play on words; a pun.

jeu d'esprit [Fr.], a display of wit; a witticism.

jeu de théâtre [Fr.], stage-trick; clap-trap.

jeunesse dorée [Fr.], gilded youth; rich young fellows.

je vis en espoir [Fr.], I live in hope.

joci causa [L.], for the sake of a joke.

joli [Fr.], pretty; fine.

jour de fête [Fr.], a feast day.

jour de l'an [Fr.], New Year's day.

jubilate Deo [L.], rejoice in God; be joyful in the Lord.

jucundi acti labores [L.], accomplished labors are pleasant.

judex damnatur cum nocens absolvitur [L.], the judge is condemned when the offender is acquitted.

judicium Dei [L.], the judgment of God.

judicium parium, aut leges terræ [L.], the judgment of our peers or the laws of the land.

juge de paix [Fr.], a justice of peace.

juniores ad labores [L.], the younger men (are fittest) for labors.

jurare in verba magistri [L.], to swear to the words of a master.

jure divino [L.], by divine law.

jure humano [L.], by human law.

juris peritus [L.], skilled in the law; one who is learned in the law.

juris utriusque doctor [L.], doctor of both the civil and canon law.

jus canonicum [L.], the canon law.

jus civile [L.], the civil law.

jus divinum [L.], the divine law.

jus et norma loquendi [L.], the law and rule of speech.

jus gentium [L.], the law of nations.

jus gladii [L.], the right of the sword.

jus possessionis [L.], right of possession.

jus proprietatis [L.], the right of property.

jus summum sæpe summa malitia est [L.], law carried to extremes is often extreme wrong.

juste milieu [Fr.], the golden mean.

justum et tenacem propositi virum [L.], a man upright and tenacious of purpose.

kein Kreuzer, kein Schweizer [G.], no money no Swiss; a proverb of the time when the Swiss were common as mercenaries.

ktema es aei [Gr.], a possession for all time.

L

la beauté sans vertu est une fleur sans parfum [Fr.], beauty without virtue is like a flower without perfume.

labitur et labetur in omne volubilis ævum [L.], it glides on, and will glide on forever. See Rusticus expectat.

laborare est orare [L.], to work is to pray.

labore et honore [L.], by labor and honor.

labor ipse voluptas [L.], labor itself is a pleasure.

labor omnia vincit [L.], labor conquers everything.

laborum dulce lenimen [L.], the sweet solace of our labors.

la bride sur le cou [Fr.], with rein on neck; at full speed.

la critique est aisée, et l'art est difficile [Fr.], criticism is easy, and art is difficult.

l'affaire s'achemine [Fr.], the business is progressing.

la fortune passe partout [Fr.], fortune passes everywhere; all suffer change or vicissitude.

l'allegro [It.], the merry man.

l'amour et la fumée ne peuvent se cacher [Fr.], love and smoke cannot conceal themselves.

lana caprina [L.], goat's wool; hence, a thing of little worth.

langage des halles [Fr.], the language of the markets, profane or foul.

la patience est amère, mais son fruit est doux [Fr.], patience is bitter, but its fruit is sweet.

lapis philosophorum [L.], the philosophers' stone.

la poverta è la madre di tutte le arti [It.], poverty is the mother of all the arts.

la propriété c'est le vol [Fr.], property is robbery.

lapsus calami [L.], a slip of the pen.

lapsus linguæ [L.], a slip of the tongue.

lapsus memoriæ [L.], a slip of the memory.

lares et penates [L.], household gods.

la reyne (or le roy) le veult [Norm. Fr.], the queen (or the king) wills it; the formula expressing the sovereign's assent to a bill.

l'argent [Fr.], money.

lasciate ogni speranza, voi ch'entrate [It.], abandon hope all ye who enter here.

lateat scintillula forsan [L.], perhaps a small spark may lie hid.

latet anguis in herba [L.], a snake lies hid in the grass.

Latine dictum [L.], spoken in Latin.

lauda la moglie e tienti donzello [It.], praise a wife and remain a bachelor.

laudari a viro laudato [L.], praised by one who is himself praised.

laudationes eorum qui sunt ab Homero laudati [L.], praises from those who were themselves praised by Homer.

laudator temporis acti [L.], one who praises time past.

laudum immensa cupido [L.], insatiable desire for praise.

laus Deo [L.], praise to God.

l'avenir [Fr.], the future.

la vertu est la seule noblesse [Fr.], virtue is the only nobility.

le beau monde [Fr.], the fashionable world.

le bon temps viendra [Fr.], the good time will come.

le coût ôte le goût [Fr.], the cost takes away the taste.

lector benevole [L.], kind or gentle reader.

le dessous des cartes [Fr.], the underside of the cards.

le diable boiteux [Fr.], the devil on two sticks or with crutches.

legalis homo [L.], a lawful person, i.e. one not outlawed, infamous, or excommunicated.

legatus a latere [L.], a papal ambassador.

le génie c'est la patience [Fr.], genius is patience.

le grand monarque [Fr.], the great monarch; a name applied to Louis XIV of France.

le grand œuvre [Fr.], the great work; the philosophers' stone.

le jeu ne vaut pas la chandelle [Fr.], the game is not worth the candle; the object is not worth the trouble.

le jour viendra [Fr.], the day will come.

le mieux est l'ennemi du bien [Fr.], the better is the enemy of the good.

le monde est le livre des femmes [Fr.], the world is woman's book.

le monde savant [Fr.], the learned world.

le mot de l'énigme [Fr.], the key to the mystery.

l'empire des lettres [Fr.], the republic (lit. empire) of letters.

leonina societas [L.], partnership with a lion.

le pas [Fr.], precedence in place or rank.

le point du jour [Fr.], daybreak.

le roi est mort, vive le roi! [Fr.], the king is dead, long live the king (his successor)!

le roi et l'état [Fr.], the king and the state.

le roi le veut [Fr.], the king wills it.

le roi s'avisera [Fr.], the king will consider or deliberate.

les absents ont toujours tort [Fr.], the absent are always in the wrong.

les affaires font les hommes [Fr.], business makes men.

les bras croisés [Fr.], with folded arms; idle.

les doux yeux [Fr.], tender glances.

lèse majesté [Fr.], high treason.

les extrêmes se touchent [Fr.], extremes meet.

les murailles ont des oreilles [Fr.], walls have ears.

les plus sages ne le sont pas toujours [Fr.], the wisest are not so always.

le style, c'est l'homme [Fr.], the style is the man.

l'état, c'est moi [Fr.], it is I who am the state.

l'étoile du nord [Fr.], the star of the north.

le tout ensemble [Fr.], the whole together.

lettre de cachet [Fr.], a sealed letter containing private orders; a royal warrant.

lettre de change [Fr.], bill of exchange.

lettre de créance [Fr.], letter of credit.

lettre de marque [Fr.], a letter of marque or reprisal.

levamen probationis [L.], relief from proving.

leve fit quod bene fertur onus [L.], the burden which is well borne becomes light.

le vrai n'est pas toujours vraisemblable [Fr.], the truth is not always probable; truth is stranger than fiction.

lex loci [L.], the law or custom of the place.

lex non scripta [L.], unwritten law; common law.

lex scripta [L.], statute (or written) law.

lex talionis [L.], the law of retaliation.

lex terræ [L.], the law of the land.

l'homme propose, et Dieu dispose [Fr.], man proposes, and God disposes.

libertas et natale solum [L.], liberty and one's native land.

liberum arbitrium [L.], free will.

libraire [Fr.], a bookseller.

licentia vatum [L.], the license of the poets; poetic license.

limæ labor et mora [L.], the labor and delay of the file; the slow and laborious polishing of a literary composition.

l'inconnu [Fr.], the unknown.

l'incroyable [Fr.], the incredible.

lingua franca [It.], the mixed language used between Europeans and orientals in the Levant.

lis litem generat [L.], strife begets strife.

lit de justice [Fr.], a bed of justice; the throne of the king in the parliament of Paris; the sitting of that parliament when the king was present.

litem lite resolvere [L.], to settle strife by strife, to remove one difficulty by introducing another.

lite pendente [L.], during the trial.

littera scripta manet [L.], the written letter remains.

l'occasion fait le larron [Fr.], opportunity makes the thief.

loci communes [L.], common places.

loco citato [L.], in the place or passage cited.

locos y niños dicen la verdad [Sp.], fools and children speak the truth.

locum tenens [L.], one occupying the place of another; a substitute.

locus classicus [L.], a classical passage.

locus criminis [L.], place of the crime.

locus in quo [L.], the place in which.

locus pænitentiæ [L.], place for repentance.

locus sigilli [L.], the place of the seal on a document.

longe aberrat scopo [L.], he goes far from the mark.

longo intervallo [L.], by or with a long interval.

loyal devoir [L.], loyal duty.

loyal en tout [Fr.], loyal in everything.

loyauté m'oblige [Fr.], loyalty binds me.

loyauté n'a honte [Fr.], loyalty has no shame.

lucidus ordo [L.], a lucid arrangement.

lucri causa [L.], for the sake of gain.

lucus a non lucendo [L.], used as typical of an absurd derivation or explanation—**lucus**, meaning *grove*, is wrongly implied to be another form of **lucere**, meaning *to shine*.

ludere cum sacris [L.], to trifle with sacred things.

lupum auribus teneo [L.], I hold a wolf by the ears, i.e. I have caught a tartar.

lupus in fabula [L.], the wolf in the fable.

lupus pilum mutat, non mentem [L.], the wolf changes his coat, not his disposition.

lusus naturæ [L.], a sport or freak of nature.

M

ma chère [Fr.], my dear (fem.).

macte virtute [L.], go on or persevere in virtue.

ma foi [Fr.], upon my faith.

maggiore fretta, minore atto [It.], the more haste the less speed.

magister cæremoniarum [L.], master of the ceremonies.

magna civitas, magna solitudo [L.], a great city is a great solitude.

magnæ spes altera Romæ [L.], another hope of great Rome.

magna est veritas et prevalebit [L.], truth is mighty and will prevail.

magna est vis consuetudinis [L.], great is the force of habit.

magnanimiter crucem sustine [L.], bear the cross nobly.

magnas inter opes inops [L.], poor in the midst of great wealth.

magni nominis umbra [L.], the shadow of a great name.

magnum bonum [L.], a great good.

magnum vectigal est parsimonia [L.], economy is itself a great income.

magnum opus [L.], a great work.

magnus Apollo [L.], great Apollo, i.e. one of great authority.
maigre [Fr.], fasting. See in Dict.
main de justice [Fr.], the hand of justice; the sceptre.
maintien le droit [Fr.], maintain the right.
maison de campagne [Fr.], a country house.
maison de santé [Fr.], a private asylum or hospital.
maison de ville [Fr.], a town-house.
maître des basses œuvres [Fr.], literally, 'master of low works'; i.e. a sewer-cleaner.
maître des hautes œuvres [Fr.], an executioner; a hangman.
maître d'hôtel [Fr.], a house-steward.
maladie du pays [Fr.], home-sickness.
mala fide [L.], with bad faith; treacherously.
mal à propos [Fr.], ill-timed. See in Dict.
mal de dents [Fr.], toothache.
mal de mer [Fr.], sea-sickness.
mal de tête [Fr.], headache.
malentendu [Fr.], a misunderstanding; a mistake.
male parta, male dilabuntur [L.], things ill gotten are consumed without doing any good.
malgré nous [Fr.], in spite of us.
malgré soi [Fr.], in spite of himself.
malheur ne vient jamais seul [Fr.], misfortunes never come singly.
mali exempli [L.], of a bad example.
mali principii malus finis [L.], bad beginnings have bad endings.
malis avibus [L.], with unlucky birds; with bad omens.
malo modo [L.], in a bad manner.
malo mori quam fœdari [L.], I would rather die than be debased.
malpropre [Fr.], slovenly; not neat and clean.
malum in se [L.], evil or an evil in itself.
malum prohibitum [L.], an evil prohibited; evil because prohibited.
malus pudor [L.], false shame.
manet alta mente repostum [L.], it remains deeply fixed in the mind.
manibus pedibusque [L.], with hands and feet.
manu forti [L.], with a strong hand.
manu propria [L.], with one's own hand.
Mardi gras [Fr.], Shrove Tuesday.
mare clausum [L.], a closed sea; a bay.
mariage de conscience [Fr.], a private marriage.
mariage de convenance [Fr.], marriage from motives of material interest rather than of love.
mariage de la main gauche [Fr.], left-handed marriage; a morganatic marriage.
Mars gravior sub pace latet [L.], a severer war lies hidden under peace.
más vale saber que haber [Sp.], better to be wise than to be rich.
más vale ser necio que porfiado [Sp.], better to be a fool than obstinate.
más vale tarde que nunca [Sp.], better late than never.
materfamilias [L.], the mother of a family.
materiam superabit opus [L.], the workmanship will prove superior to the material.
matre pulchra filia pulchrior [L.], a daughter more beautiful than her beautiful mother.
mauvaise honte [Fr.], false modesty.
mauvais goût [Fr.], bad taste.
mauvais sujet [Fr.], a bad subject; a worthless scamp.
maxima debetur puero reverentia [L.], the greatest reverence is due to a boy.
maximus in minimis [L.], very great in trifles.
mea culpa [L.], by my fault.
médecin, guéris-toi toi-même [Fr.], physician, heal thyself.
mediocria firma [L.], moderate or middle things are surest.
medio tutissimus ibis [L.], in a medium course you will be safest.
medium tenuere beati [L.], happy are they who have held the middle course.
mega biblion, mega kakon [Gr.], a great book is a great evil.
me judice [L.], I being judge; in my opinion.
memento mori [L.], remember death.
memor et fidelis [L.], mindful and faithful.
memoria in æterna [L.], in eternal remembrance.
mendacem memorem esse oportet [L.], a liar should have a good memory.
mens agitat molem [L.], mind moves matter.
mens legis [L.], the spirit of the law.
mens sana in corpore sano [L.], a sound mind in a sound body.
mens sibi conscia recti [L.], a mind conscious of its own rectitude.
meo periculo [L.], at my own risk.
meo voto [L.], according to my wish.
merum sal [L.], pure or genuine wit.
mésalliance [Fr.], marriage with one of a lower rank.
meum et tuum [L.], mine and thine.
mihi cura futuri [L.], my care is for the future.
mirabile dictu [L.], wonderful to relate.
mirabile visu [L.], wonderful to see.
mirabilia [L.], wonders.
mirum in modum [L.], in a wonderful manner.
mise en scène [Fr.], the getting up for the stage, or the putting on the stage.
miserabile vulgus [L.], a wretched crew.
miseris succurere disco [L.], I learn to succor the wretched.
mittimus [L.], we send; name of a writ in law. See in Dict.
mobile perpetuum [L.], perpetual motion.
modo et forma [L.], in manner and form.
modus operandi [L.], manner of working.
mole ruit sua [L.], it falls in ruins by its own weight.
mollia tempora fandi [L.], times favorable for speaking.
mon ami [Fr.], my friend.
mon cher [Fr.], my dear (masc.).
montani semper liberi [L.], mountaineers are always free men.
monumentum ære perennius [L.], a monument more lasting than brass.
more Hibernico [L.], after the Irish fashion.
more majorum [L.], after the manner of our ancestors.
more suo [L.], in his own way.
mors janua vitæ [L.], death is the gate of eternal life.
mors omnibus communis [L.], death is common to all.
mos pro lege [L.], custom or usage for law.
mot du guet [Fr.], a watchword.
mots d'usage [Fr.], words in common use.
motu proprio [L.], of his own accord.
mucho en el suelo, poco en el cielo [Sp.], much on earth, little in heaven.
muet comme un poisson [Fr.], dumb as a fish.
multa gemens [L.], with many a groan.
multum in parvo [L.], much in little.
mundus vult decipi [L.], the world wishes to be deceived.
munus Apolline dignum [L.], a gift worthy of Apollo.
muraglia bianca, carta di matto [It.], a white wall is the fool's paper.
murus aeneus conscientia sana [L.], a clear conscience is a firm wall.
mutare vel timere sperno [L.], I scorn to change or to fear.
mutatis mutandis [L.], with the necessary changes.
mutato nomine de te fabula narratur [L.], the name being changed the story is true of yourself.
muta est pictura poema [L.], a picture is a silent poem.
mutuus consensus [L.], mutual consent.

N

naissance [Fr.], birth.
natale solum [L.], native soil.
natura lo fece, e poi ruppe la stampa [It.], nature made him, and then broke the mould.
naturam expellas furca tamen usque recurret [L.], though you drive out Nature with a pitchfork, yet will she ever return.
natura non facit saltum [L.], nature does not make a leap; i.e. nature proceeds slowly.
naviget Anticyram [L.], let him sail to Anticyra (where he will get hellebore to cure him of madness).
nec cupias, nec metuas [L.], neither desire nor fear.
ne cede malis [L.], yield not to misfortune.
necessitas non habet legem [L.], necessity has no law.
nec mora, nec requies [L.], neither delay nor repose.
nec pluribus impar [L.], not an unequal match for numbers.
nec prece, nec pretio [L.], neither by entreaty nor by bribe.
nec quærere, nec spernere honorem [L.], neither to seek nor to contemn honors.
nec scire fas est omnia [L.], it is not permitted to know all things.
nec temere, nec timide [L.], neither rashly nor timidly.
née [Fr.], born; having as her maiden name.
nefasti dies [L.], days on which judgment could not be pronounced, nor assemblies of the people be held; hence, unlucky days.
ne fronti crede [L.], trust not to appearances.
négligé [Fr.], morning dress; an easy loose dress.
ne Jupiter quidem omnibus placet [L.], not even Jupiter pleases everybody.
nel bisogno si conoscono gli amici [It.], a friend in need is a friend indeed.
nemine contradicente [L.], no one speaking in opposition; without opposition.
nemine dissentiente [L.], no one dissenting; without a dissenting voice.
nemo bis punitur pro eodem delicto [L.], no one is twice punished for the same offence.
nemo me impune lacessit [L.], no one assails me with impunity.
nemo mortalium omnibus horis sapit [L.], no one is wise at all times.
nemo repente fuit turpissimus [L.], no one ever became a villain in an instant.
nemo solus sapit [L.], no one is wise alone (with no person to consult).
ne nimium [L.], avoid excess.
ne plus ultra [L.], nothing further; the uttermost point, perfection.
ne puero gladium [L.], intrust not a boy with a sword.
ne quid detrimenti respublica capiat [L.], lest the state receive any detriment.
ne quid nimis [L.], in nothing go too far.
nervi belli pecunia [L.], money is the sinews of war.
nervus probandi [L.], the sinews of the argument.
n'est-ce pas? [Fr.], is it not so?
ne sutor supra crepidam [L.], let not the shoemaker go beyond his last (properly sandal); let no one meddle with what lies beyond his range.
ne tentes, aut perfice [L.], either attempt it not or succeed.
netteté [Fr.], neatness.
ne vile fano [L.], let nothing vile be in the temple.
niaiserie [Fr.], silliness; simplicity.
nicht wahr? [G.], is it not so? am I not right?
ni firmes carta que no leas, ni bebas agua que no veas [Sp.], never sign a paper you have not read, nor drink water you have not examined.
nihil ad rem [L.], nothing to the point.
nihil (properly **nullum**) **quod tetigit non ornavit** [L.], he touched nothing without embellishing it.
nil admirari [L.], to be astonished at nothing.
nil conscire sibi nulla pallescere culpa [L.], to be conscious of no fault, and to turn pale at no accusation.
nil desperandum [L.], there is no reason for despair.
nil nisi cruce [L.], no dependence but on the cross.
ni l'un ni l'autre [Fr.], neither the one nor the other.
nimium ne crede colori [L.], trust not too much to looks (or externals).
n'importe [Fr.], it matters not.
nisi Dominus frustra [L.], unless God be with us all is in vain.
nitor in adversum [L.], I strive against opposition.
nobilitas sola est atque unica virtus [L.], virtue is the true and only nobility.
noblesse oblige [Fr.], rank imposes obligations; much is expected from one in good position.
no es oro todo lo quo reluce [Sp.], all is not gold that glistens.
no hay cerradura si es de oro la ganzúa [Sp.], there is no lock that a golden key will not open.
nolens volens [L.], willing or unwilling.
noli irritare leones [L.], do not irritate lions.
noli me tangere [L.], touch me not.
nolle prosequi [L.], to be unwilling to proceed. See in Dict.
nolo episcopari [L.], I do not wish to be made a bishop.
nom de guerre [Fr.], a war name; an assumed traveling name; pen name.
nom de plume [Fr.], an assumed name of a writer: an English expression formed from the French.
nomina stultorum parietibus hærent [L.], fools' names are stuck upon the walls.
non compos mentis [L.], not of sound mind.
non cuivis homini contingit adire Corinthum [L.], every man has not the fortune to go to Corinth.
non datur tertium [L.], there is not given a third one or a third chance.
non deficiente crumena [L.], the purse not failing; if the money holds out.
non est [L.], it is not; it is wanting or absent.
non est inventus [L.], he has not been found.
non est vivere sed valere vita [L.], life is not merely to live, but to be strong.
non far mai il medico tuo erede [It.], never make your physician your heir.
non ignara mali, miseris succurere disco [L.], not unacquainted with misfortune I learn to succor the wretched.
non libet [L.], it does not please me.
non liquet [L.], the case is not clear or proved.
non mi ricordo [It.], I do not remember.
non multa, sed multum [L.], not many things but much.
non nobis solum [L.], not to ourselves alone.
non nostrum est tantas componere lites [L.], it is not for us to settle such weighty disputes.
nonobstant clameur de haro [Fr.], notwithstanding the hue and cry.
non ogni fiore fa buon odore [It.], not every flower has a sweet perfume.
non omne licitum honestum [L.], not every lawful thing is honorable.
non omnia possumus omnes [L.], we cannot, all of us, do everything.
non omnis moriar [L.], I shall not wholly die.
non quis, sed quid [L.], not who but what, not the person but the deed.
non quo, sed quomodo [L.], not by whom, but in what manner.
non sequitur [L.], it does not follow.
non sibi, sed omnibus [L.], not for self, but for all.
non sibi, sed patriæ [L.], not for himself but for his country.
non sine numine [L.], not without divine aid.
non sum qualis eram [L.], I am not what I once was.
non tali auxilio [L.], not with such aid or help.
nonum prematur in annum [L.], let it be kept back (from publication) till the ninth year.
nosce te ipsum [L.], know thyself.
noscitur a (or **e**) **sociis** [L.], he is known by his companions.
nostro periculo [L.], at our risk.
nota bene [L.], mark well.
Notre Dame [Fr.], Our Lady.
n'oubliez pas [Fr.], don't forget.
nous avons changé tout cela [Fr.], we have changed all that.
nous verrons [Fr.], we shall see.
novus homo [L.], a new man; one who has raised himself from obscurity.
nuance [Fr.], shade; subtle variation.
nudis verbis [L.], in plain words.
nudum pactum [L.], a mere agreement, unconfirmed by writing.
nugæ canoræ [L.], melodious trifles.
nul bien sans peine [Fr.], no pains, no gains.
nulla dies sine linea [L.], not a day without a line; no day without something done.
nulla nuova, buona nuova [It.], no news is good news.
nulli secundus [L.], second to none.
nullius addictus jurare in verba magistri [L.], not bound to swear to the opinions of any master.
nullius filius [L.], a son of nobody; an illegitimate son.
nunc aut nunquam [L.], now or never.
nunquam minus solus, quam cum solus [L.], never less alone than when alone.
nunquam non paratus [L.], never unprepared; always ready.
nuptiæ [L.], nuptials; wedding.

O

obiit [L.], he, or she, died.
obiter dictum [L.], a thing said by the way.
obra de común, obra de ningún [Sp.], everybody's business is nobody's business.
obscurum per obscurius [L.], explaining an obscurity by something more obscure still.
observanda [L.], things to be observed.
obsta principiis [L.], resist the beginnings.
obstupui steteruntque comæ [L.], I was astonished and my hair stood on end.
occasio facit furem [L.], opportunity makes the thief.
occurrent nubes [L.], clouds will intervene.
oderint dum metuant [L.], let them hate provided they fear.
odi profanum vulgus [L.], I loathe the profane rabble.
odium medicum [L.], the hatred of physicians.
odium in longum jacens [L.], hatred long cherished.
odium theologicum [L.], the hatred of theologians.
œil de bœuf [Fr.], a bull's-eye.
œuvres [Fr.], works.
officina gentium [L.], the workshop of the world.
O fortunatos nimium sua si bona norint agricolas [L.], O too happy husbandmen if only they knew their own blessings.
ofrecer mucho especie es de negar [Sp.], to offer much is a kind of denial.
ogni bottega ha la sua malizia [It.], every shop has its tricks; tricks in all trades.
ogni medaglia ha il suo riverso [It.], every medal has its reverse side.
ogniuno per se, e Dio per tutti [It.], every one for himself, and God for all.
ohe! jam satis [L.], hold! enough.
ohne Hast, aber ohne Rast [G.], without haste, but without rest.
olet lucernam [L.], it smells of the lamp ('the midnight oil'); it is a labored production.
omen faustum [L.], a favorable omen.
omne ignotum pro magnifico [L.] whatever is unknown is held to be magnificent.
omnem movere lapidem [L.], to turn every stone; to leave no stone unturned; to make every exertion.
omne solum forti patria [L.], every soil is a brave man's country.
omne trinum perfectum [L.], every perfect thing is threefold.
omne tulit punctum qui miscuit utile dulci [L.], he gains the approval of all who mixes the useful with the agreeable.
omne vivum ex ovo [L.], every living thing comes from an egg (or germ).
omnia ad Dei gloriam [L.], all things for the glory of God.
omnia bona bonis [L.], all things are good to the good.
omnia mutantur, nos et mutamur in illis [L.], all things change, and we change with them.
omnia vincit amor [L.], love conquers all things.
omnia vincit labor [L.], labor overcomes all things.
omnis amans amens [L.], every lover is demented.
on commence par être dupe, on finit par être fripon [Fr.], one begins by being a fool, and ends in becoming a knave.
on connait l'ami au besoin [Fr.], a friend is known in time of need.
operæ pretium est [L.], it is worthwhile.
opprobrium medicorum [L.], the reproach of the doctors.
optimates [L.], men of the first rank. See in Dict.
opus operatum [L.], an effective work or operation. See **Opus**, in Dict.
ora et labora [L.], pray and work.
ora pro nobis [L.], pray for us.
orator fit, poeta nascitur [L.], an orator is made, a poet is born.
ore rotundo [L.], with round full voice.
ore tenus [L.], from the mouth merely.
origo mali [L.], origin of the evil.
oro è che oro vale [It.], that is gold that is worth gold; all is not gold that glitters.
O! si sic omnia [L.], O! if all things were so; O! if he had always so spoken or acted.
O tempora! O mores! [L.], O the times! O the manners!
otia dant vitia [L.], idleness occasions vice.
otiosa sedulitas [L.], idle industry; laborious trifling.
otium cum dignitate [L.], ease with dignity; dignified leisure.
otium sine litteris est mors [L.], leisure without literature is death.
oublier je ne puis [Fr], I can never forget.
ouï-dire [Fr.], hearsay.
ou la chèvre est attachée, il faut qu'elle broute [Fr.], where the goat is tethered, there it must browse.
ouvrage de longue haleine [Fr.], a work of long breath; a work long in being accomplished; a long-winded or tedious business.
ouvrier [Fr.], a workman; an operative.

P

pabulum Acherontis [L.], food for Acheron, or the tomb.
pace [L.], by leave of; not to give offence to.
pace tua [L.], by your leave; with your consent.
pacta conventa [L.], the conditions agreed on.
pactum illicitum [L.], an illegal agreement.
padrone [It.], a master; a landlord.
pallida mors [L.], pale death.
palmam qui meruit ferat [L.], let him who has won the palm wear it.
palma non sine pulvere [L.], the palm is not won without dust; i.e. no success without exertion.
par accès [Fr.], by fits and starts.
par accident [Fr.], by accident or chance.
par accord [Fr.], by agreement; in harmony.
par avion [Fr.], by airplane: French label for air mail.
par ci par là [Fr.], here and there.
par complaisance [Fr.], by complaisance.
par dépit [Fr.], out of spite.
pardonnez-moi [Fr.], pardon me; excuse me.
parem non fert [L.], he suffers no equal.
par excellence [Fr.], by way of eminence.
par exemple [Fr.], by example; for instance.
parfaitement bien [Fr.], perfectly well.
par faveur [Fr.], by favor; with the countenance of.
par force [Fr.], by force.
par hasard [Fr.], by chance.
pari passu [L.], with equal step; together.
paritur pax bello [L.], peace is produced by war.
par le droit du plus fort [Fr.], by the right of the strongest.
par les mêmes voies on ne va pas toujours aux mêmes fins [Fr.], by the same methods we do not always attain the same ends.
parlez du loup, et vous en verrez sa queue [Fr.], speak of the wolf, and you will see his tail; talk of the devil and he will appear.
parlez peu et bien si vous voulez qu'on vous regarde comme un homme de mérite [Fr.], speak little and well if you would be esteemed as a man of merit.
par manière d'acquit [Fr.], by way of acquittal; for form's sake.
par negotiis, neque supra [L.], neither above nor below his business.
par nobile fratrum [L.], a noble pair of brothers; two just alike; the one as good or as bad as the other.
parole d'honneur [Fr.], word of honor.
par oneri [L.], equal to the burden.
par parenthèse [Fr.], by way of parenthesis.
par pari refero [L.], I return like for like; tit for tat.
par précaution [Fr.], by way of precaution.
par privilège [Fr.], by privilege; license.
par rapport [Fr.], by reason of.
pars adversa [L.], the opposite party.
par signe de mépris [Fr.], as a token of contempt.
pars pro toto [L.], part for the whole.
parti [Fr.], a party; person.
particeps criminis [L.], an accomplice in a crime.
particulier [Fr.], a private person.—**en particulier**, in private.
partout [Fr.], everywhere; in all directions.
parturiunt montes, nascetur ridiculus mus [L.], the mountains are in travail, a ridiculous mouse will be brought forth.
parva componere magnis [L.], to compare small things with great.
parva leves capiunt animas [L.], trifles captivate small minds.
parvenu [Fr.], a person of low origin who has risen suddenly to wealth or position.
parvum parva decent [L.], trifles become a little person.
pas [Fr.], a step.
pas à pas on va bien loin [Fr.], step by step one goes a long way.
passé [Fr.], past; out of date.
passe-partout [Fr.], a master-key, passport.
pas seul [Fr.], a dance performed by one person.
passim [L.], everywhere; throughout the book or writing referred to.
pasticcio [It.], patchwork.
paté de foie gras [Fr.], goose-liver paste.
pater patriæ [L.], father of his country.
patience passe science [Fr.], patience surpasses knowledge.
pâtisserie [Fr.], pastry; pastry shop.
patois [Fr.], a provincial dialect; the language of the lower classes.
patres conscripti [L.], the conscript fathers; Roman senators.
patriis virtutibus [L.], by ancestral virtues.
paucis verbis [L.], in a few words.
paulo majora canamus [L.], let us sing of somewhat higher themes.
pax in bello [L.], peace in war.
pax vobiscum [L.], peace be with you.
peccavi [L.], I have sinned.
peine forte et dure [Fr.], strong and severe punishment; a kind of judicial torture.
penchant [Fr.], a strong liking.
pensée [Fr.], a thought.
penetralia [L.], secret or inmost recesses.
per [L.], by; by means of; through.
per [It.], for; through; by.
per ambages [L.], by circuitous ways; hence, by allegory; figuratively; metaphorically.
per angusta ad augusta [L.], through trials to triumphs.
per annum [L.], by the year; annually.
per aspera ad astra [L.], through rough ways to the stars; through suffering to renown.
per baroniam [L.], by right of barony.
per capita [L.], by the head or poll.
per centum [L.], by the hundred.
per contante [It.], for cash.
per conto [It.], upon account.
per contra [L.], contrariwise.
per curiam [L.], by the court.
per diem [L.], by the day; daily.
perdu [Fr.], lost.
pereant qui ante nos nostra dixerunt [L.], deuce take those who said our good things before us.
père de famille [Fr.], the father of a family.
pereunt et imputantur [L.], they (the hours) pass away and are laid to our charge.
per fas et nefas [L.], through right and wrong.
perfervidum ingenium Scotorum [L.], the intense earnestness of Scotsmen.
per gradus [L.], step by step.
periculum in mora [L.], there is danger in delay.
per interim [L.], in the meantime.
perjuria ridet amantium Jupiter [L.], at lovers' perjuries Jove laughs.
per mare per terras [L.], through sea and land.
per mese [It.], by the month.
permitte divis cetæra [L.], leave the rest to the gods.
per pares [L.], by one's peers.
per più strade si va a Roma [It.], there are many roads to Rome.
per saltum [L.], by a leap or jump.
per se [L.], by, or in, itself.
per stirpes [L.], by stocks.
per troppo dibatter la verità si perde [It.], truth is lost by too much controversy.
per viam [L.], by the way of.
petit chaudron, grandes oreilles [Fr.], little pitchers (have) big ears.
petitio principii [L.], a begging of the question.
petit-maître [Fr.], a fop.
peu-à-peu [Fr.], little by little; by degrees.
peu de chose [Fr.], a little thing; a trifle.
peu de gens savent être vieux [Fr.], few people know how to be old.
pezzo [It.], a piece; an Italian coin.
piccolo [It.], small.
pièce de résistance [Fr.], the chief dish of a meal; something substantial by way of entertainment; a substantial joint of meat.
pied-à-terre [Fr.], a resting-place; a temporary lodging.
pietra mossa non fa muschio [It.], a rolling stone gathers no moss.
pinxit [L.], he, or she, painted it.
pis aller [Fr.], the worst or last shift.
piuttosto mendicante che ignorante [It.], better be a beggar than be ignorant.
place aux dames [Fr.], make way for the ladies.
plebs [L.], common people; the multitude.
plein de soi-même [Fr.], full of himself.
plein pouvoir [Fr.], full power or authority.
pleno jure [L.], with full power or authority.
plus aloes quam mellis habet [L.], he has more gall than honey; sarcastic wit.
plus on est de fous, plus on rit [Fr.], the more fools, the more fun.
plus sage que les sages [Fr.], wiser than the wise.
poca barba, poca verguenza [Sp.], little beard, little shame.
poca roba, poco pensiero [It.], little wealth, little care.
poco a poco [It.], little by little.
poeta nascitur, non fit [L.], the poet is born, not made; nature, not study, must form the poet.
point d'appui [Fr.], point of support; prop.
poisson d'avril [Fr.], April fool (lit. April fish).
pondere, non numero [L.], by weight not by number.
pons asinorum [L.], an ass's bridge; a name given to the fifth proposition of the first book of Euclid.
populus vult decipi [L.], the populace wishes to be deceived.
possunt quia posse videntur [L.], they are able because they think they are.
post bellum auxilium [L.], aid after the war.
post cineres gloria venit [L.], after death comes glory.
post equitem sedet atra cura [L.], behind the rider sits black care.
poste restante [Fr.], to be left at the post office till called for: applied to letters.
post hoc ergo propter hoc [L.], after this, therefore on account of this; a non sequitur in argument.
post nubila jubila [L.], after sorrow joy.
post nubila Phœbus [L.], after clouds comes Phœbus, or the sun.
post obitum [L.], after death.
pour acquit [Fr.], received payment; paid; written at the bottom of a discharged account.
pour comble de bonheur [Fr.], as the height of happiness.
pour couper court [Fr.], to cut the matter short.
pour encourager les autres [Fr.], to encourage the others.
pour faire rire [Fr.], to excite laughter.
pour faire visite [Fr.], to pay a visit.
pour passer le temps [Fr.], to pass away the time.
pour prendre congé [Fr.], to take leave: often abbreviated p.p.c. on visiting-cards.
pour se faire valoir [Fr.], to make himself of value.
pour tout potage [Fr.], all that one gets; all that a person is allotted.
pour y parvenir [Fr.], to attain the object.
præcognita [L.], things previously known.
præmonitus, præmunitus [L.], forewarned, forearmed.
præscriptum [L.], a thing prescribed.
prendre la balle au bond [Fr.], to catch the ball as it bounds.
prendre la lune avec les dents [Fr.], to take the moon by the teeth; to aim at impossibilities.
prends moi tel que je suis [Fr.], take me just as I am.
prenez garde [Fr.], beware; look out.
presto maturo, presto marcio [It.], soon ripe, soon rotten.
prêt d'accomplir [Fr.], ready to accomplish.
prêt pour mon pays [Fr.], ready for my country.
preux chevalier [Fr.], a brave knight.
prima donna [It.], the chief female vocalist. See in Dict.

primæ viæ [L.], the first passages; the chief canals of the body.
prima facie [L.], on first sight. See in Dict.
primo [L.], in the first place.
primo uomo [It.], the chief actor or vocalist.
primum mobile [L.], the source of motion, the mainspring.
primus inter pares [L.], first among his peers.
principia, non homines [L.], principles, not men.
principiis obsta [L.], resist the beginnings.
prior tempore, prior jure [L.], first in time, first by right; first come, first served.
pro aris et focis [L.], for our altars and our hearths; for civil and religious liberty.
probatum est [L.], it is proved.
probitas laudatur, et alget [L.], honesty is praised, and is left to starve.
pro bono publico [L.], for the good of the public.
pro confesso [L.], as if conceded.
procul, O procul este, profani [L.], far, far hence, O ye profane!
pro Deo et ecclesia [L.], for God and the church.
pro et contra [L.], for and against.
profanum vulgus [L.], the profane rabble.
pro forma [L.], for the sake of form.
pro hac vice [L.], for this occasion.
proh pudor! [L.], for shame!
projet de loi [Fr.], a legislative bill.
prolétaire [Fr.], member of the lower classes; workingman.
pro memoria [L.], for a memorial.
pro nunc [L.], for the present.
propaganda [L.], the propagation of principles or views. See in Dict.
pro patria [L.], for our country.
propria quæ maribus [L.], things appropriate to males, men, or husbands (a fragment of a rule in old Latin grammars).
propriétaire [Fr.], an owner or proprietor.
pro rata [L.], according to rate or proportion.
pro rege, lege, et grege [L.], for the king, the law, and the people.
pro re nata [L.], for a particular emergency arising.
pro salute animæ [L.], for the health of the soul.
prosit! [L.], a health to you!
pro tanto [L.], for so much; for as far as it goes.
protégé [Fr.], one under the protection of another.
pro virili parte [L.], according to one's power; with all one's might.
prudens futuri [L.], thoughtful of the future.
publice [L.], publicly.
publiciste [Fr.], one who writes on national laws and customs; a publicist.
pugnis et calcibus [L.], with fists and heels; with all one's might.
punctum saliens [L.], a salient or prominent point.
Punica fides [L.], Punic or Carthaginian faith; treachery.

Q

quæ fuerunt vitia, mores sunt [L.], what were once vices are now customs.
quæ nocent, docent [L.], things which injure, instruct; we learn by what we suffer.
qualis ab incepto [L.], the same as at the beginning.
qualis rex, talis grex [L.], like king, like people.
qualis vita, finis ita [L.], as life is, so is its end.
quam diu se bene gesserit [L.], during good behavior.
quand même [Fr.], even though; nevertheless.
quand on ne trouve pas son repos en soi-même, il est inutile de le chercher ailleurs [Fr.], when a man finds no repose in himself, it is futile for him to seek it elsewhere.
quand on voit la chose, on la croit [Fr.], that which one sees he gives credit to.
quandoque bonus dormitat Homerus [L.], even good Homer sometimes nods; the wisest make mistakes.
quanti est sapere [L.], how desirable is wisdom or knowledge.
quantum libet [L.], as much as you please.
quantum meruit [L.], as much as he deserved.
uantum mutatus ab illo! [L.], how changed from what he once was!
quantum sufficit [L.], as much as suffices; a sufficient quantity.
quantum vis [L.], as much as you wish.
que la nuit parait longue à la douleur qui veille! [Fr.], to sleepless grief how long must night appear.
quelque chose [Fr.], something; a trifle.
quelqu'un [Fr.], somebody.
quem deus vult perdere prius dementat [L.], whom a god would destroy he first drives mad.
quem di diligunt adolescens moritur [L.], he whom the gods love dies young.
querelle d'Allemand [Fr.], a German quarrel; a drunken affray.
qui a bu boira [Fr.], the tippler will go on tippling.
quid faciendum? [L.], what is to be done?
qui docet discit [L.], he who teaches learns.
quid pro quo [L.], one thing for another; tit for tat; value received.
quid rides? [L.], why do you laugh?
quién sabe? [Sp.], who knows?
quieta non movere [L.], not to disturb things at rest.
qui facit per alium facit per se [L.], he who acts by another acts by himself.
qu'il soit comme il est desiré [Fr.], let it be as desired.
qui m'aime, aime mon chien [Fr.], love me, love my dog.
qui n'a point de sens à trente ans, n'en aura jamais [Fr.], he who has no sense when thirty years old, will never have any.
qui n'a santé n'a rien [Fr.], he who lacks health lacks everything.
qui nimium probat, nihil probat [L.], he proves nothing who proves too much.
qui non proficit, deficit [L.], he who does not advance goes backward.
qui perd, pèche [Fr.], he who loses, offends; an unsuccessful man is always deemed to be wrong.
quis custodiet ipsos custodes? [L.], who shall keep the keepers themselves?
qui s'excuse s'accuse [Fr.], he who excuses himself accuses himself.
qui tacet consentit [L.], he who is silent gives consent.
qui timide rogat, docet negare [L.], he who asks timidly invites denial.
qui transtulit sustinet [L.], he who transports, supports.
qui va là? [Fr.], who goes there?
qui vive? [Fr.], a challenge: 'Who goes there?'
quoad hoc [L.], to this extent.
quo animo? [L.], with what intention?
quocunque jeceris stabit [L.], wherever you throw it, it will stand.
quocunque modo [L.], in whatever manner.
quocunque nomine [L.], under whatever name.
quod avertat Deus! [L.], which may God avert!
quod bene notandum [L.], which may be especially noticed.
quod bonum, felix, faustumque sit! [L.], and may it be advantageous, fortunate, and favorable!
quod erat demonstrandum [L.], which was to be proved or demonstrated.
quod erat faciendum [L.], which was to be done.
quod non opus est, asse carum est [L.], what is not wanted (or is of no use to a person) is dear at a copper.
quod semper, quod ubique, quod ab omnibus [L.], what (has been believed) always, everywhere, by all.
quod vide [L.], which see; see that reference.
quo Fata vocant [L.], whither the Fates call.
quo jure [L.], by what right?
quo pax et gloria ducunt [L.], where peace and glory lead.
quorum pars magna fui [L.], of whom, or which, I was an important part.
quot homines, tot sententiæ [L.], many men, many minds.

R

raconteur [Fr.], a teller of stories.
railleur [Fr.], a jester; one addicted to raillery.
raison d'état [Fr.], a reason of state.
raison d'être [Fr.], the reason for a thing's existence.
rappel [Fr.], a recall.
rapprochement [Fr.], the act of bringing together.
rara avis in terris, nigroque simillima cygno [L.], a rare bird on earth, and very like a black swan (formerly believed to be nonexistent).
rari nantes in gurgite vasto [L.], swimming here and there on the vast sea.
Rathaus [G.], a townhall.
ratione soli [L.], as regards the soil.
re [L.], in the matter of; in reference to the question of.
Realschule [G.], a real school; a secondary German school giving an education more in modern subjects than in classics.
réchauffé [Fr.], lit. something warmed up; hence old literary material worked up into a new form.
recoje tu heno mientras que el sol luziere [Sp.], make hay while the sun shines.
reconnaissance [Fr.], survey. See Dict.
recte et suaviter [L.], justly and agreeably.
rectus in curia [L.], upright in court; with clean hands.
reçu [Fr.], received; a receipt.
recueil [Fr.], a collection.
reculer pour mieux sauter [Fr.], to go back in order to leap the better.
rédacteur [Fr.], an editor; one who edits or gives literary form to something.
redolet lucerna [L.], it smells of the lamp; it is a labored production.
reductio ad absurdum [L.], the reducing of a supposition or hypothesis to an absurdity.
regium donum [L.], a royal gift; the former annual grant of public money to the Presbyterian ministers of Ireland. See in Dict.
re infecta [L.], the business being unfinished.
relâche [Fr.], intermission; relaxation; respite.
relata refero [L.], I repeat the story as it was given me.
religieux [Fr.], a monk or friar. See in Dict.
religio loci [L.], the religious spirit of the place.
rem acu tetigisti [L.], you have touched the matter with a needle; you have hit the thing exactly.
rem facias, rem; recte si possis, si non quocumque modo rem [L.], make money, money; honestly if you can, if not, make it anyhow.
remisso animo [L.], with mind remiss or listless.
remis velisque [L.], with oars and sails; using every endeavor.
remuda de pasturaje haze bizerros gordos [Sp.], change of pasture makes fat calves.
renascentur [L.], they will be born again.
rencontre [Fr.], an encounter; a hostile meeting.
renommée [Fr.], renown; celebrity.
renovate animos [L.], renew your courage.
renovato nomine [L.], by a revived name.
rentes [Fr.], funds; stocks.
répertoire [Fr.], a list; a stock of songs, dramas, etc., already prepared. See in Dict.
répondez s'il vous plait [Fr.], send an answer if you please.
répondre en Normand [Fr.], to give an evasive answer.
requiescat in pace [L.], may he (or she) rest in peace; **requiescant,** may they.
rerum primordia [L.], the first elements of things.
res angusta domi [L.], narrow circumstances at home.
res est sacra miser [L.], a sufferer is a sacred thing.
res gestæ [L.], things done; exploits.
res judicata [L.], a case or suit already settled.
respice finem [L.], look to the end.
respublica [L.], the commonwealth.
résumé [Fr.], a summary or abstract. See in Dict.
resurgam [L.], I shall rise again.
revanche [Fr.], revenge.
revenons à nos moutons [Fr.], let us return to our sheep; let us return to our subject.
re vera [L.], in truth; in actual fact.
revoir [Fr.], a meeting again; **au revoir,** good-bye until we meet again.
rez-de-chaussée [Fr.], the ground-floor.
rideau d'entr'acte [Fr.], the scene let down between the acts of a play.
ridere in stomacho [L.], to laugh secretly; to laugh in one's sleeve.
ride si sapis [L.], laugh, if you are wise.
rien n'arrive pour rien [Fr.], nothing comes for nothing.
rien n'est beau que le vrai [Fr.], there is nothing beautiful except the truth.
rifacimento [It.], a remaking. See Dict.
rigueur [Fr.], strictness; strict etiquette.
rira bien, qui rira le dernier [Fr.], he laughs well who laughs last.
rire entre cuir et chair [Fr.] }
rire sous cape [Fr.] } to laugh in one's sleeve.
risum teneatis, amici? [L.], could you keep from laughing, friends?
rixatur de lana caprina [L.], he contends about goat's wool; he quarrels about trifles.
robe de chambre [Fr.], a morning-gown or dressing-gown.
robe de nuit [Fr.], a nightgown.
rôle [Fr.], a character represented on the stage. See in Dict.
rôle d'équipage [Fr.], the list of a ship's crew.
roué [Fr.], a man of fashion devoted to sensual pleasure. See in Dict.
rouge et noir [Fr.], red and black, a game of chance. See in Dict.
ruat cælum [L.], let the heavens fall.
rudis indigestaque moles [L.], a rude and undigested mass.
ruit mole sua [L.], it falls to ruin by its own weight.
ruse contre ruse [Fr.], trick against trick; diamond cut diamond.
ruse de guerre [Fr.], a stratagem of war.
rus in urbe [L.], the country in town.
rusticus expectat dum defluat amnis at ille labitur et labetur in omne volubilis ævum [L.], the rustic waits till the river flows past (and ceases to flow), but it glides on and will glide for all time.

S

sa boule est demeurée [Fr.], his bowl has stopped short of the mark; he has failed in his object.
sabreur [Fr.], a brave soldier distinguished for his use of his sabre.
sæpe stylum vertas [L.], often turn the style or pen (and make erasures with the blunt end on the waxen tablets); correct freely (if you wish to produce good literature).
saggio fanciullo è chi conosce il suo vero padre [It.], he is a wise child who knows his own father.
sal Atticum [L.], Attic salt; i.e. wit.
salle [Fr.], a hall; **salle à manger,** a dining-room; **salle de batailles,** a gallery or room decorated with pictures of martial subjects; **salle de réception,** a room in which visitors are received.
salon [Fr.], a saloon or drawing-room; a picture gallery.
salus populi suprema lex est [L.], the welfare of the people is the supreme law.
salve! [L.], hail!
salvo jure [L.], the right being safe; without prejudice to one's rights.
salvo pudore [L.], without offence to modesty.
salvo sensu [L.], the sense being preserved.
sang-froid [Fr.], coolness; indifference. See in Dict.
sang pur [Fr.], pure blood; of aristocratic birth.
sans cérémonie [Fr.], without ceremony or formality.
sans-culotte [Fr.], without breeches. See in Dict.
sans Dieu rien [Fr.], nothing without God.
sans façon [Fr.], without ceremony.
sans pain, sans vin, amour n'est rien [Fr.], without bread, without wine, love is naught.
sans pareil [Fr.], without equal.
sans peine [Fr.], without difficulty.
sans peur et sans reproche [Fr.], without fear and without reproach.
sans rime et sans raison [Fr.], without rhyme or reason.
sans souci [Fr.], without care.
sans tache [Fr.], without spot, stainless.
santé [Fr.], health; **en bonne santé,** in good health; **maison de santé,** a private hospital.
sapere aude [L.], dare to be wise.
sartor resartus [L.], the botcher re-

patched; the tailor re-tailored or mended.
sat cito, si sat bene [L.], soon enough done, if well enough done.
satis dotata si bene morata [L.], well enough dowered, if well principled.
satis eloquentiæ, sapientiæ parum [L.], eloquence enough, but little wisdom.
satis superque [L.], enough, and more than enough.
satis verborum [L.], enough of words; no more need be said.
sat pulchra, si sat bona [L.], she is handsome enough, if good enough.
sauce piquante [Fr.], a pungent sauce; a relish.
sauf et sain [Fr.], safe and sound.
sauve qui peut [Fr.], let him save himself who can.
savoir faire [Fr.], the knowing how to act; tact.
savoir vivre [Fr.], good-breeding; refined manners.
scandalum magnatum [L.], speech or writing defamatory to dignitaries.
scire facias [L.], cause it to be known. See in Dict.
scribendi recte sapere est et principium et fons [L.], the principle and source of good writing is to possess good sense.
scribimus indocti doctique [L.], learned and unlearned, we all write.
sdegno d'amante poco dura [It.], a lover's anger is short-lived.
séance [Fr.]. See in Dict.
secrétaire [Fr.], a secretary; **secrétaire d'état**, a secretary of state.
secret et hardi [Fr.], secret and bold.
secundum artem [L.], according to art or rule; scientifically.
secundum naturam [L.], according to nature.
secundum ordinem [L.], in due order.
secundum usum [L.], according to practice.
sed hæc hactenus [L.], but so far, this will suffice.
seigneur [Fr.], a lord, nobleman; a seignior (which see in Dict.).
se jeter dans l'eau de peur de la pluie [Fr.], to cast oneself into the water out of fear of rain.
selon les règles [Fr.], according to rule.
selon lui [Fr.], according to him.
semel abbas, semper abbas [L.], once an abbot, always an abbot.
semel et simul [L.], once and together.
semel insanivimus omnes [L.], we have all, at some time, been mad.
semel pro semper [L.], once for all.
semper avarus eget [L.], the avaricious is always in want.
semper fidelis [L.], always faithful.
semper idem [L.], always the same.
semper paratus [L.], always ready.
semper timidum scelus [L.], guilt is always timid.
semper vivit in armis [L.], he lives always in arms.
sempre il mal non vien per nuocere [It.], misfortune does not always come to injure.
senatus consultum [L.], a decree of the senate.
senex bis puer [L.], the old man is twice a child.
se non è vero, è ben trovato [It.], if not true, it is cleverly invented (or fabricated).
sensu bono [L.], in a good sense.
sensu malo [L.], in a bad sense.
sequiturque patrem non passibus æquis [L.], he follows his father, but not with equal steps.
sero sed serio [L.], late, but seriously.
sero venientibus ossa [L.], those who come late shall have the bones.
serus in cælum redeas [L.], late may you return to heaven; may you live long.
servabo fidem [L.], I will keep faith.
servare modum [L.], to keep within bounds.
servus servorum Dei [L.], a servant of the servants of God.
sesquipedalia verba [L.], words a foot and a half long.
sic eunt fata hominum [L.], thus go the fates of men.
sic itur ad astra [L.], such is the way to the stars, or to immortality.
sic passim [L.], so here and there throughout; so everywhere.
sic semper tyrannis [L.], ever so to tyrants.
sic transit gloria mundi [L.], thus passes away the glory of this world.
sicut ante [L.], as before.
sicut patribus, sit Deus nobis [L.], as with our fathers, so may God be with us.
sic volo sic jubeo; stat pro ratione voluntas [L.], thus I will, thus I command; let my will stand for a reason.
sic vos non vobis [L.], thus you labor but not for yourselves.
si Deus nobiscum, quis contra nos? [L.], if God be with us, who shall stand against us?
si Dieu n'existait pas, il faudrait l'inventer [Fr.], if God did not exist, it would be necessary to invent him.
si diis placet [L.], if it pleases the gods.
siècle [Fr.], an age; **siècle d'or**, the golden age; **siècles des ténèbres**, the dark ages.
siesta [Sp.], a short nap during the heat of the day.
sile et philosophus esto [L.], be silent and pass for a philosopher.
silentium altum [L.], deep silence.
silent leges inter arma [L.], amidst arms, or in war, laws are silent, or disregarded.
similia similibus curantur [L.], like things are cured by like.
similis simili gaudet [L.], like is pleased with like.
si monumentum quæris circumspice [L.], if you seek his monument, look around you.
simplex munditiis [L.], elegant in simplicity.
sine cura [L.], without charge or care.
sine die [L.], without a day being appointed.
sine dubio [L.], without doubt.
sine mora [L.], without delay.
sine præjudicio [L.], without prejudice.
sine qua non [L.], without which, not.
si nous n'avions point de défauts, nous ne prendrions pas tant de plaisir à en remarquer dans les autres [Fr.], if we had no faults we should not take so much pleasure in remarking those of others.
si parva licet componere magnis [L.], if small things may be compared with great.
siste viator [L.], stop, traveler!
sit tibi terra levis [L.], light lie the earth upon thee.
sit ut est aut non sit [L.], let it be as it is, or not at all.
sit venia verbis [L.], may the words be excused.
si vis pacem, para bellum [L.], if you wish for peace, prepare for war.
sobriquet [Fr.], a nickname. See in Dict.
sœurs de charité [Fr.], sisters of charity.
soi-disant [Fr.], self-styled.
soi-même [Fr.], oneself.
sola nobilitas virtus [L.], virtue the only nobility.
solitudinem faciunt, pacem appellant [L.], they make a wilderness and call it peace.
sottise [Fr.], absurdity; foolishness.
sotto voce [It.], in an undertone.
soubrette [Fr.], a waiting-maid; an actress who plays the part of a waiting-maid, etc.
souffler le chaud et le froid [Fr.], to blow hot and cold.
sous tous les rapports [Fr.], in all respects or relations.
soyez ferme [Fr.], be firm; persevere.
spero meliora [L.], I hope for better things.
spes sibi quisque [L.], let every one hope in himself.
spirituel [Fr.], intellectual; witty.
splendide mendax [L.], nobly untruthful; untrue for a good object.
spolia optima [L.], the choicest of the spoils.
sponte sua [L.], of one's (or its) own accord.
spretæ injuria formæ [L.], the insult of despising her beauty.
stat magni nominis umbra [L.], he stands in the shadow of a mighty name.
stat pro ratione voluntas [L.], will stands in place of reason.
statu quo ante bellum [L.], in the state in which things were before the war.
status quo [L.], the state in which.
sta viator, heroem calcas [L.], halt, traveler, thou standest on a hero's dust.
stemmata quid faciunt? [L.], of what value are pedigrees?
sternitur alieno vulnere [L.], he is slain by a blow aimed at another.
stratum super stratum [L.], layer above layer.
studium immane loquendi [L.], an insatiable desire for talking.
Sturm und Drang [G.], storm and stress.
sua cuique voluptas [L.], every man has his own pleasures.
suaviter in modo, fortiter in re [L.], gentle in manner, resolute in execution (or action).
sub colore juris [L.], under color of law.
sub hoc signo vinces [L.], under this standard you will conquer.
sub judice [L.], still before the judge; under consideration.
sublata causa, tollitur effectus [L.], the cause being removed, the effect ceases.
sub pœna [L.], under a penalty.
sub prætexto juris [L.], under the pretext of justice.
sub rosa [L.], under the rose; secretly.
sub silentio [L.], in silence.
sub specie [L.], under the appearance of.
sub voce [L.], under such or such a word.
succès d'estime [Fr.], success of esteem; success with more prestige than profit.
sufre por saber y trabaja por tener [Sp.], suffer in order to be wise, and labor in order to have.
suggestio falsi [L.], suggestion of falsehood.
sui generis [L.], of its own or of a peculiar kind.
suivez raison [Fr.], follow reason.
summa summarum [L.], the sum total.
summum bonum [L.], the chief good.
summum jus, summa injuria [L.], the rigor of the law is the height of oppression.
sumptibus publicis [L.], at the public expense.
sum quod eris; fui quod es [L.], I am what you will be (dead), I was what you are (alive): inscription on tombstones.
sunt lacrimæ rerum [L.], there are tears for misfortune.
suo Marte [L.], by his own prowess.
suppressio veri, suggestio falsi [L.], a suppression of the truth is the suggestion of a falsehood.
surgit amari aliquid [L.], something bitter arises.
sursum corda! [L.], lift up your hearts!
surtout pas de zèle! [Fr.], above all, no zeal!
suum cuique [L.], to each his own.
suus cuique mos [L.], every one has his particular habit.

T

tabagie [Fr.], a smoking-room.
table à manger [Fr.], a dining-table.
tableau vivant [Fr.], a living picture; the representation of some scene by groups of persons.
table d'hôte [Fr.], a public dinner at a hotel; a meal at a fixed price.
tabula rasa [L.], a smooth or blank tablet.
tâche sans tache [Fr.], a work (or task) without a stain.
tædium vitæ [L.], weariness of life.
taisez-vous [Fr.], be quiet; hold your tongue.
tam Marte quam Minerva [L.], as much by Mars as by Minerva; as much by courage as by skill.
tangere vulnus [L.], to touch the wound.
tantæne animis cælestibus iræ? [L.], can such anger dwell in heavenly minds?
tant mieux [Fr.], so much the better.
tanto buon che val niente [It.], so good as to be good for nothing.
tant pis [Fr.], so much the worse.
tant s'en faut [Fr.], far from it.
tantum vidit Virgilium [L.], he merely saw Virgil; he only looked on the great man.
Te, Deum, laudamus [L.], we praise Thee, O God (or rather, as God).
te judice [L.], you being the judge.
tel brille au second rang qui s'éclipse au premier [Fr.], a man may shine in the second rank, who would be eclipsed in the first.
tel est notre plaisir [Fr.], such is our pleasure.
tel maître, tel valet [Fr.], like master, like man.
tel père, tel fils [Fr.], like father, like son.
telum imbelle, sine ictu [L.], a feeble weapon thrown without effect.
tempora mutantur, nos et mutamur in illis [L.], the times are changing and we with them.
tempori parendum [L.], we must yield to the times.
tempus edax rerum [L.], time the devourer of all things.
tempus fugit [L.], time flies.
tempus ludendi [L.], the time for play.
tempus omnia revelat [L.], time reveals all things.
tenax propositi [L.], tenacious of his purpose.
tenez [Fr.], take it; hold; hark; look here.
tentanda via est [L.], a way must be attempted.
teres atque rotundus [L.], smooth and round; polished and complete.
terminus ad quem [L.], the term or limit to which.
terminus a quo [L.], the term or limit from which.
terræ filius [L.], a son of the earth.
terra firma [L.], solid earth; a secure foothold.
terra incognita [L.], an unknown or unexplored region.
tertium quid [L.], a third something; a nondescript.
tête de famille [Fr.], the head of the house; paterfamilias.
tête de fou ne blanchit jamais [Fr.], the head of a fool never becomes white.
tibi seris, tibi metis [L.], you sow for yourself, you reap for yourself.
tiens à la vérité [Fr.], maintain the truth.
tiens ta foi [Fr.], keep thy faith.
tiers-état [Fr.], the third estate. See in Dict.
timeo Danaos et dona ferentes [L.], I fear the Greeks even when they bring gifts.
tirailleur [Fr.], a sharpshooter; skirmisher. See in Dict.
toga virilis [L.], the manly toga; the dress of manhood.
to kalon [Gr.], the beautiful; the chief good.
tomava la por rosa mas devenia cardo [Sp.], I took her for a rose but she proved to be a thistle.
tombé des nues [Fr.], fallen from the clouds.
ton [Fr.], taste; fashion; high life.
to prepon [Gr.], the becoming (or proper).
tôt gagné, tôt gaspillé [Fr.], soon gained, soon spent.
tot homines, quot sententiæ [L.], so many men, so many opinions.
totidem verbis [L.], in just so many words.
toties quoties [L.], as often as.
totis viribus [L.], with all his might.
toto cælo [L.], by the whole heavens; diametrically opposite.
tôt ou tard [Fr.], sooner or later.
totus, teres, atque rotundus [L.], complete, polished, and rounded.
toujours perdrix [Fr.], always partridges; always the same thing over again.
toujours prêt [Fr.], always ready.
tour de force [Fr.], a feat of strength or skill.
tourner casaque [Fr.], to turn one's coat; to change sides.
tous frais faits [Fr.], all expenses paid.
tout-à-fait [Fr.], wholly; entirely.
tout-à-l'heure [Fr.], instantly.
tout au contraire [Fr.], on the contrary.
tout à vous [Fr.], wholly yours.
tout bien ou rien [Fr.], the whole or nothing.
tout comprendre est tout pardonner [Fr.], to understand all is to forgive all.
tout court [Fr.], quite short; abruptly.
tout de même [Fr.], quite the same.
tout de suite [Fr.], immediately.
tout ensemble [Fr.], the whole together. See in Dict.
tout frais fait [Fr.], all expenses paid.
tout le monde est sage après le coup [Fr.], everybody is wise after the event.
tout mon possible [Fr.], everything in my power.
tout vient de Dieu [Fr.], all things come from God.
traducteur [Fr.], a translator.
traduction [Fr.], a translation.
traduttori traditori [It.], translators are traitors.
trahit sua quemque voluptas [L.], every one is attracted by his own liking.
transeat in exemplum [L.], may it pass into an example or precedent.
travaux forcés [Fr.], hard labor.
tria juncta in uno [L.], three joined in one.
tristesse [Fr.], depression of spirits.
Troja fuit [L.], Troy was; Troy is no more.

Tros Tyriusque mihi nullo discrimine agetur [L.], Trojan and Tyrian—there shall be no distinction so far as I am concerned.
trottoir [Fr.], the pavement; the footway on the side of a street or road.
trouvaille [Fr.], sudden good fortune; a godsend.
truditur dies die [L.], one day is pressed onward by another.
tu ne cede malis [L.], do not thou yield to evils.
tu quoque [L.], thou also; you're another.
tu quoque, Brute! [L.], thou also, Brutus!
tutor et ultor [L.], protector and avenger.
tutte le strade conducono a Roma [It.], all roads lead to Rome.
tuum est [L.], it is your own.

U

uberrima fides [L.], superabounding faith.
ubi bene, ibi patria [L.], where it is well, there is one's country.
ubi jus incertum, ibi jus nullum [L.], where the law is uncertain, there is no law.
ubi lapsus? [L.], where have I fallen?
ubi libertas, ibi patria [L.], where liberty is, there is my country.
ubi mel, ibi apes [L.], where honey is, there are the bees.
ubique [L.], everywhere.
ubique patriam reminisci [L.], to remember our country everywhere.
ubi supra [L.], where above mentioned.
Übung macht den Meister [G.], practice makes the master; practice makes perfect.
ultima ratio regum [L.], the last argument of kings; war.
ultima Thule [L.], remotest Thule; some far distant region.
ultimus Romanorum [L.], the last of the Romans.
ultra licitum [L.], beyond what is allowable.
ultra vires [L.], transcending authority.
una scopa nuova spazza bene [It.], a new broom sweeps clean.
una voce [L.], with one voice, unanimously.
una volta furfante e sempre furfante [It.], once a knave, always a knave.
un bienfait n'est jamais perdu [Fr.], an act of kindness is never lost.
un cabello hace sombra [Sp.], a single hair makes a shadow.
und so weiter [G.], and so forth.
une affaire flambée [Fr.], a gone case.
une fois n'est pas coutume [Fr.], one act does not constitute a habit.
un fait accompli [Fr.], an accomplished fact.
unguibus et rostro [L.], with claws and beak; tooth and nail.
unguis in ulcere [L.], a claw in the wound.
un je servirai [Fr.], one I will serve.
uno animo [L.], with one mind; unanimously.
un sot à triple étage [Fr.], an egregious fool.
un sot trouve toujours un plus sot qui l'admire [Fr.], a fool always finds a greater fool to admire him.
unter vier Augen [G.], under four eyes; between ourselves.
urbem lateritiam invenit, marmoream reliquit [L.], he (Augustus) found the city (Rome) brick, and left it marble.
urbi et orbi [L.], to the city (Rome) and the world.
usque ad aras [L.], to the very altars; to the last extremity.
usque ad nauseam [L.], so as to induce disgust.
usus loquendi [L.], usage in speaking.
ut ameris, amabilis esto [L.], that you may be loved, be lovable.
ut apes geometriam [L.], as bees practice geometry.
utcunque placuerit Deo [L.], as it shall please God.
utile dulci [L.], the useful with the pleasant.
utinam noster esset [L.], would that he were of our party.
ut infra [L.], as below.
uti possidetis [L.], as you now possess; each retaining what he at present holds.
ut pignus amicitiæ [L.], as a pledge of friendship.
ut prosim [L.], that I may do good.
ut quocunque paratus [L.], prepared for every event.
ut supra [L.], as above stated.

V—W—Z

vacuus cantat coram latrone viator [L.], the traveler with an empty purse sings in presence of the highwayman.
vade in pace [L.], go in peace.
væ victis [L.], woe to the vanquished.
vale (sing.), **valete** (pl.) [L.], farewell.
valeat quantum valere potest [L.], let it pass for what it is worth.
valet anchora virtus [L.], virtue serves as an anchor.
valet de chambre [Fr.], a personal attendant; a body-servant.
valet de place [Fr.], a guide for visitors to a place.
valete et plaudite [L.], good-by and applaud us; said by Roman actors at the end of a piece.
variæ lectiones [L.], various readings.
variorum notæ [L.], the notes of various commentators.
varium et mutabile semper femina [L.], woman is ever a changeful and capricious thing.
vaudeville [Fr.], a ballad; a comic opera. See in Dict.
vaurien [Fr.], a worthless fellow.
vedi Napoli e poi muori [It.], see Naples and then die.
vehimur in altum [L.], we are carried out into the deep.
velis et remis [L.], with sails and oars; by every possible means.
vel prece, vel pretio [L.], with either entreaty or payment; for love or money.
veluti in speculum [L.], even as in a mirror.
venalis populus, venalis curia patrum [L.], the people are venal, and the senate is equally venal.
venenum in auro bibitur [L.], poison is drunk from golden vessels.
venia necessitati datur [L.], indulgence is granted to necessity; necessity has no law.
venienti occurrite morbo [L.], meet the coming of the disease; prevention is better than cure.
venit summa dies et ineluctabile tempus [L.], the last day has come, and the inevitable doom.
veni, vidi, vici [L.], I came, I saw, I conquered.
ventis secundis [L.], with favoring winds.
ventre à terre [Fr.], with belly to the ground; at full speed.
vera incessu patuit dea [L.], the real goddess was made manifest by her walk.
vera pro gratiis [L.], truth before favor.
vera prosperità è non necessità [It.], it is true prosperity to have no want.
verbatim et litteratim [L.], word for word and letter for letter.
verbum sat sapienti [L.], a word is enough for a wise man.
verdad es verde [Sp.], truth is green.
veritas odium parit [L.], truth begets hatred.
veritas prevalebit [L.], truth will prevail.
veritas vincit [L.], truth conquers.
veritatis simplex oratio est [L.], the language of truth is simple.
vérité sans peur [Fr.], truth without fear.
ver non semper viret [L.], spring is not always green; as a punning motto of the Vernons, Vernon always flourishes.
vestigia nulla retrorsum [L.], no returning footsteps; no traces backward.
vexata quæstio [L.], a disputed question.
via [L.], by way of. See in Dict.
via crucis, via lucis [L.], the way of the cross, the way of light.
via media [L.], a middle course.
via militaris [L.], a military road.
via trita, via tuta [L.], the beaten path is the safe path.
vice [L.], in the place of. **Vice versa.** See in Dict.
vide et crede [L.], see and believe.
videlicet [L.], namely.
video meliora proboque deteriora sequor [L.], I see and approve the better things, I follow the worse.
videtur [L.], it appears.
vide ut supra [L.], see what is stated above.
vidi tantum [L.], I merely saw him.
vi et armis [L.], by force and arms; by main force; by violence.
vigilate et orate [L.], watch and pray.
vigueur de dessus [Fr.], strength from on high.
vilius argentum est auro, virtutibus aurum [L.], silver is less valuable than gold, and gold than virtue.
vincit amor patriæ [L.], the love of our country prevails.
vincit omnia veritas [L.], truth conquers all things.
vincit qui patitur [L.], he who endures conquers.
vincit qui se vincit [L.], he conquers who conquers himself.
vinculum matrimonii [L.], the bond of marriage.
vindex injuriæ [L.], an avenger of injury.
vino dentro, senno fuori [It.], when the wine is in, the wit is out.
vin ordinaire [Fr.], a cheap wine commonly used in wine-growing countries.
vires acquirit eundo [L.], as it goes it acquires strength (originally said of rumor).
Virgilium vidi tantum [L.], Virgil (or some great man) I merely saw.
virginibus puerisque [L.], for girls and boys.
vir sapit qui pauca loquitor [L.] he is a wise man who says but little.
virtus in actione consistit [L.], virtue consists in action.
virtus in arduis [L.], virtue or courage in difficulties.
virtus incendit vires [L.], virtue kindles strength.
virtus laudatur, et alget [L.], virtue is praised, and suffers from cold.
virtus millia scuta [L.], virtue (or valor) is a thousand shields.
virtus semper viridis [L.], virtue is always green.
virtus sola nobilitat [L.], virtue alone ennobles.
virtus vincit invidiam [L.], virtue overcomes envy or hatred.
virtute et fide [L.], by or with virtue and faith.
virtute et labore [L.], by or with virtue and labor.
virtute non astutia [L.], by virtue (or valor), not by craft.
virtute non verbis [L.], by virtue, not by words.
virtute officii [L.], by virtue of office.
virtute quies [L.], rest or quietude in virtue.
virtute securus [L.], secure through virtue.
virtuti, non armis, fido [L.], I trust to virtue, not to weapons.
virtutis amore [L.], from love of virtue.
virtutis fortuna comes [L.], fortune is the companion of valor or virtue.
virum volitare per ora [L.], to hover on men's lips; to be in everybody's mouth.
vis-à-vis [Fr.], opposite; face to face.
vis comica [L.], comic power or talent.
vis conservatrix naturæ [L.], the preservative power of nature.
vis consili expers mole ruit sua [L.], strength without judgment falls by its own might.
vis inertiæ [L.], the power of inertia; dead resistance to force applied.
vis medicatrix naturæ [L.], the healing power of nature.
vis unita fortior [L.], united power is stronger.
vis vitæ [L.], the vigor of life.
vita brevis, ars longa [L.], life is short, art is long.
vitæ via virtus [L.], virtue, the way of life.
vitam impendere vero [L.], to stake one's life for the truth.
vita sine litteris mors est [L.], life without literature is death.
vivat regina! [L.], long live the queen!
vivat respublica! [L.], long live the republic!
vivat rex! [L.], long live the king!
viva voce [L.], by the living voice; orally.
vive la bagatelle! [Fr.], long live folly!
vive le roi! [Fr.], long live the king!
vive memor leti [L.], live ever mindful of death.
vivere est cogitare [L.], to live is to think.
vive ut vivas [L.], live that you may live.
vive, vale [L.], farewell, be happy.
vivida vis animi [L.], the living force of the mind.
vivit post funera virtus [L.], virtue survives the grave.
vivre ce n'est pas respirer, c'est agir [Fr.], life consists not in breathing, but in doing.
vix ea nostra voco [L.], I scarcely call these things our own.
vixere fortes ante Agamemnona [L.], brave men lived before Agamemnon; great men lived in previous ages.
vogue la galère! [Fr.], let come what may!
voilà! [Fr.], behold! there is; there are.
voilà tout [Fr.], that's all.
voilà une autre chose [Fr.], that's another thing; that is quite a different matter.
voir le dessous des cartes [Fr.], to see the under side of the cards; to be in the secret.
volens et potens [L.], willing and able.
volenti non fit injuria [L.], no injustice is done to the consenting person.
volo, non valeo [L.], I am willing, but unable.
volventibus annis [L.], as the years roll by.
vota vita mea [L.], my life is devoted.
vous y perdrez vos pas [Fr.], you will there lose your steps or labor.
vox et præterea nihil [L.], a voice and nothing more; sound but no sense.
vox faucibus hæsit [L.], his voice, or words, stuck in his throat; he was dumb from astonishment.
vox populi, vox Dei [L.], the voice of the people is the voice of God.
vraisemblance [Fr.], probability; apparent truth.
vulgo [L.], commonly.
vulnus immedicabile [L.], an irreparable injury.
vultus animi janua et tabula [L.], the countenance is the portal and picture of the mind.
vultus est index animi [L.], the countenance is the index of the mind.
Wahrheit gegen Freund und Feind [G.], truth in spite of friend and foe.
Wahrheit und Dichtung. See **Dichtung.**
Zeitgeist [G.], the spirit of the age.
zonam perdidit [L.], he has lost his purse; he is in straitened circumstances.
zum Beispiel [G.], for example.

A DICTIONARY OF SCRIPTURE PROPER NAMES AND FOREIGN WORDS

WITH THEIR MEANING AND PLACE IN THE BIBLE

A

Aaron (ăr'ŏn), light (?). Ex. 4. 14.

Aaronites (ăr'ŏn-īts), descendants of Aaron. 1 Chr. 12. 27.

Abaddon (ȧ-bad'ŏn), destruction. Rev. 9. 11.

Abagtha (ȧ-bag'thȧ), given by fortune. Est. 1. 10.

Abana (ab'ȧ-nȧ), stony. 2 Kin. 5. 12.

Abarim (ab'ȧ-rim), regions beyond. Num. 27. 12.

Abba (ab'ȧ), father. Mark 14. 36.

Abda (ab'dȧ), servant. 1 Kin. 4. 6.

Abdeel (ab'dē-el), same as **Abdiel.** Jer. 36. 26.

Abdi (ab'dī), servant of Jehovah. 1 Chr. 6. 44.

Abdiel (ab'di-el), s. of God. 1 Chr. 5. 15.

Abdon (ab'don), servile. Judg. 12. 13.

Abed-nego (ȧ-bed'nē-gō), servant or worshiper of Nebo. Dan. 1. 7.

Abel (ā'bel), (1) vanity. Gen. 4. 2. (2) A meadow. 2 Sam. 20. 14.

Abel-beth-maachah (ā'bel-beth-mā'-ȧ-chȧ), meadow of the house of Maachah. 1 Kin. 15. 20.

Abel-maim (ā'bel-mā'im), m. of the waters. 2 Chr. 16. 4.

Abel-meholah (ā'bel-mē-hō'lȧ), m. of dancing. Judg. 7. 22.

Abel-mizraim (ā'bel-miz-rā'im), meadow of Egypt. Gen. 50. 11.

Abel-shittim (ā'bel-shit'im), meadow of acacias. Num. 33. 49.

Abez (ā'bez), whiteness. Josh. 19. 20.

Abi (ā'bī), shortened form of **Abiah.** 2 Kin. 18. 2.

Abia (ȧ-bī'ȧ), Greek form of following. Matt. 1. 7.

Abiah (ȧ-bī'ȧ), same as **Abijah.** 2 Kin. 18. 2.

Abi-albon (ā'bī-al'bŏn), father of strength. 2 Sam. 23. 31.

Abiasaph (ȧ-bī'ȧ-saf), f. of gathering. Ex. 6. 24.

Abiathar (ȧ-bī'ȧ-thăr), f. of plenty. 1 Sam. 22. 20.

Abib (ā'bib), an ear of corn, or green ear. Ex. 13. 4.

Abidah (ȧ-bī'dȧ), father of knowledge. Gen. 25. 4.

Abidan (ȧ-bī'dan), f. of a judge. Num. 1. 11.

Abiel (ā'bi-el), f. of strength. 1 Sam. 9. 1.

Abiezer (ā-bi-ē'zẽr), f. of help. Josh. 17. 2.

Abiezrite (ā-bī-ez'rīt), a descendant of Abiezer Judg. 6. 11.

Abigail (ab'i-gāl), father of exultation. 1 Sam. 25. 14.

Abihail (ab'i-hāl), f. of strength. Num. 3. 35.

Abihu (ȧ-bī'hū), He (i.e. God) is my f. Ex. 6. 23.

Abihud (ȧ-bī'hud), f. of Judah. 1 Chr. 8. 3.

Abijah (ȧ-bī'jȧ), f. of Jehovah. 1 Kin. 14. 1.

Abijam (ȧ-bī'jăm), another mode of spelling **Abijah.** 1 Kin. 14. 31.

Abilene (ab-i-lē'nē), a grassy place (?). Luke 3. 1.

Abimael (ȧ-bim'ā-el), father of Mael. Gen. 10. 28.

Abimelech (ȧ-bim'e-lech), f. of the king. Gen. 20. 2.

Abinadab (ȧ-bin'ȧ-dab), f. of nobility. 1 Sam. 7. 1.

Abiner (ab'nẽr), same as **Abner.** 1 Sam. 14. 50.

Abinoam (ȧ-bin'ō-am), f. of pleasantness. Judg. 4. 6.

Abiram (ȧ-bī'răm), f. of loftiness. Num. 16. 1.

Abishag (ab'i-shag), f. of error (?). 1 Kin. 1. 3.

Abishai (ȧ-bish'ā-ī), f. of a gift. 1 Sam. 26. 6.

Abishalom (ȧ-bish'ȧ-lŏm), f. of peace. 1 Kin. 15. 2.

Abishua (ȧ-bish'ū-ȧ), f. of welfare. 1 Chr. 6. 4.

Abishur (ȧ-bī'shūr), f. of the wall. 1 Chr. 2. 28.

Abital (ȧ-bī'tăl), f. of dew. 2 Sam. 3. 4.

Abitub (ȧ-bī'tub), f. of goodness. 1 Chr. 8. 11.

Abiud (ȧ-bī'ud), Greek form of **Abihud.** Matt. 1. 13.

Abner (ab'nẽr), f. of light. 1 Sam. 14. 50.

Abraham (ā'brȧ-ham), f. of a great multitude. Gen. 17. 5.

Abram (ā'brăm), a high f. Gen. 11. 26.

Absalom (ab'sȧ-lŏm), f. of peace. 2 Sam. 3. 3.

Accad (ac'ad), fortress (?). Gen. 10. 10.

Accho (ac'ō), sand-heated. Judg. 1. 31.

Aceldama (ȧ-cel'dȧ-mȧ), field of blood. Acts 1. 19.

Achaia (ȧ-chā'yȧ), Greece. Acts 18. 12.

Achaicus (ȧ-chā'i-cus), belonging to Achaia. 1 Cor. 16. 17.

Achan or **Achar** (ā'chan, ā'chär), troubler. Josh. 7. 18.

Achaz (ā'chaz), Greek form of **Ahaz.** Matt. 1. 9.

Achbor (ach'bor), a mouse. Gen. 36. 38.

Achim (ā'chim), short form of **Jachin** (?). Matt. 1. 14.

Achish (ā'chish), angry (?). 1 Sam. 21. 10.

Achmetha (ach'mē-thȧ), fortress (?). Ezra 6. 2.

Achor (ā'chor), trouble. Josh. 7. 24.

Achsa (ach'sȧ), same as following. 1 Chr. 2. 49.

Achsah (ach'sȧ), anklet. Josh. 15. 16.

Achshaph (ach'shaf), enchantment. Josh. 11. 1.

Achzib (ach'zib), deceit. Josh. 15. 44.

Adadah (ad'ȧ-dȧ), festival (?). Josh. 15. 22.

Adah (ā'dȧ), ornament. Gen. 4. 19.

Adaiah (ȧ-dā'yȧ), whom Jehovah adorns. 2 Kin. 22. 1.

Adalia (ȧ-dā'li-ȧ), upright (?). Est. 9. 8.

Adam (ad'ăm), red. Gen. 2. 19.

Adamah (ad'ȧ-mȧ), red earth. Josh. 19. 36.

Adami (ad'ȧ-mī), human. Josh. 19. 33.

Adar (ā'där), fire (?). Est. 3. 7.

Adbeel (ad'bē-el), miracle of God (?). Gen. 25. 13.

Addan (ad'ăn), humble (?). Ezra 2. 59.

Addar (ad'är), greatness (?). 1 Chr. 8. 3.

Addi (ad'ī), ornament (?). Luke 3. 28.

Addon (ad'on), same as **Addan.** Neh. 7. 61.

Ader (ā'dẽr), flock. 1 Chr. 8. 15.

Adiel (ā'di-el), ornament of God. 1 Chr. 4. 36.

Adin (ā'din), slender. Ezra 2. 15.

Adina (ad'i-nȧ), same as preceding. 1 Chr. 11. 42.

Adino (ad'i-nō). 2 Sam. 23. 8.

Adithaim (ad-i-thā'im), twofold ornament. Josh. 15. 36.

Adlai (ad'lā-ī), just. 1 Chr. 27. 29.

Admah (ad'mȧ), same as **Adamah.** Gen. 10. 19.

Admatha (ad'mȧ-thȧ). Est. 1. 14.

Adna (ad'nȧ), pleasure. Ezra 10. 30.

Adnah, same as preceding. 2 Chr. 17. 14.

Adoni-bezek (ȧ-dō'nī-bē'zek), lord of Bezek. Judg. 1. 5.

Adonijah (ad-ō-nī'jȧ), Jehovah is my Lord. 2 Sam. 3. 4.

Adonikam (ad-ō-nī'kam), lord of enemies. Ezra 2. 13.

Adoniram (ad-ō-nī'răm), lord of height. 1 Kin. 4. 6.

Adoni-zedec (ȧ-dō'nī-zē'dec), lord of justice. Josh. 10. 1.

Adoraim (ad-ō-rā'im), two chiefs (?). 2 Chr. 11. 9.

Adoram (ȧ-dō'răm), contracted from **Adoniram.** 2 Sam. 20. 24.

Adrammelech (ȧ-dram'me-lech), magnificence of the king (?), king of fire (?). 2 Kin. 17. 31.

Adramyttium (ad-rȧ-myt'ti-um). Acts 27. 2.

Adria (ā'dri-ȧ). Acts 27. 27.

Adriel (ā'dri-el), flock of God. 1 Sam. 18. 19.

Adullam (ȧ-dul'ăm), justice of the people. Josh. 12. 15.

Adullamite (ȧ-dul'ȧ-mīt), a native of Adullam. Gen. 38. 1.

Adummim (ȧ-dum'im), the red (men?). Josh. 15. 7.

Æneas (ē-nē'ăs), praiseworthy (?). Acts 9. 33.

Ænon (ē'non), springs. John 3. 23.

Agabus (ag'ȧ-bus), probably Greek form of **Hagab.** Acts 11. 28.

Agag (ā'gag), flaming (?). Num. 24. 7.

Agagite (ag'ȧ-gīt). Est. 3. 1.

Agar (ā'gär), same as **Hagar.** Gal. 4. 24.

Agee (ā'gē), fugitive (?). 2 Sam. 23. 11.

Agrippa (ȧ-grip'ȧ). Acts 25. 13.

Agur (ā'gūr), an assembler. Prov. 30. 1.

Ahab (ā'hab), uncle. 1 Kin. 16. 29.

Aharah (ȧ-har'ȧ), after the brother. 1 Chr. 8. 1.

Aharhel (ȧ-här'hel), behind the breastwork. 1 Chr. 4. 8.

Ahasai (ȧ-hā'sī), probably a corruption of **Jahzerah.** Neh. 11. 13.

Ahasbai (ȧ-has'bī). 2 Sam. 23. 34.

Ahasuerus (ȧ-has'ū-ē'rus), king (?). Est. 1. 1.

Ahava (ȧ-hā'vȧ). Ezra 8. 15.

Ahaz (ā'haz), possessor. 2 Kin. 15. 38.

Ahaziah (ā'hȧ-zī'ȧ), whom Jehovah upholds. 1 Kin. 22. 40.

Ahban (ā'ban), brotherly. 1 Chr. 2. 29.

Aher (ā'hẽr), following. 1 Chr. 7. 12.

Ahi (ā'hī), brother. 1 Chr. 5. 15.

Ahiah (ȧ-hī'ȧ), brother of Jehovah. 1 Sam. 14. 3.

Ahiam (ȧ-hī'ăm), b. of the father (?). 2 Sam. 23. 33.

Ahian (ȧ-hī'ăn), brotherly. 1 Chr. 7. 19.

Ahiezer (ā'hī-ē'zẽr), brother of help. Num. 1. 12.

Ahihud (ȧ-hī'hud), b. of (?). Num. 34. 27.

Ahijah (ȧ-hī'jȧ), same as **Ahiah.** 1 Kin. 11. 29.

Ahikam (ȧ-hī'kam), b. of the enemy. 2. Kin. 22. 12.

Ahilud (ȧ-hī'lud), b. of one born. 2 Sam. 8. 16.

Ahimaaz (ȧ-him'ā-az), b. of anger. 2 Sam. 15. 27.

Ahiman (ȧ-hī'măn), b. of a gift. Num. 13. 22.

Ahimelech (ȧ-him'e-lech), b. of the king. 1 Sam. 21. 1.

Ahimoth (ȧ-hī'moth), b. of death. 1 Chr. 6. 25.

Ahinadab (ȧ-hin'ȧ-dab), b. of a nobleman. 1 Kin. 4. 14.

Ahinoam (ȧ-hin'ō-am), b. of grace. 1 Sam. 14. 50.

Ahio (ȧ-hī'ō), brotherly. 2 Sam. 6. 3.

Ahira (ȧ-hī'rȧ), b. of a wicked man. Num. 1. 15.

Ahiram (ȧ-hī'răm), b. of a tall man. Num. 26. 38.

Ahiramite (ȧ-hī'rȧ-mīt), a descendant of Ahiram. Num. 26. 38.

Ahisamach (ȧ-his'ȧ-mach), b. of aid. Ex. 31. 6.

Ahishahar (ȧ-hish'ȧ-här), b. of the dawn. 1 Chr. 7. 10.

Ahishar (ȧ-hī'shär), b. of the singer. 1 Kin. 4. 6.

Ahithophel (ȧ-hith'ō-fel), b. of impiety. 2 Sam. 15. 12.

Ahitub (ȧ-hī'tub), b. of goodness. 1 Sam. 14. 3.

Ahlab (ä'lab), fertility. Judg. 1. 31.

Ahlai (ä'lī), sweet (?). 1 Chr. 2. 31.

Ahoah (ȧ-hō'ȧ), same as **Ahijah** (?). 1 Chr. 8. 4.

Ahohite (ȧ-hō'hīt), a descendant of Ahoah. 2 Sam. 23. 9.

Aholah (ȧ-hō'lȧ), (she has) her own tent. Ezek. 23. 4.

Aholiab (ȧ-hō'li-ab), father's tent. Ex. 31. 6.

Aholibah (ȧ-hol'i-bȧ), my tent is in her. Ezek. 23. 4.

Aholibamah (ȧ-hol'i-bā'mȧ), tent of the high place. Gen. 36. 2.

Ahumai (ȧ-hū'mī), brother of (i. e. dweller near) water. 1 Chr. 4. 2.

Ahuzam (ȧ-hū'zam), their possession. 1 Chr. 4. 6.

Ahuzzath (ȧ-huz'ath), possession. Gen. 26. 26.

Ai (ā'ī), a heap of ruins. Josh. 7. 2.

Aiah (ā-ī'ȧ), hawk. 2 Sam. 3. 7.

Aiath (ā-ī'ath), ruins. Is. 10. 28.

Aija (ā-ī'jȧ), same as **Ai.** Neh. 11. 31.

Aijalon (ā'jȧ-lon), place of gazelles. Josh. 21. 24.

Aijeleth Shahar (ā'je-leth shā'här), morning hind. Ps. 22 title.

Ain (ā'īn), an eye, or fountain. Num. 34. 11.

Ajah (ā'jȧ), same as **Aiah.** Gen. 36. 24.

Ajalon (aj'ȧ-lon), same as **Aijalon.** Josh. 19. 42.

Akan (ā'kan). Gen. 36. 27.

Akkub (ak'ub), insidious. 1 Chr. 3. 24.

Akrabbim (ak-rab'im), scorpions. Num. 34. 4.

Alameth (al'ȧ-meth), covering. 1 Chr. 7. 8.

Alammelech (ȧ-lam'e-lech), king's oak. Josh. 19. 26.

Alamoth (al'ȧ-moth), virgins (?). Ps. 46 title.

Alemeth (al'ē-meth), same as **Alameth.** 1 Chr. 8. 36.

Alexander (al-eg-zan'dẽr), defending men. Mark 15. 21.

Alexandria (al-eg-zan'dri-ȧ), the city named after Alexander. Acts 18. 24.

Aliah (ȧ-lī'ȧ), same as **Alvah.** 1 Chr. 1. 51.

Alian (al'i-ăn), same as **Alvan.** 1 Chr. 1. 40.

Alleluia (al-e-lū'yȧ), praise ye the Lord. Rev. 19. 1.

Allon (al'ŏn), an oak. 1 Chr. 4. 37.

Allon-bachuth (al-ŏn-bach'uth), oak of weeping. Gen. 35. 8.

Almodad (al-mō'dad), extension (?). Gen. 10. 26.

Almon (al'mŏn), hidden. Josh. 21. 18.

Almon-diblathaim (al'mŏn-dib'lȧ-thā'im), hiding of the two cakes (?). Num. 33. 46.

Aloth (ā'loth), yielding milk (?). 1 Kin. 4. 16.

Alpha (al'fȧ), the first letter of the Greek alphabet. Rev. 1. 8.

Alphæus (al-fē'us), successor. Matt. 10. 3.

Al-taschith (al-tas'chith), do not destroy. Ps. 57 title.

Alush (ā'lush). Num. 33. 13.

Alvah (al'vȧ). Gen. 36. 40.

Alvan (al'văn), tall. Gen. 36. 23.

Amad (ā'mad), eternal people (?). Josh. 19. 26.

Amal (ā'măl), labor, sorrow. 1 Chr. 7. 35.

Amalek (am'ȧ-lek). Gen. 36. 12.

Amalekites (am'ȧ-lek-īts), descendants of Amalek. Gen. 14. 7.

Amam (ā'mam), metropolis (?). Josh. 15. 26.

Amana (ȧ-mā'nȧ), fixed (?). S. of Sol. 4. 8.

Amariah (am-ȧ-rī'ȧ), Jehovah has said. 1 Chr. 6. 7.

Amasa (am'ȧ-sȧ), burden. 2 Sam. 17. 25.

Amasai (ȧ-mas'ā-ī), burdensome. 1 Chr. 6. 25.

Amashai (ȧ-mash'ā-ī). Neh. 11. 13.

Amasiah (am-ȧ-sī'ȧ), burden of Jehovah. 2 Chr. 17. 16.

Amaziah (am-ȧ-zī'ȧ), Jehovah strengthens. 2 Kin. 14. 1.

Ami (ā'mī), probably same as **Amon.** Ezra 2. 57.

Aminadab (ȧ-min'ȧ-dab), same as **Amminadab.** Matt. 1. 4.

Amittai (ȧ-mit'ī), true. 2 Kin. 14. 25.

Ammah (am'ȧ). 2 Sam. 2. 24.

Ammi (am'ī), my people. Hos. 2. 1.

Ammiel (am'i-el), people of God. Num. 13. 12.

Ammihud (ȧ-mī'hud), p. of praise (?). Num. 1. 10.

Amminadab (ȧ-min'ȧ-dab), p. of the prince. Ex. 6. 23.

Amminadib (ȧ-min'ȧ-dib), same as preceding. S. of Sol. 6. 12.

Ammishaddai (am-i-shad'ī), p. of the Almighty. Num. 1. 12.

Ammizabad (ȧ-miz'ȧ-bad), p. of the giver (i.e. Jehovah). 1 Chr. 27. 6.
Ammon (am'ŏn), son of my p. (?). Gen. 19. 38.
Ammonites (am'ŏn-īts), a tribe descended from Ammon. Deut. 2. 20.
Ammonitess (am'ŏn-ī-tes), feminine of preceding. 2 Chr. 12. 13.
Amnon (am'non), faithful. 2 Sam. 3. 2.
Amok (ā'mok), deep. Neh. 12. 7.
Amon (ā'mon). 2 Kin. 21. 18.
Amorite (am'ō-rīt), mountaineer. Gen. 10. 16.
Amos (ā'mŏs), burden. Amos 1. 1.
Amoz (ā'moz), strong. Is. 1. 1.
Amphipolis (am-fip'ō-lis), named from the river Strymon flowing around the city. Acts 17. 1.
Amplias (am'pli-ăs), short form of Ampliatus, enlarged. Rom. 16. 8.
Amram (am'ram), people of the Highest (i. e. God). Ex. 6. 18.
Amramites (am'ram-īts), the descendants of Amram. Num. 3. 27.
Amraphel (am'rȧ-fel). Gen. 14. 1.
Amzi (am'zī), strong. 1 Chr. 6. 46.
Anab (ā'nab), place fertile in grapes. Josh. 11. 21.
Anah (ā'nȧ). Gen. 36. 2.
Anaharath (ȧ-nā'hȧ-rath). Josh. 19. 19.
Anaiah (ȧ-nī'ȧ), Jehovah has answered. Neh. 8. 4.
Anak (ā'nak), long-necked (?). Num. 13. 22.
Anakim (an'ȧ-kim), a tribe called after Anak. Deut. 1. 28.
Anamim (an'ȧ-mim). Gen. 10. 13.
Anammelech (ȧ-nam'e-leçh), idol of the king (?), or shepherd and flock (?). 2 Kin. 17. 31.
Anan (ā'nan), a cloud. Neh. 10. 26.
Anani (ȧ-nā'nī), shortened form of **Ananiah.** 1 Chr. 3. 24.
Ananiah (an-ȧ-nī'ȧ), whom Jehovah covers. Neh. 3. 23.
Ananias (an-ȧ-nī'ăs), Greek form of **Hananiah.** Acts 5. 1.
Anath (ā'nath), an answer to prayer. Judg. 3. 31.
Anathema (ȧ-nath'ē-mȧ), something accursed. 1 Cor. 16. 22.
Anathoth (an'ȧ-thoth), answers to prayer. Josh. 21. 18.
Andrew (an'drů). Mark 1. 29.
Andronicus (an-drō-nī'çus). Rom. 16. 7.
Anem (ā'nem), same as **En-gannim** (?). 1 Chr. 6. 73.
Aner (ā'nẽr), a young man (?). Gen. 14. 13.
Anethothite (an'ē-thoth-īt) or **Anetothite** (an'ē-toth-īt), a man of Anathoth. 2 Sam. 23. 27.
Aniam (ȧ-nī'ăm). 1 Chr. 7. 19.
Anim (ā'nim), fountains. Josh. 15. 50.
Anna (an'ȧ), grace. Luke 2. 36.
Annas (an'ăs), Greek form of **Hananiah.** Luke 3. 2.
Antichrist (an'ti-çhrīst), adversary to Christ. 1 John 2. 18.
Antioch (an'ti-oçh), named in honor of Antiochus. Acts 6. 5.
Antipas (an'ti-pas), contraction of Antipater. Rev. 2. 13.
Antipatris (an-tip'ȧ-tris), from the foregoing. Acts 23. 31.
Antothijah (an-tō-thī'jȧ), prayers answered by Jehovah (?). 1 Chr. 8. 24.
Antothite (an'tŏth-īt), a man of Anathoth. 1 Chr. 11. 28.
Anub (ā'nub), bound together (?). 1 Chr. 4. 8.
Apelles (ȧ-pel'ēş). Rom. 16. 10.
Apharsachites (ȧ-fär'săçh-īts). Ezra 5. 6.
Aphek (ā'fek), strength. Josh. 12. 18.
Aphekah (ȧ-fē'kȧ), same as preceding. Josh. 15. 53.
Aphiah (ȧ-fī'ȧ). 1 Sam. 9. 1.
Aphik (ā'fik), same as **Aphek.** Judg. 1. 31.
Aphrah (af'rȧ), dust. Mic. 1. 10.
Aphses (af'sēş), dispersion. 1 Chr. 24. 15.
Apollonia (ap'ŏl-ō'ni-ȧ). Acts 17. 1.
Apollos (ȧ-pol'ŏs), another form of Apollonius or Apollodorus. Acts 18. 24.
Apollyon (ȧ-pol'yŏn), one that exterminates. Rev. 9. 11.
Appaim (ap'ā-im), the nostrils. 1 Chr. 2. 30.
Apphia (af'i-ȧ), the Greek form of Appia. Philem. 2.
Appii forum (ap'i-ī fō'rum), forum or market-place of Appius. Acts 28. 15.
Aquila (ak'wil-ȧ), an eagle. Acts 18. 2.
Ar (är), city. Num. 21. 15.
Ara (ā'rȧ), lion (?). 1 Chr. 7. 38.
Arab (ā'rab), ambush. Josh. 15. 52.
Arabah (ar'ȧ-bȧ), a plain. Josh. 18. 18.
Arabia (ȧ-rā'bi-ȧ). Gal. 1. 17.
Arabian (ȧ-rā'bi-ăn), a person from Arabia. Neh. 2. 19.
Arad (ā'rad), wild ass. 1 Chr. 8. 15.
Arah (ā'rȧ), wandering. 1 Chr. 7. 39.
Aram (ā'ram), height. Gen. 10. 22.
Aramitess (ar'ȧ-mī-tes), a female inhabitant of Aram. 1 Chr. 7. 14.
Aran (ā'răn), wild goat. Gen. 36. 28.
Ararat (ar'ȧ-rat). Gen. 8. 4.
Araunah (ȧ-rą'nȧ), calf (?). 2 Sam. 24. 18.
Arba, or **Arbah** (är'bȧ). Gen. 35. 27.
Arbathite (är'bȧ-thīt). 1 Chr. 11. 32.
Arbel, see **Beth-arbel.**
Arbite (är'bīt), an inhabitant of Arab. 2 Sam. 23. 35.
Archelaus (är-çhē-lā'us), prince. Matt. 2. 22.
Archevites (är'çhē-vīts), the men of Erech (?), q. v. Ezra 4. 9.
Archi (är'çhī), an inhabitant of Erech. Josh. 16. 2.
Archippus (är-çhip'us), master of the horse. Col. 4. 17.
Archite (är'çhīt), a native of Erech. 2 Sam. 15. 32.
Arcturus (ärç-tū'rus), probably the constellations known as the Great and Little Bear. Job 9. 9.
Ard (ärd), fugitive (?). Gen. 46. 21.
Ardites (ärd'īts), descendants of Ard. Num. 26. 40.
Ardon (är'don), fugitive. 1 Chr. 2. 18.
Areli (ȧ-rē'lī), heroic. Gen. 46. 16.
Arelites (ā'rel-īts), a family descended from Areli. Num. 26. 17.
Areopagite (ar-ē-op'ȧ-ġīt), belonging to the Council held on Areopagus. Acts 17. 34.
Areopagus (ar-ē-op'ȧ-gus), hill of Mars. Acts 17. 19.
Aretas (ar'ē-tas), a husbandman (?). 2 Cor. 11. 32.
Argob (är'gob), a rocky district. Deut. 3. 4.
Aridai (ȧ-rid'ā-ī). Est. 9. 9.
Aridatha (ȧ-rid'ȧ-thȧ). Est. 9. 8.
Arieh (ȧ-rī'e), lion. 2 Kin. 15. 25.
Ariel (ār'i-el), lion of God. Ezra 8. 16.
Arimathæa (ar'i-mȧ-thē'ȧ), the same as **Ramah.** Matt. 27. 57.
Arioch (ar'i-oçh). Gen. 14. 1.
Arisai (ȧ-ris'ā-ī). Est. 9. 9.
Aristarchus (ar-is-tarçh'us), best ruling. Acts 19. 29.
Aristobulus (ȧ-ris'to-bū'lus), best counsellor. Rom. 16. 10.
Arkite (ärk'īt), fugitive (?). Gen. 10. 17.
Armageddon (är-mȧ-ged'ŏn), height of Megiddo. Rev. 16. 16.
Armenia (är-mē'ni-ȧ), land of Aram. 2 Kin. 19. 37.
Armoni (är-mō'nī), belonging to a palace. 2 Sam. 21. 8.
Arnan (är'năn), active. 1 Chr. 3. 21.
Arnon (är'non), swift. Num. 21. 13.
Arod (ā'rod), wild ass. Num. 26. 17.
Arodi (ar'ō-dī), same as preceding. Gen. 46. 16.
Arodites (ar'ō-dīts), descendants of Arod. Num. 26. 17.
Aroer (ȧ-rō'ẽr), ruins (?). Deut. 2. 36.
Aroerite (ȧ-rō'ẽr-īt), a man of Aroer. 1 Chr. 11. 44.
Arpad (är'pad). 2 Kin. 18. 34.
Arphad (är'fad), same as preceding. Is. 36. 19.
Arphaxad (är-fak'sad). Gen. 10. 22.
Artaxerxes (är-tȧ-zẽrk'sēş), honored king (?). Ezra 4. 8.
Artemas (är'tē-măs), shortened form of Artemidorus (?). Tit. 3. 12.
Aruboth (ȧ-rů'bōth), windows. 1 Kin. 4. 10.
Arumah (ȧ-rů'mȧ), elevated. Judg. 9. 41.
Arvad (är'vad), wandering. Ezek. 27. 8.
Arvadites (är'văd-īts), inhabitants of Arvad. Gen. 10. 18.
Arza (är'zȧ), earth. 1 Kin. 16. 9.
Asa (ā'sȧ), physician. 1 Kin. 15. 8.
Asahel (as'ȧ-hel), whom God made. 2 Sam. 2. 18.
Asahiah (as'ȧ-hī'ȧ). 2 Kin. 22. 12.
Asaiah (ȧ-sā'yȧ). 1 Chr. 4. 36.
Asaph (ā'saf), collector. 2 Kin. 18. 18; 1 Chr. 6. 39.
Asareel (ȧ-sā'rē-el), whom God has bound. 1 Chr. 4. 16.
Asarelah (as-ȧ-rē'lȧ), same as **Jesharelah.** 1 Chr. 25. 2.
Asenath (as'ē-nath), she who is of Neith (i.e. a goddess of the Egyptians) (?). Gen. 41. 45.
Aser (ā'sẽr), same as **Asher.** Luke 2. 36.
Ashan (ā'shăn), smoke. Josh. 15. 42.
Ashbea (ash'bē-ȧ), I conjure. 1 Chr. 4. 21.
Ashbel (ash'bel), blame (?). Gen. 46. 21.
Ashbelites (ash'bel-īts), the descendants of Ashbel. Num. 26. 38.
Ashchenaz (ash'çhē-naz), same as **Ashkenaz.** 1 Chr. 1. 6.
Ashdod (ash'dod), a strong place. Josh. 15. 46.
Ashdodites (ash'dod-īts), the inhabitants of Ashdod. Neh. 4. 7.
Ashdoth-pisgah (ash'doth-piş'gȧ), springs of Pisgah. Josh. 12. 3.
Ashdothites (ash'doth-īts), same as **Ashdodites.** Josh. 13. 3.
Asher (ash'ẽr), fortunate, happy. Gen. 30. 13.
Asherah (ȧ-shē'rȧ), the goddess Ashtoreth. 2 Kin. 17. 10.
Asherites (ash'ẽr-īts), descendants of Asher. Judg. 1. 32.
Ashima (ȧ-shī'mȧ). 2 Kin. 17. 30.
Ashkelon (ash'kē-lon), migration. Judg. 14. 19.
Ashkenaz (ash'kē-naz). Gen. 10. 3.
Ashnah (ash'nȧ), strong. Josh. 15. 33.
Ashpenaz (ash'pē-naz). Dan. 1. 3.
Ashriel (ash'ri-el), same as **Asriel.** 1 Chr. 7. 14.
Ashtaroth (ash'tȧ-roth), statues of Ashtoreth. Josh. 9. 10.
Ashterathite (ash'tē-rath-īt), a native of Ashteroth. 1 Chr. 11. 44.
Ashteroth-karnaim (ash'tē-roth-kär-nā'im), Ashteroth of the two horns. Gen. 14.5.
Ashtoreth (ash'tō-reth), she who enriches. 1 Kin. 11. 5.
Ashur (ash'ūr). 1 Chr. 2. 24.
Ashurites (ash'ūr-īts). 2 Sam. 2. 9.
Ashvath (ash'vath). 1 Chr. 7. 33.
Asia (ā'zȧ). Acts 2. 9.
Asiel (ā'si-el), created by God. 1 Chr. 4. 35.
Askelon, see **Ashkelon.** Judg. 1. 18.
Asnah (as'nȧ), bramble. Ezra 2. 50.
Asnapper (as-nap'ẽr), same as Assurbani-pal. Assur has formed a son. Ezra 4. 10.
Aspatha (as-pā'thȧ). Est. 9. 7.
Asriel (as'ri-el), the prohibition of God. Num. 26. 31.
Asrielites (as'ri-el-īts), the family of Asriel. Num. 26. 31.
Asshur (ăs'shůr), the gracious One (?). Gen. 10. 22.
Asshurim (ȧ-shůr'im). Gen. 25. 3.
Assir (as'īr), captive. Ex. 6. 24.
Assos (as'os). Acts 20. 13.
Assyria (ȧ-syr'i-ȧ), the land so named from Asshur. Gen. 2. 14.
Assyrians (ȧ-syr'i-ănş), inhabitants of Assyria. Is. 10. 5.
Astaroth (as'tȧ-roth), same as **Ashtoreth.** Deut. 1. 4.
Asuppim (ȧ-sup'im). 1 Chr. 26. 15.
Asyncritus (ȧ-siń'çri-tus), incomparable. Rom. 16. 14.
Atad (ā'tad), buckthorn. Gen. 50. 10.
Atarah (at'ȧ-rä), a crown. 1 Chr. 2. 26.
Ataroth (at'ȧ-roth), crowns. Num. 32. 3.
Ater (ā'tẽr), bound, shut up. Ezra 2. 16.
Athach (ā'thaçh), lodging-place. 1 Sam. 30. 30.
Athaiah (ȧ-thā'yȧ), whom Jehovah made (?). Neh. 11. 4.
Athaliah (ath-ȧ-lī'ȧ), whom Jehovah has afflicted. 2 Kin. 8. 26.
Athenians (ȧ-thē'ni-ănş), natives of Athens. Acts 17. 21.
Athens (ath'enş). Acts 17. 15.
Athlai (ath'lā-ī), shortened form of **Athalain.** Ezra 10. 28.
Atroth (at'roth), same as **Ataroth.** Num. 32. 35.
Attai (at'ā-ī), opportune. 1 Chr. 2. 35.
Attalia (at-ȧ-lī'ȧ), so called from Attalus, the royal founder of the city. Acts 14. 25.
Augustus (ą-gus'tus), venerable. Luke 2. 1.
Ava (ā'vȧ). 2 Kin. 17. 24.
Aven (ā'ven), nothingness. Ezek. 30. 17.
Avim (ā'vim), ruins. Josh. 18. 23.
Avith (ā'vith). Gen. 36. 35.
Azal (ā'zal), root of a mountain. Zech. 14. 5.
Azaliah (az-ȧ-lī'ȧ), whom Jehovah has reserved. 2 Kin. 22. 3.
Azaniah (az-ȧ-nī'ȧ), whom Jehovah hears. Neh. 10. 9.
Azarael (ȧ-zā'rā-el), whom God helps. Neh. 12. 36.
Azareel (ȧ-zā'rē-el), same as preceding. 1 Chr. 12. 6.
Azariah (az-ȧ-rī'ȧ), whom Jehovah aids. 2 Chr. 22. 6.
Azaz (ā'zaz), strong. 1 Chr. 5. 8.
Azaziah (az-ȧ-zī'ȧ), whom Jehovah strengthened. 1 Chr. 15. 21.
Azbuk (az'buk). Neh. 3. 16.
Azekah (ȧ-zē'kȧ), dug over. Josh. 10. 10.
Azel (ā'zel), noble. 1 Chr. 8. 37.
Azem (ā'zem), strength, bone. Josh. 15. 29.
Azgad (az'gad), strong in fortune. Ezra 2. 12.
Aziel (ā'zi-el), whom God strengthens. 1 Chr. 15. 20.
Aziza (ȧ-zī'zȧ), strong. Ezra 10. 27.
Azmaveth (az-mā'veth), strength (?). 2 Sam. 23. 31.
Azmon (az'mon), robust. Num. 34. 4.
Aznoth-tabor (az'noth-tā'bọr), ears (i.e. summits) of Tabor. Josh. 19. 34.
Azor (ā'zọr), helper. Matt. 1. 13.
Azotus (ȧ-zō'tus), the Greek form of **Ashdod.** Acts 8. 40.
Azriel (az'ri-el), help of God. 1 Chr. 5. 24.
Azrikam (az'ri-kam), help against an enemy. 1 Chr. 3. 23.
Azubah (ȧ-zū'bȧ), forsaken. 1 Kin. 22. 42.
Azur (ā'zūr), same as **Azor.** Jer. 28. 1.
Azzah (az'ȧ), strong, fortified. Deut. 2. 23.
Azzan (az'ăn), strong. Num. 34. 26.
Azzur (az'ūr), same as **Azor.** Neh. 10. 17.

B

Baal (bā'ăl), lord, master, possessor, owner. Num. 22. 41.
Baalah (bā'ȧ-lȧ), mistress. Josh. 15. 10.
Baalath (bā'ăl-ăth), same as preceding. Josh. 19. 44.
Baalath-beer (bā'ăl-ăth-bē'ẽr), having a well. Josh. 19. 8.
Baal-berith (bā'ăl-bē'rith), lord of covenant. Judg. 8. 33.
Baale (bā'ȧ-lē), plural of Baal. 2 Sam. 6. 2.
Baal-gad (bā'ăl-gad), lord of fortune. Josh. 11. 17.
Baal-hamon (bā'ăl-hā'mŏn), place of a multitude. S. of Sol. 8. 11.
Baal-hanan (bā'ăl-hā'năn), lord of benignity. Gen. 36. 38.
Baal-hazor (bā'ăl-hā'zọr), having a village. 2 Sam. 13. 23.
Baal-hermon (bā'ăl-hẽr'mŏn), place of Hermon. Judg. 3. 3.
Baali (bā'ȧ-lī), my lord. Hos. 2. 16.
Baalim (bā'ȧ-lim), lords. Judg. 2. 11.
Baalis (bā'ȧ-lis). Jer. 40. 14.
Baal-meon (bā'ăl-mē'on), place of habitation. Num. 32. 38.
Baal-peor (bā'ăl-pē'ọr), lord of the opening. Num. 25. 3.
Baal-perazim (bā'ăl-pē-rā'zim), place of breaches. 2 Sam. 5. 20.
Baal-shalisha (bā'ăl-shal'i-shȧ), lord (or place) of Shalisha. 2 Kin. 4. 42.
Baal-tamar (bā'ăl-tā'mär), place of palm trees. Judg. 20. 33.
Baal-zebub (bā'ăl-zē'bub), lord of flies. 2 Kin. 1. 2.
Baal-zephon (bā'ăl-zē'fon), place of Zephon, or sacred to Zephon. Ex. 14. 2.
Baana (bā'ȧ-nȧ). 1 Kin. 4. 12.
Baanah (bā'ȧ-nȧ). 2 Sam. 4. 2.
Baara (bā'ȧ-rȧ), foolish. 1 Chr. 8. 8.
Baaseiah (bā-ȧ-sē'yȧ), work of Jehovah. 1 Chr. 6. 40.
Baasha (bā'ȧ-shȧ), wicked (?). 1 Kin. 15. 16.
Babel (bā'bel), confusion. Gen. 11. 9.
Babylon (bab'y-lŏn), Greek form of **Babel.** 2 Kin. 20. 12.
Babylonish (bab'y-lōn-ish), of, or belonging to, Babylon. Josh. 7. 21.
Baca (bā'çȧ), weeping. Ps. 84. 6.
Bachrites (baçh'rīts), the family of Becher. Num. 26. 35.
Baharumite (bȧ-hā'rum-īt), an inhabitant of Bahurim. 1 Chr. 11. 33.
Bahurim (bȧ-hū'rim), (town of) young men. 2 Sam. 16. 5.
Bajith (bā'jith), (same as Beth), house. Is. 15. 2.
Bakbakkar (bak-bak'ăr). 1 Chr. 9. 15.
Bakbuk (bak'buk), a bottle. Ezra 2. 51.
Bakbukiah (bak-bū-kī'ȧ), emptying (i.e. wasting) of Jehovah. Neh. 11. 17.
Balaam (bā'lăm), destruction (?). Num. 22. 5.
Balac (bā'laç), same as **Balak.** Rev. 2. 14.
Baladan (bal'ȧ-dan), He has given a son. 2 Kin. 20. 12.
Balah (bā'lȧ). Josh. 19. 3.
Balak (bā'lak), to make empty. Num. 22. 2.
Bamah (bä'mä), high place. Ezek. 20. 29.
Bamoth (bā'moth), high places. Num. 21. 19.
Bamoth-baal (bā'moth-bā'ăl), h. p. of Baal. Josh. 13. 17.

Bani (bā'nī), built. 2 Sam. 23. 36.
Barabbas (bȧ-rab'ȧs), son of Abba or father. Mark 15. 7.
Barachel (bar'ȧ-çhel), whom God blessed. Job 32. 6.
Barachias (bar-ȧ-çhī'ȧs), whom Jehovah blesses. Matt. 23. 35.
Barak (bâr'ăk), thunderbolt, lightning. Judg. 4. 6.
Barhumite (bär-hū'mīt), same as **Baharumite.** 2 Sam. 23. 31.
Bariah (bȧ-rī'ȧ), a fugitive. 1 Chr. 3. 22.
Bar-jesus (bär-jē'ṣus), son of Jesus. Acts 13. 6.
Bar-jona (bär-jō'nȧ), son of Jona. Matt. 16. 17.
Barkos (bär'kos), painter (?). Ezra 2. 53.
Barnabas (bär'nȧ-bȧs), son of exhortation. Acts 4. 36.
Barsabas (bär'sȧ-bȧs), s. of Seba. Acts 1. 23
Bartholomew (bär-thol'ō-mū), s. of Talmai. Matt. 10. 3.
Bartimæus (bär-ti-mē'us), s. of Timai. Mark 10. 46.
Baruch (bâr'uçh), blessed. Jer. 32. 12.
Barzillai (bär-zil'ā-ī), of iron. 2 Sam. 17. 27.
Bashan (bā'shan), soft rich soil. Num. 21. 33.
Bashan-havoth-jair (bā'shan-hā'-voth-jā'ir), Bashan of the villages of Jair. Deut. 3. 14.
Bashemath (bash'ē-math), sweet-smelling. Gen. 26. 34.
Basmath (bas'math), same as **Bashemath.** 1 Kin. 4. 15.
Bath-rabbim (bath'rab-im), daughter of many. S. of Sol. 7. 4.
Bath-sheba (bath'shē-bȧ), d. of the oath. 2 Sam. 11. 3.
Bath-shua (bath'shū-ȧ). 1 Chr. 3. 5.
Bavai (bav'ā-ī). Neh. 3. 18.
Bazlith (baz'lith), a making naked (?). Neh. 7. 54.
Bazluth (baz'luth), same as **Bazlith.** Ezra 2. 52.
Bealiah (bē-ȧ-lī'ȧ), whom Jehovah rules. 1 Chr. 12. 5.
Bealoth (bē'ȧ-loth), citizens (?), plural of Baalah. Josh. 15. 24.
Bebai (bē'bā-ī). Ezra 8. 11.
Becher (bē'çhēr), a young camel. Gen. 46. 21.
Bechorath (bē-çhō'rath), offspring of the first birth. 1 Sam. 9. 1.
Bedad (bē'dad), separation, part. Gen. 36. 35.
Bedan (bē'dan), son of Dan (?). 1 Sam. 12. 11.
Bedeiah (bē-dē'yȧ). Ezra 10. 35.
Beeliada (bē-ē-lī'ȧ-dȧ), whom Baal has known. 1 Chr. 14. 7.
Beelzebub (bē-el'zē-bub), same as **Baal-zebub.** Matt. 10. 25.
Beer (bē'ēr), a well. Num. 21. 16.
Beera (bē-ē'rȧ), same as **Beer.** 1 Chr. 7. 37.
Beerah (bē-ē'rȧ), same as **Beer.** 1 Chr. 5. 6.
Beer-elim (bē-ēr-ē'lim), w. of heroes. Is. 15. 8.
Beeri (bē-ē'rī), man of the w. Gen. 26. 34.
Beer-lahai-roi (bē'ēr-lȧ-hī'roi), w. of vision (of God) to the living. Gen. 16. 14.
Beeroth (bē-ē'roth), wells. Josh. 9. 17.
Beerothite (bē-ē'roth-īt), a native of Beeroth. 2 Sam. 23. 37.
Beer-sheba (bē-ēr-shē'bȧ), well of the oath. Gen. 21. 31.
Beesh-terah (bē-esh'tē-rȧ), house or temple of Astarte (?). Josh. 21. 27.
Behemoth (bē-hē'moth), the water-ox. Job 40. 15.
Bekah (bē'kȧ), part, half. Ex. 38. 26.
Bel (bel), another form of **Baal.** Is. 46. 1.
Bela (bē'lȧ), destruction. Gen. 14. 2.
Belah (bē'lȧ), same as **Bela.** Gen. 46. 21.
Belaites (bē'lā-īts), descendants of Bela. Num. 26. 38.
Belial (bē'li-ăl), worthless. Deut. 13. 13.
Belshazzar (bel-shaz'ăr), Bel protects. Dan. 5. 1.
Belteshazzar (bel-tē-shaz'ăr), preserve his life. Dan. 1. 7.
Ben (ben), son. 1 Chr. 15. 18.
Benaiah (bē-nā'yȧ), whom Jehovah has built. 2 Sam. 8. 18.
Ben-ammi (ben-am'ī), son of my own kindred. Gen. 19. 38.
Bene-berak (ben-ē-bē'rak), sons of Barak, or of lightning. Josh. 19. 45.
Bene-jaakan (ben-ē-jā'ȧ-kăn), s. of Jaakan. Num. 33. 31.
Ben-hadad (ben-hā'dad), s. of Hadad. 1 Kin. 15. 18.
Ben-hail (ben-hā'il), s. of the host. 2 Chr. 17. 7.
Ben-hanan (ben-hā'năn), s. of one who is gracious. 1 Chr. 4. 20.
Beninu (bē-nī'nū), our s. Neh. 10. 13.
Benjamin (ben'jȧ-min), s. of the right hand (i.e. fortunate). Gen. 35. 18.
Benjamite (ben'jȧ-mīt), a man of the tribe of Benjamin. Judg. 20. 35.
Beno (bē'nō), his s. 1 Chr. 24. 26.
Ben-oni (ben-ō'nī), s. of my sorrow. Gen. 35. 18.
Ben-zoheth (ben-zō'heth), s. of Zoheth. 1 Chr. 4. 20.
Beon (bē'on), contracted from **Baal-meon.** Num. 32. 3.
Beor (bē'or). Gen. 36. 32.
Bera (bē'rȧ). Gen. 14. 2.
Berachah (ber'ȧ-çhä), blessing. 1 Chr. 12. 3.
Berachiah (ber-ȧ-çhī'ȧ), whom Jehovah hath blessed. 1 Chr. 6. 39.
Beraiah (ber-ā-ī'ȧ), whom Jehovah created. 1 Chr. 8. 21.
Berea (bē'rē-ȧ). Acts 17. 10.
Berechiah (ber-ē-çhī'ȧ), same as **Berachiah.** 1 Chr. 3. 20.
Bered (bē'red), hail. Gen. 16. 14.
Beri (bē'rī), man of the well. 1 Chr. 7. 36.
Beriah (bē-rī'ȧ), in evil (?). Gen. 46. 17.
Beriites (bē-rī'īts), descendants of Beriah. Num. 26. 44.
Berites (bē'rīts). 2 Sam. 20. 14.
Berith (bē'rith), a covenant. Judg. 9. 46.
Bernice (bēr-nī'cē), Victoria. Acts 25. 13.
Berodach-baladan (bē-rō'daçh-bal'ȧ-dan), Berodach (same as **Merodach**) has given a son. 2 Kin. 20. 12.
Berothah (bē-rō'thȧ), wells. Ezek. 47. 16.
Berothai (bē-rō'thī), my wells. 2 Sam. 8. 8.
Berothite (bē'roth-īt), same as **Beerothite.** 1 Chr. 11. 39.
Besai (bē'sī), sword (?), or victory (?). Ezra 2. 49.
Besodeiah (bes-ō-dē'yȧ), in the secret of Jehovah. Neh. 3. 6.
Besor (bē'sor), cool. 1 Sam. 30. 9.
Betah (bē'tȧ), confidence. 2 Sam. 8. 8.
Beten (bē'ten). Josh. 19. 25.
Bethabara (beth-ab'ȧ-rȧ), house of passage. John 1. 28.
Beth-anath (beth-ā'nath), echo. Josh. 19. 38.
Beth-anoth (beth-ā'noth), Beit Ainun. Josh. 15. 59.
Bethany (beth'ȧ-ny), house of dates. Matt. 21. 17.
Beth-arabah (beth-ar'ȧ-bȧ), house of the desert. Josh. 15. 6.
Beth-aram (beth-ā'răm), h. of the height. Josh. 13. 27.
Beth-arbel (beth-är'bel), h. of the ambush of God. Hos. 10. 14.
Beth-aven (beth-ā'ven), h. of vanity (i. e. of idols). Josh. 7. 2.
Beth-azmaveth (beth'az-mā'veth), h. of strength. Neh. 7. 28.
Beth-baal-meon (beth'bā'ăl-mē'on), h. of Baal-meon. Josh. 13. 17.
Beth-barah (beth-bâr'ȧ), same as **Bethabara.** Judg. 7. 24.
Beth-birei (beth-bir'ē-ī), h. of my creation. 1 Chr. 4. 31.
Beth-car (beth-çär'), h. of pasture. 1 Sam. 7. 11.
Beth-dagon (beth-dā'gon), h. of Dagon. Josh. 16. 41.
Beth-diblathaim (beth'dib-lȧ-thā'-im), h. of the two cakes. Jer. 48. 22.
Beth-el (beth'el), h. of God. Gen. 12. 8.
Bethelite (beth'el-īt), a native of Bethel. 1 Kin. 16. 34.
Beth-emek (beth-ē'mek), h. of the valley. Josh. 19. 27.
Bether (bē'thēr), separation. S. of Sol. 2. 17.
Bethesda (bē-theṣ'dȧ), house of mercy. John 5. 2.
Beth-ezel (beth-ē'zel), h. of firmness (?). Mic. 1. 11.
Beth-gader (beth-gā'dēr), h. of the wall. 1 Chr. 2. 51.
Beth-gamul (beth-gā'mul), h. of the weaned. Jer. 48. 23.
Beth-haccerem (beth-haç'cē-rem), h. of the vineyard. Neh. 3. 14.
Beth-haran (beth-hā'răn). Num. 32. 36.
Beth-hoglah (beth-hog'lȧ), h. of the partridge. Josh. 15. 6.
Beth-horon (beth-hō'ron), h. of the hollow. Josh. 10. 10.
Beth-jesimoth (beth-jes'i-moth), h. of the deserts. Num. 33. 49.
Beth-lebaoth (beth-lē-bā'oth), h. of lionesses. Josh. 19. 6.
Beth-lehem (beth'lē-hem), h. of bread. Gen. 35. 19.
Beth-lehem Ephratah (beth'lē-hem ef'rȧ-tȧ), B. the fruitful (?). Mic. 5. 2.
Bethlehemite (beth'lē-hem-īt), a man of Bethlehem. 1 Sam. 16. 1.
Beth-lehem-Judah (beth'lē-hem-jū'-dȧ), B. of Judah. Judg. 17. 7.
Beth-maachah (beth-mā'ȧ-çhȧ), house of Maachah. 2 Sam. 20. 14.
Beth-marcaboth (beth-mär'ça-both), h. of chariots. Josh. 19. 5.
Beth-meon (beth-mē'on), h. of habitation. Jer. 48. 23.
Beth-nimrah (beth-nim'rȧ), h. of sweet water. Num. 32. 36.
Beth-palet (beth-pā'let), h. of escape or of Palet. Josh. 15. 27.
Beth-pazzez (beth-paz'ez), h. of dispersion. Josh. 19. 21.
Beth-peor (beth-pē'or), temple of Peor. Deut. 3. 29.
Bethphage (beth'fȧ-ġē), house of unripe figs. Matt. 21. 1.
Beth-phelet (beth-fē'let), same as **Beth-palet.** Neh. 11. 26.
Beth-rapha (beth-rā'fȧ), house of Rapha. 1 Chr. 4. 12.
Beth-rehob (beth-rē'hob), h. of Rehob. Judg. 18. 28.
Bethsaida (beth-sā'i-dȧ), h. of fishing. Matt. 11. 21.
Beth-shan (beth-shan'), h. of rest. 1 Sam. 31. 10.
Beth-shean (beth-shē'ăn), same as **Bethshan.** Josh. 17. 11.
Beth-shemesh (beth-shē'mesh), h. of the sun. Josh. 15. 10.
Bethshemite (beth-shē'mīt), a native of Bethshemesh. 1 Sam. 6. 14.
Beth-shittah (beth-shit'ȧ), h. of acacias. Judg. 7. 22.
Beth-tappuah (beth-tap'ū-ȧ), h. of apples. Josh. 15. 53.
Bethuel (bē-thū'el), h. of God. Gen. 22. 22.
Bethul (beth'ul), same as **Beth-el** (?). Josh. 19. 4.
Beth-zur (beth-zūr'), house of the rock. Josh. 15. 58.
Betonim (bet'ō-nim), pistachio nuts. Josh. 13. 26.
Beulah (bū'lȧ), married. Is. 62. 4.
Bezai (bē'zā-ī). Ezra 2. 17.
Bezaleel (bē-zal'ē-el), in the shadow of God (?). Ex. 31. 2.
Bezek (bē'zek), lightning (?). Judg. 1. 4.
Bezer (bē'zēr), ore of precious metal. Deut. 4. 43.
Bichri (biçh'rī), young. 2 Sam. 20. 1.
Bidkar (bid'kär), cleaver (?). 2 Kin. 9. 25.
Bigtha (big'thȧ). Est. 1. 10.
Bigthan (big'than), given by God. Est. 2. 21.
Bigthana (big-thā'nȧ), same as **Bigthan.** Est. 6. 2.
Bigvai (big'vā-ī). Ezra 2. 2.
Bildad (bil'dad), son of contention (?). Job 2. 11.
Bileam (bil'ē-am), same as **Balaam** (?), or **Ibleam** (?). 1 Chr. 6. 70.
Bilgah (bil'gȧ), cheerfulness. 1 Chr. 24. 14.
Bilgai (bil'gā-ī), same as **Bilgah.** Neh. 10. 8.
Bilhah (bil'hȧ), modesty. Gen. 29. 29.
Bilhan (bil'han), modest. Gen. 36. 27.
Bilshan (bil'shan), seeker (?). Ezra 2. 2.
Bimhal (bim'hal). 1 Chr. 7. 33.
Binea (bin'ē-ȧ). 1 Chr. 8. 37.
Binnui (bin'ū-ī), a building. Ezra 8. 33.
Birsha (bir'shȧ). Gen. 14. 2.
Birzavith (bir-zā'vith), wounds (?). 1 Chr. 7. 31.
Bishlam (bish'lam). Ezra 4. 7.
Bithiah (bith-ī'ȧ), daughter (i.e. worshiper) of Jehovah. 1 Chr. 4. 18.
Bithron (bith'ron), a broken place. 2 Sam. 2. 29.
Bithynia (bi-thyn'i-ȧ). Acts 16. 7.
Bizjothjah (biz-joth'jȧ), contempt of Jehovah. Josh. 15. 28.
Biztha (biz'thȧ). Est. 1. 10.
Blastus (blas'tus), a shoot. Acts. 12. 20.
Boanerges (bō-ȧ-nēr'ġeṣ), sons of thunder. Mark 3. 17.
Boaz (bō'az), fleetness. Ruth 2. 1.
Bocheru (bō'çhe-rū), firstborn (?). 1 Chr. 8. 38.
Bochim (bō'çhim), weepers. Judg. 2. 1.
Bohan (bō'han), thumb (?). Josh. 15. 6.
Booz (bō'oz), same as **Boaz.** Matt. 1. 5.
Boscath (bos'çath), stony, elevated ground. 2 Kin. 22. 1.
Bosor (bō'sor), Greek and Aramaic form of **Beor.** 2. Pet. 2. 15.
Bozez (bō'zez), shining. 1 Sam. 14. 4.
Bozkath (boz'kath), same as **Boscath.** Josh. 15. 39.
Bozrah (boz'rȧ), sheepfold. Gen. 36. 33.
Bukki (buk'ī), wasting. Num. 34. 22.
Bukkiah (bu-kī'ȧ), wasting from Jehovah. 1 Chr. 25. 4.
Bul (bûl), rain. 1 Kin. 6. 38.
Bunah (bū'nȧ), prudence. 1 Chr. 2. 25.
Bunni (bun'ī), built. Neh. 9. 4.
Buz (buz), contempt. Gen. 22. 21.
Buzi (bū'zī), descended from Buz. Ezek. 1. 3.
Buzite (bū'zīt), a descendant of Buz. Job 32. 2.

C

Cabbon (çab'ŏn), cake. Josh. 15. 40.
Cabul (çā'bul), displeasing (?). Josh. 19. 27.
Cæsar (cē'ṣăr). Matt. 22. 17.
Cæsarea (ces-ȧ-rē'ȧ), named after Augustus Cæsar. Acts 8. 40.
Cæsarea Philippi (ces-ȧ-rē'ȧ fi-lip'ī), named after Philip the tetrarch. Matt. 16. 13.
Caiaphas (çā'yȧ-fȧs), depression (?). Matt. 26. 3.
Cain (çān), possession. Gen. 4. 1. Josh. 15. 57.
Cainan (çā-ī'năn), possessor. Gen. 5. 9.
Calah (çā'lȧ). Gen. 10. 11.
Calcol (çal'çol). 1 Chr. 2. 6.
Caleb (çā'leb), a dog. Num. 26. 65.
Caleb-ephratah (çā'leb-ef'rȧ-tȧ), C. the fruitful. 1 Chr. 2. 24.
Calneh (çal'ne). Gen. 10. 10.
Calno (çal'nō), same as **Calneh.** Is. 10. 9.
Calvary (çal'vȧ-ry), skull. Luke 23. 33.
Camon (çā'mŏn), abounding in stalks. Judg. 10. 5.
Cana (çā'nȧ). John 2. 1.
Canaan (çā'năn), low region. Gen. 9. 18.
Canaanite (çā'năn-īt), a zealot. Mark 3. 18.
Canaanites (çā'năn-īts), inhabitants of Canaan. Judg. 1. 1.
Canaanitess (çā'năn-īt-es), feminine of preceding. 1 Chr. 2. 3.
Candace (çan'dȧ-cē). Acts 8. 27.
Canneh (çan'e), probably same as **Calneh.** Ezek. 27. 23.
Capernaum (çȧ-pēr'nā-um), city of consolation (?). Matt. 4. 13.
Caphthorim (çaf'thō-rim), same as **Caphtorim.** 1 Chr. 1. 12.
Caphtor (çaf'tor). Deut. 2. 23.
Caphtorim (çaf'tō-rim), inhabitants of Caphtor. Gen. 10. 14.
Cappadocia (çap-ȧ-dō'çhi-ȧ). Acts 2. 9.
Carcas (çär'çȧs). Est. 1. 10.
Carchemish (çär'çhē-mish), fortress of Chemosh. Jer. 46. 2.
Careah (çȧ-rē'ȧ), bald. 2 Kin. 25. 23.
Carmel (çär'mel), park. Josh. 12. 22.
Carmelite (çär'mel-īt), a native of Carmel. 1 Sam. 30. 5.
Carmelitess (çär'mel-īt-es), feminine of preceding. 1 Sam. 27. 3.
Carmi (çär'mī), a vine-dresser. Gen. 46. 9.
Carmites (çär'mīts), descendants of Carmi. Num. 26. 6.
Carpus (çär'pus), fruit (?). 2 Tim. 4. 13.
Carshena (çär'shē-nȧ). Est. 1. 14.
Casiphia (çȧ-sif'i-ȧ), silver (?). Ezra 8. 17.
Casluhim (ças'lū-him). Gen. 10. 14.
Castor (ças'tŏr). Acts 28. 11.
Cedron (cē'drŏn), same as **Kidron.** John 18. 1.
Cenchrea (cen'çhrē-ȧ), millet, small pulse. Acts 18. 18.
Cephas (cē'fȧs), stone. John 1. 42.
Chalcol (çhal'çol), same as **Calcol.** 1 Kin. 4. 31.
Chaldea (çhal-dē'ȧ). Jer. 50. 10.
Chaldeans (çhal-dē'ănṣ), inhabitants of Chaldea. Job 1. 17.
Chaldees (çhal-dēṣ'), same as preceding. Gen. 11. 28.
Chanaan (çhā'năn), another form of **Canaan** Acts 7. 11.
Charashim (çhar'ȧ-shim), craftsmen. 1 Chr. 4. 14.
Charchemish (çhär'çhē-mish), same as **Carchemish.** 2 Chr. 35. 20.
Charran (çhar'ăn), same as **Haran.** Acts 7. 2.
Chebar (çhē'bär), great (?). Ezek. 1. 1.
Chedorlaomer (çhed'ŏr-lā-ō'mēr), glory of—(?). Gen. 14. 1.
Chelal (çhē'lal), completion. Ezra 10. 30.
Chelluh (çhel'ū). Ezra 10. 35.
Chelub (çhē'lub), bird-trap. 1 Chr. 4. 11.

Chelubai (çhē-lū'bī), same as **Caleb.** 1 Chr. 2. 9.
Chemarims (çhem'ȧ-rimș), persons dressed in black attire. Zeph. 1. 4.
Chemosh (çhē'mosh), subduer. Num. 21. 29.
Chenaanah (çhē-nā'ȧ-nä), probably fem. of Canaan. 1 Kin. 22. 11.
Chenani (çhē-nā'nī), probably same as **Chenaniah.** Neh. 9. 4.
Chenaniah (çhen-ȧ-nī'ȧ), whom Jehovah supports. 1 Chr. 15. 22.
Chephar-haammonai (çhē'fär-hā-am'ō-nī), village of the Ammonites. Josh. 18. 24.
Chephirah (çhē-fī'rȧ), same as Kefireh. Josh. 9. 17.
Cheran (çhē'răn). Gen. 36. 26.
Cherethims (çher'ē-thimș), Cretans (?). Ezek. 25. 16.
Cherethites (çher'ē-thīts), probably same as preceding. 2 Sam. 8. 18.
Cherith (çhē'rith), gorge (?). 1 Kin. 17. 3.
Cherub (cher'ub), blessing (?), strong (?). Ezra 2. 59.
Cherubim (cher'ū-bim), plural of **Cherub.** Gen. 3. 24.
Chesalon (çhes'ȧ-lon), hope. Josh. 15. 10.
Chesed (çhē'sed), conqueror (?). Gen. 22. 22.
Chesil (çhē'sil), a fool. Josh. 15. 30.
Chesulloth (çhē-sul'oth), confidences. Josh. 19. 18.
Chezib (çhē'zib), false. Gen. 38. 5.
Chidon (çhī'dŏn), javelin. 1 Chr. 13. 9.
Chileab (çhil'ē-ab), probably another form of **Caleb.** 2 Sam. 3. 3.
Chilion (çhil'i-ŏn), wasting away. Ruth 1. 2.
Chilmad (çhil'mad). Ezek. 27. 23.
Chimham (çhim'ham), longing. 2 Sam. 19. 37.
Chinnereth (çhin'ē-reth), a lyre. Josh. 19. 35.
Chinneroth (çhin'ē-roth), plural of **Chinnereth.** Josh. 11. 2.
Chios (çhī'os). Acts 20. 15.
Chisleu (çhis'lū). Neh. 1. 1.
Chislon (çhis'lon), confidence, hope. Num. 34. 21.
Chisloth-tabor (çhis'loth-tā'bŏr), flanks of Tabor. Josh. 19. 12.
Chittim (çhit'im), probably Cyprus. Num. 24. 24.
Chiun (çhī'un), image. Amos 5. 26.
Chloe (çhlō'ē). 1 Cor. 1. 11.
Chor-ashan (çhọr'ash-ăn), smoking furnace. 1 Sam. 30. 30.
Chorazin (çhō-rā'zin). Matt. 11. 21.
Chozeba (çhō-zē'bȧ), deceiver. 1 Chr. 4. 22.
Christ (çhrīst), the anointed, Greek for **Messiah.** Matt. 1. 1.
Chub (çhub). Ezek. 30. 5.
Chun (çhun), establishment. 1 Chr. 18. 8.
Chushan-rishathaim (çhū'shan-rish'ȧ-thā'im). Judg. 3. 8.
Chuza (çhū'zȧ). Luke 8. 3.
Cilicia (ci-liçh'i-ȧ). Acts 15. 23.
Cinneroth (cin'e-roth), same as **Chinneroth.** 1 Kin. 15. 20.
Cis (cis), same as **Kish.** Acts 13. 21.
Clauda (clạ'dȧ). Acts 27. 16.
Claudia (clạ'di-ȧ). 2 Tim. 4. 21.
Claudius (clạ'di-us). Acts 11. 28.
Clement (clem'ent). Phil. 4. 3.
Cleopas (clē'ō-pas), either a shortened form of Cleopatros, or a Greek form of Alphæus. Luke 24. 18.
Cleophas (clē'ō-fas), probably same as preceding. John 19. 25.
Cnidus (nī'dus), nettle (?). Acts 27. 7.
Col-hozeh (col-hō'ze), every one that seeth. Neh. 3. 15.
Colosse (cō-los'ē). Col. 1. 2.
Colossians (cō-losh'ănș), people of Colosse.
Conaniah (con-ȧ-nī'ȧ). 2 Chr. 35. 9, same as **Cononiah.**
Coniah (cō-nī'ȧ), contracted from **Jeconiah.** Jer. 22. 24.
Cononiah (con-ō-nī'ȧ), whom Jehovah has set up. 2 Chr. 31. 12.
Coos (cō'os). Acts 21. 1.
Core (cō'rē), Greek form of **Korah.** Jude 11.
Corinth (cọr'inth). Acts 18. 1.
Corinthians (cō-rin'thi-ănș), inhabitants of Corinth. Acts 18. 8.
Cornelius (cọr-nēl'yus). Acts 10. 1.
Cosam (cō'sam). Luke 3. 28.
Coz (coz), thorn. 1 Chr. 4. 8.
Cozbi (coz'bī), deceitful. Num. 25. 15.
Crescens (cres'enș), growing. 2 Tim. 4. 10.
Crete (crēt). Acts 27. 7.
Cretes or **Cretians** (crēt'i-ănș), inhabitants of Crete. Acts 2. 11. Tit. 1. 12.
Crispus (cris'pus), curled. Acts 18. 8.
Cumi (cū'mī), arise. Mark 5. 41.
Cush (cush), black. Gen. 10. 6.
Cushan (cū'shan), same meaning as **Cush.** Hab. 3. 7.
Cushi (cū'shī), same meaning as **Cush.** 2 Sam. 18. 21.
Cuth (cuth). 2 Kin. 17. 30.
Cuthah (cū'thȧ), same as **Cuth.** 2 Kin. 17. 24.
Cyprus (cȳ'prus). Acts 4. 36.
Cyrene (cȳ-rē'nē). Matt. 27. 32.
Cyrenian (cȳ-rē'ni-ăn), a native of Cyrene. Acts 6. 9.
Cyrenius (cȳ-rē'ni-us), Greek form of the Roman name Quirinus. Luke 2. 2.
Cyrus (cȳ'rus), the sun. 2 Chr. 36. 32.

D

Dabareh (dab'ȧ-re), pasture. Josh. 21. 28.
Dabbasheth (dab'ȧ-sheth), hump of a camel. Josh. 19. 11.
Daberath (dab'e-rath), same as **Dabareh.** Josh. 19. 12.
Dagon (dā'gon), fish. Judg. 16. 23.
Dalaiah (dal-ā-ī'ȧ), whom Jehovah hath delivered. 1 Chr. 3. 24.
Dalmanutha (dal-mȧ-nū'thȧ). Mark 8. 10.
Dalmatia (dal-mā'shi-ȧ). 2 Tim. 4. 10.
Dalphon (dal'fon), proud (?). Est. 9. 7.
Damaris (dam'ȧ-ris), calf (?). Acts 17. 34.
Damascenes (dam'ȧ-sēnș), people of Damascus. 2 Cor. 11. 32.
Damascus (dȧ-mas'cus), activity (?). Gen. 14. 15.
Dan (dan), judge. Gen. 30. 6.
Daniel (dan'yel), God's judge. Dan. 1. 6.
Danites (dan'īts), descendants of Dan. Judg. 13. 2.
Dan-jaan (dan-jā'ăn), woodland (?). 2 Sam. 24. 6.
Dannah (dan'ȧ). Josh. 15. 49.
Dara (dâr'ȧ), probably contracted from the next word. 1 Chr. 2. 6.
Darda (dâr'dȧ), pearl of wisdom (?). 1 Kin. 4. 31.
Darius (dȧ-rī'us), governor (?). Ezra 4. 5.
Darkon (där'kon), scatterer (?). Ezra 2. 56.
Dathan (dā'thăn). Num. 16. 1.
David (dā'vid), beloved. 1 Sam. 16. 19.
Debir (dē'bīr), a recess. Josh. 10. 3.
Deborah (deb'ọr-ȧ), bee. Judg. 4. 4.
Decapolis (dē-cap'ō-lis), ten cities. Matt. 4. 25.
Dedan (dē'dăn). Gen. 10. 7.
Dedanim (dē'dȧ-nim), inhabitants of Dedan. Is. 21. 13.
Dehavites (dē-hā'vīts). Ezra 4. 9.
Dekar (dē'kär), piercing. 1 Kin. 4. 9.
Delaiah (dē-lā'yȧ), whom Jehovah has freed. 1 Chr. 24. 18.
Delilah (dē-lī'lȧ), delicate. Judg. 16. 4.
Demas (dē'mas), probably same as following. Col. 4. 14.
Demetrius (dē-mē'tri-us), belonging to Demeter. Acts 19. 24.
Derbe (dĕr'bē), juniper (?). Acts 14. 6.
Deuel (dū'el), the same as **Reuel** (?). Num. 1. 14.
Deuteronomy (dū-tēr-on'ō-my), a recapitulation of the law.
Diana (dī-an'ȧ). Acts 19. 24.
Diblaim (dib-lā'im), two cakes. Hos. 1. 3.
Diblath (dib'lath), supposed to be the same as **Riblah.** Ezek. 6. 14.
Diblathaim (dib-lȧ-thā'im), same as **Diblaim.** Num. 33. 46.
Dibon (dī'bon), wasting. Num. 21. 30.
Dibon-gad (dī'bon-gad'), wasting of Gad. Num. 33. 45.
Dibri (dib'rī), eloquent. Lev. 24. 11.
Didymus (did'y-mus), twin. John 11. 16.
Diklah (dik'lä), a palm-tree. Gen. 10. 27.
Dilean (dil'ē-ăn), cucumber-field (?). Josh. 15. 38.
Dimnah (dim'nä), dunghill. Josh. 21. 35.
Dimon (dī'mon), same as **Dibon.** Is. 15. 9.
Dimonah (dī-mō'nȧ), probably same as preceding. Josh. 15. 22.
Dinah (dī'nȧ), vindicated. Gen. 30. 21.
Dinaites (dī'nȧ-īts). Ezra 4. 9.
Dinhabah (din'hȧ-bä). Gen. 36. 32.
Dionysius (dī-ō-nish'i-us), belonging to Dionysus. Acts 17. 34.
Diotrephes (dī-ot'rē-fēș), nourished by Zeus. 3 John 9.
Dishan (dī'shan), antelope (?). Gen. 36. 28.
Dishon (dī'shŏn), same as preceding. Gen. 36. 21.
Dizahab (dī'zȧ-hab), a place abounding in gold (?). Deut. 1. 1.
Dodai (dō'dī), loving. 1 Chr. 27. 4.
Dodanim (dō'dȧ-nim). Gen. 10. 4.
Dodavah (dō'dȧ-vȧ), love of Jehovah. 2 Chr. 20. 37.
Dodo (dō'dō), same as **Dodai.** 2 Sam. 23. 9.
Doeg (dō'eg), anxious. 1 Sam. 21. 7.
Dophkah (dof'kȧ). Num. 33. 12.
Dor (dọr), dwelling. Josh. 11. 2.
Dorcas (dọr'cȧs), gazelle. Acts 9. 36.
Dothan (dō'thăn), two wells or cisterns. Gen. 37. 17.
Drusilla (drụ-sil'ȧ). Acts 24. 24.
Dumah (dū'mȧ), silence. Gen. 25. 14.
Dura (dū'rȧ), town. Dan. 3. 1.

E—F

Ebal (ē'băl), stony (?). Gen. 36. 23.
Ebed (ē'bed), servant. Judg. 9. 26.
Ebed-melech (ē-bed-mē'leçh), servant of the king. Jer. 38. 7.
Eben-ezer (eb-en-ē'zēr), stone of help. 1 Sam. 4. 1.
Eber (ē'bēr), the region beyond. Gen. 10. 21.
Ebiasaph (ē-bī'ȧ-saf), same as **Abiasaph.** 1 Chr. 6. 23.
Ebronah (e'brō'nȧ), passage (?). Num. 33. 34.
Ecclesiastes (e-clē'şi-as'tēș), the preacher.
Ed (ed), witness. Josh. 22. 34.
Edar (ē'där), flock. Gen. 35. 21.
Eden (ē'dn), pleasantness. Gen. 2. 8.
Eder (ē'dēr), flock, same as **Edar.** 1 Chr. 23. 23.
Edom (ē'dŏm), red. Gen. 25. 30.
Edomites (ē'dŏm-īts), inhabitants of Edom. Gen. 36. 9.
Edrei (ed'rē-ī), strong. Num. 21. 33.
Eglah (eg'lȧ), heifer. 2 Sam. 3. 5.
Eglaim (eg'lā-im), two pools. Is. 15. 8.
Eglon (eg'lon). Judg. 3. 12.
Egypt (ē'ġypt), black. Gen. 12. 10.
Egyptian (ē-ġyp'shăn), a native of Egypt. 1 Sam. 30. 11.
Ehi (ē'hī), shortened from **Ahiram.** Gen. 46. 21.
Ehud (ē'hud), joined together (?). Judg. 3. 15.
Eker (ē'kēr), same as **Achar.** 1 Chr. 2. 27.
Ekron (ek'ron), eradication. Josh. 13. 3.
Ekronites (ek'ron-its), inhabitants of Ekron. Josh. 13. 3.
Eladah (el'ȧ-dȧ), whom God clothes. 1 Chr. 7. 20.
Elah (ē'lȧ), terebinth. Gen. 36. 41.
Elam (ē'lăm). Gen. 10. 22.
Elamites (ē'lăm-īts), inhabitants of Elam. Ezra 4. 9.
Elasah (el'ȧ-sȧ), whom God made. Ezra 10. 22.
Elath (ē'lath), a grove. Deut. 2. 8.
El-beth-el (el-beth'el), the house of God. Gen. 35. 7.
Eldaah (el-dā'ȧ), whom God called. Gen. 25. 4.
Eldad (el'dad), whom God loves. Num. 11. 26.
Elead (el'ē-ad), whom God praises. 1 Chr. 7. 21.
Elealeh (e-lē-ā'le), whither God ascends. Num. 32. 3.
Eleasah (el-ē-ā'sȧ), same as **Elasah.** 1 Chr. 2. 39.
Eleazar (el-ē-ā'zär), whom God aids. Ex. 6. 23.
El-elohe-Israel (el'ē-lō'he-iș'rā-el), God, the God of Israel. Gen. 33. 20.
Eleph (ē'lef), ox. Josh. 18. 28.
Elhanan (el-hā'năn), whom God gave. 2 Sam. 21. 19.
Eli (ē'lī), my God. Matt. 27. 46.
Eli (ē'lī), height. 1 Sam. 1. 3.
Eliab (ē-lī'ab), whose father is God. Num. 1. 9.
Eliada or **Eliadah** (ē-lī'ȧ-dȧ), whom God cares for. 2 Sam. 5. 16.
Eliah (ē-lī'ȧ), same name as **Elijah.** 1 Chr. 8. 27.
Eliahba (ē-lī'ȧ-bȧ), whom God hides. 2 Sam. 23. 32.
Eliakim (ē-lī'a-kim), whom God establishes. 2 Kin. 18. 18.
Eliam (ē-lī'am), same as **Ammiel.** 2 Sam. 11. 3.
Elias (ē-lī'ȧs), same as **Elijah.** John 1. 21.
Eliasaph (ē-lī'ȧ-saf), whom God added. Num. 1. 14.
Eliashib (ē-lī'ȧ-shib), whom God restores. 1 Chr. 24. 12.
Eliathah (ē-lī'ȧ-thȧ), to whom God comes. 1 Chr. 25. 4.
Elidad (ē-lī'dad), whom God loves. Num. 34. 21.
Eliel (ē'lī-el), to whom God is strength. 1 Chr. 5. 24.
Elienai (el-i-ē'nī), unto Jehovah my eyes are raised (?). 1 Chr. 8. 20.
Eliezer (el-i-ē'zēr), my God is help. Gen. 15. 2.
Elihoenai (el'i-hō-ē'nī), same as **Elioenai.** Ezra. 8. 4.
Elihoreph (el-i-hō'ref), to whom God is the reward. 1 Kin. 4. 3.
Elihu (ē-lī'hū), whose God is He. 1 Sam. 1. 1.
Elijah (ē-lī'jȧ), my God is Jehovah. 1 Kin. 17. 1.
Elika (ē-lī'kȧ), whom God purifies (?). 2 Sam. 23. 25.
Elim (ē'lim), oaks. Ex. 15. 27.
Elimelech (ē-lim'e-leçh), to whom God is king. Ruth 1. 2.
Elioenai (ē-lī'ō-ē'nī), unto Jehovah my eyes are turned. 1 Chr. 3. 23.
Eliphal (ē-lī'fal), whom God judges. 1 Chr. 11. 35.
Eliphalet (ē-lif'ȧ-let), to whom God is salvation. 2 Sam. 5. 16.
Eliphaz (el'i-faz), to whom God is strength. Gen. 36. 4.
Elipheleh (ē-lif'e-le), whom God distinguishes. 1 Chr. 15. 18.
Eliphelet (ē-lif'e-let), same as **Eliphalet.** 1 Chr. 3. 8.
Elisabeth (ē-liș'ȧ-beth), same as **Elisheba.** Luke 1. 5.
Eliseus (el-i-sē'us), Greek form of **Elisha.** Luke 4. 27.
Elisha (ē-lī'shȧ), to whom God is salvation. 1 Kin. 19. 16.
Elishah (ē-lī'shȧ). Gen. 10. 4.
Elishama (ē-lish'ȧ-mä), whom God hears. Num. 1. 10.
Elishaphat (ē-lish'ȧ-fat), whom God judges. 2 Chr. 23. 1.
Elisheba (ē-lish'ē-bä), to whom God is the oath. Ex. 6. 23.
Elishua (el-i-shū'ȧ), same as **Elisha.** 2 Sam. 5. 15.
Eliud (ē-lī'ud), God of Judah. Matt. 1. 14.
Elizaphan (el-i-zā'fan), whom God protects. Num. 3. 30.
Elizur (ē-lī'zūr), God is a rock. Num. 1. 5.
Elkanah (el-kā'nȧ), whom God possessed. Ex. 6. 24.
Elkoshite (el'kosh-īt), inhabitant of Elkosh. Nah. 1. 1.
Ellasar (el-lā'sär). Gen. 14. 1.
Elmodam (el-mō'dam), same as **Almodad.** Luke 3. 28.
Elnaam (el-nā'am), whose pleasure God is. 1 Chr. 11. 46.
Elnathan (el-nā'thăn), whom God gave. 2 Kin. 24. 8.
Eloi (ē-lō'ī), my God. Mark 15. 34.
Elon (ē'lon), oak. Gen. 26. 34.
Elon-beth-hanan (ē'lon-beth-hā'năn), oak of the house of grace. 1 Kin. 4. 9.
Elonites (ē'lŏn-īts), descendants of Elon. Num. 26. 26.
Eloth (ē'loth), same as **Elath.** 1 Kin. 9. 26.
Elpaal (el-pā'al), to whom God is the reward. 1 Chr. 8. 11.
Elpalet (el-pā'let), same as **Eliphalet.** 1 Chr. 14. 5.
El-paran (el-pā'răn), oak of Paran. Gen. 14. 6.
Eltekeh (el'tē-kē), whose fear is God. Josh. 19. 44.
Eltekon (el'tē-kon), whose foundation is God. Josh. 15. 59.
Eltolad (el-tō'lad), whose posterity is from God. Josh. 15. 30.
Elul (e-lụl'). Neh. 6. 15.
Eluzai (ē-lū'zā-ī), God is my praises. 1 Chr. 12. 5.
Elymas (el'y-mas), a wise man. Acts 13. 8.
Elzabad (el-zā'bad), whom God gave. 1 Chr. 12. 12.
Elzaphan (el-zā'fan), whom God protects. Ex. 6. 22.
Emims (ē'mimș), terrible men. Gen. 14. 5.
Emmanuel (e-man'ū-el), same as **Immanuel.** Matt. 1. 23.
Emmaus (e-mā'us), hot springs (?). Luke. 24. 13.
Emmor (em'ŏr), same as **Hamor.** Acts 7. 16.
Enam (ē'nam), two fountains. Josh. 15. 34.
Enan (ē'nan), having eyes. Num. 1. 15.
En-dor (en'dọr), fountain of Dor. Josh. 17. 11.
En-eglaim (en-eg'lā-im), f. of two calves. Ezek. 47. 10.
En-gannim (en-gan'im), f. of gardens. Josh. 15. 34.
En-gedi (en-gē'dī), f. of the kid. Josh. 15. 62.
En-haddah (en-had'ȧ), f. of sharpness (i.e. swift f.), Josh. 19. 21.

En-hakkore (en-hak'ō-rē), f. of him that calleth. Judg. 15. 19.
En-hazor (en-hā'zọr), f. of the village. Josh. 19. 37.
En-mishpat (en-mish'pat), f. of judgment. Gen. 14. 7.
Enoch (ē'nŏch), experienced (?). Gen. 4. 17.
Enos (ē'nŏs), man. Gen. 4. 26.
Enosh (ē'nosh), same as **Enos.** 1 Chr. 1. 1.
En-rimmon (en-rim'ŏn), fountain of the pomegranate. Neh. 11. 29.
En-rogel (en-rō'gel), f. of the fuller. Josh. 15. 7.
En-shemesh (en-shē'mesh), f. of the sun. Josh. 15. 7.
En-tappuah (en-tap'ū-ȧ), f. of the apple-tree. Josh. 17. 7.
Epænetus (ē-pē'nē-tus), laudable. Rom. 16. 5.
Epaphras (ep'ȧ-fras), contracted from the next word (?). Col. 1. 7.
Epaphroditus (ē-paf'rō-dī'tus), handsome. Phil. 2. 25.
Epenetus, same as **Epænetus.** Rom. 16. 5.
Ephah (ē'fȧ). Gen. 25. 4.
Ephai (ē'fī), languishing. Jer. 40. 8.
Epher (ē'fēr), calf. Gen. 25. 4.
Ephes-dammim (ē'fes-dam'im), boundary of blood. 1 Sam. 17. 1.
Ephesians (ē-fē'zăns), inhabitants of Ephesus. Acts 19. 28.
Ephesus (ef'ē-sus). Acts 18. 19.
Ephlal (ef'lal), judgment. 1 Chr. 2. 37.
Ephod (ē'fod). Num. 34. 23.
Ephphatha (ef'ȧ-thȧ), be opened. Mark 7. 34.
Ephraim (ē'frā-im), fruitful (?). Gen. 41. 52.
Ephraimites (ē'frā-im-īts), inhabitants of Ephraim. Judg. 12. 4.
Ephrain (ē'frā-in), same as **Ephron.** 2. Chr. 13. 19.
Ephrath, or **Ephratah** (ef'rȧ-tȧ), fruitful (?). 1 Chr. 2. 50. Gen. 35. 16.
Ephrathites (ef'rȧ-thīts), inhabitants of Ephrath. Ruth 1. 2.
Ephron (ē'fron), of or belonging to a calf. Gen. 23. 8.
Epicureans (ep'i-cū-rē'ăns), followers of Epicurus. Acts 17. 18.
Er (ēr), watchful. Gen. 38. 3.
Eran (ē'ran). Num. 26. 36.
Eranites (ē'ran-īts), posterity of Eran. Num. 26. 36.
Erastus (ē-ras'tus), beloved. Acts 19. 22.
Erech (ē'rech). Gen. 10. 10.
Eri (ē'rī), same as **Er.** Gen. 46. 16.
Erites (ē'rīts), descendants of Eri. Num. 26. 16.
Esaias (ē-sā'yȧs), same as **Isaiah.** Matt. 3. 3.
Esar-haddon (ē-sär-had'ŏn), Assur giveth a brother. 2 Kin. 19. 37.
Esau (ē'sạ), hairy. Gen. 25. 25.
Esek (ē'sek), strife. Gen. 26. 20.
Esh-baal (esh'bā-ăl), man of Baal. 1 Chr. 8. 33.
Eshban (esh'ban). Gen. 36. 26.
Eshcol (esh'col), cluster. Gen. 14. 13.
Eshean (esh'ē-an), support (?). Josh. 15. 52.
Eshek (ē'shek), oppression. 1 Chr. 8. 39.
Eshkalonites (esh'kȧ-lon-īts), men of Ashkalon. Josh. 13. 3.
Eshtaol (esh'tā-ol). Josh. 15. 33.
Eshtaulites (esh-tȧ-ū'līts), inhabitants of Eshtaol. 1 Chr. 2. 53.
Eshtemoa (esh-tē-mō'ȧ), obedience. Josh. 21. 14.
Eshtemoh (esh'tē-mō), same as **Eshtemoa.** Josh. 15. 50.
Eshton (esh'ton), womanly. 1 Chr. 4. 11.
Esli (es'lī), same as **Azaliah** (?). Luke 3. 25.
Esrom (es'rom), same as **Hezron.** Matt. 1. 3.
Esther (es'tēr), star. Est. 2. 7.
Etam (ē'tam), a place of ravenous creatures. Judg. 15. 8.
Etham (ē'tham), boundary of the sea (?). Ex. 13. 20.
Ethan (ē'thăn), firmness. 1 Kin. 4. 31.
Ethanim (eth'ȧ-nim), gifts (?). 1 Kin. 8. 2.
Ethbaal (eth-bā'ăl), living with Baal. 1 Kin. 16. 31.
Ether (ē'thēr), plenty. Josh. 15. 42.
Ethiopia (ē-thi-ō'pi-ȧ), (region of) burnt faces. Gen. 2. 13.
Ethiopian (ē-thi-ō'pi-ăn), a native of Ethiopia. Jer. 13. 23.
Ethnan (eth'nan), a gift. 1 Chr. 4. 7.
Ethni (eth'nī), bountiful. 1 Chr. 6. 41.
Eubulus (ū-bū'lus), good counselor. 2 Tim. 4. 21.
Eunice (ū-nī'cē). 2 Tim. 1. 5.
Euodias (ū-ō'di-as), success. Phil. 4. 2.
Euphrates (ū-frā'tēs), the fertile river (?). Gen. 2. 14.
Euroclydon (ū-roc'ly-don), storm from the east. Acts 27. 14.
Eutychus (ū'ty-chus), fortunate. Acts 20. 9.
Eve (ēv), life. Gen. 3. 20.
Evi (ē'vī). Num. 31. 8.
Evil-merodach (ē'vil-mē-rō'dach), man of Merodach. 2 Kin. 25. 27.
Exodus (ek'sō-dus), departure.
Ezar (ē'zăr), treasure. 1 Chr. 1. 38.
Ezbai (ez'bā-ī), 1 Chr. 11. 37.
Ezbon (ez'bon). Gen. 46. 16.
Ezekias (ez-ē-kī'ăs), same as **Hezekiah.** Matt. 1. 9.
Ezekiel (ē-zēk'yel), whom God will strengthen. Ezek. 1. 3.
Ezel (ē'zel), departure. 1 Sam. 20. 19.
Ezem (ē'zem), bone. 1 Chr. 4. 29.
Ezer (ē'zēr), help. 1 Chr. 4. 4.
Ezion-gaber, or **Ezion-geber** (ē'zi-on-gē'bēr), the backbone of a giant. Num. 33. 35.
Eznite (ez'nīt). 2 Sam. 23. 8.
Ezra (ez'rȧ), help. Ezra. 7. 1.
Ezrahite (ez'rȧ-hīt), a descendant of Zerah. 1 Kin. 4. 31.
Ezri (ez'rī), the help of Jehovah (?). 1 Chr. 27. 26.

Fair Havens. Acts 27. 8.
Felix (fē'liks), happy. Acts 23. 24.
Festus (fes'tus), joyful. Acts 24. 27.
Fortunatus (fọr-tū-nā'tus), prosperous. 1 Cor. 16. 17.

G

Gaal (gā'ăl), loathing. Judg. 9. 26.
Gaash (gā'ash), shaking. Josh. 24. 30.
Gaba (gā'bȧ), hill. Josh. 18. 24.
Gabbai (gab'ā-ī), a collector of tribute. Neh. 11. 8.
Gabbatha (gab'ȧ-thȧ), height. John 19. 13.
Gabriel (gā'bri-el), man of God. Dan. 8. 16.
Gad (gad), a troop, good fortune. Gen. 30. 11.
Gadarenes (gad-ȧ-rēns'), inhabitants of Gadara. Mark 5. 1.
Gaddi (gad'ī), fortunate. Num. 13. 11.
Gaddiel (gad'i-el), fortune sent from God. Num. 13. 10.
Gadi (gā'dī). 2 Kin. 15. 14.
Gadites (gad'īts), persons belonging to the tribe of Gad. Deut. 3. 12.
Gaham (gā'hăm), sunburnt (?). Gen. 22. 24.
Gahar (gā'hăr), hiding-place. Ezra 2. 47.
Gaius (gā'yus) the Greek form of Caius. Acts 19. 29.
Galal (gā'lal), worthy (?). 1 Chr. 9. 15.
Galatia (gȧ-lā'shi-ȧ), a place colonized by Gauls. Acts 16. 6.
Galatians (gȧ-lā'shăns), inhabitants of Galatia. Gal. 3. 1.
Galeed (gal'ē-ed), witness-heap. Gen. 31. 47.
Galilee (gal'i-lē), circuit. Josh. 20. 7.
Gallim (gal'im), heaps. 1 Sam. 25. 44.
Gallio (gal'i-ō). Acts 18. 12.
Gamaliel (gȧ-mā'li-el), benefit of God. Num. 1. 10.
Gammadims (gam'ȧ-dims), warriors (?). Ezek. 27. 11.
Gamul (gā'mul), weaned. 1 Chr. 24. 17.
Gareb (gā'reb), scabby. 2 Sam. 23. 38.
Garmite (gär'mīt), bony. 1 Chr. 4. 19.
Gashmu (gash'mū), same as **Geshem.** Neh. 6. 6.
Gatam (gā'tăm). Gen. 36. 11.
Gath (gath), wine-press. Josh. 11. 22.
Gath-hepher (gath-hē'fēr), the wine-press of the well. 2 Kin. 14. 25.
Gath-rimmon (gath-rim'ŏn), wine-press of the pomegranate. Josh. 19. 45.
Gaza (gā'zȧ), same as **Azzah.** Gen. 10. 19.
Gazathites (gā'zath-īts), inhabitants of Gaza. Josh. 13. 3.
Gazer (gā'zēr), place cut off. 2 Sam. 5. 25.
Gazez (gā'zez), shearer. 1 Chr. 2. 46.
Gazites (gā'zīts), inhabitants of Gaza. Judg. 16. 2.
Gazzam (gaz'ăm), eating up. Ezra 2. 48.
Geba (gē'bȧ), hill. Josh. 21. 17.
Gebal (gē'băl), mountain. Ps. 83. 7.
Geber (gē'bēr), man. 1 Kin. 4. 13.
Gebim (gē'bim), trenches. Is. 10. 31.
Gedaliah (ged-ȧ-lī'ȧ), whom Jehovah has made great. 2 Kin. 25. 22.
Gedeon (ged'ē-ŏn). Greek form of Gideon. Heb. 11. 32.
Geder (gē'dēr), wall. Josh. 12. 13.
Gederah (gē-dē'rȧ), inclosure, sheepfold. Josh. 15. 36.
Gederathite (gē-dē'rȧ-thīt), an inhabitant of Gederah. 1 Chr. 12. 4.
Gederite (ge-dēr'īt), native of Geder. 1 Chr. 27. 28.
Gederoth (ge-dē'roth), sheepfolds. Josh. 15. 41.
Gederothaim (ged'ē-rō-thā'im), two sheepfolds. Josh. 15. 36.
Gedor (gē'dọr), wall. Josh. 15. 58.
Gehazi (gē-hā'zī), valley of vision. 2 Kin. 4. 12.
Geliloth (gē-lī'loth), regions. Josh. 18. 17.
Gemalli (gē-mal'i), possessor of camels. Num. 13. 12.
Gemariah (gem-ȧ-rī'ȧ), whom Jehovah has completed. Jer. 29. 3.
Genesis (gen'ē-sis), generation, or beginning.
Gennesaret (ge-nes'ȧ-ret). Matt. 14. 34.
Gentiles (gen'tīls). Gen. 10. 5.
Genubath (gē-nū'bath). 1 Kin. 11. 20.
Gera (gē'rȧ), a grain. Gen. 46. 21.
Gerah (gē'rȧ). Ex. 30. 13.
Gerar (gē'rär), sojourning. Gen. 10. 19.
Gergesenes (gēr-ge-sēns'), inhabitants of Gerasa. Matt. 8. 28.
Gerizim (ge-rī'zim), persons living in a desert. Deut. 11. 29.
Gershom (gēr'shŏm), expulsion. Ex. 2. 22.
Gershon (gēr'shon), same as preceding. Gen. 46. 11.
Gershonites (gēr'shon-īts), descendants of Gershon. Num. 3. 21.
Gesham (gē'shăm). 1 Chr. 2. 47.
Geshem (gē'shem), stout (?). Neh. 2. 19.
Geshur (gē'shūr), bridge. 2 Sam. 3. 3.
Geshuri (gē-shū'rī), inhabitants of Geshur. Deut. 3. 14.
Geshurites (gesh'ū-rīts), same as preceding. Josh. 12. 5.
Gether (gē'thēr), dregs (?). Gen. 10. 23.
Gethsemane (geth-sem'ȧ-nē), oil-press. Matt. 26. 36.
Geuel (gē-ū'el), majesty of God. Num. 13. 15.
Gezer (gē'zēr), precipice. Josh. 10. 33.
Gezrites (gez'rīts), dwelling in a desert land. 1 Sam. 27. 8.
Giah (gī'ȧ), gushing forth. 2 Sam. 2. 24.
Gibbar (gib'är), a hero. Ezra 2. 20.
Gibbethon (gib'ē-thon), a lofty place. Josh. 19. 44.
Gibea (gib'ē-ȧ), hill. 1 Chr. 2. 49.
Gibeah (gib'ē-ȧ), hill. Josh. 15. 57.
Gibeath (gib'ē-ath), hill. Josh. 18. 28.
Gibeon (gib'ē-ŏn), pertaining to a hill. Josh. 9. 3.
Gibeonites (gib'ē-ŏn-īts), inhabitants of Gibeon. 2 Sam. 21. 1.
Giblites (gib'līts), inhabitants of Gebal. Josh. 13. 5.
Giddalti (gi-dal'tī), I have increased. 1 Chr. 25. 4.
Giddel (gid'el), gigantic. Ezra 2. 47.
Gideon (gid'ē-ŏn), one who cuts down. Judg. 6. 11.
Gideoni (gid-ē-ō'nī), cutting down. Num. 1. 11.
Gidom (gī'dom). Judg. 20. 45.
Gihon (gī'hon), a river. Gen. 2. 13.
Gilalai (gil'ȧ-lī), dungy (?). Neh. 12. 36.
Gilboa (gil-bō'ȧ), bubbling fountain. 1 Sam. 28. 4.
Gilead (gil'ē-ăd), hill of witness. Gen. 31. 21.
Gileadite (gil'ē-ăd-īt), inhabitant of Gilead. Judg. 10. 3.
Gilgal (gil'gal), a circle. Josh. 4. 19.
Giloh (gī'lō), exile. Josh. 15. 51.
Gilonite (gī'lō-nīt), an inhabitant of Giloh. 2 Sam. 15. 12.
Gimzo (gim'zō), a place abounding with sycamores. 2 Chr. 28. 18.
Ginath (gī'nath), garden. 1 Kin. 16. 21.
Ginnetho (gin'ē-thō), garden. Neh. 12. 4.
Ginnethon (gin'ē-thon), same as preceding. Neh. 10. 6.
Girgashite (gīr'gȧ-shīt), dwelling in a clayey soil. 1 Chr. 1. 14.
Girgasite (gīr'gȧ-sīt), same as preceding. Gen. 10. 16.
Gispa (gis'pȧ), flattery. Neh. 11. 21.
Gittah-hepher (git-ä-hē'fēr), wine-press of the well. Josh. 19. 13.
Gittaim (git'ā-im), two wine-presses. 2 Sam. 4. 3.
Gittites (git'īts), inhabitants of Gath. Josh. 13. 3.
Gittith (git'ith), after the manner of Gittites. Ps. 8, title.
Gizonite (gī'zō-nīt). 1 Chr. 11. 34.
Goath (gō'ath), lowing. Jer. 31. 39.
Gob (gob), pit, cistern. 2 Sam. 21. 18.
Gog (gog). 1 Chr. 5. 4.
Golan (gō'lan), exile. Deut. 4. 43.
Golgotha (gol'gō-thȧ), a skull. Matt. 27. 33.
Goliath (gō-lī'ăth), exile (?). 1 Sam. 17. 4.
Gomer (gō'mēr), complete. Gen. 10. 2.
Gomorrah (gō-mor'ȧ). Gen. 10. 19.
Gomorrha (gō-mor'ȧ), same as preceding. Matt. 10. 15.
Goshen (gō'shen). Gen. 45. 10.
Gozan (gō'zan). 2 Kin. 17. 6.
Grecia (grē'chȧ), same as **Greece.** Dan. 8. 21.
Grecian (grē'chăn), a Jew who speaks Greek. Acts 11. 20.
Greece (grēc), country of the Greeks. Acts 20. 2.
Greek (grēk), the language of Greece. Acts 21. 37.
Greeks (grēks), inhabitants of Greece. Acts 18. 17.
Gudgodah (gud-gō'dȧ), thunder (?). Deut. 10. 7.
Guni (gū'nī), painted with colors. Gen. 46. 24.
Gunites (gū'nīts), descendants of Guni. Num. 26. 48.
Gur (gūr), a young lion. 2 Kin. 9. 27.
Gur-baal (gūr-bā'ăl), Gur of Baal. 2 Chr. 26. 7.

H

Haahashtari (hā-ȧ-hash'tȧ-rī), the muleteer (?). 1 Chr. 4. 6.
Habaiah (hȧ-bā'yȧ), whom Jehovah hides. Ezra 2. 61.
Habakkuk (hȧ-bak'uk), embrace. Hab. 1. 1.
Habaziniah (hab'ȧ-zi-nī'ȧ), lamp of Jehovah (?). Jer. 35. 3.
Habor (hā'bọr), joining together. 2 Kin. 17. 6.
Hachaliah (hach-ȧ-lī'ȧ), whom Jehovah disturbs. Neh. 1. 1.
Hachilah (hȧ-chī'lȧ), dark. 1 Sam. 23. 19.
Hachmoni (hach'mō-nī), wise. 1 Chr. 27. 32.
Hachmonite (hach'mō-nīt), a descendant of Hachmoni. 1 Chr. 11. 11.
Hadad (hā'dad). Gen. 36. 35.
Hadadezer (had-ad-ē'zēr), whose help is Hadad. 2 Sam. 8. 3.
Hadadrimmon (hā-dad-rim'ŏn), named from Hadad and Rimmon. Zech. 12. 11.
Hadar (hā'där), inclosure. Gen. 25. 15.
Hadarezer (had-ȧ-rē'zēr), same as Hadadezer. 1 Chr. 18. 3.
Hadashah (hȧ-dash'ȧ), new. Josh. 15. 37.
Hadassah (hȧ-das'ȧ), myrtle. Est. 2. 7.
Hadattah (hȧ-dat'ȧ), new. Josh. 15. 25.
Hadid (hā'did), sharp. Ezra 2. 33.
Hadlai (had'lī), rest. 2 Chr. 28. 12.
Hadoram (hȧ-dō'răm). Gen. 10. 27.
Hadrach (hā'drach). Zech. 9. 1.
Hagab (hā'gab), locust. Ezra. 2. 46.
Hagaba (hag'ȧ-bä), same as **Hagab.** Neh. 7. 48.
Hagar (hā'gär), flight. Gen. 16. 3.
Hagarenes (hag'ȧ-rēns), inhabitants of Hagar. Ps. 83. 6.
Hagarites (hā'gär-īts), same as preceding. 1 Chr. 5. 10.
Hagerite (hā'gēr-īt), same as **Hagarene.** 1. Chr. 27. 31.
Haggai (hag'ā-ī), festive. Hag. 1. 1.
Haggi (hag'ī), same as preceding. Gen. 46. 16.
Haggeri (hag'e-rī). 1 Chr. 11. 38.
Haggiah (hȧ-gī'ȧ), festival of Jehovah. 1 Chr. 6. 30.
Haggites (hag'īts), the posterity of Haggi. Num. 26. 15.
Haggith (hag'ith), festive. 2 Sam. 3. 4.
Hai (hā'ī), same as **Ai.** Gen. 12. 8.
Hakkatan (hak'ȧ-tan), the small. Ezra 8. 12.
Hakkoz (hak'oz), the thorn. 1. Chr. 24. 10.
Hakupha (hȧ-kū'fȧ). Ezra 2. 51.
Halah (hā'lȧ), same as **Calah** (?). 2 Kin. 17. 6.
Halak (hā'lak), smooth. Josh. 11. 17.
Halhul (hal'hul). Josh. 15. 58.
Hali (hā'lī), necklace. Josh. 19. 25.
Hallohesh (ha-lō'hesh), same as following. Neh. 10. 24.
Halohesh (ha-lō'hesh), the enchanter. Neh. 3. 12.
Ham (ham), warm Gen. 9. 18.
Haman (hā'măn). Est. 3. 1.
Hamath (hā'math), fortress. Num. 34. 8.
Hamathite (hā'math-īt), a dweller at Hamath. Gen. 10. 18.
Hamath-zobah (hā'math-zō'bȧ), fortress of Zobah. 2 Chr. 8. 3.

Hammath (ham′ath), warm springs. Josh. 19. 35.
Hammedatha (ham-ē-dā′thȧ), given by the moon (?). Est. 3. 1.
Hammelech (ham′e-leçh), the king. Jer. 36. 26.
Hammoleketh (ha-mol′ē-keth), the queen. 1 Chr. 7. 18.
Hammon (ham′ŏn), warm. Josh. 19. 28.
Hammoth-dor (ham′oth-dọr′), warm springs of Dor. Josh. 21. 32.
Hamonah (hȧ-mō′nȧ), multitude. Ezek. 39. 16.
Hamon-gog (hā′mon-gog′), m. of Gog. Ezek. 39. 11.
Hamor (hā′mọr), ass. Gen. 33. 19.
Hamuel (ham′ū-el), heat (wrath) of God. 1 Chr. 4. 26.
Hamul (hā′mul), who has experienced mercy. Gen. 46. 12.
Hamulites (hā′mul-īts), the posterity of Hamul. Num. 26. 21.
Hamutal (hȧ-mū′tăl), refreshing like dew. 2 Kin. 23. 31.
Hanameel (hȧ-nam′ē-el), probably another form of **Hananeel**. Jer. 32. 7.
Hanan (hā′năn), merciful. 1 Chr. 8. 23.
Hananeel (hȧ-nan′ē-el), whom God graciously gave. Neh. 3. 1.
Hanani (hȧ-nā′nī), probably same as **Hananiah.** 1 Kin. 16. 1.
Hananiah (han-ȧ-nī′ȧ), whom Jehovah graciously gave. 1 Chr. 3. 19.
Hanes (hā′nēş). Is. 30. 4.
Haniel (han′i-el), favor of God. 1 Chr. 7. 39.
Hannah (han′ȧ), gracious. 1 Sam. 1. 2.
Hannathon (han′ȧ-thon), gracious. Josh. 19. 14.
Hanniel (han′i-el), same as **Haniel.** Num. 34. 23.
Hanoch (hā′noçh), same as **Enoch.** Gen. 25. 4.
Hanochites (hā′noçh-īts), descendants of Hanoch. Num. 26. 5.
Hanun (hā′nun), whom (God) pities. 2 Sam. 10. 1.
Haphraim (haf-rā′im), two pits. Josh 19. 19.
Hara (hā′rȧ), mountainous. 1 Chr. 5. 26.
Haradah (hȧ-rā′dȧ), fear. Num. 33. 24.
Haran (hā′răn), mountaineer. Gen. 11. 27.
Hararite (ha′rȧ-rīt), a mountaineer. 2 Sam. 23. 11.
Harbonah (här-bō′nȧ). Est. 7. 9.
Hareph (hā′ref), plucking. 1 Chr. 2. 51.
Hareth (hā′reth), thicket. 1 Sam. 22. 5.
Harhaiah (här-hā′yȧ), dried up (?). Neh. 3. 8.
Harhas (här′has). 2 Kin. 22. 14.
Harhur (här′hūr), inflammation. Ezra 2. 51.
Harim (hā′rim), flat-nosed. 1 Chr. 24. 8.
Hariph (hā′rif), autumnal showers. Neh. 7. 24.
Harnepher (här′ne-fĕr). 1 Chr. 7. 36.
Harod (hā′rod), terror. Judg. 7. 1.
Harodite (hā′rod-īt), inhabitant of Harod. 2 Sam. 23. 25.
Haroeh (hȧ-rō′e), the seer. 1 Chr. 2. 52.
Harorite (hā′rō-rīt), probably another form of **Harodite.** 1 Chr. 11. 27.
Harosheth (hȧ-rō′sheth), carving. Judg. 4. 2.
Harsha (här′shȧ), enchanter, magician. Ezra 2. 52.
Harum (hā′rum), high (?). 1 Chr. 4. 8.
Harumaph (hȧ-rụ′maf), flat-nosed. Neh. 3. 10.
Haruphite (hȧ-rụ′fīt). 1 Chr. 12. 5.
Haruz (hā′ruz), active. 2 Kin. 21. 19.
Hasadiah (has-ȧ-dī′ȧ), whom Jehovah loves. 1 Chr. 3. 20.
Hasenuah (has-ē-nū′ȧ), she that is hated. 1 Chr. 9. 7.
Hashabiah (hash-ȧ-bī′ȧ), whom Jehovah esteems. 1 Chr. 6. 45.
Hashabnah (hȧ-shab′nȧ), same as preceding (?). Neh. 10. 25.
Hashabniah (hash-ab-nī′ȧ), same as **Hashabiah.** Neh. 3. 10.
Hashbadana (hash-bad′ȧ-nȧ). Neh. 8. 4.
Hashem (hā′shem), fat. 1 Chr. 11. 34.
Hashmonah (hash-mō′nȧ), fatness, fat soil. Num. 33. 29.
Hashub (hā′shub), thoughtful. Neh. 3. 11.
Hashubah (hȧ-shụ′bȧ), same as preceeding. 1 Chr. 3. 20.
Hashum (hā′shum), rich. Ezra 2. 19.
Hashupha (hȧ-shụ′fȧ), another form of **Hasupha.** Neh. 7. 46.
Hasrah (haş′rȧ), probably same as **Harhas.** 2 Chr. 34. 22.
Hassenaah (has-ē-nā′ȧ), the thorny. Neh. 3. 3.
Hasshub (hash′ub), same as **Hashub.** 1 Chr. 9. 14.
Hasupha (hȧ-sū′fȧ), one of the Nethinims. Ezra 2. 43.
Hatach (hā′taçh). Est. 4. 5.
Hathath (hā′thath), terror. 1 Chr. 4. 13.
Hatipha (hȧ-tī′fȧ), seized. Ezra 2. 54.
Hatita (hȧ-tī′tȧ), digging. Ezra 2. 42.
Hattil (hat′il), wavering. Ezra 2. 57.
Hattush (hat′ush), assembled (?). 1 Chr. 3. 22.
Hauran (hä-ụ-rän′), hollow land. Ezek. 47. 6.
Havilah (hav′i-lä). Gen. 10. 7.
Havoth-jair (hā′voth-jā′ir), villages of Jair. Num. 32. 41.
Hazael (haz′ā-el), whom God watches over. 1 Kin. 19. 15.
Hazaiah (hȧ-zā′yȧ), whom Jehovah watches over. Neh. 11. 5.
Hazar-addar (hā′zär-ad′är), Addar-town. Num. 34. 4.
Hazar-enan (hā′zär-ē′năn), fountain-town. Num. 34. 9.
Hazar-gaddah (hā′zär-gad′ȧ), luck-town. Josh. 15. 27.
Hazar-hatticon (hā′zär-hat′i-çon), middle-town. Ezek. 47. 16.
Hazarmaveth (hā′zär-mā′veth), death-town. Gen. 10. 26.
Hazar-shual (hā′zär-shụ′ăl), jackal-town. Josh. 15. 28.
Hazar-susah (hā′zär-sū′sȧ), mare-town. Josh. 19. 5.
Hazar-susim (hā′zär-sū′sim), horses-town. 1 Chr. 4. 31.
Hazelelponi (haz′e-lel-pō′nī), the shadow looking on me. 1 Chr. 4. 3.
Hazerim (hȧ-zē′rim), villages. Deut. 2. 23.
Hazeroth (hȧ-zē′roth), same as **Hazerim.** Num. 11. 35.
Hazezon-tamar (haz′ē-zon-tā′măr), pruning of the palm. Gen. 14. 7.
Haziel (hā′zi-el), the vision of God, 1 Chr. 23. 9.
Hazo (hā′zō), vision. Gen. 22. 22.
Hazor (hā′zọr), castle. Josh. 11. 1.
Heber (hē′bĕr), (1) same as **Eber.** 1 Chr. 5. 13; (2) fellowship. Gen. 46. 17.
Heberites (hē′bĕr-īts), descendants of Heber. Num. 26. 45.
Hebrew (hē′brụ), (1) the language spoken by the Jews. John 19. 20. (2) a Jew. Jer. 34. 9.
Hebrewess (hē′brụ-es), a Jewess. Jer. 34. 9.
Hebrews (hē′brụş), descendants of Eber. Gen. 40. 15.
Hebron (hē′brŏn), alliance. Gen. 13. 18.
Hebronites (hē′brŏn-īts), the people of Hebron. Num. 3. 27.
Hegai (heg′ā-ī) or **Hege** (hē′gē). Est. 2. 3, 8.
Helah (hē′lä), rust. 1 Chr. 4. 5.
Helam (hē′lăm), stronghold. 2 Sam. 10. 16.
Helbah (hel′bȧ), fatness. Judg. 1. 31.
Helbon (hel′bon), fertile. Ezek. 27. 18.
Heldai (hel′dā-ī), terrestrial. 1 Chr. 27. 15.
Heleb (hē′leb), fat, fatness. 2 Sam. 23. 29.
Heled (hē′led), world. 1 Chr. 11. 30.
Helek (hē′lek), portion. Num. 26. 30.
Helekites (hē′lek-īts), descendants of Helek. Num. 26. 30.
Helem (hē′lem), another form of **Heldai.** 1 Chr. 7. 35.
Heleph (hē′lef), exchange. Josh. 19. 33.
Helez (hē′lez), liberation. 2 Sam. 23. 26.
Heli (hē′lī), the Greek form of **Eli.** Luke 3. 23.
Helkai (hel′kā-ī), another form of **Hilkiah.** Neh. 12. 15.
Helkath (hel′kath), a portion. Josh 19. 25.
Helkath-hazzurim (hel′kath-haz′ū-rim), the field of swords (?). 2 Sam. 2. 16.
Helon (hē′lon), strong. Num. 1. 9.
Hemam (hē′mam), same as **Homam.** Gen. 36. 22.
Heman (hē′măn), faithful. 1 Kin. 4. 31.
Hemath (hē′math), (1) fortress, 1 Chr. 2. 55; (2) same as **Hamath.** Amos 6. 14.
Hemdan (hem′dan), pleasant. Gen. 36. 26.
Hen (hen), favor. Zech. 6. 14.
Hena (hē′nȧ). 2 Kin. 18. 34.
Henadad (hen′ȧ-dad), favor of Hadad (?). Ezra 3. 9.
Henoch (hē′nŏçh), same as **Enoch.** 1 Chr. 1. 3.
Hepher (hē′fĕr), pit. Josh. 12. 17
Hepherites (hē′fĕr-īts), descendants of Hepher. Num. 26. 32.
Hephzi-bah (hef′zi-bȧ), in whom is my delight. 2 Kin. 21. 1.
Heres (hē′rēş), the sun. Judg. 1. 35.
Heresh (hē′resh), artificer. 1 Chr. 9. 15.
Hermas (hĕr′măs). Rom. 16. 14.
Hermes (hĕr′mēş). Rom. 16. 14.
Hermogenes (hĕr-moġ′ē-nēş). 2 Tim. 1. 15.
Hermon (hĕr′mŏn), lofty. Deut. 3. 8.
Hermonites (hĕr′mŏn-īts), the summits of Hermon. Ps. 42. 6.
Herod (her′ŏd). Matt. 2. 1.
Herodians (hē-rō′di-ănş), partisans of Herod. Matt. 22. 16.
Herodias (hē-rō′di-as). Matt. 14. 3.
Herodion (hē-rō′di-ŏn). Rom. 16. 11.
Hesed (hē′sed), mercy. 1 Kin. 4. 10.
Heshbon (hesh′bon), counting. Num. 21. 25.
Heshmon (hesh′mon), fatness. Josh. 15. 27.
Heth (heth). Gen. 10. 15.
Hethlon (heth′lon), hiding-place. Ezek. 47. 15.
Hezeki (hez′ē-kī), shortened from **Hizkiah.** 1 Chr. 8. 17.
Hezekiah (hez-ē-kī′ȧ), the might of Jehovah. 2 Kin. 18. 1.
Hezion (hē′zi-ŏn), vision. 1 Kin. 15. 18.
Hezir (hē′zīr), swine. 1 Chr. 24. 15.
Hezrai (hĕz′rā-ī), inclosed wall. 2 Sam. 23. 35.
Hezro (hez′rō), same as preceding. 1 Chr. 11. 37.
Hezron (hez′ron), same as **Hezrai.** Gen. 46. 12.
Hezronites (hez′ron-īts), descendants of Hezron. Num. 26. 6.
Hiddai (hid′ā-ī), the rejoicing of Jehovah. 2 Sam. 23. 30.
Hiddekel (hid′e-kel). Gen. 2. 14.
Hiel (hī′el), God liveth. 1 Kin. 16. 34.
Hierapolis (hī-ĕr-ap′ō-lis), a sacred or holy city. Col. 4. 13.
Higgaion (hi-gā′yon), meditation. Ps. 9. 16.
Hilen (hī′len). 1 Chr. 6. 58.
Hilkiah (hil-kī′ȧ), portion of Jehovah. 2 Kin. 18. 18.
Hillel (hil′el), praising. Judg. 12. 13.
Hinnom (hin′ŏm). Josh. 15. 8.
Hirah (hī′rȧ), nobility. Gen. 38. 1.
Hiram (hī′răm), noble (?). 2 Sam. 5. 11.
Hittites (hit′īts), descendants of Heth. Gen. 15. 20.
Hivites (hī′vīts), villagers. Ex. 3. 8.
Hizkiah (hiz-kī′ȧ), might of Jehovah. Zeph. 1. 1.
Hizkijah (hiz-kī′jȧ), same as preceding. Neh. 10. 17.
Hobab (hō′bab), beloved. Num. 10. 29.
Hobah (hō′bȧ), a hiding-place. Gen. 14. 15.
Hod (hod), splendor. 1 Chr. 7. 37.
Hodaiah (hō-dā′yȧ), praise of Jehovah. 1 Chr. 3. 24.
Hodaviah (hō-dȧ-vī′ȧ), Jehovah is his praise. 1 Chr. 5. 24.
Hodesh (hō′desh), new moon. 1 Chr. 8. 9.
Hodevah (hō-dē′vȧ), same as **Hodaviah.** Neh. 7. 43.
Hodiah (hō-dī′ȧ), same as **Hodaiah.** 1 Chr. 4. 19.
Hodijah (hō-dī′jȧ), same as preceding. Neh. 8. 7.
Hoglah (hog′lȧ), partridge. Num. 26. 33.
Hoham (hō′ham). Josh. 10. 3.
Holon (hō′lon), sandy. Josh. 15. 51.
Homam (hō′mam), destruction. 1 Chr. 1. 39.
Hophni (hof′nī), pugilist. 1 Sam. 1. 3.
Hophra (hof′rȧ), priest of the sun. Jer. 44. 30.
Hor (họr), mountain. Num. 20. 23.
Horam (hō′ram). Josh. 10. 33.
Horeb (hō′reb), desert. Ex. 3. 1.
Horem (hō′rem). Josh. 19. 38.
Hor-hagidgad (họr′ha-gid′gad), mountain of Gudgodah. Num. 33. 32.
Hori (hō′rī), cave-dweller. Gen. 36. 22.
Horims (hō′rimş), descendants of Hori. Deut. 2. 12.
Horites (hō′rīts), same as preceding. Gen. 14. 6.
Hormah (họr′mȧ), a devoting, a place laid waste. Num. 14. 45.
Horonaim (họr-ō-nā′im), two caverns. Is. 15. 5.
Horonite (họr′ō-nīt), native of Beth-horon. Neh. 2. 10.
Hosah (hō′sȧ), fleeing to Jehovah for refuge (?). Josh. 19. 29.
Hosanna (hō-şan′ȧ), save us we pray. Matt. 21. 9.
Hosea (hō-şē′ȧ), salvation. Hos. 1. 1.
Hoshaiah (hō-shā′yȧ), whom Jehovah has set free. Neh. 12. 32.
Hoshama (hosh′ȧ-mȧ). 1 Chr. 3. 18.
Hoshea (hō-shē′ȧ), same as **Hoseah.** Deut. 32. 44.
Hotham (hō′thȧm), signet ring. 1 Chr. 7. 32.
Hothan (hō′thăn). 1 Chr. 11. 44.
Hothir (hō′thīr). 1 Chr. 25. 4.
Hukkok (huk′ok), decreed. Josh. 19. 34.
Hukok (hū′kok), same as preceding. 1 Chr. 6. 75.
Hul (hul), circle. Gen. 10. 23.
Huldah (hul′dȧ), weasel. 2 Kin. 22. 14.
Humtah (hum′tȧ), fortress (?). Josh. 15. 54.
Hupham (hū′făm), inhabitant of the shore (?). Num. 26. 39.
Huphamites (hū′făm-īts), descendants of Hupham. Num. 26. 39.
Huppah (hup′ȧ), covering. 1 Chr. 24. 13.
Huppim (hup′im), same as **Hupham** (?). Gen. 46. 21.
Hur (hūr), cavern. Ex. 17. 10.
Hurai (hū′rā-ī), another way of writing **Hiddai.** 1 Chr. 11. 32.
Huram (hū′răm), the older way of spelling **Hiram.** 2 Chr. 2. 13.
Huri (hū′rī), linen-worker (?). 1 Chr. 5. 14.
Hushah (hū′shȧ), haste. 1 Chr. 4. 4.
Hushai (hū′shī), hasting. 2 Sam. 15. 32.
Husham (hū′shăm), haste. Gen. 36. 34.
Hushathite (hū′shath-īt), inhabitant of Hushah. 2 Sam. 23. 27.
Hushim (hū′shim), those who make haste. Gen. 46. 23.
Huz (huz). Gen. 22. 21.
Huzzab (huz′ăb), it is decreed. Neh. 2. 7.
Hymenæus (hȳ-me-nē′us), belonging to Hymen. 2 Tim. 2. 17.

I

Ibhar (ib′här), whom God chooses. 2 Sam. 5. 15.
Ibleam (ib′lē-am), He destroys the people. Josh. 17. 11.
Ibneiah (ib-nē′yȧ), whom Jehovah will build up. 1 Chr. 9. 8.
Ibnijah (ib-nī′jȧ), same as preceding. 1 Chr. 9. 8.
Ibri (ib′rī), Hebrew. 1 Chr. 24. 27.
Ibzan (ib′zan), active (?). Judg. 12. 8.
I-chabod (içh′ȧ-bod), inglorious. 1 Sam. 4. 21.
Iconium (ī-çō′ni-um). Acts 13. 51.
Idalah (id′ȧ-lȧ), snares (?). Josh. 19. 15.
Idbash (id′bash), honeyed. 1 Chr. 4. 3.
Iddo (id′ō), (1) loving. 1 Chr. 27. 21.; (2) Ezra 8. 17.; (3) seasonable. Zech. 1. 1.
Idumea (id-ū-mē′ȧ), same as **Edom.** Is. 34. 5.
Igal (ī′gal), whom God will avenge. Num. 13. 7.
Igdaliah (ig-dȧ-lī′ȧ), whom Jehovah shall make great. Jer. 35. 4.
Igeal (ī′gē-ăl), same as **Igal.** 1 Chr. 3. 22.
Iim (ī′im), ruins. Num. 33. 45.
Ije-abarim (ī-jē-ab′ȧ-rim), ruinous heaps of Abarim. Num. 21. 11.
Ijon (ī′jon), a ruin. 1 Kin. 15. 20.
Ikkesh (ik′esh), perverseness of mouth. 2 Sam. 23. 26.
Ilai (ī′lā-ī), most high. 1 Chr. 11. 29.
Illyricum (il-lyr′i-çum). Rom. 15. 19.
Imla (im′lȧ), same as **Imlah.** 2 Chr. 18. 7.
Imlah (im′lȧ), whom (God) will fill up. 1 Kin. 22. 8.
Immanuel (i-man′ū-el), God with us. Is. 7. 14.
Immer (im′ĕr), talkative. 1 Chr. 9. 12.
Imna (im′nȧ), whom (God) keeps back. 1 Chr. 7. 35.
Imnah (im′nȧ), whom (God) assigns (?). 1 Chr. 7. 30.
Imrah (im′rȧ), stubborn. 1 Chr. 7. 36.
Imri (im′rī), eloquent. 1 Chr. 9. 4.
India (in′di-ȧ). Est. 1. 1.
Iphedeiah (if-ē-dē′yȧ), whom Jehovah frees. 1 Chr. 8. 25.
Ir (ir), city. 1 Chr. 7. 12.
Ira (ī′rȧ), watchful. 2 Sam. 20. 26.
Irad (ī′rad). Gen. 4. 18.
Iram (ī′ram), belonging to a city. Gen. 36. 43.
Iri (ī′rī), same as **Iram.** 1 Chr. 7. 7.
Irijah (ī-rī′jȧ), whom Jehovah looks on. Jer. 37. 13.
Ir-nahash (ir-nā′hash), snake-town. 1 Chr. 4. 12.
Iron (ī′ron), reverence. Josh. 19. 38.

Irpeel (ir'pē-el), which God heals. Josh. 18. 27.

Ir-shemesh (ir-shĕ'mesh), sun-town. Josh. 19. 41.

Iru (ī'rụ), same as **Iram.** 1 Chr. 4. 15.

Isaac (ī'şa̤ç), laughter. Gen. 17. 19.

Isaiah (ī-şā'yȧ), salvation of Jehovah. Is. 1. 1.

Iscah (is'çȧ). Gen. 11. 29.

Iscariot (is-çar'i-ŏt), man of Kerioth. Matt. 10. 4.

Ishbah (ish'bȧ), praising. 1 Chr. 4. 17.

Ishbak (ish'bak). Gen. 25. 2.

Ishbi-benob (ish'bī-bē'nob), one who dwells at Nob. 2 Sam. 21. 16.

Ish-bosheth (ish-bō'sheth), man of shame. 2 Sam. 2. 8.

Ishi (ish'ī), my husband. Hos. 2. 16.

Ishi (ish'ī), salutary. 1 Chr. 2. 31.

Ishiah (ish-ī'ȧ), whom Jehovah lends. 1 Chr. 7. 3.

Ishijah (ish-ī'jȧ), same as **Ishiah.** Ezra 10. 31.

Ishma (ish'mȧ). 1 Chr. 4. 3.

Ishmael (ish'mā-el), whom God hears. Gen. 16. 15

Ishmaelites (ish'mā-el-īts), descendants of Ishmael. Judg. 8. 24.

Ishmaiah (ish-mā'yȧ), whom Jehovah hears. 1 Chr. 27. 19.

Ishmeelites (ish'mē-el-īts), same as **Ishmaelites.** Gen. 37. 25.

Ishmerai (ish'mē-rī), whom Jehovah keeps. 1 Chr. 8. 18.

Ishod (ī'shod), man of glory. 1 Chr. 7. 18.

Ishpan (ish'pan), cunning (?). 1 Chr. 8. 22.

Ish-tob (ish'tob), men of Tob. 2 Sam. 10. 6.

Ishuah (ish'ū-ȧ), level. Gen. 46. 17.

Ishuai (ish'ū-ī), same as **Isui.** 1 Chr. 7. 30.

Ishui (ish'ū-ī), same as **Ishuah.** 1 Sam. 14. 49.

Ismachiah (is-mȧ-ḉhī'ȧ), whom Jehovah upholds. 2 Chr. 31. 13.

Ismaiah (is-mā'yȧ), same as **Ishmaiah.** 1 Chr. 12. 4.

Ispah (is'pȧ), bald. 1 Chr. 8. 16.

Israel (iş'rā-el), soldier of God. Gen. 32. 28.

Israelites (iş'rā-el-īts), descendants of Israel. Ex. 9. 7.

Israelitish (iş'rā-el-īt-ish), after the fashion of an Israelite. Lev. 24. 10.

Issachar (is'ȧ-ḉhär), he is hired (?). Gen. 30. 18.

Isshiah (is-shī'ȧ), same as **Ishiah.** 1 Chr. 24. 21.

Isuah (is'ū-ȧ), same as **Ishuah.** 1 Chr. 7. 30.

Isui (is'ū-ī), same as **Ishui.** Gen. 46. 17.

Italian (i-tal'yăn), belonging to Italy. Acts 10. 1.

Italy (it'ȧ-ly). Acts 18. 2.

Ithai (ith'ā-ī), plowman. 1 Chr. 11. 31.

Ithamar (ith'ȧ-mär), island of palms. Ex. 6. 23.

Ithiel (ith'i-el), God is with me. Neh. 11. 7.

Ithmah (ith'mä), bereavedness. 1 Chr. 11. 46.

Ithnan (ith'nan). Josh. 15. 23.

Ithra (ith'rȧ), excellence. 2 Sam. 17. 25.

Ithran (ith'ran), same as **Ithra.** Gen. 36. 26.

Ithream (ith'rē-am), remainder of the people. 2 Sam. 3. 5.

Ithrite (ith'rīt), descendants of Jethor (?). 2 Sam. 23. 38.

Ittah-kazin (it-ȧ-kā'zin), time of the chief. Josh. 19. 13.

Ittai (it'ā-ī), same as **Ithai.** 2 Sam. 15. 19.

Ituraea (it-ū-rē'ȧ), a province so named from Jetur. Luke 3. 1.

Ivah (ī'vȧ). 2 Kin. 18. 34.

Izehar (iz'ē-här), oil. Num. 3. 19.

Izeharites (iz-ē-här'īts), the descendants of Izehar. Num. 3. 27.

Izhar (iz'här), same as **Izehar.** Ex. 6. 18.

Izharites (iz'här-īts), the same as **Izeharites.** 1 Chr. 26. 23.

Izrahiah (iz-rȧ-hī'ȧ), whom Jehovah brought to light. 1 Chr. 7. 3.

Izrahite (iz'rȧ-hīt), probably same as **Zarhite.** 1 Chr. 27. 8.

Izri (iz'rī), a descendant of Jezer. 1 Chr. 25. 11.

J

Jaakan (jā'ȧ-kan), one who turns. Deut. 10. 6.

Jaakobah (jā-ȧ-kō'bȧ), same as Jacob. 1 Chr. 4. 36.

Jaala (jā'ȧ-lȧ), wild she-goat. Neh. 7. 58.

Jaalah (jā'ȧ-lȧ), same as **Jaala.** Ezra 2. 56.

Jaalam (jā'ȧ-lam), whom God hides. Gen. 36. 5.

Jaanai (jā'ȧ-nī), whom Jehovah answers. 1 Chr. 5. 12.

Jaare-oregim (jā'ȧ-rē-ọr'ē-ġim), forests of the weavers. 2 Sam. 21. 19.

Jassau (jā'ȧ-sạ). Ezra 10. 37.

Jaasiel (jā-ā'si-el), whom God created. 1 Chr. 27. 21.

Jaazaniah (jā-az'ȧ-nī'ȧ), whom Jehovah hears. 2 Kin. 25. 28.

Jaazer (jā'ȧ-zēr), whom (God) aids. Num. 21. 32.

Jaaziah (jā-ȧ-zī'ȧ), whom Jehovah strengthens. 1 Chr. 24. 26.

Jaaziel (jā-ā'zi-el), whom God strengthens. 1 Chr. 15. 18.

Jabal (jā'băl). Gen. 4. 20.

Jabbok (jab'ŏk), pouring out. Gen. 32. 22.

Jabesh (jā'besh), dry. 2 Kin. 15. 10.

Jabesh-gilead (jā'besh-gil'ē-ăd), Jabesh of Gilead. Judg. 21. 8.

Jabez (jā'bez), causing pain. 1 Chr. 4. 9.

Jabin (jā'bin), whom He (God) considered. Judg. 4. 2.

Jabneel (jab'nē-el), may God cause to be built. Josh. 15. 11.

Jabneh (jab'ne), which (God) causes to be built. 2 Chr. 26. 6.

Jachan (jā'ḉhăn), troubled. 1 Chr. 5. 13.

Jachin (jā'ḉhin), whom (God) strengthens. 1 Kin. 7. 21.

Jachinites (jā'ḉhin-īts), descendants of Jachin. Num. 26. 12.

Jacob (jā'çŏb), supplanter. Gen. 25. 26.

Jada (jā'dȧ), wise. 1 Chr. 2. 28.

Jadau (jā'da̤). Ezra 10. 43.

Jaddua (jȧ-dū'ȧ), skilled. Neh. 10. 21.

Jadon (jā'dŏn), a judge. Neh. 3. 7.

Jael (jā'el), same as **Jaala.** Judg. 4. 17.

Jagur (jā'gūr), a lodging. Josh. 15. 21.

Jah (jä), poetic form of **Jehovah.** Ps. 68. 4.

Jahath (jā'hath). 1 Chr. 6. 20.

Jahaz (jā'haz), a place trodden down. Num. 21. 23.

Jahaza (jȧ-hā'zȧ), same as **Jahaz.** Josh. 13. 18.

Jahazah (jȧ-hā'zȧ), same as **Jahaza.** Josh. 21. 36.

Jahaziah (jā-hȧ-zī'ȧ), whom Jehovah watches over. Ezra 10. 15.

Jahaziel (jȧ-hā'zi-el), whom God watches over. 1 Chr. 16. 6.

Jahdai (jä'dā-ī), whom Jehovah directs. 1 Chr. 2. 47.

Jahdiel (jä'di-el), whom God makes glad. 1 Chr. 5. 24.

Jahdo (jä'dō), union. 1 Chr. 5. 14.

Jahleel (jä'lē-el), hoping in God. Num. 26. 26.

Jahleelites (jä'lē-el-īts), descendants of Jahleel. Num. 26. 26.

Jahmai (jä'mā-ī). 1 Chr. 7. 2.

Jahzah (jä'zȧ), same as **Jahaz.** 1 Chr. 6. 78.

Jahzeel (jä'zē-el), whom God allots. Gen. 46. 24.

Jahzeelites (jä'zē-el-īts), descendants of Jahzeel. Num. 26. 48.

Jahzerah (jä'ze-rȧ), may he bring back. 1 Chr. 9. 12.

Jahziel (jä'zi-el), same as **Jahzeel.** 1 Chr. 7. 13.

Jair (jā'īr), (i.e. God) enlightens. Num. 32. 41.

Jairite (jā'īr-īt), a descendant of Jair. 2 Sam. 20. 26.

Jairus (jā'i-rus), Greek form of **Jair.** Mark 5. 22.

Jakan (jā'kăn), same as **Jaakan.** 1 Chr. 1. 42.

Jakeh (jā'ke), pious (?). Prov. 30. 1.

Jakim (jā'kim), (God) sets up. 1 Chr. 8. 19.

Jalon (jā'lon), passing the night. 1 Chr. 4. 17.

Jambres (jam'brēş). 2 Tim. 3. 8.

James (jāmş), the English equivalent for Jacob in the New Testament. Matt. 4. 21.

Jamin (jā'min), right hand. Gen. 46. 10.

Jaminites (jā'min-īts), descendants of Jamin. Num. 26. 12.

Jamlech (jam'leḉh), He makes to reign. 1 Chr. 4. 34.

Janna (jan'ȧ), probably another form of John. Luke 3. 24.

Jannes (jan'ēş). 2 Tim. 3. 8.

Janoah (jȧ-nō'ȧ), rest. 2 Kin. 15. 29.

Janohah (jȧ-nō'hȧ), same as preceding. Josh. 16. 6.

Janum (jā'num), sleep. Josh. 15. 53.

Japheth (jā'feth), extension. Gen. 5. 32.

Japhia (jȧ-fī'ȧ), splendid. Josh. 19. 12.

Japhlet (jaf'let), may he deliver. 1 Chr. 7. 32.

Japhleti (jaf'lē-tī), the Japhletite, or descendant of Japhlet. Josh. 16. 3.

Japho (jā'fō), beauty. Josh. 19. 46.

Jarah (jā'rȧ), forest. 1 Chr. 9. 42.

Jareb (jā'reb), one who is contentious. Hos. 5. 13.

Jared (jā'red), descent. Gen. 5. 15.

Jaresiah (jar-ē-sī'ȧ), whom Jehovah nourishes. 1 Chr. 8. 27.

Jarha (jär'hȧ). 1 Chr. 2. 34.

Jarib (jā'rib), adversary. 1 Chr. 4. 24.

Jarmuth (jär'muth), height. Josh. 10. 3.

Jaroah (jȧ-rō'ȧ), moon (?). 1 Chr. 5. 14.

Jashen (jā'shen), sleeping. 2 Sam. 23. 32.

Jasher (jā'shēr), upright. Josh. 10. 13.

Jashobeam (jȧ-shō'bē-am), the people return. 1. Chr. 11. 11.

Jashub (jā'shub), he returns. Num. 26. 24.

Jashubi-lehem (jȧ-shụ'bī-lē'hem), giving bread (?). 1 Chr. 4. 22.

Jashubites (jā'shub-īts), descendants of Jashub. Num. 26. 24.

Jasiel (jā'si-el), whom God made. 1 Chr. 11. 47.

Jason (jā'sŏn), Greco-Judean equivalent of Joshua. Acts 17. 5.

Jathniel (jath'ni-el), God gives. 1 Chr. 26. 2.

Jattir (jat'īr), excelling. Josh. 15. 48.

Javan (jā'văn), wine (?). Gen. 10. 2.

Jazer (jā'zēr), same as **Jaazer.** Num. 32. 1.

Jaziz (jā'ziz), wanderer (?). 1 Chr. 27. 31.

Jearim (jē'ȧ-rim), forests. Josh. 15. 10.

Jeaterai (jē-at'ē-rī). 1 Chr. 6. 21.

Jeberechiah (jē-ber'ē-ḉhī'ȧ), whom Jehovah blesses. Is. 8. 2.

Jebus (jē'bus), a place trodden down (?). Judg. 19. 10.

Jebusi (jeb'ū-sī), a Jebusite. Josh. 18. 16.

Jebusites (jeb'ū-sīts), the descendants of Jebus, the son of Canaan. Num. 13. 29.

Jecamiah (jeç-ȧ-mī'ȧ). 1 Chr. 3. 18.

Jecholiah (jeḉh-ō-lī'ȧ), Jehovah is strong. 2 Kin. 15. 2.

Jechonias (jeḉh-ō-nī'ăs), the Greek way of spelling **Jeconiah.** Matt. 1. 11.

Jecoliah (jeç-ō-lī'ȧ), same as **Jecholiah.** 2 Chr. 26. 3.

Jeconiah (jeç-ō-nī'ȧ), Jehovah establishes. 1 Chr. 3. 16.

Jedaiah (jē-dā'yȧ), (1) Jehovah—(?). 1 Chr. 4. 37; (2) Jehovah knoweth. 1 Chr. 24. 7.

Jediael (jē-dī'ā-el), known of God. 1 Chr. 7. 6.

Jedidah (jē-dī'dȧ), beloved. 2 Kin. 22. 1.

Jedidiah (jed-i-dī'ȧ), beloved of Jehovah. 2 Sam. 12. 25.

Jeduthun (jē-dū'thun), friendship (?). 1 Chr. 16. 38.

Jeezer (jē-ē'zēr), contracted from **Abiezer.** Num. 26. 30.

Jeezerites (jē-ē'zēr-īts), descendants of Jeezer. Num. 26. 30.

Jegar-sahadutha (jē'gär-sā'hȧ-dū'thȧ), the heap of testimony. Gen. 31. 47.

Jehaleleel (jē-hȧ-lē'lē-el), he praises God. 1 Chr. 4. 16.

Jehalelel (jē-hal'ē-lel), same as preceding. 2 Chr. 29. 12.

Jehdeiah (jē-dē'yȧ), whom Jehovah makes glad. 1 Chr. 24. 20.

Jehezekel (jē-hez'ē-kel), same as **Ezekiel.** 1 Chr. 24. 16.

Jehiah (jē-hī'ȧ), Jehovah lives. 1 Chr. 15. 24.

Jehiel (jē-hī'el), God liveth. 1 Chr. 15. 18.

Jehieli (jē-hī'e-lī), a Jehielite. 1 Chr. 26. 21.

Jehizkiah (jē-hiz-kī'ȧ), same as **Hezekiah.** 2. Chr. 28. 12.

Jehoadah (jē-hō'ȧ-dȧ), whom Jehovah adorns. 1 Chr. 8. 36.

Jehoaddan (jē'hō-ad'ăn), Jehovah is beauteous (?). 2 Kin. 14. 2.

Jehoahaz (jē-hō'ȧ-haz), whom Jehovah holds fast. 2 Kin. 10. 35.

Jehoash (jē-hō'ash), Jehovah supports. 2 Kin. 11. 21.

Jehohanan (jē'hō-hā'năn), Jehovah is gracious. 1 Chr. 26. 3.

Jehoiachin (jē-hoi'ȧ-ḉhin), Jehovah has established. 2 Kin. 24. 6.

Jehoiada (jē-hoi'ȧ-dȧ), Jehovah knoweth. 2 Sam. 8. 18.

Jehoiakim (jē-hoi'ȧ-kim), Jehovah has set up. 2 Kin. 23. 34.

Jehoiarib (jē-hoi'ȧ-rib), Jehovah will contend. 1 Chr. 9. 10.

Jehonadab (jē-hon'ȧ-dab), Jehovah is bounteous. 2 Kin. 10. 15.

Jehonathan (jē-hon'ȧ-thăn), same as **Jonathan.** 1 Chr. 27. 25.

Jehoram (jē-hō'ram), Jehovah is high. 1 Kin. 22. 50.

Jehoshabeath (jē'hō-shab'ē-ath), Jehovah is the oath. 2 Chr. 22. 11.

Jehoshaphat (jē-hosh'ȧ-fat), whom Jehovah judges. 1 Kin. 15. 24.

Jehosheba (jē-hosh'ē-bȧ), same as **Jehoshabeath.** 2 Kin. 11. 2.

Jehoshua (jē-hosh'ū-ȧ), same as **Joshua.** Num. 13. 16.

Jehoshuah (jē-hosh'ū-ȧ), same as **Joshua.** 1 Chr. 7. 27.

Jehovah (jē-hō'vȧ), the Eternal One. Ex. 6. 3.

Jehovah-jireh (jē-hō'vȧ-jī're), Jehovah will provide. Gen. 22. 14.

Jehovah-nissi (jē-hō'vȧ-nis'ī), Jehovah my banner. Ex. 17. 15.

Jehovah-shalom (jē-hō'vȧ-shā'lom), Jehovah send peace. Judg. 6. 24.

Jehozabad (jē-hoz'ȧ-bad), Jehovah gave. 2 Kin. 12. 21.

Jehozadak (jē-hoz'ȧ-dak), Jehovah is just. 1 Chr. 6. 14.

Jehu (jē'hū), Jehovah is He (?). 1 Kin. 19. 16.

Jehubbah (jē-hub'ȧ), hidden. 1 Chr. 7. 34.

Jehucal (jē-hū'çăl), Jehovah is mighty. Jer. 37. 3.

Jehud (jē'hud), praise. Josh. 19. 45.

Jehudi (jē-hū'dī), a Jew. Jer. 36. 14.

Jehudijah (jē'hū-dī'jȧ), a Jewess. 1 Chr. 4. 18.

Jehush (jē'hush), to whom God hastens. 1 Chr. 8. 39.

Jeiel (jē-ī'el). 1 Chr. 5. 7.

Jekabzeel (jē-kab'zē-el), God gathers. Neh. 11. 25.

Jekameam (jek-ȧ-mē'am). 1 Chr. 23. 19.

Jekamiah (jek-ȧ-mī'ȧ), same as **Jecamiah.** 1. Chr. 2. 41.

Jekuthiel (jē-kū'thi-el), the fear of God. 1 Chr. 4. 18.

Jemima (jē-mī'mȧ), dove. Job 42. 14.

Jemuel (jē-mū'el), day of God. Gen. 46. 10.

Jephthae (jef'thē), Greek way of writing **Jephthah.** Heb. 11. 32.

Jephthah (jef'thȧ), God opens. Judg. 11. 1.

Jephunneh (jē-fun'e), for whom it is prepared. Num. 13. 6.

Jerah (jē'rȧ), the moon. Gen. 10. 26.

Jerahmeel (jē-rä'mē-el), whom God loves. 1 Chr. 2. 9.

Jerahmeelites (jē-rä'mē-el-īts), descendants of Jerahmeel. 1 Sam. 27. 10.

Jered (jē'red), descent. 1 Chr. 1. 2.

Jeremai (jer'ē-mī), dwelling in heights. Ezra 10. 33.

Jeremiah (jer-ē-mī'ȧ), whom Jehovah has appointed. Jer. 1. 1.

Jeremias (jer-ē-mī'ăs), Greek form of **Jeremiah.** Matt. 16. 14.

Jeremoth (jer'ē-moth), high places. 1 Chr. 8. 14.

Jeremy (jer'ē-my), shortened English form of **Jeremiah.** Matt. 2. 17.

Jeriah (jē-rī'ȧ), whom Jehovah regards (?). 1 Chr. 23. 19.

Jeribai (jer'i-bī), contentious. 1 Chr. 11. 46.

Jericho (jer'i-ḉhō), a fragrant place. Num. 22. 1.

Jeriel (jē'ri-el), founded by God. 1 Chr. 7. 2.

Jerijah (jē-rī'jȧ), same as **Jeriah.** 1 Chr. 26. 31.

Jerimoth (jer'i-moth), same as **Jeremoth.** 1 Chr. 7. 7.

Jerioth (jer'i-oth), curtains. 1 Chr. 2. 18.

Jeroboam (jer-ō-bō'ăm), whose people are many. 1 Kin. 11. 26.

Jeroham (jē-rō'ham), who is loved. 1 Sam. 1. 1.

Jerubbaal (jer-ub-bā'ăl), let Baal plead. Judg. 6. 32.

Jerubbesheth (jer'ub-bē'sheth), let shame plead, another name for **Jerubbaal.** 2 Sam. 11. 21.

Jeruel (jē-rụ'el), same as **Jeriel.** 2 Chr. 20. 16.

Jerusalem (jē-rụ'sȧ-lem), founded in peace (?). Josh. 10. 1.

Jerusha (jē-rụ'shȧ), possession. 2 Kin. 15. 33.

Jerushah (jē-rụ'shȧ), same as preceding. 2 Chr. 27. 1.

Jesaiah (jē-sā'yȧ), same as **Isaiah.** 1 Chr. 3. 21.

Jeshaiah (jē-shā'yȧ), same as preceding. 1 Chr. 25. 3.

Jeshanah (jesh'ȧ-nȧ), old. 2 Chr. 13. 19.

Jesharelah (jesh-ȧ-rē'lȧ), right before God (?). I Chr. 25. 14.

Jeshebeab (jē-sheb'ē-ab), father's seat. 1 Chr. 24. 13.

Jesher (jē'shẽr), uprightness. 1 Chr. 2. 18.
Jeshimon (jē-shī'mon), the waste. Num. 21. 20.
Jeshishai (jē-shish'ā-ī), like an old man. 1 Chr. 5. 14.
Jeshohaiah (jesh-ō-hā'yȧ), whom Jehovah humbles. 1 Chr. 4. 36.
Jeshua (jesh'ū-ȧ), Jehovah is salvation. Ezra 2. 2.
Jeshuah (jesh'ū-ȧ), help. 1 Chr. 24. 11
Jeshurun (jesh'ū-run), righteous. Deut. 32. 15.
Jesiah (jē-sī'ȧ). 1 Chr. 12. 6.
Jesimiel (jē-sim'i-el), whom God founds (?). 1 Chr. 4. 36.
Jesse (jes'ē), gift (?). Ruth 4. 17.
Jesui (jes'ū-ī), same as **Ishua.** Num. 26. 44.
Jesuites (jes'ū-īts), the posterity of Jesui. Num. 26. 44.
Jesurun (jes'ū-run), wrongly printed for **Jeshurun.** Is. 44. 2.
Jesus (jē'ṣus), Saviour. Matt. 1. 21.
Jether (jē'thẽr), same as **Ithra.** Judg. 8. 20.
Jetheth (jē'theth). Gen. 36. 40.
Jethlah (jeth'lȧ), lofty. Josh. 19. 42.
Jethro (jeth'rō), same as **Ithra.** Ex. 3. 1.
Jetur (jē'tūr), an inclosure. Gen. 25. 15.
Jeuel (jē-ū'el), same as **Jeiel.** 1 Chr. 9. 6.
Jeush (jē'ush), same as **Jehush.** Gen. 36. 5.
Jeuz (jē'uz), counselor. 1 Chr. 8. 10.
Jew (jū), an Israelite. Est. 2. 5.
Jewess (jū'es), a female Jew. Acts 16. 1.
Jewish (jū'ish), of or belonging to Jews. Tit. 1. 14.
Jewry (jū'ry), Old English name for Judea. Dan. 5. 13.
Jews (jūṣ), inhabitants of Judea. 2 Kin. 16. 6.
Jezaniah (jez-ȧ-nī'ȧ), Jehovah adorns (?). Jer. 40. 8.
Jezebel (jez'e-bel), unmarried. 1 Kin. 16. 31.
Jezer (jē'zẽr), anything made. Gen. 46. 24.
Jezerites (jē'zẽr-īts), descendants of Jezer. Num. 26. 49.
Jeziah (jē-zī'ȧ), whom Jehovah assembles. Ezra 10. 25.
Jeziel (jē'zi-el), the assembly of God. 1 Chr. 12. 3.
Jezliah (jez-lī'ȧ), deliverance (?). 1 Chr. 8. 18.
Jezoar (jē-zō'ȧr), splendid. 1 Chr. 4. 7.
Jezrahiah (jez-rȧ-hī'ȧ), Jehovah shines forth. Neh. 12. 42.
Jezreel (jez'rē-el), God scatters. 1 Chr. 4. 3.
Jezreelite (jez'rē-el-īt), an inhabitant of Jezreel. 1 Kin. 21. 6.
Jezreelitess (jez'rē-el-īt-es), feminine of preceding. 1 Sam. 27. 3.
Jibsam (jib'săm), fragrant. 1 Chr. 7. 2.
Jidlaph (jid'laf), weeping (?). Gen. 22. 22.
Jimna (jim'nȧ), same as **Imna.** Num. 26. 44.
Jimnah (jim'nȧ), same as **Imnah.** Gen. 46. 17.
Jimnites (jim'nīts), descendants of Jimnah. Num. 26. 44.
Jiphtah (jif'tȧ), same as **Jephthah.** Josh. 15. 43.
Jiphthah-el (jif'thȧ-el), which God opens. Josh. 19. 14.
Joab (jō'ab), Jehovah is father. 2 Sam. 2. 13.
Joah (jō'ȧ), Jehovah is brother. 2 Kin. 18. 18.
Joahaz (jō'ȧ-haz), whom Jehovah holds. 2 Chr. 34. 8.
Joanna (jō-an'ȧ), Greek way of writing Jehonan. Luke 3. 27.
Joash (jō'ash), whom Jehovah supports (?). 2 Kin. 11. 2.
Joatham (jō'ȧ-tham), Greek form of **Jotham.** Matt. 1. 9.
Job (jōb), (1) a desert. Gen. 46. 13; (2) one persecuted. Job 1. 1.
Jobab (jō'bab), a desert. Gen. 10. 29.
Jochebed (joch'ē-bed), Jehovah is glorious (?). Ex. 6. 20.
Joed (jō'ed), for whom Jehovah is witness. Neh. 11. 7.
Joel (jō'el), Jehovah is might. Joel 1. 1.
Joelah (jō-ē'lȧ), He helps (?). 1 Chr. 12. 7.
Joezer (jō-ē'zẽr), Jehovah is help. 1 Chr. 12. 6.
Jogbehah (jog'bē-hä), lofty. Num. 32. 35.
Jogli (jog'lī), an exile. Num. 34. 22.
Joha (jō'hȧ), Jehovah lives (?). 1 Chr. 8. 16.
Johanan (jō-hā'năn), Jehovah is gracious. 2 Kin. 25. 23.
John (jon), English way of spelling **Johanan.** Matt. 3. 1.
Joiada (joi'ȧ-dȧ), Jehovah knows. Neh. 12. 10.
Joiakim (joi'ȧ-kim), shortened from **Jehoiakim.** Neh. 12. 10.
Joiarib (joi'ȧ-rib), whom Jehovah defends. Ezra 8. 16.
Jokdeam (jok'dē-am), burning of the people. Josh. 15. 56.
Jokim (jō'kim), shortened from **Jehoiakim.** 1 Chr. 4. 22.
Jokmeam (jok'mē-am). 1 Chr. 6. 68.
Jokneam (jok'nē-am), possessed by the people. Josh. 12. 22.
Jokshan (jok'shăn), fowler. Gen. 25. 2.
Joktan (jok'tăn), small. Gen. 10. 25.
Joktheel (jok'thē-el), subdued by God. Josh. 15. 38.
Jona (jō'nȧ), a Greek way of spelling **Johanan.** John 1. 42.
Jonadab (jon'ȧ-dab), same as **Jehonadab.** 2. Sam. 13. 3.
Jonah (jō'nȧ), dove. 2 Kin. 14. 25.
Jonan (jō'nan), contracted from **Jonanan.** Luke 3. 30.
Jonas (jō'năs), same as **(1) Jona.** John 21. 15; or (2) **Jonah.** Matt. 12. 39.
Jonath-elem-rechokim (jō'nath-ē'lem-rē-chō'kim), the silent dove far off. Title of Ps. 56.
Jonathan (jon'ȧ-thăn), whom Jehovah gave. 1 Sam. 13. 2.
Joppa (jop'ȧ), beauty (?). 2 Chr. 2. 16.
Jorah (jō'rȧ), watering (?). Ezra 2. 18.
Jorai (jō'rā-ī), archer (?). 1 Chr. 5. 13.
Joram (jō'ram), same as **Jehoram.** 2 Sam. 8. 10.
Jordan (jor'dăn), flowing down. Gen. 13. 10.
Jorim (jō'rim), a form of **Joram** (?). Luke 3. 29.
Jorkoam (jor'kō-am), spreading of the people (?). 1 Chr. 2. 44.
Josabad (jos'ȧ-bad), same as **Jehozabad.** 1 Chr. 12. 4.
Josaphat (jos'ȧ-fat), Greek form of **Jehoshaphat.** Matt. 1. 8.
Josedech (jos'ē-dech), same as **Jehozadak.** Hag. 1. 1.
Joseph (jō'ṣef), he shall add. Gen. 30. 24.
Joses (jō'sēṣ). Matt. 13. 55.
Joshah (jō'shȧ), Jehovah presents (?). 1 Chr. 4. 34.
Joshaphat (josh'ȧ-fat), shortened from **Jehoshaphat.** 1 Chr. 11. 43.
Joshaviah (josh'ȧ-vī'ȧ), same as **Joshah.** 1 Chr. 11. 46.
Joshbekashah (josh-bē-kȧ'shȧ), seat of hardship (?). 1 Chr. 25. 4.
Joshua (josh'ū-ȧ), Jehovah is salvation. Num. 14. 6.
Josiah (jō-sī'ȧ), whom Jehovah heals. 2 Kin. 21. 24.
Josias (jō-sī'ȧs), Greek form of **Josiah.** Matt. 1. 10.
Josibiah (jos-i-bī'ȧ), to whom God gives a dwelling. 1 Chr. 4. 35.
Josiphiah (jos-i-fī'ȧ), whom Jehovah will increase. Ezra. 8. 10.
Jotbah (jot'bȧ), pleasantness (?). 2 Kin. 21. 19.
Jotbath (jot'bath), same as **Jotbah.** Deut. 10. 7.
Jotbathah (jot'bȧ-thȧ), same as **Jotbah.** Num. 33. 33.
Jotham (jō'thăm), Jehovah is upright. Judg. 9. 5.
Jozabad (joz'ȧ-bad), same as **Jehozabad.** 1 Chr. 12. 20.
Jozachar (joz'ȧ-chär), whom Jehovah has remembered. 2 Kin. 12. 21.
Jozadak (joz'ȧ-dak), same as **Jehozadak.** Ezra 3. 2.
Jubal (jū'băl), music (?). Gen. 4. 21.
Jucal (jū'căl), same as **Jehucal.** Jer. 38. 1.
Juda (jū'dȧ), same as **Judah.** Luke 3. 30.
Judah (jū'dȧ), praised. Gen. 29. 35.
Judas (jū'dăs), Greek form of **Judah.** Matt. 10. 4.
Jude (jūd), abbreviated from **Judas.** Jud 1.
Judea (jū-dē'ȧ), (land of Judah). Ezra 5. 8.
Judith (jū'dith), (probably from the same). Gen. 26. 34.
Julia (jūl'yȧ), feminine form of Julius. Rom. 16. 15.
Julius (jūl'yus), downy. Acts 27. 1.
Junia (jū'ni-ȧ). Rom. 16. 7.
Jupiter (jū'pi-tẽr). Acts 14. 12.
Jushab-hesed (jū'shab-hē'sed), whose love is returned. 1 Chr. 3. 20.
Justus (jus'tus), upright. Acts 1. 23.
Juttah (jut'ȧ), extended. Josh. 15. 55.

K

Kabzeel (kab'zē-el), God has gathered. Josh. 15. 21.
Kadesh (kā'desh), consecrated. Gen. 20. 1.
Kadesh-barnea (kā'desh-bär'nē-ȧ). Num. 34. 4.
Kadmiel (kad'mi-el), eternity of God (?). Ezra 2. 40.
Kadmonites (kad'mŏn-īts), Orientals. Gen. 15. 19.
Kallai (kal'ā-ī), swift. Neh. 12. 20.
Kanah (kā'nȧ), a place of reeds. Josh. 19. 28.
Kareah (kȧ-rē'ȧ), bald. Jer. 40. 8.
Karkaa (kär'kā-ȧ), floor. Josh. 15. 3.
Karkor (kär'kor), plain (?). Judg. 8. 10.
Karnaim (kär'nā-im), two horns. Gen. 14. 5.
Kartah (kär'tȧ), city. Josh. 21. 34.
Kartan (kär'tan), double city. Josh. 21. 32.
Kattath (kat'ath), small (?). Josh. 19. 15.
Kedar (kē'dăr), black-skinned. Gen. 25. 13.
Kedemah (ked'ē-mȧ), eastward. Gen. 25. 15.
Kedemoth (ked'ē-moth), eastern parts. Josh. 13. 18.
Kedesh (kē'desh), sanctuary. Josh. 12. 22.
Kehelathah (kē'hē-lā'thȧ), assembly. Num. 33. 22.
Keilah (kē-ī'lȧ), sling (?). Josh. 15. 44.
Kelaiah (kē-lā'yȧ), contempt (?). Ezra 10. 23.
Kelita (kel'i-tȧ), dwarf. Neh. 8. 7.
Kemuel (kem'ū-el), congregation of God. Gen. 22. 21.
Kenan (kē'năn), smith (?). 1 Chr. 1. 2.
Kenath (kē'nath), possession. Num. 32. 42.
Kenaz (kē'naz), hunting. Gen. 36. 11.
Kenezite (kē'nez-īt), descendant of Kenaz. Num. 32. 12.
Kenites (kē'nīts), descendants of an unknown man named Kain. Gen. 15. 19.
Kenizzite (kē'niz-īt), same as **Kenezite.** Gen. 15. 19.
Keren-happuch (ker'en-hap'uk), horn of paint. Job 42. 14.
Kerioth (kē'ri-oth), cities. Josh. 15. 25.
Keros (kē'ros), crook (?). Ezra 2. 44.
Keturah (ke-tū'rȧ), incense. Gen. 25. 1.
Kezia (ke-zī'ȧ), cassia. Job 42. 14.
Keziz (kē'ziz), cut off. Josh. 18. 21.
Kibroth-hattaavah (kib'roth-hȧ-tā'ȧ-vȧ), graves of lust. Num. 11. 34.
Kibzaim (kib-zā'im), two heaps. Josh. 21. 22.
Kidron (kid'ron), turbit. 2 Sam. 15. 23.
Kinah (kī'nȧ), song of mourning, lamentation. Josh. 15. 22.
Kir (kir), town. 2 Kin. 16. 9.
Kir-haraseth (kir'har'ȧ-seth), brick-town. 2 Kin. 3. 25.
Kir-hareseth (kir'har'ē-seth), same as preceding. Is. 16. 7.
Kir-haresh (kir'hā'resh), same as preceding. Is. 16. 11.
Kir-heres (kir'hē'res), same as preceding. Jer. 48. 31.
Kiriathaim (kir-i-ȧ-thā'im), same as **Kirjathaim.** Ezek. 25. 9.
Kirioth (kir'i-oth), cities. Amos 2. 2.
Kirjath (kir'jath), city (?). Josh. 18. 28.
Kirjathaim (kir'jath-ā'im), double city. Num. 32. 37.
Kirjath-arba (kir'jath-är'bȧ), city of Arba. Gen. 23. 2.
Kirjath-arim (kir'jath-ā'rim), contracted from **Kirjath-jearim.** Ezra 2. 25.
Kirjath-baal (kir'jath-bā'ăl), city of Baal. Josh. 15. 60.
Kirjath-huzoth (kir'jath-hū'zoth), c. of streets. Num. 22. 39.
Kirjath-jearim (kir'jath-jē'ȧ-rim), c. of woods. Josh. 9. 17.
Kirjath-sannah (kir'jath-san'ȧ), c. of thorns. Josh. 15. 49.
Kirjath-sepher (kir'jath-sē'fẽr), book-city. Josh. 15. 15.
Kish (kish), bow. 1 Sam. 9. 1.
Kishi (kish'i), bow of Jehovah. 1 Chr. 6. 44.
Kishion (kish'i-on), hardness. Josh. 19. 20.
Kishon (kī'shon), tortuous. Judg. 4. 7.
Kison (kī'son), same as **Kishon.** Ps. 83. 9.
Kithlish (kith'lish), fortified. Josh. 15. 40.
Kitron (kit'ron), burning. Judg. 1. 30.
Kittim (kit'im), same as **Chittim.** Gen. 10. 4.
Koa (kō'ȧ), prince. Ezek. 23. 23.
Kohath (kō'hath), assembly. Gen. 46. 11.
Kohathites (kō'hath-īts), descendants of Kohath. Num. 3. 27.
Kolaiah (kō-lā'yȧ), voice of **Jehovah** (?). Neh. 11. 7.
Korah (kō'rȧ), bald. Num. 16. 1.
Korahites (kō'rȧ-īts), descendants of Korah. 1 Chr. 9. 19.
Korathites (kō'rath-īts), same as preceding. Num. 26. 58.
Kore (kō'rē), partridge. 1 Chr. 9. 19.
Korhite (kor'hīt), same as **Korathite.** 2 Chr. 20. 19.
Koz (koz), thorn. Ezra 2. 61.
Kushaiah (kū-shā'yȧ), longer form of **Kishi.** 1 Chr. 15. 17.

L

Laadah (lā'ȧ-dȧ), order (?). 1 Chr. 4. 21.
Laadan (lā'ȧ-dăn), put in order (?). 1 Chr. 7. 26.
Laban (lā'băn), white. Gen. 24. 29.
Lachish (lā'chish), impregnable. Josh. 10. 3.
Lael (lā'el), (devoted) to God. Num. 3. 24.
Lahad (lā'had), oppression. 1 Chr. 4. 2.
Lahai-roi (lȧ-hī'roi), to the living is sight. Gen. 24. 62.
Lahmam (lä'mam). Josh. 15. 40.
Lahmi (lä'mī), warrior. 1 Chr. 20. 5.
Laish (lā'ish), lion. 1 Sam. 25. 44.
Lakum (lā'kum), fort (?). Josh. 19. 33.
Lama (lā'mȧ), why? Matt. 27. 46.
Lamech (lā'mech), destroyer. Gen. 4. 18.
Laodicea (lā-od'i'cē'ȧ). Col. 2. 1.
Laodiceans (lā-od'i-cē'ănṣ), inhabitants of Laodicea. Col. 4. 16.
Lapidoth (lap'i-doth), torches. Judg. 4. 4.
Lasea (lȧ-sē'ȧ). Acts 27. 8.
Lasha (lā'shȧ), fissure. Gen. 10. 19.
Lasharon (lȧ-shā'rŏn), of the plain. Josh. 12. 18.
Latin (lat'in), the language spoken by Romans. John 19. 20.
Lazarus (laz'ȧ-rus), Greek form of **Eleazar.** Luke 16. 20.
Leah (lē'ȧ), languid. Gen. 29. 16.
Lebanah (lē-bā'nȧ), white. Ezra 2. 45.
Lebanon (leb'ȧ-nŏn), the white (mountain). Deut. 1. 7.
Lebaoth (lē-bā'oth), lionesses. Josh. 15. 32.
Lebbæus (le-bē'us). Matt. 10. 3.
Lebonah (lē-bō'nȧ), frankincense. Judg. 21. 19.
Lecah (lē'cȧ), journey (?). 1 Chr. 4. 21.
Lehabim (lē-hā'bim). Gen. 10. 13.
Lehi (lē'hī), jawbone. Judg. 15. 9.
Lemuel (lem'ū-el), devoted to God. Prov. 31. 1.
Leshem (lē'shem), precious stone. Josh. 19. 47.
Letushim (lē-tū'shim), the hammered. Gen. 25. 3.
Leummim (lē-um'im), peoples. Gen. 25. 3.
Levi (lē'vī), associate (?). Gen. 29. 34.
Leviathan (lē-vī'ȧ-thăn), a water monster. Ps. 104. 26.
Levites (lē'vīts), descendants of Levi. Ex. 6. 25.
Leviticus (lē-vit'i-cus), the book which treats of the affairs of the Levitical law.
Libertines (lib'ẽr-tīnṣ), freedmen. Acts. 6. 9.
Libnah (lib'nȧ), whiteness. Num. 33. 20.
Libni (lib'nī), white. Ex. 6. 17.
Libnites (lib'nīts), descendants of Libni. Num. 3. 21.
Libya (lib'y-ȧ). Acts 2. 10.
Likhi (lik'hī), fond of learning (?). 1 Chr. 7. 19.
Linus (lī'nus), flax. 2 Tim. 4. 21.
Lo-ammi (lō-am'ī), not my people. Hos. 1. 9.
Lod (lod), strife (?). 1 Chr. 8. 12.
Lo-debar (lō-dē'bär), without pasture (?). 2 Sam. 9. 4.
Lois (lō'is). 2 Tim. 1. 5.
Lo-ruhamah (lō'rū-hä'mȧ), not having obtained mercy. Hos. 1. 6.
Lot (lot), veil. Gen. 11. 27.
Lotan (lō'tăn), veiling. Gen. 36. 20.
Lubims (lū'bimṣ), same as **Lehabim.** 2 Chr. 12. 3.
Lucas (lū'căs), same as **Luke.** Philem. 24.
Lucifer (lū'ci-fẽr), light-bearer. Is. 14. 12.
Lucius (lū'chi-us), a noble (?). Acts 13. 1.
Lud (lud), strife (?). Gen. 10. 22.
Ludim (lū'dim). Gen. 10. 13.
Luhith (lū'hith), abounding in boards. Is. 15. 5.

Luke (lūk), of or belonging to Lucania. Col. 4. 14.

Luz (luz), almond-tree. Gen. 28. 19.

Lycaonia (lyç'ā-ō'ni-à). Acts 14. 6.

Lycia (lyçh'i-à). Acts 27. 5.

Lydda (lyd'à), Greek form of **Lod** (?). Acts 9. 32.

Lydia (lyd'i-à). Acts 16. 14.

Lysanias (ly̆-sā'ni-as), ending sorrow. Luke 3. 1.

Lysias (lys'i-as), a person of Lysia. Acts 23. 26.

Lystra (lys'trà). Acts 14. 6

M

Maacah (mā'à-çà), same as **Maachah.** 2 Sam. 3. 3.

Maachah (mā'à-çhà), royal (?). 1 Kin. 2. 39.

Maachathi (mā-açh'à-thī), an inhabitant of Maachah. Deut. 3. 14.

Maachathites (mā-açh'à-thīts), plural of preceding. Josh. 12. 5.

Maadai (mā-à-dā'ī), adorned. Ezra 10. 34.

Maadiah (mā-à-dī'à), ornament of Jehovah. Neh. 12. 5.

Maai (mā-ā'ī), compassionate (?). Neh. 12. 36.

Maaleh-acrabbim (mā'à-le-à-çrab'-im), ascent of scorpions. Josh. 15. 3.

Maarath (mā'à-rath), a treeless place. Josh. 15. 59.

Maaseiah (mā-à-sē'yà), work of Jehovah. Ezra 10. 18.

Maasiai (mā-as'i-ī) same as **Amashai** (?). 1 Chr. 9. 12.

Maath (mā'ath), small (?). Luke 3. 26.

Maaz (mā'az), wrath. 1 Chr. 2. 27.

Maaziah (mā-à-zī'à). 1 Chr. 24. 18.

Macedonia (mac-ē-dō'ni-à). Acts 16. 9.

Machbanai (maçh'bà-nī), cloak. 1 Chr. 12. 13.

Machbenah (maçh-bē'nà), clad with a cloak (?). 1 Chr. 2. 49.

Machi (mā'çhī). Num. 13. 15.

Machir (mā'çhir), sold. Gen. 50. 23.

Machirites (mā'çhir-īts), the descendants of Machir. Num. 26. 29.

Machnadebai (maçh-nad'ē-bī). Ezra 10. 40.

Machpelah (maçh-pē'là), a doubling. Gen. 23. 9.

Madai (mad'ā-ī). Gen. 10. 2.

Madian (mā'di-ăn), Greek form of **Midian.** Acts 7. 29.

Madmannah (mad-man'à), dunghill. Josh. 15. 31.

Madmen (mad'men), dungheap. Jer. 48. 2.

Madmenah (mad-mē'nà), same as **Madmen.** Is. 10. 31.

Madon (mā'don), place of contention. Josh. 11. 1.

Magbish (mag'bish), congregating. Ezra 2. 30.

Magdala (mag'dà-là), tower. Matt. 15. 39.

Magdalene (mag'dà-lēn), inhabitant of Magdala. Matt. 27. 56.

Magdiel (mag'di-el), praise of God. Gen. 36. 43.

Magog (mā'gog). Gen. 10. 2.

Magor-missabib (mā'gor-mis'à-bib), fear round about. Jer. 20. 3.

Magpiash (mag'pi-ash). Neh. 10. 20.

Mahalah (mà-hā'lä), disease. 1 Chr. 7. 18.

Mahalaleel (mà-hā'là-lē'ĕl), praise of God. Gen. 5. 12.

Mahalath (mā'hà-lath), a musical instrument. Gen. 28. 9.

Mahalath Leannoth (-lē-an-oth'). Ps. 88, title.

Mahali (mā'hà-lī), weak. Ex. 6. 19.

Mahanaim (mā-hà-nā'im), two camps. Gen. 32. 2.

Mahaneh-dan (mā'hà-ne-dan'), camp of Dan. Judg. 18. 12.

Maharai (mà-har'ā-ī), impetuous. 2 Sam. 23. 28.

Mahath (mā'hath), taking hold (?). 1 Chr. 6. 35.

Mahavite (mā'hà-vīt). 1 Chr. 11. 46.

Mahazioth (mà-hā'zi-oth), visions. 1 Chr. 25. 4.

Maher-shalal-hash-baz (mā'hĕr-shal'al-hash'baz), the spoil hastens, the prey speeds. Is. 8. 1.

Mahlah (mä'là), same as **Mahalah.** Num. 26. 33.

Mahli (mä'lī), same as **Mahali.** 1 Chr. 6. 19.

Mahlites (mä'līts), the descendants of Mahli. Num. 3. 33.

Mahlon (mä'lon) a sick person. Ruth 1. 2.

Mahol (mā'hol), a dance. 1 Kin. 4. 31.

Makaz (mā'kaz), end (?). 1 Kin. 4. 9.

Makheloth (mak-hē'loth), assemblies. Num. 33. 25.

Makkedah (ma-kē'dà), place of shepherds (?). Josh. 10. 10.

Maktesh (mak'tesh), a mortar. Zeph. 1. 11.

Malachi (mal'à-çhī), the messenger of Jehovah. Mal. 1. 1.

Malcham (mal'çham), their king. 1 Chr. 8. 9.

Malchiah (mal-çhī'à), Jehovah's king. 1 Chr. 6 40.

Malchiel (mal'çhi-el), God's king. Gen. 46. 17.

Malchielites (mal'çhi-el-īts), the descendants of Malchiel. Num. 26. 45.

Malchijah (mal-çhī'jà), same as **Malchiah.** 1 Chr. 9. 12.

Malchiram (mal-çhī'ram), king of height (?). 1 Chr. 3. 18.

Malchi-shua, (mal'çhī-shū'à), king of aid. 1 Chr. 8. 33.

Malchus (mal'çhus), Greek form of **Malluch.** John 18. 10.

Maleleel (mà-lē'lē-el), same as **Mahalaleel.** Luke 3. 37.

Mallothi (mal'ō-thī). 1 Chr. 25. 4.

Malluch (mal'uçh), counselor. 1 Chr. 6. 44.

Mammon (mam'ŏn), fullness. Matt. 6. 24.

Mamre (mam'rē), fatness. Gen. 14. 13.

Manaen (man'à-en), Greek form of **Menahem.** Acts 13. 1.

Manahath (man'à-hath), rest. Gen. 36. 23.

Manahethites (mà-nā'heth'īts), inhabitants of Manahath (?). 1 Chr. 2. 52.

Manasseh (mà-nas'e), one who causes to forget. Gen. 41. 51.

Manasses (mà-nas'ēṣ), Greek form of **Manasseh.** Matt. 1. 10.

Manassites (mà-nas'īts), members of the tribe of Manasseh. Deut. 4. 42.

Maneh (mā'ne), a weight. Ezek. 45. 12.

Manoah (mà-nō'à), rest. Judg. 13. 2.

Maoch (mā'oçh), oppressed (?). 1 Sam. 27. 2.

Maon (mā'on), habitation. Josh. 15. 55.

Maonites (mā'on-īts). Judg. 10. 12.

Mara (mä'rà), sad. Ruth 1. 20.

Marah (mā'rà), bitter. Ex. 15. 23.

Maralah (mar'à-lä), trembling. Josh. 19. 11.

Maranatha (mar-à-nath'à), our Lord cometh. 1 Cor. 16. 22.

Marcus (mär'çus). Col. 4. 10.

Mareshah (mà-rē'shà), capital. Josh. 15. 44.

Mark (märk), English form of Marcus. Acts 12. 12.

Maroth (mā'roth), bitterness. Mic. 1. 12.

Mars' Hill, English name for Areopagus. Acts 17. 22.

Marsena (mär-sē'nà). Est. 1. 14.

Martha (mär'thà), lady. Luke 10. 38.

Mary, Greek form of Miriam. Matt. 1. 16.

Maschil (mäs'çhil), understanding. Ps. 53, title.

Mash. Gen. 10. 23.

Mashal (mā'shal), entreaty (?). 1 Chr. 6. 74.

Masrekah (mas-rē'kà), vineyard. Gen. 36. 36.

Massa (mas'à), burden. Gen. 25. 14.

Massah (mas'à), temptation. Ex. 17. 7.

Mathusala (mà-thū'sà-là), Greek form of **Methuselah.** Luke 3. 37.

Matred (mā'tred), pushing forward. Gen. 36. 39.

Matri (mā'trī), rainy. 1 Sam. 10. 21.

Mattan (mat'ăn), a gift. 2 Kin. 11. 18.

Mattanah (mat'à-nà), same as preceding. Num. 21. 18.

Mattaniah (mat-à-nī'à), gift of Jehovah. 2 Kin. 24. 17.

Mattatha (mat'à-thà), a Greek form of above. Luke. 3. 31.

Mattathah (mat'à-thà), gift of Jehovah. Ezra. 10. 33.

Mattathias (mat-à-thī'ăs), a Greek form of the preceding. Luke 3. 26.

Mattenai (mat-ē-nā'ī), liberal. Ezra 10. 33.

Matthan (mat'than), gift. Matt. 1. 15.

Matthat (mat'that), another form of **Matthan.** Luke 3. 24.

Matthew, English way of spelling **Mattithiah.** Matt. 9. 9

Matthias (mà-thī'ăs), another Greek form of **Mattathias.** Acts 1. 23.

Mattithiah (mat-i-thī'à), another form of **Mattathias.** 1 Chr. 9. 31.

Mazzaroth (maz'à-roth), the signs of the zodiac. Job. 38. 32.

Meah (mē'à), a hundred. Neh. 3. 1.

Mearah (mē-ā'rà), cave. Josh. 13. 4.

Mebunnai (mē-bun'ī), built (?). 2 Sam. 23. 27.

Mecherathite (mē-çhē'rath-īt), inhabitant of Mecherah (?). 1 Chr. 11. 36.

Medad (mē'dad). Num. 11. 26.

Medan (mē'dan), contention. Gen. 25. 2.

Medeba (med'ē-bà), flowing water (?). Num. 21. 30.

Medes, inhabitants of Media. 2 Kin. 17. 6.

Media (mē'di-à), Greek form of Madia. Est. 1. 3.

Megiddo (mē-gid'ō), place of troops. Josh. 12. 21.

Megiddon (mē-gid'on), same as preceding. Zech. 12. 11.

Mehetabeel (mē-het'à-bēl), lengthened form of the following. Neh. 6. 10.

Mehetabel (mē-het'à-bel), God makes happy. Gen. 36. 39.

Mehida (mē-hī'dà). Ezra. 2. 52.

Mehir (mē'hīr), price. 1 Chr. 4. 11.

Meholathite (mē-hō'lā-thīt), native of Meholah. 1 Sam. 18. 19.

Mehujael (mē-hū'jā-el), struck by God. Gen. 4. 18.

Mehuman (mē-hū'man). Est. 1. 10.

Mehunim (mē-hū'nim). Ezra 2. 50.

Mehunims (mē-hū'nimṣ), the people of Maon (?). 2 Chr. 26. 7.

Me-jarkon (mē-jär'kon), waters of yellowness. Josh. 19. 46.

Mekonah (mē-kō'nà), a base. Neh. 11. 28.

Melatiah (mel-à-tī'à), whom Jehovah freed. Neh. 3. 7.

Melchi (mel'çhī), Greek form of **Melchiah.** Luke 3. 24.

Melchiah (mel-çhī'à), Jehovah's king. Jer. 21. 1.

Melchisedec (mel-çhis'e-deç), Greek form of **Melchizedek.** Heb. 5. 6.

Melchi-shua (mel'çhī-shū'à), same as **Malchi-shua.** 1 Sam. 14. 49.

Melchizedek (mel-çhiz'e-dek), king of righteousness. Gen. 14. 18.

Melea (mē'lē-à), fullness (?). Luke 3. 31.

Melech (mē'leçh), king. 1 Chr. 8. 35.

Melicu (mel'i-çū), same as **Malluch.** Neh. 12. 14.

Melita (mel'i-tà). Acts 28. 1.

Melzar (mel'zär), steward. Dan. 1. 11.

Memphis (mem'fis). Hos. 9. 6.

Memucan (mē-mū'çăn). Est. 1. 14.

Menahem (men'à-hem), comforter. 2 Kin. 15. 14.

Menan (mē'nan). Luke 3. 31.

Mene (mē'nē), numbered. Dan. 5. 25.

Meonenim (mē-on'ē-nim). Judg. 9. 37.

Meonothai (mē-on'ō-thī), my habitations. 1 Chr. 4. 14.

Mephaath (mef'ā-ath), beauty. Josh. 13. 18.

Mephibosheth (mē-fib'ō-sheth), destroying shame. 2 Sam. 4. 4.

Merab (mē'rab), increase. 1 Sam. 14. 49.

Meraiah (mē-rā'yà), contumacy. Neh. 12. 12.

Meraioth (mē-rā'yoth), rebellions. 1 Chr. 6. 6.

Merari (mē-rā'rī), bitter. Gen. 46. 11.

Merathaim (mer-à-thā'im), rebellions. Jer. 50. 21.

Mercurius (mẽr-çū'ri-us). Acts 14. 12.

Mered (mē'red), rebellion. 1 Chr. 4. 17.

Meremoth (mer'ē-moth), elevations. Ezra 8. 33.

Meres (mē'rēṣ), worthy (?). Est. 1. 14.

Meribah (mer'i-bä), water of strife. Ex. 17. 7.

Merib-baal (mer'ib-bā'ăl), contender (?) against Baal. 1 Chr. 8. 34.

Merodach (mē-rō'daçh). Jer. 50. 2.

Merodach-baladan (mē-rō'daçh-bal'-à-dăn), Merodach gives a son. Is. 39. 1.

Merom (mē'rom), a high place. Josh. 11. 5.

Meronothite (mē-ron'ō-thīt), an inhabitant of Meronoth. 1 Chr. 27. 30.

Meroz (mē'roz), refuge (?). Judg. 5. 23.

Mesech (mē'seçh), same as **Meshech.** Ps. 120. 5.

Mesha (mē'shà), deliverance. 2 Kin. 3. 4.

Meshach (mē'shaçh). Dan. 1. 7.

Meshech (mē'sheçh), tall (?). Gen. 10. 2.

Meshelemiah (mē-shel'ē-mī'à), Jehovah repays. 1 Chr. 9. 21.

Meshezabeel (mē-shez'à-bēl), God delivers. Neh. 3. 4.

Meshillemith (mē-shil'ē-mith), recompense. 1 Chr. 9. 12.

Meshillemoth (mē-shil'ē-moth), retribution. 2 Chr. 28. 12.

Meshobab (mē-shō'bab), brought back. 1 Chr. 4. 34.

Meshullam (mē-shul'ăm), friend. 2 Kin. 22. 3.

Meshullemeth (mē-shul'ē-meth), feminine of preceding. 2 Kin. 21. 19.

Mesobaite (mē-sō'bà-īt), inhabitant of Mesoba (?). 1 Chr. 11. 47.

Mesopotamia (mes'ō-pō-tā'mi-à), amidst the rivers. Gen. 24. 10.

Messiah (me-sī'à), anointed. Dan. 9. 25.

Messias (me-sī'ăs), Greek form of the above. John 1. 41.

Metheg-ammah (mē'theg-am'à), bridle of Ammah. 2 Sam. 8. 1.

Methusael (mē-thū'sā-el), man of God. Gen. 4. 18.

Methuselah (mē-thū'ṣe-là), man of the dart (?). Gen. 5. 21.

Meunim (mē-ū'nim), same as **Mehunim.** Neh. 7. 52.

Mezahab (mez'ā-hab), water of gold. Gen. 36. 39.

Miamin (mī'à-min), on the right hand. Ezra 10. 25.

Mibhar (mib'här), choicest. 1 Chr. 11. 38.

Mibsam (mib'sam), sweet odor. Gen. 25. 13.

Mibzar (mib'zär), a fortress. Gen. 36. 42.

Micah (mī'çà), who (is) like unto Jehovah? Judg. 17. 1.

Micaiah (mī-çā'yà), fuller form of **Micah.** 1 Kin. 22. 8.

Michael (mī'çhā-el), who (is) like unto God? Dan. 10. 13.

Michah (mī'çhà), same as **Micah.** 1 Chr. 24. 24.

Michaiah (mī-çhā'yà), same as **Micaiah.** Neh. 12. 35.

Michal (mī'çhăl), brook. 1 Sam. 14. 49.

Michmas (miçh'mas), later form of **Michmash.** Ezra 2. 27.

Michmash (miçh'mash), treasured. 1 Sam. 13. 2.

Michmethah (miçh'mē-thà), hiding-place (?). Josh. 16. 6.

Michri (miçh'rī), precious (?). 1 Chr. 9. 8.

Michtam (miçh'tam), writing (?). Ps. 16, title.

Middin (mid'in), extensions. Josh. 15. 61.

Midian (mid'i-ăn), strife. Gen. 25. 2.

Midianites (mid'i-ăn-īts), people of Midian. Gen. 37. 28.

Migdal-el (mig'dal-el), tower of God. Josh. 19. 38.

Migdal-gad (mig'dal-gad), tower of Gad. Josh. 15. 37.

Migdol (mig'dol). Ex. 14. 2.

Migron (mig'ron), a precipice. Is. 10. 28.

Mijamin (mij'à-min), same as **Miamin.** 1 Chr. 24. 9.

Mikloth (mik'loth), staves, lots. 1 Chr. 8. 32.

Mikneiah (mik-nē'yà), possession of Jehovah. 1 Chr. 15. 18.

Milalai (mil-à-lā'ī), eloquent (?). Neh. 12. 36.

Milcah (mil'çà), counsel (?). Gen. 11. 29.

Milcom (mil'çom), same as **Moloch.** 1 Kin. 11. 5.

Miletum (mī-lē'tum), improper form of **Miletus.** 2 Tim. 4. 20.

Miletus (mī-lē'tus). Acts 20. 15.

Millo (mil'ō), a mound. Judg. 9. 6.

Miniamin (min'yà-min), full form of **Miamin.** 2 Chr. 31. 15.

Minni (min'ī), Armenia. Jer. 51. 27.

Minnith (min'ith), allotment. Judg. 11. 33.

Miphkad (mif'kad), place of meeting. Neh. 3. 31.

Miriam (mir'i-ăm), rebellion (?). Ex. 15. 20.

Mirma (mīr'mà), fraud. 1 Chr. 8. 10.

Misgab (mis'gab), height. Jer. 48. 1.

Mishael (mish'ā-el), who is what God is? Ex. 6. 22.

Mishal (mī'shăl), prayer. Josh. 21. 30

Misheal (mish'ē-al), same as **Mishal.** Josh. 19. 26.

Misham (mī'sham), cleansing. 1 Chr. 8. 12.

Mishma (mish'mà), report. Gen. 25. 14.

Mishmannah (mish-man'à), fatness. 1 Chr. 12. 10.

Mishraites (mish'rā-its). 1 Chr. 2. 53.

Mispereth (mis'pē-reth), number. Neh. 7. 7.

Misrephoth-maim (mis'rē-foth-mā'im), burning of waters. Josh. 11. 8.

Mithcah (mith'çà), place of sweetness. Num. 33. 28.

Mithnite (mith'nīt). 1 Chr. 11. 43.

Mithredath (mith'rē-dath), given by Mithra. Ezra 1. 8.

Mitylene (mit-y-lē'nē). Acts 20. 14.

Mizar (mī'zär), smallness. Ps. 42. 6.

Mizpah (miz'pà), a lookout. Gen. 31. 49.

Mizpar (miz'pär), number. Ezra 2. 2.

Mizpeh (miz'pe), watchtower. Josh. 11. 3.
Mizraim (miz-rā'im), fortresses. Gen. 10. 6.
Mizzah (miz'ȧ). Gen. 36. 13.
Mnason (nā'sŏn). Acts 21. 16.
Moab (mō'ab), progeny of a father. Gen. 19. 37.
Moabites (mō'ăb-īts), people of Moab. Deut. 2. 9.
Moabitess (mō'ăb-īt-es), a lady of Moab. Ruth 4. 5.
Moadiah (mō-ȧ-dī'ȧ), festival of Jehovah. Neh. 12. 17.
Moladah (mol'ȧ-dȧ), birth. Josh. 15. 26.
Molech (mō'leçh), English form for **Moloch.** Lev. 18. 21.
Moloch (mō'loçh), king. Amos 5. 26.
Molid (mō'lid), begetter. 1 Chr. 2. 29.
Morasthite (mō-ras'thīt), native of Moresheth. Jer. 26. 18.
Mordecai (mọr'dē-çī), worshiper of Merodach (?). Est. 2. 5.
Moreh (mō're), archer. Gen. 12. 6.
Moresheth-gath (mō'resh-eth-gath'), the possession of Gath. Mic. 1. 14.
Moriah (mō-rī'ȧ), provided by Jehovah. Gen. 22. 2.
Mosera (mō-sē'rȧ), bond. Deut. 10. 6.
Moseroth (mō-sē'roth), bonds. Num. 33. 30.
Moses (mō'ṣes), saved from the water. Ex. 2. 10.
Moza (mō'zȧ), fountain. 1 Chr. 2. 46.
Mozah (mō'zȧ), same as **Moza.** Josh. 18. 26.
Muppim (mup'im), probably written for **Shupham.** Gen. 46. 21.
Mushi (mū'shī), withdrawn. Ex. 6. 19.
Muth-labben (muth-lab'en), death to the son (?). Ps. 9, title.
Myra (mȳ'rȧ), balsam. Acts 27. 5.
Mysia (mish'i-ȧ). Acts 16. 7.

N

Naam (nā'am), pleasantness. 1 Chr. 4. 15.
Naamah (nā'ȧ-mȧ), pleasant. Gen. 4. 22.
Naaman (nā'ȧ-măn), pleasantness. 2 Kin. 5. 1.
Naamathite (nā'ȧ-mȧ-thīt). Job 2. 11.
Naamites (nā'ăm-īts), descendants of Naaman. Num. 26. 40.
Naarah (nā'ȧ-rȧ), a girl. 1 Chr. 4. 5.
Naarai (nā'ȧ-rī), youthful. 1 Chr. 11. 37.
Naaran (nā'ȧ-ran), same as **Naarah.** 1 Chr. 7. 28.
Naarath (nā'ȧ-rath), to Naarah. Josh. 16. 7.
Naashon (nā-ash'on), enchanter. Ex. 6. 23.
Naasson (nā-as'on), Greek form of **Naashon.** Matt. 1. 4.
Nabal (nā'băl), foolish. 1 Sam. 25. 3.
Naboth (nā'both), fruits (?). 1 Kin. 21. 1.
Nachon (nā'çhon), prepared. 2 Sam. 6. 6.
Nachor (nā'çhọr), snorting. Josh. 24. 2.
Nadab (nā'dab), liberal. Ex. 6. 23.
Nagge (nag'ē), Greek form of **Nogah.** Luke 3. 25.
Nahalal (nā'hȧ-lal), a pasture. Josh. 21. 35.
Nahaliel (nȧ-hā'li-el), valley of God. Num. 21. 19.
Nahallal (nȧ-hal'ăl), same as **Nahalal.** Josh. 19. 15.
Nahalol (nā'hȧ-lol), same as preceding. Judg. 1. 30.
Naham (nā'ham), consolation. 1 Chr. 4. 19.
Nahamani (nā-hȧ-mā'nī), comforter. Neh. 7. 7.
Naharai (nā'hȧ-rī), one who snores. 1 Chr. 11. 39.
Nahari (nā'hȧ-rī), same as preceding. 2 Sam. 23. 37.
Nahash (nā'hash), serpent. 1 Sam 11. 1.
Nahath (nā'hath), descent. Gen. 36. 13.
Nahbi (nä'bī), hidden. Num. 13. 14.
Nahor (nā'họr), another way of spelling **Nachor.** Gen. 11. 22.
Nahshon (nä'shon), same as **Naashon.** Num. 1. 7.
Nahum (nā'hum), comforter. Nah. 1. 1.
Nain (nā'in), pasture. Luke 7. 11.
Naioth (nā'yoth), habitations. 1 Sam. 19. 18.
Naomi (nā'ō-mī), pleasant. Ruth 1. 2.
Naphish (nā'fish), cheerful. Gen. 25. 15.
Naphtali (naf'tȧ-lī), my wrestling. Gen. 30. 8.
Naphtuhim (naf-tū'him). Gen. 10. 13.
Narcissus (när-cis'us), benumbing. Rom. 16. 11.
Nathan (nā'thăn), gift. 2 Sam. 7. 2.
Nathanael (nȧ-than'ā-el), gift of God. John 1. 45.
Nathan-melech (nā'thăn-mē'leçh), gift of the king. 2 Kin. 23. 11.
Naum (nā'um), same as **Nahum.** Luke 3. 25.
Nazarene (naz-ȧ-rēn'), a native of Nazareth. Matt 2. 23.
Nazareth (naz'ȧ-reth), branch. Luke 1. 26.
Nazarite (naz'ȧ-rīt), one separated. Num. 6. 2.
Neah (nē'ȧ), of a slope. Josh. 19. 13.
Neapolis (nē-ap'ō-lis), new city. Acts 16. 11.
Neariah (nē-ȧ-rī'ȧ), servant of Jehovah. 1 Chr. 3. 22.
Nebai (nē'bī), fruitful. Neh. 10. 19.
Nebaioth (nē-bā'yoth), high places. 1 Chr. 1. 29.
Nebajoth (nē-bā'joth), same as **Nebaioth.** Gen. 25. 13.
Neballat (nē-bal'at). Neh. 11. 34.
Nebat (nē'bat), aspect. 1 Kin. 11. 26.
Nebo (nē'bō), a lofty place. Deut. 32. 49.
Nebuchadnezzar (neb'ū-çhăd-nez'ăr), another way of spelling the following. 2 Kin. 24. 1.
Nebuchadrezzar (neb'ū-çhăd-rez'ăr), Nebo protect the crown. Jer. 21. 2.
Nebushasban (neb'ū-shas'ban), Nebo will save me. Jer. 39. 13.
Nebuzar-adan (neb'ū-zär-ā'dan), Nebo gives posterity. 2 Kin. 25. 8.
Necho (nē'çhō), conqueror (?). Jer. 46. 2.
Nechoh, same as **Necho.** 2 Kin. 23. 29.
Nedabiah (ned-ȧ-bī'ȧ), Jehovah is bountiful (?). 1 Chr. 3. 18.
Neginah (ne-gī'nä), a stringed instrument. Ps. 61, title.
Neginoth (neg'i-noth), stringed instruments. Ps. 4, title.
Nego (nē'gō), same as **Nebo.** Dan. 1. 7.
Nehelamite (nē-hel'ȧ-mīt). Jer. 29. 24.
Nehemiah (nē'hē-mī'ȧ), Jehovah comforts. Neh. 1. 1.
Nehiloth (nē'hil-oth), flutes. Ps. 5, title.
Nehum (nē'hum), consolation. Neh. 7. 7.
Nehushta (nē-hush'tȧ), bronze. 2 Kin. 24. 8.
Nehushtan (nē-hush'tan), brazen. 2 Kin. 18. 4.
Neiel (nē-ī'el), moved by God. Josh 19. 27.
Nekeb (nē'keb), cavern. Josh. 19. 33.
Nekoda (nē-kō'dȧ), a herdman. Ezra 2. 48.
Nemuel (nem'ū-el), same as **Jemuel** (?). Num. 26. 9.
Nemuelites (nem'ū-el-īts), descendants of Nemuel. Num. 26. 12.
Nepheg (nē'feg), sprout. Ex. 6. 21.
Nephish (nē'fish), same as **Naphish.** 1 Chr. 5. 19.
Nephishesim (nē-fish'ē-sim), expansions. Neh. 7. 52.
Nephthalim (nef'thȧ-lim), Greek form of **Naphtali.** Matt. 4. 13.
Nephtoah (nef-tō'ȧ), opened. Josh. 15. 9.
Nephusim (nē-fū'sim), a better form for **Nephishesim.** Ezra 2. 50.
Ner (nẽr), light. 1 Sam. 14. 50.
Nereus (nē'rūs), liquid (?). Rom. 16. 15.
Nergal (nẽr'gäl), lion. 2 Kin. 17. 30.
Nergal-sharezer (nẽr'gäl-shȧ-rē'zẽr), Nergal protect the king. Jer. 39. 3.
Neri (nē'rī), Greek form of **Neriah.** Luke 3. 27.
Neriah (nē-rī'ȧ), lamp of Jehovah. Jer. 32. 12.
Nethaneel (nē-than'ē-el), same as **Nathanael.** Num. 1. 8.
Nethaniah (neth-ȧ-nī'ȧ), whom Jehovah gave. 2 Kin. 25. 23.
Nethinims (neth'i-nimṣ), the appointed. Neh. 10. 28.
Netophah (nē-tō'fȧ), dropping. Ezra 2. 22.
Netophathi (nē-tō'fȧ-thī), an inhabitant of Netophah. Neh. 12. 28.
Netophathite (nē-tof'ȧ-thīt), same as the preceding. 2 Sam. 23. 28.
Neziah (nē-zī'ȧ), illustrious. Ezra 2. 54.
Nezib (nē'zib), garrison. Josh. 15. 43.
Nibhaz (nib'haz). 2 Kin. 17. 31.
Nibshan (nib'shan), level (?). Josh. 15. 62.
Nicanor (nī-çā'nọr). Acts 6. 5.
Nicodemus (niç-ō-dē'mus). John 3. 1.
Nicolaitans (niç-ō-lā'i-tanṣ), named after Nicolas. Rev. 2. 6.
Nicolas (niç'ō-lȧs). Acts 6. 5.
Nicopolis (ni-çop'ō-lis), city of victory. Tit. 3. 12.
Niger (nī'gẽr), black. Acts 13. 1.
Nimrah (nim'rȧ), limpid (water). Num. 32. 3.
Nimrim (nim'rim), clear waters. Is. 15. 6.
Nimrod (nim'rod), an inhabitant of Marad (?). Gen. 10. 8.
Nimshi (nim'shī), discloser (?). 1 Kin. 19. 16.
Nineveh (nin'e-ve), dwelling (?). Gen. 10. 11.
Ninevites (nin'ev-īts), inhabitants of Nineveh. Luke 11. 30.
Nisan (nī'san). Neh. 2. 1.
Nisroch (nis'roçh), eagle (?). 2 Kin. 19. 37.
No (nō), abode (?). Nah. 3. 8.
Noadiah (nō-ȧ-dī'ȧ), whom Jehovah meets. Neh. 6. 14.
Noah (nō'ȧ), (1) rest. Gen. 5. 29. (2) wandering. Num. 26. 33.
No-amon (nō-ā'mon), abode of Amon. Jer. 46. 25.
Nob (nōb), high place. 1 Sam. 21. 1.
Nobah (nō'bȧ), a barking. Num. 32. 42.
Nod (nod), flight wandering. Gen. 4. 16.
Nodab (nō'dab), nobility. 1 Chr. 5. 19.
Noe (nō'ē), Greek form of **Noah.** Matt. 24. 37.
Nogah (nō'gȧ), brightness. 1 Chr. 3. 7.
Nohah (nō'hȧ), rest. 1 Chr. 8. 2.
Non (non), same as **Nun.** 1 Chr. 7. 27.
Noph (nof), same as **Memphis.** Is. 19. 13.
Nophah (nō'fȧ), windy. Num. 21. 30.
Nun (nun), fish. Ex. 33. 11.
Nymphas (nim'fas), shortened form of Nymphodorus. Col. 4. 15.

O

Obadiah (ō-bȧ-dī'ȧ), worshiper of Jehovah. Obad. 1.
Obal (ō'bal), hill (?). Gen. 10. 28.
Obed (ō'bed), worshiping (God). Ruth 4. 17.
Obed-edom (ō'bed-ē'dŏm), serving Edom. 2 Sam. 6. 10.
Obil (ō'bil), camel-keeper. 1 Chr. 27. 30.
Oboth (ō'both), bottles (of skin). Num. 21. 10.
Ocran (oç'răn), troublesome. Num. 1. 13.
Oded (ō'ded), setting up (?). 2 Chr. 15. 1.
Og (og), circle (?). Num. 21. 33.
Ohad (ō'had), might. Gen. 46. 10.
Ohel (ō'hel), tent. 1 Chr. 3. 20.
Olivet (ol'i-vet), place of olives. 2 Sam. 15. 30.
Olympas (ō-lym'pas), bright (?). Rom. 16. 15.
Omar (ō'măr), talkative. Gen. 36. 11.
Omega (ō-mē'gȧ), great O. Rev. 1. 8.
Omri (om'rī), like a sheaf (?). 1 Kin. 16. 16.
On (on), the sun. Gen. 41. 45.
Onam (ō'nam), wealthy. Gen. 36. 23.
Onan (ō'nan), strong. Gen. 38. 4.
Onesimus (ō-nes'i-mus), profitable. Col. 4. 9.
Onesiphorus (on-ē-sif'ō-rus), bringing profit. 2. Tim. 1. 16.
Ono (ō'nō), strong. 1 Chr. 8. 12.
Ophel (ō'fel), a hill. 2 Chr. 27. 3.
Ophir (ō'fīr). Gen. 10. 29.
Ophni (of'nī), man of the hill. Josh. 18. 24.
Ophrah (of'rȧ), fawn. 1 Chr. 4. 14.
Oreb (ō'reb), raven. Judg. 7. 25.
Oren (ō'ren), pine-tree. 1 Chr. 2. 25.
Orion (ō-rī'ŏn). Job 9. 9.
Ornan (ọr'năn). 1 Chr. 21. 15.
Orpah (ọr'pä), hind (?). Ruth 1. 4.
Osee (ō'ṣē), same as **Hosea.** Rom. 9. 25.
Oshea (ō-shē'ȧ), same as **Joshua.** Num. 13. 8.
Othni (oth'nī), powerful (?). 1 Chr. 26. 7.
Othniel (oth'ni-el), powerful man of God. Josh. 15. 17.
Ozem (ō'zem), strength. 1 Chr. 2. 15.
Ozias (ō-zī'ăs), Greek form of **Uzziah.** Matt. 1. 8.
Ozni (oz'nī), hearing. Num. 26. 16.
Oznites (oz'nīts), descendants of Ozni. Num. 26. 16.

P—Q

Paarai (pā'ȧ-rī), devoted to Peor (?). 2 Sam. 23. 35.
Padan-aram (pā'dăn-ā'ram), the plain of Syria. Gen. 25. 20.
Padon (pā'don), redemption. Ezra 2. 44.
Pagiel (pā'gi-el), intervention of God. Num. 1. 13.
Pahath-moab (pā'hath-mō'ab), governor of Moab. Ezra 2. 6.
Pai (pā'ī). bleating. 1 Chr. 1. 50.
Palal (pā'lăl), judge. Neh. 3. 25.
Palestina (pal'es-tī-na), land of strangers (?). Ex. 15. 14.
Pallu (pal'ū), distinguished. Ex. 6. 14.
Palluites (pal'ū-īts), descendants of Pallu. Num. 26. 5.
Palti (pal'tī), deliverance of Jehovah. Num. 13. 9.
Paltiel (pal'ti-el), deliverance of God. Num. 34. 26.
Paltite (pal'tīt), a descendant of Palti. 2 Sam. 23. 26.
Pamphylia (pam-fyl'i-ȧ). Acts 27. 5.
Paphos (pā'fos). Acts 13. 6.
Parah (pā'rȧ), heifer. Josh. 18. 23.
Paran (pā'răn), cavernous. Deut. 33. 2.
Parbar (pär'bär), open apartment. 1 Chr. 26. 18.
Parmashta (pär-mash'tȧ), superior (?). Est. 9. 9.
Parmenas (pär'mē-naṣ), standing firm. Acts 6. 5.
Parnach (pär'naçh). Num. 34. 25.
Parosh (pā'rosh), flea. Ezra 2. 3.
Parshandatha (pär-shan-dā'thȧ), given to Persia. (?). Est. 9. 7.
Parthians (pär'thi-ănṣ). Acts 2. 9.
Paruah (pȧ-rū'ȧ), flourishing. 1 Kin. 4. 17.
Parvaim (pär-vā'im), Oriental regions (?). 2 Chr. 3. 6.
Pasach (pā'saçh), divider. 1 Chr. 7. 33.
Pas-dammim (pas-dam'im), shortened from **Ephes-dammim.** 1 Chr. 11. 13.
Paseah (pȧ-sē'ȧ), lame. 1 Chr. 4. 12.
Pashur (pash'ūr), prosperity round about. Jer. 20. 1.
Patara (pat'ȧ-rȧ). Acts 21. 1.
Pathros (path'ros). Is. 11. 11.
Pathrusim (path-rū'sim), people of Pathros. Gen. 10. 14.
Patmos (pat'mos). Rev. 1. 9.
Patrobas (pat'rō-băs). Rom. 16. 14.
Pau (pā'ū), older form of **Pai.** Gen. 36. 39.
Paul (pạl) or **Paulus,** little. Acts 13. 9.
Pedahel (ped'ȧ-hel), God redeemed. Num. 34. 28.
Pedahzur (pē-dä'zūr), the Rock redeemed. Num. 1. 10.
Pedaiah (pē-dā'yȧ), whom Jehovah redeemed. 1 Chr. 27. 20.
Pekah (pē'kä), open-eyed. 2 Kin. 15. 25.
Pekahiah (pek-ȧ-hī'ȧ), whose eyes Jehovah opened. 2 Kin. 15. 22.
Pekod (pē'kod), visitation. Jer. 50. 21.
Pelaiah (pē-lā'yȧ), whom Jehovah made distinguished. 1 Chr. 3. 24.
Pelaliah (pel-ȧ-lī'ȧ), whom Jehovah judged. Neh. 11. 12.
Pelatiah (pel-ȧ-tī'ȧ), whom Jehovah delivered. Ezek. 11. 1.
Peleg (pē'leg), division. Gen. 10. 25.
Pelet (pē'let), liberation. 1 Chr. 2. 47.
Peleth (pē'leth), swiftness. Num. 16. 1.
Pelethites (pel'ē-thīts), runners. 2 Sam. 8. 18.
Pelonite (pel'ō-nīt). 1 Chr. 11. 27.
Peniel (pē-nī'el), the face of God. Gen. 32. 30.
Peninnah (pē-nin'ȧ), coral. 1 Sam. 1. 2.
Pentecost (pen'tē-çost), fiftieth. Acts 2. 1.
Penuel (pē-nū'el), old form of **Peniel.** Gen. 32. 31.
Peor (pē'ọr). point. Num. 23. 28.
Perazim (per'ȧ-zim), breaches. Is. 28. 21.
Peres, (pē'res), divided. Dan. 5. 28.
Peresh (pē'resh), distinction. 1 Chr. 7. 16.
Perez (pē'rez), breach. 1 Chr. 27. 3.
Perez-uzza (pē-rez-uz'ȧ), same as following. 1 Chr. 13. 11.
Perez-uzzah (pē-rez-uz'ȧ), breach of Uzzah. 2 Sam. 6. 8.
Perga (pẽr'gȧ). Acts 13. 13.
Pergamos (pẽr'gȧ-mos), citadel (?). Rev. 1. 11.
Perida (pē-rī'dȧ), a recluse. Neh. 7. 57.
Perizzites (per'i-zīts), belonging to a village. Gen. 34. 30.
Persia (pẽr'zȧ). 2 Chr. 36. 20.
Persian (pẽr'zăn), belonging to Persia. Dan. 6. 28.
Persis (pẽr'sis), a Persian woman. Rom. 16. 12.
Peruda (pē-rū'dȧ), same as **Perida.** Ezra 2. 55.
Peter (pē'tẽr), a stone. Matt. 16. 18.
Pethahiah (peth-ȧ-hī'ȧ), whom Jehovah looses. 1 Chr. 24. 16.
Pethor (pē'thọr). Num. 22. 5.
Pethuel (pē-thū'el), God's opening (?). Joel 1. 1.

Peulthai (pē-ul'thī), deed of Jehovah. 1 Chr. 26. 5.
Phalec (fā'leç), Greek form of **Peleg.** Luke 3. 35.
Phallu (fal'ů), an English way of spelling **Pallu.** Gen. 46. 9.
Phalti (fal'tī), deliverance of Jehovah. 1 Sam. 25. 44.
Phaltiel (fal'ti-el), deliverance of God. 2 Sam. 3. 15.
Phanuel (fȧ-nū'el), Greek form of **Penuel.** Luke 2. 36.
Pharaoh (fâr'ō), the sun. Gen. 12. 15.
Phares (fā'rēş), Greek form of **Pharez.** Luke 3. 33.
Pharez (fā'rēz), breach. Gen. 38. 29.
Pharisees (far'i-sēş), the separated. Matt. 5. 20.
Pharosh (fā'rosh), same as **Parosh.** Ezra 8. 3.
Pharpar (fär'pär), swift. 2 Kin. 5. 12.
Pharzites (fär'zīts), descendants of Pharez. Num. 26. 20.
Phaseah (fȧ-sē'ȧ), same as **Paseah.** Neh. 7. 51.
Phebe (fē'bē), moon. Rom. 16. 1.
Phenice (fē-nī'cē), palm tree. Acts 27. 12.
Phenicia (fē-niçh'i-ȧ), land of palms. Acts 21. 2.
Phichol (fī'çhol), attentive (?). Gen. 21. 22.
Philadelphia (fil-ȧ-del'fi-ȧ), brotherly love. Rev. 1. 11.
Philemon (fi-lē'mŏn), affectionate. Philem. 1.
Philetus (fi-lē'tus), beloved. 2 Tim. 2. 17.
Philip (fil'ip), lover of horses. Matt. 10. 3.
Philippi (fi-lip'ī), a town so called after Philip of Macedon. Acts 16. 12.
Philippians (fi-lip'i-ănş), the people of Philippi. Phil. 4. 15.
Philistia (fi-lis'ti-ȧ), the land of the Philistines. Ps. 60. 8.
Philistim (fi-lis'tim), wanders. Gen. 10. 14.
Philistines (fi-lis'tinş), same as **Philistim.** Gen. 21. 34.
Philologus (fi-lol'ō-gus), talkative. Rom. 16. 15.
Phinehas (fin'ē-ăs), serpent's mouth. Num. 25. 7.
Phlegon (flē'gon), zealous, burning. Rom. 16. 14.
Phrygia (fryġ'i-ȧ). Acts 2. 10.
Phurah (fū'rȧ), branch (?). Judg. 7. 10.
Phut (fut). Gen. 10. 6.
Phuvah (fū'vȧ), mouth. Gen. 46. 13.
Phygellus (fȳ-ġel'us), little fugitive. 2 Tim. 1. 15.
Pi-beseth (pī-bē'seth), the city of Bast. Ezek. 30. 17.
Pi-hahiroth (pī-hȧ-hī'roth), where sedge grows. Ex. 14. 2.
Pilate (pī'lăt), armed with a javelin (?). Matt. 27. 2.
Pildash (pil'dash), steel (?). Gen. 22. 22.
Pileha (pil'ē-hä), plowman (?). Neh. 10. 24.
Piltai (pil'tī), whom Jehovah delivers. Neh. 12. 17.
Pinon (pī'non), darkness. Gen. 36. 41.
Piram (pī'răm), like a wild ass. Josh. 10. 3.
Pirathon (pir'ȧ-thon), leader. Judg. 12. 15.
Pirathonite (pir'ȧ-thŏn-īt), an inhabitant of Pirathon. Judg. 12. 13.
Pisgah (piş'gȧ), a part, boundary. Num. 21. 20.
Pisidia (pi-sid'i-ȧ). Acts 13. 14.
Pison (pī'son), flowing stream (?). Gen. 2. 11.
Pispah (pis'pä), expansion. 1 Chr. 7. 38.
Pithom (pī'thom). Ex. 1. 11.
Pithon (pī'thon), simple (?). 1 Chr. 8. 35.
Pleiades (plē'yȧ-dēş), (coming at) the sailing season (?). Job. 9. 9.
Pochereth of Zebaim (poçh'ē-reth uv zē-bā'im), offspring of gazelles (?). Ezra 2. 57.
Pollux (pol'uks). Acts 28. 11.
Pontius (pon'shus), belonging to the sea. Matt. 27. 2.
Pontus (pon'tus), sea. Acts 2. 9.
Poratha (pō-rā'thȧ), having many chariots (?). Est. 9. 8.
Porcius Festus (pǫr'çhi-us fes'tus). Acts 24. 27.
Potiphar (pot'i-făr), belonging to the sun. Gen. 37. 36.
Poti-pherah (pō-tif'ĕr-ȧ), same as **Potiphar.** Gen. 41. 45.
Prisca (pris'çȧ), ancient. 2 Tim. 4. 19.
Priscilla (pri-sil'ȧ), diminutive of **Prisca.** Acts 18. 2.
Prochorus (proçh'ō-rus), he that presides over the choir. Acts 6. 5.
Ptolemais (tol-ē-mā'is), city of Ptolemy. Acts 21. 7.
Pua (pū'ȧ), same as **Phuvah.** Num. 26. 23.
Puah, (pū'ȧ), splendor. Ex. 1. 15.
Publius (pub'li-us). Acts 28. 7.
Pudens (pū'denş), shamefaced. 2 Tim. 4. 21.
Puhites (pū'hīts). 1 Chr. 2. 53.
Pul (pul), (1) a short name for **Tiglath-Pileser** (?). 2 Kin. 15. 19. (2) son (?) Is. 66. 19.
Punites (pū'nīts), descendants of Pua. Num. 26. 23.
Punon (pū'non), same as **Pinon.** Num. 33. 42.
Pur (pūr), a lot. Est. 3. 7.
Purim (pū'rim), lots. Est. 9. 26.
Put (put), same as **Phut.** 1 Chr. 1. 8.
Puteoli (pū-tē'ō-lī), wells. Acts 28. 13.
Putiel, (pū'ti-el). Ex. 6. 25.
Quartus (kwąr'tus), the fourth. Rom. 16. 23.

R

Raamah (rā'ȧ-mȧ), trembling. Gen. 10. 7.
Raamiah (rā-ȧ-mī'ȧ), trembling of Jehovah. Neh. 7. 7.
Raamses (rā-am'sēş), son of the sun. Ex. 1. 11.
Rabbah (rab'ȧ), capital city. Josh. 13. 25.
Rabbath (rab'ath), same as **Rabbah.** Deut. 3. 11.
Rabbi (rab'ī), master. Matt. 23. 7.
Rabbith (rab'ith), populous. Josh. 19. 20.
Rabboni (ra-bō'nī), my master. John 20. 16.
Rab-mag (rab'mag), most exalted. Jer. 39. 3.
Rab-saris (rab'sȧ-ris), chief eunuch. 2 Kin. 18. 17.
Rab-shakeh (rab'shȧ-ke), chief of the cupbearers. 2 Kin. 18. 17.
Rachab (rā'çhab), Greek form of **Rahab.** Matt. 1. 5.
Rachal (rā'çhal), traffic. 1 Sam. 30. 29.
Rachel (rā'chel), ewe. Gen. 29. 6.
Raddai (rad'ā-ī), subduing. 1 Chr. 2. 14.
Ragau (rā'gạ), Greek form of **Reuben.** Luke 3. 35.
Raguel (rȧ-gū'el), friend of God. Num. 10. 29.
Rahab (rā'hab), (1) broad. Josh. 2. 1. (2) violence. Ps. 87. 4.
Raham (rā'ham). 1 Chr. 2. 44.
Rahel (rā'hel), same as **Rachel.** Jer. 31. 15.
Rakem (rā'kem), variegated. 1 Chr. 7. 16.
Rakkath (rak'ath), shore. Josh. 19. 35.
Rakkon (rak'on), same as **Rakkath.** Josh. 19. 46.
Ram (ram), high. Ruth 4. 19.
Rama (rā'mȧ), Greek form of **Ramah.** Matt. 2. 18.
Ramah (rā'mȧ), high place. Josh. 18. 25.
Ramath (rā'math), same as preceding. Josh. 19. 8.
Ramathaim (rā-mȧ-thā'im), double high place. 1 Sam. 1. 1.
Ramathite (rā'math-īt), a native of Ramah. 1 Chr. 27. 27.
Ramath-lehi (rā'math-lē'hī), heigh of Lehi. Judg. 15. 17.
Ramath-mizpeh (rā'math-miz'pe), height of Mizpeh. Josh. 13. 26.
Rameses (ram'ē-sēş), same as **Raamses.** Gen. 47. 11.
Ramiah (rȧ-mī'ȧ), Jehovah is high. Ezra 10. 25.
Ramoth (rā'moth), plural of **Ramah.** 1 Chr. 6. 73.
Ramoth-gilead (rā'moth-gil'ē-ăd), heights of Gilead. 1 Kin. 4. 13.
Rapha (rā'fȧ), giant (?). 1 Chr. 8. 37.
Raphu (rā'fū), healed. Num. 13. 9.
Reaia (rē-ā'yȧ), Jehovah has seen. 1 Chr. 5. 5.
Reaiah, correct form of **Reaia.** 1 Chr. 4. 2.
Reba (rē'bȧ), a fourth part. Num. 31. 8.
Rebecca (rē-beç'ȧ), Greek form of **Rebekah.** Rom. 9. 10.
Rebekah (rē-bek'ȧ), a noose. Gen. 22. 23.
Rechab (rē'çhab), horseman. 2 Kin. 10. 15.
Rechabites (reçh'ȧ-bīts), descendants of Rechab. Jer. 35. 2.
Rechah (rē'çhȧ), side (?). 1 Chr. 4. 12.
Reelaiah (rē-el-ā'yȧ), trembling caused by Jehovah. Ezra 2. 2.
Regem (rē'gem), friend. 1 Chr. 2. 47.
Regem-melech (rē'gem-mē'leçh), friend of the king. Zech. 7. 2.
Rehabiah (rē-hȧ-bī'ȧ), Jehovah enlarges. 1 Chr. 23. 17.
Rehob (rē'hob), street. 2 Sam. 8. 3.
Rehoboam (rē'hō-bō'am), who enlarges the people. 1 Kin. 11. 43.
Rehoboth (rē-hō'both), roominess. Gen. 10. 11.
Rehum (rē'hum), merciful. Ezra 4. 8.
Rei (rē'ī), friendly. 1 Kin. 1. 8.
Rekem (rē'kem), same as **Rakem.** Num. 31. 8.
Remaliah (rem-ȧ-lī'ȧ), whom Jehovah adorned. 2 Kin. 15. 25.
Remeth (rē'meth), a high place. Josh. 19. 21.
Remmon (rem'on), more correctly spelled **Rimmon.** Josh. 19. 7.
Remmon-methoar (rem'on-meth'ō-är), R. stretching (to Neah). Josh. 19. 13.
Remphan (rem'fan). Acts 7. 43.
Rephael (rē'fā-el), whom God healed. 1. Chr. 26. 7.
Rephah (rē'fȧ), riches. 1 Chr. 7. 25.
Rephaiah (rē-fā'yȧ), whom Jehovah healed. 1 Chr. 3. 21.
Rephaim (ref'ā-im), giants. 2 Sam. 5. 18.
Rephaims (ref'ā-imş), same as **Rephaim.** Gen. 14. 5.
Rephidim (ref'i-dim), supports. Ex. 17. 1.
Resen (rē'sen), bridle. Gen. 10. 12.
Resheph (rē'shef), flame. 1 Chr. 7. 25.
Reu (rē'ū), same as **Raguel.** Gen. 11. 18.
Reuben (rů'ben), behold a son (?). Gen. 29. 32.
Reubenites (rů'ben-īts), descendants of Reuben. Num. 26. 7.
Reuel (rů'el), friend of God. 1 Chr. 9. 8.
Reumah (rů'mȧ), exalted. Gen. 22. 24.
Rezeph (rē'zef), a stone. 2 Kin. 19. 12.
Rezia (rē-zī'ȧ), delight. 1 Chr. 7. 39.
Rezin (rē'zin), firm. 2 Kin. 15. 37.
Rezon (rē'zŏn), lean. 1 Kin. 11. 23.
Rhegium (rē'ġi-um). Acts 28. 13.
Rhesa (rē'sȧ), chieftain (?). Luke 3. 27.
Rhoda (rō'dȧ), a rose. Acts 12. 13.
Rhodes (rōdş). Acts 21. 1.
Ribai (rī'bī), contentious. 2 Sam. 23. 29.
Riblah (rib'lȧ), fertility. Num. 34. 11.
Rimmon (rim'ŏn), pomegranate. 2 Sam. 4. 2.
Rimmon-parez (rim'ŏn-pā'rēz), pomegranate of the breach. Num. 33. 19.
Rinnah (rin'ȧ), shout. 1 Chr. 4. 20.
Riphath (rī'fath). Gen. 10. 3.
Rissah (ris'ȧ), ruin. Num. 33. 21.
Rithmah (rith'mȧ), broom. Num. 33. 18.
Rizpah (riz'pä), hot coal. 2 Sam. 3. 7.
Roboam (rō-bō'ăm), Greek form of **Rehoboam.** Matt. 1. 7.
Rogelim (rō'gē-lim), fullers. 2 Sam. 17. 27.
Rohgah (rō'gȧ), outcry. 1 Chr. 7. 34.
Romamti-ezer (rō-mam'tī-ē'zĕr), I have exalted help. 1 Chr. 25. 4.
Romans (rō'mănş), inhabitants of Rome. John 11. 48.
Rome (rōm), strength (?). Acts 2. 10.
Rosh (rosh), head. Gen. 46. 21.
Rufus (rů'fus), red. Mark 15. 21.
Ruhamah (rů-hä'mȧ), compassionated. Hos. 2. 1.
Rumah (rů'mȧ), height. 2 Kin. 23. 36.
Ruth (růth), friendship (?). Ruth 1. 4.

S

Sabachthani (sȧ-baçh'thȧ-nī), thou hast forsaken me. Mark 15. 34.
Sabaoth (sab'ā-oth), hosts. Rom. 9. 29.
Sabeans (sȧ-bē'ănş), people of Seba. Is. 45. 14.
Sabtah (sab'tȧ), rest (?). Gen. 10. 7.
Sabtecha (sab'tē-çhȧ). 1 Chr. 1. 9.
Sabtechah (sab'tē-çhȧ), Gen. 10. 7.
Sacar (sā'çär), hire, reward. 1 Chr. 11. 35.
Sadducees (sad'ū-çēş), (named from Zadok, founder of the sect). Matt. 3. 7.
Sadoc (sā'doç), Greek form of **Zadok.** Matt. 1. 14.
Sala (sā'lȧ), Greek form of **Salah.** Luke 3. 35.
Salah (sā'lȧ), sprout (?). Gen. 10. 24.
Salamis (sal'ȧ-mis). Acts 13. 5.
Salathiel (sȧ-lā'thi-el), Greek form of **Shealtiel.** 1 Chr. 3. 17.
Salcah or **Salchah** (sal'çȧ), road. Deut. 3. 10.
Salem (sā'lem), perfect. Gen. 14. 18.
Salim (sā'lim), Greek form of **Salem.** John 3. 23.
Sallai (sal'ā-ī), exaltation. Neh. 11. 8.
Sallu (sal'ū), same as **Sallai.** 1 Chr. 9. 7.
Salma (sal'mȧ), garment. 1 Chr. 2. 11.
Salmon (sal'mŏn), shady. Ps. 68. 14.
Salmone (sal-mō'nē). Acts 27. 7.
Salome (sȧ-lō'mē), perfect. Mark 15. 40.
Salu (sā'lū), same as **Sallu.** Num. 25. 14.
Samaria (sȧ-mâr'i-ȧ), Greek equivalent of Shomron, which means guard. 1 Kin. 16. 24.
Samaritans (sȧ-mar'i-tanş), inhabitants of Samaria. 2 Kin. 17. 29.
Samgar-nebo (sam'gär-nē'bō), be gracious, Nebo. Jer. 39. 3.
Samlah (sam'lȧ), garment. Gen. 36. 36.
Samos (sā'mos), a height (?). Acts 20. 15.
Samothracia (sam'ō-thrā'çhi-ȧ). Acts 16. 11.
Samson (sam'sŏn), like the sun. Judg. 13. 24.
Samuel (sam'ū-el), heard of God. 1 Sam. 1. 20.
Sanballat (san-bal'ăt), Sin (the moon) giveth life (?). Neh. 2. 10.
Sansannah (san-san'ȧ), palm branch. Josh. 15. 31.
Saph (saf), threshold. 2 Sam. 21. 18.
Saphir (sā'fīr), beautiful. Mic. 1. 11.
Sapphira (sȧ-fī'rȧ), Greek form of the above (feminine). Acts 5. 1.
Sara (sâr'ȧ), Greek form of Sarah. Heb. 11. 11.
Sarah (sâr'ȧ), princess. Gen. 17. 15.
Sarai (sā'rī), contentious (?). Gen. 11. 20.
Saraph (sā'raf), burning. 1 Chr. 4. 22.
Sardis (sär'dis). Rev. 1. 11.
Sardites (särd'īts), descendants of Sered. Num. 26. 26.
Sarepta (sȧ-rep'tȧ), Greek form of Zarephath. Luke 4. 26.
Sargon (sär'gon), (God) appoints the king. Is. 20. 1.
Sarid (sā'rid), survivor. Josh. 19. 10.
Saron (sā'rŏn), Greek form of **Sharon.** Acts 9. 35.
Sarsechim (sär'sē-çhim). Jer. 39. 3.
Saruch (sā'ruçh), Greek form of **Serug.** Luke 3. 35.
Satan (sā'tăn), adversary. 1 Chr. 21. 1.
Saul (sąl), asked for. 1 Sam 9. 2.
Sceva (sē'vȧ), left-handed. Acts 19. 14.
Scythian (syth'i-ăn). Col. 3. 11.
Seba (sē'bȧ), man (?). Gen. 10. 7.
Sebat (sē'bat), rest (?). Zech. 1. 7.
Secacah (sē-çā'çȧ), inclosure. Josh. 15. 61.
Sechu (sē'çhū), watchtower. 1 Sam. 19. 22.
Secundus (sē-çun'dus), second. Acts 20. 4.
Segub (sē'gub), elevated. 1 Kin. 16. 34.
Seir (sē'ir), hairy. Gen. 36. 20.
Seirath (sē-ī'rath), well-wooded. Judg. 3. 26.
Sela (sē'lȧ), rock. Is. 16. 1.
Sela-hammahlekoth (sē'lȧ-hȧ-mä'lē-koth), rock of escapes. 1 Sam. 23. 28.
Selah (sē'lȧ), forte (?), a musical direction. Ps. 3. 2.
Seled (sē'led), exultation, or burning. 1 Chr. 2. 30.
Seleucia (sē-lū'çhi-ȧ), called after Seleucus. Acts 13. 4.
Sem, Greek form of **Shem.** Luke 3. 36.
Semachiah (sem-ȧ-çhī'ȧ), whom Jehovah sustains. 1 Chr. 26. 7.
Semei (sem'ē-ī), Greek form of **Shimei.** Luke 3. 26.
Senaah (sē-nā'ȧ), perhaps thorny. Ezra 2. 35.
Seneh (sē'ne), crag, thorn. 1 Sam. 14. 4.
Senir (sē'nir), coat of mail. 1 Chr. 5. 23.
Sennacherib (se-naçh'ĕr-ib), Sin (the moon) multiplies brethren. 2 Kin. 18. 13.
Senuah (sē-nū'ȧ), bristling (?). Neh. 11. 9.
Seorim (sē-ō'rim), barley. 1 Chr. 24. 8.
Sephar (sē'fär), a numbering. Gen. 10. 30.
Sepharad (sē-fā'rad). Obad. 20.
Sepharvaim (sef'är-vā'im). 2 Kin. 17. 24.
Serah (sē'rȧ), abundance. Gen. 46. 17.
Seraiah (sē-rā'yȧ), soldier of Jehovah (?). 2 Sam. 8. 17.
Seraphims (ser'ȧ-fimş), burning ones. Is. 6. 2.
Sered (sē'red), fear. Gen. 46. 14.
Sergius (sĕr'ġi-us). Acts 13. 7.
Serug (sē'rug), shoot. Gen. 11. 20.
Seth (seth), substitute. Gen. 4. 25.
Sethur (sē'thŭr), hidden. Num. 13. 13.
Shaalabbin (shā-ȧ-lab'in), earths of foxes. Josh. 19. 42.
Shaalbim (shā-al'bim), same as preceding. Judg. 1. 35.
Shaalbonite (shā-al'bō-nīt), inhabitant of Shaalbim. 2 Sam. 23. 32.
Shaaph (shā'af), anger (?). 1 Chr. 2. 47.
Shaaraim (shā-ȧ-rā'im), two gates. 1 Sam. 17. 52.

Shaashgaz (shā-ash'gaz), beauty's servant (?). Est. 2. 14.
Shabbethai (shab'ē-thī), born on the sabbath. Ezra 10. 15.
Shachia (shȧ-çhī'ȧ), lustful. 1 Chr. 8. 10.
Shaddai (shad'ī), Almighty. Num. 1. 6.
Shadrach (shā'draçh). Dan. 1. 7.
Shage (shā'gē), wanderer. 1 Chr. 11. 34.
Shaharaim (shā-hȧ-rā'im), two dawns. 1 Chr. 8. 8.
Shahazimah (shā-hȧ-zī'mȧ), lofty places. Josh. 19. 22.
Shalem (shā'lem), safe, perfect. Gen. 33. 18.
Shalim (shā'lim), foxes. 1 Sam. 9. 4.
Shalisha (shȧ-lī'shȧ), a third part. 1 Sam. 9. 4.
Shallecheth (shal'ē-çheth), felling. 1 Chr. 26. 16.
Shallum (shal'um), retribution. 2 Kin. 15. 10.
Shallun (shal'un), spoliation. Neh. 3. 15.
Shalmai (shal'mī), peaceful (?). Ezra 2. 46.
Shalman (shal'măn), shortened form of following. Hos. 10. 14.
Shalmaneser (shal-măn-ē'zēr), Shalman be propitious. 2 Kin. 17. 3.
Shama (shā'mȧ), obedient. 1 Chr. 11. 44.
Shamariah (sham-ȧ-rī'ȧ), whom Jehovah guards. 2 Chr. 11. 19.
Shamed (shā'med), destroyer. 1 Chr. 8. 12.
Shamer (shā'mēr), keeper. 1 Chr. 6. 46.
Shamgar (sham'gär), destroyer (?). Judg. 3. 31.
Shamhuth (sham'huth), notoriety (?). 1 Chr. 27. 8.
Shamir (shā'mir), a thorn. 1 Chr. 24. 24.
Shamma (sham'ȧ), desert. 1 Chr. 7. 37.
Shammah (sham'ȧ), same as **Shamma.** Gen. 36. 13.
Shammai (sham'ā-ī), wasted. 1 Chr. 2. 28.
Shammoth (sham'oth), deserts. 1 Chr. 11. 27.
Shammua (sha-mū'ȧ), famous. Num. 13. 4.
Shammuah (sha-mū'ȧ), same as preceding. 2 Sam. 5. 14.
Shamsherai (sham'shē-rī). 1 Chr. 8. 26.
Shapham (shā'făm), bald. 1 Chr. 5. 12.
Shaphan (shā'făn), coney. 2 Kin. 22. 3.
Shaphat (shā'fat), judge. Num. 13. 5.
Shapher (shā'fēr), pleasantness. Num. 33. 23.
Sharai (shȧ-rā'ī), free. Ezra 10. 40.
Sharaim (shȧ-rā'im), same as **Shaaraim.** Josh. 15. 36.
Sharar (shā'rär), firm. 2 Sam. 23. 33.
Sharezer (shȧ-rē'zēr), (God) protect the king. 2 Kin. 19. 37.
Sharon (shar'ŏn), plain. 1 Chr. 27. 29.
Sharonite (shar'ŏn-īt), one who lives in Sharon. 1 Chr. 27. 29.
Sharuhen (shȧ-rů'hen). Josh. 19. 6.
Shashai (shā'shī), pale. Ezra 10. 40.
Shashak (shā'shak), activity (?). 1 Chr. 8. 14.
Shaul (shā'ul), same as **Saul.** Gen. 46. 10.
Shaulites (shā'ul-īts), the family of Shaul. Num. 26. 13.
Shaveh (shā've), plain. Gen. 14. 17.
Shaveh Kiriathaim (shā've-kir'yȧ-thā'im), plain of Kiriathaim. Gen. 14. 5.
Shavsha (shav'shȧ), another name of **Seraiah.** 1 Chr. 18. 16.
Sheal (shē'ăl), prayer. Ezra 10. 29.
Shealtiel (shē-al'ti-el), I asked from God. Ezra 3. 2.
Sheariah (shē-ȧ-rī'ȧ), gate of Jehovah. 1 Chr. 8. 38.
Shear-jashub (shē'är-jā'shub), the remnant shall return. Is. 7. 3.
Sheba (shē'bȧ), an oath. 2 Sam. 20. 1.
Shebah (shē'bȧ). Gen. 26. 33.
Shebam (shē'bam), fragrance. Num. 32. 3.
Shebaniah (sheb-ȧ-nī'ȧ), whom Jehovah hides. 1 Chr. 15. 24.
Shebarim (sheb'ȧ-rim), breaches. Josh. 7. 5.
Sheber (shē'bēr), breaking. 1 Chr. 2. 48.
Shebna (sheb'nȧ), youth (?). 2 Kin. 18. 18.
Shebuel (shē-bū'el), captive of God. 1 Chr. 23. 16.
Shecaniah (sheç-ȧ-nī'ȧ), same as following. 1 Chr. 24. 11.
Shechaniah (sheçh-ȧ-nī'ȧ), Jehovah dwells. 1 Chr. 3. 21.
Shechem (shē'çhem), back, shoulder. Gen. 34. 2.
Shechemites (shē'çhem-īts), people of Shechem. Num. 26. 31.
Shedeur (shed'ē-ūr), giving forth of light. Num. 1. 5.
Shehariah (shē-hȧ-rī'ȧ), Jehovah seeks. 1 Chr. 8. 26.
Shelah (shē'lȧ), petition. Gen. 38. 5.
Shelanites (shē'lăn-īts), descendants of Shelah. Num. 26. 20.
Shelemiah (shel-ē-mī'ȧ), whom Jehovah repays. 1 Chr. 26. 14.
Sheleph (shē'lef), drawing out. Gen. 10. 26.
Shelesh (shē'lesh), triad. 1 Chr. 7. 35.
Shelomi (shē-lō'mī), peaceful. Num. 34. 27.
Shelomith (shē-lō'mith), peacefulness. Lev. 24. 11.
Shelomoth (shē-lō'moth), same as **Shelomith.** 1 Chr. 24. 22.
Shelumiel (shē-lū'mi-el), friend of God. Num. 1. 6.
Shem (shem), name. Gen. 5. 32.
Shema (shē'mȧ), (1) echo (?). Josh. 15. 26. (2) fame. 1 Chr. 2. 43.
Shemaah (shē-mā'ȧ), fame. 1 Chr. 12. 3.
Shemaiah (shē-mā'yȧ), Jehovah has heard. 1 Kin. 12. 22.
Shemariah (shem-ȧ-rī'ȧ), Jehovah guards. 1 Chr. 12. 5.
Shemeber (shem-ē'bēr), soaring on high (?). Gen. 14. 2.
Shemer (shē'mēr), guardian. 1 Kin. 16. 24.
Shemida (shē-mī'dȧ), fame of wisdom. Num. 26. 32.
Shemidah (shē-mī'dȧ), same as preceding. 1 Chr. 7. 19.
Shemidaites (shē-mī'dȧ-īts), descendants of Shemida. Num. 26. 32.
Sheminith (shem'i-nith), eighth. 1 Chr. 15. 21.
Shemiramoth (shē-mir'ȧ-moth), most high name. 1 Chr. 15. 18.
Shemuel (shē-mū'el), same as **Samuel.** Num. 34. 20.
Shen (shen), tooth. 1 Sam. 7. 12.
Shenazar (shē-nā'zär). 1 Chr. 3. 18.
Shenir (shē'nīr), same as **Senir.** Deut. 3. 9.
Shepham (shē'fam), nakedness. Num. 34. 10.
Shephathiah (shef-ȧ-thī'ȧ), an incorrect way of spelling the next word. 1 Chr. 9. 8.
Shephatiah (shef-ȧ-tī'ȧ), whom Jehovah defends. 2 Sam. 3. 4.
Shephi (shē'fī), baldness. 1 Chr. 1. 40.
Shepho (shē'fō), same as **Shephi.** Gen. 36. 23.
Shephuphan (shē-fū'fan), serpent (?). 1 Chr. 8. 5.
Sherah (shē'rȧ), consanguinity. 1 Chr. 7. 24.
Sherebiah (sher-ē-bī'ȧ), heat of Jehovah. Ezra 8. 18.
Sheresh (shē'resh), root. 1 Chr. 7. 16.
Sherezer (shē-rē'zēr), same as **Sharezer** (?). Zech. 7. 2.
Sheshach (shē'shaçh), a name for **Babel.** Jer. 25. 26.
Sheshai (shē'shī), clothed in white (?). Num. 13. 22.
Sheshan (she'shan), lily (?). 1 Chr. 2. 31.
Sheshbazzar (shesh-baz'ăr). Ezra 1. 8.
Sheth (sheth), tumult. Num. 24. 17.
Shethar (shē'thär), star. Est. 1. 14.
Shethar-boznai (shē'thär-boz'nī), bright star. Ezra 5. 3.
Sheva (shē'vȧ), vanity. 2 Sam. 20. 25.
Shibboleth (shib'ō-leth), an ear of corn, or a flood. Judg. 12. 6.
Shibmah (shib'mȧ), fragrant. Num. 32. 38.
Shicron (shiç'ron), drunkenness. Josh. 15. 11.
Shiggaion (shi-gā'yon), irregular. Ps. 7, title.
Shigionoth (shig-i-ō'noth). Hab. 3. 1.
Shihon (shī'hon), ruin. Josh. 19. 19.
Shihor (shī'hǫr), black. 1 Chr. 13. 5.
Shihor-libnath (shī'hǫr-lib'nath). Josh. 19. 26.
Shilhi (shil'hī), darter. 1 Kin. 22. 42.
Shilhim (shil'him), aqueducts. Josh. 15. 32.
Shillem (shil'em), requital. Gen. 46. 24.
Shiloah (shi-lō'ȧ), outlet of water. Is. 8. 6.
Shiloh (shī'lō), rest. Josh. 18. 1.
Shiloni (shi-lō'nī), native of Shiloh. Neh. 11. 5.
Shilonite (shī'lō-nīt), same as preceding. 1 Kin. 11. 29.
Shilshah (shil'shä), triad. 1 Chr. 7. 37.
Shimea (shim'ē-ȧ), famous. 1 Chr. 3. 5.
Shimeah (shim'ē-ȧ), same as **Shemaah.** 2 Sam. 21. 21.
Shimeam (shim'ē-am), same as preceding. 1 Chr. 9. 38.
Shimeath (shim'ē-ath), fame. 2 Kin. 12. 21.
Shimeathite (shim'ē-ath-īt). 1 Chr. 2. 55.
Shimei (shim'ē-ī), my fame. Num. 3. 18.
Shimeon (shim'ē-ŏn), a hearkening. Ezra 10. 31.
Shimhi (shim'hī), same as **Shimei.** 1 Chr. 8. 21.
Shimi (shim'ī), same as preceding. Ex. 6. 17.
Shimites (shim'īts), descendants of Shimei. Num. 3. 21.
Shimma (shim'ȧ), rumor. 1 Chr. 2. 13.
Shimon (shī'mon). 1 Chr. 4. 20.
Shimrath (shim'rath), watchfulness. 1 Chr. 8. 21.
Shimri (shim'rī), watchful. 1 Chr. 4. 37.
Shimrith (shim'rith), vigilant. 2 Chr. 24. 26.
Shimrom (shim'rom), watch-post. 1 Chr. 7. 1.
Shimron (shim'ron), watchful. Josh. 11. 1.
Shimronites (shim'ron-īts), descendants of Shimron. Num. 26. 24.
Shimron-meron (shim'ron-mē'ron). Josh. 12. 20.
Shimshai (shim'shī), sunny. Ezra 4. 8.
Shinab (shī'nab), hostile (?). Gen. 14. 2.
Shinar (shī'när). Gen. 10. 10.
Shiphi (shī'fī), abundant. 1 Chr. 4. 37.
Shiphmite (shif'mīt), a native of Shephan. 1 Chr. 27. 27.
Shiphrah (shif'rȧ), beauty. Ex. 1. 15.
Shiphtan (shif'tăn), judicial. Num. 34. 24.
Shisha (shī'shȧ), brightness. 1 Kin. 4. 3.
Shishak (shī'shak), illustrious. 1 Kin. 11. 40.
Shitrai (shit'rī), official. 1 Chr. 27. 29.
Shittim (shit'im), acacias. Num. 25. 1.
Shiza (shī'zȧ), cheerful (?). 1 Chr. 11. 42.
Shoa (shō'ä), opulent. Ezek. 23. 23.
Shobab (shō'bab), apostate. 2 Sam. 5. 14.
Shobach (shō'baçh), pouring. 2 Sam. 10. 16.
Shobai (shō'bī), bright (?). Ezra 2. 42.
Shobal (shō'bal), stream. Gen. 36. 20.
Shobek (shō'bek), forsaker. Neh. 10. 24.
Shobi (shō'bī), taking captive. 2 Sam. 17. 27.
Shocho (shō'çhō), same as the next word. 2 Chr. 28. 18.
Shochoh (shō'çhō), a hedge. 1 Sam. 17. 1.
Shoco (shō'çō), same as the preceding. 2. Chr. 11. 7.
Shoham (shō'ham), onyx. 1 Chr. 24. 27.
Shomer (shō'mēr), watchman. 2 Kin. 12. 21.
Shophach (shō'façh), same as **Shobek.** 1 Chr. 19. 16.
Shophan (shō'fan), baldness. Num. 32. 35.
Shoshannim (shō-shan'im), lilies. Ps. 45, title.
Shoshannim Eduth (-ē'duth), lilies, a testimony. Ps. 80, title.
Shua (shů'ȧ), wealth. 1 Chr. 2. 3.
Shuah (shů'ȧ), depression. Gen. 25. 2.
Shual (shů'ăl), jackal. 1 Chr. 7. 36.
Shubael (shů'bā-el), same as **Shebuel** (?). 1 Chr. 24. 20.
Shuham (shů'ham), pitman (?). Num. 26. 42.
Shuhamites (shů'ham-īts), the descendants of Shuham. Num. 26. 42.
Shuhite (shů'hīt), a descendant of Shua. Job 8. 1.
Shulamite (shů'lăm-īt), same as **Shelomith.** Cant. 6. 13.
Shumathites (shů'math-īts), people of Shumah. 1 Chr. 2. 53.
Shunammite (shů'năm-īt), an inhabitant of Shunem. 1 Kin. 1. 3.
Shunem (shů'nem), two resting places. Josh. 19. 18.
Shuni (shů'nī), quiet. Gen. 46. 16.
Shunites (shů'nīts), descendants of Shuni. Num. 26. 15.
Shupham (shů'fam), serpent. Num. 26. 39.
Shuphamites (shů'fam-īts), the descendants of Shupham. Num. 26. 39.
Shuppim (shup'im). 1 Chr. 7. 12.
Shur (shůr), a fort. Gen. 16. 7.
Shushan (shů'shan). Neh. 1. 1.
Shushan Eduth (-ē'duth), lily of the testimony. Ps. 60, title.
Shuthalhites (shů'thăl-īts), the descendants of Shuthelah. Num. 26. 35.
Shuthelah (shů-thē'lȧ), plantation (?). Num. 26. 35.
Sia (sī'ȧ), assembly. Neh. 7. 47.
Siaha (sī'ȧ-hȧ), council. Ezra 2. 44.
Sibbecai (sib'ē-çī), entangling. 1 Chr. 11. 29.
Sibbechai (sib'ē-çhī), same as preceding. 2 Sam. 21. 18.
Sibboleth (sib'ō-leth), same as **Shibboleth.** Judg. 12. 6.
Sibmah (sib'mȧ), same as **Shibmah.** Josh. 13. 19.
Sibraim (sib-rā'im), two hills (?). Ezek. 47. 16.
Sichem (sī'çhem), the shoulder-blade. Gen. 12. 6.
Siddim (sid'im), the plains. Gen. 14. 3.
Sidon (sī'dŏn), fishing. Gen. 10. 15.
Sidonians (sī-dō'ni-anş), persons living in Sidon. Deut. 3. 9.
Sihon (sī'hon), brush. Num. 21. 21.
Sihor (sī'hǫr), same as **Shihor.** Josh. 13. 3.
Silas (sī'lăs), shortened form of **Silvanus.** Acts 15. 22.
Silla (sil'ȧ), way, highway (?). 2 Kin. 12. 20.
Siloam (si-lō'ăm), same as **Shiloah.** John 9. 7.
Silvanus (sil-vā'nus), of the forest. 2 Cor. 1. 19.
Simeon (sim'ē-ŏn), same as **Shimeon.** Gen. 29. 33.
Simon (sī'mŏn), same as preceding. Matt. 10. 4.
Simri (sim'rī), same as **Shimri.** 1 Chr. 26. 10.
Sin (sin), clay. Ex. 16. 1.
Sina (sī'nȧ), Greek form of **Sinai.** Acts 7. 30.
Sinai (sī'nī), pointed. Ex. 19. 1.
Sinim (sī'nim), Chinese (?). Is. 49. 12.
Sinite (sī'nīt). Gen. 10. 17.
Sion (sī'ŏn), (1) lifted up. Deut. 4. 48. (2) Greek name for Mount Zion. Matt. 21. 5.
Siphmoth (sif'moth), bare places (?). 1 Sam. 30. 28.
Sippai (sip'ī), belonging to the doorstep (?). 1 Chr. 20. 4.
Sirah (sī'rȧ), withdrawing. 2 Sam. 3. 26.
Sirion (sir'i-on), a coat of mail. Deut. 3. 9.
Sisamai (sis'ȧ-mī), fragrant (?). 1 Chr. 2. 40.
Sisera (sis'ēr-ȧ), binding in chains (?). Judg. 4. 2.
Sitnah (sit'nȧ), contention. Gen. 26. 21.
Sivan (sī-vän'), bright. Est. 8. 9.
Smyrna (smīr'nȧ), myrrh. Rev. 1. 11.
So (sō), Hebrew form of Egyptian word Sevech. 2 Kin. 17. 4.
Socho (sō'çhō), same as **Shocho.** 1 Chr. 4. 18.
Sochoh, same as **Shochoh.** 1 Kin. 4. 10.
Socoh, same as **Shoco.** Josh. 15. 35.
Sodi (sō'dī), an acquaintance. Num. 13. 10.
Sodom (sod'ŏm), burning. Gen. 10. 19.
Sodoma (sod'ō-mȧ), Greek form of the preceding. Rom. 9. 29.
Sodomites (sod'ŏm-īts), persons who were as wicked as the men of Sodom. 1 Kin. 15. 12.
Solomon (sol'ō-mŏn), peaceable. 2 Sam. 5. 14.
Sopater (sō'pȧ-tēr). Acts 20. 4.
Sophereth (sō-fē'reth), scribe. Ezra 2. 55.
Sorek (sō'rek), choice vine. Judg. 16. 4.
Sosipater (sō-sip'ȧ-tēr). Rom. 16. 21.
Sosthenes (sos'thē-nēş). Acts 18. 17.
Sotai (sō'tī), deviator. Ezra 2. 55.
Spain. Rom. 15. 24.
Stachys (stā'çhys), an ear of corn. Rom. 16. 9.
Stephanas (stef'ȧ-nas), crowned. 1 Cor. 1. 16.
Stephen (stē'ven), English form of **Stephanas.** Acts 6. 5.
Stoics (stō'içs), philosophers whose founder taught in a famous porch or Stoa. Acts 17. 18.
Suah (sū'ȧ), sweepings. 1 Chr. 7. 36.
Succoth (suç'oth), booths. Gen. 33. 17.
Succoth-benoth (suç'oth-bē'noth). 2 Kin. 17. 30.
Suchathites (sū'çhath-īts). 1 Chr. 2. 55.
Sukkiims (suk'i-imş), nomads. 2 Chr. 12. 3.
Sur (sůr). 2 Kin. 11. 6.
Susanchites (sū-san'çhīts), inhibitants of Susa or Susinak. Ezra 4. 9.
Susanna (sū-şan'ȧ), lily. Luke 8. 3.

Susi (sū'sī), horseman. Num. 13. 11.
Sychar (sȳ'çhär), drunken (?). John 4. 5.
Sychem (sȳ'çhem), Greek form of **Shechem.** Acts 7. 16.
Syene (sȳ-ē'nē), opening. Ezek. 29. 10.
Syntyche (syn'ty-çhē), fortunate. Phil. 4. 2.
Syracuse (syr'ȧ-çūs). Acts 28. 12.
Syria (syr'i-ȧ). Judg. 10. 6.
Syrian (syr'i-ăn), inhabitant of Syria. Gen. 25. 20.
Syrophenician (sȳ'rō-fē-niçh'ăn), Phenician living in Syria. Mark 7. 26.

T

Taanach (tā'ȧ-naçh), castle (?). Josh. 12. 21.
Taanath-shiloh (tā'ȧ-nath-shī'lō), fig-tree of Shiloh (?). Josh. 16. 6.
Tabbaoth (tȧ-bā'oth), rings. Ezra 2. 43.
Tabbath (tab'ăth), pleasantness. Judg. 7. 22.
Tabeal (tā'bē-ăl), God is good. Is. 7. 6.
Tabeel (tā'bē-el), another way of writing **Tabeal.** Ezra 4. 7.
Taberah (tab'ē-rȧ), burning. Num. 11. 3.
Tabitha (tab'i-thȧ), gazelle. Acts 9. 36.
Tabor (tā'bŏr), height. Josh. 19. 22.
Tabrimon (tab'rim-on), Rimmon is good. 1 Kin. 15. 18.
Tachmonite (taçh'mō-nīt), same as **Hachmonite** (?). 2 Sam. 23. 8.
Tadmor (tad'mọr), city of palms (?). 1 Kin. 9. 18.
Tahan (tā'hăn), camp. Num. 26. 35.
Tahanites (tā'hăn-īts), descendants of Tahan. Num. 26. 35.
Tahapanes (tȧ-hap'ȧ-nēş), head of the land. Jer. 2. 16.
Tahath (tā'hath), substitute. 1 Chr. 6. 24.
Tahpanhes, same as preceding. Jer. 43. 7.
Tahpenes (tä'pē-nēş). 1 Kin. 11. 19.
Tahrea (tä'rē-ȧ), cunning (?). 1 Chr. 9. 41.
Tahtim-hodshi (tä'tim-hod'shī), nether land newly inhabited (?). 2 Sam. 24. 6.
Talitha (tal'i-thȧ), girl. Mark 5. 41.
Talmai (tal'mī), abounding in furrows. Num. 13. 22.
Talmon (tal'mon), oppressed. 1 Chr. 9. 17.
Tamah (tā'mȧ), joy. Neh. 7. 55.
Tamar (tā'măr), a palm tree. Gen. 38. 6.
Tammuz (tam'uz), son of life (?). Ezek. 8. 14.
Tanach (tā'naçh), same as **Taanach.** Josh. 21. 25.
Tanhumeth (tan-hū'meth), consolation. 2 Kin. 25. 23.
Taphath (tā'fath), a drop (?). 1 Kin. 4. 11.
Tappuah (ta-pū'ȧ), apple. 1 Chr. 2. 43.
Tarah (tā'rȧ), station. Num. 33. 27.
Taralah (tar'ȧ-lä), reeling (?). Josh. 18. 27.
Tarea (tā'rē-ȧ), same as **Tahrea.** 1. Chr. 8. 35.
Tarpelites (tär'pel-īts), people of Tarpel. Ezra 4. 9.
Tarshish (tär'shish). Gen. 10. 4.
Tarsus (tär'sus). Acts 9. 11.
Tartak (tär'tak). 2 Kin. 17. 31.
Tartan (tär'tăn), military chief. 2 Kin. 18. 17.
Tatnai (tat'nī), gift (?). Ezra 5. 3.
Tebah (tē'bȧ), slaughter. Gen. 22. 24.
Tebaliah (teb-ȧ-lī'ȧ), whom Jehovah has immersed. 1 Chr. 26. 11.
Tebeth (tē'beth). Est. 2. 16.
Tehaphnehes (tē-haf'nē-hēş), same as **Tahapanes.** Ezek. 30. 18.
Tehinnah (tē-hin'ȧ), cry for mercy. 1 Chr. 4. 12.
Tekel (te'kĕl), weighed. Dan 5. 25.
Tekoa (tē-kō'ȧ), sound of trumpet. 1 Chr. 2. 24.
Tekoah (tē-kō'ȧ), same as **Tekoa.** 2 Sam. 14. 2.
Tekoite (tē-kō'īt), inhabitant of Tekoah. 2 Sam. 23. 26.
Tel-abib (tel-ā'bib), hill of ears of corn. Ezek. 3. 15.
Telah (tē'lȧ). 1 Chr. 7. 25.
Telaim (tē-lā'im), lambs. 1 Sam. 15. 4.
Telassar (tē-las'ăr), Assyrian hill. Is. 37. 12.
Telem (tē'lem), oppression. Ezra 10. 24.
Tel-haresha (tel-hȧ-rē'shȧ), forest-hill. Neh. 7. 61.
Tel-harsa (tel-här'sȧ), same as preceding. Ezra 2. 59.
Tel-melah (tel-mē'lȧ), salt-hill. Ezra 2. 59.
Tema (tē'mȧ), a desert. Gen. 25. 15.
Teman (tē'măn), on the right hand. Gen. 36. 11.
Temani (tem'ȧ-nī), descendants of Teman. Gen. 36. 34.
Temanite (tē'măn-īt), same as preceding. Job 2. 11.
Temeni (tem'ē-nī), same as **Temani.** 1 Chr. 4. 6.
Terah (tē'rȧ), a station (?). Gen. 11. 24.
Teraphim (ter'ȧ-fim), nourishers. Judg. 17. 5.
Teresh (tē'resh), severe (?). Est. 2. 21.
Tertius (tẽr'shi-us), the third. Rom. 16. 22.
Tertullus (tẽr-tul'us), dim. of Tertius. Acts 24. 1.
Tetrarch (tē'trärçh), ruler of a fourth part of a country. Matt. 14. 1.
Thaddæus (tha-dē'us), Greek form of **Theudas.** Matt. 10. 3.
Thahash (thā'hash), seal (?). Gen. 22. 24.
Thamah (thā'mȧ), laughter. Ezra 2. 53.
Thamar (thā'mär), Greek equivalent of **Tamar.** Matt. 1. 3.
Thara (thā'rȧ), Greek form of **Terah.** Luke 3. 34.
Tharshish (thär'shish), same as **Tarshish.** 1 Kin. 10. 22.
Thebez (thē'bez), brightness. Judg. 9. 50.
Thelasar (thē-lā'săr), same as **Telassar.** 2 Kin. 19. 12.
Theophilus (thē-of'i-lus), loved of God. Luke 1. 3.
Thessalonica (thes'ȧ-lō-nī'çȧ). Acts 17. 1.
Theudas (thū'dăs), praise (?). Acts 5. 36.
Thimnathah (thim'nȧ-thä), portion. Josh. 19. 43.
Thomas (tom'ȧs), a twin. Matt. 10. 3.
Thummim (thum'im), truth (?). Ex. 28. 30.
Thyatira (thȳ-ȧ-tī'rȧ). Acts 16. 14.
Tiberias (tī-bē'ri-as), a place named after Tiberius. John 6. 1.
Tiberius (tī-bēr'i-us). Luke 3. 1.
Tibhath (tib'hath), butchery. 1 Chr. 18. 8.
Tibni (tib'nī), made of straw (?). 1 Kin. 16. 21
Tidal (tī'dal), dread. Gen. 14. 1.
Tiglath-pileser (tig'lăth-pi-lē'şẽr), the son of the temple of Sarra is a ground of confidence (?). 2 Kin. 15. 29.
Tikvah (tik'vä), expectation. 2 Kin. 22. 14.
Tikvath (tik'vath), same as **Tikvah.** 2 Chr. 34. 22.
Tilgath-pilneser (til'gath-pil-nē'şẽr), same as **Tiglath-pileser.** 1 Chr. 5. 6.
Tilon (tī'lŏn), gift (?). 1 Chr. 4. 20.
Timæus (tī-mē'us), polluted (?). Mark 10. 46.
Timna (tim'nȧ), unapproachable. Gen. 36. 12.
Timnah (tim'nȧ), a portion. Josh. 15. 10.
Timnath (tim'nath), same as **Timnah.** Gen. 38. 12.
Timnath-heres (tim'nath-hē'rēş), portion of the sun. Judg. 2. 9.
Timnath-serah (tim'nath-sē'rȧ), portion of the remainder. Josh. 19. 50.
Timnite (tim'nīt), a man of Timna. Judg. 15. 6.
Timon (tī'mon). Acts 6. 5.
Timotheus (ti-mō'thē-us), honoring God. Acts 16. 1.
Timothy (tim'ō-thy), English form of the above. 2 Cor. 1. 1.
Tiphsah (tif'sȧ), passage. 1 Kin. 4. 24.
Tiras (tī'răs), crushing (?). Gen. 10. 2.
Tirathites (tī'răth-īts). 1 Chr. 2. 55.
Tirhakah (tĩr'hȧ-kä), distance (?). 2 Kin. 19. 9.
Tirhanah (tĩr'hȧ-nä), murmuring (?). 1 Chr. 2. 48.
Tiria (tir'i-ȧ), fear. 1 Chr. 4. 16.
Tirshatha (tĩr-shā'thȧ), the feared (?). Ezra 2. 63.
Tirzah (tĩr'zȧ), pleasantness. Num. 26. 33.
Tishbite (tish'bīt), inhabitant of Tishbe. 1 Kin. 17. 1.
Titus (tī'tus), protected. 2 Cor. 2. 13.
Tizite (tī'zīt). 1 Chr. 11. 45.
Toah (tō'ȧ), low. 1 Chr. 6. 34.
Tob (tob), good. Judg. 11. 3.
Tob-adonijah (tob'ad-ō-nī'jȧ), good is my lord Jehovah. 2 Chr. 17. 8.
Tobiah (tō-bī'ȧ), Jehovah is good. Ezra 2. 60.
Tobijah (tō-bī'jȧ), same as **Tobiah.** 2 Chr. 17. 8.
Tochen (tō'çhen), a measure. 1 Chr. 4. 32.
Togarmah (tō-gär'mȧ), rugged. Gen. 10. 3.
Tohu (tō'hū), same as **Toah.** 1 Sam. 1. 1.
Toi (tō'ī), wanderer. 2 Sam. 8. 9.
Tola (tō'lȧ), worm. Gen. 46. 13.
Tolad (tō'lad), birth. 1 Chr. 4. 29.
Tolaites (tō'lȧ-īts), descendants of Tola. Num. 26. 23.
Tophel (tō'fel), lime. Deut. 1. 1.
Tophet (tō'fet), burning. Is. 30. 33.
Topheth (tō'feth), same as **Tophet.** 2 Kin. 23. 10.
Tormah (tọr'mȧ), privily. Judg. 9. 31.
Tou (tō'ū), older form of **Toi.** 1 Chr. 18. 9.
Trachonitis (traçh-ō-nī'tis), rugged. Luke 3. 1.
Troas (trō'ăs), so called from Tros. Acts 16. 8.
Trogyllium (trō-ġyl'i-um). Acts 20. 15.
Trophimus (trof'i-mus), master of the house (?). Acts 20. 4.
Tryphena (trȳ-fē'nȧ), delicate. Rom. 16. 12.
Tryphosa (trȳ-fō'sȧ), delicate. Rom. 16. 12.
Tubal (tū'băl), production (?). Gen. 10. 2.
Tubal-cain (tū'băl-çān'), producer of weapons (?). Gen. 4. 22.
Tychicus (tyçh'i-çus), fortuitous. Acts 20. 4.
Tyrannus (tȳ-ran'us), tyrant. Acts 19. 9.
Tyre (tȳr), rock. Josh. 19. 29.
Tyrus (tȳ'rus), Latin name of **Tyre.** Jer. 25. 22.

U—V

Ucal (ū'çal), I shall prevail. Prov. 30. 1.
Uel (ū'el), will of God (?). Ezra 10. 34.
Ulai (ū'lī). Dan. 8. 2.
Ulam (ū'lam), foremost. 1 Chr. 7. 16.
Ulla (ul'ȧ), yoke. 1 Chr. 7. 39.
Ummah (um'ȧ), community. Josh. 19. 30.
Unni (un'ī), depressed. 1 Chr. 15. 18.
Upharsin (ū-fär'sin), dividers. Dan. 5. 25.
Uphaz (ū'faz). Jer. 10. 9.
Ur (ūr), light. Gen. 11. 28.
Urbane (ūr'bān), pleasant. Rom. 16. 9.
Uri (ū'rī), fiery. Ex. 31. 2.
Uriah (ū-rī'ȧ), light of Jehovah. 2 Sam. 11. 3.
Urias (ū-rī'ăs), Greek form of **Uriah.** Matt. 1. 6.
Uriel (ū'ri-el), light of God. 1 Chr. 6. 24.
Urijah (ū-rī'jȧ), same as **Uriah.** 2 Kin. 16. 10.
Urim (ū'rim), light. Ex. 28. 30.
Uthai (ū'thī), helpful. 1 Chr. 9. 4.
Uz (uz), fertile. Gen. 10. 23.
Uzai (ū'zī), hoped for (?). Neh. 3. 25.
Uzal (ū'zal), wanderer. Gen. 10. 27.
Uzza (uz'ȧ), strength. 2 Kin. 21. 18.
Uzzah (uz'ȧ), another form of **Uzza.** 2 Sam. 6. 3.
Uzzen-sherah (uz'en-shē'rȧ). 1 Chr. 7. 24.
Uzzi (uz'ī), shortened form of **Uzziah.** 1 Chr. 6. 5.
Uzzia (u-zī'ȧ), another form of **Uzziah.** 1 Chr. 11. 44.
Uzziah (u-zī'ȧ), might of Jehovah. 2 Kin. 15. 13.
Uzziel (u-zī'el), power of God. Ex. 6. 18.
Uzzielites (u-zī'el-īts), descendants of Uzziel. Num. 3. 27.

Vajezatha (vȧ-jez'ȧ-thȧ), strong as the wind (?). Est. 9. 9.
Vaniah (vȧ-nī'ȧ), distress (?). Ezra 10. 36.
Vashni (vash'nī), strong (?), but perhaps not a proper name. 1 Chr. 6. 28.
Vashti (vash'tī), beautiful. Est. 1. 9.
Vophsi (vof'sī), expansion (?). Num. 13. 14.

Z

Zaanaim (zā-ȧ-nā'im), wanderings (?). Judg. 4. 11.
Zaanan (zā'ȧ-nan), place of flocks. Mic. 1. 11.
Zaanannim (zā-ȧ-nan'im), same as **Zaanaim.** Josh. 19. 33.
Zaavan (zā'ȧ-van), disturbed. Gen. 36. 27.
Zabad (zā'bad), gift. 1 Chr. 2. 36.
Zabbai (zab'ā-ī). Ezra 10. 28.
Zabbud (zab'ud), given. Ezra 8. 14.
Zabdi (zab'dī), the gift of Jehovah. Josh. 7. 1.
Zabdiel (zab'di-el), the gift of God. 1 Chr. 27. 2.
Zabud (zab'ud), same as **Zabbud.** 1 Kin. 4. 5.
Zabulon (zab'ū-lŏn), Greek form of **Zebulun.** Matt. 4. 13.
Zaccai (zaç'ā-ī), pure. Ezra 2. 9.
Zacchæus (za-çhē'us), Greek form of **Zaccai.** Luke 19. 2.
Zacchur (zaç'ūr), mindful. 1 Chr. 4. 26.
Zaccur (zaç'ūr), same as preceding. Num. 13. 4.
Zachariah (zaçh-ȧ-rī'ȧ), whom Jehovah remembers. 2 Kin. 14. 29.
Zacharias (zaçh-ȧ-rī'ăs), Greek form of preceding. Matt. 23. 35.
Zacher (zā'çhẽr), memorial. 1 Chr. 8. 31.
Zadok (zā'dok), just. 2 Sam. 8. 17.
Zaham (zā'ham), loathing. 2 Chr. 11. 19.
Zair (zā'ir), small. 2 Kin. 8. 21.
Zalaph (zā'laf), wound (?). Neh. 3. 30.
Zalmon (zal'mŏn), shady. 2 Sam. 23. 28.
Zalmonah (zal-mō'nȧ), same as preceding. Num. 33. 41.
Zalmunna (zal-mun'ȧ), shelter denied. Judg. 8. 5.
Zamzummims (zam-zum'imş). Deut. 2. 20.
Zanoah (zȧ-nō'ȧ), marsh. Josh. 15. 34.
Zaphnath-paaneah (zaf'nath-pā'ȧ-nē'ȧ), prince of the life of the age. Gen. 41. 45.
Zaphon (zā'fon), north. Josh. 13. 27.
Zara (zā'rȧ), Greek form of **Zarah.** Matt. 1. 3.
Zarah (zā'rȧ), sunrise (?). Gen. 38. 30.
Zareah (zā'rē-ȧ), honest. Neh. 11. 29.
Zareathites (zā'rē-ăth-īts), inhabitants of Zareah. 1 Chr. 2. 53.
Zared (zā'red), exuberant growth. Num. 21. 12.
Zaretan (zar'ē-tan), same as **Zarthan.** Josh. 3. 16.
Zareth-shahar (zā'reth-shā'här), the splendor of the morning. Josh. 13. 19.
Zarhites (zär'hīts), persons descended from Zerah. Num. 26. 13.
Zartanah (zär-tā'nȧ). 1 Kin. 4. 12.
Zarthan (zär'than), same as **Zaretan.** 1 Kin. 7. 46.
Zatthu (zat'thū), same as **Zattu.** Neh. 10. 14.
Zattu (zat'ū), irascible (?). Ezra 2. 8.
Zavan (zā'van), same as **Zaavan.** 1 Chr. 1. 42.
Zaza (zā'zȧ). 1 Chr. 2. 33.
Zebadiah (zeb-ȧ-dī'ȧ), full form of **Zabdi.** 1 Chr. 8. 15.
Zebah (zē'bȧ), sacrifice. Judg. 8. 5.
Zebaim (zē-bā'im), same as **Zeboim.** Ezra 2. 57.
Zebedee (zeb'ē-dē), Greek form of **Zebadiah.** Matt. 4. 21.
Zebina (zē-bī'nȧ), bought. Ezra 10. 43.
Zeboim (zē-bō'im), gazelles. Gen. 10. 19.
Zebudah (zē-bū'dȧ), given. 2 Kin. 23. 36.
Zebul (zē'bul), habitation. Judg. 9. 28.
Zebulonite (zeb'ū-lŏn-īt), a member of the tribe of Zebulun. Judg. 12. 11.
Zebulun (zeb'ū-lun). Gen. 30. 20.
Zebulunites (zeb'ū-lun-īts), a less correct way of spelling Zebulonites. Num. 26. 27.
Zechariah (zeçh-ȧ-rī'ȧ), a better way of spelling **Zachariah.** 2 Chr. 24. 20.
Zedad (zē'dad), hunting (?). Num. 34. 8.
Zedekiah (zed-ē-kī'ȧ), justice of Jehovah. 1 Kin. 22. 11.
Zeeb (zē'eb), wolf. Judg. 7. 25.
Zelah (zē'lȧ), side. Josh. 18. 28.
Zelek (zē'lek), fissure. 2 Sam. 23. 37.
Zelophehad (zē-lō'fē-had), fracture. Num. 26. 33.
Zelotes (zē-lō'tēş), Greek equivalent of **Canaanite**, an emulator. Luke 6. 15.
Zelzah (zel'zȧ), shade in the heat. 1 Sam. 10. 2.
Zemaraim (zem-ȧ-rā'im), two fleeces. Josh. 18. 22.
Zemarite (zem'ȧ-rīt). Gen. 10. 18.
Zemira (zē-mī'rȧ). 1 Chr. 7. 8.
Zenan (zē'nan), same as **Zaanan.** Josh. 15. 37.
Zenas (zē'năs), contraction of Zenodorus. Tit. 3. 13.
Zephath (zē'fath), watchtower (?). Judg. 1. 17.
Zephathah (zef'ȧ-thȧ). 2 Chr. 14. 10.
Zephi (zē'fī), same as **Zephath.** 1 Chr. 1. 36.
Zepho (zē'fō), older form of **Zephi.** Gen. 36. 11.
Zephon (zē'fon), a looking out. Num. 26. 15.
Zephonites (zē'fŏn-īts), descendants of Zephon. Num. 26. 15.
Zer (zẽr), flint (?). Josh. 19. 35.
Zerah (zē'rȧ), dawn. 2 Chr. 14. 9.

Zerahiah (zer-ȧ'hī'ȧ), whom Jehovah caused to rise. 1 Chr. 6. 6.
Zered (zē'red), same as **Zared**. Deut. 2. 13.
Zereda (zer'ē-dȧ), cool. 1 Kin. 11. 26.
Zeredathah (zer-ē-dā'thȧ), same as preceding. 2 Chr. 4. 17.
Zererath (zer'ē-rath). Judg. 7. 22.
Zeresh (zē'resh), gold. Est. 5. 10.
Zereth (zē'reth), gold (?). 1 Chr. 4. 7.
Zeri (zē'rī), same as **Izri**. 1 Chr. 25. 3.
Zeror (zē'rọr), bundle. 1 Sam. 9. 1.
Zeruah (zē-rū'a), leprous. 1 Kin. 11. 26.
Zerubbabel (ze-rub'ȧ-bel), scattered in Babylon. Hag. 1. 1.
Zeruiah (zer-ů-ī'ȧ). 1 Sam. 26. 6.
Zetham (zē'thăm), olive. 1 Chr. 23. 8.
Zethan (zē'thăn), same as **Zetham**. 1 Chr. 7. 10.
Zethar (zē'thär). Est. 1. 10.
Zia (zī'ȧ), motion. 1 Chr. 5. 13.
Ziba (zī'bȧ), planter. 2 Sam. 9. 2.
Zibeon (zib'ē-ŏn), dyed. Gen. 36. 2.
Zibia (zib'i-ȧ), roe. 1 Chr. 8. 9.
Zibiah (zib'i-ȧ), same as **Zibia**. 2 Kin. 12. 1.
Zichri (zic̦h'rī), famous. 2 Chr. 23. 1.
Ziddim (zid'im), sides. Josh. 19. 35.
Zidkijah (zid-kī'jȧ), justice of Jehovah. Neh. 10. 1.
Zidon (zī'dŏn), fishing. Gen. 49. 13.
Zidonians (zī-dō'ni-ăn̦s), inhabitants of Zidon. Judg. 10. 12.
Zif (zif), blossom. 1 Kin. 6. 1.
Ziha (zī'hȧ), drought. Ezra 2. 43.
Ziklag (zik'lag). Josh. 15. 31.
Zillah (zil'ȧ), shade. Gen. 4. 19.
Zilpah (zil'pȧ), dropping. Gen. 29. 24.
Zilthai (zil'thī), shady. 1 Chr. 8. 20.
Zimmah (zim'ȧ), planning. 1 Chr. 6. 20.
Zimran (zim'ran), celebrated. Gen. 25. 2.
Zimri (zim'rī), same as **Zimran**.
Zina (zī'nȧ), abundance (?). 1 Chr. 23. 10.
Zion (zī'ŏn), sunny. 2 Sam. 5. 7.
Zior (zī'ọr), smallness. Josh. 15. 54.
Ziph (zif), flowing. 1 Chr. 4. 16.
Ziphah (zī'fȧ), feminine of **Ziph**. 1 Chr. 4. 16.
Ziphims (zif'imṣ), inhabitants of Ziph. Ps. 54, title.
Ziphites (zif'īts), same as **Ziphims**. 1 Sam. 23. 19.
Ziphion (zif'i-on), same as **Zephon**. Gen. 46. 16.
Ziphron (zif'ron), sweet smell. Num. 34. 9.
Zippor (zip'ọr), bird. Num. 22. 2.
Zipporah (zi-pō'rȧ), fem. of **Zippor**. Ex. 2. 21.
Zithri (zith'rī), protection of Jehovah (?). Ex. 6. 22.
Ziz (ziz), a flower. 2 Chr. 20. 16.
Ziza (zī'zȧ), abundance. 1 Chr. 4. 37.
Zizah (zī'zȧ). 1 Chr. 23. 11.
Zoan (zō'an), low region. Num. 13. 22.
Zoar (zō'ăr), smallness. Gen. 13. 10.
Zoba (zō'bȧ), a plantation. 2 Sam. 10. 6.
Zobah (zō'bȧ), same as preceding. 1 Sam. 14. 47.
Zobebah (zō-bē'bȧ), walking slowly. 1 Chr. 4. 8.
Zohar (zō'här), light. Gen. 23. 8.
Zoheleth (zō'hē-leth), serpent stone. 1 Kin. 1. 9.
Zoheth (zō'heth), strong (?). 1 Chr. 4. 20.
Zophah (zō'fȧ), a cruse (?). 1 Chr. 7. 35.
Zophai (zō'fī), honeycomb. 1 Chr. 6. 26.
Zophar (zō'făr), chatterer. Job 2. 11.
Zophim (zō'fim), watchers. Num. 23. 14.
Zorah (zō'rȧ), a place of hornets. Josh. 19. 41.
Zorathites (zō'rath-īts), people of Zorah. 1 Chr. 4. 2.
Zoreah (zō'rē-ȧ), same as **Zorah**. Josh. 15. 33.
Zorites (zō'rīts), same as **Zorathites**. 1 Chr. 2. 54.
Zorobabel (zō-rob'ȧ-bel), Greek form of **Zerubbabel**. Matt. 1. 12.
Zuar (zū'ăr), same as **Zoar**. Num. 1. 8.
Zuph (zuf), flag, sedge. 1 Sam. 1. 1.
Zur (zūr), rock. Num. 25. 15.
Zuriel (zū'ri-el), God is the rock. Num. 3. 35.
Zurishaddai (zū'ri-shad'ī), whose Almighty is the rock. Num. 1. 6.

ABBREVIATIONS COMMONLY USED IN WRITING AND PRINTING

A

A, argon.
a, in algebra, known quantity, constant.
A., Absolute; Academy; acre; America; American; angstrom unit; April; Artillery.
A., a., (L. *anno*) in the year; (L. *ante*) before.
a., about; acre(s); active; adjective; alto; ampere; anonymous; answer; are (in metric system).
A. A., Associate of Arts; antiaircraft; antiaircraft artillery.
A. A. A., Amateur Athletic Association; Automobile Association of America.
A.A.A.S., American Academy of Arts and Sciences; American Association for the Advancement of Science.
A. A. G., Assistant Adjutant General.
A.A.P.S.S., American Academy of Political and Social Sciences.
A.A.S., (L. *Academiæ Americanæ Socius*) Fellow of the American Academy.
A.A.S.S., (L. *Americanæ Antiquarianæ Societatis Socius*) Member of the American Antiquarian Society.
A.B., (L. *Artium Baccalaureus*) Bachelor of Arts: see *B.A.*
A.B., able-bodied seaman.
abbr., abbrev., abbreviated; abbreviation.
A.B.C.F.M., American Board of Commissioners for Foreign Missions.
A. B. F. M., American Board of Foreign Missions.
abl., ablative.
ABM, anti-ballistic missile.
abp., archbishop.
abr., abridged; abridgment.
abs., absol., absolute.
A. B. S., American Bible Society.
abt., about.
A. C., (L. *Ante Christum*) before Christ.
A. C., a.c., alternating current.
acc., accusative.
acc., acct., account; accountant.
A.C.S., American Chemical Society; American Colonization Society.
ACW, alternating continuous waves.
a. d., after date.
ad., advertisement.
A.D., (L. *Anno Domini*) in the year of our Lord.
A. D. C., Aide-de-camp.
ad inf., (L. *ad infinitum*) to infinity.
ad int., (L. *ad interim*) in the meantime.
adj., adjective.
Adj., Adjt., Adjutant.
ad lib., ad libit., (L. *ad libitum*) at pleasure.
ad loc., (L. *ad locum*) at the place.
adm., administrator.
Adm., Admiral; Admiralty.
Adm. Co., Admiralty Court.
adv., adverb.
Adv., Advent; Advocate.
ad val., (L. *ad valorem*) according to the value.
æ., æt., (L. *ætatis*) of age; aged.
A. E. F., American Expeditionary Forces.
A. F., a. f., audio frequency.
Af., Africa; African.
A.F., Air Force; Anglo-French.
A.F.A.M., A.F. & A.M., Ancient Free and Accepted Masons.
A. F. B. S., American and Foreign Bible Society.
A. F. L., American Federation of Labor: also *A. F. of L.*
A.G., Adjutant General; Attorney General.
Ag., August.
ag., agriculture.
Ag. (L. *argentum*) silver.
A. G. O., Adjutant General's Office.
agr., agric., agriculture.
agt., agent.
A.H., (L. *Anno Hegiræ*) in the year of the Hegira.
a. h., ampere-hour.
A. H. C., Army Hospital Corps.
A. H. M. S., American Home Missionary Society.
A. H. S., (L. *Anno Humanæ Salutis*) in the year of human salvation.
A. I. A., Associate of the Institute of Actuaries.
A.I.C., American Institute of Chemists.
A.I.C.E., American Institute of Civil Engineers.
A.I.E.E., American Institute of Electrical Engineers.
A. I. M. E., American Institute of Mining Engineers; Associate of the Institute of Mechanical Engineers; Associate of the Institute of Mining Engineers.
AK, Alaska.
AL, Alabama.
A.L., American Legion.
al., (L. *alii*) other persons; (L. *alia*) other things.
Al, aluminum.
Ala., Alabama.
A. L. A., American Library Association.
Alas., Alaska.
Ald., Alderman.
Alex., Alexander.
Alf., Alfred.
alg., algebra.
alt., alternate; altitude; alto.
A. M., (L. *Anno Mundi*) in the year of the world; (L. *Artium Magister*) Master of Arts: also *M.A.*; Ave Maria.
A. M., a. m., (L. *ante meridiem*) before noon.
Am., America; American.
A.M.A., American Medical Association.
Amb., Ambassador.
Amb. Co., Ambulance Company.
A. M. D., Army Medical Department.
A.M.E., African Methodist Episcopal.
Amer., America; American.
A. M. I. C. E., Associate Member of the Institution of Civil Engineers (British).
amm., amalgama.
amp., amperage; ampere(s).
A. M. S., Army Medical Staff.
amt., amount.
A. N., Anglo-Norman.
An., (L. *anno*) in the year; anonymous.
anal., analysis.
anat., anatomical; anatomy.
A. N. C., Army Nurse Corps.
anc., ancient.
Angl., Anglican.
Ang.-Sax., Anglo-Saxon.
anon., anonymous.
ans., answer.
A. N. S. S., Associate of the Normal School of Science.
Ant., Antiq., antiquarian; antiquities.
anthrop., anthropological; anthropology.
A. O. C., Army Ordnance Corps.
A. O. D., Army Ordnance Department.
A. O. F., Ancient Order of Foresters.
A. O. H., Ancient Order of Hibernians.
aor., aorist.
A. O. U., American Ornithologists' Union.
A. O. U. W., Ancient Order of United Workmen.
Ap., Apostle; April.
A. P. A., American Protective Association.
A. P. C., Army Pay Corps.
A. P. D., Army Pay Department.
Apl., April.
A.P.O., APO, Army Post Office.
apo., apogee.
Apoc., Apocalypse; Apocrypha.
apog., apogee.
app., appendix.
approx., approximate; approximately.
Apr., April.
aq., aqua.
AR, Arkansas.
a. r., (L. *anno regni*) in the year of the reign.
A. R., Army Regulations; Autonomous Republic.
Ar., Arab., Arabic.
ar., arrival; arrive(s).
A. R. A., Associate of the Royal Academy.
Aram., Aramaic.
arch., architecture.
Archd., Archdeacon.
Archaeol., Archaeology.
Arg., Argentina.
A. R. H. A., Associate of the Royal Hibernian Academy.
A. R. I. B. A., Associate of the Royal Institute of British Architects.
arith., arithmetic; arithmetical.
Ariz., Arizona.
Ark., Arkansas.
Arm., Armenian; Armoric.
Armor., Armoric.
arr., arrival; arrive.
A. R. R., (L. *Anno Regni Regis* or *Reginæ*) in the year of the king's (or queen's) reign.
A. R. S. A., Associate of the Royal Scottish Academy.
A. R. S. L., Associate of the Royal Society of Literature.
art., article.
A.S., A.-S., Anglo-Saxon.
As, arsenic.
A.S.A., American Statistical Association.
A. S. C., Army Service Corps.
A. S. M. E., American Society of Mechanical Engineers.
ass., assistant; association; assorted.
A.S.S.R., Autonomous Soviet Socialist Republic.
asst., assistant.
A.S.S.U., American Sunday-School Union.
Assyr., Assyrian.
astrol., astrology.
astron., astronomical; astronomy.
at., atmosphere; atomic.
a.t., arch treasurer.
ats., at suit of.
A.T.S., American Tract Society; American Temperance Society.
A. T. S. Q. M. C., Army Transport Service Quartermaster Corps.
Att., Atty., Attorney.
Att. Gen., Atty. Gen., Attorney General.
at. wt., atomic weight.
A. U., angstrom unit; astronomical unit.
Au, (L. *aurum*) gold.
A. U. A., American Unitarian Association.
A. U. C., (L. *Anno Urbis Conditæ* or *Ab Urbe Condita*) in the year from the building of the city (Rome).
aug., augment; augmentative.
Aug., August.
Aust., Austria; Austria-Hungary; Austrian.
Austral., Australia; Australasia.
aux., auxil., auxiliary.
A. V., Artillery Volunteers; Authorized Version (of the Bible).
av., average; avoirdupois.
Av., Ave., Avenue.
A. V. C., American Veterans Committee.
A. V. D., Army Veterinary Department.
avdp., avoirdupois.
Av. Sec., Aviation Section.
Av. Sec. S. R. C., Aviation Section, Signal Reserve Corps.
avoir., avoirdupois.
a. w. l., absent with leave.
a. w. o. l., absent without official leave.
ax., axiom; axis.
AZ, Arizona.

B

B., Bible; British; Brotherhood; in chess, bishop; in medicine, bacillus.
B., b., bachelor; battery; bay; bicuspid; book; born; breadth; brother; in baseball, base; also, base hit; in music, bass; basso.
Ba, barium.
B. A., Bachelor of Arts; British Academy; British America.
B. A. F., British Air Force.
B. Ag., B. Agr., Bachelor of Agriculture.
bal., balance.
bank., banking.
Bap., Bapt., Baptist.
bar., barometer; barrel; barrister.
B. Ar., Bachelor of Architecture.
Barb., Barbados.
barr., barrister.
Bart., Baronet.
B. A. S., Bachelor of Agricultural Science; Bachelor of Applied Science.
bat., batt., battalion; battery.
B. B. A., Bachelor of Business Administration.
B. B. C., British Broadcasting Corporation.
bbl., barrel.—**bbls.**, barrels.
B. B. S., Bachelor of Business Science.
B. C., Bachelor of Chemistry; Bachelor of Commerce; before Christ; British Columbia.
B. C., b. c., battery commander; bass clarinet.
bch., bunch.
B. Ch., (L. *Baccalaureus Chirurgiæ*) Bachelor of Surgery.
B. C. L., Bachelor of Civil Law.
B. D., Bachelor of Divinity.
bd., board; bond; bound; bundle.
bd. ft., board foot; board feet.
bdl., bundle.—**bdls.**, bundles.
bds., boards; (bound in) boards; bundles.
Be, beryllium.
B. E., Bachelor of Education; Bachelor of Engineering; Bank of England; Board of Education.
B. E., B/E, b. e., bill of exchange.
B. E. F., British Expeditionary Forces.
Belg., Belgian; Belgic; Belgium.
bf., in printing, boldface.
B/F, in bookkeeping, brought forward.
B. F., Bachelor of Finance; Bachelor of Forestry.
B. F. A., Bachelor of Fine Arts.
bg., bag.—**bgs.**, bags.
B. G., Brigadier General.
B. I., British India.
Bi, bismuth.
Bib., Bible; Biblical.
bibliog., bibliography.
biog., biographical; biography.
biol., biological; biology.
bk., bank; book.
bkts., baskets.
bl., bale; bales; barrel; barrels; black.
B/L, bill of lading.
B. L., Bachelor of Laws; Bachelor of Letters.
B. L. E., Brotherhood of Locomotive Engineers.
B. LL., (L. *Baccalaureus Legum*) Bachelor of Laws: see *LL.B.*
B. L. R., breech-loading rifle.
bls., bales; barrels.
B. M., (L. *Baccalaureus Medicinæ*) Bachelor of Medicine.
B. Mus., (L. *Baccalaureus Musicæ*) Bachelor of Music.
B/O, in bookkeeping, brought over.
b. o., back order; box office; branch office; broker's order; buyer's option.
Boh., Bohemia; Bohemian.
B. O. T., Board of Trade.
bot., botanical; botanist; botany; bottle.
B. O. U., British Ornithologists' Union.
bp., birthplace; bishop.
B. P., bills payable.
B. P. O. E., Benevolent and Protective Order of Elks.
Br, bromine.
Br., Breton; Britain; British.
br., branch; brig; bronze; brother.
Br. Am., British America.
B. R., bills receivable.
brev., brevet.
Brig., brigade; brigadier.
Brig.-Gen., Brigadier-General.
Brit., Britain; Britannia; British; Briton.
Brit. Mus., British Museum.
B. S., Bachelor of Science; Bachelor of Surgery.
b. s., bill of sale.
B.Sc., (L. *Baccalaureus Scientiæ*) Bachelor of Science.
B. S. L., Botanical Society, London.
Bt., Baronet.
B. T. U., British thermal unit.
bu., bushel.
bu., bur., bureau.
B. V., (L. *Beata Virgo*) Blessed Virgin.
B.V.M., (L. *Beata Virgo Maria*) Blessed Virgin Mary.
bvt., brevet; brevetted.
B. W. I., British West Indies.
bx., box(es).
Bz., benzene.

C

C, carbon.
C., c., capacity; carbon; case; cent(s); centigrade; centime; centimeter; century; chapter; chief; church; circa; copper; copy; copyright; corps; cost; cubic; hundredweight.
c., catcher; city; cloudy; center.
CA, California.
Ca, calcium.
ca., cathode; centiare(s); circa.
C. A., Central America; Coast Artillery; Confederate Army.
C. A., c. a., chief accountant; commercial agent; consular agent.
C/A, credit account; current account.
CAA, Civil Aeronautics Authority.
C. A. C., Coast Artillery Corps.
Cal., California; large calorie(s).
cal., calendar; caliber; small calorie(s).
Calif., California.
Can., Canada; Canadian.
Cant., Canticles (Song of Solomon).
cap., capital; (L. *capitulum*) chapter; captain.
Capt., Captain.
Car., carat(s).
C. A. R. C., Coast Artillery Reserve Corps.
Card., Cardinal.
carp., carpentry.
cat., catalogue; catechism.
Cath., cathedral; Catholic.
caus., causative.
cav., cavalry.

C.B.S., CBS, Columbia Broadcasting System.

c.c., cubic centimeter(s).

C.C., c.c., carbon copy; cashier's check; chief clerk; company commander; county commissioner; county court.

C.C.A., Chief Clerk of the Admiralty; Circuit Court of Appeals.

C.C.D., Commander of Coast Defenses.

C.C.P., Court of Common Pleas.

Cd, cadmium.

c.d., cash discount.

C.E., Chemical Engineer; Chief Engineer; Church of England; Civil Engineer.

Ce, cerium.

C.E.F., Canadian Expeditionary Force.

Celt., Celtic.

cent., centigrade; centime; centimeter; central; centum; century.

cf., (L. *confer*) compare; in baseball, center field(er).

c/f, in bookkeeping, carried forward.

C.F., c.f., cost and freight.

C. F. A., Chief of Field Artillery.

C.G., Captain of the Guard; Commanding General; Commissary General; Consul General; Coast Guard.

c.g.m., centigram.

C.G.S., cgs, c.g.s., centimeter-gram-second.

Ch., ch., chancery; chaplain; check; chief.

c.h., customhouse.

ch., chapter.

Chal., Chald., Chaldaic; Chaldean; Chaldee.

Chanc., Chancellor.

chap., chaplain; chapter.

Ch. E., Chemical Engineer.

chem., chemical; chemistry.

chg., charge.

chgd., charged.

Chin., China; Chinese.

chm., chmn., chairman.

Chr., Christ; Christian.

Chron., Chronicles.

C.I., Channel Islands.

C.I.C., Commander in Chief.

Cic., Cicero.

C.I.E., Companion of the Order of the Indian Empire.

C. I. O., Congress of Industrial Organization.

cir., circa; circular; circulation; circumference.

cit., citizen.

civ., civil; civilian.

C.J., Chief Justice.

Cl, chlorine.

cl., centiliter(s); claim; class; clause; clearance; cloth.

clar., clarinet.

class., classical; classification.

cld., cleared.

clk., clerk.

cm., centimeter(s).

c.m., common meter; corresponding member; court-martial.

C.M.G., Companion of the Order of St. Michael and St. George.

cml., commercial.

C.M.S., Church Missionary Society.

CO, Colorado.

Co, cobalt.

Co., company; county.

C.O., Commanding Officer; Conscientious Objector.

c/o, c.o., care of; carried over.

coad., coadjutor.

C.O.D., collect on delivery.

C. of O., Chief of Ordnance.

C. of S., Chief of Staff.

cog., cogn., cognate.

Col., Colonel; Colonial; Colorado; Colossians.

col., collector; college; colony; color; column.

coll., colleague; collect; collection; college; colloquial.

colloq., colloquial; colloquialism; colloquially.

Colo., Colorado.

Col. Serg., Color Sergeant.

Com., Commander; Commissioner; Committee; Commodore; Communist.

com., comedy; comma; commentary; commerce; commercial; common; commune; communication; community.

Comdg., Commanding.

comm., commander; commerce; commission; committee; commonwealth.

comp., comparative; compare; compiler; composer; composition; compositor; compound; compounded.

compar., comparative.

compos., composition.

Com. Ver., Common Version (of the Bible).

Con., Consul; Conformist.

con., concerto; conclusion; connection; consolidate; (L. *contra*) against.

conc., concentrate; concerning.

conch., conchology.

conf., (L. *confer*) compare.

Cong., Congregation; Congregationalist; Congress.

conj., conjunction.

Conn., Connecticut.

Const., constable; constitution.

cont., continent; continued; contract.

contr., contracted; contraction; contralto; contrary; control; controller.

Cop., Copt., Coptic.

Cor., Corinthians; Coroner.

cor., corner; correct; correction; correlative; correspondence; correspondent; corresponding.

Cor. Mem., corresponding member.

Corn., Cornish; Cornwall.

corol., corollary.

Cor. Sec., corresponding secretary.

cos., cosine.

cosec., cosecant.

cot., cotangent.

cp., compare.

C.P., Chief Patriarch; Common Pleas; Common Prayer; Communist Party.

C. P. A., c. p. a., Certified Public Accountant.

Cpl., Corporal.

C. P. O., Chief Petty Officer.

C.P.S., (L. *Custos Privati Sigilli*) Keeper of the Privy Seal.

cr., created; credit; credited; creditor; crown.

Cr, chromium.

C.R., (L. *Custos Rotulorum*) Keeper of the Rolls; Costa Rica.

cres., crescendo.

crim. con., criminal conversation.

crystall., crystallography.

C.S., Civil Service; Clerk of the Signet; Court of Session.

Cs, cesium.

C.S.A., Confederate States of America.

C. S. C., Civil Service Commission.

C. S. O., Chief Signal Officer; Chief Staff Officer.

C. S. T., Central Standard Time.

CT, Connecticut.

ct., cent; (L. *centum*) a hundred; court.

Ct., Connecticut; Count.

cts., cents.

Cu, (L. *cuprum*) copper.

cu., cub., cubic.

cur., current.

cwt., hundredweight.

Cy., County.

cy., capacity; currency.

CZ, C. Z., Canal Zone.

D

D., December; Democrat; Democratic; (L. *Deus*) God; Doctor; (L. *Dominus*) Lord; Duchess; Duke; Dutch.

d., day(s); dead; delete; (L. *denarius, denarii*) penny, pennies or pence; density; diameter; died.

D.A., District Attorney.

Dak., Dakota.

Dan., Daniel; Danish.

D. A. R., Daughters of the American Revolution.

dat., dative.

DC, District of Columbia.

D.C., (It. *da capo*) in music, from the beginning; Dental Corps; District of Columbia.

D. C., d. c., direct current.

D.C.L., Doctor of Civil Law.

D. C. M., Distinguished Conduct Medal.

D.D., Doctor of Divinity.

D.D.S., Doctor of Dental Surgery.

DE, Delaware.

Dec., December.

dec., deceased; decimeter; declaration; declension; decrease.

decim., decimeter.

decl., declension.

def., defendant; defense; deferred; definite; definition.

deg., degree(s).

Del., Delaware.

del., (L. *delineavit*) he (or she) drew it; delete; delegate.

Dem., Democrat.

Den., Denmark.

dep., department; deposit; depositor; deputy.

der., derivation; derivative; derived.

Deut., Deuteronomy.

D.F., Dean of the Faculty; Defender of the Faith.

D. F. C., Distinguished Flying Cross.

dft., defendant.

dg., decigram(s).

Di, didymium.

dial., dialect; dialectic.

diam., diameter.

dict., dictator; dictionary.

dim., diminutive.

dim., dimin., diminuendo.

dis., distance; distribute.

dist., discount; distance; distinguish; district.

Dist. Atty., District Attorney.

div., divide; dividend; division; divisor; divorced.

dl., deciliter(s).

D. Lit., Doctor of Literature.

D.L.O., Dead Letter Office.

D.M., D. Mus., Doctor of Music.

dm., decimeter(s).

D. O., District Office; Doctor of Optometry; Doctor of Osteopathy.

do., ditto.

dol., dollar.

D.O.M., (L. *Deo Optimo Maximo*) To God, the Best, the Greatest.

dom. econ., domestic economy.

Dor., Doric.

doz., dozen.

D.P., displaced person.

dpt., department; deponent.

Dr., Doctor.

dr., debtor; dram(s).

D. R., Drill Regulations.

D.S., (It. *dal segno*), (repeat) from this sign.

D.Sc., Doctor of Science.

D. S. C., Distinguished Service Cross.

D. S. M., Distinguished Service Medal.

d.s.p., (L. *decessit sine prole*) died without issue.

D.S.T., Daylight Saving Time.

D. Th., D. Theol., Doctor of Theology.

Du., Dutch.

D.V., (L. *Deo volente*) God willing; Douay Version (of the Bible).

D.V.M., Doctor of Veterinary Medicine.

dwt., pennyweight(s).

dyn., dynamics.

dz., dozen(s).

E

E., Earl; Easter; English.

E, E., e, e., east.

E., e., earth; eastern; engineering; errors; electromotive force.

E. & O. E., errors and omissions excepted.

ea., each.

E. A., in psychology, educational age.

E b N, east by north.

E b S, east by south.

E.C., Engineering Corps; Established Church.

e.c., (L. *exempli causa*) for the sake of example.

Eccl., Eccles., Ecclesiastes; Ecclesiastical.

Ecclus., Ecclesiasticus.

Eclec., eclectic.

econ., economics; economy.

ed., edition; editor.

Ed. B., Bachelor of Education.

Ed. D., Doctor of Education.

E. E., Early English; Electrical Engineer.

e.e., errors excepted.

E. F., Expeditionary Forces.

e.g., (L. *exempli gratia*) for example.

Eg., Egypt., Egyptian.

E.I., East India; East Indies.

elec., elect., electric; electricity.

elem., element; elementary.

Eliz., Elizabethan.

Emp., Emperor; Empire; Empress.

enc., enclosed; enclosure; encyclopedia.

encl., enclosure.

ency., encyc., encyclopedia.

E.N.E., east-northeast.

Eng., England; English.

engin., engineering.

engr., engraved; engraver; engraving.

Ens., Ensign.

ent., entom., entomology.

Env. Ext., Envoy Extraordinary.

Eph., Ephesians.

Epiph., Epiphany.

Epis., Episcopal.

Epist., Epistle.

eq., equal; equation; equator; equivalent.

equiv., equivalent.

Er, erbium.

E.S.E., east-southeast.

esp., especially.

Esq., Esqr., Esquire.

Esth., Esther.

et al., (L. *et alibi*) and elsewhere.

et al., (L. *et alii*) and others.

etc., et cetera.

Eth., Ethiopic.

ethnol., ethnological; ethnology.

et seq., (L. *et sequentes* or *sequentia*) and the following.

etym., etymological; etymology.

Eur., Europe; European.

ex., example; except; exception; exchange; executed; executive; export; extra; extract.

Ex., Exodus.

Exc., Excellency.

exc., excellent; except; exception.

exch., exchange; exchequer.

exec., executive; executor.

execx., executrix.

ex g., (L. *exempli gratia*) by way of example, for instance.

Exod., Exodus.

exp., expenses; export; exportation; express.

exr., executor.

Ez., Ezr., Ezra.

Ezek., Ezekiel.

F

F., Fahrenheit; February; Fellow; France; French; Friday.

F., f., farad; farthing; father; fathom; feet; feminine; filly; fine; fluid; folio(s); following; foot; form; franc(s); from; forte; (L. *fiat*) in pharmacy, let there be made.

F. A., Field Artillery.

F. Amb., Field Ambulance.

F. Hosp., Field Hospital.

Fahr., Fahrenheit.

F. & A. M., Free and Accepted Masons.

fath., fathom.

fb., in football, fullback.

f. b., freight bill.

FBI, F.B.I., Federal Bureau of Investigation.

FCC, F.C.C., Federal Communications Commission.

fcp., foolscap.

F.C.S., Fellow of the Chemical Society.

F.D., (L. *Fidei Defensor*) Defender of the Faith.

Fe, (L. *ferrum*) iron.

Feb., February.

fec., (L. *fecit*) he (or she) made (it).

fem., feminine.

feud., feudal.

ff., folio; following; fortissimo.

F.F.A., f.f.a., in nautical usage, free from alongside.

F.F.I., French Forces of the Interior.

F.F.P.S., Fellow of the Faculty of Physicians and Surgeons.

F.F.V., First Families of Virginia.

F.G.S.A., Fellow of the Geological Society of America.

FHA, F.H.A., Federal Housing Administration.

Fid. Def., (L. *Fidei Defensor*) Defender of the Faith.

fig., figurative; figuratively; figure(s).

Fin., Finland.

fin., finance; financial.

Finn., Finnish.

fir., firkin(s).

FL, Florida.

Fl., Flemish.

fl., florin(s); flourished.

Fla., Florida.

Flem., Flemish.

fl. oz., fluid ounce(s).

FM, frequency modulation.

fm., fathom; from.

F.M., Field Marshal.

F.O., field officer.

fo., fol., folio(s).

f.o.b., free on board.

fol., foll., following.

for., foreign; forestry.

fort., fortification.

F. P., foot-pound.

f. p., fp, fp., freezing point.

FPC, F.P.C., Federal Power Commission.

Fr., Father; France; French.

fr., franc(s); frequent; from.

F.R.C.P., Fellow of the Royal College of Physicians.

F.R.C.S., Fellow of the Royal College of Surgeons.

F.R.G.S., Fellow of the Royal Geographical Society.

Fri., Friday.

Fris., Frs., Frisian.

F. R. S., Fellow of the Royal Society.

F.R.S.L., Fellow of the Royal Society of Literature.

F.R.S.S., Fellow of the Royal Statistical Society.

frt., freight.

F. S., Field Service; Fleet Surgeon.

FSA, F.S.A., Farm Security Administration; Federal Security Agency.

ft., feet; foot; fort.

FTC, F.T.C., Federal Trade Commission.

fth., fathom.

ft-lb, foot-pound.

fur., furlong.

fut., future.

F.Z.S., Fellow of the Zoological Society.

G

G., German; Germany; specific gravity.

G., g., gauge; gold; grain; gram(s); grand; guide; guinea(s); gulf; in electricity, conductance.

g, in physics, gravity; in psychology, general intelligence.

g., gender; genera; genitive.

GA, Ga., Georgia.

Ga, gallium.

G.A., General Assembly.

Gael., Gadhelic; Gaelic.

Gal., Galatians.

gal., gall., gallon(s).

galv., galvanic; galvanism.

G.A.R., Grand Army of the Republic.

G.B., Great Britain.

G.B. & I., Great Britain and Ireland.

g-cal., gram calorie(s).

G.C.D., g.c.d., greatest common divisor.

G.C.F., g.c.f., greatest common factor.

G.C.M., g.c.m., greatest common measure.

G.D., Grand Duchess; Grand Duke.

Gen., General; Genesis; Geneva; Genevan.

gen., generally; genitive.

Geneal., genealogical; genealogy.

Gent., gentleman; gentlemen.

geog., geographer; geographical; geography.

geol., geological; geology.
geom., geometer; geometrical; geometry.
Ger., Germ., German.
ger., gerund.
G. H. Q., General Headquarters.
gi., gill; gills (measure).
Gl, glucinum.
gloss., glossary.
gm., gram(s).
G.M., General Manager; Grand Master.
G.M.T., Greenwich Mean Time.
G. O. P., Grand Old Party (Republican Party).
Goth., Gothic.
Gov., Governor.
Gov. Gen., Governor General.
Govt., government.
G.P., g.p., general paresis; general practitioner.
G.P.O., General Post Office; Government Printing Office.
gr., grain(s); great; gross.
Gr., Greece; Greek.
gram., grammar; grammatical.
gro., gross.
GS, German silver.
G.S., general secretary; general staff.
G.S.A., Girl Scouts of America.
G.S.C., General Staff Corps.
gt., gilt; great; gutta.
Gt. Br., Great Britain.
gun., gunnery.

H

H., h., harbor; hard; hardness; height; hence; high; hour(s); hundred; husband.
H, hydrogen.
ha., hectare(s).
Hab., Habakkuk.
hab. corp., habeas corpus.
Hag., Haggai.
Haw., Hawaiian.
Hb, hemoglobin.
hb., in football, halfback.
H.B.M., His (or Her) Britannic Majesty.
H.C., Heralds' College; House of Commons.
H.C.F., h.c.f., heighest common factor.
hd., head.
hdkf., handkerchief.
hdqrs., headquarters.
H. E., high explosive; horizontal equivalent.
Heb., Hebr., Hebrew; Hebrews.
hectol., hectoliter.
hectom., hectometer.
her., heraldic; heraldry.
herp., herpetology.
Hf, hafnium.
hf., half.
H.F., high-frequency.
hf. bd., half-bound.
H. F. C., high-frequency current.
H.G., Horse Guards.
Hg, (L. *hyrargyrum*) mercury.
H.H., His (or Her) Highness; His Holiness.
hhd., hogshead.
HI, Hawaii
H.I.H., His (or Her) Imperial Highness.
H.I.M., His (or Her) Imperial Majesty.
Hind., Hindi; Hindu; Hindustan; Hindustani.
hist., historical; history.
H.J., (L. *hic jacet*) here lies.
H.L., House of Lords.
hl., hectoliter.
hm., hectometer.
H.M., His (or Her) Majesty.
H.M.S., His (or Her) Majesty's Service; His (or Her) Majesty's Ship; His (or Her) Majesty's Steamer.
Hon., honorable; honorary.
Hond., honored.
hor., horol., horological; horology.
hort., hortic., horticultural; horticulture.
Hos., Hosea.
H.P., h.p., high pressure; horsepower.
H.Q., Hq., headquarters.
hr., hrs., hour, hours.
H. R., Home Rule; House of Representatives.
H.R.E., Holy Roman Empire (or Emperor).
H.R.H., His (or Her) Royal Highness.
H.R.I.P., (L. *hic requiescit in pace*) here rests in peace.
H.S.H., His (or Her) Serene Highness.
ht., heat; height(s).
Hun., Hung., Hungarian; Hungary.
hund., hundred.
H.V., high voltage.
hyd., hydraulics; hydrostatics.
hydraul., hydraulics.
hydros., hydrostatics.
hypoth., hypothesis; hypothetical.
Hz, hz, hertz.

I

I., Idaho; Independent; Iowa.
i., incisor; interest; intransitive.
I., i., imperator; island(s); isle(s).
IA, Ia., Iowa.
i. a., (L. *in absentia*) in absence; absent.
ib., ibid., (L. *ibidem*) in the same place.
I.C., (L. *Iesus Christus*) Jesus Christ.
ICBM, intercontinental ballistic missile.
I. C. C., Interstate Commerce Commission.
Icel., Iceland; Icelandic.
ich., ichth., ichthyology.
icon., iconographic.
I. C. S., International Correspondence School.
ID, Idaho.
I. D., Intelligence Department.
id., (L. *idem*) the same.
Ida., Idaho.
I.D.N., (L. *In Dei Nomine*) In the name of God.
i.e., (L. *id est*) that is.
i.h.p., I.H.P., indicated horsepower.
I. H. S., (L. *Iesus Hominum Salvator*) Jesus, Savior of Men; (L. *In Hoc Signo* [*Vinces*]) in this sign (thou shalt conquer); (L. *In Hoc* [*Cruce*] *Salus*) in this (cross) salvation.
IL, Ill., Illinois.
ill., illus., illust., illustrated; illustration.
imag., imaginary.
imp., imperative; imperfect; imperial; impersonal; import; importer; imprimator; imprint.
imper., imperative.
impf., imperfect.
IN, Indiana
in., inch; inches.
In, indium.
inch., incho., inchoative.
incl., including; inclusive.
incog., incognito.
Ind., India; Indian; Indiana; Indies.
ind., independent; index; indicative; indigo; industrial.
I. N. D., (L. *in nomine Dei*) in the name of God.
indecl., indeclinable.
indef., indefinite.
indic., indicative.
in f., (L. *in fine*) at the end.
Inf., Infantry.
inf., infinitive; information.
in loc. cit., (L. *in loco citato*) in the place cited.
I.N.R.I., (L. *Iesus Nazarenus Rex Iudæorum*) Jesus of Nazareth, King of the Jews.
INS, I.N.S., International News Service.
Ins. Gen., Inspector General.
inst., instant; institute; institution.
insur., insurance.
int., interest; interim; interior; interjection; internal; international; intransitive.
intens., intensive.
interj., interjection.
internat., international.
interrog., interrogation; interrogatively.
intrans., intransitive.
in trans., (L. *in transitu*) on the way or passage.
introd., introduction.
Io., Iowa.
I.O.F., Independent Order of Foresters.
I.O.G.T., Independent Order of Good Templars.
I.O.O.F., Independent Order of Odd Fellows.
I. O. R. M., Improved Order of Red Men.
I.O.S.M., Independent Order of the Sons of Malta.
I.O.U., I owe you—an acknowledgment for a debt.
IPA, International Phonetic Alphabet; International Phonetic Association.
I. Q., IQ, intelligence quotient.
i.q., (L. *idem quod*) the same as.
Ir., Ireland; Irish.
Ir, iridium.
I. R., Internal Revenue.
irreg., irregular.
Is., Isa., Isaiah.
is., isl., island; isle.
It., Ital., Italian; Italic; Italy.
it., ital., italic(s).
I.T., Inner Temple.
itin., itinerary.
I.W.W., Industrial Workers of the World.

J

J., Judge; Justice.
J.A., Judge Advocate.
J.A.G., Judge Advocate General.
Jam., Jamaica.
Jan., January.
Jap., Japan; Japanese.
Jav., Javanese.
J. C., Jesus Christ; Julius Caesar; jurisconsult.
J.C.D., (L. *Juris Civilis Doctor*) Doctor of Civil Law.
J.D., (L. *Jurum Doctor*) Doctor of Laws.
Jer., Jeremiah.
j.g., jg., junior grade.
J.H.S., Jesus.
Jl., July.
Jos., Joseph.
Josh., Joshua.
jour., journal; journeyman.
J.P., Justice of the Peace.
Jr., jr., junior.
Ju., June.
Jud., Judges; Judith.
Judge Adv., Judge Advocate.
Jul., July.
Jun., June; Junior.
juris., jurisprudence.
Jus. P., Justice of the Peace.
just., justice.
Jy., July.

K

K, knit; in chess, king.
K., k., karat; kilo; kilogram; king; knight; kopeck(s); krona, kronor; krone, kronen, kroner; in electricity, capacity; in nautical usage, knot.
kal., kalends.
Kan., Kas., Kansas.
K.B., Knight Bachelor; King's Bench; Knight of the Bath.
K.B.E., Knight Commander of the British Empire.
kc., kilocycle(s).
K.C., King's Counsel; Knight Commander; Knight (or Knights) of Columbus.
K.C.B., Knight Commander of the Bath.
K.C.M.G., Knight Commander of St. Michael and St. George.
Ken., Kentucky.
kg., keg(s); kilogram(s).
K.G., Knight of the Garter.
Ki., Kings.
kil., kilometer(s).
kilo., kilogram; kilometer.
kingd., kingdom.
K. K. K., Ku Klux Klan.
KKt, in chess, king's knight.
kl., kiloliter(s).
km., kilometer(s); kingdom.
K.M., Knight of Malta.
kn., krona, kronor; krone, kronen, kroner.
knt., knight.
K. P., Kitchen Police; Knight of St. Patrick; Knight (or Knights) of Pythias.
KR, in chess, king's rook.
Kr. krypton.
KS, Kansas.
Kt, in chess, knight.
kt., carat.
K.T., Knight of the (Order of the) Thistle; Knight (or Knights) Templar.
kw., kilowatt.
kwh., kilowatt-hour.
KY, Ky., Kentucky.

L

L., l., lady; lake; land; latitude; law; leaf; league; left; length; liberal; licentiate; line; link; lira, lire; liter(s); locus; lodge; lord; low.
L., l., £, (L. *libra*) pound(s).
L., Latin.
LA, La., Louisiana.
La, lanthanum.
L.A., Law Agent; Legislative Assembly.
Lab., Laborite; Labrador.
lab., labial; labiate; laboratory.
Lam., Lamentations.
lang., language.
Lat., Latin.
lat., latitude.
lb., pound(s).
L/C, l/c, letter of credit.
L.C., Library of Congress; Lower Canada.
l.c., left center (of stage); (L. *loco citato*) in the place cited; lower case.
L.C.B., Lord Chief Baron.
L.C.D., least common denominator.
L.C.F., least common factor.
L.C.J., Lord Chief Justice.
l. c. l., less than carload lot.
L.C.M., least common multiple.
L.D., Low Dutch.
Ld., Limited; Lord.
Ldp., Lordship.
L.D.S., Licentiate in Dental Surgery.
lea., league; leather; leave.
leg., legal; legate; legato; legend; legislative; legislature.
Lev., Leviticus.
lex., lexicon.
lexicog., lexicography.
lf., in baseball, left field; left fielder.
L. F., Low Frequency.
lg., in football, left guard.
L.G., Life Guards; Low German.
L.Ger., Low German.
L. Gr., Low (or Late) Greek.
L.H.C., Lord High Chancellor.
L.H.D., (L. *Litterarum Humanarum Doctor*) Doctor of Humanities.
L.I., Light Infantry; Long Island.
Li, lithium.
Lib., Liberal; Liberia.
lib., (L. *liber*) book; librarian; library.
Lieut., Lieutenant.
Lieut. Col., Lieutenant Colonel.
Lieut. Comdr., Lieutenant Commander.
Lieut. Gen., Lieutenant General.
Lieut. Gov., Lieutenant Governor.
liq., liquid; liquor.
lit., literature; literary; literally.
Lit. D., Litt. D., (L. *Litterarum Doctor*) Doctor of Letters or Literature.
Lith., Lithuanian.
liv., livre.
LL., L.Lat., Late Latin; Low Latin.
LL.B., (L. *Legum Baccalaureus*) Bachelor of Laws.
LL.D., (L. *Legum Doctor*) Doctor of Laws.
LL.M., (L. *Legum Magister*) Master of Laws.
L.M., Licentiate in Medicine; Lord Mayor.
loc. cit., (L. *loco citato*) in the place cited.
log., logarithm.
L. O. M., Loyal Order of Moose.
Lon., Lond., London.
long., longitude.
loq., (L. *loquitur*) speaks.
L.P., Lord Provost.
Lp., Ladyship; Lordship.
L.P., l.p., long primer; low pressure.
L.R., Lloyd's Register.
L.S., Licentiate in Surgery; Linnaean Society; (L. *Locus Sigilli*) place of the seal (on a document).
l.s., left side.
l.s.c., (*loco supra citato*) in the place cited above.
L.S.D., £.s.d., (L. *Libræ Solidi, Denarii*) pounds, shillings, pence.
L. S. S., Life Saving Station.
LST, Landing Ship, Tanks.
Lt., Lieutenant.
Lt. Inf., Light Infantry.
lv., leave(s); livre(s).

M

M., Manitoba; Marshal; Master; Medieval; Monday; Monsieur.
M., m., majesty; male; manual; mark (coin); marquis; married; masculine; medicine; medium; meridian; (L. *meridies*) noon; meter(s); middle; mile(s); mill(s); minim; minute(s); month; moon; morning; mountain; in dentistry, molar; in mathematics, modulus; in mechanics, mass.
MA, Massachusetts.
M.A., Master of Arts; Military Academy.
Ma, masurium.
Mac., Macc., Maccabees.
mach., machinery.
Mad., Madm., Madam.
mag., magazine; magnetic.
Maj., Major.
Maj. Gen., Major General.
Mal., Malachi; Malay; Malayan.
Man., Manitoba.
man., manual.
manuf., manufacture; manufacturing.
Mar., March.
mar., marine; maritime.
March., Marchioness.
marg., margin; marginal.
Marq., Marquess; Marquis.
mas., masc., masculine.
Mass., Massachusetts.
math., mathematical; mathematician; mathematics.
Matt., Matthew.
M.B., (L. *Medicinæ Baccalaureus*) Bachelor of Medicine; (L. *Musicæ Baccalaureus*) Bachelor of Music.
M. C., Master Commandant, Master of Ceremonies; Medical Corps; Member of Congress; Member of Council.
M.C.L., Master of Civil Law.
MD, Md., Maryland.
M.D., (L. *Medicinæ Doctor*) Doctor of Medicine.
Mdlle., Mademoiselle.
Mdm., Madam.
Mdme., Madame.
mdse., merchandise.
ME, Me., Maine.
M.E., Methodist Episcopal; Military, Mining, or Mechanical Engineer; Most Excellent.
ME., M.E., Middle English.
meas., measure.
mech., mechanical; mechanics.
med., medical; medicine.
mem., member; memoir; memorandum; memoranda; memorial.
mer., meridian.
merc., mercantile.
Messrs., Messieurs.
met., metaphysics.
metal., metallurgy.
metaph., metaphysics.
meteor., meteorology.
Meth., Methodist.
meton., metonymy.
Mex., Mexican; Mexico.
m.f., in music, mezzo forte; microfarad; millifarad.
M.F.A., Master of Fine Arts.
mfd., manufactured.
mfg., manufacturing.
M.F.H., Master of Foxhounds.
mfr., manufacturer.
Mg, magnesium.
Mgr., Manager; Monseigneur; Monsignor.
M.H., Medal of Honor.
M.H.G., Middle High German.
M.Hon., Most Honorable.
M.H.R., Member of the House of Representatives.
MI, Michigan.

Mic., Micah.
M.I.C.E., Member of the Institution of Civil Engineers.
Mich. Michigan.
mid., middle; midshipman.
mil., **milit.**, military; militia.
M.I.M.E., Member of the Institute of Mining Engineers.
min., mineralogical; mineralogy; minutes.
Minn., Minnesota.
Min. Plen., Minister Plenipotentiary.
Miss., Mississippi.
mk., mark.
mkt., market.
ml., milliliter(s).
M.L.G., Middle Low German.
Mlle., Mademoiselle.
MM., Majesties; Messieurs.
mm., millimeter(s).
M. M., Master Mason; Master Mechanic.
M.M.E., Master of Mechanical Engineering; Master of Mining Engineering.
Mme., Madame.
m.m.f., magnetomotive force.
MN, Minnesota.
Mn, manganese.
M.N.A.S., Member of the National Academy of Sciences.
MO, Missouri.
Mo., Missouri; Monday.
mo., **mos.**, month; months.
Mo, molybdenum.
M.O., Medical Officer; money order.
mod., moderate; modern; in music, moderato; modulus.
Moham., Mohammedan.
Mon., Monday.
Mons., Monsieur.
Mont., Montana.
M. O. R. C., Medical Officers' Reserve Corps.
MP, **M.P.**, Military Police.
M.P., Member of Parliament; Methodist Protestant; Mettopolitan Police; Mounted Police.
M.P., **m.p.**, melting point.
mph, **m.p.h.**, miles per hour.
Mr., Mister.
Mrs., Mistress.
M.S., Master of Science; Master of Surgery; (L. *memoriæ sacrum*) sacred to the memory of.
MS, Mississippi.
MS., manuscript.
MSS., manuscripts.
MT, Montana.
Mt., mount; mountain.
mus., museum; music; musical.
Mus.B., (L. *Musicæ Baccalaureus*) Bachelor of Music.
Mus.D., **Mus. Doc.**, (L. *Musicæ Doctor*) Doctor of Music.
myth., **mythol.**, mythological; mythology.

N

N., National; Nationalist; Norse; November.
N., **n.**, nail; name; (L. *natus*) born; navy; neuter; new; nominative; noon; north; northern; noun; in chemistry, normal.
n., nephew; net; note; number.
N, nitrogen.
Na, (L. *natrium*) sodium.
n/a, in banking, no account.
N.A., National Academician; National Academy; National Army; North America.
N.A.A.C.P., **NAACP**, National Association for the Advancement of Colored People.
NACA, **N.A.C.A.**, National Advisory Committee for Aeronautics.
Nah., Nahum.
N.A.M., **NAM**, National Association of Manufacturers.
Nap., Napoleon.
nat., national; native; natural.
nat. hist., natural history.
nat. ord., natural order.
nat. phil., natural philosophy.
naut., nautical.
nav., naval; navigable; navigation; navy.
navig., navigation.
NB, Nebraska.
N.B., New Brunswick; North Britain; (L. *nota bene*) note well.
Nb, niobium.
NbE, north by east.
NbW, north by west.
NC, **N.C.**, North Carolina.
N. C. O., noncommissioned officer.
ND, North Dakota.
N.D., **n.d.**, no date.
N.Dak., North Dakota.
N.E., northeast; northeastern (postal district); New England.
N. E. A., National Education Association.
Neb., Nebraska.
neg., negative; negatively.
Neh., Nehemiah.
Nep, **NEP**, New Economic Policy.
Neth., Netherlands.
neut., neuter.
New M., New Mexico.
N.F., Newfoundland; Norman French.
N. G., National Guard; New Guinea; no good.
N.Gr., New Greek.
NH, **N.H.**, New Hampshire.
N.H.G., New High German.
Ni, nickel.
N.I., Northern Ireland.
NJ, **N.J.**, New Jersey.
n.l., (L. *non liquet*) it is not clear.
N.L., **N.Lat.**, north latitude.
N.L., New Latin.
NLRB, **N.L.R.B.**, National Labor Relations Board.
NM, **N.M.**, New Mexico.
N.N.E., north-northeast.
N.N.W., north-northwest.
No., Noah; north; northern; number.
nol. pros., to be unwilling to prosecute.
nom., nominative.
non obst., (L. *non obstante*) notwithstanding.
non pros., (L. *non prosequitur*) he does not prosecute.
non seq., (L. *non sequitur*) it does not follow.
Nor., Norman; North; Norway; Norwegian.
Nor. Fr., **Norm. Fr.**, Norman-French.
Norw., Norway; Norwegian.
nos., numbers.
Nov., November.
N.P., Notary Public.
NP, neuropsychiatric.
Np, neptunium.
n/p, **n.p.**, net proceeds.
nr., near.
NRA, **N.R.A.**, National Recovery Administration.
N/S, **n/s**, **N.S.F.**, in banking, not sufficient funds.
N.S., New Style; Nova Scotia.
N.S.J.C., (L. *Noster Salvator Jesus Christus*) Our Saviour Jesus Christ.
N.S.P.C.A., National Society for the Prevention of Cruelty to Animals.
N.S.P.C.C., National Society for the Prevention of Cruelty to Children.
N.S.W., New South Wales.
N.T., New Testament; Northern Territory.
Nt, niton.
Num., **Numb.**, Numbers.
numis., numismatics.
NV, Nevada.
N.V., New Version.
N.W., North Wales.
NW, **N.W.**, northwest; northwestern.
NWbN, northwest by north.
NWbW, northwest by west.
N.W.T., Northwest Territories.
NY, **N.Y.**, New York.
N.Y.H.S., New York Historical Society.
N.Z., **N.Zeal.**, New Zealand.

O

O., Ocean; October; Ohio; Ontario; Oregon.
O., **o.**, (L. *octarius*) in pharmacy, a pint; octavo; old.
o., off; only; order; in baseball, outs, put-outs.
O, oxygen.
ob., (L. *obiit*) died; oboe.
Obad., Obadiah.
obdt., obedient.
obj., object; objective.
obs., obsolete.
Obs., Observatory.
obsoles., obsolescent.
Oct., October.
O. D., Doctor of Optometry; Officer of the Day; olive drab; outside diameter; overdraft; overdrawn.
O.F., **OFr.**, Old French.
off., office; officer; official; officinal.
O.Fris., Old Frisian.
OH, Ohio.
O.H.G., Old High German.
O.H.M.S., On Her (or His) Majesty's Service.
O.Ir., Old Irish.
O.It., Old Italian.
OK, **Okla.**, Oklahoma.
O.L.G., Old Low German.
O.M., Order of Merit (British).
Ont., Ontario.
OP, **O.P.**, observation post.
op., opera; operation; opposite; opus.
O.P., **o.p.**, out of print; overproof; in philately, overprint.
OPA, **O.P.A.**, Office of Price Administration.
op. cit., (L. *opere citato*) in the work cited.
OPS, **O.P.S.**, Office of Price Stabilization.
opt., optative; optical; optician; optics.
OR, Oregon.
Or., Oregon; Oriental.
o.r., owner's risk.
O. R. C., Officers' Reserve Corps; Order of the Red Cross.
ord., ordinance; ordinary.
Ore., **Oreg.**, Oregon.
orig., original; originally.
ornith., ornithology.
O.S., Old Saxon; Old Style; Ordinary Seaman.
Os, osmium.
O.S.B., Order of St. Benedict.
O.S.F., Order of St. Francis.
O.Sl., Old Slavic.
O.T., Old Testament.
O. T. C., Officers' Training Camp.
O.W.I., Office of War Information.
Oxf., Oxford.
oz., ounce.
ozs., ounces.

P

P, phosphorus; in mechanics, power, pressure.
P., **p.**, pastor; post; power; president; pressure; priest; prince; in chess, pawn.
p., page; part; participle; past; penny; per; pint; pipe; pitcher; pole; population; pro; in music, piano.
PA, **Pa.**, Pennsylvania.
Pa, protactinium.
P.A., Passenger Agent; Post Adjutant; Purchasing Agent.
p.a., participial adjective.
paint., painting.
Pal., Palestine.
pal., **paleon.**, paleontological; paleontology.
par., paragraph; parallel; parenthesis; parish.
parl., parliament; parliamentary.
part., participle; particular.
part. adj., participial adjective.
pass., passenger; passive.
Pat., Patrick.
pathol., pathological; pathology.
payt., payment.
P.B., (L. *Pharmacopoeia Britannica*) British Pharmacopoeia; Prayer Book.
p.b., in baseball, passed ball(s).
Pb, (L. *plumbum*) lead.
P.C., Past Commander; Police Constable; Post Commander; Privy Council; Privy Councilor.
p.c., per cent; postal card.
pct., per cent.
Pd, palladium.
pd., paid.
P.D., Police Department; postal district; potential difference; per diem.
Pd. B., (L. *Pedagogiæ Baccalaureus*) Bachelor of Pedagogy.
Pd. D., Doctor of Pedagogy.
P.E., Presiding Elder; probable error; Protestant Episcopal.
P.E.I., Prince Edward Island.
pen., peninsula.
Penn., Pennsylvania.
Pent., Pentecost.
Per., Persia; Persian.
per., period; person.
per an., (L. *per annum*) by the year; yearly.
per cent., **per ct.**, per centum.
perf., perfect.
perh., perhaps.
peri., perigee.
Pers., Persia; Persian.
pers., person; personal.
persp., perspective.
pert., pertaining.
Peruv., Peruvian.
Pet., Peter.
pf., perfect; pfennig; pianoforte; preferred.
Pfc., Private First Class.
pfd., preferred.
Pg., Portugal; Portuguese.
P.G., Postgraduate.
P.G.M., Past Grand Master.
Phar., **Pharm.**, Pharmacopoeia; Pharmacy.
Ph.B., (L. *Philosophiæ Baccalaureus*) Bachelor of Philosophy.
Ph.D., (L. *Philosophiæ Doctor*) Doctor of Philosophy.
Phil., Philippians; Philippine.
phil., philosopher; philosophical; philosophy.
Philem., Philemon.
philol., philology.
philos., philosophical; philosophy.
phon., **phonet.**, phonetics.
photog., photograph; photographer; photography.
photom., photometry.
phren., phrenology.
P.H.S., Public Health Service.
phys., physical; physician; physics; physiology.
phys. ed., physical education.
physiol., physiological; physiology.
P. I., Philippine Islands.
pk., pack; park; peak; peck.
pkg., package(s).
P.L., Poet Laureate.
pl., place; plate; plural.
plff., plaintiff.
plu., plural.
plup., pluperfect.
plur., plural; plurality.
P.M., Past Master; Paymaster; Police Magistrate; Postmaster; Provost Marshall.
P.M., **p.m.**, (L. *post meridiem*) after noon; (L. *post mortem*) after death.
P.M.G., Paymaster General; Postmaster General.
p.n., promissory note.
P.O., Petty Officer; Postal Order; Post Office.
P. O. D., pay on delivery; Post Office Department.
poet., poetical; poetry.
Pol., Poland; Polish.
pol., **polit.**, political; politics.
polit. econ., political economy.
pop., popular; popularly; population.
Port., Portugal; Portuguese.
poss., possessive.
pp., pages; past participle; pianissimo.
P.P., **p.p.**, parcel post; parish priest; postpaid.
ppd., prepaid.
Pph., pamphlet.
ppr., **p.pr.**, present participle.
P.Q., previous question; Province of Quebec.
PR, Puerto Rico.
Pr, praseodymium.
PR., **Pr.**, preferred (stock).
Pr., Priest; Prince; Provençal.
pr., pair; power; preferred (stock); present; price; pronoun.
P.R., Puerto Rico; proportional representation.
prec., preceding.
pref., preface; prefix.
prep., preposition.
Pres., Presbyterian; President.
pres., present; presidency.
pret., preterit.
prim., primary; primitive.
prin., principally; principle.
print., printing.
priv., privative.
prob., probably; problem.
Prof., Professor.
pron., pronoun; pronounced; pronunciation.
pron. a., pronominal adjective.
prop., proposition.
pros., prosody.
Prot., Protestant.
pro. tem., (L. *pro tempore*) for the time being.
Prov., Proverbs; Province.
prov., provincial; provincially; provost.
prox., proximo.
Prus., Prussia; Prussian.
ps., pieces; pseudonym.
P.S., passenger steamer; permanent secretary; Privy Seal; Public School.
PS., **P.S.**, **p.s.**, postscript.
Ps. Psa., Psalm; Psalms.
P.S.T., Pacific Standard Time.
pseud., pseudonym.
psychol., psychology.
Pt, platinum.
Pt., Point; Port.
P.T., Pacific Time; pupil teacher.
p.t., past tense; pro tempore.
P.T.A., Parent-Teacher Association.
P.T.O., please turn over (leaf).
pub., public; published; publisher; publishing.
Pub. Doc., Public Documents.
Pvt., Private.
PWA, **P.W.A.**, Public Works Administration.
P.W.D., Public Works Department.
P.W.P., Past Worthy Patriarch.
pwt., pennyweight.
PX, post exchange.
pxt., (L. *pinxit*) he (or she) painted it.

Q

Q., Quebec; Queen; Question.
q., (L. *quadrans*) farthing; quart; quarter; quarterly; quarto; quasi; queen; query; question; quintal; quire; quotient.
QB, in chess, queen's bishop.
Q.B., **q.b.**, **qb**, in football, quarterback.
Q.B., Queen's Bench.
Q.C., Queen's College; Queen's Council (or Counsel).
q.d., (L. *quasi dicat*) as if he should say; (L. *quasi dictum*) as if said; (L. *quasi dixisset*) as if he had said.
q.e., (L. *quod est*) which is.
Q.E.D., (L. *quod erat demonstrandum*) which was to be demonstrated.
Q.E.F., (L. *quod erat faciendum*) which was to be done.
q.i.d., (L. *quater in die*) four times a day.
Qkt, in chess, queen's knight.
ql., quintal.
Q.M., Quartermaster.
Q.M.C., Quartermaster Corps.
Q.Mess., Queen's Messenger.
Q.M.G., Quartermaster General.
q.p., **q.pl.**, (L. *quantum placet*) as much as you please.
qr., quarter; quire; (L. *quadrans*) farthing.
qrs., quarters; quires; (L. *quadrantes*) farthings.
q.s., quarter section; (L. *quantum sufficit*) enough.
Q.S., Quarter Sessions.
Qt., quantity; quart.
qto., quarto.
qts., quantities; quarts.
qu., quart; quarter; quarterly; queen; query; question.
quad., quadrangle.
quar., **quart.**, quarter; quarterly.
Que., Quebec.
ques., **quest.**, question.
q.v., (L. *quod vide*) which see; (L. *quantum vis*) as much as you will.
qy., query.

R

R, in chemistry, radical; in electricity, resistance; in mathematics, radius, ratio.
r, roentgen(s); royal; ruble.

R., Radical; Reaumur; Republic; Republican; in ecclesiastical usage, respond, response.
R., r., rabbi; radius; railroad; railway; (L. *recipe*) take: in prescriptions; (L. *Regina*) queen; (L. *Rex*) king; right; river; road; royal; ruble; rupee; in chess, rook.
r., range; rare; received; residence; resides; retired; rod(s); rubber; in baseball and cricket, run(s); in law, rule.
Ra, radium.
R.A., Rear Admiral; Rear Artillery; Regular Army; Royal Academy; Royal Artillery; right ascension.
Rabb., Rabbinical.
rad., radial; radical; radius; radix.
R. A. F., Royal Air Force.
R.A.M., Royal Academy of Music.
Rb, rubidium.
r.b.i., rbi, RBI, in baseball, run(s) batted in.
R.C., Red Cross; Reformed Church; Roman Catholic.
R.C.A.F., Royal Canadian Air Force.
R.C.Ch., Roman Catholic Church.
rcd., received.
R.C.M.P., Royal Canadian Mounted Police.
R.C.P., Royal College of Physicians.
rcpt., receipt.
R.C.S., Royal College of Surgeons.
Rd., rd., rix-dollar; road; rod; round.
R.D., Rural Delivery.
Rd, radium.
Re, rhenium.
R.E., real estate; Reformed Episcopal; Right Excellent; Royal Engineers; Royal Exchange.
re., in football, right end; rupee.
Rec. Sec., Recording Secretary.
recd., received.
recpt., receipt.
Rect., rector; receipt.
redupl., reduplication.
ref., reformation; reformed; reformer; reference.
Ref. Ch., Reformed Church.
refl., reflexive; reflexively.
Ref. Pres., Reformed Presbyterian.
Reg., Regiment.
reg., regent; regiment; region; register; registered; registrar; registry; regular; regulation; regulator.
regr., register; registrar; regular.
Regt., Regiment.
rel., relative; religion; religious.
rel. pron., relative pronoun.
rem., remark.
Rep., Report; Reporter; Representative; Republic.
Repub., Republic; Republican.
retd., returned.
Rev., Revelation; Reverend.
rev., revenue; reverse; review; revise; revised; revision; revolution; revolving.
Revd., Reverend.
Revs., Reverends.
Rev. Ver., Revised Version (of the Bible).
rf., in baseball, right fielder.
R.F., Reserve Force.
R.F., r.f., radio-frequency; rapid-fire.
RFC, R.F.C., Reconstruction Finance Corporation.
R. F. D., Rural Free Delivery.
rg., in football, right guard.
Rh, rhodium.
R.H., Royal Highlanders; Royal Highness.
rhet., rhetoric; rhetorical.
RI, R.I., Rhode Island.
R.I.P., (L. *requiescat in pace*) may he (or she) rest in peace.
riv., river.
RM., r.m., reichsmark.
rm., ream; room.
R.M.A., Royal Marine Artillery; Royal Military Academy; Royal Military Asylum.
R.M.C., Royal Military College.
R.M.S., Railway Mail Service; Royal Mail Service; Royal Mail Steamship.
r.m.s., root mean square.
Rn, radon.
R.N., registered nurse; Royal Navy.
R. N. W. M. P., Royal Northwest Mounted Police.
ro., recto; roan; rood.
R.O., Receiving Office.
Robt., Robert.
Rom., Roman; Romance; Romanic; Romans.
rom., roman (type).
Rom. Cath., Roman Catholic.
R. O. T. C., Reserve Officers' Training Camp (or Corps).
R. P., Regius Professor.
r.p.m., revolutions per minute.
R. P. O., Railroad Post Office.
r.p.s., revolutions per second.
rpt., report.
R.R., railroad; Right Reverend.
R.S., Recording Secretary; Reformed Spelling.
R. S., Recruiting Service.
Rs., rupees.
r.s., right side.
R. S. F. S. R., RSFSR, Russian Soviet Federal Socialist Republic.
RSV, R.S.V., Revised Standard Version (of the Bible).
R.S.V.P., (Fr. *répondez, s'il vous plaît*) please reply.
rt., right.
Rt. Hon., Right Honorable.
Rt. Rev., Right Reverend.
Rt. Wpful., Right Worshipful.
Ru, ruthenium.
Russ., Russia; Russian.
R.V., Revised Version (of the Bible); Rifle Volunteers.
R.W., Right Worshipful; Right Worthy.
Rwy., Ry., Railway.
Rx., tens of rupees.

S

S, sulfur.
S., Sabbath; Saturday; Saxon; Senate; September; Signor; Socialist; Sunday.
S., s., saint; school; society; south; southern.
s., second(s); section; see; series; shilling(s); sign; silver; singular; sire; son; steamer; substantive.
Sa, samarium.
s.a., semiannual; small arms.
S.A., Salvation Army; South Africa; South America; South Australia.
Sa., Saturday.
Sab., Sabbath.
S. A. E., Society of Automotive Engineers.
SALT, Strategic Arms Limitation Talks.
S. Am., South America.
Sam., Samuel; Samaritan.
Sans., Sansk., Sanskrit.
Sar., Sardinia; Sardinian.
S. A. R., Sons of the American Revolution.
Sat., Saturday; Saturn.
S. Aust., South Australia.
Sax., Saxon; Saxony.
Sb, (L. *stibium*) antimony.
sb., substantive.
S.B., (L. *Scientiæ Baccalaureus*) Bachelor of Science; South Britain.
s.b., sb, stolen base(s).
SbE, south by east.
SbW, south by west.
SC, South Carolina.
Sc., Scotch; Scots; Scottish.
sc., scale; scene; scilicet; screw; scruple.
S.C., Sanitary Corps; Signal Corps; South Carolina; Staff Corps; Supreme Court.
Sc, scandium.
s.c., in printing, small capitals; supercalendered.
Scand., Scandinavian.
s. caps., in printing, small capitals.
Sc.B., (L. *Scientiæ Baccalaureus*) Bachelor of Science.
Sc.D., (L. *Scientiæ Doctor*) Doctor of Science.
sch., school; schooner.
sci., science; scientific.
scil., scilicet.
s.c.m., summary court-martial.
Scot., Scotch; Scotland; Scottish.
scr., scruple(s).
Script., scriptural; Scripture.
sculp., sculpt., sculptor; sculpture.
SD, South Dakota.
S.D., Senior Deacon; South Dakota; Standard Deviation.
s.d., sine die.
S. Dak., South Dakota.
S.E., southeast; southeastern.
Se, selenium.
SEbE, southeast by east.
SEbS, southeast by south.
SEC, S.E.C., Securities and Exchange Commission.
sec., secant; second(s); secondary; secretary; section(s); sector; security.
sec. leg., (L. *secundum legem*) according to law.
Sen., Senate; Senator; Senior.
Sep., September; Septuagint.
seq., (L. *sequentes* or *sequentia*) the following or the next.
ser., series; sermon.
Serb., Serbian.
Serg., Sergeant.
sess., session.
S.G., Solicitor General.
s.g., specific gravity.
Sgt., Sergeant.
Sgt. Maj., Sergeant Major.
sh., sheet; shilling(s).
Shak., Shakespeare.
shtg., shortage.
Si, silicon.
S.I., Sandwich Islands; Staten Island.
Sic., Sicilian; Sicily.
Sig., sig., signal; signature; signor.
sing., singular.
S. J., Society of Jesus.
Skr., Sanskrit.
sld., sailed.
S.Lat., South Latitude.
Slav., Slavic; Slavonian; Slavonic.
S.M., Sergeant Major; Sons of Malta; State Militia.
Sm, samarium.
S. M., Master of Science.
Sn, (L. *stannum*) tin.
S.O., Signal Officer; Special Order.
So., south; southern.
Soc., Socialist.
Soc., soc., society.
Sol., Solicitor; Solomon.
s.p., (L. *sine prole*) childless.
Sp., Spanish; Spain; Spirit.
sp., special; species; specific; specimen; spelling.
S.P., Shore Patrol; Socialist Party; Submarine Patrol.
S.P.C.A., Society for the Prevention of Cruelty to Animals.
S.P.C.C., Society for the Prevention of Cruelty to Children.
specif., specifically.
sp. gr., specific gravity.
S.P.Q.R., (L. *Senatus Populusque Romanus*) Senate and People of Rome.
spt., seaport.
Sq., Squadron.
Sq., sq., square.
sq. ft., square foot; square feet.
sq. in., square inch(es).
sq. mi., square mile(s).
sqq., (L. *sequentes* or *sequentia*) the following ones.
sq. yd., square yard(s).
Sr, strontium.
S.R.I., (L. *Sacrum Romanum Imperium*) Holy Roman Empire.
S.R.O., standing room only.
ss., in baseball, shortstop.
S.S., steamship.
S.S.E., south-southeast.
S.S.W., south-southwest.
St., Saint; Strait; Street.
st., stanza; stet; stone (weight).
s.t., short ton.
Sta., Santa; Station.
sta., stationary; stator.
S.T.D., (L. *Sacræ Theologiæ Doctor*) Doctor of Divinity.
Ste., Saint (female).
ster., stg., sterling.
Su., Sunday.
subj., subject; subjective; subjunctive.
suff., suffix.
Sun., Sund., Sunday.
sup., superior; superfine; superlative; supplement.
Sup. C., Superior Court.
Sup. Col., Supply Column.
super., superfine; superior.
superl., superlative.
Sup. O., Supply Officer.
supp., supplement.
Supt., Superintendent.
surg., surgeon; surgery.
Surg. Gen., Surgeon General.
surv., surveying; surveyor.
Surv. Gen., Surveyor General.
Sw., Sweden; Swedish.
S.W., southwest; southwestern.
Switz., Switzerland.
syn., synonym; synonymous.
synop., synopsis.
Syr., Syria; Syriac.
syr., syrup.

T

T., tablespoon(s); Testament; Tuesday; Turkish.
T., t., tenor; territorial; territory; (L. *tomus*) volume; ton(s).
t., tare; target; teaspoon(s); telephone; temperature; tempore; tense; time; tome; town; township; transit; transitive; troy.
Ta, tantalum.
tab., tables.
tan., tangent.
Tas., Tasmania.
Tb, terbium.
TB, T.B., tb., t.b., tubercle bacillus; tuberculosis.
t.b., trial balance.
Tc, technetium.
tc., tierce.
T.C.D., Trinity College, Dublin.
T/D, time deposit.
T.D., Traffic Director; Treasury Department.
Te, tellurium.
tech., technical; technically.
technol., technology.
teleg., telegram; telegraph; telegraphy.
temp., temperance; temperature; temporary; (L. *tempore*) in the time of.
Tenn., Tennessee.
ter., territory.
term., termination.
Test., Testament.
Teut., Teutonic.
Tex., Texas.
Th., Thomas; Thursday.
Th, thorium.
Th.B., (L. *Theologiæ Baccalaureus*) Bachelor of Theology.
Th.D., (L. *Theologiæ Doctor*) Doctor of Theology.
Theo., Theodore; Theodosia.
theol., theological; theology.
theor., theorem.
theos., theosophical; theosophist; theosophy.
Thess., Thessalonians.
Tho., Thos., Thomas.
Thu., Thur., Thurs., Thursday.
Ti, titanium.
tier., tierce.
Tim., Timothy.
Tit., Titus; title.
T.K.O., TKO, in boxing, technical knockout.
Tl, thallium.
TN, Tennessee.
T.N.T., trinitrotoluine; trinitrotoluol.
T. O., Telegraph Office; Transport Officer.
t.o., turn over.
Tob., Tobit.
tonn., tonnage.
topog., topographical; topography.
tp., township.
t.p., title page.
tr., trace; transitive; translated; translation; translator; transpose; treasurer.
T.R., tons registered.
Tr, terbium.
trans., transactions; translated; translation; translator.
trav., travels.
Treas., Treasurer.
trig., trigon., trigonometrical; trigonometry.
Trin., Trinity.
T. S., test solution.
T.Sgt., Technical Sergeant.
tsp., teaspoon(s).
Tu., Tuesday.
Tu, thulium.
T. U., Trade Union; Trading Unit.
Tues., Tuesday.
Turk., Turkey; Turkish.
TV, television.
TVA, T.V.A., Tennessee Valley Authority.
TX, Texas.
typ., typo., typog., typographer; typographical; typography.

U

U, uranium.
U., Uncle; Union; University.
U., u., upper.
U.B., United Brethren (in Christ).
U.C., Upper Canada.
u.c., upper case.
U.K., United Kingdom.
ult., ultimate; ultimately; ultimo.
UMT, Universal Military Training.
UN, U.N., United Nations.
Unit., Unitarian.
univ., university; universally.
up., upper.
U. P. C., United Presbyterian Church.
U.S., United States.
u.s., (L. *ut supra*) as above.
U.S.A., United States Army; United States of America.
U.S.A.F., USAF, United States Air Force.
U. of S. A., Union of South Africa.
U.S.C. & G.S., United States Coast and Geodetic Survey.
U. S. C. G., United States Coast Guard.
U.S.L., United States Legation.
U. S. M., United States Mail; United States Marine(s).
U. S. M. A., United States Military Academy.
U. S. M. C., United States Marine Corps.
U.S.N., USN, United States Navy.
U. S. N. A., United States Naval Academy.
U. S. N. G., United States National Guard.
U. S. P., U.S. Pharm., United States Pharmacopoeia.
U. S. R., United States Reserves.
U. S. S., United States Senate; United States Ship; United States Steamer; United States Steamship.
U. S. S. B., United States Shipping Board.
U.S.S.Ct., United States Supreme Court.
U.S.S.R., USSR, Union of Soviet Socialist Republics.
U.S.S.S., United States Steamship.
usu., usual; usually.
U. S. V., United States Volunteers.
u.s.w., (G. *und so weiter*) and so forth.
UT, Ut., Utah.
ut sup., (L. *ut supra*) as above.
ux., (L. *uxor*) wife.

V

V, vanadium.
V, v, velocity; volt(s); vector.
V., Venerable; Vicar; Viscount.
v., valve; ventral; verb; verse; version; verso; versus; (L. *vide*) see; village; violin; vice; vocative; voice; voltage; volume; (G. *von*) of.
VA, V.A., Veterans' Administration.
VA, Va., Virginia.
v. a., active verb; verbal adjective.
V. A., Vicar Apostolic; Vice Admiral.
var., variant; variation; variety; various.
Vat., Vatican.
v. aux., verb auxiliary.
vb., verb; verbal.
vb. n., verbal noun.

V. C., Veterinary Corps; Vice Chairman; Vice-Chancellor; Victoria Cross.
Vd, vanadium.
V.D., venereal disease.
V. D. L., Van Diemen's Land.
Ven., Venerable; Venice.
ver., verse(s).
vet., veteran; veterinarian; veterinary.
Veter., Veterinary.
V. G., Vicar General.
Vi, virginium.
VI, V.I., Virgin Islands.
v. i., intransitive verb.
Vic., Victoria.
Vice-Pres., Vice-President.
vid., (L. *vide*) see.
vil., village.
v. imp., impersonal verb.
v. irreg., irregular verb.
Vis., Visc., Viscount.
viz., (L. *videlicet*) namely.
V. M. D., Doctor of Veterinary Medicine.
v.n., neuter verb.
vo., verso.
voc., vocative.
Vol., Volunteer.
vol., volcano; volume.
vols., volumes.
V. P., Vice-President.
v.p., passive verb.
V. R., (L. *Victoria Regina*) Queen Victoria.
v.r., reflexive verb.
V. Rev., Very Reverend.
vs., versus.
V. S., Veterinary Surgeon.
v.t., transitive verb.
VT, Vt., Vermont.
Vul., Vulg., Vulgate.
vulg., vulgar; vulgarly.
vv., verses; violins.
v.v., vice versa.
vv. ll., (L. *variæ lectiones*) various readings.

W

W, watt(s); west; wolfram.
W., Wales; Washington; Welsh; Western.
W., w., warden; warehouse; watt(s); weight; west; western; width; in physics, work.
w., week(s); wide; wife; with; won.
WA, Washington.
W. A., West Africa; Western Australia.
W. A. A. C., Women's Army Auxiliary Corps (British).
W. A. C., Women's Army Corps.
W. Afr., West Africa; West African.
W.A.F.S., Women's Auxiliary Ferrying Squadron.
Wal., Walachian; Walloon.
Wash., Washington.
W.A.V.E.S., Women's Reserve of the United States Naval Reserve.
W.B., waybill.
w.b., warehouse book; westbound; in nautical usage, water ballast.
WbN, west by north.
WbS, west by south.
W.C., West Central (postal district).
w.c., water closet; without charge.
W. C. T. U., Women's Christian Temperance Union.
W. D., War Department.
wd., ward; word.
Wed., Wednesday.
Westm., Westminster.
w. f., wf, in printing, wrong font.
W.G., wire gauge.
wh., watt-hour.
whf., wharf.
WI, Wisconsin.
W. I., West Indian; West Indies.
Wis., Wisc., Wisconsin.
wk., week.
wkly., weekly.
w.l., wave length.
WLB, War Labor Board.
WMC, War Manpower Commission.
wmk., watermark.
Wm., William.
W. N. W., west-northwest.
W. O., War Office; Warrant Officer.
WPA, W.P.A., Works Project Administration.
WPB, W.P.B., War Production Board.
W.R.A.F., Women's Royal Air Force.
W. S., West Saxon.
W. S. W., west-southwest.
wt., weight.
WV, W. Va., West Virginia.
WY, Wyo., Wyoming.

X—Y—Z

X, Christ.
Xe, xenon.
Xn., Christian.
Xnty., Christianity.
Xt., Christ.
Xtian., Christian.
Y., Year.
Y, yttrium.
Y., Young Men's Christian Association.
y., yard(s); year(s).
Yb, ytterbium.
Y. B., Yearbook.
yd., yard(s).
Y. M. C. A., Young Men's Christian Association.
Y. M. Cath. A., Young Men's Catholic Association.
Y. M. C. U., Young Men's Christian Union.
Y. M. H. A., Young Men's Hebrew Association.
Y. P. S. C. E., Young People's Society of Christian Endeavor.
yr., year; younger; your.
Yt, yttrium.
Y.T., Yukon Territory.
Y. W. C. A., Young Women's Christian Association.
Y. W. H. A., Young Women's Hebrew Association.
Z., in astronomy, zenith distance; in chemistry, atomic number.
Z., z., zone.
z, in mathematics, unknown quantity.
Zach., Zachary.
Zech., Zechariah.
Zeph., Zephaniah.
Z. G., Zoological Gardens.
Zir, zirconium.
Zn, zinc.
zoochem., zoochemical; zoochemistry.
zoogeog., zoogeographical; zoogeography.
zool., zoological; zoology.
Zr, zirconium.
Z. S., Zoological Society.

PRACTICAL BUSINESS MATHEMATICS

ELEMENTS OF ARITHMETIC

With Tables and Examples of Practical Application

It would be difficult to overestimate the extent to which mathematics enters into the conditions of everyday life. In its elementary stages, as the science of number, it teaches us the relations of magnitude, and enables us to build up a system of calculation and measurement which, applied to the relations observed to exist in nature, gives results of far-reaching importance.

The properties of number are investigated in arithmetic, and methods examined by which those engaged in practical science are able to work out their results to any degree of approximation.

With the help of algebra, we arrive at a system of logarithms by which many of these results may be reached with the minimum of labor.

The measurement of lines and angles, by methods investigated in geometry and trigonometry, enables us to calculate areas and work out various problems met with in surveying, and is of the first importance in astronomy.

Arithmetic, which deals with the properties of number, forms the basis of all mathematical calculation.

COMMON FRACTIONS

A *fraction* is one or more of the equal parts into which a unit has been divided. A *common fraction* is expressed by two numbers; the one written above the line is called the *numerator*, the one below, the *denominator:* both, called the *terms*, denote the value of the fraction.

Thus, in the fraction $\frac{3}{4}$, the denominator, 4, denotes that a unit or whole thing has been divided into four equal parts; and the numerator, 3, shows that three of those parts are taken or expressed in the fraction.

A *proper fraction* is one whose numerator is less than its denominator; as $\frac{1}{2}$, $\frac{3}{4}$, $\frac{7}{8}$, etc. Its value is always less than 1.

An *improper fraction* is one whose numerator is equal to or greater than its denominator; as $\frac{5}{5}$, $\frac{9}{7}$, $\frac{30}{12}$, etc. Its value is never less than 1.

A *mixed number* is a whole number and a fraction; as $3\frac{2}{5}$, $10\frac{1}{2}$, $6\frac{2}{3}$.

The mixed number means that there are whole things taken together with a fraction of another.

A *complex fraction* is one in which the numerator or denominator, or both, are fractions.

Thus $\frac{3\frac{1}{7}}{2\frac{3}{8}}$, $\frac{1}{\frac{5}{6} \times \frac{3}{4}}$, $\frac{\frac{15}{17}}{8}$ are complex fractions.

Principles of Fractions

1. A fraction's value is the quotient obtained by dividing the numerator by the denominator.

$$\frac{6}{2} = 3 \qquad 3 \text{ is the value of } \frac{6}{2}$$

$$\frac{2}{3} = \frac{2}{3} \qquad \frac{2}{3} \text{ is the value of } \frac{2}{3}$$

2. Multiplying the denominator of a fraction divides the fraction by that number.

$$\frac{1}{2 \times 4} = \frac{1}{8} \qquad \frac{3}{7 \times 3} = \frac{3}{21} \qquad \frac{2}{3 \times 9} = \frac{2}{27}$$

3. Dividing the denominator of a fraction multiplies the fraction by that number.

$$\frac{3}{8 \div 4} = \frac{3}{2} \qquad \frac{10}{9 \div 3} = \frac{10}{3} \qquad \frac{3}{10 \div 5} = \frac{3}{2}$$

4. Multiplying the numerator of a fraction multiplies the fraction by that number.

$$\frac{2 \times 2}{3} = \frac{4}{3} \qquad \frac{1 \times 8}{9} = \frac{8}{9} \qquad \frac{5 \times 3}{8} = \frac{15}{8}$$

5. Dividing the numerator of a fraction divides the fraction by that number.

$$\frac{4 \div 2}{7} = \frac{2}{7} \qquad \frac{12 \div 12}{16} = \frac{1}{16} \qquad \frac{3 \div 3}{7} = \frac{1}{7}$$

6. Multiplying both numerator and denominator of a fraction by the same number does not change the value of the fraction.

$$\frac{1 \times 3}{3 \times 3} = \frac{3}{9} = \frac{1}{3} \qquad \frac{6 \times 2}{7 \times 2} = \frac{12}{14} = \frac{6}{7}$$

7. Dividing both numerator and denominator of a fraction by the same number does not change the value of the fraction.

$$\frac{12 \div 3}{15 \div 3} = \frac{4}{5} = \frac{12}{15} \qquad \frac{18 \div 9}{27 \div 9} = \frac{2}{3} = \frac{18}{27}$$

Reduction of Fractions

Reduction of fractions is the process of changing their forms without altering their values.

To reduce a fraction to its lowest terms:

Rule.—*Divide both terms by their greatest common divisor.*

Reduce $\frac{8}{12}$ to its lowest terms.

Work: $4)\frac{8}{12}(\frac{2}{3}$ *Ans.* $\frac{2}{3}$.

Four is the G. C. D. of 8 and 12; hence $\frac{8}{12} \div 4 = \frac{2}{3}$.

Reduce $\frac{35}{56}$ to its lowest terms.

Work: $7)\frac{35}{56}(\frac{5}{8}$ *Ans.* $\frac{5}{8}$.

Seven is the G. C. D. of 35 and 56; hence $\frac{35}{56} \div 7 = \frac{5}{8}$.

A fraction whose terms have no common divisor is in its lowest terms, as $\frac{9}{16}$.

To reduce an improper fraction to a whole or mixed number:

Rule.—*Divide the numerator by the denominator; the quotient will be the whole or mixed number.*

How many units in $\frac{30}{6}$?

Work: $30 \div 6 = 5$ *Ans.* 5.

There are as many units in 30 sixths as 6 is contained times in 30.

Reduce $\frac{75}{4}$ to a mixed number.

Work: $75 \div 4 = 18 + 3$ *Ans.* $18\frac{3}{4}$.

In 75 fourths there are 18 units, and 3 fourths over, which equals $18\frac{3}{4}$.

To reduce a mixed number to an improper fraction:

Rule.—*Multiply the whole number by the denominator of the fraction; add the numerator to the product, and write the sum over the denominator.*

Reduce $18\frac{3}{4}$ to an improper fraction.

Work $18 \times 4 = 72$ $\frac{72}{4} + \frac{3}{4} = \frac{75}{4}$ *Ans.* $\frac{75}{4}$.

In 18 are 72 fourths, plus the 3 fourths, equals 75 fourths.

To reduce two or more fractions to their least common denominator:

Rule.—*Find the least common multiple of the given denominators for a common denominator. Then for each new numerator take such a part of this common denominator as the fraction is part of 1.*

Reduce $\frac{1}{2}$, $\frac{2}{3}$, and $\frac{3}{4}$ to their L. C. D.

Work:

$$\frac{1}{2} = \frac{6}{12} \qquad \frac{2}{3} = \frac{8}{12} \qquad \frac{3}{4} = \frac{9}{12}$$

Ans. $\frac{6}{12}$, $\frac{8}{12}$ and $\frac{9}{12}$.

The L. C. M. of the denominators 2, 3, and 4 is 12. Hence, 12 is the L. C. D. to which the given fractions can be reduced. Then to change $\frac{1}{2}$ to 12ths, say $\frac{1}{2}$ of 12 is 6, and write it over 12;

to change $\frac{2}{3}$ to 12ths, say $\frac{2}{3}$ of 12 is 8, and write it over 12; to change $\frac{3}{4}$ to 12ths, say $\frac{3}{4}$ of 12 is 9, and write it over 12.

Fractions must be reduced to a common denominator to be added or subtracted.

Addition of Fractions

If two or more fractions have the same denominator, their sum is obtained by adding the numerators.

Work:

$$\frac{1}{7} + \frac{4}{7} + \frac{5}{7} = \frac{1 + 4 + 5}{7} = \frac{10}{7} = 1\frac{3}{7}$$

If the fractions have different denominators, we must first express them as equivalent fractions with the same denominator.

Example 1: Find the value of

$$\frac{1}{9} + \frac{3}{7} + \frac{5}{21} + \frac{2}{3}$$

The lowest common multiple is 63. The several denominators, when divided into 63, give 7, 9, 3, 21 respectively, for quotients. Therefore, we multiply the numerators and denominators of the fractions by 7, 9, 3, 21, and add the numerators to obtain the required sum. The result must be reduced to a mixed number or to lower terms, if necessary.

Work:

$$\frac{1}{9} + \frac{3}{7} + \frac{5}{21} + \frac{2}{3}$$

$$= \frac{7 + 27 + 15 + 42}{63}$$

$$= \frac{91}{63} = 1\frac{28}{63} = 1\frac{4}{9} \textit{ Ans.}$$

In adding mixed numbers, first add the whole numbers, then the fractions, finally adding the two results.

Example 2: Add together $3\frac{1}{8} + \frac{7}{24} + 7\frac{11}{15} + 4\frac{3}{20}$. Given expression:

$$= 3 + 7 + 4 + \frac{1}{8} + \frac{7}{24} + \frac{11}{15} + \frac{3}{20}$$

$$= 14 + \frac{15 + 35 + 88 + 18}{120}$$

$$= 14 + \frac{156}{120} = 14 + 1\frac{36}{120} = 15\frac{3}{10} \textit{ Ans.}$$

Subtraction of Fractions

The principle is the same as in addition. Reduce the fractions, if they have different denominators, to a common denominator, and then take the difference of the numerators.

Example 1: From $\frac{9}{11}$ subtract $\frac{3}{4}$.

$$\frac{9}{11} - \frac{3}{4} = \frac{36}{44} - \frac{33}{44} = \frac{3}{44}$$

Explanation.—Since the fractions are not similar they must be made similar before subtracting. The least common denominator of the given fractions is 44. $\frac{9}{11} = \frac{36}{44}$ and $\frac{3}{4} = \frac{33}{44}$. $\frac{36}{44} - \frac{33}{44} = \frac{3}{44}$.

When there are mixed numbers or integers, subtract the fractions and the integers separately.

NOTE.—Mixed numbers may be reduced to improper fractions and subtracted according to the rule above.

Example 2: From $4\frac{1}{3}$ subtract $2\frac{5}{8}$.

$$4\tfrac{1}{3} = 4\tfrac{8}{24}$$
$$2\tfrac{5}{8} = 2\tfrac{15}{24}$$
$$1\tfrac{17}{24}$$

Explanation.—Since the numbers are composed of integers and fractions, the integers and the fractions may be subtracted separately.

The fractions must be first reduced to similar fractions. It is evident that $\frac{15}{24}$ cannot be subtracted from $\frac{8}{24}$, hence 1 or $\frac{24}{24}$ is taken from 4 and united with the $\frac{8}{24}$, making $\frac{32}{24}$. $\frac{15}{24}$ from $\frac{32}{24}$ leaves $\frac{17}{24}$, and 2 from 3 (the number left after 1 has been united with the fraction $\frac{8}{24}$) leaves 1. Hence the remainder is $1\frac{17}{24}$.

Example 3: Simplify $3\frac{2}{9} + 4\frac{5}{7} - 5\frac{13}{21} + \frac{2}{35} - 1\frac{14}{15}$. Given expression:

$$= 3 + 4 - 5 - 1 + \frac{2}{9} + \frac{5}{7} - \frac{13}{21} + \frac{2}{35} - \frac{14}{15}$$

$$= 1 + \frac{70 + 225 - 195 + 18 - 294}{315}$$

$$= 1 + \frac{313 - 489^*}{315}$$

$$= \frac{628 - 489}{315} = \frac{139}{315} \textit{ Ans.}$$

* Obtained by adding all the numerators with + before them, and then all those with − before them.

Multiplication of Fractions

1. When the multiplier is a whole number: This, as in the case of whole numbers, means that we have to find the sum of a given number of repetitions of the fraction.

Example 1:

$$\frac{7}{9} \times 4 \text{ means } \frac{7}{9} + \frac{7}{9} + \frac{7}{9} + \frac{7}{9}, \textit{ i.e.}, \frac{28}{9}; \text{ or } \frac{7 \times 4}{9}$$

Hence, to multiply a fraction by a whole number, simply multiply the numerator by that number.

Since the multiplier thus becomes a factor of the numerator, we cancel any common factors contained in the multiplier and the denominator; and this may be done before we perform the actual multiplication:

Example 2: Multiply $\frac{19}{46}$ by 69.

$$\frac{19}{46} \times 69 = \frac{19 \times 69}{46} = \frac{19 \times 3}{2} \text{ (cancelling 23)}, = \frac{57}{2} = 28\tfrac{1}{2} \textit{ Ans.}$$

It follows that if the multiplier be itself a factor of the denominator, we may, to multiply a fraction by a whole number, divide the denominator by that number.

2. When the multiplier is a fraction:

Example: In performing the operation 7×9, it is plain that we do to 7 what we do to a unit to obtain 9. Similarly, $\frac{3}{5} \times \frac{4}{11}$ may be looked upon as doing to $\frac{3}{5}$ what we do to the unit to obtain $\frac{4}{11}$.

Now, to obtain $\frac{4}{11}$ from the unit, we must divide the unit into 11 equal parts and take 4 of them.

Therefore, to find the value of $\frac{3}{5} \times \frac{4}{11}$ we must divide $\frac{3}{5}$ into 11 equal parts and take 4 of them.

But $\frac{3}{5} = \frac{33}{55} = \frac{3}{55} \times 11$, which means that the eleventh part of $\frac{3}{5}$ is $\frac{3}{55}$; and, if we take 4 of these parts, we get $\frac{3}{55} \times 4$ or $\frac{12}{55}$.

Thus, $\frac{3}{5} \times \frac{4}{11} = \frac{12}{55}$. Now $12 = 3 \times 4$, and $55 = 5 \times 11$.

Hence, we have the following rule: *To multiply two fractions together, multiply the numerators for a new numerator and the denominators for a new denominator.*

As in Example 2, the work is shortened if we cancel common factors from the numerators and denominators.

Example: Multiply $\frac{22}{91}$ by $\frac{13}{77}$.

$$\text{The product } = \frac{\overset{2}{22} \times 13}{\underset{7}{91} \times \underset{7}{77}} = \frac{2}{49} \textit{ Ans.}$$

Here, the 22 of the numerator and the 77 of the denominator contain a common factor, 11. Therefore, we cross out the 22 and write 2 above it, and cross out the 77 and write 7 under it. Similarly, we cancel the factor 13 from 13 and 91. There is now 2 left for numerator and 7×7 for denominator.

To multiply more than two fractions together, we proceed in the same way.

In multiplication of fractions, mixed numbers must first be expressed as improper fractions.

Example: Simplify $5\frac{1}{7} \times 1\frac{1}{27} \times 1\frac{11}{24}$.

$$\text{Given expression } = \frac{\overset{3}{36}}{7} \times \frac{11}{\underset{9}{27}} \times \frac{\overset{5}{35}}{\underset{2}{24}} = \frac{55}{18} = 3\frac{1}{18} \textit{ Ans.}$$

Division of Fractions

1. When the divisor is a whole number:

Suppose we have to divide $\frac{7}{9}$ by 4.

We know $\frac{7}{9} = \frac{28}{36}$. This fraction means that the unit is divided into 36 equal parts, and 28 of the parts taken. If we divide the 28 parts by 4, we get 7 of them—*i.e.*, $\frac{7}{36}$. Hence $\frac{7}{9} \div 4 = \frac{7}{36}$.

Therefore, to divide a fraction by a whole number, we multiply the denominator by that number.

In the same way as already explained for multiplication, we cancel any common factors contained in the divisor and the numerator. Hence, if the numerator be exactly divisible by the divisor, we may divide a fraction by a whole number by dividing the numerator by that number.

Example 1:

$$\frac{27}{31} \div 18 = \frac{\overset{3}{27}}{31 \times \underset{2}{18}} = \frac{3}{62}\ Ans.$$

Example 2:

$$\frac{36}{41} \div 9 = \frac{\overset{4}{36}}{41 \times 9} = \frac{4}{41}\ Ans.$$

2. When the divisor is a fraction:

In the operation 24 ÷ 3, we have to find the number which, when multiplied by 3, will give 24. Similarly, to find the value of $\frac{3}{7} \div \frac{5}{9}$ we have to find the fraction which, when multiplied by $\frac{5}{9}$, will give $\frac{3}{7}$.

But $\frac{3 \times 9}{7 \times 5}$ is the fraction which gives $\frac{3}{7}$ when multiplied by $\frac{5}{9}$.

Therefore, $\frac{3}{7} \div \frac{5}{9} = \frac{3 \times 9}{7 \times 5}$.

Hence, to divide by a fraction, invert the divisor and multiply.
As in multiplication, mixed numbers must first be reduced to improper fractions.

Example 3: Divide $3\frac{1}{14}$ by $5\frac{5}{42}$.

$$3\frac{1}{14} \div 5\frac{5}{42} = \frac{43}{14} \div \frac{215}{42} = \frac{43}{14} \times \frac{\overset{3}{42}}{\underset{5}{215}} = \frac{3}{5}\ Ans.$$

DECIMAL FRACTIONS

Decimal fractions differ in form from common fractions, in not having a written denominator; and from whole numbers, by having the decimal point (.) prefixed; which also separates the integral part from the decimal. The word *decimal* is derived from the Latin word *decem*, which signifies "ten." The denominator of a decimal is always 10, or some power of 10, as 100, 1000, etc.

A *complex decimal* is a decimal with a common fraction at the right, as, .12½.

A *mixed decimal* is a whole number with a decimal fraction to its right, as, 34.5.

The denominations of United States money are based on the decimal system—the dollar occupying the unit's place, the dime the tenth's place, the cent the hundredth's place, and the mill the thousandth's place.

The rules given for addition, subtraction, and so on, also apply to decimals.

Addition in Decimals

Example: 27.295 + .0287 + 591.68 + 9.1846.

```
 27.295
   .0287
591.68
  9.1846
628.1883 Ans.
```

Write the numbers so that the same powers of 10 come under one another, or, what is the same thing, write the numbers so that the decimal points come under one another. Then, adding the ten thousandths first, 7 and 6 are 13, carry 1, etc.

Subtraction in Decimals

Example: Subtract .07295 from 21.651.

```
21.651
  .07295
21.57805 Ans.
```

Write the first number under the second, so that the point comes under the point. Remember that we may consider there are 0's above the 9 and 5, since in 21.651 there are no ten-thousandths and no hundred-thousandths.

Say, mentally, 10 minus 5 is 5,
9 minus 9 is 0,
10 minus 2 is 8, etc.

Multiplication in Decimals

Rule.—*Multiply as in whole numbers, and point off from the right of the product as many places as there are decimal places in both multiplier and multiplicand—prefixing ciphers if necessary.*

Example 1: What is the product of .417 multiplied by .34?

```
  .417
   .34
  1668
 1251
.14178 Ans.
```

Explanation.—The numbers may be multiplied as though they were integers. Since the multiplier contains 2 decimal places, and the multiplicand 3 decimal places, the product will contain 5 decimal places and the decimal point is placed before the fifth figure counting from the right.

Example 2: Multiply 7.5864 by 200.

```
     7.5864
        200
  1517.2800
= 1517.28 Ans.
```

Explanation.—Since each removal of a figure one place to the left increases its value tenfold, the removal of the decimal point one place to the right multiplies by 10, and two places by 100. The product of 7.5864 × 100 is therefore 758.64, and this multiplied by 2 gives the product of 7.5864 × 200, which is 1517.28.

NOTE.—The number of decimal places in the product will always be equal to the sum of the number of decimal places in the multiplier and the multiplicand. This is obvious in Example 1; and it is implicit in Example 2, in which the working product is 1517.2800.

To multiply a decimal by 10, 100, etc.:

Rule.—*Remove the* (.) *as many places to the right as there are ciphers in the multiplier.*

Work:

```
8.75 ×   10 =   87.5
8.75 ×  100 =  875.
8.75 × 1000 = 8750.
```

Division of Decimals

Rule.—*Divide as in whole numbers, annexing ciphers to the dividend, if necessary; then point off from the right of the quotient as many places as the decimal places in the dividend exceed those in the divisor—prefixing ciphers if necessary.*

1. Division of a decimal by a whole number:

Example 1: Divide 18.2754 by 4.

```
4)18.2754
   4.56885
```

We divide 4 into 18 (units) and have 4 (units) quotient and 2 units remainder. Since the 4 is the unit's figure of the quotient, we write the decimal point immediately after it. Then, the 2 units remainder and the 2 tenths of the dividend make 22 tenths to be divided by 4, and so on. Having reached the 4 (ten-thousandths) of the dividend, we find 8 (ten-thousandths) quotient and 2 remainder. This remainder is 20 hundred-thousandths, which when divided by 4 gives 5 (hundred-thousandths) and no further remainder

Example 2: Divide 18.2758 by 11.

```
11)18.2758
    1.66143636
```

Here we find the digits 3, 6 repeated indefinitely in the quotient. Decimals of this sort will be fully considered later.

Example 3: Divide 354.43 by 184.

```
184)354.43(1.92625 Ans.
    1704
     483
     1150*
      460
       920
```

Here we find the first figure of the quotient is obtained by dividing 184 into 354 units. Having now reached the decimal point in the dividend we also put the decimal point in the answer, and go on as before.

* At this stage there is a remainder 115 hundredths. We bring down 0 from the dividend, and obtain 1150 thousandths, etc.

2. Division of a decimal:

EXAMPLE 4: Divide 10.6603 by 7.85.

```
785)1066.03(1.358 Ans.
    2810
     4553
      6280
```

Here 7.85 is 785 hundredths, and 10.6603 is 1066.03 hundredths; so that the required quotient is obtained by dividing 1066.03 by 785.

Therefore, to divide by a decimal, move the point as many places to the right as will make the divisor a whole number; move the point in the dividend the same number of places to the right. Then proceed as in Example 3.

EXAMPLE 5: Divide 176.4 by .00012.

12)17640000
Ans. 1470000

Here, to make the divisor a whole number, we have to move the point 5 places. Therefore we also move the point 5 places to the right in the dividend, first writing enough 0's after the 176.4 to enable us to do so.

To divide a decimal by 10, 100, etc.:

RULE.—*Remove the (.) as many places to the left as there are ciphers in the divisor.*

WORK:

$$62.5 \div 10 = 6.25$$
$$62.5 \div 100 = .625$$
$$62.5 \div 1000 = .0625$$

Expression of decimal fractions as common fractions:

EXAMPLE: Express 5.375 as a common fraction.

.375 = 375 thousandths.

$$\text{Therefore } 5.375 = 5\frac{375}{1000} = 5\frac{3}{8}\ \textit{Ans.}$$

RULE.—*Take the digits of the decimal for numerator; for the denominator put down 1 followed by as many ciphers as there are digits in the decimal. Reduce this fraction to its lowest terms.*

Expression of common fractions as decimals:

We have seen that a common fraction represents the quotient of the numerator divided by the denominator. Therefore, to convert a common fraction to a decimal fraction, we divide the numerator by the denominator.

EXAMPLE: Express 3/32 as a decimal.

```
4)3.0
8) .75
  .09375 Ans.
```

It will be found in many cases that there is always a remainder, so that the quotient can be continued indefinitely.

CIRCULATING DECIMALS

The learner has already discovered that some common fractions cannot be changed to exact decimal fractions, as—

1/3 = .33333 on to infinity.
2/3 = .66666 on to infinity.
7/33 = .212121, etc.

These decimals are known as *circulates, recurring,* or *circulating* decimals.

The part which recurs is called the *repetend.*

This is marked by putting a dot over the first and last figures of it. For instance, if we write the 21 in the last case above this way: $\dot{2}\dot{1}$, it indicates that, if written out, the result would be 21212121, etc., on to infinity.

Where a circulating decimal occurs in work, it is best to reduce it to a common fraction. If need be, it may be expressed in the result as a circulate to any number of decimal places.

To change a pure circulate to a common fraction:

RULE.—*Omit the (.) and write the figures of the repetend for the numerator, and as many 9's for the denominator as there are places in the repetend.*

EXAMPLE: Change the pure circulates $.\dot{3}$, $.\dot{2}\dot{7}$, $.\dot{1}4285\dot{7}$, to common fractions.

$$.\dot{3},\ \left(\frac{3}{9} = \frac{1}{3}\right)\ \textit{Ans. } 1/3. \qquad .\dot{2}\dot{7},\ \left(\frac{27}{99} = \frac{3}{11}\right)\ \textit{Ans. } 3/11.$$

$$.\dot{1}4285\dot{7},\ \left(\frac{142857}{999999} = \frac{1}{7}\right)\ \textit{Ans. } 1/7.$$

To change a mixed circulate to a common fraction:

RULE.—*From the whole decimal subtract the finite part, and make the remainder the numerator. For the denominator, write as many 9's as there are figures in the repetend, and annex as many 0's as there are finite places.*

EXAMPLE: Change the mixed circulates .16 and .416 to common fractions.

$$16 - 1 = 15,\ \frac{15}{90} = \frac{1}{6}.\ \textit{Ans. } 1/6.$$

$$416 - 41 = 375,\ \frac{375}{900} = \frac{5}{12}.\ \textit{Ans. } 5/12.$$

To add, subtract, multiply, and divide circulates, reduce them to common fractions, then apply the respective rules.

SHORT METHODS IN MERCHANDISING

When one of the numbers is an *aliquot part* of 100, the process of multiplication and division can often be very much shortened, as shown below.

Find cost of 27 yards of goods at 16⅔¢ ($1/6) per yard. At $1 per yard, 27 yards cost $27; at $1/6, (27 ÷ 6) = $4½. *Ans.* $4½.

Find cost of a bale of cotton, 528 pounds at 8⅓¢ ($1/12) per pound. At $1 per pound, 528 pounds cost $528; at $1/12 (528 ÷ 12) = $44. *Ans.* $44.

Find cost of 1845 pounds of iron, at 3⅓¢ ($1/30) per pound. Take 1/30 of 1845, since 3⅓¢ is 1/30 of $1. (1845 ÷ 30 = 61½). *Ans.* $61½.

Find cost of 16 pounds of butter at 37½¢ ($⅜) per pound. Here we take ⅜ of 16. Say ⅛ of 16 is 2, and ⅜ is (2 × 3) 6. Or say 3 times 16 is 48, and ⅛ of 48 is 6. *Ans.* $6

Find cost of 17½ bushels of apples at 75¢ ($¾) per bushel. The shortest way to find ¾ of $17.50 is to diminish it by ¼ of itself.

```
4)17.50    at $1
   4.37½  at $¼
  13.12½  at $¾
```

Ans. $13.12½.

At 6¼¢ per pound how much sugar will $5 buy? As 6¼¢ is 1/16 of $1, evidently each dollar will buy 16 pounds. *Ans.* 80 pounds.

In multiplying by a fraction, write the quantity in a line with the numerator and cancel common factors.

Find cost of 72 yards of carpet, at 87½¢ ($⅞) a yard. Cancel 8, also 72 and write 9 instead. *Ans.* $63.

$$\frac{7}{8} \times \overset{9}{72} = 63$$

Of 28 pounds of coffee, at 18¾¢ ($3/16) per pound. Cancel 28 and 16, write 7 and 4. *Ans.* $5¼.

$$\frac{3}{\underset{4}{16}} \times \overset{7}{28} = \frac{21}{4} \text{ or } 5\tfrac{1}{4}$$

At 66⅔¢ ($⅔) per bushel, how many bushels of wheat will $34 buy? *Ans.* 51 bushels.

$$\frac{3}{2} \times \overset{17}{34} = 51$$

In division, invert terms of fraction.

How much sirup, at 41⅔¢ ($5/12) per gallon, can be bought for $15? *Ans.* 36 gallons.

$$\frac{12}{5} \times \overset{3}{15} = 36$$

TABLE OF ALIQUOT PARTS OF 100

3⅓ is 1/30	25 is ¼	50 is ½	75 is ¾
6¼ is 1/16	31¼ is 5/16	56¼ is 9/16	80 is ⅘
8⅓ is 1/12	33⅓ is ⅓	58⅓ is 7/12	81¼ is 13/16
12½ is ⅛	37½ is ⅜	60 is ⅗	83⅓ is ⅚
16⅔ is ⅙	40 is ⅖	62½ is ⅝	87½ is ⅞
18¾ is 3/16	41⅔ is 5/12	66⅔ is ⅔	91⅔ is 11/12
20 is ⅕	43¾ is 7/16	68¾ is 11/16	93¾ is 15/16

This table embodies all the aliquot parts of 100 and their

equivalent fractions which are generally used in practical calculations.

PROBLEMS IN GRAIN, STOCK, COTTON, COAL, HAY, LUMBER, ETC.

To find the value of articles sold by the unit, hundred or thousand:

RULE.—*Multiply the quantity by the price, or vice versa, and point off the proper number of decimal places in the result.*

Find the cost of a bale (518 pounds) of cotton at 7⅜¢ per pound.

518 × .07 = 36.26
518 × .00⅜ = 1.94¼
Ans. $38.20¼

At 7¢ (.07) per pound, 518 pounds cost $36.26; at ⅜¢, $1.94¼. For ⅜ of 518, multiply by 3, and divide product by 8.

Find cost of a lot of hogs, weighing 8740 pounds, at $4.35 per hundredweight.

87.40
4.35
380.1900

The price being $4.35 per 100 pounds and as in 8740 pounds there are 87.40 hundredweight, four decimal places are pointed off. *Ans.* $380.19.

Find the cost of 2864 feet of lumber, at $17¼ per 1000 feet.

Price being dollars per 1000, point off three places. (2.864 × 17¼ = 49.404.) *Ans.* $49.40.

To find the value of articles sold by the ton (2000 pounds):

RULE.—*Multiply the weight by the price and take half of the product.*

Find the cost of 2680 pounds of hay, at $11½ per ton.

Point off three places, when price is dollars; five if dollars and cents. (2680 × 11½ = 30820; 30820 ÷ 2 = 15.410.) *Ans.* $15.41.

When the long ton of 2240 pounds is used:

RULE.—*Multiply the weight by the price and divide the product by 2.240.*

Find the cost of 4800 pounds of coal, at $6¾ per long ton. (4800 × 6¾) ÷ 2.24 = $14.46, *Ans.*

To find the cost of grain, when the price per bushel and weight is given:

RULE.—*Reduce the weight to bushels, and multiply by the price.*

Find the cost of 3570 pounds of shelled corn, at 36¢ per bushel.

56)3570(63.75 bu.
.36
Ans. $22.9500

To reduce pounds of shelled corn to bushels, divide by 56. At 36¢ per bushel, 63.75 bushels come to $22.95.

Find cost of 2900 pounds of wheat, at 57¢ per bushel.

To reduce pounds of wheat to bushels divide by 60. 2900 ÷ 60 = 48⅓ bushels; 48⅓ × .57 = $27.55, *Ans.*

In computing the value of grain, the operation can often be abbreviated by cancellation:

RULE.—*Write the weight and price per bushel, on the right of a vertical line, and the number of pounds to the bushel on the left. Then cancel common factors, as explained above.*

Find the cost of 3230 pounds of wheat, at 72¢ per bushel.

60 | 3230
| 72 12
323 × 12 = 38.76

Here we cancel the 0's on both sides; then, 6 and 72, which leaves 323 and 12. Their product gives the answer.

At 28¢ per bushel, what will 4080 pounds of oats cost?

32 | 4080 510
4 | 28 7
Ans. $35.70

Oats, 32 pounds to the bushel. Cancel 32 and 4080, then, 4 and 28, leaving the factors 510 and 7.

Other short cuts for computing cost of merchandise, produce, etc.

Find cost of 26½ dozen eggs, at 18½¢ a dozen.

26 × .18 = 4.68
½ of 44 = .22
½ × ½ = ¼ 4.90¼
Ans. $4.90.

When both fractions are ½, to product of the whole numbers, add ½ of their sum, and annex ¼ to answer.

Of 53¾ pounds of butter, at 28¾¢ per pound.

53 × .28 = 14.84
¾ of 81 = .60¾
¾ × ¾ = 9/16 15.45 9/16
Ans. $15.45 9/16.

To the product of the whole numbers, add ¾ of their sum, plus the square of ¾.

Of 13¼ yards of flannel, at 31¼¢ per yard.

13 × .31 = 4.03 + .11 = 4.14, *Ans.*

To 4.03 add .11, ¼ of 44 (13 + 31). The 1/16 (¼ × ¼) is disregarded.

DENOMINATE NUMBERS

Simple denominate numbers.—When we speak of measures, whether they are of money, extension, time, or weight, we use terms like 5 dollars, 4 yards, 3 hours, or 10 pounds to express the quantity we are talking about.

Sometimes we use two or more terms or names to express the measure, as 3 hours, 15 minutes, 10 seconds; 4 gallons, 3 quarts, 1 pint. These are *compound denominate numbers.*

The chief differences between compound numbers and simple numbers is that, with the exceptions of United States money and the metric system of weights and measures, the denominations of compound numbers do not increase or decrease by the scale of ten.

REDUCTION.—Reduction of compound numbers is the process of changing them from one denomination to another without altering their value.

Reduction descending is changing the denomination of a number to another that is lower, as: 2 hours = 120 minutes; 2 feet = 24 inches.

Reduction ascending is changing the denomination of a number to another that is higher, as: 120 minutes = 2 hours; 24 inches = 2 feet.

RULES FOR ADDITION OF DENOMINATE NUMBERS

1. Write the names of the different units to be used in addition, placing them in a horizontal row, the largest to the left.

2. Write the numbers of each unit to be added, below the names of the units, each in its proper place.

3. Add and place each sum below the column added.

EXAMPLE: Add 7 hours 15 minutes 30 seconds, 9 hours 30 minutes 40 seconds, and 11 hours 40 minutes 32 seconds.

WORK:

Hours	Minutes	Seconds
7	15	30
9	30	40
11	40	32
28	26	42

EXPLANATION: 30 seconds + 40 seconds + 32 seconds = 102 seconds. But, 102 seconds = 1 minute 42 seconds. Write the 42 below and carry the 1 minute. 1 minute (carried) + 15 minutes + 30 minutes + 40 minutes = 86 minutes. But 86 minutes = 1 hour 26 minutes. Write the 26 and carry the 1 hour. 1 hour + 7 hours + 9 hours + 11 hours = 28 hours. Result = 28 hours 26 minutes 42 seconds.

SUBTRACTION OF DENOMINATE QUANTITIES

EXAMPLE: Subtract 6 tons 12 cwt. 9 pounds 10 ounces from 15 tons 7 cwt. 13 pounds 9 ounces.

WORK:

Tons	Cwt.	Pounds	Ounces
15	7	13	9
6	12	9	10
8	15	3	15

EXPLANATION: (1) Place as in addition of denominate quantities. 10 ounces cannot be taken from 9 ounces, so we must take 1 pound from the 13 pounds and add it to the nine ounces. 16 ounces + 9 ounces = 25 ounces. 25 − 10 = 15. Write the 15 below.

(2) Now there are only 12 pounds left to take the 9 from. 12 − 9 = 3. Write the 3 below.

(3) 12 is larger than 7. 1 ton + 7 cwt. = 27 cwt. 27 − 12 = 15. Write the 15 below.

(4) 14 − 6 = 8. Write the 8 below.

(5) Result = 8 tons 15 cwt. 3 pounds 15 ounces.

Multiplication of Denominate Quantities

Example: Multiply 21 yards 2 feet 11 inches by 6.

Work:

Yards	Feet	Inches
21	2	11
		6
131	2	6

Explanation: (1) 6 × 11 inches = 66 inches = 5 feet 6 inches. Write the 6 below and carry the 5.

(2) 6 × 2 feet = 12 feet. 12 feet + 5 feet (carried) = 17 feet, or 5 yards 2 feet. Write the 2 below and carry the 5.

(3) 6 × 21 yards = 126 yards. 126 yards + 5 yards = 131 yards.

(4) Result = 131 yards 2 feet 6 inches.

Division of Denominate Quantities

Problem: Divide 3 years 9 months 4 days by 12.

Work:

Years	Months	Days	Hours
12)3	9	4	0
0	3	22	20

Explanation: (1) We cannot divide 3 by 12, so we reduce 3 years to months. 3 years = 36 months. 36 months + 9 months = 45 months. 45 ÷ 12 = 3, and a remainder 9. Write the 3 and carry the remainder 9.

(2) 9 months (carried) = 270 days. 270 days + 4 days = 274 days. 274 ÷ 12 = 22, and a remainder 10. Write the 22 and carry the 10.

(3) 10 days = 240 hours. 240 ÷ 12 = 20. Write the 20.

(4) Result = 3 months 22 days 20 hours.

Rules for Reduction Ascending

1. Divide the given denomination by the number which will reduce it to the next higher denomination. Divide the quotient in the same manner, and continue the operation until the entire quantity is reduced.

2. To the last quotient, annex the several remainders in their proper order. The result will be the answer.

Example: Reduce 201458 inches to higher denominations.

Work:	
12	201458 inches
3	16788 feet 2 inches
5½	5596 yards
2	2
11	11192 half yards
320	1017 rods 5 half yards
	3 miles 57 rods
	2 yds. 1 ft. 6 in.

201458 inches = 3 miles 57 rods 2 yards 1 foot 8 inches.

Solution:

201458 inches = 16788 feet 2 inches.
16788 feet 2 inches = 5596 yards 2 inches.
5596 yards 2 inches = 1017 rods 2 yards 1 foot 8 inches.
1017 rods 2 yards 1 foot 8 inches = 3 miles 57 rods 2 yards 1 foot 8 inches.

Rules for Reduction Descending

1. Write the given quantity in the order of its denominations, beginning with the highest, and supply vacant denominations with ciphers.

2. Multiply the highest denomination by the number which will reduce it to the next lower denomination, and add to the product the units of the lower denomination, if there be any.

3. Proceed in the same manner until the entire quantity is reduced to the required denomination.

Example: Reduce 10 yards 8 feet 10 inches to inches.

Work:

Yards	Feet	Inches
10	8	10
3		
38		
12		
456		
10		
466		

Solution:

10 yards = 10 × 3 feet = 30 feet. 30 feet and 8 feet are 38 feet. 38 feet = 38 × 12 inches, or 456 inches. 456 inches + 10 inches = 466 inches.

NOTE.—To prove the above work, use reduction ascending, beginning with the result.

LONG OR LINEAR MEASURE

Long or linear measure is used in measuring lines and distances.

There are two systems in use in the United States, the *English system* and the *French system.* The English system is the one commonly used, while the French, or metric system, is used in making scientific measurements.

Table of Long Measure

12 inches (in.)	= 1 foot (ft.)
3 feet	= 1 yard (yd.)
5½ yards, or 16½ feet	= 1 rod (rd.)
320 rods, or 5280 feet	= 1 mile (mi.)
1760 yards	= 1 mile

mi.		rd.		yd.		ft.		in.
1	=	320	=	1760	=	5280	=	63360

Architects, carpenters, and mechanics frequently write ′ for foot, and ″ for inch. Thus 8′7″ means 8 feet 7 inches.

Other measures of length are:
1 hand = 4 in. Used in measuring the height of horses.
1 fathom = 6 ft. Used in measuring depths at sea.
1 knot, nautical or geographical mile = 1.1526⅔ miles or 6080 feet.

The *knot* is used in measuring distances at sea. It is equivalent to 1 minute of longitude at the equator.

Surveyor's Linear Measure

7.92 inches	= 1 link (l.)
25 links	= 1 rod (rd.)
4 rods or 100 links	= 1 chain (ch.)
80 chains	= 1 mile (mi.)

mi.		ch.		rd.		l.		in.
1	=	80	=	320	=	8000	=	63360

The linear unit commonly employed by surveyors is *Gunter's chain,* which is 4 rods or 66 feet.

An *engineer's chain,* used by civil engineers, is 100 feet long, and consists of 100 links.

Measures of Length

The following measures of length are also used:

3 barleycorns	= 1 inch. Used by shoemakers.
4 inches	= 1 hand. Used to measure the height of horses.
6 feet	= 1 fathom. Used to measure depths of sea.
3 feet	= 1 pace. } Used in pacing distances.
5 paces	= 1 rod. } Used in pacing distances.
8 furlongs	= 1 mile.
1.15 statute miles	= 1 geographical, or nautical mile.
3 geographical miles	= 1 league.
60 geographical miles } 69.16 statute miles }	= 1 degree {of Latitude on a Meridian, or of Longitude on the Equator.

The *length of a degree of latitude* varies. 69.16 miles is the average length, and is that adopted by the United States Coast Survey.

The *standard unit of length* is identical with the *imperial yard* of Great Britain.

The *standard yard,* under William IV, was declared to be fixed by dividing a pendulum which vibrates seconds in a vacuum, at the level of the sea, at 62 degrees Fahrenheit, in the latitude of London, into 391,393 equal parts, and taking 360,000 of these parts for the yard.

The following denominations also occur: The *span* = 9 inches; 1 *commom cubit* (the distance from the elbow to the end of the middle finger) = 18 inches; 1 *sacred cubit* = 21.888 inches.

Mariner's Measure

6 feet	=	1 fathom
120 fathoms	=	1 cable length (or cable)
7½ cable lengths	=	1 mile (mi.)
5280 feet	=	1 statute mile
6080 feet	=	1 nautical mile

SQUARE MEASURE

Square measure is used in measuring surfaces, such as cloth, ceilings, floors, etc.; paving, glazing, and stonecutting, by the square foot; roofing, flooring, and slating by the square of 100 feet.

A surface has two dimensions, *length* and *breadth.*

A *square* is a figure that has four equal sides and four right angles.

The unit of measure for surfaces is a *square,* each of whose sides is a linear unit. Thus, a *square inch* is a square, each side of which is one inch long; a *square foot* is a square, each of whose sides is one foot long, etc.

The *area of a square* is the product of two of its sides. Thus, the area of a surface 3 feet square is 3 × 3 = 9 square feet.

Hence, to find the area of a rectangle:

Rule.—*Multiply the length by the breadth expressed in units of the same denomination.*

As the *area of a rectangle* is found by taking the product of the numbers representing its length and breadth, it is evident that if the area be divided by either of those numbers, the quotient will be the other number. Hence, to find either side of a rectangle when its area and the other side are given:

Rule.—*Divide the area by the given side. The quotient will be the required side.*

Table of Square Measure

144 square inches (sq. in.)	=	1 square foot (sq. ft.)
9 square feet	=	1 square yard (sq. yd.)
30¼ square yards	=	1 square rod (sq. rd.)
160 square rods	=	1 acre (A.)
640 acres	=	1 square mile (sq. mi.)

Sq. ′ and sq. ″ are frequently used for square foot and square inch. Thus, 15 sq. ′ 6 sq. ″ means 15 square feet 6 square inches.

A *square* is 100 square feet. It is used in measuring roofing.

Practical Application of Square Measure

PAPERING

Facts about *wall paper:*

(1) Wall paper in this country is ½ yard wide, and comes in rolls 8 yards long, or in double rolls, 16 yards long.

(2) It is sold by the roll only.

(3) Bordering is sold by the linear yard.

(4) Make liberal allowances for waste in matching figures.

(5) If the border is wide, the strips need not extend to the ceiling.

Rules for measuring:

(1) Measure the distance around the room in feet.

(2) Deduct the width of doors and windows.

(3) Divide the difference by 1½, and the quotient will be the number of strips needed.

(4) Multiply the number of strips by the height (in yards), and the product is the number of yards needed, approximately.

(5) Divide the number of yards by 8, and the result is the number of single rolls needed.

Example: A room 12 feet high and 16 feet by 24 feet, has three windows and 2 doors, each 4 feet wide. How many rolls of paper are needed to paper the sides?

Solution:

Distance around the room	=	80 feet
Width of doors and windows	=	20 feet
After deducting for doors and windows		60 feet

60 ÷ 3/2 = 40
40 × 4 = 160
160 ÷ 8 = 20 single, or 10 double rolls.

CARPETING

Facts about *carpets:*

(1) Carpets are usually ¾ yard wide and are sold by the linear yard.

(2) Always draw a diagram of the floor or stairs to be covered.

(3) The number of yards required depends on which way the strips run—whether lengthwise or across the room. Sometimes, by running the strips lengthwise, there is less waste in matching the pattern.

(4) The part cut off in matching patterns is charged to the purchaser.

Rules for estimating:

The number of yards required will be the number of yards in a strip (including the waste for matching), multiplied by the number of strips.

Example: What is the cost of carpeting a room 16 feet by 24 feet at 85¢ per yard? The carpet is 2¼ feet wide and the strips run lengthwise.

Solution:

16 ÷ 2¼ = 7⅑. Hence, I must buy 8 strips.
24 ÷ 3 = 8, which is the number of yards in a strip.
8 × 8 yards = 64 yards.
64 yards will cost 64 × 85¢, or $54.40.

To this must be added the cost of sewing, the laying of the carpet, and the waste in matching the pattern.

LAND MEASURE

To find the number of acres in a tract of land:

Rule.—*Divide the number of square rods by 160, or number of square chains by 10.*

Example: (1) How many square rods, also acres, in a field 80 rods long and 62½ rods wide?

80 × 62½ = 5000 square rods; 5000 ÷ 160 = 31¼ acres. *Ans.* 31¼ acres.

(2) In tract, 79 chains 84 links (79.84 chains) by 41 chains 25 links (41.25 chains)?

79.84 × 41.25 = 3293.4 square chains; 3293.4 ÷ 10 = 329.34 acres. *Ans.* 329.34 acres.

Table showing one side of a square tract or lot containing:

1 acre	=	208.7 feet	=	43,560 square feet
1½ acres	=	255.6 feet	=	65,340 square feet
2 acres	=	295.2 feet	=	87,120 square feet
2½ acres	=	330 feet	=	108,900 square feet
3 acres	=	361.5 feet	=	130,680 square feet
5 acres	=	466.7 feet	=	217,800 square feet
10 acres	=	660 feet	=	435,600 square feet
1/10 acre	=	66 feet	=	4,356 square feet
⅛ acre	=	73.8 feet	=	5,445 square feet
⅙ acre	=	85.2 feet	=	7,260 square feet
¼ acre	=	104.4 feet	=	10,890 square feet
⅓ acre	=	120.5 feet	=	14,520 square feet
½ acre	=	147.6 feet	=	21,780 square feet
¾ acre	=	180.8 feet	=	32,670 square feet

Table of Surveyor's Square Measure

272¼ square feet = 1 square rod
16 square rods = 1 square chain
160 square rods, or 10 square chains = 1 acre
640 acres = 1 square mile, or section
36 square miles, or 36 sections = 1 township

CUBIC MEASURE

Just as the rectangle is the chief surface considered in arithmetic, so the rectangular solid is the chief solid body.

A *rectangular solid* is bounded by six rectangular surfaces, each opposite pair of rectangles being equal and parallel to each other.

A rectangular solid thus has three dimensions—*length, breadth,* and *thickness.*

If the length, breadth, and thickness are all equal to one another, the solid is called a *cube.* Hence, a *cubic foot,* the unit of volume, is a solid body whose length, breadth, and thickness are each a linear foot. Similarly, a *cubic inch* measures one linear inch in length, breadth, and thickness; and a *cubic yard* measures one linear yard in length, breadth, and thickness.

The number of cubic feet (or inches, or yards) in the volume of a rectangular solid is equal to the number of linear feet (or inches, or yards) in the length, multiplied by the number of linear feet (or inches, or yards) in the breadth, multiplied by the number of linear feet (or inches, or yards) in the thickness.

This is usually abbreviated into

Length × breadth × thickness = volume, or cubic content.

For, suppose the solid in the diagram to be 10 feet in length, 8 feet in breadth, and 5 feet in thickness. It is clear that this solid can be cut into five slices, each 1 foot thick, by planes parallel to the bottom. But, the bottom contains 10 × 8 square

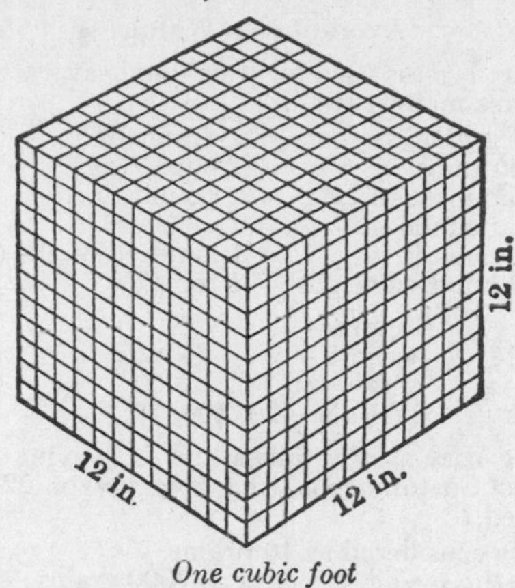

One cubic foot

feet and above each square foot there is a cubic foot. Thus, each slice contains 10 × 8 cubic feet. Therefore, since there are five slices, the whole solid contains 10 × 8 × 5, or 400 cubic feet.

Since length × breadth × thickness = cubic content, it follows that, if we know any three of these four quantities, we can find the fourth.

The student should remember that:

(a) A cubic foot of water weighs 1000 ounces (avoirdupois), approximately.

(b) A gallon of pure water (U. S. standard) weighs 8⅓ pounds.

We have thus a relation between weight, capacity, and cubic content.

Table of Cubic Measure

1728 cubic inches (cu. in.)	=	1 cubic foot (cu. ft.)
27 cubic feet	=	1 cubic yard (cu. yd.)
128 cubic feet	=	1 cord (C.)

Cubic Yard		Cubic Feet		Cubic Inches
1	=	27	=	46656

A *cord* of wood or stone is a pile 8 feet long, 4 feet wide, and 4 feet high.

A pile of wood 4 feet high, 4 feet wide, and 1 foot long makes a *cord foot.* 8 cord feet = 1 cord.

A *perch* of stone or masonry is 16½ feet long, 1½ feet thick, and 1 foot high, and contains 24¾ cubic feet.

A *cubic yard* of earth is considered a *load.*

Brick work is commonly estimated by the thousand bricks.

Bricklayers, masons, and joiners commonly make a deduction of one half the space occupied by windows and doors in the walls of buildings.

In computing the contents of walls, masons and bricklayers multiply the entire distance around on the outside of the wall by the height and thickness. The corners are thus measured twice.

A cubic foot of distilled water at the maximum density, at the level of the sea, and the barometer at 30 inches, weighs 62.4 pounds or 1000 ounces avoirdupois.

By actual measurements, it has been found that a bushel, dry measure, contains about 1¼ cubic feet. This makes it easy to estimate about how many bushels any bin will hold.

Practical Applications of Cubic Measure

Example: An open tank made of iron ¼ inch thick, is 4 feet long, 2 feet 6 inches broad, and 2 feet deep, outside measurement. Assuming that iron weighs 7.8 times as much as water, find the weight of the tank.

The external volume of the tank = 2 × 2½ × 4 cubic feet = 20 cubic feet.

Since the iron is ¼ inch thick, the inside length is ½ inch less than the outside, the inside breadth is ½ inch less than the outside, and the inside depth is ¼ inch less than the outside.

Therefore the interior volume

$$= 29\tfrac{1}{2} \times 47\tfrac{1}{2} \times 23\tfrac{3}{4} \text{ cubic inches}$$
$$= \frac{59 \times 95 \times 95}{16} \text{ cubic inches}$$
$$= 33279\tfrac{11}{16} \text{ cubic inches}$$

Therefore, volume of iron in the tank

$$= 20 \text{ cubic feet} - 33279\tfrac{11}{16} \text{ cubic inches}$$
$$= 1280\tfrac{5}{16} \text{ cubic inches.}$$

But 1 cubic foot of iron weighs as much as 7.8 cubic feet of water, *i.e.*, 7.8 × 1000 ounces, or 7800 ounces.

$$\therefore \text{Weight of tank} = \frac{1280\tfrac{5}{16} \times 7800}{1728 \times 16} \text{ pounds}$$
$$= 361.199 \text{ pounds, } Ans.$$

Example: A wood pile is 8 feet high and 40 feet long. The sticks are 4 feet long. How many cords in it?

Solution: Being 8 feet high, it is 2 cords high. 40 feet in length equal 5 cords in length. Hence, the pile contains 2 × 5 cords, or 10 cords.

To estimate a bin:

(1) Find the number of cubic feet in the bin.

(2) Divide the number of cubic feet by 1¼.

(3) The result is the number of bushels.

Example: How many bushels will a bin hold, if its inside measurements are, length 20 feet, width 12 feet, depth 8 feet?

Solution: The number of cubic feet in the bin is 8 × 12 × 20, or 1920.

If 1 bushel contains 1¼ cubic feet, in 1920 cubic feet there are as many bushels as 1¼ is contained times in 1920, or 1536.

Work:
$$8 \times 12 \times 20 = 1920$$
$$1920 \div 1\tfrac{1}{4} = 1536.$$

The work may be indicated in this way as well:—

$$8 \times 12 \times 20 \times \tfrac{4}{5} = 1536.$$

To get the number of heaped bushels of corn in the ear in a crib:

(1) Multiply the length of the crib in inches by the width in inches.

(2) Multiply the product obtained, by the height of the corn in the crib in inches.

(3) Divide the result by 2748.

Example: How much corn in the ear can I put into a crib 12 feet wide, 20 feet long, and 10 feet deep?

Solution: The number of cubic inches in the crib is 144 × 240 × 120, or 4,147,200.

Since 2748 cubic inches hold 1 bushel, 4,147,200 cubic inches hold as many bushels as 2748 is contained times in 4,147,200, or 1509+ bushels.

Work:

$$\frac{144 \times 240 \times 120}{2748} = 1509+.$$

MEASURES OF CAPACITY

Measures used in telling the extent of room in vessels are called *measures of capacity*.

There are two kinds of capacity measures, *dry measures* and *liquid measures*.

Dry measures are used to measure grain, seeds, and the like.

Liquid measures are used to measure water, milk, oils, etc.

Common Liquid Measure Table

4 gills (gi.) = 1 pint (pt.)
2 pints = 1 quart (qt.)
4 quarts = 1 gallon (gal.)
31½ gallons = 1 barrel (bbl.)
2 barrels = 1 hogshead (hhd.)

Gallon		Quarts		Pints		Gills
1	=	4	=	8	=	32

A pint, quart, or gallon, dry measure, is more than the same quantity, liquid measure; for a quart, dry measure, is $\frac{1}{32}$ of a bushel, or $\frac{1}{32}$ of 2150.4 cubic inches, which is about $67\frac{1}{5}$ cubic inches, while a quart liquid measure is ¼ of 231 cubic inches, or $57\frac{3}{4}$ cubic inches.

	Cu. In. in 1 Gal.	Cu. In. in 1 Qt.	Cu. In. in 1 Pt.	Cu. In. in 1 Gi.
Liquid measure . . .	231	$57\frac{3}{4}$	$28\frac{7}{8}$	$7\frac{7}{32}$
Dry measure	$268\frac{4}{5}$	$67\frac{1}{5}$	$33\frac{3}{5}$	$8\frac{2}{5}$

In determining the capacity of cisterns, reservoirs, etc., 31½ gallons are considered a barrel (bbl.), and 2 barrels, or 63 gallons, a hogshead (hhd.). In commerce, however, the barrel and hogshead are not fixed measures.

Casks of large size, called *tierces, pipes, butts, tuns*, etc., do not hold any fixed quantity. Their capacity is usually marked upon them.

The *standard gallon* of the United States contains 231 cubic inches, and will hold a little over $8\frac{1}{3}$ pounds of distilled water. The *imperial gallon*, now adopted by Great Britain, contains 277.274 cubic inches, or 10 pounds of distilled water, temperature 62 degrees Fahrenheit, the barometer standing at 30 inches.

Table of Apothecaries' Liquid Measure

These measures are used in mixing medicines.

60 minims (m) = 1 fluid dram (*f*ʒ)
8 fluid drams = 1 fluid ounce (*f*℥)
16 fluid ounces = 1 pint (*O.*)
8 pints = 1 gallon (*Cong.*)

A minim is about 1 drop.

Table of Dry Measure

2 pints (pt.) = 1 quart (qt.)
8 quarts = 1 peck (pk.)
4 pecks = 1 bushel (bu.)

Bushel		Pecks		Quarts		Pints
1	=	4	=	32	=	64

A *common Winchester bushel* (the standard of the United States) contains 2150.42 cubic inches. In Great Britain, the bushel contains 2218.2 cubic inches.

A *dry quart* contains 67.2 cubic inches.

A *liquid quart* contains 57.75 cubic inches.

Example 1: Reduce 5 bushels 2 pecks 4 quarts 1 pint to pints.

Operation:

```
    4    8    2
bu. pk. qt.  pts.
 5  2    4    1
 4
 22 pk.
  8
180 qt.
  2
361 pt.
```

Explanation: As there are 4 pecks in 1 bushel, any number of bushels is equal to 4 times that number of pecks. Then, 5 bushels = 20 pecks, and 2 pecks added make 22 pecks. As there are 8 quarts in 1 peck, any number of pecks is equal to 8 times that number of quarts. Then 22 pecks = 176 quarts, and 4 quarts added make 180 quarts. As there are 2 pints in 1 quart, any number of quarts is equal to 2 times that number of pints. Then, 180 quarts = 360 pints, and 1 pint added make 361 pints. Hence, 5 bushels 2 pecks 4 quarts 1 pint = 361 pints.

Example 2: Reduce 361 pints to bushels.

Operation:

```
2 | 361 pt.
8 | 180 qt. + 1 pt.
4 |  22 pk. + 4 qt.
  | 5 bu. + 2 pk.
```

Explanation: As there are 2 pints in 1 quart, 361 pints are equal to one half that number of quarts = 180 quarts, with a remainder of 1 pint. Also, 180 quarts are equal to one eighth of that number of pecks = 22 pecks, with a remainder of 4 quarts. Finally, 22 pecks are equal to one fourth of that number of bushels = 5 bushels, with a remainder of 2 pecks. Hence, 361 pints are equal to 5 bushels 2 pecks 4 quarts 1 pint.

MEASURES OF WEIGHT

Avoirdupois Weight

Avoirdupois weight is used for weighing heavy articles as grain, groceries, coarse metals, etc.

27.34 grains = 1 dram (dr.)
16 drams = 1 ounce (oz.)
16 ounces (oz.) = 1 pound (lb.)
25 pounds = 1 quarter
100 pounds = 1 hundredweight (cwt.)
20 hundredweight = 1 ton (T.)

Ton		Hundred-weight		Pounds		Ounces
1	=	20	=	2000	=	32000

Scale.—20, 100, 16.

In weighing coal at the mines and in levying duties at the United States Customhouse, the *long ton* of 2240 pounds is sometimes used.

The *ounce* is considered as 16 drams.
The unit is the *pound*. It contains 7000 grains.

The following denominations are also used:

14 pounds = 1 stone
100 pounds butter = 1 firkin
100 pounds grain or flour = 1 cental
100 pounds dried fish = 1 quintal
100 pounds nails = 1 keg
196 pounds flour = 1 barrel
200 pounds pork or beef = 1 barrel
280 pounds salt at N. Y. works = 1 barrel

Troy Weight

Troy weight is used in weighing gold, silver, and jewels.

TABLE

24 grains (gr.) = 1 pennyweight (pwt.)
20 pennyweights = 1 ounce (oz.)
12 ounces = 1 pound (lb.)

Pounds		Ounces		Penny-weights		Grains
1	=	12	=	240	=	5760

In weighing diamonds, pearls, and other jewels, the unit commonly employed is the *carat*, which is equal to 4 carat grains, or 3.168 troy grains.

The *carat* is also used to express the fineness of gold, and means $\frac{1}{24}$ part. Thus gold that is 18 carats fine is $\frac{18}{24}$ gold, and $\frac{6}{24}$ alloy.

The standard unit of weight is the *troy* pound. It is equal to the weight of 22.7944 cubic inches of distilled water at its maximum density, the barometer being at 30 inches. It is identical with the troy pound of Great Britain.

Apothecaries' Weight

Apothecaries' weight is used by pharmacists and physicians in weighing medicines for prescriptions.

TABLE

20 grains (gr.) = 1 scruple (sc. *or* ℈)
3 scruples = 1 dram (dr. *or* ʒ)
8 drams = 1 ounce (oz. *or* ℥)
12 ounces = 1 pound (lb. *or* ℔)

Pound		Ounces		Drams		Scruples		Grains
1	=	12	=	96	=	288	=	5760

In writing prescriptions, physicians express the number in Roman characters. They also write the symbol first; thus, ℥v, ʒvi, ℈ii.

Medical Signs and Abbreviations

℞ (Lat. Recipe), take; āā, of each; ℔, pound; ℥, ounce; ʒ, dram; ℈, scruple; ♏, minim, or drop; O or o, pint; f ℥, fluid ounce; f ʒ, fluid dram; as, ʒ ss, half an ounce; ℥ i, one ounce; ℥ iss, one ounce and a half; ℥ ii, two ounces; gr. grain; Q. S., as much as sufficient; Ft. Mist., let a mixture be made; Ft. Haust., let a draught be made; Ad., add to; Ad lib., at pleasure; Aq., water; M., mix; Mac., macerate; Pulv., powder; Pil., pill; Solv., dissolve; St., let it stand; Sum., to be taken; D., dose; Dil., dilute; Filt., filter; Lot., a wash; Garg., a gargle; Hor. Decub., at bed time; Inject., injection; Gtt., drops; ss, (semis) one half; Ess., essence.

Comparison of Weights

TABLE

1 pound avoirdupois	= 7000	grains
1 ounce avoirdupois	= 437½	grains
1 pound troy, or apothecary	= 5760	grains
1 ounce troy, or apothecary	= 480	grains

Time Measure

60 seconds (sec.)	= 1 minute (min.)
60 minutes	= 1 hour (hr.)
24 hours	= 1 day (da.)
7 days	= 1 week (wk.)
365 days	= 1 common year (yr.)
12 months	= 1 common year
366 days	= 1 leap year
100 years	= 1 century

Common Units

12 units	= 1 dozen (doz.)
12 dozen	= 1 gross (gr.)
144 units	= 1 gross
12 gross	= 1 great gross
20 units	= 1 score

Paper Measure

24 sheets	= 1 quire
20 quires	= 1 ream (480 sheets)
500 sheets	= 1 ream (commercial)
2 reams	= 1 bundle
5 bundles	= 1 bale

CIRCULAR MEASURES

Circular or *angular measures* are used in surveying, navigation, astronomy, geography, reckoning latitude and longitude, and computing differences in time.

A *circle* is a plane figure bounded by a curved line, every point of which is equally distant from a point within, called the center.

The *circumference* is the bounding line of a circle.

The *radius* of a circle is a straight line drawn from the circumference to the center.

The *diameter* is a straight line drawn through the center, with the ends terminating in the circumference.

An *arc* of a circle is any portion of the circumference.

An *angle* is the difference in direction between two straight lines which meet.

If two diameters divide a circle into four equal parts, these diameters make *right angles* with each other.

An angle less than a right angle is an *acute angle*.

The circumference of a circle may be divided into 360 equal parts, called *degrees*. If the circle is large, the degree is large, and if the circle is small, the degree is small; but the degree is always 1/360 part of the circumference, whatever the size of the circle.

An angle at the center of a circle is measured by the arc which bounds it.

If the angle is a right angle, it is measured by ¼ of 360 degrees, or 90 degrees; hence, any angle of 90 degrees is a right angle.

An acute angle is always less than 90 degrees.

An obtuse angle is always more than 90 degrees.

Table of Circular Measure

60 seconds (″)	= 1 minute (′)
60 minutes	= 1 degree (°)
360 degrees	= 1 circumference (cir.)

Circumference		Degrees		Minutes		Seconds
1	=	360	=	21,600	=	1,296,000

A *quadrant* is ¼ of a circumference, or 90°; a *sextant* is ⅙ of a circumference, or 60°.

The length of a degree of longitude on the earth's surface at the Equator is 69.16 miles.

In astronomical calculation, 30° are called a *sign*, and there are, therefore, 12 signs in a circle.

THE METRIC SYSTEM OF WEIGHTS AND MEASURES

Measures of length

Metric Denominations and Values	Equivalents in Denominations in Use
Megameter . . . 1,000,000 meters	
Myriameter . . . . . 10,000 meters	. . . . . .6.2137 miles
Kilometer . . . . 1,000 meters	. . . . . .0.62137 mile, or 3,280 feet and 10 inches
Hectometer . . . . 100 meters	. . . . . .328 feet and 1 inch
Dekameter. . . . . .10 meters	. . . . . .393.7 inches
Meter. . . . . .1 meter	. . . . . . .39.37 inches
Decimeter. . . . . . 1/10 of a meter	. . . . .3.937 inches
Centimeter. . . . 1/100 of a meter	. . . . 0.3937 inch
Millimeter. . . . 1/1000 of a meter	. . . . .0.0394 inch
Micron. . . 1/1,000,000 of a meter	

MEASURES OF SURFACE

Metric Denominations and Values	Equivalents in Denominations in Use
Hectare . . 10,000 square meters	. . . . 2.471 acres
Are. . . . . 100 square meters	. . . . .119.6 square yds.
Centare . . . . . . .1 square meter	. . . . .1,550 square inches

MEASURES OF CAPACITY

Metric Denominations and Values			Equivalents in Denominations in Use	
Names	No. of liters	Cubic Measure	Dry Measure	Liquid or Wine Measure
Kiloliter or Stere . . .	1,000	1 cubic meter	1.308 cubic yards. . . .	264.17 gallons
Hectoliter. .	100	1/10 of a cubic meter	2 bu. and 3.35 pks.	26.417 gallons
Dekaliter . .	10	10 cubic decimeters . .	9.08 quarts	2.6417 gallons
Liter	1	1 cubic decimeter	0.908 quart.	1.0567 quarts
Deciliter . .	1/10	1/10 of a cubic decimeter	6.1022 cubic inches . . .	0.845 gill
Centiliter . .	1/100	10 cubic centimeters .	0.6102 cubic inch	0.338 fluid oz.
Milliliter. . .	1/1000	1 cubic centimeter . .	0.061 cubic inch	0.27 fluid dram

WEIGHTS

Metric Denominations and Values			Equivalents in Denominations in Use
Names	Number of grams	Weight of what quantity of water at maximum density	Avoirdupois Weight
Millier or Ton	1,000,000	1 cubic meter	2,204.6 pounds
Quintal	100,000	1 hectoliter	220.46 pounds
Myriagram	10,000	10 liters	22.046 pounds
Kilogram or Kilo	1,000	1 liter	2.2046 pounds
Hectogram	100	1 deciliter	3.5274 ounces
Dekagram	10	10 cubic centimeters	0.3527 ounce
Gram	1	1 cubic centimeter	15.432 grains
Decigram	1/10	1/10 of a cubic centimeter	1.5432 grains
Centigram	1/100	10 cubic millimeters	0.1543 grain
Milligram	1/1000	1 cubic millimeter	0.0154 grain
Microgram	1/1,000,000		

EQUIVALENTS, ENGLISH AND METRIC

Linear Measure

One inch is 25.4 millimeters, 2.54 centimeters, .0254 meter.
One foot is 30.48 centimeters, .3048 meter.
One yard is 91.44 centimeters, .9144 meter.
One mile is 1609.3472 meters, 1.609347 kilometers.

One millimeter is .03937 inch.
One meter is 3.28083 feet, 1.093611 yards.
One kilometer is .62137 mile.

Square Measure

One square inch is 6.452 square centimeters.
One square foot is .0929 square meter.
One square yard is .8361 square meter.
One acre is .4047 hectare.
One square mile is 2.59 square kilometers.

One square centimeter is .155 square inch.
One square meter is 10.764 square feet, 1.196 square yards.
One hectare is 2.471 acres.
One square kilometer is .3861 square mile.

Cubic Measure

One cubic inch is 16.3872 cubic centimeters.
One cubic foot is .028317 cubic meter.
One cubic yard is .7646 cubic meter.

One cubic centimeter is .06102 cubic inch.
One cubic meter is 35.314 cubic feet, 1.3079 cubic yards.

Equivalent Measures of Volume and Capacity

In the metric system, the liter is the unit measure of volume. It equals a cubic decimeter, with an almost infinitesimal decimal deviation. Precisely, it is one and twenty-seven millionths cubic decimeter.
One cubic inch, dry measure, is .016386 liter.
One cubic foot, dry measure, is 28.316 liters.

One liter, dry measure, is 61.025 cubic inches.
One liter, dry measure, is .035315 cubic foot.
One U. S. liquid pint is .47317 liter.
One liquid U. S. quart is .94633 liter.
One liquid U. S. gallon is 3.78533 liters.

One liter, liquid measure, is 2.1134 pints, 1.05671 quarts, .26418 gallons.
One quart, dry measure, is 1.1012 liters.
One peck is 8.81 liters, .881 dekaliter.
One bushel is 35.2883 liters, 3.52383 dekaliters, .35238 hectoliter.
One bushel per acre is .8708 hectoliters per hectare.
One liter, dry measure, is .9081 quart, .11351 peck.
One dekaliter, dry measure, is 1.1351 pecks.
One hectoliter, dry measure, is 2.8378 bushels.
One hectoliter per hectare is 1.1484 bushels per acre.
One fluid ounce is 29.5729 milliliters, .0297 liter.
One gill is 118.292 milliliters, .118292 liter.
One pint is 473.167 milliliters, .473167 liter.
One quart is 946.333 milliliters, .946333 liter.
One gallon is 3785.332 milliliters, 3.785332 liters, 231 cubic inches.

Weights

One ounce troy weight is 31.103 grams.
One ounce avoirdupois is 28.35 grams.
One pound avoirdupois is .45359 kilogram.

One gram is .032151 troy ounce, .035274 avoirdupois ounce.
One kilogram is 2.20462 avoirdupois pounds.
One short ton, 2,000 pounds avoirdupois, is 907.18486 kilograms, .90718486 metric ton.
One long ton, 2,240 pounds avoirdupois, is 1016.04704 kilograms, 1.01604704 metric tons.

ROMAN NUMERALS

I	1	XXX	30
II	2	XL	40
III	3	L	50
IV	4	LX	60
V	5	LXX	70
VI	6	LXXX or XXC	80
VII	7	XC	90
VIII	8	C	100
IX	9	CC	200
X	10	CCC	300
XI	11	CCCC	400
XII	12	D	500
XIII	13	DC	600
XIV	14	DCC	700
XV	15	DCCC	800
XVI	16	CM	900
XVII	17	M or clc	1000
XVIII	18	MM	2000
XIX	19		
XX	20		

Note.—A dash line over a numeral multiplies the value by 1,000: thus, $\overline{X}$ = 10,000; $\overline{L}$ = 50,000; $\overline{C}$ = 100,000; $\overline{D}$ = 500,000; $\overline{M}$ = 1,000,000: $\overline{CLIX}$ = 159,000; $\overline{DLIX}$ = 559,000.

Other general rules in Roman numerals are as follows: (1) repeating a letter repeats its value—XX = 20; CCC = 300; (2) a letter placed after one of greater value adds thereto—VI = 6; DC = 600; (3) a letter placed before one of greater value subtracts therefrom—IV = 4.

Arabic numerals are those now commonly in use—0, 1, 2, 3, 4, 5, 6, 7, 8, 9, etc.

USEFUL VALUES

To find the diameter of a circle, multiply the circumference by .31831.

To find the circumference of a circle, multiply the diameter by 3.1416.

To find the area of a circle, multiply the square of the diameter by .7854.

To find the surface of a ball, multiply the square of the diameter by 3.1416.

RAPID TABLE OF MULTIPLICATION AND DIVISION

A figure in the top line (19) multiplied by a figure in the last column on the left (18) produces the figure where the top line and the side line meet (342), and so on.

A figure in the table (342) divided by the figure at the top of that column (19) results in the figure (18) at the extreme left; also, a figure in the table (342) divided by the figure (18) at the extreme left gives the figure (19) at the top of the column, and so on.

1	**2**	**3**	**4**	**5**	**6**	**7**	**8**	**9**	**10**	**11**	**12**	**13**	**14**	**15**	**16**	**17**	**18**	**19**	**20**	**21**	**22**	**23**	**24**	**25**	**1**
2	**4**	6	8	10	12	14	16	18	20	22	24	26	28	30	32	34	36	38	40	42	44	46	48	50	**2**
3	6	**9**	12	15	18	21	24	27	30	33	36	39	42	45	48	51	54	57	60	63	66	69	72	75	**3**
4	8	12	**16**	20	24	28	32	36	40	44	48	52	56	60	64	68	72	76	80	84	88	92	96	100	**4**
5	10	15	20	**25**	30	35	40	45	50	55	60	65	70	75	80	85	90	95	100	105	110	115	120	125	**5**
6	12	18	24	30	**36**	42	48	54	60	66	72	78	84	90	96	102	108	114	120	126	132	138	144	150	**6**
7	14	21	28	35	42	**49**	56	63	70	77	84	91	98	105	112	119	126	133	140	147	154	161	168	175	**7**
8	16	24	32	40	48	56	**64**	72	80	88	96	104	112	120	128	136	144	152	160	168	176	184	192	200	**8**
9	18	27	36	45	54	63	72	**81**	90	99	108	117	126	135	144	153	162	171	180	189	198	207	216	225	**9**
10	20	30	40	50	60	70	80	90	**100**	110	120	130	140	150	160	170	180	190	200	210	220	230	240	250	**10**
11	22	33	44	55	66	77	88	99	110	**121**	132	143	154	165	176	187	198	209	220	231	242	253	264	275	**11**
12	24	36	48	60	72	84	96	108	120	132	**144**	156	168	180	192	204	216	228	240	252	264	276	288	300	**12**
13	26	39	52	65	78	91	104	117	130	143	156	**169**	182	195	208	221	234	247	260	273	286	299	312	325	**13**
14	28	42	56	70	84	98	112	126	140	154	168	182	**196**	210	224	238	252	266	280	294	308	322	336	350	**14**
15	30	45	60	75	90	105	120	135	150	165	180	195	210	**225**	240	255	270	285	300	315	330	345	360	375	**15**
16	32	48	64	80	96	112	128	144	160	176	192	208	224	240	**256**	272	288	304	320	336	352	368	384	400	**16**
17	34	51	68	85	102	119	136	153	170	187	204	221	238	255	272	**289**	306	323	340	357	374	391	408	425	**17**
18	36	54	72	90	108	126	144	162	180	198	216	234	252	270	288	306	**324**	342	360	378	396	414	432	450	**18**
19	38	57	76	95	114	133	152	171	190	209	228	247	266	285	304	323	342	**361**	380	399	418	437	456	475	**19**
20	40	60	80	100	120	140	160	180	200	220	240	260	280	300	320	340	360	380	**400**	420	440	460	480	500	**20**
21	42	63	84	105	126	147	168	189	210	231	252	273	294	315	336	357	378	399	420	**441**	462	483	504	525	**21**
22	44	66	88	110	132	154	176	198	220	242	264	286	308	330	352	374	396	418	440	462	**484**	506	528	550	**22**
23	46	69	92	115	138	161	184	207	230	253	276	299	322	345	368	391	414	437	460	483	506	**529**	552	575	**23**
24	48	72	96	120	144	168	192	216	240	264	288	312	336	360	384	408	432	456	480	504	528	552	**576**	600	**24**
25	50	75	100	125	150	175	200	225	250	275	300	325	350	375	400	425	450	475	500	525	550	575	600	**625**	**25**
	2	**3**	**4**	**5**	**6**	**7**	**8**	**9**	**10**	**11**	**12**	**13**	**14**	**15**	**16**	**17**	**18**	**19**	**20**	**21**	**22**	**23**	**24**	**25**	

To find the side of an equal square, multiply the diameter by .8862.

To find the cubic inches in a ball, multiply the diameter by .5236.

Doubling the diameter of a pipe increases its capacity four times.

One cubic foot of anthracite coal weighs about 53 pounds.

One cubic foot of bituminous coal weighs 47 to 50 pounds.

One ton of coal is equivalent to two cords of wood for steam purposes.

A gallon of water (U. S. standard) weighs 8⅓ pounds and contains 231 cubic inches.

A cubic foot of water contains 7½ gallons, 1728 cubic inches, and weighs about 62½ pounds.

A horsepower is equivalent to raising 33,000 pounds one foot per minute, or 550 pounds one foot per second.

To find the pressure in pounds per square foot of water, multiply the height of column in feet by .434.

Steam rising from water at its boiling point (212 degrees) has a pressure equal to the atmosphere (14.7 pounds to the square inch).

To evaporate one cubic foot of water requires the consumption of 7½ pounds of ordinary coal or about 1 pound of coal to 1 gallon of water.

SQUARE ROOT AND CUBE ROOT

Powers and Roots.—When a product consists of the same factor repeated any number of times, it is called a *power* of that factor.

$49 = 7 \times 7$ is the second power, or the *square* of 7.
$343 = 7 \times 7 \times 7$ is the third power, or the *cube* of 7.

A power of a number is generally expressed by writing the number only once, and placing after it, above the line, a small figure to show how many factors are to be taken. The small figure is called an *index*.

Thus, $7^2 = 49$; $7^3 = 343$; $7^4 = 2401$.

A number is called the *square root* of its square.

Since $7^2 = 49$, the square root of 49 is 7.

The square root of 49 is written $\sqrt{49}$.

Again, a number is called the *cube root* of its cube. $7^3 = 343$. Therefore, the cube root of 343 is 7.

The cube root of 343 is written $\sqrt[3]{343}$.

A *perfect square* is a number whose square root is a whole number. A *perfect cube* is a number whose cube root is a whole number.

Square Root.—If a number can be put into prime factors its square root can be written down by inspection.

Example: Find the square root of 27225.
Since $27225 = 3^2 \times 5^2 \times 11^2$.
$\therefore \sqrt{27225} = 3 \times 5 \times 11 = 165$ *Ans.*

Rule for Digits.—We know that $\sqrt{1} = 1$, and $\sqrt{100} = 10$. Therefore, the square root of any number which lies between 1 and 100 lies between 1 and 10; *i. e.*, if a number contains one or two digits, its square root consists of one digit.

Similarly, since $\sqrt{100} = 10$ and $\sqrt{10000} = 100$, the square root of a number between 100 and 10000 lies between 10 and 100. That is, if a number contains three or four digits, its square root consists of two digits.

Proceeding in this way, we obtain a general result—viz., the square of a number has either twice as many digits as the number, or one less than twice as many.

Hence, to ascertain the number of digits in the square root of a perfect square, mark off the digits in pairs, beginning from the right. Each pair marked off gives a digit in the square root; and, if there is an odd digit remaining, that digit also gives a digit in the square root.

Examples: There are three digits in the square root of 546121, and four in the square root of 5774409.

For, marking off the digits from the right, we get in the first case 54.61.21, giving three digits in the square root, and in the second case 5.77.44.09, the odd digit giving the fourth in the square root.

The method of finding the square root of a given number depends on the *form* of the square of the sum of two numbers.

EXPLANATION: The square root of 144 is 12. Let us see how we found it.

$12 = 1$ ten $+ 2$ units.
12^2 is the same as $(10 + 2)^2$.

Let us square $(10 + 2)$, that is, multiply $10 + 2$ by $10 + 2$.

$$\begin{array}{l} 10 + 2 \\ 10 + 2 \\ \hline 10^2 + (10 \times 2) \\ \quad + (10 \times 2) + 2^2 \\ \hline 10^2 + 2\,(10 \times 2) + 2^2 \end{array}$$

Then, $12^2 = 10^2 + 2\,(10 \times 2) + 2^2$

RULE.—*The square of any number made up of tens and units is equal to the square of the tens, plus twice the product of the tens by the units, plus the square of the units.*

ANOTHER EXPLANATION: Find the square root of 45369.

SOLUTION:

$$\begin{array}{r|l} \multicolumn{2}{l}{\sqrt{4.53.69} = 213} \\ & 4 \\ \hline 41 & 53 \\ & 41 \\ \hline 423 & 1269 \\ & 1269 \end{array}$$

(1) Point off the number into periods of two figures each, as before.

(2) The square root of the first period is 2. $2 \times 2 = 4$. Write the 2 in the root and subtract the 4 from 4. Bring down the next period, 53.

(3) $2 \times 2 = 4$. (Remember the 4 is to be used as a trial divisor, being $2 \times$ the *tens*.)

4 is contained in 5 about 1 time.

Place 1 in the root, also on the right of the 4 in the divisor. Multiply 41 by 1. Subtract and bring down the next period.

(4) $2 \times 21 = 42$. 42 is the *trial divisor*. $126 \div 42 =$ *about* 3 times. Place the 3 in the root also at the right of the 42 in the divisor. Multiply out.
Square root $= 213$.

CUBE ROOT.—The *cube root* of a number is one of the three equal factors of that number.

Thus, 5 is the cube root of 125, because $5 \times 5 \times 5 = 125$.

The *radical sign* with a figure 3 over it ($\sqrt[3]{\quad}$) means that the cube root of the number following it is to be taken.

The cube root of 125 is written $\sqrt[3]{125}$.

If we can find the prime factors of any perfect cube, we can write down its cube root by inspection.

EXAMPLE: Find the cube root of 74088.

$$\begin{array}{r|r} 8 & 74088 \\ 9 & 9261 \\ 3 & 1029 \\ 7 & 343 \\ 7 & 49 \\ & 7 \end{array}$$

$\therefore 74088 = 8 \times 9 \times 3 \times 7 \times 7 \times 7$
$= 2^3 \times 3^3 \times 7^3$
$\therefore \sqrt[3]{74088} = 2 \times 3 \times 7$
$= 42$ *Ans.*

RULE FOR DIGITS.—Since $1^3 = 1$ and $10^3 = 1000$, therefore the cube of a number which lies between 1 and 10 lies between 1 and 1000, *i.e.*, the cube of a number of one digit contains either one, two or three digits.

Again, since $10^3 = 1000$ and $100^3 = 1{,}000{,}000$, the cube of a number of two digits contains either four, five, or six digits.

Proceeding in this way, we see that the cube of a number contains three times, or one less or two less than three times, as many digits as the number.

Hence, to find the number of digits in the cube root of a given number, we mark off the digits in sets of three, beginning at the decimal point, and marking both to the right and to the left.

Thus, 289383 will be pointed off into two periods or groups of figures—289.383—and we readily see there will be only 2 figures in the root.

The simplest method of finding the cube root of numbers whose prime factors are not known is analogous to the method of finding square root, being based upon the form of the cube of the sum of two numbers.

EXPLANATION: The cube root of 1728 is 12. Let us see how we found it.

$12 = 1$ ten $+ 2$ units
$12^3 = (10 + 2)^3$
$(10 + 2)^3$ means $10 + 2 \times 10 + 2 \times 10 + 2$

$$\begin{array}{l} 10 + 2 \\ 10 + 2 \\ \hline 10^2 + (10 \times 2) \\ \quad + (10 \times 2) + 2^2 \\ \hline 10^2 + 2\,(10 \times 2) + 2^2 \\ 10 + 2 \\ \hline 10^3 + 2\,(10^2 \times 2) + (10 \times 2^2) \\ \quad (10^2 \times 2) + 2\,(10 \times 2^2) + 2^3 \\ \hline 10^3 + 3\,(10^2 \times 2) + 3\,(10 \times 2^2) + 2^3 \end{array}$$

That is, the cube of any number made up of tens and units equals—

The cube of the tens + three times the product of the square of the tens by the units + three times the product of the tens by the units + the cube of the units, or tens^3 + 3 (tens^2 × units) + 3 (tens × units^2) + units.^{3}

After the process is understood, this short method of writing the work may be used by the pupil:

EXAMPLE: Find the cube root of .0163956, carrying the root to 3 decimal places.

WORK:

$$\begin{array}{r|l} \multicolumn{2}{l}{\sqrt[3]{.016.395.600} = .254 +} \\ & 8 \\ \hline 1200 & 8395 \\ 300 & \\ 25 & \\ \hline 1525 & 7625 \\ & \overline{770600} \\ 187500 & \\ 3000 & \\ 16 & \\ \hline 190516 & 762064 \\ & \overline{8536} \end{array}$$

PERCENTAGE

The expression *per cent*, which is an abbreviation of the Latin words *per centum*, means "for each hundred."

The symbol % is often used to denote "per cent." Thus, 7 per cent, or 7%, means 7 parts out of every 100 parts, *i. e.*, 7/100 of the whole.

Since per cent means hundredths, we may write any fraction whose denominator is 100 as so many per cent. In some cases, the corresponding common fractions are so simple that it is advisable to remember them. For example:

$$25\% = \frac{25}{100} = \frac{1}{4}, \qquad 50\% = \frac{50}{100} = \frac{1}{2},$$

$$75\% = \frac{75}{100} = \frac{3}{4}, \qquad 33\tfrac{1}{3}\% = \frac{33\frac{1}{3}}{100} = \frac{1}{3},$$

$$66\tfrac{2}{3}\% = \frac{66\frac{2}{3}}{100} = \frac{2}{3}, \qquad 5\% = \frac{5}{100} = \frac{1}{20},$$

$$2\tfrac{1}{2}\% = \frac{2\frac{1}{2}}{100} = \frac{1}{40}, \qquad 12\tfrac{1}{2}\% = \frac{12\frac{1}{2}}{100} = \frac{1}{8},$$

and so on.

TABLE OF ADDITIONAL VALUES

PER CENT		DECIMAL		100THS		COMMON FRACTION
1%	=	.01	=	1/100		
2%	=	.02	=	2/100	=	1/50
3%	=	.03	=	3/100		
4%	=	.04	=	4/100	=	1/25
5%	=	.05	=	5/100	=	1/20
6%	=	.06	=	6/100	=	3/50
7%	=	.07	=	7/100		
8%	=	.08	=	8/100	=	2/25
9%	=	.09	=	9/100		
10%	=	.10	=	10/100	=	1/10
20%	=	.20	=	20/100	=	1/5
25%	=	.25	=	25/100	=	1/4
50%	=	.50	=	50/100	=	1/2
100%	=	1.00	=	100/100	=	1

Here are a few others that should be learned:

$6\frac{2}{3}\% = \frac{1}{15}$ of 100% $16\frac{2}{3}\% = \frac{1}{6}$ of 100%
$8\frac{1}{3}\% = \frac{1}{12}$ of 100% $33\frac{1}{3}\% = \frac{1}{3}$ of 100%
$12\frac{1}{2}\% = \frac{1}{8}$ of 100% $66\frac{2}{3}\% = \frac{2}{3}$ of 100%

A Decimal as Per Cent

Write the decimal as hundredths, and the number expressing the number of hundredths is the per cent.

EXAMPLES:

$$.4 = .40 = \frac{40}{100} = 40\%$$

$$.8 = .80 = \frac{80}{100} = 80\%$$

$$.25 = \frac{25}{100} = 25\%$$

$$.33\tfrac{1}{3} = \frac{33\frac{1}{3}}{100} = 33\tfrac{1}{3}\%$$

$$.50 = \frac{50}{100} = 50\%$$

$$.87\tfrac{1}{2} = \frac{87\frac{1}{2}}{100} = 87\tfrac{1}{2}\%$$

If the decimal has more than two decimal places, the figures after the second one are written as a fraction of a per cent, as:

$$.255 = \frac{25\frac{1}{2}}{100} = 25\tfrac{1}{2}\%$$

$$.163 = \frac{16\frac{3}{10}}{100} = 16\tfrac{3}{10}\%.$$

To change a common fraction to per cent:

1. *Change the fraction to a decimal.*
2. *Express the decimal as hundredths.*
3. *The result is the per cent desired.*

EXAMPLES:

$\frac{1}{2} = .5 = .50 = 50\%$
$\frac{3}{4} = .75 = 75\%$
$\frac{2}{3} = .66\frac{2}{3} = 66\frac{2}{3}\%$
$\frac{9}{10} = .90 = 90\%$
$\frac{8}{9} = .88\frac{8}{9} = 88\frac{8}{9}\%$
$\frac{7}{8} = .87\frac{1}{2} = 87\frac{1}{2}\%$
$\frac{25}{26} = .96\frac{2}{13} = 96\frac{2}{13}\%$

Or they may be written this way:

$$\tfrac{3}{4} = \tfrac{3}{4} \text{ of } \frac{100}{100} = \frac{75}{100} = 75\%$$

$$\tfrac{2}{3} = \tfrac{2}{3} \text{ of } \frac{100}{100} = \frac{66\frac{2}{3}}{100} = 66\tfrac{2}{3}\%$$

$$\tfrac{1}{2} = \tfrac{1}{2} \text{ of } \frac{100}{100} = \frac{50}{100} = 50\%$$

Terms Used in Percentage

In percentage, there are five terms or quantities considered; namely, the base, rate per cent, percentage, amount and proceeds, or difference; any two being given, a third one may be found.

The base and rate given, to find the percentage:

RULE.—*Multiply the base by the rate per cent expressed decimally.*

EXAMPLE: How many dollars is 6% of $50?

$50, the *base*, or number on which percentage is computed.
.06, the *rate*, or term denoting number of hundredths taken.
$3.00, the *percentage*, or the product of the base and rate per cent.
$53.00, the *amount*, or the base increased by the percentage.
$47.00, the *proceeds*, or *difference*, the base less the percentage.
Ans. $3.00.

When the rate per cent is an aliquot part of 100, the percentage is readily found by taking such a part of the base as the rate per cent is part of 100. Thus, at 10%, take $\frac{1}{10}$ of base; at $12\frac{1}{2}\%$, $\frac{1}{8}$; at $16\frac{2}{3}\%$, $\frac{1}{6}$; etc.

The base and percentage given, to find the rate:

RULE.—*Divide the percentage by 1% of the base.*

EXAMPLE: Bought a watch for $15 and sold it for $18; what per cent did I make?

.15)3.00
20
Ans. 20%

Here $15 is the base, and ($18 − $15) = $3.00, the gain or percentage. Now, as 1% of 15.00 is .15, it is evident that 3.00 is as many per cent of 15.00, as the number of times .15 is contained in 3.00, which is 20.

Proof: 20% or $\frac{1}{5}$ of $15 = $3.

The percentage and rate given, to find the base:

RULE.—*Divide the percentage by the rate per cent expressed decimally.*

EXAMPLE: Received $6.40, percentage or interest, for money loaned at 4%, what was the base or principal?

.04)6.40
Ans. $160

If $1 produces .04 (4 cents) in a certain time, $6.40 must be the percentage of as many dollars as .04 is contained times in $6.40, which is 160.

Proof: 4% of $160 (160 × .04) = $6.40.

The amount and rate given, to find the base:

RULE.—*Divide the given amount by 1.00 plus the rate per cent.*

EXAMPLE: Bought a horse at a certain price, and sold him for $84, making 12% on cost; what did he cost?

1.12)84.00
Ans. $75

If I made 12% on cost, every dollar invested gained 12 cents; hence, the horse cost as many dollars as 1.12 is contained times in 84.00, which is 75.

Proof: 12% of $75 (75 × .12) = $9; $75 + $9 = $84.

The proceeds and the rate given, to find the base:

RULE.—*Divide the given proceeds by 1.00 minus the rate per cent.*

EXAMPLE: Sold a wagon for $51, which is 40% less than it cost; what did it cost?

.60)51.00
Ans. $85

If I lost 40%, or 40 cents on the dollar, I received only 60 cents for every dollar the wagon cost; hence, it cost as many dollars as .60 is contained times in 51.00, which is 85.

Proof: 40% of $85 (85 × .40) = $34; $85 − $34 = $51.

NOTE.—The principles of percentage, in one form or another, enter into nearly all commercial calculations, besides many others. It is, therefore, of the utmost importance to businessmen, clerks, accountants, bookkeepers, and others to become expert in percentage, and to adopt the easiest, simplest, and shortest methods in computing interest, partial payments, trade discount, profit and loss, commission, insurance, stocks, bonds, taxes, exchange, etc.

PROFIT AND LOSS

When a thing is sold for more than it cost the seller, it is said to be sold at a *profit*. If it is sold for less than the cost, it is sold at a *loss*. Hence,

Profit = Selling Price − Cost Price.
Loss = Cost Price − Selling Price.

A profit or loss is generally reckoned as a percentage.

It is always understood that the percentage is reckoned on the cost price.

EXAMPLE: I buy wheat at 60 cents and sell it for 75 cents. What per cent do I gain?

SOLUTION: I gain the difference between 75 cents and 60 cents, or 15 cents. 15 cents is 25% of the cost. Hence, I gain 25%.

WORK:

75 cents − 60 cents = 15 cents.
15 cents ÷ 60 cents = .25, or 25%.

EXAMPLE: I bought flour at $3.50 per barrel. For what must I sell it to gain 20%?

SOLUTION: I must sell it for 100% of the cost plus 20% of the cost, or 120% of the cost.

120% of $3.50 = $4.20.
∴ I must sell it at $4.20.

EXAMPLE: I sold my radio for 80% of its cost and received $90 for it. What was the cost?

SOLUTION:

1% of the cost is $\frac{1}{80}$ of $90, or $1.125.
100% of the cost = 100 × $1.125, or $112.50.

COMMISSION

Commission is a percentage paid for buying or selling real estate, goods, etc. A consignment is a quantity of goods sent to an agent, broker, or commission merchant, for sale. The consignor is the one who sends the goods, the consignee the one to whom they are sent.

PRINCIPLES:

1. *The commission is some number or per cent of the price of what is bought or sold.*
2. *The proceeds equal the selling price minus the commission.*
3. *The amount equals the selling price plus the commission.*

Commission presents two classes of problems. One of these classes may be called *buying problems.* The other may be called *selling problems.*

BUYING PROBLEMS: I sent my agent $1977.60 to *buy* wild farm lands in northern Wisconsin, at $3 per acre. He was to receive 3% for his work. How many acres did he buy?

WORK AND EXPLANATION:

3% of $3 = $.09.
Cost to me of 1 acre is $3 + $.09 = $3.09

For $1977.60 he buys as many acres as $3.09 is contained times in $1977.60, or 640. Hence, he buys 640 acres.

SELLING PROBLEM: My agent *sells* 360 pounds of coffee for me at 20 cents. He pays $4.20 freight charges and $9.60 for storage. His commission is 5%. What does he send me?

WORK AND EXPLANATION:

360 pounds at 20 cents = $72.00
Freight is $4.20
Storage is 9.60
Commission is 5% of $72, or 3.60
Total charges = 17.40
He sends me the difference, or $54.60

TRADE DISCOUNT

Trade discount is an allowance made by manufacturers and jobbers from their list or marking prices. When the market varies, they change the discount accordingly, or make several discounts instead of changing the list.

Trade discount is a certain per cent off from the list or marking price; while profit and loss is computed on the cost or purchase price.

The amount of the discount allowed depends sometimes upon the amount of order, and sometimes upon the terms of settlement. Very often two or more discounts are deducted in succession. Thus, 10% and 5% off; or, as it is generally expressed in business, 10 and 5 off, means a discount of 10%, and then 5% from what is left; 20, 10, and 5 off, means three successive discounts. A retailer's profit is smaller when he is allowed 10 and 5 off, than if he were allowed 15 off. The result is not affected by the order in which the discounts are taken.

EXAMPLE: I receive a bill of goods amounting to $100, 20% off. What is the net cost?

FIRST WAY:

20% of $100 = $20
$100 − $20 = $80

SECOND WAY:

100% − 20% = 80%
80% of $100 = $80

EXAMPLE: A merchant receives two bills of $200 each. On one there is a discount of 25%; on the other, 15% and 10%. What must he pay on each, net?

FIRST BILL:

100% − 25% = 75%,
or ¾
¾ of $200 = $150.

SECOND BILL:

100% − 15% = 85%
100% − 10% = 90%
90% of 85% = 76.5%
.765 × $200 = $153.

BANK DISCOUNT

The sum charged by a bank for cashing a note or time draft is called *bank discount.* This discount is the simple interest, paid in advance, for the number of days the note has to run. Wholesale business houses usually sell goods on credit and take notes from the retailers in payment. These notes are not often for a longer period than three months. Some are placed in the banks for collection, others are *discounted.* When a note is discounted at a bank, the payee *endorses* it, making it payable to the bank. Both maker and payee are then responsible to the bank for its payment. If the note is drawing interest, the discount is reckoned on and deducted from the amount due at maturity. The *time* in bank discount is always the number of days from the date of discounting to the date of maturity.

EXAMPLE: A note of $600, dated June 20, payable in three months, is discounted June 20 at 6%; find the proceeds.

EXPLANATION: This note is due in 92 days, or September 20 (see next section, *Interest*, including table for finding number of days). The interest of $600 for 92 days at 6% is $9.20. The proceeds, then, will be $600 − $9.20, or $590.80.

The *present worth* of a note or debt is a sum, which, if put at interest, will amount to that debt in the given time.

The *true discount* is the difference between the debt at maturity and its present worth.

REMEMBER: *To add the interest due at maturity to the principal, before discounting, if the note bears interest.*

EXAMPLES: Case I.—Note not bearing interest.

What are the present worth and true discount on a note of $200, if paid 6 months before due, the discount being 6%?

SOLUTION: Amount of $1 for 6 months at 6% = $1.03. If $1.03 = amount of $1, $200 is the amount of as many dollars as 200/1.03, or $194.17+.

$194.17 is the present worth. $200 − $194.17 = $5.83 true discount.

The following rule can be deduced from the foregoing solution:

RULE: 1. *To find the present worth, divide the debt by the amount of $1 for the given time.*

2. *To find the true discount, subtract the present worth from the debt.*

Case II.—Note bearing interest.

What is the present worth of a note of $300, bearing 6% interest, due in 2 years 4 months, if money is worth 10%?

SOLUTION: Interest on $300 for 2 years 4 months at 6% = $42.
$300 + $42 = $342. Amount due at maturity.
Amount of $1 for 2 years 4 months at 10% = $1.23⅓.
If $1.23⅓ = amount of $1, then $3.42 is the amount
of $\$\frac{342}{1.23\frac{1}{3}}$, or $277.29.
$277.29 = present worth.

INTEREST

If a person borrows money, he usually pays something for the loan.

The sum of money he borrows is called the *principal;* the money he pays for the use of the principal is called *interest.* Interest is generally reckoned at so much for the use of each $100 for one year. This amount is called the *rate per cent per annum.*

Thus, if we say that $200 is borrowed for three years at 4 per cent per annum, we mean that the borrower, at the end of each year, pays the lender $4 for each $100 borrowed—*i. e.*, $8 interest for each year.

In the above example, the interest is supposed to be paid to the lender at the end of each year. Interest thus reckoned is called *simple interest.*

The sum obtained by adding the interest for any given time to the principal is called the *amount* in that time.

COMMON INTEREST METHODS

If we were to find the interest on a sum of money for 3 years 4 months 5 days, we would find the interest for 1 year, then for 1 month (1⁄12 of a year), then for 1 day (1⁄360 of a year). Having the interest for 1 year 1 month 1 day, it is a simple matter of multiplication to get it for 3 years 4 months 5 days.

EXAMPLE:

What is the interest on $520 for 1 year 3 months at 6%?

WORK:

1 year 3 months = 1¼ year
$520 principal
.06
4)$31.20 interest 1 year
$7.80 interest ¼ year
$39.00 interest 1¼ year

TABLE OF SIMPLE INTEREST

Principal	Time	4%	5%	6%	7%	8%
$100.00	1 day	.011	.013	.017	.019	.022
$100.00	2 days	.022	.028	.033	.039	.044
$100.00	3 days	.033	.042	.050	.058	.067
$100.00	4 days	.044	.056	.067	.078	.089
$100.00	5 days	.056	.069	.083	.097	.111
$100.00	6 days	.067	.083	.100	.117	.133
$100.00	7 days	.078	.097	.117	.136	.156
$100.00	8 days	.089	.111	.133	.156	.178
$100.00	9 days	.100	.125	.150	.175	.200
$100.00	10 days	.111	.139	.167	.194	.222
$100.00	11 days	.122	.153	.183	.214	.244
$100.00	12 days	.133	.167	.200	.233	.267
$100.00	13 days	.144	.181	.217	.253	.289
$100.00	14 days	.156	.194	.233	.272	.311
$100.00	15 days	.167	.208	.250	.292	.333
$100.00	16 days	.178	.222	.267	.311	.356
$100.00	17 days	.189	.236	.283	.331	.378
$100.00	18 days	.200	.250	.300	.350	.400
$100.00	19 days	.211	.264	.317	.369	.422
$100.00	20 days	.222	.278	.333	.389	.444
$100.00	21 days	.233	.292	.350	.408	.467
$100.00	22 days	.244	.306	.367	.428	.489
$100.00	23 days	.256	.319	.383	.447	.511
$100.00	24 days	.267	.333	.400	.467	.533
$100.00	25 days	.278	.347	.417	.486	.556
$100.00	26 days	.289	.361	.433	.506	.578
$100.00	27 days	.300	.375	.450	.525	.600
$100.00	28 days	.311	.389	.467	.544	.622
$100.00	29 days	.322	.403	.483	.564	.644
$100.00	30 days	.333	.417	.500	.583	.667
$100.00	1 month	.333	.417	.500	.583	.667
$100.00	2 months	.667	.833	1.000	1.167	1.333
$100.00	3 months	1.000	1.250	1.500	1.750	2.000
$100.00	4 months	1.333	1.667	2.000	2.333	2.667
$100.00	5 months	1.667	2.083	2.500	2.917	3.333
$100.00	6 months	2.000	2.500	3.000	3.500	4.000
$100.00	7 months	2.333	2.917	3.500	4.083	4.667
$100.00	8 months	2.667	3.333	4.000	4.667	5.333
$100.00	9 months	3.000	3.750	4.500	5.250	6.000
$100.00	10 months	3.333	4.167	5.000	5.833	6.667
$100.00	11 months	3.667	4.583	5.500	6.417	7.333
$100.00	12 months	4.000	5.000	6.000	7.000	8.000

THE 60-DAY INTEREST METHOD

In what is called the *60-day method,* 360 days are considered one year, and 30 days one month. Upon this basis, the interest for 60 days, or two months, at any rate, will be ⅙ of the interest for one year; and when the rate is 6%, the interest for 60 days is one per cent or $\frac{1}{100}$ of the principal. Thus, the interest of $247 for 60 days at 6% is $2.47.

EXAMPLE: Find the interest of $1728 for 80 days at 6%.

WORK:

$17	28	= interest for 60 days.
5	76	= interest for 20 days.
$23	04	= interest for 80 days.

EXPLANATION: The interest of $1728 for 60 days at 6% is 1% of $1728, or $17.28; and the interest for 20 days (⅓ of 60) is ⅓ of $17.28, or $5.76. Hence for 80 days it will be $17.28 plus $5.76, or $23.04.

METHODS OF RECKONING TIME

The Common Method.—When the time is long, generally 30 days are considered a month.

The Exact Method.—When the time is short, the exact number of days is generally counted, but we sometimes find the exact number of days also when the time is long.

The Bankers' Method.—Bankers get the exact number of days between two dates, but each day is reckoned as $\frac{1}{360}$ of a year.

PROBLEM, when the time is long.
Find the time between April 12, 1935, and September 22, 1939.

BEST METHOD

From April 12, 1935, to April 12, 1939, is *4 years.*
From April 12, 1939, to Sept. 12, 1939, is *5 months.*
From Sept. 12, 1939, to Sept. 22, 1939, is *10 days.*
Time between dates = 4 years 5 months 10 days.

ANOTHER METHOD

1939	9	22
1935	4	12
4	5	10

PROBLEM, when the time is short.
Find the difference in time between April 12 and July 15, 1939.

WORK:

Number of days left in April = 18
in May = 31
in June = 30
in July = 15
Total number of days = 94

NOTE.—If the rate and principal are given, it is a simple matter to find the interest, now that we have the time.

COMPOUND INTEREST

Interest computed, at regular intervals, on the sum of the principal and any unpaid interest is called *compound interest.* In other words, as soon as interest becomes due and is unpaid, it begins to draw interest at the same rate as the principal. Compound interest is generally paid on the deposits in savings banks and is used in calculating amortization and sinking funds.

Interest may be compounded quarterly, semi-annually, annually, or at the end of any other period agreed upon. In some States, the collection of compound interest is not permitted.

EXAMPLE: Find the amount and the compound interest of $1200 at 6% for two years, interest compounded semiannually.

SOLUTION:

$1200.00	First principal
36.00	Interest for 6 months
1236.00	Principal at beginning of second 6 months
37.08	Interest for second 6 months
1273.08	Principal at beginning of third period
38.19	Interest for third period
1311.27	Principal at beginning of fourth period
39.34	Interest for fourth period
$1350.61	Amount at end of two years
$1350.61	Amount at end of two years
1200.00	Principal
$ 150.61	Compound interest.

PRINCIPLES OF EXCHANGE

To find the cost of a draft, the face and rate per cent of exchange being given:

RULE.—*Find the percentage of the given rate per cent of exchange and add it to, or subtract it from, the amount of draft.*

EXAMPLE: What is the cost, in Chicago, of a sight draft on Denver for $400 if exchange is ¾% premium; and how much if ½% discount?

$400 × .00¾ = $3; $400 + $3 = $403, at ¾% premium.
$400 × .00½ = $2; $400 − $2 = $398, at ½% discount.

To find the face of a draft, cost and rate per cent of exchange given:

RULE.—*Divide by the cost of a draft for $1, at given rate per cent of exchange.*

EXAMPLE: Find face of draft that can be bought for $1000 at 1% premium, and at 1% discount.

$1000 ÷ 1.01 = $ 990.10, at 1% premium.
$1000 ÷ .99 = $1010.10, at 1% discount.

TABLE OF COMPOUND INTEREST

(Amount of $1 principal, interest compounded annually)

Years	1½%	2%	2½%	3%	3½%	4%	5%
1	1.0150	1.0200	1.0250	1.0300	1.0350	1.0400	1.0500
2	1.0302	1.0404	1.0506	1.0609	1.0712	1.0816	1.1025
3	1.0457	1.0612	1.0769	1.0927	1.1087	1.1248	1.1576
4	1.0614	1.0824	1.1038	1.1255	1.1475	1.1699	1.2155
5	1.0773	1.1041	1.1314	1.1593	1.1877	1.2167	1.2763
6	1.0934	1.1262	1.1597	1.1941	1.2293	1.2653	1.3401
7	1.1098	1.1487	1.1887	1.2299	1.2723	1.3159	1.4071
8	1.1265	1.1717	1.2184	1.2668	1.3168	1.3686	1.4775
9	1.1434	1.1951	1.2489	1.3048	1.3629	1.4233	1.5513
10	1.1605	1.2190	1.2801	1.3439	1.4106	1.4802	1.6289
11	1.1779	1.2434	1.3121	1.3842	1.4600	1.5395	1.7103
12	1.1956	1.2682	1.3449	1.4258	1.5111	1.6010	1.7969
13	1.2136	1.2936	1.3785	1.4685	1.5639	1.6651	1.8857
14	1.2318	1.3195	1.4130	1.5126	1.6187	1.7319	1.9800
15	1.2502	1.3459	1.4483	1.5580	1.6754	1.8009	2.0789
16	1.2690	1.3727	1.4845	1.6047	1.7340	1.8729	2.2829
17	1.2880	1.4002	1.5216	1.6529	1.7949	1.9479	2.2920
18	1.3073	1.4283	1.5597	1.7024	1.8575	2.0258	2.4066
19	1.3270	1.4568	1.5987	1.7535	1.9225	2.1069	2.5269
20	1.3469	1.4860	1.6386	1.8061	1.9898	2.1911	2.6533
21	1.3671	1.5156	1.6796	1.8603	2.0594	2.2788	2.7860
22	1.3876	1.5461	1.7216	1.9161	2.1315	2.3700	2.9253
23	1.4084	1.5770	1.7646	1.9736	2.2055	2.4647	3.0715
24	1.4295	1.6076	1.8087	2.0328	2.2835	2.5633	3.2251
25	1.4509	1.6405	1.8539	2.0938	2.3628	2.6658	3.3864

Time drafts, when negotiated before maturity, are subject to discount which is computed on the face of the draft, the same as interest.

EXAMPLE: What are the proceeds of a 60-day draft for $800, at ⅝% premium, and discounted at 7%?

$805.00, face + ⅝% premium
9.33, interest (7%, 60 days)
$795.67, proceeds. *Ans.*

Foreign drafts are usually made payable in the money of the country on which they are drawn. However, since the foreign rate of exchange fluctuates from day to day, it is advisable to consult the daily newspapers, or a bank, for the prevailing rate.
To find the equivalent of foreign money in United States money and vice versa:

RULE.—*Multiply, or divide (as the case may require) the given sum, by the equivalent of a unit in United States money.*

EXAMPLE: What is the cost of a draft on London for £125, reckoning exchange at $2.80?

125 × 2.80 = 350.00. *Ans.* $350.00.

Wishing to remit $105.00 to Northern Ireland, for what amount must I buy a draft on London?

105.00 ÷ 2.80 = 37.5. *Ans.* £37½.

STOCKS AND BONDS

APPLICATION OF PERCENTAGE TO STOCKS

1. To find the value of stocks, when above or below par:

RULE.—*Multiply the price per share, by the number of shares.*

EXAMPLE: Find cost of 65 shares of bank stock, at $107 per share, or 7% premium. Also of 48 shares of railroad stock, at $87½ per share, or 12½% discount.

(1) 65 × 107 = 6955. *Ans.* $6955.
(2) 48 × 87½ = 4200. *Ans.* $4200.

2. To find what rate per cent is realized by investing in stocks or bonds when above or below par:

RULE.—*Annex two ciphers to the fixed rate per cent and divide by the cost per share.* Or by proportion: *As the cost per share is to the fixed rate, so is 100 to the required rate.*

EXAMPLE: Mr. Warren bought ten shares of Illinois Central Railroad stock at 96. What does he get when a dividend of 6% is declared? What per cent is that on his investment?

WORK AND EXPLANATION:

(1) 1 share at 6% yields $6
10 shares yield 10 × $6 = $60.

(2) Each share at 96 costs $96.
Each share yields $6.

Query? $6 is what per cent of $96?
$6 is 6/96 of 100%, or 6¼%.
∴ the investment yields 6¼%.

3. To find which is the more profitable investment:

RULE.—*Find the rate per cent that each investment yields, by rule, under item 2; then compare rates.*

EXAMPLE: Which is the better investment: 6% mortgages at 10% premium, or 5% bonds at 10% discount?

(1) 110)600 = 5 5/11%.
(2) 90)500 = 5 5/9%. 5/9 − 5/11 = 10/99, practically 1/10.

Ans. The latter, by 1/10 of 1%, nearly.

TAXES AND TAXATION

USE OF THE MILL IN TAXES.—When a tax is apportioned, it is usually found that if a few mills are paid on each dollar's worth of property in the district, the aggregate amount is equal to the whole sum of tax needed. Consequently, we often hear of tax levies of so many *mills* on the *dollar*, as, 2 mills on the dollar, 5 mills on the dollar, etc.

The denomination of our money system called the *mill* has practically its only use in the levy of taxes.

Assessors make use of a table like the one following. This table is based on a tax levy of 9 mills on the dollar.

PROPERTY VALUE	TAX	PROPERTY VALUE	TAX	PROPERTY VALUE	TAX
$ 1	$0.009	$ 40	$0.36	$ 700	$ 6.30
2	0.018	50	0.45	800	7.20
3	0.027	60	0.54	900	8.10
4	0.036	70	0.63	1,000	9.00
5	0.045	80	0.72	2,000	18.00
6	0.054	90	0.81	3,000	27.00
7	0.063	100	0.90	4,000	36.00
8	0.072	200	1.80	5,000	45.00
9	0.081	300	2.70	6,000	54.00
10	0.09	400	3.60	7,000	63.00
20	0.18	500	4.50	8,000	72.00
30	0.27	600	5.40	9,000	81.00

The following tax rates are equivalent:

16 mills (on the dollar);
1.6%;
$1.60 (on each hundred dollars).

EXPLANATION OF TABLE. The table shows the tax at nine mills on the dollar, for values of $1 to $30; the fourth column shows the tax for values of $40 and multiples of ten, to $600; the sixth column shows the tax for values of $700 and multiples of one hundred, to $9,000.

THE AMOUNT OF TAX.—To find the amount of tax to be paid by any property owner:

RULE.—*Multiply the assessed value of the property by the tax rate.*

EXAMPLE: Taylor's property is assessed at $3800. The rate is 24 mills.

SOLUTION: $3800 assessed valuation
.024 tax rate in mills
$91.20 tax.

EXAMPLE: The town of Grant is to raise $4725 in tax. The property in the town has an assessed valuation of $395,140. What is the rate?

INTEREST CALCULATIONS

RULE.—Multiply the principal by as many one hundredths as there are days, and then divide as follows:

Per cent...........	4	5	6	7	8	9	10	12
Divide by..........	90	72	60	52	45	40	36	30

Table Showing the Number of Days From Any Date in One Month to the Same Date in Any Other Month

From To	Jan.	Feb.	Mar.	Apr.	May	June	July	Aug.	Sept.	Oct.	Nov.	Dec.
Jan.............	365	31	59	90	120	151	181	212	243	273	304	334
Feb.............	334	365	28	59	89	120	150	181	212	242	273	303
Mar.............	306	337	365	31	61	92	122	153	184	214	245	275
April............	275	306	334	365	30	61	91	122	153	183	214	244
May.............	245	276	304	335	365	31	61	92	123	153	184	214
June............	214	245	274	304	334	365	30	61	92	122	153	183
July.............	184	215	243	273	304	335	365	31	62	92	123	153
Aug.............	153	184	212	243	273	304	334	365	31	61	92	122
Sept............	122	153	181	212	242	273	303	334	365	30	61	91
Oct.............	92	123	151	182	212	243	273	304	335	365	31	61
Nov.............	61	92	120	151	181	212	242	273	304	334	365	30
Dec.............	31	62	90	121	151	182	212	243	274	304	335	365

EXAMPLE: How many days from May 5 to October 5? Look for May at left hand and October at the top; in the angle is 153. In Leap Year add 1 day if February is included.

If on \$395,140 a tax of \$4725 is to be raised, on \$1 as much tax must be raised as \$395,140 is contained times in \$4725, which is .0119+, or about \$.0119. This would be called \$0.012, or 12 mills on the dollar.

EXAMPLE: Finch's property is assessed at \$5470. The tax rate is \$1.95.

SOLUTION:

\$ 1.95 the rate per hundred dollars
54.70 the number of hundreds of dollars assessed value
\$106.67 the tax.

Tare is an allowance made for the weight of bags, barrels, or cases, in which merchandise is shipped.

Leakage is an allowance made for loss of liquids from casks, barrels, etc., in shipping.

Breakage is an allowance made for the loss of liquids from bottles in shipping.

EXAMPLE: Find the duty on 4 dozen bottles of cologne, allowing 4% for leakage and 3% for tare. The invoice value is 90 cents a bottle and the duty is 25% ad valorem and 20 cents specific. Find the total cost per bottle.

WORK AND EXPLANATION:

Leakage and tare are 4% + 3% = 7%.
4 dozen bottles = 48 bottles.
The invoice value of 48 bottles is
48 × 90 cents = \$43.20
Tare and leakage are 7% of \$43.20 = \$ 3.024
Value on which duty is paid........\$40.176
Ad valorem duty is 25% of \$40.176 = \$10.044
Specific duty is 48 × 20 cents = 9.60
Total duty \$19.644
The total cost is:
Invoice value \$43.20
Ad valorem duty.................... 10.04
Specific duty...................... 9.60
\$62.84

The total cost per bottle is 1/48 of \$62.84, or \$1.31.

FORMS OF ADDRESS

Person Being Addressed	*Envelope Address*	*Salutation*		*In Speaking*
		Formal	*Less Formal*	
Ambassador (United States)	The Honorable (full name), The Ambassador of the United States of America, (city and country)	Sir (*or* Madam):	My dear Mr. (*or* Madam) Ambassador:	Mr. Ambassador (*or* Madam Ambassador)
Ambassador (Foreign)	His (*or* Her) Excellency (full name), Ambassador of (country), Washington, D. C.	Excellency:	My dear Mr. (*or* Madam) Ambassador:	Excellency *or* Mr. Ambassador (*or* Madam Ambassador) *or* Sir (*or* Madam)
Archbishop (Roman Catholic)	The Most Reverend (full name), Archbishop of (city), (city and State, etc.)	Your Excellency: *or* Most Reverend Sir:	Most Reverend and dear Sir:	Your Excellency
Bishop (Methodist)	Bishop (full name), (city and State, etc.)	My dear Bishop (surname):	Dear Bishop (surname):	Bishop (surname)
Bishop (Protestant Episcopal)	The Right Reverend (full name), Bishop of (diocese), (city and State, etc.)	Right Reverend Sir:	My dear Bishop (surname):	Bishop (surname)
Bishop (Roman Catholic)	The Most Reverend (full name), (church), (city and State, etc.)	Most Reverend Sir:	My dear Bishop (surname):	Bishop (surname)
Brother (of a religious order)	Brother (religious name plus initials of his order), (address, city, and State)	My dear Brother:	Dear Brother (religious name):	Brother (religious name)
Cabinet Officer of the U. S.	The Honorable (full name), (title), Washington, D. C.	Sir (*or* Madam): *or* Dear Sir (*or* Dear Madam):	My dear Mr. (*or* Madam) Secretary: *or* Dear Mr. (*or* Mrs. *or* Ms. *or* Miss) (surname):	Mr. (*or* Madam) Secretary *or* Sir (*or* Madam)
Cardinal (Roman Catholic)	His Eminence (given name) Cardinal (surname), Archbishop of (city, etc.), (city and State, etc.)	Your Eminence:		Your Eminence
Common Form (Man)	Mr. (full name), (address, city, and State)	My dear Mr. (surname): *or* My dear Sir: *in plural*, Gentlemen:	Dear Mr. (surname): *or* Dear Sir:	Mr. (surname)
Common Form (Woman)	Mrs. (*or* Miss *or* Ms.) (full name), (address, city, and State)	My dear Mrs. (*or* Miss *or* Ms.) (surname): *or* My dear Madam: *in plural*, Ladies: *or* Mesdames:	Dear Mrs. (*or* Miss *or* Ms.) (surname): *or* Dear Madam:	Miss (*or* Mrs. *or* Ms.) (surname)
Consul (United States or **other)**	(full name), Esq., American (*or* other) Consul, (city and country, or State)	Sir (*or* Madam): *or* My dear Sir (*or* My dear Madam):	Dear Mr. (*or* Mrs. *or* Ms. *or* Miss) (surname):	Mr. (*or* Mrs. *or* Ms. *or* Miss) (surname)
Doctor (of Philosophy, Medicine, Divinity, etc.)	(full name), Ph.D., M.D., D.D., etc. *or* Dr. (full name), (address, city, and State)	My dear Dr. (surname): *or* My dear Sir (*or* My dear Madam):	Dear Dr. (surname):	Dr. (surname)
Governor (of a State)	The Honorable (*or in some states* His *or* Her Excellency) (full name), Governor of (State), (capital city and State)	Sir (*or* Madam):	Dear Governor (surname):	Governor (surname) *or* Sir (*or* Madam)
Judge (see also **Supreme Court)**	The Honorable (full name), Justice (name of court), (city and State)	Sir (*or* Madam):	Dear Judge (surname):	Judge (surname)
King (or **Queen)**	His (Her) Most Gracious Majesty, King, (Queen) (name)	May it please Your Majesty:		*Initially*, Your Majesty; *thereafter*, Sir (*or* Ma'am)
Mayor	His (*or* Her) Honor, The Mayor, City Hall (city and State)	Sir (*or* Madam):	My dear Mr. (*or* Madam) Mayor: *or* My dear Mayor (surname):	Mr. (or Madam) Mayor
Military Enlisted Personnel (American)	(title of rank), (full name), (address)	Sir (*or* Madam): *or* Dear Sir (*or* Dear Madam):	Dear Private (*or* Airman, etc.) (surname):	Private (*or* Airman, etc.) (surname)
Military Officer (American)	(title of rank), (full name), (address)	Sir (*or* Madam): *or* Dear Sir (or Dear Madam):	Dear General (*or* Colonel, Major, Captain, etc.) (surname):	General (*or* Colonel, Major, Captain, etc.) (surname)
Minister (Protestant)	The Reverend (full name plus D.D. if applicable), (address, city, and State)	My dear Sir (*or* My dear Madam): *or* Sir (*or* Madam):	Dear Mr. (*or* Mrs. *or* Ms. *or* Miss *or* Dr.) (surname):	Mr. (or Mrs. *or* Ms. *or* Miss *or* Dr. *or, if a Lutheran*, Pastor) (surname)

Forms of Address

Person Being Addressed	Envelope Address	Salutation: Formal	Salutation: Less Formal	In Speaking
Monsignor (Roman Catholic)	The Right Reverend Monsignor (surname), (city and State)	Right Reverend and dear Monsignor (surname):	Reverend and dear Monsignor (surname):	Monsignor (surname)
Naval Enlisted Personnel (American)	(title of rank), (full name), (address)	Sir (*or* Madam): *or* Dear Sir (*or* Dear Madam):	Dear Seaman (*or* Quartermaster, etc.) (surname):	Seaman (*or* Quartermaster, etc.) (surname)
Naval Officer (American)	(title of rank), (full name), (address)	Sir (*or* Madam): *or* Dear Sir (*or* Dear Madam):	Dear Admiral (*or* Commodore, Captain, etc.) (surname):	Admiral (*or* Commodore, Captain, etc.) (surname)
Pope	His Holiness the Pope, Vatican City, Italy	Your Holiness:		Your Holiness (*or* Most Holy Father)
President (of the United States)	The President, The White House, Washington, D.C. 20500	Sir: *or* Mr. President:	My dear Mr. President: *or* Dear President (surname):	Mr. President *or* Sir
Priest (Roman Catholic)	The Reverend (full name plus initials of his order), (address, city, and State)	Reverend Father:	Dear Father (surname):	Father (surname) *or* Father
Prince (or Princess)	His (Her) Royal Highness, Prince(ss) (given name)	Your Royal Highness:	Sir (*or* Madam):	Your Royal Highness
Rabbi	Rabbi (full name plus D.D. if applicable), (address, city, and State)	Dear Sir: *or* Dear Rabbi:	Dear Rabbi (*or* Dr.):	Rabbi (*or* Dr.) (surname)
Representative (of the United States Congress)	The Honorable (full name), United States House of Representatives, Washington, D.C. 20515	Sir (*or* Madam):	My dear Mr. (*or* Mrs. *or* Ms. *or* Miss) (surname):	Mr. (*or* Mrs. *or* Ms. *or* Miss) (surname)
Representative (of a State legislature)	The Honorable (full name), Member of Assembly (or other name of the legislature), (capital city and State)	Sir (*or* Madam):	My dear Mr. (*or* Mrs. *or* Ms. *or* Miss) (surname):	Mr. (*or* Mrs. *or* Ms. *or* Miss) (surname)
Senator (of the United States)	The Honorable (full name), United States Senate, Washington, D.C. 20510	Sir (*or* Madam):	My dear Senator (surname):	Senator (surname) *or* Mr. (*or* Madam) Senator
Senator (of a State)	The Honorable (full name), The Senate of (State), (capital city and State)	Sir (*or* Madam):	Dear Senator (*or* My dear Senator) (surname):	Senator (surname) *or* Mr. (*or* Madam) Senator
Sister (of a religious order)	Sister (religious name plus initials of her order), (address, city, and State)	My Dear Sister:	Dear Sister (religious name):	Sister (religious name)
Supreme Court (of the United States) (Associate Justice)	The Honorable (full name), Associate Justice, Supreme Court of the United States, Washington, D.C. 20543	My Dear Justice (surname):		Justice (surname) or Sir (*or* Madam)
Supreme Court (of the United States) (Chief Justice)	The Honorable (full name), The Chief Justice, Supreme Court of the United States, Washington, D.C. 20543	My Dear Chief Justice (surname):		Chief Justice (surname)
Supreme Court (of a State) (Associate Justice)	The Honorable (full name), Associate Justice of the Supreme Court of (State), (address)	Sir (*or* Madam):	Dear Justice (surname):	Mr. (*or* Madam) Justice (surname) *or* Judge (surname)
Supreme Court (of a State) (Chief Justice)	The Honorable (full name), Chief Justice of the Supreme Court of (State), (address)	Sir (*or* Madam):	Dear Mr. (*or* Madam) Chief Justice:	Mr. (*or* Madam) Chief Justice *or* Chief Justice (surname) *or* Judge (surname)
United Nations Delegate (other than U.S.)	His (*or* Her) Excellency, (country) Representative to the United Nations, United Nations, New York 10017	Sir (*or* Madam): *or* Your Excellency:	My Dear Mr. (*or* Madam) Ambassador: *or* My dear Mr. (*or* Ms. *or* Miss *or* Mrs.) (surname):	Your Excellency
United Nations Delegate (United States)	The Honorable (full name), United States Permanent Representative to the United Nations, United Nations, New York 10017	Sir (*or* Madam):	My dear Mr. (*or* Madam) Ambassador: *or* My dear Mr. (*or* Ms. *or* Miss *or* Mrs.) (surname):	Mr. Ambassador (*or* Madam Ambassador)
Vice President (of the United States)	The Vice President, United States Senate, Washington, D.C. 20510	Sir:	My dear Mr. Vice President:	Mr. Vice President *or* Sir
Warrant Officer	Warrant Officer (*or* Chief Warrant Officer) (full name), (address)	Sir (*or* Madam): *or* Dear Sir (*or* Dear Madam):	Dear Mr. (*or* Mrs. *or* Ms. *or* Miss) (surname):	Mr. (*or* Mrs. *or* Ms. *or* Miss) (surname)

TABLES OF WEIGHTS AND MEASURES

Linear Measure

1 inch		= 2.54 centimeters
12 inches	= 1 foot	= 0.3048 meter
3 feet	= 1 yard	= 0.9144 meter
5½ yards or 16½ feet	= 1 rod (or pole or perch)	= 5.029 meters
40 rods	= 1 furlong	= 201.17 meters
8 furlongs or 1,760 yards or 5,280 feet	= 1 (statute) mile	= 1,609.3 meters
3 miles	= 1 (land) league	= 4.83 kilometers

Square Measure

1 square inch		= 6.452 square centimeters
144 square inches	= 1 square foot	= 929 square centimeters
9 square feet	= 1 square yard	= 0.8361 square meter
30¼ square yards	= 1 square rod (or square pole or square perch)	= 25.29 square meters
160 square rods or 4,840 square yards or 43,560 square feet	= 1 acre	= 0.4047 hectare
640 acres	= 1 square mile	= 259 hectares or 2.59 square kilometers

Cubic Measure

1 cubic inch		= 16.387 cubic centimeters
1,728 cubic inches	= 1 cubic foot	= 0.0283 cubic meter
27 cubic feet	= 1 cubic yard	= 0.7646 cubic meter
(in units for cordwood, etc.)		
16 cubic feet	= 1 cord foot	
8 cord feet	= 1 cord	= 3.625 cubic meters

Chain Measure

(for Gunter's, or surveryor's, chain)		
7.92 inches	= 1 link	= 20.12 centimeters
100 links or 66 feet	= 1 chain	= 20.12 meters
10 chains	= 1 furlong	= 201.17 meters
80 chains	= 1 mile	= 1,609.3 meters
(for engineer's chain)		
1 foot	= 1 link	= 0.3048 meter
100 feet	= 1 chain	= 30.48 meters
52.8 chains	= 1 mile	= 1,609.3 meters

Surveyor's (Square) Measure

625 square links	= 1 square pole	= 25.29 square meters
16 square poles	= 1 square chain	= 404.7 square meters
10 square chains	= 1 acre	= 0.4047 hectare
640 acres	= 1 square mile or 1 section	= 259 hectares or 2.59 square kilometers
36 square miles	= 1 township	= 9,324.0 hectares or 93.24 square kilometers

Nautical Measure

6 feet	= 1 fathom	= 1.829 meters
100 fathoms	= 1 cable's length (ordinary) (In the U.S. Navy 120 fathoms or 720 feet = 1 cable's length; in the British Navy, 608 feet = 1 cable's length.)	
10 cables' lengths	= 1 nautical mile (6,076.10333 feet,	= 1.852 kilometers by international agreement, 1954)
1 nautical mile	= 1.1508 statute miles (the length of a minute of longitude at the equator) (Also called geographical, sea, or air mile, and, in Great Britain, Admiralty mile.)	
3 nautical miles	= 1 marine league (3.45 statute miles)	= 5.56 kilometers
60 nautical miles	= 1 degree of a great circle of the earth	

Dry Measure

1 pint		= 33.60 cubic inches	= 0.5505 liter
2 pints	= 1 quart	= 67.20 cubic inches	= 1.1012 liters
8 quarts	= 1 peck	= 537.61 cubic inches	= 8.8096 liters
4 pecks	= 1 bushel	= 2,150.42 cubic inches	= 35.2383 liters

1 British dry quart = 1.032 U.S. dry quarts.

According to United States government standards, the following are the weights avoirdupois for single bushels of the specified grains: for wheat, 60 pounds; for barley, 48 pounds; for oats, 32 pounds; for rye, 56 pounds; for corn, 56 pounds. Some states have specifications varying from these.

Liquid Measure

1 gill	= 4 fluid ounces (see next table)	= 7.219 cubic inches	= 0.1183 liter
4 gills	= 1 pint	= 28.875 cubic inches	= 0.4732 liter
2 pints	= 1 quart	= 57.75 cubic inches	= 0.9463 liter
4 quarts	= 1 gallon	= 231 cubic inches	= 3.7853 liters

The British imperial gallon (4 imperial quarts) = 277.42 cubic inches = 4.546 liters. The barrel in Great Britain equals 36 imperial gallons, in the United States, usually 31½ gallons.

Apothecaries' Fluid Measure

1 minim		= 0.0038 cubic inch	= 0.0616 milliliter
60 minims	= 1 fluid dram	= 0.2256 cubic inch	= 3.6966 milliliters
8 fluid drams	= 1 fluid ounce	= 1.8047 cubic inches	= 0.0296 liter
16 fluid ounces	= 1 pint	= 28.875 cubic inches	= 0.4732 liter

See table immediately preceding for quart and gallon equivalents.
The British pint = 20 fluid ounces.

Circular (or Angular) Measure

60 seconds (″)	= 1 minute (′)
60 minutes	= 1 degree (°)
90 degrees	= 1 quadrant or 1 right angle
4 quadrants or 360 degrees	= 1 circle

Avoirdupois Weight

(The grain, equal to 0.0648 gram, is the same in all three tables of weight)

1 dram or 27.34 grains		= 1.772 grams
16 drams or 437.5 grains	= 1 ounce	= 28.3495 grams
16 ounces or 7,000 grains	= 1 pound	= 453.59 grams
100 pounds	= 1 hundredweight	= 45.36 kilograms
2,000 pounds	= 1 ton	= 907.18 kilograms

In Great Britain, 14 pounds (6.35 kilograms) = 1 stone, 112 pounds (50.80 kilograms) = 1 hundredweight, and 2,240 pounds (1,016.05 kilograms) = 1 long ton.

Troy Weight

(The grain, equal to 0.0648 gram, is the same in all three tables of weight)

3.086 grains	= 1 carat	= 200 milligrams
24 grains	= 1 pennyweight	= 1.5552 grams
20 pennyweights or 480 grains	= 1 ounce	= 31.1035 grams
12 ounces or 5,760 grains	= 1 pound	= 373.24 grams

Apothecaries' Weight

(The grain, equal to 0.0648 gram, is the same in all three tables of weight)

20 grains	= 1 scruple	= 1.296 grams
3 scruples	= 1 dram	= 3.888 grams
8 drams or 480 grains	= 1 ounce	= 31.1035 grams
12 ounces or 5,760 grains	= 1 pound	= 373.24 grams

THE METRIC SYSTEM

Linear Measure

10 millimeters	= 1 centimeter	= 0.3937 inch
10 centimeters	= 1 decimeter	= 3.937 inches
10 decimeters	= 1 meter	= 39.37 inches or 3.28 feet
10 meters	= 1 decameter	= 393.7 inches
10 decameters	= 1 hectometer	= 328 feet 1 inch
10 hectometers	= 1 kilometer	= 0.621 mile
10 kilometers	= 1 myriameter	= 6.21 miles

Square Measure

100 square millimeters	= 1 square centimeter	= 0.15499 square inch
100 square centimeters	= 1 square decimeter	= 15.499 square inches
100 square decimeters	= 1 square meter	= 1,549.9 square inches or 1.196 square yards
100 square meters	= 1 square decameter	= 119.6 square yards
100 square decameters	= 1 square hectometer	= 2.471 acres
100 square hectometers	= 1 square kilometer	= 0.386 square mile

Land Measure

1 square meter	= 1 centiare	= 1,549.9 square inches
100 centiares	= 1 are	= 119.6 square yards
100 ares	= 1 hectare	= 2.471 acres
100 hectares	= 1 square kilometer	= 0.386 square mile

Volume Measure

1,000 cubic millimeters	= 1 cubic centimeter	= .06102 cubic inch
1,000 cubic centimeters	= 1 cubic decimeter	= 61.02 cubic inches
1,000 cubic decimeters	= 1 cubic meter	= 35.314 cubic feet

(the unit is called a *stere* in measuring firewood)

Capacity Measure

10 milliliters	= 1 centiliter	= .338 fluid ounce
10 centiliters	= 1 deciliter	= 3.38 fluid ounces
10 deciliters	= 1 liter	= 1.0567 liquid quarts or 0.9081 dry quart
10 liters	= 1 decaliter	= 2.64 gallons or 0.284 bushel
10 decaliters	= 1 hectoliter	= 26.418 gallons or 2.838 bushels
10 hectoliters	= 1 kiloliter	= 264.18 gallons or 35.315 cubic feet

Weights

10 milligrams	= 1 centigram	= 0.1543 grain
10 centigrams	= 1 decigram	= 1.5432 grains
10 decigrams	= 1 gram	= 15.432 grains
10 grams	= 1 decagram	= 0.3527 ounce
10 decagrams	= 1 hectogram	= 3.5274 ounces
10 hectograms	= 1 kilogram	= 2.2046 pounds
10 kilograms	= 1 myriagram	= 22.046 pounds
10 myriagrams	= 1 quintal	= 220.46 pounds
10 quintals	= 1 metric ton	= 2,204.6 pounds

SPECIAL SIGNS AND SYMBOLS

ASTRONOMY

1. SUN, MOON, PLANETS, ETC.

☉ (1) The Sun. (2) Sunday.

☾ *or* ☽ (1) The Moon. (2) Monday

● New Moon.

☽, ◐, *or* ☽ First Quarter.

○ Full Moon.

☾, ◑, *or* ☾ Last Quarter.

✱ *or* ✳ Fixed Star.

☿ (1) Mercury. (2) Wednesday.

♀ (1) Venus. (2) Friday

⊕, ⊖, *or* ♁ The Earth.

♂ (1) Mars. (2) Tuesday.

♃ (1) Jupiter. (2) Thursday.

♄ (1) Saturn. (2) Saturday.

♅ *or* ♅ Uranus.

♆ Neptune.

♇ Pluto.

☄ Comet.

①, ③, ⓢ, *etc.* Asteroids in the order of their discovery.

α, β, γ, etc. The stars (of a constellation) in the order of their brightness; the Greek letter is followed by the Latin genitive of the name of the constellation.

2. SIGNS OF THE ZODIAC

Spring Signs

1. ♈ Aries (the Ram).
2. ♉ Taurus (the Bull).
3. ♊ *or* Π Gemini (the Twins).

Summer Signs

4. ♋ *or* ⊗ Cancer (the Crab).
5. ♌ Leo (the Lion).
6. ♍ Virgo (the Virgin).

Autumn Signs

7. ♎ Libra (the Balance).
8. ♏ Scorpio (the Scorpion).
9. ♐ Sagittarius (the Archer).

Winter Signs

10. ♑ *or* ♑ Capricorn (the Goat).
11. ♒ Aquarius (the Water Bearer).
12. ♓ Pisces (the Fish).

3. ASPECTS AND NODES

☌ Conjunction;—with reference to bodies having the same longitude, or right ascension.

✱ Sextile;—being 60° apart in longitude, or right ascension.

□ Quadrature;—being 90° apart in longitude, or right ascension.

△ Trine;—being 120° apart in longitude, or right ascension.

☍ Opposition;—being 180° apart in longitude, or right ascension.

☊ Ascending Node.

☋ Descending Node.

4. SIGNS AND ABBREVIATIONS USED IN ASTRONOMICAL NOTATION

a. Mean distance.

A.R. Right ascension.

β Celestial latitude.

D. Diameter.

δ Declination.

△ Distance.

E. East.

e Eccentricity.

h. *or* ʰ Hours: as, 5h. or 5ʰ.

i Inclination to the ecliptic.

L, l, *or* ε Mean longitude in orbit.

λ Longitude.

M. Mass.

m. *or* ᵐ Minutes of time: as, 5m. or 5ᵐ.

μ or n Mean daily motion.

+ *or* N. North.

N. P. D. North polar distance.

ν, ☊, *or* L. Longitude of ascending node.

π or ω Longitude of perihelion.

q. Perihelion distance.

ρ or R. Radius or radius vector.

— *or* S. South.

s. *or* ˢ Seconds of time: as, 16s. or 16ˢ.

T. Periodic time.

W. West.

φ Angle of eccentricity; also, geographical latitude.

° Degrees of arc.

′ Minutes of arc.

″ Seconds of arc.

BIOLOGY

○, ☉, ① Annual plant.

②, ☉☉, ♂ Biennial plant.

♃ Perennial herb.

△ Evergreen plant.

☉ Monocarpic plant, that bears fruit but once.

♄ Shrub.

♄ Treelike shrub.

♄ Tree.

⌒ Climbing plant.

♂, ♂ (1) Male organism or cell. (2) Staminate plant or flower.

♀ (1) Female organism or cell. (2) Pistillate plant or flower.

☿ Perfect, or hermaphroditic, plant or flower.

○ Individual, especially female, organism.

□ Individual, especially male, organism.

♂ ♀ Unisexual; having male and female flowers separate.

♂—♀ Monoecious; having male and female flowers on the same plant.

♂ : ♀ Dioecious; having male and female flowers on different plants.

♀ ♂ ♀ Polygamous; having hermaphroditic and unisexual flowers on the same or different plants.

∞ Indefinite number, as of stamens when there are more than twenty.

0 Lacking or absent, as a part.

) Turning or winding to the left.

(Turning or winding to the right.

× Crossed with: used of a hybrid.

P Parental (generation).

F Filial (generation); offspring.

F_1, F_2, F_3, *etc.* Offspring of the first, second, third, etc. filial generation.

+ Possessing a (specified) characteristic.

− Lacking a (specified) characteristic.

✱̲ Northern hemisphere.

✱̄ Southern hemisphere.

|✱ Old World.

✱| New World.

°, ′, ″ Feet, inches, lines.

′, ″, ‴ Feet, inches, lines (in European usage).

CHEMISTRY

The symbol for each of the chemical elements is formed of the initial or an abbreviation of its English, Latin, or Modern Latin name, as C for carbon, K for potassium (Mod. L. *kalium*), Mn for manganese, Au for gold (L. *aurum*). A complete list of the symbols of elements can be found on p. 586.

The formula for a chemical compound is expressed by combining the symbols of its constituent elements, with a small subscript at the right of each specifying the number of atoms of each element in a molecule of the compound. Where only one atom is involved, no subscript is used. Examples: MgO (magnesium oxide), a compound in which one atom of magnesium is combined with one atom of oxygen; H_2O (water), a compound in which two atoms of hydrogen are combined with one atom of oxygen; $NaHCO_3$ (sodium bicarbonate), a compound in which one atom each of sodium, hydrogen, and carbon, and three atoms of oxygen are combined.

In equations, the number of molecules of the element or compound entering into a reaction is indicated by a figure placed before the symbol or formula (unless there is only one molecule), as $3O_2$, three molecules of oxygen; 2NaCl, two molecules of sodium chloride.

· separates radicals, as in $CH_3{\cdot}CHO$ (acetaldehyde, C_2H_4O), or the water of crystallization, as in $CaSO_4{\cdot}2H_2O$ (gypsum, or hydrated calcium sulfate).

, indicates elements which are interchangeable; for example, (Er, Y) PO_4 means $ErPO_4$ and YPO_4 in proportions that vary.

() indicates a radical within a compound, as in $(NH_4)_2S$, ammonium sulfide, or is used to set off elements that are interchangeable, as in the example for the preceding symbol.

[] is used together with parentheses to indicate certain radicals, as in $Fe_3[Fe(CN)_6]_2$, ferrous ferricyanide, or in co-ordination formulas to indicate relationship to the central atom.

⬡ is used in structural formulas to indicate the benzene ring.

+, ++, +++, *etc.* or ¹⁺, ²⁺, ³⁺, *etc.* indicate the unit charges of positive electricity, as Al^{+++}, an aluminum ion with three positive charges.

−, −−, −−−, *etc.* or ¹⁻, ²⁻, ³⁻, *etc.* indicate the unit charges of negative electricity, as S^{--}, a sulfide ion with two negative charges.

—, =, ≡, *etc.* indicate (1) the same as the symbols immediately preceding, as S=; (2) a single, double, or triple bond, as in HC≡CH, acetylene.

., :, ⁝, *etc.* indicate a single, double, or triple bond, as in $C_6H_5C⁝CH$, phenylacetylene.

′, ″, ‴, *etc.* indicate (1) a valence of one, two, three, etc., as Fe‴, trivalent iron; (2) the unit charges of negative electricity, as SO_4'', a sulfate ion with two negative charges.

1−, 2−, 3−, *etc.* or *α*−, *β*−, *γ*−, *etc.* used in names of compounds to designate one of the several possible positions of substituting groups in a parent compound, as in 2-ethylnaphthalene, *γ*-resorcylic acid.

— indicates levorotation, as —130°.

+ (1) means "with the addition of, or together with," and is used in chemical equations between the formulas of the reacting substances: see example under the next symbol. (2) indicates dextrorotation as +130°.

= means "form, or result in," and is used in chemical equations between the formulas of the reacting substances and those of the reaction products. Example: $H_2SO_4 + 2NaCl = Na_2SO_4 + 2HCl$, meaning one molecule of sulfuric acid together with two molecules of sodium chloride will form one molecule of sodium sulfate and two molecules of hydrogen chloride.

→ indicates the direction of the reaction.

⇄ indicates a reversible reaction; i.e., one that can proceed in either direction, or in both directions at the same time, in a state of equilibrium.

↓ indicates that the specified reaction product (after which it is written) appears as a precipitate.

↑ indicates that the specified reaction product (after which it is written) appears as a gas.

≡ *or* ⇔ means "is equivalent to" and is used in quantitative equations to indicate the quantities of specified substances that will react with each other completely, so as to leave no excess matter.

COMMERCE AND FINANCE

$ Dollar or dollars: as, $100.

¢ Cent or cents: as, 13¢.

£ Pound or pounds sterling: as, £100.

/ Shilling or shillings: as, 2/6, two shillings and sixpence.

℔ Pound (in weight).

@ (1) At: as, 200 @ $1 each. (2) To: as, shoes per pr. $10 @ $15.

℘ Per.

% (1) Per cent: as, 5%. (2) Order of.

a/c Account.

B/L Bill of Lading.

B/S Bill of Sale.

c/d, C/D Carried down (in bookkeeping).

c/f, C/F Carried forward (in bookkeeping).

c/o (1) Care of. (2) Carried over (in bookkeeping).

d/a Days after acceptance.

d/s Days after sight.

L/C Letter of Credit.

(1) Number (before a figure): as, #5 can. (2) Pounds (after a figure): as, 25#.

MATHEMATICS

1. NUMERATION

Arabic	*Greek*	*Roman*
0	. . .	. . .
1	α	I
2	β	II
3	γ	III
4	δ	IV *or* IIII
5	ε	V
6	ς	VI
7	ζ	VII
8	η	VIII *or* IIX
9	θ	IX *or* VIIII
10	ι	X
11	ια	XI
12	ιβ	XII
13	ιγ	XIII *or* XIIV
14	ιδ	XIV *or* XIIII
15	ιε	XV
16	ις	XVI
17	ιζ	XVII
18	ιη	XVIII *or* XIIX
19	ιθ	XIX *or* XVIIII
20	κ	XX
30	λ	XXX
40	μ	XL *or* XXXX
50	ν	L
60	ξ	LX
70	ο	LXX
80	π	LXXX *or* XXC
90	ϙ	XC *or* LXXXX
100	ρ	C
200	σ	CC
300	τ	CCC
400	υ	CD *or* CCCC
500	φ	D *or* IↃ
600	χ	DC *or* IↃC
700	ψ	DCC *or* IↃCC
800	ω	DCCC *or* IↃCCC
900	. . .	CM, DCCCC, *or* IↃCCCC
1,000	. . .	M *or* CIↃ
2,000	. . .	MM *or* CIↃCIↃ

Capital letters were sometimes used for the Greek numerals, and lower-case letters are often used for the Roman. In the Roman notation, the value of a character to the right of a larger numeral is added to that of the numeral: as, VI = V + I = 6. I, X, and sometimes C, are also placed to the left of larger numerals and when so situated their value is subtracted from that of such numerals: as, IV, that is, V − I = 4. After the sign IↃ for D, when the character Ↄ was repeated, each repetition had the effect of multiplying IↃ by ten: as, IↃↃ, 5,000; IↃↃↃ, 50,000; and the like. In writing numbers twice as great as these, C was placed as many times before the stroke I as the Ↄ was written after it. Sometimes a line was drawn over a numeral to indicate thousands: as, $\overline{C}$ = 100,000.

2. CALCULATION

+ (1) Plus, the sign of addition; used also to indicate that figures are only approximately exact, some figures being omitted at the end: as, 2.1557+. (2) Positive.

− (1) Minus, the sign of subtraction; used also to indicate that figures have been left off from the end of a number, and that the last figure has been increased by one: as, 2.9378 = 2.94−. (2) Negative.

± *or* ∓ Plus or minus; indicating that either of the signs + or − may properly be used; also used to introduce the probable error after a figure obtained by experimentation, etc.

× Multiplied by: 5 × 4 = 20; multiplication is also indicated by a centered dot (5 · 4 = 20) or by placing the factors in immediate juxtaposition ($2ab = 2 \times a \times b$).

÷ Divided by; division is also indicated by the sign: ($x \div y = x : y$), by a straight line between the dividend and the divisor $\left(\frac{x}{y}\right)$, or by an oblique line (x/y).

= Is equal to; equals.

≠ Is not equal to.

> Is greater than: as, $x > y$; that is, x is greater than y.

< Is less than: as, $x < y$; that is, x is less than y.

≮, ≧, *or* ≥ Is not less than; is equal to or greater than.

≯, ≦, *or* ≤ Is not greater than; is equal to or less than.

⇔ Is equivalent to; applied to magnitudes or quantities that are equal in area or volume, but are not of the same form.

≡ Is identical with.

≅ Is congruent to.

∼ The difference between; used to designate the difference between two quantities without indicating which is the greater; as, $x \sim z$ = the difference between x and z.

∝ Varies as; is directly proportional to: as, $x \propto y$; that is, x varies as y.

∺ Geometric proportion: as, ∺ $x : y :: a : b$; that is, the geometric proportion, x is to y as a is to b.

: Is to; the ratio of.

: : As; equals: used between ratios.

∞ Indefinitely great: the symbol for infinity.

! *or* ⌊ The factorial of, or the continued product of numbers from one upward: as, 5! = 5 × 4 × 3 × 2 × 1.

∴ Therefore.

∵ Since; because.

. . . And so on.

∠ Angle: as, ∠XYZ.

∟ Right angle.

⊥ The perpendicular; is perpendicular to: as, EF ⊥ MN = EF is perpendicular to MN.

∥ Parallel; is parallel to: as, EF ∥ DG.

○ Circle; circumference; 360°.

⌒ Arc of a circle.

△ Triangle.

□ Square.

▭ Rectangle.

▱ Parallelogram.

√‾ *or* √ Radical sign; root, indicating, when used without a figure placed above it, the square root: as, $\sqrt{9} = 3$. When any other than the square root is meant, a figure (called the *index*) expressing the degree of the required root, is placed above the sign: as, $\sqrt[3]{27} = 3$.

¹, ², ³, *etc.* Exponents, placed above and to the right of a quantity to indicate that it is raised to the first, second, third, etc. power: as, a^2, $(a + b)^3$.

′, ″, ‴, *etc.* Prime, double (or second) prime, triple (or third) prime, etc., used to distinguish between different values of the same variable: as, x', x'', x''', etc.

These signs indicate that the quantities connected or enclosed by them are to be taken together, as a single quantity:

— Vinculum: as, $\overline{x + y}$

( ) Parentheses: as, $2(x + y)$

[ ] Brackets: as, $a[2(x + y)]$

{ } Braces: as, $b + \{2 - a[2(x + y)]\}$

f or F Function; function of: as, $f(a)$, a function of a.

d Differential of: as, da.

δ Variation of: as, δa.

Δ Finite difference, or increment.

D Differential coefficient, or derivative.

∫ Integral; integral of, indicating that the expression following it is to be integrated: as, $\int f(x)dx$ indicates the indefinite integral of $f(x)$ with respect to x.

$\int_a^b$ Definite integral, indicating the limits of integration: as, $\int_a^b f(x)dx$ indicates the integral of $f(x)$ with respect to x, between the limits a and b.

Σ Sum; algebraic sum; when used to indicate the summation of finite differences, it has a sense similar to that of the symbol ∫.

Π The continued product of all terms such as (those indicated).

π Pi, the number 3.14159265+; the ratio of the circumference of a circle to its diameter, of a semicircle to its radius, and of the area of a circle to the square of its radius.

e or ε The number 2.7182818+; the base of the Napierian system of logarithms; also, the eccentricity of a conic section.

M The modulus of a system of logarithms, especially of the common system of logarithms, where it is equal to 0.4342944819+.

g The acceleration of gravity.

° Degrees: as, 90°.

′ (1) Minutes of arc. (2) Feet.

″ (1) Seconds of arc. (2) Inches.

h Hours.

m Minutes of time.

s Seconds of time.

MEDICINE AND PHARMACY

A̅A̅, A̅ *or* a̅a̅ [Gr. *ana*], of each.

a.c. [L. *ante cibum*], before meals.

ad [L.], up to; so as to make: as, *ad* ℥ij, so as to make two drams.

ad. [L. *adde*], let there be added; add.

ad lib. [L. *ad libitum*], at pleasure; as needed or desired.

aq. [L. *aqua*], water.

b. (i.) d. [L. *bis (in) die*], twice daily.

C. [L. *congius*], a gallon.

coch. [L. *cochleare*], a spoonful.

D. [L. *dosis*], a dose.

dil. [L. *dilue*], dilute or dissolve.

ess. [L. *essentia*], essence.

ft. mist. [L. *fiat mistura*], let a mixture be made.

ft. pulv. [L. *fiat pulvis*], let a powder be made.

gr. [L. *granum*], a grain.

gtt. [L. *guttae*], drops.

guttatim [L.], drop by drop.

haust. [L. *haustus*], a draft.

hor. decub. [L. *hora decubitus*], at bedtime.

lot. [L. *lotio*], a lotion.

M. [L. *misce*], mix.

mac. [L. *macera*], macerate.

O. *or* o. [L. *octarius*], a pint.

p.c. [L. *post cibum*], after meals.

pil. [L. *pilula(e)*], pill(s).

p.r.n. [L. *pro re nata*], as circumstances may require.

pulv. [L. *pulvis*], powder.

q. (i.) d. [L. *quater (in) die*], four times daily.

q.l. [L. *quantum libet*], as much as you please.

q.s. [L. *quantum sufficit*], as much as will suffice.

q.v. [L. *quantum vis*], as much as you like.

℞ [L. *recipe*], take: used at the beginning of a prescription.

S *or* **Sig.** [L. *signa*], write: used in prescriptions to indicate the directions to be placed on the label of the medicine.

t. (i.) d. [L. *ter (in) die*], three times daily.

℥ ounce; ℥i = one ounce; ℥ij = two ounces; ℥ss = half an ounce; ℥iss = one ounce and a half, etc.; *f*℥ = a fluid ounce.

ʒ dram; ʒi = one dram; ʒij = two drams; ʒss = half a dram; ʒiss = one dram and a half, etc.; *f*ʒ = a fluid dram.

℈ scruple; ℈i = one scruple; ℈ij = two scruples; ℈ss = half a scruple; ℈iss = one scruple and a half, etc.

♏ *or* **♍** minim.

MISCELLANEOUS

& *or* **&** (the ampersand) and: as, A. B. Smith & Co.

&c. [L. *et cetera*], and others; and so forth.

© copyrighted.

℟ response: in religious services, used to mark the part to be uttered by the congregation in answer to the officiant.

***** in Roman Catholic service books, a mark used to divide each verse of a psalm into two parts, indicating where the response begins.

℣, V', or V̸ versicle: in religious services, used to mark the part to be uttered by the officiant.

✠ (1) a sign of the cross used by the pope, by archbishops, and by bishops, before their names. (2) in religious services, used to mark the places where the sign of the cross is to be made.

† died: used in genealogies, etc.

× (1) by: used in dimensions, as paper 8 × 11 inches. (2) a mark representing a signature, as on a legal document, made by someone unable to write; the name is added by someone else; e.g.

his
John × *Doe*
mark

7ber September.

8ber October.

9ber November

10ber December.

f° folio.

4to *or* **4°** quarto; four leaves (eight pages) to a sheet.

8vo *or* **8°** octavo; eight leaves (sixteen pages) to a sheet.

12mo *or* **12°** twelvemo, or duodecimo; twelve leaves (twenty-four pages) to a sheet.

16mo *or* **16°** sixteenmo, or sextodecimo; sixteen leaves (thirty-two pages) to a sheet.

18mo *or* **18°** eighteenmo, or octodecimo; eighteen leaves (thirty-six pages) to a sheet.

24mo *or* **24°** twenty-fourmo; twenty-four leaves (forty-eight pages) to a sheet.

32mo *or* **32°** thirty-twomo; thirty-two leaves (sixty-four pages) to a sheet.

48mo *or* **48°** forty-eightmo; forty-eight leaves (ninety-six pages) to a sheet.

PRESIDENTS OF THE UNITED STATES

No.	Name	Life Dates	Politics	Place of Birth	Dates of Term
1	George Washington	1732-1799	Federalist	Virginia	1789-1797
2	John Adams	1735-1826	Federalist	Massachusetts	1797-1801
3	Thomas Jefferson	1743-1826	Dem.-Rep.	Virginia	1801-1809
4	James Madison	1751-1836	Dem.-Rep.	Virginia	1809-1817
5	James Monroe	1758-1831	Dem.-Rep.	Virginia	1817-1825
6	John Quincy Adams	1767-1848	Dem.-Rep.	Massachusetts	1825-1829
7	Andrew Jackson	1767-1845	Democrat	South Carolina	1829-1837
8	Martin Van Buren	1782-1862	Democrat	New York	1837-1841
9	William Henry Harrison	1773-1841	Whig	Virginia	1841
10	John Tyler	1790-1862	Democrat	Virginia	1841-1845
11	James Knox Polk	1795-1849	Democrat	North Carolina	1845-1849
12	Zachary Taylor	1784-1850	Whig	Virginia	1849-1850
13	Millard Fillmore	1800-1874	Whig	New York	1850-1853
14	Franklin Pierce	1804-1869	Democrat	New Hampshire	1853-1857
15	James Buchanan	1791-1868	Democrat	Pennsylvania	1857-1861
16	Abraham Lincoln	1809-1865	Republican	Kentucky	1861-1865
17	Andrew Johnson	1808-1875	Republican	North Carolina	1865-1869
18	Ulysses Simpson Grant	1822-1885	Republican	Ohio	1869-1877
19	Rutherford Birchard Hayes	1822-1893	Republican	Ohio	1877-1881
20	James Abram Garfield	1831-1881	Republican	Ohio	1881
21	Chester Alan Arthur	1830-1886	Republican	Vermont	1881-1885
22	Grover Cleveland	1837-1908	Democrat	New Jersey	1885-1889
23	Benjamin Harrison	1833-1901	Republican	Ohio	1889-1893
24	Grover Cleveland	1837-1908	Democrat	New Jersey	1893-1897
25	William McKinley	1843-1901	Republican	Ohio	1897-1901
26	Theodore Roosevelt	1858-1919	Republican	New York	1901-1909
27	William Howard Taft	1857-1930	Republican	Ohio	1909-1913
28	Woodrow Wilson	1856-1924	Democrat	Virginia	1913-1921
29	Warren Gamaliel Harding	1865-1923	Republican	Ohio	1921-1923
30	Calvin Coolidge	1872-1933	Republican	Vermont	1923-1929
31	Herbert Clark Hoover	1874-1964	Republican	Iowa	1929-1933
32	Franklin Delano Roosevelt	1882-1945	Democrat	New York	1933-1945
33	Harry S. Truman	1884-1972	Democrat	Missouri	1945-1953
34	Dwight David Eisenhower	1890-1969	Republican	Texas	1953-1961
35	John Fitzgerald Kennedy	1917-1963	Democrat	Massachusetts	1961-1963
36	Lyndon Baines Johnson	1908-1973	Democrat	Texas	1963-1969
37	Richard Milhous Nixon	1913-	Republican	California	1969-1974
38	Gerald Rudolph Ford	1913-	Republican	Nebraska	1974-1977
39	James Earl Carter, Jr.	1924-	Democrat	Georgia	1977-1981
40	Ronald Wilson Reagan	1911-	Republican	Illinois	1981-

VICE-PRESIDENTS AND CABINET OFFICERS OF THE UNITED STATES

VICE-PRESIDENTS OF THE UNITED STATES

	Name	Term Began	Politics
1	John Adams	1789	Fed.
2	Thomas Jefferson	1797	Rep.
3	Aaron Burr	1801	Rep.
4	George Clinton	1805	Rep.
5	Elbridge Gerry	1813	Rep.
6	Daniel D. Tompkins	1817	Rep.
7	John C. Calhoun	1825	Rep.
8	Martin Van Buren	1833	Dem.
9	Richard M. Johnson	1837	Dem.
10	John Tyler	1841	Dem.
11	George M. Dallas	1845	Dem.
12	Millard Fillmore	1849	Whig
13	William R. King	1853	Dem.
14	John C. Breckinridge	1857	Dem.
15	Hannibal Hamlin	1861	Rep.
16	Andrew Johnson	1865	Rep.
17	Schuyler Colfax	1869	Rep.
18	Henry Wilson	1873	Rep.
19	William A. Wheeler	1877	Rep.
20	Chester A. Arthur	1881	Rep.
21	Thomas A. Hendricks	1885	Rep.
22	Levi P. Morton	1889	Dem.
23	Adlai E. Stevenson	1893	Rep.
24	Garrett A. Hobart	1897	Dem.
25	Theodore Roosevelt	1901	Rep.
26	Charles W. Fairbanks	1905	Rep.
27	James S. Sherman	1909	Rep.
28	Thomas R. Marshall	1913	Dem.
29	Calvin Coolidge	1921	Rep.
30	Charles G. Dawes	1925	Rep.
31	Charles Curtis	1929	Rep.
32	John Nance Garner	1933	Dem.
33	Henry Agard Wallace	1941	Dem.
34	Harry S. Truman	1945	Dem.
35	Alben W. Barkley	1949	Dem.
36	Richard M. Nixon	1953	Rep.
37	Lyndon B. Johnson	1961	Dem.
38	Hubert Horatio Humphrey	1965	Dem.
39	Spiro T. Agnew	1969	Rep.
40	Gerald R. Ford	1973	Rep.
41	Nelson A. Rockefeller	1974	Rep.
42	Walter F. Mondale	1977	Dem.
43	George Bush	1981	Rep.

SECRETARIES OF STATE

Presidents	Cabinet Officers	Appointed
Washington	John Jay (unofficial)	....
"	Thomas Jefferson	1789
"	Edmund Randolph	1794
"	Timothy Pickering	1795
J. Adams	"	1797
"	John Marshall	1800
Jefferson	James Madison	1801
Madison	Robert Smith	1809
"	James Monroe	1811
Monroe	John Quincy Adams	1817
J. Q. Adams	Henry Clay	1825
Jackson	Martin Van Buren	1829
"	Edward Livingston	1831
"	Louis McLane	1833
"	John Forsyth	1834
Van Buren	"	1837
W. H. Harrison	Daniel Webster	1841
Tyler	"	1841
"	Hugh S. Legaré	1843
"	Abel P. Upshur	1843
"	John C. Calhoun	1844
Polk	James Buchanan	1845
Taylor	John M. Clayton	1849
Fillmore	Daniel Webster	1850
Fillmore	Edward Everett	1852
Pierce	William L. Marcy	1853
Buchanan	Lewis Cass	1857
"	Jeremiah S. Black	1860
Lincoln	William H. Seward	1861
Johnson	"	1865
Grant	Elihu B. Washburne	1869
"	Hamilton Fish	1869
Hayes	William M. Evarts	1877
Garfield	James G. Blaine	1881
Arthur	"	1881
"	F. T. Frelinghuysen	1881
Cleveland	Thomas F. Bayard	1885
B. Harrison	James G. Blaine	1889
"	John W. Foster	1892
Cleveland	Walter Q. Gresham	1893
"	Richard Olney	1895
McKinley	John Sherman	1897
"	William R. Day	1898
"	John Hay	1898
T. Roosevelt	"	1901
"	Elihu Root	1905
"	Robert Bacon	1909
Taft	Philander C. Knox	1909
Wilson	William J. Bryan	1913
"	Robert Lansing	1915
"	Bainbridge Colby	1920
Harding	Charles E. Hughes	1921
Coolidge	"	1923
"	Frank B. Kellogg	1925
Hoover	Henry L. Stimson	1929
F. D. Roosevelt	Cordell Hull	1933
"	E. R. Stettinius, Jr.	1944
Truman	James F. Byrnes	1945
"	George C. Marshall	1947
"	Dean G. Acheson	1949
Eisenhower	John Foster Dulles	1953
"	Christian A. Herter	1959
Kennedy	Dean Rusk	1961
Johnson	"	1963
Nixon	William P. Rogers	1969
"	Henry A. Kissinger	1973
Ford	"	1974
Carter	Cyrus R. Vance	1977
"	Edmund S. Muskie	1980
Reagan	Alexander M. Haig, Jr.	1981

SECRETARIES OF THE TREASURY

Presidents	Cabinet Officers	Appointed
Washington	Alexander Hamilton	1789
"	Oliver Wolcott, Jr.	1795
J. Adams	"	1797
"	Samuel Dexter	1801
Jefferson	"	1801
"	Albert Gallatin	1801
Madison	"	1809
"	George W. Campbell	1814
"	Alexander J. Dallas	1814
"	William H. Crawford	1816
Monroe	"	1817
J. Q. Adams	Richard Rush	1825
Jackson	Samuel D. Ingham	1829
"	Louis McLane	1831
"	William J. Duane	1833
"	Roger B. Taney	1833
"	Levi Woodbury	1834
Van Buren	"	1837
W. H. Harrison	Thomas Ewing	1841
Tyler	"	1841
"	Walter Forward	1841
"	John C. Spencer	1843
"	George M. Bibb	1844
Polk	Robert J. Walker	1845
Taylor	William M. Meredith	1849
Fillmore	Thomas Corwin	1850
Pierce	James Guthrie	1853
Buchanan	Howell Cobb	1857
"	Philip F. Thomas	1860
"	John A. Dix	1861
Lincoln	Salmon P. Chase	1861
"	William P. Fessenden	1864
"	Hugh McCulloch	1865
Johnson	"	1865
Grant	George S. Boutwell	1869
"	William A. Richardson	1873
"	Benjamin H. Bristow	1874
"	Lot M. Morrill	1876
Hayes	John Sherman	1877
Garfield	William Windom	1881
Arthur	"	1881
"	Charles J. Folger	1881
"	Walter Q. Gresham	1884
"	Hugh McCulloch	1884
Cleveland	Daniel Manning	1885
"	Charles S. Fairchild	1887
B. Harrison	William Windom	1889
"	Charles Foster	1891
Cleveland	John G. Carlisle	1893
McKinley	Lyman J. Gage	1897
T. Roosevelt	Lyman J. Gage	1901
"	Leslie M. Shaw	1902
T. Roosevelt	George B. Cortelyou	1907
Taft	Franklin MacVeagh	1909
Wilson	William G. McAdoo	1913
"	Carter Glass	1919
"	David F. Houston	1920
Harding	Andrew W. Mellon	1921
Coolidge	"	1923
Hoover	"	1929
"	Ogden L. Mills	1932
F. D. Roosevelt	William H. Woodin	1933
"	Henry Morgenthau, Jr.	1934
Truman	Fred M. Vinson	1945
"	John W. Snyder	1946
Eisenhower	George M. Humphrey	1953
"	Robert Anderson	1957
Kennedy	C. Douglas Dillon	1961
Johnson	"	1963
"	Henry Hamill Fowler	1965
Nixon	David M. Kennedy	1969
"	John B. Connally	1970
"	George P. Schultz	1972
"	William E. Simon	1974
Ford	"	1974
Carter	W. Michael Blumenthal	1977
"	G. William Miller	1979
Reagan	Donald T. Regan	1981

SECRETARIES OF WAR

Presidents	Cabinet Officers	Appointed
Washington	Henry Knox	1789
"	Timothy Pickering	1795
"	James McHenry	1796
J. Adams	"	1797
"	Samuel Dexter	1800
Jefferson	Henry Dearborn	1801
Madison	William Eustis	1809
"	John Armstrong	1813
"	James Monroe	1814
"	William H. Crawford	1815
Monroe	George Graham *(ad. in.)*	1817
"	John C. Calhoun	1817
J. Q. Adams	James Barbour	1825
"	Peter B. Porter	1828
Jackson	John H. Eaton	1829
"	Lewis Cass	1831
"	Benjamin F. Butler	1837
Van Buren	Joel R. Poinsett	1837
W. H. Harrison	John Bell	1841
Tyler	John C. Spencer	1841
"	James M. Porter	1843
"	William Wilkins	1844
Polk	William L. Marcy	1845
Taylor	George W. Crawford	1849
Fillmore	Charles M. Conrad	1850
Pierce	Jefferson Davis	1853
Buchanan	John B. Floyd	1857
"	Joseph Holt	1861
Lincoln	Simon Cameron	1861
"	Edwin M. Stanton	1862
Johnson	"	1865
"	U. S. Grant *(ad. in.)*	1867
"	Lorenzo Thomas *(ad in.)*	1868
"	John M. Schofield	1868
Grant	John A. Rawlins	1869
"	William T. Sherman	1869
"	William W. Belknap	1869
"	Alphonso Taft	1876
"	James D. Cameron	1876
Hayes	George W. McCrary	1877
"	Alexander Ramsey	1879
Garfield	Robert T. Lincoln	1881
Arthur	"	1881
Cleveland	William C. Endicott	1885
B. Harrison	Redfield Proctor	1889
"	Stephen B. Elkins	1891
Cleveland	Daniel S. Lamont	1893
McKinley	Russell A. Alger	1897
"	Elihu Root	1899
T. Roosevelt	"	1901
"	William H. Taft	1904
"	Luke E. Wright	1908
Taft	Jacob M. Dickinson	1909
"	Henry L. Stimson	1911
Wilson	Lindley M. Garrison	1913
"	Newton D. Baker	1916
Harding	John W. Weeks	1921
Coolidge	"	1923
"	Dwight F. Davis	1925
Hoover	James W. Good	1929
"	Patrick J. Hurley	1929
F. D. Roosevelt	George H. Dern	1933
"	Harry H. Woodring	1936
"	Henry L. Stimson	1940
Truman	Robert P. Patterson	1945
"	Kenneth C. Royall	1947

See also Secretaries of Defense.

SECRETARIES OF THE INTERIOR

Presidents	Cabinet Officers	Appointed
Taylor	Thomas Ewing	1849
Fillmore	T. M. T. McKennan	1850
"	Alexander H. H. Stuart	1850
Pierce	Robert McClelland	1853
Buchanan	Jacob Thompson	1857
Lincoln	Caleb B. Smith	1861
"	John P. Usher	1863
Johnson	"	1865
"	James Harlan	1865
"	Orville H. Browning	1866
Grant	Jacob D. Cox	1869
"	Columbus Delano	1870
"	Zachariah Chandler	1875
Hayes	Carl Schurz	1877
Garfield	Samuel J. Kirkwood	1881
Arthur	Henry M. Teller	1882
Cleveland	Lucius Q. C. Lamar	1885
Cleveland	William F. Vilas	1888
B. Harrison	John W. Noble	1889
Cleveland	Hoke Smith	1893
"	David R. Francis	1896
McKinley	Cornelius N. Bliss	1897
"	Ethan A. Hitchcock	1898
T. Roosevelt	"	1901
"	James R. Garfield	1907
Taft	Richard A. Ballinger	1909
"	Walter L. Fisher	1911
Wilson	Franklin K. Lane	1913
"	John B. Payne	1920
Harding	Albert B. Fall	1921
"	Hubert Work	1923
Coolidge	"	1923
"	Roy O. West	1928
Hoover	Ray Lyman Wilbur	1929
F. D. Roosevelt	Harold L. Ickes	1933
Truman	"	1945
"	Julius A. Krug	1946
"	Oscar L. Chapman	1949
Eisenhower	Douglas McKay	1953
"	Frederick A. Seaton	1956
Kennedy	Stewart L. Udall	1961
Johnson	"	1963
Nixon	Walter J. Hickel	1969
"	Rogers C. B. Morton	1971
Ford	"	1974
"	Stanley K. Hathaway	1975
"	Thomas S. Kleppe	1975
Carter	Cecil D. Andrus	1977
Reagan	James G. Watt	1981

ATTORNEYS GENERAL

Presidents	Cabinet Officers	Appointed
Washington	Edmund Randolph	1789
"	William Bradford	1794
"	Charles Lee	1795
J. Adams	"	1797
Jefferson	Levi Lincoln	1801
"	John Breckenridge	1805
"	Caesar A. Rodney	1807
Madison	"	1809
"	William Pinkney	1811
"	*Richard Rush	1814
Monroe	"	1817
"	William Wirt	1817
J. Q. Adams	"	1825
Jackson	John McP. Berrien	1829
"	Roger B. Taney	1831
"	Benjamin F. Butler	1833
Van Buren	"	1837
"	Felix Grundy	1838
"	Henry D. Gilpin	1840
W. H. Harrison	John J. Crittenden	1841
Tyler	"	1841
"	Hugh S. Legaré	1841
"	John Nelson	1843
Polk	John Y. Mason	1845
"	Nathan Clifford	1846
"	Isaac Toucey	1848
Taylor	Reverdy Johnson	1849
Fillmore	John J. Crittenden	1850
Pierce	Caleb Cushing	1853
Buchanan	Jeremiah S. Black	1857
"	Edwin M. Stanton	1860
Lincoln	Edward Bates	1861
"	James Speed	1864
Johnson	"	1865
"	Henry Stanbery	1866
"	William M. Evarts	1868
Grant	Ebenezer R. Hoar	1869
"	Amos T. Akerman	1870
"	George H. Williams	1871
"	Edwards Pierrepont	1875
"	Alphonso Taft	1876
Hayes	Charles Devens	1877
Garfield	Wayne MacVeagh	1881
Arthur	Benjamin H. Brewster	1881
Cleveland	August H. Garland	1885
B. Harrison	William H. H. Miller	1889
Cleveland	Richard Olney	1893
"	Judson Harmon	1895
McKinley	Joseph McKenna	1897
"	John W. Griggs	1898
"	Philander C. Knox	1901
T. Roosevelt	"	1901
"	William H. Moody	1904
"	Charles J. Bonaparte	1906
Taft	George E. Wickersham	1909
Wilson	J. C. McReynolds	1913
Wilson	Thomas E. Gregory	1914
"	A. M. Palmer	1919
Harding	H. M. Daugherty	1921
Coolidge	"	1923
"	Harlan F. Stone	1924
"	John G. Sargent	1925
Hoover	William D. Mitchell	1929
F. D. Roosevelt	Homer S. Cummings	1933
"	Frank Murphy	1939
"	Robert H. Jackson	1940
"	Francis Biddle	1941
Truman	Tom C. Clark	1945
"	J. Howard McGrath	1949
"	James P. McGranery	1952
Eisenhower	Herbert Brownell, Jr.	1953
"	William P. Rogers	1957
Kennedy	Robert F. Kennedy	1961
Johnson	"	1963
"	Nicholas deB. Katzenbach	1965
"	Ramsey Clark	1967
Nixon	John N. Mitchell	1969
"	Richard G. Kleindienst	1972
"	Elliot L. Richardson	1973
"	William B. Saxbe	1974
Ford	"	1974
"	Edward H. Levi	1975
Carter	Griffin B. Bell	1977
"	Benjamin R. Civiletti	1979
Reagan	William French Smith	1981

*First Attorney General to be a member of the Cabinet.

*POSTMASTERS GENERAL

Presidents	Cabinet Officers	Appointed
Washington	Samuel Osgood	1789
"	Timothy Pickering	1791
"	Joseph Habersham	1795
J. Adams	"	1797
Jefferson	"	1801
"	Gideon Granger	1801
Madison	"	1809
"	Return J. Meigs, Jr.	1814
Monroe	"	1817
"	John McLean	1823
J. Q. Adams	"	1825
Jackson	‡William T. Barry	1829
"	Amos Kendall	1835
Van Buren	"	1837
"	John M. Niles	1840
W. H. Harrison	Francis Granger	1841
Tyler	"	1841
"	Charles A. Wickliff	1841
Polk	Cave Johnson	1845
Taylor	Jacob Collamer	1849
Fillmore	Nathan K. Hall	1850
"	Samuel D. Hubbard	1852
Pierce	James Campbell	1853
Buchanan	Aaron V. Brown	1857
"	Joseph Holt	1859
"	Horatio King	1861
Lincoln	Montgomery Blair	1861
"	William Dennison	1864
Johnson	"	1865
"	Alexander W. Randall	1866
Grant	John A. J. Creswell	1869
"	James W. Marshall	1874
"	Marshall Jewell	1874
"	James N. Tyner	1876
Hayes	David McK. Key	1877
"	Horace Maynard	1880
Garfield	Thomas L. James	1881
Arthur	Timothy O. Howe	1881
"	Walter Q. Gresham	1883
"	Frank Hatton	1884
Cleveland	William F. Vilas	1885
"	Don M. Dickinson	1888
B. Harrison	John Wanamaker	1889
Cleveland	Wilson S. Bissel	1893
"	William L. Wilson	1895
McKinley	James A. Gary	1897
McKinley	Charles E. Smith	1898
T. Roosevelt	"	1901
"	Henry C. Payne	1902
"	Robert J. Wynne	1904
"	George B. Cortelyou	1905
"	George von L. Meyer	1907
Taft	F. H. Hitchcock	1909
Wilson	Albert S. Burleson	1913
Harding	Will S. Hays	1921
"	Hubert Work	1922
"	Harry S. New	1923
Coolidge	"	1923
Hoover	Walter F. Brown	1929
F. D. Roosevelt	James A. Farley	1933
"	Frank C. Walker	1940
Truman	Robert E. Hannegan	1945
"	Jesse M. Donaldson	1947
Eisenhower	Arthur E. Summerfield	1953
Kennedy	J. Edward Day	1961
"	John A. Gronouski	1963
Johnson	"	1963
"	Lawrence Francis O'Brien	1965
"	W. Marvin Watson	1968
Nixon	Winton M. Blount	1969

‡First Postmaster General to be a member of the Cabinet.

*Discontinued as a Cabinet Office when the Postal Reform Act of 1970 replaced the Post Office Department with the Postal Service, an independent federal agency.

SECRETARIES OF THE NAVY

Presidents	Cabinet Officers	Appointed
J. Adams	Benjamin Stoddert	1798
Jefferson	"	1801
"	Robert Smith	1802
Madison	"	1802
"	Paul Hamilton	1809
"	William Jones	1813
"	B. W. Crowninshield	1814
Monroe	"	1817
"	Smith Thompson	1818
"	Samuel L. Southard	1823
J. Q. Adams	"	1825
Jackson	John Branch	1829
"	Levi Woodbury	1831
"	Mahlon Dickerson	1834
Van Buren	"	1837
"	James K. Paulding	1838
W. H. Harrison	George E. Badger	1841
Tyler	"	1841
"	Abel P. Upshur	1841
"	David Henshaw	1843
Tyler	Thomas W. Gilmer	1844
"	John Y. Mason	1844
Polk	George Bancroft	1845
"	John Y. Mason	1845
Taylor	William B. Preston	1849
Fillmore	William A. Graham	1850
"	John P. Kennedy	1852
Pierce	James C. Dobbin	1853
Buchanan	Isaac Toucey	1857
Lincoln	Gideon Welles	1861
Johnson	"	1865
Grant	Adolph E. Borie	1869
"	George M. Robeson	1869
Hayes	Richard W. Thompson	1877
"	Nathan Goff, Jr.	1881
Garfield	William H. Hunt	1881
Arthur	William E. Chandler	1882
Cleveland	William C. Whitney	1885
B. Harrison	Benjamin F. Tracy	1889
Cleveland	Hilary A. Herbert	1893
McKinley	John D. Long	1897
T. Roosevelt	"	1901
"	William H. Moody	1902
"	Paul Morton	1904
"	Charles J. Bonaparte	1905
"	Victor H. Metcalf	1906
"	Truman H. Newberry	1908
Taft	George von L. Meyer	1909
Wilson	Josephus Daniels	1913
Harding	Edward Denby	1921
Coolidge	"	1923
"	Curtis D. Wilbur	1924
Hoover	Charles Francis Adams	1929
F. D. Roosevelt	Claude A. Swanson	1933
"	Charles Edison	1940
"	Frank Knox	1940
"	James V. Forrestal	1944
Truman	"	1945

See also Secretaries of Defense.

SECRETARIES OF AGRICULTURE

Presidents	Cabinet Officers	Appointed
Cleveland	Norman J. Colman	1889
B. Harrison	Jeremiah M. Rusk	1889
Cleveland	J. Sterling Morton	1893
McKinley	James Wilson	1897
T. Roosevelt	"	1901
Taft	James Wilson	1909
Wilson	David F. Houston	1913
"	Edward T. Meredith	1920
Harding	Henry C. Wallace	1921
Coolidge	Howard M. Gore	1924
"	W. M. Jardine	1925
Hoover	Arthur M. Hyde	1929
F. D. Roosevelt	Henry A. Wallace	1933
"	Claude R. Wickard	1940
Truman	Clinton P. Anderson	1945
"	Charles F. Brannan	1948
Eisenhower	Ezra Taft Benson	1953
Kennedy	Orville L. Freeman	1961
Johnson	"	1963
Nixon	Clifford M. Hardin	1969
"	Earl L. Butz	1971
Ford	"	1974
"	*John A. Knebel	1976
Carter	Robert S. Bergland	1977
Reagan	John R. Block	1981

*Acting

SECRETARIES OF COMMERCE

Presidents	Cabinet Officers	Appointed
Wilson	William C. Redfield	1913
"	Joshua W. Alexander	1919
Harding	Herbert C. Hoover	1921
Coolidge	"	1923
"	William F. Whiting	1929
Hoover	Robert P. Lamont	1929
"	Roy D. Chapin	1932
F. D. Roosevelt	Daniel C. Roper	1933
"	Harry L. Hopkins	1939
"	Jesse Jones	1940
"	Henry A. Wallace	1945
Truman	Henry A. Wallace	1945
"	W. Averell Harriman	1946
"	Charles W. Sawyer	1948
Eisenhower	Sinclair Weeks	1953
"	Frederick Henry Mueller	1959
Kennedy	Luther H. Hodges	1961
Johnson	"	1963
"	John T. Connor	1965
"	Alexander B. Trowbridge	1967
Johnson	C. R. Smith	1968
Nixon	Maurice H. Stans	1969
"	Peter G. Peterson	1972
"	Frederick B. Dent	1973
Ford	"	1974
"	Rogers C. B. Morton	1975
"	Elliot L. Richardson	1976
Carter	Juanita M. Kreps	1977
"	Philip M. Klutznick	1979
Reagan	Malcom Balridge	1981

SECRETARIES OF LABOR

Presidents	Cabinet Officers	Appointed
Wilson	William B. Wilson	1913
Harding	James J. David	1921
Coolidge	"	1923
Hoover	"	1929
"	William N. Doak	1930
F. D. Roosevelt	Frances Perkins	1933
Truman	L. B. Schwellenbach	1945
Truman	Maurice J. Tobin	1948
Eisenhower	Martin P. Durkin	1953
"	James P. Mitchell	1953
Kennedy	Arthur J. Goldberg	1961
"	W. Willard Wirtz	1962
Johnson	"	1963
Nixon	George P. Schultz	1969
Nixon	James D. Hodgson	1970
"	Peter J. Brennan	1973
Ford	"	1974
"	John T. Dunlop	1975
"	W. J. Usery	1976
Carter	F. Ray Marshall	1977
Reagan	Raymond J. Donovan	1981

*SECRETARIES OF COMMERCE AND LABOR

Presidents	Cabinet Officers	Appointed
T. Roosevelt	George B. Cortelyou	1903
"	Victor H. Metcalf	1904
"	Oscar S. Straus	1906
Taft	Charles Nagel	1909

*The Department of Commerce and Labor was divided into two departments in 1913.

*SECRETARIES OF DEFENSE

Presidents	Cabinet Officers	Appointed
Truman	James V. Forrestal	1947
"	Louis A. Johnson	1949
"	George C. Marshall	1950
"	Robert A. Lovett	1951
Eisenhower	Charles E. Wilson	1953
"	Thomas S. Gates, Jr.	1959
Kennedy	Robert S. McNamara	1961
Johnson	"	1963
"	Clark M. Clifford	1968
Nixon	Melvin R. Laird	1969
"	Elliot L. Richardson	1973
"	James R. Schlesinger	1973
Ford	"	1974
"	Donald H. Rumsfeld	1975
Carter	Harold Brown	1977
Reagan	Caspar W. Weinberger	1981

*The Departments of War and Navy were combined into the Department of Defense in 1947.

*SECRETARIES OF HEALTH, EDUCATION, AND WELFARE

Presidents	Cabinet Officers	Appointed
Eisenhower	Oveta Culp Hobby	1953
"	Marion B. Folsom	1955
"	Arthur S. Fleming	1958
Kennedy	Abraham A. Ribicoff	1961
"	Anthony J. Celebrezze	1962
Johnson	"	1963
"	John W. Gardner	1965
"	Wilbur J. Cohen	1968
Nixon	Robert H. Finch	1969
"	Elliot L. Richardson	1970
"	Caspar W. Weinberger	1973
Ford	"	1974
"	Forrest D. Mathews	1975
Carter	Joseph A. Califano, Jr.	1977

*The Department of Health, Education, and Welfare was divided into two departments in 1979.

SECRETARIES OF HEALTH AND HUMAN SERVICES

Presidents	Cabinet Officers	Appointed
Carter	Patricia Roberts Harris	1979
Reagan	Richard S. Schweicker	1981

SECRETARIES OF EDUCATION

Presidents	Cabinet Officers	Appointed
Carter	Shirley M. Hufstedler	1979
Reagan	Terrel Bell	1981

SECRETARIES OF HOUSING AND URBAN DEVELOPMENT

Presidents	Cabinet Officers	Appointed
Johnson	Robert C. Weaver	1966
Nixon	George W. Romney	1969
"	James T. Lynn	1973
Ford	"	1974
"	Carla A. Hills	1975
Carter	Patricia R. Harris	1977
"	Moon Landrieu	1979
Reagan	Samuel R. Pierce, Jr.	1981

SECRETARIES OF TRANSPORTATION

Presidents	Cabinet Officers	Appointed
Johnson	Alan S. Boyd	1967
Nixon	John A. Volpe	1969
"	Claude S. Brinegar	1973
Ford	"	1974
"	William T. Coleman, Jr.	1975
Carter	Brockman Adams	1977
"	Neil E. Goldschmidt	1979
Reagan	Drew Lewis	1981

SECRETARIES OF ENERGY

Presidents	Cabinet Officers	Appointed
Carter	James R. Schlesinger	1977
"	Charles W. Duncan, Jr.	1979
Reagan	James B. Edwards	1981

DECLARATION OF INDEPENDENCE

The Declaration of Independence was adopted by the Continental Congress, in Philadelphia, on July 4, 1776, and was signed by John Hancock as President and by Charles Thomson as Secretary. It was published first on July 6 in the Pennsylvania Evening Post. A copy of the Declaration, engrossed on parchment, was signed by members of Congress on and after Aug. 2, 1776.

When in the Course of human events, it becomes necessary for one people to dissolve the political bands which have connected them with another, and to assume among the Powers of the earth, the separate and equal station to which the Laws of Nature and of Nature's God entitle them, a decent respect to the opinions of mankind requires that they should declare the causes which impel them to the separation.

We hold these truths to be self-evident, that all men are created equal, that they are endowed by their Creator with certain unalienable Rights, that among these are Life, Liberty and the pursuit of Happiness. That to secure these rights, Governments are instituted among Men, deriving their just powers from the consent of the governed, That whenever any Form of Government becomes destructive of these ends, it is the Right of the People to alter or to abolish it, and to institute new Government, laying its foundation on such principles and organizing its powers in such form, as to them shall seem most likely to effect their Safety and Happiness. Prudence, indeed, will dictate that Governments long established should not be changed for light and transient causes; and accordingly all experience hath shown, that mankind are more disposed to suffer, while evils are sufferable, than to right themselves by abolishing the forms to which they are accustomed. But when a long train of abuses and usurpations, pursuing invariably the same Object, evinces a design to reduce them under absolute Despotism, it is their right, it is their duty, to throw off such Government, and to provide new Guards for their future security. —Such has been the patient sufferance of these Colonies; and such is now the necessity which constrains them to alter their former Systems of Government. The history of the present King of Great Britain is a history of repeated injuries and usurpations, all having in direct object the establishment of an absolute Tyranny over these States. To prove this, let Facts be submitted to a candid world.

He has refused his Assent to Laws, the most wholesome and necessary for the public good.

He has forbidden his Governors to pass Laws of immediate and pressing importance, unless suspended in their operation till his Assent should be obtained; and when so suspended, he has utterly neglected to attend to them.

He has refused to pass other Laws for the accommodation of large districts of people, unless those people would relinquish the right of Representation in the Legislature, a right inestimable to them and formidable to tyrants only.

He has called together legislative bodies at places unusual, uncomfortable, and distant from the depository of their public Records, for the sole purpose of fatiguing them into compliance with his measures.

He has dissolved Representative Houses repeatedly, for opposing with manly firmness his invasions on the rights of the people.

He has refused for a long time, after such dissolutions, to cause others to be elected; whereby the Legislative powers, incapable of Annihilation, have returned to the People at large for their exercise; the State remaining in the mean time exposed to all the dangers of invasion from without, and convulsions within.

He has endeavoured to prevent the population of these States; for that purpose obstructing the Laws of Naturalization of Foreigners; refusing to pass others to encourage their migrations hither, and raising the conditions of new Appropriations of Lands.

He has obstructed the Administration of Justice, by refusing his Assent to Laws for establishing Judiciary Powers.

He has made Judges dependent on his Will alone, for the tenure of their offices, and the amount and payment of their salaries.

He has erected a multitude of New Offices, and sent hither swarms of Officers to harass our People, and eat out their substance.

He has kept among us, in times of peace, Standing Armies without the Consent of our legislature.

He has affected to render the Military independent of and superior to the Civil Power.

He has combined with others to subject us to a jurisdiction foreign to our constitution, and unacknowledged by our laws; giving his Assent to their Acts of pretended Legislation: For quartering large bodies of armed troops among us: For protecting them, by a mock Trial, from punishment for any Murders which they should commit on the inhabitants of these States: For cutting off our Trade with all parts of the world: For imposing taxes on us without our Consent: For depriving us in many cases, of the benefits of Trial by Jury: For transporting us beyond Seas to be tried for pretended offenses: For abolishing the free System of English Laws in a neighbouring Province, establishing therein an Arbitrary government, and enlarging its Boundaries so as to render it at once an example and fit instrument for introducing the same absolute rule into these Colonies: For taking away our Charters, abolishing our most valuable Laws, and altering fundamentally the Forms of our Government: For suspending our own Legislature, and declaring themselves invested with Power to legislate for us in all cases whatsoever.

He has abdicated Government here, by declaring us out of his Protection and waging War against us.

He has plundered our seas, ravaged our Coasts, burnt our towns, and destroyed the lives of our people.

He is at this time transporting large armies of foreign mercenaries to compleat the works of death, desolation and tyranny, already begun with circumstances of Cruelty and perfidy scarcely paralleled in the most barbarous ages, and totally unworthy the Head of a civilized nation.

He has constrained our fellow Citizens taken Captive on the high Seas to bear Arms against their Country, to become the executioners of their friends and Brethren, or to fall themselves by their Hands.

He has excited domestic insurrections amongst us, and has endeavoured to bring on the inhabitants of our frontiers, the merciless Indian Savages, whose known rule of warfare, is an undistinguished destruction of all ages, sexes and conditions. In every stage of these Oppressions We have Petitioned for Redress in the most humble terms: Our repeated Petitions have been answered only by repeated injury. A Prince, whose character is thus marked by every act which may define a Tyrant, is unfit to be the ruler of a free people. Nor have We been wanting in attention to our British brethren. We have warned them from time to time of attempts by their legislature to extend an unwarrantable jurisdiction over us. We have reminded them of the circumstances of our emigration and settlement here. We have appealed to their native justice and magnanimity, and we have conjured them by the ties of our common kindred to disavow these usurpations, which would inevitably interrupt our connections and correspondence. They too have been deaf to the voice of justice and of consanguinity. We must, therefore, acquiesce in the necessity, which denounces our Separation, and hold them, as we hold the rest of mankind, Enemies in War, in Peace Friends.

We, therefore, the Representatives of the United States of America, in General Congress, Assembled, appealing to the Supreme Judge of the world for the rectitude of our intentions, do, in the Name, and by authority of the good People of these Colonies, solemnly publish and declare, That these United Colonies are, and of Right ought to be Free and Independent States; that they are Absolved from all Allegiance to the British Crown, and that all political connection between them and the State of Great Britain, is and ought to be totally dissolved; and that as Free and Independent States, they have full Power to levy War, conclude Peace, contract Alliances, establish Commerce, and to do all other Acts and Things which Independent States may of right do. And for the support of this Declaration, with a firm reliance on the Protection of Divine Providence, we mutually pledge to each other our Lives, our Fortunes, and our sacred Honor.

The Declaration was signed by the following delegates to the Congress:

John Adams (Mass.)
Samuel Adams (Mass.)
Josiah Bartlett (N.H.)
Carter Braxton (Va.)
Charles Carroll (Md.)
Samuel Chase (Md.)
Abraham Clark (N.J.)
George Clymer (Penn.)
William Ellery (R.I.)
William Floyd (N.Y.)
Benjamin Franklin (Penn.)
Elbridge Gerry (Mass.)
Button Gwinnett (Ga.)
Lyman Hall (Ga.)
John Hancock (Mass.)
Benjamin Harrison (Va.)
John Hart (N.J.)
Joseph Hewes (N.C.)
Thomas Heyward, Jr. (S.C.)
William Hooper (N.C.)
Stephen Hopkins (R.I.)
Francis Hopkinson (N.J.)
Samuel Huntington (Conn.)
Thomas Jefferson (Va.)
Richard Henry Lee (Va.)
Francis Lightfoot Lee (Va.)
Francis Lewis (N.Y.)
Philip Livingston (N.Y.)
Thomas Lynch, Jr. (S.C.)
Thomas McKean (Del.)
Arthur Middleton (S.C.)
Lewis Morris (N.Y.)
Robert Morris (Penn.)
John Morton (Penn.)
Thomas Nelson, Jr. (Va.)
William Paca (Md.)
Robert Treat Paine (Mass.)
John Penn (N.C.)
George Read (Del.)
Caesar Rodney (Del.)
George Ross (Penn.)
Benjamin Rush (Penn.)
Edward Rutledge (S.C.)
Roger Sherman (Conn.)
James Smith (Penn.)
Richard Stockton (N.J.)
Thomas Stone (Md.)
George Taylor (Penn.)
Matthew Thornton (N.H.)
George Walton (Ga.)
William Whipple (N.H.)
William Williams (Conn.)
James Wilson (Penn.)
John Witherspoon (N.J.)
Oliver Wolcott (Conn.)
George Wythe (Va.)

CONSTITUTION OF THE UNITED STATES

The Constitution originally consisted of a Preamble and seven Articles, and in that form was ratified by a convention of the States, Sept. 17, 1787. The Government under the Constitution was declared in effect on the first Wednesday in March, 1789. The signers of the original Constitution, by virtue of their membership in Congress, were:

Geo. Washington, President and deputy from Virginia. New Hampshire—John Langdon, Nicholas Gilman, Massachusetts—Nathaniel Gorham, Rufus King. Connecticut—Wm. Saml. Johnson, Roger Sherman. New York—Alexander Hamilton. New Jersey—Wil. Livingston, David Brearley, Wm. Patterson, Jona. Dayton. Pennsylvania—B. Franklin, Robt. Morris, Thos. Fitzsimons, James Wilson, Thomas Mifflin, Geo. Clymer, Jared Ingersoll, Gouv. Morris. Delaware—Geo. Read, John Dickinson, Jaco. Broom, Gunning Bedford jun., Richard Basset. Maryland—James McHenry, Danl. Carroll, Dan. of St. Thos. Jenifer. Virginia—John Blair, James Madison, Jr. North Carolina—Wm. Blount, Hu. Williamson, Richd. Dobbs Spaight. South Carolina—J. Rutledge, Charles Pinckney, Charles Cotesworth Pinckney, Pierce Butler. Georgia—William Few, Abr. Baldwin. Attest: William Jackson, Secretary.

The Constitution was ratified by the thirteen original States in the following order:

Delaware, December 7, 1787 (yeas, 30), unanimous.
Pennsylvania, December 12, 1787, vote 43 to 23.
New Jersey, December 18, 1787 (yeas, 38), unanimous.
Georgia, January 2, 1788 (yeas, 26), unanimous.
Connecticut, January 9, 1788, vote 128 to 40.
Massachusetts, February 6, 1788, vote 187 to 168.
Maryland, April 28, 1788, vote 63 to 11.
South Carolina, May 23, 1788, vote 149 to 73.
New Hampshire, June 21, 1788, vote 57 to 46.
Virginia, June 26, 1788, vote 89 to 79.
New York, July 26, 1788, vote 30 to 27.
North Carolina, November 21, 1789, vote 194 to 77.
Rhode Island, May 29, 1790, vote 34 to 32.
(Vermont, by convention, ratified Jan. 10, 1791; and Congress, Feb. 18, 1791, admitted that State into the Union.)

THE CONSTITUTION

PREAMBLE

We, the people of the United States, in order to form a more perfect Union, establish justice, insure domestic tranquillity, provide for the common defence, promote the general welfare, and secure the blessings of liberty to ourselves and our posterity, do ordain and establish this Constitution for the United States of America.

ARTICLE I.

Section 1—(Legislative powers: in whom vested:)

All legislative powers herein granted shall be vested in a Congress of the United States, which shall consist of a Senate and House of Representatives.

Section 2—(House of Representatives, how and by whom chosen. Qualifications of a Representative. Representatives and direct taxes, how apportioned. Enumeration. Vacancies to be filled. Power of choosing officers, and of impeachment.)

1. The House of Representatives shall be composed of members chosen every second year by the people of the several States, and the electors in each State shall have the qualifications requisite for electors of the most numerous branch of the State Legislature.

2. No person shall be a Representative who shall not have attained to the age of twenty-five years and been seven years a citizen of the United States, and who shall not, when elected, be an inhabitant of that State in which he shall be chosen.

3. Representatives and direct taxes shall be apportioned among the several States which may be included within this Union according to their respective numbers, which shall be determined by adding to the whole number of free persons, including those bound to service for a term of years, and excluding Indians not taxed, three-fifths of all other persons. The actual enumeration shall be made within three years after the first meeting of the Congress of the United States, and within every subsequent term of ten years, in such manner as they shall by law direct. The number of Representatives shall not exceed one for every thirty thousand, but each State shall have at least one Representative: and until such enumeration shall be made, the State of New Hampshire shall be entitled to choose 3; Massachusetts, 8; Rhode Island and Providence Plantations, 1; Connecticut, 5; New York, 6; New Jersey, 4; Pennsylvania, 8; Delaware 1; Maryland, 6; Virginia, 10; North Carolina, 5; South Carolina, 5, and Georgia, 3.*

4. When vacancies happen in the representation from any State, the Executive Authority thereof shall issue writs of election to fill such vacancies.

5. The House of Representatives shall choose their Speaker and other officers, and shall have the sole power of impeachment.

Section 3—(Senators, how and by whom chosen. How classified. State Executive, when to make temporary appointments, in case, etc. Qualifications of a Senator. President of the Senate, his right to vote. President pro tem., and other officers of the Senate, how chosen. Power to try impeachments. When President is tried, Chief Justice to preside. Sentence.)

1. The Senate of the United States shall be composed of two Senators from each State, chosen by the Legislature thereof, for six years; and each Senator shall have one vote.

2. Immediately after they shall be assembled in consequence of the first election, they shall be divided as equally as may be into three classes. The seats of the Senators of the first class shall be vacated at the expiration of the second year, of the second class at the expiration of the fourth year, and of the third class at the expiration of the sixth year, so that one-third may be chosen every second year; and if vacancies happen by resignation, or otherwise, during the recess of the Legislature of any State, the Executive thereof may make temporary appointment until the next meeting of the Legislature, which shall then fill such vacancies.

3. No person shall be a Senator who shall not have attained to the age of thirty years, and been nine years a citizen of the United States, and who shall not, when elected, be an inhabitant of that State for which he shall be chosen.

4. The Vice-President of the United States shall be President of the Senate, but shall have no vote unless they be equally divided.

5. The Senate shall choose their other officers, and also a President pro tempore, in the absence of the Vice-President, or when he shall exercise the office of President of the United States.

6. The Senate shall have the sole power to try all impeachments. When sitting for that purpose, they shall be on oath or affirmation. When the President of the United States is tried, the Chief Justice shall preside; and no person shall be convicted without the concurrence of two-thirds of the members present.

7. Judgment of cases of impeachment shall not extend further than to removal from office, and disqualification to hold and enjoy any office of honor, trust, or profit under the United States; but the party convicted shall nevertheless be liable and subject to indictment, trial judgment and punishment, according to law.

Section 4—(Times, etc., of holding elections, how prescribed. One session in each year.)

1. The times, places, and manner of holding elections for Senators and Representatives shall be prescribed in each State by the Legislature thereof; but the Congress may at any time by law make or alter such regulations, except as to places of choosing Senators.

2. The Congress shall assemble at least once in every year, and such meeting shall be on the first Monday in December, unless they shall by law appoint a different day.

Section 5—(Membership, Quorum, Adjournments. Rules. Power to punish or expel. Journal. Time of adjournments, how limited, etc.)

1. Each House shall be the judge of the elections, returns, and qualifications of its own members, and a majority of each shall constitute a quorum to do business; but a small number may adjourn from day to day, and may be authorized to compel the attendance of absent members in such manner and under such penalties as each House may provide.

2. Each House may determine the rules of its proceedings, punish its members for disorderly behavior, and with the concurrence of two-thirds expel a member.

3. Each House shall keep a journal of its proceedings, and from time to time publish the same, excepting such parts as may in their judgment require secrecy; and the yeas and nays of the members of either House on any question shall, at the desire of one-fifth of those present, be entered on the journal.

4. Neither House, during the session of Congress shall, without the consent of the other, adjourn for more than three days, nor to any other place than that in which the two Houses shall be sitting.

Section 6—(Compensation. Privileges. Disqualification in certain cases.)

1. The Senators and Representatives shall receive a compensation for their services to be ascertained by law, and paid out of the Treasury of the United States. They shall in all cases, except treason, felony, and breach of the peace, be privileged from arrest during their attendance at the session of their respective Houses, and in going to and returning from the same; and for any speech or debate in either House they shall not be questioned in any other place.

2. No Senator or Representative shall, during the time for which he was elected, be appointed to any civil office under the authority of the United States which shall have been created, or the emoluments whereof shall have been increased during such time; and no person holding any office under the United States shall be a member of either House during his continuance in office.

Section 7—(House to originate all revenue bills. Veto. Bill may be passed by two-thirds of each House, notwithstanding, etc. Bill, not returned in ten days, to become a law. Provisions as to orders, concurrent resolutions, etc.)

1. All bills for raising revenue shall originate in the House of Representatives, but the Senate may propose or concur with amendments, as on other bills.

2. Every bill which shall have passed the House of Representatives and the Senate shall, before it becomes a law, be presented to the President of the United States; if he approve, he shall sign it, but if not, he shall return it, with his objections, to that House in which it shall have originated, who shall enter the objections at large on their journal, and proceed to reconsider it. If after such reconsideration two-thirds of that House shall agree to pass the bill, it shall be sent, together with the objections, to the other House, by which it shall likewise be reconsidered; and if approved by two-thirds of that House it shall become a law. But in all such cases the votes of both Houses shall be determined by yeas and nays, and the names of the persons voting for and against the bill shall be entered on the journal of each House respectively. If any bill shall not be returned by the President within ten days (Sundays excepted) after it shall have been presented to him, the same shall be a law in like manner as if he had signed it, unless the Congress by their adjournment prevent its return; in which case it shall not be a law.

3. Every order, resolution, or vote to which the concurrence of the Senate and House of Representatives may be necessary (except on a question of adjournment) shall be presented to the President of the United States; and before the same shall take effect shall be approved by him, or being disapproved by him, shall be repassed by two-thirds of the Senate and the House of Representatives, according to the rules and limitations prescribed in the case of a bill.

Section 8—(Powers of Congress.)

1. The Congress shall have power:

To lay and collect taxes, duties, imposts, and excises, to pay the debts and provide for the common defence and general welfare of the United States; but all duties, imposts, and excises shall be uniform throughout the United States.

2. To borrow money on the credit of the United States.

3. To regulate commerce with foreign nations, and among the several States, and with the Indian tribes.

* See Article XIV, Amendments.

4. To establish an uniform rule of naturalization and uniform laws on the subject of bankruptcies throughout the United States.
5. To coin money, regulate the value thereof, and of foreign coin, and fix the standards of weights and measures.
6. To provide for the punishment of counterfeiting the securities and current coin of the United States.
7. To establish post-offices and post-roads.
8. To promote the progress of science and useful arts by securing for limited times to authors and inventors the exclusive rights to their respective writings and discoveries.
9. To constitute tribunals inferior to the Supreme Court.
10. To define and punish piracies and felonies committed on the high seas, and offences against the laws of nations.
11. To declare war, grant letters of marque and reprisal, and make rules concerning captures on land and water.
12. To raise and support armies, but no appropriation of money to that use shall be for a longer term than two years.
13. To provide and maintain a navy.
14. To make rules for the government and regulation of the land and naval forces.
15. To provide for calling forth the militia to execute the laws of the Union, suppress insurrections, and repel invasions.
16. To provide for organizing, arming, and disciplining the militia, and for governing such part of them as may be employed in the service of the United States, reserving to the States respectively the appointment of the officers, and the authority of training the militia according to the discipline prescribed by Congress.
17. To exercise exclusive legislation in all cases whatsoever over such district (not exceeding ten miles square) as may, by cession of particular States and the acceptance of Congress, become the seat of Government of the United States, and to exercise like authority over all places purchased by the consent of the Legislature of the State in which the same shall be, for the erection of forts, magazines, arsenals, drydocks, and other needful buildings.
18. To make all laws which shall be necessary and proper for carrying into execution the foregoing powers and all other powers vested by this constitution in the Government of the United States, or in any department or officer thereof.

Section 9—(Provision as to migration or importation of certain persons. Habeas Corpus. Bills of attainder, etc. Taxes, how apportioned. No export duty. No commercial preference. Money, how drawn from Treasury, etc. No titular nobility. Officers not to receive presents, etc.)
1. The migration or importation of such persons as any of the States now existing shall think proper to admit shall not be prohibited by the Congress, prior to the year one thousand eight hundred and eight, but a tax or duty may be imposed on such importation, not exceeding ten dollars for each person.
2. The privilege of the writ of habeas corpus shall not be suspended, unless when in cases of rebellion or invasion the public safety may require it.
3. No bill of attainder or ex post facto law shall be passed.
4. No capitation or other direct tax shall be laid, unless in proportion to the census or enumeration hereinbefore directed to be taken.
5. No tax or duty shall be laid on articles exported from any State.
6. No preference shall be given by any regulation of commerce or revenue to the ports of one State over those of another, nor shall vessels bound to or from one State be obliged to enter, clear, or pay duties in another.
7. No money shall be drawn from the Treasury but in consequence of appropriations made by law; and a regular statement and account of the receipts and expenditures of all public money shall be published from time to time.
8. No title of nobility shall be granted by the United States. And no person holding any office of profit or trust under them shall, without the consent of the Congress, accept of any present, emolument, office, or title of any kind whatever from any king, prince, or foreign state.

Section 10—(States prohibited from the exercise of certain powers.)
1. No State shall enter into any treaty, alliance, or confederation, grant letters of marque and reprisal, coin money, emit bills of credit, make anything but gold and silver coin a tender in payment of debts, pass any bill of attainder, ex post facto law, or law impairing the obligation of contracts, or grant any title of nobility.
2. No State shall, without the consent of the Congress, lay any impost or duties on imports or exports, except what may be absolutely necessary for executing its inspection laws, and the net produce of all duties and imposts, laid by any State on imports or exports, shall be for the use of the Treasury of the United States; and all such laws shall be subject to the revision and control of the Congress.
3. No State shall, without the consent of Congress, lay any duty of tonnage, keep troops or ships of war in time of peace, enter into agreement or compact with another State, or with a foreign power, or engage in war, unless actually invaded, or in such imminent danger as will not admit of delay.

ARTICLE II.

Section 1—(President; his term of office. Electors of President; number and how appointed. Electors to vote on same day. Qualification of President. On whom his duties devolve in case of his removal, death, etc. President's compensation. His oath of office.)
1. The Executive power shall be vested in a President of the United States of America. He shall hold his office during the term of four years, and, together with the Vice-President, chosen for the same term, be elected as follows:
2. Each State shall appoint, in such manner as the Legislature thereof may direct, a number of electors equal to the whole number of Senators and Representatives to which the State may be entitled in the Congress; but no Senator or Representative or person holding an office of trust or profit under the United States shall be appointed an elector.
3. The electors shall meet in their respective States and vote by ballot for two persons, of whom one at least shall not be an inhabitant of the same State with themselves. And they shall make a list of all the persons voted for, and of the number of votes for each, which list they shall sign and certify and transmit, sealed, to the seat of the Government of the United States, directed to the President of the Senate. The President of the Senate shall, in the presence of the Senate, and House of Representatives, open all the certificates, and the votes shall then be counted. The person having the greatest number of votes shall be the President, if such number be a majority of the whole number of electors appointed, and if there be more than one who have such a majority, and have an equal number of votes, then the House of Representatives shall immediately choose by ballot one of them for President; and if no person have a majority, then from the five highest on the list the said House shall in like manner choose the President. But in choosing the President, the vote shall be taken by States, the representation from each State having one vote. A quorum, for this purpose, shall consist of a member or members from two-thirds of the States, and a majority of all the States shall be necessary to a choice. In every case, after the choice of the President, the person having the greatest number of votes of the electors shall be the Vice-President. But if there should remain two or more who have equal votes, the Senate shall choose from them by ballot the Vice-President.*
4. The Congress may determine the time of choosing the electors and the day on which they shall give their votes, which day shall be the same throughout the United States.
5. No person except a natural born citizen, or a citizen of the United States, at the time of the adoption of this Constitution, shall be eligible to the office of President; neither shall any person be eligible to that office who shall not have attained to the age of thirty-five years and been fourteen years a resident within the United States.
6. In case of the removal of the President from office, or of his death, resignation, or inability to discharge the powers and duties of the said office, the same shall devolve on the Vice President, and the Congress may by law provide for the case of removal, death, resignation, or inability, both of the President and Vice President, declaring what officer shall then act as President, and such officer shall act accordingly, until the disability be removed or a President shall be elected.
7. The President shall, at stated times, receive for his services a compensation which shall neither be increased nor diminished during the period for which he shall have been elected, and he shall not receive within that period any other emolument from the United States, or any of them.
8. Before he enter on the execution of his office he shall take the following oath or affirmation:
"I do solemnly swear (or affirm) that I will faithfully execute the office of President of the United States, and will, to the best of my ability, preserve, protect, and defend the Constitution of the United States."

Section 2—(President to be Commander-in-Chief. He may require opinions of Cabinet Officers, etc., may pardon. Treaty-making power. Nomination of certain officers. When President may fill vacancies.)
1. The President shall be Commander-in-Chief of the Army and Navy of the United States, and of the militia of the several States when called into the actual service of the United States; he may require the opinion, in writing, of the principal officer in each of the executive departments upon any subject relating to the duties of their respective offices, and he shall have power to grant reprieves and pardons for offences against the United States except in cases of impeachment.
2. He shall have power, by and with the advice and consent of the Senate to make treaties, provided two-thirds of the Senators present concur, and he shall nominate and by and with the advice and consent of the Senate shall appoint ambassadors, other public ministers and consuls, judges of the Supreme Court, and all other officers of the United States whose appointments are not herein otherwise provided for, and which shall be established by law; but the Congress may by law vest the appointment of such inferior officers as they think proper in the President alone, in the courts of law, or in the heads of departments.
3. The President shall have power to fill up all vacancies that may happen during the recess of the Senate by granting commissions, which shall expire at the end of their next session.

Section 3—(President shall communicate to Congress. He may convene and adjourn Congress, in case of disagreement, etc. Shall receive Ambassadors, execute laws, and commission officers.)
He shall from time to time give to the Congress information of the state of the Union, and recommend to their consideration such measures as he shall judge necessary and expedient; he may, on extraordinary occasions, convene both Houses, or either of them, and in case of disagreement between them with respect to the time of adjournment, he may adjourn them to such time as he shall think proper; he shall receive ambassadors and other public ministers; he shall take care that the laws be faithfully executed, and shall commission all the officers of the United States.

Section 4—(All civil offices forfeited for certain crimes.)
The President, Vice-President, and all civil officers of the United States shall be removed from office on impeachment for and conviction of treason, bribery or other high crimes and misdemeanors.

ARTICLE III.

Section 1—(Judicial powers. Tenure. Compensation.)
The judicial power of the United States shall be vested in one Supreme Court, and in such inferior courts as the Congress may from time to time ordain and establish. The judges, both of the Supreme and inferior courts, shall hold their offices during good behavior, and shall at stated times receive for their services a compensation which shall not be diminished during their continuance in office.

Section 2—(Judicial power; to what cases it extends. Original jurisdiction of Supreme Court. Appellate. Trial by jury, etc. Trial, where.)
1. The judicial power shall extend to all cases in law and equity arising under this Constitution, the laws of the United States, and treaties made, or which shall be made, under their authority; to all cases affecting ambassadors, other public ministers and consuls; to all cases of admiralty and maritime jurisdiction; to controversies to which the United States shall be a party: to controversies between two or more States, between a State and citizens of another State, between citizens of different States, between citizens of the same State claiming lands under grants of different States, and between a State, or the citizens thereof, and foreign states, citizens, or subjects.
2. In all cases affecting ambassadors, other public ministers, and consuls, and those in which a State shall be party, the Supreme Court shall have original jurisdiction. In all the other cases before mentioned the Supreme Court shall have appellate jurisdiction both as to law and fact, with such exceptions and under such regulations as the Congress shall make.
3. The trial of all crimes, except in cases of impeachment, shall be by jury, and such trial shall be held in the State where the said crimes shall have been committed; but when not committed within any State the trial shall be at such place or places as the Congress may by law have directed.

Section 3—(Treason defined. Proof of. Punishment of.)
1. Treason against the United States shall consist only in levying war against them, or in adhering to their enemies, giving them aid and comfort. No person shall be convicted of treason unless on the testimony of two witnesses to the same overt act, or on confession in open court.
2. The Congress shall have power to declare the punishment of treason, but no attainder of treason shall work corruption of blood or forfeiture except during the life of the person attained.

ARTICLE IV.

Section 1—(Each State to give credit to the public acts, etc., of every other State.)
Full faith and credit shall be given in each State to the public acts, records, and judicial proceedings of every other State. And the Congress may by general

* This clause is superseded by Article XII, Amendments.

laws prescribe the manner in which such acts, records, and proceedings shall be proved, and the effect thereof.

Section 2—(Privileges of citizens of each State. Fugitives from justice to be delivered up. Persons held to service having escaped, to be delivered up.)

1. The citizens of each State shall be entitled to all privileges and immunities of citizens in the several States.

2. A person charged in any State with treason, felony, or other crime, who shall flee from justice, and be found in another State, shall on demand of the Executive authority of the State from which he fled, be delivered up, to be removed to the State having jurisdiction of the crime.

3. No person held to service or labor in one State under the laws thereof, escaping into another shall in consequence of any law or regulation therein, be discharged from such service or labor, but shall be delivered up on claim of the party to whom such service or labor may be due.

Section 3—(Admission of new States. Power of Congress over territory and other property.)

1. New States may be admitted by the Congress into this Union; but no new State shall be formed or erected within the jurisdiction of any other State, nor any State be formed by the junction of two or more States, or parts of States, without the consent of the Legislatures of the States concerned, as well as of the Congress.

2. The Congress shall have power to dispose of and make all needful rules and regulations respecting the territory or other property belonging to the United States; and nothing in this Constitution shall be so construed as to prejudice any claims of the United States, or of any particular State.

Section 4—(Republican form of government guaranteed. Each State to be protected.)

The United States shall guarantee to every State in this Union a Republican form of government, and shall protect each of them against invasion; and, on application of the Legislature, or of the Executive (when the Legislative cannot be convened), against domestic violence.

ARTICLE V.

(Constitution; how amended. Proviso.)

The Congress, whenever two-thirds of both Houses shall deem it necessary, shall propose amendments to this Constitution, or, on the application of the Legislatures of two-thirds of the several States, shall call a convention for proposing amendments, which, in either case, shall be valid to all intents and purposes, as part of this Constitution, when ratified by the Legislatures of three-fourths of the several States, or by conventions in three-fourths thereof, as the one or the other mode of ratification may be proposed by the Congress; provided that no amendment which may be made prior to the year one thousand eight hundred and eight shall in any manner affect the first and fourth clauses in the Ninth Section of the First Article; and that no State, without its consent, shall be deprived of its equal suffrage in the Senate.

ARTICLE VI.

(Certain debts, etc., declared valid. Supremacy of Constitution, treaties, and laws of the United States. Oath to support Constitution, by whom taken. No religious test.)

1. All debts contracted and engagements entered into before the adoption of this Constitution shall be as valid against the United States under this Constitution as under the Confederation.

2. This Constitution and the laws of the United States which shall be made in pursuance thereof and all treaties made or which shall be made, under the authority of the United States, shall be the supreme law of the land, and the judges in every State shall be bound thereby, anything in the Constitution or laws of any State to the contrary notwithstanding.

3. The Senators and Representatives before mentioned, and the members of the several State Legislatures, and all executive and judicial officers, both of the United States, and of the several States, shall be bound by oath or affirmation to support this Constitution; but no religious test shall ever be required as a qualification to any office or public trust under the United States.

ARTICLE VII.

(What ratification shall establish Constitution.)

The ratification of the Conventions of nine States shall be sufficient for the establishment of this Constitution between the States so ratifying the same.

AMENDMENTS TO THE CONSTITUTION OF THE UNITED STATES

Opposition in and out of Congress to the Constitution, in that it was not sufficiently explicit as to individual and State rights, led to an agreement to submit to the people immediately after the adoption of the Constitution a number of safeguarding amendments.

And so it was that the First Congress, at its first session, in the City of New York, Sept. 25, 1789, adopted and submitted to the States twelve proposed amendments—A Bill of Rights as it was then and ever since has been popularly called. Ten of these amendments (now commonly known as one to ten inclusive, but in reality three to twelve inclusive) were ratified by the States as follows—New Jersey, Nov. 20, 1789; Maryland, Dec. 19, 1789; North Carolina, Dec. 22, 1789; South Carolina, Jan. 19, 1790; New Hampshire, Jan. 25, 1790; Delaware, Jan. 28, 1790; Pennsylvania, March 10, 1790; New York, March 27, 1790; Rhode Island, June 15, 1790; Vermont, Nov. 3, 1791; Virginia, Dec. 15, 1791. No ratification by Connecticut, Georgia or Massachusetts is on record. These original ten ratified amendments appear in order below as Articles I. to X. inclusive.

The two of the original proposed amendments which were not ratified by the necessary number of States related, the first to apportionment of Representatives; the second, to compensation of members of Congress.

THE BILL OF RIGHTS

(Declared in force December 15, 1791)

ARTICLE I.

Religious Establishment Prohibited. Freedom of Speech, of the Press, and Right to Petition.

Congress shall make no law respecting an establishment of religion, or prohibiting the free exercise thereof; or abridging the freedom of speech or of the press; or the right of the people peaceably to assemble and to petition the Government for a redress of grievances.

ARTICLE II.

Right to Keep and Bear Arms.

A well-regulated militia being necessary to the security of a free State, the right of the people to keep and bear arms shall not be infringed.

ARTICLE III.

No Soldier to Be Quartered in Any House, Unless, Etc.

No soldier shall, in time of peace, be quartered in any house without the consent of the owner, nor in time of war but in a manner to be prescribed by law.

ARTICLE IV.

Right of Search and Seizure Regulated.

The right of the people to be secure in their persons, houses, papers, and effects, against unreasonable searches and seizures, shall not be violated, and no warrants shall issue but upon probable cause, supported by oath or affirmation, and particularly describing the place to be searched, and the persons or things to be seized.

ARTICLE V.

Provisions Concerning Prosecution, Trial and Punishment—Private Property Not to Be Taken for Public Use, Without Compensation.

No person shall be held to answer for a capital or other infamous crime unless on a presentment or indictment of a Grand Jury, except in cases arising in the land or naval forces, or in the militia, when in actual service, in time of war or public danger; nor shall any person be subject for the same offense to be twice put in jeopardy of life or limb; nor shall be compelled in any criminal case to be a witness against himself, nor be deprived of life, liberty, or property, without due process of law; nor shall private property be taken for public use without just compensation.

ARTICLE VI.

Right to Speedy Trial, Witnesses, Etc.

In all criminal prosecutions, the accused shall enjoy the right to a speedy and public trial, by an impartial jury of the State and district wherein the crime shall have been committed, which districts shall have been previously ascertained by law, and to be informed of the nature and cause of the accusation; to be confronted with the witnesses against him; to have compulsory process for obtaining witnesses in his favor, and to have the assistance of counsel for his defense.

ARTICLE VII.

Right of Trial by Jury.

In suits at common law, where the value in controversy shall exceed twenty dollars, the right of trial by jury shall be preserved, and no fact tried by a jury shall be otherwise re-examined in any court of the United States than according to the rules of the common law.

ARTICLE VIII.

Excessive Bail or Fines and Cruel Punishment Prohibited.

Excessive bail shall not be required, nor excessive fines imposed, nor cruel and unusual punishments inflicted.

ARTICLE IX.

Rule of Construction of Constitution.

The enumeration in the Constitution of certain rights shall not be construed to deny or disparage others retained by the people.

ARTICLE X.

Rights of States Under Constitution.

The powers not delegated to the United States by the Constitution, nor prohibited by it to the States, are reserved to the States respectively, or to the people.

ARTICLE XI.

Judicial Powers Construed.

The following amendment was proposed to the Legislatures of the several States by the Third Congress on the 5th of March, 1794, and was declared to have been ratified in a message from the President to Congress, dated Jan. 8, 1798.

The judicial power of the United States shall not be construed to extend to any suit in law or equity, commenced or prosecuted against one of the United States, by citizens of another State, or by citizens or subjects of any foreign state.

ARTICLE XII.

Manner of Choosing President and Vice-President.

The following amendment was proposed to the Legislatures of the several States by the Eighth Congress on the 12th of December, 1803, and was declared to have been ratified in a proclamation by the Secretary of State, dated September 25, 1804. It was ratified by all the States except Connecticut, Delaware, Massachusetts, and New Hampshire.

The Electors shall meet in their respective States, and vote by ballot for President and Vice-President, one of whom at least shall not be an inhabitant of the same State with themselves; they shall name in their ballots the person voted for as President, and in distinct ballots the person voted for as Vice-President; and they shall make distinct list of all persons voted for as President, and of all persons voted for as Vice-President, and of the number of votes for each, which list they shall sign and certify, and transmit, sealed, to the seat of the Government of the United States, directed to the President of the Senate; the President of the Senate shall, in the presence of the Senate and House of Representatives, open all the certificates and the votes shall then be counted; the person having the greatest number of votes for President shall be the President, if such number be a majority of the whole number of Electors appointed; and if no person have such majority, then from the persons having the highest number, not exceeding three, on the list of those voted for as President, the House of Representatives shall choose immediately, by ballot, the President. But in choosing the President, the votes shall be taken by States, the representation from each State having one vote; a quorum for this purpose shall consist of a member or members from two-thirds of the States, and a majority of all the States shall be necessary to a choice. And if the House of Representatives shall not choose a President, whenever the right of choice shall devolve upon them, before the fourth day of March next following, then the Vice-President shall act as President, as in the case of the death or other constitutional disability of the President. The person having the greatest number of votes as Vice-President shall be the Vice-President, if such number be a majority of the whole number of Electors appointed, and if no person have a majority, then from the two highest numbers on the list the Senate shall choose the Vice-President; a quorum for the purpose shall consist of two-thirds of the whole number of Senators, and a majority of the whole number shall be necessary to a choice. But no person constitutionally ineligible to the office of President shall be eligible to that of Vice-President of the United States.

ARTICLE XIII.

Slavery Abolished.

The following amendment was proposed to the Legislatures of the several States by the Thirty-eighth Congress on the 1st of February, 1865, and was declared to have been ratified in a proclamation by the Secretary of State dated December 18, 1865. It was rejected by Delaware and Kentucky: was conditionally ratified by Alabama and Mississippi; and Texas took no action.

1. Neither slavery nor involuntary servitude, except as a punishment for crime whereof the party shall have been duly convicted, shall exist within the United States, or any place subject to their jurisdiction.

2. Congress shall have power to enforce this article by appropriate legislation.

ARTICLE XIV.

Citizenship Rights Not to Be Abridged.

The following, popularly known as the Reconstruction Amendment, was proposed to the Legislatures of the several States by the Thirty-ninth Congress on the 16th of June, 1866, and was declared to have been ratified in a proclamation by the Secretary of State, dated July 23, 1868. The amendment got the support of 23 Northern States: it was rejected by Delaware, Kentucky, Maryland, and 10 Southern States. California took no action. Subsequently it was ratified by the 10 Southern States.

1. All persons born or naturalized in the United States, and subject to the jurisdiction thereof, are citizens of the United States and of the State wherein they reside. No State shall make or enforce any law which shall abridge the privileges or immunities of citizens of the United States; nor shall any State deprive any person of life, liberty, or property without due process of law, nor deny to any person within its jurisdiction the equal protection of the laws.

Apportionment of Representatives in Congress.

2. Representatives shall be apportioned among the several States according to their respective numbers counting the whole number of persons in each State excluding Indians not taxed. But when the right to vote at any election for the choice of Electors for President and Vice-President of the United States, Representatives in Congress, the executive and judicial officers of a State, or the members of the Legislature thereof, is denied to any of the male inhabitants of such State, being twenty-one years of age, and citizens of the United States, or in any way abridged, except for participation in rebellion, or other crime, the basis of representation therein shall be reduced in the proportion which the number of such male citizens shall bear to the whole number of male citizens twenty-one years of age in such State.

Power of Congress to Remove Disabilities of United States Officials for Rebellion.

3. No person shall be a Senator or Representative in Congress, or Elector of President and Vice-President or holding any office, civil or military, under the United States, or under any State, who, having previously taken an oath, as a member of Congress, or as an officer of the United States, or as a member of any State Legislature or as an executive or judicial officer of any State, to support the Constitution of the United States, shall have engaged in insurrection or rebellion against the same, or given aid and comfort to the enemies thereof. But Congress may, by a vote of two-thirds of each House, remove such disability.

What Public Debts Are Valid.

4. The validity of the public debt of the United States, authorized by law, including debts incurred for payment of pensions and bounties for services in suppressing insurrection and rebellion, shall not be questioned. But neither the United States nor any State shall assume or pay any debt or obligation incurred in aid of insurrection or rebellion against the United States, or any claim for the loss or emancipation of any slave; but all such debts, obligations, and claims shall be held illegal and void.

5. The Congress shall have power to enforce by appropriate legislation the provisions of this article.

ARTICLE XV.

Equal Rights for White and Colored Citizens.

The following amendment was proposed to the Legislatures of the several States by the Fortieth Congress on the 27th of February, 1869, and was declared to have been ratified in a proclamation by the Secretary of State, dated March 30, 1870. It was not acted on by Tennessee: it was rejected by California, Delaware, Kentucky, Maryland, and Oregon: ratified by the remaining 30 States. New York rescinded its ratification January 5, 1870. New Jersey rejected it in 1870 but ratified it in 1871.

1. The right of the citizens of the United States to vote shall not be denied or abridged by the United States or by any State on account of race, color, or previous condition of servitude.

2. The Congress shall have power to enforce the provisions of this article by appropriate legislation.

ARTICLE XVI.

Income Taxes Authorized.

The following amendment was proposed to the Legislatures of the several States by the Sixty-first Congress on the 12th day of July, 1909, and was declared to have been ratified in a proclamation by the Secretary of State, dated February 25, 1913. The income tax amendment was ratified by all the States except Connecticut, Florida, Pennsylvania, Rhode Island, Utah, and Virginia.

The Congress shall have power to lay and collect taxes on incomes, from whatever sources derived, without apportionment among the several States and without regard to any census or enumeration.

ARTICLE XVII.

United States Senators to Be Elected by Direct Popular Vote.

The following amendment was proposed to the Legislatures of the several States by the Sixty-second Congress on the 16th day of May, 1912, and was declared to have been ratified in a proclamation by the Secretary of State, dated May 31, 1913. It got the vote of all the States except Alabama, Delaware, Florida, Georgia, Kentucky, Louisiana, Maryland, Mississippi, Rhode Island, South Carolina, Utah, and Virginia.

1. The Senate of the United States shall be composed of two Senators from each State, elected by the people thereof, for six years; and each Senator shall have one vote. The electors in each State shall have the qualifications requisite for electors of the most numerous branch of the State Legislatures.

Vacancies in Senatorships, When Governor May Fill by Appointment.

2. When vacancies happen in the representation of any State in the Senate, the executive authority of such State shall issue writs of election to fill such vacancies: Provided, That the Legislature of any State may empower the Executive thereof to make temporary appointment until the people fill the vacancies by election as the Legislature may direct.

3. This amendment shall not be so construed as to affect the election or term of any Senator chosen before it becomes valid as part of the Constitution.

ARTICLE XVIII.

Liquor Prohibition Amendment.

The following amendment was proposed to the Legislatures of the several States by the Sixty-fifth Congress, December 18, 1917: and on January 29, 1919, the United States Secretary of State proclaimed its adoption by 36 States, and declared it in effect on January 16, 1920.

The amendment ultimately was adopted by all the States except Connecticut and Rhode Island. New Jersey ratified on March 10, 1922.

Enforcement of the National Prohibition Act was in effect at 12 P. M., January 16, 1920, except as to certain sections of Title II. wherein other dates were specified.

Early in 1920, the validity of the Eighteenth Amendment was upheld by the Supreme Court of the United States, in suits to void, brought by the States of Rhode Island and New Jersey, and by various brewers and distillers.

1. After one year from the ratification of this article the manufacture, sale, or transportation of intoxicating liquors within, the importation thereof into, or the exportation thereof from the United States and all territory subject to the jurisdiction thereof for beverage purposes is hereby prohibited.

2. The Congress and the several States shall have concurrent power to enforce this article by appropriate legislation.

3. This article shall be inoperative unless it shall have been ratified as an amendment to the Constitution by the Legislatures of the several States, as provided in the Constitution, within seven years from the date of the submission hereof to the States by the Congress.

ARTICLE XIX.

Giving Nation-Wide Suffrage to Women.

The following amendment was proposed to the Legislatures of the several States by the Sixty-fifth Congress, having been adopted by the House of Representatives, May 21, 1919, and by the Senate June 4, 1919. On August 26, 1920, the United, States Secretary of State proclaimed it in effect, having been adopted (June 10, 1919-August 18, 1920) by three-quarters of the States. The Tennessee House, August 31, rescinded its ratification, 47 to 24.

1. The right of citizens of the United States to vote shall not be denied or abridged by the United States or by any State on account of sex.

2. Congress shall have power, by appropriate legislation, to enforce the provisions of this article.

ARTICLE XX.

Terms of President and Vice-President to begin on January 20; those of Senators and Representatives, on January 3.

The following amendment was proposed to the Legislatures of the several States by the Seventy-second Congress, in March, 1932, a joint resolution to that effect having been adopted, first by the House, and then, on March 2, by the Senate. On Feb. 6, 1933, the Secretary of State proclaimed it in effect, 39 of the 48 States having ratified. By Oct. 15, 1933, it had been ratified by all of the 48 States.

Section 1—The terms of the President and Vice-President shall end at noon on the 20th day of January, and the terms of Senators and Representatives at noon on the 3rd day of January, of the years in which such terms would have ended if this article had not been ratified; and the terms of their successors shall then begin.

Section 2—The Congress shall assemble at least once in every year, and such meeting shall begin at noon on the 3rd day of January, unless they shall by law appoint a different day.

Section 3—If, at the time fixed for the beginning of the term of the President, the President elect shall have died the Vice-President elect shall become President. If a President shall not have been chosen before the time fixed for the beginning of his term, or if the President elect shall have failed to qualify, then the Vice-President elect shall act as President until a President shall have qualified; and the Congress may by law provide for the case wherein neither a President elect nor a Vice-President elect shall have qualified, declaring who shall then act as President, or the manner in which one who is to act shall be selected, and such person shall act accordingly until a President or Vice-President shall have qualified.

Section 4—The Congress may by law provide for the case of the death of any of the persons from whom the House of Representatives may choose a President whenever the right of choice shall have devolved upon them, and for the case of the death of any of the persons from whom the Senate may choose a Vice-President whenever the right of choice shall have devolved upon them.

Section 5—Sections 1 and 2 shall take effect on the 15th day of October following the ratification of this article (Oct., 1933).

Section 6—This article shall be inoperative unless it shall have been ratified as an amendment to the Constitution by the legislatures of three-fourths of the several States within seven years from the date of its submission.

ARTICLE XXI.

Repeal of the Eighteenth (Prohibition) Amendment by Conventions in the States.

The following proposed amendment to the Constitution, embodied in a joint resolution of the 72nd Congress (Senate Feb. 16, 1933, by 63 to 23; House, Feb. 20, 1933, by 289 to 121), was transmitted to the Secretary of State on Feb. 21 and he at once sent to the governors of the States copies of the resolution. The amendment went into effect on Dec. 5, 1933, having been adopted by 36 of the 48 States—three-quarters of the entire number. The amendment is:

Section 1—The eighteenth article of amendment to the Constitution of the United States is hereby repealed.

Section 2—The transportation or importation into any State, Territory, or Possession of the United States for delivery or use therein of intoxicating liquors, in violation of the laws thereof, is hereby prohibited.

Section 3—This article shall be inoperative unless it shall have been ratified as an amendment to the Constitution by conventions in the several States, as provided in the Constitution, within seven years from the date of the submission hereof to the States by the Congress.

ARTICLE XXII.

Presidents Barred from Serving More than Two Elective Terms.

The following proposed amendment was approved by the Eightieth Congress on March 26, 1947, and transmitted to the Secretary of State who sent copies of the resolution to the governors of the States. The amendment went into effect on February 26, 1951, having been adopted by 36 of the 48 States.

Section 1—No person shall be elected to the office of the President more than twice, and no person who has held the office of President, or acted as President, for more than two years of a term to which some other person was elected President shall be elected to the office of the President more than once. But this article shall not apply to any person holding the office of President when this article was proposed by the Congress, and shall not prevent any person who may be holding the office of President, or acting as President, during the term within which this article becomes operative from holding the office of President or acting as President during the remainder of such term.

Section 2—This article shall be inoperative unless it shall have been ratified as an amendment to the Constitution by the Legislatures of three-fourths of the several states within seven years from the date of its submission to the States by the Congress.

ARTICLE XXIII.

Citizens of District of Columbia Granted Right to Vote in Presidential Elections.

The following proposed amendment was approved by the Eighty-seventh Congress on March 29, 1961, when it was ratified by 34 of the 50 States. The amendment was approved 286 days after its submission to the States.

Section 1—The District constituting the seat of Government of the United States shall appoint in such manner as the Congress may direct:

A number of electors of President and Vice-President equal to the whole number of Senators and Representatives in Congress to which the District would be entitled if it were a State, but in no event more than the least populous State; they shall be in addition to those appointed by the States, but they shall be considered, for the purposes of the election of President and Vice-President, to be electors appointed by a State; and they shall meet in the District and perform such duties as provided by the twelfth article of the amendment.

Section 2—The Congress shall have power to enforce this article by appropriate legislation.

ARTICLE XXIV.

Poll Tax Barred as Prerequisite in Federal Elections.

The following proposed amendment was approved by the Eighty-eighth Congress on Jan. 23, 1964, when it was ratified by 38 of the 50 States. It had been submitted to the States by Congress Aug. 27, 1962.

Section 1—The right of citizens of the United States to vote in any primary or other election for President or Vice-President, for electors for President or Vice-President, or for Senator or Representative in Congress, shall not be denied or abridged by the United States or any State by reason of failure to pay any poll tax or other tax.

Section 2—The Congress shall have the power to enforce this article by appropriate legislation.

ARTICLE XXV.

Procedures to be Followed in the Event of the Death or Disability of the President.

The following proposed amendment was approved by the Ninetieth Congress on Feb. 10, 1967, when it was ratified by 38 of the 50 States. It had been submitted to the States by Congress July 6, 1965.

Section 1—In case of the removal of the President from office or his death or resignation, the Vice-President shall become President.

Section 2—Whenever there is a vacancy in the office of the Vice-President, the President shall nominate a Vice-President who shall take the office upon confirmation by a majority vote of both houses of Congress.

Section 3—Whenever the President transmits to the President pro tempore of the Senate and the Speaker of the House of Representatives his written declaration that he is unable to discharge the powers and duties of his office, and until he transmits to them a written declaration to the contrary, such powers and duties shall be discharged by the Vice-President as Acting President.

Section 4—Whenever the Vice-President and a majority of either the principal officers of the executive department or of such other body as Congress may by law provide, transmit to the President pro tempore of the Senate and the Speaker of the House of Representatives their written declaration that the President is unable to discharge the powers and duties of his office, the Vice-President shall immediately assume the powers and duties of the office as Acting President.

Thereafter, when the President transmits to the President pro tempore of the Senate and the Speaker of the House of Representatives his written declaration that no inability exists, he shall resume the powers and duties of his office unless the Vice-President and a majority of either the principal officers of the executive department or of such other body as Congress may by law provide, transmit within four days to the President pro tempore of the Senate and the Speaker of the House of Representatives their written declaration that the President is unable to discharge the powers and duties of his office. Thereupon Congress shall decide the issue, assembling within 48 hours for that purpose if not in session. If the Congress, within 21 days after receipt of the latter written declaration, or, if Congress is not in session, within 21 days after Congress is required to assemble, determines by two-thirds vote of both houses that the President is unable to discharge the powers and duties of his office, the Vice-President shall continue to discharge the same as Acting President; otherwise, the President shall resume the powers and duties of his office.

ARTICLE XXVI.

Voting Age Lowered to Eighteen Years.

The following proposed amendment was approved by the Ninety-second Congress on June 30, 1971, when it was ratified by 38 of the 50 States. It had been submitted to the States by Congress March 23, 1971.

Section 1—The right of citizens of the United States who are 18 years of age or older, to vote shall not be denied or abridged by the United States or any State on account of age.

Section 2—The Congress shall have the power to enforce this article by appropriate legislation.

HISTORY OF CANADA

A CHRONOLOGY OF THE MOST IMPORTANT EVENTS

1497. June 24, Eastern coast of North America discovered by John Cabot.
1498. Cabot discovered Hudson strait.
1501. Gaspar Corte Real visited Newfoundland and Labrador.
1524. Verrazano explored the coast of Nova Scotia.
1534. June 21, Landing of Jacques Cartier at Esquimaux bay.
1535. Cartier's second voyage. He ascended the St. Lawrence to Stadacona (Quebec), (Sept. 14), and Hochelaga (Montreal), (Oct. 2).
1541. Cartier's third voyage. He planted wheat, cabbages, turnips and lettuces near Cape Rouge river.
1542–3. De Roberval and his party wintered at Cape Rouge, and were rescued by Cartier on his fourth voyage.
1557. Sept. 1, Death of Cartier at St. Malo, France.
1592. Straits of Juan de Fuca discovered by de Fuca.
1603. June 22, Champlain's first landing in Canada, at Quebec.
1604. De Monts settled colony on island in the St. Croix river.
1605. Founding of Port Royal (Annapolis, N.S.)
1608. Champlain's second visit. July 3, Founding of Quebec.
1609. July, Champlain discovered Lake Champlain.
1610–11. Hudson explored Hudson bay and James bay.
1611. Brûlé ascended the Ottawa river.
1612. Oct. 15, Champlain made Lieutenant-General of New France.
1613. June, Champlain ascended the Ottawa river.
1615. Champlain explored lakes Nipissing, Huron and Ontario (discovered by Brûlé and Le Caron).
1616. First schools opened at Tadoussac and on the site of the city of Three Rivers.
1617. Arrival at Quebec of the first colonist, Louis Hébert and his family.
1620. Population of Quebec, 60 persons.
1621. Code of laws issued and register of births, deaths and marriages opened in Quebec. Nova Scotia granted to Sir William Alexander by King James I.
1622. Lake Superior discovered by Brûlé.
1623. First British settlement of Nova Scotia.
1627. New France and Acadia granted to the Company of 100 Associates.
1628. Port Royal taken by Sir David Kirke.
1629. April 24, Treaty of Susa between France and England. July 20, Quebec taken by Sir David Kirke.
1632. Mar. 29, Canada and Acadia restored to France by the Treaty of St. Germain-en-Laye.
1633. May 23, Champlain made first Governor of New France.
1634. July 4, Founding of Three Rivers.
1634–35. Exploration of the Great Lakes by Nicolet.
1635. Dec. 25, Death of Champlain at Quebec. Founding of the first college at Quebec.
1638. June 11, First recorded earthquake in Canada.
1640. Discovery of lake Erie by Chaumonot and Brébeuf.
1641. Resident population of New France, 240.
1642. May 17, Founding of Ville-Marie (Montreal) by Maisonneuve.
1646. Exploration of the Saguenay by Dablon.
1647. Lake St. John discovered by de Quen.
1648. Mar. 5, Council of New France created.
1649. Mar. 16–17, Murder of Fathers Brébeuf and Lalemant by Indians and massacre of the Hurons.
1654. August, Acadia taken by an expedition from New England.
1656. Acadia granted by Cromwell to La Tour, Temple and Crowne.
1659. June 16, François de Laval arrived in Canada as Vicar-Apostolic.
1660. May 21, Dollard des Ormeaux and sixteen companions killed by Iroquois at the Long Sault, Ottawa river.
1663. Company of 100 Associates dissolved. Feb. 5, severe earthquake. April, Sovereign Council of New France established. Population of New France, 2,500, of whom 800 were in Quebec. Foundation of the 'Grand Seminary' at Quebec, by Laval.
1664. May, Company of the West Indies founded.
1665. Mar. 23, Talon appointed Intendant.
1666. Feb.–Mar., First census. Population of New France, 3,215.
1667. July 21, Acadia restored to France by the Treaty of Breda. Sept.–Oct., Second census; white population of New France, 3,918.
1668. Foundation of the 'Little Seminary' at Quebec by Laval. Mission at Sault Ste. Marie founded by Marquette.
1670. May 2, Charter of the Hudson's Bay Company granted.
1671. Population of Acadia, 441.
1672. Population of New France, 6,705. April 6, Comte de Frontenac, Governor.
1673. June 13, Cataraqui (Kingston) founded.
1674. Oct. 1, Laval became first Bishop of Quebec.
1675. Population of New France, 7,832.
1678. Niagara falls visited by Hennepin.
1679. Ship *Le Griffon* built on Niagara river above the falls by La Salle. Third census; population of New France, 9,400; of Acadia, 515.
1681. Fourth census; population of New France, 9,677.
1682. Frontenac recalled.
1683. Population of New France, 10,251.
1685. First issue of card money. Fifth census; population of New France, 12,263, including 1,538 settled Indians.
1686. Population of New France, 12,373; of Acadia, 885.
1687. Mar. 18, La Salle assassinated.
1688. Sixth census; population of New France, 11,562, including 1,259 settled Indians.
1689. June 7, Frontenac re-appointed Governor. Aug. 5, Massacre of whites by Indians at Lachine.
1690. May 21, Sir William Phips captured Port Royal, but was repulsed in an attack on Quebec (Oct. 16–21).
1692. Seventh census; population of New France, 12,431. Oct. 22, Defence of Vèrcheres against Indians by Madeleine de Vèrcheres.
1693. Population of Acadia, 1,009.
1695. Eighth census; population of New France, 13,639, including 853 settled Indians.
1697. Sept. 20, By the treaty of Ryswick, places taken during the war were mutually restored. D'Iberville defeated the Hudson's Bay Co.'s ships on Hudson bay.
1698. Nov. 28, Death of Frontenac. Ninth census; population of New France, 15,355.
1701. La Motte Cadillac built a fort at Detroit.
1703. June 16, Sovereign Council of Canada became Superior Council and membership increased from 7 to 12.
1706. Tenth census; population of New France, 16,417.
1708. Death of Laval.
1709. British invasion of Canada.
1710. Oct. 13, Port Royal taken by Nicholson.
1711. Sept. 1, Part of Sir H. Walker's fleet, proceeding against Quebec, wrecked off the Seven Islands.
1713. April 11, Treaty of Utrecht; Hudson Bay, Acadia and Newfoundland ceded to Great Britain. August, Louisbourg founded by the French. Population of New France, 18,119.
1718. Foundation of New Orleans in carrying out French plan to control the Mississippi as well as the St. Lawrence.
1719. Census population of New France, 22,530.
1720. Population of New France, 24,234; of Île St. Jean (P.E.I.), about 100. April 25, Governor and Council of Nova Scotia appointed.
1721. June 19, Burning of about one half of Montreal. Census population of New France, 24,951.
1727. Population of New France, 30,613.
1728. Population of Île St. Jean (P.E.I.), 830.
1731. Population of the north of the peninsula of Acadia, 6,000.
1733. Discovery of lake Winnipeg by La Vérendrye.
1734. Road opened from Quebec to Montreal. Census population of New France, 37,716.
1737. Iron smelted on St. Maurice. French population of the north of the Acadia peninsula, 7,598.
1739. Census population of New France, 42,701.
1743. The younger La Vérendrye discovered the Rocky mountains.
1745. June 17, Taking of Louisbourg by Pepperell and Warren.
1748. Oct. 18, Treaty of Aix-la-Chapelle. Louisbourg restored to France in exchange for Madras.
1749. June 21, Founding of Halifax—British immigrants brought to Nova Scotia by Governor Cornwallis, 2,544 persons. Fort Rouillé (Toronto) built.
1750. St. Paul's Church, Halifax (oldest Anglican church in Canada), built.
1752. Mar. 25, Issue of the Halifax *Gazette*, first paper in Canada. British and German population of Nova Scotia, 4,203.
1754. Census population of New France, 55,009.
1755. Establishment at Halifax of first post office in what is now Canada, together with direct mail communication with Great Britain. June 16, Surrender of Fort Beauséjour on the isthmus of Chignecto to the British. Sept. 10, Expulsion of the Acadians from Nova Scotia.
1756. Seven Years' War between Great Britain and France began.
1758. July 26, Final capture of Louisbourg by the British. Oct. 7, First meeting of the Legislature of Nova Scotia.
1759. July 25, Taking of Fort Niagara by the British. July 26, Beginning of the siege of Quebec. July 31, French victory at Beauport Flats. Sept. 13, Defeat of the French on the Plains of Abraham. Death of Wolfe. Sept. 14, Death of Montcalm. Sept. 18, Surrender of Quebec.
1760. April 28, Victory of the French under Lévis at Ste. Foy. Sept. 8, Surrender of Montreal. Military rule set up in Canada.
1762. British population of Nova Scotia, 8,104. First British settlement in New Brunswick.
1763. Feb. 10, Treaty of Paris, by which Canada and its dependencies were ceded to the British. May, Rising of Indians under Pontiac, who took a number of forts and defeated the British at Bloody Run (July 31). Oct. 7, Civil government proclaimed. Cape Breton and Île St. Jean annexed to Nova Scotia; Labrador, Anticosti and Magdalen islands to Newfoundland. Nov. 21, General James Murray appointed Governor in Chief. First Canadian post offices established at Montreal, Three Rivers and Quebec.
1764. June 21, First issue of the Quebec *Gazette*. Aug. 13, Civil government established.
1765. Publication of the first book printed in Canada, 'Catéchisme du Diocèse de Sens.' May 18, Montreal nearly destroyed by fire. Population of Canada, 69,810.
1766. July 24, Peace made with Pontiac at Oswego.
1768. Charlottetown, P.E.I., founded. April 11, Great fire at Montreal. April 12, Sir Guy Carleton (Lord Dorchester) Governor in Chief.
1769. Île St. Jean (P.E.I.) separated from Nova Scotia.
1770–72. Hearne's journey to the Coppermine and Slave rivers and Great Slave lake.
1773. Suppression of the order of Jesuits in Canada and escheat of their estates.
1774. June 22, The Quebec Act passed.
1775. May 1, The Quebec Act came into force. Outbreak of the American Revolution. Montgomery and Arnold invaded Canada. Nov. 12, Montgomery took Montreal; Dec. 31, was defeated and killed in an attack on Quebec.
1776. The Americans were defeated and driven from Canada by Carleton.
1777. Sept. 18, General Frederick Haldimand Governor in Chief.
1778. Captain Jas. Cook explored Nootka sound and claimed the northwest coast of America for Great Britain. June 3, First issue of the Montreal *Gazette*.
1783. Sept. 3, Treaty of Versailles, recognizing the independence of the United States. Organization of the Northwest Company at Montreal. Kingston, Ont., and Saint John, N.B., founded by the United Empire Loyalists.
1784. Population of Canada, 113,012. Aug. 16, New Brunswick and (Aug. 26) Cape Breton separated from Nova Scotia.
1785. May 18, Incorporation of Parrtown (Saint John, N.B.).
1786. April 22, Lord Dorchester again Governor in Chief. Oct. 23, Government of New Brunswick moved from Saint John to Fredericton.
1787. C. Inglis appointed Anglican Bishop of Nova Scotia—the first colonial bishopric in the British Empire.
1788. King's College, Windsor, N.S., opened. Sailing packet service restored between Great Britain and Halifax.
1789. Quebec and Halifax Agricultural Societies established.
1790. Spain surrendered her exclusive rights on the Pacific coast. Population of Canada, 161,311. (This census did not include what became, in the next year, Upper Canada.)
1791. The Constitutional Act divided the province of Quebec into Upper and Lower Canada, each with a lieutenant-governor and legislature. The Act went into force Dec. 26. Sept. 12, Colonel J. G. Simcoe, first Lieutenant-Governor of Upper Canada.
1792. Sept. 17, First Legislature of Upper Canada opened at Newark (Niagara). Dec. 17, First Legislature of Lower Canada opened at Quebec.

Vancouver island circumnavigated by Vancouver.

1793. April 18, First issue of the *Upper Canada Gazette*. June 28, Jacob Mountain appointed first Anglican Bishop of Quebec. July 9, Importation of slaves into Upper Canada forbidden. Rocky mountains crossed by (Sir) Alexander Mackenzie, who reached the Pacific ocean. York (Toronto) founded by Simcoe.

1794. Nov. 19, Jay's Treaty between Great Britain and the United States.

1795. Pacific coast of Canada finally given up by Spaniards.

1796. Government of Upper Canada moved from Niagara to York (Toronto).

1798. St. John's island (Ile St. Jean, population 4,500) renamed Prince Edward Island.

1800. Founding of New Brunswick College, Fredericton (now University of N.B.). The Rocky mountains crossed by David Thompson.

1803. Settlers sent by Lord Selkirk to Prince Edward Island.

1806. Nov. 22, Issue of *Le Canadien*—first wholly French newspaper. Population—Upper Canada, 70,718; Lower Canada, 250,000; New Brunswick, 35,000; P.E.I., 9,676.

1807. Simon Fraser explored the Fraser river. Estimated population of Nova Scotia, 65,000.

1809. Nov. 4, First Canadian steamer ran from Montreal to Quebec.

1811. Lord Selkirk's Red River settlement founded on land granted by Hudson's Bay Company.

1812. June 18, Declaration of war by the United States. July 12, Americans under Hull crossed the Detroit river. Aug. 16, Detroit surrendered by Hull to Brock. Oct. 13, Defeat of the Americans at Queenston Heights and death of General Brock.

1813. Jan. 22, British victory at Frenchtown. April 27, York (Toronto) taken and burned by the Americans. June 5, British victory at Stoney Creek. June 24, British, warned by Laura Secord, captured an American force at Beaver Dam. Sept. 10, Commodore Perry destroyed the British flotilla on lake Erie. Oct. 5, Americans under Harrison defeated the British at Moraviantown. Tecumseh killed. Oct. 26, Victory of French-Canadian troops under de Salaberry at Châteauguay. Nov. 11, Defeat of the Americans at Crysler's Farm. British stormed Fort Niagara and burned Buffalo.

1814. Mar. 30, Americans repulsed at La Colle. May 6, Capture of Oswego by the British. July 5, American victory at Chippawa. July 25, British victory at Lundy's Lane. July, British from Nova Scotia invaded and occupied northern Maine. Sept. 11, British defeat at Plattsburg on lake Champlain. Dec. 24, Treaty of Ghent ended the war. Population—Upper Canada, 95,000; Lower Canada, 335,000.

1815. July 3, Treaty of London regulated trade with the United States. The Red River settlement destroyed by the Northwest Company but restored by Governor Semple.

1816. June 19, Governor Semple killed. The Red River settlement again destroyed.

1817. July 18, First Treaty with the Northwest Indians. Lord Selkirk restored the Red River settlement. Opening of the Bank of Montreal; first note issue Oct. 1. Population of Nova Scotia, 81,351. Rush-Bagot Convention with the United States, limiting naval armament on the Great Lakes, signed.

1818. Oct. 20, Convention at London regulating North American fisheries. Dalhousie College, Halifax, founded. Bank of Quebec founded.

1819–22. Franklin's overland Arctic expedition.

1820. Oct. 16, Cape Breton re-annexed to Nova Scotia.

1821. Mar. 26, The Northwest Company absorbed by the Hudson's Bay Company. Charter given to McGill College.

1822. Population of Lower Canada, 427,465.

1824. Population of Upper Canada, 150,066; of New Brunswick, 74,176.

1825. Oct. 6, Great fire in the Miramichi district, N.B. Opening of the Lachine canal. Population of Lower Canada, 479,288.

1826. Founding of Bytown (Ottawa).

1827. Sept. 29, Convention of London relating to the territory west of the Rocky mountains. Population of Nova Scotia (including Cape Breton), 123,630.

1828. The Methodist Church of Upper Canada separated from that of the United States.

1829. Nov. 27, First Welland canal opened. McGill University opened. Upper Canada College founded.

1831. June 1, The North Magnetic Pole discovered by (Sir) James Ross. Population—Upper Canada, 236,702; Lower Canada, 553,131; Assiniboia, 2,390.

1832. Outbreak of cholera in Canada. Incorporation of Quebec and Montreal. Bank of Nova Scotia founded. May 30, Opening of the Rideau canal.

1833. Aug. 18, The steamer *Royal William*, built at Quebec, crossed the Atlantic from Pictou to England.

1834. Feb. 21, The Ninety-Two Resolutions on public grievances passed by the Assembly of Lower Canada. Mar. 6, Incorporation of Toronto. Population of Upper Canada, 321,145; of New Brunswick, 119,457; of Assiniboia, 3,356.

1836. July 21, Opening of the first railway in Canada, from Laprairie to St. John's, Que. Victoria University opened at Cobourg (afterwards moved to Toronto).

1837. Report of the Canada Commissioners. Rebellion in Lower Canada (Papineau) and Upper Canada (W. L. Mackenzie). Nov. 23, Gas lighting first used in Montreal.

1838. Feb. 10, Constitution of Lower Canada suspended and Special Council created. Mar. 30, The Earl of Durham, Governor in Chief. April 27, Martial law revoked. June 28, Amnesty to political prisoners proclaimed. Nov. 1, Lord Durham, censured by British Parliament, resigned. Population—Upper Canada, 339,442; Assiniboia, 3,966; Nova Scotia, 202,575.

1839. Feb. 11, Lord Durham's report submitted to Parliament. John Strachan ordained first Anglican Bishop of Toronto.

1840. July 23, Passing of the Act of Union. First ship of the Cunard line arrived at Halifax. July 28, Death of Lord Durham.

1841. Feb. 10, Union of the two provinces as the Province of Canada, with Kingston as capital. Feb. 13, Draper-Ogden Administration. April 10, Halifax incorporated. June 13, Meeting of the first United Parliament. Sept. 19, Death of Lord Sydenham. Population of Upper Canada, 455,668; of P.E.I., 47,042.

1842. Mar. 10, Opening of Queen's University, Kingston. Aug. 9, The Ashburton Treaty. Sept. 16, Baldwin-Lafontaine Administration.

1843. June 4, Victoria, B.C., founded. Dec. 12, Draper-Viger Administration. King's (now University) College, Toronto, opened.

1844. May 10, Capital moved from Kingston to Montreal. Knox College, Toronto, founded. Population of Lower Canada, 697,084.

1845. May 28 and June 28, Great fires at Quebec. Franklin started on his last Arctic expedition.

1846. May 18, Kingston incorporated. June 15, Oregon Boundary Treaty. June 18, Draper-Papineau Administration. First telegraph line, operated by the Toronto, Hamilton and Niagara Electro-Magnetic Telegraph Co., opened.

1847. May 29, Sherwood-Papineau Administration. Nov. 25, Montreal-Lachine Railway opened.

1848. Mar. 11, Lafontaine-Baldwin Administration. May 30, Fredericton incorporated. Responsible government granted to Nova Scotia and New Brunswick. St. Lawrence canals opened to navigation.

1849. April 25, Signing of the Rebellion Losses Act; rioting in Montreal and burning of the Parliament Buildings. Nov. 14, Toronto made the capital. Vancouver Island granted to the Hudson's Bay Company. Population of Assiniboia, 5,391.

1851. April 6, Transfer of the postal system from the British to the Provincial Government; uniform rate of postage introduced. April 23, Postage stamps issued. Aug. 2, Incorporation of Trinity College, Toronto. Sept. 22, Quebec became the capital. Oct. 28, Hincks-Morin Administration. Responsible government granted to Prince Edward Island. Population—Upper Canada, 952,004; Lower Canada, 890,261; New Brunswick, 193,800; Nova Scotia, 276,854.

1852. July 8, Great fire at Montreal. Dec. 8, Laval University, Quebec, opened. Grand Trunk Railway chartered.

1853. Opening of G.T.R. from Montreal to Portland.

1854. June 5, Reciprocity Treaty with the United States. Sept. 11, MacNab-Morin Ministry. Seigneurial tenure in Lower Canada abolished. Secularization of the clergy reserves.

1855. Jan. 1, Incorporation of Ottawa. Jan. 27, MacNab-Taché Administration. Mar. 9, Opening of the Niagara Railway suspension bridge. April 17, Incorporation of Charlottetown. Oct. 20, Government moved to Toronto.

1856. The Legislative Council of Canada made elective. First meeting of the Legislature of Vancouver Island. May 24, Taché-J. A. Macdonald Administration. Oct. 27, Opening of the Grand Trunk Railway from Montreal to Toronto. Population of Assiniboia, 6,691.

1857. Nov. 26, J. A. Macdonald-Cartier Administration. Dec. 31, Ottawa chosen by Queen Victoria as future capital of Canada.

1858. February, Discovery of gold in Fraser River valley. July 1, Introduction of Canadian decimal currency. Aug. 2, Brown-Dorien Administration. Aug. 5, Completion of Atlantic cable; first message sent. Aug. 6, Cartier-J. A. Macdonald Administration. Aug. 20, Colony of British Columbia established. Control of Vancouver Island surrendered by Hudson's Bay Company.

1859. January, Canadian silver coinage issued. Sept. 24, Government moved to Quebec.

1860. Aug. 8, The Prince of Wales (King Edward VII) arrived at Quebec. Sept. 1, Laying of the cornerstone of the Parliament Building at Ottawa by the Prince of Wales. Prince of Wales College, Charlottetown, founded.

1861. Aug. 14, Great flood at Montreal. Sept. 10, Meeting of the first Anglican provincial synod. Population—Upper Canada, 1,396,091; Lower Canada, 1,111,566; New Brunswick, 252,047; Nova Scotia, 330,857; Prince Edward Island, 80,857.

1862. May 24, Sandfield Macdonald-Sicotte Administration. Aug. 2, Victoria, B.C., incorporated.

1863. May 16, Sandfield Macdonald-Dorion Administration.

1864. Mar. 30, Taché-J. A. Macdonald Administration. Conferences on confederation of British North America; Sept. 1, at Charlottetown; Oct. 10–29, at Quebec. Oct. 19, Raid of American Confederates from Canada on St. Albans, Vermont.

1865. Feb. 3, The Canadian Legislature resolved on an address to the Queen praying for union of the provinces of British North America. Aug. 7, Belleau-J. A. Macdonald Administration. Oct. 20, Proclamation fixing the seat of government at Ottawa.

1866. Mar. 17, Termination of the Reciprocity Treaty by the United States. May 31, Raid of Fenians from the United States into Canada; they were defeated at Ridgeway (June 2) and retreated across the border (June 3). June 8, First meeting at Ottawa of the Canadian Legislature. Nov. 17, Proclamation of the union of Vancouver Island with British Columbia.

1867. Mar. 29, Royal Assent given to the British North America Act. July 1, The Act came into force; Union of the provinces of Canada, Nova Scotia and New Brunswick as the Dominion of Canada; Upper and Lower Canada made separate provinces as Ontario and Quebec; Viscount Monck first Governor General; Sir John A. Macdonald, Premier. Nov. 6, Meeting of the first Dominion Parliament.

1868. April 7, Murder of D'Arcy McGee at Ottawa. July 31, The Rupert's Land Act authorized the acquisition by the Dominion of the Northwest territories.

1869. June 22, Act providing for the government of the Northwest Territories. Nov. 19, Deed of surrender to the Crown of the Hudson's Bay Company's territorial rights in the Northwest. Outbreak of the Red River Rebellion under Riel.

1870. May 12, Act to establish the province of Manitoba. July 15, Northwest Territories transferred to the Dominion and Manitoba admitted into Confederation. Aug. 24, Wolseley's expedition reached Fort Garry (Winnipeg); end of the rebellion.

1871. April 2, First Dominion Census: population, 3,689,257. April 14, Act establishing uniform currency in the Dominion. May 8, Treaty of Washington, dealing with questions outstanding between the United Kingdom and the United States. July 20, British Columbia entered Confederation.

1873. May 23, Act establishing the North West Mounted Police. July 1, Prince Edward Island entered Confederation. Nov. 8, Incorporation of Winnipeg.

1874. May, Ontario Agricultural College, Guelph, opened.

1875. April 8, The Northwest Territories Act established a Lieutenant-Governor and a Northwest Territories Council. April-May, Letting of first contract and commencement of work upon the Canadian Pacific railway as a Government line; work commenced at Fort William. June 15. Formation of the Presbyterian Church of Canada.

1876. June 1, Opening of the Royal Military College, Kingston. June 5, First sitting of the Supreme Court of Canada. July 3, Opening of the Intercolonial Railway from Quebec to Halifax. Branch of Laval University established at Montreal.

1877. June 20, Great fire at Saint John, N.B. October, First exportation of wheat from Manitoba to the United Kingdom. Founding of the University of Manitoba.

1878. July 1, Canada joined the International Postal Union.

1879. May 15, Adoption of a protective tariff ('The National Policy').

1880. Royal Canadian Academy of Arts founded; first meeting and exhibition, Mar. 6. May 11, Sir A. T. Galt appointed first Canadian High Commissioner in London. Sept. 1, All British possessions in North America and adjacent Islands except Newfoundland and its dependencies annexed to Canada by Imperial Order in Council of July 31. Oct. 21, Signing of the contract with the present Canadian Pacific Railway Co. for the completion of the Canadian Pacific railway.

1881. April 4, Second Dominion Census: population, 4,324,810. May 2, First sod of the Canadian Pacific railway as a company line turned.

1882. May 8, Provisional districts of Assiniboia, Saskatchewan, Athabaska and Alberta formed. May 25, First meeting of the Royal Society of Canada. Aug. 23, Regina established as seat of government of Northwest Territories.

1883. Sept. 5, Formation of the Methodist Church in Canada; united conference.

1884. May 24, Sir Charles Tupper, High Commissioner in London. Aug. 11, Order in Council settling the boundary of Ontario and Manitoba.

1885. Mar. 26, Outbreak of Riel's second rebellion in the Northwest. April 24, Engagement at Fish Creek. May 2, Engagement at Cut Knife. May

12, Taking of Batoche. May 16, Surrender of Riel. Aug. 24, First census of the Northwest Territories. Nov. 7, Last spike of Canadian Pacific Railway main line driven at Craigellachie. Nov. 16, Execution of Riel.

1886. April 6, Incorporation of Vancouver. June 7, Archbishop Taschereau of Quebec made first Canadian Cardinal. June 13, Vancouver destroyed by fire. June 28, First through train of the Canadian Pacific Railway left Montreal for Port Moody.

1887. Interprovincial Conference at Quebec. April 4, First Colonial Conference in London.

1888. Feb. 15, Signing of Fishery Treaty between United Kingdom and United States at Washington. August, Rejection of Fishery Treaty by United States' Senate.

1890. Mar. 31, The Manitoba School Act abolished separate schools.

1891. April 5, Third Dominion Census. June 6, Death of Sir John A. Macdonald.

1892. Feb. 29, Washington Treaty, providing for arbitration of the Bering Sea Seal Fisheries question. July 22, Boundary Convention between Canada and United States.

1893. April 4, First sitting of the Bering Sea Arbitration Court. Dec. 18, Archbishop Machray, of Rupert's Land, elected first Anglican Primate of all Canada.

1894. Dec. 12, Death of Sir John Thompson at Windsor Castle.

1895. Sept. 10, Opening of new Sault Ste. Marie canal. Oct. 2, Proclamation naming the Ungava, Franklin, Mackenzie and Yukon districts of Northwest Territories.

1896. April 24, Sir Donald Smith (Lord Strathcona) High Commissioner in London. August, Gold discovered in the Klondyke.

1897. June 22, Celebration throughout the Empire of Diamond Jubilee of Queen Victoria. Dec. 17, Award of Bering Sea Arbitration Court.

1898. June 13, The Yukon district established as a separate Territory. Aug. 1, British Preferential Tariff went into force. Aug. 23. Meeting at Quebec of the Joint High Commission between Canada and the United States. Dec. 25, British Imperial penny (2 cent) postage introduced.

1899. Oct. 1, Mgr. Diomède Falconio arrived at Quebec as first permanent Apostolic Delegate to Canada. Oct. 11, Beginning of the South African War. Oct. 29, First Canadian contingent left Quebec for South Africa.

1900. Feb. 27, Battle of Paardeberg. April 26, Great fire at Ottawa and Hull.

1901. Jan. 22, Death of Queen Victoria and accession of King Edward VII.

1902. May 31, End of South African War; peace signed at Vereeniging.

1903. Jan. 24, Signing of the Alaskan Boundary Convention. June 19, Incorporation of Regina. Oct. 20. Award of the Alaskan Boundary Commission.

1904. Feb. 1, Dominion Railway Commission established. April 19, Great fire in Toronto. Oct. 8, Incorporation of Edmonton.

1905. Sept. 1, Creation of the provinces of Alberta and Saskatchewan.

1906. University of Alberta founded.

1907. April 15–May 14, Fifth Colonial Conference in London. New customs tariff, including introduction of intermediate tariff. Sept. 19, New commercial convention with France signed at Paris. Oct. 17, First message by wireless telegraphy between Canada and the United Kingdom. University of Saskatchewan founded.

1908. Jan. 2, Establishment of Ottawa Branch of Royal Mint. June 21–23, Bicentenary of Bishop Laval celebrated at Quebec. July 20–31, Quebec tercentenary celebrations. Visit of Prince of Wales to Quebec. Aug. 2, Great fire in Kootenay valley, B.C. University of British Columbia founded.

1909. Jan. 11, Signing of International Boundary Waters Convention between Canada and United States. July 28, Conference on Imperial defence in London.

1910. May 6, Death of King Edward VII and accession of King George V. Sept. 7, North Atlantic Coast Fisheries Arbitration Award of The Hague Tribunal. New trade agreements made with Germany, Belgium, Holland, and Italy. Oct. 11, Inauguration at Kitchener of Ontario hydro-electric power transmission system.

1911. May 23–June 20, Imperial Conference in London. July 11, Disastrous fires in Porcupine district. Sept. 21, General election.

1912. April 15, Loss of the steamship *Titanic*. May 15 Extension of the boundaries of Quebec, Ontario and Manitoba.

1913. April 10, Japanese Treaty Act assented to. June 2, Trade agreement with West Indies came into force.

1914. May 20, Loss of the steamship *Empress of Ireland*. Aug. 4, War with Germany; Aug. 12, with Austria-Hungary; Nov. 5, with Turkey. Aug. 18–22, Special war session of Canadian Parliament. Oct. 16, First Canadian contingent of over 33,000 troops landed at Plymouth, England.

1915. February, First Canadian contingent landed in France and proceeded to Flanders. April 22, Second Battle of Ypres. April 24, Battle of St. Julien. May 20–26, Battle of Festubert. June 15, Battle of Givenchy.

1916. Jan. 12, Order in Council authorizing increase in number of Canadian troops to 500,000. Feb. 3, Destruction of the Houses of Parliament at Ottawa by fire. April 3–20, Battle of St. Eloi. June 1–3, Battle of Sanctuary Wood. July 1, Commencement of the Battle of the Somme. Sept. 1, Cornerstone of new Houses of Parliament laid by Duke of Connaught.

1917. Feb. 12–May 15, Imperial Conference. Mar. 20–May 2, Meetings in London of Imperial War Cabinet. Mar. 21–April 27, Imperial War Conference. April 6, United States declared war against Germany. April 9, Capture of Vimy Ridge. June 21, Appointment of Food Controller. Aug. 15, Battle of Loos, capture of Hill 70. Aug. 29, Passing of Military Service Act. Sept. 20, Completion of Quebec Bridge; Parliamentary franchise extended to women. Oct. 26–Nov. 10, Battle of Passchendaele. Dec. 6, Serious explosion at Halifax, N.S.

1918. Mar. 31, Germans launched critical offensive on West Front. March–April, Second Battle of the Somme. April 17, Secret Session of Parliament. June–July, Prime Minister and colleagues attended Imperial War Conference in London. July 18, Allies assumed successful offensive on West Front. Aug. 12, Battle of Amiens. Aug. 26–28, Capture of Monchy le Preux. Sept. 2–4, Breaking of Drocourt-Quéant line. Sept. 16, Austrian peace note. Sept. 27–29, Capture of Bourlon Wood. Sept. 30, Bulgaria surrendered and signed armistice. October, Serious influenza epidemic. Oct. 1–9, Capture of Cambrai. Oct. 6, First German peace note. Oct. 20, Capture of Denain. Oct. 25–Nov. 2, Capture of Valenciennes. Oct. 31, Turkey surrendered and signed armistice. Nov. 4, Austria-Hungary surrendered and signed armistice. Nov. 11, Capture of Mons. Germany surrendered and signed armistice.

1919. Feb. 17, Death of Sir Wilfrid Laurier. May 1–June 15, General strike at Winnipeg and other western cities. June 28, Signing at Versailles of Peace Treaty and Protocol. Aug. 15, Arrival of the Prince of Wales for official tour in Canada. Aug. 22, Formal opening of Quebec Bridge by the Prince. Sept. 1, The Prince laid foundation stone of Peace Tower, Parliament Buildings, Ottawa. Dec. 20, Organization of 'Canadian National Railways' by Order in Council.

1920. Jan. 10, Ratifications of the Treaty of Versailles. Feb. 19, Shareholders ratified agreement for sale of the Grand Trunk Railway to the Dominion Government. May 31–June 18, Trade Conference at Ottawa between Dominion and West Indian Governments. July 10, Sir Robert Borden succeeded by Arthur Meighen as Prime Minister. July 16, Ratifications of the Treaty of St. Germain-en-Laye. Aug. 9, Ratifications of the Treaty of Neuilly-sur-Seine.

1921. May 10, Preferential tariff arrangement with British West Indies became effective. Dec. 6, Dominion general election.

1922. Feb. 1, Arms Conference at Washington approved 5-power treaty. Dec. 15, Signing of trade agreement between Canada and France.

1923. Jan. 4, Signing of trade agreement between Canada and Italy. April 1, Removal of British embargo on Canadian cattle effective.

1924. July 3, Trade agreement between Canada and Belgium signed at Ottawa. Aug. 6–16, Meeting of the British Association for the Advancement of Science at Toronto.

1925. June 10, Inauguration of the United Church of Canada. July 6, signing at Ottawa of trade agreement between Canada and British West Indies.

1926. June 1, Census of Prairie Provinces. July 1, Two-cent domestic rate of postage restored. Nov. 26, Vincent Massey appointed Envoy Extraordinary and Minister Plenipotentiary to United States.

1927. June 1, Wm. Phillips, first U.S. Minister to Canada, reached Ottawa. July 1–3, Diamond Jubilee of Confederation celebrated throughout the Dominion. July 30, The Prince of Wales, Prince George, the Rt. Hon. Stanley Baldwin and party, arrived at Quebec on a visit to Canada.

1928. Jan. 30, President Cosgrave of the Irish Free State visited Ottawa. April 25, Sir Wm. H. Clark appointed first British High Commissioner to Canada. May 31, Legislative Council of Nova Scotia ceased to exist, leaving Quebec as the only province with a bicameral legislature.

1929. Oct. 15–25, Ramsay MacDonald, Prime Minister of Great Britain, visited Canada.

1930. Jan. 21, Five-power naval arms conference opened at London. Aug. 1, H.M. Airship *R-100* arrived at Montreal, being the first transatlantic lighter-than-air craft to reach Canada. Dec. 20, Viscount Willingdon, Governor General of Canada, appointed Viceroy of India by the King.

1931. June 11, Remembrance Day (Nov. 11) proclaimed a general holiday by Act of Parliament. June 30, The Statute of Westminster exempting the Dominion and the provinces from the operation of the Colonial Laws Validity Act and the Merchant Shipping Act approved by the House of Commons. Great Britain suspended specie payments, following which Canada restricted the export of gold. Nov. 21, Abnormal Importations Act, extending preference to Empire products, assented to in the United Kingdom. Dec. 12, Statute of Westminster establishing complete legislative equality of the Parliament of Canada with that of the United Kingdom became effective.

1932. July 21–Aug. 20, Imperial Economic Conference at Ottawa. Aug. 6, Official opening of the Welland Ship Canal.

1933. Jan. 17–19, Dominion-Provincial Conference. Signs of economic depression, from 1930 on, were abating.

1934. Canada again on way to prosperity.

1935. Mar. 11, Bank of Canada commenced business. May 6, Celebrations throughout the Empire of the 25th anniversary of the accession of King George V. Nov. 2, Lord Tweedsmuir assumed office as Governor General of Canada.

1936. Jan. 20, Death of King George V and accession of King Edward VIII. July 15, Sanctions against Italy removed. July 30, President Roosevelt visited Lord Tweedsmuir at the Citadel, Quebec —the first official visit of a U. S. President to a Governor General of Canada. Dec. 11, Abdication of King Edward VIII and accession of King George VI.

1937. Jan. 28, Decision of the Judicial Committee of the Privy Council declaring certain legislation, passed by the former Administration, on unemployment insurance, hours of labour, minimum wages, and marketing, 'ultra vires' of the Dominion Parliament.

1938. Aug. 18, Joint dedication of Thousand Islands Bridge by Canada and United States. President Roosevelt promised armed assistance to Canada in case of invasion.

1939. Jan. 1, The revised three-year reciprocal trade agreement between Canada and United States went into effect, replacing the agreement of 1936. May, King George VI and Queen Elizabeth visited Canada and United States. Sept., The War Measures Act of 1914, giving the government dictatorial power, was revived. Sept. 10, Canada legally declared war against Germany.

1940. Mar. 26, Liberal party returned to power with increased majority. June 21, Lord Athlone succeeded the late Lord Tweedsmuir as Governor General. May 16, Parliament adopted the National Registration Act, and the National Resources Mobilization Act.

1941. Mar. 19, Canadian-United States agreement on co-operative development and utilization of the Great Lakes-St. Lawrence river basin was signed. March, April and Oct., Prime Minister Mackenzie King made three important visits to President Roosevelt regarding hemisphere defense and aid to Britain.

1942. Apr. 27, A plebiscite was held in which Canadian voters released the administration from its anticonscription pledge. Sept. 30, Compulsory military service extended to include 19-year-old males and all unmarried men of military age except enemy aliens. Nov. 9, Canadian relations with the Vichy Government were broken.

1943. Aug. 21, Canadian-United States Joint War Aid committee set up. Aug. 10–24, Quebec Conference of President Roosevelt, Prime Minister Churchill, and Canadian Prime Minister King. Dec. 5, Prime Minister King outlined his anti-inflationary plan. Canadian troops fought in Sicily, Italy and Attu, while the Navy reduced submarine losses in the Atlantic and St. Lawrence.

1944. June 6, the Canadian 1st Army landed in Normandy on D-Day and fought to the Dutch border by the year's end. June 26, Soldiers' insurance was increased and extended and a new Reconstruction Department created by Parliament. Sept. 12, Second Quebec Conference held by Roosevelt, Churchill and King.

1945. Jan.–May, Canadian 1st Army held north flank of Allied line in Germany. May 8, Germany surrendered. June 11, Prime Minister Mackenzie King returned to power in General Election. Canada shared with the U. S. and Britain in development of atom bombs dropped on Japan. Sept. 2, Japan surrendered. Oct. 12, a tax reduction of **$100,000,000** voted by Parliament.

1946. Mar. 4, a Royal Commission charged 13 men and women with seeking atom and radar secrets for Soviet Embassy; among those convicted was Fred Rose, Communist M.P. April 12, Viscount Alexander became Governor General.

1947. Canadian Citizenship Act went into force.

1948. July 22, Newfoundland decided, by national referendum, for confederation with Canada. Nov. 15, Louis Stephen St. Laurent became Prime Minister, following the resignation of Mackenzie King.

1949. Mar. 31, Newfoundland became 10th Canadian province. Apr. 4, Canada and 11 other nations signed North Atlantic Treaty.

1950. Co-operation with the U.S. was close during the tense international situation. Canada contributed naval and other units to support of the U. N. in the Korean war.

1951. Census population: 14,009,429. Three-year rearmament program to cost $5 billion begun. July, Government proclamation ended state of war with Germany. Sept., Canada signed the peace treaty with Japan.

1952. Feb. 6, Death of King George VI, and accession of Queen Elizabeth II. Feb. 28, Vincent Massey succeeded Earl Alexander as Governor General. Lester B. Pearson, Secretary of State for External Affairs, president of U. N. General Assembly. Canada continued donations of military and industrial aid to other NATO members.

1953. June 2, Coronation of Queen Elizabeth. Aug. 10, Fifth successive general election victory of Liberal party, headed by Prime Minister St. Laurent. Military co-operation with U.S. continued, including development of radar defense network. In a year of record prosperity, both taxes and the national debt were reduced.

1954. Trade agreement with Japan was approved. May, Legislation at last authorized the U.S. to join Canada in development of St. Lawrence Seaway Project. Aug. 10, Work begun on St. Lawrence Power Project, near Cornwall, Ont., and Massena, N.Y.

1955. March, Foreign Secretary Pearson said that a Communist-Nationalist clash over Quemoy and Matsu should not require any Canadian intervention. Over nine million bushels of wheat sold to Poland; largest transaction in Canadian history involving an eastern Eurpoean country.

1956. Census population: 16,080,791. Major capital projects under way, besides the St. Lawrence Seaway, including the trans-Canada pipeline, which is to bring natural gas from Alberta to central Canada, and the uranium development of the Blind River area of Ontario. April, Merger of two major labor organizations, Trades and Labor Congress of Canada and Canadian Congress of Labor.

1957. A large nickel-mining project was begun in northern Manitoba. New copper mines were developed north of Lake Superior. June 10, Liberals were defeated in general elections and the Progressive Conservative party formed the new government with John Diefenbaker as Prime Minister. Oct. 14, Queen Elizabeth II officially opened parliament; the first time a reigning monarch had done so.

1958. Louis St. Laurent retired as Liberal leader and Lester Pearson succeeded him. March 31, General elections gave the Progressive Conservatives their greatest margin of victory in Canadian history. Sept., Commonwealth Trade Conference was held at Montreal.

1959. April 25, St. Lawrence Seaway opened. May 27, South Saskatchewan power and irrigation project begun. June-July, 45-day tour of the Provinces by Queen Elizabeth II and Prince Philip. Sept. 15, Major General George Vanier succeeded Vincent Massey as Governor General.

1960. The economy experienced a mild recession. July, Provinces demanded more tax-sharing agreements. Aug. 4, Bill of Rights approved by the House of Commons. Oct. 11, With a federal election possible a major reorganization of the cabinet was announced.

1961. Census population: 18,238,247. Feb. 3, Merger of the Canadian Bank of Commerce and the Imperial Bank of Canada approved. June, NATO-strengthening agreement reached between the U.S. and Canada by which the U.S. gave Canada jet aircraft in exchange for Canada's promise to operate and maintain the Pinetree line of radar stations in Northwest Territories. Oct. 1, Establishment of the Organization for Economic Co-operation and Development, which includes Canada, U.S., and 18 European nations. Nov., Completion of a natural gas line from Alberta to Idaho, Washington, Oregon, and California.

1962. April 2, 400-mile microwave system opened between Alberta and Northwest Territories. June 18, General elections were held; the Progressive Conservatives stayed in power but lost nearly 100 seats in parliament. July, Saskatchewan's medical-care plan was launched. Aug., Trans-Canada, highway, begun in 1949, was completed.

1963. Jan., Diefenbaker opposed Canada's acceptance of U.S. nuclear weapons. Feb., Progressive Conservative leadership overthrown by a no-confidence vote. Feb. 6, Parliament dissolved. April 8, Liberals won a plurality in the general elections. April 17, Diefenbaker resigned; Lester Pearson succeeded him as Prime Minister. An intensification of the separatist movement in Quebec was marked by terrorist activities. Increased exports and a record wheat crop (719,000,000 bushels) kept the economic activity at a high level.

1964. U.S.-Canada treaty (Sept.) for the joint development of the power sources of the Columbia River. Oct., Queen Elizabeth visits in recognition of the centennial celebration of the union of the British colonies of North America. Dec., Approval of a new national flag, a red maple leaf on a white field with a vertical red bar on each side.

1965. Feb., Several cabinet changes were announced in the wake of opposition charges of bribery involving cabinet members. Nov., In a general election Lester Pearson's minority government stayed in power but failed to increase its strength in parliament.

1966. Prime Minister Pearson's Liberal Party continued to hold office. Several important social welfare measures were passed in parliament—a plan to consolidate and extend public assistance programs, an old-age assistance plan, a plan to increase financial aid to education, a plan for construction of medical facilities. Sept., Quebec premier seeks more internal self-government. Nov., Direct air link established between Montreal and Moscow.

1967. Apr., Daniel Michener replaces Georges Vanier, who died in March, as governor general. Army, navy, and air force merged into a single unit. Apr.-Oct., A "Universal and International Exhibition," called *Expo 67*, was held in Montreal in celebration of Canada's 100th anniversary. July, French President de Gaulle speaks out for a "Free Quebec."

1968. Feb., Evidence of Norse settlement in Newfoundland about 1000 A.D. revealed by archaeologists. Apr., Pierre Trudeau elected Prime Minister succeeding Lester Pearson. May, National League baseball franchise awarded to Montreal. Oct., The U.S. delivered $52,100,000 to Canada for flood-control benefits on American portion of Arrow Lake dam project on Columbia River in British Columbia.

1969. Mar., Satellite-tracking station opened in Nova Scotia, for use in commercial communications traffic. New Government Organization Act established, setting up new departments, abolishing and consolidating others, and rearranging duties, all for the purpose of providing better service to the public. July, Parliament passes Official Languages Act declaring English and French to be official languages, providing for services in both to the public. Nov., Government announced $50,000,000 program to promote nationwide language training including grants to the provinces for teaching French or English as a second language.

1970. June, Legal voting age in federal elections lowered to 18. Oct., British Trade Commissioner kidnapped and held for ransom by members of FLQ (Quebec Liberation Front). FLQ members kidnapped Canadian Minister of Labor who was found strangled a week later. Armed forces called to deal with danger of insurrection in Quebec.

1971. Feb., First incident of hijacking of a foreign aircraft to Canada. Mar., Canada's first ambassador to People's Republic of China appointed. June, Department of the Environment established. July, Arrival of first ambassador from People's Republic of China. Oct., Premier Kosygin visits Canada; 1st head of government of the Soviet Union to do so. Dec., Legislation passed authorizing a complete revision of the federal income tax system, including, for the first time, a tax on capital gains.

1972. Apr., President Nixon visits Canada, addresses parliament, and signs a bill providing for construction and improvement of sewage treatment facilities along the Great Lakes. Aug., A trade delegation to Peking secures an increase in exports to China. In return the Chinese put on a large exhibit at the National Exhibition. Oct., Prime Minister Trudeau reelected, but the Liberals were reduced to holding only two more seats than the Conservatives in the House of Commons.

1973. Inflation is the chief economic problem as the cost of living increases 9%. The government reluctantly provides troops for an international truce force in Vietnam; later, with popular support, the troops are pulled out. Oct., Prime Minister Trudeau visits China to foster relations and increase trade agreements.

1974. Mar., Quebec Parliament makes French the official language of the province. July, Prime Minister Trudeau is reelected and his Liberal Party wins an unexpected majority of 141 seats in Parliament, up from the 109 seats won in 1972. Oct., In an effort to control U.S. ownership of Canadian industry, Parliament passes a law requiring that foreign investments be screened by the cabinet before being permitted.

1975. Mar., Prime Minister Trudeau visits Europe in order to strengthen ties with the European Community. Oct., Parliament passes a strong Anti-inflation Act to control escalating wages and prices. The implementation program set up by the Act meets vigorous opposition from both business and organized labor. The Canadian Labour Congress stages a massive demonstration in protest. Nov., separatist Parti Quebecois elected to office in Quebec.

1976. May, In action exacerbating the U.S. during the energy crisis, export prices on oil and gas are raised. The government unilaterally extends (effective Jan. 1, 1977) jurisdiction of its fisheries to 200 miles offshore. June, Parliament approves government proposal to abolish the death penalty. July, The Olympic Games, the most expensive in history, are held in Montreal; controversy marks the Games as 31 nations boycott them. Oct., Joseph Clark of Alberta is elected leader of the Conservative Party replacing Robert Stanfield who was resigning.

1977. Parti Quebecois victory led to language controversy as Prime Minister Trudeau proposed constitutional changes to make French-language education available across the country. Economy depressed with low growth rate and high unemployment. May, Liberals gained in federal by-elections but Conservatives gained in two provincial elections. Sep., federal cabinet reshuffled. Canada and U.S. agree to an $8 billion pipeline for bringing natural gas from Alaska to U.S. Oct., revelations of misconduct by Royal Canadian Mounted Police.

1978. Two cabinet ministers resigned as a result of revelations of personal misconduct. The economy continued in a sluggish state. Jan., Soviet satellite falls in northern regions spreading radioactive debris. Feb., 13 Soviet officials expelled for plotting to infiltrate Royal Canadian Mounted Police security service. Apr., Canada supplies personnel to U.N. peacekeeping mission in southern Lebanon. Oct., Liberal Party loses 10 of 15 seats to Progressive Conservatives in by-election; federal-provincial conference failed to agree on Prime Minister Trudeau's constitutional reforms.

1979. Mar., Treaties were signed with the U.S. concerning reciprocal fishing in border waters. May, Prime Minister Pierre Elliott Trudeau lost to Charles Joseph Clark in a general election after dominating Canadian politics for 11 years. July, Clark is first Canadian Prime Minister to visit Africa. Aug., Despite pending treaties, Canadian authorities seized U.S. tuna fishing boats, leading to a U.S. ban on tuna imports from Canada. Dec., The Clark government was defeated on a budget vote in the House of Commons and resigned.

1980. Feb., Election returns Trudeau as prime minister as Liberals return to power. Mar., Bank of Canada announces move to floating bank rate. Apr., Canadian boycott of Olympic Games is confirmed; government announces it will buy military aircraft from U.S. May, Separatism is defeated in Quebec referendum. Aug., Canada and U.S. agree to study pollution problems. Oct., Opposition forms to Trudeau's plan to transfer the authority to make constitutional changes from the British parliament to the Canadian parliament.

CHARTER OF THE UNITED NATIONS

We, the peoples of the United Nations
Determined to save succeeding generations from the scourge of war, which twice in our lifetime has brought untold sorrow to mankind, and
To reaffirm faith in fundamental human rights, in the dignity and worth of the human person, in the equal right of men and women and of nations large and small, and
To establish conditions under which justice and respect for the obligations arising from treaties and other sources of international law can be maintained, and
To promote social progress and better standards of life in larger freedom, and for these ends
To practice tolerance and live together in peace with one another as good neighbors, and
To unite our strength to maintain international peace and security, and
To ensure, by the acceptance of principles and the institution of methods, that armed force shall not be used, save in the common interest, and
To employ international machinery for the promotion of the economic and social advancement of all people, have resolved to combine our efforts to accomplish these aims.
Accordingly, our respective governments, through representatives assembled in the city of San Francisco, who have exhibited their full powers found to be in good and due form, have agreed to the present Charter of the United Nations and do hereby establish an international organization to be known as the United Nations.

CHAPTER I

Purposes

Article 1—The purposes of the United Nations are:
1. To maintain international peace and security, and to that end: to take effective collective measures for the prevention and removal of threats to the peace and for the suppression of acts of aggression or other breaches of the peace, and to bring about by peaceful means, and in conformity with the principles of justice and international law, adjustment or settlement of international disputes or situations which might lead to a breach of the peace;
2. To develop friendly relations among nations based on respect for the principle of equal rights and self-determination of peoples, and to take other appropriate measures to strengthen universal peace;
3. To achieve international cooperation in solving international problems of an economic, social, cultural or humanitarian character, and in promoting and encouraging respect for human rights and for the fundamental freedoms for all without distinction as to race, sex, language or religion; and
4. To be a center for harmonizing the actions of nations in the attainment of these common ends.

Principles

Article 2—The organization and its members, in pursuit of the purposes stated in Article 1, shall act in accordance with the following principles:
1. The organization is based on the principle of the sovereign equality of all its members.
2. All members, in order to insure to all of them the rights and benefits resulting from membership, shall fulfill in good faith the obligations assumed by them in accordance with the present Charter.
3. All members shall settle their international disputes by peaceful means in such a manner that international peace, and security, and justice, are not endangered.
4. All members shall refrain in their international relations from the threat or use of force against the territorial integrity or political independence of any member or state, or in any other manner inconsistent with the purposes of the United Nations.
5. All members shall give the United Nations every assistance in any action it takes in accordance with the provisions of the present Charter, and shall refrain from giving assistance to any state against which the United Nations is taking preventive or enforcement action.
6. The organization shall insure that states not members act in accordance with these principles so far as may be necessary for the maintenance of international peace and security.
7. Nothing contained in the present Charter shall authorize the United Nations to intervene in matters which are essentially within the domestic jurisdiction of any state or shall require the members to submit such matters to settlement under the present Charter; but this principle shall not prejudice the application of enforcement measures under Chapter VII.

CHAPTER II

Membership

Article 3—The original members of the United Nations shall be the states which, having participated in the United Nations Conference on International Organization at San Francisco, or have previously signed the declaration of the United Nations on Jan. 1, 1942, sign the present Charter and ratify it in accordance with Article 110.

Article 4—1. Membership in the United Nations is open to all other peace-loving states which accept the obligations contained in the present Charter and which, in the judgment of the organization, are able and willing to carry out these obligations.
2. The admission of any such state to membership in the United Nations will be effected by a decision of the General Assembly upon the recommendation of the Security Council.

Article 5—A member of the United Nations against which preventive or enforcement action has been taken by the Security Council may be suspended from the exercise of the rights and privileges of membership by the General Assembly upon the recommendation of the Security Council. The exercise of these rights and privileges may be restored by the Security Council.

Article 6—A member of the United Nations which has persistently violated the principles contained in the present charter may be expelled from the organization by the General Assembly upon the recommendation of the Security Council.

CHAPTER III

Organs

Article 7—1. There are established as the principal organs of the United Nations: A General Assembly, a Security Council, an Economic and Social Council, an International Court of Justice, a Trusteeship Council and a Secretariat.
2. Such subsidiary organs as may be found necessary may be established in accordance with the present Charter.

Article 8—The United Nations shall place no restrictions on the eligibility of men and women to participate in any capacity and under conditions of equality in the principal and subsidiary organs.

CHAPTER IV

The General Assembly Composition

Article 9—The General Assembly shall consist of all the members of the United Nations.
Each member shall not have more than five representatives in the General Assembly.

Functions and Powers

Article 10—The General Assembly may discuss any questions or any matters within the scope of the present Charter or relating to the powers and functions of any organs provided in the present Charter, and, except as provided in Article 12, may make recommendations to the members of the United Nations or to the Security Council, or both, on any such questions or matters.

Article 11—1. The General Assembly may consider the general principles of cooperation in the maintenance of international peace and security, including the principles governing disarmament and the regulations of armaments, and may make recommendations with regard to such principles to the members or to the Security Council or both.
2. The General Assembly may discuss any questions relating to the maintenance of international peace and security brought before it by any member of the United Nations, or by the Security Council, or by a state, which is not a member of the United Nations, in accordance with the provisions of Article 35, Paragraph 2, and, except as provided in Article 12, may make recommendations with regard to any such questions to the state or states concerned or to the Security Council, or both. A question on which action is necessary shall be referred to the Security Council by the General Assembly either before or after discussion.
3. The General Assembly may call the attention of the Security Council to situations which are likely to endanger international peace and security.
4. The powers of the General Assembly set out in this article shall not limit the general scope of Article 10.

Article 12—1. While the Security Council is exercising in respect of any dispute or situation the functions assigned to it in the present Charter, the General Assembly shall not make any recommendation with regard to that dispute or situation unless the Security Council so requests.
2. The Secretary General, with the consent of the Security Council, shall notify the General Assembly at each session of any matters relative to the maintenance of international peace and security which are being dealt with by the Security Council and shall similarly notify the General Assembly, or the members of the United Nations if the General Assembly is not in session, immediately the Security Council ceases to deal with such matters.

Article 13—1. The General Assembly shall initiate studies and make recommendations for the purpose of:
(a) Promoting international cooperation in the political field and encouraging the progressive development of international law and its codification;
(b) Promoting international cooperation in the economic, social, cultural, educational and health fields and assisting in the realization of human rights and basic freedoms for all without distinctions as to race, sex, language or religion.
2. The further responsibilities, functions and powers of the General Assembly with respect to matters mentioned in Paragraph (b) above are set forth in Chapters IX and X.

Article 14—Subject to the provisions of Article 12, the General Assembly may recommend measures for the peaceful adjustment of any situation, regardless of origin, which it deems likely to impair the general welfare or friendly relations among nations, including situations resulting from a violation of the provisions of the present Charter setting forth the purposes and principles of the United Nations.

Article 15—1. The General Assembly shall receive and consider annual and special reports from the Security Council; these reports shall include an account of the measures that the Security Council has adopted or applied to maintain international peace and security.
2. The General Assembly shall receive and consider reports from the other bodies of the organization.

Article 16—The General Assembly shall perform such functions with respect to the international trusteeship system, as are assigned to it under Chapters XII and XIII, including the approval of the trusteeship agreements for areas not designated as strategic.

Article 17—1. The General Assembly shall consider and approve the budget of the organization.
2. The General Assembly shall consider and approve any financial and budgetary arrangements with specialized agencies referred to in Article 57 and shall examine the administrative budgets of such specialized agencies with a view to making recommendations to the agencies concerned.

3. The expenses of the organization shall be borne by the members as apportioned by the General Assembly.

Voting

Article 18—1. Each member of the United Nations shall have one vote in the General Assembly.

2. Decisions of the General Assembly on important questions shall be made by a two-thirds majority of those present and voting. These questions shall include: recommendations with respect to the maintenance of international peace and security, the election of the non-permanent members of the Security Council, the election of the members of the Economic and Social Council, the election of the members of the United Nations which are to designate the members on the Trusteeship Council in accordance with the provisions of Article 86 (c), the admission of new members to the United Nations, the expulsion of members, the suspension of the rights and privileges of members, questions relating to the operations of the trusteeship system, and budgetary questions.

3. Decisions on other questions—including the determination of additional categories of questions to be decided by a two-thirds majority—shall be made by a majority of those present and voting.

Article 19—A member which is in arrears in the payments of its financial contributions to the organization shall have no vote if the amount of its arrears equals or exceeds the amount of the contributions due from it for the preceding two full years. The General Assembly may, nevertheless, permit such a member to vote if it is satisfied that the failure to pay is due to conditions beyond the control of the member.

Procedure

Article 20—The General Assembly shall meet in regular annual sessions and in such special sessions as occasion may require. Special sessions shall be convoked by the Secretary General at the request of the Security Council or of a majority of the members of the United Nations.

Article 21—The General Assembly shall adopt its own rules of procedure. It shall elect its president for each session.

Article 22—The General Assembly may establish such subsidiary organs as it deems necessary for the performance of its functions.

CHAPTER V

The Security Council Composition

Article 23—1. The Security Council shall consist of eleven members of the United Nations. The United States of America, the United Kingdom of Great Britain and Northern Ireland, the Union of Soviet Socialist Republics, the Republic of China, and France, shall be permanent members of the Security Council. The General Assembly shall elect six other members of the United Nations to be non-permanent members of the Security Council, due regard being specially paid, in the first instance to the contribution of members of the United Nations to the maintenance of international peace and security and to the other purposes of the organization, and also to equitable geographical distribution.

2. The non-permanent members of the Security Council shall be elected for a term of two years. In the first election of the non-permanent members, however, three shall be chosen for a term of one year. A retiring member shall not be eligible for immediate re-election.

3. Each member of the Security Council shall have one representative.

Primary Responsibility

Article 24—1. In order to insure prompt and effective action by the United Nations, its members confer on the Security Council primary responsibility for the maintenance of international peace and security, and agree that in carrying out its duties under this responsibility the Security Council acts on their behalf.

2. In discharging these duties the Security Council shall act in accordance with the purposes and principles of the United Nations. The specific powers granted to the Security Council for the discharge of these duties are laid down in Chapters VI, VII, VIII and XII.

3. The Security Council shall submit annual and, when necessary, special reports to the General Assembly for its consideration.

Article 25—The members of the United Nations agree to accept and carry out the decisions of the Security Council in accordance with the provisions of the present Charter.

Article 26—In order to promote the establishment and maintenance of international peace and security with the least diversion for armaments of the world's human and economic resources, the Security Council shall be responsible for formulating, with the assistance of the Military Staff Committee referred to in Article 47, plans to be submitted to the members of the United Nations for the establishment of a system for the regulation of armaments.

Voting

Article 27—1. Each member of the Security Council shall have one vote.

2. Decisions of the Security Council on procedural matters shall be made by an affirmative vote of seven members.

3. Decisions of the Security Council on all other matters shall be made by an affirmative vote of seven members including the concurring votes of the permanent members; provided that, in decisions under Chapter VI and under Paragraph 3 of Article 52 a party to a dispute shall abstain from voting.

Procedure

Article 28—1. The Security Council shall be so organized as to be able to function continuously. Each member of the Security Council shall for this purpose be represented at all times at the seat of the organization.

2. The Security Council shall hold periodic meetings at which each of its members may, if it so desires, be represented by a member of the Government or by some other specially designated representative.

3. The Security Council may hold meetings at such places other than the seat of the organization as in its judgment may best facilitate its work.

Article 29—The Security Council may establish such subsidiary organs as it deems necessary for the performance of its functions.

Article 30—The Security Council shall adopt its own rules of procedure, including the method of selecting its president.

Article 31—Any member of the United Nations which is not a member of the Security Council may participate without a vote in the discussion of any question brought before the Security Council whenever the latter considers that the interests of that member are specially affected.

Article 32—Any member of the United Nations which is not a member of the Security Council or any state not a member of the United Nations, if it is a party to a dispute under consideration by the Security Council, shall be invited to participate in the discussion relating to the dispute. The Security Council shall lay down such conditions as it may deem just for the participation of a state which is not a member of the United Nations.

CHAPTER VI

Pacific Settlement of Disputes

Article 33—1. The parties to any dispute, the continuance of which is likely to endanger the maintenance of international peace and security, shall, first of all, seek a solution by negotiation, inquiry, mediation, conciliation, arbitration, judicial settlement, resort to regional agencies or arrangements, or other peaceful means of their own choice.

2. The Security Council shall, when it deems necessary, call upon the parties to settle their dispute by such means.

Article 34—The Security Council may investigate any dispute, or any situation which might lead to international friction or give rise to a dispute, in order to determine whether its continuance is likely to endanger the maintenance of international peace and security.

Article 35—1. Any member of the United Nations may bring any dispute or any situation of the nature referred to in Article 34 to the attention of the Security Council, or of the General Assembly.

2. A state which is not a member of the United Nations may bring to the attention of the Security Council or of the General Assembly any dispute to which it is a party, if it accepts in advance, for the purposes of the dispute, the obligations of pacific settlement provided in the present Charter.

3. The proceedings of the General Assembly in respect of matters brought to its attention under this article will be subject to the provisions of Articles 11 and 12.

Article 36—1. The Security Council may, at any stage of a dispute of the nature referred to in Article 33 or of a situation of like nature, recommend appropriate procedures or methods of adjustment.

2. The Security Council should take into consideration any procedures for the settlement of the dispute which have already been adopted by the parties.

3. In making recommendations under this article the Security Council should take into consideration that legal disputes should as a general rule be referred by the parties to the International Court of Justice in accordance with the provisions of the statute of the court.

Article 37—1. Should the parties to a dispute of the nature referred to in Article 33 fail to settle it by the means indicated in that article, they shall refer it to the Security Council.

2. If the Security Council deems that the continuance of the dispute is in fact likely to endanger the maintenance of international peace and security, it shall decide whether to take action under Article 36 or to recommend such terms of settlement as it may consider appropriate.

Article 38—Without prejudice to the provisions of Articles 33–37 of this chapter, the Security Council may, if all the parties to any dispute so request, make recommendations to the parties with a view to a peaceful settlement of the dispute.

CHAPTER VII

Action with Respect to Threats to the Peace, Breaches of the Peace and Acts of Aggression

Article 39—The Security Council shall determine the existence of any threat to the peace, breach of the peace, or act of aggression and shall make recommendations, or decide what measures shall be taken in accordance with the provisions of Articles 41 and 42, to maintain or restore international peace and security.

Article 40—In order to prevent an aggravation of the situation, the Security Council may, before making the recommendations or deciding upon the measures provided for in Article 41, call upon the parties concerned to comply with such provisional measures as it deems necessary or desirable. Such provisional measures shall be without prejudice to the rights, claims, or position of the parties concerned. The Security Council shall duly take account of failure to comply with such provisional measures.

Article 41—The Security Council may decide what measures not involving the use of armed force are to be employed to give effect to its decisions, and it may call upon members of the United Nations to apply such measures. These may include complete or partial interruptions of economic relations and of rail, sea, air, postal, telegraphic, radio, and other means of communication, and the severance of diplomatic relations.

Article 42—Should the Security Council consider that measures provided for in Article 41, would be inadequate, or have proved to be inadequate, it may take such action by air, sea or land forces as may be necessary to maintain or restore international peace and security. Such actions may include demonstrations, blockade, and other operations by air, sea or land forces of members of the United Nations.

Article 43—1. All members of the United Nations, in order to contribute to the maintenance of international peace and security, undertake to make available to the Security Council, on its call and in accordance with a special agreement or agreements, armed forces, assistance, and facilities, including rights of passage, necessary for the purpose of maintaining international peace and security.

2. Such agreement or agreements shall govern the numbers and types of forces, their degree of readiness and general location, and the nature of the facilities and assistance to be provided.

3. The agreement or agreements shall be negotiated as soon as possible on the initiative of the Security Council. They shall be concluded between the Security Council and member states or between the Security Council and groups of member states and shall be subject to ratification by the signatory states in accordance with their constitutional processes.

Article 44—When the Security Council has decided to use force it shall, before calling upon a member not represented on it to provide armed forces in fulfillment of the obligations assumed under Article 43, invite that member, if the member so desires, to participate in the decisions of the Security Council concerning the employment of contingents of that member's armed forces.

Article 45—In order to enable the United Nations to take urgent military measures, members shall hold immediately available national air force contingents for combined international enforcement action. The strength and degree of readiness of these contingents and plans for their combined action shall be determined, within the limits laid down in the special agreement or agreements referred to in Article 43, by the Security Council with the assistance of the Military Staff Committee.

Article 46—Plans for the application of armed force shall be made by the Security Council with the assistance of the Military Staff Committee.

Article 47—1. There shall be established a Military Staff Committee to advise and assist the Security Council on all questions relating to the Security Council's military requirements for the maintenance of international peace and security, the employment and command of forces placed at its disposal, the regulation of armaments, and possible disarmament.

2. The Military Staff Committees shall consist of the Chiefs of Staff of the permanent members of the Security Council or their representatives. Any member of the United Nations not permanently represented on the committee shall be invited by the committee to be associated with it when the efficient discharge of the committee's responsibilities requires the participation of that member in its work.

3. The Military Staff Committee shall be responsible, under the Security Council, for the strategic direction of any armed forces placed at the disposal of the Security Council. Questions relating to the command of such forces shall be worked out subsequently.

4. The Military Staff Committee, with the authorization of the Security Council and after consultation with appropriate regional agencies, may establish regional subcommittees.

Article 48—1. The action required to carry out the decisions of the Security Council for the maintenance of international peace and security shall be taken by all the members of the United Nations, or by some of them, as the Security Council may determine.

2. Such decisions shall be carried out by the members of the United Nations directly and through their action in the appropriate international agencies of which they are members.

Article 49—The members of the United Nations shall join in affording mutual assistance in carrying out the measures decided upon by the Security Council.

Article 50—If preventive or enforcement measures against any state are taken by the Security Council, any other state, whether a member of the United Nations or not, which finds itself confronted with special economic problems arising from the carrying out of those measures shall have the right to consult the Security Council with regard to a solution of those problems.

Article 51—Nothing in the present Charter shall impair the inherent right of individual or collective self-defense, if an armed attack occurs against a member of the organization, until the Security Council has taken the measures necessary to maintain international peace and security. Measures taken by members in the exercise of this right of self-defense shall be immediately reported to the Security Council and shall not in any way affect the authority and responsibility of the Security Council under the present Charter to take at any time such action as it may deem necessary in order to maintain or restore international peace and security.

CHAPTER VIII

Regional Arrangements

Article 52—1. Nothing in the present Charter precludes the existence of regional arrangements or agencies for dealing with such matters relating to the maintenance of international peace and security as are appropriate for regional action, provided that such arrangements or agencies and their activities are consistent with the purposes and principles of the organization.

2. The members of the United Nations entering into such arrangements or constituting such agencies shall make every effort to achieve peaceful settlement of local disputes through such regional arrangements or by such regional agencies before referring them to the Security Council.

3. The Security Council should encourage the development of peaceful settlement of local disputes through such regional arrangements or by such regional agencies either on the initiative of the states concerned or by reference from the Security Council.

4. This article in no way impairs the application of Articles 34 and 35.

Article 53—1. The Security Council shall, where appropriate, utilize such arrangements or agencies for enforcement action under its authority. But no enforcement action shall be taken under regional arrangement or by regional agencies without the authorization of the Security Council, with the exception of measures against any enemy state, as described below, provided for pursuant to Article 107, or in regional arrangements directed against renewal of aggressive policy on the part of any such state, until such time as the organization may, on request of the governments concerned, be charged with the responsibility for preventing further aggression by such a state.

2. The term "enemy state" as used in Paragraph 1 of this article applies to any state which during the second World War has been an enemy of any signatory of the present charter.

Article 54—The Security Council shall at all times be kept fully informed of activities undertaken, or in contemplation, under regional arrangements or by regional agencies for the maintenance of international peace and security.

CHAPTER IX

International Economic and Social Cooperation

Article 55—With a view to the creation of conditions of stability and well-being which are necessary for peaceful and friendly relations among nations based on respect for the principle of equal rights and self-determination of people, the United Nations shall promote:

(a) Higher standards of living, full employment, and conditions of economic and social progress and development;

(b) Solutions of international economic, social, health, and related problems and international cultural and educational cooperation and

(c) Universal respect for, and observance of, human rights and fundamental freedoms for all without distinction as to race, sex, language, or religion.

Article 56—All members pledge themselves to take joint and separate action in cooperation with the organization for the achievement of the purposes set forth in Article 55.

Article 57—1. The various specialized agencies established by intergovernmental agreement, and having wide international responsibilities as defined in their basic instruments in economic, social, cultural, educational, health and related fields, shall be brought into relationship with the United Nations in accordance with the provisions of Article 63.

2. Specialized agencies thus brought into relationship with the organization are hereinafter referred to as "the specialized agencies."

Article 58—The organization shall make recommendations for the coordination of the policies and activities of the specialized agencies.

Article 59—The organization shall, where appropriate, initiate negotiations among the states concerned for the creation of any new specialized agency required for the accomplishment of the purposes set forth in Article 55.

Article 60—Responsibility for the discharge of the organization's functions set forth in this chapter shall be vested in the General Assembly and, under the authority of the General Assembly, in the Economic and Social Council, which shall have for this purpose the powers set forth in Chapter X.

CHAPTER X

Economic and Social Council Composition

Article 61—1. The Economic and Social Council shall consist of eighteen members of the United Nations elected by the General Assembly.

2. Subject to the provisions of Paragraph 3, six members of the Economic and Social Council shall be elected each year for a term of three years. A retiring member shall be eligible for immediate re-election.

3. At the first election, eighteen members of the Economic and Social Council shall be chosen. The term of office of six members so chosen shall expire at the end of one year, and of six other members at the end of two years, in accordance with arrangements made by the General Assembly.

4. Each member of the Economic and Social Council shall have one representative.

Functions and Powers

Article 62—1. The Economic and Social Council may make or initiate studies and reports with respect to international economic, social, cultural, educational, health, and related matters and may make recommendations with respect to any such matters to the General Assembly, to the members of the United Nations, and to the specialized agencies concerned.

2. It may make recommendations for the purpose of promoting respect for, and observance of, human rights and fundamental freedoms for all.

3. It may prepare draft conventions for submission to the General Assembly, with respect to matters falling within its competence.

4. It may call, in accordance with the rules prescribed by the United Nations, international conferences on matters falling within its competence.

Article 63—1. The Economic and Social Council may enter into an agreement, approved by the General Assembly, with any of the agencies referred to in Article 57, defining the terms on which the agency concerned shall be brought into relationship with the United Nations.

2. It may coordinate the activities of the specialized agencies through consultation with and recommendations to such agencies and through recommendations to the General Assembly and to the members of the United Nations.

Article 64—1. The Economic and Social Council is authorized to take appropriate steps to obtain regular reports from the specialized agencies. It may make arrangements with the members of the United Nations and with the specialized agencies to obtain reports on the steps taken to give effect to its own recommendations and falling within its competence which are made by the General Assembly.

2. It may communicate its observance on these reports to the General Assembly.

Article 65—The Economic and Social Council may furnish information to the Security Council and shall assist the Security Council upon its request.

Article 66—1. The Economic and Social Council shall perform such functions as fall within its competence, in connection with the carrying out of the recommendations of the General Assembly.

2. It may, with the approval of the General Assembly, perform services at the request of the members of the United Nations and at the request of the specialized agencies.

3. It may perform such other functions as are specified elsewhere in the present Charter and such functions as may be assigned to it by the General Assembly.

Voting

Article 67—1. Each member of the Economic and Social Council shall have one vote.

2. Decisions of the Economic and Social Council shall be taken by a majority of the members present and voting.

Procedure

Article 68—The Economic and Social Council shall set up commissions in economic and social fields and for the promotion of human rights, and such other commissions as may be required for the performance of its functions.

Article 69—The Economic and Social Council shall invite any member of the United Nations to participate, without vote, in its deliberations on any matter of particular concern to that member.

Article 70—The Economic and Social Council may make arrangements for representatives of the specialized agencies to participate, without vote, in its deliberations and in those of the commissions established by it, and for its representatives to participate in the deliberations of the specialized agencies.

Article 71—The Economic and Social Council may make suitable arrangements for consultation with nongovernmental organizations which are concerned with matters within its competence. Such arrangements may be made with international organizations, and, where appropriate, with national organizations after consultation with the member of the United Nations concerned.

Article 72—1. The Economic and Social Council shall adopt its own rules of procedure, including the method of selecting its president.
2. The Economic and Social Council shall meet as required in accordance with its rules, which shall include provision for the convening of meetings on request of a majority of its members.

CHAPTER XI

Declaration Regarding Non-self-governing Territories

Article 73—Members of the United Nations which have or assume responsibilities for the administration of territories whose peoples have not yet attained a full measure of self-government recognize the principle that the interests of the inhabitants of these territories are paramount, and accept as a sacred trust the obligation to promote to the utmost, within the system of international peace and security established by the present Charter, the well-being of the inhabitants of these territories, and, to this end:
(a) To insure, with due respect for the culture of the peoples concerned, their political, economic, social, and educational advancement, their just treatment, and their protection against abuses;
(b) To develop self-government, to take due account of the political aspirations of the peoples, and to assist them in the progressive development of their free political institutions, according to the particular circumstances of each territory and its peoples and their varying stages of advancement;
(c) To further international peace and security;
(d) To promote constructive measures of development, to encourage research, and to cooperate with one another and with appropriate international bodies with a view to the practical achievement of the social, economic, and scientific purposes set forth in this paragraph; and
(e) To transmit regularly to the secretary general for information purposes, subject to such limitation as security and constitutional considerations may require, statistical and other information of a technical nature relating to economic, social, and educational conditions in the territories for which they are respectively responsible other than those territories to which Chapters XII and XIII apply.

Article 74—Members of the United Nations agree that their policy in respect to the territories, to which this chapter applies, no less than in respect of their metropolitan areas, must be based on the general principle of good-neighborliness, due account being taken of the interests of well-being of the rest of the world, in social, economic and commerical matters.

CHAPTER XII

International Trusteeship System

Article 75—The United Nations shall establish under its authority an international trusteeship system for the administration and supervision of such territories as may be placed thereunder by subsequent individual agreements. These territories are hereafter referred to as trust territories.

Article 76—The basic objectives of the trusteeship system in accordance with the purposes of the United Nations laid down in Article 1 of the present Charter, shall be:
(a) To further international peace and security;
(b) To promote the political, economic, social and educational advancement of the inhabitants of the trust territories, and their progressive development toward self-government or independence as may be appropriate to the particular circumstances of each territory and its peoples and the freely expressed wishes of the peoples concerned, and as may be provided by the terms of each trusteeship agreement;
(c) To encourage respect for human rights and for fundamental freedoms for all without distinction as to race, sex, language or religion, and to encourage recognition of the interdependence of the peoples of the world; and
(d) To insure equal treatment in social, economic and commerical matters for all members of the United Nations and their nationals, and also equal treatment of the latter in the administration of justice, without prejudice to the attainment of the foregoing objectives, and subject to the provisions of Article 80.

Article 77—1. The trusteeship system shall apply to such territories in the following categories as may be placed thereunder by means of trusteeship agreements:
(a) Territories now held under mandate;
(b) Territories which may be detached from enemy states as a result of the second World War; and
(c) Territories voluntarily placed under the system by states responsible for their administration.
2. It will be a matter for subsequent agreement as to which territories in the foregoing categories will be brought under the trusteeship system and upon what terms.

Article 78—The trusteeship system shall not apply to territories which have become members of the United Nations, relationship among which should be based on respect for the principle of sovereign equality.

Article 79—The terms of trusteeship for each territory to be placed under the trusteeship system, including any alteration or amendment, shall be agreed upon by the states directly concerned including the mandatory power in the case of territories held under mandate by a member of the United Nations, and shall be approved as provided for in Articles 83 and 85.

Article 80—1. Except as may be agreed upon in individual trusteeship agreements made in accordance with the provisions of this chapter, placing each territory under the trusteeship system, and until such agreements have been concluded, nothing in this chapter shall be construed in or of itself to alter in any manner the rights whatsoever of any states or any peoples or the terms of existing international instruments to which members of the United Nations may respectively be parties.
2. Paragraph 1 of this article shall not be interpreted as giving grounds for delay or postponement of the negotiation and conclusion of such agreements for placing mandated and other territories under the trusteeship system as provided for in Article 77.

Article 81—The trusteeship agreement shall in each case include the terms under which the trust territory will be administered and designate the authority which shall exercise the administration of the trust territory. Such authority, hereafter called the administering authority, may be one or more states of the United Nations itself.

Article 82—There may be designated, in any trusteeship agreement, a strategic area or areas which may include part or all of the trust territory to which the agreement applies, without prejudice to any special agreement or agreements made under Article 43.

Article 83—1. All functions of the United Nations relating to strategic areas, including the approval of the terms of the trusteeship agreements and of their alteration or amendment, shall be exercised by the Security Council.
2. The basic objectives set forth in Article 76 shall be applicable to the people of each strategic area.
3. The Security Council shall, subject to the provisions of the trusteeship agreements and without prejudice to security considerations, avail itself of the assistance of the Trusteeship Council to perform those functions of the United Nations under the trusteeship system relating to political, economic, social and educational matters in the strategic areas.

Article 84—It shall be the duty of the administering authority to insure that the trust territory shall play its part in the maintenance of international peace and security. To this end the administering authority may make use of volunteer forces, facilities, and assistance from the trust territory in carrying out the obligations toward the Security Council undertaken in this regard by the administering authority, as well as for local defense and the maintenance of law and order within the trust territory.

Article 85—1. The functions of the United Nations with regard to trusteeship agreements for all areas not designated as strategic, including the approval of the terms of the trusteeship agreements and of their alteration or amendment, shall be exercised by the General Assembly.
2. The Trusteeship Council, operating under the authority of the General Assembly, shall assist the General Assembly in carrying out these functions.

CHAPTER XIII

The Trusteeship Council Composition

Article 86—1. The Trusteeship Council shall consist of the following members of the United Nations:
(a) Those members administering trust territories;
(b) Such of those members mentioned by name in Article 23 as are not administering trust territories; and
(c) As many other members elected for three-year terms by the General Assembly as may be necessary to insure that the total number of members of the Trusteeship Council is equally divided between those members of the United Nations which administer trust territories and those which do not.
2. Each member of the Trusteeship Council shall designate one specially qualified person to represent it therein.

Functions and Powers

Article 87—The General Assembly and, under its authority, the Trusteeship Council, in carrying out their functions, may:
(a) Consider reports submitted by the administering authority;
(b) Accept petitions and examine them in consultation with the administering authority;
(c) Provide for periodic visits to the respective trust territories at times agreed upon within the administering authority; and
(d) Take these and other actions in conformity with the terms of the trusteeship agreements.

Article 88—The Trusteeship Council shall formulate a questionnaire on the political, economic, social and educational advancement of the inhabitants of each trust territory, and the administering authority for each trust territory within the competence of the General Assembly shall make an annual report to the General Assembly upon the basis of such questionnaire.

Voting

Article 89—1. Each member of the Trusteeship Council shall have one vote.
2. Decisions of the Trusteeship Council shall be taken by a majority of the members present and voting.

Procedure

Article 90—1. The Trusteeship Council shall adopt its own rules of procedure, including the method of selecting its president.
2. The Trusteeship Council shall meet as required in accordance with its rules, which shall include provisions for the convening of meetings on the request of a majority of its members.

Article 91—The Trusteeship Council shall, when appropriate, avail itself of the assistance of the Economic and Social Council and of the specialized agencies in regard to matters with which they are respectively concerned.

CHAPTER XIV

The International Court of Justice

Article 92—The International Court of Justice shall be the principal judicial organ of the United Nations. It shall function in accordance with the annexed statute, which is based upon the statute of the Permanent Court of International Justice and forms an integral part of the present chapter.

Article 93—1. All members of the United Nations are ipso facto parties to the statute of the International Court of Justice.
2. A state which is not a member of the United Nations may become party to the statute of the International Court of Justice on conditions to be determined in each case by the General Assembly upon recommendation of the Security Council.

Article 94—1. Each member of the United Nations undertakes to comply with the decision of the International Court of Justice in any case to which it is a party.
2. If any party to a case fails to perform the obligations incumbent upon it under a judgment rendered by the court, the other party may have recourse to the Security Council, which may, if it deems necessary, make recommendations or decide upon measures to be taken to give effect to the judgment.

Article 95—Nothing in the present Charter shall prevent members of the United Nations from entrusting the solution of their differences to other tribunals by virtue of agreements already in existence or which may be concluded in the future.

Article 96—1. The General Assembly or the Security Council may request the International Court of Justice to give an advisory opinion on any legal question.
2. Other organs of the United Nations and specialized agencies which may at any time be so authorized by the General Assembly, may also request advisory opinions of the court on legal questions arising within the scope of their activities.

CHAPTER XV

The Secretariat

Article 97—There shall be a secretariat comprising a secretary general and such staff as the organization may require. The secretary general shall be appointed by the General Assembly on the recommendation of the Security Council. He shall be the chief administrative officer of the organization.

Article 98—The secretary general shall act in that capacity in all meetings of the General Assembly, of the Security Council, of the Economic and Social Council and of the Trusteeship Council, and shall perform such other functions as are entrusted to him by these organs. The secretary general shall make an annual report to the General Assembly on the work of the organization.

Article 99—The secretary general may bring to the attention of the Security Council any matter which in his opinion may threaten the maintenance of international peace and security.

Article 100—1. In the performance of their duties the secretary general and the staff shall not seek or receive instructions from any Government or from any other authority external to the organization. They shall refrain from any action which might reflect on their position as international officials responsible only to the organization.
2. Each member of the United Nations undertakes to respect the exclusively international character of the responsibilities of the secretary general and the staff, and not to seek to influence them in the discharge of their responsibilities.

Article 101—1. The staff shall be appointed by the secretary general under regulations established by the General Assembly.
2. Appropriate staffs shall be permanently assigned to the Economic and Social Council, the Trusteeship Council, and, as required, to other organs of the United Nations. These staffs shall form a part of the Secretariat.
3. The paramount consideration in the employment of the staff and in the determination of the conditions of service shall be the necessity of securing the highest standards of efficiency, competence and integrity. Due regard shall be paid to the importance of recruiting the staff on as wide a geographical basis as possible.

CHAPTER XVI

Miscellaneous Provisions

Article 102—1. Every treaty and every international agreement entered into by any member of the United Nations after the present Charter comes into force shall as soon as possible be registered with the Secretariat and published by it.
2. No party to any such treaty or international agreement which has not been registered in accordance with the provisions of Paragraph 1 of this article may invoke that treaty or agreement before any organ of the United Nations.

Article 103—In the event of a conflict between the obligations of the members of the United Nations under the present Charter and any other international obligations to which they are subject, their obligations under the present Charter shall prevail.

Article 104—The organization shall enjoy in the territory of each of its members such legal capacity as may be necessary for the exercise of its functions and the fulfillment of its purposes.

Article 105—1. The organization shall enjoy in the territory of each of its members such privileges and immunities as are necessary for the fulfillment of its purposes.
2. Representatives of the members of the United Nations and officials of the organization shall similarly enjoy such privileges and immunities as are necessary for the independent exercise of their functions in connection with the organization.
3. The General Assembly may make recommendations with a view to determining the details of the application of Paragraphs 1 and 2 of this article or may propose conventions to the members of the United Nations for this purpose.

CHAPTER XVII

Transitional Security Arrangements

Article 106—Pending the coming into force of such special agreements referred to in Article 43, as in the opinion of the Security Council enable it to begin the exercise of its responsibilities under Article 42, the parties to the four-nation declaration signed at Moscow, Oct. 30, 1943, and France, shall, in accordance with the provisions of Paragraph 5 of that declaration, consult with one another and, as occasion requires, with other members of the organization with a view to such joint action on behalf of the organization as may be necessary for the purpose of maintaining international peace and security.

Article 107—Nothing in the present Charter shall invalidate or preclude action in relation to any state which during the second World War has been an enemy of any signatory to the present Charter, taken or authorized as a result of that war by the governments having responsibility for such action.

CHAPTER XVIII

Amendments

Article 108—Amendments to the present Charter shall come into force for all members of the organization when they have been adopted by a vote of two-thirds of the members of the General Assembly and ratified in accordance with their respective constitutional processes by two-thirds of the members of the United Nations, including all the permanent members of the Security Council.

Article 109—1. A general conference of the members of the United Nations for the purpose of reviewing the present Charter may be held at a date and place to be fixed by a two-thirds vote of the General Assembly and by a vote of any seven members of the Security Council. Each member of the United Nations shall have one vote in the conference.
2. Any alteration of the present Charter recommended by a two-thirds vote of the conference shall take effect when ratified in accordance with their respective constitutional processes by two-thirds of the members of the United Nations including all the permanent members of the Security Council.
3. If such a conference has not been held before the tenth annual session of the General Assembly following the coming into force of the present Charter the proposal to call such a conference shall be placed on the agenda of that session of the General Assembly, and the conference shall be held if so decided by a majority vote of the members of the General Assembly and by a vote of any seven members of the Security Council.

CHAPTER XIX

Ratification and Signature

Article 110—1. The present Charter shall be ratified by the signatory states in accordance with their respective constitutional processes.
2. The ratifications shall be deposited with the Government of the United States of America, which shall notify all the signatory states of each deposit as well as the secretary general of the organization when he has been elected.
3. The present Charter shall come into force upon the deposit of ratifications by the Republic of China, France, the Union of Soviet Socialist Republics, the United Kingdom of Great Britain and Northern Ireland, and the United States of America, and by a majority of the other signatory states.
4. The states signatory to the present Charter which ratify it after it has come into force will become original members of the United Nations on the date of the deposit of their respective ratifications.

Article 111—The present Charter, of which the Chinese, English, French, Russian and Spanish texts are equally authentic, shall remain deposited in the archives of the Government of the United States of America. Duly certified copies thereof shall be transmitted by that Government to the Governments of the other signatory states.
In faith whereof the representatives of the United Nations have signed the present Charter.
Done in the city of San Francisco, the twenty-sixth day of June, one thousand nine hundred and forty-five.

AIR DISTANCES BETWEEN PRINCIPAL CITIES OF THE UNITED STATES

	Amarillo, Tex.	Atlanta, Ga.	Billings, Mont.	Boston, Mass.	Buffalo, N. Y.	Charleston, S. C.	Cheyenne, Wyo.	Chicago, Ill.	Cincinnati, Ohio	Cleveland, Ohio	Dallas, Tex.	Denver, Colo.	Detroit, Mich.	El Paso, Tex.	Houston, Tex.	Indianapolis, Ind.	Jacksonville, Fla.	Kansas City, Mo.	Los Angeles, Calif.	Louisville, Ky.	Memphis, Tenn.	Miami, Fla.	Minneapolis, Minn.	New Orleans, La.	New York, N. Y.	Philadelphia, Pa.	Phoenix, Ariz.	Pittsburgh, Pa.	Portland, Ore.	St. Louis, Mo.	Salt Lake City, Utah	San Francisco, Calif.	Seattle, Wash.	Tulsa, Okla.	Washington, D. C.
Amarillo, Tex.		999	809	1722	1338	1266	440	894	992	1173	334	358	1124	358	533	915	1219	481	937	915	667	1441	812	776	1560	1494	598	1244	1304	685	668	1157	1359	335	1391
Atlanta, Ga.	999		1519	937	697	267	1229	587	369	554	721	1212	596	1291	701	426	285	676	1936	319	337	604	907	424	748	666	1592	521	2172	467	1583	2139	2182	678	543
Billings, Mont.	809	1519		1861	1473	1761	370	1073	1304	1369	1092	453	1283	973	1315	1204	1796	846	959	1275	1213	2085	742	1479	1760	1727	872	1479	686	1057	387	904	668	930	1669
Boston, Mass.	1722	937	1861		400	820	1735	851	740	551	1551	1769	613	2072	1605	807	1017	1251	2596	826	1137	1255	1123	1359	188	271	2300	483	2540	1038	2099	2699	2493	1398	393
Buffalo, N. Y.	1338	697	1473	400		699	1335	454	393	173	1198	1370	216	1692	1286	435	879	861	2198	483	803	1181	731	1086	292	279	1906	178	2156	662	1699	2300	2117	1023	292
Charleston, S. C.	1266	267	1761	820	699		1486	757	506	609	981	1474	681	1552	936	594	197	928	2203	500	604	482	1104	630	641	562	1857	528	2425	704	1845	2405	2428	945	453
Cheyenne, Wyo.	440	1229	370	1735	1335	1486		891	1082	1199	726	96	1125	653	947	986	1493	560	882	1033	902	1763	642	1131	1604	1556	663	1298	947	795	371	967	973	588	1477
Chicago, Ill.	894	587	1073	851	454	757	891		252	308	803	920	238	1252	940	165	863	414	1745	269	482	1188	355	833	713	666	1453	410	1758	262	1260	1858	1737	598	597
Cincinnati, Ohio	992	369	1304	740	393	506	1082	252		222	814	1094	235	1335	892	100	626	541	1897	90	410	952	605	706	570	503	1581	257	1985	309	1453	2043	1972	661	404
Cleveland, Ohio	1173	554	1369	551	173	609	1199	308	222		1025	1227	90	1525	1114	263	770	700	2049	311	630	1087	630	924	405	360	1749	115	2055	492	1568	2166	2026	853	306
Dallas, Tex.	334	721	1092	1551	1198	981	726	803	814	1025		663	999	572	225	763	908	451	1240	726	420	1111	862	443	1374	1299	887	1070	1633	547	999	1483	1681	236	1185
Denver, Colo.	358	1212	453	1769	1370	1474	96	920	1094	1227	663		1156	557	879	1000	1467	558	831	1038	879	1726	700	1082	1631	1579	586	1320	982	796	371	949	1021	550	1494
Detroit, Mich.	1124	596	1283	613	216	681	1125	238	235	90	999	1156		1479	1105	240	831	645	1983	316	623	1152	543	939	482	443	1690	205	1969	455	1492	2091	1938	813	396
El Paso, Tex.	358	1291	973	2072	1692	1552	653	1252	1335	1525	572	557	1479		676	1264	1473	839	701	1254	976	1643	1157	983	1905	1836	346	1590	1286	1034	689	995	1376	674	1728
Houston, Tex.	533	701	1315	1605	1286	936	947	940	892	1114	225	879	1105	676		865	821	644	1374	803	484	968	1056	318	1420	1341	1017	1137	1836	679	1200	1645	1891	442	1220
Indianapolis, Ind.	915	426	1204	807	435	594	986	165	100	263	763	1000	240	1264	865		699	453	1809	107	384	1024	511	712	646	585	1499	330	1885	231	1356	1949	1872	591	494
Jacksonville, Fla.	1219	285	1796	1017	879	197	1493	863	626	770	908	1467	831	1473	821	699		950	2147	594	590	326	1191	504	838	758	1794	703	2439	751	1837	2374	2455	921	647
Kansas City, Mo.	481	676	846	1251	861	928	560	414	591	700	451	558	645	839	644	453	950		1356	480	369	1241	413	680	1097	1038	1049	781	1497	238	925	1506	1506	216	945
Los Angeles, Calif.	937	1936	959	2596	2198	2203	882	1745	1897	2049	1240	831	1983	701	1374	1809	2147	1356		1829	1603	2339	1524	1673	2451	2394	357	2136	825	1589	579	347	959	1266	2300
Louisville, Ky.	915	319	1275	826	483	500	1033	269	90	311	726	1038	316	1254	803	107	594	480	1829		320	919	605	623	652	582	1508	344	1950	242	1402	1986	1943	582	476
Memphis, Tenn.	667	337	1213	1137	803	604	902	482	410	630	420	879	623	976	484	384	590	369	1603	320		872	699	358	957	881	1263	660	1849	240	1250	1802	1867	341	765
Miami, Fla.	1441	604	2085	1255	1181	482	1763	1188	952	1087	1111	1726	1152	1643	968	1024	326	1241	2339	919	872		1511	669	1092	1019	1982	1010	2708	1061	2089	2594	2734	1176	923
Minneapolis, Minn.	812	907	742	1123	731	1104	642	355	605	630	862	700	543	1157	1056	511	1191	413	1524	605	699	1511		1051	1018	985	1280	743	1427	466	987	1584	1395	626	934
New Orleans, La.	776	424	1479	1359	1086	630	1131	833	706	924	443	1082	939	983	318	712	504	680	1673	623	358	669	1051		1171	1089	1316	919	2063	598	1434	1926	2101	548	966
New York, N. Y.	1560	748	1760	188	292	641	1604	713	570	405	1374	1631	482	1905	1420	646	838	1097	2451	652	957	1092	1018	1171		83	2145	317	2445	875	1972	2571	2408	1231	205
Philadelphia, Pa.	1494	666	1727	271	279	562	1556	666	503	360	1299	1579	443	1836	1341	585	758	1038	2394	582	881	1019	985	1089	83		2083	259	2412	811	1925	2523	2380	1163	123
Phoenix, Ariz.	598	1592	872	2300	1906	1857	663	1453	1581	1749	887	586	1690	346	1017	1499	1794	1049	357	1508	1263	1982	1280	1316	2145	2083		1828	1005	1272	504	653	1114	932	1983
Pittsburgh, Pa.	1244	521	1479	483	178	528	1298	410	257	115	1070	1320	205	1590	1137	330	703	781	2136	344	660	1010	743	919	317	259	1828		2165	559	1668	2264	2138	917	192
Portland, Ore.	1304	2172	686	2540	2156	2425	947	1758	1985	2055	1633	982	1969	1296	1836	1885	2439	1497	825	1950	1849	2708	1427	2063	2445	2412	1005	2165		1723	636	534	145	1531	2354
St. Louis, Mo.	685	467	1057	1038	662	704	795	262	309	492	547	796	455	1034	679	231	751	238	1589	242	240	1061	466	598	875	811	1272	559	1723		1162	1744	1724	361	712
Salt Lake City, Utah	668	1583	387	2099	1699	1845	371	1260	1453	1568	999	371	1492	689	1200	1356	1837	925	579	1402	1250	2089	987	1434	1972	1925	504	1668	636	1162		600	701	917	1848
San Francisco, Calif.	1157	2139	904	2699	2300	2405	967	1858	2043	2166	1483	949	2091	995	1645	1949	2374	1506	347	1986	1802	2594	1584	1926	2571	2523	653	2264	534	1744	600		678	1461	2442
Seattle, Wash.	1359	2182	668	2493	2117	2428	973	1737	1972	2026	1681	1021	1938	1376	1891	1872	2455	1506	959	1943	1867	2734	1395	2101	2408	2380	1114	2138	145	1724	701	678		1560	2329
Tulsa, Okla.	335	678	930	1398	1023	945	588	598	661	853	236	550	813	674	442	591	921	216	1266	582	341	1176	626	548	1231	1163	932	917	1531	361	917	1461	1560		1058
Washington, D. C.	1391	543	1669	393	292	453	1477	597	404	306	1185	1494	396	1728	1220	494	647	945	2300	476	765	923	934	966	205	123	1983	192	2354	712	1848	2442	2329	1058	

AIR DISTANCES BETWEEN PRINCIPAL CITIES OF THE WORLD

	Berlin, Ger.	Bombay, Ind.	Buenos Aires, Arg.	Calcutta, Ind.	Cape Town, S. Afr.	Darwin, Australia	Gibraltar	Hong Kong	Honolulu, H. I.	Istanbul, Turk.	Juneau, Alas.	London, Eng.	Los Angeles, U. S. A.	Manila, P. I.	Melbourne, Australia	Mexico City, Mex.	Moscow, U. S. S. R.	New York, U. S. A.	Nome, Alas.	Oslo, Norw.	Panama, Pan.	Paris, Fr.	Peking, Ch.	Port Said, Eg.	Quebec, Can.	Reykjavik, Ice.	Rio de Janeiro, Bras.	Rome, It.	Seattle, U. S. A.	Shanghai, Ch.	Singapore	Tokyo, Jap.	Valparaiso, Chile	Wellington, N. Z.	Zanzibar, Afr.
Berlin, Ger.		3910	7376	4376	5977	8036	1453	5500	7305	1078	4560	574	5782	6128	9919	6037	996	3961	4342	515	5849	542	4567	1747	3583	1479	6114	734	5041	5215	6166	5538	7795	11265	4309
Bombay, Ind.	3910		9273	1041	5134	4503	4814	2673	8020	2991	6866	4462	8701	3148	6097	9722	3131	7794	5901	4130	9742	4359	2964	2659	7371	5191	8257	3843	7741	3133	2429	4188	10037	7677	2855
Buenos Aires, Arg.	7376	9273		10242	4270	9127	5963	11463	7558	7568	7759	6918	6118	11042	7234	4633	8375	5297	8848	7613	3381	6877	11974	7362	5680	7099	1218	6929	6913	12197	9864	11400	761	6260	6421
Calcutta, Ind.	4376	1041	10242		6026	3744	5521	1534	7037	3646	6326	4954	8148	2189	5547	9495	3447	7921	5271	4459	10114	4889	2024	3506	7481	5409	9376	4496	7224	2112	1791	3187	10993	7042	3859
Cape Town, S. Afr.	5977	5134	4270	6026		6947	5076	7372	11532	5219	10330	6005	9969	7525	6412	8511	6294	7801	10107	6494	7014	5841	8045	4590	7857	7111	3769	5249	10199	8059	6016	9071	4998	7019	2346
Darwin, Australia	8036	4503	9127	3744	6947		9265	2642	5355	7390	7105	8598	7835	1979	1964	9081	7046	9959	6235	8022	10352	8575	3728	7159	9724	8631	9960	8190	7619	3142	2075	3367	8961	3310	6409
Gibraltar	1453	4814	5963	5521	5076	9265		6828	8075	1874	5273	1094	5936	7483	10798	5629	2413	3627	5398	1791	4926	964	6009	2179	3383	2047	4775	1034	5462	6646	7231	6988	6408	12060	4103
Hong Kong	5500	2673	11463	1534	7372	2642	6828		5537	4980	5634	5981	7240	693	4607	8776	4439	8051	4547	5337	10084	5956	1226	4975	7650	6031	10995	5768	6471	772	1652	1796	11607	5853	5414
Honolulu, H. I.	7305	8020	7558	7037	11532	5355	8075	5537		8104	2815	7226	2557	5296	5513	3781	7033	4959	3004	6784	5248	7434	5067	8738	5000	6084	8190	8022	2678	4934	6710	3850	6793	4708	10869
Istanbul, Turk.	1078	2991	7568	3646	5219	7390	1874	4980	8104		5498	1551	6843	5659	9088	7102	1088	5009	5101	1518	6750	1401	4379	693	4644	2558	6395	854	6063	4959	5373	5556	8172	10663	3312
Juneau, Alas.	4560	6866	7759	6326	10330	7105	5273	5634	2815	5498		4418	1842	5869	8035	3219	4534	2854	1094	4045	4460	4628	4522	6215	2660	3268	7598	5247	899	4869	7235	4011	7271	7475	8795
London, Eng.	574	4462	6918	4954	6005	8598	1094	5981	7226	1551	4418		5439	6667	10501	5541	1549	3459	4381	714	5278	213	5054	2154	3101	1171	5772	887	4782	5710	6744	5938	7263	11682	4604
Los Angeles, U. S. A.	5782	8701	6118	8148	9969	7835	5936	7240	2557	6843	1842	5439		7269	7931	1542	6068	2451	2876	5325	3001	5601	6250	7528	2579	4306	6296	6326	959	6477	8767	5470	5527	6714	10021
Manila, P. I.	6128	3148	11042	2189	7525	1979	7483	693	5296	5659	5869	6667	7269		3941	8829	5130	8493	4817	6016	10283	6673	1770	5619	8124	6651	11254	6457	6641	1152	1479	1863	10930	5162	5763
Melbourne, Australia	9919	6097	7234	5547	6412	1964	10798	4607	5513	9088	8035	10501	7931	3941		8422	8963	10355	7558	9926	9022	10396	5667	8658	10497	10544	8186	9934	8186	5005	3761	5089	6998	1595	6802
Mexico City, Mex.	6037	9722	4633	9495	8511	9081	5629	8776	3781	7102	3219	5591	1542	8829	8422		6688	2085	4309	5706	1495	5706	7733	7671	2454	4622	4770	6353	2337	8039	10307	7035	4053	6899	9484
Moscow, U. S. S. R.	996	3131	8375	3447	6294	7046	2413	4439	7033	1088	4534	1549	6068	5130	8963	6688		4662	4036	1016	6711	1541	3597	1710	4242	2056	7179	1474	5199	4235	5238	4650	8792	10279	4270
New York, U. S. A.	3961	7794	5297	7921	7801	9959	3627	8051	4959	5009	2854	3459	2451	8493	10355	2085	4662		3769	3672	2231	3622	6823	5590	439	2576	4820	4273	2408	7357	9630	6735	5094	8946	7698
Nome, Alas.	4342	5901	8848	5271	10107	6235	5398	4547	3004	5101	1094	4381	2876	4817	7558	4309	4036	3739		3836	5541	4574	3428	5745	3489	3366	8586	5082	1976	3784	6148	2983	8360	7383	8209
Oslo, Norw.	515	4130	7613	4459	6494	8022	1791	5337	6784	1518	4045	714	5325	6016	9926	5706	1016	3672	3836		5691	832	4360	2211	3263	1083	6482	1243	4591	5020	6246	5221	7914	10974	4803
Panama, Pan.	5849	9742	3381	10114	7014	10352	4926	10084	5245	6750	4460	5278	3001	10283	9022	1495	6711	2231	5541	5691		5382	8906	7146	2659	4706	3294	5903	3651	9324	11687	8423	2943	7433	8245
Paris, Fr.	542	4359	6877	4889	5841	8575	964	5956	7434	1401	4628	213	5601	6673	10396	5706	1541	3622	4574	832	5382		5101	1975	3235	1380	5703	682	4993	5752	6671	6033	7251	11791	4396
Peking, Ch.	4567	2964	11974	2024	8045	3728	6009	1226	5067	4379	4522	5054	6250	1770	5667	7733	3597	6823	3428	4360	8906	5101		4584	6423	4903	10768	5047	5396	662	2774	1307	11774	6698	5803
Port Said, Eg.	1747	2659	7362	3506	4590	7159	2179	4975	8738	693	6215	2154	7528	5619	8658	7671	1710	5590	5745	2211	7146	1975	4584		5250	3227	6244	1317	6759	5132	5088	5842	8088	10249	2729
Quebec, Can.	3583	7371	5680	7481	7857	9724	3383	7650	5000	4644	2660	3101	2579	8124	10497	2454	4242	439	3489	3263	2659	3235	6423	5250		2189	5125	3943	2353	6981	9097	6417	5504	9228	7443
Reykjavik, Ice.	1479	5191	7099	5409	7111	8631	2047	6031	6084	2558	3268	1171	4306	6651	10544	4622	2056	2576	3366	1083	4706	1380	4903	3227	2189		6118	2044	3614	5559	7160	5472	7225	10724	5757
Rio de Janeiro, Braz.	6144	8257	1218	9376	3769	9960	4775	10995	8190	6395	7598	5772	6296	11254	8186	4770	7179	4820	8586	6482	3294	5703	10768	6244	5125	6118		5684	6891	11340	9774	11535	1855	7349	5589
Rome, It.	734	3843	6929	4496	5249	8190	1034	5768	8022	854	5247	887	6326	6457	9934	6353	1474	4273	5082	1243	5903	682	5047	1317	3943	2044	5684		5659	5677	6232	6124	7420	11524	3712
Seattle, U. S. A.	5041	7741	6913	7224	10199	7619	5462	6471	2678	6063	899	4782	959	6641	8186	2337	5199	2408	1976	4591	3651	4993	5396	6759	2353	3614	6891	5659		5703	8057	4777	6230	7242	9359
Shanghai, Ch.	5215	3133	12197	2112	8059	3142	6646	772	4934	4959	4869	5710	6477	1152	5005	8039	4235	7357	3784	5020	9324	5752	662	5132	6981	5559	11340	5677	5703		2377	1094	11650	6054	5971
Singapore	6166	2429	9864	1791	6016	2075	7231	1652	6710	5373	7235	6744	8767	1479	3761	10307	5238	9630	6148	6246	11687	6671	2774	5088	9097	7160	9774	6232	8057	2377		3304	10226	5292	4480
Tokyo, Jap.	5538	4188	11400	3186	9071	3367	6988	1796	3850	5556	4011	5938	5470	1863	5089	7035	4650	6735	2983	5221	8423	6033	1307	5842	6417	5472	11535	6124	4777	1094	3304		10635	5760	7040
Valparaiso, Chile	7795	10037	761	10993	4998	8961	6408	11607	6793	8172	7271	7263	5527	10930	6998	4053	8792	5094	8360	7914	2943	7251	11774	8088	5504	7225	1855	7420	6230	11650	10226	10635		5785	7184
Wellington, N. Z.	11265	7677	6260	7042	7019	3310	12060	5853	4708	10663	7475	11682	6714	5162	1595	6899	10279	8946	7383	10974	7433	11791	6698	10249	9228	10724	7349	11524	7242	6054	5292	5760	5785		8122
Zanzibar, Afr.	4309	2855	6421	3859	2346	6409	4103	5414	10869	3312	8795	4604	10021	5763	6802	9484	4270	7693	8209	4803	8245	4396	5803	2729	7443	5757	5589	3712	9359	5971	4480	7040	7184	8122	

PRINCIPAL GEOGRAPHIC FEATURES OF THE WORLD

Principal Mountains of the World

Name	*Location*	*Mountain Range*	*Height* (in feet)
Everest	Tibet-Nepal	Himalayas	29,002
Godwin-Austen or K2	India	Karakorum	28,250
Kanchenjunga	Nepal-India	Himalayas	28,146
Makalu	Nepal	Himalayas	27,790
Dhaulagiri	Nepal	Himalayas	26,795
Nanga Parbat	India	Himalayas	26,620
Gosainthan	Tibet	Himalayas	26,291
Nanda Devi	India	Himalayas	25,645
Kamet	India	Himalayas	25,447
Namcha Barwa	Tibet	Himalayas	25,445
Gurla Mandhata	Tibet	Himalayas	25,355
Tirach Mir	Pakistan	Hindu Kush	25,263
Kula Kangri	Tibet	Himalayas	24,740
Stalin	Tadzhik S.S.R.	Pamir Mountains	24,590
Muztagh Ata	China	Muztagh Ata	24,388
Minya Kanka	China		24,000
Chomo Lhari	Bhutan-Tibet	Himalayas	23,930
Api	Nepal	Himalayas	23,899
Tengri Khan	Khirgiz S.S.R.	Tien Shan	23,622
Lenin	Kirghiz S.S.R.-Tadzhik S.S.R.	Pamir Mountains	23,382
Aconcagua (volcanic)	Argentina	Andes	23,080
Ojos del Salado	Argentina		22,572
Mercedario	Argentina		22,211
Huascarán	Peru	Andes	22,180
Llullaillaco (volcanic)	Chile	Andes	22,057
Kailas	Tibet	Himalayas	22,000
Tupungato	Argentina-Chile	Andes	21,810
Incahuasi	Argentina		21,719
Sajama	Bolivia		21,491
Illampu	Bolivia	Andes	21,489
Neradas de Cachí	Argentina		21,325
Illimani	Bolivia	Andes	21,280
Antofalla (volcanic)	Argentina		21,129
Chimborazo (volcanic)	Ecuador	Andes	20,702
Cumbre de la Mejicana	Argentina	Andes	20,500
McKinley	Alaska	Alaska	20,300
Copiapo or Azufre	Chile	Andes	19,950
Logan	Yukon, Canada	St. Elias	19,850
Cotopaxi (volcanic)	Ecuador	Andes	19,498
Kilimanjaro (volcanic)	Tanzania		19,321
Ollagüe	Chile-Bolivia	Andes	19,260
Misti (volcanic)	Peru	Andes	19,200
Cayambe	Ecuador	Andes	19,170
Cerro del Potro	Argentina-Chile	Andes	19,125
Huila (volcanic)	Colombia	Andes	18,865
Orizaba or Citlaltepetl (volcanic)	Mexico		18,701
Demavend	Iran	Elburz	18,603
Elbruz (volcanic)	Georgian S.S.R.	Caucasus	18,468
Tolima (volcanic)	Colombia	Andes	18,438
St. Elias (volcanic)	Alaska-Canada	St. Elias	18,008
Popocatepetl (volcanic)	Mexico		17,888
Cerro Lejía	Chile		17,585
Maipo (volcanic)	Argentina-Chile	Andes	17,388
Lucania	Yukon, Canada	St. Elias	17,147
Dykh Tau	European R.S.F.S.R.	Caucasus	17,085
Kenya	Kenya		17,040
Foraker	Alaska	Alaska	17,000
Ixtacihuatl (volcanic)	Mexico		16,960
Ararat	Turkey		16,915
Kazbek (volcanic)	Georgian S.S.R.	Caucasus	16,547
Jaja	West Irian, Indonesia	Nassau	16,500
Sanford	Alaska	Wrangell	16,206
Blackburn	Alaska	Wrangell	16,140
Klyuchevskaya (volcanic)	Khabarovsk Territory, U.S.S.R.	Kamchatka	15,912
Mont Blanc	France-Italy	Alps	15,781
Vancouver	Alaska-Yukon, Canada	St. Elias	15,696
Trikora	West Irian, Indonesia	Orange	15,580
Domuyo (volcanic)	Argentina	Andes	15,500
Fairweather	Alaska-British Columbia, Canada		15,399
Monte Rosa	Switzerland-Italy	Alps	15,196
Ras Dashan	Ethiopia	Simyen	15,158
Belukha	Kazak S.S.R.	Altai	15,157
Markham	Antarctica		15,100
Siple	Antarctica		15,000
Hubbard	Alaska-Yukon, Canada	St. Elias	14,986
Meru (volcanic)	Tanzania		14,979
Weisshorn	Switzerland	Alps	14,804
Karisimbi (volcanic)	Congo	Virunga	14,787
Matterhorn or Mont Cervin	Switzerland-Italy	Alps	14,780
Kirkpatrick	Antarctica	Queen Alexandra	14,600
Whitney	California	Sierra Nevada	14,501
Elbert	Colorado	Sawatch, Rocky Mountains	14,431
Massive Mount	Colorado	Sawatch, Rocky Mountains	14,424
Rainier or Tacoma	Washington	Cascade	14,408
Harvard	Colorado	Sawatch, Rocky Mountains	14,399
Blanca Peak	Colorado	Sangre de Cristo, Rocky Mountains	14,390
Williamson	California	Sierra Nevada	14,384
La Plata	Colorado	Sawatch, Rocky Mountains	14,340
Uncompahgre	Colorado	San Juan, Rocky Mountains	14,306
Crestone	Colorado	Sangre de Cristo, Rocky Mountains	14,291
Lincoln	Colorado	Park, Rocky Mountains	14,284
Grays	Colorado	Front, Rocky Mountains	14,274
Evans	Colorado	Front, Rocky Mountains	14,260
Longs	Colorado	Front, Rocky Mountains	14,255
White	California	Sierra Nevada	14,242
Colima (volcanic)	Mexico		14,219

Principal Mountains of the World (Continued)

Name	*Location*	*Mountain Range*	*Height* (in feet)
Princeton	Colorado	Sawatch, Rocky Mountains	14,196
Shavano	Colorado	Sawatch, Rocky Mountains	14,179
Yale	Colorado	Sawatch, Rocky Mountains	14,172
Grand Combin	Switzerland	Alps	14,163
Shasta (volcanic)	California	Sierra Nevada	14,162
San Luis	Colorado		14,149
Elgon (volcanic)	Uganda-Kenya		14,136
Pikes Peak	Colorado	Front, Rocky Mountains	14,110
Snowmass	Colorado	Sangre de Cristo, Rocky Mountains	14,077
Culebra	Colorado	San Juan, Rocky Mountains	14,070
Sunlight	Colorado	San Juan, Rocky Mountains	14,053
Split	California	Sierra Nevada	14,051
Redcloud	Colorado		14,050
Finsteraarhorn	Switzerland	Alps	14,026
Wrangell	Alaska	Wrangell	14,005
Morrison	Taiwan		14,000
Mount of the Holy Cross	Colorado	Sawatch, Rocky Mountains	13,996
Humphreys	California	Sierra Nevada	13,972
Ouray	Colorado	Sawatch, Rocky Mountains	13,955
Guna	Ethiopia		13,881
Mauna Kea (volcanic)	Hawaii		13,825
Gannett	Wyoming	Wind River, Rocky Mountains	13,785
Hayes	Alaska	Alaska	13,740
Fremont	Wyoming	Wind River, Rocky Mountains	13,730
Mauna Loa (volcanic)	Hawaii		13,675
Jungfrau	Switzerland	Alps	13,667
Kings	Utah	Uinta, Rocky Mountains	13,498
Barre des Écrins	France	Alps	13,461
Kinabalu	Sabah		13,451
Tala	Ethiopia		13,451
Lister	Antarctica	Royal Society	13,350
Cameroon (volcanic)	Cameroun		13,349
Tacaná (volcanic)	Mexico-Guatemala		13,333
Truchas	New Mexico		13,306
Bernina	Switzerland	Alps	13,304
Summit	Colorado	San Juan, Rocky Mountains	13,272
Waddington	British Columbia, Canada	Coast Mountains	13,260
Erebus (volcanic)	Antarctica		13,202
Cloud Peak	Wyoming	Bighorn, Rocky Mountains	13,165
Fridtjof Nansen	Antarctica		13,156
Wheeler	Nevada	Snake	13,058
Robson	British Columbia, Canada	Canadian Rockies, Rocky Mountains	12,972
Granite	Montana	Beartooth	12,850
Borah	Idaho	Lost River	12,655
Baldy	New Mexico		12,623
Monte Viso	Italy	Alps	12,602
Ulmer	Antarctica	Sentinel	12,500
Adams	Washington	Cascade	12,470
Kerintji (volcanic)	Sumatra	Barisan	12,467
Grossglockner	Austria		12,460
Excelsior	California	Sierra Nevada	12,440
Fujiyama (volcanic)	Japan		12,395
Cook	New Zealand	Southern Alps	12,349
Lanín (volcanic)	Argentina-Chile	Andes	12,300
Teyde or Tenerife (volcanic)	Canary Islands		12,192
Mahameru (volcanic)	Java	Semeru	12,060
Sidley	Antarctica		12,000
Assiniboine	British Columbia-Alberta, Canada	Canadian Rockies, Rocky Mountains	11,870
Hood (volcanic)	Oregon	Cascade	11,245
Reinwaldhorn	Switzerland	Alps	11,173
Pico de Aneto	Spain	Pyrenees	11,168
Perdido	Spain	Pyrenees	10,997
Baker	Washington	Cascade	10,750
Etna (volcanic)	Sicily		10,741
Lassen (volcanic)	California	Sierra Nevada	10,453
Dempo (volcanic)	Sumatra	Barisan	10,364
Montcalm	France	Pyrenees	10,105
Haleakala (volcanic)	Hawaii		10,032
Tahat	Algeria	Ahaggar	9,850
St. Helens	Washington		9,671
Pulog	Philippines		9,606
Shishaldin (volcanic)	Aleutian Islands		9,500
Ruapehu (volcanic)	New Zealand		9,175
Katherine	Egypt		8,651
Roraima	Brazil-Venezuela-Guyana	Serra Pacaraima	8,620
Doi Inthanon	Thailand		8,452
Galdhöpiggen	Norway	Jotunheimen	8,097
Parnassus	Greece		8,070
Olympus	Washington	Olympic	7,954
Kosciusko	Australia	Australian Alps	7,352
Harney	South Dakota	Black Hills	7,242
Mitchell	North Carolina	Appalachian	6,711
Clingmans Dome	North Carolina-Tennessee	Great Smoky Mountains	6,642
Washington	New Hampshire	White Mountains	6,288
Rogers	Virginia		5,719
Cirque	Labrador	Torngat	5,500
Marcy	New York	Adirondacks	5,344
Pelée (volcanic)	Martinique		4,430
Ben Nevis	Scotland	Grampian	4,405
Vesuvius (volcanic)	Italy		3,858

Principal Lakes of the World

Name	*Location*	*Area* (in square miles)	*Length* (in miles)	*Maximum Depth* (in feet)
Caspian (salt)	Asia-Europe	169,000	760	3,104
Superior	North America	31,810	350	1,290
Victoria	Africa	26,200	250	270
Aral (slightly salty)	Asia	24,400	280	225
Huron	North America	23,010	206	750

Principal Lakes of the World (Continued)

Name	*Location*	*Area* (in square miles)	*Length* (in miles)	*Maximum Depth* (in feet)
Michigan	North America	22,400	307	923
Nyasa	Africa	14,000	350	2,316
Baikal	Asia	13,300	385	5,400
Tanganyika	Africa	12,700	450	4,700
Great Bear	North America	11,800	195	
Great Slave	North America	11,172	325	2,015
Erie	North America	9,940	240	210
Winnipeg	North America	8,550	260	70
Ontario	North America	7,540	193	778
Balkhash (slightly salty)	Asia	7,200	440	36
Ladoga	Europe	7,000	120	730
Chad	Africa	6,500	130	24
Eyre (salt)	Australia	4,000	115	
Onega	Europe	3,764	145	408
Rudolf	Africa	3,475	180	
Titicaca	South America	3,200	130	1,000
Nicaragua	Central America	3,089	100	200
Athabaska	North America	3,085	200	300
Reindeer	North America	2,435	155	
Torrens (salt)	Australia	2,400	130	
Great Salt Lake (salt)	North America	2,360	75	60
Issyk-Kul (slightly salty)	Asia	2,230	115	2,297
Koko Nor	Asia	2,200	68	
Väner	Europe	2,149	87	292
Winnipegosis	North America	2,000	122	38
Bangweulu	Africa	1,900	60	15
Lake of the Woods	North America	1,850	70	36
Urmia (salt)	Asia	1,750	80	50
Nipigon	North America	1,730	70	540
Manitoba	North America	1,711	120	
Albert Nyanza	Africa	1,640	100	55
Van (salt)	Asia	1,425	80	
Dead Sea (salt)	Asia	370	46	

Principal Rivers of the World

Name	*Location*	*Empties Into*	*Length* (in miles)
(Mississippi-Missouri)	North America	Gulf of Mexico	4,240
Nile	Africa	Mediterranean Sea	4,000
Amazon	South America	Atlantic Ocean	c.4,000
Ob	Asia	Gulf of Ob	3,200
Yangtze	Asia	East China Sea	3,000
Congo	Africa	Atlantic Ocean	3,000
Amur	Asia	Tartary Strait	2,900
Yenisei	Asia	Arctic Ocean	c.2,800
Lena	Asia	Arctic Ocean	2,800
Hwang Ho	Asia	Yellow Sea	2,700
Mekong	Asia	South China Sea	2,600
Niger	Africa	Gulf of Guinea	2,600
Mississippi	North America	Gulf of Mexico	2,560
Mackenzie	North America	Beaufort Sea	2,500
Missouri	North America	Mississippi River	2,475
Paraná	South America	Plata River	2,450
Yukon	North America	Bering Sea	2,300
Volga	Europe	Caspian Sea	2,300
Irtish	Asia	Ob River	2,250
St. Lawrence	North America	Gulf of St. Lawrence	2,100
Madeira	South America	Amazon River	c.2,000
Indus	Asia	Arabian Sea	2,000
Parús	South America	Amazon River	1,850
Rio Grande	North America	Gulf of Mexico	1,800
São Francisco	South America	Atlantic Ocean	1,800
Darling	Australia	Murray River	c.1,750
Salween	Asia	Gulf of Martaban	1,750
Danube	Europe	Black Sea	1,725
Brahmaputra	Asia	Bay of Bengal	1,700
Euphrates	Asia	Persian Gulf	1,700
Tocantins	South America	Para River	1,700
Murray	Australia	Encounter Bay	c.1,600
Orinoco	South America	Atlantic Ocean	1,600
Zambezi	Africa	Indian Ocean	1,600
Ganges	Asia	Bay of Bengal	1,550
Amu Darya	Asia	Lake Aral	1,500
Paraguay	South America	Paraná River	1,500
Arkansas	North America	Mississippi River	1,460
Ural	Asia	Caspian Sea	1,400
Dnepr	Europe	Black Sea	1,400
Negro	South America	Amazon River	1,400
Syr Darya	Asia	Lake Aral	1,300
Angara	Asia	Yenisei River	1,300
Aldan	Asia	Lena River	1,300
Orange	Africa	Atlantic Ocean	1,300
Irrawaddy	Asia	Bay of Bengal	1,250
Xingú	South America	Amazon River	1,250
Si-Kiang	Asia	South China Sea	1,250
Ucayali	South America	Amazon River	1,220
Columbia	North America	Pacific Ocean	1,214
Juruá	South America	Amazon River	1,200
Saskatchewan	North America	Lake Winnipeg	1,200
Tigris	Asia	Euphrates River	1,150
Don	Europe	Sea of Azov	1,100
Kama	Europe	Volga River	1,100
Kolyma	Asia	Arctic Ocean	1,100
Northern Dvina	Europe	White Sea	1,100
Araguaya	South America	Tocantins River	1,100
Peace	North America	Slave River	1,050
Snake	North America	Columbia River	1,038
Red	North America	Mississippi River	1,018

Principal Rivers of the World (Continued)

Name	*Location*	*Empties Into*	*Length (in miles)*
Pilcomayo	South America	Paraguay River	**1,000**
Churchill	North America	Hudson Bay	**1,000**
Uruguay	South America	Plata River	**1,000**
Ohio	North America	Mississippi River	**981**
Pechora	Europe	Barents Sea	**975**
Oka	Europe	Volga River	**950**
Magdalena	South America	Caribbean Sea	**950**
Canadian	North America	Arkansas River	**906**
Godavari	Asia	Bay of Bengal	**900**
Brazos	North America	Gulf of Mexico	**870**
Salado	South America	Colorado River	**850**
Parnahyba	South America	Atlantic Ocean	**850**
Colorado	North America	Gulf of Mexico	**840**
Dnestr	Europe	Black Sea	**800**
Narbada	Asia	Arabian Sea	**800**
Tisza	Europe	Danube	**800**
Tobol	Asia	Irtish River	**800**
Athabaska	North America	Lake Athabaska	**765**
Marañón	South America	Amazon River	**750**
Pecos	North America	Rio Grande	**735**
Green	North America	Colorado River	**730**
Elbe	Europe	North Sea	**725**
Rhine	Europe	North Sea	**700**
Fraser	North America	Georgia Strait	**695**
White	North America	Mississippi River	**690**
Cumberland	North America	Ohio River	**687**
Ottawa	North America	St. Lawrence River	**685**
Donets	Europe	Don River	**675**
Yellowstone	North America	Missouri River	**671**
Tennessee	North America	Ohio River	**652**
Gila	North America	Colorado River	**630**
Vistula	Europe	Baltic Sea	**630**
Loire	Europe	Bay of Biscay	**625**
North Platte	North America	Platte River	**618**
Cimarron	North America	Arkansas River	**600**
Tagus	Europe	Atlantic Ocean	**565**
Oder	Europe	Baltic Sea	**c.550**
Ouachita	North America	Red River	**545**
Niemen	Europe	Baltic Sea	**500**
Gambia	Africa	Atlantic Ocean	**500**
Sava	Europe	Danube River	**450**

Principal Waterfalls of the World

Name	*Location*	*Height (in feet)*
Angel	Venezuela	3,700
Yosemite (including upper, central, and lower falls, and rapids)	California	2,525
Kukenaäm	Guyana	2,000
Sutherland	New Zealand	1,904
Tugela	South Africa	1,800
Wollomombie	Australia	1,700
Ribbon	California	1,612
Gavarnie	France	1,515
Upper Yosemite	California	1,430
Takkakau	British Columbia	1,200
Staubbach	Switzerland	980
Trümmelbach	Switzerland	950
Middle Cascade	California	910
Vettisfoss	Norway	850
King Edward VIII	Guyana	840
Gersoppa	India	830
Kalambo	Zambia	786
Kaieteur	Guyana	741
Skykjefos	Norway	650
Maradalsfos	Norway	650
Maletsunyane	South Africa	630
Multnomah	Oregon	620
Bridalveil	California	620
Nevada	California	594
Terni	Italy	590
Vöringfoss	Norway	535
Skjeggedalsfoss	Norway	525
Marina	Guyana	500

Name	*Location*	*Height (in feet)*
Tequendama	Colombia	**450**
Aughrabies	**South Africa**	**450**
Guaíra	**Brazil-Paraguay**	**374**
Illilouette	**California**	**370**
Kegon-no-taki	**Japan**	**350**
Victoria	**Zambia and Rhodesia**	**343**
Lower Yosemite	**California**	**320**
Cauvery	India	**320**
Vernal	California	**317**
Virginia	Northwest Territories	**315**
Lower Yellowstone	Wyoming	**308**
Grand	Labrador	**302**
Sluiskin	Washington	**300**
Reichenbach	Switzerland	**300**
Lower Gastein	Austria	**280**
Paulo Alfonso	Brazil	**275**
Snoqualmie	Washington	**268**
Seven	Colorado	**266**
Montmorency	Quebec	**265**
Handegg	Switzerland	**250**
Taughannock	New York	**215**
Iguassú	Brazil	**210**
Shoshone	Idaho	**210**
Upper Gastein	Austria	**207**
Comet	Washington	**200**
Narada	Washington	**168**
Niagara	New York-Ontario	**167**
Tower	Wyoming	**132**
Stora Sjöfallet	Sweden	**121**
Murchison	Uganda	**118**
Upper Yellowstone	Wyoming	**109**

Principal Dams of the World

Name	*Location*	*Height (in feet)*	*Year Completed*	*Total Volume of Material Used (in cubic yards)*
Hoover or Boulder	Colorado River, Nevada-Arizona	727	1936	4,400,000
Shasta	Sacramento River, California	602	1945	6,541,000
Grand Coulee	Columbia River, Washington	550	1942	10,585,000
Ross	Skagit River, Washington	545		(incomplete)
Fontana	Little Tennessee River, North Carolina	480	1944	2,812,000
Anderson Ranch	Boise River, Idaho	456		(incomplete)
Chambon	Romanche River, France	452	1934	392,000
O'Shaughnessy	Tuolumne River, California	430	1923 (addition, 1938)	935,000
Mud Mountain or Stevens	White River, Washington	425		(incomplete)
Owyhee	Owyhee River, Oregon	417	1932	537,200
Sautet	Drac River, France	414	1934	130,400

Principal Dams of the World (Continued)

Name	*Location*	*Height* (in feet)	*Year Completed*	*Total Volume of Material Used* (in cubic yards)
Diablo	Skagit River, Washington	386	1930	350,000
San Gabriel No. 1	San Gabriel River, California	381	1938	10,641,000
Grimsel	Aar River, Switzerland	377	1931	445,000
Pacoima	Pacoima River, California	372	1928	225,300
Pardee	Mokelumne River, California	358	1929	615,000
Arrowrock	Boise River, Idaho	350	1915 (addition, 1937)	636,000
Camarasa	Pallaresa River, Spain	333	1920	283,000
Salt Springs	Mokelumne River, California	328	1931	3,171,500
Esla	Spain	328		
Morris	San Gabriel River, California	328	1934	446,000
Exchequer	Merced River, California	326	1926	390,600
Buffalo Bill or Shoshone	Shoshone River, Wyoming	325	1910	82,900
Friant	San Joaquin River, California	320	1944	2,135,000
Parker	Colorado River, California-Arizona	320	1938	380,000
Ariel	Lewis River, Washington	313	1931	307,000
Green Mountain	Blue River, Colorado	309	1943	4,406,000
Kensico	Bronx River, New York	307	1916	900,000
Hiwassee	Hiwassee River, North Carolina	307	1940	807,200
Elephant Butte	Rio Grande, New Mexico	301	1916	629,400
Horse Mesa	Salt River, Arizona	300	1927	162,900
Seminoe	North Platte River, Wyoming	295	1939	210,000
Jandula	Spain	295		
New Croton	Croton River, New York	294	1906	855,000
San Gabriel No. 2	San Gabriel River, California	290	1935	1,200,000
Don Pedro	Tuolumne River, California	284	1923	296,600
Roosevelt	Salt River, Arizona	280	1911	355,800
Cushman	Skokomish River, Washington	280	1926	90,000
Morena	Cottonwood Creek, California	279	1930	335,000
Barberine	Switzerland	271		
Harrodsburg	Dix River, Kentucky	270	1925	1,747,000
Marshall Ford	Colorado River, Texas	270	1942	3,389,000
El Capitan	San Diego River, California	270	1935	2,679,700
Norris	Clinch River, Tennessee	265	1936	1,184,000
Alcova	North Platte River, Wyoming	265	1938	1,635,300
Cobble Mountain	Little River, Massachusetts	263	1932	1,779,200
Shannon	Baker River, Washington	263	1925	132,000
Upper Narrows	Yuba River, California	260	1941	380,000
Lake Pleasant	Aqua Fria River, Arizona	256	1927	98,400
Ashokan	Esopus Creek, New York	252	1912	2,471,900
Nantahala	Nantahala River, North Carolina	250	1942	1,829,000
Fort Peck	Missouri River, Montana	250	1940	128,000,000
Coolidge	Gila River, Arizona	250	1928	204,000
Burrinjuck	Murrumbidgee River, Australia	247	1927	408,000
Mettur	Cauvery River, India	230	1934	2,000,000
Saluda	Saluda River, South Carolina	208	1930	11,160,800
Dnepr	Dnepr River, U.S.S.R.	200	1932	291,800
Hartebeestpoort	South Africa	193		
Hume	Murray River, Australia	172	1936	
Aswan	Nile River, Egypt	170	1902	1,732,000
Bonneville	Columbia River, Washington-Oregon	170	1937	596,500
Denison	Red River, Oklahoma-Texas	165	1944	15,475,000
Kingsley	North Platte River, Nebraska	162	1941	26,000,000
Wilson	Tennessee River, Alabama	137	1925	1,331,500
Sennar	Blue Nile River, Sudan	128		
Krishnaraja	India	124		
Sardis	Little Tallahatchie River, Mississippi	117	1940	16,842,000
Gatun	Chagres River, Panama Canal Zone	115	1912	22,958,000
Don Martin	Mexico	111		
Jerry O'Connell	Brazil	110		
Hansen	Tujunga Wash, California	100	1940	14,000,000
Ottmachau	Germany	57		

PRINCIPAL COMMERCIAL AND FINANCIAL TERMS IN EIGHT LANGUAGES

English	Dutch	French	German	Italian	Portuguese	Russian	Spanish
A							
abrogate, to	opheffen	abroger	abschaffen	abolire	abrogar	unichtojat'	abrogar
abstract	uittreksel	abrégé	Auszug	astratto	abstracto	izvlechenie	abstracto
acceptance	acceptatie	acceptation	Accept	accettazione	aceitação	prinyatie	aceptación
account	rekening	compte	Rechnung	conto	conta	schot	cuenta
addition	bijvoeging	addition	Zusatg	addizione	addição	dobavlenie	adición
adjustment	vereffening	ajustement	Regulierung	aggiustamento	ajuste	popravlenie	ajuste
admit, to	toelaten	admettre	einlassen	ammettere	admittir	vpuskat	admitir
advance	voorschot	avance	Vorschuss	avanzo	avanço	zadatok	avance
advice	raad	conseil	Rat	avviso	aviso	sovet	consejo
advise, to	raden	conseiller	raten	avvisare	aconselhar	sovetovat'	aconsejar
affidavit	beëedigde verklaring	déposition	beschworene Aussage	deposizione	deposição	klatvenoe svidetel'stvo	declaración
affirmation	bevestiging	affirmation	Bestätigung	affermazione	affirmação	utverjdenie	afirmación
agent	agent	agent	Agent	agente	agente	agent	agente
agreement	overeenkomst	accord	Abkommen	accordo	accordo	soglashenie	acuerdo
agriculture	landbouw	agriculture	Landwirtschaft	agricoltura	agricultura	zemledelie	agricultura
alcohol	alcohol	alcool	Alkohol	alcool	alcool	chisti spirt	alcohol
allotment	aandeel	répartition	Anteil	assegnazione	partilha	otdelenie	asignación
allowance	rabat	remise	Abzug	sconto	abono	skidka	concesión
aluminium	aluminium	aluminium	Aluminium	alluminio	aluminio	alumini	aluminio
ambassador	gezant	ambassadeur	Gesandte	ambaciatore	embaixador	poslanik	embajador
amount	bedrag	montant	Betrag	montante	importe	itog	importe
answer	antwoord	réponse	Antwort	risposta	resposta	otvet	contestación
appeal	beroep	appel	Berufung	appellazione	appellação	appelatsia	apelación
application	aanvraag	application	Anmeldung	applicazione	applicação	proshonie	aplicación
appraise, to	schatten	évaluer	schätzen	apprezzare	avaliar	otsenit'	valuar
appraisement	schatting	estimation	Schätzung	estimazione	estimação	otsenka	avalúo
appraiser	schatter	estimateur	Schätzer	apprezzatore	avaliador	otsenshchik	avaluador
apprise, to	onderrichten	informer	unterrichten	informare	informar	uvedomlat'	informar
appropriation	toeeigening	appropriation	Zueignung	appropriazione	apropriação	opredelenie	apropriación
approval	goedkeuring	approbation	Billigung	approvazione	approvação	odobrenie	aprobación
approximate	benaderend	approximatif	annähernd	prossimo	approximativo	priblizitel'no	aproximativo
arbitration	arbitrage	arbitrage	Schiedsspruch	arbitrato	arbitramento	treteiski sud	arbitramento
arbitrator	scheidsrechter	arbitre	Schiedsrichter	arbitro	arbitrador	posrednitsa	arbitrador
arrears	achterstand	arrérages	Rückstand	debito	atrazado	nedoimka	atraso
arrival	aankomst	arrivée	Ankunft	arrivo	chegada	pribytie	llegada
article	artikel	article	Artikel	articulo	artigo	tovar	articulo
artificial	kunstig	artificiel	künstlich	artificiale	artificial	iskustveny	artificial
assess, to	belasten	taxer	besteuern	tassare	taxar	oblojit'	amillarar
assets	actief	actif	Aktiva	attivo	activo	aktiv	activo
assign, to	aanwijzen	assigner	anweisen	assegnare	assignar	naznachat'	asignar
assignment	aanwijzing	assignation	Anweisung	assegnazione	assignação	naznachenie	asignación
assortment	sortering	assortiment	Assortiment	assortimento	sortimento	podbiranie	surtido
attachment	beslag	saisie-arrêt	Beschlagnahme	sequestro	penhora	zapreshchenie	secuestro
attest, to	betuigen	attester	bezeugen	attestare	attestar	zasvidetelstvovat'	atestiguar
audit	rekening	audition	Rechnungsprüfung	esame d'un conto	audição	raschot	intervención de una cuenta
authenticate	bekrachtigen	légaliser	beglaubigen	autenticare	authenticar	udostoveryat'	autenticar
authorize	machtigen	autoriser	bevollmächtigen	autorizzare	autorisar	upolnomchivat'	autorizar
average	doorsnee	moyenne	Durchschnitt	medio	medio	sredneye	medio
average price	middenprijs	prix moyen	Durchschnittspreis	prezzo medio	preço modio	srednyaya tsena	precio medio
avoidable	vermijdelijk	évitable	vermeidlich	evitabile	evitavel	izbejny	evitable
B							
balance	balans	balance	Bilanz	bilancia	balança	balans	balanza
bale	baal	balle	Ballen	balla	bala	kip	bala
bank	bank	banque	Bank	banco	banco	bank	banco
bankruptcy	bankroet	banqueroute	Bankerott	fallimento	falimento	bankrotstvo	bancarrota
barrel	vat	baril	Fass	barile	barril	bochka	barril
bidder	bieder	offrant	Bieter	offerente	lançador	kto predlagaet tsenu	pujador
bill	rekening	compte	Rechnung	fattura	conta	schot	cuenta
bill of exchange	wissel	lettre de change	Wechsel	lettera di cambio	letra de cambio	veksel	letra de cambio
bill of lading	vrachtbrief	connaissement	Frachtbrief	polizza di carico	conhecimento	nakladnaya	conocimiento
book trade	boekhandel	commerce de livres	Buchhandel	commercio di libri	commercio de livros	knijnaya torgozhlya	comercio de libros
boxes	dosen	boîtes	Schachteln	scatole	caixas	korobki	cajas
broker	makelaar	courtier	Makler	sensale	corretor	makler	corredor
brokerage	makelaardij	courtage	Maklergebühr	senseria	corretagem	koortaj	corretaje
bullion	muntmetaal	or-argent en lingots	Gold oder Silber in Barren	verga d'oro o d'argente	ouro, prata em barra	zoloto ile serebro v slitkakh	oro o plata en barras
business	bezigheid	affaire	Geschäft	affare	occupação	zanyatie	empleo
buy, to	koopen	acheter	kaufen	comprare	comprar	pokupat'	comprar
buyer	kooper	acheteur	Käufer	compratore	comprador	pokupatel'	comprador
C							
cable	kabel	câble	Kabel	gomena	cabo	kabel	cable
calculation	berekening	calcul	Berechnung	computo	calculo	vychislenie	calculo
cancel, to	herroepen	annuler	annullieren	cancellare	annullar	otmenyat'	cancelar
capacity	ruimte	capacité	Kapazität	capacità	capacidade	vmestitelnost'	capacidad
capital	kapitaal	capital	Kapital	capitale	capital	kapital	capital
car	wagen	wagon	Wagen	carretta	carro	vagon	carro
cargo	lading	cargaison	Fracht	carico	carga	gruz	carga
cash	kas	argent comptant	Kasse	danaro contante	dinheiro de contado	kasa	dinero contante
cashier	kassier	caissier	Kassierer	cassiere	caixero	kasir	cajero
cask	vat	baril	Fass	barile	barril	bochka	barril
catalogue	catalogus	catalogue	Katalog	catalogo	catalogo	katalog	catálogo
certificate	getuigschrift	certificat	Zeugnis	certificato	certificado	svidetelstvo	certificado
chain	ketting	chaîne	Kette	catena	cadeia	tsep'	cadena
charge, to	in rekening brengen	porter au débit	belasten	caricare	debitar	schitat'	cargar
charges	kosten	frais	Kosten	spese	gastos	raskhody	gastos
chattels	roerend goed	biens mobiliers	Mobilien	mobili	bens moveis	dvijimoe imushchestvo	bienes muebles
check	cheque	chèque	Check	scecche	cheque	chek	cheque
chemical	scheikundig	chimique	chemisch	chimico	quimico	khimicheski	químico
circular	circulaire	circulaire	Rundschreiben	circolare	circular	tsirkulyarnoe pis'mo	circular
claim	eisch	reclamation	Anspruch	pretensione	pretensão	trebovanie	pretensión
coast trade	kusthandel	petit cabotage	Küstenhandel	cabotaggio	cabotagem	kabotaj	cabotaje

English	Dutch	French	German	Italian	Portuguese	Russian	Spanish
code	wetboek	code	Gesetzbuch	codice	codigo	ulojenie	código
coin	munt	monnaie	Münze	moneta	moeda	moneta	moneda
collect, to	incasseeren	encaisser	einkassieren	incassare	cobrar	poluchat'	cobrar
collector	ontvanger	receveur	Einnchmer	collettore	cobrador	sborshchik	colector
combine, to	verbinden	combiner	vereinigen	combinare	combinar	soedinyat'	combinar
combination	verbinding	combinaison	Vereinigung	combinazione	combinação	soedinenie	combinación
commerce	handel	commerce	Handel	commercio	commercio	torgovlya	comercio
commercial	commercieel	commercial	Handels	commerciale	commercial	komercheski	comercial
commission	commissie	commission	Kommission	commissione	commissão	komisiya	comisión
commission merchant	commissie koopman	commissionnaire	Kommissionär	commissionario	commissionista	komisioner	comisionista
compromise	compromis	compromis	Kompromiss	compromesso	compromisso	kompromis	compromiso
consignee	adressant	consignataire	Warenempfänger	consegnatario	consignatario	tovaropoluchatel	consignatario
consignment	consignatie	consignation	Konsignation	consegna	consignação	otpravlenie tovarov	consignación
consignor	afzender	consignateur	Warenversender	speditore	consignador	otpavitel' tovarov	consignador
consul	consul	consul	Konsul	console	consul	konsul	consul
contract	verdrag	contrat	Kontrakt	contratto	contrato	kontrakt	contrato
corporation	corporatie	corporation	Körperschaft	corporazione	corporação	korporatsia	corporación
correspondent	correspondent	correspondant	Geschäftsfreund	corrispondente	correspondente	korespondent	correspondiente
cost	prijs	coût	Kosten	costo	custo	stoimost'	costo
credit	crediet	crédit	Kredit	credito	credito	kredit	crédito
creditor	schuldeischer	créancier	Gläubiger	creditore	credor	kreditor	acreedor
currency	munt	monnaie	Währung	moneta	moeda	moneta	moneda
custom house	douane	douane	Zollhaus	dogana	alfandega	tamojnya	aduana
D							
damage	schade	dommage, avarie	Schaden	danno	damno	ubytok	daño
date	datum	date	Datum	data	data	chislo	data
dealer	handelaar	marchand	Händler	mercante	mercador	kupets	traficante
debt	schuld	dette	Schuld	debito	debito	dolg	deuda
debtor	schuldenaar	débiteur	Schuldner	debitore	devedor	doljnik	deudor
declaration	verklaring	déclaration	Erklärung	dichiarazione	declaração	zayavlenie	declaración
deed	akte	contrat	Urkunde	contratto	escriture	dokument	escritura
defraud, to	bedriegen	frauder	betrügen	defraudare	fraudar	obmanivat'	defraudar
delivery	levering	livraison	Lieferung	consegna	entrega	dostavka	entrega
demand	eisch	demande	Forderung	domanda	demanda	trebovanie	demanda
deposit	deposito	dépôt	Anzahlung	deposito	deposito	depozit	depósito
depreciation	waarde vermindering	dépréciation	Entwertung	deprezzamento	depreciação	obeztsenivanie	depreciación
depression	slapte	dépression	Flauheit	depressione	depressao	depresia	depresión
designation	aanwijzing	désignation	Bezeichnung	designazione	designação	naznachenie	designación
despatch	afdoening	dépêche	Abfertigung	dispaccio	despacho	otpravlenie	despacho
detention	terughouding	détention	Zurückhaltung	detenzione	detenção	zaderjaniye	detención
director	bestuurder	directeur	Direktor	direttore	director	direktor	director
disapproval	afkeuring	désapprobation	Missbilligung	disapprovazione	desapprovação	neodobrenie	desaprobación
disburse, to	uitgeven	débourser	auszahlen	sborsare	desembolsar	izderjivat'	desembolsar
discount	korting	escompte	Disconto	sconto	desconto	skidka	descuento
dispute	geschil	dispute	Streit	disputa	disputa	spor	disputa
dissolution	oplossing	dissolution	Auflösung	dissoluzione	dissolução	raspuskanie	disolución
dividend	dividend	dividende	Gewinnanteil	dividendo	dividendo	dividend	dividendo
dock	dok	bassin	Dock	darsena	darsena	dok	dársena
document	bewijsstuk	document	Beweisschrift	documento	documento	dokument	documento
dozen	dozijn	douzaine	Dutzend	dozzina	duzia	dyujina	docena
draft	traite	traite	Tratte	tratta	saque	veksel'	letra de cambio
due	vervallen	dû	fällig	dovuto	vencido	podlejashchi uplate	vencido
duty	tol	impôt	Zoll	tassa	imposto	poshlina	impuesto
E							
earn, to	verdienen	gagner	verdienen	guadagnare	ganhar	zarabotat'	ganar
economy	besparing	economie	Ersparnis	economia	economia	ekonomiya	economia
embargo	embargo	embargo	Handelssperre	embargo	embargo	ambargo	embargo
embezzlement	ontvreemding	détournement	Veruntreuung	malversazione	malversação	prisvoenie	desfalco
employ, to	in dienst hebben	employer	anstellen	impiegare	empregar	dat' slujbu	emplear
empower, to	machtigen	autoriser	ermächtigen	autorizzare	autorizar	upolnomochit'	autorizar
enclosure	bijlage	pièce jointe	Beilage	acclusa	inclusa	prilojenie	incluso
engagement	verpligting	engagement	Verpflichtung	obbligo	obrigação	obyazatel'stvo	obligación
entry	boeking	entrée, inscription	Eintragung	iscrizione	partida	zapiska	partida
error	fout	erreur	Irrtum	errore	erro	oshibka	error
estimate	schatting	estimation	Schätzung	estimazione	orçamento	smeta	presupuesto
examination	onderzoeking	examen	Untersuchung	esame	exame	osmotr	examen
exchange	omwisseling	échange	Austausch	cambio	cambio	obmen	cambio
excise	accijns	accise	Accise	assisa	siza	aktsiz	sisa
exports	uitvoer	exportation	Ausfuhr	esportazione	exportação	vyvos	exportación
F							
failure	failisse	faillité	Bankerott	bancarrota	bancarotta	neudacha	falta
fee	honorarium	honoraire	Gebühr	onorario	honorario	plata	honorarios
firm	firma	firme	Firma	ditta	firma	firma	firma
free trade	vrijhandel	libre échange	Freihandel	libero scambio	livre cambio	svobodnaya torgovlya	libre cambio
freight	vracht	frêt	Fracht	nolo	frete	frakht	flete
funds	fonds	fonds	Geldmittel	fondi	fundos	sredstva	fondos
G							
gold	goud	or	Gold	oro	ouro	zoloto	oro
gross (12 doz.)	gros	grosse	Gross	grossa	grosa	gros	gruesa
gross (weight)	bruto	brut	Brutto	brutto	bruto	brutto	bruto
H							
hundred	honderd	cent	Hundert	cento	cento	sto	ciento
I							
import	invoer	importation	Einfuhr	importazione	importação	vvoz	importación
import duty	invoerrechten	droit d'entrée	Einfuhrzoll	dazio d'introduzione	direito de entrada	vvoznaya poshlina	derechos de entrada
income	inkomsten	revenu	Einkommen	rendita	renda	dochod	renta
income tax	inkomstenbelasting	impôt sur le revenu	Einkommensteuer	tassa sulla rendita	imposte sobre a renda	nalog na dokhod	impuesto sobre las rentas
indemnification	schadeloosstelling	indemnité	Schadenersatz	indennizzazione	indemnização	voznagrajdenie	indemnización
inland trade	binnenhandel	commerce intérieur	Binnenhandel	commercio interiore	commercio interior	domashnyaya torgovlya	comercio interior

English	Dutch	French	German	Italian	Portuguese	Russian	Spanish
insolvency	onvermogen tot betaling	**insolvabilité**	Zahlungsunfähigkeit	**insolvibilità**	**insolvencia**	**nesostoyatel'nost'**	**insolvencia**
insurance	verzekering	**assurance**	Versicherung	**assicurazione**	**seguro**	**strakhovanie**	**seguro**
interest	interest	intérêt	Zinsen	interesse	juro	protzent	interes
inventory	inventaris	inventaire	Inventur	inventario	inventario	inventar	inventario
invoice	factuur	facture	Faktura	fattura	factura	faktura	factura
J							
judgment	oordeel	jugement	Urteil	giudizio	sentença	reshenie suda	juicio
L							
letter of credit	credietbrief	lettre de crédit	Kreditbrief	lettera di credito	carta de credito	kreditnoe pis'mo	letra de crédito
license	**vergunning**	licence	Erlaubnisschein	licenza	licença	privilegiya	licencia
lighterage	**lichtergeld**	gabarage	Lichtergeld	spesa d'alleggio	transporte em barcacas	perevoz likhterom	gabarraje
M							
mail	**brievenpost**	poste, courrier	Post	corriere	correio	pochta	correo
manifest	**manifest**	manifeste	Ladungsverzeichniss	manifesto	manifesto	manifest	manifiesto
manufacture	manufactuur	fabrication	Fabrikation	manifattura	manufactura	manufaktura	manufactura
marine insurance	zeeverzekering	assurance maritime	Seeversicherung	assicuranza marittima	seguro maritimo	morskoe strakhovanie	seguro de mar
market	markt	marché	Markt	mercato	mercado	rynok	mercado
market price	markt prijs	prix courant	Marktpreis	prezzo corrente	preco corrente	rynochnaya tzena	precio corriente
measure	maat	mesure	Masz	misura	medida	mera	medida
merchandise	waren	marchandises	Ware	mercanzie	mercancias	tovar	mercancías
merchant	koopman	marchand	Kaufmann	mercante	commerciante	kupets	comerciante
monetary	munt-	monétaire	Geld-	monetario	monetario	denejny	monetario
money	geld	argent	Geld	danaro	dinheiro	den'gi	dinero
monopoly	monopolie	monopole	Monopol	monopolio	monopolio	monopolia	monopolio
mortgage	hypotheek	hypotèque	**Hypothek**	ipoteca	hypotheca	zakladnaya	hipoteca
N							
navigation	zeevaart	navigation	Schiffahrt	navigazione	navegação	sudokhodstvo	navegación
negotiation	onderhandeling	négociation	Unterhandlung	negoziazione	negociação	peregovory	negociación
net proceeds	netto provenu	net produit	Reinertrag	prodotto netto	produto neto	chisty dokhod	producto neto
net weight	netto gewicht	poids net	Nettogewicht	peso netto	peso neto	chisty ves	peso neto
notary	notaris	notaire	Notar	notaio	notario	notarius	escribano publico
notification	kennisvening	notification	Benachrichtigung	notificazione	notificação	povestka	notificación
number	aantal	nombre	**Zahl**	numero	numero	chislo	número
O							
obligation	verplichting	obligation	Verpflichtung	obligazione	obligaçoo	obligatziya	obligación
obtain	verkrijgen	obtenir	erlangen	ottenere	obter	dostavat	obtener
open port	vrijhaven	port franc	Freihafen	porto franco	porto franco	svobodnaya gavan'	puerto franco
option	optie	option	Wahl	scelta	opção	vybor	opción
order	order	ordre	Bestellung	ordine	ordem	zakaz	orden
organization	organisatie	organisation	Organisation	organizzazione	organização	organizatsiya	organización
overcharge, to	te veel berekenen	faire payer trop cher	zu viel berechnen	caricare troppo	sobrecarregar	obschitat'	sobrecargar
P							
paper money	papierengeld	papier-monnaie	Papiergeld	carta-moneta	papel-moeda	bumajnie den'gi	papel moneda
par	pari	pair	pari	pari	par	alpari	par
parcel	pakket	paquet	Paket	paco	pacote	paket	paquete
partner	deelhebber	associé	Teilhaber	socio	associado	kompanion	socio
partnership	vennootschap-	société	Kompagnie	società	associação	tovarishchestvo	sociedad
passport	paspoort	passeport	Pass	passaporto	passaporte	pasport	pasaporte
payable	betaalbaar	payable	zahlbar	pagabile	pagavel	platimy	pagadero
payment	betaling	paiement	Zahlung	pagamento	pagamento	plata	paga
percentage	percentage	tantième	Prozent	percento	percentagem	protsenty	porcentaje
pilotage	loodsgeld	pilotage	Lotsengeld	pilotaggio	pilotogem	plata lotsmanu	pilotaje
port	haven	port	Hafen	porto	porto	gavan'	puerto
postage	port	port de lettre	Porto	porto	franqueo	pochtovyia raskhody	porte de correo
premium	premie	prime	Prämie	premio	premio	premia	premio
price	prijs	prix	Preis	prezzo	preço	tsena	precio
price list	prijscourant	prix-courant	Preisliste	lista de prezzi	lista de preços	preiskurent	lista de precios
proceeds	opbrengst	produit	Erlös	prodotto	producto	vyruchka	producto
produce	product	produits	Erzeugnis	prodotto	producto	produkt	producto
profit	winst	profit	Gewinn	profitto	lucro	pribyl'	lucro
promissory note	promesse	billet à ordre	Schuldschein	paghero	nota promissoria	prostoi veksel	pagaré
protest	protest	protêt	**Protest**	protesto	protesto	protest	protesto
provisions	levensmiddelen	comestibles	Lebensmittel	viveri	viveres	pripasy	víveres
Q							
quality	kwaliteit	qualité	Güte	qualità	qualidade	kachestvo	calidad
quantity	hoeveelheid	quantité	Menge	quantità	quantidade	kolichestvo	cantidad
quarantine	quarantaine	quarantaine	**Quarantäne**	quarantina	quarentena	karantin	cuarentena
quotation	prijs-noteering	cote	**Preisnotierung**	corso	cotação	kotirovka	cotización
R							
railroad	spoorweg	chemin de fer	Eisenbahn	ferrovia	caminho de ferro	jeleznaya doroga	ferrocarril
rate of exchange	koers	cours	Kurs	tassa del cambio	cambio	kurs	tipo de cambio
ratification	bekrachtiging	ratification	Bestätigung	ratificazione	ratificação	utverjdenie	ratificación
raw materials	grondstoffen	matieres premières	Rohstoffe	materie crude	materia prima	syr'yo	materia prima
receipt	kwitantie	quittance	Empfangschein	ricevuta	recepção	rospiska	recibo
receipt	ontvangst	réception	Erhalt	ricevuta	recepcao	poluchenie	recibo
receiver	ontvanger	receveur	Empfänger	ricevitore	recebedor	poluchatel	recibidor
reciprocity	wederkeerigheid	reciprocité	Gegenseitigkeit	reciprocità	reciprocidade	vzaimnost	reciprocidad
reckon, to	rekenen	compter	rechnen	calcolare	calcular	schitat'	calcular
recommendation	aanbeveling	recommandation	Empfehlung	raccomandazione	recommendação	rekomendatsiya	recomendación
reconsider, to	weder overwegen	reconsidérer	wiedererwägen	riconsiderare	considerar de novo	snova razsmatrivat'	considerar de nuevo
record	register	registre	Urkunde	registro	registro	zapiski	registro
recover, to	herkrijgen	recouvrer	wiedererlangen	ricuperare	recuperar	poluchat' obratno	recobrar
rectification	verbetering	rectification	Berichtigung	rettificazione	rectificação	ispravlenie	rectificación

English	Dutch	French	German	Italian	Portuguese	Russian	Spanish
redemption	inlossing	rédemption	Einlösung	redenzione	redempção	vykup	redención
reduction	reductie	réduction	Preisverminderung	riduzione	reducção	sbavka	reducción
referee	scheidsman	arbitre	Schiedsmann	arbitro	arbitro	treteiski sud'ya	árbitro
refusal	weigering	refus	Weigerung	rifiuto	recusa	otkaz	negativa
reimburse	vergoeden	rembourser	vergüten	rimborsare	reembolsar	vozvrashchat'	reembolsar
remittance	remise	remise	Überweisung	rimessa	remessa	rimes	remesa
renewal	vernieuwing	renouvellement	Erneuerung	rinnovellamento	prorroga	vozobnovlenie	prorroga
repayment	wederbetaling	remboursement	Rückzahlung	rimborso	reembolso	vozvrat	devolucion
repudiation	verwerping	répudiation	Nichtanerkennung	ripudio	repudiação	otverjenie	repudiación
responsibility	verantwoordelijkheid	responsabilité	Verantwortlichkeit	responsabilità	responsabilidada	otvetstvennost'	responsabilidad
resumption	herneming	reprise	Wiederufnahme	repigliamento	resunção	vozobnovlenie	reasunción
retailer	kleinhandelaar	detailleur	Kleinhändler	venditore a minuto	retalheiro	torgovets v roznitsu	detallista
revenue	inkomsten	revenu	Einkünfte	rendita	renda	dokhod	reditos
revocation	herroeping	révocation	Widerruf	rivocazione	revocação	otmena	revocación
S							
salary	salaris	salaire	Gehalt	salario	salario	jalovanie	salario
sale	verkoop	vente	Verkauf	vendita	venda	prodaja	venta
salesman	verkooper	vendeur	Verkäufer	venditore	vendedor	prodavets	vendedor
salvage	berging	sauvetage	Bergung	salvataggio	salvamento	spasenie korablia	salvamento
sample	staal	échantillon	Muster	campione	amostra	obrazets	muestra
satisfaction	voldoening	satisfaction	Befriedigung	sodisfazione	satisfação	udovletvorenie	satisfacción
sell, to	verkoopen	vendre	verkaufen	vendere	vender	prodavat'	vender
seller	verkooper	vendeur	Verkäufer	venditore	vendedor	prodavets	vendedor
seaman	zeeman	marin	Seemann	marinaio	marinheiro	moryak	marinero
seaport	zeehaven	port de mer	Seehafen	porto di mare	porto de mar	morskaya gavan'	puerto de mar
ship	schip	navire	Schiff	vascello	navio	parokhod, korabl'	buque
ship broker	scheeps makelaar	courtier de navires	Schiffmakler	sensale marittimo	corretor de navios	sudovoi makler	corredor de buques
shipper	verscheper	chargeur	Schiffer	caricatore	exportador	otpravitel'	cargador
shipping	verscheping	embarquement	Verschiffung	imbarco	transporte	otpravlenie	embarque
speculation	speculatie	spéculation	Spekulation	speculazione	especulação	spekulatsiya	especulación
standard	standaard	étalon	Normal-	norma	norma	norma	norma
stipulation	bedinging	stipulation	Bestimmung	stipulazione	estipulação	uslovie	estipulación
stock	voorraad	stock	Vorrat	esistenze	mercancias disponiveis	zapas	surtido
storehouse	magazijn	entrepôt	Vorratshaus	magazzino	armazem	sklad	almacén
T							
tare	tarra	tare	Tara	tara	tara	tara	tara
tariff	tarief	tarif	Tarif	tariffa	tarifa	tarif	tarifa
tax	schatting	taxe	Steuer	tassa	taxa	nalog	impuesto
telegraph	telegraaf	télégraphe	Telegraph	telegrafo	telegrafo	telegraf	telégrafo
tentative	beproevend	tentatif	versuchsweise	di tentativo	tentativo	na probu	de ensayo
termination	beëindiging	terminaison	Ablauf	terminazione	terminação	okonchanie	terminación
testimony	getuigenis	témoignage	Zeugnis	testimonio	testemunho	pokazanie	testimonio
trade	handel	commerce	Handel	commercio	commercio	torgovlya	comercio
transfer, to	overdragen	transférer	versetzen	trasferire	transferir	perevesti	transferir
transit	doorgang	transit	Durchgang	transito	transito	transit	tránsito
transmit, to	overzenden	transmettre	übersenden	trasmettere	transmitir	peredavat'	transmitir
transport	transport	transport	Transport	trasporto	transporte	perevoz	transporte
treasury	schatkamer	tresorerie	Schatzkammer	tesoreria	tesouro	kazna	tesorería
tribunal	rechtbank	tribunal	Gericht	tribunale	tribunal	sud	tribunal
U							
unauthorised	onbevoegd	sans autorité	unbefugt	non autorizzato	sem autorisação	nedozvoleny	sin autorización
useless	nutteloos	inutile	nutzlos	inutile	inutil	bezpolezny	inútil
unavoidable	onvermijdelijk	inevitable	unvermeidlich	inevitabile	inevitavel	neizbejny	inevitable
unclaimed	onafgehaald	non reclamé	unbestellbar	non-reclamato	não reclamado	nevostrebovanny	sin reclamación
unconditional	onvoorwaardelijk	sans condition	bedingungslos	senza condizione	incondicional	bezuslovny	incondicional
undertaking	onderneming	entreprise	Unternehmen	impresa	empresa	predpriatie	empresa
underwriter	assuradeur	assureur	Versicherer	assicuratore	segurador	strakhovshchik	asegurador
unfounded	ongegrond	sans fondement	unbegründet	infondato	sem fundamento	bez osnovania	sin fundamento
unlawful	onwettig	illégal	ungesetzlich	illecito	ilegal	nezakony	ilegal
unlimited	onbegrensd	illimité	unbegrenzt	illimitato	illimitado	neogranichenny	ilimitado
unload, to	ontladen	décharger	ausladen	scaricare	descarregar	vygrujat'	descargar
unpaid	onbetaald	non payé	unbezahlt	non pagato	não pago	neplachenny	no pagado
usage	gebruik	usage	Brauch	uso	uso	obychai	uso
V							
validity	geldigheid	validité	Gültigkeit	validità	validade	sila	validez
valuation	schatting	évaluation	Schätzung	stima	avaliação	otsenka	valuación
value	waarde	valeur	Wert	valore	valor	stoimost'	valor
verbal	mondeling	verbal	mündlich	verbale	verbal	ustny	verbal
verification	bevestiging	vérification	Prüfung	verificazione	verificação	poverka	verificación
vessel	schip	vaisseau	Schiff	bastimento	navio	sudno	buque
voucher	bewijsstuk	pièce justificative	Belegschein	scontrino	peca justificativa	opravdatel'ny dokument	documento justificativo
W							
wages	loon	gages	Lohn	salario	salario	jalovanie	salario
waive, to	opgeven	renoncer	verzichten	rinunciare	renunciar	otkazat'sia	renunciar
warehouse	magazijn	magasin	Warenlager	magazzino	armazem	magazin	almacén
way bill	vrachtbrief	lettre de voiture	Frachtbrief	polizza di carico	guia das fazendas	nakladnaya	hoja de ruta
weigh, to	wegen	peser	wiegen	pesare	pesar	vesit'	pesar
weigher	weger	peseur	Wieger	pesatore	pesador	vesovshchik	pesar
weight	gewicht	poids	Gewicht	peso	peso	ves	peso
wharf	kaai	quai	Werft	molo	cais	pristan'	muelle
wharfage	kaaigeld	droits de quai	Werftgeld	diritto di ripaggio	direito de cais	poshlina za pristan'	muellaje
wholesale	en gros	vente en gros	Grosshandel	vendita all'ingrosso	por grosso	optom	por mayor
wholesaler	grossier	marchand en gros	Grosshändler	venditore all'ingrosso	negociante por grosso	optovshchtik	vendedor por mayor
Y & Z							
yield	opbrengst	rendement	Ertrag	prodotto	rendimento	dokhod	rendimiento
zone	zone	zone	Zone	zona	zona	zona	zona

THE WORLD
MERCATOR PROJECTION
Capitals of Countries
Copyright by C.S. HAMMOND & Co., N.Y.
Longitude East of Greenwich
Longitude West of Greenwich
Longitude West of Greenwich
Longitude East of Greenwich
ARCTIC OCEAN
NORTH PACIFIC OCEAN
SOUTH PACIFIC OCEAN
NORTH ATLANTIC OCEAN
SOUTH ATLANTIC OCEAN
INDIAN OCEAN
Tropic of Cancer
Tropic of Capricorn
Equator
Arctic Circle
International Date Line
SEVERNAYA ZEMLYA
C. Chelyuskin
LAPTEV SEA
NEW SIBERIAN ISLANDS
EAST SIBERIAN SEA
UNION OF SOVIET SOCIALIST REPUBLICS
ASIA
EUROPE
NORTH AMERICA
SOUTH AMERICA
AFRICA
AUSTRALIA
Nordvik
Srednekolymsk
Yakutsk
Magadan
Anadyr
Krasnoyarsk
Irkutsk
Khabarovsk
Sakhalin Island
SEA OF OKHOTSK
Kuril Is.
BERING SEA
ALEUTIAN IS.
Bering Str.
Ulaanbaatar
MONGOLIA
GOBI
CHINA
Peking
Tianjin
Shenyang
Nanjing
Shanghai
Chongqing
Lhasa
Canton
Dhaka
BURMA
Rangoon
Bangkok
THAI.
LAOS
VIETNAM
Ho Chi Minh City
HONG KONG (Br.)
Taipei
Taiwan (Formosa)
PHILIPPINES
Manila
South China Sea
East China Sea
Sea of Japan
N. KOR.
S. KOR.
JAPAN
Tokyo
Osaka
MALAYSIA
SINGAPORE
Sumatra
Borneo
Celebes
INDONESIA
Jakarta
Java
New Guinea
PAPUA NEW GUINEA
Mariana Is. (U.S.)
Guam (U.S.)
Caroline Is. (U.S.)
Wake I. (U.S.)
Marshall (U.S.) Is.
NAURU
SOLOMON IS.
TUVALU
KIRIBATI
W. SAMOA
Samoa
FIJI
TONGA
VANUATU
New Caledonia (Fr.)
CORAL SEA
TASMAN SEA
Darwin
Townsville
Brisbane
Sydney
Canberra
Melbourne
Adelaide
Perth
Tasmania
Hobart
NEW ZEALAND
Auckland
Wellington
Midway Is. (U.S.)
HAWAIIAN IS
U.S. HAWAII
Honolulu
Kiritimati
Marquesas Is. (Fr.)
Society Is. (Fr.)
Tahiti
TUAMOTU ARCH. (Fr.)
Easter I. (Chile)
Pr. Patrick I.
QUEEN ELIZABETH IS.
SVERDRUP IS.
Axel Heiberg I.
Ellesmere Island
Lincoln Sea
Devon I.
Melville I.
McClure Str.
Parry Channel
Banks I.
Victoria I.
Amundsen G.
BEAUFORT SEA
Pt. Barrow
UNITED STATES
ALASKA
Nome
Fairbanks
Anchorage
Yukon
G. of Alaska
Juneau
Mackenzie
Gt. Bear L.
Gt. Slave L.
CANADA
Edmonton
Vancouver
Seattle
Winnipeg
HUDSON BAY
Foxe Basin
Baffin Island
G. of Boothia
BAFFIN BAY
Thule Air Base
GREENLAND (KALAALLIT NUNAAT) (Den.)
Qaqortoq
C. Farewell
Str. of Denmark
Montréal
Ottawa
Minneapolis
Chicago
Denver
San Francisco
Los Angeles
UNITED STATES
Washington
New York
Boston
Philadelphia
Atlanta
Houston
Halifax
Newfoundland
St. John's
C. Race
G. of Mexico
MEXICO
Mexico City
CENTRAL AMERICA
BAHAMAS
WEST INDIES
CUBA
Hispaniola
PUERTO RICO (U.S.)
Caribbean Sea
Panama
Caracas
VEN.
GUYANA
SUR.
FR. G.
Bogota
COL.
Quito
ECU.
Galápagos Is. (Ec.)
Amazon
Manaus
Belém
Natal
Salvador
BRAZIL
PERU
Lima
La Paz
BOLIVIA
Brasília
PAR.
Asunción
Antofagasta
Rio de Janeiro
São Paulo
Córdoba
URU.
Montevideo
Buenos Aires
Santiago
CHILE
ARGENTINA
Punta Arenas
Cape Horn
FALKLAND IS. (Br.)
S. Georgia (Br.)
SCOTIA SEA
SOUTH SANDWICH IS. (Br.)
SOUTH ORKNEY IS. (Br.)
GREENLAND SEA
Jan Mayen (Nor.)
NORWEGIAN SEA
ICELAND
Reykjavík
Faerøe Is. (Den.)
SVALBARD (Nor.)
FRANZ JOSEF LAND (U.S.S.R.)
BARENTS SEA
NOVAYA ZEMLYA
KARA SEA
North Cape
Murmansk
Archangel
Salekhard
Dudinka
Yenisey
Ob'
NORWAY
SWEDEN
FINLAND
Oslo
Stockholm
Helsinki
Leningrad
Baltic Sea
North Sea
UNITED KINGDOM
IRELAND
Glasgow
London
DEN.
BEL.
NE.
GER.
POL.
Berlin
Warsaw
Moscow
Volga
Sverdlovsk
Omsk
Novosibirsk
Paris
FRANCE
SWITZ.
AUS.
HUN.
ROM.
YUGO.
BUL.
GR.
ITALY
Rome
Kharkov
Volgograd
Black Sea
Caspian Sea
Aral Sea
Tashkent
Ürümqi
XINJIANG
PORTUGAL
Madrid
SPAIN
Lisbon
Algiers
Rabat
MOROCCO
ALGERIA
TUNISIA
Tripoli
LIBYA
Mediterranean Sea
Istanbul
TURKEY
SYRIA
ISR.
JOR.
IRAQ
IRAN
Tehran
Baku
Cairo
EGYPT
Nile
Red Sea
SAUDI ARABIA
Mecca
Persian G.
OMAN
AFGH.
PAK.
Kabul
Islamabad
TIBET
Karachi
New Delhi
INDIA
BANG.
Calcutta
Bombay
ARABIAN SEA
B. of Bengal
Madras
SRI LANKA (CEYLON)
MALDIVES
Azores (Port.)
Canary Is. (Sp.)
W. SAHARA
SAHARA
MAURITANIA
MALI
NIGER
CHAD
SUDAN
CAPE VERDE
Dakar
SEN.
GUINEA
SIERRA LEONE
LIBERIA
IVORY COAST
GHANA
TOGO
B. FASO
NIGERIA
Lagos
CAM.
CENT. AFR. REP.
DJIBOUTI
ETHIOPIA
Addis Ababa
G. of Aden
SOMALIA
Mogadishu
UGANDA
KENYA
Nairobi
GABON
CONGO
Brazzaville
Kinshasa
ZAIRE
TANZANIA
Dar es Salaam
SEYCHELLES
Luanda
ANGOLA
ZAMBIA
MAL.
MOZAMBIQUE
Mozambique Chan.
ZIM.
NAMIBIA (S.-W. AFRICA)
Windhoek
BOTS.
Johannesburg
Maputo
SOUTH AFRICA
LESOTHO
Cape Town
C. of Good Hope
MADAGASCAR
MAURITIUS
Reunion (Fr.)
Ascension (Br.)
St. Helena (Br.)
Tristan da Cunha (Br.)
Gough I. (Br.)
Bouvet I. (Nor.)
Pr. Edward Is. (S. Afr.)
Crozet Is. (Fr.)
Kerguélen (Fr.)
McDonald Is. (Australia)
Heard I. (Australia)
Amsterdam I. (Fr.)
St. Paul I. (Fr.)

NORTH AMERICA
LAMBERT AZIMUTHAL EQUAL-AREA PROJECTION
SCALE OF MILES
0 200 400 600 800 1000
SCALE OF KILOMETRES
0 200 400 600 800 1000
Capitals of Countries
International Boundaries
Canals
Copyright by C.S.HAMMOND & Co., N.Y.
North Pole
ARCTIC OCEAN
ASIA
Anadyr'
Arctic Circle
Wrangel I.
BERING SEA
St. Lawrence I.
Bering Str.
Norton Sd.
Nome
Seward Pen.
Koyukuk
Yukon
Kuskokwim
Bristol Bay
Alaska Pen.
Kodiak I.
Anchorage
Fairbanks
UNITED STATES
ALASKA
Pt. Barrow
BEAUFORT SEA
G. of Alaska
ALEXANDER ARCH.
Juneau
Ketchikan
Dixon Entr.
QUEEN CHARLOTTE IS.
Prince Rupert
Whitehorse
Dawson
Aklavik
Inuvik
Norman Wells
Mackenzie
Ft. Simpson
Liard
Port Radium
Great Bear L.
Yellowknife
Great Slave L.
Ft. Smith
L. Athabasca
Fort McMurray
Peace
Athabasca
Reindeer L.
Churchill
Chesterfield Inlet
Prince Patrick I.
Melville I.
McClure Str.
Banks I.
Amundsen Gulf
Victoria I.
Viscount Melville Sd.
McClintock Chan.
Dease Str.
Boothia Pen.
G. of Boothia
Melville Pen.
Wager Bay
Southampton I.
Coats I.
Mansel I.
Hudson Bay
BELCHER IS.
James Bay
Axel Heiberg I.
SVERDRUP IS.
QUEEN ELIZABETH IS.
Ellesmere I.
Devon I.
Lancaster Sd.
Baffin Bay
Baffin I.
Foxe Basin
Pangnirtung
Cumberland Sd.
Hudson Str.
C. Chidley
Ungava Bay
Labrador
Hamilton Inlet
Battle Harbour
Str. of Belle Isle
Newfoundland
Goose Bay
Gt. Whale
Ft. George
Nottaway
St. John's
C. Race
LINCOLN SEA
PEARY LAND
GREENLAND SEA
GREENLAND (KALAALLIT NUNAAT) (Den.)
KING CHRISTIAN X LAND
KING CHRISTIAN IX LAND
PRUDHOE LAND
Thule Air Base
FREDERICK VI COAST
Disko I.
Davis Strait
Nuuk (Godthåb)
Qaqortoq
C. Farewell
Ammassalik
Jan Mayen (Nor.)
ICELAND
Reykjavík
Str. of Denmark
ATLANTIC OCEAN
CANADA
Edmonton
Calgary
Saskatchewan
Saskatoon
Prince Albert
Lethbridge
Regina
Medicine Hat
L. Manitoba
Winnipeg
L. Winnipeg
Nelson
Albany
Moosonee
L. Nipigon
Timmins
Thunder Bay
L. Superior
Sault-Ste-Marie
Québec
St. Lawrence
G. of St. Lawrence
Montréal
Ottawa
Charlottetown
Saint John
Halifax
Sydney
C. Breton I.
C. Sable
Vancouver I.
Victoria
Vancouver
Str. of Juan de Fuca
Fraser
Tacoma
Seattle
Spokane
Portland
Columbia
Butte
Great Falls
Yellowstone
Fargo
Bismarck
Duluth
St. Paul
Minneapolis
Boise
Snake
Pocatello
Pierre
Missouri
Milwaukee
L. Michigan
L. Huron
Detroit
Toronto
L. Ontario
Buffalo
L. Erie
Albany
Boston
C. Cod
Providence
New York
Philadelphia
Baltimore
Pittsburgh
Cleveland
Columbus
Chicago
Des Moines
Peoria
Omaha
Sioux City
Casper
Cheyenne
Salt Lake City
Great Salt Lake
Platte
C. Mendocino
Reno
Sacramento
San Francisco
Oakland
Denver
Pueblo
Kansas City
St. Louis
Indianapolis
Cincinnati
Ohio
Louisville
Washington
Richmond
Norfolk
C. Hatteras
Colorado
UNITED STATES
Los Angeles
San Diego
Wichita
Tulsa
Oklahoma City
Arkansas
Nashville
Chattanooga
Winston-Salem
Charlotte
Albuquerque
Amarillo
Phoenix
Little Rock
Memphis
Atlanta
Birmingham
Charleston
Savannah
Tucson
El Paso
Fort Worth
Dallas
Red
Mississippi
Jackson
Mobile
Jacksonville
Brazos
Austin
Houston
San Antonio
New Orleans
C. Canaveral
Tampa
Miami
Bermuda (Br.) Hamilton
BAHAMAS
Nassau
Strs. of Florida
Gulf of Mexico
I. Guadalupe (Mex.)
I. Cedros
Tropic of Cancer
Lower California
Gulf of California
Ciudad Juárez
Hermosillo
Yaqui
Chihuahua
Rio Grande
Monterrey
Torreón
Durango
MEXICO
C. Falso
Mazatlán
San Luis Potosí
Tampico
Aguascalientes
Guadalajara
C. Corrientes
Santiago
Mexico City
Veracruz
Revillagigedo Is. (Mex.)
Balsas
Villahermosa
Acapulco
Oaxaca
Mérida
Yucatán Pen.
Belmopan
BELIZE
HONDURAS
Tegucigalpa
C. Gracias a Dios
Guatemala
GUATEMALA
San Salvador
EL SALVADOR
Managua
NICARAGUA
CENTRAL AMERICA
San José
COSTA RICA
Panamá
PANAMA
G. Panamá
Clipperton I. (Fr.)
Cocos I. (C.R.)
GALÁPAGOS IS. (Ecuador)
Equator
Havana
CUBA
Yucatán Chan.
I. de la Juventud
Camagüey
Santiago de Cuba
JAMAICA
Kingston
WEST INDIES
HAITI
Port-au-Prince
Windward Pass.
DOMINICAN REP.
Santo Domingo
Mona Pass.
San Juan
PUERTO RICO (U.S.)
CARIBBEAN SEA
Maracaibo
Medellín
Bogotá
SOUTH AMERICA
Quito
Guayaquil
PACIFIC OCEAN
120° 110° Longitude 100° West of Greenwich 90° 80°